Table of Contents

See the following volumes for other country listings:
Volume 1A: United States, United Nations, Abu Dhabi-Australia; Volume 1B: Austria-B
Volume 2A: C-Cur; Volume 2B: Cyp-F
Volume 3B: H-I
Volume 4A: J-L; Volume 4B: M
Volume 5A: N-Phil; Volume 5B: Pit-Sam
Volume 6A: San-Tete; Volume 6B: Thai-Z

Scott Catalogue Mission Statement

The Scott Catalogue Team exists to serve the recreational, educational and commercial hobby needs of stamp collectors and dealers.

We strive to set the industry standard for philatelic information and products by developing and providing goods that help collectors identify, value, organize and present their collections.

Quality customer service is, and will continue to be, our highest priority. We aspire toward achieving total customer satisfaction.

Copyright Notice

Trademark Notice

ISBN 978-0-89487-565-6

Library of Congress Card No. 2-3301

Acknowledgments

Our appreciation and gratitude go to the following individuals who have assisted us in preparing information included in this year's Scott Catalogues. Some helpers prefer anonymity. These individuals have generously shared their stamp knowledge with others through the medium of the Scott Catalogue.

Those who follow provided information that is in addition to the hundreds of dealer price lists and advertisements and scores of auction catalogues and realizations that were used in producing the catalogue values. It is from those noted here that we have been able to obtain information on items not normally seen in published lists and advertisements. Support from these people goes beyond data leading to catalogue values, for they also are key to editorial changes.

A special acknowledgment to Liane and Sergio Sismondo of The Classic Collector for their assistance and knowledge sharing that have aided in the preparation of this year's Standard and Classic Specialized Catalogues.

Roland Austin (United States Stamp Society)
Michael & Cecilia Ball (A To Z Stamps)
Jim Bardo (Bardo Stamps)
Jules K. Beck (Latin American Philatelic Society)
John Birkinbine II
Helmut Blaschczyk
James A. Booth
Les Bootman
Roger S. Brody
Peter Bylen
Tina & John Carlson (JET Stamps)
Carlson Chambliss
Tony L. Crumbley (Carolina Coin and Stamp, Inc.)
Ubaldo Del Toro
Bob and Rita Dumaine (Sam Houston Duck Co.)
Mark Eastzer
Paul G. Eckman
Robert Finder (Korea Stamp Society)
Jeffrey M. Forster
Robert S. Freeman
Ernest E. Fricks (France & Colonies Philatelic Society)
Bob Genisol (Sultan Stamp Center)
Stan Goldfarb
Dan Harding
Bruce Hecht (Bruce L. Hecht Co.)
Peter Hoffman
John M. Hotchner
Armen Hovsepian (ArmenStamp)
Eric Jackson
John I. Jamieson (Saskatoon Stamp and Coin)
Peter C. Jeannopoulos
William A. (Bill) Jones
Allan Katz (Ventura Stamp Co.)
Patricia A. Kaufmann (Confederate Stamp Alliance)
Jon Kawaguchi (Ryukyu Philatelic Specialist Society)
William V. Kriebel (Brazil Philatelic Association)
George Krieger
John R. Lewis (The William Henry Stamp Co.)
Ulf Lindahl (Ethiopian Philatelic Society)
Ignacio Llach (Filatelia Llach, S.L.)
Dennis Lynch (Eire Philatelic Association)
Kevin MacKeown (Korea Stamp Society)
Marilyn Mattke
William K. McDaniel
Gary Morris (Pacific Midwest Co.)
Peter Mosiondz, Jr.
Bruce M. Moyer (Moyer Stamps & Collectables)
Scott Murphy
Leonard Nadybal
Dr. Tiong Tak Ngo
Nik & Lisa Oquist
Dr. Everett L. Parker
John E. Pearson
Don Peterson (International Philippine Philatelic Society)
Stanley M. Piller (Stanley M. Piller & Associates)
Virgil Pirvulescu
Todor Drumev Popov
Dr. Charles Posner
Bob Prager (Gary Posner, Inc.)
Ed Reiser (Century Stamp Co.)
Ghassan D. Riachi
Peter A. Robertson
Omar Rodriguez
Mehrdad Sadri (Persiphila)
Dennis W. Schmidt
Michael Schreiber
Christian Schunck
Guy Shaw (Mexico-Elmhurst Philatelic Society International)
Jeff Siddiqui (Pakistan Philatelic Study Circle)
Sergio & Liane Sismondo (The Classic Collector)
Jay Smith
Telah Smith
Ivo Spanjersberg (Korea Stamp Society)
Earl Toops
Dan Undersander
Steven Unkrich
Philip T. Wall
Yong S. Yi (Korea Stamp Society)
Ralph Yorio
Val Zabijaka (Zabijaka Auctions)
Dr. Michal Zika (Album)
Steven Zirinsky (Zirinsky Stamps)
Alfonso G. Zulueta, Jr.

2020 STANDARD POSTAGE STAMP CATALOGUE

ONE HUNDRED AND SEVENTY-SIXTH EDITION IN SIX VOLUMES

VOLUME 3A

G

Released June 2019
Includes New Stamp Listings through the April 2019 *Linn's Stamp News Monthly* Catalogue Update

AMOS MEDIA

911 S. Vandemark Road, Sidney, OH 45365-4129
Publishers of *Linn's Stamp News, Linn's Stamp News Monthly, Coin World* and *Coin World Monthly.*

SCOTT

What's new for 2020 Scott Standard Volume 3A?

Another catalog season is upon us as we continue the journey of the 151-year history of the Scott catalogs. The 2020 volumes are the 176th edition of the Scott *Standard Postage Stamp Catalogue*. Vol. 3A includes listings for countries of the world beginning with the letter G. Listings for countries of the world H through I can be found in Vol. 3B.

Frequent users of the catalogs may notice a new look for the covers. Highlighted are single stamps from a postal entity found in that catalog. The Vol. 3A catalog shows the Germany 1952 10-pfennig Thurn and Taxis Postilion stamp (Scott 692).

Collectors will want to take note of and look closely at the Germany listings. An exhaustive review resulted in thousands of value changes. Overall, we see a mix of increases and decreases. The 1933 President von Hindenburg booklet pane of three (Scott 415b) increased from $21 to $42.50 in unused condition, and from $37.50 to $75 in used condition.

A couple hundred value changes were made for Great Britain. The sheet of David Bowie stamps (Scott 3591E) that originally sold for £12.95 (approximately U.S. $16.75) increased noticeably in value. This issue appears for the first time in the 2020 Vol. 3A catalog, with a value of $85. It was originally listed and valued at $32.50 in the Scott New Listings Update *in Linn's*.

For Alderney, almost all of the more than 400 recorded value changes are drops of 10 percent to 15 percent. Dealer stocks are mostly complete, often with multiple quantities of sets in stock. Several early commemorative sets rise modestly in value. The 1992 set of four honoring the 300th anniversary of the Battle of La Houge moves up $1 both mint and used, from $8.25 to $9.25.

Declines predominated among the hundreds of value changes made for Greenland, but a handful of values trend upward modestly. The 1953 dark blue 30-ore Frederik IX rises $4, from $36 in mint condition in 2019 to $40 this year. Scattered increases standout a bit more for modern issues such as the 2003 Sled Dogs booklet panes (411a and 411b), which advance from $12 each to $15. A few modern semipostal issues also increase in value.

A couple hundred value changes were recorded for the stamps of Guatemala. The 2009 Native Costumes set of seven (Scott 607-613) increased from $6.50 mint and used in 2019 to $21 both ways this year. The souvenir sheet from the same issue (614) also increased in value, from $2.75 to $30 both mint and used.

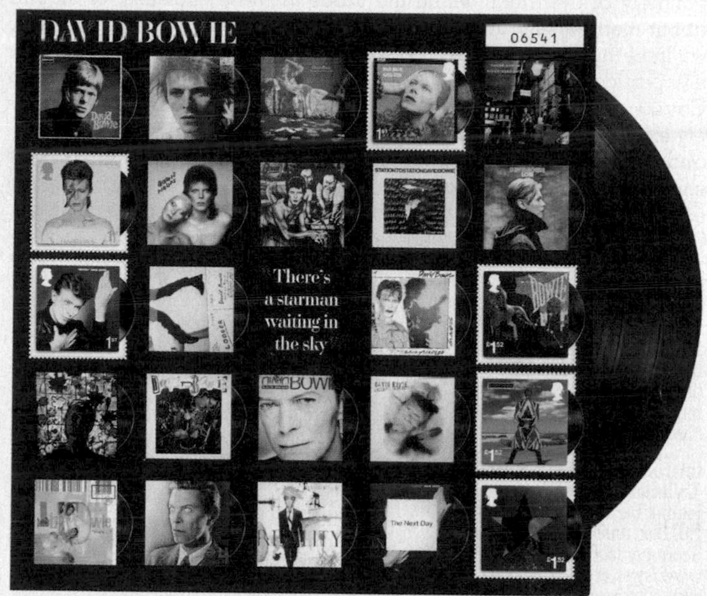

Great Britain David Bowie souvenir sheet (Scott 3591E) that increased in value from $32.50 to $85.

A mixed bag of value increases and value decreases were recorded for the stamps of Guinea-Bissau. Most of the value changes trend down for unused stamps, while scattered used stamps rise a bit in value. One notable increase is seen for the 1974 5-peso Proclamation of Independence (Scott 347), which advances from $14 mint and $6 used in the 2019 catalog to $22.50 and $8, respectively, this year.

Editorial enhancements for Vol. 3A

For Guyana a dozen new watermark varieties have been added to the 1985-87 Orchids series. Each of these minor listings show the multiple lotus bud watermark (No. 364).

Issue dates for most of the 1979-82 Guinea-Bissau sets were clarified with the addition of the month and day of issue.

An editorial note was added in the Germany semipostal section to draw attention to the unissued 60-pfennig+30pf 1980 Olympics stamp. Several of the stamps were used by a postal official, which is why the issue exists in collector hands.

And lastly, we encourage you to pay special attention to the Number Additions, Deletions & Changes found on page 915 in this volume. We also suggest reading the catalog introduction, which includes an abundance of useful information.

Best wishes in your stamp collecting pursuits!

Jay Bigalke, Scott catalog editor-in-chief

Addresses, Telephone Numbers, Web Sites, E-Mail Addresses of General & Specialized Philatelic Societies

Collectors can contact the following groups for information about the philately of the areas within the scope of these societies, or inquire about membership in these groups. Aside from the general societies, we limit this list to groups that specialize in particular fields of philately, particular areas covered by the Scott Standard Postage Stamp Catalogue, and topical groups. Many more specialized philatelic society exist than those listed below. These addresses are updated yearly, and they are, to the best of our knowledge, correct and current. Groups should inform the editors of address changes whenever they occur. The editors also want to hear from other such specialized groups not listed. Unless otherwise noted all website addresses begin with http://

General Societies

American Philatelic Society
100 Match Factory Place
Bellefonte, PA 16823-1367
(814) 933-3803
https://stamps.org
apsinfo@stamps.org

International Society of Worldwide Stamp Collectors
Joanne Berkowitz, M.D.
P.O. Box 19006
Sacramento, CA 95819
www.iswsc.org
executivedirector@iswsc.org

Royal Philatelic Society of Canada
P.O. Box 69080
St. Clair Post Office
Toronto, ON M4T 3A1
CANADA
(888) 285-4143
www.rpsc.org
info@rpsc.org

Royal Philatelic Society, London
41 Devonshire Place
London W1G 6JY
UNITED KINGDOM
020 7486 1044
www.rpsl.org.uk
secretary@rpsl.org.uk

Libraries, Museums, and Research Groups

American Philatelic Research Library
Scott Tiffney
100 Match Factory Place
Bellefonte, PA 16823
(814) 933-3803
www.stamplibrary.org
library@stamps.org

V. G. Greene Philatelic Research Foundation
P.O. Box 69100
St. Clair Post Office
Toronto, ON M4T 3A1
CANADA
(416) 921-2073
info@greenefoundation.ca

Aero/Astro Philately

American Air Mail Society
Stephen Reinhard
P.O. Box 110
Mineola, NY 11501
www.americanairmailsociety.org
sreinhard1@optonline.net

Postal History

Auxiliary Markings Club
Jerry Johnson
6621 W. Victoria Ave.
Kennewick, WA 99336
www.postal-markings.org
membership-2016@postal-markings.org

Cover Collectors Circuit Club
P.O. Box 316
Clallam Bay, WA 98320-0316
www.covercollectors.org
adirondack.stamps@gmail.com

Postage Due Mail Study Group
Bob Medland
Camway Cottage
Nanny Hurn's Lane
Cameley, Bristol BS39 5AJ
UNITED KINGDOM
01761 45959
www.postageduemail.org.uk
secretary.pdmsg@gmail.com

Postal History Society
Yamil Kouri
405 Waltham St. #347
Lexington, MA 02421
www.postalhistorysociety.org
yhkouri@massmed.org

Post Mark Collectors Club
Bob Milligan
7014 Woodland Oaks Drive
Magnolia, TX 77354
(281) 259-2735
www.postmarks.org
bob.milligan@gmail.com

Precancel Stamp Society
Dick Kalmbach
2658 Ironworks Drive
Buford, GA 30519-7070
www.precancels.com
promo@precancels.com

U.S. Cancellation Club
Roger Curran
20 University Ave.
Lewisburg, PA 17837
rcurran@dejazzd.com

Postal Stationery

United Postal Stationery Society
Stuart Leven
1659 Branham Lane, Suite F-307
San Jose, CA 95118-2291
www.upss.org
postat@gmail.com

Revenues & Cinderellas

American Revenue Association
Lyman Hensley
473 E. Elm St.
Sycamore, IL 60178-1934
www.revenuer.org
ilrno2@netzero.net

Christmas Seal & Charity Stamp Society
John Denune Jr. & Sr.
234 E. Broadway
Granville, OH 43023
(740) 814-6031
www.seal-society.org
john@christmasseals.net

National Duck Stamp Collectors Society
Anthony J. Monico
P.O. Box 43
Harleysville, PA 19438-0043
www.ndscs.org
ndscs@ndscs.org

State Revenue Society
Kent Gray
P.O. Box 67842
Albuquerque, NM 87193
www.staterevenue.org
srssecretary@comcast.net

Thematic Philately

Americana Unit
Dennis Dengel
17 Peckham Road
Poughkeepsie, NY 12603-2018
www.americanaunit.org
ddengel@americanaunit.org

American Topical Association
Vera Felts
P.O. Box 8
Carterville, IL 62918-0008
(618) 985-5100
www.americantopicalassn.org
americantopical@msn.com

Astronomy Study Unit
Leonard Zehr
1009 Treverton Crescent
Windsor, ON N8P 1K2
CANADA
(416) 833-9317
www.astronomystudyunit.net
lenzehr@gmail.com

Bicycle Stamps Club
Steve Andreasen
2000 Alaskan Way, Unit 157
Seattle, WA 98121
www.bicyclestampsclub.org
steven.w.andreasen@gmail.com

Biology Unit
Chris Dahle
1401 Linmar Drive NE
Cedar Rapids, IA 52402-3724
www.biophilately.org
chris-dahle@biophilately.org

Bird Stamp Society
Mr. S. A. H. (Tony) Statham
Ashlyns Lodge
Chesham Road
Berkhamsted, Herts HP4 2ST
UNITED KINGDOM
www.bird-stamps.org/bss
tony.statham@sky.com

Captain Cook Society
Jerry Yucht
8427 Leale Ave.
Stockton, CA 95212
www.captaincooksociety.com
us@captaincooksociety.com

The CartoPhilatelic Society
Marybeth Sulkowski
2885 Sanford Ave., SW, #32361
Grandville, MI 49418-1342
www.mapsonstamps.org
secretary@mapsonstamps.org

Casey Jones Railroad Unit
Jeff Lough
2612 Redbud Land, Apt. C
Lawrence, KS 66046
www.uqp.de/cjr
jeffydplaugh@gmail.com

Cats on Stamps Study Unit
Robert D. Jarvis
2731 Teton Lane
Fairfield, CA 94533
www.catstamps.info
bobmarci@aol.com

Chemistry & Physics on Stamps Study Unit
Dr. Roland Hirsch
20458 Water Point Lane
Germantown, MD 20874
(301) 903-9009
www.cpossu.org
rfhirsch@cpossu.org

Chess on Stamps Study Unit
Barry Keith
555 Rolling Valley Court
Charlottesville, VA 22902-8257
www.chessonstamps.org
keithfam@embarqmail.com

Cricket Philatelic Society
A. Melville-Brown
11 Weppons, Ravens Road
Shorham-by-Sea
West Sussex BN43 5AW
UNITED KINGDOM
www.cricketstamp.net
mel.cricket.100@googlemail.com

Ebony Society of Philatelic Events and Reflections (ESPER)
Don Neal
P.O. Box 5245
Somerset, NJ 08875-5245
www.esperstamps.org
esperdon@verizon.net

Earth's Physical Features Study Group
Fred Klein
515 Magdalena Ave.
Los Altos, CA 94024
http://epfsu.jeffhayward.com
epfsu@jeffhayward.com

Europa Study Unit
Tonny E. Van Loij
3002 S. Xanthia St.
Denver, CO 80231-4237
(303) 752-0189
www.europastudyunit.org
tvanloij@gmail.com

Fire Service in Philately
John Zaranek
81 Hillpine Road
Cheektowaga, NY 14227-2259
(716) 668-3352
jczaranek@roadrunner.com

Gay & Lesbian History on Stamps Club
Joe Petronie
P.O. Box 190842
Dallas, TX 75219-0842
www.glhsonline.org
glhsc@aol.com

Gems, Minerals & Jewelry Study Unit
Fred Haynes
10 Country Club Drive
Rochester, NY 14618-3720
fredmhaynes55@gmail.com

Graphics Philately Association
Larry Rosenblum
1030 E. El Camino Real
PMB 107
Sunnyvale, CA 94087-3759
www.graphics-stamps.org
larry@graphics-stamps.org

Journalists, Authors and Poets on Stamps
Christopher D. Cook
7222 Hollywood Rd.
Berrien Springs, MI 49103
cdcook2@gmail.com

Lighthouse Stamp Society
Dalene Thomas
1805 S. Balsam St., #106
Lakewood, CO 80232
(303) 986-6620
www.lighthousestampsociety.org
dalene@lighthousestampsociety.org

Lions International Stamp Club
David McKirdy
s-Gravenwetering 248
3062 SJ Rotterdam
NETHERLANDS
31(0) 10 212 0313
www.lisc.nl
davidmckirdy@aol.com

Masonic Study Unit
Gene Fricks
25 Murray Way
Blackwood, NJ 08012-4400
genefricks@comcast.net

Mathematical Study Unit
Monty J. Strauss
4209 88th Street
Lubbock, TX 79423-2941
www.mathstamps.org
montystrauss@gmail.com

Medical Subjects Unit
Dr. Frederick C. Skvara
P.O. Box 6228
Bridgewater, NJ 08807
fcskvara@optonline.net

Napoleonic Age Philatelists
Ken Berry
4117 NW 146th St.
Oklahoma City, OK 73134-1746
(405) 748-8646
www.nap-stamps.org
krb4117@att.net

Old World Archaeological Study Unit
Caroline Scannell
14 Dawn Drive
Smithtown, NY 11787-1761
www.owasu.org
editor@owasu.org

Petroleum Philatelic Society International
Feitze Papa
922 Meander Drive
Walnut Creek, CA 94598-4239
www.ppsi.org.uk
oildad@astound.net

Rotary on Stamps Fellowship
Gerald L. Fitzsimmons
105 Calle Ricardo
Victoria, TX 77904
www.rotaryonstamps.org
glfitz@suddenlink.net

Scouts on Stamps Society International
Woodrow (Woody) Brooks
498 Baldwin Road
Akron, OH 44312
(330) 612-1294
www.sossi.org
secretary@sossi.org

Ships on Stamps Unit
Erik Th. Matzinger
Voorste Havervelden 30
4822 AL Breda
NETHERLANDS
www.shipsonstamps.org
erikships@gmail.com

Space Topic Study Unit
David Blog
P.O. Box 174
Bergenfield, NJ 07621
www.space-unit.com
davidblognj@gmail.com

Stamps on Stamps Collectors Club
Michael Merritt
73 Mountainside Road
Mendham, NJ 07945
www.stampsonstamps.org
stampsonstamps@yahoo.com

Windmill Study Unit
Walter J. Hallien
607 N. Porter St.
Watkins Glenn, NY 14891-1345
(607) 229-3541
www.windmillworld.com

Youth Philately
Young Stamp Collectors of America
100 Match Factory Place
Bellefonte, PA 16823
(814) 933-3803
https://stamps.org/stamps.org/Learn/youth-in-philately
ysca@stamps.org

United States

American Air Mail Society
Stephen Reinhard
P.O. Box 110
Mineola, NY 11501
www.americanairmailsociety.org
sreinhard1@optonline.net

American First Day Cover Society
Douglas Kelsey
P.O. Box 16277
Tucson, AZ 85732-6277
(520) 321-0880
www.afdcs.org
afdcs@afdcs.org

American Plate Number Single Society
Rick Burdsall
APNSS Secretary
P.O. BOX 1023
Palatine, IL 60078-1023
www.apnss.org
apnss.sec@gmail.com

American Revenue Association
Lyman Hensley
473 E. Elm St.
Sycamore, IL 60178-1934
www.revenuer.org
ilrno2@netzero.net

American Society for Philatelic Pages and Panels
Ron Walenciak
P.O. Box 1042
Washington TWP, NJ 07676
www.asppp.org
rwalenciak@aol.com

Auxiliary Markings Club
Jerry Johnson
6621 W. Victoria Ave.
Kennewick, WA 99336
www.postal-markings.org
membership-2016@postal-markings.org

Canal Zone Study Group
Mike Drabik
P.O. Box 281
Bolton, MA 01740
www.canalzonestudygroup.com
czsgsecretary@gmail.com

Carriers and Locals Society
John Bowman
14409 Pentridge Drive
Corpus Christi, TX 78410
(361) 933-0757
www.pennypost.org
jbowman@stx.rr.com

Christmas Seal & Charity Stamp Society
John Denune Jr. & Sr.
234 E. Broadway
Granville, OH 43023
(740) 814-6031
www.seal-society.org
john@christmasseals.net

Confederate Stamp Alliance
Patricia A. Kaufmann
10194 N. Old State Road
Lincoln, DE 19960-3644
(302) 422-2656
www.csalliance.org
trishkauf@comcast.net

Cover Collectors Circuit Club
P.O. Box 316
Clallam Bay, WA 98326-0316
www.covercollectors.org
adirondack.stamps@gmail.com

Error, Freaks, and Oddities Collectors Club
Scott Shaulis
P.O. Box 549
Murrysville, PA 15668-0549
(724) 733-4134
www.efocc.org
scott@shaulisstamps.com

National Duck Stamp Collectors Society
Anthony J. Monico
P.O. Box 43
Harleysville, PA 19438-0043
www.ndscs.org
ndscs@ndscs.org

Plate Number Coil Collectors Club (PNC3)
Gene Trinks
16415 W. Desert Wren Court
Surprise, AZ 85374
(623) 322-4619
www.pnc3.org
gctrinks@cox.net

Post Mark Collectors Club
Bob Milligan
7014 Woodland Oaks Drive
Magnolia, TX 77354
(281) 259-2735
www.postmarks.org
bob.milligan@gmail.com

Souvenir Card Collectors Society
William V. Kriebel
1923 Manning St.
Philadelphia, PA 19103-5728
www.souvenircards.org
kriebewv@drexel.edu

U.S. Cancellation Club
Roger Curran
20 University Ave.
Lewisburg, PA 17837
rcurran@dejazzd.com

U.S. Philatelic Classics Society
Rob Lund
2913 Fulton
Everett, WA 98201-3733
www.uspcs.org
membershipchairman@uspcs.org

US Possessions Philatelic Society
Daniel F. Ring
P.O. Box 113
Woodstock, IL 60098
http://uspps.tripod.com
danielfring@hotmail.com

United States Stamp Society
Larry Ballantyne
P.O. Box 6634
Katy, TX 77491-6634
www.usstamps.org
webmaster@usstamps.org

North America (excluding United States)

Bermuda Collectors Society
John Pare
405 Perimeter Road
Mount Horeb, WI 53572
(608) 852-7358
www.bermudacollectorssociety.com
pare16@mhtc.net

British Caribbean Philatelic Study Group
Bob Stewart
7 West Dune Lane
Long Beach Township, NJ 08008
(941) 379-4108
www.bcpsg.com
bcpsg@comcast.net

British North America Philatelic Society
Andy Ellwood
10 Doris Ave.
Gloucester, ON K1T 3W8
CANADA
www.bnaps.org
secretary@bnaps.org

British West Indies Study Circle
John Seidl
4324 Granby Way
Marietta, GA 30062
(404) 229-6863
www.bwisc.org
john.seidl@gmail.com

Haiti Philatelic Society
Ubaldo Del Toro
5709 Marble Archway
Alexandria, VA 22315
www.haitiphilately.org
u007ubi@aol.com

Hawaiian Philatelic Society
Gannon Sugimura
P.O. Box 10115
Honolulu, HI 96816-0115
www.stampshows.com/hps.html
hiphilsoc@gmail.com

Latin America

Brazil Philatelic Association
William V. Kriebel
1923 Manning St.
Philadelphia, PA 19103-5728
www.brazilphilatelic.org
info@brazilphilatelic.org

Canal Zone Study Group
Mike Drabik
P.O. Box 281
Bolton, MA 01740
www.canalzonestudygroup.com
czsgsecretary@gmail.com

Colombia-Panama Philatelic Study Group
Thomas P. Myers
P.O. Box 522
Gordonsville, VA 22942
www.copaphil.org
tpmphil@hotmail.com

Association Filatelic de Costa Rica
Giana Wayman (McCarty)
#SJO 4935
P.O. Box 025723
Miami, FL 33102-5723
011-506-2-228-1947
scotland@racsa.co.cr

International Cuban Philatelic Society (ICPS)
Ernesto Cuesta
P.O. Box 34434
Bethesda, MD 20827
(301) 564-3099
www.cubafil.org
ecuesta@philat.com

Falkland Islands Philatelic Study Groups
Morva White
42 Colton Road
Shrivenham
Swindon SN6 8AZ
UNITED KINGDOM
44(0) 1793 783245
www.fipsg.org.uk
morawhite@supanet.com

International Society of Guatemala Collectors
Jaime Marckwordt
449 St. Francis Blvd.
Daly City, CA 94015-2136
(415) 997-0295
www.guatemalastamps.com
president@guatamalastamps.com

Federacion Filatelica de la Republica de Honduras
Mauricio Mejia
Apartado Postal 1465
Tegucigalpa, D.C.
HONDURAS
504 3399-7227
www.facebook.com/filateliadehonduras
ffrh@hotmail.com

Asociacion Mexicana de Filatelia (AMEXFIL)
Alejandro Grossmann
Jose Maria Rico, 129
Col. Del Valle
3100 Mexico City, DF
MEXICO
www.amexfil.mx
amexfil@gmail.com

Mexico-Elmhurst Philatelic Society International
Eric Stovner
P.O. Box 10097
Santa Ana, CA 92711-0097
www.mepsi.org
treasurer@mepsi.org

Nicaragua Study Group
Erick Rodriguez
11817 S. W. 11th St.
Miami, FL 33184-2501
nsgsec@yahoo.com

Asociación Filatélica de Panamá
Edward D. Vianna B
ASOFILPA
0819-03400
El Dorado, Panama
PANAMA
http://asociacionfilatelicadepanama.blogspot.com
asofilpa@gmail.com

Associated Collectors of El Salvador
Joseph D. Hahn
301 Rolling Ridge Drive, Apt. 111
State College, PA 16801-6149
www.elsalvadorphilately.org
joehahn100@hotmail.com

Africa

Bechuanalands and Botswana Society
Otto Peetoom
Roos
East Yorkshire HU12 0LD
UNITED KINGDOM
44(0)1964 670239
www.bechuanalandphilately.com
info@bechuanalandphilately.com

Egypt Study Circle
Mike Murphy
11 Waterbank Road
Bellingham
London SE6 34DJ
UNITED KINGDOM
(44) 0203 6737051
www.egyptstudycircle.org.uk
secretary@egyptstudycircle.org.uk

Ethiopian Philatelic Society
Ulf Lindahl
21 Westview Place
Riverside, CT 06878
(203) 722-0769
https://ethiopianphilatelicsociety.weebly.com
ulindahl@optonline.net

Liberian Philatelic Society
Travis Searls
P.O. Box 1570
Parker, CO 80134
www.liberiastamps.org
liberiastamps@comcast.net

Society for Moroccan and Tunisian Philately
S.P.L.M.
206, Bld Pereire
75017 PARIS
FRANCE
http://splm-philatelie.org
splm206@aol.com

Sudan Study Group
Andy Neal
Bank House, Coedway
Shrewsbury SY5 9AR
UNITED KINGDOM
www.sudanstamps.org
andywneal@gmail.com

Orange Free State Study Circle
J. R. Stroud, RDPSA
24 Hooper Close
Burnham-on-sea
Somerset TA8 1JQ
UNITED KINGDOM
44 1278 782235
www.orangefreestatephilately.org.uk
richard@richardstroud.plus.com

Rhodesian Study Circle
William R. Wallace
P.O. Box 16381
San Francisco, CA 94116
(415) 564-6069
www.rhodesianstudycircle.org.uk
bwall8rscr@earthlink.net

Philatelic Society for Greater Southern Africa
Alan Hanks
34 Seaton Drive
Aurora, ON L4G 2K1
CANADA
www.psgsa.org
alan.hanks@sympatico.ca

South Sudan Philatelic Society
William Barclay
1370 Spring Hill Road
South Londonderry, VT 05155
barclayphilatelics@gmail.com

Transvaal Study Circle
c/o 9 Meadow Road
Gravesend, Kent DA11 7LR
UNITED KINGDOM
www.transvaalstamps.org.uk
transvaalstudycircle@aol.co.uk

West Africa Study Circle
Martin Bratzel
1233 Virginia Ave.
Windsor, ON N8S 2Z1
CANADA
www.wasc.org.uk
marty_bratzel@yahoo.ca

Europe

Andorran Philatelic Study Circle
David Hope
17 Hawthorn Drive
Stalybridge
Cheshire SK15 1UE
UNITED KINGDOM
www.andorranpsc.org.uk
andorranpsc@btinternet.com

Austria Philatelic Society
Ralph Schneider
P.O. Box 978
Iowa Park, TX 76376
(940) 213-5004
www.austriaphilatelicsociety.com
rschneiderstamps@att.net

Channel Islands Specialists Society
Richard Flemming
Burbage, 64 Falconers Green
Hinckley
Leicestershire LE102SX
UNITED KINGDOM
www.ciss1950.org.uk
secretary@ciss1950.org.uk

Cyprus Study Circle
Rob Wheeler
47 Drayton Ave.
London W13 0LE
UNITED KINGDOM
www.cyprusstudycircle.org
robwheeler47@aol.com

Society for Czechoslovak Philately
Tom Cossaboom
P.O. Box 4124
Prescott, AZ 86302
(928) 771-9097
www.csphilately.org
klfck1@aol.com

Danish West Indies Study Unit of Scandinavian Collectors Club
Arnold Sorensen
7666 Edgedale Drive
Newburgh, IN 47630
(812) 480-6532
www.scc-online.org
valbydwi@hotmail.com

Eire Philatelic Association
John B. Sharkey
1559 Grouse Lane
Mountainside, NJ 07092-1340
www.eirephilatelicassoc.org
jsharkeyepa@me.com

Estonian Philatelic Society
Eo Vaher
39 Clafford Lane
Melville, NY 11747
www.eestipost.com

Faroe Islands Study Circle
Norman Hudson
40 Queen's Road
Vicar's Cross
Chester CH3 5HB
UNITED KINGDOM
www.faroeislandssc.org
jntropics@hotmail.com

France & Colonies Philatelic Society
Edward Grabowski
111 Prospect St., 4C
Westfield, NJ 07090
(908) 233-9318
www.franceandcolsps.org
edjjg@alum.mit.edu

Germany Philatelic Society
P.O. Box 6547
Chesterfield, MO 63006-6547
www.germanyphilatelicusa.org
info@germanyphilatelicsocietyusa.org

Gibraltar Study Circle
Susan Dare
22, Byways Park, Strode Road
Clevedon
North Somerset BS21 6UR
UNITED KINGDOM
www.gibraltarstudycircle.wordpress.com
smldare@yahoo.co.uk

Great Britian Collector's Club
Steve McGill
10309 Brookhollow Circle
Highlands Ranch, CO 80129
(303) 594-7029
www.gbphilately.org
steve.mcgill@comcast.net

Society for Hungarian Philately
Alan Bauer
P.O. Box 3024
Andover, MA 01810
(978) 682-0242
www.hungarianphilately.org
alan@hungarianstamps.com

Italy and Colonies Study Circle
Richard Harlow
7 Duncombe House
8 Manor Road
Teddington, Middlesex TW118BE
UNITED KINGDOM
44 208 977 8737
www.icsc-uk.com
richardharlow@outlook.com

Liechtenstudy USA
Paul Tremaine
410 SW Ninth St.
Dundee, OR 97115-9731
(503) 538-4500
www.liechtenstudy.org
tremaine@liechtenstudy.org

Lithuania Philatelic Society
Audrius Brazdeikis
9915 Murray Landing
Missouri City, TX 77459
(281) 450-6224
www.lithuanianphilately.com/lps
audrius@lithuanianphilately.com

Luxembourg Collectors Club
Gary B. Little
7319 Beau Road
Sechelt, BC V0N 3A8
CANADA
(604) 885-7241
http://lcc.luxcentral.com
gary@luxcentral.com

American Society for Netherlands Philately
Hans Kremer
50 Rockport Court
Danville, CA 94526
(925) 820-5841
www.asnp1975.com

Plebiscite-Memel-Saar Study Group of the German Philatelic Society
Clayton Wallace
100 Lark Court
Alamo, CA 94507
claytonwallace@comcast.net

Polonus Polish Philatelic Society
Daniel Lubelski
P.O. Box 2212
Benicia, CA 94510
(419) 410-9115
www.polonus.org
info@polonus.org

International Society for Portuguese Philately
Clyde Homen
1491 Bonnie View Road
Hollister, CA 95023-5117
www.portugalstamps.com
ispp1962@sbcglobal.net

Rossica Society of Russian Philately
Alexander Kolchinsky
1506 Country Lake Drive
Champaign, IL 61821-6428
www.rossica.org
alexander.kolchinsky@rossica.org

Scandinavian Collectors Club
Steve Lund
P.O. Box 16213
St. Paul, MN 55116
www.scc-online.org
steve88h@aol.com

Spanish Study Circle
Edith Knight
www.spaincircle.wixsite.com/spainstudycircle
spaincircle@gmail.com

American Helvetia Philatelic Society
Richard T. Hall
P.O. Box 15053
Asheville, NC 28813-0053
www.swiss-stamps.org
secretary2@swiss-stamps.org

Ukrainian Philatelic & Numismatic Society
Martin B. Tatuch
5117 8th Road N
Arlington, VA 22205-1201
www.upns.org
treasurer@upns.org
hkremer@usa.net

Vatican Philatelic Society
Joseph Scholten
1436 Johnston St. SE
Grand Rapids, MI 49507-2029
www.vaticanphilately.org
jscholten@vaticanphilately.org

Yugoslavia Study Group
Michael Chant
1514 N. Third Ave.
Wausau, WI 54401
0208-748-9919
www.yugosg.org
membership@yugosg.org

Middle East

Aden & Somaliland Study Group
Gary Brown
P.O. Box 106
Briar Hill, VIC 3088
AUSTRALIA
www.stampdomain.com/aden
garyjohn951@optushome.com.au

Iran Philatelic Study Circle
Nigel Gooch
Marchwood, 56, Wickham Ave.
Bexhill on-Sea
East Sussex TN39 3ER
UNITED KINGDOM
www.iranphilately.org
nigelmgooch@gmail.com

Society of Israel Philatelists, Inc.
Jacqueline Baca
100 Match Factory Place
Bellefonte, PA 16823-1367
(814) 933-3803 ext. 212
www.israelstamps.com
israelstamps@gmail.com

Pakistan Philatelic Study Circle
Jeff Siddiqui
P.O. Box 7002
Lynnwood, WA 98046
jeffsiddiqui@msn.com

Ottoman and Near East Philatelic Society
Rolfe Smith
201 SE Verada Ave.
Port St. Lucie, FL 34983
(772) 240-8937
www.oneps.org
xbow2@mac.com

Asia

Burma (Myanmar) Philatelic Study Circle
Michael Whittaker
1, Ecton Leys, Hillside
Rugby
Warwickshire CV22 5SL
UNITED KINGDOM
https://burmamyanmarphilately.wordpress.com/burma-myanmar-philatelic-study-circle
manningham8@mypostoffice.co.uk

Ceylon Study Circle
Rodney W. P. Frost
42 Lonsdale Road
Cannington
Bridgwater, Somerset TA5 2JS
UNITED KINGDOM
01278 652592
www.ceylonsc.org
rodney.frost@tiscali.co.uk

China Stamp Society
H. James Maxwell
1050 W. Blue Ridge Blvd.
Kansas City, MO 64145-1216
www.chinastampsociety.org
president@chinastampsociety.org

Hong Kong Philatelic Society
John Tang
G.P.O. Box 446
HONG KONG
www.hkpsociety.com
hkpsociety@outlook.com

Hong Kong Study Circle
Robert Newton
www.hongkongstudycircle.com/index.html
newtons100@gmail.com

India Study Circle
John Warren
P.O. Box 7326
Washington, DC 20044
(202) 488-7443
https://indiastudycircle.org
jw-kbw@earthlink.net

Society of Indo-China Philatelists
Ron Bentley
2600 N. 24th St.
Arlington, VA 22207
(703) 524-1652
www.sicp-online.org
ron.bentley@verizon.net

International Society for Japanese Philately
William Eisenhauer
P.O. Box 230462
Tigard, OR 97281
(503) 496-2634
www.isjp.org
secretary@isjp.org

Korea Stamp Society
John E. Talmage, Jr.
P.O. Box 6889
Oak Ridge, TN 37831
(865) 482-5226
https://koreastampsociety.org
jtalmage@usit.net

Nepal & Tibet Philatelic Study Group
Colin T. Hepper
2238 Greiner St.
Eugene, OR 97405
www.fuchs-online.com/ntpsc
ntpsc@fuchs-online.com

International Philippine Philatelic Society
James R. Larot, Jr.
4990 Bayleaf Court
Martinez, CA 94553
(925) 260-5425
www.theipps.info
jlarot@ccwater.com

Australasia and Oceana

Australian States Study Circle of the Royal Sydney Philatelic Club
Ben Palmer
G.P.O. 1751
Sydney, NSW 2001
AUSTRALIA
http://club.philas.org.au/states

Society of Australasian Specialists / Oceania
David McNamee
P.O. Box 37
Alamo, CA 94507
www.sasoceania.org
treasurer@sosoceania.org

Malaya Study Group
David Tett
4 Amenbury Court
Harpenden Herts
Wheathampstead, Herts AL5 2BU
UNITED KINGDOM
www.m-s-g.org.uk
davidtett@aol.com

New Zealand Society of Great Britain
Michael Wilkinson
121 London Road
Sevenoaks
Kent TN13 1BH
UNITED KINGDOM
01732 456997
www.nzsgb.org.uk
mwilkin799@aol.com

Pacific Islands Study Circle
John Ray
24 Woodvale Ave.
London SE25 4AE
UNITED KINGDOM
www.pisc.org.uk
secretary@pisc.org.uk

Papuan Philatelic Society
Steven Zirinsky
P.O. Box 49, Ansonia Station
New York, NY 10023
(718) 706-0616
www.papuanphilatelicsociety.com
szirinsky@cs.com

Pitcairn Islands Study Group
Dr. Everett L. Parker
207 Corinth Road
Hudson, ME 04449-3057
(207) 573-1686
www.pisg.net
eparker@hughes.net

Ryukyu Philatelic Specialist Society
Laura Edmonds
P.O. Box 240177
Charlotte, NC 28224-0177
(336) 509-3739
www.ryukyustamps.org
secretary@ryukyustamps.org

Fellowship of Samoa Specialists
Trevor Shimell
18 Aspen Drive, Newton Abbot
Devon TQ12 4TN
UNITED KINGDOM
www.samoaexpress.org
trevor.shimell@gmail.com

Sarawak Specialists' Society
Stephen Schumann
2417 Cabrallo Drive
Hayward, CA 94545
(510) 785-4794
www.britborneostamps.org.uk
vpnam@s-s-s.org.uk

Western Australia Study Group
Brian Pope
P.O. Box 423
Claremont, WA 6910
AUSTRALIA
(61) 419 843 943
www.wastudygroup.com
wastudygroup@hotmail.com

Interregional Societies

American Society of Polar Philatelists
Alan Warren
P.O. Box 39
Exton, PA 19341-0039
(610) 321-0740
www.polarphilatelists.org
alanwar@att.net

First Issues Collector's Club
Kurt Streepy
3128 E. Mattatha Drive
Bloomington, IN 47401
www.firstissues.org
secretary@firstissues.org

France & Colonies Philatelic Society
Edward Grabowski
111 Prospect St., 4C
Westfield, NJ 07090
(908) 233-9318
www.franceandcolsps.org
edjjg@alum.mit.edu

Former French Colonies Specialist Society
Col.fra
BP 628
75367 PARIS Cedex 08
FRANCE
www.colfra.org
postmaster@colfra.org

International Society of Reply Coupon Collectors
Peter Robin
P.O. Box 353
Bala Cynwyd, PA 19004
peterrobin@verizon.net

Italy and Colonies Study Circle
Richard Harlow
7 Duncombe House
8 Manor Road
Teddington, Middlesex TW118BE
UNITED KINGDOM
44 208 977 8737
www.icsc-uk.com
richardharlow@outlook.com

Joint Stamp Issues Society
Richard Zimmermann
29A, Rue Des Eviats
67220 LALAYE
FRANCE
www.philarz.net
richard.zimmermann@club-internet.fr

The King George VI Collectors Society
Brian Livingstone
21 York Mansions
Prince of Wales Drive
London SW11 4DL
UNITED KINGDOM
www.kg6.info
livingstone484@btinternet.com

St. Helena, Ascension & Tristan Da Cunha Philatelic Society
Dr. Everett L. Parker
207 Corinth Road
Hudson, ME 04449-3057
(207) 573-1686
www.shatps.org
eparker@hughes.net

United Nations Philatelists
Blanton Clement, Jr.
P.O. Box 146
Morrisville, PA 19067-0146
www.unpi.com
bclemjunior@gmail.com

Stamp Dealer Associations

American Stamp Dealers Association, Inc.
P.O. Box 692
Leesport, PA 19553
(800) 369-8209
www.americanstampdealer.com
asda@americanstampdealer.com

National Stamp Dealers Association
Sheldon Ruckens, President
3643 Private Road 18
Pinckneyville, IL 62274-3426
(618) 357-5497
www.nsdainc.org
nsda@nsdainc.org

Expertizing Services

The following organizations will, for a fee, provide expert opinions about stamps submitted to them. Collectors should contact these organizations to find out about their fees and requirements before submiting philatelic material to them. The listing of these groups here is not intended as an endorsement by Amos Media Co.

General Expertizing Services

American Philatelic Expertizing Service (a service of the American Philatelic Society)
100 Match Factory Place
Bellefonte PA 16823-1367
(814) 933-3803 ext. 206
https://stamps.org/stamp-authentication
twhorn@stamps.org
Areas of Expertise: Worldwide

B. P. A. Expertising, Ltd.
P.O. Box 1141
Guildford
Surrey, GU5 0WR
UNITED KINGDOM
www.bpaexpertising.com
sec@bpaexpertising.org
Areas of Expertise: British Commonwealth, Great Britain, Classics of Europe, South America and the Far East

Philatelic Foundation
22 E. 35th St., 4th Floor
New York, NY 10016
(212) 221-6555
www.philatelicfoundation.org
philatelicfoundation@verizon.net
Areas of Expertise: U.S. & Worldwide

Philatelic Stamp Authentication and Grading, Inc.
P.O. Box 41-0880
Melbourne, FL 32941-0880
(305) 345-9864
www.psaginc.com
info@psaginc.com
Areas of Expertise: U.S., Canal Zone, Hawaii, Philippines, Canada & Provinces

Professional Stamp Experts
P.O. Box 539309
Henderson, NV 89053-9309
(702) 776-6522
www.gradingmatters.com
www.psestamp.com
info@gradingmatters.com
Areas of Expertise: Stamps and covers of U.S., U.S. Possessions, British Commonwealth

Royal Philatelic Society Expert Committee
41 Devonshire Place
London, W1N 1PE
UNITED KINGDOM
44 (0) 20 7935 7332
www.rpsl.limited/experts.aspx
experts@rpsl.limited
Areas of Expertise: Worldwide

Specialized Expertizing Services

China Stamp Society Expertizing Service
1050 W. Blue Ridge Blvd.
Kansas City, MO 64145
(816) 942-6300
www.chinastampsociety.org/expertization-and-identification-procedure
expertizing@chinastampsociety.org
Areas of Expertise: China

Confederate Stamp Alliance Authentication Service
John L. Kimbrough
P.O. Box 278
Capshaw, AL 35742-0396
(302) 422-2656
www.csalliance.org/CSAAS.shtml
authentication@csalliance.org
Areas of Expertise: Confederate stamps and postal history

Estonian Philatelic Society Expertizing Service
39 Clafford Lane
Melville NY 11747
(516) 421-2078
esto4@aol.com
Areas of Expertise: Estonia

Hawaiian Philatelic Society Expertizing Service
P.O. Box 10115
Honolulu HI 96816-0115
Areas of Expertise: Hawaii

International Association of Philatelic Experts United States Associate members:

Paul Buchsbayew
119 W. 57th St.
New York, NY 10019
Ph: (212) 977-7734
paulb@cherrystoneauctions.com
Areas of Expertise: Russia, Soviet Union

William T. Crowe
P.O. Box 2090
Danbury CT 06813-2090
E-mail: wtcrowe@aol.com
Areas of Expertise: United States

Robert Odenweller
P.O. Box 401
Bernardsville NJ 07924-0401
(908) 766-5460
odenwelleraiep@verizon.net
Areas of Expertise: New Zealand, Samoa to 1900

Sergio Sismondo
The Regency Tower, Suite 1109
770 James Street
Syracuse NY 13203
Ph: (315) 422-2331
Fax: (315) 422-2956
Areas of Expertise: British East Africa, Camerouns, Cape of Good Hope, Canada, British North America

International Society for Japanese Philately Expertizing Committee
Florian Eichhorn
Adolfsallee 17
D-65185 Wiesbaden
GERMANY
www.isjp.org/expertizing
minatobay@t-online.de
Areas of Expertise: Japan and related areas, except WWII Japanese Occupation issues

International Society for Portuguese Philately Expertizing Service
P.O. Box 43146
Philadelphia PA 19129-3146
(215) 843-2106
www.portugalstamps.com/expert.html
s.s.washburne@worldnet.att.net
Areas of Expertise: Portugal and Colonies

Mexico-Elmhurst Philatelic Society International Expert Committee
Expert Committee Administrator
Marc E. Gonzales
P.O. Box 29040
Denver CO 80229-0040
www.mepsi.org/expertization
Areas of Expertise: Mexico

Ukrainian Philatelic & Numismatic Society Expertizing Service
Jerry G. Tkachuk
7266 Dibrova Drive
Brighton, MI 48116
www.upns.org/expertization
Areas of Expertise: Ukraine, Western Ukraine

V. G. Greene Philatelic Research Foundation
P.O. Box 69100, St. Clair Post Office
Toronto, ON, M4T 3A1
CANADA
(416) 921-2073
www.greenefoundation.ca
info@greenefoundation.ca
Areas of Expertise: British North America

Information on Catalogue Values, Grade and Condition

Catalogue Value

The Scott Catalogue value is a retail value; that is, an amount you could expect to pay for a stamp in the grade of Very Fine with no faults. Any exceptions to the grade valued will be noted in the text. The general introduction on the following pages and the individual section introductions further explain the type of material that is valued. The value listed for any given stamp is a reference that reflects recent actual dealer selling prices for that item.

Dealer retail price lists, public auction results, published prices in advertising and individual solicitation of retail prices from dealers, collectors and specialty organizations have been used in establishing the values found in this catalogue. Amos Media Co. values stamps, but Amos Media is not a company engaged in the business of buying and selling stamps as a dealer.

Use this catalogue as a guide for buying and selling. The actual price you pay for a stamp may be higher or lower than the catalogue value because of many different factors, including the amount of personal service a dealer offers, or increased or decreased interest in the country or topic represented by a stamp or set. An item may occasionally be offered at a lower price as a "loss leader," or as part of a special sale. You also may obtain an item inexpensively at public auction because of little interest at that time or as part of a large lot.

Stamps that are of a lesser grade than Very Fine, or those with condition problems, generally trade at lower prices than those given in this catalogue. Stamps of exceptional quality in both grade and condition often command higher prices than those listed.

Values for pre-1900 unused issues are for stamps with approximately half or more of their original gum. Stamps with most or all of their original gum may be expected to sell for more, and stamps with less than half of their original gum may be expected to sell for somewhat less than the values listed. On rarer stamps, it may be expected that the original gum will be somewhat more disturbed than it will be on more common issues. Post-1900 unused issues are assumed to have full original gum. From breakpoints in most countries' listings, stamps are valued as never hinged, due to the wide availability of stamps in that condition. These notations are prominently placed in the listings and in the country information preceding the listings. Some countries also feature listings with dual values for hinged and never-hinged stamps.

Grade

A stamp's grade and condition are crucial to its value. The accompanying illustrations show examples of Very Fine stamps from different time periods, along with examples of stamps in Fine to Very Fine and Extremely Fine grades as points of reference. When a stamp seller offers a stamp in any grade from fine to superb without further qualifying statements, that stamp should not only have the centering grade as defined, but it also should be free of faults or other condition problems.

FINE stamps (illustrations not shown) have designs that are quite off center, with the perforations on one or two sides very close to the design but not quite touching it. There is white space between the perforations and the design that is minimal but evident to the unaided eye. Imperforate stamps may have small margins, and earlier issues may show the design just touching one edge of the stamp design. Very early perforated issues normally will have the perforations slightly cutting into the design. Used stamps may have heavier than usual cancellations.

FINE-VERY FINE stamps will be somewhat off center on one side, or slightly off center on two sides. Imperforate stamps will have two margins of at least normal size, and the design will not touch any edge. For perforated stamps, the perfs are well clear of the design, but are still noticeably off center. *However, early issues of a country may be printed in such a way that the design naturally is very close to the edges. In these cases, the perforations may cut into the design very slightly.* Used stamps will not have a cancellation that detracts from the design.

VERY FINE stamps will be just slightly off center on one or two sides, but the design will be well clear of the edge. The stamp will present a nice, balanced appearance. Imperforate stamps will be well centered within normal-sized margins. *However, early issues of many countries may be printed in such a way that the perforations may touch the design on one or more sides. Where this is the case, a boxed note will be found defining the centering and margins of the stamps being valued.* Used stamps will have light or otherwise neat cancellations. This is the grade used to establish Scott Catalogue values.

EXTREMELY FINE stamps are close to being perfectly centered. Imperforate stamps will have even margins that are slightly larger than normal. Even the earliest perforated issues will have perforations clear of the design on all sides.

Amos Media Co. recognizes that there is no formally enforced grading scheme for postage stamps, and that the final price you pay or obtain for a stamp will be determined by individual agreement at the time of transaction.

Condition

Grade addresses only centering and (for used stamps) cancellation. *Condition* refers to factors other than grade that affect a stamp's desirability.

Factors that can increase the value of a stamp include exceptionally wide margins, particularly fresh color, the presence of selvage, and plate or die varieties. Unusual cancels on used stamps (particularly those of the 19th century) can greatly enhance their value as well.

Factors other than faults that decrease the value of a stamp include loss of original gum, regumming, a hinge remnant or foreign object adhering to the gum, natural inclusions, straight edges, and markings or notations applied by collectors or dealers.

Faults include missing pieces, tears, pin or other holes, surface scuffs, thin spots, creases, toning, short or pulled perforations, clipped perforations, oxidation or other forms of color changelings, soiling, stains, and such man-made changes as reperforations or the chemical removal or lightening of a cancellation.

Grading Illustrations

On the following two pages are illustrations of various stamps from countries appearing in this volume. These stamps are arranged by country, and they represent early or important issues that are often found in widely different grades in the marketplace. The editors believe the illustrations will prove useful in showing the margin size and centering that will be seen on the various issues.

In addition to the matters of margin size and centering, collectors are reminded that the very fine stamps valued in the Scott catalogues also will possess fresh color and intact perforations, and they will be free from defects.

Examples shown are computer-manipulated images made from single digitized master illustrations.

Stamp Illustrations Used in the Catalogue

It is important to note that the stamp images used for identification purposes in this catlaogue may not be indicative of the grade of stamp being valued. Refer to the written discussion of grades on this page and to the grading illustrations on the following two pages for grading information.

Fine-Very Fine
SCOTT
CATALOGUES
VALUE
STAMPS IN
THIS GRADE
Very Fine
Extremely Fine

Fine-Very Fine
SCOTT
CATALOGUES
VALUE
STAMPS IN
THIS GRADE
Very Fine
Extremely Fine

Fine-Very Fine
SCOTT CATALOGUES VALUE STAMPS IN THIS GRADE
Very Fine
Extremely Fine
Fine-Very Fine
SCOTT CATALOGUES VALUE STAMPS IN THIS GRADE
Very Fine
Extremely Fine

For purposes of helping to determine the gum condition and value of an unused stamp, Scott presents the following chart which details different gum conditions and indicates how the conditions correlate with the Scott values for unused stamps. Used together, the Illustrated Grading Chart on the previous pages and this Illustrated Gum Chart should allow catalogue users to better understand the grade and gum condition of stamps valued in the Scott catalogues.

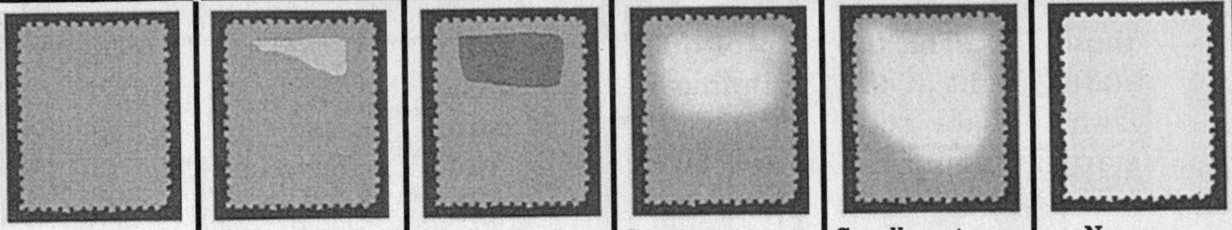

Gum Categories:	MINT N.H.	ORIGINAL GUM (O.G.)				NO GUM
	Mint Never Hinged *Free from any disturbance*	**Lightly Hinged** *Faint impression of a removed hinge over a small area*	**Hinge Mark or Remnant** *Prominent hinged spot with part or all of the hinge remaining*	**Large part o.g.** *Approximately half or more of the gum intact*	**Small part o.g.** *Approximately less than half of the gum intact*	**No gum** *Only if issued with gum*
Commonly Used Symbol:	★★	★	★	★	★	(★)
Pre-1900 Issues (Pre-1881 for U.S.)	*Very fine pre-1900 stamps in these categories trade at a premium over Scott value*			Scott Value for "Unused"		Scott "No Gum" listings for selected unused classic stamps
From 1900 to breakpoints for listings of never-hinged stamps	Scott "Never Hinged" listings for selected unused stamps	Scott Value for "Unused" (Actual value will be affected by the degree of hinging of the full o.g.)				
From breakpoints noted for many countries	Scott Value for "Unused"					

Never Hinged (NH; ★★): A never-hinged stamp will have full original gum that will have no hinge mark or disturbance. The presence of an expertizer's mark does not disqualify a stamp from this designation.

Original Gum (OG; ★): Pre-1900 stamps should have approximately half or more of their original gum. On rarer stamps, it may be expected that the original gum will be somewhat more disturbed than it will be on more common issues. Post-1900 stamps should have full original gum. Original gum will show some disturbance caused by a previous hinge(s) which may be present or entirely removed. The actual value of a post-1900 stamp will be affected by the degree of hinging of the full original gum.

Disturbed Original Gum: Gum showing noticeable effects of humidity, climate or hinging over more than half of the gum. The significance of gum disturbance in valuing a stamp in any of the Original Gum categories depends on the degree of disturbance, the rarity and normal gum condition of the issue and other variables affecting quality.

Regummed (RG; (★)): A regummed stamp is a stamp without gum that has had some type of gum privately applied at a time after it was issued. This normally is done to deceive collectors and/or dealers into thinking that the stamp has original gum and therefore has a higher value. A regummed stamp is considered the same as a stamp with none of its original gum for purposes of grading.

Catalogue Listing Policy

It is the intent of Amos Media Co. to list all postage stamps of the world in the *Scott Standard Postage Stamp Catalogue*. The only strict criteria for listing is that stamps be decreed legal for postage by the issuing country and that the issuing country actually have an operating postal system. Whether the primary intent of issuing a given stamp or set was for sale to postal patrons or to stamp collectors is not part of our listing criteria. Scott's role is to provide basic comprehensive postage stamp information. It is up to each stamp collector to choose which items to include in a collection.

It is Scott's objective to seek reasons why a stamp should be listed, rather than why it should not. Nevertheless, there are certain types of items that will not be listed. These include the following:

1. Unissued items that are not officially distributed or released by the issuing postal authority. If such items are officially issued at a later date by the country, they will be listed. Unissued items consist of those that have been printed and then held from sale for reasons such as change in government, errors found on stamps or something deemed objectionable about a stamp subject or design.
2. Stamps "issued" by non-existent postal entities or fantasy countries, such as Nagaland, Occusi-Ambeno, Staffa, Sedang, Torres Straits and others. Also, stamps "issued" in the names of legitimate, stamp-issuing countries that are not authorized by those countries.
3. Semi-official or unofficial items not required for postage. Examples include items issued by private agencies for their own express services. When such items are required for delivery, or are valid as prepayment of postage, they are listed.
4. Local stamps issued for local use only. Postage stamps issued by governments specifically for "domestic" use, such as Haiti Scott 219-228, or the United States non-denominated stamps, are not considered to be locals, since they are valid for postage throughout the country of origin.
5. Items not valid for postal use. For example, a few countries have issued souvenir sheets that are not valid for postage. This area also includes a number of worldwide charity labels (some denominated) that do not pay postage.
6. Egregiously exploitative issues such as stamps sold for far more than face value, stamps purposefully issued in artificially small quantities or only against advance orders, stamps awarded only to a selected audience such as a philatelic bureau's standing order customers, or stamps sold only in conjunction with other products. All of these kinds of items are usually controlled issues and/or are intended for speculation. These items normally will be included in a footnote.
7. Items distributed by the issuing government only to a limited group, club, philatelic exhibition or a single stamp dealer or other private company. These items normally will be included in a footnote.
8. Stamps not available to collectors. These generally are rare items, all of which are held by public institutions such as museums. The existence of such items often will be cited in footnotes.

The fact that a stamp has been used successfully as postage, even on international mail, is not in itself sufficient proof that it was legitimately issued. Numerous examples of so-called stamps from non-existent countries are known to have been used to post letters that have successfully passed through the international mail system.

There are certain items that are subject to interpretation. When a stamp falls outside our specifications, it may be listed along with a cautionary footnote.

A number of factors are considered in our approach to analyzing how a stamp is listed. The following list of factors is presented to share with you, the catalogue user, the complexity of the listing process.

Additional printings — "Additional printings" of a previously issued stamp may range from an item that is totally different to cases where it is impossible to differentiate from the original. At least a minor number (a small-letter suffix) is assigned if there is a distinct change in stamp shade, noticeably redrawn design, or a significantly different perforation measurement. A major number (numeral or numeral and capital-letter combination) is assigned if the editors feel the "additional printing" is sufficiently different from the original that it constitutes a different issue.

Commemoratives — Where practical, commemoratives with the same theme are placed in a set. For example, the U.S. Civil War Centennial set of 1961-65 and the Constitution Bicentennial series of 1989-90 appear as sets. Countries such as Japan and Korea issue such material on a regular basis, with an announced, or at least predictable, number of stamps known in advance. Occasionally, however, stamp sets that were released over a period of years have been separated. Appropriately placed footnotes will guide you to each set's continuation.

Definitive sets — Blocks of numbers generally have been reserved for definitive sets, based on previous experience with any given country. If a few more stamps were issued in a set than originally expected, they often have been inserted into the original set with a capital-letter suffix, such as U.S. Scott 1059A. If it appears that many more stamps than the originally allotted block will be released before the set is completed, a new block of numbers will be reserved, with the original one being closed off. In some cases, such as the U.S. Transportation and Great Americans series, several blocks of numbers exist. Appropriately placed footnotes will guide you to each set's continuation.

New country — Membership in the Universal Postal Union is not a consideration for listing status or order of placement within the catalogue. The index will tell you in what volume or page number the listings begin.

"No release date" items — The amount of information available for any given stamp issue varies greatly from country to country and even from time to time. Extremely comprehensive information about new stamps is available from some countries well before the stamps are released. By contrast some countries do not provide information about stamps or release dates. Most countries, however, fall between these extremes. A country may provide denominations or subjects of stamps from upcoming issues that are not issued as planned. Sometimes, philatelic agencies, those private firms hired to represent countries, add these later-issued items to sets well after the formal release date. This time period can range from weeks to years. If these items were officially released by the country, they will be added to the appropriate spot in the set. In many cases, the specific release date of a stamp or set of stamps may never be known.

Overprints — The color of an overprint is always noted if it is other than black. Where more than one color of ink has been used on overprints of a single set, the color used is noted. Early overprint and surcharge illustrations were altered to prevent their use by forgers.

Personalized Stamps — Since 1999, the special service of personalizing stamp vignettes, or labels attached to stamps, has been offered to customers by postal administrations of many countries. Sheets of these stamps are sold, singly or in quantity, only through special orders made by mail, in person, or through a sale on a computer website with the postal administrations or their agents for which an extra fee is charged, though some countries offer to collectors at face value personalized stamps having generic images in the vignettes or on the attached labels. It is impossible for any catalogue to know what images have been chosen by customers. Images can be 1) owned or created by the customer, 2) a generic image, or 3) an image pulled from a library of stock images on the stamp creation website. It is also impossible to know the quantity printed for any stamp having a particular image. So from a valuing standpoint, any image is equivalent to any other image for any personalized stamp having the same catalogue number. Illustrations of personalized stamps in the catalogue are not always those of stamps having generic images.

Personalized items are listed with some exceptions. These include:

1. Stamps or sheets that have attached labels that the customer cannot personalize, but which are nonetheless marketed as "personalized," and are sold for far more than the franking value.
2. Stamps or sheets that can be personalized by the customer, but where a portion of the print run must be ceded to the issuing country for sale to other customers.
3. Stamps or sheets that are created exclusively for a particular commercial client, or clients, including stamps that differ from any similar stamp that has been made available to the public.
4. Stamps or sheets that are deliberately conceived by the issuing authority that have been, or are likely to be, created with an excessive number of different face values, sizes, or other features that are changeable.
5. Stamps or sheets that are created by postal administrations using the same system of stamp personalization that has been put in place for use by the public that are printed in limited quantities and sold above face value.
6. Stamps or sheets that are created by licensees not directly affiliated or controlled by a postal administration.

Excluded items may or may not be footnoted.

Se-tenants — Connected stamps of differing features (se-tenants) will be listed in the format most commonly collected. This includes pairs, blocks or larger multiples. Se-tenant units are not always symmetrical. An example is Australia Scott 508, which is a block of seven stamps. If the stamps are primarily collected as a unit, the major number may be assigned to the multiple, with minors going to each component stamp. In cases where continuous-design or other unit se-tenants will receive significant postal use, each stamp is given a major Scott number listing. This includes issues from the United States, Canada, Germany and Great Britain, for example.

Understanding the Listings

On the opposite page is an enlarged "typical" listing from this catalogue. Below are detailed explanations of each of the highlighted parts of the listing.

1 Scott number — Scott catalogue numbers are used to identify specific items when buying, selling or trading stamps. Each listed postage stamp from every country has a unique Scott catalogue number. Therefore, Germany Scott 99, for example, can only refer to a single stamp. Although the Scott catalogue usually lists stamps in chronological order by date of issue, there are exceptions. When a country has issued a set of stamps over a period of time, those stamps within the set are kept together without regard to date of issue. This follows the normal collecting approach of keeping stamps in their natural sets.

When a country issues a set of stamps over a period of time, a group of consecutive catalogue numbers is reserved for the stamps in that set, as issued. If that group of numbers proves to be too few, capital-letter suffixes, such as "A" or "B," may be added to existing numbers to create enough catalogue numbers to cover all items in the set. A capital-letter suffix indicates a major Scott catalogue number listing. Scott generally uses a suffix letter only once. Therefore, a catalogue number listing with a capital-letter suffix will seldom be found with the same letter (lower case) used as a minor-letter listing. If there is a Scott 16A in a set, for example, there will seldom be a Scott 16a. However, a minor-letter "a" listing may be added to a major number containing an "A" suffix (Scott 16Aa, for example).

Suffix letters are cumulative. A minor "b" variety of Scott 16A would be Scott 16Ab, not Scott 16b.

There are times when a reserved block of Scott catalogue numbers is too large for a set, leaving some numbers unused. Such gaps in the numbering sequence also occur when the catalogue editors move an item's listing elsewhere or have removed it entirely from the catalogue. Scott does not attempt to account for every possible number, but rather attempts to assure that each stamp is assigned its own number.

Scott numbers designating regular postage normally are only numerals. Scott numbers for other types of stamps, such as air post, semi-postal, postal tax, postage due, occupation and others have a prefix consisting of one or more capital letters or a combination of numerals and capital letters.

2 Illustration number — Illustration or design-type numbers are used to identify each catalogue illustration. For most sets, the lowest face-value stamp is shown. It then serves as an example of the basic design approach for other stamps not illustrated. Where more than one stamp use the same illustration number, but have differences in design, the design paragraph or the description line clearly indicates the design on each stamp not illustrated. Where there are both vertical and horizontal designs in a set, a single illustration may be used, with the exceptions noted in the design paragraph or description line.

When an illustration is followed by a lower-case letter in parentheses, such as "A2(b)," the trailing letter indicates which overprint or surcharge illustration applies.

Illustrations normally are 70 percent of the original size of the stamp. Oversized stamps, blocks and souvenir sheets are reduced even more. Overprints and surcharges are shown at 100 percent of their original size if shown alone, but are 70 percent of original size if shown on stamps. In some cases, the illustration will be placed above the set, between listings or omitted completely. Overprint and surcharge illustrations are not placed in this catalogue for purposes of expertizing stamps.

3 Paper color — The color of a stamp's paper is noted in italic type when the paper used is not white.

4 Listing styles — There are two principal types of catalogue listings: major and minor.

Major listings are in a larger type style than minor listings. The catalogue number is a numeral that can be found with or without a capital-letter suffix, and with or without a prefix.

Minor listings are in a smaller type style and have a small-letter suffix or (if the listing immediately follows that of the major number) may show only the letter. These listings identify a variety of the major item. Examples include perforation and shade differences, multiples (some souvenir sheets, booklet panes and se-tenant combinations), and singles of multiples.

Examples of major number listings include 16, 28A, B97, C13A, 10N5, and 10N6A. Examples of minor numbers are 16a and C13Ab.

5 Basic information about a stamp or set — Introducing each stamp issue is a small section (usually a line listing) of basic information about a stamp or set. This section normally includes the date of issue, method of printing, perforation, watermark and, sometimes, some additional information of note. *Printing method, perforation and watermark apply to the following sets until a change is noted.* Stamps created by overprinting or surcharging previous issues are assumed to have the same perforation, watermark, printing method and other production characteristics as the original. Dates of issue are as precise as Scott is able to confirm and often reflect the dates on first-day covers, rather than the actual date of release.

6 Denomination — This normally refers to the face value of the stamp; that is, the cost of the unused stamp at the post office at the time of issue. When a denomination is shown in parentheses, it does not appear on the stamp. This includes the non-denominated stamps of the United States, Brazil and Great Britain, for example.

7 Color or other description — This area provides information to solidify identification of a stamp. In many recent cases, a description of the stamp design appears in this space, rather than a listing of colors.

8 Year of issue — In stamp sets that have been released in a period that spans more than a year, the number shown in parentheses is the year that stamp first appeared. Stamps without a date appeared during the first year of the issue. Dates are not always given for minor varieties.

9 Value unused and Value used — The Scott catalogue values are based on stamps that are in a grade of Very Fine unless stated otherwise. Unused values refer to items that have not seen postal, revenue or any other duty for which they were intended. Pre-1900 unused stamps that were issued with gum must have at least most of their original gum. Later issues are assumed to have full original gum. From breakpoints specified in most countries' listings, stamps are valued as never hinged. Stamps issued without gum are noted. Modern issues with PVA or other synthetic adhesives may appear ungummed. Unused self-adhesive stamps are valued as appearing undisturbed on their original backing paper. Values for used self-adhesive stamps are for examples either on piece or off piece. For a more detailed explanation of these values, please see the "Catalogue Value," "Condition" and "Understanding Valuing Notations" sections elsewhere in this introduction.

In some cases, where used stamps are more valuable than unused stamps, the value is for an example with a contemporaneous cancel, rather than a modern cancel or a smudge or other unclear marking. For those stamps that were released for postal and fiscal purposes, the used value represents a postally used stamp. Stamps with revenue cancels generally sell for less.

Stamps separated from a complete se-tenant multiple usually will be worth less than a pro-rated portion of the se-tenant multiple, and stamps lacking the attached labels that are noted in the listings will be worth less than the values shown.

10 Changes in basic set information — Bold type is used to show any changes in the basic data given for a set of stamps. These basic data categories include perforation gauge measurement, paper type, printing method and watermark.

11 Total value of a set — The total value of sets of three or more stamps issued after 1900 are shown. The set line also notes the range of Scott numbers and total number of stamps included in the grouping. The actual value of a set consisting predominantly of stamps having the minimum value of 25 cents may be less than the total value shown. Similarly, the actual value or catalogue value of se-tenant pairs or of blocks consisting of stamps having the minimum value of 25 cents may be less than the catalogue values of the component parts.

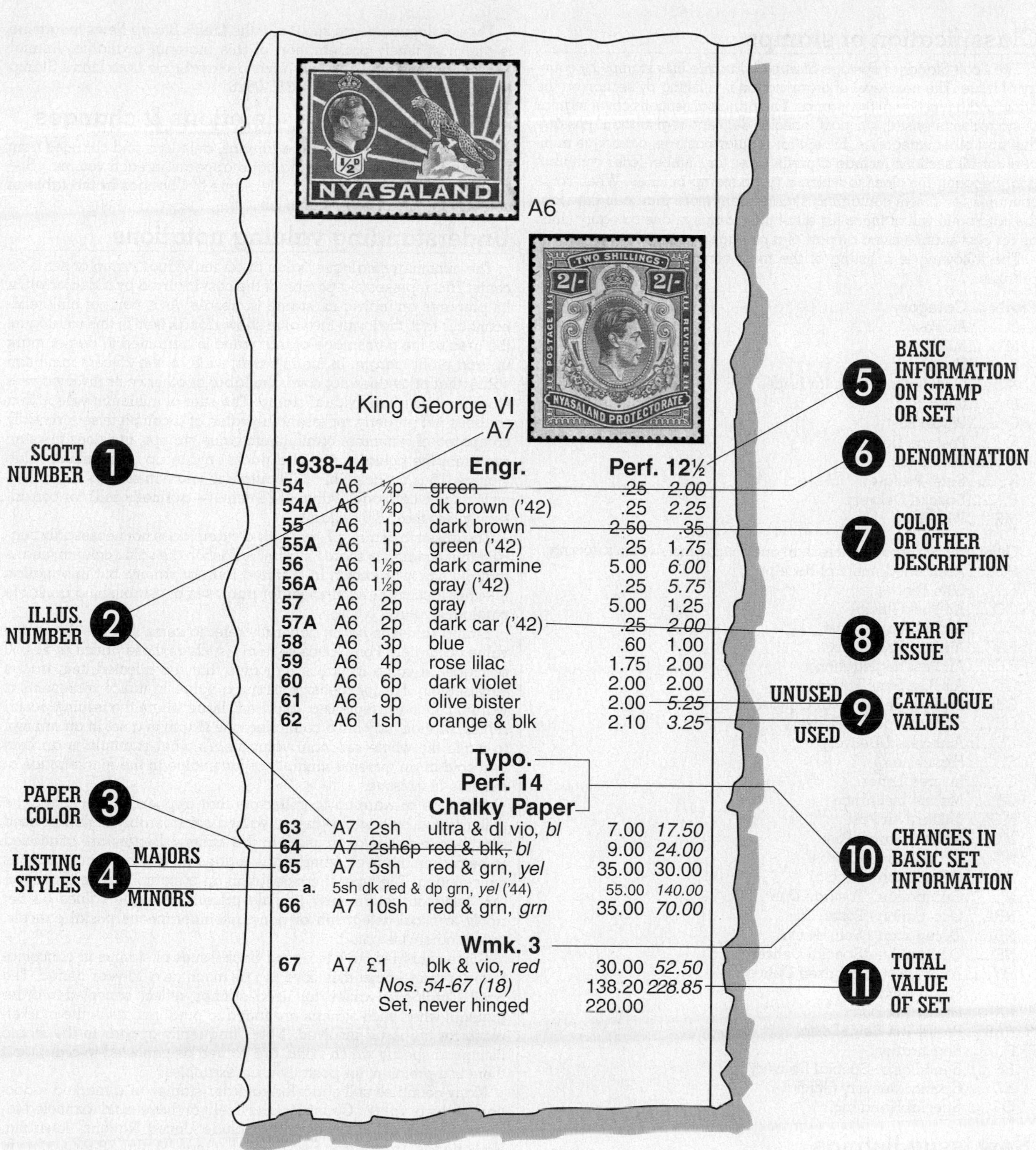

1938-44 Engr. Perf. 12½

54	A6	½p	green	.25	*2.00*
54A	A6	½p	dk brown ('42)	.25	*2.25*
55	A6	1p	dark brown	2.50	.35
55A	A6	1p	green ('42)	.25	*1.75*
56	A6	1½p	dark carmine	5.00	*6.00*
56A	A6	1½p	gray ('42)	.25	*5.75*
57	A6	2p	gray	5.00	1.25
57A	A6	2p	dark car ('42)	.25	*2.00*
58	A6	3p	blue	.60	1.00
59	A6	4p	rose lilac	1.75	2.00
60	A6	6p	dark violet	2.00	2.00
61	A6	9p	olive bister	2.00	*5.25*
62	A6	1sh	orange & blk	2.10	*3.25*

Typo.
Perf. 14
Chalky Paper

63	A7	2sh	ultra & dl vio, *bl*	7.00	*17.50*
64	A7	2sh6p	red & blk, *bl*	9.00	*24.00*
65	A7	5sh	red & grn, *yel*	35.00	30.00
a.			5sh dk red & dp grn, *yel* ('44)	55.00	*140.00*
66	A7	10sh	red & grn, *grn*	35.00	*70.00*

Wmk. 3

67	A7	£1	blk & vio, *red*	30.00	*52.50*
			Nos. 54-67 (18)	138.20	*228.85*
			Set, never hinged	220.00	

Special Notices

Classification of stamps

The *Scott Standard Postage Stamp Catalogue* lists stamps by country of issue. The next level of organization is a listing by section on the basis of the function of the stamps. The principal sections cover regular postage, semi-postal, air post, special delivery, registration, postage due and other categories. Except for regular postage, catalogue numbers for all sections include a prefix letter (or number-letter combination) denoting the class to which a given stamp belongs. When some countries issue sets containing stamps from more than one category, the catalogue will at times list all of the stamps in one category (such as air post stamps listed as part of a postage set).

The following is a listing of the most commonly used catalogue prefixes.

Prefix .... Category
C........ Air Post
M........ Military
P........ Newspaper
N........ Occupation - Regular Issues
O........ Official
Q........ Parcel Post
J........ Postage Due
RA...... Postal Tax
B........ Semi-Postal
E........ Special Delivery
MR...... War Tax

Other prefixes used by more than one country include the following:
H........ Acknowledgment of Receipt
I.......... Late Fee
CO...... Air Post Official
CQ...... Air Post Parcel Post
RAC.... Air Post Postal Tax
CF...... Air Post Registration
CB...... Air Post Semi-Postal
CBO... Air Post Semi-Postal Official
CE...... Air Post Special Delivery
EY...... Authorized Delivery
S........ Franchise
G........ Insured Letter
GY...... Marine Insurance
MC..... Military Air Post
MQ..... Military Parcel Post
NC...... Occupation - Air Post
NO...... Occupation - Official
NJ....... Occupation - Postage Due
NRA.... Occupation - Postal Tax
NB...... Occupation - Semi-Postal
NE...... Occupation - Special Delivery
QY...... Parcel Post Authorized Delivery
AR...... Postal-fiscal
RAJ..... Postal Tax Due
RAB.... Postal Tax Semi-Postal
F........ Registration
EB....... Semi-Postal Special Delivery
EO...... Special Delivery Official
QE...... Special Handling

New issue listings

Updates to this catalogue appear each month in the *Linn's Stamp News* monthly magazine. Included in this update are additions to the listings of countries found in the *Scott Standard Postage Stamp Catalogue* and the *Specialized Catalogue of United States Stamps and Covers*, as well as corrections and updates to current editions of this catalogue.

From time to time there will be changes in the final listings of stamps from the *Linn's Stamp News* magazine to the next edition of the catalogue. This occurs as more information about certain stamps or sets becomes available.

The catalogue update section of the *Linn's Stamp News* magazine is the most timely presentation of this material available. Annual subscriptions to *Linn's Stamp News* are available from Linn's Stamp News, Box 926, Sidney, OH 45365-0926.

Number additions, deletions & changes

A listing of catalogue number additions, deletions and changes from the previous edition of the catalogue appears in each volume. See Catalogue Number Additions, Deletions & Changes in the table of contents for the location of this list.

Understanding valuing notations

The *minimum catalogue value* of an individual stamp or set is 25 cents. This represents a portion of the cost incurred by a dealer when he prepares an individual stamp for resale. As a point of philatelic-economic fact, the lower the value shown for an item in this catalogue, the greater the percentage of that value is attributed to dealer mark up and profit margin. In many cases, such as the 25-cent minimum value, that price does not cover the labor or other costs involved with stocking it as an individual stamp. The sum of minimum values in a set does not properly represent the value of a complete set primarily composed of a number of minimum-value stamps, nor does the sum represent the actual value of a packet made up of minimum-value stamps. Thus a packet of 1,000 different common stamps — each of which has a catalogue value of 25 cents — normally sells for considerably less than 250 dollars!

The *absence of a retail value* for a stamp does not necessarily suggest that a stamp is scarce or rare. A dash in the value column means that the stamp is known in a stated form or variety, but information is either lacking or insufficient for purposes of establishing a usable catalogue value.

Stamp values in *italics* generally refer to items that are difficult to value accurately. For expensive items, such as those priced at $1,000 or higher, a value in italics indicates that the affected item trades very seldom. For inexpensive items, a value in italics represents a warning. One example is a "blocked" issue where the issuing postal administration may have controlled one stamp in a set in an attempt to make the whole set more valuable. Another example is an item that sold at an extreme multiple of face value in the marketplace at the time of its issue.

One type of warning to collectors that appears in the catalogue is illustrated by a stamp that is valued considerably higher in used condition than it is as unused. In this case, collectors are cautioned to be certain the used version has a genuine and contemporaneous cancellation. The type of cancellation on a stamp can be an important factor in determining its sale price. Catalogue values do not apply to fiscal, telegraph or non-contemporaneous postal cancels, unless otherwise noted.

Some countries have released back issues of stamps in canceled-to-order form, sometimes covering as much as a 10-year period. The Scott Catalogue values for used stamps reflect canceled-to-order material when such stamps are found to predominate in the marketplace for the issue involved. Notes frequently appear in the stamp listings to specify which items are valued as canceled-to-order, or if there is a premium for postally used examples.

Many countries sell canceled-to-order stamps at a marked reduction of face value. Countries that sell or have sold canceled-to-order stamps at *full* face value include United Nations, Australia, Netherlands, France and Switzerland. It may be almost impossible to identify such stamps if the gum has been removed, because official government canceling devices are used. Postally used examples of these items on cover, however, are usually worth more than the canceled-to-order stamps with original gum.

Abbreviations

Scott uses a consistent set of abbreviations throughout this catalogue to conserve space, while still providing necessary information.

COLOR ABBREVIATIONS

amb. amber	crim. crimson	ol ..... olive
anil.. aniline	cr ..... cream	olvn . olivine
ap.... apple	dk .... dark	org... orange
aqua aquamarine	dl ..... dull	pck .. peacock
az .... azure	dp .... deep	pnksh pinkish
bis ... bister	db .... drab	Prus . Prussian
bl ..... blue	emer emerald	pur... purple
bld... blood	gldn. golden	redsh reddish
blk ... black	gryshgrayish	res ... reseda
bril... brilliant	grn... green	ros ... rosine
brn... brown	grnsh greenish	ryl .... royal
brnsh brownish	hel ... heliotrope	sal ... salmon
brnz. bronze	hn .... henna	saph sapphire
brt.... bright	ind... indigo	scar . scarlet
brnt . burnt	int .... intense	sep .. sepia
car ... carmine	lav ... lavender	sien . sienna
cer ... cerise	lem .. lemon	sil.... silver
chlky chalky	lil ..... lilac	sl...... slate
chamchamois	lt ..... light	stl ..... steel
chnt . chestnut	mag. magenta	turq.. turquoise
choc chocolate	man. manila	ultra ultramarine
chr ... chrome	mar.. maroon	Ven .. Venetian
cit .... citron	mv ... mauve	ver ... vermilion
cl...... claret	multi multicolored	vio ... violet
cob .. cobalt	mlky milky	yel ... yellow
cop .. copper	myr .. myrtle	yelsh yellowish

When no color is given for an overprint or surcharge, black is the color used. Abbreviations for colors used for overprints and surcharges include: "(B)" or "(Blk)," black; "(Bl)," blue; "(R)," red; and "(G)," green.

Additional abbreviations in this catalogue are shown below:

Adm. .... Administration
AFL............... American Federation of Labor
Anniv. .... Anniversary
APS .... American Philatelic Society
Assoc. .... Association
ASSR. .... Autonomous Soviet Socialist Republic
b. .... Born
BEP............... Bureau of Engraving and Printing
Bicent. .... Bicentennial
Bklt. .... Booklet
Brit................ British
btwn. .... Between
Bur................ Bureau
c. or ca.......... Circa
Cat. .... Catalogue
Cent. .... Centennial, century, centenary
CIO .... Congress of Industrial Organizations
Conf. .... Conference
Cong. .... Congress
Cpl. .... Corporal
CTO .... Canceled to order
d. .... Died
Dbl. .... Double
EDU.............. Earliest documented use
Engr. .... Engraved
Exhib............. Exhibition
Expo.............. Exposition
Fed. .... Federation
GB .... Great Britain
Gen. .... General
GPO .... General post office
Horiz. .... Horizontal
Imperf. .... Imperforate
Impt.............. Imprint
Intl. .... International
Invtd.............. Inverted
L .... Left
Lieut., lt......... Lieutenant
Litho.............. Lithographed
LL .... Lower left
LR .... Lower right
mm .... Millimeter
Ms. .... Manuscript
Natl. .... National
No.................. Number
NY .... New York
NYC .... New York City
Ovpt. .... Overprint
Ovptd............. Overprinted
P .... Plate number
Perf................ Perforated, perforation
Phil. .... Philatelic
Photo.............. Photogravure
PO .... Post office
Pr. .... Pair
P.R................. Puerto Rico
Prec. .... Precancel, precanceled
Pres. .... President
PTT .... Post, Telephone and Telegraph
R .... Right
Rio................. Rio de Janeiro
Sgt................. Sergeant
Soc. .... Society
Souv. .... Souvenir
SSR .... Soviet Socialist Republic, see ASSR
St.................. Saint, street
Surch. .... Surcharge
Typo. .... Typographed
UL.................. Upper left
Unwmkd. ...... Unwatermarked
UPU .... Universal Postal Union
UR .... Upper Right
US .... United States
USPOD .... United States Post Office Department
USSR .... Union of Soviet Socialist Republics
Vert................ Vertical
VP .... Vice president
Wmk.............. Watermark
Wmkd. .... Watermarked
WWI .... World War I
WWII .... World War II

Examination

Amos Media Co. will not comment upon the genuineness, grade or condition of stamps, because of the time and responsibility involved. Rather, there are several expertizing groups that undertake this work for both collectors and dealers. Neither will Amos Media Co. appraise or identify philatelic material. The company cannot take responsibility for unsolicited stamps or covers sent by individuals.

All letters, E-mails, etc. are read attentively, but they are not always answered due to time considerations.

How to order from your dealer

When ordering stamps from a dealer, it is not necessary to write the full description of a stamp as listed in this catalogue. All you need is the name of the country, the Scott catalogue number and whether the desired item is unused or used. For example, "Japan Scott 422 unused" is sufficient to identify the unused stamp of Japan listed as "422 A206 5y brown."

Basic Stamp Information

A stamp collector's knowledge of the combined elements that make a given stamp issue unique determines his or her ability to identify stamps. These elements include paper, watermark, method of separation, printing, design and gum. On the following pages each of these important areas is briefly described.

Paper

Paper is an organic material composed of a compacted weave of cellulose fibers and generally formed into sheets. Paper used to print stamps may be manufactured in sheets, or it may have been part of a large roll (called a web) before being cut to size. The fibers most often used to create paper on which stamps are printed include bark, wood, straw and certain grasses. In many cases, linen or cotton rags have been added for greater strength and durability. Grinding, bleaching, cooking and rinsing these raw fibers reduces them to a slushy pulp, referred to by paper makers as "stuff." Sizing and, sometimes, coloring matter is added to the pulp to make different types of finished paper.

After the stuff is prepared, it is poured onto sieve-like frames that allow the water to run off, while retaining the matted pulp. As fibers fall onto the screen and are held by gravity, they form a natural weave that will later hold the paper together. If the screen has metal bits that are formed into letters or images attached, it leaves slightly thinned areas on the paper. These are called watermarks.

When the stuff is almost dry, it is passed under pressure through smooth or engraved rollers - dandy rolls - or placed between cloth in a press to be flattened and dried.

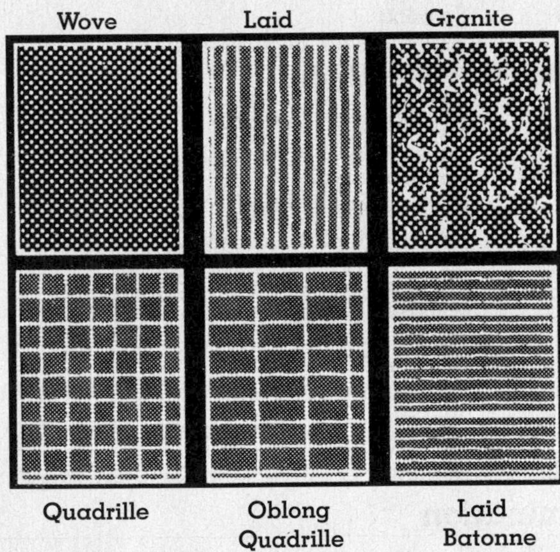

Stamp paper falls broadly into two types: wove and laid. The nature of the surface of the frame onto which the pulp is first deposited causes the differences in appearance between the two. If the surface is smooth and even, the paper will be of fairly uniform texture throughout. This is known as *wove paper*. Early papermaking machines poured the pulp onto a continuously circulating web of felt, but modern machines feed the pulp onto a cloth-like screen made of closely interwoven fine wires. This paper, when held to a light, will show little dots or points very close together. The proper name for this is "wire wove," but the type is still considered wove. Any U.S. or British stamp printed after 1880 will serve as an example of wire wove paper.

Closely spaced parallel wires, with cross wires at wider intervals, make up the frames used for what is known as *laid paper*. A greater thickness of the pulp will settle between the wires. The paper, when held to a light, will show alternate light and dark lines. The spacing and the thickness of the lines may vary, but on any one sheet of paper they are all alike. See Russia Scott 31-38 for examples of laid paper.

Batonne, from the French word meaning "a staff," is a term used if the lines in the paper are spaced quite far apart, like the printed ruling on a writing tablet. Batonne paper may be either wove or laid. If laid, fine laid lines can be seen between the batons.

Quadrille is the term used when the lines in the paper form little squares. *Oblong quadrille* is the term used when rectangles, rather than squares, are formed. Grid patterns vary from distinct to extremely faint. See Mexico-Guadalajara Scott 35-37 for examples of oblong quadrille paper.

Paper also is classified as thick or thin, hard or soft, and by color. Such colors may include yellowish, greenish, bluish and reddish.

Brief explanations of other types of paper used for printing stamps, as well as examples, follow.

Colored — Colored paper is created by the addition of dye in the paper-making process. Such colors may include shades of yellow, green, blue and red. *Surface-colored papers*, most commonly used for British colonial issues in 1913-14, are created when coloring is added only to the surface during the finishing process. Stamps printed on surface-colored paper have white or uncolored backs, while true colored papers are colored through. See Jamaica Scott 71-73.

Pelure — Pelure paper is a very thin, hard and often brittle paper that is sometimes bluish or grayish in appearance. See Serbia Scott 169-170.

Native — This is a term applied to handmade papers used to produce some of the early stamps of the Indian states. Stamps printed on native paper may be expected to display various natural inclusions that are normal and do not negatively affect value. Japanese paper, originally made of mulberry fibers and rice flour, is part of this group. See Japan Scott 1-18.

Manila — This type of paper is often used to make stamped envelopes and wrappers. It is a coarse-textured stock, usually smooth on one side and rough on the other. A variety of colors of manila paper exist, but the most common range is yellowish-brown.

Silk — Introduced by the British in 1847 as a safeguard against counterfeiting, silk paper contains bits of colored silk thread scattered throughout. The density of these fibers varies greatly and can include as few as one fiber per stamp or hundreds. U.S. revenue Scott R152 is a good example of an easy-to-identify silk paper stamp.

Silk-thread paper has uninterrupted threads of colored silk arranged so that one or more threads run through the stamp or postal stationery. See Great Britain Scott 5-6 and Switzerland Scott 14-19.

Granite — Filled with minute cloth or colored paper fibers of various colors and lengths, granite paper should not be confused with either type of silk paper. Austria Scott 172-175 and a number of Swiss stamps are examples of granite paper.

Chalky — A chalk-like substance coats the surface of chalky paper to discourage the cleaning and reuse of canceled stamps, as well as to provide a smoother, more acceptable printing surface. Because the designs of stamps printed on chalky paper are imprinted on what is often a water-soluble coating, any attempt to remove a cancellation will destroy the stamp. *Do not soak these stamps in any fluid.* To remove a stamp printed on chalky paper from an envelope, wet the paper from underneath the stamp until the gum dissolves enough to release the stamp from the paper. See St. Kitts-Nevis Scott 89-90 for examples of stamps printed on this type of chalky paper.

India — Another name for this paper, originally introduced from China about 1750, is "China Paper." It is a thin, opaque paper often used for plate and die proofs by many countries.

Double — In philately, the term double paper has two distinct meanings. The first is a two-ply paper, usually a combination of a thick and a thin sheet, joined during manufacture. This type was used experimentally as a means to discourage the reuse of stamps.

The design is printed on the thin paper. Any attempt to remove a cancellation would destroy the design. U.S. Scott 158 and other Banknote-era stamps exist on this form of double paper.

The second type of double paper occurs on a rotary press, when the end of one paper roll, or web, is affixed to the next roll to save time feeding the paper through the press. Stamp designs are printed over the joined paper and, if overlooked by inspectors, may get into post office stocks.

Goldbeater's Skin — This type of paper was used for the 1866 issue of Prussia, and was a tough, translucent paper. The design was printed in reverse on the back of the stamp, and the gum applied over the printing. It is impossible to remove stamps printed on this type of paper from the paper to which they are affixed without destroying the design.

Ribbed — Ribbed paper has an uneven, corrugated surface made by passing the paper through ridged rollers. This type exists on some copies of U.S. Scott 156-165.

Various other substances, or substrates, have been used for stamp manufacture, including wood, aluminum, copper, silver and gold foil, plastic, and silk and cotton fabrics.

Watermarks

Watermarks are an integral part of some papers. They are formed in the process of paper manufacture. Watermarks consist of small designs, formed of wire or cut from metal and soldered to the surface of the mold or, sometimes, on the dandy roll. The designs may be in the form of crowns, stars, anchors, letters or other characters or symbols. These pieces of metal - known in the paper-making industry as "bits" - impress a design into the paper. The design sometimes may be seen by holding the stamp to the light. Some are more easily seen with a watermark detector. This important tool is a small black tray into which a stamp is placed face down and dampened with a fast-evaporating watermark detection fluid that brings up the watermark image in the form of dark lines against a lighter background. These dark lines are the thinner areas of the paper known as the watermark. Some watermarks are extremely difficult to locate, due to either a faint impression, watermark location or the color of the stamp. There also are electric watermark detectors that come with plastic filter disks of various colors. The disks neutralize the color of the stamp, permitting the watermark to be seen more easily.

Multiple watermarks of Crown Agents and Burma

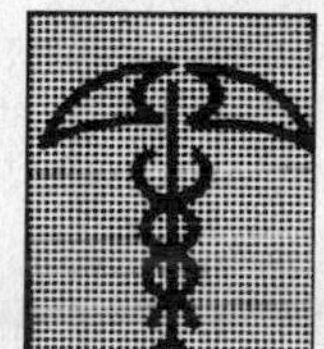

Watermarks of Uruguay, Vatican City and Jamaica

WARNING: Some inks used in the photogravure process dissolve in watermark fluids (Please see the section on Soluble Printing Inks). Also, see "chalky paper."

Watermarks may be found normal, reversed, inverted, reversed and inverted, sideways or diagonal, as seen from the back of the stamp. The relationship of watermark to stamp design depends on the position of the printing plates or how paper is fed through the press. On machine-made paper, watermarks normally are read from right to left. The design is repeated closely throughout the sheet in a "multiple-watermark design." In a "sheet watermark," the design appears only once on the sheet, but extends over many stamps. Individual stamps may carry only a small fraction or none of the watermark.

"Marginal watermarks" occur in the margins of sheets or panes of stamps. They occur on the outside border of paper (ostensibly outside the area where stamps are to be printed). A large row of letters may spell the name of the country or the manufacturer of the paper, or a border of lines may appear. Careless press feeding may cause parts of these letters and/or lines to show on stamps of the outer row of a pane.

Soluble Printing Inks

WARNING: Most stamp colors are permanent; that is, they are not seriously affected by short-term exposure to light or water. Many colors, especially of modern inks, fade from excessive exposure to light. There are stamps printed with inks that dissolve easily in water or in fluids used to detect watermarks. Use of these inks was intentional to prevent the removal of cancellations. Water affects all aniline inks, those on so-called safety paper and some photogravure printings - all such inks are known as fugitive colors. *Removal from paper of such stamps requires care and alternatives to traditional soaking.*

Separation

"Separation" is the general term used to describe methods used to separate stamps. The three standard forms currently in use are perforating, rouletting and die-cutting. These methods are done during the stamp production process, after printing. Sometimes these methods are done on-press or sometimes as a separate step. The earliest issues, such as the 1840 Penny Black of Great Britain (Scott 1), did not have any means provided for separation. It was expected the stamps would be cut apart with scissors or folded and torn. These are examples of imperforate stamps. Many stamps were first issued in imperforate formats and were later issued with perforations. Therefore, care must be observed in buying single imperforate stamps to be certain they were issued imperforate and are not perforated copies that have been altered by having the perforations trimmed away. Stamps issued imperforate usually are valued as singles. However, imperforate varieties of normally perforated stamps should be collected in pairs or larger pieces as indisputable evidence of their imperforate character.

PERFORATION

The chief style of separation of stamps, and the one that is in almost universal use today, is perforating. By this process, paper between the stamps is cut away in a line of holes, usually round, leaving little bridges of paper between the stamps to hold them together. Some types of perforation, such as hyphen-hole perfs, can be confused with roulettes, but a close visual inspection reveals that paper has been removed. The little perforation bridges, which project from the stamp when it is torn from the pane, are called the teeth of the perforation.

As the size of the perforation is sometimes the only way to differentiate between two otherwise identical stamps, it is necessary to be able to accurately measure and describe them. This is done with a perforation gauge, usually a ruler-like device that has dots or graduated lines to show how many perforations may be counted in the space of two centimeters. Two centimeters is the space universally adopted in which to measure perforations.

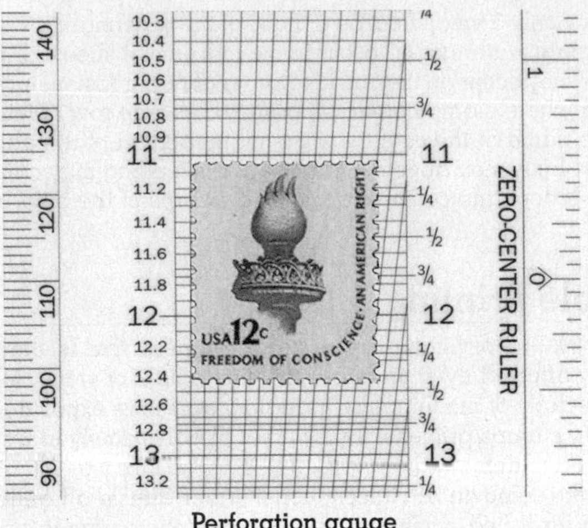

Perforation gauge

To measure a stamp, run it along the gauge until the dots on it fit exactly into the perforations of the stamp. If you are using a graduated-line perforation gauge, simply slide the stamp along the surface until the lines on the gauge perfectly project from the center of the bridges or holes. The number to the side of the line of dots or lines that fit the stamp's perforation is the measurement. For example, an "11" means that 11 perforations fit between two centimeters. The description of the stamp therefore is "perf. 11." If the gauge of the perforations on the top and bottom of a stamp differs from that on the sides, the result is what is known as *compound perforations.* In measuring compound perforations, the gauge at top and bottom is always given first, then the sides. Thus, a stamp that measures 11 at top and bottom and 10½ at the sides is "perf. 11 x 10½." See U.S. Scott 632-642 for examples of compound perforations.

Stamps also are known with perforations different on three or all four sides. Descriptions of such items are clockwise, beginning with the top of the stamp.

A perforation with small holes and teeth close together is a "fine perforation." One with large holes and teeth far apart is a "coarse perforation." Holes that are jagged, rather than clean-cut, are "rough perforations." *Blind perforations* are the slight impressions left by the perforating pins if they fail to puncture the paper. Multiples of stamps showing blind perforations may command a slight premium over normally perforated stamps.

The term *syncopated perfs* describes intentional irregularities in the perforations. The earliest form was used by the Netherlands from 1925-33, where holes were omitted to create distinctive patterns. Beginning in 1992, Great Britain has used an oval perforation to help prevent counterfeiting. Several other countries have started using the oval perfs or other syncopated perf patterns.

A new type of perforation, still primarily used for postal stationery, is known as microperfs. Microperfs are tiny perforations (in some cases hundreds of holes per two centimeters) that allows items to be intentionally separated very easily, while not accidentally breaking apart as easily as standard perforations. These are not currently measured or differentiated by size, as are standard perforations.

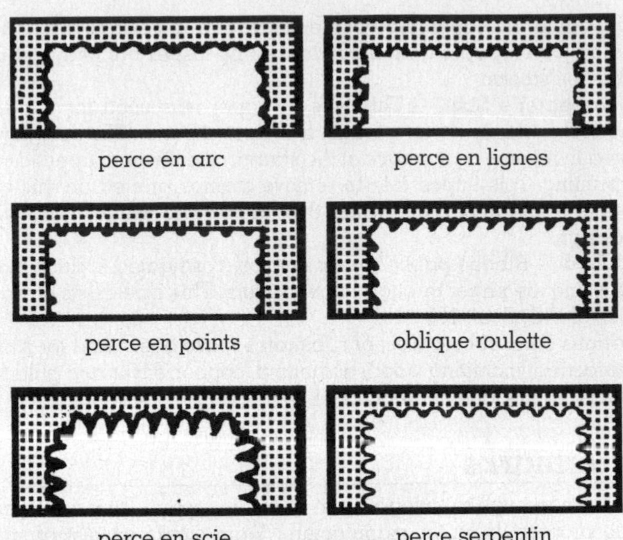

ROULETTING

In rouletting, the stamp paper is cut partly or wholly through, with no paper removed. In perforating, some paper is removed. Rouletting derives its name from the French roulette, a spur-like wheel. As the wheel is rolled over the paper, each point makes a small cut. The number of cuts made in a two-centimeter space determines the gauge of the roulette, just as the number of perforations in two centimeters determines the gauge of the perforation.

The shape and arrangement of the teeth on the wheels varies. Various roulette types generally carry French names:

Perce en lignes - rouletted in lines. The paper receives short, straight cuts in lines. This is the most common type of rouletting. See Mexico Scott 500.

Perce en points - pin-rouletted or pin-perfed. This differs from a small perforation because no paper is removed, although round, equidistant holes are pricked through the paper. See Mexico Scott 242-256.

Perce en arc and *perce en scie* - pierced in an arc or saw-toothed designs, forming half circles or small triangles. See Hanover (German States) Scott 25-29.

Perce en serpentin - serpentine roulettes. The cuts form a serpentine or wavy line. See Brunswick (German States) Scott 13-18.

Once again, no paper is removed by these processes, leaving the stamps easily separated, but closely attached.

DIE-CUTTING

The third major form of stamp separation is die-cutting. This is a method where a die in the pattern of separation is created that later cuts the stamp paper in a stroke motion. Although some standard stamps bear die-cut perforations, this process is primarily used for self-adhesive postage stamps. Die-cutting can appear in straight lines, such as U.S. Scott 2522, shapes, such as U.S. Scott 1551, or imitating the appearance of perforations, such as New Zealand Scott 935A and 935B.

Printing Processes

ENGRAVING (Intaglio, Line-engraving, Etching)

Master die — The initial operation in the process of line engraving is making the master die. The die is a small, flat block of softened steel upon which the stamp design is recess engraved in reverse.

Master die

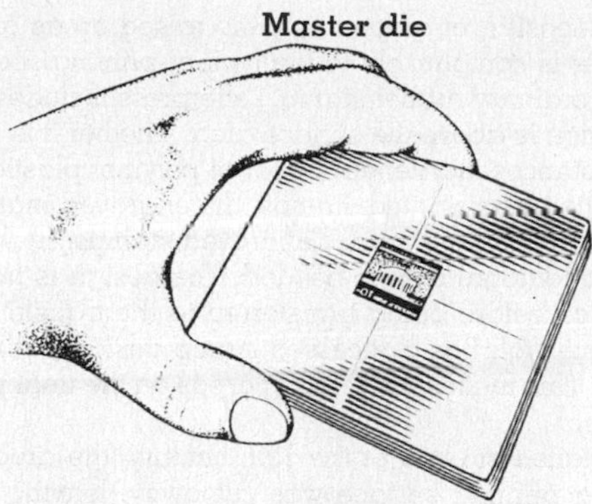

Photographic reduction of the original art is made to the appropriate size. It then serves as a tracing guide for the initial outline of the design. The engraver lightly traces the design on the steel with his graver, then slowly works the design until it is completed. At various points during the engraving process, the engraver hand-inks the die and makes an impression to check his progress. These are known as progressive die proofs. After completion of the engraving, the die is hardened to withstand the stress and pressures of later transfer operations.

Transfer roll

Transfer roll — Next is production of the transfer roll that, as the name implies, is the medium used to transfer the subject from the master die to the printing plate. A blank roll of soft steel, mounted on a mandrel, is placed under the bearers of the transfer press to allow it to roll freely on its axis. The hardened die is placed on the bed of the press and the face of the transfer roll is applied to the die, under pressure. The bed or the roll is then rocked back and forth under increasing pressure, until the soft steel of the roll is forced into every engraved line of the die. The resulting impression on the roll is known as a "relief" or a "relief transfer." The engraved image is now positive in appearance and stands out from the steel. After the required number of reliefs are "rocked in," the soft steel transfer roll is hardened.

Different flaws may occur during the relief process. A defective relief may occur during the rocking in process because of a minute piece of foreign material lodging on the die, or some other cause. Imperfections in the steel of the transfer roll may result in a breaking away of parts of the design. This is known as a relief break, which will show up on finished stamps as small, unprinted areas. If a damaged relief remains in use, it will transfer a repeating defect to the plate. Deliberate alterations of reliefs sometimes occur. "Altered reliefs" designate these changed conditions.

Plate — The final step in pre-printing production is the making of the printing plate. A flat piece of soft steel replaces the die on the bed of the transfer press. One of the reliefs on the transfer roll is positioned over this soft steel. Position, or layout, dots determine the correct position on the plate. The dots have been lightly marked on the plate in advance. After the correct position of the relief is determined, the design is rocked in by following the same method used in making the transfer roll. The difference is that this time the image is being transferred from the transfer roll, rather than to it. Once the design is entered on the plate, it appears in reverse and is recessed. There are as many transfers entered on the plate as there are subjects printed on the sheet of stamps. It is during this process that double and shifted transfers occur, as well as re-entries. These are the result of improperly entered images that have not been properly burnished out prior to rocking in a new image.

Modern siderography processes, such as those used by the U.S. Bureau of Engraving and Printing, involve an automated form of rocking designs in on preformed cylindrical printing sleeves. The same process also allows for easier removal and re-entry of worn images right on the sleeve.

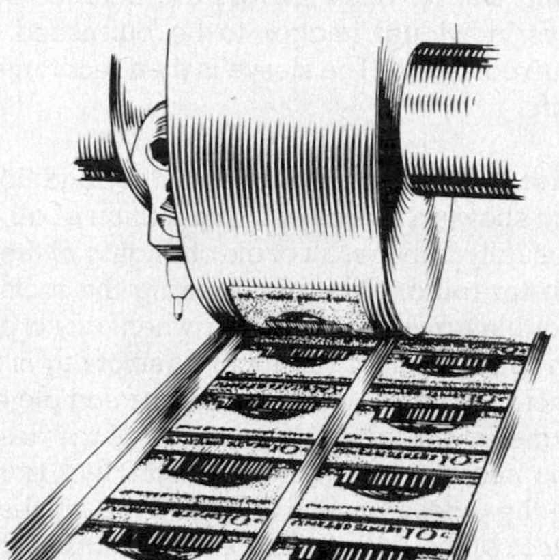

Transferring the design to the plate

Following the entering of the required transfers on the plate, the position dots, layout dots and lines, scratches and other markings generally are burnished out. Added at this time by the siderographer are any required *guide lines, plate numbers* or other *marginal markings.* The plate is then hand-inked and a proof impression is taken. This is known as a plate proof. If the impression is approved, the plate is machined for fitting onto the press, is hardened and sent to the plate vault ready for use.

On press, the plate is inked and the surface is automatically wiped clean, leaving ink only in the recessed lines. Paper is then forced under pressure into the engraved recessed lines, thereby receiving the ink. Thus, the ink lines on engraved stamps are slightly raised, and slight depressions (debossing) occur on the back of the stamp. Prior to the advent of modern high-speed presses and more advanced ink formulations, paper had to be dampened before receiving the ink. This sometimes led to uneven shrinkage by the time the stamps were perforated, resulting in improperly perforated stamps, or misperfs. Newer presses use drier paper, thus both *wet* and *dry printings* exist on some stamps.

Rotary Press — Until 1914, only flat plates were used to print engraved stamps. Rotary press printing was introduced in 1914, and slowly spread. Some countries still use flat-plate printing.

After approval of the plate proof, older *rotary press plates* require additional machining. They are curved to fit the press cylinder. "Gripper slots" are cut into the back of each plate to receive the "grippers," which hold the plate securely on the press. The plate is then hardened. Stamps printed from these bent rotary press plates are longer or wider than the same stamps printed from flat-plate presses. The stretching of the plate during the curving process is what causes this distortion.

Re-entry — To execute a re-entry on a flat plate, the transfer roll is re-applied to the plate, often at some time after its first use on the press. Worn-out designs can be resharpened by carefully burnishing out the original image and re-entering it from the transfer roll. If the original impression has not been sufficiently removed and the transfer roll is not precisely in line with the remaining impression, the resulting double transfer will make the re-entry obvious. If the registration is true, a re-entry may be difficult or impossible to distinguish. Sometimes a stamp printed from a successful re-entry is identified by having a much sharper and clearer impression than its neighbors. With the advent of rotary presses, post-press re-entries were not possible. After a plate was curved for the rotary press, it was impossible to make a re-entry. This is because the plate had already been bent once (with the design distorted).

However, with the introduction of the previously mentioned modern-style siderography machines, entries are made to the preformed cylindrical printing sleeve. Such sleeves are dechromed and softened. This allows individual images to be burnished out and re-entered on the curved sleeve. The sleeve is then rechromed, resulting in longer press life.

Double Transfer — This is a description of the condition of a transfer on a plate that shows evidence of a duplication of all, or a portion of the design. It usually is the result of the changing of the registration between the transfer roll and the plate during the rocking in of the original entry. Double transfers also occur when only a portion of the design has been rocked in and improper positioning is noted. If the worker elected not to burnish out the partial or completed design, a strong double transfer will occur for part or all of the design.

It sometimes is necessary to remove the original transfer from a plate and repeat the process a second time. If the finished re-worked image shows traces of the original impression, attributable to incomplete burnishing, the result is a partial double transfer.

With the modern automatic machines mentioned previously, double transfers are all but impossible to create. Those partially doubled images on stamps printed from such sleeves are more than likely re-entries, rather than true double transfers.

Re-engraved — Alterations to a stamp design are sometimes necessary after some stamps have been printed. In some cases, either the original die or the actual printing plate may have its "temper" drawn (softened), and the design will be re-cut. The resulting impressions from such a re-engraved die or plate may differ slightly from the original issue, and are known as "re-engraved." If the alteration was made to the master die, all future printings will be consistently different from the original. If alterations were made to the printing plate, each altered stamp on the plate will be slightly different from each other, allowing specialists to reconstruct a complete printing plate.

Dropped Transfers — If an impression from the transfer roll has not been properly placed, a dropped transfer may occur. The final stamp image will appear obviously out of line with its neighbors.

Short Transfer — Sometimes a transfer roll is not rocked its entire length when entering a transfer onto a plate. As a result, the finished transfer on the plate fails to show the complete design, and the finished stamp will have an incomplete design printed. This is known as a "short transfer." U.S. Scott No. 8 is a good example of a short transfer.

TYPOGRAPHY (Letterpress, Surface Printing, Flexography, Dry Offset, High Etch)

Although the word "Typography" is obsolete as a term describing a printing method, it was the accepted term throughout the first century of postage stamps. Therefore, appropriate Scott listings in this catalogue refer to typographed stamps. The current term for this form of printing, however, is "letterpress."

As it relates to the production of postage stamps, letterpress printing is the reverse of engraving. Rather than having recessed areas trap the ink and deposit it on paper, only the raised areas of the design are inked. This is comparable to the type of printing seen by inking and using an ordinary rubber stamp. Letterpress includes all printing where the design is above the surface area, whether it is wood, metal or, in some instances, hardened rubber or polymer plastic.

For most letterpress-printed stamps, the engraved master is made in much the same manner as for engraved stamps. In this instance, however, an additional step is needed. The design is transferred to another surface before being transferred to the transfer roll. In this way, the transfer roll has a recessed stamp design, rather than one done in relief. This makes the printing areas on the final plate raised, or relief areas.

For less-detailed stamps of the 19th century, the area on the die not used as a printing surface was cut away, leaving the surface area raised. The original die was then reproduced by stereotyping or electrotyping. The resulting electrotypes were assembled in the required number and format of the desired sheet of stamps. The plate used in printing the stamps was an electroplate of these assembled electrotypes.

Once the final letterpress plates are created, ink is applied to the raised surface and the pressure of the press transfers the ink impression to the paper. In contrast to engraving, the fine lines of letterpress are impressed on the surface of the stamp, leaving a debossed surface. When viewed from the back (as on a typewritten page), the corresponding line work on the stamp will be raised slightly (embossed) above the surface.

PHOTOGRAVURE (Gravure, Rotogravure, Heliogravure)

In this process, the basic principles of photography are applied to a chemically sensitized metal plate, rather than photographic paper. The design is transferred photographically to the plate through a halftone, or dot-matrix screen, breaking the reproduction into tiny dots. The plate is treated chemically and the dots form depressions, called cells, of varying depths and diameters, depending on the degrees of shade in the design. Then, like engraving, ink is applied to the plate and the surface is wiped clean. This leaves ink in the tiny cells that is lifted out and deposited on the paper when it is pressed against the plate.

Gravure is most often used for multicolored stamps, generally using the three primary colors (red, yellow and blue) and black. By varying the dot matrix pattern and density of these colors, virtually any color can be reproduced. A typical full-color gravure stamp will be created from four printing cylinders (one for each color). The original multicolored image will have been photographically separated into its component colors.

Modern gravure printing may use computer-generated dot-matrix screens, and modern plates may be of various types including metal-coated plastic. The catalogue designation of Photogravure (or "Photo") covers any of these older and more modern gravure methods of printing.

For examples of the first photogravure stamps printed (1914), see Bavaria Scott 94-114.

LITHOGRAPHY (Offset Lithography, Stone Lithography, Dilitho, Planography, Collotype)

The principle that oil and water do not mix is the basis for lithography. The stamp design is drawn by hand or transferred from engraving to the surface of a lithographic stone or metal plate in a greasy (oily) substance. This oily substance holds the ink, which will later be transferred to the paper. The stone (or plate) is wet with an acid fluid, causing it to repel the printing ink in all areas not covered by the greasy substance.

Transfer paper is used to transfer the design from the original stone or plate. A series of duplicate transfers are grouped and, in turn, transferred to the final printing plate.

Photolithography — The application of photographic processes to lithography. This process allows greater flexibility of design, related to use of halftone screens combined with line work. Unlike photogravure or engraving, this process can allow large, solid areas to be printed.

Offset — A refinement of the lithographic process. A rubber-covered blanket cylinder takes the impression from the inked lithographic plate. From the "blanket" the impression is *offset* or transferred to the paper. Greater flexibility and speed are the principal reasons offset printing has largely displaced lithography. The term "lithography" covers both processes, and results are almost identical.

EMBOSSED (Relief) Printing

Embossing, not considered one of the four main printing types, is a method in which the design first is sunk into the metal of the die. Printing is done against a yielding platen, such as leather or linoleum. The platen is forced into the depression of the die, thus forming the design on the paper in relief. This process is often used for metallic inks.

Embossing may be done without color (see Sardinia Scott 4-6); with color printed around the embossed area (see Great Britain Scott 5 and most U.S. envelopes); and with color in exact registration with the embossed subject (see Canada Scott 656-657).

HOLOGRAMS

For objects to appear as holograms on stamps, a model exactly the same size as it is to appear on the hologram must be created. Rather than using photographic film to capture the image, holography records an image on a photoresist material. In processing, chemicals eat away at certain exposed areas, leaving a pattern of constructive and destructive interference. When the photoresist is developed, the result is a pattern of uneven ridges that acts as a mold. This mold is then coated with metal, and the resulting form is used to press copies in much the same way phonograph records are produced.

A typical reflective hologram used for stamps consists of a reproduction of the uneven patterns on a plastic film that is applied to a reflective background, usually a silver or gold foil. Light is reflected off the background through the film, making the pattern present on the film visible. Because of the uneven pattern of the film, the viewer will perceive the objects in their proper three-dimensional relationships with appropriate brightness.

The first hologram on a stamp was produced by Austria in 1988 (Scott 1441).

FOIL APPLICATION

A modern technique of applying color to stamps involves the application of metallic foil to the stamp paper. A pattern of foil is applied to the stamp paper by use of a stamping die. The foil usually is flat, but it may be textured. Canada Scott 1735 has three different foil applications in pearl, bronze and gold. The gold foil was textured using a chemical-etch copper embossing die. The printing of this stamp also involved two-color offset lithography plus embossing.

THERMOGRAPHY

In the 1990s stamps began to be enhanced with thermographic printing. In this process, a powdered polymer is applied over a sheet that has just been printed. The powder adheres to ink that lacks drying or hardening agents and does not adhere to areas where the ink has these agents. The excess powder is removed and the sheet is briefly heated to melt the powder. The melted powder solidifies after cooling, producing a raised, shiny effect on the stamps. See Scott New Caledonia C239-C240.

COMBINATION PRINTINGS

Sometimes two or even three printing methods are combined in producing stamps. In these cases, such as Austria Scott 933 or Canada 1735 (described in the preceding paragraph), the multiple-printing technique can be determined by studying the individual characteristics of each printing type. A few stamps, such as Singapore Scott 684-684A, combine as many as three of the four major printing types (lithography, engraving and typography). When this is done it often indicates the incorporation of security devices against counterfeiting.

INK COLORS

Inks or colored papers used in stamp printing often are of mineral origin, although there are numerous examples of organic-based pigments. As a general rule, organic-based pigments are far more subject to varieties and change than those of mineral-based origin.

The appearance of any given color on a stamp may be affected by many aspects, including printing variations, light, color of paper, aging and chemical alterations.

Numerous printing variations may be observed. Heavier pressure or inking will cause a more intense color, while slight interruptions in the ink feed or lighter impressions will cause a lighter appearance. Stamps printed in the same color by water-based and solvent-based inks can differ significantly in appearance. This affects several stamps in the U.S. Prominent Americans series. Hand-mixed ink formulas (primarily from the 19th century) produced under different conditions (humidity and temperature) account for notable color variations in early printings of the same stamp (see U.S. Scott 248-250, 279B, for example). Different sources of pigment can also result in significant differences in color.

Light exposure and aging are closely related in the way they affect stamp color. Both eventually break down the ink and fade colors, so that a carefully kept stamp may differ significantly in color from an identical copy that has been exposed to light. If stamps are exposed to light either intentionally or accidentally, their colors can be faded or completely changed in some cases.

Papers of different quality and consistency used for the same stamp printing may affect color appearance. Most pelure papers, for example, show a richer color when compared with wove or laid papers. See Russia Scott 181a, for an example of this effect.

The very nature of the printing processes can cause a variety of differences in shades or hues of the same stamp. Some of these shades are scarcer than others, and are of particular interest to the advanced collector.

Luminescence

All forms of tagged stamps fall under the general category of luminescence. Within this broad category is fluorescence, dealing with forms of tagging visible under longwave ultraviolet light, and phosphorescence, which deals with tagging visible only under shortwave light. Phosphorescence leaves an afterglow and fluorescence does not. These treated stamps show up in a range of different colors when exposed to UV light. The differing wavelengths of the light activates the tagging material, making it glow in various colors that usually serve different mail processing purposes.

Intentional tagging is a post-World War II phenomenon, brought about by the increased literacy rate and rapidly growing mail volume. It was one of several answers to the problem of the need for more automated mail processes. Early tagged stamps served the purpose of triggering machines to separate different types of mail. A natural outgrowth was to also use the signal to trigger machines that faced all envelopes the same way and canceled them.

Tagged stamps come in many different forms. Some tagged stamps have luminescent shapes or images imprinted on them as a form of security device. Others have blocks (United States), stripes, frames (South Africa and Canada), overall coatings (United States), bars (Great Britain and Canada) and many other types. Some types of tagging are even mixed in with the pigmented printing ink (Australia Scott 366, Netherlands Scott 478 and U.S. Scott 1359 and 2443).

The means of applying taggant to stamps differs as much as the intended purposes for the stamps. The most common form of tagging is a coating applied to the surface of the printed stamp. Since the taggant ink is frequently invisible except under UV light, it does not interfere with the appearance of the stamp. Another common application is the use of phosphored papers. In this case the paper itself either has a coating of taggant applied before the stamp is printed, has taggant applied during the papermaking process (incorporating it into the fibers), or has the taggant mixed into the coating of the paper. The latter method, among others, is currently in use in the United States.

Many countries now use tagging in various forms to either expedite mail handling or to serve as a printing security device against counterfeiting. Following the introduction of tagged stamps for public use in 1959 by Great Britain, other countries have steadily joined the parade. Among those are Germany (1961); Canada and Denmark (1962); United States, Australia, France and Switzerland (1963); Belgium and Japan (1966); Sweden and Norway (1967); Italy (1968); and Russia (1969). Since then, many other countries have begun using forms of tagging, including Brazil, China, Czechoslovakia, Hong Kong, Guatemala, Indonesia, Israel, Lithuania, Luxembourg, Netherlands, Penrhyn Islands, Portugal, St. Vincent, Singapore, South Africa, Spain and Sweden to name a few.

In some cases, including United States, Canada, Great Britain and Switzerland, stamps were released both with and without tagging. Many of these were released during each country's experimental period. Tagged and untagged versions are listed for the aforementioned countries and are noted in some other countries' listings. For at least a few stamps, the experimentally tagged version is worth far more than its untagged counterpart, such as the 1963 experimental tagged version of France Scott 1024.

In some cases, luminescent varieties of stamps were inadvertently created. Several Russian stamps, for example, sport highly fluorescent ink that was not intended as a form of tagging. Older stamps, such as early U.S. postage dues, can be positively identified by the use of UV light, since the organic ink used has become slightly fluorescent over time. Other stamps, such as Austria Scott 70a-82a (varnish bars) and Obock Scott 46-64 (printed quadrille lines), have become fluorescent over time.

Various fluorescent substances have been added to paper to make it appear brighter. These optical brightners, as they are known, greatly affect the appearance of the stamp under UV light. The brightest of these is known as Hi-Brite paper. These paper varieties are beyond the scope of the Scott Catalogue.

Shortwave UV light also is used extensively in expertizing, since each form of paper has its own fluorescent characteristics that are impossible to perfectly match. It is therefore a simple matter to detect filled thins, added perforation teeth and other alterations that involve the addition of paper. UV light also is used to examine stamps that have had cancels chemically removed and for other purposes as well.

Gum

The Illustrated Gum Chart in the first part of this introduction shows and defines various types of gum condition. Because gum condition has an important impact on the value of unused stamps, we recommend studying this chart and the accompanying text carefully.

The gum on the back of a stamp may be shiny, dull, smooth, rough, dark, white, colored or tinted. Most stamp gumming adhesives use gum arabic or dextrine as a base. Certain polymers such as polyvinyl alcohol (PVA) have been used extensively since World War II.

The *Scott Standard Postage Stamp Catalogue* does not list items by types of gum. The *Scott Specialized Catalogue of United States Stamps and Covers* does differentiate among some types of gum for certain issues.

Reprints of stamps may have gum differing from the original issues. In addition, some countries have used different gum formulas for different seasons. These adhesives have different properties that may become more apparent over time.

Many stamps have been issued without gum, and the catalogue will note this fact. See, for example, United States Scott 40-47. Sometimes, gum may have been removed to preserve the stamp. Germany Scott B68, for example, has a highly acidic gum that eventually destroys the stamps. This item is valued in the catalogue with gum removed.

Reprints and Reissues

These are impressions of stamps (usually obsolete) made from the original plates or stones. If they are valid for postage and reproduce obsolete issues (such as U.S. Scott 102-111), the stamps are *reissues.* If they are from current issues, they are designated as *second, third,* etc., *printing*. If designated for a particular purpose, they are called *special printings.*

When special printings are not valid for postage, but are made from original dies and plates by authorized persons, they are *official reprints. Private reprints* are made from the original plates and dies by private hands. An example of a private reprint is that of the 1871-1932 reprints made from the original die of the 1845 New Haven, Conn., postmaster's provisional. *Official reproductions* or imitations are made from new dies and plates by government authorization. Scott will list those reissues that are valid for postage if they differ significantly from the original printing.

The U.S. government made special printings of its first postage stamps in 1875. Produced were official imitations of the first two stamps (listed as Scott 3-4), reprints of the demonetized pre-1861 issues (Scott 40-47) and reissues of the 1861 stamps, the 1869 stamps and the then-current 1875 denominations. Even though the official imitations and the reprints were not valid for postage, Scott lists all of these U.S. special printings.

Most reprints or reissues differ slightly from the original stamp in some characteristic, such as gum, paper, perforation, color or watermark. Sometimes the details are followed so meticulously that only a student of that specific stamp is able to distinguish the reprint or reissue from the original.

Remainders and Canceled to Order

Some countries sell their stock of old stamps when a new issue replaces them. To avoid postal use, the *remainders* usually are canceled with a punch hole, a heavy line or bar, or a more-or-less regular-looking cancellation. The most famous merchant of remainders was Nicholas F. Seebeck. In the 1880s and 1890s, he arranged printing contracts between the Hamilton Bank Note Co., of which he was a director, and several Central and South American countries. The contracts provided that the plates and all remainders of the yearly issues became the property of Hamilton. Seebeck saw to it that ample stock remained. The "Seebecks," both remainders and reprints, were standard packet fillers for decades.

Some countries also issue stamps *canceled-to-order (CTO),* either in sheets with original gum or stuck onto pieces of paper or envelopes and canceled. Such CTO items generally are worth less than postally used stamps. In cases where the CTO material is far more prevalent in the marketplace than postally used examples, the catalogue value relates to the CTO examples, with postally used examples noted as premium items. Most CTOs can be detected by the presence of gum. However, as the CTO practice goes back at least to 1885, the gum inevitably has been soaked off some stamps so they could pass as postally used. The normally applied postmarks usually differ slightly from standard postmarks, and specialists are able to tell the difference. When applied individually to envelopes by philatelically minded persons, CTO material is known as *favor canceled* and generally sells at large discounts.

Cinderellas and Facsimiles

Cinderella is a catch-all term used by stamp collectors to describe phantoms, fantasies, bogus items, municipal issues, exhibition seals, local revenues, transportation stamps, labels, poster stamps and many other types of items. Some cinderella collectors include in their collections local postage issues, telegraph stamps, essays and proofs, forgeries and counterfeits.

A *fantasy* is an adhesive created for a nonexistent stamp-issuing authority. Fantasy items range from imaginary countries (Occusi-Ambeno, Kingdom of Sedang, Principality of Trinidad or Torres Straits), to non-existent locals (Winans City Post), or nonexistent transportation lines (McRobish & Co.'s Acapulco-San Francisco Line).

On the other hand, if the entity exists and could have issued stamps (but did not) or was known to have issued other stamps, the items are considered *bogus* stamps. These would include the Mormon postage stamps of Utah, S. Allan Taylor's Guatemala and Paraguay inventions, the propaganda issues for the South Moluccas and the adhesives of the Page & Keyes local post of Boston.

Phantoms is another term for both fantasy and bogus issues.

Facsimiles are copies or imitations made to represent original stamps, but which do not pretend to be originals. A catalogue illustration is such a facsimile. Illustrations from the Moens catalogue of the last century were occasionally colored and passed off as stamps. Since the beginning of stamp collecting, facsimiles have been made for collectors as space fillers or for reference. They often carry the word "facsimile," "falsch" (German), "sanko" or "mozo" (Japanese), or "faux" (French) overprinted on the face or stamped on the back. Unfortunately, over the years a number of these items have had fake cancels applied over the facsimile notation and have been passed off as genuine.

Forgeries and Counterfeits

Forgeries and counterfeits have been with philately virtually from the beginning of stamp production. Over time, the terminology for the two has been used interchangeably. Although both forgeries and counterfeits are reproductions of stamps, the purposes behind their creation differ considerably.

Among specialists there is an increasing movement to more specifically define such items. Although there is no universally accepted terminology, we feel the following definitions most closely mirror the items and their purposes as they are currently defined.

Forgeries (also often referred to as *Counterfeits*) are reproductions of genuine stamps that have been created to defraud collectors. Such spurious items first appeared on the market around 1860, and most old-time collections contain one or more. Many are crude and easily spotted, but some can deceive experts.

An important supplier of these early philatelic forgeries was the Hamburg printer Gebruder Spiro. Many others with reputations in this craft included S. Allan Taylor, George Hussey, James Chute, George Forune, Benjamin & Sarpy, Julius Goldner, E. Oneglia and L.H. Mercier. Among the noted 20th-century forgers were Francois Fournier, Jean Sperati and the prolific Raoul DeThuin.

Forgeries may be complete replications, or they may be genuine stamps altered to resemble a scarcer (and more valuable) type. Most forgeries, particularly those of rare stamps, are worth only a small fraction of the value of a genuine example, but a few types, created by some of the most notable forgers, such as Sperati, can be worth as much or more than the genuine. Fraudulently produced copies are known of most classic rarities and many medium-priced stamps.

In addition to rare stamps, large numbers of common 19th- and early 20th-century stamps were forged to supply stamps to the early packet trade. Many can still be easily found. Few new philatelic forgeries have appeared in recent decades. Successful imitation of well-engraved work is virtually impossible. It has proven far easier to produce a fake by altering a genuine stamp than to duplicate a stamp completely.

Counterfeit (also often referred to as *Postal Counterfeit* or *Postal Forgery*) is the term generally applied to reproductions of stamps that have been created to defraud the government of revenue. Such items usually are created at the time a stamp is current and, in some cases, are hard to detect. Because most counterfeits are seized when the perpetrator is captured, postal counterfeits, particularly used on cover, are usually worth much more than a genuine example to specialists. The first postal counterfeit was of Spain's 4-cuarto carmine of 1854 (the real one is Scott 25). Apparently, the counterfeiters were not satisfied with their first version, which is now very scarce, and they soon created an engraved counterfeit, which is common. Postal counterfeits quickly followed in Austria, Naples, Sardinia and the Roman States. They have since been created in many other countries as well, including the United States.

An infamous counterfeit to defraud the government is the 1-shilling Great Britain "Stock Exchange" forgery of 1872, used on telegraph forms at the exchange that year. The stamp escaped detection until a stamp dealer noticed it in 1898.

Fakes

Fakes are genuine stamps altered in some way to make them more desirable. One student of this part of stamp collecting has estimated that by the 1950s more than 30,000 varieties of fakes were known. That number has grown greatly since then. The widespread existence of fakes makes it important for stamp collectors to study their philatelic holdings and use relevant literature. Likewise, collectors should buy from reputable dealers who guarantee their stamps and make full and prompt refunds should a purchased item be declared faked or altered by some mutually agreed-upon authority. Because fakes always have some genuine characteristics, it is not always possible to obtain unanimous agreement among experts regarding specific items. These students may change their opinions as philatelic knowledge increases. More than 80 percent of all fakes on the philatelic market today are regummed, reperforated (or perforated for the first time), or bear forged overprints, surcharges or cancellations.

Stamps can be chemically treated to alter or eliminate colors. For example, a pale rose stamp can be re-colored to resemble a blue shade of high market value. In other cases, treated stamps can be made to resemble missing color varieties. Designs may be changed by painting, or a stroke or a dot added or bleached out to turn an ordinary variety into a seemingly scarcer stamp. Part of a stamp can be bleached and reprinted in a different version, achieving an inverted center or frame. Margins can be added or repairs done so deceptively that the stamps move from the "repaired" into the "fake" category.

Fakers have not left the backs of the stamps untouched either. They may create false watermarks, add fake grills or press out genuine grills. A thin India paper proof may be glued onto a thicker backing to create the appearance an issued stamp, or a proof printed on cardboard may be shaved down and perforated to resemble a stamp. Silk threads are impressed into paper and stamps have been split so that a rare paper variety is added to an otherwise inexpensive stamp. The most common treatment to the back of a stamp, however, is regumming.

Some in the business of faking stamps have openly advertised fool-proof application of "original gum" to stamps that lack it, although most publications now ban such ads from their pages. It is believed that very few early stamps have survived without being hinged. The large number of never-hinged examples of such earlier material offered for sale thus suggests the widespread extent of regumming activity. Regumming also may be used to hide repairs or thin spots. Dipping the stamp into watermark fluid, or examining it under longwave ultraviolet light often will reveal these flaws.

Fakers also tamper with separations. Ingenious ways to add margins are known. Perforated wide-margin stamps may be falsely represented as imperforate when trimmed. Reperforating is commonly done to create scarce coil or perforation varieties, and to eliminate the naturally occurring straight-edge stamps found in sheet margin positions of many earlier issues. Custom has made straight-edged stamps less desirable. Fakers have obliged by perforating straight-edged stamps so that many are now uncommon, if not rare.

Another fertile field for the faker is that of overprints, surcharges and cancellations. The forging of rare surcharges or overprints began in the 1880s or 1890s. These forgeries are sometimes difficult to detect, but experts have identified almost all. Occasionally, overprints or cancellations are removed to create non-overprinted stamps or seemingly unused items. This is most commonly done by removing a manuscript cancel to make a stamp resemble an unused example. "SPECIMEN" overprints may be removed by scraping and repainting to create non-overprinted varieties. Fakers use inexpensive revenues or pen-canceled stamps to generate unused stamps for further faking by adding other markings. The quartz lamp or UV lamp and a high-powered magnifying glass help to easily detect removed cancellations.

The bigger problem, however, is the addition of overprints, surcharges or cancellations - many with such precision that they are very difficult to ascertain. Plating of the stamps or the overprint can be an important method of detection.

Fake postmarks may range from many spurious fancy cancellations to a host of markings applied to transatlantic covers, to adding normally appearing postmarks to definitives of some countries with stamps that are valued far higher used than unused. With the increased popularity of cover collecting, and the widespread interest in postal history, a fertile new field for fakers has come about. Some have tried to create entire covers. Others specialize in adding stamps, tied by fake cancellations, to genuine stampless covers, or replacing less expensive or damaged stamps with more valuable ones. Detailed study of postal rates in effect at the time a cover in question was mailed, including the analysis of each handstamp used during the period, ink analysis and similar techniques, usually will unmask the fraud.

Restoration and Repairs

Scott bases its catalogue values on stamps that are free of defects and otherwise meet the standards set forth earlier in this introduction. Most stamp collectors desire to have the finest copy of an item possible. Even within given grading categories there are variances. This leads to a controversial practice that is not defined in any universal manner: stamp *restoration.*

There are broad differences of opinion about what is permissible when it comes to restoration. Carefully applying a soft eraser to a stamp or cover to remove light soiling is one form of restoration, as is washing a stamp in mild soap and water to clean it. These are fairly accepted forms of restoration. More severe forms of restoration include pressing out creases or removing stains caused by tape. To what degree each of these is acceptable is dependent upon the individual situation. Further along the spectrum is the freshening of a stamp's color by removing oxide build-up or the effects of wax paper left next to stamps shipped to the tropics.

At some point in this spectrum the concept of *repair* replaces that of restoration. Repairs include filling thin spots, mending tears by reweaving or adding a missing perforation tooth. Regumming stamps may have been acceptable as a restoration or repair technique many decades ago, but today it is considered a form of fakery.

Restored stamps may or may not sell at a discount, and it is possible that the value of individual restored items may be enhanced over that of their pre-restoration state. Specific situations dictate the resultant value of such an item. Repaired stamps sell at substantial discounts from the value of sound stamps.

Terminology

Booklets — Many countries have issued stamps in small booklets for the convenience of users. This idea continues to become increasingly popular in many countries. Booklets have been issued in many sizes and forms, often with advertising on the covers, the panes of stamps or on the interleaving.

The panes used in booklets may be printed from special plates or made from regular sheets. All panes from booklets issued by the United States and many from those of other countries contain stamps that are straight edged on the sides, but perforated between. Others are distinguished by orientation of watermark or other identifying features. Any stamp-like unit in the pane, either printed or blank, that is not a postage stamp, is considered to be a *label* in the catalogue listings.

Scott lists and values booklet panes. Modern complete booklets also are listed and valued. Individual booklet panes are listed only when they are not fashioned from existing sheet stamps and, therefore, are identifiable from their sheet stamp counterparts.

Panes usually do not have a used value assigned to them because there is little market activity for used booklet panes, even though many exist used and there is some demand for them.

Cancellations — The marks or obliterations put on stamps by postal authorities to show that they have performed service and to prevent their reuse are known as cancellations. If the marking is made with a pen, it is considered a "pen cancel." When the location of the post office appears in the marking, it is a "town cancellation." A "postmark" is technically any postal marking, but in practice the term generally is applied to a town cancellation with a date. When calling attention to a cause or celebration, the marking is known as a "slogan cancellation." Many other types and styles of cancellations exist, such as duplex, numerals, targets, fancy and others. See also "precancels," below.

Coil Stamps — These are stamps that are issued in rolls for use in dispensers, affixing and vending machines. Those coils of the United States, Canada, Sweden and some other countries are perforated horizontally or vertically only, with the outer edges imperforate. Coil stamps of some countries, such as Great Britain and Germany, are perforated on all four sides and may in some cases be distinguished from their sheet stamp counterparts by watermarks, counting numbers on the reverse or other means.

Covers — Entire envelopes, with or without adhesive postage stamps, that have passed through the mail and bear postal or other markings of philatelic interest are known as covers. Before the introduction of envelopes in about 1840, people folded letters and wrote the address on the outside. Some people covered their letters with an extra sheet of paper on the outside for the address, producing the term "cover." Used airletter sheets, stamped envelopes and other items of postal stationery also are considered covers.

Errors — Stamps that have some major, consistent, unintentional deviation from the normal are considered errors. Errors include, but are not limited to, missing or wrong colors, wrong paper, wrong watermarks, inverted centers or frames on multicolor printing, inverted or missing surcharges or overprints, double impressions, missing perforations, unintentionally omitted tagging and others. Factually wrong or misspelled information, if it appears on all examples of a stamp, are not considered errors in the true sense of the word. They are errors of design. Inconsistent or randomly appearing items, such as misperfs or color shifts, are classified as freaks.

Color-Omitted Errors — This term refers to stamps where a missing color is caused by the complete failure of the printing plate to deliver ink to the stamp paper or any other paper. Generally, this is caused by the printing plate not being engaged on the press or the ink station running dry of ink during printing.

Color-Missing Errors — This term refers to stamps where a color or colors were printed somewhere but do not appear on the finished stamp. There are four different classes of color-missing errors, and the catalog indicates with a two-letter code appended to each such listing what caused the color to be missing. These codes are used only for the United States' color-missing error listings.

FO = A *foldover* of the stamp sheet during printing may block ink from appearing on a stamp. Instead, the color will appear on the back of the foldover (where it might fall on the back of the selvage or perhaps on the back of the stamp or another stamp). FO also will be used in the case of foldunders, where the paper may fold underneath the other stamp paper and the color will print on the platen.

EP = A piece of *extraneous paper* falling across the plate or stamp paper will receive the printed ink. When the extraneous paper is removed, an unprinted portion of stamp paper remains and shows partially or totally missing colors.

CM = A misregistration of the printing plates during printing will result in a *color misregistration*, and such a misregistraion may result in a color not appearing on the finished stamp.

PS = *A perforation shift* after printing may remove a color from the finished stamp. Normally, this will occur on a row of stamps at the edge of the stamp pane.

Measurements – When measurements are given in the Scott catalogues for stamp size, grill size or any other reason, the first measurement given is always for the top and bottom dimension, while the second measurement will be for the sides (just as perforation gauges are measured). Thus, a stamp size of 15mm x 21mm will indicate a vertically oriented stamp 15mm wide at top and bottom, and 21mm tall at the sides. The same principle holds for measuring or counting items such as U.S. grills. A grill count of 22x18 points (B grill) indicates that there are 22 grill points across by 18 grill points down.

Overprints and Surcharges — Overprinting involves applying wording or design elements over an already existing stamp. Overprints can be used to alter the place of use (such as "Canal Zone" on U.S. stamps), to adapt them for a special purpose ("Porto" on Denmark's 1913-20 regular issues for use as postage due stamps, Scott J1-J7) or to commemorate a special occasion (United States Scott 647-648).

A *surcharge* is a form of overprint that changes or restates the face value of a stamp or piece of postal stationery.

Surcharges and overprints may be handstamped, typeset or, occasionally, lithographed or engraved. A few hand-written overprints and surcharges are known.

Personalized Stamps — In 1999, Australia issued stamps with se-tenant labels that could be personalized with pictures of the customer's choice. Other countries quickly followed suit, with some offering to print the selected picture on the stamp itself within a frame that was used exclusively for personalized issues. As the picture used on these stamps or labels vary, listings for such stamps are for any picture within the common frame (or any picture on a se-tenant label), be it a "generic" image or one produced especially for a customer, almost invariably at a premium price.

Precancels — Stamps that are canceled before they are placed in the mail are known as precancels. Precanceling usually is done to expedite the handling of large mailings and generally allow the affected mail pieces to skip certain phases of mail handling.

In the United States, precancellations generally identified the point of origin; that is, the city and state. This information appeared across the face of the stamp, usually centered between parallel lines. More recently, bureau precancels retained the parallel lines, but the city and state designations were dropped. Recent coils have a service inscription that is present on the original printing plate. These show the mail service paid for by the stamp. Since these stamps are not intended to receive further cancellations when used as intended, they are considered precancels. Such items often do not have parallel lines as part of the precancellation.

In France, the abbreviation *Affranchts* in a semicircle together with the word *Postes* is the general form of precancel in use. Belgian precancellations usually appear in a box in which the name of the city appears. Netherlands precancels have the name of the city enclosed between concentric circles, sometimes called a "lifesaver." Precancellations of other countries usually follow these patterns, but may be any arrangement of bars, boxes and city names.

Precancels are listed in the Scott catalogues only if the precancel changes the denomination (Belgium Scott 477-478); if the precanceled stamp is different from the non-precanceled version (such as untagged U.S. precancels); or if the stamp exists only precanceled (France Scott 1096-1099, U.S. Scott 2265).

Proofs and Essays — Proofs are impressions taken from an approved die, plate or stone in which the design and color are the same as the stamp issued to the public. Trial color proofs are impressions taken from approved dies, plates or stones in colors that vary from the final version. An essay is the impression of a design that differs in some way from the issued stamp. "Progressive die proofs" generally are considered to be essays.

Provisionals — These are stamps that are issued on short notice and intended for temporary use pending the arrival of regular issues. They usually are issued to meet such contingencies as changes in government or currency, shortage of necessary postage values or military occupation.

During the 1840s, postmasters in certain American cities issued stamps that were valid only at specific post offices. In 1861, postmasters of the Confederate States also issued stamps with limited validity. Both of these examples are known as "postmaster's provisionals."

Se-tenant — This term refers to an unsevered pair, strip or block of stamps that differ in design, denomination or overprint.

Unless the se-tenant item has a continuous design (see U.S. Scott 1451a, 1694a) the stamps do not have to be in the same order as shown in the catalogue (see U.S. Scott 2158a).

Specimens — The Universal Postal Union required member nations to send samples of all stamps they released into service to the International Bureau in Switzerland. Member nations of the UPU received these specimens as samples of what stamps were valid for postage. Many are overprinted, handstamped or initial-perforated "Specimen," "Canceled" or "Muestra." Some are marked with bars across the denominations (China-Taiwan), punched holes (Czechoslovakia) or back inscriptions (Mongolia).

Stamps distributed to government officials or for publicity purposes, and stamps submitted by private security printers for official approval, also may receive such defacements.

The previously described defacement markings prevent postal use, and all such items generally are known as "specimens."

Tete Beche — This term describes a pair of stamps in which one is upside down in relation to the other. Some of these are the result of intentional sheet arrangements, such as Morocco Scott B10-B11. Others occurred when one or more electrotypes accidentally were placed upside down on the plate, such as Colombia Scott 57a. Separation of the tete-beche stamps, of course, destroys the tete beche variety.

Pronunciation Symbols

ə .... banana, collide, abut

ˈə, ˌə .... humdrum, abut

ə .... immediately preceding \l\, \n\, \m\, \ŋ\, as in battle, mitten, eaten, and sometimes open \ˈō-pᵊm\, lock and key \-ᵊŋ-\; immediately following \l\, \m\, \r\, as often in French table, prisme, titre

ər .... further, merger, bird

ˈər- / ˈə-r .... as in two different pronunciations of hurry \ˈhər-ē, ˈhə-rē\

a .... mat, map, mad, gag, snap, patch

ā .... day, fade, date, aorta, drape, cape

ä .... bother, cot, and, with most American speakers, father, cart

ȧ .... father as pronounced by speakers who do not rhyme it with *bother*; French patte

au̇ .... now, loud, out

b .... baby, rib

ch .... chin, nature \ˈnā-chər\

d .... did, adder

e .... bet, bed, peck

ˈē, ˌē .... beat, nosebleed, evenly, easy

ē .... easy, mealy

f .... fifty, cuff

g .... go, big, gift

h .... hat, ahead

hw .... whale as pronounced by those who do not have the same pronunciation for both *whale* and *wail*

i .... tip, banish, active

ī .... site, side, buy, tripe

j .... job, gem, edge, join, judge

k .... kin, cook, ache

k̲ .... German ich, Buch; one pronunciation of loch

l .... lily, pool

m .... murmur, dim, nymph

n .... no, own

ⁿ .... indicates that a preceding vowel or diphthong is pronounced with the nasal passages open, as in French *un bon vin blanc* \œⁿ -bōⁿ -vaⁿ -bläⁿ\

ŋ .... sing \ˈsiŋ\, singer \ˈsiŋ-ər\, finger \ˈfiŋ-gər\, ink \ˈiŋk \

ō .... bone, know, beau

ȯ .... saw, all, gnaw, caught

œ .... French boeuf, German Hölle

œ̄ .... French feu, German Höhle

ȯi .... coin, destroy

p .... pepper, lip

r .... red, car, rarity

s .... source, less

sh .... as in shy, mission, machine, special (actually, this is a single sound, not two); with a hyphen between, two sounds as in *grasshopper* \ˈgras-ˌhä-pər\

t .... tie, attack, late, later, latter

th .... as in thin, ether (actually, this is a single sound, not two); with a hyphen between, two sounds as in *knighthood* \ˈnīt-ˌhu̇d\

t̲h̲ .... then, either, this (actually, this is a single sound, not two)

ü .... rule, youth, union \ˈyün-yən\, few \ˈfyü\

u̇ .... pull, wood, book, curable \ˈkyu̇r-ə-bəl\, fury \ˈfyu̇r-ē\

ue .... German füllen, hübsch

ue̅ .... French rue, German fühlen

v .... vivid, give

w .... we, away

y .... yard, young, cue \ˈkyü\, mute \ˈmyüt\, union \ˈyün-yən\

ʸ .... indicates that during the articulation of the sound represented by the preceding character the front of the tongue has substantially the position it has for the articulation of the first sound of *yard*, as in French *digne* \dēnʸ\

z .... zone, raise

zh .... as in vision, azure \ˈa-zhər\ (actually, this is a single sound, not two); with a hyphen between, two sounds as in *hogshead* \ˈhȯgz-ˌhed, ˈhägz-\

\ .... slant line used in pairs to mark the beginning and end of a transcription: \ˈpen\

ˈ .... mark preceding a syllable with primary (strongest) stress: \ˈpen-mən-ˌship\

ˌ .... mark preceding a syllable with secondary (medium) stress: \ˈpen-mən-ˌship\

\- .... mark of syllable division

() .... indicate that what is symbolized between is present in some utterances but not in others: *factory* \ˈfak-t(ə-)rē\

÷ .... indicates that many regard as unacceptable the pronunciation variant immediately following: *cupola* \ˈkyü-pə-lə, ÷-ˌlō\

Currency Conversion

Country	Dollar	Pound	S Franc	Yen	HK $	Euro	Cdn $	Aus $
Australia	1.3742	1.7957	1.3840	0.0126	0.1751	1.5774	1.0475	—
Canada	1.3119	1.7143	1.3213	0.0120	0.1672	1.5095	—	0.9547
European Union	0.8712	1.1384	0.8774	0.0080	0.1110	—	0.6641	0.6340
Hong Kong	7.8476	10.254	7.9037	0.0720	—	9.0078	5.9819	5.7107
Japan	109.02	142.46	109.80	—	13.892	125.14	83.101	79.333
Switzerland	0.9929	1.2974	—	0.0091	0.1265	1.1397	0.7568	0.7225
United Kingdom	0.7653	—	0.7708	0.0070	0.0975	0.8784	0.5833	0.5569
United States	—	1.3067	1.0072	0.0092	0.1274	1.1478	0.7623	0.7277

Country	Currency	U.S. $ Equiv.
Gabon	Community of French Africa (CFA) franc	.0018
Gambia	dalasy	.0202
Georgia	lari	.3766
Germany	euro	1.1478
Ghana	cedi	.2012
Gibraltar	pound	1.3067
Great Britain	pound	1.3067
Alderney	pound	1.3067
Guernsey	pound	1.3067
Jersey	pound	1.3067
Isle of Man	pound	1.3067
Greece	euro	1.1478
Mount Athos	euro	1.1478
Greenland	Danish krone	.1538
Grenada	East Caribbean dollar	.3704
Grenada Grenadines	East Caribbean dollar	.3704
Guatemala	quetzal	.1296
Guinea	franc	.0001
Guinea-Bissau	CFA franc	.0018
Guyana	dollar	.0048

Source: ***xe.com****, Feb. 1, 2019. Figures reflect values as of Feb. 1, 2019.*

COMMON DESIGN TYPES

Pictured in this section are issues where one illustration has been used for a number of countries in the Catalogue. Not included in this section are overprinted stamps or those issues which are illustrated in each country. Because the location of Never Hinged breakpoints varies from country to country, some of the values in the listings below will be for unused stamps that were previously hinged.

EUROPA

Europa, 1956

The design symbolizing the cooperation among the six countries comprising the Coal and Steel Community is illustrated in each country.

Belgium	*496-497*
France	*805-806*
Germany	*748-749*
Italy	*715-716*
Luxembourg	*318-320*
Netherlands	*368-369*

Nos. 496-497 (2)	9.00	.50
Nos. 805-806 (2)	5.25	1.00
Nos. 748-749 (2)	7.40	1.10
Nos. 715-716 (2)	9.25	1.25
Nos. 318-320 (3)	65.50	42.00
Nos. 368-369 (2)	25.75	1.50
Set total (13) Stamps	122.15	47.35

Europa, 1958

"E" and Dove — CD1

European Postal Union at the service of European integration.

1958, Sept. 13

Belgium	527-528
France	889-890
Germany	790-791
Italy	750-751
Luxembourg	341-343
Netherlands	375-376
Saar	317-318

Nos. 527-528 (2)	3.75	.60
Nos. 889-890 (2)	1.65	.55
Nos. 790-791 (2)	2.95	.60
Nos. 750-751 (2)	1.05	.60
Nos. 341-343 (3)	1.35	.90
Nos. 375-376 (2)	1.25	.75
Nos. 317-318 (2)	1.05	2.30
Set total (15) Stamps	13.05	6.30

Europa, 1959

6-Link Enless Chain — CD2

1959, Sept. 19

Belgium	536-537
France	929-930
Germany	805-806
Italy	791-792
Luxembourg	354-355
Netherlands	379-380

Nos. 536-537 (2)	1.55	.60
Nos. 929-930 (2)	1.40	.80
Nos. 805-806 (2)	1.35	.60
Nos. 791-792 (2)	.80	.50
Nos. 354-355 (2)	2.65	1.00
Nos. 379-380 (2)	2.10	1.85
Set total (12) Stamps	9.85	5.35

Europa, 1960

19-Spoke Wheel CD3

First anniverary of the establishment of C.E.P.T. (Conference Europeenne des Administrations des Postes et des Telecommunications.) The spokes symbolize the 19 founding members of the Conference.

1960, Sept.

Belgium	553-554
Denmark	379
Finland	376-377
France	970-971
Germany	818-820
Great Britain	377-378
Greece	688
Iceland	327-328
Ireland	175-176
Italy	809-810
Luxembourg	374-375
Netherlands	385-386
Norway	387
Portugal	866-867
Spain	941-942
Sweden	562-563
Switzerland	400-401
Turkey	1493-1494

Nos. 553-554 (2)	1.25	.55
No. 379 (1)	.55	.50
Nos. 376-377 (2)	1.70	1.80
Nos. 970-971 (2)	.50	.50
Nos. 818-820 (3)	1.90	1.35
Nos. 377-378 (2)	8.00	5.00
No. 688 (1)	5.00	2.00
Nos. 327-328 (2)	1.30	1.85
Nos. 175-176 (2)	47.50	27.50
Nos. 809-810 (2)	.50	.50
Nos. 374-375 (2)	1.00	.80
Nos. 385-386 (2)	2.00	2.00
No. 387 (1)	1.25	1.25
Nos. 866-867 (2)	3.00	1.75
Nos. 941-942 (2)	1.50	.75
Nos. 562-563 (2)	1.05	.55
Nos. 400-401 (2)	1.75	.75
Nos. 1493-1494 (2)	2.10	1.35
Set total (34) Stamps	81.85	50.75

Europa, 1961

19 Doves Flying as One — CD4

The 19 doves represent the 19 members of the Conference of European Postal and Telecommunications Administrations C.E.P.T.

1961-62

Belgium	572-573
Cyprus	201-203
France	1005-1006
Germany	844-845
Great Britain	382-384
Greece	718-719
Iceland	340-341
Italy	845-846
Luxembourg	382-383
Netherlands	387-388
Spain	1010-1011
Switzerland	410-411
Turkey	1518-1520

Nos. 572-573 (2)	.75	.50
Nos. 201-203 (3)	*2.10*	*1.20*
Nos. 1005-1006 (2)	.50	.50
Nos. 844-845 (2)	.60	.75
Nos. 382-384 (3)	.75	.75
Nos. 718-719 (2)	.80	.50
Nos. 340-341 (2)	1.10	1.60
Nos. 845-846 (2)	.50	.50
Nos. 382-383 (2)	.55	.55
Nos. 387-388 (2)	.50	.50
Nos. 1010-1011 (2)	.70	.55
Nos. 410-411 (2)	1.90	.60
Nos. 1518-1520 (3)	2.45	1.30
Set total (29) Stamps	13.20	9.80

Europa, 1962

Young Tree with 19 Leaves CD5

The 19 leaves represent the 19 original members of C.E.P.T.

1962-63

Belgium	582-583
Cyprus	219-221
France	1045-1046
Germany	852-853
Greece	739-740
Iceland	348-349
Ireland	184-185
Italy	860-861
Luxembourg	386-387
Netherlands	394-395
Norway	414-415
Switzerland	416-417
Turkey	1553-1555

Nos. 582-583 (2)	.65	.65
Nos. 219-221 (3)	*76.25*	*6.75*
Nos. 1045-1046 (2)	.60	.50
Nos. 852-853 (2)	.65	.75
Nos. 739-740 (2)	2.25	1.15
Nos. 348-349 (2)	.85	.85
Nos. 184-185 (2)	2.00	.50
Nos. 860-861 (2)	1.00	.55
Nos. 386-387 (2)	.75	.55
Nos. 394-395 (2)	1.35	.90
Nos. 414-415 (2)	2.25	2.25
Nos. 416-417 (2)	1.65	1.00
Nos. 1553-1555 (3)	*3.00*	1.55
Set total (28) Stamps	93.25	17.95

Europa, 1963

Stylized Links, Symbolizing Unity — CD6

1963, Sept.

Belgium	598-599
Cyprus	229-231
Finland	419
France	1074-1075
Germany	867-868
Greece	768-769
Iceland	357-358
Ireland	188-189
Italy	880-881
Luxembourg	403-404
Netherlands	416-417
Norway	441-442
Switzerland	429
Turkey	1602-1603

Nos. 598-599 (2)	1.60	.55
Nos. 229-231 (3)	*64.00*	*9.40*
No. 419 (1)	1.25	.55
Nos. 1074-1075 (2)	.60	.50
Nos. 867-868 (2)	.50	.55
Nos. 768-769 (2)	5.25	1.90
Nos. 357-358 (2)	1.20	1.20
Nos. 188-189 (2)	4.75	3.25
Nos. 880-881 (2)	.50	.50
Nos. 403-404 (2)	.75	.55
Nos. 416-417 (2)	1.30	1.00
Nos. 441-442 (2)	4.75	3.00
No. 429 (1)	.90	.60
Nos. 1602-1603 (2)	1.40	.60
Set total (27) Stamps	88.75	24.15

Europa, 1964

Symbolic Daisy — CD7

5th anniversary of the establishment of C.E.P.T. The 22 petals of the flower symbolize the 22 members of the Conference.

1964, Sept.

Austria	738
Belgium	614-615
Cyprus	244-246
France	1109-1110
Germany	897-898
Greece	801-802
Iceland	367-368
Ireland	196-197
Italy	894-895
Luxembourg	411-412
Monaco	590-591
Netherlands	428-429
Norway	458
Portugal	931-933
Spain	1262-1263
Switzerland	438-439
Turkey	1628-1629

No. 738 (1)	1.20	.80
Nos. 614-615 (2)	1.40	.60
Nos. 244-246 (3)	*32.25*	*5.10*
Nos. 1109-1110 (2)	.50	.50
Nos. 897-898 (2)	.50	.50
Nos. 801-802 (2)	5.00	1.90
Nos. 367-368 (2)	1.40	1.15
Nos. 196-197 (2)	17.00	4.25
Nos. 894-895 (2)	.50	.50
Nos. 411-412 (2)	.75	.55
Nos. 590-591 (2)	2.50	.70
Nos. 428-429 (2)	.75	.60
No. 458 (1)	4.50	4.50
Nos. 931-933 (3)	*10.00*	*2.00*
Nos. 1262-1263 (2)	1.30	.80
Nos. 438-439 (2)	1.65	.50
Nos. 1628-1629 (2)	2.65	1.35
Set total (34) Stamps	83.85	26.30

Europa, 1965

Leaves and "Fruit" CD8

1965

Belgium	636-637
Cyprus	262-264
Finland	437
France	1131-1132
Germany	934-935
Greece	833-834
Iceland	375-376
Ireland	204-205
Italy	915-916
Luxembourg	432-433
Monaco	616-617
Netherlands	438-439
Norway	475-476
Portugal	958-960
Switzerland	469
Turkey	1665-1666

Nos. 636-637 (2)	.50	.50
Nos. 262-264 (3)	*25.35*	*6.00*
No. 437 (1)	1.25	.55
Nos. 1131-1132 (2)	.70	.55
Nos. 934-935 (2)	.50	.50
Nos. 833-834 (2)	2.25	1.15
Nos. 375-376 (2)	2.50	1.75
Nos. 204-205 (2)	16.00	3.35
Nos. 915-916 (2)	.50	.50
Nos. 432-433 (2)	.75	.55
Nos. 616-617 (2)	3.25	1.65
Nos. 438-439 (2)	.55	.50
Nos. 475-476 (2)	4.00	3.10
Nos. 958-960 (3)	*10.00*	*2.75*
No. 469 (1)	1.15	.50
Nos. 1665-1666 (2)	3.50	2.10
Set total (32) Stamps	72.75	26.00

Europa, 1966

Symbolic Sailboat — CD9

1966, Sept.

Andorra, French	172
Belgium	675-676
Cyprus	275-277
France	1163-1164
Germany	963-964

Greece 862-863
Iceland 384-385
Ireland 216-217
Italy 942-943
Liechtenstein 415
Luxembourg 440-441
Monaco 639-640
Netherlands 441-442
Norway 496-497
Portugal 980-982
Switzerland 477-478
Turkey 1718-1719

No. 172 (1)	3.00	3.00
Nos. 675-676 (2)	.80	.50
Nos. 275-277 (3)	4.75	2.75
Nos. 1163-1164 (2)	.55	.50
Nos. 963-964 (2)	.50	.55
Nos. 862-863 (2)	2.25	1.05
Nos. 384-385 (2)	4.50	3.50
Nos. 216-217 (2)	6.75	2.00
Nos. 942-943 (2)	.50	.50
No. 415 (1)	.40	.35
Nos. 440-441 (2)	.70	.55
Nos. 639-640 (2)	2.00	.65
Nos. 441-442 (2)	.85	.50
Nos. 496-497 (2)	5.00	3.00
Nos. 980-982 (3)	9.75	2.25
Nos. 477-478 (2)	1.40	.60
Nos. 1718-1719 (2)	3.35	1.75
Set total (34) Stamps	47.05	24.00

Europa, 1967

Cogwheels
CD10

1967

Andorra, French 174-175
Belgium 688-689
Cyprus 297-299
France 1178-1179
Germany 969-970
Greece 891-892
Iceland 389-390
Ireland 232-233
Italy 951-952
Liechtenstein 420
Luxembourg 449-450
Monaco 669-670
Netherlands 444-447
Norway 504-505
Portugal 994-996
Spain 1465-1466
Switzerland 482
Turkey B120-B121

Nos. 174-175 (2)	10.75	6.25
Nos. 688-689 (2)	1.05	.55
Nos. 297-299 (3)	4.25	2.50
Nos. 1178-1179 (2)	.55	.50
Nos. 969-970 (2)	.55	.55
Nos. 891-892 (2)	3.75	1.00
Nos. 389-390 (2)	3.00	2.00
Nos. 232-233 (2)	5.90	2.30
Nos. 951-952 (2)	.60	.50
No. 420 (1)	.45	.40
Nos. 449-450 (2)	1.00	.70
Nos. 669-670 (2)	2.75	.70
Nos. 444-447 (4)	2.70	2.05
Nos. 504-505 (2)	3.25	2.75
Nos. 994-996 (3)	9.50	1.85
Nos. 1465-1466 (2)	.50	.50
No. 482 (1)	.60	.30
Nos. B120-B121 (2)	3.50	2.75
Set total (38) Stamps	54.65	28.15

Europa, 1968

Golden Key with C.E.P.T. Emblem
CD11

1968

Andorra, French 182-183
Belgium 705-706
Cyprus 314-316
France 1209-1210
Germany 983-984
Greece 916-917
Iceland 395-396
Ireland 242-243
Italy 979-980
Liechtenstein 442
Luxembourg 466-467
Monaco 689-691
Netherlands 452-453
Portugal 1019-1021
San Marino 687
Spain 1526
Switzerland 488
Turkey 1775-1776

Nos. 182-183 (2)	16.50	10.00
Nos. 705-706 (2)	1.25	.50
Nos. 314-316 (3)	2.90	2.50
Nos. 1209-1210 (2)	.85	.55
Nos. 983-984 (2)	.50	.55
Nos. 916-917 (2)	3.75	1.65
Nos. 395-396 (2)	3.00	2.20
Nos. 242-243 (2)	3.30	2.25
Nos. 979-980 (2)	.50	.50
No. 442 (1)	.45	.40
Nos. 466-467 (2)	.80	.70
Nos. 689-691 (3)	5.40	.95
Nos. 452-453 (2)	1.05	.70
Nos. 1019-1021 (3)	9.75	2.10
No. 687 (1)	.55	.35
No. 1526 (1)	.25	.25
No. 488 (1)	.40	.25
Nos. 1775-1776 (2)	5.00	2.00
Set total (35) Stamps	56.20	28.40

Europa, 1969

"EUROPA" and "CEPT"
CD12

Tenth anniversary of C.E.P.T.

1969

Andorra, French 188-189
Austria 837
Belgium 718-719
Cyprus 326-328
Denmark 458
Finland 483
France 1245-1246
Germany 996-997
Great Britain 585
Greece 947-948
Iceland 406-407
Ireland 270-271
Italy 1000-1001
Liechtenstein 453
Luxembourg 475-476
Monaco 722-724
Netherlands 475-476
Norway 533-534
Portugal 1038-1040
San Marino 701-702
Spain 1567
Sweden 814-816
Switzerland 500-501
Turkey 1799-1800
Vatican 470-472
Yugoslavia 1003-1004

Nos. 188-189 (2)	18.50	12.00
No. 837 (1)	.65	.30
Nos. 718-719 (2)	.75	.50
Nos. 326-328 (3)	3.00	2.25
No. 458 (1)	.75	.75
No. 483 (1)	3.50	.75
Nos. 1245-1246 (2)	.55	.50
Nos. 996-997 (2)	.70	.50
No. 585 (1)	.25	.25
Nos. 947-948 (2)	5.00	1.50
Nos. 406-407 (2)	4.20	2.40
Nos. 270-271 (2)	3.50	2.00
Nos. 1000-1001 (2)	.50	.50
No. 453 (1)	.45	.45
Nos. 475-476 (2)	.95	.50
Nos. 722-724 (3)	10.50	2.00
Nos. 475-476 (2)	1.35	1.00
Nos. 533-534 (2)	3.75	2.35
Nos. 1038-1040 (3)	17.75	2.40
Nos. 701-702 (2)	.90	.90
No. 1567 (1)	.25	.25
Nos. 814-816 (3)	4.00	2.85
Nos. 500-501 (2)	1.85	1.00
Nos. 1799-1800 (2)	3.85	2.25
Nos. 470-472 (3)	.75	.75
Nos. 1003-1004 (2)	4.00	4.00
Set total (51) Stamps	92.20	44.90

Europa, 1970

Interwoven Threads
CD13

1970

Andorra, French 196-197
Belgium 741-742
Cyprus 340-342
France 1271-1272
Germany 1018-1019
Greece 985, 987
Iceland 420-421
Ireland 279-281
Italy 1013-1014
Liechtenstein 470
Luxembourg 489-490
Monaco 768-770
Netherlands 483-484
Portugal 1060-1062
San Marino 729-730
Spain 1607
Switzerland 515-516
Turkey 1848-1849
Yugoslavia 1024-1025

Nos. 196-197 (2)	20.00	8.50
Nos. 741-742 (2)	1.10	.55
Nos. 340-342 (3)	2.70	2.75
Nos. 1271-1272 (2)	.65	.50
Nos. 1018-1019 (2)	.60	.50
Nos. 985,987 (2)	7.75	2.00
Nos. 420-421 (2)	6.00	4.00
Nos. 279-281 (3)	7.50	2.50
Nos. 1013-1014 (2)	.50	.50
No. 470 (1)	.45	.45
Nos. 489-490 (2)	.80	.55
Nos. 768-770 (3)	6.35	2.10
Nos. 483-484 (2)	1.30	1.15
Nos. 1060-1062 (3)	9.75	2.35
Nos. 729-730 (2)	.90	.55
No. 1607 (1)	.25	.25
Nos. 515-516 (2)	1.85	.70
Nos. 1848-1849 (2)	5.00	2.25
Nos. 1024-1025 (2)	.80	.80
Set total (40) Stamps	74.25	32.95

Europa, 1971

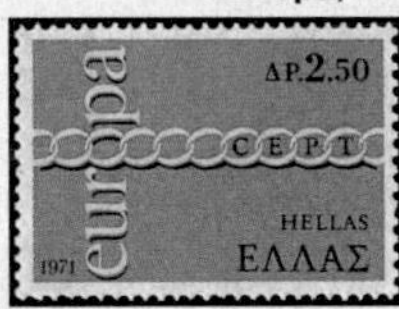

"Fraternity, Cooperation, Common Effort"
CD14

1971

Andorra, French 205-206
Belgium 803-804
Cyprus 365-367
Finland 504
France 1304
Germany 1064-1065
Greece 1029-1030
Iceland 429-430
Ireland 305-306
Italy 1038-1039
Liechtenstein 485
Luxembourg 500-501
Malta 425-427
Monaco 797-799
Netherlands 488-489
Portugal 1094-1096
San Marino 749-750
Spain 1675-1676
Switzerland 531-532
Turkey 1876-1877
Yugoslavia 1052-1053

Nos. 205-206 (2)	20.00	7.75
Nos. 803-804 (2)	1.30	.55
Nos. 365-367 (3)	2.60	3.25
No. 504 (1)	5.00	.75
No. 1304 (1)	.45	.40
Nos. 1064-1065 (2)	.60	.50
Nos. 1029-1030 (2)	4.00	1.80
Nos. 429-430 (2)	5.00	3.75
Nos. 305-306 (2)	4.50	1.50
Nos. 1038-1039 (2)	.65	.50
No. 485 (1)	.45	.45
Nos. 500-501 (2)	1.00	.65
Nos. 425-427 (3)	.80	.80
Nos. 797-799 (3)	15.00	2.80
Nos. 488-489 (2)	1.20	.95
Nos. 1094-1096 (3)	9.75	1.75
Nos. 749-750 (2)	.65	.55
Nos. 1675-1676 (2)	.75	.55
Nos. 531-532 (2)	1.85	.65
Nos. 1876-1877 (2)	5.60	2.50
Nos. 1052-1053 (2)	.50	.50
Set total (43) Stamps	81.65	32.90

Europa, 1972

Sparkles, Symbolic of Communications
CD15

1972

Andorra, French 210-211
Andorra, Spanish 62
Belgium 825-826
Cyprus 380-382
Finland 512-513
France 1341
Germany 1089-1090
Greece 1049-1050
Iceland 439-440
Ireland 316-317
Italy 1065-1066
Liechtenstein 504
Luxembourg 512-513
Malta 450-453
Monaco 831-832
Netherlands 494-495
Portugal 1141-1143
San Marino 771-772
Spain 1718
Switzerland 544-545
Turkey 1907-1908
Yugoslavia 1100-1101

Nos. 210-211 (2)	21.00	7.00
No. 62 (1)	60.00	60.00
Nos. 825-826 (2)	.95	.55
Nos. 380-382 (3)	5.95	4.25
Nos. 512-513 (2)	7.00	1.40
No. 1341 (1)	.50	.35
Nos. 1089-1090 (2)	1.10	.50
Nos. 1049-1050 (2)	2.00	1.55
Nos. 439-440 (2)	2.90	2.65
Nos. 316-317 (2)	13.00	4.50
Nos. 1065-1066 (2)	.55	.50
No. 504 (1)	.45	.45
Nos. 512-513 (2)	.95	.65
Nos. 450-453 (4)	1.05	1.40
Nos. 831-832 (2)	5.00	1.40
Nos. 494-495 (2)	1.20	.90
Nos. 1141-1143 (3)	9.75	1.50
Nos. 771-772 (2)	.70	.50
No. 1718 (1)	.50	.40
Nos. 544-545 (2)	1.65	.60
Nos. 1907-1908 (2)	7.50	3.00
Nos. 1100-1101 (2)	1.20	1.20
Set total (44) Stamps	144.90	95.25

Europa, 1973

Post Horn and Arrows
CD16

1973

Andorra, French 219-220
Andorra, Spanish 76
Belgium 839-840
Cyprus 396-398
Finland 526
France 1367
Germany 1114-1115
Greece 1090-1092
Iceland 447-448
Ireland 329-330
Italy 1108-1109
Liechtenstein 528-529
Luxembourg 523-524
Malta 469-471
Monaco 866-867
Netherlands 504-505
Norway 604-605
Portugal 1170-1172
San Marino 802-803
Spain 1753
Switzerland 580-581
Turkey 1935-1936
Yugoslavia 1138-1139

Nos. 219-220 (2)	20.00	11.00
No. 76 (1)	1.25	.85
Nos. 839-840 (2)	1.00	.65
Nos. 396-398 (3)	4.25	3.85
No. 526 (1)	1.25	.55
No. 1367 (1)	1.25	.75
Nos. 1114-1115 (2)	.85	.50
Nos. 1090-1092 (3)	2.10	1.40
Nos. 447-448 (2)	6.65	3.35

Nos. 329-330 (2)	5.25	2.00
Nos. 1108-1109 (2)	.50	.50
Nos. 528-529 (2)	.60	.60
Nos. 523-524 (2)	.90	.75
Nos. 469-471 (3)	.90	1.20
Nos. 866-867 (2)	15.00	2.40
Nos. 504-505 (2)	1.20	.95
Nos. 604-605 (2)	6.25	2.40
Nos. 1170-1172 (3)	*13.00*	2.15
Nos. 802-803 (2)	*1.00*	.60
No. 1753 (1)	.35	.25
Nos. 580-581 (2)	1.55	.60
Nos. 1935-1936 (2)	10.00	4.50
Nos. 1138-1139 (2)	1.15	1.10
Set total (46) Stamps	96.25	42.90

Europa, 2000

CD17

2000

Albania 2621-2622
Andorra, French 522
Andorra, Spanish 262
Armenia 610-611
Austria 1814
Azerbaijan 698-699
Belarus 350
Belgium 1818
Bosnia & Herzegovina (Moslem) 358
Bosnia & Herzegovina (Serb) 111-112
Croatia 428-429
Cyprus 959
Czech Republic 3120
Denmark 1189
Estonia 394
Faroe Islands 376
Finland 1129
Aland Islands 166
France 2771
Georgia 228-229
Germany 2086-2087
Gibraltar 837-840
Great Britain (Jersey) 935-936
Great Britain (Isle of Man) 883
Greece 1959
Greenland 363
Hungary 3699-3700
Iceland 910
Ireland 1230-1231
Italy 2349
Latvia 504
Liechtenstein 1178
Lithuania 668
Luxembourg 1035
Macedonia 187
Malta 1011-1012
Moldova 355
Monaco 2161-2162
Poland 3519
Portugal 2358
Portugal (Azores) 455
Portugal (Madeira) 208
Romania 4370
Russia 6589
San Marino 1480
Slovakia 355
Slovenia 424
Spain 3036
Sweden 2394
Switzerland 1074
Turkey 2762
Turkish Rep. of Northern Cyprus 500
Ukraine 379
Vatican City 1152

Nos. 2621-2622 (2)	11.00	11.00
No. 522 (1)	2.00	1.00
No. 262 (1)	1.75	.80
Nos. 610-611 (2)	4.75	4.75
No. 1814 (1)	1.40	1.40
Nos. 698-699 (2)	6.00	6.00
No. 350 (1)	1.75	1.75
No. 1818 (1)	1.40	.60
No. 358 (1)	4.75	4.75
Nos. 111-112 (2)	110.00	110.00
Nos. 428-429 (2)	6.25	6.25
No. 959 (1)	2.10	1.40
No. 3120 (1)	1.20	.40
No. 1189 (1)	3.50	2.25
No. 394 (1)	1.25	1.25
No. 376 (1)	2.40	2.40
No. 1129 (1)	2.00	.60
No. 166 (1)	2.00	1.10
No. 2771 (1)	1.25	.40
Nos. 228-229 (2)	9.00	9.00
Nos. 2086-2087 (2)	4.35	2.10
Nos. 837-840 (4)	5.50	5.30
Nos. 935-936 (2)	2.40	2.40
No. 883 (1)	1.75	1.75
No. 363 (1)	1.90	1.90
Nos. 3699-3700 (2)	6.50	2.50
No. 910 (1)	1.60	1.60
Nos. 1230-1231 (2)	4.35	4.35
No. 2349 (1)	1.50	.40
No. 504 (1)	5.00	2.40
No. 1178 (1)	2.25	1.75
No. 668 (1)	1.50	1.50
No. 1035 (1)	1.40	.85
No. 187 (1)	3.00	3.00
Nos. 1011-1012 (2)	4.35	4.35
No. 355 (1)	3.50	3.50
Nos. 2161-2162 (2)	2.80	1.40
No. 3519 (1)	1.25	.75
No. 2358 (1)	1.25	.65
No. 455 (1)	1.25	.50
No. 208 (1)	1.25	.50
No. 4370 (1)	2.50	1.25
No. 6589 (1)	2.00	.85
No. 1480 (1)	1.00	1.00
No. 355 (1)	1.60	.80
No. 424 (1)	3.25	3.25
No. 3036 (1)	.75	.40
No. 2394 (1)	3.00	2.25
No. 1074 (1)	2.10	1.05
No. 2762 (1)	2.00	2.00
No. 500 (1)	2.50	2.50
No. 379 (1)	4.50	3.00
No. 1152 (1)	1.25	1.25
Set total (68) Stamps	260.85	230.15

The Gibraltar stamps are similar to the stamp illustrated, but none have the design shown above. All other sets listed above include at least one stamp with the design shown, but some include stamps with entirely different designs. Bulgaria Nos. 4131-4132, Guernsey Nos. 802-803 and Yugoslavia Nos. 2485-2486 are Europa stamps with completely different designs.

PORTUGAL & COLONIES

Vasco da Gama

Fleet Departing CD20

Fleet Arriving at Calicut — CD21

Embarking at Rastello CD22

Muse of History CD23

San Gabriel, da Gama and Camoens CD24

Archangel Gabriel, the Patron Saint CD25

Flagship San Gabriel — CD26

Vasco da Gama — CD27

Fourth centenary of Vasco da Gama's discovery of the route to India.

1898

Azores 93-100
Macao 67-74
Madeira 37-44
Portugal 147-154
Port. Africa 1-8
Port. Congo 75-98
Port. India 189-196
St. Thomas & Prince Islands ... 170-193
Timor 45-52

Nos. 93-100 (8)	122.00	76.25
Nos. 67-74 (8)	136.00	96.75
Nos. 37-44 (8)	44.55	34.00
Nos. 147-154 (8)	155.00	50.25
Nos. 1-8 (8)	27.00	17.75
Nos. 75-98 (24)	41.50	34.45
Nos. 189-196 (8)	20.25	12.95
Nos. 170-193 (24)	38.75	34.30
Nos. 45-52 (8)	19.50	8.75
Set total (104) Stamps	604.55	365.45

Pombal POSTAL TAX POSTAL TAX DUES

Marquis de Pombal — CD28

Planning Reconstruction of Lisbon, 1755 — CD29

Pombal Monument, Lisbon — CD30

Sebastiao Jose de Carvalho e Mello, Marquis de Pombal (1699-1782), statesman, rebuilt Lisbon after earthquake of 1755. Tax was for the erection of Pombal monument. Obligatory on all mail on certain days throughout the year. Postal Tax Dues are inscribed "Multa."

1925

Angola RA1-RA3, RAJ1-RAJ3
Azores RA9-RA11, RAJ2-RAJ4
Cape Verde RA1-RA3, RAJ1-RAJ3
Macao RA1-RA3, RAJ1-RAJ3
Madeira RA1-RA3, RAJ1-RAJ3
Mozambique RA1-RA3, RAJ1-RAJ3
Nyassa RA1-RA3, RAJ1-RAJ3
Portugal RA11-RA13, RAJ2-RAJ4
Port. Guinea RA1-RA3, RAJ1-RAJ3
Port. India RA1-RA3, RAJ1-RAJ3
St. Thomas & Prince Islands RA1-RA3, RAJ1-RAJ3
Timor RA1-RA3, RAJ1-RAJ3

Nos. RA1-RA3,RAJ1-RAJ3 (6)	6.60	6.60
Nos. RA9-RA11,RAJ2-RAJ4 (6)	6.60	9.30
Nos. RA1-RA3,RAJ1-RAJ3 (6)	4.50	3.90
Nos. RA1-RA3,RAJ1-RAJ3 (6)	21.25	10.50
Nos. RA1-RA3,RAJ1-RAJ3 (6)	4.35	12.45
Nos. RA1-RA3,RAJ1-RAJ3 (6)	2.40	2.55
Nos. RA1-RA3,RAJ1-RAJ3 (6)	52.50	38.25
Nos. RA11-RA13,RAJ2-RAJ4 (6)	5.95	5.20
Nos. RA1-RA3,RAJ1-RAJ3 (6)	3.30	2.70
Nos. RA1-RA3,RAJ1-RAJ3 (6)	3.45	3.45
Nos. RA1-RA3,RAJ1-RAJ3 (6)	3.60	3.60
Nos. RA1-RA3,RAJ1-RAJ3 (6)	2.10	3.90
Set total (72) Stamps	116.60	102.40

Vasco da Gama CD34

Mousinho de Albuquerque CD35

Dam CD36

Prince Henry the Navigator CD37

Affonso de Albuquerque CD38

Plane over Globe CD39

1938-39

Angola 274-291, C1-C9
Cape Verde 234-251, C1-C9
Macao 289-305, C7-C15
Mozambique 270-287, C1-C9
Port. Guinea 233-250. C1-C9
Port. India 439-453, C1-C8
St. Thomas & Prince Islands ... 302-319, 323-340, C1-C18
Timor 223-239, C1-C9

Nos. 274-291,C1-C9 (27)	132.90	22.85
Nos. 234-251,C1-C9 (27)	87.00	27.15
Nos. 289-305,C7-C15 (26)	589.45	145.25
Nos. 270-287,C1-C9 (27)	63.45	11.20
Nos. 233-250,C1-C9 (27)	88.05	30.70
Nos. 439-453,C1-C8 (23)	74.75	25.50
Nos. 302-319,323-340,C1-C18 (54)	319.25	190.35
Nos. 223-239,C1-C9 (26)	149.25	73.15
Set total (237) Stamps	1,504.	526.15

Lady of Fatima

Our Lady of the Rosary, Fatima, Portugal — CD40

1948-49

Angola 315-318
Cape Verde 266
Macao 336
Mozambique 325-328
Port. Guinea 271
Port. India 480
St. Thomas & Prince Islands 351
Timor 254

Nos. 315-318 (4)	68.00	17.25
No. 266 (1)	8.50	4.50
No. 336 (1)	42.50	12.00
Nos. 325-328 (4)	73.25	16.85
No. 271 (1)	3.25	3.00
No. 480 (1)	2.50	2.25
No. 351 (1)	7.25	6.50
No. 254 (1)	2.75	2.75
Set total (14) Stamps	208.00	65.10

A souvenir sheet of 9 stamps was issued in 1951 to mark the extension of the 1950 Holy Year. The sheet contains: Angola No. 316, Cape Verde No. 266, Macao No. 336, Mozambique No. 325, Portuguese Guinea No. 271, Portuguese India Nos. 480, 485, St. Thomas & Prince Islands No. 351, Timor No. 254. The sheet also contains a portrait of Pope Pius XII and is inscribed "Encerramento do

Ano Santo, Fatima 1951." It was sold for 11 escudos.

Holy Year

Church Bells and Dove
CD41

Angel Holding Candelabra
CD42

Holy Year, 1950.

1950-51

Angola 331-332
Cape Verde 268-269
Macao 339-340
Mozambique 330-331
Port. Guinea 273-274
Port. India 490-491, 496-503
St. Thomas & Prince Islands 353-354
Timor 258-259

Nos. 331-332 (2)	7.60	1.35
Nos. 268-269 (2)	5.50	3.50
Nos. 339-340 (2)	60.00	14.00
Nos. 330 331 (2)	3.00	1.10
Nos. 273-274 (2)	3.50	2.60
Nos. 490-491,496-503 (10)	12.80	5.40
Nos. 353-354 (2)	7.50	4.40
Nos. 258-259 (2)	3.75	3.25
Set total (24) Stamps	103.65	35.60

A souvenir sheet of 8 stamps was issued in 1951 to mark the extension of the Holy Year. The sheet contains: Angola No. 331, Cape Verde No. 269, Macao No. 340, Mozambique No. 331, Portuguese Guinea No. 275, Portuguese India No. 490, St. Thomas & Prince Islands No. 354, Timor No. 258, some with colors changed. The sheet contains doves and is inscribed 'Encerramento do Ano Santo, Fatima 1951.' It was sold for 17 escudos.

Holy Year Conclusion

Our Lady of Fatima — CD43

Conclusion of Holy Year. Sheets contain alternate vertical rows of stamps and labels bearing quotation from Pope Pius XII, different for each colony.

1951

Angola 357
Cape Verde 270
Macao 352
Mozambique 356
Port. Guinea 275
Port. India 506
St. Thomas & Prince Islands 355
Timor 270

No. 357 (1)	5.25	1.50
No. 270 (1)	1.50	1.25
No. 352 (1)	45.00	10.00
No. 356 (1)	2.25	1.00
No. 275 (1)	1.00	.65
No. 506 (1)	1.60	1.00
No. 355 (1)	2.50	2.00
No. 270 (1)	2.00	1.75
Set total (8) Stamps	61.10	19.15

Medical Congress

CD44

First National Congress of Tropical Medicine, Lisbon, 1952. Each stamp has a different design.

1952

Angola 358
Cape Verde 287
Macao 364
Mozambique 359
Port. Guinea 276
Port. India 516
St. Thomas & Prince Islands 356
Timor 271

No. 358 (1)	1.50	.50
No. 287 (1)	.75	.60
No. 364 (1)	10.00	6.00
No. 359 (1)	1.25	.55
No. 276 (1)	.45	.35
No. 516 (1)	4.75	2.00
No. 356 (1)	.30	.30
No. 271 (1)	1.00	1.00
Set total (8) Stamps	20.00	11.30

Postage Due Stamps

CD45

1952

Angola J37-J42
Cape Verde J31-J36
Macao J53-J58
Mozambique J51-J56
Port. Guinea J40-J45
Port. India J47-J52
St. Thomas & Prince Islands J52-J57
Timor J31-J36

Nos. J37-J42 (6)	4.05	3.15
Nos. J31-J36 (6)	2.80	2.30
Nos. J53-J58 (6)	17.45	6.85
Nos. J51-J56 (6)	1.80	1.55
Nos. J40-J45 (6)	2.55	2.55
Nos. J47-J52 (6)	6.10	6.10
Nos. J52-J57 (6)	4.15	4.15
Nos. J31-J36 (6)	6.20	3.50
Set total (48) Stamps	45.10	30.15

Sao Paulo

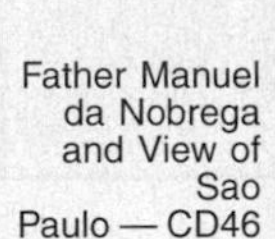

Father Manuel da Nobrega and View of Sao Paulo — CD46

Founding of Sao Paulo, Brazil, 400th anniv.

1954

Angola 385
Cape Verde 297
Macao 382
Mozambique 395
Port. Guinea 291
Port. India 530
St. Thomas & Prince Islands 369
Timor 279

No. 385 (1)	.80	.50
No. 297 (1)	.70	.60
No. 382 (1)	15.00	6.00
No. 395 (1)	.40	.30
No. 291 (1)	.35	.25
No. 530 (1)	.80	.40
No. 369 (1)	.80	.60
No. 279 (1)	.85	.70
Set total (8) Stamps	19.70	9.35

Tropical Medicine Congress

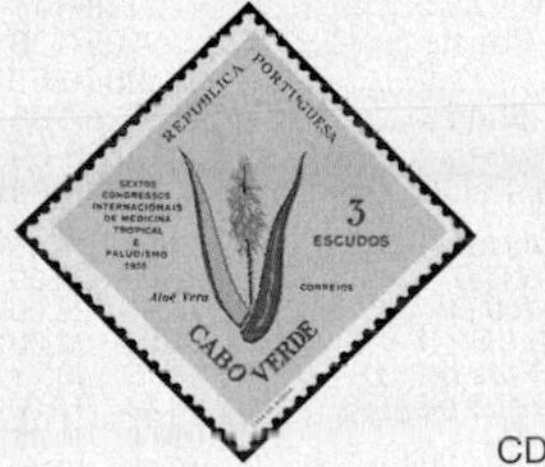

CD47

Sixth International Congress for Tropical Medicine and Malaria, Lisbon, Sept. 1958. Each stamp shows a different plant.

1958

Angola 409
Cape Verde 303
Macao 392
Mozambique 404
Port. Guinea 295
Port. India 569
St. Thomas & Prince Islands 371
Timor 289

No. 409 (1)	3.50	1.10
No. 303 (1)	5.50	2.10
No. 392 (1)	10.00	5.00
No. 404 (1)	2.50	.85
No. 295 (1)	2.75	1.10
No. 569 (1)	1.75	.75
No. 371 (1)	2.75	2.25
No. 289 (1)	3.00	2.75
Set total (8) Stamps	31.75	15.90

Sports

CD48

Each stamp shows a different sport.

1962

Angola 433-438
Cape Verde 320-325
Macao 394-399
Mozambique 424-429
Port. Guinea 299-304
St. Thomas & Prince Islands 374-379
Timor 313-318

Nos. 433-438 (6)	5.50	3.20
Nos. 320-325 (6)	15.25	5.20
Nos. 394-399 (6)	68.65	14.60
Nos. 424-429 (6)	5.70	2.45
Nos. 299-304 (6)	4.95	2.15
Nos. 374-379 (6)	6.75	3.20
Nos. 313-318 (6)	6.40	3.70
Set total (42) Stamps	113.20	34.50

Anti-Malaria

Anopheles Funestus and Malaria Eradication Symbol — CD49

World Health Organization drive to eradicate malaria.

1962

Angola 439
Cape Verde 326
Macao 400
Mozambique 430
Port. Guinea 305
St. Thomas & Prince Islands 380
Timor 319

No. 439 (1)	1.75	.90
No. 326 (1)	1.40	.90
No. 400 (1)	7.00	2.25
No. 430 (1)	1.40	.40
No. 305 (1)	1.25	.45
No. 380 (1)	2.00	1.50
No. 319 (1)	.75	.60
Set total (7) Stamps	15.55	7.00

Airline Anniversary

Map of Africa, Super Constellation and Jet Liner — CD50

Tenth anniversary of Transportes Aereos Portugueses (TAP).

1963

Angola 490
Cape Verde 327
Mozambique 434
Port. Guinea 318
St. Thomas & Prince Islands 381

No. 490 (1)	1.00	.35
No. 327 (1)	1.10	.70
No. 434 (1)	.40	.25
No. 318 (1)	.65	.35
No. 381 (1)	.70	.60
Set total (5) Stamps	3.85	2.25

National Overseas Bank

Antonio Teixeira de Sousa — CD51

Centenary of the National Overseas Bank of Portugal.

1964, May 16

Angola 509
Cape Verde 328
Port. Guinea 319
St. Thomas & Prince Islands 382
Timor 320

No. 509 (1)	.90	.30
No. 328 (1)	1.10	.75
No. 319 (1)	.65	.40
No. 382 (1)	.70	.50
No. 320 (1)	.75	.60
Set total (5) Stamps	4.10	2.55

ITU

ITU Emblem and the Archangel Gabriel — CD52

International Communications Union, Cent.

1965, May 17

Angola 511
Cape Verde 329
Macao 402
Mozambique 464
Port. Guinea 320
St. Thomas & Prince Islands 383
Timor 321

No. 511 (1)	1.25	.65
No. 329 (1)	2.10	1.40
No. 402 (1)	6.00	2.25
No. 464 (1)	.45	.25
No. 320 (1)	1.90	.75
No. 383 (1)	1.50	1.00
No. 321 (1)	1.50	.90
Set total (7) Stamps	14.70	7.20

National Revolution

CD53

40th anniv. of the National Revolution. Different buildings on each stamp.

1966, May 28

Angola 525
Cape Verde 338
Macao 403
Mozambique 465
Port. Guinea 329
St. Thomas & Prince Islands 392
Timor 322

No. 525 (1)	.50	.25
No. 338 (1)	.60	.45
No. 403 (1)	9.00	2.25
No. 465 (1)	.50	.30
No. 329 (1)	.55	.35
No. 392 (1)	.75	.50
No. 322 (1)	1.50	.90
Set total (7) Stamps	13.40	5.00

Navy Club

CD54

Centenary of Portugal's Navy Club. Each stamp has a different design.

1967, Jan. 31

Angola 527-528
Cape Verde 339-340
Macao 412-413
Mozambique 478-479
Port. Guinea 330-331
St. Thomas & Prince Islands 393-394
Timor 323-324

Nos. 527-528 (2)	1.75	.75
Nos. 339-340 (2)	2.00	1.40
Nos. 412-413 (2)	11.25	4.00
Nos. 478-479 (2)	1.40	.65
Nos. 330-331 (2)	1.20	.90
Nos. 393-394 (2)	3.20	1.25
Nos. 323-324 (2)	4.00	2.00
Set total (14) Stamps	24.80	10.95

Admiral Coutinho

CD55

Centenary of the birth of Admiral Carlos Viegas Gago Coutinho (1869-1959), explorer and aviation pioneer. Each stamp has a different design.

1969, Feb. 17

Angola 547
Cape Verde 355
Macao 417
Mozambique 484
Port. Guinea 335
St. Thomas & Prince Islands 397
Timor 335

No. 547 (1)	.85	.35
No. 355 (1)	.50	.25
No. 417 (1)	5.00	1.75
No. 484 (1)	.25	.25
No. 335 (1)	.35	.25
No. 397 (1)	.50	.35
No. 335 (1)	1.10	.85
Set total (7) Stamps	8.55	4.05

Administration Reform

Luiz Augusto Rebello da Silva — CD56

Centenary of the administration reforms of the overseas territories.

1969, Sept. 25

Angola 549
Cape Verde 357
Macao 419
Mozambique 491
Port. Guinea 337
St. Thomas & Prince Islands 399
Timor 338

No. 549 (1)	.35	.25
No. 357 (1)	.50	.25
No. 419 (1)	6.00	1.00
No. 491 (1)	.25	.25
No. 337 (1)	.25	.25
No. 399 (1)	.45	.45
No. 338 (1)	.40	.25
Set total (7) Stamps	8.20	2.70

Marshal Carmona

CD57

Birth centenary of Marshal Antonio Oscar Carmona de Fragoso (1869-1951), President of Portugal. Each stamp has a different design.

1970, Nov. 15

Angola 563
Cape Verde 359
Macao 422
Mozambique 493
Port. Guinea 340
St. Thomas & Prince Islands 403
Timor 341

No. 563 (1)	.45	.25
No. 359 (1)	.55	.35
No. 422 (1)	2.00	1.00
No. 493 (1)	.40	.25
No. 340 (1)	.35	.25
No. 403 (1)	.75	.45
No. 341 (1)	.25	.25
Set total (7) Stamps	4.75	2.80

Olympic Games

CD59

20th Olympic Games, Munich, Aug. 26-Sept. 11. Each stamp shows a different sport.

1972, June 20

Angola 569
Cape Verde 361
Macao 426
Mozambique 504
Port. Guinea 342
St. Thomas & Prince Islands 408
Timor 343

No. 569 (1)	.65	.25
No. 361 (1)	.85	.30
No. 426 (1)	4.25	1.00
No. 504 (1)	.30	.25
No. 342 (1)	.45	.25
No. 408 (1)	.35	.25
No. 343 (1)	.50	.50
Set total (7) Stamps	7.35	2.80

Lisbon-Rio de Janeiro Flight

CD60

50th anniversary of the Lisbon to Rio de Janeiro flight by Arturo de Sacadura and Coutinho, March 30-June 5, 1922. Each stamp shows a different stage of the flight.

1972, Sept. 20

Angola 570
Cape Verde 362
Macao 427
Mozambique 505
Port. Guinea 343
St. Thomas & Prince Islands 409
Timor 344

No. 570 (1)	.35	.25
No. 362 (1)	1.50	.30
No. 427 (1)	22.50	8.50
No. 505 (1)	.25	.25
No. 343 (1)	.25	.25
No. 409 (1)	.35	.25
No. 344 (1)	.25	.40
Set total (7) Stamps	25.45	10.20

WMO Centenary

WMO Emblem — CD61

Centenary of international meterological cooperation.

1973, Dec. 15

Angola 571
Cape Verde 363
Macao 429
Mozambique 509
Port. Guinea 344
St. Thomas & Prince Islands 410
Timor 345

No. 571 (1)	.45	.25
No. 363 (1)	.65	.30
No. 429 (1)	6.00	1.75
No. 509 (1)	.30	.25
No. 344 (1)	.45	.35
No. 410 (1)	.60	.50
No. 345 (1)	1.75	2.00
Set total (7) Stamps	10.20	5.40

FRENCH COMMUNITY

Upper Volta can be found under Burkina Faso in Vol. 1
Madagascar can be found under Malagasy in Vol. 3

Colonial Exposition

People of French Empire CD70

Women's Heads CD71

France Showing Way to Civilization CD72

"Colonial Commerce" CD73

International Colonial Exposition, Paris.

1931

Cameroun 213-216
Chad 60-63
Dahomey 97-100
Fr. Guiana 152-155
Fr. Guinea 116-119
Fr. India 100-103
Fr. Polynesia 76-79
Fr. Sudan 102-105
Gabon 120-123
Guadeloupe 138-141
Indo-China 140-142
Ivory Coast 92-95
Madagascar 169-172
Martinique 129-132
Mauritania 65-68
Middle Congo 61-64
New Caledonia 176-179
Niger 73-76
Reunion 122-125
St. Pierre & Miquelon 132-135
Senegal 138-141
Somali Coast 135-138
Togo 254-257
Ubangi-Shari 82-85
Upper Volta 66-69
Wallis & Futuna Isls. 85-88

Nos. 213-216 (4)	23.00	18.25
Nos. 60-63 (4)	22.00	22.00
Nos. 97-100 (4)	26.00	26.00
Nos. 152-155 (4)	22.00	22.00
Nos. 116-119 (4)	19.75	19.75
Nos. 100-103 (4)	18.00	*18.00*
Nos. 76-79 (4)	30.00	30.00
Nos. 102-105 (4)	19.00	19.00
Nos. 120-123 (4)	17.50	17.50
Nos. 138-141 (4)	19.00	19.00
Nos. 140-142 (3)	12.00	11.50
Nos. 92-95 (4)	22.50	22.50
Nos. 169-172 (4)	7.90	5.00
Nos. 129-132 (4)	21.00	21.00
Nos. 65-68 (4)	22.00	22.00
Nos. 61-64 (4)	20.00	18.50
Nos. 176-179 (4)	24.00	24.00
Nos. 73-76 (4)	21.50	21.50
Nos. 122-125 (4)	22.00	22.00
Nos. 132-135 (4)	24.00	24.00
Nos. 138-141 (4)	20.00	20.00
Nos. 135-138 (4)	22.00	22.00
Nos. 254-257 (4)	22.00	22.00
Nos. 82-85 (4)	21.00	21.00
Nos. 66-69 (4)	19.00	19.00
Nos. 85-88 (4)	31.00	35.00
Set total (103) Stamps	548.15	542.50

Paris International Exposition
Colonial Arts Exposition

"Colonial Resources"
CD74 CD77

Overseas Commerce CD75

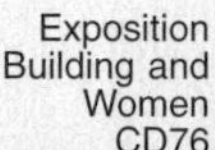

Exposition Building and Women CD76

"France and the Empire" CD78

Cultural Treasures of the Colonies CD79

Souvenir sheets contain one imperf. stamp.

1937

Cameroun 217-222A
Dahomey 101-107
Fr. Equatorial Africa 27-32, 73
Fr. Guiana 162-168
Fr. Guinea 120-126
Fr. India 104-110
Fr. Polynesia 117-123
Fr. Sudan 106-112
Guadeloupe 148-154
Indo-China 193-199
Inini 41
Ivory Coast 152-158
Kwangchowan 132
Madagascar 191-197
Martinique 179-185
Mauritania 69-75
New Caledonia 208-214
Niger 77-83
Reunion 167-173
St. Pierre & Miquelon 165-171
Senegal 172-178
Somali Coast 139-145
Togo 258-264
Wallis & Futuna Isls. 89

Nos. 217-222A (7)	18.80	20.30
Nos. 101-107 (7)	23.60	27.60
Nos. 27-32, 73 (7)	28.10	32.10
Nos. 162-168 (7)	22.50	24.50
Nos. 120-126 (7)	24.00	28.00
Nos. 104-110 (7)	21.15	36.50
Nos. 117-123 (7)	58.50	75.00
Nos. 106-112 (7)	23.60	27.60
Nos. 148-154 (7)	19.55	21.05
Nos. 193-199 (7)	17.70	19.70
No. 41 (1)	21.00	27.50
Nos. 152-158 (7)	22.20	26.20
No. 132 (1)	9.25	11.00
Nos. 191-197 (7)	19.25	21.75
Nos. 179-185 (7)	19.95	21.70
Nos. 69-75 (7)	20.50	24.50
Nos. 208-214 (7)	39.00	50.50
Nos. 73-83 (11)	42.70	46.70
Nos. 167-173 (7)	21.70	23.20
Nos. 165-171 (7)	49.60	64.00
Nos. 172-178 (7)	21.00	23.80
Nos. 139-145 (7)	25.60	32.60
Nos. 258-264 (7)	20.40	20.40
No. 89 (1)	19.00	37.50
Set total (154) Stamps	608.65	743.70

Curie

Pierre and Marie Curie CD80

40th anniversary of the discovery of radium. The surtax was for the benefit of the Intl. Union for the Control of Cancer.

1938

Cameroun	B1
Cuba	B1-B2
Dahomey	B2
France	B76
Fr. Equatorial Africa	B1
Fr. Guiana	B3
Fr. Guinea	B2
Fr. India	B6
Fr. Polynesia	B5
Fr. Sudan	B1
Guadeloupe	B3
Indo-China	B14
Ivory Coast	B2
Madagascar	B2
Martinique	B2
Mauritania	B3
New Caledonia	B4
Niger	B1
Reunion	B4
St. Pierre & Miquelon	B3
Senegal	B3
Somali Coast	B2
Togo	B1

No. B1 (1)	10.00	10.00
Nos. B1-B2 (2)	12.00	3.35
No. B2 (1)	9.50	9.50
No. B76 (1)	21.00	12.50
No. B1 (1)	24.00	24.00
No. B3 (1)	13.50	13.50
No. B2 (1)	8.75	8.75
No. B6 (1)	10.00	10.00
No. B5 (1)	20.00	20.00
No. B1 (1)	12.50	12.50
No. B3 (1)	11.00	10.50
No. B14 (1)	12.00	12.00
No. B2 (1)	11.00	7.50
No. B2 (1)	11.00	11.00
No. B2 (1)	13.00	13.00
No. B3 (1)	7.75	7.75
No. B4 (1)	16.50	17.50
No. B1 (1)	15.00	15.00
No. B4 (1)	14.00	14.00
No. B3 (1)	21.00	22.50
No. B3 (1)	10.50	10.50
No. B2 (1)	7.75	7.75
No. B1 (1)	20.00	20.00
Set total (24) Stamps	311.75	293.10

Caillie

Rene Caillie and Map of Northwestern Africa — CD81

Death centenary of Rene Caillie (1799-1838), French explorer. All three denominations exist with colony name omitted.

1939

Dahomey	108-110
Fr. Guinea	161-163
Fr. Sudan	113-115
Ivory Coast	160-162
Mauritania	109-111
Niger	84-86
Senegal	188-190
Togo	265-267

Nos. 108-110 (3)	1.20	3.60
Nos. 161-163 (3)	1.20	3.20
Nos. 113-115 (3)	1.20	3.20
Nos. 160-162 (3)	1.05	2.55
Nos. 109-111 (3)	1.05	3.80
Nos. 84-86 (3)	1.05	2.35
Nos. 188-190 (3)	1.05	2.90
Nos. 265-267 (3)	1.05	3.30
Set total (24) Stamps	8.85	24.90

New York World's Fair

Natives and New York Skyline CD82

1939

Cameroun	223-224
Dahomey	111-112
Fr. Equatorial Africa	78-79
Fr. Guiana	169-170
Fr. Guinea	164-165
Fr. India	111-112
Fr. Polynesia	124-125
Fr. Sudan	116-117
Guadeloupe	155-156
Indo-China	203-204
Inini	42-43
Ivory Coast	163-164
Kwangchowan	133-134
Madagascar	209-210
Martinique	186-187
Mauritania	112-113
New Caledonia	215-216
Niger	87-88
Reunion	174-175
St. Pierre & Miquelon	205-206
Senegal	191-192
Somali Coast	179-180
Togo	268-269
Wallis & Futuna Isls.	90-91

Nos. 223-224 (2)	2.80	2.40
Nos. 111-112 (2)	1.60	3.20
Nos. 78-79 (2)	1.60	3.20
Nos. 169-170 (2)	2.60	2.60
Nos. 164-165 (2)	1.60	3.20
Nos. 111-112 (2)	3.00	*8.00*
Nos. 124-125 (2)	4.80	4.80
Nos. 116-117 (2)	1.60	3.20
Nos. 155-156 (2)	2.50	2.50
Nos. 203-204 (2)	2.05	2.05
Nos. 42-43 (2)	7.50	9.00
Nos. 163-164 (2)	1.50	3.00
Nos. 133-134 (2)	2.50	2.50
Nos. 209-210 (2)	1.50	2.50
Nos. 186-187 (2)	2.35	2.35
Nos. 112-113 (2)	1.40	2.80
Nos. 215-216 (2)	3.35	3.35
Nos. 87-88 (2)	1.40	2.80
Nos. 174-175 (2)	2.80	2.80
Nos. 205-206 (2)	4.80	6.00
Nos. 191-192 (2)	1.40	2.80
Nos. 179-180 (2)	1.40	2.80
Nos. 268-269 (2)	1.40	2.80
Nos. 90-91 (2)	5.00	6.00
Set total (48) Stamps	62.45	86.65

French Revolution

Storming of the Bastille CD83

French Revolution, 150th anniv. The surtax was for the defense of the colonies.

1939

Cameroun	B2-B6
Dahomey	B3-B7
Fr. Equatorial Africa	B4-B8, CB1
Fr. Guiana	B4-B8, CB1
Fr. Guinea	B3-B7
Fr. India	B7-B11
Fr. Polynesia	B6-B10, CB1
Fr. Sudan	B2-B6
Guadeloupe	B4-B8
Indo-China	B15-B19, CB1
Inini	B1-B5
Ivory Coast	B3-B7
Kwangchowan	B1-B5
Madagascar	B3-B7, CB1
Martinique	B3-B7
Mauritania	B4-B8
New Caledonia	B5-B9, CB1
Niger	B2-B6
Reunion	B5-B9, CB1
St. Pierre & Miquelon	B4-B8
Senegal	B4-B8, CB1
Somali Coast	B3-B7
Togo	B2-B6
Wallis & Futuna Isls.	B1-B5

Nos. B2-B6 (5)	60.00	60.00
Nos. B3-B7 (5)	47.50	47.50
Nos. B4-B8,CB1 (6)	120.00	120.00
Nos. B4-B8,CB1 (6)	79.50	79.50
Nos. B3-B7 (5)	47.50	47.50
Nos. B7-B11 (5)	28.75	*32.50*
Nos. B6-B10,CB1 (6)	122.50	122.50
Nos. B2-B6 (5)	50.00	50.00
Nos. B4-B8 (5)	50.00	50.00
Nos. B15-B19,CB1 (6)	85.00	85.00
Nos. B1-B5 (5)	80.00	100.00
Nos. B3-B7 (5)	43.75	43.75
Nos. B1-B5 (5)	46.25	46.25
Nos. B3-B7,CB1 (6)	65.50	65.50
Nos. B3-B7 (5)	52.50	52.50
Nos. B4-B8 (5)	42.50	42.50
Nos. B5-B9,CB1 (6)	101.50	101.50
Nos. B2-B6 (5)	60.00	60.00
Nos. B5-B9,CB1 (6)	87.50	87.50
Nos. B4-B8 (5)	67.50	72.50
Nos. B4-B8,CB1 (6)	56.50	56.50
Nos. B3-B7 (5)	45.00	45.00
Nos. B2-B6 (5)	42.50	42.50
Nos. B1-B5 (5)	80.00	110.00
Set total (128) Stamps	1,562.	1,621.

Plane over Coastal Area CD85

All five denominations exist with colony name omitted.

1940

Dahomey	C1-C5
Fr. Guinea	C1-C5
Fr. Sudan	C1-C5
Ivory Coast	C1-C5
Mauritania	C1-C5
Niger	C1-C5
Senegal	C12-C16
Togo	C1-C5

Nos. C1-C5 (5)	4.00	4.00
Nos. C1-C5 (5)	4.00	4.00
Nos. C1-C5 (5)	4.00	4.00
Nos. C1-C5 (5)	3.80	3.80
Nos. C1-C5 (5)	3.50	3.50
Nos. C1-C5 (5)	3.50	3.50
Nos. C12-C16 (5)	3.50	3.50
Nos. C1-C5 (5)	3.15	3.15
Set total (40) Stamps	29.45	29.45

Defense of the Empire

Colonial Infantryman — CD86

1941

Cameroun	B13B
Dahomey	B13
Fr. Equatorial Africa	B8B
Fr. Guiana	B10
Fr. Guinea	B13
Fr. India	B13
Fr. Polynesia	B12
Fr. Sudan	B12
Guadeloupe	B10
Indo-China	B19B
Inini	B7
Ivory Coast	B13
Kwangchowan	B7
Madagascar	B9
Martinique	B9
Mauritania	B14
New Caledonia	B11
Niger	B12
Reunion	B11
St. Pierre & Miquelon	B8B
Senegal	B14
Somali Coast	B9
Togo	B10B
Wallis & Futuna Isls.	B7

No. B13B (1)	1.60
No. B13 (1)	1.20
No. B8B (1)	3.50
No. B10 (1)	1.40
No. B13 (1)	1.40
No. B13 (1)	1.25
No. B12 (1)	3.50
No. B12 (1)	1.40
No. B10 (1)	1.00
No. B19B (1)	1.60
No. B7 (1)	1.75
No. B13 (1)	1.25
No. B7 (1)	.85
No. B9 (1)	1.50
No. B9 (1)	1.40
No. B14 (1)	.95
No. B12 (1)	1.40
No. B11 (1)	1.60
No. B8B (1)	4.50
No. B14 (1)	1.25
No. B9 (1)	1.60
No. B10B (1)	1.10
No. B7 (1)	1.75
Set total (23) Stamps	38.75

Each of the CD86 stamps listed above is part of a set of three stamps. The designs of the other two stamps in the set vary from country to country. Only the values of the Common Design stamps are listed here.

Colonial Education Fund

CD86a

1942

Cameroun	CB3
Dahomey	CB4
Fr. Equatorial Africa	CB5
Fr. Guiana	CB4
Fr. Guinea	CB4
Fr. India	CB3
Fr. Polynesia	CB4
Fr. Sudan	CB4
Guadeloupe	CB3
Indo-China	CB5
Inini	CB3
Ivory Coast	CB4
Kwangchowan	CB4
Malagasy	CB5
Martinique	CB3
Mauritania	CB4
New Caledonia	CB4
Niger	CB4
Reunion	CB4
St. Pierre & Miquelon	CB3
Senegal	CB5
Somali Coast	CB3
Togo	CB3
Wallis & Futuna	CB3

No. CB3 (1)	1.10	
No. CB4 (1)	.80	5.50
No. CB5 (1)	.80	
No. CB4 (1)	1.10	
No. CB4 (1)	.40	5.50
No. CB3 (1)	.90	
No. CB4 (1)	2.00	
No. CB4 (1)	.40	5.50
No. CB3 (1)	1.10	
No. CB5 (1)	1.10	
No. CB3 (1)	1.25	
No. CB4 (1)	1.00	5.50
No. CB4 (1)	1.00	
No. CB5 (1)	.65	
No. CB3 (1)	1.00	
No. CB4 (1)	.80	
No. CB4 (1)	2.25	
No. CB4 (1)	.35	
No. CB4 (1)	.90	
No. CB3 (1)	7.00	
No. CB5 (1)	.80	6.50
No. CB3 (1)	.70	
No. CB3 (1)	.35	
No. CB3 (1)	2.00	
Set total (24) Stamps	29.75	28.50

Cross of Lorraine & Four-motor Plane CD87

1941-5

Cameroun	C1-C7
Fr. Equatorial Africa	C17-C23
Fr. Guiana	C9-C10
Fr. India	C1-C6
Fr. Polynesia	C3-C9
Fr. West Africa	C1-C3
Guadeloupe	C1-C2
Madagascar	C37-C43

Martinique	C1-C2
New Caledonia	C7-C13
Reunion	C18-C24
St. Pierre & Miquelon	C1-C7
Somali Coast	C1-C7

Nos. C1-C7 (7)	6.30	6.30
Nos. C17-C23 (7)	10.40	6.35
Nos. C9-C10 (2)	3.80	3.10
Nos. C1-C6 (6)	9.30	*15.00*
Nos. C3-C9 (7)	13.75	10.00
Nos. C1-C3 (3)	9.50	3.90
Nos. C1-C2 (2)	3.75	2.50
Nos. C37-C43 (7)	5.60	3.80
Nos. C1-C2 (2)	3.00	1.60
Nos. C7-C13 (7)	8.85	7.30
Nos. C18-C24 (7)	7.05	5.00
Nos. C1-C7 (7)	11.60	9.40
Nos. C1-C7 (7)	13.95	11.10
Set total (71) Stamps	106.85	85.35

Somali Coast stamps are inscribed "Djibouti".

Transport Plane CD88

Caravan and Plane CD89

1942

Dahomey	C6-C13
Fr. Guinea	C6-C13
Fr. Sudan	C6-C13
Ivory Coast	C6-C13
Mauritania	C6-C13
Niger	C6-C13
Senegal	C17-C25
Togo	C6-C13

Nos. C6-C13 (8)	7.15
Nos. C6-C13 (8)	5.75
Nos. C6-C13 (8)	8.00
Nos. C6-C13 (8)	11.15
Nos. C6-C13 (8)	9.75
Nos. C6-C13 (8)	6.90
Nos. C17-C25 (9)	9.45
Nos. C6-C13 (8)	6.75
Set total (65) Stamps	64.90

Red Cross

Marianne CD90

The surtax was for the French Red Cross and national relief.

1944

Cameroun	B28
Fr. Equatorial Africa	B38
Fr. Guiana	B12
Fr. India	B14
Fr. Polynesia	B13
Fr. West Africa	B1
Guadeloupe	B12
Madagascar	B15
Martinique	B11
New Caledonia	B13
Reunion	B15
St. Pierre & Miquelon	B13
Somali Coast	B13
Wallis & Futuna Isls.	B9

No. B28 (1)	2.00	1.60
No. B38 (1)	1.60	1.20
No. B12 (1)	1.75	1.25
No. B14 (1)	1.50	1.25
No. B13 (1)	2.00	1.60
No. B1 (1)	6.50	4.75
No. B12 (1)	1.40	1.00
No. B15 (1)	.90	.90
No. B11 (1)	1.20	1.20
No. B13 (1)	1.50	1.50
No. B15 (1)	1.60	1.10
No. B13 (1)	2.60	2.60
No. B13 (1)	1.75	2.00
No. B9 (1)	3.00	3.00
Set total (14) Stamps	29.30	24.95

Eboue

CD91

Felix Eboue, first French colonial administrator to proclaim resistance to Germany after French surrender in World War II.

1945

Cameroun	296-297
Fr. Equatorial Africa	156-157
Fr. Guiana	171-172
Fr. India	210-211
Fr. Polynesia	150-151
Fr. West Africa	15-16
Guadeloupe	187-188
Madagascar	259-260
Martinique	196-197
New Caledonia	274-275
Reunion	238-239
St. Pierre & Miquelon	322-323
Somali Coast	238-239

Nos. 296-297 (2)	2.40	1.95
Nos. 156-157 (2)	2.55	2.00
Nos. 171-172 (2)	2.45	2.00
Nos. 210-211 (2)	2.20	1.95
Nos. 150-151 (2)	3.60	2.85
Nos. 15-16 (2)	2.40	2.40
Nos. 187-188 (2)	2.05	1.60
Nos. 259-260 (2)	2.00	1.45
Nos. 196-197 (2)	2.05	1.55
Nos. 274-275 (2)	3.40	3.00
Nos. 238-239 (2)	2.40	2.00
Nos. 322-323 (2)	4.40	3.45
Nos. 238-239 (2)	2.45	2.10
Set total (26) Stamps	34.35	28.30

Victory

Victory — CD92

European victory of the Allied Nations in World War II.

1946, May 8

Cameroun	C8
Fr. Equatorial Africa	C24
Fr. Guiana	C11
Fr. India	C7
Fr. Polynesia	C10
Fr. West Africa	C4
Guadeloupe	C3
Indo-China	C19
Madagascar	C44
Martinique	C3
New Caledonia	C14
Reunion	C25
St. Pierre & Miquelon	C8
Somali Coast	C8
Wallis & Futuna Isls.	C1

No. C8 (1)	1.60	1.20
No. C24 (1)	1.60	1.25
No. C11 (1)	1.75	1.25
No. C7 (1)	1.00	4.00
No. C10 (1)	2.75	2.00
No. C4 (1)	1.60	1.20
No. C3 (1)	1.25	1.00
No. C19 (1)	1.00	.55
No. C44 (1)	1.00	.35
No. C3 (1)	1.30	1.00
No. C14 (1)	1.50	1.25
No. C25 (1)	1.10	.90
No. C8 (1)	2.10	2.10
No. C8 (1)	1.75	1.40
No. C1 (1)	2.25	1.90
Set total (15) Stamps	23.55	21.35

Chad to Rhine

Leclerc's Departure from Chad — CD93

Battle at Cufra Oasis — CD94

Tanks in Action, Mareth — CD95

Normandy Invasion — CD96

Entering Paris — CD97

Liberation of Strasbourg — CD98

"Chad to the Rhine" march, 1942-44, by Gen. Jacques Leclerc's column, later French 2nd Armored Division.

1946, June 6

Cameroun	C9-C14
Fr. Equatorial Africa	C25-C30
Fr. Guiana	C12-C17
Fr. India	C8-C13
Fr. Polynesia	C11-C16
Fr. West Africa	C5-C10
Guadeloupe	C4-C9
Indo-China	C20-C25
Madagascar	C45-C50
Martinique	C4-C9
New Caledonia	C15-C20
Reunion	C26-C31
St. Pierre & Miquelon	C9-C14
Somali Coast	C9-C14
Wallis & Futuna Isls.	C2-C7

Nos. C9-C14 (6)	12.05	9.70
Nos. C25-C30 (6)	14.70	10.80
Nos. C12-C17 (6)	12.65	10.35
Nos. C8-C13 (6)	12.80	*15.00*
Nos. C11-C16 (6)	17.55	13.40
Nos. C5-C10 (6)	16.05	11.95
Nos. C4-C9 (6)	12.00	9.60
Nos. C20-C25 (6)	6.40	6.40
Nos. C45-C50 (6)	10.30	8.40
Nos. C4-C9 (6)	8.85	7.30
Nos. C15-C20 (6)	13.40	11.90
Nos. C26-C31 (6)	10.25	6.55
Nos. C9-C14 (6)	17.30	14.35
Nos. C9-C14 (6)	18.10	12.65
Nos. C2-C7 (6)	13.75	10.45
Set total (90) Stamps	196.15	158.80

UPU

French Colonials, Globe and Plane — CD99

Universal Postal Union, 75th anniv.

1949, July 4

Cameroun	C29
Fr. Equatorial Africa	C34
Fr. India	C17
Fr. Polynesia	C20
Fr. West Africa	C15
Indo-China	C26
Madagascar	C55
New Caledonia	C24
St. Pierre & Miquelon	C18
Somali Coast	C18
Togo	C18
Wallis & Futuna Isls.	C10

No. C29 (1)	8.00	4.75
No. C34 (1)	16.00	12.00
No. C17 (1)	11.50	8.75
No. C20 (1)	20.00	15.00
No. C15 (1)	12.00	8.75
No. C26 (1)	4.75	4.00
No. C55 (1)	4.00	2.75
No. C24 (1)	7.50	5.00
No. C18 (1)	20.00	12.00
No. C18 (1)	14.00	10.50
No. C18 (1)	8.50	7.00
No. C10 (1)	11.00	8.25
Set total (12) Stamps	137.25	98.75

Tropical Medicine

Doctor Treating Infant CD100

The surtax was for charitable work.

1950

Cameroun	B29
Fr. Equatorial Africa	B39
Fr. India	B15
Fr. Polynesia	B14
Fr. West Africa	B3
Madagascar	B17
New Caledonia	B14
St. Pierre & Miquelon	B14
Somali Coast	B14
Togo	B11

No. B29 (1)	7.25	5.50
No. B39 (1)	7.25	5.50
No. B15 (1)	6.00	4.00
No. B14 (1)	10.50	8.00
No. B3 (1)	9.50	7.25
No. B17 (1)	5.50	5.50
No. B14 (1)	6.75	5.25
No. B14 (1)	16.00	15.00
No. B14 (1)	7.75	6.25
No. B11 (1)	5.00	3.50
Set total (10) Stamps	81.50	65.75

Military Medal

Medal, Early Marine and Colonial Soldier — CD101

Centenary of the creation of the French Military Medal.

1952

Cameroun	322
Comoro Isls.	39
Fr. Equatorial Africa	186

Fr. India 233
Fr. Polynesia 179
Fr. West Africa 57
Madagascar 286
New Caledonia 295
St. Pierre & Miquelon 345
Somali Coast 267
Togo 327
Wallis & Futuna Isls. 149

No. 322 (1)	7.25	3.25
No. 39 (1)	45.00	37.50
No. 186 (1)	8.00	5.50
No. 233 (1)	5.50	7.00
No. 179 (1)	13.50	10.00
No. 57 (1)	8.75	6.50
No. 286 (1)	3.75	2.50
No. 295 (1)	6.50	6.00
No. 345 (1)	16.00	15.00
No. 267 (1)	9.00	8.00
No. 327 (1)	5.50	4.75
No. 149 (1)	7.25	7.25
Set total (12) Stamps	136.00	113.25

Liberation

Allied Landing, Victory Sign and Cross of Lorraine — CD102

Liberation of France, 10th anniv.

1954, June 6

Cameroun C32
Comoro Isls. C4
Fr. Equatorial Africa C38
Fr. India C18
Fr. Polynesia C22
Fr. West Africa C17
Madagascar C57
New Caledonia C25
St. Pierre & Miquelon C19
Somali Coast C19
Togo C19
Wallis & Futuna Isls. C11

No. C32 (1)	7.25	4.75
No. C4 (1)	32.50	19.00
No. C38 (1)	12.00	8.00
No. C18 (1)	11.00	8.00
No. C22 (1)	10.00	8.00
No. C17 (1)	12.00	5.50
No. C57 (1)	3.25	2.00
No. C25 (1)	7.50	5.00
No. C19 (1)	19.00	12.00
No. C19 (1)	10.50	8.50
No. C19 (1)	7.00	5.50
No. C11 (1)	11.00	8.25
Set total (12) Stamps	143.00	94.50

FIDES

Plowmen CD103

Efforts of FIDES, the Economic and Social Development Fund for Overseas Possessions (Fonds d' Investissement pour le Developpement Economique et Social). Each stamp has a different design.

1956

Cameroun 326-329
Comoro Isls. 43
Fr. Equatorial Africa 189-192
Fr. Polynesia 181
Fr. West Africa 65-72
Madagascar 292-295
New Caledonia 303
St. Pierre & Miquelon 350
Somali Coast 268-269
Togo 331

Nos. 326-329 (4)	6.90	3.20
No. 43 (1)	2.25	1.60
Nos. 189-192 (4)	3.20	1.65
No. 181 (1)	4.00	2.00
Nos. 65-72 (8)	16.00	6.35
Nos. 292-295 (4)	2.25	1.20
No. 303 (1)	1.90	1.10
No. 350 (1)	6.00	4.00
Nos. 268-269 (2)	5.35	3.15
No. 331 (1)	4.25	2.10
Set total (27) Stamps	52.10	26.35

Flower

CD104

Each stamp shows a different flower.

1958-9

Cameroun 333
Comoro Isls. 45
Fr. Equatorial Africa 200-201
Fr. Polynesia 192
Fr. So. & Antarctic Terr. 11
Fr. West Africa 79-83
Madagascar 301-302
New Caledonia 304-305
St. Pierre & Miquelon 357
Somali Coast 270
Togo 348-349
Wallis & Futuna Isls. 152

No. 333 (1)	1.60	.80
No. 45 (1)	5.25	4.25
Nos. 200-201 (2)	3.60	1.60
No. 192 (1)	6.50	4.00
No. 11 (1)	8.75	7.50
Nos. 79-83 (5)	10.45	5.60
Nos. 301-302 (2)	1.60	.60
Nos. 304-305 (2)	8.00	3.00
No. 357 (1)	4.50	2.25
No. 270 (1)	4.25	1.40
Nos. 348-349 (2)	1.10	.50
No. 152 (1)	3.25	3.25
Set total (20) Stamps	58.85	34.75

Human Rights

Sun, Dove and U.N. Emblem CD105

10th anniversary of the signing of the Universal Declaration of Human Rights.

1958

Comoro Isls. 44
Fr. Equatorial Africa 202
Fr. Polynesia 191
Fr. West Africa 85
Madagascar 300
New Caledonia 306
St. Pierre & Miquelon 356
Somali Coast 274
Wallis & Futuna Isls. 153

No. 44 (1)	9.00	9.00
No. 202 (1)	2.40	1.25
No. 191 (1)	13.00	8.75
No. 85 (1)	2.40	2.00
No. 300 (1)	.80	.40
No. 306 (1)	2.00	1.50
No. 356 (1)	3.50	2.50
No. 274 (1)	3.50	2.10
No. 153 (1)	4.50	4.50
Set total (9) Stamps	41.10	32.00

C.C.T.A.

CD106

Commission for Technical Cooperation in Africa south of the Sahara, 10th anniv.

1960

Cameroun 339
Cent. Africa 3
Chad 66
Congo, P.R. 90
Dahomey 138
Gabon 150
Ivory Coast 180
Madagascar 317
Mali 9
Mauritania 117
Niger 104
Upper Volta 89

No. 339 (1)	1.60	.75
No. 3 (1)	1.60	.75
No. 66 (1)	1.90	.50
No. 90 (1)	1.00	1.00
No. 138 (1)	.50	.25
No. 150 (1)	1.40	1.10
No. 180 (1)	1.10	.50
No. 317 (1)	.60	.30
No. 9 (1)	1.20	.50
No. 117 (1)	.75	.40
No. 104 (1)	.85	.45
No. 89 (1)	.65	.40
Set total (12) Stamps	13.15	6.90

Air Afrique, 1961

Modern and Ancient Africa, Map and Planes — CD107

Founding of Air Afrique (African Airlines).

1961-62

Cameroun C37
Cent. Africa C5
Chad C7
Congo, P.R. C5
Dahomey C17
Gabon C5
Ivory Coast C18
Mauritania C17
Niger C22
Senegal C31
Upper Volta C4

No. C37 (1)	1.00	.50
No. C5 (1)	1.00	.65
No. C7 (1)	1.00	.25
No. C5 (1)	1.75	.90
No. C17 (1)	.80	.40
No. C5 (1)	11.00	6.00
No. C18 (1)	2.00	1.25
No. C17 (1)	2.50	1.25
No. C22 (1)	1.75	.90
No. C31 (1)	.80	.30
No. C4 (1)	3.50	1.75
Set total (11) Stamps	27.10	14.15

Anti-Malaria

CD108

World Health Organization drive to eradicate malaria.

1962, Apr. 7

Cameroun B36
Cent. Africa B1
Chad B1
Comoro Isls. B1
Congo, P.R. B3
Dahomey B15
Gabon B4
Ivory Coast B15
Madagascar B19
Mali B1
Mauritania B16
Niger B14
Senegal B16
Somali Coast B15
Upper Volta B1

No. B36 (1)	1.00	.45
No. B1 (1)	1.40	1.40
No. B1 (1)	1.25	.50
No. B1 (1)	3.50	3.50
No. B3 (1)	1.40	1.00
No. B15 (1)	.75	.75
No. B4 (1)	1.00	1.00
No. B15 (1)	1.25	1.25
No. B19 (1)	.75	.50
No. B1 (1)	1.25	.60
No. B16 (1)	.80	.80
No. B14 (1)	.60	.60
No. B16 (1)	1.10	.65
No. B15 (1)	7.00	7.00
No. B1 (1)	.75	.70
Set total (15) Stamps	23.80	20.70

Abidjan Games

CD109

Abidjan Games, Ivory Coast, Dec. 24-31, 1961. Each stamp shows a different sport.

1962

Cent. Africa 19-20, C6
Chad 83-84, C8
Congo, P.R. 103-104, C7
Gabon 163-164, C6
Niger 109-111
Upper Volta 103-105

Nos. 19-20,C6 (3)	4.15	2.85
Nos. 83-84,C8 (3)	6.30	1.55
Nos. 103-104,C7 (3)	3.85	1.80
Nos. 163-164,C6 (3)	5.00	3.00
Nos. 109-111 (3)	2.60	1.10
Nos. 103-105 (3)	2.80	1.75
Set total (18) Stamps	24.70	12.05

African and Malagasy Union

Flag of Union CD110

First anniversary of the Union.

1962, Sept. 8

Cameroun 373
Cent. Africa 21
Chad 85
Congo, P.R. 105
Dahomey 155
Gabon 165
Ivory Coast 198
Madagascar 332
Mauritania 170
Niger 112
Senegal 211
Upper Volta 106

No. 373 (1)	2.00	.75
No. 21 (1)	1.25	.75
No. 85 (1)	1.25	.25
No. 105 (1)	1.50	.50
No. 155 (1)	1.25	.90
No. 165 (1)	1.60	1.25
No. 198 (1)	2.10	.75
No. 332 (1)	.80	.80
No. 170 (1)	.75	.50
No. 112 (1)	.80	.40
No. 211 (1)	.80	.50
No. 106 (1)	1.10	.75
Set total (12) Stamps	15.20	8.10

Telstar

Telstar and Globe Showing Andover and Pleumeur-Bodou — CD111

First television connection of the United States and Europe through the Telstar satellite, July 11-12, 1962.

1962-63

Andorra, French 154
Comoro Isls. C7
Fr. Polynesia C29
Fr. So. & Antarctic Terr. C5
New Caledonia C33
St. Pierre & Miquelon C26
Somali Coast C31
Wallis & Futuna Isls. C17

No. 154 (1)	2.00	1.60
No. C7 (1)	4.50	2.75
No. C29 (1)	11.50	8.00

No. C5 (1)	29.00	21.00
No. C33 (1)	25.00	18.50
No. C26 (1)	7.25	4.50
No. C31 (1)	1.00	1.00
No. C17 (1)	3.75	3.75
Set total (8) Stamps	84.00	61.10

Freedom From Hunger

World Map and Wheat Emblem CD112

U.N. Food and Agriculture Organization's "Freedom from Hunger" campaign.

1963, Mar. 21

Cameroun....B37-B38
Cent. Africa....B2
Chad....B2
Congo, P.R....B4
Dahomey....B16
Gabon....B5
Ivory Coast....B16
Madagascar....B21
Mauritania....B17
Niger....B15
Senegal....B17
Upper Volta....B2

Nos. B37-B38 (2)	2.25	.75
No. B2 (1)	1.25	1.25
No. B2 (1)	2.00	.50
No. B4 (1)	1.40	1.00
No. B16 (1)	.80	.80
No. B5 (1)	1.00	1.00
No. B16 (1)	1.50	1.50
No. B21 (1)	.60	.45
No. B17 (1)	.80	.80
No. B15 (1)	.60	.60
No. B17 (1)	.80	.50
No. B2 (1)	.75	.70
Set total (13) Stamps	13.75	9.85

Red Cross Centenary

CD113

Centenary of the International Red Cross.

1963, Sept. 2

Comoro Isls....55
Fr. Polynesia....205
New Caledonia....328
St. Pierre & Miquelon....367
Somali Coast....297
Wallis & Futuna Isls....165

No. 55 (1)	7.50	6.00
No. 205 (1)	15.00	12.00
No. 328 (1)	8.00	6.75
No. 367 (1)	12.00	5.50
No. 297 (1)	6.25	6.25
No. 165 (1)	4.00	4.00
Set total (6) Stamps	52.75	40.50

African Postal Union, 1963

UAMPT Emblem, Radio Masts, Plane and Mail CD114

Establishment of the African and Malagasy Posts and Telecommunications Union.

1963, Sept. 8

Cameroun....C47
Cent. Africa....C10
Chad....C9
Congo, P.R....C13
Dahomey....C19
Gabon....C13
Ivory Coast....C25
Madagascar....C75
Mauritania....C22
Niger....C27
Rwanda....36
Senegal....C32
Upper Volta....C9

No. C47 (1)	2.25	1.00
No. C10 (1)	1.90	.90
No. C9 (1)	2.40	.60
No. C13 (1)	1.40	.75
No. C19 (1)	.75	.25
No. C13 (1)	1.90	.80
No. C25 (1)	2.50	1.50
No. C75 (1)	1.25	.80
No. C22 (1)	1.50	.60
No. C27 (1)	1.25	.60
No. 36 (1)	1.00	.75
No. C32 (1)	1.75	.50
No. C9 (1)	1.50	.75
Set total (13) Stamps	21.35	9.80

Air Afrique, 1963

Symbols of Flight — CD115

First anniversary of Air Afrique and inauguration of DC-8 service.

1963, Nov. 19

Cameroun....C48
Chad....C10
Congo, P.R....C14
Gabon....C18
Ivory Coast....C26
Mauritania....C26
Niger....C35
Senegal....C33

No. C48 (1)	1.25	.40
No. C10 (1)	2.40	.60
No. C14 (1)	1.60	.60
No. C18 (1)	1.40	.65
No. C26 (1)	1.00	.50
No. C26 (1)	.70	.25
No. C35 (1)	.90	.50
No. C33 (1)	2.00	.65
Set total (8) Stamps	11.25	4.15

Europafrica

Europe and Africa Linked — CD116

Signing of an economic agreement between the European Economic Community and the African and Malagasy Union, Yaounde, Cameroun, July 20, 1963.

1963-64

Cameroun....402
Cent. Africa....C12
Chad....C11
Congo, P.R....C16
Gabon....C19
Ivory Coast....217
Niger....C43
Upper Volta....C11

No. 402 (1)	2.25	.60
No. C12 (1)	2.50	1.75
No. C11 (1)	2.00	.50
No. C16 (1)	1.60	1.00
No. C19 (1)	1.40	.75
No. 217 (1)	1.10	.35
No. C43 (1)	.85	.50
No. C11 (1)	1.50	.80
Set total (8) Stamps	13.20	6.25

Human Rights

Scales of Justice and Globe CD117

15th anniversary of the Universal Declaration of Human Rights.

1963, Dec. 10

Comoro Isls....56
Fr. Polynesia....206
New Caledonia....329
St. Pierre & Miquelon....368
Somali Coast....300
Wallis & Futuna Isls....166

No. 56 (1)	7.50	6.00
No. 205 (1)	15.00	12.00
No. 329 (1)	7.00	6.00
No. 368 (1)	7.00	3.50
No. 300 (1)	8.50	8.50
No. 166 (1)	7.00	7.00
Set total (6) Stamps	52.00	43.00

PHILATEC

Stamp Album, Champs Elysees Palace and Horses of Marly CD118

Intl. Philatelic and Postal Techniques Exhibition, Paris, June 5-21, 1964.

1963-64

Comoro Isls....60
France....1078
Fr. Polynesia....207
New Caledonia....341
St. Pierre & Miquelon....369
Somali Coast....301
Wallis & Futuna Isls....167

No. 60 (1)	4.00	3.50
No. 1078 (1)	.25	.25
No. 206 (1)	15.00	10.00
No. 341 (1)	6.50	6.50
No. 369 (1)	11.00	8.00
No. 301 (1)	7.75	7.75
No. 167 (1)	3.00	3.00
Set total (7) Stamps	47.50	39.00

Cooperation

CD119

Cooperation between France and the French-speaking countries of Africa and Madagascar.

1964

Cameroun....409-410
Cent. Africa....39
Chad....103
Congo, P.R....121
Dahomey....193
France....1111
Gabon....175
Ivory Coast....221
Madagascar....360
Mauritania....181
Niger....143
Senegal....236
Togo....495

Nos. 409-410 (2)	2.50	.50
No. 39 (1)	.90	.50
No. 103 (1)	1.00	.25
No. 121 (1)	.80	.35
No. 193 (1)	.80	.35
No. 1111 (1)	.25	.25
No. 175 (1)	.90	.60
No. 221 (1)	1.10	.35
No. 360 (1)	.60	.25
No. 181 (1)	.60	.35
No. 143 (1)	.80	.40
No. 236 (1)	1.60	.85
No. 495 (1)	.70	.25
Set total (14) Stamps	12.55	5.25

ITU

Telegraph, Syncom Satellite and ITU Emblem CD120

Intl. Telecommunication Union, Cent.

1965, May 17

Comoro Isls....C14
Fr. Polynesia....C33
Fr. So. & Antarctic Terr....C8
New Caledonia....C40
New Hebrides....124-125
St. Pierre & Miquelon....C29
Somali Coast....C36
Wallis & Futuna Isls....C20

No. C14 (1)	18.00	9.00
No. C33 (1)	80.00	52.50
No. C8 (1)	200.00	160.00
No. C40 (1)	10.00	8.00
Nos. 124-125 (2)	40.50	34.00
No. C29 (1)	24.00	11.50
No. C36 (1)	15.00	9.00
No. C20 (1)	16.00	16.00
Set total (9) Stamps	403.50	300.00

French Satellite A-1

Diamant Rocket and Launching Installation — CD121

Launching of France's first satellite, Nov. 26, 1965.

1965-66

Comoro Isls....C16a
France....1138a
Reunion....359a
Fr. Polynesia....C41a
Fr. So. & Antarctic Terr....C10a
New Caledonia....C45a
St. Pierre & Miquelon....C31a
Somali Coast....C40a
Wallis & Futuna Isls....C23a

No. C16a (1)	9.00	9.00
No. 1138a (1)	.65	.65
No. 359a (1)	3.50	3.00
No. C41a (1)	14.00	14.00
No. C10a (1)	29.00	24.00
No. C45a (1)	7.00	7.00
No. C31a (1)	14.50	14.50
No. C40a (1)	7.00	7.00
No. C23a (1)	8.50	8.50
Set total (9) Stamps	93.15	87.65

French Satellite D-1

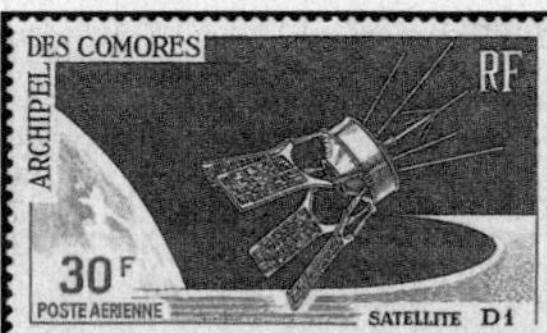

D-1 Satellite in Orbit — CD122

Launching of the D-1 satellite at Hammaguir, Algeria, Feb. 17, 1966.

1966

Comoro Isls....C17
France....1148

Fr. Polynesia.................................. C42
Fr. So. & Antarctic Terr. C11
New Caledonia.................................. C46
St. Pierre & Miquelon...................... C32
Somali Coast..................................... C49
Wallis & Futuna Isls. C24

No. C17 (1) 4.00 4.00
No. 1148 (1) .25 .25
No. C42 (1) 7.00 4.75
No. C11 (1) 57.50 40.00
No. C46 (1) 2.25 2.00
No. C32 (1) 9.00 6.00
No. C49 (1) 4.25 2.75
No. C24 (1) 3.50 3.50
Set total (8) Stamps 87.75 63.25

Air Afrique, 1966

Planes and Air Afrique Emblem — CD123

Introduction of DC-8F planes by Air Afrique.

1966

Cameroun.. C79
Cent. Africa C35
Chad.. C26
Congo, P.R....................................... C42
Dahomey C42
Gabon.. C47
Ivory Coast C32
Mauritania.. C57
Niger.. C63
Senegal C47
Togo.. C54
Upper Volta...................................... C31

No. C79 (1) .80 .25
No. C35 (1) 1.00 .50
No. C26 (1) 1.00 .25
No. C42 (1) 1.00 .25
No. C42 (1) .75 .25
No. C47 (1) .90 .35
No. C32 (1) 1.00 .60
No. C57 (1) .80 .30
No. C63 (1) .65 .35
No. C47 (1) .80 .30
No. C54 (1) .80 .25
No. C31 (1) .75 .50
Set total (12) Stamps 10.25 4.15

African Postal Union, 1967

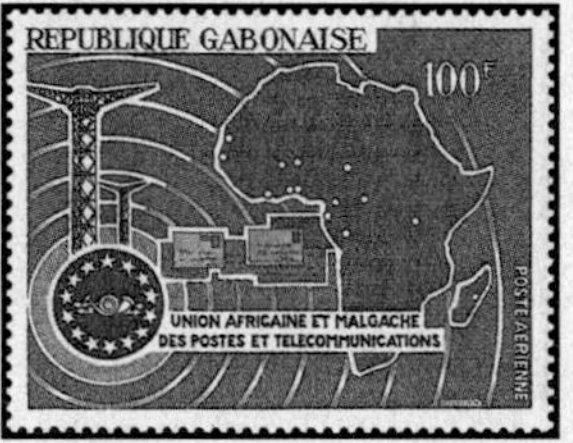

Telecommunications Symbols and Map of Africa — CD124

Fifth anniversary of the establishment of the African and Malagasy Union of Posts and Telecommunications, UAMPT.

1967

Cameroun.. C90
Cent. Africa C46
Chad.. C37
Congo, P.R....................................... C57
Dahomey C61
Gabon.. C58
Ivory Coast C34
Madagascar...................................... C85
Mauritania.. C65
Niger.. C75
Rwanda C1-C3
Senegal C60
Togo.. C81
Upper Volta...................................... C50

No. C90 (1) 2.40 .65
No. C46 (1) 2.25 .85
No. C37 (1) 2.00 .60
No. C57 (1) 1.60 .60
No. C61 (1) 1.75 .95
No. C58 (1) 2.25 .95
No. C34 (1) 3.50 1.50
No. C85 (1) 1.25 .60
No. C65 (1) 1.25 .60
No. C75 (1) 1.40 .60
Nos. C1-C3 (3) 2.30 1.25
No. C60 (1) 1.75 .50
No. C81 (1) 1.90 .30
No. C50 (1) 1.80 .70
Set total (16) Stamps 27.40 10.65

Monetary Union

Gold Token of the Ashantis, 17-18th Centuries — CD125

West African Monetary Union, 5th anniv.

1967, Nov. 4

Dahomey 244
Ivory Coast 259
Mauritania...238
Niger...204
Senegal 294
Togo..623
Upper Volta.......................................181

No. 244 (1) .65 .65
No. 259 (1) .85 .40
No. 238 (1) .45 .25
No. 204 (1) .45 .25
No. 294 (1) .60 .25
No. 623 (1) .60 .25
No. 181 (1) .65 .35
Set total (7) Stamps 4.25 2.40

WHO Anniversary

Sun, Flowers and WHO Emblem CD126

World Health Organization, 20th anniv.

1968, May 4

Afars & Issas 317
Comoro Isls. 73
Fr. Polynesia..............................241-242
Fr. So. & Antarctic Terr. 31
New Caledonia..................................367
St. Pierre & Miquelon........................377
Wallis & Futuna Isls. 169

No. 317 (1) 3.00 3.00
No. 73 (1) 2.40 1.75
Nos. 241-242 (2) 22.00 12.75
No. 31 (1) 62.50 47.50
No. 367 (1) 4.00 2.25
No. 377 (1) 12.00 9.00
No. 169 (1) 5.75 5.75
Set total (8) Stamps 111.65 82.00

Human Rights Year

Human Rights Flame — CD127

1968, Aug. 10

Afars & Issas 322-323
Comoro Isls. 76
Fr. Polynesia..............................243-244
Fr. So. & Antarctic Terr. 32
New Caledonia..................................369
St. Pierre & Miquelon........................382
Wallis & Futuna Isls. 170

Nos. 322-323 (2) 6.75 4.00
No. 76 (1) 3.25 3.25
Nos. 243-244 (2) 24.00 14.00
No. 32 (1) 55.00 47.50
No. 369 (1) 2.75 1.50
No. 382 (1) 8.00 5.50
No. 170 (1) 3.25 3.25
Set total (9) Stamps 103.00 79.00

2nd PHILEXAFRIQUE

CD128

Opening of PHILEXAFRIQUE, Abidjan, Feb. 14. Each stamp shows a local scene and stamp.

1969, Feb. 14

Cameroun...................................... C118
Cent. Africa C65
Chad.. C48
Congo, P.R....................................... C77
Dahomey C94
Gabon.. C82
Ivory Coast C38-C40
Madagascar...................................... C92
Mali.. C65
Mauritania.. C80
Niger.. C104
Senegal C68
Togo.. C104
Upper Volta...................................... C62

No. C118 (1) 3.25 1.25
No. C65 (1) 1.75 1.75
No. C48 (1) 2.40 1.00
No. C77 (1) 2.00 1.75
No. C94 (1) 2.25 2.25
No. C82 (1) 2.25 2.25
Nos. C38-C40 (3) 14.50 14.50
No. C92 (1) 1.75 .85
No. C65 (1) 1.75 1.00
No. C80 (1) 1.90 .75
No. C104 (1) 2.75 1.90
No. C68 (1) 2.00 1.40
No. C104 (1) 2.25 .45
No. C62 (1) 4.00 3.25
Set total (16) Stamps 44.80 34.35

Concorde

Concorde in Flight CD129

First flight of the prototype Concorde supersonic plane at Toulouse, Mar. 1, 1969.

1969

Afars & Issas C56
Comoro Isls. C29
France.. C42
Fr. Polynesia.................................... C50
Fr. So. & Antarctic Terr. C18
New Caledonia.................................. C63
St. Pierre & Miquelon...................... C40
Wallis & Futuna Isls. C30

No. C56 (1) 26.00 16.00
No. C29 (1) 18.00 12.00
No. C42 (1) .75 .35
No. C50 (1) 55.00 35.00
No. C18 (1) 55.00 37.50
No. C63 (1) 27.50 20.00
No. C40 (1) 32.50 11.00
No. C30 (1) 15.00 10.00
Set total (8) Stamps 229.75 141.85

Development Bank

Bank Emblem — CD130

African Development Bank, fifth anniv.

1969

Cameroun..499
Chad..217
Congo, P.R.................................181-182
Ivory Coast 281
Mali...127-128
Mauritania...267
Niger...220
Senegal 317-318
Upper Volta.......................................201

No. 499 (1) .80 .25
No. 217 (1) .70 .25
Nos. 181-182 (2) .80 .50
No. 281 (1) .70 .40
Nos. 127-128 (2) 1.00 .50
No. 267 (1) .60 .25
No. 220 (1) .60 .30
Nos. 317-318 (2) 1.55 .50
No. 201 (1) .65 .30
Set total (12) Stamps 7.40 3.25

ILO

ILO Headquarters, Geneva, and Emblem — CD131

Intl. Labor Organization, 50th anniv.

1969-70

Afars & Issas 337
Comoro Isls. 83
Fr. Polynesia..............................251-252
Fr. So. & Antarctic Terr. 35
New Caledonia..................................379
St. Pierre & Miquelon........................396
Wallis & Futuna Isls. 172

No. 337 (1) 2.75 2.00
No. 83 (1) 1.25 .75
Nos. 251-252 (2) 24.00 12.50
No. 35 (1) 15.00 10.00
No. 379 (1) 2.25 1.10
No. 396 (1) 10.00 5.50
No. 172 (1) 2.75 2.75
Set total (8) Stamps 58.00 34.60

ASECNA

Map of Africa, Plane and Airport CD132

10th anniversary of the Agency for the Security of Aerial Navigation in Africa and Madagascar (ASECNA, Agence pour la Securite de la Navigation Aerienne en Afrique et a Madagascar).

1969-70

Cameroun..500
Cent. Africa 119
Chad..222
Congo, P.R..197
Dahomey 269
Gabon..260
Ivory Coast 287
Mali...130
Niger...221
Senegal 321
Upper Volta.......................................204

No. 500 (1) 2.00 .60
No. 119 (1) 2.00 .80
No. 222 (1) 1.00 .25
No. 197 (1) 2.00 .40
No. 269 (1) .90 .55
No. 260 (1) 1.75 .75
No. 287 (1) .90 .40
No. 130 (1) .90 .40
No. 221 (1) 1.25 .70
No. 321 (1) 1.60 .50
No. 204 (1) 1.75 1.00
Set total (11) Stamps 16.05 6.35

U.P.U. Headquarters

CD133

New Universal Postal Union headquarters, Bern, Switzerland.

1970

Afars & Issas 342
Algeria 443
Cameroun 503-504
Cent. Africa 125
Chad 225
Comoro Isls. 84
Congo, P.R. 216
Fr. Polynesia 261-262
Fr. So. & Antarctic Terr. 36
Gabon 258
Ivory Coast 295
Madagascar 444
Mali 134-135
Mauritania 283
New Caledonia 382
Niger 231-232
St. Pierre & Miquelon 397-398
Senegal 328-329
Tunisia 535
Wallis & Futuna Isls. 173

No. 342 (1)	2.50	1.40
No. 443 (1)	1.10	.40
Nos. 503-504 (2)	2.60	.55
No. 125 (1)	1.75	.70
No. 225 (1)	1.00	.25
No. 84 (1)	5.50	2.00
No. 216 (1)	.00	.05
Nos. 261-262 (2)	20.00	10.00
No. 36 (1)	40.00	27.50
No. 258 (1)	.90	.55
No. 295 (1)	1.10	.50
No. 444 (1)	.55	.25
Nos. 134-135 (2)	1.05	.50
No. 283 (1)	.60	.30
No. 382 (1)	3.00	1.50
Nos. 231-232 (2)	1.20	.60
Nos. 397-398 (2)	34.00	16.25
Nos. 328-329 (2)	1.55	.55
No. 535 (1)	.60	.25
No. 173 (1)	3.25	3.25
Set total (26) Stamps	123.05	67.55

De Gaulle

CD134

First anniversary of the death of Charles de Gaulle, (1890-1970), President of France.

1971-72

Afars & Issas 356-357
Comoro Isls. 104-105
France 1325a
Fr. Polynesia 270-271
Fr. So. & Antarctic Terr. 52-53
New Caledonia 393-394
Reunion 380a
St. Pierre & Miquelon 417-418
Wallis & Futuna Isls. 177-178

Nos. 356-357 (2)	12.50	7.50
Nos. 104-105 (2)	9.00	5.75
No. 1325a (1)	3.00	2.50
Nos. 270-271 (2)	51.50	29.50
Nos. 52-53 (2)	40.00	29.50
Nos. 393-394 (2)	23.00	11.75
No. 380a (1)	9.25	8.00
Nos. 417-418 (2)	56.50	31.00
Nos. 177-178 (2)	20.00	16.25
Set total (16) Stamps	224.75	141.75

African Postal Union, 1971

UAMPT Building, Brazzaville, Congo — CD135

10th anniversary of the establishment of the African and Malagasy Posts and Telecommunications Union, UAMPT. Each stamp has a different native design.

1971, Nov. 13

Cameroun C177
Cent. Africa C89
Chad C94
Congo, P.R. C136
Dahomey C146
Gabon C120
Ivory Coast C47
Mauritania C113
Niger C164
Rwanda C8
Senegal C105
Togo C166
Upper Volta C97

No. C177 (1)	2.00	.50
No. C89 (1)	2.25	.85
No. C94 (1)	1.50	.50
No. C136 (1)	1.60	.75
No. C146 (1)	1.75	.80
No. C120 (1)	1.75	.70
No. C47 (1)	2.00	1.00
No. C113 (1)	1.20	.65
No. C164 (1)	1.25	.60
No. C8 (1)	2.75	2.50
No. C105 (1)	1.60	.50
No. C166 (1)	1.25	.40
No. C97 (1)	1.50	.70
Set total (13) Stamps	22.40	10.45

West African Monetary Union

African Couple, City, Village and Commemorative Coin — CD136

West African Monetary Union, 10th anniv.

1972, Nov. 2

Dahomey 300
Ivory Coast 331
Mauritania 299
Niger 258
Senegal 374
Togo 825
Upper Volta 280

No. 300 (1)	.65	.25
No. 331 (1)	1.00	.50
No. 299 (1)	.75	.25
No. 258 (1)	.55	.30
No. 374 (1)	.50	.30
No. 825 (1)	.60	.25
No. 280 (1)	.60	.25
Set total (7) Stamps	4.65	2.10

African Postal Union, 1973

Telecommunications Symbols and Map of Africa — CD137

11th anniversary of the African and Malagasy Posts and Telecommunications Union (UAMPT).

1973, Sept. 12

Cameroun 574
Cent. Africa 194
Chad 294
Congo, P.R. 289
Dahomey 311
Gabon 320
Ivory Coast 361
Madagascar 500
Mauritania 304
Niger 287
Rwanda 540
Senegal 393
Togo 849
Upper Volta 297

No. 574 (1)	1.75	.40
No. 194 (1)	1.25	.75
No. 294 (1)	1.75	.40
No. 289 (1)	1.60	.50
No. 311 (1)	1.25	.55
No. 320 (1)	1.40	.75
No. 361 (1)	2.50	1.00
No. 500 (1)	1.10	.35
No. 304 (1)	1.10	.40
No. 287 (1)	.90	.60
No. 540 (1)	4.00	2.00
No. 393 (1)	1.60	.50
No. 849 (1)	1.00	.35
No. 297 (1)	1.25	.70
Set total (14) Stamps	22.45	9.25

Philexafrique II — Essen

CD138

CD139

Designs: Indigenous fauna, local and German stamps. Types CD138-CD139 printed horizontally and vertically se-tenant in sheets of 10 (2x5). Label between horizontal pairs alternately commemoratives Philexafrique II, Libreville, Gabon, June 1978, and 2nd International Stamp Fair, Essen, Germany, Nov. 1-5.

1978-1979

Benin C286a
Central Africa C201a
Chad C239a
Congo Republic C246a
Djibouti C122a
Gabon C216a
Ivory Coast C65a
Mali C357a
Mauritania C186a
Niger C292a
Rwanda C13a
Senegal C147a
Togo C364a

No. C286a (1)	9.00	8.50
No. C201a (1)	7.50	7.50
No. C239a (1)	8.00	4.00
No. C246a (1)	7.00	7.00
No. C122a (1)	8.50	8.50
No. C216a (1)	6.50	4.00
No. C65a (1)	9.00	9.00
No. C357a (1)	5.00	3.00
No. C186a (1)	4.50	4.00
No. C292a (1)	6.00	5.00
No. C13a (1)	4.00	4.00
No. C147a (1)	10.00	4.00
No. C364a (1)	3.00	1.50
Set total (13) Stamps	88.00	70.00

BRITISH COMMONWEALTH OF NATIONS

The listings follow established trade practices when these issues are offered as units by dealers. The Peace issue, for example, includes only one stamp from the Indian state of Hyderabad. The U.P.U. issue includes the Egypt set. Pairs are included for those varieties issued with bilingual designs se-tenant.

Silver Jubilee

Windsor Castle and King George V CD301

Reign of King George V, 25th anniv.

1935

Antigua 77-80
Ascension 33-36
Bahamas 92-95
Barbados 186-189
Basutoland 11-14
Bechuanaland Protectorate 117-120
Bermuda 100-103
British Guiana 223-226
British Honduras 108-111
Cayman Islands 81-84
Ceylon 260-263
Cyprus 136-139
Dominica 90-93
Falkland Islands 77-80
Fiji 110-113
Gambia 125-128
Gibraltar 100-103
Gilbert & Ellice Islands 33-36
Gold Coast 108-111
Grenada 124-127
Hong Kong 147-150
Jamaica 109-112
Kenya, Uganda, Tanzania 42-45
Leeward Islands 96-99
Malta 184-187
Mauritius 204-207
Montserrat 85-88
Newfoundland 226-229
Nigeria 34-37
Northern Rhodesia 18-21
Nyasaland Protectorate 47-50
St. Helena 111-114
St. Kitts-Nevis 72-75
St. Lucia 91-94
St. Vincent 134-137
Seychelles 118-121
Sierra Leone 166-169
Solomon Islands 60-63
Somaliland Protectorate 77-80
Straits Settlements 213-216
Swaziland 20-23
Trinidad & Tobago 43-46
Turks & Caicos Islands 71-74
Virgin Islands 69-72

The following have different designs but are included in the omnibus set:

Great Britain 226-229
Offices in Morocco (Sp. Curr.) 67-70
Offices in Morocco (Br. Curr.) 226-229
Offices in Morocco (Fr. Curr.) 422-425
Offices in Morocco (Tangier) 508-510
Australia 152-154
Canada 211-216
Cook Islands 98-100
India 142-148
Nauru 31-34
New Guinea 46-47
New Zealand 199-201
Niue 67-69
Papua 114-117
Samoa 163-165
South Africa 68-71
Southern Rhodesia 33-36
South-West Africa 121-124

Nos. 77-80 (4)	20.25	23.25
Nos. 33-36 (4)	58.50	127.50
Nos. 92-95 (4)	25.00	46.00
Nos. 186-189 (4)	30.00	50.30
Nos. 11-14 (4)	11.60	21.25
Nos. 117-120 (4)	15.75	36.00
Nos. 100-103 (4)	16.80	58.50
Nos. 223-226 (4)	18.35	35.50
Nos. 108-111 (4)	15.25	16.35
Nos. 81-84 (4)	21.60	24.50
Nos. 260-263 (4)	10.40	21.60
Nos. 136-139 (4)	39.75	34.40
Nos. 90-93 (4)	18.85	19.85
Nos. 77-80 (4)	55.00	14.75
Nos. 110-113 (4)	20.25	34.00
Nos. 125-128 (4)	12.20	25.25
Nos. 100-103 (4)	28.75	42.75
Nos. 33-36 (4)	36.80	67.00
Nos. 108-111 (4)	25.75	78.10
Nos. 124-127 (4)	16.70	40.60
Nos. 147-150 (4)	59.00	18.75
Nos. 109-112 (4)	17.00	39.00
Nos. 42-45 (4)	8.75	11.00
Nos. 96-99 (4)	35.75	49.60
Nos. 184-187 (4)	22.00	33.70
Nos. 204-207 (4)	47.60	58.25
Nos. 85-88 (4)	10.25	30.25
Nos. 226-229 (4)	17.50	12.05
Nos. 34-37 (4)	17.50	70.00
Nos. 18-21 (4)	17.00	15.00
Nos. 47-50 (4)	39.75	80.25
Nos. 111-114 (4)	31.15	33.25
Nos. 72-75 (4)	10.80	18.65
Nos. 91-94 (4)	16.00	20.80
Nos. 134-137 (4)	9.45	21.25
Nos. 118-121 (4)	17.50	32.50
Nos. 166-169 (4)	24.25	56.00
Nos. 60-63 (4)	29.00	38.00
Nos. 77-80 (4)	17.00	48.25
Nos. 213-216 (4)	15.00	25.10
Nos. 20-23 (4)	6.80	18.25
Nos. 43-46 (4)	14.05	27.75
Nos. 71-74 (4)	8.40	14.50
Nos. 69-72 (4)	25.00	55.25
Nos. 226-229 (4)	5.15	4.40

Nos. 67-70 (4)	14.35	*26.10*
Nos. 226-229 (4)	8.20	*28.90*
Nos. 422-425 (4)	3.90	2.00
Nos. 508-510 (3)	18.80	*23.85*
Nos. 152-154 (3)	49.50	45.35
Nos. 211-216 (6)	23.85	13.35
Nos. 98-100 (3)	9.65	*12.00*
Nos. 142-148 (7)	28.85	14.00
Nos. 31-34 (4)	9.90	*9.90*
Nos. 46-47 (2)	4.35	1.70
Nos. 199-201 (3)	21.75	*31.75*
Nos. 67-69 (3)	11.80	*26.50*
Nos. 114-117 (4)	9.20	*17.00*
Nos. 163-165 (3)	4.40	5.50
Nos. 68-71 (4)	57.50	*153.00*
Nos. 33-36 (4)	27.75	*45.25*
Nos. 121-124 (4)	10.00	*30.10*
Set total (245) Stamps	1,336.	2,142.

Coronation

Queen Elizabeth and King George VI
CD302

1937

Aden....13-15
Antigua....81-83
Ascension....37-39
Bahamas....97-99
Barbados....190-192
Basutoland....15-17
Bechuanaland Protectorate....121-123
Bermuda....115-117
British Guiana....227-229
British Honduras....112-114
Cayman Islands....97-99
Ceylon....275-277
Cyprus....140-142
Dominica....94-96
Falkland Islands....81-83
Fiji....114-116
Gambia....129-131
Gibraltar....104-106
Gilbert & Ellice Islands....37-39
Gold Coast....112-114
Grenada....128-130
Hong Kong....151-153
Jamaica....113-115
Kenya, Uganda, Tanzania....60-62
Leeward Islands....100-102
Malta....188-190
Mauritius....208-210
Montserrat....89-91
Newfoundland....230-232
Nigeria....50-52
Northern Rhodesia....22-24
Nyasaland Protectorate....51-53
St. Helena....115-117
St. Kitts-Nevis....76-78
St. Lucia....107-109
St. Vincent....138-140
Seychelles....122-124
Sierra Leone....170-172
Solomon Islands....64-66
Somaliland Protectorate....81-83
Straits Settlements....235-237
Swaziland....24-26
Trinidad & Tobago....47-49
Turks & Caicos Islands....75-77
Virgin Islands....73-75

The following have different designs but are included in the omnibus set:

Great Britain....234
Offices in Morocco (Sp. Curr.)....82
Offices in Morocco (Fr. Curr.)....439
Offices in Morocco (Tangier)....514
Canada....237
Cook Islands....109-111
Nauru....35-38
Newfoundland....233-243
New Guinea....48-51
New Zealand....223-225
Niue....70-72
Papua....118-121
South Africa....74-78
Southern Rhodesia....38-41
South-West Africa....125-132

Nos. 13-15 (3)	2.70	*5.65*
Nos. 81-83 (3)	1.85	*8.00*
Nos. 37-39 (3)	2.75	*2.75*
Nos. 97-99 (3)	1.05	*3.05*
Nos. 190-192 (3)	1.10	1.95
Nos. 15-17 (3)	1.15	*3.00*
Nos. 121-123 (3)	.95	3.35
Nos. 115-117 (3)	1.25	5.00
Nos. 227-229 (3)	1.45	3.05
Nos. 112-114 (3)	1.20	2.40
Nos. 97-99 (3)	1.10	2.70
Nos. 275-277 (3)	8.25	10.35
Nos. 140-142 (3)	3.75	6.50
Nos. 94-96 (3)	.85	2.40
Nos. 81-83 (3)	2.90	*2.30*
Nos. 114-116 (3)	1.35	*5.75*
Nos. 129-131 (3)	.95	3.95
Nos. 104-106 (3)	2.25	6.45
Nos. 37-39 (3)	.85	*2.15*
Nos. 112-114 (3)	3.10	*10.00*
Nos. 128-130 (3)	1.00	.85
Nos. 151-153 (3)	23.00	12.50
Nos. 113-115 (3)	1.25	1.25
Nos. 60-62 (3)	1.00	2.35
Nos. 100-102 (3)	1.55	4.00
Nos. 188-190 (3)	1.25	1.60
Nos. 208-210 (3)	2.05	3.75
Nos. 89-91 (3)	1.00	3.05
Nos. 230-232 (3)	7.00	2.80
Nos. 50-52 (3)	3.25	8.50
Nos. 22-24 (3)	.95	2.25
Nos. 51-53 (3)	1.05	1.30
Nos. 115-117 (3)	1.45	2.05
Nos. 76-78 (3)	.95	2.15
Nos. 107-109 (3)	1.05	2.05
Nos. 138-140 (3)	.80	*4.75*
Nos. 122-124 (3)	1.20	*1.90*
Nos. 170-172 (3)	1.95	5.65
Nos. 64-66 (3)	.90	2.00
Nos. 81-83 (3)	1.10	*3.50*
Nos. 235-237 (3)	3.25	1.60
Nos. 24-26 (3)	1.05	1.75
Nos. 47-49 (3)	1.00	1.00
Nos. 75-77 (3)	1.30	1.15
Nos. 73-75 (3)	2.20	6.90
No. 234 (1)	.25	.25
No. 82 (1)	.80	.80
No. 439 (1)	.35	.25
No. 514 (1)	.55	.55
No. 237 (1)	.35	.25
Nos. 109-111 (3)	.85	.80
Nos. 35-38 (4)	1.10	*5.50*
Nos. 233-243 (11)	41.90	30.40
Nos. 48-51 (4)	1.40	*7.90*
Nos. 223-225 (3)	1.40	*2.75*
Nos. 70-72 (3)	.80	*2.05*
Nos. 118-121 (4)	1.60	*5.25*
Nos. 74-78 (5)	7.60	9.35
Nos. 38-41 (4)	3.55	15.50
Nos. 125-132 (8)	5.00	8.40
Set total (189) Stamps	170.85	261.70

Peace

King George VI and Parliament Buildings, London
CD303

Return to peace at the close of World War II.

1945-46

Aden....28-29
Antigua....96-97
Ascension....50-51
Bahamas....130-131
Barbados....207-208
Bermuda....131-132
British Guiana....242-243
British Honduras....127-128
Cayman Islands....112-113
Ceylon....293-294
Cyprus....156-157
Dominica....112-113
Falkland Islands....97-98
Falkland Islands Dep....1L9-1L10
Fiji....137-138
Gambia....144-145
Gibraltar....119-120
Gilbert & Ellice Islands....52-53
Gold Coast....128-129
Grenada....143-144
Jamaica....136-137
Kenya, Uganda, Tanzania....90-91
Leeward Islands....116-117
Malta....206-207
Mauritius....223-224
Montserrat....104-105
Nigeria....71-72
Northern Rhodesia....46-47
Nyasaland Protectorate....82-83
Pitcairn Islands....9-10
St. Helena....128-129
St. Kitts-Nevis....91-92
St. Lucia....127-128
St. Vincent....152-153
Seychelles....149-150
Sierra Leone....186-187
Solomon Islands....80-81
Somaliland Protectorate....108-109
Trinidad & Tobago....62-63
Turks & Caicos Islands....90-91
Virgin Islands....88-89

The following have different designs but are included in the omnibus set:

Great Britain....264-265
Offices in Morocco (Tangier)....523-524
Aden
  Kathiri State of Seiyun....12-13
  Qu'aiti State of Shihr and Mukalla....12-13
Australia....200-202
Basutoland....29-31
Bechuanaland Protectorate....137-139
Burma....66-69
Cook Islands....127-130
Hong Kong....174-175
India....195-198
  Hyderabad....51-53
New Zealand....247-257
Niue....90-93
Pakistan-Bahawalpur....O16
Samoa....191-194
South Africa....100-102
Southern Rhodesia....67-70
South-West Africa....153-155
Swaziland....38-40
Zanzibar....222-223

Nos. 28-29 (2)	.95	2.50
Nos. 96-97 (2)	.50	*.80*
Nos. 50-51 (2)	.80	*2.00*
Nos. 130-131 (2)	.50	1.40
Nos. 207-208 (2)	.50	1.10
Nos. 131-132 (2)	.55	.55
Nos. 242-243 (2)	1.05	*1.40*
Nos. 127-128 (2)	.50	.50
Nos. 112-113 (2)	.80	.80
Nos. 293-294 (2)	.60	*2.10*
Nos. 156-157 (2)	.90	.70
Nos. 112-113 (2)	.50	.50
Nos. 97-98 (2)	.90	1.35
Nos. 1L9-1L10 (2)	1.30	1.00
Nos. 137-138 (2)	.75	*1.75*
Nos. 144-145 (2)	.50	.95
Nos. 119-120 (2)	.75	*1.00*
Nos. 52-53 (2)	.50	*1.10*
Nos. 128-129 (2)	1.85	*3.75*
Nos. 143-144 (2)	.50	*.95*
Nos. 136-137 (2)	.80	*12.50*
Nos. 90-91 (2)	.65	.65
Nos. 116-117 (2)	.50	1.50
Nos. 206-207 (2)	.65	2.00
Nos. 223-224 (2)	.50	1.05
Nos. 104-105 (2)	.50	.50
Nos. 71-72 (2)	.70	*2.75*
Nos. 46-47 (2)	1.25	*2.00*
Nos. 82-83 (2)	.50	.50
Nos. 9-10 (2)	1.40	1.40
Nos. 128-129 (2)	.65	.70
Nos. 91-92 (2)	.50	.50
Nos. 127-128 (2)	.50	.60
Nos. 152-153 (2)	.50	.50
Nos. 149-150 (2)	.55	.50
Nos. 186-187 (2)	.50	.50
Nos. 80-81 (2)	.50	1.50
Nos. 108-109 (2)	.70	.50
Nos. 62-63 (2)	.50	.50
Nos. 90-91 (2)	.50	.50
Nos. 88-89 (2)	.50	.50
Nos. 264-265 (2)	.50	.50
Nos. 523-524 (2)	1.50	3.00
Nos. 12-13 (2)	.50	.90
Nos. 12-13 (2)	.50	*1.25*
Nos. 200-202 (3)	1.60	*1.25*
Nos. 29-31 (3)	2.10	2.60
Nos. 137-139 (3)	2.05	*4.75*
Nos. 66-69 (4)	1.50	1.25
Nos. 127-130 (4)	2.00	1.85
Nos. 174-175 (2)	6.75	3.15
Nos. 195-198 (4)	5.60	5.50
Nos. 51-53 (3)	1.50	1.70
Nos. 247-257 (11)	3.85	3.80
Nos. 90-93 (4)	1.70	*2.20*
No. O16 (1)	5.50	*7.00*
Nos. 191-194 (4)	2.05	1.00
Nos. 100-102 (3)	1.00	3.25
Nos. 67-70 (4)	1.40	1.75
Nos. 153-155 (3)	1.85	3.25
Nos. 38-40 (3)	2.40	*5.50*
Nos. 222-223 (2)	.65	1.00
Set total (151) Stamps	75.05	114.30

Silver Wedding

King George VI and Queen Elizabeth
CD304 CD305

1948-49

Aden....30-31
  Kathiri State of Seiyun....14-15
  Qu'aiti State of Shihr and Mukalla....14-15
Antigua....98-99
Ascension....52-53
Bahamas....148-149
Barbados....210-211
Basutoland....39-40
Bechuanaland Protectorate....147-148
Bermuda....133-134
British Guiana....244-245
British Honduras....129-130
Cayman Islands....116-117
Cyprus....158-159
Dominica....114-115
Falkland Islands....99-100
Falkland Islands Dep....1L11-1L12
Fiji....139-140
Gambia....146-147
Gibraltar....121-122
Gilbert & Ellice Islands....54-55
Gold Coast....142-143
Grenada....145-146
Hong Kong....178-179
Jamaica....138-139
Kenya, Uganda, Tanzania....92-93
Leeward Islands....118-119
Malaya
  Johore....128-129
  Kedah....55-56
  Kelantan....44-45
  Malacca....1-2
  Negri Sembilan....36-37
  Pahang....44-45
  Penang....1-2
  Perak....99-100
  Perlis....1-2
  Selangor....74-75
  Trengganu....47-48
Malta....223-224
Mauritius....229-230
Montserrat....106-107
Nigeria....73-74
North Borneo....238-239
Northern Rhodesia....48-49
Nyasaland Protectorate....85-86
Pitcairn Islands....11-12
St. Helena....130-131
St. Kitts-Nevis....93-94
St. Lucia....129-130
St. Vincent....154-155
Sarawak....174-175
Seychelles....151-152
Sierra Leone....188-189
Singapore....21-22
Solomon Islands....82-83
Somaliland Protectorate....110-111
Swaziland....48-49
Trinidad & Tobago....64-65
Turks & Caicos Islands....92-93
Virgin Islands....90-91
Zanzibar....224-225

The following have different designs but are included in the omnibus set:

Great Britain....267-268
  Offices in Morocco (Sp. Curr.)....93-94
  Offices in Morocco (Tangier)....525-526
Bahrain....62-63
Kuwait....82-83
Oman....25-26
South Africa....106
South-West Africa....159

Nos. 30-31 (2)	45.40	56.50
Nos. 14-15 (2)	17.85	*16.00*
Nos. 14-15 (2)	18.55	*12.50*
Nos. 98-99 (2)	13.55	*15.75*
Nos. 52-53 (2)	55.55	50.45
Nos. 148-149 (2)	45.25	40.30
Nos. 210-211 (2)	18.35	13.55
Nos. 39-40 (2)	52.80	*55.25*
Nos. 147-148 (2)	42.85	*47.75*
Nos. 133-134 (2)	47.75	*55.25*
Nos. 244-245 (2)	24.25	*28.45*
Nos. 129-130 (2)	25.25	*53.20*
Nos. 116-117 (2)	25.25	*33.50*
Nos. 158-159 (2)	58.50	*78.05*
Nos. 114-115 (2)	25.25	*32.75*
Nos. 99-100 (2)	110.10	70.10
Nos. 1L11-1L12 (2)	4.25	6.00
Nos. 139-140 (2)	18.20	11.50
Nos. 146-147 (2)	21.25	21.25
Nos. 121-122 (2)	61.00	*78.00*
Nos. 54-55 (2)	14.25	*26.25*
Nos. 142-143 (2)	35.25	48.20
Nos. 145-146 (2)	21.75	21.75
Nos. 178-179 (2)	283.50	96.50
Nos. 138-139 (2)	27.85	*60.25*
Nos. 92-93 (2)	50.25	*67.75*
Nos. 118-119 (2)	7.00	8.25
Nos. 128-129 (2)	29.25	*53.25*
Nos. 55-56 (2)	35.25	*50.25*
Nos. 44-45 (2)	35.75	*62.75*
Nos. 1-2 (2)	35.40	*49.75*
Nos. 36-37 (2)	28.10	*38.20*
Nos. 44-45 (2)	28.00	*38.05*
Nos. 1-2 (2)	40.50	37.80

Nos. 99-100 (2)	27.80	37.75
Nos. 1-2 (2)	33.50	58.00
Nos. 74-75 (2)	30.25	25.30
Nos. 47-48 (2)	32.75	61.75
Nos. 223-224 (2)	40.55	45.25
Nos. 229-230 (2)	17.75	45.25
Nos. 106-107 (2)	8.75	17.25
Nos. 73-74 (2)	17.85	22.80
Nos. 238-239 (2)	35.30	45.75
Nos. 48-49 (2)	100.30	90.25
Nos. 85-86 (2)	18.25	30.25
Nos. 11-12 (2)	44.75	48.50
Nos. 130-131 (2)	32.80	42.80
Nos. 93-94 (2)	11.25	10.50
Nos. 129-130 (2)	22.25	45.25
Nos. 154-155 (2)	27.75	30.25
Nos. 174-175 (2)	50.40	52.90
Nos. 151-152 (2)	16.25	45.75
Nos. 188-189 (2)	24.75	26.25
Nos. 21-22 (2)	116.00	45.40
Nos. 82-83 (2)	13.40	13.40
Nos. 110-111 (2)	8.40	8.75
Nos. 48-49 (2)	40.30	47.75
Nos. 64-65 (2)	32.75	38.25
Nos. 92-93 (2)	11.25	16.25
Nos. 90-91 (2)	16.25	22.25
Nos. 224-225 (2)	29.60	38.00
Nos. 267-268 (2)	30.40	25.25
Nos. 93-94 (2)	20.10	25.35
Nos. 525-526 (2)	23.10	29.25
Nos. 62-63 (2)	38.50	57.75
Nos. [illegible] (2)	45.50	45.50
Nos. 25-26 (2)	46.00	47.50
No. 106 (1)	.80	1.00
No. 159 (1)	1.10	.35
Set total (136) Stamps	2,472.	2,685.

U.P.U.

Mercury and Symbols of Communications — CD306

Plane, Ship and Hemispheres — CD307

Mercury Scattering Letters over Globe CD308

U.P.U. Monument, Bern CD309

Universal Postal Union, 75th anniversary.

1949

Aden ... 32-35
Kathiri State of Seiyun ... 16-19
Qu'aiti State of Shihr and Mukalla ... 16-19
Antigua ... 100-103
Ascension ... 57-60
Bahamas ... 150-153
Barbados ... 212-215
Basutoland ... 41-44
Bechuanaland Protectorate ... 149-152
Bermuda ... 138-141
British Guiana ... 246-249
British Honduras ... 137-140
Brunei ... 79-82
Cayman Islands ... 118-121
Cyprus ... 160-163
Dominica ... 116-119
Falkland Islands ... 103-106
Falkland Islands Dep. ... 1L14-1L17
Fiji ... 141-144
Gambia ... 148-151
Gibraltar ... 123-126
Gilbert & Ellice Islands ... 56-59
Gold Coast ... 144-147
Grenada ... 147-150
Hong Kong ... 180-183
Jamaica ... 142-145
Kenya, Uganda, Tanzania ... 94-97
Leeward Islands ... 126-129
Malaya
Johore ... 151-154
Kedah ... 57-60
Kelantan ... 46-49
Malacca ... 18-21
Negri Sembilan ... 59-62
Pahang ... 46-49
Penang ... 23-26
Perak ... 101-104
Perlis ... 3-6
Selangor ... 76-79
Trengganu ... 49-52
Malta ... 225-228
Mauritius ... 231-234
Montserrat ... 108-111
New Hebrides, British ... 62-65
New Hebrides, French ... 79-82
Nigeria ... 75-78
North Borneo ... 240-243
Northern Rhodesia ... 50-53
Nyasaland Protectorate ... 87-90
Pitcairn Islands ... 13-16
St. Helena ... 132-135
St. Kitts-Nevis ... 95-98
St. Lucia ... 131-134
St. Vincent ... 170-173
Sarawak ... 176-179
Seychelles ... 153-156
Sierra Leone ... 190-193
Singapore ... 23-26
Solomon Islands ... 84-87
Somaliland Protectorate ... 112-115
Southern Rhodesia ... 71-72
Swaziland ... 50-53
Tonga ... 87-90
Trinidad & Tobago ... 66-69
Turks & Caicos Islands ... 101-104
Virgin Islands ... 92-95
Zanzibar ... 226-229

The following have different designs but are included in the omnibus set:

Great Britain ... 276-279
Offices in Morocco (Tangier) ... 546-549
Australia ... 223
Bahrain ... 68-71
Burma ... 116-121
Ceylon ... 304-306
Egypt ... 281-283
India ... 223-226
Kuwait ... 89-92
Oman ... 31-34
Pakistan-Bahawalpur 26-29, O25-O28
South Africa ... 109-111
South-West Africa ... 160-162

Nos. 32-35 (4)	5.85	8.45
Nos. 16-19 (4)	2.75	8.00
Nos. 16-19 (4)	2.60	8.00
Nos. 100-103 (4)	3.60	7.70
Nos. 57-60 (4)	11.10	9.00
Nos. 150-153 (4)	5.35	9.30
Nos. 212-215 (4)	4.40	14.85
Nos. 41-44 (4)	4.75	10.00
Nos. 149-152 (4)	3.35	7.25
Nos. 138-141 (4)	4.75	6.15
Nos. 246-249 (4)	2.75	4.20
Nos. 137-140 (4)	3.30	6.35
Nos. 79-82 (4)	9.50	8.45
Nos. 118-121 (4)	3.60	7.25
Nos. 160-163 (4)	4.60	10.70
Nos. 116-119 (4)	2.30	5.65
Nos. 103-106 (4)	14.00	17.10
Nos. 1L14-1L17 (4)	14.60	14.50
Nos. 141-144 (4)	3.35	15.75
Nos. 148-151 (4)	3.10	7.10
Nos. 123-126 (4)	5.90	8.75
Nos. 56-59 (4)	4.30	13.00
Nos. 144-147 (4)	2.55	10.35
Nos. 147-150 (4)	2.15	3.55
Nos. 180-183 (4)	57.25	18.25
Nos. 142-145 (4)	2.25	2.45
Nos. 94-97 (4)	2.90	3.40
Nos. 126-129 (4)	3.05	9.60
Nos. 151-154 (4)	4.70	8.90
Nos. 57-60 (4)	4.80	12.00
Nos. 46-49 (4)	4.25	12.65
Nos. 18-21 (4)	4.25	17.30
Nos. 59-62 (4)	3.50	10.75
Nos. 46-49 (4)	3.00	7.25
Nos. 23-26 (4)	5.10	11.75
Nos. 101-104 (4)	3.65	10.75
Nos. 3-6 (4)	3.95	14.25
Nos. 76-79 (4)	4.90	12.30
Nos. 49-52 (4)	5.55	12.25
Nos. 225-228 (4)	4.50	4.85
Nos. 231-234 (4)	4.35	6.70
Nos. 108-111 (4)	3.30	4.35
Nos. 62-65 (4)	1.60	4.25
Nos. 79-82 (4)	24.25	24.25
Nos. 75-78 (4)	2.80	9.25
Nos. 240-243 (4)	7.15	6.50
Nos. 50-53 (4)	5.00	6.50
Nos. 87-90 (4)	4.05	4.05
Nos. 13-16 (4)	18.50	16.50
Nos. 132-135 (4)	4.85	7.10
Nos. 95-98 (4)	3.35	5.55
Nos. 131-134 (4)	2.55	3.85
Nos. 170-173 (4)	2.20	5.05
Nos. 176-179 (4)	8.15	10.85
Nos. 153-156 (4)	3.25	4.10
Nos. 190-193 (4)	3.00	5.10
Nos. 23-26 (4)	19.00	13.70
Nos. 84-87 (4)	4.05	4.90
Nos. 112-115 (4)	3.95	8.70
Nos. 71-72 (2)	1.95	2.25
Nos. 50-53 (4)	2.80	4.65
Nos. 87-90 (4)	3.00	5.25
Nos. 66-69 (4)	3.15	3.15
Nos. 101-104 (4)	2.70	4.10
Nos. 92-95 (4)	2.60	5.90
Nos. 226-229 (4)	5.45	13.50
Nos. 276-279 (4)	1.35	1.00
Nos. 546-549 (4)	3.20	10.15
No. 223 (1)	.40	.40
Nos. 68-71 (4)	4.75	16.50
Nos. 116-121 (6)	7.30	5.35
Nos. 304-306 (3)	3.35	4.25
Nos. 281-283 (3)	5.75	2.70
Nos. 223-226 (4)	27.25	10.50
Nos. 89-92 (4)	6.10	10.25
Nos. 31-34 (4)	5.55	15.75
Nos. 26-29,O25-O28 (8)	2.00	42.00
Nos. 109-111 (3)	2.00	2.70
Nos. 160-162 (3)	3.00	5.50
Set total (313) Stamps	461.10	707.20

University

Arms of University College CD310

Alice, Princess of Athlone CD311

1948 opening of University College of the West Indies at Jamaica.

1951

Antigua ... 104-105
Barbados ... 228-229
British Guiana ... 250-251
British Honduras ... 141-142
Dominica ... 120-121
Grenada ... 164-165
Jamaica ... 146-147
Leeward Islands ... 130-131
Montserrat ... 112-113
St. Kitts-Nevis ... 105-106
St. Lucia ... 149-150
St. Vincent ... 174-175
Trinidad & Tobago ... 70-71
Virgin Islands ... 96-97

Nos. 104-105 (2)	1.35	3.75
Nos. 228-229 (2)	1.75	2.65
Nos. 250-251 (2)	1.10	1.25
Nos. 141-142 (2)	1.40	2.20
Nos. 120-121 (2)	1.40	1.75
Nos. 164-165 (2)	1.20	1.60
Nos. 146-147 (2)	.90	.70
Nos. 130-131 (2)	1.35	4.00
Nos. 112-113 (2)	.85	2.00
Nos. 105-106 (2)	.90	2.25
Nos. 149-150 (2)	1.40	1.50
Nos. 174-175 (2)	1.00	2.15
Nos. 70-71 (2)	.75	.75
Nos. 96-97 (2)	1.50	3.75
Set total (28) Stamps	16.85	30.30

Coronation

Queen Elizabeth II — CD312

1953

Aden ... 47
Kathiri State of Seiyun ... 28
Qu'aiti State of Shihr and Mukalla ... 28
Antigua ... 106
Ascension ... 61
Bahamas ... 157
Barbados ... 234
Basutoland ... 45
Bechuanaland Protectorate ... 153
Bermuda ... 142
British Guiana ... 252
British Honduras ... 143
Cayman Islands ... 150
Cyprus ... 167
Dominica ... 141
Falkland Islands ... 121
Falkland Islands Dependencies ... 1L18
Fiji ... 145
Gambia ... 152
Gibraltar ... 131
Gilbert & Ellice Islands ... 60
Gold Coast ... 160
Grenada ... 170
Hong Kong ... 184
Jamaica ... 153
Kenya, Uganda, Tanzania ... 101
Leeward Islands ... 132
Malaya
Johore ... 155
Kedah ... 82
Kelantan ... 71
Malacca ... 27
Negri Sembilan ... 63
Pahang ... 71
Penang ... 27
Perak ... 126
Perlis ... 28
Selangor ... 101
Trengganu ... 74
Malta ... 241
Mauritius ... 250
Montserrat ... 127
New Hebrides, British ... 77
Nigeria ... 79
North Borneo ... 260
Northern Rhodesia ... 60
Nyasaland Protectorate ... 96
Pitcairn Islands ... 19
St. Helena ... 139
St. Kitts-Nevis ... 119
St. Lucia ... 156
St. Vincent ... 185
Sarawak ... 196
Seychelles ... 172
Sierra Leone ... 194
Singapore ... 27
Solomon Islands ... 88
Somaliland Protectorate ... 127
Swaziland ... 54
Trinidad & Tobago ... 84
Tristan da Cunha ... 13
Turks & Caicos Islands ... 118
Virgin Islands ... 114

The following have different designs but are included in the omnibus set:

Great Britain ... 313-316
Offices in Morocco (Tangier) ... 579-582
Australia ... 259-261
Bahrain ... 92-95
Canada ... 330
Ceylon ... 317
Cook Islands ... 145-146
Kuwait ... 113-116
New Zealand ... 280-284
Niue ... 104-105
Oman ... 52-55
Samoa ... 214-215
South Africa ... 192
Southern Rhodesia ... 80
South-West Africa ... 244-248
Tokelau Islands ... 4

No. 47 (1)	1.25	1.25
No. 28 (1)	.75	1.50
No. 28 (1)	1.10	.60
No. 106 (1)	.40	.75
No. 61 (1)	1.25	2.75
No. 157 (1)	1.40	.75
No. 234 (1)	1.00	.25
No. 45 (1)	.50	.60
No. 153 (1)	.75	.35
No. 142 (1)	.85	.50
No. 252 (1)	.45	.25
No. 143 (1)	.60	.40
No. 150 (1)	.40	1.75
No. 167 (1)	1.60	.75
No. 141 (1)	.40	.40
No. 121 (1)	.90	1.50
No. 1L18 (1)	1.80	1.40
No. 145 (1)	1.00	.60
No. 152 (1)	.50	.50
No. 131 (1)	.50	.50
No. 60 (1)	.65	2.25
No. 160 (1)	1.00	.25

No. 170 (1)	.30	.25
No. 184 (1)	6.00	.35
No. 153 (1)	.70	.25
No. 101 (1)	.40	.25
No. 132 (1)	1.00	*2.25*
No. 155 (1)	1.40	.30
No. 82 (1)	2.25	.60
No. 71 (1)	1.60	1.60
No. 27 (1)	1.10	*1.50*
No. 63 (1)	1.40	.65
No. 71 (1)	2.25	.25
No. 27 (1)	1.75	.30
No. 126 (1)	1.60	.25
No. 28 (1)	1.75	*4.00*
No. 101 (1)	1.75	.25
No. 74 (1)	1.50	1.00
No. 241 (1)	.50	.25
No. 250 (1)	1.00	.25
No. 127 (1)	.60	.45
No. 77 (1)	.75	.60
No. 79 (1)	.45	.25
No. 260 (1)	2.00	1.00
No. 60 (1)	.70	.25
No. 96 (1)	.75	.75
No. 19 (1)	2.25	2.25
No. 139 (1)	1.25	1.25
No. 119 (1)	.35	.25
No. 156 (1)	.70	.35
No. 185 (1)	.50	.30
No. 196 (1)	2.00	*1.75*
No. 172 (1)	.80	.80
No. 194 (1)	.40	.40
No. 27 (1)	2.50	.40
No. 88 (1)	1.00	1.00
No. 127 (1)	.40	.25
No. 54 (1)	.30	.25
No. 84 (1)	.25	.25
No. 13 (1)	1.00	1.75
No. 118 (1)	.40	*1.10*
No. 114 (1)	.40	*1.00*
Nos. 313-316 (4)	16.35	5.95
Nos. 579-582 (4)	7.40	5.20
Nos. 259-261 (3)	3.60	2.75
Nos. 92-95 (4)	15.25	12.75
No. 330 (1)	.25	.25
No. 317 (1)	1.40	.25
Nos. 145-146 (2)	2.65	2.65
Nos. 113-116 (4)	16.00	8.50
Nos. 280-284 (5)	5.75	5.60
Nos. 104-105 (2)	1.60	1.60
Nos. 52-55 (4)	15.25	6.50
Nos. 214-215 (2)	2.10	1.00
No. 192 (1)	.45	.30
No. 80 (1)	7.25	7.25
Nos. 244-248 (5)	3.00	2.35
No. 4 (1)	2.75	2.75
Set total (106) Stamps	168.10	116.70

Separate designs for each country for the visit of Queen Elizabeth II and the Duke of Edinburgh.

Royal Visit 1953

1953

Aden	62
Australia	267-269
Bermuda	163
Ceylon	318
Fiji	146
Gibraltar	146
Jamaica	154
Kenya, Uganda, Tanzania	102
Malta	242
New Zealand	286-287

No. 62 (1)	.65	4.00
Nos. 267-269 (3)	2.75	2.05
No. 163 (1)	.50	.25
No. 318 (1)	1.00	.25
No. 146 (1)	.65	.35
No. 146 (1)	.50	.30
No. 154 (1)	.50	.25
No. 102 (1)	.50	.25
No. 242 (1)	.35	.25
Nos. 286-287 (2)	.50	.50
Set total (13) Stamps	7.90	8.45

West Indies Federation

Map of the Caribbean CD313

Federation of the West Indies, April 22, 1958.

1958

Antigua	122-124
Barbados	248-250
Dominica	161-163
Grenada	184-186
Jamaica	175-177
Montserrat	143-145
St. Kitts-Nevis	136-138
St. Lucia	170-172
St. Vincent	198-200
Trinidad & Tobago	86-88

Nos. 122-124 (3)	5.80	3.80
Nos. 248 250 (3)	1.60	*2.90*
Nos. 161-163 (3)	1.95	1.85
Nos. 184-186 (3)	1.50	1.20
Nos. 175-177 (3)	2.65	3.45
Nos. 143-145 (3)	2.35	1.35
Nos. 136-138 (3)	3.00	3.10
Nos. 170-172 (3)	2.05	2.80
Nos. 198-200 (3)	1.50	1.75
Nos. 86-88 (3)	.75	.90
Set total (30) Stamps	23.15	23.10

Freedom from Hunger

Protein Food CD314

U.N. Food and Agricultural Organization's "Freedom from Hunger" campaign.

1963

Aden	65
Antigua	133
Ascension	89
Bahamas	180
Basutoland	83
Bechuanaland Protectorate	194
Bermuda	192
British Guiana	271
British Honduras	179
Brunei	100
Cayman Islands	168
Dominica	181
Falkland Islands	146
Fiji	198
Gambia	172
Gibraltar	161
Gilbert & Ellice Islands	76
Grenada	190
Hong Kong	218
Malta	291
Mauritius	270
Montserrat	150
New Hebrides, British	93
North Borneo	296
Pitcairn Islands	35
St. Helena	173
St. Lucia	179
St. Vincent	201
Sarawak	212
Seychelles	213
Solomon Islands	109
Swaziland	108
Tonga	127
Tristan da Cunha	68
Turks & Caicos Islands	138
Virgin Islands	140
Zanzibar	280

No. 65 (1)	1.50	1.75
No. 133 (1)	.35	.35
No. 89 (1)	1.00	.50
No. 180 (1)	.65	.65
No. 83 (1)	.50	.25
No. 194 (1)	.50	.50
No. 192 (1)	1.00	.50
No. 271 (1)	.45	.25
No. 179 (1)	.60	.25
No. 100 (1)	3.25	2.25
No. 168 (1)	.55	.30
No. 181 (1)	.30	.30
No. 146 (1)	10.50	2.50
No. 198 (1)	3.50	2.25
No. 172 (1)	.50	.25
No. 161 (1)	4.00	2.25
No. 76 (1)	1.40	.40
No. 190 (1)	.30	.25
No. 218 (1)	47.50	7.50
No. 291 (1)	2.00	2.00
No. 270 (1)	.50	.50
No. 150 (1)	.55	.35
No. 93 (1)	.60	.25
No. 296 (1)	1.90	.75
No. 35 (1)	10.00	4.50
No. 173 (1)	2.25	1.10
No. 179 (1)	.40	.40
No. 201 (1)	.90	.50
No. 212 (1)	1.60	*1.75*
No. 213 (1)	.85	.35
No. 109 (1)	3.00	.85
No. 108 (1)	.50	.50
No. 127 (1)	.60	.35
No. 68 (1)	.75	.35
No. 138 (1)	.50	.25
No. 140 (1)	.50	.50
No. 280 (1)	1.50	.80
Set total (37) Stamps	107.25	39.30

Red Cross Centenary

Red Cross and Elizabeth II CD315

1963

Antigua	134-135
Ascension	90-91
Bahamas	183-184
Basutoland	84-85
Bechuanaland Protectorate	195-196
Bermuda	193-194
British Guiana	272-273
British Honduras	180-181
Cayman Islands	169-170
Dominica	182-183
Falkland Islands	147-148
Fiji	203-204
Gambia	173-174
Gibraltar	162-163
Gilbert & Ellice Islands	77-78
Grenada	191-192
Hong Kong	219-220
Jamaica	203-204
Malta	292-293
Mauritius	271-272
Montserrat	151-152
New Hebrides, British	94-95
Pitcairn Islands	36-37
St. Helena	174-175
St. Kitts-Nevis	143-144
St. Lucia	180-181
St. Vincent	202-203
Seychelles	214-215
Solomon Islands	110-111
South Arabia	1-2
Swaziland	109-110
Tonga	134-135
Tristan da Cunha	69-70
Turks & Caicos Islands	139-140
Virgin Islands	141-142

Nos. 134-135 (2)	1.00	*2.00*
Nos. 90-91 (2)	6.75	3.35
Nos. 183-184 (2)	2.30	2.80
Nos. 84-85 (2)	1.20	.90
Nos. 195-196 (2)	.95	.85
Nos. 193-194 (2)	3.00	2.80
Nos. 272-273 (2)	1.05	.80
Nos. 180-181 (2)	1.00	2.50
Nos. 169-170 (2)	1.10	*3.00*
Nos. 182-183 (2)	.70	*1.05*
Nos. 147-148 (2)	18.00	5.50
Nos. 203-204 (2)	3.25	2.80
Nos. 173-174 (2)	.75	1.00
Nos. 162-163 (2)	6.25	5.40
Nos. 77-78 (2)	2.00	*3.50*
Nos. 191-192 (2)	.80	.50
Nos. 219-220 (2)	35.00	7.35
Nos. 203-204 (2)	.75	*1.65*
Nos. 292-293 (2)	2.50	4.75
Nos. 271-272 (2)	.90	.90
Nos. 151-152 (2)	1.00	.75
Nos. 94-95 (2)	1.00	.50
Nos. 36-37 (2)	6.50	5.50
Nos. 174-175 (2)	1.70	2.30
Nos. 143-144 (2)	.90	.90
Nos. 180-181 (2)	1.25	1.25
Nos. 202-203 (2)	.90	.90
Nos. 214-215 (2)	1.10	.90
Nos. 110-111 (2)	1.25	1.15
Nos. 1-2 (2)	1.25	1.25
Nos. 109-110 (2)	1.10	1.10
Nos. 134-135 (2)	1.00	1.25
Nos. 69-70 (2)	1.15	.80
Nos. 139-140 (2)	.85	.75
Nos. 141-142 (2)	.80	1.25
Set total (70) Stamps	111.00	73.95

Shakespeare

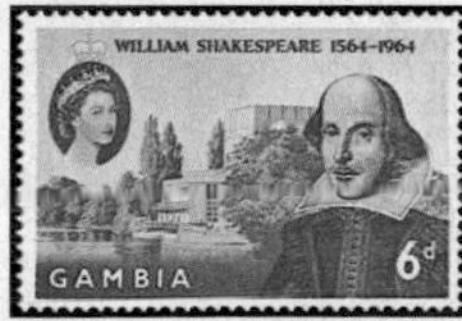

Shakespeare Memorial Theatre, Stratford-on-Avon — CD316

400th anniversary of the birth of William Shakespeare.

1964

Antigua	151
Bahamas	201
Bechuanaland Protectorate	197
Cayman Islands	171
Dominica	184
Falkland Islands	149
Gambia	192
Gibraltar	164
Montserrat	153
St. Lucia	196
Turks & Caicos Islands	141
Virgin Islands	143

No. 151 (1)	.35	.25
No. 201 (1)	.60	.35
No. 197 (1)	.35	.35
No. 171 (1)	.35	.30
No. 181 (1)	.35	.35
No. 149 (1)	1.60	.50
No. 192 (1)	.35	.25
No. 164 (1)	.65	.55
No. 153 (1)	.35	.25
No. 196 (1)	.45	.25
No. 141 (1)	.40	.25
No. 143 (1)	.45	.45
Set total (12) Stamps	6.25	4.10

ITU

ITU Emblem CD317

Intl. Telecommunication Union, cent.

1965

Antigua	153-154
Ascension	92-93
Bahamas	219-220
Barbados	265-266
Basutoland	101-102
Bechuanaland Protectorate	202-203
Bermuda	196-197
British Guiana	293-294
British Honduras	187-188
Brunei	116-117
Cayman Islands	172-173
Dominica	185-186
Falkland Islands	154-155
Fiji	211-212
Gibraltar	167-168
Gilbert & Ellice Islands	87-88
Grenada	205-206
Hong Kong	221-222
Mauritius	291-292
Montserrat	157-158
New Hebrides, British	108-109
Pitcairn Islands	52-53
St. Helena	180-181
St. Kitts-Nevis	163-164
St. Lucia	197-198
St. Vincent	224-225
Seychelles	218-219
Solomon Islands	126-127
Swaziland	115-116
Tristan da Cunha	85-86
Turks & Caicos Islands	142-143
Virgin Islands	159-160

Nos. 153-154 (2)	1.45	1.35
Nos. 92-93 (2)	1.90	1.30
Nos. 219-220 (2)	1.35	1.50
Nos. 265-266 (2)	1.50	1.25
Nos. 101-102 (2)	.85	.65
Nos. 202-203 (2)	1.10	.75
Nos. 196-197 (2)	2.15	*2.25*
Nos. 293-294 (2)	.60	.55
Nos. 187-188 (2)	.75	.75
Nos. 116-117 (2)	1.75	1.75
Nos. 172-173 (2)	1.00	.85
Nos. 185-186 (2)	.55	.55
Nos. 154-155 (2)	6.75	3.15
Nos. 211-212 (2)	2.00	1.05
Nos. 167-168 (2)	9.00	5.95
Nos. 87-88 (2)	.85	.60
Nos. 205-206 (2)	.50	.50
Nos. 221-222 (2)	24.50	3.80
Nos. 291-292 (2)	1.20	.65
Nos. 157-158 (2)	1.05	1.15
Nos. 108-109 (2)	.65	.50
Nos. 52-53 (2)	6.25	4.30
Nos. 180-181 (2)	.80	.60
Nos. 100-104 (2)	.60	.60
Nos. 197-198 (2)	1.25	1.25
Nos. 224-225 (2)	.80	.90
Nos. 218-219 (2)	.90	.60
Nos. 126-127 (2)	.70	.55
Nos. 115-116 (2)	.75	.75
Nos. 85-86 (2)	1.00	.65
Nos. 142-143 (2)	.75	.50
Nos. 159-160 (2)	.85	.85
Set total (64) Stamps	76.10	42.40

Intl. Cooperation Year

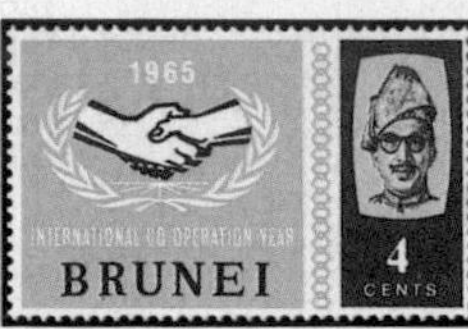

ICY Emblem CD318

1965

Antigua 155-156
Ascension 94-95
Bahamas 222-223
Basutoland 103-104
Bechuanaland Protectorate 204-205
Bermuda 199-200
British Guiana 295-296
British Honduras 189-190
Brunei 118-119
Cayman Islands 174-175
Dominica 187-188
Falkland Islands 156-157
Fiji 213-214
Gibraltar 169-170
Gilbert & Ellice Islands 104-105
Grenada 207-208
Hong Kong 223-224
Mauritius 293-294
Montserrat 176-177
New Hebrides, British 110-111
New Hebrides, French 126-127
Pitcairn Islands 54-55
St. Helena 182-183
St. Kitts-Nevis 165-166
St. Lucia 199-200
Seychelles 220-221
Solomon Islands 143-144
South Arabia 17-18
Swaziland 117-118
Tristan da Cunha 87-88
Turks & Caicos Islands 144-145
Virgin Islands 161-162

Nos. 155-156 (2)	.55	.50
Nos. 94-95 (2)	1.30	1.40
Nos. 222-223 (2)	.65	1.90
Nos. 103-104 (2)	.75	.85
Nos. 204-205 (2)	.85	1.00
Nos. 199-200 (2)	2.05	1.25
Nos. 295-296 (2)	.65	.60
Nos. 189-190 (2)	.60	.55
Nos. 118-119 (2)	.85	.85
Nos. 174-175 (2)	1.00	.75
Nos. 187-188 (2)	.55	.55
Nos. 156-157 (2)	6.00	1.65
Nos. 213-214 (2)	1.95	1.25
Nos. 169-170 (2)	1.25	*2.75*
Nos. 104-105 (2)	.85	.60
Nos. 207-208 (2)	.50	.50
Nos. 223-224 (2)	22.00	3.10
Nos. 293-294 (2)	.70	.70
Nos. 176-177 (2)	.80	.65
Nos. 110-111 (2)	.50	.50
Nos. 126-127 (2)	12.00	12.00
Nos. 54-55 (2)	6.35	4.50
Nos. 182-183 (2)	.95	.50
Nos. 165-166 (2)	.80	.60
Nos. 199-200 (2)	.55	.55
Nos. 220-221 (2)	.90	.65
Nos. 143-144 (2)	.70	.60
Nos. 17-18 (2)	1.20	.50
Nos. 117-118 (2)	.75	.75
Nos. 87-88 (2)	1.05	.65
Nos. 144-145 (2)	.65	.50
Nos. 161-162 (2)	.65	.50
Set total (64) Stamps	70.90	44.20

Churchill Memorial

Winston Churchill and St. Paul's, London, During Air Attack CD319

1966

Antigua 157-160
Ascension 96-99
Bahamas 224-227
Barbados 281-284
Basutoland 105-108
Bechuanaland Protectorate 206-209
Bermuda 201-204
British Antarctic Territory 16-19
British Honduras 191-194
Brunei 120-123
Cayman Islands 176-179
Dominica 189-192
Falkland Islands 158-161
Fiji 215-218
Gibraltar 171-174
Gilbert & Ellice Islands 106-109
Grenada 209-212
Hong Kong 225-228
Mauritius 295-298
Montserrat 178-181
New Hebrides, British 112-115
New Hebrides, French 128-131
Pitcairn Islands 56-59
St. Helena 184-187
St. Kitts-Nevis 167-170
St. Lucia 201-204
St. Vincent 241-244
Seychelles 222-225
Solomon Islands 145-148
South Arabia 19-22
Swaziland 119-122
Tristan da Cunha 89-92
Turks & Caicos Islands 146-149
Virgin Islands 163-166

Nos. 157-160 (4)	3.05	3.05
Nos. 96-99 (4)	10.00	6.40
Nos. 224-227 (4)	2.30	*3.20*
Nos. 281-284 (4)	3.00	4.95
Nos. 105-108 (4)	2.80	3.25
Nos. 206-209 (4)	2.50	2.50
Nos. 201-204 (4)	4.00	*4.75*
Nos. 16-19 (4)	41.20	18.00
Nos. 191-194 (4)	2.45	1.30
Nos. 120-123 (4)	7.65	6.55
Nos. 176-179 (4)	3.10	3.65
Nos. 189-192 (4)	1.15	1.15
Nos. 158-161 (4)	12.75	9.55
Nos. 215-218 (4)	4.40	3.00
Nos. 171-174 (4)	3.05	5.30
Nos. 106-109 (4)	1.50	1.30
Nos. 209-212 (4)	1.10	1.10
Nos. 225-228 (4)	52.50	11.40
Nos. 295-298 (4)	4.05	4.05
Nos. 178-181 (4)	1.60	1.55
Nos. 112-115 (4)	2.30	1.00
Nos. 128-131 (4)	10.25	10.25
Nos. 56-59 (4)	11.00	6.75
Nos. 184-187 (4)	1.85	1.95
Nos. 167-170 (4)	1.50	1.70
Nos. 201-204 (4)	1.50	1.50
Nos. 241-244 (4)	1.50	1.75
Nos. 222-225 (4)	3.20	3.60
Nos. 145-148 (4)	1.50	1.60
Nos. 19-22 (4)	2.95	2.20
Nos. 119-122 (4)	1.70	2.55
Nos. 89-92 (4)	5.95	2.70
Nos. 146-149 (4)	1.60	1.75
Nos. 163-166 (4)	1.90	1.90
Set total (136) Stamps	212.85	137.20

Royal Visit, 1966

Queen Elizabeth II and Prince Philip CD320

Caribbean visit, Feb. 4 - Mar. 6, 1966.

1966

Antigua 161-162
Bahamas 228-229
Barbados 285-286
British Guiana 299-300
Cayman Islands 180-181
Dominica 193-194
Grenada 213-214
Montserrat 182-183
St. Kitts-Nevis 171-172
St. Lucia 205-206
St. Vincent 245-246
Turks & Caicos Islands 150-151
Virgin Islands 167-168

Nos. 161-162 (2)	3.50	2.60
Nos. 228-229 (2)	3.05	3.05
Nos. 285-286 (2)	3.00	2.00
Nos. 299-300 (2)	3.35	1.60
Nos. 180-181 (2)	3.45	1.80
Nos. 193-194 (2)	3.00	.60
Nos. 213-214 (2)	.80	.50
Nos. 182-183 (2)	2.00	1.00
Nos. 171-172 (2)	.90	.75
Nos. 205-206 (2)	1.50	1.35
Nos. 245-246 (2)	2.75	1.35
Nos. 150-151 (2)	1.20	.55
Nos. 167-168 (2)	1.75	1.75
Set total (26) Stamps	30.25	18.90

World Cup Soccer

Soccer Player and Jules Rimet Cup CD321

World Cup Soccer Championship, Wembley, England, July 11-30.

1966

Antigua 163-164
Ascension 100-101
Bahamas 245-246
Bermuda 205-206
Brunei 124-125
Cayman Islands 182-183
Dominica 195-196
Fiji 219-220
Gibraltar 175-176
Gilbert & Ellice Islands 125-126
Grenada 230-231
New Hebrides, British 116-117
New Hebrides, French 132-133
Pitcairn Islands 60-61
St. Helena 188-189
St. Kitts-Nevis 173-174
St. Lucia 207-208
Seychelles 226-227
Solomon Islands 167-168
South Arabia 23-24
Tristan da Cunha 93-94

Nos. 163-164 (2)	.80	.85
Nos. 100-101 (2)	2.50	2.00
Nos. 245-246 (2)	.65	.65
Nos. 205-206 (2)	1.75	1.75
Nos. 124-125 (2)	1.30	1.25
Nos. 182-183 (2)	.75	.65
Nos. 195-196 (2)	1.20	.75
Nos. 219-220 (2)	1.70	.60
Nos. 175-176 (2)	1.85	1.75
Nos. 125-126 (2)	.70	.60
Nos. 230-231 (2)	.65	*.95*
Nos. 116-117 (2)	1.00	1.00
Nos. 132-133 (2)	7.00	7.00
Nos. 60-61 (2)	5.50	5.00
Nos. 188-189 (2)	1.25	.60
Nos. 173-174 (2)	.85	.80
Nos. 207-208 (2)	1.15	.90
Nos. 226-227 (2)	.85	.85
Nos. 167-168 (2)	1.10	1.10
Nos. 23-24 (2)	1.90	.55
Nos. 93-94 (2)	1.25	.80
Set total (42) Stamps	35.70	30.40

WHO Headquarters

World Health Organization Headquarters, Geneva — CD322

1966

Antigua 165-166
Ascension 102-103
Bahamas 247-248
Brunei 126-127
Cayman Islands 184-185
Dominica 197-198
Fiji 224-225
Gibraltar 180-181
Gilbert & Ellice Islands 127-128
Grenada 232-233
Hong Kong 229-230
Montserrat 184-185
New Hebrides, British 118-119
New Hebrides, French 134-135
Pitcairn Islands 62-63
St. Helena 190-191
St. Kitts-Nevis 177-178
St. Lucia 209-210
St. Vincent 247-248
Seychelles 228-229
Solomon Islands 169-170
South Arabia 25-26
Tristan da Cunha 99-100

Nos. 165-166 (2)	1.15	.55
Nos. 102-103 (2)	6.60	3.35
Nos. 247-248 (2)	.80	.80
Nos. 126-127 (2)	1.35	1.35
Nos. 184-185 (2)	2.25	1.20
Nos. 197-198 (2)	.75	.75
Nos. 224-225 (2)	4.70	3.30
Nos. 180-181 (2)	6.50	4.50
Nos. 127-128 (2)	.80	.70
Nos. 232-233 (2)	.80	.50
Nos. 229-230 (2)	11.25	2.30
Nos. 184-185 (2)	1.00	1.00
Nos. 118-119 (2)	.75	.50
Nos. 134-135 (2)	8.75	8.75
Nos. 62-63 (2)	7.25	6.50
Nos. 190-191 (2)	3.50	1.50
Nos. 177-178 (2)	.60	.60
Nos. 209-210 (2)	.80	.80
Nos. 247-248 (2)	1.15	1.05
Nos. 228-229 (2)	1.25	.75
Nos. 169-170 (2)	.95	.80
Nos. 25-26 (2)	2.10	.70
Nos. 99-100 (2)	1.90	1.25
Set total (46) Stamps	66.95	43.50

UNESCO Anniversary

"Education" — CD323

"Science" (Wheat ears & flask enclosing globe). "Culture" (lyre & columns). 20th anniversary of the UNESCO.

1966-67

Antigua 183-185
Ascension 108-110
Bahamas 249-251
Barbados 287-289
Bermuda 207-209
Brunei 128-130
Cayman Islands 186-188
Dominica 199-201
Gibraltar 183-185
Gilbert & Ellice Islands 129-131
Grenada 234-236
Hong Kong 231-233
Mauritius 299-301
Montserrat 186-188
New Hebrides, British 120-122
New Hebrides, French 136-138
Pitcairn Islands 64-66
St. Helena 192-194
St. Kitts-Nevis 179-181
St. Lucia 211-213
St. Vincent 249-251
Seychelles 230-232
Solomon Islands 171-173
South Arabia 27-29
Swaziland 123-125
Tristan da Cunha 101-103
Turks & Caicos Islands 155-157
Virgin Islands 176-178

Nos. 183-185 (3)	1.90	*2.50*
Nos. 108-110 (3)	11.00	5.80
Nos. 249-251 (3)	2.35	2.35
Nos. 287-289 (3)	2.35	2.15
Nos. 207-209 (3)	3.80	*3.90*
Nos. 128-130 (3)	4.65	5.40
Nos. 186-188 (3)	2.50	1.50
Nos. 199-201 (3)	1.60	.75
Nos. 183-185 (3)	6.50	3.25
Nos. 129-131 (3)	2.50	*2.45*
Nos. 234-236 (3)	1.10	1.20
Nos. 231-233 (3)	69.50	17.50
Nos. 299-301 (3)	2.10	1.50
Nos. 186-188 (3)	2.40	2.40
Nos. 120-122 (3)	1.90	1.90
Nos. 136-138 (3)	7.75	7.75
Nos. 64-66 (3)	7.10	4.75
Nos. 192-194 (3)	5.25	3.65
Nos. 179-181 (3)	.90	.90
Nos. 211-213 (3)	1.15	1.15
Nos. 249-251 (3)	2.30	1.35
Nos. 230-232 (3)	2.40	2.40
Nos. 171-173 (3)	2.00	1.50
Nos. 27-29 (3)	5.50	5.50
Nos. 123-125 (3)	1.45	1.45
Nos. 101-103 (3)	2.00	1.40
Nos. 155-157 (3)	1.05	.90
Nos. 176-178 (3)	1.40	1.30
Set total (84) Stamps	156.40	88.55

Silver Wedding, 1972

Queen Elizabeth II and Prince Philip — CD324

Designs: borders differ for each country.

1972

Anguilla 161-162
Antigua 295-296
Ascension 164-165
Bahamas 344-345
Bermuda 296-297
British Antarctic Territory 43-44
British Honduras 306-307
British Indian Ocean Territory 48-49

Brunei	186-187
Cayman Islands	304-305
Dominica	352-353
Falkland Islands	223-224
Fiji	328-329
Gibraltar	292-293
Gilbert & Ellice Islands	206-207
Grenada	466-467
Hong Kong	271-272
Montserrat	286-287
New Hebrides, British	169-170
New Hebrides, French	188-189
Pitcairn Islands	127-128
St. Helena	271-272
St. Kitts-Nevis	257-258
St. Lucia	328-329
St.Vincent	344-345
Seychelles	309-310
Solomon Islands	248-249
South Georgia	35-36
Tristan da Cunha	178-179
Turks & Caicos Islands	257-258
Virgin Islands	241-242

Nos. 161-162 (2)	1.10	*1.50*
Nos. 295-296 (2)	.50	.50
Nos. 164-165 (2)	.70	.70
Nos. 344-345 (2)	.60	.60
Nos. 296-297 (2)	.50	*.65*
Nos. 43-44 (2)	6.50	5.65
Nos. 306-307 (2)	.80	.80
Nos. 48-49 (2)	2.00	1.00
Nos. 186-187 (2)	.70	.70
Nos. 304-305 (2)	.75	.75
Nos. 352-353 (2)	.65	.65
Nos. 223-224 (2)	1.00	1.15
Nos. 328-329 (2)	.70	.70
Nos. 292-293 (2)	.50	.50
Nos. 206-207 (2)	.50	.50
Nos. 466-467 (2)	.70	.70
Nos. 271-272 (2)	1.70	1.50
Nos. 286-287 (2)	.50	.50
Nos. 169-170 (2)	.50	.50
Nos. 188-189 (2)	1.05	1.05
Nos. 127-128 (2)	.90	.85
Nos. 271-272 (2)	.70	1.20
Nos. 257-258 (2)	.65	.50
Nos. 328-329 (2)	.75	.75
Nos. 344-345 (2)	.55	.55
Nos. 309-310 (2)	.95	.95
Nos. 248-249 (2)	.50	.50
Nos. 35-36 (2)	1.40	1.40
Nos. 178-179 (2)	.70	.70
Nos. 257-258 (2)	.50	.50
Nos. 241-242 (2)	.50	.50
Set total (62) Stamps	30.05	29.00

Princess Anne's Wedding

Princess Anne and Mark Phillips — CD325

Wedding of Princess Anne and Mark Phillips, Nov. 14, 1973.

1973

Anguilla	179-180
Ascension	177-178
Belize	325-326
Bermuda	302-303
British Antarctic Territory	60-61
Cayman Islands	320-321
Falkland Islands	225-226
Gibraltar	305-306
Gilbert & Ellice Islands	216-217
Hong Kong	289-290
Montserrat	300-301
Pitcairn Islands	135-136
St. Helena	277-278
St. Kitts-Nevis	274-275
St. Lucia	349-350
St. Vincent	358-359
St. Vincent Grenadines	1-2
Seychelles	311-312
Solomon Islands	259-260
South Georgia	37-38
Tristan da Cunha	189-190
Turks & Caicos Islands	286-287
Virgin Islands	260-261

Nos. 179-180 (2)	.55	.55
Nos. 177-178 (2)	.60	.60
Nos. 325-326 (2)	.50	.50
Nos. 302-303 (2)	.50	.50
Nos. 60-61 (2)	1.10	1.10
Nos. 320-321 (2)	.50	.50
Nos. 225-226 (2)	.70	.60
Nos. 305-306 (2)	.55	.55
Nos. 216-217 (2)	.50	.50
Nos. 289-290 (2)	2.65	2.00
Nos. 300-301 (2)	.55	.55
Nos. 135-136 (2)	.70	.60
Nos. 277-278 (2)	.50	.50
Nos. 274-275 (2)	.50	.50
Nos. 349-350 (2)	.50	.50
Nos. 358-359 (2)	.50	.50
Nos. 1-2 (2)	.50	.50
Nos. 311-312 (2)	.70	.70
Nos. 259-260 (2)	.70	.70
Nos. 37-38 (2)	.75	.75
Nos. 189-190 (2)	.50	.50
Nos. 286-287 (2)	.50	.50
Nos. 260-261 (2)	.50	.50
Set total (46) Stamps	15.55	14.70

Elizabeth II Coronation Anniv.

CD326

CD327

CD328

Designs: Royal and local beasts in heraldic form and simulated stonework. Portrait of Elizabeth II by Peter Grugeon. 25th anniversary of coronation of Queen Elizabeth II.

1978

Ascension	229
Barbados	474
Belize	397
British Antarctic Territory	71
Cayman Islands	404
Christmas Island	87
Falkland Islands	275
Fiji	384
Gambia	380
Gilbert Islands	312
Mauritius	464
New Hebrides, British	258
New Hebrides, French	278
St. Helena	317
St. Kitts-Nevis	354
Samoa	472
Solomon Islands	368
South Georgia	51
Swaziland	302
Tristan da Cunha	238
Virgin Islands	337

No. 229 (1)	2.00	2.00
No. 474 (1)	1.35	1.35
No. 397 (1)	1.40	1.75
No. 71 (1)	6.00	6.00
No. 404 (1)	2.00	2.00
No. 87 (1)	3.50	*4.00*
No. 275 (1)	4.00	5.50
No. 384 (1)	1.75	1.75
No. 380 (1)	1.50	1.50
No. 312 (1)	1.25	1.25
No. 464 (1)	2.75	2.75
No. 258 (1)	1.75	1.75
No. 278 (1)	3.50	3.50
No. 317 (1)	1.75	1.75
No. 354 (1)	1.00	1.00
No. 472 (1)	2.00	2.00
No. 368 (1)	2.50	2.50
No. 51 (1)	3.00	3.00
No. 302 (1)	1.75	1.75
No. 238 (1)	1.50	1.50
No. 337 (1)	1.80	1.80
Set total (21) Stamps	48.05	50.40

Queen Mother Elizabeth's 80th Birthday

CD330

Designs: Photographs of Queen Mother Elizabeth. Falkland Islands issued in sheets of 50; others in sheets of 9.

1980

Ascension	261
Bermuda	401
Cayman Islands	443
Falkland Islands	305
Gambia	412
Gibraltar	393
Hong Kong	364
Pitcairn Islands	193
St. Helena	341
Samoa	532
Solomon Islands	426
Tristan da Cunha	277

No. 261 (1)	.40	.40
No. 401 (1)	.45	.75
No. 443 (1)	.40	.40
No. 305 (1)	.40	.40
No. 412 (1)	.40	.50
No. 393 (1)	.35	.35
No. 364 (1)	1.10	1.25
No. 193 (1)	.60	.60
No. 341 (1)	.50	.50
No. 532 (1)	.55	.55
No. 426 (1)	.50	.50
No. 277 (1)	.45	.45
Set total (12) Stamps	6.10	6.65

Royal Wedding, 1981

Prince Charles and Lady Diana — CD331

CD331a

Wedding of Charles, Prince of Wales, and Lady Diana Spencer, St. Paul's Cathedral, London, July 29, 1981.

1981

Antigua	623-627
Ascension	294-296
Barbados	547-549
Barbuda	497-501
Bermuda	412-414
Brunei	268-270
Cayman Islands	471-473
Dominica	701-705
Falkland Islands	324-326
Falkland Islands Dep.	1L59-1L61
Fiji	442-444
Gambia	426-428
Ghana	759-764
Grenada	1051-1055
Grenada Grenadines	440-443
Hong Kong	373-375
Jamaica	500-503
Lesotho	335-337
Maldive Islands	906-909
Mauritius	520-522
Norfolk Island	280-282
Pitcairn Islands	206-208
St. Helena	353-355
St. Lucia	543-549
Samoa	558-560
Sierra Leone	509-518
Solomon Islands	450-452
Swaziland	382-384
Tristan da Cunha	294-296
Turks & Caicos Islands	486-489
Caicos Island	8-11
Uganda	314-317
Vanuatu	308-310
Virgin Islands	406-408

Nos. 623-627 (5)	6.55	2.55
Nos. 294-296 (3)	1.00	1.00
Nos. 547-549 (3)	.90	.90
Nos. 497-501 (5)	10.95	10.95
Nos. 412-414 (3)	2.00	2.00
Nos. 268-270 (3)	2.15	*4.50*
Nos. 471-473 (3)	1.20	1.30
Nos. 701-705 (5)	8.35	2.35
Nos. 324-326 (3)	1.65	1.70
Nos. 1L59-1L61 (3)	1.45	1.45
Nos. 442-444 (3)	1.35	1.35
Nos. 426-428 (3)	.80	.80
Nos. 759-764 (9)	6.20	6.20
Nos. 1051-1055 (5)	9.85	1.85
Nos. 440-443 (4)	2.35	2.35
Nos. 373-375 (3)	3.05	2.85
Nos. 500-503 (4)	1.45	1.05
Nos. 335-337 (3)	.90	.90
Nos. 906-909 (4)	1.55	1.55
Nos. 520-522 (3)	2.75	2.75
Nos. 280-282 (3)	1.35	1.35
Nos. 206-208 (3)	1.10	1.10
Nos. 353-355 (3)	.85	.85
Nos. 543-549 (5)	8.50	8.50
Nos. 558-560 (3)	.85	.85
Nos. 509-518 (10)	15.50	15.50
Nos. 450-452 (3)	1.25	1.25
Nos. 382-384 (3)	1.30	1.25
Nos. 294-296 (3)	.90	.90
Nos. 486-489 (4)	2.20	2.20
Nos. 8-11 (4)	5.00	5.00
Nos. 314-317 (4)	3.30	3.00
Nos. 308-310 (3)	1.15	1.15
Nos. 406-408 (3)	1.10	1.10
Set total (131) Stamps	110.80	94.65

Princess Diana

CD332

CD333

Designs: Photographs and portrait of Princess Diana, wedding or honeymoon photographs, royal residences, arms of issuing country. Portrait photograph by Clive Friend. Souvenir sheet margins show family tree, various people related to the princess. 21st birthday of Princess Diana of Wales, July 1.

1982

Antigua	663-666
Ascension	313-316
Bahamas	510-513
Barbados	585-588
Barbuda	544-547
British Antarctic Territory	92-95
Cayman Islands	486-489
Dominica	773-776
Falkland Islands	348-351
Falkland Islands Dep.	1L72-1L75
Fiji	470-473
Gambia	447-450
Grenada	1101A-1105
Grenada Grenadines	485-491
Lesotho	372-375
Maldive Islands	952-955
Mauritius	548-551
Pitcairn Islands	213-216
St. Helena	372-375
St. Lucia	591-594
Sierra Leone	531-534
Solomon Islands	471-474
Swaziland	406-409
Tristan da Cunha	310-313
Turks and Caicos Islands	531-534
Virgin Islands	430-433

Nos. 663-666 (4)	8.25	7.35
Nos. 313-316 (4)	3.50	3.50
Nos. 510-513 (4)	6.00	3.85
Nos. 585-588 (4)	3.40	3.25
Nos. 544-547 (4)	9.75	7.70
Nos. 92-95 (4)	4.25	3.45
Nos. 486-489 (4)	*4.75*	*2.70*
Nos. 773-776 (4)	7.05	7.05
Nos. 348-351 (4)	2.95	2.95
Nos. 1L72-1L75 (4)	2.50	2.60
Nos. 470-473 (4)	3.25	2.95
Nos. 447-450 (4)	2.85	2.85
Nos. 1101A-1105 (7)	16.05	15.55

Nos. 485-491 (7)	17.65	17.65
Nos. 372-375 (4)	4.00	4.00
Nos. 952-955 (4)	5.50	3.90
Nos. 548-551 (4)	5.50	5.50
Nos. 213-216 (4)	2.15	2.15
Nos. 372-375 (4)	2.95	2.95
Nos. 591-594 (4)	9.90	9.90
Nos. 531-534 (4)	7.20	7.20
Nos. 471-474 (4)	2.90	2.90
Nos. 406-409 (4)	3.85	2.25
Nos. 310-313 (4)	3.65	1.45
Nos. 486-489 (4)	2.20	2.20
Nos. 430-433 (4)	3.00	3.00
Set total (110) Stamps	145.00	130.80

250th anniv. of first edition of Lloyd's List (shipping news publication) & of Lloyd's marine insurance.

CD335

Designs: First page of early edition of the list; historical ships, modern transportation or harbor scenes.

1984

Ascension	351-354
Bahamas	555-558
Barbados	627-630
Cayes of Belize	10-13
Cayman Islands	522-526
Falkland Islands	404-407
Fiji	509-512
Gambia	519-522
Mauritius	587-590
Nauru	280-283
St. Helena	412-415
Samoa	624-627
Seychelles	538-541
Solomon Islands	521-524
Vanuatu	368-371
Virgin Islands	466-469

Nos. 351-354 (4)	2.90	2.55
Nos. 555-558 (4)	4.15	2.95
Nos. 627-630 (4)	6.10	5.15
Nos. 10-13 (4)	2.65	2.65
Nos. 522-526 (5)	9.30	8.45
Nos. 404-407 (4)	3.50	3.65
Nos. 509-512 (4)	5.30	4.90
Nos. 519-522 (4)	4.20	4.30
Nos. 587-590 (4)	8.95	8.95
Nos. 280-283 (4)	2.40	2.35
Nos. 412-415 (4)	2.40	2.40
Nos. 624-627 (4)	2.75	2.55
Nos. 538-541 (4)	5.25	5.25
Nos. 521-524 (4)	4.65	3.95
Nos. 368-371 (4)	2.40	2.40
Nos. 466-469 (4)	4.25	4.25
Set total (65) Stamps	71.15	66.70

Queen Mother 85th Birthday

CD336

Designs: Photographs tracing the life of the Queen Mother, Elizabeth. The high value in each set pictures the same photograph taken of the Queen Mother holding the infant Prince Henry.

1985

Ascension	372-376
Bahamas	580-584
Barbados	660-664
Bermuda	469-473
Falkland Islands	420-424
Falkland Islands Dep.	1L92-1L96
Fiji	531-535
Hong Kong	447-450
Jamaica	599-603
Mauritius	604-608
Norfolk Island	364-368
Pitcairn Islands	253-257
St. Helena	428-432
Samoa	649-653
Seychelles	567-571
Zil Elwannyen Sesel	101-105
Solomon Islands	543-547
Swaziland	476-480
Tristan da Cunha	372-376
Vanuatu	392-396

Nos. 372-376 (5)	4.65	4.65
Nos. 580-584 (5)	7.70	6.45
Nos. 660-664 (5)	8.00	6.70
Nos. 469-473 (5)	9.40	9.40
Nos. 420-424 (5)	7.35	6.65
Nos. 1L92-1L96 (5)	8.00	8.00
Nos. 531-535 (5)	6.15	6.15
Nos. 447-450 (4)	9.50	8.50
Nos. 599-603 (5)	6.15	7.00
Nos. 604-608 (5)	11.80	11.80
Nos. 364-368 (5)	5.05	5.05
Nos. 253-257 (5)	5.25	5.95
Nos. 428-432 (5)	5.25	5.25
Nos. 649-653 (5)	8.65	7.80
Nos. 567-571 (5)	8.70	8.70
Nos. 101-105 (5)	7.15	7.15
Nos. 543-547 (5)	3.95	3.95
Nos. 476-480 (5)	8.00	7.50
Nos. 372-376 (5)	5.40	5.40
Nos. 392-396 (5)	5.25	5.25
Set total (99) Stamps	141.35	137.30

Queen Elizabeth II, 60th Birthday

CD337

1986, April 21

Ascension	389-393
Bahamas	592-596
Barbados	675-679
Bermuda	499-503
Cayman Islands	555-559
Falkland Islands	441-445
Fiji	544-548
Hong Kong	465-469
Jamaica	620-624
Kiribati	470-474
Mauritius	629-633
Papua New Guinea	640-644
Pitcairn Islands	270-274
St. Helena	451-455
Samoa	670-674
Seychelles	592-596
Zil Elwannyen Sesel	114-118
Solomon Islands	562-566
South Georgia	101-105
Swaziland	490-494
Tristan da Cunha	388-392
Vanuatu	414-418
Zambia	343-347

Nos. 389-393 (5)	2.80	3.30
Nos. 592-596 (5)	2.75	*3.70*
Nos. 675-679 (5)	3.25	3.10
Nos. 499-503 (5)	4.65	*5.15*
Nos. 555-559 (5)	4.55	5.60
Nos. 441-445 (5)	3.95	*4.95*
Nos. 544-548 (5)	3.00	3.00
Nos. 465-469 (5)	8.75	6.75
Nos. 620-624 (5)	2.75	2.70
Nos. 470-474 (5)	2.10	2.10
Nos. 629-633 (5)	3.70	3.70
Nos. 640-644 (5)	4.50	4.50
Nos. 270-274 (5)	2.70	2.70
Nos. 451-455 (5)	3.05	3.05
Nos. 670-674 (5)	2.90	2.90
Nos. 592-596 (5)	2.70	2.70
Nos. 114-118 (5)	2.25	2.25
Nos. 562-566 (5)	2.90	2.90
Nos. 101-105 (5)	3.30	3.65
Nos. 490-494 (5)	2.30	2.30
Nos. 388-392 (5)	3.00	3.00
Nos. 414-418 (5)	3.10	3.10
Nos. 343-347 (5)	1.75	1.75
Set total (115) Stamps	76.70	78.85

Royal Wedding

Marriage of Prince Andrew and Sarah Ferguson CD338

1986, July 23

Ascension	399-400
Bahamas	602-603
Barbados	687-688
Cayman Islands	560-561
Jamaica	629-630
Pitcairn Islands	275-276
St. Helena	460-461
St. Kitts	181-182
Seychelles	602-603
Zil Elwannyen Sesel	119-120
Solomon Islands	567-568
Tristan da Cunha	397-398
Zambia	348-349

Nos. 399-400 (2)	1.60	1.60
Nos. 602-603 (2)	2.75	2.75
Nos. 687-688 (2)	2.00	1.25
Nos. 560-561 (2)	1.70	*2.35*
Nos. 629-630 (2)	1.35	1.35
Nos. 275-276 (2)	2.40	2.40
Nos. 460-461 (2)	1.05	1.05
Nos. 181-182 (2)	1.50	2.25
Nos. 602-603 (2)	2.50	2.50
Nos. 119-120 (2)	2.30	2.30
Nos. 567-568 (2)	1.00	1.00
Nos. 397-398 (2)	1.40	1.40
Nos. 348-349 (2)	1.10	1.30
Set total (26) Stamps	22.65	23.50

Queen Elizabeth II, 60th Birthday

Queen Elizabeth II & Prince Philip, 1947 Wedding Portrait — CD339

Designs: Photographs tracing the life of Queen Elizabeth II.

1986

Anguilla	674-677
Antigua	925-928
Barbuda	783-786
Dominica	950-953
Gambia	611-614
Grenada	1371-1374
Grenada Grenadines	749-752
Lesotho	531-534
Maldive Islands	1172-1175
Sierra Leone	760-763
Uganda	495-498

Nos. 674-677 (4)	8.00	8.00
Nos. 925-928 (4)	5.50	6.20
Nos. 783-786 (4)	23.15	23.15
Nos. 950-953 (4)	7.25	7.25
Nos. 611-614 (4)	8.25	7.90
Nos. 1371-1374 (4)	6.80	6.80
Nos. 749-752 (4)	6.75	6.75
Nos. 531-534 (4)	5.25	5.25
Nos. 1172-1175 (4)	6.25	6.25
Nos. 760-763 (4)	6.30	6.30
Nos. 495-498 (4)	8.50	8.50
Set total (44) Stamps	92.00	92.35

Royal Wedding, 1986

CD340

Designs: Photographs of Prince Andrew and Sarah Ferguson during courtship, engagement and marriage.

1986

Antigua	939-942
Barbuda	809-812
Dominica	970-973
Gambia	635-638
Grenada	1385-1388
Grenada Grenadines	758-761
Lesotho	545-548
Maldive Islands	1181-1184
Sierra Leone	769-772
Uganda	510-513

Nos. 939-942 (4)	7.00	*8.75*
Nos. 809-812 (4)	14.55	14.55
Nos. 970-973 (4)	7.25	7.25
Nos. 635-638 (4)	8.55	8.55
Nos. 1385-1388 (4)	8.30	8.30
Nos. 758-761 (4)	9.00	9.00
Nos. 545-548 (4)	7.45	7.45
Nos. 1181-1184 (4)	8.45	8.45
Nos. 769-772 (4)	5.35	5.35
Nos. 510-513 (4)	9.25	10.00
Set total (40) Stamps	85.15	87.65

Lloyds of London, 300th Anniv.

CD341

Designs: 17th century aspects of Lloyds, representations of each country's individual connections with Lloyds and publicized disasters insured by the organization.

1986

Ascension	454-457
Bahamas	655-658
Barbados	731-734
Bermuda	541-544
Falkland Islands	481-484
Liberia	1101-1104
Malawi	534-537
Nevis	571-574
St. Helena	501-504
St. Lucia	923-926
Seychelles	649-652
Zil Elwannyen Sesel	146-149
Solomon Islands	627-630
South Georgia	131-134
Trinidad & Tobago	484-487
Tristan da Cunha	439-442
Vanuatu	485-488

Nos. 454-457 (4)	5.00	5.00
Nos. 655-658 (4)	8.90	4.95
Nos. 731-734 (4)	12.50	8.35
Nos. 541-544 (4)	8.00	*6.60*
Nos. 481-484 (4)	5.45	3.85
Nos. 1101-1104 (4)	4.25	4.25
Nos. 534-537 (4)	11.00	7.85
Nos. 571-574 (4)	8.35	8.35
Nos. 501-504 (4)	8.70	7.15
Nos. 923-926 (4)	9.40	9.40
Nos. 649-652 (4)	13.10	13.10
Nos. 146-149 (4)	11.25	11.25
Nos. 627-630 (4)	7.00	4.45
Nos. 131-134 (4)	6.30	3.70
Nos. 484-487 (4)	10.25	6.35
Nos. 439-442 (4)	7.60	7.60
Nos. 485-488 (4)	5.90	5.90
Set total (68) Stamps	142.95	118.10

Moon Landing, 20th Anniv.

CD342

Designs: Equipment, crew photographs, spacecraft, official emblems and report profiles created for the Apollo Missions. Two stamps in each set are square in format rather than like the stamp shown; see individual country listings for more information.

1989

Ascension	468-472
Bahamas	674-678
Belize	916-920
Kiribati	517-521
Liberia	1125-1129
Nevis	586-590
St. Kitts	248-252
Samoa	760-764
Seychelles	676-680
Zil Elwannyen Sesel	154-158
Solomon Islands	643-647
Vanuatu	507-511

Nos. 468-472 (5)	9.40	8.60
Nos. 674-678 (5)	23.00	19.70
Nos. 916-920 (5)	22.85	18.10
Nos. 517-521 (5)	12.50	12.50
Nos. 1125-1129 (5)	8.50	8.50
Nos. 586-590 (5)	7.50	7.50

Nos. 248-252 (5)	8.00	8.25
Nos. 760-764 (5)	9.60	9.05
Nos. 676-680 (5)	16.05	16.05
Nos. 154-158 (5)	26.85	26.85
Nos. 643-647 (5)	9.00	6.75
Nos. 507-511 (5)	9.90	9.90
Set total (60) Stamps	163.15	151.75

Queen Mother, 90th Birthday

CD343

CD344

Designs: Portraits of Queen Elizabeth, the Queen Mother. See individual country listings for more information.

1990

Ascension 491-492
Bahamas 698-699
Barbados 782-783
British Antarctic Territory 170-171
British Indian Ocean Territory 106-107
Cayman Islands 622-623
Falkland Islands 524-525
Kenya 527-528
Kiribati 555-556
Liberia 1145-1146
Pitcairn Islands 336-337
St. Helena 532-533
St. Lucia 969-970
Seychelles 710-711
Zil Elwannyen Sesel 171-172
Solomon Islands 671-672
South Georgia 143-144
Swaziland 565-566
Tristan da Cunha 480-481

Nos. 491-492 (2)	4.75	4.75
Nos. 698-699 (2)	5.25	5.25
Nos. 782-783 (2)	4.00	3.70
Nos. 170-171 (2)	6.00	6.00
Nos. 106-107 (2)	18.00	18.50
Nos. 622-623 (2)	4.00	*5.50*
Nos. 524-525 (2)	4.75	4.75
Nos. 527-528 (2)	7.00	7.00
Nos. 555-556 (2)	4.75	4.75
Nos. 1145-1146 (2)	3.25	3.25
Nos. 336-337 (2)	4.25	4.25
Nos. 532-533 (2)	5.25	5.25
Nos. 969-970 (2)	5.25	5.25
Nos. 710-711 (2)	6.60	6.60
Nos. 171-172 (2)	8.25	8.25
Nos. 671-672 (2)	5.00	*5.30*
Nos. 143-144 (2)	5.50	6.50
Nos. 565-566 (2)	4.35	4.35
Nos. 480-481 (2)	5.60	5.60
Set total (38) Stamps	111.80	114.80

Queen Elizabeth II, 65th Birthday, and Prince Philip, 70th Birthday

CD345

CD346

Designs: Portraits of Queen Elizabeth II and Prince Philip differ for each country. Printed in sheets of 10 + 5 labels (3 different) between. Stamps alternate, producing 5 different triptychs.

1991

Ascension 506a
Bahamas 731a
Belize 970a
Bermuda 618a
Kiribati 572a
Mauritius 734a
Pitcairn Islands 349a
St. Helena 555a
St. Kitts 319a
Samoa 791a
Seychelles 724a
Zil Elwannyen Sesel 178a
Solomon Islands 689a
South Georgia 150a
Swaziland 587a
Vanuatu 541a

No. 506a (1)	3.50	3.75
No. 731a (1)	4.00	4.00
No. 970a (1)	3.75	3.75
No. 618a (1)	3.50	*4.00*
No. 572a (1)	4.00	4.00
No. 734a (1)	3.75	3.75
No. 349a (1)	3.25	3.25
No. 555a (1)	2.75	2.75
No. 319a (1)	3.00	3.00
No. 791a (1)	4.25	4.25
No. 724a (1)	5.00	5.00
No. 178a (1)	6.50	6.50
No. 689a (1)	3.75	3.75
No. 150a (1)	4.75	7.00
No. 587a (1)	4.25	4.25
No. 541a (1)	2.50	2.50
Set total (16) Stamps	62.50	65.50

Royal Family Birthday, Anniversary

CD347

Queen Elizabeth II, 65th birthday, Charles and Diana, 10th wedding anniversary: Various photographs of Queen Elizabeth II, Prince Philip, Prince Charles, Princess Diana and their sons William and Henry.

1991

Antigua 1446-1455
Barbuda 1229-1238
Dominica 1328-1337
Gambia 1080-1089
Grenada 2006-2015
Grenada Grenadines 1331-1340
Guyana 2440-2451
Lesotho 871-875
Maldive Islands 1533-1542
Nevis 666-675
St. Vincent 1485-1494
St. Vincent Grenadines 769-778
Sierra Leone 1387-1396
Turks & Caicos Islands 913-922
Uganda 918-927

Nos. 1446-1455 (10)	21.70	20.05
Nos. 1229-1238 (10)	125.00	119.50
Nos. 1328-1337 (10)	30.20	30.20
Nos. 1080-1089 (10)	24.65	24.40
Nos. 2006-2015 (10)	25.45	22.10
Nos. 1331-1340 (10)	23.85	23.35
Nos. 2440-2451 (12)	21.40	21.15
Nos. 871-875 (5)	13.55	13.55
Nos. 1533-1542 (10)	28.10	28.10
Nos. 666-675 (10)	25.65	25.65
Nos. 1485-1494 (10)	26.75	25.90
Nos. 769-778 (10)	25.40	25.40
Nos. 1387-1396 (10)	26.55	26.55
Nos. 913-922 (10)	27.50	25.30
Nos. 918-927 (10)	26.60	26.60
Set total (147) Stamps	472.35	457.80

Queen Elizabeth II's Accession to the Throne, 40th Anniv.

CD348

Various photographs of Queen Elizabeth II with local Scenes.

1992

Antigua 1513-1518
Barbuda 1306-1311
Dominica 1414-1419
Gambia 1172-1177
Grenada 2047-2052
Grenada Grenadines 1368-1373
Lesotho 881-885
Maldive Islands 1637-1642
Nevis 702-707
St. Vincent 1582-1587
St. Vincent Grenadines 829-834
Sierra Leone 1482-1487
Turks and Caicos Islands 978-987
Uganda 990-995
Virgin Islands 742-746

Nos. 1513-1518 (6)	15.00	*15.10*
Nos. 1306-1311 (6)	125.25	83.65
Nos. 1414-1419 (6)	12.50	12.50
Nos. 1172-1177 (6)	16.60	16.35
Nos. 2047-2052 (6)	15.95	15.95
Nos. 1368-1373 (6)	17.00	15.35
Nos. 881-885 (5)	11.90	11.90
Nos. 1637-1642 (6)	17.55	17.55
Nos. 702-707 (6)	13.80	13.80
Nos. 1582-1587 (6)	14.40	14.40
Nos. 829-834 (6)	19.65	19.65
Nos. 1482-1487 (6)	22.50	22.50
Nos. 913-922 (10)	27.50	25.30
Nos. 990-995 (6)	19.50	19.50
Nos. 742-746 (5)	15.50	15.50
Set total (92) Stamps	364.60	319.00

CD349

1992

Ascension 531-535
Bahamas 744-748
Bermuda 623-627
British Indian Ocean Territory 119-123
Cayman Islands 648-652
Falkland Islands 549-553
Gibraltar 605-609
Hong Kong 619-623
Kenya 563-567
Kiribati 582-586
Pitcairn Islands 362-366
St. Helena 570-574
St. Kitts 332-336
Samoa 805-809
Seychelles 734-738
Zil Elwannyen Sesel 183-187
Solomon Islands 708-712
South Georgia 157-161
Tristan da Cunha 508-512
Vanuatu 555-559
Zambia 561-565

Nos. 531-535 (5)	6.10	6.10
Nos. 744-748 (5)	6.90	4.70
Nos. 623-627 (5)	7.40	*7.55*
Nos. 119-123 (5)	22.75	19.25
Nos. 648-652 (5)	7.60	6.60
Nos. 549-553 (5)	5.95	5.90
Nos. 605-609 (5)	5.15	*5.50*
Nos. 619-623 (5)	5.10	5.25
Nos. 563-567 (5)	9.10	9.10
Nos. 582-586 (5)	3.85	3.85
Nos. 362-366 (5)	5.35	5.35
Nos. 570-574 (5)	5.70	5.70
Nos. 332-336 (5)	6.60	5.50
Nos. 805-809 (5)	8.10	6.15
Nos. 734-738 (5)	10.80	10.80
Nos. 183-187 (5)	9.40	9.40
Nos. 708-712 (5)	5.00	5.30
Nos. 157-161 (5)	5.60	5.90
Nos. 508-512 (5)	8.75	8.30
Nos. 555-559 (5)	3.65	3.65
Nos. 561-565 (5)	5.60	5.60
Set total (105) Stamps	154.45	145.45

Royal Air Force, 75th Anniversary

CD350

1993

Ascension 557-561
Bahamas 771-775
Barbados 842-846
Belize 1003-1008
Bermuda 648-651
British Indian Ocean Territory 136-140
Falkland Is. 573-577
Fiji 687-691
Montserrat 830-834
St. Kitts 351-355

Nos. 557-561 (5)	15.60	14.60
Nos. 771-775 (5)	24.65	21.45
Nos. 842-846 (5)	14.15	12.85
Nos. 1003-1008 (6)	16.55	16.50
Nos. 648-651 (4)	9.65	*10.45*
Nos. 136-140 (5)	16.10	16.10
Nos. 573-577 (5)	10.85	10.85
Nos. 687-691 (5)	17.75	17.40
Nos. 830-834 (5)	14.10	14.10
Nos. 351-355 (5)	22.80	23.55
Set total (50) Stamps	162.20	157.85

Royal Air Force, 80th Anniv.

Design CD350 Re-inscribed

1998

Ascension 697-701
Bahamas 907-911
British Indian Ocean Terr 198-202
Cayman Islands 754-758
Fiji 814-818
Gibraltar 755-759
Samoa 957-961
Turks & Caicos Islands 1258-1265
Tuvalu 763-767
Virgin Islands 879-883

Nos. 697-701 (5)	16.10	16.10
Nos. 907-911 (5)	13.60	12.65
Nos. 136-140 (5)	16.10	16.10
Nos. 754-758 (5)	15.25	15.25
Nos. 814-818 (5)	14.00	12.75
Nos. 755-759 (5)	9.70	9.70
Nos. 957-961 (5)	16.70	15.90
Nos. 1258-1265 (2)	27.50	27.50
Nos. 763-767 (5)	9.75	9.75
Nos. 879-883 (5)	15.00	15.00
Set total (47) Stamps	153.70	150.70

End of World War II, 50th Anniv.

CD351

CD352

1995

Ascension 613-617
Bahamas 824-828
Barbados 891-895
Belize 1047-1050
British Indian Ocean Territory 163-167
Cayman Islands 704-708
Falkland Islands 634-638
Fiji 720-724
Kiribati 662-668
Liberia 1175-1179
Mauritius 803-805
St. Helena 646-654
St. Kitts 389-393
St. Lucia 1018-1022
Samoa 890-894
Solomon Islands 799-803
South Georgia 198-200
Tristan da Cunha 562-566

Nos. 613-617 (5)	21.50	21.50

Nos. 824-828 (5) 22.00 18.70
Nos. 891-895 (5) 14.20 11.90
Nos. 1047-1050 (4) 6.05 5.90
Nos. 163-167 (5) 16.25 16.25
Nos. 704-708 (5) 17.65 13.95
Nos. 634-638 (5) 18.65 17.15
Nos. 720-724 (5) 17.50 14.50
Nos. 662-668 (7) 16.30 16.30
Nos. 1175-1179 (5) 15.25 11.15
Nos. 803-805 (3) 7.50 7.50
Nos. 646-654 (9) 26.10 26.10
Nos. 389-393 (5) 16.40 16.40
Nos. 1018-1022 (5) 14.25 11.15
Nos. 890-894 (5) 14.25 13.50
Nos. 799-803 (5) 14.75 14.75
Nos. 198-200 (3) 14.50 15.50
Nos. 562-566 (5) 20.10 20.10
Set total (91) Stamps 293.20 272.30

UN, 50th Anniv.

CD353

1995

Bahamas 839-842
Barbados 901-904
Belize 1055-1058
Jamaica 847-851
Liberia 1187-1190
Mauritius 813-816
Pitcairn Islands 436-439
St. Kitts 398-401
St. Lucia 1023-1026
Samoa 900-903
Tristan da Cunha 568-571
Virgin Islands 807-810

Nos. 839-842 (4) 7.15 6.40
Nos. 901-904 (4) 7.00 5.75
Nos. 1055-1058 (4) 4.70 4.70
Nos. 847-851 (5) 5.40 5.45
Nos. 1187-1190 (4) 9.65 9.65
Nos. 813-816 (4) 3.90 3.90
Nos. 436-439 (4) 8.15 8.15
Nos. 398-401 (4) 6.15 7.15
Nos. 1023-1026 (4) 7.50 7.25
Nos. 900-903 (4) 9.35 8.20
Nos. 568-571 (4) 13.50 13.50
Nos. 807-810 (4) 7.45 7.45
Set total (49) Stamps 89.90 87.55

Queen Elizabeth, 70th Birthday

CD354

1996

Ascension 632-635
British Antarctic Territory 240-243
British Indian Ocean Territory 176-180
Falkland Islands 653-657
Pitcairn Islands 446-449
St. Helena 672-676
Samoa 912-916
Tokelau 223-227
Tristan da Cunha 576-579
Virgin Islands 824-828

Nos. 632-635 (4) 5.30 5.30
Nos. 240-243 (4) 9.45 8.15
Nos. 176-180 (5) 11.50 11.50
Nos. 653-657 (5) 13.55 11.20
Nos. 446-449 (4) 8.60 8.60
Nos. 672-676 (5) 12.70 12.70
Nos. 912-916 (5) 11.50 11.50
Nos. 223-227 (5) 10.50 10.50
Nos. 576-579 (4) 8.35 8.35
Nos. 824-828 (5) 11.30 11.30
Set total (46) Stamps 102.75 99.10

Diana, Princess of Wales (1961-97)

CD355

1998

Ascension 696
Bahamas 901A-902
Barbados 950
Belize 1091
Bermuda 753
Botswana 659-663
British Antarctic Territory 258
British Indian Ocean Terr. 197
Cayman Islands 752A-753
Falkland Islands 694
Fiji 819-820
Gibraltar 754
Kiribati 719A-720
Namibia 909
Niue 706
Norfolk Island 644-645
Papua New Guinea 937
Pitcairn Islands 487
St. Helena 711
St. Kitts 437A-438
Samoa 955A-956
Seycelles 802
Solomon Islands 866-867
South Georgia 220
Tokelau 252B-253
Tonga 980
  Niuafo'ou 201
Tristan da Cunha 618
Tuvalu 762
Vanuatu 718A-719
Virgin Islands 878

No. 696 (1) 5.25 5.25
Nos. 901A-902 (2) 5.30 5.30
No. 950 (1) 6.25 6.25
No. 1091 (1) 5.00 5.00
No. 753 (1) 5.00 5.00
Nos. 659-663 (5) 8.25 8.80
No. 258 (1) 5.50 5.50
No. 197 (1) 5.50 5.50
Nos. 752A-753 (3) 7.40 7.40
No. 694 (1) 5.00 5.00
Nos. 819-820 (2) 5.25 5.25
No. 754 (1) 4.75 4.75
Nos. 719A-720 (2) 4.85 4.85
No. 909 (1) 1.75 1.75
No. 706 (1) 5.50 5.50
Nos. 644-645 (2) 5.25 5.25
No. 937 (1) 6.50 6.50
No. 487 (1) 4.75 4.75
No. 711 (1) 4.25 4.25
Nos. 437A-438 (2) 5.15 5.15
Nos. 955A-956 (2) 7.00 7.00
No. 802 (1) 6.25 6.25
Nos. 866-867 (2) 5.40 5.40
No. 220 (1) 4.50 5.00
Nos. 252B-253 (2) 6.00 6.00
No. 980 (1) 5.75 5.75
No. 201 (1) 6.50 6.50
No. 618 (1) 5.00 5.00
No. 762 (1) 4.00 4.00
Nos. 718A-719 (2) 8.00 8.00
No. 878 (1) 4.50 4.50
Set total (46) Stamps 169.35 170.40

Wedding of Prince Edward and Sophie Rhys-Jones

CD356

1999

Ascension 729-730
Cayman Islands 775-776
Falkland Islands 729-730
Pitcairn Islands 505-506
St. Helena 733-734
Samoa 971-972
Tristan da Cunha 636-637
Virgin Islands 908-909

Nos. 729-730 (2) 4.50 4.50
Nos. 775-776 (2) 4.95 4.95
Nos. 729-730 (2) 14.00 14.00
Nos. 505-506 (2) 7.00 7.00
Nos. 733-734 (2) 5.00 5.00
Nos. 971-972 (2) 5.00 5.00
Nos. 636-637 (2) 7.50 7.50
Nos. 908-909 (2) 7.50 7.50
Set total (16) Stamps 55.45 55.45

1st Manned Moon Landing, 30th Anniv.

CD357

1999

Ascension 731-735
Bahamas 942-946
Barbados 967-971
Bermuda 778
Cayman Islands 777-781
Fiji 853-857
Jamaica 889-893
Kirbati 746-750
Nauru 465-469
St. Kitts 460-464
Samoa 973-977
Solomon Islands 875-879
Tuvalu 800-804
Virgin Islands 910-914

Nos. 731-735 (5) 12.80 12.80
Nos. 942-946 (5) 14.10 14.10
Nos. 967-971 (5) 9.45 8.25
No. 778 (1) 9.00 9.00
Nos. 777-781 (5) 9.25 9.25
Nos. 853-857 (5) 9.25 8.45
Nos. 889-893 (5) 8.30 7.18
Nos. 746-750 (5) 8.85 8.85
Nos. 465-469 (5) 9.25 8.00
Nos. 460-464 (5) 11.35 11.65
Nos. 973-977 (5) 13.45 13.30
Nos. 875-879 (5) 7.50 7.50
Nos. 800-804 (5) 7.45 7.45
Nos. 910-914 (5) 11.75 11.75
Set total (66) Stamps 141.75 137.53

Queen Mother's Century

CD358

1999

Ascension 736-740
Bahamas 951-955
Cayman Islands 782-786
Falkland Islands 734-738
Fiji 858-862
Norfolk Island 688-692
St. Helena 740-744
Samoa 978-982
Solomon Islands 880-884
South Georgia 231-235
Tristan da Cunha 638-642
Tuvalu 805-809

Nos. 736-740 (5) 15.50 15.50
Nos. 951-955 (5) 13.75 12.65
Nos. 782-786 (5) 8.35 8.35
Nos. 734-738 (5) 30.00 28.25
Nos. 858-862 (5) 12.80 13.25
Nos. 688-692 (5) 10.30 10.30
Nos. 740-744 (5) 16.15 16.15
Nos. 978-982 (5) 12.50 12.10
Nos. 880-884 (5) 7.50 7.00
Nos. 231-235 (5) 29.75 30.00
Nos. 638-642 (5) 18.00 18.00
Nos. 805-809 (5) 8.65 8.65
Set total (60) Stamps 183.25 180.20

Prince William, 18th Birthday

CD359

2000

Ascension 755-759
Cayman Islands 797-801
Falkland Islands 762-766
Fiji 889-893
South Georgia 257-261
Tristan da Cunha 664-668
Virgin Islands 925-929

Nos. 755-759 (5) 15.50 15.50
Nos. 797-801 (5) 11.15 10.90
Nos. 762-766 (5) 24.60 22.50
Nos. 889-893 (5) 12.90 12.90
Nos. 257-261 (5) 29.00 28.75
Nos. 664-668 (5) 21.50 21.50
Nos. 925-929 (5) 14.50 14.50
Set total (35) Stamps 129.15 126.55

Reign of Queen Elizabeth II, 50th Anniv.

CD360

2002

Ascension 790-794
Bahamas 1033-1037
Barbados 1019-1023
Belize 1152-1156
Bermuda 822-826
British Antarctic Territory 307-311
British Indian Ocean Territory 239-243
Cayman Islands 844-848
Falkland Islands 804-808
Gibraltar 896-900
Jamaica 952-956
Nauru 491-495
Norfolk Island 758-762
Papua New Guinea 1019-1023
Pitcairn Islands 552
St. Helena 788-792
St. Lucia 1146-1150
Solomon Islands 931-935
South Georgia 274-278
Swaziland 706-710
Tokelau 302-306
Tonga 1059
  Niuafo'ou 239
Tristan da Cunha 706-710
Virgin Islands 967-971

Nos. 790-794 (5) 14.10 14.10
Nos. 1033-1037 (5) 15.25 15.25
Nos. 1019-1023 (5) 12.90 12.90
Nos. 1152-1156 (5) 12.65 12.25
Nos. 822-826 (5) 18.00 18.00
Nos. 307-311 (5) 23.00 23.00
Nos. 239-243 (5) 19.40 19.40
Nos. 844-848 (5) 13.25 13.25
Nos. 804-808 (5) 23.00 22.00
Nos. 896-900 (5) 6.65 6.65
Nos. 952-956 (5) 16.65 16.65
Nos. 491-495 (5) 17.75 17.75
Nos. 758-762 (5) 19.50 19.50
Nos. 1019-1023 (5) 14.50 14.50
No. 552 (1) 9.25 9.25
Nos. 788-792 (5) 19.75 19.75
Nos. 1146-1150 (5) 12.25 12.25
Nos. 931-935 (5) 12.40 12.40
Nos. 274-278 (5) 28.00 28.50
Nos. 706-710 (5) 12.75 12.75
Nos. 302-306 (5) 14.50 14.50
No. 1059 (1) 8.50 8.50
No. 239 (1) 8.75 8.75
Nos. 706-710 (5) 18.50 18.50
Nos. 967-971 (5) 16.50 16.50
Set total (113) Stamps 387.75 386.85

Queen Mother Elizabeth (1900-2002)

CD361

2002

Ascension 799-801
Bahamas 1044-1046
Bermuda 834-836
British Antarctic Territory 312-314
British Indian Ocean Territory 245-247
Cayman Islands 857-861
Falkland Islands 812-816
Nauru 499-501
Pitcairn Islands 561-565
St. Helena 808-812
St. Lucia 1155-1159
Seychelles 830
Solomon Islands 945-947
South Georgia 281-285
Tokelau 312-314
Tristan da Cunha 715-717
Virgin Islands 979-983

Nos. 799-801 (3)	8.85	8.85
Nos. 1044-1046 (3)	9.10	9.10
Nos. 834-836 (3)	12.25	12.25
Nos. 312-314 (3)	18.75	18.75
Nos. 245-247 (3)	17.35	17.35
Nos. 857-861 (5)	15.00	15.00
Nos. 812-816 (5)	28.50	28.50
Nos. 499-501 (3)	14.00	14.00
Nos. 561-565 (5)	15.25	15.25
Nos. 808-812 (5)	12.00	12.00
Nos. 1155-1159 (5)	13.00	13.00
No. 830 (1)	6.50	6.50
Nos. 945-947 (3)	9.25	9.25
Nos. 281-285 (5)	19.50	19.50
Nos. 312-314 (3)	11.85	11.85
Nos. 715-717 (3)	16.25	16.25
Nos. 979-983 (5)	23.50	23.50
Set total (63) Stamps	250.90	250.90

Head of Queen Elizabeth II

CD362

2003

Ascension 822
Bermuda 865
British Antarctic Territory 322
British Indian Ocean Territory 261
Cayman Islands 878
Falkland Islands 828
St. Helena 820
South Georgia 294
Tristan da Cunha 731
Virgin Islands 1003

No. 822 (1)	12.50	12.50
No. 865 (1)	50.00	50.00
No. 322 (1)	9.50	9.50
No. 261 (1)	11.00	11.00
No. 878 (1)	14.00	14.00
No. 820 (1)	9.00	9.00
No. 820 (1)	9.00	9.00
No. 294 (1)	8.50	8.50
No. 731 (1)	10.00	10.00
No. 1003 (1)	10.00	10.00
Set total (10) Stamps	143.50	143.50

Coronation of Queen Elizabeth II, 50th Anniv.

CD363

2003

Ascension 823-825
Bahamas 1073-1075
Bermuda 866-868
British Antarctic Territory 323-325
British Indian Ocean Territory 262-264
Cayman Islands 879-881
Jamaica 970-972
Kiribati 825-827
Pitcairn Islands 577-581
St. Helena 821-823
St. Lucia 1171-1173
Tokelau 320-322
Tristan da Cunha 732-734
Virgin Islands 1004-1006

Nos. 823-825 (3)	12.50	12.50
Nos. 1073-1075 (3)	13.00	13.00
Nos. 866-868 (2)	14.25	14.25
Nos. 323-325 (3)	23.00	23.00
Nos. 262-264 (3)	28.00	28.00
Nos. 879-881 (3)	19.25	19.25
Nos. 970-972 (3)	10.00	10.00
Nos. 825-827 (3)	13.50	13.50
Nos. 577-581 (5)	14.40	14.40
Nos. 821-823 (3)	7.25	7.25
Nos. 1171-1173 (3)	8.75	8.75
Nos. 320-322 (3)	17.25	17.25
Nos. 732-734 (3)	16.75	16.75
Nos. 1004-1006 (3)	25.00	25.00
Set total (43) Stamps	222.90	222.90

Prince William, 21st Birthday

CD364

2003

Ascension 826
British Indian Ocean Territory 265
Cayman Islands 882-884
Falkland Islands 829
South Georgia 295
Tokelau 323
Tristan da Cunha 735
Virgin Islands 1007-1009

No. 826 (1)	7.25	7.25
No. 265 (1)	8.00	8.00
Nos. 882-884 (3)	6.95	6.95
No. 829 (1)	13.50	13.50
No. 295 (1)	8.50	8.50
No. 323 (1)	7.25	7.25
No. 735 (1)	6.00	6.00
Nos. 1007-1009 (3)	10.00	10.00
Set total (12) Stamps	67.45	67.45

British Commonwealth of Nations

Dominions, Colonies, Territories, Offices and Independent Members

Comprising stamps of the British Commonwealth and associated nations.

A strict observance of technicalities would bar some or all of the stamps listed under Burma, Ireland, Kuwait, Nepal, New Republic, Orange Free State, Samoa, South Africa, South-West Africa, Stellaland, Sudan, Swaziland, the two Transvaal Republics and others but these are included for the convenience of collectors.

1. Great Britain

Great Britain: Including England, Scotland, Wales and Northern Ireland.

2. The Dominions, Present and Past

AUSTRALIA

The Commonwealth of Australia was proclaimed on January 1, 1901. It consists of six former colonies as follows:

New South Wales
Queensland
South Australia
Victoria
Tasmania
Western Australia

The following islands and territories are, or have been, administered by Australia: Australian Antarctic Territory, Christmas Island, Cocos (Keeling) Islands, Nauru, New Guinea, Norfolk Island, Papua.

CANADA

The Dominion of Canada was created by the British North America Act in 1867. The following provinces were former sepa- rate colonies and issued postage stamps:

British Columbia and Vancouver Island
New Brunswick
Newfoundland
Nova Scotia
Prince Edward Island

FIJI

The colony of Fiji became an independent nation with dominion status on Oct. 10, 1970.

GHANA

This state came into existence Mar. 6, 1957, with dominion status. It consists of the former colony of the Gold Coast and the Trusteeship Territory of Togoland. Ghana became a republic July 1, 1960.

INDIA

The Republic of India was inaugurated on January 26, 1950. It succeeded the Dominion of India which was proclaimed August 15, 1947, when the former Empire of India was divided into Pakistan and the Union of India. The Republic is composed of about 40 predominantly Hindu states of three classes: governor's provinces, chief commissioner's provinces and princely states. India also has various territories, such as the Andaman and Nicobar Islands.

The old Empire of India was a federation of British India and the native states. The more important princely states were autonomous. Of the more than 700 Indian states, these 43 are familiar names to philatelists because of their postage stamps.

CONVENTION STATES

Chamba
Faridkot
Gwalior
Jhind
Nabha
Patiala

FEUDATORY STATES

Alwar
Bahawalpur
Bamra
Barwani
Bhopal
Bhor
Bijawar
Bundi
Bussahir
Charkhari
Cochin
Dhar
Dungarpur
Duttia
Faridkot (1879-85)
Hyderabad
Idar
Indore
Jaipur
Jammu
Jammu and Kashmir
Jasdan
Jhalawar
Jhind (1875-76)
Kashmir
Kishangarh
Kotah
Las Bela
Morvi
Nandgaon
Nowanuggur
Orchha
Poonch
Rajasthan
Rajpeepla
Sirmur
Soruth
Tonk
Travancore
Wadhwan

NEW ZEALAND

Became a dominion on September 26, 1907. The following islands and territories are, or have been, administered by New Zealand:

Aitutaki
Cook Islands (Rarotonga)
Niue
Penrhyn
Ross Dependency
Samoa (Western Samoa)
Tokelau Islands

PAKISTAN

The Republic of Pakistan was proclaimed March 23, 1956. It succeeded the Dominion which was proclaimed August 15, 1947. It is made up of all or part of several Moslem provinces and various districts of the former Empire of India, including Bahawalpur and Las Bela. Pakistan withdrew from the Commonwealth in 1972.

SOUTH AFRICA

Under the terms of the South African Act (1909) the self-governing colonies of Cape of Good Hope, Natal, Orange River Colony and Transvaal united on May 31, 1910, to form the Union of South Africa. It became an independent republic May 3, 1961.

Under the terms of the Treaty of Versailles, South-West Africa, formerly German South-West Africa, was mandated to the Union of South Africa.

SRI LANKA (CEYLON)

The Dominion of Ceylon was proclaimed February 4, 1948. The island had been a Crown Colony from 1802 until then. On May 22, 1972, Ceylon became the Republic of Sri Lanka.

3. Colonies, Past and Present; Controlled Territory and Independent Members of the Commonwealth

Aden
Aitutaki
Anguilla
Antigua
Ascension
Bahamas
Bahrain
Bangladesh
Barbados
Barbuda
Basutoland
Batum
Bechuanaland
Bechuanaland Prot.
Belize
Bermuda
Botswana
British Antarctic Territory
British Central Africa
British Columbia and Vancouver Island
British East Africa
British Guiana

British Honduras
British Indian Ocean Territory
British New Guinea
British Solomon Islands
British Somaliland
Brunei
Burma
Bushire
Cameroons
Cape of Good Hope
Cayman Islands
Christmas Island
Cocos (Keeling) Islands
Cook Islands
Crete,
 British Administration
Cyprus
Dominica
East Africa & Uganda
 Protectorates
Egypt
Falkland Islands
Fiji
Gambia
German East Africa
Gibraltar
Gilbert Islands
Gilbert & Ellice Islands
Gold Coast
Grenada
Griqualand West
Guernsey
Guyana
Heligoland
Hong Kong
Indian Native States
 (see India)
Ionian Islands
Jamaica
Jersey
Kenya
Kenya, Uganda & Tanzania
Kuwait
Labuan
Lagos
Leeward Islands
Lesotho
Madagascar
Malawi
Malaya
 Federated Malay States
 Johore
 Kedah
 Kelantan
 Malacca
 Negri Sembilan
 Pahang
 Penang
 Perak
 Perlis
 Selangor
 Singapore
 Sungei Ujong
 Trengganu
Malaysia
Maldive Islands
Malta
Man, Isle of
Mauritius
Mesopotamia
Montserrat
Muscat
Namibia
Natal
Nauru
Nevis
New Britain
New Brunswick
Newfoundland
New Guinea
New Hebrides
New Republic
New South Wales
Niger Coast Protectorate
Nigeria
Niue
Norfolk Island
North Borneo
Northern Nigeria
Northern Rhodesia
North West Pacific Islands
Nova Scotia
Nyasaland Protectorate
Oman
Orange River Colony
Palestine
Papua New Guinea
Penrhyn Island
Pitcairn Islands
Prince Edward Island
Queensland
Rhodesia
Rhodesia & Nyasaland
Ross Dependency
Sabah
St. Christopher
St. Helena
St. Kitts
St. Kitts-Nevis-Anguilla
St. Lucia
St. Vincent
Samoa
Sarawak
Seychelles
Sierra Leone
Solomon Islands
Somaliland Protectorate
South Arabia
South Australia
South Georgia
Southern Nigeria
Southern Rhodesia
South-West Africa
Stellaland
Straits Settlements
Sudan
Swaziland
Tanganyika
Tanzania
Tasmania
Tobago
Togo
Tokelau Islands
Tonga
Transvaal
Trinidad
Trinidad and Tobago
Tristan da Cunha
Trucial States
Turks and Caicos
Turks Islands
Tuvalu
Uganda
United Arab Emirates
Victoria
Virgin Islands
Western Australia
Zambia
Zanzibar
Zululand

POST OFFICES IN FOREIGN COUNTRIES

Africa
 East Africa Forces
 Middle East Forces
Bangkok
China
Morocco
Turkish Empire

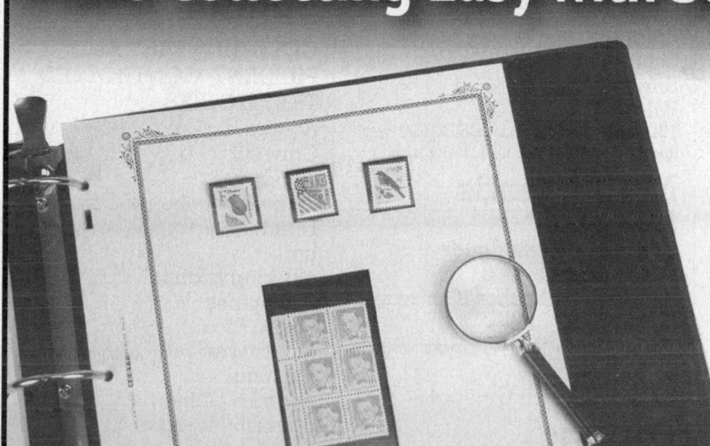

Colonies, Former Colonies, Offices, Territories Controlled by Parent States

Belgium

Belgian Congo
Ruanda-Urundi

Denmark

Danish West Indies
Faroe Islands
Greenland
Iceland

Finland

Aland Islands

France

COLONIES PAST AND PRESENT, CONTROLLED TERRITORIES

Afars & Issas, Territory of
Alaouites
Alexandretta
Algeria
Alsace & Lorraine
Anjouan
Annam & Tonkin
Benin
Cambodia (Khmer)
Cameroun
Castellorizo
Chad
Cilicia
Cochin China
Comoro Islands
Dahomey
Diego Suarez
Djibouti (Somali Coast)
Fezzan
French Congo
French Equatorial Africa
French Guiana
French Guinea
French India
French Morocco
French Polynesia (Oceania)
French Southern & Antarctic Territories
French Sudan
French West Africa
Gabon
Germany
Ghadames
Grand Comoro
Guadeloupe
Indo-China
Inini
Ivory Coast
Laos
Latakia
Lebanon
Madagascar
Martinique
Mauritania
Mayotte
Memel
Middle Congo
Moheli
New Caledonia
New Hebrides
Niger Territory
Nossi-Be
Obock
Reunion
Rouad, Ile
Ste.-Marie de Madagascar
St. Pierre & Miquelon
Senegal
Senegambia & Niger
Somali Coast
Syria
Tahiti
Togo
Tunisia
Ubangi-Shari
Upper Senegal & Niger
Upper Volta
Viet Nam
Wallis & Futuna Islands

POST OFFICES IN FOREIGN COUNTRIES

China
Crete
Egypt
Turkish Empire
Zanzibar

Germany

EARLY STATES

Baden
Bavaria
Bergedorf
Bremen
Brunswick
Hamburg
Hanover
Lubeck
Mecklenburg-Schwerin
Mecklenburg-Strelitz
Oldenburg
Prussia
Saxony
Schleswig-Holstein
Wurttemberg

FORMER COLONIES

Cameroun (Kamerun)
Caroline Islands
German East Africa
German New Guinea
German South-West Africa
Kiauchau
Mariana Islands
Marshall Islands
Samoa
Togo

Italy

EARLY STATES

Modena
Parma
Romagna
Roman States
Sardinia
Tuscany
Two Sicilies
  Naples
  Neapolitan Provinces
  Sicily

FORMER COLONIES, CONTROLLED TERRITORIES, OCCUPATION AREAS

Aegean Islands
  Calimno (Calino)
  Caso
  Cos (Coo)
  Karki (Carchi)
  Leros (Lero)
  Lipso
  Nisiros (Nisiro)
  Patmos (Patmo)
  Piscopi
  Rodi (Rhodes)
  Scarpanto
  Simi
  Stampalia
Castellorizo
Corfu
Cyrenaica
Eritrea
Ethiopia (Abyssinia)
Fiume
Ionian Islands
  Cephalonia
  Ithaca
  Paxos
Italian East Africa
Libya
Oltre Giuba
Saseno
Somalia (Italian Somaliland)
Tripolitania

POST OFFICES IN FOREIGN COUNTRIES

"ESTERO"*
Austria
China
  Peking
  Tientsin
Crete
Tripoli
Turkish Empire
  Constantinople
  Durazzo
  Janina
Jerusalem
Salonika
Scutari
Smyrna
Valona

*Stamps overprinted "ESTERO" were used in various parts of the world.

Netherlands

Aruba
Caribbean Netherlands
Curacao
Netherlands Antilles (Curacao)
Netherlands Indies
Netherlands New Guinea
St. Martin
Surinam (Dutch Guiana)

Portugal

COLONIES PAST AND PRESENT, CONTROLLED TERRITORIES

Angola
Angra
Azores
Cape Verde
Funchal
Horta
Inhambane
Kionga
Lourenco Marques
Macao
Madeira
Mozambique
Mozambique Co.
Nyassa
Ponta Delgada
Portuguese Africa
Portuguese Congo
Portuguese Guinea
Portuguese India
Quelimane
St. Thomas & Prince Islands
Tete
Timor
Zambezia

Russia

ALLIED TERRITORIES AND REPUBLICS, OCCUPATION AREAS

Armenia
Aunus (Olonets)
Azerbaijan
Batum
Estonia
Far Eastern Republic
Georgia
Karelia
Latvia
Lithuania
North Ingermanland
Ostland
Russian Turkestan
Siberia
South Russia
Tannu Tuva
Transcaucasian Fed. Republics
Ukraine
Wenden (Livonia)
Western Ukraine

Spain

COLONIES PAST AND PRESENT, CONTROLLED TERRITORIES

Aguera, La
Cape Juby
Cuba
Elobey, Annobon & Corisco
Fernando Po
Ifni
Mariana Islands
Philippines
Puerto Rico
Rio de Oro
Rio Muni
Spanish Guinea
Spanish Morocco
Spanish Sahara
Spanish West Africa

POST OFFICES IN FOREIGN COUNTRIES

Morocco
Tangier
Tetuan

Dies of British Colonial Stamps

DIE A:

1. The lines in the groundwork vary in thickness and are not uniformly straight.
2. The seventh and eighth lines from the top, in the groundwork, converge where they meet the head.
3. There is a small dash in the upper part of the second jewel in the band of the crown.
4. The vertical color line in front of the throat stops at the sixth line of shading on the neck.

DIE B:

1. The lines in the groundwork are all thin and straight.
2. All the lines of the background are parallel.
3. There is no dash in the upper part of the second jewel in the band of the crown.
4. The vertical color line in front of the throat stops at the eighth line of shading on the neck.

DIE I:

1. The base of the crown is well below the level of the inner white line around the vignette.
2. The labels inscribed "POSTAGE" and "REVENUE" are cut square at the top.
3. There is a white "bud" on the outer side of the main stem of the curved ornaments in each lower corner.
4. The second (thick) line below the country name has the ends next to the crown cut diagonally.

DIE Ia.	DIE Ib.
1 as die II.	1 and 3 as die II.
2 and 3 as die I.	2 as die I.

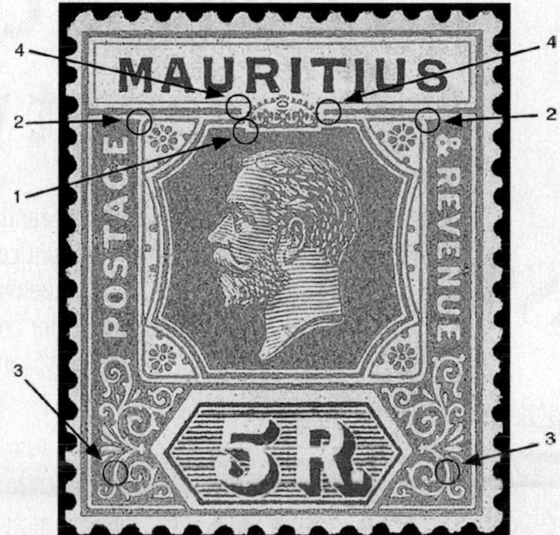

DIE II:

1. The base of the crown is aligned with the underside of the white line around the vignette.
2. The labels curve inward at the top inner corners.
3. The "bud" has been removed from the outer curve of the ornaments in each corner.
4. The second line below the country name has the ends next to the crown cut vertically.

Wmk. 1
Crown and C C

Wmk. 2
Crown and C A

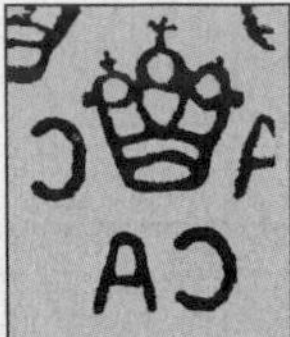
Wmk. 3
Multiple Crown and C A

Wmk. 4
Multiple Crown and Script C A

Wmk. 4a

Wmk. 46

Wmk. 314
St. Edward's Crown and C A Multiple

Wmk. 373

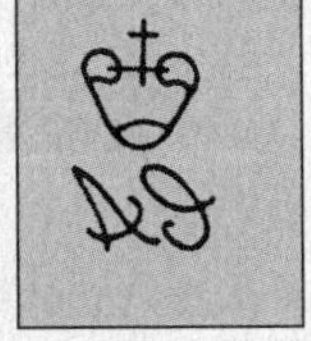
Wmk. 384

Wmk. 406

British Colonial and Crown Agents Watermarks

Watermarks 1 to 4, 314, 373, 384 and 406, common to many British territories, are illustrated here to avoid duplication.

The letters "CC" of Wmk. 1 identify the paper as having been made for the use of the Crown Colonies, while the letters "CA" of the others stand for "Crown Agents." Both Wmks. 1 and 2 were used on stamps printed by De La Rue & Co.

Wmk. 3 was adopted in 1904; Wmk. 4 in 1921; Wmk. 46 in 1879; Wmk. 314 in 1957; Wmk. 373 in 1974; Wmk. 384 in 1985; Wmk 406 in 2008.

In Wmk. 4a, a non-matching crown of the general St. Edwards type (bulging on both sides at top) was substituted for one of the Wmk. 4 crowns which fell off the dandy roll. The non-matching crown occurs in 1950-52 printings in a horizontal row of crowns on certain regular stamps of Johore and Seychelles, and on various postage due stamps of Barbados, Basutoland, British Guiana, Gold Coast, Grenada, Northern Rhodesia, St. Lucia, Swaziland and Trinidad and Tobago. A variation of Wmk. 4a, with the non-matching crown in a horizontal row of crown-CA-crown, occurs on regular stamps of Bahamas, St. Kitts-Nevis and Singapore.

Wmk. 314 was intentionally used sideways, starting in 1966. When a stamp was issued with Wmk. 314 both upright and sideways, the sideways varieties usually are listed also – with minor numbers. In many of the later issues, Wmk. 314 is slightly visible.

Wmk. 373 is usually only faintly visible.

GABON

ga-'bōⁿ

LOCATION — West coast of Africa, at the equator
GOVT. — Republic
AREA — 102,089 sq. mi.
POP. — 1,225,853 (1999 est.)
CAPITAL — Libreville

Gabon originally was under the control of French West Africa. In 1886, it was united with French Congo. In 1904, Gabon was granted a certain degree of colonial autonomy which prevailed until 1934, when it merged with French Equatorial Africa. Gabon Republic was proclaimed November 28, 1958.

100 Centimes = 1 Franc

Catalogue values for unused stamps in this country are for Never Hinged items, beginning with Scott 148 in the regular postage section, Scott B4 in the semi-postal section, Scott C1 in the airpost section, Scott CB1 in the airpost semi-postal section, Scott J34 in the postage due section, and Scott O1 in the officials section.

Watermark

Wmk. 385

For detailed listings of overprint and surcharge varieties of Gabon Nos. 1-15, see the *Scott Classic Specialized Catalogue of Stamps and Covers.*

Stamps of French Colonies of 1881-86 Handstamp Surcharged in Black

a

b

1886 Unwmk. *Perf. 14x13½*

No.	Type	Description	Unused	Used
1	A9 (a)	5c on 20c red, *grn*	575.00	*625.00*
2	A9 (b)	10c on 20c red, *grn*	550.00	*575.00*
3	A9 (b)	25c on 20c red, *grn*	100.00	75.00
e.		56-dot diamond grid around "GAB"	*6,750.*	2,100.
4	A9 (b)	50c on 15c bl	1,500.	*2,100.*
5	A9 (b)	75c on 15c bl	1,900.	*2,300.*

Nos. 1-3 exist with double surcharge of numeral; No. 3 with "GAB" double or inverted, or with "25" double.

On Nos. 3 and 5 the surcharge slants down; on No. 4 it slants up. The number of dots varies.

Counterfeits of Nos. 1-15 exist.

Handstamp Surcharged in Black — c

1888-89

No.	Type	Description	Unused	Used
6	A9	15c on 10c blk, *lav*	*6,000.*	1,500.
7	A9	15c on 1fr brnz grn, *straw*	*2,400.*	1,200.
8	A9	25c on 5c grn, *grnsh*	1,500.	325.00
a.		Double surcharge	*4,000.*	*4,000.*
9	A9	25c on 10c blk, *lav*	*6,000.*	1,900.
10	A9	25c on 75c car, *rose*	*4,000.*	2,100.

Official reprints exist.

Postage Due Stamps of French Colonies Handstamp Surcharged in Black — d

1889 *Imperf.*

No.	Type	Description	Unused	Used
11	D1	15c on 5c black	325.00	275.00
12	D1	15c on 30c black	*5,000.*	*3,800.*
13	D1	25c on 20c black	150.00	120.00

Nos. 11 and 13 exist with "GABON," "TIMBRE" or "25" double; "TIMBRE" or "15" omitted, etc.

A8

1889 Typeset

No.	Type	Description	Unused	Used
14	A8	15c blk, *rose*	1,900.	1,200.
15	A8	25c blk, *green*	1,200.	950.

Ten varieties of each. Nos. 14-15 exist with "GAB" inverted, double or omitted, and with small "f" in "Francaise."

Navigation and Commerce — A9

Name of Colony in Blue or Carmine

1904-07 Typo. *Perf. 14x13½*

No.	Type	Description	Unused	Used
16	A9	1c blk, *lil bl*	1.40	1.40
a.		"GABON" double	360.00	360.00
17	A9	2c brn, *buff*	2.10	1.40
18	A9	4c claret, *lav*	2.75	2.10
19	A9	5c yellow green	3.25	2.40
20	A9	10c rose	10.00	7.50
21	A9	15c gray	11.00	7.50
22	A9	20c red, *grn*	15.00	14.00
23	A9	25c blue	14.00	7.50
24	A9	30c yel brn	16.00	15.00
25	A9	35c blk, *yel* ('06)	24.00	24.00
26	A9	40c red, *straw*	25.00	20.00
27	A9	45c blk, *gray grn* ('07)	37.50	32.50
28	A9	50c brn, *az*	16.00	14.00
29	A9	75c dp vio, *org*	25.00	25.00
30	A9	1fr brnz grn, *straw*	40.00	40.00
31	A9	2fr vio, *rose*	80.00	80.00
32	A9	5fr lil, *lav*	127.50	127.50
		Nos. 16-32 (17)	450.50	421.80

Perf. 13½x14 stamps are counterfeits.
For surcharges see Nos. 72-84.

Fang Warrior — A10

Fang Woman — A12

Libreville A11

Inscribed: "Congo Français"

1910 *Perf. 13½x14*

No.	Type	Description	Unused	Used
33	A10	1c choc & org	2.00	2.00
34	A10	2c black & choc	2.75	2.75
35	A10	4c vio & dp bl	2.50	2.50
36	A10	5c ol gray & grn	4.00	4.00
37	A10	10c red & car	5.75	5.75
38	A10	20c choc & dk vio	8.00	8.00
39	A11	25c dp bl & choc	8.00	8.00
40	A11	30c gray blk & red	40.00	40.00
41	A11	35c dk vio & grn	24.00	24.00
42	A11	40c choc & ultra	32.50	32.50
43	A11	45c car & vio	52.50	52.50
44	A11	50c bl grn & gray	75.00	75.00
45	A11	75c org & choc	130.00	130.00
46	A12	1fr dk brn & bis	130.00	130.00
47	A12	2fr car & brn	325.00	325.00
48	A12	5fr blue & choc	325.00	325.00
		Nos. 33-48 (16)	1,167.	1,167.

Inscribed: "Afrique Equatoriale"

1910-22 Dull Cream Paper

No.	Type	Description	Unused	Used
49	A10	1c choc & org	.35	*.40*
50	A10	2c black & choc	.35	*.40*
b.		2c gray black & deep olive	.65	*.80*
51	A10	4c vio & dp bl	.35	*.50*
52	A10	5c ol gray & grn	.95	.55
53	A10	5c gray blk & ocher ('22)	1.40	1.40
54	A10	10c red & car	1.40	1.00
55	A10	10c yel grn & bl grn ('22)	1.40	1.40
56	A10	15c brn vio & rose ('18)	1.25	.80
57	A10	20c ol brn & dk vio	6.50	5.50
58	A11	25c dp bl & choc	1.40	1.00
59	A11	25c Prus bl & blk ('22)	1.60	1.60
60	A11	30c gray blk & red	1.60	1.60
61	A11	30c rose & red ('22)	2.00	*2.40*
62	A11	35c dk vio & grn	1.40	1.25
63	A11	40c choc & ultra	1.60	1.60
64	A11	45c carmine & vio	1.60	1.60
65	A11	45c blk & red ('22)	2.75	*3.25*
66	A11	50c bl grn & gray	2.00	2.00
67	A11	50c dk bl & bl ('22)	1.60	1.60
68	A11	75c org & choc	7.00	5.00
69	A12	1fr dk brn & bis	3.50	2.75
70	A12	2fr car & brn	7.00	*6.50*
71	A12	5fr blue & choc	7.00	*8.50*
		Nos. 49-71 (23)	56.00	52.60

Nos. 49-51, 54, 62, 64 and 66 also exist on white paper. See the *Scott Classic Specialized Catalogue of Stamps and Covers* for listings.

For overprints and surcharges, see Nos 85-119, B1-B3.

Stamps of 1904-07 Surcharged in Black or Carmine

Spacing between figures of surcharge 1.5mm (5c), 2mm (10c)

1912

No.	Type	Description	Unused	Used
72	A9	5c on 2c brn, *buff*	1.60	*2.00*
73	A9	5c on 4c cl, *lav* (C)	1.60	*2.00*
74	A9	5c on 15c gray (C)	1.25	1.25
75	A9	5c on 20c red, *grn*	1.25	*1.60*
76	A9	5c on 25c bl (C)	1.25	*1.60*
77	A9	5c on 30c pale brn (C)	1.60	*2.00*
78	A9	10c on 40c red, *straw*	1.25	*1.60*
a.		Double surcharge	2,400.	
79	A9	10c on 45c blk, *gray grn* (C)	1.25	*1.60*
80	A9	10c on 50c brn, *az* (C)	1.60	*2.00*
81	A9	10c on 75c dp vio, *org*	1.60	*2.00*
82	A9	10c on 1fr brnz grn, *straw*	1.60	*2.00*
83	A9	10c on 2fr vio, *rose*	1.60	*2.00*
a.		Inverted surcharge	340.00	340.00
84	A9	10c on 5fr lil, *lav*	4.00	*4.25*
		Nos. 72-84 (13)	21.45	25.90

Two spacings between the surcharged numerals are found on Nos. 72 to 84. For detailed listings, see the *Scott Classic Specialized Catalogue of Stamps and Covers.*

Stamps of 1910-22 Overprinted in Black, Blue or Carmine

On A10, A12

On A11

1924-31

No.	Type	Description	Unused	Used
85	A10	1c brn & org	.35	*.35*
86	A10	2c blk & choc (Bl)	.35	*.70*
87	A10	4c violet & ind	.25	*.35*
88	A10	5c gray blk & ocher	.35	*.70*
89	A10	10c yel grn & bl grn	.70	1.10
a.		Double overprint (Bk & Bl)	175.00	
90	A10	10c dk bl & brn ('26) (C)	.40	.40
a.		Overprint omitted	350.00	350.00
b.		Double overprint		475.00
91	A10	15c brn vio & rose (Bl)	1.00	1.00
92	A10	15c rose & brn vio ('31) (Bl)	1.25	1.25
a.		Overprint omitted	250.00	
93	A10	20c ol brn & dk vio (C)	.70	1.10
a.		Inverted overprint	180.00	180.00
b.		Double overprint		400.00
c.		Double overprint, both inverted	525.00	
94	A11	25c Prus bl & blk (C)	.70	1.10
95	A11	30c rose & red (Bl)	.70	*1.10*
96	A11	30c blk & org ('26)	.70	.85
a.		Overprint omitted	—	
97	A11	30c dk grn & bl grn ('28)	1.25	1.25
a.		Overprint omitted	1,800.	
98	A11	35c dk vio & grn (Bl)	.70	*1.10*
99	A11	40c choc & ultra (C)	.75	*.75*
100	A11	45c blk & red (Bl)	1.50	2.10
101	A11	50c dk bl & bl (C)	1.00	1.00
102	A11	50c car & grn ('26)	.70	.90
103	A11	65c dp bl & red org ('27)	3.50	3.50
104	A11	75c org & brn (Bl)	2.25	2.25
105	A11	90c brn red & rose ('30)	2.75	2.75
106	A12	1fr dk brn & bis	1.40	1.75
107	A12	1.10fr dl grn & rose red ('28)	6.00	*7.50*
108	A12	1.50fr pale bl & dk bl ('30)	1.25	1.25
a.		Overprint omitted	290.00	
109	A12	2fr rose & brn	2.25	*2.75*
110	A12	3fr red vio ('30)	7.00	7.00
a.		Overprint omitted	275.00	
111	A12	5fr dp bl & choc	7.00	5.50
		Nos. 85-111 (27)	46.75	51.35

Types of 1924-31 Issues Surcharged with New Values in Black or Carmine

1925-28

No.	Type	Description	Unused	Used
112	A12	65c on 1fr ol grn & brn	1.25	1.25
113	A12	85c on 1fr ol grn & brn	1.25	1.25
114	A11	90c on 75c brn red & cer ('27)	1.75	1.75
a.		"90" omitted	240.00	
115	A12	1.25fr on 1fr dk bl & ultra (C)	1.25	1.25
116	A12	1.50fr on 1fr lt bl & dk bl ('27)	2.00	2.00
117	A12	3fr on 5fr mag & ol brn	7.00	8.00
118	A12	10fr on 5fr org brn & grn ('27)	12.00	*12.50*

119 A12 20fr on 5fr red vio & org red ('27) 16.00 *17.50*
Nos. 112-119 (8) 42.50 45.50

Bars cover the old denominations on Nos. 114-119.

Common Design Types pictured following the introduction.

Colonial Exposition Issue
Common Design Types

1931 ***Perf. 12½***
Name of Country in Black

120 CD70 40c dp green 4.00 4.00
121 CD71 50c violet 4.00 4.00
122 CD72 90c red orange 4.00 4.00
123 CD73 1.50fr dull blue 5.50 5.50
Nos. 120-123 (4) 17.50 17.50

Timber Raft on Ogowe River A16

Count Savorgnan de Brazza — A17

Village of Setta Kemma A18

1932-33 **Photo.** ***Perf. 13x13½***
124 A16 1c brown violet .25 .25
125 A16 2c blk, *rose* .25 .25
126 A16 4c green .30 .30
127 A16 5c grnsh blue .70 .50
128 A16 10c red, *yel* .55 .55
129 A16 15c red, *grn* .70 .65
130 A16 20c deep red .70 .65
131 A16 25c brown red .70 .50
132 A17 30c yellow grn 2.00 1.60
133 A17 40c brown vio 2.25 1.10
134 A17 45c blk, *dl grn* 3.50 2.40
135 A17 50c red brown 1.60 1.25
136 A17 65c Prus blue 6.50 6.50
137 A17 75c blk, *red org* 4.00 3.25
138 A17 90c rose red 4.00 3.25
139 A17 1fr yel grn, *bl* 27.50 24.00
140 A18 1.25fr dp vio ('33) 2.25 2.00
141 A18 1.50fr dull blue 11.00 7.25
142 A18 1.75fr dp grn ('33) 2.50 2.00
143 A18 2fr brn red 52.50 45.00
144 A18 3fr yel grn, *bl* 6.00 4.50
145 A18 5fr red brown 15.00 13.50
146 A18 10fr blk, *red org* 32.50 27.50
147 A18 20fr dk violet 47.50 40.00
Nos. 124-147 (24) 224.75 188.75

For overprints see French Equatorial Africa Nos. 1-10.

See French Equatorial Africa No. 192 for stamp inscribed "Gabon" and "Afrique Equatoriale Francaise."

Catalogue values for all unused stamps in this section, from this point to the end of the section, are for Never Hinged items.

Republic

Prime Minister Leon Mba — A19

Unwmk.
1959, Nov. 28 **Engr.** ***Perf. 13***
148 A19 15fr shown .40 .25
149 A19 25fr Mba, profile .40 .25

Proclamation of the Republic, 1st anniv.

Imperforates
Most Gabon stamps from 1959 onward exist imperforate in issued and trial colors, and also in small presentation sheets in issued colors.

C.C.T.A. Issue
Common Design Type

1960, May 21 **Engr.** ***Perf. 13***
150 CD106 50fr vio brn & Prus bl 1.40 1.10

Flag & Map of Gabon & UN Emblem — A20

1961, Feb. 9
151 A20 15fr multi .35 .25
152 A20 25fr multi .55 .25
153 A20 85fr multi 1.90 1.10
Nos. 151-153 (3) 2.80 1.60

Gabon's admission to United Nations.

Combretum A21

1fr, 5fr, Tulip tree, vert. 2fr, 3fr, Yellow cassia.

1961, July 4 **Unwmk.** ***Perf. 13***
154 A21 50c rose red & grn .25 .25
155 A21 1fr sl grn, red & bis .25 .25
156 A21 2fr dk grn & yel .25 .25
157 A21 3fr ol grn & yel .55 .55
158 A21 5fr multi .60 .60
159 A21 10fr grn & rose red .60 .60
Nos. 154-159 (6) 2.50 2.50

President Leon Mba — A22

1962 **Engr.**
160 A22 15fr indigo, car & grn .35 .25
161 A22 20fr brn blk, car & grn .50 .25
162 A22 25fr brn, car & grn .70 .25
Nos. 160-162 (3) 1.55 .75

Issued: 15fr, 2/9; 20fr, 11/15; 25fr, 8/17.

Abidjan Games Issue
Common Design Type

1962, July 21 **Photo.** ***Perf. 12½x12***
163 CD109 20fr Foot race, start .75 .50
164 CD109 50fr Soccer 1.25 1.00
Nos. 163-164,C6 (3) 5.00 3.00

African-Malgache Union Issue
Common Design Type

1962, Sept. 8 ***Perf. 12½x12***
165 CD110 30fr emer, bluish grn, red & gold 1.60 1.25

Captain Ntchorere and Flags of France and Gabon A23

1962, Nov. 23 ***Perf. 12***
166 A23 80fr multi 1.60 1.10

Capt. Ntchorere, who died for France, 6/7/40.

Waves Around Globe A23a

Design: 100fr, Orbit patterns around globe.

1963, Sept. 19 **Photo.** ***Perf. 12½***
167 A23a 25fr ultra, grn & org .55 .55
168 A23a 100fr grn, ultra & red brn 2.10 1.75

Issued to publicize space communications.

UNESCO Emblem, Scales and Tree A23b

1963, Dec. 10 **Engr.** ***Perf. 13***
169 A23b 25fr grn, dk gray & red brn .70 .25

15th anniv. of the Universal Declaration of Human Rights.

Barograph and WMO Emblem A23c

1964, Mar. 23 **Unwmk.** ***Perf. 13***
170 A23c 25fr ol bis, sl grn & ultra .90 .60

UN's 4th World Meteorological Day, Mar. 23.

Arms of Gabon — A24

1964, June 15 **Photo.** ***Perf. 13x12½***
171 A24 25fr ocher & multi .90 .45

Tarpon A25

Designs: 60fr, Gorilla, vert. 80fr, Buffalo.

1964, July 15 **Engr.** ***Perf. 13***
172 A25 30fr brn red, bl & blk 1.25 .70
173 A25 60fr brn, grn & brn red 2.25 .90
174 A25 80fr dk bl, grn & red brn 2.40 1.25
Nos. 172-174 (3) 5.90 2.85

Cooperation Issue
Common Design Type

1964, Nov. 7
175 CD119 25fr gray, dk brn & lt bl .90 .60

Dissotis Rotundifolia — A26

5fr, Gloriosa superba. 15fr, Eulophia horsfallii.

1964, Nov. 16 **Photo.** ***Perf. 12x12½***
Flowers in Natural Colors

176 A26 3fr deep grn .30 .25
177 A26 5fr green .50 .30
178 A26 15fr dark brn .75 .50
Nos. 176-178 (3) 1.55 1.05

Sun and IQSY Emblem A27

1965, Feb. 25 ***Perf. 12½x12***
179 A27 85fr multi 1.40 .80

International Quiet Sun Year, 1964-65.

Morse Telegraph A28

1965, May 17 **Engr.** ***Perf. 13***
180 A28 30fr multi .75 .60

Cent. of the ITU.

Manganese Crusher, Moanda A29

Design: 60fr, Uranium mining, Mounana.

1965, June 15 **Unwmk.** ***Perf. 13***
181 A29 15fr brt bl, pur & red .55 .30
182 A29 60fr brn, brt bl & red 1.90 .90

Issued to publicize Gabon's mineral wealth.

Field Ball — A30

1965, July 15 **Engr.** ***Perf. 13***
183 A30 25fr brt grn, blk & red .75 .35

1st African Games, Brazzaville, 7/18-25. See No. C35.

Okoukoue Dance — A31

Design: 60fr, Mukudji dance.

1965, Sept. 15 ***Perf. 13***
184 A31 25fr brn, grn & yel .40 .25
185 A31 60fr blk, dk red & brn 1.50 .60

Abraham Lincoln A32

1965, Sept. 28 Photo. ***Perf. 12½x13***
186 A32 50fr vio bl, blk, gold & buff .90 .40

Centenary of death of Abraham Lincoln.

Old & New Post Offices and Mail Transport A33

1965, Dec. 18 Engr. ***Perf. 13***
187 A33 30fr bl, brt grn & choc .90 .50

Issued for Stamp Day, 1965.

Balumbu Mask — A34

Intl. Negro Arts Festival, Dakar, Senegal, Apr. 1-24 — 10fr, Fang ancestral figure, Byeri. 25fr, Fang mask. 30fr, Okuyi mask, Myene. 85fr, Bakota leather mask.

1966, Apr. 18 Photo. ***Perf. 12x12½***
188 A34 5fr red, brn, blk & buff .25 .25
189 A34 10fr brt grnsh bl, dk brn & yel .30 .25
190 A34 25fr multicolored .80 .30
191 A34 30fr mar, yel & blk 1.10 .50
192 A34 85fr multicolored 2.50 1.25
Nos. 188-192 (5) 4.95 2.55

WHO Headquarters, Geneva — A35

1966, May 3 Photo. ***Perf. 12½x13***
193 A35 50fr org yel, ultra & blk 1.20 .60

Inauguration of the WHO Headquarters, Geneva.

Mother Learning to Write — A36

1966, June 22 Photo. ***Perf. 12x12½***
194 A36 30fr multi .90 .45

UNESCO literacy campaign.

Soccer Player — A37

Design: 90fr, Player facing left.

1966, July 15 Engr. ***Perf. 13***
195 A37 25fr brn, grn & ultra 1.20 .25
196 A37 90fr ultra & dk pur 2.00 .75
Nos. 195-196,C45 (3) 5.45 1.85

8th World Cup Soccer Championship, Wembley, England, July 11-30.

Timber Industry — A38

Economic development: 85fr, Offshore oil rigs.

1966, Aug. 17 ***Perf. 13***
197 A38 20fr red brn, lil & dk grn .45 .35
198 A38 85fr dk brn, brt bl & brt grn 3.25 1.25

Woman with Children at Bank Window A39

1966, Sept. 23 Engr. ***Perf. 13***
199 A39 25fr brt bl, vio brn & sl grn .85 .45

Issued to publicize Savings Banks.

Scouts Around Campfire A40

50fr, Boy Scout pledging ceremony, vert.

1966, Oct. 17 Engr. ***Perf. 13***
200 A40 30fr sl bl, car & dk brn .85 .40
201 A40 50fr Prus bl, brn red & dk brn 1.25 .50

Issued to honor Gabon's Boy Scouts.

Sikorsky S-43 Seaplane and Map of West Africa A41

1966, Dec. 17 Photo. ***Perf. 12½x12***
202 A41 30fr multi 1.90 .60

Stamp Day and for the 30th anniv. of the 1st air-mail service from Libreville to Port Gentil.

Hippopotami — A42

Animals: 2fr, African crocodiles. 3fr, Water chevrotain. 5fr, Chimpanzees. 10fr, Elephants. 20fr, Leopards.

1967, Jan. 5 Photo. ***Perf. 13x14***
203 A42 1fr multi .25 .25
204 A42 2fr multi .45 .25
205 A42 3fr multi .45 .25
206 A42 5fr multi .50 .25
207 A42 10fr multi 1.50 .80
208 A42 20fr multi 3.50 .80
Nos. 203-208 (6) 6.65 2.60

Lions International Emblem — A43

50fr, Lions emblem, map of Gabon and globe.

1967, Jan. 14 ***Perf. 12½x13***
209 A43 30fr multicolored .80 .25
210 A43 50fr blue & multi 1.00 .50
a. Strip of 2, #209-210 + label 3.00 1.50

50th anniv. of Lions Intl.

Carnival Masks — A44

1967, Feb. 4 Photo. ***Perf. 12x12½***
211 A44 30fr brn, yel bis & bl 1.10 .45

Libreville Carnival, Feb. 4-7.

"Transportation" and Tourist Year Emblem — A45

1967, Feb. 15 ***Perf. 12½x13***
212 A45 30fr multi 1.10 .45

International Tourist Year, 1967.

Olympic Diving Tower, Mexico City — A46

1968 Olympic Games: 30fr, Sun, snow crystals and Olympic rings. 50fr, Ice skating rink and view of Grenoble.

1967, Mar. 18 Engr. ***Perf. 13***
213 A46 25fr dk vio, grnsh bl & ultra .50 .25
214 A46 30fr grn, red lil & mar .90 .45
215 A46 50fr ultra, grn & brn 1.25 .75
Nos. 213-215 (3) 2.65 1.45

Symbolic of Atomic Energy Agency — A47

1967, Apr. 15 Engr. ***Perf. 13***
216 A47 30fr red brn, dk grn & ultra .90 .25

International Atomic Energy Agency.

Pope Paul VI, Papal Arms and Libreville Cathedral A48

1967, June 1 Engr. ***Perf. 13***
217 A48 30fr ultra, grn & blk 1.10 .50

"Populorum progressio" encyclical by Pope Paul VI concerning underdeveloped countries.

Flags, Tree, Logger, Map of Gabon and Mask — A49

1967, June 24 Engr. ***Perf. 13***
218 A49 30fr multi .80 .45

EXPO '67, International Exhibition, Montreal, Apr. 28-Oct. 27, 1967.

Europafrica Issue

Map of Europe and Africa and Products A50

1967, July 18 Photo. ***Perf. 12½x12***
219 A50 50fr multi 1.50 .60

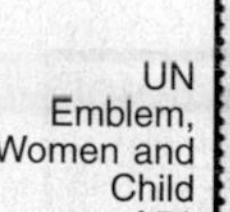

UN Emblem, Women and Child A51

1967, Aug. 10 Engr. ***Perf. 13***
220 A51 75fr brt blue, dk brn & emer 1.60 .80

United Nations Commission for Women.

19th Century Mail Ships — A52

Design: No. 222, Modern mail ships.

1967, Nov. 17 Photo. *Perf. 12½*

221 30fr multi 1.90 .95
222 30fr multi 1.90 .95
a. A52 Pair, #221-222 5.00 5.00

Stamp Day. No. 222a has continuous design.

Draconea Fragrans — A53

Trees: 10fr, Pycnanthus angolensis. 20fr, Disthemonanthus benthamianus.

1967, Dec. 5 Engr. *Perf. 13*
Size: 22x36mm

223 A53 5fr bl, emer & brn .75 .35
224 A53 10fr grn, dk grn & bl .90 .45
225 A53 20fr rose red, grn & ol 1.20 .70
Nos. 223-225,C61-C62 (5) 7.20 4.50

For booklet pane see No. C62a.

WHO Regional Office A54

1968, Apr. 8 Engr. *Perf. 13*

226 A54 20fr multi .85 .50

20th anniv. of the WHO.

Dam, Power Station and UNESCO Emblem A55

1968, June 18 Engr. *Perf. 13*

227 A55 15fr lake, org & Prus bl .75 .40

Hydrological Decade (UNESCO), 1965-74.

Pres. Albert Bernard Bongo — A56

30fr, Pres. Bongo & arms of Gabon in background.

1968, June 24 Photo. *Perf. 12x12½*

228 A56 25fr grn, buff & blk .65 .25
229 A56 30fr rose lil, lt bl & blk .75 .25

Tanker, Refinery, and Map of Area Served — A56a

1968, July 30 Photo. *Perf. 12½*

230 A56a 30fr multi .85 .50

Port Gentil (Gabon) Refinery opening, 6/12/68.

Open Book, Child and UNESCO Emblem A57

1968, Sept. 10 Engr. *Perf. 13*

231 A57 25fr vio bl, dl red & brn 1.25 .25

Issued for International Literacy Day.

A58

1968, Oct. 15 Engr. *Perf. 13*

232 A58 20fr Coffee 2.00 .75
233 A58 40fr Cacao 1.25 .50

A59

1968, Nov. 23 Engr. *Perf. 13*

234 A59 30fr "La Junon" 1.75 .70

Issued for Stamp Day.

A60

Lawyer, globe and human rights flame.

1968, Dec. 10

235 A60 20fr blk, bl grn & car .75 .45

International Human Rights Year.

Okanda Gap — A61

Designs: 15fr, Barracuda. 25fr, Kinguele Waterfall, vert. 30fr, Sitatunga trophies, vert.

1969, Mar. 28 Engr. *Perf. 13*

236 A61 10fr brn, bl & sl grn .35 .25
237 A61 15fr brn red, emer & ind 2.25 .35
238 A61 25fr bl, pur & ol .65 .30
239 A61 30fr multi 1.40 .50
Nos. 236-239 (4) 4.65 1.40

Year of African Tourism, 1969.

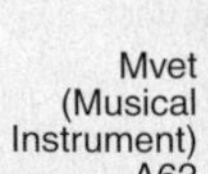

Mvet (Musical Instrument) A62

Musical Instruments: 30fr, Ngombi harp. 50fr, Ebele and Mbe drums. 100fr, Medzang xylophone.

1969, June 6 Engr. *Perf. 13*

240 A62 25fr plum, ol & dp car .50 .25
241 A62 30fr red brn, ol & dk brn .50 .25
242 A62 50fr plum, ol & dp car 1.10 .65
243 A62 100fr red brn, ol & dk brn 2.40 1.00
a. Min. sheet of 4, #240-243 6.50 6.50
Nos. 240-243 (4) 4.50 2.15

Aframomum Polyanthum (Zingiberaceae) A63

African Plants: 2fr, Chlamydocola chlamydantha (Sterculiaceae). 5fr, Costus dinklagei (Zingiberaceae). 10fr, Cola rostrata (Sterculiaceae). 20fr, Dischistocalyx grandifolius (Acanthaceae).

1969, July 15 Photo. *Perf. 12x12½*

244 A63 1fr multi .25 .25
245 A63 2fr lt ol & multi .30 .25
246 A63 5fr multi .35 .25
247 A63 10fr slate & multi .80 .35
248 A63 20fr yel & multi 1.20 .70
Nos. 244-248 (5) 2.90 1.80

Tree of Life — A64

1969, Aug. 17 Photo.

249 A64 25fr multi .60 .50

National renovation.

Drilling for Oil on Land — A65

Design: 50fr, Offshore drilling station.

1969, Sept. 13 *Perf. 12x12½*

250 A65 25fr multi .75 .25
251 A65 50fr multi 1.50 .25
a. Strip of 2, #250-251 + label 3.00 1.50

20th anniv. of the ELF-SPAFE oil operations in Gabon.

Workers and ILO Emblem — A66

1969, Oct. 29 Engr. *Perf. 13*

252 A66 30fr bl, sl grn & dp car .90 .45

50th anniv. of the ILO.

Arms of Port Gentil — A67

Coats of Arms: 20fr, Lambarene. 30fr, Libreville.

1969, Nov. 19 Photo. *Perf. 12*

253 A67 20fr red, gold, sil & blk .85 .25
254 A67 25fr bl, blk & gold 1.10 .25
255 A67 30fr bl & multi 1.40 .45
Nos. 253-255 (3) 3.35 .95

See Nos. 267-269, 291-293, 321-326, 340-348, 409-417, 492-501.

Canoe Mail Transport A68

1969, Dec. 18 Engr. *Perf. 13*

256 A68 30fr brt grn, grnsh bl & red brn 1.25 .80

Issued for Stamp Day 1969.

Satellite, Globe, TV Screen and ITU Emblem A69

1970, May 17 Engr. *Perf. 13*

257 A69 25fr dk bl, dk red brn & blk .80 .40

International Telecommunications Day.

UPU Headquarters Issue
Common Design Type

1970, May 20 Engr. *Perf. 13*

258 CD133 30fr brt grn, brt rose lil & brn .90 .55

Geisha and African Drummer A70

1970, May 27 Photo. *Perf. 12½x12*

259 A70 30fr ultra & multi .90 .40

EXPO '70 Intl. Exhibition, Osaka, Japan, 3/15-9/13.

ASECNA Issue
Common Design Type

1970, Aug. 26 Engr. *Perf. 13*

260 CD132 100fr brt grn & bl grn 1.75 .75

UN Emblem, Globe, Dove and Charts A71

1970, Oct. 24 Photo. *Perf. 12½x12*

261 A71 30fr Prus bl & multi .90 .60

25th anniversary of the United Nations.

Bushbucks A72

Designs: 15fr, Pels scaly-tailed flying squirrel. 25fr, Gray-cheeked monkey, vert. 40fr, African golden cat. 60fr, Sevaline genet.

1970, Dec. 14 Photo. *Perf. 12½x13*

262 A72 5fr yel grn & multi .45 .30
263 A72 15fr red org & blk .70 .40
264 A72 25fr vio & multi 1.40 .60
265 A72 40fr red & multi 2.75 1.10
266 A72 60fr bl & multi 4.00 2.10
Nos. 262-266 (5) 9.30 4.50

Arms Type of 1969

20fr, Mouila. 25fr, Bitam. 30fr, Oyem.

1971, Feb. 16 Photo. *Perf. 12*

267	A67	20fr ver, blk, sil & gold	.90	.25
268	A67	25fr emer, gold & blk	1.00	.25
269	A67	30fr emer, gold, blk & red	1.25	.25
		Nos. 267-269 (3)	3.15	.75

Men of Four Races and Emblem — A73

1971, Mar. 21 Engr. *Perf. 13*

270	A73	40fr multi	.90	.45

Intl. year against racial discrimination.

Map of Africa and Telecommunications System — A74

1971, Apr. 30 Photo. *Perf. 13*

271	A74	30fr org & multi	.90	.45

Pan-African telecommunications system.

Charaxes Smaragdalis — A75

Butterflies: 10fr, Euxanthe crossleyi. 15fr, Epiphora rectifascia. 25fr, Imbrasia bouvieri.

1971, May 26 Photo. *Perf. 13*

272	A75	5fr yel & multi	2.25	.45
273	A75	10fr bl & multi	3.75	.60
274	A75	15fr grn & multi	7.50	.70
275	A75	25fr ol & multi	8.50	1.10
		Nos. 272-275 (4)	22.00	2.85

Hertzian Center, Nkol Ogoum A76

1971, June 17 Engr. *Perf. 13*

276	A76	40fr grn, blk & dk car	.90	.40

3rd World Telecommunications Day.

Mother Nursing Child A77

1971, Aug. 17 Engr. *Perf. 13*

277	A77	30fr lil rose, sep & ocher	.90	.45

Gabonese social security system, 15th anniv.

UN Headquarters and Emblem — A78

1971, Sept. 30 Photo. *Perf. 13*

278	A78	30fr red & multi	.90	.45

10th anniv. of Gabon's admission to the UN.

Large Egret — A79

Birds: 40fr, African gray parrot. 50fr, Woodland Kingfisher. 75fr, Cameroon bareheaded rock-fowl. 100fr, Gold Coast touraco.

1971, Oct. 12 Litho. *Perf. 13*

279	A79	30fr multi	1.25	.75
280	A79	40fr multi	2.10	1.00
281	A79	50fr multi	2.75	1.20
282	A79	75fr multi	3.75	1.25
283	A79	100fr multi	5.25	1.50
		Nos. 279-283 (5)	15.10	5.70

Asystasia Volgeliana A80

Designs: Flowers of Acanthus Family after paintings by Noel Hallé.

1972, Apr. 4 Photo. *Perf. 13*

284	A80	5fr pale cit & multi	.25	.25
285	A80	10fr multi	.40	.25
286	A80	20fr multi	.65	.40
287	A80	30fr lil rose & multi	1.00	.50
288	A80	40fr dk grn & multi	1.40	.75
289	A80	65fr red & multi	2.25	1.10
		Nos. 284-289 (6)	5.95	3.25

Louis Pasteur — A81

1972, May 15 Engr. *Perf. 13*

290	A81	80fr dp org, pur & grn	1.25	.60

Sesquicentennial of the birth of Louis Pasteur (1822-1895), scientist and bacteriologist.

Arms Type of 1969

30fr, Franceville. 40fr, Makokou. 60fr, Tchibanga.

1972, June 2 Photo. *Perf. 12*

291	A67	30fr sil & multi	.75	.25
292	A67	40fr grn & multi	.75	.50
293	A67	60fr blk, grn & sil	1.60	.75
		Nos. 291-293 (3)	3.10	1.50

Globe and Telecommunications Symbols — A81a

1972, July 25 *Perf. 13x12½*

294	A81a	40fr blk, yel & org	.90	.45

4th World Telecommunications Day.

Nat King Cole — A82

Black American Jazz Musicians: 60fr, Sidney Bechet. 100fr, Louis Armstrong.

1972, Sept. 1 Photo. *Perf. 13x13½*

295	A82	40fr bl & multi	1.60	.35
296	A82	60fr org & multi	2.40	.70
297	A82	100fr multi	4.00	1.10
		Nos. 295-297 (3)	8.00	2.15

Blanding's Rear-fanged Snake — A83

Designs: 2fr, Beauty snake. 3fr, Eggeating snake. 15fr, Striped ground snake. 25fr, Jameson's mamba. 50fr, Gabon viper.

1972, Oct. 2 Litho. *Perf. 13*

298	A83	1fr lem & multi	.25	.25
299	A83	2fr red brn & multi	.40	.25
300	A83	3fr brn org & multi	.40	.25
301	A83	15fr multi	2.25	.40
302	A83	25fr grn & multi	3.25	.45
303	A83	50fr multi	5.00	.75
		Nos. 298-303 (6)	11.55	2.35

See Nos. 330-332, 354-357.

Dr. Armauer G. Hansen, Lambarene Leprosarium — A84

1973, Jan. 28 Engr. *Perf. 13*

304	A84	30fr Prus grn, sl grn & brn	1.10	.55

Centenary of the discovery of the Hansen bacillus, the cause of leprosy.

Charaxes Candiope — A85

Various butterflies: 15fr, Eunica pechueli. 20fr, Cyrestis camillus. 30fr, Charaxes castor. 40fr, Charaxes ameliae. 50fr, Pseudacrea boisduvali.

1973, Feb. 23 Litho. *Perf. 13*

305	A85	10fr shown	1.90	.40
306	A85	15fr multicolored	2.25	.40
307	A85	20fr multicolored	3.75	.85
308	A85	30fr multicolored	5.00	1.25
309	A85	40fr multicolored	6.00	1.75
310	A85	50fr multicolored	6.50	2.10
		Nos. 305-310 (6)	25.40	6.75

Balloon of Santos Dumont, 1901 — A86

History of Aviation: 1fr, Montgolfier's balloon, 1783, vert. 3fr, Octave Chanute's biplane, 1896. 4fr, Clement Ader's Plane III, 1897. 5fr, Louis Bleriot crossing the Channel, 1909. 10fr, Fabre's hydravion, 1910.

1973, May 3 Engr. *Perf. 13*

311	A86	1fr grn, sl grn & dk red	.25	.25
312	A86	2fr sl grn & brt bl	.25	.25
313	A86	3fr bl, sl & org	.25	.25
314	A86	4fr lil & dk pur	.75	.25
315	A86	5fr slate grn & org	1.10	.35
316	A86	10fr rose lil & Prus bl	2.10	.50
		Nos. 311-316 (6)	4.70	1.85

1977 Coil Stamp

316A	A86	10fr aqua	3.50	.25

No. 316A has red control numbers on back of every 10th stamp.

INTERPOL Emblem — A87

1973, June 26 Engr. *Perf. 13*

317	A87	40fr magenta & ultra	.90	.40

50th anniversary of the International Criminal Police Organization (INTERPOL).

Earth Station "2 Decembre" A88

1973, July 2 Engr. *Perf. 13*

318	A88	40fr slate grn, bl & brn	.90	.40

Party Headquarters, Libreville — A89

1973, Aug. 17 Photo.

319	A89	30fr multi	.90	.25

African Postal Union Issue

Common Design Type

1973, Sept. 12 Engr. *Perf. 13*

320	CD137	100fr red lil, pur & bl	1.40	.75

Arms Type of 1969

5fr, Gamba. 10fr, Ogowe-Lolo. 15fr, Fougamou. 30fr, Kango. 40fr, Booue. 60fr, Koula-Moutou.

1973-74 Photo. *Perf. 12*

321	A67	5fr bl & multi ('74)	.65	.25
322	A67	10fr blk, red & gold ('74)	.65	.25
323	A67	15fr grn & multi ('74)	.90	.25
324	A67	30fr red & multi	1.60	.35
325	A67	40fr red & multi	1.90	.55
326	A67	60fr emer & multi	3.00	.70
		Nos. 321-326 (6)	8.70	2.35

Issued Nos. 321-323, 2/13; Nos. 324-326, 10/4.

St. Teresa of Lisieux — A90

40fr, St. Teresa and Jesus carrying cross.

1973, Dec. 4 **Photo.** ***Perf. 13***
327 A90 30fr blk & multi .90 .25
328 A90 40fr blk & multi 1.10 .35

St. Teresa of the Infant Jesus (Thérèse Martin, 1873-97), Carmelite nun.

Human Rights Flame — A91

1973, Dec. 10 **Engr.**
329 A91 20fr grn, red & ultra .60 .25

25th anniversary of the Universal Declaration of Human Rights.

Wildlife Type of 1972

Monkeys: 40fr, Mangabey. 60fr, Cercopithecus cephus. 80fr, Mona monkey.

1974, Mar. 20 **Litho.** ***Perf. 14***
330 A83 40fr gray grn & multi 1.20 .45
331 A83 60fr lt bl & multi 2.00 .50
332 A83 80fr lil rose & multi 3.25 .80
Nos. 330-332 (3) 6.45 1.75

Ogowe River at Lambarene A93

50fr, Cape Estérias. 75fr, Poubara rope bridge.

1974, July 30 **Photo.** ***Perf. 13x13½***
333 A93 30fr multi .60 .25
334 A93 50fr multi .80 .25
335 A93 75fr multi 1.75 .90
Nos. 333-335 (3) 3.15 1.40

Manioc A94

Design: 50fr, Palms and dates.

1974, Nov. 13 **Photo.** ***Perf. 13x12½***
336 A94 40fr org red & multi .90 .30
337 A94 50fr bister & multi 1.10 .30

UDEAC Issue

Presidents and Flags of Cameroun, CAR, Congo, Gabon and Meeting Center — A95

1974, Dec. 8 **Photo.** ***Perf. 13***
338 A95 40fr multi .80 .30

See No. C156.

Hôtel du Dialogue — A96

1975, Jan. 20 **Photo.** ***Perf. 13***
339 A96 50fr multi .90 .45

Opening of Hôtel du Dialogue.

Arms Type of 1969

5fr, Ogowe-Ivindo. 10fr, Moabi. No. 342, Moanda. No. 343, Nyanga. 25fr, Mandji. No. 345, Mekambo. No. 346, Omboué. 60fr, Minvoul. 90fr, Mayumba.

1975-77 **Photo.** ***Perf. 12***
340 A67 5fr red & multi .25 .25
341 A67 10fr gold & multi .25 .25
342 A67 15fr red, sil & blk .45 .25
343 A67 15fr bl & multi .35 .25
344 A67 25fr grn & multi .45 .25
345 A67 50fr blk, gold & red 1.40 .35
346 A67 50fr multi 1.50 .60
347 A67 60fr multi 1.40 .60
348 A67 90fr multi 1.90 .75
Nos. 340-348 (9) 7.95 3.55

Issued: Nos. 340-342, Jan. 21, 1975; Nos. 343-345, Aug. 17, 1976; Nos. 346-348, July 12, 1977.

Map of Africa with Lion's Head, and Lions Emblem — A97

1975, May 2 **Typo.** ***Perf. 13***
349 A97 50fr grn & multi 1.40 .50

Lions Club 17th congress, District 403, Libreville.

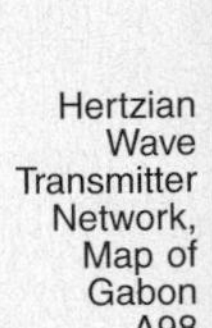

Hertzian Wave Transmitter Network, Map of Gabon A98

1975, July 8 **Engr.** ***Perf. 13***
350 A98 40fr multi .90 .60

City and Rural Women, Car, Train and Building — A99

1975, July 22 **Engr.** ***Perf. 13***
351 A99 50fr car, bl & brn 2.10 .80

International Women's Year 1975.

Scoutmaster Ange Mba, Emblems and Rope — A100

Design: 50fr, Hand holding rope, Scout, camp, Boy Scout and Nordjamb 75 emblems.

1975, July 29
352 A100 40fr multi .60 .30
353 A100 50fr grn, red & dk brn .90 .40

Nordjamb 75, 14th Boy Scout Jamboree, Lillehammer, Norway, July 29-Aug. 7.

Wildlife Type of 1972

Fish: 30fr, Lutjanus goreensis. 40fr, Galeoides decadactylus. 50fr, Sardinella aurita. 120fr, Scarus hoefleri.

1975, Sept. 22 **Litho.** ***Perf. 14***
354 A83 30fr multi .55 .30
355 A83 40fr multi 1.00 .50
356 A83 50fr multi 1.60 .50
357 A83 120fr multi 2.50 1.00
Nos. 354-357 (4) 5.65 2.30

Agro-Industrial Complex — A102

1975, Dec. 15 **Litho.** ***Perf. 12½***
358 A102 60fr multi .90 .40

Inauguration of Agro-Industrial Complex, Franceville.

Tchibanga Bridge — A103

Bridges of Gabon: 10fr, Mouila. 40fr, Kango. 50fr, Lambaréné, vert.

1976, Jan. 30 **Engr.** ***Perf. 13***
359 A103 5fr multi .35 .25
360 A103 10fr multi .45 .25
361 A103 40fr multi 1.00 .30
362 A103 50fr multi 1.25 .45
Nos. 359-362 (4) 3.05 1.25

Telephones 1876 and 1976, Satellite, A. G. Bell — A104

1976, Mar. 10 **Engr.** ***Perf. 13***
363 A104 60fr dk bl, grn & sl grn .90 .40

Centenary of first telephone call by Alexander Graham Bell, Mar. 10, 1876.

Msgr. Jean Remy Bessieux — A105

1976, Apr. 30 **Engr.** ***Perf. 13***
364 A105 50fr grn, bl & sepia .90 .45

Death centenary of Msgr. Bessieux.

Athletes, Torch, Map of Africa, Games Emblem — A106

1976, June 25 **Photo.** ***Perf. 13x12½***
365 A106 50fr multi .70 .25
366 A106 60fr org & multi .90 .30

First Central African Games (Zone 5), Libreville, June-July.

Motobécane, France — A107

Motorcycles: 5fr, Bultaco, Spain. 10fr, Suzuki, Japan. 20fr, Kawasaki, Japan. 100fr, Harley-Davidson, US.

1976, July 20 **Litho.** ***Perf. 12½***
367 A107 3fr multi .40 .25
368 A107 5fr org & multi .40 .25
369 A107 10fr bl & multi .70 .30
370 A107 20fr multi 1.25 .30
371 A107 100fr car & multi 4.50 1.00
Nos. 367-371 (5) 7.25 2.10

Rice A108

1976, Oct. 15 **Litho.** ***Perf. 13x13½***
372 A108 50fr shown .70 .35
373 A108 60fr Pepper plants 1.00 .50

1977, Apr. 22 **Litho.** ***Perf. 13x13½***

50fr, Banana plantation. 60fr, Peanut market.

374 A108 50fr multi .70 .35
375 A108 60fr multi 1.00 .50

Telecommunications Emblem and Telephone — A109

1977, May 17 *Perf. 13*
376 A109 60fr multi .90 .50

World Telecommunications Day.

View of Oyem A110

50fr, Cape Lopez. 70fr, Lebamba Cave.

1977, June 9 **Litho.** *Perf. 12½*
377 A110 50fr multi .70 .30
378 A110 60fr multi .75 .40
379 A110 70fr multi .85 .45
Nos. 377-379 (3) 2.30 1.15

Conference Hall — A111

1977, June 23 **Photo.** *Perf. 13x12½*
380 A111 100fr multi 1.40 .75

Meeting of the OAU, Libreville.

Arms of Gabon — A112

Size: 23x36mm

1977 **Engr.** *Perf. 13*
381 A112 50fr blue 1.25 .50

Size: 17x23mm

382 A112 60fr orange 1.10 .50
a. Booklet pane of 5 6.00
383 A112 80fr red 1.60 .65
Nos. 381-383 (3) 3.95 1.65

No. 381 issued in coils, No. 382 in booklets only.

Issued: Nos. 381-382, June 23; No. 383, Sept.

Modern Buildings, Libreville — A113

1977, Aug. 17 **Litho.** *Perf. 12*
387 A113 50fr multi .90 .25

National Festival 1977.

Paris to Vienna, 1902 — A114

Renault Automobiles: 10fr, Coupé 1 2 CV, 1921. 30fr, Torpédo Scaphandrier, 1925. 40fr, Reinastella 10 CV, 1929. 100fr, Nerva Grand Sport, 1937. 150fr, Voiturette 1 CV, 1899. 200fr, Alpine Renault V6, 1977.

1977, Aug 30 **Engr.** *Perf. 13*
388 A114 5fr multi .50 .35
389 A114 10fr multi .50 .35
390 A114 30fr multi 1.25 .50
391 A114 40fr multi 2.10 .60
392 A114 100fr multi 5.25 2.25
Nos. 388-392 (5) 9.60 4.05

Miniature Sheet

393 Sheet of 2 + label 18.00 18.00
a. A114 150fr multi 5.25 5.25
b. A114 200fr multi 7.00 7.00

Louis Renault, French automobile pioneer, birth centenary. Nos. 383a-393b are perf. on 3 sides, without perforation between stamps and center label showing dark brown portrait of Renault.

See Nos. 395-400.

Globe A115

1978, Feb. 21 **Engr.** *Perf. 13x12½*
394 A115 80fr multi .90 .60

World Leprosy Day.

Automobile Type of 1977

Citroen Cars: 10fr, Cabriolet, 1922. 50fr, Taxi, 1927. 60fr, Berline, 1932. 80fr, Berline, 1934. 150fr, Torpedo, 1919. 200fr, Berline, 1948. 250fr, Pallas, 1975.

1978, May 9 **Engr.** *Perf. 13*
395 A114 10fr multi .80 .35
396 A114 50fr multi 1.50 .45
397 A114 60fr multi 2.50 .95
398 A114 80fr multi 2.50 .95
399 A114 200fr multi 6.75 2.25
Nos. 395-399 (5) 14.05 4.95

Miniature Sheet

400 Sheet of 2 18.00 18.00
a. A114 150fr multi 5.25 5.25
b. A114 250fr multi 7.00 7.00

Andre Citroen (1878-1935), automobile designer and manufacturer.

Ndjole on Ogowe River — A116

Views: 40fr, Lambarene lake district. 50fr, Owendo Harbor.

1978, May 17 **Litho.** *Perf. 12½*
401 A116 30fr multi .40 .25
402 A116 40fr multi .70 .25
403 A116 50fr multi .90 .35
Nos. 401-403 (3) 2.00 .85

Sternotomis Mirabilis — A117

Various Coleopteras.

1978, June 21 **Photo.** *Perf. 12½x13*
404 A117 20fr multi .00 .25
405 A117 60fr multi 2.25 .65
406 A117 75fr multi 3.00 .75
407 A117 80fr multi 3.75 .90
Nos. 404-407 (4) 9.80 2.55

Anti-Apartheid Emblem — A118

1978, July 25 **Engr.** *Perf. 13*
408 A118 80fr multi .75 .40

Arms Type of 1969

No. 409, Oyem. No. 410, Ogowe-Maritime ('79). No. 411, Lastoursville ('79). No. 412, Haut-Ogooue ('80). No. 413, M'Digou ('79). No. 414, Estuaire ('80). No. 415, Bitam ('80). No. 416, Okondja. No. 417, Mimongo.

1978-80 **Photo.** *Perf. 12*
409 A67 5fr multicolored .25 .25
410 A67 5fr multicolored .25 .25
411 A67 10fr multicolored .25 .25
412 A67 10fr multicolored .25 .25
413 A67 15fr multicolored .25 .25
414 A67 20fr multicolored .25 .25
415 A67 30fr multicolored .25 .25
416 A67 40fr multicolored .80 .25
417 A67 60fr multicolored 1.60 .40
Nos. 409-417 (9) 4.15 2.40

Issued: Nos. 409, 416-417, 8/17; Nos. 410-411, 413, 3/21/79; Nos. 412, 414, 415, 8/13/80.

A119

1978, Oct. 24 **Engr.** *Perf. 13*
419 A119 80fr multi 1.00 .40

UNESCO campaign to save the Acropolis.

Penicillin Formula, — A120

1978, Nov. 21 **Engr.** *Perf. 13*
420 A120 90fr multi 3.00 1.10

Alexander Fleming's discovery of antibiotics, 50th anniversary.

The Visitation — A121

80fr, Massacre of the Innocents. Woodcarvings from St. Michael's Church, Libreville.

1978, Dec. 15 **Photo.**
421 A121 60fr gold & multi .90 .40
422 A121 80fr gold & multi 1.10 .50

Christmas 1978. See Nos. 437-438.

Train and Map A122

1978, Dec. 27 **Litho.** *Perf. 12½*
423 A122 60fr multi 1.75 .60

Inauguration of Trans-Gabon Railroad, Libreville to Njolé.

A123

Pre-Olympic Year (Kremlin Towers, Olympic Emblem, Ancestral Figure and): 80fr, Long jump, vert. 100fr, Yachts.

1979, May 15 **Engr.** *Perf. 13*
424 A123 60fr multi .60 .30
425 A123 80fr multi .75 .40
426 A123 100fr multi .95 .55
a. Miniature sheet of 3, #424-426 3.75 3.75
Nos. 424-426 (3) 2.30 1.25

Rowland Hill, Messenger and Gabon No. O9 — A124

Allamanda Schottii A125

Designs: 80fr, Bakota mask and tulip tree flowers, vert. 150fr, Pigeon, UPU emblem, truck and canoe. No. 430b, Gloriosa superba. No. 430c, Phaeomeria magnifica, vert. No. 430d, Berlinia bracteosa, vert.

1979, June 8 **Photo.** *Perf. 13*
427 A124 50fr multi 1.10 1.10
428 A124 80fr multi 2.00 1.25

Engr.

429 A124 150fr multi 3.25 2.00
Nos. 427-429 (3) 6.35 4.35

Souvenir Sheet

Photo. *Perf. 14*
430 Sheet of 4 11.00 11.00
a. A125 100fr multicolored 2.00
b. A125 100fr multicolored 2.00
c. A125 100fr multicolored 2.00
d. A125 100fr multicolored 2.00

Philexafrique II, Libreville, June 8-17. Nos. 427-429 each printed in sheets of 10 with 5 labels showing exhibition emblem. No. 427 also commemorates Sir Rowland Hill (1795-1879), originator of penny postage. No. 430 has label with exhibition emblem.

IYC Emblem, Globe, Child with Bird — A126

1979, June 15 Engr. *Perf. 13*

431 A126 100fr multi 1.40 .70

International Year of the Child.

"TELECOM 79" — A127

1979, Sept. 18 Litho. *Perf. 13x12½*

432 A127 80fr multi 1.00 .40

3rd World Telecommunications Exhibition, Geneva, Sept. 20-26.

Sugar Cane Harvest — A128

1979, Oct. 9 Photo. *Perf. 12½x13*

433 A128 25fr shown .45 .25
434 A128 30fr Yams .65 .25

Judo Throw — A129

1979, Oct. 23 Engr. *Perf. 13*

435 A129 40fr multi 1.90 .75

World Judo Championships, Paris, Dec.

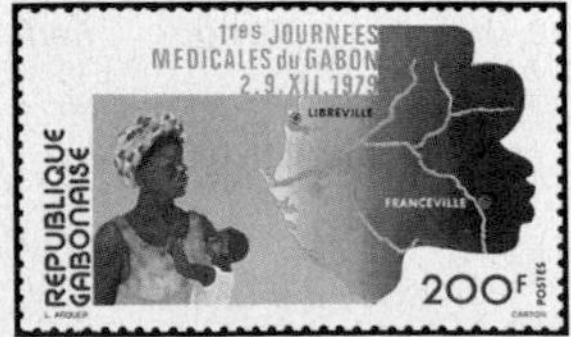

Mother and Child, Map of Congo River Basin — A130

1979, Dec. 2 Litho. *Perf. 12*

436 A130 200fr multi 2.50 .80

Medical Week, Dec. 2-9.

Christmas Type of 1978

Wood Carvings, St. Michael's Church, Libreville: 60fr, Flight into Egypt. 80fr, The Circumcision.

1979, Dec. 12 Photo. *Perf. 13*

437 A121 60fr multi .90 .40
438 A121 80fr multi 1.10 .40

Pres. Omar Bongo — A131

1979-80 Litho. *Perf. 12½*

439 A131 60fr multi .90 .40
440 A131 80fr multi 2.50 1.25

Bongo's 44th birthday (No. 439); re-election and inauguration (No. 440).
Issued: 60fr, 12/30/79; 80fr, 2/27/80.

OPEC, 20th Anniv. — A132

1980, Mar. 27 Litho. *Perf. 13½x13*

441 A132 50fr multi .90 .35

Donguila Church — A133

80fr, Bizengobibere Church.

1980 Apr. 3 Litho. *Perf. 12½*

442 A133 60fr shown .65 .30
443 A133 80fr multicolored .85 .35

Easter 1980.

De Brazza (1852-1905), Map of Gabon with Franceville — A134

1980, June 30 Litho. *Perf. 12½*

444 A134 165fr multi 2.50 1.10

Franceville Foundation centenary, founded by Savorgnan De Brazza.

20th Anniversary of Independence — A135

60cr, Leon Mba and Omar Bongo.

1980, Aug. 17 Photo. *Perf. 13*

445 A135 60fr multicolored .90 .25

World Tourism Conference, Manila, Sept. 27 — A136

1980, Sept. 10 Engr.

446 A136 80fr multi .90 .35

20th Anniversary of OPEC A137

120fr, Men Holding OPEC emblem, vert.

1980, Sept. 15 Litho. *Perf. 12½*

447 A137 80fr shown 1.00 .40
448 A137 120fr multicolored 1.50 .60

Pseudochelidon Eurystomina A138

1980, Oct. 15 Photo. *Perf. 14x14½*

449 A138 50fr shown 2.00 .50
450 A138 60fr multi 2.50 .75
451 A138 80fr Pitta angolensis 3.50 1.00
452 A138 150fr Scotopelia peli 7.00 2.00
Nos. 449-452 (4) 15.00 4.25

Statue of Bull, Bizangobibere Church — A139

1980, Dec. 10 Photo. *Perf. 14x14½*

453 A139 60fr shown .90 .30
454 A139 80fr Male statue 1.40 .45

Christmas 1980.

Heinrich von Stephan — A140

1981, Jan. 7 Engr. *Perf. 13*

455 A140 90fr brn & dk brn .90 .35

Von Stephan (1831-97), UPU founder.

13th Anniversary of National Renovation Movement — A141

1981, Mar. 12 Litho. *Perf. 13x12½*

456 A141 60fr multi .80 .25

Lion Statue, Bizangobibere A142

1981, Apr. 12 Photo. *Perf. 14x14½*

457 A142 75fr multi .90 .40
458 A142 100fr multi 1.10 .55

Easter 1981.

Port Gentil Lions Club Banner — A143

75fr, District 403. 80fr, Libreville Cocotiers. 100fr, Libreville Hibiscus. 165fr, Ekwata. 200fr, Haut-Ogooue.

1981, May 1 Litho. *Perf. 12½*

459 A143 60fr shown .75 .25
460 A143 75fr multi .85 .30
461 A143 80fr multi 1.10 .35
462 A143 100fr multi 1.40 .40
463 A143 165fr multi 2.10 .70
464 A143 200fr multi 2.40 .90
Nos. 459-464 (6) 8.60 2.90

Lions International, 23rd Congress of District 403, Libreville, May 1-3.

13th World Telecommunications Day — A144

1981, May 17 Photo. *Perf. 13*

465 A144 125fr multi 1.60 .55

Unity, Work and Justice — A145

1981-96? Photo. *Perf. 13*

466	A145	5fr beige & blk	.25	.25
467	A145	10fr pale lil & blk	.25	.25
468	A145	15fr brt yel grn & blk	.25	.25
469	A145	20fr pink & blk	.25	.25
470	A145	25fr vio & blk	.25	.25
471	A145	40fr red org & blk	.45	.25
472	A145	50fr bluish grn & blk	.55	.25
473	A145	75fr bis brn & blk	.70	.25
473A	A145	90fr lt bl & blk ('83)	.70	.25
474	A145	100fr yel & blk	1.00	.40
474A	A145	125fr grn & blk ('83)	1.10	.35
474B	A145	150fr brt pink & blk ('86)	1.25	.40
474C	A145	175fr grnish bl & blk ('96)	.65	.55
		Nos. 466-474B (12)	7.00	3.40

Issued: 5fr, 10fr, 15fr, 20fr, 25fr, 40fr, 50fr, 75fr, 100fr, 7/1. See Nos. 862-871, 959-960.

R.P. Klaine (Missionary), 70th Death Anniv. — A146

90fr, Archbishop Walker, 110th birth anniv.

1981, July 2 Litho.

475 A146	70fr multi	.80	.30
476 A146	90fr multi	1.25	.35

Map of Gabon and Scout Sign — A147

1981, July 16 *Perf. 12½*

477 A147	75fr multi	1.00	.35

4th Pan-African Scouting Congress, Abidjan, Aug.

No. 477 Overprinted: DAKAR / 28e CONFERENCE / MONDIALE DU / SCOUTISME

1981, July 23

478 A147	75fr multi	1.50	.45

28th World Scouting Conf., Dakar, Aug.

Intl. Year of the Disabled — A148

1981, Aug. 6 Engr. *Perf. 13*

479 A148	100fr multi	1.50	.65

Hypolimnas Salmacis A149

100fr, Euphaedra themis. 150fr, Amauris niavius. 250fr, Cymothoe lucasi.

1981, Sept. 10 Litho. *Perf. 14½x14*

480 A149	75fr shown	1.75	.60
481 A149	100fr multicolored	2.25	.75
482 A149	150fr multicolored	2.75	1.00
483 A149	250fr multicolored	3.75	1.75
	Nos. 480-483 (4)	10.50	4.10

Paul as Harlequin, by Pablo Picasso (1881-1973) A150

1981, Sept. 25 *Perf. 14½x13½*

484 A150	500fr multi	7.00	2.50

World Food Day — A151

1981, Oct. 16 Engr. *Perf. 13*

485 A151	350fr multi	4.00	1.60

Traditional Hairstyle — A152

Designs: Various hairstyles.

1981, Nov. 12 Litho. *Perf. 14½x15*

486 A152	75fr multi	.90	.55
487 A152	100fr multi	1.00	.50
488 A152	125fr multi	1.60	.80
489 A152	200fr multi	2.50	1.10
a.	Souvenir sheet of 4, #486-489	6.50	6.50
	Nos. 486-489 (4)	6.00	2.95

See Nos. 609A-609B, 676.

Christmas 1981 A153

Designs: Children's drawings.

1981, Dec. 10 *Perf. 14½x14*

490 A153	75fr Girls dancing	.90	.35
491 A153	100fr Dinner	1.25	.50

Arms Type of 1969

No. 492, Moyen-Ogooue. No. 493, Cocobeach. No. 494, Woleu-N'tem. No. 495, Lambarene. No. 496, Port Gentil District. No. 497, Medouneu. No. 498, Mouila. No. 499, N'Djole. No. 500, N'Gounle. No. 501, Leconi.

Perf. 12, 13 (#495-497)

1982-92 Photo.

492	A67	75fr multicolored	.70	.25
493	A67	90fr multicolored	.90	.25
494	A67	100fr multicolored	1.00	.25
495	A67	100fr multicolored	.90	.30
496	A67	100fr multicolored	.90	.35
497	A67	100fr multicolored	.90	.35
498	A67	125fr multicolored	1.25	.35
499	A67	135fr multicolored	1.40	.40
500	A67	150fr multicolored	1.50	.40
501	A67	160fr multicolored	1.40	.60
		Nos. 492-501 (10)	10.85	3.50

Issued: Nos. 492, 494, 500, 1/13/82; Nos. 493, 498, 499, 8/7/84; Nos. 495, 501, 8/11/86; No. 496, 4/17/91; No. 497, 8/12/92.

A154

1982, Feb. 16 Litho. *Perf. 13*

502 A154	100fr multi	2.40	1.10

Visit of Pope John Paul II, Feb. 17-19.

A155

1982, Mar. 31 Engr. *Perf. 13*

503 A155	75fr black	1.50	.75

Alfred de Musset (1810-1857), writer.

Merchant Navy Ships A156

1982, Apr. 7 Litho. *Perf. 14½x14*

504 A156	75fr multicolored	.75	.30
505 A156	100fr Freighter	1.00	.40
506 A156	200fr Oil tanker	2.00	.85
	Nos. 504-506 (3)	3.75	1.55

See Nos. 588, 599.

TB Bacillus Centenary — A157

1982, Apr. 24 Litho. *Perf. 13*

507 A157	100fr multi	1.75	.75

PHILEXFRANCE '82 Stamp Exhibition, Paris, June 11-21 — A158

1982, Apr. 28 *Perf. 12½*

508 A158	100fr Rope bridge	.85	.40
509 A158	200fr Sculptured head	1.90	.55
a.	Pair, #508-509 + label	4.00	2.75

14th World Telecommunications Day — A159

1982, May 17 *Perf. 13*

510 A159	75fr multi	.90	.40

1982 World Cup — A160

Designs: Various soccer players.

1982, May 19 *Perf. 14x14½*

511 A160	100fr multi	1.00	.40
512 A160	125fr multi	1.10	.45
513 A160	200fr multi	2.10	.75
a.	Souvenir sheet of 3, #511-513, perf. 14½	5.00	5.00
	Nos. 511-513 (3)	4.20	1.60

For overprints see Nos. 516-518.

2nd UN Conf. on Peaceful Uses of Outer Space, Vienna, Aug. 9-21 — A161

1982, July 7 Engr. *Perf. 13*

514 A161	250fr Satellites	2.75	1.25

White Carnations A162

Designs: Various carnations.

1982, June 9 Photo. *Perf. 14½x14*

515	Strip of 3	4.50	1.75
a.	A162 75fr multi	.90	.45
b.	A162 100fr multi	1.10	.50
c.	A162 175fr multi	2.25	1.00

Nos. 511-513a Overprinted in Red with Semi-Finalists or Finalists

1982, Aug. 19 Litho. *Perf. 14x14½*

516 A160	100fr multi	1.00	.35
517 A160	125fr multi	1.10	.45
518 A160	200fr multi	2.10	.75
a.	Souvenir sheet of 3	5.00	5.00
	Nos. 516-518 (3)	4.20	1.55

Italy's victory in 1982 World Cup.

Phyllonotus Duplex A163

100fr, Chama crenulata. 125fr, Cardium hians.

1982, Sept. 22 *Perf. 14½x14*

519 A163	75fr shown	1.25	.50
520 A163	100fr multi	1.50	.65
521 A163	125fr multi	2.25	1.25
	Nos. 519-521 (3)	5.00	2.40

Okouyi Mask — A164

100fr, Ondoumbo reliquary. 150fr, Tsogho statuette. 250fr, Fang bellows.

1982, Oct. 13 Litho. *Perf. 14x14½*

522 A164 75fr shown .65 .30
523 A164 100fr multi 1.10 .40
524 A164 150fr multi 1.90 .55
525 A164 250fr multi 2.75 .95
Nos. 522-525 (4) 6.40 2.20

St. Francis Xavier Church — A165

1982, Dec. 15 Litho. *Perf. 14x14½*

526 A165 100fr multicolored .90 .35

Christmas 1982.

Trans-Gabon Railroad Inauguration — A166

1983, Jan. 18 *Perf. 12½*

527 A166 75fr multi 2.00 .50

5th African Highway Conference, Libreville, Feb. 6-11 — A167

1983, Feb. 2 *Perf. 13*

528 A167 100fr multi .90 .35

15th Anniv. of Natl. Renewal — A168

Provincial Symbols: a. Bakota mask, Ogowe Ivindo. b. Butterfly, Ogowe Lolo. c. Buffalo, Nyanga. d. Isogho hairdo, Ngounie. e. Tarpon, Ogowe Maritime. f. Manganese, Haut Ogowe. g. Crocodiles, Moyen Ogowe. h. Coffee plant. i. Epitorium trochiformis.

1983, Mar. 12 Litho. *Perf. 13x13½*

529 Strip of 9 + label 17.50 15.00
a. A168 75fr multi 1.00 .45
b. A168 90fr multi 1.25 .50
c. A168 90fr multi 1.25 .50
d. A168 100fr multi 1.40 .60
e. A168 125fr multi 1.60 .75
f. A168 125fr multi 1.60 .75
g. A168 125fr multi 1.60 .75
h. A168 135fr multi 1.90 .85
i. A168 135fr multi 1.90 .85

25th Anniv. of Intl. Maritime Org. — A169

1983, Mar. 17 *Perf. 13*

530 A169 125fr multi 1.40 .50

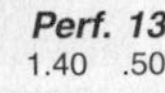

Pelican A170

90fr, Water musk deer. 225fr, Elephant. 400fr, Iguana.

1983, Apr. 20 Litho. *Perf. 15x14½*

531 A170 90fr multi .90 .35
532 A170 125fr shown 1.25 .45
533 A170 225fr multi 3.25 .85
534 A170 400fr multi 4.50 1.50
a. Souv. sheet of 4, #531-534 16.00 16.00
Nos. 531-534 (4) 9.90 3.15

25th Anniv. of UN Economic Commission for Africa A171

1983, Apr. 29 Litho. *Perf. 12½*

535 A171 125fr multi 1.25 .50

15th World Telecommunications Day — A172

1983, May 17 Litho. *Perf. 13*

536 A172 90fr multi 1.40 .55
537 A172 90fr multi 1.40 .55
a. Pair, #536-537 4.00 4.00

Denomination of No. 536 in lower right, No. 537, upper left.

Nkoltang Earth Satellite Station — A173

1983, July 2

538 A173 125fr multi 1.50 .60

10th anniv. of station; WCY.

Ivindo River Rapids — A174

125fr, Ogooue River. 185fr, Wonga Wongue Preserve. 350fr, Coastal view.

1983, Sept. 7 Engr. *Perf. 13*

539 A174 90fr shown .85 .35
540 A174 125fr multicolored 1.40 .60
541 A174 185fr multicolored 2.00 .80
542 A174 350fr multicolored 3.75 1.50
Nos. 539-542 (4) 8.00 3.25

Hand Drum, Mahongwe A175

125fr, Okoukoue dancer. 135fr, Four-stringed fiddle. 260fr, Ndoumou dancer.

1983, Oct. 12 Litho. *Perf. 14x14½*

543 A175 90fr shown .90 .35
544 A175 125fr multicolored 1.40 .45
545 A175 135fr multicolored 1.50 .60
546 A175 260fr multicolored 3.00 1.10
Nos. 543-546 (4) 6.80 2.50

Harmful Insects — A176

90fr, Glossinidae. 125fr, Belonogaster junceus. 300fr, Aedes aegypti. 350fr, Mylabris.

1983, Nov. 9

547 A176 90fr multicolored 1.60 .80
548 A176 125fr multicolored 2.00 1.10
549 A176 300fr multicolored 4.25 1.60
550 A176 350fr multicolored 5.25 2.10
Nos. 547-550 (4) 13.10 5.60

Christmas 1983 — A177

Wood Carvings, St. Michael's Church, Libreville — 90fr, Adultress. 125fr, Good Samaritan.

Perf. 14½x13½

1983, Dec. 14 Litho.

551 A177 90fr multicolored .80 .35
552 A177 125fr multicolored 1.40 .65

Boeing 737, No. 202 — A178

225fr, Lufthansa jet, Germany No. C2.

1984, Jan. 12 *Perf. 13x12½*

553 A178 125fr shown 1.50 .40
554 A178 225fr org & multi 3.00 .70
a. Pair, #553-554 + label 5.50 4.75

19th World UPU Congress, Hamburg, June 19-26.

3rd Anniv. of Africa 1 Radio Transmitter — A179

1984, Feb. 7 Litho. *Perf. 12½*

555 A179 125fr multi 1.50 .65

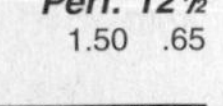

Local Flowers — A180

Various flowers.

1984, Apr. 18 Litho. *Perf. 14x15*

556 A180 90fr multi 1.25 .45
557 A180 125fr multi 1.40 .55
558 A180 135fr multi 1.90 .65
559 A180 350fr multi 4.00 1.60
Nos. 556-559 (4) 8.55 3.25

Fruit Trees A181

1984, Mar. 1 Litho. *Perf. 14½x14*

560 A181 90fr Coconut 1.15 .45
561 A181 100fr Papaya 1.40 .55
562 A181 125fr Mango 1.60 .65
563 A181 250fr Banana 3.75 1.25
Nos. 560-563 (4) 7.90 2.90

World Telecommunications Day — A182

1984, May 17 *Perf. 13x13½*

564 A182 125fr multi 1.50 .65

Black Jazz Musicians A183

1984, July 5 *Perf. 12½*

565 A183 90fr Lionel Hampton 1.75 .70
566 A183 125fr Charlie Parker 2.40 .70
567 A183 260fr Erroll Garner 3.75 1.75
Nos. 565-567 (3) 7.90 3.15

View of Medouneu — A184

125fr, Canoes, Ogooue River. 165fr, Railroad.

1984, Sept. 1 Litho. *Perf. 13*

568	A184	90fr shown	.95	.40
569	A184	125fr multi	1.50	.55
570	A184	165fr multi	2.50	1.25
		Nos. 568-570 (3)	4.95	2.20

15th World UPU Day — A185

125fr, UPU emblem, globe, mail.

1984, Oct. 9 Litho. *Perf. 13½*

571 A185 125fr multi 1.40 .50

40th Anniv., International Civil Aviation Organization — A186

1984, Dec. 1 Litho. *Perf. 13½*

572 A186 125fr Icarus 1.50 .65

Masks — A186a

90fr, Kouele. 125fr, Eventail Pounou. 150fr, Reliquaire Mahongoue. 250fr, Kota du Sud.

1984, Oct. 30 Litho. *Perf. 14x15*

572A	A186a	90fr multicolored	—	—
572B	A186a	125fr multicolored	—	—
572C	A186a	150fr multicolored	—	—
572D	A186a	250fr multicolored	—	—

Christmas — A187

90fr, St. Michael's Church Libreville. 125fr, St. Michael's, diff.

1984, Dec. 14 Litho. *Perf. 12½*

573		90fr multi	.90	.45
574		125fr multi	1.40	.65
a.		A187 Pair, #573-574	3.00	2.50

World Leprosy Day — A188

1985, Jan. 27 Litho. *Perf. 12½*

575 A188 125fr Hospital, Libreville 1.50 .55

International Youth Year — A189

1985, Feb. 6 Litho. *Perf. 13x12½*

576 A189 125fr Silhouttes, wreath 1.40 .50

Birds A190

1984, Nov. 16 Litho. *Perf. 15x14*

577	A190	90fr Crowned crane	1.25	.75
578	A190	125fr Hummingbird	2.00	1.00
579	A190	150fr Toucan	2.50	1.25
		Nos. 577-579 (3)	5.75	3.00

Silhouettes, Emblem — A191

1985, Mar. 20 Wmk. 385 *Perf. 12½*

580 A191 125fr brt ultra, red & bl 1.50 .75

Cultural and Technical Cooperation Agency, 15th anniv.

Wildlife A192

1985, Apr. 17 Unwmk. *Perf. 15x14*

581	A192	90fr Aulacode	1.50	.50
582	A192	100fr Porcupine	1.50	.50
583	A192	125fr Giant pangolin	2.00	1.00
584	A192	350fr Antelope	5.00	2.25
a.		Souvenir sheet of 4, #581-584	13.00	13.00
		Nos. 581-584 (4)	10.00	4.25

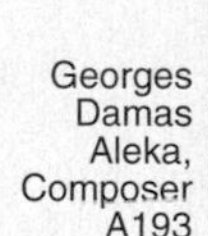

Georges Damas Aleka, Composer A193

90fr, Portrait, La Concorde score.

1985, Apr. 30 *Perf. 13*

585 A193 90fr multicolored 1.20 .35

ITU, 120th Anniv. — A194

1985, May 17 *Perf. 13½*

586 A194 125fr multi 1.50 .65

World Telecommunications Day.

A195

1985, June 9

587 A195 90fr Emblem 1.10 .60

Christian Youth Workers' Movement (J.O.C.) in Gabon, 30th anniv.

Merchant Navy Ships Type of 1982

1985, July 1 *Perf. 15x14*

588 A156 185fr Freighter Mpassa 2.25 .80

Posts and Telecommunications Administration, 20th Anniv. — A196

1985, July 25 *Perf. 13*

589 A196 90fr Headquarters 1.10 .50

President Bongo — A197

1000fr, View of Libreville.

1985, Aug. 17 *Perf. 14*

590	A197	250fr multi	3.50	1.60
591	A197	500fr multi	7.75	4.00
a.		Pair, #590-591 + 3 labels	14.00	14.00

Imperf

Size: 120x90mm

592	A197	1000fr multi	14.00	14.00
		Nos. 590-592 (3)	25.25	19.60

Natl. Independence, 25th anniv.

No. 592 has non-denominated vignettes of Nos. 590-591.

Org. of Petroleum Exporting Countries, 25th Anniv. — A198

1985, Sept. 25 Wmk. 385 *Perf. 13½*

593 A198 350fr multi 4.00 1.90

Intl. Center of the Bantu Civilizations — A199

Perf. 15x14

1985, Nov. 16 Litho. Unwmk.

594 A199 185fr multi 2.00 .95

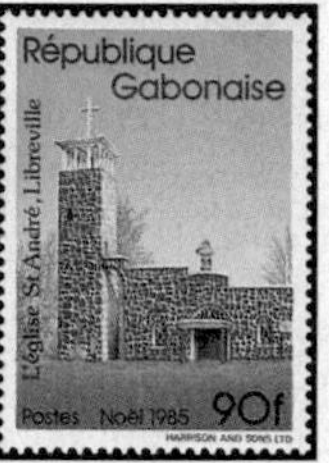

St. Andrew's Church, Libreville — A199a

Design: 125fr, Church interior, horiz.

Perf. 14x15, 15x14

1985, Dec. 16 Litho.

594A	A199a	90fr multicolored	—	—
594B	A199a	125fr multicolored		—

Christmas.

UNESCO, 25th Anniv. — A200

1986, Jan. 5 Litho. *Perf. 12½*

595 A200 100fr multi 1.10 .45

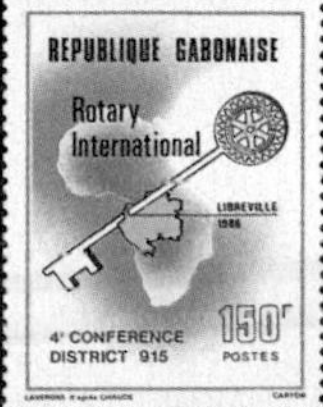

A201

1986, May 1 Litho. *Perf. 13½*

596 A201 150fr multi 1.75 .60

Rotary Intl. District 915, 4th conf.

A202

1986, June 16 Litho. *Perf. 12½*
597 A202 150fr multi 1.75 .60

Natl. Week of Cartography, Libreville, June 16-20.

Coffee Flowers, Berries, Beans — A203

1986, Aug. 27 Litho. *Perf. 12½*
598 A203 125fr multi 1.50 .90

Organization of African and Madagascar Coffee Producers, 25th anniv.

Merchant Navy Ships Type of 1982

250fr, Merchantman L'Abanga.

1986, June 24 Litho. *Perf. 15x14*
599 A156 250fr multicolored 3.00 1.25

Natl. Postage Stamp, Cent. — A205

1986, July 10 *Perf. 13½x14½*
600 A205 500fr Boats, No. 4 7.00 3.50

Flowering Plants — A206

100fr, Allamanda neriifolia. 150fr, Musa cultivar. 160fr, Dissotis decumbens. 350fr, Campylospermum laeve.

1986, July 23 *Perf. 14½x15*
601 A206 100fr multicolored 1.25 .50
602 A206 150fr multicolored 1.90 .80
603 A206 160fr multicolored 2.10 .85
604 A206 350fr multicolored 4.75 2.10
Nos. 601-604 (4) 10.00 4.25

Butterflies A207

1986, Sept. 18 Litho. *Perf. 15x14*
605 A207 150fr Machaon 2.40 .60
606 A207 290fr Urania 4.75 1.40

St. Pierre Church, Libreville A208

1986, Dec. 23 Litho. *Perf. 15x14½*
607 A208 500fr multi 4.50 1.50

Christmas.

Trans-Gabon Railway from Owendo to Franceville, Inauguration — A209

1986, Dec. 30 *Perf. 13*
608 A209 90fr multi 1.40 .50

Souvenir Sheet

609 A209 250fr multi 4.50 4.50

Traditional Hairstyles Type of 1981

1986, Nov. 10 Litho. *Perf. 14x15*
609A A152 100fr blk, gray & yell *150.00 7.50*
609B A152 150fr tan, blk & red brn 5.00 1.50

Fish A210

90fr, Adioryx bastatus. 125fr, Scarus boefleri. 225fr, Cephalacanthus volitans. 350fr, Dasyatis marmorata.

1987, Jan. 15 *Perf. 15x14½*
610 A210 90fr multicolored 1.25 .60
611 A210 125fr multicolored 1.75 .85
612 A210 225fr multicolored 2.25 1.25
613 A210 350fr multicolored 3.25 1.90
a. Souv. sheet of 4, Nos. 610-613 11.50 11.50
Nos. 610-613 (4) 8.50 4.60

No. 613a issued Oct. 1987.

Raoul Follereau (1903-1977) A211

1987, Jan. 23 *Perf. 12½*
614 A211 125fr multi 1.75 .85

World Leprosy Day.

Pres. Bongo Accepting the 1986 Dag Hammarskjold Peace Prize — A212

1987, Mar. 31 Litho. *Perf. 13*
615 A212 125fr multi 1.25 .60

World Telecommunications Day — A213

1987, May 17 Litho. *Perf. 13½*
616 A213 90fr multi 1.10 .40

Lions Club of Gabon, 30th Anniv. — A214

1987, July 18 Litho. *Perf. 12x12½*
617 A214 90fr multi 1.10 .40

Pierre de Coubertin, Father of the Modern Olympics A215

1987, Aug. 29
618 A215 200fr multi 2.10 .85

Lions Club Intl., 70th Anniv. — A216

1987, Oct. 1
619 A216 165fr multi 1.75 .65

World Post Day — A217

1987, Oct. 9 Litho. *Perf. 13½*
620 A217 125fr multi 1.50 .75

Seashells A218

1987, Feb. 20 *Perf. 15x14*
621 A218 90fr Natica fanel 1.20 .35
622 A218 125fr Natica fulminea cruentata 2.60 .45
a. Souv. sheet of 2, Nos. 621-622 7.00 7.00

Intl. Year of Shelter for the Homeless — A219

1987, Oct. 5 *Perf. 12½*
623 A219 90fr multi 1.10 .40

Solidarity with the South West African Peoples' Organization (SWAPO) — A220

225fr, Pres. Bongo, SWAPO leader.

1987, Sept. 15 Litho. *Perf. 14½x15*
624 A220 225fr multicolored 2.10 .95

St. Anna of Odimba Mission — A221

1987, Nov. 2 *Perf. 13½*
625 A221 90fr multi 1.00 .30

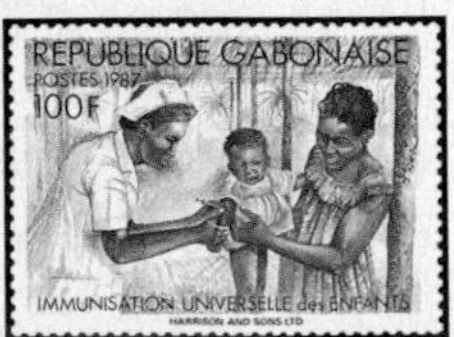

Universal Child Immunization — A222

1987, Nov. 16 *Perf. 15x14½*
626 A222 100fr multi 1.25 .40

20th Anniv. of the Presidency of Omar Bongo
A223

1987, Dec. 2 *Perf. 14½x13½*
627 A223 1000fr multi 10.00 5.50

Christmas
A224

90fr, St. Therese Church, Oyem.

1987, Dec. 15 *Perf. 15x14½*
628 A224 90fr multicolored 1.00 .30

1988 Winter Olympics, Calgary — A225

1987, Dec. 30 *Perf. 13½x14½*
629 A225 125fr multi 1.25 .50

Medicinal Plants — A226

90fr, Cassia occidentalis. 125fr, Tabernanthe iboga. 225fr, Cassia alata. 350fr, Anthocleista schweinfurthii.

1988, Jan. 26 **Litho.** *Perf. 14x15*
630 A226 90fr multicolored 1.10 .55
631 A226 125fr multicolored 1.50 .55
632 A226 225fr multicolored 2.75 1.10
633 A226 350fr multicolored 5.00 2.75
a. Miniature sheet of 4, #630-633 12.00 12.00
Nos. 630-633 (4) 10.35 4.95

World Wildlife Fund — A227

African forest elephant, Loxodonta africana cyclotis.

1988, Feb. 29 **Litho.** *Perf. 13½*
634 A227 25fr multi 2.25 .75
635 A227 40fr multi, diff. 3.00 1.50
636 A227 50fr multi, diff. 5.00 1.75
637 A227 100fr multi, diff. 8.25 3.25
Nos. 634-637 (4) 18.50 7.25

Traditional Musical Instruments — A228

90fr, Obamba hochet. 100fr, Fang sanza, vert. 125fr, Mitsogho harp, vert. 165fr, Fang xylophone.

1988, Feb. 17 *Perf. 14*
638 A228 90fr multicolored 1.10 .70
639 A228 100fr multicolored 1.20 .70
640 A228 125fr multicolored 1.50 .90
641 A228 165fr multicolored 2.40 1.00
a. Souv. sheet of 4, Nos. 638-641 7.00 7.00
Nos. 638-641 (4) 6.20 3.30

World Cup Rugby — A229

Perf. 13½x14½
1987, June 10 **Litho.**
642 A229 350fr multi 4.25 1.90

Delta Post Office Inauguration — A230

1988, Mar. 9
643 A230 90fr multi 1.00 .30

World Telecommunications Day — A231

1988, May 17 *Perf. 13½*
644 A231 125fr multi 1.25 .45

Storming of the Bastille, July 14, 1789 — A232

1988, May 30 **Litho.** *Perf. 13*
645 A232 125fr multi 1.60 .50

PHILEXFRANCE '89.

Intl. Fund for Agricultural Development (IFAD), 10th Anniv. — A233

1988, June 20 *Perf. 13½*
646 A233 350fr multi 4.25 1.60

Intl. Red Cross and Red Crescent Organizations, 125th Annivs. — A234

1988, July 15 **Litho.** *Perf. 12½*
647 A234 125fr multi 1.25 .45

1988 Summer Olympics, Seoul
A235

1988, Sept. 17 **Litho.** *Perf. 15x14*
648 A235 90fr Tennis 1.00 .35
649 A235 100fr Swimming 1.00 .45
650 A235 350fr Running 3.75 1.60
651 A235 500fr Hurdles 5.75 2.00
a. Souv. sheet of 4, #648-651 13.00 13.00
Nos. 648-651 (4) 11.50 4.40

World Post Day
A236

1988, Oct. 9 *Perf. 13½*
652 A236 125fr blk, brt yel & brt blue 1.25 .45

Christmas
A237

200fr, Medouneu Church.

1988, Dec. 20 **Litho.** *Perf. 15x14*
653 A237 200fr multi 2.00 .70

Natica Fanel — A237a

1988, July 1 **Litho.** *Perf. 15x14*
653A A237a 90fr shown *24.00 5.00*
653B A237a 125fr Natica sp. *24.00 7.50*
c. Souv. sheet of 2, #653A-653B *60.00* —

A238

1989, Feb. 21 *Perf. 13½*
654 A238 175fr multi 1.50 .60

Chaine des Rotisseurs in Gabon, 10th anniv.

A239

1989, Mar. 6 **Litho.** *Perf. 13½*
655 A239 125fr multi 1.40 .55

Rabi Kounga oil field. See No. 707.

REPUBLIQUE GABONAISE

Traditional Games — A240

Perf. 13½x14½
1989, Mar. 20 **Litho.**
656 A240 90fr multicolored 1.10 .55

Birds — A241

100fr, White-tufted bittern. 175fr, Gabon gray parakeet. 200fr, Pygmy hornbill. 500fr, Pope's martin.

1989, Apr. 17 **Litho.** *Perf. 14x15*
657 A241 100fr multicolored 1.00 .35
658 A241 175fr multicolored 1.50 .65
659 A241 200fr multicolored 1.90 .70
660 A241 500fr multicolored 4.75 2.10
a. Souv. sheet of 4, Nos. 657-660 11.00 11.00
Nos. 657-660 (4) 9.15 3.80

See Nos. 750-753.

A242

1989, Apr. 27 *Perf. 13*
661 A242 125fr multi 1.25 .45

8th Convention of Lions Intl. District 403, Libreville, Apr. 27-29.

World Telecommunications Day — A243

1989, May 17 Wmk. 385 ***Perf. 13½***
662 A243 300fr multi 3.25 1.10

PHILEXFRANCE '89 — A244

Symbols of the French revolution, 1789.

Wmk. 385
1989, July 7 Litho. ***Perf. 13***
663 A244 175fr multi 2.10 .80

French Revolution, Bicent. — A245

1989, July 14 Wmk. 385
664 A245 500fr multi 6.50 3.25

Fruit — A246

Perf. 14½x15
1989, May 30 Litho. Unwmk.

665 A246	90fr Coconuts	1.00	.45
666 A246	125fr Cabosse	1.50	.50
667 A246	175fr Pineapple	2.25	.80
668 A246	250fr Breadfruit	2.75	1.25
a.	Souv. sheet of 4, #665-668	8.50	8.50
	Nos. 665-668 (4)	7.50	3.00

A247

1989, July 27 Litho. ***Perf. 13***
669 A247 100fr multi 1.25 .50

International Association of Francophone Mayors (AIMF), 10th anniv.

African Development Bank, 25th Anniv. — A248

1989, Aug. 2 Litho. ***Perf. 13***
670 A248 100fr multi 1.00 .40

Apples and Oranges, by Cezanne (1839-1906) — A249

Perf. 13½x14½
1989, June 22 Litho.
671 A249 500fr multicolored 6.00 3.25

1990 World Cup Soccer Championships, Italy — A250

Various athletes.

Perf. 15x14½
1989, Aug. 23 Litho. Unwmk.

672 A250	100fr shown	.95	.35
673 A250	175fr multi, diff.	1.75	.65
674 A250	300fr multi, diff.	3.00	1.25
675 A250	500fr multi, diff.	4.75	1.90
a.	Souv. sheet of 4, #672-675	11.00	11.00
	Nos. 672-675 (4)	10.45	4.15

Traditional Hairstyles Type of 1981

1989, Sept. 16 ***Perf. 14½x15***
676 A152 175fr gray, black & vio 2.00 .85

Post Day — A252

Granite Paper

1989, Sept. 10 Litho. ***Perf. 12***
677 A252 175fr multicolored 1.75 .80

Postal Service, 125th Anniv. (in 1987) — A255

Perf. 13½x14½
1989 Litho. Unwmk.
681 A255 90fr multicolored 10.00 2.75

Dated 1988.

St. Louis Church, Port Gentil A256

1989, Dec. 15 Litho. ***Perf. 15x14***
682 A256 100fr multicolored 1.00 .40

Christmas. See Nos. 725-726, 757.

L'Ogooue', N'Gomo

1989, Nov. 18 Litho. ***Perf. 15x14***
682A A256a 100fr multicolored — —

Libreville Coat of Arms — A257

Wmk. 385
1990, Mar. 12 Litho. ***Perf. 13½***
683 A257 100fr multicolored 1.10 .55

World Health Day — A258

Unwmk.
1990, Apr. 7 Litho. ***Perf. 13***
684 A258 400fr multicolored 4.50 2.10

Prehistoric Tools A259

Designs: 100fr, Hand axe. 175fr, Knife blade. 300fr, Arrowhead. 400fr, Double-bladed hand axe.

1990, Feb. 14 Litho. ***Perf. 15x14***

685 A259	100fr multi	1.25	.60
685A A259	175fr multi	2.10	1.40
685B A259	300fr multi	3.75	1.50
685C A259	400fr multi	6.25	4.50
d.	Souvenir sheet of 4, #685-685C	30.00	30.00
	Nos. 685-685C (4)	13.35	8.00

See Nos. 727-730.

Fauna — A260

Designs: No. 686, 100fr, Cercopitheque. No. 686A, 175fr, Potamochoerus porcus, horiz. No. 686B, 200fr, Antilope du Gabon, horiz. No. 686C, 500fr, Papio mandrillus sphinx.

1990, Apr. 13 ***Perf. 14***
686-686C A260 Set of 4 14.00 8.00
686Cd Souvenir sheet of 4, #686-686C, + label *15.00 15.00*

First Postage Stamps, 150th Anniv. — A261

1991, Jan. 9 ***Perf. 13½x14½***
687 A261 500fr multicolored 7.00 3.50

Independence, 30th Anniv. — A263

1990, Aug. 17 Litho. ***Perf. 13***
693 A263 100fr multicolored 1.10 .50

Mushrooms — A263a

Various mushrooms.

1990, Sept. 12 Litho. ***Perf. 15x14***

693A A263a	100fr multicolored	*6.00*	*1.10*
693B A263a	175fr multicolored	*12.00*	*2.25*
693C A263a	300fr multicolored	*17.50*	*4.25*
693D A263a	500fr multicolored	*24.50*	*6.50*
	Nos. 693A-693D (4)	*60.00*	*14.10*

Organization of Petroleum Exporting Countries (OPEC), 30th anniv. — A264

1990, Sept. 19 Litho. ***Perf. 13***
694 A264 200fr multicolored 2.00 1.00

1990 World Cup Soccer Championships, Italy — A264a

100fr, Goalie making save. 175fr, Four players, ball. 300fr, Goalie reaching for ball. 500fr, Player celebrating.

1990, June 8 Litho. *Perf. 15x14*

694A A264a 100fr multi *10.00 5.00*
694B A264a 175fr multi *10.00 5.00*
694C A264a 300fr multi — —
694D A264a 500fr multi *10.00 5.00*
e. Souvenir sheet, #604A-694D — —

World Post Day — A265

1990, Oct. 9 *Perf. 13½*

695 A265 175fr blue, yel & blk 2.00 1.00

Traditional Bwiti Dancer — A265a

100fr, Ndjembe dancers.

1990, Apr. 25 Litho. *Perf. 15x14*

695A A265a 100fr multi —
695B A265a 175fr shown —

Flowers A266

100fr, Frangipanier. 175fr, Boule de feu. 200fr, Flamboyant. 300fr, Rose de porcelaine.

1991, Jan. 9 Litho. *Perf. 15x14*

696 A266 100fr multi 1.25 .60
697 A266 175fr multi 2.10 1.00
698 A266 200fr multi 2.40 1.10
699 A266 300fr multi 3.75 1.75
a. Souvenir sheet of 4, #696-699 10.00 10.00
Nos. 696-699 (4) 9.50 4.45

Petroglyphs — A267

100fr, Lizard figure. 175fr, Triangular figure. 300fr, Incused lines. 500fr, Concentric circles, circles in lines.

1991, Feb. 26 Litho. *Perf. 15x14*

700 A267 100fr multi 1.25 .60
701 A267 175fr multi 2.00 1.25
702 A267 300fr multi 3.50 1.50
703 A267 500fr multi 5.75 3.00
a. Souvenir sheet of 4, #700-703 75.00 75.00
Nos. 700-703 (4) 12.50 6.35

Rubber Trees — A268

1991, Mar. 20 Litho. *Perf. 14x15*

705 A268 100fr multicolored 1.00 .45

World Telecommunications Day — A269

1991, May 17 Litho. *Perf. 13½*

706 A269 175fr multicolored 1.90 .95

Rabi Kounga Oil Field Type of 1989

1991 Litho. *Perf. 13½*

707 A239 175fr multicolored *150.00*

Ngounie Women Washing Clothes A271

1991, July 17 Litho. *Perf. 13½*

708 A271 100fr multicolored 1.00 .45

Craftsmen A272

1991, June 19 *Perf. 14x15*

709 A272 100fr Basket maker 1.10 .55
710 A272 175fr Wood carver 1.90 .95
711 A272 200fr Weaver 2.25 1.10
712 A272 500fr Thatch maker 5.75 2.75
a. Souvenir sheet of 4, #709-712 — —
Nos. 709-712 (4) 11.00 5.35

A273

Gabonese Medals: 100fr, Equatorial Knight's Star. 175fr, Equatorial Officer's Star. 200fr, Equatorial Commander's Star.

1991, Aug. 18 Litho. *Perf. 14x15*
Gray Background

713 A273 100fr multicolored 1.00 .50
714 A273 175fr multicolored 1.75 .90
715 A273 200fr multicolored 2.00 1.00
Nos. 713-715 (3) 4.75 2.40

See Nos. 735-737.

Fishing in Gabon A274

100fr, Bow-net fishing. 175fr, Trammel fishing. 200fr, Net fishing. 300fr, Seine fishing.

1991, Sept. 18 *Perf. 15x14*

716 A274 100fr multi 1.25 .55
717 A274 175fr multi 1.60 .95
718 A274 200fr multi 2.25 1.10
719 A274 300fr multi 3.25 1.75
a. Souvenir sheet of 4, #716-719 9.50 9.50
Nos. 716-719 (4) 8.35 4.35

World Post Day — A275

1991, Oct. 9 *Perf. 13½*

720 A275 175fr blue & multi 2.00 .95

See Nos. 749, 786.

Termite Mounds — A276

1991, Nov. 6 *Perf. 14x15*

721 A276 100fr Phallic 1.50 .60
722 A276 175fr Cathedral 2.50 1.00
723 A276 200fr Mushroom 3.00 1.10
724 A276 300fr Arboreal 4.00 1.75
Nos. 721-724 (4) 11.00 4.45

Church Type of 1989

No. 725, Church of Makokou. No. 726, Church of Dibwangui.

1991, Dec. 18 Litho. *Perf. 15x14*

725 A256 100fr multicolored 1.00 .40
726 A256 100fr multicolored 1.00 .40

Christmas. No. 725 inscribed 1990.

Prehistoric Tools Type of 1990

Pottery: 100fr, Neolithic pot. 175fr, Bottle, 8th cent. 200fr, Vase, 8th cent. 300fr, Vase, 8th cent, diff.

1992, Jan. 9 Litho. *Perf. 14x15*

727 A259 100fr multi, vert. 1.10 .40
728 A259 175fr multi, vert. 1.90 .75
729 A259 200fr multi, vert. 2.50 .85
730 A259 300fr multi, vert. 3.00 1.25
a. Sheet of 4, #727-730 9.50 9.50
Nos. 727-730 (4) 8.50 3.25

Occupations A277

1992, Feb. 5

731 A277 100fr Basket maker 1.10 .55
732 A277 175fr Blacksmith 1.90 .95
733 A277 200fr Boat builder 2.10 1.10
734 A277 300fr Hairdresser 3.25 1.75
a. Souvenir sheet of 4, #731-734 9.50 9.50
Nos. 731-734 (4) 8.35 4.35

No. 734a issued Feb. 9.

Gabonese Medals Type of 1991

Designs: 100fr, Equatorial Grand Officer's Star. 175fr, Grand Cross of Dignity and Equatorial Star. 200fr, Order of Merit.

1992, Mar. 18 Litho. *Perf. 14x15*
Aquamarine Background

735 A273 100fr multicolored .95 .50
736 A273 175fr multicolored 1.90 .90
737 A273 200fr multicolored 2.25 1.00
Nos. 735-737 (3) 5.10 2.40

A278

1992, Apr. 19 *Perf. 13*

738 A278 500fr multicolored 6.00 3.00

Konrad Adenauer (1876-1967), German Statesman.

A279

1992, May 17 *Perf. 13½*

739 A279 175fr multicolored 2.00 .95

World Telecommunications Day.

Butterflies A280

100fr, Graphium policenes. 175fr, Acraea egina.

1992, June 10 Litho. *Perf. 15x14*

740 A280 100fr multi 1.90 1.25
741 A280 175fr multi 2.75 1.75

A281

1992, July 25 *Perf. 14x15*

742 A281 100fr Cycling 1.10 .55
743 A281 175fr Boxing 2.00 1.00
744 A281 200fr Pole vault 2.25 1.10
Nos. 742-744 (3) 5.35 2.65

1992 Summer Olympics, Barcelona.

Tribal Masks — A282

1992, Sept. 16 Litho. *Perf. 14x15*

745 A282 100fr Fang 1.00 .50
746 A282 175fr Mpongwe 1.90 .95
747 A282 200fr Kwele 2.10 1.00
748 A282 300fr Pounou 3.25 1.60
a. Souvenir sheet of 4, #745-748 9.50 9.50
Nos. 745-748 (4) 8.25 4.05

World Post Day Type of 1991 Inscribed 1992

1992, Oct. 9 Litho. *Perf. 13½*

749 A275 175fr bl grn & multi 2.00 .95

Bird Type of 1989

100fr, African owl. 175fr, Coliou strie. 200fr, Vulture. 300fr, Giant kingfisher.

1992, Nov. 4 Litho. *Perf. 14x15*

750	A241 100fr multi		2.10	.50
751	A241 175fr multi		3.50	1.00
752	A241 200fr multi		4.50	1.20
753	A241 300fr multi		6.75	1.50
a.	Souvenir sheet of 4, #750-753		22.50	22.50
	Nos. 750-753 (4)		16.85	4.20

Cattle A283

Various scenes of cattle in pasture.

1992, Dec. 10 *Perf. 15x14*

754	A283 100fr multicolored	1.00	.50
755	A283 175fr multicolored	1.75	.90
756	A283 200fr multicolored	2.00	1.00
	Nos. 754-756 (3)	4.75	2.40

Church Type of 1989

100fr, Tchibanga Church.

1992, Dec. 16

757	A256 100fr multi	1.00	.40

Christmas.

Intl. Conference on Nutrition, Rome — A284

1992, Dec. 20 *Perf. 13½*

758	A284 100fr multicolored	1.00	.40

Shells A285

1993, Jan. 6 Litho. *Perf. 15x14*

759	A285 100fr Pugilina	.90	.40
760	A285 175fr Conus pulcher	1.90	.70
761	A285 200fr Fusinus	2.25	.80
762	A285 300fr Cymatium	3.50	1.25
a.	Souvenir sheet, #759-762	*14.00*	*14.00*
	Nos. 759-762 (4)	8.55	3.15

World Leprosy Day A286

1993, Jan. 28 *Perf. 13½*

763	A286 175fr multicolored	2.00	.95

Fernan-Vaz Mission A287

1993, Feb. 3 *Perf. 15x14*

764	A287 175fr multicolored	2.50	1.25

Chappe's Semaphore Telegraph, Bicent. — A288

Designs: 100fr, Claude Chappe (1763-1805), engineer and inventor. 175fr, Chappe's signaling device and code. 200fr, Emile Baudot (1845-1903), devising telegraph code, early telegraph equipment. 300fr, Modern satellite, electronic chip and fiber optics.

1993, Mar. 10 Litho. *Perf. 13½*

765	A288 100fr multicolored	1.00	.50
766	A288 175fr multicolored	1.75	.90
767	A288 200fr multicolored	2.00	1.10
768	A288 300fr multicolored	3.25	1.60
a.	Souvenir sheet of 4, #765-768	9.50	9.50
	Nos. 765-768 (4)	8.00	4.10

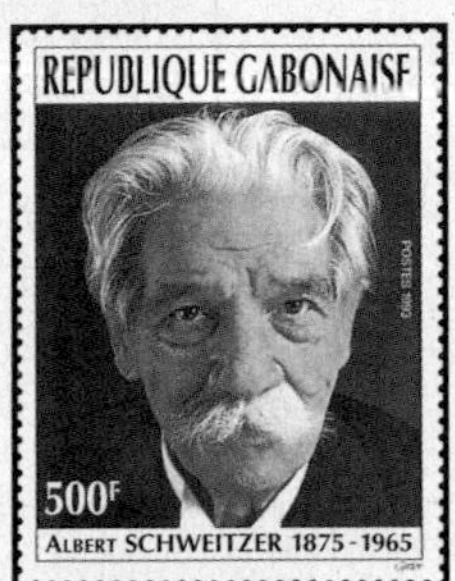

Albert Schweitzer's Arrival in Lambarene, 80th Anniv. — A289

No. 770, Feeding chickens. No. 771, Holding babies.

1993, Apr. 6 Litho. *Perf. 13*

769	A289 500fr multicolored	6.00	2.75
a.	Booklet pane of 1	6.50	

Booklet Stamps
Size: 26x37mm
Perf. 13½

770	A289 250fr multi	3.50	1.40
a.	Booklet pane of 4	20.00	
771	A289 250fr multi	3.50	1.40
a.	Booklet pane of 4	20.00	
	Nos. 769-771 (3)	13.00	5.55

Booklet containing one of each pane sold for 3000fr. Value $40.

Nicolaus Copernicus, Heliocentric Solar System A290

1993, May 5 Litho. *Perf. 15x14*

772	A290 175fr multicolored	1.60	.75

Polska '93.

A291

1993, May 17 *Perf. 13½*

773	A291 175fr multicolored	1.60	.75

World Telecommunications Day.

A292

Traditional Wine Making: 100fr, Still. 175fr, Extracting juice from palm roots. 200fr, Man in palm tree.

1993, June 9 Litho. *Perf. 14*

774	A292 100fr multicolored	1.00	.45
775	A292 175fr multicolored	1.60	.80
776	A292 200fr multicolored	1.90	.95
a.	Souvenir sheet of 3, #774-776	6.00	6.00
	Nos. 774-776 (3)	4.50	2.20

Crustaceans — A293

1993, July 21 Litho. *Perf. 15x14*

777	A293 100fr Spiny lobster	.90	.60
778	A293 175fr Violin crab	1.45	.95
779	A293 200fr Crayfish	1.90	1.10
780	A293 300fr Spider crab	2.75	1.60
a.	Souvenir sheet of 4, #777-780	—	—
	Nos. 777-780 (4)	7.00	4.25

Paris '94 — A294

1993, Aug. 10 Litho. *Perf. 13*

781	A294 100fr multicolored	1.10	.50

Animal Traps A295

1993, Sept. 15 Litho. *Perf. 15x14*

782	A295 100fr Squirrel	1.10	.25
783	A295 175fr Small game	1.75	.55
784	A295 200fr Large game	1.90	.90
785	A295 300fr Palm rat	3.25	1.40
a.	Souvenir sheet of 4, #782-785	6.00	6.00
	Nos. 782-785 (4)	8.00	3.10

World Post Day Type of 1991
Inscribed 1993

1993, Oct. 9 *Perf. 13½*

786	A275 175fr yellow & multi	1.75	.75

Making Bamboo Toys — A296

1993, Oct. 20 *Perf. 11½*

787	A296 100fr multicolored	1.10	.55

Tourism A297

1993, Nov. 16

788	A297 100fr Leconi Canyon	1.00	.25
789	A297 175fr La Lope Valley	1.60	.50

Christmas A298

100fr, Catholic Mission, Mandji.

1993, Dec. 20 *Perf. 15x14*

790	A298 100fr multi	1.10	.55

Provincial Map — A299

1993-94 Litho. *Perf. 14½*

791	A299 5fr yel & multi ('94)	—	*6.00*
792	A299 10fr gray & multi ('93)	—	*6.00*
a.	Dated 1994	—	6.00
793	A299 25fr pink & multi ('93)	—	*6.00*
a.	Dated 1994	—	6.00
794	A299 50fr grn & multi ('93)	—	*6.00*
795	A299 75fr lilac & multi ('94)	—	*6.00*
796	A299 100fr brnsh pink & multi ('94)	—	*6.00*
797	A299 175fr multi ('94)	—	*6.00*

Issued: 10fr, 25fr, 50fr, 3/25; 5fr, 75fr, 100fr, 175fr, 1/28/94.

Nos. 792 and 793 are dated 1993.

Vision of Gabon's Future — A300

1994, Oct. 5 Litho. *Perf. 14½*

798	A300 500fr multicolored	*3.00*	*1.50*

1994 World Cup Soccer Championships, US — A301

Designs: a, 100fr, Hands on soccer ball. b, 175fr, Two players, ball in air. c, 200fr, Legs of players. d, 300fr, Player, ball.

1994, Apr. 5 *Perf. 15x14*

799	A301 Sheet of 4, #a.-d.	*35.00*	*35.00*

UN, 50th Anniv. — A301a

1995, July 5 Litho. *Perf. 11¾x11½*

799E	A301a 500fr multi	30.00	15.00

Prehistoric Wildlife — A302

No. 800: a, Sordes. b, Diplodocus (d-e, g-h). c, Eudimorphodon (b). d, Dimetrodon (a). e, Anuroenathus. f, Deinonychus, pachycephalosaurus (e). g, Triceratops (j). h, Hadrosaur (i, k-l). i, Genus Meganeura. j, Longisquama. k, Oviraptor. l, Monoclonius.

No. 801: a, Pistosaurus (d-e, h). b, Pteranodon (c). c, Coelophysis. d, Xenacanthus (g). e, Ischyodus (f, h-i). f, Placochelys. g, Dunkleosteus (j). h, Cymbospondylus (i). i, Enchodus. j, Paracybeloides (k). k, Nautiliod (h). l, Palaeospondylus.

No. 802: a, Tyrannosaurus rex (d). b, Apatosaurus (a, d-e). c, Dimorphodon. d, Stegasaurus (a, e). e, Archaeopteryx. f, Protoceratops. g, Ichthyosaur. h, Phobosuchus, deltoptychius. i, Parasaurolophus (f). j, Scapanorhynchus (g). k, Spathobathis, plesiosaurus (j, l). l, Cladoselacho.

1995, Sept. 4 Litho. *Perf. 14*

800 A302 125fr Sheet of 12, #a.-l. 8.00 8.00
801 A302 225fr Sheet of 12, #a.-l. 13.50 13.50
802 A302 260fr Sheet of 12, #a.-l. 16.00 16.00
Nos. 800-802 (3) 37.50 37.50

Singapore '95 (No. 800).

Nobel Prize Fund Established, Cent. — A303

No. 803 — Nobel Prize recipients: a, Walter H. Brattain, physics, 1956. b, Carl F. Cori, medicine, 1947. c, Gerty T. Cori, medicine, 1947. d, Owen Chamberlain, physics, 1959. e, Christian Anfinsen, chemistry, 1972. f, George de Hevesy, chemistry, 1943. g, Kenichi Fukui, chemistry, 1981. h, Elie Wiesel, peace, 1986. i, Carl F. Braun, physics, 1909.

No. 804: a, Georg Wittig, chemistry, 1979. b, Charles Dawes, peace, 1925. c, Frederic Mistral, literature, 1904. d, Juan Jimenez, literature, 1956. e, Michael S. Brown, medicine, 1985. f, Guglielmo Marconi, physics, 1909. g, Werner Forssmann, medicine, 1956. h, Francis W. Aston, chemistry, 1922. i, Martin Ryle, physics, 1974.

No. 805: a, Leon Jouhaux, peace, 1951. b, Rudolf L. Mossbauer, physics, 1961. c, George Seferis, literature, 1963. d, James Chadwick, physics, 1935. e, Aung San Suu Kyi, peace, 1991. f, John H. Nothrop, chemistry, 1946. g, Eduard Buchner, chemistry, 1907. h, Hans A. Bethe, physics, 1967. i, Nils Dalen, physics, 1912.

No. 806, 1500fr, Hermann Hesse, literature, 1946. No. 807, 1500fr, Albert Schweitzer, peace, 1952. No. 808, 1500fr, Nelson Mandela, peace, 1993.

1995, Oct. 18 Litho. *Perf. 14*

803 A303 125fr Sheet of 9, #a.-i. 6.75 6.75
804 A303 225fr Sheet of 9, #a.-i. 9.00 9.00
805 A303 260fr Sheet of 9, #a.-i. 14.00 14.00
Nos. 803-805 (3) 29.75 29.75

Souvenir Sheets

806-808 A303 Set of 3 27.00 27.00

Monseigneur Bessieux (1803-76), Evangelist A306

1995, Dec. 25 Litho. *Perf. 13*

811 A306 500fr multicolored 2.75 1.40

Louis Pasteur (1822-95), Microbiologist — A306a

Perf. 14¼x14¾

1995, Dec. 12 Litho.

811A A306a 500fr multi *45.00 10.00*

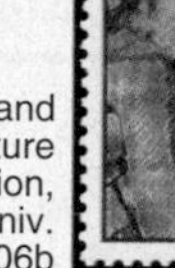

Food and Agriculture Organization, 50th Anniv. — A306b

1995, Sept. 20 Litho. *Perf. 11¾*

811B A306b 500fr multi *10.00 10.00*

Mbigou Rock Sculptor — A306c

Perf. 14¼x14¾

1995, Nov. 15 Litho.

811C A306c 500fr multi *30.00* —

Miniature Sheet of 8

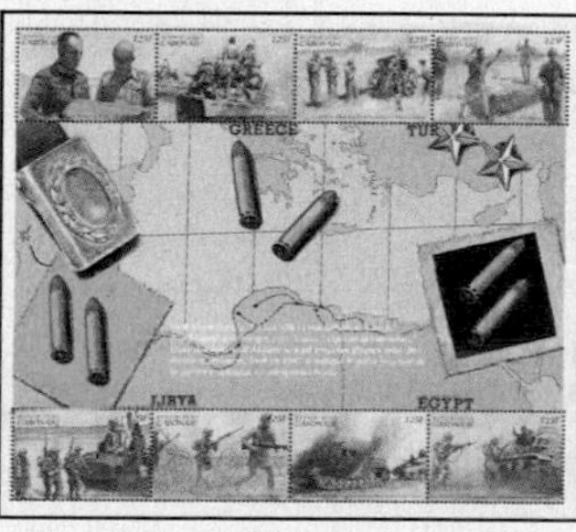

World War II, 50th Anniv. — A307

No. 812: a, German generals planning attack. b, Afrika Korps troops ride tanks into El Agheila. c, German artillary fires on British positions in Tobruk. d, British soldiers surrender. e, British soldiers break siege of Tobruk. f, Allies advancing though barbed wire, El Alamein. g, German tanks retreat to Tunis. h, German tank surrenders.

1996, Jan. 29 *Perf. 14*

812 A307 125fr Sheet of 8, #a.-h. + label 6.50 2.75

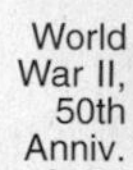

World War II, 50th Anniv. A308

No. 813: a, Pres. Franklin D. Roosevelt. b, Pres. Harry S Truman. c, Gen. George Marshall.

1000fr, Flags of US, Great Britain, USSR.

1996, Jan. 26 Litho. *Perf. 14*

813 A308 225fr Strip of 3, #a.-c. 4.50 4.50

Souvenir Sheet

814 A308 1000fr multicolored 6.50 6.50

No. 813 was issued in sheets of 9 stamps.

Dogs — A309

No. 815: a, Dalmatian. b, Basset hound. c, Harrier. d, German Shepherd. e, Bernese bouvier. f, Pug. g, West highland white terrier. h, Akita.

1996, May 13 Litho. *Perf. 14*

815 A309 125fr Sheet of 8, #a.-h. 6.00 6.00

China '96 Philatelic Exhibition.

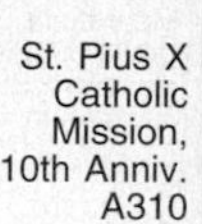

St. Pius X Catholic Mission, 10th Anniv. A310

Mgr. Marcel Lefebvre, interior of mission.

1996, Mar. 4 *Perf. 13½*

816 A310 100fr yellow & multi .90 .30
817 A310 125fr blue & multi 1.00 .50

Rotary, Intl. A311

Rotary emblem and: 125fr, UN flag. 225fr, Natl. flag of Gabon. 260fr, Rotary, Intl. flag.
1500fr, Olympic flag.

1996, July 3 Litho. *Perf. 14*

818-820 A311 Set of 3 4.00 3.00

Souvenir Sheet

821 A311 1500fr multicolored 9.00 9.00

Boy Scouts — A312

Designs: 125fr, Scout sign. 225fr, Constructing a lean-to. 260fr, Camping.
1500fr, Lord Baden-Powell.

1996, July 15

822-824 A312 Set of 3 4.00 3.25

Souvenir Sheet

825 A312 1500fr multicolored 9.00 9.00

Cercopithecus Solatus — A313

1996, Mar. 6 *Perf. 13½x13*

826 A313 500fr multicolored 3.25 1.75

Fight Against AIDS — A314

1996, Apr. 3 *Perf. 13½x13*

827 A314 500fr multicolored 3.25 1.75

Shells — A315

Designs: 100fr, Fusinus caparti. 260fr, Hexaplex rosarium. 500fr, Conus pulcher, horiz.

1996 *Perf. 13½x13, 13x13½*

828-830 A315 Set of 3 5.25 3.50

1996 Summer Olympic Games, Atlanta A316

1996, May 8 *Perf. 11½*

831 A316 225fr Boxing 1.25 .75
832 A316 500fr Relay race 2.50 1.60

Campaign Against Use of Illegal Drugs A317

1996, Aug. 6 Litho. *Perf. 11½*

833 A317 500fr multicolored 2.75 1.25

Contemporary Paintings, by H. Moundounga A318

1996, Sept. 10

834 A318 100fr Girl .65 .25
835 A318 125fr Three faces .85 .40
836 A318 225fr Eyes 1.50 .75
a. Souvenir sheet, #834-836 3.25 3.25
Nos. 834-836 (3) 3.00 1.40

Souvenir Sheet

Temple in Winter — A319

1996, May 13 Litho. *Perf. 14*

837 A319 500fr multicolored 4.50 2.25

China '96 Philatelic Exhibition, No. 837 was not available until March 1997.

Environmental Protection — A320

Endangered species: 100fr, Galago alleni, vert. 125fr, Perodicticus potto. 225fr, Orycteropus afer. 260fr, Manis gigantea.

1996, June 5 *Perf. 13½*

838-841 A320 Set of 4 5.00 3.25

Children's Paintings A321

Designs: 100fr, Woman's arms encircling world, vert. 125fr, People forming circle around animals. 225fr, Slaughtering of elephants, vert.

1996, Dec. 25 Litho. *Perf. 11½*

842-844 A321 Set of 3 1.75 1.25

Dated 1996.

Traditional Houses A322

Designs: 100fr, Mud & stick cabin. 125fr, Pygmy hut. 225fr, Bark-sided cabins. 260fr, Wood-sided cabins.

1996, Nov. 6

845-848 A322 Set of 4 4.50 2.75

a. Souvenir sheet, #845-848 5.00 5.00

A323

1996, Oct. 10

849 A323 500fr multicolored 2.00 1.25

Investiture of Pres. Nelson Mandela, 3rd anniv.

A324

UNICEF, 50th Anniv.: No. 850: a, Boy holding cup. b, Girl holding cup. c, Boy eating. 1500fr, Boy holding plate.

1997, Apr. 9 Litho. *Perf. 14*

850 A324 260fr Sheet of 3, #a.-c. 4.00 4.00

Souvenir Sheet

851 A324 1500fr multicolored 8.50 8.50

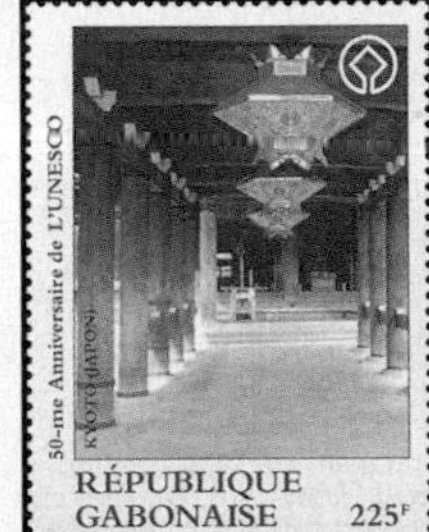

UNESCO, 50th Anniv. A325

No. 852, 225fr: a, Kyoto, Japan. b, Puma, Los Katios Natl. Park, Colombia. c, Abu Simbel Monument, Egypt. d, Old Rauma, Finland. e, Rotunda, City of Vicenza, Italy. f, Homes, China. g, Port of Salvador, Brazil. h, Delos Ruins, Greece.

No. 853, 225fr: a, Fasil Ghebbi Monument, Gondar Region, Ethiopia. b, Victoria Falls, Zambia. c, Zambezi Plains, Chewore Safari Areas, Zimbabwe. d, Nature Reserve, Niger. e, Banc D'Arguin Natl. Park, Mauritania. f, Gorée Island, Senegal. g, Djémila Ruins, Algeria. h, Mosque, Medina of Fez, Morocco.

1000fr, Terracotta warriors, Mausoleum of first Qin Emperor, China.

1997, Apr. 16

Sheets of 8, #a-h, + Label

852-853 A325 Set of 2 15.00 15.00

Souvenir Sheet

854 A325 1000fr multicolored 7.50 7.50

City Arms — A326

1997, Mar. 12 Litho. *Perf. 11½x12*

855 A326 100fr N'Dendé .65 .25

856 A326 125fr Libreville .85 .35

857 A326 225fr Mitzic 1.50 .80

Nos. 855-857 (3) 3.00 1.40

Return of Hong Kong to China — A327

Designs: 125fr, Skyline. 225fr, Skyline, diff. 260fr, Skyline at night, horiz. 500fr, Skyline at night, Deng Xiaoping (1904-97), horiz.

1997, July 1 *Perf. 14*

858-861 A327 Set of 4 6.00 4.00

Nos. 858-859 were each issued in sheets of 4. Nos. 860-861 are 59x28mm and were issued in sheets of 3.

Unity, Work and Justice Type of 1981

1994-95 Litho. *Perf. 11¾*

Granite Paper

862 A145 5fr grn blue & blk .30 .25

863 A145 10fr orange & black .30 .25

864 A145 25fr grey lilac & black .30 .25

865 A145 50fr salmon & black .45 .25

866 A145 75fr tan & blk .30 .25

867 A145 100fr pink & black .40 .25

868 A145 125fr yell grn & blk .70 .35

869 A145 175fr yellow & black — —

870 A145 225fr green & black — —

871 A145 260fr lt blue & black 1.60 .75

Nos. 862-871 (10) 4.35 2.60

Issued: 50fr, 125fr, 9/30/95; others, 9/20/94.

Paintings — A328

1995, Oct. 10 Litho. *Perf. 14*

872 A328 100fr Woman *1.00* .45

873 A328 125fr Stylized women *1.50* .65

873A A328 225fr Masked Face *2.00* *1.10*

b. Souvenir sheet of 3, #872-873A 65.00 65.00

Raponda Walker, 25th Death Anniv. — A329

1995, June 7 *Perf. 13½*

874 A329 500fr multicolored *10.00* *5.00*

Masks — A330

1995, Feb. 15

875 A330 100fr Bateke — —

876 A330 125fr Bavili — —

877 A330 225fr Fang — *10.00*

878 A330 260fr Bandjabi *80.00* *12.00*

a. Souvenir sheet of 4, #875-878 150.00 150.00

Shells A331

100fr, Cymbium glans. 125fr, Muricidae murey. 225fr, Siliquaria. 260fr, Strombus latus.

1995, Apr. 4

879 A331 100fr multi *30.00* *10.00*

880 A331 125fr multi *30.00* *10.00*

880A A331 225fr multi *30.00* *10.00*

881 A331 260fr multi *30.00* *10.00*

a. Souvenir sheet of 4, #879-880A, 881 175.00 175.00

Saint-Exupery French Cultural Center — A332

1996, May 12 *Perf. 13x13½*

883 A332 100fr black & multi — —

884 A332 125fr blue & multi — —

885 A332 225fr red & multi — *12.00*

Inter-Continental Hotel, 50th Anniv. — A333

1996, Apr. 4 *Perf. 13½*

886 A333 125fr creme & blue — *10.00*

886A A333 225fr lt yel & blue — *10.00*

Early Post Offices — A333a

100fr, Port Gentil, 1917. 125fr, Cap-Lopez, 1888. 225fr, Libreville, 1862.

1996, July 20 Litho. *Perf. 12x11½*

886B A333a 100fr multi *1.00* *.50*

886C A333a 125fr multi *1.00* *.65*

886D A333a 225fr multi *1.45* *1.10*

Flowers, Butterflies, Moths, Insects A334

Designs, vert: 125fr, Rubra tigridia pauonia, pieridae. 225fr, Acraeidae, strelitzia reginae. 260fr, Zautedeschia aethiopica, zonabris oculata. 500fr, Bee orchid, iron prominent moth caterpillar.

No. 891, 260fr: a, Liliaceae. b, Macrophylla, phoebis philea. c, Theaceae amugashita. d, Lilium american cultivars, vanessa atalanta. e, Hybrids, hippodamia convergens. f, Sibine stimulea, iridaceae.

No. 892, 260fr: a, Kalmialati. b, G. gandavensis, calopteryx maculata. c, Narcissus pseudonarcissus. d, Ipheton uniflorum, Tlemaris thysbe. e, Rudbackia hirta. f, Tritida grandiflora, danaus plexippus.

No. 893, 1500fr, Papilion zellicaon, geranium pelargonium, vert. No. 894, 1500fr, Anax jumus, gladstoniana, vert.

1997, Aug. 11 Litho. *Perf. 14*

887-890 A334 Set of 4 7.25 5.00

Sheets of 6, #a-f

891-892 A334 Set of 2 16.00 16.00

Souvenir Sheets

893-894 A334 Set of 2 15.00 15.00

Protection of Indigenous Animals — A335

Designs: 100fr, Dendrohyrax arboreus. 125fr, Galago elegantulus. 225fr, Stephanoaetus coronatus.

1997, June 5 ***Perf. 13½x13***
895-897 A335 Set of 3 3.00 2.00
897a Souvenir sheet of 3, #895-897 6.50 6.50

Gabonese Art — A336

Designs: 100fr, Droits de Creatures, vert. 125fr, Ambassadeur, vert. 225fr, Hallucinations.

1997, May 8 ***Perf. 13½x13, 13x13½***
898-900 A336 Set of 3 3.00 3.00
900a Souvenir sheet of 1, #900 1.50 1.50

Air Gabon, 20th Anniv. A337

1997, June 1 ***Perf. 13x13½***
901 A337 125fr multicolored .90 .50
902 A337 225fr multicolored 1.60 .80

First ACP Summit, Libreville — A338

1997, Nov. 6 **Litho.** ***Perf. 13½x13***
903 A338 225fr multicolored 1.40 .70

Lions Club in Gabon, 40th Anniv. — A339

1997, Oct. 8 ***Perf. 13½x13***
904 A339 225fr multicolored 1.40 .70

AIPLF, 30th Anniv. A340

1997, Oct. 30 ***Perf. 12x11½***
905 A340 260fr multicolored 1.40 .65

Paul Gondjout, 1st Pres. of the Natl. Assembly — A341

1997, Nov. 11 ***Perf. 14x14½***
906 A341 500fr multicolored 2.75 1.25

Heinrich von Stephan (1831-97) — A342

1997, Nov. 17 ***Perf. 11½x12***
907 A342 500fr multicolored 2.75 1.25

Princess Diana (1961-97) — A343

No. 908: a, 500fr. b, 300fr. c, 260fr. d, 225fr. e, f, 125fr.
3000fr, Diana in white dress.

1998, Feb. 10 **Litho.** ***Perf. 13½***
908 A343 Sheet of 6, #a.-f. 8.50 8.50

Souvenir Sheet

909 A343 3000fr multicolored 15.00 15.00

District Arms — A344

Designs: 100fr, Akieni. 125fr, Pana. 225fr, Lebamba.

1998, June 4 **Litho.** ***Perf. 13½x13***
910-912 A344 Set of 3 3.00 1.50

Traditional Tools A345

Designs: 100fr, Yanghe. 125fr, Ikanga. 225fr, Ivedili.

1997, Nov. 5 **Litho.** ***Perf. 14***
913-915 A345 Set of 3 3.00 1.90

New Horizons Foundation A346

1998, May 15 **Litho.** ***Perf. 13x13½***
916 A346 225fr multicolored 1.40 .70

Protected Animals — A347

Designs: 100fr, Hippopotamus amphibius. 125fr, Sylvicapra grimmia. 225fr, Pelecanus rufescens.

1998, Apr. 17 ***Perf. 13½x13***
917 A347 100fr multicolored .75 .40
918 A347 125fr multicolored 1.25 .70
919 A347 225fr multicolored 1.50 .85
a. Souvenir sheet, #917-919 30.00 30.00

1998 World Cup Soccer Championships, France — A348

Various soccer plays, country flags in background: 100fr, 125fr, 225fr, 260fr.

1998, July 10 **Litho.** ***Perf. 13½x13***
920-923 A348 Set of 4 4.75 2.75
923a Sheet of 4, #920-923 5.00 5.00

ACCT, 26th Anniv. — A349

1998, Oct. 10
924 A349 260fr multicolored 1.40 .65

Elimination of Land Mines — A350

1998, May 15 **Litho.** ***Perf. 11½x12***
925 A350 260fr multicolored 1.60 .80

Gandhi — A351

1998, Oct. 9
926 A351 260fr multicolored 1.60 .80

Mother Teresa (1910-97) — A352

1998, June 30
927 A352 500fr multicolored 2.75 1.40

Deng Xiaoping (1904-97) A353

1998, Sept. 14
928 A353 500fr multicolored 2.75 1.40

Intl. Year of the Ocean A354

1999, Oct. 19 **Litho.** ***Perf. 11½***
929 A354 125fr multicolored 2.50 .85

Dated 1998.

Wooden Tools — A355

1999
930 A355 100fr Mortier .70 .55
931 A355 125fr Pilon 1.00 .80

Dated 1998.

Universal Declaration of Human Rights A356

1999, Aug. 10
932 A356 225fr multicolored 1.40 .80

Dated 1998.

Space Exploration — A357

Designs: No. 933, 225fr, Gemini 7. No. 934, 225fr, Skylab. No. 935, 225fr, Atlas Moon Explorer. No. 936, 225fr, Space Shuttle.

No. 937: a, Venera 4. b, TDRS. c, Sputnik II. d, Zond II. e, Untethered walk. f, Intelsat 6. g, Luna 16. h, Sputnik III. i, Vostok V. j, Lunar explorer. k, 2nd lunar landing. l, Conrad and Surveyor.

No. 938: a, Sputnik. b, Mariner 2. c, Apollo 11 Lunar Module. d, Gemini 7. e, Mir. f, Atlas Moon Explorer. g, Space Shuttle Orbit. h, Hubbell. i, Soyuz. j, Apollo 11 re-entry. k, Skylab. l, Venture Star.

No. 939: a, Lunar landing II. b, Gemini 7. c, Venture Star. d, Hubbell.

No. 940, 1500fr, Shuttle launch. No. 941, 1500fr, Untethered walk. No. 942, 1500fr, Apollo II. No. 943, 1500fr, Lunar landing module.

1999, Apr. 30 **Litho.** ***Perf. 14***
933-936 A357 Set of 4 3.75 2.00
937 A357 100fr Sheet of 12, #a.-l. 6.00 6.00
938 A357 125fr Sheet of 12, #a.-l. 8.50 8.50

Sheet of 4

939 A357 225fr Sheet of 4, #a.-d. 4.00 4.00

Souvenir Sheets

940-943 A357 Set of 4 35.00 35.00

Moon landing, 30th anniv.

Traditional Weapons — A358

Designs: 100fr, Sagaie. 125fr, Arbalète. 225fr, Couteau et jet.

1999, Nov. 10 *Perf. 13*

944-946 A358 Set of 3 3.00 1.60

Folklore — A358a

Designs: 125fr, Mitsogho reliquary. 225fr, Bwèri Fang sculpture.

1999, July 2 Litho. *Perf. 13¼*

946A A358a 125fr multi *125.00 10.00*

946B A358a 225fr multi *145.00 —*

Democracy A359

1999, Dec. 12 Litho. *Perf. 11¾*

947 A359 100fr multicolored .75 .50

UPU, 125th Anniv. A360

Designs: 100fr, People, map. 225fr, Emblem, letters, vert. 260fr, Great Wall of China, vert.

1999, Aug. 21

948 A360 100fr multicolored .60 .40

949 A360 225fr multicolored 1.00 .75

950 A360 260fr multicolored 1.50 1.00

Nos. 948-950 (3) 3.10 2.15

Manufacture of Aspirin, Cent. — A361

1999, July 6

951 A361 225fr multicolored 1.40 .70

Mushrooms — A361a

Designs: 100fr, Amanite panthère. 125fr, Basidomycetes, horiz. 225fr, Basidomycetes, diff., horiz. 260fr, Amanite tue-mouches.

Perf. 13¼x13, 13x13¼

1999, Apr. 30 Litho.

951A-951D A361a Set of 4 *8.00 8.00*

951De Souvenir sheet of 4, #951A-951D *120.00 120.00*

PhilexFrance '99 — A362

1999, July 2 Litho. *Perf. 13*

952 A362 225fr multi *3.00 1.40*

No. 952 has a holographic image. Soaking in water may affect hologram.

Elephants A363

1999 *Perf. 13x13¼*

953 A363 100fr multi 3.00 1.25

PhilexFrance '99 World Philatelic Exhibition, Paris.

Central African Economic and Monetary Community Days — A364

Map of Africa and: 125fr, Circle of member's flags. 225fr, Rows of member's flags.

1999, Nov. 23 Litho. *Perf. 14½*

954-955 A364 Set of 2 2.40 2.40

Pope John XXIII, St. Peter's Basilica A365

1999, Dec. 12 Litho. *Perf. 11¾*

956 A365 100fr multi 1.00 .75

Announcement of 2nd Vatican Council, 40th anniv., Christmas.

Unity, Work and Justice Type of 1981

1999, Dec. 12 Litho. *Perf. 11¾*

Granite Paper

959 A145 40fr lil & blk 1.00 .25

960 A145 90fr olive grn & blk — —

Shells A365a

Designs: 100fr, Harpa doris. 125fr, Thais haemastoma. 225fr, Cassis tessellata.

1999, June 25 Litho. *Perf. 13x13½*

964-966 A365a Set of 3 5.00 5.00

Fish A365b

Designs: 100fr, Epinephelus marginatus, mugil cephalus. 125fr, Brycinus macrolepidotus. 225fr, Oreochromis schwebischi. 260fr, Pomadasys peroteti, caranx hippos, ethmalosa fimbriata.

1999, Apr. 26

967-970 A365b Set of 4 5.50 5.50

970a Souvenir sheet of 4, #967-970 *125.00 —*

Expo 2000, Hanover A366

Perf. 11¾x11½

2000, Feb. 16 Litho.

971 A366 225fr multi 2.00 1.00

Protected Animals A367

Designs: 125fr, Haliaetus vocifer. 225fr, Panthera pardus. 260fr, Panthera leo.

2000, June 5

972-974 A367 Set of 3 8.00 2.50

974a Souvenir sheet of 3, #972-974 *17.50 17.50*

Events of the 20th Century A368

Designs: 100fr, Universal Declaration of Human Rights, vert. 125fr, World War II. 225fr, First man on the moon.

Perf. 11½x11¾, 11¾x11½

2000, July 20

975-977 A368 Set of 3 3.00 3.00

Scientific Achievements of the 20th Century — A369

Designs: 100fr, Microprocessor, 1971. 125fr, Nuclear reactor, 1942. 225fr, Structure of DNA, 1953.

2000, Nov. 28 *Perf. 11¾x11½*

978-980 A369 Set of 3 3.00 3.00

See Nos. 1040-1042.

Tourism A370

100fr, Pygmy village. 125fr, Lake region. 225fr, Poubara Waterfall. 260fr, Mt. Brazza.

2000, Sept. 29 *Perf. 13x13½*

981-984 A370 Set of 4 5.50 5.50

984a Miniature sheet of 4, #981-984 *15.00 15.00*

Y2K Bug — A371

2000, Dec. 11 *Perf. 11½x11¾*

985 A371 225fr multi 1.40 1.40

Dr. Albert Schweitzer (1875-1965) A372

2000, Jan. 14 *Perf. 13¼x13*

986 A372 260fr multi 4.00 1.60

A373

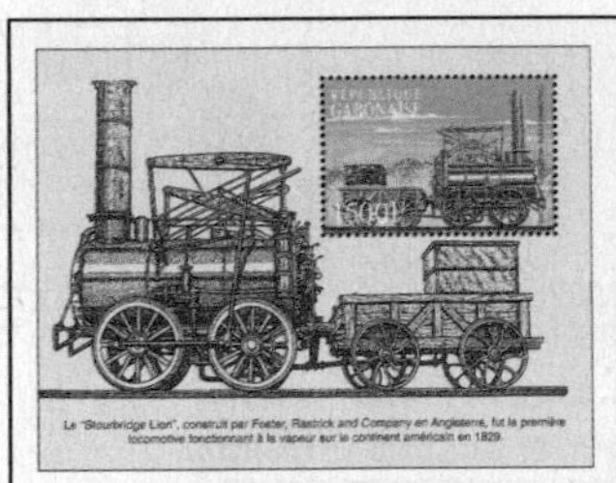

Trains — A374

Designs: No. 987, 100fr, Japanese Hikari trains. 125fr, Hungarian Bo-Bo electric locomotive. No. 989, 500fr, Pakistani electric locomotive. No. 990, 500fr, Belgian locomotive.

No. 991: a, 100fr, Korean Bo-Bo locomotive. b, 100fr, Moroccan electric locomotive. c, 100fr, Spanish electric locomotive. d, 500fr, Yugoslavian Type J2-441. e, 500fr, Chinese electric locomotive. f, 500fr, Norwegian Type E115.

No. 992: a, 100fr, Portuguese Diesel-electric locomotive. b, 100fr, Japanese mag-lev train. c, 100fr, Long Island Railroad diesel car. d, 500fr, German Type 103. e, 500fr, Romanian Co-Co locomotive. f, 500fr, English HST.

No. 993, 1500fr, English train "The Advanced." No. 994, 1500fr, French TGV 001. No. 995, 1500fr, Austrian Transalpine train. No. 996, 1500fr, Stourbridge Lion. No. 997, 1500fr, Puffing Billy, vert. No. 998, 1500fr, Union Pacific 4-8-8-4 Big Boy, vert. No. 999, French TGV, vert.

Perf. 13¼x13¾, 13¾x13¼

2000, Dec. 10 Litho.

987-990 A373 Set of 4 6.00 6.00

Sheets of 6, #a-f

991-992 A373 Set of 2 20.00 20.00

Souvenir Sheets

993-995 A373 Set of 3 24.00 24.00
996-999 A374 Set of 4 30.00 30.00

See Nos. 1024-1027, 1032-1033, 1036-1037.

A375

Prehistoric Animals — A376

Designs: No. 1000, 100fr, Archaeopteryx. No. 1001, 100fr, Velociraptor, vert. No. 1002, 125fr, Torosaurus. No. 1003, 125fr, Corythosaurus, vert. No. 1004, 225fr, Pachycephalosaurus, vert. No. 1005, 500fr, Parasaurolophus.

No. 1006, 100fr, Pterodactylus. No. 1007, 125fr, Allosaurus. No. 1008, 125fr, Struthiomimus, vert. No. 1009, 225fr, Psittacosaurus, vert. No. 1010, 260fr, Parasauraolophus, vert. No. 1011, 500fr, Acanthostega.

No. 1012: a, 125fr, Camarasaurus. b, 125fr, Rhamphorhynchus. c, 125fr, Saltasaurus. d, 225fr, Camptosaurus. e, 225fr, Megalosaurus. f, 225fr, Allosaurus. g, 260fr, Anchisaurus. h, 260fr, Dilophosaurus. i, 260fr, Massospondylus.

No. 1013: a, 100fr, Stegosaurus. b, 100fr, Pteranodon. c, 100fr, Carnotaurus. d, 125fr, Iguanodon. e, 125fr, Pentaceratops. f, 125fr, Styracosaurus. g, 500fr, Deinonychus. h, 500fr, Stegoceras. i, 500fr, Struthiomimus.

No. 1014: a, 125fr, Volcano. b, 125fr, Pterodactylus. c, 125fr, Dimorphodon. d, 125fr, Alamosaurus. e, 225fr, Psittacosaurus. f, 225fr, Deinonychus. g, 225fr, Dromiceiomimus. h, 225fr, Yangchuanosaurus. i, 260fr, Protorosaurus. j, 260fr, Triceratops. k, 260fr, Daspletosaurus. l, 260fr, Pentaceratops.

No. 1015: a, 125fr, Brachiosaurus. b, 125fr, Scaphognathus. c, Mountain and sun. d, 125fr, Pteranodon. e, 225fr, Tyrannosaurus. f, 225fr, Ichthyosaurus. g, 225fr, Macroplata. h, 225fr, Dilophosaurus. i, 500fr, Stegosaurus. j, 500fr, Thecodontosaurus. k, 500fr, Saltosaurus. l, 500fr, Pachyrhinosaurus.

No. 1016, 225fr: a, Tyrannosaurus. b, Criorhynchus. c, Pterodactylus. d, Albertosaurus. e, Dromiceiomimus. f, Opisthocoelicaudia. g, Brachiosaurus. h, Pachycephalosaurus. i, Parasaurolophus. j, Edmontosaurus. k, Pentaceratops. l, Corythosaurus.

No. 1017, 260fr: a, Peteinosaurus. b, Volcanoes. c, Acanthostega. d, Ceresiosaurus. e, Pliosaur. f, Stethacanthus. g, Ichthyosaur. h, Pholidogaster. i, Gerrothorax. j, Diplocaulus. k, Mixosaurus. l, Echinoceras raricostatum.

No. 1018, 1500fr, Tyrannosaurus Rex. No. 1019, 1500fr, Arrhinoceratops. No. 1020, 1500fr, Argentinosaurus, vert. No. 1021, 1500fr, Cetiosaurus, vert. No. 1022, 1500fr, Archaeopteryx. No. 1023, Saltasaurus, vert.

2000, Dec. 20

1000-1005 A376 Set of 6 8.00 8.00
1006-1011 A376 Set of 6 8.00 8.00

Sheets of 9, #a-i

1012-1013 A375 Set of 2 20.00 20.00

Sheets of 12, #a-l

1014-1015 A375 Set of 2 30.00 30.00
1016-1017 A376 Set of 2 30.00 30.00

Souvenir Sheets

1018-1021 A375 Set of 4 30.00 30.00
1022-1023 A376 Set of 2 16.00 16.00

No. 1021 contains one 42x56mm stamp.

Train Type of 2000 and

A377

Designs: 100fr, German Type 201. No. 1025, 225fr, German Type 112. No. 1026, 225fr, ICT. No. 1027, 260fr, ICE.

No. 1028, 260fr, French Electric BB9004. No. 1029, 260fr, French Type 232U 4-8-2. No. 1030, 500fr, French Type 241C 4-8-2 "Mountain." No. 1031, 500fr, German TEE.

No. 1032: a, 125fr, German Type 41. b, 125fr, Type 39. c, 125fr, German Type 10. d, 500fr, German Type 99. e, 500fr, German Type 58. f, 500fr, German Type 44.

No. 1033: a, 225fr, German Type 229. b, 225fr, Type 152. c, 225fr, German Type 101. d, 500fr, German Type 250. e, 500fr, German Type 232. f, 500fr, Type 216.

No. 1034: a, 125fr, Prussian Type P8 4-6-0. b, 125fr, Bavarian Type S3/6 4-6-2. c, 125fr, German Type 01 4-6-2. d, 500fr, German Electric "Crocodile." e, 500fr, Swiss Electric Type Be 4/6. f, 500fr, Swiss Electric Type Ae 6/6.

No. 1035: a, 125fr, Stirling 8ft Single 4-2-2 "No. 1," UK. b, 125fr, Greeley Pacific Type A3 4-6-2 "Flying Scotsman," UK. c, 125fr, Stanier Coronation Type 4-6-2 "Coronation Scot," UK. d, 500fr, Baldwin 4-4-0 "The General," US. e, Class J1 Hudson 4-8-4, US. f, "Super Chief" Diesel-electric, US.

No. 1036, 1500fr, Type 91. No. 1037, 1500fr, Type 57. No. 1038, Greeley Pacific Type A4 4-6-2 "Silver Link," UK. No. 1039, J Type 4-8-4, US.

Perf. 13¼x13½, 13½x13¼

2000? **Litho.**

1024-1027 A374 Set of 4 4.00 4.00
1028-1031 A377 Set of 4 8.00 8.00

Sheets of 6, #a-f

1032-1033 A374 Set of 2 20.00 20.00
1034-1035 A377 Set of 2 19.00 19.00

Souvenir Sheets

1036-1037 A374 Set of 2 16.00 16.00
1038-1039 A377 Set of 2 16.00 16.00

Nos. 1038-1039 each contain one 56x42mm stamp.

Raponda Walker Foundation A378

2000, Dec. 25 **Litho.** ***Perf. 11½***

1039A A378 225fr multi 1.10 1.10

End of the Millennium A379

2000, Dec. 11

1039B A379 225fr multi 1.20 1.20

Scientific Achievements of the 20th Century Type of 2000

Designs: 100fr, Isolation of insulin, 1921. 125fr, Invention of television, 1921. 225fr, Invention of the calculator, 1951.

Perf. 11¾x11½

2000, Nov. 28 **Litho.**

1040-1042 A369 Set of 3 3.00 3.00

Dancers A380

Designs: 100fr, Mengane dancers. 130fr, Maghouba dancers. 225fr, Ndjobi dancers.

2001, Apr. 24 **Litho.** ***Perf. 11¾***

1043 A380 100fr multi .50 .30
1044 A380 130fr multi .50 .30
1045 A380 225fr multi 1.00 .50
a. Souvenir sheet of 3, #1043-1045 3.00 2.50
Nos. 1043-1045 (3) 2.00 1.10

Flowers — A381

Design: 100fr, Pseudogardenia kallreyeri. 125fr, Ouratea turnerae. 225fr, Strophantus gratus. 260fr, Spathodea campanulata.

2001 **Litho.** ***Perf. 11¾***

1046-1049 A381 Set of 4 3.50 3.50
1049a Miniature sheet of 4, #1046-1049 3.50 3.50

Gabon Poste Emblem A382

Color of denomination: 125fr, Green. 225fr, Blue.

2003, Apr. 5 **Litho.** ***Perf. 13x13¼***

1050-1051 A382 Set of 2 1.75 1.75

Orchids — A383

Designs: 100fr, Plectrelmintus caudatus. 125fr, Eulophia. 225fr, Jacinthe d'eau.

2004, Feb. 20 ***Perf. 13¼x13***

1052-1054 A383 Set of 3 3.00 2.25
1054a Souvenir sheet, #1052-1054 6.00 4.00

Cooperation Between Gabon and People's Republic of China, 30th Anniv. — A384

No. 1055: a, 125fr, Chinese Prime Minister Wen Jiabao, Gabon Pres. Omar Bongo and flags. b, 225fr, Coats of arms of People's Republic of China and Gabon. No. 1056, 2500fr, Like No. 1055a. No. 1057, 2500fr, Like No. 1055b.

2004, Apr. 20 ***Perf. 12***

1055 A384 Horiz. pair, #a-b 2.00 2.00

Souvenir Sheets

Printed on Wood Veneer

Self-Adhesive

1056-1057 A384 Set of 2 120.00 —

Nos. 1056 and 1057 are airmail and each contains one 90x50mm stamp.

FIFA (Fédération Internationale de Football Association), Cent. — A385

Background color: 125fr, Blue. 225fr, Green.

2004, Apr. 24 **Litho.** ***Perf. 13x13¼***

1058-1059 A385 Set of 2 2.00 1.75

Biodiversity — A386

Designs: 100fr, Hyperolius kuligae. 125fr, Chameleon, vert. 225fr, Merops malimbicus. 260fr, Owl.

2004, June 5 ***Perf. 13x13¼, 13¼x13***

1060-1063 A386 Set of 4 5.50 5.50
1063a Souvenir sheet of 4, #1060-1063 4.00 3.00

Rotary International, Cent. — A387

2005, Feb. 23 **Litho.** ***Perf. 13x13¼***

1064 A387 125fr multi 2.00 1.00

Souvenir Sheet

1065 A387 2500fr multi 12.00 12.00

Souvenir Sheet

Lake Evaro — A388

2005 **Litho.** ***Perf. 13¾x13½***

1066 A388 225fr multi 3.00 2.00

Souvenir Sheet

1067 A388 500fr multi 12.00 —

Christmas A389

No. 1068 — Carved wooden toys: a, 260fr, Antique car. b, 350fr, Logging truck.

2005 ***Perf. 13x13¼***

1068 A389 Pair, #a-b *25.00* —
c. Souvenir sheet of 4, 2 each #1068a-1068b *50.00* —

Soccer Players and Flag A390

2005 ***Perf. 13x13¼***

1069 A390 225fr multi 2.00 1.25

No. 1069 issued in sheets of 4.

Central African Network of Protected Areas — A391

2007, May 28 ***Perf. 13¼***
1070 A391 500fr multi 2.10 2.10

Petroleum Exploration in Gabon, 80th Anniv. A392

Designs: No. 1071, 250fr, Ship and offshore drilling platform. No. 1072, 250fr, Oil drilling complex in jungle. No. 1073, 250fr, Oil workers. No. 1074, 500fr, Oil tanker at dock. No. 1075, 500fr, Elephants and oil drilling complex in jungle, vert. No. 1076, 500fr, Oil workers, vert.

Perf. 13x13¼, 13¼x13

2008, May 5 **Litho.**
1071-1076 A392 Set of 6 11.00 11.00
1076a Sheet of 6, #1071-1076 11.00 11.00

Souvenir Sheet

Children's Drawings of Petroleum Industry — A393

No. 1077: a, Workers at Shell Gabon Terminal. b, Petroleum and Biodiversity.

2008, Sept. 25 **Litho.** ***Perf. 13x13¼***
1077 A393 250fr Sheet of 2, #a-b 2.25 2.25

Rule of Pres. Omar Bongo, 41st Anniv. A394

Litho. & Embossed

2008, Dec. 5 ***Perf. 13½x13***
1078 A394 500fr multi 2.25 2.25

Litho. & Embossed With Foil Application

1079 A394 5000fr gold & multi 22.50 22.50

Nos. 1078-1079 each were printed in sheets of 4.

Rotary International, 50th Anniv. in Gabon (in 2009) — A396

2010 **Litho.** ***Perf. 13x13¼***
1082 A396 250fr multi 1.00 .50

Gabon Numerique 2010 A397

2010, July
1083 A397 500fr multi 2.00 1.25

A398

A399

Prize-winning Art in 50th Anniversary of Gabon Art Contest — A400

2010, Aug. ***Perf. 13¼x13, 13x13¼***
1084 A398 250fr multi 1.00 .50
1085 A399 250fr multi 1.00 .50
1086 A400 250fr multi 1.00 .50

Pres. Ali Bongo Ondimba — A401

2010, Aug. ***Perf. 13¼x13***
1087 A401 500fr multi 2.00 1.25

Gabon Presidents Léon Mba (1902-67), Omar Bongo (1935-2009) and Ali Bongo — A402

2010, Aug.
1088 A402 500fr multi 2.00 1.25

Souvenir Sheet

1089 A402 1500fr multi 20.00 15.00

A403

A404

Intl. Widows Day — A405

2011, June 23 **Litho.** ***Perf. 13x13¼***
1090 A403 250fr multi *2.50 2.50*
1091 A404 250fr multi *2.50 2.50*

Perf. 13¼x13

1092 A405 250fr multi *2.50 2.50*

2012 African Cup of Nations Soccer Championships, Gabon and Equatorial Guinea — A406

Flags of Gabon and Equatorial Guinea and mascot: 250fr, Holding ball on ground. 500fr, Dribbling ball.

2012 ***Perf. 13x13¼***
1093-1094 A406 Set of 2 6.00 6.00

SEMI-POSTAL STAMPS

No. 37 Surcharged in Red

1916 **Unwmk.** ***Perf. 13½x14***
B1 A10 10c + 5c red & car 30.00 30.00
a. Double surcharge 200.00 225.00
d. In pair with unsurcharged stamp 550.00

Same Surcharge on No. 54 in Red

B2 A10 10c + 5c red & car 37.50 37.50
a. Double surcharge 200.00 225.00
b. Inverted surcharge 175.00
c. Double surcharge, one inverted 175.00 200.00
d. In pair with unsurcharged stamp 550.00

No. 54 Surcharged in Red

1917
B3 A10 10c + 5c red & car 2.40 2.40

Catalogue values for unused stamps in this section, from this point to the end of the section, are for Never Hinged items.

Republic
Anti-Malaria Issue
Common Design Type

1962, Apr. 7 **Engr.** ***Perf. 12½x12***
B4 CD108 25fr + 5fr yel grn 1.00 1.00

WHO drive to eradicate malaria.

Freedom from Hunger Issue
Common Design Type

1963, Mar. 21 **Unwmk.** ***Perf. 13***
B5 CD112 25fr + 5fr dk red, grn & brn 1.00 1.00

Red Cross — SP1

1997, May 8 **Litho.** ***Perf. 13½x13***
B6 SP1 150fr +75fr multi 1.40 1.10

AIR POST STAMPS

Catalogue values for unused stamps in this section are for Never Hinged items.

Dr. Albert Schweitzer — AP1

Unwmk.

1960, July 23 **Engr.** ***Perf. 13***
C1 AP1 200fr grn, dl red brn & ultra 7.50 3.75

For surcharge see No. C11.

Workmen Felling Tree — AP2

1960, Oct. 8
C2 AP2 100fr red brn, grn & blk 4.00 1.50

5th World Forestry Cong., Seattle, WA, Aug. 29-Sept. 10.

Olympic Games Issue

French Equatorial Africa No. C37 Surcharged in Red Like Chad No. C1

1960, Dec. 15

C3 AP8 250fr on 500fr grnsh blk, blk & slate 8.00 8.00

17th Olympic Games, Rome, 8/25-9/11.

Lyre-tailed Honey Guide — AP3

1961, May 30 *Perf. 13*

C4 AP3 50fr sl grn, red brn & ultra 4.00 1.00

See Nos. C14-C17.

Air Afrique Issue

Common Design Type

1962, Feb. 17 Engr. *Perf. 13*

C5 CD107 500fr sl grn, blk & bis 11.00 6.00

Long Jump — AP3a

1962, July 21 Photo. *Perf. 12x12½*

C6 AP3a 100fr dk & lt bl, brn & blk 3.00 1.50

Issued to publicize the Abidjan Games.

Breguet 14, 1928 — AP4

Development of air transport: 20fr, Dragon biplane transport. 60fr, Caravelle jet. 85fr, Rocket-propelled aircraft.

1962, Sept. 4 Engr. *Perf. 13*

C7 AP4 10fr dl red brn & sl .65 .25
C8 AP4 20fr dk bl, sl & ocher .90 .35
C9 AP4 60fr dk sl grn, blk & brn 2.25 .90
C10 AP4 85fr dk bl, blk & org 3.25 1.60
a. Souv. sheet of 4, #C7-C10 9.00 11.00
Nos. C7-C10 (4) 7.05 3.10

Gabon's 1st phil. exhib., Libreville, Sept. 2-9.

No. C1 Surcharged in Red: "100F/JUBILE GABONAIS/1913-1963"

1963, Apr. 18

C11 AP1 100fr on 200fr 4.00 2.10

50th anniv. of Dr. Albert Schweitzer's arrival in Gabon.

Post Office, Libreville — AP5

1963, Apr. 28 Photo. *Perf. 13x12*

C12 AP5 100fr multi 3.00 .90

African Postal Union Issue

Common Design Type

1963, Sept. 8 Unwmk. *Perf. 12½*

C13 CD114 85fr brt car, ocher & red 1.90 .80

Bird Type of 1961

Birds: 100fr, Johanna's sunbird. 200fr, Blue-headed bee-eater, vert. 250fr, Crowned hawk-eagle, vert. 500fr, Narina trogon, vert.

1963-64 Engr. *Perf. 13*

C14 AP3 100fr dk grn, vio bl & car 3.75 1.25
C15 AP3 200fr ol, vio bl & red 8.00 3.00
C16 AP3 250fr grn, blk & dk brn ('64) 15.00 4.00
C17 AP3 500fr multi 15.00 7.00
Nos. C14-C17 (4) 41.75 15.25

Issued: Nos. C14-C15, C17, 10/7; No. C16, 9/23/64.

1963 Air Afrique Issue

Common Design Type

1963, Nov. 19 Photo. *Perf. 13x12*

C18 CD115 50fr lt vio, gray, blk & grn 1.40 .65

Europafrica Issue

Common Design Type

1963, Nov. 30 *Perf. 12x13*

C19 CD116 50fr vio, yel & dk brn 1.40 .75

Chiefs of State Issue

Map and Presidents of Chad, Congo, Gabon and CAR — AP5a

1964, June 23 *Perf. 12½*

C20 AP5a 100fr multi 2.10 .90

See note after Central African Republic No. C19.

Europafrica Issue

Globe and Emblems of Industry and Agriculture — AP6

1964, July 20 *Perf. 12x13*

C21 AP6 50fr red, olive & blue 1.60 .75

See note after Cameroun No. 402.

Start of Race — AP7

Athletes (Greek): 50fr, Massage at gymnasium, vert. 100fr, Anointing with oil before game, vert. 200fr, Four athletes.

1964, July 30 Engr. *Perf. 13*

C22 AP7 25fr sl grn, dk brn & org .75 .40
C23 AP7 50fr dk brn, sl grn & org brn 1.20 .45
C24 AP7 100fr vio bl, ol grn & dk brn 2.40 .90
C25 AP7 200fr dk brn, mag & org red 4.00 2.50
a. Min. sheet of 4, #C22-C25 12.00 12.00
Nos. C22-C25 (4) 8.35 4.25

18th Olympic Games, Tokyo, Oct. 10-25.

Communications Symbols — AP7a

1964, Nov. 2 Litho. *Perf. 12½x13*

C26 AP7a 25fr lt grn, dk brn & lt red brn .90 .25

See note after Chad No. C19.

John F. Kennedy (1917-63) — AP8

1964, Nov. 23 Photo. *Perf. 12½*

C27 AP8 100fr grn, org & blk 1.75 1.50
a. Souv. sheet of 4 9.00 9.00

Telephone Operator, Nurse and Police Woman — AP9

1964, Dec. 5 Engr. *Perf. 13*

C28 AP9 50fr car, bl & chocolate 1.40 .40

Social evolution of Gabonese women.

World Map and ICY Emblem — AP10

1965, Mar. 25 Unwmk. *Perf. 13*

C29 AP10 50fr org, Prus bl & grnsh bl 1.40 .70

International Cooperation Year.

Merchant Ship, 17th Century — AP11

25fr, Galleon, 16th cent., vert. 85fr, Frigate, 18th cent., vert. 100fr, Brig, 19th cent.

1965, Apr. 22 Photo. *Perf. 13*

C30 AP11 25fr lilac & multi 1.00 .55
C31 AP11 50fr yellow & multi 2.00 .80
C32 AP11 85fr multi 3.25 1.50
C33 AP11 100fr multi 4.50 2.00
Nos. C30-C33 (4) 10.75 4.85

Red Cross Nurse Carrying Sick Child — AP12

1965, June 25 Engr. *Perf. 13*

C34 AP12 100fr brn, slate grn & red 2.25 .75

Issued for the Gabonese Red Cross.

Women's Basketball AP13

1965, July 15 Unwmk.

C35 AP13 100fr sep, red org & brt lil 2.40 .90

African Games, Brazzaville, July 18-25.

Maps of Europe and Africa — AP14

1965, July 26 Photo. *Perf. 13x12*

C36 AP14 50fr multi 1.60 .50

See note after Cameroun No. 421.

Pres. Leon Mba AP15

1965, Aug. 17 *Perf. 12½*

C37 AP15 25fr multi .90 .50

Fifth anniversary of independence.

Sir Winston Churchill and Microphones — AP16

1965, Sept. 28 Photo. *Perf. 12½*
C38 AP16 100fr gold, blk & bl 2.00 .75

Sir Winston Spencer Churchill (1874-1965), statesman and World War II leader.

Dr. Albert Schweitzer — AP17

Embossed on Gold Foil

Die-cut Perf. 14½, Approx.

1965, Dec. 4
C39 AP17 1000fr gold 55.00 55.00

Dr. Albert Schweitzer (1875-1965), medical missionary, theologian and musician.

Pope John XXIII and St. Peter's — AP18

1965, Dec. 10 Photo. *Perf. 13x12½*
C40 AP18 85fr multi 1.60 .75

Issued in memory of Pope John XXIII.

Anti-Malaria Treatment AP19

1966, Apr. 8 Photo. *Perf. 12½*
C41 AP19 50fr shown 1.00 .60
a. Min. sheet of 4 7.00 7.00
C42 AP19 100fr First aid 2.10 1.00
a. Min. sheet of 4 10.00 10.00

Issued for the Red Cross.

Diamant Rocket, A-1 Satellite and Map of Africa — AP20

90fr, FR-1 satellite, Diamant rocket and earth.

1966, May 18 Engr. *Perf. 13*
C43 AP20 30fr dk pur, brt bl & red brn .75 .35
C44 AP20 90fr brt lil, red & pur 1.50 .65

French achievements in space.

Soccer and World Map — AP21

1966, July 15 Engr. *Perf. 13*
C45 AP21 100fr slate & brn red 2.25 .85

8th World Soccer Cup Championship, Wembley, England, July 11-30.

Symbols of Industry and Transportation AP22

1966, July 26 Photo. *Perf. 12x13*
C46 AP22 50fr multi 1.50 .65

3rd anniv. of the economic agreement between the European Economic Community and the African and Malgache Union.

Air Afrique Issue, 1966
Common Design Type

1966, Aug. 31 Photo. *Perf. 13*
C47 CD123 30fr org, blk & gray .90 .35

Student and UNESCO Emblem — AP23

1966, Nov. 4 Engr. *Perf. 13*
C48 AP23 100fr dl bl, ocher & blk 1.90 .85

20th anniv. of UNESCO.

Libreville Airport — AP24

1966, Nov. 21 Engr. *Perf. 13*
C49 AP24 200fr dp bl & red brn 4.50 1.50

Inauguration of Libreville Airport.

Farman 190 — AP25

Planes: 300fr, De Havilland Heron. 500fr, Potez 56.

1967, Apr. 1 Engr. *Perf. 13*
C50 AP25 200fr ultra, lil & bl grn 4.00 1.75
C51 AP25 300fr brn, lil & brt bl 6.50 2.10
C52 AP25 500fr brn car, dk grn & indigo 11.00 4.75
Nos. C50-C52 (3) 21.50 8.60

For surcharge see No. C128.

Planes, Runways and ICAO Emblem — AP26

1967, May 19 Engr. *Perf. 13*
C53 AP26 100fr plum, brt bl & yel grn 2.00 1.10

International Civil Aviation Organization.

Blood Donor and Bottles — AP27

100fr, Human heart and transfusion apparatus.

1967, June 26 Photo. *Perf. 12½*
C54 AP27 50fr ocher, red & sl 1.50 .55
a. Souvenir sheet of 4 7.50 7.50
C55 AP27 100fr yel grn, red & gray 3.00 1.25
a. Souvenir sheet of 4 12.50 12.50

Issued for the Red Cross. Nos. C54a, C55a each contain 2 vertical tête bêche pairs.

Jamboree Emblem and Symbols of Orientation AP28

Design: 100fr, Jamboree emblem, maps and Scouts of Africa and America.

1967, Aug. 1 Engr. *Perf. 13*
C56 AP28 50fr multi 1.60 .80
C57 AP28 100fr brt grn, dp car & bl 2.40 1.60

12th Boy Scout World Jamboree, Farragut State Park, Idaho, Aug. 1-9.

African Postal Union Issue, 1967
Common Design Type

1967, Sept. 9 Engr. *Perf. 13*
C58 CD124 100fr dl bl, ol & red brn 2.25 .95

Mission Church — AP29

1967, Oct. 18 Engr. *Perf. 13*
C59 AP29 100fr brt bl, dk grn & blk 2.75 1.25

125th anniv. of the arrival of American Protestant missionaries in Baraka-Libreville.

UN Emblem, Sword, Book and People — AP30

1967, Nov. 7 Photo. *Perf. 13*
C60 AP30 60fr dk red, vio bl & bis 1.10 .65

UN Commission on Human Rights.

Tree Type of Regular Issue

Designs: 50fr, Baillonella toxisperma. 100fr, Aucoumea klaineana.

1967, Dec. 5 Engr. *Perf. 13*
Size: 26½x47½mm
C61 A53 50fr grn, brt bl & brn 1.60 1.10
C62 A53 100fr multi 2.75 1.90
a. Bklt. pane of 5, #223-225, C61-C62 with gutter btwn. 8.00 8.00

Konrad Adenauer AP31

1968, Feb. 20 Photo. *Perf. 12½*
C63 AP31 100fr blk, dl org & red 2.50 1.10
a. Souvenir sheet of 4 10.00 10.00

Issued in memory of Konrad Adenauer (1876-1967), chancellor of West Germany (1949-63). No. C63a includes 1967 CEPT (Europa) emblem.

Madonna of the Rosary by Murillo AP32

90fr, Christ in Bonds, by Luis de Morales. 100fr, St. John on Patmos, by Juan Mates.

1968, July 9 Photo. *Perf. 12½x12*
C64 AP32 60fr multi 1.20 .55
C65 AP32 90fr multi 1.40 .95
C66 AP32 100fr multi, horiz. 1.90 1.10
Nos. C64-C66 (3) 4.50 2.60

See Nos. C77, C102-C102B, C132-C133, C146-C148.

Europafrica Issue

Stylized Knot — AP32a

1968, July 23 Photo. *Perf. 13*

C67 AP32a 50fr yel brn, emer & lt ultra 1.10 .45

See note after Congo Republic No. C69.

Support for Red Cross — AP33

50fr, Distribution of Red Cross gifts.

1968, Aug. 13

C68 AP33 50fr multi 1.40 .65
C69 AP33 100fr multi 2.75 1.40
a. Bklt. pane of 2, #C68, C69 with gutter btwn. 6.50 6.50

Issued for the Red Cross.

High Jump — AP34

1968, Sept. 3 Engr.

C70 AP34 25fr shown .70 .50
C71 AP34 30fr Bicycling, vert. .85 .55
C72 AP34 100fr Judo, vert. 2.25 1.25
C73 AP34 200fr Boxing 4.25 2.10
a. Bklt. pane of 4, #C70-C71, C72-C73 with gutter btwn. 11.00 11.00
Nos. C70-C73 (4) 8.05 4.40

Issued to publicize the 19th Summer Olympic Games, Mexico City, Oct. 12-27.

Pres. Mba, Flag and Arms of Gabon AP35

Embossed on Gold Foil

1968, Nov. 28 *Perf. 14½*

C74 AP35 1000fr gold, grn, yel & dk bl 25.00 25.00

Death of Pres. Léon Mba (1902-67), 1st anniv.

Pres. Bongo, Maps of Gabon and Owendo Harbor — AP36

1968, Dec. 16 Photo. *Perf. 12½*

C75 AP36 25fr shown 1.25 .25
C76 AP36 30fr Owendo Harbor 1.25 .25
a. Strip of 2, #C75-C76 + label 3.00 3.00

Laying of the foundation stone for Owendo Harbor, June 24, 1968.

PHILEXAFRIQUE Issue
Painting Type of 1968

Design: 100fr, The Convent of St. Mary of the Angels, by Francois Marius Granet.

1969, Jan. 8 Photo. *Perf. 12½x12*

C77 AP32 100fr multi 3.50 3.50

Issued to publicize PHILEXAFRIQUE Philatelic Exhibition in Abidjan, Feb. 14-23. Printed with alternating brown label.

Mahatma Gandhi — AP37

Portraits: 30fr, John F. Kennedy. 50fr, Robert F. Kennedy. 100fr, Martin Luther King, Jr.

1969, Jan. 15 *Perf. 12½*

C78 AP37 25fr peach & blk .75 .45
C79 AP37 30fr lt yel grn & blk .75 .45
C80 AP37 50fr lt bl & blk 1.10 .45
C81 AP37 100fr brt rose lil & blk 2.25 .90
a. Souv. sheet of 4, #C78-C81 6.00 6.00
Nos. C78-C81 (4) 4.85 2.25

Issued to honor exponents of non-violence.

2nd PHILEXAFRIQUE Issue
Common Design Type

1969, Feb. 14 Engr. *Perf. 13*

C82 CD128 50fr grn, ind & red brn 2.25 2.25

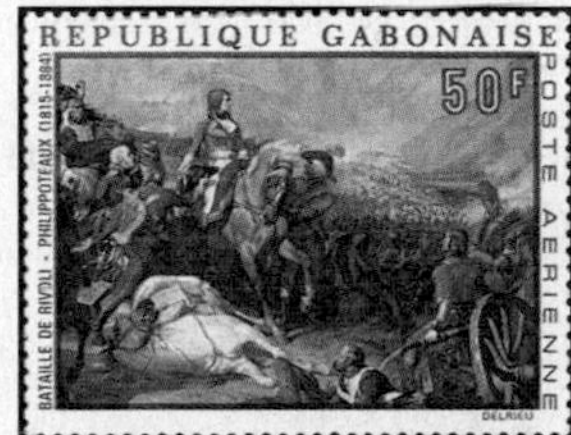

Battle of Rivoli, by Henri Philippoteaux — AP39

100fr, The Oath of the Army, by Jacques Louis David. 250fr, Napoleon with the Children on the Terrace in St. Cloud, by Louis Ducis.

1969, Apr. 23 Photo. *Perf. 12½x12*

C83 AP39 50fr brn & multi 2.10 1.10
C84 AP39 100fr grn & multi 2.50 2.00
C85 AP39 250fr lil & multi 10.00 6.00
Nos. C83-C85 (3) 14.60 9.10

Birth bicentenary of Napoleon I.

Red Cross Plane, Nurse and Biafran Children — AP40

20fr, Dispensary, ambulance & supplies. 25fr, Physician & nurse in children's ward. 30fr, Dispensary & playing children.

1969, June 20 Photo. *Perf. 14x13½*

C86 AP40 15fr lt ultra, dk brn & red .55 .25
C87 AP40 20fr emer, blk, brn & red .75 .45
C88 AP40 25fr grnsh bl, dk brn & red .75 .45
C89 AP40 30fr org yel, dk brn & red .90 .45
Nos. C86-C89 (4) 2.95 1.60

Red Cross help for Biafra.

A souvenir sheet contains four stamps similar to Nos. C86-C89, but lithographed and rouletted 13x13½. Gray margin with red inscription and Red Cross. Size: 118x75mm. Sold in cardboard folder. Value $4.

Astronauts and Lunar Landing Module, Apollo 11 — AP41

Embossed on Gold Foil

1969, July 25 *Die-cut Perf. 10½x10*

C90 AP41 1000fr gold 20.00 20.00

See note after Algeria No. 427.

Europafrica Issue

African and European Heads and Symbols — AP42

1970, June 5 Photo. *Perf. 12x13*

C91 AP42 50fr multi 1.25 .50

Icarus and Sun — AP43

Designs: 100fr, Leonardo da Vinci's flying man, 1519. 200fr, Jules Verne's space shell approaching moon, 1865.

1970, June 10 Engr. *Perf. 13*

C92 AP43 25fr ultra, red & org .60 .45
C93 AP43 100fr ocher, plum & sl grn 1.50 .75
C94 AP43 200fr gray, ultra & dk car 3.50 1.50
a. Min. sheet of 3, #C92-C94 6.50 6.50
Nos. C92-C94 (3) 5.60 2.70

UAMPT Emblem AP44

Embossed on Gold Foil

1970, June 18 *Die-cut Perf. 12½*

C95 AP44 200fr gold, yel grn & bl 3.00 1.50

Meeting of the Afro-Malagasy Union of Posts & Telecommuncations (UAMPT), Libreville, 6/17-23.

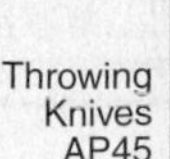

Throwing Knives AP45

Gabonese Weapons: 30fr, Assegai and crossbow, vert. 50fr, War knives, vert. 90fr, Dagger and sheath.

1970, July 10 Engr. *Perf. 13*

C96 AP45 25fr multi .60 .35
C97 AP45 30fr multi .70 .40
C98 AP45 50fr multi 1.00 .50
C99 AP45 90fr multi 2.00 .75
a. Min. sheet of 4, #C96-C99 6.00 6.00
Nos. C96-C99 (4) 4.30 2.00

Japanese Masks, Mt. Fuji and Torii at Miyajima — AP46

Embossed on Gold Foil

1970, July 31 *Die-cut Perf. 10*

C100 AP46 1000fr multi 20.00 20.00

Issued to publicize EXPO '70 International Exhibition, Osaka, Japan, Mar. 15-Sept. 13.

Pres. Albert Bernard Bongo — AP47

Lithographed; Gold Embossed

1970, Aug. 17 *Perf. 12½*

C101 AP47 200fr multi 5.00 2.25

10th anniversary of independence.

Painting Type of 1968

Paintings: 50fr, Portrait of a Young Man, School of Raphael. 100fr, Portrait of Jeanne d'Aragon, by Raphael. 200fr, Madonna with Blue Diadem, by Raphael.

1970, Oct. 16 Photo. *Perf. 12½x12*

C102 AP32 50fr multi 1.10 .50
C102A AP32 100fr blue & multi 2.25 .95
C102B AP32 200fr brn & multi 4.50 2.50
Nos. C102-C102B (3) 7.85 3.95

Raphael (1483-1520).

Miniature Sheets

AP47a

Hugo Junkers — AP47b

1970, Dec. 5 Litho. *Perf. 12*

C103 AP47a Sheet of 8 10.00 10.00
- *a.* 15fr Sikorsky S-32
- *b.* 25fr Fokker "Southern Cross"
- *c.* 40fr Dornier DO-18
- *d.* 60fr Dornier DO-X
- *e.* 80fr Breguet "Bizerte"
- *f.* 125fr Douglas "Cloudster"
- *g.* 150fr De Havilland DH-2
- *h.* 200fr Vickers "Vimi"

C104 Sheet of 4 15.00 15.00
- *a.* AP47b 200fr shown
- *b.* AP47b 300fr Claude Dornier
- *c.* AP47b 400fr Anthony Fokker
- *d.* AP47b 500fr Igor Sikorsky

Imperf

C105 AP47a Sheet of 8 10.00 10.00
- *a.* 10fr Dornier "Spatz"
- *b.* 20fr Douglas DC-3
- *c.* 30fr Dornier DO-7 "Wal"
- *d.* 50fr Sikorsky S-38
- *e.* 75fr De Havilland "Moth"
- *f.* 100fr Supermarine "Spitfire"
- *g.* 125fr Breguet XIX
- *h.* 150fr Fokker "Universal"

Size: 80x90mm

C106 AP47b 1000fr Claude Dornier 15.00 15.00

Claude Dornier (1884-1969), aviation pioneer. No. C104 exists imperf. Value $17.

Presidents Bongo and Pompidou — AP48

1971, Feb. 11 Photo. *Perf. 13*

C107 AP48 50fr multi 1.75 .85

Visit of Georges Pompidou, Pres. of France.

Apollo 14 — AP48a

15fr, Lift off. 25fr, Achieving orbit. 40fr, Lunar module descent. 55fr, Lunar landing. 75fr, Lunar liftoff. 120fr, Earth re-entry.

1971, Feb. 19 *Perf. 14*

Yellow Inscriptions

C108	15fr multi	.25	.25
C108A	25fr multi	.45	.30
C108B	40fr multi	.80	.60
C108C	55fr multi	1.00	.65
C108D	75fr multi	1.50	1.00
C108E	120fr multi	2.50	1.50
	Nos. C108-C108E (6)	6.50	4.30

Souvenir Sheet

C108F Sheet of 2 7.50 4.25
- *g.* AP48a 100fr Modules attached 3.00 1.75
- *h.* AP48a 100fr like #C108E 3.00 1.75

Nos. C108-C108F exist imperf. with white inscriptions. Same values.

Flowers and Plane — AP49

25fr, Carnations. 40fr, Roses. 55fr, Daffodils. 75fr, Orchids. 120fr, Tulips.

1971, May 7 Litho. *Perf. 13½x14*

C109	AP49	15fr yellow & multi	.35	.25
C109A	AP49	25fr multi	.55	.25
C109B	AP49	40fr pink & multi	.90	.30
C109C	AP49	55fr blue & multi	1.20	.35
C110	AP49	75fr multi	2.00	.60
C111	AP49	120fr green & multi	2.40	.85
a.		Souv. sheet of 2, #C110-C111	6.00	6.00
		Nos. C109-C111 (6)	7.40	2.60

"Flowers by air."

Napoleon's Death Mask AP50

Designs: 200fr, Longwood, St. Helena, by Jacques Marchand, horiz. 500fr, Sarcophagus in Les Invalides, Paris.

1971, May 12 Photo. *Perf. 13*

C112	AP50 100fr gold & multi	2.75	.70
C113	AP50 200fr gold & multi	4.25	1.50
C114	AP50 500fr gold & multi	10.00	3.50
	Nos. C112-C114 (3)	17.00	5.70

Napoleon Bonaparte (1769-1821).

Souvenir Sheet

Charles de Gaulle — AP51

Designs: 40fr, President de Gaulle. 80fr, General de Gaulle. 100fr, Quotation.

1971, June 18 Photo. *Perf. 12½*

C115 AP51 Sheet of 5 9.00 9.00
- *a.* 40fr dark red & multi .75 .75
- *b.* 80fr dark green & multi .75 .75
- *c.* 100fr green, brown & yel 2.00 2.00

In memory of Gen. Charles de Gaulle (1890-1970), Pres. of France.

For surcharge see No. C126.

Red Crosses AP52

1971, June 29

C116 AP52 50fr multicolored 1.40 .40

For the Red Cross of Gabon.

For surcharge see No. C143.

Uranium — AP53

1971, July 20 Photo. *Perf. 13x12½*

C117	AP53 85fr shown	7.00	3.50
C118	AP53 90fr Manganese	8.00	4.00

Landing Module over Moon — AP54

Embossed on Gold Foil

1971, July 30 *Die-cut Perf. 10*

C119 AP54 1500fr multi 25.00 25.00

Apollo 11 and 15 US moon missions.

African Postal Union Issue, 1971

Common Design Type

Design: 100fr, Bakota copper mask and UAMPT building, Brazzaville, Congo.

1971, Nov. 13 Photo. *Perf. 13x13½*

C120 CD135 100fr bl & multi 1.75 .70

Ski Jump and Miyajima Torii AP55

130fr, Speed skating and Japanese temple.

1972, Jan. 31 Engr. *Perf. 13*

C121	AP55 40fr hn brn, sl grn & vio bl	1.40	.50
C122	AP55 130fr hn brn, sl grn & vio bl	2.00	.75
a.	Souvenir sheet of 2, #C121-C122 + label	5.00	5.00

11th Winter Olympic Games, Sapporo, Japan, Feb. 3-13.

The Basin and Grand Canal, by Vanvitelli — AP56

Paintings: 70fr, Rialto Bridge, by Canaletto (erroneously inscribed Caffi), vert. 140fr, Santa Maria della Salute, by Vanvitelli, vert.

1972, Feb. 7 Photo. *Perf. 13*

C123	AP56 60fr gold & multi	2.10	.70
C124	AP56 70fr gold & multi	3.25	1.00
C125	AP56 140fr gold & multi	5.75	1.50
	Nos. C123-C125 (3)	11.10	3.20

UNESCO campaign to save Venice.

No. C115 Surcharged in Brown and Gold

Souvenir Sheet

1972, Feb. 11 *Perf. 12½*

C126 AP51 Sheet of 5 15.00 15.00
- *a.* 60fr on 40fr multi 2.00 2.00
- *b.* 120fr on 80fr multi 3.00 3.00
- *c.* 180fr on 100fr multi 6.25 6.25

Publicity for the erection of a memorial for Charles de Gaulle. Nos. C126a-C126b have surcharge and Cross of Lorraine in gold, 2 bars obliterating old denomination in brown; No. C126c has surcharge, cross and bars in brown. Two Lorraine Crosses and inscription (MEMORIAL DU GENERAL DE GAULLE) in brown added in margin.

Hotel Inter-Continental, Libreville — AP57

1972, Feb. 26 Engr. *Perf. 13*

C127 AP57 40fr bl, sl grn & org brn 1.10 .35

No. C51 Surcharged

1972, Mar. 3

C128 AP25 50fr on 300fr multi 1.40 .50

Official visit of the Grand Master of the Knights of Malta, March 3.

Discobolus, by Alcamenes AP58

Designs: 100fr, Doryphoros, by Polycletus. 140fr, Borghese gladiator, by Agasias.

1972, May 10 Engr. *Perf. 13*

C129	AP58 30fr rose cl & gray	.80	.40
C130	AP58 100fr rose cl & gray	1.75	.50
C131	AP58 140fr rose cl & gray	2.25	.70
a.	Min. of sheet of 3, #C129-C131	6.00	6.00
	Nos. C129-C131 (3)	4.80	1.60

20th Olympic Games, Munich, 8/26-9/10.

For surcharges see Nos. C134-C136.

Painting Type of 1968

Paintings: 30fr, Adoration of the Magi, by Peter Brueghel, the Elder, horiz. 40fr, Madonna and Child, by Marco Basaiti.

1972, Oct. 30 Photo. *Perf. 13*

C132	AP32 30fr gold & multi	1.10	.25
C133	AP32 40fr gold & multi	1.60	.25

Christmas 1972.

Nos. C129-C131 Surcharged with New Value, Two Bars and Names of Athletes.

1972, Dec. 5 Engr. *Perf. 13*
C134 AP58 40fr on 30fr 1.00 .35
C135 AP58 120fr on 100fr 2.00 .65
C136 AP58 170fr on 140fr 3.00 1.00
Nos. C134-C136 (3) 6.00 2.00

Gold medal winners in 20th Olympic Games: Daniel Morelon, France, Bicycling (C134); Kipchoge Keino, Kenya, steeplechase (C135); Mark Spitz, US, swimming (C136).

Globe with Space Orbits, Simulated Stamps — AP59

1973, Feb. 20 Photo. *Perf. 13*
C137 AP59 100fr multi 2.25 .50
a. Souv. sheet of 4, perf. 12x12½ 25.00 25.00

PHILEXGABON 1973, Phil. Exhib., Libreville, Feb. 19-26. No. C137a exists imperf.

DC10-30 "Libreville" over Libreville Airport — AP60

1973, Mar. 19 Typo. *Perf. 13*
C138 AP60 40fr blue & multi 3.00 1.50

Kinguélé Hydroelectric Station — AP61

Design: 40fr, Kinguélé Dam.

1973, June 19 Engr. *Perf. 13*
C139 AP61 30fr slate grn & dk ol .80 .25
C140 AP61 40fr slate grn, dk ol & bl 1.10 .25
a. Strip of 2, #C139-C140 + label 2.75 1.25

Hydroelectric installations at Kinguélé.

M'Bigou Stone Sculpture, Woman's Head — AP62

Design: 200fr, Sculpture, man's head.

1973, July 5
C141 AP62 100fr blk, bl & grn 1.60 .70
C142 AP62 200fr grn, sep & sl grn 3.00 1.25

No. C116 Srchd. and Ovptd. in Ultramarine

1973, Aug. 16 Photo. *Perf. 12½*
C143 AP52 100fr on 50fr multi 2.25 .65

African solidarity in drought emergency.

Astronauts and Lunar Rover on Moon — AP63

1973, Sept. 6 Engr. *Perf. 13*
C144 AP63 500fr multi 8.50 4.00

Apollo 17 US moon mission, 12/7-19/73.

Presidents Houphouet Boigny (Ivory Coast) and De Gaulle — AP64

1974, Apr. 30 Engr. *Perf. 13*
C145 AP64 40fr rose lilac & indigo 2.00 .75

30th anniv. of the Conf. of Brazzaville.

Painting Type of 1968

Impressionist Paintings: 40fr, Pleasure Boats, by Claude Monet, horiz. 50fr, Ballet Dancer, by Edgar Degas. 130fr, Young Girl with Flowers, by Auguste Renoir.

1974, June 11 Photo. *Perf. 13*
C146 AP32 40fr gold & multi 3.25 .50
C147 AP32 50fr gold & multi 5.00 .70
C148 AP32 130fr gold & multi 8.00 1.10
Nos. C146-C148 (3) 16.25 2.30

Astronaut on Moon, Eagle and Emblems AP65

1974, July 20 Engr. *Perf. 13*
C149 AP65 200fr multi 2.75 .90

First men on the moon, 5th anniversary.

UPU Emblem, Letters, Pigeon AP66

UPU cent.: 300fr, UPU emblem, letters, pigeons, diff.

1974, Oct. 9 Engr. *Perf. 13*
C150 AP66 150fr lt bl & Prus bl 2.50 .90
C151 AP66 300fr org & claret 5.00 1.75

Space Docking, US and USSR Crafts AP67

1974, Oct. 23 Engr. *Perf. 13*
C152 AP67 1000fr grn, red & sl 11.00 5.25

Russo-American space cooperation. For overprint see No. C169.

Soccer and Games Emblem — AP68

Designs: Soccer actions.

1974, Oct. 25
C153 AP68 40fr grn, red & brn .70 .25
C154 AP68 65fr red, brn & grn 1.00 .35
C155 AP68 100fr grn, red & brn 1.50 .60
a. Souv. sheet of 3, #C153-C155 + 3 labels 4.50 4.50
Nos. C153-C155 (3) 3.20 1.20

World Cup Soccer Championship, Munich, June 13-July 7.

UDEAC Issue

Presidents and Flags of Cameroun, CAR, Gabon and Congo — AP68a

1974, Dec. 8 Photo. *Perf. 13*
C156 AP68a 100fr gold & multi 1.40 .45

Annunciation, Tapestry, 15th Century — AP69

Christmas: 40fr, Visitation from 15th century tapestry, Notre Dame de Beaune, vert.

1974, Dec. 11
C157 AP69 40fr gold & multi 1.10 .30
C158 AP69 50fr gold & multi 1.25 .35

Dr. Schweitzer and Lambarene Hospital — AP70

1975, Jan. 14 Engr. *Perf. 13*
C159 AP70 500fr multi 9.00 3.00

Dr. Albert Schweitzer (1875-1965), medical missionary, birth centenary.

Crucifixion, by Bellini — AP71

Paintings: 150fr, Resurrection, Burgundian School, c. 1500.

1975, Apr. 8 Photo. *Perf. 13½*
Size: 26x45mm
C160 AP71 140fr gold & multi 2.10 .60
Size: 36x48mm
Perf. 13
C161 AP71 150fr gold & multi 2.50 .70

Easter 1975.

Marc Seguin Locomotive, 1829 — AP72

Locomotives: 25fr, The Iron Duke, 1847. 40fr, Thomas Rogers, 1895. 50fr, The Soviet 272, 1934.

1975, Apr. 8 Engr. *Perf. 13*
C162 AP72 20fr multi 1.75 .40
C163 AP72 25fr multi 2.25 .40
C164 AP72 40fr multi 3.00 .65
C165 AP72 50fr lil & multi 4.00 .75
Nos. C162-C165 (4) 11.00 2.20

Swimming Pool, Montreal Olympic Games' Emblem — AP73

Designs: 150fr, Boxing ring and emblem. 300fr, Stadium, aerial view, and emblem.

1975, Sept. 30 Litho. *Perf. 13x12½*
C166 AP73 100fr multi 1.50 .30
C167 AP73 150fr multi 1.90 .60
C168 AP73 300fr multi 3.75 1.10
a. Min. sheet of 3, #C166-C168 8.00 8.00
Nos. C166-C168 (3) 7.15 2.00

Pre-Olympic Year 1975.

No. C152 Surcharged in Violet Blue: "JONCTION / 17 Juillet 1975"

1975, Oct. 20 Engr. *Perf. 13*
C169 AP67 1000fr multi 9.50 4.50

Apollo-Soyuz link-up in space, July 17, 1975.

Annunciation, by Maurice Denis — AP74

Painting: 50fr, Virgin and Child with Two Saints, by Fra Filippo Lippi.

1975, Dec. 9 Photo. *Perf. 13*
C170 AP74 40fr gold & multi 1.25 .40
C171 AP74 50fr gold & multi 1.60 .55

Christmas 1975.

Concorde and Globe — AP75

1975, Dec. 29 Engr. Perf. 13
C172 AP75 500fr bl, vio bl & red 10.00 3.75

For overprint see No. C198.

No. C172 Surcharged

1976, Jan. 21
C173 AP75 1000fr on 500fr 16.00 8.00

Nos. C172-C173 for the 1st commercial flight of supersonic jet Concorde from Paris to Rio, Jan. 21.

Slalom and Olympic Games Emblem — AP76

Design: 250fr, Speed skating and Winter Olympic Games emblem.

1976, Apr. 22 Engr. Perf. 13
C174 AP76 100fr blk, bl & red 1.50 .40
C175 AP76 250fr blk, bl & red 3.25 1.40
a. Souvenir sheet 6.50 6.50

12th Winter Olympic Games, Innsbruck, Austria, Feb. 4-15. No. C175a contains 100fr and 250fr stamps in continuous design with additional inscription and skier between, but without perforations between the design elements.

Size of perforated area: 125x27mm; size of sheet: 169x90mm.

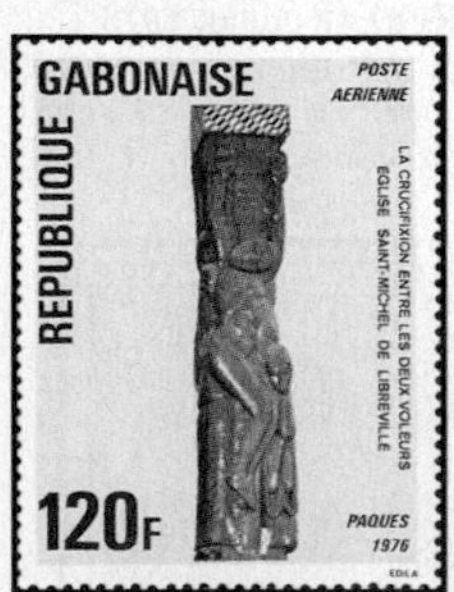
Jesus Between the Thieves AP77

Design: 130fr, St. Thomas putting finger into wounds of Jesus. Both designs after wood carvings in Church of St. Michael, Libreville.

1976, Apr. 28 Litho. Perf. 12½x13
C176 AP77 120fr multi 1.60 .65
C177 AP77 130fr multi 2.25 .95

Easter 1976. See Nos. C188-C189, C220-C221.

Boston Tea Party — AP78

Designs: 150fr, Battle of New York. 200fr, Demolition of statue of George III.

1976, May 3 Engr. Perf. 13
C178 AP78 100fr multi 1.00 .50
C179 AP78 150fr multi 1.90 .70
C180 AP78 200fr multi 2.40 .80
a. Triptych, #C178-C180 + 2 labels 8.00 6.50

American Bicentennial.

Nos. C178-C180 Overprinted: "4 JUILLET 1976"

1976, July 4 Engr. Perf. 13
C181 AP78 100fr multi 1.00 .50
C182 AP78 150fr multi 1.90 .70
C183 AP78 200fr multi 2.40 .80
a. Triptych, #C181-C183 + 2 labels 8.00 6.50

Independence Day.

Running — AP79

200fr, Soccer. 260fr, High jump.

1976, July 27 Litho. Perf. 12½
C184 AP79 100fr multi 1.10 .35
C185 AP79 200fr multi 2.50 .65
C186 AP79 260fr multi 3.25 .90
a. Souv. sheet of 3, #C184-C186, perf. 13 8.00 3.75
Nos. C184-C186 (3) 6.85 1.90

21st Olympic Games, Montreal, Canada, July 17-Aug. 1.

Presidents Giscard d'Estaing and Bongo — AP80

1976, Aug. 5 Photo. Perf. 13
C187 AP80 60fr blue & multi 1.25 .30

Visit of Pres. Valèrie Giscard d'Estaing of France.

Sculpture Type of 1976

Christmas: 50fr, Presentation at the Temple. 60fr, Nativity. Designs after wood Carvings in Church of St. Michael, Libreville.

1976, Dec. 6 Litho. Perf. 12½x13
C188 AP77 50fr multi 1.00 .25
C189 AP77 60fr multi 1.10 .35

Oklo Fossil Reactor — AP81

1976, Dec. 15 Litho. Perf. 13
C190 AP81 60fr red & multi 1.10 .30

The Last Supper, by Juste de Gand — AP82

100fr, The Deposition, by Nicolas Poussin.

1977, Mar. 25 Litho. Perf. 12½
C191 AP82 50fr gold & multi 1.10 .25
C192 AP82 100fr gold & multi 2.25 .65

Easter 1977.

Air Gabon Plane and Insigne — AP83

1977, June 3 Litho. Perf. 12½
C193 AP83 60fr multi 1.40 .50

Air Gabon's first intercontinental route.

Beethoven, Piano and Score — AP84

1977, June 15 Engr. Perf. 13
C194 AP84 260fr slate 3.00 .95

Ludwig van Beethoven (1770-1827).

Lindbergh and Spirit of St. Louis — AP85

1977, Sept. 13 Engr. Perf. 13
C195 AP85 500fr multi 8.00 2.75

Charles A. Lindbergh's solo transatlantic flight from NY to Paris, 50th anniv.

Soccer — AP86

1977, Oct. 18 Photo. Perf. 13x12½
C196 AP86 250fr multi 3.25 1.10

Elimination games, World Soccer Cup, Buenos Aires, 1978.

Viking on Mars AP87

1977, Nov. 17 Engr. Perf. 13
C197 AP87 1000fr multi 10.00 8.00

Viking, US space probe.

No. C172 Overprinted: "PARIS NEW-YORK / PREMIER VOL / 22.11.77"

1977, Nov. 22 Engr. Perf. 13
C198 AP75 500fr multi 9.00 5.00

Concorde, 1st commercial flight, Paris to NYC.

Lion Hunt, by Rubens — AP88

Rubens Paintings: 80fr, Hippopotamus Hunt. 200fr, Head of Black Man, vert.

1977, Nov. 24 Litho. Perf. 13
C199 AP88 60fr gold & multi .95 .35
C200 AP88 80fr gold & multi 1.25 .45
C201 AP88 200fr gold & multi 3.00 1.10
a. Souv. sheet of 3, #C199-C201 6.50 6.50
Nos. C199-C201 (3) 5.20 1.90

Peter Paul Rubens (1577-1640).

Adoration of the Kings, by Rubens — AP89

Design: 80fr, Flight into Egypt, by Rubens.

1977, Dec. 15 Litho. Perf. 12½
C202 AP89 60fr gold & multi 1.10 .30
C203 AP89 80fr gold & multi 1.25 .45

Christmas 1977; Peter Paul Rubens.

Paul Gauguin, Self-Portrait AP90

150fr, Flowers in vase and Maori statuette.

1978, Feb. 8 Litho. Perf. 12½x12
C204 AP90 150fr multi 3.00 .60
C205 AP90 300fr multi 5.50 1.10

Paul Gauguin (1848-1903), French painter.

Pres. Bongo, Map of Gabon, Plane and Train
AP91

Lithographed; Gold Embossed

1978, Mar. 12 ***Perf. 12½***
C206 AP91 500fr multi 7.00 1.75

10th anniversary of national renewal.

Soccer and Argentina '78 Emblem — AP92

Argentina '78 Emblem and: 120fr, Three soccer players. 200fr, Jules Rimet Cup, vert.

1978, July 18 **Engr.** ***Perf. 13***
C207 AP92 100fr red, grn & brn 1.10 .25
C208 AP92 120fr grn, red & brn 1.25 .40
C209 AP92 200fr brn & red 2.40 .55
a. Min. sheet of 3, #C207-C209 6.50 3.00
Nos. C207-C209 (3) 4.75 1.20

11th World Cup Soccer Championship, Argentina, June 1-25.

Nos. C207-C209a Overprinted in Ultramarine or Black

a

b

c

1978, July 21 **Engr.** ***Perf. 13***
C210 AP92(a) 100fr multi 1.00 .30
C211 AP92(b) 120fr multi 1.25 .40
C212 AP92(c) 200fr multi 2.10 .65
a. Min. sheet of 3 (Bk) 6.00 6.00
Nos. C210-C212 (3) 4.35 1.35

Argentina's World Cup victory.

Albrecht Dürer (age 13), Self-portrait
AP93

Design: 250fr, Lucas de Leyde, by Dürer.

1978, Sept. 15 **Engr.** ***Perf. 13***
C213 AP93 100fr red brn & slate 1.25 .30
C214 AP93 250fr blk & red brn 3.50 .80

Dürer (1474-1528), German painter.

Philexafrique II-Essen Issue
Common Design Types

Designs: No. C215, Gorilla and Gabon No. 280. No. C216, Stork and Saxony No. 1.

1978, Nov. 1 **Litho.** ***Perf. 13x12½***
C215 CD138 100fr multi 2.00 1.40
C216 CD139 100fr multi 2.00 1.40
a. Pair, #C215-C216 + label 6.50 4.00

No. C216a exists with two different labels: one for PHILEXAFRIQUE II and one for ESSEN '78.

Wright Brothers and Flyer
AP94

1978, Dec. 19 **Engr.** ***Perf. 13***
C217 AP94 380fr multi 5.00 1.10

75th anniversary of 1st powered flight.

Pope John Paul II
AP95

Design: 200fr, Popes Paul VI and John Paul I, St. Peter's Basilica and Square, horiz.

1979, Jan. 24 **Litho.** ***Perf. 12½***
C218 AP95 100fr multi 2.50 .35
C219 AP95 200fr multi 5.50 .80

Sculpture Type of 1976

Easter: 100fr, Disciples recognizing Jesus in the breaking of the bread. 150fr, Jesus appearing to Mary Magdalene. Designs after wood carvings in Church of St. Michael, Libreville.

1979, Apr. 10 **Litho.** ***Perf. 12½x13***
C220 AP77 100fr multi 1.25 .45
C221 AP77 150fr multi 2.25 .65

Capt. Cook and Ships
AP96

1979, July 10 **Engr.** ***Perf. 13***
C222 AP96 500fr multi 5.50 2.00

Capt. James Cook (1728-1779), explorer, death bicentenary.

Flags and Map of England and France, Bleriot, Bleriot XI — AP97

Aviation Retrospect: 1000fr, Astronauts walking on moon (gold embossed inset).

Perf. 12½x12, 12

1979, Aug. 8 **Litho.**
C223 AP97 250fr multi 3.25 1.00
C224 AP97 1000fr multi 11.00 3.75

1st flight over English Channel, 70th anniv.; Apollo 11 moon landing, 10th anniv.

Rotary Emblem, Map of Africa, Head — AP98

1979, Sept. 25 **Photo.** ***Perf. 13***
C225 AP98 80fr multi 1.50 .35

Rotary International, 75th anniversary.

Eugene Jamot, Tsetse Fly — AP99

1979, Nov. 23 **Engr.** ***Perf. 13***
C226 AP99 300fr multi 4.50 1.50

Eugene Jamot (1879-1937), discoverer of sleeping sickness cure.

Bobsledding, Lake Placid '80 Emblem
AP100

1980, Feb. 25 **Litho.** ***Perf. 12½***
C227 AP100 100fr shown 1.00 .40
C228 AP100 200fr Ski jump 2.10 .75
a. Souv. sheet of 2, #C227-C228 4.00 1.90

13th Winter Olympic Games, Lake Placid, NY, Feb. 12-24.

Jean Ingres
AP101

200fr, Jacques Offenbach. 360fr, Gustave Flaubert.

1980, May 14 **Engr.** ***Perf. 13***
C229 AP101 100fr shown 1.50 .50
C230 AP101 200fr multi 3.00 .95
C231 AP101 360fr multi 4.50 1.75
Nos. C229-C231 (3) 9.00 3.20

12th World Telecommunications Day — AP102

1980, May 17 **Litho.** ***Perf. 12½***
C232 AP102 80fr multi 1.10 .35

Costes, Bellonte and Plane — AP103

Design: 1000fr, Mermoz, sea plane.

1980, July 16 **Engr.** ***Perf. 13***
C233 AP103 165fr multi 1.40 .70
C234 AP103 1000fr multi 9.00 4.50

1st North Atlantic crossing, 50th anniv.; 1st South Atlantic air mail service, 50th anniv.

Running, Moscow '80 Emblem
AP104

1980, July 25 **Litho.**

C235 AP104 50fr shown .55 .25
C236 AP104 100fr Pole vault 1.10 .45
C237 AP104 250fr Boxing 2.90 1.00
a. Souv. sheet of 3, #C235-C237 8.50 4.00
Nos. C235-C237 (3) 4.55 1.70

22nd Summer Olympic Games, Moscow, July 19-Aug. 3.

Nos. C235-C237a Overprinted in Red, Brown, Ultramarine or Black

No. C238

No. C239

No. C240

1980, Sept. 25 **Litho.** ***Perf. 13***

C238 AP104 50fr (R, vert. & horiz.) .50 .25
C239 AP104 100fr (Br) .95 .40
C240 AP104 250fr (U) 2.50 .85
a. Souv. sheet of 3 (Blk) 8.50 4.00
Nos. C238-C240 (3) 3.95 1.50

Pres. Charles de Gaulle AP105

200fr, Pres. & Mrs. de Gaulle.

1980, Nov. 9 **Photo.** ***Perf. 13***

C241 AP105 100fr shown 1.25 .35
C242 AP105 200fr multi 2.40 .70
a. Souv. sheet of 2, #C241-C242 6.50 3.25

Pres. Charles de Gaulle (1890-1970).

AP106

60fr, Soccer Players. 190fr, Soccer player.

1981, Feb. 19 **Litho.** ***Perf. 13***

C243 AP106 60fr multi .65 .25
C244 AP106 190fr multi 2.10 .75

ESPANA '82 World Cup Soccer Championship.

AP107

Spacecraft and Astronauts: 250fr, Yuri Gagarin. 500fr, Alan B. Shepard.

1981, Mar. 26 **Litho.** ***Perf. 13***

C245 AP107 150fr multi 1.40 .55
C246 AP107 250fr multi 2.40 .85
C247 AP107 500fr multi 4.75 1.75
a. Souv. sheet of 3, #C245-C247, perf. 12½ 9.00 4.50
Nos. C245-C247 (3) 8.55 3.15

200th anniv. of discovery of Uranus by William Herschel (1738-1822).

Map of Africa and Emblems AP108

1981, June 1 **Litho.** ***Perf. 12½***

C248 AP108 100fr multi 1.00 .40

Electric Power Distribution Union, 7th Congress, Libreville, June 1-5.

D-51 Steam Locomotive, Japan, and SNCF Turbotrain TGV-001, France — AP109

200th Birth Anniv. of George Stephenson: 100fr, B&O Mallet 7100, US, Prussian T3 steam locomotive. 350fr, Stephenson and his Rocket, BB Alsthom electric locomotive, Central Africa.

1981, June 4 **Engr.** ***Perf. 13***

C249 AP109 75fr multi 1.10 .35
C250 AP109 100fr multi 1.60 .45
C251 AP109 350fr multi 5.25 1.50
a. Souvenir sheet of 3 7.50 3.25
Nos. C249-C251 (3) 7.95 2.30

No. C251a contains No. C249-C251 in changed colors.

No. C251a Overprinted in 1 line across 3 stamps: "26 fevrier 1981-Record du monde de vitesse 380 km a l'heure"

Souvenir Sheet

1981, June 13 **Engr.** ***Perf. 13***

C252 AP109 Sheet of 3 6.50 3.25

New world railroad speed record, set Feb. 26.

Intl. Letter Writing Week, Oct. 9-16 — AP110

1981, Oct. 9 **Photo.** ***Perf. 13***

C253 AP110 200fr multi 2.25 .90

Souvenir Sheet

22nd Anniv. of Independence — AP110a

1982 **Typo.** ***Perf. 13x12½***

Self-Adhesive

C253A AP110a 2000fr multi 40.00 40.00

Printed on wood.

Still Life with a Mandolin, by George Braque (1882-1963) — AP111

Design: 350fr, Boy Blowing Bubbles, by Edouard Manet (1832-1883), vert.

Perf. 13x12½, 12½x13

1982, Oct. 5 **Litho.**

C254 AP111 300fr multi 3.75 1.10
C255 AP111 350fr multi 6.00 1.25

Pre-olympic Year — AP112

1983, Feb. 16 **Litho.** ***Perf. 13***

C256 AP112 90fr Gymnast .70 .30
C257 AP112 350fr Wind surfing 4.00 1.10

Manned Flight Bicentenary AP113

Balloons: 100fr, Transatlantic flight, 5th anniv. 125fr, Montgolfiere, 1783. 350fr, Rozier's balloon, 1783.

1983, June 1 **Engr.** ***Perf. 13***

C258 AP113 100fr multicolored 1.00 .40
C259 AP113 125fr multicolored 1.25 .45
C260 AP113 350fr multicolored 3.75 1.50
Nos. C258-C260 (3) 6.00 2.35

Lady with Unicorn, by Raphael (1483-1520) AP114

1983, June 19 ***Perf. 12½x13***

C261 AP114 1000fr multi 10.00 4.50

1984 Winter Olympics — AP115

1984, Feb. 8 **Litho.** ***Perf. 12½***

C262 AP115 125fr Hockey 1.40 .25
C263 AP115 350fr Figure skaters 3.75 .70

See No. C268.

Paris-Libreville-Paris Air Race, Mar. 15-28 — AP116

500fr, Planes, emblem.

1984, Mar. 15 **Litho.** ***Perf. 13x12½***

C264 AP116 500fr multi 4.50 1.25

The Racetrack, by Edgar Degas — AP117

1984, Mar. 21 ***Perf. 13***

C265 AP117 500fr multi 7.50 3.00

1984 Summer Olympics AP118

1984, May 31 Litho. *Perf. 12½*

C266	AP118	90fr Basketball	.80	.25
C267	AP118	125fr Running	1.25	.25

Nos. C262-C263, C266-C267 with Added Inscriptions

Souvenir Sheet

1984, Oct. 3 Litho. *Perf. 13*

C268	Sheet of 4	7.50	5.00
a.	AP118 90fr MEDAILLE D'OR: U.S.A.	.65	.25
b.	AP118 125fr MEDAILLE D'OR: KORIR	.95	.25
c.	AP115 125fr Hockey sur glace: U.R.S.S.	.95	.25
d.	AP115 350fr Danse couple: J. Torvill-C. Dean	2.75	.55

Souvenir Sheet

Hamburg '84 Philatelic Exhibition — AP119

1984 Typo. *Perf. 13x12½*
Self-Adhesive

C268A	AP119	1000fr multi	21.00	21.00

Printed on wood.

Dr. Albert Schweitzer (1875-1965) — AP119a

1985, Sept. 5 Litho. *Perf. 12½*

C269	AP119a	350fr multi	4.25	.70

Flags of Gabon, UN AP120

1985, Sept. 20

C270	AP120	225fr multi	2.50	.40

Admission of Gabon to UN, 25th anniv.

Central Post Office, Libreville, UPU and Gabon Postal Emblems — AP121

1985, Oct. 9

C271	AP121	300fr multi	3.25	.60

World Post Day.

UN, 40th Anniv. — AP122

1985, Oct. 24 Litho. *Perf. 12½*

C272	AP122	350fr multi	3.75	.70

PHILEXAFRICA '85, Lome, Togo — AP123

100fr, Scout campsite. 150fr, Telecommunications, transportation.

1985, Oct. 30 *Perf. 13*

C273	AP123	100fr multicolored	2.00	.25
C274	AP123	150fr multicolored	3.50	.50
a.		Pair, #C273-C274 + label	6.50	2.00

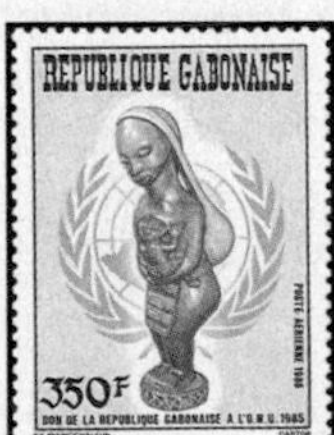
Gabon's Gift to the UN — AP124

Design: Mother and Child, carved wood statue, and UN emblem.

1986, Mar. 15 Litho. *Perf. 13½*

C275	AP124	350fr multi	3.75	1.10

Lastour Arriving in Gabon — AP125

1986, Mar. 25 Litho. *Perf. 12½*

C276	AP125	100fr multi	1.50	.45

Lastoursville, cent.

World Telecommunications Day — AP126

1986, May 17 *Perf. 13½*

C277	AP126	300fr multi	3.00	.95

1986 World Cup Soccer Championships, Mexico — AP127

100fr, Goal. 150fr, Dribbling, religious carving. 250fr, Players, map, soccer cup. 350fr, Stadium, flags.

1986, May 31 *Perf. 12½*

C278	AP127	100fr multi	1.00	.35
C279	AP127	150fr multi	1.50	.45
C280	AP127	250fr multi	2.50	.80
C281	AP127	350fr multi	3.25	1.10
a.		Souv. sheet of 4, #C278-C281	10.00	4.75
		Nos. C278-C281 (4)	8.25	2.70

For overprints see Nos. C283-C286.

World Post Day — AP128

1986, Oct. 9 Litho. *Perf. 12½*

C282	AP128	500fr multi	5.00	1.50

Nos. C278-C281 Ovptd. "ARGENTINA 3 -R.F.A 2" in One or Two Lines in Red

1986, Oct. 23 Litho. *Perf. 12½*

C283	AP127	100fr multi	1.00	.35
C284	AP127	150fr multi	1.50	.45
C285	AP127	250fr multi	2.50	.80
C286	AP127	350fr multi	3.25	1.10
		Nos. C283-C286 (4)	8.25	2.70

The Renewal, 19th Anniv. AP129

1987, Mar. 12 Litho. *Perf. 13*

C287	AP129	500fr multi	6.00	2.00

Konrad Adenauer (1876-1967), West German Chancellor AP130

1987, Apr. 15 *Perf. 12x12½*

C288	AP130	300fr mar, chlky bl & blk	4.50	1.25

Schweitzer and Medical Settlement — AP131

1988, Apr. 17 Litho. *Perf. 12½x12*

C289	AP131	500fr multi	6.50	2.25

Dr. Albert Schweitzer (1875-1965), missionary physician and founder of the hospital and medical settlement, Lambarene, Gabon.

Port Gentil Refinery, 20th Anniv. — AP132

1988, Sept. 1 Litho. *Perf. 13½*

C290	AP132	350fr multi	4.00	1.75

De Gaulle's Call for French Resistance, 50th Anniv. — AP133

1990, June 18 Litho. *Perf. 13*

C291	AP133	500fr multicolored	7.50	2.50

Port of Marseilles by J. B. Jongkind (1819-1891) — AP134

1991, Feb. 9 Litho. *Perf. 13*

C292	AP134	500fr multicolored	6.00	2.75

Discovery of America, 500th Anniv. — AP135

1992, Oct. 12 Litho. *Perf. 13*
C293 AP135 500fr multicolored 5.50 2.50

Antoine de Saint-Exupery (1900-44) — AP136

1994 Litho. *Perf. 13*
C294 AP136 500fr multicolored *3.25 1.60*

Opening of the Channel Tunnel — AP137

1994, Sept. 5
C295 AP137 500fr multicolored *3.00 1.50*

AIR POST SEMI-POSTAL STAMPS

Catalogue values for unused stamps in this section are for Never Hinged items.

Ramses II Paying Homage to Four Gods, Wadi-es-Sabua — SPAP1

Unwmk.
1964, Mar. 9 Engr. *Perf. 13*
CB1 SPAP1 10fr + 5fr dk bl & bis brn 1.00 1.00
CB2 SPAP1 25fr + 5fr dk car rose & vio bl 1.25 1.25
CB3 SPAP1 50fr + 5fr sl grn & claret 2.10 2.10
Nos. CB1-CB3 (3) 4.35 4.35

UNESCO world campaign to save historic monuments in Nubia.

POSTAGE DUE STAMPS

Postage Due Stamps of France Overprinted

1928 Unwmk. *Perf. 14x13½*
J1 D2 5c light blue .40 *.55*
J2 D2 10c gray brown .40 *.65*
J3 D2 20c olive green 1.05 *1.60*
J4 D2 25c bright rose 1.05 *1.40*
J5 D2 30c light red 1.60 *2.00*
J6 D2 45c blue green 2.00 *2.40*
J7 D2 50c brown violet 3.00 *3.25*
J8 D2 60c yellow brown 3.00 *3.25*
J9 D2 1fr red brown 3.00 *3.25*
J10 D2 2fr orange red 3.50 4.25
J11 D2 3fr bright violet 4.25 5.00
Nos. J1-J11 (11) 23.25 27.60

Chief Makoko, de Brazza's Aide — D3

Count Savorgnan de Brazza — D4

1930 Typo. *Perf. 13½x14*
J12 D3 5c dk bl & olive .70 1.10
J13 D3 10c dk red & brn .70 1.10
J14 D3 20c green & brn 1.40 1.40
J15 D3 25c lt bl & brn 1.40 1.40
J16 D3 30c bis brn & Prus bl 2.25 2.00
J17 D3 45c Prus bl & ol 2.75 3.25
J18 D3 50c red vio & brn 3.50 4.00
J19 D3 60c gray lil & bl blk 7.00 6.50
J20 D4 1fr bis brn & bl blk 7.00 10.00
J21 D4 2fr violet & brn 10.50 14.00
J22 D4 3fr dp red & brn 17.50 15.00
Nos. J12-J22 (11) 54.70 59.75

Fang Woman — D5

1932 Photo. *Perf. 13x13½*
J23 D5 5c dk bl, *bl* 1.10 1.40
J24 D5 10c red brown 1.40 1.75
J25 D5 20c chocolate 1.75 2.00
J26 D5 25c yel grn, *bl* 1.75 2.00
J27 D5 30c car rose 1.75 2.10
J28 D5 45c red org, *yel* 7.00 7.00
J29 D5 50c dk violet 2.75 2.75
J30 D5 60c dull blue 3.75 3.75
J31 D5 1fr blk, *red org* 8.50 9.50
J32 D5 2fr dark green 11.00 12.00
J33 D5 3fr rose lake 9.00 11.50
Nos. J23-J33 (11) 49.75 55.75

Catalogue values for unused stamps in this section, from this point to the end of the section, are for Never Hinged items.

Republic

Pineapple — D6

Unwmk.
1962, Dec. 10 Engr. *Perf. 11*
J34 D6 50c shown .25 .25
J35 D6 50c Mangoes .25 .25
a. Pair, #J34-J35 .35
J36 D6 1fr Avocados .25 .25
J37 D6 1fr Tangerines .25 .25
a. Pair, #J36-J37 .50
J38 D6 2fr Coconuts .25 .25
J39 D6 2fr Grapefruit .25 .25
a. Pair, #J38-J39 .50
J40 D6 5fr Oranges .35 .35
J41 D6 5fr Papaya .35 .35
a. Pair, #J40-J41 1.00
J42 D6 10fr Breadfruit .75 .75
J43 D6 10fr Guavas .75 .75
a. Pair, #J42-J43 2.25
J44 D6 25fr Lemons 1.00 1.00
J45 D6 25fr Bananas 1.00 1.00
a. Pair, #J44-J45 3.50
Nos. J34-J45 (12) 5.70 5.70

Pairs se-tenant at the base.

Charaxes Candiope — D7

Butterflies: 10fr, Charaxes ameliae. 25fr, Cyrestis camillus. 50fr, Charaxes castor. 100fr, Pseudacrea boisduvali.

1978, July 4 Litho. *Perf. 13*
J46 D7 5fr multi .30 .25
J47 D7 10fr multi .30 .25
J48 D7 25fr multi .65 .30
J49 D7 50fr multi 1.25 .50
J50 D7 100fr multi 2.00 .95
Nos. J46-J50 (5) 4.50 2.25

OFFICIAL STAMPS

Catalogue values for unused stamps in this section are for Never Hinged items.

Map of Gabon — O1

Designs: 25fr, 30fr, Flag of Gabon. 50fr, 85fr, 100fr, 200fr, Coat of Arms.

1968 Unwmk. Photo. *Perf. 14*
O1 O1 1fr olive & multi .25 .25
O2 O1 2fr multi .25 .25
O3 O1 5fr lilac & multi .25 .25
O4 O1 10fr emer & multi .25 .25
O5 O1 25fr brn & multi .50 .25
O6 O1 30fr org & multi .50 .25
O7 O1 50fr multi .95 .25
O8 O1 85fr multi 1.75 .35
O9 O1 100fr yel & multi 2.10 .45
O10 O1 200fr gray & multi 4.00 1.10
Nos. O1-O10 (10) 10.80 3.65

Flag of Gabon — O2

1971-84 Typo. *Perf. 13x14*
O11 O2 5fr multi ('81) .25 .25
O12 O2 10fr multi .30 .25
O13 O2 20fr multi ('81) .30 .25
O14 O2 25fr multi ('84) .50 .25
O15 O2 30fr multi ('78) .40 .25
O16 O2 40fr multi ('72) .75 .25
O17 O2 50fr multi ('76) .85 .25
O18 O2 60fr multi ('77) 1.10 .25
O19 O2 75fr multi ('81) .75 .25
O20 O2 80fr multi ('77) 1.50 .40
O21 O2 100fr multi ('78) 1.25 .25
O22 O2 500fr multi ('78) 6.25 1.25
Nos. O11-O22 (12) 14.20 4.15

GAMBIA

'gam-bē-ə

LOCATION — Extending inland from the mouth of the Gambia River on the west coast of Africa
GOVT. — Republic in British Commonwealth
AREA — 4,068 sq. mi.
POP. — 1,087,000 (1995 est.)
CAPITAL — Banjul

The British Crown Colony and Protectorate of Gambia became independent in 1965 and a republic in 1970.

12 Pence = 1 Shilling
100 Bututs = 1 Dalasy (1971)

Catalogue values for unused stamps in this country are for Never Hinged items, beginning with Scott 144.

Queen Victoria — A1

Typographed and Embossed
1869, Jan. Unwmk. *Imperf.*
1 A1 4p pale brown 575.00 240.00
No gum 400.00
a. 4p brown 675.00 240.00
No gum 475.00
2 A1 6p blue 675.00 240.00
No gum 450.00
a. 6p deep blue *625.00* 240.00
No gum 425.00
b. 6p pale blue *3,400.* *1,250.*
No gum 2,500.

1874, Aug. Wmk. 1
3 A1 4p brown 450.00 240.00
No gum 300.00
a. 4p pale brown 475.00 250.00
No gum 300.00
4 A1 6p blue 425.00 240.00
No gum 290.00
a. 6p deep blue 450.00 250.00
No gum 290.00
b. Panel sloping down from left to right 975.00 525.00
No gum 650.00

Nos. 1-4 are often seen with flat embossing. Unused values for are for fine-very fine examples with sharp, detailed embossing. Values for unused stamps without gum and used stamps are for examples with average embossing.

The name panel sloping down variety, No. 4b, is from a top right corner position. A top left corner position exists with a less noticeable sloping of the panel down from right to left; it is worth less.

1880, June *Perf. 14*
5 A1 ½p orange 19.00 *27.50*
6 A1 1p maroon 11.00 *7.00*
7 A1 2p rose 67.50 12.50
8 A1 3p ultra 80.00 37.50
9 A1 4p pale brown 350.00 25.00
a. 4p brown 350.00 26.00
10 A1 6p blue 140.00 52.50
a. Panel sloping down from left to right 375.00 175.00
11 A1 1sh green 300.00 165.00
a. 1sh deep green 400.00 200.00
Nos. 5-11 (7) 967.50 327.00

The watermark on Nos. 5-11 exists both upright and sideways.
See footnote following No. 4.

1886-93 Wmk. 2 Sideways
12 A1 ½p gray grn 6.50 3.50
13 A1 1p rose car ('87) 10.50 *12.50*
14 2p dp org 4.50 *10.50*
b. 2p orange 15.00 5.75
15 A1 2½p dp brt blue 12.50 1.75
16 A1 3p gray 14.00 *17.00*
17 A1 4p dp brown 13.00 2.50
18 A1 6p sl grn ('93) 20.00 *67.50*
a. 6p pale olive green ('86) 110.00 60.00
b. 6p bronze green ('89) 47.50 *72.50*
c. As "a," panel sloping down from left to right 325.00 150.00
d. As "b," panel sloping down from left to right 95.00 *180.00*
19 A1 1sh violet 10.00 *24.00*
a. 1sh purple 5.00 *22.50*
Nos. 12-19 (8) 91.00 *139.25*

See footnote following No. 4.

Queen Victoria — A2

1898, Jan. Typo. Wmk. 2
20 A2 ½p gray green 3.25 2.00
21 A2 1p carmine rose 3.50 .85
22 A2 2p brn org & pur 7.00 4.00
23 A2 2½p ultramarine 5.25 *2.75*
24 A2 3p red vio & ultra 50.00 14.00
25 A2 4p brown & ultra 20.00 *37.50*
26 A2 6p ol grn & car rose 19.00 *50.00*
27 A2 1sh vio & green 45.00 *85.00*
Nos. 20-27 (8) 153.00 *196.10*

King Edward VII — A3

1902-05 *Perf. 14*

No.	Type	Description	Unused	Used
28	A3	½p green	7.25	2.75
29	A3	1p car rose	15.00	1.10
30	A3	2p org & pur	3.75	2.25
31	A3	2½p ultramarine	52.50	20.00
32	A3	3p red vio & ultra	23.00	4.00
33	A3	4p brn & ultra	10.00	42.50
34	A3	6p ol grn & rose	19.50	14.50
35	A3	1sh bluish vio & green	50.00	92.50
36	A3	1sh6p grn & red, *yel*	13.00	26.00
37	A3	2sh black & org	55.00	75.00
38	A3	2sh6p pur & brn, *yel*	16.00	75.00
39	A3	3sh red & grn, *yel*	22.50	72.50
		Nos. 28-39 (12)	287.50	428.10

Numerals of 5p, 7½p, 10p, 1sh6p, 2sh, 2sh6p and 3sh of type A3 are in color on plain tablet.

Issue dates: 1p, Mar. 13. ½p, 3p, Apr. 19. 2p, 2½p, 4p, 6p, 1sh, 2sh, June 14. 1sh6p, 2sh6p, 3sh, Apr. 6, 1905.

For surcharges, see Nos. 65-66.

1904-09 **Wmk. 3**

No.	Type	Description	Unused	Used
41	A3	½p green	5.25	.35
a.		½p blue green ('09)	15.00	7.00
42	A3	1p car rose	5.25	.25
a.		1p carmine ('09)	17.50	.25
43	A3	2p org & pur ('06)	14.00	2.50
44	A3	2p gray ('09)	2.25	12.50
45	A3	2½p brt blue ('05)	17.50	5.50
46	A3	3p red vio & ultra	20.00	3.00
47	A3	3p vio, *yel* ('09)	7.50	1.10
48	A3	4p brn & ultra ('06)	25.00	50.00
49	A3	4p blk & red, *yel* ('09)	3.75	.75
50	A3	5p gray & black	19.00	30.00
51	A3	5p org & vio ('09)	3.75	1.60
52	A3	6p ol grn & rose ('06)	26.00	75.00
53	A3	6p dull vio ('09)	3.75	2.50
54	A3	7½p blue grn & red	21.00	65.00
55	A3	7½p brn & ultra ('09)	5.00	2.75
56	A3	10p ol bis & red	32.50	52.50
57	A3	10p ol grn & car rose ('09)	7.00	8.00
58	A3	1sh violet & grn	42.50	65.00
59	A3	1sh blk, *grn* ('09)	7.50	20.00
60	A3	1sh 6p vio & grn ('09)	32.50	80.00
61	A3	2sh black & org	100.00	125.00
62	A3	2sh vio & bl, *bl* ('09)	16.00	22.50
63	A3	2sh 6p blk & red, *bl* ('09)	25.00	22.50
64	A3	3sh yel & grn ('09)	50.00	55.00
		Nos. 41-64 (24)	492.00	703.30

Nos. 38-39 Surcharged in Black

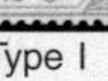
Type I

Type II

Type I — The word "PENNY" is 5mm from the horizontal bars.

Type II — "PENNY" is 4mm from the bars.

1906, Apr. **Wmk. 2**

No.	Type	Description	Unused	Used
65	A3	½p on 2sh6p, type I	57.50	70.00
a.		Type II	62.50	75.00
66	A3	1p on 3sh	62.50	35.00
a.		Double surcharge	2,150.	5,750.

King George V — A4

1912-22 **Wmk. 3**

No.	Type	Description	Unused	Used
70	A4	½p dp green	3.75	1.75
71	A4	1p carmine	3.00	1.25
a.		1p scarlet ('16)	11.00	1.00
72	A4	1½p ol brn & grn	.85	.35
73	A4	2p gray	.85	3.25
74	A4	2½p dp brt blue	5.00	3.50
75	A4	3p violet, *yel*	2.25	.35
76	A4	4p blk & red, *yel*	1.10	11.50
77	A4	5p orange & vio	2.00	2.25
78	A4	6p dl vio & red violet	3.00	2.75
79	A4	7½p brn & ultra	6.00	16.00
80	A4	10p ol grn & car rose	6.25	20.00
81	A4	1sh blk, *green*	4.25	1.10
a.		1sh black, *emerald*	3.75	28.00
82	A4	1sh6p vio & green	22.50	11.50
83	A4	2sh vio & bl, *bl*	10.00	7.00
84	A4	2sh6p blk & red, *bl*	10.00	16.00
85	A4	3sh yel & green	18.00	50.00
86	A4	5sh grn & red, *yel* ('22)	130.00	200.00
		Nos. 70-86 (17)	228.80	348.55

Numerals of 1½p, 5p, 7½p, 10p, 1sh6p, 2sh, 2sh6p, 3sh, 4sh and 5sh of type A3 are in color on colorless tablet. No. 86 is on chalky paper.

1921-22 **Wmk. 4**

No.	Type	Description	Unused	Used
87	A4	½p green	.35	22.50
88	A4	1p carmine	2.75	11.00
89	A4	1½p ol grn & bl grn	3.00	24.00
90	A4	2p gray	1.50	2.75
91	A4	2½p ultramarine	.75	13.00
92	A4	5p org & violet	2.00	26.00
93	A4	6p dl vio & red vio	3.50	22.50
94	A4	7½p brn & ultra	3.25	57.50
95	A4	10p yel grn & car rose	12.00	27.50
96	A4	4sh gray & red ('22)	110.00	225.00
		Nos. 87-96 (10)	139.10	431.75

No. 96 is on chalky paper.

George V and Elephant — A5

George V — A6

1922-27 **Engr.** **Wmk. 4**

Head and Shield in Black

No.	Type	Description	Unused	Used
102	A5	½p green	.65	.65
103	A5	1p brown	1.10	.30
104	A5	1½p carmine	1.10	.30
105	A5	2p gray	2.25	5.00
106	A5	2½p orange	3.50	15.00
107	A5	3p ultramarine	1.10	.25
108	A5	4p car, *org* ('27)	29.00	40.00
109	A5	5p yellow green	4.50	18.50
110	A5	6p claret	1.50	1.00
111	A5	7½p vio, *yel* ('27)	26.00	95.00
112	A5	10p blue	7.50	24.00
113	A6	1sh vio, *org* ('24)	5.75	2.50
114	A6	1sh6p blue	25.00	23.00
115	A6	2sh vio, *blue*	15.00	8.50
116	A6	2sh6p dark green	17.00	14.00
117	A6	3sh aniline vio	34.00	95.00
a.		3sh black purple	300.00	475.00
118	A6	4sh brown	22.50	26.00
119	A6	5sh dk grn, *yel* ('26)	52.50	82.50
120	A6	10sh yellow green	85.00	150.00
		Nos. 102-120 (19)	334.95	601.50

1922, Sept. 1 **Wmk. 3**

Head & Shield in Black

No.	Type	Description	Unused	Used
121	A5	4p carmine, *yel*	8.00	7.25
122	A5	7½p violet, *yel*	9.50	11.50
123	A6	1sh violet, *orange*	42.50	52.50
124	A6	5sh dk green, *yel*	77.50	260.00
		Nos. 121-124 (4)	137.50	331.25

Common Design Types pictured following the introduction.

Silver Jubilee Issue

Common Design Type

1935, May 6 **Wmk. 4** ***Perf. 11x12***

No.	Type	Description	Unused	Used
125	CD301	1½p carmine & bl	.55	2.75
126	CD301	3p ultra & brn	1.00	2.50
127	CD301	6p ol grn & lt bl	1.90	7.00
128	CD301	1sh brn vio & ind	8.75	13.00
		Nos. 125-128 (4)	12.20	25.25
		Set, never hinged	22.50	

Coronation Issue

Common Design Type

1937, May 12 ***Perf. 11x11½***

No.	Type	Description	Unused	Used
129	CD302	1p brown	.25	1.10
130	CD302	1½p dark carmine	.25	1.10
131	CD302	3p deep ultra	.45	1.75
		Nos. 129-131 (3)	.95	3.95
		Set, never hinged	1.45	

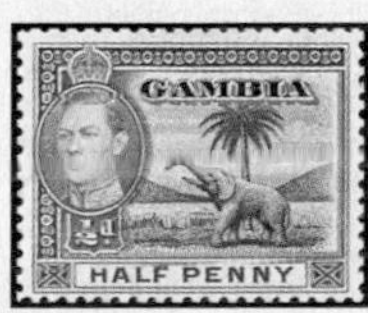

King George VI and Elephant Badge of Gambia — A7

1938-46 ***Perf. 12***

No.	Type	Description	Unused	Used
132	A7	½p bl grn & blk	.25	.70
133	A7	1p brn & red vio	.25	.55
134	A7	1½p rose red & brn lake	.25	2.00
134A	A7	1½p gray blk & ultra ('44)	.25	1.50
135	A7	2p gray blk & ultra	8.50	3.50
135A	A7	2p rose red & brn lake ('43)	.95	2.25
136	A7	3p blue & brt bl	.25	.25
136A	A7	5p dk vio brn & olive ('41)	.45	.60
137	A7	6p plum & ol grn	1.75	.40
138	A7	1sh vio & sl blk	2.75	.25
138A	A7	1sh3p bl & choc ('46)	2.25	2.50
139	A7	2sh bl & dp rose	7.50	3.25
140	A7	2sh6p sl grn & sep	9.50	2.50
141	A7	4sh dk vio & red orange	21.00	2.50
142	A7	5sh org red & dk blue	21.00	4.00
143	A7	10sh blk & yel org	22.50	8.50
		Nos. 132-143 (16)	99.40	35.25
		Set, never hinged	170.00	

Issued: 5p, 3/13; No. 135A, 10/1; No. 134A, 1/22; 1sh3p, 11/28; others, 4/1.

Catalogue values for unused stamps in this section, from this point to the end of the section, are for Never Hinged items.

Peace Issue

Common Design Type

1946, Aug. 6 **Engr.** ***Perf. 13½***

No.	Type	Description	Unused	Used
144	CD303	1½p black	.25	.50
145	CD303	3p deep blue	.25	.45

Silver Wedding Issue

Common Design Types

1948, Dec. 24 **Photo.** ***Perf. 14x14½***

No.	Type	Description	Unused	Used
146	CD304	1½p black	.25	.25

Perf. 11½x11

Engr.; Name Typo.

No.	Type	Description	Unused	Used
147	CD305	£1 purple	21.00	21.00

UPU Issue

Common Design Types

Engr.; Name Typo. on 3p, 6p

Perf. 13½, 11x11½

1949, Oct. 10 **Wmk. 4**

No.	Type	Description	Unused	Used
148	CD306	1½p slate	.35	1.50
149	CD307	3p indigo	1.50	2.00
150	CD308	6p red lilac	.75	3.00
151	CD309	1sh violet	.50	.60
		Nos. 148-151 (4)	3.10	7.10

Coronation Issue

Common Design Type

1953, June 2 **Engr.** ***Perf. 13½x13***

No.	Type	Description	Unused	Used
152	CD312	1½p dk blue & black	.50	.50

Palm Wine Tapping — A8

Designs: 1p, 1sh3p, Cutter. 1½p, 5sh, Wolof woman. 2½p, 2sh, Barra canoe. 3p, 10sh, "Lady Wright." 4p, 4sh, James Island. 1sh, 2sh6p, Woman farming. £1, Elephant badge of Gambia.

1953, Nov. 2 ***Perf. 13½***

No.	Type	Description	Unused	Used
153	A8	½p dk green & car	.50	.30
154	A8	1p dk brn & ultra	1.25	.45
155	A8	1½p gray & dk brn	.25	.80
156	A8	2½p car & black	.45	.75
157	A8	3p pur & indigo	.30	.25
158	A8	4p dp blue & blk	1.25	2.50
159	A8	6p dp plum & brn	.75	.25
160	A8	1sh green & yel brn	.85	.55
161	A8	1sh3p blue & vio bl	11.00	.55
162	A8	2sh car & indigo	6.00	4.00
163	A8	2sh6p brn & bl grn	7.25	2.25
164	A8	4sh brn org & dp bl	12.50	3.50
165	A8	5sh ultra & red brn	4.00	3.00
166	A8	10sh dk yel green & ultra	21.00	11.00
167	A8	£1 black & bl grn	22.50	12.00
		Nos. 153-167 (15)	89.85	42.15

Palm Leaf and Elizabeth II, by Annigoni — A9

Design: 3p, 6p, Map of West Africa.

Wmk. 314

1961, Dec. 2 **Engr.** ***Perf. 11½***

No.	Type	Description	Unused	Used
168	A9	2p lilac & green	.25	.40
169	A9	3p brown & Prus grn	.80	.25
170	A9	6p car rose & dk blue	.80	.65
171	A9	1sh3p green & violet	.80	2.00
		Nos. 168-171 (4)	2.65	3.30

Visit of Elizabeth II to Gambia, Dec., 1961.

Freedom from Hunger Issue

Common Design Type

1963, June 4 **Photo.** ***Perf. 14x14½***

No.	Type	Description	Unused	Used
172	CD314	1sh3p car rose	.50	.25

Red Cross Centenary Issue

Common Design Type

1963, Sept. 2 **Litho.** ***Perf. 13***

No.	Type	Description	Unused	Used
173	CD315	2p black & red	.25	.25
174	CD315	1sh3p ultra & red	.50	.75

Beautiful Long-tailed Sunbird — A10

Birds: 1p, Yellow-mantled whydah. 1½p, Cattle egret. 2p, Yellow-bellied parrot. 3p, Ring-necked parakeet. 4p, Amethyst starling. 6p, Village weaver. 1sh, Rufous-crowned roller. 1sh3p, Red-eyed turtle dove. 2sh6p, Double-spurred francolin. 5sh, Palm-nut vulture. 10sh, Orange-cheeked waxbill. £1, Emerald cuckoo.

Perf. 12½x13

1963, Nov. 4 **Photo.** **Wmk. 314**

Multicolored Design & Inscription

No.	Type	Description	Unused	Used
175	A10	½p rose buff	.60	.90
176	A10	1p gray green	.60	.25
177	A10	1½p pale violet	1.75	.70
178	A10	2p buff	1.75	.70
179	A10	3p light gray	1.75	.95
180	A10	4p lt yel green	1.75	.80
181	A10	6p light blue	1.75	.25
182	A10	1sh pale grysh grn	1.75	.25
183	A10	1sh3p light blue	9.00	2.25
184	A10	2sh6p pale green	6.50	2.00
185	A10	5sh blue	6.50	3.00
186	A10	10sh tan	9.00	9.00
187	A10	£1 pale rose	22.50	13.00
		Nos. 175-187 (13)	65.20	34.05

For overprints see Nos. 188-191, 193-205.

Nos. 176, 179, 182 and 183 Overprinted: "SELF GOVERNMENT/1963"

1963, Nov. 7

No.	Type	Description	Unused	Used
188	A10	1p multicolored	.25	.35
189	A10	3p multicolored	.35	.25
190	A10	1sh multicolored	.35	.35
a.		Double overprint		5,000.
191	A10	1sh3p multicolored	.45	.45
		Nos. 188-191 (4)	1.40	1.40

Shakespeare Issue

Common Design Type

1964, Apr. 23 **Photo.** ***Perf. 14x14½***

No.	Type	Description	Unused	Used
192	CD316	6p ultramarine	.35	.25

Nos. 175-187 Overprinted: "INDEPENDENCE / 1965"

Perf. 12½x13

1965, Feb. 18 **Photo.** **Wmk. 314**

Multicolored Design & Inscription

No.	Type	Description	Unused	Used
193	A10	½p rose buff	.30	.85
194	A10	1p gray green	.35	.25
195	A10	1½p pale violet	.50	.85
196	A10	2p buff	.65	.30
197	A10	3p light gray	.65	.25
198	A10	4p lt yel green	.65	1.50
199	A10	6p light blue	.65	.25
200	A10	1sh pale grysh grn	.65	.25
201	A10	1sh3p light blue	.65	.25
202	A10	2sh6p pale green	.65	.60
203	A10	5sh blue	.65	.65
204	A10	10sh tan	1.50	3.50
205	A10	£1 pale rose	7.75	8.50
		Nos. 193-205 (13)	15.60	18.00

In the overprint, "1965" is flush at left side under "Independence" on the ½p, 1½p, 6p, 1sh3p and 2sh6p; it is centered on the others.

Flag of Gambia over Gambia River — A11

Design: 2p, 1sh6p, Coat of arms.

1965, Feb. 18 Unwmk. *Perf. 14*

206 A11 ½p slate & multi .25 .25
207 A11 2p lt brown & multi .25 .25
208 A11 7½p dk brown & multi .40 .40
209 A11 1sh6p lt green & multi .55 .30
Nos. 206-209 (4) 1.45 1.20

Gambia's Independence.

ITU Emblem, Old and New Communication Equipment — A12

1965, May 17 Photo. *Perf. 14½x14*

210 A12 1p dull blue & silver .40 .25
211 A12 1sh6p violet & gold 1.25 .30

Cent. of the ITU.

Winston Churchill and Parliament — A13

1966, Jan. 24 *Perf. 14x14½*

212 A13 1p multicolored .25 .25
213 A13 6p multicolored .40 .25
214 A13 1sh6p multicolored .60 *.60*
Nos. 212-214 (3) 1.25 1.10

Sir Winston Leonard Spencer Churchill, statesman and WWII leader.

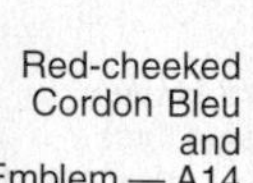

Red-cheeked Cordon Bleu and Emblem — A14

Birds: 1p, White-faced tree duck. 1½p, Red-throated bee eater. 2p, Pied kingfisher. 3p, Yellow-crowned bishop. 4p, Fish eagle. 6p, Bruce's green pigeon. 1sh, Blue-bellied roller. 1sh6p, African pigmy kingfisher. 2sh6p, Spur-winged goose. 5sh, Little woodpecker. 10sh, Violet plantain eater. £1, Pintailed whydah, vert.

Perf. 12½x13

1966, Feb. 18 Photo. Unwmk.

Size: 29x25mm

Multicolored Design & Inscription

215 A14 ½p gray .75 .30
216 A14 1p bluish green .25 *.45*
217 A14 1½p yel green .25 *.35*
218 A14 2p rose lilac 4.00 .70
219 A14 3p lilac .25 .25
220 A14 4p blue .40 .30
221 A14 6p gray .30 .25
222 A14 1sh light green .30 .25
223 A14 1sh6p bright blue .60 .25
224 A14 2sh6p tan .60 .60
225 A14 5sh gray green .60 .75
226 A14 10sh ocher .75 *2.50*

Perf. 14x14½

Size: 25x39mm

227 A14 £1 pink 1.00 *6.00*
Nos. 215-227 (13) 10.05 *12.95*

Coat of Arms, Old and New Views of Bathurst — A15

Photo.; Silver Impressed (Arms)

1966, June 24 *Perf. 14½x14*

228 A15 1p orange & dk brn .25 .25
229 A15 2p lt ultra & dk brn .25 .25
230 A15 6p emer & dk brown .25 .25
231 A15 1sh6p brt pink & dk brn .25 .25
Nos. 228-231 (4) 1.00 1.00

150th anniv. of the founding of Bathurst.

Adonis and Atlantic Hotels and ITY Emblem — A16

Photo.; Silver Impressed (Emblem)

1967, Dec. 20 *Perf. 14½x14*

232 A16 2p lt yel green & brn .25 .25
233 A16 1sh orange & brown .25 .25
234 A16 1sh6p lilac rose & brn .25 .25
Nos. 232-234 (3) .75 .75

International Tourist Year.

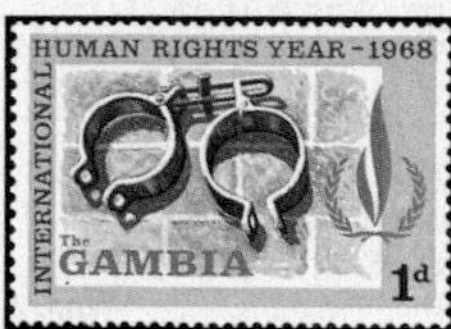

Handcuffs and Human Rights Flame A17

Intl. Human Rights Year: 1sh, Fort Bullen. 5sh, Methodist Church.

1968, July 15 Photo. *Perf. 14x13*

235 A17 1p gold & multi .25 .25
236 A17 1sh gold & multi .25 .25
237 A17 5sh gold & multi .30 *1.00*
Nos. 235-237 (3) .80 1.50

Gambia #1, Victoria and Elizabeth II — A18

Designs: 6p, Gambia #2, Victoria & Elizabeth II. 2sh6p, Gambia #1-2, Elizabeth II.

Photo. and Embossed

Perf. 14x13½

1969, Jan. 20 Wmk. 314

238 A18 4p dull yel & dk brn .30 .25
239 A18 6p dp yel grn & bl .30 .25
240 A18 2sh6p dk bl gray, brn & bl .90 *1.40*
Nos. 238-240 (3) 1.50 1.90

Centenary of Gambian postage stamps.

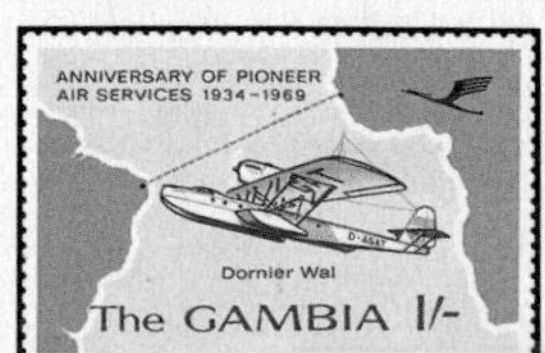

Dornier Wal, Route Gambia to Brazil and Lufthansa Emblem — A19

2p, Plane & ship Westfalen, route Gambia to Brazil & Lufthansa emblem. 1sh6p, Zeppelin, route Gambia to Brazil & Lufthansa emblem.

Perf. 13½x14

1969, Dec. 15 Litho. Unwmk.

241 A19 2p pink, org red & blk .75 .25
242 A19 1sh buff, dl yel & blk .75 .25
243 A19 1sh6p lt bl, ultra & blk .85 *1.40*
Nos. 241-243 (3) 2.35 1.90

35th anniversary of pioneer air services.

Runner, Flag and Arms of Gambia A20

1970, July 16 *Perf. 14½x14*

Flag in Red, Blue & Green

244 A20 1p pink & brown .25 .25
245 A20 1sh ultra & brown .25 .25
246 A20 5sh green & brown .30 *.80*
Nos. 244-246 (3) .80 1.30

9th Commonwealth Games, Edinburgh, Scotland, July 16-25.

Pres. Jawara and State House A21

Republic Day, Apr. 24, 1970: 1sh, Pres. Sir Dauda Kairaba Jawara, vert. 1sh6p, Pres. Jawara and Gambia flag, vert.

1970, Nov. 2 Litho. *Perf. 14*

247 A21 2p gray & multi .25 .25
248 A21 1sh multicolored .25 .25
249 A21 1sh6p pink & multi .50 .70
Nos. 247-249 (3) 1.00 1.20

Methodist Church, Georgetown — A22

Designs: 1sh, Map of Africa and cross, vert. 1sh6p, John Wesley.

1971, Apr. 16 Unwmk. *Perf. 14*

250 A22 2p multicolored .25 .25
251 A22 1sh vio blue & multi .25 .25
252 A22 1sh6p green & multi .60 .80
Nos. 250-252 (3) 1.10 1.30

Establishment of Methodist Mission, 150th anniv.

Yellowfin Tuna A23

Fish from Gambian Waters: 4b, Peters' mormyrid. 6b, Tropical two-wing flying fish. 8b, African sleeper goby. 10b, Yellowtail snapper. 13b, Rock hind. 25b, West African eel cat. 38b, Tiger shark. 50b, Electric catfish. 63b, Swamp eel. 1.25d, Smalltooth sawfish. 2.50d, Barracuda. 5d, Brown bullhead.

1971, July 1 Litho. *Perf. 14*

Fish in Natural Colors

253 A23 2b blue .25 *.70*
254 A23 4b lemon .25 .25
255 A23 6b lt blue green .25 *.70*
256 A23 8b orange brown .25 .25
257 A23 10b lt Prus blue .25 *.70*
258 A23 13b orange yel .25 .25
259 A23 25b green .40 .50
260 A23 38b brick red .70 .40
261 A23 50b Prus blue .80 .55
262 A23 63b bister .90 *1.75*
263 A23 1.25d yel green 1.50 *3.00*
264 A23 2.50d deep rose 2.50 *4.50*
265 A23 5d ultramarine 4.00 *7.50*
Nos. 253-265 (13) 12.30 *21.05*

Mungo Park, Scottish Landscape, Map of Gambia Basin — A24

Map of Gambia River Basin and: 25b, Park traveling in dugout canoe. 37b, Park's death under attack at Busa Rapids.

Perf. 13½x14

1971, Sept. 10 Litho. Unwmk.

270 A24 4b ultra & multi .35 .25
271 A24 25b yel green & multi 1.05 .45
272 A24 37b brick red & multi 1.70 *2.00*
Nos. 270-272 (3) 3.10 2.70

Mungo Park (1771-1806), Scottish explorer of the Gambia and Niger Rivers.

Radio Gambia and Pres. Jawara A25

Designs: 25b, Map showing area reached by Radio Gambia. 37b, Like 4b.

1972, July 1 *Perf. 14*

273 A25 4b black & dull yel .25 .25
274 A25 25b black, blue & red .25 *.25*
275 A25 37b black & yel green .30 *.75*
Nos. 273-275 (3) .80 1.25

Radio Gambia, 10th anniv., May 1.

High Jump A26

1972, Aug. 31 *Perf. 13½*

276 A26 4b emerald & multi .25 .25
277 A26 25b lt ultra & multi .25 .25
278 A26 37b red & multi .40 .40
Nos. 276-278 (3) .90 .90

20th Olympic Games, Munich, 8/26-9/11.

Mandingo Woman — A27

Designs: 25b, Musician playing Mandingo 21-stringed lute (kora). 37b, Map of Mali empire and area of Mandingo language.

1972, Oct. 18 Litho. *Perf. 14x14½*

279 A27 2b rose red & multi .25 .25
280 A27 25b lt ultra & multi .30 .30
281 A27 37b emerald & multi .40 .40
Nos. 279-281 (3) .95 .95

International Conference on Mandingo Studies, London, June 30-July 3.

Ship Model with Lanterns A28

Christmas: 2b, Lighted ship (lantern) carried by boys.

1972, Dec. 1 Litho. *Perf. 13x13½*

282	A28	2b	violet & multi	.25	.25
283	A28	1.25d	blue & multi	.65	.65

Peanuts, FAO Emblem — A29

1973, Mar. 31 Litho. *Perf. 14½x14*

284	A29	2b	red & multi	.25	.25
285	A29	25b	lt blue & multi	.25	.25
286	A29	37b	emerald & multi	.30	.30
			Nos. 284-286 (3)	.80	.80

Freedom from Hunger, 2nd UN development campaign.

Planting and Drying Rice — A30

25b, Sorghum (Guinea corn). 37b, Rice crop.

1973, Apr. 30 *Perf. 14½x14*

287	A30	2b	shown	.25	.25
288	A30	25b	multicolored	.25	.25
289	A30	37b	multicolored	.40	.30

Oil Palms — A31

1973, July 16

290	A31	2b	shown	.25	.25
291	A31	25b	Limes	.25	.25
292	A31	37b	Oil palm fruits	.55	.45

Cassava A32

1973, Oct. 15

293	A32	2b	shown	.25	.25
294	A32	50b	Cotton	.55	.45
			Nos. 287-294 (8)	2.75	2.45

Gambian agriculture.

OAU Emblem — A33

1973, Nov. 1 Unwmk. *Perf. 13½x13*

295	A33	4b	green, yel & black	.25	.25
296	A33	25b	dp mag, yel & black	.25	.25
297	A33	37b	blue, yel & black	.25	.25
			Nos. 295-297 (3)	.75	.75

10th anniv. of the OAU.

Red Cross — A34

Perf. 14½x14

1973, Nov. 30 Wmk. 314

298	A34	4b	red & black	.25	.25
299	A34	25b	ultra, red & black	.25	.25
300	A34	37b	emer, red & black	.25	.25
			Nos. 298-300 (3)	.75	.75

25th anniv. of Gambia Red Cross Soc.

Flag of Gambia and Arms of Banjul — A35

Perf. 13½x13

1973, Dec. 17 Litho. Unwmk.

301	A35	4b	yel green & multi	.25	.25
302	A35	25b	ver & multi	.25	.25
303	A35	37b	lt ultra & multi	.25	.25
			Nos. 301-303 (3)	.75	.75

Change of name of Bathurst to Banjul and of St. Mary's Island to Banjul Island.

UPU Emblem — A36

1974, Aug. 24 Litho. *Perf. 13½x13*

304	A36	4b	lilac & multi	.25	.25
305	A36	37b	blue & multi	.45	.45

Centenary of Universal Postal Union.

Churchill at Harrow — A37

Churchill in Uniform of 4th Hussars — A38

Designs: 50b, Churchill as Prime Minister.

1974, Nov. 30 Litho. *Perf. 13½*

306	A37	4b	multicolored	.25	.25
307	A38	37b	multicolored	.30	.25
308	A38	50b	multicolored	.35	*.65*
			Nos. 306-308 (3)	.90	*1.15*

Sir Winston Churchill (1874-1965).

WPY Emblem, Races of Man A39

Symbolic Designs and WPY Emblem: 37b, Races multiplying and dividing like atom. 50b, World population.

1974, Dec. 16 Litho. *Perf. 14*

309	A39	4b	multicolored	.25	.25
310	A39	37b	multicolored	.25	.25
311	A39	50b	multicolored	.25	.25
			Nos. 309-311 (3)	.75	.75

World Population Year.

Dr. Schweitzer and Hospital, Lambarene — A40

50b, Dr. Schweitzer examining patient. 1.25d, Dr. Schweitzer in boat on Ogowe River.

1975, Jan. 14 Litho. *Perf. 14*

312	A40	10b	multicolored	.25	.25
313	A40	50b	multicolored	.60	.25
314	A40	1.25d	multicolored	1.10	.75
			Nos. 312-314 (3)	1.95	1.25

Dr. Albert Schweitzer (1875-1965), medical missionary, birth centenary.

Peace Dove A41

10b, Gambia flag. 50b, Gambia coat of arms. 1.25d, Map of Gambia & Gambia River.

1975, Feb. 18 *Perf. 13*

315	A41	4b	multicolored	.25	.25
316	A41	10b	multicolored	.25	.25
317	A41	50b	multicolored	.25	.25
318	A41	1.25d	multicolored	.25	.40
			Nos. 315-318 (4)	1.00	1.15

10th anniversary of independence.

Public Services Graph, A.D.B. Emblem — A42

African Development Bank Emblem and: 50b, Plant symbolizing growth of Africa, fed by Development Bank. 1.25d, A.D.B. emblem surrounded by symbols of water, education, roads and hospitals.

1975, Mar. 31 Litho. *Perf. 14*

319	A42	10b	multicolored	.25	.25
320	A42	50b	multicolored	.25	.25
321	A42	1.25d	multicolored	.40	.40
			Nos. 319-321 (3)	.90	.90

African Development Bank, 10th anniv.

David, by Michelangelo A43

Bas-reliefs by Michelangelo: 50b, Madonna of the Steps. 1.25d, Battle of the Centaurs, horiz.

1975, Nov. 14 *Perf. 14½*

322	A43	10b	dull blue & multi	.25	.25
323	A43	50b	sepia & multi	.35	.35
324	A43	1.25d	green & multi	.80	.80
			Nos. 322-324 (3)	1.40	1.40

Michelangelo Buonarroti (1475-1564), Italian painter, sculptor and architect.

Gambia High School A44

Designs: 50b, Pupil in laboratory and school emblem. 1.50d, School emblem.

1975, Nov. 17

325	A44	10b	multicolored	.25	.25
326	A44	50b	multicolored	.25	.25
327	A44	1.50d	multicolored	.40	.40
			Nos. 325-327 (3)	.90	.90

Gambia High School, centenary.

Teacher and IWY Emblem A45

IWY: 10b, Women planting rice. 50b, Nurse holding baby. 1.50d, Woman traffic officer.

1975, Dec. 15 Litho. *Perf. 14½*

328	A45	4b	yellow & multi	.25	.25
329	A45	10b	multicolored	.25	.25
330	A45	50b	multicolored	.35	.25
331	A45	1.50d	blue & multi	.60	.30
			Nos. 328-331 (4)	1.45	1.05

Woman Golfer A46

Designs: 50b, Golfer addressing ball. 1.50d, Golfer finishing iron shot.

1976, Feb. 18 Litho. *Perf. 14½*

332	A46	10b	multicolored	.80	.25
333	A46	50b	multicolored	1.60	.35
334	A46	1.50d	multicolored	2.75	1.00
			Nos. 332-334 (3)	5.15	1.60

11th anniversary of independence.

American Militiaman — A47

American Bicent.: 50b, Continental Army soldier. 1.25d, Declaration of Independence.

1976, May 15 Litho. *Perf. 14x13½*

335	A47	25b	multicolored	.25	.25
336	A47	50b	multicolored	.40	.40
337	A47	1.25d	multicolored	.75	.75
a.			Souvenir sheet of 3, #335-337	1.75	*3.00*
			Nos. 335-337 (3)	1.40	1.40

Mother and Child, Christmas Decoration — A48

1976, Oct. 28 Litho. *Perf. 14*

338	A48	10b	lt ultra & multi	.25	.25
339	A48	50b	rose & multi	.25	.25
340	A48	1.25d	yel grn & multi	.30	.40
			Nos. 338-340 (3)	.80	.90

Christmas.

Serval Cat and Wildlife Fund Emblem — A49

Designs: 25b, Harnessed antelope. 50b, Sitatunga. 1.25d, Leopard.

1976, Nov. 29 ***Perf. 13½x14***

341	A49	10b multicolored	*6.00*	*.50*
342	A49	25b multicolored	*8.00*	*.50*
343	A49	50b multicolored	*14.00*	*1.00*
344	A49	1.25d multicolored	*22.50*	*6.00*
a.		Souvenir sheet of 4, #341-344	*85.00*	*20.00*
		Nos. 341-344 (4)	*50.50*	*8.00*

Abuko Nature Reserve.

Queen's Visit, 1961 — A50

Designs: 50b, The spurs and jeweled sword. 1.25d, The oblation of the sword.

1977, Feb. 7 **Litho.** ***Perf. 13½x14***

345	A50	25b multicolored	.25	.25
346	A50	50b multicolored	.25	.25
347	A50	1.25d multicolored	.30	.40
		Nos. 345-347 (3)	.80	.90

25th anniv. of the reign of Elizabeth II.

Festival Emblem and Weaver A51

1977, Jan. 12 **Litho.** ***Perf. 14***

348	A51	25b multicolored	.25	.25
349	A51	50b multicolored	.30	.30
350	A51	1.25d multicolored	.70	.70
a.		Souvenir sheet of 3, #348-350	2.40	*3.50*
		Nos. 348-350 (3)	1.25	1.25

2nd World Black and African Festival, Lagos, Nigeria, Jan. 15-Feb. 12.

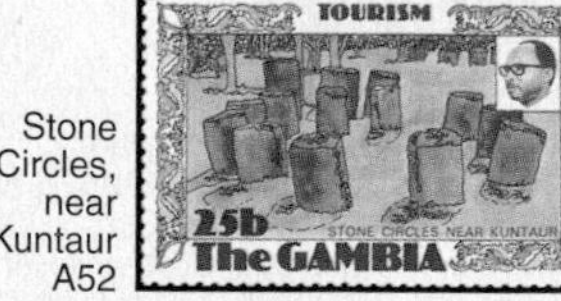

Stone Circles, near Kuntaur A52

Tourism: 50b, Ruins of Fort on James Island. 1.25d, Mungo Park Monument.

1977, Feb. 18 **Litho.** ***Perf. 14½***

351	A52	25b multicolored	.25	.25
352	A52	50b multicolored	.30	.30
353	A52	1.25d multicolored	.70	.70
		Nos. 351-353 (3)	1.25	1.25

Clerodendrum Splendens — A53

Flowers and Shrubs: 4b, White water lily. 6b, Fireball lily. 8b, Mussaenda elegans. 10b, Broad-leaved ground orchid. 13b, Fiber plant. 25b, False kapok. 38b, Baobab. 50b, Coral tree. 63b, Gloriosa lily. 1.25d, Bell-flowered mimosa. 2.50d, Kindin dolo. 5d, African tulip tree. 6b, 8b, 10b, 13b, 25b, 38b, 1.25d, 2.50d, vertical.

1977, July 1 **Litho.** ***Perf. 14½***

354	A53	2b multicolored	.25	.25
355	A53	4b multicolored	.25	*.30*
356	A53	6b multicolored	.25	*.30*
357	A53	8b multicolored	.25	.25
358	A53	10b multicolored	2.25	.40
359	A53	13b yellow & multi	.75	*.75*
a.		Pale olive background	*2.75*	*4.25*
360	A53	25b multicolored	.25	.25
361	A53	38b multicolored	.25	*.70*
362	A53	50b multicolored	.40	.55
363	A53	63b multicolored	.45	*.75*
364	A53	1.25d multicolored	.65	*1.50*
365	A53	2.50d multicolored	.75	*1.50*
366	A53	5d multicolored	.90	*2.50*
		Nos. 354-366 (13)	7.65	*10.00*

For surcharges see Nos. 390A-390C.

Crowned Crane, Nile Crocodile, Bush Buck — A54

Designs: 25b, Banjul Declaration, excerpt, flag colors. 50b, Banjul Declaration. 1.25d, Climbing lily, butterfly and moth.

1977, Oct. 15 **Litho.** ***Perf. 14***

367	A54	10b lt blue & black	.25	.25
368	A54	25b multicolored	.35	.25
369	A54	50b multicolored	.60	.25
370	A54	1.25d red & black	2.00	.75
		Nos. 367-370 (4)	3.20	1.50

Banjul Declaration, for the conservation of flora and fauna, Feb. 18, 1977.

Madonna, Flight into Egypt, by Rubens — A55

Rubens Paintings: 25b, Education of Mary by St. Ann. 50b, Child's head. 1d, Madonna surrounded by saints.

1977, Dec. 15 **Litho.** ***Perf. 14x13½***

371	A55	10b multicolored	.25	.25
372	A55	25b multicolored	.25	.25
373	A55	50b multicolored	.45	.35
374	A55	1d multicolored	.65	*.85*
		Nos. 371-374 (4)	1.60	1.70

Peter Paul Rubens (1577-1640). Nos. 371-374 printed in sheets of 5 stamps and decorative label.

Dome of the Rock, Jerusalem — A56

1978, Jan. 3 **Litho.** ***Perf. 14½***

375	A56	8b olive green & multi	*1.00*	*.60*
376	A56	25b red & multi	*3.25*	*2.00*

Palestinian fighters and their families.

Walking on Greased Pole — A57

Designs: 50b, Pillow fight on greased pole. 1.25d, Rowers in long boat.

1978, Feb. 18 ***Perf. 14***

377	A57	10b multicolored	.25	.25
378	A57	50b multicolored	.25	.25
379	A57	1.25d multicolored	.30	.30
		Nos. 377-379 (3)	.80	.80

Independence Regatta celebrating 13th anniversary of independence.

Elizabeth II Coronation Anniversary Issue

Souvenir Sheet

Common Design Types

1978, Apr. 15 **Litho.** ***Perf. 15***

380		Sheet of 6	1.50	1.50
a.		CD326 1d White grayhound of Richmond	.30	.30
b.		CD327 1d Elizabeth II	.30	.30
c.		CD328 1d Lion	.30	.30

No. 380 contains 2 se-tenant strips of Nos. 380a-380c, separated by horizontal gutter with commemorative and descriptive inscriptions.

Verreaux's Eagle Owl — A58

Birds of Prey and Wildlife Fund Emblem: 25b, Lizard buzzard. 50b, West African harrier hawk. 1.25d, Long-crested hawk eagle.

1978, Oct. 28 **Litho.** ***Perf. 14x13½***

381	A58	20b multicolored	*20.00*	*1.00*
382	A58	25b multicolored	*20.00*	*1.00*
383	A58	50b multicolored	*25.00*	*4.00*
384	A58	1.25d multicolored	*37.50*	*14.00*
		Nos. 381-384 (4)	*102.50*	*20.00*

Abuko Nature Reserve.

MV Lady Wright A59

New river vessels: 25b, River vessel Lady Chilel Jawara. 1d, Cross section of Lady Chilel Jawara.

1978, Dec. 1 **Litho.** ***Perf. 14½***

385	A59	8b multicolored	.25	.25
386	A59	25b multicolored	.40	.40
387	A59	1d multicolored	1.40	1.40
		Nos. 385-387 (3)	2.05	2.05

Motorized Police A60

1979, Feb. 18 **Litho.** ***Perf. 14***

388	A60	10b shown	.80	.25
389	A60	50b Fire engine	1.50	.30
390	A60	1.25d Ambulance	2.40	1.10
		Nos. 388-390 (3)	4.70	1.65

14th anniversary of independence.

Nos. 359, 363-364 Surcharged

1979 **Litho.** ***Perf. 14½***

390A	A53	25b on 13b multi	.25	*.35*
390B	A53	25b on 63b multi	.25	.25
390C	A53	25b on 1.25d multi	.25	.25
		Nos. 390A-390C (3)	.75	.85

Issued: No. 390A, 3/5; others, 3/26.

Ramsgate Sands, by William P. Frith — A61

Designs: 10b, 25b, IYC emblem and details from painting shown on 1d. 25b, vert.

1979, May 25 **Litho.** ***Perf. 14***

Size: 38x21mm, 21x38mm

391	A61	10b multicolored	.25	.25
392	A61	25b multicolored	.25	.25

Size: 56x21mm

393	A61	1d multicolored	.75	.75
		Nos. 391-393 (3)	1.25	1.25

International Year of the Child.

Gambia No. 15, Maltese Cross Postmark A62

Gambian Stamps and Maltese Cross Postmark: 25b, #1. 50b, #208. 1.25d, #125.

1979, Aug. 16 **Litho.** ***Perf. 14½***

394	A62	10b multicolored	.25	.25
395	A62	25b multicolored	.25	.25
396	A62	50b multicolored	.25	.25
397	A62	1.25d multicolored	.25	*.45*
a.		Souvenir sheet of 1	*.75*	*1.25*
		Nos. 394-397 (4)	1.00	1.20

Sir Rowland Hill (1795-1879), originator of penny postage.

Abuko Earth Station, Construction — A63

Telecommunications: 50b, Newly opened station. 1d, Intelsat satellites orbiting earth.

1979, Sept. 20 **Litho.** ***Perf. 14***

398	A63	25b multicolored	.25	.25
399	A63	50b multicolored	.30	.30
400	A63	1d multicolored	.50	.50
		Nos. 398-400 (3)	1.05	1.05

Apollo 11 Lift-off — A64

1979, Oct. 17 **Litho.** ***Perf. 14***

401	A64	25b shown	.25	.25
402	A64	38b Orbiting moon	.25	.25
403	A64	50b Splashdown	.50	.50
a.		Souvenir booklet	4.75	
b.		Pane, 2 each 25b, 38b, 50b	1.75	
c.		Pane of 1 (2d Lunar module)	1.50	
		Nos. 401-403 (3)	1.00	1.00

Apollo 11 moon landing, 10th anniversary. No. 403a contains Nos. 403b-403c printed on peelable, self-adhesive paper backing with Apollo 11 emblems on back. Stamps and panes are die-cut and have 1 to 3 sides rouletted 9½.

Large Spotted Acraea, Wildlife Fund Emblem — A65

Wildlife Fund Emblem and Butterflies: 50b, Yellow pansy. 1d, Veined swallowtail. 1.25d, Foxy charaxes.

1980, Jan. 3 Litho. *Perf. 13½x14*

404 A65 25b multicolored 11.00 .50
405 A65 50b multicolored 14.00 1.00
406 A65 1d multicolored 18.00 2.50
407 A65 1.25d multicolored 22.00 3.00
a. Souvenir sheet of 4, #404-407 97.50 20.00
Nos. 404-407 (4) 65.00 7.00

Abuko Nature Reserve.

Steam Launch "Vampire" — A66

1980, May 6 Litho. *Perf. 14½*

408 A66 10b shown .25 .25
409 A66 25b "Lady Denham" .35 .25

Perf. 13½x14½

Size: 49x21mm

410 A66 50b "Mansa Kila Ba" .50 .50
411 A66 1.25d "Prince of Wales" .65 *.85*
Nos. 408-411 (4) 1.75 1.85

London 80 Intl. Stamp Exhib., May 6-14.
For surcharge see No. 497A.

Queen Mother Elizabeth Birthday Issue

Common Design Type

1980, Aug. 4 Litho. *Perf. 14*

412 CD330 67b multicolored .40 *.50*

Phoenician Trading Vessel — A67

67b, Egyptian seagoing ship. 75b, Portuguese caravel. 1d, Spanish galleon.

1980, Oct. 2 Litho. *Perf. 14½*

413 A67 8b shown .25 .25
414 A67 67b multicolored .70 .60
415 A67 75b multicolored .80 .70
416 A67 1d multicolored 1.00 .90
Nos. 413-416 (4) 2.75 2.45

Virgin and Child, by Francesco de Mura — A68

Christmas: 67b, Praying Virgin with Crown of Stars, by Correggio. 75b, Rest on the Flight, after Correggio.

1980, Dec. 18 Litho. *Perf. 14*

417 A68 8b multicolored .25 .25
418 A68 67b multicolored .25 .25
419 A68 75b multicolored .25 .25
Nos. 417-419 (3) .75 .75

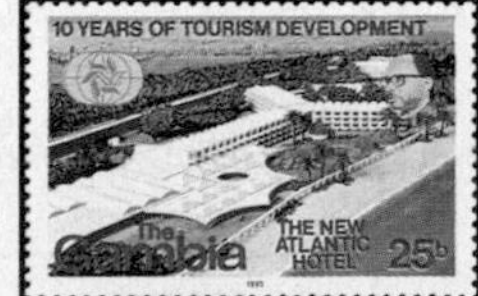

New Atlantic Hotel, Conference Emblem — A69

1981, Feb. 18 Litho. *Perf. 14*

420 A69 25b shown .25 .25
421 A69 75b Ancient stone circle .40 .40
422 A69 85b Conference emblem .55 .55
Nos. 420-422 (3) 1.20 1.20

World Tourism Conference, Manila, Sept. 27 and 16th anniversary of independence.

13th World Telecomunications Day — A70

1981, May 17 Litho. *Perf. 14*

423 A70 50b No. 399 .50 .35
424 A70 50b No. 313 .50 .35
425 A70 85b ITU, WHO emblems .75 .60
Nos. 423-425 (3) 1.75 1.30

Royal Wedding Issue

Common Design Type

1981, July 22 Litho. *Perf. 13½x13*

426 CD331 75b Bouquet .25 .25
427 CD331 1d Charles .25 .25
428 CD331 1.25d Couple .30 .30
Nos. 426-428 (3) .80 .80

For surcharges see Nos. 439, 497C.

Planting Rice Seedlings A71

50b, Spraying. 85b, Winnowing and drying.

1981, Sept. 4 Litho. *Perf. 14*

429 A71 10b shown .25 .25
430 A71 50b multicolored .25 *.30*
431 A71 85b multicolored .25 *.35*
Nos. 429-431 (3) .75 *.90*

West African Rice Development Assoc., 10th anniv.

Abuko Nature Reserve A72

Designs: Wildlife Fund emblem and reptiles.

1981, Nov. 17 Litho. *Perf. 14*

432 A72 40b Bosc's monitor 15.00 *.75*
433 A72 60b Dwarf crocodile 17.50 *1.50*
434 A72 80b Royal python 20.00 *2.50*
435 A72 85b Chameleon 22.50 *3.00*
Nos. 432-435 (4) 75.00 *7.75*

30th Anniv. of West African Examinations Council — A73

1982, Mar. 16 Litho. *Perf. 14*

436 A73 60b Test room .55 .40
437 A73 85b 1st high school .65 .55
438 A73 1.10d Council office .85 .75
Nos. 436-438 (3) 2.05 1.70

No. 426 Surcharged

1982, Apr. 19 Litho. *Perf. 13½x13*

439 CD331 60b on 75b multi *5.00 3.00*

Scouting Year A74

1982, May *Perf. 14*

440 A74 85b Tree planting 2.25 1.25
441 A74 1.25d Woodworking 2.50 2.25
442 A74 1.27d Baden-Powell 2.75 3.00
Nos. 440-442 (3) 7.50 6.50

1982 World Cup A75

1982, June 13 Litho. *Perf. 14*

443 A75 10b Team .25 .25
444 A75 1.10d Players 1.50 .75
445 A75 1.25d Stadium 1.50 .80
446 A75 1.55d Cup 1.75 1.00
a. Souvenir sheet of 4, #443-446 6.00 6.00
Nos. 443-446 (4) 5.00 2.80

For surcharge see No. 497B.

Princess Diana Issue

Common Design Type

1982, July 1 *Perf. 14½x14*

447 CD333 10b Arms .25 .25
448 CD333 85b Diana .60 .60
449 CD333 1.10d Wedding .75 .75
450 CD333 2.50d Portrait 1.25 1.25
Nos. 447-450 (4) 2.85 2.85

For surcharge see No. 479D.

Economic Community of West African States Development A76

Designs: 10b, Yundum Experimental Farm. 60b, Banjul/Kaolack Microwave Tower. 90b, Soap Factory, Denton Bridge Banjul. 1.25d, Control Tower, Yundum.

1982, Nov. 5 Litho. *Perf. 14x14½*

451 A76 10b multicolored .30 .25
452 A76 60b multicolored 2.10 *2.40*
453 A76 90b multicolored 2.10 *3.25*
454 A76 1.25d multicolored 3.00 *3.75*
Nos. 451-454 (4) 7.50 9.65

Kassina Cassinoides — A77

20b, Hylarana galamensis. 85b, Euphlyctis occipitalis. 2d, Kassina senegalensis.

1982, Dec. Litho. *Perf. 14*

455 A77 10b shown 2.25 .25
456 A77 20b multicolored 4.25 .45
457 A77 85b multicolored 7.25 4.50
458 A77 2d multicolored 9.50 *12.00*
Nos. 455-458 (4) 23.25 17.20

A78

10b, Globe showing Gambia. 60b, Batik cloth. 1.10d, Bagging peanuts. 2.10d, Flag.

1983, Mar. 14 Wmk. 373 *Perf. 12*

459 A78 10b multicolored .25 .25
460 A78 60b multicolored .25 *.35*
461 A78 1.10d multicolored .35 *.60*
462 A78 2.10d multicolored .60 *1.10*
Nos. 459-462 (4) 1.45 2.30

Commonwealth Day.

Sisters of St. Joseph of Cluny Centenary — A79

10b, Founder Anne Marie Javouhey, vert. 85b, Javouhey with children, house.

1983, Apr. 8 Litho. *Perf. 14*

463 A79 10b multicolored .25 .25
464 A79 85b multicolored .45 .45

River Boats A80

1b, Canoes. 2b, Upstream ferry. 3b, Dredging vessel. 4b, Harbor launch. 5b, Freighter. 10b, 60-foot launch. 20b, Multi-purpose vessel. 30b, Large sailing canoe. 40b, Passenger-cargo ferry. 50b, Cargo liner, diff. 75b, Fishing boats. 1d, Peanut river train. 1.25d, Groundnutter. 2.50d, Banjul-Barra ferry. 5d, Binlang Bolong. 10d, Passenger-cargo ferry, diff.

1983, July 11 Litho. *Perf. 14*

465 A80 1b multicolored .25 .25
466 A80 2b multicolored .25 .25
467 A80 3b multicolored .25 .25
468 A80 4b multicolored .30 .30
469 A80 5b multicolored .30 .30
470 A80 10b multicolored .30 .30
471 A80 20b multicolored .40 .40
472 A80 30b multicolored .40 .40
473 A80 40b multicolored .40 .40
474 A80 50b multicolored .45 .45
475 A80 75b multicolored .55 .50
476 A80 1d multicolored .80 .60
477 A80 1.25d multicolored .85 *1.25*
478 A80 2.50d multicolored 1.50 *2.25*
479 A80 5d multicolored 2.75 *4.50*
480 A80 10d multicolored 5.75 *7.25*
Nos. 465-480 (16) 15.50 *19.65*

For overprints see Nos. 523-524.

World Communications Year — A81

10b, Local ferry. 85b, GPO telex, Banjul. 90b, Radio Gambia. 1.10d, Loading mail, Yundum Airport.

1983, Oct. 10

481 A81 10b multi .25 .25
482 A81 85b multi .55 .55
483 A81 90b multi .75 .75
484 A81 1.10d multi 1.25 1.00
Nos. 481-484 (4) 2.80 2.55

Osprey, Breeding Range A82

Designs. Birds, Maps of Europe and Africa.

1983, Sept. 12 Litho. *Perf. 14*

485 A82 10b multicolored 2.75 .65
486 A82 60b multicolored 4.50 4.25
487 A82 85b multicolored 5.25 4.75
488 A82 1.10d multicolored 6.00 *7.25*
Nos. 485-488 (4) 18.50 16.90

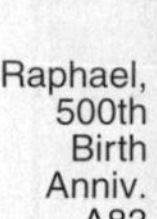

Raphael, 500th Birth Anniv. A83

Details from St. Paul Preaching at Athens.

1983, Nov. 1 Litho. *Perf. 14*

489 A83 60b multicolored .55 .55
490 A83 85b multicolored .65 .65
491 A83 1d multicolored .70 .70
Nos. 489-491 (3) 1.90 1.90

Souvenir Sheet

492 A83 2d multi, vert. 1.75 1.75

Manned Flight, 200th Anniv. A84

Flown covers and: 60b, Montgolfier Balloon. 85b, British Caledonian Aircraft. 96b, Junkers Airplane. 1.25d, Lunar module. 4d, Zeppelin.

1983, Dec. 12 Litho. *Perf. 14*

493 A84 60b multicolored .35 .35
494 A84 85b multicolored .45 .45
a. Bklt. pane, 2 each #493, 494 3.75
495 A84 90b multicolored .45 .45
496 A84 1.25d multicolored .50 .50
a. Bklt. pane, 2 each #495, 496 4.50
Nos. 493-496 (4) 1.75 1.75

Souvenir Sheet

497 A84 4d multicolored 7.50 7.50

No. 497 issued in booklet containing Nos. 497, 494a, 496a.

Nos. 411, 445, 428 and 449 Surcharged with Black Bars and New Value

Perfs. as before

1983, Dec. 14 Litho.

497A A66 1.50d on 1.25d, #411 *40.00*
497B A75 1.50d on 1.25d, #445 *40.00*
497C CD331 2d on 1.25d, #428 *40.00*
497D CD333 2d on 1.10d, #449 *40.00*

The status of Nos. 497A-497D is questioned.

Easter A85

Various Disney characters painting Easter eggs.

1984, Apr. 15 Litho. *Perf. 11*

498 A85 1b multicolored .25 .25
499 A85 2b multicolored .25 .25
500 A85 3b multicolored .25 .25
501 A85 4b multicolored .25 .25
502 A85 5b multicolored .25 .25
503 A85 10b multicolored .25 .25
504 A85 60b multicolored .35 .35
505 A85 90b multicolored .70 .70
506 A85 5d multicolored 2.75 2.75
Nos. 498-506 (9) 5.30 5.30

Souvenir Sheet

Perf. 14

507 A85 5d multicolored 5.50 5.50

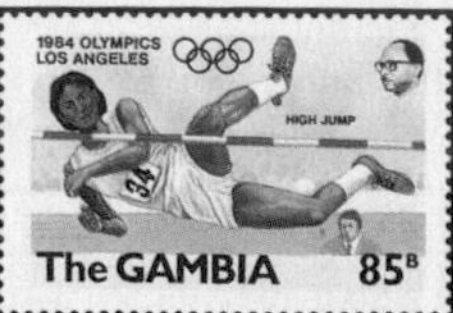

1984 Summer Olympics A86

60b, Shot put, vert. 85b, High jump. 90b, Wrestling, vert. 1d, Gymnastics, vert. 1.25d, Swimming. 2d, Diving.
5d, Yachting, vert.

1984, Mar. 30 Litho. *Perf. 14*

508 A86 60b multi .30 .30
509 A86 85b multi .45 .45
510 A86 90b multi .45 .45
511 A86 1d multi .50 .50
512 A86 1.25d multi .60 .60
513 A86 2d multi 1.00 1.00
Nos. 508-513 (6) 3.30 3.30

Souvenir Sheet

514 A86 5d multi 3.00 3.00

For overprints see Nos. 570-576.

Nile Crododile A87

4b, Young hatching. 6b, Adult carrying young. 90b, Adult. 1.50d, Adult, diff.
No. 518A as Nos. 515-518, without WWF emblem.

1984, May 23

515 A87 4b multi *3.25* *.75*
516 A87 6b multi *3.25* *.75*
517 A87 90b multi *18.00* *3.75*
518 A87 1.50d multi *22.50* *7.50*
Nos. 515-518 (4) *47.00* *12.75*

Souvenir Sheet

518A A87 Sheet of 4 *8.50* *6.00*
b.-e. each single *2.00* *1.50*

Lloyd's List Issue

Common Design Type

60b, Banjul Port. 85b, Bulk cargo carrier. 90b, Sinking of the Dagomba. 1.25d, 19th-cent. frigate.

1984, June 1 Litho. *Perf. 14*

519 CD335 60b multicolored .75 .60
520 CD335 85b multicolored .95 .95
521 CD335 90b multicolored 1.00 1.00
522 CD335 1.25d multicolored 1.50 *1.75*
Nos. 519-522 (4) 4.20 4.30

Nos. 478-479 Overprinted: "19th UPU / CONGRESS HAMBURG"

1984, June 19 Litho. *Perf. 14*

523 A80 2.50d multicolored 1.50 *1.75*
524 A80 5d multicolored 2.75 *3.50*

1984 Summer Olympics A88

1984, July 28 Litho. *Perf. 14*

525 A88 60b Running .50 .40
526 A88 85b Long jump .60 .55
527 A88 90b Running, diff. .60 .55
528 A88 1.25d Long jump, diff. .80 .70
Nos. 525-528 (4) 2.50 2.20

Gambia-South America Transatlantic Flight, 50th Anniv. — A89

60b, Graf Zeppelin D-LZ127. 85b, Dornier Wal on S.S. Westfalen. 90b, Dornier DO-18 D-ABYM. 1.25d, Dornier Wal D-2069.

1984, Nov. 1 Litho. *Perf. 14*

529 A89 60b multicolored 1.40 1.10
530 A89 85b multicolored 2.10 *1.90*
531 A89 90b multicolored 2.50 *2.75*
532 A89 1.25d multicolored 2.50 *3.00*
Nos. 529-532 (4) 8.50 *8.75*

Butterflies A90

10b, Antanartia hippomene. 85b, Pseudacraea eurytus. 90b, Charaxes lactitinctus. 3d, Graphium pylades.
5d, Eurema hapale.

1984, Nov. 27

533 A90 10b multicolored .35 .25
534 A90 85b multicolored 1.00 1.00
535 A90 90b multicolored 1.25 1.00
536 A90 3d multicolored 3.25 *4.25*
Nos. 533-536 (4) 5.85 *6.50*

Souvenir Sheets

537 A90 5d multicolored 12.50 12.50

Marine Life — A90a

55b, Penaeus duorarum. 75b, Caretta caretta. 1.50d, Physalia. 2.35d, Uca pugilator.
5d, Cowrie snail.

1984, Nov. 27

538 A90a 55b multicolored .40 .35
539 A90a 75b multicolored .60 .50
540 A90a 1.50d multicolored .95 .95
541 A90a 2.35d multicolored 1.60 1.60
Nos. 538-541 (4) 3.55 *3.40*

Souvenir Sheets

542 A90a 5d multicolored 4.75 4.75

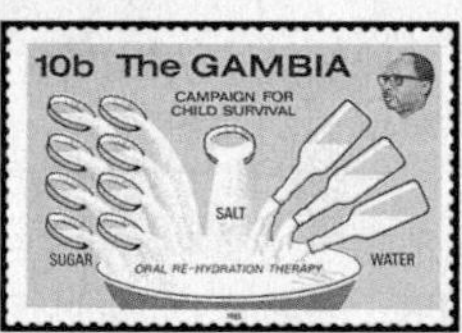

UN Child Survival Campaign A91

10b, Oral rehydration therapy. 85b, Growth monitoring. 1.10d, Breast-feeding. 1.50d, Universal immunization.

1985, Feb. 27

543 A91 10b multicolored .25 .25
544 A91 85b multicolored .45 .45
545 A91 1.10d multicolored .60 .60
546 A91 1.50d multicolored .70 .70
Nos. 543-546 (4) 2.00 2.00

UN Decade for Women A92

Design: 1d, 1.25d, Woman working in office.

1985, Mar. 11

547 A92 60b multicolored .30 .30
548 A92 85b multicolored .45 .45
549 A92 1d multicolored .60 .60
550 A92 1.25d multicolored .65 .65
Nos. 547-550 (4) 2.00 2.00

Audubon Birth Bicent. — A93

Illustrations of North American bird species by John J. Audubon (1785-1851): 60b, Cathartes aura. 85b, Anhinga anhinga. 1.50d, Butoroides striatus. 5d, Aix sponsa.
10d, Gavia immer.

1985, July 15

551 A93 60b multicolored 1.60 .75
552 A93 85b multicolored 2.00 1.50
553 A93 1.50d multicolored 2.25 2.60
554 A93 5d multicolored 3.50 *4.50*
Nos. 551-554 (4) 9.35 9.35

Souvenir Sheet

555 A93 10d multicolored 8.50 8.50

Queen Mother, 85th Birthday — A94

85b, Inspecting troops. 3d, Portrait. 5d, Portrait, diff.
10d, On parade with Prince Charles.

1985, July 24

556 A94 85b multicolored .45 .45
557 A94 3d multicolored 1.40 1.40
558 A94 5d multicolored 2.40 2.40
Nos. 556-558 (3) 4.25 4.25

Souvenir Sheet

559 A94 10d multicolored 5.00 5.00

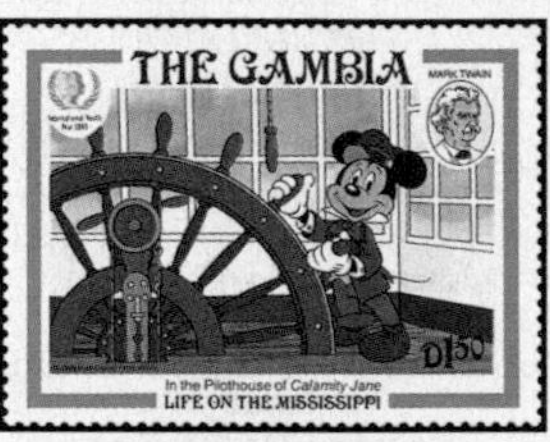

Life on the Mississippi, by Mark Twain (1835-1910) — A95

Walt Disney characters: 60b, Portrait. 85b, Treasure. 1.50d, Helm of Calamity Jane. 2d, Antebellum Mansion, Missouri Shore. 2.35d, Music. 2.50d, Measuring Channel Depth, Natchez. 3d, Card Game aboard the Gold Dust. 5d, Statue. No. 568, Landing, St. Louis. No. 569, Goofy.
The 60b, 85b, 2.35d, 5d and No. 569 show scenes from "Faithful John" by the brothers Grimm.

1985, Oct. 30

560 A95 60b multicolored .80 .80
561 A95 85b multicolored 1.00 1.00
562 A95 1.50d multicolored 2.10 2.10
563 A95 2d multicolored 2.25 2.25
564 A95 2.35d multicolored 2.25 2.25
565 A95 2.50d multicolored 2.75 2.75
566 A95 3d multicolored 3.00 3.00
567 A95 5d multicolored 4.00 4.00
Nos. 560-567 (8) 18.15 18.15

Souvenir Sheet

568 A95 10d multicolored 10.00 10.00
569 A95 10d multicolored 10.00 10.00

Nos. 508-514 Ovptd. "GOLD MEDALIST" or "GOLD MEDAL," Name of Winner and Country

60b, Claudia Losch, West Germany, women's shot put. 85b, Ulrike Meyfarth, West Germany, women's high jump. 90b, Pasquale Passarelli, West Germany, 126-pound Greco-Roman wrestling. 1d, Li Ning, China, men's gymnastic floor exercises. 1.25d, Michael Gross, West Germany, men's 100-meter butterfly and 200-meter freestyle swimming. 2d, Sylvie Bernier, Canada, women's springboard diving. 5d, US, Star Class yachting.

1985, Nov. 11 *Perf. 14*

570 A86 60b multicolored .60 .30
571 A86 85b multicolored .70 .40
572 A86 90b multicolored .75 .45
573 A86 1d multicolored .80 .50
574 A86 1.25d multicolored 1.00 .65
575 A86 2d multicolored 1.25 1.00
Nos. 570-575 (6) 5.10 3.30

Souvenir Sheet

576 A86 5d multicolored 2.60 2.60

UN 40th Anniv. A97

Views of Banjul: 85b, Independence Stadium. 2d, Central Bank. 4d, Port. 6d, Oyster Creek Bridge.

1985, Nov. 15

577 A97 85b multicolored .65 .65
578 A97 2d multicolored 1.50 1.50
579 A97 4d multicolored 3.75 3.75
580 A97 6d multicolored 5.00 5.00
Nos. 577-580 (4) 10.90 10.90

Natl. independence, 20th anniv.

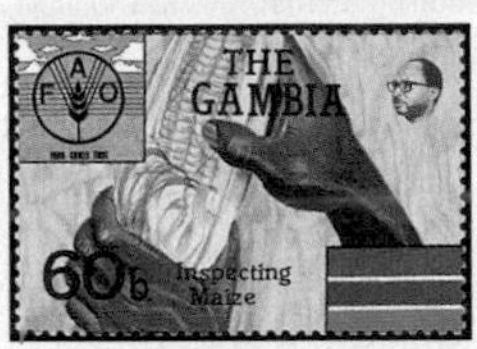

UN FAO, 40th Anniv. A98

1985, Nov. 15

581 A98 60b Corn .80 .80
582 A98 1.10d Paddy 1.25 1.25
583 A98 3d Cow, calf 3.50 3.50
584 A98 5d Fruit 4.50 4.50
Nos. 581-584 (4) 10.05 10.05

Diocese of Gambia and Guinea, 50th Anniv. A99

Designs: 60b, Fishermen, Fotoba, Guinea. 85b, St. Mary's Primary School, Banjul. 1.10d, St. Mary's Cathedral, Banjul. 1.50d, Mobile Dispensary at Christy, Kunda, 1935-45.

1985, Dec. 24

585 A99 60b multicolored .35 .30
586 A99 85b multicolored .60 .45
587 A99 1.10d multicolored .65 .60
588 A99 1.50d multicolored 1.00 .90
Nos. 585-588 (4) 2.60 2.25

Girl Guides, 75th Anniv. — A100

60b, Application, horiz. 85b, 2nd Bathurst, horiz. 1.50d, Lady Baden-Powell. 5d, Rosamond Fowlis, leader.
10d, Guides.

1985, Dec. 27

589 A100 60b multicolored .35 .35
590 A100 85b multicolored .55 .55
591 A100 1.50d multicolored 1.10 1.10
592 A100 5d multicolored 3.50 3.50
Nos. 589-592 (4) 5.50 5.50

Souvenir Sheet

593 A100 10d multicolored 6.50 6.50

Christmas — A101

Painting details: 60b, Virgin and Child, by Dirck Bouts (c. 1400-1475). 85b, The Annunciation, by Robert Campin (c. 1378-1444). 1.50d, Adoration of the Shepherds, by Gerard David (c. 1460-1523). 5d, The Nativity, by Gerard David. 10d, Adoration of the Magi, by Hieronymus Bosch (1450-1516).

1985, Dec. 27 *Perf. 15*

594 A101 60b multicolored .25 .25
595 A101 85b multicolored .40 .40
596 A101 1.50d multicolored .80 .80
597 A101 5d multicolored 1.50 1.50
Nos. 594-597 (4) 2.95 2.95

Souvenir Sheet

598 A101 10d multicolored 5.25 5.25

Intl. Youth Year A102

1985, Dec. 31 *Perf. 14*

599 A102 60b Mother's helper .30 .30
600 A102 85b Wrestling .45 .45
601 A102 1.10d Griot storyteller .55 *1.00*
602 A102 1.50d Crocodile pool .90 *1.25*
Nos. 599-602 (4) 2.20 3.00

Souvenir Sheet

603 A102 5d Cow herder 3.00 3.00

A103

Halley's Comet — A104

Designs: 10b, Maria Mitchell (1818-1889), American astronomer, Kitt Peak Natl. Observatory, Papago Indian Reservation, Arizona. 20b, Apollo 11, Neil Armstrong steps on moon, 1969. 75b, Skylab 4, Kohoutek Comet, 1973. 1d, NASA Infrared Astronomical Satellite, 1983. 2d, Comet sighting, 1577, Turkish art. No. 609, NASA Intl. Cometary Explorer satellite. No. 610, Comet.

1986, Mar.

604 A103 10b multicolored .35 .25
605 A103 20b multicolored .65 .25
606 A103 75b multicolored .90 .55
607 A103 1d multicolored 1.25 .80
608 A103 2d multicolored 1.75 1.40
609 A103 10d multicolored 4.75 5.00
Nos. 604-609 (6) 9.65 8.25

Souvenir Sheet

610 A104 10d multicolored 7.50 7.50

For overprints see Nos. 650-656.

Queen Elizabeth II, 60th Birthday
Common Design Type

Designs: 1d, Royal family at Royal Tournament, 1936. 2.50d, Christening, 1983. No. 613, State visit to West Germany, 1978. No. 614, At Balmoral, 1935.

1986, Apr. 21

611 CD339 1d lt yel bis & blk .50 .40
612 CD339 2.50d pale grn & multi 1.00 .75
613 CD339 10d dl lil & multi 3.00 3.00
Nos. 611-613 (3) 4.50 4.15

Souvenir Sheet

614 CD339 10d tan & black 3.75 3.75

1986 World Cup Soccer Championships, Mexico — A105

75b, Block. 1d, Kneeing the ball. 2.50d, Kick. No. 618, Heading the ball. No. 619, Goalie catching ball.

1986, May 2

615 A105 75b multicolored .60 .60
616 A105 1d multicolored .85 .85
617 A105 2.50d multicolored 2.50 2.50
618 A105 10d multicolored 6.00 6.00
Nos. 615-618 (4) 9.95 9.95

Souvenir Sheet

619 A105 10d multicolored 10.00 10.00

For overprints see Nos. 639-643.

AMERIPEX '86 — A106

Exhibition emblem, automobiles and flags: 25b, 1986 Mercedes 500, Germany. 75b, 1935 Cord 810, US. 1d, 1957 Borgward Isabella Coupe, Germany. 1.25d, 1985-6 Lamborghini Countach, Italy. 2d, 1955 Ford Thunderbird, US. 2.25d, 1956 Citroen DS19, France. 5d, 1936 Bugatti Atlante, France. 10d, 1936 Horch 853, Germany. No. 628, 1913 Benz 8/20, Germany. No. 629, 1924 Steiger 10/50, Germany.

1986, May 22 *Perf. 15*

620 A106 25b multi .25 .25
621 A106 75b multi .40 .35
622 A106 1d multi .45 .55
623 A106 1.25d multi .50 .65
624 A106 2d multi .60 *1.00*
625 A106 2.25d multi .70 *1.10*
626 A106 5d multi 1.00 *2.25*
627 A106 10d multi 2.50 *4.00*
Nos. 620-627 (8) 6.40 *10.15*

Souvenir Sheets

628 A106 12d multi 4.75 4.75
629 A106 12d multi 4.75 4.75

Karl Benz automobile cent.

Statue of Liberty, Cent. A107

Statue and famous emigrants: 20b, John Jacob Astor (1763-1848), financier. 1d, Jacob Riis (1849-1914), journalist. 1.25d, Igor Sikorsky (1889-1972), aeronautics engineer. 5d, Charles Boyer (1899-1978), actor. 10d, Statue, vert.

1986, June 10 *Perf. 14*

630 A107 20b multicolored .25 .25
631 A107 1d multicolored .60 .60
632 A107 1.25d multicolored .65 .65
633 A107 5d multicolored 2.75 2.75
Nos. 630-633 (4) 4.25 4.25

Souvenir Sheet

634 A107 10d multicolored 5.50 5.50

Royal Wedding Issue, 1986
Common Design Type

1d, Engagement of Prince Andrew and Sarah Ferguson. 2.50d, Andrew. 4d, Andrew in flight uniform, other helicopter pilot. 7d, Couple, diff.

1986, July 23

635 CD340 1d multi .45 .45
636 CD340 2.50d multi 1.10 1.10
637 CD340 4d multi 2.25 2.25
Nos. 635-637 (3) 3.80 3.80

Souvenir Sheet

638 CD340 7d multi 4.75 4.75

Nos. 615-619 Overprinted "WINNERS / Argentina 3 / W. Germany 2" in Gold

1986, Sept. 16 **Litho.** *Perf. 14*

639 A105 75b multicolored .40 .40
640 A105 1d multicolored .60 .60
641 A105 2.50d multicolored 1.25 1.25
642 A105 10d multicolored 5.00 5.00
Nos. 639-642 (4) 7.25 7.25

Souvenir Sheet

643 A105 10d multicolored 6.50 6.50

Christmas, STOCKHOLMIA '86 — A108

Disney characters mailing letters in various countries.

1986, Nov. 4 *Perf. 11*

644 A108 1d Great Britain 1.00 .50
645 A108 1.25d United States 1.10 .70
646 A108 2d France 1.75 1.25
647 A108 2.35d Australia 2.00 1.40
648 A108 5d Germany 2.25 2.25
Nos. 644-648 (5) 8.10 6.10

Souvenir Sheet

649 A108 10d Sweden 8.75 8.75

Nos. 604-610 Ovptd. in Silver

1986, Oct. 21 **Litho.** *Perf. 14*

650 A103 10b multicolored .25 .25
651 A103 20b multicolored .65 .25
652 A103 75b multicolored 1.00 .50
653 A103 1d multicolored 1.10 .60
654 A103 2d multicolored 1.40 1.50
655 A103 10d multicolored 4.25 4.50
Nos. 650-655 (6) 8.65 7.60

Souvenir Sheet

656 A104 10d multicolored 5.00 5.00

Marc Chagall (1887-1985), Artist A109

Paintings, ceramicware, sculpture: 75b, Snowing. 85b, The Boat, 1957. 1d, Maternity, 1913. 1.25d, The Flute Player. 2.35d, Lovers and the Beast, 1957. 4d, Fishes at Saint Jean. 5d, Entering the Ring, 1968. 10d, Three Acrobats, 1956. No. 665, The Sabbath. No. 666, The Cattle Driver.

1987, Feb. 6 **Litho.**

657 A109 75b multi .45 .25
658 A109 85b multi .55 .30
659 A109 1d multi .65 .40
660 A109 1.25d multi .85 .50
661 A109 2.35d multi 1.10 1.10
662 A109 4d multi 1.75 1.75
663 A109 5d multi 2.25 2.25
664 A109 10d multi 4.00 2.50

Sizes: 110x95mm, 110x68mm

Imperf

665 A109 12d multi 5.75 5.75
666 A109 12d multi 5.75 5.75
Nos. 657-666 (10) 23.10 20.55

Musical Instruments — A110

Various instruments from the Mandingo Empire: 75b, Bugarab, tabala. 1d, Balaphong, fiddle. 1.25d, Bolongbato, konting. 10d, Koras. 12d, Sabarrs.

1987, Jan. 21 Litho. *Perf. 15*

No.	Type	Value		Unused	Used
667	A110	75b	multicolored	.25	.25
668	A110	1d	multicolored	.30	.30
669	A110	1.25d	multicolored	.35	.35
670	A110	10d	multicolored	2.00	2.00
			Nos. 667-670 (4)	2.90	2.90

Souvenir Sheet

No.	Type	Value		Unused	Used
671	A110	12d	multicolored	3.00	3.00

Nos. 669-670 vert.
For overprints see Nos. 750, 856-860.

America's Cup A111

20b, America, 1851. 1d, Courageous, 1974. 2.50d, Volunteer, 1887. 10d, Intrepid, 1967. 12d, Australia II, 1983.

1987, Apr. 3 *Perf. 14*

No.	Type	Value		Unused	Used
672	A111	20b	multi	.25	.25
673	A111	1d	multi	.35	.35
674	A111	2.50d	multi	.90	.90
675	A111	10d	multi	4.00	4.00
			Nos. 672-675 (4)	5.50	5.50

Souvenir Sheet

No.	Type	Value		Unused	Used
676	A111	12d	multi	5.75	5.75

For overprint see No. 751.

Statue of Liberty, Cent. A112

Photographs of restoration and unveiling in 1986: 1b, Shoulder, torch. 2b, Operation Sail flotilla. 3b, Tall ship, ships. 5b, Luxury liner, aircraft carrier. 50b, Statue's coiffure. 75b, Coiffure, diff. 1d, Workmen scaling statue. 1.25d, Back of statue. 10d, Front of Statue. 12d, Side of statue.

1987, Apr. 9 Litho.

No.	Type	Value		Unused	Used
677	A112	1b	multicolored	.25	.25
678	A112	2b	multicolored	.25	.25
679	A112	3b	multicolored	.25	.25
680	A112	5b	multicolored	.25	.25
681	A112	50b	multicolored	.50	.50
682	A112	75b	multicolored	.70	.70
683	A112	1d	multicolored	.85	.85
684	A112	1.25d	multicolored	1.00	1.00
685	A112	10d	multicolored	5.00	5.00
686	A112	12d	multicolored	5.25	5.25
			Nos. 677-686 (10)	14.30	14.30

Nos. 677, 681-686 vert.

Flowers from Abuko Nature Reserve — A113

75b, Lantana camara. 1d, Clerodendrum thomsoniae. 1.50d, Haemanthus multiflorus. 1.70d, Gloriosa simplex. 1.75d, Combretum microphyllum. 2.25d, Eulophia guineensis. 5d, Erythrina senegalensis. 15d, Dichrostachys glomerata.

No. 691, Costus spectabilis. No. 691A, Strophanthus preussii.

1987, May 25

No.	Type	Value		Unused	Used
687	A113	75b	multi	.25	.25
687A	A113	1d	multi	.25	.25
688	A113	1.50d	multi	.45	.40
688A	A113	1.70d	multi	.50	.45
689	A113	1.75d	multi	.50	.45
689A	A113	2.25d	multi	.65	.60
689B	A113	5d	multi	1.40	1.40
690	A113	15d	multi	3.25	3.25
			Nos. 687-690 (8)	7.25	7.05

Souvenir Sheets

No.	Type	Value		Unused	Used
691	A113	15d	shown	3.75	3.75
691A	A113	15d	multi	3.75	3.75

Nos. 691-691A are continuous designs.
For overprint see No. 752.

CAPEX '87 A115

Various buses.

1987, June 15

No.	Type	Value		Unused	Used
692	A115	20b	multi, vert.	.55	.25
693	A115	75b	multi	.75	.25
694	A115	1d	multi	1.60	.75
695	A115	10d	multi, vert.	4.00	4.00
			Nos. 692-695 (4)	6.90	5.25

Souvenir Sheet

No.	Type	Value		Unused	Used
696	A115	12d	multi	7.00	7.00

For overprint see No. 749.

1988 Summer Olympics, Seoul A116

50b, Women's basketball. 1d, Volleyball. 3d, Field hockey. 10d, Handball.
15d, Soccer.

1987, July 3

No.	Type	Value		Unused	Used
697	A116	50b	multicolored	.25	.25
698	A116	1d	multicolored	.60	.30
699	A116	3d	multicolored	1.10	.90
700	A116	10d	multicolored	3.50	3.00
			Nos. 697-700 (4)	5.45	4.45

Souvenir Sheet

No.	Type	Value		Unused	Used
701	A116	15d	multicolored	5.00	5.00

Nos. 697-698 vert.

A117

The Twelve Days of Christmas, Medieval Counting Song — A118

Designs: 20b, Partridge in a pear tree. 40b, 2 turtle doves. 60b, 3 French hens. 75b, 4 calling birds. 1d, 5 golden rings. 1.25d, 6 geese a-laying. 1.50d, 7 swans a-swimming. 2d, 8 maids a-milking. 3d, 9 ladies dancing. 5d, 10 lords a-leaping. 10d, 11 pipers piping. 12d, 12 drummers drumming.

Miniature Sheet

1987, Nov. 2 Litho. *Perf. 14*

No.	Type	Value		Unused	Used
702			Sheet of 12	14.50	14.50
a.	A117	20b	multicolored	.25	.25
b.	A117	40b	multicolored	.25	.25
c.	A117	60b	multicolored	.25	.25
d.	A117	75b	multicolored	.25	.25
e.	A117	1d	multicolored	.40	.40
f.	A117	1.25d	multicolored	.45	.45
g.	A117	1.50d	multicolored	.60	.60
h.	A117	2d	multicolored	.75	.75
i.	A117	3d	multicolored	1.25	1.25
j.	A117	5d	multicolored	1.90	1.90
k.	A117	10d	multicolored	3.50	3.50
l.	A117	12d	multicolored	4.25	4.25

Souvenir Sheet

No.	Type	Value		Unused	Used
703	A118	15d	multi	4.50	4.50

16th Boy Scout Jamboree, Australia, 1987-88 A119

75b, Singing around campfire. 1d, Nature study, African katydid. 1.25d, Bird watching, red-tailed tropicbird. 12d, Boarding bus.
15d, Nature study.

1987, Nov. 9

No.	Type	Value		Unused	Used
704	A119	75b	multicolored	.55	.30
705	A119	1d	multicolored	.85	.40
706	A119	1.25d	multicolored	1.60	1.00
707	A119	12d	multicolored	4.75	4.75
			Nos. 704-707 (4)	7.75	6.45

Souvenir Sheet

No.	Type	Value		Unused	Used
708	A119	15d	multicolored	7.75	7.75

Mickey Mouse, 60th Anniv. — A120

Disney animated characters and historic locomotives: 60b, Richard Trevithick's locomotive, 1804. 75b, Empire State Express 999, 1893. 1d, George Stephenson's Rocket, 1829. 1.25d, Santa Fe Mountain 2-10-2, 1920. 2d, Class GG-1 Pennsylvania, 1933. 5d, Stourbridge Lion, 1829. 10d, Best Friend of Charleston, 1830. 12d, M10001 Union Pacific, 1934. No. 717, Tres Grande Vitesse-SNCF, 1981, France. No. 718, The General, Western & Atlantic, 1855.

1987, Dec. 9 Litho. *Perf. 14x13½*

No.	Type	Value		Unused	Used
709	A120	60b	multicolored	.35	.35
710	A120	75b	multicolored	.40	.40
711	A120	1d	multicolored	.50	.50
712	A120	1.25d	multicolored	.60	.60
713	A120	2d	multicolored	.90	.90
714	A120	5d	multicolored	2.00	2.00
715	A120	10d	multicolored	3.75	3.75
716	A120	12d	multicolored	4.25	4.25
			Nos. 709-716 (8)	12.75	12.75

Souvenir Sheets

No.	Type	Value		Unused	Used
717	A120	15d	multicolored	6.25	6.25
718	A120	15d	multicolored	6.25	6.25

Fauna and Flora A121

50b, Duiker, acacia. 75b, Red-billed hornbill, casuarina. 90b, West African dwarf crocodile, rice. 1d, Leopard, papyrus. 1.25d, Crested cranes, millet. 2d, Waterbuck, baobab tree. 3d, Oribi, Senegal palm. 5d, Hippopotamus, papaya.

No. 727, Great white pelican. No. 728, Red-throated bee-eater.

1988, Feb. 9 Litho. *Perf. 15*

No.	Type	Value		Unused	Used
719	A121	50b	multicolored	.25	.25
720	A121	75b	multicolored	.90	.90
721	A121	90b	multicolored	.45	.45
722	A121	1d	multicolored	.45	.45
723	A121	1.25d	multicolored	.90	.90
724	A121	2d	multicolored	.50	.50
725	A121	3d	multicolored	.75	.75
726	A121	5d	multicolored	1.25	1.25
			Nos. 719-726 (8)	5.45	5.45

Souvenir Sheets

No.	Type	Value		Unused	Used
727	A121	12d	multicolored	2.25	2.25
728	A121	12d	multicolored	2.25	2.25

Nos. 720, 722, 724, 726 and 728 vert.

40th Wedding Anniv. of Queen Elizabeth II and Prince Philip — A122

75b, Wedding portrait, 1947. 1d, Couple at leisure. 3d, Wedding portrait, diff. 10d, Couple, c. 1987.
15d, Wedding party.

1988, Mar. 15 *Perf. 14*

No.	Type	Value		Unused	Used
729	A122	75b	multicolored	.25	.25
730	A122	1d	multicolored	.25	.25
731	A122	3d	multicolored	.75	.75
732	A122	10d	multicolored	3.00	3.00
			Nos. 729-732 (4)	4.25	4.25

Souvenir Sheet

No.	Type	Value		Unused	Used
733	A122	15d	multicolored	3.25	3.25

1988 Summer Olympics, Seoul A123

1d, Archery, vert. 1.25d, Boxing, vert. 5d, Gymnastics, vert. 10d, 100-Meter sprint.
15d, Award ceremony, Olympic stadium.

1988, May 3 Litho. *Perf. 14*

No.	Type	Value		Unused	Used
734	A123	1d	multi	.25	.25
735	A123	1.25d	multi	.25	.25
736	A123	5d	multi	1.50	1.25
737	A123	10d	multi	3.00	2.50
			Nos. 734-737 (4)	5.00	4.25

Souvenir Sheet

No.	Type	Value		Unused	Used
738	A123	15d	multi	3.75	3.75

Anniversaries & Events — A124

Designs: 50b, Red Cross flag. 75b, Friendship 7, piloted by John Glenn, 1963. 1d, British Airways Concorde jet. 1.25d, Spirit of St. Louis, piloted by Charles Lindbergh, 1927. 2d, X-15, piloted by Major William Knight, 1967. 3d, Bell X-1, piloted by Capt. Charles Yeager, 1947. 10d, Spanish galleon, British warship, 1588. 12d, The Titanic. No. 747, Kangaroo and joey. No. 748, Cathedral, modern church, vert.

1988, May 15

No.	Type	Value		Unused	Used
739	A124	50b	multicolored	1.25	.75
740	A124	75b	multicolored	.75	.75
741	A124	1d	multicolored	2.50	1.00
742	A124	1.25d	multicolored	1.25	1.25
743	A124	2d	multicolored	1.75	1.75
744	A124	3d	multicolored	2.00	2.00
745	A124	10d	multicolored	4.00	4.00
746	A124	12d	multicolored	6.50	6.50
			Nos. 739-746 (8)	20.00	18.00

Souvenir Sheets

No.	Type	Value		Unused	Used
747	A124	15d	multicolored	4.00	4.00
748	A124	15d	multicolored	4.00	4.00

Intl. Red Cross, 125th anniv. (50b); first American in space, 25th anniv. in 1987 (75b); 1st London-New York scheduled Concorde flight, 10th anniv. in 1987 (1d); first solo transatlantic flight, 60th anniv. in 1987 (1.25d); fastest speed flown, 6.72 Mach, 20th anniv. in 1987 (2d); 1st supersonic flight, 40th anniv. in 1987 (3d); defeat of the Spanish Armada, 400th anniv. (10d); maiden voyage of the Titanic, 75th anniv. in 1987 (12d); founding of Australia, bicentennial (No. 747); and founding of Berlin, 750th anniv. in 1987 (No. 748).

Nos. 694, 670, 675 and 690 Ovptd. for Philatelic Exhibitions

a

b

c

d

1988, Apr. 19 Litho. *Perf. 14, 15*

No.	Type	Value	Description	Unused	Used
749	A115(a)	1d	multi	.50	.50
750	A110(b)	10d	multi	3.00	3.00
751	A111(c)	10d	multi	3.00	3.00
752	A113(d)	15d	multi	3.50	3.50
			Nos. 749-752 (4)	10.00	10.00

Paintings by Titian A125

Designs: 25b, Emperor Charles V, 1549. 50b, St. Margaret and the Dragon, 1565. 60b, Ranuccio Farnese, 1542. 75b, Tarquin and Lucretia, 1570. 1d, The Knight of Malta, c. 1550. 5d, Spain Succouring Faith, 1571. 10d, Doge Francesco Venier, 1555. 12d, Doge Grimani Before the Faith, c. 1555-1576. No. 761, Jealous Husband, 1511. No. 762, Venus Blindfolding Cupid, 1560.

1988, July 7 Litho. *Perf. 13½x14*

No.	Type	Value	Description	Unused	Used
753	A125	25b	multicolored	.25	.25
754	A125	50b	multicolored	.50	.50
755	A125	60b	multicolored	.50	.50
756	A125	75b	multicolored	.70	.70
757	A125	1d	multicolored	.80	.80
758	A125	5d	multicolored	2.75	2.75
759	A125	10d	multicolored	4.50	4.50
760	A125	12d	multicolored	5.00	5.00
			Nos. 753-760 (8)	15.00	15.00

Souvenir Sheets

No.	Type	Value	Description	Unused	Used
761	A125	15d	multicolored	3.75	3.75
762	A125	15d	multicolored	3.75	3.75

Tribute to John F. Kennedy A126

75b, Sailing. 1d, Peace Corps enactment. 1.25d, Public address, vert. 12d, Grave, Arlington Natl. Cemetery. 15d, Kennedy, vert.

1988, Sept. 1 Litho. *Perf. 14*

No.	Type	Value	Description	Unused	Used
763	A126	75b	multicolored	.25	.25
764	A126	1d	multicolored	.30	.30
765	A126	1.25d	multicolored	.40	.40
766	A126	12d	multicolored	2.75	2.75
			Nos. 763-766 (4)	3.70	3.70

Souvenir Sheet

No.	Type	Value	Description	Unused	Used
767	A126	15d	multicolored	4.00	4.00

Entertainers — A127

20b, Emmett Lee Kelly (1898-1979), clown. 1d, Gambia Natl. Ensemble. 1.25d, Jackie Gleason (1916-87), comedian, & The Honeymooners cast. 1.50d, Stan Laurel (1890-1965) & Oliver Hardy (1892-1957), film comedy team. 2.50d, Yul Brynner (c. 1920-85), actor. 3d, Cary Grant (1904-86), actor. 10d, Danny Kaye (1918-87), comedian, actor. 20d, Charlie Chaplin (1889-1977), comedian, actor. No. 776, Harpo (1893-1964), Chico (1891-1961), Zeppo (1901-79) & Groucho (1890-1977) Marx, comedy team. No. 777, Fred Astaire (1899-1987) & Rita Hayworth (1918-87), dancers & film stars. Nos. 768-775 vert.

1988, Nov. 9 Litho.

No.	Type	Value	Description	Unused	Used
768	A127	20b	multi	.25	.25
769	A127	1d	multi	.50	.50
770	A127	1.25d	multi	.60	.60
771	A127	1.50d	multi	.65	.65
772	A127	2.50d	multi	1.00	1.00
773	A127	3d	multi	1.25	1.25
774	A127	10d	multi	3.75	3.75
775	A127	20d	multi	6.50	6.50
			Nos. 768-775 (8)	14.50	14.50

Souvenir Sheets

No.	Type	Value	Description	Unused	Used
776	A127	15d	multi	7.00	7.00
777	A127	15d	multi	7.00	7.00

Kelly's name is spelled incorrectly; Brynner's and Grant's dates are incorrect.

Zeppelin LZ7 Deutschland, 1910 — A128

Transportation innovations: 50b, Stephenson's Locomotion, 1825. 75b, General Motors Sun Racer, 1987. 1d, Sprague's Premiere, 1888. 1.25d, Gold Rush bicycle, 1986. 2.50d, 1st Liquid-fuel rocket, invented by Robert Goddard, 1925. 10d, Orukter Amphibolos, 1805. 12d, Sovereign of the Seas, 1988. No. 786, USS Nautilus, 1954, vert. No. 787, Fulton's Nautilus, early 19th cent.

1988, Nov. 21 Litho. *Perf. 14*

No.	Type	Value	Description	Unused	Used
778	A128	25b	multi	.60	.25
779	A128	50b	multi	1.00	.40
780	A128	75b	multi	1.10	.55
781	A128	1d	multi	1.50	.70
782	A128	1.25d	multi	1.50	.75
783	A128	2.50d	multi	2.25	1.25
784	A128	10d	multi	5.75	3.50
785	A128	12d	multi	6.75	4.00
			Nos. 778-785 (8)	20.45	11.40

Souvenir Sheets

No.	Type	Value	Description	Unused	Used
786	A128	15d	multi	5.00	5.00
787	A128	15d	multi	5.00	5.00

Discovery of America, 500th Anniv. (in 1992) A129

Designs: 50b, Caravel, Henry the Navigator (1394-1460), Prince of Portugal, and coat of arms, vert. 75b, Jesse Ramsden's sextant, map of Africa, arms, vert. 1d, Hour glass, 15th cent., and map, vert. 1.25d, Henry and Vasco da Gama, vert. 2.50d, Da Gama and 15th cent. caravel, vert. 5d, Mungo Park (1771-1806), Scottish explorer, arms and map of Gambia River. 10d, Map of west African coast, 1563. 12d, Portuguese caravel, arms. No. 796, Caravel off the Gambian coast, 15th cent., vert. No. 797, European ship off Gambian coast, 15th cent., vert.

1988, Dec. 1 Litho. *Perf. 14*

No.	Type	Value	Description	Unused	Used
788	A129	50b	multi	.95	.95
789	A129	75b	multi	1.10	1.10
790	A129	1d	multi	1.40	1.40
791	A129	1.25d	multi	1.60	1.60
792	A129	2.50d	multi	1.90	1.90
793	A129	5d	shown	3.25	3.25
794	A129	10d	multi	5.50	5.50
795	A129	12d	multi	5.75	5.75
			Nos. 788-795 (8)	21.45	21.45

Souvenir Sheets

No.	Type	Value	Description	Unused	Used
796	A129	15d	multi	5.25	5.25
797	A129	15d	multi	5.25	5.25

Space Achievements — A130

Galileo and: 50b, Futuristic aerospace plane and Ernst Mach (1838-1916), Austrian physicist, vert. 75b, OAO III astronomical satellite and Niels Bohr (1885-1962), Danish physicist and Nobel lauerate in 1922, vert. 1d, NASA space shuttle, future space station and Robert Goddard (1882-1945), American rocket scientist. 1.25d, Flyby of probe past Jupiter, 1979, and Edward Barnard (1857-1923), American astronomer who discovered Jupiter's 5th satellite in 1892. 2d, Hubble Space Telescope and George Hale (1868-1938), American astronomer, vert. 3d, Precision measurement of the distance between the Earth and the Moon by laser and Albert A. Michelson (1852-1931), Nobel lauerate in 1907 for research on the speed of light. 10d, HEAO-2 Einstein orbital satellite and Albert Einstein, vert. 20d, Voyager, 1st circumnavigation of the world without refueling, 1987, and the Wright Brothers. No. 806, Moon Ganymede passing the Great Red Spot on Jupiter. No. 807, Apollo and Neil Armstrong, 1st man on the Moon, July 20, 1969, vert.

1988, Dec. 12 *Perf. 14*

No.	Type	Value	Description	Unused	Used
798	A130	50b	multi	.50	.30
799	A130	75b	multi	.60	.40
800	A130	1d	multi	.75	.55
801	A130	1.25d	multi	.90	.75
802	A130	2d	multi	1.25	1.10
803	A130	3d	multi	1.50	1.50
804	A130	10d	multi	3.50	3.50
805	A130	20d	multi	6.00	6.00
			Nos. 798-805 (8)	15.00	14.10

Souvenir Sheets

No.	Type	Value	Description	Unused	Used
806	A130	15d	multi	4.75	4.75
807	A130	15d	multi	4.75	4.75

350th anniv. of the publication of Discourses, by Galileo.

Army Day A131

75b, Troops on parade. 1d, Regimental flags. 1.25d, Drummer, vert. 10d, Atlantic Shooting Cup winner, vert. 15d, Assault course, vert. 20d, 105-mm gun.

1989, Feb. 10 Litho. *Perf. 14*

No.	Type	Value	Description	Unused	Used
808	A131	75b	multicolored	.30	.30
809	A131	1d	multicolored	.35	.35
810	A131	1.25d	multicolored	.45	.45
811	A131	10d	multicolored	2.25	2.25
812	A131	15d	multicolored	3.25	3.25
813	A131	20d	multicolored	4.00	4.00
			Nos. 808-813 (6)	10.60	10.60

Miniature Sheet

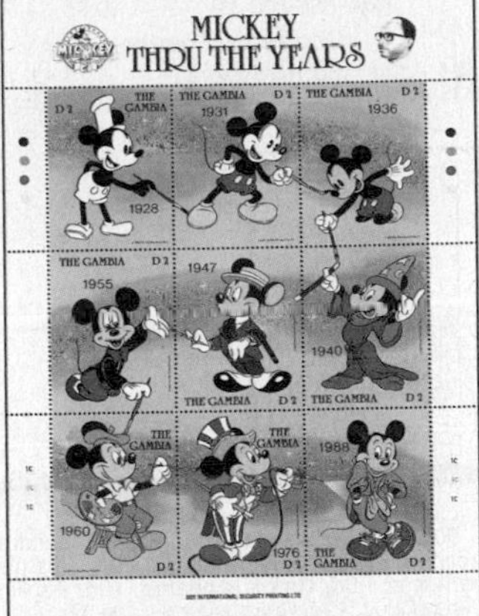

Mickey Mouse, 60th Anniv. (in 1988) — A132

Mickey Mouse through the years: a, 1928. b, 1931. c, 1936. d, 1955. e, 1947. f, 1940. g, 1960. h, 1976. i, 1988. 15d, Birthday party.

1989, Apr. 6 Litho. *Perf. 13x13½*

No.	Type	Value	Description	Unused	Used
814	A132		Sheet of 9	12.50	12.50
a.-i.		2d	any single	1.00	.90

Size: 139x110mm

Imperf

No.	Type	Value	Description	Unused	Used
815	A132	15d	multi	7.50	7.50

Easter A133

Paintings by Rubens: 50b, Le Coup de Lance, 1620. 75b, The Flagellation of Christ, 1617. 1d, The Lamentation for Christ, c. 1617. 1.25d, Descent from the Cross, c. 1611. 2d, The Holy Trinity, c. 1617. 5d, The Doubting Thomas. 10d, Lamentation over Christ, 1614. 12d, Lamentation over Christ with the Virgin and St. John, c. 1613. No. 824, The Last Supper, c. 1631. No. 825, The Raising of the Cross, c. 1610.

1989, Apr. 14 *Perf. 13½x14*

No.	Type	Value	Description	Unused	Used
816	A133	50b	multi	.45	.25
817	A133	75b	multi	.55	.35
818	A133	1d	multi	.55	.35
819	A133	1.25d	multi	.60	.50
820	A133	2d	multi	1.00	.80
821	A133	5d	multi	1.75	1.75
822	A133	10d	multi	2.75	2.75
823	A133	12d	multi	3.00	3.00
			Nos. 816-823 (8)	10.65	9.75

Souvenir Sheets

No.	Type	Value	Description	Unused	Used
824	A133	15d	multi	4.75	4.75
825	A133	15d	multi	4.75	4.75

Indigenous Birds — A134

20b, African emerald cuckoo. 60b, Gray-headed bush shrike. 75b, Crowned crane. 1d, Secretary bird. 2d, Red-billed hornbill. 5d, Superb sunbird. 10d, Little owl. 12d, Bateleur eagle.

No. 834, Red-billed fire finch. No. 835, Ostriches.

1989, Apr. 24 *Perf. 14*

No.	Type	Value	Description	Unused	Used
826	A134	20b	multicolored	.90	.30
827	A134	60b	multicolored	1.25	.55
828	A134	75b	multicolored	1.40	.60
829	A134	1d	multicolored	1.60	.70
830	A134	2d	multicolored	1.75	1.00
831	A134	5d	multicolored	3.00	3.00

832 A134 10d multicolored 5.00 4.00
833 A134 12d multicolored 5.75 4.50
Nos. 826-833 (8) 20.65 14.65

Souvenir Sheets

834 A134 15d multicolored 5.75 5.75
835 A134 15d multicolored 5.75 5.75

Indigenous Butterflies — A135

50b, Papilio antimachus. 75b, Euphaedra neophron. 1d, Aterica rabena. 1.25d, Salamis parhassus. 5d, Precis rhadama. 10d, Papilio demodocus. 12d, Charaxes etesippe. No. 843, 15d, Danaus formosa.

No. 844, Euphaedra ceres. No. 845, Cymothoe pluto.

1989, May 15

836 A135 50b multicolored .60 .25
837 A135 75b multicolored .75 .45
838 A135 1d multicolored .75 .45
839 A135 1.25d multicolored .90 .90
840 A135 5d multicolored 2.25 2.25
841 A135 10d multicolored 3.75 3.75
842 A135 12d multicolored 4.25 4.25
843 A135 15d multicolored 4.75 4.75
Nos. 836-843 (8) 18.00 17.05

Souvenir Sheets

844 A135 15d multicolored 8.00 8.00
845 A135 15d multicolored 8.00 8.00

Trains of Africa A136

Designs: 50b, Nigerian coal train, 1959. 75b, 14A Class 2-6-6-2 Garratt. 1d, British (Pacific) in Sudan. 1.25d, American 0-8-0, 1925. 5d, Scottish 4-8-2, 1955. 7d, Scottish 4-8-2, 1926. 10d, British 4-6-0. 12d, American-made 2-6-0 in Ghana. No. 854, British 2-8-2 Class 25 facing forward, vert. No. 855, Class 25 facing left, vert.

1989, June 15 Litho. *Perf. 14*

846 A136 50b multi .55 .30
847 A136 75b multi .65 .40
848 A136 1d multi .70 .50
849 A136 1.25d multi .85 .80
850 A136 5d multi 2.25 2.25
851 A136 7d multi 2.50 2.50
852 A136 10d multi 4.00 4.00
853 A136 12d multi 4.50 4.50
Nos. 846-853 (8) 16.00 15.25

Souvenir Sheets

854 A136 15d multi 6.00 6.00
855 A136 15d multi 6.00 6.00

Nos. 667-671 Ovptd. "PHILEXFRANCE / '89"

1989, June 23 Litho. *Perf. 15*

856 A110 75b multi .25 .25
857 A110 1d multi .30 .30
858 A110 1.25d multi .40 .40
859 A110 10d multi 1.75 1.75
Nos. 856-859 (4) 2.70 2.70

Souvenir Sheet

860 A110 12d multi 3.00 3.00

Paintings by Japanese Artists A137

Paintings by Hiroshige unless noted otherwise: 50b, Sparrow and Bamboo. 75b, Peonies and a Canary, by Hokusai. 1d, Crane and Marsh Grasses. 1.25d, Crossbill and Thistle, by Hokusai. 2d, Cuckoo and Azalea, by Hokusai. 5d, Parrot on a Pine Branch. 10d, Mandarin Ducks in a Stream. 12d, Bullfinch and Drooping Cherry, by Hokusai. No. 869, Tit and Peony, horiz. No. 870, Peony and Butterfly, by Shigenobu, horiz.

1989, July 7 *Perf. 13½x14, 14x13½*

861 A137 50b multi .60 .30
862 A137 75b multi .80 .40
863 A137 1d multi 1.00 .50
864 A137 1.25d multi 1.10 .60
865 A137 2d multi 1.50 .90
866 A137 5d multi 2.00 2.00
867 A137 10d multi 3.25 3.25
868 A137 12d multi 3.50 3.50
Nos. 861-868 (8) 13.75 11.45

Souvenir Sheets

869 A137 15d multi 5.50 5.50
870 A137 15d multi 5.50 5.50

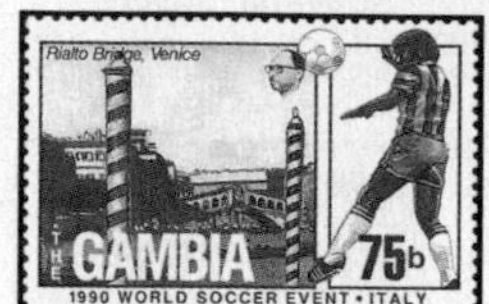

1990 World Cup Soccer Championships, Italy — A138

Various athletes and Italian landmarks: 75b, Rialto Bridge, Venice. 1.25d, The Baptistery, Pisa. 7d, Casino San Remo. 12d, The Colosseum, Rome. No. 875, St. Mark's Cathedral, Venice. No. 876, Piazza Colonna, Rome.

1989, Aug 25 *Perf. 14*

871 A138 75b multi .55 .55
872 A138 1.25b multi .70 .70
873 A138 7d multi 2.75 2.75
874 A138 12d multi 4.25 4.25
Nos. 871-874 (4) 8.25 8.25

Souvenir Sheets

875 A138 15d multi 5.75 5.75
876 A138 15d multi 5.75 5.75

Medicinal Plants — A139

20b, Vitex doniana. 50b, Ricinus communis. 75b, Palisota hirsuta. 1d, Smilax kraussiana. 1.25d, Aspilia africana. 5d, Newbouldia laevis. 8d, Monodora tenuifolia. 10d, Gossypium arboreum.

No. 885, Kigelia africana. No. 886, Spathodea campanulata.

1989, Sept. 18 Litho. *Perf. 14*

877 A139 20b multicolored .25 .25
878 A139 50b multicolored .25 .25
879 A139 75b multicolored .35 .35
880 A139 1d multicolored .45 .45
881 A139 1.25d multicolored .55 .55
882 A139 5d multicolored 1.90 1.90
883 A139 8d multicolored 3.00 3.00
884 A139 10d multicolored 3.50 3.50
Nos. 877-884 (8) 10.25 10.25

Souvenir Sheets

885 A139 15d multicolored 6.00 6.00
886 A139 15d multicolored 6.00 6.00

Fish A140

20b, Lookdown. 75b, Boarfish. 1d, Gray triggerfish. 1.25d, Skipjack tuna. 2d, Bermuda chub. 4d, Atlantic manta. 5d, Striped mullet. 10d, Ladyfish.

No. 895, Porcupinefish. No. 896, Shortfin makos.

1989, Oct. 19 Litho. *Perf.*

887 A140 20b multicolored .25 .25
888 A140 75b multicolored .65 .65
889 A140 1d multicolored .70 .70
890 A140 1.25d multicolored .80 .80
891 A140 2d multicolored 1.00 1.00
892 A140 4d multicolored 2.00 2.00
893 A140 5d multicolored 2.50 2.50
894 A140 10d multicolored 3.50 3.50
Nos. 887-894 (8) 11.40 11.40

Souvenir Sheet

895 A140 15d multicolored 7.25 7.25
896 A140 15d multicolored 7.25 7.25

Souvenir Sheet

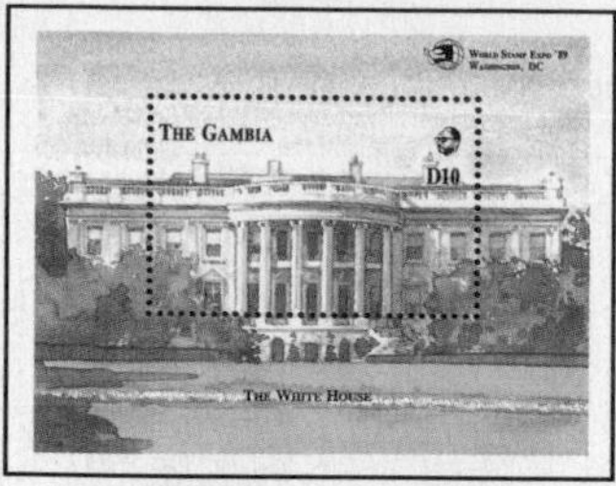

The White House, Washington, D.C. — A141

1989, Nov. 17 Litho. *Perf. 14*

897 A141 10d multicolored 2.50 2.50

World Stamp Expo '89.

World Stamp Expo '89, Washington, D.C. — A142

Disney characters riding carousel horses: 20b, Daniel Muller Indian pony. 50b, Herschell-Spillman steed. 75b, Gustav Dentzel stander. 1d, Muller armored stander. 1.25d, Jumper from the Smithsonian Collection. 2d, Illion "American Beauty." 8d, Zalar jumper. 10d, Parker buckling. No. 906, Philadelphia Tobaggan Co. Carousel, Elitch Gardens, Denver, CO. No. 907, PTC Roman chariot.

1989, Nov. 29 Litho. *Perf. 14x13½*

898 A142 20b multicolored .70 .30
899 A142 50b multicolored .90 .50
900 A142 75b multicolored .95 .60
901 A142 1d multicolored 1.00 .70
902 A142 1.25d multicolored 1.10 .80
903 A142 2d multicolored 1.60 1.10
904 A142 8d multicolored 4.50 4.50
905 A142 10d multicolored 4.75 4.75
Nos. 898-905 (8) 15.50 13.25

Souvenir Sheets

906 A142 12d multicolored 7.25 7.25
907 A142 12d multicolored 7.25 7.25

Nobel Prize Winners for Physiology and Great Medical Pioneers — A143

20b, Charles Nicolle (1866-1936), France, 1928 Prize, discovered transmission of typhus by body lice. 50b, Paul Ehrlich (1854-1915), Germany, 1908 Prize, immunology research. 75b, Selman Waksman (1888-1973), Russian-American, 1952 Prize, discovered antibiotic streptomycin, used to treat tuberculosis. 1d, Edward Jenner (1749-1823), Great Britain, discovered smallpox vaccine. 1.25d, Robert Koch (1843-1910), 1905 Prize, isolated the tubercle bacillus. 5d, Sir Alexander Fleming (1881-1955), Scotland, 1945 Prize, developed penicillin. 8d, Max Theiler (1899-1972), US, 1951 Prize, developed yellow fever vaccine. 10d, Louis Pasteur (1822-95), France, proved the germ theory of infection.

#916, C-9 Nightingale Aeromedical Airlift. #917, Hughes Vicking helicopter used in airlift.

1989, Dec. 12 *Perf. 14*

908 A143 20b multicolored 1.00 .30
909 A143 50b multicolored 1.10 .35
910 A143 75b multicolored 1.25 .45
911 A143 1d multicolored 1.40 .55
912 A143 1.25d multicolored 1.50 .75
913 A143 5d multicolored 2.25 2.25
914 A143 8d multicolored 3.25 3.25
915 A143 10d multicolored 3.50 3.50
Nos. 908-915 (8) 15.25 11.40

Souvenir Sheets

916 A143 15d multicolored 5.50 5.50
917 A143 15d multicolored 5.50 5.50

Orchids — A144

20b, Bulbophyllum lepidum. 75b, Tridactyle tridactylites. 1d, Vanilla imperialis. 1.25d, Oeceoclades maculata. 2d, Polystachya affinis. 4d, Ancistrochilus rothschildianus. 5d, Angraecum distichum. 10d, Liparis guineensis.

No. 926, Eulophia guineensis. No. 927, Plectrelminthus caudatus.

1989, Dec. 18 *Perf. 14*

918 A144 20b multicolored .35 .30
919 A144 75b multicolored .60 .60
920 A144 1d multicolored .90 .90
921 A144 1.25d multicolored 1.00 1.00
922 A144 2d multicolored 1.50 1.50
923 A144 4d multicolored 2.50 2.50
924 A144 5d multicolored 3.00 3.00
925 A144 10d multicolored 4.75 4.75
Nos. 918-925 (8) 14.60 14.55

Souvenir Sheets

926 A144 15d multicolored 6.50 6.50
927 A144 15d multicolored 6.50 6.50

Christmas — A145

Disney characters and classic automobiles: 20b, 1922 Pierce Arrow. 50b, 1919 Spyker. 75b, 1929 Packard. 1d, 1920 Daimler. 1.25d, 1924 Hispano Suiza. 2d, Opel Laubfrosch, 1924-27. 10d, 1927 Vauxhall 30/98. 12d, 1923 Peerless. No. 936, 1930 Bentley Supercharged, Santa Claus. No. 937, 1928 Stutz Blackhawk Speedster, picnic.

1989, Dec. 19 Litho. *Perf. 14*

928 A145 20b multicolored .75 .25
929 A145 50b multicolored 1.00 .40
930 A145 75b multicolored 1.10 .55
931 A145 1d multicolored 1.25 .65
932 A145 1.25d multicolored 1.40 .90
933 A145 2d multicolored 1.75 1.25
934 A145 10d multicolored 4.00 4.00
935 A145 12d multicolored 4.25 4.25
Nos. 928-935 (8) 15.50 12.25

Souvenir Sheets

936 A145 15d multicolored 7.75 7.75
937 A145 15d multicolored 7.75 7.75

Wimbledon Tennis Champions — A146

No. 938, John Newcombe. No. 939, G.W. Hillyard. No. 940, Roy Emerson. No. 941, Dorothy Chambers. No. 942, Donald Budge. No. 943, Suzanne Lenglen. No. 944, Laurence Doherty. No. 945, Helen Wills Moody. No. 946, Bjorn Borg. No. 947, Maureen Connolly. No. 948, Jean Borotra. No. 949, Maria Bueno. No. 950, Anthony Wilding. No. 951, Louise Brough. No. 952, Fred Perry. No. 953, Margaret Court. No. 954, Bill Tilden. No. 955, Billie Jean King. No. 956, Rod Laver. No. 957, Martina Navratilova.

No. 958, Rod Laver, diff. No. 959, Martina Navratilova, diff.

1990, Jan. 2 Litho. *Perf. 15x14½*

938 A146 20b multicolored .25 .25
939 A146 20b multicolored .25 .25
a. Pair, #938-939 .40 .40
940 A146 50b multicolored .30 .30
941 A146 50b multicolored .30 .30
a. Pair, #940-941 .65 .65
942 A146 75b multicolored .40 .40
943 A146 75b multicolored .40 .40
a. Pair, #942-943 .85 .85
944 A146 1d multicolored .45 .45
945 A146 1d multicolored .45 .45
a. Pair, #944-945 .95 .95
946 A146 1.25d multicolored .50 .50
947 A146 1.25d multicolored .50 .50
a. Pair, #946-947 1.10 1.10
948 A146 4d multicolored 1.10 1.10
949 A146 4d multicolored 1.10 1.10
a. Pair, #948-949 2.50 2.50
950 A146 5d multicolored 1.40 1.40
951 A146 5d multicolored 1.40 1.40
a. Pair, #950-951 3.00 3.00
952 A146 7d multicolored 1.60 1.60
953 A146 7d multicolored 1.60 1.60
a. Pair, #952-953 4.00 4.00
954 A146 10d multicolored 2.25 2.25
955 A146 10d multicolored 2.25 2.25
a. Pair, #954-955 5.75 5.75
956 A146 12d multicolored 2.50 2.50
957 A146 12d multicolored 2.50 2.50
a. Pair, #956-957 6.25 6.25
Nos. 938-957 (20) 21.50 21.50

Souvenir Sheets

958 A146 15d multicolored 6.75 6.75
959 A146 15d multicolored 6.75 6.75

1st Moon Landing, 20th Anniv. (in 1989) — A147

Designs: 20b, Eagle lunar module descending, horiz. 50b, Apollo 11 liftoff. 75b, Astronaut descending ladder, horiz. 1d, Astronaut, US flag over Sea of Tranquillity, horiz. 1.25d, Mission emblem. 1.75d, Crew, horiz. 8d, Lunar module, Sea of Tranquillity, horiz. 12d, Recovery of command module Columbia after splashdown. No. 968, Neil Armstrong returning to Eagle. No. 969, View of Earth.

1990, Feb. 16 *Perf. 14*

960 A147 20b multicolored .70 .25
961 A147 50b multicolored .90 .30
962 A147 75b multicolored 1.00 .45
963 A147 1d multicolored 1.10 .55
964 A147 1.25d multicolored 1.25 .60
965 A147 1.75d multicolored 1.40 1.25
966 A147 8d multicolored 3.75 3.75
967 A147 12d multicolored 5.00 5.00
Nos. 960-967 (8) 15.10 12.15

Souvenir Sheets

968 A147 15d multicolored 5.00 5.00
969 A147 15d multicolored 5.00 5.00

Miniature Sheet

Birds of Africa — A148

No. 970: a, White-faced owl. b, Village weaver. c, Red-throated bee eater. d, Brown harrier eagle. e, Red bishop. f, Scarlet-chested sunbird. g, Red-billed hornbill. h, Mosque swallow. i, White-faced tree duck. j, African fish eagle. k, Great white pelican. l, Carmine bee eater. m, Hadada ibis. n, Crocodile plover. o, Yellow-bellied sunbird. p, African skimmer. q, Woodland kingfisher. r, Jacana. s, Pygmy goose. t, Hamerkop.

1990, Apr. 12 Litho. *Perf. 14*

970 A148 Sheet of 20 17.50 17.50
a.-t. 1.25d any single .80 .80

RAF World War II Planes A149

Designs: 10b, Bristol Blenheim Mk-1. 20b, Battle. 50b, Blenheim 4. 60b, Wellington 1C. 75b, Whitley 5. 1d, Hampden Mk-1. 1.25d, Spitfire 1A and Hurricane 1. 2d, Avro Manchester. 3d, Stirling. 5d, Handley Page Halifax B-2. 10d, Lancaster B-3. 12d, Mosquito B-4. No. 983, Lancaster B-3 over Hamburg. No. 984, Spitfire 1, Battle of Britain.

1990, Apr. 18 *Perf. 14*

971 A149 10b multicolored 1.00 .50
972 A149 20b multicolored 1.10 .50
973 A149 50b multicolored 1.15 .50
974 A149 60b multicolored 1.20 .50
975 A149 75b multicolored 1.30 .50
976 A149 1d multicolored 1.35 .50
977 A149 1.25d multicolored 1.40 .55
978 A149 2d multicolored 1.50 .80
979 A149 3d multicolored 1.75 1.25
980 A149 5d multicolored 2.50 2.50
981 A149 10d multicolored 3.50 3.50
982 A149 12d multicolored 4.00 4.00
Nos. 971-982 (12) 21.75 15.60

Souvenir Sheets

983 A149 15d multicolored 5.75 5.75
984 A149 15d multicolored 5.75 5.75

Independence, 25th Anniv. — A150

Designs: 3d, Sir Dawda Jawara, President. 12d, Jet and map showing airport. 18d, National arms.

1990, June 5 Litho. *Perf. 14*

985 A150 1d multicolored .25 .25
986 A150 3d multicolored 1.10 1.10
987 A150 12d multicolored 5.00 5.00
Nos. 985-987 (3) 6.35 6.35

Souvenir Sheet

988 A150 18d multicolored 5.50 5.50

Baobab Tree A151

10b, Woodcarving. 20b, Pres. Jawara. 50b, Map. 75b, Batik fabric. 1d, Bakau Beach Resort. 1.25d, Tendaba Camp. 2d, Shrimp industry. 5d, Peanut oil mill. 10d, Pottery, kora. 15d, Ansellia Africana orchid. 30d, Ancient stone rings, Euryphene gambiae.

1990, June 14 Litho. *Perf. 14*

989 A151 5b shown .75 *.85*
990 A151 10b multicolored .25 .30
991 A151 20b multicolored .25 .25
992 A151 50b multicolored 2.00 .25
993 A151 75b multicolored .35 .25
994 A151 1d multicolored .40 .25
995 A151 1.25d multicolored .40 .30
996 A151 2d multicolored .45 .45
997 A151 5d multicolored 1.25 *1.25*
998 A151 10d multicolored 1.75 1.75
999 A151 15d multicolored 7.00 7.00
1000 A151 30d multicolored 10.00 10.00
Nos. 989-1000 (12) 24.85 22.90

Nos. 990, 999 vert.

Penny Black, 150th Anniv. A152

1990, June 18

1001 A152 1.25d brt bl & blk 1.50 .50
1002 A152 12d dark red & blk 4.75 4.75

Souvenir Sheet

1003 A152 15d sil, bis & blk 7.00 7.00

Mickey Visits England — A153

Walt Disney characters at: 20b, 10 Downing Street. 50b, Trafalgar Square. 75b, Cliffs of Dover. 1d, Tower of London. 5d, Hampton Court Palace. 8d, Magdalen Tower, Oxford University. 10d, Old London Bridge. 12d, Rosetta Stone, British Museum. No. 1012, Picadilly Circus. No. 1013, Houses of Parliament and Big Ben on the River Thames.

1990, June 19 *Perf. 14x13½*

1004 A153 20b multicolored .45 .30
1005 A153 50b multicolored .65 .35
1006 A153 75b multicolored .85 .40
1007 A153 1d multicolored 1.10 .45
1008 A153 5d multicolored 2.50 2.50
1009 A153 8d multicolored 3.00 3.00
1010 A153 10d multicolored 3.75 3.75
1011 A153 12d multicolored 4.75 4.75
Nos. 1004-1011 (8) 17.05 15.50

Souvenir Sheets

1012 A153 18d multicolored 8.50 8.50
1013 A153 18d multicolored 8.50 8.50

Stamp World London '90. Nos. 1004-1005, 1007, 1009 vert.

A154

1990, July 19 *Perf. 14*

1014 6d Girl facing left 1.50 1.50
1015 6d Young girl, diff. 1.50 1.50
1016 6d Seated in chair 1.50 1.50
a. A154 Strip of 3, #1014-1016 5.75 5.75

Souvenir Sheet

1017 A154 18d like No. 1014 5.50 5.50

A156

Players from participating countries.

1990, Sept. 24 Litho. *Perf. 14*

1018 A156 1d Italy .45 .45
1019 A156 1.25d Argentina .55 .55
1020 A156 3d Costa Rica 1.10 1.10
1021 A156 5d UAE 1.60 1.60
Nos. 1018-1021 (4) 3.70 3.70

Souvenir Sheets

1022 A156 18d Holland 7.50 7.50
1023 A156 18d Romania 7.50 7.50

World Cup Soccer Championships, Italy.

A157

20b, Men's discus. 50b, Men's 100-meter race. 75b, Women's 400-meter race. 1d, Men's 200-meter race. 1.25d, Rhythmic gymnastics. 3d, Soccer. 10d, Men's marathon. 12d, Tornado class sailing.

No. 1032, Parade of flags. No. 1033, Stadium, card section.

1990, Nov. 1 Litho. *Perf. 14*

1024 A157 20b multicolored .40 .25
1025 A157 50b multicolored .45 .25
1026 A157 75b multicolored .50 .30
1027 A157 1d multicolored .55 .55
1028 A157 1.25d multicolored .45 .45
1029 A157 3d multicolored 1.60 1.60
1030 A157 10d multicolored 4.25 4.25
1031 A157 12d multicolored 5.25 5.25
Nos. 1024-1031 (8) 13.45 12.90

Souvenir Sheets

1032 A157 15d multicolored 6.75 6.75
1033 A157 15d multicolored 6.75 6.75

1992 Summer Olympics, Barcelona.

Christmas A158

Entire paintings or different details from: 20b, 7d, The Annunciation with St. Emidius by Crivelli. 50b, The Annunciation by Campin. 75b, The Solly Madonna by Raphael. 1.25d, The Tempi Madonna by Raphael. 2d, Madonna of the Linen Window by Raphael. 10d, The Orleans Madonna by Raphael. 15d, Madonna and Child by Crivelli. No. 1042, The Niccolini-Cowper Madonna by Raphael.

1990, Dec. 24 Litho. *Perf. 13½x14*

1034 A158 20b multicolored .45 .25
1035 A158 50b multicolored .55 .25
1036 A158 75b multicolored .70 .25
1037 A158 1.25d multicolored .80 .65
1038 A158 2d multicolored .90 .90
1039 A158 7d multicolored 2.50 2.50
1040 A158 10d multicolored 3.00 3.00
1041 A158 15d multicolored 4.75 4.75
Nos. 1034-1041 (8) 13.65 12.55

Souvenir Sheet

1042 A158 15d multicolored 8.00 8.00

Peter Paul Rubens (1577-1640), Painter — A159

Entire paintings or different details from: 20b, 75b, 10d, No. 1054, The Lion Hunt. 1d, 1.25d, 3d, 15d, The Tiger Hunt. 5d, No. 1055, The Boar Hunt. No. 1056, The Crocodile and Hippopotamus Hunt. No. 1057, Saint George Slays the Dragon, vert.

1990, Dec. 24 Litho. *Perf. 14x13½*

1046 A159 20b multicolored .25 .25
1047 A159 75b multicolored .35 .25
1048 A159 1d multicolored .40 .40
1049 A159 1.25d multicolored .55 .55
1050 A159 3d multicolored 1.25 1.25
1051 A159 5d multicolored 1.60 1.60
1052 A159 10d multicolored 2.75 2.75
1053 A159 15d multicolored 3.75 3.75
Nos. 1046-1053 (8) 10.90 10.80

Souvenir Sheets

1054 A159 15d multicolored 4.25 4.25
1055 A159 15d multicolored 4.25 4.25
1056 A159 15d multicolored 4.25 4.25
1057 A159 15d multicolored 4.25 4.25

World Summit for Children A160

1991, Jan. 7 Litho. *Perf. 14*

1058	A160	1d multicolored	.80	.80

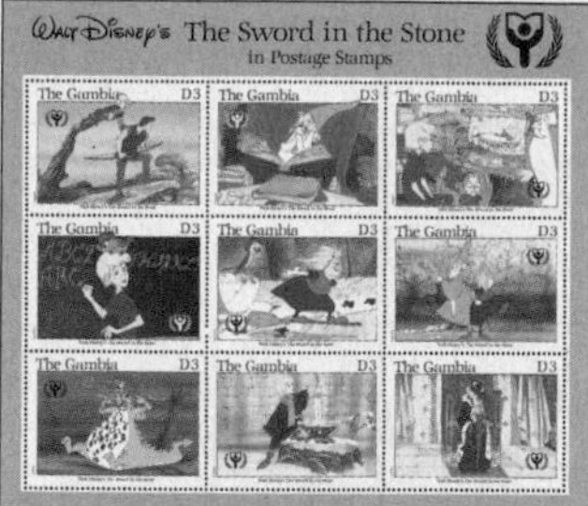

Intl. Literacy Year — A161

Walt Disney characters in "The Sword in the Stone": No. 1059a, Wart and Sir Kay. b, Merlin reading book. c, Wart learning geography. d, Wart writing on blackboard. e, Wart as bird, Madam Mim. f, Merlin and Madam Mim. g, Mim as dragon. h, Wart pulling sword from stone. i, Wart as King of England. No. 1060, Merlin, Wart in forest, vert. No. 1061, Knight trying to remove sword from stone, vert.

1991, Feb. 14 Litho. *Perf. 14x13½*

1059	A161	3d Sheet of 9, #a.-i	15.00	15.00

Souvenir Sheets

1060	A161	20d multicolored	9.00	9.00
1061	A161	20d multicolored	9.00	9.00

Miniature Sheets

Wildlife — A162

No. 1062: a, Bebearia senegalensis. b, Graphium ridleyanus. c, Precis antilope. d, Charaxes ameliae. e, Addax. f, Sassaby. g, Civet. h, Green monkey. i, Spurwing goose. j, Red-billed hornbill. k, Osprey. l, Glossy ibis. m, Egyptian plover. n, Golden-tailed woodpecker. o, Green woodhoopoe. p, Gaboon viper.

No. 1063: a, Red-billed firefinch. b, Leaflove. c, Piacpiac. d, Emerald cuckoo. e, Red colobus monkey. f, African elephant. g, Duiker. h, Giant eland. i, Oribi. j, West African dwarf crocodile. k, Crowned crane. l, Jackal. m, Yellow-throated longclaw. n, Abyssinian ground hornbill. o, Papilio hesperus. p, Papilio antimachus.

No. 1064: a, Martial eagle. b, Red-cheeked cordon-bleu. c, Red bishop. d, Great white pelican. e, Patas monkey. f, Vervet monkey. g, Roan antelope. h, Western hartebeest. i, Waterbuck. j, Warthog. k, Spotted hyena. l, Olive baboon. m, Palla decius. n, Acraea pharsalus. o, Neptidopsis ophione. p, Acraea caecilia.

No. 1065, African spoonbill, vert. No. 1066, Lion, vert. No. 1067, Buffalo weaver, vert.

1991, May 31 Litho. *Perf. 14*

1062	A162	1d Sheet of 16, #a.-p.	6.50	6.50
1063	A162	1.50d Sheet of 16, #a.-p.	9.00	9.00
1064	A162	5d Sheet of 16, #a.-p.	25.00	25.00
		Nos. 1062-1064 (3)	40.50	40.50

Souvenir Sheets

1065	A162	18d multicolored	6.00	6.00
1066	A162	18d multicolored	6.00	6.00
1067	A162	18d multicolored	6.00	6.00

Butterflies — A163

Designs: 20b, Papilio dardanus. 50b, Bematistes poggei. 1d, Vanessa cardiu. 1.50d, Amphicallia tigris. 3d, Hypolimnes dexithea. 8d, Acraea egina. 10d, Salmis temora. 15d, Precis octavia. No. 1076, Danaus chrysippus. No. 1077, Charaxes jasius. No. 1078, Papilio demodocus. No. 1079, Papilio nireus.

1991, June 1 Litho. *Perf. 14*

1068	A163	20b multicolored	.60	.35
1069	A163	50b multicolored	.85	.40
1070	A163	1d multicolored	.95	.55
1071	A163	1.50d multicolored	1.00	.85
1072	A163	3d multicolored	1.50	1.25
1073	A163	8d multicolored	2.50	2.50
1074	A163	10d multicolored	3.25	3.25
1075	A163	15d multicolored	5.00	5.00
		Nos. 1068-1075 (8)	15.65	14.15

Souvenir Sheets

1076	A163	18d multicolored	5.00	5.00
1077	A163	18d multicolored	5.00	5.00
1078	A163	18d multicolored	5.00	5.00
1079	A163	18d multicolored	5.00	5.00

While Nos. 1078-1079 have same release date as Nos. 1068-1077, the dollar value of Nos. 1078-1079 were lower when they were released.

Royal Family Birthday, Anniversary

No. 1088, Elizabeth, Philip. No. 1089, Diana, sons, Charles.

Common Design Type

1991, Aug. 12 Litho. *Perf. 14*

1080	CD347	20b multi	.35	.25
1081	CD347	50b multi	.40	.30
1082	CD347	75b multi	.45	.40
1083	CD347	1d multi	.50	.50
1084	CD347	1.25d multi	.65	.65
1085	CD347	1.50d multi	.80	.80
1086	CD347	12d multi	4.50	4.50
1087	CD347	15d multi	6.00	6.00
		Nos. 1080-1087 (8)	13.65	13.40

Souvenir Sheets

1088	CD347	18d multi	4.50	4.50
1089	CD347	18d multi	6.50	6.50

20b, 75b, 1.50d, 15d, No. 1089, Charles and Diana, 10th wedding anniversary. Others, Queen Elizabeth II, 65th birthday.

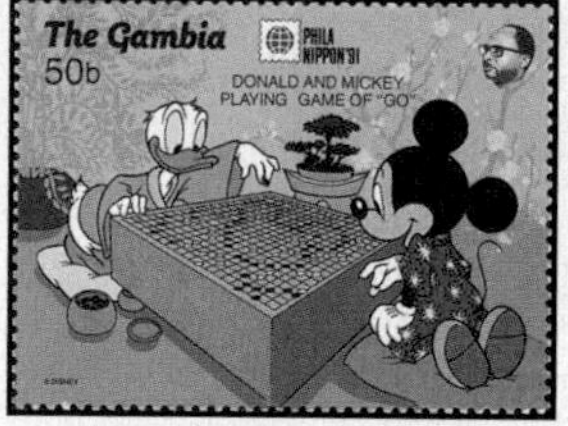

Phila Nippon '91 — A164

Walt Disney characters playing Japanese games and sports: 50b, Donald Duck and Mickey Mouse playing Go. 75b, Morty, Ferdie and Pete sumo wrestling. 1d, Minnie Mouse, Clarabelle, Daisy Duck playing battledore and shuttlecock. 1.25d, Goofy, Mickey at Okinawa bullfight, vert. 5d, Mickey as a Hawk Hunter Tagari, vert. 7d, Mickey, Minnie, and Donald play Jan-Ken-Pon, vert. 10d, Goofy as archer. 15d, Morty, Ferdie fly Japanese kites, vert. No. 1098, Goofy batting in Japanese baseball game, vert. No. 1099, Mickey, Scrooge McDuck playing Japanese football, vert. No. 1100, Mickey fly fishing, vert. No. 1101, Mickey climbing Mt. Fuji, vert.

Perf. 14x13½, 13½x14

1991, Aug. 22 Litho.

1090	A164	50b multicolored	.50	.30
1091	A164	75b multicolored	.60	.40
1092	A164	1d multicolored	.70	.45
1093	A164	1.25d multicolored	.80	.55
1094	A164	5d multicolored	2.25	2.25
1095	A164	7d multicolored	3.00	3.00
1096	A164	10d multicolored	4.00	4.00
1097	A164	15d multicolored	5.75	5.75
		Nos. 1090-1097 (8)	17.60	16.70

Souvenir Sheets

1098	A164	20d multicolored	5.50	5.50
1099	A164	20d multicolored	5.50	5.50
1100	A164	20d multicolored	5.50	5.50
1101	A164	20d multicolored	5.50	5.50

Intl. Literacy Year — A165

Walt Disney characters in scenes from Rudyard Kipling's "Just So Stories": 50b, How the Whale Got His Throat. 75b, How the Camel Got His Hump. 1d, How the Leopard Got His Spots. 1.25d, The Elephant's Child. 1.50d, Singsong of Old Man Kangaroo. 7d, The Crab that Played with the Sea. 10d, The Cat that Walked by Himself. 15d, The Butterfly that Stamped. No. 1110, How the Alphabet was Made, vert. No. 1111, The Beginning of the Armadillos. No. 1112, How the First Letter was Written, vert. No. 1113, How the Rhinoceros Got His Skin.

1991, Aug. 28 Litho. *Perf. 14x13½*

1102	A165	50b multicolored	.80	.30
1103	A165	75b multicolored	.90	.40
1104	A165	1d multicolored	1.00	.45
1105	A165	1.25d multicolored	1.25	.55
1106	A165	1.50d multicolored	1.40	1.40
1107	A165	7d multicolored	3.25	3.25
1108	A165	10d multicolored	4.50	4.50
1109	A165	15d multicolored	6.50	6.50
		Nos. 1102-1109 (8)	19.60	17.35

Souvenir Sheets

Perf. 13½x14, 14x13½

1110	A165	20d multicolored	6.75	6.75
1111	A165	20d multicolored	6.75	6.75
1112	A165	20d multicolored	6.75	6.75
1113	A165	20d multicolored	6.75	6.75

Train Cabooses — A166

No. 1114: a, Steel cupola, Canadian Pacific. b, Four-wheel, Cumberland and Pennsylvania. c, Mexican slim gauge. d, All steel cupola, Northern Pacific. e, Four-wheel, Morristown & Erie. f, Streamlined cupola, Burlington Northern. g, Caboose coach, McCloud River. h, Wide vision, Santa Fe. i, Wide vision, Frisco.

No. 1115: a, Narrow gauge, Oahu Railway. b, Standard brake-van, British Railways. c, Wide view steel, Union Pacific. d, Four-wheel, Belt Railway of Chicago. e, Four-wheel, McCloud River. f, Logging, Angelina County Lumber Co. g, Narrow gauge, Coahuila & Zacatecas. h, Three-foot gauge, United Railways of Yucatan. i, Steel cupola, Rio Grande.

No. 1116: a, Four-wheel, Colorado & Southern. b, Transfer, Santa Fe. c, Wooden cupola, Canadian National. d, Transfer steel, Union Pacific. e, Caboose coach, Virginia & Truckee. f, Standard brake-van, British. g, Narrow gauge, Intl. Railways of Central America. h, Steel cupola, Northern Pacific. i, Wood, Burlington Northern.

No. 1117, Pennsylvania electric, vert. No. 1118, Unidentified caboose, trainman with flag, vert. No. 1119, Unidentified green wooden caboose behind yellow freight car.

Sheets of 9

1991, Sept. 12 Litho. *Perf. 14x13½*

1114	A166	1d #a.-i.	6.75	6.75
1115	A166	2d #a.-i.	6.75	6.75
1116	A166	1.50d #a.-i.	6.75	6.75
		Nos. 1114-1116 (3)	20.25	20.25

Souvenir Sheets

Perf. 12x13, 13x12

1117	A166	20d multicolored	6.25	6.25
1118	A166	20d multicolored	6.25	6.25
1119	A166	20d multicolored	6.25	6.25

While Nos. 1115-1116 and 1118-1119 have the same issue date as Nos. 1114 and 1117, the dollar value of Nos. 1115-1116 and 1118-1119 was lower when they were released.

Fish — A167

20b, Tiger shark. 25b, Common jewel fish. 50b, Five spot fish. 75b, Smalltooth sawfish. 1d, Five spot tilapia. 1.25d, Dwarf jewel fish. 1.50d, Five spot jewel fish. 3d, Bumphead. 10d, Egyptian mouthbrooder. 15d, Burton's mouthbrooder.

No. 1130, Great barracuda. No. 1131, Yellowtail snapper.

1991, Oct. 28 Litho. *Perf. 14x14½*

1120	A167	20b multicolored	.25	.25
1121	A167	25b multicolored	.25	.25
1122	A167	50b multicolored	.45	.45
1123	A167	75b multicolored	.45	.45
1124	A167	1d multicolored	.45	.45
1125	A167	1.25d multicolored	.55	.55
1126	A167	1.50d multicolored	.65	.65
1127	A167	3d multicolored	1.00	1.00
1128	A167	10d multicolored	3.00	3.00
1129	A167	15d multicolored	4.25	4.25
		Nos. 1120-1129 (10)	11.30	11.30

Souvenir Sheets

1130	A167	18d multicolored	8.50	8.50
1131	A167	18d multicolored	8.50	8.50

While Nos. 1120-1122, 1125, 1129-1131 have the same issue date as Nos. 1123-1124, 1126-1128 the dollar value of Nos. 1120-1122, 1125, 1129-1130 was lower when they were released.

Hummel Figurines — A168

20b, No. 1141a, Girl and boy waving handkerchiefs. 75b, No. 1140a, Boy and girl under umbrella. 1d, No. 1140b, Two girls wearing scarfs. 1.50d, No. 1140c, Girl and boy in window with flower box. 2.50d, No. 1141b, Two girls with basket. 5d, No. 1141c, Boy wearing long pants, boy wearing shorts. 10d, No. 1141d, Two girls on fence. 15d, No. 1140d, Boy with stick, girl with bag.

1991, Nov. 4 Litho. *Perf. 14*

1132	A168	20b multicolored	.25	.25
1133	A168	75b multicolored	.25	.25
1134	A168	1d multicolored	.25	.25
1135	A168	1.50d multicolored	.50	.50
1136	A168	2.50d multicolored	.70	.70
1137	A168	5d multicolored	1.25	1.25
1138	A168	10d multicolored	2.50	2.50
1139	A168	15d multicolored	3.25	3.25
		Nos. 1132-1139 (8)	8.95	8.95

Souvenir Sheets

1140	A168	4d Sheet of 4, #a.-d.	4.25	4.25
1141	A168	5d Sheet of 4, #a.-d.	5.25	5.25

Paintings by Vincent Van Gogh A169

Designs: 20b, The Old Cemetery Tower at Nuenen in the Snow, horiz. 25b, Head of a Peasant Woman with White Cap. 50b, The Green Parrot. 75b, Vase with Carnations. 1d, Vase with Red Gladioli. 1.25b, Beach at Scheveningen in Calm Weather, horiz. 1.50d, Boy Cutting Grass with a Sickle, horiz. 2d, Coleus Plant in a Flowerpot. 3d, Self-portrait, spring-summer 1887. 4d, Self-portrait. 5d, Self-portrait, diff. 6d, Self-portrait, spring 1887. 8d, Still Life with a Bottle, Two Glasses, Cheese and Bread. 10d, Still Life with Cabbage, Clogs and

Potatoes, horiz. 12d, Montmartre: The Street Lamps. 15d, Head of a Peasant Woman with Brownish Cap. No. 1158, Arles: View From the Wheat Fields. No. 1159, Autumn Landscape. No. 1160, Montmartre: Quarry, The Mills, horiz. No. 1161, The Potato Eaters, horiz.

Perf. 13½x14, 14x13½

1991, Dec. 5 **Litho.**

1142	A169	20b multicolored	.40	.25
1143	A169	25b multicolored	.45	.25
1144	A169	50b multicolored	.50	.25
1145	A169	75b multicolored	.55	.30
1146	A169	1d multicolored	.60	.35
1147	A169	1.25d multicolored	.65	.45
1148	A169	1.50d multicolored	.70	.55
1149	A169	2d multicolored	.75	.65
1150	A169	3d multicolored	.90	.90
1151	A169	4d multicolored	1.25	1.25
1152	A169	5d multicolored	1.50	1.50
1153	A169	6d multicolored	2.00	2.00
1154	A169	8d multicolored	2.75	2.75
1155	A169	10d multicolored	3.25	3.25
1156	A169	12d multicolored	4.25	4.25
1157	A169	15d multicolored	4.50	4.50

Size: 127x102mm

Imperf

1158	A169	20d multicolored	6.25	6.25
1159	A169	20d multicolored	6.25	6.25
1160	A169	20d multicolored	6.25	6.25
1161	A169	20d multicolored	6.25	6.25
		Nos. 1142-1161 (20)	50.00	48.45

While Nos. 1142-1143, 1146, 1148, 1150, 1153, 1155-1156, 1160-1161 have the same issue date as Nos. 1144-1145, 1147, 1149, 1151-1152, 1154, 1157-1159, the dollar value of Nos. 1142-1143, 1146, 1148, 1150, 1153, 1155-1156, 1160-1161 was lower when they were released.

Christmas A170

Paintings by Fra Angelico: 20b, The Madonna of Humility. 50b, Madonna and Child with Angels. 75b, The Virgin and Child with Angels. 1d, Annunciation. 1.25d, Presentation in the Temple. 5d, Annunciation, diff. 10d, Madonna della Stella. 15d, Naming of St. John the Baptist. No. 1170, Annunciation and Adoration of the Magi. No. 1171, Coronation of the Virgin.

1991, Dec. 23 ***Perf. 12***

1162	A170	20b multicolored	.25	.25
1163	A170	50b multicolored	.25	.25
1164	A170	75b multicolored	.30	.25
1165	A170	1d multicolored	.35	.30
1166	A170	1.25d multicolored	.45	.45
1167	A170	5d multicolored	1.40	1.40
1168	A170	10d multicolored	2.50	2.50
1169	A170	15d multicolored	4.00	4.00
		Nos. 1162-1169 (8)	9.50	9.40

Souvenir Sheets

Perf. 14½

1170	A170	20d multicolored	5.25	5.25
1171	A170	20d multicolored	5.25	5.25

Queen Elizabeth II's Accession to the Throne, 40th Anniv.

No. 1176, Queen at left, yacht. No. 1177, Queen at right, boat.

Common Design Type

1992, Feb. 6 **Litho.** ***Perf. 14***

1172	CD348	20b multicolored	.25	.25
1173	CD348	50b multicolored	.35	.25
1174	CD348	1d multicolored	.50	.35
1175	CD348	15d multicolored	5.00	5.00
		Nos. 1172-1175 (4)	6.10	5.85

Souvenir Sheets

1176	CD348	20d multicolored	5.25	5.25
1177	CD348	20d multicolored	5.25	5.25

Famous Blues Musicians — A171

20b, Son House. 25b, W. C. Handy. 50b, Muddy Waters. 75b, Lightnin Hopkins. 1d, Ma Rainey. 1.25d, Mance Lipscomb. 1.50d, Mahalia Jackson. 2d, Ella Fitzgerald. 3d, Howlin Wolf. 5d, Bessie Smith. 7d, Leadbelly. 10d, Joe Willie Wilkins.

No. 1190, Gambian string drummer. No. 1191, Elvis Presley. No. 1192, Billie Holiday.

1992, Feb. 12 ***Perf. 14***

1178	A171	20b multicolored	.25	.25
1179	A171	25b multicolored	.25	.25
1180	A171	50b multicolored	.40	.40
1181	A171	75b multicolored	.55	.55
1182	A171	1d multicolored	.60	.60
1183	A171	1.25d multicolored	.70	.70
1184	A171	1.50d multicolored	.80	.80
1185	A171	2d multicolored	.85	.85
1186	A171	3d multicolored	.90	.90
1187	A171	5d multicolored	1.50	1.50
1188	A171	7d multicolored	2.00	2.00
1189	A171	10d multicolored	3.00	3.00
		Nos. 1178-1189 (12)	11.80	11.80

Souvenir Sheets

1190	A171	20d multicolored	5.75	5.75
1191	A171	20d multicolored	5.75	5.75
1192	A171	20d multicolored	5.75	5.75

While all stamps have the same issue date the dollar value of some was lower when they actually were released.

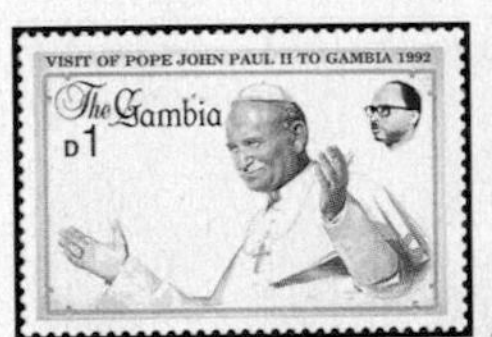

A172

Papal Visit, 1992 — A172a

Designs: 1d, Pope John Paul II. 1.25d, Pope, Pres. Dwada Jawara. 20d, Flags, Papal arms. 25d, Pope at Mass.

1992, Feb. 23 **Litho.** ***Perf. 14***

1193	A172	1d multicolored	.65	.65
1194	A172	1.25d multicolored	.80	.80
1195	A172	20d multicolored	6.00	6.00
		Nos. 1193-1195 (3)	7.45	7.45

Souvenir Sheet

1196	A172	25d multicolored	8.00	8.00

Embossed

Perf. 12

Without Gum

Size: 65x43mm

1196A	A172a	50d gold	*35.00*

No. 1196A was not available until late 1993, exists imperf on large card.

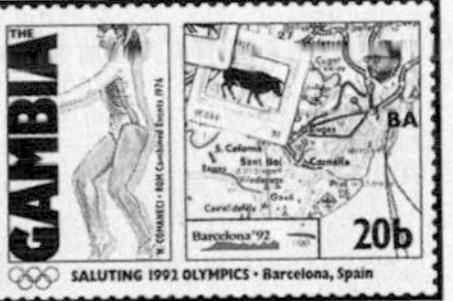

1992 Summer Olympics, Barcelona A173

20b, Map & Nadia Comaneci, gymnastics, Romania, 1976. 50b, D. Moorcraft, 5000 meters, Great Britain, 1984. 75b, M. Nemeth, javelin, Hungary, 1976. 1d, J. Pedraza, 20k walking, Mexico, 1968. 1.25d, Map, Spanish Arms & flag, Yachting soling class, Brazil, 1984. 1.50d, Spanish building, Field hockey, East Germany, 1984. 12d, Map & Michael Jordan, basketball, US, 1984. 15d, V. Borzov, 100 meters, USSR, 1972. No. 1205, Flamenco dancer, vert. No. 1206, Map & Bull.

1992, Mar. 6 **Litho.** ***Perf. 14***

1197	A173	20b multicolored	.30	.25
1198	A173	50b multicolored	.40	.30
1199	A173	75b multicolored	.45	.40
1200	A173	1d multicolored	.50	.50
1201	A173	1.25d multicolored	.70	.70
1202	A173	1.50d multicolored	.75	.75
1203	A173	12d multicolored	3.00	3.00
1204	A173	15d multicolored	5.00	5.00
		Nos. 1197-1204 (8)	11.10	10.90

Souvenir Sheet

1205	A173	20d multicolored	6.25	6.25
1206	A173	20d multicolored	6.25	6.25

While Nos. 1197, 1201-1203, 1206 have the same issue date as Nos. 1198-1200, 1204-1205, the value of Nos. 1197, 1201-1203, 1206 was lower when they were released.

Easter A174

Paintings: 20b, Christ Presented to the People, by Rembrandt. 50b, Christ Carrying the Cross, by Mathias Grunewald. 75b, The Crucifixion, by Mathias Grunewald. 1d, The Crucifixion, by Rubens. 1.25d, The Road to Calvary (detail), by Tintoretto. 1.50d, The Road to Calvary (entire), by Tintoretto. 15d, The Crucifixion, by Masaccio. 20d, Descent from the Cross (detail), by Rembrandt. No. 1215, Crowning with Thorns (detail), by Titian. No. 1216, Crowning with Thorns, by Anthony Van Dyck.

1992, Apr. 16 **Litho.** ***Perf. 13½***

1207	A174	20b multicolored	.25	.25
1208	A174	50b multicolored	.25	.25
1209	A174	75b multicolored	.25	.25
1210	A174	1d multicolored	.30	.25
1211	A174	1.25d multicolored	.45	.35
1212	A174	1.50d multicolored	.55	.40
1213	A174	15d multicolored	3.75	3.75
1214	A174	20d multicolored	4.75	4.75
		Nos. 1207-1214 (8)	10.55	10.25

Souvenir Sheets

1215	A174	25d multicolored	6.25	6.25
1216	A174	25d multicolored	6.25	6.25

World Columbian Stamp Expo, Chicago A175

Walt Disney characters in Chicago: 50b, Mickey at Navy pier. 1d, Mickey floats by Wrigley Building. 1.25d, Donald graduates from University of Chicago. 12d, Goofy at Chicago's Adler Planetarium. No. 1221, Goofy above Chicago at the Hancock Center, horiz.

1992, Apr. 8 **Litho.** ***Perf. 13½x14***

1217	A175	50b multicolored	.50	.25
1218	A175	1d multicolored	.65	.50
1219	A175	1.25d multicolored	.80	.75
1220	A175	12d multicolored	5.00	5.00
		Nos. 1217-1220 (4)	6.95	6.50

Souvenir Sheet

Perf. 14x13½

1221	A175	18d multicolored	7.50	7.50

No. 1220 has name spelled "Alder."

Granada '92 — A176

Mickey Mouse as Columbus: 20b, With map. 75b, Ideas rejected. 1.50d, Explores America. 15d, Returns to Spain. No. 1231, Embarks for America.

1992, Apr. 8 ***Perf. 13½x14***

1227	A176	20b multicolored	.60	.60
1228	A176	75b multicolored	.80	.80
1229	A176	1.50d multicolored	1.00	1.00
1230	A176	15d multicolored	4.75	4.75
		Nos. 1227-1230 (4)	7.15	7.15

Souvenir Sheet

1231	A176	18d multicolored	7.00	7.00

Flowers — A177

20b, Hibiscus. 50b, Calabash nutmeg. 75b, Silk cotton tree. 1d, Oncoba. 1.25d, Paintbrush plant. 1.50d, Tree gardenia. 2d, Glory bower. 5d, Ashanti blood. 10d, African peach. 12d, Butterfly bush. 15d, Crepe ginger. 18d, Spider tresses.

No. 1249, Water lily. No. 1250, Bougainvillea. No. 1251, Baobab tree. No. 1252, Climbing pea.

1992, July 21 **Litho.** ***Perf. 14***

1237	A177	20b multicolored	.25	.25
1238	A177	50b multicolored	.25	.25
1239	A177	75b multicolored	.30	.30
1240	A177	1d multicolored	.40	.40
1241	A177	1.25d multicolored	.50	.50
1242	A177	1.50d multicolored	.55	.55
1243	A177	2d multicolored	.70	.70
1244	A177	5d multicolored	1.30	1.30
1245	A177	10d multicolored	2.25	2.25
1246	A177	12d multicolored	2.50	2.50
1247	A177	15d multicolored	3.00	3.00
1248	A177	18d multicolored	3.25	3.25
		Nos. 1237-1248 (12)	15.25	15.25

Souvenir Sheets

1249	A177	20d multicolored	4.25	4.25
1250	A177	20d multicolored	4.25	4.25
1251	A177	20d multicolored	4.25	4.25
1252	A177	20d multicolored	4.25	4.25

While Nos. 1240, 1242, 1244, 1247, 1250 have the same release date as Nos. 1237, 1241, 1243, 1248-1249, their values in relation to the dollar were higher when they were released.

Riverboats — A178

Riverboat and waterway: 20b, Joven Antonia, Gambia River. 50b, Dresden, Elbe River. 75b, Medway Queen, Medway River. 1d, Lady Wright, Gambia River. 1.25d, Devin, Vltava River. 1.50d, Lady Chilel, Gambia River. 5d, Robert Fulton, Hudson River. 10d, Coonawarra, Murray River. 12d, Nakusp, Columbia River. 15d, Lucy Ashton, Firth of Clyde. No. 1263, Rudesheim, Rhine River. No. 1264, City of Cairo, Mississippi River.

1992, Aug. 3 **Litho.** ***Perf. 14***

1253	A178	20b multicolored	.25	.25
1254	A178	50b multicolored	.25	.25
1255	A178	75b multicolored	.30	.30
1256	A178	1d multicolored	.40	.40
1257	A178	1.25d multicolored	.50	.50
1258	A178	1.50d multicolored	.60	.60

1259 A178 5d multicolored 1.50 1.50
1260 A178 10d multicolored 2.40 2.40
1261 A178 12d multicolored 2.60 2.60
1262 A178 15d multicolored 3.50 3.50
Nos. 1253-1262 (10) 12.30 12.30

Souvenir Sheets

1263 A178 20d multicolored 6.50 6.50
1264 A178 20d multicolored 6.50 6.50

Miniature Sheet

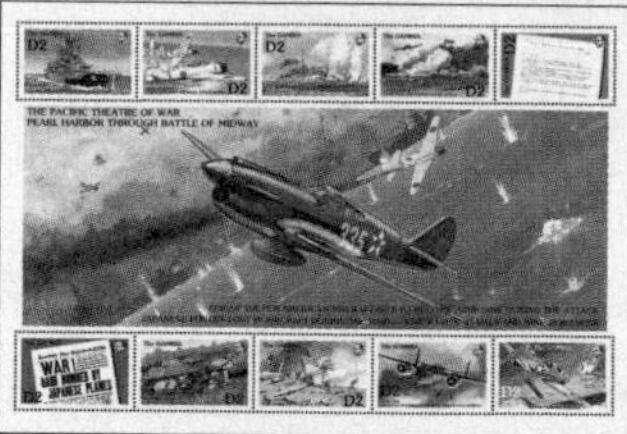

World War II in the Pacific — A179

Designs: a, USS Pennsylvania. b, Japanese attack begins. c, USS Ward sinking Japanese submarine. d, Ford Naval Air Station under attack. e, News bulletin announcing attack. f, Front page of Honolulu Star-Bulletin. g, Japanese invade Guam. h, US recovers Wake Island. i, Doolittle raids Japan from USS Hornet. j, Battle of Midway.

1992 Litho. *Perf. 14½x15*

1265 A179 2d Sheet of 10, #a.-j. 13.00 13.00

1992 Summer Olympics, Barcelona A180

Designs: 20b, Women's double sculls. 50b, Kayak, vert. 75b, Women's precision rapid-fire shooting. 1d, Judo, vert. 1.25d, Javelin, vert. 1.50d, Gymnastics, vault, vert. 3d, Windsurfing, vert. 5d, High jump. No. 1274, Women's 200-meter backstroke. No. 1275, Table tennis.

1992, Aug. 10 Litho. *Perf. 14*

1266 A180 20b multicolored .30 .30
1267 A180 50b multicolored .50 .50
1268 A180 75b multicolored .70 .70
1269 A180 1d multicolored .80 .80
1270 A180 1.25d multicolored 1.00 1.00
1271 A180 1.50d multicolored 1.25 1.25
1272 A180 3d multicolored 2.00 2.00
1273 A180 5d multicolored 3.00 3.00
Nos. 1266-1273 (8) 9.55 9.55

Souvenir Sheets

1274 A180 18d multicolored 6.25 6.25
1275 A180 18d multicolored 6.25 6.25

1992 Winter Olympics, Albertville — A181

Designs: 2d, Downhill skiing, vert. 10d, Four-man bobsled, vert. 12d, Ski jumping, vert. 15d, Slalom skiing.

No. 1280, 18d, Men's 500-meter speedskating. No. 1281, 18d, Pairs figure skating, vert.

1992, Aug. 10 Litho. *Perf. 14*

1276-1279 A181 Set of 4 18.00 18.00

Souvenir Sheets

1280-1281 A181 Set of 2 14.00 14.00

Dinosaurs — A182

20b, Dryosaurus. 25b, Saurolophus. 50b, No. 1291, Allosaurus. 75b, Fabrosaurus. 1d, Deinonychus. 1.25d, No. 1292A, Cetiosaurus. 1.50d, Camptosaurus. 2d, No. 1292, Ornithosuchus. 3d, Spinosaurus. 5d, Ornithomimus. 10d, Kentrosaurus. 12d, Schlermochus.

1992, Sept. 21 Litho. *Perf. 14*

1283 A182 20b multi .45 .45
1284 A182 25b multi .45 .45
1284A A182 50b multi .55 .55
1284B A182 75b multi .65 .65
1284C A182 1d multi .65 .65
1285 A182 1.25d multi .75 .75
1286 A182 1.50d multi .75 .75
1286A A182 2d multi .75 .75
1287 A182 3d multi .80 .80
1288 A182 5d multi 1.25 1.25
1289 A182 10d multi 2.25 2.25
1290 A182 12d multi 2.75 2.75
Nos. 1283-1290 (12) 12.05 12.05

Souvenir Sheets

1291 A182 25d multi 6.50 6.50
1292 A182 25d multi 6.50 6.50
1292A A182 25d multi 6.50 6.50

Genoa '92.

Walt Disney's Goofy, 60th Anniv. — A183

Scenes from Disney cartoon films: 50b, Orphan's Benefit, 1934, 1941. 75b, Moose Hunters, 1937. 1d, Mickey's Amateurs, 1937. 1.25d, Lonesome Ghosts, 1937. 5d, Boat Builders, 1938. 7d, The Whalers, 1938. 10d, Goofy and Wilbur, 1939. 15d, Saludos Amigos, 1941. No. 1301, The Band Concert, 1935, vert. No. 1302, Goofy today, vert.

1992 Litho. *Perf. 14x13½*

1293 A183 50b multicolored .45 .45
1294 A183 75b multicolored .65 .65
1295 A183 1d multicolored .80 .80
1296 A183 1.25d multicolored .80 .80
1297 A183 5d multicolored 2.00 2.00
1298 A183 7d multicolored 2.50 2.50
1299 A183 10d multicolored 2.50 2.50
1300 A183 15d multicolored 3.00 3.00
Nos. 1293-1300 (8) 12.70 12.70

Souvenir Sheets

Perf. 13½x14

1301 A183 20d multicolored 8.00 8.00
1302 A183 20d multicolored 8.00 8.00

Discovery of America, 500th Anniv. A184

5d, Santa Maria. 12d, Pinta, Santa Maria, and Nina. 18d, Tree branch, green-winged macaw.

1992, Oct. Litho. *Perf. 14*

1303 A184 5d multi 1.25 1.25
1304 A184 12d multi 2.25 2.25

Souvenir Sheet

1305 A184 18d multi, vert. 8.00 8.00

Golf — A186

Pres. Jarwara playing golf and: 20b, Map, flag of Australia. 1d, Trophy, Gambian flag. 1.50d, Gambian flag. 2d, Map, flag of Japan. 3d, Map, flag of US. 5d, Trophy, 1985, Gambian flag (small portrait only). No. 1312, Map, flag of Scotland. 12d, Map, flag of Italy. No. 1312B, Pres. Jawara about to tee off. No. 1312C, Gambian flag (small portrait).

1992 Litho. *Perf. 14*

1306 A186 20b multi .70 .70
1307 A186 1d multi .90 .90
1308 A186 1.50d multi 1.10 1.10
1309 A186 2d multi 1.40 1.40
1310 A186 3d multi 1.75 1.75
1311 A186 5d multi 2.40 2.40
1312 A186 10d multi 3.50 3.50
1312A A186 12d multi 4.25 4.25
Nos. 1306-1312A (8) 16.00 16.00

Souvenir Sheets

1312B A186 10d multi 8.00 8.00
1312C A186 18d multi, horiz. 8.00 8.00

No. 1306, Royal Melbourne Golf Course, Australia. No. 1309, Shinonoseki Golf Course, Japan. No. 1310, US Open, Pebble Beach. No. 1312, St. Andrew's Golf Course, Scotland. No. 1312A, Italian Open, Monticello, Milan.

Issued: 20b, 2d, 5d, Nos. 1312, 1312B, Dec. 8; others, Oct.

Souvenir Sheet

Ellis Island, New York City — A187

1992, Oct. 28 Litho. *Perf. 14*

1313 A187 18d multicolored 5.75 5.75

Postage Stamp Mega Event '92, New York City.

Christmas A188

Details or entire paintings: 50b, The Holy Family, by Raphael. 75b, Madonna and Child with St. Elizabeth and the Infant St. John (Small Holy Family), by Raphael. 1d, The Holy Family as the Little Holy Family, by Raphael. 1.25d, Escape to Egypt, by Broederlam. 1.50d, Flight Into Egypt, by Isenbrant. No. 1319, The Flight into Egypt, by Cosimo Tura. No. 1320, Flight into Egypt, by Master of Hoogstraelen. No. 1321, The Holy Family, by El Greco. 4d, The Holy Family, by Bernard Van Orley. 5d, Holy Family with Infant Jesus Sleeping, by Charles Le Brun. 10d, Rest on the Flight to Egypt, by Gentileschi. 12d, Rest on the Flight to Egypt, by Orazio Gentileschi. No. 1326, The Holy Family, by Giorgione. No. 1327, Rest on the Flight to Egypt, by Simone Cantarino. No. 1328, The Flight to Egypt, by Vittore Carpaccio.

1992, Nov. 3 Litho. *Perf. 13½x14*

1314 A188 50b multicolored .25 .25
1315 A188 75b multicolored .35 .35
1316 A188 1d multicolored .45 .45
1317 A188 1.25d multicolored .60 .60
1318 A188 1.50d multicolored .60 .60
1319 A188 2d multicolored .85 .85
1320 A188 2d multicolored .85 .85
1321 A188 2d multicolored .85 .85
1322 A188 4d multicolored 1.30 1.30
1323 A188 5d multicolored 1.60 1.60
1324 A188 10d multicolored 3.00 3.00
1325 A188 12d multicolored 3.25 3.25
Nos. 1314-1325 (12) 13.95 13.95

Souvenir Sheets

1326 A188 25d multicolored 4.50 4.50
1327 A188 25d multicolored 4.50 4.50
1328 A188 25d multicolored 4.50 4.50

A189

A190

A191

A192

A193

A194

Anniversaries and Events — A195

Designs: No. 1329, Ariane 4 rocket. No. 1330, Berlin airlift, Konrad Adenauer. No. 1331, LZ127 Graf Zeppelin. 6d, Jentink's duiker. 7d, World map. 9d, Wolfgang Amadeus Mozart. No. 1335, America's Cup yacht Enterprise, 1930. No. 1336, Imperial parrot. No. 1337, Lions Intl. emblem. No. 1338, American Space shuttle. 15d, Prisoners of war returning home, Adenauer. 18d, First rigid airship, LZ1. No. 1341, European Space Agency's Hermes space shuttle. No. 1342, Scene from "The Marriage of Figaro." No. 1343, Face of Adenauer. No. 1344, Count Ferdinand von Zeppelin. No. 1345, Earth as seen from space.

1992-93 Litho. *Perf. 14*

1329 A189 2d multicolored 1.00 1.00
1330 A191 2d multicolored 1.25 1.25
1331 A191 2d multicolored 1.00 1.00
1332 A192 6d multicolored 2.25 2.25
1333 A193 7d multicolored 2.50 2.50
1334 A190 9d multicolored 4.25 4.25
1335 A194 10d multicolored 3.50 3.50
1336 A192 10d multicolored 2.75 2.75
1337 A195 10d multicolored 2.50 2.50
1338 A189 12d multicolored 2.50 2.50
1339 A191 15d multicolored 4.75 4.75
1340 A191 18d multicolored 3.00 3.00
Nos. 1329-1340 (12) 31.25 31.25

Souvenir Sheets

1341	A189 18d multicolored	5.75	5.75
1342	A190 18d multicolored	7.50	7.50
1343	A191 18d multicolored	7.50	7.50
1344	A191 18d multicolored	5.75	5.75
1345	A192 18d multicolored	5.75	5.75

Intl. Space Year (Nos. 1329, 1338, 1341). Wolfgang Amadeus Mozart, bicent. of death (Nos. 1334, 1342). Konrad Adenauer, 25th anniv. of death (Nos. 1330, 1339, 1343). Count Zeppelin, 75th anniv. of death (Nos. 1331, 1340, 1344). Earth Summit, Rio de Janeiro (Nos. 1332, 1336, 1345). Intl. Conf. on Nutrition, Rome (No. 1333). America's Cup yacht race (No. 1335). Lions Intl., 75th anniv. (No. 1337).

Issued: Nos. 1333, 1335, 1339, 1343, 1/93; others, 12/92.

Peace Corps, 25th Anniv. A196

1993, Feb.

1346 A196 2d multicolored 1.40 1.40

Elvis Presley, 15th Anniv. of Death (in 1992) — A197

No. 1347: a, Portrait. b, With guitar. c, Holding microphone.

1993

1347 A197 3d Strip of 3, #a.-c. 2.75 2.75

Miniature Sheets

Baseball Films — A198

No. 1348 — Movie and stars: a, Casey at the Bat, Wallace Beery, 1927, Elliott Gould, 1986. b, Babe Comes Home, Anna Q. Nilsson, Babe Ruth, 1927. c, Elmer the Great, Joe E. Brown, 1933. d, The Naughty Nineties, Bud Abbott and Lou Costello, 1945. e, Take Me Out to the Ball Game, Frank Sinatra, Gene Kelly, Esther Williams, 1949. f, Damn Yankees, Tab Hunter, Gwen Verdon, 1958. g, The Pride of St. Louis, Dan Dailey, 1952. h, Brewster's Millions, John Candy, Richard Pryor, 1985.

No. 1349: a, The Jackie Robinson Story, Jackie Robinson, Ruby Dee, 1950. b, Bang the Drum Slowly, Robert DeNiro, 1973. c, The Bingo Long Traveling All-Stars & Motor Kings, James Earl Jones, Billy Dee Williams, 1976. d, Bull Durham, Kevin Costner, Susan Sarandon, 1988. e, Eight Men Out, eight actors, 1988. f, Field of Dreams, Ray Liotta, 1989. g, Major League, Charlie Sheet, 1989. h, Mr. Baseball, Tom Selleck, 1992.

No. 1350, The Babe, John Goodman, 1992. No. 1351, The Natural, Robert Redford. No. 1351A, The Winning Team, Ronald Reagan. No. 351B, A League of Their Own, Tom Hanks, Madonna.

1993, Mar. 25 Litho. *Perf. 13*

1348 A198 3d Sheet of 8, #a.-h. 7.50 7.50

1349 A198 3d Sheet of 8, #a.-h. 7.50 7.50

Souvenir Sheet

1350	A198 20d multi	5.00	5.00
1351	A198 20d multi, vert.	5.00	5.00
1351A	A198 20d multi	5.00	5.00
1351B	A198 20d multi, vert.	5.00	5.00

Miniature Sheets

Louvre Museum, Bicent. — A199

Details from paintings, by Jacques-Louis David (1748-1825): Nos. 1352a-b, Oath of the Horatii (diff. details). c, The Love of Paris & Helen. d, Rape of the Sabine Women. e, Leonidas of Thermopylae. f-h, Napoleon Crowning Josephine (left, center, right).

Details from paintings, by Antoine (c. 1588-1648) and Louis (1593-1648) Le Nain: No. 1353a, Inside Home of Peasants. b-c, The Tobacco Smokers (diff. details). d, The Cart. e, Peasants' Meal. f-g, Interior Portraits (diff. details). h, The Forge.

Details or entire paintings, by Leonardo Da Vinci: No. 1354a, St. John the Baptist. b, Virgin of the Rocks. c, Bacchus. d, Woman from the Court of Milan. e, The Virgin of the Rocks (detail). f, Mona Lisa. g, Mona Lisa (detail of hands). h, Two Horsemen, Study of the Horse.

No. 1355, Allegory of Victory, by Mathieu Le Nain (1607-1677). No. 1356, The Artist and Her Daughter, by Elisabeth Vigee-Lebrun (1755-1842).

1993, Jan. 7 Litho. *Perf. 12*

1352 A199 3d Sheet of 8, #a.-h. 7.50 7.50

1353 A199 3d Sheet of 8, #a.-h. 7.50 7.50

1354 A199 3d Sheet of 8, #a.-h. 7.50 7.50

Souvenir Sheets

Perf. 14½

1355 A199 20d multicolored 8.25 8.25

1356 A199 20d multicolored 8.25 8.25

Nos. 1355-1356 each contain one 55x88mm stamp.

Miniature Sheet

Animals of West Africa — A200

No. 1358: a, Giraffe. b, Baboon. c, Caracal. d, Large-spotted genet. e, Bushbuck. f, Red-fronted gazelle. g, Red-flanked duiker. h, Cape buffalo. i, African civet. j, Side-striped jackal. k, Ratel. l, Striped polecat.

No. 1359: a, Vervet. b, Blackish-green guenon. c, Long-tailed pangolin. d, Leopard. e, Elephant. f, Hunting dog. g, Spotted hyena. h, Lion. i, Hippopotamus. j, Nile crocodile. k, Aardvark. l, Warthog.

1993, Apr. 5 Litho. *Perf. 14*

1358 A200 2d Sheet of 12, #a.-l. 10.00 10.00

1359 A200 5d Sheet of 12, #a.-l. 14.00 14.00

Souvenir Sheet

1360 A200 20d like #1359b 8.25 8.25

No. 1360 printed in continuous design with black frameline around stamp. A number has been reserved for an additional value in this set.

Long-Tailed Pangolin — A201

Pangolin in various positions on tree limb.

1993, Apr. 5

1362	A201 1.25d multicolored	.70	.70
1363	A201 1.50d multicolored	.80	.80
1364	A201 2d multicolored	1.00	1.00
1365	A201 5d multicolored	2.50	2.50
	Nos. 1362-1365 (4)	5.00	5.00

Souvenir Sheet

1366 A201 20d like #1363 7.50 7.50

World Wildlife Federation.

Nos. 1362-1365 exist imperf. Value, set of 4 $40. No. 1366 exists imperf. Value, $35.

Birds

A202 A203

Designs: 1.25d, Osprey. 1.50d, Egyptian vulture, horiz. 2d, Martial eagle. 3d, Ruppell's griffon vulture, horiz. 5d, Auger buzzard. 8d, Greater kestrel. 10d, Secretary bird. 15d, Bateleur eagle, horiz.

No. 1375a, Rose-ringed parakeet. b, Variable sunbird. c, Red-billed hornbill. d, Red-billed fire-finch. e, Common go-away bird. f, Crimson-breasted shrike. g, Gray-headed bush-shrike. h, Nicator. i, Egyptian plover. j, Congo peacock. k, Greater painted snipe. l, Crowned crane.

#1376, Verreaux's eagle. #1377, Tawny owl.

1993, Apr. 15 Litho. *Perf. 14*

1367	A202 1.25d multicolored	1.00	.80
1368	A202 1.50d multicolored	1.25	1.00
1369	A202 2d multicolored	1.60	1.20
1370	A202 3d multicolored	2.00	1.60
1371	A202 5d multicolored	2.00	2.00
1372	A202 8d multicolored	2.75	2.75
1373	A202 10d multicolored	2.75	2.75
1374	A202 15d multicolored	3.50	3.50
	Nos. 1367-1374 (8)	16.85	15.60

Miniature Sheet

1375 A203 2d Sheet of 12, #a.-l. 18.50 18.50

Souvenir Sheets

1376 A202 20d multicolored 8.50 8.50

1377 A202 20d multicolored 8.50 8.50

Nos. 1376-1377 each contain 1 56x42mm stamp.

Aviation Anniversaries — A204

Designs: No. 1379, Guyot balloon, 1785, vert. No. 1380, Dr. Hugo Eckener, zeppelin LZ3 in flight. No. 1381, Sopwith Snipe. No. 1382, Eckener, LZ3 moored to ground. 8d, Eckener, Graf Zeppelin. 10d, Balloon, Comte D'Artois, 1785, vert. 15d, Royal Aircraft Factory S.E.5. No. 1386, Avro 504K. No. 1387, Eckener, LZ3 in flight, diff. No. 1388, Blanchard's flying ship, 1785, vert.

1993, May Litho. *Perf. 14*

1379	A204 2d multicolored	.70	.70
1380	A204 2d multicolored	.70	.70
1381	A204 5d multicolored	1.25	1.25
1382	A204 5d multicolored	1.25	1.25
1383	A204 8d multicolored	2.00	2.00
1384	A204 10d multicolored	2.25	2.25
1385	A204 15d multicolored	3.00	3.00
	Nos. 1379-1385 (7)	11.15	11.15

Souvenir Sheets

1386	A204 20d multicolored	7.00	7.00
1387	A204 20d multicolored	7.00	7.00
1388	A204 20d multicolored	7.00	7.00

Dr. Hugo Eckener, 125th birth anniv. (Nos. 1380, 1382, 1383, 1387). Royal Air Force, 75th anniv. (Nos. 1381, 1385, 1386).

Nos. 1379, 1384, 1388 are airmail.

Miniature Sheet

Coronation of Queen Elizabeth II, 40th Anniv. — A205

Designs: a, 2d, Official coronation photograph. b, 5d, Orb and Scepter. c, 8d, Winston Churchill. d, 10d, Queen during Trooping of the Color.

20d, Portrait, by Joe King, 1972.

1993, June 2 *Perf. 13½x14*

1389 A205 Sheet of 8, 2 each #a.-d. 15.00 15.00

Souvenir Sheet

Perf. 14

1390 A205 20d multicolored 8.00 8.00

No. 1390 contains one 28x42mm stamp.

Miniature Sheet

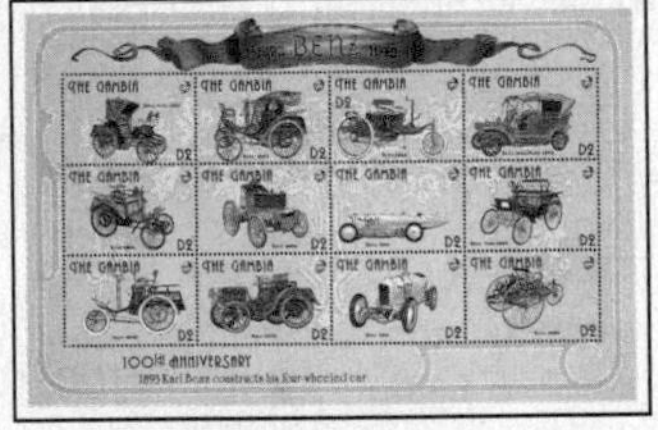

A206

No. 1391 — Benz Automobiles: a, 1894 Benz Velo. b, 1894 Benz. c, 1885 Benz. d, 1905 Benz Mannheim. e, 1892 Benz. f, 1900 Benz, blue. g, 1911 Benz. h, 1893 Benz Velo. i, 1900 Benz, black. j, 1900 Benz, red. k, 1911 Benz, front view. l, 1885 Benz, rear view.

No. 1393, 20d, 1900 Benz, diff.

No. 1392 — Ford automobiles: a, Henry Ford, age 30, 1910 Model T. b, 1896, green seat. c, Henry Ford with Barney Oldfield and 1902 racing car, 999. d, 1896, Henry Ford with bicycle. e, 1903 Model A. f, 1908 Model T, top down. g, 1908 Model T, top up. h, 1906 Model K. i, 1931 Model A. j, 1906 Model A. k, 1906 Model N. l, 1905 Model F.

No. 1393, 1900 Benz, diff. No. 1394, 1896 Ford with red seat.

1993, June 7 *Perf. 14*

1391 A206 2d Sheet of 12, #a.-l. 7.50 7.50

1392 A206 2d Sheet of 12, #a.-l. 7.50 7.50

Souvenir Sheets

1393 A206 20d multicolored 6.00 6.00

1394 A206 20d multicolored 6.00 6.00

1st Benz 4-wheel automobile, cent. (Nos. 1391, 1393).

1st engine by Henry Ford, cent. (Nos. 1392, 1394).

Miniature Sheets

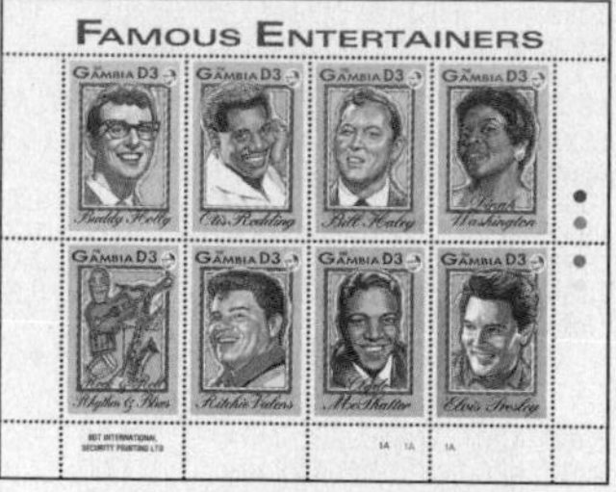

Entertainers — A207

No. 1395: a, Buddy Holly. b, Otis Redding. c, Bill Haley. d, Dinah Washington. e, Musical instruments. f, Ritchie Valens. g, Clyde McPhatter. h, Elvis Presley.

No. 1396: a-i, Various pictures of Madonna.

No. 1397: a-i, Various pictures of Elvis Presley.

No. 1398: a-i, Various pictures of Marilyn Monroe.

1993, July 26 Litho. *Perf. 14*

1395 A207 3d Sheet of 8, #a.-h. 11.50 11.50
1396 A207 3d Sheet of 9, #a.-i. 11.50 11.50
1397 A207 3d Sheet of 9, #a,-i. 11.50 11.50
1398 A207 3d Sheet of 9, #a.-i. 11.50 11.50
Nos. 1395-1398 (4) 46.00 46.00

Cats and Dogs A208

No. 1399 — Cats, Siamese. b, Colorpoint longhair. c, Burmese. d, Birman. e, Snowshoe. f, Tonkinese. g, Foreign shorthair. h, Balinese. i, Oriental shorthair. j, Foreign shorthair, diff. k, Colorpoint longhair, diff. l, Colorpoint longhair, diff.

Dogs: No. 1400a, Shih tzu. b, Skye terrier. c, Berner laufhund. d, Boxer. e, Welsh corgi (Queen Elizabeth II). f, Dumfrieshire. g, Lurcher. h, Welsh corgi (Princess Anne). i, Pekinese. j, Papillon. k, Otterhound. l, Pug.

No. 1401, Colorpoint shorthair, vert. No. 1402, Burmese, vert. No. 1403, Long-haired dachshund. No. 1404, Cairn terrier.

1993, Sept. 13 Litho. *Perf. 14*

1399 A208 2d Sheet of 12, #a.-l. 15.00 15.00
1400 A208 2d Sheet of 12, #a.-i. 14.00 14.00

Souvenir Sheets

1401 A208 20d multicolored 6.50 6.50
1402 A208 20d multicolored 6.50 6.50
1403 A208 20d multicolored 6.50 6.50
1404 A208 20d multicolored 6.50 6.50

Taipei '93 — A209

Designs: No. 1405, Fawang Si Pagoda, Song Shan Mt., Henan. No. 1406, Wanshoubao Pagoda, Shashi. No. 1407, Red Pavilion, Shibaozhai. No. 1408, Songyue Si Pagoda, Song Shan Mt., Henan. No. 1409, Bond Center, Hong Kong. No. 1410, Tianning Si Pagoda, Beijing. No. 1411, Xuanzhuang Pagoda, Xian, Shenxi. No. 1412, Forbidden City, Beijing.

No. 1413 — Tang Dynasty funerary objects: a, Camel. b, Horse and female rider. c, Camel, diff. d, Yellow-glazed horse. e, Camel, diff. f, Horse with saddle.

No. 1414 — Pottery: a, Vase. b, Small wine cup. c, Fahua type Mei-ping vase. d, Urn vase, export ware. e, Tureen. f, Lidded Potiche.

No. 1415, Standing Buddhas,Hallway of Upper Huayan Si Temple, Datong, horiz. No. 1416, Seated Buddha, Main Hall, Shanhua Si Temple, Datong.

1993, Sept. 27 Litho. *Perf. 14*

1405 A209 20b multicolored .25 .25
1406 A209 20b multicolored .25 .25
1407 A209 2d multicolored .80 .80
1408 A209 2d multicolored .80 .80
1409 A209 5d multicolored 1.75 1.75
1410 A209 5d multicolored 1.75 1.75
1411 A209 15d multicolored 3.25 3.25
1412 A209 15d multicolored 3.25 3.25
Nos. 1405-1412 (8) 12.10 12.10

Miniature Sheets

1413 A209 5d Sheet of 6, #a.-f. 13.00 13.00
1414 A209 5d Sheet of 6, #a.-f. 13.00 13.00

Souvenir Sheets

1415 A209 18d multicolored 5.50 5.50
1416 A209 18d multicolored 5.50 5.50

With Bangkok '93 Emblem

No. 1417, Sanctuary of Prasat Phanom Wan. No. 1418, Lai Kham Vihan, Chiang Mai. No. 1419, Spirit Shrine, Bangkok. No. 1420, Walking Buddha, Wat Phra Si Ratana Mahathat. No. 1421, Buddha, Sukhothai's Wat Mahathat. No. 1422, Gopura of Prasat Phanom Rung. No. 1423, Prang of Prasat Hin Phimai. No. 1424, Slender Chedis, Wat Yai Chai, Mongkon.

No. 1425 — Thai painting: a, Early Fruit Stand. b, Scene in Chinese Style, Wat Bovornivet. c, Buddha Descends from Tauatimsa. d, Sang Thong Tales, Lai Kham Vihan. e, The Damned in Hell, Wah Suthat. f, King Sanjaya Travels on Elephant, Wat Suwannaram.

No. 1426 — Thai Buddha sculpture: a, U Thong C, 14th-15th cent. b, Adorned Seated, 17th cent. c, Phra Chai, 19th cent. d, Bronze, 14th cent. e, U Thong A, bronze. f, Crowned, 14th-15th cent.

No. 1427, Ceramics, horiz. No. 1428, Character in Khon, dance drama.

1993

1417 A209 20b multicolored .25 .25
1418 A209 20b multicolored .25 .25
1419 A209 2d multicolored .80 .80
1420 A209 2d multicolored .80 .80
1421 A209 5d multicolored 1.75 1.75
1422 A209 5d multicolored 1.75 1.75
1423 A209 15d multicolored 3.25 3.25
1424 A209 15d multicolored 3.25 3.25
Nos. 1417-1424 (8) 12.10 12.10

Miniature Sheets

1425 A209 5d Sheet of 6, #a.-f. 13.00 13.00
1426 A209 5d Sheet of 6, #a.-f. 13.00 13.00

Souvenir Sheets

1427 A209 18d multicolored 5.50 5.50
1428 A209 18d multicolored 5.50 5.50

With Indopex '93 Emblem

Designs: No. 1429, Pura Taman Ayun (garden temple), Mengwi, Bali. No. 1430, Natl. monument with statue of Prince Diponegoro, Jakarta. No. 1431, Candi Jawi, East Java. No. 1432, Guardian at Singosari Palace, East Java. No. 1433, Monument of Irian Jaya, (liberation), Jakarta. No. 1434, Central Temple, Prambanan complex, Lara Djonggrang. No. 1435, "Date of the Year Temple," Panataran complex, East Java. No. 1436, Brahma & Siva Temples, Loro Jonggrang, Java.

No. 1437 — Masks: a, Telek Luh. b, Jero Gde. c, Barong Macan. d, Monkey. e, Mata Gde. f, Jauk Kras.

No. 1438 — Paintings: a, Tree Mask, Soedibio, 1978. b, Dry Lizard, Hendra Gunawan, 1977. c, The Corn Eater, Sudjana Kerton, 1988. d, Night Watchman, Djoko Pekik, 1988. e, Hunger, Kerton, 1984. f, Arje Player, Soedjojono, 1971.

No. 1439, Stone carving, Brahma & Gods, Borobudur, Java, horiz. No. 1440, Effigies of the Dead, Torajaland, horiz.

1993, Sept. 27 Litho. *Perf. 14*

1429 A209 20b multicolored .25 .25
1430 A209 20b multicolored .25 .25
1431 A209 2d multicolored .80 .80
1432 A209 2d multicolored .80 .80
1433 A209 5d multicolored 1.75 1.75
1434 A209 5d multicolored 1.75 1.75
1435 A209 15d multicolored 3.25 3.25
1436 A209 15d multicolored 3.25 3.25
Nos. 1429-1436 (8) 12.10 12.10

Miniature Sheets

1437 A209 5d Sheet of 6, #a.-f. 13.00 13.00
1438 A209 5d Sheet of 6, #a.-f. 13.00 13.00

Souvenir Sheets

1439 A209 18d multicolored 5.50 5.50
1440 A209 18d multicolored 5.50 5.50

Miniature Sheet

Casey at the Bat — A210

Nos. 1441-1443: Characters and scenes from Disney's animated film Casey at the Bat.

1993, Oct. 25 Litho. *Perf. 14x13½*

1441 A210 2d Sheet of 9, #a.-i. 10.00 10.00

Souvenir Sheets

1442 A210 20d multicolored 7.00 7.00

Perf. 13½x14

1443 A210 20d multi, vert. 7.00 7.00

Picasso — A211

Paintings: 2d, Woman with a Comb, 1906. 5d, The Mirror, 1932. 7d, Woman on a Pillow, 1969. 18d, The Three Dancers, 1925.

1993, Oct. 7 Litho. *Perf. 14*

1444-1446 A211 Set of 3 4.50 4.50

Souvenir Sheet

1447 A211 18d multicolored 6.00 6.00

Copernicus A212

5d, Early astronomical instrument. 10d, Telescope.
18d, Copernicus.

1993, Oct. 7 *Perf. 14*

1448-1449 A212 Set of 2 4.50 4.50

Souvenir Sheet

Perf. 12x13

1450 A212 18d multi 6.00 6.00

Polska '93 A213

Paintings: 2d, Pont-Neuf, Paris, by Rudzka-Cybisowa, 1932. No. 1452, 10d, Honegger's Liturgical Symphony, by Bogusz, 1973. No. 1453, 10d, Niedzica castle. 18d, When You Enter Here, Whisper My Name Soundlessly, by Waniek, 1973.

1993, Oct. 7 *Perf. 14*

1451-1453 A213 Set of 3 6.75 6.75

Souvenir Sheet

1454 A213 18d multicolored 6.00 6.00

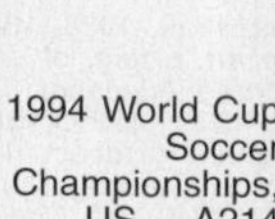

1994 World Cup Soccer Championships, US — A214

Players, country: 1.25d, Hannich, Hungary; Stopyra, France. 1.50d, Labd, Morocco; Lineker, England. 2d, Segota, Canada; Morozov, Russia. 3d, Roger Milla, Cameroun. 5d, Rodax, Australia; Weiss, Czech Republic. 10d, Claesen, Belgium; Bossis & Amoros, France. 12d, Candida, Brazil; Ramirez, Costa Rica. 15d, Silva, Brazil; Platini, France. No. 1463, Muller, Brazil; McDonald, Ireland, horiz. No. 1463A, Buchwald and Matthaeus, Germany; Maradona, Argentina, horiz.

1993, Nov. 22 *Perf. 13½x14*

1455 A214 1.25d multi .60 .60
1456 A214 1.50d multi .65 .65
1457 A214 2d multi .90 .90
1458 A214 3d multi 1.60 1.60
1459 A214 5d multi 2.25 2.25
1460 A214 10d multi 3.25 3.25
1461 A214 12d multi 3.50 3.50
1462 A214 15d multi 4.50 4.50
Nos. 1455-1462 (8) 17.25 17.25

Souvenir Sheets

Perf. 13

1463 A214 25d multi 8.50 8.50
1463A A214 25d multi 8.50 8.50

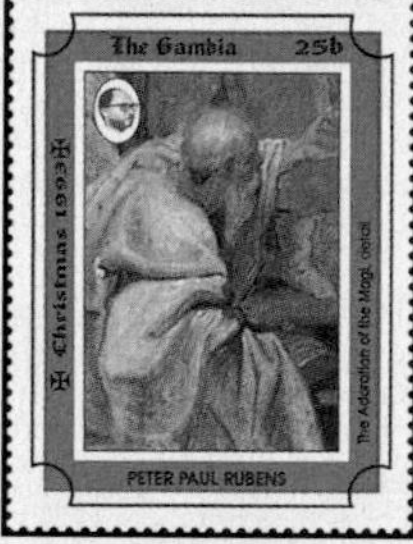

Christmas A215

Designs: No. 1464, 25b, No. 1467, 2d, No. 1471, 15d, Details or entire painting, Adoration of the Magi, by Rubens.

Details or entire woodcut by Durer: No. 1465, 1d, Holy Family with Joachim & Anna. No. 1466, 1.50d, The Annunciation, Life of the Virgin. No. 1468, 2d, The Virgin Mary Worshipped by Albrecht Bonstetten. No. 1469, 7d, Virgin on a Throne, Crowned by an Angel. No. 1470, 10d, The Holy Family with Two Angels in a Portico (detail).

No. 1472, 20d, Adoration of the Magi, by Rubens. No. 1473, 20d, The Holy Family with Two Angels in a Portico, (entire), by Durer, horiz.

1993, Dec. 1 *Perf. 13½x14, 14x13½*

1464-1471 A215 Set of 8 14.00 14.00

Souvenir Sheets

1472-1473 A215 Set of 2 12.00 12.00

Fine Art — A216

Paintings by Rembrandt: 50b, A Man in a Cap. No. 1476, Man with a Gold Helmet. 7d, A Franciscan Monk. 15d, The Apostle Paul. 20d, Dr. Tulp Demonstrating the Anatomy of the Arm, horiz.

Paintings by Matisse: 1.50d, Portrait of Pierre Matisse. No. 1477, Portrait of Auguste Pellerin (II). 5d, Andre Derain. 12d, The Young Sailor (II). No. 1483, Pianist and Checker Players, horiz.

1993, Dec. 15 *Perf. 13½x14*

1474 A216	50b multicolored	.75	.75
1475 A216	1.50d multicolored	1.25	1.25
1476 A216	2d multicolored	1.40	1.40
1477 A216	2d multicolored	1.50	1.50
1478 A216	5d multicolored	2.25	2.25
1479 A216	7d multicolored	3.00	3.00
1480 A216	12d multicolored	3.00	3.00
1481 A216	15d multicolored	3.50	3.50
	Nos. 1474-1481 (8)	16.65	16.65

Souvenir Sheets

Perf. 14x13½

1482 A216	20d multicolored	7.50	7.50
1483 A216	20d multicolored	7.50	7.50

Winter Sports A217

Disney characters portraying sports: 50b, Ski ballet. 75b, Pairs figure skating. 1d, Speed skating. 1.25d, Biathlon. 4d, 4-Man bobsled. 5d, Luge. 7d, Figure skating. 10d, Downhill skiing. 15d, Ice hockey.

No. 1493, 20d, Cross country skiing. No. 1494, 20d, Mogul skiing.

1993, Dec. 20 *Perf. 13½x14*

1484-1492 A217 Set of 9 16.00 16.00

Souvenir Sheets

1493-1494 A217 20d Set of 2 13.00 13.00

A218

Hong Kong '94 — A219

Stamps, painting, Spring Garden-1846, by M. Bruce: No. 1495, Hong Kong #357, left detail. No. 1496, Right detail, #1000.

No. 1497 — Museum of Qin Figures, Shaanxi Province, Tomb of First Emperor: a, Qin warriors, horses. b, Warrior in battle dress. c, Armor clad warrior. d, Chariot driver. e, Dog. f, Qin warriors.

No. 1498, Show emblem, Hong Kong #253, vert.

1994, Feb. 18 **Litho.** *Perf. 14*

1495 A218	1.50d multicolored	.70	.40
1496 A218	1.50d multicolored	.70	.40
a.	Pair, #1495-1496	2.00	2.00
1497 A219	1.50d Sheet of 6, #a.-f.	5.00	5.00

Souvenir Sheet

1498 A218 20d multicolored 5.75 5.75

Nos. 1495-1496 issued in sheets of 5 pairs. No. 1496a is a continuous design.

New Year 1994 (Year of the Dog) (Nos. 1497e, 1498).

New Year 1994 (Year of the Dog) A220

Disney characters: 25b, Pluto the Racer. 50b, Fifi. 75b, Pluto, Jr. 1.25d, Goofy and Bowser. 1.50d, Butch. 2d, Toliver. 3d, Ronnie. 5d, Primo. 8d, Pluto's kid brother. 10d, Army mascot. 12d, Pluto and Dinah's pups. 18d, Bent Tail, Junior.

No. 1511, Pluto, Dinah. No. 1512, Eega Beeva, Dog Pflip, Goofy, horiz. No. 1513, Dinah's pups, Pluto.

1994, Apr. 11 **Litho.** *Perf. 13½x14*

1499-1510 A220 Set of 12 20.00 20.00

Souvenir Sheets

1511 A220 20d multicolored 5.50 5.50

Perf. 14x13½, 13½x14

1512 A220	20d multicolored	5.50	5.50
1513 A220	20d multicolored	5.50	5.50

Orchids A221

Designs: 1d, Oeceoclades maculata. 1.25d, Angraecum distichum. 2d, Plectrelminthus caudatus. 5d, Tridactyle tridactylites. 8d, Bulbophyllum lepidum. 10d, Angraecum eburneum. 12d, Eulophia guineensis. 15d, Angraecum eichleranum.

No. 1522, Ancistrochilus rothschildianus. No. 1523, Vanilla imperialis.

1994, May 1 *Perf. 14*

1514 A221	1d multicolored	.50	.30
1515 A221	1.25d multicolored	.60	.30
1516 A221	2d multicolored	.70	.50
1517 A221	5d multicolored	1.25	1.25
1518 A221	8d multicolored	2.00	2.00
1519 A221	10d multicolored	2.25	2.25
1520 A221	12d multicolored	2.50	2.50
1521 A221	15d multicolored	3.00	3.00
	Nos. 1514-1521 (8)	12.80	12.10

Souvenir Sheets

1522 A221	25d multicolored	6.50	6.50
1523 A221	25d multicolored	6.50	6.50

Easter A222

Disney characters celebrate Easter: No. 1524, 25b, No. 1527, 4d, No. 1529, 8d, No. 1531, 12d, Ludwig von Drake. No. 1525, 50b, Minnie Mouse, Daisy Duck. No. 1526, 3d, Mickey Mouse. No. 1528, 5d, Donald Duck. No. 1530, 10d, Goofy.

No. 1532, 20d, Von Drake. No. 1533, 20d, Mickey, Minnie.

1994, Apr. 11 **Litho.** *Perf. 13½x14*

1524-1531 A222 Set of 8 16.50 16.50

Souvenir Sheets

1532-1533 A222 Set of 2 13.00 13.00

Sierra Club, Cent. A223

No. 1534, 5d — Various views of: a-b, Prince William Sound. c-d, The Serengeti. e-f, Ross Island.

No. 1535, 5d: a-c, Briksdal Fjord, vert. d-f, Yosemite, vert.

No. 1536, 5d: a-b, Tibetan Plateau, vert. c-d, Yellowstone, vert. e, Ross Island, vert. f, The Serengeti, vert. g, Mount Erebus, vert. h, Ansel Adams Wilderness, vert.

No. 1537, 5d: a-b, Ansel Adams Wilderness. c-d, Mount Erebus. e, Prince William Sound. f, Yellowstone. g, Tibetan Plateau. h, Sierra Club emblem.

1994, Apr. 25 *Perf. 14*

Miniature Sheets of 6, #a-f

1534-1535 A223 Set of 2 18.50 18.50

Miniature Sheets of 8, #a-h

1536-1537 A223 Set of 2 22.50 22.50

Paintings of Cats A224

No. 1538, 5d: a, The Arena, by Harold Weston. b, Cat Killing a Bird, by Picasso. c, Cat and Butterfly, by Hokusai. d, Winter: Cat on a Cushion, by Steinlen. e, Rattown Tigers, by Prang. f, Cat on the Floor, by Steinlen. g, Cat and Kittens. h, Cats Looking Over a Fence, by Prang. i, Little White Kittens into Mischief, by Ives. j, Cat Bathing, by Hiroshige. k, Playtime, by Tuck. l, Summer: Cat on a Balustrade, by Steinlen.

No. 1539, 5d, vert.: a, Girl with a Kitten, by Perronneau. b, Still Life with Cat and Fish, by Chardin. c, Tinkle a Cat. d, Naughty Puss! e, Cats, by Steinlen. f, Girl in Red with Cat and Dog, by Phillips. g, Cat, Butterfly and Begonia, by Haronobu. h, Cat and Kitten, by Higgins. i, Woman with a Cat, by Renoir. j, Minnie from Outskirts of Village, by Thrall. k, The Fisher, by Tuck. l, Artist and His Family, by Vaenius.

No. 1540, 20d, The Morning Rising, by Lepicie. No. 1541, 20d, The Graham Children, by Hogarth, vert.

1994, July 11 **Litho.** *Perf. 14*

Sheets of 12, #a-l

1538-1539 A224 Set of 2 42.50 42.50

Souvenir Sheets

1540-1541 A224 Set of 2 12.50 12.50

Monkeys — A225

Designs: 1d, Patas. 1.50d, Collared mangabey. 2d, Black and white colobus. 5d, Mona. 8d, Kirk's colobus. 10d, Vervet. 12d, Red colobus. 15d, Guinea baboon.

Heads of: No. 1550, 25d, Collared mangabey. No. 1551, 25d, Guinea baboon.

1994, Aug. 1 **Litho.** *Perf. 14*

1542-1549 A225 Set of 8 15.00 15.00

Souvenir Sheets

1550-1551 A225 25d Set of 2 16.00 16.00

D-Day, 50th Anniv. A226

Designs: 50b, Free Dutch sloop Soema joins attack. 75b, HMS Belfast fires on beach defenses. 1d, USS Texas hits Point Du Hoc. 2d, Free French cruiser George Leygues.

20d, HMS Ramillies.

1994, Aug. 16

1552-1555 A226 Set of 4 4.00 4.00

Souvenir Sheet

1556 A226 20d multicolored 6.50 6.50

First Manned Moon Landing, 25th Anniv. — A227

No. 1557: a, Yuri Gagarin. b, Valentina Tereshkova. c, Ham (chimpanzee). d, Alexei Leonov. e, Neil Armstrong. f, Svetlana Y. Savitskaya. g. Marc Garneau. h, Vladimir Komarov. i, Ulf Merbold.

30d, Neil Armstrong, Edwin "Buzz" Aldrin, Michael Collins at press conference.

1994, Aug. 16

1557 A227 2d Sheet of 9, #a.-i. 8.00 8.00

Souvenir Sheet

1558 A227 30d multicolored 10.00 10.00

A228

PHILAKOREA '94 — A229

Designs: 50b, Kungnakchon Hall, Naejangsa. 2d, Kettle of Popchusa. 3d, Pomun Tourist Resort.

Paper screen panels, episode from Sanguozhi, 18th cent. Choson Dynasty: a, Warriors on horseback. b, Soldiers atop fort. c, Shooting with bows and arrows. d, Bowing before horse & rider. e, Fight on horseback. f, h, Charging on horses. g, Trudging through valley. i, j, Living peacefully.

20d, Traditional tombstone guardian, Taenung, vert.

1994, Aug. 16 *Perf. 14, 13½ (#1562)*

1559-1561 A228	Set of 3	2.00	2.00
1562 A229	1d Sheet of 10, #a.-j.	12.00	12.00

Souvenir Sheet

1563 A228 20d multicolored 7.50 7.50

A230

Intl. Olympic Committee, Cent. — A231

Designs: 1.50d, Daley Thompson, Great Britain, decathalon, 1980, 1984. 5d, Heide Marie Rosendohl, Germany, long jump, 1972. 20d, Team Sweden, ice hockey, 1994.

1994, Aug. 16 ***Perf. 14***

1564 A230 1.50d multicolored .75 .75
1565 A230 5d multicolored 1.75 1.75

Souvenir Sheet

1566 A231 20d multicolored 7.00 7.00

Butterflies A232

Designs: 1d, Mylothris rhodope. 1.25d, Iolaphilus menas. 2d, Neptis nemetes. 5d, Antanartia delius. 8d, Acraea caecilia. 10d, Papilio nireus. 12d, Pipilio menestheus. 15d, Iolaphilus julus.

No. 1575, 25d, Colotis evippe. No. 1576, 25d, Bematistes epaea.

1994, Aug. 18 ***Perf. 14***

1567-1574 A232 Set of 8 15.00 15.00

Souvenir Sheets

1575-1576 A232 Set of 2 15.00 15.00

1994 World Cup Soccer Championships, US — A233

Designs: 50b, Bobby Charlton, England. 75b, Ferenc Puskas, Hungary. 1d, Paolo Rossi, Italy. 2d, Biri Biri, Gambian playing for Spain. 3d, Diego Maradona, Argentina. 8d, Johan Cruyff, Netherlands. 10d, Franz Beckenbauer, Germany. 15d, Thomas Dooley, US.

No. 1585, 25d, Pele, Brazil. No. 1586, 25d, Gordon Banks, England.

1994, Sept. 1

1577-1584 A233 Set of 8 12.50 12.50

Souvenir Sheets

1585-1586 A233 Set of 2 15.00 15.00

Mushrooms A234

No. 1587, 5d: a, Agaricus campestris. b, Lepista nuda. c, Podaxis pistillaris. d, Oudemansiella radicata. e, Schizophyllum commune. f, Chlorophyllum molybdites. g, Hypholoma fasciculare. h, Mycena pura. i, Ganoderma lucidum.

No. 1588, 5d: a, Suillus luteus. b, Bolbitius vitellinus. c, Clitocybe nebularis. d, Omphalotus olearius. e, Auricularia auricula. f, Macrolepiota rhacodes. g, Volvariella volvacea. h, Psilocybe coprophila. i, Suillus granulatus.

No. 1589, 20d, Cyathus striatus. No. 1590, 20d, Leucoagaricus naucina.

1994, Sept. 30 **Sheets of 9, #a-i**

1587-1588 A234 Set of 2 22.50 22.50

Souvenir Sheets

1589-1590 A234 Set of 2 14.00 14.00

Christmas A235

French paintings: 50b, Expectant Madonna with St. Joseph, by unknown artist. 75b, Rest of the Holy Family, by Louis Le Nain. 1d, Rest on the Flight into Egypt, by Antoine Watteau. No. 1594, 2d, Noon, by Claude Lorrain. No. 1595, 2d, Rest on the Flight into Egypt, by Francois Boucher. No. 1596, 2d, Rest on the Flight into Egypt, by Jean-Honore Fragonard. 10d, The Holy Family, by Nicolas Poussin. 12d, Mystical Marriage of St. Catherine, by Pierre-Francois Mignard.

No. 1599, 25d, The Nativity by Torchlight, by Louis Le Nain. No. 1600, 25d, Adoration of the Shepherds, by Mathieu Le Nain.

1994, Dec. 5 **Litho.** ***Perf. 13½x14***

1591-1598 A235 Set of 8 11.00 11.00

Souvenir Sheets

1599-1600 A235 Set of 2 14.00 14.00

Marilyn Monroe (1926-62), Actress — A236

No. 1601: a-i, Various portraits.

No. 1602, 25d, Wearing red dress. No. 1603, 25d, Wearing long, dangling earrings.

1995, Jan. 8 **Litho.** ***Perf. 14***

1601 A236 4d Sheet of 9, #a.-i. 11.00 11.00

Souvenir Sheets

1602-1603 A236 Set of 2 12.00 12.00

Elvis Presley (1935-77), Entertainer A237

No. 1604: a, As child. b, Singing, later years. c, With mother. d, With wife, Priscilla. e, With gold medallion. f, Wearing army uniform. g, Singing, younger years. h, Wearing hat. i, With daughter, Lisa Marie.

1995, Jan. 8

1604 A237 4d Sheet of 9, #a.-i. 13.00 13.00

Dinosaurs — A238

No. 1605: a, Pteranodon. b, Archaeopteryx. c, Rhamphorhynchus. d, Ornithomimus. e, Stegosaurus. f, Heterodontosaurus. g, Lystrosaurus. h, Euoplocephalus. i, Coelophysis. j, Staurilosaurus. k, Giantoperis. l, Diarthrognathus.

No. 1606: a, Archaeopteryx, diff. b, Vangehuanosaurus. c, Ceolophysis, diff. d, Plateosaurus. e, Baryonyx. f, Ornitholestes. g, Dryosaurus. h, Estemmenosuchus. i, Macroplata. j, Shonisaurus. k, Muraeonosaurus. l, Archelon.

20d, Bactrosaurus. 22d, Tyrannosaurus, vert. No. 1609, 25d, Triceratops, vert. No. 1610, 25d, Spinosaurus.

1995 **Litho.** ***Perf. 14***

1605 A238 2d Sheet of 12, #a.-l. 9.50 9.50
1606 A238 3d Sheet of 12, #a.-l. 9.50 9.50

Souvenir Sheets

1607 A238 20d multi 7.50 7.50
1608 A238 22d multi 7.50 7.50
1609-1610 A238 Set of 2 15.00 15.00

New Year 1995 (Year of the Boar) — A239

No. 1611: Stylized boars with Chinese inscriptions in: a, Green. b, Blue violet. c, White. d, Black.

10d, Three boars.

1995, May 4 ***Perf. 14½***

1611 A239 3d Sheet of 4, #a.-d. 3.50 3.50

Souvenir Sheet

1612 A239 10d multicolored 3.50 3.50

Water Birds A240

Designs: 2d, Great white egret. 8d, Hammerkop. 10d, Shoveler. 12d, Crowned crane.

No. 1617: a, Pintail. b, Fulvous tree duck (a). c, Garganey. d, White-faced tree duck. e, White-backed duck. f, Egyptian goose. g, Pigmy goose. h, Little bittern (k). i, Redshank. j, Ringed plover. k, Black-winged stilt. l, Squacco heron (k).

No. 1618, 25d, Ferruginous duck. No. 1619, 25d, Moorhen.

1995, May 8 ***Perf. 14***

1613-1616 A240 Set of 4 10.00 10.00
1617 A240 3d Sheet of 12, #a.-l. 11.00 11.00

Souvenir Sheets

1618-1619 A240 Set of 2 15.00 15.00

ECOWAS — A241

Designs: 2d, Free movement of people in Gambia. 5d, Captain Yaya AJJ Jammeh, Chairman of Arm Force Provisional Ruling Council, Head of State.

1995, May 30 **Litho.** ***Perf. 14***

1620 A241 2d multicolored .55 .55
1621 A241 5d multicolored 1.40 1.40

Marine Life A242

No. 1622, vert: a, Multicolored parrot fish. b, Sparisoma viride. c, Queen parrot fish. d, Bicolor parrot fish.

No. 1623: a, Leatherback turtle. b, Tiger shark. c, Surgeon fish. d, Emperor angelfish. e, Blue parro fish. f, Triggerfish. g, Sea horse. h, Lionfish. i, Moray eel. j, Red fin butterflyfish. k, Octopus. l, Ray.

No. 1624, 25d, Holacanthus ciliaris. No. 1625, 25d, Angelichthys isabelita.

1995, June 20

1622 A242 8d Strip of 4, #a.-d. 9.00 9.00
1623 A242 3d Sheet of 12, #a.-l. 10.00 10.00

Souvenir Sheets

1624-1625 A242 Set of 2 19.00 19.00

UN, 50th Anniv. — A243

No. 1626: a, 3d, Girls. b, 5d, Woman helping girl at blackboard. c, 8d, Girl writing on blackboard.

25d, Nurse holding baby on scales.

1995, July 6

1626 A243 Strip of 3, #a.-c. 3.50 3.50

Souvenir Sheet

1627 A243 25d multicolored 6.50 6.50

World War II Motion Pictures A244

No. 1628 — Movie stars: a, Peter Lawford. b, Gene Tierney, Dana Andrews. c, Groucho, Gummo Marx. d, James Stewart. e, Chico, Harpo Marx. f, Tyrone Power. g, Cary Grant, Ingrid Bergman. h, Veronica Lake.

Motion pictures: No. 1629, 25d, A Lady Fights Back. No. 1630, 25d, Desert Victory.

1995, July 6

1628 A244 3d Sheet of 8, #a.-h. + label 11.00 11.00

Souvenir Sheets

1629-1630 A244 Set of 2 11.50 11.50

VJ Day, 50th Anniv. A245

No. 1631: a, Fairey Firefly. b, Fairey Barracuda II. c, Vickers Supermarine Seafire II. d, HMS Repulse. e, HMS Illustrious. f, HMS Exeter.

25d, Bomber being shot down by 3-stack cruiser.

1995, Aug. 1
1631 A245 5d Sheet of 6, #a.-f. + label 9.25 9.25

Souvenir Sheet
1632 A245 25d multicolored 7.50 7.50

A246

Carrying sacks of grain: No. 1633a, 3d, Woman in pink. b, 5d, Two people. c, 8d, Man. 25d, Fisherman with net.

1995, Aug. 1 Litho. *Perf. 14*
1633 A246 Strip of 3, #a.-c. 3.75 3.75

Souvenir Sheet
1634 A246 25d multicolored 6.50 6.50

FAO, 50th Anniv. No. 1633 is a continuous design.

A247

Nobel Prize Winners: 2d, Kenichi Fukui, chemistry, 1981. 3d, Gustav Stresemann, peace, 1929. 5d, Thomas Mann, literature, 1929. 8d, Albert Schweitzer, peace, 1952. 12d, Leo Esaki, physics, 1973. 15d, Lech Walsea, peace, 1983.

No. 1635: a, Marie Curie, chemistry, 1911. b, Adolf Butenandt, chemistry, 1939. c, Tonegawa Susumu, medicine, 1987. d, Nelly Sachs, literature, 1966. e, Kawabata Yasunari, literature, 1968. f, Yukawa Hideki, physics, 1949. g, Paul Ehrlich, medicine, 1908. h, Sato Eisaku, peace, 1974. i, Carl von Ossietzky, peace, 1935.

25d, Willy Brandt, peace, 1971.

1995, Aug. 1
1634A-1634F A247 Set of 6 9.50 9.50
1635 A247 5d Sheet of 9, #a.-i. 10.50 10.50

Souvenir Sheet
1636 A247 25d multicolored 7.00 7.00

Rotary Intl., 90th Anniv. A248

Designs: 15d, Paul Haris, Rotary emblem. 20d, Natl. flag, Rotary emblem.

1995, Aug. 1
1637 A248 15d multicolored 3.25 3.25

Souvenir Sheet
1638 A248 20d multicolored 5.25 5.25

Miniature Sheets of 3

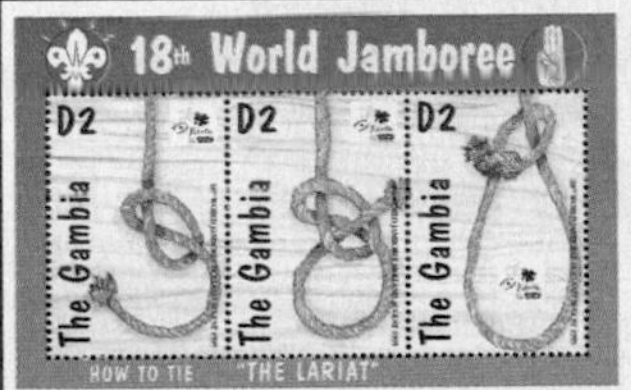
1995 Boy Scout Jamboree, Holland — A249

No. 1639 — How to tie the lariat: a, First step. b, Second step. c, Completed.

No. 1640 — How to tie bowline: a, 12d, First step. b, 10d, Second step. c, 5d, Completed.

No. 1641, 25d, Bowline used to lift injured scout. No. 1642, 25d, Hitch used in lifesaving lift.

1995, Aug. 1
1639 A249 2d Sheet of 3, #a.-c. 1.75 1.75
1640 A249 Sheet of 3, #a.-c. 8.00 8.00

Souvenir Sheets
1641-1642 A249 Set of 2 10.00 10.00

Queen Mother, 95th Birthday A250

No. 1643: a, Drawing. b, Bright blue hat, dress. c, Formal portrait. d, Green hat, dress. 25d, Pale blue & white dress, blue hat.

1995, Aug. 1 *Perf. 13½14*
1643 A250 5d Strip or block of 4, #a.-d. 4.50 4.50

Souvenir Sheet
1644 A250 25d multicolored 5.50 5.50

No. 1643 was issued in sheets of 8 stamps.

Nos. 1643-1644 exist with black frame and overprint in sheet margin "In Memoriam 1900-2002" in one or two lines.

1996 Summer Olympics, Atlanta A251

Designs: 1d, Bruce Jenner, US, decathlon. 1.25d, Greg Louganis, US, diving. 1.50d, Michael Gross, Germany 50-meter butterfly. 2d, Vasily Alexeev, USSR, weight lifting. 3d, Patrick Ewing, US, Juan Antonio Corbalan, Spain, basketball. 5d, Men's volleyball, US v. Brazil. 10d, John Svenden, West Germany, Armando Fernandez, US, water polo. 15d, Pertti Karppinen, Finland, single sculls.

No. 1653, vert: a, Stefano Cerioni, Italy, fencing. b, Alberto Covo, Italy, 10,000-meter run. c, Mary Lou Retton, US, women's gymnastics. d, Vladimir Artemov, USSR, men's gymnastics. e, Florence Griffith-Joyner, US, 400-meter relay. f, Brazil, soccer. g, Nelson Valis, US, 1000-meter sprint cycling. h, Cheryl Miller, US, women's basketball.

No. 1654, 25d, Karen Stives, US, equestrian. No. 1655, 25d, Edwin Moses, US, 400-meter hurdles, vert.

1995, Aug. 17
1645-1652 A251 Set of 8 11.00 11.00
1653 A251 3d Sheet of 8, #a.-h. 7.50 7.50

Souvenir Sheets
1654-1655 A251 Set of 2 15.00 15.00

Volleyball, cent. (No. 1650).

Rotary, Intl., 90th Anniv., 1995 Boy Scout Jamboree, Holland — A252

Designs: 2d, Gambia Rotary contributing to education. No. 1657, 5d, Wood Badge course, Yundum, 1980. No. 1658, 5d, M.J.E. Sambou, organizing scout commissioner, vert.

1995, Sept. 5
1656-1658 A252 Set of 3 3.50 3.50

Flowers — A253

Designs: 2d, Zantedeschia rehmannii. 5d, Eulophia eminens. 10d, Passiflora vitifolia. 15d, Dietes grandiflora.

No. 1663, 3d: a, Canarina abyssinica. b, Nerine bowdenii. c, Zantedeschia aethiopica. d, Aframomum sceptrum. e, Schotia brachypetala. f, Catharanthus roseus. g, Protea grandiceps. h, Plumbago capensis. i, Uncarina grandidieri.

No. 1664, 3d: a, Kigelia africana. b, Hibiscus schizopetalus. c, Dombeya mastersii. d, Agapanthus orientalis. e, Strelitzia reginae. f, Spathodea campanulata. g, Rhodolaena bakeriana. h, Gazania rigens. i, Ixianthes retzioides.

No. 1665, 25d, Eulophia quartiniana. No. 1666, 25d, Gloriosa simplex.

1995, Oct. 2 Litho. *Perf. 14*
1659-1662 A253 Set of 4 8.00 8.00

Sheets of 9, #a-i
1663-1664 A253 Set of 2 14.50 14.50

Souvenir Sheets
1665-1666 A253 Set of 2 15.00 15.00

SOS Children's Villages A254

Designs: No. 1667, 2d, Children playing near houses. No. 1668, 2d, Aid worker with child, vert. 5d, Children.

1995, Oct. 9 Litho. *Perf. 14*
1667-1669 A254 Set of 3 2.50 2.50

Entertainers A255

No. 1670: a, Roy Orbison. b, Mick Jagger. c, Bruce Springsteen. d, Jimi Hendrix. e, Bill Haley. f, Gene Vincent. g, Buddy Holly. h, Jerry Lee Lewis. i, Chuck Berry.

No. 1671: a-i, Various pictures of James Dean.

No. 1672, 25d, James Dean. No. 1673, 25d, Elvis Presley.

1995, Dec. 1 Litho. *Perf. 13½x14*
1670 A255 3d Sheet of 9, #a.-i. 9.00 9.00
1671 A255 3d Sheet of 9, #a.-i. 8.25 8.25

Souvenir Sheets
1672-1673 A255 Set of 2 16.00 16.00

Motion pictures, cent. (Nos. 1671-1672).

Christmas A256

Details or entire paintings: 75b, Madonna of the, Valley. 1d, Madonna, by Giotto. 2d, The Flight into Egypt, by Luca Giordano. 5d, The Epiphany, by Bondone. 8d, Virgin & Child, by Burgkmair. 12d, Madonna, by Bellini.

No. 1680, 25d, Mother and Child, by Rubens. No. 1681, 25d, The Christ, by Carpaccio.

1995, Dec. 18
1674-1679 A256 Set of 6 10.00 10.00

Souvenir Sheets
1680-1681 A256 Set of 2 16.00 16.00

Banjul Intl. Airport A257

Denominations: 1d, 2d, 3d, 5d.

1995, Dec. 21 Litho. *Perf. 14*
1682-1685 A257 Set of 4 3.50 3.50

UPU, 121st Anniv. — A258

Denominations: 1d, 2d, 3d, 7d.

1995, Dec. 21
1686-1689 A258 Set of 4 4.25 4.25

Marine Life A259

Designs: 2d, Commerson's dolphin. 5d, Narwhal. 8d, True's beaked whale. 10d, Rough-toothed dolphin.

No. 1694, 3d — Dolphins:a, Northern rightwhale. b, Spotted. c, Common. d, Pacific white-sided. e, Atlantic humpbacked. f, Atlantic white-sided. g, White-beaked. h, Striped. i, Risso's.

No. 1695, 3d — Whales: a, Bryde's. b, Sperm. c, Humpback. d, Sei. e, Blue. f, Gray. g, Fin. h, Killer. i, Right.

No. 1696, 25d, Beluga, clymene dolphin. No. 1697, 25d, Bowhead whale, dall's porpoise, blue shark.

1995, Dec. 22
1690-1693 A259 Set of 4 6.25 6.25

Sheets of 9, #a-i
1694-1695 A259 Set of 2 15.00 15.00

Souvenir Sheets
1696-1697 A259 Set of 2 13.50 13.50

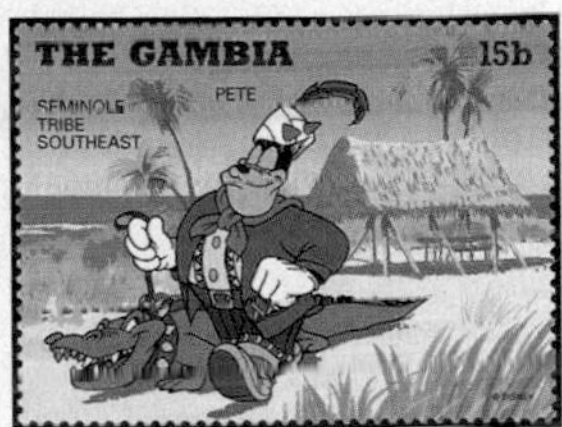
Cowboys and American Indians — A260

Disney characters portraying Amerian Indians or in western scenes: 15b, Pete, Seminole. 20b, Donald, Chinook. 25b, Huey, Dewey, Louie, Blackfoot. 30b, Sharp shooter Minnie. 40b, Bull-riding Donald. 50b, Cattle-branding Mickey. 2d, Donald, Tlingit. 3d, Bronco-busting Mickey. 12d, Trick-roping Grandma Duck. No. 1707, 15d, Goofy the ranch hand. No. 1708, 15d, Mickey, Pomo. 20d, Minnie, Goofy, Navaho.

No. 1710, 25d, Minnie, Massachusetts Tribe. No. 1711, 25d, Pluto singing, vert. No.

1712, 25d, Donald with rope around neck, vert. No. 1713, 25d, Minnie, Shoshoni, vert.

1995, Dec. 22 *Perf. 14x13½*
1698-1709 A260 Set of 12 18.50 18.50

Souvenir Sheets

1710-1713 A260 Set of 4 28.00 28.00

New Year 1996 (Year of the Rat) — A261

No. 1714 — Various stylized rats: a, 63b. b, 75b. c, 1.50d. d, 4d.
No. 1715: a, Like #1714a. b, Like #1714d. c, Like #1714c. d, Like #1714b.
No. 1716, Two rats.

1996, Jan. 2 *Perf. 14½*
1714 A261 Strip of 4, #a.-d. 3.00 3.00
1715 A261 3d Sheet of 4, #a.-d. 3.25 3.25

Souvenir Sheet

1716 A261 10d multicolored 4.50 4.50

No. 1714 issued in sheets of 16 stamps.

Paintings from Metropolitan Museum of Art — A262

No. 1717, 4d: a, Don Tiburcio Pérez y Cuervo, by Goya. b, Jean Antoine Moltedo, by J.A.D. Ingres. c, The Letter, by Corot. d, General Etienne Maurice Gerard, by J.L. David. e, Portrait of the Artist, by Van Gogh. f, Joseph Henri Altés, by Degas. g, Princess de Broglie, by Ingres. h, Lady at the Table, by Cassatt.
No. 1718, 4d: a, Broken Eggs, by Greuze. b, Johann Joachim Winckelmann, by Mengs. c, Col. George K.H. Coussmaker, by Reynolds. d, Self Portrait with Pupils, by Labille-Guiard. e, Courtesan Holding a Fan, by Utamaro. f, The Woodgatherers, by Gainsborough. g, Mr. Grace D. Elliott, by Gainsborough. h, The Drummond Children, by Raeburn.
No. 1719, 4d: a, Sunflowers, by Monet. b, Still Life with Pansies, by Fantin-Latour. c, Parisians Enjoying the Park, by Monet. d, La Mére Larchevêque, by Pissarro. e, Rue de L'Epicerie, Rouen, by Pissarro. f, The Abduction of Rebecca, by Delacroix. g, Daughter, Abraham-Ben-Chimol, by Delacroix. h, Christ on Lake of Gennesaret, by Delacroix.
No. 1720, 4d: a, Henry Frederick, Prince of Wales, by Peake. b, Saints Peter, Martha, Mary & Leonard, by Correggio. c, Marriage Feast at Cana, by Juan de Flandes. d, Portrait of one of Wedigh Family, by Holbein. e, Guilluame Budé, by Clouet. f, Portrait of a Cardinal, by El Greco. g, St. Jerome as a Cardinal, by El Greco. h, Portrait of a Man, by Titian.
No. 1721, 25d, The Harvesters, by Bruegel. No. 1722, 25d, The Creation of the World and the Expulsion from Paradise, by Giovanni de Paolo. No. 1723, 25d, Henry IV at the Battle of Ivry, by Rubens. No. 1724, 25d, The Israelites Gathering Manna in the Desert, by Rubens.

1996, Jan. 29 Litho. *Perf. 13½x14*

Sheets of 8, #a-h

1717-1720 A262 Set of 4 32.50 32.50

Souvenir Sheets

Perf. 14

1721-1724 A262 Set of 4 25.00 25.00

Nos. 1721-1724 each contain one 85x57mm stamp.
No. 1723 is actually in the Uffizi Gallery in Florence; No. 1724 in the Los Angeles County Museum of Art.
Nos. 1717-1724 exist imperf. Value, set of 8 sheets *$100.*

Traditional Fire Dance A263

Designs: 1d, Blowing fire from mouth, vert. 2d, Like 1d, diff. 3d, Holding sticks of fire at leg, vert. 7d, Holding out two sticks of fire.

1996, Jan. 29 Litho. *Perf. 14*
1725-1728 A263 Set of 4 4.50 4.50

Disney Characters Performing Good Deeds — A264

Designs: 1d, Community blood drive. 4d, Adopt-a-pet. 5d, Christmas giving for the needy. 10d, Teaching outdoor skills. 15d, Teaching reading. 20d, Volunteer fire fighters.
No. 1735, 25d, Highway volunteers. No. 1736, 25d, Counting whales.

1996, Apr. 12 Litho. *Perf. 13½x14*
1729-1734 A264 Set of 6 12.00 12.00

Souvenir Sheets

1735-1736 A264 Set of 2 12.00 12.00

Bruce Lee (1940-73), Martial Arts Expert — A265

No. 1737: Various portraits. 25d, In fighting stance.

1996, Apr. 1 Litho. *Perf. 14*
1737 A265 3d Sheet of 9, #a.-i. 8.00 8.00

Souvenir Sheet

1738 A265 25d multicolored 9.00 9.00

China '96, 9th Asian Intl. Philatelic Exhibition (No. 1737).

African Wildlife A266

15d, African civet.
No. 1740: a, Roan antelope. b, Lesser bush baby. c, Leopard. d, Guinea forest red colobus. e, Kob. f, Common eland.
No. 1741: a, African buffalo. b, Topi. c, Vervet. d, Hippopotamus. e, Waterbuck. f, Senegal chameleon. g, Western green mamba. h, Slender snouted crocodile (i). i, Adanson's mud turtle.
No. 1742, 25d, Lion. No. 1743, 25d, Chimpanzee.

1996, Apr. 15 Litho. *Perf. 14*
1739 A266 15d multicolored 3.25 3.25
1740 A266 3d Block of 6, #a.-f. 5.00 5.00
1741 A266 4d Sheet of 9, #a.-i. 7.50 7.50

Souvenir Sheets

1742-1743 A266 Set of 2 11.50 11.50

No. 1740 issued in sheets of 12 stamps.

Queen Elizabeth II, 70th Birthday A267

No. 1744: a, Portrait wearing blue dress. b, Wearing white dress, crown. c, Younger picture, crown.
25d, Buckingham Palace, horiz.

1996, May 9 Litho. *Perf. 13½x14*
1744 A267 8d Strip of 3, #a.-c. 4.75 4.75

Souvenir Sheet

Perf. 14x13½

1745 A267 25d multicolored 5.50 5.50

No. 1744 was issued in sheets of 9 stamps with each strip in a different order.

Classic Cars and Fire Engines A268

No. 1746, 4d — Classic cars: a, 1912 Fiat Tipo 510, Italy. b, 1936 Toyota Model 4B Phaeton, Japan. c, 1924 NAG C4B, Germany. d, 1903 Cadillac, US. e, 1925 Bentley, Great Britain. f, 1909 Renault Model AX, France.
No. 1747, 4d — Fire engines: a, 1850 Pumper Hose Cart, US. b, 1891 Steam Fire Engine, US. c, 1864 Lausitzer, Germany. d, 1902 Chemical Engine, Great Britain. e, 1904 Motor Fire Engine, Great Britain. f, 1860 Colonia No. 5, Germany.
No. 1748, 25d, 1917 Mitsubishi Model A, Japan. No. 1749, 25d, 1865 Amoskeag steamer, US.

1996, May 27 *Perf. 14*

Sheets of 6, #a-f

1746-1747 A268 Set of 2 11.50 11.50

Souvenir Sheets

1748-1749 A268 Set of 2 12.00 12.00

Euro '96, 1996 European Soccer Championships, England — A269

Team pictures: No. 1750, 2d, Bulgaria. No. 1751, 2d, Croatia. No. 1752, 2d, Czech Republic. No. 1753, 2d, Denmark. No. 1754, 2d, England. No. 1755, 2d, France. No. 1756, 2d, Germany. No. 1757, 2d, Holland. No. 1758, 2d, Italy. No. 1759, 2d, Portugal. No. 1760, 2d, Romania. No. 1761, 2d, Russia. No. 1762, 2d, Scotland. No. 1763, 2d, Spain. No. 1764, 2d, Switzerland. No. 1765, 2d, Turkey.
No. 1766, 25d,Hristo Stoitchkov, Bulgaria, vert. No. 1767, 25d, Davor Suker, Croatia, vert. No. 1768, 25d, Pavel Hapal, Czech Republic. No. 1769, 25d, 1992 Denmark team, European championship winners. No. 1770, 25d, Bryan Robson, England, vert. No. 1771, 25d, 1984 Championship cup won by French team, vert. No. 1772, 25d, Jüegen Klinsmann, Germany. No. 1773, 25d, Ruud Gullit, Holland, vert. No. 1774, 25d, Roberto Baggio, Italy, vert. No. 1775, 25d, Eusebio, Portugal, vert. No. 1776, 25d, Gheorge Hagi, Romania, vert. No. 1777, 25d, Oleg Salenko, Russia, vert.No. 1778, 25d, Gary McAllister, Scotland, vert. No. 1779, 25d, Juan Goikoetxea, Spain, vert. No. 1780, 25d, Christophe Ohrel, Switzerland, vert. No. 1781, 25d, Hami Mandirali, Turkey, vert.

1996, June 8 Litho. *Perf. 14*
1750-1765 A269 Set of 16 10.00 10.00

Souvenir Sheets

1766-1781 A269 Set of 16 100.00 100.00

Nos. 1750-1765 each exist in miniature sheets of 8 + 1 label.
See Nos. 1808-1819.

1996 Summer Olympic Games, Atlanta — A270

1912 Olympics, Stockholm: 1d, Ray Ewry, standing high jump. 2d, Fanny Durack, freestyle swimming. 5d, Stadium, scenes in Stocholm. 10d, Jim Thorpe, decathlon, pentathlon.
No. 1786, 3d — Winners in past Olympics: a, Japanese volleyball team, 1964. b, Li Neng, floor exercises, 1984. c, Sergei Bubka, pole vault, 1988. d, Nadia Comaneci, all around gymnastics, 1976. e, Edwin Moses, 400-meter hurdles, 1984. f, Vitaly Shcherbo, all around gymnastics, 1992. g, Evelyn Ashford, 100-meters, 1984. h, Muhammad Ali, light heavyweight boxing, 1960. i, Carl Lewis, C. Smith, 400-meters relay, 1984.
No. 1787, 3d — 1992 Olympians: a, Fu Mingxia, platform diving. b, Heike Henkel, high jump. c, Spanish soccer team. d, Jackie Joyner-Kersee, heptathlon. e, Tatiana Gutsu, all around gymnastics. f, Michael Johnson, 400-meters. g, Lin Li, 200-meter individual medley. h, Gail Devers, 100-meters. i, Mike Powell, long jump.
No. 1788, 25d, Michael Gross, swimming, 1984, 1988, horiz. No. 1789, 25d, Ulrike Meyfarth, high jump, 1972, 1984.

1996, July 18 Litho. *Perf. 14*
1782-1785 A270 Set of 4 3.25 3.25

Sheets of 9, #a-i

1786-1787 A270 Set of 2 8.00 8.00

Souvenir Sheets

1788-1789 A270 Set of 2 10.00 10.00

Jerusalem, 3000th Anniv. — A271

Designs: 1.50d, Roman costume, Pillar of Absalem. 2d, Turkish costume, Gate of Mercy. 3d, Greek costume, Church of the Holy Sepulcher. 10d, Western Wall of the Temple Mount, Hasidic costume.
25d, Emblem, King David Tower, vert.

1996, July 25
1790-1793 A271 Set of 4 5.00 5.00

Souvenir Sheet

1794 A271 25d multicolored 5.50 5.50

Radio, Cent. A272

Designs: 1d, Glenn Miller. 4d, Louis Armstrong. 5d, Nat King Cole. 10d, Andrews Sisters.
25d, Harry S Truman.

1996, July 25 *Perf. 13½x14*
1795-1798 A272 Set of 4 5.00 5.00

Souvenir Sheet

1799 A272 25d multicolored 5.50 5.50

UNICEF, 50th Anniv. — A273

Designs: 63b, Boy holding shoes. 3d, Girl receiving vaccination. 8d, Boy with soup ladle. 10d, Girl with blanket.
25d, Boy receiving vaccination, horiz.

1996, July 25 ***Perf. 14***
1800-1803 A273 Set of 4 4.25 4.25

Souvenir Sheet
1804 A273 25d multicolored 5.00 5.00

A274

A275

No. 1805: a, John F. Kennedy. b, Jacqueline Kennedy Onassis. c, Willy Brandt. d, Marilyn Monroe. e, Mao Tse Tung. f, Sung Ching Ling. g, Charles de Gaulle. h, Marlene Dietrich.
Nos. 1806-1807: Various portraits of Jacqueline Kennedy Onassis (1929-94).

1996, Aug. 22
1805 A274 5d Sheet of 8, #a.-h. 9.50 9.50
1806 A275 5d Sheet of 9, #a.-i. 11.00 11.00

Souvenir Sheet
1807 A274 25d multicolored 5.75 5.75

Nos. 1751-1752, 1754, 1756, 1758, 1761, 1767-1768, 1770, 1772, 1774, 1777 With Added Inscriptions

1996, Aug. 26
1808-1813 A269 Set of 6 3.50 3.50

Souvenir Sheets
1814-1819 A269 Set of 6 34.00 34.00

Nos. 1808-1813, each of which are 2d stamps, were issued in sheets of 8 + 1 label. Inscriptions on Nos. 1808-1813 and in sheet margins of Nos. 1814-1819, each of which are 25d stamps, show date of game, teams competing, and final score. Margin of the miniature sheets show additional information about individual games, and name of Germany as winner.
Team or team player shown as follows: Croatia (Nos. 1808, 1814), Czech Republic (Nos. 1809, 1815), England (Nos. 1810, 1816), Germany (Nos. 1811, 1817), Italy (Nos. 1812, 1818), Russia (Nos. 1813, 1819).

Richard Petty, NASCAR Driving Champion A276

No. 1820: a, 1969 Ford. b, Richard Petty. c, 1978 Dodge Magnum. d, 1987 Pontiac. e, 1989 Pontiac. f, 1975 Dodge Daytona.
25d, 1972 Plymouth.

1996, Aug. 27
1820 A276 5d Sheet of 6, #a.-f. 6.75 6.75

Souvenir Sheet
1821 A276 25d multicolored 5.00 5.00

No. 1821 contains one 85x28mm stamp.

Elvis Presley's 1st "Hit" Year, 40th Anniv. A277

Designs: Various portraits.

1996, Sept. 8 **Litho.** ***Perf. 13½x14***
1822 A277 5d Sheet of 6, #a.-f. 7.25 7.25

Supermarine S6B's Schneider Trophy Victory, 65th Anniv. — A278

No. 1823 — Spitfire aircraft: a, PR XIX, Royal Swedish Air Force. b, MK VB, US Army Air. c, MK VC, French Air Force. d, MK VB, Soviet Air Force. e, MK IXE, Netherlands East Indies Air Force. f, MK IXE, Israeli Defense Force. g, MK VIII, Royal Australian Air Force. h, MK VB, Turkish Air Force. i, PR XI, Royal Danish Air Force.
No. 1823J: k, K5054, first prototype aircraft. l, K9787, first production aircraft. m, MK 1A, "Battle of Britain." n, LF MK IXE, D-Day invasion markings. o, MK XII, first "Griffon" engined model. p, MK XIVC, SEAC markings. q, PR XIX, Royal Swedish Air Force. r, PR MK XIX. s, FMK 22/24 final variant.
No. 1824, The Supermarine S.6B S1595. No. 1824A, Supermarine S.6B S1595 seaplane.

1996, Sept. 13 **Litho.** ***Perf. 14***
1823 A278 4d Sheet of 9, #a.-i. 9.00 9.00
1823J A278 4d Sheet of 9, #k.-s. 9.00 9.00

Souvenir Sheets
1824 A278 25d multicolored 7.25 7.25
1824A A278 25d multicolored 7.25 7.25

Bob Dylan, Singer — A279

1996, Sept. 8 **Litho.** ***Perf. 14***
1825 A279 5d multicolored 1.60 1.60

Issued in sheets of 16.

Birds — A280

Designs: 50b, Egyptian plover. 63b, Painted snipe. 75b, Golden-breasted bunting. 1d, Bateleur. 1.50d, Didric cuckoo. 2d, European turtle dove. 3d, Village weaver. 4d, European roller. 5d, Cut-throat. 10d, Hoopoe. 15d, White-faced scops-owl. 20d, Narina trogan. 25d, Pied kingfisher. 30d, Common kestrel.

1996, Oct. 22 **Litho.** ***Perf. 14***
1826 A280 50b multicolored .40 .40
1827 A280 63b multicolored .45 .40
1828 A280 75b multicolored .50 .40
1829 A280 1d multicolored .75 .50
1830 A280 1.50d multicolored .90 .60
1831 A280 2d multicolored 1.00 .60
1832 A280 3d multicolored 1.10 .60
1833 A280 4d multicolored 1.25 .60
1834 A280 5d multicolored 1.40 .75
1835 A280 10d multicolored 1.50 1.00
1836 A280 15d multicolored 3.25 3.25
1837 A280 20d multicolored 4.50 4.50
1838 A280 25d multicolored 5.50 5.50
1839 A280 30d multicolored 8.00 8.00
Nos. 1826-1839 (14) 30.50 27.10

See Nos. 1898-1900.

Christmas A281

Details of painting, Assumption of the Madonna, by Titian: 1d, Watching assumption, cherub, clouds. 1.50d, Cherubs. 2d, Cherub. 3d, Cherub holding up cloud, outstretched arms below. 10d, People watching assumption. 15d, Cherubs pointing.
No. 1846, 25d, Madonna and Child with Two Angels, by Filippo Lippi, horiz. No. 1847, 25d, Virgin and Child with Infant St. John, by Raphael.

1996, Nov. 18 ***Perf. 13½x14***
1840-1845 A281 Set of 6 6.75 6.75

Souvenir Sheets
1846-1847 A281 Set of 2 10.00 10.00

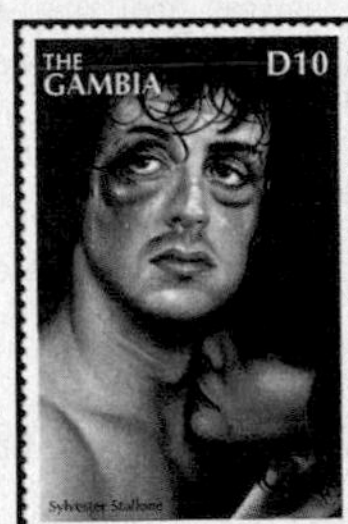

Sylvester Stallone in Movie, "Rocky" — A282

1996, Nov. 21 **Litho.** ***Perf. 14***
1848 A282 10d multicolored 2.00 2.00

Issued in sheets of 3.

Development Projects — A283

Designs: No. 1849, 63b, No. 1852, 2d, Arch 22, vert. 1d, Tractor, rice development project. 1.50d, Worker in rice paddy, vert. 3d, Banjul Intl. Airport Terminal Building. 5d, Chamoi Bridge.
20d, Workers in rice paddy. 25d, Statue in front of Arch 22, vert.

1996 **Litho.** ***Perf. 14***
1849-1854 A283 Set of 6 3.75 3.75

Souvenir Sheets
1855 A283 20d multicolored 4.00 4.00
1856 A283 25d multicolored 5.00 5.00

New Year 1997 (Year of the Ox) — A284

Nos. 1857-1858 — Various stylized oxen, background color: a, 63b, orange. b, 75b, purple. c, 1.50d, blue green. d, 4d, yellow orange. All stamps in No. 1858 are 3d.
10d, Ox with baby lying on its back.

1997, Jan. 16 ***Perf. 15***
1857 A284 Strip of 4, #a.-d. 2.00 2.00
1858 A284 3d Sheet of 4, #a.-d. 2.75 2.75

Souvenir Sheet
Perf. 14
1859 A284 10d multicolored 3.00 3.00

No. 1859 contains one 43x29mm stamp.

Mickey's Journey to the West — A285

Nos. 1860-1861: a-f, Scenes from Disney's "Monkey King."
No. 1862, Donald, Mickey, vert. No. 1863, Wu-Kong Sun (The Monkey King), monkeys, Mickey. No. 1864, Mickey, Intelligent Tortoise, Master San Tang. No. 1865, Mickey, Minnie obtaining Buddhist scriptures.

1997, Jan. 28 ***Perf. 14x13½***
1860 A285 2d Sheet of 6, #a.-f. 5.50 5.50
g. No. 1860 overprinted 5.50 5.50
1861 A285 3d Sheet of 6, #a.-f. 6.25 6.25
g. No. 1861 overprinted 7.00 7.00

Souvenir Sheets
1862 A285 5d multi 4.75 4.75
a. With marginal overprint 5.00 5.00
1863 A285 10d multi 4.75 4.75
a. With marginal overprint 5.00 5.00
1864 A285 10d multi 4.75 4.75
a. With marginal overprint 5.00 5.00
1865 A285 15d multi 4.75 4.75
a. With marginal overprint 5.00 5.00

Nos. 1860g, 1861g are overprinted in red in sheet margin: "70TH ANNIVERSARY OF MICKEY & MINNIE," and in black with "Happy Birthday," Mickey Mouse, and "1998" in emblem. Nos. 1862a, 1863a, 1864a, 1865a are overprinted in black in sheet margin with just "Happy Birthday" emblem.

Souvenir Sheet

Deng Xiaoping — A286

No. 1867, Like No. 1866.

1996, May 13 **Litho.** ***Perf. 13***
1866 A286 5d shown 5.25 5.25

Litho. & Embossed
Die Cut Perf. 9
Size: 95x56mm
1867 A286 300d gold

China '96. Nos. 1866-1867 were not available until March 1997.

Jackie Chan, Action Film Actor — A287

A287a

Various portraits.

1997, Feb. 12 *Perf. 14*

1868 A287 4d Sheet of 8, #a.-h. 8.00 8.00

Souvenir Sheet

1869 A287 25d multi, horiz. 7.00 7.00

Litho. & Embossed

Die Cut Perf. 9

Without Gum

1869A A287a 300d gold & multi

Endangered Species — A288

No. 1870, 1.50d: a, Clouded leopard. b, Audouin's gull. c, Leatherback turtle. d, White-eared pheasant. e, Kakapo. f, Right whale. g, Black-footed ferret. h, Dwarf lemur. i, Peacock pheasant. j, Brown hyena. k, Cougar. l, Gharial. m, Monk seal. n, Mountain gorilla. o, Blyth's tragopan. p, Malayan tapir. q, Black rhinoceros. r, Polar bear. s, Red colobus. t, Tiger.

No. 1871, 1.50d: a, Arabian oryx. b, Baiji. c, Ruffed lemur. d, California condor. e, Blue-headed quail-dove. f, Numbat. g, Congo peacock. h, White uakari. i, Eskimo curlew. j, Gouldian finch. k, Coelacanth. l, Toucan barbet. m, Snow leopard. n, Queen Alexandra's birdwing. o, Dalmatian pelican. p, Chaco tortoise. q, Medong catfish. r, Helmeted hornbill. s, White-eyed river martin. t, Fluminense swallowtail.

No. 1872, 25d, Giant panda. No. 1873, 25d, Humpback whale. No. 1874, 25d, Japanese crane.

1997, Feb. 24 **Sheets of 20, #a-t**

1870-1871 A288 Set of 2 18.50 18.50

Souvenir Sheets

1872-1874 A288 Set of 3 18.00 18.00

Hong Kong '97 (Nos. 1870-1871).

Jungle Book — A289

No. 1875: a, Monkey facing right. b, Bear. c, Elephant. d, Monkey facing left. e, Panther, butterfly. f, Buffalo. g, Mandrill. h, Tiger. i, Wolf. j, Cobra. k, Mongoose. l, Child's face, flower.

1997

1875 A289 3d Sheet of 12, #a.-l. 8.25 8.25

Mushrooms — A290

Designs: 1d, Polyporus squamosus. 3d, Armillaria tabescens. 5d, Collybia velutipes. 10d, Sarcoscypha coccinea.

No. 1880, vert: a, Amanita caesarea. b, Lepiota procera. c, Hygophorus psittacinus. d, Russula xerampelina. e, Laccaria amethystina. f, Coprinus micaceus. g, Boletus edulis. h, Morchella esculenta. i, Otidea auricula.

25d, Volvariella bombycina.

1997, Mar. 10 **Litho.** *Perf. 14*

1876-1879 A290 Set of 4 4.50 4.50

1880 A290 4d Sheet of 9, #a.-i. 7.75 7.75

Souvenir Sheet

1881 A290 25d multicolored 7.00 7.00

UNESCO, 50th Anniv. — A291

World Heritage sites: 1d, Horyu-Ji, Japan. 2d, Great Wall, China. 3d, City of Ayutthaya, Thailand. 4d, Ascension Convent, Santa Maria, Philippines. 10d, Dragons, Komodo Natl. Park, Indonesia. 15d, Timbuktu, Mali.

No. 1888, 4d, vert. — Various sites in Japan: a, g, h. Kyoto. b, Himeji-Jo. c, d, Horyu-Ji. e, f, Yakushma.

No. 1889, 4d, vert. — Various sites in China: a, b, c, Mogao Caves. d, e, Great Wall. f, g, h, Imperial Palace.

No. 1890, 4d, vert. — Various sites: a, Mt. Nimba Strict Nature Reserve, Guinea. b, Banc D'Argun Natl. Park, Mauritania. c, Marrakesh, Morocco. d, Ichkeul Natl. Park, Tunisia. e, Mali. f, Salonga Natl. Park, Zaire. g, Timgad, Algeria. h, Benin.

No. 1891, 5d — Various sites in Germany: a, b, c, Bamberg. d, e, Maulbronn.

No. 1892, 5d — Various sites in Greece: a, d, e, Ruins in Delphi. b, c, City of Rhodes.

No. 1893, 5d — Various sites in Japan: a, b, Shirakami-Sanchi. c, d, e, Himeji-Jo.

No. 1894, 25d, Cloisters, Santa Maria de Alcobaca, Portugal, No. 1895, 25d, Kyoto, Japan. No. 1896, 25d, Ruins of Kilwa Kisiwani, Tanzania. No. 1897, 25d, Plitvice Lakes Natl. Park, Croatia.

1997, Mar. 24

1882-1887 A291 Set of 6 7.25 7.25

Sheets of 8, #a-h, + Label

1888-1890 A291 Set of 3 20.00 20.00

Sheets of 5, #a-e, + Label

1891-1893 A291 Set of 3 15.50 15.50

Souvenir Sheets

1894-1897 A291 Set of 4 18.50 18.50

Bird Type of 1996

Designs: 40d, Temminck's courser. 50d, European bee-eater. 100d, Green-winged teal.

1997, Mar. 25 **Litho.** *Perf. 14*

1898 A280 40d multicolored 7.50 7.50

1899 A280 50d multicolored 9.50 9.50

1900 A280 100d multicolored 18.50 18.50

Nos. 1898-1900 (3) 35.50 35.50

Disney's 101 Dalmatians — A293

No. 1901, vert.1: a, Dipstick. b, Fidget. c, Jewel. d, Lucky. e, Two-Tone. f, Wizzer.

No. 1902: a-i, Various "Playful Puppies."

No. 1903: a-i, Various "Mischievous puppies."

No. 1904, 25d, Hiding under sheep. No. 1905, 25d, Cruella. No. 1906, 25d, Looking at picture. No. 1907, 25d, Distributing mail, vert. No. 1908, 25d, Into paint. No. 1909, 25d, Playing video game.

1997, May 1 *Perf. 13½x14, 14x13½*

1901 A293 50b Sheet of 6, #a.-f. 3.00 3.00

1902 A293 2d Sheet of 9, #a.-i. 6.00 6.00

1903 A293 3d Sheet of 9, #a.-i. 8.00 8.00

Souvenir Sheets

1904-1909 A293 Set of 6 42.50 42.50

Minnie Thru the Years — A294

No. 1910 — Minnie in various scenes dated: a, 1928. b, 1933. c, 1934. d, 1937. e, 1938. f, 1941. g, 1950. h, 1990. i, 1997.

25d, 1987.

1997, May 1 *Perf. 13½x14*

1910 A294 4d Sheet of 9, #a.-i. 12.00 12.00

Souvenir Sheet

1911 A294 25d multicolored 9.00 9.00

Juventus (World Club Soccer Champions), Cent. — A295

No. 1912: a, Juventus, 1897. b, Player from early years, emblems. c, Giampiero Boniperti. d, Roberto Bettega. e, European/ South American Cup, 1996. f, Drawing in celebration of cent.

1997, May 9 **Litho.** *Perf. 14x13½*

1912 A295 5d Sheet of 6, #a.-f. 6.50 6.50

Queen Elizabeth II, Prince Philip, 50th Wedding Anniv. A296

No. 1913: a, Queen. b, Royal Arms. c, Queen, Prince Philip. d, Queen holding flowers, Prince saluting. e, Royal Yacht Britannia. f, Prince Philip.

20d, Queen in red hat.

1997, May 20 *Perf. 14*

1913 A296 4d Sheet of 6, #a.-f. 6.00 6.00

Souvenir Sheet

1914 A296 20d multicolored 5.50 5.50

Paul P. Harris (1868-1947), Founder of Rotary Intl. — A297

Rotary emblem, portrait of Harris and: 10d, Tree of friendship planted by Sydney W. Pascall, Rotary Pres. 1931-32.

25d, Emblem, preserve planet earth.

1997, May 20 **Litho.** *Perf. 14*

1915 A297 10d multicolored 1.75 1.75

Souvenir Sheet

1916 A297 25d multicolored 5.00 5.00

Heinrich von Stephan (1831-97), Founder of UPU A298

No. 1917 — Portrait of von Stephan and: a, Otto von Bismarck. b, UPU emblem. c, Two-horse team and wagon, Boston, 1900.

25d, Hamburg-Lübeck postilion, 1828.

1997, May 20

1917 A298 5d Sheet of 3, #a.-c. 3.25 3.25

Souvenir Sheet

1918 A298 25d multicolored 5.50 5.50

PACIFIC 97.

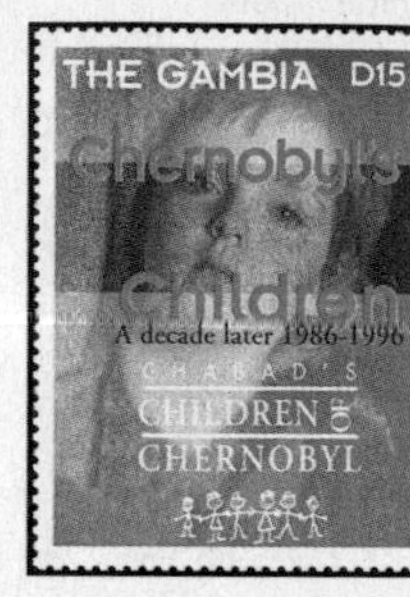

Chernobyl Disaster, 10th Anniv. A299

Designs: No. 1919, Chabad's Children of Chernobyl. No. 1920, UNESCO.

1997, May 20 **Litho.** *Perf. 13½x14*

1919 A299 15d multicolored 2.75 2.75

1920 A299 15d multicolored 2.75 2.75

Grimm's Fairy Tales A300

Mother Goose — A301

No. 1921 — Scenes from "Little Red Riding Hood": a, Grandmother's house. b, Little Red Riding Hood. c, Wolf.

No. 1922, Little Red Riding Hood, wolf, horiz. No. 1923, Girl seated on chair from "I'll Tell You a Story."

1997, May 20 *Perf. 13½x14*

1921 A300 10d Sheet of 3, #a.-c. 6.25 6.25

Souvenir Sheets

Perf. 14x13½

1922 A300 10d multicolored 4.00 4.00

Perf. 14

1923 A301 25d multicolored 4.75 4.75

Paintings, by Hiroshige (1797-1858)
A302

No. 1924, 4d: a, Morning Glory and Cricket. b, Dragonfly and Begonia. c, Two Ducks Swimming among Reeds. d, A Black-Naped Oriole Perched on a Stem of Rose Mallow. e, A Pheasant on a Snow-covered Pine. f, A Cuckoo Flying through the Rain.

No. 1925, 4d: a, An Egret among Rushes. b, Peacock and Peonies. c, Three Wild Geese Flying across the Moon. d, A Cock in the Snow. e, A Pheasant and Bracken. f, Peonies.

No. 1926, 4d: a, Sparrow and Bamboo. b, Mandarin Ducks on an Icy Pond with Brown Leaves Falling. c, Blossoming Plum Tree. d, Java Sparrow and Magnolia. e, Chinese Bell-flowers and Miscanthus. f, A Small Black Bird Clinging to a Tendril of Ivy.

No. 1927, 5d: a, Sparrows and Camellia in Snow. b, Parrot on a Branch of Pine. c, A Long-tailed Blue Bird on a Branch of Flowering Plum. d, Sparrow and Bamboo. e, Bird in a Tree. f, A Wild Duck Swimming beneath Snow-laden Reeds.

No. 1928, 5d: a, Kingfisher above a Yellow-flowered Water Plant. b, Wagtail and Roses. c, A Mandarin Duck on a Snowy Bank. d, A Japanese White-eye on a Persimmon Branch. e, Sparrows and Camellia in Snow. f, Kingfisher and Moon above a Yellow-flowered Water Plant.

No. 1929, 5d: a, Sparrow and Bamboo. b, Birds Flying over Waves. c, Blossoming Plum Tree with Full Moon. d, Kingfisher and Iris. e, A Blue-and-white Flycatcher on a Hibiscus Flower. f, Mandarin Ducks in Snowfall.

Unidentified paintings of: No. 1930, 25d, Falcon on perch. No. 1931, 25d, Two birds seated on branch. No. 1932, 25d, Kingfisher above Iris. No. 1933, 25d, Like #1925c. No. 1934, 25d, Bird on grapevine. No. 1935, 25d, Small bird in flowering tree.

1997, May 20 ***Perf. 14***

Sheets of 6, #a-f

1924-1926 A302 Set of 3 15.00 15.00
1927-1929 A302 Set of 3 19.00 19.00

Souvenir Sheets

1930-1935 A302 Set of 6 35.00 35.00

Return of Hong Kong & Macao to China — A303

No. 1936: a, Signing of joint declaration on question of Macao, 1987. b, Deng Xiaoping sharing toast with Portugal's Prime Minister Anibal Cavaco Silva after signing declaration. c, Deng Xiaoping, Britain's Prime Minister Margaret Thatcher sharing toast after signing Sino-British Declaration, 1984. d, Signing of the Sino-British Joint Declaration on question of Hong Kong, 1984.

No. 1937: a, Sir Henry Pottinger, 1st governor of Hong Kong, 1841-44, Hong Kong Island ceded to Britain, 1843. b, Sir Hercules Robinson, governor 1859-65, Kowloon ceded to Britain, 1860. c, Sir Henry Blake, governor 1898-1903, New Territories leased to Britain, 1899.

No. 1938: a, Ships in harbor, Sir Henry Pottinger. b, Suspension bridge, Chris Patten, governor of Hong Kong, 1992-1997. c, Skyline at night, C.H. Tung, first Chinese chief executive, 1997.

No. 1939: a, Signing of Treaty of Nanking, 1842. b, Signing of Japanese surrender document, 1945. c, Signing of Sino-British Joint Declaration on question of Hong Kong, 1984, diff.

1997, July 1

1936 A303 3d Sheet of 4, #a.-d. 2.75 2.75
1937 A303 4d Sheet of 3, #a.-c. 2.75 2.75
1938 A303 5d Sheet of 3, #a.-c. 3.00 3.00
1939 A303 6d Sheet of 3, #a.-c. 3.50 3.50

Wonders of the World — A304

Designs: 63b, Great Mosque at Samarra, Iraq, vert. (24x38mm). 75b, Moai stone faces, Easter Island. 1d, Golden Gate Bridge, San Francisco. 1.50d, Statue of Liberty, New York, vert. (24x38mm). 2d, Parthenon, Greece. 3d, Pyramid of the Sun, Teotihuacán, Mexico.

No. 1946, 5d: a, Rock of Gibraltar. b, St. Peter's Basilica, Vatican City. c, Santa Sophia, Istanbul. d, Gateway Arch, St. Louis. e, Great Wall of China. f, Carcassonne, France.

No. 1947, 5d: a, Stonehenge, England. b, Hughes HK-1 Hercules "Spruce Goose" airplane. c, Hoverspeed catamaran, Great Britain. d, Jet powered "Thrust 2." e, Djoser Step Pyramid, Egypt. f, Mallard steam locomotive.

No. 1948, 25d, Grand Canyon of the Colorado River, Arizona. No. 1949, 25d, Mt. Everest, Nepal. No. 1950, 25d, Washington Monument, Washington, DC.

1997, July 15

1940-1945 A304 Set of 6 4.00 4.00

Sheets of 6, #a-f

1946-1947 A304 Set of 2 16.00 16.00

Souvenir Sheets

1948-1950 A304 Set of 3 16.00 16.00

1998 Winter Olympics, Nagano
A305

Designs: 5d, Downhill skiing. 10d, Luge. 15d, Speed skating. 20d, Ice hockey.

No. 1955, 5d: a, Luge, diff. b, Ice hockey (goalie). c, 4-man bobsled. d, Ski jumping. e, Curling. f, Women's figure skating. g, Speed skating, diff. h, Biathlon. i, Downhill skiing, diff.

No. 1956, 5d, vert: a, 2-man bobsled. b, Free-style skiing. c, Speed skating, diff. d, Downhill skiing, diff. e, Women's figure skating, diff. f, Slalom skiing. g, Pairs figure skating. h, Cross-country skiing. i, Ski jumping, diff.

No. 1957, 25d, Female figure skater, vert. No. 1958, 25d, 2-man bobsled, diff.

1997, July 21 **Litho.** ***Perf. 14***

1951-1954 A305 Set of 4 10.00 10.00

Sheets of 9, #a-i

1955-1956 A305 Set of 2 20.00 20.00

Souvenir Sheets

1957-1958 A305 Set of 2 13.00 13.00

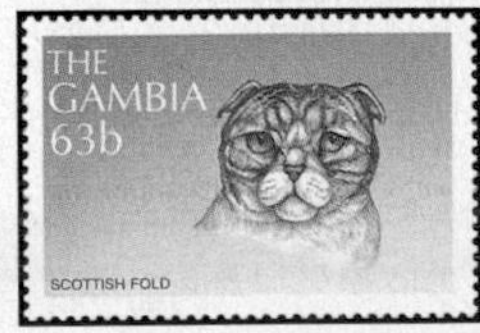

Cats
A306

Designs: 63b, Scottish fold. 1.50d, American curl. 2d, British bi-color. 3d, Devon rex. 6d, Silver tabby 20d, Abyssinian.

No. 1965: a, Burmilla. b, Blue Burmese. c, Korat. d, British tabby. e, Foreign white. f, Somali.

No. 1966, 25d, Cornish rex. No. 1967, 25d, Siamese.

1997, Aug. 12

1959-1964 A306 Set of 6 8.25 8.25
1965 A306 5d Sheet of 6, #a.-f. 7.50 7.50

Souvenir Sheets

1966-1967 A306 Set of 2 11.50 11.50

Dinosaurs
A307

Designs: 50b, Coelophysis, ornitholestes. 63b, Spinosaurus. 75b, Kentrosaurus. 1d, Ceratosaurus. 1.50d, Stygimoloch. 2d, Troodon. 3d, Velociraptor. 4d, Triceratops. 5d, Protoceratops. 10d, Ornithomimus. 15d, Stegosaurus. 20d, Ankylosaurus saichania.

No. 1980, 4d: a, Anurognathus. b, Pteranodon. c, Pterosaurus. d, Saltasaurus. e, Agathaumus. f, Stegosaurus. g, Albertosaurus libratus. h, 4 Lesothosaurus. i, 7 Lesothosaurus.

No. 1981, 4d: a, Tarbosaurus bataar. b, Brachiosaurus. c, Styracosasaurus. d, Baryonyx. e, Coelophysis. f, Carnotaurus. g, Compsognathus longipes. h, Compsognathus-elegant jaw. i, Stenonychosaurus.

No. 1982, 25d, Deinonychus. No. 1983, 25d, Seismosaurus.

1997, June 23 **Litho.** ***Perf. 14***

1968-1979 A307 Set of 12 16.00 16.00

Sheets of 9, #a-i

1980-1981 A307 Set of 2 13.50 13.50

Souvenir Sheets

1982-1983 A307 Set of 2 12.00 12.00

No. 1982 contains one 50x38mm stamp. No. 1983 contains one 89x28mm stamp.

Dogs
A308

Designs: 75b, Dalmatian. 1d, Rottweiler. 3d, Newfoundland. 4d, Great Dane. 10d, Old English sheepdog. 15d, Queensland heeler.

No. 1990: a, Akita. b, Welsh corgi. c, German shepherd. d, St. Bernard. e, Bullmastiff. f, Malamute.

No. 1991, 25d, Doberman pinscher. No. 1992, 25d, Boxer.

1997, Aug. 12

1984-1989 A308 Set of 6 8.25 8.25
1990 A308 5d Sheet of 6, #a.-f. 7.50 7.50

Souvenir Sheets

1991-1992 A308 Set of 2 11.50 11.50

1998 World Cup Soccer Championships, France — A309

Winning teams: 1d, Uruguay, 1950. 1.50d, W. Germany, 1954. 2d, Brazil, 1970. 3d, Brazil, 1962. 5d, Italy, 1938. 10d, Uruguay, 1930.

No. 1999, 4d: a, Brazil, 1994. b, Argentina, 1986. c, Brazil, 1970. d, Italy, 1934. e, Uruguay, 1958. f, England, 1966. g, Brazil, 1962. h, W. Germany, 1990.

No. 2000, 4d: a, Mario Kempes, Argentina, 1978. b, Ademir, Brazil, 1950. c. Muller, W. Germany, 1970. d, Lineker, England, 1986. e, Eusebio, Portugal, 1966. f, Schillaci, Italy, 1990. g, Lata, Poland, 1974. h, Rossi, Italy, 1982.

No. 2001, 4d, vert: a, Kinkladze, Georgia. b, Shearer, England. c, Dani, Portugal. d, Weah, Liberia. e, Ravanelli, Italy. f, Raducioiu, Romania. g, Peter Schmeichel, Denmark. h, Bergkamp, Holland.

No. 2002, 4d, vert: a, Moore, England, 1966. b, Fritzwalter, W. Germany, 1954. c, Beckenbauer, W. Germany, 1974. d, Zoff, Italy, 1982. e, Maradona, Argentina, 1986. f, Passarella, Argentina, 1978. g, Matthäus, W. Germany, 1990. h, Dunga, Brazil, 1994.

No. 2003, 25d, Pele, Brazil. No. 2004, 25d, Eusebio, Portugal. No. 2005, 25d, Juninho, Brazil. No. 2006, 25d, Philippe Albert, Belgium.

1997, Sept. 4 ***Perf. 14x13½, 13½x14***

1993-1998 A309 Set of 6 4.00 4.00

Sheets of 8, #a-h, + Label

1999-2002 A309 Set of 4 27.50 27.50

Souvenir Sheets

2003-2006 A309 Set of 4 22.50 22.50

Sea Birds
A310

Designs: 5d, Red-legged cormorant. 10d, Roseate tern. 15d, Blue-footed booby. 20d, Sanderling.

No. 2011: a, Brown pelican. b, Galapagos penguin. c, Red billed tropic bird. d, Little tern. e, Dunlin. f, Kittiwake. g, Atlantic puffin. h, Wandering albatross. i, Masked booby. j, Glaucous winged gull. k, Artic tern. l, Piping plover.

No. 2012, 23d, Osprey. No. 2013, 23d, Long-tailed skua.

1997, Aug. 4 **Litho.** ***Perf. 14***

2007-2010 A310 Set of 4 11.00 11.00
2011 A310 3d Sheet of 12, #a.-l. 9.50 9.50

Souvenir Sheets

2012-2013 A310 Set of 2 10.00 10.00

A311

Diana, Princess of Wales (1961-97) — A312

Various portraits.

1997, Nov. 26 **Litho.** ***Perf. 14***

2014 A311 10d Sheet of 4, #a.-d. 8.50 8.50

Souvenir Sheet

2015 A312 25d multicolored 5.25 5.25

Christmas
A313

Entire paintings or details: 1d, Angel, by Rembrandt. 1.50d, Initiation into the Rites of

Dionysus, in Villa dei Misteri, Pompeii. 2d, Pair of Erotes with Purple Cloaks. 3d, The Ecstasy of Saint Teresa, by Gianlorenzo Bernini (carving). 5d, Annunciation, by Mathias Grunewald. 10d, Angel Playing the Organ, by Stefan Lochner.

No. 2022, 25d, The Rest on the Flight into Egypt, by Caravaggio. No. 2023, 25d, Education of Cupid, by Titian.

1997, Dec. 8

2016-2021 A313 Set of 6 7.75 7.75

Souvenir Sheets

2022-2023 A313 Set of 2 9.50 9.50

New Year 1998 (Year of the Tiger) — A314

No. 2024 — Various stylized tigers with: a, Yellow brown background. b, Purple background. c, Brown background. d, Orange background.

10d, Tiger, landscape.

1998, Jan. 5 Litho. *Perf. 14½*

2024 A314 3d Sheet of 4, #a.-d. 2.75 2.75

Souvenir Sheet

Perf. 14

2025 A314 10d multicolored 2.75 2.75

No. 2025 contains one 38x24mm stamp.

Trains A315

No. 2026, 5d: a, Electric Train, Scotland. b, Beaconsfield, China. c, TGV, France. d, People Mover, England. e, ICE train, Germany. f, Montmartre Funicular, France.

No. 2027, 5d: a, SD70 Burlington Northern, US. b, Mallard, England. c, Baldwin 4-8-0, Peru. d, Sweden Rail. e, Rack Train, Amberawa-Java. f, Beyer-Peacock, Pakistan.

No. 2028, 25d, Monorail, England. No. 2029, 25d, Southern Pacific, US.

1998, May 19 Litho. *Perf. 14*

Sheets of 6, #a-f

2026-2027 A315 Set of 2 13.00 13.00

Souvenir Sheets

2028-2029 A315 Set of 2 9.50 9.50

Flowers A316

Designs, vert: 75b, Daffodil. 1.50d, Transvaal daisy. 3d, Torchlily. 4d, Ancistrochilus rothschildianus. 10d, Polystachya vulcanica. 15d, Gladiolus.

No. 2036: a, Adenium multiflorum. b, Huernia namaquensis. c, Gloriosa superba. d, Strelitzia reginae. e, Passiflora mollissima. f, Bauhinia variegata.

No. 2037, 25d, Aerangis rhodosticta, vert. No. 2038, 25d, Ansella gigantea, vert.

1998, June 2 Litho. *Perf. 14*

2030-2035 A316 Set of 6 8.00 8.00

2036 A316 5d Sheet of 6, #a.-f. 7.00 7.00

Souvenir Sheets

2037-2038 A316 Set of 2 11.00 11.00

Historical Aircraft A317

No. 2039, 5d: a, Short Type 38, 1913. b, Fokker F.VII B 3m, 1925. c, Junkers F-13, 1919. d, Pitcairn "Mailwing," 1927. e, Douglas, 1920. f, Curtiss "Condor," 1934.

No. 2040, 5d: a, Wright Brothers, 1903. b, Curtiss, 1910. c, Farman, 1907. d, Bristol, 1911. e, Antoinette, 1908. f, Sopwith "Bat Boat," 1912.

No. 2041, 25d, Albatross, 1913. No. 2042, 25d, Boeing 247, 1932.

1998, June 10 Sheets of 6, #a-f

2039-2040 A317 Set of 2 14.00 14.00

Souvenir Sheets

2041-2042 A317 Set of 2 11.00 11.00

Nos. 2041-2042 each contain one 85x28mm stamp.

Disney's "Mulan" A318

Characters from the animated movie — No. 2043: a, Mulan. b, Mushu. c, Little Brother. d, Cri-Kee. e, Grandmother Fa. f, Fa Li. g, Fa Zhou. h, Mulan and Khan.

No. 2044: a, Mulan riding Khan. b, Shang. c, Chi Fu. d, Chien-Po. e, Yao. f, Ling. g, Shan-Yu. h, Mulan, Shang & Mushu.

No. 2045, 25d, Mulan. No. 2046, 25d, Mulan riding Khan, diff. No. 2047, 25d, Mulan jumping in air. No. 2048, 25d, Mulan looking at Shang (in margin).

1998, July 1 Litho. *Perf. 13½x14*

2043 A318 4d Sheet of 8, #a.-h. 10.00 10.00

2044 A318 5d Sheet of 8, #a.-h. 10.50 10.50

Souvenir Sheets

2045-2048 A318 Set of 4 27.50 27.50

Ferrari Automobiles — A318a

No. 2048A: c, 365 GTB/4. d, Daytona. e, 1966 275 GTB.

25d, 365 GTB/4, diff.

1998, Oct. 29 Litho. *Perf. 14*

2048A A318a 10d Sheet of 3, #c-e 5.25 5.25

Souvenir Sheet

Perf. 13¾x14¼

2048B A318a 25d multi 4.50 4.50

No. 2048A contains three 39x25mm stamps.

Famous People — A319

No. 2049, 4d — Jazz musicians: a, Sidney Bechet (1897-1959). b, Bechet playing clarinet. c, "Duke" Ellington conducting band. d, Ellington (1899-1974). e, Louis Armstrong (1900-71). f, Armstrong playing trumpet. g, Charlie "Bird" Parker playing saxophone. h, Parker (1920-55).

No. 2050, 4d — Composers: a, Cole Porter (1893-1964). b, "Born to Dance," by Porter. c, "Porgy and Bess," by George Gershwin. d, Gershwin (1898-1937). e, Richard Rodgers (1902-79) & Oscar Hammerstein II (1895-1960). f, "The King and I," by Rodgers & Hammerstein. g, "West Side Story," by Leonard Bernstein. h, Bernstein (1918-90).

No. 2051, 25d, Ella Fitzgerald (1917-96). No. 2052, 25d, Irving Berlin (1888-1989), "Oh How I Hate to Get Up in the Morning."

1998, Oct. 12 Litho. *Perf. 14*

Sheets of 8, #a-h

2049-2050 A319 Set of 2 14.00 14.00

Souvenir Sheets

2051-2052 A319 Set of 2 13.00 13.00

Nos. 2049b-2049c, 2049f-2049g, 2050b-2050c, 2050f-2050g are 53x38mm.

Sinking of the Titanic — A320

No. 2053: a, Capt. Edward J. Smith. b, Molly Brown. c, News of the disaster breaks. d, Benjamin Guggenheim. e, Isidor Strauss. f, Ida Strauss.

No. 2054, 25d, Picture of ship on postcard. No. 2055, 25d, Ship sinking. No. 2056, 25d, Remains of ship lying on bottom of ocean years later.

1998, Oct. 25

2053 A320 5d Sheet of 6, #a.-f. 7.75 7.75

Souvenir Sheets

2054-2056 A320 Set of 3 18.00 18.00

Diana, Princess of Wales (1961-97) A321

No. 2057: a, Inscription panel at left. b, Panel at right.

1998, Oct. 29 *Perf. 14½x14*

2057 A321 10d Horiz. pair, a-b 3.50 3.50

Issued in sheets of 3 pairs.

Pablo Picasso (1881-1973) — A322

Paintings: 3d, Death of Casagemas, 1901. 5d, Seated Woman, 1920, vert. 10d, Mother and Child, 1907, vert.

25d, Child Playing with a Toy Truck, 1953, vert.

1998, Oct. 29 *Perf. 14½*

2058-2060 A322 Set of 3 3.25 3.25

Souvenir Sheet

2061 A322 25d multicolored 4.50 4.50

A323

No. 2062 — Mahatma Gandhi (1869-1948) : a, Age 62, 1932. b, Age 60, 1930, with Sarojini Naidu. c, Age 61, 1931, spinning yarn. d, Age 47, 1916.

25d, Age 61, 1931.

1998, Oct. 29 *Perf. 14*

2062 A323 10d Sheet of 4, #a.-d. 7.50 7.50

Souvenir Sheet

2063 A323 25d multicolored 5.00 5.00

Nos. 2062b-2062c are 53x39mm.

A324

Ships: 2d, Chinese Junk. 3d, HMS Victory. 10d, County Class Destroyer. 15d, Viking Longboat.

No. 2068, 5d, horiz: a, HMS Dreadnought. b, Truxton Class Cruiser. c, Queen Mary. d, Canberra. e, Queen Elizabeth. f, Queen Elizabeth 2.

No. 2069, 5d: a, Santa Maria. b, Mary Rose. c, Mayflower. d, Ark Royal. e, HMS Beagle. f, HMS Bounty.

No. 2070, 25d, Cutty Sark. No. 2071, 25d, Sovereign of the Seas.

1998

2064-2067 A324 Set of 4 5.50 5.50

Sheets of 6, #a-f

2068-2069 A324 Set of 2 11.00 11.00

Souvenir Sheets

2070-2071 A324 Set of 2 9.00 9.00

No. 2070 contains one 42x56mm stamp; No. 2071, one 56x42mm stamp.

1998 World Scouting Jamboree, Chile — A325

No. 2072: a, Scout handclasp. b, Small boat sailing. c, Scout salute.

No. 2073, Lord Robert Baden-Powell.

1998, Oct. 29 Litho. *Perf. 14*

2072 A325 10d Sheet of 3, #a.-c. 5.50 5.50

Souvenir Sheet

2073 A325 25d multicolored 4.50 4.50

Royal Air Force, 80th Anniv. A326

No. 2074, 5d: a, Sepecat Jaguar GR1. b, BAe Harrier GR7. c, Panavia Tornado GR1 firing Sidewinder AIM 9-L missle. d, Panavia Tornado GR1 on afterburner.

No. 2075, 5d: a, Sepecat Jaguar GR1A in low visibility gray finish. b, Panavia Tornado GR1A. c, Sepecat Jaguar GR1A in Bosnia theater camouflage finish. d, BAe Hawk 200.

No. 2076, 7d: a, Panavia Tornado GR1 flying left. b, BAe Hawk TIA. c, Sepecat Jaguar GR1A. d, Panavia Tornado GR1 flying right.

No. 2077, 20d, Eurofighters. No. 2078, 25d, Biplane, hawk's head. No. 2079, 25d, Lightning, Eurofighter. No. 2080, 25d, Biplane, hawk in flight. No. 2081, 25d, Lancaster, Eurofighter. No. 2082, 25d, Biplane, hawk perched.

1998, Oct. 29 Sheets of 4, #a-d

2074-2076 A326 Set of 3 12.50 12.50

Souvenir Sheets

2077-2082 A326 Set of 6 27.50 27.50

Paintings by Eugène Delacroix (1798-1863) — A327

No. 2083, 4d: a, Mule Drivers from Tetuan, b, Encampment of Arab Mule Drivers. c, An Orange Seller. d, The Banks of the River. e, View of Tangier from the Seashore. f, Arab Horses Fighting in a Stable. g, Horses at the Trough. h, The Combat of the Giaour and Hassan.

No. 2084, 4d, vert: a, Moroccan from Tangier Standing. b, A Man of Tangier. c, Young Arab Standing with a Rifle. d, Moroccan Chieftan. e, Jewish Bride of Tangiers. f, Seated Jewess from Morocco. g, A seated Arab. h, Young Arab Seated by a Wall.

No. 2085, 4d: a, Turk Seated on a Sofa Smoking. b, View of Tangier from North African and Spanish Album. c, The Spanish Coast at Salobrena from North African and Spanish Album. d, The Aissaouas. e, Sea View from the Heights of Dieppe. f, An Arab Fantasy. g, Arab Comic Fantasy. h, An Arab Camp at Night.

Details: No. 2086, 25d, Self-portrait, vert. No. 2087, 25d, Two Women of Algiers in Their Apartment. No. 2088, 25d, Massacre of Chios.

1998, Oct. 29 — Sheets of 8, #a-h

2083-2085 A327 Set of 3 19.50 19.50

Souvenir Sheets

2086-2088 A327 Set of 3 14.00 14.00

Christmas — A328

Designs: 1d, Beagle in sock. 2d, Giraffe, wreath. 3d, Rainbow bee eater, ribbon, ornament. 4d, Adult deer. 5d, Fawn. 10d, Irish red and white setter in package.

No. 2095, 25d, Brown classic tabby kitten. No. 2096, 25d, Basset hound, rough collie.

1998, Nov. 23

2089-2094 A328 Set of 6 5.00 5.00

Souvenir Sheets

2095-2096 A328 Set of 2 9.00 9.00

New Year 1999 (Year of the Rabbit) — A329

No. 2097 — Stylized rabbits, background color: a, Olive brown. b, Green blue. c, Red brown. d, Pale orange.

1999, Jan. 4 Litho. *Perf. 14½*

2097 A329 3d Sheet of 4, #a.-d. 2.40 2.40

Souvenir Sheet

2098 A329 10d multicolored 2.25 2.25

No. 2098 contains one 39x24mm stamp.

Disney's Jungle Book A330

No. 2099: a, Mowgli, King Louie (bear). b, Mowgli, snake, c, Flunky Monkey. d, Monkey singing. e, Girl. f, Mowgli, Flunky Monkey. g, Mowgli, buzzards. h, Shere Khan (tiger).

No. 2100, 25d, Baby elephant, horiz. No. 2101, 25d, King Louie, horiz.

1999, Mar. 11 Litho. *Perf. 13½x14*

2099 A330 5d Sheet of 8, #a.-h. 11.00 11.00

Souvenir Sheets

2100-2101 A330 Set of 2 11.00 11.00

Australia '99, World Stamp Expo A331

No. 2102, 6d — African butterflies: a, Golden piper. b, Citrus swallowtail. c, Azure hairstreak. d, Two-tailed pasha. e, Blue pansy. f, African leaf butterfly.

No. 2103, 6d: a, Plain tiger. b, Blue swallowtail. c, Papilio mnesheus. d, Common opal. e, Forest green. f, Boisduval's false acraea.

No. 2104, 25d, Pirate butterfly, vert. No. 2105, 25d, Two-tailed pasha, vert.

1999, Apr. 12 Litho. *Perf. 14*

Sheets of 6, #a-f

2102-2103 A331 Set of 2 13.00 13.00

Souvenir Sheets

2104-2105 A331 Set of 2 9.00 9.00

Wedding of Prince Edward and Sophie Rhys-Jones A332

No. 2106 — Various portraits of couple showing Sophie with: a, Blue collar. b, Long hair. c, Red collar.

25d, Couple, horiz.

1999, June 19 Litho. *Perf. 13½*

2106 A332 10d Sheet of 3, #a.-c. 5.00 5.00

Souvenir Sheet

2107 A332 25d multicolored 4.50 4.50

IBRA '99, World Philatelic Exhibition, Nuremberg — A333

Exhibition emblem, Adler 2-3-2 steam engine and: 4d, Samoa #104d. 5d, Samoa #55.

Emblem, sailing ship Friedrech August and: 10d, Samoa #64, #65. 15d, Samoa #67.

25d, Cover with Samoa #67 (part), 68.

1999, July 6 *Perf. 14x14¼*

2108-2111 A333 Set of 4 6.50 6.50

Souvenir Sheet

2112 A333 25d multicolored 4.50 4.50

No. 2112 contains one 60x40mm stamp.

Apollo 11 Moon Landing, 30th Anniv. — A334

No. 2113: a, Bell X-14A VTOL aircraft. b, Lunar landing practice rig. c, Early prototype lander. d, Zero gravity training. c, Jet pack training. f, Lunar lander pilot training.

No. 2114, 25d, Apollo 11 Eagle, horiz. No. 2115, 25d, Apollo 11 splash down, horiz.

1999, July 6 *Perf. 14*

2113 A334 6d Sheet of 6, #a.-f. 6.50 6.50

Souvenir Sheets

2114-2115 A334 Set of 2 10.00 10.00

Souvenir Sheets

PhilexFrance '99, World Philatelic Exhibition — A335

Early railroads: No. 2116, 25d, Road-railer carriage. No. 2117, 25d, 2-2-2 Passenger locomotive, 1846.

1999, July 6 *Perf. 13¾*

2116-2117 A335 Set of 2 10.00 10.00

Roots Homecoming Festival — A336

Designs: 1d, Cannon, Freedom Post, Jufureh. 2d, Fort Bullen, Barra. 3d, James Fort Island.

1999, June 21 Litho. *Perf. 14*

2118-2120 A336 Set of 3 1.25 1.25

UN Rights of the Child, 10th Anniv. — A337

No. 2121 — Children: a, With head down on table. b, Drinking from cup. c, Drawing on paper.

25d, Child smiling under umbrella.

1999, July 6

2121 A337 10d Sheet of 3, #a.-c. 5.50 5.50

Souvenir Sheet

2122 A337 25d multicolored 4.50 4.50

Johann Wolfgang von Goethe (1749-1832), Poet — A338

No. 2123: a, Faust quaffs the spirit's nectar. b, Portraits of Goethe and Friedrich von Schiller (1759-1805). c, Faust contemplates mortality.

25d, Portrait of Goethe, vert.

1999, July 6

2123 A338 15d Sheet of 3, #a.-c. 8.00 8.00

Souvenir Sheet

2124 A338 25d multicolored 4.50 4.50

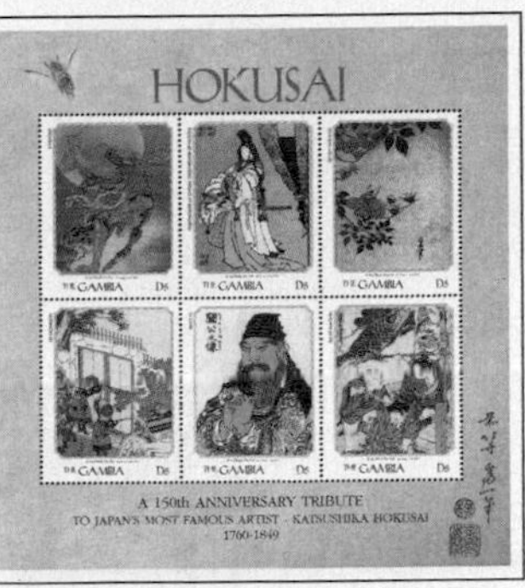

Paintings by Hokusai (1760-1849) — A339

No. 2125, 5d — Details or entire paintings: a, Bunshosei. b, Overthrower of Castles, Overthrower of Nations. c, Bee on Wild Rose. d, Sei Shonagon. e, Kuan-Yu. f, The Fifth Month.

No. 2126, 5d: a, Exotic Beauty. b, Wind (2 people). c, Dancing Monkey. d, Lady and Maiden on an Outing. e, Wind (3 people). f, Courtesan with Fan.

No. 2127, 25d, People on the Balcony of Sazaido. No. 2128, 25d, Caocao before the Battle of Chibi.

1999, July 6 *Perf. 13¾*

Sheets of 6, #a-f

2125-2126 A339 Set of 2 12.00 12.00

Souvenir Sheets

2127-2128 A339 Set of 2 10.00 10.00

Sea Birds A340

Designs: 2d, American oystercatcher. 3d, Blue-footed booby. 10d, Western gull. 15d, Brown pelican.

No. 2133, 4d: a, Atlantic puffin. b, Red-tailed tropicbird. c, Reddish egret. d, Laughing gull. e, Great white egret. f, Northern gannet. g, Forster's tern. h, Great cormorant. i, Razor bill.

No. 2134, 4d: a, Adélie penguin. b, Black skimmer. c, Erect-crested penguin. d, Heerman's gull. e, Glaucous-winged gull. f, Layson albatross. g, White pelican. h, Tufted puffin. i, Black guillemot.

No. 2135: a, Razor bill. b, Shelduck. c, Sandwich tern. d, Arctic skua. e, Gannet. f, Common gull.

No. 2136, 25d, Pelicans. No. 2137, 25d, California gull. No. 2138, 25d, Gentoo penguin.

1999, Aug. 1 *Perf. 14*

2129-2132 A340 Set of 4 5.50 5.50

Sheets of 9, #a-i

2133-2134 A340 Set of 2 14.50 14.50

2135 A340 5d Sheet of 6, #a.-f. 10.00 10.00

Souvenir Sheets

2136-2138 A340 Set of 3 15.00 15.00

Nos. 2135-2138 have continuous designs.

Prehistoric Amimals — A341

No. 2139, 3d: a, Diatryma. b, Pteranodon. c, Stegodon. d, Icaronycteris. e, Archaeopteryx. f, Chasmatosaurus. g, Tytthostonyx. h, Hyaenodon. i, Uintatherium. j, Hesperocyon. k, Ambelodon. l, Indricotherium.

No. 2140, 3d: a, Carnotaurus. b, Quetzalcoatlus. c, Peteinosaurus. d, Prenocephale. e, Hesperornis. f, Coelophysis. g,

Camptosaurus. h, Panderichthys. i, Garudimimus. j, Cacops. k, Ichthyostega. l, Scutellosaurus.

No. 2141, 25d, Lepisosteus. No. 2142, 25d, Sabertooth cat. No. 2143, 25d, Deinonychus. No. 2144, 25d, Microceratops.

1999, Aug. 1 Sheets of 12, #a-l

2139-2140 A341 Set of 2 12.00 12.00

Souvenir Sheets

2141-2144 A341 Set of 4 19.00 19.00

Queen Mother, 100th Birthday (in 2000) — A342

No. 2145: a, Duchess of York, Princess Elizabeth, 1928. b, Lady Elizabeth Bowles-Lyon, 1923. c, Queen Elizabeth, 1946. d, Queen Mother, Prince Harry.

25d, Queen Mother celebrating 89th birthday, 1989.

1999, Aug. 4

2145 A342 10d Sheet of 4, #a.-d. + label 7.25 7.25

Souvenir Sheet

Perf. 13¾

2146 A342 25d multicolored 5.00 5.00

No. 2146 contains one 38x51mm stamp. Margins of sheets are embossed.

See Nos. 2555-2556.

Orchids — A343

Designs: 2d, Sophrocattleya. 3d, Cattleya. 4d, Brassolaeliocattleya. 5d, Brassoepidendrum. 10d, Sophrolaeliocattleya. 15d, Iwanagaara.

No. 2153, 6d: a, Brassolaeliocattleya (yellow). b, Cattleytonia. c, Laeliocattleya (yellow). d, Miltonia. e, Cattleya forbesii. f, Odontoglossum cervantesii.

No. 2154, 6d: a, Lycaste macrobulbon. b, Laeliocattleya (red). c, Brassocattleya (pink). d, Cattleya, diff. e, Brassocattleya (speckled). f, Brassolaeliocattleya (yellow & red).

No. 2155, 25d, Unnamed. No. 2156, 25d, Brassolaeliocattleya (white & red).

1999, Aug. 1 Litho. *Perf. 14*

2147-2152 A343 Set of 6 7.25 7.25

Sheets of 6, #a-f

2153-2154 A343 Set of 2 14.00 14.00

Souvenir Sheets

2155-2156 A343 Set of 2 11.00 11.00

Marine Fauna A344

Designs: 1d, Sea gull. 1.50d, Portuguese man-of-war. 5d, Walrus. 10d, Manatee.

No. 2161, 3d: a, Anglefish. b, Leafy sea dragon. c, Hawksbill turtle. d, Mandarin fish. e, Candy cane sea star. f, Plate coral. g. Butterflyfish. h, Coral polyp. i, Hermit crab. j, Strawberry shrimp. k, Giant blue clam. l, Sea cucumber.

No. 2162, 3d: a, Whale shark. b, Gray reef shark. c, New ZEngland octopus. d, Puffer fish. e, Lionfish. f, Squid. g, Chambered nautilus. h, Clown fish. i, Moray eel. j, Spiny lobster. k, Sotted ray. l, Clown anemone.

25d, Common dolphin.

1999, Aug. 1

2157-2160 A344 Set of 4 3.50 3.50

Sheets of 12, #a-l

2161-2162 A344 Set of 2 13.00 13.00

2163 A344 25d multicolored 5.00 5.00

Galapagos Islands Marine Fauna — A345

No. 2164: a, Swallow-tailed gull. b, Frigate bird. c, Red-footed booby. d, Galapagos hawk. e, Great blue heron. f, Masked booby. g, Bottlenose dolphins. h, Black grunts. i, Surgeonfish. j, Stingray. k, Pilot whales. l, Pacific green sea turtle. m, Shark. n, Sea lion. o, Marine iguana. p, Pacific manta ray. q, Moorish idol. r, Galapagos penguin. s, Silver grunts. t, Sea urchin. u, Wrasse. v, Almaco amberjack. w, Blue-chin parrotfish. x, Yellow sea urchin. y, Lobster. z, Grouper. aa, Coer pionfish. ab, Squirrelfish. ac, Octopus. ad, King angelfish. ae, Horned shark. af, Galapagos hogfish. ag, Puffer fish. ah, Moray eel. ai, Orange tube corals. aj, Whitestripe chromis. ak, Longnose hawkfish. al, Sea cucumber, am, Spotted hawkfish. an, Zebra moray eel.

25d, Emperor penguins.

1999, Aug. 1

2164 A345 1.50d Sheet of 40, #a.-an. 15.00 15.00

Souvenir Sheet

2165 A345 25d multicolored 5.25 5.25

Souvenir Sheet

1999 Return of Macao to People's Republic of China — A346

No. 2166: a, Temple of A-ma. b, Border gate. c, Ruins of St. Paul's Cathedral.

1999, Aug. 20 Litho. *Perf. 14*

2166 A346 7d Sheet of 3, #a-c 4.00 4.00

Space Exploration A347

Designs: 1d, Telstar I, horiz. 1.50d, Skylab. 2d, Mars 3 orbiter and lander. 3d, COBE. 10d, Astronaut Bruce McCandless. 15d, Apollo 13.

No. 2173, 6d: a, German V-2 rocket. b, Delta Straight 8. c, Ariane 4. d, Mercury on Atlas rocket. e, Saturn 1B. f, Cassini.

No. 2174, 6d, horiz.: a, Mariner 4. b, Viking Mars orbiter and lander. c, Giotto. d, Luna 9. e, Voyager. f, Galileo.

No. 2175, 6d, horiz.: a, Soviet Vostok 1. b, Apollo command and service modules. c, Mecury capsule. d, Apollo 16 lunar module. e, Gemini 8. f, Soviet Soyuz.

No. 2176, 25d, Apollo-Soyuz, horiz. No. 2177, 25d, Mars Pathfinder, horiz.

1999

2167-2172 A347 Set of 6 6.00 6.00

Sheets of 6, #a-f

2173-2175 A347 Set of 3 20.00 20.00

2176-2177 A347 Set of 2 12.00 12.00

Nos. 2176-2177 each contain one 57x43mm stamp.

John F. Kennedy, Jr. (1960-99) A348

No. 2178: a, In 1961. b, In 1970s. c, In 1997.

1999, Dec. 7

2178 A348 15d Sheet of 3, #a.-c. 7.25 7.25

Flowers A349

Various flower photographs making up a photomosaic of Princess Diana.

1999, Dec. 31 Litho. *Perf. 13¾*

2179 A349 3d Sheet of 8, #a.-h. 5.00 5.00

See No. 2290.

Millennium A350

No. 2180, 3d — Highlights of 1450-1500: a, Da Vinci designs 1st flying machine. b, Gutenberg prints the Bible. c, 1st book in color printed. d, Ivan III becomes Grand Prince of Moscow. e, Ottomans capture Constantinople. f, Ming emperors rebuild Great Wall of China. g, Lorenzo de Medici begins rule in Florence. h, Henry VII becomes first Tudor king of England. i, Vasco da Gama sails to India. j, Aragon and Castile unite. k, Birth of Desiderius Erasmus. l, Cabot explores No. America. m, Henry VI wages War of the Roses. n, Bartholomeu Dias discovers Cape of Good Hope. o, Matthias Corvinus (Hunyadi) becomes king of Hungary. p, Columbus sails to America (60x40mm). q, Girolamo Savonarola burned at stake.

No. 2181, 3d — Highlights of 1900-1910: a, Max Planck develops quantum theory. b, Graf Ferdinand von Zeppelin constructs first airship. c, Marconi sends 1st transatlantic message. d, Queen Victoria dies. e, 1st Nobel Prize. f, Boer War ends. g, Wright Brothers' 1st flight. h, 1st teddy bears made in Germany. i, Work begins on Panama Canal. j, Einstein develops theory of relativity. k, 1905 revolution in Russia. l, San Francisco earthquake. m, Color photography developed by Louis Lumière. n, Picasso paints "Les Demoiselles d'Avignon." o, Peary reaches North Pole. p, Model T appears (60x40mm). q, 1st kibbutz founded in Holy Land.

2000, Feb. 1 *Perf. 12¾x12½*

Sheets of 17, #a-q

2180-2181 A350 Set of 2 19.00 19.00

Inscriptions are misspelled on several stamps on No. 2181.

New Year 2000 (Year of the Dragon) A351

No. 2182 — Various dragons and Chinese characters with background colors: a, Blue green. b, Brownish gray. c, Red orange (purple dragon). d, Orange.

15d, Dull orange.

2000, Feb. 5 *Perf. 14x14½*

2182 A351 5d Sheet of 4, #a.-d. 4.25 4.25

Souvenir Sheet

Perf. 14

2183 A351 15d multi 3.00 3.00

No. 2183 contains one 42x28mm stamp.

African Wildlife A352

Designs: 50b, Indri. 75b, Nubian ibex. 1d, Grevy's zebra, vert. 2d, Bongo, vert. 3d, White rhinoceros. 4d, Lesser galago. 5d, Okapi, vert. 10d, Mhorr gazelle, vert.

No. 2192, 5d: a, Giant sable antelope. b, Greater kudu. c, Somali wild ass. d, Dorcas gazelle. e, Addax. f, Pelzeln's gazelle.

No. 2193, 6d: a, Cheetah. b, Chimpanzee. c, Angwantibo. d, Black rhinoceros. e, Bontebok. f, Giant eland.

No. 2194, 7d: a, Mountain gorilla. b, Black-faced impala. c, Crowned lemur. d, Long-tailed ground roller. e, Brown hyena. f, Mountain zebra.

No. 2195, 7d: a, Sacred ibis. b, Mauritius kestrel. c, Barbary leopard. d, Radiated tortoise. e, Pygmy hippopotamus. f, Bald ibis.

No. 2196, 25d, Aye-aye. No. 2197, 25d, Black lechwe, vert. No. 2198, 25d, Nile crocodile. No. 2199, 25d, African elephant.

2000, Feb. 18 *Perf. 14*

2184-2191 A352 Set of 8 4.50 4.50

Sheets of 6, #a.-f.

2192-2195 A352 Set of 4 27.50 27.50

Souvenir Sheets

2196-2199 A352 Set of 4 22.50 22.50

AmeriStamp Expo, Portland, Ore. (No. 2194).

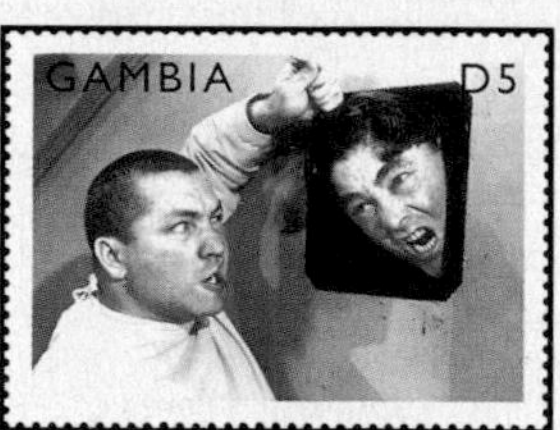

The Three Stooges — A353

No. 2200: a, Curly pulling Moe's hair. b, Curly caught in wringer. c, Curly, Moe with drill. d, Moe pulling Larry's hair. e, Moe. f, Moe sticking finger in Curly's nose. g, Stooges pointing. h, Skull biting Curly's nose. i, Shemp.

No. 2201, 25d, Larry with crown. No. 2202, 25d, Curly on telephone, vert.

2000, Jan. 14 Litho. *Perf. 13¼*

2200 A353 5d Sheet of 9, #a.-i. 8.50 8.50

Souvenir Sheets

2201-2202 A353 Set of 2 9.00 9.00

See Nos. 2446-2448.

I Love Lucy — A354

No. 2203: a, Lucy on sofa. b, Lucy, Ricky. c, Fred, Lucy, and Ethel. d, Lucy standing. e, Lucy, Ricky embracing. f, Lucy looking in mirror. g, Lucy with fists clenched. h, Lucy, Ricky on sofa. i, Lucy and Ethel.

No. 2204, 25d, Lucy, Ricky embracing, vert. No. 2205, 25d, Lucy looking in mirror, vert.

2000, Jan. 14 Litho. *Perf. 13¼*

2203 A354 5d Sheet of 9, #a.-i. 9.00 9.00

Souvenir Sheets

2204-2205 A354 Set of 2 9.00 9.00

See Nos. 2440-2442, 2449-2451.

Betty Boop A355

No. 2206: a, In green and yellow outfit. b, In red dress. c, In red shirt and blue jeans. d, In green and brown outfit. e, Seated in chair. f, In orange shirt and blue jeans. g, In fur coat. h, In pink dress. i, With dumbbell and water bottle.

No. 2207, 25d, In yellow flowered dress. No. 2208, 25d, In bathtub.

2000, Jan. 14 Litho. *Perf. 13¼*

2206 A355 5d Sheet of 9, #a.-i. 9.50 9.50

Souvenir Sheets

2207-2208 A355 Set of 2 9.50 9.50

Paintings of Anthony Van Dyck — A356

No. 2209: a, Samson and Delilah, c. 1619-20. b, Samson and Delilah sketch, 1618-20. c, Samson and Delilah, c. 1628-30.

No. 2210, 5d: a, The Adoration of the Shepherds. b, The Rest on the Flight to Egypt, The Virgin of the Partridges. c, Suffer the Little Children to Come Unto Me. d, Christ and the Moneychangers. e, Feast at the House of Simon the Pharisee. f, The Lamentation Over the Dead Christ.

No. 2211, 5d, vert.: a, Anton Giulo Brignole-Sale. b, Paolina Adorno Brignole-Sale. c, Battina Balbi Durazzo. d, Portrait of a Man of the Cattaneo Family. e, Portrait of a Woman. f, Elena Grimaldi Cattaneo.

No. 2212, 5d, vert.: a, A Genoese Senator. b, A Seated Gentlewoman. c, The Senator's Wife. d, A Genoese Lady, The Marchesa Balbi. e, Polyxena Spinola, Marchesa de Legones. f, Agostino Pallavicini.

No. 2213, 5d, vert.: a, A Prince Rupert of the Palatinate. b, William II of Nassau and Orange. c, Prince Charles Louis of the Palatinate. d, Prince Rupert, Count Palatine. e, The Princess Mary. f, Prince Charles Louis, Count Palatine.

No. 2214, 5d, vert.: a, Sir George Villiers and Lady Katherine Manners as Adonis and Venus. b, Lady Mary Villiers with Lord Arran. c, Rachel de Ruvigny, Countess Southampton as Fortune. d, Venus at Forge of Vulcan. e, Daedalus and Icarus. f, The Clipping of Cupid's Wing.

No. 2215, 25d, A Man with His Son. No. 2216, 25d, Prince Charles Louis, Elector Palatine and His Brother, Prince Rupert of the Palatinate, vert. No. 2217, 25d, Venetia, Lady Digby, as Prudence, vert. No. 2218, 25d, Drunken Silenus, vert. No. 2219, 25d, Portrait of a Genoese Lady, vert. No. 2220, 25d, Charles II as Prince of Wales, vert. No. 2221, 25d, William II, Prince of Orange, and His Bride, Mary, Princess Royal of England, vert. No. 2222, 25d, The Three Eldest Children of Charles I, vert.

2000, May 1 *Perf. 13¾*

2209 A356 5d Sheet of 3, #a.-c. 2.75 2.75

Sheets of 6, #a.-f.

2210-2214 A356 Set of 5 27.50 27.50

Souvenir Sheets

2215-2222 A356 Set of 8 42.50 42.50

Papal Visits — A357

No. 2223, 6d — 1991-92 Visits: a, Portugal. b, Poland. c, Hungary. d, Brazil. e, Senegal. f, Gambia. g, Guinea. h, Angola. i, Sao Tomé. j, Dominican Republic.

No. 2224, 6d — 1993 Visits: a, Benin. b, Uganda. c, Sudan. d, Albania. e, Spain. f, Jamaica. g, Mexico. h, United States. i, Lithuania. j, Latvia.

No. 2225, 6d — 1993-95 Visits: a, Estonia. b, Croatia. c, Philippines. d, Papua New Guinea. e, Australia. f, Sri Lanka. g, Czech Republic. h, Belgium. i, Slovakia. j, Cameroon.

No. 2226, 6d — 1995-96 Visits: a, South Africa. b, Kenya. c, United States. d, United Nations. e, Guatemala. f, Nicaragua. g, El Salvador. h, Venezuela. i, Tunisia. j, Slovenia.

No. 2227, 6d — 1996-98 Visits: a, Germany. b, Hungary. c, France, 1996. d, Bosnia. e, Czech Republic. f, Lebanon. g, Poland. h, France, 1997. i, Brazil. j, Cuba.

No. 2228, 6d — 1998-99 Visits: a, Nigeria. b, Austria. c, Croatia. d, Mexico. e, United States. f, Romania. g, Poland. h, Slovenia. i, India. j, Georgia.

No. 2229, 25d, Pope rekindles Eternal Flame. No. 2230, 25d, Pope blesses Holy Land. No. 2231, 25d, Pope places prayer on Western Wall. No. 2232, 25d, Pope assisted by Israeli president and prime minister. No. 2233, 25d, Pope prays at Western Wall. No. 2234, 25d, Pope receives Bible from chief rabbis. No. 2235, 25d, Pope touches bowl of soil. No. 2236, 25d, Pope at Yad Vashem, horiz.

2000, May 15 Litho. *Perf. 13¾*

Sheets of 10, #a.-j, + 2 labels

2223-2228 A357 Set of 6 57.50 57.50

Souvenir Sheets

Perf. 14½x14¾, 14¾x14½ (#2236)

2229-2236 A357 Set of 8 33.00 33.00

Stamps from Nos. 2223-2228 are 28x47mm.

Mushrooms A358

Designs: 4d, Morel. 5d, Chanterelle. 15d, Knight cap. 20d, Spindle.

No. 2241, 7d: a, Yellow parasol. b, Mottle-gill. c, Poplar field cap. d, Caesar's. e, Flame shield-cap. f, Lilac bonnet.

No. 2242, 7d: a, Common puffball. b, Earth star. c, Silky volvar. d, Stump puffball. e, Spindle-stemmed bolete. f, Fox-orange cort.

No. 2243, 25d, Red-stemmed tough shank. No. 2244, 25d, St. George's.

2000, May 15 *Perf. 14*

2237-2240 A358 Set of 4 7.50 7.50

Sheets of 6, #a.-f.

2241-2242 A358 Set of 2 15.00 15.00

Souvenir Sheets

2243-2244 A358 Set of 2 10.00 10.00

First Zeppelin Flight, Cent. — A359

No. 2245: a, LZ-10. b. LZ-127. c, LZ-129. 25d, LZ-130.

2000, May 1 Litho. *Perf. 14*

2245 A359 15d Sheet of 3, #a-c 8.25 8.25

Souvenir Sheet

2246 A359 25d multi 5.25 8.25

No. 2246 contains one 50x38mm stamp.

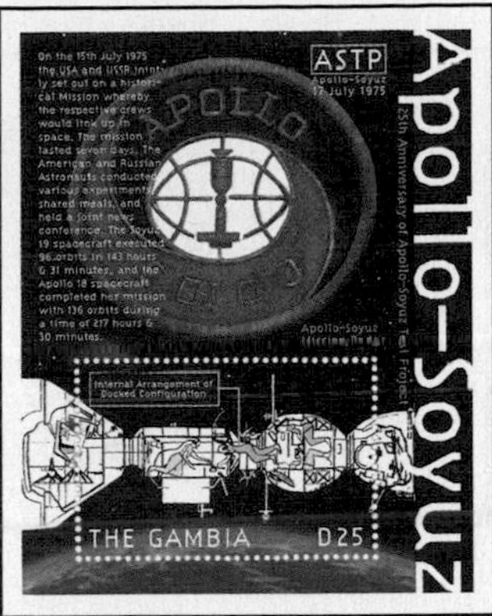

Prince William, 18th Birthday — A360

No. 2247: a, As child. b, In sweater. c, In suit, with flowers. d, In suit.

25d, With Prince Harry.

2000, May 1 *Perf. 14*

2247 A360 7d Sheet of 4, #a-d 5.00 5.00

Souvenir Sheet

Perf. 13¾

2248 A360 25d multi 4.50 4.50

No. 2248 contains one 38x50mm stamp.

Berlin Film Festival, 50th Anniv. — A361

No. 2249: a, Pane. Amore e Fantasia. b, Richard III. c, Smultronstället (Wild Strawberries). d, The Defiant Ones. e, The Living Desert. f, A Bout de Souffle.

25d, Twelve Angry Men.

2000, May 1 *Perf. 14*

2249 A361 7d Sheet of 6, #a-f 7.25 7.25

Souvenir Sheet

2250 A361 25d multi 4.50 4.50

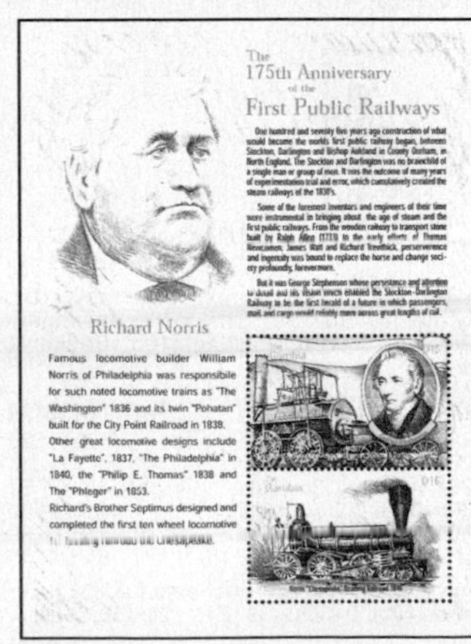

Apollo-Soyuz Mission, 25th Anniv. — A362

No. 2251: a, Donald K. Slayton. b, Thomas P. Stafford. c, Vance D. Brand.

25d, Diagram of docked spacecraft.

2000, May 1

2251 A362 15d Sheet of 3, #a-c 8.50 8.50

Souvenir Sheet

2252 A362 25d multi 4.50 4.50

Souvenir Sheet

2000 Summer Olympics, Sydney — A363

No. 2253: a, Paavo Nurmi. b, Basketball. c, Panathenian Stadium, Athens and Greek flag. d, Ancient Greek chariot racing.

2000, May 1

2253 A363 6d Sheet of 4, #a-d 5.00 5.00

Public Railways, 175th Anniv. — A364

No. 2254: a, Locomotion No. 1, George Stephenson. b, Chesapeake.

2000, May 1

2254 A364 15d Sheet of 2, #a-b 5.50 5.50

Souvenir Sheet

Johann Sebastian Bach (1685-1750) — A365

2000, May 1

2255 A365 25d multi		4.25	4.25

Popes — A366

No. 2256, 7d: a, Pope Felix IV, 526-30. b, Gelasius I, 492-96. c, Gregory I, 590-604. d, Gregory IX, 1227-41. e, Gregory XII, 1406-15. f, Honorius III, 1216-27.

No. 2257, 7d: a, Gregory XIII, 1572-85. b, Urban II, 1088-99. c, Sixtus I, 115-125. d, Pius IX, 1846-78. e, Pius IV, 1559-65. f, Paschal I, 817-24.

No. 2258, 7d: a, Alexander VII, 1655-67. b, Benedict XI, 1303-04. c, Calixtus III, 1455-58. d, Celestine V, 1294. e, Clement IX, 1667-69. f, Fabian, 236-50.

No. 2259, 25d, Peter, 33-64. No. 2260, 25d, Damasus I, 366-384. No. 2261, 25d, John I, 523-526.

2000, July 26 Litho. *Perf. 13¾*

Sheets of 6, #a-f

2256-2258 A366 Set of 3		24.00	24.00

Souvenir Sheets

2259-2261 A366 Set of 3		14.50	14.50

Butterflies — A367

Designs: 1.50d, Amphicalia tigris. 2d, Myrina silenus. 3d, Chrysiridia madagascarensis. 5d, Papilionidae. 10d, Dasiothia medea.

2000, Aug. 7 *Perf. 14¾x14*

2262 A367 1.50d multi		.40	.25
2263 A367 2d multi		.50	.35
2264 A367 3d multi		1.25	.50
2265 A367 5d multi		1.50	.80
2266 A367 10d multi		2.10	1.60
Nos. 2262-2266 (5)		5.75	3.50

Nos. 2264-2266 exist dated 2003.

See Nos. 2436-2439, 2452-2452B, 2699.

Souvenir Sheet

Albert Einstein (1879-1955) — A368

2000, May 1 Litho. *Perf. 14¼*

2267 A368 25d multi		5.00	5.00

Space — A369

No. 2268, 7d: a, Uhuru. b, Rosat. c, I.U.E. d, Astro E. e, Exosat. f, Chandra.

No. 2269, 7d, vert.: a, Helios. b, Solar Max. c, SOHO. d, O.S.O. e, Special rocket launch. f, I.M.P.

No. 2270, 25d, XMM. No. 2271, 25d, Cassini Huygens.

2000, May 1 *Perf. 14*

Sheets of 6, #a-f

2268-2269 A369 Set of 2		14.00	14.00

Souvenir Sheets

2270-2271 A369 Set of 2		8.25	8.25

The Stamp Show 2000, London; World Stamp Expo 2000, Anaheim.

Monarchs — A370

No. 2272: a, Charles I of Great Britain, 1625-49. b, Clovis III, king of the Franks (691-95).

No. 2273, 7d: a, Charles II of France, 885-887. b, Catherine de Medici of France, 1547-59. c, Boris Godunov of Russia, 1598-1605. d, Basil III of Russia, 1505-33. e, Anne of Great Britain, 1702-14. f, Charles IX of France, 1560-74.

No. 2274, 7d: a, James IV of Scotland, 1488-1513. b, James V of Scotland, 1513-42. c, James VI of Scotland, 1567-1625. d, Mary of Scotland, 1542-67. e, Mary of Great Britain, 1689-94. f, Elizabeth II, of Great Britain, 1952-present.

No. 2275, 25d, James Francis Edward Stuart. No. 2276, 25d, Robert I, the Bruce of Scotland. No. 2277, 25d, Bahadur Shah of India, 1837-57.

2000, July 26 *Perf. 13¾*

2272 A370 7d Sheet of 2, #a-b		2.50	2.50

Sheets of 6, #a-f

2273-2274 A370 Set of 2		14.00	14.00

Souvenir Sheets

2275-2277 A370 Set of 3		11.00	11.00

Puppies — A371

Designs: 1d, West Highland terrier. 1.50d, Bernese mountain dog. 3d, Yorkshire terrier. 4d, West Highland terrrier, diff. 10d, Chow chow. 15d, Poodle.

No. 2284: a, Border collie (brown and white). b, Border collie (black, brown and white). c, Yorkshire terrier. d, German shepherd. e, Beagle. f, Spaniel.

2000, Aug. 7 *Perf. 14¼*

2278-2283 A371 Set of 6		5.25	5.25
2284 A371 7d Sheet of 6, #a-f		7.00	7.00

Souvenir Sheet

2285 A371 25d Boxer		4.50	4.50

The Stamp Show 2000, London (Nos. 2284-2285).

Cats — A372

No. 2286, 4d: a, Egyptian mau. b, Singapura. c, American shorthair. d, Cornish rex. e, Birman. f, Scottish fold. g, Turkish angora. h, Turkish van.

No. 2287, 5d: a, Ragdoll. b, Bombay. c, Korat. d, Somali. e, British shorthair. f, American curl. g, Maine coon cat. h, Like No. 2286h.

No. 2288, 25d, Cat and kitten. No. 2289, 25d, Cat.

2000, Aug. 7 Sheets of 8, #a-h

2286-2287 A372 Set of 2		11.50	11.50

Souvenir Sheets

2288-2289 A372 Set of 2		9.50	9.50

The Stamp Show 2000, London.

Flower Photomosaic Type of 1999 and

Queen Mother, 100th Birthday — A373

Designs: No. 2090, Various flower photographs making up a photomosaic of the Queen Mother.

No. 2290I: Various photos of religious scenes making up a photomosaic of Pope John Paul II.

2000, Aug. 7 Litho. *Perf. 13¾*

2290 A349 5d Sheet of 8, #a-h		7.50	7.50
2290I A349 6d Sheet of 8, #j-q		10.00	10.00

Litho. & Embossed

Without Gum

Die Cut 9x8¾

2291 A373 85d multi		*22.50*	*22.50*

Issued: Nos. 2290, 2291 8/7. No. 2290I, 8/8.

European Soccer Championships — A374

No. 2292, horiz. — Czech Republic: a, Nedved. b, Team photo. c, Maier. d, Antonin Panenka. e, Selessin Stadium, Liege. f, Patrik Berger.

No. 2293, horiz. — England: a, Alan Shearer. b, Team photo. c, David Seaman. d, Sol Campbell. e, Philips Stadium, Eindhoven. f, Southgate.

No. 2294, horiz. — Norway: a, Leonardsen. b, Team photo. c, Mykland. d, Solbakken. e, Rekdal.

No. 2295, horiz. — Slovenia: a, Aleksander Knavs. b, Team photo. c, Zlatko Zahovic. d, Ales Ceh. e, Stade Communal, Charleroi. f, Miran Pavlin.

No. 2296, horiz. — Sweden: a, Ljungberg. b, Team photo. c, Andersson. d, Nilsson. e, Schwarz.

No. 2297, horiz. — Turkey: a, Yalcin. b, Team photo. c, Buruk. d, Erdem. e, King Baudouin Stadium. f, Korkut.

No. 2298, 25d, Czech Republic coach, Jozef Chovanec. No. 2299, 25d, England coach Kevin Keegan. No. 2300, 25d, Norway coach Nils-Johan Semb. No. 2301, 25d, Slovenia coach Srecko Katanec. No. 2302, 25d, Sweden coaches, Söderberg and Lagerbäck. No. 2303, 25d, Turkey coach Mustafa Denizli.

2000, Aug. 7 Litho. *Perf. 13¾*

2292 A374 7d Sheet of 6, #a-f		7.50	7.50
2293 A374 7d Sheet of 6, #a-f		7.50	7.50
2294 A374 7d Sheet of 6, #a-e, 2292e		7.50	7.50
2295 A374 7d Sheet of 6, #a-f		7.50	7.50
2296 A374 7d Sheet of 6, #a-e, 2293e		7.50	7.50
2297 A374 7d Sheet of 6, #a-f		7.50	7.50
Nos. 2292-2297 (6)		45.00	45.00

Souvenir Sheets

2298-2303 A374 Set of 6		28.50	28.50

Paintings of Birds — A375

Designs: 1.50d, A White Pheasant and Other Fowl in a Classical Landscape, by Abraham Bisschop. 3d, Salmon-crested Cockatoo, by Bartolomeo Bimbi. 4d, A Great Bustard Cock and Other Birds, by Ludger Tom Ring. 15d, A Great Black-backed Gull and Other Birds, by Jokob Bogdani.

No. 2308, 5d: a, Peacocks, Hens and Mouse, by Tobias Stranover. b, Lady in a Red Jacket Feeding a Parrot, by Frans van Mieris. c, Birds by a Pool, by Melchior de Hondecoeter. d, Ganymede and the Eagle, by Peter Paul Rubens. e, Leda and the Swan, by Cesare de Sesto. f, Ducks and Ducklings at the Foot of a Tree in a Mediterranean Landscape, by Adriaen van Oolen. g, Portrait of the Falconer Robert Cheseman Carrying a Hooded Falcon, by Hans Holbein. h, A Golden Pheasant on a Stone Plinth, with Other Birds, by Jacobus Vonck.

No. 2309, 5d, horiz.: a, Still Life of Birds, by Caravaggio (hanging dead birds, basket). b, Turkeys with Young and Rock Doves, by Johan Wenzel Peter. c, The Threatened Swan, by Jan Asselyn. d, Still Life of Fruit and Birds in a Landscape, by Jakab Bogdany. e, Mobbing the Owl, by Tobias Stranover (owl at right, other birds). f, A Concert of Birds, by Hondecoeter (owl, cockatoo at center). g, Owls and Young Ones, by William Tomkins. h, Birds by a Stream, by Jean Baptiste Oudry.

No. 2310, 25d, The King Eagle Pursued to the Sun, by Philip Reinagle. No. 2311, 25d, Still Life of Birds, by Georg Flegl, horiz.

2000, Oct. 2 *Perf. 13½*

2304-2307 A375 Set of 4		4.75	4.75

Sheets of 8, #a-h

2308-2309 A375 Set of 2 14.00 14.00

Souvenir Sheets

2310-2311 A375 Set of 2 10.00 10.00

Descriptions of paintings are in margins on Nos. 2308-2311.

Paintings from the Prado — A376

No. 2312, 6d: a, The Madonna of the Fish, by Raphael. b, The Holy Family with a Lamb, by Raphael. c, The Madonna of the Stair, by Andrea del Sarto. d, Moneychanger from The Moneychanger and his Wife, by Marinus van Reymerswaele. e, Madonna and Child by Jan Gossaert. f, Wife from The Moneychanger and his Wife.

No. 2313, 6d: a, Bearded man from St. Benedict's Supper, by Juan Andres Ricci. b, Our Lady of the Immaculate Conception, by Francisco de Zurbarán. c, Monk with candle from St. Benedict's Supper. d, The Penitient Magdalen, by José de Ribera. e, Christ as Man of Sorrows, by Antonion de Pereda. f, St. Jerome, by Pereda.

No. 2314, 6d: a, Children with a Shell, by Bartolomé Esteban Murillo. b, Our Lady of the Immaculate Conception, by Murillo. c, The Good Shepherd, by Murillo. d, Woman with red headdress from The Parasol, by Francisco de Goya. e, A Rural Gift, by Ramon Bayeu. f, Woman with blue headdress from The Parasol.

No. 2315, 6d: a, Queen Isabella Farnese, by Jean Ranc. b, Young Woman Seen from the Back, by Jean-Baptiste Greuze. c, Charles III as a Child, by Ranc. d, James Bourdieu, by Sir Joshua Reynolds. e, Dr. Isaac Henrique Sequeira, by Thomas Gainsborough. f, Portrait of a Clergyman, by Reynolds.

No. 2316, 6d: a, Portrait of a Young Woman, by Zacarias González Velázquez. b, The Painter Francisco de Goya, by Vicente Lopez Portaña. c, Portrait of a Girl, by Rafael Tejeo Diaz. d, Mary, from The Nativity, by Federico Barocci. e, Madonna and Child with St. John, by Correggio. f, Jesus, from The Nativity.

No. 2317, 6d: a, St. Andrew, by Francisco Rizi. b, Christ Crucified, by Diego Velázquez. c, St. Onuphrius, by Francisco Collantes. d, Charles II, by Juan Carreño de Miranda. e, St. Sebastian, by Carreño de Miranda. f, Peter Ivanovich Potemkin, by Carreño de Miranda.

No. 2318, 25d, The Defense of Cádiz Against the English, by Zurbarán. No. 2319, 25d, The Surrender of Juliers, by Jusepe Leonardo. No. 2320, 25d, The Holy Family with a Bird, by Murillo. No. 2321, 25d, Danäe, by Titian, horiz. No. 2322, 25d, Venus and Adonis, by Paolo Veronese, horiz. No. 2323, 25d, Jacob's Dream, by Ribera.

2000, Oct. 6 ***Perf. 12x12¼, 12¼x12***

Sheets of 6, #a-f

2312-2317 A376 Set of 6 40.00 40.00

Souvenir Sheets

2318-2323 A376 Set of 6 28.50 28.50

Espana 2000, Intl. Philatelic Exhibition.

Battle of Britain, 60th Anniv. — A377

No. 2324, 5d, horiz.: a, Hurricane downing German BF109. b, Spitfire over River Thames. c, Flight Lt. Denys E. Gilliam attacking German Dornier 217 planes. d, Hurricanes heading to intercept Luftwaffe bombers. e, Hurricanes returning to Croydon. f, G.A. Langley in combat with BF109. g, Bristol Blenheim IV over English Channel. h, Spitfires taking off from Hornchurch.

No. 2325, 5d, horiz.: a, Plane from 29th Blenheim Squadron heading to Norwegian coast. b, Luftwaffe pilot Helmut Wick downs RAF pilot John Cock. c, Spitfire downs Dornier 217 off Dover. d, Bristol Beaufighter IIF on patrol. e, Bolton-Paul Defiants intercept Luftwaffe bombers. f, Spitfire in dogfite with German Stuka JU-87 divebomber. g, Spitfire and Hurricane fly over London and River Thames. h, Gloster Gladiator.

No. 2326, 25d, Group Captain Frank Carey. No. 2327, 25d, German Commander Adolf Joseph Ferdinand Galland.

2000, Oct. 16 ***Perf. 14***

Sheets of 8, #a-h

2324-2325 A377 Set of 2 14.00 14.00

Souvenir Sheets

2326-2327 A377 Set of 2 9.00 9.00

Composers — A378

No. 2328, 7d: a, Antonio Vivaldi. b, Giacomo Puccini. c, Franz Joseph Haydn. d, Leopold Stokowski. e, Felix Mendelssohn. f, Gaetano Donizetti.

No. 2329, 7d: a, Witold Lutoslawski. b, William Sterndale Bennett. c, Wolfgang Amadeus Mozart. d, Ludwig van Beethoven. e, Sergei Rachmaninoff. f, Peter Ilich Tchaikovsky.

No. 2330, 25d, Manuel de Falla. No. 2331, 25d, Fréderic Chopin.

2000, Oct. 2 Litho. ***Perf. 13¾x13¼***

Sheets of 6, #a-f

2328-2329 A378 Set of 2 16.00 16.00

Souvenir Sheets

2330-2331 A378 Set of 2 10.00 10.00

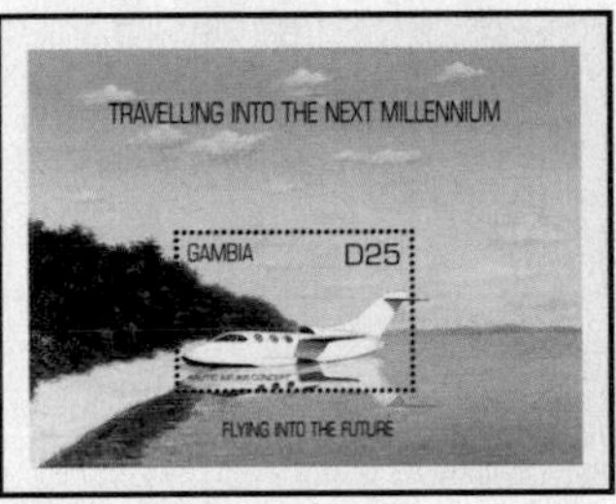

Transportation of the Future — A379

No. 2332 — Automobiles: b, Mazda RX-Evolv. c, Isuzu Kai. d, Ford 021C. e, Pontiac GTO. f, Chevrolet CERV III. g, Toyota Will VI.

No. 2333 — Aircraft: a, Blended wing body, BWB-1. b, Boeing 767-400 ERX. c, Lockheed concept. d, Boeing X. e, American National Aerospace plane X-30 concept. f, Hotol taking off from Russian AN-225.

No. 2334 — Trains: a, Maglev train MLU-002. b, Magnetic rail car. c, Monorail above ground concept. d, Seattle Monorail. e, Monorail above cabin concept. f, Monorail concept.

No. 2335 — Watercraft: h, Pendolare concept boat. i, Planesail boat. j, Airfoil concept. k, Ferry Sea Coaster concept. l, Shinaitoku Matu new sail technology. m, Supersport luxury yacht concept.

No. 2335G, 25d, Nautic Air 400 concept. No. 2335H, 25d, Maglev train. No. 2335I, 25d, Honda Sprocket concept. No. 2335J, 25d, Triton, US Coast Guard concept.

2000, Oct. 2 ***Perf. 14***

Sheets of 6, #a-f

2332 A379 7d Sheet of 6, #b-g 8.00 8.00
2333 A379 7d Sheet of 6, #a-f 8.00 8.00
2334 A379 8d Sheet of 6, #a-f 9.00 9.00
2335 A379 8d Sheet of 6, #h-m 9.00 9.00

Souvenir Sheets

2335G-2335J A379 Set of 4 16.00 16.00

Nos. 2335 and 2335A contain one 56x41mm stamp.

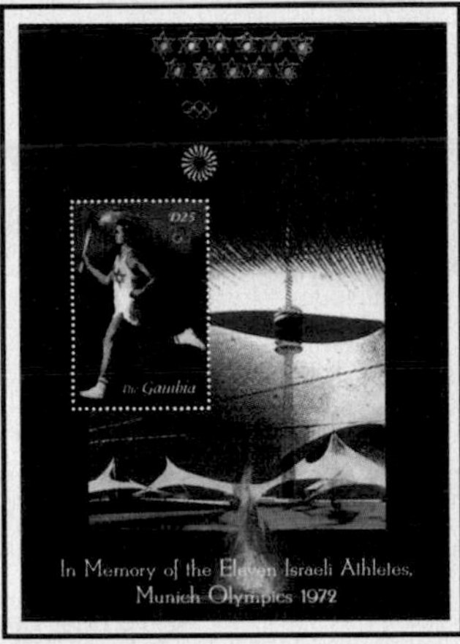

Massacre of Israeli Olympic Athletes, 1972 — A380

No. 2336, horiz.: a, Moshe Weinberg. b, Eliezer Halffin. c, Mark Slavin. d, Ze'ev Friedman. e, Joseph Romano. f, Kahat Shor. g, David Berger. h, Joseph Gottfreund. i, Andrei Schpitzer. j, Amitsur Shapira. k, Yaakov Springer. l, Olympic poster.

2000, Nov. 9

2336 A380 4d Sheet of 12, #a-l 9.00 9.00

Souvenir Sheet

2337 A380 25d Torchbearer 5.00 5.00

Ships A381

Designs: 5d, Spanish Armada. 10d, Brazilian river gunboat Colombo. 15d, Russian Navy mine carrier Jenissel. 20d, Japanese battleship Yamato.

No. 2342, 7d: a, British first-rate battleship, 18th cent. b, Spanish galleon, 16th cent. c, Russian four-masted barque, 20th cent. d, Henri Grace à Dieu with flag on stern, 16th cent. e, Frontispiece of John Dee's Arte of Navigation, 16th cent. f, British ironclad, 19th cent.

No. 2343, 7d: a, Chinese junk, 18th cent. b, Two-masted cog, 15th cent. c, Henri Grace à Dieu, no flag on stern, 16th cent. d, St. Brendan and monks at sea, 6th cent. e, Figurehead. f, British carrack, 16th cent.

No. 2344, 25d, Challenger, 19th cent. No. 2345, 25d, Golden Hind, 16th cent.

2000, Oct. 2 Litho. ***Perf. 14***

2338-2341 A381 Set of 4 9.00 9.00

Sheets of 6, #a-f

2342-2343 A381 Set of 2 16.00 16.00

Souvenir Sheets

2344-2345 A381 Set of 2 9.50 9.50

Birds — A382

No. 2346, 7d, vert.: a, Pied flycatcher. b, Blackcap. c, Stonechat. d, Nightingale. e, Black-headed tchagra. f, Yellow wagtail.

No. 2347, 7d, vert.: a, Gray parrot. b, Great spotted cuckoo. c, Bar-tailed trogon. d, African hobby. e, Green turaco. f, Trumpeter hornbill.

No. 2348, 7d, vert.: a, Yellow-rumped tinkerbird. b, Greater honeyguide. c, Hoopoe. d, European roller. e, Carmine bee-eater. f, White-throated bee-eater.

No. 2349, 25d, European bee-eater. No. 2350, 25d, Bateleur. No. 2351, 25d, Secretary bird.

2000, Oct. 2 ***Perf. 13¾x13¼***

Sheets of 6, #a-f

2346-2348 A382 Set of 3 24.00 24.00

Souvenir Sheets

2349-2351 A382 Set of 3 13.50 13.50

Ferrari Automobiles — A383

Designs: 4d, 3335P. 5d, 5125. 10d, 312P. 25d, 330P4.

2000, Nov. 15 ***Perf. 14***

2352-2355 A383 Set of 4 8.00 8.00

12th Classic Automobile Marathon — A384

No. 2356, 5d: a, Morgan. b, Rover. c, Marmon. d, Rolls Royce Silver Cloud. e, Rolls Royce Phantom. f, Mercedes 680S. g, Mercedes 74. h, Invicta.

No. 2357, 5d: a, Allard. b, Ford coupe. c, Citroen Pilot. d, Packard (white). e, Austin A90. f, Bentley. g, Packard (red). h, Aston Martin.

No. 2358, 25d, Cadillac. No. 2359, 25d, Morris Minor.

2000, Nov. 15 **Sheets of 8, #a-h**

2356-2357 A384 Set of 2 10.50 10.50

Souvenir Sheets

2358-2359 A384 Set of 2 10.00 10.00

Queen Mother, 100th Birthday — A385

2000, Aug. 7 Litho. *Perf. 14*

2360 A385 7d multi 1.50 1.50

Printed in sheets of 6.

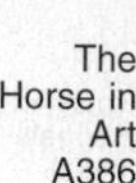

The Horse in Art A386

Designs: 4d, At Full Stretch, by John Skeaping. 5d, The Burton, by Lionel Edwards. 10d, A Game of Polo, by Li Lin. 15d, St. George and the Dragon, by Raphael, vert.

No. 2365, 7d: a, Horses Emerging From the Sea, by Eugène Delacroix. b, The Ninth Duke of Marlborough on a Grey Horse, by Sir Alfred Munnings. c, Ovid in Exile Amongst the Scythians, by Delacroix. d, Early Morning Gallop, by Skeaping. e, Mare and Foal, by Munnings. f, Detail from Three-a-side Polo at Simla, by Edwards.

No. 2366, 7d, vert.: a, A Lady Hawking, by E. J. H. Vernet. b, Captain Robert Orme, by Sir Joshua Reynolds. c, Napoleon Crossing the Alps, by Jacques-Louis David. d, Nobby Gray, by Munnings. e, Amateur Jockeys Near a Carriage, by Edgar Degas. f, Detail from Three-a-side Polo at Simla, diff.

No. 2367, 25d, The Reckoning, by George Morland. No. 2368, 25d, One of the Family, by Frederic G. Cotman.

2000, Oct. 2

2361-2364 A386 Set of 4 5.75 5.75

Sheets of 6, #a-f

2365-2366 A386 Set of 2 15.00 15.00

Souvenir Sheets

2367-2368 A386 Set of 2 9.00 9.00

New Year 2001 (Year of the Snake) — A387

No. 2369: a, Vermilion background. b, Purple background. c, Dark blue background. d, Light green background.

2001, Jan. 2

2369 A387 4d Sheet of 4, #a-d 2.75 2.75

Souvenir Sheet

2370 A387 15d Snake 3.00 3.00

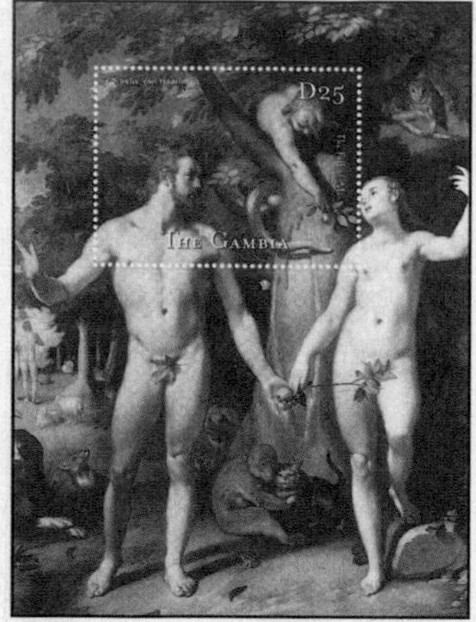

Rijksmuseum, Amsterdam, Bicent. (in 2000) — A388

No. 2371, 7d, vert.: a, Vessels in a Strong Wind, by Jan Porcellis. b, Seascape in the Morning, by Simon de Vlieger. c, Travelers at a Country Inn, by Isaack van Ostade. d, Orpheus with Animals in a Landscape, by Aelbert Cuyp. e, Italian With a Mountain Plateau, by Cornelis van Poelenburch. f, Boatmen and hill from Boatman Moored on a Lake Shore, by Adam Pynacker.

No. 2372, 7d, vert.: a, Cow, boatmen and sailboat from Boatmen Moored on a Lake Shore. b, The Ford in the River, by Jan Baptist Weenix. c, Two Horses Near a Gate in a Meadow, by Paulus Potter. d, Cows and Sheep at a Stream, by Karel Dujardin. e, Violin player from The Duet, by Cornelis Saftleven. f, Lute player from The Duet.

No. 2373, 7d, vert.: a, Teapot from Still Life With Turkey Pie, by Pieter Claesz. b, Bouquet of Flowers in a Vase, by Ambrosius Bosschaert. c, Vase from Still Life With Flowers, Fruit and Shells, by Balthasar van der Ast. d, Flowers and fruit from Still Life With Flowers, Fruit and Shells. e, Tulips in a Vase, by Hans Boulenger. f, Laid Table With Cheese and Fruit, by Floris van Dijck.

No. 2374, 7d, vert.: a, Turkey, from Still Life With Turkey Pie. b, Still Life With Gilt Goblet, by Willem Claesz Heda. c, Still Life With Lobster and Nautilus Cup, by Jan Davidsz de Heem. d, Bacchanal, by Moses van Uyttenbroeck. e, The Anatomy Lesson of Dr. Nicolaes Tulp, by Rembrandt. f, Johannes Lutma, by Jacob Backer.

No. 2375, 7d, vert.: a, The Meagre Company, by Frans Hals and Pieter Codde. b, The Twins Clara and Aelbert de Bray, by Salomon de Bray. c, Self-portrait, by Ferdinand Bol. d, Ambulatory of the New Church in Delft, with the Tomb of Willem the Silent, by Gerard Houckgeest. e, View of the Tomb of Willem in the New Church in Delft, by Emanuel de Witte. f, Mountainous Landscape, by Hercules Segers.

No. 2376, 7d, vert.: a, Lute player from Gallant Company by Codde. b, Men and archway from Gallant Company. c, Man on bended knee from The Marriage of Willem van Loon and Margaretha Bas, by Jan Miense Molenaer. d, Crowd from The Marriage of Willem van Loon and Margaretha Bas. e, Woman in black robe from The Marriage of Willem van Loon and Margaretha Bas. f, Johanna Le Maire, by Nicolaes Eliasz Pickenoy.

No. 2377, 25d, The Fall of Man, by Cornelis van Haarlem. No. 2378, 25d, The Art Gallery of Jan Gildemeester Jansz, by Jan Ekels II. No. 2379, 25d, View of the Nieuwe Kerk and the Rear of the Town Hall in Amsterdam, by Isaak Outwater. No. 2380, 25d, The Spendthrift, by Cornelis Troost. No. 2381, 25d, Morning Ride on the Beach, by Anton Mauve. No. 2382, 25d, Meadow Landscape With Cattle, by Willen Roelofs.

2001, Jan. 15 *Perf. 13¾*

Sheets of 6, #a-f

2371-2376 A388 Set of 6 42.50 42.50

Souvenir Sheets

2377-2382 A388 Set of 6 28.00 28.00

The Wizard of Oz, Cent. (in 2000) — A389

No. 2383, 7d: a, Witch of the North. b, Poppies. c, Dorothy's house. d, Witch of the East. e, Dorothy. f, The Wizard.

No. 2384, 7d: a, Witch's wolf. b, Witch's forest. c, Witch's monkeys. d, Dorothy in poppies. e, Queen Mouse. f, Witch and evil bees.

No. 2385, 7d: a, Cowardly Lion. b, Land of Oz. c, Tin Man. d, Scarecrow. e, Toto. f, Munchkins.

No. 2386, 27d, Green Maiden. No. 2387, 27d, Gate keeper. No. 2388, 27d, Dorothy at crossroads, horiz.

2001, Jan. 30 Sheets of 6, #a-f

2383-2385 A389 Set of 3 24.00 24.00

Souvenir Sheets

2386-2388 A389 Set of 3 15.00 15.00

History of the Theater — A390

No. 2389, 6d: a, Terra cotta statue. b, Tragic masks of King Priam. c, Euripides. d, Terra cotta statues of actors portraying drunks. e, Scene from Chinese play. f, Indian actors. g, Scene from Noh play, Japan. h, Scene from Clytemnestra.

No. 2390, 6d: a, William Shakespeare. b, Johann Wolfgang von Goethe. c, Moliere. d, Henrik Ibsen. e, George Bernard Shaw. f, Anton Chekhov. g, Sholom Aleichem. h, Tennessee Williams.

No. 2391, 25d, Sarah Bernhardt, vert. No. 2392, 25d, John Barrymore, vert.

2001, Jan. 30 *Perf. 14*

Sheets of 8, #a-h

2389-2390 A390 Set of 2 20.00 20.00

Souvenir Sheet

2391-2392 A390 Set of 2 10.00 10.00

Pokémon — A391

No. 2393: a, Beedrill. b, Arbok. c, Machop. d, Vileplume. e, Clefairy. f, Poliwhirl.

2001, Feb. 1 *Perf. 13¾*

2393 A391 7d Sheet of 6, #a-f 6.00 6.00

Souvenir Sheet

2394 A391 25d Articuno 4.75 4.75

Orchids — A392

Designs: 1.50d, Encyclia alata. 2d, Dendrobium lasiantherum. 3d, Cymbidiella pardalina. No. 2398, 4d, Cymbidium lowianum. 5d, Cypripedium irapeanum. 15d, Doritas pulcherrima.

No. 2401: a, Epidendrum pseudepidendrum. b, Eriopsis biloba. c, Masdevallia coccinea. d, Odontoglossum lindleyanum. e, Oerstedella wallisii. f, Paphiopedilum acmodontum. g, Laelia rubescens. h, Huntleya wallisii. i, Lycaste longiscapa. j, Maxillaria variabilis. k, Mexicoa ghiesbrechtiana. l, Miltoniopsis phalaenopsis.

No. 2402: a, Sobralia candida. b, Phragmipedium basseae. c, Phaius tankervilleae. d, Vanda rothchildiana. e, Telipogon pulchera. f, Rossioglossum insleayi.

No. 2403, 25d, Chaubardia heteroclita. No. 2404, 25d, Cychnoches loddigesii. No. 2405, 25d, Cattleya dowiana.

2001, Feb. 1 Litho. *Perf. 14*

2395-2400 A392 Set of 6 6.00 6.00

2401 A392 4d Sheet of 12, #a-l 11.00 11.00

2402 A392 7d Sheet of 6, #a-f 9.00 9.00

Souvenir Sheets

2403-2405 A392 Set of 3 16.50 16.50

Hong Kong 2001 Stamp Exhibition (Nos. 2401-2405).

Medicinal Plants — A393

Designs: 3d, Pokeweed. 5d, Bay laurel. 10d, Coltsfoot. 15d, Marshmallow.

No. 2410, 8d, vert.: a, Restharrow. b, White willow. c, Sweet serge. d, Passion flower. e, Rosemary. f, Pepper.

No. 2411, 8d, vert.: a, Succory. b, Dandelion. c, Garlic. d, Hemp agrimony. e, Star thistle. f, Cypress.

No. 2412, 25d, Arbutus, vert. No. 2413, 25d, Olive, vert.

2001, Mar. 1

2406-2409 A393 Set of 4 5.75 5.75

Sheets of 6, #a-f

2410-2411 A393 Set of 2 18.00 18.00

Souvenir Sheets

2412-2413 A393 Set of 2 11.00 11.00

Japanese Art — A394

Designs: 1d, Mount Fuji and Tea Fields, by Matsuoka Eikyu. 2d, One heron from Herons and Flowers, by Okamoto Shuki. No. 2416, 3d, Two herons from Herons and Flowers. No. 2417, 3d, The Realm of Gods in Yingzhou, by Tomioka Tessai. No. 2418, 4d, Peach Blossom Spring in Wuling, by Tessai. No. 2419, 4d, Egret, by Takeuchi Seiho. No. 2420, 5d, Spring Colors of the Lake and Mountains, by Shoda Gyokan. No. 2421, 5d, Sparrows, by Seiho. No. 2422, 10d, Red Lotus and White Goose, by Goun Saku. No. 2423, 10d, Portrait of Ushiwakamaru, by Kano Osanobu. 15d, Woman Selling Flowers, by Ito Shoha. 20d, The Sound of the Ocean, by Matsumoto Ichiyo.

No. 2426, 5d — Birds and Flowers of the Twelve Months, by Sakai Hoitsu: a, Red and white flowers, bird on branch. b, Yellow flowers, bird flying. c, White flowers, bird on branch. d, Blue flowers. e, Sun, white and blue flowers. f, Red and white flowers.

No. 2427, 5d — Birds and Flowers of the Twelve Months, by Hoitsu: a, Insect in sky, red pink and white flowers. b, Blue irises. c, Red, white light blue flowers. d, Fruit on tree. e, Bird standing in water. f, Snow-covered tree.

No. 2428, 7d — Birds and Flowers, by Soga Chokuan: a, White flowers. b, Rooster at R. c, Roosters at L, red flower at R. d, Rooster at R, white flowers. e, Birds in sky. f, Roosters at L and R, white and red flowers. g, Roosters at L and R. h, Rooster at L, tree and red flowers.

No. 2429, 7d — The Four Accomplishments, by Kaiho Yusho: a, Table. b, Two people near tree. c, Rock and hill. d, Two people. e, Rock and tree. f, One person. g, Three people. h, Three people, table.

No. 2430 — Book of Lacquer Paintings, by Shibata Zeshin: a, Flower. b, Birds. c, Butterfly on flower. d, Lobster.

No. 2431, 30d, Untitled painting (Yanagibashi at Ryogoku), by Utagawa Kuniyoshi, horiz. No. 2432, 30d, Poppies, by Tsuchida Bakusen, horiz. No. 2433, 30d, Puppies and Morning Glories, by Yamaguchi Soken, horiz. No. 2434, 30d, Deep Pool, by Nishimura Goun, horiz. No. 2435, 30d, Spring Farming Near a Riverside Village, by Mori Getsujo, horiz.

2001, Apr. 17

2414-2425 A394 Set of 12 15.00 15.00

Sheets of 6, #a-f

2426-2427 A394 Set of 2 12.00 12.00

Sheets of 8, #a-h

2428-2429 A394 Set of 2 21.00 21.00

2430 A394 10d Sheet of 4, #a-d 7.50 7.50

Imperf.

Size: 118x88mm

2431-2435 A394 Set of 5 27.50 27.50

Nos. 2428-2430 contain 28x42mm stamps. Phila Nippon '01, Japan.

Butterflies Type of 2000

Designs: 7d, Salamis temora. 8d, Cyrestus camillus. 20d, Papilio demodocus. 25d, Danaus chrysippus.

2001 ***Perf. 14¾x14***

2436-2439 A367 Set of 4 11.50 11.50

No. 2439 exists dated 2003.

I Love Lucy Type of 2000

No. 2440: a, Lucy singing. b, Lucy with tambourine. c, Lucy with Ricky and Ethel. d, Lucy. e, Ethel and Ricky at piano. f, Ethel and Ricky on bench. g, Lucy at typewriter. h, Ethel singing. i, Lucy on bench.

No. 2441, 25d, Like No. 2440a, vert. No. 2442, 25d, Like No. 2440d, vert.

2001 ***Perf. 13¾***

2440 A354 5d Sheet of 9, #a-i 8.75 8.75

Souvenir Sheets

2441-2442 A354 Set of 2 9.50 9.50

Horses — A395

No. 2443, 7d, Head of: a, Akhal-Teke. b, Palomino. c, Kladruber. d, Paint Horse. e, Pinto. f, Kabardin.

No. 2444, 7d, horiz: a, Akhal-Teke. b, Kladruber. c, Palomino. d, Pinto. e, Paint Horse. f, Kabardin.

No. 2445, Palomino.

2001 **Litho.** ***Perf. 14***

Sheets of 6, #a-f

2443-2444 A395 Set of 2 14.50 14.50

Souvenir Sheet

2445 A395 25d multi 4.00 4.00

Three Stooges Type of 2000

No. 2446: a, Shemp as angel. b, Larry, Moe, Shemp, wearing feathered hats. c, Moe, Shemp and Larry wearing hospital uniforms. d, Larry with hammer, Shemp with gun, Moe. e, Moe, Larry, Shemp with woman. f, Moe and Shemp wearing tams. g, Moe, Larry, wagon wheel. h, Shemp, Moe, Larry in bus driver uniforms. i, Shemp hitting Larry and Moe.

No. 2447, 25d, Curly with telephone, skull, vert. No. 2448, 25d, Shemp on Moe's back, vert.

2001 ***Perf. 13¾***

2446 A353 5d Sheet of 9, #a-i 6.00 6.00

Souvenir Sheets

2447-2448 A353 Set of 2 7.00 7.00

I Love Lucy Type of 2000

No. 2449 : a, Lucy crawling on building ledge. b, Lucy standing against wall, arms outstretched. c, Lucy in apartment. d, Lucy reclining on ledge. e, Lucy with hand on forehead. f, Lucy reclining against wall. g, Ricky, bound and gagged Lucy. h, Lucy on sofa. i, Lucy, robber.

No. 2450, 25d, Lucy, robber, vert. No. 2451, 25d, Bound and gagged Lucy, seated Ethel, vert.

2001

2449 A354 5d Sheet of 9, #a-i 6.00 6.00

Souvenir Sheets

2450-2451 A354 Set of 2 7.00 7.00

Butterfly Type of 2000

50d, Coeliades forestan. 75d, Ornithoptera alexandrae. 100d, Morpho cypris.

2001 ***Perf. 14¾x14***

2452 A367 50d multicolored 6.00 6.00

2452A A367 75d multicolored 11.00 11.00

2452B A367 100d multicolored 13.00 13.00

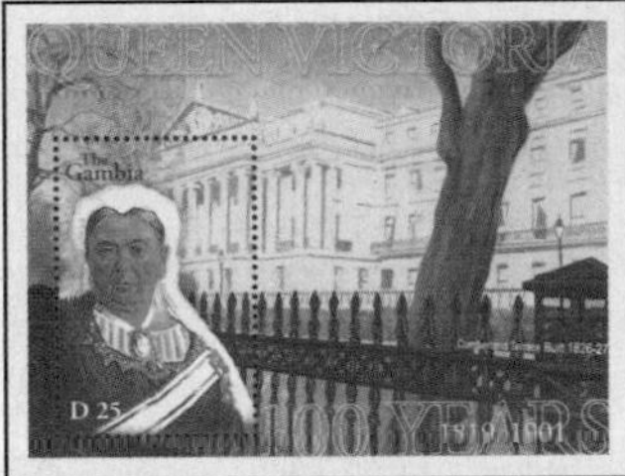

Queen Victoria (1819-1901) — A396

No. 2453, horiz.: a, Reading speech from throne. b, Benjamin Disraeli. c, Riding in procession from Parliament.

2001, Apr. 26 ***Perf. 14***

2453 A396 15d Sheet of 3, #a-c 9.00 9.00

Souvenir Sheet

2454 A396 25d Portrait 5.00 5.00

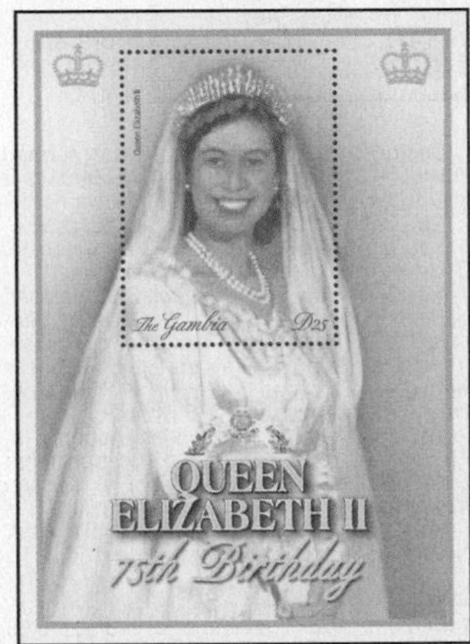

Queen Elizabeth II, 75th Birthday — A397

No. 2456: a, In uniform. b, In pink hat. c, Wearing crown, facing R. d, Wearing crown, facing L.

2001, Apr. 26 ***Perf. 14***

2455 A397 15d Sheet of 4, #a-d 9.00 9.00

Souvenir Sheet

2456 A397 25d In wedding dress 6.00 6.00

Flowers — A398

Designs: 1d, Disa uniflora. 4d, Monodora myristica. 6d, Clappertonia ficifolia. 20d, Calanthe rosea.

No. 2461, 7d: a, Vanilla planifolia. b, Strelitzia reginae. c, Gladiolus cardinalis. d, Arctotis venusta. e, Protea obtusifolia. f, Geissorhiza rochensis.

No. 2462, 7d: a, Canarina abyssinica. b, Amorphophallus abyssinicus. c, Calanthe rosea, diff. d, Gloriosa simplex. e, Clappertonia ficifolia, diff. f, Ansellia gigantea.

No. 2463, 25d, Arctotis venusta, diff. No. 2464, 25d, Geissorhiza rochensis, horiz.

2001, Mar. 1 **Litho.** ***Perf. 14***

2457-2460 A398 Set of 4 5.00 5.00

Sheets of 6, #a-f

2461-2462 A398 Set of 2 15.00 15.00

Souvenir Sheets

2463-2464 A398 Set of 2 8.50 8.50

Photomosaic of Queen Elizabeth II — A399

2001, Apr. 26

2465 A399 8d multi 1.50 1.50

Printed in sheets of 8, with and without marginal inscription "In Celebration of the 50th Anniversary of H. M. Queen Elizabeth II's Accession to the Throne.'

Marlene Dietrich — A400

No. 2466: a, With head on forearm. b, With bare shoulder. c, With arms crossed. d, Wearing hat.

2001, Apr. 26 ***Perf. 13¾***

2466 A400 10d Sheet of 4, #a-d 7.50 7.50

Mao Zedong (1893-1976) — A401

No. 2467: a, In 1935. b, In 1949. c, In 1951. 25d, In 1928.

2001, Apr. 26 ***Perf. 14***

2467 A401 15d Sheet of 3, #a-c 7.50 7.50

Souvenir Sheet

2468 A401 25d multi 4.50 4.50

Giuseppe Verdi (1813-1901), Opera Composer — A402

No. 2469: a, Verdi with gray hair. b, Score and perfromers from La Traviata. c, Score and performer from Aida. d, Verdi with brown hair.
25d, Verdi and scores of Don Carlos and Rigoletto.

2001, Apr. 26

2469 A402	10d Sheet of 4, #a-d		8.00	8.00

Souvenir Sheet

2470 A402	25d multi		5.50	5.50

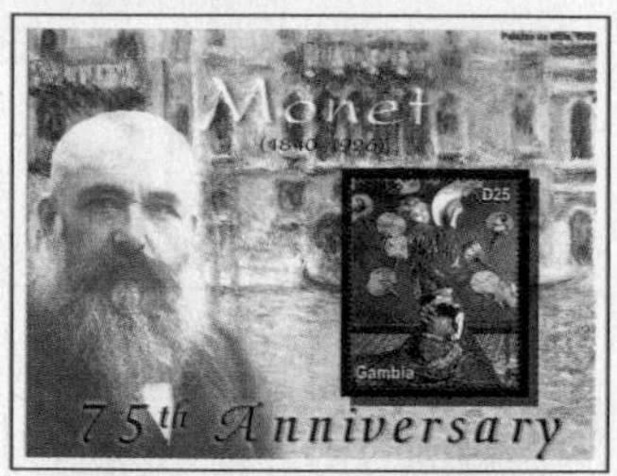

Monet Paintings — A403

No. 2471, horiz.: a, Madame Monet on the Sofa. b, The Picnic. c, The Luncheon. d, Jean Monet on His Mechanical Horse.
25d, La Japonaise.

2001, Apr. 26 ***Perf. 13¾***

2471 A403	10d Sheet of 4, #a-d		8.00	8.00

Souvenir Sheet

2472 A403	25d multi		5.00	5.00

Toulouse-Lautrec Paintings — A404

No. 2473: a, At Le Rat Mort. b, The Milliner. c, Messaline.
25d, Napoleon.

2001, Apr. 26

2473 A404	7d Sheet of 3, #a-c		4.50	4.50

Souvenir Sheet

2474 A404	25d multi		5.50	5.50

Orchids — A405

Designs: 3d, Orchis morio. 4d, Fulophia speciosa. 5d, Angraecum leonis. 15d, Oeceoclades maculata.
No. 2479, 8d: a, Ceratostylis retisquama. b, Rangaeris rhipsalisocia. c, Phaius hybrid. d, Disa hybrid. e, Disa uniflora. f, Angraecum leonis.
No. 2480, 8d, horiz.: a, Satyrium erectum. b, Aeranthes grandiose. c, Aerangis somasticta. d, Polystachya bella. e, Eulophia guineensis. f, Disa blackii.
No. 2482, 25d, Disa kirstenbosch pride. No. 2482A, 25d, Aerangis eurnowiana

2001, June 15 ***Perf. 14***

2475-2478 A405	Set of 4		5.00	5.00

Sheets of 6, #a-f

2479-2480 A405	Set of 2		16.00	16.00

Souvenir Sheets

2482	A405	multi	5.50	5.50
2482A	A405	multi	5.50	5.50

Belgica 2001 Intl. Stamp Exhibition, Brussels (Nos. 2479-2480).

SOS Children's Village A406

2001, July 2

2483 A406	10d multi		2.00	2.00

Flora & Fauna A407

Designs: 2d, Hoopoe. 3d, Great spotted cuckoo. 4d, Plain tiger butterfly. 5d, Zebra duiker. 10d, Sooty managbey. 20d, Greater kudu.
No. 2490, 8d: a, Hippopotamus. b, Elephant. c, Parusta simplex. d, Gray heron. e, Charaxes imperialis. f, Gloriosa simplex.
No. 2491, 8d: a, Alpine swift. b, Blotched genet. c, Thomas' galago. d, Carmine bee-eater. e, Tree pangolin. f, Campbell's monkey.
No. 2492, 8d: a, Gray parrot. b, Rachel's weaver. c, European bee-eater. d, River kingfisher. e, Red river hog. f, Bushbuck.
No. 2493, 8d: a, Blue diadem butterfly. b, Fire-footed rope squirrel. c, Clappertonia ficifolia. d, Costus spectabilis. e, African migrant butterfly. f, Giant African snail.
No. 2494, 25d, Long-tailed pangolin, vert. No. 2495, 25d, Eurasian kestrel, vert.

2001, July 16

2484-2489 A407	Set of 6		8.50	8.50

Sheets of 6, #a-f

2490-2493 A407	Set of 4		36.00	36.00

Souvenir Sheets

2494-2495 A407	Set of 2		9.00	9.00

A408

Ducks and Geese — A409

Designs: 2d, Blue-winged teal. No. 2497, 3d, Red-crested pochard. No. 2498, 4d, Falcated teal. No. 2499, 5d, Mandarin duck. No. 2500, 10d, King eider. 15d, Hooded merganser.
No. 2502, 3d, Wood duck. No. 2503, 4d, Mallard. No. 2504, 5d, Barrow's goldeneye. No. 2505, 10d, Bufflehead.
No. 2506, 7d, horiz.: a, Barrow's goldeneye. b, Harlequin duck. c, Pintail. d, Black-bellied whistling duck. e, Cinnamon teal. f, Surf scoter.
No. 2507, 7d, horiz.: a, Black scoter. b, Black duck. c, Green-winged teal. d, Bufflehead. e, Red-breasted merganser. f, Fulvous whistling duck.
No. 2508, 8d: a, European wigeon. b, Mallard. c, Garganey. d, Pintail, diff. e, Shoveler. f, Green-winged teal.
No. 2509, 8d: a, Black duck. b, Bufflehead. c, Cinnamon teal, diff. d, Goldeneye. e, Ruddy shelduck. f, Ferruginous duck.
No. 2510, 8d: a, Masked duck. b, Old squaw. c, Ring-necked duck. d, Harlequin duck, diff. e, Redhead. f, Canvasback.
No. 2511, 25d, American wigeon. No. 2512, 25d, Wood duck. No. 2513, 25d, Baikal teal.
No. 2514, 25d, Green-winged teal, horiz. No. 2515, 25d, Canada geese, horiz.

2001, July 16

2496-2501	A408	Set of 6	8.00	8.00
2502-2505	A409	Set of 4	5.00	5.00

Sheets of 6, #a-f

2506-2507	A409	Set of 2	16.00	16.00
2508-2510	A408	Set of 3	26.00	26.00

Souvenir Sheets

2511-2513	A408	Set of 3	15.00	15.00
2514-2515	A409	Set of 2	10.00	10.00

Cetaceans — A410

No. 2516, 7d: a, Killer whale (denomination at UR). b, Sperm whale (denomination at UR). c, Strap-toothed whale. d, Humpback whale. e, Southern right whale. f, Beluga.
No. 2517, 7d: a, Killer whale (denomination at LR). b, Sperm whale (denomination at LR). c, Narwhal. d, Gray whale. e, Blue whale. f, Northern right whale.
No. 2518, 25d, Killer whale. No. 2519, 25d, Humpback whale.

2001, July 16 **Sheets of 6, #a-f**

2516-2517 A410	Set of 2		18.00	18.00

Souvenir Sheets

2518-2519 A410	Set of 2		12.00	12.00

A411

Trains A412

Designs: 2d, Rheingold Express. No. 2521, 10d, Amtrak train. No. 2522, 15d, The Blue Train. 20d, Cisalpino.
4d, Eurostar. No. 2525, 7d, Mallard. No. 2526, 10d, Rocket. No. 2527, 15d, TGV.
No. 2528, 7d: a, Eurostar, diff. b, Flying Hamburger. c, Coast Starlight. d, Tres Grande Vitesse. e, Golden Arrow. f, Shinkanzen "Max."
No. 2529, 7d: a, Siliguri to Darjeeling, India train. b, California Zephyr. c, Flying Scotsman. d, Trans-Siberian Express. e, Indian-Pacific. f, Thunersee.
No. 2530, 8d: a, Le Shuttle. b, Nord Express. c, 2-6-0, Switzerland. d, Duchess. e, Balkan Express. f, Class 44 2-10-0, Germany.
No. 2531, 8d: a, 7029 Clun Castle. b, Puffing Billy. c, ICE Electric. d, 4-4-2 S, Belgium. e, 2-8-2, Germany. f, PLM Coupe-Vents.
No. 2532, 25d, Cape Town to Victoria Falls train. No. 2533, 25d, The Southerner.
No. 2534, 25d, Stanier Class 5 4-6-0. No. 2535, 25d, Flying Scotsman, diff.

2001, July 31 ***Perf. 14***

2520-2523	A411	Set of 4	7.50	7.50
2524-2527	A412	Set of 4	6.00	6.00

Sheets of 6, #a-f

2528-2529	A411	Set of 2	17.00	17.00
2530-2531	A412	Set of 2	19.00	19.00

Souvenir Sheets

2532-2533	A411	Set of 2	10.00	10.00
2534-2535	A412	Set of 2	10.00	10.00

British Royal Navy — A413

Designs: 3d, St. Andrew, 1600s. 4d, Fleet maneuvers, 1914. 10d, HMS Illustrious, 1899. 15d, Battle of North Foreland, 1666.
No. 2540, 7d, horiz.: a, Mary Rose, 1512. b, Attack off Quebec, 1759. c, Armada campaign, 1588. d, Battle of Scheveningen, 1653. e, Blanche captures La Pique, 1795. f, Embarkation at Dover, 1520.
No. 2541, 7d, horiz. — Battles: a, Quiberon Bay, 1759. b, Barfleur, 1692. c, Nile, 1798. d, Trafalgar, 1805. e, Jutland, 1916. f, Camperdown, 1797.
No. 2542, 7d, horiz.: a, Battle of Navarino, 1827. b, Sinking of Eurydice, 1878. c, HMS Pantaloon captures Borboleta, 1845. d, Dardanelles, 1915. e, HMS Pickle captures Bolodora, 1829. f, HMS Invincible and Inflexible, Battle of the Falklands, 1914.
No. 2543, 25d, Ark Royal, 1582, horiz. No. 2544, 25d, Sovereign of the Seas, 1637, horiz.

2001, Sept. 6 **Litho.**

2536-2539 A413	Set of 4		7.00	7.00

Sheets of 6, #a-f

2540-2542 A413	Set of 3		27.00	27.00

Souvenir Sheets

2543-2544 A413	Set of 2		10.00	10.00

2002 World Cup Soccer Championships, Japan and Korea — A414

Jules Rimet Trophy and: 2d, Netherlands flag and player. 3d, Argentina flag and player. 4d, Ibaraki Kashima Stadium, Japan, horiz. 5d, George Best and Northern Ireland flag. 10d, Dino Zoff and Italian flag. 15d, Poster for 1938 tournament, France.
25d, Pat Bonner making save for Ireland.

2001, Sept. 6

2545-2550 A414	Set of 6		7.50	7.50

Souvenir Sheet

2551 A414	25d multi		5.00	5.00

No. 2551 contains one 56x42mm stamp.

European Royalty — A415

No. 2552: a, King Harald V, Queen Sonja, Norway. b, Queen Margrethe II, Denmark. c, King Carl XVI Gustaf and Queen Silvia, Sweden. d, King Juan Carlos, Queen Sofia, Spain. e, Queen Beatrix, Netherlands. f, King Albert II, Queen Paola, Belgium.
No. 2553, 25d, Crown Prince Haakon, Princess Mette-Marit, Norway. No. 2554, 25d, King Juan Carlos, Spain, vert.

Perf. 14¼x14½, 14½x14¼

2001, Nov. 15

2552 A415 7d Sheet of 6, #a-f 9.00 9.00

Souvenir Sheets

2553-2554 A415 Set of 2 11.00 11.00

Queen Mother Type of 1999

No. 2555: a, Duchess of York, Princess Elizabeth, 1928. b, Lady Elizabeth Bowes-Lyon, 1923. c, Queen Elizabeth, 1946. d, Queen Mother, Prince Harry.

40d, Queen Mother celebrating 89th birthday, 1989.

2001, Dec. 13 ***Perf. 14***

2555 A342 15d Sheet of 4, #a-d + label 13.00 13.00

Souvenir Sheet

Perf. 13¾

2556 A342 40d multi 8.00 8.00

No. 2556 contains one 38x50mm stamp.

Oriental Actors and Actresses — A416

No. 2557, 15d: a, Alex Fong. b, William So. c, Flora Chan. d, Rain Li.

No. 2558, 15d — Kelly Chen: a, Close-up. b, As child, with cherry. c, On swing. d, As child, with hand above eyes.

No. 2559, 15d — Jacky Cheung: a, At L, laughing, looking to R. b, Looking forward, mouth open. c, At R, laughing, looking L. d, Looking forward, mouth closed.

No. 2560, 15d — Andy Hui, and Chinese characters at: a, L (pink suit). b, R (yellow suit). c, L (yellow suit). d, R (pink suit).

No. 2561, 15d — Miriam Yeung, with roses and petals at: a, LR. b, LL. c, UR. d, UL.

2001, Nov. 5 Litho. ***Perf. 13¾x13¼***

Sheets of 4, #a-d

2557-2561 A416 Set of 5 40.00 40.00

New Year 2002 (Year of the Horse) — A417

No. 2562 — Denomination at: a, UR. b, UL. c, LR. d, LL.

20d, African zebra.

2001, Dec. 26 ***Perf. 13***

2562 A417 6d Miniature sheet of 4, #a-d 5.00 5.00

Souvenir Sheet

Perf. 12½x13

2563 A417 20d multi 5.00 5.00

No. 2563 contains one 68x31mm triangular stamp.

Jacqueline Kennedy Onassis (1929-94) — A418

No. 2564: a, As baby. b, At age 6. c, Engagement to J.F.K. d, In wedding gown, 1955. e, In 1960. f, In 1980.

30d, At wedding to Aristotle Onassis.

2002, Jan. 24 ***Perf. 14***

2564 A418 7d Sheet of 6, #a-f 5.50 5.50

Souvenir Sheet

2565 A418 30d multi 4.50 4.50

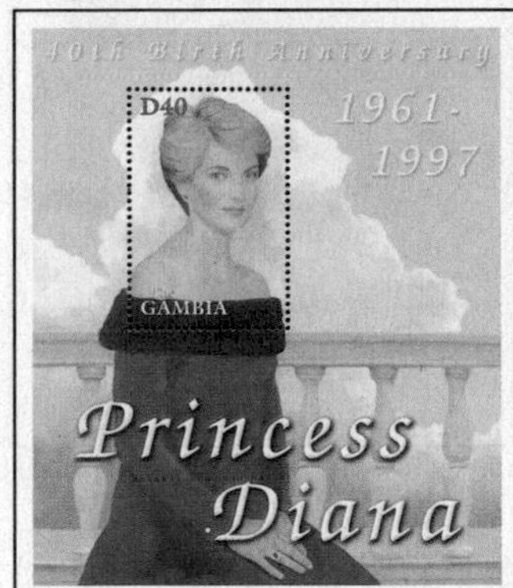

Princess Diana (1961-97) — A419

No. 2566 — Diana and: a, Coral rose. b, White rose. c, Yellow rose. d, Purple rose.

40d, Portrait.

2002, Jan. 24

2566 A419 15d Sheet of 4, #a-d 12.00 12.00

Souvenir Sheet

2567 A419 40d multi 6.50 6.50

Moths A420

Designs: 2d, Tiger moth. 3d, Hawk moth. No. 2570, 10d, Pericopid moth. 15d, Spurge hawk.

No. 2572, 10d (50x38mm): a, Sloane's urania. b, Saturniid moth. c, Black witch moth. d, Burnet moth on plant. e, Day-flying moth. f, Lime hawk moth.

No. 2573, 10d (50x38mm): a, Emperor moth. b, Millar's tiger. c, Hawk moth, diff. d, Phrygionis privignara. e, Burnet moth, waterfall. f, Urania leilus.

No. 2574, 40d, Emerald moth. No. 2575, 40d, Red under-wing moth, vert.

Perf. 14, 13¾ (#2572-2573)

2002, Jan. 24

2568-2571 A420 Set of 4 6.75 6.75

Sheets of 6, #a-f

2572-2573 A420 Set of 2 25.00 25.00

Souvenir Sheets

2574-2575 A420 Set of 2 17.50 17.50

United We Stand — A421

2002, Feb. 6 ***Perf. 13¾x13¼***

2576 A421 20d multi 2.75 2.75

Issued in sheets of 4.

Reign of Queen Elizabeth II, 50th Anniv. — A422

No. 2577: a, With beige hat. b, With red hat. c, With blue hat. d, Near vehicle.

40d, Wearing uniform.

2002, Feb. 6 ***Perf. 14½***

2577 A422 15d Sheet of 4, #a-d 12.00 12.00

Souvenir Sheet

2578 A422 40d multi 8.50 8.50

See No. 2704.

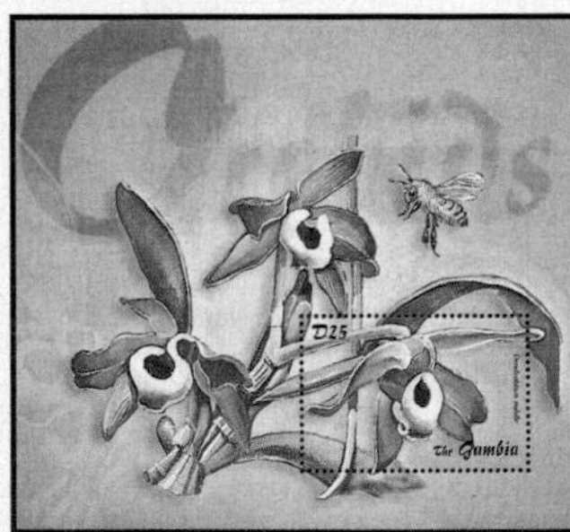

A423

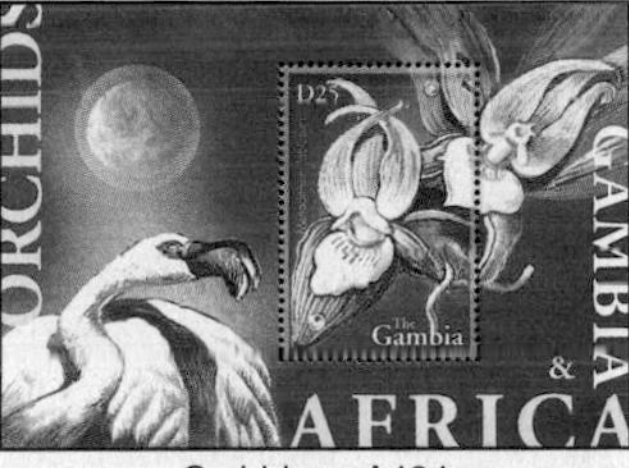

Orchids — A424

No. 2579, vert.: a, Machu piechu. b, Masdevallia copper angel. c, Masdevallia hirtzi. d, Tuakau canoy.

No. 2580: a, Eriopsis sceptrum. b, Sarcanthopsis muellem. c, Bougainville white. d, Telipogon klotzchianus.

No. 2581, 7d: a, Richard Mueller. b, Colmanara wildcat. c, Cycnoches chlorochilon. d, Vanda coerylea. e, Disa blackii. f, Unnamed.

No. 2582, 7d: a, Seagulls beaulu queen. b, Hazel Boyd. c, Costa Rica. d, Dendrobium infudibulum. e, Disa hybrid. f, Chysis.

No. 2583, 6d, horiz.: a, Spathoglottis portusfinschii. b, Dendrobium macrophyllum. c, Grammanels ellisii. d, Stanhopea wardii. e, Dendrobium nindi. f, Dendrobium williamsianum.

No. 2584, 7d: a, Seutieama steeli. b, Dendrobium inaequale. c, Dendrobium lasiathera. d, Calypso bulbosa. e, Vanda hindsii. f, Dendrobium violaceoflavens.

No. 2585, 8d, horiz.: a, Phaleonopsis rosenstomii. b, Cypripedium guttatum. c, Cypripedium reginae. d, Dendrobium engae. e, Diplocaulobium hydrophilum. f, Dendrobium cuthbertsonii.

No. 2586, 25d, Dendrobium nobile. No. 2587, 25d, Ancidium alliance, vert.

No. 2588, 25d, Menadenium labiosum. No. 2589, 25d, Dendrobium spectabile. No. 2590, 25d, Dendrobium canaliculatum, horiz.

2001, June 15 Litho. ***Perf. 14***

2579 A423 7d Sheet of 4, #a-d 9.00 9.00

2580 A424 10d Sheet of 4, #a-d 8.00 8.00

Sheets of 6, #a-f

2581-2582 A423 Set of 2 17.00 17.00

2583-2585 A424 Set of 3 27.00 27.00

Souvenir Sheets

2586-2587 A423 Set of 2 14.00 14.00

2588-2590 A424 Set of 3 27.00 27.00

Nos. 2579-2590 were not available until 2002. Belgica 2001 Intl. Stamp Exhibition (No. 2579).

Wildlife A425

Designs: 2d, Martial eagle. 4d, Lion. 5d, Aardvark. 10d, Lion cub, vert.

No. 2595, 7d: a, Lion cub. b, Water buffalo. c, Topi. d, Hyena. e, Secretary bird. f, Genet.

No. 2596, 7d: a, Reedbuck. b, Hippopotamus. c, Waterbuck and malachite kingfisher. d, Hoopoe. e, White pelican. f, Waterbuck.

No. 2597, 25d, Hippopotamus. No. 2598, 25d, Crocodile.

2001, July 16

2591-2594 A425 Set of 4 5.50 5.50

Sheets of 6, #a-f

2595-2596 A425 Set of 2 18.00 18.00

Souvenir Sheets

2597-2598 A425 Set of 2 13.00 13.00

Nos. 2591-2598 were not available until 2002.

Pres. Theodore Roosevelt (1858-1919) — A426

No. 2599: a, Wearing hat and uniform. b, Close-up. c, With hand on chair. d, Wearing hat and neckerchief.

40d, Close-up, diff.

2002, Jan. 24

2599 A426 15d Sheet of 4, #a-d 9.00 9.00

Souvenir Sheet

2600 A426 40d multi 6.50 6.50

Betty Boop — A427

No. 2602, 40d, With gray ribbon in hair, horiz. No. 2603, 40d, With ice cream sundae.

2002, Feb. 13 ***Perf. 13¾***

2601 A427 7d shown 1.10 1.10

Souvenir Sheets

2602-2603 A427 Set of 2 9.50 9.50

No. 2601 was issued in sheets of 9.

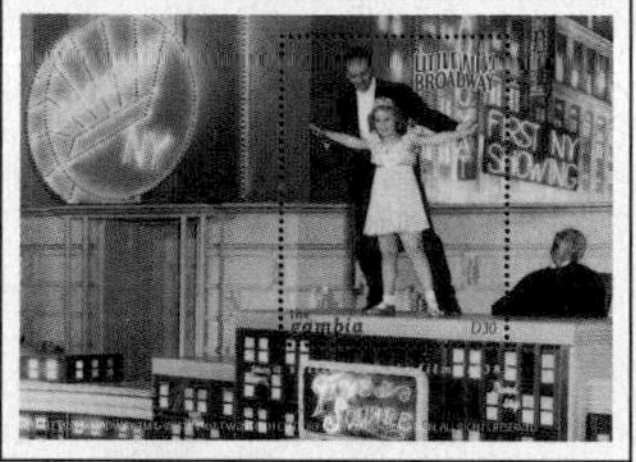

Shirley Temple in "Little Miss Broadway" — A428

No. 2604, horiz.: a, With man and old woman. b, Close-up. c, Waving. d, Holding man's tie. e, At hotel desk with men. f, Woman watching Temple point to tooth.

No. 2605: a, Dancing with young man. b, Dancing with old man with hat. c, Sitting with boy. d, Holding hands with old man.

30d, Wearing tiara and dancing with young man.

2002, Feb. 13

2604 A428 8d Sheet of 6, #a-f 6.00 6.00
2605 A428 10d Sheet of 4, #a-d 5.50 5.50

Souvenir Sheet

2606 A428 30d multi 4.25 4.25

2002 Winter Olympics, Salt Lake City — A429

Designs: No. 2607, 20d, Curling. No. 2608, 20d, Ski jumping.

2002, Mar. 18 ***Perf. 14***

2607-2608 A429 Set of 2 7.00 7.00
a. Souvenir sheet, #2607-2608 7.50 7.50

Chiune Sugihara, Japanese Diplomat Who Saved Jews in World War II — A430

2002, Apr. 29 ***Perf. 13½x13¼***

2609 A430 10d multi 1.75 1.75

Printed in sheets of 4.

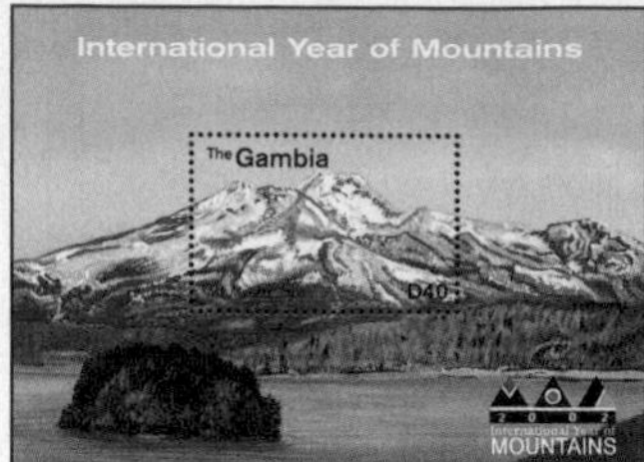

Intl. Year of Mountains — A431

No. 2610: a, Winkler Tower, Italy. b, Mt. Huanstan Chico, Peru. c, Hodaka Mountains, Japan. d, Mustagh Ata, Kashmir.

40d, Mt. Myoko, Japan.

2002, July 1 ***Perf. 13¼x13½***

2610 A431 15d Sheet of 4, #a-d 9.50 9.50

Souvenir Sheet

2611 A431 40d multi 6.50 6.50

2002 World Cup Soccer Championships, Japan and Korea — A432

Players, dates and locations of matches — No. 2612, 9d: a, France v. Senegal. b, Uruguay v. Denmark. c, France v. Uruguay. d, Denmark v. Senegal. e, Denmark v. France. f, Senegal v. Uruguay.

No. 2613, 9d: a, Paraguay v. South Africa. b, Spain v. Slovenia. c, Spain v. Paraguay. d, South Africa v. Slovenia. e, South Africa v. Spain. f, Slovenia v. Paraguay.

No. 2614, 9d: a, Brazil v. Turkey. b, China v. Costa Rica. c, Brazil v. China. d, Costa Rica v. Turkey. e, Costa Rica v. Brazil. f, Turkey v. China.

No. 2615, 9d: a, South Korea v. Poland. b, US v. Portugal. c, South Korea v. US. d, Portugal v. Poland. e, Portugal v. South Korea. f, Poland v. US.

No. 2616, 9d: a, Germany v. Saudi Arabia. b, Ireland v. Cameroun. c, Germany v. Ireland. d, Cameroun v. Saudi Arabia. e, Cameroun v. Germany. f, Saudi Arabia v. Ireland.

No. 2617, 9d: a, England v. Sweden. b, Argentina v. Nigeria. c, Sweden v. Nigeria. d, Argentina v. England. e, Sweden v. Argentina. f, Nigeria v. England.

No. 2618, 9d: a, Croatia v. Mexico. b, Italy v. Ecuador. c, Italy v. Croatia. d, Mexico v. Ecuador. e, Mexico v. Italy. f, Ecuador v. Croatia.

No. 2619, 9d: a, Japan v. Belgium. b, Russia v. Tunisia. c, Japan v. Russia. d, Tunisia v. Belgium. e, Tunisia v. Japan. f, Belgium v. Russia.

Stadia and dates of matches between — No. 2620, 20d: a, France v. Senegal. b, Uruguay v. Denmark.

No. 2621, 20d: a, France v. Uruguay. b, Denmark v. Senegal.

No. 2622, 20d: a, Denmark v. France. b, Senegal v. Uruguay.

No. 2623, 20d: a, Paraguay v. South Africa. b, Spain v. Slovenia.

No. 2624, 20d: a, Spain v. Paraguay. b, South Africa v. Slovenia.

No. 2625, 20d, a, South Africa v. Spain. b, Slovenia v. Paraguay.

No. 2626, 20d: a, Brazil v. Turkey. b, China v. Costa Rica.

No. 2627, 20d: a, Brazil v. China. b, Costa Rica v. Turkey.

No. 2628, 20d: a, Costa Rica v. Brazil. b, Turkey v. China.

No. 2629, 20d: a, South Korea v. Poland. b, US v. Portugal.

No. 2630, 20d: a, South Korea v. US. b, Portugal v. Poland.

No. 2631, 20d: a, Portugal v. South Korea. b, Poland v. US.

No. 2632, 20d: a, Germany v. Saudi Arabia. b, Ireland v. Cameroun.

No. 2633, 20d: a, Germany v. Ireland. b, Cameroun v. Saudi Arabia.

No. 2634, 20d: a, Cameroun v. Germany. b, Saudi Arabia v. Ireland.

No. 2635, 20d: a, England v. Sweden. b, Argentina v. Nigeria.

No. 2636, 20d: a, Sweden v. Nigeria. b, Argentina v. England.

No. 2637, 20d: a, Sweden v. Argentina. b, Nigeria v. England.

No. 2638, 20d: a, Croatia v. Mexico. b, Italy v. Ecuador.

No. 2639, 20d: a, Italy v. Croatia. b, Mexico v. Ecuador.

No. 2640, 20d: a, Mexico v. Italy. b, Ecuador v. Croatia.

No. 2641, 20d: a, Japan v. Belgium. b, Russia v. Tunisia.

No. 2642, 20d: a, Japan v. Russia. b, Tunisia v. Belgium.

No. 2643, 20d: a, Tunisia v. Japan. b, Belgium v. Russia.

2002, July 1 ***Perf. 13¼***

Sheets of 6, #a-f

2612-2619 A432 Set of 8 55.00 55.00

Souvenir Sheets

2620-2643 A432 Set of 24 110.00 110.00

See Nos. 2654-2656 for sheets with match results.

Popeye — A433

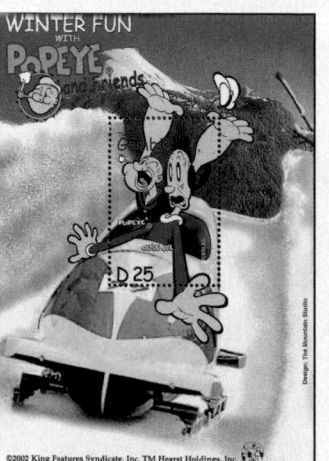

No. 2644, 10d: a, Popeye on cross-country skis. b, Popeye ski jumping. c, Popeye slaloming. d, Popeye snowboarding.

No. 2645, 10d: a, Swee'Pea on sled. b, Olive Oyl on skis. c, Brutus. d, Wimpy on ice skates.

No. 2646, 25d, Popeye and Olive in bobsled. No. 2647, 25d, Brutus playing hockey. No. 2648, 25d, Olive on ice skates. No. 2649, 25d, Popeye speed skating, horiz.

2002, June 17 **Litho.** ***Perf. 14***

Sheets of 4, #a-d

2644-2645 A433 Set of 2 10.00 10.00

Souvenir Sheets

2646-2649 A433 Set of 4 14.00 14.00

20th World Scout Jamboree, Thailand — A434

No. 2650: a, Scout with bugle. b, Scout making fire. c, Scout fishing.

40d, Scout tying knot.

2002, July 1 ***Perf. 13½x13¼***

2650 A434 15d Sheet of 3, #a-c 8.00 8.00

Souvenir Sheet

2651 A434 40d multi 6.50 6.50

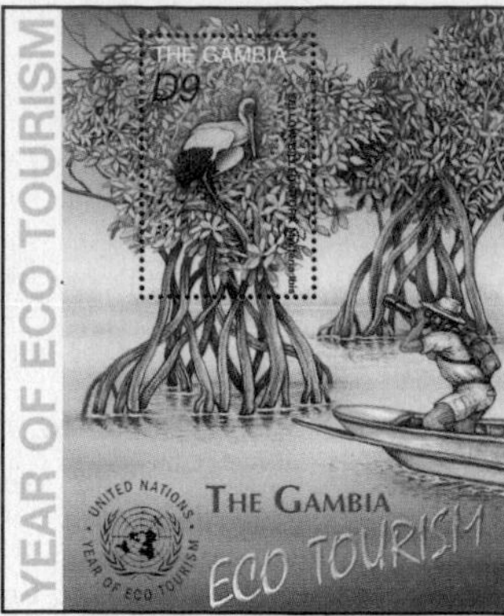

Intl. Year of Ecotourism — A435

No. 2652: a, Bird-of-Paradise flower. b, Goliath heron. c, Baobab tree. d, Roan antelope. e, Red tip butterfly. f, Egyptian cobra.

No. 2653, Yellow-billed stork.

2002, July 1

2652 A435 9d Sheet of 6, #a-d 10.00 10.00

Souvenir Sheet

2653 A435 9d multi 2.00 2.00

Nos. 2616, 2617 and 2619 Redrawn With Match Scores

No. 2654, 9d: a, Germany 8, Saudi Arabia 0. b, Ireland 1, Cameroun 1. c, Germany 1, Ireland 1. d, Cameroun 1, Saudi Arabia 0. e, Cameroun 0, Germany 2. f, Saudi Arabia 0, Ireland 3

No. 2655, 9d: a, England 1, Sweden 1. b, Argentina 1, Nigeria 0. c, Sweden 2, Nigeria 1. d, Argentina 0, England 1. e, Sweden 1, Argentina 1. f, Nigeria 0, England 0.

No. 2656, 9d: a, Japan 2, Belgium 2. b, Russia 2, Tunisia 0. c, Japan 1, Russia 0. d, Tunisia 1, Belgium 1. e, Japan 2, Tunisia 0. f, Belgium 3, Russia 2.

2002, July 15 ***Perf. 13¼***

Sheets of 6, #a-f

2654-2656 A432 Set of 3 24.00 24.00

Elvis Presley (1935-77) A436

2002, Aug. 19 ***Perf. 13½x13¾***

2657 A436 5d multi 1.00 1.00

Things from the Netherlands — A437

Netherlands Lighthouses — A438

Netherlands Postage Stamps, 150th Anniv. — A439

Women's Traditional Costumes of the Netherlands — A440

No. 2658: a, Farm. b, Porcelain. c, Building. d, Ice skaters. e, Cheese, flowers and wooden shoes. f, Prince Willem-Alexander and his bride.

No. 2659: a, Den Helder. b, Terschelling. c, Maasvlakte. d, Ijmuiden. e, Westkapelle. f, Breskens.

No. 2660: a, Netherlands #1. b, Netherlands #B72. c, Netherlands #279. d, Netherlands #586. e, Netherlands #620. f, Netherlands #1108a.

No. 2661: a, Woman from Friesland (plaid headdress). b, Back of woman from Utrecht. c, Woman and child from Noord-Holland.

2002, Aug. 30 ***Perf. 13½x13¼***

2658	A437 10d Sheet of 6, #a-f		10.00	10.00
2659	A438 10d Sheet of 6, #a-f		12.00	12.00

Perf. 13¼x13½

2660	A439 10d Sheet of 6, #a-f	10.00	10.00

Perf. 13¼

2661	A440 20d Sheet of 3, #a-c	11.00	11.00

Amphilex 2002 Intl. Stamp Exhibition, Amsterdam.

Marine Mammals and Flowers — A441

No. 2662, 10d: a, Blue whale. b, Pan-tropical spotted dolphin. c, Killer whale. d, Minke whale. e, Sperm whale. f, Pilot whale.

No. 2663, 10d: a, Juba-jamba. b, Devil's tongue. c, Rattle box. d, Vernonia purpurea. e, Seaside purslane. f, Fireball lily.

No. 2664, 50d, Humpback whale. No. 2665, 50d, Cape weed, swamp arum, vert.

2002, Sept. 23 ***Perf. 14***

Sheets of 6, #a-f

2662-2663	A441	Set of 2	24.00	24.00

Souvenir Sheets

2664-2665	A441	Set of 2	20.00	20.00

See Nos. 2763-2764.

A442

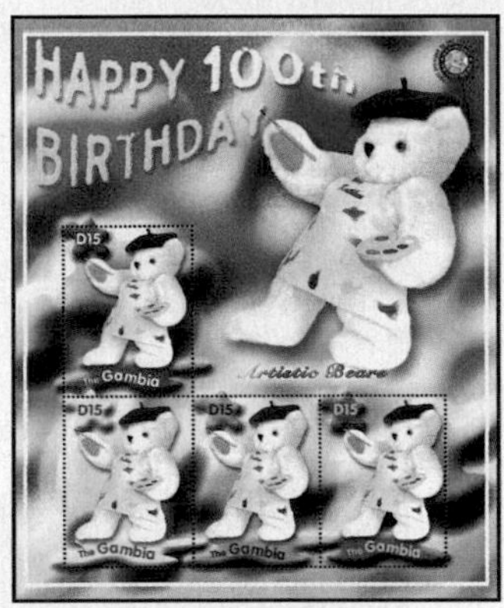

Teddy Bears, Cent. — A443

No. 2666: a, Bear with green feathered cap. b, Bear with beer stein. c, Bear with flower bouquet. d, Bear with mountain hat.

No. 2667 — Color of denomination and country name: a, White. b, Red violet. c, Blue violet. d, Green.

2002, Oct. 21 ***Perf. 14***

2666	A442 15d Sheet of 4, #a-d	7.00	7.00

Perf. 14¼

2667	A443 15d Sheet of 4, #a-d	7.00	7.00

Christmas — A444

Designs: 3d, Madonna of Loreto, by Perugino. 5d, Madonna della Consolazione, by Perugino. 7d, Adoration of the Shepherds, by Perugino. 15d, Transfiguration of Christ, by Giovanni Bellini. 35d, Adoration of the Magi, by Perugino.
45d, Christ Blessing, by Bellini.

2002, Nov. 4 ***Perf. 14***

2668-2672	A444	Set of 5	11.00	11.00

Souvenir Sheet

2673	A444 45d multi	7.50	7.50

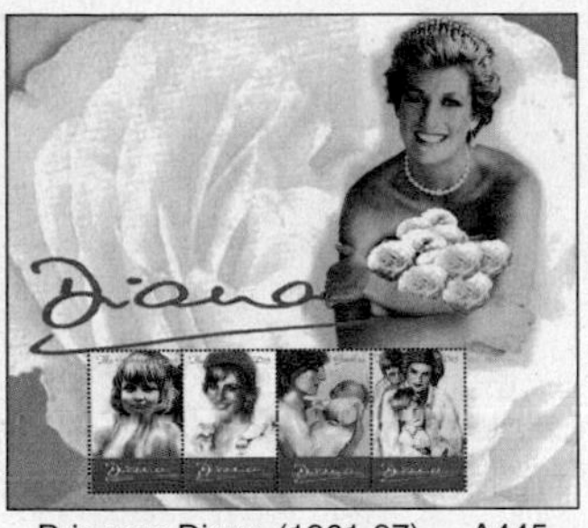

Princess Diana (1961-97) — A445

No. 2674, 15d — With red panel at bottom: a, As child. b, Wearing tiara. c, Holding baby. d, With children.

No. 2675, 15d: a, Wearing red hat. b, Wearing red and white hat. c, Wearing white gown. d, Wearing black gown and choker.

2002, Nov. 18 **Sheets of 4, #a-d**

2674-2675	A445	Set of 2	20.00	20.00

Souvenir Sheet

Gold-banded Forester Butterfly — A446

2002 **Litho.** ***Perf. 14***

2676	A446 60d multi	11.00	11.00

Birds — A447

No. 2677: a, Black-crowned crane. b, Barn owl. c, African pygmy kingfisher. d, Audouin's gull. e, Royal tern. f, Blue-bellied roller.

2002

2677	A447 7d Sheet of 6, #a-f	10.00	10.00

Pres. John F. Kennedy (1917-63) — A448

No. 2678, 15d: a, With daughter Caroline. b, At typewriter. c, At wedding to Jacqueline. d, With Jacqueline.

No. 2679, 15d, vert: a, In naval uniform. b, As child. c, Wearing shirt with open collar. d, At microphone.

2002, Nov. 8 **Sheets of 4, #a-d**

2678-2679	A448	Set of 2	17.50	17.50

A449

Trains A450

Designs: 2d, Paris, Lyon & Mediterranean Railway. 3d, Zugspitz rack train, Germany. No. 2682, 10d, Austrian State Railway Class 210. 15d, State Railway of Saxony.

4d, 1922 Great Britain Class A1 4-6-2. 5d, 1957 Tee four car train. No. 2686, 7d, 1928 German Rheingold Mitropa car. 8d, 1900 German Gerda 4-4-0.

No. 2688, 7d: a, French Natl. Railway Series 68. b, French Natl. Railway Mistral. c, Prussian State Railway. d, Austrian Southern Railway. e, Paris-Orleans Railway. f, German Federal Railway E10.

No. 2689, 7d: a, Royal Prussian Union Railway. b, Austrian Federal Railway. c, German Rugen steam locomotive. d, Rh B Ge 2/4 electric locomotive. e, Panoramic Express, Switzerland. f, Brunig steam engine, Swiss Natl. Railway.

No. 2690, 10d: a, 1813 Puffing Billy, Great Britain. b, Adler, Germany, 1836. c, 1906 German 4-6-0. d, Class 132 Co-Co, Germany.

No. 2691, 10d: a, 1832 Brother Jonathan 4-2-0, US. b, Medoc Class 2-4-0, Germany and Switzerland, 1857. c, 1908 German Class S 3/6 4-6-2. d, 1959 German Class VT 11.5.

No. 2692, 10d: a, 1843 Beuth 2-2-2, Germany. b, 1852 Crampton 4-2-0, France. c, 1932 Sut 877 Flying Hamburger, Germany. d, 1970 Class 103.1 Co-Co, Germany.

No. 2693, 25d, German Federal Railway V200. No. 2694, 25d, German Federal Railway Trans-Europe Express.

No. 2695, 25d, 1953 VT10.5, Germany. No. 2696, 25d,1973 Class ET 403 four-car electric, Germany.

2002

2680-2683	A449	Set of 4	9.50	9.50
2684-2687	A450	Set of 4	8.50	8.50

Sheets of 6, #a-f

2688-2689	A449	Set of 2	18.00	18.00

Sheets of 4, #a-d

2690-2692	A450	Set of 3	25.00	25.00

Souvenir Sheets

2693-2694	A449	Set of 2	10.00	10.00
2695-2696	A450	Set of 2	10.00	10.00

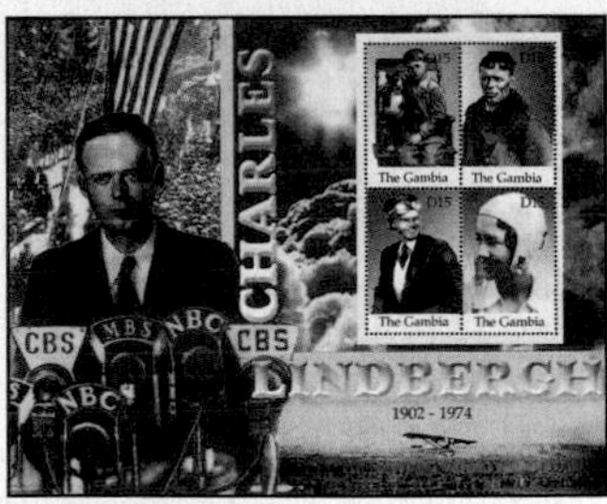

Charles A. Lindbergh (1902-74), Aviator — A451

No. 2697, 15d: a, As child, with dog. b, As young man, brown violet background. c, With aviator goggles. d, Anne Morrow Lindbergh.

No. 2698, 15d: a, As child. b, As young man, blue background. c, Wearing uniform. d, Wearing suit and tie.

2002, Nov. 18 **Litho.** ***Perf. 14***

Sheets of 4, #a-d

2697-2698	A451	Set of 2	22.00	22.00

Butterfly Type of 2000

Designs: 4d, Amphicalia tigris.

2003, Jan. 14 ***Perf. 14¾x14***

2699	A367 4d multi	.40	.40

New Year 2003 (Year of the Ram) — A452

No. 2697: a, Tan background, brown ram. b, Purple background. c, Brown background, orange ram. d, Orange background, purple and red ram.

2003, Jan. 27 ***Perf. 13¾***

2701 A452 10d Sheet of 4, #a-d 6.00 6.00

A453

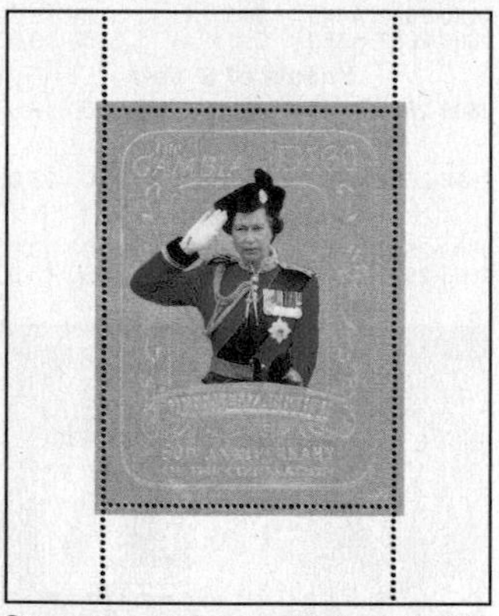

Coronation of Queen Elizabeth II, 50th Anniv. — A454

No. 2702: a, Wearing tiara. b, Wearing blue hat. c, Wearing cape and hat.

2003 **Litho.** ***Perf. 14***

2702 A453 20d Sheet of 3, #a-c 10.00 10.00

Souvenir Sheet

2703 A453 45d shown 7.50 7.50

Miniature Sheet

Litho. & Embossed

Perf. 13¼x13

2704 A454 130d shown 25.00 25.00

Issued: Nos. 2702-2703, 5/13; 130d, 2/2.

Art by Yoshitoshi Taiso (1839-92) A455

Designs: 5d, Concubine Washing Her Hands Under an Ornate Faucet. 10d, Housewife in an Inner Chamber Fanning a Fire. 15d, Geisha Catching a Firefly. 25d, A Young Geisha Dressed as an Elegant Young Man While Taking Part in the Niwaka Celebration.

No. 2709: a, Music Teacher Playing on a Samisen. b, An "Okamisan," or Proprietress of a Tea House, at Work. c, A City Merchant's Widow Absorbed in a Novelette. d, Busy Young Waitress Preoccupied With Her Responsibilities.

45d, A "Saikun," or Wife of a Government Official, Lighting an Oil Lamp.

2003, Mar. 10 **Litho.** ***Perf. 14¼***

2705-2708 A455 Set of 4 6.75 6.75

2709 A455 20d Sheet of 4, #a-d 10.00 10.00

Souvenir Sheet

2710 A455 45d multi 4.75 4.75

Paintings by the Cranachs A456

Paintings by Lucas Cranach the Elder (1472-1553) or Lucas Cranach the Younger (1515-86) (Y): 5d, Portrait of Johannes Scheyring. 7d, Rudolph Agricola. 10d, Portrait Head of a Gentleman (Y). 20d, Hans von Lindau (Y).

No. 2715: a, Margravine Elizabeth von Ansbach (Y). b, Elector Joachim II of Brandenburg (Y). c, Portrait of a Nobleman (Y). d, Portrait of a Noblewoman (Y).

40d, The Ill-matched Couple.

2003, Mar. 10

2711-2714 A456 Set of 4 6.00 6.00

2715 A456 15d Sheet of 4, #a-d 9.50 9.50

Souvenir Sheet

2716 A456 40d multi 5.00 5.00

Paintings by Wassily Kandinsky (1866-1944) — A457

Designs: 2d, Composition X. 4d, Arrow Towards the Circle. 5d, Yellow-Red-Blue. 7d, Accompanied Middle. 10d, In Blue. 20d, Round and Pointed.

No. 2723, vert.: a, Picture with Archer. b, Light. c, Picture in the Picture. d, White Stroke.

No. 2724, 45d, Improvisation XIX. No. 2725, 45d, On the Points.

2003, Mar. 10 ***Perf. 14¼***

2717-2722 A457 Set of 6 7.25 7.25

2723 A457 15d Sheet of 4, #a-d 10.00 10.00

Size: 97x78mm

Imperf

2724-2725 A457 Set of 2 11.50 11.50

A458

Astronauts Killed In Space Shuttle Columbia Accident — A459

No. 2726, 15d — Michael P. Anderson: a, Columbia crew, brown background, country name at UL. b, Anderson and jet. c, Shuttle lifting off. d, Shuttle in orbit, Space Station.

No. 2727, 15d — Kalpana Chawla: a, Like No. 2726a, country name at LL. b, Shuttle being transported by jet. c, Shuttle glowing in re-entry. d, Chawla, astronaut spacewalking.

No. 2728, 15d — Laurel Blair Salton Clark: a, Like No. 2727a, green and red background. b, Shuttle in orbit, moon in background. c, Shuttle on launch pad. d, Clark and jet.

No. 2729, 15d — Ilan Ramon: a, Columbia crew, purple and yellow background. b, Ramon in jet. c, Shuttle with engines firing at launch pad. d, Shuttle in orbit.

No. 2730: a, Mission Specialist David M. Brown. b, Commander Rick D. Husband. c, Mission Specialist 4 Laurel Blair Salton Clark. d, Mission Specialist 4 Kalpana Chawla. e, Payload Commander, Michael P. Anderson. f, Pilot William C. McCool. g, Payload Specialist 4 Ilan Ramon.

2003, Apr. 7 ***Perf. 14¼***

Sheets of 4, #a-d

2726-2729 A458 Set of 4 35.00 35.00

Souvenir Sheet

2730 A459 10d Sheet of 7, #a-g 10.00 10.00

A460

Teddy Bears — A461

No. 2732, 15d — Bears with flags and soccer uniforms of: a, England. b, Brazil. c, Germany. d, Spain.

No. 2733, 15d — Bears with soocer uniforms of German teams: a, Schalke 04. b, FC Bayern Munich. c, Bayer Leaerkusen. d, Hertha Berlin.

No. 2734, 45d, FC Bayern Munich, white uniform. No. 2735, 45d, FC Bayern Munich red uniform, horiz.

2003 **Embroidered** ***Imperf.***

Self-Adhesive (#2731)

2731 A460 150d shown 20.00 20.00

Sheets of 4, #a-d

Litho.

Perf. 13¼

2732-2733 A461 Set of 2 16.00 16.00

Souvenir Sheets

2734-2735 A461 Set of 2 9.50 9.50

Issued: No. 2731, Apr.; Nos. 2732-2735, 7/1.

No. 2731 was issued in sheets of 4.

Prince William, 21st Birthday — A462

No. 2736: a, Wearing suit, no tie. b, Wearing suit and tie. c, Wearing blue shirt, no suit.

45d, Wearing polo uniform.

2003, May 13 **Litho.** ***Perf. 14***

2736 A462 20d Sheet of 3, #a-c 9.00 9.00

Souvenir Sheet

2737 A462 45d multi 6.50 6.50

Intl. Year of Fresh Water — A463

No. 2738 — Gambia River: a, Foliage at top. b, Foliage at top, silhouette of far shore at center. c, Trees at right.

45d, Gambia River rapids.

2003, July 1 ***Perf. 13¼***

2738 A463 20d Sheet of 3, #a-c 8.50 8.50

Souvenir Sheet

2739 A463 45d multi 6.75 6.75

Tour de France Bicycle Race, Cent. — A464

No. 2740, 15d: a, Henri Pelissier, 1923. b, Ottavio Bottecchia, 1924. c, Bottecchia, 1925. d, Lucien Buysse, 1926.
No. 2741, 15d: a, Nicholas Frantz, 1927. b, Frantz, 1928. c, Maurice de Waele, 1929. d, André Leducq, 1930.
No. 2742, 15d: a, Antonin Magne, 1931. b, Leducq, 1932. c, Georges Speicher, 1933. d, Magne, 1934.

2003, July 1 ***Perf. 13¼***

Sheets of 4, #a-d

2740-2742 A464 Set of 3 30.00 30.00

General Motors Automobiles — A465

No. 2743, 15d — Cadillacs: a, 1937 Series 60. b, 1927 La Salle. c, 1930 V-16. d, 1931 V-16 Convertible.
No. 2744, 15d — Corvettes: a, 1960 Shark. b, 1964 Sting Ray Convertible. c, 1956 Convertible. d, 1967.
No. 2745, 45d, 1954 Cadillac Eldorado. No. 2746, 45d, 1964 Corvette Sting Ray.

2003, July 1 ***Perf. 13¼x13½***

Sheets of 4, #a-d

2743-2744 A465 Set of 2 18.00 18.00

Souvenir Sheets

2745-2746 A465 Set of 2 13.00 13.00

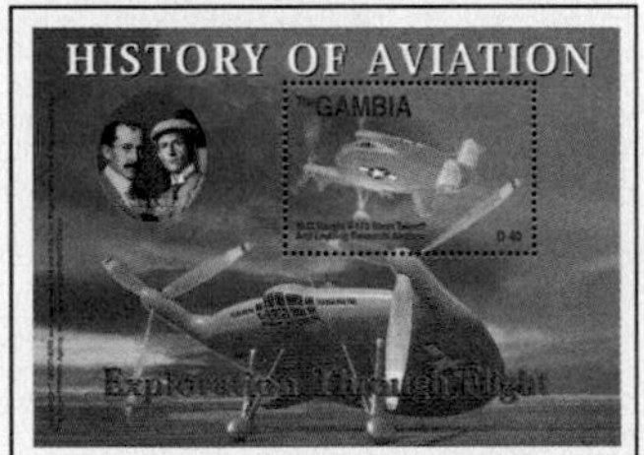

History of Aviation — A466

No. 2747, 15d: a, First powered flight by Wright Brothers, 1903. b, Goupy I, first full-size triplane, 1908. c, Deutschland LZ-7, first commercial airship, 1909. d, Lt. Col. Richard Byrd's flight over North Pole, 1926.
No. 2748, 15d: a, Granville Gee Bee, world speed record, 1932. b, Boeing 247D with all-metal construction retractable landing gear, 1933. c, Douglas DC 3, 1935. d, Amelia Earhart's solo flight from Hawaii to California, 1935.
No. 2749, 15d: a, First solar powered flight, by MacCready Solar Challenger, 1981. b, Voyager 2 space probe explores Saturn, 1981. c, Space Shuttle Columbia, 1981. d, First non-stop non-refueled around the world flight, by Voyager, 1986.
No. 2750, 40d, Vought V-173 Short Takeoff and Landing research airplane, 1942. No. 2751, 40d, Pioneer 10 space probe, 1972. No. 2752, 40d, AD-1 scissors-wing SST, 1979.

2003, July 14 ***Perf. 14***

Sheets of 4, #a-d

2747-2749 A466 Set of 3 24.00 24.00

Souvenir Sheets

2750-2752 A466 Set of 3 17.50 17.50

Ferrari Race Cars — A467

Designs: 2d, 126 C2. 3d, 312 T2. 5d, 312 T4. 7d, 126 C3. 10d, F399. 15d, F1-2000. 20d, F2001. 25d, F2002.

2003, July 28 ***Perf. 14¼***

2753-2760 A467 Set of 8 11.00 11.00

Circus Performers — A468

No. 2761, 15d: a, Francesco Caroli. b, Lou Jacobs. c, Frankie Saluto. d, Gingernut.
No. 2762, 15d: a, Evgeny Maranogli. b, Saby. c, Colonel Joe. d, Puma.

2003, Sept. 1 ***Perf. 14***

Sheets of 4, #a-d

2761-2762 A468 Set of 2 13.00 13.00

Marine Mammals and Flowers Type of 2002

No. 2763 — Insects and flowers: a, Colored shield-backed bug, Waltheria indica. b, Dragonfly, Red mangrove. c, Cotton stainer bug, Baissea multiflora. d, Harpagomantis. Mimosa pigra. e, Katydid, Coia cordifolia. f, African grasshopper, Urena labata.
50d, Giant swallowtail butterfly, Ipomoea cairica.

2003 ***Perf. 14***

2763 A441 10d Sheet of 6, #a-f 12.00 12.00

Souvenir Sheet

2764 A441 50d multi 10.00 10.00

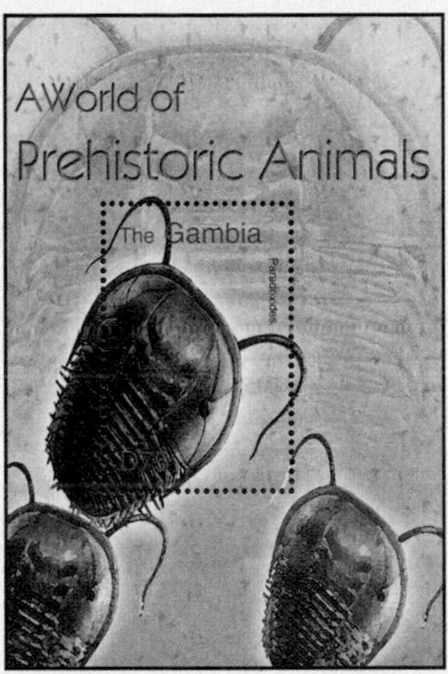

Prehistoric Animals — A469

No. 2765, 30d: a, Peteinosaurus. b, Pachycephalosaurus. c, Ichthyosaur. d, Anomalocaris.
No. 2766, 30d, horiz.: a, Criorhynchus. b, Seismosaurus. c, Triceratops. d, Stegosaurus.
No. 2767, 75d, Paradoxides. No. 2768, 75d, Edmontosaurus, horiz.

2003, Nov. 4 **Litho.** ***Perf. 14***

Sheets of 4, #a-d

2765-2766 A469 Set of 2 25.00 25.00

Souvenir Sheets

2767-2768 A469 Set of 2 18.00 18.00

Christmas A470

Paintings: 3d, Madonna of the Grand Duke, by Raphael. 5d, Madonna della Impannata, by Raphael. 7d, Adoration of the Magi, by Filippo Lippi. 60d, Adoration in the Woods, by Lippi.
75d, Madonna del Carmelo, by Giambattista Tiepolo.

2003, Nov. 17 ***Perf. 14¼***

2769-2772 A470 Set of 4 10.00 10.00

Souvenir Sheet

2773 A470 75d multi 10.00 10.00

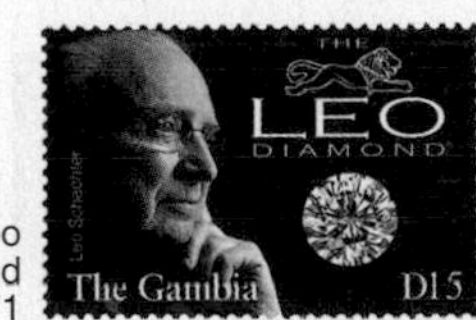

Leo Diamond A471

2003, Nov. 18 ***Perf. 13¼x13½***

2774 A471 15d multi 1.75 1.75

Souvenir Sheet

2775 A471 60d multi 9.00 9.00

No. 2774 issued in sheets of six.

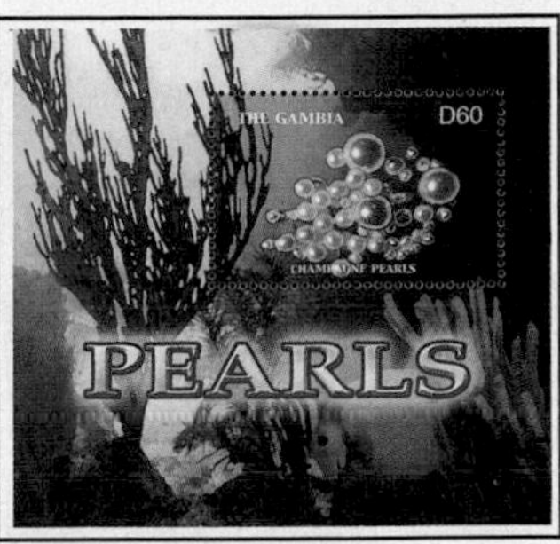

Pearls — A472

No. 2776: a, South Sea pearls. b, Mabe pearls. c, Pinctada maxima. d, Australian pearls. e, Pearls on ocean floor. f, South Sea white pearls.
60d, Champagne pearls.

2003, Nov. 18

2776 A472 15d Sheet of 6, #a-f 14.00 14.00

Souvenir Sheet

2777 A472 60d multi 8.50 8.50

James Cagney (1899-1986) — A473

No. 2778: a, With solid tie. b, With hat. c, With gun. d, With lapel handkerchief. e, With plaid tie. f, With woman.

2003 ***Perf. 14***

2778 A473 10d Sheet of 6, #a-f 8.00 8.00

Clark Gable (1901-60) — A474

No. 2779: a, Wearing tuxedo and bow tie, hand showing. b, Wearing suit and tie, no mustache, no hand showing. c, Wearing tuxedo and bow tie, no hand showing. d, Wearing suit and tie, hand showing. e, Wearing suit and solid tie, with mustache. f, Wearing suit and striped tie, with mustache.

2003

2779 A474 10d Sheet of 6, #a-f 8.00 8.00

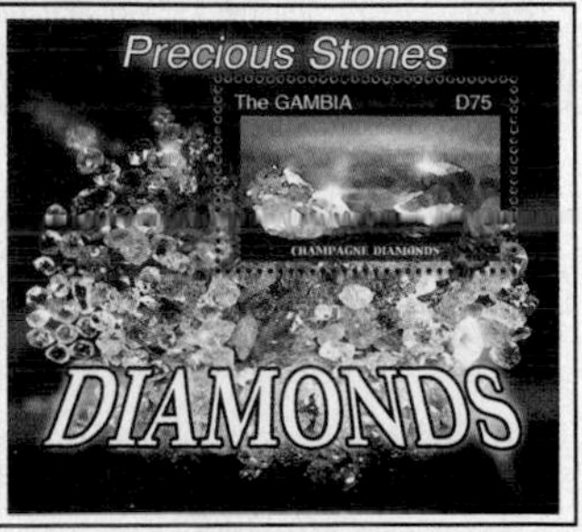

Diamonds — A475

No. 2780: a, Rough diamonds. b, Yellow diamonds. c, Pink diamonds. d, Blue diamonds. e, White diamonds. f, Green diamonds.
75d, Champagne diamonds.

Perf. 13¼x13½

2003, Nov. 18 **Litho.**

2780 A475 20d Sheet of 6, #a-f 13.00 13.00

Souvenir Sheet

2781 A475 75d multi 8.00 8.00

Minerals — A476

No. 2782: a, Stilbite. b, Smoky quartz. c, Lapis lazuli. d, Amethyst. e, Black opals. f, Rubies.
60d, Quartz.

2003, Nov. 18

2782 A476 15d Sheet of 6, #a-f 12.00 12.00

Souvenir Sheet

2783 A476 60d multi 6.50 6.50

New Year 2004 (Year of the Monkey) — A477

No. 2784: a, Monkey with white and brown face, white ears. b, Monkey with white and blue gray face. c, Monkey with white and brown face. d, Monkey with orange and white face.

2004, Jan. 5 *Perf. 13¼*

2784 A477 15d Sheet of 4, #a-d 7.50 7.50

Paintings by Xu Beihong (1895-1953) — A478

No. 2785, vert.: a, Four Magpies. b, Cormorants. c, Under the Banyan Tree. d, Citrus Tree. e, Double Happiness. f, Rooster in Bamboo Garden.
No. 2786: a, Bird on the Kapok Tree. b, Twin Pines.

2004, Jan. 21 **Litho.** *Perf. 13½x13¼*

2785 A478 10d Sheet of 6, #a-f 7.75 7.75

Perf. 13¼

2786 A478 25d Sheet of 2, #a-b 6.50 6.50

2004 Hong Kong Stamp Expo. No. 2785 contains six 28x42mm stamps.

FIFA (Fédération Internationale de Football Association), Cent. — A479

FIFA cups: No. 2787, 10d, World Cup. No. 2788, 10d, Jules Rimet Cup. No. 2789, 10d, Women's World Cup. No. 2790, 10d, Under 17 World Championship Cup. No. 2791, 10d, Under 19 Women's World Championship Cup. No. 2792, 10d, Club World Championship Cup. No. 2793, 10d, Confederations Cup. No. 2794, 10d, World Youth Championship Cup. No. 2795, 10d, Fustal (Indoor Soccer) World Championship Cup.

2004, Feb. 16 *Perf. 13¼*

2787-2795 A479 Set of 9 9.50 9.50

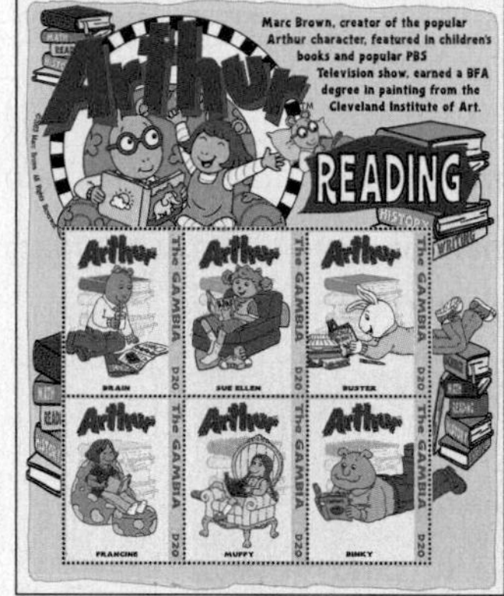

Arthur and Friends — A480

No. 2796 — Characters reading: a, Brain. b, Sue Ellen. c, Buster. d, Francine. e, Muffy. f, Binky.
No. 2797, 30d: a, Brain playing clarinet. b, Francine playing banjo. c, Buster playing flute. d, Sue Ellen playing violin.
No. 2798, 30d: a, Brain playing bass. b, Francine playing drum. c, Buster playing tuba. d, Sue Ellen playing saxophone.

2004, Feb. 16

2796 A480 20d Sheet of 6, #a-f 12.00 12.00

Sheets of 4, #a-d

2797-2798 A480 Set of 2 21.00 21.00

Concorde and Queen Elizabeth 2 — A481

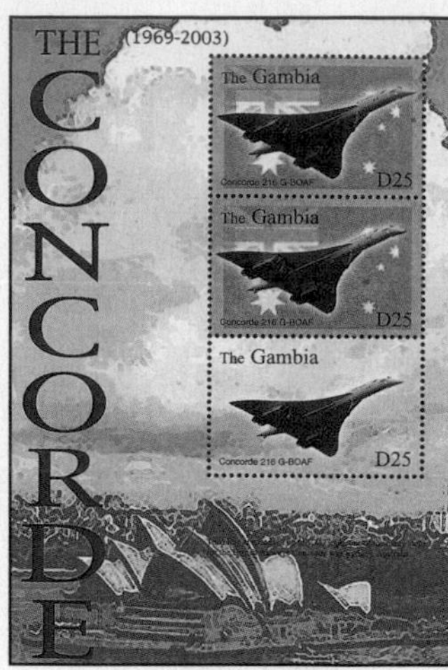

Concorde — A482

No. 2800, 25d — Concorde 216 G-BOAF and: a, British flag, with dots of blue at UR. b, British flag, no dots at UR. c, Clouds.
No. 2801, 25d — Concorde 216 G-BOAF and: a, Statue of Liberty. b, Field of US flag. c, Stripes of US flag.
No. 2802, 25d — Concorde 213 F-BTSD and: a, Top of Eiffel Tower. b, French flag, middle part of Eiffel Tower. c, French flag, first and second landings of Eiffel Tower.

2004, Feb. 17 *Perf. 14*

2799 A481 60d multi 8.50 8.50

Sheets of 3, #a-c

Perf. 13¼x13½

2800-2802 A482 Set of 3 24.00 24.00

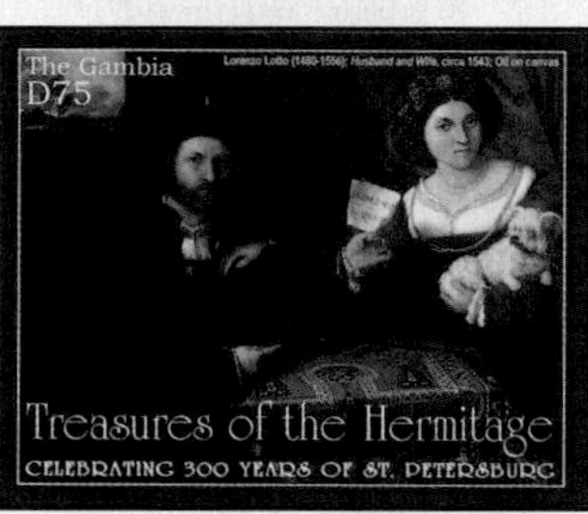

Paintings in the Hermitage, St. Petersburg, Russia — A483

No. 2803, vert.: a, Portrait of a Gentleman, by Domenico Capriolo. b, Sybil, by Dosso Dossi. c, A Woman in a Turban, by Anne-Louis Girodet-Trioson. d, Portrait of a Gentleman, by Ambrosius Holbein.
75d, Husband and Wife, by Lorenzo Lotto.

2004, Feb. 17 *Perf. 13¼*

2803 A483 30d Sheet of 4, #a-d 12.50 12.50

Imperf

2804 A483 75d multi 8.50 8.50

St. Petersburg, 300th anniv. No. 2803 contains four 37x50mm stamps.

Paintings by Pablo Picasso — A484

No. 2805, vert.: a, Girl in Chemise. b, Portrait of Jacinto Salvadó as Harlequin. c, Tumblers. d, Woman with a Crow.
75d, The Siesta.

2004, Feb. 17 *Perf. 13¼*

2805 A484 30d Sheet of 4, #a-d 13.50 13.50

Imperf

2806 A484 75d multi 9.00 9.00

No. 2805 contains four 37x50mm stamps.

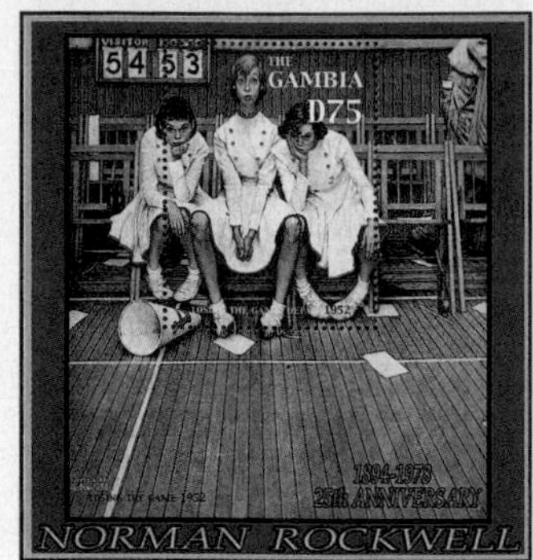

Paintings by Norman Rockwell — A485

No. 2807: a, Detail of 1957 Saturday Evening Post Illustration. b, Girl at Mirror. c, After the Prom. d, The Prom Dress.
75d, Losing the Game.

2004, Feb. 17 *Perf. 13¼*

2807 A485 30d Sheet of 4, #a-d 12.50 12.50

Souvenir Sheet

2808 A485 75d multi 7.50 7.50

Paintings by Kunichika Toyohara (1835-1900) A486

Designs: 10d, The Actor Kikugoro Onoe V as Moronao with the Late Sojuro Nakamura I as Hangan Enya. 15d, The Actor Kikugoro Onoe V as Kunimoto Shinohara with Danjuro Ichikawa IX as Takamori. 20d, The Actor Kikugoro Onoe V as Kansuke Yamamoto with Sadanji Ichikawa I as Daizo Ushikubo. 35d, The Actor Kikugoro Onoe V as the Ghost Seigen with Fukusuke Nakamura IV as Sakurahime.
No. 2813: a, The Actor Sadanji Ichikawa I as the Fishmonger Fukashichi. b, The Actor Sadanji Ichikawa I as Umeomaru. c, The Actor Kuzo Ichikawa III as Shihei Fujiwara. d, The Actor Shikan Nakamura IV as Motome.
75d, The Actor Udanji Ichikawa as Saihei Koya (Ozawa Keifu Tomofusa), horiz.

2004, Feb. 17

2809-2812 A486 Set of 4 8.00 8.00

2813 A486 30d Sheet of 4, #a-d 12.50 12.50

Souvenir Sheet

2814 A486 75d multi 5.25 5.25

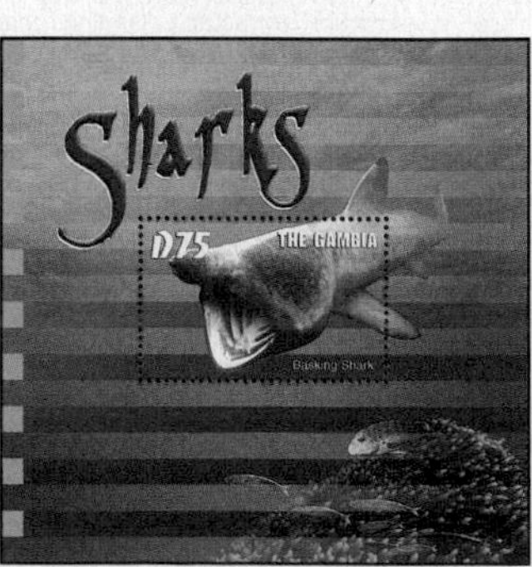

Sharks — A487

No. 2815: a, Lemon shark. b, Nurse shark. c, Leopard shark. d, Starry smoothhound sharks.
75d, Basking shark.

2004, Mar. 8 *Perf. 13¼x13½*
2815 A487 30d Sheet of 4, #a-d 14.00 14.00

Souvenir Sheet

2816 A487 75d multi 8.50 8.50

Cats — A488

No. 2817, vert.: a, Black and white bicolor American shorthair. b, Brown and white Sphinx. c, Copper-eyed white Persian. d, Blue mackerel tabby Oriental longhair.
75d, Copper-eyed cameo Persian.

2004, Mar. 8 *Perf. 13½x13¼*
2817 A488 30d Sheet of 4, #a-d 13.00 13.00

Souvenir Sheet
Perf. 13¼x13½

2818 A488 75d multi 7.50 7.50

Dogs — A489

No. 2819, vert.: a, Bracco. b, Shih tzu. c, Boston terrier. d, Chihuahua.
75d, Borzoi.

2004, Mar. 8 *Perf. 13½x13¼*
2819 A489 30d Sheet of 4, #a-d 13.00 13.00

Souvenir Sheet
Perf. 13¼x13½

2820 A489 75d multi 7.50 7.50

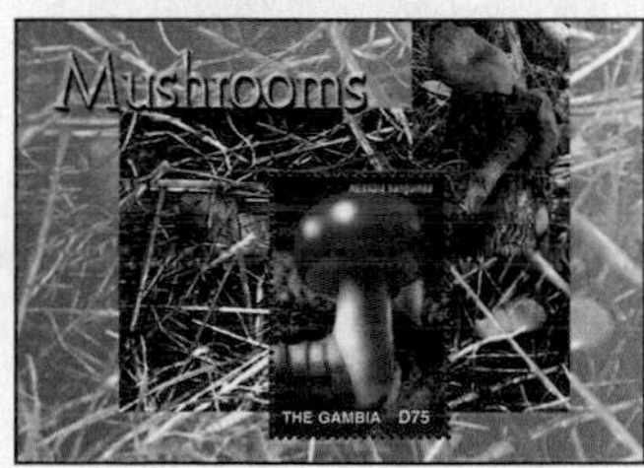

Mushrooms — A490

No. 2821, 30d: a, Hydrocybe conica. b, Laccaria fraterna. c, Gomphus clavatus. d, Hydrocybe psittacina.
No. 2822, 30d, horiz.: a, Steel blue entoloma. b, Caged stinkhorn. c, Flowerpot depiota. d, Singeri dodge.
75d, Russula sanguinea.

Perf. 13½x13¼, 13¼x13½
2004, Mar. 8 **Sheets of 4, #a-d**
2821-2822 A490 Set of 2 26.00 26.00

Souvenir Sheet

2823 A490 75d multi 8.00 8.00

Orchid Cacti — A491

No. 2824, 30d: a, Echinocerus. b, Harrisia. c, Stapelia. d, Matucana.
No. 2825, 30d: a, Epiphyllum crenatum. b, Isopogon latifolius. c, Banksia ericifolia. d, Echinopsis.
75d, Epiphyllum.

2004, Mar. 8 *Perf. 13¼x13½*

Sheets of 4, #a-d

2824-2825 A491 Set of 2 24.00 24.00

Souvenir Sheet

2826 A491 75d multi 8.50 8.50

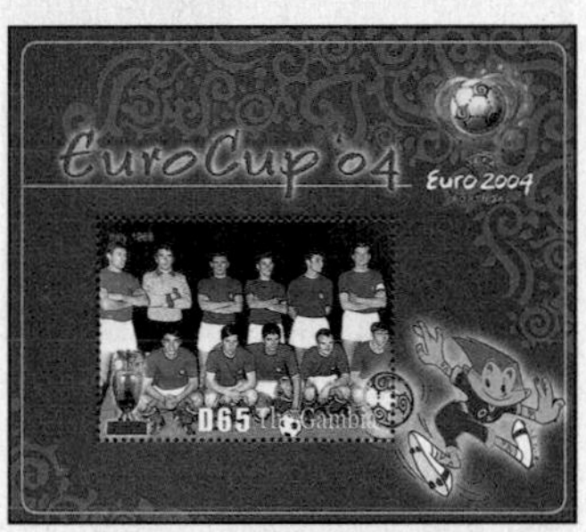

European Soccer Championships, Portugal — A492

No. 2827 — Teams from: a, Bulgaria. b, Croatia. c, Czech Republic. d, Denmark. e, England. f, France. g, Germany. h, Greece. i, Italy. j, Latvia. k, Netherlands. l, Portugal (no country name). m, Russia. n, Spain. o, Sweden. p, Switzerland.
No. 2828, vert.: a, Angelo Domenghini. b, Dragan Dzajic. c, Luigi Riva. d, Stadio Olimpico.
65d, 1968 champions, Italy.

Perf. 13¼, 13½x13¼ (#2828)
2004, Mar. 26
2827 A492 6d Sheet of 16, #a-p 9.50 9.50
2828 A492 25d Sheet of 4, #a-d 9.50 9.50

Souvenir Sheet

2829 A492 65d multi 4.75 4.75

No. 2828 contains four 28x42mm stamps.

2004 Summer Olympics, Athens — A493

Designs: 10d, Swimming. 15d, Henri de Baillet-Latour (1876-1942), Intl. Olympic Committee President, vert. 20d, Gold medal of 1896 Olympics, vert. 30d, Pentathlon.

2004, Apr. 19 *Perf. 13¼*
2830-2833 A493 Set of 4 7.00 7.00

Trains, Bridges, Tunnels and Stations — A494

No. 2834, 12d: a, Mallard locomotive. b, North British 4-8-2T locomotive. c, Russian P36 4-8-4 locomotive. d, Forth Rail Bridge. e, Lune Viaduct. f, Lambley Viaduct. g, Alston Arches Viaduct. h, Royal Albert Bridge. i, Blackfriar's Bridge.
No. 2835, 12d: a, City of Truro train. b, Sharp Stewart 4-4-0 locomotive. c, Indian Railways WT Class locomotive. d, Charing Cross Station. e, Linlithgow Station. f, Hellifield Station. g, Kings Cross Station. h, Paddington Station. i, Victoria Station.
No. 2836, 12d: a, Virgin Pendolino train. b, Mountain Class Garratt locomotive. c, 2-8-8-4 No. 227 locomotive. d, Kilsby Tunnel. e, Box Tunnel. f, Willersley Tunnel. g, Stansted Airport Tunnel. h, Clayton Tunnel. i, Severn Tunnel.
No. 2837, 65d, West Highland Line train. No. 2838, 65d, Darjeeling-Himalaya train. No. 2839, 65d, Eurostar.

2004, Apr. 19 *Perf. 13¼x13½*

Sheets of 9, #a-i

2834-2836 A494 Set of 3 36.00 36.00

Souvenir Sheets

2837-2839 A494 Set of 3 20.00 20.00

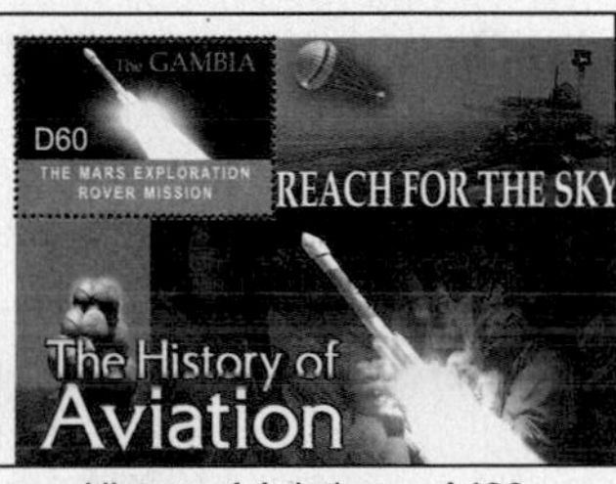

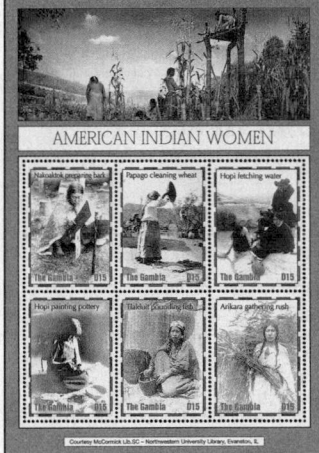

American Indians — A495

No. 2840: a, Nakoaktok preparing bark. b, Papago cleaning wheat. c, Hopi fetching water. d, Hopi painting pottery. e, Tlakluit pounding fish. f, Arikara gathering rush.
No. 2841, horiz.: a, Apsaroke Indians and teepee. b, Pigean Indians. c, Apsaroke Indians. d, Sioux chiefs.

2004, May 3 *Perf. 14¼x14¾*
2840 A495 15d Sheet of 6, #a-f 9.00 9.00

Perf. 13¾

2841 A495 30d Sheet of 4, #a-d 11.00 11.00

No. 2841 contains four 38x30mm stamps.

History of Aviation — A496

No. 2842: a, Leonardo da Vinci. b, Count Ferdinand von Zeppelin. c, William E. Boeing. d, Capt. John Cunningham. e, Capt. Edwin C. Musick. f, Capt. Jock Lowe. g, William Lear. h, Jenny Murray.
60d, Mars Rover mission.

2004, May 3 *Perf. 14*
2842 A496 12d Sheet of 8, #a-h 12.00 12.00

Souvenir Sheet

2843 A496 60d multi 7.50 7.50

A497

Marilyn Monroe (1926-62) — A498

No. 2844: a, Wearing necklace. b, No necklace.
No. 2845 — Background color: a, Orange. b, Green. c, Bright lilac rose. d, Bright yellow. e, Bright blue. f, Bright red. g, Dull blue. h, Bright yellow green. i, Blue green. j, Yellow. k, Red orange. l, Purple. m, Red lilac. n, Light blue. o, Dark blue. p, Rose pink.
No. 2846 — Black background and: a, Hand on face. b, Wearing necklace. c, Wearng red dress. d, Wearing blouse with collar.

2004, May 3 *Perf. 14*
2844 A497 25d Pair, #a-b 4.25 4.25
2845 A498 7d Sheet of 16, #a-p 14.50 14.50
2846 A498 25d Sheet of 4, #a-d 9.00 9.00

No. 2844 was printed in sheets containing two pairs.

D-Day, 60th Anniv. A499

Designs: 7d, Jim Wallwork, 6th Airborne Division. 10d, Major Gen. Richard Gale. 15d, Winston Churchill. 30d, J.K. "Paddy" Byrne, 197th Typhoon Squadron.
No. 2851, 25d: a, Bombers over coast of Normandy. b, RAF Mitchell bomber dropping bombs. c, British Horsa gliders behind enemy lines. d, Paratroopers dropping into Normandy.
No. 2852, 25d: a, British paratroopers prepare for mission. b, British paratroopers secure Pegasus Bridge. c, American paratroopers drop into Sainte-Mère-Eglise area. d, American paratroopers enter town of Sainte-Mère-Eglise.
No. 2853, 60d, RAF bombers under construction. No. 2854, 60d, Troops disembarking from landing craft.

2004, May 3 **Litho.**
2847-2850 A499 Set of 4 + labels 8.50 8.50

Sheets of 4, #a-d

2851-2852 A499 Set of 2 18.00 18.00

Souvenir Sheets

2853-2854 A499 Set of 2 14.00 14.00

Election of Pope John Paul II, 25th Anniv. (in 2003) — A500

No. 2855 — Pope in: a, 1988. b, 1989. c, 1990. d, 1991. e, 1992. f, 1993. g, 1994. h, 1995. i, 1996. j, 1997. k, 1998. l, 1999. m, 2000. n, 2001. o, 2002.

No. 2856 — Pope in: a, 1978. b, 1979. c, 1980. d, 1981. e, 1982. f, 1983. g, 1984. h, 1985. i, 1986. j, 1987.

2004, May 13 *Perf. 13½x13¼*

2855 A500 7d Sheet of 15, #a-o 12.00 12.00
2856 A500 10d Sheet of 10, #a-j 10.00 10.00

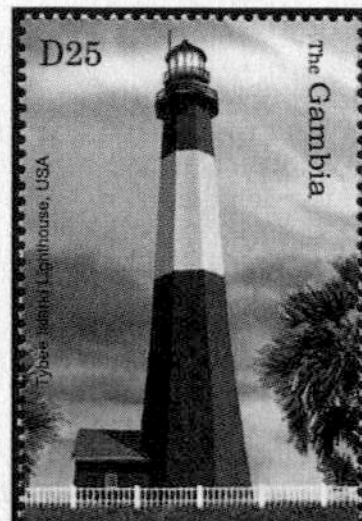

American Lighthouses A501

Designs: 25d, Tybee Island, Georgia. 30d, Old Cape Henry, Virginia. 35d, Morris Island, South Carolina. 40d, Hillsboro Inlet, Florida. 50d, Cape Lookout, North Carolina.

2004, May 27 *Perf. 14¾x14¼*

2857-2861 A501 Set of 5 17.50 17.50

See Nos. 2911A-2911G.

Gambian postal authorities have declared the following items as "illegal";

Sheet of nine 25d stamps: Oceans;

Sheets of six 25d stamps: Birds of Prey with Rotary emblem, Orchids with Rotary emblem, New Cinema, Vincent van Gogh Paintings, Monuments of Egypt, Fire Engines;

Sheets of four 25d stamps: Pope John Paul II, Nude Art, Great Composers, Lighthouses with Rotary emblem, Aircraft with Rotary emblem, Actresses, Pin-up Art;

Sheet of three 25d stamps: Polar Birds with Rotary emblem;

Sheets of two 25d stamps: Prehistoric World, Chinese New Year, Looney Tunes, Games and Sports.

Paintings by Joan Miró A502

Designs: 20d, Woman, 1934, pastel on paper. 25d, Woman, 1934, pastel and pencil on emery paper. 35d, Self-portrait. No. 2865, 75d, Man with Pipe.

No. 2866: a, Portrait IV. b, Seated Woman. c, Painting on Ingres Paper. d, Portrait II.

No. 2867, 75d, Composition with Personages in the Burning Forest, horiz. No. 2868, 75d, Bird, horiz.

2004, Feb. 17 **Litho.** *Perf. 13¼*

2862-2865 A502 Set of 4 13.50 13.50
2866 A502 30d Sheet of 4, #a-d 13.00 13.00

Size: 100x80mm

Imperf

2867-2868 A502 Set of 2 14.50 14.50

Souvenir Sheet

Deng Xiaoping (1904-97), Chinese Leader — A503

2004, May 3 *Perf. 13½*

2869 A503 75d multi 6.25 6.25

Miniature Sheet

Intl. Year of Peace — A504

No. 2870: a, Dalai Lama. b, European nuclear disarmament banner. c, Woodstock music festival.

2004, May 3 *Perf. 14*

2870 A504 35d Sheet of 3, #a-c 10.00 10.00

Miniature Sheet

Rare and Famous Postage Stamps — A505

No. 2871: a, British Guiana #13. b, Great Britain #1. c, United States #85A. d, United States #C3a. e, United States #1.

2004, June 24 *Perf. 13*

2871 A505 20d Sheet of 5, #a-e, + label 11.00 11.00

Flowers — A506

Designs: 1d, Babiana rubrocyanaea. 2d, Protea. 3d, Lithops bromfieldii. 5d, Saintpaulia ionantha. 6d, Monopsis lutea. 7d, Dudleya lanceolata. 9d, Euphorbia punicea. 10d, Oxalis violacea. 25d, Helichrysum bracteatum. 50d, Senecio obovatus. 75d, Mesembryanthemum acinaciforme. 100d, Montbretia crocosmiiflora. 200d, Gladiolus colvillei.

2004, July 1 *Perf. 14¾x14*

2872	A506	1d multi	.25	.25
2873	A506	2d multi	.30	.30
2874	A506	3d multi	.40	.40
2875	A506	5d multi	.60	.60
2876	A506	6d multi	.75	.75
2877	A506	7d multi	.90	.90
2878	A506	9d multi	1.10	1.10
2879	A506	10d multi	1.25	1.25
2880	A506	25d multi	2.50	2.50
2881	A506	50d multi	4.50	4.50
2882	A506	75d multi	6.00	6.00
2883	A506	100d multi	8.00	8.00
2884	A506	200d multi	15.00	15.00
		Nos. 2872-2884 (13)	41.55	41.55

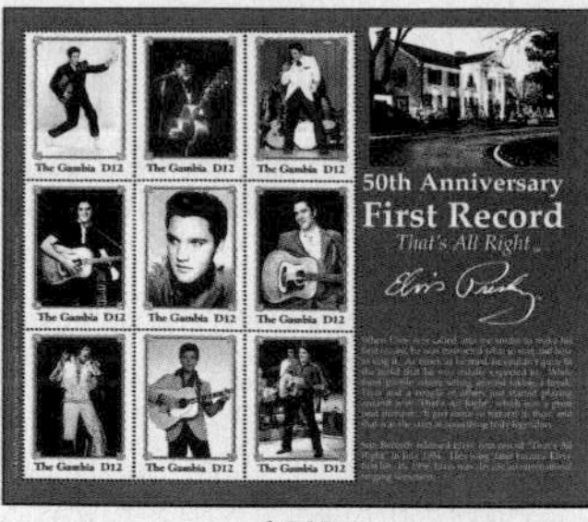

A507

First Elvis Presley Record, 50th Anniv. — A508

Various portraits of Elvis Presley.

2004, Aug. 2 *Perf. 13¼*

2885 A507 12d Sheet of 9, #a-i 13.00 13.00
2886 A508 12d Sheet of 9, #a-i 13.00 13.00

Miniature Sheet

George Herman "Babe" Ruth (1895-1948), Baseball Player — A509

No. 2887: a, Swinging, legs spread apart. b, Standing. c, Swinging, legs together. d, Holding bat.

2004, Sept. 3 *Perf. 13½*

2887 A509 25d Sheet of 4, #a-d 9.25 9.25

Pres. Ronald Reagan (1911-2004) — A510

No. 2888: a, With wife, Nancy and Pope John Paul II. b, With Israeli Prime Minister Shimon Peres.

No. 2889: a, With window in background. b, Before microphones. c, Holding glass.

2004, Oct. 13

2888 A510 15d Pair, #a-b 4.00 4.00
2889 A510 15d Vert. strip of 3, #a-c 5.75 5.75

No. 2888 was printed in sheets of three pairs. No. 2889 was printed in sheets of two strips.

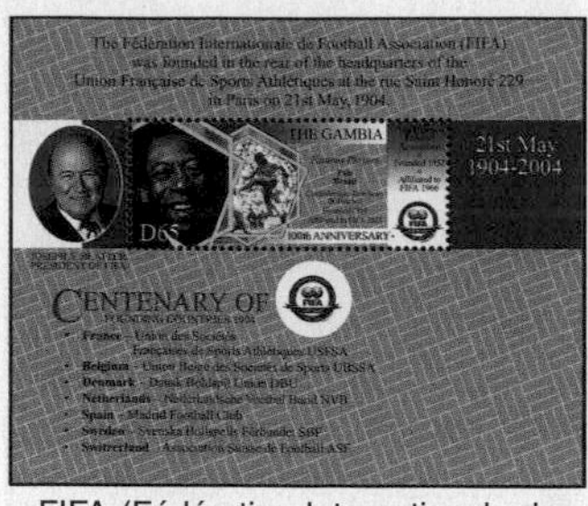

FIFA (Fédération Internationale de Football Association), Cent. — A511

No. 2890: a, Dixie Dean. b, Ruud Gullit. c, Karl-Heinz Rummenigge. d, Luis Enrique Martinez.

65d, Pele.

2004, Oct. 27 *Perf. 12¾x12½*

2890 A511 25d Sheet of 4, #a-d 10.00 10.00

Souvenir Sheet

2891 A511 65d multi 6.50 6.50

National Basketball Association Players — A512

Designs: No. 2892, 10d, Darko Milicic, Detroit Pistons. No. 2893, 10d, Chris Kaman, Los Angeles Clippers. No. 2894, 10d, Andrei Kirilenko, Utah Jazz. No. 2895, 10d, T. J. Ford, Milwaukee Bucks.

2004 *Perf. 14*

2892-2895 A512 Set of 4 4.00 4.00

Issued: No. 2892, 11/2; Nos. 2893-2894, 11/3; No. 2895, 11/6. Each stamp printed in sheets of 12.

See Nos. 2916-2917.

Ocean Liners — A513

Designs: 7d, Bremen. 10d, RMS Queen Mary. 15d, Queen Mary II. 20d, RMS Queen Elizabeth 2. 25d, Britannic. 35d, RMS Majestic.

90d, RMS Aquitania.

2004, Nov. 5 *Perf. 14¼*

2896-2901 A513 Set of 6 13.00 13.00

Souvenir Sheet

2902 A513 90d multi 10.00 10.00

Miniature Sheet

Elvis Presley and Teddy Bears — A514

No. 2903: a, Presley in dark red suit. b, Teddy bear, plaid sleeve in background. c, Presley with guitar. d, Teddy bear, dark red suit in background. e, Presley in pink suit and tie. f, Teddy bear, guitar in background.

2004, Nov. 29 *Perf. 14*
2903 A514 20d Sheet of 6, #a-f 11.00 11.00

Christmas A515

Designs: 7d, Greek Madonna, by Giovanni Bellini. 10d, Madonna in the Church, by Jan van Eyck. 20d, Conestabile Madonna, by Raphael. 25d, Madonna and Child, by Sandro Botticelli.
65d, Madonna and Child with Chancellor Rolin, by van Eyck.

2004, Dec. 13 *Perf. 12*
2904-2907 A515 Set of 4 7.00 7.00

Souvenir Sheet

2908 A515 65d multi 7.00 7.00

Pres. Ronald Reagan (1911-2004) — A516

No. 2909, 25d: a, With Margaret Thatcher, 1986. b, With Pope John Paul II, 1982. c, Signing Missing Children's Act and Victim Witness Protection Act, 1992. d, With wife, Nancy, 1987.
No. 2910, 25d, horiz.: a, First Family, 1982. b, Signing treaty with Mikhail Gorbachev, 1987. c, Assassination attempt, 1981. d, With Deng Xiaoping, 1984.
60d, Portrait.

2004, Oct. 13 **Litho.** *Perf. 14*

Sheets of 4, #a-d

2909-2910 A516 Set of 2 22.50 22.50

Souvenir Sheet

2911 A516 60d multi 6.00 6.00

Lighthouse Type of 2004

Designs: 5d, Isla de Flores Lighthouse, Uruguay. 7d, Punta Brava Lighthouse, Uruguay. 15d, Boston Lighthouse, US. No. 2911D, 20d, Cabo Polonio Lighthouse, Uruguay. No. 2911E, 20d, Bass Harbor Head Lighthouse, US. 45d, Punta del Este Lighthouse, Uruguay. 60d, Portland Head Lighthouse, US.

2004 **Litho.** *Perf. 14¾x14*
2911A-2911G A501 Set of 7 17.50 17.50

Elvis Presley (1935-77) — A517

No. 2912, 15d: a, Standing, with guitar, 1956. b, Wearing army hat, 1957. c, Holding guitar, 1968. d, Holding guitar, 1970. e, Playing guitar, 1972. f, Singing, 1973.
No. 2913, 15d: a, Seated, with guitar, 1956. b, With guitar, 1958. c, Playing guitar, 1964. d, Playing drums, 1966. e, On horse, 1968. f, Playing guitar, 1969.

2005, Jan. 8 **Sheets of 6, #a-f**
2912-2913 A517 Set of 2 20.00 20.00

New Year 2005 (Year of the Rooster) A518

Paintings by Xu Beihong: 10d, Rooster. 40d, Black Rooster, horiz.

2005, Jan. *Perf. 11½*
2914 A518 10d multi 1.25 1.25

Souvenir Sheet

2915 A518 40d multi 4.00 4.00

No. 2914 printed in sheets of 4. No. 2915 contains one 46x36mm stamp.

Basketball Players Type of 2004

Designs: No. 2916, 25d, Steve Nash, Dallas Mavericks. No. 2917, 25d, Shaquille O'Neal, Los Angeles Lakers.

2005, Feb. 10 *Perf. 14*
2916-2917 A512 Set of 2 4.00 4.00

Both players were on different teams when stamps were released.

Intl. Year of Rice (in 2004) — A519

No. 2918, vert.: a, Rice terraces. b, Woman holding rice plants. c, Two people holding rice plants.
60d, Rice farmers.

2005, Feb. 10
2918 A519 30d Sheet of 3, #a-c 7.25 7.25

Souvenir Sheet

2919 A519 60d multi 6.50 6.50

Butterflies — A520

Designs: 1d, Belenois solilucis. 2d, Colotis evippe. 3d, Acraea cepheus. 5d, Bebearia senegalensis. 6d, Danaus chrysippus. 7d, Papilio dardanus. 10d, Graphium agamedes. 15d, Papilio hesperus. 25d, Charaxes bouell. 30d, Cymothoe egesta. 50d, Amauris albimaculata. 75d, Charaxes lucretius. 100d, Papilio zalmoxis. 200d, Papilio antimachus.

Perf. 13¼x13½, 14¾x14¼ (7d, 30d)

2005, Apr. 4

2920	A520	1d	multi	.25	.25
2921	A520	2d	multi	.35	.35
2922	A520	3d	multi	.40	.40
2923	A520	5d	multi	.50	.50
2924	A520	6d	multi	.55	.55
2924A	A520	7d	multi	.75	.75
2925	A520	10d	multi	1.00	1.00
2926	A520	15d	multi	1.50	1.50
2927	A520	25d	multi	2.00	2.00
2927A	A520	30d	multi	2.50	2.50
2928	A520	50d	multi	3.75	3.75
2929	A520	75d	multi	6.00	6.00
2929A	A520	100d	multi	8.50	8.50
2929B	A520	200d	multi	15.00	15.00
	Nos. 2920-2929B (14)			43.05	43.05

Battle of Trafalgar, Bicent. — A521

Designs: 5d, Santisima Trinidad. 10d, Victory firing at French flagship Bucentaure, horiz. 15d, Lord Horatio Nelson. 30d, French sailors from the Redoubtable boarding Victory.
60d, Vice-admiral Horatio Nelson.

2005, Apr. 4 *Perf. 14*
2930-2933 A521 Set of 4 7.00 7.00

Souvenir Sheet

2934 A521 60d multi 7.50 7.50

Souvenir Sheet

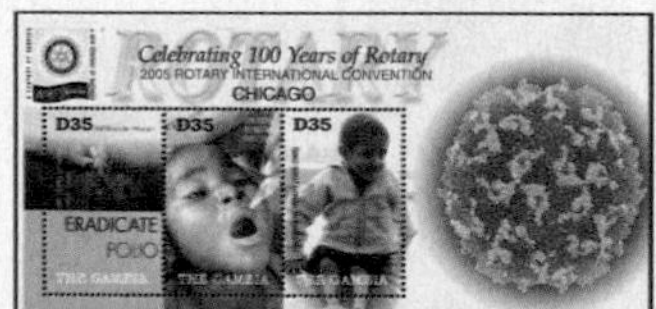

Rotary International, Cent. — A522

No. 2935: a, "Eradicate Polio," child receiving polio vaccine. b, Child receiving polio vaccine, diff. c, Child seated.

2005, Apr. 4
2935 A522 35d Sheet of 3, #a-c 9.50 9.50

Blondie, by Dean Young and Denis LeBrun — A523

No. 2936, 40d: a, "I have a date with Cookie." b, "Wait one second, please." c, "Wow, Cookie! I didn't know your family was wealth enough to have a chauffeur!"
No. 2937, 40d: a, "Listen up, everybody. . ." b, "Then after he leaves you can get back to normal." c, "I want to see this place humming with activity and enthusiasm!"

2005, Apr. 4 *Perf. 13¼*

Sheets of 3, #a-c

2936-2937 A523 Set of 2 22.00 22.00

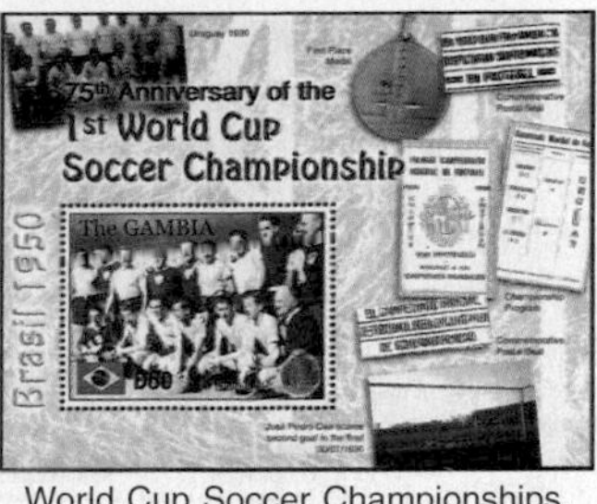

World Cup Soccer Championships, 75th Anniv. — A524

No. 2938 — Brazilian flag and scenes from 1950 World Cup: a, 1950 Uruguay team. b, Goal from Uruguay-Brazil championship game. c, Maracanã Municipal Stadium, Brazil. d, Alcide Edgardo Ghiggia.
60d, 1950 Uruguay team, diff.

2005, Apr. 4 *Perf. 14¼*
2938 A524 25d Sheet of 4, #a-d 10.00 10.00

Souvenir Sheet

2939 A524 60d multi 5.50 5.50

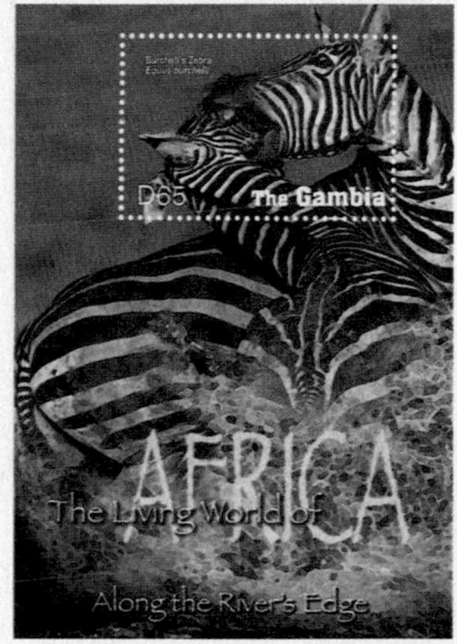

African Fauna — A525

No. 2940, 25d: a, African fish eagle. b, Hummingbird hawkmoth. c, Nile crocodile. d, Blue wildebeest.
No. 2941, 25d: a, Bateleur eagle. b, Green mamba. c, Chimpanzee. d, Yellow pansy butterfly.
No. 2942, 25d: a, Jackass penguins. b, Leatherback turtle. c, Scaevola thunbergii. d, Cancrid crab.
No. 2943, 25d: a, Mediterranean monk seal. b, Horned boxfish. c, Scorpion fish. d, Cnidarians.
No. 2944, Burchell's zebra. No. 2945, 65d, Greater galago. No. 2946, 65d, Bottlenose dolphin, vert. No. 2947, 65d, Gerbera daisies, vert.

2005, Apr. 4 *Perf. 13¼x13½*

Sheets of 4, #a-d

2940-2943 A525 Set of 4 32.50 32.50

Souvenir Sheets

2944-2947 A525 Set of 4 22.50 22.50

Hans Christian Andersen (1805-75), Author — A526

No. 2942, horiz.: a, The Ugly Duckling. b, The Little Match Girl. c, The Rose Tree Regiment.
60d, The Emperor's New Clothes.

2005, Apr. 4 ***Perf. 14***

2948 A526 35d Sheet of 3, #a-c 11.50 11.50

Souvenir Sheet

2949 A526 60d multi 7.00 7.00

Wedding of Prince Charles and Camilla Parker Bowles — A527

Various photos of couple with oval color of: No. 2950, 2d, Brown. No. 2951, 2d, Purple. No. 2952, 2d, Red brown.

2005, Apr. 9 ***Perf. 13½***

2950-2952 A527 Set of 3 2.00 2.00

Each stamp printed in sheets of 4.

Friedrich von Schiller (1759-1805), Writer — A528

No. 2953: a, Statue of Schiller. b, Painting of Schiller. c, Bust of Schiller.
60d, Cameo of Schiller.

2005, Apr. 4 **Litho.** ***Perf. 14***

2953 A528 35d Sheet of 3, #a-c 10.00 10.00

Souvenir Sheet

2954 A528 60d multi 6.00 6.00

Miniature Sheet

End of World War II, 60th Anniv. — A529

No. 2955 — Prince Bernhard of the Netherlands: a, And Prime Minister Pieter Gerbrandy. b, And Queen Wilhelmina. c, And Generals Bernard Montgomery and Hendrik Kruls. d, And people of Nimwegen. e, At German surrender. f, Returning home with family.

2005, Apr. 14 **Litho.** ***Perf. 12¾***

2955 A529 12d Sheet of 6, #a-f 5.00 5.00

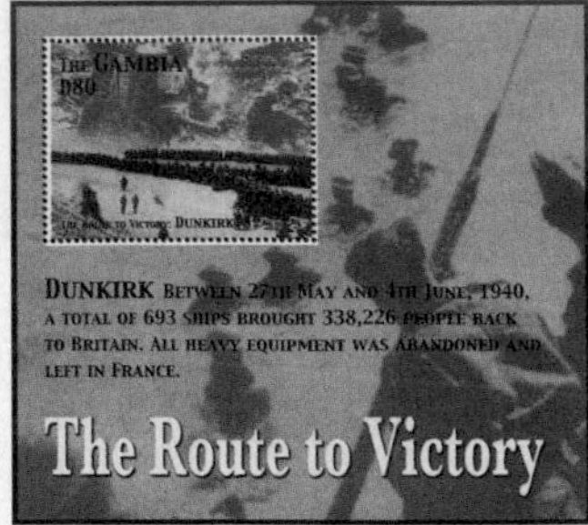

End of World War II, 60th Anniv. — A530

No. 2956, 20d — Dunkirk: a, Germans advance across France. b, Anthony C. Bartley. c, Ships and boats. d, Rescued soldiers.
No. 2957, 20d — D-Day: a, Allied troops hit the beaches of Normandy. b, Germans blast Sword Beach. c, Allied troops advance inland. d, Germans begin to surrender.
No. 2958, 80d, Operation Dynamo. No. 2959, 80d, Royal Navy lands on Gold Beach.

2005, May 9 ***Perf. 13¼x13½***

Sheets of 4, #a-d

2956-2957 A530 Set of 2 20.00 20.00

Souvenir Sheets

2958-2959 A530 Set of 2 16.00 16.00

Souvenir Sheet

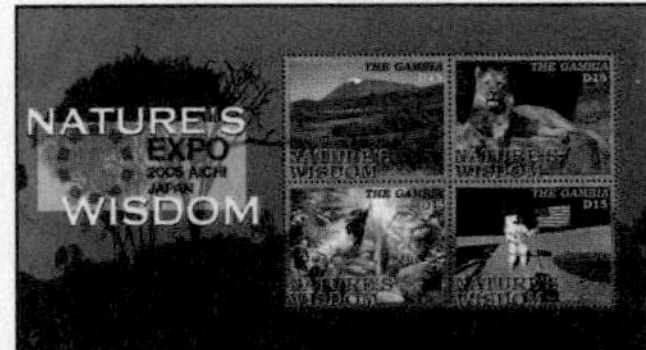

Expo 2005, Aichi, Japan — A531

No. 2960: a, Mt. Kilimanjaro. b, Lion. c, Splitting of the Red Sea. d, Astronaut on Moon.

2005, May 16 ***Perf. 12***

2960 A531 15d Sheet of 4, #a-d 8.00 8.00

Pope John Paul II (1920-2005) and Mother Teresa (1910-97) — A532

2005, June 1 ***Perf. 14***

2961 A532 30d multi 3.50 3.50

Printed in sheets of 6.

Maimonides (1135-1204) — A533

No. 2962: a, Denomination in white. b, Denomination in red.

2005, July 12 ***Perf. 12***

2962 A533 25d Pair, #a-b 5.50 5.50

Printed in sheets of 2 pairs.

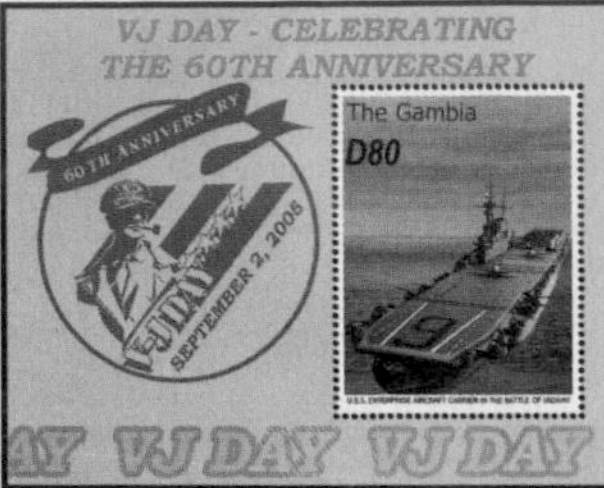

VJ Day, 60th Anniv. — A534

No. 2963, horiz. — Paintings by Jean Masterly: a, B-29 Flies Over the Missouri. b, Enola Gay Over Hiroshima. c, Dogfight Over the Pacific. d, Hellcat Fury Engages the Enemy.
80d, USS Enterprise Aircraft Carrier in the Battle of Midway.

2005, July 12 ***Perf. 12¾***

2963 A534 25d Sheet of 4, #a-d 11.00 11.00

Souvenir Sheet

2964 A534 80d multi 8.00 8.00

No. 2963 contains four 40x31mm stamps.

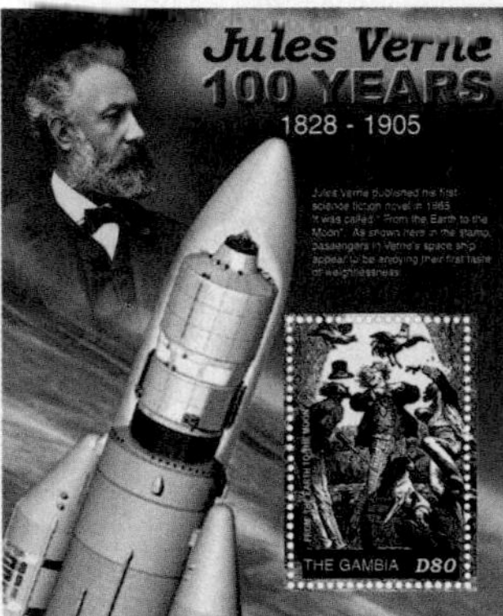

Jules Verne (1828-1905), Writer — A535

No. 2965, horiz.: a, Hungary #C287. b, Monaco #1100. c, France #770.
80d, Scene from "From the Earth to the Moon."

2005, July 12

2965 A535 35d Sheet of 3, #a-c 10.00 10.00

Souvenir Sheet

2966 A535 80d multi 8.00 8.00

Souvenir Sheet

Albert Einstein (1879-1955), Physicist — A536

No. 2967: a, Einstein, country name in red. b, Einstein, country name in white. c, Israel #117.

2005, July 28

2967 A536 35d Sheet of 3, #a-c 11.00 11.00

American First Day Cover Society, 50th Anniv. A537

2005, July 29

2968 A537 25d multi 2.75 2.75

Souvenir Sheet

Taipei 2005 Stamp Exhibition — A538

No. 2969: a, Presidential Palace, Taipei. b, Chiang Kai-Shek Memorial, Taipei. c, Queen's Head, Yehliu. d, National Palace Museum, Taipei.

2005, Aug. 19 ***Perf. 14***

2969 A538 35d Sheet of 4, #a-d 13.00 13.00

First Europa Stamps, 50th Anniv. (in 2006) A539

Designs: 35d, Mailman, Luxembourg #318. 40d, Stars, "50," France #806. 50d, Map of Europe, France #805.

2005, Oct. 20

2970-2972 A539 Set of 3 10.00 10.00
2972a Souvenir sheet, #2970-2972 + label 10.00 10.00

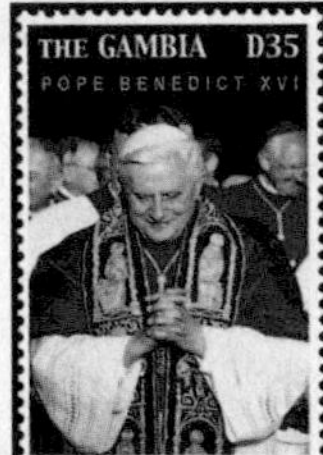

Election of Pope Benedict XVI — A540

2005, Nov. 15 ***Perf. 13½***

2973 A540 35d multi 3.50 3.50

Printed in sheets of 4.

Pope John Paul II (1920-2005) A541

Pope John Paul II: No. 2974, 40d, Looking right. No. 2975, 40d, With arm raised. No. 2976, 40d, With hand to face. No. 2977, 40d, Praying with four men at side. No. 2978, 40d, Surrounded by praying clergymen. No. 2979, With praying hands of other people. No. 2980, 40d, Wearing miter, with crowd. No. 2981, 40d, Praying at church. No. 2982, 40d, With arms outstretched at church. No. 2983, 40d, Praying with rosary. No. 2984, 40d, Holding crucifix, round globe. No. 2985, 40d, Holding crucifix, oval world map. No. 2986, 40d, Holding crucifix, and at doorway. No. 2987, 40d, With crucifix at side of face. No. 2988, 40d, Holding crucifix in front of his face. No. 2989, 40d, Holding crucifix, with other arm raised. No. 2990, 40d, With crucifix, Papal arms. No. 2991, 40d, With Good Shepherd. No. 2992, 40d, Holding child. No. 2993, 40d, With UN emblem. No. 2994, 40d, Being assisted.
No. 2995, 80d, Bowing with crucifix. No. 2996, 80d, Wearing miter in front of church. No. 2997, 80d, With kneeling bishop. No. 2998, 80d, Holding microphone. No. 2999, 80d, With raised hands, Papal arms. No. 3000, 80d, With Virgin Mary.

Embossed on Metal

2005 ***Die Cut Perf. 12½***

Self-Adhesive

Silver-Colored Metal

2974-2994 A541 Set of 21 120.00 120.00

Gold-Colored Metal

2995-3000 A541 Set of 6 55.00 55.00

Miniature Sheet

American Indian Chiefs — A542

No. 3001: a, Hiawatha. b, Chief Joseph. c, Sitting Bull. d, Red Cloud. e, Powhatan. f, Sequoyah. g, Crazy Horse. h, Cochise. i, Geronimo. j, Tecumseh.

2005, Nov. 15 Litho. ***Perf. 13½***
3001 A542 12d Sheet of 10, #a-j 11.00 11.00

Christmas — A543

Designs: 7d, The Annunciation, by Lorenzo di Credi. 10d, The Holy Family, by di Credi. 25d, The Adoration of the Magi, by Filippo Lippi. 30d, Marriage of St. Catherine, by Lippi. 65d, The Annunciation, by Fra Angelico.

2005, Dec. 19 ***Perf. 13½x13¼***
3002-3005 A543 Set of 4 6.50 6.50

Souvenir Sheet

3006 A543 65d multi 6.00 6.00

New Year 2006 (Year of the Dog) A544

2006, Jan. 3 ***Perf. 13¼***
3007 A544 15d multi 1.75 1.75

Printed in sheets of 4.

Elvis Presley (1935-77) — A545

Serpentine Die Cut 7¾
2006, Jan. 24 Litho. & Embossed
3008 A545 200d multi 16.00 16.00

Children's Drawings — A546

No. 3009, 25d — Cats: a, Kitty, by Raquel Bobolia. b, Jaguar, by Megan Albe. c, Quazy Jaguar, by Nick Abrams. d, Chelsy Cheetah, by Carly Bowerman.

No. 3010, 25d — Reptiles: a, Stripey, by Christopher Bowerman. b, Sea Turtle, by Tyler Overton. c, Hungry Lizard, by Jessica Shutt. d, Frogs, by Elyse Bobczynski.

No. 3011, 25d — Flowers: a, Three Flowers, by Lauren Van Way. b, Blossoms, by Michelle Malachowsky. c, Flower Pot, by Van Way. d, Red Flower Pot, by Anne Wilks.

2006, Jan. 24 Litho. ***Perf. 13¼***
Sheets of 4, #a-d
3009-3011 A546 Set of 3 25.00 25.00

Queen Elizabeth II, 80th Birthday — A547

No. 3012: a, Wearing military uniform. b, At coronation. c, On Time Magazine cover. d, Wearing wedding gown.
65d, Wearing robe and crown.

2006, Feb. 27 ***Perf. 13¼***
3012 A547 30d Sheet of 4, #a-d 11.00 11.00

Souvenir Sheet
Perf. 12

3013 A547 65d multi 7.50 7.50

Worldwide Fund for Nature (WWF) — A548

No. 3014 — Black-crowned crane: a, Head. b, Standing on one leg. c, Birds in wild. d, Chick.

2006, Feb. 27 ***Perf. 12¾***
3014 A548 30d Block or strip of 4, #a-d 9.50 9.50
e. Souvenir sheet, 2 each #3014a-3014d 19.00 19.00

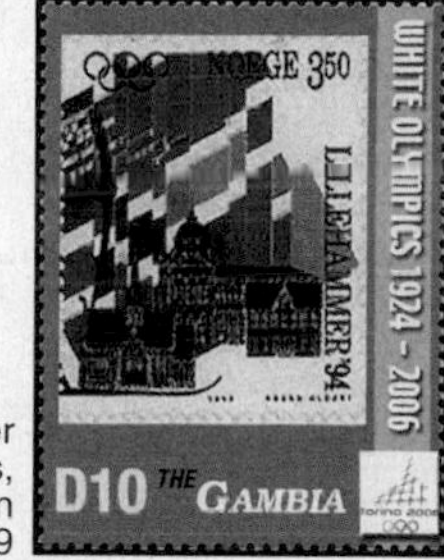

2006 Winter Olympics, Turin A549

Designs: No. 3015, Norway #1048. No. 3015A, Poster for 1992 Albertville Winter Olympics. 15d, Norway #1047. No. 3017, Poster for 2002 Salt Lake City Winter Olympics. No. 3017A, France #B611, horiz. 25d, Poster for 1994 Lillehammer Winter Olympics.

2006, Mar. 23 ***Perf. 13¼***

3015	A549	10d multicolored	1.00	1.00
3015A	A549	10d multicolored	1.00	1.00
3016	A549	15d multicolored	1.50	1.50
3017	A549	20d multicolored	2.00	2.00
3017A	A549	20d multicolored	2.25	2.25
3018	A549	25d multicolored	2.50	2.50
		Nos. 3015-3018 (6)	10.25	10.25

Marilyn Monroe (1926-62), Actress — A550

2006, Apr. 6
3019 A550 30d multi 2.50 2.50

Printed in sheets of 4.

Dr. Martin Luther King, Jr. (1929-68), Civil Rights Activist — A551

2006, May 27 ***Perf. 11½x12***
3020 A551 40d multi 3.25 3.25

Printed in sheets of 3.

Miniature Sheet

American Philatelic Society, 120th Anniv. — A552

No. 3021 — United States stamps: a, #1120. b, #E14. c, #114. d, #C3. e, #894. f, #E2. g, #294. h, #Q2.

2006, May 27 ***Perf. 13¼***
3021 A552 17d Sheet of 8, #a-h 12.00 12.00

Washington 2006 World Philatelic Exhibition.

Souvenir Sheet

Ludwig Durr (1878-1956), Engineer, and Zeppelins — A553

No. 3022 — Durr and: a, Zeppelin NT. b, Zeppelin ZR-3 (U.S.S. Los Angeles). c, Zeppelin ZRS (U.S.S. Macon)

2006, June 22 ***Perf. 12¾***
3022 A553 40d Sheet of 3, #a-c 11.00 11.00

Souvenir Sheet

Wolfgang Amadeus Mozart (1756-91), Composer — A554

No. 3023: a, Mozart's Memorial, Vienna. b, Portrait of Mozart, by Barbara Kraft. c, Portrait of Mozart by unknown artist. d, Mozart family graves, Salzburg.

2006, June 22
3023 A554 30d Sheet of 4, #a-d 12.75 12.75

Rembrandt (1606-69), Painter A555

Details from paintings: 10d, Jacob Blessing the Sons of Joseph. 12d, Jacob Blessing the Sons of Joseph, diff. 15d, Jacob Blessing the Sons of Joseph, diff. No. 3027, 25d, Jacob Wrestling with the Angel.

No. 3028, 25d — The Staalmeesters: a, Man wearing hat, leaning to right, "Rembrandt" in white. b, Man wearing hat, "Rembrandt" in white. c, Man without hat. d, Man wearing hat, "Rembrandt" in black.

No. 3029, 25d: a, Young Girl at Open Half-Door. b, Self-portrait, 1632-39. c, Self-portrait, 1640. d, Portrait of a Young Woman.

No. 3030, 25d — A Married Couple with Their Children: a, Man. b, Child, "Rembrandt" in white. c, Child, "Rembrandt" in black. d, Woman.

No. 3031, 65d — A Polish Nobleman. No. 3032, 65d, The Knight with the Falcon. No. 3033, 65d, A Young Woman in Fancy Dress. No. 3034, 65d, Portrait of a Lady with a Lap Dog.

2006, Aug. 23 Litho. ***Perf. 14¼***
3024-3027 A555 Set of 4 6.00 6.00

Sheets of 4, #a-d

3028-3030 A555 Set of 3 25.00 25.00

Imperf
Size: 76x106mm

3031-3034 A555 Set of 4 22.50 22.50

Queen Juliana of the Netherlands A556

2006, July 24 Litho. ***Perf. 13¼***
3035 A556 15d multi 1.25 1.25

Printed in sheets of 6.

Princess Maxima of the Netherlands — A557

No. 3036: a, Head. b, Head and torso.

2006, Dec. 6

3036 A557 30d Pair, #a-b 4.75 4.75

Printed in sheets containing 3 of each stamp.

Christmas — A558

Designs: No. 3037, 25d, Gingerbread man. 30d, Christmas tree. 45d, Bell. 50d, Mittens.

No. 3041: a, 15d, Gingerbread man. b, 18d, Christmas tree. c, 25d, Bell.

2006, Dec. 8 ***Perf. 14***

3037-3040 A558 Set of 4 11.00 11.00

Souvenir Sheet

3041 A558 Sheet of 4, #3041a-3041c, 3040 7.75 7.75

Miniature Sheet

2006 World Cup Soccer Championships, Germany — A559

No. 3042 — World Cup and soccer ball with flag of: a, 10d, Australia. b, 20d, Germany. c, 25d, Sweden. d, 30d, Brazil.

2006, Dec. 20 ***Perf. 13¼***

3042 A559 Sheet of 4, #a-d 6.75 6.75

Concorde A560

No. 3043, 15d: a, Concorde arriving at Filton. b, Concorde G-BOAF in flight.

No. 3044, 15d: a, Concorde taking off from Toulouse. b, Concorde test pilot Andre Turcat.

2006, Dec. 20 ***Perf. 13¼x13½***

Pairs, #a-b

3043-3044 A560 Set of 2 8.00 8.00

Nos. 3043-3044 were each printed in sheets containing three pairs.

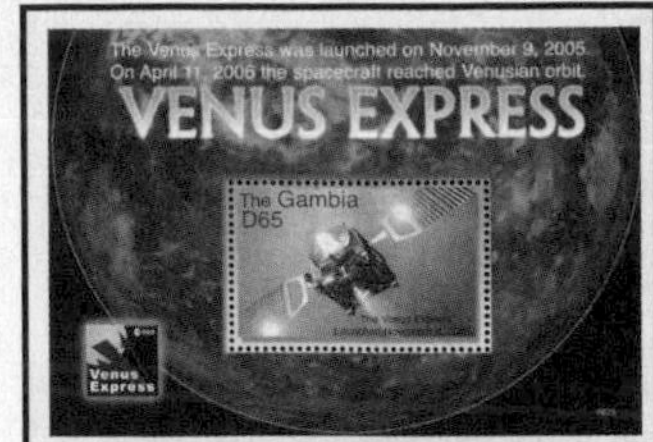

Space Achievements — A561

No. 3045, 20d — Various views of Mars Reconnaissance Orbiter.

No. 3046, 20d — Space Shuttle Columbia: a, Columbia attached to rocket boosters in flight. b, Lift-off of Columbia. c, Shuttle mission simulator. d, Mission control. e, Capt. John W. Young. f, Capt. Robert L. Crippen.

No. 3047, 25d — Giotto Comet Probe: a, Halley's Comet. b, Giotto Comet Probe, green and orange lines. c, Giotto Comet Probe. d, Comet and Giotto Comet Probe.

No. 3048, 25d — Viking 1: a, Viking 1 in flight. b, Viking 1 on Mars, text in black, denomination at UL. c, Viking 1 on Mars, text in black, denomination at UR. d, Viking 1 on Mars, "Viking 1" in white.

No. 3049, 65d, Venus Express. No. 3050, 65d, Hayabusa spacecraft. No. 3051, 65d, Luna 9, vert. No. 3052, 65d, Space Shuttle Discovery returns to space, vert.

2006, Dec. 20 ***Perf. 14***

Sheets of 6, #a-f

3045-3046 A561 Set of 2 27.50 27.50

Sheets of 4, #a-d

3047-3048 A561 Set of 2 16.00 16.00

Souvenir Sheets

3049-3052 A561 Set of 4 24.00 24.00

New Year 2007 (Year of the Pig) A562

2007, Feb. 15 ***Perf. 13x13½***

3053 A562 20d multi 2.00 2.00

Printed in sheets of 4.

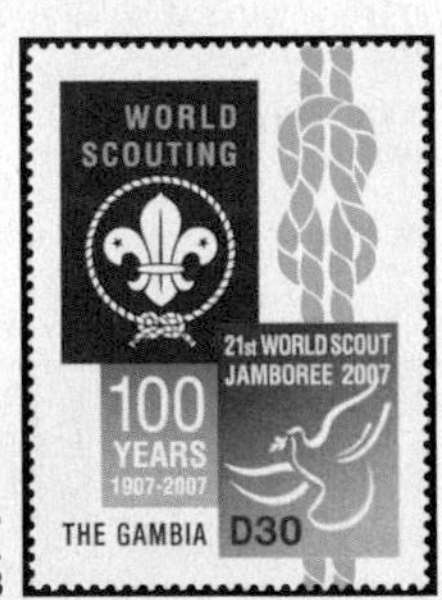

Scouting, Cent. A563

Knot in: 30d, Green. 65d, Orange.

2007, Feb. 15 ***Perf. 13¼***

3054 A563 30d multi 2.75 2.75

Souvenir Sheet

3055 A563 65d multi 5.50 5.50

No. 3054 printed in sheets of 4.

Miniature Sheets

Programs of Pres. John F. Kennedy — A564

No. 3056, 25d — Peace Corps: a, Kennedy greeting Peace Corps volunteers at White House. b, R. Sargent Shriver, first director of Peace Corps. c, Kennedy signing executive order creating Peace Corps. d, Kennedy greeting Peace Corps volunteers.

No. 3057, 25d — Alliance for Progress: a, Kennedy in rocking chair. b, Kennedy and Cabinet. c, Volunteer Ida Shoatz in Peru. d, Kennedy speaking at University of Michigan.

2007, Feb. 15 ***Perf. 12¾***

Sheets of 4, #a-d

3056-3057 A564 Set of 2 17.50 17.50

Betty Boop — A565

No. 3058 — Betty Boop: a, With hands at side. b, Holding flowers. c, With dog biting swimsuit. d, Wearing long red dress. e, With hands clasped. f, Holding top hat and cane.

No. 3059 — Betty Boop in: a, Red. b, Purple.

2007, Feb. 15 **Litho.**

3058 A565 15d Sheet of 6, #a-f 9.00 9.00

Souvenir Sheet

3059 A565 40d Sheet of 2, #a-b 6.00 6.00

Pope Benedict XVI — A566

2007, May 1 ***Perf. 13¼***

3060 A566 12d multi 1.40 1.40

Printed in sheets of 8.

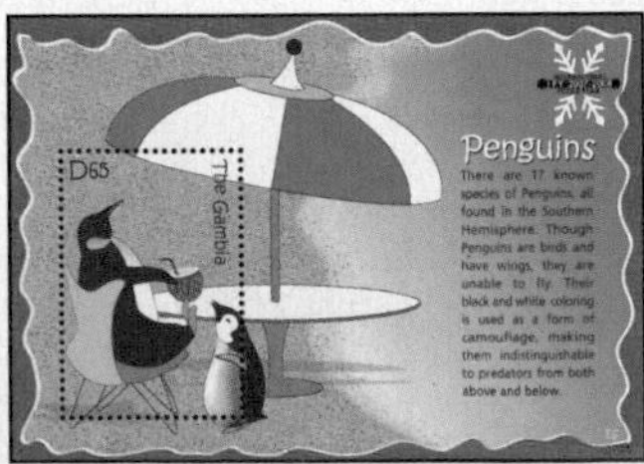

Intl. Polar Year — A567

No. 3061 — Penguin: a, At bongo drums. b, With lei and grass skirt. c, At drum set. d, With purple guitar. e, At microphone. f, With yellow and orange guitar.

65d, Penguin in chair at table.

2007, May 1 **Litho.**

3061 A567 15d Sheet of 6, #a-f 10.00 10.00

Souvenir Sheet

3062 A567 65d multi 8.50 8.50

Wedding of Queen Elizabeth II and Prince Philip, 60th Anniv. — A568

No. 3063, vert. — Photos of Queen and Prince: a, On wedding day, gray brown frame. b, As older couple, gray brown frame. c, As older couple, pink frame. d, On wedding day, pink frame. e, On wedding day, blue gray frame. f, As older couple, blue gray frame.

65d, Queen and Prince, diff.

2007, May 1

3063 A568 15d Sheet of 6, #a-f 10.00 10.00

Souvenir Sheet

3064 A568 65d multi 7.00 7.00

Princess Diana (1961-97) — A569

No. 3065, vert. — Diana wearing: a, Tiara, close-up. b, Light blue dress, close-up. c, Maroon dress, close-up. d, Tiara, from distance. e, Light blue dress, from distance. f, Maroon dress, from distance.

No. 3066, vert. — Diana wearing: a, Blue and white hat. b, Lilac and purple hat. c, Black dress. d, Red and white hat.

65d, Painting of Diana.

2007, May 1

3065 A569 15d Sheet of 6, #a-f 9.50 9.50

3066 A569 25d Sheet of 4, #a-d 10.00 10.00

Souvenir Sheet

3067 A569 65d multi 7.50 7.50

1986 Halley's Comet Merchandising Emblem — A570

No. 3068: a, Light olive green frame. b, Light blue frame. c, Violet black frame. d, Brown frame.

65d, Black background.

2007, June 20 *Perf. 13¼*
3068 A570 20d Sheet of 4, #a-d 7.50 7.50

Souvenir Sheet

3069 A570 65d black 6.50 6.50

Ferrari Automobiles, 60th Anniv. — A571

No. 3070: a, 1970 512 S. b, 1996 F 310. c, 1950 195 S. d, 1965 275 P2. e, 1980 Mondial 8. f, 1975 312 T. g, 1952 500 F2. h, 1986 GTB Turbo.

2007, June 20 *Perf. 13½x13¼*
3070 A571 12d Sheet of 8, #a-h 9.50 9.50

Paintings by Qi Baishi (1864-1957) — A572

No. 3071: a, Autumn Leaves and Magpie. b, Camellias. c, Pomegranates. d, Mynahs and Amaranthus.
65d, Magpie and Plum Blossoms.

2007, July 16 *Perf. 12½*
3071 A572 25d Sheet of 4, #a-d 9.50 9.50

Souvenir Sheet

Perf. 11¼x11½

3072 A572 65d multi 6.75 6.75

First Helicopter Flight, Cont. A573

No. 3073: a, UH-1B/C. b, S-65/RH-53B. c, UH-1. d, BK 117. e, Autogyro. f, AS-61.
65d, AH-1 Huey Cobra.

2007, July 16 *Perf. 13¼*
3073 A573 15d Sheet of 6, #a-f 9.50 9.50

Souvenir Sheet

3074 A573 65d multi 8.00 8.00

Wives of United States Presidents and First Ladies — A574

No. 3075: a, Martha Washington. b, Abigail Adams. c, Dolley Madison. d, Elizabeth Monroe. e, Louisa Adams. f, Emily Donelson. g, Angelica Van Buren. h, Anna Harrison. i, Letitia Tyler. j, Julia Tyler. k, Sarah Polk. l, Margaret Taylor. m, Abigail Fillmore. n, Jane Pierce. o, Eagle, flags, White House.

No. 3076: a, Harriet Johnston. b, Mary Lincoln. c, Eliza Johnson. d, Julia Grant. e, Lucy Hayes. f, Lucretia Garfield. g, Mary Arthur McElroy. h, Frances Cleveland. i, Caroline Harrison. j, Ida McKinley. k, Edith Roosevelt. l, Helen Taft. m, Ellen Wilson. n, Edith Wilson.

No. 3077: a, Florence Harding. b, Grace Coolidge. c, Lou Hoover. d, Eleanor Roosevelt. e, Bess Truman. f, Mamie Eisenhower. g, Jacqueline Kennedy. h, Lady Bird Johnson. i, Pat Nixon. j, Betty Ford. k, Rosalynn Carter. l, Nancy Reagan. m, Barbara Bush. n, Hillary Clinton. o, Laura Bush.

No. 3078, 65d, Martha Washington. No. 3079, 65d, Abigail Adams. No. 3080, 65d, Martha Jefferson. No. 3081, 65d, Martha Washington Jefferson Randolph. No. 3082, 65d, Dolley Madison. No. 3083, 65d, Elizabeth Monroe. No. 3084, 65d, Louisa Adams. No. 3085, 65d, Rachael Jackson. No. 3086, 65d, Emily Donelson. No. 3087, 65d, Hannah Van Buren. No. 3088, 65d, Angelica Van Buren. No. 3089, 65d, Anna Harrison. No. 3090, 65d, Letitia Tyler. No. 3091, 65d, Priscilla Tyler. No. 3092, 65d, Julia Tyler. No. 3093, 65d, Sarah Polk. No. 3094, 65d, Margaret Taylor. No. 3095, 65d, Mary Taylor. No. 3096, 65d, Abigail Fillmore. No. 3097, 65d, Jane Pierce. No. 3098, 65d, Harriet Johnston. No. 3099, 65d, Mary Lincoln. No. 3100, 65d, Eliza Johnson. No. 3101, 65d, Julia Grant. No. 3102, 65d, Lucy Hayes. No. 3103, 65d, Lucretia Garfield. No. 3104, 65d, Ellen Arthur. No. 3105, 65d, Mary Arthur McElroy. No. 3106, 65d, Frances Cleveland. No. 3107, 65d, Caroline Harrison. No. 3108, 65d, Mary Lord Harrison. No. 3109, 65d, Ida McKinley. No. 3110, 65d, Edith Roosevelt. No. 3111, 65d, Helen Taft. No. 3112, 65d, Ellen Wilson. No. 3113, 65d, Edith Wilson. No. 3114, 65d, Florence Harding. No. 3115, 65d, Grace Coolidge. No. 3116, 65d, Lou Hoover. No. 3117, 65d, Eleanor Roosevelt. No. 3118, 65d, Bess Truman. No. 3119, 65d, Mamie Eisenhower. No. 3120, 65d, Jacqueline Kennedy. No. 3121, 65d, Lady Bird Johnson. No. 3122, 65d, Pat Nixon. No. 3123, 65d, Betty Ford. No. 3124, 65d, Rosalynn Carter. No. 3125, 65d, Nancy Reagan. No. 3126, 65d, Barbara Bush. No. 3127, 65d, Hillary Clinton. No. 3128, 65d, Laura Bush.

2007 *Perf. 13¼*

3075	A574	10d Sheet of 15, #a-o		14.00	14.00
3076	A574	10d Sheet of 15, #a-n, 3075o		14.00	14.00
3077	A574	10d Sheet of 15, #a-o		14.00	14.00
		Nos. 3075-3077 (3)		42.00	42.00

Souvenir Sheets

3078-3128	A574	Set of 51	250.00	250.00
3078a		Perf. 14¼	6.25	6.25

Issued: Nos. 3075-3077, 7/31. Nos. 3078-3128, 10/24. Nos. 3075-3077 each contain fifteen 25x37mm stamps.

No. 3078a was not issued in a souvenir sheet.

See No. 3293.

Miniature Sheet

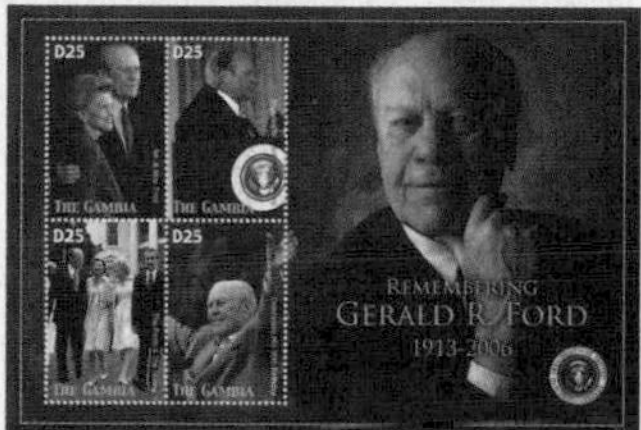

Pres. Gerald R. Ford (1913-2006) — A575

No. 3129 — Ford: a, With wife, Betty. b, At Presidential inauguration ceremony. c, With Betty, Pres. Richard Nixon and Pat Nixon. d, At 90th birthday celebration.

2007, Aug. 9 **Litho.** *Perf. 13¼*
3129 A575 25d Sheet of 4, #a-d 8.75 8.75

Miniature Sheet

Elvis Presley (1935-77) — A576

No. 3130 — Presley, guitar and background color of: a, Green. b, Tan. c, Orange. d, Black (white suit). e, Brown. f, Black (black jacket).

2007, Sept. 6
3130 A576 15d Sheet of 6, #a-f 8.25 8.25

Miniature Sheets

Intl. Holocaust Remembrance Day — A577

No. 3131, 14d — United Nations diplomats and delegates: a, Ronaldo Mota Sardenberg, Brazil. b, Alisher Vohidov, Uzbekistan. c, Martin Belinga-Eboutou, Cameroun. d, Fernand Poukre-Kono, Central African Republic. e, Heraldo Muñoz, Chile. f, Wang Guangya, China. g, Elbio O. Rosselli, Uruguay. h, Shashi Tharoor, Undersecretary General.

No. 3132, 14d: a, Basile Ikouebe, Republic of the Congo. b, Saul Weisleder, Costa Rica. c, Alcicle Djedje, Ivory Coast. d, Andreas D. Mavroiannis, Cyprus. e, Martin Palous, Czech Republic. f, Atoki Ileka, Democratic Republic of the Congo. g, Crispin S. Gregoire, Dominica. h, Parfait Onanga-Anyanga, Ambassador and Special Advisor of the 61st UN General Assembly.

No. 3133, 14d: a, Hoya Rashed Al-Khalifa, President of 61st UN General Assembly. b, Denis Dangue Rewaka, Gabon. c, Crispin Grey-Johnson, Gambia. d, Irakli Alasania, Georgia. e, Nana Effah-Apenteng, Ghana. f, Adamantios Vassilakis, Greece. g, Jorge Skinner-Klee Arenales, Guatemala. h, Jean-Maurice Ripert, France.

No. 3134, 14d: a, Hilari G. Davide, Jr., Philippines. b, Andrzej Towpik, Poland. c, Joao Manuel Guerra Salgueiro, Portugal. d, Alexei Tulbure, Moldova. e, Mihnea I. Motoc, Romania. f, Vitaly I. Churkin, Russia. g, Joseph Nsengimana, Rwanda. h, Augustine P. Mahiga, Tanzania.

2007, Nov. 28 **Litho.** *Perf. 13½*

Sheets of 8, #a-h

3131-3134 A577 Set of 4 42.50 42.50

2008 Summer Olympics, Beijing — A578

Die Cut Perf. 8½x8¼

2007, Nov. 29 **Litho. & Embossed**

Without Gum

3135 A578 40d multi *20.00 20.00*

Christmas A579

Designs: 25d, Girl at manger scene. 30d, Children eating holiday dishes. 45d, Boy with Madonna and Child sculptures. 50d, Christmas celebrations with music.

2007, Dec. 3 **Litho.** *Perf. 12*
3136-3139 A579 Set of 4 14.00 14.00

Souvenir Sheet

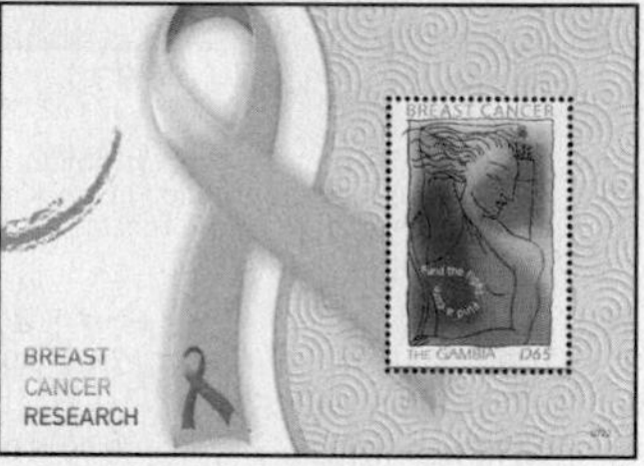

Breast Cancer Prevention — A580

2007, Dec. 10 *Perf. 14*
3140 A580 65d multi 6.00 6.00

America's Cup Yacht Races A581

No. 3141 — Various yachts with wide panels in: a, Blue. b, Yellow orange. c, Red. d, Orange.

2007, Dec. 28 *Perf. 13¼*

3141	Strip of 4	7.75	7.75
a.	A581 10d multi	.90	.90
b.	A581 15d multi	1.50	1.50
c.	A581 20d multi	1.90	1.90
d.	A581 30d multi	3.00	3.00

Miniature Sheet

National Basketball Association Players — A582

No. 3142: a, Carmelo Anthony, Denver Nuggets. b, Kobe Bryant, Los Angeles Lakers. c, Vince Carter, New Jersey Nets. d, Allen Iverson, Denver Nuggets. e, LeBron James, Cleveland Cavaliers. f, Yao Ming, Houston Rockets. g, Steve Nash, Phoenix Suns. h, Shaquille O'Neal, Miami Heat. i, Dwayne Wade, Miami Heat.

2007, Dec. 28 *Perf. 13¼*
3142 A582 10d Sheet of 9, #a-i 9.50 9.50

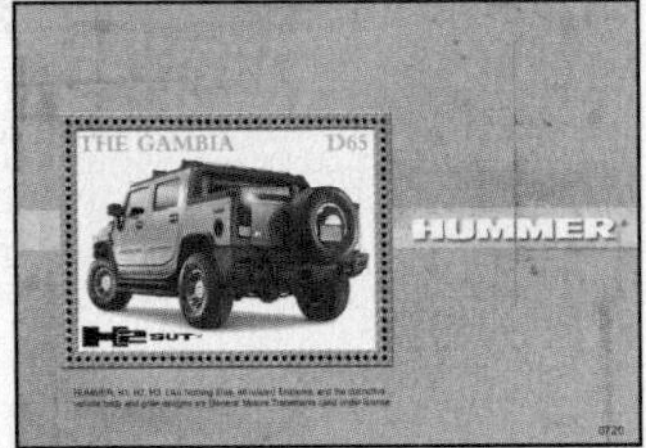

Hummer Vehicles — A583

No. 3143: a, H2 on road, denomination in white. b, H2 on road, denomination in black. c, H2, white background. d, H2 on rocks.
65d, H2 SUT.

2007, Dec. 28 *Perf. 13½*
3143 A583 25d Sheet of 4, #a-d 9.00 9.00

Souvenir Sheet

3144 A583 65d multi 6.00 6.00

New Year 2008 (Year of the Rat) A584

2008, Jan. 28 **Litho.** *Perf. 12*
3145 A584 30d multi 3.00 3.00

Printed in sheets of 4.

2008 Taipei Intl. Stamp Exhibition — A585

No. 3146, horiz. — Taipei landmarks: a, Temple and garden. b, Dr. Sun Yat-sen Memorial Hall. c, Natl. Opera House. d, Temple.
45d, Lover's Bridge, Tamsui.

2008, Apr. 11 *Perf. 13¼*
3146 A585 12d Sheet of 4, #a-d 5.00 5.00

Souvenir Sheet

Perf. 13¼x13½

3147 A585 45d multi 4.50 4.50

No. 3146 contains four 42x28mm stamps.

Pioneer Satellites — A586

No. 3148: a, Pioneer 1 in orbit, Moon in background. b, Pioneer 1 in nose cone. c, Pioneer 1.
No. 3149, horiz.: a, Technicians and Pioneer 3. b, Pioneer 3 in orbit. c, Pioneer 3 on launch pad.
No. 3150: a, Pioneer 1 on launch pad. b, Pioneer 1 in orbit, diff.
No. 3151: a, Pioneer 3. b, Pioneer 3 in orbit, Moon in background.
No. 3152, Pioneer 1, horiz. No. 3153, Pioneer 3, horiz.

2008, Apr. 11 *Perf. 13¼*

3148	A586	15d Horiz. strip of 3, #a-c	6.75	6.75
3149	A586	15d Vert. strip of 3, #a-c	6.75	6.75
3150	A586	20d Pair, #a-b	5.00	5.00
3151	A586	20d Pair, #a-b	5.00	5.00

Souvenir Sheets

3152 A586 65d multi 7.50 7.50

Perf. 13¼x13½

3153 A586 65d multi 7.50 7.50

No. 3153 contains one 51x38mm stamp. Nos. 3148-3151 were issued in sheets containing two strips or pairs.

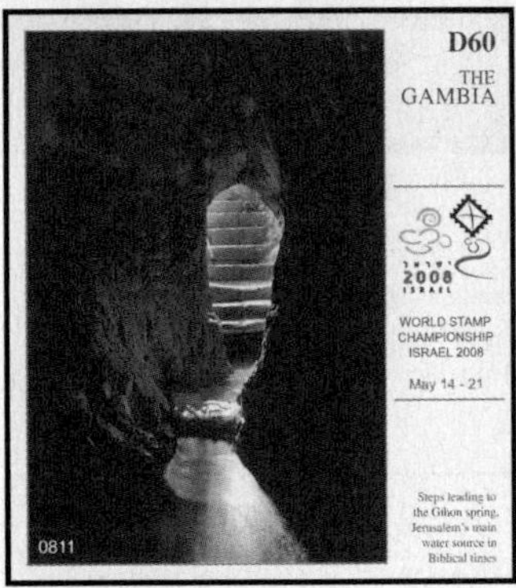

2008 World Stamp Championship, Israel — A587

2008, May 14 *Imperf.*
3154 A587 60d multi 6.25 6.25

Miniature Sheet

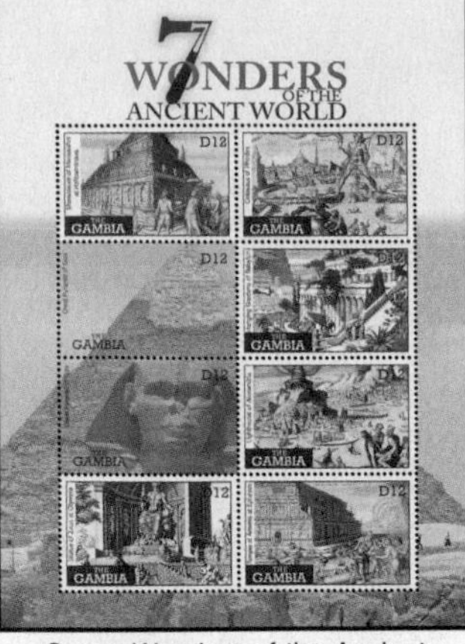

Seven Wonders of the Ancient World — A588

No. 3155: a, Mausoleum of Maussollos, Halicarnassus. b, Colossus of Rhodes. c, Tip of Giant Pyramid, Giza. d, Hanging Gardens of Babylon. e, Sphinx and Giant Pyramid. f, Lighthouse of Alexandria. g, Statue of Zeus, Olympia. h, Temple of Artemis, Ephesus.

2008, May 16 *Perf. 13¼*
3155 A588 12d Sheet of 8, #a-h 10.00 10.00

Miniature Sheet

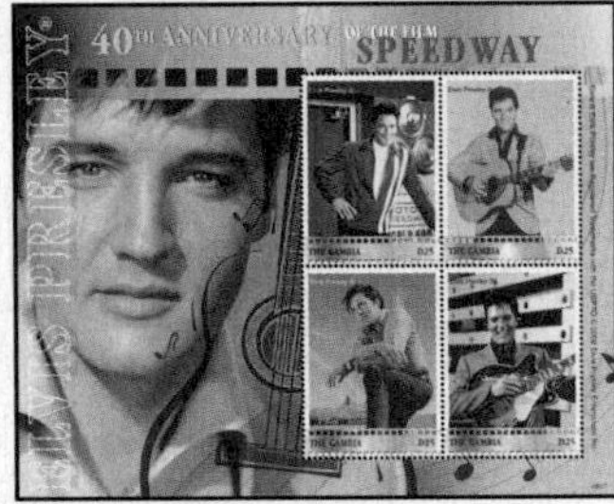

Elvis Presley (1935-77) — A589

No. 3156 — Presley: a, Wearing striped jacket. b, With acoustic guitar. c, With arms on knee. d, With electric guitar.

2008, May 16
3156 A589 25d Sheet of 4, #a-d 9.50 9.50

Miniature Sheet

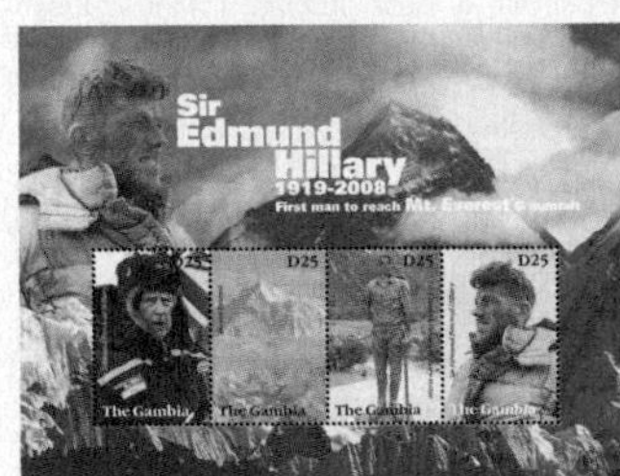

Sir Edmund Hillary (1919-2008), Mountaineer — A590

No. 3157: a, Hillary and flag. b, Mt. Everest. c, Statue of Hillary. d, Hillary as young man.

2008, May 16
3157 A590 25d Sheet of 4, #a-d 9.50 9.50

Miniature Sheet

2008 Summer Olympics, Beijing — A591

No. 3158: a, Suzanne Lenglen, 1920 Tennis gold medalist. b, Duke Kahanamoku, 1920 Swimming gold medalist. c, Nedo Nadi, 1920 Fencing gold medalist. d, Olympic rings and text "Olympex 2008."

2008, May 28 *Perf. 12*
3158 A591 10d Sheet of 4, #a-d 4.00 4.00

Visit of Pope Benedict XVI to United States — A592

2008, June 12 *Perf. 13¼*
3159 A592 25d multi 2.50 2.50

Printed in sheets of 4.

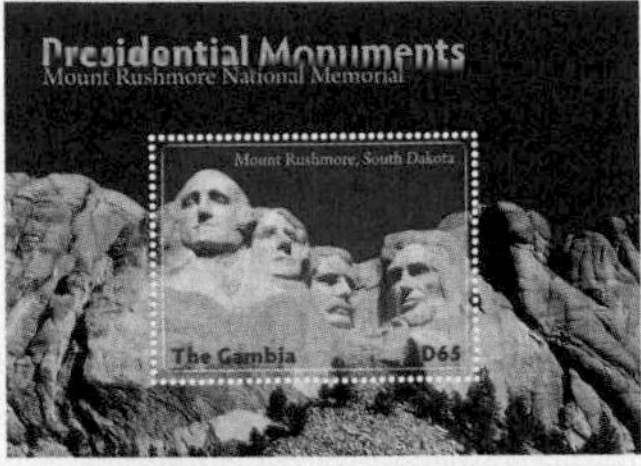

United States Landmarks — A593

No. 3160, vert.: a, Grant's Tomb, New York. b, Jefferson Memorial, Washington, DC. c, Kennedy Eternal Flame, Arlington, Virginia. d, Capitol, Washington, DC. e, Lincoln Memorial, Washington, DC. f, Washington Monument, Washington, DC.
65d, Mount Rushmore, South Dakota.

2008, June 12
3160 A593 15d Sheet of 6, #a-f 8.50 8.50

Souvenir Sheet

3161 A593 65d multi 6.50 6.50

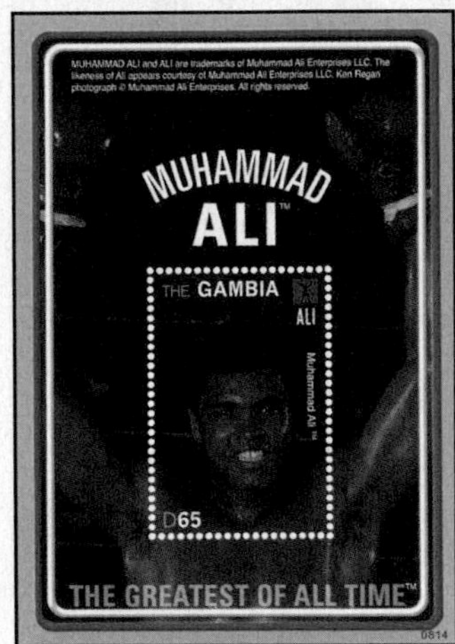

Muhammad Ali, Boxer — A594

No. 3162, 25d — Ali: a, With white trunks, fists in front of chest. b, Seated. c, With white trunks, arm extended. d, Wearing drawstring shorts.
No. 3163, 25d, horiz. — Ali: a, Behind microphone. b, With hand on chin. c, With fist raised. d, Running.
No. 3164, 65d, Head of Ali in color. No. 3165, 65d, Head of Ali in black and white.

2008, July 21 *Perf. 11½*

Sheets of 4, #a-d

3162-3163 A594 Set of 2 20.00 20.00

Souvenir Sheets

Perf. 13¼

3164-3165 A594 Set of 2 13.00 13.00

No. 3162 contains four 30x40mm stamps. No. 3163 contains four 40x30mm stamps.

Gambia Coat of Arms — A595

2008, Sept. 15 Litho. *Perf. 14x15*
3166 A595 40d blk & mar + label 3.50 3.50

Printed in sheets of 8 stamps + 8 labels.

Miniature Sheet

Marilyn Monroe (1926-62), Actress — A596

No. 3167 — Monroe: a, Facing forward, eyes open. b, Facing left. c, Facing right. d, Facing forward, eyes shut.

2008, Sept. 22 *Perf. 13¼*
3167 A596 25d Sheet of 4, #a-d 9.00 9.00

Miniature Sheets

A597

End of World War I, 90th Anniv. — A598

No. 3168: a, Generals talking. b, Soldier and trench. c, Pilot. d, Pilot and propeller. e, Soldier wearing helmet. f, Officers standing in row.

No. 3169: a, Soldiers at air field. b, Tanks. c, Two soldiers. d, Soldiers at cannon.

2008, Nov. 11 Litho. *Perf. 11½x12*
3168 A597 15d Sheet of 6, #a-f 11.00 11.00
3169 A598 25d Sheet of 4, #a-d 11.50 11.50

Miniature Sheet

Prince Charles, 60th Birthday — A599

No. 3170: a, Wearing black suit. b, Wearing top hat. c, Wearing gray suit. d, Wearing military uniform.

2008, Nov. 14 *Perf. 11¼x11½*
3170 A599 25d Sheet of 4, #a-d 10.00 10.00

Christmas A600

Designs: 25d, Map of West Africa, ribbon and bow. 30d, Red, blue and green bows. 45d, Woman carrying gift on head, flag, vert. 50d, Gifts, flag.

2008, Dec. 1 *Perf. 14¾x14, 14x14¾*
3171-3174 A600 Set of 4 12.50 12.50

Miniature Sheet

Signing of Limited Nuclear Test Ban Treaty — A601

No. 3175: a, Pres. John F. Kennedy. b, Kennedy and Soviet Premier Nikita Khrushchev. c, Kennedy at American University commencement. d, Atomic bomb test, Bikini Atoll, 1946.

2008, Dec. 4 *Perf. 11½x12*
3175 A601 25d Sheet of 4, #a-d 9.00 9.00

Miniature Sheet

Pres. Abraham Lincoln (1809-65) — A602

No. 3176: a, Lincoln with son, Tad. b, Lincoln wih beard in profile. c, Lincoln without beard. d, Lincoln with beard.

2008, Dec. 4 *Perf. 13¼*
3176 A602 25d Sheet of 4, #a-d 9.00 9.00

A603

A604

A605

Flowers — A606

No. 3177: a, Calotropis procera. b, Calliandra surinamensis. c, Plumeria alba. d, Quisqualis indica.

No. 3178: a, Adansonia digitata. b, Commelina benghalensis. c, Heliconia psittacorum. d, Tabebuia rosea.

2008, Dec. 31 *Perf. 12½*
3177 A603 25d Sheet of 4, #a-d 8.75 8.75

Perf. 12
3178 A604 25d Sheet of 4, #a-d 8.75 8.75

Souvenir Sheets
3179 A605 65d multi 6.50 6.50
3180 A606 65d multi 6.50 6.50

New Year 2009 (Year of the Ox) A607

2009, Jan. 5 *Perf. 12*
3181 A607 25d multi 2.50 2.50

Printed in sheets of 4.

Inauguration of US Pres. Barack Obama — A608

No. 3183: a, Pres. Obama. b, Vice-president Joseph Biden.

2009, Jan. 20 *Perf. 14x14¾*
3182 A608 16d shown 1.50 1.50

Souvenir Sheet
3183 A608 60d Sheet of 2, #a-b 10.00 10.00

No. 3182 was printed in sheets of 9.

Miniature Sheet

Pope John Paul II (1920-2005) — A609

No. 3184 — Pope John Paul II at: a, Inaugural Mass, 1978. b, United Nations, 1979. c, Warsaw, 1983. d, Denver, Colorado, 1993.

2009, Feb. 4 *Perf. 13¼*
3184 A609 25d Sheet of 4, #a-d 11.00 11.00

A610

A611

A612

A613

Elvis Presley (1935-77) — A614

No. 3185 — Presley wearing: a, Black suit and tie, white shirt. b, Black suit and shirt, no tie. c, Red sweater. d, Brown shirt and gray tie. e, Blue shirt. f, Gray sweater and white shirt.

2009 *Perf. 13¼*
3185 A610 20d Sheet of 6, #a-f 11.00 11.00

Souvenir Sheets

3186 A611 60d multi 6.00 6.00
3187 A612 60d multi 6.00 6.00
3188 A613 60d multi 6.00 6.00
3189 A614 60d multi 6.00 6.00

Issued: No. 3185, 4/30; others, 2/25.

Miniature Sheet

Jet Li One Foundation — A615

No. 3190: a, Education. b, Jet Li. c, Poverty. d, Health. e, Environment. f, Disaster relief.

2009, Apr. 1 *Perf. 12¾*
3190 A615 40d Sheet of 6, #a-f 22.50 22.50

Souvenir Sheet

Great Wall of China — A616

2009, Apr. 10 *Perf. 12*
3191 A616 80d multi 7.50 7.50

China 2009 Intl. Philatelic Exhibition.

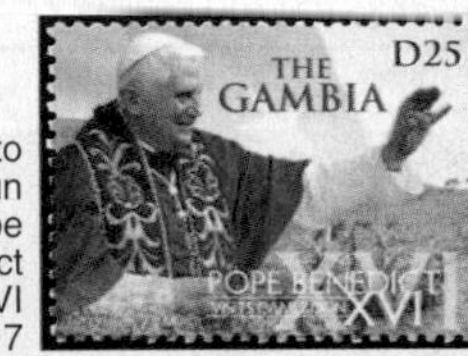

Visit to Cameroun of Pope Benedict XVI
A617

2009, Apr. 30 *Perf. 11½x11¼*
3192 A617 25d multi 2.25 2.25

Printed in sheets of 4.

Miniature Sheet

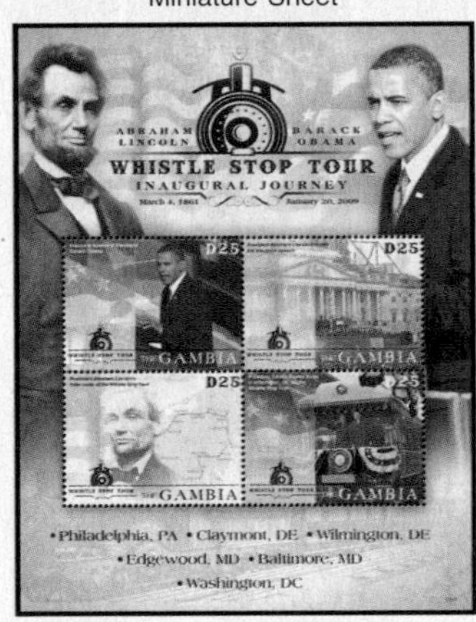

Whistle-stop Inaugural Journeys of US Presidents Abraham Lincoln and Barack Obama — A618

No. 3193: a, Inaugural speech of Pres. Obama. b, Inaugural speech of Pres. Lincoln. c, Lincoln, map of train route. d, Pres. Obama and Vice-president Joseph Biden on train in Wilmington, Delaware.

2009, Apr. 30 *Perf. 14¾x14*
3193 A618 25d Sheet of 4, #a-d 7.50 7.50

American Military Aviation, Cent. — A619

No. 3194, horiz.: a, B-17 and P-51 Escort. b, Doolittle's B-25. c, B-24. d, P-47D. e, F-86F. f, AT-6. g, F-80. h, F-15. i, T-38 and F-117.
80d, P-38 and ME-262.

2009, June 12 *Perf. 11½x11¼*
3194 A619 15d Sheet of 9, #a-i 13.00 13.00

Souvenir Sheet

Perf. 13¼

3195 A619 80d multi 8.50 8.50

No. 3194 contains nine 40x30mm stamps. National Topical Stamp Show, Dayton, Ohio.

Miniature Sheets

Michael Jackson (1958-2009), Singer — A620

No. 3196: a, 20d, Holding microphone. b, 20d, Wearing white jacket and hat. c, 30d, As "b." d, 30d, As "a."
No. 3197, horiz.: a, 20d, Wearing black jacket and hat. b, 20d, Wearing white jacket. c, 30d, As "a." d, 30d, As "b."

Perf. 12x11½, 11½ (#3197)

2009, July 7 **Litho.**

Sheets of 4, #a-d

3196-3197 A620 Set of 2 20.00 20.00

Miniature Sheet

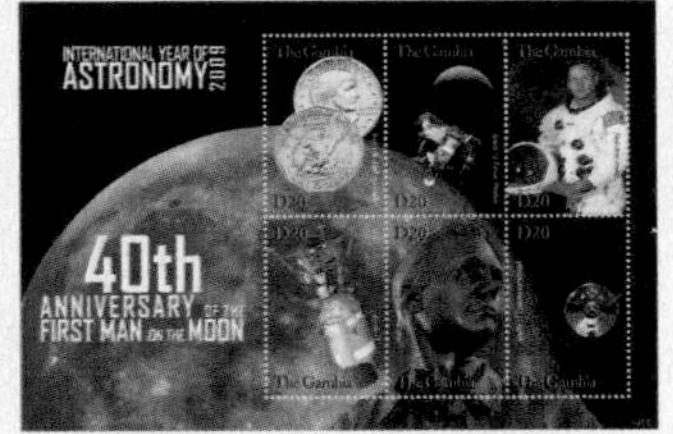

First Man on the Moon, 40th Anniv. — A621

No. 3198: a, Obverse and reverse of US Susan B. Anthony dollar coin. b, Apollo 11 Lunar Module. c, Neil Armstrong. d, Apollo 11. e, Statue of Armstrong. f, Apollo 11 Command Module.

2009, July 20 *Perf. 13¼*
3198 A621 20d Sheet of 6, #a-f 11.50 11.50

Miniature Sheets

Dogs — A622

No. 3199, 25d — Pembroke Welsh corgi: a, Jumping. b, Sitting in leaves. c, Sitting in front of flower basket. d, Sitting on lawn.
No. 3200, 25d — West Highland white terrier and: a, Upright basket. b, Beach ball. c, Gift boxes. d, Yellow flowers and basket on side.

2009, Aug. 29 *Perf. 12*

Sheets of 4, #a-d

3199-3200 A622 Set of 2 20.00 20.00

Birds
A623

Designs: 15d, Hamerkop. 20d, Pied kingfisher. No. 3203, 25d, Black-capped babbler. No. 3204, 40d, African darter.
No. 3205, 25d, vert.: a, Malachite kingfisher. b, Common bulbul. c, Black-crowned night heron. d, Wire-tailed swallow.
No. 3206, 40d: a, Sacred ibis. b, Little grebe.

2009, Aug. 29 *Perf. 11½*
3201-3204 A623 Set of 4 9.00 9.00
3205 A623 25d Sheet of 4, #a-d 9.00 9.00

Souvenir Sheet

3206 A623 40d Sheet of 2, #a-b 8.00 8.00

Miniature Sheet

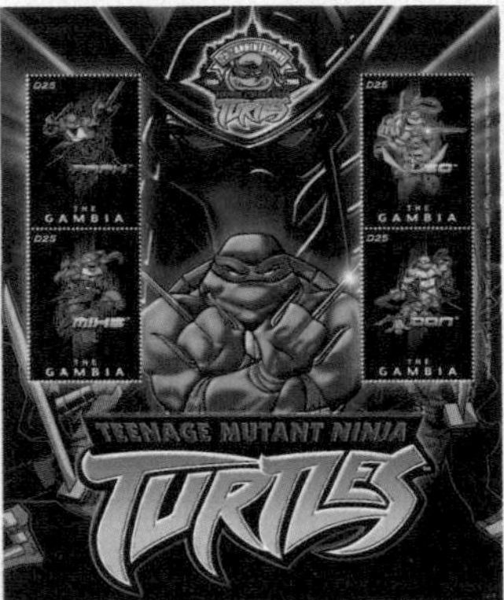

Teenage Mutant Ninja Turtles, 25th Anniv. — A624

No. 3207: a, Raphael. b, Leonardo. c, Michelangelo. d, Donatello.

2009, Aug. 29 *Perf. 13¼*
3207 A624 25d Sheet of 4, #a-d 9.00 9.00

Pres. Barack Obama and Queen Elizabeth II — A625

No. 3208, horiz.: a, Pres. Obama. b, Queen Elizabeth II. c, Michelle Obama.
80d, Pres. Obama and Queen Elizabeth II at G20 World Leader Reception.

2009, Aug. 29 *Perf. 11½x12*
3208 A625 25d Sheet of 3, #a-c 7.00 7.00

Souvenir Sheet

Perf. 11½

3209 A625 80d multi 7.50 7.50

Pres. Barack Obama in Germany — A626

No. 3210: a, Obama, Bishop Jochen Bohl, German Chancellor Angela Merkel. b, Obama. c, Merkel. d, Obama and Merkel.
65d, Obama, Merkel, Elie Wiesel and Bertrand Herz at Buchenwald Concentration Camp.

2009, Oct. 22 ***Perf. 11½***
3210 A626 25d Sheet of 4, #a-d 9.00 9.00

Souvenir Sheet
Perf. 13¼
3211 A626 65d multi 6.50 6.50

No. 3210 contains four 30x40mm stamps.

Methodist Church Conference A627

Cross and map of: 25d, The Gambia. 35d, Africa, vert.

2009 ***Perf. 11½***
3212-3213 A627 Set of 2 5.50 5.50

Miniature Sheet

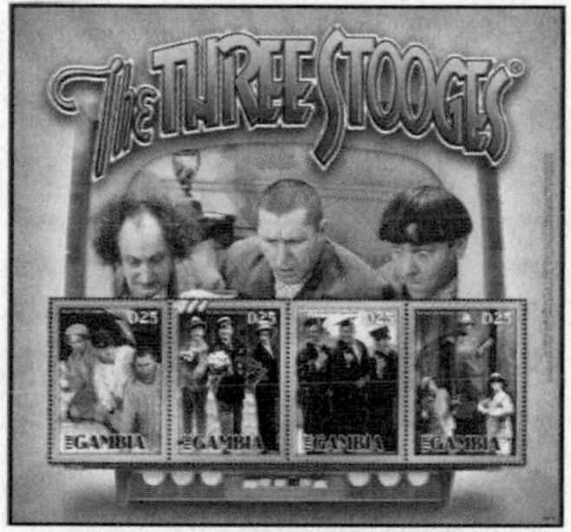

The Three Stooges — A628

No. 3214 — Scenes from: a, Rockin' Thru the Rockies. b, The Sitter Downers. c, Violent is the Word for Curly. d, We Want Our Mummy.

2009 ***Perf. 13¼***
3214 A628 25d Sheet of 4, #a-d 8.50 8.50

Miniature Sheet

Pres. Barack Obama, 2009 Nobel Peace Laureate — A629

No. 3215 — Pres. Obama with: a, Microphones at LR. b, Microphones at LL. c, Foliage at right. d, Flag at right.

2009, Dec. 30 **Litho.** ***Perf. 13x13¼***
3215 A629 25d Sheet of 4, #a-d 8.50 8.50

Mushrooms A630

Designs: 10d, Panaeolus bispora. No. 3217, 15d, Panaeolus tropicalis. 25d, Psilocybe mairei. 30d, Gymnopilus aeruginosus.
No. 3220, 15d, horiz.: a, Panaeolus retirugis. b, Gymnopilus junionius. c, Psilocybe natalensis. d, Panaeolus africanus. e, Panaeolus cinctulus. f, Panaeolus subbalteatus.

2009, Dec. 30 ***Perf. 14x14¾***
3216-3219 A630 Set of 4 7.50 7.50

Perf. 14¾x14
3220 A630 15d Sheet of 6, #a-f 8.00 8.00

Butterflies A631

Designs: 10d, Elegant acraea. No. 3222, 15d, Bamboo charaxes. 25d, Green-veined charaxes. 30d, Pink acraea.
No. 3225, 15d, horiz.: a, Abadima acraea. b, African common white. c, Cream-bordered charaxes. d, African caper white. e, Large spotted acraea. f, Tiny orange tip.

2009, Dec. 30 ***Perf. 14x14¾***
3221-3224 A631 Set of 4 7.50 7.50

Perf. 14¾x14
3225 A631 15d Sheet of 6, #a-f 8.50 8.50

Christmas — A632

Designs: 10d, Map of Africa with stocking cap. 15d, Cane-shaped cookies. 25d, Christmas light display. 30d, Candle and poinsettia.

2009, Dec. 30 ***Perf. 14x14¾***
3226-3229 A632 Set of 4 7.00 7.00

Ferraris and Their Parts A633

No. 3230, 12d: a, Chassis of 1999 360 Modena. b, 1999 360 Modena.
No. 3231, 12d: a, Engine and drive train of 2003 F2003-GA. b, 2003 F2003-GA.
No.3232, 12d: a, Convertible roof of 2005 Superamerica. b, 2005 Superamerica.
No. 3233, 12d: a, Engine of 2008 California. b, 2008 California.

2010, Feb. 24 ***Perf. 12***
Vert. Pairs, #a-b
3230-3233 A633 Set of 4 8.50 8.50

Whales and Dolphins A634

Designs: 10d, Common dolphin. 15d, Pygmy killer whale. No. 3236, 25d, Short-finned pilot whale. 30d, Clymene dolphin.
No. 3228, 25d: a, Southern bottlenose whale. b, Fraser's dolphin. c, Atlantic humpbacked dolphin. d, Ginkgo-toothed beaked whale.
No. 3239, 35d: a, Blainville's beaked whalen. b, Atlantic spotted dolphin.

2010, Feb. 24 ***Perf. 11½x11¼***
3234-3237 A634 Set of 4 7.50 7.50

Perf. 11½x12
3238 A634 25d Sheet of 4, #a-d 8.50 8.50

Souvenir Sheet
Perf. 11½x11¼
3239 A634 35d Sheet of 2, #a-b 6.75 6.75

Miniature Sheet

Charles Darwin (1809-82), Naturalist — A635

No. 3240 — Birds: a, Warbler finch. b, Common cactus finch. c, Large cactus finch. d, Small ground finch.

2010, Feb. 24 ***Perf. 13¼***
3240 A635 25d Sheet of 4, #a-d 9.00 9.00

Miniature Sheet

Pres. John F. Kennedy (1917-63) — A636

No. 3241 — Kennedy: a, Curtainin background at left. b, At inauguration ceremony. c, With flag in background at right. d, With family.

2010, Apr. 15 ***Perf. 12x11½***
3241 A636 30d Sheet of 4, #a-d 11.00 11.00

Miniature Sheets

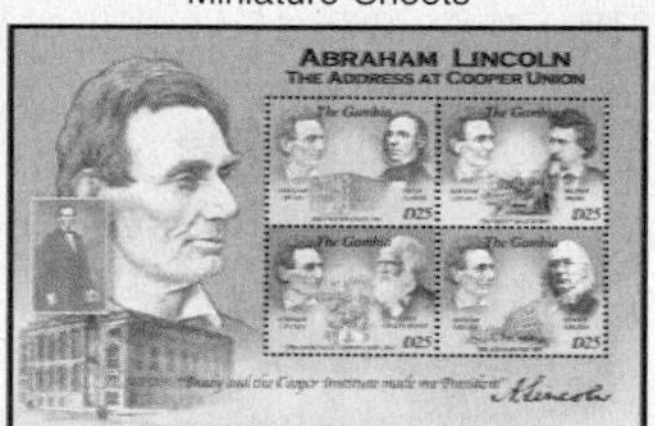

Pres. Abraham Lincoln (1809-65) — A637

No. 3242, 25d — Lincoln and: a, Peter Cooper, Cooper Union. b, Mathew Brady, Brady Gallery. c, William Cullen Bryant, Great Hall, Cooper Union. d, Horace Greeley, Astor House.
No. 3243, 25d — Lincoln and: a, Brady, photograph of Lincoln by Brady. b, Alexander Gardner, photographs of Lincoln by Gardner. c, Victor David Brenner, Lincoln cent, Pres. Theodore Roosevelt. d, Daniel Chester French, statue of Lincoln in Lincoln Memorial.

2010, Apr. 15 ***Perf. 11½x12***
Sheets of 4, #a-d
3242-3243 A637 Set of 2 18.00 18.00

Miniature Sheets

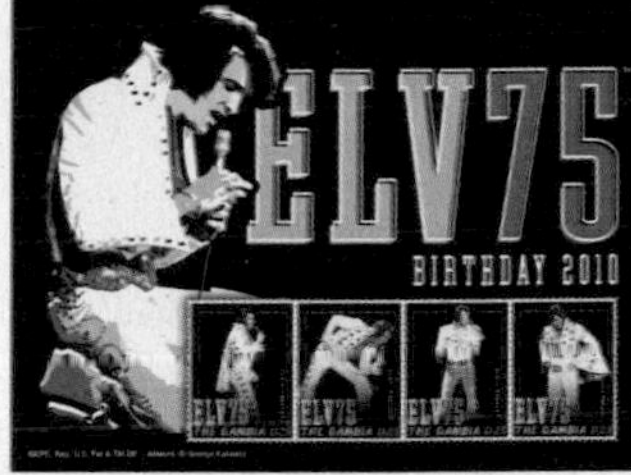

A638

Elvis Presley (1935-77) — A639

No. 3244 — Presley: a, Holding microphone, facing right, cape and microphone cord visible. b, Holding microphone, leaning. c, Holding microphone, no cord visible. d, Standing with arms akimbo.
No. 3245 — Presley: a, With guitar. b, With microphone near mouth. c, With guitar, pointing, and holding microphone on stand. d, Holding microphone on stand, with guitar strap on shoulder.

2010, Apr. 15 ***Perf. 11¼x11½***
3244 A638 25d Sheet of 4, #a-d 8.50 8.50

Perf. 13¼
3245 A639 30d Sheet of 4, #a-d 11.00 11.00

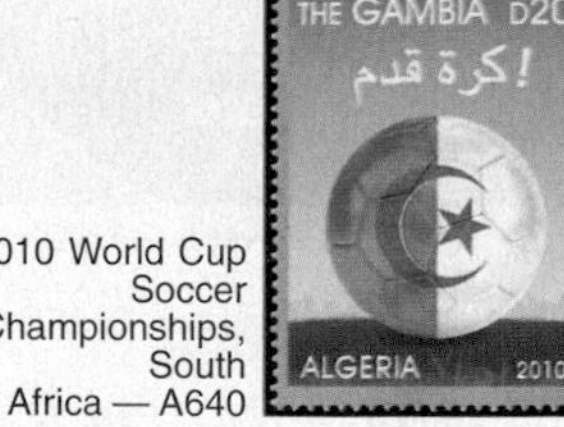

2010 World Cup Soccer Championships, South Africa — A640

Soccer ball with flag of participating nations: No. 3246, 20d, Algeria. No. 3247, 20d, Argentina. No. 3248, 20d, Australia. No. 3249, 20d, Brazil. No. 3250, 20d, Cameroon. No. 3251, 20d, Chile. No. 3252, 20d, Denmark. No. 3253, 20d, England. No. 3254, 20d, France. No. 3255, 20d, Germany. No. 3256, 20d, Ghana. No. 3257, 20d, Greece. No. 3258, 20d, Honduras. No. 3259, 20d, Italy. No. 3260, 20d, Ivory Coast (Côte d'Ivoire). No. 3261, 20d, Japan. No. 3262, 20d, Korea DPR (North Korea). No. 3263, 20d, Korea Republic (South Korea). No. 3264, 20d, Mexico. No. 3265, 20d, Netherlands. No. 3266, 20d, New Zealand. No. 3267, 20d, Nigeria. No. 3268, 20d, Paraguay. No. 3269, 20d, Portugal. No. 3270, 20d, Serbia. No. 3271, 20d, Slovakia. No. 3272, 20d, Slovenia. No. 3273, 20d, South Africa. No. 3274, 20d, Spain. No. 3275, 20d, Switzerland. No. 3276, 20d, United States. No. 3277, 20d, Uruguay.

2010, May 24 ***Perf. 14x14¾***
3246-3277 A640 Set of 32 50.00 50.00

Nos. 3246-3277 each were printed in sheets of 6.

Traditional Musical Instruments
A641

Designs: 2d, 25d, Wollof tabala. 3d, 30d, Jola bugarab. 5d, 35d, Fula rilty. 6d, 50d, Mandinka kontingo. 7d, 65d, Mandinka bolongbato. 10d, 100d, Mandinka kora. 15d, 200d, Mandinka kora, diff. 18d, Mandinka balafongo, horiz.

Perf. 11¼x11½, 11½x11¼

2010, June 8

3278	A641	2d multi	.25	.25
3279	A641	3d multi	.25	.25
3280	A641	5d multi	.35	.35
3281	A641	6d multi	.40	.40
3282	A641	7d multi	.50	.50
3283	A641	10d multi	.70	.70
3284	A641	15d multi	1.00	1.00
3285	A641	18d multi	1.25	1.25
3286	A641	25d multi	1.75	1.75
3287	A641	30d multi	2.00	2.00
3288	A641	35d multi	2.40	2.40
3289	A641	50d multi	3.25	3.25
3290	A641	65d multi	4.00	4.00
3291	A641	100d multi	6.00	6.00
3292	A641	200d multi	10.00	10.00
	Nos. 3278-3292 (15)		34.10	34.10

US First Ladies Type of 2007

Souvenir Sheet

No. 3293, Michelle Obama.

2010, June 8 ***Perf. 13¼***

3293 A574 65d multi 5.00 5.00

Miniature Sheet

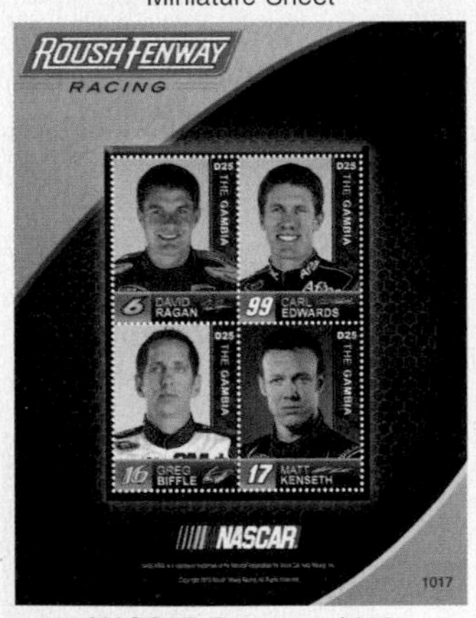

NASCAR Drivers — A642

No. 3294: a, David Ragan. b, Carl Edwards. c, Greg Biffle. d, Matt Kenseth.

2010, June 8 ***Perf. 13¼x13***

3294 A642 25d Sheet of 4, #a-d 8.50 8.50

Souvenir Sheet

Elvis Presley (1935-77) — A643

No. 3295 — Presley wearing: a, Black jacket. b, White jacket.

2010, June 11 ***Imperf.***

3295 A643 140d Sheet of 2, #a-b *27.50 27.50*

Miniature Sheet

Elvis Presley (1935-77) — A644

No. 3296 — Presley wearing: a, Checked shirt. b, Jacket and tie. c, Sweater. d, White shirt with open collar.

2010, Apr. 15 Litho. ***Perf. 13¼***

3296 A644 30d Sheet of 4, #a-d 11.00 11.00

Lech Kaczynski (1949-2010), President of Poland — A645

2010, July 14 ***Perf. 12x11½***

3297 A645 30d multi 2.50 2.50

Printed in sheets of 4.

Miniature Sheet

Accession to the Throne by King George V, Cent. — A646

No. 3298: a, 1917 cartoon of King George V. b, King George V. c, King Edward VIII. d, Badge of the House of Windsor. e, King George VI. f, Queen Elizabeth II.

2010, July 14 Litho. ***Perf. 11¼x11½***

3298 A646 20d Sheet of 6, #a-f 11.00 11.00

Visit of Pope Benedict XVI to Malta A647

Pope Benedict XVI wearing: No. 3299, 30d, Miter. No. 3300, 30d, Zucchetto.

2010, Aug. 26 ***Perf. 13¼***

3299-3300 A647 Set of 2 5.50 5.50

Nos. 3299-3300 each were printed in sheets of 5.

Miniature Sheet

Paintings by Sandro Botticelli (1445-1510) — A648

No. 3301: a, Lamentation. b, Madonna del Magnificat. c, The Return of Judith to Bethulia. d, Venus from Venus and Mars. e, Mars from Venus and Mars. f, The Punishment of Korah.

2010, Aug. 26 ***Perf. 11¼x11½***

3301 A648 20d Sheet of 6, #a-f 11.00 11.00

Miniature Sheets

Mother Teresa (1910-97), Humanitarian — A649

No. 3302, 30d — Mother Teresa at left, Princess Diana at right, with: a, Princess Diana bending to talk to Mother Teresa. b, Princess Diana with hands clasped at waist and Mother Teresa with hands clasped below chin. c, Mother Teresa and Princess Diana holding hands, Mother Teresa's arm at side. d, Mother Teresa and Princess Diana holding hands, Mother Teresa's arm extended.

No. 3303, 30d — Mother Teresa with: a, Pres. Ronald Reagan. b, Archbishop Desmond Tutu. c, Pope John Paul II. d, Queen Elizabeth II.

2010, Aug. 26 ***Perf. 11½x12***

Sheets of 4, #a-d

3302-3303 A649 Set of 2 22.50 22.50

Robert Schumann (1810-56), Composer — A650

No. 3304, horiz. — Schumann and: a, Birthplace. b, His wife, Clara. c, Schumann Monument, Zwickau, Germany. d, Grave marker, Bonn, Germany.

65d, Robert and Clara Schumann.

2010, Aug. 26 ***Perf. 11½x12***

3304 A650 30d Sheet of 4, #a-d 12.00 12.00

Souvenir Sheet

Perf. 11¼x11½

3305 A650 65d multi 6.50 6.50

Posters for Films Directed by Akira Kurosawa (1910-98) — A651

No. 3306, 30d, vert.: a, Nora Inu (Stray Dog). b, Zoku Sugata Sanshiro (Sanshiro Sugata Part II). c, Shichinin no Samurai (Seven Samurai). d, Shizukanaru Ketto (The Quiet Duel).

No. 3307, 30d, vert.: a, Donzoko (The Lower Depths). b, Hakuchi (The Idiot). c, Ikimono no Kiroku (I Live in Fear). d, Ikiru.

80d, Ichiban Utsukushiku (The Most Beautiful).

2010, Aug. 26 ***Perf. 13¼***

Sheets of 4, #a-d

3306-3307 A651 Set of 2 21.00 21.00

Souvenir Sheet

3308 A651 80d multi 8.00 8.00

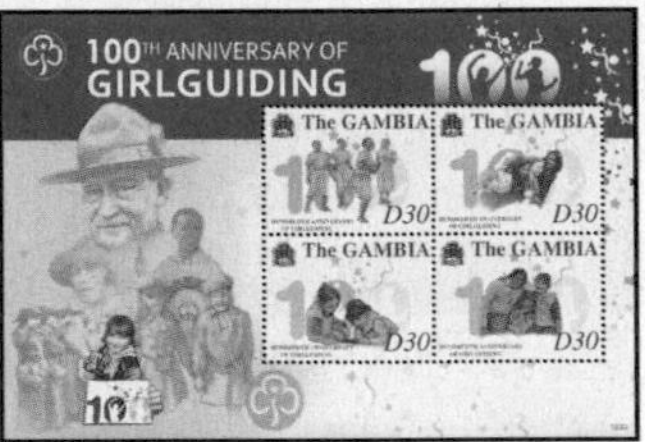

Girl Guides, Cent. — A652

No. 3309 — Girl Guides emblem, centenary emblem and: a, Four Girl Guides in green uniforms. b, Four Girl Guides not wearing uniforms. c, Two Girl Guides. d, Three Girl Guides.

80d, Two Girl Guides with backpacks, vert.

2010, Oct. 15 ***Perf. 11½x12***

3309 A652 30d Sheet of 4, #a-d 8.50 8.50

Souvenir Sheet

Perf. 11¼x11½

3310 A652 80d multi 5.75 5.75

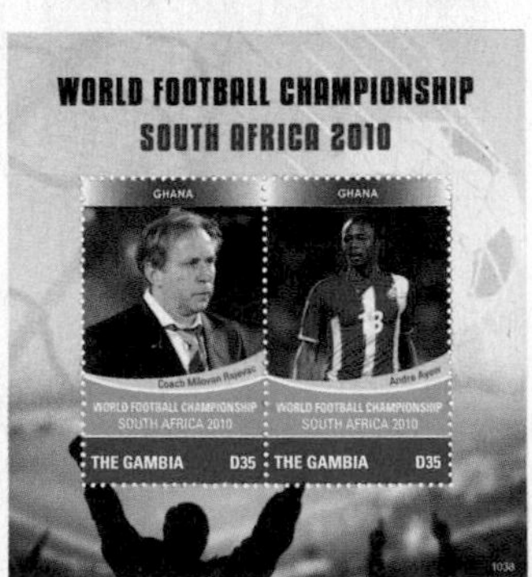

Players and Coaches in Second Round Matches of 2010 World Cup Soccer Championships — A653

No. 3311, 15d — United States vs. Ghana: a, Jay Demerit. b, Asamoah Gyan. c, Robbie Findley. d, Samuel Inkoom. e, Ricardo Clark. f, Stephen Appiah.

No. 3312, 15d — Uruguay vs. South Korea: a, Fernando Musiera. b, Lee Chung-Yong. c, Jorge Fucile. d, Cha Du-Ri. e, Maximiliano Pereira. f, Park Chu-Young.

No. 3313, 15d — Argentina vs. Mexico: a, Gabriel Heinze. b, Efrain Juarez. c, Carlos Tevez. d, Carlos Salcido. e, Lionel Messi. f, Andres Guardado.

No. 3314, 15d — Germany vs. England: a, Sami Khedira. b, Steven Gerrard. c, Philipp

Lahm. d, Joe Cole. e, Lukas Podolski. f, Ashley Cole.
No. 3315, 35d — Ghana: a, Coach Milovan Rajevac. b, Andre Ayew.
No. 3316, 35d — Uruguay: a, Coach Oscar Tabarez. b, Diego Forlan.
No. 3317, 35d — Argentina: a, Coach Diego Maradona. b, Nicolas Otramendi.
No. 3318, 35d — Germany: a, Coach Joachim Loew. b, Thomas Mueller.

2010, Oct. 15 ***Perf. 12***
Sheets of 6, #a-f
3311-3314 A653 Set of 4 30.00 30.00
Souvenir Sheets of 2, #a-b
3315-3318 A653 Set of 4 20.00 20.00

Miniature Sheets

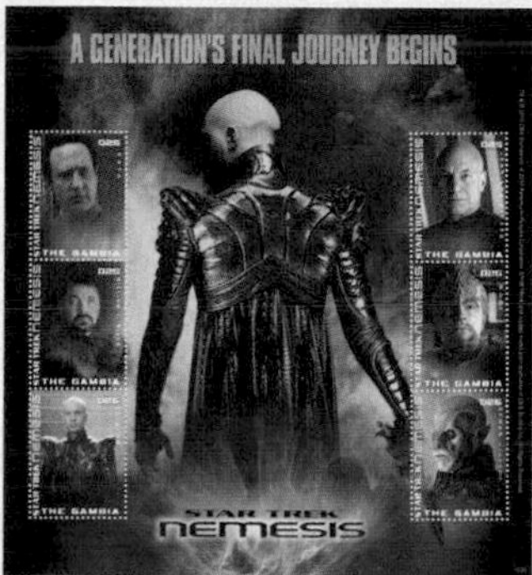

Characters From Star Trek Movies — A654

No. 3319, 25d — Characters from *Star Trek: Nemesis*: a, Lt. Commander Data. b, Capt. Jean-Luc Picard. c, Commander William T. Riker. d, Lt. Commander Worf. e, Praetor Shinzon. f, Reman Viceroy Vkruk.
No. 3320, 25d, horiz. — Characters from *Star Trek: First Contact*: a, Worf. b, Riker and Picard. c, Data and Borg Queen. d, Dr. Zefram Cochrane. e, Lt. Commander Geordi La Forge. f, Picard and Dr. Beverly Crusher.

2010, Nov. 5 **Litho.** ***Perf. 12***
Sheets of 6, #a-f
3319-3320 A654 Set of 2 18.00 18.00

Christmas A655

Paintings: 15d, Madonna with Child, by Carlo Crivelli. 25d, Nativity, Birth of Jesus, by Giotto di Bondone. 30d, The Journey of the Magi, by Stefano di Giovanni. 40d, Nativity, by Bernardo Daddi.

2010, Dec. 25
3321-3324 A655 Set of 4 7.75 7.75

Souvenir Sheets

A656

Designs: No. 3325: a, Pope Leo XIII (1810-1903). b, Coat of arms of Pope Leo XIII. No. 3325C: d, St. Pius X (1835-1914). e, Arms of St. Pius X.

2010, Dec. 25 **Litho.** ***Imperf.***
Without Gum
3325 A656 100d Sheet of 2, #a-b 22.50 22.50
3325C A656 100d Sheet of 2, #a-b 22.50 22.50

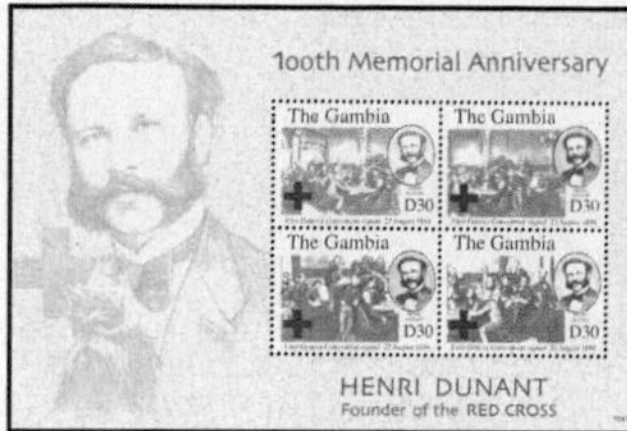

Henri Dunant (1828-1910), Founder of Red Cross — A657

No. 3326 — Red Cross, depictions of First Geneval Convention negotiations and portrait of Dunant in: a, Green blue. b, Brown. c, Purple. d, Blue.
65d, Portrait of Dunant, portraits of 1863 members of International Committee of the Red Cross.

2010, Dec. 30 ***Perf. 12***
3326 A657 30d Sheet of 4, #a-d 8.50 8.50
Souvenir Sheet
3327 A657 65d multi 4.75 4.75

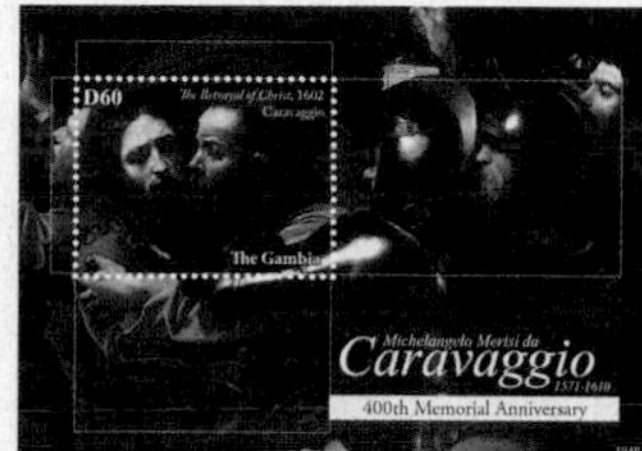

Paintings by Michelangelo Merisi da Caravaggio (1573-1610) — A658

No. 3328, vert.: a, The Seven Works of Mercy. b, The Conversion on the Way to Damascus. c, Alof de Wignacourt. d, David and Goliath. e, The Death of the Virgin. f, The Raising of Lazarus.
60d, The Betrayal of Christ.

2010, Dec. 30
3328 A658 20d Sheet of 6, #a-f 8.50 8.50
Souvenir Sheet
3329 A658 60d multi 4.25 4.25

Pres. John F. Kennedy (1917-63) A659

No. 3330, 30d — Pres. Kennedy and wife, Jacqueline: a, Standing. b, Sitting in limousine.
No. 3331, 30d — Pres. Kennedy and: a, Jacqueline, watching America's Cup race. b, Daughter Caroline.
No. 3332, 60d, Pres. Kennedy standing in limousine. No. 3333, 60d, With Jacqueline, leaving Air Force One, horiz.

2010, Dec. 30 ***Perf. 12***
Vert. Pairs, #a-b
3330-3331 A659 Set of 2 8.50 8.50
Souvenir Sheets
3332-3333 A659 Set of 2 11.50 11.50

Nos. 3330-3331 each were printed in sheets containing two pairs.

A660

No. 3334, 30d — Denomination in black, Princess Diana wearing: a, Red hat. b, Black hat. c, White dress. d, Hooded raincoat.
No. 3335, 30d — Denomination in white, Princess Diana wearing: a, Tiara. b, Black hat with veil. c, Red hat. d, Black hat with bow.
80d, Princess Diana wearing white dress.

2010, Dec. 30 **Litho.**
Sheets of 4, #a-d
3334-3335 A660 Set of 2 15.00 15.00
Souvenir Sheet
3336 A660 80d multi 5.75 5.75

Bengal Tiger — A661

No. 3337, vert. — Tiger with: a, Paws visible. b, Paws not shown.

Perf. 13 Syncopated
2011, Feb. 8 **Litho.**
3337 A661 30d Sheet of 4, 2 each #a-b 9.00 9.00
Souvenir Sheet
Perf. 12
3338 A661 120d shown 9.00 9.00

Indipex 2011 World Philatelic Exhibition, New Delhi.

Miniature Sheets

A662

Princess Diana (1961-97) — A663

No. 3339 — Princess Diana wearing: a, Black dress. b, Red and white polka dot dress. c, Red and black plaid blouse. d, Black dress and hat.
No. 3340 — Princess Diana wearing: a, Black dress and necklace. b, Red dress and tiara. c, Tiara and necklace. d, Black dress and headband.

2011, Feb. 8 ***Perf. 12***
3339 A662 30d Sheet of 4, #a-d 9.00 9.00
3340 A663 30d Sheet of 4, #a-d 9.00 9.00

Engagement of Prince William and Catherine Middleton A664

Designs: No. 3341, Couple. No. 3343, Couple, horiz.
No. 3342: a, Middleton. b, Prince William.
No. 3344, horiz.: a, Prince William. b, Middleton.

2011, Feb. 8 ***Perf. 13 Syncopated***
3341 A664 30d multi 2.25 2.25
3342 A664 30d Horiz. pair, #a-b 4.50 4.50
Perf. 12
3343 A664 40d multi 3.00 3.00
Souvenir Sheet
3344 A664 40d Sheet of 2, #a-d 6.00 6.00

No. 3341 was printed in sheets of 4. No. 3342 was printed in sheets containing two pairs. No. 3343 was printed in sheets of 2.

Miniature Sheets

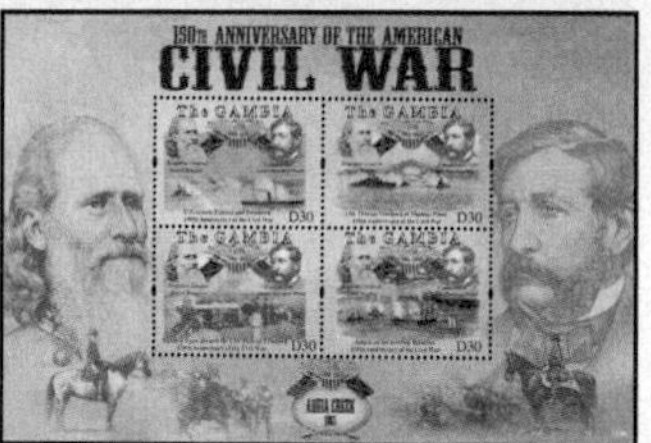

U.S. Civil War Battles, 150th Anniv. — A665

No. 3345, 30d — Eagle, shield, Union and Confederate flags, Brigadier General Daniel Ruggles and Commander James Harmon Ward from Battle of Aquia Creek, May 29, 1861, and: a, Union vessels Pawnee and Thomas Freeborn. b, USS Thomas Freeborn at Mathias Point. c, Sighting a gun aboard the USS Thomas Freeborn. d, Attack on the Confederate batteries.
No. 3346, 30d — Eagle, shield, Union and Confederate flags, Colonel John B. Magruder and Brigadier General Ebenezer W. Peirce from Battle of Big Bethel, June 10, 1861, and: a, Fort Monroe wounded. b, Rodman gun battery at Fort Monroe. c, New York 5th Regiment (Duryee's Zouaves). d, New York 5th Regiment's charge on Big Bethel.
No. 3347, 30d — Eagle, shield, Union and Confederate flags, Colonel John S. Marmaduke and Brigadier General Nathaniel Lyon from Battle of Boonville, June 17, 1861, and: a, St. Louis riot. b, General Lyon departing Boonville. c, Battle scene. d, Confederates retreat from Union forces.
No. 3348, 30d — Eagle, shield, Union and Confederate flags, Colonel Stonewall Jackson and Major General Robert Patterson from Battle of Hoke's Run, July 2, 1861, and: a, General Patterson's division crossing the Potomac.

b, Union soldiers skirmish at Hoke's Run. c, Union scout at Shenandoah Valley. d, Union forces advance near Martinsburg.

No. 3349, 30d — Eagle, shield, Union and Confederate flags, Governor Claiborne Fox Jackson and Colonel Franz Sigel from Battle of Carthage, July 5, 1861, and: a, The Wide Wakes Demonstration. b, Colonel Sigel at the Missouri River. c, Battle scene. d, Union forces retreat to Sarcoxie.

2011, Feb. 8 ***Perf. 13 Syncopated***

Sheets of 4, #a-d

3345-3349 A665 Set of 5 45.00 45.00

Pres. Ronald Reagan (1911-2004) — A666

No. 3350, horiz. — Pres. Reagan and: a, Flags. b, Wife, Nancy. c, Helicopter. d, Horse.

2011, Feb. 8 ***Perf. 12***

3350 A666 30d Sheet of 4, #a-d 9.00 9.00

Souvenir Sheet

3351 A666 65d shown 5.00 5.00

Miniature Sheet

Jewish South African Anti-Apartheid Leaders — A667

No. 3352: a, Hilda Bernstein (1915-2006). b, Lionel "Rusty" Bernstein (1920-2002). c, Ruth First (1925-82). d, Ronald Segal (1932-2008).

2011, Mar. 1 **Litho.**

3352 A667 25d Sheet of 4, #a-d 7.25 7.25

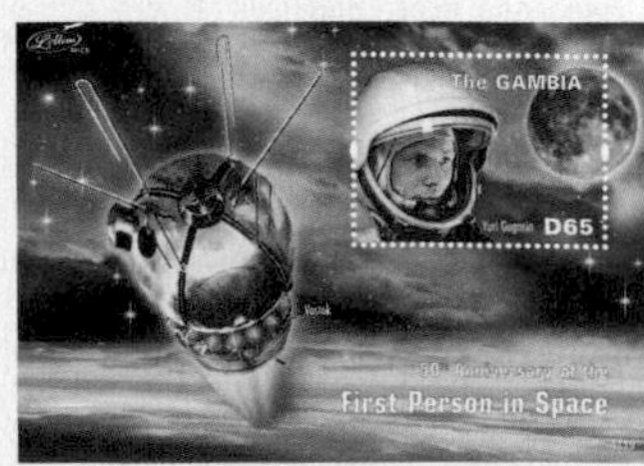

First Man in Space, 50th Anniv. — A668

No. 3353, 30d: a, Raising to vertical of Vostok rocket. b, Tracking ship Yuri Gagarin. c, U.S. astronaut John Glenn. d, Monument to Conquerors of Space, Moscow.

No. 3354, 30d, vert.: a, Yuri Gagarin, first man in space. b, U.S. astronaut Scott Carpenter. c, Vostok spaceship. d, Titanium statue.

No. 3355, 65d, Gagarin and Moon. No. 3356, 65d, Gagarin.

2011, Mar. 29 ***Perf. 12***

Sheets of 4, #a-d

3353-3354 A668 Set of 2 17.50 17.50

Souvenir Sheets

Perf. 13 Syncopated

3355-3356 A668 Set of 2 9.50 9.50

Souvenir Sheets

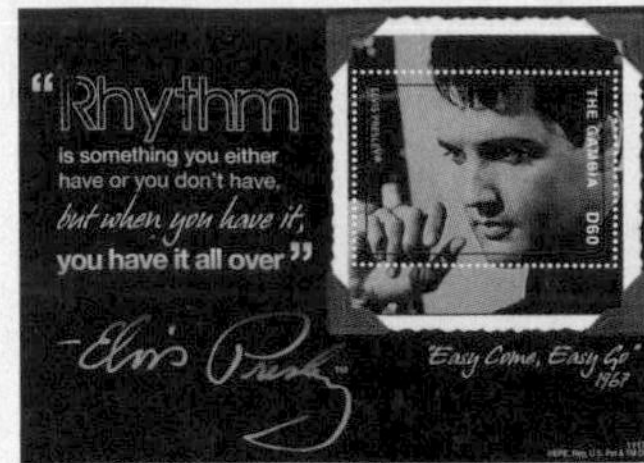

A669

A670

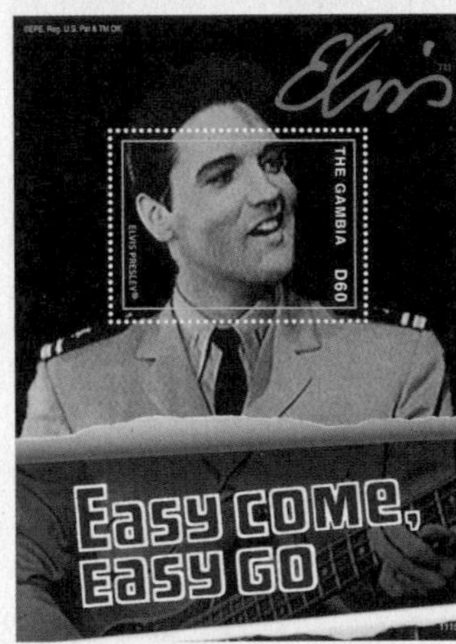

A671

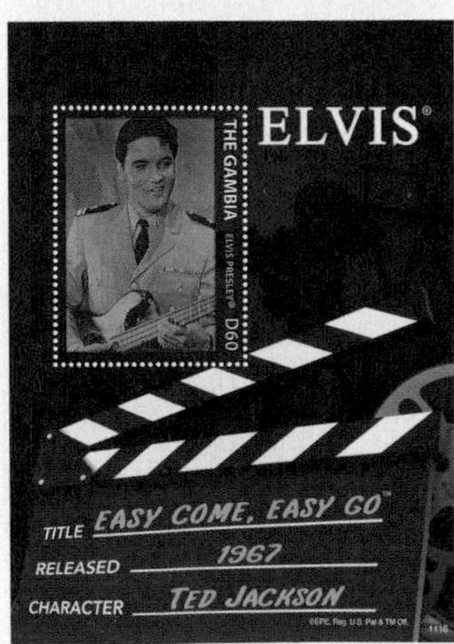

Elvis Presley (1935-77) — A672

2011, Mar. 29 ***Perf. 12¾***

3357 A669 60d multi 4.50 4.50
3358 A670 60d multi 4.50 4.50
3359 A671 60d multi 4.50 4.50
3360 A672 60d multi 4.50 4.50
Nos. 3357-3360 (4) 18.00 18.00

Wedding of Prince William and Catherine Middleton A673

Designs: No. 3361, Couple.

No. 3362: a, Prince William. b, Middleton. 65d, Couple, diff.

2011, Apr. 29 ***Perf. 12***

3361 A673 30d multi 2.25 2.25
3362 A673 30d Sheet of 4, 2 each #a-b 8.75 8.75

Souvenir Sheet

3363 A673 65d multi 4.75 4.75

No. 3361 was printed in sheets of 4.

Miniature Sheet

Discovery of Machu Picchu by Hiram Bingham, Cent. — A674

No. 3364: a, Aerial view of Machu Picchu. b, Stonework. c, Stone buildings as seen through hole in wall. d, Bingham.

2011, May 16 ***Perf. 13 Syncopated***

3364 A674 30d Sheet of 4, #a-d 8.75 8.75

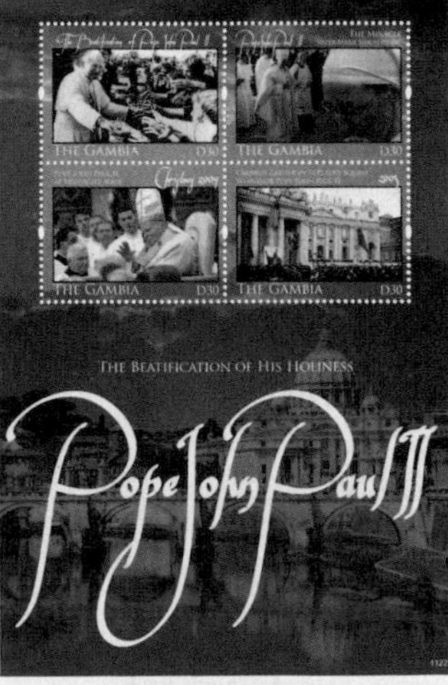

Beatification of Pope John Paul II — A675

No. 3365: a, Pope John Paul II greeting crowd. b, Pope John Paul II in procession, Sister Marie Simon Pierre. c, Pope John Paul II at Midnight mass. d, Crowd in St. Peter's Square honoring Pope John Paul II.

60d, Pope John Paul II and Mother Teresa.

2011, May 16 ***Perf. 13 Syncopated***

3365 A675 30d Sheet of 4, #a-d 8.75 8.75

Souvenir Sheet

Perf. 12¾

3366 A675 60d multi 4.25 4.25

No. 3366 contains one 50x38mm stamp.

Cats — A676

No. 3367: a, Munchkin. b, Ragamuffin. c, Chinchilla. d, Burman.

70d, Turkish Van.

2011, May 16 ***Perf. 13 Syncopated***

3367 A676 30d Sheet of 4, #a-d 8.75 8.75

Souvenir Sheet

Perf. 12

3368 A676 70d multi 5.00 5.00

A677

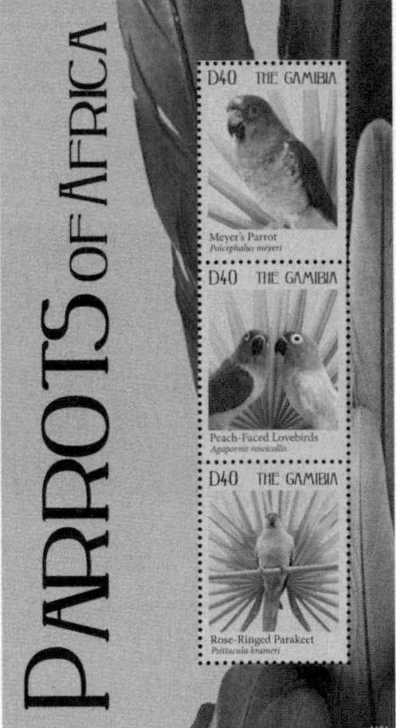

A678

Parrots — A679

No. 3369: a, Masked lovebird. b, Madagascar lovebird. c, Red-fronted macaw. d, Senegal parrot.

No. 3370: a, Meyer's parrot. b, Peach-faced lovebirds. c, Rose-ringed parakeet.

No. 3371, 70d, Fischer's lovebird. No. 3372, 70d, African gray parrot.

2011, May 16 ***Perf. 13 Syncopated***

3369 A677 30d Sheet of 4, #a-d 8.75 8.75
3370 A678 40d Sheet of 3, #a-c 8.75 8.75

Souvenir Sheets

Perf.

3371-3372 A679 Set of 2 10.00 10.00

A680

PhilaNippon '11, Yokohama — A681

No. 3373 — Origami: a, Brown elephant. b, Green frog. c, Red crab. d, Bright pink and blue cranes. e, Yellow and orange pinwheel. f, Light green praying mantis. g, Orange flower. h, Purple flowers.

No. 3374: a, Two cherry blossoms. b, Cherry blossom petals. c, Three cherry blossoms.

No. 3375, Crane. No. 3376, Cherry blossom and bud.

Perf. 12. Perf. (A681)

2011, May 16 **Litho.**

3373 A680 15d Sheet of 8, #a-h 8.75 8.75
3374 A681 40d Sheet of 3, #a-c 8.75 8.75

Souvenir Sheets

3375 A680 65d multi 4.75 4.75
3376 A681 65d multi 4.75 4.75

Jane Goodall Institute, Gombe, Tanzania, 50th Anniv. — A682

No. 3377: a, Jane Goodall. b, Baby chimpanzee hanging from tree. c, Head of chimpanzee. d, Goodall and chimpanzee.

No. 3378, horiz.: a, Goodall looking at hills through binoculars. b, Chimpanzee. c, Goodall, diff.

No. 3379, horiz.: a, Baby chimpanzee pointing. b, Goodall holding binoculars. c, Chimpanzee in tree.

80d, Adult and juvenile chimpanzee.

Perf. 13¼x13, 12 (#3378-3379)

2011, May 26

3377 A682 30d Sheet of 4, #a-d 8.75 8.75
3378 A682 35d Sheet of 3, #a-c 7.50 7.50
3379 A682 35d Sheet of 3, #a-c 7.50 7.50
Nos. 3377-3379 (3) 23.75 23.75

Souvenir Sheet

3380 A682 80d multi 5.75 5.75

Worldwide Fund for Nature (WWF) — A683

No. 3381 — Yellow-billed storks: a, Two birds in flight. b, Two birds in water. c, One bird landing, heads of two birds. d, Three birds in water.

2011, June 30 ***Perf. 12¾***

3381 Horiz. strip of 4 5.75 5.75
a.-d. A683 20d Any single 1.40 1.40
e. Souvenir sheet of 8, 2 each #3381a-3381d 11.50 11.50

A684

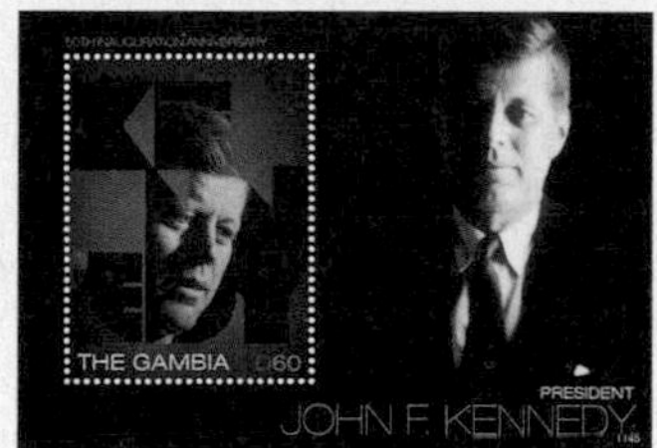

Pres. John F. Kennedy (1917-63) — A685

No. 3382 — Kennedy: a, At microphone, pointing. b, At microphone. c, At microphone, with arms extended. d, In front of White House.

2011, July 6 ***Perf. 12***

3382 A684 30d Sheet of 4, #a-d 8.25 8.25

Souvenir Sheet

Perf. 12¾x12½

3383 A685 60d multi 4.25 4.25

Visit of U.S. Pres. Barack Obama to the United Kingdom — A686

No. 3384, 30d: a, Pres. Barack Obama. b, First Lady Michelle Obama. c, Prince William. d, Catherine, Duchess of Cambridge.

No. 3385, 30d, horiz. — Obama with: a, Queen Elizabeth II and Prince Philip. b, John Hall, Dean of Westminster Abbey. c, Prince William and Catherine, Duchess of Cambridge. d, Prime Minister David Cameron and his wife, Samantha.

No. 3386: a, Cameron. b, Pres. Obama.

65d, Queen Elizabeth II and Pres. Obama, horiz.

2011, July 25 ***Perf. 12, 12½ (#3387)***

Sheets of 4, #a-d

3384-3385 A686 Set of 2 18.50 18.50
3386 A686 35d Sheet of 2, #a-b 5.50 5.50

Souvenir Sheet

3387 A686 65d multi 5.00 5.00

No. 3387 contains one 51x38mm stamp.

British Royalty — A687

Designs: No. 3388, 30d, King George V (1865-1936). No. 3389, 30d, King George VI (1895-1952). No. 3390, 30d, Queen Elizabeth II. No. 3391, 30d, Prince Philip.

2011, Oct. 11 ***Perf. 13¼x13***

3388-3391 A687 Set of 4 8.00 8.00

Nos. 3388-3391 each were printed in sheets of 4.

Miniature Sheet

Sept. 11, 2001 Terrorist Attacks, 10th Anniv. — A688

No. 3392 — Color of stripe at upper left corner: a, Dark blue. b, Orange. c, Red violet. d, Green.

2011, Oct. 11

3392 A688 30d Sheet of 4, #a-d 8.00 8.00

Miniature Sheet

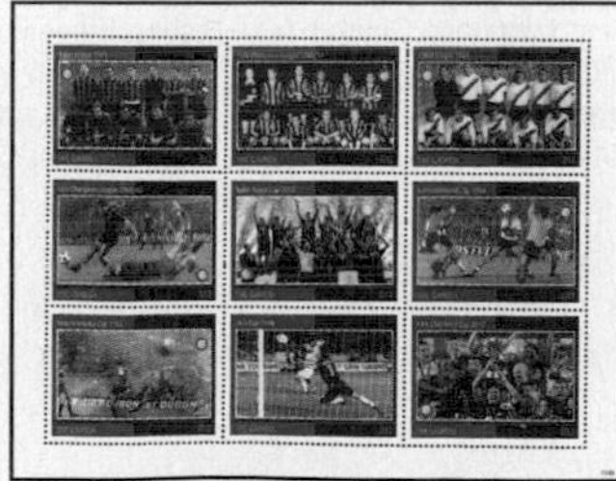

Inter Milan Soccer Team — A689

No. 3393 — Team emblem and photos: a, Italian League, 1963. b, UEFA Champions League, 1963-64. c, Italian League, 1965. d, UEFA Champions League, 1964-65. e, Italian Super Cup, 2010. f, Intercontinental Cup, 1964. g, Intercontinental Cup, 1965. h, UEFA Cup, 1998. i, FIFA Club World Cup, 2010.

2011, Oct. 11 ***Perf. 12½***

3393 A689 12d Sheet of 9, #a-i 7.25 7.25

Miniature Sheets

A690

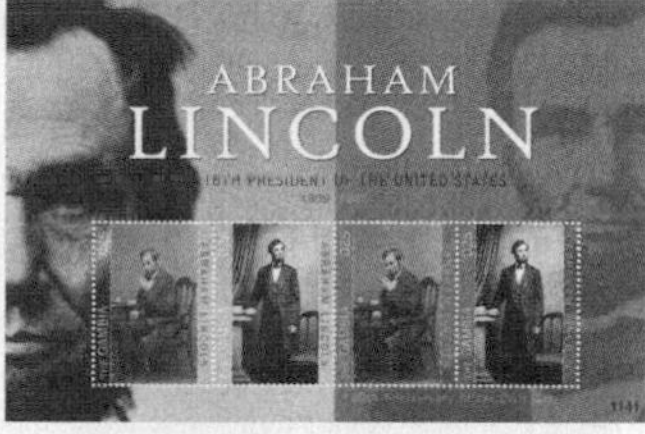

Pres. Abraham Lincoln (1809-65) — A691

No. 3394 — Lincoln: a, Facing right. b, Standing, with hand on book. c, Facing left. d, Standing, with both arms best.

No. 3395 — Lincoln: a, Seated, name in brown. b, Standing, name in brown. c, Seated, name in tan. d, Standing, name in tan.

2011, Oct. 11 ***Perf. 13¼x13***

3394 A690 25d Sheet of 4, #a-d 6.75 6.75
3395 A691 25d Sheet of 4, #a-d 6.75 6.75

Birds — A692

No. 3396, 16d: a, Bald eagle. b, European bee-eater. c, Keel-billed toucan. d, Red-crowned crane. e, Emperor penguin. f, Australian pelican.

No. 3397, 16d: a, African gray parrot. b, African darter. c, African fish eagle. d, African penguin. e, Reed cormorant. f, Spotted eagle-owl.

No. 3398, 80d, Lesser flamingo. No. 3399, 80d, African gray hornbill.

2011, Oct. 11 ***Perf. 13x12¾***

Sheets of 6, #a-f, + label

3396-3397 A692 Set of 2 13.00 13.00

Souvenir Sheets

Perf. 13x13¼

3398-3399 A692 Set of 2 10.50 10.50

Orchids — A693

No. 3400: a, Cephalanthera rubra. b, Aerangis biloba. c, Angreacum angustum. d, Ancistrochilus thomsonianus. e, Aerangis luteoalba. f, Polystacha carnosa.

No. 3401, vert.: a, Ansellia africana. b, Bulbophyllum falcatum. c, Angraecopsis ischnopus. d, Angraecum moandense.
No. 3402, 80d, Ancistrochilus rothschildianus. No. 3403, 80d, Bulbophyllum cochleatum, vert.

2011, Oct. 11 *Perf. 13 Syncopated*
3400 A693 20d Sheet of 6, #a-f 8.00 8.00
3401 A693 30d Sheet of 4, #a-d 8.00 8.00

Souvenir Sheets

3402-3403 A693 Set of 2 10.50 10.50

Statue of Liberty, 125th Anniv. (in 2011) — A694

No. 3404: a, Frederic Auguste Bartholdi, sculptor of Statue of Liberty. b, Statue's torch under construction. c, Statue's head under construction. d, Statue.
70d, Statue, diff.

2012, Feb. 24 *Perf. 13 Syncopated*
3404 A694 30d Sheet of 4, #a-d 8.00 8.00

Souvenir Sheet

3405 A694 70d multi 4.75 4.75

Visit of Pope Benedict XVI to Germany — A695

No. 3406 — Pope Benedict XVI: a, Waving at Brandenburg Gate. b, Holding censer. c, Facing left, with Berlin skyline in background.
90d, Pope Benedict XVI wearing miter.

2012, Feb. 24 *Perf. 12*
3406 A695 30d Sheet of 3, #a-c 6.00 6.00

Souvenir Sheet

3407 A695 90d multi 6.00 6.00

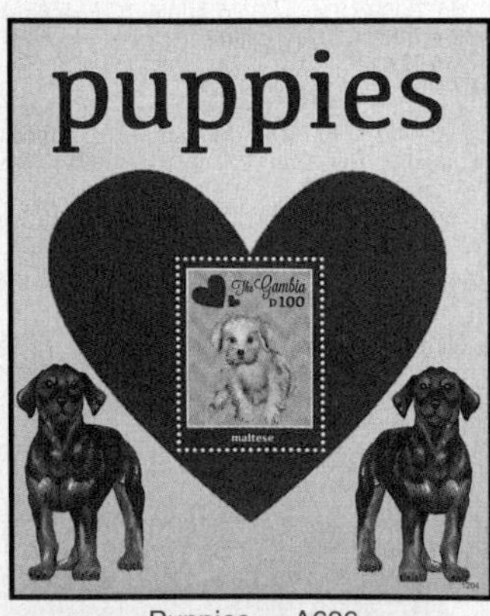

Puppies — A696

No. 3408: a, Toy poodle. b, Yorkshire terrier. c, Beagle.
No. 3409: a, Rottweiler. b, Chihuahua. c, Golden retriever. d, German shepherd.
No. 3410, 100d, Maltese. No. 3411, 100d, Pomeranian.

2012, Feb. 29
3408 A696 40d Sheet of 3, #a-c 8.00 8.00
3409 A696 40d Sheet of 4, #a-d 11.00 11.00

Souvenir Sheets

3410-3411 A696 Set of 2 13.50 13.50

Christmas 2011 A697

Paintings: 15d, Adoration of the Shepherds, by Gerard van Honthorst. 25d, Adoraton of the Shepherds, by Agnolo Bronzino. 30d, The Adoration of the Magi, by Peter Paul Rubens. 40d, The Journey of the Magi, by James Jacques Joseph Tissot.

2012, Mar. 3 *Perf. 14*
3412-3415 A697 Set of 4 7.50 7.50

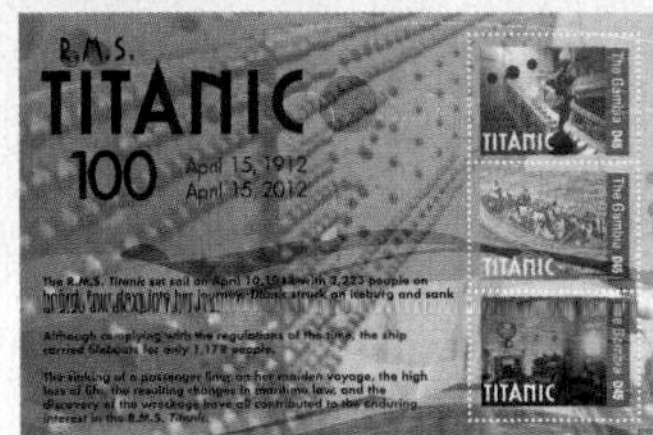

Sinking of the Titanic, Cent. — A698

No. 3416: a, Staircase. b, Lifeboat. c, Parlor.
100d, Titanic.

2012, Mar. 2 *Perf. 12*
3416 A698 45d Sheet of 3, #a-c 9.00 9.00

Souvenir Sheet

3417 A698 100d multi 6.75 6.75

Miniature Sheet

Ferrari Race Cars — A699

No. 3418: a, 150 Italia. b, F10. c, F60. d, F2008.

2012, Mar. 13 *Perf. 12*
3418 A699 30d Sheet of 4, #a-d 8.25 8.25

Souvenir Sheets

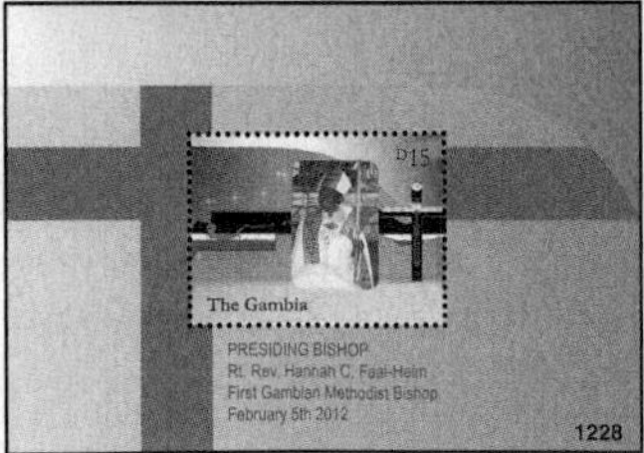

Bishop Hannah C. Faal-Heim, Gambian Methodist Presiding Bishop — A700

Bishop Faal-Heim, cross and: 15d, Map of Gambia. 25d, Church. 35d, Emblem of Gambian Methodist Church. 50d, Bishop Emeritus Peter Stephens.

2012, Feb. 2 *Perf. 13x13¼*
3419-3422 A700 Set of 4 8.25 8.25

Wild Cats — A701

No. 3423: a, Caracal. b, Cheetah. c, Jungle cat.
100d, Lion.

2012, May 16 *Perf. 13¾*
3423 A701 40d Sheet of 3, #a-c 7.75 7.75

Souvenir Sheet

3424 A701 100d multi 6.50 6.50

British Monarchs A702

Designs: No. 3425, 20d, King William I. No. 3426, 20d, King Henry II. No. 3427, 20d, King Henry IV. No. 3428, 20d, King Henry VI. No. 3429, 20d, King Richard III. No. 3430, 20d, Queen Elizabeth I. No. 3431, 20d, King James I. No. 3432, 20d, King Edward VII.

2012, June 27 *Perf. 13¼x13*
3425-3432 A702 Set of 8 10.50 10.50

Nos. 3425-3432 each were printed in sheets of 8 + central label.

Miniature Sheet

2012 Summer Olympics, London — A703

No. 3433: a, High jump. b, Gymnastics. c, Uneven bars. d, Long jump.

2012, June 27 *Perf. 14*
3433 A703 25d Sheet of 4, #a-d 6.50 6.50

Pres. Yahya A. J. J. Jammeh — A704

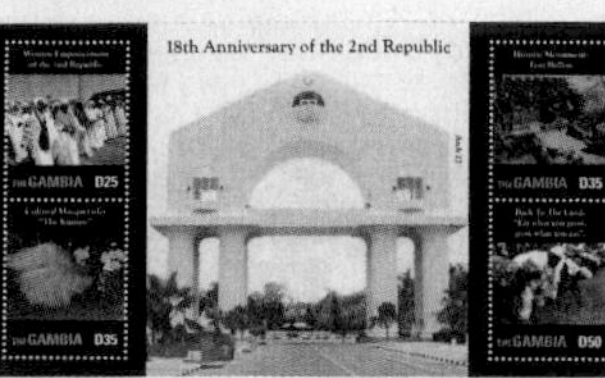

Gambian Second Republic, 18th Anniv. — A705

No. 3435: a, 25d, Women empowerment of the Second Republic. b, 35d, Fort Bullen Historic Monument. c, 35d, Cultural masquerade, The Kumpo. d, 50d, Back to the land.
75d, Pres. Jammeh, diff.

2012, July 22 *Perf. 14*
3434 A704 150d shown 9.75 9.75

Perf. 12

3435 A705 Sheet of 4, #a-d 9.50 9.50

Souvenir Sheet

3436 A704 75d multi 5.00 5.00

Miniature Sheet

Reign Of Queen Elizabeth II, 60th Anniv. — A706

No. 3437 — Photographs of Queen Elizabeth II from: a, 1937. b, 1946. c, 1953. d, 1952. e, 1962. f, 2004.

2012, July 31 *Perf. 13 Syncopated*
3437 A706 30d Sheet of 6, #a-f 11.50 11.50

Whales — A707

No. 3438: a, Humpback whale. b, Bryde's whale. c, Southern right whale. d, Blue whale. e, Killer whale. f, Sperm whale.
100d, Minke whale.

2012, Aug. 2 *Perf. 14*
3438 A707 30d Sheet of 6, #a-f 11.50 11.50

Souvenir Sheet

Perf. 12

3439 A707 100d multi 6.50 6.50

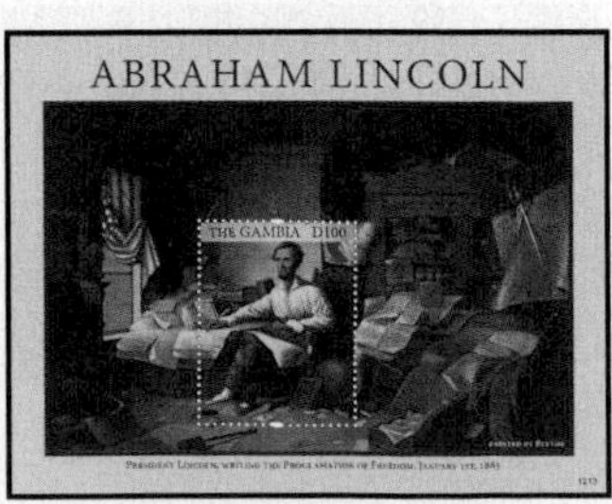

Drafting of the Emancipation Proclamation by Pres. Abraham Lincoln, 150th Anniv. — A708

No. 3440: a, Drawing of Lincoln seated at desk. b, Text of preliminary draft of the Emancipation Proclamation. c, Drawing of Lincoln writing the Emancipation Proclamation, d, First reading of the Emancipation Proclamation.
100d, Lincoln writing, vert.

2012, Aug. 2 *Perf. 13 Syncopated*
3440 A708 40d Sheet of 4, #a-d 10.50 10.50

Souvenir Sheet

3441 A708 100d multi 6.50 6.50

Premiere of *The Three Stooges The Movie* — A709

No. 3442: a, Moe grabbing heads of Larry and Curly, denomination in purple. b, Stooges on bicycle. c, Moe grabbing heads of Larry and Curly, denomination in orange. d, Stooges standing.
100d, Silhouette of Stooges, vert.

2012, Aug. 2 *Perf. 12¾*
3442 A709 40d Sheet of 4, #a-d 10.50 10.50

Souvenir Sheet

3443 A709 100d multi 6.50 6.50

Souvenir Sheets

Record Covers of Elvis Presley — A710

Record: No. 3444, 100d, Elvis Presley. No. 3445, 100d, All Shook Up and That's When Your Heartaches Begin. No. 3446, 100d, 50,000,000 Elvis Fans Can't Be Wrong. No. 3447, 100d, A Big Hunk O'Love and My Wish Came True. No. 3448, 100d, (You're the) Devil in Disguise and Please Don't Drag That String Around.

2012, Aug. 2 *Perf. 12¾*
3444-3448 A710 Set of 5 32.50 32.50

Greek Olympic Stamps of 1896 — A711

Designs: No. 3449, 100d, Greece #125 (1d stamp). No. 3450, 300d, Greece #117 (1 l stamp). No. 3451, 300d, Greece #118 (2 l stamp). No. 3452, 300d, Greece #119 (5 l stamp). No. 3453, 300d, Greece #120 (10 l stamp). No. 3454, 300d, Greece #121 (20 l stamp). No. 3455, 300d, Greece #122 (25 l stamp). No. 3456, 300d, Greece #123 (40 l stamp). No. 3457, 300d, Greece #124 (60 l stamp). No. 3458, 300d, Greece #126 (2d stamp). No. 3459, 300d, Greece #127 (5d stamp). No. 3460, 300d, Greece #128 (10d stamp).

Litho. & Embossed With Foil Application

2012, Aug. 2 *Die Cut Perf. 7¾*

Without Gum

3449-3460 A711 Set of 12 220.00 220.00

Christmas A712

Paintings: 5d, The Virgin of the Green Cushion, by Andrea Solario. 15d, The Adoration of the Magi, by Peter Paul Rubens. 25d, Bridgewater Madonna, by Raphael. 50d, The Nativity, by Domenico Ghirlandaio. 75d, Nativity and Adoration of Shepherds, by Bartolo di Fredi.
100d, Holy Family, by Rembrandt.

Perf. 12¾x12½

2012, Sept. 25 **Litho.**
3461-3465 A712 Set of 5 11.00 11.00

Souvenir Sheet

3466 A712 100d multi 6.50 6.50

Miniature Sheets

A713

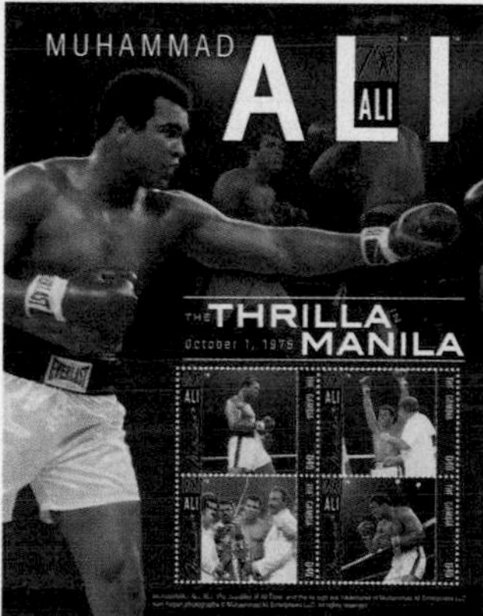

Oct. 1, 1975 Boxing Match Between Muhammad Ali and Joe Frazier, Manila, Philippines — A714

No. 3467: a, Ali at left, no lights at top. b, Frazier at left, ropes straight. c, Ali at left, lights at top, corner of ring in background. d, Frazier at left, corner of ring in background.
No. 3468: a, Ali in ring, facing right. b, Ali with arms raised. c, Ali and handlers with trophy. d, Ali, facing left, against ropes.

2012, July 27 **Litho.** *Perf. 12½x13¼*
3467 A713 40d Sheet of 4, #a-d 10.50 10.50

Perf. 12½x12

3468 A714 40d Sheet of 4, #a-d 10.50 10.50

Miniature Sheet

Primates — A715

No. 3469: a, Bonobo. b, Bornean orangutan. c, Chimpanzee. d, Mountain gorilla.

2012, Nov. 28 **Litho.** *Perf. 14x13¾*
3469 A715 40d Sheet of 4, #a-d 11.00 11.00

Miniature Sheets

NASA Achievements — A716

Hubble Space Telescope — A717

No. 3470: a, John Glenn, Jr., first U.S. astronaut to orbit Earth, 1962. b, Edwin A. "Buzz" Aldrin on Moon, 1969. c, Space Shuttle Discovery, 1984. d, Hubble Space Telescope, 1990.
No. 3471 — Hubble Space Telescope: a, Black background, denomination at LL. b, Black background, denomination at UR. c, Earth in background, denomination at LL. d, Earth in background, denomination at UR.

Perf. 13 Syncopated

2012, Nov. 28 **Litho.**
3470 A716 35d Sheet of 4, #a-d 9.50 9.50
3471 A717 35d Sheet of 4, #a-d 9.50 9.50

Nos. 3470-3471 exist imperf. Value, set of 2 sheets *$25.*

Castles — A718

No. 3472: a, Alnwick Castle, Scotland. b, Dover Castle, England. c, Edinbugh Castle, Scotland. d, Eilean Donan Castle, Scotland. e, Neuschwanstein Castle, Germany.
100d, Alcázar of Segovia, Spain.

2012, Nov. 28 **Litho.** *Perf. 12*
3472 A718 30d Sheet of 5, #a-e 10.00 10.00

Souvenir Sheet

Perf. 12½

3473 A718 100d multi 6.75 6.75

No. 3473 contains one 38x51mm. Inscription on No. 3472c incorrectly states that Edinburgh Castle is in England.

Insects — A719

No. 3474: a, Fiery searcher beetle. b, Blue milkweed beetle. c, Locust borer beetle. d, Grapevine beetle.
100d, Banded alder borer.

2012, Dec. 31 **Litho.** *Perf. 12*
3474 A719 40d Sheet of 4, #a-d 9.50 9.50

Souvenir Sheet

3475 A719 100d multi 6.00 6.00

World Radio Day — A721

No. 3477: a, Red orange radio with handle. b, Pink radio. c, Black radio. d, Tan and gray radio.
110d, Tan radio with dial.

Perf. 13 Syncopated

2013, Feb. 4 **Litho.**
3477 A721 35d Sheet of 4, #a-d 8.25 8.25

Souvenir Sheet

3478 A721 110d multi 6.50 6.50

Completion of Painting of Sistine Chapel Ceiling by Michelangelo, 500th Anniv. (in 2012) — A722

No. 3479: a, The Expulsion from Paradise. b, Creation of Eve. c, The Virgin and Child with Saint John and Angels. d, Drunkenness of Noah.
110d, The Torment of Saint Anthony, vert.

2013, Feb. 4 **Litho.** *Perf. 12½*
3479 A722 35d Sheet of 4, #a-d 8.25 8.25

Souvenir Sheet

3480 A722 110d multi 6.50 6.50

Shells — A723

No. 3481: a, Chicoreus clausii. b, Tympanotonus. c, Distorsio smithi. d, Nerita senegalensis.
110d, Xenophora crispa senegalensis.

2013, Feb. 20 Litho. *Perf. 12*
3481 A723 35d Sheet of 4, #a-d 8.25 8.25

Souvenir Sheet
3482 A723 110d multi 6.50 6.50

Turtles — A724

No. 3483: a, Aldabra giant tortoise. b, African spurred tortoise. c, Leopard tortoise. d, Radiated tortoise.
110d, African helmeted turtle.

Perf. 13 Syncopated
2013, Feb. 20 Litho.
3483 A724 35d Sheet of 4, #a-d 8.25 8.25

Souvenir Sheet
3484 A724 110d multi 6.50 6.50

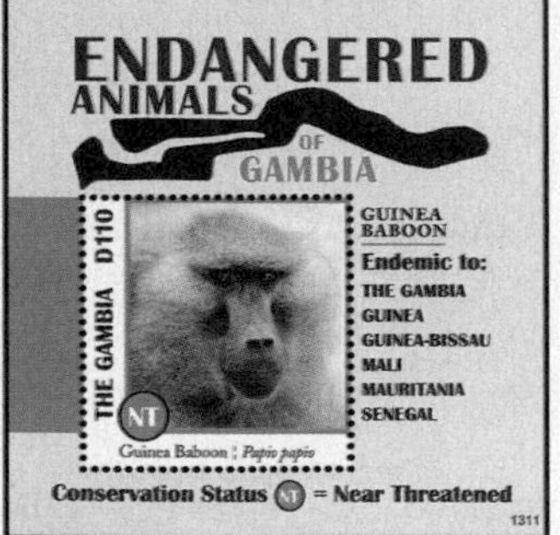

Endangered Animals — A725

No. 3485, 35d: a, Crowned lemur. b, Giant eland. c, African elephant. d, Lion. e, Black rhinoceros.
No. 3486, 35d: a, Nubian ibex. b, Gerenuk. c, Fossa. d, Striped hyena. e, Coquerel's sifaka.
No. 3487, 110d, Guinea baboon. No. 3488, 110d, Western red colobus.

2013, Mar. 20 Litho. *Perf. 13¾*
Sheets of 5, #a-e
3485-3486 A725 Set of 2 21.00 21.00

Souvenir Sheets
3487-3488 A725 Set of 2 13.50 13.50

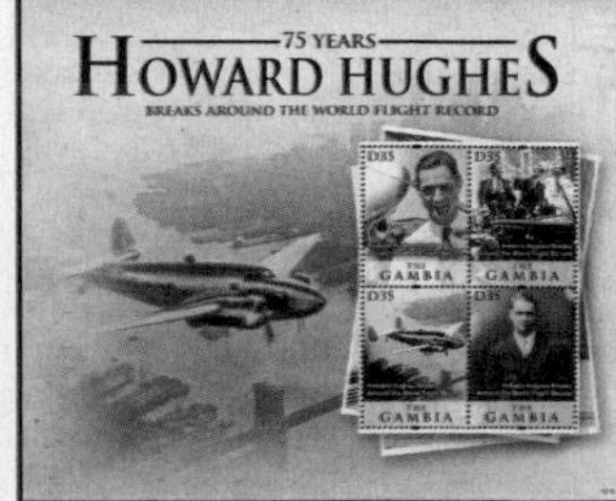

Setting of Around-the-World Flight Record by Howard Hughes, 75th Anniv. — A726

No. 3489: a, Hughes without suit in front of airplane. b, Hughes in car in ticker-tape parade. c, Airplane over Brooklyn Bridge. d, Hughes in suit in front of airplane.
110d, Crowd of people around airplane, horiz.

Perf. 13 Syncopated
2013, Apr. 3 Litho.
3489 A726 35d Sheet of 4, #a-d 8.50 8.50

Souvenir Sheet
3490 A726 110d multi 6.75 6.75

First Flight of Boeing 314 Clipper Flying Boats, 75th Anniv. — A727

No. 3491: a, View of front of airplane in water. b, Side view of airplane just above water. c, Eddie Allen, first pilot. d, Overhead view of airplane just above water.
110d, Airplane moving through water.

Perf. 13 Syncopated
2013, Apr. 3 Litho.
3491 A727 35d Sheet of 4, #a-d 8.50 8.50

Souvenir Sheet
3492 A727 110d multi 6.75 6.75

A728

Coronation of Queen Elizabeth II, 60th Anniv. — A729

No. 3493 — Yellow bister panel and black-and-white photograph of Queen Elizabeth II: a, Wearing flowered hat, facing right. b, With Prince Philip. c, Wearing hat, facing left. d, Wearing crown in coach.
No. 3494 — Blue panel and photograph of Queen Elizabeth: a, With dark hair, facing forward. b, With dark hair, facing right. c, With gray hair. d, With dark hair, facing left.
No. 3495, 110d, Portrait of Queen Elizabeth II wearing crown. No. 3496, 110d, Flags and Queen Elizabeth II, horiz.

2013, Apr. 3 Litho. *Perf. 14*
3493 A728 35d Sheet of 4, #a-d 8.50 8.50
3494 A729 35d Sheet of 4, #a-d 8.50 8.50

Souvenir Sheets
Perf. 12
3495-3496 A729 Set of 2 13.50 13.50

No. 3495 contains one 30x50mm stamp. No. 3496 contains one 50x30mm stamp.

Pres. John F. Kennedy (1917-63) — A730

No. 3497 — Pres. Kennedy: a, On telephone. b, Facing right. b, Facing left. c, In crowd.
110d, Pres. Kennedy and flag.

2013, Apr. 4 Litho. *Perf. 12*
3497 A730 35d Sheet of 4, #a-d 8.50 8.50

Souvenir Sheet
3498 A730 110d multi 6.75 6.75

History of Art — A731

No. 3499, 45d — Lascaux Cave Paintings: a, Horned animal. b, Animals without horns. c, Three horned animals, animal without horns.
No. 3500, 45d — Art of Ancient Greece: a, Hercules and Athena, c. 470 B.C. b, Venus de Milo statue, c. 130-100 B.C. c, Panathenaic amphora featuring runners, c. 520 B.C.
No. 3501, 110d, Bust of Nefertiti, c. 1345 B.C. No. 3502, 110d, Stonehenge, horiz.

2013, Apr. 4 Litho. *Perf. 12½*
Sheets of 3, #a-c
3499-3500 A731 Set of 2 16.50 16.50

Souvenir Sheets
3501-3502 A731 Set of 2 13.50 13.50

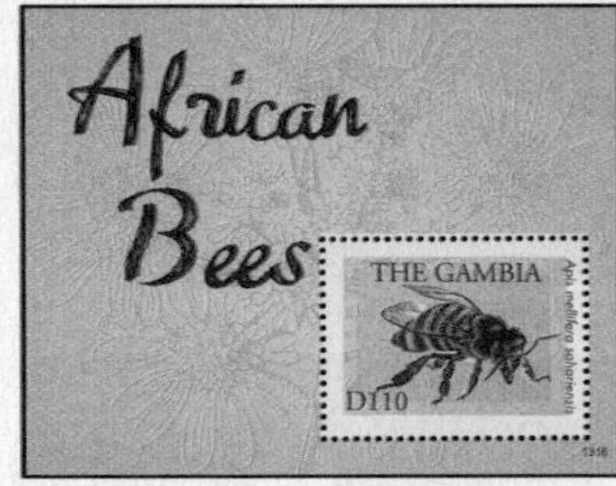

Bees — A732

No. 3503: a, Apis mellifera. b, Apis mellifera intermissa. c, Apis mellifera scutellata. d, Apis mellifera sahariensis.
110d, Apis mellifera sahariensis, diff.

2013, Apr. 29 Litho. *Perf. 12*
3503 A732 35d Sheet of 4, #a-d 8.50 8.50

Souvenir Sheet
3504 A732 110d multi 6.75 6.75

Aircraft Carriers — A733

No. 3505: a, Hosho, Japan. b, ARA Veinticinco de Mayo, Argentina. c, Graf Zeppelin, Germany. d, USS Saipan, U.S.
110d, USS Hornet, U.S.

2013, Apr. 29 Litho. *Perf. 12*
3505 A733 35d Sheet of 4, #a-d 8.50 8.50

Souvenir Sheet
Perf. 12½
3506 A733 110d multi 6.75 6.75

No. 3506 contains one 51x38mm stamp.

A734

Pope Benedict XVI — A735

No. 3507 — Photographs of Pope Benedict XVI at 2005 inauguration: a, On balcony with crowd in background. b, Facing forward with arms raised, both hands visible. c, Facing left with arms raised. d, Facing forward with arms raised, one hand visible.
No. 3508 — Photographs of Pope Benedict XVI at World Youth Day, Cologne, Germany, 2005: a, With German Pres. Horst Köhler. b, Behind microphone, holding paper. c, Behind microphone, holding paper, with other clergy. d, Praying near candles.
No. 3509, Pope Benedict XVI waving. No. 3510, 110d, Pope Benedict XVI with youths.

Perf. 13 Syncopated
2013, Apr. 29 Litho.
3507 A734 35d Sheet of 4, #a-d 8.50 8.50
3508 A735 35d Sheet of 4, #a-d 8.50 8.50

Souvenir Sheets
3509 A734 110d multi 6.75 6.75
3510 A735 110d multi 6.75 6.75

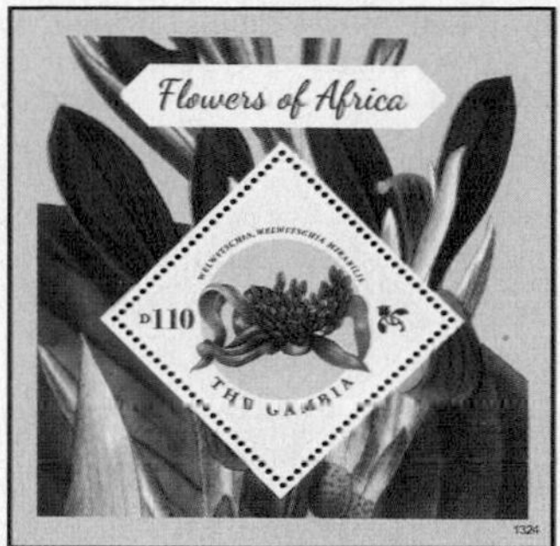

Flowers — A736

No. 3511, 35d: a, Broadleaf beechwood. b, Red daisy. c, Wagon tree. d, River beechwood.
No. 3512, 35d: a, Thistle protea. b, African violet. c, Common protea. d, King protea.
No. 3513, 110d, Welwitschia. No. 3514, 110d, Cape African queen.

2013, May 7 Litho. *Perf. 13¾*

Sheets of 4, #a-d

3511-3512 A736 Set of 2 15.50 15.50

Souvenir Sheets

3513-3514 A736 Set of 2 12.00 12.00

Lady Margaret Thatcher (1925-2013), British Prime Minister — A737

No. 3515 — Thatcher: a, With hand on chin. b, With hand raised. c, With roses. d, Facing left.
110d, Thatcher facing right.

Perf. 13 Syncopated

2013, June 3 Litho.

3515 A737 35d Sheet of 4, #a-d 7.75 7.75

Souvenir Sheet

3516 A737 110d multi 6.00 6.00

A738

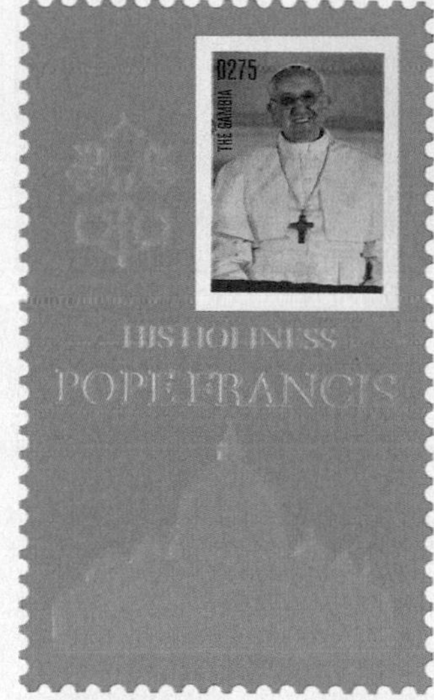

Election of Pope Francis — A739

No. 3517 — Pope Francis: a, Waving to crowd. b, Delivering first "Urbi et Orbi" blessing during Easter Mass. c, Greeting crowd in St. Peter's Square. d, Celebrating Mass during Lent.

2013, June 3 Litho. *Perf. 12*

3517 A738 35d Sheet of 4, #a-d 7.75 7.75

Litho., Margin Embossed With Foil Application

Souvenir Sheet Without Gum

Imperf

3518 A739 275d multi 15.00 15.00

Souvenir Sheet

Elvis Presley (1935-77) — A740

Litho., Margin Embossed With Foil Application

2013, July 22 *Imperf.*

Without Gum

3519 A740 300d multi 16.50 16.50

Fruits — A741

No. 3520: a, Mangos. b, Baobab. c, Marulas. d, Kiwanos.
110d, Tamarinds.

2013, Aug. 7 Litho. *Perf. 12*

3520 A741 35d Sheet of 4, #a-d 7.75 7.75

Souvenir Sheet

3521 A741 110d multi 6.00 6.00

Record New York to London Flight of Concorde, 25th Anniv. — A742

No. 3522 — Concorde: a, And New York City skyline. b, And Prince Charles, Princess Diana and dignitaries. c, Taking off. d, And Big Ben.
110d, Concorde and military jets.

Perf. 12¾x12½

2013, Aug. 26 Litho.

3522 A742 35d Sheet of 4, #a-d 8.00 8.00

Souvenir Sheet

Perf. 12½x12¾

3523 A742 110d multi 6.25 6.25

Animals of Thailand — A743

No. 3524, vert.: a, Asian elephant. b, Agile gibbon. c, Water buffalo.
No. 3525: a, Indochinese tiger. b, Dhole.

2013, Aug. 26 Litho. *Perf. 12*

3524 A743 45d Sheet of 3, #a-c 7.75 7.75

Souvenir Sheet

3525 A743 55d Sheet of 2, #a-b 6.25 6.25

2013 World Stamp Exhibition, Bangkok, Thailand.

Birth of Prince George of Cambridge — A744

No. 3526: a, Duchess of Cambridge holding Prince George. b, Duke and Duchess of Cambridge, Prince George. c, Duke of Cambridge holding Prince George. d, Prince George.
110d, Duke and Duchess of Cambridge, Prince George, horiz.

2013, Sept. 10 Litho. *Perf. 12½*

3526 A744 35d Sheet of 4, #a-d 8.00 8.00

Souvenir Sheet

Perf. 13¼

3527 A744 110d multi 6.25 6.25

No. 3527 contains one 51x38mm stamp.

Mushrooms — A745

No. 3528: a, Golden-edge bonnets. b, Common bonnets.
110d, Sickeners.

2013, Sept. 30 Litho. *Perf. 14*

3528 A745 35d Pair, #a-b 4.00 4.00

Souvenir Sheet

Perf. 12¾x12½

3529 A745 110d multi 6.25 6.25

No. 3528 was printed in sheets containing two pairs. No. 3529 contains one 38x51mm stamp.

Miniature Sheet

Princess Diana (1961-97) — A746

No. 3530 — Princess Diana holding flowers and wearing: a, White dress. b, Hooded raincoat. c, Jacket with striped lapels. d, Pink hat.

2013, Oct. 7 Litho. *Perf. 12*

3530 A746 35d Sheet of 4, #a-d 8.00 8.00

Trains — A747

No. 3531: a, GEA Locomotive Number 4009. b, GEA Locomotive Number 4048. c, Garratt Locomotive Number 81. d, GEA Locomotive Number 4047.
110d, 15F Class Locomotive Number 3150.

2013, Oct. 7 Litho. *Perf. 12*

3531 A747 35d Sheet of 4, #a-d 8.00 8.00

Souvenir Sheet

Perf. 14

3532 A747 110d multi 6.25 6.25

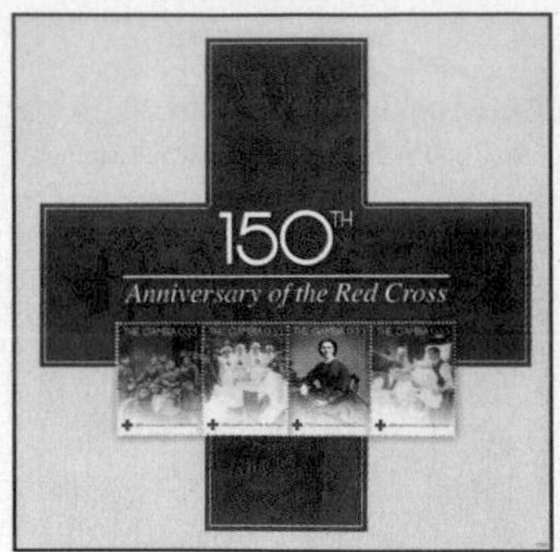

International Red Cross, 150th Anniv. — A748

No. 3533: a, Members of American Red Cross in Great Britain. b, Participants in Birmingham, Alabama American Red Cross Parade. c, Clara Barton, founder of American Red Cross. d, Red Cross workers doing laundry during World War I.
110d, Jean-Henri Dunant, co-founder of Intl. Red Cross.

2013, Nov. 18 Litho. *Perf. 14*
3533 A748 35d Sheet of 4, #a-d 7.50 7.50

Souvenir Sheet

3534 A748 110d multi 5.75 5.75

Miniature Sheet

Birds of Brazil — A749

No. 3535: a, Blue-fronted amazon. b, Toco toucan. c, Hyacinth macaw. d, Scarlet ibis.

2013, Nov. 18 Litho. *Perf. 12½*
3535 A749 35d Sheet of 4, #a-d 7.50 7.50

2013 Brasiliana Intl. Philatelic Exhibition, Rio de Janeiro.

Coronation of Queen Elizabeth II, 60th Anniv. — A750

2013, Nov. 18 Embroidered *Imperf.*
Self-Adhesive

3536 A750 270d multi 14.00 14.00

Christmas A751

Paintings: 5d, Adoration of the Shepherds, by Ghirlandaio. 25d, Annunciation, by Masolino da Panicale. 75d, Madonna and Child with Angels, by Bernardo Daddi. 100d, Nativity Scene from Vyssí Brod Altarpiece, by Master of Vyssí Brod.

2013, Dec. 2 Litho. *Perf. 12¾*
3537-3540 A751 Set of 4 11.00 11.00

Pres. Barack Obama — A752

No. 3541: a, Head of Pres. Obama. b, Pres. Obama and U.S. flag.
No. 3542, 110d, Pres. Obama on telephone. No. 3543, 110d, Pres. Obama on airplane steps.

2013, Dec. 9 Litho. *Perf. 13¾*
3541 A752 45d Sheet of 3, #3541a, 2 #3541b 7.00 7.00

Souvenir Sheets
Perf. 12½

3542-3543 A752 Set of 2 11.50 11.50

Nos. 3542-3543 each contain one 38x51mm stamp.

A753

Nelson Mandela (1918-2013), President of South Africa — A754

No. 3545 — Mandela: a, Wearing black, red and gray patterned shirt. b, In black-and-white photograph with arms raised. c, In color photograph with arms raised. d, Wearing white shirt. e, Wearing blue and white shirt. f, With fist raised.
No. 3546, 110d, Wearing gray shirt with floral design, vert. No. 3547, 110d, Wearing suit and tie with arm raised, vert.

2013, Dec. 15 Litho. *Perf. 13¾*
3544 A753 30d multi 1.60 1.60
3545 A754 30d Sheet of 6, #a-f 9.50 9.50

Souvenir Sheets
Perf. 12¾

3546-3547 A754 Set of 2 11.50 11.50

No. 3544 was printed in sheets of 6. Nos. 3546-3547 each contain one 38x51mm stamp.

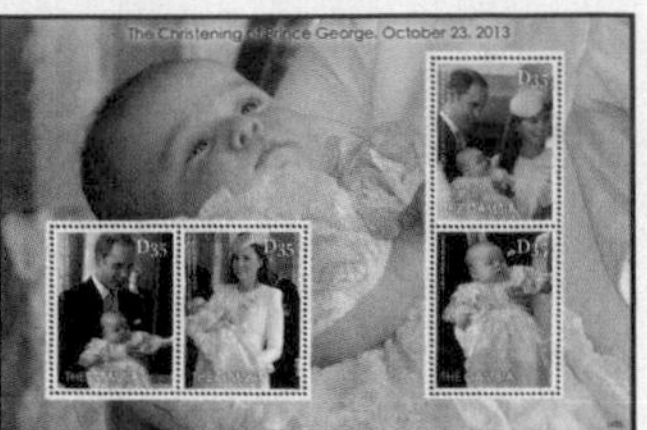

Christening of Prince George of Cambridge — A755

No. 3548: a, Duke and Duchess of Cambridge holding Prince George. b, Duke of Cambridge holding Prince George. c, Duchess of Cambridge holding Prince George. d, Close-up of Prince George.
110d, Prince George, diff.

2013, Dec. 31 Litho. *Perf. 14*
3548 A755 35d Sheet of 4, #a-d 7.25 7.25

Souvenir Sheet

3549 A755 110d multi 5.75 5.75

No. 3549 contains one 38x51mm stamp.

Butterflies — A756

No. 3550: a, Tailed orange butterfly. b, Queen butterfly. c, Caribbean sailor butterfly. d, Tiger mimic queen butterfly. e, Caribbean sailor butterfly, green at bottom of stamp. f, Caribbean hairstreak butterfly. g, Lophanus pyrrhias. h, Caribbean banner butterfly. i, Caribbean skipper butterfly.
No. 3551, 135d: a, Thick-rimmed sailor butterfly. b, Caribbean sailor butterfly, diff.
No. 3552, 135d: a, American painted lady butterfly with light brown thorax. b, American painted lady butterfly with black thorax.

2014, Feb. 26 Litho. *Perf. 13¾*
3550 A756 30d Sheet of 9, #a-i 14.00 14.00

Souvenir Sheets of 2, #a-b

3551-3552 A756 Set of 2 27.00 27.00

World War I, Cent. — A757

No. 3553, 65d: a, Russian officer leading his troops. b, Russian soldiers taking aim. c, Russian troops marching off to war. d, Russian soldier charging the enemy.
No. 3554, 65d — Zeppelins: a, LZ-10 Schwaben. b, L3. c, LZ-127 Graf Zeppelin. d, LZ-13 Hansa.
No. 3555, 270d, Cannon and Czar Nicholas II of Russia (1868-1918). No. 3556, 270d, L3 Zeppelin, diff.

2014, Feb. 26 Litho. *Perf. 14*
Sheets of 4, #a-d

3553-3554 A757 Set of 2 27.00 27.00

Souvenir Sheets
Perf. 12½

3555-3556 A757 Set of 2 28.00 28.00

Nos. 3555-3556 each contain one 51x38mm stamp.

A758

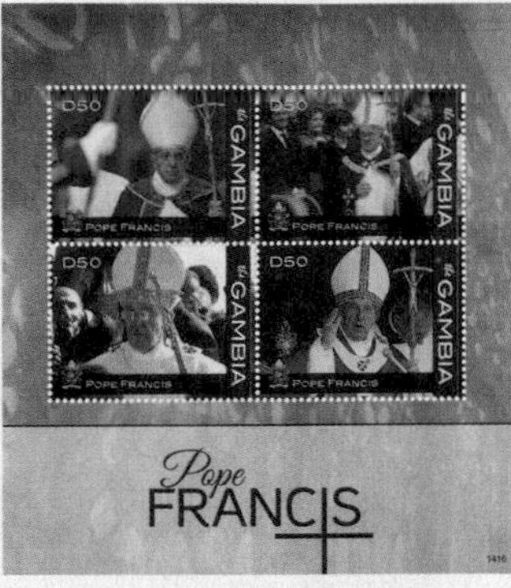

A759

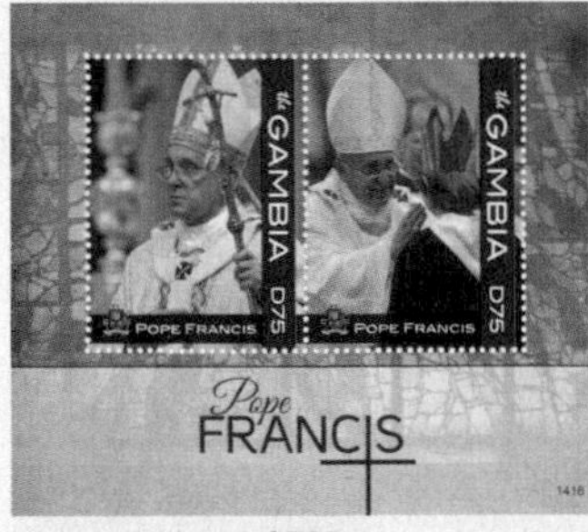

A760

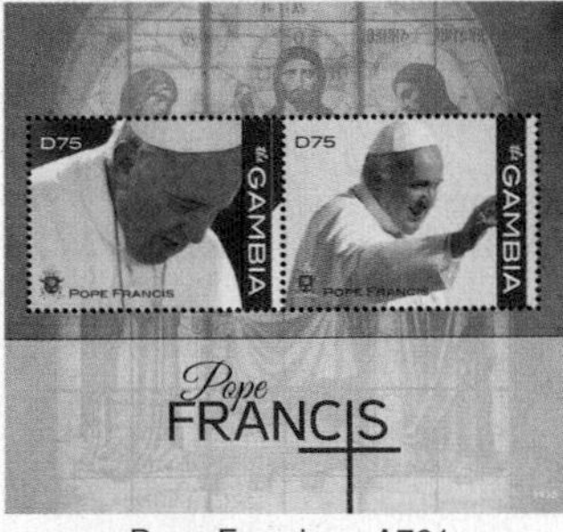

Pope Francis — A761

No. 3557 — Pope Francis wearing: a, Miter and green vestments. b, Zucchetto, steeple in background. c, Zucchetto, greeting crowd. d, Miter and white vestments.
No. 3558 — Pope Francis wearing: a, Red vestments. b, Purple vestments. c, White vestments. d, Green vestments.
No. 3559 — Pope Francis: a, Holding crucifix. b, Blessing person wearing crown.
No. 3560 — Pope Francis: a, Arms not visible. b, With arm extended.

2014, Mar. 24 Litho. *Perf. 14*
3557 A758 50d Sheet of 4, #a-d 10.50 10.50
3558 A759 50d Sheet of 4, #a-d 10.50 10.50

Souvenir Sheets

3559 A760 75d Sheet of 2, #a-b 8.00 8.00
3560 A761 75d Sheet of 2, #a-b 8.00 8.00

A762

A763

A764

African Penguins — A765

Various photographs.

2014, Apr. 2 Litho. *Perf. 13¾*

3561 A762 50d Sheet of 3, #a-c 8.00 8.00
3562 A763 50d Sheet of 4, #a-d 10.50 10.50

Souvenir Sheets

3563 A764 150d multi 8.00 8.00
3564 A765 150d multi 8.00 8.00

Worldwide Fund for Nature (WWF) — A766

Nos. 3565 and 3566: a, Two African darters on branch. b, African darter in water. c, One African darter on branch. d, African darter with wings extended.

2014, Apr. 2 Litho. *Perf. 14*

3565 A766 32d Block or vert. strip of 4, #a-d 6.75 6.75
3566 A766 35d Block or vert. strip of 4, #a-d 7.50 7.50

Paintings — A767

No. 3567, 50d — Paintings by Henri Rousseau: a, Tiger in a Tropical Storm. b, The Sleeping Gypsy. c, Carnival Evening.

No. 3568, 50d: a, Le Rifain Assis, by Henri Matisse. b, The Dance II, by Matisse. c, Judith and the Head of Holofernes, by Gustav Klimt.

No. 3569, 150d, Water Lilies, by Claude Monet. No. 3570, 150d, The Bed, by Henri de Toulouse-Lautrec.

2014, Mar. 10 Litho. *Perf. 12¾*

Sheets of 3, #a-c

3567-3568 A767 Set of 2 16.00 16.00

Imperf

Size: 99x99mm

3569-3570 A767 Set of 2 16.00 16.00

A768

A769

A770

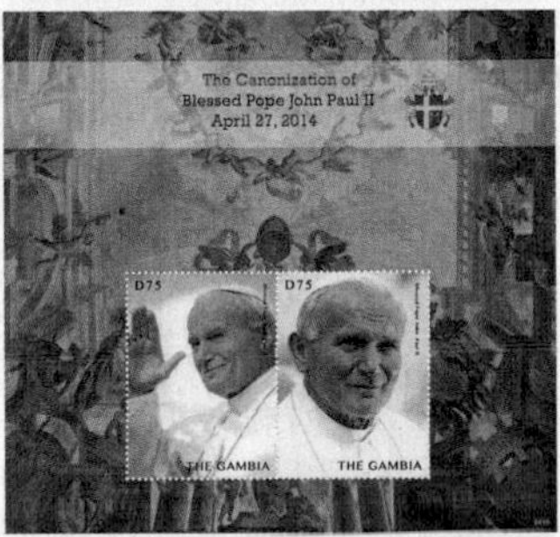
Canonization of Pope John Paul II — A771

No. 3571 — Pope John Paul II wearing miter: a, Waving, entire hand visible. b, Miter 24mm wide. c, Miter 21mm wide. d, Waving, hand partially visible.

No. 3572 — Pope John Paul II wearing zucchetto: a, Praying. b, Smiling, top of zucchetto not visible. c, Smiling, top of zucchetto visible. d, Seated, surrounded by Swiss Guards.

No. 3573 — Pope John Paul II wearing miter, blessing crowd: a, Back of hand visible. b, Palm of hand visible.

No. 3574 — Pope John Paul II wearing zucchetto: a, Waving, b, Not waving.

2014, May 8 Litho. *Perf. 14*

3571 A768 50d Sheet of 4, #a-d 10.00 10.00
3572 A769 50d Sheet of 4, #a-d 10.00 10.00

Souvenir Sheets

Perf. 12¾

3573 A770 75d Sheet of 2, #a-b 7.50 7.50
3574 A771 75d Sheet of 2, #a-b 7.50 7.50

Hibiscus, National Flower of South Korea — A772

2014, May 12 Litho. *Die Cut*

Self-Adhesive

3575 A772 30d multi 1.50 1.50

No. 3575 was printed in sheets of 9.

Paintings by Paul Cézanne (1839-1906) — A773

No. 3576, 50d: a, Self-portrait with White Turban. b, Flowers in a Vase. c, The Boy in the Red Vest. d, Still Life with Pomegranate and Pears.

No. 3577, 50d: a, Self-portrait with Palette. b, The Bathers. c, Madame Cézanne in a Red Dress. d, The Card Players.

No. 3578, 75d, horiz. — Details from Paul Alexis Reading at Zola's House: a. Zola holding quill pen. b, Alexis reading.

No. 3579, 75d, horiz. — Details from The Card Players: a, Player facing right, smoking pipe. b, Player facing left.

2014, May 12 Litho. *Perf. 12¾*

Sheets of 4, #a-d

3576-3577 A773 Set of 2 20.00 20.00

Souvenir Sheets of 2, #a-b

3578-3579 A773 Set of 2 15.00 15.00

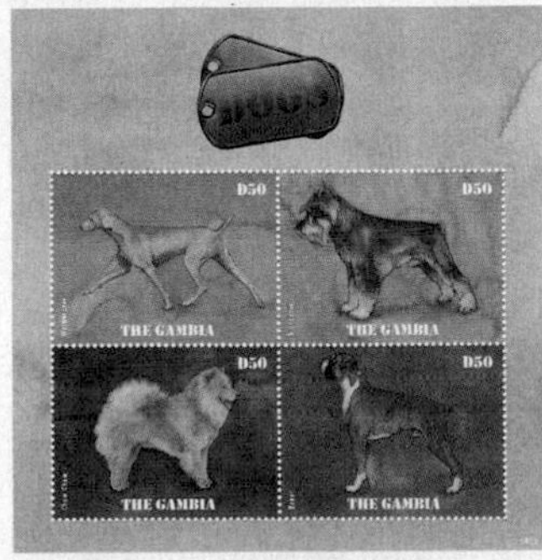
Dogs — A774

No. 3580: a, Weimaraner. b, Schnauzer. c, Chow chow. d, Boxer.

150d, Doberman pinscher.

2014, June 23 Litho. *Perf. 12¾*

3580 A774 50d Sheet of 4, #a-d 10.00 10.00

Souvenir Sheet

3581 A774 150d multi 7.50 7.50

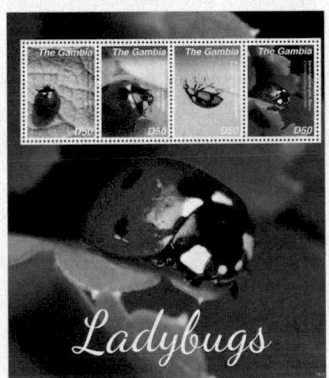

Ladybugs — A775

No. 3582: a, Seven-spotted ladybug on veined leaf. b, Seven-spotted ladybug on leaf, yellow area at UR. c, Multicolored Asian ladybug. d, Seven-spotted ladybug on leaf.

No. 3583: a, Ten-spotted lady bug. b, Spotless ladybug.

2014, July 1 Litho. *Perf. 12*

3582 A775 50d Sheet of 4, #a-d 10.00 10.00

Souvenir Sheet

Perf. 14

3583 A775 75d Sheet of 2, #a-b 7.50 7.50

See Nos. 3594-3595.

A776

A777

A778

Berlin Wall Graffiti — A779

No. 3584: a, People reading newspaper. b, Person jumping wall. c, Archway between legs. d, Zipper and Gernan text.

No. 3585: a, Automobile smashing through wall. b, Stylized faces with connected eyes, c, Stylized faces with large lips. d, Doves and Brandenburg Gate.

No. 3586: a, Crowd, wall at left. b, Crowd, wall at right.

No. 3587: a, Shackled hand in prison window. b, Dove carrying ball and chain.

2014, July 1 Litho. *Perf. 14*

3584 A776 50d Sheet of 4, #a-d 10.00 10.00
3585 A777 50d Sheet of 4, #a-d 10.00 10.00

Souvenir Sheets

Perf. 12

3586 A778 75d Sheet of 2, #a-b 7.50 7.50
3587 A779 75d Sheet of 2, #a-b 7.50 7.50

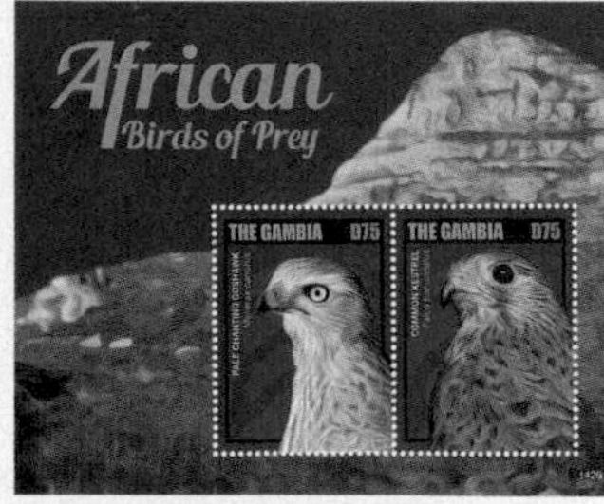

Birds of Prey — A780

No. 3588: a, Crowned eagle. b, Pearl-spotted owlet. c, Steppe eagle. d, Peregrine falcon.

No. 3589: a, Pale chanting goshawk. b, Common kestrel.

2014, Sept. 4 Litho. *Perf. 14*

3588 A780 50d Sheet of 4, #a-d 10.00 10.00

Souvenir Sheet

3589 A780 75d Sheet of 2, #a-b 7.50 7.50

See Nos. 3614-3615.

Meerkats — A781

No. 3590 — Meerkat facing: a, Right, brown background. b, Right, black background. c, Left, black background. d, Left, brown background.

110d, Six meerkats, horiz.

2014, Sept. 4 Litho. *Perf. 14*

3590 A781 50d Sheet of 4, #a-d 10.00 10.00

Souvenir Sheet

Perf. 12

3591 A781 110d multi 5.50 5.50

See Nos. 3596-3597.

Space Exploration — A782

No. 3592: a, Cosmonaut Yuri Gagarin and Vostok 1. b, Vostok 1, large crescent moon at UL. c, Vostok 1, small crescent moon at top. b, Rocket designer Sergei Korolev, schematic drawings.

150d, Sputnik 1.

2014, Sept. 4 Litho. *Perf. 14*

3592 A782 50d Sheet of 4, #a-d 10.00 10.00

Souvenir Sheet

Perf. 12

3593 A782 150d multi 7.50 7.50

Ladybugs Type of 2014

No. 3594: a, Two-spotted ladybug. b, Multicolored Asian ladybug (black with red spots), amidst plant matter. c, Multicolored Asian ladybug (brown with black spots) on bare ground. d, Spotless ladybug, diff.

No. 3595: a, Ten-spotted ladybug on branch. b, Multicolored Asian ladybug (brown with black spots) on leaf.

2014 Litho. *Perf. 12*

3594 A775 50d Sheet of 4, #a-d 10.00 10.00

Souvenir Sheet

3595 A775 75d Sheet of 2, #a-b 7.50 7.50

Meerkats Type of 2014

Designs: 45d, Meerkat standing on rear legs.

110d, Meerkat on four legs, horiz.

2014 Litho. *Perf. 12*

Size of No. 3596: 30x50mm

3596 A781 45d multi 2.25 2.25

Souvenir Sheet

3597 A781 110d multi 5.50 5.50

No. 3596 was printed in sheets of 6. No. 3597 contains one 40x30mm stamp.

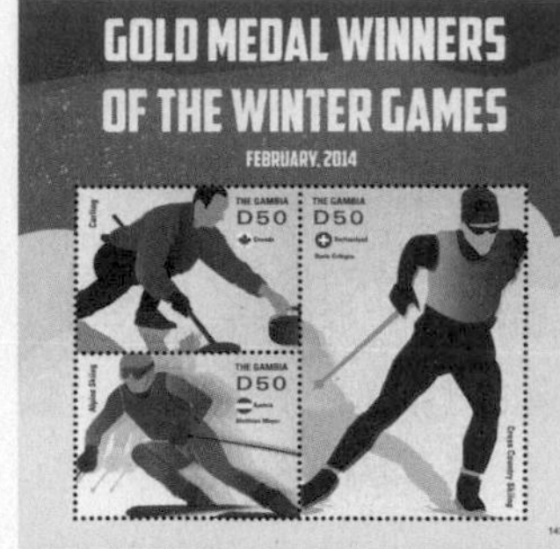

Gold Medalists at 2014 Winter Olympics — A783

No. 3598: a, Canadian men's curling team (40x30mm). b, Matthias Mayer, Alpine skiing (40x30mm). c, Dario Cologna, cross-country skiing, vert. (40x60mm).

No. 3600, vert.: a, Adelina Sotnikova, figure skating. b, Martin Fourcade, biathlon.

2014, Sept. 15 Litho. *Perf. 14*

3598 A783 50d Sheet of 3, #a-c 7.50 7.50

Souvenir Sheet

3599 A783 75d Sheet of 2, #a-b 7.50 7.50

Dinosaurs — A784

No. 3600, 50d: a, Pteranodon longiceps. b, Archaeoceratops. c, Ampelosaurus. d, Apatosaurus.

No. 3601, 50d: a, Stegosaurus. b, Albertaceratops. c, Spinosaurus. d, Nedoceratops.

No. 3602, 150d, Kentrosaurus. No. 3603, 150d, Compsognathus.

2014, Sept. 15 Litho. *Perf. 14*

Sheets of 4, #a-d

3600-3601 A784 Set of 2 20.00 20.00

Souvenir Sheet

3602-3603 A784 Set of 2 15.00 15.00

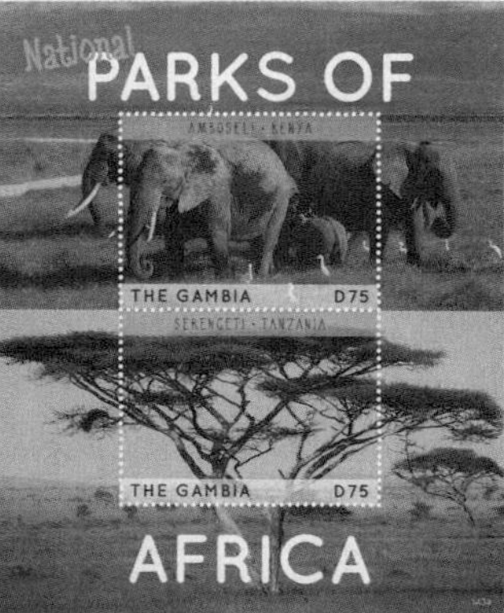

National Parks in Africa — A785

No. 3604: a, Augrabies Falls, South Africa. b, Kiang West, Gambia. c, Black River Gorges, Mauritius. d, Kakum, Ghana. e, Al Hoceim, Morocco. f, Bénoué, Cameroun.

No. 3605: a, Chobe, Botswana. b, Day Forest, Djibouti. c, Murchison Falls, Uganda. d, Arusha, Tanzania.

No. 3606, 75d: a, Amboseli, Kenya. b, Serengeti, Tanzania.

No. 3607, 75d: a, Andringitra, Madagascar. b, Nyika, Malawi.

2014, Sept. 15 Litho. *Perf. 12½*

3604 A785 45d Sheet of 6, #a-f 13.50 13.50
3605 A785 50d Sheet of 4, #a-d 10.00 10.00

Souvenir Sheets of 2, #a-b

3606-3607 A785 Set of 2 15.00 15.00

Miniature Sheets

Downton Abbey Television Series — A786

No. 3608, 45d: a, Downton Abbey, buff background at top. b, Earl of Grantham. c, Mr. Carson. d, Anna Bates. e, Lady Mary Crawley.

No. 3609, 45d: a, Downton Abbey, white background at top. b, Mrs. Hughes. c, Countess of Grantham. d, Tom Branson. e, Thomas Barrow.

2014, Oct. 14 Litho. *Perf. 14*

Sheets of 5, #a-e

3608-3609 A786 Set of 2 21.00 21.00

Christmas A787

Cross and paintings: 5d, Adoration of the Shepherds, by Domenico Ghirlandaio. 25d, The Archangel Gabriel, by Masolino da Panicale. 75d, Madonna and Child with Angels, by Bernardo Daddi. 100d, Nativity Scene, by Meister von Hohenfurth.

2014, Nov. 24 Litho. *Perf. 12¾*

3610-3613 A787 Set of 4 9.50 9.50

Birds of Prey Type of 2014

No. 3614: a, Bateleur. b, Red kite. c, African scops owl. d, Osprey.

No. 3615: a, Montagu's harrier. b, Secretary bird.

2014 Litho. *Perf. 14*

3614 A780 50d Sheet of 4, #a-d 10.00 10.00

Souvenir Sheet

Perf. 12

3615 A780 75d Sheet of 2, #a-b 7.50 7.50

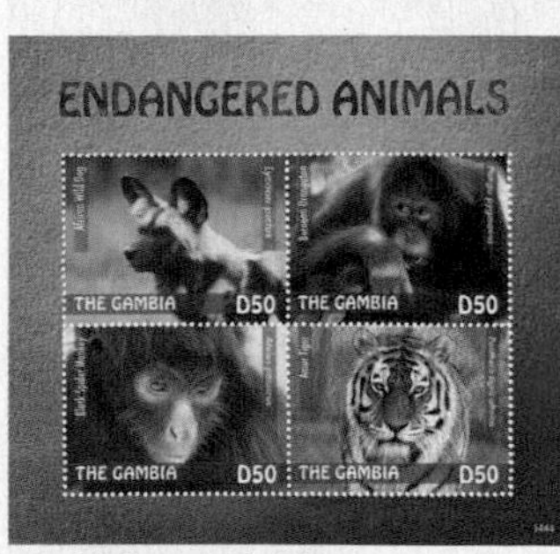

Endangered Animals — A788

No. 3616, 50d: a, African wild dog. b, Bornean orangutan. c, Black spider monkey. d, Amur tiger, denomination in white.

No. 3617, 50d: a, Two African wild dogs. b, Eastern lowland gorilla. c, Amur tiger, denomination in black. d, Chimpanzee.

No. 3618, 75d: a, Chimpanzee, diff. b, Cross River gorilla.

No. 3619, 75d: a, Sumatran rhinoceroses. b, Amur leopard.

2014, Oct. 14 Litho. *Perf. 14*

Sheets of 4, #a-d

3616-3617 A788 Set of 2 18.50 18.50

Souvenir Sheets of 2, #a-b

Perf. 12½

3618-3619 A788 Set of 2 14.00 14.00

Nos. 3618-3619 both contain two 51x38mm stamps.

Butterflies — A789

No. 3620, 50d: a, African map butterfly. b, Green-banded swallowtail. c, Gold-banded forester. d, African caper white.

No. 3621, 50d: a, Citrus swallowtail. b, Angola white lady. c, African monarch. d, African swallowtail.

No. 3622, 150d, Blood red glider. No. 3623, 150d, Giant blue swallowtail.

2014, Oct. 20 Litho. *Perf. 14*

Sheets of 4, #a-d

3620-3621 A789 Set of 2 18.50 18.50

Souvenir Sheets

Perf. 12

3622-3623 A789 Set of 2 14.00 14.00

Souvenir Sheets

Elvis Presley (1935-77) — A790

Photographs of Presley with inscriptions: No. 3624, 150d, Elvis' debut album tops charts. No. 3625, 150d, Elvis donates yacht to St. Jude's Children's Research Hospital. No. 3626, 150d, Elvis receives first guitar. No. 3627, 150d, Elvis wins first Grammy award.

2014, Oct. 14 Litho. *Perf. 14*

3624-3627 A790 Set of 4 28.00 28.00

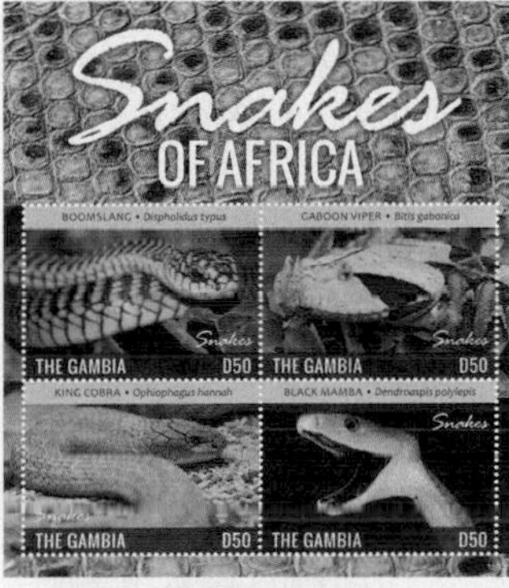

Snakes — A791

No. 3628, 50d: a, Boomslang. b, Gaboon viper. c, King cobra. d, Black mamba.

No. 3629, 50d: a, Leaf viper. b, Egg eating snake. c, Puff adder. d, Green mamba.

No. 3630, 150d, Red spitting cobra. No. 3631, 150d, Cape cobra, vert.

2014, Dec. 31 Litho. *Perf. 12½*

Sheets of 4, #a-d

3628-3629 A791 Set of 2 18.50 18.50

Souvenir Sheets

3630-3631 A791 Set of 2 14.00 14.00

Taiwan Lantern Festival — A792

No. 3632: a, Dragon lantern. b, Archer lantern. c, Boar lantern. d, Flower lantern. e, Horse lantern.

150d, Flying lantern.

2015, Jan. 15 Litho. *Perf. 14*

3632 A792 45d Sheet of 5, #a-e 10.50 10.50

Souvenir Sheet

Perf. 12

3633 A792 150d multi 7.00 7.00

Taipei 2015 International Stamp Exhibition.

World War I Posters From Australia — A793

World War I Posters From Italy — A794

No. 3634: a, Woman, damaged Australian flag. b, Bandaged soldier with rifle with bayonet. c, Soldier holding gun with arm extended towards battle. d, Monster with German helmet and bloody hands reaching for globe. e, Soldiers, bugler calling recruits. f, Bandaged soldier saluting.

No. 3635: a, Two women near woman with crown and sword. b, Woman and soldier with medals on suit lapel. c, Man wearing top hat, man wearing German helmet and bloody apron. d, Soldier with dagger, woman and child. e, Soldier and young girl. f, Soldier pointing.

No. 3636, Red Cross nurse. No. 3637, Cannon.

2015, Mar. 2 Litho. *Perf. 12½*

3634 A793 45d Sheet of 6, #a-f 12.50 12.50

3635 A794 45d Sheet of 6, #a-f 12.50 12.50

Souvenir Sheets

3636 A793 150d multi 7.00 7.00

3637 A794 150d multi 7.00 7.00

Pres. Abraham Lincoln (1809-65) — A795

No. 3638: a, Lincoln with his family. b, Lincoln reading Emancipation Proclamation. c, Inauguration. d, Funeral of Lincoln.

150d, Lincoln family log cabin.

2015, Apr. 1 Litho. *Perf. 14*

3638 A795 50d Sheet of 4, #a-d 9.50 9.50

Souvenir Sheet

Perf. 12

3639 A795 150d multi 7.00 7.00

Sir Winston Churchill (1874-1965), British Prime Minister — A796

No. 3640 — Churchill: a, Holding cane. b, As young man, wearing top hat. c, At lectern. d, Waving. e, On horse. f, Wearing military cap.

150d, Churchill wearing glasses.

2015, Apr. 1 Litho. *Perf. 14*

3640 A796 45d Sheet of 6, #a-f 12.50 12.50

Souvenir Sheet

Perf. 12½

3641 A796 150d black 7.00 7.00

No. 3641 contains one 38x51mm stamp.

Paintings by Vincent van Gogh (1853-90) — A797

No. 3642: a, Vase with Irises. b, La Berceuse. c, Field with Poppies. d, Sunflowers.

150d, The Bedroom, horiz.

2015, Apr. 1 Litho. *Perf. 12*

3642 A797 50d Sheet of 4, #a-d 9.50 9.50

Souvenir Sheet

Perf. 12½

3643 A797 150d multi 7.00 7.00

No. 3643 contains one 51x38mm stamp.

Roses — A798

No. 3644 — Color of roses: a, Dark pink. b, Red. c, Pale pink. d, Red violet.

150d, Grayish pink roses

2015, Apr. 13 Litho. *Perf. 12*

3644 A798 50d Sheet of 4, #a-d 9.50 9.50

Souvenir Sheet

Perf. 12

3645 A798 150d multi 7.00 7.00

2015 Europhilex Stamp Exhibition, London.

Akatsuki (Venus Climate Orbiter) — A799

No. 3646 — Akatsuki and inscription: a, Venus orbiter mission. b, Closed approach, December 6, 2010. c, Solar magnetic field. d, Planetary meteorology.

150d, Launch of probe, May 20, 2010, vert.

2015, July 1 Litho. *Perf. 12½x12*

3646 A799 50d Sheet of 4, #a-d 10.50 10.50

Souvenir Sheet

Perf. 12x12½

3647 A799 150d multi 7.75 7.75

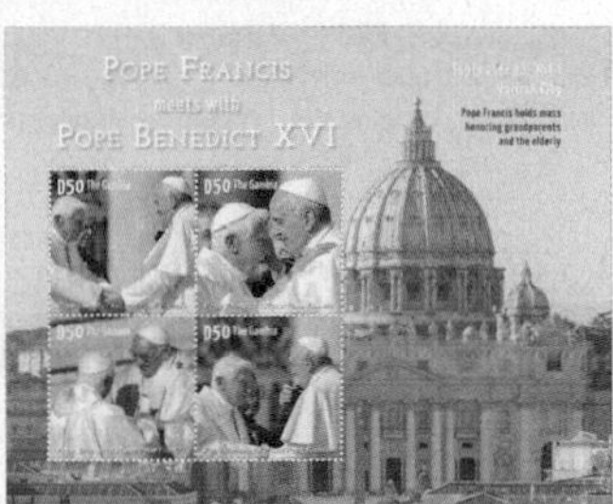

Popes Benedict XVI and Francis — A800

No. 3648: a, Popes clasping hands. b, Popes with hands on each other's shoulders. c, Popes clasping hands, face of Pope Benedict XVI not visible. d, Popes clasping hands, Pope Francis with hand near chin.

No. 3649, Pope Benedict XVI and Pope Francis getting ready to clasp hands, not touching.

2015, July 13 Litho. *Perf. 13¾*

3648 A800 50d Sheet of 4, #a-d 10.00 10.00

Souvenir Sheet

Perf. 12

3649 A800 150d multi 7.50 7.50

No. 3649 contains one 40x30mm stamp.

House of Windsor — A801

No. 3650: a, Queen Mother holding Princess Elizabeth. b, Queen Elizabeth II, Prince Philip, Prince Charles and Princess Anne. c, Duke and Duchess of Cambridge, Prince George. d, Duchess of Cambridge holding Princess Charlotte.
150d, Duke and Duchess of Cambridge, Princess Charlotte.

2015, July 13 Litho. *Perf. 14*
3650 A801 50d Sheet of 4, #a-d 10.00 10.00

Souvenir Sheet
Perf. 12
3651 A801 150d multi 7.50 7.50

Birth of Princess Charlotte.

International Year of Light — A802

No. 3652 — Photograph of city lights in a, Asia. b, North America. c, South America. d, Africa and Europe.
150d, City lights of Europe, Africa and Asia.

2015, July 13 Litho. *Perf. 14*
3652 A802 50d Sheet of 4, #a-d 10.00 10.00

Souvenir Sheet
Perf. 12½
3653 A802 150d multi 7.50 7.50

No. 3653 contains one 38x51mm stamp.

Fruits of Singapore — A803

No. 3654: a, Guavas. b, Custard apples. c, Chikus. d, Rose apples. e, Pomegranates. f, Soursops.
150d, Durians.

2015, Aug. 3 Litho. *Perf. 14*
3654 A803 45d Sheet of 6, #a-f 14.00 14.00

Souvenir Sheet
Perf. 12
3655 A803 150d multi 7.75 7.75

Singapore 2015 World Stamp Exhibition.

International Telecommunication Union, 150th Anniv. — A804

No. 3656 — 150th anniv. emblem, sine wave and: a, Satellite above earth. b, Tower and satellite dish, orange sky. c, Satellite dish. d, Radio tower and clouds at botton, blue sky. e, Communications tower at twilight.
150d, 150th anniv. emblem, sine wave, globe showing telecommunication connections.

2015, Aug. 3 Litho. *Perf. 12*
3656 A804 45d Sheet of 5, #a-e 11.50 11.50

Souvenir Sheet
3657 A804 150d multi 7.75 7.75

Magna Carta, 800th Anniv. — A805

No. 3658: a, King John. b, Magna Carta issued by Henry III, 1225. c, Original Magna Carta manuscript, 1215. d, King John signing Magna Carta, 1215.
150d, Original seal of Magna Carta, 1215, horiz.

2015, Aug. 3 Litho. *Perf. 13¼x12½*
3658 A805 50d Sheet of 4, #a-d 10.00 10.00

Souvenir Sheet
Perf. 12½x12
3659 A805 150d multi 7.75 7.75

Miniature Sheet

Orchids — A806

No. 3660: a, Ansellia africana. b, Paniculate polystachya. c, Polystachya galeata. d, Ancistrochilus rothschildianus.

2015, Sept. 8 Litho. *Perf. 13¼x12½*
3660 A806 45d Sheet of 4, #a-d 9.25 9.25

Animals — A807

No. 3661: a, African savanna hare. b, Bohor reedbuck. c, Striped polecat. d, Lesser spot-nosed monkey. e, Leopard. f, African wild dog.
150d, Four-toed hedgehog.

2015, Sept. 30 Litho. *Perf. 13¾*
3661 A807 45d Sheet of 6, #a-f 14.00 14.00

Souvenir Sheet
3662 A807 150d multi 7.75 7.75

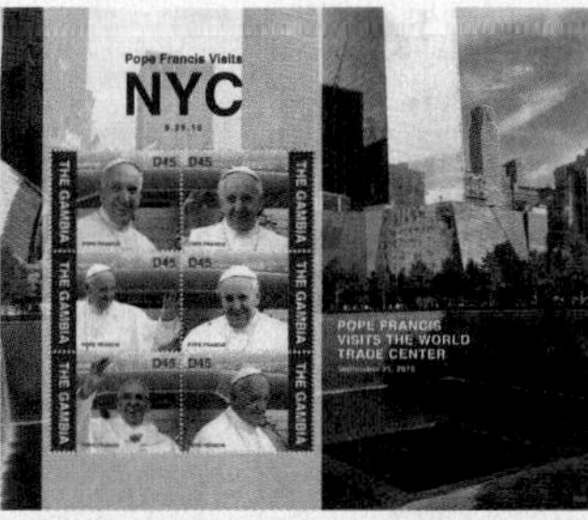

Visit of Pope Francis To New York City — A808

No. 3663 — World Trade Center Memorial and: a, Pope not waving, rose at LR. b, Pope waving, hand at left, 2 roses behind head. c, Pope waving, hand at right, rose at LR. d, Pope not waving, rose at LL and at right. e, Pope waving, hand at left, rose at left and LR. f, Pope not waving, rose stem at right.
150d, Pope Francis waving, buildings.

2015, Nov. 1 Litho. *Perf. 14*
3663 A808 45d Sheet of 6, #a-f 14.00 14.00

Souvenir Sheet
Perf. 12
3664 A808 150d multi 7.75 7.75

Christmas A809

Paintings by Sandro Botticelli: 5d, Adoration of the Magi, 1475. 25d, Adoration of the Kings, 1470. 75d, Adoration of the Kings, 1470-75. 100d, Cestello Annunciation, 1489.

2015, Nov. 2 Litho. *Perf. 12½*
3665-3668 A809 Set of 4 10.50 10.50

Queen Elizabeth II, Longest-Reigning British Monarch — A810

No. 3669 — Hat color: a, Carmine red. b, Peach. c, Beige. d, Blue.
150d, Queen Elizabeth II wearing pale yellow and black hat.

2015, Nov. 25 Litho. *Perf. 14*
3669 A810 50d Sheet of 4, #a-d 10.00 10.00

Souvenir Sheet
Perf. 12
3670 A810 150d multi 7.75 7.75

Snakes — A811

No. 3671, 50d: a, Milk snake. b, Bush viper. c, Female Bush viper. d, Mandarin rat snake.
No. 3672, 50d: a, Mangrove snake. b, Corn snake. c, Green tree python. d, Garter snake.
No. 3673: a, Grass snake. b, Boa constrictor.
150d, Green pit viper.

2015, Dec. 7 Litho. *Perf. 14*
Sheets of 4, #a-d
3671-3672 A811 Set of 2 20.00 20.00

Souvenir Sheets
Perf. 12
3673 A811 75d Sheet of 2, #a-b 7.75 7.75

Perf. 12½
3674 A811 150d multi 7.75 7.75

No. 3674 contains one 51x38mm stamp.

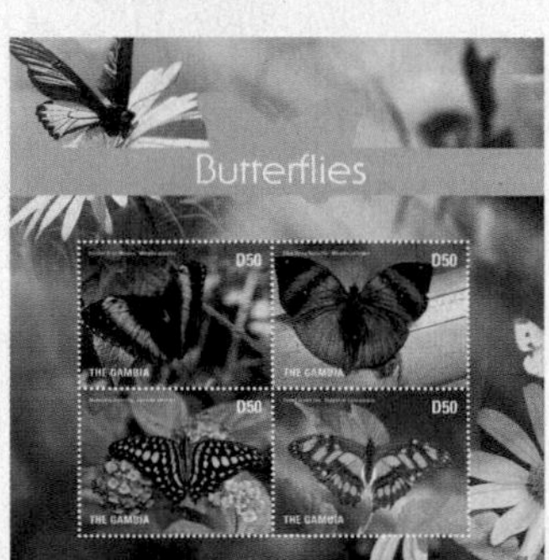

Butterflies — A812

No. 3675, 50d: a, Banded blue morpho. b, Blue shiny butterfly. c, Malachite butterfly. d, Tailed green jay.
No. 3676, 50d: a, Red postman. b, Postman butterfly. c, Protographium marcellus. d, Common cruiser butterfly.
No. 3677, 75d: a, Emerald swallowtail. b, Thoas swallowtail.
No. 3678, 75d: a, Paper kite butterfly. b, Piano key butterfly.

2015, Dec. 7 Litho. *Perf. 12½*
Sheets of 4, #a-d
3675-3676 A812 Set of 2 20.00 20.00

Sheets of 2, #a-b
3677-3678 A812 Set of 2 15.50 15.50

Orchids — A813

No. 3679, 50d: a, Orchipedum plantaginifolium. b, Satyrium coriifolium. c, Cattleya guttata. d, Cattleya granulosa.
No. 3680, 50d: a, Aganisia cyanea. b, Disa cernua. c, Coilostylis ciliaris. d, Masdevallia coccinea.

No. 3681, 75d: a, Disa uniflora. b, Ancistrochilus rothschildianus.
No. 3682, 75d: a, Satyrium erectum. b, Liparis nervosa.

2015, Dec. 7 Litho. *Perf. 14*

Sheets of 4, #a-d

3679-3680 A813 Set of 2 20.00 20.00

Sheets of 2, #a-b

3681-3682 A813 Set of 2 15.50 15.50

Kingfishers — A814

No. 3683: a, Striped kingfisher. b, Blue-breasted kingfisher. c, Malachite kingfisher. d, Pied kingfisher.
150d, Woodland kingfisher, vert.

2015, Dec. 31 Litho. *Perf. 12*

3683 A814 50d Sheet of 4, #a-d 10.00 10.00

Souvenir Sheet

Perf. 12½

3684 A814 150d multi 7.75 7.75

No. 3684 contains one 38x51mm stamp.

Pres. Dwight D. Eisenhower (1890-1969) — A815

No. 3685 — Eisenhower as General in World War II: a, Seated with other officers. b, Getting into vehicle. c, Seated, holding pencil. d, Talking with combat soldiers. e, Seated, flag in background. f, Standing with other officers.
150d, Eisenhower in uniform, flag in background, vert.

2015, Dec. 31 Litho. *Perf. 14*

3685 A815 45d Sheet of 6, #a-f 14.00 14.00

Souvenir Sheet

Perf. 12½

3686 A815 150d multi 7.75 7.75

No. 3686 contains one 38x51mm stamp.

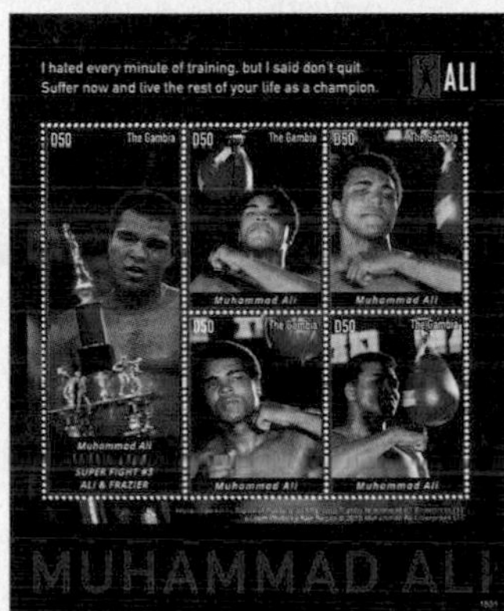

Muhammad Ali (1942-2016), Boxer — A816

No. 3687 — Ali with: a, Trophy (30x80mm). b, Punching bag at UL (30x40mm). c, Part of punching bag at right (30x40mm). d, Part of punching bag at upper right (30x40mm). e, Entire punching bag at right (30x40mm).
150d, Ali with boxing gloves.

2015, Dec. 31 Litho. *Perf. 14*

3687 A816 50d Sheet of 5, #a-e 13.00 13.00

Souvenir Sheet

Perf. 12

3688 A816 150d multi 7.75 7.75

No. 3688 contains one 30x50mm stamp.

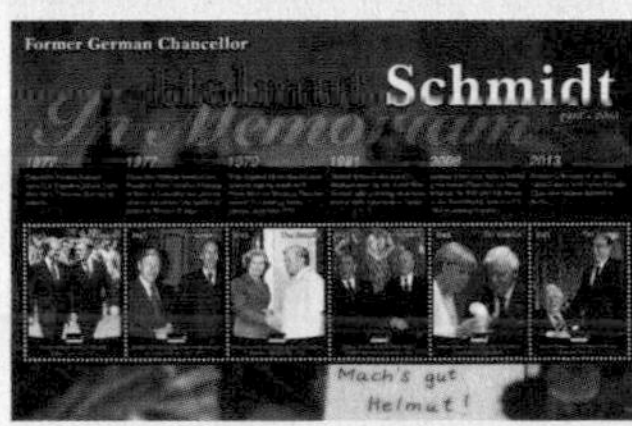

Helmut Schmidt (1918-2013), German Chancellor — A817

No. 3689 — German flag, Schmidt and: a, U.S. Pres. Jimmy Carter, 1977. b, French Pres. Valéry Giscard d'Estaing, 1977. c, British Prime Minister Margaret Thatcher, 1979. d, Soviet General Secretary Leonid Brezhnev, 1981. e, German Chancellor Angela Merkel, 2008. f, Chinese Premier Li Keqiang, 2013.
150d, Schmidt and German flag.

2015, Dec. 31 Litho. *Perf. 14*

3689 A817 45d Sheet of 6, #a-f 14.00 14.00

Souvenir Sheet

Perf. 12

3690 A817 150d multi 7.75 7.75

No. 3690 contains one 30x50mm stamp.

Minerals — A818

No. 3691: a, Chalcopyrite. b, Topaz. c, Dioptase. d, Pyrite. e, Tetrahedrite. f, Cassiterite.
No. 3692: a, Amethyst. b, Vivianite. c, Stibnite. d, Garnet.
150d, Rhodochrosite.

2015, Dec. 31 Litho. *Perf. 13¾*

3691 A818 45d Sheet of 6, #a-f 14.00 14.00
3692 A818 50d Sheet of 4, #a-d 10.00 10.00

Souvenir Sheet

3693 A818 150d multi 7.75 7.75

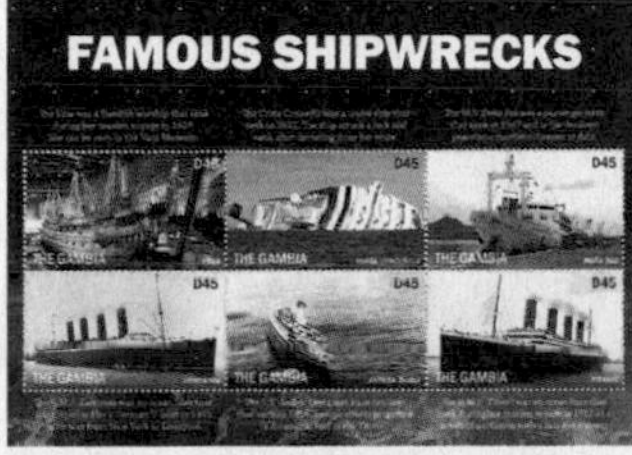

Famous Shipwrecks — A819

No. 3694: a, Vasa. b, Costa Concordia. c, Doña Paz. d, Lusitania. e, Andrea Doria. f, Titanic.
150d, U.S.S. Arizona Memorial.

2016, Feb. 20 Litho. *Perf. 13½*

3694 A819 45d Sheet of 6, #a-f 13.50 13.50

Souvenir Sheet

Perf. 12½x12

3695 A819 150d multi 7.50 7.50

No. 3695 contains one 80x30mm stamp.

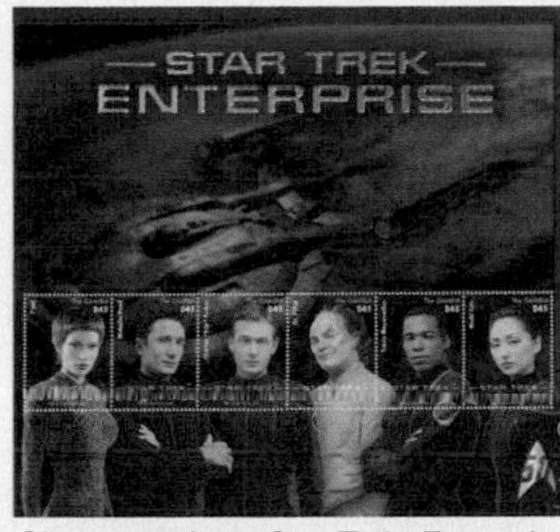

Characters from *Star Trek: Enterprise* Television Series — A820

No. 3696: a, T'pol. b, Malcolm Reed. c, Charles "Trip" Tucker. d, Dr. Phlox. e, Travis Mayweather. f, Hoshi Sato.
150d, Jonathan Archer.

2016, Feb. 20 Litho. *Perf. 14*

3696 A820 45d Sheet of 6, #a-f 14.00 14.00

Souvenir Sheet

Perf. 13¾

3697 A820 150d multi 7.50 7.50

No. 3697 contains one 35x35mm stamp.

Bougainvillea Flowers — A821

Oleander Flowers — A822

No. 3698 — Various bougainvillea flowers, as shown.
No. 3699 — Various oleander flowers, as shown.
150d, Yellow cassia flowers.

2016, Feb. 20 Litho. *Perf. 13¾*

3698 A821 45d Sheet of 6, #a-f 14.00 14.00
3699 A822 50d Sheet of 4, #a-d 10.00 10.00

Souvenir Sheet

3700 A822 150d multi 7.50 7.50

Queen Elizabeth II, 90th Birthday — A823

No. 3701 — Queen Elizabeth II wearing: a, Blue green and black coat and hat. b, Patterned coat, no hat. c, Dark blue coat and light blue hat. d, Pale blue coat and hat.
195d, Queen Elizabeth II wearing sash and tiara.

2016, Apr. 1 Litho. *Perf. 12*

3701 A823 50d Sheet of 4, #a-d 9.25 9.25

Souvenir Sheet

Perf. 12½

3702 A823 195d multi 9.00 9.00

No. 3702 contains one 38x51mm stamp.

New York City Landmarks — A824

No. 3703: a, Flatiron Building (30x80mm). b, Grand Central Terminal (30x40mm). c, New York Stock Exchange (30x40mm). d, United Nations Headquarters (30x40mm). e, Statue of Liberty (30x40mm).
195d, New York City skyline, horiz.

2016, Apr. 1 Litho. *Perf. 14*

3703 A824 40d Sheet of 5, #a-e 9.25 9.25

Souvenir Sheet

Perf. 12

3704 A824 195d multi 9.00 9.00

2016 World Stamp Show, New York. No. 3704 contains one 80x60mm stamp.

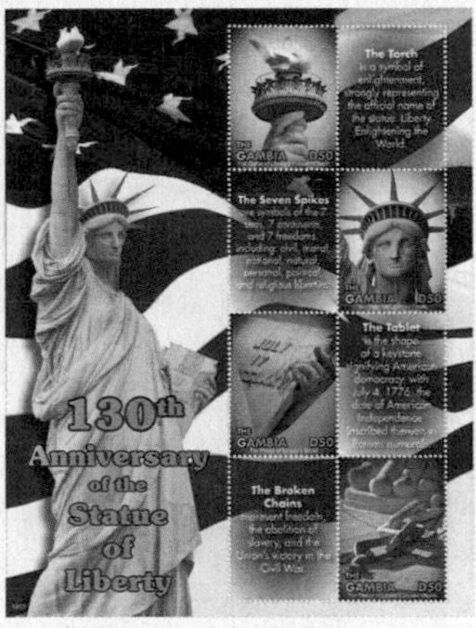

Statue of Liberty, 130th Anniv. — A825

No. 3705: a, Torch. b, Head and crown. c, Tablet. d, Broken chains.
195d, Head, diff.

2016, May 30 Litho. *Perf. 14*

3705 A825 50d Sheet of 4, #a-d, + 4 labels 9.50 9.50

Souvenir Sheet

Perf. 12¾

3706 A825 195d multi 9.25 9.25

No. 3706 contains one 38x51mm stamp.

Terrorist Attack on World Trade Center, 15th Anniv. — A826

No. 3707 — World Trade Center: a, At left, clear blue skies. b, With Brooklyn Bridge in foreground. c, At twilight, cloudy skies. d, At right, partly cloudy blue skies. e, At center, with gray skies, sun in background. f, At left, with gray brown skies.

No. 3708, vert. — World Trade Center: a, Daytime view. b, Twilight view.

195d, World Trade Center, Statue of Liberty.

2016, May 30 Litho. *Perf. 14*

3707 A826 45d Sheet of 6, #a-f 13.00 13.00

Souvenir Sheets

Perf. 12

3708 A826 100d Sheet of 2, #a-b 9.50 9.50

Perf. 12½

3709 A826 195d multi 9.25 9.25

No. 3709 contains one 38x51mm stamp.

Souvenir Sheets

A827

A828

A829

Elvis Presley (1935-77) — A830

2016, June 30 Litho. *Perf. 13x13½*

3710 A827 150d multi 7.00 7.00

Perf. 13½x13

3711 A828 150d multi 7.00 7.00

3712 A829 150d multi 7.00 7.00

3713 A830 150d multi 7.00 7.00

Nos. 3710-3713 (4) 28.00 28.00

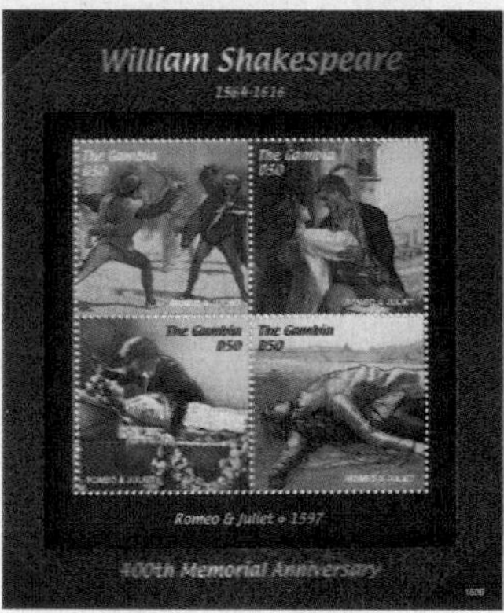

William Shakespeare (1564-1616), Writer — A831

No. 3714 — Scenes from *Romeo and Juliet*: a, Sword fight. b, Romeo and Juliet embracing. c, Romeo embracing comatose Juliet. d, Dead bodies of Romeo and Juliet.

150d, Shakespeare, vert.

2016, July 14 Litho. *Perf. 13¾*

3714 A831 50d Sheet of 4, #a-d 9.50 9.50

Souvenir Sheet

Perf. 12½

3715 A831 150d multi 7.00 7.00

No. 3715 contains one 38x51mm stamp.

Duke and Duchess of Cambridge, 5th Wedding Anniversary — A832

No. 3716: a, Duke waving. b, Prince George. c, Duchess. d, Duchess wearing white blouse. e, Princess Charlotte. f, Duke, hands not visible.

No. 3717, horiz.: a, Duke and Duchess at wedding. b, Duke, Duchess, Prince George and Princess Charlotte.

2016, Aug. 15 Litho. *Perf. 13¾*

3716 A832 45d Sheet of 6, #a-f 13.00 13.00

Souvenir Sheet

Perf. 14

3717 A832 75d Sheet of 2, #a-b 7.00 7.00

No. 3717 contains two 60x40mm stamps.

Luna 9, 50th Anniv. — A833

No. 3718: a, Luna 10, Moon at LR. b, Luna 2, Moon at LL. c, Luna 9, Moon at UR. d, Luna 3, Moon at UL.

200d, Luna 9 Molniya Rocket launch, vert.

2016, Sept. 9 Litho. *Perf. 14*

3718 A833 75d Sheet of 4, #a-d 14.50 14.50

Souvenir Sheet

Perf. 12

3719 A833 200d multi 9.50 9.50

No. 3718b is erroneously inscribed "Luna 10." The lauch date of Luna 2 is Sept. 12, 1959, not 1966.

Volcanoes — A834

No. 3720: a, Eyjafjallajökull, Iceland. b, Mt. St. Helens, U.S. c, Krakatoa, Indonesia. d, Mt. Fuji, Japan. e, Cotopaxi, Ecuador. f, Kilauea, U.S.

170d, Mt. Vesuvius, Italy, vert.

2016, Nov. 14 Litho. *Perf. 14*

3720 A834 55d Sheet of 6, #a-f 15.00 15.00

Souvenir Sheet

Perf. 12½

3721 A834 170d multi 7.75 7.75

No. 3721 contains one 38x51mm stamp.

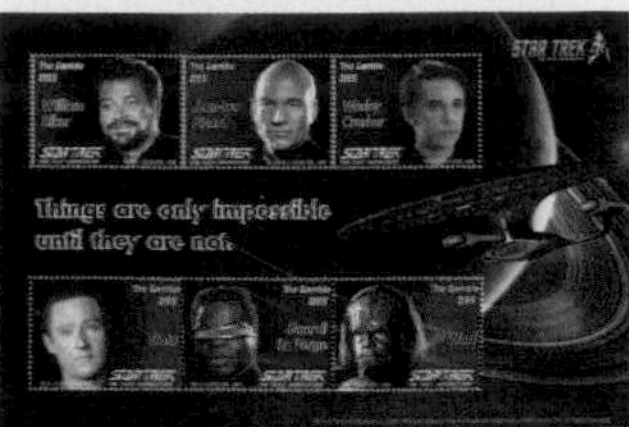

Characters From *Star Trek: The Next Generation* Television Series — A835

No. 3722: a, William Riker. b, Jean-Luc Picard. c, Wesley Crusher. d, Data. e, Geordi La Forge. f, Worf.

No. 3723: a, Beverly Crusher. b, Deanna Troi. c, Guinan.

No. 3724: a, La Forge, Data, Worf, Riker, Troi, Beverly Crusher, and Picard. b, U.S.S. Enterprise NCC-1701-D.

2016, Nov. 3 Litho. *Perf. 14*

3722 A835 55d Sheet of 6, #a-f 15.00 5.00

Perf.

3723 A835 85d Sheet of 3, #a-c 12.00 12.00

Souvenir Sheet

Perf. 12¾

3724 A835 125d Sheet of 2, #a-b 11.50 11.50

No. 3723 contains three 38mm diameter stamps. No. 3724 contains two 51x38mm stamps.

On No. 3723b the last name "TROI" is spelled incorrectly.

Worldwide Fund for Nature (WWF) — A836

No. 3725 — Temminck's red colobus: a, With tree branch at left. b, Sitting. c, With tree branch at right. d, Head.

2016, Nov. 14 Litho. *Perf. 12*

3725 A836 85d Block or horiz. strip of 4, #a-d 16.00 16.00

e. Miniature sheet of 8, 2 each #3725a-3725d 32.00 32.00

Paintings by Hieronymus Bosch (c. 1450-1516) — A837

No. 3726 — Details from The Garden of Earthly Delights: a, Flock of birds from left panel. b, Water from center panel. c, Owl from center panel. d, Ear from right panel.

No. 3727 — Adoration of the Magi from circa: a, 1475 (Jesus on lap). b, 1499 (Jesus lifted).

2016, Nov. 14 Litho. *Perf. 12*

3726 A837 85d Sheet of 4, #a-d 16.00 16.00

Souvenir Sheet

3727 A837 125d Sheet of 2, #a-b 11.50 11.50

Christmas A838

Christmas tree ornaments: No. 3728, 85d, Rocking horse. No. 3729, 85d, Angel. No. 3730, 170d, Reindeer. No. 3731, 170d, Snowman.

2016, Dec. 1 Litho. *Perf. 12¾*

3728-3731 A838 Set of 4 23.50 23.50

King Bhumibol Adulyadej of Thailand (1927-2016) — A839

No. 3732 — King Bhumibol Adulyadej: a, As young man, without hat, denomination at UR. b, As older man, wearing suit, denomination at UL. c, With Queen Sirikit, denomination at UR. d, With Queen Sirikit, denomination at UL. d, As young man wearing military hat, denomination at UR. e, As older man, wearing military uniform, denomination at UL.

No. 3733: a, Wearing ceremonial crown. b, Wearing military hat. c, Wearing suit aand tie, with Queen Sirikit. d, Wearing military uniform, with Queen Sirikit.

2016, Dec. 28 Litho. *Perf. 14*

3732 A839 55d Sheet of 6, #a-f 16.00 16.00

3733 A839 85d Sheet of 4, #a-d 16.00 16.00

Miniature Sheets

A840

Pres. John F. Kennedy (1917-63) — A841

No. 3734 — Pres. Kennedy in Navy in World War II: a, 60d, Wearing cap, in front of flat brick wall (40x30mm). b, 60d, Wearing cap, foliage in background (40x30mm). c, 60d, Without cap (40x30mm). d, 60d, Wearing cap, near corner of brick wall (40x30mm). e, 100d, With fellow crew members (80x30mm).

No. 3735 — Pres. Kennedy in Navy in World War II: a, Wearing dress cap. b, Without cap. c, In boat, wearing cap, facing right. d, In boat, wearing cap, facing left.

2017, Feb. 7 Litho. *Perf. 14*

3734 A840 Sheet of 5, #a-e 15.50 15.50

3735 A841 75d Sheet of 4, #a-d 13.50 13.50

Mammals — A842

Designs: 2000d, Guinea baboon. 3000d, Spotted hyena. 5000d, Lion.

2017, Mar. 8 Litho. *Perf. 12½x13¼*

3736 A842 2000d multi 90.00 90.00

3737 A842 3000d multi 130.00 130.00

3738 A842 5000d multi 220.00 220.00

Nos. 3736-3738 (3) 440.00 440.00

A843

First Ladies of the United States — A844

No. 3739, 20d: a, Martha Washington. b, Abigail Adams. c, Martha Jefferson. d, Dolley Madison. e, Elizabeth Monroe. f, Louisa Adams. g, Emily Donelson. h, Angelica Van Buren. i, Anna Harrison. j, Letitia Tyler. k, Julia Tyler. l, Sarah Polk. m, Margaret Taylor. n, Abigail Fillmore. o, Jane Pierce. p, Harriet Johnson.

No. 3740, 20d: a, Mary Lincoln. b, Eliza Johnson. c, Julia Grant. d, Lucy Hayes. e, Lucretia Garfield. f, Mary McElroy. g, Frances Cleveland (gray green portrait). h, Caroline Harrison. i, Frances Cleveland (gray portrait). j, Ida McKinley. k, Edith Roosevelt. l, Helen Taft. m, Ellen Wilson. n, Edith Wilson. o, Florence Harding. p, Grace Coolidge.

No. 3741, 20d: a, Lou Hoover. b, Eleanor Roosevelt. c, Bess Truman. d, Mamie Eisenhower. e, Jacqueline Kennedy. f, Claudia Johnson. g, Thelma Nixon. h, Elizabeth Ford. i, Eleanor Carter. j, Nancy Reagan. k, Barbara Bush. l, Hillary Clinton. m, Laura Bush. n, Michelle Obama. o, Melania Trump. p, White House and Seal of the Executive Office.

145d, Melania Trump.

2017 Litho. *Perf. 14*

Sheets of 16, #a-p

3739-3741 A843 Set of 3 42.00 42.00

Souvenir Sheet

Perf. 13¼

3742 A844 145d multi 6.50 6.50

Issued: Nos. 3739-3741, 7/10; No. 3742, 3/8.

Miniature Sheet

Princess Diana (1961-97) — A845

Various depictions of Princess Diana, as shown.

2017, Apr. 14 Litho. *Perf. 13¾*

3743 A845 85d Sheet of 4, #a-d 15.00 15.00

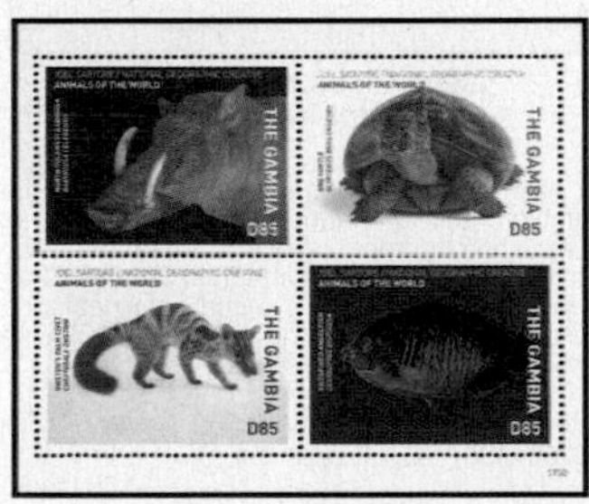

Animals — A846

No. 3744: a, North Sulawesi babirusa. b, Bog turtle. c, Owston's palm civet. d, Twospined angelfish.

200d, Red panda, vert.

2017, June 7 Litho. *Perf. 12½*

3744 A846 85d Sheet of 4, #a-d 15.00 15.00

Souvenir Sheet

3745 A846 200d multi 8.75 8.75

A847

Sunflowers — A848

Various photographs of sunflowers, as shown.

2017, June 26 Litho. *Perf. 13¾*

3746 A847 85d Sheet of 4, #a-d 15.00 15.00

Souvenir Sheet

3747 A848 125d Sheet of 2, #a-b 11.00 11.00

Miniature Sheet

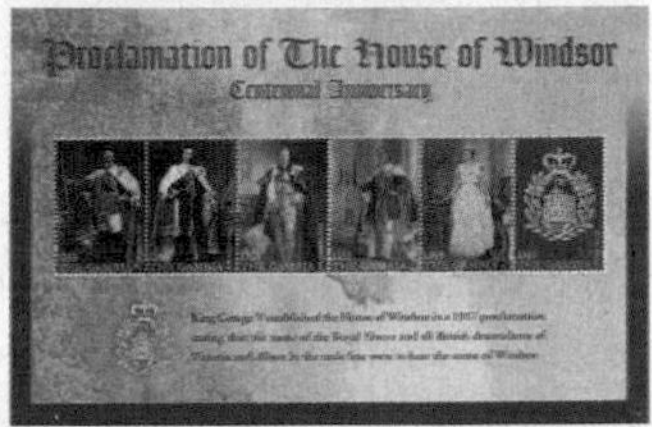

Proclamation of the House of Windsor, Cent. — A849

No. 3748, 55d: a, King Edward VII. b, King George V. c, King Edward VIII. d, King George VI. e, Queen Elizabeth II. f, Royal badge.

2017, July 10 Litho. *Perf. 13¼*

3748 A849 Sheet of 6, #a-f 14.50 14.50

Meerkats — A850

No. 3749: a, Meerkat on rock, front paws at left. b, Meerkat facing forward, rocks in background. c, Meerkat facing forward, foliage in background. d, Two meerkats.

No. 3750: a, Meerkat behind rock. b, Meerkat, rocks in background.

2017, Aug. 2 Litho. *Perf. 14*

3749 A850 90d Sheet of 4, #a-d 16.00 16.00

Souvenir Sheet

3750 A850 150d Sheet of 2, #a-b 13.50 13.50

Paintings of Dogs by Lang Shining (Giuseppe Castiglione) (1688-1766) — A851

No. 3751, 85d: a, Heavenly Lion. b, Young Black Dragon. c, Dog in the Bamboo Shade. d, Yellow Leopard.

No. 3752, 85d: a, Young Gray Dragon. b, Golden-Winged Face. c, Star-Glancing Wolf. d, Flying Magpie.

2017, Aug. 2 Litho. *Perf. 12*
Sheets of 4, #a-d

3751-3752 A851 Set of 2 30.00 30.00

New Year 2018 (Year of the Dog).

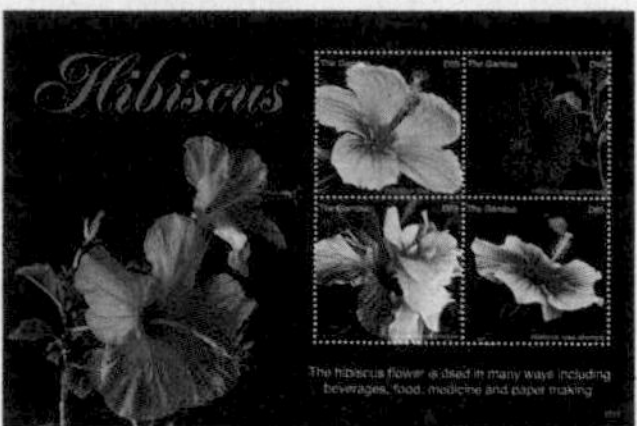

A852

Hibiscus Flowers — A853

Various photographs of hibiscus flowers, as shown.

2017, Aug. 9 Litho. *Perf. 13¾*

3753 A852 85d Sheet of 4, #a-d 15.00 15.00

Souvenir Sheet
Perf. 12

3754 A853 125d Sheet of 2, #a-b 11.00 11.00

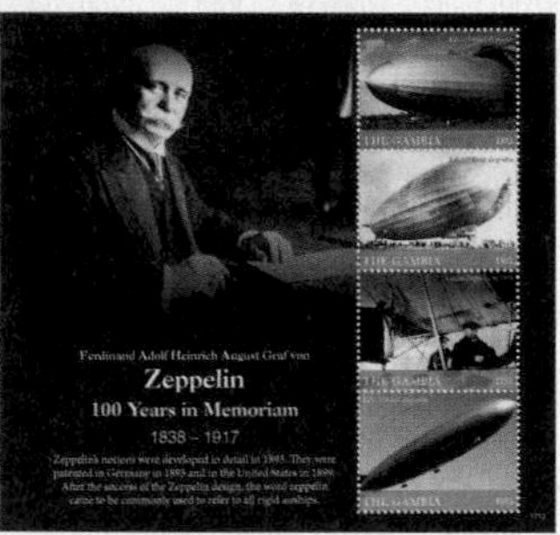

Zeppelins — A854

No. 3755: a, LZ-127 Graf Zeppelin in hangar. b, People and automobiles near LZ-127 Graf Zeppelin. c, Count Ferdinand von Zeppelin in 1914. d, LZ-130 Graf Zeppelin II in flight.

170d, Count Ferdinand von Zepplein (1838-1917), vert.

2017, Oct. 12 Litho. *Perf. 12*

3755 A854 85d Sheet of 4, #a-d 14.50 14.50

Souvenir Sheet
Perf. 12½

3756 A854 170d multi 7.25 7.25

No. 3756 contains one 38x51mm stamp.

Souvenir Sheets

Elvis Presley (1935-77) — A855

Inscriptions: No. 3757, 170d, Breaks concert attendance record. No. 3758, 170d, Jamming with the Fab Four. No. 3759, 170d, Buys first Stutz Blackhawk. No. 3760, 170d, Introudces his jumpsuits, vert.

2017, Nov. 17 Litho. *Perf. 12½*

3757-3760 A855 Set of 4 29.00 29.00

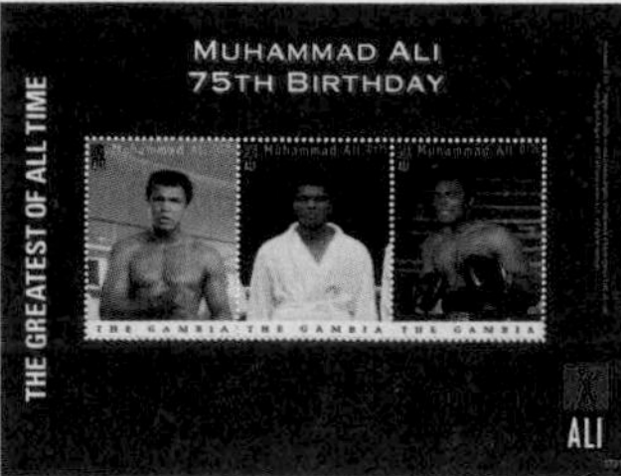

Muhammad Ali (1942-2016), Boxer — A856

No. 3761 — Ali: a, With bare fists. b, Wearing white robe. c, Wearing boxing gloves.

250d, Ali wearing suit and tie.

2017, Dec. 17 Litho. *Perf. 14*

3761 A856 175d Sheet of 3, #a-c 22.00 22.00

Souvenir Sheet
Perf. 12½

3762 A856 250d multi 10.50 10.50

No. 3762 contains one 38x51mm stamp.

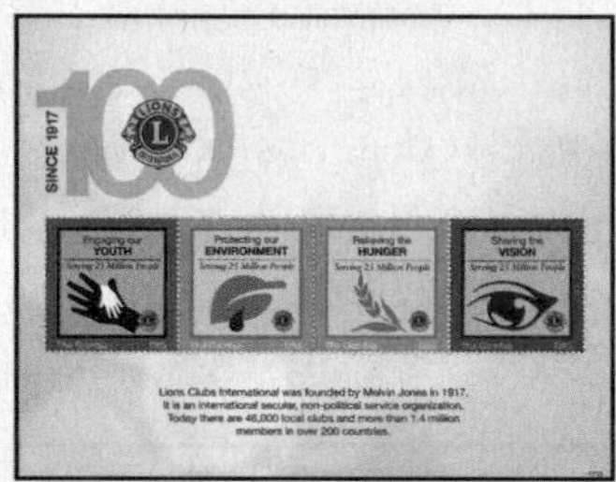

Lions Clubs International, Cent. — A857

No. 3763 — Lions Clubs International emblem and: a, Hands of adult and child. b, Leaf and raindrop. c, Stalk of wheat. d, Eye.

No. 3764, vert. — Centennial Service Challenge emblem, hands, eye, stalk of wheat, and leaf, with frame color of: a, Yellow. b, Bluish violet.

2017, Dec. 17 Litho. *Perf. 13¾*

3763 A857 85d Sheet of 4, 3a-d 14.50 14.50

Souvenir Sheet
Perf. 12½

3764 A857 85d Sheet of 2, #a-b 7.25 7.25

No. 3764 contains two 38x51mm stamps.

Miniature Sheet

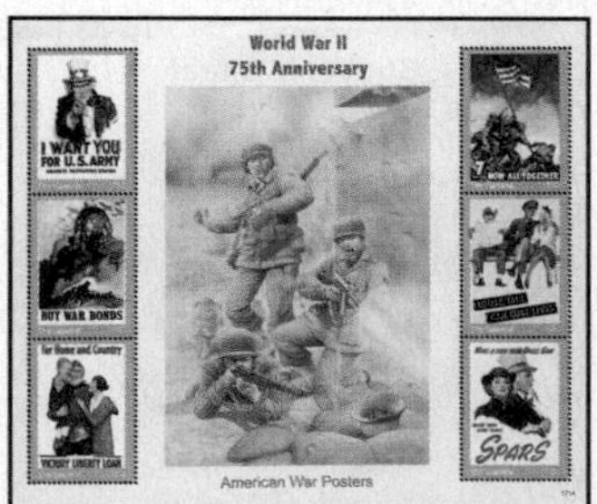

World War II, 75th Anniv. — A858

No. 3765 — American posters: a, Uncle Sam Army recruitment poster. b, 7th War Loan poster. c, Buy War Bonds poster. d, Loose Talk Can Cost Lives poster. e, Victory Liberty Loan poster. f, SPARS recruiting poster.

2017, Dec. 17 Litho. *Perf. 14*

3765 A858 55d Sheet of 6, #a-f 14.00 14.00

GEORGIA

ˈjor-jə

LOCATION — South of Russia, bordering on the Black Sea and occupying the entire western part of Trans-Caucasia
GOVT. — Republic
AREA — 26,900 sq. mi.
POP. — 5,066,499 (1999 est.)
CAPITAL — Tbilisi (Tiflis)

Georgia was formerly a province of the Russian Empire and later a part of the Transcaucasian Federation of Soviet Republics. Stamps of Georgia were replaced in 1923 by those of Transcaucasian Federated Republics.

On Mar. 1, 1994, Georgia joined the Commonwealth of Independent States.

100 Kopecks = 1 Ruble
100 Kopecks = 1 Coupon (1993)
100 Tetri = 1 Lari (Sept. 25, 1995)

Catalogue values for unused stamps in this country are for Never Hinged items, beginning with Scott 75 in the regular postage section, and Scott B10 in the semi-postal section.

Tiflis

A 6k local stamp, imperforate and embossed without color on white paper, was issued in November, 1857, at Tiflis by authority of the viceroy. The square design shows a coat of arms.

National Republic

St. George
A1 A2

1919 Litho. Unwmk. *Perf. 11½*

1 A1 10k blue .85 .85
2 A1 40k red orange .85 .85
a. Tête bêche pair 30.00 30.00
3 A1 50k emerald .85 .85
4 A1 60k red .85 .85
5 A1 70k claret .85 *.85*
6 A2 1r orange brown .85 *.85*
Nos. 1-6 (6) 5.10 5.10

Imperf

7 A1 10k blue .85 .85
8 A1 40k red orange .85 .85
a. Tête bêche pair 50.00 50.00
9 A1 50k emerald .85 .85
10 A1 60k red .85 .85
11 A1 70k claret .85 *.85*
12 A2 1r orange brown .85 *.85*
Nos. 7-12 (6) 5.10 5.10

Queen Thamar — A3

1920 *Perf. 11½*

13 A3 2r red brown .65 1.40
14 A3 3r gray blue .65 1.40
15 A3 5r orange .65 1.40
Nos. 13-15 (3) 1.95 4.20

Imperf

16 A3 2r red brown .65 1.40
17 A3 3r gray blue .65 1.40
18 A3 5r orange .65 1.40
Nos. 16-18 (3) 1.95 4.20

Nos. 1-18 with parts of design inverted, sideways or omitted are fraudulent varieties.

Overprints reading "Day of the National Guard, 12, 12, 1920" (5 lines) and "Recognition of Independence, 27, 1, 1921" (4 lines) were applied, probably in Italy, to remainders taken by government officials who fled when Russian forces occupied Georgia. Value, set $30.

"Constantinople" and new values were unofficially surcharged on stamps of 1919-20 by a consul in Turkey.

Soviet Socialist Republic

Soldier with Flag — A5

Peasant Sowing Grain — A6

Industry and Agriculture — A7

1922 Unwmk. *Perf. 11½*

26 A5 500r rose 8.00 5.25
27 A6 1000r bister brown 8.00 5.25
28 A7 2000r slate 11.50 8.25
29 A7 3000r brown 11.50 8.25
30 A7 5000r green 11.50 8.25
Nos. 26-30 (5) 50.50 35.25

Forgeries exist of Nos. 26-30.

Nos. 26 to 30 exist imperforate but were not so issued. Value for set, $200.

Nos. 26-30 Handstamped with New Values in Violet

1923

36 A6 10,000r on 1000r 8.75 6.50
a. Black surcharge 35.00 *35.00*
b. 20,000r on 1000r 200.00
37 A7 15,000r on 2000r, blk surch. 9.25 *8.50*
a. Violet surcharge 40.00 40.00
38 A5 20,000r on 500r 9.25 *8.50*
a. Black surcharge 20.00 15.00
39 A7 40,000r on 5000r 8.75 5.50
a. Black surcharge 20.00 *20.00*
40 A7 80,000r on 3000r 9.25 *8.50*
a. Black surcharge 20.00 *25.00*
Nos. 36-40 (5) 45.25 *37.50*

There were two types of the handstamped surcharges, with the numerals 5½mm and 6½mm high. The impressions are often too indistinct to measure or even to distinguish the numerals.

Double and inverted surcharges exist, as is usual with handstamps.

Surcharged in Black

43 A6 10,000r on 1000r 7.00 7.00
44 A7 15,000r on 2000r 4.50 4.50
a. Double surcharge 100.00
45 A5 20,000r on 500r 2.25 2.25
a. Inverted surcharge 50.00
46 A7 40,000r on 5000r 4.50 4.50
47 A7 80,000r on 3000r 4.50 4.50
Nos. 43-47 (5) 22.75 *22.75*

Nos. 43, 45, 46 and 47 exist imperforate but were not so issued. Value $25 each.

Russian Stamps of 1909-18 Handstamp Surcharged

Type I — Surcharge 20x5½mm.
Type II — Surcharge 22x7¼mm.

1923 *Perf. 14½x15*

48 A14 10,000r on 7k lt bl 150.00 150.00
49 A11 15,000r on 15k red brn & bl (I) 15.00 15.00
a. Type II 10.00 10.00
b. As "a," surcharge inverted 25.00

Type I Surcharge Handstamped on Armenia No. 141

50 A11 15,000r on 5r on 15k red brn & bl 500.00 *500.00*
a. Type II 500.00
Nos. 48-50 (3) 665.00 *665.00*

Russian Stamps and Types of 1909-18 Surcharged in Dark Blue or Black

1923 *Perf. 11½, 14½x15*

51 A14 75,000r on 1k org 3.50 *4.25*
a. Imperf. 150.00 *150.00*
52 A14 200,000r on 5k cl 4.00 *5.00*
53 A8 300,000r on 20k bl & car (Bk) 4.00 *5.00*
a. Dark blue surcharge 70.00 *100.00*
54 A14 350,000r on 3k red 7.00 *8.00*
a. Imperf. 7.00 *7.25*
b. Horiz. pair, imperf. btwn. 100.00

Imperf

55 A14 700,000r on 2k grn 7.00 *10.00*
a. Perf. 14½x15 27.50 *32.50*
Nos. 51-55 (5) 25.50 *32.25*

Catalogue values for unused stamps in this section, from this point to the end of the section, are for Never Hinged items.

Republic

Admission to UN, 1st Anniv. A20

Map, flag, UN emblem.

1993, July 31 **Litho.** *Perf. 13¼*

73 A20 25r green & multi .75 .75
74 A20 50r brown & multi 1.10 1.10
75 A20 100r violet & multi 1.75 1.75
a. Souvenir sheet of 3, #73-75 + label 4.00 4.00
Nos. 73-75 (3) 3.60 3.60

For overprint, see Nos. 327-328.

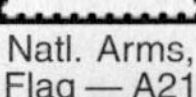

Natl. Arms, Flag — A21

Fresco, 18th Cent. — A22

Apostle Simon, 11th Cent. — A23

Three Women, by Lado Gudiashvili A24

1993, Oct. 11 **Photo.** *Perf. 12x11½*

76 A21 50k multicolored .50 .50

Litho.

Perf. 12x12½

77 A22 50k multicolored 1.10 1.10
78 A23 1c multicolored .90 .90
79 A24 1c multicolored 1.40 1.40
Nos. 76-79 (4) 3.90 3.90

Nos. 76, 78-79 dated 1992.

For surcharges see Nos. 80-83, 93-95, 404, 458.

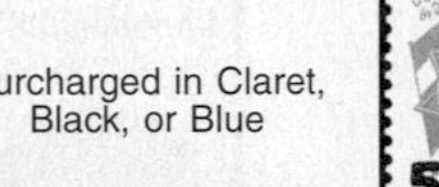

Surcharged in Claret, Black, or Blue

1994, May 31 **Photo.** *Perf. 12x11½*

80 A21 5000c on 50k #76 (C) .65 .65

Litho.

Perf. 12x12½

81 A22 5000c on 50k #77 (Blk) .65 .65
82 A23 10,000c on 1c #78 (Bl) .90 .90
83 A24 10,000c on 1c #79 (C) .90 .90
Nos. 80-83 (4) 3.10 3.10

Size and location of surcharge varies.

Places of Worship — A25

30c, Mtskheta Church. 40c, Gelati Church. 50c, Nikortsminda Church. 60c, Ikorta Church. 70c, Samtavisi Church. 80c, Bolnisi Zion Synagogue. 90c, Gremi Citadel Church.

1993, Oct. 11 **Litho.** *Perf. 13½*

84 A25 30c blue .35 .35
85 A25 40c red brown .45 .45
86 A25 50c olive brown .55 .55
87 A25 60c rose carmine .65 .65
88 A25 70c rose lake .85 .85
89 A25 80c green 1.00 1.00
90 A25 90c slate 1.10 1.10
Nos. 84-90 (7) 4.95 4.95

See Nos. 111-120.

Niko Nikoladze (1843-1928) — A26

1994, May 31 **Litho.** *Perf. 13½*

91 A26 150c black & gold 1.00 1.00

UPU, 120th Anniv. A27

1994, May 30

92 A27 200c multicolored 1.00 1.00

Nos. 77-79 Surcharged in Green or Red

1994 **Litho.** *Perf. 12x12½*

93 A22 200c on 50k #77 .50 .50
94 A23 300c on 1c #78 (R) .55 .55
95 A24 500c on 1c #79 1.25 1.25
Nos. 93-95 (3) 2.30 2.30

Set exists with inverted surcharges. Value $10.

A27a

1994, Oct. 9 **Litho.** *Perf. 14*

95A A27a 100c shown 2.75 2.75
95B A27a 200c Monument 5.00 5.00

All Georgian Congress.

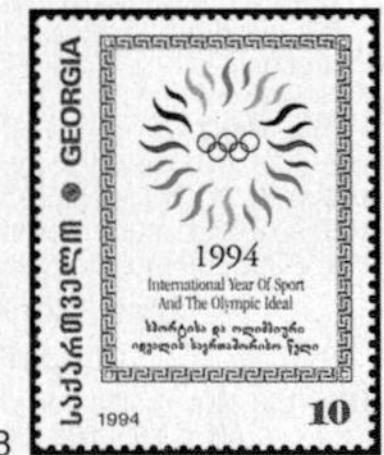

A28

Georgia Natl. Olympic Committee: 10c, Intl. year of sport & Olympic ideal. 15c, Olympic congress, cent. 20c, Intl. Olympic Committee, cent. 25c, Olympic truce.

1995, Mar. 28 **Litho.** *Perf. 14½*

96-99 A28 Set of 4 7.50 7.50

Dated 1994.

Paintings by Niko Piromanashvili (1862-1918) — A29

No. 100, Three Princes Carousing on the Grass. No. 101, Still life. No. 102, Georgian Woman with a Tambourine, vert. No. 103, Bear on a Moonlit Night, vert. No. 104, Woman with a Tankard of Beer, vert. No. 105, Deer, vert. No. 106, Fisherman, vert. No. 107, Giraffe, vert. No. 108, Boy on a Donkey, vert. No. 109, Brooder with Chicks.
No. 110, Family Picnicking.

1995, Mar. 29 **Litho.** *Perf. 14*

100-109 A29 20c Set of 10 10.00 10.00

Souvenir Sheet

110 A29 100c multicolored 5.00 5.00

Churches Type of 1993

10c

20c

400c

1c, No. 120, Metechi, 1278-1289. 2c, No. 117, Alaverdi, 11th cent. 3c, No. 116, Dranda, 8th cent. No. 114, Sveti-Zchoveli, 1010-1019. No. 115, Kumurdo, 964. No. 118, Anauri, 17th cent. No. 119, Bitschvinta, 10th cent.

Size: 25½x39mm

1995 **Litho.** *Perf. 14*

111 A25 1c black & violet 1.50 1.50
112 A25 2c black & sepia 1.50 1.50
113 A25 3c black & red brn 1.50 1.50
114 A25 10c black & violet 1.50 1.50
115 A25 10c black & sepia 1.50 1.50
116 A25 10c black & grn blue 1.50 1.50
117 A25 20c black & slate 1.50 1.50
118 A25 20c black & olive grn 1.50 1.50
119 A25 400c black & org brn 1.50 1.50
120 A25 400c black & red brn 1.50 1.50
Nos. 111-120 (10) 15.00 15.00

Paolo Iashvili (1894-1937) — A30

1995, Apr. 1

125 A30 300c multicolored 1.25 1.25

Prehistoric Animals — A31

No. 126, Brontosaurus. No. 127, Saurolophus. No. 128, Scolosaurus. No. 129, Triceratops. No. 130, Parasaurolophus. No. 131, Ceratosaurus. No. 132, Deinonichus. No. 133, Tyrannosaurus. No. 134, Stegosaurus.
No. 135: a, Pterodactylus (d). b, Rhamphophynghus (c, e). c, Pteranodon. d, Spinosaurus. e, Tyrannosaurus (f, h, i). f, Velociraptor. g, Monoklonius. h, Ornithomimus. i, Mastodon.
100c, Deinonychus.

1995 **Litho.** *Perf. 14*

126-134 A31 15c Set of 9 6.25 6.25

Miniature Sheet of 9

135 A31 15c #a.-i. 7.25 7.25

Souvenir Sheet

136 A31 100c multicolored 5.25 5.25

Issued: Nos. 126-134, 5/12.

UNESCO World Heritage Sites A32

100c, Bagrati Cathedral. 500c, Jvari of Mtskhetha.

1995, Aug. 30 Litho. *Perf. 14*

137 A32 100c multi 1.00 1.00

Souvenir Sheet

138 A32 500c multi, vert. 6.00 6.00

Miniature Sheet

Wildlife Painting A33

Design: Nos. a.-p., Various animals and birds.

1995, Aug. 4

139 A33 15c Sheet of 16, #a.-p. 9.75 9.75

Miniature Sheets

Birds — A34

Designs: Each 15t: Nos. 140a-140p, Various songbirds. Nos. 141a-141p, Various raptors.

Each 100t: No. 142, Songbird. No. 143, Owl.

1996, Feb. 26 Litho. *Perf. 14*

140-141 A34 Set of 2 *22.50 22.50*

Souvenir Sheets

142-143 A34 Set of 2 *12.50 12.50*

Miniature Sheet

Fauna and Flora — A35

a, Stork's head. b, Stork's body (a, f), berries. c, Snake (d, g, h). d, Moth. e, Lizard. f, Songbirds. g, Insect, flowers. h, Bee on flower. i, Butterfly, flower. j, Frog, lily (f). k, Snail. l, Turtle (p). m. Lobster. n, Sea plant, eel (o). o, Fish. p, Salamander.

1996, Mar. 14 Litho. *Perf. 14*

144 A35 10t Sheet of 16, #a.-p. 12.00 12.00

Dinosaurs — A36

1996, Apr. 24 Litho. *Perf. 14*

145 A36 10t Sheet of 9, #a.-i. 7.50 7.50

Intl. Olympic Committee, Cent. — A37

Georgian Olympians, landmarks from earlier Summer Olympic Games: 1t, Helsinki, 1952. 2t, Melbourne, 1956. 3t, Rome, 1960. 4t, Tokyo, 1964. 5t, Mexico City, 1968. 6t, Munich, 1972. 7t, Montreal, 1976. 8t, Moscow, 1980. 9t, Seoul, 1988. 10t, Barcelona, 1992.

Early Greek: 50t, Wrestlers. 70t, Runner.

1996, Aug. 16 Litho. *Perf. 14*

146-155 A37 Set of 10 7.50 7.50

Souvenir Sheets

156 A37 50t multicolored 7.00 7.00

157 A37 70t multicolored 8.50 8.50

Olymphilex '96 (No. 157).

Paintings — A38

Designs: 10t, Citizens of Paris, by Lado Gudiashvili. 20t, Abstract, by Wassily Kandinsky. 30t, Still Life, by David Kakabadze. 50t, Three Painters, by Shalva Kikodze.

80t, Portrait of Niko Pirosmani, by Pablo Picasso.

1996, Aug. 2 Litho. *Perf. 14*

158 A38 10t multicolored .40 .40

159 A38 20t multicolored .70 .70

160 A38 30t multicolored 1.00 1.00

161 A38 50t multicolored 1.40 1.40

Size: 72x90mm

Imperf

162 A38 80t multicolored 3.00 3.00

Nos. 158-162 (5) 6.50 6.50

A39

1996, Dec. 25 Litho. *Perf. 13x14*

163 A39 30t Anton I (1720-88) 1.25 1.25

Ivan Javakhishvili (1876-1940), Writer — A40

1997, Mar. 6 *Perf. 14*

164 A40 50t multicolored 1.50 1.50

UN, 50th Anniv. A41

1997, Mar. 5 Litho. *Perf. 14*

165 A41 30t purple & blue 1.25 1.25

166 A41 125t red & blue 3.50 3.50

Dogs — A42

Designs: 10t, Rottweiler. 30t, Gordon setter. 50t, St. Bernard. 60t, English bulldog. 70t, Caucasian sheep dog.

125t, Caucasian sheep dog, diff.

1997, June 2 Litho. *Perf. 14*

167 A42 10t multicolored .35 .35

168 A42 30t multicolored .85 .85

169 A42 50t multicolored 1.40 1.40

170 A42 60t multicolored 1.60 1.60

171 A42 70t multicolored 2.00 2.00

a. Sheet of 6, #167-172 8.00

Nos. 167-171 (5) 6.20 6.20

Souvenir Sheet

172 A42 125t multicolored 3.75 3.75

No. 171a contains stamp from No. 172 without the continuous design. Issued: 2/27/98.

Animated Film Characters — A43

Designs: a, 20t, Two mice talking. b, 30t, Man in bed. c, 40t, Balloons, bear, girl on cloud. d, 50t, Animals dancing, tree. e, 60t, Duck dressed as woman, tree.

1997, July 15 Litho. *Perf. 14*

173 A43 Strip of 5, #a.-e. 9.00 9.00

Georgian Women's Team, Winners of 1996 World Chess Olympiad — A44

No. 174: a, Maia Chiburdanidze, Nona Gaprindashvili, Nana Ioseliani, Nino Gurieli, 1992 winners. b, Chiburdanidze, Ioseliani, Ketevan Arakhamia, Gurieli, 1994 winners. c, Chiburdanidze, Ioseliani, Arakhamia, Gurieli, 1996 winners.

No. 175: a, 20t, Vice-Champion Nana Alexandria, 1975, 1981. b, 40t, Chiburdanidze, 1978, 1981 (Vice-Champion), 1984, 1986, 1991. c, 20t, Ioseliani, 1988, 1993. d, 50t, Gaprindashvili, 1962, 1965, 1969, 1972, 1975 (Vice-Champion).

1997, July 21 Litho. *Imperf.*

174 A44 30t Sheet of 3, #a.-c.+ label 3.25 3.25

175 A44 Sheet of 4, #a.-d. 4.25 4.25

Nos. 174-175 have simulated perforations.

A45

1998 Winter Olympic Games, Nagano — A46

Stylized skier — No. 176: a, 20t. b, 30t. c, 40t. d, 50t.

Early hand-made winter apparel, equipment — No. 177: a, 20t, Snow shoe, hat, gloves. b, 30t, Scarf, snow shoe. c, 40t, Sled, gloves. d, 50t, Scarf, snow shoe.

No. 178, Stylized skier, diff. No. 179, Man's feet with snow shoes.

1998, Feb. 8 Litho. *Perf. 14*

176 A45 Sheet of 4, #a.-d. 4.00 4.00

177 A46 Sheet of 4, #a.-d. 4.00 4.00

Souvenir Sheets

178 A45 70t multicolored 2.75 2.75

179 A46 70t multicolored 2.75 2.75

Moscow '97 — A47

Tiflis local postage stamp of 1857.

1997, Oct. 17 Litho. *Perf. 13x14*

180 A47 80t multicolored 2.00 2.00

Souvenir Sheet

181 A47 1 l multicolored 3.00 3.00

Prince Vakhushti Bagrationi (1696-1758) — A48

40t, Map of Georgia, 1745, portrait. 80t, Portrait.

1997, Oct. 9

182 A48 40t multi 1.00 1.00
183 A48 80t multi, vert. 2.00 2.00

World Delphic Congress — A49

40t, Symbols of education, art & music, 1st World Junior Delphics. 80t, Building on mountaintop, 2nd World Delphic Cong.

1997, Nov. 24 Litho. ***Perf. 14***

184 A49 40t multicolored 1.50 1.50
185 A49 80t multicolored 3.00 3.00

Voyage of Jason and the Argonauts A50

Plate and Vase Paintings: a, 30t, Greek galley from Rhodes, terracotta plate, 700-650BC. b, 40t, Preparation for Battle, vase painting, 460BC. c, 50t, Boreades, Phineus & Harpy, vase painting, 6th cent. d, 60t, Punishment of King Amicus, vase painting, 420-400BC. e, 70t, Argonauts in Colchis, vase painting, 4th cent. BC. f, 80t, The Dragon Vomiting Jason, vase painting, 490-485BC.

1998, June 23 Litho. ***Perf. 13x13½***

186 A50 Sheet of 6, #a.-f. 7.50 7.50

Independence, 80th Anniv. — A51

1998, Dec. 25 Litho. ***Perf. 14***

187 A51 80t multicolored 3.00 3.00

Horses A52

Various breeds.

1998, Dec. 22

188 A52 10t multicolored .65 .65
189 A52 40t multicolored 1.75 1.75
190 A52 70t multicolored 3.00 3.00
191 A52 80t multicolored 3.50 3.50
Nos. 188-191 (4) 8.90 8.90

Souvenir Sheet

Imperf

192 A52 100t multicolored 5.00 5.00

No. 192 has simulated perfs.

Locomotives — A53

Various locomotives built at Tbilisi Locomotives Works.

1998, Dec. 24

193 A53 10t multicolored .40 .40
194 A53 30t multicolored 1.10 1.10
195 A53 40t multicolored 1.40 1.40
196 A53 50t multicolored 1.60 1.60
197 A53 80t multicolored 2.75 2.75
Nos. 193-197 (5) 7.25 7.25

Souvenir Sheet

198 A53 100t multicolored 4.00 4.00

Europa A54

(80t), Berikaoba. (100t), Chiakokonoba.

1998, Dec. 31 Litho. ***Perf. 13x12¾***

199 A54 (80t) multi *1.60 1.60*
200 A54 (100t) multi *2.10 2.10*

Wildlife A55

10t, Vormela peregusna guld. 40t, Hyaena hyaena. 80t, Ursus aegactos syriacus. 100t, Capra aegagrus erxleber.

1999, Feb. Litho. ***Perf. 14x13½***

201 A55 10t multicolored .40 .40
202 A55 40t multicolored 1.25 1.25
203 A55 80t multicolored 2.50 2.50
Nos. 201-203 (3) 4.15 4.15

Souvenir Sheet

Imperf

204 A55 100t multicolored 3.25 3.25

Dated 1998. No. 204 has simulated perfs.

Ancient and Modern Bridges of Tbilisi — A56

Bridges: a, 10t, Michael. b, 40t, Saarbruken. c, 50t, N. Baratashvili. d, 60t, Mukhrani. e, 70t, Avlabari. f, 80t, Metekhi.

1999, Feb. ***Perf. 13½x14***

205 A56 Sheet of 6, #a.-f. 11.00 11.00

Mustela Lutreola, Worldwide Fund for Wildlife A57

(10t), Standing in water. (20t), Feeding. (30t), Two standing. (60t), In burrow.

1999, Apr. 27 Litho. ***Perf. 13x12¾***

206 A57 (10t) multi *1.25 1.25*
207 A57 (20t) multi *1.25 1.25*
208 A57 (30t) multi *1.25 1.25*
209 A57 (60t) multi *1.25 1.25*
b. Strip of 4, #206-209 14.00 14.00

Nos. 206-209 were issued in sheets of 10 of each denomination and as se-tenant blocks of 4 in sheets of 20. The stamps from the se-tenant sheets have thicker lettering in the country and Latin names. Singles from the se-tenant sheets of 20 and from the individual sheetlets of 10 are of equal value.

Europa — A58

(80t), Batsara-Babaneury Reserve. (100t), Lagodekhy Reserve.

1999, Apr. 28 Litho. ***Perf. 12¾x13***

210 A58 (80t) multi *2.50 2.50*
211 A58 (100t) multi *3.00 3.00*

Council of Europe, 50th Anniv. — A59

1999, Nov. Litho. ***Perf. 12¾***

212 A59 50t shown *1.45 1.45*
213 A59 80t Latin letters *2.00 2.00*

Georgian Olympic Committee, 10th Anniv. A60

1999, Nov. ***Perf. 13¾***

214 A60 20t multi .90 .90
215 A60 50t multi 2.00 2.00

Butterflies A61

Designs: 10t, Iphiclides podalirius. 20t, Parnassius apollo. 50t, Colias aurorina herrich-schaffer. 80t, Tomares romanovi.

1999, Nov.

216 A61 10t multi .50 .50
217 A61 20t multi .85 .85
218 A61 50t multi 1.60 1.60
219 A61 80t multi 3.50 3.50
Nos. 216-219 (4) 6.45 6.45

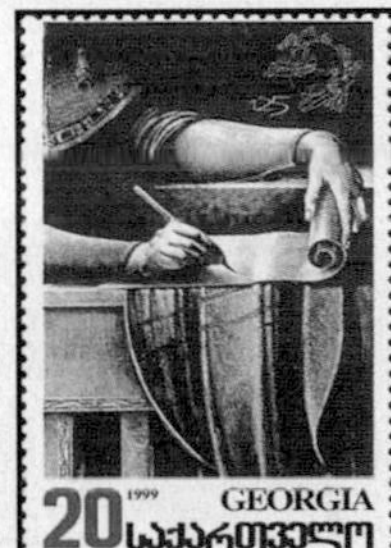

UPU, 125th Anniv. — A62

1999, Nov. ***Perf. 13¼x13½***

220 A62 20t shown .75 .75
221 A62 80t Letter writer 2.75 2.75

Trucks A63

1999, Dec. ***Perf. 13¾***

Color of Truck

222 A63 20t green .75 .75
223 A63 40t red & yellow 1.40 1.40
224 A63 50t blue & white 1.75 1.75
225 A63 80t red & white 3.00 3.00
Nos. 222-225 (4) 6.90 6.90

Souvenir Sheet

226 A63 100t red 4.25 4.25

Souvenir Sheet

Svaneti, World Heritage Site — A64

1999, Dec. ***Perf. 12¾***

227 A64 100t multi 3.00 3.00

Europa, 2000

Common Design Type

Denominations: 80t, 100t.

2000, Mar. 31 Litho. ***Perf. 12¾x13***

228 CD17 multi *4.50 4.50*
229 CD17 multi *4.50 4.50*

Scenes from "The Knight in a Tiger's Skin," by Shota Rustaveli A65

Denominations: 10t, 20t, 30t, 50t, 60t.

2000, May 8 ***Perf. 14¼x13¾***

230-234 A65 Set of 5 5.50 5.50

Souvenir Sheet

235 A65 80t multi + label 4.00 4.00

Nos. 230-235 also issued imperf. Value, set $10.

Christianity, 2000th Anniv. — A66

Icons: 20t, St. Nino the Preacher. 50t, The Savior. 80t, The Virgin Hodigitria.

2000, May 10 ***Perf. 13¾***

236-238 A66 Set of 3 *5.00 5.00*

Souvenir Sheet

Georgian State System, 3000th Anniv. — A67

2000, May 11 ***Perf. 13***
239 A67 100t multi *5.00 5.00*

Fish — A68

Various fish: 10t, 20t, 30t, 50t, 80t.

2000, May 12 ***Perf. 13¾x13¼***
240-244 A68 Set of 5 7.25 7.25

David Saradjishvili (1848-1911), Brandy Maker A69

2000, Sept. 20 Litho. ***Perf. 14¼x14***
245 A69 80t multi 2.00 2.00

2000 Summer Olympics, Sydney — A70

No. 246: a, 20t, Runner at left. b, 50t, Runner at center. c, 80t, Runner at right.

2000 Sept. 20 ***Perf. 13¾***
246 A70 Strip of 3, #a-c 5.00 5.00

Millennium — A71

No. 247: a, 20t, "1999." b, 50t, "2000." c, 80t, "2001."

2000, Sept. 20
247 A71 Strip of 3, #a-c *6.00 6.00*

Joint Georgia-Russia Space Reflector Project — A72

Designs: 20t, Astronauts at work. 80t, Reflector.

2000, Dec. 11 Litho. ***Perf. 13¾***
248-249 A72 Set of 2 4.00 4.00

Human Rights in Europe, 50th Anniv. A73

Denomination colors: 50t, Orange brown. 80t, Blue.

2000, Dec. 12 ***Perf. 14¼x14***
250-251 A73 Set of 2 3.75 3.75

Mushrooms A74

Designs: 10t, Cantharellus cibarius. 20t, Agaricus campestris. 30t, Armillariella mella. 50t, Russula adusta. 80t, Cortinarus violaceus.

2000, Dec. 14 ***Perf. 13¼x13½***
252-256 A74 Set of 5 7.50 7.50

UN High Commissioner for Refugees, 50th Anniv. — A75

2000, Dec. 14 ***Perf. 13½x14***
257 A75 50t multi 1.50 1.50

Houses of Worship Type of 1993

Unidentified buildings. Colors: 10t, Brown. 50t, Blue.

Size: 24x32mm

2000, Dec. 18 ***Perf. 13¼x13***
258-259 A25 Set of 2 2.25 2.25

Writers — A76

Designs: 30t, Alexander Kazbegi (1848-93). 40t, Jakob Gogebashvili (1840-1912). 50t, Vadja Pshavela (1861-1915). 70t, Akaki Tsereteli (1840-1915). 80t, Ilia Chavchavadze (1837-1907).

2000, Dec. 19 ***Perf. 13¼x13¾***
260-264 A76 Set of 5 6.50 6.50

Alexander Kartveli (1896-1977), Aircraft Designer — A77

Designs: 10t, P-47D Thunderbolt. 20t, F-84. 80t, F-105D Thunderchief.

2000, Dec. 20 ***Perf. 13¾x14***
265-267 A77 Set of 3 4.00 4.00

Souvenir Sheet

Perf. 13

268 A77 100t Portrait, vert. 3.50 3.50

Fire Fighting Service, 175th Anniv. — A78

2000, Dec. 24 ***Perf. 13¾x14***
269 A78 50t multi 2.25 2.25

Europa — A79

Designs: 40t, Ritsa Lake. 80t, Borjomi Park.

2001, Sept. 10 Litho. ***Perf. 12½x13***
270-271 A79 Set of 2 *5.75 5.75*
a. Booklet pane, 2 each #270-271, perf. 12½x13 on 3 sides *11.00*
Booklet, #271a *12.00*

Great Silk Route A80

2001, Sept. 20 ***Perf. 13x12½***
272 A80 20t shown .75 .75

Souvenir Sheet

273 A80 80t Like 20t, no emblem 3.00 3.00

Kutaisi Synagogue — A81

2001, Sept. 13 Litho. ***Perf. 13x14***
274 A81 140t multi 4.50 4.50

First Europe-Asia Chess Match — A82

2001, Sept. 18 Litho. ***Perf. 13¾***
275 A82 1 l multi 4.00 4.00

Poets — A83

No. 276: a, Taras Shevchenko (1814-61), Ukrainian poet. b, Akaki Tsereteli (1840-1915), Georgian poet.

2001, Dec. 19 ***Perf. 13***
276 A83 50t Horiz. pair, #a-b 3.25 3.25

See Ukraine No. 445.

Georgian National Ballet — A84

Designs: 30t, Dancers Iliko Sukhishvili (1907-85) and Nino Ramishvili (1910-2000), sketch for dance "Mtiuluri." 50t, Dancers, sketch for dance "Samaya." 80t, Sukhishvili, Ramishvili, and sketch for dance "Jeirani."

2002, Feb. 11 ***Perf. 13¼x13¼***
277-279 A84 Set of 3 5.25 5.25

Port of Poti, 140th Anniv. — A85

No. 280: a, Map, ship (black and white photograph). b, Mobile container crane, containers. c, Ship and tugboat, cargo hauler. d, Cargo hauler, small boat, container crane lifting container (black and white photograph). e, Ship, cargo hauler (black and white photograph). f, Cargo hauler, large ship.

2002, Feb. 11 ***Perf. 13¼x13½***
280 A85 30t Sheet of 6, #a-f 6.00 6.00

A86

Ashot Kurapalatl Opiza — A87

2002, Feb. 11 ***Perf. 13¼x13½***
281 A86 100t blue 2.50 2.50

Perf. 13¼

282 A87 5 l brown 9.50 9.50

Europa — A88

Designs: 40t, Georgian Circus. 80t, Tbilisi Circus.

2002, Mar. 22 ***Perf. 13½x13¼***
283-284 A88 Set of 2 *3.75 3.75*
a. Booklet pane, 2 each #283-284, perf. 13½x13¼ on 3 sides *8.75*
Booklet, #284a *9.75*

Convention on Status of Refugees, 50th Anniv. — A89

2002, May 15 **Litho.** ***Perf. 13¼***
285 A89 50t multi 1.25 1.25

Dinamo Tbilisi, Winner of 1981 European Soccer Cup — A90

2002, Sept. 23 ***Perf. 13¾***
286 A90 20t multi 2.50 2.50

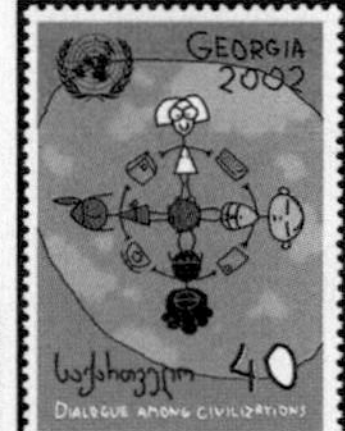

Year of Dialogue Among Civilizations A91

2002, Sept. 23 ***Perf. 13x13¾***
287 A91 40t multi 1.75 1.75

Intl. Federation of Stamp Dealers Associations, 50th Anniv. — A92

2002, Sept. 23 ***Perf. 13¼x13***
288 A92 100t No. 12 3.00 3.00

Fighter Aircraft A93

Designs: 30t, SU-25 Scorpio. 80t, MiG 21U.

2002, Sept. 23 ***Perf. 13¾x13***
289-290 A93 Set of 2 3.25 3.25

Traditional Costumes A94

Men and women in various costumes: 20t, 30t, 50t.

2002, Sept. 23 ***Perf. 13¾***
291-293 A94 Set of 3 4.00 4.00

Church Murals A95

Murals from: 10t, 14th cent., vert. 30t, 16th-17th cent. 80t, 18th cent., vert.

Perf. 13½x13, 13x13½
2002, Sept. 23
294-296 A95 Set of 3 5.25 5.25

Pectoral Crosses A96

Designs: 10t, Crucifixion, 10th cent. 20t, Cross from Martvili, 7th-9th cent. 50t, Cross from Martvili, 10th cent. 80t, Cross of King Tamari, 12th cent.

2002, Sept. 23 ***Perf. 14¼x14***
297-300 A96 Set of 4 6.00 6.00

Flowers — A97

Designs: 20t, Bellflower. 30t, Caucasia rhododendron. 50t, Anemone. 80t, Marsh marigold.

2002, Sept. 23 ***Perf. 13x13¾***
301-304 A97 Set of 4 6.00 6.00

Souvenir Sheet

Alexandre Dumas (Père) (1802-70), French Novelist — A98

2002, Sept. 23 ***Perf. 14x13¾***
305 A98 120t multi 4.25 4.25

Europa — A99

Poster art: 40t, Three men and donkey. 80t, Four people.

2003, Mar. 10 ***Perf. 13½x13¼***
306-307 A99 Set of 2 *4.00 4.00*
307a Booklet pane, 2 each #306-307, perf. 13½x13¼ on 3 sides 8.75 —
Complete booklet, #307a 9.75

Souvenir Sheet

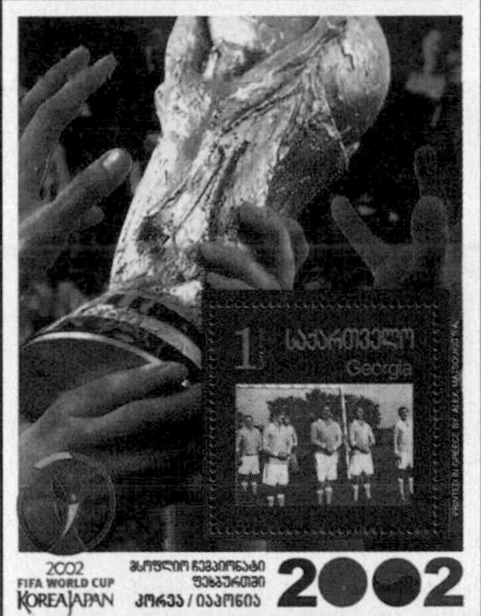

2002 World Cup Soccer Championships, Japan and Korea — A100

2003, Apr. 25 ***Perf. 13¾***
308 A100 1 l multi 3.25 3.25

Souvenir Sheet

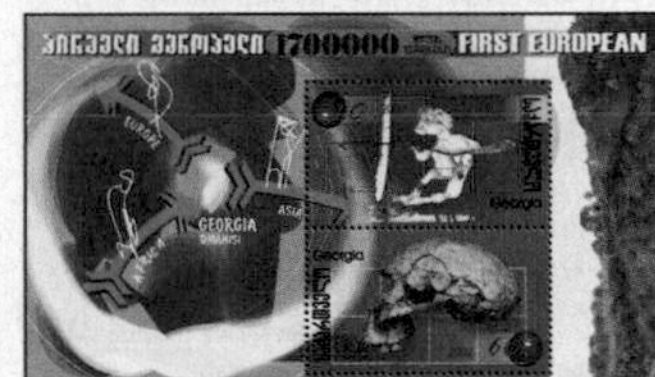

Paleontology — A101

No. 309: a, Stylized drawing of ancient European man. b, Skull.

2003, Apr. 25 ***Perf. 12¾***
309 A101 60t Sheet of 2, #a-b 5.00 5.00

Margin of No. 309 has "1700000 YEARS OLD" overprinted in red brown on silver oval that is an overprint over an inscription that reads "17000000 YEARS OLD". Examples exist without the red brown overprint.

Youth — A102

2003, June 20 **Litho.** ***Perf. 14x14¼***
310 A102 50t multi 1.50 1.50

Women for Peace A103

2003, June 20 ***Perf. 13¾x13***
311 A103 50t multi 1.50 1.50

Zoo Animals — A104

Animals at Tbilisi Zoo: 20t, Elephant. 30t, Wolf. 40t, Ostrich. 50t, Bear.

2003, Aug. 25 ***Perf. 14x13¾***
312-315 A104 Set of 4 4.75 4.75
315a Miniature sheet, 2 each #312-315 12.00 12.00

No. 315a was sold in a booklet cover but unattached, and is comprised of two tete-beche blocks of Nos. 312-315.

Minerals — A105

Minerals: 10t, Rock crystal. 20t, Agate with amethyst. 30t, Orpiment rose. 50t, Realgar with orpiment.

2003, Aug. 25 ***Perf. 13¼x13***
316-319 A105 Set of 4 3.75 3.75
319a Miniature sheet, 2 each #316-319 9.00 9.00

No. 319a was sold in a booklet cover but unattached, and is composed of two tete-beche blocks of Nos. 316-319.

Fruit — A106

Designs: 10t, Prunus spinosa. 20t, Laurocerasus officinalis. 30t, Cydonia oblonga. 50t, Punica granatum. 80t, Pyrus caucasica.

2003, Aug. 25 ***Perf. 14x13¾***
320-324 A106 Set of 5 6.00 6.00

Souvenir Sheet

Old Tbilisi, by Elene Akhvlediani (1901-75) — A107

2003, Aug. 25
325 A107 80t multi 3.00 3.00

Souvenir Sheet

Self-portrait, by Vincent van Gogh (1853-90) — A108

2003, Aug. 25 ***Perf. 13x12¾***
326 A108 100t multi 4.00 4.00

Nos. 73, 75a Overprinted

2003, Oct. 6 Litho. ***Perf. 13¼***
327 A20 25t green & multi .85 .85

Souvenir Sheet

328 Sheet, #327, 328a, 328b 6.00 6.00
a. A20 50t brown & multi 1.60 1.60
b. A20 100t violet & multi 3.50 3.50

First postage stamps, 10th anniv.

Intl. Association of Academies of Science, 10th Anniv. — A109

2003, Nov. 28 ***Perf. 13¾x13¼***
329 A109 30t multi 1.10 1.10

East-West Energy Corridor — A110

2003, Nov. 28 ***Perf. 13¼x13¾***
330 A110 80t multi 2.50 2.50

Tourism — A111

Designs: 10t, Skiers, Bakuriani. 20t, Caves, Vardzia. 30t, Harbor, Batum. 50t, Lake Ritsa.

2003, Nov. 28 ***Perf. 13¾x13¼***
331-334 A111 Set of 4 3.50 3.50
334a Booklet pane, 2 each #331-334 7.00 —
Complete booket, #334a 7.50

No. 334a is composed of two tete-beche blocks of Nos. 331-334.

Grapes A112

Designs: 10t, Aladasturi. 20t, Rkhatsiteli. 30t, Ojaleshi. 50t, Goruli Mtsvane. 80t, Aleksandrouli (Khvanchkhara).

2003, Nov. 28
335-339 A112 Set of 5 7.00 7.00

Europa A113

Designs: 40t, Merry Christmas. 80t, Happy Easter.

2004, Jan. 28 Litho. ***Perf. 13¼x13½***
340-341 A113 Set of 2 *5.00 5.00*
341a Booklet pane, 4 each #340-341, perf. 13¼x13½ on 2 or 3 sides *17.50* —
Complete booklet, #341a *20.00*

A114

Design: Georgi Tsereteli (1904-73), Director of Institute of Oriental Studies.

2004, Nov. 5 Litho. ***Perf. 13¼x13¾***
342 A114 30t multi 1.10 1.10

Souvenir Sheet

Rose Revolution, 1st Anniv. — A115

No. 343: a, Crowd with flags. b, Protestors with flag sprayed with water.

2004, Nov. 5 ***Perf. 13¼x13***
343 A115 50t Sheet of 2, #a-b 3.75 3.75

FIFA (Fédération Internationale de Football Association), Cent. — A116

Caricatures of soccer players: 20t, Boris Paichadze. 30t, Avtandil Gogoberidze. 50t, Mikheil Meskhi. 80t, David Kipiani.

2004, Nov. 5 ***Perf. 13¾x13¼***
344-347 A116 Set of 4 5.00 5.00

2004 Summer Olympics, Athens — A117

Sculptures of athletes by: 20t, B. Skhulukhia. 30t, V. Cherkezishvili. 50t, N. Jikia. 80t, L. Vardosanidze.

2004, Nov. 5 ***Perf. 13¼x13¾***
348-351 A117 Set of 4 5.50 5.50

Ancient Jewelry — A118

Designs: 20t, Belt and buckle, 3rd-4th cent. 30t, Necklace and belt buckle, 3rd-4th cent. 40t, Necklace and pins, 2000-1500 B.C. 80t, Necklace, 5th cent. B.C., double-voluted pins, 3rd millennium B.C.

2004, Nov. 5
352-355 A118 Set of 4 5.00 5.00

UNESCO World Heritage Sites A119

Designs: 20t, Ushguli. 30t, Bagrati. 50t, Gelati. 60t, Samtavro. 70t, Svetitskhoveli. 80t, Jvari.

2004, Nov. 5 Litho. ***Perf. 14x13¼***
356-361 A119 Set of 6 *9.50 9.50*

Flag of Georgia A120

2005, Feb. 11 Litho. ***Perf. 14x13¼***
362 A120 50t multi 1.75 1.75

Europa — A121

Loaves of bread and: 20t, Girl. 80t, Bakers.

2005, May 27 ***Perf. 14x13¾***
363 A121 20t multi *.80 .80*
364 A121 80t multi *4.25 4.25*

Booklet Stamps

Size: 29x41mm

Perf. 13¾ on 2, 3 or 4 Sides

365 A121 20t multi *1.00 1.00*
366 A121 80t multi *4.25 4.25*
a. Booklet pane, 2 each #365-366 *10.50* —
b. Booklet pane, 3 each #365-366 *16.00* —
Complete booklet, #366a, 366b *27.50*

For overprints see Nos. 402-403.

Rabbi Abraam Khvoles — A122

2005, June 1 ***Perf. 12***
367 A122 1 l multi 3.00 3.00

2008 Summer Olympics, Beijing A123

2005, Dec. 28 Litho. ***Perf. 12***
368 A123 80t multi 2.40 2.40

2006 World Cup Soccer Championships, Germany — A124

2005, Dec. 28
369 A124 100t multi 3.00 3.00

Georgian Ballet — A125

Designs: 40t, V. Tsiguadze. 50t, V. Chabukiani.

2005, Dec. 28
370-371 A125 Set of 2 3.00 3.00

Orchids — A126

Designs: 20t, Dactylorhiza euxina. 40t, Dactylorhiza iberica. 50t, Oprys caucasica. 80t, Orchis caucasica.

2005, Dec. 28
372-375 A126 Set of 4 6.00 6.00

Theaters — A127

Designs: No. 376, 30t, Georgian Drama Theater, Batumi. No. 377, 30t, Georgian Drama Theater, Kutaisi. No. 378, 30t, Abkhazian Drama Theater, Sukhumi. No. 379, 30t, Georgian Academic Theater, Tbilisi. No. 380, 30t, Georgian Drama Theater, Tbilisi. No.

381, 30t, Georgian Opera and Ballet Theater, Tbilisi. No. 382, 30t, Armenian Drama Theater, Tbilisi. No. 383, 30t, Ossetian Drama Theater, Tskhinvali.

2005, Dec. 28
376-383 A127 Set of 8 7.50 7.50

2006 Winter Olympics, Turin A128

Designs: 10t, Speed skating. 20t, Biathlon. 30t, Ski jumping. 40t, Figure skating. 80t, Downhill skiing.

2005, Dec. 29
384-388 A128 Set of 5 5.00 5.00

Souvenir Sheet

Tbilisi Funicular, Cent. — A129

2005, Dec. 30
389 A129 100t multi 3.00 3.00

Europa Stamps, 50th Anniv. A130

Designs: 10t, Various Georgian Europa stamps. 20t, Person inserting postcard in mail slot. 30t, France #805, Germany #748, magnifying glass, newspaper. 40t, Earth in ripped newspaper wrapper.

No. 394, 80t, Like 10t. No. 395, 80t, Like 20t. No. 396, 80t, Like 30t. No. 397, 80t, Like 40t.

2006, Jan. 30 ***Perf. 12¾x13***
390-393 A130 Set of 4 *3.75 3.75*

Souvenir Sheets
394-397 A130 Set of 4 *12.50 12.50*

Europa — A131

Stars and: 20t, People holding flags. 80t, Earth, Georgian flag.

Perf. 13½x13¼
2006, June 30 **Litho.**
398-399 A131 Set of 2 *4.50 4.50*
399a Booklet pane, 4 each #398-399, perf. 13½x13¼ on 3 sides *22.00* —
Complete booklet, #399a *23.00*

No. 399a contains two tete-beche pairs of Nos. 398-399.

Nos. 365-366 Overprinted

Perf. 13¾ on 2, 3 or 4 Sides
2006, Oct. 23 **Litho.**
402 A121 20t multi *.90 .90*
403 A121 80t multi *3.75 3.75*
a. Sheet of 4, 2 each #402-403 *9.50 9.50*
b. Sheet of 6, 3 each #402-403 *14.50 14.50*

Europa stamps, 50th anniv. Nos. 403a and 403b are Nos. 366a and 366b removed from the booklet and overprinted on the stamps and margin.

No. 79 Surcharged in Gray and Silver

Method and Perf. As Before
2006, Nov. 2
404 A24 10t on 1c #79 .40 .40

A132

Design: Nikola Tesla (1856-1943), Electrical Engineer, and Wireless Transmission Tower.

2006, Nov. 15 Litho. ***Perf. 12x12¼***
405 A132 50t multi 1.50 1.50

Souvenir Sheet

Georgian Wild West Show Horsemen — A133

2007, Jan. 25 Litho. ***Perf. 12¼***
406 A133 100t multi 3.50 3.50

Tbilisi State University, Cent. A134

2007, Jan. 25 Litho. ***Perf. 12¼x12***
407 A134 40t multi 1.10 1.10

Prince David Guramishvili (1705-92), Poet A135

2007, July 11 ***Perf. 13¾x13¼***
408 A135 50t multi 1.40 1.40

2006 Chess Olympics, Turin A136

2007, July 11
409 A136 200t multi 5.50 5.50

Famous Men A137

Designs: No. 410, Rembrandt (1606-69), painter. No. 411, Wolfgang Amadeus Mozart (1756-91), composer.

2007, July 11 ***Perf. 13¾x13¼***
410 A137 100t multi 2.75 2.75

Perf. 13¾x14
Size: 39x27mm
411 A137 100t multi 2.75 2.75

Worldwide Fund for Nature (WWF) — A138

Aquila clanga: 30t, In flight. 40t, On branch. 50t, With prey. 60t, Head.

2007, July 11 ***Perf. 13¼x13¾***
412-415 A138 Set of 4 5.50 5.50

Eagles — A139

Designs: 10t, Aquila rapax. 30t, Haliaeetus albicilla. 50t, Circaetus gallicus. 70t, Aquila chryaetus.

2007, July 11
416-419 A139 Set of 4 4.50 4.50

Georgian Military A140

Designs: 20t, Tanks. 30t, Soldiers. 40t, Ship. 50t, Helicopters.

2007, July 11 ***Perf. 14¼x14***
420-423 A140 Set of 4 3.75 3.75

Ancient Ships A141

Various ships: 20t, 30t, 50t, 70t.

2007, July 11
424-427 A141 Set of 4 4.75 4.75

Souvenir Sheets

Guns from National Museum — A142

Sculpture from National Museum — A143

No. 428 — Various guns with background color of: a, Yellow. b, Buff. c, Light blue. d, Light green.

2007, July 11 ***Perf. 13x13¼***
428 A142 50t Sheet of 4, #a-d 5.00 5.00
429 A143 100t multi 2.75 2.75

Souvenir Sheet

Magician, Cards and Dove — A144

Perf. 13¼x13¾
2008, Mar. 14 **Litho.**
430 A144 1 l multi 3.50 3.50

Europa — A145

Designs: 90t, Scouts in boat and near tent. 1 l, Scouts around campfire.

2008, Mar. 14 ***Perf. 14x13¾***
431-432 A145 Set of 2 *6.00 6.00*
432a Booklet pane, 4 each #431-432 *24.00* —
Complete booklet, #432a *24.00*

Scouting, cent. (in 2007). No. 432a contains two tete-beche pairs of Nos. 431-432.

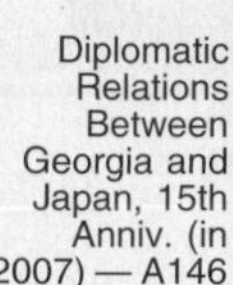

Diplomatic Relations Between Georgia and Japan, 15th Anniv. (in 2007) — A146

2008, Mar. 14 Litho. *Perf. 13¾*
433 A146 1 l multi 3.50 3.50

Dated 2007.

Mountains A147

Designs: 20t, Mt. Ushba. 30t, Mt. Ushba, diff. 50t, Mt. Kazbeg. 70t, Mt. Shkhara.

2008 Litho. *Perf. 13¼x13¾*
434-437 A147 Set of 4 6.25 6.25

Issued: 30t, 6/1; others, 3/14. Bottom panel with mountain name on No. 435 was overprinted in silver and black to correct inscription. No. 435 was not issued without overprint.

King David IV (1073-1125) A148

2008, Dec. 5 Litho. *Perf. 13¾x14¼*
438 A148 50t multi 1.75 1.75

Europa A149

Dove and: 90t, Georgia #398, cover with Georgia #213. 1 l, Letter, pencil, eyeglasses, Georgia #399.

2008, Dec. 5 *Perf. 13¾x14*
439-440 A149 Set of 2 *7.00 7.00*
440a Booklet pane of 8, 4 each #439-440, perf. 13¾x13¼ on 3 sides *28.00*

No. 440a was sold with but not attached to a booklet cover.

2008 Summer Olympics, Beijing A150

Designs: 10t, Shooting. 30t, Wrestling. 60t, Weight lifting. 80t, Judo.

2008, Dec. 5 *Perf. 14¼x14*
441-444 A150 Set of 4 6.75 6.75

Prince Sulkhan-Saba Orbeliani (1658-1725), Monk — A151

2009, Mar. 20 *Perf. 13¼*
445 A151 60t multi 1.75 1.75

Kakutsa Cholokhashvili (1888-1930), Military Leader — A152

2009, Mar. 20
446 A152 80t multi 2.10 2.10

Port of Poti, 150th Anniv. A153

2009, Mar. 20
447 A153 1 l multi 2.75 2.75

Grape Varieties A154

Designs: 10t, Chkhaveri. 20t, Aleksandrouli. 30t, Rkatsiteli. 40t, Ojaleshi. 50t, Tsolikouri. 70t, Tavkveri. 90t, Saperavi.

2009, Mar. 20
448-454 A154 Set of 7 7.25 7.25

Souvenir Sheet

Anti-war Movement in Georgia — A155

No. 455: a, 30t, Flowers. b, 50t, Hands, Georgian flags. c, 70t, Demonstrators.

2009, Mar. 20
455 A155 Sheet of 3, #a-c 4.50 4.50

European Court of Human Rights, 50th Anniv. A156

Council of Europe, 60th Anniv. A157

2009, Aug. 10 Litho. *Perf. 13¼*
456 A156 1 l multi 2.50 2.50
457 A157 2 l multi 5.00 5.00

No. 79 Surcharged in Gold and Black

Method and Perf. As Before

2010, Sept. 9
458 A24 1 l on 1c #79 2.50 2.50

Georgian National Rugby Team, 2009 European Champions A158

2010, Oct. 15 Litho. *Perf. 13¼*
459 A158 5 l multi *9.00 9.00*

Nodar Kumaritashvili (1988-2010), Luger Killed in Winter Olympics Practice Accident — A159

2010, Oct. 15 *Perf. 13¼x13½*
460 A159 5 l multi *9.00 9.00*

Georgian Women's Chess Team, Four-time Chess Olympics Champion — A160

2010, Oct. 15 *Perf. 13¼*
461 A160 7 l multi *12.00 12.00*

Flowers — A161

2010, Oct. 15 *Perf. 14x14¼*

462	A161	1 l	Iris	*1.50*	*1.50*
463	A161	1.20 l	Lilium	*1.75*	*1.75*
464	A161	2 l	Viola	*3.00*	*3.00*
465	A161	3 l	Colchicum	*4.50*	*4.50*
	Nos. 462-465 (4)			*10.75*	*10.75*

Birds A162

Designs: 20t, Grus grus. 40t, Perdix perdix. 50t, Tetraogallus caspius. 60t, Lyrurus mlokosiewiczi. 1 l, Tetrax tetrax.

2010, Oct. 15 *Perf. 13¼*
466-470 A162 Set of 5 *6.00 6.00*

Latin names on 40t, 60t and 1 l are misspelled.

Souvenir Sheet

David Gareji Monastery Complex — A163

No. 471: a, Monastery complex. b, Frescoes on walls.

2010, Oct. 15 Litho.
471 A163 60t Sheet of 2, #a-b *2.75 2.75*

Souvenir Sheet

Georgian Alphabet — A164

No. 472 — Columns of letters and: a, Numerals 1-40. b, Numerals 50-700. c, Numerals 800-10,000.

2010, Oct. 15 *Perf. 13¼*
472 A164 40t Sheet of 3, #a-c *2.75 2.75*

Europa — A165

Planets and: 2 l, Orbital diagram. 3 l, Pectoral of priestess depicting Sun.

2010, Oct. 15 *Perf. 13½x13¼*
473-474 A165 Set of 2 10.00 10.00
474a Souvenir sheet of 2, #473-474 10.00 10.00
474b Booklet pane of 8, 4 each #473-474 40.00 —

Intl. Year of Astronomy. No. 474b was sold with, but unattached to, a booklet cover.

Flowers — A166

2012, Apr. 11 ***Perf. 13¼***

475 A166 10t Daisy .25 .25
476 A166 25t Carnation .60 .60
477 A166 50t Rose 1.25 1.25
478 A166 1 l Lilac 2.40 2.40
Nos. 475-478 (4) 4.50 4.50

Dated 2011.

Souvenir Sheet

Georgian Illuminated Manuscripts — A167

No. 479 — Various manuscripts: a, 1 l. b, 1.50 l. c, 2.50 l.

2012, Apr. 11

479 A167 Sheet of 3, #a-c 12.50 12.50

Dated 2011.

Past Olympic Champions of Georgia — A168

Georgian flag, Olympic rings, list of winners and: 1.50 l, Parthenon, Athens. 2.50 l, Temple of Heaven, Beijing.

2012, Apr. 11 ***Perf. 12¾x13¼***

480-481 A168 Set of 2 10.00 10.00

A169

2012, Apr. 11 ***Perf. 13¼***

482 A169 4 l multi 10.00 10.00

United Nations High Commissioner for Refugees, 60th anniv. (in 2011).

Europa — A170

Designs: 3 l, Gergeti Glacier.

No. 484: a, 10t, Kolkheti Reserve. b, 10t, Tetnulkdi. c, 20t, Bakuriani Ski Resort. d, 20t, Alazani Valley. e, 30t, Imereti Caves. f, 30t, Gudauri Ski Resort. g, 40t, Borjomi-Kharagauli Reserve. h, 40t, Tusheti. i, 50t, Black Sea Coast. j, 50t, Keli Lake. k, 70t, Mountains in Adjara.

2013, Apr. 15

483 A170 3 l multi 6.50 6.50

Miniature Sheet

484 A170 Sheet of 12, #483, 484a-484k, + central label 14.50 14.50

Niko Pirosmani (1862-1918), Painter — A171

2013, Apr. 15 ***Perf. 13¼x13***

485 A171 1.80 l multi 4.00 4.00

Miniature Sheet

Cultural Heritage — A172

No. 486: a, 1 l, Gold bracelets, 5th-4th cent. B.C. b, 2 l, Gold bowl, 2nd-1st cent, B.C. c, 3 l, Gold lion figurine, 4th-3rd cent. B.C. d, 4 l, Gold earrings, 5th-4th cent. B.C.

2013, Apr. 15 ***Perf. 14½***

486 A172 Sheet of 4, #a-d 21.50 21.50

Souvenir Sheet

Baku-Tbilisi-Kars Railway — A173

2013, Apr. 15 ***Perf. 12½***

487 A173 3 l multi 6.50 6.50

First Rules of Soccer, 150th Anniv. A174

2014, Dec. 22 **Litho.** ***Perf. 13x13¼***

488 A174 1 l multi 2.25 2.25

Dated 2013.

Smiling Children A175

2014, Dec. 22 **Litho.** ***Perf. 13x13¼***

489 A175 1 l multi 2.25 2.25

Dated 2013.

Smiling Man — A176

2014, Dec. 22 **Litho.** ***Perf. 14¼***

490 A176 1 l multi 2.25 2.25

Dated 2013.

Diplomatic Relations With Latvia, 20th Anniv. — A177

2014, Dec. 22 **Litho.** ***Perf. 13¾***

491 A177 2 l multi 4.25 4.25

See Latvia No. 871.

Swallows and Flowers — A178

2014, Dec. 22 **Litho.** ***Perf. 13¼***

492 A178 3 l multi 6.25 6.25

Dated 2013.

Europa — A179

Designs: No. 493, 1.50 l, No. 495a, 2 l, Horse-drawn postal wagon. No. 494, 1.50 l, No. 495b, 2 l, Postal automobile.

2014, Dec. 22 **Litho.** ***Perf. 13¼x13***

493-494 A179 Set of 2 6.50 6.50

Souvenir Sheet

495 A179 2 l Sheet of 2, #a-b 8.75 8.75

Dated 2013.

Miniature Sheet

Love — A180

No. 496 — Wall with graffiti, flowers, butterfly and/or bird and country name in: a, Green. b, Purple. c, Red. d, Blue.

2014, Dec. 22 **Litho.** ***Perf. 13¾x14***

496 A180 2 l Sheet of 4, #a-d 16.50 16.50

Dated 2013.

Miniature Sheet

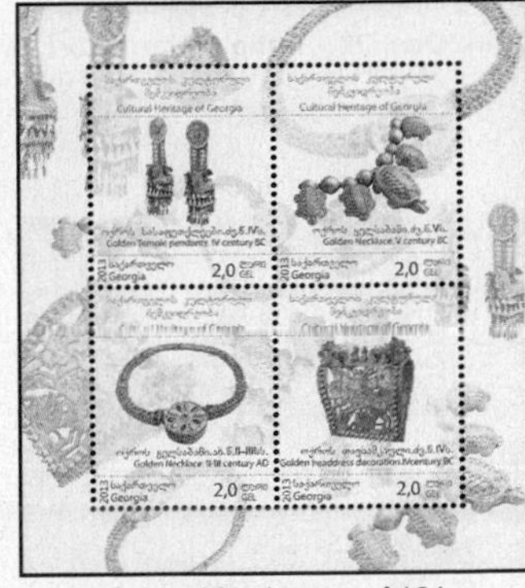

Cultural Heritage — A181

No. 497: a, Golden temple pendants, 4th cent., B. C. b, Golden necklace, 5th cent., B. C. c, Golden necklace, 2nd-3rd cent. B. C. d, Golden headdress decoration, 4th cent. B. C.

2014, Dec. 22 **Litho.** ***Perf. 13¾***

497 A181 2 l Sheet of 4, #a-d 16.50 16.50

Dated 2013.

Miniature Sheet

Four Seasons — A182

No. 498 — Tree in: a, Winter. b, Spring. c, Summer. d, Autumn.

2014, Dec. 22 **Litho.** ***Perf. 14¼***

498 A182 2 l Sheet of 4, #a-d 16.50 16.50

Dated 2013.

Miniature Sheet

Views of Old Tbilisi — A183

No. 499: a, Statue and church on hilltop. b, Tower. c, Aerial view of buildings. d, Street scene.

2014, Dec. 22 **Litho.** ***Perf. 13¾***

499 A183 5 l Sheet of 4, #a-d 41.00 41.00

Dated 2013.

Miniature Sheet

Georgian Kings — A184

No. 500: a, Pharnavaz (ruled 304-239 B. C.). b, Mirian (ruled 332-306 B. C.). c, Tamar (ruled 1184-1213). d, Vakhtang I Gorgasali (ruled 449-94). e, Aghmashenebeli (ruled

1089-1125). f, Giorgi (ruled 1314-46). g, Bagrat (ruled 975-1014).

2014, Dec. 22 Litho. ***Perf. 13x13¼***
500 A184 1 l Sheet of 7, #a-g 14.50 14.50

Dated 2013.

Souvenir Sheet

Carrier Pigeon — A185

Perf. 13¼x13½
2014, Dec. 22 Litho.
501 A185 3 l multi 6.25 6.25

Dated 2013.

Souvenir Sheet

Tbilisi Tram — A186

Perf. 13½x13¼
2014, Dec. 22 Litho.
502 A186 3 l multi 6.25 6.25

Dated 2013.

Souvenir Sheet

Tbilisi Doorway — A187

2014, Dec. 22 Litho. ***Perf. 13¾***
503 A187 3 l multi 6.25 6.25

Dated 2013.

Souvenir Sheet

Time — A188

Perf. 13¼x13½
2014, Dec. 22 Litho.
504 A188 3 l multi 6.25 6.25

Dated 2013.

Souvenir Sheet

Ekvtime Takaishvili (1863-1953), Historian — A189

2014, Dec. 22 Litho. ***Perf. 13x13¼***
505 A189 7 l multi 14.50 14.50

Dated 2013.

Souvenir Sheet

Giorgi Eristavi (1813-64), Playwright — A190

2014, Dec. 22 Litho. ***Perf. 13¾***
506 A190 7 l multi 14.50 14.50

Dated 2013.

National Musical Instruments A191

2015, Feb. 10 Litho. ***Perf. 13x13¼***
Stamp With White Frame
507 A191 1.50 l multi 3.50 3.50

Souvenir Sheet
Stamp With Tan Frame
508 A191 1.50 l multi 3.50 3.50

Europa. Dated 2014.

International Telecommunication Union, 150th Anniv. — A192

2015, July 22 Litho. ***Perf. 13x13¼***
509 A192 1.50 l bright blue 2.50 2.50

European Youth Olympics Festival, Tbilisi — A193

Designs: No. 510, 2 l, Mascot. No. 511, 2 l, Emblem.

2015, July 22 Litho. ***Perf. 13¼x13***
510-511 A193 Set of 2 6.75 6.75
511a Souvenir sheet of 2, #510-511 6.75 6.75

Europa — A194

Old toys: No. 512, 2 l, Wooden horse on wheels. No. 513, 2 l, Doll.

2015, July 22 Litho. ***Perf. 13¼x13***
512-513 A194 Set of 2 6.75 6.75
513a Souvenir sheet of 2, #512-513 6.75 6.75

Souvenir Sheet

Boris Paichadze (1915-90), Soccer Player — A195

2015, July 22 Litho. ***Perf. 13x13¼***
514 A195 1.50 l multi 2.50 2.50

Souvenir Sheet

Poets — A196

No. 515: a, Vazha-Pshavela (1861-1915). b, Akaki Tsereteli (1840-1915).

2015, July 22 Litho. ***Perf. 13x13¼***
515 A196 2 l Sheet of 2, #a-b 6.75 6.75

Independence, 25th Anniv. — A197

Litho. With Foil Application
2016, Oct. 24 ***Perf. 13x13¼***
516 A197 2.90 l multi 3.25 3.25

Europa A198

2016, Oct. 24 Litho. ***Perf. 13x13¼***
517 A198 2.90 l multi 3.25 3.25

Think Green Issue.

A199

Fairy Tale Characters A200

Serpentine Die Cut 13x12¼
2016, Oct. 24 Litho.
Self-Adhesive
518 A199 30t multi .55 .55

Serpentine Die Cut 12¼x13
519 A200 40t multi .70 .70

Souvenir Sheet

Georgian Connections With the European Union — A201

2016, Oct. 24 Litho. ***Perf. 13¼x13***
520 A201 2 l multi 2.25 2.25

2016 Summer Olympics, Rio de Janeiro A202

2016, Oct. 24 Litho. ***Perf. 13¼x13***
521 A202 2 l multi 3.25 3.25

Fauna A203

Designs: 10t, Panurus biarmicus. 15t, Phoenicurus erythrogastrus. 20t, Panthera pardus.

Serpentine Die Cut 12½
2016, Oct. 24 Litho.
Self-Adhesive
522-524 A203 Set of 3 .85 .85

Staphylea Colchica — A204

2016, Dec. 15 Litho. *Perf. 13¼x13*
525 A204 35t multi .85 .85

Souvenir Sheet

Ivane Javakhishvili (1876-1940), Historian — A205

2016, Dec. 15 Litho. *Perf. 13x13¼*
526 A205 2.50 l multi 3.75 3.75

Souvenir Sheet

Georgian Architecture and Art — A206

No. 527: a, 2 l, Alaverdi Cathedral. b, 3 l, Religious painting from Alaverdi Cathedral.

2016, Dec. 15 Litho. *Perf. 13¼*
527 A206 Sheet of 2, #a-b 7.00 7.00

Souvenir Sheet

Mountain Resorts — A207

No. 528: a, Mestia. b, Bakuriani. c, Gudauri.

Perf. 13¼x13¾
2016, Dec. 15 Litho.
528 A207 1.25 l Sheet of 3, #a-c 5.50 5.50

Europa — A208

Designs: No. 529, 2.50 l, Narikala Fortress. No. 530, 2.50 l, Rabati Castle.

2017, Oct. 5 Litho. *Perf. 13¼x13*
529-530 A208 Set of 2 8.50 8.50
530a Souvenir sheet of 2, #529-530 8.50 8.50

Democratic Republic of Georgia, Cent. — A209

No. 531: a, Georgian people on Independence Day, 1918. b, Coat of arms of Democratic Republic of Georgia.

No. 532, 3.50 l, Flag of Democratic Republic of Georgia. No. 533, 3.50 l. Democratic Republic of Georgia soldiers.

2018, May 31 Litho. *Perf. 14*
531 A209 2.50 l Sheet of 2, #a-b 8.75 8.75

Souvenir Sheets

532-533 A209 Set of 2 12.50 12.50

Prince Vakhushti Batonishvili (1696-1757), Geographer and Historian — A210

2018, June 14 Litho. *Perf. 13x13¼*
534 A210 80t multi 1.50 1.50

43rd World Chess Olympiad, Batumi A211

2018, June 14 Litho. *Perf. 13*
535 A211 80t multi 1.60 1.60

Prince Ilia Chavchavadze (1837-1907), Writer — A212

2018, June 14 Litho. *Perf. 14*
536 A212 1 l multi 1.75 1.75

Nato Vachnadze (1904-53), Actress A213

2018, June 14 Litho. *Perf. 13x13¼*
537 A213 1 l multi 1.75 1.75

Nodar Dumbadze (1928-84), Writer A214

2018, June 14 Litho. *Perf. 13x13¼*
538 A214 1 l multi 1.75 1.75

Zakaria Paliashvili (1871-1933), Composer — A215

2018, June 14 Litho. *Perf. 13x13¼*
539 A215 1 l multi 1.75 1.75

Noe Zhordania (1868-1953), Journalist and Politician — A216

2018, June 14 Litho. *Perf. 13¼x13*
540 A216 1 l multi 1.75 1.75

Diplomatic Relations Between Georgia and Brazil, 25th Anniv. A217

2018, June 14 Litho. *Perf. 13¼*
541 A217 1.50 l multi 2.75 2.75

2018 Winter Olympics, Pyeongchang, South Korea — A218

2018, June 14 Litho. *Perf. 13¼x13*
542 A218 2 l multi 3.50 3.50

2018 Summer Youth Olympics, Buenos Aires — A219

2018, June 14 Litho. *Perf. 14½*
543 A219 2 l multi 3.50 3.50

Europa A220

Designs: No. 544, 2.90 l, Besleti Bridge. No. 545, 2.90 l, Freedom Bridge.

2018, June 14 Litho. *Perf. 13x13¼*
544-545 A220 Set of 2 10.50 10.50

Souvenir Sheets

National Heroes — A221

Designs: No. 546, 2.50 l, Gen. Giorgi Mazniashvili (1870-1937). No. 547, 2.50 l, Merab Kostava (1939-89), musician and poet.

2018, June 14 Litho. *Perf. 13¼x13*
546-547 A221 Set of 2 9.00 9.00

Souvenir Sheet

Prince Nikoloz Baratashvili (1817-45), Poet — A222

2018, June 14 Litho. *Perf. 14¼*
548 A222 1.50 l multi 2.75 2.75

Souvenir Sheet

Diplomatic Relations Between Georgia and Various Countries, 25th Anniv. — A223

2018, June 14 Litho. ***Perf. 13¾***
549 A223 3 l multi 5.50 5.50

Souvenir Sheet

Self-Portrait, by David Kakabadze (1889-1952) — A224

2018, June 14 Litho. ***Perf. 13¼x13***
550 A224 3 l multi 5.50 5.50

Miniature Sheet

Endangered Animals in Red Book of Georgia — A225

No. 551: a, Lynx lynx. b, Sciurus anomalus. c, Cervus elaphus. d, Ursus arctos linnaeus.

2018, July 6 Litho. ***Perf. 13½***
551 A225 50t Sheet of 4, #a-d 3.50 3.50

Petre Otskheli (1907-37), Theater Set and Costume Designer — A226

No. 552 — Costumes from: a, 10t, Beatrice Cenci. b, 20t, Othello. c, 30t, Flying Decorator (man with brush). d, 40t, Flying Decorator (aviator). e, 50t, Surami Fortress.
1.50 l, Otskheli portrait.

2018, July 6 Litho. ***Perf. 14x13¾***
552 A226 Sheet of 5, #a-e, + label 2.75 2.75

Souvenir Sheet

553 A226 1.50 l multi 2.75 2.75

SEMI-POSTAL STAMPS

Surcharge in Red or Black

SP1

SP2

SP3

SP4

1922 Unwmk. ***Perf. 11½***
B1 SP1 1000r on 50r vio (R) .75 *3.00*
B2 SP2 3000r on 100r brn red .75 *3.00*
B3 SP3 5000r on 250r gray grn .75 *3.00*
B4 SP4 10,000r on 25r blue (R) .75 *3.00*
Nos. B1-B4 (4) 3.00 *12.00*

Nos. B1-B4 exist imperf but were not so issued. Value slightly more than perforated examples.

Georgian Natl. Olympic Committee SP10

1994, May 27 Litho. ***Perf. 13½***
B10 SP10 100c +50c multi 1.10 1.10

UNICEF, 50th Anniv. SP11

Children's paintings: 20t+5t, People on ladder above rainbow, vert. 30t+10t, Animal character.

Perf. 13x14, 14x13
1996, Dec. 20 Litho.
B11 SP11 20t +5t multi 1.40 1.40
B12 SP11 30t +10t multi 1.90 1.90

In Remembrance of Sept. 11, 2001 Terrorist Attacks — SP12

2001, Dec. 31 Litho. ***Perf. 13x13¼***
B13 SP12 30t +10t multi 1.60 1.60

Souvenir Sheet

B14 SP12 120t +10t multi 5.50 5.50

GERMAN EAST AFRICA

'jər-mən 'ēst 'a-fri-kə

LOCATION — In East Africa, bordering on the Indian Ocean
GOVT. — German Colony
AREA — 384,180 sq. mi.
POP. — 7,680,132 (1913)
CAPITAL — Dar-es Salaam

Following World War I, the greater part of this German Colonial possession was mandated to Great Britain. The British ceded to the Belgians the provinces of Ruanda and Urundi (Belgian East Africa). The Kionga triangle was awarded to the Portuguese and became part of the Mozambique Colony. The remaining area became the British Mandated Territory of Tanganyika.

64 Pesa = 1 Rupee
100 Heller = 1 Rupee (1905)
100 Centimes = 1 Franc (1916)
12 Pence = 1 Shilling (1916)
100 Cents = 1 Rupee (1917)
12 Pence = 1 Shilling 100 Cents = 1 Rupee (1917)

Stamps of Germany Surcharged in Black

1893 Unwmk. ***Perf. 13½x14½***

Surcharge 15¼mm long

1 A9 2pes on 3pf brown 47.50 *47.50*
2 A9 3pes on 5pf green 55.00 *47.50*
3 A10 5pes on 10pf car 40.00 27.50

Surcharge 16¼mm long

4 A10 10pes on 20pf ultra 32.50 14.00

Surcharge 16¾mm long

5 A10 25pes on 50pf red brn 47.50 27.50
Nos. 1-5 (5) 222.50 164.00

The surcharge also comes 16¾mm on No. 1; 14¼ or 16¼mm on Nos. 2-3; 17½mm on No. 5. See the *Scott Classic Catalogue* for listings of these spacings.

Stamps of Germany Surcharged in Black

1896
6 A9 2pes on 3pf dk brn 2.40 *37.50*
a. 2pes on 3pf light brown 28.00 *45.00*
b. 2pes on 3pf grayish brown 12.00 11.50
c. 2pes on 3pf reddish brown 115.00 *200.00*
7 A9 3pes on 5pf green 3.25 *4.50*
8 A10 5pes on 10pf car 6.50 4.50
9 A10 10pes on 20pf ultra 6.50 5.25
10 A10 25pes on 50pf red brn 32.50 *28.00*
Nos. 6-10 (5) 51.15 *79.75*

A5

Kaiser's Yacht "Hohenzollern" — A6

1900 Typo. ***Perf. 14***
11 A5 2p brown 2.75 1.60
12 A5 3p green 2.75 2.00
13 A5 5p carmine 3.25 2.50
14 A5 10p ultra 5.25 4.75
15 A5 15p org & blk, *sal* 5.25 *6.50*
16 A5 20p lake & blk 7.25 *14.50*
17 A5 25p pur & blk, *sal* 7.25 *14.50*
18 A5 40p lake & blk, *rose* 9.50 *22.50*

Engr.

Perf. 14½x14

19 A6 1r claret 20.00 *47.50*
20 A6 2r yel green 9.50 *80.00*
21a A6 3r red & slate 120.00 *185.00*
Nos. 11-21a (11) 192.75 *381.35*

Value in Heller

1905 Typo. ***Perf. 14***
22 A5 2½h brown 5.50 1.75
23 A5 4h dk olive green 24.00 5.50
a. 4h green 16.00 1.60
b. 4h dark yellowish green 32.50 *20.00*
24 A5 7½h carmine 16.00 1.60
25 A5 15h ultra 28.00 6.00
a. 15h violet blue 52.50 16.00
26 A5 20h org & blk, *yel* 16.00 *16.00*
27 A5 30h lake & blk 16.00 6.00
28 A5 45h pur & blk 32.50 *35.00*
29 A5 60h lake & blk, *rose* 47.50 *95.00*
Nos. 22-29 (8) 185.50 *166.85*

1905-16 Wmk. Lozenges (125)
31 A5 2½h brn ('06) .95 .06
32 A5 4h grn ('06) .95 .65
b. Booklet pane of 4 + 2 labels 45.00
c. Booklet pane of 5 + label *400.00*
33 A5 7½h car ('06) 1.10 *1.60*
b. Booklet pane of 4 + 2 labels 45.00
c. Booklet pane of 5 + label *400.00*
34 A5 15h dk blue ('08) 2.25 1.50
35 A5 20h org & blk, *yel* ('11) 2.50 *20.00*
36 A5 30h lake & blk ('09) 2.60 *8.00*
37 A5 45h pur & blk ('06) 5.50 *55.00*
38 A5 60h lake & blk, *rose* 30.00 *190.00*

Engr.

Perf. 14½x14

39 A6 1r red ('16) 13.00 *25,000.*
40 A6 2r yel grn 47.50
41 A6 3r car & sl ('08) 47.50 *240.00*
a. 3r red & blackish green ('08) 160.00 *400.00*
Nos. 31-41 (11) 153.85 25,518.

No. 40 was never placed in use.

The frame of No. 41a fluoresces bright orange under ultra-violet light.

Forged cancellations are found on #35-39, 41.

In early 1916, German East African authorities ordered supplies of provisional stamps, printed by the press of the Evangelical Mission in Wuga. Three values in denominations most urgently needed were produced in March, but before they could be issued, new stocks of regular stamps were received from Germany. To prevent their capture by the British, the provisionals were buried until 1922, when they were retrieved by the German government and sold at auction. Because of their long storage in the tropical climate, 90-95% of the stamps were destroyed and those surviving are usually brittle and somewhat faded.

Values: 2½h violet brown, $55; 7½h, carmine, $25; 1r pink, $1,400.

OCCUPATION STAMPS

Issued Under Belgian Occupation
Stamps of Belgian Congo, 1915, Handstamped "RUANDA" in Black, Blue or Red Violet

1916 Unwmk. ***Perf. 13½ to 15***
N1 A29 5c green & blk 65.00
N2 A30 10c carmine & blk 65.00
N3 A21 15c blue grn & blk 125.00
N4 A31 25c blue & blk 65.00
N5 A23 40c brown red & blk 65.00
N6 A24 50c brown lake & blk 75.00
N7 A25 1fr olive bis & blk 400.00
N8 A27 5fr ocher & blk *4,000.*
Nos. N1-N7 (7) 860.00

Stamps of Belgian Congo, 1915, Handstamped "URUNDI" in Black, Blue or Red Violet

N9	A29	5c green & blk	65.00
N10	A30	10c carmine & blk	65.00
N11	A21	15c bl grn & blk	125.00
N12	A31	25c blue & blk	65.00
N13	A23	40c brn red & blk	65.00
N14	A24	50c brn lake & blk	75.00
N15	A25	1fr ol bis & blk	400.00
N16	A27	5fr ocher & blk	*4,000.*
		Nos. N9-N15 (7)	860.00

Stamps of Belgian Congo overprinted "Karema," "Kigoma" and "Tabora" were not officially authorized.

Nos. N1-N16 exist with forged overprint.

Stamps of Belgian Congo, 1915, Ovptd. in Dark Blue

1916 ***Perf. 12½ to 15***

N17	A29 5c green & blk	1.00	.30
b.	Inverted overprint	225.00	—
N18	A30 10c carmine & blk	1.25	.50
a.	Inverted overprint	225.00	
N19	A21 15c bl grn & blk	1.00	.30
N20	A31 25c blue & blk	7.25	1.75
N21	A23 40c brn red & blk	20.00	6.00
N22	A24 50c brn lake & blk	27.50	6.00
N23	A25 1fr olive bis & blk	3.00	.75
a.	Double overprint		
N24	A27 5fr ocher & blk	3.50	1.75
	Nos. N17-N24 (8)	64.50	17.35
	Set, never hinged	90.00	

Nos. N17-N18, N20-N22 Surcharged in Black or Red

1922

N25	A24 5c on 50c brn lake & blk	.60	.45
N26	A29 10c on 5c grn & blk (R)	.60	.40
N27	A23 25c on 40c brn red & blk (R)	3.75	2.75
N28	A30 30c on 10c car & blk	.60	.30
N29	A31 50c on 25c bl & blk (R)	.60	.30
	Nos. N25-N29 (5)	6.15	4.20
	Set, never hinged	21.50	

No. N25 has the surcharge at each side.

ISSUED UNDER BRITISH OCCUPATION

Stamps of Nyasaland Protectorate, 1913-15 Overprinted

1916 **Wmk. 3** ***Perf. 14***

N101	A3 ½p green	1.75	*9.50*
a.	Double overprint (R & Bk)		
N102	A3 1p carmine	1.75	*3.75*
N103	A3 3p violet, *yel*	27.50	18.00
a.	Double overprint		*26,000.*
N104	A3 4p scar & blk, *yel*	52.50	42.00
N105	A3 1sh black, *green*	72.50	*72.50*
	Nos. N101-N105 (5)	156.00	*145.75*

"N.F." stands for "Nyasaland Force."

Stamps of East Africa and Uganda, 1912-14, Overprinted in Black or Red

1917

N106	A3 1c black (R)	.25	*.95*
N107	A3 3c blue green	.25	.25
N108	A3 6c carmine	.25	.25
N109	A3 10c brown orange	.60	*.70*
N110	A3 12c gray	.60	*3.00*
N111	A3 15c ultramarine	1.90	*3.50*
N112	A3 25c scar & blk, *yel*	.90	*4.50*
N113	A3 50c violet & blk	2.50	*5.00*
N114	A3 75c blk, *bl grn,* olive back (R)	1.25	*4.50*
a.	75c black, *emerald* (R)	3.75	*52.50*

Overprinted

N115	A4 1r blk, *green* (R)	6.50	*8.00*
a.	1r black, *emerald* (R)	14.00	*65.00*
N116	A4 2r blk & red, *bl*	15.00	*62.50*
N117	A4 3r gray grn & vio	17.50	*95.00*
N118	A4 4r grn & red, *yel*	27.50	*120.00*
N119	A4 5r dl vio & ultra	52.50	*140.00*
N120	A4 10r grn & red, *grn*	160.00	*450.00*
a.	10r grn & red, *emerald*	210.00	*700.00*
N121	A3 20r vio & blk, *red*	325.00	*700.00*
N122	A3 50r gray grn & red	750.00	*1,200.*
	Nos. N106-N120 (15)	287.50	*898.15*

See Tanganyika for "G.E.A." overprints on stamps inscribed "East Africa and Uganda Protectorates" with watermark 4.

SEMI-POSTAL STAMPS

Issued under Belgian Occupation

Semi-Postal Stamps of Belgian Congo, 1915, Overprinted

1918 **Unwmk.** ***Perf. 14, 15***

NB1	A29 5c + 10c grn & bl	.50	.50
NB2	A30 10c + 15c car & bl	.80	.50
NB3	A21 15c + 20c bl grn & bl	1.00	.50
NB4	A31 25c + 25c dp & pale bl	1.50	.50
NB5	A23 40c + 40c brn red & bl	1.00	.75
NB6	A24 50c + 50c brn lake & bl	1.50	1.00
NB7	A25 1fr + 1fr ol bis & bl	3.00	3.00
NB8	A27 5fr + 5fr ocher & bl	10.00	10.00
NB9	A28 10fr + 10fr grn & bl	95.00	95.00
	Nos. NB1-NB9 (9)	114.30	111.75

The letters "A.O." are the initials of "Afrique Orientale" (East Africa).

GERMAN NEW GUINEA

ˈjər-mən ˈnü ˈgi-nē

LOCATION — A group of islands in the west Pacific Ocean, including a part of New Guinea and adjacent islands of the Bismarck Archipelago.

GOVT. — German Protectorate

AREA — 93,000 sq. mi.

POP. — 601,427 (1913)

CAPITAL — Herbertshohe (later Kokopo)

The islands were occupied by Australian troops during World War I and renamed "New Britain." By covenant of the League of Nations they were made a mandated territory of Australia in 1920. The old name of "New Guinea" has since been restored. Postage stamps were issued under all regimes. For other listings see New Britain (1914-15), North West Pacific Islands (1915-22) and New Guinea in Vol. 4.

100 Pfennig = 1 Mark

Stamps of Germany Overprinted in Black

1897-99 **Unwmk.** ***Perf. 13½x14½***

1	A9 3pf brown	8.00	*8.00*
a.	3pf reddish brown ('99)	135.00	*240.00*
b.	3pf yellow brown ('98)	30.00	*57.50*
2	A9 5pf green	5.50	5.00
3	A10 10pf carmine	6.50	*8.00*
4	A10 20pf ultra	9.00	*12.00*
5	A10 25pf orange ('98)	25.00	*52.50*
a.	Inverted overprint	*2,250.*	
6	A10 50pf red brown	32.50	*50.00*
	Nos. 1-6 (6)	86.50	*135.50*

A3

Kaiser's Yacht "Hohenzollern" — A4

1901 **Typo.** ***Perf. 14***

7	A3 3pf brown	1.25	1.25
8	A3 5pf green	6.50	1.25
9	A3 10pf carmine	20.00	3.00
10	A3 20pf ultra	1.50	*3.00*
11	A3 25pf org & blk, *yel*	1.75	*16.00*
12	A3 30pf org & blk, *sal*	1.75	*20.00*
13	A3 40pf lake & blk	1.75	*23.00*
14	A3 50pf pur & blk, *sal*	2.00	*20.00*
15	A3 80pf lake & blk, *rose*	3.75	*27.50*

Engr.

Perf. 14½x14

16	A4 1m carmine	9.50	*52.50*
17	A4 2m blue	9.50	*77.50*
18	A4 3m blk vio	12.00	*150.00*
19	A4 5m slate & car	175.00	*500.00*
	Nos. 7-19 (13)	246.25	*895.00*

Fake cancellations exist on Nos. 10-19.

The stamps of German New Guinea overprinted "G.R.I." and new values in British currency were all used in New Britain and are listed under that country as Nos. 1-29C, O1-2.

A5

A6

Nos. 21-23 have "NEUGUINEA" as one word without a hyphen.

Wmk. Lozenges (125)

1914-19 **Typo.** ***Perf. 14***

20	A3 3pf brown ('19)	1.75
21	A5 5pf green	1.75
22	A5 10pf carmine	1.75

Engr.

Perf. 14½x14

23	A6 5m slate & carmine	32.50
	Nos. 20-23 (4)	37.75

Nos. 20-23 were never placed in use.

GERMAN SOUTH WEST AFRICA

'jər-mən 'sauth 'west 'a-fri-kə

LOCATION — In southwest Africa, bordering on the South Atlantic
GOVT. — German Colony
AREA — 322,450 sq. mi. (1913)
POP. — 94,372 (1913)
CAPITAL — Windhoek

The Colony was occupied by South African troops during World War I and in 1920 was mandated to the Union of South Africa by the League of Nations. See South West Africa in Vol. 6.

100 Pfennig = 1 Mark

Stamps of Germany Overprinted

1897 Unwmk. ***Perf. 13½x14½***

1	A9	3pf dark brown	8.25	*12.00*
a.		3pf yellow brown	50.00	*2,800.*
2	A9	5pf green	4.50	4.75
3	A10	10pf carmine	21.00	16.00
4	A10	20pf ultra	8.00	5.75
5	A10	25pf orange	225.00	*28,000.*
6	A10	50pf red brown	225.00	*28,000.*
		Nos. 1-4 (4)	41.75	38.50

Nos. 5 and 6 were prepared for issue but were not sent to the Colony. However, a small number were postally used from the Colony. Used values for Nos. 5 and 6 are for expertized stamps bearing genuine, contemporaneous Colony postmarks.

Overprinted in Black on 2 lines

1898-99

7	A9	3pf dark brown	4.00	*20.00*
a.		3pf reddish brown	52.50	*160.00*
b.		3pf yellow brown	8.00	*12.00*
8	A9	5pf green	4.00	3.25
9	A10	10pf carmine	4.00	4.00
10	A10	20pf ultra	16.00	15.00
11	A10	25pf orange	350.00	400.00
12	A10	50pf red brown	20.00	12.00

Kaiser's Yacht "Hohenzollern"
A3 A4

1901 Typo. ***Perf. 14***

13	A3	3pf brown	4.00	1.60
14	A3	5pf green	20.00	1.60
15	A3	10pf carmine	14.00	.80
16	A3	20pf ultra	30.00	1.50
17	A3	25pf org & blk, *yel*	1.50	*5.50*
18	A3	30pf org & blk, *sal*	80.00	2.75
19	A3	40pf lake & blk	1.75	*3.25*
20	A3	50pf pur & blk, *sal*	2.10	2.10
21	A3	80pf lake & blk, *rose*	2.10	*9.00*

Engr.

Perf. 14½x14

22	A4	1m carmine	125.00	30.00
23	A4	2m blue	30.00	*37.50*
24	A4	3m blk vio	32.50	*50.00*
25	A4	5m slate & car	200.00	160.00
		Nos. 13-25 (13)	542.95	*305.60*

Wmk. Lozenges (125)

1906-19 Typo. ***Perf. 14***

26	A3	3pf dk brn ('07)	.80	*3.75*
27	A3	5pf green	.80	*1.50*
b.		Bklt. pane of 6 (2 #27, 4 #28)	65.00	
c.		Booklet pane of 5 + label	*600.00*	
28	A3	10pf lt rose	1.00	*1.50*
b.		Booklet pane of 5 + label	*600.00*	
29	A3	20pf ultra ('11)	1.00	*3.75*
30	A3	30pf org & blk, *pale yel* ('11)	16.00	*52.50*

Engr.

Perf. 14½x14

31	A4	1m carmine ('12)	13.00	*80.00*
32	A4	2m blue ('11)	13.00	*80.00*
33	A4	3m blk vio ('19)	15.00	
a.		3m gray violet	75.00	
34	A4	5m slate & car	37.50	*325.00*
a.		5m slate & rose red	100.00	*300.00*
		Nos. 26-34 (9)	98.10	548.00

Nos. 33, 33a, 34a were never placed in use.
Forged cancellations are found on #30-32, 34.

GERMAN STATES

'jər-mən 'stāts

Watermarks

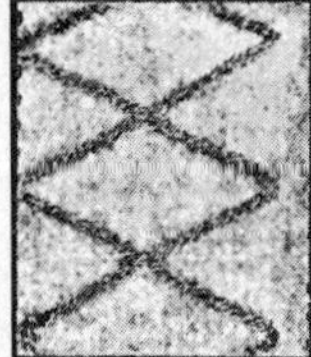
Wmk. 92 — 17mm wide

Wmk. 93 — 14mm wide

Wmk. 94 — Horiz. Wavy Lines Wide Apart

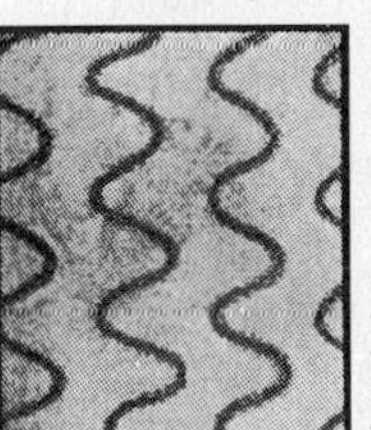
Wmk. 95v — Vert. Wavy Lines Close Together

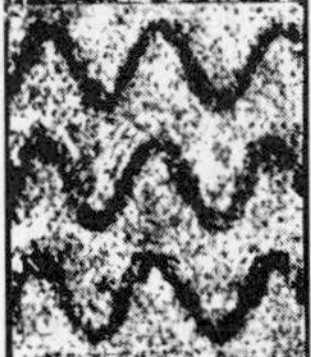
Wmk. 95h — Horiz. Wavy Lines Close Together

Wmk. 102 — Post Horn

Wmk. 116 — Crosses and Circles

Wmk. 128 — Wavy Lines

Wmk. 130 — Wreath of Oak Leaves

Wmk. 148 — Small Flowers

Wmk. 162 — Laurel Wreath

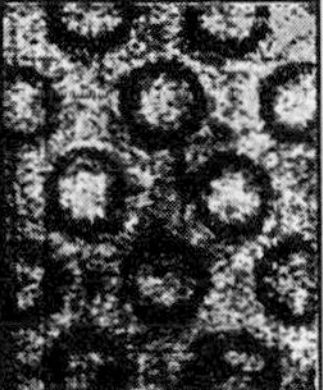
Wmk. 192 — Circles

BADEN

LOCATION — In southwestern Germany
GOVT. — Former Grand Duchy
AREA — 5,817 sq. mi.
POP. — 1,432,000 (1864)
CAPITAL — Karlsruhe (Principal city)

Baden was a member of the German Confederation. In 1870 it became part of the German Empire.

60 Kreuzer = 1 Gulden

Values for unused stamps are for examples with original gum as defined in the catalogue introduction except for Nos. 1-9 which are valued without gum. Very fine examples of Nos. 1-9 will have one or two margins touching the framelines due to the very narrow spacing of the stamps on the plates. Stamps with margins clear of the framelines on all four sides are scarce and sell for considerably more.

A1

1851-52 Unwmk. Typo. *Imperf.*

No.	Type	Description	Unused	Used
1	A1	1kr blk, *dk buff*	275.00	250.00
2	A1	3kr blk, *yellow*	140.00	16.00
3	A1	6kr blk, *yel grn*	440.00	45.00
4	A1	9kr blk, *lil rose*	90.00	26.00
		Nos. 1-4 (4)	945.00	337.00

Thin Paper (First Printing, 1851)

No.	Type	Description	Unused	Used
1a	A1	1kr black, *buff*	2,000.	800.00
2a	A1	3kr blk, *org*	675.00	35.00
3a	A1	6kr blk, *blue grn*	2,250.	90.00
4a	A1	9kr blk, *dp rose*	2,800.	160.00

No. 4b

No.	Type	Description	Unused	Used
4b	A1	9kr blk, *bl grn* (error)		1,300,000.

1853-58

No.	Type	Description	Unused	Used
6	A1	1kr black	160.00	27.50
a.		Tête bêche gutter pair		*35,000.*
7	A1	3kr black, *green*	160.00	14.00
8	A1	3kr black, *bl* ('58)	675.00	30.00
a.		Printed on both sides		
9	A1	6kr black, *yellow*	250.00	27.50
		Nos. 6-9 (4)	1,245.	99.00

The paper of No. 6 is 0.06-0.095mm thick.

Reissues (1865) of Nos. 1, 2, 3, 6, 7 and 8 exist on thick paper and No. 9 on thin paper; the color of the last is brighter than that of the original.

Coat of Arms — A2

1860-62 *Perf. 13½*

No.	Type	Description	Unused	Used
10	A2	1kr black	87.50	30.00
12	A2	3kr ultra ('61)	87.50	22.00
a.		3kr Prussian blue	275.00	72.50
13	A2	6kr red org ('61)	95.00	72.50
a.		6kr yellow orange ('62)	180.00	87.50
14	A2	9kr rose ('61)	250.00	175.00
		Nos. 10-14 (4)	520.00	299.50

Examples of Nos. 10-14 and 18 with all perforations intact sell for considerably more.

Coat of Arms — A3

1862 *Perf. 10*

No.	Type	Description	Unused	Used
15	A2	1kr black	65.00	87.50
a.		1kr silver gray	6,500.	*6,500.*
16	A2	6kr Prus bl ('62)	125.00	235.00
17	A2	9kr brown	80.00	72.50
a.		9kr dark brown	325.00	250.00

Perf. 13½

No.	Type	Description	Unused	Used
18	A3	3kr rose	2,250.	290.00

1862-65 *Perf. 10*

No.	Type	Description	Unused	Used
19	A3	1kr black ('64)	47.50	15.00
a.		1kr silver gray		*2,250.*
20	A3	3kr rose	62.50	4.00
a.		Imperf.	*40,000.*	*40,000.*
22	A3	6kr ultra ('65)	11.00	*27.50*
a.		6kr Prussian blue ('64)	*575.00*	70.00
23	A3	9kr brn ('64)	16.00	30.00
a.		9kr bister	375.00	90.00
b.		Printed on both sides		*6,500.*
24	A3	18kr green	400.00	575.00
25	A3	30kr dp org	32.50	*2,250.*
a.		30kr yellow orange	140.00	*2,400.*

Forged cancellations are known on No. 25.

A4

1868

No.	Type	Description	Unused	Used
26	A4	1kr green	4.00	*9.00*
27	A4	3kr rose	2.75	4.50
28	A4	7kr dull blue	20.00	*35.00*
a.		7kr sky blue	42.50	*100.00*
		Nos. 26-28 (3)	26.75	48.50

Forged cancellations are known on No. 28a.

The postage stamps of Baden were superseded by those of the German Empire on Jan. 1, 1872, but Official stamps were used during the year 1905.

Stamps of the Baden sector of the French Occupation Zone of Germany, issued in 1947-49, are listed under Germany, Occupation Issues.

RURAL POSTAGE DUE STAMPS

RU1

1862 Unwmk. *Perf. 10*

Thin Paper

No.	Type	Description	Unused	Used
LJ1	RU1	1kr blk, *yellow*	5.00	*325.00*
a.		Thick paper	140.00	*600.00*
LJ2	RU1	3kr blk, *yellow*	2.75	*125.00*
a.		Thick paper	120.00	*400.00*
LJ3	RU1	12kr blk, *yellow*	35.00	*13,500.*
a.		Half used as 6kr on cover		*25,000.*
b.		Quarter used as 3kr on cover		—
		Nos. LJ1-LJ3 (3)	42.75	13,950.

On No. LJ3, "LAND-POST" is a straight line.

Paper of #LJ1a, LJ2a is darker yellow.

Forged cancellations abound on Nos. LJ1-LJ3.

OFFICIAL STAMPS

See Germany Nos. OL16-OL21.

BAVARIA

LOCATION — In southern Germany
GOVT. — Kingdom
AREA — 30,562 sq. mi. (1920)
POP. — 7,150,146 (1919)
CAPITAL — Munich

Bavaria was a member of the German Confederation and became part of the German Empire in 1870. After World War I, it declared itself a republic. It lost its postal autonomy on Mar. 31, 1920.

60 Kreuzer = 1 Gulden
100 Pfennig = 1 Mark (1874)

Values for unused stamps are for examples with original gum as defined in the catalogue introduction. Unused examples of the 1849-78 issues without gum sell for about 50-60% of the figures quoted.

A1

Broken Circle — A1a

1849 Unwmk. Typo. *Imperf.*

No.	Type	Description	Unused	Used
1	A1	1kr black	1,000.	*2,250.*
a.		1kr deep black	2,800.	*3,000.*
b.		Tête bêche pair	*125,000.*	

With Silk Thread

No.	Type	Description	Unused	Used
2	A1a	3kr blue	60.00	3.50
a.		3kr greenish blue	60.00	3.50
b.		3kr deep blue	60.00	3.50
3	A1a	6kr brown	*7,000.*	240.00

No. 1 exists with silk thread, from a single proof sheet, value about $4,000.

Complete circle — A2

1850-58 With Silk Thread

No.	Type	Description	Unused	Used
4	A2	1kr pink	95.00	22.50
5	A2	6kr brown	50.00	6.50
a.		Half used as 3kr on cover		*16,000.*
6	A2	9kr yellow green	70.00	16.00
a.		9kr blue green ('53)	*11,000.*	150.00
7	A2	12kr red ('58)	150.00	*140.00*
8	A2	18kr yel ('54)	140.00	*190.00*
		Nos. 4-8 (5)	505.00	375.00

1862

No.	Type	Description	Unused	Used
9	A2	1kr yellow	80.00	20.00
10	A1a	3kr rose	140.00	4.00
a.		3kr carmine	52.50	6.00
11	A2	6kr blue	70.00	12.00
a.		6kr ultra	*2,400.*	*9,000.*
b.		Half used as 3kr on cover		*10,000.*
12	A2	9kr bister	110.00	16.00
13	A2	12kr yel grn	95.00	70.00
a.		Half used as 6kr on cover		*32,000.*
14	A2	18kr ver red	900.00	140.00
a.		18kr pale red	190.00	*450.00*
		Nos. 9-14 (6)	1,395.	262.00

No. 11a was not put in use.

Coat of Arms — A3

1867-68 Embossed

No.	Type	Description	Unused	Used
15	A3	1kr yel grn	65.00	12.00
a.		1kr dark blue green	300.00	52.50
16	A3	3kr rose	70.00	2.40
a.		Printed on both sides		*5,000.*
17	A3	6kr ultra	45.00	19.00
a.		Half used as 3kr on cover		*75,000.*
18	A3	6kr bis ('68)	80.00	50.00
a.		Half used as 3kr on cover		*32,000.*
19	A3	7kr ultra ('68)	400.00	16.00
20	A3	9kr bister	45.00	35.00

No.	Type	Description	Unused	Used
21	A3	12kr lilac	350.00	95.00
22	A3	18kr red	140.00	175.00
		Nos. 15-22 (8)	1,195.	404.40

The paper of the 1867-68 issues often shows ribbed or laid lines.

1870-72 Wmk. 92 *Perf. 11½*

Without Silk Thread

No.	Type	Description	Unused	Used
23	A3	1kr green	12.00	1.60
24	A3	3kr rose	24.00	1.60
25	A3	6kr bister	30.00	30.00
26	A3	7kr ultra	3.50	*4.50*
a.		7kr Prussian blue	20.00	14.00
27	A3	9kr pale brn ('72)	5.50	4.00
28	A3	10kr yellow	6.50	*15.00*
29	A3	12kr lilac	1,200.	*4,800.*
30	A3	18kr dull brick red	16.00	*16.00*
b.		18kr dark brick red	120.00	70.00

The paper of the 1870-75 issues frequently appears to be laid with the lines either close or wide apart.

See Nos. 33-37.

Reprints exist.

Wmk. 93

No.	Type	Description	Unused	Used
23a	A3	1kr green	100.00	9.50
24a	A3	3kr rose	95.00	2.40
25a	A3	6kr bister	175.00	70.00
26b	A3	7kr ultra	140.00	35.00
27a	A3	9kr pale brown	290.00	*475.00*
28a	A3	10kr yellow	240.00	*360.00*
29a	A3	12kr lilac	360.00	*1,125.*
30a	A3	18kr dull brick red	300.00	190.00
c.		18kr dark brick red	400.00	225.00

A4

1874-75 Wmk. 92 *Imperf.*

No.	Type	Description	Unused	Used
31	A4	1m violet	675.00	85.00

Perf. 11½

No.	Type	Description	Unused	Used
32	A4	1m violet ('75)	200.00	55.00

See Nos. 46-47, 54-57, 73-76.

1875 Wmk. 94

No.	Type	Description	Unused	Used
33	A3	1kr green	.80	*24.00*
34	A3	3kr rose	.80	*8.00*
35	A3	7kr ultra	5.25	*275.00*
36	A3	10kr yellow	30.00	*250.00*
37	A3	18kr red	24.00	*60.00*
		Nos. 33-37 (5)	60.85	617.00

A5

1876-78 Embossed *Perf. 11½*

No.	Type	Description	Unused	Used
38	A5	3pf lt grn	35.00	1.60
39	A5	5pf dk grn	90.00	16.00
40	A5	5pf lilac ('78)	160.00	20.00
41	A5	10pf rose	190.00	1.25
42	A5	20pf ultra	190.00	3.25
43	A5	25pf yel brn	175.00	6.50
44	A5	50pf scarlet	55.00	7.25
45	A5	50pf brn ('78)	800.00	27.50
46	A4	1m violet	1,900.	90.00
47	A4	2m orange	24.00	12.00

The paper of the 1876-78 issue often shows ribbed lines.

See Nos. 48-53, 58-72. For overprints and surcharge see Nos. 237, O1-O5.

1881-1906 Wmk. 95v *Perf. 11½*

No.	Type	Description	Unused	Used
48	A5	3pf green	12.00	.80
a.		Imperf.	400.00	*2,000.*
49	A5	5pf lilac	17.50	1.25
50	A5	10pf carmine	12.50	.65
a.		Imperf.	*400.00*	2,000.
51	A5	20pf ultramarine	14.00	.80
52	A5	25pf yellow brown	125.00	3.50
53	A5	50pf deep brown	145.00	3.25
54	A4	1m rose lil, *white* ('00)	4.50	3.50
a.		1m brownish lilac, toned paper	52.50	4.00
55	A4	2m orange ('01)	5.50	*8.00*
a.		Toned paper ('90)	90.00	14.00
56	A4	3m olive gray ('00)	24.00	*30.00*
a.		White paper ('06)	175.00	*400.00*
57	A4	5m yel grn ('00)	24.00	*30.00*
a.		White paper ('06)	150.00	*350.00*
		Nos. 48-57 (10)	384.00	81.75

Nos. 54-55 are on white paper. Nos. 56-57 are on toned paper. A 2m lilac was not regularly issued.

1888-1900 Wmk. 95h *Perf. 14x14½*

No.	Type	Description	Unused	Used
58	A5	2pf gray ('00)	2.40	.55
59	A5	3pf green	9.25	2.10
60	A5	3pf brown ('00)	.30	*.65*
61	A5	5pf lilac	24.00	5.50
62	A5	5pf dk grn ('00)	.30	*.65*
63	A5	10pf carmine	.40	*.80*
64	A5	20pf ultra	.40	*.80*
65	A5	25pf yel brn	32.50	6.75
66	A5	25pf orange ('00)	.60	*1.10*
67	A5	30pf ol grn ('00)	.80	*1.40*
68	A5	40pf yellow ('00)	.80	*1.10*
69	A5	50pf dp brn	60.00	6.75
70	A5	50pf maroon ('00)	.50	*1.60*
71	A5	80pf lilac ('00)	3.25	*4.00*
		Nos. 58-71 (14)	193.00	33.75

Nos. 59, 61, 65, 69 and 70 are on toned paper; Nos. 67-68 on white.

1888-99 Toned Paper

No.	Type	Description	Unused	Used
58a	A5	2pf gray ('99)	12.00	5.25
60a	A5	3pf dk ocher brn ('90)	9.25	.40
62a	A5	5pf dk green ('90)	10.00	.65
63a	A5	10pf car red	6.75	.80
b.		Imperf.	72.50	*175.00*
64a	A5	20pf ultra	10.00	1.25
66a	A5	25pf org ('90)	16.50	1.60
70a	A5	50pf mar ('90)	47.50	2.40
71a	A5	80pf lilac ('99)	32.50	12.00

1911, Jan. 23 Wmk. 95v

No.	Type	Description	Unused	Used
72	A5	5pf dark green	.65	*13.50*

1911, Jan. Wmk. 95h *Perf. 11½*

No.	Type	Description	Unused	Used
73	A4	1m rose lilac	4.00	*27.50*
74	A4	2m orange	17.00	*37.50*
75	A4	3m olive gray	17.00	*57.50*
76	A4	5m pale yel grn	17.00	*57.50*
		Nos. 73-76 (4)	55.00	180.00

See note after No. 91 concerning used values.

A6

A7

A8

Prince Regent Luitpold

Perf. 14x14½

1911 Wmk. 95h Litho.

No.	Type	Description	Unused	Used
77	A6	3pf brn, *gray brn*	.30	.30
a.		"911" for "1911"	*325.00*	*325.00*
78	A6	5pf dk grn, *grn*	.30	.30
a.		Tête bêche pair	4.50	*10.50*
b.		Booklet pane of 4 + 2 labels	100.00	*150.00*
c.		Bklt. pane of 5 + label	225.00	*375.00*
d.		Bklt. pane of 6	35.00	
79	A6	10pf scar, *buff*	.30	.30
a.		Tête bêche pair	5.75	*62.50*
b.		"911" for "1911"	15.00	15.00
d.		Booklet pane of 5 + label	65.00	30.00
80	A6	20pf dp bl, *bl*	2.00	.75
81	A6	25pf vio brn, *buff*	3.25	1.25

Perf. 11½

Wmk. 95v

No.	Type	Description	Unused	Used
82	A7	30pf org buff, *buff*	2.25	1.25
83	A7	40pf ol grn, *buff*	4.00	1.25
84	A7	50pf cl, *gray brn*	3.25	*3.25*
84A	A7	60pf dk grn, *buff*	3.25	*3.25*
85	A7	80pf vio, *gray brn*	9.00	*11.00*
86	A8	1m brn, *gray brn*	3.25	*4.00*
87	A8	2m dk grn, *grn*	4.75	*12.00*
88	A8	3m lake, *buff*	13.00	*65.00*
89	A8	5m dk bl, *buff*	13.00	*45.00*
90	A8	10m org, *yel*	22.50	*65.00*
91	A8	20m blk brn, *yel*	25.00	*32.50*
		Nos. 77-91 (16)	109.40	*246.40*

90th birthday of Prince Regent Luitpold.

All values exist in 2 types except No. 84A.

Nos. 77-84, 85-91 exist imperf.

Used values: Nos. 73-76 and 77-91 often were canceled en masse for accounting purposes. These cancels are perfectly clear, and used values are for stamps canceled thus. Postally used examples are worth about twice as much.

Prince Regent Luitpold — A9

1911, June 10 Unwmk.

No.	Type	Description	Unused	Used
92	A9	5pf grn, yel & blk	.80	*1.40*
b.		Horiz. pair, imperf. btwn.	140.00	*225.00*
93	A9	10pf rose, yel & blk	1.25	*2.40*
b.		Pair, imperf. between	140.00	*225.00*

Silver Jubilee of Prince Regent Luitpold.

Used values of Nos. 94-275, B1-B3 are for postally used stamps. Canceled-to-order stamps, which abound, sell for same prices as unused.

A10

A11

King Ludwig III — A12

Perf. 14x14½

1914-20 Wmk. 95h Photo.

No.	Type	Description	Unused	Used
94	A10	2pf gray ('18)	.25	*2.00*
95	A10	3pf brown	.25	*2.00*
96	A10	5pf yellow grn	1.10	*2.00*
a.		5pf dark green	1.10	*2.00*
b.		Tête bêche pair	3.50	*16.50*
c.		Booklet pane of 5 + 1 label	16.00	*60.00*
97	A10	7½pf dp grn ('16)	.25	*2.00*
a.		Tête bêche pair	2.40	*11.00*
b.		Booklet pane of 6	16.00	
98	A10	10pf vermilion	1.40	*2.00*
a.		Tête bêche pair	3.50	*16.50*
b.		Booklet pane of 5 + 1 label	16.00	*60.00*
99	A10	10pf car rose ('16)	.25	*2.00*
100	A10	15pf ver ('16)	.25	*2.00*
a.		Tête bêche pair	2.40	*11.00*
b.		Booklet pane of 5 + 1 label	6.75	*24.00*
101	A10	15pf car ('20)	1.50	*27.50*
102	A10	20pf blue	.25	*2.00*
103	A10	25pf gray	.25	*2.00*
104	A10	30pf orange	1.25	*2.00*
105	A10	40pf olive grn	.25	*2.00*
106	A10	50pf red brn	.25	*2.00*
107	A10	60pf blue grn	.80	*2.00*
108	A10	80pf violet	.25	*2.00*

Perf. 11½

Wmk. 95v

No.	Type	Description	Unused	Used
109	A11	1m brown	.25	*2.00*
110	A11	2m violet	.30	*2.75*
111	A11	3m scarlet	.40	*5.50*

Wmk. 95h

No.	Type	Description	Unused	Used
112	A12	5m deep blue	.55	*20.00*
113	A12	10m yellow grn	1.75	*55.00*
114	A12	20m brown	3.25	*80.00*
		Nos. 94-114 (21)	15.05	*220.75*

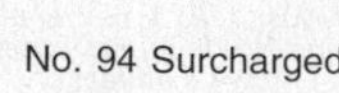
No. 94 Surcharged

1916 Wmk. 95h *Perf. 14x14½*

No.	Type	Description	Unused	Used
115	A10	2½pf on 2pf gray	.25	*2.00*
a.		Double surcharge		

Ludwig III Types of 1914-20

1916-20 *Imperf.*

No.	Type	Description	Unused	Used
117	A10	2pf gray	.25	*14.50*
118	A10	3pf brown	.25	*14.50*
119	A10	5pf pale yel grn	.25	*14.50*
120	A10	7½pf dp green	.25	*14.50*
a.		Tête bêche pair	3.25	*25.00*
121	A10	10pf car rose	.25	*14.50*
122	A10	15pf vermilion	.25	*14.50*
a.		Tête bêche pair	3.25	*25.00*
123	A10	20pf blue	.25	*14.50*
124	A10	25pf gray	.25	*14.50*
125	A10	30pf orange	.25	*14.50*
126	A10	40pf olive grn	.25	*14.50*
127	A10	50pf red brown	.25	*14.50*
128	A10	60pf dark green	.25	*16.00*
129	A10	80pf violet	.25	*16.00*
130	A11	1m brown	.35	*16.00*
131	A11	2m violet	.35	*20.00*
132	A11	3m scarlet	.50	*27.50*
133	A12	5m deep blue	.95	*45.00*
134	A12	10m yellow green	1.60	*65.00*
135	A12	20m brown	2.25	*110.00*
		Nos. 117-135 (19)	9.25	*475.00*

Stamps and Type of 1914-20 Overprinted

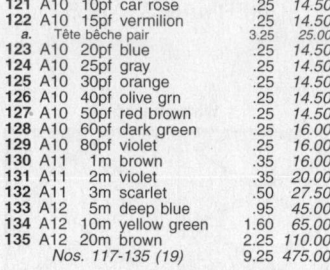

a

b

Wmk. 95h or 95v

1919 *Perf. 14x14½*

Overprint "a"

No.	Type	Description	Unused	Used
136	A10	3pf brown	.25	*2.00*
137	A10	5pf yellow grn	.25	*2.00*
138	A10	7½pf deep green	.25	*2.00*
139	A10	10pf car rose	.25	*2.00*
140	A10	15pf vermilion	.25	*2.00*
141	A10	20pf blue	.25	*2.00*
142	A10	25pf gray	.25	*2.00*
143	A10	30pf orange	.25	*2.00*
144	A10	35pf orange	.25	*2.50*
a.		Without overprint	100.00	
145	A10	40pf olive grn	.25	*2.00*
146	A10	50pf red brown	.25	*2.00*
147	A10	60pf dark green	.25	*2.00*
148	A10	75pf red brown	.25	*2.00*
a.		Without overprint	22.50	*225.00*
149	A10	80pf violet	.25	*2.00*

Perf. 11½

Overprint "a"

No.	Type	Description	Unused	Used
150	A11	1m brown	.25	*2.00*
151	A11	2m violet	.25	*2.00*
152	A11	3m scarlet	.45	*4.75*

Overprint "b"

No.	Type	Description	Unused	Used
153	A12	5m deep blue	.90	*12.00*
154	A12	10m yellow green	1.40	*50.00*
155	A12	20m dk brown	2.50	*50.00*
		Nos. 136-155 (20)	9.25	149.25

Inverted overprints exist on Nos. 137-143, 145-147, 149. Value, each $15.

Double overprints exist on Nos. 137, 139, 143, 145, 150. Values, $30-$75.

Imperf

Overprint "a"

No.	Type	Description	Unused	Used
156	A10	3pf brown	.25	*20.00*
157	A10	5pf pale yel grn	.25	*20.00*
158	A10	7½pf dp green	.25	*20.00*
159	A10	10pf car rose	.25	*20.00*
160	A10	15pf vermilion	.25	*20.00*
161	A10	20pf blue	.25	*20.00*
162	A10	25pf gray	.25	*20.00*
163	A10	30pf orange	.25	*20.00*
164	A10	35pf orange	.25	*20.00*
a.		Without overprint	13.00	
165	A10	40pf olive grn	.25	*20.00*
166	A10	50pf red brown	.25	*20.00*
167	A10	60pf dk green	.25	*20.00*
168	A10	75pf red brown	.25	*20.00*
a.		Without overprint	190.00	
169	A10	80pf violet	.25	*20.00*
170	A11	1m brown	.25	*24.00*
171	A11	2m violet	.50	*27.50*
172	A11	3m scarlet	.70	*45.00*

Overprint "b"

No.	Type	Description	Unused	Used
173	A12	5m deep blue	.95	*55.00*
174	A12	10m yellow grn	1.40	*80.00*
175	A12	20m brown	2.75	*80.00*
		Nos. 156-175 (20)	10.05	591.50

Stamps of Germany 1906-19 Overprinted

1919 Wmk. 125 *Perf. 14, 14½*

No.	Type	Description	Unused	Used
176	A22	2½pf gray	.25	*2.00*
177	A16	3pf brown	.25	*2.00*
178	A16	5pf green	.25	*2.00*
179	A22	7½pf orange	.25	*2.00*

180 A16 10pf carmine .25 2.00
181 A22 15pf dk violet .25 2.00
a. Double overprint 375.00 1,050.
182 A16 20pf ultra .25 2.00
183 A16 25pf org & blk, *yel* .25 2.00
184 A22 35pf red brown .25 2.00
185 A16 40pf lake & blk .40 2.00
186 A16 75pf green & blk .55 2.40
187 A16 80pf lake & blk, *rose* .55 3.25
188 A17 1m car rose 1.25 4.75
189 A21 2m dull blue 1.60 11.00
190 A19 3m gray violet 1.60 13.00
191 A20 5m slate & car 1.60 13.00
a. Inverted overprint 3,575.
Nos. 176-191 (16) 9.80 67.40

Bavarian Stamps of 1914-16 Overprinted

c

d

Wmk. 95h or 95v

1919-20 ***Perf. 14x14½***

Overprint "c"

193 A10 3pf brown .25 2.00
194 A10 5pf yellow grn .25 2.00
195 A10 7½pf dp green .25 16.00
196 A10 10pf car rose .25 2.00
197 A10 15pf vermilion .25 2.00
198 A10 20pf blue .25 2.00
199 A10 25pf gray .25 2.00
200 A10 30pf orange .25 2.00
201 A10 40pf olive grn .25 14.50
202 A10 50pf red brown .25 2.00
203 A10 60pf dk green .25 14.50
204 A10 75pf olive bister .40 14.50
205 A10 80pf violet .25 3.50

Perf. 11½

Overprint "c"

206 A11 1m brown .25 3.50
207 A11 2m violet .25 4.25
208 A11 3m scarlet .35 6.00

Overprint "d"

209 A12 5m deep blue 1.10 17.50
210 A12 10m yellow grn 2.00 35.00
211 A12 20m dk brown 2.40 60.00
Nos. 193-211 (19) 9.75 205.25

Imperf

Overprint "c"

212 A10 3pf brown .25 12.00
213 A10 5pf pale yel grn .25 12.00
214 A10 7½pf deep green .25 22.50
215 A10 10pf car rose .25 12.00
216 A10 15pf vermilion .25 12.00
217 A10 20pf blue .25 12.00
a. Double overprint 50.00
218 A10 25pf gray .25 12.00
219 A10 30pf orange .25 13.50
220 A10 40pf olive grn .25 14.50
221 A10 50pf red brn .25 14.50
222 A10 60pf dk green .25 14.50
223 A10 75pf olive bis .25 35.00
a. Without overprint 5.00
224 A10 80pf violet .25 14.50
225 A11 1m brown .25 22.50
226 A11 2m violet .25 22.50
227 A11 3m scarlet .65 27.50

Overprint "d"

228 A12 5m deep blue 1.10 40.00
229 A12 10m yellow grn 2.00 70.00
230 A12 20m brown 2.40 110.00
Nos. 212-230 (19) 9.90 493.50

Ludwig Type of 1914, Printed in Various Colors and Surcharged

1919 ***Perf. 11½***

231 A11 1.25m on 1m yel grn .25 2.40
232 A11 1.50m on 1m orange .25 3.25
233 A11 2.50m on 1m gray .45 6.50
Nos. 231-233 (3) .95 12.15

1920 ***Imperf.***

234 A11 1.25m on 1m yel grn .30 35.00
a. Without surcharge 400.00
235 A11 1.50m on 1m org .30 35.00
a. Without surcharge 8.00
236 A11 2.50m on 1m gray .65 35.00
a. Without surcharge 8.00
Nos. 234-236 (3) 1.25 105.00

No. 60 Surcharged in Dark Blue

1920 ***Perf. 14½***

237 A5 20pf on 3pf brown .25 2.00
a. Inverted surcharge 9.00 30.00
b. Double surcharge 95.00 225.00

Plowman
A14

"Electricity" Harnessing Light to a Water Wheel
A15

Sower — A16

Madonna and Child — A17

von Kaulbach's "Genius" — A18

TWENTY PFENNIG
Type I — Foot of "2" turns downward.
Type II — Foot of "2" turns upward.

Perf. 14x14½

1920 **Wmk. 95h** **Typo.**

238 A14 5pf yellow grn .25 2.40
239 A14 10pf orange .25 2.40
240 A14 15pf carmine .25 2.40
241 A15 20pf violet (I) .25 2.40
a. 20pf violet (II) 10.00 1,400.
242 A15 30pf dp blue .25 3.25
243 A15 40pf brown .25 2.40
244 A16 50pf vermilion .25 2.40
245 A16 60pf blue green .25 2.40
246 A16 75pf lilac rose .25 2.40

Perf. 12x11½

Wmk. 95v

247 A17 1m car & gray .35 2.40
248 A17 1¼m ultra & ol bis .25 2.40
249 A17 1½m dk grn & gray .25 3.25
250 A17 2½m blk & gray .25 32.50

Perf. 11½x12

Wmk. 95h

251 A18 3m pale blue .55 14.50
252 A18 5m orange .55 14.50
253 A18 10m deep green .95 25.00
254 A18 20m black 1.40 32.50
Nos. 238-254 (17) 6.80 149.50

Imperf. Pairs

238a A14 5pf yellow grn 65.00 450.00
239a A14 10pf orange 160.00
241b A15 20pf violet (I) 65.00
243a A15 40pf brown 140.00
244a A16 50pf vermilion 80.00
245a A16 60pf blue green 47.50
246a A16 75pf lilac rose 47.50
247a A17 1m car & gray 8.00 32.50
248a A17 1¼m ultra & ol bis 8.00 32.50
249a A17 1½m dk grn & gray 8.00 32.50
250a A17 2½m blk & gray 18.00 160.00
251a A18 3m pale blue 14.00 80.00
252a A18 5m orange 14.00 80.00
253a A18 10m deep green 14.00 95.00
254a A18 20m black 14.00 125.00

Perf. 12x11½

1920 **Litho.** **Wmk. 95v**

255 A17 2½m black & gray .50 65.00

On No. 255 the background dots are small, hazy and irregularly spaced. On No. 250 they are large, clear, round, white and regularly spaced in rows. The backs of the typo. stamps usually show a raised impression of parts of the design.

Stamps and Types of Preceding Issue Overprinted

1920

256 A14 5pf yellow green .25 1.60
a. Inverted overprint 30.00
b. Imperf., pair 37.50 375.00
257 A14 10pf orange .25 1.60
a. Imperf., pair 37.50 375.00
b. Inverted overprint 30.00 600.00
258 A14 15pf carmine .25 1.60
a. Inverted overprint 30.00
259 A15 20pf violet .25 1.60
a. Inverted overprint 30.00 750.00
b. Double overprint 13.00
c. Imperf., pair 50.00
260 A15 30pf deep blue .25 1.60
a. Inverted overprint 30.00
b. Imperf., pair 50.00 375.00
261 A15 40pf brown .25 1.60
a. Inverted overprint 30.00 750.00
b. Imperf., pair 50.00
262 A16 50pf vermilion .25 2.40
a. Inverted overprint 30.00 900.00
263 A16 60pf blue green .50 1.40
264 A16 75pf lilac rose .40 5.25
a. Inverted overprint 30.00
265 A16 80pf dark blue .40 2.75
a. Without overprint 100.00
b. Imperf., pair 50.00

Overprinted in Black or Red

266 A17 1m car & gray .50 2.75
a. Imperf., pair 50.00 375.00
b. Inverted overprint 52.50
267 A17 1¼m ultra & ol bis .50 2.75
a. Imperf., pair 47.50
268 A17 1½m dk grn & gray .50 3.50
a. Imperf., pair 47.50
269 A17 2m vio & ol bis .80 4.00
a. Without overprint 32.50
b. Imperf., pair 50.00
270 A17 2½m (#250) (R) .25 2.75
c. Imperf., pair 50.00
270A A17 2½m (#255) (R) .95 95.00
b. Imperf., pair 50.00

Nos. 251-254 Overprinted

271 A18 3m pale blue 3.25 9.50
272 A18 4m dull red 3.25 10.00
a. Without overprint 47.50
273 A18 5m orange 3.25 9.50
274 A18 10m dp green 5.25 16.00
275 A18 20m black 6.00 13.00
Nos. 256-275 (21) 27.55 190.15

Nos. 256-275 were available for postage through all Germany, but were used almost exclusively in Bavaria.

SEMI-POSTAL STAMPS

Regular Issue of 1914-20 Surcharged in Black

1919 **Wmk. 95h** ***Perf. 14x14½***

B1 A10 10pf + 5pf car rose .40 2.00
a. Inverted surcharge 26.00 65.00
b. Surcharge on back 50.00
c. Imperf., pair 325.00
B2 A10 15pf + 5pf ver .40 2.00
a. Inverted surcharge 26.00 65.00
b. Imperf., pair 190.00
B3 A10 20pf + 5pf blue .40 2.40
a. Inverted surcharge 26.00 65.00
b. Imperf., pair 375.00
Nos. B1-B3 (3) 1.20 6.40

Surtax was for wounded war veterans.

POSTAGE DUE STAMPS

D1

With Silk Thread

1862 **Typeset** **Unwmk.** ***Imperf.***

J1 D1 3kr black 125.00 325.00
a. "Empfange" 375.00 1,000.

Without Silk Thread

1870 **Typo.** **Wmk. 93** ***Perf. 11½***

J2 D1 1kr black 12.00 800.00
a. Wmk. 92 55.00 1,750.
J3 D1 3kr black 12.00 475.00
a. Wmk. 92 55.00 960.00

Type of 1876 Regular Issue Overprinted in Red "Vom Empfänger zahlbar"

D2

1876 **Wmk. 94**

J4 D2 3pf gray 16.00 40.00
J5 D2 5pf gray 10.00 17.00
J6 D2 10pf gray 3.25 1.25
a. Vert. half used as 5pt on cover 2,800.
Nos. J4-J6 (3) 29.25 58.25

1883 **Wmk. 95v**

J7 D2 3pf gray 90.00 100.00
J8 D2 5pf gray 55.00 70.00
J9 D2 10pf gray 2.40 .80
a. "Empfanper" 140.00 140.00
b. "zahlhar" 80.00 80.00
c. Imperf. 95.00
Nos. J7-J9 (3) 147.40 170.80

1895-1903 **Wmk. 95h** ***Perf. 14½***

J10 D2 2pf gray .80 2.40
J11 D2 3pf gray ('03) .80 2.50
J12 D2 5pf gray ('03) 1.00 1.75
J13 D2 10pf gray ('03) .60 .90
Nos. J10-J13 (4) 3.20 7.55

1888 **Rose-toned Paper**

J10a D2 2pf gray 2.00 4.75
J11a D2 3pf gray 2.60 2.40
b. Inverted overprint 2,200.
J12a D2 5pf gray 2.60 2.60
J13a D2 10pf gray 2.60 1.25
b. As "a," double overprint 2,200.
Nos. J10a-J13a (4) 9.80 11.00

No. J13b was used at Pirmasens.

Surcharged in Red in Each Corner

1895

J14 D2 2pf on 3pf gray *150,000.*

Six used examples of No. J14 exist, all used in Aichach. There are two covers (each bearing two examples) and two loose stamps.

OFFICIAL STAMPS

Nos. 77-81, 84, 95-96, 98-99, 102 perforated with a large E were issued for official use in 1912-16.

Regular Issue of 1888-1900 Overprinted

1908 Wmk. 95h *Perf. 14½*

No.	Type	Description	Unused	Used
O1	A5	3pf dk brown (R)	.75	*4.50*
O2	A5	5pf dk green (R)	.25	.40
O3	A5	10pf carmine (G)	.25	.40
O4	A5	20pf ultra (R)	.50	.80
O5	A5	50pf maroon	4.50	*8.00*
		Nos. O1-O5 (5)	6.25	*14.10*

Nos. O1-O5 were issued for the use of railway officials. "E" stands for "Eisenbahn."

Coat of Arms — O1

1916-20 Typo. *Perf. 11½*

No.	Type	Description	Unused	Used
O6	O1	3pf bister brn	.25	*.80*
O7	O1	5pf yellow grn	.25	*.80*
O8	O1	7½pf grn, *grn*	.25	*.50*
O9	O1	7½pf grn	.25	*1.20*
O10	O1	10pf deep rose	.25	*1.20*
O11	O1	15pf red, *buff*	.30	*1.20*
O12	O1	15pf red	.25	*1.20*
O13	O1	20pf dp bl, *bl*	2.00	*2.25*
O14	O1	20pf dp blue	.25	*1.20*
O15	O1	25pf gray	.25	*.65*
O16	O1	30pf orange	.25	*.65*
O17	O1	60pf dark green	.25	*1.25*
O18	O1	1m dl vio, *gray*	.95	*3.25*
O19	O1	1m maroon ('20)	2.75	*475.00*
		Nos. O6-O19 (14)	8.50	491.15

Used values of Nos. O6-O69 are for postally used stamps. Canceled-to-order stamps, which abound, sell for same prices as unused.

Official Stamps and Type of 1916-17 Overprinted

1918

No.	Type	Description	Unused	Used
O20	O1	3pf bister brn	.25	*13.50*
O21	O1	5pf yellow green	.25	*2.00*
O22	O1	7½pf gray green	.25	*13.00*
O23	O1	10pf deep rose	.25	*2.25*
O24	O1	15pf red	.25	*2.25*
O25	O1	20pf blue	.25	*2.25*
O26	O1	25pf gray	.25	*2.25*
O27	O1	30pf orange	.25	*2.25*
O28	O1	35pf orange	.25	*2.25*
O29	O1	50pf olive gray	.25	*2.50*
O30	O1	60pf dark green	.30	*13.50*
O31	O1	75pf red brown	.35	*3.50*
O32	O1	1m dl vio, *gray*	1.10	*14.50*
O33	O1	1m maroon	4.00	*375.00*
		Nos. O20-O33 (14)	8.25	451.00

O2

O3

O4

1920 Typo. *Perf. 14x14½*

No.	Type	Description	Unused	Used
O34	O2	5pf yellow grn	.25	*6.50*
O35	O2	10pf orange	.25	*6.50*
O36	O2	15pf carmine	.25	*6.50*
O37	O2	20pf violet	.25	*6.50*
O38	O2	30pf dark blue	.25	*7.25*
O39	O2	40pf bister	.25	*7.25*

Perf. 14½x14

Wmk. 95v

No.	Type	Description	Unused	Used
O40	O3	50pf vermilion	.25	*22.50*
O41	O3	60pf blue green	.25	*9.50*
O42	O3	70pf dk violet	.25	*27.50*
a.		Imperf., pair	26.00	
O43	O3	75pf deep rose	.25	*35.00*
O44	O3	80pf dull blue	.25	*35.00*
O45	O3	90pf olive green	.25	*55.00*
O46	O4	1m dark brown	.25	*50.00*
a.		Imperf., pair	72.50	
O47	O4	1¼m green	.25	*65.00*
O48	O4	1½m vermilion	.25	*65.00*
a.		Imperf. pair	25.00	
O49	O4	2½m deep blue	.25	*70.00*
a.		Imperf. pair	72.50	
O50	O4	3m dark red	.25	*100.00*
a.		Imperf. pair	20.00	
O51	O4	5m black	1.50	*125.00*
a.		Imperf., pair	72.50	
		Nos. O34-O51 (18)	5.75	700.00

Stamps of Preceding Issue Overprinted

1920, Apr. 1

No.	Type	Description	Unused	Used
O52	O2	5pf yellow green	.25	*3.25*
a.		Imperf., pair	26.00	
O53	O2	10pf orange	.25	*1.90*
O54	O2	15pf carmine	.25	*2.00*
O55	O2	20pf violet	.25	*1.60*
O56	O2	30pf dark blue	.25	*1.60*
O57	O2	40pf bister	.25	*1.60*
O58	O3	50pf vermilion	.25	*2.00*
a.		Imperf., pair	26.00	
O59	O3	60pf blue green	.25	*1.60*
O60	O3	70pf dark violet	2.00	*2.75*
O61	O3	75pf deep rose	.35	*1.40*
O62	O3	80pf dull blue	.25	*1.40*
O63	O3	90pf olive green	1.60	*3.50*

Similar Ovpt., Words 8mm apart

No.	Type	Description	Unused	Used
O64	O4	1m dark brown	.25	*2.00*
a.		Imperf., pair	26.00	
O65	O4	1¼m green	.25	*2.00*
O66	O4	1½m vermilion	.25	*2.00*
O67	O4	2½m deep blue	.25	*2.00*
a.		Imperf., pair	37.50	
O68	O4	3m dark red	.25	*2.00*
O69	O4	5m black	8.75	*25.00*
		Nos. O52-O69 (18)	16.20	59.60

Nos. O52-O69 could be used in all parts of Germany, but were almost exclusively used in Bavaria.

BERGEDORF

LOCATION — A town in northern Germany.
POP. — 2,989 (1861)

Originally Bergedorf belonged jointly to the Free City of Hamburg and the Free City of Lübeck. In 1867 it was purchased by Hamburg.

16 Schillings = 1 Mark

Values for unused stamps are for examples with original gum as defined in the catalogue introduction. Copies without gum sell for about 40% of the figures quoted. Values for used stamps are for examples canceled with parallel bars. Copies bearing dated town postmarks sell for more.

Combined Arms of Lübeck and Hamburg

A1 A2 A3

A4

A5

1861-67 Unwmk. Litho. *Imperf.*

No.	Type	Description	Unused	Used
1	A1	½s blk, *pale bl*	45.00	*725.00*
a.		½s black, *blue* ('67)	125.00	*4,750.*
2	A3	1s blk, *white*	45.00	*375.00*
a.		Tête bêche pair, vert.	225.00	
b.		Tête bêche pair, horiz.	300.00	
3	A4	1½s blk, *yellow*	20.00	*1,600.*
a.		Tête bêche pair	*125.00*	
4	A2	3s blue, *pink*	25.00	*2,000.*
5	A5	4s blk, *brown*	25.00	*2,250.*
		Nos. 1-5 (5)	160.00	6,950.

Full margins Nos. 1-3 = 1½mm; No. 4 = ¾mm; No. 5 = 1mm. There are vertical dividing lines between stamps.

Counterfeit cancellations are plentiful.

No. 3 exists in a tête bêche gutter pair. Value, unused $310.

The ½s on violet and 3s on rose, listed previously, as well as a 1s and 1½s on thick paper and 4s on light rose brown, come from proof sheets and were never placed in use.

Color proofs on white paper exist for each denomination in colors of green, red, blue, brown and black. Value $100 each.

A 1½ "SCHILLINGE" (instead of SCHILLING) was produced in limited quantities on original paper by the Belgian dealer Moens in the late 1860s. Se-tenant pairs of 1½ "SCHILLINGE" and 1½ "SCHILLING" exist from this printing.

REPRINTS

½ SCHILLING

There is a dot in the upper part of the right branch of "N" *of* "EIN." *The upper part of the shield is blank or almost blank. The horizontal bar of* "H" *in* "HALBER" *is generally defective.*

1 SCHILLING

The "I" *in the corners is generally with foot. The central horizontal bar of the* "E" *of* "EIN" *is separated from the vertical branch by a black line. The* "A" *of* "POSTMARKE" *has the horizontal bar incomplete or missing. The horizontal bar of the* "H" *of* "SCHILLING" *is separated from the vertical branches by a dark line at each side, sometimes the bar is missing.*

1½ SCHILLINGE

There is a small triangle under the right side of the tower, exactly over the "R" *of* "POSTMARKE."

3 SCHILLINGE

The head of the eagle is not shaded. The horizontal bar of the second "E" *of* "BERGEDORF" *is separated from the vertical branch by a thin line. There is generally a colored dot in the lower half of the* "S" *of* "POSTMARKE."

4 SCHILLINGE

The upper part of the shield is blank or has two or three small dashes. In most of the reprints there is a diagonal dash across the wavy lines of the groundwork at the right of "I" *and* "E" *of* "VIER."

Reprints, value $1 each.

These stamps were superseded by those of the North German Confederation in 1868.

BREMEN

LOCATION — In northwestern Germany
AREA — 99 sq. mi.
POP. — 122,402 (1871)

Bremen was a Free City and member of the German Confederation. In 1870 it became part of the German Empire.

22 Grote = 10 Silbergroschen.

Values for unused stamps are for examples with original gum as defined in the catalogue introduction. Stamps without gum sell for about 50-60% the figures quoted.

Coat of Arms — A1

I

II

III

Type I. The central part of the scroll below the word Bremen is crossed by one vertical line.

Type II. The center of the scroll is crossed by two vertical lines.

Type III. The center of the scroll is crossed by three vertical lines.

1855 Unwmk. Litho. *Imperf.*

Horizontally Laid Paper

No.	Type	Description	Unused	Used
1	A1	3gr black, *blue*	200.00	*290.00*

Vertically Laid Paper

No.	Type	Description	Unused	Used
1A	A1	3gr black, *blue*	450.00	*600.00*

No. 1 can be found with parts of a papermaker's watermark, consisting of lilies. Value: unused $700; unused, no gum, $400; used $1,000.

See Nos. 9-10.

A2

A3

FIVE GROTE

Type I. The shading at the left of the ribbon containing "funf Grote" runs downward from the shield.

Type II. The shading at the left of the ribbon containing "funf Grote" runs upward.

1856-60 Wove Paper

No.	Type	Description	Unused	Used
2	A2	5gr blk, *rose*	150.00	*300.00*
a.		Printed on both sides		4,000.
b.		"Marken" (not issued)	12.00	
3	A2	7gr blk, *yel* ('60)	240.00	*725.00*
4	A3	5sgr green ('59)	500.00	*300.00*
a.		Chalky paper	60.00	*2,000.*
b.		5sgr yellow green	160.00	*300.00*

See Nos. 6, 8, 12-13, 15.

A4

A5

1861-63 *Serpentine Roulette*

No.	Type	Description	Unused	Used
5	A4	2gr orange ('63)	400.00	*2,000.*
a.		2gr red orange	800.00	*3,500.*
b.		Chalky paper	350.00	*3,250.*
c.		as "a," chalky paper	800.00	*3,500.*
6	A2	5gr blk, *rose* ('62)	350.00	*225.00*
a.		Horiz. pair, imperf between		—
7	A5	10gr black	700.00	*950.00*
8	A3	5sgr yellow green ('63)	1,100.	200.00
a.		Chalky paper	600.00	450.00
b.		5sgr green	925.00	225.00

See Nos. 11, 14.

1863

Horizontally (H) or Vertically (V) Laid Paper

No.	Type	Description	Unused	Used
9	A1	3gr blk, *blue* (V)	650.00	725.00
a.		3gr black, *blue* (H)	2,250.	*4,000.*

1866-67 *Perf. 13*

No.	Type	Description	Unused	Used
10	A1	3gr black, *blue*	80.00	*325.00*

Wove Paper

No.	Type	Description	Unused	Used
11	A4	2gr orange	95.00	*325.00*
a.		2gr red orange	450.00	*800.00*
b.		Horiz. pair, imperf. btwn.	3,250.	
12	A2	5gr blk, *rose*	125.00	*325.00*
a.		Horiz. pair, imperf. btwn.	1,250.	—
13	A2	7gr blk, *yel* ('67)	150.00	*4,500.*
14	A5	10gr black ('67)	190.00	*1,125.*
15	A3	5sgr green	140.00	*3,750.*
a.		5sgr yellow green	450.00	175.00
b.		As "a," chalky paper	450.00	275.00

The stamps of Bremen were superseded by those of the North German Confederation on Jan. 1, 1868.

BRUNSWICK

LOCATION — In northern Germany
GOVT. — Former duchy
AREA — 1,417 sq. mi.
POP. — 349,367 (1880)
CAPITAL — Brunswick

Brunswick was a member of the German Confederation and, in 1870 became part of the German Empire.

12 Pfennigs = 1 Gutegroschen
30 Silbergroschen (Groschen) = 24 Gutegroschen = 1 Thaler

Values for unused stamps are for examples with original gum as defined in the catalogue introduction except for Nos. 1-3 which are valued without gum. Nos. 1-3 with original gum sell for much higher prices, and Nos. 4-26 without gum sell for about 50-60% of the figures quoted.

The "Leaping Saxon Horse" — A1

The ½gr has white denomination and "Gr" in right oval.

1852 Unwmk. Typo. *Imperf.*
1 A1 1sgr rose 2,200. 300.00
2 A1 2sgr blue 1,450. 250.00
 a. Half used as 1sgr on cover —
3 A1 3sgr vermilion 1,450. 250.00

See Nos. 4-11, 13-22.

1853-63 Wmk. 102
4 A1 ¼ggr blk, *brn* ('56) 800.00 250.00
5 A1 ⅓sgr black ('56) 140.00 325.00
6 A1 ½gr blk, *grn* ('63) 25.00 *240.00*
7 A1 1sgr blk, *orange* 400.00 55.00
 a. 1sgr black, *orange buff* 400.00 65.00
8 A1 1sgr blk, *yel* ('61) 400.00 50.00
 a. Diagonal half used as ½sgr on cover *18,000.*
9 A1 2sgr blk, *blue* 325.00 65.00
 a. Diagonal half used as 1sgr on cover *9,600.*
 b. Vertical half used as 1sgr on cover *18,000.*
10 A1 3sgr blk, *rose* 475.00 80.00
11 A1 3sgr rose ('62) 600.00 200.00

A3

1857
12 A3 Four ¼ggr blk, *brn* ('57) 40.00 95.00
 a. Four ¼ggr blk, *yel brown* — 210.00

The bister on white paper was not issued. Value $6.

1864 *Serpentine Roulette 16*
13 A1 ⅓sgr black 475.00 *2,250.*
14 A1 ½gr blk, *green* 190.00 *3,000.*
15 A1 1sgr blk, *yellow* *2,850.* *1,425.*
16 A1 1sgr yellow 400.00 145.00
17 A1 2sgr blk, *blue* 400.00 340.00
 a. Half used as 1sgr on cover *12,000.*
18 A1 3sgr rose 800.00 525.00

Rouletted 12
20 A1 1sgr blk, *yellow* *11,000.*
21 A1 1sgr yellow 600.00 325.00
22 A1 3sgr rose — 2,500.

Nos. 13, 16, 18, 21-22 are on white paper.
Faked roulettes of Nos. 13-22 exist.

A4

Serpentine Roulette
1865 Embossed Unwmk.
23 A4 ⅓gr black 27.50 *350.00*
24 A4 1gr carmine 3.00 *50.00*
25 A4 2gr ultra 8.75 *125.00*
 a. 2gr gray blue 8.75 *125.00*
 c. Half used as 1sgr on cover *20,000.*
26 A4 3gr brown 8.00 *160.00*
 Nos. 23-26 (4) 47.25 685.00

Faked cancellations of Nos. 5-26 exist.

Imperf., Pairs
23a A4 ⅓gr 110.00
24a A4 1gr 32.50
25b A4 2gr 92.50
26a A4 3gr 110.00

Stamps of Brunswick were superseded by those of the North German Confederation on Jan. 1, 1868.

HAMBURG

LOCATION — Northern Germany
GOVT. — A former Free City
AREA — 160 sq. mi.
POP. — 453,869 (1880)
CAPITAL — Hamburg

Hamburg was a member of the German Confederation and became part of the German Empire in 1870.

16 Schillings = 1 Mark

Values for unused stamps are for examples with original gum as defined in the catalogue introduction. Stamps without gum sell for about 50-60% of the figures quoted.

Value Numeral on Arms — A1

1859 Typo. Wmk. 128 *Imperf.*
1 A1 ½s black 100.00 *600.00*
2 A1 1s brown 100.00 *95.00*
3 A1 2s red 100.00 *100.00*
4 A1 3s blue 100.00 *125.00*
5 A1 4s yellow green 80.00 *1,450.*
 a. 4s green 125.00 *1,300.*
 b. Double impression —
6 A1 7s orange 100.00 47.50
7 A1 9s yellow 200.00 *2,000.*

See Nos. 13-21.

A2

A3

1864 Litho.
9 A2 1¼s gray 90.00 80.00
 a. 1¼s lilac 150.00 85.00
 b. 1¼s red lilac 125.00 72.50
 c. 1¼s blue 425.00 *850.00*
 d. 1¼s greenish gray 110.00 *200.00*
12 A3 2½s green 140.00 *140.00*

See Nos. 22-23.

The 1¼s and 2½s have been reprinted on watermarked and unwatermarked paper.

1864-65 Typo. *Perf. 13½*
13 A1 ½s black 8.00 *12.00*
 a. Horiz. pair, imperf between 72.50
14 A1 1s brown 13.00 *17.50*
 a. Half used as ½s on cover *16,000.*
 b. Horiz. pair, imperf between 450.00 *650.00*
15 A1 2s red 16.00 *20.00*
17 A1 3s ultra 40.00 40.00
 a. Imperf., pair 140.00
 b. Horiz. pair, imperf. vert. —
 c. 3s blue 42.50 29.00
18 A1 4s green 12.00 20.00
19 A1 7s orange 160.00 125.00
20 A1 7s vio ('65) 11.50 16.00
 a. Imperf, pair 275.00
21 A1 9s yellow 25.00 *2,000.*
 a. Vert. pair, imperf btwn. 400.00

Litho.
22 A2 1¼s lilac 95.00 12.00
 a. 1¼s red lilac 95.00 12.00
 b. 1¼s violet 95.00 12.00
23 A3 2½s yel grn, blurred printing 125.00 35.00
 a. 2½s blue green 125.00 35.00

The 1¼s has been reprinted on watermarked and unwatermarked paper; the 2½s on unwatermarked paper.

A4

A5

Rouletted 10
1866 Unwmk. Embossed
24 A4 1¼s violet 40.00 35.00
 a. 1¼s red violet 72.50 72.50
25 A5 1½s rose 12.50 *125.00*

REPRINTS

1¼s: The rosettes between the words of the inscription have a well-defined open circle in the center of the originals, while in the reprints this circle is filled up.

In the upper part of the top of the "g" of "Schilling", there is a thin vertical line which is missing in the reprints.

The two lower lines of the triangle in the upper left corner are of different thicknesses in the originals while in the reprints they are of equal thickness.

The labels at the right and left containing the inscriptions are 2¾mm in width in the originals while they are 2½mm in reprints.

1½s: The originals are printed on thinner paper than the reprints. This is easily seen by turning the stamps over, when on the originals the color and impression will clearly show through, which is not the case in the reprints.

The vertical stroke of the upper part of the "g" in Schilling is very short on the originals, scarcely crossing the top line, while in the reprints it almost touches the center of the "g."

The lower part of the "g" of Schilling in the originals, barely touches the inner line of the frame, in some stamps it does not touch it at all, while in the reprints the whole stroke runs into the inner line of the frame.

A6

1867 Typo. Wmk. 128 *Perf. 13½*
26 A6 2½s dull green 12.50 *80.00*
 a. 2½s dark green 65.00 *100.00*
 b. Imperf., pair 225.00
 c. Horiz. pair, imperf between 92.50

Forged cancellations exist on almost all stamps of Hamburg, especially on Nos. 4, 7, 21 and 25.

Nos. 1-23 and 26 exist without watermark, but they come from the same sheets as the watermarked stamps.

The stamps of Hamburg were superseded by those of the North German Confederation on Jan. 1, 1868.

HANOVER

LOCATION — Northern Germany
GOVT. — A former Kingdom
AREA — 14,893 sq. mi.
POP. — 3,191,000
CAPITAL — Hanover

Hanover was a member of the German Confederation and became in 1866 a province of Prussia.

10 Pfennigs = 1 Groschen
24 Gute Groschen = 1 Thaler
30 Silbergroschen = 1 Thaler (1858)

Values for unused stamps are for examples with original gum as defined in the catalogue introduction. Examples without gum sell for about 50-60% of the figures quoted.

Coat of Arms — A1

Wmk. Square Frame
1850 Rose Gum Typo. *Imperf.*
1 A1 1gg blk, *gray bl* 3,250. 50.00

See Nos. 2, 11.

The reprints have white gum and no watermark.

Coat of Arms — A2

1851-55 Wmk. 130
2 A1 1gg blk, *gray grn* 80.00 9.00
 a. 1gg black, *yellow green* 950.00 32.50
3 A2 1/30th blk, *salmon* 95.00 50.00
 a. 1/30th black, *crimson* ('55) 95.00 50.00
 b. Bisect on cover —
5 A2 1/15th blk, *gray bl* 160.00 80.00
 a. Bisect on cover —
6 A2 1/10th blk, *yellow* 240.00 60.00
 a. 1/10th black, *orange* 240.00 60.00
 Nos. 2-6 (4) 575.00 199.00

Bisects Nos. 3b, 5a, 12a and 13a were used for ½g.

See Nos. 8, 12-13.

The 1/10th has been reprinted on unwatermarked paper, with white gum.

Crown and Numeral — A3

1853 Wmk. 130
7 A3 3pf rose 400.00 300.00

See Nos. 9, 16-17, 25.

The reprints of No. 7 have white gum.

Fine Network in Second Color
1855 Unwmk.
8 A2 1/10th blk & org 200.00 160.00
 a. 1/10th black & yellow 400.00 275.00

No. 8 with olive yellow network and other values with fine network are essays.

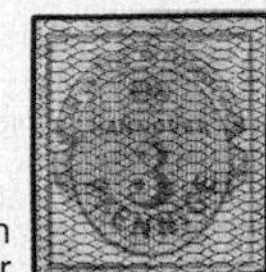
Large Network in Second Color

1856-57
9 A3 3pf rose & blk 275.00 275.00
 a. 3pf rose & gray 400.00 350.00
11 A1 1gg blk & grn 55.00 12.00
12 A2 1/30th blk & rose 125.00 32.50
 a. Bisect on cover *13,500.*
13 A2 1/15th blk & bl 95.00 72.50
 a. Bisect on cover *12,000.*
14 A2 1/10th blk & org ('57) 725.00 55.00

The reprints have white gum, and the network does not cover all the outer margin.

1859-63 Without Network
16 A3 3pf pink 140.00 *100.00*
 a. 3pf carmine rose 80.00 *90.00*
17 A3 3pf grn (Drei Zehntel) ('63) 400.00 *950.00*

Examples of No. 25 with rouletting trimmed off are sometimes offered as No. 17. Minimum size of No. 17 acknowledged as genuine: 21½x24½mm.

The reprints of No. 16 have pink gum instead of red; the extremities of the banderol point downward instead of outward.

Crown and Post Horn — A7

King George V — A8

1859-61 *Imperf.*
18 A7 ½g black ('60) 120.00 200.00
 a. Rose gum 400.00 *325.00*

19 A8 1g rose 4.00 4.50
 a. 1g vio rose 20.00 20.00
 b. 1g carmine 80.00 32.50
 c. Half used as ½g on cover *12,000.*
20 A8 2g ultra 16.00 40.00
 a. Half used as 1g on cover *8,000.*
22 A8 3g yellow 260.00 60.00
 a. 3g orange yellow 160.00 95.00
23 A8 3g brown ('61) 27.50 50.00
 a. One third used as 1g on cover —
24 A8 10g green ('61) 275.00 875.00

Reprints of ½g are on thick toned paper with yellowish gum. Originals are on white paper with rose or white gum. Reprints exist tête bêche.

Reprints of 3g yellow and 3g brown have white or pinkish gum. Originals have rose or orange gum.

1864 White Gum ***Perce en Arc 16***

25 A3 3pf grn (Drei Zehntel) 30.00 60.00
26 A7 ½g black 275.00 275.00
27 A8 1g rose 12.00 8.00
28 A8 2g ultra 125.00 60.00
 a. Half used as 1g on cover 16,000.
29 A8 3g brown 70.00 70.00
 Nos. 25-29 (5) 512.00 473.00

Reprints of 3g are percé en arc 13½.

Rose Gum

25a A3 3pf green 80.00 80.00
26a A7 ½g black 475.00 450.00
27a A8 1g rose 40.00 25.00
29a A8 3g brown *1,200.* *1,200.*

Used examples of Nos. 25a-29a retain the rose color on the reverse after the gum has been removed.

The stamps of Prussia superseded those of Hanover on Oct. 1, 1866.

LUBECK

LOCATION — Situated on an arm of the Baltic Sea between the former German States of Holstein and Mecklenburg.
GOVT. — Former Free City and State
AREA — 115 sq. mi.
POP. — 136,413
CAPITAL — Lubeck

Lubeck was a member of the German Confederation and became part of the German Empire in 1870.

16 Schillings = 1 Mark

Values for Nos. 1-7 unused are for stamps without gum. Nos. 6 and 7 with gum sell for about twice the figures quoted. Values for Nos. 8-14 unused are for examples with original gum as defined in the catalogue introduction. Nos. 8-14 without gum sell for about 50-60% of the figures quoted.

Coat of Arms — A1

1859 Litho. Wmk. 148 ***Imperf.***

1 A1 ½g gray lilac 475.00 *2,000.*
2 A1 1s orange 475.00 *2,000.*
3 A1 2s brown 27.50 *240.00*
 a. Value in words reads "ZWEI EIN HALB" 400.00 *7,200.*
4 A1 2½s rose 50.00 *800.00*
5 A1 4s green 27.50 *600.00*

The 1872 reprints of the 1859 issue are unwatermarked and printed in bright colors. Values: unused, $240 each; never hinged, $550 each.

1862 **Unwmk.**

6 A1 ½s lilac 17.50 *1,600.*
7 A1 1s yellow orange 30.00 *1,600.*

A2

1863 ***Rouletted 11½***

Eagle embossed

8 A2 ½s green 50.00 *72.50*
9 A2 1s orange 125.00 *160.00*
 a. Rouletted 10 200.00 *475.00*
10 A2 2s rose 27.50 *65.00*
11 A2 2½s ultra 125.00 *400.00*
12 A2 4s bister 55.00 *100.00*
 Nos. 8-12 (5) 382.50 *797.50*

The 1872 reprints are imperforate and without embossing. Values: unused, $120 each; never hinged, $225 each.

A3

1864 **Litho.** ***Imperf.***

13 A3 1¼s dark brown 45.00 *55.00*
 a. 1¼s reddish brown 32.50 *125.00*

A4

1865 ***Rouletted 11½***

Eagle embossed

14 A4 1⅓s red lilac 30.00 *85.00*

The 1872 reprints are imperforate and without embossing. Values: unused, $120; never hinged, $225.

Counterfeit cancellations are found on Nos. 1-14.

The stamps of Lübeck were superseded by those of the North German Confederation on Jan. 1, 1868.

MECKLENBURG-SCHWERIN

LOCATION — In northern Germany, bordering on the Baltic Sea.
GOVT. — Grand Duchy
AREA — 5,065 sq. mi. (approx.)
POP. — 674,000 (approx.)
CAPITAL — Schwerin

Mecklenburg-Schwerin was a member of the German Confederation and became part of the German Empire in 1870.

48 Schillings = 1 Thaler

Values for unused stamps are for examples with original gum as defined in the catalogue introduction. Examples without gum sell for about 70% of the figures quoted.

Coat of Arms
A1 A2

A1 has dots in background.

1856 Unwmk. Typo. ***Imperf.***

1 A1 Four ¼s red 150.00 125.00
 a. ¼s red 14.50 12.00
2 A2 3s yellow 95.00 55.00
3 A2 5s blue 225.00 275.00
 Nos. 1-3 (3) 470.00 455.00

See Nos. 4, 6-8.

A3

A3 has no dots in background.

1864-67 ***Rouletted 11½***

4 A1 Four ¼s red *2,800.* *1,900.*
 a. ¼s red 175.00 240.00
5 A3 Four ¼s red 70.00 60.00
 a. ¼s red 9.50 9.50
6 A2 2s gray lil ('67) 140.00 *1,600.*
 a. 2s red violet ('66) 240.00 240.00
7 A2 3s org yel, wide margin ('67) 45.00 *300.00*
 a. Narrow margin ('65) 160.00 125.00
8 A2 5s bister brn 160.00 *240.00*
 a. Thick paper 240.00 *340.00*

The overall size of No. 7, including margin, is 24½x24½mm. That of No. 7a is 23½x23mm.

The bister on white paper was not issued. Value $12.

Counterfeit cancellations exist on those stamps valued higher used than unused.

These stamps were superseded by those of the North German Confederation on Jan. 1, 1868.

MECKLENBURG-STRELITZ

LOCATION — In northern Germany, divided by Mecklenburg-Schwerin
GOVT. — Grand Duchy
AREA — 1,131 sq. mi.
POP. — 106,347
CAPITAL — Neustrelitz

Mecklenburg-Strelitz was a member of the German Confederation and became part of the German Empire in 1870.

30 Silbergroschen = 48 Schillings = 1 Thaler

Values for unused stamps are for examples with original gum as defined in the catalogue introduction. Examples without gum sell for about 50% of the figures quoted.

Coat of Arms
A1 A2

Rouletted 11½

1864 Unwmk. Embossed

1 A1 ¼sg orange 175.00 *2,400.*
 a. ¼sg yellow orange 340.00 *4,000.*
2 A1 ⅓sg green 80.00 *1,350.*
 a. ⅓sg dark green 140.00 *2,400.*
3 A1 1sch violet 290.00 *3,200.*
4 A2 1sg rose 140.00 190.00
5 A2 2sg ultra 40.00 *800.00*
6 A2 3sg bister 40.00 *1,275.*

Counterfeit cancellations abound.

These stamps were superseded by those of the North German Confederation in 1868.

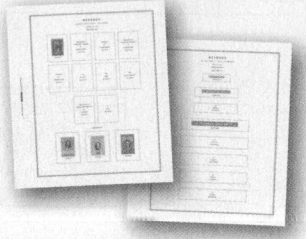

OLDENBURG

LOCATION — In northwestern Germany, bordering on the North Sea.
GOVT. — Grand Duchy
AREA — 2,482 sq. mi.
POP. — 483,042 (1910)
CAPITAL — Oldenburg

Oldenburg was a member of the German Confederation and became part of the German Empire in 1870.

30 Silbergroschen = 1 Thaler
30 Groschen = 1 Thaler

Values for unused stamps are for examples with original gum as defined in the catalogue introduction. Examples without gum sell for about 50% of the figures quoted.

A1 A2

1852-55 Unwmk. Litho. *Imperf.*

1	A1	1/30th blk, *blue*	350.00	27.50
2	A1	1/15th blk, *rose*	800.00	80.00
3	A1	1/10th blk, *yellow*	800.00	95.00
4	A2	1/3sgr blk, *grn* ('55)	1,275.	1,100.

There are three types of Nos. 1 and 2.

A3

1859

5	A3	1/3g blk, *green*	2,600.	*2,900.*
6	A3	1g blk, *blue*	725.00	45.00
7	A3	2g blk, *rose*	1,050.	600.00
8	A3	3g blk, *yellow*	1,050.	600.00
a.		"OLBENBURG"	1,600.	1,200.

See Nos. 10, 13-15.

A4

1861

9	A4	1/4g orange	300.00	*4,000.*
10	A3	1/3g green	475.00	*875.00*
a.		1/3g bluish green	475.00	*875.00*
b.		1/3g moss green	1,600.	*2,800.*
c.		"OLDEIBURG"	*875.00*	*1,450.*
d.		"Dritto"	*875.00*	*1,450.*
e.		"Drittd"	*875.00*	*1,450.*
f.		Printed on both sides		*5,000.*
12	A4	1/2g redsh brn	450.00	525.00
a.		1/2g dark brown	450.00	525.00
13	A3	1g blue	240.00	160.00
a.		1g gray blue	475.00	250.00
b.		Printed on both sides		*3,750.*
14	A3	2g red	450.00	450.00
15	A3	3g yellow	450.00	450.00
a.		"OLDEIBURG"	*000.00*	*875.00*
b.		Printed on both sides		*5,000.*

Forged cancellations are found on Nos. 9, 10, 12 and their minor varieties.

Coat of Arms — A5

1862 Embossed *Rouletted 11½*

16	A5	1/3g green	200.00	190.00
17	A5	1/2g orange	200.00	110.00
a.		1/2g orange red	250.00	160.00
18	A5	1g rose	110.00	16.00
19	A5	2g ultra	200.00	50.00
20	A5	3g bister	210.00	52.50

1867 *Rouletted 10*

21	A5	1/3g green	32.50	*725.00*
22	A5	1/2g orange	40.00	*360.00*
23	A5	1g rose	20.00	*55.00*
a.		Half used as 1/2g on cover		—
24	A5	2g ultra	20.00	*475.00*
25	A5	3g bister	45.00	*400.00*
		Nos. 21-25 (5)	157.50	*2,015.*

Forged cancellations are found on Nos. 21-25.

The stamps of Oldenburg were replaced by those of the North German Confederation on Jan. 1, 1868.

PRUSSIA

LOCATION — The greater part of northern Germany.
GOVT. — Independent Kingdom
AREA — 134,650 sq. mi.
POP. — 40,165,219 (1910)
CAPITAL — Berlin

Prussia was a member of the German Confederation and became part of the German Empire in 1870.

12 Pfennigs = 1 Silbergroschen
60 Kreuzer = 1 Gulden (1867)

Values for unused stamps are for examples with original gum as defined in the catalogue introduction. Examples without gum sell for about 50% of the figures quoted.

King Frederick William IV
A1 A2

1850-56 Engr. Wmk. 162 *Imperf.*
Background of Crossed Lines

1	A1	4pf yel grn ('56)	110.00	72.50
a.		4pf dark green	160.00	125.00
2	A1	6pf (1/2sg) red org	90.00	52.50
3	A2	1sg black, *rose*	80.00	14.00
a.		1sg black, *bright red*	*20,000.*	450.00
4	A2	2sg black, *blue*	110.00	16.00
a.		Half used as 1sg on cover		—
5	A2	3sg black, *yellow*	110.00	16.00
a.		3sg black, *orange buff*	325.00	37.50
		Nos. 1-5 (5)	500.00	171.00

See Nos. 10-13.

Reprints exist on watermarked and unwatermarked paper.

A3

Solid Background

1857 Typo. Unwmk.

6	A3	1sg rose	325.00	35.00
a.		1sg carmine rose	360.00	50.00
7	A3	2sg blue	1,280.	90.00
a.		2sg dark blue	1,750.	125.00
b.		Half used as 1sg on cover		—
8	A3	3sg orange	160.00	40.00
a.		3sg yellow	1,600.	95.00
b.		3sg deep orange	800.00	120.00
		Nos. 6-8 (3)	1,765.	165.00

The reprints of Nos. 6-8 have a period instead of a colon after "SILBERGR."

A4

Background of Crossed Lines

1858-60 Typo.

9	A4	4pf green	80.00	32.50

Engr.

10	A1	6pf (1/2sg) org ('59)	190.00	160.00
a.		6pf (1/2sg) brick red	275.00	225.00

Typo.

11	A2	1sg rose	32.50	4.00
12	A2	2sg blue	110.00	17.50
a.		2sg dark blue	160.00	42.50
b.		Half used as 1sg on cover		—
13	A2	3sg orange	95.00	16.00
a.		3sg yellow	140.00	20.00
		Nos. 9-13 (5)	507.50	230.00

Coat of Arms
A6 A7

1861-67 Embossed *Rouletted 11½*

14	A6	3pf red lilac ('67)	27.50	45.00
a.		3pf red violet ('65)	325.00	275.00
15	A6	4pf yellow green	12.00	12.00
a.		4pf green	42.50	55.00
16	A6	6pf orange	12.00	14.50
a.		6pf vermilion	125.00	65.00
17	A7	1sg rose	3.50	1.60
18	A7	2sg ultra	12.00	1.60
a.		2sg blue	400.00	27.50
20	A7	3sg bister	8.75	2.00
a.		3sg gray brown ('65)	—	29.00
		Nos. 14-20 (6)	75.75	76.70

A8 A9

Typographed in Reverse on Paper Resembling Goldbeater's Skin

1866 *Rouletted 10*

21	A8	10sg rose	95.00	*105.00*
22	A9	30sg blue	110.00	*225.00*

Perfect examples of Nos. 21-22 are extremely rare.

A10

1867 Embossed *Rouletted 16*

23	A10	1kr green	30.00	*45.00*
24	A10	2kr orange	45.00	*95.00*
25	A10	3kr rose	24.00	*27.50*
26	A10	6kr ultra	24.00	*45.00*
27	A10	9kr bister brown	27.50	*47.50*
		Nos. 23-27 (5)	150.50	*260.00*

Imperforate stamps of the above sets are proofs.

The stamps of Prussia were superseded by those of the North German Confederation on Jan. 1, 1868.

OFFICIAL STAMPS
See Germany Nos. OL1-OL15.

SAXONY

LOCATION — In central Germany
GOVT. — Kingdom
AREA — 5,787 sq. mi.
POP. — 2,500,000 (approx.)
CAPITAL — Dresden

Saxony was a member of the German Confederation and became a part of the German Empire in 1870.

10 Pfennings = 1 Neu-Groschen
30 Neu-Groschen = 1 Thaler

Values for unused stamps are for examples with original gum as defined in the catalogue introduction. Examples without gum sell for about 50-60% of the figures quoted.

A1

1850 Unwmk. Typo. *Imperf.*

1	A1	3pf brick red	*8,000.*	*6,500.*
a.		3pf cherry red	*12,000.*	*13,600.*
b.		3pf brown red	*12,000.*	*10,500.*

There are vertical dividing lines between stamps.

Coat of Arms — A2

1851

2	A2	3pf green	125.00	95.00
a.		3pf yellow green	1,750.	800.00

Nos. 2 and 2a are valued with the margin just touching the design in one or two places. Stamps with margins all around sell for considerably more.

Stamps with very fine impressions, from the first printing, command substantial premiums.

Frederick Augustus II — A3

1851-52 Engr.

3	A3	1/2ng black, *gray*	72.50	12.00
a.		1/2ng black, *pale blue* (error)	*20,000.*	
5	A3	1ng black, *rose*	95.00	12.00
6	A3	2ng black, *pale bl*	250.00	70.00
7	A3	2ng blk, *dk bl* ('52)	725.00	55.00
8	A3	3ng black, *yellow*	160.00	25.00
		Nos. 3-8 (5)	1,303.	174.00

The error No. 3a occurred when paper meant for printing No. 6 was inadvertently placed in the stack of paper for printing No. 3.

King John I — A4

1855-60

9	A4	1/2ng black, *gray*	16.00	8.00
a.		"1 1/20" at left or right	—	—
10	A4	1ng black, *rose*	16.00	8.00
11	A4	2ng black, *dark blue*	24.00	20.00
a.		2ng black, *blue*	72.50	47.50
12	A4	3ng black, *yellow*	24.00	16.00
13	A4	5ng ver ('56)	90.00	65.00
a.		5ng orange brown ('60)	325.00	*325.00*
b.		5ng deep brown ('57)	*725.00*	175.00
14	A4	10ng milky blue ('56)	225.00	225.00

A5 A6

Typo.; Arms Embossed

1863 *Perf. 13*

15	A5	3pf blue green	4.00	*40.00*
a.		3pf yellow green	95.00	*125.00*
16	A5	1/2ng orange	4.00	*2.75*
a.		1/2ng red orange	24.00	6.00
17	A6	1ng rose	1.60	2.40
a.		Vert. pair, imperf. between	*225.00*	
b.		Horiz. pair, imperf. between	*375.00*	
18	A6	2ng blue	2.75	8.00
a.		2ng dark blue	12.00	32.50
19	A6	3ng red brown	4.50	12.00
a.		3ng bister brown	24.00	9.50
20	A6	5ng dull violet	30.00	*47.50*
a.		5ng gray violet	16.00	*450.00*
b.		5ng gray blue	30.00	*72.50*
c.		5ng slate	22.50	*250.00*

The stamps of Saxony were superseded on Jan. 1, 1868, by those of the North German Confederation.

SCHLESWIG-HOLSTEIN

LOCATION — In northern Germany.
GOVT. — Duchies
AREA — 7,338 sq. mi.
POP. — 1,519,000 (approx.)
CAPITAL — Schleswig

Schleswig-Holstein was an autonomous territory from 1848 to 1851 when it came under Danish rule. In 1864, it was occupied by Prussia and Austria, and in 1866 it became a province of Prussia.

16 Schillings = 1 Mark

Values for unused stamps are for examples with original gum as defined in the catalogue introduction. Stamps without gum sell for about 50% of the figures quoted.

Coat of Arms — A1

Typographed; Arms Embossed

1850 Unwmk. *Imperf.*

With Silk Threads

No.	Type	Description	Unused	Used
1	A1	1s dl bl & grnsh bl	325.00	*5,600.*
a.		1s Prussian blue	725.00	
2	A1	2s rose & pink	560.00	*7,200.*
a.		2s deep pink & rose	725.00	
b.		Double embossing	*3,100.*	

Forged cancellations are found on Nos. 1-2, 5-7, 9, 16 and 19.

A2

A3

1865 Typo. *Rouletted 11½*

No.	Type	Description	Unused	Used
3	A2	½s rose	40.00	*45.00*
4	A2	1¼s green	20.00	*20.00*
5	A3	1⅓s red lilac	45.00	*125.00*
6	A2	2s ultra	50.00	*240.00*
7	A3	4s bister	65.00	*1,300.*
		Nos. 3-7 (5)	220.00	1,730.

Schleswig

A4

1864 Typo. *Rouletted 11½*

No.	Type	Description	Unused	Used
8	A4	1¼s green	45.00	20.00
9	A4	4s carmine	95.00	*450.00*

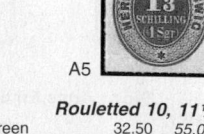

A5

1865 *Rouletted 10, 11½*

No.	Type	Description	Unused	Used
10	A4	½s green	32.50	*55.00*
11	A4	1¼s red lilac	55.00	25.00
a.		1¼s gray lilac ('67)	255.00	47.50
b.		Half of #11a used as ½s on cover		*32,000.*
12	A5	1⅓s rose	27.50	*60.00*
13	A4	2s ultra	27.50	*60.00*
14	A4	4s bister	32.50	*80.00*
		Nos. 10-14 (5)	175.00	*280.00*

Holstein

A6

Type I — Small lettering in frame. Wavy lines in spandrels close together.
Type II — Small lettering in frame. Wavy lines wider apart.
Type III — Larger lettering in frame and no periods after "H R Z G." Wavy lines as II.

1864 Litho. *Imperf.*

No.	Type	Description	Unused	Used
15	A6	1¼s bl & gray, I	52.50	*55.00*
a.		Half used as ½s on cover		*9,500.*
16	A6	1¼s bl & gray, II	800.00	*2,400.*
a.		Half used as ½s on cover		*24,000.*
17	A6	1¼s bl & gray, III	45.00	*55.00*
a.		Half used as ½s on cover		*8,000.*

A7

1864 Typo. *Rouletted 8*

No.	Type	Description	Unused	Used
18	A7	1¼s blue & rose	45.00	20.00
a.		Half used as ½s on cover		*2,000.*

A8

1865 *Rouletted 8*

No.	Type	Description	Unused	Used
19	A8	½s green	65.00	*95.00*
20	A8	1¼s red lilac	47.50	25.00
21	A8	2s blue	52.50	47.50
		Nos. 19-21 (3)	165.00	167.50

A9

A10

1865-66 *Rouletted 7 and 8*

No.	Type	Description	Unused	Used
22	A9	1¼s red lilac ('66)	72.50	25.00
a.		Half used as ½s on cover		*24,000.*
23	A10	1⅓s carmine	60.00	45.00
24	A9	2s blue ('66)	145.00	*160.00*
25	A10	4s bister	65.00	*80.00*
		Nos. 22-25 (4)	342.50	310.00

These stamps were superseded by those of North German Confederation on Jan. 1, 1868.

THURN AND TAXIS

A princely house which, prior to the formation of the German Empire, enjoyed the privilege of a postal monopoly. These stamps were superseded on July 1, 1867, by those of Prussia, followed by those of the North German Postal District on Jan. 1, 1868, and later by stamps of the German Empire on Jan. 1, 1872.

Values are for stamps with four complete margins just clear of the framelines. Stamps with margins just touching the framelines on one or two sides are worth approximately 60% of the values quoted. Stamps with four large margins are rare and command premiums of up to 500% over the values quoted.

Values for unused stamps are for examples with original gum as defined in the catalogue introduction. Stamps without gum sell for about 50% of the figures quoted.

NORTHERN DISTRICT

30 Silbergroschen or Groschen = 1 Thaler

A1

1852-58 Unwmk. Typo. *Imperf.*

No.	Type	Description	Unused	Used
1	A1	¼sgr blk, *red brn* ('54)	265.00	60.00
2	A1	⅓sgr blk, *buff* ('58)	125.00	250.00
3	A1	½sgr blk, *green*	725.00	40.00
4	A1	1sgr blk, *dk bl*	1,325.	140.00
5	A1	1sgr blk, *lt bl* ('53)	800.00	22.50
6	A1	2sgr blk, *rose*	850.00	32.50
a.		Half used as 1sgr on cover		*10,000.*
7	A1	3sgr blk, *brownish yellow*	1,000.	30.00
a.		3sgr blk, *pale orange yellow*	1,000.	80.00

Reprints of Nos. 1-12, 15-20, 23-24, were made in 1910. They have "ND" in script on the back. Value, $6.50 each.

A2

1859-60

No.	Type	Description	Unused	Used
8	A1	¼sgr red ('60)	67.50	67.50
9	A1	½gr green	300.00	95.00
10	A1	1sgr blue	300.00	45.00
11	A1	2sgr rose ('60)	145.00	80.00
12	A1	3sgr red brn ('60)	145.00	110.00
13	A2	5sgr lilac	2.75	*400.00*
14	A2	10sgr orange	2.75	*875.00*

Excellent forged cancellations exist on Nos. 13 and 14. For reprints, see note after No. 7.

1862-63

No.	Type	Description	Unused	Used
15	A1	¼sgr black ('63)	35.00	*75.00*
16	A1	⅓sgr green ('63)	50.00	*250.00*
17	A1	½sgr org yel	100.00	47.50
18	A1	1sgr rose ('63)	67.50	27.50
19	A1	2sgr blue ('63)	60.00	*100.00*
20	A1	3sgr bister ('63)	27.50	*55.00*
		Nos. 15-20 (6)	340.00	*555.00*

For reprints, see note after No. 7.

1865 *Rouletted*

No.	Type	Description	Unused	Used
21	A1	¼sgr black	7.50	*400.00*
22	A1	⅓sgr green	11.00	*240.00*
23	A1	½sgr yellow	22.50	*37.50*
24	A1	1sgr rose	25.00	25.00
25	A1	2sgr blue	1.50	*67.50*
26	A1	3sgr bister	2.75	*27.50*
		Nos. 21-26 (6)	70.25	*797.50*

For reprints, see note after No. 7.

1866 *Rouletted in Colored Lines*

No.	Type	Description	Unused	Used
27	A1	¼sgr black	2.00	*1,250.*
28	A1	⅓sgr green	2.00	*600.00*
29	A1	½sgr yellow	2.00	*120.00*
30	A1	1sgr rose	1.50	*60.00*
a.		Horizontal pair without rouletting between	150.00	1,500.
b.		Half used as ½sgr on cover		*52,500.*
31	A1	2sgr blue	1.50	*600.00*
32	A1	3sgr bister	1.50	*150.00*
		Nos. 27-32 (6)	10.50	*2,780.*

Forged cancellations on Nos. 2, 13-14, 15-16, 21-22, 25-32 are plentiful.

SOUTHERN DISTRICT

60 Kreuzer = 1 Gulden

A1

1852-53 Unwmk. *Imperf.*

No.	Type	Description	Unused	Used
42	A1	1kr blk, *lt grn*	240.00	15.00
43	A1	3kr blk, *dk bl*	925.00	50.00
44	A1	3kr blk, *bl* ('53)	800.00	20.00
45	A1	6kr blk, *rose*	800.00	11.00
46	A1	9kr blk, *brnish yell*	875.00	17.50
a.		9kr blk, *pale orange yellow*	750.00	45.00

Reprints of Nos. 42-50, 53-56 were made in 1910. Each has "ND" in script on the back. Value, each $6.50.

A2

1859

No.	Type	Description	Unused	Used
47	A1	1kr green	25.00	10.00
48	A1	3kr blue	560.00	25.00
49	A1	6kr rose	560.00	67.50
50	A1	9kr yellow	560.00	67.50
51	A2	15kr lilac	2.75	*175.00*
52	A2	30kr orange	2.75	*475.00*

Forged cancellations exist on Nos. 51 and 52. For reprints, see note after No. 46.

1862

No.	Type	Description	Unused	Used
53	A1	3kr rose	13.50	30.00
54	A1	6kr blue	13.50	30.00
55	A1	9kr bister	13.50	35.00
		Nos. 53-55 (3)	40.50	95.00

For reprints, see note after No. 46.

1865 *Rouletted*

No.	Type	Description	Unused	Used
56	A1	1kr green	12.50	13.50
57	A1	3kr rose	18.50	7.50
58	A1	6kr blue	1.50	*20.00*
59	A1	9kr bister	2.25	*22.50*
		Nos. 56-59 (4)	34.75	*63.50*

For reprint of No. 56, see note after No. 46.

1866 *Rouletted in Colored Lines*

No.	Type	Description	Unused	Used
60	A1	1kr green	1.50	*22.50*
61	A1	3kr rose	1.50	*20.00*
62	A1	6kr blue	1.50	*37.50*
63	A1	9kr bister	1.50	*32.50*
		Nos. 60-63 (4)	6.00	*112.50*

Forged cancellations exist on Nos. 51-52, 58-63.

The Thurn & Taxis Stamps, Northern and Southern Districts, were replaced on July 1, 1867, by those of Prussia.

WURTTEMBERG

LOCATION — In southern Germany
GOVT. — Kingdom
AREA — 7,530 sq. mi.
POP. — 2,580,000 (approx.)
CAPITAL — Stuttgart

Württemberg was a member of the German Confederation and became a part of the German Empire in 1870. It gave up its postal autonomy on March 31, 1902, but official stamps were issued until 1923.

16 Kreuzer = 1 Gulden
100 Pfennigs = 1 Mark (1875)

Values for unused stamps are for examples with original gum as defined in the catalogue introduction. Unused stamps without gum of Nos. 1-46 sell for about 60-70% of the figures quoted. Unused stamps without gum of Nos. 47-54 sell for about 50% of the figures quoted.

A1

A1a

1851-52 Unwmk. Typo. *Imperf.*

No.	Type	Description	Unused	Used
1	A1	1kr blk, *buff*	1,125.	95.00
a.		1kr black, *straw*	3,500.	500.00
2	A1	3kr blk, *yellow*	275.00	7.25
a.		3kr black, *orange*	3,000.	300.00
4	A1	6kr blk, *yel grn*	1,450.	32.50
a.		6kr black, *blue green*	2,600.	50.00
5	A1	9kr blk, *rose*	*4,800.*	37.50
6	A1a	18kr blk, *dl vio* ('52)	1,750.	725.00

On the "reprints" the letters of "Württemberg" are smaller, especially the first "e"; the right branch of the "r's" of Württemberg runs upward in the reprints and downward in the originals.

Coat of Arms — A2

With Orange Silk Threads Typographed and Embossed

1857
7 A2 1kr yel brn 800.00 80.00
a. 1kr dark brown 1,100. 225.00
9 A2 3kr yel org 400.00 14.00
10 A2 6kr green 800.00 65.00
11 A2 9kr car rose 1,925. 70.00
12 A2 18kr blue 3,350. 1,350.

Very fine examples of Nos. 7-12 with have one or two margins touching, but not cutting, the frameline.

See Nos. 13-40, 53.

The reprints have red or yellow silk threads and are printed 2mm apart, while the originals are ¾mm apart.

1859 **Without Silk Threads**
13 A2 1kr brown 650.00 100.00
a. 1kr dark brown 2,000. 725.00
15 A2 3kr yel org 275.00 14.00
16 A2 6kr green *9,600.* 125.00
17 A2 9kr car rose 1,275. 80.00
18 A2 18kr dark blue 3,000. 1,450.

The colors of the reprints are brighter; they are also printed 2mm apart instead of 1¼mm.

1860 ***Perf. 13½***
19 A2 1kr brown 1,125. 125.00
20 A2 3kr yel org 325.00 9.50
21 A2 6kr green 3,000. 100.00
22 A2 9kr carmine 1,200. 120.00

1861 **Thin Paper**
23 A2 1kr brown 950.00 275.00
a. 1kr black brown 1,000. 250.00
25 A2 3kr yel org 200.00 65.00
26 A2 6kr green 400.00 110.00
27 A2 9kr rose 1,275. 275.00
a. 9kr claret 1,500. 350.00
29 A2 18kr dark blue 3,000 2,250.

Examples of Nos. 23-29 with all perforations intact sell for considerably more.

1862 ***Perf. 10***
30 A2 1kr blk brn 650.00 440.00
31 A2 3kr yel org 800.00 47.50
32 A2 6kr green 525.00 160.00
33 A2 9kr claret 4,000. 800.00

1863
34 A2 1kr yel grn 45.00 13.50
a. 1kr green 400.00 95.00
36 A2 3kr rose 325.00 5.50
a. 3kr dark claret 1,600. 275.00
37 A2 6kr blue 160.00 55.00
39 A2 9kr yel brn 750.00 175.00
a. 9kr red brown 260.00 52.50
b. 9kr black brown 1,200. 190.00
40 A2 18kr orange 1,200. 400.00

1865-68 ***Rouletted 10***
41 A2 1kr yel grn 45.00 12.00
a. 1kr dark green 575.00 275.00
42 A2 3kr rose 45.00 3.25
a. 3kr claret 1,900. 2,250.
43 A2 6kr blue 275.00 52.50
44 A2 7kr slate bl ('68) 960.00 125.00
45 A2 9kr bis brn 1,500. 120.00
a. 9kr red brown 1,150. 80.00
46 A2 18kr orange ('67) 1,800. 950.00

A3

1869-73 **Typo. & Embossed**
47 A3 1kr yel grn 32.50 2.40
48 A3 2kr orange 175.00 140.00
49 A3 3kr rose 16.00 1.60
50 A3 7kr blue 67.50 17.50
51 A3 9kr lt brn ('73) 80.00 40.00
52 A3 14kr orange 88.00 45.00
a. 14kr lemon yellow 1,500. 1,500.
Nos. 47-52 (6) 459.00 246.50

See No. 54.

1873 ***Imperf.***
53 A2 70kr red violet 1,750. 4,000.
a. 70kr violet 2,900. 5,250.

Nos. 53 and 53a have single or double lines of fine black dots printed in the gutters between the stamps.

1874 ***Perf. 11½x11***
54 A3 1kr yellow green 110.00 40.00

A4

A5

1875-1900 **Typo.**
55 A4 2pf sl gray ('93) 2.00 .95
56 A4 3pf green 20.00 1.60
57 A4 3pf brn ('90) .80 .55
a. Imperf., pair 160.00
58 A4 5pf violet 9.50 .80
59 A4 5pf grn ('90) 1.60 .55
a. 5pf blue green 300.00 24.00
b. Imperf., pair 175.00
60 A4 10pf carmine 1.60 .80
a. 10pf rose 85.00 1.25
b. Imperf., pair 80.00
61 A4 20pf ultra 1.60 1.60
a. 20pf dull blue 1.60 1.60
b. Imperf., pair 175.00
62 A4 25pf red brn 125.00 12.00
63 A4 25pf org ('90) 2.75 1.60
a. Imperf., pair 175.00
64 A5 30pf org & blk ('00) 4.00 5.50
65 A5 40pf dp rose & blk ('00) 4.00 6.50
66 A4 50pf gray 725.00 40.00
67 A4 50pf gray grn 65.00 6.50
68 A4 50pf pur brn ('90) 3.25 .95
a. 50pf red brown 640.00 65.00
b. As #68, imperf., pair 175.00
69 A4 2m yellow 800.00 260.00
70 A4 2m ver, *buff* ('79) 2,800. 125.00
71 A5 2m org & blk ('86) 8.00 12.00
Telegraph cancel 4.50
a. 2m yellow & black 450.00 72.50
b. Imperf., pair 125.00
72 A5 5m bl & blk ('81) 45.00 *160.00*
Telegraph cancel 72.50
a. Double impression of figure of value 200.00

No. 70 has "Unverkauflich" (not for sale) printed on its back to remind postal clerks that it, like No. 69, was for their use and not to be sold to the public.

The regular postage stamps of Württemberg were superseded by those of the German Empire in 1902. Official stamps were in use until 1923.

WURTTEMBERG OFFICIAL STAMPS

For the Communal Authorities

O1

Perf. 11½x11
1875-1900 **Typo.** **Unwmk.**
O1 O1 2pf sl gray ('00) 3.00 2.00
O2 O1 3pf brn ('96) 3.00 2.00
O3 O1 5pf violet 37.50 2.40
a. Imperf., pair *3,000.*
O4 O1 5pf bl grn ('90) 1.60 2.00
a. Imperf., pair 55.00
O5 O1 10pf rose 7.50 2.25
a. Imperf., pair 90.00
O6 O1 25pf org ('00) 22.50 8.00
Nos. O1-O6 (6) 75.10 18.65

See Nos. O12-O32. For overprints and surcharges see Nos. O7-O11, O40-O52, O59-O93.

Used Values

When italicized, used values for Nos. O7-O183 are for favor-canceled stamps. Postally used stamps command a premium.

Stamps of Previous Issues Overprinted in Black

1906, Jan. 30
O7 O1 2pf slate gray 45.00
O8 O1 3pf dk brown 14.00 *9.25*
O9 O1 5pf green 6.50 *4.75*
O10 O1 10pf deep rose 6.50 *4.75*
O11 O1 25pf orange 47.50 *72.50*
Nos. O7-O11 (5) 119.50 *91.25*

Centenary of Kingdom of Württemberg.

Nos. O7-O11 also exist imperf but it is doubtful if they were ever issued in that condition.

1906-21 **Wmk. 116**
O12 O1 2pf slate gray 4.00 .40
O13 O1 2½pf gray blk ('16) .80 .25
O14 O1 3pf dk brown .95 .40
O15 O1 5pf green .80 .40
O16 O1 7½pf orange ('16) .80 .25
O17 O1 10pf dp rose .80 .40
O18 O1 10pf orange ('21) .30 *.30*
O19 O1 15pf yellow brn ('16) 2.40 .25
O20 O1 15pf purple ('17) 1.25 .25
O21 O1 20pf dp ultra ('11) 1.60 .40
O22 O1 20pf dp green ('21) .30 .30
O23 O1 25pf orange .95 .40
O24 O1 25pf brn & blk ('17) 1.25 .25
O25 O1 35pf brown ('19) 1.60 .95
O26 O1 40pf rose red ('21) .30 .30
O27 O1 50pf rose lake ('11) 14.50 .40
O28 O1 50pf vio brn ('21) .30 .30
O29 O1 60pf olive grn ('21) .50 .30
O30 O1 1.25m emerald ('21) .30 .30
O31 O1 2m gray ('21) .30 .30
O32 O1 3m brown ('21) .50 .30
Nos. O12-O32 (21) 34.50 7.40

No. O24 contains solid black numerals.

Nos. O12-O32 exist imperf. Value, each pair, $6-$16.

O3

Perf. 14½x14
1916, Oct. 6 **Typo.** **Unwmk.**
O33 O3 2½pf slate 1.60 1.60
O34 O3 7½pf orange 1.60 1.60
O35 O3 10pf car rose 1.60 1.60
O36 O3 15pf yellow brn 1.60 1.60
O37 O3 20pf blue 1.60 1.60
O38 O3 25pf gray blk 4.00 1.60
O39 O3 50pf red brown 8.00 1.60
Nos. O33-O39 (7) 20.00 11.20

25th year of the reign of King Wilhelm II.

Stamps of 1900-06 Surcharged

Perf. 11½x11
1916, Sept. 10 **Wmk. 116**
O40 O1 25pf on 25pf orange 4.00 .95

No. O13 Surcharged in Blue

1919 **Wmk. 116**
O42 O1 2pf on 2½pf gray blk .80 .50

Official Stamps of 1906-19 Overprinted

1919
O43 O1 2½pf gray blk .40 *.60*
O44 O1 3pf dk brown 12.00 .60
O45 O1 5pf green .30 .60
O46 O1 7½pf orange 1.00 .60
O47 O1 10pf rose .30 .60
O48 O1 15pf purple .30 .60
O49 O1 20pf ultra .40 .60
O50 O1 25pf brown & blk .40 .60
O51 O1 35pf brown 4.00 .60
O52 O1 50pf red brown 5.50 .60
Nos. O43-O52 (10) 24.60 *6.00*

Stag — O4

Wmk. 192
1920, Mar. 19 **Litho.** ***Perf. 14½***
O53 O4 10pf maroon 1.45 *1.00*
O54 O4 15pf brown 1.45 *1.60*
O55 O4 20pf indigo 1.45 *1.60*
O56 O4 30pf deep green 1.45 *1.60*
O57 O4 50pf yellow 3.25 *1.60*
O58 O4 75pf bister 3.25 *1.60*
Nos. O53-O58 (6) 12.30 *9.60*

Official Stamps of 1906-19 Overprinted

Perf. 11½x11
1920, Apr. 1 **Wmk. 116**
O59 O1 5pf green 4.00 10.00
O60 O1 10pf deep rose 2.40 4.75
O61 O1 15pf dp violet 2.40 5.25
O62 O1 20pf ultra 4.00 8.75
a. Wmk. 192 4.75 8.75
O63 O1 50pf red brown 6.50 20.00
Nos. O59-O63 (5) 19.30 48.75

Nos. O59 to O63 were available for official postage throughout all Germany but were used almost exclusively in Württemberg.

Stamps of 1917-21 Surcharged in Black, Red or Blue

1923
O64 O1 5m on 10pf orange .25 *.50*
O65 O1 10m on 15pf dp violet .25 *.50*
O66 O1 12m on 40pf rose red .25 *.50*
O67 O1 20m on 10pf orange .80 *.50*
O68 O1 25m on 20pf green .25 *.50*
O69 O1 40m on 20pf green .25 *.50*
O70 O1 50m on 60pf olive grn .25 *.50*

Surcharged

O71 O1 60m on 1.25m emer .25 *.50*
O72 O1 100m on 40pf rose red .25 *.50*
O73 O1 200m on 2m gray (R) .25 *.50*
O74 O1 300m on 50pf red brn (Bl) .25 *.50*
O75 O1 400m on 3m brn (Bl) .25 *.50*
O76 O1 1000m on 60pf ol grn .25 *.50*
O77 O1 2000m on 1.25m emer .25 *.50*
Nos. O64-O77 (14) 4.05 *7.00*

Abbreviations:
Th = (Tausend) Thousand
Mil = (Million) Million
Mlrd = (Milliarde) Billion

Surcharged

1923
O78 O1 5th m on 10pf orange .25 *.50*
O79 O1 20th m on 40pf rose red .25 *.50*
O80 O1 50th m on 15pf violet 1.00 .50
O81 O1 75th m on 2m gray 1.60 .50
O82 O1 100th m on 20pf green .25 *.50*
O83 O1 250th m on 3m brown .25 .60

Surcharged

O84 O1 1mil m on 60pf ol grn 1.25 .50
O85 O1 2mil m on 50pf red brn .25 *.50*
O86 O1 5mil m on 1.25m emer .35 *.50*

Surcharged

O87	O1	4 mlrd m on 50pf red brn	4.50	.50
O88	O1	10 mlrd m on 3m brn	3.25	.50
		Nos. O78-O88 (11)	13.20	5.50

No. O23 Surcharged in Rentenpfennig as

1923, Dec.

O89	O1	3pf on 25pf orange	.50	.40
O90	O1	5pf on 25pf orange	.40	.40
O91	O1	10pf on 25pf orange	.40	.40
O92	O1	20pf on 25pf orange	.50	.40
O93	O1	50pf on 25pf orange	.40	.40
		Nos. O89-O93 (5)	2.20	2.00

For the State Authorities

O6

Perf. 11½x11

1881-1902 Typo. Unwmk.

O94	O6	2pf sl gray ('96)	1.60	1.60
O95	O6	3pf green	25.00	4.50
O96	O6	3pf dk brn ('90)	1.60	2.00
		Never hinged	2.50	
O97	O6	5pf violet	8.00	2.00
O98	O6	5pf green ('90)	2.40	2.00
O99	O6	10pf rose	8.00	1.90
O100	O6	20pf ultra	1.00	2.40
O101	O6	25pf brown	35.00	6.50
O102	O6	25pf orange ('90)	5.25	1.40
O103	O6	30pf org & blk ('02)	2.00	3.25
O104	O6	40pf dp rose & blk ('02)	2.25	3.25
O105	O6	50pf gray grn	6.50	8.75
O106	O6	50pf maroon ('91)	1.60	4.00
a.		50pf red brown ('90)	240.00	*1,750.*
O107	O6	1m yellow	72.50	175.00
O108	O6	1m violet ('90)	5.50	16.00
		Nos. O94-O108 (15)	178.20	234.55

See #O119-O135. For overprints & surcharges see #O109-O118, O146-O164, O176-O183.

Overprinted in Black

1906

O109	O6	2pf slate gray	27.00	5.00
O110	O6	3pf dk brown	5.50	*5.00*
O111	O6	5pf green	4.75	*5.00*
O112	O6	10pf dp rose	4.50	*5.00*
O113	O6	20pf ultra	4.75	*5.00*
O114	O6	25pf orange	11.00	6.00
O115	O6	30pf org & blk	9.50	7.50
O116	O6	40pf dp rose & blk	32.50	7.50
O117	O6	50pf red brown	32.50	7.50
O118	O6	1m purple	65.00	7.50
		Nos. O109-O118 (10)	197.00	*61.00*

Cent. of the kingdom of Wüttemberg.

Nos. O109 to O118 are also found imperforate, but it is doubtful if they were ever issued in that condition. Value, each: unused $45; never hinged $90.

1906-19 Wmk. 116

O119	O6	2pf slate gray	.50	.40
O120	O6	2½pf gray blk ('16)	.55	.40
O121	O6	3pf dk brown	.50	.40
O122	O6	5pf green	.50	.40
O123	O6	7½pf orange ('16)	.55	.40
O124	O6	10pf deep rose	.50	.40
O125	O6	15pf yel brn ('16)	.65	.40
O126	O6	15pf purple ('17)	1.25	.40
O127	O6	20pf ultra	.65	.40
O128	O6	25pf orange	.60	.40
O129	O6	25pf brn & blk ('17)	.50	.40
O130	O6	30pf org & blk	.50	.40
O131	O6	35pf brown ('19)	1.60	*2.40*
O132	O6	40pf dp rose & blk	.50	.40
O133	O6	50pf red brown	.65	.40
O134	O6	1m purple	5.50	.40
O135	O6	1m sl & blk ('17)	11.00	1.55
		Nos. O119-O135 (17)	26.50	*9.95*

King Wilhelm II — O8

1916 Unwmk. Typo. *Perf. 14*

O136	O8	2½pf slate	.80	.65
O137	O8	7½pf orange	.80	.45
O138	O8	10pf carmine	.80	.45
O139	O8	15pf yellow brn	.80	.45
O140	O8	20pf blue	.80	.45
O141	O8	25pf gray blk	1.60	.65
O142	O8	30pf green	1.60	1.25
O143	O8	40pf claret	2.40	1.25
O144	O8	50pf red brn	3.25	1.85
O145	O8	1m violet	3.25	2.50
		Nos. O136-O145 (10)	16.10	9.95

25th year of the reign of King Wilhelm II.

Stamps of 1890-1906 Surcharged

1916-19 Wmk. 116 *Perf. 11½x11*

O146	O6	25pf on 25pf org	2.75	.80
a.		Without watermark	35.00	13,400.
O147	O6	50pf on 50pf red brn	1.60	1.10
a.		Inverted surcharge	32.50	

Beware of fake cancels on No. O146a.
No. O147a is considered a proof.

No. O120 Surcharged in Blue

1919 Wmk. 116

O149	O6	2pf on 2½pf gray blk	1.60	1.60

Official Stamps of 1890-1919 Overprinted

1919

O150	O6	2½pf gray blk	.55	.40
O151	O6	3pf dk brown	7.25	.80
a.		Without watermark	52.50	
O152	O6	5pf green	.40	.40
O153	O6	7½pf orange	.40	.40
O154	O6	10pf rose	.40	.40
O155	O6	15pf purple	.40	.40
O156	O6	20pf ultra	.40	.40
O157	O6	25pf brn & blk	.40	.40
a.		Inverted overprint	95.00	240.00
O158	O6	30pf org & blk	.80	.40
a.		Inverted overprint	475.00	—
O159	O6	35pf brown	.55	.40
O160	O6	40pf rose & blk	.55	.40
O161	O6	50pf claret	.80	.65
		Never hinged	1.25	
		Postally used		5.00
O162	O6	1m slate & blk	.80	.80
		Nos. O150-O162 (13)	13.70	6.25

Nos. O151, O151a Surcharged in Carmine

1920 Wmk. 116

O164	O6	75pf on 3pf dk brn	1.25	1.25
a.		Without watermark	80.00	*20.00*

View of Stuttgart O9

10pf, 50pf, 2.50m, 3m, View of Stuttgart. 15pf, 75pf, View of Ulm. 20pf, 1m, View of Tubingen. 30pf, 1.25m, View of Ellwangen.

Wmk. 192

1920, Mar. 25 Typo. *Perf. 14½*

O166	O9	10pf maroon	.55	*1.20*
O167	O9	15pf brown	.55	*1.20*
O168	O9	20pf indigo	.55	*1.20*
O169	O9	30pf blue grn	.55	*1.20*
O170	O9	50pf yellow	.55	*1.20*
O171	O9	75pf bister	.55	*1.20*
O172	O9	1m orange red	.80	*1.20*
O173	O9	1.25m dp violet	.80	*1.20*
O174	O9	2.50m dark ultra	2.00	1.20
O175	O9	3m yellow grn	2.40	1.20
		Nos. O166-O175 (10)	9.30	*12.00*

Official Stamps of 1906-19 Overprinted

1920 Wmk. 116 *Perf. 11½x11*

O176	O6	5pf green	2.40	4.00
O177	O6	10pf deep rose	1.00	0.25
O178	O6	15pf purple	1.60	3.25
O179	O6	20pf ultra	1.60	1.60
a.		Wmk. 192	125.00	325.00
O180	O6	30pf orange & blk	1.60	4.00
O181	O6	40pf dp rose & blk	1.60	3.25
O182	O6	50pf red brown	1.60	4.00
O183	O6	1m slate & blk	2.40	8.00
		Nos. O176-O183 (8)	14.40	31.35

The note after No. O63 will also apply to Nos. O176-O183.

NORTH GERMAN CONFEDERATION

Northern District
30 Groschen = 1 Thaler
Southern District
60 Kreuzer = 1 Gulden
Hamburg
16 Schillings = 1 Mark

Values for unused stamps are for examples with original gum as defined in the catalogue introduction. Stamps without gum sell for about 50% of the figures quoted.

A1

A2

Rouletted 8½ to 10, 11 to 12½ and Compound

1868 Typo. Unwmk.

1	A1	¼gr violet	15.00	15.00
2	A1	⅓gr green	30.00	4.00
3	A1	½gr orange	30.00	2.50
4	A1	1gr rose	20.00	1.60
b.		Half used as ½gr on cover		—
5	A1	2gr ultra	80.00	3.25
6	A1	5gr bister	80.00	9.50
7	A2	1kr green	35.00	8.00
8	A2	2kr orange	55.00	55.00
9	A2	3kr rose	35.00	3.25
10	A2	7kr ultra	160.00	11.00
11	A2	18kr bister	35.00	65.00
		Nos. 1-11 (11)	575.00	178.10

See Nos. 13-23.

Imperf

1a	A1	¼gr red lilac	200.00	—
2a	A1	⅓gr green	95.00	—
3a	A1	½gr orange	140.00	—
4a	A1	1gr rose	80.00	—
5a	A1	2gr ultra	275.00	—
6a	A1	5gr bister	275.00	—
7a	A2	1kr green	72.50	*125.00*
8a	A2	2kr orange	200.00	95.00
9a	A2	3kr rose	80.00	100.00
10a	A2	7kr ultra	350.00	*675.00*
11a	A2	18kr bister	350.00	*675.00*

A3

1868

12	A3	(½s) lilac brown	110.00	55.00
d.		Imperf	200.00	

See No. 24.

1869 *Perf. 13½x14*

13	A1	¼gr lilac	14.50	16.00
a.		¼gr red violet	25.00	20.00
14	A1	⅓gr green	5.25	2.75
15	A1	½gr orange	5.25	3.50
16	A1	1gr rose	4.00	1.60
17	A1	2gr ultra	7.25	2.00
18	A1	5gr bister	8.75	10.00
19	A2	1kr green	12.75	10.00
20	A2	2kr orange	40.00	*110.00*
21	A2	3kr rose	7.25	3.25
22	A2	7kr ultra	11.00	12.00
23	A2	18kr bister	150.00	*1,750.*
		Nos. 13-23 (11)	266.00	1,921.

Counterfeit cancels exist on No. 23.

1869

24	A3	(½s) dull violet brown	4.75	8.75

A4

A5

Perf. 14x13½

25	A4	10gr gray	325.00	400.00
		Pen cancellation		65.00
26	A5	30gr blue	240.00	*960.00*
		Pen cancellation		*140.00*

Counterfeit cancels exist on No. 26.

See Germany designs A2, A3 and A8 for similar stamps.

OFFICIAL STAMPS

O1

1870 Unwmk. Typo. *Perf. 14½x14*

O1	O1	¼gr black & buff	27.50	*45.00*
O2	O1	⅓gr black & buff	9.50	*20.00*
O3	O1	½gr black & buff	2.75	*4.00*
O4	O1	1gr black & buff	2.75	2.00
O5	O1	2gr black & buff	7.25	4.75
O6	O1	1kr black & gray	32.50	*250.00*
O7	O1	2kr black & gray	80.00	*875.00*
O8	O1	3kr black & gray	25.00	*47.50*
O9	O1	7kr black & gray	45.00	*275.00*
		Nos. O1-O9 (9)	232.25	1,523.

Counterfeit cancels exist on Nos. O6-O9.

The stamps of the North German Confederation were replaced by those of the German Empire on Jan. 1, 1872.

GERMANY

'jər-mə-nē

LOCATION — In northern Europe bordering on the Baltic and North Seas
AREA — 182,104 sq. mi. (until 1945)
POP. — 67,032,242 (1946)
CAPITAL — Berlin

In 1949 the Russian occupied areas became a separate country, the German Democratic Republic. The country was reunified Oct. 3, 1990.

30 Silbergroschen or Groschen = 1 Thaler
60 Kreuzer = 1 Gulden
100 Pfennigs = 1 Mark (1875)
100 Pfennigs = 1 Deutsche Mark (1948)
100 Cents = 1 Euro (2002)

Catalogue values for unused stamps in this country are for Never Hinged items, beginning with Scott 722 in the regular postage section, Scott B338 in the semi-postal section, Scott C61 in the airpost section, Scott 9N103 in the Berlin regular postage section and Scott 9NB12 in the Berlin semi-postal section.

Watermarks

Wmk. 48 — Diagonal Zigzag Lines

Wmk. 116 — Crosses and Circles

Wmk. 125 — Lozenges

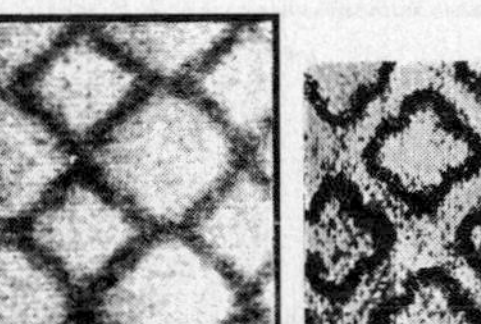

Wmk. 126 — Network

Wmk. 127 — Quatrefoils

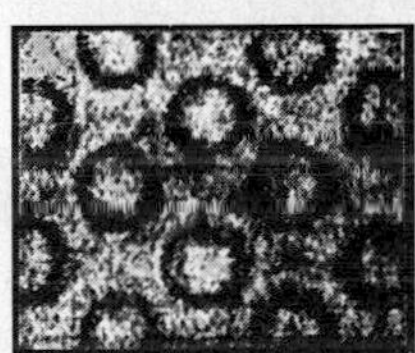

Wmk. 192 — Circles

Wmk. 223 — Eagle

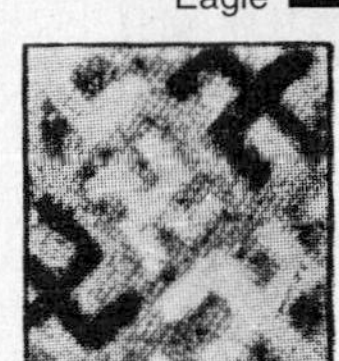

Wmk. 237 — Swastikas

Wmk. 241 — Cross

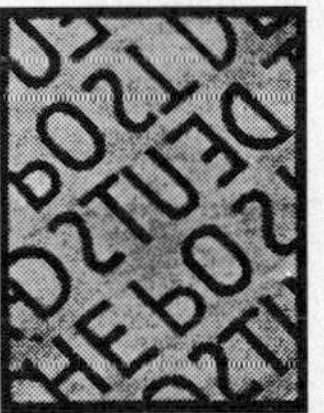

Wmk. 284 — "DEUTSCHE POST" Multiple

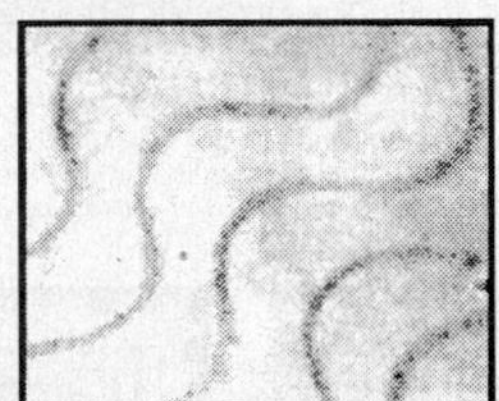

Wmk. 285 — Marbleized Pattern

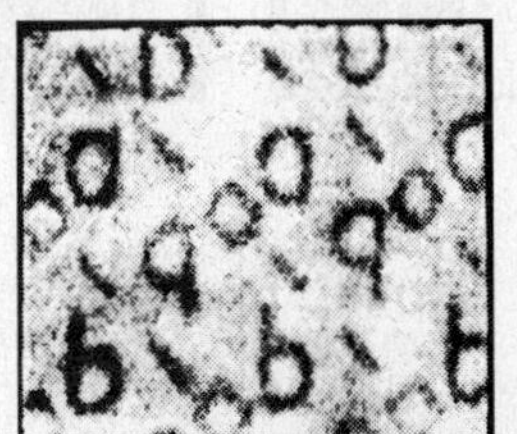

Wmk. 286 — D P Multiple

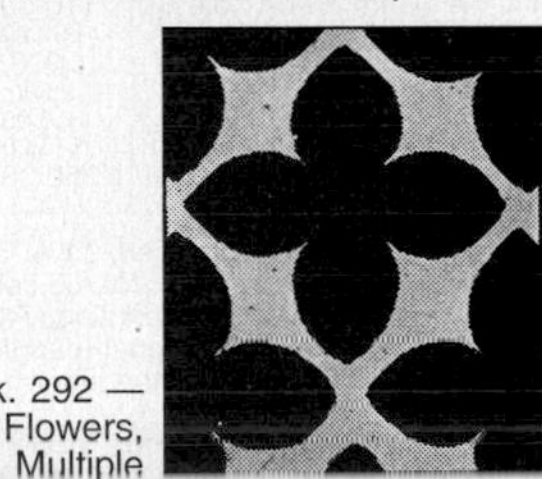

Wmk. 292 — Flowers, Multiple

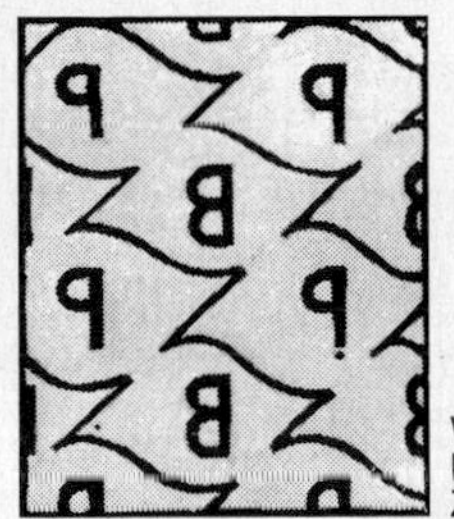

Wmk. 295 — B P and Zigzag Lines

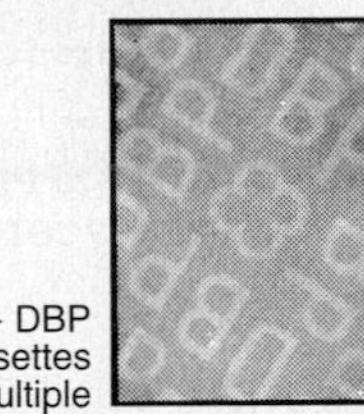

Wmk. 304 — DBP and Rosettes Multiple

Empire

Values for unused stamps are for examples with original gum as defined in the catalogue introduction. Any exceptions are specifically mentioned.

Imperial Eagle — A1

Typographed, Center Embossed

1872 Unwmk. ***Perf. 13½x14½***

Eagle with small shield

1	A1	¼gr violet	200.00	85.00
2	A1	⅓gr green	475.00	36.00
a.		Imperf.		—
3	A1	½gr red orange	950.00	40.00
a.		½gr orange yellow	1,100.	47.50
4	A1	1gr rose	290.00	7.25
a.		Imperf.		—
b.		Half used as ½gr on cover		*50,000.*
5	A1	2gr ultra	1,500.	13.50
a.		Imperf.		*8,500.*
6	A1	5gr bister	825.00	85.00
a.		Imperf.		*10,000.*
7	A1	1kr green	650.00	50.00
8	A1	2kr orange	35.00	*165.00*
a.		2kr red orange	590.00	285.00
9	A1	3kr rose	1,700.	14.50
10	A1	7kr ultra	2,350.	85.00
11	A1	18kr bister	475.00	360.00

Values for imperforates are for stamps postmarked at Leipzig (⅓gr), Coblenz (1gr), Hoengen (2gr) and Leutersdorf (5gr).

A2

A3

1872 Typo. ***Perf. 14½x13½***

12	A2	10gr gray	50.00	*1,300.*
		Pen cancellation		165.00
13	A3	30gr blue	95.00	*2,500.*
		Pen cancellation		*540.00*

For similar designs see A8, North German Confederation A4, A5.

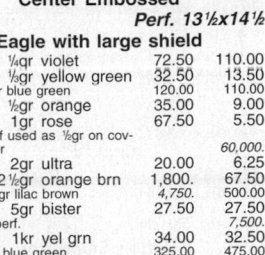

A4

Center Embossed

1872 ***Perf. 13½x14½***

Eagle with large shield

14	A4	¼gr violet	72.50	110.00
15	A4	⅓gr yellow green	32.50	13.50
a.		⅓gr blue green	120.00	110.00
16	A4	½gr orange	35.00	9.00
17	A4	1gr rose	67.50	5.50
b.		Half used as ½gr on cover		*60,000.*
18	A4	2gr ultra	20.00	6.25
19	A4	2½gr orange brn	1,800.	67.50
a.		2½gr lilac brown	*4,750.*	500.00
20	A4	5gr bister	27.50	27.50
a.		Imperf.		*7,500.*
21	A4	1kr yel grn	34.00	32.50
a.		1kr blue green	325.00	475.00
22	A4	2kr orange	450.00	*2,250.*
23	A4	3kr rose	20.00	6.25
24	A4	7kr ultra	30.00	*60.00*
25	A4	9kr red brown	400.00	375.00
a.		9kr lilac brown	1,350.	400.00
26	A4	18kr bister	32.50	*1,900.*

Values for Nos. 17a and 20a are for stamps postmarked at Potsdam (1gr), Damgarten or Anklam (5gr).

Nos. 14-26 with embossing inverted are fraudulent.

A5

1874 **Brown Surcharge**

27	A5	2½gr on 2½gr brn	40.00	42.50
28	A5	9kr on 9kr brown	82.50	*425.00*

A6

A7

"Pfennige"

1875-77 **Typo.**

29	A6	3pf blue green	57.50	5.25
30	A6	5pf violet	97.50	3.75

Center Embossed

31	A7	10pf rose	42.50	1.50
32	A7	20pf ultra	450.00	1.90
33	A7	25pf red brown	500.00	18.00
34	A7	50pf gray	1,650.	11.00
35	A7	50pf ol gray ('77)	1,900.	14.00
		Nos. 29-35 (7)	4,698.	55.40

See Nos. 37-42. For surcharges see Offices in Turkey Nos. 1-6.

A8

1875-90 Typo. *Perf. 14½x13½*

36 A8 2m brnsh pur ('90) 75.00 6.00
a. 2m purple ('75) 1,900. 340.00
b. 2m dull vio pur ('89) 1,500. 60.00

No. 36a used is valued as a stamp with cds cancel dated between Jan. 1875 and November 17, 1884.

Types of 1875-77, "Pfennig" without final "e"

1880-83 *Perf. 13½x14½*

37 A6 3pf yel green 3.00 1.50
a. Imperf. —
38 A6 5pf violet 2.25 2.00

Center Embossed

39 A7 10pf red 21.00 1.50
a. Imperf. *300.00*
40 A7 20pf brt ultra 6.00 1.50
41 A7 25pf dull rose brn 17.50 5.25
a. 25pf red brown, thick paper 175.00 6.00
42 A7 50pf dp grayish ol grn 15.00 1.50
a. 50pf olive green 200.00 1.50
Nos. 37-42 (6) 64.75 13.25

Values for Nos. 37-42 are for stamps on thin paper. Those on thick paper sell for considerably more.

A9

A10

1889-1900 *Perf. 13½x14½*

45 A9 2pf gray ('00) .90 *.90*
a. "REIGHSPOST" 60.00 *140.00*
46 A9 3pf brown 3.00 1.40
a. 3pf yellow brown 9.00 1.40
b. Imperf. 600.00 —
c. 3pf reddish brown 52.50 8.25
47 A9 5pf blue green 3.00 1.40
48 A10 10pf carmine 4.50 1.50
a. Imperf. 225.00
49 A10 20pf ultra 7.50 1.40
a. 20pf Prus blue 2,250. 115.00
50 A10 25pf orange ('90) 30.00 2.00
a. Imperf. 260.00
51 A10 50pf chocolate 30.00 1.40
a. 50pf copper brown 375.00 9.75
b. Imperf. 450.00
Nos. 45-51 (7) 78.90 10.00
Set, never hinged 341.25

For surcharges and overprints see Offices in China Nos. 1-6, 16, Offices in Morocco 1-6, Offices in Turkey 8-12.

Germania — A11

1900, Jan. 1 *Perf. 14*

52 A11 2pf gray .85 .60
a. Imperf. 400.00
53 A11 3pf brown .85 1.00
a. Imperf. 400.00
54 A11 5pf green 1.60 .90
55 A11 10pf carmine 2.40 .75
a. Imperf. 60.00
56 A11 20pf ultra 11.00 .90
57 A11 25pf org & blk, *yel* 15.00 4.50
58 A11 30pf org & blk, *sal* 22.50 .90
59 A11 40pf lake & black 26.00 1.50
60 A11 50pf pur & blk, *sal* 27.50 1.20
61 A11 80pf lake & blk, *rose* 37.50 2.25
Nos. 52-61 (10) 145.20 14.50
Set, never hinged 650.00

Early printings of Nos. 57-61 had "REICHSPOST" in taller and thicker letters than on the ordinary stamps.

For surcharges see Nos. 65B, Offices in China 17-32, Offices in Morocco 7-15, 32A, Offices in Turkey 13-20, 25-27.

"REICHSPOST" Larger

57a A11 25pf 1,900. 6,500.
58a A11 30pf 1,900. 4,250.
59a A11 40pf 1,900. 4,250.
60a A11 50pf 1,900. 4,250.
61a A11 80pf 1,900. 4,250.

General Post Office in Berlin — A12

"Union of North and South Germany" A13

Unveiling Kaiser Wilhelm I Memorial, Berlin — A14

Wilhelm II Speaking at Empire's 25th Anniversary Celebration A15

Type I

Type II

Two types of 3m:
I — The rein is loose, curved. The horse is looking to left. The emperor's face is defined by a curved line. The bottoms of the foot and stirrup are mostly flat.
II — The rein is tight, straight. The horse is looking straight ahead. The emperor's face is defined by an angular line like an inverted "V." The bottoms of the foot and stirrup have two protrusions.

Type I

Type II

Two types of 5m:
I — "5" is thick; "M" has slight serifs.
II — "5" thinner; "M" has distinct serifs.

Engr. *Perf. 14½x14*

62 A12 1m carmine rose 100.00 3.25
Never hinged 400.00
63 A13 2m gray blue 100.00 7.25
Never hinged 425.00
64 A14 3m black violet (I) 110.00 45.00
Never hinged 600.00
65 A15 5m slate & car, I 1,200. 2,100.
Never hinged 5,000.
d. Red and white retouched 350.00 *360.00*
e. White only retouched 575.00 *575.00*
65A A15 5m slate & car, II 350.00 *360.00*
Never hinged 1,325.

Nos. 62-65 exist perf. 11½.

The vignette and frame of No. 65 usually did not align perfectly during printing. Red paint was used to retouch the vignette and/or white paint was used to retouch the inner frame.

No. 62a is without gum.

For surcharges see Offices in China Nos. 33-36A, Offices in Morocco 16-19A, Offices in Turkey 21-24B, 28-30.

Half of No. 54 Handstamp Surcharged in Violet

3PF

1901 *Perf. 14*

65B A11 3pf on half of 5pf *9,000. 7,000.*
Never hinged *25,000.*

This provisional was produced aboard the German cruiser Vineta. The purser, with the ship commander's approval, surcharged and bisected 300 5pf stamps so the ship's post office could meet the need for a 3pf (printed matter rate). The crew wanted to send home U.S. newspapers reporting celebrations of the Kaiser's birthday.

Forgeries exist and improper usages as well.

A16

1902 Typo.

65C A16 2pf gray 1.50 .60
66 A16 3pf brown .75 *1.00*
a. "DFUTSCHES" 9.75 *42.50*
67 A16 5pf green 4.00 1.00
68 A16 10pf carmine 9.00 1.00
69 A16 20pf ultra 30.00 1.00
70 A16 25pf org & blk, *yel* 45.00 2.10
71 A16 30pf org & blk, *sal* 60.00 .60
72 A16 40pf lake & blk 90.00 1.00
73 A16 50pf pur & blk, *buff* 70.00 1.10
74 A16 80pf lake & blk, *rose* 200.00 3.00
Nos. 65C-74 (10) 510.25 12.40
Set, never hinged 1,890.

Nos. 65C-74 exist imperf. Value, set: unused $1,600; never hinged $3,750.

See Nos. 80-91, 118-119, 121-132, 169, 174, 210. For surcharges see Nos. 133-136, B1, Offices in China 37-42, 47-52, Offices in Morocco 20-28, 33-41, 45-53, Offices in Turkey 31-38, 43-50, 55-59. For overprints, see Bavaria Nos. 177-178, 180, 182-183, 185-187. Poland Nos. 15, 17-19, 21, 24-26.

A17

A18

A19

A20

Perf. 14¼-14½ (26x17 holes)
Engr.

75 A17 1m car rose 240.00 2.75
a. Imperf. 900.00 *10,000.*
76 A18 2m gray blue 87.50 *97.50*
77 A19 3m black violet 225.00 19.00
a. Imperf. 900.00 *10,000.*
78 A20 5m slate & car 200.00 19.00
a. Imperf. 900.00 *2,500.*

See Nos. 92, 94-95, 102, 111-113. For surcharges see Nos. 115-116, Offices in China 43, 45-46, 53, 55-56, Offices in Morocco 29, 31-32, 42, 44, 54, 56-57, Offices in Turkey 39, 41-42, 51, 53-54. For overprints, see Bavaria Nos. 188, 190-191.

A21

79 A21 2m gray blue 120.00 5.00
a. Imperf. 900.00 *10,000.*
Nos. 75-79 (5) 872.50 143.25
Set, never hinged 4,060.

See Nos. 93, 114. For surcharges see Nos. 117, Offices in China 44, 54, Offices in Morocco 30, 43, 55, Offices in Turkey 40, 52. For overprint, see Bavaria No. 189.

1905-19 Typo. Wmk. 125 *Perf. 14*
80 A16 2pf gray ('05) 1.60 2.60
81 A16 3pf brown ('15) .60 *1.50*
82 A16 5pf grn (shades) .60 *1.50*
b. Bklt. pane of 5 + label ('11) 250.00 500.00
c. Bklt. pane of 4 + 2 labels ('10) 400.00 800.00
d. Bklt. pane of 2 + 4 labels ('12) 250.00 500.00
e. Bklt. pane, #82 + 5 #83 ('17) 75.00 190.00
f. Bklt. pane, 2 #82 + 4 #83 ('20) 21.00 50.00
g. Bklt. pane, 4 #82 + 2 #83 ('19) 21.00 50.00
83 A16 10pf red .75 *1.50*
b. Bklt. pane of 5 + label ('10) 325.00 650.00
c. Bklt. pane of 4 + 2 labels ('12) 300.00 625.00
d. 10pf carmine red 2.00 1.75
84 A16 20pf bl vio ('18) 1.50 *1.50*
a. 20pf light blue 12.00 3.75
b. 20pf ultramarine 8.00 1.50
c. Imperf. 5,250. *2,750.*
d. Half used as 10pf on cover 750.00
85 A16 25pf org & blk, *yel* .60 *1.50*
86 A16 30pf org & blk, *buff* 2.00 *1.50*
a. 30pf org & blk, *cr* 26.00 *90.00*
87 A16 40pf lake & black 1.50 *1.50*
88 A16 50pf pur & blk, *buff* .75 *1.50*
89 A16 60pf magenta 2.00 1.50
a. 60pf red violet 22.50 13.50
90 A16 75pf grn & blk ('19) .25 *2.25*
a. 75pf dk bluish grn & greenish blk 1.10 *3.00*
91 A16 80pf lake & blk, *rose* 1.10 *1.90*

Perf. 14½ (25x17 holes)
Engr.
92 A17 1m car rose 2.60 2.25
93 A21 2m brt blue 5.25 4.75
a. 2m gray blue ('16) 47.50 *42.50*
94 A19 3m violet gray 3.00 *4.25*
b. 3m blk violet 50.00 26.00
95 A20 5m slate & car 3.00 *4.75*
a. Center inverted *45,000.* *65,000.*
Nos. 80-95 (16) 27.10 36.25
Set, Never Hinged 73.00

Pre-war printings of Nos. 80-91 have brighter colors and white instead of yellow gum. They sell for considerably more than the wartime printings which are valued here. No. 80 exists only from a pre-war printing.

Nos. 92-95 exist only from a wartime printing. The 1m-5m also exist perf 14¼-14¾ (26x17 holes) in both pre-war and wartime printings. Both of these printings are much more expensive than Nos. 92-95. See the *Scott Classic Specialized Catalogue* for detailed listings.

Labels in No. 82c contain an "X." The version with advertising is worth 3 times as much. No. 82f has three 10pf stamps in the top row. The version with 3 on the bottom row is worth 4 times as much.

No. 84d was used at Field Post Office No. 107 in 1915, and at Field Post Office No. 766 during 1917.

Surcharged and overprinted stamps of designs A16-A22 are listed under Allenstein, Belgium, Danzig, France, Latvia, Lithuania, Marienwerder, Memel, Poland, Romania, Saar, Upper Silesia and German States-Bavaria.

A22

1916-19 Typo.
96 A22 2pf lt gray ('18) .30 *3.75*
97 A22 2½pf lt gray .25 *1.90*
98 A22 7½pf red orange .50 2.25
b. Bklt. pane, 4 #98 + 2 #100 110.00 275.00
c. Bklt. pane, 2 #98 + 4 #99 125.00 300.00
d. Bklt. pane, 2 #98 + 4 #100 110.00 275.00
e. Bklt. pane, 2 #82 + 4 #98 37.50 90.00
f. 7½pf yellow orange 3.50 2.25
99 A22 15pf yellow brown 3.00 2.25
100 A22 15pf dk violet ('17) .35 *2.00*
b. Bklt. pane, 4 #82 + 2 #100 110.00 275.00
c. Bklt. pane, 2 #83 + 4 #100 82.50 210.00
101 A22 35pf red brn ('19) .30 *2.25*
Nos. 96-101 (6) 4.70 *14.40*
Set, never hinged 18.40

See No. 120. For surcharge see No. B2. For overprints, see Bavaria Nos. 176, 179, 184, Poland Nos. 16, 20, 23.

Nos. 98e and 100c have the 2 stamps first in the bottom row.

Type of 1902
1920 Engr. Wmk. 192 *Perf. 14½*
102 A19 3m black violet 1,875. *3,750.*
Never hinged 4,500.

Republic
National Assembly Issue

A23

A24

Rebuilding Germany — A25

Designs: A23, Live Stump of Tree Symbolizing that Germany will Survive her Difficulties. A24, New Shoots from Oak Stump Symbolical of New Government.

Perf. 13x13½
1919-20 Unwmk. Typo.
105 A23 10pf carmine rose .25 1.50
106 A24 15pf choc & blue .25 1.50
107 A25 25pf green & red .25 1.50
108 A25 30pf red vio & red ('20) .25 2.25
Nos. 105-108 (4) 1.00 *6.75*
Set, never hinged 3.50

Types of 1902
Perf. 15x14½
1920 Wmk. 125 Offset
111 A17 1m red 3.75 *2.40*
a. Double impression 120.00 *600.00*
112 A17 1.25m green 3.75 *1.90*
a. Double impression 900.00
113 A17 1.50m yellow brown .50 *1.90*
c. As "a," double impression 100.00 *725.00*
114 A21 2.50m lilac rose .50 *2.50*
a. 2.50m magenta 1.50 *2.25*
b. 2.50m brown lilac .75 *2.75*
c. Double impression 100.00 *650.00*
d. As "a," double impression 140.00 *550.00*
e. As "b," double impression 140.00 *675.00*
Nos. 111-114 (4) 8.50 *8.70*
Set, never hinged 27.00

Nos. 111, 112 and 113 differ from the illustration in many minor respects. The numerals of Nos. 75 and 92 are outlined, with shaded background. Those of No. 111 are plain, with solid background and flags have been added to the top of the building, at right and left.

Types of 1902 Surcharged

1920 Engr. *Perf. 14½*
115 A17 1.25m on 1m green .40 *6.00*
116 A17 1.50m on 1m org brn .40 *7.25*
117 A21 2.50m on 2m lilac rose 8.75 *180.00*
Nos. 115-117 (3) 9.55 *193.25*
Set, never hinged 31.00

Germania Types of 1902-16
1920 Typo. *Perf. 14, 14½*
118 A16 5pf brown .25 *2.00*
119 A16 10pf orange .25 *1.50*
a. Tête bêche pair 1.75 *7.00*
d. Bklt. pane, 4 #119 + 2 #123 8.25 13.50
120 A22 15pf violet brn .25 *1.90*
a. Imperf. 67.50
c. Bklt. pane, 4 #84 + 2 #120 22.50 30.00
121 A16 20pf green .25 *2.25*
a. Imperf. *1,200.*
123 A16 30pf dull blue 2.40 *27.50*
a. Tête bêche pair 3.50 *13.50*
d. Bklt. pane, 2 #123 + 4 #124 8.25 15.00
124 A16 40pf carmine rose .25 *1.90*
a. Tête bêche pair 1.90 *7.00*
b. Imperf. 150.00 900.00
d. Bklt. pane, 2 #124 + 4 #126 12.00 75.00
125 A16 50pf red lilac .60 *2.25*
126 A16 60pf olive green .25 *1.60*
a. Tête bêche pair 2.75 *20.00*
c. Imperf. 160.00
127 A16 75pf red violet .60 *1.90*
128 A16 80pf blue violet .25 *2.25*
a. Imperf. 175.00
129 A16 1m violet & grn .25 *2.25*
a. Imperf. 77.50
130 A16 1¼m ver & mag .25 *1.90*
131 A16 2m carmine & bl .60 *1.50*
132 A16 4m black & rose .25 *2.25*
Nos. 118-132 (14) 6.70 *52.95*
Set, never hinged 20.00

Stamps of 1920 Surcharged

No. 133

No. 135

Nos. 134, 136

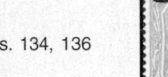

1921, Aug.
133 A16 1.60m on 5pf .25 *2.25*
134 A16 3m on 1¼m .25 *2.60*
135 A16 5m on 75pf (G) .25 *2.25*
136 A16 10m on 75pf .40 *2.25*
Nos. 133-136 (4) 1.15 *9.35*
Set, never hinged 4.50

In 1920 the current stamps of Bavaria were overprinted "Deutsches Reich". These stamps were available for postage throughout Germany, but because they were used almost exclusively in Bavaria, they are listed among the issues of that state.

A26

Iron Workers A27

Miners A28

Farmers A29

Post Horn A30

Numeral of Value — A31

Plowing A32

Wmk. Lozenges (125)
1921 Typo. *Perf. 14*
137 A26 5pf claret .25 *2.00*
138 A26 10pf olive green .25 *2.00*
a. Tête bêche pair 5.50 *37.50*
b. Bklt. pane, 5 #138 + 1 #141 12.00 —
139 A26 15pf grnsh blue .25 *1.60*
140 A26 25pf dark brown .25 *1.60*
141 A26 30pf blue green .25 *1.60*
a. Tête bêche pair 5.50 *37.50*
b. Bklt. pane, 2 #124 + 4 #141 12.00 75.00

142 A26 40pf red orange .25 *1.60*
143 A26 50pf violet .30 *1.60*
144 A27 60pf red violet .25 *1.60*
145 A27 80pf carmine rose .25 *5.25*
146 A28 100pf yellow grn .30 *2.00*
147 A28 120pf ultra .25 *1.60*
148 A29 150pf orange .25 *2.00*
149 A29 160pf slate grn .25 *8.50*
150 A30 2m dp vio & rose .40 *3.50*
151 A30 3m red & yel .40 *15.00*
152 A30 4m dp grn & yel grn .25 *3.50*

Engr.

153 A31 5m orange .35 *2.25*
154 A31 10m carmine rose .50 *3.00*
155 A32 20m indigo & grn 3.00 *2.75*
a. Green background inverted 190.00 *1,050.*
Nos. 137-155 (19) 8.25 *62.95*
Set, never hinged 24.00

See Nos. 156-209, 211, 222-223, 225, 227. For surcharges and overprints see Nos. 241-245, 247-248, 261-262, 273-276, B6-B7, O24.

1922 Litho. *Perf. 14½x14*

156 A31 100m brown vio, *buff* .25 *1.40*
157 A31 200m rose, *buff* .25 *1.40*
158 A31 300m green, *buff* .25 *1.40*
159 A31 400m bis brn, *buff* .55 *2.25*
160 A31 500m orange, *buff* .25 *1.40*
Nos. 156-160 (5) 1.55 *7.85*
Set, never hinged 3.70

Postally Used vs. CTO

Values quoted for canceled stamps of the 1921-1923 issues are for postally used stamps. These bring higher prices than the plentiful canceled-to-order stamps made by applying genuine handstamps to remainders. C.T.O. examples sell for about the same price as unused stamps. Certification of postal usage by competent authorities is necessary.

Perf. 14, 14½

1921-22 Typo. Wmk. 126

161 A26 5pf claret .75 *200.00*
162 A26 10pf olive grn 7.00 *190.00*
163 A26 15pf grnsh blue .55 *225.00*
164 A26 25pf dark brown .25 *3.75*
165 A26 30pf blue green .85 *325.00*
166 A26 40pf red orange .25 *3.75*
167 A26 50pf violet ('21) .25 *1.50*
168 A27 60pf red violet .25 *20.00*
169 A16 75pf red violet .40 *2.75*
170 A26 75pf deep ultra .25 *3.00*
171 A27 80pf car rose .40 *57.50*
172 A28 100pf olive green .25 *1.50*
a. Imperf. 60.00 *1,500.*
173 A28 120pf ultra .70 *110.00*
174 A16 1¼m ver & mag .25 *1.50*
175 A29 150pf orange .25 *1.50*
a. Imperf. 37.50
Never hinged 110.00
176 A29 160pf slate green .70 *175.00*
177 A30 2m violet & rose .25 *1.50*
178 A30 3m red & yel ('21) .25 *1.50*
a. Imperf. 37.50 *375.00*
Never hinged 110.00
179 A30 4m dp grn & yel grn .25 *1.50*
180 A30 5m org & yel .30 *2.00*
a. Imperf. 135.00
181 A30 10m car & pale rose .30 *2.25*
a. Pale rose (background) omitted 45.00 *975.00*
182 A30 20m violet & org .35 *3.00*
183 A30 30m brown & yel .25 *1.50*
184 A30 50m dk grn & vio .25 *1.50*
Nos. 161-184 (24) 15.55 *1,337.*
Set, never hinged 49.00

1922-23

SIX MARKS:
Type I — Numerals upright.
Type II — Numerals leaning toward the right and slightly thinner.

EIGHT MARKS:
Type I — Numerals 2½mm wide with thick strokes.
Type II — Numerals 2mm wide with thinner strokes.

185 A30 2m blue violet .25 *1.50*
a. Imperf. 100.00
186 A30 3m red .25 *1.50*
187 A30 4m dark green .25 *1.50*
a. Imperf. 30.00
b. 4m deep blue green 1.50 5.25
188 A30 5m orange .25 *1.50*
a. Imperf. 80.00
189 A30 6m dark blue (II) .25 *1.50*
a. Type I .25 *1.90*
b. Imperf. 70.00
190 A30 8m olive green (I) .25 *1.50*
a. Type II .40 *37.50*
191 A30 20m dk violet ('23) .25 *1.50*
192 A30 30m pur brn ('23) .25 *7.50*
193 A30 40m lt green .25 *2.25*

Engr.

194 A31 5m orange .25 *1.75*
a. Imperf. 125.00 *2,750.*
195 A31 10m carmine rose .55 *2.25*
196 A32 20m indigo & grn .25 *3.50*
a. Imperf. 160.00 *2,100.*
b. Green background inverted 32.50 *675.00*
Nos. 185-196 (12) 3.30 *27.75*
Set, never hinged 10.00

1922-23 Litho. *Perf. 14½x14*

198 A31 50m indigo .25 *1.50*
199 A31 100m brn vio, *buff* ('23) .25 *1.40*
200 A31 200m rose, *buff* ('23) .25 *1.90*
201 A31 300m grn, *buff* ('23) .25 *1.35*
202 A31 400m bis brn, *buff* ('23) .25 *1.35*
203 A31 500m org, *buff* ('23) .25 *1.35*
204 A31 1000m gray ('23) .25 *1.35*
205 A31 2000m bl ('23) .30 *1.90*
206 A31 3000m brn ('23) .25 *1.50*
207 A31 4000m vio ('23) .25 *1.50*
a. Imperf. 37.50 *190.00*
208 A31 5000m gray grn ('23) .30 *1.50*
a. Imperf. 52.50 *225.00*
209 A31 100,000m ver ('23) .25 *1.40*
a. Imperf. 52.50 225.00
Nos. 198-209 (12) 3.10 *18.00*
Set, never hinged 6.00

1920-22 Wmk. 127 Typo.

210 A16 1¼m ver & mag 450.00 *975.00*
Never hinged 1,350.
211 A30 50m grn & vio ('22) 2.25 *825.00*
Never hinged 5.25

Wmk. 127 was intended for use only in printing revenue stamps.

Arms of Munich — A33

Wmk. Network (126)

1922, Apr. 22 Typo. *Perf. 13x13½*

212 A33 1¼m claret .25 *1.90*
213 A33 2m dark violet .25 *1.90*
214 A33 3m vermilion .25 *1.90*
215 A33 4m deep blue .25 *1.90*
a. Imperf. 75.00 *225.00*

Wmk. Lozenges (125)

216 A33 10m brown, *buff* .60 *2.60*
217 A33 20m lilac rose, *pink* 3.75 *13.00*
Nos. 212-217 (6) 5.35 *23.20*
Set, never hinged 18.00

Munich Industrial Fair.

Type of 1921 and

Miners — A34

A35

1922-23 Wmk. 126 *Perf. 14*

221 A34 5m orange .25 *12.00*
222 A29 10m dull blue ('22) .25 *1.50*
223 A29 12m vermilion ('22) .25 *1.50*
224 A34 20m red lilac .25 *1.50*
225 A29 25m olive brown .25 *1.50*
226 A34 30m olive green .25 *2.25*
227 A29 40m green .25 *1.50*
228 A34 50m grnsh blue .40 *115.00*
229 A35 100m violet .25 *1.50*
230 A35 200m carmine rose .25 *1.50*
231 A35 300m green .25 *1.50*
232 A35 400m dark brown .25 *5.75*
233 A35 500m red orange .25 *6.00*
234 A35 1000m slate .25 *1.50*
Nos. 221-234 (14) 3.65 *154.50*
Set, never hinged 6.50

The 50m was issued only in vertical coils.
Nos. 222-223 exist imperf.
For surcharges and overprints see Nos. 246, 249-260, 263-271, 277, 310, B5, O22-O23, O25-O28.

Wartburg Castle — A36

Cathedral of Cologne — A37

1923 Engr.

237 A36 5000m deep blue .30 *3.00*
a. Imperf. 300.00 *1,200.*
238 A37 10,000m brn ol .30 *3.75*
Set, never hinged 1.90

Abbreviations:
Th = (Tausend) Thousand
Mil = (Million) Million
Mlrd = (Milliarde) Billion

A38

1923 Typo.

238A A38 5th m grnsh blue .25 *16.50*
b. Imperf. 90.00
239 A38 50th m bister .25 *1.50*
a. Imperf. 22.50 *3,750.*
240 A38 75th m dark violet .25 *10.50*
Nos. 238A-240 (3) .75 28.50
Set, never hinged 1.15

For surcharges see Nos. 272, 278.

Stamps and Types of 1922-23 Surcharged in Black, Blue, Green or Brown

No. 241

No. 243

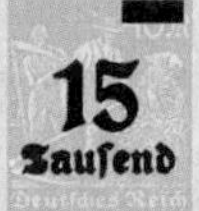

No. 246

No. 253

No. 269

Wmk. Lozenges (125)

1923 *Perf. 14*

241 A26 8th m on 30pf .25 *1.50*
a. "8" inverted 21.00 *340.00*
Never hinged 57.50

Wmk. Network (126)

242 A26 5th m on 40pf .25 *1.60*
b. Double surcharge 150.00
242A A26 8th m on 30pf 22.50 *6,000.*
243 A29 15th m on 40m .25 *1.90*
a. Inverted surcharge 600.00
b. Pair, one with surcharge omitted 375.00
244 A29 20th m on 12m .25 *1.50*
a. Inverted surcharge 115.00
b. Pair, one with surcharge omitted 300.00
245 A29 20th m on 25m .25 *2.25*
246 A35 20th m on 200m .25 *2.25*
a. Inverted surcharge 57.50 750.00
247 A29 25th m on 25m .25 *13.50*
248 A29 30th m on 10m dp bl .25 *1.50*
a. Inverted surcharge 67.50
249 A35 30th m on 200m pale bl (Bl) .25 *1.50*
a. Without surcharge 115.00
250 A35 75th m on 300m yel grn .25 *13.50*
a. Imperf. 45.00
b. Double surcharge 150.00
251 A35 75th m on 400m yel grn .25 *1.50*
252 A35 75th m on 1000m yel grn .25 *1.90*
a. Without surcharge 115.00
b. Double surcharge 67.50
253 A35 100th m on 100m .25 *2.25*
a. Double surcharge 37.50 *450.00*
b. Inverted surcharge 13.50 *600.00*
254 A35 100th m on 400m bluish grn (G) .25 *1.50*
a. Imperf. 42.50 750.00
b. Without surcharge 115.00
Never hinged 225.00
255 A35 125th m on 1000m sal .25 *1.90*
256 A35 250th m on 200m .25 *5.25*
a. Inverted surcharge 34.00
b. Double surcharge 52.50
257 A35 250th m on 300m dp grn .25 *16.50*
a. Inverted surcharge 34.00
258 A35 250th m on 400m .25 *19.00*
a. Inverted surcharge 26.00

259 A35 250th m on 500m pink .25 1.50
a. Imperf. 52.50 900.00
260 A35 250th m on 500m red org .25 19.00
a. Double surcharge 30.00 975.00
b. Inverted surcharge 37.50
261 A20 800th m on 5pf lt grn (G) .25 4.25
a. Imperf. 34.00 150.00
Never hinged 90.00
262 A26 800th m on 10pf lt grn (G) .25 5.00
a. Imperf. 30.00
263 A35 800th m on 200m .25 75.00
a. Double surcharge 75.00 975.00
b. Inverted surcharge 37.50 —
264 A35 800th m on 300m lt grn (G) .25 5.00
a. Black surcharge 30.00
265 A35 800th m on 400m dk brn .25 12.00
a. Inverted surcharge 42.50 —
b. Double surcharge 75.00
266 A35 800th m on 400m lt grn (G) .25 3.75
267 A35 800th m on 500m lt grn (G) .25 1,500.
a. 800th m on 500m red org (Bk) 30.00
268 A35 800th m on 1000m lt grn (G) .25 1.50
269 A35 2mil m on 200m rose red .25 2.10
b. 2mil m on 200m car rose (#230) 1,500.
270 A35 2mil m on 300m dp grn .25 2.10
a. Inverted surcharge 42.50 —
b. Double surcharge 75.00 —
271 A35 2mil m on 500m dl rose .25 6.00
272 A38 2mil m on 5th m dl rose .25 1.50
b. Imperf. 37.50 150.00

Nos. 264a, 267a were not put in use.

Serrate Roulette 13½

273 A26 400th m on 15pf bis (Br) .25 4.50
a. Imperf. 52.50 260.00
274 A26 400th m on 25pf bis (Br) .25 4.50
a. Imperf. 90.00 260.00
275 A26 400th m on 30pf bis (Br) .25 4.50
a. Imperf. 45.00
b. Double surcharge 90.00
276 A26 400th m on 40pf bis (Br) .25 4.50
a. Imperf. 45.00 —
b. Double surcharge 90.00
277 A35 2mil m on 200m rose red .25 150.00
278 A38 2mil m on 5th m dull rose .25 9.00
Nos. 241-278 (39) 32.00 *7,907.*
Set, never hinged 51.00

Nos. 272-276 exist without surcharge. Value each, $150 unused, $375 never hinged.

A39

A39a

The stamps of types A39 and A39a usually have the value darker than the rest of the design.

1923 Wmk. 126 *Perf. 14*

280 A39 500th m brown .25 2.60
281 A39 1mil m grnsh bl .25 1.60
a. Imperf. 52.50 1,500.
Never hinged 115.00
282 A39 2mil m dull vio .25 19.50
284 A39 4mil m yel grn .25 1.50
a. Value double 45.00
b. Imperf. 42.50
285 A39 6mil m rose .25 1.50
286 A39 10mil m red .25 1.50
a. Value double 45.00 3,750.
287 A39 20mil m ultra .25 1.90
288 A39 30mil m red brn .25 9.00
289 A39 50mil m dull ol grn .25 1.90
a. Imperf. 52.50 340.00
b. Value inverted 45.00
290 A39 100mil m gray .25 1.50
a. Imperf. 67.50 375.00
b. Value double 45.00
291 A39 200mil m bis brn .25 1.50
a. Imperf. 42.50
Never hinged 97.50
293 A39a 500mil m ol grn .25 1.50
294 A39a 1mlrd m choc .30 1.90
295 A39a 2mlrd m pale brn & grn .25 1.90
296 A39a 5mlrd m yellow & brn .25 1.50
297 A39a 10mlrd m ap grn & grn .25 1.50
a. Imperf. 45.00 260.00
298 A39a 20mlrd m bluish grn & brn .25 1.90
299 A39a 50mlrd m bl & dp bl .25 34.00
Nos. 280-299 (18) 4.55 *88.20*
Set, never hinged 11.50

The variety "value omitted" exists on Nos. 280-281, 284-287, 290-291, 293-294, 296 and 298-299. Values $37.50 to $100 hinged, $75 to $190 never hinged.

See Nos. 301-309. For surcharges and overprints see Nos. 311-321, O40-O46.

Serrate Roulette 13½

301 A39 10mil m red .55 45.00
302 A39 20mil m ultra .55 300.00
303 A39 50mil m dull grn .55 6.00
304 A39 200mil m bis brn .55 11.50
305 A39a 1mlrd m choc .55 7.50
306 A39a 2mlrd m pale brn & grn .55 3.50
307 A39a 5mlrd m yel & brn .75 2.25
308 A39a 20mlrd m bluish grn & brn .75 11.50
309 A39a 50mlrd m bl & dp bl 1.90 675.00
Nos. 301-309 (9) 6.70 *1,062.*
Set, never hinged 18.50

Stamps and Types of 1923 Surcharged with New Values

1923 *Perf. 14*

Design Type A35

310 1mlrd m on 100m vio .25 29.00
a. Inverted surcharge 115.00

Design Type A39

311 5mlrd m on 2mil m .25 130.00
a. Inverted surcharge 19.00
b. Double surcharge 45.00
Never hinged 110.00
312 5mlrd m on 4mil m .25 22.50
a. Inverted surcharge 37.50 1,200.
b. Double surcharge 37.50
313 5mlrd m on 10mil m .25 2.60
a. Inverted surcharge 19.00 1,100.
b. Double surcharge 37.50
314 10mlrd m on 20mil m .25 4.50
a. Double surcharge 45.00
b. Inverted surcharge 26.00
315 10mlrd m on 50mil m .25 4.50
a. Inverted surcharge 19.00 900.00
b. Double surcharge 45.00
316 10mlrd m on 100mil m .25 7.50
a. Inverted surcharge 26.00 1,500.
b. Double surcharge 45.00
Nos. 310-316 (7) 1.75 *200.60*
Set, never hinged 5.25

No. 310b was issued in Bavaria only and is known as the Hitler provisional. Excellent forgeries exist.

Serrate Roulette 13½

Design Type A39

319 5mlrd m on 10mil m 1.90 180.00
a. Inverted surcharge 26.00 1,100.
b. Double surcharge 45.00
320 10mlrd m on 20mil m 3.75 105.00
321 10mlrd m on 50mil m 1.90 37.50
a. Inverted surcharge 26.00 1,100.
Nos. 319-321 (3) 7.55 *322.50*
Set, never hinged 22.50

A40

1923 *Perf. 14*

323 A40 3pf brown .40 .25
324 A40 5pf dark green .40 .25
325 A40 10pf carmine .40 .25
326 A40 20pf deep ultra 1.15 .40
327 A40 50pf orange 2.60 1.00
328 A40 100pf brn vio 8.25 1.10
Nos. 323-328 (6) 13.20 3.25
Set, never hinged 85.00

For overprints see Nos. O47-O52.

Imperf

323a A40 3pf 105.00 *260.00*
324a A40 5pf 97.50 —
325a A40 10pf 135.00 260.00
326a A40 20pf 135.00 *260.00*
327a A40 50pf 975.00 —
328a A40 100pf 170.00 260.00
Nos. 323a-328a (6) 1,618. *1,040.*
Set, never hinged 3,650.

Value Omitted

323b A40 3pf 180.00 *300.00*
324b A40 5pf 150.00 *300.00*
325b A40 10pf 150.00 *300.00*
326b A40 20pf 165.00 *300.00*
327b A40 50pf 150.00
328b A40 100pf 150.00
Nos. 323b-328b (6) 945.00
Set, never hinged 2,475.

German Eagle — A41

1924 Wmk. 126

330 A41 3pf lt brown .30 .40
331 A41 5pf lt green .30 .40
332 A41 10pf vermilion .40 .40
333 A41 20pf dull blue 1.90 .40
334 A41 30pf rose lilac 1.90 .45
335 A41 40pf olive green 13.00 .70
336 A41 50pf orange 15.00 1.15
Nos. 330-336 (7) 32.80 3.90
Set, never hinged 277.50

The values above 5pf have "Pf" in the upper right corner.

For overprints see Nos. O53-O61.

Imperf.

330a A41 3pf 115.00 *375.00*
331a A41 5pf 150.00 *375.00*
332a A41 10pf 190.00
333a A41 20pf 130.00
334a A41 30pf 130.00
335a A41 40pf 170.00
Nos. 330a-335a (6) 885.00
Set, never hinged 2,500.

Rheinstein Castle — A43

View of Cologne A44

Marienburg Castle — A45

1924 Engr. Wmk. 126

337 A43 1m green 10.00 3.50
a. Watermark sideways ('27) 26.00 12.00
338 A44 2m blue 13.50 3.50
339 A45 3m claret 18.50 6.00
Nos. 337-339 (3) 42.00 13.00
Set, never hinged 155.00

See No. 387.

Dr. Heinrich von Stephan
A46 A47

1924-28 Typo.

340 A46 10pf dark green .75 .30
a. Imperf —
341 A46 20pf dark blue 1.50 .75
342 A47 60pf red brown 3.75 .75
a. Chalky paper ('28) 22.50 13.50
343 A47 80pf slate 9.75 1.50
Nos. 340-343 (4) 15.75 3.30
Set, never hinged 79.00

Universal Postal Union, 50th anniversary.

Traffic Wheel — A48

1925, May 30 *Perf. 13½x13*

345 A48 5pf deep green 3.75 5.25
346 A48 10pf vermilion 3.75 9.75
Set, never hinged 42.50

German Traffic Exhibition, Munich, May 30-Oct. 11, 1925.

German Eagle Watching Rhine Valley — A49

1925 *Perf. 14*

347 A49 5pf green 1.00 .40
348 A49 10pf vermilion 1.00 .40
349 A49 20pf deep blue 5.75 1.05
Nos. 347-349 (3) 7.75 1.85
Set, never hinged 45.00

1000 years' union of the Rhineland with Germany.

Speyer Cathedral A50

1925, Sept. 11 **Engr.**

350 A50 5m dull green 35.00 15.00
Never hinged 130.00

Johann Wolfgang von Goethe — A51

Designs: 3pf, 25pf, Goethe. 5pf, Friedrich von Schiller. 8pf, 20pf, Ludwig van Beethoven. 10pf, Frederick the Great. 15pf, Immanuel Kant. 30pf, Gotthold Ephraim Lessing. 40pf, Gottfried Wilhelm Leibnitz. 50pf, Johann Sebastian Bach. 80pf, Albrecht Durer.

1926-27 **Typo.** ***Perf. 14***

351 A51 3pf olive brown 1.15 .40
352 A51 3pf bister ('27) 1.15 .40
353 A51 5pf dark green 1.15 .40
354 A51 8pf blue grn ('27) 1.50 .40
355 A51 10pf carmine 1.50 .40
356 A51 15pf vermilion 2.25 .40
a. Booklet pane of 8 + 2 labels 1,100. 3,250.
357 A51 20pf myrtle grn 10.50 1.15
358 A51 25pf blue 3.50 .90
359 A51 30pf olive grn 6.50 .60
360 A51 40pf dp violet 11.50 .60
361 A51 50pf brown 14.50 7.50
362 A51 80pf chocolate 30.00 5.00
Nos. 351-362 (12) 85.20 18.15
Set, never hinged 875.00

Nos. 351-354, 356 and 357 exist imperf. See *Scott Classic Specialized Catalogue of Stamps & Covers* for detailed listing.

Nos. 354, 356 and 358 Overprinted

1927, Oct. 10

363 A51 8pf blue green 16.50 *65.00*
364 A51 15pf vermilion 16.50 *65.00*
365 A51 25pf blue 16.50 *65.00*
Nos. 363-365 (3) 49.50 *195.00*
Set, never hinged 180.00

"I.A.A." stands for "Internationales Arbeitsamt," (Intl. Labor Bureau), an agency of the League of Nations. Issued in connection with a meeting of the I.A.A. in Berlin, Oct. 10-15, 1927, they were on sale to the public.

Pres. Friedrich Ebert A60

Pres. Paul von Hindenburg A61

1928-32 **Typo.** ***Perf. 14***

366 A60 3pf bister .25 .60
367 A61 4pf lt blue ('31) 1.10 1.20
a. Tête bêche pair 22.50 37.50
b. Bklt. pane of 9 + label 97.50 180.00
368 A61 5pf lt green .40 .60
[illegible] Tête bêche pair 18.00 30.00
[illegible]rf. 105.00
[illegible]ane of 6 + 4 labels 82.50 120.00
[illegible]ne, 4 #368 + 6 [illegible] 97.50 180.00
[illegible]t olive grn [illegible]'32) .75 .70
[illegible]369 + 8 [illegible] 97.50 180.00
[illegible] 165.00
3[illegible]en .25 .60
a. [illegible] 18.00 30.00
[illegible] 1.90 2.25
b. [illegible]
[illegible] 1.75 .75
[illegible] 1.50 .70
[illegible] 22.50 37.50
[illegible] .60 .60
[illegible] 18.00 30.00
[illegible] 30.00
[illegible] 82.50 120.00

375 A60 20pf Prus green 6.25 3.75
a. Imperf. 260.00
376 A60 20pf gray ('30) 6.00 .75
377 A61 25pf blue 7.50 .90
378 A60 30pf olive green 5.25 .90
379 A61 40pf violet 15.00 .90
380 A60 45pf orange 9.00 3.00
381 A61 50pf brown 9.75 2.60
382 A60 60pf orange brn 11.50 3.00
383 A61 80pf chocolate 22.50 6.75
384 A61 80pf yel bis ('30) 7.50 2.25
Nos. 366-384 (19) 108.75 32.80
Set, never hinged 1,025.

Stamps of 1928 Overprinted

1930, June 30

385 A60 8pf dark green 2.25 .90
386 A61 15pf carmine rose 2.25 .90
Set, never hinged 16.00

Issued in commemoration of the final evacuation of the Rhineland by the Allied forces.

View of Cologne A63

1930 **Engr.** **Wmk. 126**

Inscribed: "Reichsmark"

387 A63 2m dark blue 26.00 14.50
Never hinged 105.00

A type of design A43 in green exists with "Reichsmark" instead of "Mark." It was not issued, though some examples are known in private hands. Value $15,000.

Pres. von Hindenburg — A64

1932, Oct. 1 **Typo.** **Wmk. 126**

391 A64 4pf blue .55 .60
392 A64 5pf brt green .85 .60
393 A64 12pf dp orange 5.00 .60
394 A64 15pf dk red 3.00 *9.75*
395 A64 25pf ultra 2.40 .75
396 A64 40pf violet 20.50 1.50
397 A64 50pf dk brown 3.75 *10.50*
Nos. 391-397 (7) 36.05 24.30
Set, never hinged 130.00

85th birthday of von Hindenburg.

See Nos. 401-431, 436-441. For surcharges and overprints see France N27-N58, Luxembourg N1-N16 and Poland N17-N29.

Frederick the Great — A65

1933, Apr. 12 **Photo.**

398 A65 6pf dk green .80 .90
a. Tête bêche pair 18.00 30.00
399 A65 12pf carmine 1.20 .90
a. Tête bêche pair 18.00 30.00
b. Bklt. pane of 5 + label 37.50 65.00
400 A65 25pf ultra 42.50 21.00
Nos. 398-400 (3) 44.50 22.80
Set, never hinged 246.25

Celebration of Potsdam Day.

Hindenburg Type of 1932

1933 **Typo.**

401 A64 3pf olive bister 16.50 .75
402 A64 4pf dull blue 3.75 .75
403 A64 6pf dk green 1.90 .75
404 A64 8pf dp orange 6.00 .75
a. Bklt. pane, 3 #404 + 5 #406 110.00 *150.00*
b. Open "D" 19.00 3.75
405 A64 10pf chocolate 3.75 .75
406 A64 12pf dp carmine 2.25 .75
a. Bklt. pane, 4 #392 + 4 #406 82.50 *150.00*
407 A64 15pf maroon 5.25 *26.00*
408 A64 20pf brt blue 6.75 1.50
409 A64 30pf olive grn 6.75 1.35
410 A64 40pf red violet 30.00 2.60
411 A64 50pf dk grn & blk 15.00 2.25
412 A64 60pf claret & blk 30.00 1.00
413 A64 80pf dk blue & blk 9.00 1.15
414 A64 100pf orange & blk 26.00 13.00
Nos. 401-414 (14) 162.90 *53.35*
Set, never hinged 950.00

Hindenburg Type of 1932

1933-36 **Wmk. 237** ***Perf. 14***

415 A64 1pf black .25 .40
a. Bklt. pane, 4 #415, 3 #417, label 15.00 *16.50*
b. Bklt. pane, 3 #415, 3 #416 + 2 #418 42.50 *75.00*
c. Bklt. pane, 2 #415, 5 #420, label 22.50 *42.50*
d. Bklt. pane, 4 #415 + 4 #422 21.00 *37.50*
416 A64 3pf olive bis ('34) .25 .40
a. Bklt. pane, 4 #416 + 4 #418 22.50 *42.50*
b. Bklt. pane, 4 #416 + 4 #419 21.00 *37.50*
c. Bklt. pane, 6 #416, 1 #422, label 11.50 *16.50*
417 A64 4pf dull blue ('34) .25 .40
a. Bklt. pane, 3 #417, 4 #422, label 21.00 *37.50*
418 A64 5pf brt green ('34) .25 .40
a. Bklt. pane, 2 #418, 5 #419, label 15.00 *16.50*
b. Bklt. pane, 2 #418, 3 #419 + 3 #420 21.00 *37.50*
c. Bklt. pane, 4 #418 + 4 #420 42.50 *75.00*
419 A64 6pf dk green ('34) .25 .40
b. Bklt. pane of 7 + label 9.00 *16.50*
c. Bklt. pane, 1 #419, 6 #422, label 67.50 *105.00*
420 A64 8pf dp orange ('34) .25 .40
a. Bklt. pane, 3 #420, 4 #422, label 15.00 *16.50*
b. Open "D" 4.25 4.50
421 A64 10pf choc ('34) .25 .40
422 A64 12pf dp car ('34) .25 .40
a. Bklt. pane of 7 + label 22.50 *42.50*
423 A64 15pf maroon ('34) .30 .40
424 A64 20pf brt blue ('34) .45 .40
425 A64 25pf ultra ('34) .45 .40
426 A64 30pf olive grn ('34) .75 .40
427 A64 40pf red violet ('34) 1.50 .40
428 A64 50pf dk grn & blk ('34) 3.00 .40
429 A64 60pf claret & blk ('34) .75 .40
430 A64 80pf dk bl & blk ('36) 2.25 1.20
431 A64 100pf org & blk ('34) 3.00 1.15
Nos. 415-431 (17) 14.45 8.35
Set, never hinged 65.00

Karl Peters — A66

Designs: 3pf, Franz Adolf E. Lüderitz. 6pf, Dr. Gustav Nachtigal. 12pf, Karl Peters. 25pf, Hermann von Wissmann.

1934, June 30 ***Perf. 13x13½***

432 A66 3pf brown & choc 2.60 *6.00*
433 A66 6pf dk grn & choc .95 1.50
434 A66 12pf dk car & choc 3.00 1.50
435 A66 25pf brt blue & choc 9.50 *19.50*
Nos. 432-435 (4) 16.05 28.50
Set, never hinged 145.00

Issued in remembrance of the lost colonies of Germany.

Hindenburg Memorial Issue
Type of 1932
With Black Border

1934, Sept. 4 ***Perf. 14***

436 A64 3pf olive bister .45 .45
437 A64 5pf brt green .45 .55
438 A64 6pf dk green .90 .45
439 A64 8pf vermilion 2.25 .45
440 A64 12pf deep carmine 2.75 .45
441 A64 25pf ultra 6.75 *8.25*
Nos. 436-441 (6) 13.55 10.60
Set, never hinged 115.00

Swastika, Sun and Nuremberg Castle — A70

1934, Sept. 1 **Photo.**

442 A70 6pf dark green 3.00 .60
443 A70 12pf dark carmine 4.00 .60
Set, never hinged 65.00

Nazi Congress at Nuremberg.

Imperfs exist. Value never hinged, each $750.

Allegory "Saar Belongs to Germany" A71

German Eagle A72

1934, Aug. 26 **Typo.** **Wmk. 237**

444 A71 6pf dark green 3.00 .60
445 A72 12pf dark carmine 3.75 .60
Set, never hinged 67.50

Issued to mark the Saar Plebiscite.

Friedrich von Schiller — A73

1934, Nov. 5

446 A73 6pf green 2.00 .60
447 A73 12pf carmine 4.75 .60
Set, never hinged 75.00

175th anniv. of the birth of von Schiller.

Germania Welcoming Home the Saar — A74

1935, Jan. 16 **Photo.**

448 A74 3pf brown .35 1.15
449 A74 6pf dark green .35 .75
450 A74 12pf lake 2.00 .75
451 A74 25pf dark blue 7.50 8.25
Nos. 448-451 (4) 10.20 10.90
Set, never hinged 90.00

Return of the Saar to Germany.

German Soldier — A75

1935, Mar. 15

452 A75 6pf dark green 1.50 1.50
453 A75 12pf copper red 1.60 1.50
Set, never hinged 16.00

Issued to commemorate War Heroes' Day.

Wreath and Swastika — A76

1935, Apr. 26 **Unwmk.**

454 A76 6pf dark green 1.05 1.35
455 A76 12pf crimson 1.60 1.35
Set, never hinged 19.00

Young Workers' Professional Competitions.

Heinrich Schütz — A77

Wmk. Swastikas (237)

1935, June 21 Engr. *Perf. 14*

456 A77 6pf shown 1.10 .75
457 A77 12pf Bach 1.10 .75
458 A77 25pf Handel 1.60 .90
Nos. 456-458 (3) 3.80 2.40
Set, never hinged 26.00

Schutz-Bach-Handel celebration.

"The Eagle" — A80

Designs: 12pf, Modern express train. 25pf, "The Hamburg Flyer." 40pf, Streamlined locomotive.

1935, July 10 *Perf. 14*

459 A80 6pf dark green .95 .75
460 A80 12pf copper red .95 .75
461 A80 25pf ultra 5.25 1.75
462 A80 40pf red violet 8.75 1.75
Nos. 459-462 (4) 15.90 5.00
Set, never hinged 97.50

Centenary of railroad in Germany.
Exist impert. Values: Nos. 459-462, $475 each.

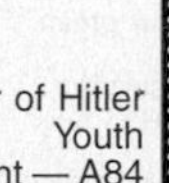

Bugler of Hitler Youth Movement — A84

1935, July 25 Photo.

463 A84 6pf deep green 1.15 2.25
464 A84 15pf brown lake 2.25 3.00
Set, never hinged 22.50

Hitler Youth Meeting.

Eagle and Swastika over Nuremberg — A85

1935, Aug. 30 Engr.

465 A85 6pf gray green 1.35 .55
466 A85 12pf dark carmine 2.00 .55
Set, never hinged 19.00

1935 Nazi Congress at Nuremberg.

Nazi Flag Bearer and Feldherrnhalle at Munich — A86

1935, Nov. 5 Photo. *Perf. 13½*

467 A86 3pf brown .25 .70
468 A86 12pf dark carmine .60 .70
Set, never hinged 12.00

12th anniv. of the 1st Hitler "Putsch" at Munich, Nov. 9, 1923.

Airplane — A87

1936, Jan. 6

469 A87 40pf sapphire 6.00 3.00
Never hinged 50.00

10th anniv. of the Lufthansa air service.

Gottlieb Daimler — A88

Carl Benz — A89

1936, Feb. 15 *Perf. 14*

470 A88 6pf dark green .70 1.00
471 A89 12pf copper red .90 1.00
Set, never hinged 13.50

The 50th anniv. of the automobile; Intl. Automobile and Motorcycle Show, Berlin.

Otto von Guericke — A90

1936, May 4

472 A90 6pf dark green .30 .55
Never hinged 1.20

250th anniv. of the death of the German inventor, Otto von Guericke, May 11, 1686.

Symbolical of Municipalities A91

1936, June 3

473 A91 3pf dark brown .50 .30
474 A91 5pf deep green .70 .30
475 A91 12pf lake .85 .60
476 A91 25pf dark ultra 1.75 1.05
Nos. 473-476 (4) 3.80 2.25
Set, never hinged 15.00

6th Intl. Cong. of Municipalities, June 7-13.

Allegory of Recreation Congress — A92

1936, June 30

477 A92 6pf dark green .65 .55
478 A92 15pf deep claret 1.25 1.00
Set, never hinged 13.50

World Congress for Vacation and Recreation held at Hamburg.

Salute to Swastika — A93

1936, Sept. 3 *Perf. 14*

479 A93 6pf deep green .55 .60
480 A93 12pf copper red .95 .60
Set, never hinged 10.50

The 1936 Nazi Congress.

Shield Bearer — A94

1937, Mar. 3 Engr. Unwmk.

481 A94 3pf brown .45 .40
482 A94 6pf green .60 .40
483 A94 12pf carmine 1.20 .75
Nos. 481-483 (3) 2.25 1.55
Set, never hinged 11.50

The Reich's Air Protection League.

German and Austrian Carrying Nazi Flag — A95

Wmk. Swastikas (237)

1938, Apr. 8 Photo. *Perf. 14x13½*

Size: 23x28mm

484 A95 6pf dark green .75 .60
Never hinged 1.50

Unwmk. *Perf. 12½*

Size: 21½x26mm

485 A95 6pf deep green .75 1.30
Never hinged 1.50

Union of Austria and Germany.

Cathedral Island A96

Hermann Goering Stadium A97

Town Hall, Breslau — A98

Centennial Hall, Breslau — A99

1938, June 21 Engr. *Perf. 14*

486 A96 3pf dark brown .30 .55
487 A97 6pf deep green .30 .55
488 A98 12pf copper red .75 .55
489 A99 15pf violet brown 1.75 .75
Nos. 486-489 (4) 3.10 2.40
Set, never hinged 12.00

16th German Gymnastic and Sports Festival held at Breslau, July 23-31, 1938.

Nazi Emblem — A100

1939, Apr. 4 Photo. Wmk. 237

490 A100 6pf dark green 1.75 3.75
491 A100 12pf deep carmine 2.25 3.75
Set, never hinged 19.00

Young Workers' Professional Competitions.

St. Mary's Church — A101

The Krantor, Danzig — A102

1939, Sept. 18

492 A101 6pf dark green .45 .75
493 A102 12pf orange red .65 .75
Set, never hinged 3.75

Unification of Danzig with the Reich.

Johannes Gutenberg and Library at Leipzig — A103

Designs: 6pf, "High House," Leipzig. 12pf, Old Town Hall, Leipzig. 25pf, View of Leipzig Fair.

Inscribed "Leipziger Messe"

Perf. 10½

1940, Mar. 3 Photo. Unwmk.

494 A103 3pf dark brown .45 .45
495 A103 6pf dk gray green .45 .45
496 A103 12pf henna brown .45 .45
497 A103 25pf ultra .90 1.15
Nos. 494-497 (4) 2.25 2.50
Set, never hinged 7.50

Leipzig Fair.

House of Nations, Leipzig — A107

6pf, Concert Hall, Leipzig. 12pf, Leipzig Fair Office. 25pf, Railroad Terminal, Leipzig.

Inscribed: "Reichsmesse Leipzig, 1941"

1941, Mar. 1 *Perf. 14x13½*

498 A107 3pf brown .30 1.00
499 A107 6pf green .30 1.00
500 A107 12pf dark red .30 1.00
501 A107 25pf bright blue .70 1.00
Nos. 498-501 (4) 1.60 4.00
Set, never hinged 9.75

Leipzig Fair.

Fashion Allegory — A111

Vienna Fair Hall — A112

"Burgtheater" A113

Monument to Prince Eugene A114

1941, Mar. 8 *Perf. 13½x14*

502 A111 3pf dark red brown .45 .55
503 A112 6pf brt bluo grn .45 .55
504 A113 12pf scarlet .45 .60
505 A114 25pf bright blue 1.25 1.50
Nos. 502-505 (4) 2.60 3.20
Set, never hinged 10.50

Vienna Fair.

A115

Adolf Hitler — A

1941-44 Typo.

Size: 18½x22½

506 A115 1pf gray black
a. Bklt. pane, 4 #506 + 4 #509
Never hinged

540
541

507 A115 3pf lt brown .25 .30
a. Bklt. pane, 6 #507 + 2 #510 6.75 *15.00*
Never hinged 11.50
508 A115 4pf slate .25 .30
a. Bklt. pane, 4 #508, 2 #511 + 2 labels 6.75 *15.00*
Never hinged 11.50
509 A115 5pf dp yel grn .25 .30
510 A115 6pf purple .25 .30
a. Bklt. pane of 7 + label 13.50 *30.00*
Never hinged 22.50
511 A115 8pf red .25 .30
511A A115 10pf dk brn ('42) .25 .45
511B A115 12pf car ('42) .25 .45

Engr.

512 A115 10pf dark brown .40 .30
513 A115 12pf brt carmine .40 .30
a. Bklt. pane of 6 + 2 labels 4.50 *15.00*
Never hinged 7.50
514 A115 15pf brown lake .30 1.50
515 A115 16pf peack grn .25 1.50
516 A115 20pf blue .25 .40
517 A115 24pf org brn .25 1.50

Size: 21½x26mm

518 A115 25pf brt ultra .25 .45
519 A115 30pf olive green .25 .45
520 A115 40pf brt red vio .25 .45
521 A115 50pf myrtle green .25 .45
522 A115 60pf dk red brn .25 .45
523 A115 80pf indigo .25 .45
524 A116 1m dk slate grn ('44) .45 5.25
a. Perf. 12½ ('42) 1.50 6.00
525 A116 2m violet ('44) 1.50 67.50
a. Perf. 12½ ('42) 1.20 6.00

Perf. 12½

526 A116 3m cop red ('42) 1.50 15.00
a. Perf. 14 ('44) 9.00 450.00
527 A116 5m dk bl ('42) 3.00 50.00
a. Perf. 14 ('44) 4.50 1,050.
Nos. 506-527 (24) 11.80 148.65
Set, #506-527, never hinged 30.00
Set, #524a-527a, never hinged 42.50

Nos. 507, 510, 511, 511A, 511B, 520, 524-526 exist imperf.

For surcharge see No. MQ3. For overprints see Austria Nos. 390-393, 398-403, 405-431, Russia Nos. N9-N48.

Storm Trooper Emblem — A117

1942, Aug. 8 Photo. *Perf. 14*

528 A117 6pf purple .25 .75
Never hinged .75

War Effort Day of the Storm Troopers.

Adolf Hitler — A118

1944 Engr.

529 A118 42pf bright green .25 1.90
Never hinged .30

Exists imperf. Value $750 hinged.
For overprint see Austria No. 404.

A119

1946 Typo. Wmk. 284 *Perf. 14*

Size: 18x22mm

530 A119 1pf black .25 *3.00*
531 A119 2pf black .25 .25
532 A119 3pf yellow brn .25 *3.75*
533 A119 4pf slate .25 *4.50*
534 A119 5pf yellow grn .25 *.60*
535 A119 6pf purple .25 .25
536 A119 8pf dp ver .25 .25
537 A119 10pf chocolate .25 .60
538 A119 12pf bright red .25 .25
539 A119 12pf slate gray .25 .25
a. Bklt. pane, 5 #539 + 3 #542 9.00 *115.00*
Never hinged 20.50
540 A119 15pf violet brn .25 *7.50*
541 A119 15pf lt yel grn .25 .40
542 A119 16pf slate green .25 .40
543 A119 20pf lt blue .25 .40
544 A119 24pf orange brn .25 .40
a. Bklt. pane, 8 #544 9.00 *115.00*
Never hinged 20.50
545 A119 25pf brt ultra .25 *7.50*
546 A119 25pf orange yel .25 *1.15*
547 A119 30pf olive .25 .25
548 A119 40pf red violet .25 .40
549 A119 42pf emerald .75 *30.00*
550 A119 45pf brt red .25 *.40*
551 A119 50pf dk ol grn .25 .25
552 A119 60pf brown red .25 .25
553 A119 75pf deep ultra .25 .25
554 A119 80pf dark blue .25 .40
555 A119 84pf emerald .25 .25

Size: 24½x29½mm

556 A119 1m olive green .25 .40
Nos. 530-556 (27) *64.30*
Set, never hinged 5.75

Imperf. examples of Nos. 543, 544 and 548 are usually from the souvenir sheet No. B295. Most other denominations exist imperf.

For overprints see Nos. 585A-599, 9N64, 10N17-10N21.

Planting Olive A120

Laborer A122

Reaping Wheat A123

Sower A121

Germany Reaching for Peace — A124

1947-48 *Perf. 14*

557 A120 2pf brown blk .25 .40
558 A120 6pf purple .25 .25
559 A121 8pf red .25 .40
560 A121 10pf yel grn ('48) .25 .60
561 A122 12pf gray .25 .25
562 A120 15pf choc ('48) .25 *3.75*
563 A123 16pf dk bl grn .25 .40
564 A121 20pf blue .25 *1.50*
565 A123 24pf brown org .25 .40
566 A120 25pf orange yel .25 *1.50*
567 A122 30pf red ('48) .25 *3.00*
568 A121 40pf red vio .25 .60
569 A123 50pf ultra ('48) .25 *1.90*
571 A122 60pf red brn ('48) .25 .75
a. 60pf brown red .25 .40
572 A122 80pf blue gray .25 *1.50*
573 A123 84pf emerald .25 *2.25*

Engr.

574 A124 1m olive .25 .40
575 A124 2m dk brown vio .25 *1.50*
576 A124 3m copper red .25 *19.00*
577 A124 5m dk blue ('48) .75 *45.00*
Nos. 557-577 (20) *85.35*
Set, never hinged 7.50

Used examples of Nos. 576-577 with expertized postal cancellations sell for much more.

For overprints see Nos. 600-633, 9N1-9N34, 9N65-9N67, 10N1-10N16.

Heinrich von Stephan — A125

1947, May 15 Litho.

578 A125 24pf orange brown .25 *1.50*
579 A125 75pf dark blue .25 *1.50*
Set, never hinged .75

50th anniv. of the death of Heinrich von Stephan, 1st postmaster general of the German Empire.

Leipzig Fair Issues

Type of Semi-Postal Stamp of 1947

12pf, Maximilian I granting charter, 1497.
75pf, Estimating and collecting taxes, 1365.

Perf. 13½x13

1947, Sept. 2 Litho. Wmk. 284

580 SP252 12pf carmine .25 1.90
581 SP252 75pf dk vio blue .25 1.90
Set, never hinged .90

Type of Semi-Postal Stamp of 1947, Dated 1948

50pf, Merchants at customs barrier, 1388.
84pf, Arranging stocks of merchandise, 1433.

1948, Mar. 2 Engr.

582 SP252 50pf deep blue .25 1.50
583 SP252 84pf green .25 2.25
Set, never hinged .90

Exist imperf. Value, each, $450.

Hanover Fair Issue

Weighing Goods for Export — A126

1948, May 22 Typo. *Perf. 14*

584 A126 24pf deep carmine .25 1.50
585 A126 50pf ultra .25 2.25
c. Pair, #584-585 2.25 19.00
Pair, never hinged 7.50
Set, never hinged .75

For Use in the United States and British Zones

Stamps of Germany 1946-47 Overprinted in Black

a

b

Overprint Type "a" on 1946 Numeral Issue

1948 Wmk. 284 *Perf. 14*

585A A119 2pf black 2.25 *32.00*
585B A119 8pf dp ver 4.50 *65.00*
586 A119 10pf chocolate .30 *5.00*
586A A119 12pf bright red 3.75 *52.50*
586B A119 12pf slate gray 65.00 *575.00*
586C A119 15pf violet brn 3.75 *52.50*
587 A119 15pf lt yel grn 1.20 *16.50*
587A A119 16pf slate green 10.00 *200.00*
587B A119 24pf orange brn 35.00 *210.00*
587C A119 25pf brt ultra 6.00 *65.00*
588 A119 25pf orange yel .60 *11.50*
589 A119 30pf olive .90 *11.50*
589A A119 40pf red violet 29.00 *210.00*
590 A119 45pf brt red 1.20 *11.50*
591 A119 50pf dk olive grn .75 *7.50*
592 A119 75pf dp ultra 2.25 *24.00*
593 A119 84pf emerald 2.25 *24.00*
Nos. 585A-593 (17) 185.05
Set, never hinged 375.00

Same, Overprinted Type "b"

593A A119 2pf black 10.50 *67.50*
593B A119 8pf dp ver 18.00 *190.00*
593C A119 10pf chocolate 16.50 *190.00*
593D A119 12pf bright red 5.25 *67.50*
593E A119 12pf slate gray 130.00 *1,050.*
593F A119 15pf violet brown 5.25 *52.50*
594 A119 15pf lt yel grn .55 *8.25*
594A A119 16pf slate grn 19.00 *170.00*
594B A119 24pf org brn 21.00 *210.00*
594C A119 25pf brt ultra 5.25 *65.00*
594D A119 25pf orange yel 19.00 *200.00*
595 A119 30pf olive .75 *6.75*
595A A119 40pf red violet 26.00 *250.00*
596 A119 45pf bright red 1.50 *12.00*
597 A119 50pf dk ol grn 1.50 *12.00*
598 A119 75pf dp ultra 1.15 *12.00*
599 A119 84pf emerald 1.15 *13.00*
Nos. 593A-599 (17) 295.25
Set, never hinged 600.00

Nine other denominations of type A119 (1, 3, 4, 5, 6, 20, 42, 60 and 80pf) were also overprinted with types "a" and "b." These overprints were not authorized, but the stamps were sold at post offices and tolerated for postal use. Forgeries exist.

The overprints on Nos. 585A-599 have been extensively counterfeited.

Overprint Type "a" on Stamps and Types of 1947 Pictorial Issue

600 A120 2pf brown black .25 *.55*
601 A120 6pf purple .25 *.40*
602 A121 8pf dp vermilion .25 *.40*
603 A121 10pf yellow green .25 .40
604 A122 12pf slate gray .25 .40
605 A120 15pf chocolate 2.60 *15.00*
606 A123 16pf dk blue green .55 *2.60*
607 A121 20pf blue .25 *1.00*
608 A123 24pf brown orange .25 *.40*
609 A120 25pf orange yellow .25 *.40*
610 A122 30pf red 1.00 *4.50*
611 A121 40pf red violet .30 *2.00*
612 A123 50pf ultra .35 *1.60*
614 A122 60pf red brown .35 *.80*
a. 60pf brown red 22.50 *225.00*
Never hinged 60.00
615 A122 80pf dark blue .55 *2.00*
616 A123 84pf emerald 1.60 *6.00*
Nos. 600-616 (16) 9.30 *38.45*
Set, never hinged 24.00

Same, Overprinted Type "b"

617 A120 2pf brown black .35 *2.60*
618 A120 6pf purple .35 *1.30*
619 A121 8pf red .35 *1.60*
620 A121 10pf yellow green .25 *.65*
621 A122 12pf gray .35 *1.60*
622 A120 15pf chocolate .25 *1.00*
623 A123 16pf dk blue green .60 *2.25*
624 A121 20pf blue .25 *.65*
625 A123 24pf brown orange .25 *1.30*
626 A120 25pf orange yel 3.00 *15.00*
627 A122 30pf red .25 *1.30*
628 A121 40pf red violet .25 *.65*
629 A123 50pf ultra .25 *.65*
631 A122 60pf red brown .25 *1.00*
a. 60pf brown red .95 *3.75*
Never hinged 2.50
632 A122 80pf dark blue .25 *1.00*
633 A123 84pf emerald .40 *1.30*
Nos. 617-633 (16) 7.65 *33.85*
Set, never hinged 22.50

Most of Nos. 585A-633 exist with inverted and double overprints.

Frankfurt Town Hall A127

Our Lady's Church, Munich A128

Cologne Cathedral A129

Brandenburg Gate, Berlin A130

Holsten Gate, Lübeck — A131

Type I

Type II

Two types of mark values:
Type I — Four horiz. lines in stairs inside arch.
Type II — Seven horizontal lines in stairs inside arch.

Perf. 11½x11, 11

1948-51 Litho. Wmk. 286

634 A127 2pf black .25 *.40*
a. Perf. 14 1.00 *5.00*
635 A128 4pf orange brown .25 *.40*
a. Perf. 14 .55 .40
636 A129 5pf blue .25 *.40*
a. Perf. 14 .65 .40
637 A128 6pf orange brown .25 *.40*
638 A128 6pf orange .25 *.40*
a. Perf. 14 6.00 4.50
639 A127 8pf orange yel .25 *.40*
640 A128 8pf dk slate blue .25 *.40*
641 A129 10pf green .25 *.40*
a. Perf. 14 .65 .40
642 A128 15pf orange .80 *4.50*
643 A127 15pf violet .50 .40
a. Perf. 14 4.50 .40
644 A127 16pf bluish green .30 *.55*
645 A127 20pf blue .40 *2.60*
646 A130 20pf carmine .30 *.40*
a. Perf. 14 1.60 .40
647 A130 24pf carmine .25 *.40*
648 A129 25pf vermilion .40 .40
a. Perf. 14 7.50 *30.00*
649 A130 30pf blue .55 .40
a. Perf. 14 11.00 .40
650 A128 30pf scarlet 1.00 *5.25*
651 A129 40pf rose lilac .65 .40
a. Perf. 14 7.50 .40
652 A130 50pf ultra .55 *1.60*
653 A128 50pf bluish green .65 .40
a. Perf. 14 67.50 .40
654 A129 60pf violet brn 30.00 .40
a. Perf. 14 1.00 .40
655 A130 80pf red violet 1.05 .40
a. Perf. 14 45.00 .40
656 A128 84pf rose violet .65 6.00
657 A129 90pf rose lilac 1.05 .40
a. Perf. 14 60.00 .40

Perf. 11, 11x11½

658 A131 1m yellow grn (I) 15.00 .55
a. Perf. 14 (II) ('51) 60.00 .40
b. Perf. 11 (II) 90.00 .40
659 A131 2m violet (I) 13.50 .55
a. Type II 22.50 .40
660 A131 3m car rose (I) 15.00 2.25
a. Type II 75.00 .95
661 A131 5m blue (I) 22.50 21.00
a. Type II 90.00 3.00
Nos. 634-661 (28) 107.10 52.05
Set, never hinged 225.00
Set, 634a-658a, never hinged 550.00
Set, 658b-661a, never hinged 375.00

Imperforates of many values exist.

Specialists collect Nos. 634-661 with watermark in four positions: upright, D's facing left; upright, D's facing right; sideways, D's facing up; sideways, D's facing down.

Two types of perforation: line and comb. Nos. 634-657 are found both perf. 11 and 11½x11.

Herman Hildebrant Wedigh — A132

Wmk. 116

1949, Apr. 22 Engr. *Perf. 14*

662 A132 10pf green 1.00 *2.25*
663 A132 20pf carmine rose 1.00 *2.00*
664 A132 30pf blue 1.30 3.00
a. Sheet of 3, #662-664 34.00 *260.00*
Sheet, never hinged 105.00
Nos. 662-664 (3) 3.30 7.25
Set, never hinged 10.50

Hanover Export Fair, 1949.
No. 664a sold for 1 mark.

Federal Republic

AREA — 95,520 sq. mi.
POP. — 62,040,000 (1974 est.)
CAPITAL — Bonn

"Reconstruction" A133

1949, Sept. 7 Litho. Wmk. 286

665 A133 10pf blue green 14.50 *15.00*
666 A133 20pf rose carmine 16.00 *19.00*
Set, never hinged 75.00

Opening of the first Federal Assembly.
Exist imperf. Value, each $875.

Bavaria Stamp — A134

Design: 30pf, Bavaria 6kr.

Wmk. 285

1949, Sept. 30 Litho. *Perf. 14*

667 A134 20pf red & dull blue 13.00 *34.00*
668 A134 30pf dull blue & choc 16.00 *52.50*
Set, never hinged 67.50

Cent. of German postage stamps. See No. B309.

Heinrich von Stephan, General Post Office and Guild House, Bern A135

1949, Oct. 9 Wmk. 286

669 A135 30pf ultra 19.50 *35.00*
Never hinged 52.50

75th anniv. of the UPU.

Numeral and Post Horn — A136

1951-52 Typo. Wmk. 295

670 A136 2pf yellow grn .35 .85
671 A136 4pf yellow brn .55 .30
a. Booklet pane, 3 #671 + 3 #673 + 4 #677 110.00 900.00
Never hinged 280.00
672 A136 5pf dp rose vio 1.60 .30
673 A136 6pf orange 4.50 2.60
674 A136 8pf gray 4.50 6.00
675 A136 10pf dk green 1.30 .30
a. Booklet pane, 4 #675 + 5 #677 + label 110.00 900.00
Never hinged 280.00
676 A136 15pf purple 9.00 .85
677 A136 20pf carmine 1.00 .30
678 A136 25pf dk rose lake 19.00 5.25

Engr.

Size: 20x24½mm

679 A136 30pf blue 11.50 .55
680 A136 40pf rose lilac ('52) 26.00 .55
681 A136 50pf blue gray ('52) 37.50 .55
682 A136 60pf brown ('52) 26.00 .55
683 A136 70pf dp yel ('52) 135.00 14.50
684 A136 80pf carmine ('52) 135.00 2.00
685 A136 90pf yel grn ('52) 150.00 2.25
Nos. 670-685 (16) 562.80 37.70
Set, never hinged 1,700.

Imperfs. exist of Nos. 671, 673, 675, 681 & 684.

W. K. Roentgen — A137

1951, Dec. 10

686 A137 30pf blue 24.00 15.00
Never hinged 60.00

50th anniv. of the awarding of the Nobel prize in physics to Wilhelm K. Roentgen.

Mona Lisa — A138

Wmk. 285

1952, Apr. 15 Litho. *Perf. 13½*

687 A138 5pf multicolored .40 *2.00*
Never hinged 1.05

500th anniv. of the birth of Leonardo da Vinci.

N. A. Otto — A139

Wmk. 295

1952, July 25 Engr. *Perf. 14*

688 A139 30pf deep blue 10.50 12.00
Never hinged 24.00

75th anniv. of the four-cycle gas engine.

Martin Luther — A140

1952, July 25

689 A140 10pf green 3.75 *4.50*
Never hinged 11.50

Issued to publicize the Lutheran World Federation Assembly, Hanover, 1952.

Freighter Off Heligoland — A141

1952, Sept. 6

690 A141 20pf red 4.50 5.25
Never hinged 11.50

Return of Heligoland, Mar. 1, 1952.

Carl Schurz — A142

Wmk. 285

1952, Sept. 17 Litho. *Perf. 13½*

691 A142 20pf blue, blk & brn org 6.50 *7.50*
Never hinged 15.00

Centenary of Carl Schurz's arrival in America.

Thurn and Taxis Postilion A143

1952, Oct. 25

692 A143 10pf multicolored 1.50 2.25
Never hinged 4.50

1st Thurn and Taxis stamp, cent.

Philipp Reis — A144

1952, Oct. 27 Photo. *Perf. 14*

693 A144 30pf blue 16.50 13.50
Never hinged 42.50

75 years of telephone service in Germany.

"Prevent Traffic Accidents" — A145

1953, Mar. 30 Litho. Wmk. 285

694 A145 20pf blk, red & bl grn 5.25 4.50
Never hinged 13.50

Justus von Liebig — A146

1953, May 12 Engr. Wmk. 295

695 A146 30pf dark blue 9.00 *19.00*
Never hinged 26.00

150th anniv. of the birth of Justus von Liebig, chemist.

Red Cross and Compass — A147

Perf. 14x13½

1953, May 8 Litho. Wmk. 285

696 A147 10pf dp ol grn & red 4.50 *5.75*
Never hinged 16.50

125th anniv. of the birth of Henri Dunant, founder of the Red Cross.

War Prisoner and Barbed Wire — A148

Typographed and Embossed

1953, May 9 Unwmk. *Perf. 14*

697 A148 10pf gray & black 1.60 .35
Never hinged 5.25

Issued in memory of the prisoners of war.

Train and Hand Signal — A149

Designs: 10pf, Pigeon and planes. 20pf, Automobiles and traffic signal. 30pf, Ship, barges and buoy.

Wmk. 295

1953, June 20 Engr. *Perf. 14*

698 A149 4pf brown	1.60	*3.75*
699 A149 10pf deep green	4.00	*6.00*
700 A149 20pf red	4.50	*7.50*
701 A149 30pf deep ultra	13.00	*15.00*
Nos. 698-701 (4)	23.10	32.25
Set, never hinged	65.00	

Exhibition of Transport and Communications, Munich, 1953.

Pres. Theodor Heuss — A150

1954-60 Typo. *Perf. 14*

Size: 18½x22mm

702 A150 2pf citron	.25	.25
a. Booklet pane, 5 #702, 4 #704 + label ('55)	22.50	130.00
Never hinged	45.00	
b. Booklet pane, 3 #702, 6 #704 + label ('56)	3.75	60.00
Never hinged	11.50	
c. Booklet pane, 3 #702, 1 #707, 5 #708 + label ('56)	7.50	75.00
Never hinged	16.50	
703 A150 4pf orange brn	.25	.25
704 A150 5pf rose lilac	.25	.25
a. Booklet pane, 2 #704, 7 #708 + label ('55)	22.50	130.00
Never hinged	45.00	
705 A150 6pf lt brown	.25	.65
706 A150 7pf bluish green	.25	.30
707 A150 8pf gray	.25	.55
708 A150 10pf green	.25	.25
a. Booklet pane, 4 #708, 5 #710 + label ('55)	22.50	130.00
Never hinged	45.00	
709 A150 15pf ultra	.25	.40
710 A150 20pf dk car rose	.25	.25
711 A150 25pf red brown	.25	.55

Engr.

Size: 19½x24mm

712 A150 30pf blue	3.75	4.50
713 A150 40pf red violet	1.30	.30
714 A150 50pf gray	57.50	.40
715 A150 60pf red brown	11.50	.55
716 A150 70pf olive	4.50	1.60
717 A150 80pf deep rose	.65	.65
718 A150 90pf deep green	3.75	2.00

Size: 24½x29½mm

719 A150 1m olive green	.50	.30
720 A150 2m lt vio blue	.65	1.00
721 A150 3m deep plum	1.60	2.00
Nos. 702-721 (20)	88.20	17.00
Set, never hinged	225.00	

Coils and sheets of 100 were issued of the 5, 7, 10, 15, 20, 25, 40 and 70pf. Every fifth coil stamp has a control number on the back.

Printings of Nos. 704, 706, 708-711 and 708b were made on fluorescent paper beginning in 1960.

Nos. 702, 709, 714 exist imperf. Value about $425 each.

See Nos. 737Ab, 755-761.

Catalogue values for unused stamps in this section, from this point to the end of the section, are for Never Hinged items.

Paul Ehrlich and Emil von Behring — A151

Wmk. 285

1954, Mar. 13 Litho. *Perf. 13½*

722 A151 10pf dark green 9.00 3.00

Centenary of the births of Paul Ehrlich and Emil von Behring, medical researchers.
Exists imperf. Value $800.

15th Century Printer — A152

1954, May 5 Typo. Wmk. 295

723 A152 4pf chocolate 1.20 .55

500th anniversary of the publication of Gutenberg's 42-line Bible. Design from woodcut by Jost Amman.

Bishop's Miter and Sword — A153

Engraved; Center Embossed

1954, June 5 Unwmk. *Perf. 13½x14*

724 A153 20pf gray & red 6.75 3.75

Martyrdom of Saint Boniface, 1200th anniv.

Carl F. Gauss — A154

Wmk. 295

1955, Feb. 23 Engr. *Perf. 14*

725 A154 10pf deep green 4.50 .55

Cent. of the death of Carl Friedrich Gauss, mathematician.

A155

Wmk. 304

1955, May 7 Litho. *Perf. 13½*

726 A155 10pf green 4.50 1.20

Cent. of the birth of Oskar von Miller, electrical engineer.

A156

Engraved and Embossed

1955, May 9 Unwmk. *Perf. 13½x14*

727 A156 40pf blue 13.50 5.00

Friedrich von Schiller, poet, 150th death anniv.

1906 Automobile A157

Wmk. 304

1955, June 1 Typo. *Perf. 13½*

728 A157 20pf red & black 9.00 4.25

German postal motor-bus service, 50th anniv.

Arms of Baden-Württemberg — A158

Perf. 13x13½

1955, June 15 Litho. Wmk. 295

729 A158 7pf lemon, blk & brn red	4.25	2.60
730 A158 10pf lemon, blk & grn	5.00	2.00

Baden-Wurttemberg Exhibition, Stuttgart, 1955.

Globe and Atomic Symbol — A159

1955, June 24 Photo. *Perf. 13½x14*

731 A159 20pf rose brown 9.00 .85

Issued to encourage scientific research.

Orb and Symbols of Battle — A160

Photogravure and Embossed

Perf. 14x13½

1955, Aug. 10 Unwmk.

732 A160 20pf red lilac 7.50 2.60

Issued in honor of Augsburg and the millenium of the Battle on the Lechfeld.

Family in Flight — A161

1955, Aug. 2 Engr. Wmk. 304

733 A161 20pf org brown 3.00 .50

Ten years of German expatriation. See No. 930.

Railroad Signal, Tracks — A162

Perf. 13½x14

1955, Oct. 5 Litho. Wmk. 304

734 A162 20pf red & black 7.50 2.00

European Timetable conf. at Wiesbaden, Oct. 5-15, 1955.

A163

Stifter monument and sylized Trees.

1955, Oct. 22 Engr.

735 A163 10pf dark green 3.00 2.00

150th anniv. of the birth of Adalbert Stifter, poet.

A164

Lithographed and Embossed

Perf. 14x13½

1955, Oct. 24 Unwmk.

736 A164 10pf UN emblem 3.00 3.75

United Nations Day, Oct. 24, 1955.

Numeral — A165

1955-58 Wmk. 304 Typo. *Perf. 14*

737 A165 1pf gray .25 .35

Wmk. 295

737A A165 1pf gray ('58)	7.50	*15.00*
b. Bklt. pane of 10 (#707, 2 each #737A, #704, #708, 3 #710)	22.50	52.50

No. 737A was issued only in the booklet pane, No. 737b. No. 737 was issued on fluorescent paper in 1963.

Numeral and Signature A166

1956, Jan. 7 Engr. Wmk. 304

738 A166 20pf dark red 6.00 2.00

125th anniv. of the birth of Heinrich von Stephan, co-founder of the UPU.

Clavichord A167

1956, Jan. 27 Litho.

739 A167 10pf dull lilac .80 .35

200th anniv. of the birth of Wolfgang Amadeus Mozart, composer.

Heinrich Heine, Poet, Death Cent. — A168

Perf. 13x13½

1956, Feb. 17 **Wmk. 295**
740 A168 10pf ol grn & blk 2.25 2.60

Old Buildings, Lüneburg A169

Wmk. 304
1956, May 2 **Engr.** ***Perf. 14***
741 A169 20pf dull red 6.50 7.50

Millenary of Lüneburg.

Olympic Rings — A170

1956, June 9 ***Perf. 13½x14***
742 A170 10pf slate green .65 .55

Issued to publicize the Olympic year, 1956.

Robert Schumann — A171

1956, July 28 **Litho.** **Unwmk.**
743 A171 10pf citron, blk & red .65 .40

Schumann, composer, death cent.

Synod Emblem — A172

Perf. 13½x13

1956, Aug. 8 **Wmk. 304**
744 A172 10pf green 2.60 3.00
745 A172 20pf brown carmine 3.75 4.50

Meeting of German Protestants (Evangelical Synod), Frankfurt on Main, Aug. 8-12.

Thomas Mann — A173

1956, Aug. 11 **Engr.** ***Perf. 13½x14***
746 A173 20pf pale rose vio 2.25 1.75

1st anniv. of the death of Thomas Mann, novelist.

Maria Laach Abbey — A174

1956, Aug. 24 **Photo.** ***Perf. 13x13½***
747 A174 20pf brn lake & gray 1.75 1.75

800th anniv. of the dedication of the Maria Laach Abbey.

Europa Issue

"Rebuilding Europe" — A175

1956, Sept. 15 **Engr.** ***Perf. 14***
748 A175 10pf green *.65* *.25*
749 A175 40pf blue *6.75* *.85*

Issued to symbolize the cooperation among the six countries comprising the Coal and Steel Community.

Plan of Cologne Cathedral and Hand — A176

1956, Aug. 29 **Litho.** ***Perf. 13x13½***
750 A176 10pf gray grn & red brn 2.25 2.25

77th meeting of German Catholics, Cologne, Aug. 29.

Map of the World and Policeman's Hand — A177

1956, Sept. 1 ***Perf. 13½x13***
751 A177 20pf red org, grn & blk 2.25 2.25

Issued on the occasion of the International Police Show, Essen, Sept. 1-23.

Pigeon Holding Letter — A178

1956, Oct. 27 **Engr.** ***Perf. 14***
752 A178 10pf green 1.30 .60

Issued to publicize the Day of the Stamp.

Cemetery Crosses — A179

1956, Nov. 17 ***Perf. 14x13½***
753 A179 10pf slate 1.30 .60

Issued to commemorate the people of Germany who died during WWII and to promote the Society for the Care of Military Cemeteries.

Saar Coat of Arms — A180

1957, Jan. 2 **Litho.** ***Perf. 13x13½***
754 A180 10pf bluish grn & brn .50 .40

Return of the Saar to Germany. See Saar No. 262.

Heuss Type of 1954

1956-57 **Wmk. 304** **Engr.** ***Perf. 14***
Size: 18½x22mm

755	A150 30pf slate green	.35	.55
756	A150 40pf lt ultra	1.30	.30
757	A150 50pf olive	.85	.30
758	A150 60pf lt brown	2.50	.40
759	A150 70pf violet	8.25	.40
760	A150 80pf red orange	5.25	1.60
761	A150 90pf bluish green	13.50	.85
	Nos. 755-761 (7)	32.00	4.40

Nos. 755-756 were printed on both ordinary and fluorescent paper; Nos. 757-761 only on ordinary paper. Issue dates: 40pf, 1956. Others, 1957.

The 40pf and 70pf were also issued in coils. Every fifth coil stamp has control number on back.

Heinrich Hertz — A181

1957, Feb. 22 **Litho.** ***Perf. 14***
762 A181 10pf lt green & blk 1.15 .55

Heinrich Hertz, physicist, birth cent.

Paul Gerhardt — A182

1957, May 18 **Engr.**
763 A182 20pf carmine lake .55 .50

350th anniv. of the birth of Paul Gerhardt, Lutheran clergyman and hymn writer.

Tulip and Post Horn — A183

1957, June 8
764 A183 20pf red orange .55 .50

Flora & Philately Exhib., Cologne, June 8-10.

Arms of Aschaffenburg, 1332 — A184

Perf. 13x13½

1957, June 15 **Wmk. 304**
765 A184 20pf dp salmon & blk .55 .50

1000th anniv. of the founding of the Abbey and town of Aschaffenburg.

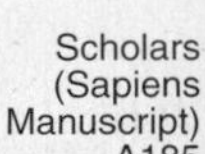
Scholars (Sapiens Manuscript) A185

1957, June 24 ***Perf. 13½x13***
766 A185 10pf blk, bl grn & red org .40 .35

Founding of Freiburg University, 500th anniv.

Modern Passenger Freighter — A186

1957, June 25 ***Perf. 13½x14***
767 A186 15pf brt blue, blk & red .95 .95

Merchant Marine Day, June 25.

Liebig Laboratory A187

1957, July 3 **Engr.** ***Perf. 14x13½***
768 A187 10pf dark green .40 .40

350th anniv. of the Justus Liebig School at Ludwig University, Giessen.

Albert Ballin — A188

Perf. 13½x14

1957, Aug. 15 **Litho.** **Wmk. 304**
769 A188 20pf dk car rose & blk 1.15 .40

Cent. of the birth of Albert Ballin, founder of the Hamburg-America Steamship Line.

Television Screen — A189

1957, Aug. 23 **Engr.** ***Perf. 14x13½***
770 A189 10pf blue vio & grn .40 .40

Issued to publicize the television industry.

Europa Issue

"United Europe" A190

Lithographed; Tree Embossed

1957-58 **Unwmk.** ***Perf. 14x13½***
771 A190 10pf yel grn & lt bl .35 .25
a. Imperf. *300.00* *300.00*
772 A190 40pf dk bl & lt bl *4.50* *3.75*

Wmk. 304

772A A190 10pf yel grn & lt bl *6.50* 10
Nos. 771-772A (3) 11.35 1

A united Europe for peace and pro
Issued: Nos. 771-772, 9/16; No
8/1958.

Water Lily — A191

European Robin — A192

Wmk. 304

1957, Oct. 4 Litho. *Perf. 14*

773 A191 10pf yel grn & org yel .50 .40

774 A192 20pf multicolored .50 .40

Protection of wild animals and plants.

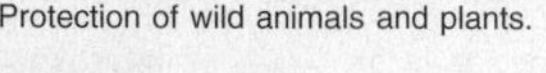

Carrier Pigeons — A193

1957, Oct. 5

775 A193 20pf dp car & blk .75 .50

Intl. Letter Writing Week, Oct. 6-12.

Baron vom Stein — A194

1957, Oct. 26 Engr. *Perf. 13½x14*

776 A194 20pf red 1.20 .55

200th anniv. of the birth of Baron Heinrich Friedrich vom und zum Stein, Prussian statesman.

Leo Baeck — A195

1957, Nov. 2

777 A195 20pf dark red 1.20 .55

1st anniv. of the death of Rabbi Leo Baeck of Berlin.

Landschaft Building, Stuttgart — A196

Perf. 13x13½

1957, Nov. 16 Litho. Wmk. 304

778 A196 10pf dk grn & yel grn .75 .50

500th anniversary of the Wurttemberg Landtag (Assembly).

Coach — A197

1957, Nov. 26 Engr. *Perf. 14*

779 A197 10pf olive green .65 .50

Centenary of the death of Joseph V. Eichendorff, poet.

"Max and Moritz" — A198

Design: 20pf, Wilhelm Busch.

1958, Jan. 9 Litho. *Perf. 13½x13*

780 A198 10pf lt ol grn & blk .25 .25

781 A198 20pf red & black .65 .55

50th anniv. of the death of Wilhelm Busch, humorist.

"Prevent Forest Fires" — A199

1958, Mar. 5 *Perf. 14*

782 A199 20pf brt red & blk .60 .50

Rudolf Diesel A200

1958, Mar. 18 Engr. *Perf. 14*

783 A200 10pf dk blue grn .35 .35

Centenary of the birth of Rudolf Diesel, inventor.

Giraffe and Lion — A201

Perf. 13x13½

1958, May 7 Litho. Wmk. 304

784 A201 10pf brt yel grn & blk .50 .35

Zoo at Frankfort on the Main, cent. Exists imperf. Value $225.

View of Old Munich — A202

1958, May 22 Engr. *Perf. 14x13½*

785 A202 20pf dark red .50 .35

800th anniversary of Munich.

Market Cross, Trier — A203

1958, June 3

786 A203 20pf dark red & black .50 .35

Millennium of the market of Trier (Treves).

Heraldic Eagle 5m Coin — A204

1958, June 20 Litho. *Perf. 13x13½*

787 A204 20pf red & black .60 .60

10th anniv. of the German currency reform. Exists imperf. Value $300.

Turner Emblem and Oak Leaf — A205

Perf. 13½x14

1958, July 21 Wmk. 304

788 A205 10pf gray, blk & dl grn .35 .40

150 years of German Turners and on the occasion of the 1958 Turner festival.

Schulze-Delitzsch A206

1958, Aug. 29 Engr. *Perf. 13½x14*

789 A206 10pf yellow green .40 .35

150th anniv. of the birth of Hermann Schulze-Delitzsch, founder of German trade organizations.

Common Design Types pictured following the introduction.

Europa Issue, 1958

Common Design Type

1958, Sept. 13 Litho.

Size: 24½x30mm

790 CD1 10pf yel grn & blue *.35* .25

791 CD1 40pf lt blue & red *2.60* *.35*

Nicolaus Cusanus (Nikolaus Krebs) — A207

1958, Dec. 3 Litho. *Perf. 14x13½*

792 A207 20pf dk car rose & blk .40 .35

500th anniv. of the Cusanus Hospice at Kues, founded by Cardinal Nicolaus (1401-64).

Exists imperf. Value $300, mint or used.

Pres. Theodor Heuss — A208

1959 Wmk. 304 *Perf. 14*

793 A208 7pf blue green .25 .25

794 A208 10pf green .35 .25

795 A208 20pf dk car rose .35 .25

Engr.

796 A208 40pf blue 10.50 .80

797 A208 70pf deep purple 3.75 .65

Nos. 793-797 (5) 15.20 2.20

Nos. 793-795 were issued in sheets of 100 and in coils. Every fifth coil stamp has a control number on the back.

An experimental booklet containing one pane of 10 of No. 794 was sold at Darmstadt in 1960. Value $750.

Jakob Fugger — A209

1959, Mar. 6 *Perf. 13x13½*

798 A209 20pf dk red & black .35 .40

500th anniversary of the birth of Jakob Fugger the Rich, businessman and banker.

Adam Riese — A210

1959, Mar. 28 *Perf. 13½x13*

799 A210 10pf ol grn & blk .35 .40

Adam Riese (c. 1492-1559), arithmetic teacher, 400th death anniversary.

Alexander von Humboldt — A211

1959, May 6 Engr. *Perf. 13½x14*

800 A211 40pf blue 1.45 1.15

Alexander von Humboldt (1769-1859), naturalist and geographer, death centenary.

Buildings, Buxtehude A212

1959, June 20 Litho. *Perf. 14*

801 A212 20pf lt blue, ver & blk .40 .40

Millennium of town of Buxtehude.

Holy Coat of Trier — A213

Lithographed; Coat Embossed

1959, July 18 Wmk. 304 *Perf. 14*

802 A213 20pf dull cl, buff & blk .35 .35

Showing of the seamless robe of Christ at the Cathedral of Trier, July 19-Sept. 20.

Synod Emblem — A214

1959, Aug. 12 **Litho.**
803 A214 10pf grn, brt vio & blk .35 .35

Meeting of German Protestants (Evangelical Synod), Munich, Aug. 12-16.

Souvenir Sheet

A215

Portraits: 10pf, George Friedrich Handel. 15pf, Louis Spohr. 20pf, Ludwig van Beethoven. 25pf, Joseph Haydn. 40pf, Felix Mendelssohn-Bartholdy.

Perf. 14x13½
1959, Sept. 8 **Engr.** **Wmk. 304**
804 A215 Sheet of 5 19.00 *37.50*
a. 10pf deep green 2.60 *5.75*
b. 15pf blue 2.60 *5.75*
c. 20pf dark carmine 2.60 *3.75*
d. 25pf brown 2.60 *7.50*
e. 40pf dark blue 2.60 *5.75*

Opening of Beethoven Hall in Bonn and to honor various anniversaries of German composers.

Europa Issue, 1959
Common Design Type
1959, Sept. 19 **Litho.** ***Perf. 13½x14***
Size: 24x29½mm
805 CD2 10pf olive green .30 .25
806 CD2 40pf dark blue *1.05* *.35*

Uprooted Oak Emblem — A216

1960, Apr. 7 ***Perf. 13½x13***
807 A216 10pf grn, blk & lil .25 .25
808 A216 40pf bl, blk & org 1.75 1.75

World Refugee Year, 7/1/59-6/30/60.

Philipp Melanchthon A217

1960, Apr. 19 ***Perf. 13½x14***
809 A217 20pf dk car rose & blk 1.00 1.00

400th anniversary of the death of Philipp Melanchthon, co-worker of Martin Luther in the German Reformation.

Symbols of Christ's Sufferings A218

1960, May 17 ***Perf. 14x13½***
810 A218 10pf Prus grn, gray & ocher .30 .30

1960 Passion Play, Oberammergau, Bavaria.

Dove, Chalice and Crucifix — A219

1960, July 30 **Engr.** ***Perf. 14x13½***
811 A219 10pf dull green .50 .35
812 A219 20pf maroon .65 .65

37th Eucharistic World Congress, Munich.

Wrestlers and Olympic Rings — A220

Sport scenes from Greek urns: 10pf, Sprinters. 20pf, Discus and Javelin throwers. 40pf, Chariot race.

1960, Aug. 8 **Wmk. 304**
813 A220 7pf red brown .25 .25
814 A220 10pf olive green .30 .25
815 A220 20pf vermilion .30 .25
816 A220 40pf dark blue 1.00 1.00
Nos. 813-816 (4) 1.85 1.75

17th Olympic Games, Rome, 8/25-9/11.

Hildesheim Cathedral, Miters, Cross and Crosier — A221

1960, Sept. 6 **Engr.** ***Perf. 13½x14***
817 A221 20pf claret .65 .40

St. Bernward (960-1022) and St. Godehard (960-1038), bishops.

Europa Issue, 1960
Common Design Type
1960, Sept. 19 **Wmk. 304**
Size: 30x25mm
818 CD3 10pf ol grn & yel grn .25 .25
819 CD3 20pf brt red & lt red *.65* .25
820 CD3 40pf bl & lt bl *1.00* *.85*
Nos. 818-820 (3) 1.90 1.35

George C. Marshall — A222

1960, Oct. 15 **Litho.** ***Perf. 13x13½***
821 A222 40pf dp blue & blk 2.25 1.75

Issued to honor George C. Marshall, US general and statesman.

Steam Locomotive — A223

1960, Dec. 7 ***Perf. 13½x14***
822 A223 10pf ol bis & blk .30 .35

125th anniversary of German railroads.

St. George — A224

Wmk. 304
1961, Apr. 23 **Engr.** ***Perf. 14***
823 A224 10pf green .25 .30

Honoring Boy Scouts of the world on St. George's Day (patron saint of Boy Scouts).

Albrecht Dürer — A225

Portraits: 5pf, Albertus Magnus. 7pf, St. Elizabeth of Thuringia. 8pf, Johann Gutenberg. 15pf, Martin Luther. 20pf, Johann Sebastian Bach. 25pf, Balthasar Neumann. 30pf, Immanuel Kant. 40pf, Gotthold Ephraim Lessing. 50pf, Johann Wolfgang von Goethe. 60pf, Friedrich von Schiller. 70pf, Ludwig van Boethoven. 80pf, Heinrich von Kleist. 90pf, Prof. Franz Oppenheimer. 1m, Annette von Droste-Hülshoff. 2m, Gerhart Hauptmann.

1961-64 **Typo.** ***Perf. 14***
Fluorescent or Ordinary Paper
824 A225 5pf olive .25 .25
b. Tête bêche pair ('63) .60 .90
825 A225 7pf dark bister .25 .25
826 A225 8pf lilac .25 .25
827 A225 10pf olive green .25 .25
b. Tête bêche pair .55 1.30
828 A225 15pf blue .25 .25
b. Tête bêche pair ('63) .80 1.75
829 A225 20pf dk red .25 .25
b. Tête bêche pair ('63) .55 1.60
830 A225 25pf orange brn .25 .25

Engr.
831 A225 30pf gray .25 .25
832 A225 40pf blue .25 .25
833 A225 50pf red brown .25 .25
834 A225 60pf dk car rose ('62) .30 .25
835 A225 70pf grnsh black .25 .25
a. 70pf deep green .55 .25
836 A225 80pf brown .35 .35
837 A225 90pf yel ol ('64) .30 .25
838 A225 1m violet blue .50 .25
839 A225 2m yel grn ('62) 2.25 .50
Nos. 824-839 (16) 6.45 4.35

Nos. 824-825, 827-830, 832, 834-835, 835a were issued in coils as well as in sheets. Every fifth coil stamp has a black control number on the back.

Nos. 824-839, including booklet panes and tête bêche pairs, were printed on fluorescent paper. Nos. 824-829 and 832 were also printed on ordinary paper.

Gottlieb Daimler's Car of 1886 and Signature A226

Design: 20pt, Carl Benz's 3-wheel car of 1886 and signature.

1961, July 3 **Litho.**
840 A226 10pf green & blk .25 .25
841 A226 20pf brick red & blk .30 .30

75 years of motorized traffic.

Messenger, Nuremberg, 18th Century — A227

Photogravure and Engraved
1961, Aug. 31 **Wmk. 304** ***Perf. 14***
842 A227 7pf brown red & blk .30 .30

Issued to publicize the exhibition "The Letter in Five Centuries," Nuremberg.

Cathedral, Speyer — A228

1961, Sept. 2 **Engr.**
843 A228 20pf vermilion .30 .40

900th anniversary of Speyer Cathedral.

Europa Issue, 1961
Common Design Type
1961, Sept. 18 **Litho.**
Size: 28½x18½mm
844 CD4 10pf olive green .25 .25
845 CD4 40pf violet blue *.35* *.50*

No. 844 was printed on both ordinary and fluorescent paper.

Reis Telephone A229

Wmk. 304
1961, Oct. 26 **Engr.** ***Perf. 14***
846 A229 10pf green .30 .35

Cent. of the demonstration of the 1st telephone by Philipp Reis.

Wilhelm Emanuel von Ketteler — A230

1961, Dec. 22 **Litho.**
847 A230 10pf olive grn & blk .30 .35

Sesquicentennial of the birth of von Ketteler, Bishop of Mainz and pioneer in social development.

Fluorescent Paper

was introduced for all stamps, starting with No. 848. Of the stamps before No. 848, those issued on both ordinary and fluorescent paper include Nos. 704, 706, 708-711, 737, 755-756, 824-829, 832, 844. Those issued only on fluorescent paper (up to No. 848) include Nos. 708b, 830-831, 833-839 and 842.

Drusus Stone and Old View of Mainz — A231

1962, May 10 **Engr.** **Wmk. 304**
848 A231 20pf deep claret .30 .35

The 2000th anniversary of Mainz.

Notes and Tuning Fork — A232

1962, July 12 **Litho.** ***Perf. 14***
849 A232 20pf red & black .30 .40

Issued to show appreciation of choral singing. The music is from the choral movement for three voices "In dulci jubilo" from "Musa Sioniae" by Michael Praetorius.

"Faith, Thanksgiving, Service" A233

1962, Aug. 22 Engr. Unwmk.

850 A233 20pf magenta .30 .40

79th meeting of German Catholics, Hanover, Aug. 22-29.

Open Bible, Chrismon and Chalice — A234

1962, Sept. 11 Litho. Wmk. 304

851 A234 20pf vermilion & blk .30 .40

Württemberg Bible Society, 150th anniv.

Europa Issue, 1962

Common Design Type

1962, Sept. 17 Engr.

Size: 28x23mm

852 CD5 10pf green .25 .25
853 CD5 40pf blue *.40* *.50*

"Bread for the World" — A235

Lithographed and Embossed

1962, Nov. 23 ***Perf. 14***

854 A235 20pf brown red & blk .30 .40

Issued in connection with the Advent Collection of the Protestant Church in Germany.

Mother and Child Receiving Gift Parcel — A236

1963, Feb. 9 Engr.

855 A236 20pf dark carmine .30 .35

Issued to express gratitude to the American organizations, CRALOG (Council of Relief Agencies Licensed to Operate in Germany) and CARE (Cooperative for American Remittances to Everywhere), for help during 1946-1962.

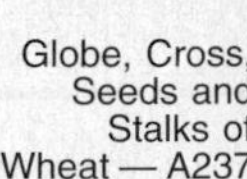

Globe, Cross, Seeds and Stalks of Wheat — A237

Lithographed and Engraved

1963, Feb. 27 Wmk. 304 ***Perf. 14***

856 A237 20pf gray, blk & red .30 .35

German Catholic "Misereor" (I have compassion) campaign against hunger and illness.

Checkered Lily — A238

Flowers: 15pf, Lady's slipper. 20pf, Columbine. 40pf, Beach thistle.

1963, Apr. 28 Litho. Unwmk.

857 A238 10pf multicolored .25 .25
858 A238 15pf multicolored .25 .25
859 A238 20pf multicolored .25 .25
860 A238 40pf multicolored .25 .25
Nos. 857-860 (4) 1.00 1.00

Flora and Philately Exhibition, Hamburg.

Heidelberg Catechism A239

1963, May 2 Litho. & Engr.

861 A239 20pf dp org, brn org & blk .30 .35

400th anniv. of the Heidelberg Catechism, containing the doctrine of the reformed church.

Cross of Golgotha, Darkened Sun and Moon — A240

1963, May 4 Litho. Wmk. 304

862 A240 10pf grn, dp car, blk & vio .25 .30

Consecration of the Regina Martyrum Church, Berlin-Plötzensee, in memory of the victims of Nazism.

Arms of 18 Participating Countries, Paris Conference, 1863 — A241

1963, May 7 Engr.

863 A241 40pf violet blue .35 .50

1st Intl. Postal Conf., Paris, 1863, cent.

Map Showing New Railroad Link, German and Danish Flags — A242

1963, May 14 Litho. Unwmk.

864 A242 20pf multi .30 .30

Inauguration of the "Bird Flight Line" railroad link between Germany and Denmark.

Cross — A243

Lithographed and Embossed

1963, May 24 Unwmk. ***Perf. 14***

865 A243 20pf magenta, red & yel .30 .30

Cent. of the founding of the Intl. Red Cross in connection with the German Red Cross cent. celebrations, Munster, May 24-26.

Synod Emblem and Crown of Barbed Wire — A244

Perf. 13½x13

1963, July 24 Litho. Wmk. 304

866 A244 20pf dp orange & blk .30 .35

Meeting of German Protestants (Evangelical Synod), Dortmund, July 24-28.

Europa Issue, 1963

Common Design Type

1963, Sept. 14 Engr. ***Perf. 14***

Size: 28x23½mm

867 CD6 15pf green .25 .30
868 CD6 20pf red .25 .25

Old Town Hall, Hanover A245

State Capitals: No. 870, Hamburg harbor, 775th anniv. No. 871, North Ferry pier, Kiel. No. 872, National Theater, Munich. No. 873, Fountain & building, Wiesbaden. No. 874, Reichstag Building,Berlin. No. 875, Gutenberg Museum, Mainz. No. 876, Jan Wellem (Johann Wilhelm II, 1658-1716) statue, Dusseldorf. No. 877, City Hall, Bonn. No. 878, City Hall, Bremen. No. 879, View of Stuttgart. No. 879A, Ludwig's Church, Saarbrucken.

Perf. 14, 13½x13 (#873, 876, 877)

1964-65 Litho. Unwmk.

869 A245 20pf gray, blk & red .25 .30
870 A245 20pf multicolored .25 .30
871 A245 20pf multicolored .25 .30
872 A245 20pf multicolored .25 .30
873 A245 20pf multicolored .25 .30
874 A245 20pf blue, blk, & grn .25 .30
875 A245 20pf multicolored .25 .30
876 A245 20pf multicolored .25 .30
877 A245 20pf multi ('65) .25 .30
878 A245 20pf multi ('65) .25 .30
879 A245 20pf multi ('65) .25 .30
879A A245 20pf multi ('65) .25 .30
Nos. 869-879A (12) 3.00 3.60

View of Ottobeuren Abbey — A246

Lithographed and Engraved

1964, May 29 ***Perf. 14***

880 A246 20pf pink, red & blk .25 .30

Ottobeuren Benedictine Abbey, 1200th anniv.

Pres. Heinrich Lübke — A247

1964, July 1 Litho. ***Perf. 14***

881 A247 20pf carmine .25 .25
882 A247 40pf ultra .25 .30

Lübke's re-election. See Nos. 974-975.

Sophie Scholl — A248

Designs: No. 884, Ludwig Beck. No. 885, Dietrich Bonhoeffer. No. 886, Alfred Delp. No. 887, Karl Friedrich Goerdeler. No. 888, Wilhelm Leuschner. No. 889, Count James von Moltke. No. 890, Count Claus Schenk von Stauffenberg.

1964, July 20 Litho. & Engr.

883 A248 20pf blue gray & blk .55 1.00
884 A248 20pf blue gray & blk .55 1.00
885 A248 20pf blue gray & blk .55 1.00
886 A248 20pf blue gray & blk .55 1.00
887 A248 20pf blue gray & blk .55 1.00
888 A248 20pf blue gray & blk .55 1.00
889 A248 20pf blue gray & blk .55 1.00
890 A248 20pf blue gray & blk .55 1.00
Nos. 883-890 (8) 4.40 8.00

Issued to honor the German resistance to the Nazis, 1943-45. Printed in sheet of eight, containing one each of Nos. 883-890, se-tenant. Size: 148x105mm. The stamps were valid; the sheet was not, though widely used. Values: mint $6; used $11.

John Calvin — A249

1964, Aug. 3 Litho. ***Perf. 14***

891 A249 20pf red & black .25 .30

Issued to honor the meeting of the International Union of the Reformed Churches in Germany, Frankfort on the Main, Aug. 3-13.

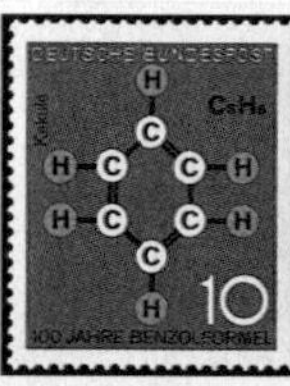

Benzene Ring, Kekulé's Formula — A250

Designs: 15pf, Cerenkov radiation, reactor in operation. 20pf, German gas engine.

1964, Aug. 14 Unwmk. ***Perf. 14***

892 A250 10pf dk brn, brt grn & blk .25 .25
893 A250 15pf brt grn, ultra & blk .25 .25
894 A250 20pf red, grn & blk .25 .25
Nos. 892-894 (3) .75 .75

Progress in science and technology: 10pf, centenary of benzene formula by August Friedrich Kekulé; 15pf, 25 years of nuclear fission, Hahn and Strassmann; 20pf, centenary of German internal combustion engine, Nikolaus August Otto and Eugen Langen.

Ferdinand Lasalle — A251

1964, Aug. 31 Litho.

895 A251 20pf slate bl & blk .25 .30

Cent. of the death of Ferdinand Lasalle, a founder of the German Labor Movement.

Radiating Sun — A252

1964, Sept. 2 Engr. Wmk. 304

896 A252 20pf gray & red .25 .30

80th meeting of German Catholics, Stuttgart, Sept. 2-6. The inscription from Romans 12:2: ". . . be ye transformed through the renewing of your mind."

Europa Issue, 1964

Common Design Type

1964, Sept. 14 Litho. Unwmk.

Size: 23x29mm

897 CD7 15pf yellow grn & lil .25 .25
898 CD7 20pf rose & lilac .25 .25

Judo — A253

1964, Oct. 10
899 A253 20pf multicolored .25 .30

18th Olympic Games, Tokyo, Oct. 10-25.

Prussian Eagle — A254

Lithographed and Embossed

1964, Oct. 30 Unwmk. *Perf. 14*
900 A254 20pf brown org & blk .25 .30

250 years of the Court of Accounts in Germany, founded as the Royal Prussian Upper Chamber of Accounts.

John F. Kennedy (1917-63) — A255

1964, Nov. 21 Engr. Wmk. 304
901 A255 40pf dark blue .30 .30

Castle Gate, Ellwangen — A256

Designs: (German buildings through 12 centuries): 10pf, Wall pavilion, Zwinger, Dresden. 15pf, Tegel Castle, Berlin. 20pf, Portico, Lorsch. 40pf, Trifels Fortress, Palatinate. 60pf, Treptow Gate, Neubrandenburg. 70pf, Osthofen Gate, Soest. 80pf, Elling Gate, Weissenburg.

1964-66 Typo. Unwmk.
903 A256 10pf brown ('65) .35 .25
904 A256 15pf dk green ('65) .35 .25
b. Tête bêche pair ('65) 1.00 2.00
905 A256 20pf brown red ('65) .35 .25
b. Tête bêche pair ('66) 1.00 1.30

Engr.
908 A256 40pf violet bl ('65) .35 .25
909 A256 50pf olive bister .65 .25
910 A256 60pf rose red 1.00 .35
911 A256 70pf dark green ('65) 1.00 .35
912 A256 80pf chocolate 1.00 .35
Nos. 903-912 (8) 5.05 2.30

Nos. 903-905, 908, 910-912 were issued in sheets of 100 and in coils. Every fifth coil stamp has a black control number on the back.

Illustrations from the Works of Matthias Claudius A257

1965, Jan. 21 Engr. *Perf. 14*
917 A257 20pf black & red .25 .30

150th anniv. of the death of Matthias Claudius, poet and editor of the "Wandsbecker Bothe." Exists imperf. Value $225.

Otto von Bismarck by Franz von Lenbach — A258

1965, Apr. 1 Litho. *Perf. 14*
918 A258 20pf black & dull red .25 .30

Prince Otto von Bismarck (1815-1898), Prussian statesman and 1st chancellor of the German Empire.
Exists imperf. Value $750.

Jet Plane and Space Capsule — A259

Designs: 5pf, Traffic lights and signs. 10pf, Communications satellite and ground station. 15pf, Old and new post buses. 20pf, Semaphore telegraph and telecommunication tower. 40pf, Old and new railroad engines. 70pf, Sailing ship and ocean liner.

1965
919 A259 5pf gray & multi .25 .30
920 A259 10pf multicolored .25 .30
921 A259 15pf multicolored .25 .30
922 A259 20pf maroon & multi .25 .30
923 A259 40pf dk blue & multi .25 .30
924 A259 60pf dull vio, yel & lt bl .25 .30
925 A259 70pf multicolored .30 .30
Nos. 919-925 (7) 1.80 2.10

Intl. Transport and Communications Exhib., Munich, June 25-Oct. 30. No. 924 also for the 10th anniv. of the reopening of air service by Lufthansa. Issued: 60pf, 4/1; others, 6/25.
No. 919 exists imperf. Value $225.

Bouquet of Flowers — A260

1965, May 1 Litho.
926 A260 15pf multicolored .25 .25

75th anniv. of May Day celebration in Germany.

ITU Emblem — A261

1965, May 17 Unwmk. *Perf. 14*
927 A261 40pf dp blue & blk .30 .35

Cent. of the ITU.

Adolph Kolping — A262

1965, May 26 Typo.
928 A262 20pf black, gray & red .25 .30

Kolping (1813-65). founder of the Catholic Unions of Journeymen, the Kolpingwork.

Rescue Ship — A263

1965, May 29 Litho. & Engr.
929 A263 20pf red & black .25 .30

Cent. of the German Sea Rescue Service.

Type of 1955 Dated "1945-1965"
Perf. 14x13½

1965, July 28 Engr. Wmk. 304
930 A161 20pf gray .25 .30

20 years of German expatriation.

Synod Emblem and Labyrinth — A264

Lithographed and Engraved
Perf. 13½x14

1965, July 28 Unwmk.
931 A264 20pf dp bl, grnsh bl & blk .25 .30

12th meeting of German Protestants (Evangelical Synod), Cologne, July 28-Aug. 1.

Waves and Stuttgart Television Tower — A265

1965, July 28 Litho. *Perf. 13½x13*
932 A265 20pf dp bl, blk & brt pink .25 .30

Issued to publicize the German Radio Exhibition, Stuttgart, Aug. 27-Sept. 5.

Stamps of Thurn and Taxis, 1852-59 A266

1965, Aug. 28 *Perf. 14*
933 A266 20pf multicolored .25 .30

125th anniv. of the introduction of postage stamps in Great Britain.

Europa Issue, 1965
Common Design Type
Perf. 14x13½

1965, Sept. 27 Engr. Wmk. 304
Size: 28x23mm
934 CD8 15pf green .25 .25
935 CD8 20pf dull red .25 .25

Nordertor, Flensburg — A267

Designs: 5pf, Berlin Gate, Stettin. 10pf, Wall Pavilion, Zwinger, Dresden. 20pf, Portico, Lorsch. 40pf, Trifels Fortress, Palatinate. 50pf, Castle Gate, Ellwangen. 60pf, Treptow Gate, Neubrandenburg. 70pf, Osthofen Gate, Soest. 80pf, Elling Gate, Weissenburg. 90pf, Zschocke Ladies' Home, Königsberg. 1m, Melanchthon House, Wittenberg. 1.10m, Trinity Hospital, Hildesheim. 1.30m, Tegel Castle, Berlin. 2m, Löwenberg, Town Hall, interior view.

1966-69 Unwmk. Engr. *Perf. 14*
936 A267 5pf olive .25 .25
937 A267 10pf dk brn ('67) .25 .25
939 A267 20pf dk grn ('67) .25 .25
940 A267 30pf yellow green .25 .25
941 A267 30pf red ('67) .25 .25
942 A267 40pf olive bis ('67) .30 .25
943 A267 50pf blue ('67) .35 .25
944 A267 60pf dp org ('67) 2.50 1.30
945 A267 70pf slate grn ('67) 1.05 .25
946 A267 80pf red brown ('67) 2.00 1.30
947 A267 90pf black .75 .30
948 A267 1m dull blue .75 .25
949 A267 1.10m red brown .75 .30
950 A267 1.30m green ('69) 2.00 1.20
951 A267 2m purple 2.00 .55
Nos. 936-951 (15) 13.70 7.20

Brandenburg Gate — A268

1966-68 Typo. *Perf. 14*
952 A268 10pf chocolate .30 .25
a. Bklt. pane, 4 #952, 2 #953, 4 #954 ('67) 4.50 15.00
b. Tête bêche pair .65 .65
c. Bklt. pane, 2 #952, 4 #953 2.25 7.50
953 A268 20pf deep green .30 .25
a. Tête bêche pair ('68) .80 .85
b. Bklt. pane, 2 #953, 2 #954 1.60 6.00
954 A268 30pf red .30 .25
a. Tête bêche pair ('68) .85 1.20
955 A268 50pf dark blue 1.05 .35
956 A268 100pf dark blue ('67) 9.75 .55
Nos. 952-956 (5) 11.70 1.65

Nos. 952-956 were issued in sheets of 100 and in coils. Every fifth coil stamp has a black control number on the back.

Nathan Söderblom — A269

1966, Jan. 15 Litho. *Perf. 13x13½*
959 A269 20pf dull lilac & blk .25 .30

Soderblom (1866-1931),Swedish Protestant theologian, who worked for the union of Christian churches and received 1930 Nobel Peace Prize.

Cardinal von Galen — A270

1966, Mar. 22 Litho. *Perf. 14*
960 A270 20pf dp lil rose, sal pink & blk .25 .30

Clemens August Cardinal Count von Galen (1878-1946), anti-Nazi Bishop of Munster.

"The Miraculous Draught" — A271

1966, July 13 Litho. *Perf. 14*
961 A271 30pf dp orange & blk .25 .30

81st meeting of German Catholics, Bamberg, July 13-17.

G. W. Leibniz — A272

1966, Aug. 24 Unwmk. *Perf. 14*

962 A272 30pf rose car, pink & blk .25 .30

Gottfried Wilhelm Leibniz (1646-1716), philosopher and mathematician.

Europa Issue, 1966

Common Design Type

1966, Sept. 24 *Perf. 14*

Size: 23x28½mm

963 CD9 20pf multicolored *.25 .30*
964 CD9 30pf multicolored .25 .25

Diagram of Three-Phase Transmission A273

1966, Sept. 28 Litho.

965 A273 20pf shown .25 .25
966 A273 30pf Dynamo .25 .25

Progress in science and technology: 20pf, 75th anniv. of three-phase power transmission; 30pf, cent.y of discovery by Werner von Siemens of the dynamoelectric principle.

UNICEF Emblem — A274

1966, Oct. 24 Litho. *Perf. 14*

967 A274 30pf red, blk & gray .25 .30

Awarding of the 1965 Nobel Peace Prize to UNICEF.

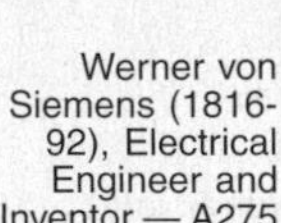

Werner von Siemens (1816-92), Electrical Engineer and Inventor — A275

1966, Dec. 13 Engr. *Perf. 14*

968 A275 30pf maroon .25 .30

Europa Issue, 1967

Common Design type

1967, May 2 Photo. *Perf. 14*

Size: 23x28mm

969 CD10 20pf multi .30 .30
970 CD10 30pf multi .25 .25

Franz von Taxis — A276

Lithographed and Engraved

1967, June 3 *Perf. 14*

971 A276 30pf dp orange & blk .25 .30

450th anniv. of the death of Franz von Taxis, founder of the Taxis (Thurn and Taxis) postal system.

"Peace Is Among Us" — A277

1967, June 21

972 A277 30pf brt pink & blk .25 .30

13th meeting of German Protestants (Evangelical Synod), Hanover, June 21-25.

Friedrich von Bodelschwingh A278

Perf. 13½x13

1967, July 1 Litho. Unwmk.

973 A278 30pf redsh brown & blk .25 .30

Cent. of Bethel Institution (for the incurable). Friedrich von Bodelschwingh (1877-1946), manager of Bethel (1910-46) & son of the founder.

Lübke Type of 1964

1967, Oct. 14 Litho. *Perf. 14*

974 A247 30pf carmine .25 .30
975 A247 50pf ultra .35 .35

Re-election of President Heinrich Lübke.

The Wartburg, Eisenach A279

1967, Oct. 31 Engr. *Perf. 14*

976 A279 30pf red .30 .35

450th anniversary of the Reformation.

Cross and Map of South America — A280

1967, Nov. 17 Photo. *Perf. 14*

977 A280 30pf multicolored .25 .30

"Adveniat," aid movement of German Catholics for the Latin American church.

Koenig Printing Press — A281

Designs: 20pf, Zinc sulfide and lead sulfide crystals. 30pf, Schematic diagram of a microscope.

1968, Jan. 12 Litho. *Perf. 14*

978 A281 10pf multicolored .25 .25
979 A281 20pf multicolored .25 .25
980 A281 30pf multicolored .25 .25
Nos. 978-980 (3) .75 .75

Progress in science and technology: 10pf, 150th anniv. of the Koenig printing press; 20pf, 1000th anniv. of mining in the Harz Mountains; 30pf, cent. of scientific microscope construction.

Symbols of Various Crafts A282

1968, Mar. 8 Litho. *Perf. 14*

981 A282 30pf multicolored .30 .35

Traditions and progress of the crafts. Exists imperf. Value $250.

Souvenir Sheet

Adenauer, Churchill, de Gasperi and Schuman — A283

Portraits: 10pf, Winston S. Churchill. 20pf, Alcide de Gasperi. 30pf, Robert Schuman. 50pf, Konrad Adenauer.

1968, Apr. 19 Litho. *Perf. 14*

Black Inscriptions

982 A283 Sheet of 4 2.00 2.00
a. 10pf dark red brown .50 .35
b. 20pf green .50 .40
c. 30pf dark red .50 .50
d. 50pf bright blue .50 .65

1st anniv. of the death of Konrad Adenauer (1876-1967), chancellor of West Germany (1949-63), and honoring leaders in building a united Europe.

Europa Issue, 1968

Common Design Type

1968, Apr. 29 Photo.

Size: 29x24½mm

983 CD11 20pf green, yel & brn .25 .30
984 CD11 30pf car, yel & brn .25 .25

Karl Marx (1818-83) A284

Lithgraphed and Engraved

1968, Apr. 29 *Perf. 14*

985 A284 30pf red, black & gray .25 .30

Pierre de Coubertin — A285

1968, June 6 Unwmk. *Perf. 14*

986 A285 30pf lilac & dk pur .55 .35
Nos. 986,B434-B437 (5) 3.65 2.70

19th Olympic Games, Mexico City, 10/12-27.

Opening Bars, "Die Meistersinger von Nurnberg," by Wagner — A286

Lithographed and Photogravure

1968, June 21

987 A286 30pf gray, blk & fawn .25 .30

Cent. of the 1st performance of Richard Wagner's "Die Meistersinger von Nurnberg."

Konrad Adenauer (1876-1967) A287

1968, July 19 Litho. *Perf. 14*

988 A287 30pf dp orange & blk .30 .30

Cross and Dove in Center of Universe A288

1968, July 19 Litho. & Engr.

989 A288 20pf brt grn, bl blk & yel .30 .30

Issued to publicize the 82nd meeting of German Catholics, Essen, Sept. 4-8.

North German Confederation Nos. 4 and 10 — A289

1968, Sept. 5 Engr. *Perf. 14*

990 A289 30pf cop red, gray vio & blk .25 .30

Cent. of the stamps of the North German Confederation.

Arrows Symbolizing Determination A290

1968, Sept. 26 Photo. *Perf. 14*

991 A290 30pf multicolored .25 .30

Centenary of the German trade unions.

Human Rights Flame — A291

1968, Dec. 10 Photo. *Perf. 14*

992 A291 30pf multicolored .25 .30

International Human Rights Year.

Junkers 52 A292

Design: 30pf, Boeing 707.

1969, Feb. 6 Litho. *Perf. 14*

993 A292 20pf green & multi .35 .25
994 A292 30pf red & multi .55 .25

50th anniv. of German airmail service.

Five-pointed Star — A293

1969, Apr. 28 Litho. *Perf. 13½x13*

995 A293 30pf red & multi .40 .30

50th anniv. of the ILO.

Europa Issue, 1969

Common Design Type

1969, Apr. 28 Photo. *Perf. 14*

Size: 29x23mm

996 CD12 20pf green, blue & yel .35 .25
997 CD12 30pf red brn, yel & blk .35 .25

Heraldic Eagles of Federal and Weimar Republics A294

1969, May 23 Photo. *Perf. 14*

998 A294 30pf red, black & gold 1.00 .40

German Basic Law, 20th anniv., and the proclamation of the Weimar Constitution, 50th anniv.

Crosses — A295

1969, June 4 Litho. & Engr.

999 A295 30pf dk violet bl & cream .40 .30

German War Graves Commission, 50th anniv.

Seashore A296

1969, June 4 *Perf. 14*

1000 A296 10pf shown .25 .25
1001 A296 20pf Foothills .55 .35
1002 A296 30pf Mountains .25 .25
1003 A296 50pf Riverbed .65 .50
Nos. 1000-1003 (4) 1.70 1.35

Issued to publicize Nature Protection.

"Hungry for Justice" — A297

1969, July 7 Litho. *Perf. 14*

1004 A297 30pf multicolored .40 .30

14th meeting of German Protestants (Evangelical Synod), Stuttgart, July 16-20.

Electromagnetic Field — A298

1969, Aug. 11 Litho. *Perf. 14*

1005 A298 30pf red & multi .40 .30

Issued to publicize the German Radio Exhibition, Stuttgart, Aug. 29-Sept. 7.

Maltese Cross — A299

1969, Aug. 11 *Perf. 13x13½*

1006 A299 30pf red & black .40 .30

Maltese Relief Service, founded 1955, world-wide activities in social services, first aid and disaster assistance.

Souvenir Sheet

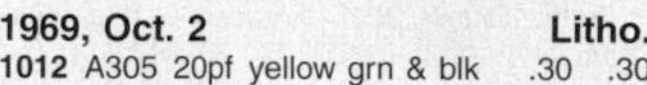

Marie Juchacz, Marie-Elisabeth Lüders and Helene Weber — A300

1969, Aug. 11 Engr. *Perf. 14*

1007 A300 Sheet of 3 1.20 .80
a. 10pf olive .30 .25
b. 20pf dark green .30 .25
c. 30pf lake .30 .25

50th anniv. of universal women's suffrage, Marie Juchacz (1879-1956), Marie-Elisabeth Lüders (1878-1966) and Helene Weber (1881-1962) were members of the German Reichstag.

Bavaria No. 16 — A301

1969, Sept. 4 Litho. & Embossed

1008 A301 30pf gray & rose .40 .30

23rd meeting of the Federation of German Philatelists, Sept. 6, the 70th Philatelists' Day, Sept. 7, and the phil. exhib. "120 Years of Bavarian Stamps" in Garmisch Partenkirchen, Sept. 4-7.

Brine Pipe Line — A302

1969, Sept. 4 Litho. *Perf. 13½x13*

1009 A302 20pf multicolored .40 .30

350th anniversary of the Brine Pipe Line from Traunstein to Bad Reichenhall.

Rothenburg ob der Tauber — A303

Lithographed and Engraved

1969, Sept. 4 *Perf. 14*

1010 A303 30pf dark red & blk .40 .30

See Nos. 1047-1049, 1067-1069A, 1106-1110.

Pope John XXIII (1881-1963) A304

1969, Oct. 2 Engr. *Perf. 13½x14*

1011 A304 30pf dark red .35 .30

Mahatma Gandhi (1869-1948) A305

1969, Oct. 2 Litho.

1012 A305 20pf yellow grn & blk .30 .30

Ernst Moritz Arndt — A306

1969, Nov. 13 Litho. & Engr.

1013 A306 30pf gray & maroon .35 .30

Arndt (1769-1860), historian, poet and member of German National Assembly.

Ludwig van Beethoven — A307

Portraits: 20pf, Georg Wilhelm Hegel (1770-1831), philosopher. 30pf, Friedrich Hölderlin (1770-1843), poet.

1970, Mar. 20 *Perf. 13½x14*

1014 A307 10pf pale vio & blk .65 .25
1015 A307 20pf olive & blk .40 .25
1016 A307 30pf rose & blk .40 .25
Nos. 1014-1016 (3) 1.45 .75

Saar No. 171 A308

1970, Apr. 29 Photo. *Perf. 14x13½*

1017 A308 30pf blk, red & gray grn .35 .30

Issued to publicize the SABRIA National Stamp Exhibition, Saarbrucken, Apr. 29-May 4. No. 1017 was issued Apr. 29 at the SABRIA post office in Saarbrucken, on May 4 throughout Germany.

Europa Issue, 1970

Common Design Type

1970, May 4 Engr. *Perf. 14x13½*

Size: 28x23mm

1018 CD13 20pf green .30 .25
1019 CD13 30pf red .30 .25

Münchhausen on His Severed Horse — A309

1970, May 11 Litho. *Perf. 13½x13*

1020 A309 20pf multicolored .35 .30

Soldier and storyteller Count Hieronymus C. F. von Münchhausen (1720-97).

Seagoing Vessel and Underpass A310

1970, June 18 Litho. *Perf. 14*

1021 A310 20pf multicolored .35 .30

North Sea-Baltic Sea Canal, 75th anniv.

Nurse Assisting Elderly Woman — A311

5pf, Welder (industrial protection). 10pf, Mountain climbers (rescuer bringing down casualty). 30pf, Fireman. 50pf, Stretcher bearer, casualty & ambulance. 70pf, Rescuer & drowning boy.

1970 Photo.

1022 A311 5pf dull blue & multi .25 .25
1023 A311 10pf brown & multi .25 .25
1024 A311 20pf green & multi .30 .25
1025 A311 30pf red & multi .65 .25
1026 A311 50pf blue & multi .65 .35
1027 A311 70pf green & multi .80 .65
Nos. 1022-1027 (6) 2.90 2.00

Honoring various voluntary services.
Issued: 20pf, 30pf, 6/18; others, 9/21.

Pres. Gustav Heinemann — A312

1970-73 Engr. *Perf. 14*

1028 A312 5pf dark gray .30 .25
1029 A312 10pf brown .30 .25
1030 A312 20pf green .30 .25
1030A A312 25pf dp yel grn .40 .25
1031 A312 30pf red brown .35 .25
1032 A312 40pf brown org .35 .25
1033 A312 50pf dark blue 1.30 .25
1034 A312 60pf blue .75 .25
1035 A312 70pf dark brown .65 .30
1036 A312 80pf slate grn .65 .30
1037 A312 90pf magenta 1.30 1.00
1038 A312 1m olive 1.00 .30
1038A A312 110pf olive gray 1.00 .65
1039 A312 120pf ocher 1.45 .65
1040 A312 130pf ocher 1.50 .65
1040A A312 140pf dk blue grn 1.50 .80
1041 A312 150pf purple 1.50 .65
1042 A312 160pf orange 2.10 .95
1042A A312 170pf orange 1.75 .65
1043 A312 190pf deep claret 2.25 .65
1044 A312 2m deep violet 2.25 .30
Nos. 1028-1044 (21) 23.15 9.85

Issued: 5pf, 1m, 7/23/70; 10, 20pf, 10/23/70; 30, 90pf, 2m, 1/7/71; 40, 50, 70, 80pf, 4/8/71; 60pf, 6/25/71; 25pf, 8/27/71; 120, 160pf, 3/8/72; 130pf, 6/20/72; 150pf, 7/5/72; 170pf, 9/11/72; 110, 140, 190pf, 1/16/73.

Cross Seen through Glass — A313

1970, Aug. 25 **Litho.**
1045 A313 20pf emerald & yellow .30 .25

Issued to publicize the world mission of Catholic missionaries who bring the Gospel to all peoples.

Cross — A314

1970, Sept. 4 *Perf. 13x13½*
1046 A314 20pf multicolored .30 .25

Issued to publicize the 83rd meeting of German Catholics, Trier, Sept. 9-13.

Town Type of 1969

Designs: No. 1047, View of Cochem and Moselle River. No. 1048, Cathedral and view of Freiburg im Breisgau. No. 1049, View of Oberammergau.

1970 **Litho.** *Perf. 14*
1047 A303 20pf apple grn & blk .40 .30
1048 A303 20pf green & dk brn .40 .30
1049 A303 30pf dp orange & blk .35 .30
Nos. 1047-1049 (3) 1.15 .90

Issued: No. 1047, 9/21; No. 1048, 11/4; No. 1049, 5/11.

Comenius — A315

1970, Nov. 12 *Perf. 13½x14*
1050 A315 30pf dark red & blk .40 .30

John Amos Comenius (1592-1670), theologian and educator.

Friedrich Engels — A316

1970, Nov. 27 **Litho.** *Perf. 14*
1051 A316 50pf red & vio blue 1.20 .65

Engels (1820-95), socialist, collaborator with Marx.

Imperial Eagle, 1872 — A317

1971, Jan. 18 **Litho.** *Perf. 13½x14*
1052 A317 30pf multicolored 1.20 .30

Centenary of the German Empire.

Friedrich Ebert (Germany No. 378) — A318

1971, Jan. 18 *Perf. 13*
1053 A318 30pf red brn, ol & blk 1.20 .30

Ebert (1871-1925), 1st Pres. of the German Republic.

Molecule Diagram Textile Pattern — A319

1971, Feb. 18 **Litho.** *Perf. 13½x13*
1054 A319 20pf brt grn, red & blk .30 .25

Synthetic textile fiber research, 125th anniversary.

School Crossing — A320

Traffic Signs: 20pf, Proceed with caution. 30pf, Stop. 50pf, Pedestrian crossing.

1971, Feb. 18 *Perf. 14*
1055 A320 10pf black, ultra & red .25 .25
1056 A320 20pf black, red & grn .30 .25
1057 A320 30pf black, gray & red .40 .25
1058 A320 50pf black, ultra & red .65 .40
Nos. 1055-1058 (4) 1.60 1.15

New traffic rules, effective Mar. 1, 1971.

Signal to Pass — A321

Traffic Signs: 10pf, Warning signal. 20pf, Drive at right. 30pf, "Observe pedestrian crossings."

1971, Apr. 16 **Photo.** *Perf. 14*
1059 A321 5pf blue, blk & car .30 .25
1060 A321 10pf multicolored .30 .25
1061 A321 20pf brt grn, blk & car .35 .25
1062 A321 30pf car & multi .60 .25
Nos. 1059-1062 (4) 1.55 1.00

New traffic rules, effective Mar. 1, 1971.

Luther Facing Charles V, Woodcut by Rabus — A322

1971, Mar. 18 *Perf. 14*
1063 A322 30pf red & black .55 .30

450th anniversary of the Diet of Worms.

Europa Issue, 1971
Common Design Type

1971, May 3 **Photo.** *Perf. 14*
Size: 28½x23mm
1064 CD14 20pf green, gold & blk .30 .25
1065 CD14 30pf dp car, gold & blk .30 .25

Thomas à Kempis — A323

1971, May 3 **Engr.**
1066 A323 30pf red & black .50 .30

500th anniversary of the death of Thomas à Kempis (1379-1471), Augustinian monk, author of "The Imitation of Christ."

Town Type of 1969

20pf, View of Goslar. No. 1068, View of Nuremberg. No. 1069, Heligoland. 40pf, Heidelberg.

1971-72 **Litho. & Engr.** *Perf. 14*
1067 A303 20pf brt green & blk .40 .35
1068 A303 30pf vermilion & blk .40 .30
1069 A303 30pf lt grn & blk ('72) .40 .25
1069A A303 40pf org & blk ('72) .50 .25
Nos. 1067-1069A (4) 1.70 1.15

Issued: 20pf, 9/15; No. 1068, 5/21; Nos. 1069, 1069A, 10/20.

Dürer's Signature A324

1971, May 21 **Engr.**
1070 A324 30pf copper red & blk 1.05 .30

500th anniversary of the birth of Albrecht Dürer (1471-1528), painter and engraver.

Congress Emblem — A325

1971, May 28 **Litho.** *Perf. 13½x13*
1071 A325 30pf red, orange & blk .40 .30

Ecumenical Meeting at Pentecost of the German Evangelical and Catholic Churches, Augsburg, June 2-5.

Illustration from New Astronomy, by Kepler — A326

1971, June 25 **Photo.** *Perf. 14*
1072 A326 30pf brt car, gold & blk .50 .30

Johannes Kepler (1571-1630), astronomer.

Dante Alighieri — A327

1971, Sept. 3 **Engr.** *Perf. 14*
1073 A327 10pf black .25 .25

650th anniversary of the death of Dante Alighieri (1265-1321), poet.

Accident Prevention — A328

Designs: 5pf, "Matches Cause Fires". 10pf, Broken ladder. 20pf, Hand and circular saw. 25pf, "Alcohol and automobile." 30pf, Safety helmets prevent injury. 40pf, Defective plug. 50pf, Nail sticking from board. 60pf, 70pf, Traffic safety (ball rolling before car). 1m, Hoisted cargo. 1.50m, Fenced-in open manhole.

1971-74 **Typo.** *Perf. 14*
1074 A328 5pf orange .30 .25
a. Bklt. pane, 2 each #1074, 1077-1079 ('74) 5.25 11.00
1075 A328 10pf dark brown .30 .25
a. Bklt. pane, 4 #1075, 2 #1078 2.60 2.60
b. Bklt. pane, 2 each #1075-1076, 1078-1079 ('75) 6.75 11.00
c. Bklt. pane, 2 each #1079, 1075, 1078, 1076 13.50 16.50
1076 A328 20pf purple .35 .25
1077 A328 25pf green .40 .25
1078 A328 30pf dark red .40 .25
1079 A328 40pf rose claret .40 .25
1080 A328 50pf Prus blue 1.60 .25
1081 A328 60pf violet blue 1.00 .40
1082 A328 70pf grn & vio bl 1.00 .30
1083 A328 100pf olive 1.60 .25
1085 A328 150pf red brown 5.00 1.00
Nos. 1074-1085 (11) 12.35 3.70

Accident prevention.

Issued in sheets of 100 and in coils. Every fifth coil stamp has a control number on the back.

Issued: 25pf, 60pf, 9/10; 5pf, 10/29; 10pf, 30pf, 3/8/72; 40pf, 6/20/72; 20pf, 100pf, 7/5/72; 150pf, 9/11/72; 50pf, 1/16/73; 70pf, 6/5/73.

Deaconesses A329

1972, Jan. 20 **Litho.** *Perf. 13x13½*
1087 A329 25pf green, blk & gray .40 .30

Wilhelm Löhe (1808-1872), founder of the Deaconesses Training Institute at Neuendettelsau.

Senefelder's Lithography Press — A330

1972, Apr. 14 **Litho.** *Perf. 13½x13*
1088 A330 25pf multicolored .40 .30

175th anniv. of the invention of the lithographic printing process by Alois Senefelder in 1796.

Europa Issue 1972
Common Design Type

1972, May 2 **Photo.** *Perf. 13½x14*
Size: 23x29mm
1089 CD15 25pf yel grn, dk bl & yel .55 .25
1090 CD15 30pf pale rose, dk & lt bl .55 .25

Lucas Cranach, by Dürer — A331

Lithographed and Engraved
1972, May 18 *Perf. 14*
1091 A331 25pf green, buff & blk .50 .30

Cranach (1472-1553), painter and engraver.

Archer in Wheelchair — A332

1972, July 18 Litho. *Perf. 14*

1092 A332 40pf yel, blk & red brn .55 .30

21st Stoke-Mandeville Games for the Paralyzed, Heidelberg, Aug. 1-10.

Kurt Schumacher A333

1972, Aug. 18 Litho. & Engr.

1093 A333 40pf red & black .95 .30

Schumacher (1895-1952), 1st chairman of the German Social Democratic Party.

Post Horn and Decree — A334

1972, Aug. 18 Photo.

1094 A334 40pf gold, car & blk .65 .30

Centenary of the German Postal Museum, Berlin. Design shows page from Heinrich von Stephan's decree establishing the museum.

Open Book — A335

1972, Sept. 11 Photo. *Perf. 13x13½*

1095 A335 40pf red & multi .55 .30

International Book Year 1972.

Music by Heinrich Schütz — A336

Lithographed and Engraved

1972, Sept. 29 *Perf. 14*

1096 A336 40pf multicolored .55 .30

300th anniversary of the death of Heinrich Schütz (1585-1672), composer.

Carnival Dancers A337

1972, Nov. 10 Litho. *Perf. 14*

1097 A337 40pf red & multi .80 .30

Cologne Carnival sesquicentennial.

Heinrich Heine (1797-1856), Poet — A338

1972, Dec. 13 Litho. *Perf. 14*

1098 A338 40pf rose, blk & red .80 .30

"Bread for the World" A339

1972, Dec. 13 Photo. *Perf. 14*

1099 A339 30pf green & red .40 .40

14th "Bread for the World-Developing Peace" campaign of the Protestant Church in Germany.

Würzburg Cathedral, 13th Century Seal — A340

1972, Dec. 13 Litho.

1100 A340 40pf dp car, lil rose & blk .50 .30

Synod 72, meeting of Catholic bishoprics, Würzburg.

Colors of France and Germany Interlaced — A340a

1973, Jan. 22 Litho. *Perf. 14*

Size: 51x28mm

1101 A340a 40pf multicolored .95 .35

10th anniversary of the Franco-German Cooperation Treaty.

Meteorological Map — A341

1973, Feb. 19 Litho. *Perf. 14*

1102 A341 30pf multicolored .40 .30

Cent. of intl. meteorological cooperation.

Radio Tower and "Interpol" A342

1973, Feb. 19 *Perf. 13½x13*

1103 A342 40pf blk & red .40 .30

50th anniversary of International Criminal Police Organization (INTERPOL).

Nicolaus Copernicus and Solar System — A343

1973, Feb. 19 *Perf. 14*

1104 A343 40pf blk & red .95 .30

Festival Poster — A344

1973, Mar. 15 Photo. *Perf. 14*

1105 A344 40pf multicolored .40 .30

German Turner Festival, Stuttgart, 6/12-17.

Town Type of 1969

Designs: 30pf, Saarbrücken. No. 1107, Ship in Hamburg Harbor. No. 1108, Rüdesheim. No. 1109, Aachen. No. 1110, Ships, Bremen Harbor.

1973 Lithographed and Engraved

1106 A303 30pf yel grn & blk .50 .25
1107 A303 40pf red & blk .65 .25
1108 A303 40pf org & blk .65 .25
1109 A303 40pf brn red & blk .50 .25
1110 A303 40pf red & blk .50 .25
Nos. 1106-1110 (5) 2.80 1.25

Issued: Nos. 1107-1108, 3/15; others 10/19.

Europa Issue 1973

Common Design Type

Size: 38½x21mm

1973, Apr. 30 Photo. *Perf. 13½x14*

1114 CD16 30pf grn, lt grn & yel .35 .25
1115 CD16 40pf dp mag, lil & yel .50 .25

Maximilian Kolbe — A345

1973, May 25 Litho. *Perf. 14*

1116 A345 40pf red, blk & brn .50 .30

Maximilian Kolbe (1894-1941), Polish priest who died in Auschwitz and was beatified in 1971.

"R" for Roswitha — A346

1973, May 25

1117 A346 40pf red, blk & yel .50 .30

Millenary of the death of Roswitha of Gandersheim, Germany's first poetess.

"Not by Bread Alone" — A347

1973, May 25 Photo.

1118 A347 30pf multicolored .35 .30

15th meeting of German Protestants (Evangelical Synod), Dusseldorf, June 27-July 1.

Environment Emblem and "Waste" — A348

30pf, "Water." 40pf, "Noise." 70pf, "Air."

1973, June 5 Litho.

1119 A348 25pf multicolored .35 .25
1120 A348 30pf multicolored .35 .25
1121 A348 40pf org & multi .80 .25
1122 A348 70pf ultra & multi 1.20 .60
Nos. 1119-1122 (4) 2.70 1.35

International environment protection and Environment Day, June 5.

Reconstructed Model of Schickard's Calculator A349

1973, June 12

1123 A349 40pf org & multi .55 .35

350th anniv. of the calculator built by Prof. Wilhelm Shickard, University of Tubingen.

Otto Wels (1873-1939), Leader of German Social Democratic Party — A350

1973, Sept. 14 Litho. *Perf. 14*

1124 A350 40pf magenta & lilac .60 .30

Lubeck Cathedral — A351

1973, Sept. 14 Litho. & Engr.

1125 A351 40pf blk & multi .80 .30

800th anniversary of Lubeck Cathedral.

Emblems from UN and German Flags A352

1973, Sept. 21 Litho.

1126 A352 40pf multicolored 1.00 .30

Germany's admission to the UN.

Radio and Speaker, 1923 — A353

1973, Oct. 19 Photo. *Perf. 14*

1127 A353 30pf brt grn & multi .35 .25

50 years of German broadcasting.

Luise Otto-Peters A354

1974, Jan. 15 Litho. & Engr.

1128	A354 40pf shown	.55	.40
1129	A354 40pf Helene Lange	.55	.40
1130	A354 40pf Gertrud Bäumer	.55	.40
1131	A354 40pf Rosa Luxemburg	.55	.40
	Nos. 1128-1131 (4)	2.20	1.60

Honoring German women writers and leaders in political and women's movements.

Drop of Blood and Police Car Light A355

1974, Feb. 15 Photo. *Perf. 14*

1132 A355 40pf carmine & ultra .65 .30

Blood donor service in conjunction with accident emergency service.

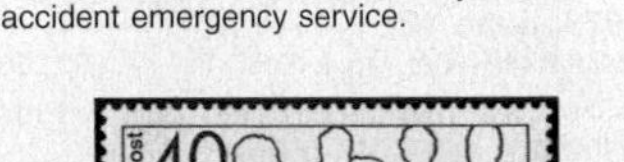

Handicapped People — A356

1974, Feb. 15 Litho. *Perf. 14*

1133 A356 40pf red & blk .65 .30

Rehabilitation of the handicapped.

Thomas Aquinas Teaching A357

1974, Feb. 15

1134 A357 40pf blk & red .50 .30

St. Thomas Aquinas (1225-1274), scholastic philosopher.

Girls under Trees, by August Macke — A358

Paintings: No. 1135, Deer in Red, by Franz Marc. 40pf, Portrait in Blue, by Alexej von Jawlensky, vert. 50pf, Pechstein (man) Asleep, by Erich Heckel, vert. 70pf, "Big Still-life," by Max Beckmann. 120pf, Old Farmer, by Ernst Ludwig Kirchner, vert.

1974 Photo.

1135	A358 30pf multicolored	.40	.25
1136	A358 30pf multicolored	.65	.25
1137	A358 40pf multicolored	.50	.25
1138	A358 50pf multicolored	.65	.30
1139	A358 70pf multicolored	.80	.65
1140	A358 120pf multicolored	1.60	1.30
	Nos. 1135-1140 (6)	4.60	3.00

German expressionist painters.

Issued: Nos. 1135, 1137, Feb. 15; Nos. 1136, 1138, Aug. 16; Nos. 1139-1140, Oct. 29.

Young Man, by Lehmbruck — A359

Europa: 40pf, Kneeling Woman, by Wilhelm Lehmbruck.

1974, Apr. 17 Litho. *Perf. 14*

1141	A359 30pf multicolored	.50	.25
1142	A359 40pf multicolored	.50	.25

Immanuel Kant — A360

1974 Litho. and Engr. *Perf. 14*

1143 A360 40pf Klopstock .50 .30

Engr.

1144 A360 90pf shown 1.60 .40

Friedrich Gottlieb Klopstock (1724-1803), poet, and Immanuel Kant (1724-1804), philosopher.

Issue dates: 40pf, May 15; 90pf, Apr. 17.

Souvenir Sheet

Federal Eagle and Flag — A361

1974, May 15 Litho. & Embossed

1145 A361 40pf gray & multi 1.15 1.60

Federal Republic of Germany, 25th anniv.

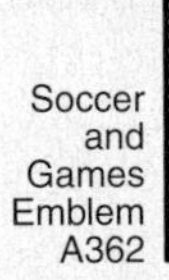

Soccer and Games Emblem A362

Design: 40pf, Three soccer players.

1974, May 15 Litho.

1146	A362 30pf grn & multi	.80	.25
1147	A362 40pf org & multi	1.60	.25

World Cup Soccer Championship, Munich, June 13-July 7.

Crowned Cross Emblem of Diaconate — A363

1974, May 15

1148 A363 40pf multicolored .50 .30

125th anniversary of the Diaconal Association of the German Protestant Church.

Landscape — A364

1974, May 15

1149 A364 30pf multicolored .35 .30

To promote hiking and youth hostels.

Broken Bars of Prison Window — A365

1974, July 16 Litho. *Perf. 14x13½*

1150 A365 70pf violet bl & blk .85 .40

"Amnesty International," an organization for the protection of the rights of political, non-violent, prisoners.

Hans Holbein, Self-portrait A366

Lithographed and Engraved

1974, July 16 *Perf. 13½x14*

1151 A366 50pf multicolored .65 .30

Hans Holbein the Elder (c. 1470-1524), painter.

Man and Woman Looking at Moon, by Friedrich — A367

1974, Aug. 16 Photo. *Perf. 14*

1152 A367 50pf multicolored .85 .30

Caspar David Friedrich (1774-1840), German Romantic painter.

Swiss and German 19th Century Mail Boxes — A368

1974, Oct. 29 Litho. *Perf. 14*

1153 A368 50pf red & multi .95 .35

Centenary of Universal Postal Union.

Mothers and Foundation Emblem — A369

1975, Jan. 15 Litho. *Perf. 13*

1154 A369 50pf multicolored .65 .30

Convalescent Mothers' Foundation, 25th anniversary.

Annette Kolb (1875-1967), Writer — A370

German women writers: 40pf, Ricarda Huch (1864-1947), writer. 50pf, Else Lasker-Schüler (1869-1945), poetess. 70pf, Gertrud von Le Fort (1876-1971), writer.

Lithographed and Engraved

1975, Jan. 15 *Perf. 14*

1155	A370 30pf brown & multi	.55	.30
1156	A370 40pf multicolored	.50	.30
1157	A370 50pf claret & multi	.50	.30
1158	A370 70pf blue & multi	.80	.80
	Nos. 1155-1158 (4)	2.35	1.70

Dr. Albert Schweitzer — A371

Design: 40pf, Hans Böckler.

1975 Engr.

1159	A371 40pf grn & blk	.65	.30
1160	A371 70pf bl & blk	1.50	.65

Böckler (1875-1951), German Workers' Union leader, and of Dr. Albert Schweitzer (1875-1965), medical missionary. Issued: 40pf, Feb. 14; 70pf, Jan. 15.

Head, by Michelangelo A372

1975, Feb. 14 Photo. *Perf. 14*

1161 A372 70pf vio bl & blk 1.30 1.20

Michelangelo Buonarroti (1475-1564), Italian sculptor, painter and architect.

Plan of St. Peter's, Rome — A373

1975, Feb. 14

1162 A373 50pf red & multi .65 .30

Holy Year 1975, the "Year of Reconciliation."

Ice Hockey A374

1975, Feb. 14 Litho. *Perf. 14*

1163 A374 50pf bl & multi .85 .30

Ice Hockey World Championship, Munich and Düsseldorf, Apr. 3-19.

Concentric Group, by Oskar Schlemmer — A375

Europa: 50pf, Bauhaus Staircase, painting by Oskar Schlemmer (1888-1943) and CEPT emblem.

1975, Apr. 15 Litho. & Engr.

1164 A375 40pf gray & multi *.40* .25
1165 A375 50pf gray & multi *.60* .25

Eduard Mörike, Weather Vane, Quill and Signature A376

1975, May 15

1166 A376 40pf multicolored .35 .30

Eduard Mörike (1804-75), pastor and poet.

Joust, from Jousting Book of William IV A377

1975, May 15 Photo. *Perf. 14*

1167 A377 50pf multicolored .80 .30

500th anniv. of the Wedding of Landshut, (last Duke of Landshut married the daughter of King of Poland, now a yearly local festival).

Cathedral of Mainz A378

1975, May 15 Litho. & Engr.

1168 A378 40pf multicolored .80 .30

Millennium of the Cathedral of Mainz.

View of Neuss, Woodcut — A379

1975, May 15

1169 A379 50pf multicolored .55 .30

500th anniv. of the unsuccessful siege of Neuss by Duke Charles the Bold of Burgundy.

Satellite — A380

10pf, Electric train. 20pf, Old Weser lighthouse. 30pf, Rescue helicopter. 40pf, Space shuttle. 50pf, Radar station. 60pf, X-ray machine. 70pf, Shipbuilding. 80pf, Tractor. 100pf, Bituminous coal excavator. 110pf, Color TV camera. 120pf, Chemical plant. 130pf, Brewery. 140pf, Heating plant, Licterfelde. 150pf, 190pf, Power shovel. 160pf, Blast furnace. 180pf, Payloader. 200pf, Oil drilling. 230pf, Frankfurt Airport. 250pf, Airport. 300pf, Electro. RR. 500pf, Effelsberg radio telescope.

1975-82 Engr. *Perf. 14*

1170	A380	5pf	olive grn	.25	.25
1171	A380	10pf	red lilac	.25	.25
1172	A380	20pf	red org	.25	.25
1173	A380	30pf	dp vio	.25	.25
1174	A380	40pf	pck blue	.30	.25
1175	A380	50pf	rose	.35	.25
1176	A380	60pf	red	.65	.25
1177	A380	70pf	blue	.55	.25
1178	A380	80pf	blue grn	.55	.25
1179	A380	100pf	brown	.55	.25
1180	A380	110pf	dp clar	1.30	.55
1181	A380	120pf	blue vio	.65	.30
1182	A380	130pf	carmine	1.60	.55
1183	A380	140pf	red	.80	.35
1184	A380	150pf	red brown	2.00	.65
1185	A380	160pf	dull green	1.05	.55
1186	A380	180pf	brown	2.00	.65
1187	A380	190pf	org brn	2.00	.55
1188	A380	200pf	dp clar	1.30	.30
1189	A380	230pf	lilac	2.60	.80
1190	A380	250pf	green	3.00	1.25
1191	A380	300pf	bister	3.75	1.25
1192	A380	500pf	dark blue	3.75	1.00
	Nos. 1170-1192 (23)			29.75	11.25

Issued: 40, 50, 100pf, 5/15; 10, 30, 70pf, 8/14; 80, 120, 160pf, 10/15; 5, 140, 200pf, 11/14; 20, 500pf, 2/17/76; 60pf, 11/16/78; 230pf, 5/17/79; 150, 180pf, 7/12/79; 110, 130, 300pf, 6/16/82; 190, 250pf, 7/15/82.

Market and Town Hall, Alsfeld A381

No. 1197, Plönlein Corner, Siebers Tower and Kobolzeller Gate, Rothenburg. No. 1198, Town Hall (Steipe), Trier. No. 1199, View of Xanten.

1975, July 15 Litho. & Engr.

1196	A381	50pf	multicolored	.65	.50
1197	A381	50pf	multicolored	.65	.50
1198	A381	50pf	multicolored	.65	.50
1199	A381	50pf	multicolored	.65	.50
	Nos. 1196-1199 (4)			2.60	2.00

European Architectural Heritage Year.

Three Stages of Drug Addiction A382

1975, Aug. 14 Photo. *Perf. 14*

1200 A382 40pf multicolored .35 .30

Fight against drug abuse.

Matthias Erzberger A383

1975, Aug. 14 Engr.

1201 A383 50pf red & black .55 .30

Erzberger (1875-1921), statesman, signer of Compiègne Armistice (1918) at end of World War I.

Sign of Royal Prussian Post, 1776 — A384

1975, Aug. 14 Litho.

1202 A384 10pf blue & multi .35 .25

Stamp Day, 1975, and 76th German Philatelists' Day, Sept. 21.

Souvenir Sheet

Gustav Stresemann, Ludwig Quidde, Carl von Ossietzky — A385

1975, Nov. 14 Engr. *Perf. 14*

1203 A385 Sheet of 3 2.00 1.60
a.-c. 50pf, single stamp .60 .50

German winners of Nobel Peace Prize. No. 1203 has litho. marginal inscription.

Olympic Rings, Symbolic Mountains A386

1976, Jan. 5 Litho. & Engr.

1204 A386 50pf red & multi 1.30 .65

12th Winter Olympic Games, Innsbruck, Austria, Feb. 4-15.

Konrad Adenauer — A387

1976, Jan. 5 Engr.

1205 A387 50pf dark slate green 1.75 .30

Konrad Adenauer (1876-1967), Chancellor (1949-63).

Books by Hans Sachs — A388

1976, Jan. 5 Litho.

1206 A388 40pf multicolored .55 .30

Hans Sachs (1494-1576), poet (meistersinger), 400th death anniversary.

Junkers F 13, 1926 — A389

1976, Jan. 5

1207 A389 50pf multicolored .80 .30

Lufthansa, 50th anniversary.

German Eagle — A390

1976, Feb. 17 Photo. *Perf. 14*

1208 A390 50pf red, blk & gold .65 .30

Federal Constitutional Court, 25th anniv.

"EG" A391

1976, Apr. 6 Photo. *Perf. 14*

1209 A391 40pf red & multi .65 .30

European Coal and Steel Community, 25th anniversary.

Wuppertal Suspension Train — A392

1976, Apr. 6 Litho.

1210 A392 50pf multicolored .65 2.60

Wuppertal suspension railroad, 75th anniv.

Girl Selling Trinkets and Prints — A393

Europa: 50pf, Boy selling copperplate prints, and CEPT emblem. Ludwigsburg china figurines, c. 1765.

1976, May 13 Photo.

1211 A393 40pf olive & multi *.50* .25
1212 A393 50pf scarlet & multi *.50* .25

Dr. Carl Sonnenschein A394

1976, May 13 Litho.

1213 A394 50pf carmine & multi .55 .30

Sonnenschein (1876-1929), Roman Catholic clergyman and social reformer.

Weber Conducting "Freischutz" in Covent Garden — A395

1976, May 13

1214 A395 50pf red brown & blk .65 .30

Carl Maria von Weber (1786-1826), composer, 150th death anniversary.

Hymn, by Paul Gerhardt A396

1976, May 13 **Engr. & Litho.**

1215 A396 40pf multicolored .40 .30

Gerhardt (1607-76), Lutheran hymn writer.

Carl Schurz, American Flag, Capitol A397

1976, May 13 **Litho.**

1216 A397 70pf multicolored .85 .35

American Bicentennial.

Modern Stage A398

1976, July 14 **Litho.** ***Perf. 14***

1217 A398 50pf multicolored 1.05 .30

Bayreuth Festival, centenary.

Bronze Ritual Chariot c. 1000 B.C. A399

Archaeological Treasures: 40pf, Celtic gold vessel, 5th-4th centuries B.C. 50pf, Celtic silver torque, 2nd-1st centuries B.C. 120pf, Roman cup with masks, 1st century A.D.

1976, July 14

1218	A399	30pf multicolored	.35	.30
1219	A399	40pf multicolored	.50	.30
1220	A399	50pf multicolored	.65	.40
1221	A399	120pf multicolored	1.45	1.45
		Nos. 1218-1221 (4)	2.95	2.45

Golden Plover — A400

1976, Aug. 17

1222 A400 50pf multicolored .95 .30

Protection of birds.

"Simplicissimus Teutsch" — A401

1976, Aug. 17

1223 A401 40pf multicolored .95 .30

Johann Jacob Christoph von Grimmelshausen, 300th birth anniversary; author of the "Adventures of Simplicissimus Teutsch."

Imperial Post Emblem, Höchst am Main, 18th Cent. — A402

1976, Oct. 14 **Litho.** ***Perf. 14***

1224 A402 10pf brown & multi .30 .25

Stamp Day.

Caroline Neuber as Medea — A403

German Actresses: 40pf, Sophie Schröder (1781-1868) as Sappho. 50pf, Louise Dumont (1862-1932) as Hedda Gabler. 70pf, Hermine Körner (1878-1960) as Lady Macbeth.

1976, Nov. 16 **Photo.**

1225	A403	30pf multicolored	.55	.25
1226	A403	40pf multicolored	.55	.25
1227	A403	50pf multicolored	.55	.30
1228	A403	70pf multicolored	1.05	.80
		Nos. 1225-1228 (4)	2.70	1.60

Palais de l'Europe, Strasbourg — A404

1977, Jan. 13 **Engr.** ***Perf. 14***

1229 A404 140pf green & blk 1.45 .50

Inauguration of the new Council of Europe Headquarters, Jan. 28.

Scenes from Till Eulenspiegel A405

1977, Jan. 13 **Litho.**

1230 A405 50pf multicolored .50 .30

Till Eulenspiegel (d. 1350), roguish fool and hero, his adventures reported in book of same name.

Pfaueninsel Castle — A406

10pf, Glucksburg. 25pf, Gemen. 30pf, Ludwigstein. 40pf, Eltz. 50pf, Neuschwanstein. 60pf, Marksburg. 70pf, Mespelbrunn. 90pf, Vischerenburg. 190pf, Pfaueninsel. 200pf, Burresheim. 210pf, Schwanenburg. 230pf, Lichtenberg.

1977-79 **Typo.** ***Perf. 14***

1231	A406	10pf dark blue	.25	.25
a.		Bklt. pane, 4 #1231, 2 each #1234, 1236	4.25	6.75
b.		Bklt. pane, 4 #1231, 2 #1234, 2 #1310	2.60	3.75
c.		Bklt. pane, 4 #1231, 2 #1310, 2 #1312	6.00	6.50
d.		Bklt. pane, 2 each #1231, 1234, 1310-1311	9.50	13.50
1232	A406	20pf orange	.25	.25
1233	A406	25pf red	.35	.25
1234	A406	30pf olive brown	.30	.25
1235	A406	40pf blue green	.40	.25
1236	A406	50pf carmine	.50	.25
1237	A406	60pf brown	.65	.25
1238	A406	70pf blue	.65	.25
1239	A406	90pf blue lilac	1.00	.35
1240	A406	190pf org brown	1.60	.65
1240A	A406	200pf green	2.00	.65
1241	A406	210pf red brown	2.60	1.00
1242	A406	230pf green	2.60	1.00
		Nos. 1231-1242 (13)	13.15	5.65

See Nos. 1308-1315.

Issued in sheets of 100 and in coils. Every fifth coil stamp has control number on the back.

Issued: 60, 200pf, 1/13; 40, 190pf, 2/16; 10, 30pf, 4/14; 50, 70pf, 5/17; 230pf, 11/16/78; 25, 90pf, 1/11/79; 20, 210pf, 2/14/79.

Souvenir Sheet

German Art Nouveau — A407

Designs: 30pf, Floral ornament. 70pf, Athena, poster by Franz von Stuck. 90pf, Chair, c. 1902.

1977, Feb. 16 **Litho.** ***Perf. 14***

1243	A407	Sheet of 3	2.10	1.30
a.		30pf multicolored	.65	.25
b.		70pf multicolored	.65	.40
c.		90pf multicolored	.75	.65

1st German Art Nouveau Exhib., 75th anniv.

Jean Monnet A408

1977, Feb. 16

1244 A408 50pf black & yellow .55 .30

Jean Monnet (1888-1979), French proponent of unification of Europe, became first Honorary Citizen of Europe in Apr. 1976.

Flower Show Emblem — A409

1977, Apr. 14

1245 A409 50pf green & multi .65 .30

25th Federal Horticultural Show, Stuttgart, Apr. 29-Oct. 23.

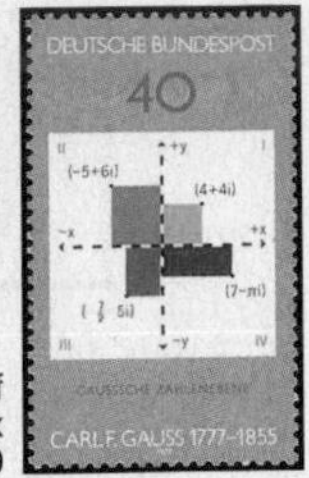

Gauss Plane of Complex Numbers — A410

1977, Apr. 14

1246 A410 40pf silver & multi 1.05 .30

Carl Friedrich Gauss (1777-1855), mathematician, 200th birth anniversary.

Barbarossa Head, Cappenberg Reliquary — A411

1977, Apr. 14

1247 A411 40pf multicolored 1.00 .30

Staufer Year 1977. "Time of the Hohenstaufen" Exhibition, Stuttgart, Mar. 25-June 5, in connection with the 25th anniversary of Baden-Wurttemberg.

Rhön Highway A412

Europa: 50pf, Rhine, Siebengebirge and train.

1977, May 7 **Litho. & Engr.**

1248	A412	40pf brt green & blk	*.55*	*.25*
1249	A412	50pf brt red & blk	*.55*	*.25*

Rubens, Self-portrait — A413

1977, May 17 **Engr.**

1250 A413 30pf brown black .65 .30

Peter Paul Rubens (1577-1640), Flemish painter, 400th birth anniversary.

Ulm Cathedral — A414

1977, May 17 **Litho. & Engr.**

1251 A414 40pf blue & sepia .55 .30

600th anniversary of Ulm Cathedral.

Madonna, Oldest Rector's Seal
A415

Landgrave Philipp, Great Seal of University
A416

1977, May 17 **Photo.**

1252 A415 50pf indigo & org red .65 .30
1253 A416 50pf indigo & org red .65 .30

Mainz University, 500th anniv. (No. 1252); Marburg University, 450th anniv. (No. 1253).

Morning, by Runge — A417

1977, July 13 **Litho.** ***Perf. 14***

1254 A417 60pf blue & multi 1.00 .35

Philipp Otto Runge (1777-1810), painter.

Bishop Ketteler's Coat of Arms — A418

1977, July 13

1255 A418 50pf multicolored .55 .30

Wilhelm Emmanuel von Ketteler (1811-1877), Bishop of Mainz, Reichstag member and social reformer, death centenary.

Fritz von Bodelschwingh
A419

1977, July 13 **Litho. & Engr.**

1256 A419 50pf multicolored .65 .30

Pastor Fritz von Bodelschwingh (1877-1946), manager of Bethel Institute (for the incurable sick), birth centenary.

Jesus as Teacher, Great Seal of University — A420

1977, Aug. 16 **Photo.**

1257 A420 50pf multicolored .80 .30

Tübingen University, 500th anniversary.

Golden Hat, Schifferstadt, Bronze Age — A421

Archaeological heritage: 120pf, Gilt helmet, from Prince's Tomb, Krefeld-Gellep. 200pf, Bronze Centaur's head, Schwarzenacker.

1977, Aug. 16 **Litho.**

1258 A421 30pf multicolored .35 .30
1259 A421 120pf multicolored 1.30 1.00
1260 A421 200pf multicolored 1.75 1.45
Nos. 1258-1260 (3) 3.40 2.75

Telephone Operator and Switchboard, 1881 — A422

1977, Oct. 13 **Litho.** ***Perf. 14***

1261 A422 50pf multicolored .95 .30

German telephone centenary.

Arms of Hamburg, Post Emblem, c. 1861 — A423

1977, Oct. 13

1262 A423 10pf multicolored .35 .30

Stamp Day.

Wilhelm Hauff — A424

1977, Nov. 10 **Photo.** ***Perf. 14***

1263 A424 40pf multicolored .40 .30

Wilhelm Hauff (1802-1827), writer and fabulist, 150th death anniversary.

Traveling Surgeon — A425

1977, Nov. 10 **Litho.**

1264 A425 50pf multicolored .65 .30

Dr. Johann Andreas Eisenbarth (1663-1727), traveling surgeon and adventurer.

Book Cover, by Alexander Schröder — A426

1978, Jan. 12 **Litho.** ***Perf. 14***

1265 A426 50pf multicolored .55 .30

Rudolf Alexander Schröder (1878-1962), writer, designer, Lutheran minister.

"Refugees" — A427

1978, Jan. 12 **Photo.**

1266 A427 50pf multicolored .55 .30

Friedland Aid Society for displaced Germans, 20th anniversary.

Souvenir Sheet

Gerhart Hauptmann, Hermann Hesse, Thomas Mann — A428

1978, Feb. 16 **Litho.** ***Perf. 14***

1267 A428 Sheet of 3 2.10 1.20
a. 30pf multicolored .60 .30
b. 50pf multicolored .60 .30
c. 70pf multicolored .65 .50

German winners of Nobel Literature Prize.

Martin Buber (1878-1965), Writer and Philosopher
A429

1978, Feb. 16

1268 A429 50pf multicolored .60 .30

Museum Tower and Observatory — A430

1978, Apr. 13 **Litho.** ***Perf. 14***

1269 A430 50pf multicolored .60 .30

German Museum for Natural Sciences and Technology, Munich, 75th anniversary.

Old City Halls
A431

Europa: 40pf, Bamberg. 50pf, Regensburg. 70pf, Esslingen on Neckar.

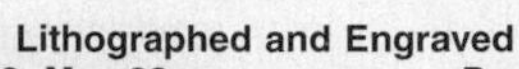

Lithographed and Engraved

1978, May 22 ***Perf. 14***

1270 A431 40pf multicolored *.55* .30
1271 A431 50pf multicolored *.80* .30
1272 A431 70pf multicolored *1.00* *.55*
Nos. 1270-1272 (3) 2.35 1.15

Pied Piper of Hamelin
A432

1978, May 22 **Litho.**

1273 A432 50pf multicolored .65 .30

The Pied Piper led 130 children of Hamelin away never to be seen again.

Janusz Korczak — A433

1978, July 13 **Litho.** ***Perf. 14***

1274 A433 90pf multicolored .95 .50

Dr. Janusz Korczak (1878-1942), physician, educator, proponent of children's rights.

Fossil Bat — A434

200pf, Eohippus (primitive horse), horiz.

1978, July 13

1275 A434 80pf multicolored 1.45 1.20
1276 A434 200pf multicolored 1.45 1.30

Archaeological heritage from Messel opencast mine, c. 50 million years old.

Parliament, Bonn — A435

1978, Aug. 17 **Litho.** ***Perf. 14***

1277 A435 70pf multicolored .95 .35

65th Interparliamentary Conf., Bonn, Sept. 3-14.

A436

Rose Window, Freiburg Cathedral.

1978, Aug. 17

1278 A436 40pf multicolored .40 .30

85th Congress of German Catholics, Freiburg, Sept. 13-17.

A437

Brentano as Butterfly, by Luise Duttenhofer.

1978, Aug. 17
1279 A437 30pf multicolored .40 .30

Clemens Brentano (1778-1842), poet.

A438

1978, Aug. 17
1280 A438 50pf multicolored .65 .30

European Human Rights Convention, 25th anniversary.

Baden Posthouse Sign, c. 1825 — A439

Saxony No. 1 with "World Philatelic Movement" Cancel — A440

1978, Oct. 12 **Litho.** ***Perf. 14***
1281 A439 40pf multicolored .40 .25
1282 A440 50pf multicolored .40 .25
a. Pair, #1281-1282 1.00 1.05

Stamp Day and German Philatelists' Meeting, Frankfurt am Main, Oct. 12-15.

Easter at Walchensee, by Lovis Corinth — A441

Impressionist Paintings: 70pf, Horseman on Shore, by Max Liebermann, vert. 120pf, Lady with Cat, by Max Slevogt, vert.

1978, Nov. 16 **Photo.** ***Perf. 14***
1283 A441 50pf multicolored .65 .40
1284 A441 70pf multicolored 1.00 .55
1285 A441 120pf multicolored 1.30 1.20
Nos. 1283-1285 (3) 2.95 2.15

Child and Building A442

1979, Jan. 11 **Photo.**
1286 A442 60pf black & rose .80 .30

International Year of the Child and 20th anniv. of Declaration of Children's Rights.

Agnes Miegel — A443

1979, Feb. 14 **Photo.** ***Perf. 14***
1287 A443 60pf multicolored .55 .30

Agnes Miegel (1879-1964), poet.

Film — A444

1979, Feb. 14 **Litho.**
1288 A444 50pf black & green .65 .30

25th German Short-Film Festival, Oberhausen, Apr. 23-28.

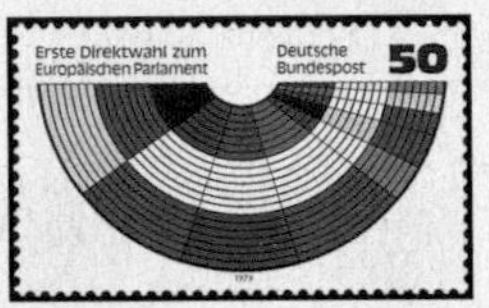

Parliament Benches in Flag Colors of Members — A445

1979, Feb. 14
1289 A445 50pf multicolored .80 .30

European Parliament, first direct elections, June 7-10, 1979.

Emblems of Road Rescue Services A446

1979, Feb. 14
1290 A446 50pf multicolored .65 .30

A447

Europa: 50pf, Telegraph office, 1863. 60pf, Post Office window, 1854.

1979, May 17 **Litho.** ***Perf. 14***
1291 A447 50pf multicolored *.55* .25
1292 A447 60pf multicolored *.65* .25

A448

1979, May 17 **Photo.**
1293 A448 60pf red & black .80 .30

Anne Frank (1929-45), author, Nazi victim.

First Electric Train, 1879 Berlin Exhibition A449

1979, May 17 **Litho.**
1294 A449 60pf multicolored .80 .30

Intl. Transportation Exhib., Hamburg.

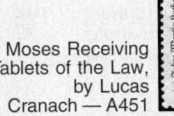

Hand Setting Radio Dial A450

1979, July 12 **Litho.** ***Perf. 14***
1295 A450 60pf multicolored .80 .30

World Administrative Radio Conference, Geneva, Sept. 24-Dec. 1.

Moses Receiving Tablets of the Law, by Lucas Cranach — A451

1979, July 12 **Litho. & Engr.**
1296 A451 50pf black & blue grn .80 .30

450th anniv. of Martin Luther's Catechism.

Cross and Charlemagne's Emblem — A452

1979, July 12 **Litho. & Embossed**
1297 A452 50pf multicolored .55 .30

1979 pilgrimage to Aachen.

Hildegard von Bingen with Manuscript A453

1979, Aug. 9 **Litho.**
1298 A453 110pf multicolored .95 .50

Hildegard von Bingen, Benedictine nun, mystic and writer, 800th death anniversary.

Diagram of Einstein's Photoelectric Effect — A454

Designs: No. 1300, Otto Hahn's diagram of the splitting of the uranium nucleus. No. 1301, Max von Laue's atom arrangement in crystals.

1979, Aug. 9 **Photo.**
1299 A454 60pf multicolored .65 .35
1300 A454 60pf multicolored 1.30 .35
1301 A454 60pf multicolored .65 .35
Nos. 1299-1301 (3) 2.60 1.05

Birth centenaries of German Nobel Prize winners: Albert Einstein, physics, 1921; Otto Hahn, chemistry, 1944; Max von Laue, physics, 1914.

Pilot on Board — A455

Lithographed and Engraved

1979, Oct. 11 ***Perf. 14***
1302 A455 60pf multicolored .55 .30

Three centuries of pilots' regulations.

Birds in Garden, by Paul Klee — A456

1979, Nov. 14 **Photo.**
1303 A456 90pf multicolored .85 .50

Paul Klee (1879-1940), Swiss artist.

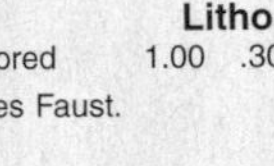

Mephistopheles and Faust — A457

1979, Nov. 14 **Litho.**
1304 A457 60pf multicolored 1.00 .30

Doctor Johannes Faust.

Energy Conservation A458

1979, Nov. 14 ***Perf. 13x13½***
1305 A458 40pf multicolored .55 .30

Castle Type A406 of 1977-79

1979-82 **Typo.** ***Perf. 14***

1308	35pf	Lichtenstein	.50	.35
1309	40pf	Wolfsburg	.55	.25
1310	50pf	Inzlingen	.60	.25
1311	60pf	Rheydt	.60	.30
1312	80pf	Wilhelmsthal	.85	.30
1313	120pf	Charlottenburg	1.30	.50
1314	280pf	Ahrensburg	2.75	.80
1315	300pf	Herrenhausen	3.25	.65
		Nos. 1308-1315 (8)	10.40	3.40

Issued: 60pf, 11/14; 40pf, 50pf, 2/14/80; 35pf, 80pf, 300pf, 6/16/82; 120pf, 280pf, 7/15/82.

Iphigenia, by Anselm Feuerbach — A459

1980, Jan. 10 **Litho.**
1321 A459 50pf multicolored .95 .30

Anselm Feuerbach (1829-1880), historical and portrait painter.

Flags of NATO and Members A460

1980, Jan. 10
1322 A460 100pf multicolored 1.30 .65

Germany's membership in NATO, 25th anniv.

Osnabruck, 1,200th Anniversary — A461

1980, Jan. 10 **Litho. & Engr.**
1323 A461 60pf multicolored .65 .30

Götz von Berlichingen, Painting on Glass — A462

1980, Jan. 10 **Litho.**
1324 A462 60pf multicolored .65 .30

Götz von Berlichingen (1480-1562), knight.

Duden Dictionary, Old and New Editions — A463

1980, Jan. 14
1325 A463 60pf multicolored .65 .30

Konrad Duden's German Language Dictionary, centenary of publication.

German Association for Public and Private Social Welfare Centenary — A464

1980, Apr. 10
1326 A464 60pf multicolored .65 .30

A465

Emperor Frederick I (Barbarossa) and Sons, Welf Chronicles, 12th century.

1980, Apr. 10
1327 A465 60pf multicolored .85 .30

Imperial Diet of Geinhausen, 800th anniv.

A466

Europa: 50pf, Albertus Magnus (1193-1280), saint and doctor of the Church. 60pf, Gottfried Wilhelm Leibniz (1646-1716), philosopher.

1980, May 8 **Litho.** ***Perf. 14***
1328 A466 50pf multicolored *.75 .25*
1329 A466 60pf multicolored *.75 .25*

Confession of Augsburg, Engraving, 1630 — A467

1980, May 8
1330 A467 50pf multicolored .60 .30

Reading of Confession of Augsburg to Charles V (first official creed of Lutheran Church), 450th anniversary.

Nature Preserves A468

1980, May 8 **Photo.**
1331 A468 40pf multicolored .85 .30

Oscillogram Pulses and Ear — A469

Lithographed and Embossed

1980, July 10 ***Perf. 14***
1332 A469 90pf multicolored 1.00 .35

16th Intl. Cong. for the Training and Education of the Hard of Hearing, Hamburg, 8/4-8.

A470

Design: Book of Daily Bible Readings, Title Page, 1731.

1980, July 10 **Litho.**
1333 A470 50pf multicolored .60 .30

Moravian Brethren's Book of Daily Bible Readings, 250th edition.

St. Benedict of Nursia, 1500th Birth Anniv. — A471

1980, July 10 ***Perf. 13x13½***
1334 A471 50pf multicolored .55 .30

Helping Hand — A472

1980, Aug. 14 **Litho. & Engr.**
1335 A472 60pf multicolored .65 .30

Dr. Friedrich Joseph Haass (1780-1853), physician and philanthropist.

Marie von Ebner-Eschenbach (1830-1916), Writer — A473

1980, Aug. 14 **Photo.**
1336 A473 60pf multicolored .65 .30

Ship's Rigging A474

1980, Aug. 14 **Litho.**
1337 A474 60pf multicolored 1.30 .30

Gorch Fock (pen name of Johan Kinau) (1880-1916), poet and dramatist.

A475

Design: Hoeing, Pressing Grapes, Wine Cellar, 14th Century Woodcuts.

1980, Oct. 9 **Litho.** ***Perf. 14***
1338 A475 50pf multicolored .65 .30

Wine production in Central Europe, 2000th anniversary.

Setting Final Stone in South Tower, Cologne Cathedral — A476

1980, Oct. 9
1339 A476 60pf multicolored 1.30 .30

Completion of Cologne Cathedral, cent.

Landscape with Fir Trees, by Altdorfer — A477

Lithographed and Engraved

1980, Nov. 13 ***Perf. 14***
1340 A477 40pf multicolored .55 .30

Albrecht Altdorfer (1480-1538), painter and engraver.

Elly Heuss-Knapp A478

1981, Jan. 15 **Photo.**
1341 A478 60pf multicolored .65 .30

Elly Heuss-Knapp (1881-1951), founded Elly Heuss-Knapp Foundation (Rest and Recuperation for Mothers).

International Year of the Disabled — A479

1981, Jan. 15 **Litho.**
1342 A479 60pf multicolored .65 .30

European Urban Renaissance — A480

1981, Jan. 15 **Litho. & Engr.**
1343 A480 60pf multicolored .75 .30

Georg Philipp Telemann, Title Page of "Singet dem Herrn" Cantata — A481

1981, Feb. 12 **Photo.**
1344 A481 60pf multicolored .65 .30

Georg Telemann (1681-1767), composer.

Foreign Guest Worker Integration — A482

1981, Feb. 12 **Litho.**
1345 A482 50pf multicolored .65 .30

Preservation of the Environment A483

1981, Feb. 12
1346 A483 60pf multicolored 1.05 .30

European Patent Office Centenary A484

1981, Feb. 12
1347 A484 60pf multicolored .65 .30

Chest Scintigram — A485

1981, Feb. 12 ***Perf. 13x13½***
1348 A485 40pf multi .55 .30

Early examination for the prevention of cancer.

A486

50pf, South German couple dancing in regional costumes. 60pf, Northern couple.

1981, May 7 **Litho.** ***Perf. 14***
1349 A486 50pf multicolored *.55* .25
1350 A486 60pf multicolored *.65* .25

Europa.

19th German Protestant Convention, Hamburg, June 17-21 — A487

1981, May 7 **Photo.**
1351 A487 50pf multicolored .65 .30

A488

1981, May 7 **Litho.**
1352 A488 60pf Altar figures .65 .30

Tilman Riemenschneider (1460-1531), sculptor, 450th death anniversary.

A489

1981, July 16 **Litho.** ***Perf. 14***
1353 A489 110pf multicolored 1.45 .40

Georg von Neumayer polar research station.

Energy Conservation Research — A490

1981, July 16
1354 A490 50pf Solar generator .85 .30

Wildlife Protection A491

1981, July 16
1355 A491 60pf Baby coot .95 .30

Cooperation in Third World Development — A492

1981, July 16
1356 A492 90pf multicolored 1.05 .40

Wilhelm Raabe (1831-1910), Poet — A493

1981, Aug. 13 **Litho. & Engr.**
1357 A493 50pf dk green & green .65 .30

Statement of Constitutional Freedom (Fundamental Concept of Democracy) — A494

50pf, Separation of powers. 60pf, Sovereignty of the people.

1981, Aug. 13 **Litho.** ***Perf. 14***
1358 A494 40pf shown .75 .25
1359 A494 50pf multicolored .75 .25
1360 A494 60pf multicolored .95 .25
Nos. 1358-1360 (3) 2.45 .75

A495

People by Mailcoach, lithograph, 1855.

1981, Oct. 8 **Litho.**
1361 A495 60pf multicolored .95 .30

Stamp Day, Oct. 25.

Antarctic Treaty, 20th Anniv. — A496

1981, Nov. 12 **Litho.** ***Perf. 14***
1362 A496 100pf multicolored 1.20 .40

St. Elizabeth of Thuringia, 750th Anniv. of Death — A497

1981, Nov. 12
1363 A497 50pf multicolored .85 .30

Karl von Clausewitz, by W. Wach — A498

1981, Nov. 12 **Photo.**
1364 A498 60pf multicolored .85 .30

Prussian general and writer, (1780-1831).

Social Insurance Centenary — A499

1981, Nov. 12
1365 A499 60pf multicolored .65 .30

Pear-shaped Pot with Lid, 1715 — A500

1982, Jan. 13 **Litho.**
1366 A500 60pf multicolored .65 .30

Johann Friedrich Bottger (1682-1719), originator of Dresden china, 300th birth anniv.

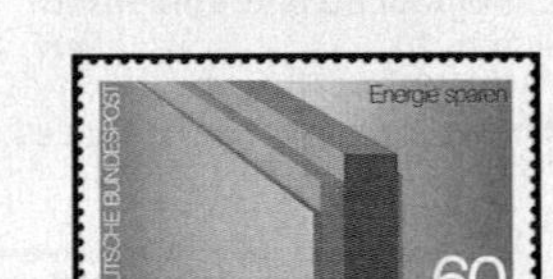

Energy Conservation — A501

1982, Jan. 13
1367 A501 60pf multicolored .65 .30

A502

Illustration from The Town Band of Bremen (folktale).

1982, Jan. 13
1368 A502 40pf red & black .55 .30

A503

1982, Feb. 18 **Photo.**
1369 A503 60pf multicolored 1.75 .30

Johann Wolfgang von Goethe (1749-1832), by Georg Melchior Kraus, 1776.

Robert Koch (1843-1910), Discoverer of Tubercle Bacillus, (1882) — A504

1982, Feb. 18
1370 A504 50pf multicolored 2.10 .30

Die Fromme Helene, by Wilhelm Busch (1832-1908) A505

1982, Apr. 15 **Litho.** ***Perf. 13½x14***
1371 A505 50pf multicolored .85 .30

Europa 1982 A506

50pf, Hambach Meeting sesquicentennial. 60pf, Treaties of Rome, 1957-1982.

1982, May 5 **Litho.** ***Perf. 14***
1372 A506 50pf multicolored *.85* *.25*
1373 A506 60pf multicolored *1.15* *.25*

Kiel Regatta Week Centenary — A507

1982, May 5
1374 A507 60pf multicolored .85 .30

Young Men's Christian Assoc. (YMCA) Centenary — A508

1982, May 5
1375 A508 50pf multicolored .65 .30

"Don't Drink and Drive" A509

1982, July 15 **Photo.**
1376 A509 80pf red & black .85 .30

25th Anniv. of German Lepers' Org. — A510

1982, July 15 **Photo.**
1377 A510 80pf multicolored .85 .30

Prevent Water Pollution A511

1982, July 15
1378 A511 120pf multicolored 2.25 .40

Urea Model and Synthesis Formula A512

1982, Aug. 12 **Photo.**
1379 A512 50pf multicolored .80 .30

Friedrich Wohler (1800-1882), chemist, discoverer of organic chemistry.

St. Francis Preaching to the Birds, by Giotto — A513

1982, Aug. 12 **Litho.**
1380 A513 60pf multicolored .80 .30

800th birth anniv. of St. Francis of Assisi and 87th German Catholics Cong., Dusseldorf, 9/1-5.

James Franck, Max Born — A514

1982, Aug. 12 **Litho. & Engr.**
1381 A514 80pf multicolored 1.05 .30

James Franck (1882-1964) and Max Born (1882-1970), Nobel Prize physicists, developed quantum theory.

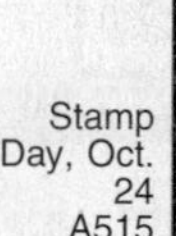
Stamp Day, Oct. 24 A515

1982, Oct. 14 **Photo.** ***Perf. 14***
1382 A515 80pf Poster 1.20 .30

400th Anniv. of the Gregorian Calendar — A516

Design: Calendar illumination, by Johannes Rasch, 1586.

1982, Oct. 14 **Litho.**
1383 A516 60pf multicolored .80 .30

A517

Presidents: a, Theodor Heuss, 1949-59. b, Heinrich Lubke, 1959-69. c, Gustav Heinemann, 1969-74. d, Walter Scheel, 1974-79. e, Karl Carstens, 1979-84.

1982, Nov. 10
1384 A517 Sheet of 5 5.00 4.50
a.-e. 80pf, single stamp .65 .65

A518

1983, Jan. 13 **Litho.** ***Perf. 14***
1385 A518 80pf gray & black 1.30 .40

Edith Stein (d. 1942), philospher and Carmelite Nun.

Persecution and Resistance, 1933-1945 — A519

1983, Jan. 13
1386 A519 80pf multicolored 1.30 .40

Light Space Modulator, 1930 — A520

Walter Gropius (1883-1969), Founder of Bauhaus Architecture: 60pf, Sanctuary, zinc lithograph, 1942. 80pf, Bauhaus Archives, Berlin, 1979.

1983, Feb. 8
1387 A520 50pf multicolored .65 .30
1388 A520 60pf multicolored .80 .30
1389 A520 80pf multicolored .95 .30
Nos. 1387-1389 (3) 2.40 .90

Federahannes, Swabian-Alemannic Carnival — A521

1983, Feb. 8
1390 A521 60pf multicolored .85 .30

4th Intl. Horticultural Show, Munich, Apr. 28-Oct. 9 — A522

1983, Apr. 12 **Litho.** ***Perf. 14***
1391 A522 60pf multicolored .85 .30

Europa 1983 A523

Discoveries: 60pf, Movable type, printing press by Johannes Guttenburg. 80pf, Resonant circuit, electric flux lines, electromagnetic waves by Heinrich Hertz.

1983, May 5 **Litho.** ***Perf. 14***
1392 A523 60pf multicolored *1.60* *.35*
1393 A523 80pf multicolored *1.00* *.35*

Johannes Brahms (1833-1897), Composer A524

1983, May 5 **Photo.**
1394 A524 80pf multicolored 1.30 .40

Franz Kafka (1883-1924), Writer — A525

80pf, Signature, Tyn Church, Prague.

1983, May 5
1395 A525 80pf multicolored 1.30 .40

Beer Pureness Law, 450th Anniv. A526

80pf, Brewers, engraving, 1677.

1983, May 5 **Litho.**
1396 A526 80pf multicolored 1.30 .40

300th Anniv. of Immigration to US — A527

1983, May 5 **Litho. & Engr.**
1397 A527 80pf Concord 1.30 .40

See US No. 2040.

Children and Road Safety A528

1983, July 14 **Litho.** ***Perf. 14***
1398 A528 80pf multicolored 1.30 .40

50th Intl. Auto Show, Frankfurt, Sept. 15-25 A529

1983, July 14
1399 A529 60pf multicolored .65 .30

Otto Warburg — A530

1983, Aug. 11 **Photo.** ***Perf. 14***
1400 A530 50pf multicolored .80 .40

Warburg (1883-1970), pioneer of modern biochemistry, 1931 Nobel prize winner in medicine.

Christoph Martin Wieland (1733-1813), Poet — A531

1983, Aug. 11 **Litho.**
1401 A531 80pf multicolored 1.05 .40

10th Anniv. of UN Membership — A532

1983, Aug. 11 **Photo.**
1402 A532 80pf multicolored 1.45 .40

Rauhe Haus Orphanage Sesquicentennial — A533

1983, Aug. 11 **Litho.**
1403 A533 80pf multicolored 1.15 .40

Survey and Measuring Maps — A534

1983, Aug. 11
1404 A534 120pf multicolored 1.30 .50

Intl. Union of Geodesy and Geophysics Gen. Assembly, Hamburg, Aug. 15-26.

Stamp Day — A535

1983, Oct. 13 **Litho.** ***Perf. 13½***
1405 A535 80pf Postrider 1.20 .40

Martin Luther (1483-1546)
A536

80pf, Engraving by G. Konig.

1983, Oct. 13 *Perf. 14*
1406 A536 80pf multi 2.00 .40

Customs Union Sesquicentennial — A537

1983, Nov. 10
1407 A537 60pf multicolored 1.30 .30

Territorial Authorities (Federation, Land, Communities) — A538

1983, Nov. 10 **Litho.**
1408 A538 80pf multicolored 1.30 .40

Trier, 2000th Anniv.
A539

80pf, Black Gate, 175 A.D.

1984, Jan. 12 **Litho. & Engr.**
1409 A539 80pf multi 1.45 .40

Philipp Reis (1834-1874) Physicist and Inventor — A540

1984, Jan. 12 **Litho.**
1410 A540 80pf multicolored 1.45 .40

Gregor Mendel (1822-1884), Basic Laws of Heredity — A541

1984, Jan. 12 **Litho.**
1411 A541 50pf multicolored .85 .30

500th Anniv. of Michelstadt Town Hall — A542

1984, Feb. 16 **Litho.**
1412 A542 60pf multicolored .85 .30

350th Anniv. of Oberammergau Passion Play — A543

1984, Feb. 16 **Photo.**
1413 A543 60pf multicolored .85 .30

Second Election of Parliament, June 17 — A544

1984, Apr. 12 **Litho.** *Perf. 13½*
1414 A544 80pf multicolored 1.75 .50

Europa (1959-1984)
A545

1984, May 8 **Photo.** *Perf. 14*
1415 A545 60pf multicolored *1.05 .35*
1416 A545 80pf multicolored *1.05 .35*

A546

1984, May 8 **Engr.**
1417 A546 60pf multicolored .65 .30

Nursery Rhyme Illustration, by Ludwig Richter (1803-84).

Statue, 1693 — A547

1984, May 8
1418 A547 80pf grn & dk grn 1.05 .40

St. Norbert von Xanten (1080-1134).

Barmer Theological Declaration, 50th Anniv. — A548

1984, May 8 **Litho.**
1419 A548 80pf Cross, text 1.05 .40

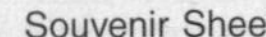

Souvenir Sheet

1984 UPU Congress — A549

a, Letter sorting, 19th cent. b, Scanner. c, H. von Stephan, founder.

1984, June 19 **Litho.** *Perf. 14*
1420 A549 Sheet of 3 3.00 2.50
a. 60pf multicolored .80 .65
b. 80pf multicolored .80 .65
c. 120pf multicolored 1.30 1.20

City of Neuss Bimillenium
A550

1984, June 19 **Litho. & Engr.**
1421 A550 80pf Tomb of Oclatius 1.05 .40

Friedrich Wilhelm Bessel (1784-1846), Astronomer
A551

80pf, Bessel function diagram.

1984, June 19
1422 A551 80pf multicolored 1.05 .40

88th German Catholic Convention, Munich, July 4-8 — A552

1984, June 19 **Photo.**
1423 A552 60pf Pope Pius XII .85 .30

Town Hall, Duderstadt — A553

1984, Aug. 21 **Litho.** *Perf. 14*
1424 A553 60pf multicolored .80 .30

Medieval Document, Computer — A554

1984, Aug. 21
1425 A554 70pf multicolored 1.00 .40

10th Intl. Archives Congress, Bonn.

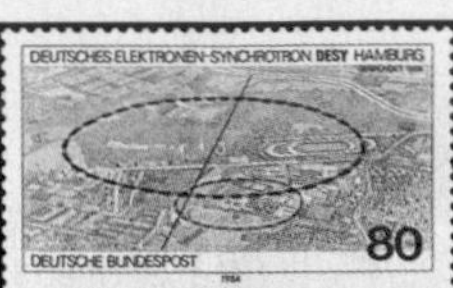

German Electron Synchrotron (DESY) Research Center, Hamburg — A555

1984, Aug. 21 **Photo.**
1426 A555 80pf multicolored 1.30 .40

Schleswig-Holstein Canal Bicentenary — A556

1984, Aug. 21 **Litho.**
1427 A556 80pf Knoop lock 1.20 .40

Stamp Day
A557

80pf, Imperial Taxis Posthouse, Augsburg.

1984, Oct. 18 **Litho.** *Perf. 14*
1428 A557 80pf multicolored 1.30 .55

Anti-smoking Campaign — A558

1984, Nov. 8 **Litho.**
1429 A558 60pf Match, text .95 .30

Equal Rights for Men and Women — A559

80pf, Male & female symbols.

1984, Nov. 8
1430 A559 80pf multicolored 1.20 .40

Peace and Understanding — A560

1984, Nov. 8
1431 A560 80pf Text .95 .40

Augsburg, 2000th Anniv. — A561

80pf, Roman Emperor Augustus, Augsburg buildings.

1985, Jan. 10 **Litho.**
1432 A561 80pf multicolored 1.20 .35

Philipp Jakob Spener, Religious Leader (1635-1705) A562

1985, Jan. 10 **Litho.**
1433 A562 80pf multicolored 1.05 .40

Deutches Wortebuch — A563

1985, Jan. 10 **Litho.**
1434 A563 80pf Bros. Grimm, text 1.30 1.00

Romano Guardini, Theologist (1885-1968) A564

1985, Jan. 10 **Litho.**
1435 A564 80pf multicolored 1.05 .40

Market and Coinage Rights in Verden, 1000th Anniv. A565

1985, Feb. 21 **Litho.**
1436 A565 60pf multicolored 1.45 .30

German-Danish Border Areas and Flags — A566

1985, Feb. 21
1437 A566 80pf multicolored 1.60 .55

Bonn-Copenhagen declarations on mutual minorities, 30th anniv.

Johann Peter Hebel (1760-1826), Poet — A567

1985, Apr. 16 **Litho.**
1438 A567 80pf multicolored .95 .40

Egon Erwin Kisch (1885-1948), Journalist A568

60pf, Kisch using telephone.

1985, Apr. 16 **Litho.**
1439 A568 60pf multicolored .85 .30

Europa 1985 — A569

European Music Year: 60pf, Georg Friedrich Handel, portrait of Handel. 80pf, Johann Sebastian Bach, portrait of Bach.

1985, May 7 **Photo.**
1440 A569 60pf multicolored *1.50 .35*
1441 A569 80pf multicolored *1.50 .35*

Dominikus Zimmermann (1685-1766), Architect — A570

1985, May 7 **Photo.**
1442 A570 70pf Stucco column .95 .40

St. George's Cathedral, 750th Anniv. — A571

60pf, Cathedral, Limburg.

1985, May 7 **Litho.** ***Perf. 14***
1443 A571 60pf multicolored .80 .40

Father Josef Kentenich (1885-1968) — A572

1985, May 7 **Litho.**
1444 A572 80pf Portrait .95 .40

Forest Conservation A573

1985, July 16 **Litho.** ***Perf. 14***
1445 A573 80pf Clock, forest 1.50 .40

Intl. Youth Year A574

60pf, Scouts, scouting and IYY emblems.

1985, July 16 ***Perf. 14***
1446 A574 60pf multicolored .95 .40

30th World Scouting Conf., Munich, 7/15-19.

Frankfurt Stock Exchange, 400th Anniv. — A575

Design: Bourse, est. 1879, and Frankfurt Eagle, the exchange emblem.

1985, Aug. 13 ***Perf. 14x14½***
1447 A575 80pf multicolored 1.20 .40

The Sunday Walk, by Carl Spitzweg (1808-85) A576

1985, Aug. 13
1448 A576 60pf multicolored 1.30 .40

Fritz Reuter (1810-1874), Dialect Author — A577

1985, Oct. 15 **Litho.** ***Perf. 14***
1449 A577 80pf Portrait, manuscript 1.00 .40

Departure of the 1st Train from Nuremberg to Furth, 1835 — A578

1985, Nov. 12 **Litho.** ***Perf. 14x14½***
1450 A578 80pf Adler locomotive 1.60 .40

Founder Johannes Scharrer (1785-1844), German Railways 150th anniv.

Reintegration of German World War II Refugees, 40th Anniv. — A579

1985, Nov. 12 ***Perf. 14***
1451 A579 80pf multicolored 1.50 .40

Natl. Armed Forces, 30th Anniv. A580

80pf, Iron Cross, natl. colors.

1985, Nov. 12 ***Perf. 14x14½***
1452 A580 80pf multicolored 2.25 .40

Benz Tricycle, Saloon Car, 1912, and Modern Automobile — A581

1986, Jan. 16 **Litho.** ***Perf. 14***
1453 A581 80pf multicolored 1.60 .40

Automobile cent.

Bad Hersfeld, 1250th Anniv. A582

1986, Feb. 13 **Litho.** ***Perf. 14***
1454 A582 60pf multicolored .95 .40

Bach Contata, Detail, by Oskar Kokoschka (1886-1980) A583

1986, Feb. 13
1455 A583 80pf Self portrait .95 .40

Halley's Comet A584

1986, Feb. 13
1456 A584 80pf multicolored 1.60 .50

Europa 1986 A585

Details from Michelangelo's David: 60pf, Mouth (pure water). 80pf, Nose, (pure air).

1986, May 5 **Photo.** ***Perf. 14***
1457 A585 60pf multicolored *1.00 .35*
1458 A585 80pf multicolored *1.00 .35*

St. Johannis Monastery, Walsrode — A586

1986, May 5 **Litho. & Engr.**
1459 A586 60pf multicolored 1.05 .40

Monastery millennium and town of Walsrode, 603rd anniv.

King Ludwig II of Bavaria (1845-1886), Neuschwanstein Castle — A587

1986, May 5 **Litho.**
1460 A587 60pf multicolored 1.75 .40

Karl Barth (1886-1968), Protestant Theologian A588

1986, May 5 **Engr.**
1461 A588 80pf blk, dk red & red lil 1.20 .40

Religion, Science, Friendship and Fatherland — A589

1986, May 5 **Litho.**
1462 A589 80pf multicolored 1.20 .40

Union of German Catholic Students, 100th assembly, Frankfurt, June 12-15.

Carl Maria von Weber (1786-1826), Mass in E-flat Major — A590

1986, June 20 **Litho.** ***Perf. 14***
1463 A590 80pf multicolored 1.60 .40

Franz Liszt and Signature A591

1986, June 20
1464 A591 80pf dk blue & dk org 1.50 .40

Intl. Peace Year A592

1986, June 20
1465 A592 80pf multicolored 1.45 .40

Souvenir Sheet

Reichstag, Berlin — A593

Historic buildings: b, Koening Museum, Bonn. c, Parliament, Bonn.

1986, June 20
1466 A593 Sheet of 3 3.75 3.25
a.-c. 80pf, any single .95 .95

European Satellite Technology — A594

Design: TV-SAT/TDF-1 over Europe.

1986, June 20
1467 A594 80pf multicolored 1.60 .50

Augsburg Cathedral Stained Glass Window A595

1986, Aug. 14 ***Perf. 14***
1468 A595 80pf multicolored 1.60 .40

Monuments protection.

King Frederick the Great (1712-1786) A596

1986, Aug. 14
1469 A596 80pf multicolored 2.25 .40

German Skat Congress, Cent. — A597

1986, Aug. 14
1470 A597 80pf Tournament card 1.60 .40

Organization for Economic Cooperation and Development, 25th Anniv. — A598

1986, Aug. 14
1471 A598 80pf multicolored 1.20 .40

Heidelberg University, 600th Anniv. — A599

1986, Oct. 16 **Litho.**
1472 A599 80pf multicolored 1.30 .40

Stagecoach, Stamps from 1975-1984 — A600

1986, Oct. 16
1473 A600 80pf multicolored 1.30 .40

Stamp Day, 50th Anniv.

A601

1986, Nov. 13 **Litho.** ***Perf. 14***
1474 A601 70pf multicolored .85 .40

Mary Wigman (1886-1973), dancer.

Famous Women — A602

Designs: 5pf, Emma Ihrer (1857-1911), politician, labor leader. 10pf, Paula Modersohn-Becker (1876-1907), painter. 20pf, Cilly Aussem (1909-63), tennis champion. 30pf, Kathe Kollwitz (1867-1945), painter, graphic artist. 40pf, Maria Sibylla Merian (1647-1717), naturalist, painter. 50pf, Christine Teusch (1888-1968), minister of education and cultural affairs. 60pf, Dorothea Erxleben (1715-62), physician. 70pf, Elisabet Boehm (1859-1943), social organizer. 80pf, Clara Schumann (1819-96), pianist, composer. 100pf, Therese Giehse (1898-1975), actress. 120pf, Elisabeth Selbert (1896-1986), politician. 130pf, Lise Meitner (1878-1968), physicist. 140pf, Cecile Vogt (1875-1962), neurologist. 150pf, Sophie Scholl (1921-43), member of anti-Nazi resistance. 170pf, Hannah Arendt (1906-75), American political scientist. 180pf, Lotte Lehmann (1888-1976), soprano. 200pf, Bertha von Suttner (1843-1914), 1905 Nobel Peace Prize winner. 240pf, Mathilde Franziska Anneke, (1817-84), American author. 250pf, Queen Louise of Prussia (1776-1810). 300pf, Fanny Hensel (1805-47), composer-conductor. 350pf, Hedwig Dransfeld (1871-1925), women's rights activist. 500pf, Alice Salomon (1872-1948), feminist and social activist.

1986-91		**Engr.**		***Perf. 14***	
1475	A602	5pf	multi	.30	.30
1476	A602	10pf	multi	.40	.35
1477	A602	20pf	multi	.65	.35
1478	A602	30pf	multi	.35	.30
1479	A602	40pf	multi	.65	.25
1480	A602	50pf	multi	.65	.25
1481	A602	60pf	multi	.80	.25
1482	A602	70pf	multi	1.00	.55
1483	A602	80pf	multi	.80	.25
1484	A602	100pf	multi	1.00	.35
1485	A602	120pf	multi	1.30	.80
1486	A602	130pf	multi	2.00	.65
1487	A602	140pf	multi	2.25	1.20
1488	A602	150pf	multi	2.25	1.20
1489	A602	170pf	multi	1.60	1.00
1490	A602	180pf	multi	2.00	1.00
1491	A602	200pf	multi	1.60	.65
1492	A602	240pf	multi	2.25	1.60
1493	A602	250pf	multi	3.75	1.60
1493A	A602	300pf	multi	2.00	1.00
1494	A602	350pf	multi	4.25	2.00
1494A	A602	500pf	multi	5.25	2.60
	Nos. 1475-1494A (22)			37.10	18.50

Issued: 50pf, 80pf, 11/18; 40pf, 60pf, 9/17/87; 120pf, 11/7/87; 10pf, 4/14/88; 20pf, 130pf, 5/5/88; 100pf, 170pf, 240pf, 350pf, 11/10/88; 500pf, 1/12/89; 5pf, 2/9/89; 180pf, 250pf, 7/13/89; 140pf, 300pf, 8/10/89; 30pf, 70pf, 1/8/91; 150pf, 200pf, 2/14/91.

See Nos. 1723/1735, 2185-2188, Berlin Nos. 9N516-9N532.

A603

1986, Nov. 13 **Litho.** ***Perf. 14***
1495 A603 80pf multicolored .85 .40

Advent Collection for Church Projects in Latin America, 25th Anniv.

Berlin, 750th Anniv. — A604

1987, Jan. 15 **Litho.**
1496 A604 80pf multicolored 1.60 .55

See Berlin No. 9N536.

Archbishop's Residence at Wurzburg, 1719-44 A605

1987, Jan. 15 **Photo.**
1497 A605 80pf multicolored 1.30 .40

Balthasar Neumann (1687-1753), Baroque architect.

Ludwig Erhard (1897-1977), Economist, Chancellor 1963-66 A606

1987, Jan. 15
1498 A606 80pf multicolored 1.60 .35

1987 Census — A607

1987, Jan. 15 **Litho.**
1499 A607 80pf Federal Eagle 1.45 .40

Clemenswerth Hunting Castle, 250th Anniv. — A608

1987, Feb. 12 **Litho.**
1500 A608 60pf multicolored 1.15 .40

Joseph von Fraunhofer (1787-1826), Optician, Physicist — A609

80pf, Light spectrum diagram.

1987, Feb. 12 **Litho. & Engr.**
1501 A609 80pf multicolored 1.15 .40

Karl May (1842-1912), Novelist — A610

80pf, Apache Chief Winnetou.

1987, Feb. 12 **Photo.**
1502 A610 80pf multicolored 1.25 .40

Papal Arms, Madonna and Child, Buildings in Kevelaer — A611

1987, Apr. 9 **Litho.**
1503 A611 80pf multicolored 1.45 .40

State visit of Pope John Paul II, Apr. 30-May 4; 17th Marian and 10th Mariological World Congress, Kevelaer, Sept. 11-20.

German Choral Soc., 125th Anniv. A612

1987, Apr. 9
1504 A612 80pf multicolored 1.15 .40

Europa 1987 A613

Modern architecture: 60pf, German Pavilion, designed by Ludwig Mies van der Rohe, 1928 World's Fair, Barcelona. 80pf, Kohlbrand Bridge, 1974, Hamburg, designed by Thyssen Engineering.

1987, May 5 **Litho.**
1505 A613 60pf multicolored *1.05* *.35*
1506 A613 80pf multicolored *1.30* *.35*

Organ Pipes, Signature A614

1987, May 5
1507 A614 80pf multicolored .85 .40

Dietrich Buxtehude (c. 1637-1707), composer.

Wilhelm Kaisen (1887-1979), Bremen City Senate President — A615

1987, May 5
1508 A615 80pf multicolored 1.05 .40

Johann Albrecht Bengel (1687-1752), Lutheran Theologian — A616

1987, May 5 **Photo.** ***Perf. 14***
1509 A616 80pf multicolored 1.00 .40

Kurt Schwitters (1887-1948), Artist — A617

1987, May 5 **Litho.**
1510 A617 80pf multicolored 1.05 .40

Rotary Intl. Convention, Munich, June 7-10 — A618

1987, May 5 **Photo.**
1511 A618 70pf multicolored 1.05 .40

A619

Design: Dulmen's Wild Horses, Merfelder Bruch Nature Reserve.

1987, May 5
1512 A619 60pf multicolored 1.45 .40

European Environmental Conservation Year.

Bishopric of Bremen, 1200th Anniv. A620

Design: Charlemagne, Bremen Cathedral, city arms, Bishop Willehad.

1987, July 16 **Litho.** ***Perf. 14***
1513 A620 80pf multicolored 1.00 .40

7th European Rifleman's Festival, Lippstadt, Sept. 12-13 — A621

1987, Aug. 20 **Litho.** ***Perf. 14***
1514 A621 80pf multicolored 1.00 .40

Stamp Day — A622

1987, Oct. 15 **Litho.**
1515 A622 80pf Postmen, 1897 .95 .75

Historic Sites and Objects — A623

Designs: 5pf, Brunswick Lion. 10pf, Frankfurt Airport. 20pf, No. 1526, Queen Nefertiti of Egypt, bust, Egyptian Museum, Berlin. 30pf, Corner tower, Celle Castle, 14th cent. 33pf, 120pf, Schleswig Cathedral. 38pf, 280pf, Statue of Roland, Bremen. 40pf, Chile House, Hamburg. 41pf, 170pf, Russian church, Wiesbaden. 45pf, Rastatt Castle. 50pf, Filigree tracery on spires, Freiburg Cathedral. 60pf, Bavaria Munich, bronze statue above the Theresienwiese, Hall of Fame. No. 1527, Heligoland. 80pf, Entrance to Zollern II coal mine, Dortmund. 90pf, 140pf, Bronze flagon from Reinheim. 100pf, Altotting Chapel, Bavaria. 200pf, Magdeburg Cathedral. 300pf, Hambach Castle. 350pf, Externsteine Bridge near Horn-Bad Meinberg. 400pf, Opera House, Dresden. 450pf, New Gate, Neubrandenburg. 500pf, State Theatre, Cottbus. 700pf, German Theater, Berlin.

1987-96 **Typo.** ***Perf. 14***

1515A	A623	5pf	multi	.35	.30
1516	A623	10pf	multi	.40	.25
1517	A623	20pf	multi	.40	.30
1518	A623	30pf	multi	.65	.25
1519	A623	33pf	multi	.40	.30
1520	A623	38pf	multi	.65	.40
1521	A623	40pf	multi	.40	.40
1522	A623	41pf	multi	.65	.35
1523	A623	45pf	multi	.40	.35
1524	A623	50pf	multi	.65	.25
1525	A623	60pf	multi	.65	.25
1526	A623	70pf	multi	.75	.25
1527	A623	70pf	multi	.40	.30
1528	A623	80pf	multi	.65	.25
a.	Bklt. pane, 4 10pf, 2 50pf, 2 80pf ('89)			5.00	4.25
b.	Bklt. pane, 2 each 20pf, 80pf			4.25	5.75
1529	A623	90pf	multi	1.20	1.60
1530	A623	100pf	multi	2.25	.30
a.	Bklt. pane, 2 each 10, 60, 80, 100pf			8.25	9.00
b.	Bklt. pane, 2 each 20, 50, 80, 100pf			9.50	10.50
c.	Booklet pane, 10 #1530			19.00	16.50
	Complete booklet, #1530c			19.00	
d.	Booklet pane, 4 #1516, 2 each #1524, 1528, 1530			9.00	9.00
	Complete booklet, #1530d			9.00	
1531	A623	120pf	multi	1.30	.60
1532	A623	140pf	multi	1.60	.55
1533	A623	170pf	multi	1.60	.65
1534	A623	200pf	multi	1.75	.60
1535	A623	280pf	multi	3.75	3.75
1536	A623	300pf	multi	2.25	.40
1537	A623	350pf	multi	2.60	.55
1538	A623	400pf	multi	3.00	.55
1539	A623	450pf	multi	3.75	1.00
1540	A623	500pf	multi	4.25	1.20
1540A	A623	700pf	multi	6.00	2.00
	Nos. 1515A-1540A (27)			42.70	17.95

Issued: 30, 50, 60, 80pf, 11/6/87; 10, 300pf, 1/14/88; 120pf, No. 1526, 7/14/88; 40, 90, 280pf, 8/11/88; 20, 33, 38, 140pf, 1/12/89; 100, 350pf, 2/9/89; 5pf, 2/15/90; 45p, No. 1527, 6/21/90; 170pf, 6/4/91; 400pf, 10/10/91; 450pf, 8/13/92; 200pf, 4/15/93; 500pf, 6/17/93; 41pf, 8/12/93; 700pf, 9/16/93; No. 1530b, 11/9/94; No. 1530d, 8/14/96.

See Nos. 1655-1663, 1838-60, 2199-2216, Berlin Nos. 9N543-9N557.

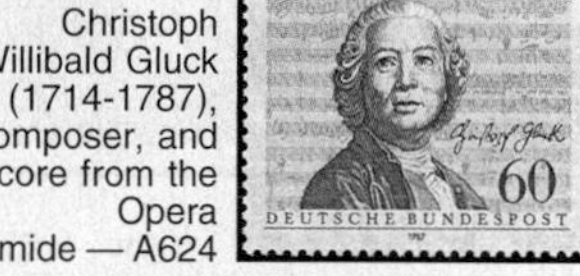

Christoph Willibald Gluck (1714-1787), Composer, and Score from the Opera Armide — A624

1987, Nov. 6 ***Perf. 14***
1541 A624 60pf car lake & dk gray .80 .35

Gerhart Hauptmann (1862-1946), Playwright — A625

1987, Nov. 6 **Litho.**
1542 A625 80pf blk & brk red 1.20 .40

German Agro Action Organization, 125th Anniv. — A626

1987, Nov. 6 **Photo.**
1543 A626 80pf Rice field 1.20 .40

Mainz Carnival, 150th Anniv. — A627

1988, Jan. 14 **Litho.** ***Perf. 14***
1544 A627 60pf Jester .95 .40

Jacob Kaiser (1888-1961), Labor Leader — A628

1988, Jan. 14 **Litho. & Engr.**
1545 A628 80pf black .85 .40

Franco-German Cooperation Treaty, 25th Anniv. — A629

80pf, Adenauer, De Gaulle.

1988, Jan. 14
1546 A629 80pf multicolored 1.30 .55

See France No. 2086.

Beatification of Edith Stein and Rupert Mayer by Pope John Paul II in 1987 — A630

1988, Jan. 14 **Photo.**
1547 A630 80pf brown, blk & ver .95 .40

A631

Woodcut (detail) by Ludwig Richter.

1988, Feb. 18 **Litho.**
1548 A631 60pf multicolored .95 .40

Woodcut inspired by poem Solitude of the Green Woods, by Baron Joseph von Eichendorff (1788-1857).

A632

1988, Feb. 18 **Photo.**
1549 A632 80pf dk red & brn blk 1.20 .40

Arthur Schopenhauer (1788-1860), philosopher.

Friedrich Wilhelm Raiffeisen (1818-1888), Economist — A633

1988, Feb. 18 **Litho.**
1550 A633 80pf black & brt yel grn 1.30 .40

The German Raiffeisen Assoc., an agricultural cooperative credit soc., was founded by Raiffeisen.

Ulrich Reichsritter von Hutten (1488-1523), Humanist — A634

Design: Detail from an engraving published with Hutten's *Conquestiones.*

1988, Apr. 14 **Litho. & Engr.**
1551 A634 80pf multicolored .95 .50

Europa 1988 A635

Transport and communication: 60pf, Airbus A320. 80pf, Integrated Services Digital Network (ISDN) system.

1988, May 5 **Litho.**
1552 A635 60pf multicolored *.95 .40*
1553 A635 80pf multicolored *.95 .40*

City of Dusseldorf, 700th Anniv. — A636

1988, May 5
1554 A636 60pf multicolored 1.05 .40

Cologne University, 600th Anniv. — A637

1988, May 5
1555 A637 80pf multicolored .95 .40

Jean Monnet (1888-1979), French Statesman A638

1988, May 5
1556 A638 80pf multicolored .95 .40

Theodor Storm (1817-1888), Poet, Novelist — A639

1988, May 5
1557 A639 80pf multicolored .95 .40

German Volunteer Service, 25th Anniv. — A640

1988, May 5
1558 A640 80pf multicolored .95 .40

Town of Meersburg, Millennium — A641

1988, July 14 **Litho.** ***Perf. 14***
1559 A641 60pf multicolored .80 .40

Leopold Gmelin (1788-1853), Chemist A642

1988, July 14 **Litho. & Engr.**
1560 A642 80pf multicolored .85 .40

Vernier Scale as a Symbol of Precision and Quality — A643

1988, July 14 **Litho.**
1561 A643 140pf multicolored 1.60 .80

Made in Germany.

August Bebel (1840-1913), Founder of the Social Democratic Party — A644

1988, Aug. 11 **Photo.**
1562 A644 80pf multicolored 1.20 .40

Intl. Red Cross, 125th Anniv. — A645

1988, Oct. 13 **Litho. & Engr.**
1563 A645 80pf scarlet & black 1.20 .40

Stamp Day — A646

1988, Oct. 13 **Litho.**
1564 A646 20pf Carrier pigeon .55 .35

1st Nazi Pogrom, Nov. 9, 1938 A647

Star, "Remembering is the secret of redemption," & burning synagogue in Baden-Baden.

1988, Oct. 13 **Photo.**
1565 A647 80pf dull pale pur & blk .85 .40

Postage Stamps for Bethel, Cent. A648

1988, Nov. 10 **Litho.**
1566 A648 60pf multicolored .95 .40

The Postage Stamps for Bethel program was founded by Pastor Friedrich V. Bodelschwingh to employ disabled residents of Bethel.

Samaritan Association of Workers (ASB) Rescue Service, Cent. — A649

1988, Nov. 10
1567 A649 80pf multicolored .95 .40

Bonn Bimillennium — A650

1989, Jan. 12 **Litho.**
1568 A650 80pf multicolored 1.30 .60

Bonn as capital of the federal republic, 40th anniv.

Bluxao I, 1955, by Willi Baumeister (1889-1955) — A651

1989, Jan. 12
1569 A651 60pf multicolored .85 .40

Misereor and Brot fur die Welt, 30th Annivs. A652

1989, Jan. 12 **Photo.**
1570 A652 80pf Barren and verdant soil 1.00 .40

Church organizations helping Third World nations to become self-sufficient in food production.

Cats in the Attic, Woodcut by Gerhard Marcks (1889-1981) — A653

1989, Feb. 9 **Litho.** ***Perf. 14***
1571 A653 60pf multicolored .85 .40

European Parliament 3rd Elections, June 18 — A654

Flags of member nations.

1989, Apr. 20 **Litho.**
1572 A654 100pf multicolored 1.75 .80

Europa 1989 A655

1989, May 5
1573 A655 60pf Kites *1.00 .30*
1574 A655 100pf Puppets *1.30 .35*

Hamburg Harbor, 800th Anniv. A656

1989, May 5
1575 A656 60pf multicolored 1.20 .40

Cosmas Damian Asam (1686-1739), Painter, Architect A657

1989, May 5 **Litho. & Engr.**
1576 A657 60pf Fresco .65 .40

Federal Republic of Germany, 40th Anniv. — A658

100pf, Natl. crest, flag, presidents' signatures.

1989, May 5 **Photo.**
1577 A658 100pf multicolored 1.60 .60

Council of Europe, 40th Anniv. — A659

100pf, Parliamentary Assembly, stars.

1989, May 5 ***Perf. 14***
1578 A659 100pf multicolored 1.45 .65

Franz Xaver Gabelsberger (1789-1849), Inventor of a German Shorthand — A660

1989, May 5 **Litho.**
1579 A660 100pf multicolored 1.45 .50

Sts. Kilian, Colman and Totnan (d. 689), Martyred Missionaries, and Clover — A661

1989, June 15 **Litho.**
1580 A661 100pf multicolored 1.30 .55

See Ireland No. 748.

Friedrich Silcher (1789-1860), Composer, and *Lorelai* Score — A662

1989, June 15
1581 A662 80pf multicolored .85 .40

Social Security Pension Insurance, Cent. — A663

1989, June 15
1582 A663 100pf dull ultra, bl & ver 1.20 .50

Friedrich List (1789-1846), Economist — A664

1989, July 13 **Engr.** ***Perf. 14***
1583 A664 170pf black & dark red 2.00 .80

Summer Evening, 1905, by Heinrich Vogler — A665

1989, July 13 **Litho.**
1584 A665 60pf multicolored .75 .40

Worpswede Artists' Village, cent.

A666

1989, July 13 **Photo.**
1585 A666 100pf slate grn, blk & gray 1.00 .50

Reverend Paul Schneider (d. 1939), martyr of Buchenwald concentration camp.

A667

1989, Aug. 10 **Litho.**
1586 A667 60pf multicolored .95 .40

Frankfurt Cathedral, 750th anniv.

Child Welfare A668

1989, Aug. 10 ***Perf. 14***
1587 A668 100pf multicolored 1.15 .50

Trade Union of the Mining and Power Industries, Cent. — A669

1989, Aug. 10 ***Perf. 14***
1588 A669 100pf multicolored .95 .50

Reinhold Maier (1889-1971), Politician A670

1989, Oct. 12 **Litho.**
1589 A670 100pf multicolored 1.15 .50

Restoration of St. James Church Organ, Constructed by Arp Schnitger, 1689 — A671

1989, Nov. 16
1590 A671 60pf multicolored .95 .40

Speyer, 2000th Anniv. A672

1990, Jan. 12 **Litho.** ***Perf. 14x14½***
1591 A672 60pf multicolored .95 .40

A673

Design: *The Young Post Rider*, an Engraving by Albrecht Durer.

Litho. & Engr.

1990, Jan. 12 ***Perf. 14***
1592 A673 100pf blksh pur, gray brn, beige 1.75 .55

Postal communications in Europe, 500th anniv. See Austria No. 1486, Belgium No. 1332, Berlin 9N584, and DDR No. 2791.

A674

1990, Jan. 12 **Litho.**
1593 A674 100pf multicolored .95 .55

Riesling Vineyards, 500th anniv.

A675

1990, Jan. 12 **Litho. & Engr.**
1594 A675 100pf multicolored 1.20 .55

Addition of Lubeck to the UNESCO World Heritage List, 1987.

Seal of Col. Spittler, 1400, and Teutonic Order Heraldic Emblem A676

1990, Feb. 15 **Litho.**
1595 A676 100pf multicolored 1.30 .55

Teutonic Order, 800th anniv.

A677

Design: Seal of Frederick II and Galleria Reception Hall at the Frankfurt Fair.

1990, Feb. 15
1596 A677 100pf multicolored 1.30 .55

Granting of fair privileges to Frankfurt by Frederick II, 750th anniv.

Youth Science and Technology Competition, 25th Anniv. — A678

1990, Feb. 15
1597 A678 100pf multicolored 1.30 .55

Nature and Environmental Protection — A679

1990, Feb. 15
1598 A679 100pf North Sea 1.60 .55

Labor Day, Cent. A680

1990, Apr. 19 **Photo.** ***Perf. 14***
1599 A680 100pf dark red & blk 1.05 .55

German Assoc. of Housewives, 75th Anniv. — A681

1990, Apr. 19 **Litho.**
1600 A681 100pf multicolored 1.05 .55

Europa A682

Post offices in Frankfurt am Main: 60pf, Thurn and Taxis Palace. 100pf, Modern Giro office.

1990, May 3 **Litho.**
1601 A682 60pf multicolored *1.20* *.40*
1602 A682 100pf multicolored *1.20* *.40*

German Students' Fraternity, 175th Anniv. — A683

1990, May 3 **Litho. & Engr.**
1603 A683 100pf multicolored 1.30 .55

Intl. Telecommunication Union, 125th Anniv. — A684

1990, May 3 **Litho.**
1604 A684 100pf multicolored 1.05 .55

German Life Boat Institution, 125th Anniv. — A685

1990, May 3
1605 A685 60pf multicolored .95 .50

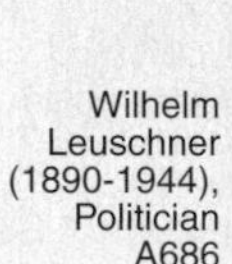

Wilhelm Leuschner (1890-1944), Politician A686

1990, May 3 **Litho. & Engr.**
1606 A686 100pf lt gray violet 1.30 .55

Rummelsberg Diaconal Institution, Cent. — A687

1990, May 3 **Litho.**
1607 A687 100pf multicolored .95 .55

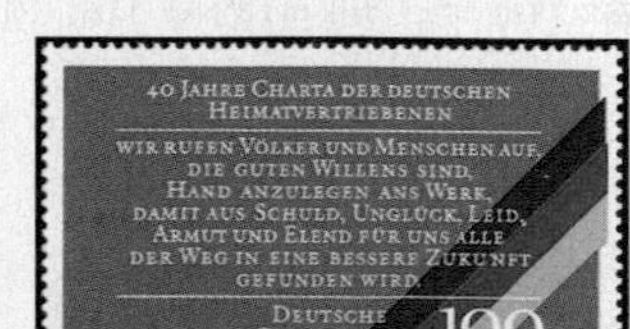

Charter of German Expellees, 40th Anniv. — A688

1990, June 21 **Photo.**
1608 A688 100pf multicolored 1.20 .50

Intl. Chamber of Commerce, 30th Universal Congress — A689

1990, June 21 **Litho.**
1609 A689 80pf multicolored .95 .65

Matthias Claudius (1740-1815), Writer — A691

1990, Aug. 9 **Litho.**
1611 A691 100pf multicolored 1.20 .40

Reunified Germany
AREA — 137,179 sq. mi.
POP. — 82,087,361 (1999 est.)
CAPITAL — Berlin

German Reunification — A692

1990, Oct. 3 **Litho.** ***Perf. 14***
1612 A692 50pf black, red & yel 1.30 .50
1613 A692 100pf black, red & yel 2.25 .80

First Postage Stamps, 150th Anniv. — A693

1990, Oct. 11 **Litho.**
1614 A693 100pf multicolored 1.20 .40

Heinrich Schliemann (1822-1890), Archaeologist — A694

1990, Oct. 11
1615 A694 60pf multicolored 1.05 .40

See Greece No. 1705.

Kathe Dorsch (1912-1957), Actress — A695

1990, Nov. 6 **Photo.**
1616 A695 100pf red & violet 1.20 .55

Opening of Berlin Wall, 1st Anniv. — A696

1990, Nov. 6 **Photo.** ***Perf. 14***
1617 A696 50pf shown 1.00 .60
1618 A696 100pf Brandenburg Gate 1.60 .60

Souvenir Sheet

1619 Sheet of 2 3.00 2.75
a. A696 50pf like No. 1617 1.00 1.00
b. A696 100pf like No. 1618 1.60 1.60

Rainbow continuous on stamps from No. 1619.

Pharmacy Profession, 750th Anniv. — A697

1991, Jan. 8 **Litho.**
1620 A697 100pf multicolored 1.30 .55

Hanover, 750th Anniv. — A698

1991, Jan. 8
1621 A698 60pf multicolored .95 .40

Brandenburg Gate, Bicentennial — A699

1991, Jan. 8 **Litho. & Engr.**
1622 A699 100pf gray, dk bl & red 1.45 .40

A700

1991, Jan. 8 **Photo.**
1623 A700 60pf multicolored .80 .40

Erich Buchholz (1891-1972), painter and architect.

A701

1991, Jan. 8 **Litho.**
1624 A701 100pf multicolored 1.15 .55

Walter Eucken (1891-1950), economist.

25th Intl. Tourism Exchange, Berlin — A702

1991, Jan. 8
1625 A702 100pf multicolored 1.20 .40

Souvenir Sheet

World Bobsled Championships, Altenberg — A703

1991, Jan. 8 ***Perf. 12½x13***
1626 A703 100pf multicolored 1.60 2.00

Friedrich Spee von Langenfeld (1591-1635), Poet — A704

1991, Feb. 14 **Litho.** ***Perf. 14***
1627 A704 100pf multicolored 1.20 .40

A705

1991, Mar. 12
1628 A705 100pf multicolored 1.20 .40

Ludwig Windthorst (1812-1891), politician.

A706

1991, Mar. 12
1629 A706 60pf multicolored .80 .40

Jan von Werth (1591-1652), general.

Flowers A707

30pf, Schweizer mannschild. 50pf, Wulfens primel (primula). 80pf, Sommerenzian (gentian). 100pf, Preiselbeere (cranberry). 350pf, Alpenedelweiss.

1991, Mar. 12 ***Perf. 13***
1630 A707 30pf multicolored .35 .35
1631 A707 50pf multicolored .50 .50
1632 A707 80pf multicolored .80 .35
1633 A707 100pf multicolored 1.15 .35
1634 A707 350pf multicolored 3.75 2.60
Nos. 1630-1634 (5) 6.55 4.15

Battle of Legnica, 750th Anniv. A708

Litho. & Engr.

1991, Apr. 9 *Perf. 14*

1635 A708 100pf multicolored 1.30 .80

See Poland No. 3019.

Choral Singing Academy of Berlin, Bicent. A709

1991, Apr. 9

1636 A709 100pf multicolored 1.20 .55

Lette Foundation, 125th Anniv. — A710

1991, Apr. 9 **Photo.**

1637 A710 100pf multicolored 1.20 .40

Historic Aircraft A711

30pf, Junkers F13, 1930. 50pf, Grade Eindecker, 1909. 100pf, Fokker FIII, 1922. 165pf, Graf Zeppelin LZ 127, 1928.

1991, Apr. 9

1638 A711 30pf multicolored .35 .35
1639 A711 50pf multicolored .50 .30
1640 A711 100pf multicolored 1.30 .35
1641 A711 165pf multicolored 2.00 1.75
Nos. 1638-1641 (4) 4.15 2.75

Europa A712

Satellites: 60pf, ERS-1. 100pf, Copernicus.

1991, May 2 **Litho.** *Perf. 14*

1642 A712 60pf multicolored *1.00* .35
1643 A712 100pf multicolored *1.60* .35

Town Charters, 700th Anniv. — A713

Design: Arms of Bernkastel, Mayen, Montabaur, Saarburg, Welschbillig, and Wittlich.

1991, May 2

1644 A713 60pf multicolored .80 .40

Max Reger (1873-1916), Composer — A714

1991, May 2

1645 A714 100pf multicolored 1.30 .40

Inter-City Express Railway A715

1991, May 2

1646 A715 60pf multicolored .80 .40

18th World Gas Congress, Berlin — A716

Designs: 60pf, Wilhelm August Lampadius (1772-1842), chemist. 100pf, Gas street lamp.

1991, June 4 **Litho.** *Perf. 13x12½*

1647 60pf lt blue & black .85 .40
1648 100pf lt blue & black 1.00 .40
a. A716 Pair, #1647-1648 + label 2.10 2.25

Sea Birds — A717

Designs: 60pf, Kampflaufer, Philomachus pugnax. 80pf, Zwergseeschwalbe, Sterna albifrons. 100pf, Ringelgans, Branta bernicla. 140pf, Seeadler, Haliaeetus albicilla.

1991, June 4 **Litho.** *Perf. 14*

1649 A717 60pf multicolored .65 .40
1650 A717 80pf multicolored 1.00 .65
1651 A717 100of multicolored 1.00 .65
1652 A717 140pf multicolored 1.75 1.60
Nos. 1649-1652 (4) 4.40 3.30

Paul Wallot (1841-1912), Architect — A718

Litho. & Engr.

1991, June 4 *Perf. 14*

1653 A718 100pf multicolored 1.30 .40

Historic Sites Type of 1987

Designs: No. 1655, Frankfurt Airport. No. 1656, Wernigerode Town Hall. 60pf, Munich, Bavaria. 80pf, Zech Zollern II Dortmund. No. 1663, Wallfahrtskapelle Alloting. No. 1664, Schwerin Castle. 110pf, Regensburg Stone Bridge.

Die Cut perf 10¼x10¾ on 3 sides (#1656, 1664, 1666), Die Cut Imperf

1991-2001 **Litho.**

Self-Adhesive

1655 A623 10pf multi 2.00 2.00
1656 A623 10pf multi 2.60 2.25
1659 A623 60pf multi 2.00 2.00
1661 A623 80pf multi 2.00 2.00
1663 A623 100pf multi 2.00 2.00
a. Bklt. pane, 2 each #1655, 1659, 1661, 1663 16.00
1664 A623 100pf multi 2.60 2.60
1666 A623 110pf multi 1.30 1.30
a. Booklet, 2 each #1656, 1664, 8 #1666 27.00
Nos. 1655-1666 (7) 14.50 14.15

Issued: Nos. 1655, 1659, 1661, 1663, 6/4. Nos. 1656, 1664, 110pf, 5/25/01.

Nos. 1655, 1659, 1661, 1663 issued on peelable paper backing serving as booklet cover.

Dragonflies A719

50pf, No. 1671, Libellula depressa. No. 1672, 70pf, Sympetrum sanguineum. No. 1673, 80pf, Cordulegaster boltonii. No. 1674, 100pf, Aeshna viridis.

1991, July 9 **Photo.** *Perf. 14*

1670 A719 50pf multicolored .55 .30
1671 A719 60pf multicolored 1.00 .55
1672 A719 60pf multicolored 1.00 .55
1673 A719 60pf multicolored 1.00 .55
1674 A719 60pf multicolored 1.00 .55
a. Block of 4, #1671-1674 5.00 4.25
1675 A719 70pf multicolored .80 .65
1676 A719 80pf multicolored .85 .65
1677 A719 100pf multicolored .95 .65
Nos. 1670-1677 (8) 7.15 4.45

Traffic Safety A720

1991, July 9 **Litho.**

1678 A720 100pf multicolored 1.30 .55

Geneva Convention on Refugees, 40th Anniv. — A721

1991, July 9

1679 A721 100pf blk, gray & pink 1.20 .40

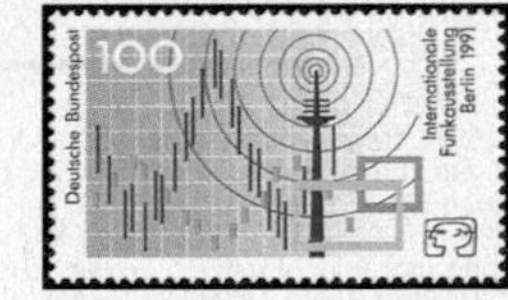

Intl. Radio Exhibition, Berlin — A722

1991, July 9

1680 A722 100pf multicolored 1.30 .40

Reinold von Thadden-Trieglaff (1891-1976), Founder of German Protestant Convention — A723

1991, Aug. 8 **Litho.** *Perf. 14*

1681 A723 100pf multicolored 1.20 .40

August Heinrich Hoffman von Fallersleben (1798-1874), Poet and Philologist — A724

1991, Aug. 8

1682 A724 100pf multicolored 1.20 .40

German national anthem, 150th anniv.

3-Phase Energy Transmission, Cent. — A725

1991, Aug. 8

1683 A725 170pf multicolored 2.00 1.00

Rhine-Ruhr Harbor, Duisburg, 275th Anniv. — A726

1991, Sept. 12 **Litho.** *Perf. 14*

1684 A726 100pf multicolored 1.20 .40

Souvenir Sheet

Theodor Korner (1791-1813), Poet — A727

1991, Sept. 12 *Perf. 13x12½*

1685 A727 Sheet of 2 2.00 2.60
a. 60pf Sword and pen 1.00 1.05
b. 100pf Portrait 1.00 1.05

Hans Albers (1891-1960), Actor — A728

1991, Sept. 12 **Photo.** *Perf. 14*

1686 A728 100pf multicolored 1.60 .40

Postman, Spreewald Region A729

1991, Oct. 10 Litho. ***Perf. 14***
1687 A729 100pf multicolored 1.20 .40

Stamp Day.

Bird Monument by Max Ernst — A730

1991, Oct. 10
1688 A730 100pf multicolored 1.20 .40

Sorbian Legends A731

60pf, Fiddler, water sprite. 100pf, Midday woman, woman from Nochten.

1991, Nov. 5 ***Perf. 13***
1689 A731 60pf multicolored .80 .40
1690 A731 100pf multicolored 1.20 .40

Souvenir Sheet

Wolfgang Amadeus Mozart, Death Bicent. — A732

1991, Nov. 5 Litho. ***Perf. 14***
1691 A732 100pf multicolored 2.00 2.25

Otto Dix (1891-1969), Painter — A733

Designs: 60pf, Portrait of the Dancer Anita Berber. 100pf, Self-portrait.

1991, Nov. 5 Photo. ***Perf. 14***
1692 A733 60pf multicolored .65 .40
1693 A733 100pf multicolored 1.30 .40

Julius Leber (1891-1945), Politician A734

1991, Nov. 5 Litho.
1694 A734 100pf black & red 1.20 .40

Nelly Sachs (1891-1970), Writer — A735

1991, Nov. 5
1695 A735 100pf violet 1.20 .50

City of Koblenz, 2000th Anniv. A736

1992, Jan. 9 ***Perf. 13x12½***
1696 A736 60pf multicolored 1.45 .50

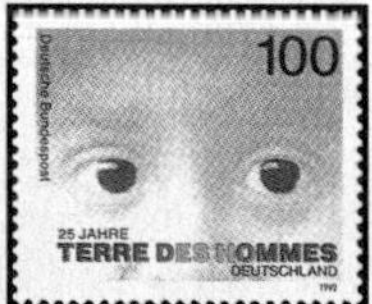

Terre Des Hommes Child Welfare Organization, 25th Anniv. — A737

1992, Jan. 9 Litho. ***Perf. 14***
1697 A737 100pf multicolored 1.30 .55

Martin Niemoller (1892-1984), Theologian A738

1992, Jan. 9
1698 A738 100pf multicolored .95 .40

Coats of Arms of States of the Federal Republic of Germany A739

No. 1699, Baden-Wurttemberg. No. 1700, Bavaria. No. 1701, Berlin. No. 1702, Brandenburg. No. 1703, Bremen. No. 1704, Hamburg. No. 1705, Hesse. No. 1706, Mecklenburg-Western Pomerania. No. 1707, Lower Saxony. No. 1708, North Rhine - Westphalia. No. 1709, Rhineland-Palatinate. No. 1710, Saar. No. 1711, Saxony. No. 1712, Saxony-Anhalt. No. 1713, Schleswig-Holstein. No. 1714, Thuringia.

1992-94 ***Perf. 13½***
1699 100pf multicolored 1.30 .60
1700 100pf multicolored 1.30 .60
1701 100pf multicolored 1.30 .60
1702 100pf multicolored 1.30 .60
1703 100pf multicolored 1.30 .60
1704 100pf multicolored 1.30 .60
1705 100pf multicolored 1.05 .60
1706 100pf multicolored 1.05 .60
1707 100pf multicolored 1.05 .60
1708 100pf multicolored 1.05 .60
1709 100pf multicolored 1.05 .60
1710 100pf multicolored 1.15 .60
1711 100pf multicolored 1.15 .60
1712 100pf multicolored 1.15 .60
1713 100pf multicolored 1.15 .60
1714 100pf multicolored 1.15 .60
Nos. 1699-1714 (16) 18.80 9.60

See No. B818.

Issued: No. 1699, 1/9/92; No. 1700, 3/12/92; No. 1701, 6/11/92; No. 1702, 7/16/92; No. 1703, 8/13/92; No. 1704, 9/10/92; No. 1705, 3/11/93; No. 1706, 6/17/93; No. 1707, 7/15/93; No. 1708, 8/12/93; No. 1709, 9/16/93; No. 1710, 1/13/94; No. 1711, 3/10/94; No. 1712, 6/16/94; No. 1713, 7/14/94; No. 1714, 9/8/94.

Famous Women Type of 1986

80pf, Rahel Varnhagen von Ense (1771-1833), pioneer in women's movement. No. 1724, Elisabeth Schwarzhaupt (1901-86), politician. No. 1725, Louise Henriette of Orange (1627-67), mother of Frederick, King of Prussia. No. 1726, Grethe Weiser (1903-70), actress. No. 1727, Marlene Dietrich (1901-92), actress. No. 1728, Käte Strobel (1907-96), government minister. No. 1729, Marie-Elisabeth Lüders (1878-1966), politician. No. 1730, Marieluise Fleisser (1901-74), writer. No. 1731, Maria Probst (1902-67), politician. No. 1732, Nelly Sachs (1891-1970), writer. 400pf, Charlotte von Stein (1742-1827), confidant of Goethe. 440pf, Gret Palucca (1902-93), dancer. 450pf, Hedwig Courths-Mahler (1867-1950), novelist.

1992-2001 Engr. ***Perf. 14***
1723 A602 80pf blue & brn .75 .40
1724 A602 100pf grn & org brn .85 .65
1725 A602 100pf vio & bis .75 .40
1726 A602 100pf ol bis & bl grn .75 .65
1727 A602 110pf vio & dk brn .85 .55
1728 A602 110pf ol & red brn .80 .65
1729 A602 220pf grn bl & vio bl 1.60 1.60
1730 A602 220pf grn & brn 1.30 1.30
1731 A602 300pf dp blue & brn 2.00 1.60
1732 A602 300pf brn & vio 2.00 2.00
1733 A602 400pf lake & blk 4.50 3.00
1734 A602 440pf dp vio & dk car 5.00 5.00
1735 A602 450pf brt blue & blue 5.00 3.75
Nos. 1723-1735 (13) 26.15 21.55

Issued: 400pf, 1/9/92; 450pf, 6/11/92; 80pf, No. 1725, 10/13/94; No. 1727, 8/14/97; No. 1729, 8/28/97; Nos. 1724, 1731, 10/16/97; 440pf, 10/8/98; Nos. 1726, 1728, 11/9/00; Nos. 1730, 1732, 1/11/01.

Arthur Honegger (1892-1955), Composer A740

1992, Feb. 6 Photo. ***Perf. 14***
1736 A740 100pf sepia & black 1.30 .60

Ferdinand von Zeppelin (1838-1917), Airship Builder — A741

1992, Feb. 6 Litho.
1737 A741 165pf multicolored 2.00 1.05

City of Kiel, 750th Anniv. A742

1992, Mar. 12
1738 A742 60pf multicolored .95 .50

Konrad Adenauer A743

1992, Mar. 12 Photo.
1739 A743 100pf black & dull org 1.60 .50

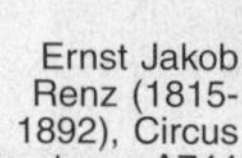

Ernst Jakob Renz (1815-1892), Circus Director — A744

1992, Mar. 12 Litho.
1740 A744 100pf multicolored 1.50 .50

Berlin Sugar Institute, 125th Anniv. A745

1992, Mar. 12 ***Perf. 13x12½***
1741 A745 100pf multicolored 1.50 .70

Johann Adam Schall von Bell (1592-1666), Astronomer and Missionary — A746

1992, Apr. 9 Litho. ***Perf. 13x12½***
1742 A746 140pf multicolored 2.00 1.00

Erfurt, Capital of Thuringia, 1250th Anniv. — A747

1992, May 7 Litho. ***Perf. 14***
1743 A747 60pf multicolored 1.05 .50

Discovery of America, 500th Anniv. — A748

Europa: 60pf, Woodcut illustrating letters from Columbus, 1493. 100pf, Rene de Laudonniere and Chief Athore by Jacques le Moyne de Morgues, 1564.

1992, May 7 ***Perf. 13½***
1744 A748 60pf multicolored *.75 .40*
1745 A748 100pf multicolored *1.50 .40*

Order of Merit, 150th Anniv. — A749

1992, May 7 ***Perf. 13***
1746 A749 100pf multicolored 1.35 .50

St. Ludgerus, 1250th Birth Anniv. — A750

1992, May 7 Litho. ***Perf. 14***
1747 A750 100pf multicolored 1.35 .60

Adam Riese (1492-1559), Mathematician — A751

1992, May 7
1748 A751 100pf multicolored 1.50 .55

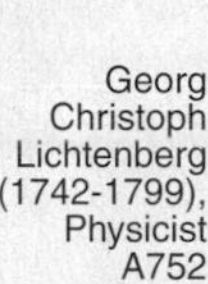

Georg Christoph Lichtenberg (1742-1799), Physicist A752

1992, June 11 Litho. *Perf. 14*
1749 A752 100pf multicolored 1.35 .60

20th Century Paintings — A753

Designs: 60pf, Landscape with a Horse, by Franz Marc (1880-1916). 100pf, Fashion Shop, by August Macke (1887-1914). 170pf, Murnau with a Rainbow, by Wassily Kandinsky (1866-1944).

1992, June 11 Litho. *Perf. 14*
1750 A753 60pf multicolored .75 .60
1751 A753 100pf multicolored 1.15 .60
1752 A753 170pf multicolored 1.90 1.60
Nos. 1750-1752 (3) 3.80 2.80

See Nos. 1878-1880.

Leipzig Botanical Garden A754

1992, July 16 Litho. *Perf. 13x12½*
1753 A754 60pf multicolored .90 .50

Family Living — A755

1992, July 16 *Perf. 13½*
1754 A755 100pf multicolored 1.50 .50

17th World Congress on Home Economics, Hanover — A756

1992, July 16 Photo. *Perf. 14*
1755 A756 100pf multicolored 1.35 .60

Egid Quirin Asam (1692-1750), Architect and Sculptor — A757

1992, Aug. 13 Litho. *Perf. 14*
1756 A757 60pf multicolored 1.15 .50

German State Opera, Berlin, 250th Anniv. A758

1992, Aug. 13
1757 A758 80pf multicolored 1.30 .50

Federation of German Amateur Theaters, Cent. — A759

1992, Aug. 13
1758 A759 100pf multicolored 1.35 .50

Construction of First Globe by Martin Behaim, 500th Anniv. — A760

1992, Sept. 10 *Perf. 13½*
1759 A760 60pf multicolored 1.05 .50

Opening of Main-Danube Canal — A761

1992, Sept. 10 *Perf. 14*
1760 A761 100pf multicolored 1.20 .50

Werner Bergengruen (1892-1964), Writer — A762

1992, Sept. 10
1761 A762 100pf blk, bl & gray 1.20 .50

Jewelry & Watch Industries in Pforzheim, 225th Anniv. — A763

1992, Sept. 10
1762 A763 100pf multicolored 1.20 .50

Balloon Post — A764

1992, Oct. 15 Litho. *Perf. 14*
1763 A764 100pf multicolored 1.35 .60

Stamp Day.

Hugo Distler (1908-1942), Composer A765

1992, Oct. 15
1764 A765 100pf violet & black 1.35 .50

Association of German Plant and Machine Builders, Cent. — A766

1992, Oct. 15 Litho. & Engr.
1765 A766 170pf multicolored 1.75 1.05

Single European Market A767

1992, Nov. 5 Litho. *Perf. 14*
1766 A767 100pf multicolored 1.75 .60

Jochen Klepper (1903-1942), Writer — A768

Litho. & Engr.
1992, Nov. 5 *Perf. 14*
1767 A768 100pf multicolored 1.35 .50

A769

1992, Nov. 5 Photo.
1768 A769 100pf sepia & black 1.35 .50

Werner von Siemens (1816-1892), electrical engineer.

A770

1992, Nov. 5 Litho.
1769 A770 100pf multicolored 1.35 .50

Gebhard Leberecht von Blucher (1742-1819), Commander of Prussian Army.

City of Munster, 1200th Anniv. — A771

1993, Jan. 14 Litho. *Perf. 14*
1770 A771 60pf multicolored .90 .50

Sir Isaac Newton, Scientist A772

1993, Jan. 14 Litho. & Engr.
1771 A772 100pf multicolored 1.30 .50

North German Naval Observatory, Hamburg, 125th Anniv. — A773

1993, Jan. 14 Litho. *Perf. 13x12½*
1772 A773 100pf multicolored 1.05 .50

Health and Safety in Workplace — A774

1993, Jan. 14 Photo. *Perf. 14*
1773 A774 100pf blk, yel & bl 1.15 .50

Association of German Electrical Engineers, Cent. — A775

1993, Jan. 14
1774 A775 170pf multicolored 1.75 1.00

Leipzig Gewandhaus Orchestra, 250th Anniv. — A776

1993, Feb. 11 Litho. *Perf. 13x12½*
1775 A776 100pf black & gold 1.05 .50

St. John of Nepomuk, 600th Death Anniv. — A777

1993, Mar. 11
1776 A777 100pf multicolored 1.20 .50

New Postal Codes A778

1993, Mar. 11 ***Perf. 14***
1777 A778 100pf multicolored 1.50 .50

20th Century German Paintings — A779

Designs: No. 1778, Cafe, by George Grosz (1893-1959). No. 1779, Sea and Sun, by Otto Pankok (1893-1966). No. 1780, Audience, by A. Paul Weber (1893-1980).

1993, Mar. 11
1778 A779 100pf multicolored 1.30 .75
1779 A779 100pf multicolored 1.30 .75
1780 A779 100pf multicolored 1.30 .75
Nos. 1778-1780 (3) 3.90 2.25

See Nos. 1863-1865, 1922-1924.

Benedictine Abbeys of Maria Laach and Bursfelde, 900th Anniv. — A780

Litho. & Engr.
1993, Apr. 15 ***Perf. 14***
1781 A780 80pf multicolored 1.30 .55

5th Intl. Horticultural Show, Stuttgart — A781

1993, Apr. 15 Litho. ***Perf. 13x12½***
1782 A781 100pf multicolored 1.05 .55

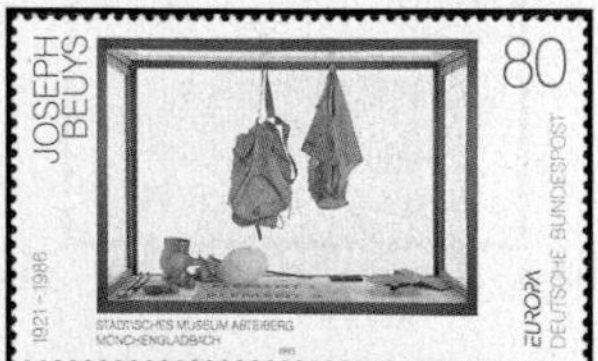

Contemporary Art — A782

Europa: 80pf, Storage Place, by Joseph Beuys (1921-1986). 100pf, Homage to the Square, by Joseph Albers (1888-1976).

1993, May 5 Litho. ***Perf. 13½x14***
1783 A782 80pf multicolored *1.15* *.70*
1784 A782 100pf multicolored *1.15* *.70*

Dahlwitz Hoppegarten (Hippodrome), Berlin, 125th Anniv. — A783

1993, May 5 Litho. ***Perf. 14***
1785 A783 80pf multicolored 1.05 .60

Lake Constance Steamer Hohentwiel — A784

1993, May 5 **Photo.**
1786 A784 100pf multicolored 1.30 .55

See Austria No. 1618, Switzerland No. 931.

Schulpforta School for Boys, 450th Anniv. — A785

1993, May 5 **Litho.**
1787 A785 100pf multicolored 1.05 .55

Coburger Convent, 125th Anniv. A786

1993, May 5 **Litho. & Engr.**
1788 A786 100pf black, green & red 1.05 .55

City of Potsdam, 1000th Anniv. A787

1993, June 17 Litho. ***Perf. 13x12½***
1789 A787 80pf multicolored 1.30 .55

German UNICEF Committee, 40th Anniv. — A788

1993, June 17 Litho. ***Perf. 14***
1790 A788 100pf multicolored 1.05 .50

Friedrich Holderlin (1770-1843), Writer — A789

1993, June 17 Photo. ***Perf. 14***
1791 A789 100pf multicolored 1.30 .50

Hans Fallada (1893-1947), Novelist — A790

1993, July 15
1792 A790 100pf multicolored 1.35 .50

Scenic Regions in Germany — A791

No. 1793, Rugen Island. No. 1794, Harz Mountains. No. 1795, Rhon Mountains. No. 1796, Bavarian Alps. No. 1797, Ore Mountains. No. 1798, Main River Valley. No. 1799, Mecklenburg lake district. No. 1800, Franconian Switzerland. No. 1801, Upper Lusatia. No. 1802, Sauerland. No. 1803, Havel River, Berlin. No. 1804, Holstein Switzerland. No. 1805, Saale. No. 1806, Spreewald. No. 1807, Eifel.

1993-96 Litho. ***Perf. 14***
Denominations 100pf
1793 A791 multicolored 1.40 .75
1794 A791 multicolored 1.40 .75
1795 A791 multicolored 1.40 .75
1796 A791 multicolored 1.10 .80
1797 A791 multicolored 1.10 .80
1798 A791 multicolored 1.10 .80
1799 A791 multicolored 1.10 .80
1800 A791 multicolored .80 .80
1801 A791 multicolored .80 .80
1802 A791 multicolored .80 .80
1803 A791 multicolored .80 .80
1804 A791 multicolored 1.00 .80
1805 A791 multicolored 1.00 .80
1806 A791 multicolored 1.00 .80
1807 A791 multicolored 1.00 .80
Nos. 1793-1807 (15) 15.80 11.85

Issued: Nos. 1793-1795, 7/15/93; Nos. 1796-1799, 7/14/94; Nos. 1800-1803, 7/6/95; Nos. 1804-1807, 4/11/96.

See Nos. 1938, 1974-1976, 2072-2073.

Mathias Klotz (1653-1743), Violin Maker — A792

1993, Aug. 12 Litho. ***Perf. 13x12½***
1808 A792 80pf multicolored 1.10 .50

Heinrich George (1893-1946), Actor — A793

1993, Aug. 12 ***Perf. 14***
1809 A793 100pf multicolored 1.10 .60

Intl. Radio Exhibition, Berlin — A794

1993, Aug. 12
1810 A794 100pf multicolored 1.30 .60

Hans Leip (1893-1983), Poet and Painter A795

1993, Sept. 16 Litho. ***Perf. 13***
1811 A795 100pf red, black & blue 1.60 .60

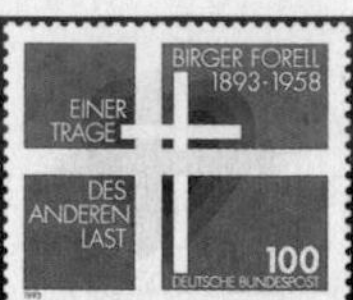

Birger Forell (1893-1958), Swedish Priest — A796

1993, Sept. 16 ***Perf. 14***
1812 A796 100pf multicolored 1.60 .60

Souvenir Sheet

For the Children — A797

1993, Sept. 16
1813 A797 100pf multicolored 2.00 1.75

Peter I. Tchaikovsky (1840-93), Composer — A798

1993, Oct. 14
1814 A798 80pf multicolored 1.40 .60

Max Reinhardt (1873-1943), Theatrical Director — A799

1993, Oct. 14
1815 A799 100pf buff, blk & red 1.50 .55

St. Hedwig of Silesia, 750th Death Anniv. — A800

1993, Oct. 14
1816 A800 100pf multicolored 1.60 .50

See Poland No. 3176.

Paracelsus (1493-1541), Physician, Teacher — A801

Litho. & Engr.
1993, Nov. 10 ***Perf. 14***
1817 A801 100pf multicolored 1.50 .55

Claudio Monteverdi (1567-1643), Composer — A802

1993, Nov. 10 Litho. *Perf. 13x12½*
1818 A802 100pf multicolored 1.50 .55

Willy Brandt (1913-92), Statesman A803

1993, Nov. 10 *Perf. 14*
1819 A803 100pf multicolored 2.10 .90

Staade, 1000th Anniv. A804

Litho. & Engr.

1994, Jan. 13. *Perf. 14*
1820 A804 80pf multicolored 1.10 .50

Intl. Year of the Family A805

1994, Jan. 13 Litho.
1821 A805 100pf multicolored 1.45 .70

Heinrich Hertz (1857-94), Physicist — A806

1994, Jan. 13 *Perf. 13x12½*
1822 A806 200pf multicolored 2.60 1.05

Frankfurt Am Main, 1200th Anniv. A807

1994, Feb. 10
1823 A807 80pf multicolored 1.10 .55

Fulda, 1250th Anniv. A808

1994, Mar. 10 *Perf. 14*
1824 A808 80pf multicolored 1.25 .55

German Women's Associations, German Women's Council, Cent. — A809

1994, Mar. 10 *Perf. 13x12½*
1825 A809 100pf blk, red & yel 1.45 .60

Fourth European Parliamentary Elections — A810

1994, Mar. 10 *Perf. 14*
1826 A810 100pf multicolored 1.60 .70

Foreigners in Germany: Living Together — A811

1994, Mar. 10
1827 A811 100pf multicolored 1.15 .70

Church of Our Lady, Munich, 500th Anniv. A812

1994, Apr. 14 Litho. *Perf. 14*
1828 A812 100pf multicolored 1.90 .75

Europa A813

Designs: 80pf, Ohm's Law, by Georg Simon Ohm. 100pf, Quantum theory, by Max Planck.

1994, May 5 Photo.
1829 A813 80pf multicolored *1.05* .45
1830 A813 100pf multicolored *1.05* .45
Bklt. of 10, #1830 14.00 13.00

Souvenir Sheet

Carl Hagenbeck (1844-1913), Circus Director, Animal Trainer, and Berlin Zoo, 150th Anniv. — A814

Designs: a, Hagenbeck, circus animals, zoo entrance. b, Zoo entrance, animals.

1994, May 5 Litho.
1831 A814 Sheet of 2 3.75 4.25
a. 100pf multicolored 1.60 1.50
b. 200pf multicolored 2.00 1.90

Hans Pfitzner (1869-1949), Composer, Conductor — A815

1994, May 5
1832 A815 100pf multicolored 1.45 .60

Spandau Fortress, 400th Anniv. A816

1994, June 16 Litho. *Perf. 14*
1833 A816 80pf multicolored 1.20 .55

Herzogsagmuhle, Social Welfare Organization, Cent. — A817

1994, June 16 *Perf. 13*
1834 A817 100pf blue, yel & blk 1.20 .60

Emperor Frederick II (1194-1250) A818

1994, June 16 *Perf. 13½x14*
1835 A818 400pf multicolored 4.50 3.75

Souvenir Sheet

Attempt to Assassinate Hitler, 50th Anniv. — A819

1994, July 20 Litho. *Perf. 14*
1836 A819 100pf multicolored 2.00 2.60

Historic Sites Type of 1987

No. 1838, Wernigerode Town Hall. No. 1839, Böttcherstrasse, Bremen. No. 1840, Berus Monument, Uberherrn. No. 1841, Wilhelmshöhe Hillside Park, Kassel. No. 1842, Kirchheim Castle. No. 1843, St. Reinoldi Church, Dortmund. No. 1844, Goethe-Schiller Monument. No. 1845, Schwerin Castle, Weimar. No. 1846, Bellevue Castle, Berlin. No. 1847, EXPO 2000, Hanover. No. 1848, Regensburg Stone Bridge. No. 1849, Brühl's Terrace, Dresden. No. 1850, St. Nikolai Cathedral, Greifswald. No. 1851, Grimma Town Hall. No. 1852, Wartburg Castle, Eisenach. No. 1853, Town hall, Bremen. No. 1854, Cologne Cathedral. No. 1855, Holsten Gate, Lübeck. No. 1856, Heidelberg Castle. No. 1857, Town Hall, Suhl-Heinrichs. No. 1858, Speyer Cathedral. No. 1859, St. Michael's Church, Hamburg. No. 1860, Hildesheim Town Hall.

1994-2001 Typo. *Perf. 14*
1838 A623 10pf multi .50 .40
1839 A623 20pf dk bl & brn org .80 .75
1840 A623 47pf grn & gray .50 .45
1841 A623 47pf dk grn & gray .50 .45
1842 A623 50pf vio brn & beige .80 .75
1843 A623 80pf dull grn & sepia .75 .60
1844 A623 100pf bl & blk .80 .75
a. Booklet pane of 10 9.00 8.25
Complete booklet, #1844a 9.75
1845 A623 100pf multi 1.20 1.10
1846 A623 110pf dk gray & buff .90 .40
a. Booklet pane of 10 9.00 8.25
Complete booklet, #1846a 9.75
1847 A623 110pf org & bl 1.05 .60
a. Booklet pane of 10 11.50 10.50
Complete booklet, #1847a 11.50
1848 A623 110pf multi 1.10 1.10
a. Booklet pane of 10 12.00 11.50
Booklet, #1848a 13.00
1849 A623 220pf grn & blk 1.60 .75
1850 A623 220pf multi 2.00 1.90
1851 A623 300pf brn & ind 2.40 2.25
1852 A623 400pf vio brn & beige 3.25 3.00
1853 A623 440pf multi 4.00 3.50
1854 A623 440pf blk & gray 4.00 3.75
1855 A623 510pf red brn & ind 4.00 3.75
1856 A623 510pf brn & bls brn 4.50 4.25
1857 A623 550pf multi 5.25 2.25
1858 A623 640pf rose brn & gray bl 7.00 3.75
1859 A623 690pf blk & grn 5.75 3.00
1860 A623 720pf dk gray & lil 6.50 6.00
Nos. 1838-1860 (23) 59.15 45.50

Issued: 550pf, 8/11/94; 640pf, 8/10/95; 690pf, 6/13/96; 47pf, 7/17/97; Nos. 1846, 1849, 1853, 8/14/97: Nos. 1844, 1855, 8/28/97; No. 1847, 9/10/98; 10pf, No. 1848, 300pf, 9/28/00; No. 1845, 1/11/01. No. 1841, 80pf, 4/5/01. 720pf, 7/2/01. Nos. 1850, 1854, 8/9/01. 50pf, No. 1852, 9/5/01. 20pf, No. 1856, 11/8/01.

Nos. 1839, 1841, 1842, 1845, 1850, 1852, 1854, 1856 and 1860 are denominated in pfennigs and euros.

Johann Gottfried Herder (1744-1803), Theologian A820

1994, Aug. 11 Photo. *Perf. 14*
1862 A820 80pf multicolored 1.00 .50

Paintings Type of 1993

Designs: 100pf, Maika, by Christian Schad. 200pf, Landscape, by Erich Heckel. 300pf, Couple Lying on Grass, by Gabriele Munter.

1994, Aug. 11 Litho. *Perf. 14*
1863 A779 100pf multicolored 1.00 .60
1864 A779 200pf multicolored 1.75 1.50
1865 A779 300pf multicolored 2.60 2.40
Nos. 1863-1865 (3) 5.35 4.50

Ethnological Museum, Leipzig, 125th Anniv. — A821

1994, Sept. 8 Litho. *Perf. 13x12½*
1866 A821 80pf multicolored 1.00 .55

Hermann von Helmholtz (1821-94), Scientist — A822

Litho. & Engr.

1994, Sept. 8 *Perf. 13½x14*
1867 A822 100pf multicolored 1.45 .55

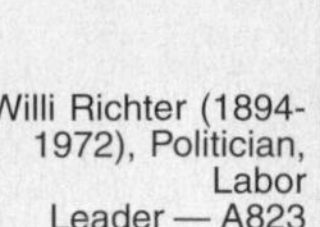

Willi Richter (1894-1972), Politician, Labor Leader — A823

1994, Sept. 8 **Litho.**
1868 A823 100pf multicolored 1.20 .50

Souvenir Sheet

For the Children — A824

1994, Sept. 8 ***Perf. 14***
1869 A824 100pf multicolored 2.00 1.90

Hans Sachs (1494-1576), Singer & Poet — A825

1994, Oct. 13 **Engr.** ***Perf. 13½x14***
1870 A825 100pf olive & maroon 1.20 .60

St. Wolfgang (924-94), Bishop of Regensburg A826

1994, Oct. 13 **Litho.** ***Perf. 14***
1871 A826 100pf multicolored 1.20 .60

Mail Delivery, Spreewald Region, c. 1900 — A827

1994, Oct. 13
1872 A827 100pf multicolored 1.45 .60

Stamp Day.

Quedlinburg, 1000th Anniv. — A828

Litho. & Engr.

1994, Nov. 9 ***Perf. 14***
1873 A828 80pf multicolored 1.00 .55

Opening of the Berlin Wall, 5th Anniv. A829

1994, Nov. 9 **Litho.** ***Perf. 13x12½***
1874 A829 100pf black, org & yel 1.20 .60

Natl. Assoc. for Preservation of German Graves Abroad, 75th Anniv. — A830

1994, Nov. 9 ***Perf. 14***
1875 A830 100pf black & red 1.20 .60

Theodore Fontane (1819-98), Poet — A831

1994, Nov. 9 ***Perf. 13½x14***
1876 A831 100pf multicolored 1.20 .60

Baron Friedrich von Steuben (1730-94) A832

1994, Nov. 9 ***Perf. 14***
1877 A832 100pf multicolored 1.20 .60

Paintings Type of 1992

Designs: 100pf, The Water Tower in Bremen, by Franz Radziwill. 200pf, Still Life with a Cat, by Georg Schrimpf. 300pf, An Estate in Dangast, by Karl Schmidt-Rottluff.

1995, Jan. 12 **Litho.** ***Perf. 14***
1878 A753 100pf multicolored 1.20 .55
1879 A753 200pf multicolored 1.90 1.50
1880 A753 300pf multicolored 3.00 2.25
Nos. 1878-1880 (3) 6.10 4.30

Province of Gera, 1000th Anniv. — A833

1995, Jan. 12 ***Perf. 13½x13***
1881 A833 80pf multicolored 1.20 .55

Diet of Worms, 500th Anniv. A834

1995, Jan. 12 ***Perf. 13x12½***
1882 A834 100pf multicolored 1.20 .60

Frederick William of Brandenburg, the Great Elector (1620-88) A835

1995, Feb. 9 **Litho.** ***Perf. 14***
1883 A835 300pf multicolored 3.25 2.40

Conf. of General Convention on Climate, Berlin — A836

1995, Mar. 9 **Litho.** ***Perf. 14***
1884 A836 100pf multicolored 1.00 .60

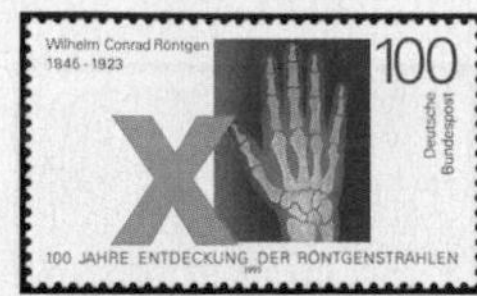

W.K. Roentgen (1845-1923) — A837

1995, Mar. 9
1885 A837 100pf multicolored 1.00 .60

Carolo-Wilhelmina Technical University, Braunschweig, 250th Anniv. — A838

1995, Mar. 9
1886 A838 100pf multicolored 1.15 .60

Former State of Mecklenburg, 1000th Anniv. — A839

1995, Mar. 9
1887 A839 100pf multicolored 1.00 .60

City of Regensburg, 750th Anniv. — A840

1995, Apr. 6 **Litho.** ***Perf. 14***
1888 A840 80pf multicolored .90 .55

Freedom of Expression A841

1995, Apr. 6 **Photo.**
1889 A841 100pf multicolored 1.00 .60

Dietrich Bonhoeffer (1906-45), Protestant Theologian — A842

1995, Apr. 6
1890 A842 100pf multicolored 1.00 .60

Johann Conrad Schlaun (1695-1773), Architect A843

1995, Apr. 6 **Litho.** ***Perf. 13***
1891 A843 200pf multicolored 2.00 1.60

Vincent Conferences in Germany, 150th Anniv. — A844

1995, May 5 **Litho.** ***Perf. 14***
1892 A844 100pf multicolored 1.00 .70

Schiller Society, Cent. — A845

1995, May 5 **Photo.**
1893 A845 100pf multicolored 1.00 .60

End of World War II, 50th Anniv. — A846

Designs: No. 1894, End of the war. 200pf, Moving towards United Europe.

No. 1896, Liberation of concentration camps. No. 1897: a, Destruction of buildings. b, Refugees.

1995, May 5 **Litho.** ***Perf. 14***
1894 A846 100pf red & black *1.20* *.75*
1895 A846 200pf bl, gray, yel & blk *1.75* *1.50*

Souvenir Sheets

1896 A846 100pf multicolored 1.60 *1.90*
1897 Sheet of 2 3.00 *3.00*
a.-b. A846 100pf any single 1.40 1.30

Europa (Nos. 1894-1895).

Kiel Canal, Cent. — A847

1995, June 8 **Litho.** ***Perf. 14***
1898 A847 80pf multicolored 1.20 .50

UN, 50th Anniv. — A848

1995, June 8
1899 A848 100pf gold, lil & gray 1.00 .60

Radio, Cent. A849

100pf, Marconi, wireless apparatus.

1995, June 8
1900 A849 100pf multicolored .90 .85

See Ireland Nos. 973-974, Italy 2038-2039, San Marino Nos. 1336-1337, Vatican City Nos. 978-979.

Carl Orff (1895-1982), Composer — A850

1995, July 6 Litho. *Perf. 13x13½*
1901 A850 100pf multicolored 1.10 .60

Henry the Lion, Duke of Bavaria (1129-95) A851

1995, July 6 *Perf. 14*
1902 A851 400pf multicolored 3.75 3.00

Kaiser Wilhelm Memorial Church, Berlin, Cent. — A852

1995, Aug. 10 Photo. *Perf. 14*
1903 A852 100pf multicolored 1.25 .60

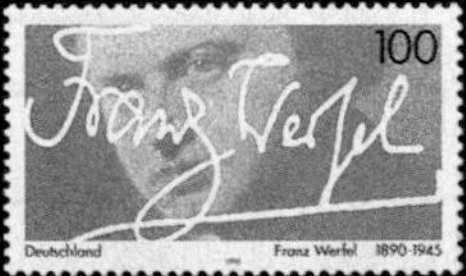

Franz Werfel (1890-1945), Author — A853

1995, Aug. 10 Litho.
1904 A853 100pf multicolored 1.10 .60

Franz Josef Strauss (1915-88), Politician A854

1995, Sept. 6 Photo. *Perf. 14x13½*
1905 A854 100pf multicolored 1.35 .75

Souvenir Sheet

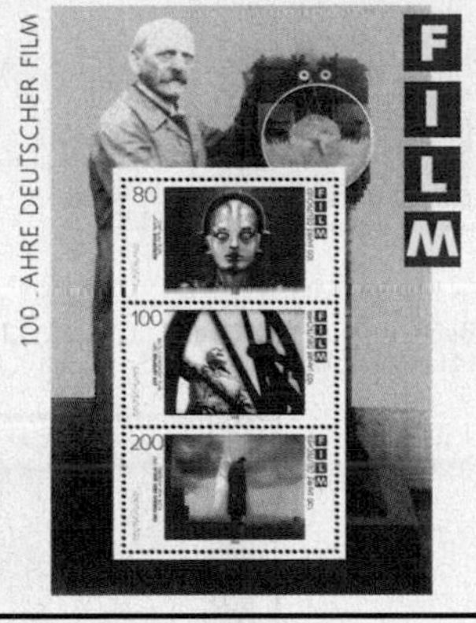

German Film, Cent. — A855

1995, Sept. 6 *Perf. 14*
1906 A855 Sheet of 3 5.50 *7.50*
a. 80pf Metropolis 1.35 1.50
b. 100pf Little Superman 1.35 1.50
c. 200pf The Sky Over Berlin 2.50 3.00

Kurt Schumacher (1895-1952), Politician A856

1995, Oct. 12 Litho. *Perf. 13*
1907 A856 100pf multicolored 1.10 .60

Souvenir Sheet

For the Children — A857

1995, Oct. 12 *Perf. 14*
1908 A857 100pf multicolored 2.25 *3.00*

Leopold von Ranke (1795-1886), Historian A858

1995, Nov. 9 Litho. *Perf. 14*
1909 A858 80pf multicolored .90 .55

Paul Hindemith (1895-1963), Composer A859

1995, Nov. 9
1910 A859 100pf multicolored 1.10 .60

Nobel Prize Fund Established, Cent. — A860

1995, Nov. 9 Litho. & Engr.
1911 A860 100pf Nobel, last will 1.45 .90

See Sweden Nos. 2155-2158.

CARE, 50th Anniv. A861

1995, Nov. 9 Litho. *Perf. 13x12½*
1912 A861 100pf multicolored 1.10 .60

Victims of a Divided Germany, 1945-89 A862

1995, Nov. 9 *Perf. 14*
1913 A862 100pf Berlin Wall 1.20 .60

Borussia Dortmund, Soccer Champions — A863

1995, Dec. 6 Photo. *Perf. 14*
1914 A863 100pf multicolored 1.50 .75

Children's Missionary Work in Germany, Cent. — A864

1996, Jan. 11 Litho. *Perf. 14*
1915 A864 100pf multicolored 1.10 .70

Friedrich von Bodelschwingh (1877-1946), Protestant Theologian A865

1996, Jan. 11 *Perf. 13½*
1916 A865 100pf black & red 1.10 .70

Martin Luther (1483-1546), Theologian A866

1996, Feb. 8 Litho. *Perf. 14*
1917 A866 100pf multicolored 1.20 .85

Philipp Franz von Siebold (1796-1866), Physician and Diplomat — A867

1996, Feb. 17 *Perf. 13x12½*
1918 A867 100pf multicolored 1.20 .85

Cathedral Square, Halberstadt, 1000th Anniv. — A868

1996, Mar. 7 Litho. *Perf. 13*
1919 A868 80pf multicolored .90 .45

August Cardinal Graf von Galen (1878-1946) A869

1996, Mar. 7 *Perf. 13½*
1920 A869 100pf bl, gray & bis 1.10 .60

Giovanni Battista Tiepolo (1696-1770), Painter — A870

1996, Mar. 7 *Perf. 13*
1921 A870 200pf multicolored 2.00 1.45

20th Century German Paintings Type of 1993

Designs: 100pf, Sitting Female Nude, by Max Pechstein (1881-1955). 200pf, Abstract For Wilhelm Runge, by Georg Muche (1895-1987). 300pf, Still Life with Guitar, Book and Vase, by Helmut Kolle (1899-1931).

1996, Mar. 7 *Perf. 14*
1922 A779 100pf multicolored 1.10 .75
1923 A779 200pf multicolored 2.10 1.50
1924 A779 300pf multicolored 2.75 2.25
Nos. 1922-1924 (3) 5.95 4.50

Souvenir Sheet

For the Children — A871

100pf, Racing messenger.

1996, Apr. 11 Litho. *Perf. 14*
1925 A871 100pf multi 2.00 1.75

Famous Women — A872

Europa: 80pf, Self-portrait, by Paula Modersohn-Becker (1876-1907). 100pf, Self-portrait, by Käthe Kollwitz (1867-1945).

1996, May 3

1926 A872 80pf multicolored *1.20* *.40*
1927 A872 100pf red & black *1.20* *.75*

Freising's Right to Hold Markets, 1000th Anniv. A873

1996, May 3

1928 A873 100pf multicolored .90 .70

Wolfgang Borchert (1921-47), Writer — A874

1996, May 3 *Perf. 13*

1929 A874 100pf multicolored .90 .70

Ruhr Festival, Recklinghausen, 50th Anniv. — A875

1996, May 3

1930 A875 100pf multicolored .90 .70

German Theater Assoc., 150th Anniv. — A876

1996, May 3 **Photo.** *Perf. 14*

1931 A876 200pf multicolored 1.75 1.10

Academy of Arts in Berlin, 300th Anniv. A877

1996, June 13 **Litho.** *Perf. 13*

1932 A877 100pf multicolored .90 .70

Gottfried Wilhelm Leibniz (1646-1716), Mathematician, Philosopher — A878

1996, June 13 *Perf. 14*

1933 A878 100pf multicolored .90 .70

City of Heidelberg, 800th Anniv. — A879

1996, July 18 **Litho.** *Perf. 14*

1934 A879 100pf multicolored .90 .70
Complete booklet, 10 #1934 13.00

UNICEF, 50th Anniv. A880

1996, July 18

1935 A880 100pf multicolored .90 .70

Ludwig Thoma (1867-1921), Satirist A881

1996, July 18 *Perf. 13x13½*

1936 A881 100pf multicolored .90 .70

Souvenir Sheet

German Natl. Parks — A882

1996, July 18 *Perf. 14*

1937 A882 Sheet of 3 7.25 6.00
a. 100pf Coastal 1.75 1.50
b. 200pf Mudflat 1.75 1.50
c. 300pf Sea-inlet 3.25 2.60

Scenic Regions Type of 1993

"Gendarmenmarkt," central district of Berlin.

1996, Aug. 14 **Litho.** *Perf. 14*

1938 A791 100pf multicolored .90 .70

Assoc. of German Philatelists, 50th Anniv. — A883

1996, Aug. 14 **Photo.** *Perf. 14*

1939 A883 100pf multicolored .90 .70

Paul Lincke (1866-1946), Musician, Composer A884

1996, Aug. 14 **Litho.** *Perf. 13*

1940 A884 100pf multicolored .90 .70

UNESCO World Cultural Heritage A885

Design: Closed blast furnace, Völklingen.

1996, Aug. 14 *Perf. 13½*

1941 A885 100pf multicolored .90 .70

German Civil Code, Cent. — A886

1996, Aug. 14

1942 A886 300pf multicolored 3.00 2.25

Borussia Dortmund, Champion Soccer Club — A887

1996, Aug. 27

1943 A887 100pf multicolored 1.20 .70

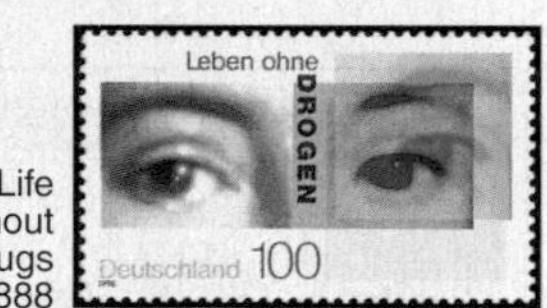

Life Without Drugs A888

1996, Sept. 12 **Photo.** *Perf. 14*

1944 A888 100pf multicolored 1.00 .70

UNESCO World Cultural Heritage A889

Design: Old Town, Bamberg

1996, Sept. 12 **Litho.** *Perf. 14*

1945 A889 100pf multicolored 1.00 .70

Homeopathic Medicine, Bicent. — A890

Samuel Hahnemann (1755-1843), physician.

1996, Sept. 12 **Litho.** *Perf. 14*

1946 A890 400pf multicolored 3.75 3.25

Anton Bruckner (1824-96), Composer A891

1996, Oct. 9 **Litho.** *Perf. 13*

1947 A891 100pf multicolored 1.00 .70

Donaueschingen Music Festival, 75th Anniv. — A892

1996, Oct. 18 **Litho.** *Perf. 13½*

1948 A892 100pf multicolored 1.00 .70

Baron Ferdinand von Mueller (1825-96), Botanist — A893

Litho. & Engr.

1996, Oct. 18 *Perf. 14*

1949 A893 100pf multicolored 1.00 .70

See Australia No. 1566.

Carl Zuckmayer (1896-1977), Playwright A894

1996, Nov. 14 **Litho.** *Perf. 13*

1950 A894 100pf red, gray & blue 1.00 .70

Carlo Schmid (1896-1979), Politician, Scholar & Writer — A895

1996, Dec. 3 **Photo.** *Perf. 14*

1951 A895 100pf multicolored .90 .70

Franz Schubert (1797-1828), Composer A896

1997, Jan. 16 **Litho.** *Perf. 14*

1952 A896 100pf multicolored 1.00 .70

Sepp Herberger (1897-1977), Soccer Coach — A897

1997, Jan. 16

1953 A897 100pf multicolored 1.10 .70

Traffic Safety for Children A898

1997, Jan. 16

1954 A898 100pf multicolored 1.00 .70

See No. 1979.

Philipp Melanchthon (1497-1560), Protestant Reformer A899

1997, Feb. 4 Litho. *Perf. 14*

1955 A899 100pf multicolored 1.00 .70

Cologne Carnival, 175th Anniv. — A900

1997, Feb. 4

1956 A900 100pf multicolored 1.00 .70

Chancellor Ludwig Erhard (1897-1977) A901

1997, Feb. 4 Photo.

1957 A901 100pf multicolored 1.10 .70

Leipzig Fair, 500th Anniv. A902

1997, Mar. 6 *Perf. 13x12½*

1958 A902 100pf red, sil & blue 1.00 .70

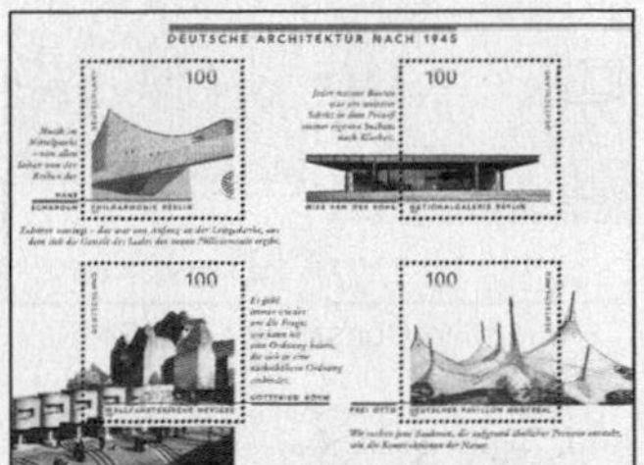

German Architecture after 1945 — A903

Building, architect: a, Berlin Philharmonic, by Hans Scharoun. b, New National Gallery, Berlin, by Ludwig Mies van der Rohe. c, St. Mary, Queen of Peace Church, Neviges, by Gottfried Böhm. d, German Pavilion, 1967 World's Fair, Montreal, by Frei Otto.

1997, Mar. 6 Litho. *Perf. 14*

1959 A903 Sheet of 4 5.50 6.00

a.-d. 100pf any single 1.25 1.20

City of Straubing, 1100th Anniv. — A904

1997, Mar. 10 *Perf. 13x12½*

1960 A904 100pf multicolored 1.10 .70

Heinrich von Stephan (1831-97) — A905

1997, Apr. 8 Litho. *Perf. 14*

1961 A905 100pf multicolored 1.20 .70

Augustusburg and Falkenlust Castles, UNESCO World Heritage Sites — A906

1997, Apr. 8

1962 A906 100pf multicolored 1.00 .70

Idar-Oberstein Gem & Jewelry Industry, 500th Anniv. — A907

1997, Apr. 8 *Perf. 13½*

1963 A907 300pf multicolored 3.25 2.60

St. Adalbert (956-997) — A908

1997, Apr. 23 Engr. *Perf. 14*

1964 A908 100pf deep violet 1.00 .70

See Poland No. 3337, Czech Republic No. 3012, Hungary No. 3569, Vatican City No. 1040.

Stories and Legends A909

Europa: 80pf, Fisherman and his Wife. 100pf, Rübezahl of Riesengebirge (Giant Mountains).

1997, May 5 Litho. *Perf. 14*

1965 A909 80pf multicolored *1.25 .60*

1966 A909 100pf multicolored *1.25 .75*

Sister Cities Movement, 50th Anniv. — A910

1997, May 5

1967 A910 100pf multicolored 1.10 .70

Souvenir Sheet

Society for Protection of German Forests, 50th Anniv. — A911

1997, May 5

1968 A911 Sheet of 2 4.00 3.75

a. 100pf multicolored 1.75 1.50

b. 200pf multicolored 1.75 1.50

Fr. Sebastian Kneipp (1821-97), Hydrotherapist A912

1997, June 9 *Perf. 13*

1969 A912 100pf multicolored 1.20 .70

Marshall Plan, 50th Anniv. A913

1997, June 9 *Perf. 13*

1970 A913 100pf multicolored 1.10 .70

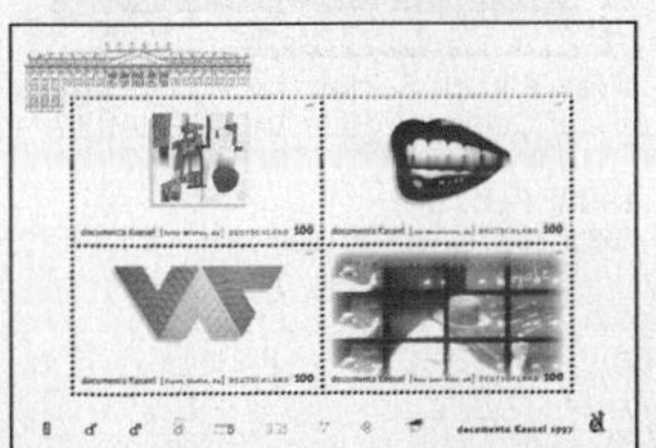
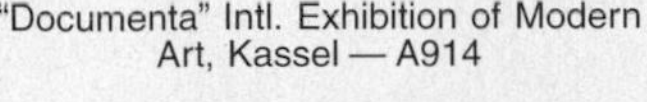

"Documenta" Intl. Exhibition of Modern Art, Kassel — A914

Designs: a, Composition, by Fritz Winter, 1956. b, Mouth No. 15, by Tom Wesselmann, 1968. c, Quathlamba, by Frank Stella, 1964. d, Video sculpture, Beuys/Bois, by Nam June Paik.

1997, June 20 Litho. *Perf. 14*

1971 A914 100pf Sheet of 4, #a.-d. 5.50 5.75

a.-d. 100pf any single

Müngsten Bridge, Cent. — A915

1997, June 20 Litho. *Perf. 13½*

1972 A915 100pf multicolored 1.00 .70

Souvenir Sheet

For the Children — A916

1997, July 17 Photo. *Perf. 13½*

1973 A916 100pf multicolored 2.00 1.90

Scenic Regions Type of 1993

No. 1974, Bavarian Forest. No. 1975, Lüneburg Heath. No. 1976, North German Moorland.

1997, Aug. 28 Litho. *Perf. 14*

1974 A791 110pf multicolored 1.20 .75

1975 A791 110pf multicolored 1.20 .75

1976 A791 110pf multicolored 1.20 .75

Nos. 1974-1976 (3) 3.60 2.25

Centenary of Rudolf Diesel's Engine A917

1997, Aug. 28 *Perf. 13*

1977 A917 300pf blue & gray 3.25 2.25

Cultivation of Potatoes in Germany, 350th Anniv. — A918

1997, Sept. 17 Litho. *Perf. 13*

1978 A918 300pf multicolored 2.75 2.25

Traffic Safety for Children Type

1997, Oct. 9 Litho. *Perf. 14*

1979 A898 10pf like #1954 .40 .25

Felix Mendelssohn-Bartholdy (1809-47), Composer — A919

1997, Oct. 9 ***Perf. 13x13½***
1980 A919 110pf multicolored 1.10 .75

FC Bayern Munchen, 1997 German Soccer Champions — A920

1997, Oct. 16 **Photo.** ***Perf. 14***
1981 A920 110pf multicolored 1.20 .75

Third Saar-Lorraine-Luxembourg Summit — A921

1997, Oct. 16 **Litho.**
1982 A921 110pf multicolored 1.20 .75

See Luxembourg No. 972, France No. 2613.

Charitable Assoc. of the German Catholic Church, Cent. — A922

1997, Nov. 6 **Photo.** ***Perf. 14***
1983 A922 110pf multicolored 1.10 .75

Heinrich Heine (1797-1856), Poet — A923

1997, Nov. 6 **Litho.** ***Perf. 13***
1984 A923 110pf multicolored *1.10* *.75*

No. 1984 was sold in sheets of 10. It was withdrawn from sale 11/18/97, because runes associated with Nazi Germany were printed on the decorative selvage of the sheet. Value of withdrawn sheet of 10, $35. It was again placed on sale in sheets with runes removed.

Gerhard Tersteegen (1697-1769), Author of Religious Hymns, Booklets — A924

1997, Nov. 6 ***Perf. 14***
1985 A924 110pf multicolored 1.10 .75

Thomas Dehler (1897-1967), Politician — A925

1997, Nov. 6
1986 A925 110pf multicolored 1.10 .75

Cistercian Monastery Maulbronn, UNESCO World Heritage Site — A926

1998, Jan. 22 **Litho.** ***Perf. 14***
1987 A926 100pf multicolored 1.10 .75

Glienicke Bridge, Berlin — A927

1998, Jan. 22
1988 A927 110pf multicolored 1.10 .75

City of Nördlingen, 1100th Anniv. — A928

1998, Jan. 22
1989 A928 110pf multicolored 1.10 .75
a. Booklet pane of 10 12.00 9.75
Complete booklet, #1989a + 20 self-adhesive labels 13.00

Bertolt Brecht (1898-1956), Playwright A929

1998, Feb. 5
1990 A929 110pf multicolored 1.10 .75

Max Planck Society for Advancement of Science, 50th Anniv. — A930

1998, Feb. 5
1991 A930 110pf multicolored 1.10 .75

Town of Bad Frankenhausen, 1000th Anniv. — A931

1998, Mar. 12 **Litho.** ***Perf. 13***
1992 A931 110pf multicolored 1.10 .75

Peace of Westphalia, End of Thirty Years' War, 350th Anniv. — A932

1998, Mar. 12 ***Perf. 14***
1993 A932 110pf black & red 1.10 .75

German State Parliament Buildings — A933

Designs: No. 1994, Baden-Württemberg. No. 1995, Bavaria. No. 1996, Chamber of Deputies, Berlin. No. 1997, Brandenburg.

1998, Mar. 12
1994 A933 110pf multicolored 1.20 .75
1995 A933 110pf multicolored 1.20 .75
1996 A933 110pf multicolored 1.20 .75
1997 A933 110pf multicolored 1.20 .75
Nos. 1994-1997 (4) 4.80 3.00

See Nos. 2027, 2029-2031, 2074-2077, 2113-2116.

Hildegard von Bingen (1098-1179), Christian Mystic — A934

1998, Apr. 16
1998 A934 100pf multicolored 1.10 .75

Cistercian Abbey of St. Marienstern, Panschwitz-Kuckau, 750th Anniv. — A935

1998, Apr. 16 ***Perf. 13x12½***
1999 A935 110pf multicolored 1.10 .75

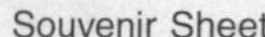
Souvenir Sheet

For the Children — A936

1998, Apr. 16 ***Perf. 14***
2000 A936 110pf multicolored 2.25 1.90

Bayreuth Opera, 250th Anniv. — A937

1998, Apr. 16 ***Perf. 13½***
2001 A937 300pf multicolored 3.25 2.40

Ernst Jünger (1895-1998), Writer — A938

1998, Apr. 22 ***Perf. 14***
2002 A938 110pf multicolored 1.20 .75

German Rural Women's Assoc. A939

1998, May 7 **Litho.** ***Perf. 13***
2003 A939 110pf multicolored 1.20 .75

Europa and German Reunification Day — A940

1998, May 7 ***Perf. 14½x14***
2004 A940 110pf multicolored 1.50 .75

Souvenir Sheet

German Constitution — A941

Designs: a, Parliamentary Council, Bonn, 1948, convening to draw up constitution. b, Natl. Assembly, St. Paul's Church, Frankfurt, 1848, electing pan-German constitutional Parliament.

1998, May 7 ***Perf. 14***
2005 A941 Sheet of 2 4.50 5.25
a. 110pf multicolored 2.25 2.25
b. 220pf multicolored 2.25 2.25

Congress of German Catholics, 150th Anniv. — A942

1998, June 10 Litho. ***Perf. 13x13½***
2006 A942 110pf multicolored 1.20 .70

Deutsche Mark, 50th Anniv. — A943

1998, June 19 ***Perf. 13***
2007 A943 110pf multicolored 2.00 .90

German Cultivation of Hops — A944

1998, July 16 Litho. ***Perf. 13***
2008 A944 110pf multicolored 1.20 .75

Founding of the European Central Bank, Frankfurt am Main — A945

1998, July 16 Photo. ***Perf. 14***
2009 A945 110pf multicolored 2.00 1.05

Souvenir Sheet

Saxon Switzerland Natl. Park — A945a

1998, July 16 Litho. ***Perf. 14***
2009A A945a Sheet of 2 4.50 4.25
b. 110pf multicolored 2.00 1.50
c. 220pf multicolored 2.40 1.90

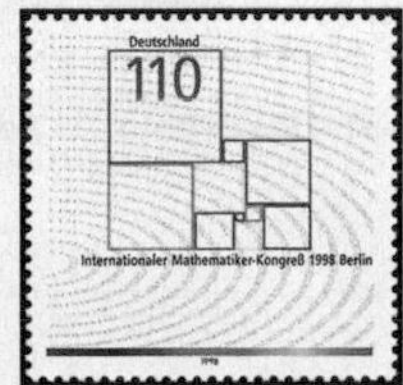

1998 Intl. Congress of Mathematicians, Berlin — A946

1998, Aug. 20 Photo. ***Perf. 14x13½***
2010 A946 110pf multicolored 1.20 .75

Grube Messel Fossil Beds A947

Würzburg Palace, Germany — A948

UNESCO World Heritage Sites: No. 2013, Puning Temple, Chengde, People's Republic of China.

1998, Aug. 20 Litho. ***Perf. 13x12½***
2011 A947 100pf multicolored 1.20 .70
Perf. 13½x14
2012 A948 110pf multicolored 1.50 .70
2013 A948 110pf multicolored 1.50 .70

See China People's Republic Nos. 2887-2888.

Souvenir Sheet

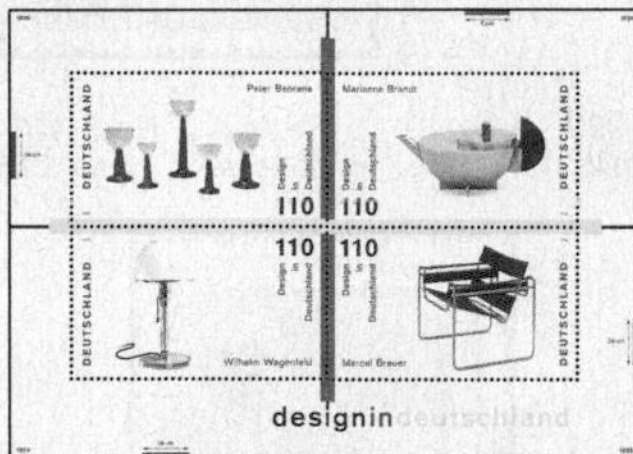

20th Cent. German Design — A949

Designs: a, Glassware, by Peter Behrens, 1910. b, Teapot, by Marianne Brandt, 1924. c, Desk lamp, by Wilhelm Wagenfeld, 1924. d, "Wassily" chair, by Marcel Breuer, 1926.

1998, Aug. 20 ***Perf. 14***
2014 A949 Sheet of 4 7.00 6.75
a.-d. 110pf any single 1.60 1.50

See No. 2051.

Manfred Hausmann (1898-1986), Author — A950

1998, Sept. 10 Litho. ***Perf. 14***
2015 A950 110pf multicolored 1.20 .75

A951

1998, Sept. 10
2016 A951 110pf multicolored 1.40 .75

Team 1 FC Kaiserslautern, 1998 German soccer champions.

Prevent Child Abuse — A952

1998, Sept. 10
2017 A952 110pf black & red 1.20 .75

Francke Charitable Institutions, Halle, 300th Anniv. — A953

1998, Sept. 10 ***Perf. 13***
2018 A953 110pf Building 1.20 .75

Mail Boat, "Hiorten" A954

1998, Oct. 8 Litho. ***Perf. 14***
2019 A954 110pf multicolored 1.20 .75

Stamp Day.

Telephone Help Lines for People in Distress — A955

1998, Oct. 8 ***Perf. 13x12½***
2020 A955 110pf multicolored 1.20 .75

Günther Ramin (1898-1956), Organist, Choir Leader — A956

1998, Oct. 8 Photo. ***Perf. 14x14½***
2021 A956 300pf multicolored 3.25 2.25

Saxony State Orchestra, Dresden, 450th Anniv. — A957

1998, Nov. 12 Litho. ***Perf. 14***
2022 A957 300pf multicolored 3.50 2.25

Universal Delcaration of Human Rights, 50th Anniv. — A958

1998, Nov. 12 ***Perf. 13x12½***
2023 A958 110pf multicolored 1.20 .75

See No. B848.

Weimar, 1999 European City of Culture, 1100th Anniv. — A959

1999, Jan. 14 Litho. ***Perf. 14***
2024 A959 100pf multicolored 1.20 .85
a. Booklet pane of 10 13.00 9.75
Complete booklet, #2024a + 20 labels 13.00

The self-adhesive labels are part of the booklet cover.

International Year of the Elderly A960

1999, Jan. 14 ***Perf. 13***
2025 A960 110pf multicolored 1.30 .85

Katharina von Bora (1499-1552), Wife of Martin Luther, from Painting by Lucas Cranach A961

1999, Jan. 14 ***Perf. 14***
2026 A961 110pf multicolored 1.30 .85

State Parliaments Type of 1998

The Hessian Parliament.

1999, Jan. 14
2027 A933 110pf multicolored 1.30 .85

Erich Kästner (1899-1974), Writer — A963

1999, Feb. 18 Litho. ***Perf. 13***
2028 A963 300pf multicolored 3.25 2.40

State Parliaments Type of 1998

Buildings: No. 2029, Hamburg. No. 2030, Mecklenburg-Western Pomerania. No. 2031, Bremen City Parliament.

1999 Litho. ***Perf. 14***
2029 A933 110pf multicolored 1.30 .85
2030 A933 110pf multicolored 1.30 .85
2031 A933 110pf multicolored 1.30 .85
Nos. 2029-2031 (3) 3.90 2.55

Issued: Nos. 2029-2030, 3/11; No. 2031, 4/27.

NATO, 50th Anniv. A963a

1999, Mar. 11 **Photo.**
2032 A963a 110pf multicolored 1.30 .85

Fraunhofer Society, 50th Anniv. — A964

1999, Mar. 11 **Litho.** ***Perf. 13***
2033 A964 110pf multicolored 1.30 .85

Expo 2000, Hanover A965

1999, Apr. 27
2034 A965 110pf multicolored 1.30 .85

See No. 2083.

German Automobile Club, Cent. — A966

1999, Apr. 27 **Photo.**
2035 A966 110pf multicolored 1.30 .85

German Cancer Relief Organization, 25th Anniv. — A967

1999, Apr. 27 **Litho.** ***Perf. 13***
2036 A967 110pf multicolored 1.30 .85

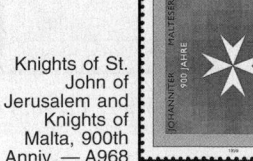

Knights of St. John of Jerusalem and Knights of Malta, 900th Anniv. — A968

1999, May 4
2037 A968 110pf multicolored 1.30 .85

Berlin Airlift, 1948-49 A969

1999, May 4 **Photo.** ***Perf. 14***
2038 A969 110pf multicolored 1.30 .85

Council of Europe, 50th Anniv. — A970

1999, May 4 **Litho.** ***Perf. 13***
2039 A970 110pf multicolored 1.50 .85

Souvenir Sheet

Berchtesgaden Natl. Park — A971

1999, May 4 ***Perf. 14***
2040 A971 110pf multicolored *3.00 3.00*

Europa.

Souvenir Sheet

Basic Law, 50th Anniv. — A972

1999, May 21 **Litho.** ***Perf. 14***
2041 A972 110pf multicolored 2.00 3.00

Souvenir Sheet

Federal Republic of Germany, 50th Anniv. — A973

Scenes from 1949, 1999: a, Leaders gathering, session of Parliament. b, Child carrying wood, child picking flower. c, Building "The Wall," people walking where "The Wall" has been removed. d, Soldiers, government assembly.

1999, May 21
2042 A973 Sheet of 4 6.50 6.75
a.-d. 110pf any single 1.50 1.50

SOS Children's Village, 50th Anniv. — A974

1999, June 10 **Litho.** ***Perf. 13¾x14***
2043 A974 110pf multicolored 1.30 .75

Paderborn Bishopric, 1200th Anniv. — A975

1999, June 10 ***Perf. 14***
2044 A975 110pf multicolored 1.30 .75

Johann Strauss, the Younger (1825-99) A976

1999, June 10 **Photo.** ***Perf. 13¾***
2045 A976 300pf multicolored 3.50 2.25

Dominikus-Ringeisen Institution, Ursberg, 115th Anniv. — A977

1999, July 15 **Litho.**
2046 A977 110pf multicolored 1.30 .75

Pres. Gustav Heinemann (1899-1976) A978

1999, July 15
2047 A978 110pf multicolored 1.30 .75

Cultural Foundation of the Federal States — A979

Sculpture: 110pf, Old Woman Smiling, by Ernst Barlach (1870-1938). 220pf, Bust of a Thinker, by Wilhelm Lehmbruck (1881-1919).

1999, July 15 **Photo.** ***Perf. 14***
2048 A979 110pf multicolored 1.30 .75
2049 A979 220pf multicolored 2.25 1.50

First Peace Conference in The Hague, Cent. — A980

1999, July 15 **Litho.** ***Perf. 13¼x13***
2050 A980 300pf multicolored 3.50 2.10

20th Cent. German Design Type of 1998

Souvenir Sheet

Designs: a, HF1 Television set, by Herbert Hirche, 1958. b, Knife, fork, spoon and teaspoon, by Peter Raacke, 1959. c, Pearl bottle, by Günter Kupetz, 1969. d, "Transrapid," Maglev train, by Alexander Neumeister, 1982.

1999, Aug. 12 **Litho.** ***Perf. 14***

Souvenir Sheet

2051 Sheet of 4 6.50 6.00
a.-d. A949 110pf any single 1.60 1.35

Johann Wolfgang von Goethe (1749-1832), Poet — A981

1999, Aug. 12 ***Perf. 13¾***
2052 A981 110pf multicolored 1.30 .85

See Korea Nos. 1964-1965.

Souvenir Sheet

For the Children — A982

1999, Aug. 12 ***Perf. 13¼***
2053 A982 110pf multicolored 2.00 2.00

Bayern München, 1999 German Soccer Champions — A983

1999, Sept. 16 **Litho.** ***Perf. 14***
2054 A983 110pf multicolored 1.30 .85

Federal Association of German Book Traders Peace Prize, 50th Anniv. — A984

1999, Sept. 16 **Photo.** ***Perf. 13¾***
2055 A984 110pf multicolored 1.20 .85

Richard Strauss (1864-1949), Composer A985

1999, Sept. 16 Litho. *Perf. 13¼*
2056 A985 300pf multicolored 3.50 2.40

Göltzsch Valley Bridge A986

1999, Oct. 14 Litho. *Perf. 14*
2057 A986 110pf multicolored 1.20 .85

German Federation of Trade Unions, 50th Anniv. — A987

1999, Oct. 14
2058 A987 110pf red & black 1.20 .85

Endangered Species A988

1999, Nov. 4 Litho. *Perf. 13¾*
2059 A988 100pf Large horse-shoe bat 1.20 .85

EXPO 2000, Hanover A989

2000, Jan. 13 Litho. *Perf. 14x14¼*
2060 A989 100pf multi 1.20 .85

See No. 2094.

Holy Year 2000 — A990

2000, Jan. 13 *Perf. 13¾*
2061 A990 110pf multi 1.30 .85

Completion of Aachen Cathedral, 1200th Anniv. — A991

2000, Jan. 13
2062 A991 110pf Charlemagne 1.30 .85

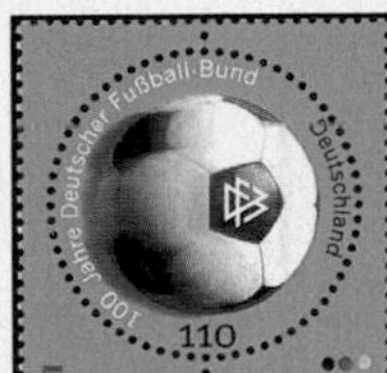

German Soccer Assoc., Cent. — A992

2000, Jan. 13 Photo.
2063 A992 110pf multi 1.60 .85

Value is for stamp with surrounding selvage.

Herbert Wehner (1906-90), Politician A993

2000, Jan. 13
2064 A993 110pf multi 1.30 .85

Albert Schweitzer (1875-1965), Humanitarian A994

2000, Jan. 13 Litho. *Perf. 14x13¾*
2065 A994 110pf multi 1.30 .85

Prevention of Violence Against Women — A995

2000, Jan. 13 *Perf. 14*
2066 A995 110pf multi 1.30 .85

Berlin Intl. Film Festival, 50th Anniv. A996

2000, Feb. 17 Litho. *Perf. 14*
2067 A996 100pf multi 1.20 .85

Johannes Gutenberg (c. 1400-1468) A997

2000, Feb. 17 *Perf. 13¾*
2068 A997 110pf red & black 1.30 .85

Friedrich Ebert (1871-1925), President of German Reich — A998

2000, Feb. 17 Photo.
2069 A998 110pf multi 1.30 .85

Düsseldorf Carnival, 175th Anniv. — A999

2000, Feb. 17 Litho. *Perf. 13x13½*
2070 A999 110pf multi 1.40 .85

Kurt Weill (1900-50), Composer — A1000

2000, Feb. 17 *Perf. 14*
2071 A1000 300pf multi 3.50 2.40

Scenic Regions Type of 1993

Designs: No. 2072, Passau. No. 2073, Saar River bend, Mettlach.

2000 Litho. *Perf. 13¾x14*
2072 A791 110pf multi 1.30 .85
2073 A791 110pf multi 1.30 .85

Issued: No. 2072, 3/16.

State Parliament Building Type

No. 2074, Lower Saxony. No. 2075, North Rhine-Westphalia. No. 2076, Rhineland-Palatinate. No. 2077, Saarland.

2000 Litho. *Perf. 13¾x14*
2074 A933 110pf multi 1.30 .85
2075 A933 110pf multi 1.40 .85
2076 A933 110pf multi 1.40 .90

Perf. 14
2077 A933 110pf multi 1.20 .90
Nos. 2074-2077 (4) 5.30 3.50

Issued: No. 2074, 3/16; No. 2075, 4/13; No. 2076, 8/14; No. 2077, 11/9.

Pinwheel A1001

2000, Mar. 16 Litho. *Perf. 13¾*
2078 A1001 110pf multi 1.60 1.20

Souvenir Sheet

Hainich National Park — A1002

2000, Mar. 16 *Perf. 13¼*
2079 A1002 110pf multi 2.00 2.00

Blue Wonder Bridge, Dresden A1003

2000, Apr. 13 Litho. *Perf. 13¼*
2080 A1003 100pf multi 1.20 .75

Cultural Foundation Type of 1999

Designs: 110pf, The Expulsion from Paradise, sculpture by Leonhard Korn. 220pf, Silver table fountain, 1652-53, by Melchior Gelb.

2000, Apr. 13 *Perf. 14x14¼*
2081 A979 110pf multi 1.50 1.05
2082 A979 220pf multi 2.25 1.60

Expo 2000 Type of 1999

2000, Apr. 13 *Die Cut Perf. 11*
Booklet Stamp
Self-Adhesive

2083 A965 110pf multi 6.50 3.75
a. Booklet pane of 10 65.00

No. 2083a is a complete booklet.

Griefswald, 750th Anniv. — A1004

Litho. & Engr.
2000, Apr. 13 *Perf. 14x14¼*
2084 A1004 110pf multi 1.30 .85

Nikolaus Ludwig von Zinzendorf (1700-60), Religious Leader A1005

2000, May 12 Photo. *Perf. 13¾*
2085 A1005 110pf multi 1.30 .75

Europa, 2000
Common Design Type

2000, May 12 Litho. *Perf. 13¾*
2086 CD17 110pf multi *1.75 .90*

Booklet Stamp
Self-Adhesive
Die Cut Perf. 10¾

2087 CD17 110pf multi *2.60 1.20*
a. Complete booklet of 10 *27.00*

Einkommende Zeitungen, First Daily Newspaper, 350th Anniv. — A1006

2000, June 8 Litho. *Perf. 13¾x14*
2088 A1006 110pf multi 1.40 .85

Chambers of Handicrafts in Germany, Cent. — A1007

2000, June 8 *Perf. 14*
2089 A1007 300pf gray & org 3.50 2.40

Zugspitze Weather Station, Cent. — A1008

2000, July 13 Litho. ***Perf. 13¾x14***
2090 A1008 100pf multi 1.50 .85

Federal Disaster Relief Organization, 50th Anniv. — A1009

2000, July 13 ***Perf. 14***
2091 A1009 110pf multi 1.50 .85

Johann Sebastian Bach (1685-1750) A1010

2000, July 13 ***Perf. 13¼***
2092 A1010 110pf multi 1.50 .85

First Zeppelin Flight, Cent. — A1011

2000, July 13
2093 A1011 110pf multi 1.50 .85

Expo 2000 Type of 2000

110pf, Expo emblem, Earth, fingerprint.

2000, Aug. 14 Litho. ***Perf. 14x14¼***
2094 A989 110pf multi 1.50 .85

Friedrich Nietzsche (1844-1900), Philosopher A1012

2000, Aug. 14 ***Perf. 13¼***
2095 A1012 110pf multi 1.50 .85

Ernst Wiechert (1887-1950), Writer A1013

2000, Aug. 14 ***Perf. 13¾***
2096 A1013 110pf multi 1.60 .85

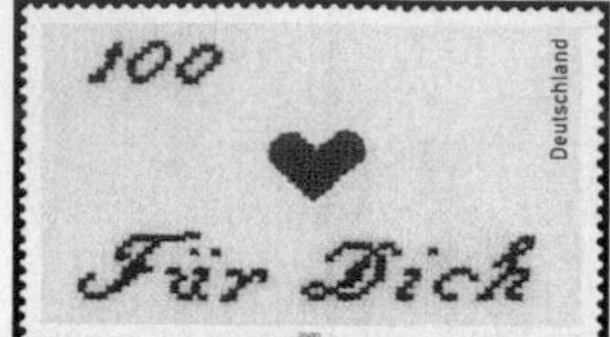

"For You" — A1014

2000, Sept. 14 Litho. ***Perf. 13x13¼***
2097 A1014 100pf multi 1.20 .85

Souvenir Sheet

For the Children — A1015

2000, Sept. 14 ***Perf. 13¾x14***
2098 A1015 110pf multi 2.00 2.00

Adolph Kolping (1813-65) A1016

2000, Sept. 14 ***Perf. 13¼***
2099 A1016 110pf multi 1.30 .85

Kolping Society, 150th anniv.

Federal Court of Justice, 50th Anniv. A1017

Litho. & Engr.

2000, Sept. 14 ***Perf. 14x14¼***
2100 A1017 110pf multi 1.40 .85

Bernhard Nocht Institute for Tropical Medicine, Cent. — A1018

2000, Sept. 14 Litho. ***Perf. 13¾x14***
2101 A1018 300pf multi 4.25 2.60

Reunification of Germany, 10th Anniv. A1019

2000, Sept. 28 ***Perf. 13¼***
2102 A1019 110pf multi 1.50 .85

Stamp Day — A1020

2000, Oct. 12 Litho. ***Perf. 13x13¼***
2103 A1020 110pf multi 1.40 .85

Rainer Maria Rilke (1875-1926), Poet — A1021

2000, Nov. 9 Litho. ***Perf. 13¼x13½***
2104 A1021 110pf multi 1.40 .90

Arnold Bode (1900-77), Artist — A1022

2000, Nov. 9 ***Perf. 13¼***
2105 A1022 110pf red & black 1.40 1.15

Leonhart Fuchs (1501-66), Botanist A1023

2001, Jan. 11 Litho. ***Perf. 13¾***
2106 A1023 100pf multi 1.30 .75

Kingdom of Prussia, 300th Anniv. A1024

2001, Jan. 11 ***Perf. 14***
2107 A1024 110pf multi 1.30 .75

Association of Disabled War Veterans, 50th Anniv. — A1025

2001, Jan. 11 Photo. ***Perf. 14***
2108 A1025 110pf multi 1.30 .75

Youth Helpline Federation — A1026

2001, Jan. 11 Litho. ***Perf. 13¾x14***
2109 A1026 110pf multi 1.30 .75

Albert Lortzing (1801-51), Opera Composer A1027

2001, Jan. 11 ***Perf. 13¾***
2110 A1027 110pf multi 1.30 .75

Martin Bucer (1491-1551), Theologian A1028

2001, Feb. 8 Litho. ***Perf. 13¾***
2111 A1028 110pf multi 1.40 .90

Johann Heinrich Voss (1751-1826), Translator of Greek Classics A1029

2001, Feb. 8 ***Perf. 13¼***
2112 A1029 300pf multi 4.00 2.60

See No. 2157.

State Parliament Type of 1998

Design: No. 2113, Saxony. No. 2114, Saxony-Anhalt. No. 2115, Schleswig-Holstein. No. 2116, Thuringia.

2001 Litho. ***Perf. 13¾x14***
2113 A933 110pf multi 1.30 .75
2114 A933 110pf multi 1.30 .75
2115 A933 110pf multi 1.30 .75
2116 A933 110pf multi 1.30 .75
Nos. 2113-2116 (4) 5.20 3.00

Issued: No. 2113, 3/8/01. No. 2114, 5/10. No. 2115, 7/12. No. 2116, 9/5.

Erich Ollenhauer (1901-63), Politician — A1030

2001, Mar. 8 Litho. ***Perf. 14***
2117 A1030 110pf multi 1.60 .75

Karl Arnold (1901-58), Politician A1031

2001, Mar. 8 *Perf. 13¼*
2118 A1031 110pf multi 1.30 .75

Federal Border Police, 50th Anniv. A1032

2001, Mar. 8 Litho. *Perf. 13¾*
2119 A1032 110pf multi 1.30 .75

Rendsburg Railway Bridge — A1033

2001, Apr. 5 Litho. *Perf. 14*
2120 A1033 100pf multi 1.50 .75

Folk Music — A1034

2001, Apr. 5 *Perf. 13x13½*
2121 A1034 110pf multi 1.30 .75

"Post!" A1035

2001, Apr. 5 Photo. *Perf. 14*
2122 A1035 110pf multi 1.30 .75

Goethe Institute, 50th Anniv. — A1036

2001, Apr. 5 Litho.
2123 A1036 300pf multi 3.50 2.25

Endangered Species — A1037

Designs: No. 2124, Mountain gorilla. No. 2125, Indian rhinoceros.

2001, May 10 Litho. *Perf. 14*
2124 A1037 110pf multi 1.40 .90
2125 A1037 110pf multi 1.40 .90

See Nos. 2132-2133.

Europa A1038

2001, May 10 *Perf. 13¾*
2126 A1038 110pf multi 1.75 .85

Werner Egk (1901-83), Composer — A1039

2001, May 10 *Perf. 14*
2127 A1039 110pf multi 1.50 .75

St. Catherine's Monastery, 750th Anniv., Oceanographic Museum, 50th Anniv. — A1040

2001, June 13 Litho. *Perf. 13x13¼*
2128 A1040 110pf multi 1.30 .75

Catholic Court Church, Dresden, 250th Anniv. A1041

2001, June 13 *Perf. 13¼*
2129 A1041 110pf multi 1.30 .75

Canzow Village Church A1042

2001, July 12 Photo. *Perf. 14x14¼*
2130 A1042 110pf multi 1.30 .75

Conservation of sacred monuments.

Souvenir Sheet

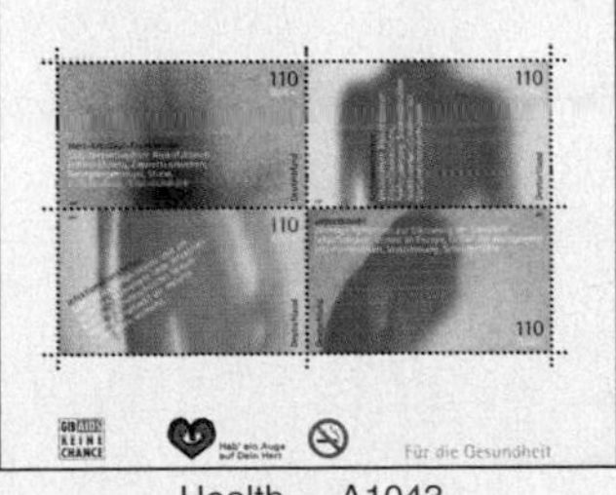

Health — A1043

No. 2131: a, Hand (circulatory diseases). b, Chest (cancer). c, Abdomen (infectious diseases). d, Head (depression).

2001, July 12 Litho. *Perf. 13x13½*
2131 A1043 Sheet of 4 7.50 5.00
a.-d. 110pf Any single 1.75 1.15

Endangered Species Type of 2001
Die Cut Perf. 11¼x11
2001, July 12 Litho.
Booklet Stamps
Self-Adhesive

2132 A1037 110pf Like #2124 2.10 1.30
2133 A1037 110pf Like #2125 2.10 1.30
a. Booklet, 5 each #2132-2133 29.00

Furth Dragon Lancing Festival A1044

2001, Aug. 9 Litho. *Perf. 13¼*
2134 A1044 100pf multi 1.15 .70

Himmelsberg Lime Tree Natural Monument — A1045

2001 *Perf. 13¾x14*
2135 A1045 110pf multi 1.30 .75

Booklet Stamp
Self-Adhesive
Die Cut Perf. 9¾x10½
2135A A1045 110pf multi 3.50 1.50
b. Booklet of 20 70.00

Issued: No. 2135, 8/9; No. 2135A, 9/13.

Lifelong Learning A1046

2001, Aug. 9 *Perf. 14*
2136 A1046 110pf multi 1.30 .75

Federal Constitutional Court, 50th Anniv. — A1047

2001, Sept. 5
2137 A1047 110pf multi 1.30 .75

First World Congress of Union Network International — A1048

2001, Sept. 5 *Perf. 13x13½*
2138 A1048 110pf multi 1.30 .75

Opening of Jewish Museum, Berlin — A1049

2001, Sept. 5 Photo. *Perf. 13¾*
2139 A1049 110pf multi 1.30 .75

Souvenir Sheet

For Children — A1050

2001, Sept. 5 Litho. *Perf. 13¾x14*
2140 A1050 110pf multi 1.75 1.35

"For You" — A1051

2001, Oct. 11 *Perf. 13x13¼*
2141 A1051 110pf multi 1.30 .75

Werner Heisenberg (1901-76), Physicist A1052

2001, Nov. 8 Litho. *Perf. 13¾*
2142 A1052 300pf multi 4.25 2.40

Souvenir Sheet

German Antarctic Expeditions, Cent. — A1053

Expedition vessels: a, Gauss. b, Polarstern.

2001, Nov. 8 *Perf. 13¾x14*
2143 A1053 Sheet of 2, #a-b 5.00 3.50
a. 110pf multi 1.75 1.15
b. 220pf multi 3.00 1.90

Introduction of the Euro, Jan. 1 — A1054

2002, Jan. 10 Litho. *Perf. 13¾*
2144 A1054 56c multi 2.00 1.30

Coil Stamp
Perf. 10½
Self-Adhesive

2144A A1054 56c multi 4.75 2.25

Hans von Dohnanyi (1902-45), Documenter of Nazi Atrocities A1055

2002, Jan. 10 **Photo.**
2145 A1055 56c multi 1.30 .75
2145A A1055 56c multi *350.00* 225.00

No. 2145A has "2002" in upper right corner and colored face and name. Approximately 320 small panes of 10 of No. 2145A were accidentally mixed in with approved stock of No. 2145 and sold over post office counters.

Bautzen, 1000th Anniv. A1056

2002, Jan. 10 **Litho.** ***Perf. 13¾***
2146 A1056 56c multi 1.30 .75

Die Cut Perf. 11
Litho.
Booklet Stamp
Self-Adhesive

2146A A1056 56c multi 5.75 3.00
b. Booklet of 10 35.00

More Tolerance — A1057

2002, Jan. 10 ***Perf. 13¾x14***
2147 A1057 56c multi 1.30 .75

Adolph Freiherr Knigge (1762-96), Writer — A1058

2002, Feb. 7 **Litho.** ***Perf. 13¾***
2148 A1058 56c multi 1.40 .85

Berlin Subway System, Cent. — A1059

2002, Feb. 7 ***Perf. 13¼***
2149 A1059 56c multi 1.75 .85

Johann Christoph Schuster's Mechanical Calculator — A1060

2002, Mar. 7 **Litho.** ***Perf. 14***
2150 A1060 56c multi 1.40 .85

Cultural Foundation of the Federal States.

Deggendorf, 1000th Anniv. — A1061

2002, Mar. 7
2151 A1061 56c multi 1.30 .75

Ecksberg Foundation for the Mentally Handicapped, 150th Anniv. — A1062

Litho. & Engr.

2002, Apr. 4 ***Perf. 14x13¾***
2152 A1062 56c multi 1.30 .75

Freemason's Museum, Cent. — A1063

2002, Apr. 4 **Litho.** ***Perf. 14***
2153 A1063 56c multi 1.40 .85

Baden-Württemberg, 50th Anniv. — A1064

2002, Apr. 4 ***Perf. 13¼***
2154 A1064 56c multi 1.40 .85

"Post" — A1065

2002, Apr. 4 ***Perf. 13x13½***
2155 A1065 56c multi 1.30 .75

Federal Employment Services, 50th Anniv. — A1066

2002, Apr. 4 ***Perf. 14***
2156 A1066 153c black & red 3.75 2.25

Voss Type of 2001
Die Cut Perf. 10¼

2002, Apr. 4 **Litho.**

Coil Stamp
Self-Adhesive

2157 A1029 €1.53 multi 5.75 3.50

Dated 2001. No. 2157 was sold only for euro currency.

Europa A1067

2002 **Litho.** ***Perf. 13¼***
2158 A1067 56c multi *1.30* *.75*

Self-Adhesive
Coil Stamp
Die Cut Perf. 10¼

2158A A1067 56c multi 3.50 2.25

Issued: No. 2158, 5/2; No. 2158A, 7/4.

Garden Kingdom of Dessau-Wörlitz, UNESCO World Heritage Site — A1068

2002 ***Perf. 13¾x14***
2159 A1068 56c multi 1.40 .85

Booklet Stamp
Self-Adhesive
Die Cut Perf. 10¾

2159A A1068 56c multi 2.25 1.05
b. Booklet of 20 52.50

Issued: No. 2159, 5/2; No. 2159A, 8/8.

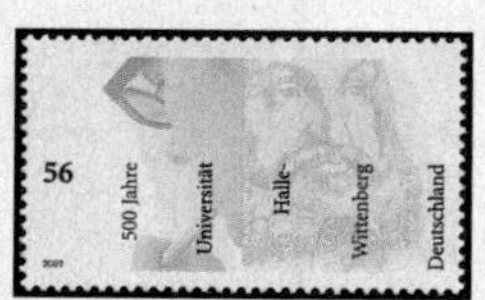

Halle-Wittenberg University, 500th Anniv. — A1069

2002, May 2 ***Perf. 14***
2160 A1069 56c multi 1.30 .75

Children's Church, 150th Anniv. A1070

2002, May 2 ***Perf. 13¼***
2161 A1070 56c multi 1.40 .85

Souvenir Sheet

Documenta 11 Art Exhibition — A1071

2002, May 2 ***Perf. 13¾x14***
2162 A1071 56c multi 2.25 1.50

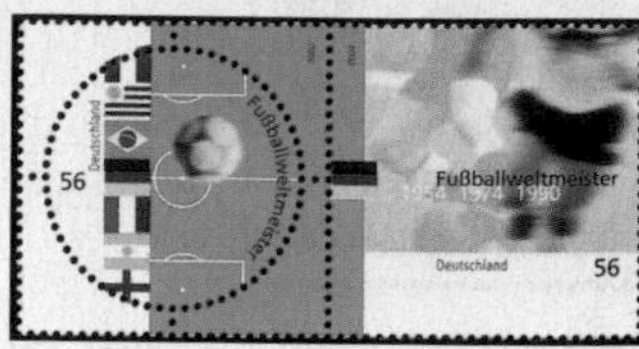

2002 World Cup Soccer Championships, Japan and Korea — A1072

No. 2163: a, Flags, soccer ball and field (28mm diameter). b, Soccer players, years of German championships.

2002, May 2 ***Perf. 13¾***
2163 A1072 Horiz. pair 3.00 1.75
a.-b. 56c Any single 1.40 .90

See Argentina No. 2184, Brazil No. 2840, France No. 2891, Italy No. 2526 and Uruguay No. 1946.

Albrecht Daniel Thaer (1752-1828), Agronomist — A1073

2002, May 2 ***Perf. 13x13½***
2164 A1073 225c multi 5.75 3.75

Yellow Feather in Red, by Ernst Wilhelm Nay (1902-68) — A1074

2002, June 6 **Litho.** ***Perf. 13¾x14***
2165 A1074 56c multi 1.30 .75

Endangered Species — A1075

Designs: 51c, Desmoulins whorl snail. 56c, Freshwater pearl mussel.

2002, June 6 ***Perf. 14x14¼***
2166 A1075 51c multi 1.40 .75
2167 A1075 56c multi 1.40 .75

See Czech Republic No. 3173.

World Hunger Help — A1076

2002, July 4 Litho. *Perf. 13¾x14*
2168 A1076 51c multi 1.15 .75

Natl. Germanic Museum, 150th Anniv. — A1077

2002, July 4
2169 A1077 56c multi 1.30 .75

Hermann Hesse (1877-1962), Writer — A1078

2002, July 4 *Perf. 14*
2170 A1078 56c multi 1.30 .75

Souvenir Sheet

Hochharz Natl. Park — A1079

2002, July 4 *Perf. 13¾x14*
2171 A1079 56c multi 1.75 1.15

Josef Felder (1900-2000), Politician, Journalist A1080

2002, Aug. 8 Litho. *Perf. 13*
2172 A1080 56c multi 1.40 .85

Volunteer Fire Brigades A1081

2002, Aug. 8 *Perf. 14*
2173 A1081 56c multi 1.40 .85

A1082

Litho. & Engr.

2002, Aug. 8 *Perf. 13¾x14*
2174 A1082 56c blk & Prus blue 1.40 .85

Museum Island, Berlin, UNESCO World Heritage Site.

Communications Museum, Berlin — A1083

2002, Aug. 8 Litho. *Perf. 14*
2175 A1083 153c multi 3.50 2.25

Foundation Walls of Roman Villa Bathhouse, Wurmlingen — A1084

2002, Sept. 5 Litho. *Perf. 13¾x14*
2176 A1084 51c multi 1.15 .75

Rotes Elisabeth-Ufer, by Ernst Ludwig Kirchner (1880-1938) — A1085

2002, Sept. 5
2177 A1085 112c multi 2.50 1.50

Souvenir Sheet

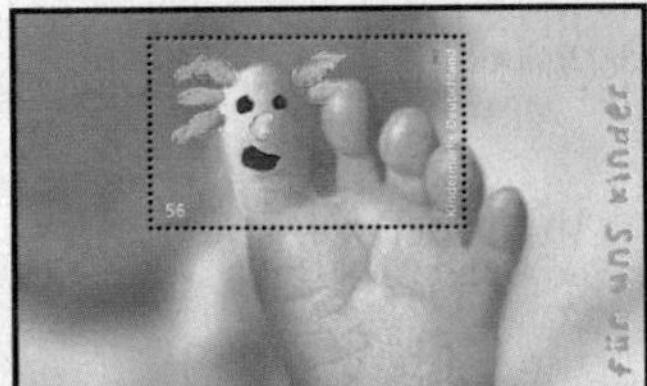

For Children — A1086

2002, Sept. 5 *Perf. 13x13½*
2178 A1086 56c multi 1.75 1.75

Heinrich von Kleist (1777-1811), Writer — A1087

2002, Oct. 10 Litho. *Perf. 13*
2179 A1087 56c multi 1.30 .75

Eugen Jochum (1902-87), Conductor A1088

2002, Oct. 10 *Perf. 14x14¼*
2180 A1088 56c multi 1.30 .75

Otto von Guericke (1602-86), Physicist — A1089

2002, Oct. 10 *Perf. 14*
2181 A1089 153c multi 4.25 2.40

Federal Agency for Civic Education, 50th Anniv. A1090

2002, Nov. 7 Litho. *Perf. 13¼*
2182 A1090 56c blk, red & org 1.30 .75

German Television, 50th Anniv. — A1091

2002, Nov. 7 *Perf. 14*
2183 A1091 56c multi 1.50 .75

Halle Market Church, by Lyonel Feininger (1871-1956) — A1092

2002, Dec. 5 Litho. *Perf. 13¾x14*
2184 A1092 55c multi 1.30 .75

Famous Women Type of 1986 With Euro Denominations Only

Designs: 45c, Annette von Droste-Hülshoff (1797-1848), poet. 55c, Hildegard Knef (1925-2002), actress. €1, Marie Juchacz (1879-1956), politician. €1.44, Esther von Kirchbach (1894-1946), writer.

2002-03 Engr. *Perf. 14*
2185 A602 45c ol grn & Prus bl 1.15 .75
2186 A602 55c car & blk 1.15 .75
2187 A602 €1 dk bl & claret 2.25 1.35
2188 A602 €1.44 dk bl & ocher 3.00 2.00
Nos. 2185-2188 (4) 7.55 4.85

Issued: 45c, 55c, €1.44, 12/27/02; €1, 1/16/03.

Historic Sites Type of 1987 With Euro Denominations Only

Designs: 25c, Prince's Residence, Arolsen. 40c, Bach Statue, Leipzig.44c, Berlin Philharmonic Hall. 45c, Tönninger Packhaus (Warehouse, Tönning). 55c, Old Opera House, Frankfurt. €1, Porta Nigra, Trier. €1.44, Birthplace of Ludwig van Beethoven, Bonn. €1.60, Bauhaus, Dessau. €1.80, Stuttgart Staatsgalerie. €2, Equestrian statue, Bamberg. €2.20, Monument to Theodor Fontane, Neuruppin. €2.60, Barque "Seute Deern," Bremerhaven. €4.10, Gabled houses, Wismar.

2002-04 Litho. *Perf. 14*
2199 A623 5c olive & turq .35 .25
2200 A623 25c multi .60 .40
2201 A623 40c pur & grn .95 .60
2202 A623 44c blk & yel 1.15 .60
2203 A623 45c gray blk & brick red 1.15 .75
2204 A623 55c blk & yel 1.15 .75
2205 A623 €1 blk & greenish gray 2.25 1.35
2206 A623 €1.44 gray grn & pink 4.25 2.60
2207 A623 €1.60 slate & org 3.50 2.25
2208 A623 €1.80 dull grn & brn 4.75 2.60
2209 A623 €2 brn blk & lake 4.75 3.00
2210 A623 €2.20 blue blk & gray bl 5.75 3.75
2211 A623 €2.60 blue & red 7.00 3.75
2212 A623 €4.10 bl grn & red vio 10.50 6.00

Coil Stamps
Self-Adhesive
Die Cut Perf. 10¼x11
Photo.
2213 A623 €1.44 gray grn & pink 4.75 2.60
Litho.
2214 A623 55c blk & yel 1.15 .75

Booklet Stamps
Die Cut Perf. 10¼x11 on 3 Sides
2215 A623 45c gray blk & brick red 3.00 1.90
2216 A623 55c blk & yel 1.40 .90
a. Booklet 4 #2215, 8 #2216 25.00
Nos. 2199-2216 (18) 58.40 34.80

Issued: 44c, 45c, 55c, €1, €1.60, 12/27/02; €1.44, €2.20, 1/16/03; €1.80, €2, 2/13/03; €2.60, €4.10, 3/6/03; No. 2213, June 2003. 25c, 40c, 1/8/04; 5c, 2/5/04.

Kronach, 1000th Anniv. — A1093

2003, Jan. 16 Litho. *Perf. 14*
2222 A1093 45c multi 1.15 .70

Georg Elser (1903-45), Failed Assassin of Hitler — A1094

2003, Jan. 16 *Perf. 13¼*
2223 A1094 55c multi 1.40 .85

Treaty for German-French Cooperation, 40th Anniv. A1095

2003, Jan. 16 *Perf. 13¾*
2224 A1095 55c multi 1.40 .85

Bible Year A1096

2003, Jan. 16 *Perf. 14x14¼*
2225 A1096 55c multi 1.40 .85

Proun 30t, by El Lissitzky (1890-1941) — A1097

2003, Jan. 16
2226 A1097 144c multi 3.50 2.00

Cultural Foundation of the Federal States.

Rose A1098

2003, Feb. 13 Litho. *Perf. 14*
2227 A1098 55c multi 1.30 .75

Booklet Stamp
Self-Adhesive
Die Cut Perf. 10x10¼
2228 A1098 55c multi 1.60 .85
a. Booklet pane of 10 16.50

Junger Argentinier, by Max Beckmann — A1099

Composition, by Adolf Hölzel — A1100

2003, Feb. 13 *Perf. 13¾x14*
2229 A1099 55c multi 1.40 .75
2230 A1100 100c multi 2.10 1.35

Souvenir Sheet

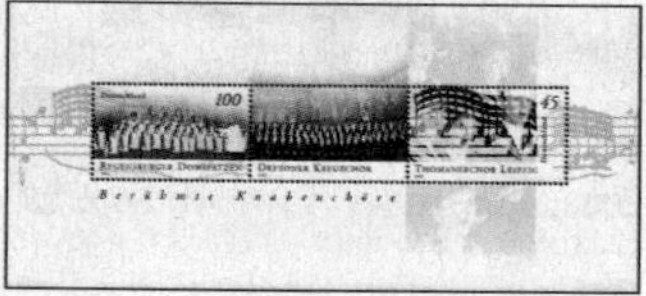
Boys' Choirs — A1101

No. 2231: a, Thomanerchor Leipzig. b, Dredner Kreuzchor. c, Regensburger Domspatzen.

2003, Feb. 13 *Perf. 14x14¼*
2231 A1101 Sheet of 3 5.25 3.75
a. 45c multi 1.50 1.00
b. 55c multi 1.50 1.00
c. 100c multi 2.10 1.35

Cologne Cathedral, UNESCO World Heritage Site — A1102

2003, Mar. 6 *Perf. 13¼*
2232 A1102 55c multi 1.40 .85

Self-Adhesive
Coil Stamp
Die Cut Perf. 10¼
2233 A1102 55c multi 1.60 .85

Intl. Horticultural Exhibition 2003, Rostock A1103

2003, Apr. 10 Litho. *Perf. 13¼*
2234 A1103 45c multi 1.30 .75

German Museum, Munich, Cent. A1104

2003, Apr. 10 Photo. *Perf. 14x14¼*
2235 A1104 55c multi 1.40 .85

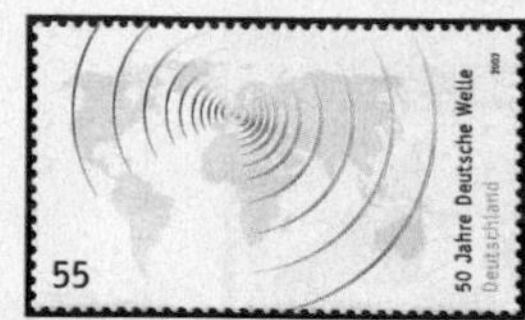
Deutsche Welle Radio, 50th Anniv. — A1105

2003, Apr. 10 Litho. *Perf. 14*
2236 A1105 55c multi 1.40 .85

German Society for the Protection of Children, 50th Anniv. A1106

2003, Apr. 10 *Perf. 13¼*
2237 A1106 55c multi 1.40 .85

Reinhold Schneider (1903-58), Writer — A1107

2003, May 8 Litho. *Perf. 13¼*
2238 A1107 55c multi 1.30 .85

Ecumenical Church Conference, Berlin — A1108

2003, May 8 *Perf. 14*
2239 A1108 55c multi 1.40 .85

Justus von Liebig (1803-73), Chemist — A1109

2003, May 8
2240 A1109 55c multi 1.40 .85

German General Automobile Club, Cent. — A1110

2003, May 8 *Perf. 13¼x13½*
2241 A1110 55c multi 1.40 .85

Europa — A1111

2003, May 8
2242 A1111 55c multi *1.40 .85*

Hans Jonas (1903-93), Philosopher — A1112

2003, May 8 *Perf. 13¾x14*
2243 A1112 220c multi 5.25 3.25

Five Digit Postal Codes, 10th Anniv. A1113

2003, June 12 Litho. *Perf. 14*
2244 A1113 55c multi 1.40 .85

Salzach River Bridge, Laufen, Germany - Oberndorf, Austria, Cent. — A1114

2003, June 12
2245 A1114 55c multi 1.40 .85

Die Cut Perf 14
Booklet Stamp
Self-Adhesive
2245A A1114 55c multi 2.25 1.00
b. Booklet pane of 20 47.50

See Austria No. 1922.

Souvenir Sheet

Unteres Odertal National Park — A1115

2003, June 12 *Perf. 13x13½*
2246 A1115 55c multi 1.50 1.15

German Music Council, 50th Anniv. A1116

2003, June 12 *Perf. 14*
2247 A1116 144c multi 3.50 2.10

Self-Adhesive
Booklet Stamp
Die Cut Perf. 11¼x11
2247A A1116 144c multi 3.50 2.10
b. Booklet pane of 10 42.50

Issued: No. 2247, 6/12/03; No. 2247A, 1/8/04.

Scenic Regions in Germany — A1117

2003, July 10 Litho. *Perf. 13x13½*
2248 A1117 55c Ruhr Region 1.40 .85

Andreas Hermes (1878-1964), Politician — A1118

2003, July 10 Photo. *Perf. 14x14¼*
2258 A1118 55c multi 1.30 .75

Petrified Forest, Chemnitz A1119

2003, Aug. 7 Litho. *Perf. 13¼*
2259 A1119 144c multi 3.50 2.25

City Views

Market, Munich A1120

Buildings in Old City, Görlitz — A1121

2003, Aug. 7 Litho. *Perf. 13¼*
2260 A1120 45c multi 1.30 .75

Perf. 13x13½
2261 A1121 55c multi 1.30 .75

Self-Adhesive
Booklet Stamp
Die Cut Perf. 11x 10¾
2261A A1120 45c multi 1.50 .70
b. Booklet pane of 10 16.50

Issued: Nos. 2260, 2261, 8/7/03; No. 2261A, 1/8/04.

Theodor W. Adorno (1903-69), Philosopher — A1122

2003, Sept. 11 ***Perf. 14***
2262 A1122 55c multi 1.30 .75

Bietigheim Enzviadukt, 150th Anniv. — A1123

2003, Sept. 11 ***Perf. 13x13½***
2263 A1123 55c multi 1.40 .85

Souvenir Sheet

For Children — A1124

2003, Sept. 11 ***Perf. 13¾x14***
2264 A1124 55c multi 1.60 1.15

Mailbox A1125

2003, Oct. 9 **Litho.** ***Perf. 13¼***
2265 A1125 55c multi 1.40 .85

German Lifesaving Association — A1126

2003, Oct. 9 ***Perf. 13¾***
2266 A1126 144c multi 3.50 2.10

Opera House, Dresden, by Gottfried Semper (1803-79), Architect — A1127

2003, Nov. 13 **Litho.** ***Perf. 13x13½***
2267 A1127 55c multi 1.30 .75

German Catholic Women's Organization, Cent. — A1128

2003, Nov. 13 ***Perf. 14***
2268 A1128 55c multi 1.30 .75

Ratification of Maastricht Treaty, 10th Anniv. — A1129

2003, Nov. 13
2269 A1129 55c multi 1.40 .85

Landshut, 800th Anniv. — A1130

2004, Jan. 8 **Litho.** ***Perf. 14***
2270 A1130 45c multi 1.05 .70

Schleswig, 1200th Anniv. A1131

2004, Jan. 8 ***Perf. 13¼***
2271 A1131 55c multi 1.30 .75

Arnstadt, 1300th Anniv. A1132

2004, Feb. 5 **Litho.** ***Perf. 13¼***
2272 A1132 55c multi 1.40 .85

Greetings — A1133

2004, Feb. 5 ***Perf. 14***
2273 A1133 55c multi 1.40 .85

Joseph Schmidt (1904-42), Singer — A1134

2004, Mar. 11 **Litho.** ***Perf. 14***
2274 A1134 55c multi 1.40 .85

Paul Ehrlich (1854-1915) and Emil von Behring (1854-1917), Physicians — A1135

2004, Mar. 11
2275 A1135 144c multi 3.50 2.10

Souvenir Sheet

Classical Theater — A1136

No. 2276: a, Premiere of *William Tell,* by Friedrich von Schiller, bicent. b, Premiere of *Faust,* by Johann Wolfgang von Goethe, 150th anniv.

2004, Mar. 11 ***Perf. 13¾***
2276 A1136 Sheet of 2 3.75 2.60
a. 45c multi 1.40 .90
b. 100c multi 2.25 1.35

Bauhaus World Heritage Sites, Weimar and Dessau — A1137

2004, Apr. 7 **Litho.** ***Perf. 14***
2277 A1137 55c multi 1.40 .85

White Stork A1138

2004, Apr. 7
2278 A1138 55c multi 1.40 .85

Kurt Georg Kiesinger (1904-88), Chancellor A1139

2004, Apr. 7 ***Perf. 13¾***
2279 A1139 55c multi 1.30 .75

Electric Light Bulb of Heinrich Göbel, 150th Anniv. A1140

2004, Apr. 7
2280 A1140 220c red & blue 5.25 3.50

Europa A1141

2004, May 6 **Litho.** ***Perf. 13¼***
2281 A1141 45c multi *1.15* .70

Expansion of the European Union A1142

2004, May 6
2282 A1142 55c multi 1.15 .70

St. Boniface of Mainz (c. 675-754) A1143

2004, May 6 ***Perf. 13¾***
2283 A1143 55c multi 1.30 .75

Reinhard Schwarz-Schilling (1904-85), Composer — A1144

2004, May 6 ***Perf. 14***
2284 A1144 55c multi 1.30 .75

Ludwigsburg Castle, 300th Anniv. — A1145

2004, May 6
2285 A1145 144c multi 3.50 2.10

Wattenmeer National Park A1146

2004, June 3 **Litho.** ***Perf. 13***
2286 A1146 55c multi 1.30 .75

German - Russian Youth Meeting A1147

2004, June 3 *Perf. 13¾*
2287 A1147 55c multi 1.30 .75

See Russia No. 6845.

Transatlantic Speed Record-Breaking Voyage of the Steamship "Bremen," 75th Anniv. — A1148

2004, July 8 **Litho.** *Perf. 14*
2288 A1148 55c multi 1.30 .75

Booklet Stamp
Self-Adhesive
Die Cut Perf. 14

2288A A1148 55c multi 1.30 .75
b. Booklet pane of 20 35.00

Ludwig Feuerbach (1804-72), Philosopher A1149

2004, July 8 *Perf. 13¾*
2289 A1149 144c multi 3.50 2.10

Lighthouses A1150

2004, July 8 *Perf. 13¾*
2290 A1150 45c Griefswalder Oie 1.30 .75
2291 A1150 55c Roter Sand 1.30 .75

Die Cut Perf. 10¼
Coil Stamp
Self-Adhesive

2291A A1150 55c Roter Sand 1.30 .75

See Nos. 2344-2345B, 2390-2391, 2447-2448, 2491-2494, 2537-2538, 2574-2575, 2629-2632, 2673, 2680-2681, 2737-2738, 2793-2794, 2847-2848, 2928-2929, 2978-2979, 3040-3042.

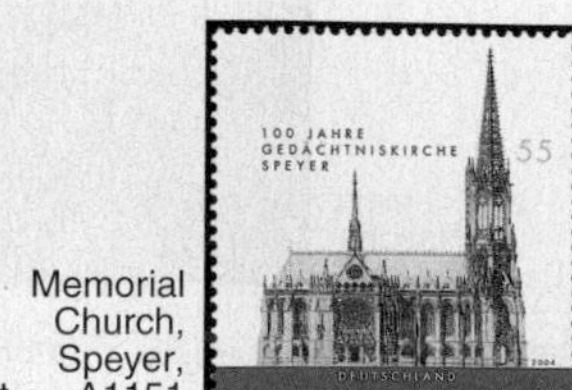

Memorial Church, Speyer, Cent. — A1151

2004, Aug. 12 **Litho.** *Perf. 13¾*
2292 A1151 55c multi 1.40 .85

Camellia — A1152

2004, Aug. 12 *Perf. 14*
2293 A1152 55c multi 1.30 .75

Booklet Stamp
Self-Adhesive
Die Cut Perf. 10x10¼

2294 A1152 55c multi 1.60 .90
a. Booklet pane, 5 each #2228, 2294 16.50

Engelbert Humperdinck (1854-1921), Composer — A1153

2004, Sept. 9 **Litho.** *Perf. 14*
2295 A1153 45c multi 1.15 .70

Eduard Mörike (1804-75), Poet — A1154

2004, Sept. 9
2296 A1154 55c multi 1.30 .75

For Children A1155

2004, Sept. 9 *Perf. 13¾*
2297 A1155 55c multi 1.30 .75

Egon Eiermann (1904-70), Architect — A1156

2004, Sept. 9 *Perf. 14*
2298 A1156 100c multi 2.25 1.35

Federal Social Court, 50th Anniv. A1157

Litho. & Embossed

2004, Sept. 9 *Perf. 13¾*
2299 A1157 144c multi 3.50 2.10

Dornier Do X A1158

2004, Oct. 7 **Litho.** *Perf. 14*
2300 A1158 55c multi 1.30 .75

Stamp Day.

Winter Scene A1159

2004, Nov. 4
2301 A1159 55c multi 1.30 .75

International Space Station — A1160

2004, Nov. 4
2302 A1160 55c multi 1.30 .75

The Secret, by Felix Nussbaum (1904-44) — A1161

2004, Nov. 4
2303 A1161 55c multi 1.30 .75

Forchheim, 1200th Anniv. A1162

2005, Jan. 3 **Litho.** *Perf. 13¼*
2304 A1162 45c multi 1.05 .60

Adoration of the Magi, St. Clara's Church, Cologne A1163

2005, Jan. 3
2305 A1163 55c multi 1.30 .75

See No. 2509.

Sculpture of Celtic Prince Found in Glauberg A1164

2005, Jan. 3 *Perf. 13¾*
2306 A1164 144c multi 3.50 2.10

Flowers — A1165

Designs: 5c, Krokus (crocus). 10c, Tulpe (tulip). 20c, Tagetes (marigold). 25c, Malve (mallow). 35c, Dahlie (dahlia). 40c, Leberblümchen (hepatica). 45c, Margerite (daisy). 50c, Aster. 55c, Klatschmohn (red poppy). 65c, Sonnenhut (rudbeckia). 70c, Kartaüsernelke (clusterhead pink). 90c, Narzisse (narcissus). 95c, Sonnenblume (sunflower). 100c, Tränendes herz (Bleeding heart). 145c, Schwertlilie (iris). 220c, Edelweiss. 390c, Feuerlilie (tiger lily). 430c, Rittersporn (larkspur).

2005-06 **Litho.** *Perf. 14*
2307 A1165 5c multi .35 .25
2308 A1165 10c multi .35 .25
2309 A1165 20c multi .50 .30
a. Miniature sheet, 4 each #2307-2308, 2 each #2309 2.75 2.75
2310 A1165 25c multi .70 .40
2311 A1165 35c multi .85 .55
2312 A1165 40c multi .95 .60
2313 A1165 45c multi 1.05 .60
2314 A1165 50c multi 1.15 .70
2315 A1165 55c multi 1.40 .75
2316 A1165 65c multi 1.60 1.00
2317 A1165 70c multi 1.75 1.00
2318 A1165 90c multi 2.00 1.30
2319 A1165 95c multi 3.50 1.50
2320 A1165 100c multi 2.25 1.35
2321 A1165 145c multi 3.00 2.00
2322 A1165 220c multi 5.25 3.25
2323 A1165 390c multi 10.50 6.75
2324 A1165 430c multi 13.00 8.25
Nos. 2307-2324 (18) 50.15 30.80

Coil Stamp
Self-Adhesive
Die Cut Perf. 10¼x10

2325 A1165 25c multi .60 .40
2326 A1165 35c multi .85 .55
2326A A1165 55c multi 1.50 .75
2326B A1165 90c multi 2.00 1.30
a. Booklet pane of 10 25.00

Issued: 95c, 430c, 1/3. 45c, 4/7. No. 2310, 50c, 6/2. 20c, No. 2315, 7/7. 5c, 8/11.10c, 40c, 9/8; No. 2326A, 7/7. No. 2325, 35c, 90c, 145c, 1/2/06. 65c, 3/2/06. 70c, 220c, 4/13/06. 390c, 5/4/06. 100c, 7/13/06. No. 2309a, 3/1/07.

See Nos. 2405-2423, 2814-2819, 2880-2886, 2968-2971, 2986, 3009-3012, 3058-3062.

Advertising Pillars, 150th Anniv. A1166

2005, Feb. 10 **Litho.** *Perf. 13¾*
2327 A1166 55c multi 1.35 .75

Berlin Cathedral, Cent. — A1167

2005, Feb. 10 *Perf. 13*
2328 A1167 95c multi 2.25 1.30

Booklet Stamp
Self-Adhesive
Die Cut Perf. 11

2329 A1167 95c multi 2.60 1.30
a. Booklet pane of 10 30.00

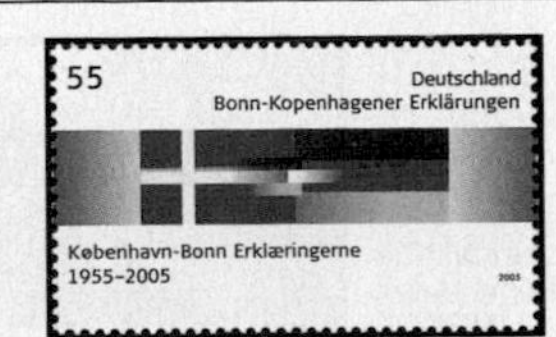

Bonn-Copenhagen Declaration, 50th Anniv. — A1168

2005, Mar. 3 *Perf. 14*
2330 A1168 55c multi 1.35 .75

See Denmark No. 1322.

Resumption of Regulated Civil Aviation, 50th Anniv. — A1169

2005, Mar. 3
2331 A1169 155c multi 3.75 2.10

Postal Workers A1170

Designs: No. 2332, Postman on bicycle. No. 2333, Postman on snowy hillside.

2005, Mar. 3 *Perf. 13¾*
2332 A1170 55c multi 1.50 .75
2333 A1170 55c multi 1.50 .75

See Nos. 2348-2349.

Mittelland Canal, Cent. — A1171

2005, Apr. 7 **Litho.** *Perf. 14*
2334 A1171 45c multi 1.20 .75

Bavarian Forest National Park — A1172

2005, Apr. 7 *Perf. 13¾*
2335 A1172 55c multi 1.35 .75

Hans Christian Andersen (1805-75), Author — A1173

2005, Apr. 7 *Perf. 14*
2336 A1173 144c multi 3.75 2.25

Coil Stamp
Self-Adhesive
Die Cut Perf. 10¼

2336A A1173 144c multi 4.25 2.60

Founding of Die Brücke Expressionist Group, Cent. — A1174

2005, May 12 **Litho.** *Perf. 13¾*
2337 A1174 55c buff, blk & red 1.35 .75

Paris Treaty, 50th Anniv. A1175

2005, May 12
2338 A1175 55c black & red 1.35 .75

Friedrich von Schiller Year — A1176

2005, May 12 *Perf. 14*
2339 A1176 55c multi 1.35 .75

Pope John Paul II (1920-2005) — A1177

2005, May 12
2340 A1177 55c multi 1.35 .75

Europa A1178

2005, May 12
2341 A1178 55c multi *1.35 .75*

Sixth Congress of European Organization of Supreme Audit Institutions, Bonn — A1179

2005, June 2 **Litho.** *Perf. 13¾*
2342 A1179 55c multi 1.35 .75

20th World Youth Day A1180

2005, June 2 *Perf. 14*
2343 A1180 55c multi 1.35 .75

See Vatican City No. 1298.

Lighthouse Type of 2004

Designs: Nos. 2344, 2345B, Brunsbüttel, Jetty 1. No. 2345A, Griefswalde Oie. 55c, Westerheversand.

2005, July 7 **Litho.** *Perf. 13¾*
2344 A1150 45c multi 1.10 .60
2345 A1150 55c multi 1.35 .75

Booklet Stamps
Self-Adhesive
Die Cut Perf. 10¾

2345A A1150 45c multi 1.20 .60
2345B A1150 45c multi 1.20 .60
c. Booklet pane, 5 each #2345A-2345B 12.00

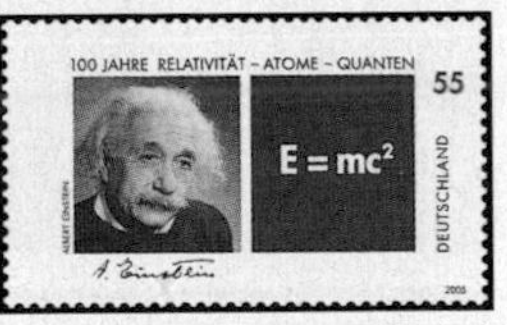

Albert Einstein's Theory of Relativity, Cent. — A1181

2005, July 7 *Perf. 14*
2346 A1181 55c multi 1.35 .75

Souvenir Sheet

Prussian Castles and Gardens — A1182

2005, July 7 *Perf. 13x13½*
2347 A1182 220c multi 5.50 3.50

Self-Adhesive
Booklet Stamp
Die Cut Perf. 11

2347A A1182 220c multi 5.50 3.50
b. Booklet pane of 10 60.00 —

Issued: No. 2347, 7/7. No. 2347A, 11/3.

Postal Workers Type of 2005

Designs: No. 2348, Postman on punt. No. 2349, Postman with handcart.

2005, Aug. 11 **Litho.** *Perf. 13¾*
2348 A1170 55c multi 1.35 .75
2349 A1170 55c multi 1.35 .75

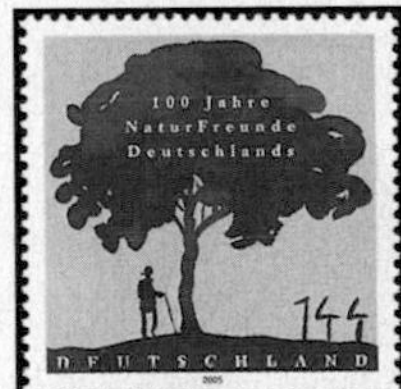

German Friends of Nature, Cent. A1183

2005, Aug. 11 *Perf. 13¼*
2350 A1183 144c multi 3.75 2.10

Magdeburg, 1200th Anniv. — A1184

2005, Sept. 8 **Litho.** *Perf. 14*
2351 A1184 55c multi 1.35 .75

For Children — A1185

2005, Sept. 8
2352 A1185 55c multi 1.35 .75

Peace of Augsburg, 450th Anniv. A1186

2005, Sept. 8 *Perf. 13¾*
2353 A1186 55c multi 1.35 .75

See No. 2508.

Max Schmeling (1905-2005), Boxer — A1187

2005, Sept. 8 *Perf. 14*
2354 A1187 55c multi 1.35 .75

Dedication of Rebuilt Church of Our Lady, Dresden — A1188

2005, Oct. 13 **Litho.** *Perf. 14*
2355 A1188 55c multi 1.35 .75

Adalbert Stifter (1805-68), Writer A1189

2005, Oct. 13 *Perf. 13¾*
2356 A1189 95c multi 2.40 1.50

St. Leonhard's Day Procession, Bad Tölz — A1190

2005, Nov. 3 **Litho.** *Perf. 13¼*
2357 A1190 45c multi 1.10 .60

Federal Armed Forces, 50th Anniv. A1191

2005, Nov. 3 ***Perf. 13¾***
2358 A1191 55c multi 1.35 .75

Diplomatic Relations With Israel, 40th Anniv. A1192

2005, Nov. 3
2359 A1192 55c multi 1.35 .75

See Israel No. 1619.

Awarding of Nobel Peace Prize to Bertha von Suttner, Cent. — A1193

2005, Nov. 3 ***Perf. 14***
2360 A1193 55c multi 1.35 .75

Awarding of Nobel Physiology or Medicine Prize to Robert Koch, Cent. — A1194

2005, Nov. 3 ***Perf. 13¼***
2361 A1194 144c multi 3.75 2.10

Halle, 1200th Anniv. A1195

2006, Jan. 2 **Litho.** ***Perf. 14***
2362 A1195 45c multi 1.10 .60

Winter A1196

2006, Jan. 2 **Litho.** ***Perf. 14***
2363 A1196 55c multi 1.35 .75

See No. 2400.

Spring A1197

2006, Apr. 13 **Litho.** ***Perf. 14***
2364 A1197 55c multi 1.35 .75

See No. 2397.

Summer — A1198

2006, July 13 **Litho.** ***Perf. 14***
2365 A1198 55c multi 1.35 .75

See No. 2398.

Autumn — A1199

2006, Oct. 5 **Litho.** ***Perf. 14***
2366 A1199 55c multi 1.35 .75

See No. 2399.

Wolfgang Amadeus Mozart (1756-91), Composer A1200

2006, Jan. 2 **Litho.** ***Perf. 13¼***
2367 A1200 55c multi 1.35 .75

Golden Bull of Emperor Charles IV — A1201

2006, Jan. 2 ***Perf. 14***
2368 A1201 145c multi 3.75 2.25

Self-Adhesive
Booklet Stamp
Die Cut Perf. 10

2369 A1201 145c multi 4.25 2.25
a. Booklet pane of 10 42.50

St. Michael's Church, Schwäbisch Hall, 850th Anniv. — A1202

2006, Feb. 9 **Litho.** ***Perf. 14***
2370 A1202 55c multi 1.35 .75

Frisian Council, 50th Anniv. A1203

2006, Feb. 9
2371 A1203 90c multi 2.10 1.30

Ingolstadt, 1200th Anniv. A1204

2006, Mar. 2 **Litho.** ***Perf. 13¼***
2372 A1204 55c multi 1.35 .75

Karl Friedrich Schinkel (1781-1841), Architect — A1205

2006 ***Perf. 14***
2373 A1205 55c multi 1.35 .75

Coil Stamp
Self-Adhesive
Die Cut Perf. 10x10¼

2373A A1205 55c multi 1.75 1.00

Issued: No. 2373, 3/2. No. 2373A, 7/13.

Care for the Blind — A1206

Litho. & Embossed

2006, Mar. 2 ***Perf. 13x13½***
2374 A1206 55c black & gray 1.35 .75

Berlin School for the Blind, 200th Anniv., Nikolaus Care Foundation, 150th Anniv.

Pres. Johannes Rau (1931-2006) — A1207

2006, Mar. 2 **Litho.** ***Perf. 14***
2375 A1207 55c multi 1.35 .75

Viadrina Universtiy, Frankfurt an der Oder, 500th Anniv. A1208

Litho. & Embossed

2006, Apr. 13 ***Perf. 13¾***
2376 A1208 55c multi 1.35 .75

Self-Portrait in Fur Coat, by Albrecht Dürer A1209

2006, Apr. 13 **Litho.**
2377 A1209 145c multi 3.50 2.00

Upper Middle Rhine Valley UNESCO World Heritage Site — A1210

2006, May 4 **Litho.** ***Perf. 13¾***
2378 A1210 55c multi 1.35 .75

Self-Adhesive
Booklet Stamp
Die Cut Perf. 11

2379 A1210 55c multi 1.45 .90
a. Booklet pane of 10 14.50

Europa A1211

2006, May 4 ***Perf. 14***
2380 A1211 55c multi 1.35 .75

Gerd Bucerius (1906-95), Publisher and Politician — A1212

2006, May 4
2381 A1212 85c multi 2.10 1.20

Stefan Andres (1906-70), Writer A1213

2006, June 8
2382 A1213 55c multi 1.35 .75

John Augustus Roebling (1806-69), Bridge Designer — A1214

2006, June 8 ***Perf. 14***
2383 A1214 145c multi 3.75 2.10

Self-Adhesive
Coil Stamp
Die Cut Perf. 11

2384 A1214 145c multi 4.25 2.60

Standardized Motor Vehicle Identification, Cent. — A1215

2006, July 13 **Litho.** ***Perf. 14***
2385 A1215 45c multi 1.20 .60

Burghausen Castle, Burghausen — A1216

2006, July 13
2386 A1216 55c multi 1.35 .75

Saskia van Uylenburgh, by Rembrandt (1606-69) A1217

2006, July 13 ***Perf. 13¾***
2387 A1217 70c multi 1.75 1.00

See Netherlands No. 1253. The design of No. 2387 was reproduced without the permission of the German authorities in a Netherlands booklet pane that also contains a similar Netherlands stamp.

Discovery of Neanderthal Man Bones, 150th Anniv. — A1218

2006, Aug. 10 **Litho.** ***Perf. 14***
2388 A1218 220c multi 5.50 3.50

Souvenir Sheet

Black Forest — A1219

2006, Aug. 10 ***Perf. 13¾***
2389 A1219 55c multi 1.60 1.00

Lighthouses Type of 2004

Designs: 45c, Neuland. 55c, Hohe Weg.

2006, Aug. 10 ***Perf. 13¾***
2390 A1150 45c multi 1.10 .60
2391 A1150 55c multi 1.35 .75

"Captain of Köpenick" A1220

2006, Sept. 7 **Litho.** ***Perf. 13¼***
2392 A1220 55c multi 1.45 .85

Theft of town funds and arrest of mayor in Köpenick by petty thief Friedrich Wilhelm Voigt, who masqueraded as an army officer, cent.

For Children A1221

2006, Sept. 7
2393 A1221 55c multi 1.35 .75

Hanseatic League, 650th Anniv. — A1222

Litho. & Engr.

2006, Sept. 7 ***Perf. 14***
2394 A1222 70c multi 1.75 1.15

See Sweden No. 2541

Stamp Day A1223

2006, Oct. 5 **Litho.** ***Perf. 14***
2395 A1223 55c multi 1.35 .75

Hannah Arendt (1906-75), Political Scientist — A1224

2006, Oct. 5 ***Perf. 13¾x14***
2396 A1224 145c multi 4.50 2.25

Seasons Types of 2006
Die Cut Perf. 14

2006, Nov. 9 **Litho.**

Booklet Stamps
Self-Adhesive

2397 A1197 55c Spring 1.50 .75
2398 A1198 55c Summer 1.50 .75
2399 A1199 55c Autumn 1.50 .75
2400 A1196 55c Winter 1.50 .75
a. Booklet pane, 5 each #2397-2400 30.00

Eugen Bolz (1881-1945), Politician A1225

2006, Nov. 9 ***Perf. 13¼***
2401 A1225 45c multi 1.20 .60

Joseph Cardinal Höffner (1906-87) A1226

2006, Nov. 9 ***Perf. 13¼***
2402 A1226 55c multi 1.35 .75

Werner Forssmann (1904-79), 1956 Physiology or Medicine Nobel Laureate — A1227

2006, Nov. 9 ***Perf. 14***
2403 A1227 90c multi 2.40 1.50

Flowers Type of 2005

Designs: 25c, Gartennelke (carnation). 28c, Tausendgüldenkraut (centaury). 45c, Maiglöckchen (lily of the valley). 55c, Gartenrose (rose). 58c, Kuhschelle (pasque flower). 60c, Kaiserkrone (kaiser's crown). 65c, Sonnenhut (rudbeckia). 70c, Kartäusernelke (clusterhead pink). 75c, Ballonblume (balloon flower). 100c, Tränendes herz (bleeding heart). 180c, Akelei (columbine). 200c, Goldmohn (California poppy). 240c, Prachtkerze (white gaura). 410c, Frauenschuh (lady's slipper). 500c, Enzian (gentian).

2006-14 **Litho.** ***Perf. 14***

2404	A1165	25c multi	.75	.40
2405	A1165	28c multi	.75	.45
2406	A1165	45c multi	1.20	.70
2407	A1165	55c multi	1.35	.75
2408	A1165	58c multi	1.50	.90
2409	A1165	60c multi	1.45	.90
2410	A1165	75c multi	1.75	1.05
2411	A1165	180c multi	4.50	2.75
2412	A1165	200c multi	5.00	2.75
2413	A1165	240c multi	6.00	3.75
2414	A1165	410c multi	10.25	6.50
2415	A1165	500c multi	11.00	6.75
	Nos. 2404-2415 (12)		45.50	27.65

Coil Stamps
Self-Adhesive
Die Cut Perf. 10¼x10

2416	A1165	25c multi	.75	.40
2417	A1165	28c multi	.75	.45
2418	A1165	58c multi	1.50	.90

Booklet Stamps

2419	A1165	45c multi	1.10	.70
a.		Booklet pane of 10	12.50	
2420	A1165	55c multi	1.35	.75
a.		Booklet pane of 10	17.50	
2421	A1165	60c multi	1.45	.90
f.		Booklet pane of 10	17.50	
2422	A1165	65c multi	1.45	.90
a.		Booklet pane of 5 + 5 etiquettes	8.75	
2423	A1165	70c multi	1.60	1.00
b.		Booklet pane of 5 + 5 etiquettes	9.50	
c.		Booklet pane of 10	19.00	
2423A	A1165	100c multi	2.40	1.50
d.		Booklet pane of 10	27.50	
	Nos. 2416-2423A (9)		12.35	7.50

Issued: 200c, 11/9/06; 55c, 6/12/08. 25c, 10/9/08. No. 2416, 6/12/08; No. 2420, 6/12/08, No. 2420a, 3/11/10; Nos. 2422-2423, 1/2/09. No. 2414, 1/2/10. No. 2406, 5/6/10; No. 2423c, 6/10/2010; 75c, 1/3/11; No. 2419, 3/1/11, 500c, 7/7/11. 58c, 240c, 12/6/12; No. 2418, 12/6/12; 60c, 12/5/13; 100c, 10/10/13; 180c, 6/5/14. 28c, 7/3/14.

No. 2420 was also issued in coils.

Fürth, 1000th Anniv. A1228

2007, Jan. 2 **Litho.** ***Perf. 13¼***
2424 A1228 45c multi 1.20 .70

Booklet Stamp
Self-Adhesive
Die Cut Perf. 11

2425 A1228 45c multi 1.20 .70
a. Booklet pane of 10 12.00

Germany, 2007 President of the European Union A1229

Litho. & Embossed

2007, Jan. 2 ***Perf. 13¾***
2426 A1229 55c multi 1.35 .75

Bamberg Bishopric, 1000th Anniv. A1230

2007, Jan. 2 **Litho.** ***Perf. 13¼***
2427 A1230 55c multi 1.35 .75

Admission of Saarland into Federal Republic, 50th Anniv. — A1231

2007, Jan. 2 ***Perf. 14***
2428 A1231 55c multi 2.10 1.35

Booklet Stamp
Self-Adhesive
Die Cut Perf. 10x10¼

2428A A1231 55c multi 1.35 .75
b. Booklet pane of 10 14.50

Wankel Rotary Engine, 50th Anniv. — A1232

2007, Jan. 2
2429 A1232 145c multi 3.50 2.10

Johann Christian Senckenberg (1707-72), Founder of Hospital, Frankfurt am Main — A1233

2007, Feb. 8 **Litho.** ***Perf. 14***
2430 A1233 90c multi 2.10 1.35

Munich Jewish Center A1234

2007, Mar. 1 **Litho.** ***Perf. 14***
2431 A1234 55c multi 1.35 .75

Paul Gerhardt (1607-76), Hymn Writer — A1235

2007, Mar. 1
2432 A1235 55c multi 1.35 .75

The Unearthing of the Cross, by Adam Elsheimer A1236

2007, Mar. 1 ***Perf. 13¼***
2433 A1236 55c multi 1.45 .75

Rome Treaty, 50th Anniv. A1237

2007, Mar. 1 ***Perf. 13¾***
2434 A1237 55c multi 1.35 .75

Leaders of Anti-Nazi Resistance Movement — A1238

2007, Mar. 1 ***Perf. 13¾x14***
2435 A1238 55c multi 1.35 .75

Claus Schenk Graf von Stauffenberg (1907-44), Hitler assassination plotter, and Helmuth James Graf von Moltke (1907-45), founding member of Kreisau Circle resistance group.

Pope Benedict XVI, 80th Birthday — A1239

2007, Apr. 12 **Litho.** ***Perf. 14***
2436 A1239 55c multi 1.35 .75

Letter Writing A1240

No. 2437, Boy writing letter. No. 2438, Boy mailing letter.

2007, Apr. 12 ***Perf. 13¾***
2437 A1240 55c multi 1.20 .75
2438 A1240 55c multi 1.20 .75

See Nos. 2454-2455.

Publication of World Map of Martin Waldseemuller, 500th Anniv. — A1241

Litho. & Engr.

2007, Apr. 12 ***Perf. 14***
2439 A1241 220c multi 6.75 4.25

Europa A1242

2007, May 3 **Litho.** ***Perf. 14***
2440 A1242 45c multi 1.10 .60

Scouting, cent.

Bellevue Palace, Presidential Residence — A1243

2007, May 3
2441 A1243 55c multi 1.45 .85

Coil Stamp
Self-Adhesive
Die Cut Perf. 10x10¼

2441A A1243 55c multi 1.60 .85

Moyland Castle, 700th Anniv. — A1244

2007, May 3
2442 A1244 85c multi 1.35 .75

Hambacher Fest, 175th Anniv. — A1245

2007, May 3 ***Perf. 14***
2443 A1245 145c multi 3.50 2.00

Booklet Stamp
Self-Adhesive
Die Cut Perf. 10x10¼

2444 A1245 145c multi 3.75 2.00
a. Booklet pane of 10 35.00

Karl Valentin (1882-1948), Writer A1246

2007, June 14 **Litho.** ***Perf. 13¾***
2445 A1246 45c multi 1.20 .70

Paul Klinger (1907-71), Film Actor A1247

2007, June 14
2446 A1247 55c multi 3.00 1.90

Lighthouses Type of 2004

Designs: 45c, Bremerhaven Oberfeuer. 55c, Hörnum.

2007, July 12 ***Perf. 13¾***
2447 A1150 45c multi 1.20 .60
2448 A1150 55c multi 1.35 .75

UNESCO World Heritage Sites — A1248

Designs: 65c, Historic Center of Riga, Latvia. 70c, Historic Centers of Straslund and Wismar, Germany.

2007, July 12 ***Perf. 14***
2449 A1248 65c multi 1.45 .90
2450 A1248 70c multi 1.60 1.00

See Latvia Nos. 679-680.

Saale Valley Dam and Lake Bleiloch, 75th Anniv. — A1249

2007, Aug. 9 **Litho.** ***Perf. 14***
2451 A1249 55c multi 1.35 .75

German Federal Bank, 50th Anniv. A1250

2007, Aug. 9
2452 A1250 55c multi 1.45 .75

Kaiser Wilhelm Bridge, Wilhelmshaven, Cent. — A1251

2007, Aug. 9 **Litho. & Engr.**
2453 A1251 145c multi 3.75 2.25

Letter Writing Type of 2007

Designs: No. 2454, Postman delivering letter to woman. No. 2455, Woman reading letter.

2007, Sept. 20 **Litho.** ***Perf. 13¾***
2454 A1240 55c multi 1.20 .75
2455 A1240 55c multi 1.20 .75

For Children — A1252

2007, Sept. 20 ***Perf. 14***
2456 A1252 55c multi 1.35 .75

Science Advisory Committee, 50th Anniv. — A1253

2007, Sept. 20
2457 A1253 90c multi 2.40 1.50

German Work Federation (Architecture Group), Cent. A1254

2007, Oct. 11 **Litho.** ***Perf. 13¼***
2458 A1254 55c multi 1.35 .75

Souvenir Sheet

Frontiers of the Roman Empire UNESCO World Heritage Site — A1255

2007, Oct. 11 ***Perf. 14***
2459 A1255 55c multi 2.10 1.35

Heinrich Friedrich Carl Freiherr vom und zum Stein (1757-1831), Prussian Statesman — A1256

2007, Oct. 11 ***Perf. 13¾x14***
2460 A1256 145c multi 3.50 2.10

St. Elizabeth of Hungary (1207-31) A1257

2007, Nov. 8 **Litho.** ***Perf. 13¾***
2461 A1257 55c multi 1.75 1.00

Astrid Lindgren (1907-2002), Writer — A1258

Litho. & Engr.

2007, Nov. 8 ***Perf. 13¾x14***
2462 A1258 100c multi 2.40 1.50

See Sweden No. 2572.

Brandenburg Gate, Designed by Carl Gotthard Langhans (1732-1808) — A1259

2007, Dec. 27 **Litho.** ***Perf. 14***
2463 A1259 55c multi 1.45 .75

Self-Adhesive
Booklet Stamp
Die Cut Perf. 10x10¼

2464 A1259 55c multi 1.75 .75
a. Booklet pane of 10 17.00

Reichenau Monastic Island UNESCO World Heritage Site — A1260

2008, Jan. 2 **Litho.** ***Perf. 13***
2465 A1260 45c multi 1.10 .60

Booklet Stamp
Self-Adhesive
Die Cut Perf. 10¾

2466 A1260 45c multi 1.20 .70
a. Booklet pane of 10 12.00

Heinrich Zille (1858-1929), Illustrator A1261

2008, Jan. 2 ***Perf. 13¾***
2467 A1261 55c multi 1.20 .75

Federal Cartel Office, 50th Anniv. A1262

2008 ***Perf. 14***
2468 A1262 90c multi 2.00 1.30

Booklet Stamp
Self-Adhesive
Die Cut Perf. 11¼x11

2468A A1262 90c multi 2.40 1.35
b. Booklet pane of 10 26.00

Issued: No. 2468, 1/2; No. 2468A, 3/13.

Eichstätt, 1100th Anniv. A1263

2008, Jan. 2 ***Perf. 13¾***
2469 A1263 145c multi 3.50 2.10

Coil Stamp
Self-Adhesive
Die Cut Perf. 10¼

2469A A1263 145c multi 3.75 2.25

Wenzel Jamnitzer (1508-85), Goldsmith — A1264

2008, Jan. 2 ***Perf. 13¾x14***
2470 A1264 220c multi 5.50 3.50

"Congratulations" — A1265

"All the Best" A1266

2008, Feb. 7 ***Perf. 14***
2471 A1265 55c multi 1.20 .75
2472 A1266 55c multi 1.20 .75

See Nos. 2487-2488.

Carl Spitzweg (1808-85), Painter A1267

2008, Feb. 7 **Litho.** ***Perf. 13¾***
2473 A1267 55c multi 1.35 .75

Coil Stamp
Self-Adhesive
Die Cut Perf. 10¼

2474 A1267 55c multi 1.45 .75

Village Church, Bochum-Stiepel, 1000th Anniv. — A1268

2008, Feb. 7 **Litho.** ***Perf. 13¾***
2475 A1268 145c multi 3.75 2.25

Helmut Käutner (1908-80), Film Director — A1269

2008, Mar. 13 **Litho.** ***Perf. 14***
2476 A1269 55c multi 1.35 .75

Frankfurt Zoo, 150th Anniv. A1270

2008, Mar. 13 ***Perf. 13¼***
2477 A1270 65c multi 1.45 .90

Seebach Bird Sanctuary, Cent. — A1271

2008, Apr. 10 **Litho.** ***Perf. 14***
2478 A1271 45c multi 1.35 .60

Johann Hinrich Wichern (1808-81), Theologian — A1272

2008, Apr. 10
2479 A1272 55c multi 1.35 .75

Max Planck (1858-1947), Physicist A1273

2008, Apr. 10 ***Perf. 13¾***
2480 A1273 55c multi 1.35 .75

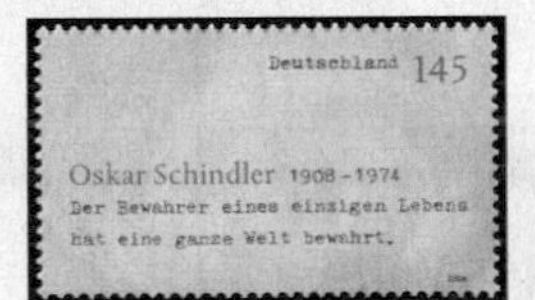

Oskar Schindler (1908-74), Industrialist Who Saved Jews From Holocaust — A1274

2008, Apr. 10 ***Perf. 14x14¼***
2481 A1274 145c multi 3.25 2.00

First International Match of German Soccer Team, Cent. A1275

2008, Apr. 10 ***Perf. 13¾***
2482 A1275 170c multi 5.00 3.00

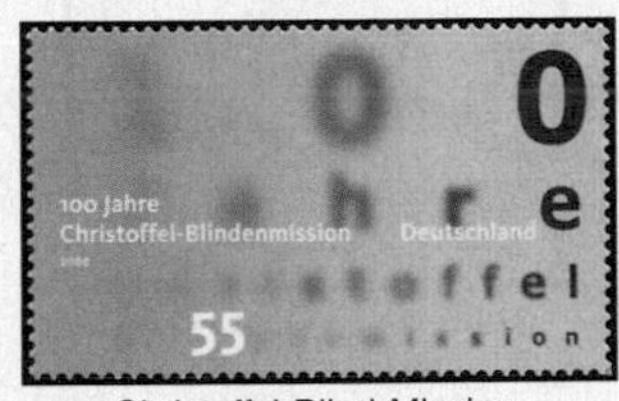

Christoffel Blind Mission, Cent. — A1276

2008, May 8 **Litho.** ***Perf. 13x13½***
2483 A1276 55c multi 1.35 .75

Greetings Types of 2008 and

"Kind Regards" — A1277

"Thank You" A1278

2008, May 8 ***Perf. 14***
2484 A1277 55c multi 1.35 .75
2485 A1278 55c multi 1.35 .75

Booklet Stamps
Self-Adhesive
Die Cut Perf. 14

2486 A1277 55c multi 1.35 .75
2487 A1265 55c multi 1.35 .75
2488 A1266 55c multi 1.35 .75
2489 A1278 55c multi 1.35 .75
a. Booklet pane of 20, 5 each #2486-2489 35.00
Nos. 2486-2489 (4) 5.40 3.00

Europa (Nos. 2484, 2486).

Honorary Offices — A1279

2008, June 12 **Litho.** ***Perf. 14***
2490 A1279 55c multi 1.35 .75

Lighthouses Type of 2004

Designs: No. 2491, 45c, Warnemünde. Nos. 2492, 2494, 55c, Amrum. No. 2493, 55c, Hörnum.

2008, July 3 **Litho.** ***Perf. 13¾***
2491 A1150 45c multi 1.20 .60
2492 A1150 55c multi 1.20 .75

Booklet Stamps
Self-Adhesive
Die Cut Perf. 11

2493 A1150 55c multi 1.35 .75
2494 A1150 55c multi 1.35 .75
a. Booklet pane of 10, 5 each #2493-2494 14.50

See No. 2632 for self-adhesive version of 45c.

Drachenfels Railway, 125th Anniv. — A1280

2008, July 3 *Perf. 14*

2495 A1280 45c multi 1.10 .60

Franz Kafka (1883-1924), Writer — A1281

2008, July 3

2496 A1281 55c black 1.35 .75

Self-portrait With Model, by Lovis Corinth (1858-1925) — A1282

2008, July 3 *Perf. 13x13½*

2497 A1282 145c multi 3.75 2.25

Training Ship Gorch Fock, 50th Anniv. A1283

2008, Aug. 7 **Litho.** *Perf. 13¼*

2498 A1283 55c multi 1.35 .75

Joachim Ringelnatz (1883-1934), Writer and Painter A1284

2008, Aug. 7 *Perf. 13¾*

2499 A1284 85c pur & black 1.90 1.20

Hermann Schulze-Delitzsch (1808-83), Economist — A1285

2008, Aug. 7 *Perf. 14*

2500 A1285 90c multi 1.90 1.20

Stamp Day — A1286

2008, Sept. 4 **Litho.** *Perf. 13¼*

2501 A1286 55c multi 1.35 .75

For Children A1287

2008, Sept. 4 *Perf. 14*

2502 A1287 55c multi 1.35 .75

Old Rhine Bridge, Bad Sackingen, Germany - Stein, Switzerland — A1288

2008, Sept. 4

2503 A1288 70c multi 1.60 1.00

See Switzerland No. 1319.

Gallimarkt (Livestock Market) of Leer, 500th Anniv. — A1289

2008, Oct. 9 **Litho.** *Perf. 14*

2504 A1289 45c multi 1.35 .60

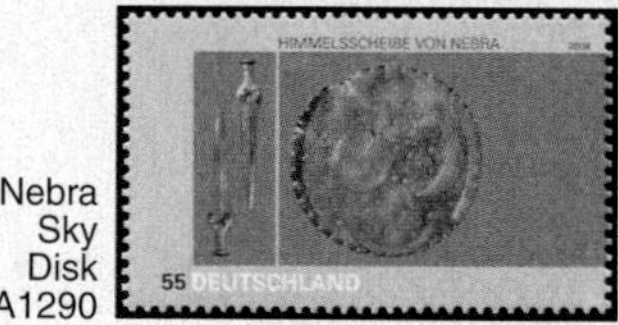

Nebra Sky Disk A1290

2008, Oct. 9

2505 A1290 55c multi 1.35 .75

Lorenz Werthmann (1858-1921), Founder of Caritas Charity A1291

2008, Oct. 9 *Perf. 13¾*

2506 A1291 55c multi 1.35 .75

First Powered Flight Over Germany, by Hans Grade, Cent. — A1292

2008, Oct. 9 *Perf. 14*

2507 A1292 145c multi 3.25 2.00

Peace of Augsburg and Adoration of the Magi Types of 2005

Die Cut Perf. 11¼

2008, Nov. 1 **Litho.**

Booklet Stamps

Self-Adhesive

2508 A1186 55c multi 1.35 .85
2509 A1163 55c multi 1.35 .85
a. Booklet pane of 10, 5 each #2508-2509 13.50

Lebenshilfe (Organization for the Mentally Handicapped), 50th Anniv. — A1293

2008, Nov. 13 *Perf. 14*

2510 A1293 55c multi 1.35 .75

A Heart for Children Charity, 30th Anniv. A1294

2008, Nov. 13 *Perf. 13¼*

2511 A1294 55c black & red 1.35 .75

Nils Holgersson on Goose A1295

2008, Nov. 13 *Perf. 13¾*

2512 A1295 100c multi 2.40 1.50

Selma Lagerlöf (1858-1940), author of *Nils Holgersson's Wonderful Journey Through Sweden.*

Frankenberg City Hall, 500th Anniv. A1296

2009, Jan. 2 **Litho.** *Perf. 13¾*

2513 A1296 45c multi 1.10 .60

Booklet Stamp

Self-Adhesive

Die Cut Perf. 10¾

2514 A1296 45c multi 1.10 .60
a. Booklet pane of 10 12.00

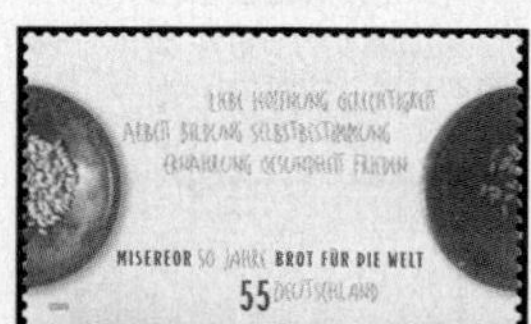

Misereor and Bread for the World Charities, 50th Anniv. — A1297

2009, Jan. 2 *Perf. 14*

2515 A1297 55c multi 1.20 .75

Tangermünde, 1000th Anniv. — A1298

2009, Jan. 2

2516 A1298 90c multi 1.90 1.20

Pres. Theodor Heuss (1884-1963) A1299

2009, Jan. 2 *Perf. 13¾*

2517 A1299 145c multi 3.25 2.00

Heinz Erhardt (1909-79), Comedian A1300

2009, Feb. 12 **Litho.** *Perf. 13¾*

2518 A1300 55c multi 1.20 .75

Felix Mendelssohn Bartholdy (1809-47), Composer A1301

2009, Feb. 12 *Perf. 13¼*

2519 A1301 65c multi 1.45 .90

Munich Propylaea, by Architect Leo von Klenze (1784-1864) A1302

2009, Feb. 12 *Perf. 13¾*

2520 A1302 70c multi 1.60 1.00

Der Feuervogel (Firebird), Woodcut by Helmut Andreas Paul Grieshaber (1909-81) A1303

2009, Feb. 12 *Perf. 13¼*

2521 A1303 165c multi 3.75 2.25

Golo Mann (1909-94), Historian A1304

2009, Mar. 12 Litho. *Perf. 13¾*
2522 A1304 45c multi 1.10 .60

1889 Daimler Automobile A1305

2009, Mar. 12 *Perf. 13¾x14*
2523 A1305 170c multi 3.75 2.25

Gottlieb Daimler (1834-1900), automobile engineer and manufacturer.

The Post — A1306

Designs: No. 2524, Hand affixing stamp on letter. No. 2525, Postal clerk serving customer. No. 2526, Postal truck. No. 2527, Postman carrying mail.

2009 *Perf. 13*
2524 A1306 55c multi 1.20 .75
2525 A1306 55c multi 1.20 .75
2526 A1306 55c multi 1.20 .75
2527 A1306 55c multi 1.20 .75

Issued: Nos. 2524-2525, 3/12. Nos. 2526-2527, 5/7.

Bernhard Grzimek (1909-87), Zoologist A1307

2009, Apr. 9
2528 A1307 55c multi 1.20 .75

Europa A1308

2009, May 7 *Perf. 14*
2529 A1308 55c multi 1.20 .75

Intl. Year of Astronomy.

Luther Memorials in Eisleben and Wittenberg UNESCO World Heritage Sites — A1309

2009, May 7 *Perf. 13¾x14*
2530 A1309 145c multi 3.25 2.00

Battle of the Teutoberg Forset, 2000th Anniv. A1310

2009, June 4 *Perf. 13¼*
2531 A1310 55c multi 1.20 .75

Booklet Stamp
Self-Adhesive
Serpentine Die Cut 10¾

2532 A1310 55c multi 1.35 .75
a. Booklet pane of 20 30.00

Frankfurt Intl. Aeronautical Exposition, Cent. A1311

2009, June 4 *Perf. 13¾*
2533 A1311 55c multi 1.20 .75

Coil Stamp
Self-Adhesive
Die Cut Perf. 10¼

2534 A1311 55c multi 1.35 .75

Heinrich Hoffmann (1809-94), Writer — A1312

2009, June 4 *Perf. 13¼*
2535 A1312 85c multi 1.90 1.20

Souvenir Sheet

Eifel National Park — A1313

2009, June 4 *Perf. 13¾*
2536 A1313 220c multi 5.00 3.00

Lighthouses Type of 2004

Designs: 45c, Norderney. 55c, Dornbusch.

2009, July 2
2537 A1150 45c multi 1.00 .60
2538 A1150 55c multi 1.20 .75

See No. 2631 for self-adhesive version of 45c.

Leipzig University, 600th Anniv. — A1314

2009, July 2 *Perf. 14*
2539 A1314 55c multi 1.20 .75

Booklet Stamp
Self-Adhesive
Size: 39x22mm
Die Cut Perf. 10

2540 A1314 55c multi 1.45 .75
a. Booklet pane of 10 16.00

John Calvin (1509-64), Theologian and Religious Reformer A1315

2009, July 2 *Perf. 13¼*
2541 A1315 70c black 1.60 1.00

Rail Ferry From Sassnitz to Trelleborg, Sweden, Cent. — A1316

2009, July 2 *Perf. 13¾x14*
2542 A1316 145c multi 3.25 2.00

Youth Hostels in Germany, Cent. — A1317

2009, Aug. 13 *Perf. 14*
2543 A1317 55c multi 1.20 .75

Consecration of Mainz Cathedral, 1000th Anniv. A1318

2009, Aug. 13 *Perf. 13¾*
2544 A1318 90c multi 1.90 1.20

Souvenir Sheet

Historical Motor Sports — A1319

2009, Aug. 13 *Perf. 14*
2545 A1319 85c multi 2.10 1.35

For Children — A1320

2009, Sept. 3
2546 A1320 55c multi 1.20 .75

People Waving German Flags — A1321

2009, Sept. 3
2547 A1321 55c multi 1.20 .75

Opening of Border Between Austria and Hungary, 20th Anniv. A1322

2009, Sept. 3 *Perf. 13¾*
2548 A1322 70c multi 1.60 1.00

See Austria No. 2219, Hungary No. 4136.

Souvenir Sheet

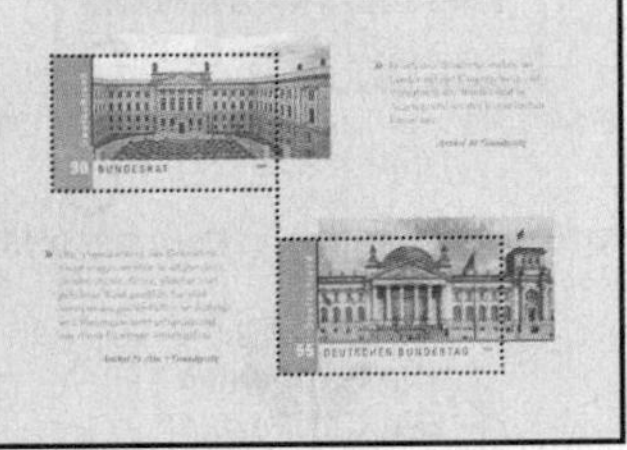
Federal Government Buildings, Berlin — A1323

2009, Sept. 3 *Perf. 14*
2549 A1323 Sheet of 2 3.50 2.10
a. 55c Bundestag 1.20 .75
b. 90c Bundesrat 2.00 1.30

Still Life with Cheese and Cherries, by Georg Flegel A1324

2009, Oct. 8 *Perf. 13¼*
2550 A1324 45c multi 1.10 .60

Crowd at St. Nicholas' Church, Leipzig A1325

2009, Oct. 8
2551 A1325 55c multi 1.35 .75

Peaceful political protest in East Germany, 20th anniv.

Marion Gräfin Dönhoff (1909-2002), Journalist — A1326

2009, Nov. 12 *Perf. 14*
2552 A1326 55c multi 1.20 .75

Badger
A1327

2009, Nov. 12 ***Perf. 13¾***
2553 A1327 55c multi 1.20 .75

Friedrich von Schiller (1759-1805), Writer
A1328

2009, Nov. 12
2554 A1328 145c multi 3.25 2.00

Berlin Natural History Museum, 200th Anniv. — A1329

2010, Jan. 2 Litho. ***Perf. 13½x13¾***
2555 A1329 45c multi 1.00 .60

Booklet Stamp
Self-Adhesive
Die Cut Perf. 10

2556 A1329 45c multi 1.20 .70
a. Booklet pane of 10 14.00

Ruhr Valley, 2010 European Cultural Capital — A1330

2010, Jan. 2 ***Perf. 13½x13¾***
2557 A1330 55c multi 1.20 .75

Limburg an der Lahn, 1100th Anniv.
A1331

2010, Jan. 2 ***Perf. 13½x13¾***
2558 A1331 145c multi 3.50 2.10

Booklet Stamp
Self-Adhesive
Die Cut Perf. 10

2559 A1331 145c multi 3.25 2.00
a. Booklet pane of 10 42.50

St. Michael's Church, Hildesheim UNESCO World Heritage Site — A1332

2010, Jan. 2 ***Perf. 13¼***
2560 A1332 220c multi 5.00 3.00

Booklet Stamp
Self-Adhesive
Die Cut Perf. 10¾

2561 A1332 220c multi 5.50 3.00
a. Booklet pane of 10 50.00

Mensch Argere Dich Nicht Board Game
A1333

Perf. 13½x13¾

2010, Feb. 11 **Litho.**
2562 A1333 55c multi 1.20 .75

Jewish Wedding Ring — A1334

2010, Feb. 11 ***Perf. 13¼***
2563 A1334 90c multi 2.00 1.30

Ariadne Abandoned by Theseus, by Angelica Kauffmann (1741-1807)
A1335

2010, Mar. 11 Litho. ***Perf. 13¾***
2564 A1335 260c multi 6.00 3.75

Greetings — A1336

2010 **Litho.** ***Perf. 13¾***
2565 A1336 55c Rainbow 1.35 .75
2566 A1336 55c Ship 1.35 .75
2567 A1336 55c Dove 1.35 .75
2568 A1336 55c Angel with heart 1.35 .75
Nos. 2565-2568 (4) 5.40 3.00

Issued: Nos. 2565-2566, 3/11; Nos. 2567-2568, 4/8. See Nos. 2596-2597, 2605-2606.

Souvenir Sheet

Heligoland Bird Station, Cent. — A1337

2010, Apr. 8 ***Perf. 14***
2569 A1337 145c multi 3.75 2.00

Coil Stamp
Die Cut Perf. 11
Self-Adhesive

2570 A1337 145c multi 3.75 2.00

Robert Schumann (1810-56), Composer — A1338

2010, May 6 Litho. ***Perf. 13½x13¾***
2571 A1338 55c multi 1.20 .75

Bee on Flower
A1339

2010, May 6 ***Perf. 13¾***
2572 A1339 55c multi 1.20 .75

Self-Adhesive
Die Cut Perf. 10¼

2572A A1339 55c multi 1.35 .75
2572Ab Booklet pane of 10 13.50

Issued: No. 2572Ab, 7/2/12.

Europa
A1340

2010, May 6 ***Perf. 13¼***
2573 A1340 55c multi 1.20 .75

Lighthouses Type of 2004

Designs: 45c, Neuwerk. 55c, Falshöft.

2010, June 10 Litho. ***Perf. 13¾***
2574 A1150 45c multi 1.00 .60
2575 A1150 55c multi 1.20 .75

Konrad Zuse (1910-95), Computer Engineer — A1341

2010, June 10 ***Perf. 13½x13¾***
2576 A1341 55c multi 1.20 .75

Porcelain Manufacturing in Germany, 300th Anniv. — A1342

2010, July 1 Litho. ***Perf. 13½x13¾***
2577 A1342 55c multi 1.20 .75

Booklet Stamp
Self-Adhesive
Die Cut Perf. 9¾x10

2577A A1342 55c multi 1.20 .75
b. Booklet pane of 20 28.00

Four-seat Mail Coach, 1858 — A1343

2010, July 1 ***Perf. 13¾***
2578 A1343 145c multi 3.25 2.00

Andrea Doria
A1344

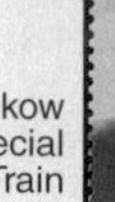

Pankow Special Train
A1345

2010, July 1 ***Perf. 13½x13¾***
2579 A1344 45c multi 1.20 .75
2580 A1345 55c multi 1.20 .75

Booklet Stamps
Self-Adhesive
Die Cut Perf. 10

2581 A1344 45c multi 1.00 .60
a. Booklet pane of 10 11.00
2582 A1345 55c multi 1.20 .75
a. Booklet pane of 10 14.00

Drawings on stamps are subjects of songs by the stamp designer, Udo Lindenberg.

Elly Beinhorn (1907-2007), Pilot — A1346

Perf. 13½x13¾

2010, Aug. 12 **Litho.**
2583 A1346 55c multi 1.20 .75

Mother Teresa (1910-97), Humanitarian
A1347

2010, Aug. 12 ***Perf. 13¼***
2584 A1347 70c multi 1.60 1.00

Jorge Luis Borges (1899-1986), Writer — A1348

2010, Aug. 12 ***Perf. 13¾x13½***
2585 A1348 170c multi 3.75 2.25

2010 Frankfurt Book Fair. See Argentina No. 2585.

For Children
A1349

2010, Sept. 9 **Litho.** ***Perf. 13¾***
2586 A1349 55c multi 1.20 .75

Octoberfest, 200th Anniv. A1350

2010, Sept. 9 *Perf. 13¼*
2587 A1350 55c multi 1.20 .75

Stamp Day — A1351

2010, Sept. 9
2588 A1351 55c multi 1.20 .75

Reunification of Germany, 20th Anniv. A1352

2010, Sept. 9 **Litho.** *Perf. 13¾*
2589 A1352 55c multi 1.20 .75

Coil Stamp
Self-Adhesive
Die Cut Perf. 10¼

2590 A1352 55c multi 1.20 .75

St. John's Foundation, 150th Anniv. A1353

2010, Sept. 9 **Litho.** *Perf. 13¾*
2591 A1353 90c multi 2.00 1.30

Old Buildings A1354

Buildings in: 45c, Eppingen, 1582. 55c, Trebel-Dänsche, 1734.

2010, Oct. 7 **Litho.** *Perf. 13¾*
2592 A1354 45c multi 1.00 .60
2593 A1354 55c multi 1.20 .75

See Nos. 2617-2618, 2669, 2702.

Thanksgiving A1355

2010, Oct. 7
2594 A1355 55c multi 1.20 .75

Friedrich Loeffler (1852-1915), Bacteriologist, Virus and Microscope — A1356

2010, Oct. 7 *Perf. 13½x13¾*
2595 A1356 85c multi 1.90 1.20

Friedrich Loeffler Institute, Cent.

Greetings Type of 2010

No. 2596, Dove. No. 2597, Angel with heart.

Die Cut Perf. 10

2010, Nov. 11 **Litho.**

Booklet Stamps
Self-Adhesive

2596 A1336 55c multi 1.20 .75
2597 A1336 55c multi 1.20 .75
a. Booklet pane of 10, 5 each #2596-2597 15.00

Railroads in Germany, 175th Anniv. A1357

Litho. & Engr.

2010, Nov. 11 *Perf. 13¾*
2598 A1357 55c multi 1.20 .75

2010 World Alpine Skiing Championships, Garmisch-Partenkirchen — A1358

Perf. 13½x13¾

2010, Nov. 11 **Litho.**
2599 A1358 55c multi 1.20 .75

Fritz Reuter (1810-74), Writer A1359

2010, Nov. 11 *Perf. 13¼*
2600 A1359 100c multi 2.10 1.35

German Miners' Guild, 750th Anniv. A1360

2010, Nov. 11 *Perf. 13½x13¾*
2601 A1360 145c black & red 3.25 2.00

Glider Flights from Wasserkuppe, Cent. — A1361

2011, Jan. 3 **Litho.** *Perf. 13½x13¾*
2602 A1361 45c multi 1.00 .60

The Wanderer Above the Mists, by Caspar David Friedrich A1362

2011 *Perf. 13¾*
2603 A1362 55c multi 1.50 .75

Coil Stamp
Self-Adhesive
Die Cut Perf. 10¼

2603A A1362 55c multi 1.60 .80

Issued: No. 2603, 1/3; No. 2603A, 5/5.

Kellerwald-Edersee National Park — A1363

2011 *Perf. 13½x13¾*
2604 A1363 145c multi 4.00 2.00

Booklet Stamp
Self-Adhesive
Die Cut Perf. 10

2604A A1363 145c multi 4.00 2.00
b. Booklet pane of 10 40.00

Issued: No. 2604, 1/3; No. 2604A, 4/7.

Greetings Type of 2010

Die Cut Perf. 10

2011, Feb. 3 **Litho.**

Booklet Stamps
Self-Adhesive

2605 A1336 55c Ship 1.50 .75
2606 A1336 55c Rainbow 1.50 .75
a. Booklet pane of 10, 5 each #2605-2606 15.00

Franz Liszt (1811-86), Composer — A1364

2011, Feb. 3 *Perf. 13½x13¾*
2607 A1364 55c multi 1.50 .75

Werra Valley View of Ludwigstein Castle and Ruins of Hanstein Castle — A1365

2011, Feb. 3 *Perf. 13½x13¾*
2608 A1365 90c multi 2.50 1.25

Booklet Stamp
Self-Adhesive
Die Cut Perf. 9¾

2609 A1365 90c multi 2.50 1.25
a. Booklet pane of 10 25.00

UNESCO World Heritage Sites — A1366

Designs: 55c, Historic Monuments of Ancient Nara, Japan. 75c, Old Town, Regensburg, Germany.

2011, Feb. 3 *Perf. 13½x13¾*
2610 A1366 55c multi 1.50 .75
2611 A1366 75c multi 2.10 1.10

Booklet Stamp
Self-Adhesive
Die Cut Perf. 10

2612 A1366 75c multi 2.10 1.10
a. Booklet pane of 10 21.00

See Japan No. 3301.

The Four Elements — A1367

Designs: No. 2613, Earth (sand dune). No. 2614, Wind (bird and clouds). No. 2615, Fire (volcano). No. 2616, Water (droplets on leaf).

2011, Mar. 3 *Perf. 13½x13¾*
2613 A1367 55c multi 1.60 .80
2614 A1367 55c multi 1.60 .80
2615 A1367 55c multi 1.60 .80
2616 A1367 55c multi 1.60 .80
Nos. 2613-2616 (4) 6.40 3.20

Old Buildings Type of 2010

Buildings in: 45c, Alsfeld, 1512-16. 55c, Hartenstein, Saxony, 1625.

2011, Apr. 7 **Litho.** *Perf. 13¾*
2617 A1354 45c multi 1.25 .65
2618 A1354 55c multi 1.60 .80

Europa A1368

2011, May 5 **Litho.** *Perf. 13½x13¾*
2619 A1368 55c multi 1.60 .80

Intl. Year of Forests.

Automobiles, 125th Anniv. — A1369

2011, May 5
2620 A1369 55c multi 1.60 .80

Wallraf-Richartz Museum, Cologne, 150th Anniv. — A1370

2011, May 5 ***Perf. 13¾***
2621 A1370 85c multi 2.50 1.25

German Chamber of Commerce and Industry, 150th Anniv. — A1371

2011, May 5 ***Perf. 13½x13¾***
2622 A1371 145c multi 4.25 2.10

National Insurance System, Cent. — A1372

2011, May 5
2623 A1372 205c multi 6.00 3.00

Mecklenburg "Molli" Rail Line, 125th Anniv. — A1373

2011, June 9
2624 A1373 45c multi 1.40 .70

Amnesty International, 50th Anniv. — A1374

2011, June 9
2625 A1374 55c multi 1.60 .80

Berlin Open-Air Gymnasium of Friedrich Ludwig Jahn, 200th Anniv. — A1375

Litho. & Engr.

2011, June 9 ***Perf. 12¾***
2626 A1375 165c multi 5.00 2.50

Souvenir Sheet

Steam Navigation in Saxony, 175th Anniv. — A1376

2011, June 9 Litho. ***Perf. 13¼***
2627 A1376 220c multi 6.50 3.25

Booklet Stamp
Self-Adhesive

Die Cut Perf. 10¾

2628 A1376 220c multi 6.50 3.25
a. Booklet pane of 10 65.00

Lighthouses Type of 2004

Designs: 55c, Arngast. 90c, Dahmeshöved. No. 2631, Norderney. No. 2632, Warnemünde.

2011 Litho. ***Perf. 13¾***
2629 A1150 55c multi 1.60 .80
2630 A1150 90c multi 2.60 1.25

Booklet Stamps
Self-Adhesive

Die Cut Perf. 10¾

2631 A1150 45c multi 1.25 .65
2632 A1150 45c multi 1.25 .65
a. Booklet pane of 10, 5 each #2631-2632 12.50

Issued: Nos. 2629-2630, 7/7; Nos. 2631-2632, 7/1.

First Publishing of Till Eulenspiegel Folk Tales, 500th Anniv. — A1377

2011, July 7 ***Perf. 13¼***
2633 A1377 55c multi 1.60 .80

German Shooting Federation, 150th Anniv. A1378

2011, July 7 ***Perf. 13¾***
2634 A1378 145c multi 4.25 2.10

Discovery of Archaeopteryx Fossil, 150th Anniv. A1379

2011, Aug. 11
2635 A1379 55c multi 1.60 .80

Elbe River Tunnel, Hamburg, Cent. — A1380

2011, Sept. 15 ***Perf. 13½x13¾***
2636 A1380 55c blue & black 1.50 .75

For Children A1381

2011, Sept. 15 ***Perf. 13¼***
2637 A1381 55c multi 1.50 .75

Biertan Church Castle UNESCO World Heritage Site, Romania A1382

2011, Sept. 15 ***Perf. 13¼***
2638 A1382 75c multi 2.10 1.10

See Romania No. 5299.

Calla Lily — A1383

2011, Oct. 13
2639 A1383 55c multi 1.50 .75

German Innovations and Inventions — A1384

Designs: 45c, Thermos bottle, currywurst, two-part teabag. 55c, Emil Berliner's gramophone, reel-to-reel tape recorder, mp3.

2011, Oct. 3 ***Perf. 13½x13¾***
2640 A1384 45c multi 1.25 .60
2641 A1384 55c multi 1.50 .75

Pinakothek Art Museum, Munich, 175th Anniv. — A1385

2011, Oct. 13
2642 A1385 145c multi 4.00 2.00

Adveniat Charity, 50th Anniv. A1386

2011, Nov. 10 ***Perf. 13½x13¾***
2643 A1386 55c multi 1.50 .75

Kaiser Wilhelm Memorial Church, Berlin, 50th Anniv. A1387

2011, Nov. 10 ***Perf. 13¼***
2644 A1387 55c multi 1.50 .75

Emil Wiechert (1861-1928), Geophysicist A1388

2011, Nov. 10 ***Perf. 13¾***
2645 A1388 90c multi 2.50 1.25

Skiers in Winter A1389

2012, Jan. 2 ***Perf. 13½x13¾***
2646 A1389 45c multi 1.25 .60

King Frederick II (the Great) of Prussia (1712-86) A1390

2012, Jan. 2 ***Perf. 13***
2647 A1390 55c multi 1.50 .75

Jasmund National Park — A1391

2012, Jan. 2 ***Perf. 13½x13¾***
2648 A1391 55c multi 1.50 .75

Booklet Stamp
Self-Adhesive
Size: 39x23mm

Die Cut Perf. 10

2649 A1391 55c multi 1.50 .75
a. Booklet pane of 10 15.00

Spectrum of Sun with Fraunhofer Lines — A1392

2012 *Perf. 13½x13¾*
2650 A1392 90c multi 2.40 1.25

Booklet Stamp
Self-Adhesive
Size:39x23mm

Die Cut Perf. 10

2651 A1392 90c multi 2.40 1.25
a. Booklet pane of 10 24.00

Joseph von Fraunhofer (1787-1826), physicist. Issued: No. 2650, 1/2; No. 2651, 4/12.

Zwinger, Dresden, Designed by Matthäus Daniel Pöppelmann (1662-1736), Architect — A1393

2012 *Perf. 13½x13¾*
2652 A1393 145c multi 3.75 1.90

Booklet Stamp
Self-Adhesive
Size: 39x23mm

Die Cut Perf. 10

2653 A1393 145c multi 3.75 1.90
a. Booklet pane of 10 37.50

Issued: No. 2652, 1/2; No. 2653, 2/9.

Harz Mountains Narrow-Gauge Railway, 125th Anniv. — A1394

2012, Feb. 9 *Perf. 13½x13¾*
2654 A1394 45c multi 1.25 .60

Booklet Stamp
Self-Adhesive
Size: 39x23mm

Die Cut Perf. 10

2655 A1394 45c multi 1.25 .60
a. Booklet pane of 10 12.50

Biathlon World Championships, Ruhpolding — A1395

2012, Feb. 9 *Perf. 13½x13¾*
2656 A1395 55c multi 1.50 .75

Blue Horse I, by Franz Marc A1396

2012, Feb. 9 **Litho.** *Perf. 13¾*
2657 A1396 145c multi 4.00 2.00

Der Blaue Reiter (Blue Rider) art movement, cent.

Reintroduction of Endangered Animals into Native Habitats — A1397

Designs: Nos. 2658, 2660, Lynx (luchs). Nos. 2659, 2661, Elk (elch).

2012 *Perf. 13½x13¾*
2658 A1397 55c multi 1.50 .75
2659 A1397 55c multi 1.50 .75

Booklet Stamps
Self-Adhesive
Size: 39x23mm

Die Cut Perf. 10

2660 A1397 55c multi 1.50 .75
2661 A1397 55c multi 1.50 .75
a. Booklet pane of 20, 10 each #2660-2661 30.00

Issued: Nos. 2658-2659, 2/9; Nos. 2660-2661, 3/1.

Tree in Spring A1398

2012, Mar. 1 *Perf. 13½x13¾*
2662 A1398 55c multi 1.50 .75

Booklet Stamp
Self-Adhesive
Size: 39x23mm

Die Cut Perf. 10

2663 A1398 55c multi 1.50 .75
a. Booklet pane of 10 15.00

Trees at Dusk A1399

2012, Mar. 1 *Perf. 13½x13¾*
2664 A1399 55c multi 1.50 .75

Gerardus Mercator (1512-94), Cartographer A1400

2012, Mar. 1 *Perf. 13¼*
2665 A1400 220c multi 6.00 3.00

Souvenir Sheet

Sistine Madonna, by Raphael, 500th Anniv. — A1401

2012, Mar. 1 *Perf. 13¾*
2666 A1401 55c multi 1.50 .75

See Vatican City Nos. 1496, 1498.

Welthungerhilfe (World Hunger Help) Charity, 50th Anniv. — A1402

2012, Apr. 12 **Litho.** *Perf. 13¼*
2667 A1402 55c multi 1.50 .75

Axel Springer (1912-85), Journalist and Publisher A1403

2012, Apr. 12 *Perf. 13¾*
2668 A1403 55c multi 1.50 .75

Old Buildings Type of 2010

Design: Building in Bad Münstereifel, 1644-64.

2012, May 2 *Perf. 13¾*
2669 A1354 165c multi 4.50 2.25

Soccer Fans with German Flags A1404

2012, May 2 *Perf. 13¾*
2670 A1404 55c multi 1.50 .75

Booklet Stamp
Self-Adhesive

Die Cut Perf. 11

2671 A1404 55c multi 1.50 .75
a. Booklet pane of 10 + 5 stickers 15.00

Johann Gottlieb Fichte (1762-1814), Philosopher A1405

2012, May 2 *Perf. 13¾*
2672 A1405 70c multi 1.90 .95

Lighthouse Type of 2004

2012, May 2 ***Die Cut Perf. 10¼***

Coil Stamp
Self-Adhesive

2673 A1150 55c Arngast 1.50 .75

Europa A1406

2012, May 2 *Perf. 13½x13¾*
2674 A1406 55c multi 1.50 .75

Grimm's Fairy Tales, 200th Anniv. A1407

2012, June 14 *Perf. 13¾*
2675 A1407 55c multi 1.40 .70

Pfälzer Hutte Mountain Lodge, Liechtenstein — A1408

Perf. 13½x13¾

2012, June 14 **Litho.**
2677 A1408 75c multi 1.90 .95

See Liechtenstein No. 1542.

German Choir Association, 150th Anniv. A1409

2012, June 14 *Perf. 13¼*
2678 A1409 85c multi 2.10 1.10

Balcony Room, by Adolph Menzel A1410

2012, June 14 *Perf. 13¾*
2679 A1410 260c multi 6.50 3.25

Lighthouses Type of 2012

Designs: 45c, Little Borkum Lighthouse (Kleiner Leuchtturm Borkum). 55c, Arkona.

2012, July 12
2680 A1150 45c multi 1.10 .55
2681 A1150 55c multi 1.40 .70

Apartment Intercom with Names of Different Nationalities — A1411

2012, July 12 *Perf. 13½x13¾*
2682 A1411 55c multi 1.40 .70

Muskauer Park UNESCO World Heritage Site, Germany and Poland — A1412

2012, July 12
2683 A1412 90c multi 2.25 1.10

See Poland No. 4050.

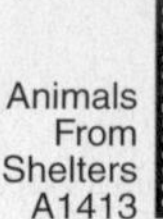

Animals From Shelters A1413

2012, July 12
2684 A1413 145c multi 3.75 1.90

King Otto the Great (912-73) A1414

2012, Aug. 9 ***Perf. 13¾***
2685 A1414 45c multi 1.25 .60

Gäubodenvolksfest (Folk Festival), Straubing, 200th Anniv. — A1415

2012, Aug. 9 ***Perf. 13½x13¾***
2686 A1415 55c multi 1.40 .70

Mittenwald Railroad, Cent. — A1416

2012, Aug. 9
2687 A1416 75c multi 2.00 1.00

Valley in Autumn A1417

2012, Sept. 13
2688 A1417 55c multi 1.50 .75

Stamp Day A1418

2012, Sept. 13
2689 A1418 55c multi 1.50 .75

First official airmail flight in Germany, cent.

National Library, Cent. A1419

2012, Sept. 13
2690 A1419 55c multi 1.50 .75

For Children A1420

2012, Sept. 13
2691 A1420 55c multi 1.50 .75

German Bible Association, Cent. — A1421

2012, Sept. 13
2692 A1421 85c multi 2.25 1.10

Second Vatican Council, 50th Anniv. A1422

2012, Oct. 11 ***Perf. 13¾***
2693 A1422 45c multi 1.25 .60

Chancellor Helmut Kohl, Honorary Citizen of Europe A1423

2012, Oct. 11
2694 A1423 55c multi 1.40 .70

Castles in Gleichen, Mühlburg and Wachsenburg — A1424

2012, Oct. 11
2695 A1424 55c multi 1.40 .70

Domowina (Society of Sorbs and Wends), Cent. — A1425

2012, Oct. 11
2696 A1425 145c multi 3.75 1.90

Numeral — A1426

2012, Nov. 2 ***Perf. 14x13½***
2697 A1426 3c multi .25 .25

Self-Adhesive
Die Cut Perf. 9¾

2698 A1426 3c multi .25 .25

See Nos. 2758-2759, 2871-2872.

Protest of the Göttingen Seven, 175th Anniv. A1427

2012, Nov. 2 ***Perf. 13¾***
2699 A1427 55c multi 1.40 .70

Gerhart Hauptmann (1862-1946), 1912 Nobel Literature Laureate — A1428

2012, Nov. 2
2700 A1428 55c multi 1.40 .70

Sistine Madonna, by Raphael, 500th Anniv. A1429

2012, Nov. 2 ***Die Cut Perf. 11***
Booklet Stamp
Self-Adhesive

2701 A1429 55c multi 1.40 .70
a. Booklet pane of 10 + 4 stickers 14.00

Old Buildings Type of 2010

Design: Building in Dinkelbühl, 1600.

2012, Dec. 6 ***Perf. 13¾***
2702 A1354 58c multi 1.50 .75

Elysée Treaty, 50th Anniv. A1430

2013, Jan. 2 **Litho.** ***Perf. 13½x13¾***
2703 A1430 75c multi 2.00 1.00

See France No. 4314.

Museum Treasures A1431

Designs: 58c, Bust of Queen Nefertiti, from Neues Museum, Berlin. 145c, Ishtar Gate, from Pergamon Museum, Berlin.

2013, Jan. 2 ***Perf. 14x13¾***
2704 A1431 58c multi 1.60 .80
2705 A1431 145c multi 4.00 2.00

See Nos. 2716, 2724.

Castles and Palaces A1432

Designs: 45c, Glücksburg Castle (Schloss Glücksburg). 58c, Nuremberg Castle (Kaiserburg Nürnberg).

2013, Jan. 2 ***Perf. 13½x13¾***
2706 A1432 45c multi 1.25 .60
2707 A1432 58c multi 1.60 .80

Booklet Stamp
Self-Adhesive
Size: 39x23mm
Die Cut Perf. 10

2708 A1432 58c multi 1.60 .80
a. Booklet pane of 10 16.00

See No. 2734.

The Bleaching, by Max Liebermann (1847-1935) A1433

2013, Jan. 2 ***Perf. 13¼***
2709 A1433 240c multi 6.50 3.25

Booklet Stamp
Self-Adhesive
Die Cut Perf. 11

2710 A1433 240c multi 6.50 3.25
a. Booklet pane of 10 65.00

Treaty of Hubertusburg, 250th Anniv. A1434

2013, Feb. 7 **Litho.** ***Perf. 13¾***
2711 A1434 90c multi 2.40 1.25

Gendarmenmarkt, Berlin — A1435

Designs: Nos. 2712, 2714, Streetlights, Concert House, denomination at UL. Nos. 2713, 2715, German Cathedral and French Cathedral, denomination at UR.

2013, Feb. 7 ***Perf. 13½x13¾***
2712 A1435 58c multi 1.50 .75
2713 A1435 58c multi 1.50 .75
a. Horiz. pair, #2712-2713 3.00 1.50

Booklet Stamps
Self-Adhesive
Size:39x23mm
Die Cut Perf. 9¾ on 3 Sides

2714 A1435 58c multi 1.50 .75
2715 A1435 58c multi 1.50 .75
a. Booklet pane of 20, 10 each #2714-2715 30.00

Museum Treasures Type of 2013

Design: 58c, Bust of Queen Nefertiti.

2013, Mar. 1 ***Die Cut Perf. 11½x11¼***
Coil Stamp
Self-Adhesive

2716 A1431 58c multi 1.50 .75

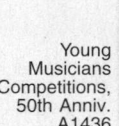

Young Musicians Competitions, 50th Anniv. A1436

2013, Mar. 1 *Perf. 13¾*
2717 A1436 58c multi 1.50 .75

Friedrich Hebbel (1813-63), Writer A1437

2013, Mar. 1 **Litho.**
2718 A1437 100c multi 2.60 1.40

August Hermann Francke (1663-1727), Theologist A1438

2013, Mar. 1
2719 A1438 205c multi 5.50 2.75

Illustrations by Janosch — A1439

Animals: 45c, In sailboat. 58c, With Easter eggs.

2013, Mar. 1 *Perf. 13½x13¾*
2720 A1439 45c multi 1.25 .60
2721 A1439 58c multi 1.50 .75

Booklet Stamps
Self-Adhesive
Size: 39x23mm
Die Cut Perf. 9¾

2722 A1439 45c multi 1.25 .60
a. Booklet pane of 10 12.50
2723 A1439 58c multi 1.50 .75
a. Booklet pane of 10 15.00

Museum Treasures Type of 2013

Design: 145c, Ishtar Gate.

Die Cut Perf. 11½x11¼
2013, Apr. 4 **Litho.** **Coil Stamp**
Self-Adhesive

2724 A1431 145c multi 3.75 1.90

Intl. Red Cross, 150th Anniv. A1440

2013, Apr. 4 *Perf. 13¾*
2725 A1440 58c black & red 1.50 .75

German Sports Badge, Cent. — A1441

2013, Apr. 4
2726 A1441 58c multi 1.50 .75

General German Workers' Association, 150th Anniv. A1442

2013, Apr. 4
2727 A1442 145c multi 3.75 1.90

Fehmarn Sound Bridge A1443

2013, Apr. 4 *Perf. 13¾*
2728 A1443 75c multi 2.00 1.00

Booklet Stamp
Self-Adhesive
Size: 39x23mm
Die Cut Perf. 10

2729 A1443 75c multi 2.00 1.00
a. Booklet pane of 10 20.00

Möhne Reservoir Dam — A1444

2013 *Perf. 13¾*
2730 A1444 90c multi 2.40 1.25

Booklet Stamp
Self-Adhesive
Size: 39x23mm
Die Cut Perf. 10

2731 A1444 90c multi 2.40 1.25
a. Booklet pane of 10 24.00

Issued: No. 2730, 4/4; No. 2731, 5/2.

Richard Wagner (1813-83), Composer — A1445

2013, May 2 *Perf. 13¾*
2732 A1445 58c multi 1.50 .75

Europa A1446

2013, May 2 **Litho.**
2733 A1446 58c multi 1.50 .75

Castles and Palaces Type of 2013

Design: 45c, Glücksburg Castle (Schloss Glücksburg).

2013, June 6 ***Die Cut Perf. 10***
Booklet Stamp
Self-Adhesive
Size: 39x23mm

2734 A1432 45c multi 1.25 .60
a. Booklet pane of 10 12.50

German Rose Show, Forst, Cent. A1447

2013, June 6 *Perf. 13¾*
2735 A1447 45c multi 1.25 .60

German Armed Forces A1448

2013, June 6
2736 A1448 58c multi 1.60 .80

Lighthouses Type of 2004

Designs: 45c, Flügge Lighthouse. 58c, Büsum Lighthouse.

2013, June 6 *Perf. 13¾*
2737 A1150 45c multi 1.25 .60
2738 A1150 58c multi 1.60 .80

Temple of the Sun, Bayreuth A1449

Gyeongbokgung Palace, Seoul, South Korea — A1450

2013, June 6 **Litho.**
2739 A1449 75c multi 2.00 1.00
2740 A1450 150c multi 4.00 2.00

See South Korea No. 2406.

Dessau, 800th Anniv. A1451

2013, July 1
2741 A1451 45c multi 1.25 .60

Berchtesgaden National Park — A1452

Wadden Sea A1453

2013, July 1 *Perf. 13¾*
2742 A1452 58c multi 1.50 .75
2743 A1453 58c multi 1.50 .75

Seascape, by Gerhard Richter — A1454

2013, July 1 *Perf. 13¾*
2744 A1454 145c multi 3.75 1.90

Booklet Stamp
Self-Adhesive
Size: 39x23mm
Die Cut Perf. 10

2745 A1454 145c multi 3.75 1.90
a. Booklet pane of 10 37.50

Julius Cardinal Dopfner (1913-76) A1455

2013, Aug. 8 *Perf. 13¾*
2746 A1455 58c multi 1.60 .80

Skat Card Game, 200th Anniv. A1456

2013, Sept. 5 **Litho.** *Perf. 13½x13¾*
2747 A1456 90c multi 2.40 1.25

Heidelberg — A1457

Designs: No. 2748, Heidelberg Castle and Old Bridge, denomination at UL. No. 2749, Old town, denomination at UR.

2013, Sept. 5
2748 58c multi 1.60 .80
2749 58c multi 1.60 .80
a. A1457 Horiz. pair, #2748-2749 3.20 1.60

Monument to the Battle of the Nations (Battle of Leipzig), Leipzig, Cent. — A1458

2013, Oct. 10 **Litho.** *Perf. 13¾*
2750 A1458 45c multi 1.25 .60

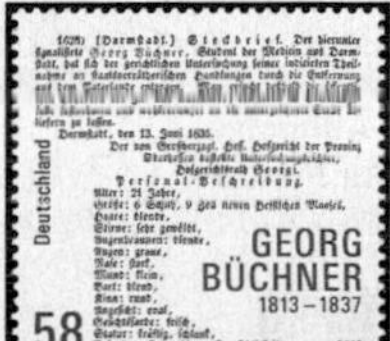

Arrest Warrant for Georg Büchner (1813-37), Playwright A1459

2013, Oct. 10 **Litho.** *Perf. 13¾*
2751 A1459 58c blk & red 1.60 .80

Ludwig Leichhardt (1813-48), Explorer of Australian Outback Region A1460

2013, Oct. 10 Litho. *Perf. 13¾*
2752 A1460 75c multi 2.10 1.10

See Australia No. 4004.

Willy Brandt (1913-92), Chancellor of Germany — A1461

2013, Nov. 2 Litho. *Perf. 13¾*
2753 A1461 58c multi 1.60 .80

Discovery of Radio Waves by Heinrich Hertz, 125th Anniv. — A1462

2013, Nov. 2 Litho. *Perf. 14x13¾*
2754 A1462 58c multi 1.60 .80

Rahel Hirsch (1870-1953), First Female Physician in Prussia — A1463

2013, Nov. 2 Litho. *Perf. 13¾*
2755 A1463 145c multi 4.00 2.00

Christmas A1464

2013, Nov. 2 Litho. *Perf. 14x13¾*
2756 A1464 58c multi 1.60 .80

Booklet Stamp
Self-Adhesive
Die Cut Perf. 11½x11¼

2757 A1464 58c multi 1.60 .80
a. Booklet pane of 10 16.00

Numeral Type of 2012

2013, Dec. 5 Litho. *Perf. 14x13½*
2758 A1426 2c multi .25 .25

Self-Adhesive
Die Cut Perf. 9¾

2759 A1426 2c multi .25 .25

Clouds in Sky A1465

2013, Dec. 5 Litho. *Perf. 13¾*
2760 A1465 60c multi 1.75 .85

Reintroduction of Atlantic Salmon to German Rivers — A1466

2014, Jan. 2 Litho. *Perf. 13½x13¾*
2761 A1466 45c multi 1.25 .60

Juvenile Animals A1467

Designs: Nos. 2762, 2764, Fox kits (fuchs). Nos. 2763, 2764, Hedgehog hoglets (igel).

2014, Jan. 2 Litho. *Perf. 13½x13¾*
2762 A1467 60c multi 1.75 .85
2763 A1467 60c multi 1.75 .85

Booklet Stamps
Self-Adhesive
Size: 39x23mm
Die Cut Perf. 10

2764 A1467 60c multi 1.75 .85
2765 A1467 60c multi 1.75 .85
a. Booklet pane of 20, 10 each #2764-2765 35.00

Lorsch Abbey UNESCO World Heritage Site — A1468

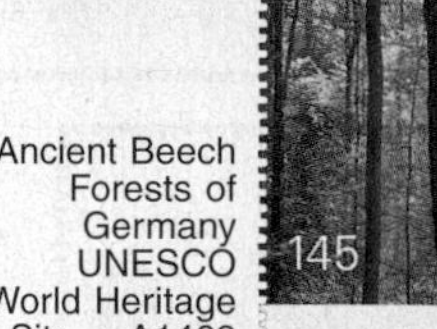

Ancient Beech Forests of Germany UNESCO World Heritage Site — A1469

2014, Jan. 2 Litho. *Perf. 13¾*
2766 A1468 60c multi 1.75 .85
2767 A1469 145c multi 4.00 2.00

Coil Stamp
Self-Adhesive
Die Cut Perf. 10¼

2768 A1468 60c multi 1.75 .85

Lorsch Abbey, 1250th anniv. See No. 2788.

Stolzenfels Castle — A1470

2014, Jan. 2 Litho. *Perf. 13½x13¾*
2769 A1470 75c multi 2.10 1.10

Lower Oder Valley Floodplain — A1471

Devil's Table, Palatinate Forest — A1472

2014, Feb. 6 Litho. *Perf. 13½x13¾*
2770 A1471 60c multi 1.75 .85
2771 A1472 60c multi 1.75 .85

See Nos. 2784-2785.

Albrechtsburg Castle, Meissen — A1473

2014, Mar. 1 Litho. *Perf. 13½x13¾*
2772 A1473 90c multi 2.50 1.25

Protestant Brass Choirs — A1474

2014, Mar. 1 Litho. *Perf. 14x13¾*
2773 A1474 215c multi 6.00 3.00

"Happy Easter" A1475

"For You" A1476

2014, Mar. 1 Litho. *Perf. 13½x13¾*
2774 A1475 45c multi 1.25 .60
2775 A1476 60c multi 1.75 .85

Booklet Stamp
Self-Adhesive
Size: 39x22mm
Die Cut Perf. 10

2776 A1476 60c multi 1.75 .85
a. Booklet pane of 10 17.50

A1477

2014, Apr. 3 Litho. *Perf. 13¾*
2777 A1477 60c multi 1.75 .85

Aktion Mensch (Action Man) Charity, 50th Anniv.

Max Weber (1864-1920), Sociologist A1478

2014, Apr. 3 Litho. *Perf. 13¾*
2778 A1478 60c multi 1.75 .85

Dresden A1479

Boats on the Elbe River and: Nos. 2779, 2781, Crescent moon, Frauenkirche, denomination at UL. Nos. 2780, 2782, Hofkirche, Zwinger Palace and Semper Opera, denomination at UR

2014, Apr. 3 Litho. *Perf. 13¾*
2779 A1479 45c multi 1.25 .60
2780 A1479 45c multi 1.25 .60
a. Horiz. pair, #2779-2780 2.50 1.25

Booklet Stamps
Self-Adhesive
Size: 39x23mm
Die Cut Perf. 9¾ on 3 Sides

2781 A1479 45c multi 1.25 .60
2782 A1479 45c multi 1.25 .60
a. Booklet pane of 10, 5 each #2781-2782 12.50

First Long Distance Railway Line in Germany, 175th Anniv. — A1480

2014, Apr. 3 Litho. *Perf. 13¾*
2783 A1480 145c multi 4.00 2.00

Lower Oder Valley Floodplain and Devil's Table Types of 2014
Booklet Stamps
Self-Adhesive Size:39x23mm

2014, May 8 Litho. *Die Cut Perf. 10*
2784 A1471 60c multi 1.75 .85
2785 A1472 60c multi 1.75 .85
a. Booklet pane of 10, 5 each #2784-2785 17.50

Two Women, Watercolor by Johann Gottfried Schadow (1764-1850) — A1481

2014, May 8 Litho. *Perf. 13¾*
2786 A1481 60c multi 1.75 .85

Clarinet A1482

2014, May 8 Litho. *Perf. 13¾*
2787 A1482 60c multi 1.75 .85

Europa.

Ancient Beech Forests Type of 2014

Die Cut Perf. 10¼

2014, June 5 **Litho.**

Coil Stamp
Self-Adhesive

2788 A1469 145c multi 4.00 2.00

Orchestral Instruments and Silhouette of Richard Strauss (1864-1949), Composer A1483

2014, June 5 **Litho.** ***Perf. 13¾***
2789 A1483 60c multi 1.75 .85

Creation of the Animals, Detail of Altarpiece by Master Bertram (c. 1340-c. 1414) — A1484

2014, June 5 **Litho.** ***Perf. 13¾***
2790 A1484 240c multi 6.75 3.50

See No. 2849.

Market Square, Bremen A1485

Designs: No. 2791, Deutsches Haus and adjoining buildings, denomination at UL. No. 2792, Town Hall, Statue of Roland, St. Peter's Cathedral, denomination at UR.

2014, June 5 **Litho.** ***Perf. 13¾***
2791 A1485 60c multi 1.75 .85
2792 A1485 60c multi 1.75 .85
a. Horiz. pair, #2791-2792 3.50 1.75

Lighthouses Type of 2004

Designs: 45c, Buk Lighthouse. 60c, Pellworm Lighthouse.

2014, July 3 **Litho.** ***Perf. 13¾***
2793 A1150 45c multi 1.25 .60
2794 A1150 60c multi 1.60 .80

Council of Constance, 600th Anniv. — A1486

2014, July 3 **Litho.** ***Perf. 13¾***
2795 A1486 60c multi 1.60 .80

Opera Glasses and Silhouette of Christoph Willibald Gluck (1714-87), Opera Composer A1487

2014, July 3 **Litho.** ***Perf. 13¾***
2796 A1487 90c multi 2.40 1.25

Ricarda Huch (1864-1947), Writer A1488

2014, July 3 **Litho** ***Perf. 13¾***
2797 A1488 145c blk & brt org 4.00 2.00

Victory of German Team at 2014 World Cup Soccer Championships — A1489

2014, July 17 **Litho.** ***Perf. 14***
2798 A1489 60c multi 1.60 .80

Youth Fire Brigades, 50th Anniv. — A1490

2014, Aug. 7 **Litho.** ***Perf. 13½x13¾***
2799 A1490 60c multi 1.60 .80

Never Again War, Poster by Käthe Kollwitz (1867-1945) A1491

2014, Aug. 7 **Litho.** ***Perf. 13¾***
2800 A1491 75c multi 2.00 1.00

World War I, cent.

Coach of Lindau Messenger Courier Service — A1492

2014, Sept. 1 **Litho.** ***Perf. 13½x13¾***
2801 A1492 60c multi 1.60 .80

Stamp Day.

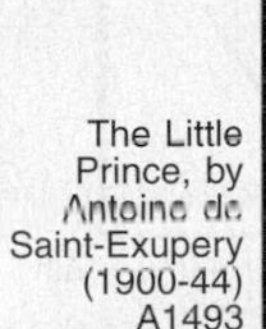

The Little Prince, by Antoine de Saint-Exupery (1900-44) A1493

2014, Sept. 1 **Litho.** ***Perf. 13¾***
2802 A1493 60c multi 1.60 .80

Booklet Stamp
Self-Adhesive

Die Cut Perf. 10¼

2803 A1493 60c multi 1.60 .80
a. Booklet pane of 10 16.00

Sunny Road, by August Macke — A1494

2014, Sept. 1 **Litho.** ***Perf. 14***
2804 A1494 100c multi 2.75 1.40

Mittelland Canal Lock, Minden, Cent. — A1495

2014, Oct. 2 **Litho.** ***Perf. 14***
2805 A1495 45c multi 1.25 .60

Fagus Factory UNESCO World Heritage Site — A1496

2014, Oct. 2 **Litho.** ***Perf. 13½x13¾***
2806 A1496 60c multi 1.50 .75

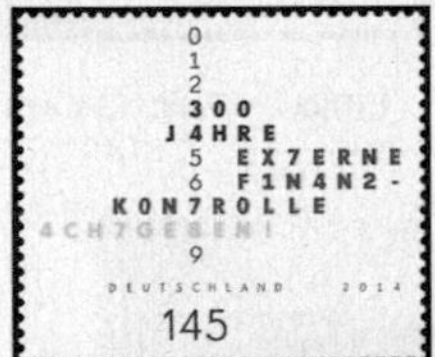

External Auditing, 300th Anniv. A1497

2014, Oct. 2 **Litho.** ***Perf. 13¾x14***
2807 A1497 145c multi 3.75 1.90

Fahrenheit Temperature Scale, 300th Anniv. — A1498

2014, Nov. 3 **Litho.** ***Perf. 13¾***
2808 A1498 60c multi 1.50 .75

Julius Robert von Mayer (1814-78), Physicist — A1499

2014, Nov. 3 **Litho.** ***Perf. 13¾***
2809 A1499 90c multi 2.25 1.10

Snowman A1500

2014, Nov. 3 **Litho.** ***Perf. 13¾x14***
2810 A1500 60c multi 1.50 .75

Booklet Stamp
Self-Adhesive

Serpentine Die Cut

2811 A1500 60c multi 1.50 .75
a. Booklet pane of 10 15.00

Reintroduction of Sea Trout to German Rivers — A1501

2014, Dec. 4 **Litho.** ***Perf. 13¾***
2812 A1501 45c multi 1.10 .55

Visitation, by Rogier van der Weyden A1502

2014, Dec. 4 **Litho.** ***Perf. 14***
2813 A1502 145c multi 3.50 1.75

Flowers Type of 2005

Designs: 62c, Pfingstrose (peony). 80c, Kugelprimel (drumstick primrose). 85c, Federnelke (pink). 395c, Purpurglöckchen (coral bells). 440c, Türkenbund (Turk's cap lily).

2014, Dec. 4 **Litho.** ***Perf. 14***
2814 A1165 62c multi 1.50 .75
2815 A1165 80c multi 2.00 1.00
2816 A1165 85c multi 2.10 1.10
2817 A1165 395c multi 9.50 4.75
2818 A1165 440c multi 11.00 5.50
Nos. 2814-2818 (5) 26.10 13.10

Self-Adhesive

Die Cut Perf. 10¼x10

2819 A1165 62c multi 1.50 .75
a. Booklet pane of 10 15.00

Western Pomerania Lagoon National Park — A1503

2015, Jan. 2 **Litho.** ***Perf. 13½x13¾***
2820 A1503 85c multi 2.10 1.10

Booklet Stamp
Self-Adhesive
Size: 39x23mm

Die Cut Perf. 9¾

2821 A1503 85c multi 2.10 1.10
a. Booklet pane of 10 21.00

Juvenile Animals A1504

Designs: Nos. 2822, 2824, Squirrels (eichhörnchen). Nos. 2823, 2825, Wildcats (wildkatze).

2015, Jan. 2 **Litho.** ***Perf. 13½x13¾***
2822 A1504 62c multi 1.50 .75
2823 A1504 62c multi 1.50 .75

Booklet Stamps
Self-Adhesive
Size: 39x23mm

Die Cut Perf. 9¾

2824 A1504 62c multi 1.50 .75
2825 A1504 62c multi 1.50 .75
a. Booklet pane of 20, 10 each #2824-2825 30.00

Marksburg Castle — A1505

Ludwigslust Castle — A1506

2015, Jan. 2 Litho. *Perf. 13½x13¾*

2826 A1505 62c multi 1.50 .75
2827 A1506 80c multi 2.00 1.00

Coil Stamp
Self-Adhesive
Die Cut Perf. 10¾

2828 A1506 62c multi 1.50 .75

Booklet Stamp
Size: 39x22mm
Die Cut Perf. 9¾

2829 A1506 80c multi 2.00 1.00
a. Booklet pane of 10 20.00

Karl Leisner (1915-45), Priest Ordained While Interned at Dachau Concentration Camp — A1507

2015, Feb. 5 Litho. *Perf. 13½x13¾*

2830 A1507 62c blue & blk 1.40 .70

Hildesheim Diocese, 1200th Anniv. — A1508

2015, Mar. 2 Litho. *Perf. 14*

2831 A1508 62c blk & gold 1.40 .70

Felix the Rabbit, Children's Book Character by Annette Landen — A1509

Designs: 45c, Felix in open suitcase. 62c, Felix writing letter.

2015, Mar. 2 Litho. *Perf. 13½x13¾*

2832 A1509 45c multi 1.00 .50
2833 A1509 62c multi 1.40 .70

Booklet Stamp
Self-Adhesive
Size: 39x22mm
Die Cut Perf. 9¾

2834 A1509 62c multi 1.40 .70
a. Booklet pane of 10 14.00

University of Kiel, 350th Anniv. — A1510

2015 Litho. *Perf. 13½x13¾*

2835 A1510 62c multi 1.40 .70

Booklet Stamp
Self-Adhesive
Size: 39x22mm
Die Cut Perf. 9¾

2836 A1510 62c multi 1.40 .70
a. Booklet pane of 10 14.00

Issued: No. 2835, 3/2; No. 2836, 5/7.

City of Köthen, 900th Anniv. A1511

2015, Mar. 2 Litho. *Perf. 13½x13¾*

2837 A1511 240c multi 5.50 2.75

Otto von Bismarck (1815-98), Chancellor — A1512

2015, Apr. 2 Litho. *Perf. 13½x13¾*

2838 A1512 62c multi 1.40 .70

Max and Moritz, by Wilhelm Busch, 150th Anniv. A1513

2015, Apr. 2 Litho. *Perf. 13¾x14*

2839 A1513 62c multi 1.40 .70

Automobiles — A1514

Designs: Nos. 2840, 2842, 1956-59 BMW 507. Nos. 2841, 2843, Mercedes-Benz 220 S (W111).

2015, Apr. 2 Litho. *Perf. 13½x13¾*

2840 A1514 145c multi 3.25 1.60
2841 A1514 145c multi 3.25 1.60

Booklet Stamps
Self-Adhesive
Size: 39x22mm
Die Cut Perf. 9¾

2842 A1514 145c multi 3.25 1.60
2843 A1514 145c multi 3.25 1.60
a. Booklet pane of 10, 5 each #2842-2843 32.50

German Maritime Search and Rescue Association, 150th Anniv. A1515

2015, May 7 Litho. *Perf. 13¾*

2844 A1515 62c multi 1.40 .70

Europa A1516

2015, May 7 Litho. *Perf. 13¾*

2845 A1516 62c multi 1.40 .70

Diplomatic Relations Between Germany and Israel, 50th Anniv. A1517

2015, May 7 Litho. *Perf. 14*

2846 A1517 80c multi 1.75 .90

See Israel No. 2062

Lighthouses Type of 2004

Designs: 45c, Moritzburg Lighthouse. 62c, Lindau Lighthouse.

2015, June 11 Litho. *Perf. 13¾*

2847 A1150 45c multi 1.00 .50
2848 A1150 62c multi 1.40 .70

Master Bertram Altarpiece Type of 2014
Die Cut Perf. 11½

2015, June 11 Litho.

Booklet Stamp
Self-Adhesive

2849 A1484 240c multi 5.25 2.60
a. Booklet pane of 10 52.50

Young Scientists Competition, 50th Anniv. — A1518

2015, June 11 Litho. *Perf. 14*

2850 A1518 62c multi 1.40 .70

First Bavarian Traditional Costume Association, 125th Anniv. A1519

2015, June 11 Litho. *Perf. 13¾*

2851 A1519 62c multi 1.40 .70

Kindergartens in Germany, 175th Anniv. — A1520

2015, June 11 Litho. *Perf. 14*

2852 A1520 215c multi 4.75 2.40

Leipzig, 1000th Anniv. A1521

2015, July 1 Litho. *Perf. 13½x13¾*

2853 A1521 62c org & red 1.40 .70

Pina Bausch (1940-2009), Choreographer — A1522

2015, July 1 Litho. *Perf. 13½x13¾*

2854 A1522 85c multi 1.90 .95

Philipp Scheidemann (1865-1939), Chancellor A1523

2015, July 1 Litho. *Perf. 13¾*

2855 A1523 145c black & red 3.25 1.60

Chiemsee — A1524

Designs: Nos. 2856, 2858, Boat on Chiemsee (denomination at UL). Nos. 2857, 2859, Mountains near Chiemsee (denomination at UR).

2015, July 1 Litho. *Perf. 13½x13¾*

2856 A1524 45c multi 1.00 .50
2857 A1524 45c multi 1.00 .50
a. Horiz. pair, #2856-2857 2.00 1.00

Booklet Stamps
Self-Adhesive
Size: 39x22mm
Die Cut Perf. 9¾ on 3 Sides

2858 A1524 45c multi 1.00 .50
2859 A1524 45c multi 1.00 .50
a. Booklet pane of 10, 5 each #2858-2859 10.00

International Windjammer Festival, Bremerhaven A1525

2015, Aug. 6 Litho. *Perf. 13¾*

2860 A1525 62c multi 1.40 .70

Helmut Schön (1915-96), Soccer Coach A1526

2015, Sept. 1 Litho. *Perf. 13¾*

2861 A1526 62c multi 1.40 .70

Asterix, Comic Strip by René Goscinny and Albert Uderzo — A1527

Characters: No. 2862a, Dogmatix carrying bone (35x35mm). Nos. 2862b, 2863, Obelix carrying boar (33x39mm). Nos. 2862c, 2864, Asterix the Gaul (33x39mm).

Perf. 13¾ (21c), 14x13¾ (62c)

2015, Sept. 1 **Litho.**

2862 A1527 Sheet of 3 3.25 3.25
a. 21c multi .45 .25
b.-c. 62c Either single 1.40 .70

Booklet Stamps
Self-Adhesive

Die Cut Perf. 11¾x11¼

2863 A1527 62c multi 1.40 .70
2864 A1527 62c multi 1.40 .70
a. Booklet pane of 10, 5 each #2863-2864 14.00

Altarpiece, St. Mary's Church, Wittenberg, by Lucas Cranach the Younger (1515-86) — A1528

2015, Oct. 1 **Litho.** ***Perf. 13½x13¾***
2865 A1528 45c multi 1.00 .50

Reunification of Germany, 25th Anniv. A1529

2015, Oct. 1 **Litho.** ***Perf. 13¾***
2866 A1529 62c multi 1.40 .70

Grieving Women, Sculpture by Tilman Riemenschneider (c. 1460-1531) — A1530

Nativity with Adoration of the Shepherds, by Martin Schongauer (c. 1444-91) A1531

2015 **Litho.** ***Perf. 14***
2867 A1530 62c multi 1.40 .70
2868 A1531 145c multi 3.25 1.60

Issued: 62c, 10/1; 145c, 11/2.

Christmas — A1532

2015, Nov. 2 **Litho.** ***Perf. 13½x13¾***
2869 A1532 62c multi 1.40 .70

Booklet Stamp
Self-Adhesive
Size: 39x23mm

Die Cut Perf. 9¾

2870 A1532 62c multi 1.40 .70
a. Booklet pane of 10 14.00

Numeral Type of 2012

2015, Dec. 3 **Litho.** ***Perf. 14x13½***
2871 A1426 8c multi .25 .25

Self-Adhesive

Die Cut Perf. 9¾

2872 A1426 8c multi .25 .25

Freiberg Universtiy of Mining and Technology, 250th Anniv. — A1533

2015, Dec. 3 **Litho.** ***Perf. 13½x13¾***
2873 A1533 70c multi 1.60 .80

Booklet Stamp
Self-Adhesive
Size: 39x23mm

Die Cut Perf. 10

2874 A1533 70c multi 1.60 .80
a. Booklet pane of 10 16.00

Microscopic View of Diatom A1534

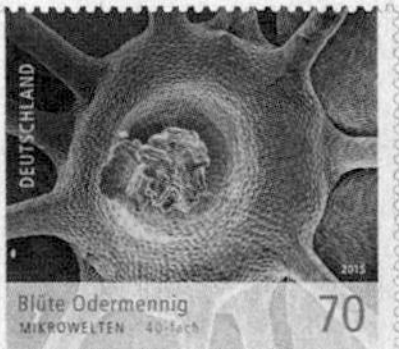

Microscopic View of Agrimony Flower A1535

2015-16 **Litho.** ***Perf. 14***
2875 A1534 70c multi 1.60 .80
2876 A1535 70c multi 1.60 .80

Coil Stamps
Self-Adhesive

Die Cut Perf. 11x11½

2877 A1534 70c multi 1.60 .80
2878 A1535 70c multi 1.60 .80
a. Horiz. pair, #2877-2878 3.20

Issued: Nos. 2875-2876, 12/3; Nos. 2877-2878, 1/2/16.

Sky Flowers Above the Yellow House, by Paul Klee (1879-1940) A1536

2015, Dec. 3 **Litho.** ***Perf. 14x13¾***
2879 A1536 240c multi 5.25 2.60

Flowers Type of 2005

Designs: 5c, Phlox. 70c, Schokoladen-kosmee (chocolate cosmos). 250c, Alpendistel (Alpine thistle). 260c, Madonnenlilie (Madonna lily). 400c, Fuchsie (fuschia). 450c, Bienenragwurz (bee orchid).

2015-17 **Litho.** ***Perf. 14***
2880 A1165 5c multi .25 .25
2881 A1165 70c multi 1.60 .80
2882 A1165 250c multi 5.50 2.75
2883 A1165 260c multi 5.75 3.00
2884 A1165 400c multi 8.75 4.50
2885 A1165 450c multi 10.00 5.00
Nos. 2881-2885 (5) 31.60 16.05

Coil Stamp
Self-Adhesive

Die Cut Perf. 10¼x10

2886 A1165 70c multi 1.60 .80

Issued: 70c, 400c, 450c, No. 2886, 12/3/15; 250c, 1/2/16; 260c, 2/11/16; 5c, 4/13/17.

Löwenburg Castle, Kassel — A1537

2016, Jan. 2 **Litho.** ***Perf. 13½x13¾***
2887 A1537 90c multi 2.00 1.00

Bavarian Forest A1538

2016, Jan. 2 **Litho.** ***Perf. 13½x13¾***
2888 A1538 85c multi 1.90 .95

Automobiles — A1539

Designs: Nos. 2889, 2891, 1965 Porsche 911 Targa. Nos. 2890, 2892, 1969-73 Ford Capri 1.

2016 **Litho.** ***Perf. 13½x13¾***
2889 A1539 70c multi 1.60 .80
2890 A1539 70c multi 1.60 .80

Booklet Stamps
Self-Adhesive
Size: 39x22mm

Die Cut Perf. 9¾

2891 A1539 70c multi 1.60 .80
2892 A1539 70c multi 1.60 .80
a. Booklet pane of 20, 10 each #2891-2892 32.00

Issued: Nos. 2889-2890, 1/2; Nos. 2891-2892, 2/11.

Schwetzingen, 1250th Anniv. — A1540

2016 **Litho.** ***Perf. 13½x13¾***
2893 A1540 145c multi 3.25 1.60

Booklet Stamp
Self-Adhesive
Size: 39x22mm

Die Cut Perf. 9¾

2894 A1540 145c multi 3.25 1.60
a. Booklet pane of 10 32.50

Issued: No. 2893, 1/2; No. 2894, 3/1.

112 European Emergency Number, 25th Anniv. A1541

2016, Feb. 11 **Litho.** ***Perf. 13¾***
2895 A1541 45c red & dp ultra 1.00 .50

Ernst Litfass (1816-74), Creator of Advertising Pillars A1542

2016, Feb. 11 **Litho.** ***Perf. 13¾***
2896 A1542 70c multi 1.60 .80

Corvey Abbey UNESCO World Heritage Site — A1543

2016, Mar. 1 **Litho.** ***Perf. 13½x13¾***
2897 A1543 70c multi 1.60 .80

Juvenile Animals A1544

Designs: Nos. 2898, 2900, Leverets. Nos. 2899, 2901, Greylag goslings.

2016, Mar. 1 **Litho.** ***Perf. 13½x13¾***
2898 A1544 70c multi 1.60 .80
2899 A1544 70c multi 1.60 .80

Booklet Stamps
Self-Adhesive
Size: 39x22mm

Die Cut Perf. 9¾

2900 A1544 70c multi 1.60 .80
2901 A1544 70c multi 1.60 .80
a. Booklet pane of 8, 4 each #2900-2901 13.00

Sanssouci Palace, Potsdam — A1545

2016 **Litho.** ***Perf. 13½x13¾***
2902 A1545 85c multi 1.90 .95

Booklet Stamp
Self-Adhesive
Size: 39x22mm

Die Cut Perf. 9¾

2903 A1545 85c multi 2.00 1.00
a. Booklet pane of 10 20.00

Issued: No. 2902, 3/1; No. 2903, 4/7.

Dresden Frauenkirche, Designed by George Bähr (1666-1738) A1546

2016, Mar. 1 Litho. *Perf. 13¾*
2904 A1546 260c multi 5.75 3.00

Booklet Stamp
Self-Adhesive
Die Cut Perf. 10¼

2905 A1546 260c multi 5.75 3.00
a. Booklet pane of 10 57.50

Bavarian Beer Purity Laws, 500th Anniv. — A1547

2016, Apr. 7 Litho. *Perf. 14*
2906 A1547 45c multi 1.10 .55

Nelly Sachs (1891-1970), 1966 Nobel Laureate in Literature A1548

2016, Apr. 7 Litho. *Perf. 13¾*
2907 A1548 70c multi 1.60 .80

Charles V, Holy Roman Emperor, by Titian — A1549

Ivory Frigate Carried by Neptune, by Jacob Zeller — A1550

2016 Litho. *Perf. 14*
2908 A1549 70c multi 1.60 .80
2909 A1550 145c multi 3.50 1.75

Coil Stamp
Self-Adhesive
Die Cut Perf. 11½x11¼

2910 A1550 145c multi 3.25 1.60

Issued: Nos. 2908-2909, 4/7; No. 2910, 6/2.

Bend in Moselle River Near Kröv A1551

Designs: Nos. 2911, 2913, River bend and bridge, denomination at UL. Nos. 2912, 2914, River bend, no bridge, denomination at UR.

2016 Litho. *Perf. 13½x13¾*
2911 A1551 90c multi 2.10 1.10
2912 A1551 90c multi 2.10 1.10
a. Horiz. pair, #2911-2912 4.25 2.25

Booklet Stamps
Self-Adhesive
Size: 39x22mm
Die Cut Perf. 9¾ on 3 Sides

2913 A1551 90c multi 2.10 1.10
2914 A1551 90c multi 2.10 1.10
a. Booklet pane of 10, 5 each #2913-2914 21.00

Issued: Nos. 2911-2912, 4/7; Nos. 2913-2914, 5/2.

Europa A1552

2016, May 2 Litho. *Perf. 13½x13¾*
2915 A1552 70c multi 1.60 .80

Think Green Issue.

German Catholics' Day, Cent. — A1553

2016, May 2 Litho. *Perf. 13¾*
2916 A1553 70c multi 1.60 .80

Wedding Shoes A1554

Birthday Cake A1555

Flowers A1556

2016, May 2 Litho. *Perf. 13½x13¾*
2917 A1554 70c multi 1.60 .80
2918 A1555 70c multi 1.60 .80
2919 A1556 70c multi 1.60 .80
Nos. 2917-2919 (3) 4.80 2.40

Booklet Stamps
Self-Adhesive
Size: 39x22mm
Die Cut Perf. 9¾

2920 A1555 70c multi 1.60 .80
2921 A1556 70c multi 1.60 .80
a. Booklet pane of 10, 5 each #2920-2921 16.00

Black Madonna and Shrine of Our Lady of Altötting A1557

2016, May 2 Litho. *Perf. 13½x13¾*
2922 A1557 85c multi 2.00 1.00

Microscopic View of Moth's Antenna A1558

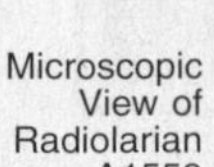

Microscopic View of Radiolarian A1559

2016, June 2 Litho. *Perf. 14*
2923 A1558 70c multi 1.60 .80
2924 A1559 250c multi 5.75 3.00

Schrammsteine Rock Formation, Saxon Switzerland National Park — A1560

2016, June 2 Litho. *Perf. 13½x13¾*
2925 A1560 45c multi 1.00 .50

Booklet Stamp
Self-Adhesive
Size:39x22mm
Die Cut Perf. 9¾

2926 A1560 45c multi 1.00 .50
a. Booklet pane of 10 10.00

Polish-German Youth Office, 25th Anniv. — A1561

2016, June 2 Litho. *Perf. 13½x13¾*
2927 A1561 90c multi 2.00 1.00

See Poland No. 4229

Lighthouses Type of 2004

Designs: 45c, Staberhuk Lighthouse. 70c, Kampen Lighthouse.

2016, July 7 Litho. *Perf. 13¾*
2928 A1150 45c multi 1.00 .50
2929 A1150 70c multi 1.60 .80

First Glider of Otto Lilienthal (1848-96), 125th Anniv. — A1562

2016, July 7 Litho. *Perf. 14*
2930 A1562 145c multi 3.25 1.60

Münsterschwarzach Abbey, 1200th Anniv. — A1563

2016, Aug. 4 Litho. *Perf. 13½x13¾*
2931 A1563 70c multi 1.60 .80

Stamp Day — A1564

2016, Sept. 1 Litho. *Perf. 14*
2932 A1564 70c red & ol brown 1.60 .80

German Television Series *Space Patrol,* 50th Anniv. — A1565

2016, Sept. 1 Litho. *Perf. 13½x13¾*
2933 A1565 145c multi 3.25 1.60

Souvenir Sheet

Livestock Breeds — A1566

No. 2934: a, Rhön sheep. b, German saddle pig.

2016, Sept. 1 Litho. *Perf. 13½x13¾*
2934 A1566 Sheet of 2 3.50 1.75
a. 70c multi 1.60 .80
b. 85c multi 1.90 .85

Naumburg Cathedral — A1567

2016, Oct. 6 Litho. *Perf. 13½x13¾*
2935 A1567 45c multi 1.00 .50

"Song of Germany," German National Anthem, 175th Anniv. A1568

2016, Oct. 6 Litho. *Perf. 13¾*
2936 A1568 70c gold & multi 1.60 .80

Electric Vehicles and Wind Generators A1569

2016, Oct. 6 Litho. *Perf. 14*
2937 A1569 190c multi 4.25 2.10

To Beauty, Painting by Otto Dix (1891-1969) — A1570

2016, Nov. 2 Litho. *Perf. 13½x13¾*
2938 A1570 85c multi 1.90 .95

Christmas — A1571

2016, Nov. 2 Litho. *Perf. 13½x13¾*
2939 A1571 70c multi 1.50 .75

Booklet Stamp
Self-Adhesive
Size:39x22mm
Die Cut Perf. 9¾

2940 A1571 70c multi 1.50 .75
a. Booklet pane of 10 15.00

Steamship *Die Weser,* 200th Anniv. — A1572

2016, Dec. 8 Litho. *Perf. 13½x13¾*
2941 A1572 70c multi 1.50 .75

See No. 2944.

German Product Design A1573

Designs: 70c, Loops Chair, by Luigi Colani. 145c, Glassware, by Hans Theo Baumann.

2016, Dec. 8 Litho. *Perf. 14*
2942 A1573 70c multi 1.50 .75
2943 A1573 145c multi 3.00 1.50

See No. 2989.

Steamship Die Weser Type of 2016
Die Cut Perf. 9¾
2017, Jan. 2 Litho.

Booklet Stamp
Self-Adhesive
Size: 39x22mm

2944 A1572 70c multi 1.50 .75
a. Booklet pane of 10 15.00

Topography of Terror Museum Foundation, 25th Anniv. A1574

2017, Jan. 2 Litho. *Perf. 14*
2945 A1574 45c black .95 .45

Martin Luther's German Translation of the Bible — A1575

2017, Jan. 2 Litho. *Perf. 14*
2946 A1575 260c multi 5.50 2.75

Protestant Reformation, 500th anniv.

Demoiselle Crane, Toucan and Tufted Crane, by Jean-Baptiste Oudry (1686-1755) — A1576

The Girl with the Wine Glass, by Johannes Vermeer (1632-75) A1577

2017, Jan. 2 Litho. *Perf. 14*
2947 A1576 70c multi 1.50 .75
2948 A1577 70c multi 1.50 .75

Coil Stamps
Self-Adhesive
Die Cut Perf. 11¼x11½

2949 A1576 70c multi 1.50 .75

Die Cut Perf. 11½x11¼

2950 A1577 70c multi 1.50 .75
a. Pair, #2949-2950 3.00

Opening of the Elbe Philharmonic Hall, Hamburg — A1578

2017 Litho. *Perf. 13½x13¾*
2951 A1578 145c multi 3.00 1.50

Booklet Stamp
Self-Adhesive
Size: 39x22mm
Die Cut Perf. 10

2952 A1578 145c multi 3.00 1.50
a. Booklet pane of 10 30.00

Issued: No. 2951, 1/2; No. 2952, 2/9.

Ludwigsburg Palace, Ludwigsburg — A1579

2017, Feb. 9 Litho. *Perf. 13½x13¾*
2953 A1579 70c multi 1.50 .75

See No. 2974.

Neunburg vorm Wald, 1000th Anniv. — A1580

2017, Mar. 1 Litho. *Perf. 13½x13¾*
2954 A1580 45c blue & red vio .95 .45

2017 German Presidency of G20 — A1581

2017, Mar. 1 Litho. *Perf. 13¾*
2955 A1581 70c multi 1.50 .75

Gray Ottifant, Cartoon Elephant by Otto Waalkes A1582

2017, Mar. 1 Litho. *Perf. 13½x13¾*
2956 A1582 70c multi 1.50 .75

Booklet Stamp
Self-Adhesive
Size: 39x22mm
Die Cut Perf. 9¾

2957 A1582 70c multi 1.50 .75
a. Booklet pane of 10 15.00

Juvenile Animals A1583

Designs: Nos. 2958, 2960, Wild boar squeakers (wildschwein). Nos. 2959, 2961, European polecat kits (iltis).

2017, Mar. 1 Litho. *Perf. 13½x13¾*
2958 A1583 85c multi 1.90 .95
2959 A1583 85c multi 1.90 .95

Booklet Stamp
Self-Adhesive
Size: 39x22mm
Die Cut Perf. 9¾

2960 A1583 85c multi 1.90 .95
2961 A1583 85c multi 1.90 .95
a. Booklet pane of 10, 5 each #2960-2961 19.00

Martin Luther (1483-1546), Religious Reformer — A1584

2017, Apr. 13 Litho. *Perf. 13½x13¾*
2962 A1584 70c multi 1.60 .80

Protestant Reformation, 500th anniv. See Brazil No. 3351.

Automobiles — A1585

Designs: Nos. 2963, 2965, 1974-83 Volkswagen Golf Series 1. Nos. 2964, 2966, 1970-75 Opel Manta A.

2017, Apr. 13 Litho. *Perf. 13½x13¾*
2963 A1585 90c multi 2.00 1.00
2964 A1585 90c multi 2.00 1.00

Booklet Stamps
Self-Adhesive
Size: 39x22mm
Die Cut Perf. 9¾

2965 A1585 90c multi 2.00 1.00
2966 A1585 90c multi 2.00 1.00
a. Booklet pane of 10, 5 each #2965-2966 20.00

Mines of Rammelsberg, Historic Town of Goslar, and Upper Harz Water Management System UNESCO World Heritage Sites — A1586

2017, Apr. 13 Litho. *Perf. 13¾x14*
2967 A1586 145c multi 3.25 1.60

Flowers Type of 2005

Designs: 10c, Winterling (winter aconite). 20c, Hasenglöckchen (bluebells). 45c, Seerose (water lily). 90c, Johanniskraut (St. John's wort).

2017 Litho. *Perf. 14*
2968 A1165 10c multi .25 .25
2969 A1165 20c multi .45 .25
2970 A1165 45c multi 1.00 .50
2971 A1165 90c multi 2.00 1.00

Issued: 45c, 90c, 5/11. 10c, 20c, 6/8.

Ludwigsburg Castle Type of 2017 and

Wartburg Castle A1587

2017, May 11 Litho. *Perf. 13½x13¾*
2972 A1587 70c multi 1.60 .80
a. Booklet pane of 8, 4each #2962, 2972 13.00 —
Complete booklet, #2972a 13.00

Booklet Stamp
Self-Adhesive
Size: 39x22mm
Die Cut Perf. 9¾

2973 A1587 70c multi 1.60 .80
2974 A1579 70c multi 1.60 .80
a. Booklet pane of 20, 10 each #2973-2974 32.00

Europa (Nos, 2972-2973). Issued: No. 2972a, 8/10.

Party Foods and Drinks A1588

Lily A1589

2017, May 11 Litho. *Perf. 13½x13¾*
2975 A1588 70c multi 1.60 .80
2976 A1589 70c multi 1.60 .80

Booklet Stamp
Self-Adhesive
Size: 39x22mm
Die Cut Perf. 9¾

2977 A1589 70c multi 1.60 .80
a. Booklet pane of 10 16.00

Lighthouse Type of 2004

Designs: 45c, Kiel-Holtenau Lighthouse. 70c, Bremerhaven Unterfeuer Lighthouse.

2017, June 8 Litho. *Perf. 13¾*
2978 A1150 45c multi 1.10 .55
2979 A1150 70c multi 1.60 .80

Heiunz Sielmann (1917-2006), Biologist and Wildlife Documentary Filmmaker — A1590

2017, June 8 Litho. *Perf. 13½x13¾*
2980 A1590 45c multi 1.10 .55

Booklet Stamp
Self-Adhesive
Size: 39x22mm
Die Cut Perf. 9¾

2981 A1590 45c multi 1.10 .55
a. Booklet pane of 10 11.00

Invention of the Draisine by Karl Drais (1785-1851), 200th Anniv. A1591

2017, July 13 Litho. *Perf. 13¾*
2982 A1591 70c multi 1.75 .85

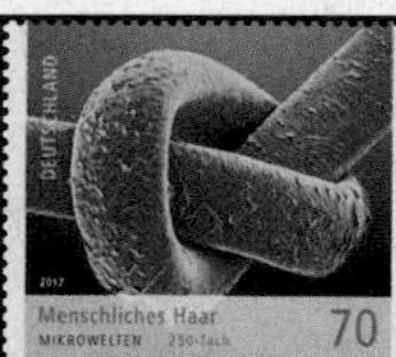

Microscopic View of Knotted Human Hair A1592

Microscopic View of Vitamin C Crystal A1593

2017-18 Litho. *Perf. 14*
2983 A1592 70c multi 1.75 .85
2984 A1593 85c multi 2.00 1.00

Coil Stamp
Self-Adhesive
Die Cut Perf. 11¼x11½

2984A A1593 85c multi 2.10 1.10

Issued: Nos. 2983, 2984, 7/13; No. 2984A, 2/1/18.

North German Confederation, 150th Anniv. A1594

2017, July 13 Litho. *Perf. 13¾*
2985 A1594 320c multi 7.75 4.00

Flowers Type of 2005

Design: 345c, Vergissmeinnicht (forget-me-not).

2017, Aug. 10 Litho. *Perf. 14*
2986 A1165 345c multi 8.25 4.25

Color Television Broadcasting in Germany, 50th Anniv. — A1595

Perf. 13½x13¾
2017, Aug. 10 Litho.
2987 A1595 70c multi 1.75 .85

Fruitbearing Society, 400th Anniv. — A1596

Perf. 13½x13¾
2017, Aug. 10 Litho.
2988 A1596 145c multi 3.50 1.75

German Product Design Type of 2016

Design: Glassware, by Hans Theo Baumann.

Die Cut Perf. 11½x11¼
2017, Aug. 10 Litho.
Coil Stamp
Self-Adhesive

2989 A1573 145c multi 3.50 1.75

Wine Grapes A1597

2017, Sept. 7 Litho. *Perf. 13¾*
2990 A1597 70c multi 1.75 .85

August Wilhelm Schlegel (1767-1845), Poet — A1598

2017, Sept. 7 Litho. *Perf. 13¾*
2991 A1598 85c multi 2.00 1.00

Walther Rathenau (1867-1922), Foreign Minister A1599

2017, Sept. 7 Litho. *Perf. 13¾*
2992 A1599 250c multi 6.00 3.00

Baden Wine Route A1600

Designs: No. 2993, Fields in valley (denomination at UL). No. 2994, Ölberg Chapel, Ehrenstetten (denomination at UR).

2017, Oct. 12 Litho. *Perf. 13½x13¾*
2993 A1600 45c multi 1.10 .55
2994 A1600 45c multi 1.10 .55
a. Horiz. pair, #2993-2994 2.20 1.10

Das Millionenspiel (The Millions Game), 1970 Television Movie — A1601

2017, Oct. 12 Litho. *Perf. 13½x13¾*
2995 A1601 70c multi 1.60 .80

Johann Joachim Winckelmann (1717-68), Archaeologist and Art Historian A1602

2017, Oct. 12 Litho. *Perf. 14*
2996 A1602 70c multi 1.60 .80

German Justitia et Pax Commission, 50th Anniv. — A1603

2017, Oct. 12 Litho. *Perf. 14*
2997 A1603 145c multi 3.50 1.75

Mecklenburg Lake District — A1604

Reinhardswald — A1605

2017, Nov. 2 Litho. *Perf. 13½x13¾*
2998 A1604 70c multi 1.75 .85
2999 A1605 90c multi 2.25 1.10

Theodor Mommsen (1817-1903), 1902 Nobel Laureate for Literature A1606

2017, Nov. 2 Litho. *Perf. 13¾*
3000 A1606 190c multi 4.50 2.25

Maria Rast Chapel, Krün A1607

2017, Nov. 2 Litho. *Perf. 13½x13¾*
3001 A1607 70c multi 1.75 .85

Booklet Stamp
Self-Adhesive
Size: 39x22mm
Die Cut Perf. 9¾

3002 A1607 70c multi 1.75 .85
a. Booklet pane of 10 17.50

Christmas.

Heinrich Böll (1917-85), 1972 Nobel Laureate in Literature A1608

2017, Dec. 7 Litho. *Perf. 13½*
3003 A1608 70c multi 1.75 .85

Stuttgart Light Rail Train, Designed by Herbert Lindinger A1609

2017-18 Litho. *Perf. 14*
3004 A1609 145c multi 3.50 1.75

Coil Stamp
Self-Adhesive
Die Cut Perf. 11½x11¼

3005 A1609 145c multi 3.75 1.90

Issued: No. 3004, 12/7/17; No. 3005, 2/1/18.

Gaia Space Observatory — A1610

Gravitational Waves — A1611

Litho. With Foil Application
2017-18 *Perf. 13¾*
3006 A1610 45c sil & multi 1.10 .55

Litho.
3007 A1611 70c multi 1.75 .85

Booklet Stamp
Self-Adhesive
Size: 39x22mm
Die Cut Perf. 9¾x10

3008 A1611 70c multi 1.75 .85
a. Booklet pane of 10 17.50

Isssued: Nos. 3006, 3007, 12/7; No. 3008, 1/2/18.

Flowers Type of 2005

Designs: 45c, Seerose (water lily). 100c, Alpenveilchen (cyclamen). 145c, Jungfer im Grünen (love-in-a-mist). 379c, Kokardenblume (Indian blanket).

2018 Litho. *Perf. 14*
3009 A1165 100c multi 2.50 1.25
3010 A1165 145c multi 3.50 1.75
3011 A1165 379c multi 9.00 4.50
Nos. 3009-3011 (3) 15.00 7.50

Die Cut Perf. 10¼x10
Coil Stamp
Self-Adhesive

3012 A1165 45c multi 1.10 .55

Issued: 45c, 4/12, 100c, 3/1; 145c, 1/2; 379c, 7/12.

Falkenlust Palace, Brühl — A1612

Friedenstein Palace, Gotha — A1613

2018 Litho. *Perf. 13½x13¾*
3013 A1612 70c multi 1.75 .85
3014 A1613 70c multi 1.75 .85

Booklet Stamps
Self-Adhesive
Size: 39x22mm
Die Cut Perf. 9¾

3015 A1613 70c multi 1.75 .85
3016 A1612 70c multi 1.75 .85
a. Booklet pane of 20, 10 each #3015-3016 35.00

Issued: No. 3013, 1/2; No. 3014, 3/1; Nos. 3015-3016, 5/3.

Juvenile Animals A1614

Designs: Nos. 3017, 3019, Fawn (reh). No. 3018, Seal pups (seehund).

2018 Litho. *Perf. 13½x13¾*
3017 A1614 85c multi 2.10 1.10
3018 A1614 85c multi 2.10 1.10

Booklet Stamp
Self-Adhesive
Size: 39x22mm
Die Cut Perf. 9¾

3019 A1614 85c multi 2.10 1.10
a. Booklet pane of 10 21.00

Issued: Nos. 3017-3018, 1/2; No. 3019, 4/12.

Five Slices of German Bread A1615

2018 Litho. *Perf. 13¾*
3020 A1615 260c multi 6.25 3.25

Booklet Stamp
Self-Adhesive
Die Cut Perf. 10¼

3021 A1615 260c multi 6.25 3.25
a. Booklet pane of 10 62.50

Issued: No. 3020, 1/2; No. 3021, 5/3.

University of Bonn (Rheinisch Friedrich-Wilhelms-Universität Bonn), 200th Anniv. — A1616

2018, Feb. 1 Litho. *Perf. 13¾*
3022 A1616 45c multi 1.10 .55

Tafel Charity, 25th Anniv. — A1617

2018, Feb. 1 Litho. *Perf. 14*
3023 A1617 70c multi 1.75 .85

Characters From *Peanuts* Comic Strip — A1618

Designs: 70c, Woodstock and Snoopy. 90c, Sally, Lucy, Woodstock, Snoopy, Linus, and Charlie Brown.

2018, Mar. 1 Litho. *Perf. 13½x13¾*
3024 A1618 70c multi 1.75 .85
3025 A1618 90c multi 2.25 1.10
a. Souvenir sheet of 2, #3024-3025 4.00 2.00

Booklet Stamps
Self-Adhesive
Size:39x22mm
Die Cut Perf. 9¾

3026 A1618 70c multi 1.75 .85
a. Booklet pane of 10 17.50
3027 A1618 90c multi 2.25 1.10
a. Booklet pane of 10 22.50

Automobiles — A1619

Designs: Nos. 3028, 3030, 1988-91 Wartburg 13. Nos. 3029, 3031 1980-91 Audi Quattro.

2018 Litho. *Perf. 13½x13¾*
3028 A1619 145c sil & multi 3.50 1.75
3029 A1619 145c sil & multi 3.50 1.75

Die Cut Perf. 9¾
Booklet Stamps
Self-Adhesive
Size:39x22mm

3030 A1619 145c multi 3.50 1.75
3031 A1619 145c multi 3.50 1.75
a. Booklet pane of 10, 5 each #3030-3031 35.00

Issued: Nos. 3028-3029, 3/1. Nos. 3030-3031, 4/12.

Peter Behrens (1868-1940), Architect and Designer — A1620

2018, Apr. 12 Litho. *Perf. 13½x13¾*
3032 A1620 70c multi 1.75 .85

Technical University of Munich, 150th Anniv. — A1621

2018, Apr. 12 Litho. *Perf. 13½x13¾*
3033 A1621 150c multi 3.75 1.90

A1622

Design: Elisabeth Mann Borgese (1918-2002), expert on maritime law and environmental protection.

2018, Apr. 12 Litho. *Perf. 13½x13¾*
3034 A1622 370c multi 9.00 4.50

Karl Marx (1818-83), Philosopher and Political Theorist — A1623

2018, May 3 Litho. *Perf. 13½x13¾*
3035 A1623 70c multi 1.75 .85

Rheinknicbrücke and Oberkassler Bridge, Düsseldorf — A1624

2018, May 3 Litho. *Perf. 13½x13¾*
3036 A1624 70c multi 1.75 .85

Europa.

Gewandhaus Orchestra, Leipzig, 275th Anniv. A1625

2018, May 3 Litho. *Perf. 13¾*
3037 A1625 70c multi 1.75 .85

Music Day.

Four-Leaf Clover and Paper Boat — A1626

Gift A1627

2018, May 3 Litho. *Perf. 13½x13¾*
3038 A1626 70c multi 1.75 .85
3039 A1627 70c multi 1.75 .85
a. Booklet pane of 7, #2917-2919, 2975-2976, 3038-3039 + label 12.50 —
Complete booklet, #3039a 12.50

Lighthouses Type of 2004

Designs: 45c, Darsser Ort Lighthouse. 70c, Wangerooge Lighthouse.

2018, June 7 Litho. *Perf. 13¾*
3040 A1150 45c multi 1.10 .55
3041 A1150 70c multi 1.75 .85

Coil Stamp
Self-Adhesive
Die Cut Perf. 10¼

3042 A1150 70c multi 1.75 .85

Rostock, 800th Anniv. — A1628

2018, June 7 Litho. *Perf. 14*
3043 A1628 70c gold & brt blue 1.75 .85

Consecration of the Catherdral of Worms, 1000th Anniv. — A1629

2018, June 7 Litho. *Perf. 13½x13¾*
3044 A1629 90c gold & brn gray 2.10 1.10

Booklet Stamp
Self-Adhesive
Size:39x22mm
Die Cut Perf. 9¾

3045 A1629 90c gold & brn gray 2.10 1.10
a. Booklet pane of 10 21.00

Goethe in the Campagna, by Johann Heinrich Wilhelm Tischbein (1751-1829) A1630

2018, June 7 Litho. *Perf. 14*
3046 A1630 145c multi 3.50 1.75

Die Cut Perf. 11¼x11½
Coil Stamp
Self-Adhesive

3047 A1630 145c multi 3.50 1.75

Garden Kingdom of Dessau-Wörlitz UNESCO World Heritage Site — A1631

Buildings and: No. 3048, Boat on water. No. 3049, Boat and swan on water. No. 3050, Boat on water. No. 3051, Boat and swan on water.

2018, July 12 Litho. *Perf. 13½x13¾*
3048 A1631 45c multi 1.10 .55
3049 A1631 45c multi 1.10 .55
a. Horiz. pair, #3048-3049 2.20 1.10

Booklet Stamps
Self-Adhesive
Size: 39x22mm
Die Cut Perf. 9¾ on 3 Sides

3050 A1631 45c multi 1.10 .55
3051 A1631 45c multi 1.10 .55
a. Booklet pane of 10, 5 each #3050-3051 11.00

Nelson Mandela (1918-2013), President of South Africa — A1632

2018, July 12 Litho. *Perf. 13½x13¾*
3052 A1632 70c multi 1.75 .85

See South Africa No.

Magnus Hirschfeld (1868-1935), Sexologist A1633

2018, July 12 Litho. *Perf. 14*
3053 A1633 70c multi 1.75 .85

Braun World Receiver T1000, Designed by Dieter Rams — A1634

2018, July 12 Litho. *Perf. 14*
3054 A1634 345c multi 8.00 4.00

Harz Mountain Spruce Forest A1635

2018, Aug. 9 Litho. *Perf. 13½x13¾*
3055 A1635 70c multi 1.75 .85

North German Confederation Nos. 4, 10, 15 and 19 — A1636

2018, Sept. 13 Litho. *Perf. 13¾*
3056 A1636 70c multi 1.75 .85

North German Confederation postage stamps, 150th anniv., Stamp Day.

Microscopic View of Carbon Fibers A1637

2018, Sept. 13 Litho. *Perf. 14*
3057 A1637 90c multi 2.10 1.10

Flowers Type of 2005

Design: 10c, Winterling (winter aconite). 15c, Wiesenschaumkraut (cuckoo flower). 20c, Hasenglöckchen (bluebells). 220c, Hauswurz (amaranth).

2018 Litho. *Perf. 14*
3058 A1165 15c multi .35 .35
3059 A1165 220c multi 5.00 2.50

Booklet Stamps Self-Adhesive

Die Cut Perf. 10¼x10

3060 A1165 10c multi .25 .25
a. Booklet pane of 10 2.40
3061 A1165 15c multi .35 .25
a. Booklet pane of 10 3.50
3062 A1165 20c multi .45 .25
a. Booklet pane of 10 4.50
Nos. 3060-3062 (3) 1.05 .75

Issued: 10c, 15c, 20c, 12/18; 220c, 10/11.

Dinner for One, 1963 Television Show — A1638

2018, Oct. 11 Litho. *Perf. 13½x13¾*
3063 A1638 45c multi 1.10 .55

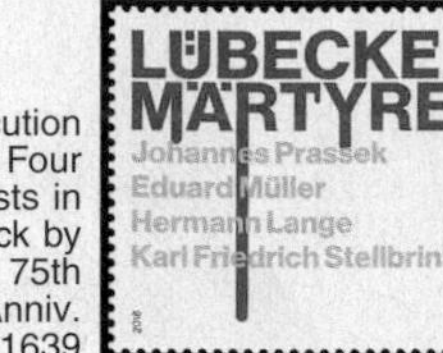

Execution of Four Priests in Lübeck by Nazis, 75th Anniv. A1639

2018, Oct. 11 Litho. *Perf. 14*
3064 A1639 70c multi 1.60 .80

Die Prinzessinnengrupe (Prussian Princesses Louise and Frederica), Sculpture by Johann Gottfried Schadow (1764-1850) — A1640

2018, Oct. 11 Litho. *Perf. 14*
3065 A1640 85c multi 2.00 1.00

Friedrich Schleiermacher (1768-1834), Theologian — A1641

2018, Nov. 2 Litho. *Perf. 13½x13¾*
3066 A1641 70c multi 1.60 .80

Ernst Otto Fischer (1918-2007), 1973 Nobel Laureate in Chemistry A1642

2018, Nov. 2 Litho. *Perf. 13¾*
3067 A1642 70c multi 1.60 .80

Christmas — A1643

2018, Nov. 2 Litho. *Perf. 13½x13¾*
3068 A1643 70c multi 1.60 .80

Booklet Stamp Self-Adhesive Size: 39x22mm

Die Cut Perf. 9¾

3069 A1643 70c multi 1.60 .80
a. Booklet pane of 10 16.00

Moor on Hornisgrinde — A1644

2018, Dec. 18 Litho. *Perf. 13¾*
3070 A1644 70c multi 1.60 .80

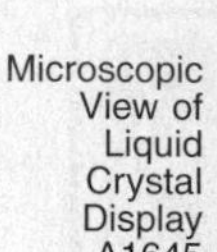

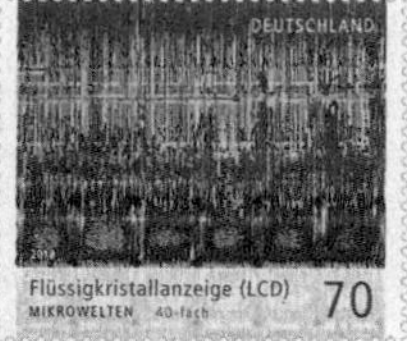

Microscopic View of Liquid Crystal Display A1645

2018, Dec. 18 Litho. *Perf. 14*
3071 A1645 70c multi 1.60 .80

Helmut Schmidt (1918-2015), Chancellor A1646

2018, Dec. 18 Litho. *Perf. 13¾*
3072 A1646 70c multi 1.60 .80

Atacama Large Millimeter Array Observatory, Chile — A1647

Illustris Project Simulation of the Evolution of the Universe — A1648

2018, Dec. 18 Litho. *Perf. 13¾*
3073 A1647 145c multi 3.25 1.60
3074 A1648 145c multi 3.25 1.60

SEMI-POSTAL STAMPS

Issues of the Republic

Nos. 83, 83d, 100, 100a, 100d Surcharged

1919, May 1 Wmk. 125 *Perf. 14*
B1 A16 10pf + 5pf on #83d .75 *4.25*
B2 A22 15pf + 5pf on #100 .75 *4.50*
Set, never hinged 5.25

The surtax was for the war wounded.

"Planting Charity" — SP1

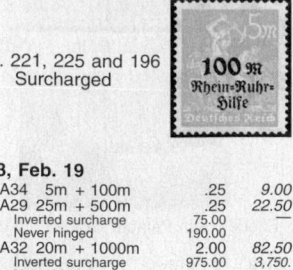

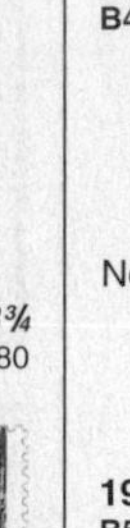

1922, Dec. 11 Litho. Wmk. 126
B3 SP1 6m + 4m ultra & brn .25 *22.50*
B4 SP1 12m + 8m red org & bl gray .25 *22.50*
Set, never hinged 1.75

Nos. 221, 225 and 196 Surcharged

1923, Feb. 19
B5 A34 5m + 100m .25 *9.00*
B6 A29 25m + 500m .25 *22.50*
a. Inverted surcharge 75.00 —
Never hinged 190.00
B7 A32 20m + 1000m 2.00 *82.50*
a. Inverted surcharge 975.00 *3,750.*
Never hinged 2,100.
b. Green background inverted 375.00 1,700.
Never hinged 750.00
Nos. B5-B7 (3) 2.50 *114.00*
Set, never hinged 7.50

Note following No. 160 applies to Nos. B1-B7.

Feeding the Hungry — SP2

Designs: 10pf+30pf, Giving drink to the thirsty. 20pf+60pf, Clothing the naked. 50pf+1.50m, Healing the sick.

1924, Feb. 25 Typo. *Perf. 14½x15*
B8 SP2 5pf + 15pf dk grn 1.75 *3.50*
B9 SP2 10pf + 30pf ver 1.75 *3.50*
B10 SP2 20pf + 60pf dk blue 5.75 *8.25*
B11 SP2 50pf + 1.50m red brn 22.50 *65.00*
Nos. B8-B11 (4) 31.75 *80.25*
Set, never hinged 120.00

The surtax was used for emergency aid. See No. B58.

Prussia — SP6

1925, Dec. 15 *Perf. 14*

Inscribed: "1925"

B12 SP6 5pf + 5pf shown .60 *1.90*
B13 SP6 10pf + 10pf Bavaria 1.75 *1.90*
B14 SP6 20pf + 20pf Saxony 9.00 *13.50*
a. Bklt. pane of 2 + 2 labels 350.00 1,050.
Never hinged 600.00
Nos. B12-B14 (3) 11.35 *17.30*
Set, never hinged 37.50

1926, Dec. 1 Inscribed: "1926"
B15 SP6 5pf + 5pf Wurttemberg 1.75 *2.25*
B16 SP6 10pf + 10pf Baden 2.25 *3.00*
a. Bklt. pane of 6 + 2 labels 270.00 650.00
Never hinged 450.00
B17 SP6 25pf + 25pf Thuringia 9.25 *19.00*
B18 SP6 50pf + 50pf Hesse 42.50 *97.50*
Nos. B15-B18 (4) 55.75 *121.75*
Set, never hinged 175.00

Nos. B15-B16 are usually found with sideways watermarks. Both exist with an upright watermark, which is very scarce. No. B18 is usually found with an upright watermark. Examples of No. B18 with a sideways watermark are scarce.

See Nos. B23-B32.

Pres. Paul von Hindenburg — SP13

1927, Sept. 26 Photo.

B19 SP13 8pf dark green .75 *1.50*
a. Bklt. pane, 4 #B19, 3 #B20 + label 110.00 190.00
Never hinged 180.00
B20 SP13 15pf scarlet 1.15 *2.25*
B21 SP13 25pf deep blue 9.50 *21.00*
B22 SP13 50pf bister brown 11.50 *24.00*
Nos. B19-B22 (4) 22.90 *48.75*
Set, never hinged 90.00

80th birthday of Pres. Hindenburg. The stamps were sold at double face value. The surtax was given to a fund for War Invalids.

Arms Type of 1925

Design: 8pf+7pf, Mecklenburg-Schwerin.

1928, Nov. 15 Typo.

Design Type SP6
Inscribed: "1928"

B23 5pf + 5pf Hamburg .55 *3.75*
B24 8pf + 7pf multi .45 *3.75*
a. Bklt. pane, 4 #B24, 3 #B25 + label 225.00 450.00
Never hinged 400.00
B25 15pf + 15pf Oldenburg .70 *3.75*
B26 25pf + 25pf Brunswick 14.50 *50.00*
B27 50pf + 50pf Anhalt 37.50 *90.00*
Nos. B23-B27 (5) 53.70 *151.25*
Set, never hinged 180.00

Nos. B23-B26 are valued with sideways watermark. All exist with upright watermark, which is scarce to very rare.

1929, Nov. 4 Inscribed: "1929"

Coats of Arms: 8pf+4pf, Lippe-Detmold. 25pf+10pf, Mecklenburg-Strelitz. 50pf+40pf, Schaumburg-Lippe.

B28 SP6 5pf + 2pf Bremen .75 *1.90*
a. Bklt. pane of 6 + 2 labels 90.00 135.00
Never hinged 150.00
B29 SP6 8pf + 4pf multi .85 *1.90*
a. Bklt. pane, 4 #B29, 3 #B30 + label 115.00 210.00
Never hinged 190.00
B30 SP6 15pf + 5pf Lubeck 1.20 1.50
B31 SP6 25pf + 10pf multi 16.50 *50.00*
B32 SP6 50pf + 40pf choc, ocher & red 37.50 *90.00*
a. "PE" for "PF" 150.00 375.00
Never hinged 450.00
Nos. B28-B32 (5) 56.80 *145.30*
Set, never hinged 180.00

Cathedral of Aachen — SP24

Brandenburg Gate, Berlin — SP25

Castle of Marienwerder SP26

Statue of St. Kilian and Marienburg Fortress at Würzburg SP27

Souvenir Sheet

Wmk. 223

1930, Sept. 12 Engr. *Perf. 14*

B33 Sheet of 4 425.00 *1,500.*
Never hinged 1,200.
a. SP24 8pf + 4pf dark green 30.00 *105.00*
Never hinged 82.50
b. SP25 15pf + 5pf carmine 30.00 *105.00*
Never hinged 82.50
c. SP26 25pf + 10p dark blue 30.00 *105.00*
Never hinged 82.50
d. SP27 50pf + 40pf dark brown 30.00 *105.00*
Never hinged 82.50

Intl. Phil. Exhib., Berlin Sept 12-21, 1930.

No. B33 is watermarked Eagle on each stamp and "IPOSTA"-"1930" in the margins. Size: approximately 105x150. Each holder of an admission ticket was entitled to purchase one sheet. The ticket cost 1m and the sheet 1.70m (face value 98pf, charity 59pf, special paper 13pf).

The margin of the souvenir sheet is ungummed.

Types of International Philatelic Exhibition Issue

1930, Nov. 1 Wmk. 126

B34 SP24 8 + 4pf dp green .90 1.90
a. Bklt. pane of 7 + label 82.50 170.00
Never hinged 145.00
b. Bklt. pane, 3 #B34, 4 #B35 + label 105.00 180.00
Never hinged 175.00
B35 SP25 15 + 5pf car 1.10 *2.25*
B36 SP26 25 + 10pf dk blue 7.75 *22.50*
B37 SP27 50 + 40pf dp brn 21.00 *82.50*
Nos. B34-B37 (4) 30.75 *109.15*
Set, never hinged 105.00

The surtax was for charity.

The Zwinger at Dresden SP28

Breslau City Hall SP29

Heidelberg Castle SP30

Holsten Gate, Lübeck SP31

1931, Nov. 1

B38 SP28 8 + 4pf dk grn .55 *2.25*
a. Bklt. pane of 7 + label 90.00 170.00
Never hinged 150.00
b. Bklt. pane, 3 #B38, 4 #B39 + label 97.50 180.00
Never hinged 170.00
B39 SP29 15 + 5pf carmine .55 *2.25*
B40 SP30 25 + 10pf dk blue 9.50 *30.00*
B41 SP31 50 + 40pf dp brown 27.50 *75.00*
Nos. B38-B41 (4) 38.10 *109.50*
Set, never hinged 180.00

The surtax was for charity.

Nos. B38-B39 Surcharged

1932, Feb. 2

B42 SP28 6 + 4pf on 8+4pf 4.25 *9.75*
B43 SP29 12 + 3pf on 15+5pf 5.00 *11.50*
Set, never hinged 45.00

Wartburg Castle — SP32

Stolzenfels Castle — SP33

Nuremberg Castle — SP34

Lichtenstein Castle — SP35

Marburg Castle — SP36

1932, Nov. 1 Engr.

B44 SP32 4 + 2pf lt blue .80 1.90
a. Bklt. pane, 5 #B44, 5 #B45 45.00 85.00
Never hinged 75.00
B45 SP33 6 + 4pf olive grn 1.00 1.90
B46 SP34 12 + 3pf lt red .65 1.90
b. Bklt. pane of 8 + 2 labels 45.00 85.00
Never hinged 75.00
B47 SP35 25 + 10pf dp blue 8.00 *18.00*
B48 SP36 40 + 40pf brn vio 27.50 *65.00*
Nos. B44-B48 (5) 37.95 *88.70*
Set, never hinged 145.00

The surtax was for charity.

"Tannhäuser" SP37

Designs: 4pf+2pf, "Der Fliegende Hollander." 5pf+2pf, "Das Rheingold." 6pf+4pf, "Die Meistersinger." 8pf+4pf, "Die Walkure." 12pf+3pf, "Siegfried." 20pf+10pf, "Tristan und Isolde." 25pf+15pf, "Lohengrin." 40pf+35pf, "Parsifal."

Wmk. Swastikas (237)

1933, Nov. 1 *Perf. 13½x13*

B49 SP37 3 + 2pf bis brn 3.75 *5.75*
B50 SP37 4 + 2pf dk blue 2.50 *2.25*
b. Bklt. pane, 5 #B50, 5 #B52 135.00 250.00
Never hinged 225.00
B51 SP37 5 + 2pf brt grn 6.25 *6.75*
B52 SP37 6 + 4pf gray grn 2.50 *2.25*
B53 SP37 8 + 4pf dp org 3.75 3.75
b. Bklt. pane, 5 #B53, 4 #B54 + label 135.00 250.00
Never hinged 225.00
B54 SP37 12 + 3pf brn red 3.75 2.60
B55 SP37 20 + 10pf blue 190.00 *190.00*
B56 SP37 25 + 15pf ultra 45.00 *37.50*
B57 SP37 40 + 35pf mag 130.00 *130.00*
Nos. B49-B57 (9) 387.50 380.85
Set, never hinged 2,360.

Perf. 13½x14

B50a SP37 4 + 2pf dark blue 2.75 *3.00*
B52a SP37 6 + 4pf gray grn 2.75 *5.00*
B53a SP37 8 + 4pf dp org 3.50 *4.25*
B54a SP37 12 + 3pf brn red 3.50 *6.50*
B55a SP37 20 + 10pf blue 135.00 *97.50*
Nos. B50a-B55a (5) 147.50 116.25
Set, never hinged 822.00

Types of Semi-Postal Stamps of 1924 Issue Overprinted

Souvenir Sheet

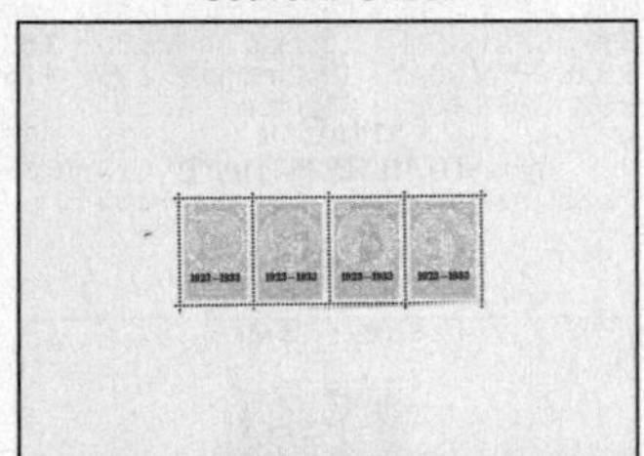

1933, Nov. 29 Typo. *Perf. 14½*

B58 Sheet of 4 1,150. *7,500.*
Never hinged 4,500.
a. SP2 5 + 15pf dark green 90.00 *375.00*
b. SP2 10 + 30pf vermilion 90.00 *375.00*
c. SP2 20 + 60pf dark blue 90.00 *375.00*
d. SP2 50pf + 1.50m dk brown 90.00 *375.00*
Any single, never hinged 225.00

The Swastika watermark covers the four stamps and above them appears a further watermark "10 Jahre Deutsche Nothilfe" and "1923-1933" below. Sheet size: 208x148mm.

The margin of the souvenir sheet is ungummed.

Businessman SP46

Judge SP54

Designs: 4pf+2pf, Blacksmith. 5pf+2pf, Mason. 6pf+4f, Miner. 8pf+4pf, Architect. 12pf+3pf, Farmer. 20pf+10pf, Agricultural Chemist. 25pf+15pf, Sculptor.

1934, Nov. 5 Engr. *Perf. 13x13½*

B59 SP46 3 + 2pf brown 1.30 *1.50*
B60 SP46 4 + 2pf black .75 *1.50*
a. Bklt. pane, 5 #B60, 5 #B62 52.50 102.50
Never hinged 90.00
B61 SP46 5 + 2pf green 5.75 *7.50*
B62 SP46 6 + 4pf dull grn .75 *.60*
B63 SP46 8 + 4pf org brn 1.30 *1.90*
a. Bklt. pane, 5 #B63, 4 #B64 + label 82.50 150.00
Never hinged 135.00
B64 SP46 12 + 3pf hn brn .75 *.60*
B65 SP46 20 + 10pf Prus bl 15.00 *21.00*
B66 SP46 25 + 15pf ultra 16.50 *21.00*
B67 SP54 40 + 35pf plum 35.00 *67.50*
Nos. B59-B67 (9) 77.10 *123.10*
Set, never hinged 450.00

Souvenir Sheet

SP55

1935, June 23 Wmk. 241 *Perf. 14*

B68 SP55 Sheet of 4 975.00 825.00
a. 3pf red brown 34.00 37.50
b. 6pf dark green 34.00 37.50
c. 12pf dark carmine 34.00 37.50
d. 25pf dark blue 34.00 37.50

Watermarked cross on each stamp and "OSTROPA 1935" in the margins of the sheet. Size: 148x104mm. 1.70m was the price of a ticket of admission to the Intl. Exhib., Königsberg, June 23-July 3, 1935.

Because the gum on No. B68 contains sulphuric acid and tends to damage the sheet, most collectors prefer to remove it. **Catalogue unused values are for sheet and singles without gum.**

East Prussia — SP59

Designs (Costumes of Various Sections of Germany): 4pf+3pf, Silesia. 5pf+3pf, Rhineland. 6pf+4pf, Lower Saxony. 8pf+4pf, Brandenburg. 12pf+6pf, Black Forest. 15pf+10pf, Hesse. 25pf+15pf, Upper Bavaria. 30pf+20pf, Friesland. 40pf+35pf, Franconia.

Wmk. Swastikas (237)

1935, Oct. 4 ***Perf. 14x13½***

B69 SP59 3 + 2pf dk brown .35 *.40*
a. Bklt. pane, 4 #B69, 5 #B74 + label 42.50 75.00
Never hinged 67.50
B70 SP59 4 + 3pf gray 1.20 *1.50*
B71 SP59 5 + 3pf emerald .35 *1.00*
a. Bklt. pane, 5 #B71, 5 #B72 27.00 50.00
Never hinged 45.00
B72 SP59 6 + 4pf dk green .25 *.40*
B73 SP59 8 + 4pf yel brn 1.75 1.50
B74 SP59 12 + 6pf dk car .25 *.40*
B75 SP59 15 + 10pf red brn 4.25 *5.75*
B76 SP59 25 + 15pf ultra 8.25 6.00
B77 SP59 30 + 20pf olive brn 9.25 *19.50*
B78 SP59 40 + 35p plum 8.50 *14.50*
Nos. B69-B78 (10) 34.40 *50.95*
Set, never hinged 135.00

Skating — SP69

12+6pf, Ski jump. 25+15pf, Bobsledding.

1935, Nov. 25 ***Perf. 13½***

B79 SP69 6 + 4pf green .90 *1.35*
B80 SP69 12 + 6pf carmine 1.75 1.20
B81 SP69 25 + 15pf ultra 7.50 *7.50*
Nos. B79-B81 (3) 10.15 10.05
Set, never hinged 50.00

Winter Olympic Games held in Bavaria, Feb. 6-16, 1936.

1936, May 8

Designs: 3pf+2pf, Horizontal bar. 4pf+3pf, Diving. 6pf+4pf, Soccer. 8pf+4pf, Throwing javelin. 12pf+6pf, Torch runner. 15pf+10pf, Fencing. 25pf+15pf, Sculling. 40pf+35pf, Equestrian.

B82 SP69 3 + 2pf brown .30 *.45*
a. Bklt. pane, 5 #B82, 5 #B86 27.00 50.00
Never hinged 45.00
B83 SP69 4 + 3pf indigo .25 *.75*
a. Bklt. pane, 5 #B83, 5 #B84 27.00 50.00
Never hinged 45.00
B84 SP69 6 + 4pf green .25 *.45*
B85 SP69 8 + 4pf red org 3.00 1.30
B86 SP69 12 + 6pf carmine .40 *.45*
B87 SP69 15 + 10pf brn vio 5.50 3.00
B88 SP69 25 + 15pf ultra 3.00 *3.75*
B89 SP69 40 + 35pf violet 5.50 *7.50*
Nos. B82-B89 (8) 18.20 *17.65*
Set, never hinged 105.00

Summer Olympic Games, Berlin, 8/1-16/36.
See Nos. B91-B92.

Souvenir Sheet

Horse Race — SP80

1936, June 22 Wmk. 237 ***Perf. 14***

B90 SP80 42pf brown 12.00 *13.50*
Never hinged 24.00

A surtax of 1.08m was to provide a 100,000m sweepstakes prize. Wmk. 237 appears on the stamp, with "Munchen Riem 1936" watermarked on sheet margin.

For overprint see No. B105.

Types of 1936

Souvenir Sheets

1936, Aug. 1 ***Perf. 14x13½***

B91 SP69 Sheet of 4 37.50 *67.50*
B92 SP69 Sheet of 4 37.50 *67.50*
Set, never hinged 200.00

11th Olympic Games, Berlin. No. B91 contains Nos. B82-B84, B89. No. B92 contains Nos. B85-B88.

Wmk. 237 appears on each stamp with "XI Olympische Spiele-Berlin 1936" watermarked on sheet margin. Sold for 1m each.

Frontier Highway, Munich — SP81

Designs: 4pf+3pf, Ministry of Aviation. 5pf+3pf, Nuremberg Memorial. 6pf+4pf, Bridge over the Saale, Saxony. 8pf+4pf, Germany Hall, Berlin. 12pf+6pf, German Alpine highway. 15pf+10pf, Fuhrer House, Munich. 25pf+15pf, Bridge over the Mangfall. 40pf+35pf, Museum of German Art, Munich.

Perf. 13½x14

1936, Sept. 21 Unwmk.

B93 SP81 3pf + 2pf blk brn .25 *.40*
a. Bklt. pane, 4 #B93 + 5 #B98 + label 27.50 55.00
Never hinged 45.00
B94 SP81 4pf + 3pf black .25 *.45*
B95 SP81 5pf + 3pf brt grn .25 *.40*
a. Bklt. pane, 5 #B95, 5 #B96) 14.00 26.00
Never hinged 22.50
B96 SP81 6pf + 4pf dk grn .25 *.40*
B97 SP81 8pf + 4pf brown .95 *1.30*
B98 SP81 12pf + 6pf brn car .25 *.40*
B99 SP81 15pf + 10pf vio brn 3.50 *3.50*
B100 SP81 25pf + 15pf indigo 2.25 *3.75*
B101 SP81 40pf + 35pf rose vio 3.75 *5.75*
Nos. B93-B101 (9) 11.70 *16.35*
Set, never hinged 60.00

Souvenir Sheets

Adolf Hitler — SP90

Wmk. 237

1937, Apr. 5 Photo. ***Perf. 14***

B102 SP90 Sheet of 4 18.00 12.00
Never hinged 52.50
a. 6pf dark green 1.15 *1.50*
Never hinged 4.25

48th birthday of Adolf Hitler. Sold for 1m.

See Nos. B103-B104. For overprint see No. B106.

1937, Apr. 16 ***Imperf.***

B103 SP90 Sheet of 4 37.50 22.50
Never hinged 170.00
a. 6pf dark green 3.75 3.00
Never hinged 12.00

German Natl. Phil. Exhib., Berlin, June 16-18, 1937 and the Phil. Exhib. of the Stamp Collectors Group of the Strength Through Joy Organization at Hamburg, Apr. 17-20, 1937.

Sold at the Exhib. post offices for 1.50m.

No. B102 with Marginal Inscriptions

Perf. 14 and Rouletted

1937, June 10 Wmk. 237

B104 SP90 Sheet of 4 75.00 *67.50*
Never hinged 240.00
a. 6pf dark grn + 25pf label 3.75 6.75
Never hinged 15.00

No. B104 inscribed in the margin beside each stamp "25 Rpf. einschliesslich Kulturspende" in three lines.

The sheets were rouletted to allow for separation of each stamp with its component label. Sold at the post office as individual stamps with labels attached or in complete sheets.

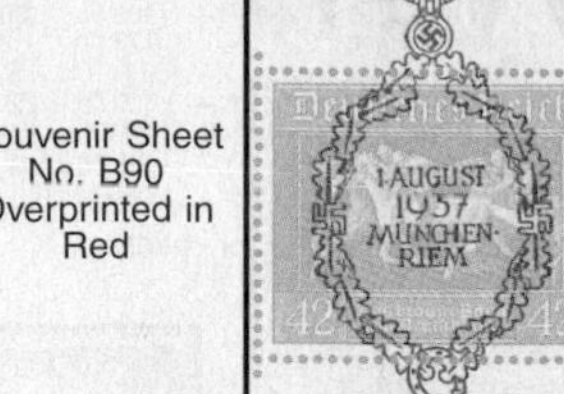

Souvenir Sheet No. B90 Overprinted in Red

1937, Aug. 1 ***Perf. 14***

B105 SP80 42pf brown 52.50 *97.50*
Never hinged 135.00
a. Inverted overprint *14,500.*

4th running of the "Brown Ribbon" horse race at the Munich-Riem Race Course, Aug. 1, 1937.

Souvenir Sheet No. B104 Overprinted in Black on Each Stamp

Perf. 14 and Rouletted

1937, Sept. 3 Wmk. 237

B106 SP90 Sheet of 4 67.50 45.00
Never hinged 240.00
a. 6pf dark grn + 25pf label 4.50 5.75
Never hinged 13.50

1937 Nazi Congress at Nuremburg.

Lifeboat — SP91

Designs: 4pf+3pf, Lightship "Elbe I." 5pf+3pf, Fishing smacks. 6pf+4pf, Steamer. 8pf+4pf, Sailing vessel. 12pf+6pf, The "Tannenberg." 15pf+10pf, Sea-Train "Schwerin." 25pf+15pf, S. S. Hamburg. 40pf+35pf, S. S. Bremen.

Perf. 13½

1937, Nov. 4 Engr. Unwmk.

B107 SP91 3pf + 2pf dk brwn .25 .40
a. Bklt. pane, 4 #B107 + 5 #B112 + label 27.00 *50.00*
Never hinged 45.00
B108 SP91 4pf + 3pf black .85 *1.15*
B109 SP91 5pf + 3pf yel grn .25 *.40*
a. Bklt. pane, 5 #B109, 5 #B110 13.50 *26.00*
Never hinged 22.50
B110 SP91 6pf + 4pf bl grn .25 *.40*
B111 SP91 8pf + 4pf orange .55 *1.15*
B112 SP91 12pf + 6pf car lake .25 .40
B113 SP91 15pf + 10pf vio brn 1.10 *3.75*
B114 SP91 25pf + 15pf ultra 2.50 *3.75*
B115 SP91 40pf + 35pf red vio 4.25 *7.50*
Nos. B107-B115 (9) 10.25 *18.90*
Set, never hinged 75.00

No. B115 actually pictures the S.S. Europa.

Youth Carrying Torch and Laurel — SP100

Wmk. 237

1938, Jan. 28 Photo. ***Perf. 14***

B116 SP100 6 + 4pf dk green 1.15 *1.90*
B117 SP100 12 + 8pf brt car 1.15 *1.90*
Set, never hinged 15.00

Assumption of power by the Nazis, 5th anniv.

Adolf Hitler — SP101

1938, Apr. 13 Engr. Unwmk.

B118 SP101 12 + 38pf copper red 1.90 *2.60*
Never hinged 9.75

Hitler's 49th birthday.

Horsewoman SP102

1938, July 20

B119 SP102 42 + 108pf dp brn 21.00 *45.00*
Never hinged 115.00

5th "Brown Ribbon" at Munich.

Adolf Hitler — SP103

1938, Sept. 1

B120 SP103 6 + 19pf deep grn 2.25 *4.25*
Never hinged 18.00

1938 Nazi Congress at Nuremberg. The surtax was for Hitler's National Culture Fund.

Theater at Saarbrücken SP104

1938, Oct. 9 Photo. Wmk. 237

B121 SP104 6 + 4pf blue grn 1.40 *1.90*
B122 SP104 12 + 8pf dk car 1.75 *2.60*
Set, never hinged 19.50

Inauguration of the theater of the District of Saarpfalz at Saarbrücken. The surtax was for Hitler's National Culture Fund.

Castle of Forchtenstein SP105

Designs (scenes in Austria and various flowers): 4pf+3pf, Flexenstrasse in Vorarlberg. 5pf+3pf, Zell am See, Salzburg. 6pf+4pf, Grossglockner. 8pf+4pf, Ruins of Aggstein. 12pf+6pf, Prince Eugene Monument, Vienna. 15pf+10pf, Erzberg. 25pf+15pf, Hall, Tyrol. 40pf+35pf, Braunau.

Unwmk.

1938, Nov. 18 Engr. ***Perf. 14***

B123 SP105 3 + 2pf ol brn .25 *.45*
a. Bklt. pane, 4 #B123, 5 #B128 + label 27.00 50.00
Never hinged 45.00
B124 SP105 4 + 3pf indigo 1.60 1.15
B125 SP105 5 + 3pf emer .25 *.45*
a. Bklt. pane, 5 #B125, 5 #B126 13.50 26.00
Never hinged 22.50
B126 SP105 6 + 4pf dk grn .25 .40
B127 SP105 8 + 4pf red org 1.60 1.15
B128 SP105 12 + 6pf dk car .25 *.45*

B129 SP105 15 + 10pf dp cl 3.00 *4.50*
B130 SP105 25 + 15pf dk bl 2.60 *4.50*
B131 SP105 40 + 35pf plum 6.00 *7.50*
Nos. B123-B131 (9) 15.80 *20.55*
Set, never hinged 75.00

The surtax was for "Winter Help."

Sudeten Couple — SP114

1938, Dec. 2 Photo. Wmk. 237
B132 SP114 6 + 4pf blue grn 1.50 *3.00*
B133 SP114 12 + 8pf dk car 2.25 *3.00*
Set, never hinged 30.00

Annexation of the Sudeten Territory. The surtax was for Hitler's National Culture Fund.

Early Types of Automobiles SP115

Designs: 12pf+8pf, Racing cars. 25pf+10pf, Modern automobile.

1939
B134 SP115 6 + 4pf dk grn 3.50 3.50
B135 SP115 12 + 8pf brt car 3.50 3.50
B136 SP115 25 + 10pf dp blue 6.00 *6.00*
Nos. B134-B136 (3) 13.00 13.00
Set, never hinged 82.50

Berlin Automobile and Motorcycle Exhibition. The surtax was for Hitler's National Culture Fund. For overprints see Nos. B141-B143.

Adolf Hitler — SP118

Unwmk.
1939, Apr. 13 Engr. *Perf. 14*
B137 SP118 12 + 38pf carmine 1.50 *4.50*
Never hinged 8.25

Hitler's 50th birthday. The surtax was for Hitler's National Culture Fund.

Exhibition Building — SP119

1939, Apr. 22 Photo. *Perf. 12½*
B138 SP119 6 + 4pf dk green 1.20 *3.00*
B139 SP119 15 + 5pf dp plum 1.75 *3.75*
Set, never hinged 15.00

Horticultural Exhib. held at Stuttgart. Surtax for Hitler's National Culture Fund.

Adolf Hitler — SP120

Perf. 14x13½
1939, Apr. 28 Wmk. 237
B140 SP120 6 + 19pf black brn 3.75 *5.00*
Never hinged 12.00

Day of National Labor. The surtax was for Hitler's National Culture Fund.
See No. B147.

Nos. B134-B136 Overprinted in Black

1939, May 18 *Perf. 14*
B141 SP115 6 + 4pf dk grn 18.00 *26.00*
B142 SP115 12 + 8pf brt car 18.00 *26.00*
B143 SP115 25 + 10pf dp bl 18.00 *26.00*
Nos. B141-B143 (3) 54.00 *78.00*
Set, never hinged 210.00

Nurburgring Auto Races, 5/21, 7/23/39.

Racehorse "Investment" and Jockey SP121

1939, June 18 Engr. Unwmk.
B144 SP121 25 + 50pf ultra 15.00 15.00
Never hinged 60.00

70th anniv. of the German Derby. The surtax was divided between Hitler's National Culture Fund and the race promoters.

Man Holding Rearing Horse — SP122

1939, July 12
B145 SP122 42 + 108pf dp brn 15.00 *24.00*
Never hinged 60.00

6th "Brown Ribbon" at Munich.

"Venetian Woman" by Albrecht Dürer — SP123

1939, July 12 Photo. Wmk. 237
B146 SP123 6 + 19pf dk grn 5.25 *9.75*
Never hinged 26.00

Day of German Art. The surtax was used for Hitler's National Culture Fund.

Hitler Type of 1939
Inscribed "Reichsparteitag 1939"
1939, Aug. 25 *Perf. 14x13½*
B147 SP120 6 + 19pf blk brn 4.25 *9.00*
Never hinged 18.00

1939 Nazi Congress at Nuremberg.

Meeting in German Hall, Berlin SP124

Designs: 4pf+3pf, Meeting of postal and telegraph employees. 5pf+3pf, Professional competitions. 6pf+4pf, 6pf+9pf, Professional camp. 8pf+4pf, 8pf+12pf, Gold flag competitions. 10pf+5pf, Awarding prizes. 12&f+6pf, 12pf+18pf, Automobile race. 15pf+10pf, Sports. 16pf+10pf, 16pf+24pf, Postal police. 20pf+10pf, 20pf+30pf, Glider workshops. 24pf+10pf, 24pf+36pf, Mail coach. 25pf+15pf, Convalescent home, Konigstein.

Perf. 13½x14
1939-41 Unwmk. Photo.
B148 3 + 2pf bister brn 2.25 *5.25*
B149 4 + 3pf slate blue 2.00 *5.25*
B150 5 + 3pf brt bl grn .60 *1.50*
B151 6 + 4pf myrtle grn .75 *1.50*
B151A 6 + 9pf dk grn ('41) .70 *2.25*
B152 8 + 4pf dp org .75 *1.50*
B152A 8 + 12pf hn brn ('41) 1.05 *1.50*
B153 10 + 5pf dk brown .75 *2.00*
B154 12 + 6pf rose brown .85 *2.00*
B154A 12 + 18pf dk car rose ('41) 1.05 *1.90*
B155 15 + 10pf dp red lilac .75 *2.25*
B156 16 + 10pf slate grn .75 *2.25*
B156A 16 + 24pf black ('41) 1.05 *3.75*
B157 20 + 10pf ultra .75 *2.25*
B157A 20 + 30pf ultra ('41) 1.40 *3.75*
B158 24 + 10pf ol grn 1.90 *3.75*
B158A 24 + 36pf pur ('41) 3.50 *11.50*
B159 25 + 15pf dk blue 1.75 *3.00*
Nos. B148-B159 (18) 22.75 *57.15*
Set, never hinged 110.00

The surtax was used for Hitler's National Culture Fund and the Postal Employees' Fund.
See Nos. B273, B275-B277.

Elbogen Castle — SP136

Buildings: 4pf+3pf, Drachenfels on the Rhine. 5pf+3pf, Kaiserpfalz at Goslar. 6pf+4pf, Clocktower at Graz. 8pf+4pf, Town Hall, Frankfurt. 12pf+6pf, Guild House, Klagenfurt. 15pf+10pf, Ruins of Schreckenstein Castle. 25pf+15pf, Fortress of Salzburg. 40pf+35pf, Castle of Hohentwiel.

1939 Unwmk. Engr. *Perf. 14*
B160 SP136 3 + 2pf dk brn .25 *.45*
a. Bklt. pane, 4 #B160, 5 #B165 + label 27.00 *50.00*
B161 SP136 4 + 3pf gray blk 1.50 *1.90*
B162 SP136 5 + 3pf emerald .35 *.55*
a. Bklt. pane, 5 #B162, 5 #B163 13.50 26.00
B163 SP136 6 + 4pf slate grn .25 *.40*
B164 SP136 8 + 4pf red org 1.50 *1.60*
B165 SP136 12 + 6pf dk car .65 *1.50*
B166 SP136 15 + 10pf brn vio 2.25 *4.50*
B167 SP136 25 + 15pf ultra 1.75 *4.50*
B168 SP136 40 + 35pf rose vio 2.50 *6.00*
Nos. B160-B168 (9) 11.00 *21.40*
Set, never hinged 45.00

Hall of Honor at Chancellery, Berlin — SP145

1940, Mar. 28
B169 SP145 24 + 76pf dk grn 6.00 *16.50*
Never hinged 27.00

2nd National Stamp Exposition, Berlin.

Child Greeting Hitler — SP146

Perf. 14x13½
1940, Apr. 10 Photo. Wmk. 237
B170 SP146 12 + 38pf cop red 3.00 *6.00*
Never hinged 12.00

51st birthday of Adolf Hitler.

Armed Warrior — SP147

1940, Apr. 30 Unwmk. *Perf. 14*
B171 SP147 6 + 4pf sl grn & lt grn .30 *1.30*
Never hinged 1.35

Issued to commemorate May Day.

Horseman SP148

Perf. 14x13½
1940, June 22 Wmk. 237
B172 SP148 25 + 100pf dp ultra 4.25 *11.00*
Never hinged 19.50

Blue Ribbon race, Hamburg, June 30, 1940. Surtax for Hitler's National Culture Fund.

Chariot SP149

Unwmk.
1940, July 20 Engr. *Perf. 14*
B173 SP149 42 + 108pf brown 22.50 *26.00*
Never hinged 90.00

7th "Brown Ribbon" at Munich.
The surtax was for Hitler's National Culture Fund and the promoters of the race.

View of Malmedy SP150

Design: 12pf+8pf, View of Eupen.

Perf. 14x13½
1940, July 25 Photo. Wmk. 237
B174 SP150 6 + 4pf dk green 1.15 *3.00*
B175 SP150 12 + 8pf org red 1.15 *3.00*
Set, never hinged 9.75

Issued on the occasion of the reunion of Eupen-Malmedy with the Reich.

Rocky Cliffs of Heligoland SP152

1940, Aug. 9 Unwmk.
B176 SP152 6 + 94pf brt bl grn & red org 5.75 *11.50*
Never hinged 22.50

Heligoland's 50th year as part of Germany.

Artushof in Danzig — SP153

Buildings: 4pf+3pf, Town Hall, Thorn. 5pf+3pf, Castle at Kaub. 6pf+4pf, City Theater, Poznan. 8pf+4pf, Castle at Heidelberg.

12pf+6pf, Porta Nigra Trier. 15pf+10pf, New German Theater, Prague. 25pf+15pf, Town Hall, Bremen. 40pf+35pf, Town Hall, Munster.

1940, Nov. 5 Engr. *Perf. 14*

B177	SP153	3 + 2pf dk brn	.30	*.45*
a.		Bklt. pane, 4 #B177 + 5 #B182 + label	27.00	50.00
		Never hinged	45.00	
B178	SP153	4 + 3pf bluish blk	.90	*.75*
B179	SP153	5 + 3pf yel grn	.30	*.45*
a.		Bklt. pane, 5 #B179, 5 #B180	13.50	26.00
		Never hinged	22.50	
B180	SP153	6 + 4pf dk grn	.35	*.45*
B181	SP153	8 + 4pf dp org	1.35	.85
B182	SP153	12 + 6pf carmine	.35	*.45*
B183	SP153	15 + 10pf dk vio brn	1.50	*2.60*
B184	SP153	25 + 15pf dp ultra	1.90	*2.60*
B185	SP153	40 + 35pf red lil	3.75	*6.00*
		Nos. B177-B185 (9)	10.70	*14.60*
		Set, never hinged	30.00	

von Behring — SP162

1940, Nov. 26 Photo.

B186	SP162	6 + 4pf dp green	1.20	*2.25*
B187	SP162	25 + 10pf brt ultra	1.75	*2.25*
		Set, never hinged	11.50	

Dr. Emil von Behring (1854-1917), bacteriologist.

Postilion — SP163

1941, Jan. 12 *Perf. 14x13½*

B188	SP163	6 +24pf dp green	1.15	*3.00*
		Never hinged	5.00	

Postage Stamp Day. The surtax was for Hitler's National Culture Fund.

Benito Mussolini and Adolf Hitler SP164

Perf. 13½x14

1941, Jan. 30 Wmk. 237

B189	SP164	12 + 38pf rose brn	1.15	*4.25*
		Never hinged	6.50	

Issued as propaganda for the Rome-Berlin Axis. The surtax was for Hitler's National Culture Fund.

Adolf Hitler — SP165

1941, Apr. 17 *Perf. 14x13½*

B190	SP165	12 + 38pf dk red	1.15	*3.00*
		Never hinged	7.50	

52nd birthday of Adolf Hitler. The surtax was for Hitler's National Culture Fund.

Race Horse — SP166

Perf. 13½x14

1941, June 20 Engr. Unwmk.

B191	SP166	25 + 100pf sapphire	3.00	*7.50*
		Never hinged	13.00	

Issued in commemoration of the Blue Ribbon race held at Hamburg, June 29, 1941.

Amazons SP167

1941, July 20 *Perf. 14*

B192	SP167	42 + 108pf brown	1.90	*5.00*
		Never hinged	9.00	

8th "Brown Ribbon" at Munich.

Brandenburg Gate, Berlin — SP168

1941, Sept. 9

B193	SP168	25 + 50pf dp ultra	2.60	*6.75*
		Never hinged	10.50	

Issued in honor of the Berlin races.

Marburg SP169

Veldes SP170

Pettau — SP171

Triglav — SP172

1941, Sept. 29 Photo.

B194	SP169	3 + 7pf brown	.75	*2.25*
B195	SP170	6 + 9pf purple	.75	*2.25*
B196	SP171	12 + 13pf rose brn	.75	*2.60*
B197	SP172	25 + 15pf dk blue	1.45	*2.60*
		Nos. B194-B197 (4)	3.70	*9.70*
		Set, never hinged	15.00	

Annexation of Styria and Carinthia.

View from Belvedere Palace, Vienna — SP173

Belvedere Gardens, Vienna SP174

1941, Sept. 16 Engr.

B198	SP173	12 + 8pf dp red	1.25	*3.75*
B199	SP174	15 + 10pf violet	1.45	*3.75*
		Set, never hinged	9.75	

Issued to commemorate the Vienna Fair.

Mozart — SP175

1941, Nov. 28

B200	SP175	6 + 4pf dk rose vio	.25	*.90*
		Never hinged	.75	

Wolfgang Amadeus Mozart (1756-91).

Philatelist SP176

1942, Jan. 11 Photo.

B201	SP176	6 + 24pf dp purple	.55	*3.00*
		Never hinged	3.00	

To commemorate Stamp Day.

Soldier's Head — SP177

1942, Mar. 10 *Perf. 14x13½*

B202	SP177	12 + 38pf slate blk	.45	*1.60*
		Never hinged	1.75	

To commemorate Hero Memorial Day.

Adolf Hitler — SP178

1942, Apr. 13

B203	SP178	12 + 38pf lake	1.50	*6.00*
		Never hinged	11.50	

To commemorate Hitler's 53rd birthday.

Racing Three-year-old SP179

1942, June 16 Engr. *Perf. 14*

B204	SP179	25 + 100pf dk bl	4.50	*11.50*
		Never hinged	16.50	

73rd Hamburg Derby.

Race Horses SP180

1942, July 14

B205	SP180	42 + 108pf brown	1.50	*5.25*
		Never hinged	7.50	

9th "Brown Ribbon" at Munich.

Lüneburg Lion and Nuremberg Betrothal Cup — SP181

1942, Aug. 8 Photo. *Perf. 14x13½*

B206	SP181	6 + 4pf copper red	.35	*1.50*
B207	SP181	12 + 88pf green	.45	*2.25*
		Set, never hinged	3.50	

10th anniv. of the German Goldsmiths' Society and the 1st Goldsmiths' Day in Germany.
For overprint see Austria No. 394.

Henlein Monument, Nuremberg — SP182

1942, Aug. 29 *Perf. 14*

B208	SP182	6 + 24pf rose vio	.45	*1.50*
		Never hinged	1.60	

400th anniversary of the death of Peter Henlein, inventor of the pocket watch.

Postilion and Map of Europe SP183

Postilion and Globe — SP184

Postilion SP185

Perf. 13½x14, 14x13½

1942, Oct. 12 Photo.

B209	SP183	3 + 7pf dull blue	.25	*1.50*
		Engr.		
B210	SP184	6 + 14pf ultra & dp brn	.35	*1.50*
B211	SP185	12 + 38pf rose red & dp brn	.60	*2.60*
		Nos. B209-B211 (3)	1.20	*5.60*
		Set, never hinged	3.75	

European Postal Congress, Vienna.
For overprints see Austria Nos. 395, 397.

Nos. B209 to B211 Overprinted in Black

1942, Oct. 19

B212 SP183 3 + 7pf .70 *2.60*
B213 SP184 6 + 14pf .70 *2.60*
B214 SP185 12 + 30pf .90 *4.50*
Nos. B212-B214 (3) 2.30 *9.70*
Set, never hinged 7.50

To commemorate the signing of the European postal-telegraph agreement at Vienna.

Mail Coach SP186

1943, Jan. 10 **Engr.**

B215 SP186 6 + 24pf gray, brn & yel .25 *.90*
Never hinged .75

To commemorate Stamp Day. The surtax went to Hitler's National Culture Fund.

Brandenburg Gate — SP187

1943, Jan. 26 **Photo.**

B216 SP187 54 + 96pf cop red .45 *2.25*
Never hinged 2.60

10th anniversary of the assumption of power by the Nazis.

Nazi Emblem — SP188

1943, Jan. 26

B217 SP188 3 + 2pf olive bister .25 *.90*
Never hinged .70

Used to secure special philatelic cancellations.

Submarine SP189

Designs: 4pf+3pf, Schutz-Staffel Troops. 5pf+4pf, Motorized marksmen. 6pf+9pf, Signal Corps. 8pf+7pf, Engineer Corps. 12pf+8pf, Grenade assault. 15pf+10pf, Heavy artillery. 20pf+14pf, Anti-aircraft units in action. 25pf+15pf, Dive bombers. 30pf+30pf, Paratroops. 40pf+40pf, Tank. 50pf+50pf, Speed boat.

1943, Mar. 21 **Engr.**

B218 SP189 3 + 2pf dk brn .50 *1.20*
B219 SP189 4 + 3pf brown .50 *1.20*
B220 SP189 5 + 4pf dk grn .40 *1.20*
B221 SP189 6 + 9pf dp violet .40 *1.20*
B222 SP189 8 + 7pf brn org .40 *1.20*
B223 SP189 12 + 8pf car lake .60 *1.20*
B224 SP189 15 + 10pf vio brn .60 *1.20*
B225 SP189 20 + 14pf slate bl .60 *1.20*
B226 SP189 25 + 15pf indigo .75 *1.20*
B227 SP189 30 + 30pf green .60 *1.90*
B228 SP189 40 + 40pf red lil .60 *1.90*
B229 SP189 50 50pf grnsh blk .60 *3.00*
Nos. B218-B229 (12) 6.55 *17.60*
Set, never hinged 16.50

Army Day and Hero Memorial Day. Nos. B220 and B224 exist imperf. Value, each $75.

Nazi Flag and Children SP201

1943, Mar. 26 **Photo.**

B230 SP201 6 + 4pf dk green .25 *1.30*
Never hinged 1.05

To commemorate the Day of Youth Obligation when all German boys and girls had to take an oath of allegiance to Hitler.

Adolf Hitler SP202

1943, Apr. 13

B231 SP202 3 + 7pf brown blk .70 *1.50*
B232 SP202 6 + 14pf dk grn .45 *1.50*
B233 SP202 8 + 22pf dk chlky bl .45 *1.50*
B234 SP202 12 + 38pf cop red .45 *1.50*
B235 SP202 24 + 76pf vio brn .95 *3.50*
B236 SP202 40 + 160pf dk ol grn .95 *3.50*
Nos. B231-B236 (6) 3.95 *13.00*
Set, never hinged 10.50

Hitler's 54th birthday. No. B231 exists imperf. Value $100.

Reich Labor Service Corpsmen SP203 SP204

Designs: 6pf+14pf, Corpsman chopping. 12pf+18pf, Corpsman with implements.

1943, June 26 **Engr.**

B237 SP203 3 + 7pf bis brn .25 *.75*
B238 SP204 5 + 10pf pale ol grn .25 *.75*
B239 SP204 6 + 14pf dp blue .25 *.75*
B240 SP204 12 + 18pf dk red .30 *1.35*
Nos. B237-B240 (4) 1.05 *3.60*
Set, never hinged 3.00

Anniversary of Reich Labor Service. Nos. B237-B238, B240 exist imperf. Values: Nos. B237-B238, $45 each; No. B240, $60.

Rosegger's Birthplace, Upper Styria — SP207

Peter Rosegger SP208

Perf. 13½x14, 14x13½

1943, July 27 **Photo.**

B241 SP207 6 + 4pf green .25 *.90*
B242 SP208 12 + 8pf copper red .25 *.90*
Set, never hinged 1.50

Centenary of the birth of Peter Rosegger, Austrian writer.

Hunter SP209

1943, July 27 **Engr.**

B243 SP209 42 + 108pf brown .25 *1.20*
Never hinged .90

10th "Brown Ribbon" at Munich. No. B243 exists imperf. Value $200.

Race Horse — SP210

1943, Aug. 14

B244 SP210 6 + 4pf vio blk .25 *1.20*
B245 SP210 12 + 88pf dk car .25 *1.20*
Set, never hinged 1.60

Grand Prize of the Freudenau, the Vienna race track, Aug. 15, 1943.

Mother and Children — SP211

1943, Sept. 1

B246 SP211 12 + 38pf dark red .25 *1.20*
Never hinged .85

10th anniversary of Winter Relief.

St. George in Gold — SP212

1943, Oct. 1

B247 SP212 6 + 4pf dk ol grn .25 *.75*
B248 SP212 12 + 88pf vio brn .25 *1.10*
Set, never hinged 1.15

German Goldsmiths' Society.

Ancient Lübeck — SP213

1943, Oct. 24 **Photo.**

B249 SP213 12 + 8pf copper red .25 *1.15*
Never hinged .70

Hanseatic town of Lubeck, 800th anniv. No. B249 exists imperf. Value, $110.

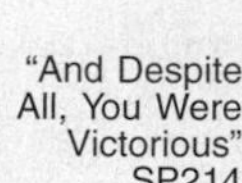

"And Despite All, You Were Victorious" SP214

1943, Nov. 5

B250 SP214 24 + 26pf henna .25 *1.50*
Never hinged 1.15

20th anniv. of the Nazis' Munich beer-hall putsch and to honor those who died for the Nazi movement. No. B250 exists imperf; value, $100.

Dr. Robert Koch — SP215

1944, Jan. 25 **Engr.** **Unwmk.**

B251 SP215 12 + 38pf sepia .25 *1.15*
Never hinged .75

Centenary of the birth of the bacteriologist, Robert Koch (1843-1910).

Hitler and Nazi Emblems SP216

1944, Jan. 29 **Photo.**

B252 SP216 54 + 96pf yel brn .25 *2.25*
Never hinged 1.50

Assumption of power by the Nazis, 11th anniv.

Airport Scene — SP217

Seaplane SP218

Plane Seen from Above — SP219

Perf. 14x13½, 13½x14

1944, Feb. 11 **Photo.** **Unwmk.**

B252A SP217 6 + 4pf dk grn .25 *1.10*
B252B SP218 12 + 8pf maroon .25 *1.10*
B252C SP219 42 + 108pf dp slate bl .30 *2.25*
Nos. B252A-B252C (3) .80 *4.45*
Set, never hinged 2.25

25th anniv. of German air mail. The surtax was for the National Culture Fund.

Infant's Crib — SP220

6pf+4pf, Public nurse. 12pf+8pf, "Mother & Child" clinic. 15pf+10pf, Expectant mothers.

1944, Mar. 2

B253 SP220 3 + 2pf dk brn .25 *.75*
B254 SP220 6 + 4pf dk grn .25 *.75*
B255 SP220 12 + 8pf dp car .25 *.75*
B256 SP220 15 + 10pf vio brn .25 *.75*
Nos. B253-B256 (4) 1.00 *3.00*
Set, never hinged 1.50

10th anniv. of "Mother and Child" aid.

Assault Boat — SP221

Designs: 4pf+3pf, Chain-wheel vehicle. 5pf+3pf, Paratroops. 6pf+4pf, Submarine officer. 8pf+4pf, Schutz-Staffel grenade throwers. 10pf+5pf, Searchlight. 12pf+6pf, Infantry. 15pf+10pf, Self-propelled gun. 16pf+10pf, Speed boat. 20pf+10pf, Sea raider. 24pf+10pf, Railway artillery. 25pf+15pf, Rockets. 30pf+20pf, Mountain trooper.

Inscribed: "Grossdeutsches Reich"

1944, Mar. 11

B257 SP221 3 + 2pf yel brn .30 *1.15*
B258 SP221 4 + 3pf royal bl .30 *1.15*
B259 SP221 5 + 3pf dp yel grn .25 *.55*
B260 SP221 6 + 4pf dp vio .25 *.55*
B261 SP221 8 + 4pf org ver .25 *.60*
B262 SP221 10 + 5pf choc .25 *.55*
B263 SP221 12 + 6pf carmine .25 *.55*
B264 SP221 15 + 10pf dp clar .25 *.75*
B265 SP221 16 + 10pf dk bl grn .25 *1.20*
B266 SP221 20 + 10pf brt bl .35 *1.90*
B267 SP221 24 + 10pf dl org brn .35 *1.90*
B268 SP221 25 + 15pf vio bl .70 *3.75*
B269 SP221 30 + 20pf ol grn .70 *3.75*
Nos. B257-B269 (13) 4.45 *18.35*
Set, never hinged 16.50

To commemorate Hero Memorial Day.

Flora Statue in Fulda's Schloss Garden — SP234

1944, Mar. 11

B270 SP234 12 + 38pf dp brown .25 *.90*
Never hinged .60

1,200th anniversary of town of Fulda.

Adolf Hitler — SP235

1944, Apr. 14 Engr. Unwmk.

B271 SP235 54 + 96pf rose car .30 *3.00*
Never hinged 1.75

To commemorate Hitler's 55th birthday.

Type of 1939-41 and

Woman Mail Carrier SP236

Field Post in the East — SP237

Designs: 8pf+12pf, Mail coach. 16pf+24pf, Automobile race. 20pf+30pf, Postal police. 24pf+36pf, Glider workshops.

1944, May 3 Photo.
Designs measure 29½x24½mm

B272 SP236 6 + 9pf vio bl .25 *.75*
B273 SP124 8 + 12pf gray blk .25 *.75*
B274 SP237 12 + 18pf dp plum .25 *.75*
B275 SP124 16 + 24pf dk grn .25 *.75*
B276 SP124 20 + 30pf blue .25 *1.35*
B277 SP124 24 + 36pf dk pur .25 *1.35*
Nos. B272-B277 (6) 1.50 *5.70*
Set, never hinged 3.00

Surtax for the Postal Employees' Fund.

Soldier and Tirolese Rifleman — SP238

1944, July

B278 SP238 6 + 4pf dp grn .25 *.85*
B279 SP238 12 + 8pf brn lake .25 *.85*
Set, never hinged .85

7th National Shooting Matches at Innsbruck.

Albert I, Duke of Prussia — SP239

1944, July

B280 SP239 6 + 4pf dk bl grn .25 *1.20*
Never hinged .75

400th anniv. of Albert University, Königsberg.

Labor Corps Girl SP240

Labor Corpsman SP241

1944, June Engr.

B281 SP240 6 + 4pf green .25 *.70*
B282 SP241 12 + 8pf carmine .25 *.70*
Set, never hinged .85

Issued to honor an exhibit of the Reich Labor Service.

Race Horse and Foal — SP242

1944, July 23 *Perf. 14x13½*

B283 SP242 42 + 108pf brown .25 *2.00*
Never hinged 1.05

11th "Brown Ribbon" at Munich.
For overprint see Austria No. 396.

Race Horse's Head in Oak Wreath — SP243

1944, Aug. Photo. *Perf. 14*

B284 SP243 6 + 4pf Prus green .25 *1.05*
B285 SP243 12 + 88pf car lake .25 *1.05*
Set, never hinged 1.05

Vienna Grand Prize Race.

Nautilus Cup in Green Vault, Dresden — SP244

1944, Sept. 11

B286 SP244 6 + 4pf dk grn .25 *1.05*
B287 SP244 12 + 88pf car brn .25 *1.05*
Set, never hinged 1.00

German Goldsmiths' Society.
No. B287 exists imperf. Value $175.

Post Horn and Letter — SP245

1944, Oct. 2

B288 SP245 6 + 24pf dk green .25 *1.20*
Never hinged .70

To commemorate Stamp Day.

Eagle and Serpent — SP246

1944, Nov. 9

B289 SP246 12 + 8pf rose red .25 *1.20*
Never hinged .75

21st anniv. of the Munich putsch.

Count Anton Günther — SP247

1945, Jan. 6 Typo. *Perf. 13½x14*

B290 SP247 6 + 14pf brown vio .25 *1.20*
Never hinged .75

600th anniv. of municipal law in Oldenburg. Exists imperf. Value, $75.

People's Army — SP248

1945, Feb. Photo. *Perf. 14x13½*

B291 SP248 12 + 8pf rose car .30 *2.60*
Never hinged 1.35

Proclamation of the People's Army (Volkssturm) in East Prussia to fight the Russians.

Elite Storm Trooper (S. S.) — SP249

Storm Trooper (S. A.) — SP250

1945, Apr. 21 *Perf. 13½x14*

B292 SP249 12 + 38pf brt car 9.00 *900.00*
B293 SP250 12 + 38pf brt car 6.00 *900.00*
Set, never hinged 60.00

12th anniv. of the assumption of power by the Nazis. Nos. B292-B293 were on sale in Berlin briefly before the collapse of that city.
Exist imperf unused. Value same as perf.
Forged cancels abound. Certificates of authenticity mandatory for used examples.

Two stamps were prepared, but not issued, recognizing the National Socialist Motor Corps (NSKK) and the National Socialist Flyers Corps (NSFK). Value $15,000 each.

Souvenir Sheets

SP251

Wmk. 284

1946, Dec. 8 Typo. *Perf. 14*

B294 SP251 Sheet of 3 19.00 *130.00*
Never hinged 45.00

Imperf

B295 SP251 Sheet of 3 19.00 *150.00*
Never hinged 45.00
a. A119 20pf light blue 4.50 *37.50*
b. A119 24pf orange brown 4.50 *37.50*
c. A119 40pf red violet 4.50 *37.50*

No. B294 contains Nos. 543, 544 and 548.
Nos. B294-B295 sold for 5m each. Surtax for refugees and the aged.

Leipzig Proclaimed Market Place, 1160 — SP252

Design: 60pf+40pf, Foreign merchants displaying their wares, 1268.

Wmk. 48

1947, Mar. 5 **Engr.** ***Perf. 13***
B296 SP252 24 +26pf chestnut brn .25 *5.00*
B297 SP252 60 + 40pf dp vio blue .25 *5.00*
Set, never hinged 2.25

1947 Leipzig Fairs.
No. B296 exists imperf. Value $150.
See Nos. 580-583, 10NB1-10NB2, 10NB4-10NB5, 10NB12-10NB13 and German Democratic Republic Nos. B15-B16.

Madonna SP254

Cathedral Towers SP255

Designs: 12pf+8pf, Three Kings. 24pf+16pf, Cologne Cathedral.

Wmk. 286

1948, Aug. 15 **Typo.** ***Perf. 11***
B298 SP254 6 + 4pf org brn .30 *.75*
a. "1948-1248" 4.25 *19.00*
Never hinged 11.50
B299 SP254 12 + 8pf grnsh blue .55 *1.90*
a. "1948-1948" 5.75 *22.50*
Never hinged 15.00
B300 SP254 24 + 16pf car 1.15 *3.75*
B301 SP255 50 + 50pf blue 2.60 *9.00*
Nos. B298-B301 (4) 4.60 *15.40*
Set, never hinged 12.00

700th anniv. of the laying of the cornerstone of Cologne Cathedral. The surtax was to aid in its reconstruction.
Specialists collect Nos. B298-B301 with watermark in four positions: upright, D's facing left; upright, D's facing right; sideways, D's facing up; sideways, D's facing down. Two types of perforation: line and comb.

Brandenburg Gate, Berlin — SP256

Perf. 10½x11½, 11

1948, Dec. **Litho.**
B302 SP256 10 + 5pf green 2.40 *6.75*
B303 SP256 20 + 10pf rose car 2.40 *6.75*
Set, never hinged 12.00

The surtax was for aid to Berlin.

Bicycle Racers — SP257

Wmk. 116

1949, May 15 **Engr.** ***Perf. 14***
B304 SP257 10 + 5pf green 1.60 *6.00*
B305 SP257 20 + 10pf brn org 4.50 *15.00*
Set, never hinged 16.50

1949 Bicycle Tour of Germany.

Goethe at Rome — SP258

Goethe — SP259

30pf+15pf, Goethe portrait facing left.

1949, Aug. 15
B306 SP258 10 + 5pf green .80 *4.25*
B307 SP259 20 + 10pf red 1.20 *7.50*
B308 SP259 30 + 15pf blue 7.50 *22.50*
Nos. B306-B308 (3) 9.50 *34.25*
Set, never hinged 32.00

Bicentenary of the birth of Johann Wolfgang von Goethe.
The surtax was for the reconstruction of Goethe House, Frankfurt-on-Main.

Federal Republic

Bavaria Stamp of 1849 — SP260

1949, Sept. 30 **Litho.** **Wmk. 285**
B309 SP260 10 + 2pf grn & blk 5.75 *22.50*
Never hinged 13.00

Centenary of German postage stamps.

St. Elisabeth — SP261

Designs: 10pf+5pf, Paracelsus. 20pf+10pf, F. W. A. Froebel. 30pf+15pf, J. H. Wichern.

1949, Dec. 14 **Engr.** **Wmk. 286**
B310 SP261 8 + 2pf brn vio 5.50 *19.00*
B311 SP261 10 + 5pf yel grn 4.50 *10.50*
B312 SP261 20 + 10pf red 4.50 *10.50*
B313 SP261 30 + 15pf vio bl 23.00 *90.00*
Nos. B310-B313 (4) 37.50 *130.00*
Set, never hinged 82.50

The surtax was for welfare organizations.

Seal of Johann Sebastian Bach — SP262

1950, July 28 ***Perf. 14***
B314 SP262 10 + 2pf dk grn 17.50 *37.50*
B315 SP262 20 + 3pf dk car 17.50 *42.50*
Set, never hinged 82.50

Bicentenary of the death of Bach

Frescoes from Marienkirche SP263

1951, Aug. 30 **Photo.** **Wmk. 286**
Center in Gray
B316 SP263 10 + 5pf green 28.00 *60.00*
B317 SP263 20 + 5pf brn lake 28.00 *65.00*
Set, never hinged 170.00

Construction of Marienkirche, Lübeck, 700th anniv.
The surtax aided in its reconstruction.

Stamps Under Magnifying Glass — SP264

Wmk. 295

1951, Sept. 14 **Typo.** ***Perf. 14***
B318 SP264 10 + 2pf multi 13.50 *37.50*
B319 SP264 20 + 3pf multi 15.00 *42.50*
Set, never hinged 67.50

Natl. Philatelic Exposition, Wuppertal, 1951.

St. Vincent de Paul — SP265

Portraits: 10pf+3pf, Friedrich von Bodelschwingh. 20pf+5pf, Elsa Brandstrom. 30pf+10pf, Johann Heinrich Pestalozzi.

1951, Oct. 23 **Engr.**
B320 SP265 4 + 2pf brown 3.00 *7.50*
B321 SP265 10 + 3pf green 4.50 *6.00*
B322 SP265 20 + 5pf rose red 4.50 *6.00*
B323 SP265 30 + 10pf dp blue 37.50 *90.00*
Nos. B320-B323 (4) 49.50 *109.50*
Set, never hinged 105.00

The surtax was for charitable purposes.

Nuremberg Madonna — SP266

1952, Aug. 9
B324 SP266 10 + 5pf green 4.50 *15.00*
Never hinged 13.00

Centenary of the founding of the Germanic National Museum, Nuremberg. The surtax was for the museum.

Boy Hikers and Youth Hostel — SP267

Design: 20pf+3pf, Girls and Hostel.

1952, Sept. 17 ***Perf. 13½x14***
B325 SP267 10 + 2pf green 7.50 *17.50*
B326 SP267 20 + 3pf dp car 7.50 *17.50*
Set, never hinged 34.00

The surtax was to aid the youth program of the Federal Republic.

Elizabeth Fry — SP268

10pf+5pf, Dr. Carl Sonnenschein. 20pf+10pf, Theodor Fliedner. 30pf+10pf, Henri Dunant.

1952, Oct. 1
B327 SP268 4 + 2pf org brn 4.00 *6.00*
B328 SP268 10 + 5pf green 4.00 *6.00*
B329 SP268 20 + 10pf brn car 5.25 *9.00*
B330 SP268 30 + 10pf dp bl 30.00 *60.00*
Nos. B327-B330 (4) 43.25 *81.00*
Set, never hinged 97.50

The surtax was for welfare organizations.

Owl and Cogwheel SP269

1953, May 7 **Wmk. 295** ***Perf. 14***
B331 SP269 10 + 5pf dp grn 10.50 *24.00*
Never hinged 22.50

50th anniv. of the founding of the German Museum in Munich.

Thurn and Taxis Palace Gate — SP270

Design: 20pf+3pf, Telecommunications Bldg., Frankfurt-on-Main.

Wmk. 285

1953, July 29 **Litho.** ***Perf. 13½***
B332 SP270 10 + 2pf yel grn, bl & fawn 6.75 *21.00*
B333 SP270 20 + 3pf fawn, blk & gray 6.75 *21.00*
Set, never hinged 37.50

The surtax was for the International Stamp Exhibition, Frankfurt-on-Main, 1953.

August Hermann Francke — SP271

Designs: 10pf+5pf, Sebastian Kneipp. 20pf+10pf, Dr. Johann Christian Senckenberg. 30pf+10pf, Fridtjof Nansen.

Wmk. 295

1953, Nov. 2 **Engr.** ***Perf. 14***
B334 SP271 4 + 2pf choc 1.60 *7.50*
B335 SP271 10 + 5pf bl grn 2.25 *7.50*
B336 SP271 20 + 10pf red 5.00 *7.50*
B337 SP271 30 + 10pf blue 17.50 *57.50*
Nos. B334-B337 (4) 26.35 *80.00*
Set, never hinged 75.00

The surtax was for welfare organizations.

Catalogue values for unused stamps in this section, from this point to the end of the section, are for Never Hinged items.

Käthe Kollwitz — SP272

Portraits: 10pf+5pf, Lorenz Werthmann. 20pf+10pf, Johann Friedrich Oberlin. 40pf+10pf, Bertha Pappenheim.

1954, Dec. 28 *Perf. 13½x14*

B338 SP272 7pf + 3pf brown 2.60 2.60
B339 SP272 10pf + 5pf green 1.30 1.30
B340 SP272 20pf + 10pf red 9.00 4.50
B341 SP272 40pf + 10pf blue 28.00 *34.00*
Nos. B338-B341 (4) 40.90 *42.40*

The surtax was for welfare organizations.

Carrier Pigeon and Magnifying Glass — SP273

20pf+3pf, Post horn and stamp tongs.

1955, Sept. 14 Wmk. 304 *Perf. 14*

B342 SP273 10pf + 2pf green 4.25 *5.25*
B343 SP273 20pf + 3pf red 9.00 *9.75*

WESTROPA, 1955, philatelic exhibition at Dusseldorf. The surtax aided the Society of German Philatelists.

Amalie Sieveking — SP274

Portraits: 10pf+5pf, Adolph Kolping. 20pf+10pf, Dr. Samuel Hahnemann. 40pf+10pf, Florence Nightingale.

1955, Nov. 15 Photo. & Litho.

B344 SP274 7 + 3pf olive bis 2.60 2.60
B345 SP274 10 + 5pf dk green 2.00 1.30
B346 SP274 20 + 10pf red org 2.00 1.30
B347 SP274 40 + 10pf grnsh blue 22.50 *30.00*
Nos. B344-B347 (4) 29.10 *35.20*

Surtax for independent welfare organizations.

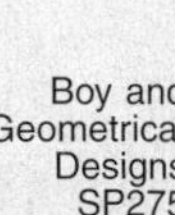

Boy and Geometrical Designs SP275

Design: 10pf+5pf, Girl playing flute.

Unwmk.

1956, July 21 Litho. *Perf. 14*

B348 SP275 7pf + 3pf multi 1.75 *2.60*
B349 SP275 10pf + 5pf multi 5.75 *7.50*

The surtax was for the Youth Hostel Organization.

The Midwife SP276

10+5pf, Ignaz Philipp Semmelweis. 20+10pf, The mother. 40+10pf, The children's nurse.

1956, Oct. 1 Photo.

Design and Inscription in Black

B350 SP276 7pf + 3pf org brn 1.30 *2.00*
B351 SP276 10pf + 5pf green 1.00 .65
B352 SP276 20pf + 10pf brt red 1.00 .65
B353 SP276 40pf + 10pf brt blue 11.50 13.00
Nos. B350-B353 (4) 14.80 *16.30*

Issued to honor Ignaz Philipp Semmelweis, the discoverer of the cause of puerperal fever. Surtax for independent welfare organizations.

Children Leaving SP277

Design: 20pf+10pf, Child arriving.

1957, Feb. 1 Litho. *Perf. 13½x13*

B354 SP277 10pf + 5pf gray grn & red org 1.00 *1.60*
B355 SP277 20pf + 10pf red org & lt bl 2.25 *3.75*

The surtax was for vacations for the children of Berlin.

Young Miner — SP278

10+5pf, Miner with drill. 20+10pf, Miner & conveyor. 40+10pf, Miner & coal elevator.

1957, Oct. 1 Wmk. 304 *Perf. 14*

B356 SP278 7pf + 3pf bis brn & blk 1.00 *1.30*
B357 SP278 10pf + 5pf blk & yel grn .65 .65
B358 SP278 20pf + 10pf black & red 1.00 .65
B359 SP278 40pf + 10pf black & blue 13.50 *16.50*
Nos. B356-B359 (4) 16.15 *19.10*

Surtax for independent welfare organizations.

"A Hunter from the Palatinate." SP279

10pf + 5pf, "The Fox who Stole the Goose"

1958, Apr. 1 Litho.

B360 SP279 10pf + 5pf brn red, grn & blk 1.30 *1.60*
B361 SP279 20pf + 10pf multi 2.25 *3.00*

The surtax was to finance young peoples' study trips to Berlin.

Friedrich Wilhelm Raiffeisen SP280

Dairy Maid SP281

Designs: 20pf+10pf, Girl picking grapes. 40pf+10pf, Farmer with pitchfork.

1958, Oct. 1 Wmk. 304 *Perf. 14*

B362 SP280 7pf + 3pf gldn brn & dk brn .40 .40
B363 SP281 10pf + 5pf grn, red & yel .40 .40
B364 SP281 20pf + 10pf red, yel & bl .40 .40
B365 SP281 40pf + 10pf blue & ocher 6.00 *7.25*
Nos. B362-B365 (4) 7.20 *8.45*

Surtax for independent welfare organizations.

Stamp of Hamburg, 1859 — SP282

Design: 20pf+10pf, Stamp of Lübeck, 1859.

1959 Engr. Wmk. 304

B366 SP282 10pf + 5pf yel green & brown .25 *.65*
a. 10pf + 5pf green & brown .65 *1.75*
B367 SP282 20pf + 10pf red org & red brn .25 *.65*
a. 20pf + 10pf maroon & red brown 1.00 *1.75*

"Interposta" Philatelic Exhibition, Hamburg, May 22-31, 1959 for the cent. of the 1st stamps of Hamburg and Lübeck.

The surtax on Nos. B366, B367 was for vacations for the children of Berlin.

Issued: Nos. B366-B367, 8/22; Nos. B366a-B367a, 5/22.

Girl Giving Bread to Beggar SP283

Jacob and Wilhelm Grimm SP284

Designs (from "Star Dollars" fairy tale): 10pf+5pf, Girl giving coat to boy, 20pf+10pf, Star-Money from Heaven.

1959, Oct. 1 Litho. *Perf. 14*

B368 SP283 7pf + 3pf brn & yel .25 *.35*
B369 SP283 10pf + 5pf grn & yel .25 *.35*
B370 SP283 20pf + 10pf brick red & yel .30 *.35*
B371 SP284 40pf + 10pf bl, blk, ocher & emer 2.60 *4.50*
Nos. B368-B371 (4) 3.40 *5.55*

Surtax for independent welfare organizations.

Little Red Riding Hood and the Wolf — SP285

Various Scenes from Little Red Riding Hood.

1960, Oct. 1 Wmk. 304 *Perf. 14*

B372 SP285 7pf + 3pf brn ol, red & blk .40 .40
B373 SP285 10pf + 5pf grn, red & blk .40 .35
B374 SP285 20pf + 10pf brick red, emer & blk .40 .35
B375 SP285 40pf + 20pf brt bl, red & blk 1.60 *3.75*
Nos. B372-B375 (4) 2.80 *4.85*

Surtax for independent welfare organizations.

1961, Oct. 2

Various Scenes from Hansel and Gretel.

B376 SP285 7pf + 3pf multi .25 *.30*
B377 SP285 10pf + 5pf multi .25 *.30*
B378 SP285 20pf + 10pf multi .25 *.30*
B379 SP285 40pf + 20pf multi .80 *1.60*
Nos. B376-B379 (4) 1.55 *2.50*

Surtax for independent welfare organizations. See B384-B387, B392-B395, B400-B403.

Fluorescent Paper was introduced for semipostal stamps, starting with No. B380.

Apollo — SP286

10pf+5pf, Camberwell beauty. 20pf+10pf, Tortoise-shell. 40pf+20pf, Tiger swallowtail.

Wmk. 304

1962, May 25 Litho. *Perf. 14*

Butterflies in Natural Colors, Black Inscriptions

B380 SP286 7pf + 3pf bis brn .35 *.55*
B381 SP286 10pf + 5pf brt green .35 *.55*
B382 SP286 20pf + 10pf dp crim .65 *1.00*
B383 SP286 40pf + 20pf brt blue 1.00 *1.60*
Nos. B380-B383 (4) 2.35 *3.70*

Issued for the benefit of young people.

Nos. B381-B383 exist without watermark. Value, each $900 unused, $975 used.

Fairy Tale Type of 1960

Scenes from Snow White (Schneewittchen).

1962, Oct. 10 *Perf. 14*

B384 SP285 7pf + 3pf multi .25 *.25*
B385 SP285 10pf + 5pf multi .25 *.25*
B386 SP285 20pf + 10pf multi .25 *.25*
B387 SP285 40pf + 20pf multi .65 *1.05*
Nos. B384-B387 (4) 1.40 *1.80*

Surtax for independent welfare organizations.

Hoopoe — SP287

Birds: 15pf+5pf, European golden oriole. 20pf+10pf, Bullfinch. 40pf+20pf, European kingfisher.

1963, June 12 Unwmk. *Perf. 14*

B388 SP287 10pf + 5pf multi .40 *.55*
B389 SP287 15pf + 5pf multi .35 *.55*
B390 SP287 20pf + 10pf multi .35 *.55*
B391 SP287 40pf + 20pf multi 1.45 *2.10*
Nos. B388-B391 (4) 2.55 *3.75*

Issued for the benefit of young people.

Fairy Tale Type of 1960

Various Scenes from the Grimm Brothers' "The Wolf and the Seven Kids."

1963, Sept. 23 Litho.

B392 SP285 10pf + 5pf multi .25 *.25*
B393 SP285 15pf + 5pf multi .25 *.25*
B394 SP285 20pf + 10pf multi .25 *.25*
B395 SP285 40pf + 20pf multi .40 *1.00*
Nos. B392-B395 (4) 1.15 *1.75*

Surtax for independent welfare organizations.

Herring SP288

Fish: 15pf+5pf, Rosefish. 20pf+10pf, Carp. 40pf+20pf, Cod.

1964, Apr. 10 Unwmk. *Perf. 14*

B396 SP288 10pf + 5pf multi .25 *.30*
B397 SP288 15pf + 5pf multi .25 *.30*
B398 SP288 20pf + 10pf multi .30 *.40*
B399 SP288 40pf + 20pf multi .80 *1.60*
Nos. B396-B399 (4) 1.60 *2.60*

Issued for the benefit of young people.

Fairy Tale Type of 1960

Various Scenes from Sleeping Beauty (Dornroschen).

1964, Oct. 6 Litho. *Perf. 14*

B400	SP285	10pf + 5pf multi	.25	*.25*
B401	SP285	15pf + 5pf multi	.25	*.25*
B402	SP285	20pf + 10pf multi	.25	*.25*
B403	SP285	40pf + 20pf multi	.25	*.80*
		Nos. B400-B403 (4)	1.00	*1.55*

Surtax for independent welfare organizations.
See Berlin Nos. 9NB25-9NB28.

Woodcock
SP289

Birds: 15pf+5pf, Ring-necked pheasant. 20pf+10pf, Black grouse. 40pf+20pf, Capercaillie.

1965, Apr. 1 Unwmk. *Perf. 14*

B404	SP289	10pf + 5pf multi	.25	*.30*
B405	SP289	15pf + 5pf multi	.25	*.30*
B406	SP289	20pf + 10pf multi	.25	*.30*
B407	SP289	40pf + 20pf multi	.25	*.80*
		Nos. B404-B407 (4)	1.00	*1.70*

Issued for the benefit of young people.
See Berlin Nos. 9NB29-9NB32.

Cinderella
Feeding
Pigeons
SP290

Various Scenes from Cinderella.

1965, Oct. 6 Litho. *Perf. 14*

B408	SP290	10pf + 5pf multi	.25	*.25*
B409	SP290	15pf + 5pf multi	.25	*.25*
B410	SP290	20pf + 10pf multi	.25	*.25*
B411	SP290	40pf + 20pf multi	.30	*.60*
		Nos. B408-B411 (4)	1.05	*1.35*

Surtax for independent welfare organizations.
See Nos. B418-B421, B426-B429; Berlin Nos. 9NB33-9NB36.

Roe
Deer — SP291

Designs: 20pf+10pf, Chamois. 30pf+15pf, Fallow deer. 50pf+25pf, Red deer.

1966, Apr. 22 Litho. *Perf. 14*

B412	SP291	10pf + 5pf multi	.25	.30
B413	SP291	20pf + 10pf multi	.25	.30
B414	SP291	30pf + 15pf multi	.25	*.30*
B415	SP291	50pf + 25pf multi	.55	*.80*
		Nos. B412-B415 (4)	1.30	*1.70*

Issued for the benefit of young people.
See Nos. B422-B425; Berlin Nos. 9NB37-9NB40.

Prussian Letter
Carrier — SP292

Design: 30pf+15pf, Bavarian mail coach.

1966 Litho. *Perf. 14*

B416	SP292	30pf + 15pf multi	.35	*.60*
B417	SP292	50pf + 25pf multi	.50	*.60*

Meeting of the Federation Internationale de Philatélie (FIP), Munich, Sept. 26-29, and stamp exhibition, Municipal Museum, Sept. 24-Oct. 1. The surcharge was for the Foundation for the Promotion of Philately and Postal History.
Issued: No. B416, 9/24; No. B417, 7/13.

Fairy Tale Type of 1965

Various Scenes from The Princess and the Frog.

1966, Oct. 5 Litho. *Perf. 14*

B418	SP290	10pf + 5pf multi	.25	*.25*
B419	SP290	20pf + 10pf multi	.25	*.25*
B420	SP290	30pf + 15pf multi	.25	*.25*
B421	SP290	50pf + 25pf multi	.30	*.80*
		Nos. B418-B421 (4)	1.05	*1.55*

Surtax for independent welfare organizations.
See Berlin Nos. 9NB41-9NB44.

Animal Type of 1966

10pf+5pf, Rabbit. 20pf+10pf, Ermine. 30pf+15pf, Hamster. 50pf+25pf, Red fox.

1967, Apr. 4 Litho. *Perf. 14*

B422	SP291	10pf + 5pf multi	.25	*.35*
B423	SP291	20pf + 10pf multi	.25	*.35*
B424	SP291	30pf + 15pf multi	.40	*.65*
B425	SP291	50pf + 25pf multi	.85	*1.30*
		Nos. B422-B425 (4)	1.75	*2.65*

Issued for the benefit of young people.
See Berlin Nos. 9NB45-9NB48.

Fairy Tale Type of 1965

Various Scenes from Frau Holle.

1967, Oct. 3 Litho. *Perf. 14*

B426	SP290	10pf + 5pf multi	.25	*.25*
B427	SP290	20pf + 10pf multi	.25	*.25*
B428	SP290	30pf + 15pf multi	.25	*.25*
B429	SP290	50pf + 25pf multi	.40	*1.00*
		Nos. B426-B429 (4)	1.15	*1.75*

Surtax for independent welfare organizations.
See Berlin Nos. 9NB49-9NB52.

Wildcat
SP293

Animals: 20pf+10pf, Otter. 30pf+15pf, Badger. 50pf+25pf, Beaver.

1968, Feb. 2 Photo. Unwmk.

B430	SP293	10pf + 5pf multi	.25	*.40*
B431	SP293	20pf + 15pf multi	.35	*.65*
B432	SP293	30pf + 15pf multi	.50	*.95*
B433	SP293	50pf + 25pf multi	1.30	*2.60*
		Nos. B430-B433 (4)	2.40	*4.60*

The surtax was for the benefit of young people.
See Berlin Nos. 9NB53-9NB56.

Olympic Games Type of Regular Issue

10pf+5pf, Karl-Friedrich Freiherr von Langen, equestrian. 20pf+10pf, Rudolf Harbig, runner. 30pf+15pf, Helene Mayer, fencer. 50pf+25pf, Carl Diem, sports organizer.

Lithographed and Engraved

1968, June 6 Unwmk. *Perf. 14*

B434	A285	10 + 5pf ol & dk brn	.55	.35
B435	A285	20 + 10pf dp emer & dk grn	.55	.35
B436	A285	30 + 15pf dp rose & dk red	1.00	.65
B437	A285	50 + 25pf brt bl & dk bl	1.00	*1.00*
		Nos. B434-B437 (4)	3.10	2.35

The surtax was for the Foundation for the Promotion of the 1972 Olympic Games in Munich.

Doll, c.
1878 — SP294

Various 19th Cent. Dolls. Nos. B438-B440 are from Germanic Natl. Museum, Nuremberg; No. B441 is from Altona Museum, Hamburg.

1968, Oct. 3 Litho. *Perf. 14*

B438	SP294	10pf + 5pf multi	.25	*.25*
B439	SP294	20pf + 10pf multi	.25	*.25*
B440	SP294	30pf + 15pf multi	.25	*.25*
B441	SP294	50pf + 25pf multi	.50	*.80*
		Nos. B438-B441 (4)	1.25	*1.55*

Surtax for independent welfare organizations.
See Berlin Nos. 9NB57-9NB60.

Pony — SP295

Horses: 20pf+10pf, Work horse. 30pf+15pf, Hotblood. 50pf+25pf, Thoroughbred.

1969, Feb. 6 Litho. *Perf. 14*

B442	SP295	10pf + 5pf multi	.30	*.40*
B443	SP295	20pf + 10pf multi	.30	*.40*
B444	SP295	30pf + 15pf multi	.50	*.65*
B445	SP295	50pf + 25pf multi	1.45	1.30
		Nos. B442-B445 (4)	2.55	*2.75*

Surtax for the benefit of young people.
See Berlin Nos. 9NB61-9NB64.

SP296

Olympic Rings and: 10pf+5pf, Track. 20pf+10pf, Hockey. 30pf+15pf, Archery. 50pf+25pf, Sailing.

1969, June 4 Photo. *Perf. 14*

B446	SP296	10pf + 5pf dk brn & lem	.65	.50
B447	SP296	20pf + 10pf bl grn & emer	.65	.55
B448	SP296	30pf + 15pf mag & dp lil rose	1.00	.65
B449	SP296	50pf + 25pf dp bl & brt bl	1.60	1.30
		Nos. B446-B449 (4)	3.90	3.00

1972 Olympic Games in Munich. The surtax was for the German Olympic Committee.

SP297

Tin Toys: 10pf+5pf, Locomotive. 20pf+10pf, Gardener. 30pf+15pf, Bird seller. 50pf+25pf, Knight on horseback.

1969, Oct. 2 Litho. *Perf. 13½x14*

B450	SP297	10pf + 5pf multi	.25	.25
B451	SP297	20pf + 10pf multi	.25	.25
B452	SP297	30pf + 15pf multi	.30	.30
B453	SP297	50pf + 25pf multi	.75	*1.00*
		Nos. B450-B453 (4)	1.55	1.80

Surtax for independent welfare organizations.
See Berlin Nos. 9NB65-9NB68.

Tin Toy — SP297a

Christmas. 10pf+5pf, Jesus in Manger.

1969, Nov. 13 *Perf. 13½x14*

B454	SP297a	10pf + 5pf multi	.35	.30

See Berlin No. 9NB69.
Inscribed: "Weihnachtsmarke 1969"

Heinrich von
Rugge — SP298

Minnesingers: 20pf+10pf, Wolfram von Eschenbach. 30pf+15pf, Walther von Metz. 50pf+25pf, Walther von der Vogelweide.

1970, Feb. 5 Photo. *Perf. 13½x14*

B455	SP298	10pf + 5pf multi	.35	.30
B456	SP298	20pf + 10pf multi	.55	.35
B457	SP298	30pf + 15pf multi	.65	.55
B458	SP298	50pf + 25pf multi	1.45	1.30
		Nos. B455-B458 (4)	3.00	2.50

Surtax was for benefit of young people.
See Berlin Nos. 9NB70-9NB73.

Residenz
(Palace),
Munich
SP299

Munich Buildings: 20pf+10pf, Propylaea. 30pf+15pf, Glyptothek. 50pf+25pf, Bavaria Statue and Colonnade.

1970, June 5 Engr. *Perf. 14*

B459	SP299	10pf + 5pf olive bis	.50	.35
B460	SP299	20pf + 10pf dk bl grn	.50	.35
B461	SP299	30pf + 15pf carmine	1.00	1.00
B462	SP299	50pf + 25pf dk blue	1.30	1.30
		Nos. B459-B462 (4)	3.30	3.00

The surtax was for the Foundation for the Promotion of the 1972 Olympic Games in Munich.

Jester — SP300

Puppets: 20pf+10pf, "Hanswurst." 30pf+15pf, Clown. 50pf+25pf, Harlequin.

1970, Oct. 6 Litho. *Perf. 13½x14*

B463	SP300	10pf + 5pf multi	.25	.25
B464	SP300	20pf + 10pf multi	.25	*.30*
B465	SP300	30pf + 15pf multi	.35	.35
B466	SP300	50pf + 25pf multi	.85	*.85*
		Nos. B463-B466 (4)	1.70	*1.75*

Surtax for independent welfare organizations.
See Berlin Nos. 9NB74-9NB77.

1970, Nov. 12

Christmas: 10pf+5pf, Rococo Angel, from Ursuline Sisters' Convent, Innsbruck.

B467	SP300	10pf + 5pf multi	.35	.30

See Berlin Nos. 9NB78.

King
Caspar — SP301

Children's Drawings: 20pf+10pf, Flea. 30pf+15pf, Puss-in-Boots. 50pf+25pf, Snake.

1971, Feb. 5 Litho. *Perf. 14*

B468	SP301	10pf + 5pf multi	.30	.30
B469	SP301	20pf + 10pf multi	.35	.35
B470	SP301	30pf + 15pf multi	.55	.55
B471	SP301	50pf + 25pf multi	.95	.95
		Nos. B468-B471 (4)	2.15	2.15

Surtax for the benefit of young people.
See Berlin Nos. 9NB79-9NB82.

Ski Jump — SP302

20pf+10pf, Figure skating. 30pf+15pf, Downhill skiing. 50pf+25pf, Ice hockey.

"1971" at Lower Right

1971, June 4 **Litho.** ***Perf. 14***

B472	SP302	10pf + 5pf brn org & blk	.30	.30
B473	SP302	20pf + 10pf grn & blk	.55	.40
B474	SP302	30pf + 15pf rose red & blk	.80	.65
B475	SP302	50pf + 25pf bl & blk	1.45	1.30
a.		Souvenir sheet of 4	3.00	2.60
b.		10pf + 5pf brown org & blk	.30	.30
c.		20pf + 10pf green & black	.55	.40
d.		30pf + 15pf rose red & black	.80	.65
e.		50pf + 25pf blue & black	1.45	1.20
		Nos. B472-B475 (4)	3.10	2.65

Olympic Games 1972.

No. B475a contains No. B475b-B475e which lack the small date ("1971") at lower right.

Women Churning Butter — SP303

Wooden Toys: 25pf+10pf, Horseback rider. 30pf+15pf, Nutcracker. 60pf+30pf, Dovecot.

1971, Oct. 5 **Litho.** ***Perf. 14***

B476	SP303	20pf + 10pf multi	.25	.25
B477	SP303	25pf + 10pf multi	.25	.25
B478	SP303	30pf + 15pf multi	.40	.40
B479	SP303	60pf + 30pf multi	1.05	1.05
		Nos. B476-B479 (4)	1.95	1.95

Surtax for independent welfare organizations.
See Berlin Nos. 9NB83-9NB86.

1971, Nov. 11

Christmas: Christmas angel with lights.

B480	SP303	20pf + 10pf multi	.55	.35

See Berlin No. 9NB87.

Ducks Crossing Road — SP304

Designs: 25pf+10pf, Hunter chasing deer and rabbits. 30pf+15pf, Girl protecting birds from cat. 60pf+30pf, Boy annoying swans.

1972, Feb. 4 **Litho.** ***Perf. 14***

B481	SP304	20pf + 10pf multi	.50	.40
B482	SP304	25pf + 10pf multi	.50	.40
B483	SP304	30pf + 15pf multi	.65	.65
B484	SP304	60pf + 30pf multi	1.20	1.20
		Nos. B481-B484 (4)	2.85	2.65

Animal protection. Surtax for the benefit of young people.
See Berlin Nos. 9NB88-9NB91.

Olympic Rings and Wrestling — SP305

25pf+10pf, Sailing. 30pf+15pf, Gymnastics. 60pf+30pf, Swimming.

1972, June 5 **Photo.** ***Perf. 14***

B485	SP305	20pf + 10pf multi	1.30	.65
B486	SP305	25pf + 10pf multi	1.30	.65
B487	SP305	30pf + 15pf multi	1.30	.65
B488	SP305	60pf + 30pf multi	2.10	2.00
		Nos. B485-B488 (4)	6.00	3.95

20th Olympic Games, Munich, Aug. 26 Sept. 10. See No. B490.

Souvenir Sheet

Olympic Games Site, Munich — SP306

a, Gymnastics stadium. b, Soccer stadium. c, Tent and lake. d, Television tower, vert.

1972, July 5 **Litho.** ***Perf. 14***

B489	SP306	Sheet of 4	5.00	5.00
a.		25pf + 10pf multi	1.00	1.00
b.		30pf + 15pf multi	1.00	1.00
c.		40pf + 20pf multi	1.00	1.00
d.		70pf + 35pf multi	1.00	1.00

20th Olympic Games, Munich. Surcharge was for the Foundation for the Promotion of the Munich Olympic Games.

Olympic Games Type of 1972

a, Long jump, women's. b, Basketball. c, Discus, women's. d, Canoeing.

Souvenir Sheet

1972, Aug. 18 **Litho.** ***Perf. 14***

B490	Sheet of 4	4.50	4.50
a.	SP305 25pf + 5pf multi	.40	.40
b.	SP305 30pf + 10pf multi	1.05	1.05
c.	SP305 40pf + 10pf multi	1.45	1.45
d.	SP305 70pf + 10pf multi	.75	.75
e.	Bklt. pane of 4, #B490a-B490d	7.50	7.50

20th Olympic Games, Munich.

Knight — SP307

1972, Oct. 5

B491	SP307	25pf + 10pf shown	.30	.30
B492	SP307	30pf + 15pf Rook	.30	.25
B493	SP307	40pf + 20pf Queen	.50	.25
B494	SP307	70pf + 35pf King	1.60	1.60
		Nos. B491-B494 (4)	2.70	2.40

19th cent. chess pieces made by Faience Works, Gien, France; now in Hamburg Museum. Surtax for independent welfare organizations.
See Berlin Nos. 9NB92-9NB95.

Adoration of the Kings — SP308

1972, Nov. 10 **Litho.**

B495	SP308	30pf + 15pf multi	.80	.50

Christmas.
See Berlin No. 9NB96.

Osprey — SP309

Birds of Prey: 30pf+15pf, Buzzard. 40pf+20pf, Red kite. 70pf+35pf, Montagu's harrier.

1973, Feb. 6 **Photo.** ***Perf. 14***

B496	SP309	25pf + 10pf multi	.65	.65
B497	SP309	30pf + 15pf multi	.80	.80
B498	SP309	40pf + 20pf multi	1.20	1.20
B499	SP309	70pf + 35pf multi	3.00	3.00
		Nos. B496-B499 (4)	5.65	5.65

Surtax was for benefit of young people.
See Berlin Nos. 9NB97-9NB100.

Hesse-Kassel SP310

Posthouse Signs: No. B501, Prussia. No. B502a, Württemberg. No. B502b, Bavaria.

1973, Apr. 5 **Litho.** ***Perf. 14***

B500	SP310	40pf + 20pf multi	.60	.60
B501	SP310	70pf + 35pf multi	1.05	1.05

Souvenir Sheet

B502	Sheet of 2	3.00	3.00
a.	SP310 40pf + 20pf multi	1.30	1.30
b.	SP310 70pf + 35pf multi	1.30	1.30

IBRA München 1973 International Philatelic Exhibition, Munich, May 11-20. No. B502 sold for 2.20 mark.

French Horn, 19th Century — SP311

Musical Instruments: 30pf+15pf, Pedal piano, 18th century. 40pf+20pf, Violin, 18th century. 70pf+35pf, Pedal harp, 18th century.

1973, Oct. 5 **Litho.** ***Perf. 14***

B503	SP311	25pf + 10pf multi	.50	.35
B504	SP311	30pf + 15pf multi	.55	.35
B505	SP311	40pf + 20pf multi	.65	.40
B506	SP311	70pf + 35pf multi	1.30	1.30
		Nos. B503-B506 (4)	3.00	2.40

Surtax was for independent welfare organizations.
See Berlin Nos. 9NB101-9NB104.

Christmas Star — SP312

1973, Nov. 9 **Litho. & Engr.**

B507	SP312	30pf + 15pf multi	.80	.50

Christmas.
See Berlin No. 9NB105.

Young Builder — SP313

30+15pf, Girl in national costume. 40+20pf, Boy studying. 70+35pf, Girl with microscope.

1974, Apr. 17 **Photo.** ***Perf. 14***

B508	SP313	25pf + 10pf multi	.50	.40
B509	SP313	30pf + 15pf multi	.80	.65
B510	SP313	40pf + 20pf multi	1.30	1.20
B511	SP313	70pf + 35pf multi	2.40	2.40
		Nos. B508-B511 (4)	5.00	4.65

Surtax was for benefit of young people.
See Berlin Nos. 9NB106-9NB109.

Campion — SP314

Flowers: 40pf+20pf, Foxglove. 50pf+25pf, Mallow. 70pf+35pf, Bellflower.

1974, Oct. 15 **Litho.** ***Perf. 14***

B512	SP314	30pf + 15pf multi	.30	.30
B513	SP314	40pf + 20pf multi	.35	.30
B514	SP314	50pf + 25pf multi	.40	.35
B515	SP314	70pf + 35pf multi	1.15	1.15
		Nos. B512-B515 (4)	2.20	2.10

Surtax was for independent welfare organizations.
See Berlin Nos. 9NB110-9NB113.

1974, Oct. 29

Christmas: 40pf+20pf, Advent decoration.

B516	SP314	40pf + 20pf multi	.80	.50

See Berlin No. 9NB114.

Diesel Locomotive Class 218 — SP315

Locomotives: 40pf+20pf, Electric engine Class 103. 50pf+25pf, Electric rail motor train Class 403. 70pf+35pf, Magnetic suspension train "Transrapid" (model).

1975, Apr. 15 **Litho.** ***Perf. 14***

B517	SP315	30pf + 15pf multi	.30	.30
B518	SP315	40pf + 20pf multi	.50	.40
B519	SP315	50pf + 25pf multi	.65	.60
B520	SP315	70pf + 35pf multi	1.25	1.00
		Nos. B517-B520 (4)	2.70	2.30

Surtax was for benefit of young people.
See Berlin Nos. 9NB115-9NB118.

Edelweiss — SP316

Alpine Flowers: 40pf+20pf, Trollflower. 50pf+25pf, Alpine rose. 70pf+35pf, Pasqueflower.

1975, Oct. 15 **Litho.** ***Perf. 14***

B521	SP316	30pf + 15pf multi	.35	.30
B522	SP316	40pf + 20pf multi	.35	.30
B523	SP316	50pf + 25pf multi	.55	.40
B524	SP316	70pf + 35pf multi	1.20	1.20
		Nos. B521-B524 (4)	2.45	2.20

Surtax was for independent welfare organizations.
See Berlin Nos. 9NB119-9NB122.

1975, Nov. 14

Christmas: Snow rose.

B525	SP316	40pf + 20pf multi	1.15	.80

See Berlin No. 9NB123.

Basketball SP317

Designs: 40pf+20pf, Rowing. 50pf+25pf, Gymnastics, women's. 70pf+35pf, Volleyball.

1976, Apr. 6 Litho. *Perf. 14*

B526	SP317	30pf + 15pf multi	.40	.30
B527	SP317	40pf + 20pf multi	.75	.55
B528	SP317	50pf + 25pf multi	.95	.80
B529	SP317	70pf + 35pf multi	1.25	1.15
		Nos. B526-B529 (4)	3.35	2.80

Youth training for Olympic Games. Surtax was for benefit of young people.
See Berlin Nos. 9NB124-9NB127.

Swimmer and Olympic Rings — SP318

30pf+15pf, Hockey. 50pf+25pf, High jump. 70pf+35pf, Rowing, coxed four.

1976, Apr. 6

B530	SP318	40pf + 20pf multi	1.00	.65
B531	SP318	50pf + 25pf multi	1.30	1.00

Souvenir Sheet

B532		Sheet of 2	2.00	1.60
a.		SP318 30pf + 15pf multi	.80	.65
b.		SP318 70pf + 35pf multi	1.05	1.00

21st Olympic Games, Montreal, Canada, July 17-Aug. 1. The surtax was for the German Sports Aid Foundation.

Phlox SP319

Flowers: 40pf+20pf, Marigolds. 50pf+25pf, Dahlias. 70pf+35pf, Pansies.

1976, Oct. 14 Litho. *Perf. 14*

B533	SP319	30pf + 15pf multi	.40	.35
B534	SP319	40pf + 20pf multi	.55	.50
B535	SP319	50pf + 25pf multi	.60	.55
B536	SP319	70pf + 35pf multi	1.00	1.00
		Nos. B533-B536 (4)	2.55	2.40

Surtax was for independent welfare organizations.

Souvenir Sheet

Nativity, Window, Frauenkirche, Esslingen — SP320

1976, Nov. 16 Litho. & Engr.

B537	SP320	50pf + 25pf multi	.80	.75

Christmas.
See Berlin No. 9NB132.

Wapen von Hamburg, c. 1730 SP321

Historic Ships: 40pf+20pf, Preussen, 5-master, 1902. 50pf+25pf, Bremen, 1929. 70pf+35pf, Freighter Sturmfels, 1972.

1977, Apr. 14 Litho. *Perf. 14*

B538	SP321	30pf + 15pf multi	.50	.50
B539	SP321	40pf + 20pf multi	.60	.55
B540	SP321	50pf + 25pf multi	.80	.75
B541	SP321	70pf + 35pf multi	1.15	1.15
		Nos. B538-B541 (4)	3.05	2.95

Surtax was for benefit of young people.
See Berlin Nos. 9NB133-9NB136.

Caraway — SP322

Meadow Flowers: 40pf+20pf, Dandelion. 50pf+25pf, Red clover. 70pf+35pf, Meadow sage.

1977, Oct. 13 Litho. *Perf. 14*

B542	SP322	30pf + 15pf multi	.60	.30
B543	SP322	40pf + 20pf multi	.60	.35
B544	SP322	50pf + 25pf multi	.60	.40
B545	SP322	70pf + 35pf multi	1.20	*1.00*
		Nos. B542-B545 (4)	3.00	*2.05*

Surtax was for independent welfare organizations.
See Nos. B553-B556; Berlin Nos. 9NB137-9NB140.

Souvenir Sheet

King Caspar Offering Gold, Window, St. Gereon's, Cologne — SP323

1977, Nov. 10

B546	SP323	50pf + 25pf multi	.75	.75

Christmas.
See Berlin No. 9NB141.

Giant Slalom SP324

Design: No. B548, Steeplechase.

1978 Litho. *Perf. 14*

B547	SP324	50pf + 25pf multi	1.20	1.00
B548	SP324	70pf + 35pf multi	2.60	2.25

Issued: No. B547, Jan. 12, No. B548, Apr. 13.
Surtax was for the German Sports Foundation.
See Berlin Nos. 9NB146-9NB147.

Balloon Ascent, Oktoberfest, Munich, 1820 — SP325

Designs: 40pf+20pf, Airship LZ 1, 1900. 50pf+25pf, Blériot monoplane, 1909. 70pf+35pf, Grade monoplane, 1909.

1978, Apr. 13 Litho. *Perf. 14*

B549	SP325	30pf + 15pf multi	.40	.40
B550	SP325	40pf + 20pf multi	.55	.55
B551	SP325	50pf + 25pf multi	.75	.75
B552	SP325	70pf + 35pf multi	1.00	1.00
		Nos. B549-B552 (4)	2.70	2.70

Surtax was for benefit of young people.
See Berlin Nos. 9NB142-9NB145.

Flower Type of 1977

Woodland Flowers: 30pf+15pf, Arum. 40pf+20pf, Weaselsnout. 50pf+25pf, Turk's-cap lily. 70pf+35pf, Liverwort.

1978, Oct. 12 Litho. *Perf. 14*

B553	SP322	30pf + 15pf multi	.35	.30
B554	SP322	40pf + 20pf multi	.50	.40
B555	SP322	50pf + 25pf multi	.65	.60
B556	SP322	70pf + 35pf multi	.85	.85
		Nos. B553-B556 (4)	2.35	2.15

Surtax was for independent welfare organizations.
See Berlin Nos. 9NB148-9NB151.

Souvenir Sheet

Christ Child, Window, Frauenkirche, Munich — SP326

1978, Nov. 16 Litho. *Perf. 14*

B557	SP326	50pf + 25pf multi	.95	.65

Christmas.
See Berlin No. 9NB152.

Dornier Wal, 1922 SP327

Airplanes: 50pf+25pf, Heinkel HE70, 1932. 60pf+30pf, Junkers W33 Bremen, 1928. 90pf+45pf, Focke-Wulf FW61, 1936.

1979, Apr. 5 Litho. *Perf. 14*

B558	SP327	40pf + 20pf multi	.50	.50
B559	SP327	50pf + 25pf multi	.65	.65
B560	SP327	60pf + 30pf multi	.80	.80
B561	SP327	90pf + 45pf multi	1.05	1.05
		Nos. B558-B561 (4)	3.00	3.00

Surtax was for benefit of young people.
See Nos. B570-B573; Berlin Nos. 9NB153-9NB156.

Handball SP328

Design: 90pf+45pf, Canoeing.

1979, Apr. 5

B562	SP328	60pf + 30pf multi	.80	.75
B563	SP328	90pf + 45pf multi	1.20	1.05

Surtax was for German Sports Foundation.
See Berlin Nos. 9NB157-9NB158.

Post House Sign, Altheim, Saar, 1754 — SP329

1979, Oct. 11 Litho. *Perf. 14*

B564	SP329	60pf + 30pf multi	.95	.95

Stamp Day. Surtax was for Foundation of Promotion of Philately and Postal History.
Issued in sheet of 10.

Red Beech SP330

Woodland Plants: 50pf+25pf, English oak. 60pf+30pf, Hawthorn. 90pf+45pf, Mountain pine.

1979, Oct. 11 Litho. *Perf. 14*

B565	SP330	40pf + 20pf multi	.65	.40
B566	SP330	50pf + 25pf multi	.65	.55
B567	SP330	60pf + 30pf multi	.65	.60
B568	SP330	90pf + 45pf multi	1.00	1.00
		Nos. B565-B568 (4)	2.95	2.55

Surtax was for independent welfare organizations.
See Berlin Nos. 9NB159-9NB162.

Nativity, Medieval Manuscript SP331

1979, Nov. 14 Litho. *Perf. 13½*

B569	SP331	60pf + 30pf multi	.80	.80

Christmas.
See Berlin No. 9NB163.

Aviation Type of 1979

40+20pf, FS 24 Phoenix, 1957. 50+25pf, Lockheed Super Constellation, 1950. 60+30pf, Airbus A300, 1972. 90+45pf, Boeing 747, 1969.

1980, Apr. 10 Litho. *Perf. 14*

B570	SP327	40 + 20pf multi	.35	.35
B571	SP327	50 + 25pf multi	.55	.55
B572	SP327	60 + 30pf multi	.75	.75
B573	SP327	90 + 45pf multi	1.05	1.05
		Nos. B570-B573 (4)	2.70	2.70

Surtax was for benefit of young people.
See Berlin Nos. 9NB164-9NB167.

Soccer SP332

Designs: 60pf+30pf, Equestrian. 90pf+45pf, Cross-country skiing.

1980, May 8 Photo. *Perf. 14*

B574 SP332 50 + 25pf multi .50 .40
B575 SP332 60 + 30pf multi .65 .55
B576 SP332 90 + 45pf multi 1.20 1.20
Nos. B574-B576 (3) 2.35 2.15

Surtax was for German Sports Foundation.
See Berlin Nos. 9NB168-9NB170.

Because of Germany's boycott of the 1980 Olympics in Russia, the postal administration pulled the planned 60+30pf semipostal before it was issued. A postal official used several examples, releasing them to collectors.

Ceratocephalus — SP333

Wildflowers: 50pf+25pf, Climbing meadow pea. 60pf+30pf, Corn cockle. 90pf+45pf, Grape hyacinth.

1980, Oct. 9 Litho. *Perf. 14*

B577 SP333 40 + 20pf multi .50 .40
B578 SP333 50 + 25pf multi .60 .55
B579 SP333 60 + 30pf multi .65 .65
B580 SP333 90 + 45pf multi 1.05 1.05
Nos. B577-B580 (4) 2.80 2.65

Surtax was for independent welfare organizations.
See Berlin Nos. 9NB171-9NB174.

Post House Sign, 1754, Altheim, Saar — SP334

1980, Nov. 13 Litho. *Perf. 14*

B581 SP334 60 + 30pf multi .65 .60

49th FIP Congress (Federation Internationale de Philatelie), Essen, Nov. 12-13.

Nativity, Altomunster Manuscript, 12th Century SP335

1980, Nov. 13 *Perf. 14x13½*

B582 SP335 60 + 30pf multi .85 .80

Christmas.
See Berlin No. 9NB175.

Borda Circle, 1800 — SP336

Historic Optical Instruments: 50pf+25pf, Reflecting telescope, 1770. 60pf+30pf, Binocular microscope, 1860. 90pf+45pf, Octant, 1775.

1981, Apr. 10 Litho. *Perf. 13½*

B583 SP336 40 + 20pf multi .50 .35
B584 SP336 50 + 25pf multi .80 .65
B585 SP336 60 + 30pf multi .80 .65
B586 SP336 90 + 45pf multi 1.15 1.15
Nos. B583-B586 (4) 3.25 2.80

Surtax was for benefit of young people.
See Berlin Nos. 9NB176-9NB179.

Rowing SP337

1981, Apr. 10 *Perf. 14*

B587 SP337 60 + 30pf shown .65 .65
B588 SP337 90 + 45pf Gliding 1.05 1.05

Surtax was for the German Sports Foundation.
See Berlin Nos. 9NB180-9NB181.

Water Nut — SP338

Endangered Species: 50pf+25pf, Floating heart. 60pf+30pf, Water gillyflower. 90pf+45pf, Water lobelia.

1981, Oct. 8 Litho.

B589 SP338 40 + 20pf multi .40 .35
B590 SP338 50 + 25pf multi .55 .50
B591 SP338 60 + 30pf multi .65 .65
B592 SP338 90 + 45pf multi 1.20 1.20
Nos. B589-B592 (4) 2.80 2.70

Surtax was for independent welfare organizations.
See Berlin Nos. 9NB182-9NB185.

Nativity, 19th Cent. Painting SP339

1981, Nov. 12 Litho.

B593 SP339 60 + 30pf multi .85 .75

Christmas.
See Berlin No. 9NB186.

Antique Cars SP340

Designs: 40+20pf, Benz, 1886. 50+25pf, Mercedes, 1913. 60+30pf, Hanomag, 1925. 90+45pf, Opel Olympia, 1937.

1982, Apr. 15 Litho.

B594 SP340 40 + 20pf multi .50 .40
B595 SP340 50 + 25pf multi .60 .55
B596 SP340 60 + 30pf multi .80 .65
B597 SP340 90 + 45pf multi 1.45 1.45
Nos. B594-B597 (4) 3.35 3.05

Surtax was for benefit of young people.
See Berlin Nos. 9NB187-9NB190.

Jogging SP341

1982, Apr. 15 Litho.

B598 SP341 60 + 30pf shown .75 .75
B599 SP341 90 + 45pf Archery 1.15 1.15

Surtax was for the German Sports Foundation.
See Berlin Nos. 9NB191-9NB192.

Tea-rose Hybrid — SP342

60+30pf, Floribunda. 80f+40pf, Bourbon rose. 120+60pf, Polyantha hybrid.

1982, Oct. 14 Litho. *Perf. 14*

B600 SP342 50 + 20pf multi .50 .40
B601 SP342 60 + 30pf multi .60 .55
B602 SP342 80 + 40pf multi .95 .85
B603 SP342 120 + 60pf multi 1.30 1.20
Nos. B600-B603 (4) 3.35 3.00

Surtax was for independent welfare organizations.
See Berlin Nos. 9NB193-9NB196.

Christmas SP343

Designs: Nativity, Oak altar, St. Peter's Church, Hamburg, 1380.

1982, Nov. 10

B604 SP343 80 + 40pf multi 1.30 .95

See Berlin No. 9NB197.

Historic Motorcycles — SP344

Designs: 50pf+20pf, Daimler-Maybach, 1885. 60pf+30pf, NSU, 1901. 80pf+40pf, Megola-Sport, 1922. 120pf+60pf, BMW, 1936.

1983, Apr. 12 Litho. *Perf. 14*

B605 SP344 50 + 20pf multi .50 .40
B606 SP344 60 + 30pf multi .60 .55
B607 SP344 80 + 40pf multi 1.05 1.00
B608 SP344 120 + 60pf multi 1.60 1.45
Nos. B605-B608 (4) 3.75 3.40

Surtax was for benefit of young people.
See Berlin Nos. 9NB198-9NB201.

1983 Sports Championships — SP345

80+40pf, Gymnastics Festival. 120+60pf, Modern Pentathlon World Championships.

1983, Apr. 12

B609 SP345 80 + 40pf multi 1.00 .85
B610 SP345 120 + 60pf multi 1.60 1.45

Surtax was for German Sports Foundation.
See Berlin Nos. 9NB202-9NB203.

Swiss Androsace SP346

60+30pf, Krain groundsel. 80+40pf, Fleischer's willow herb. 120+60pf, Alpine sowthistle.

1983, Oct. 13 Litho. *Perf. 14*

B611 SP346 50 + 20pf multi .40 .40
B612 SP346 60 + 30pf multi .55 .55
B613 SP346 80 + 40pf multi 1.00 1.00
B614 SP346 120 + 60pf multi 1.45 1.45
Nos. B611-B614 (4) 3.40 3.40

Surtax was for welfare organizations.
See Berlin Nos. 9NB204-9NB207.

Christmas SP347

1983, Nov. 10 Litho.

B615 SP347 80 + 40pf Carolers 1.30 1.05

Surtax was for free welfare work.
See Berlin No. 9NB208.

Insects — SP348

Designs: 50pf+20pf, Trichodes apoarius. 60pf+30pf, Vanessa atalanta. 80pf+40pf, Apis mellifera. 120pf+60pf, Chrysotoxum festivum.

1984, Apr. 12 Litho.

B616 SP348 50 + 20pf multi .50 .50
B617 SP348 60 + 30pf multi .85 .85
B618 SP348 80 + 40pf multi 1.15 1.15
B619 SP348 120 + 60pf multi 1.75 1.75
Nos. B616-B619 (4) 4.25 4.25

Surtax was for German Youth Stamp Foundation.
See Berlin Nos. 9NB209-9NB212.

Women's Discus SP349

Olympic Sports: 80pf+40pf, Rhythmic gymnastics. 120pf+60pf, Wind surfing.

1984, Apr. 12

B620 SP349 60 + 30pf multi 1.30 1.00
B621 SP349 80 + 40pf multi 2.00 1.60
B622 SP349 120 + 60pf multi 3.75 2.60
Nos. B620-B622 (3) 7.05 5.20

Surtax was for German Sports Foundation.
See Berlin Nos. 9NB213-9NB215.

Orchids SP350

Designs: 50pf+20pf, Aceras anthropophorum. 60pf+30pf, Orchis ustulata. 80pf+40pf, Limodorum abortivum. 120+60pf, Dactylorhiza sambucina.

1984, Oct. 18 Litho. *Perf. 14*

B623 SP350 50 + 20pf multi .60 .60
B624 SP350 60 + 30pf multi .60 .60
B625 SP350 80 + 40pf multi .95 .95
B626 SP350 120 + 60pf multi 2.00 2.00
Nos. B623-B626 (4) 4.15 4.15

Surtax was for welfare organizations.
See Berlin Nos. 9NB216-9NB219.

Christmas 1984 — SP351

No. B627, St. Martin.

1984, Nov. 8 **Litho.**
B627 SP351 80pf + 40pf multi 1.05 1.05

Surtax was for welfare organizations.
See Berlin No. 9NB220.

Bowling SP352

No. B629, Kayaking.

1985, Feb. 21 **Photo.**
B628 SP352 80pf + 40pf multi 1.05 .95
B629 SP352 120pf + 60pf multi 1.75 1.60

Surtax was for German Sports Foundation.
See Berlin Nos. 9NB221-9NB222.

Antique Bicycles SP353

50pf+20pf, Draisienne, 1817. 60pf+30pf, NSU Germania, 1886. 80pf+40pf, Cross-frame, 1887. 120pf+60pf, Adler tricycle, 1888.

1985, Apr. 16 **Litho.**
B630 SP353 50pf + 20pf multi .65 .65
B631 SP353 60pf + 30pf multi .80 .80
B632 SP353 80pf + 40pf multi 1.05 1.05
B633 SP353 120pf + 60pf multi 2.10 2.10
Nos. B630-B633 (4) 4.60 4.60

Surtax was for benefit of young people. Each stamp shows the Intl. Youth Year emblem.
See Berlin Nos. 9NB223-9NB226.

MOPHILA '85, Hamburg, Sept. 11-15 SP354

No. B634, Coachman, horses. No. 635, Stagecoach.

1985, Aug. 13 **Litho.** ***Perf. 14x14½***
B634 SP354 60 + 20pf multi 2.00 1.60
B635 SP354 80 + 20pf multi 2.00 1.60
a. Pair, #B634-B635 4.50 3.75

Surtax for the benefit of the Philatelic & Postal History Foundation. No. B635a has continuous design.

SP355

Various ornamental borders, medieval prayer book, Prussian State Library, Berlin.

1985, Oct. 15 **Litho.** ***Perf. 14***
B636 SP355 50pf + 20pf multi .80 .55
B637 SP355 60pf + 30pf multi .80 .65
B638 SP355 80pf + 40pf multi .95 .85
B639 SP355 120pf + 60pf multi 1.60 1.60
Nos. B636-B639 (4) 4.15 3.65

Surtax for welfare organizations.
See Berlin Nos. 9NB227-9NB230.

Christmas 1985 — SP356

Woodcut: The Birth of Christ, by Hans Baldung Grien (1485-1545), Freiburg Cathedral High Altar.

1985, Nov. 12 **Litho.** ***Perf. 14***
B640 SP356 80pf + 40pf multi 1.25 .125

Surtax for welfare organizations.
See Berlin No. 9NB231.

European World Sports Championships — SP357

No. B641, Running. No. B642, Bobsledding.

1986, Feb. 13 **Litho.** ***Perf. 14***
B641 SP357 80 + 40pf multi 1.30 1.30
B642 SP357 120 + 55pf multi 2.00 2.00

Surtax for the Natl. Sports Promotion Foundation.
See Berlin Nos. 9NB232-9NB233.

Vocational Training — SP358

No. B643, Optician. No. B644, Mason. No. B645, Beautician. No. B646, Baker.

1986, Apr. 10
B643 SP358 50 + 25pf multi .85 .85
B644 SP358 60 + 30pf multi 1.00 1.00
B645 SP358 70 + 35pf multi 1.15 1.15
B646 SP358 80 + 40pf multi 1.45 1.45
Nos. B643-B646 (4) 4.45 4.45

Surtax for German Youth Stamp Foundation.
See Berlin Nos. 9NB234-9NB237.

Glassware in German Museums — SP359

No. B647, Ornamental flask, c. 300. No. B648, Goblet, c. 1650. No. B649, Imperial eagle tankard, c. 1662. No. B650, Engraved goblet, c. 1720.

1986, Oct. 16 **Litho.**
B647 SP359 50 + 25pf multi .60 .55
B648 SP359 60 + 30pf multi .80 .75
B649 SP359 70 + 35pf multi .95 .80
B650 SP359 80 + 40pf multi 1.05 1.00
Nos. B647-B650 (4) 3.40 3.10

Surtax for public welfare organizations.
See Berlin Nos. 9NB238-9NB241.

Christmas SP360

Adoration of the Infant Jesus, Ortenberg Altarpiece, c. 1430, Hesse Museum, Darmstadt.

1986, Nov. 13 **Litho.** ***Perf. 14***
B651 SP360 80 + 40pf multi 1.20 1.15

Surtax for public welfare organizations.
See Berlin No. 9NB242.

World Championships — SP361

No. B652, Sailing. No. B653, Cross-country skiing.

1987, Feb. 12 **Litho.**
B652 SP361 80 + 40pf multi 1.15 1.15
B653 SP361 120 + 55pf multi 1.75 1.75

Surtax for the benefit of the national Sports Promotion Foundation.
See Berlin Nos. 9NB243-9NB244.

Youth in Industry SP362

No. B654, Plumber. No. B655, Dental technician. No. B656, Butcher. No. B657, Bookbinder.

1987, Apr. 9 **Litho.**
B654 SP362 50 + 25pf multi 1.00 .95
B655 SP362 60 + 30pf multi 1.20 1.15
B656 SP362 70 + 35pf multi 1.30 1.20
B657 SP362 80 + 40pf multi 1.75 1.75
Nos. B654-B657 (4) 5.25 5.05

Surtax for youth organizations.
See Berlin Nos. 9NB245-9NB248.

Gold and Silver Artifacts SP363

No. B658, Roman bracelet, 4th cent. No. B659, Gothic buckle, 6th cent. No. B660, Merovingian disk fibula, 7th cent. No. B661, Purse-shaped reliquary, 8th cent.

1987, Oct. 15
B658 SP363 50 + 25pf multi 1.00 1.00
B659 SP363 60 + 30pf multi 1.00 1.00
B660 SP363 70 + 35pf multi 1.00 1.00
B661 SP363 80 + 40pf multi 1.30 1.30
Nos. B658-B661 (4) 4.30 4.30

Surtax for welfare organizations sponsoring free museum exhibitions.
See Berlin Nos. 9NB249-9NB252.

Christmas SP364

Illustration from Book of Psalms, 13th cent., Bavarian Natl. Museum: Birth of Christ.

1987, Nov. 6
B662 SP364 80 + 40pf multi 1.20 1.20

Surtax for public welfare organizations.
See Berlin No. 9NB253.

Sports SP365

1988, Feb. 18 **Litho.**
B663 SP365 60 + 30pf Soccer 2.25 1.60
B664 SP365 80 + 40pf Tennis 2.25 2.00
B665 SP365 120 + 55pf Diving 3.75 3.00
Nos. B663-B665 (3) 8.25 6.60

Surtax for Stiftung Deutsche Sporthilfe, a foundation for the promotion of sports in Germany.
See Berlin Nos. 9NB254-9NB256.

Rock Stars SP366

No. B666, Buddy Holly (1936-59). No. B667, Elvis Presley (1935-77). No. B668, Jim Morrison (1943-71). No. B669, John Lennon (1940-80).

1988, Apr. 14 **Litho.** ***Perf. 14***
B666 SP366 50 + 25pf multi 1.00 1.20
B667 SP366 60 + 30pf multi 2.25 2.00
B668 SP366 70 + 35pf multi 1.20 1.30
B669 SP366 80 + 40pf multi 2.10 1.75
Nos. B666-B669 (4) 6.55 6.25

Surtax for German Youth Stamp Foundation.
See Berlin Nos. 9NB257-9NB260.

Gold and Rock Crystal Reliquary, c. 1200, Schnutgen Museum, Cologne SP367

Gold and silver artifacts: No. B671, Bust of Charlemagne, 14th cent., Aachen cathedral. No. B672, Crown of Otto III, 10th cent., Essen cathedral. No. B673, Flower bouquet, c. 1620, Schmuck Museum, Pforzheim.

1988, Oct. 13 **Litho.**
B670 SP367 50 + 25pf multi .55 .55
B671 SP367 60 + 30pf multi .80 .80
B672 SP367 70 + 35pf multi .80 .80
B673 SP367 80 + 40pf multi 1.20 1.20
Nos. B670-B673 (4) 3.35 3.35

Surtax for welfare organizations.
See Berlin Nos. 9NB261-9NB264.

Christmas SP368

Illumination from *The Gospel Book of Henry the Lion*, Helmarshausen, 1188, Prussian Cultural Museum, Bavaria: Adoration of the Magi.

1988, Nov. 10 **Litho.**
B674 SP368 80 + 40pf multi 1.20 1.05

Surtax for public welfare organizations.
See Berlin No. 9NB265.

World Championship Sporting Events Hosted by Germany — SP369

No. B675, Table tennis. No. B676, Gymnastics.

1989, Feb. 9 **Litho.**
B675 SP369 100pf + 50pf multi 1.45 1.45
B676 SP369 140pf + 60pf multi 2.25 2.25

Surtax for the Natl. Sports Promotion Foundation.
See Berlin Nos. 9NB266-9NB267.

IPHLA Philatelic Literature Exhibition, Frankfurt, Apr. 19-23 — SP370

1989, Apr. 20 **Litho.**
B677 SP370 100 + 50pf multi 2.25 2.10

Surtax benefited the Foundation for the Promotion of Philately and Postal History.

Circus SP371

No. B678, Elephants. No. B679, Bareback rider. No. B680, Clown. No. B681, Caravans, big top.

1989, Apr. 20
B678 SP371 60 + 30pf multi 1.30 1.30
B679 SP371 70 + 30pf multi 1.60 1.60
B680 SP371 80 + 35pf multi 2.25 2.00
B681 SP371 100 + 50pf multi 3.75 2.25
Nos. B678-B681 (4) 8.90 7.15

Surtax for natl. youth welfare organizations.
See Berlin Nos. 9NB268-9NB271.

Mounted Courier of Thurn and Taxis, 18th Cent. SP372

History of mail carrying: No. B683, Hamburg postal service messenger, 1808. No. B684, Bavarian mail coach, c. 1900.

1989, Oct. 12 **Litho.**
B682 SP372 60 + 30pf multi 1.00 .95
B683 SP372 80 + 35pf multi 1.60 1.30
B684 SP372 100 + 50pf multi 2.60 2.10
Nos. B682-B684 (3) 5.20 4.35

Surtax for the benefit of Free Welfare Work.
See Berlin Nos. 9NB272-9NB274.

Christmas SP373

Wood carvings by Veit Stoss in St. Lawrence's Church, Nuremburg, 1517-18: No. B685, Angel. No. B686, Adoration of the Kings.

1989, Nov. 16 **Litho.**
B685 SP373 60 + 30pf multi 1.05 .95
B686 SP373 100 + 50pf multi 1.30 1.20

Surtax for benefit of the Federal Working Assoc. of Free Welfare Work.
See Berlin Nos. 9NB275-9NB276.

Popular Sports SP374

No. B687, Handball. No. B688, Physical fitness.

1990, Feb. 15 **Litho.**
B687 SP374 100 + 50pf multi 2.10 1.30
B688 SP374 140 + 60pf multi 2.50 2.00

Surtax for the Natl. Sports Promotion Foundation.
See Berlin Nos. 9NB277-9NB278.

Max and Moritz, by Wilhelm Busch, 125th Anniv. SP375

No. B689, Widow Bolte. No. B690, Max. No. B691, Max and Moritz. No. B692, Max and Moritz, diff.

1990, Apr. 19 **Litho.**
B689 SP375 60 + 30pf multi .75 .75
B690 SP375 70 + 30pf multi 1.05 1.05
B691 SP375 80 + 35pf multi 1.45 1.30
B692 SP375 100 + 50pf multi 1.75 1.60
Nos. B689-B692 (4) 5.00 4.70

Surcharge for the German Youth Stamp Foundation.
See Berlin Nos. 9NB279-9NB282.

Souvenir Sheet

Dusseldorf '90 — SP376

1990, June 21 **Litho.**
B693 SP376 Sheet of 6 16.50 *19.00*
a. 100pf + 50pf multi 2.25 2.25

Surtax for the Foundation for Promotion of Philately and Postal History. 10th Intl. Philatelic Exhibition of Youth and 11th Natl. Philatelic Exhibition of Youth.

Post and Telecommunications — SP377

Designs: 60pf+30pf, Postal vehicle, 1900. 80pf+35pf, Telephone exchange, 1890. 100pf+50pf, Post office, 1900.

1990, Sept. 27 **Litho.** ***Perf. 13½x14***
B694 SP377 60pf + 30pf multi .75 .75
B695 SP377 80pf + 35pf multi 1.20 1.20
B696 SP377 100pf + 50pf multi 1.75 1.75
Nos. B694-B696 (3) 3.70 3.70

Surtax for welfare organizations.
See Berlin Nos. 9NB283-9NB285.

Christmas SP378

No. B698, Smoking manikin. No. B699, Nutcracker. No. B700, Angel, diff.

1990, Nov. 6 **Litho.** ***Perf. 14***
B697 SP378 50pf + 20pf shown .65 .65
B698 SP378 60pf + 30pf multi .80 .80
B699 SP378 70pf + 30pf multi 1.05 1.05
B700 SP378 100pf + 50pf multi 1.60 1.60
Nos. B697-B700 (4) 4.10 4.10

Surtax for welfare organizations.

Sports SP379

No. B701, Weight lifting. No. B702, Cycling. No. B703, Basketball. No. B704, Wrestling.

1991, Feb. 14 **Litho.** ***Perf. 14***
B701 SP379 70 +30pf multi 1.30 1.30
B702 SP379 100 +50pf multi 1.30 1.30
B703 SP379 140 +60pf multi 2.00 2.00
B704 SP379 170 +80pf multi 2.00 2.00
Nos. B701-B704 (4) 6.60 6.60

Surtax for the Foundation for the Promotion of Sports.

Endangered Butterflies SP380

No. B705, Alpen gelbling, alpine sulphur. No. B706, Grosser eisvogel, Viceroy. No. B707, Grosser schillerfalter, purple emperor. No. B708, Blauschillernder beuerfalter, bluish copper. No. B709,Schwalben-schwanz, swallowtail. No. B710, Alpen apollo, alpine apollo. No. B711, Hochmoor gelbling, moor sulphur. No. B712, Grosser feuerfalter, large copper.

1991, Apr. 9 **Litho.** ***Perf. 13½***
B705 SP380 30 +15pf multi .35 .35
B706 SP380 50 +25pf multi .40 .40
B707 SP380 60 +30pf multi .80 .80
B708 SP380 70 +30pf multi .85 .85
B709 SP380 80 +35pf multi 1.05 1.05
B710 SP380 90 +45pf multi 1.30 1.30
B711 SP380 100 +50pf multi 1.60 1.60
B712 SP380 140 +60pf multi 2.00 2.00
Nos. B705-B712 (8) 8.35 8.35

Surtax for German Youth Stamp Foundation.
See Nos. B728-B732.

Souvenir Sheet

Otto Lilienthal's First Glider Flight, Cent. — SP381

1991, July 9 **Litho.** ***Perf. 14***
B713 SP381 100pf +50pf multi 2.75 2.40

Surtax benefited Foundation of Philately and Postal History.

Post Offices SP382

30pf+15pf, Bethel. 60pf+30pf, Budingen postal station. 70pf+30pf, Stralsund. 80pf+35pf, Lauscha. 100pf+50pf, Bonn. 140pf+60pf, Weilburg.

1991, Oct. 10 **Litho.** ***Perf. 14***
B714 SP382 30pf +15pf multi .55 .55
B715 SP382 60pf +30pf multi .80 .80
B716 SP382 70pf +30pf multi 1.00 1.00
B717 SP382 80pf +35pf multi 1.20 1.20
B718 SP382 100pf +50pf multi 1.60 1.60
B719 SP382 140pf +60pf multi 2.25 2.00
Nos. B714-B719 (6) 7.40 7.15

Christmas SP383

Paintings by Martin Schongauer (c. 1450-1491): 60pf+30pf, Angel of the Annunciation. 70pf+30pf, The Annunciation. 80pf+35pf, Angel. 100pf+50pf, Nativity.

1991, Nov. 5 **Litho.** ***Perf. 14***
B720 SP383 60pf +30pf multi .85 .85
B721 SP383 70pf +30pf multi 1.05 1.00
B722 SP383 80pf +35pf multi 2.10 1.75
B723 SP383 100pf +50pf multi 2.60 2.25
Nos. B720-B723 (4) 6.60 5.85

Surtax for Federal Working Association of Free Welfare Work.

Olympic Sports SP384

No. B724, Women's fencing. No. B725, Rowing coxed eights. No. B726, Dressage. No. B727, Men's slalom skiing.

1992, Feb. 6 **Litho.** ***Perf. 14***
B724 SP384 60pf +30pf multi .95 .95
B725 SP384 80pf +40pf multi 1.10 1.10
B726 SP384 100pf +50pf multi 2.25 2.40
B727 SP384 170pf +80pf multi 4.25 4.25
Nos. B724-B727 (4) 8.55 8.70

Endangered Butterfly Type of 1991

60+30pf, Purpurbar. 70+30pf, Labkraut schwarmer. 80+40pf, Silbermonch. 100+50pf, Schwarzer bar. 170+80pf, Rauschbeerenfleckenspanner.

1992, Apr. 9 **Litho.** ***Perf. 13½***
B728 SP380 60pf +30pf multi 1.20 1.20
B729 SP380 70pf +30pf multi 1.30 1.30
B730 SP380 80pf +40pf multi 1.75 1.75
B731 SP380 100pf +50pf multi 1.75 1.75
B732 SP380 170pf +80pf multi 2.10 2.10
Nos. B728-B732 (5) 8.10 8.10

Surtax for German Youth Stamp Foundation.

Preservation of Tropical Rain Forests SP385

1992, June 11 **Litho.** ***Perf. 13***
B733 SP385 100pf +50pf multi 1.60 1.75

Antique Clocks SP386

Antique clocks: 60pf+30pf, Turret, c. 1400. 70pf+30pf, Astronomical geographical mantelpiece, 1738. 80pf+40pf, Fluted, c. 1790. 100fpf+50pf, Figurine, c. 1580. 170pf+80pf, Table, c. 1550.

1992, Oct. 15 Litho. *Perf. 14*

B734	SP386	60pf +30pf multi	.95	.95
B735	SP386	70pf +30pf multi	1.20	1.20
B736	SP386	80pf +40pf multi	1.20	1.20
B737	SP386	100pf +50pf multi	1.45	1.45
B738	SP386	170pf +80pf multi	2.00	2.00
	Nos. B734-B738 (5)		6.80	6.80

Surtax for welfare organizations.

Christmas SP387

Carvings from Church of St. Anne, Annaberg-Buchholz, by Franz Maidburg: 60pf + 30pf, Adoration of the Magi. 100pf + 50pf, The Nativity.

1992, Nov. 5

B739	SP387	60pf +30pf multi	.95	.95
B740	SP387	100pf +50pf multi	1.20	1.20

Surtax for benefit of free welfare work.

Sports SP388

Designs: 60pf+30pf, Olympic ski jump, Garmisch-Partenkirchen. 80pf+40pf, Olympic Park, Munich. 100pf+50pf, Olympic Stadium, Berlin. 170pf+80pf, Olympic harbor, Kiel.

1993, Feb. 11 Litho. *Perf. 13½*

B741	SP388	60pf +30pf multi	2.00	1.60
B742	SP388	80pf +40pf multi	2.25	1.60
B743	SP388	100pf +50pf multi	3.00	2.60
B744	SP388	170pf +80pf multi	4.50	4.50
	Nos. B741-B744 (4)		11.75	10.30

Surtax for Natl. Sports Promotion Foundation.

Beetles SP389

Designs: No. B745, Alpenbock (Alpine sawyer). No. B746, Rosenkafer (rose chafer). No. B747, Hirschkafer (stag beetle). No. B748, Sandlaufkafer (tiger beetle). 200pf + 50pf, Maikafer (cockchafer).

1993, Apr. 15 Litho. *Perf. 14*

B745	SP389	80pf +40pf multi	1.50	1.50
B746	SP389	80pf +40pf multi	1.50	1.50
B747	SP389	100pf +50pf multi	1.90	1.75
B748	SP389	100pf +50pf multi	1.90	1.75
B749	SP389	200pf +50pf multi	3.00	3.00
	Nos. B745-B749 (5)		9.80	9.50

Surtax for German Youth Stamp Foundation.

Stamp Day — SP390

1993, Sept. 16 Litho. *Perf. 13½x14*

B750	SP390	100pf +50pf multi	1.60	1.75

Surtax for the Foundation for Promotion of Philately and Postal History.

Traditional Costumes SP391

Costumes from: No. B751, Rugen, Mecklenburg, Western Pomerania. No. B752, Fohr, Schleswig-Holstein. No. B753, Schwalm, Hesse. No. B754, Oberndorf, Bavaria. 200pf + 40pf, Ernstroda, Thuringia.

1993, Oct. 14 *Perf. 14*

B751	SP391	80pf +40pf multi	1.60	1.60
B752	SP391	80pf +40pf multi	1.60	1.60
B753	SP391	100pf +50pf multi	1.60	1.60
B754	SP391	100pf +50pf multi	1.60	1.60
B755	SP391	200pf +40pf multi	2.00	2.00
	Nos. B751-B755 (5)		8.40	8.40

Surtax for welfare organizations. See Nos. B768-B772.

Christmas SP392

Wings of high altar in choir of Blaubeuren Monastery: 80pf+40pf, Adoraration of Magi. 100pf+50pf, Nativity.

1993, Nov. 10 Litho. *Perf. 14*

B756	SP392	80pf +40pf multi	1.00	1.00
B757	SP392	100pf +50pf multi	1.75	1.75

Surtax for welfare organizations.

Figure Skating SP393

Sports: No. B759, Olympic Flame. No. B760, Soccer ball, World Cup Trophy. 200pf+80pf, Skiier.

1994, Feb. 10 Litho. *Perf. 14x13½*

B758	SP393	80pf +40pf multi	3.00	1.60
B759	SP393	100pf +50pf multi	3.00	1.60
B760	SP393	100pf +50pf multi	3.00	1.60
B761	SP393	200pf +80pf multi	4.00	3.25
	Nos. B758-B761 (4)		13.00	8.05

1994 Winter Olympics, Lillehammer (No. B758). Intl. Olympic Committee, Cent. (No. B759). 1994 World Cup Soccer Championships, US (No. B760). 1994 Paralympics, Lillehammer (No. B761).

Heinrich Hoffmann (1809-94), Physician, Writer of Children's Books SP394

Characters from "Slovenly Peter:" No. B762, Little Pauline. No. B763, Johnny Head-in-the-air. No. B764, Slovenly Peter. No. B765, Naughty Frederick. 200pf+80pf, The Fidget.

1994, Apr. 14 Litho. *Perf. 13½*

B762	SP394	80pf +40pf multi	2.25	2.00
B763	SP394	80pf +40pf multi	2.25	2.00
B764	SP394	100pf +50pf multi	2.25	2.00
B765	SP394	100pf +50pf multi	2.25	2.00
B766	SP394	200pf +80pf multi	3.25	2.60
	Nos. B762-B766 (5)		12.25	10.60

Surtax for German Youth Stamp Foundation.

Environmental Protection SP395

1994, June 16 Litho. *Perf. 13*

B767	SP395	100pf +50pf blk & grn	1.60	1.60

Traditional Costume Type 1993

Costumes from. No. B768, Buckeburg. No. B769, Halle an der Saale. No. B770, Hoyerswerda. No. B771, Minden. 200pf+70pf, Betzingen.

1994, Oct. 13 Litho. *Perf. 13½*

B768	SP391	80pf +40pf multi	1.20	1.20
B769	SP391	80pf +40pf multi	1.20	1.20
B770	SP391	100pf +50pf multi	1.60	1.60
B771	SP391	100pf +50pf multi	1.60	1.60
B772	SP391	200pf +70pf multi	2.60	2.60
	Nos. B768-B772 (5)		8.20	8.20

Surtax for welfare organizations.

Christmas SP396

Paintings by Hans Memling: 80pf+40pf, Adoration of the Magi. 100pf+50pf, Nativity Scene.

1994, Nov. 9 Litho. *Perf. 13½*

B773	SP396	80pf +40pf multi	1.30	1.45
B774	SP396	100pf +50pf multi	1.60	1.60

Sports SP397

No. B775, Rowing. No. B776, Gymnastics. No. B777, Boxing. No. B778, Volleyball.

1995, Feb. 9 Photo. *Perf. 13½*

B775	SP397	80pf +40pf multi	1.20	1.45
B776	SP397	100pf +50pf multi	1.20	1.45
B777	SP397	100pf +50pf multi	1.20	1.45
B778	SP397	200pf +80pf multi	2.40	3.25
	Nos. B775-B778 (4)		6.00	7.60

World Kayaking Championships, Duisburg (No. B775). Intl. Gymnastics Festival, Berlin (No. B776). World Amateur Boxing Championships, Berlin (No. B777). Volleyball, cent. (No. B778).

Dogs SP398

No. B779, Munsterlander. No. B780, Schnauzer. No. B781, German shepherd. No. B782, Wire haired dachshund. 200pf+80pf, Wolf spitz.

1995, June 8 Litho. *Perf. 13½*

B779	SP398	80pf +40pf multi	1.20	1.40
B780	SP398	80pf +40pf multi	1.20	1.40
B781	SP398	100pf +50pf multi	1.20	1.40
B782	SP398	100pf +50pf multi	1.20	1.40
B783	SP398	200pf +80pf multi	2.40	3.00
	Nos. B779-B783 (5)		7.20	8.60

Surtax for benefit of German Youth Stamp Foundation.

See Nos. B792-B796.

Stamp Day — SP399

1995, Sept. 6 Litho. *Perf. 13*

B784	SP399	200pf +100pf multi	3.00	3.25

Surtax for Foundation for Promotion of Philately and Postal History.

Farmhouses — SP400

No. B785, Eifel region. No. B786, Saxony. No. B787, Lower Germany. No. B788, Upper Bavaria. 200pf+70pf, Mecklenburg.

1995, Oct. 12 Litho. *Perf. 14*

B785	SP400	80pf +40pf multi	1.35	1.35
B786	SP400	80pf +40pf multi	1.35	1.35
B787	SP400	100pf +50pf multi	1.35	1.35
B788	SP400	100pf +50pf multi	1.35	1.35
B789	SP400	200pf +70pf multi	2.25	2.25
	Nos. B785-B789 (5)		7.65	7.65

Surtax for welfare organizations.

See Nos. B802-B806.

Christmas SP401

Stained glass windows, Augsburg Cathedral: 80pf+40pf, Annunciation. 100pf+50pf, Nativity.

1995, Nov. 9 Litho. *Perf. 14*

B790	SP401	80pf +40pf multi	1.35	1.35
B791	SP401	100pf +50pf multi	1.75	1.75

Surtax for welfare organizations.

Dog Type of 1995

No. B792, Borzoi. No. B793, Chow chow. No. B794, St. Bernard. No. B795, Collie. 200pf+80pf, Briard.

1996, Feb. 8 Litho. *Perf. 13½*

B792	SP398	80pf +40pf multi	1.45	1.75
B793	SP398	80pf +40pf multi	1.45	1.75
B794	SP398	100pf +50pf multi	1.75	1.75
B795	SP398	100pf +50pf multi	1.75	1.75
B796	SP398	200pf +80pf multi	2.75	2.75
	Nos. B792-B796 (5)		9.15	9.75

Surtax for benefit of German Youth Stamp Foundation.

Modern Olympic Games, Cent. SP402

Olympic champions: 80pf+40pf, Carl Schuhmann (1869-1946), pommel horse. No. B798, Annie Hübler Horn (1885-1976), pairs figure skating. No. B799, Josef Neckermann (1912-92), equestrian. 200pf+80pf, Alfred Flatow (1869-1942), Gustav Felix Flatow (1875-1945), gymnastics.

1996, June 13 Photo. *Perf. 13½*

B797 SP402 80pf +40pf multi 2.75 1.75
B798 SP402 100pf +50pf multi 3.75 2.75
B799 SP402 100pf +50pf multi 3.75 2.75
B800 SP402 200pf +80pf multi 4.50 3.75
Nos. B797-B800 (4) 14.75 11.00

Preservation of Tropical Habitats — SP403

1996, July 18 Photo. *Perf. 14*

B801 SP403 100pf +50pf multi 1.75 1.75

Farmhouse Type of 1995

Location: No. B802, Spree Forest. No. B803, Thuringia. No. B804, Black Forest. No. B805, Westphalia. 200pf+70pf, Schleswig-Holstein.

1996, Oct. 9 Litho. *Perf. 14*

B802 SP400 80pf +40pf multi 1.10 .90
B803 SP400 80pf +40pf multi 1.10 .90
B804 SP400 100pf +50pf multi 1.35 1.10
B805 SP400 100pf +50pf multi 1.35 1.10
B806 SP400 200pf +70pf multi 2.40 2.40
Nos. B802-B806 (5) 7.30 6.40

Christmas SP404

Illuminated pages from Henry II's book of pericopes (Gospels), 11th cent.: 80pf+40pf, Adoration of the Magi. 100pf+50pf, Nativity.

1996, Nov. 14 Litho. *Perf. 14*

B807 SP404 80pf +40pf multi 1.25 1.45
B808 SP404 100pf +50pf multi 1.45 1.75

Surtax for welfare organizations.

Sports SP405

No. B809, Aerobics. No. B810, Inline skating. No. B811, Streetball. No. B812, Free climbing.

1997, Feb. 4 Litho. *Perf. 14x13½*

B809 SP405 80pf +40pf multi 1.25 2.10
B810 SP405 100pf +50pf multi 1.60 2.10
B811 SP405 100pf +50pf multi 1.60 2.10
B812 SP405 200pf +80pf multi 2.75 4.50
Nos. B809-B812 (4) 7.20 10.80

Horses SP406

No. B813, Rheno-German draft. No. B814, Shetland pony. No. B815, Friesian. No. B816, Haflinger. No. B817, Hanoverian.

1997, June 9 Litho. *Perf. 14*

B813 SP406 80pf + 40pf multi 2.25 1.75
B814 SP406 80pf + 40pf multi 2.25 1.75
B815 SP406 100pf + 50pf multi 2.25 1.75
B816 SP406 100pf + 50pf multi 2.25 1.75
B817 SP406 200pf + 80pf multi 4.50 3.75
Nos. B813-B817 (5) 13.50 10.75

Arms Type of 1992 Redrawn and Inscribed "Hochwasserhilfe 1997" and "DEUTSCHLAND"

1997, Aug. 19 Litho. *Perf. 13½*

B818 A739 110pf +90pf lilac #1702 2.10 3.25

Souvenir Sheet

Stamp Day — SP407

1997, Sept. 17 Litho. *Perf. 14*

B819 SP407 440pf +220pf multi 6.50 7.75

Mills — SP408

Designs: 100pf+50pf, Black Forest. No. B821, Hesse. No. B822, Windmill, lower Rhine. No. B823, Scoop windmill, Schleswig-Holstein. 220pf+80pf, Dutch windmill.

1997, Oct. 9 Litho. *Perf. 13½x14*
Background Color

B820 SP408 100pf +50pf grn 2.10 2.10
B821 SP409 110pf +50pf brn 2.40 2.40
B822 SP408 110pf +50pf blue 2.40 2.40
B823 SP408 110pf +50pf yel 2.40 2.40
B824 SP408 220pf +80pf pink 3.25 3.75
Nos. B820-B824 (5) 12.55 13.05

Christmas SP409

1997, Nov. 6 Litho. *Perf. 14*

B825 SP409 100pf +50pf Magi 1.45 1.45
B826 SP409 110pf +50pf Nativity 1.75 1.75

Surtax for Federal Assoc. of Free Welfare Work in Bonn.

Sports SP410

1998 Sporting events: 100pf+50pf, World Cup Soccer Championships, France. No. B828, Winter Olympic Games, Nagano. No. B829, Rowing Championships, Cologne. 300pf+100pf, Winter Paralympics, Nagano.

1998, Feb. 5 Photo. *Perf. 14*

B827 SP410 100pf +50pf multi 3.25 2.25
B828 SP410 110pf +50pf multi 3.25 2.25
B829 SP410 110pf +50pf multi 3.25 2.25
B830 SP410 300pf +100pf multi 7.25 7.25
Nos. B827-B830 (4) 17.00 14.00

Environmental Protection — SP411

1998, May 7 Litho. *Perf. 14*

B831 SP411 110pf +50pf multi 2.25 3.00

See No. B907, B1078.

Cartoon Figures SP412

No. B832, Mouse, Little Yellow Duck, Elephant. No. B833, Sandman. No. B834, Maja the Bee. No. B835, Captain Bluebear. No. B836, Pumuckl.

1998, June 10 Litho. *Perf. 14*

B832 SP412 100pf +50pf multi 1.75 1.75
B833 SP412 100pf +50pf multi 1.75 1.75
B834 SP412 110pf +50pf multi 1.75 1.75
B835 SP412 110pf +50pf multi 1.75 1.75
B836 SP412 220pf +50pf multi 3.00 3.00
Nos. B832-B836 (5) 10.00 10.00

Surtax for the German Youth Stamp Foundation.

Welfare Stamps SP413

Birds: 100pf+50pf, Hen-harrier. No. B838, Great bustard. No. B839, White-eyed duck. No. B840, Sedge warbler. 220pf+80pf, Woodchat shrike.

1998, Oct. 8 Litho. *Perf. 14*
Background Colors

B837 SP413 100pf +50pf tan 1.75 1.75
B838 SP413 110pf +50pf gray grn 1.75 1.75
B839 SP413 110pf +50pf gray blue 1.75 1.75
B840 SP413 110pf +50pf blue grn 1.75 1.75
B841 SP413 220pf +80pf lilac 2.75 3.25
Nos. B837-B841 (5) 9.75 10.25

Christmas SP414

No. B842, Shepherds. No. B843, Holy Child.

1998, Nov. 12

B842 SP414 100pf +50pf multi 1.45 1.45
B843 SP414 110pf +50pf multi 1.45 1.45

Racing Sports SP415

No. B844, Bicycles. No. B845, Cars. No. B846, Horses. No. B847, Motorcycles.

1999, Feb. 18 Photo. *Perf. 14*

B844 SP415 100pf +50pf multi 1.75 2.25
B845 SP415 110pf +50pf multi 1.75 2.25
B846 SP415 110pf +50pf multi 1.75 2.25
B847 SP415 300pf +100pf multi 3.75 4.25
Nos. B844-B847 (4) 9.00 11.00

Declaration of Human Rights Type of 1998 Inscribed "KOSOVO-HILFE 1999"

1999, Apr. 27 Litho. *Perf. 14*

B848 A958 110pf +100pf multi 2.10 2.10

Sutax for aid to refugees from Kosovo.

Souvenir Sheet

IBRA '99, Intl. Stamp Exhibition, Nuremberg — SP416

Design: Bavaria #1 & Saxony #1.

1999, Apr. 27 *Perf. 13½*

B849 SP416 300pf +110pf multi 5.50 7.75

German postage stamps, 150th anniv.

Cartoons SP417

No. B850, The Little Polar Bear. No. B851, Rudi the Crow. No. B852, Mecki (hedgehog). No. B853, Twipsy, mascot of Expo 2000, Hanover. 220pf+80pf, Tabaluga (green dragon).

1999, June 10 Litho. *Perf. 13¾*

B850 SP417 100pf +50pf multi 1.75 2.10
B851 SP417 100pf +50pf multi 1.75 2.10
B852 SP417 110pf +50pf multi 1.75 2.10
B853 SP417 110pf +50pf multi 1.75 2.10
B854 SP417 220pf +80pf multi 2.75 4.50
Nos. B850-B854 (5) 9.75 12.90

Surtax for the German Youth Stamp Foundation.

The Cosmos — SP418

No. B855, Andromeda galaxy. No. B856, Cygnus constellation. No. B857, X-ray image of exploding star. No. B858, Collision of Comet Shoemaker-Levy 9 and Jupiter. 300pf + 100pf, Gamma ray image of entire sky, satellite.

1999, Oct. 14 Litho. *Perf. 14*

B855	SP418	100pf +50pf multi	1.45	1.45
B856	SP418	100pf +50pf multi	1.45	1.45
B857	SP418	110pf +50pf multi	1.60	1.60
B858	SP418	110pf +50pf multi	1.60	1.60
B859	SP418	300pf +100pf multi	4.00	4.00
		Nos. B855-B859 (5)	10.10	10.10

Surtax for the Federal Association of Free Welfare Work. Nos. B858-B859 have a holographic image. Soaking in water may affect hologram.

Christmas SP419

1999, Nov. 4 Litho. *Perf. 13¾*

B860	SP419	100pf +50pf Angel	1.45	1.60
B861	SP419	110pf +50pf Manger	1.50	1.60

Sports — SP420

Ancient art and: 100pf + 50pf, Swimmer. No. B863, Gymnast. No. B864, Sprinters. 300pf + 100pf, Hands.

2000, Feb. 17 Litho. *Perf. 13¾x14*

B862	SP420	100pf + 50pf multi	2.40	2.10
B863	SP420	110pf + 50pf multi	2.40	2.10
B864	SP420	110pf + 50pf multi	2.40	2.10
B865	SP420	300pf + 100pf multi	4.00	3.75
		Nos. B862-B865 (4)	11.20	10.05

Surtax was for German Sports Federation.

Environmental Protection — SP421

2000, May 12 Litho. *Perf. 13¾x14*

B866	SP421	110pf +50pf multi	2.25	2.75

Expo 2000, Hanover — SP422

No. B867, 4 backpackers. No. B868, Crowd. No. B869, Map of Africa, words "see, come, hear, feel." No. B870, Eye. No. B871, Abstract with Chinese characters. No. B872, Abstract.

2000, June 8 Litho. *Perf. 13¾x14*

B867	SP422	100pf +50pf multi	1.75	1.75
B868	SP422	100pf +50pf multi	1.75	1.75
B869	SP422	110pf +50pf multi	1.75	1.75
B870	SP422	110pf +50pf multi	1.75	1.75
B871	SP422	110pf +50pf multi	1.75	1.75
B872	SP422	300pf +100pf multi	2.75	2.75
		Nos. B867-B872 (6)	11.50	11.50

Surtax for German Youth Stamp Foundation.

Actors and Actresses — SP423

No. B873, Curd Jürgens (1915-82). No. B874, Lilli Palmer (1914-86). No. B875, Heinz Rühmann (1902-94). No. B876, Romy Schneider (1938-82). No. B877, Gert Fröbe (1913-88).

2000, Oct. 12 Litho. *Perf. 14*

B873	SP423	100pf +50pf multi	1.75	1.75
B874	SP423	100pf +50pf multi	1.75	1.75
B875	SP423	110pf +50pf multi	1.75	1.75
B876	SP423	110pf +50pf multi	1.75	1.75
B877	SP423	300pf +100pf multi	3.75	3.75
		Nos. B873-B877 (5)	10.75	10.75

Surtax was for Federal Association of Welfare Work.

Christmas SP424

Designs: 100pf+50pf, Birth of Christ, by Conrad von Soest. 110pf+50pf, Nativity scene.

2000, Nov. 9 Litho. *Perf. 13¾*

B878	SP424	100pf +50pf multi	1.45	1.45
B879	SP424	110pf +50pf multi	1.45	1.45

Surtax for the Federal Association of Voluntary Welfare Work.

See Spain Nos. 3071-3072.

Sports — SP425

Designs: 100pf+50pf, Sports for schools. No. B881, Sports for the disabled. No. B882, Popular and leisure sports. 300pf+100pf, Sports for senior citizens.

2001, Feb. 8 Litho. *Perf. 13¾x14*

B880	SP425	100pf +50pf multi	1.75	1.75
B881	SP425	110pf +50pf multi	1.75	1.75
B882	SP425	110pf +50pf multi	1.75	1.75
B883	SP425	300pf +100pf multi	4.50	4.50
		Nos. B880-B883 (4)	9.75	9.75

Surtax for German Sports Federation.

Nos B880-B883 with the text bar in turquoise blue were unissued. Value $20,000 each.

Wuppertal Suspension Railway SP426

2001, Mar. 8

B884	SP426	110pf +50pf multi	2.25	2.00

Surtax for the Foundation for Promotion of Philately and Postal History.

Characters from Children's Stories SP427

Designs: No. B885, Pinocchio. No. B886, Pippi Longstockings. No. B887, Jim Knopf. No. B888, Heidi. 300pf +100pf, Tom Sawyer and Huckleberry Finn.

2001, June 13 Litho. *Perf. 13¾*

B885	SP427	100pf +50pf multi	2.00	2.00
B886	SP427	100pf +50pf multi	2.00	2.00
B887	SP427	110pf +50pf multi	2.00	2.00
B888	SP427	110pf +50pf multi	2.00	2.00
B889	SP427	300pf +100pf multi	4.50	4.50
		Nos. B885-B889 (5)	12.50	12.50

Surtax for the German Youth Stamp Foundation.

Film Stars SP428

Designs: No. B890, Marilyn Monroe. No. B891, Charlie Chaplin. No. B892, Film reel. No. B893, Greta Garbo. 300pf+100pf, Jean Gabin.

2001, Oct. 11 Litho. *Perf. 14*

B890	SP428	100pf +50pf multi	2.00	2.00
a.		Perf. 13x13¼x13½x13¼	4.00	4.00
B891	SP428	100pf +50pf multi	2.00	2.00
a.		Perf. 13½x13¼	4.00	4.00
B892	SP428	110pf +50pf multi	2.00	2.00
a.		Perf. 13½x13¼	4.00	4.00
B893	SP428	110pf +50pf multi	2.00	2.00
a.		Perf. 13x13¼	4.00	4.00
B894	SP428	300pf +100pf multi	4.50	4.50
a.		Perf. 13x13¼	9.00	9.00
b.		Booklet pane, #B890a-B894a	16.00	16.00
		Booklet, #B894b	20.00	
		Nos. B890-B894 (5)	12.50	12.50

Surtax for the Federal Association of Voluntary Welfare Work.

A stamp picturing Audrey Hepburn originally was to have been included in this set but was withdrawn. It was never officially issued, nor were any examples sold over post office counters. However, 30 examples from the original printing were not recovered and destroyed as ordered by the post office. Four of the stamps have been found used on German mail. Value, $150,000.

Christmas SP429

Designs: 100pf+50pf, Madonna and Child, by Alfredo Roldán. 110pf+50pf, Adoration of the Shepherds, by José de Ribera.

2001, Nov. 8 Litho. *Perf. 13¼*

B895	SP429	100pf +50pf multi	1.90	1.90
B896	SP429	110pf +50pf multi	1.90	1.90
a.		Souvenir sheet (see footnote)	6.50	6.50

No. B896a contains Nos. B895-B896 and lithographed and perf. 13¼ examples of Spain Nos. 3123-3124. No. B896a sold for 4.45m.

See Spain Nos. 3123-3124.

Intl. Year of Mountains — SP430

2002, Jan. 10 Litho. *Perf. 14*

B897	SP430	56c +26c multi	2.00	1.90

Winter Olympic Sports — SP431

Designs: 51c+26c, Biathlon. No. B899, 56c+26c, Ski jumping. No. B900, 56c+26c, Speed skating. 153c+51c, Luge.

2002, Feb. 7 Litho. *Perf. 13¾x14*

B898	SP431	51c +26c multi	2.00	2.00
B899	SP431	56c +26c multi	2.00	2.00
B900	SP431	56c +26c multi	2.00	2.00
B901	SP431	153c +51c multi	4.75	4.75
a.		Booklet pane, #B898-B901	11.50	11.50
		Booklet, #B901a	14.00	
		Nos. B898-B901 (4)	10.75	10.75

Surtax for German Sports Promotion Foundation.

Toys and Games SP432

Designs: No. B902, Chess pieces. No. B903, Toy truck. No. B904, Doll. No. B905, Teddy bear. 153c+51c, Toy train.

2002, June 6 Litho. *Perf. 13¾*

B902	SP432	51c +26c multi	2.10	2.10
B903	SP432	51c +26c multi	2.10	2.10
B904	SP432	56c +26c multi	2.10	2.10
B905	SP432	56c +26c multi	2.10	2.10
B906	SP432	153c +51c multi	4.75	4.75
		Nos. B902-B906 (5)	13.15	13.15

Surtax for German Youth Stamp Foundation.

Environmental Protection Type of 1998 Inscribed "Hochwasserhilfe 2002"

2002, Aug. 30 Litho. *Perf. 13x13½*

B907	SP411	56c +44c multi	3.00	2.50
a.		Perf. 13x14		

Surtax for flood victims relief.

Christmas SP433

Details from paintings by Rogier van der Weyden: 51c+26c, Annunciation to the Virgin. 56c+26c, Miraflores Altarpiece.

2002, Nov. 7 Litho. *Perf. 13¾*

B908	SP433 51c +26c multi	1.90	1.75
B909	SP433 56c +26c multi	1.90	1.75

Surtax for Federal Working Party on Independent Welfare.

Automobiles — SP434

Designs: 45c+20c, 1960 BMW Isetta 300. No. B911, 55c+25c, 1961 VEB Sachsenring Trabant P50. No. B912, 55c+25c, 1949 Volkswagen Beetle. No. B913, 55c+25c, 1954 Mercdes-Benz 300 SL. 144c+56c, 1957 Borgward Isabella Coupe.

2002, Dec. 5 Litho. *Perf. 14*

B910	SP434 45c +20c multi	1.90	1.90
B911	SP434 55c +25c multi	2.00	2.00
B912	SP434 55c +25c multi	2.00	2.00
B913	SP434 55c +25c multi	2.00	2.00
B914	SP434 144c +56c multi	5.25	5.25
	Nos. B910-B914 (5)	13.15	13.15

Surtax for Federal Working Party on Independent Welfare.
See Nos. B923-B927.

2006 World Cup Soccer Championships, Germany — SP435

Designs: 45c+20c, Player kicking ball. No. B916, Player heading ball. No. B917, Four children playing soccer. No. B918, Fan celebrating. 144c+56c, Child and adult playing soccer.

2003, Mar. 6 Litho. *Perf. 13x13½*

B915	SP435 45c +20c multi	2.10	2.10
B916	SP435 55c +25c multi	2.10	2.10
B917	SP435 55c +25c multi	2.10	2.10
B918	SP435 55c +25c multi	2.10	2.10
B919	SP435 144c +56c multi	4.75	4.75
	Nos. B915-B919 (5)	13.15	13.15

Surtax for German Sports Promotion Foundation.

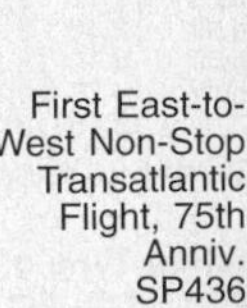

First East-to-West Non-Stop Transatlantic Flight, 75th Anniv. SP436

2003, Apr. 10 *Perf. 13¾*

B920	SP436 144c +56c multi	5.25	5.00

Surtax for German Organization for the Enhancement of Philately and Postal History.

June 17, 1953 Uprising in East Germany, 50th Anniv. SP437

2003, June 12 Photo. *Perf. 14x14¼*

B921	SP437 55c +25c multi	2.10	2.10

Souvenir Sheet

Father and Son, Cartoons by Ehrich Ohser — SP438

No. B922: a, Father and son running in same direction. b, Father and son falling. c, Son running, father seated. d, Father and son running in different directions. e, Father and son with arms extended.

2003, July 10 Litho. *Perf. 13x13½*

B922	SP438 Sheet of 5	13.00	13.00
a.	45c +20c multi	2.10	2.10
b.-d.	55c +25c any single	2.10	2.10
e.	144c +56c multi	4.25	4.25

Automobile Type of 2002

Designs: 45c+20c, Wartburg 311 Coupe. No. B924, Olympia Rekord P1. No. B925, 356 B Coupe. No. B926, 55c+25c, Taunus 17 M P3. 144c+56c, Auto Union 1000 S.

2003, Oct. 9 Litho. *Perf. 14*

B923	SP434 45c +20c multi	1.90	1.90
B924	SP434 55c +25c multi	2.00	2.00
B925	SP434 55c +25c multi	2.00	2.00
B926	SP434 55c +25c multi	2.00	2.00
B927	SP434 144c +56c multi	5.25	5.25
	Nos. B923-B927 (5)	13.15	13.15

Christmas SP439

Designs: 45c+20c, Adoration of the Shepherds. 55c+25c, Holy Family.

2003, Nov. 13 Litho. *Perf. 13¾*

B928	SP439 45c +20c multi	1.75	1.75
B929	SP439 55c +25c multi	1.75	1.75

Wind Energy SP440

2004, Jan. 8 Litho. *Perf. 13¾*

B930	SP440 55c +25c multi	2.10	2.00

Sporting Events and Anniversaries — SP441

Designs: 45c+20c, European Soccer Championships, June 12-July 4, 2004. No. B932, Summer Olympic Games, Athens, Greece. No. B933, Paralympics, Athens, Greece. No. B934, First German World Cup Championship, 50th anniv. 144c+56c, FIFA (Fédération Internationale de Football Association), cent.

2004, Feb. 5 Litho. *Perf. 13x13½*

B931	SP441 45c +20c multi	1.90	1.90
B932	SP441 55c +25c multi	2.00	2.00
B933	SP441 55c +25c multi	2.00	2.00
B934	SP441 55c +25c multi	2.00	2.00
B935	SP441 144c +56c multi	5.25	5.25
	Nos. B931-B935 (5)	13.15	13.15

Cats — SP442

Designs: 45c+20c, Two cats playing with ball of string. No. B937, Cat, two kittens playing with ball. No. B938, Kitten on cat. No. B939, Cat licking paw. 144c+56c, Two cats sleeping.

2004, June 3 Litho. *Perf. 13¾x14*

B936	SP442 45c +20c multi	1.90	1.90
B937	SP442 55c +25c multi	2.00	2.00
B938	SP442 55c +25c multi	2.00	2.00
B939	SP442 55c +25c multi	2.00	2.00
B940	SP442 144c +56c multi	5.25	5.25
	Nos. B936-B940 (5)	13.15	13.15

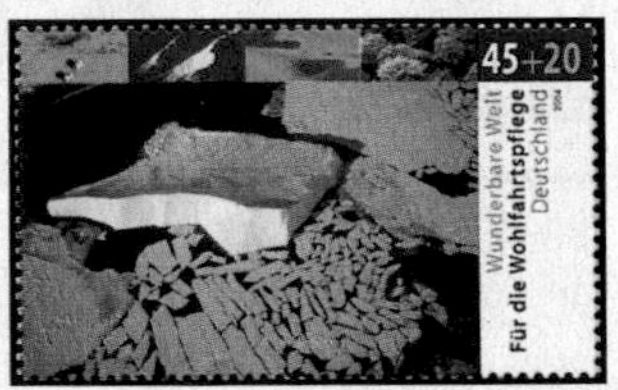
Landscapes — SP443

Designs: 45c+20c, Iceberg and pack ice. No. B942, Mountains and clouds. No. B943, Islands. No. B944, Sand dunes. 144c+56c, Tree tops.

2004, Oct. 7 Litho. *Perf. 14*

B941	SP443 45c +20c multi	1.90	1.90
B942	SP443 55c +25c multi	2.00	2.00
B943	SP443 55c +25c multi	2.00	2.00
B944	SP443 55c +25c multi	2.00	2.00
B945	SP443 144c +56c multi	5.25	5.25
	Nos. B941-B945 (5)	13.15	13.15

Christmas SP444

Paintings by Peter Paul Rubens: 45c+20c, The Flight Into Egypt. 55c+25c, Adoration of the Magi.

2004, Nov. 4 *Perf. 13¾*

B946	SP444 45c +20c multi	1.60	1.50
B947	SP444 55c +25c multi	1.90	1.75

See Belgium Nos. 2051-2053.

Sports — SP445

Designs: 45c+20c, Soccer fans, mascot of 2006 World Cup Soccer Championships. No. B949, Soccer players, soccer ball globe. No. B950, Gymnasts, Brandenburg Gate, Berlin. No. B951, Ski jumper and ski jump. 144c+56c, Fencers, Leipzig Arena.

2005, Feb. 10 Litho. *Perf. 13¾x14*

B948	SP445 45c +20c multi	1.90	1.90
B949	SP445 55c +25c multi	2.00	2.00
B950	SP445 55c +25c multi	2.00	2.00
B951	SP445 55c +25c multi	2.00	2.00
B952	SP445 144c +56c multi	5.25	5.25
	Nos. B948-B952 (5)	13.15	13.15

2006 World Cup Soccer Championships (Nos. B948-B949), Intl. Gymnastics Exhibition, Berlin (No. B950), Nordic Skiing World Championships, Oberstdorf (No. B951), Fencing World Championships, Leipzig (No. B952).

Stamp Day SP446

2005, May 12 Litho. *Perf. 14*

B953	SP446 55c +25c multi	2.00	2.00

Sailing Ships — SP447

Designs: 45c+20c, Greif. No. B955, Rickmer Rickmers. No. B956, Passat. No. B957, Grossherzogin Elisabeth. 144c+56c, Deutschland.

2005, June 2 Litho. *Perf. 13¾x14*

B954	SP447 45c +20c multi	1.90	1.90
B955	SP447 55c +25c multi	2.00	2.00
B956	SP447 55c +25c multi	2.00	2.00
B957	SP447 55c +25c multi	2.00	2.00
B958	SP447 144c +56c multi	5.25	5.25
	Nos. B954-B958 (5)	13.15	13.15

Christmas SP448

Paintings by Stefan Lochner: 45c+20c, Adoration of the Child. 55c+25c, Madonna and Child in Rose Garden.

2005, Nov. 3 Litho. *Perf. 13¾*

B959	SP448 45c +20c multi	1.60	1.50
B960	SP448 55c +25c multi	2.00	1.75

Butterflies — SP449

Designs: 45c+20c, Zitronenfalter. No. B962, Russischer Bär. Nos. B963, B965, Tagpfauenauge. 145c+55c, Weisser Waldportier.

2005, Dec. 1 Litho. *Perf. 14*

B961 SP449 45c +20c multi 1.75 1.75
B962 SP449 55c +25c multi 1.75 1.75
B963 SP449 55c +25c multi 1.75 1.75
B964 SP449 145c +55c multi 5.25 5.25
Nos. B961-B964 (4) 10.50 10.50

Self-Adhesive

Die Cut Perf. 11

B965 SP449 55c +25c multi 2.10 2.00
a. Booklet pane of 10 21.00

Protection of the Ozone Layer — SP450

2006, Jan. 2 *Perf. 14*

B966 SP450 55c +25c multi 2.10 2.00

Sports — SP451

Designs: 45c+20c, Crowd waving German flags, stadium lights. No. B968, Stadium exterior, blurred athlete. No. B969, Stadium interior, players holding World Cup. No. B970, Horse and rider, rider's leg. 145c+55c, Emblem of 2006 World Cup Soccer Championships, blurred picture of soccer player kicking ball.

2006, Feb. 9 Litho. *Perf. 13x13½*

B967 SP451 45c +20c multi 1.75 1.75
B968 SP451 55c +25c multi 1.75 1.75
B969 SP451 55c +25c multi 1.75 1.75
B970 SP451 55c +25c multi 1.75 1.75
B971 SP451 145c +55c multi 4.75 4.75
a. Souvenir sheet, #B967-B969, B971 10.00 10.00
Nos. B967-B971 (5) 11.75 11.75

2006 World Cup Soccer Championships (Nos. B967-B969, B971), World Equestrian Championships, Aachen (No. B970).
No. B971a issued 5/4.

Mammals — SP452

Designs: 45c+20c, Pine marten. No. B973, Doe and fawn. No. B974, Hares. No. B975, Squirrel. 145c+55c, Wild pig and piglets.

2006, June 8 Litho. *Perf. 14*

B972 SP452 45c +20c multi 1.50 1.50
B973 SP452 55c +25c multi 1.90 1.90
B974 SP452 55c +25c multi 1.90 1.90
B975 SP452 55c +25c multi 1.90 1.90
B976 SP452 145c +55c multi 4.75 4.75
Nos. B972-B976 (5) 11.95 11.95

Surtax for the German Youth Stamp Foundation.

Trains — SP453

Designs: 45c+20c, Fliegender Hamburger (VT 877). No. B978, Trans Europ Express (VT 11.5). Nos. B979, B981, InterCityExpress (ET403). 145c+55c, Henschel-Wegmann train (61 001).

2006, Oct. 5 Litho. *Perf. 13¾x14*

B977 SP453 45c +20c multi 1.75 1.75
B978 SP453 55c +25c multi 1.75 1.75
B979 SP453 55c +25c multi 1.75 1.75
B980 SP453 145c +55c multi 4.75 4.75
Nos. B977-B980 (4) 10.00 10.00

Self-Adhesive

Die Cut Perf. 11

B981 SP453 55c +25c multi 2.50 2.10
a. Booklet pane of 10 23.00

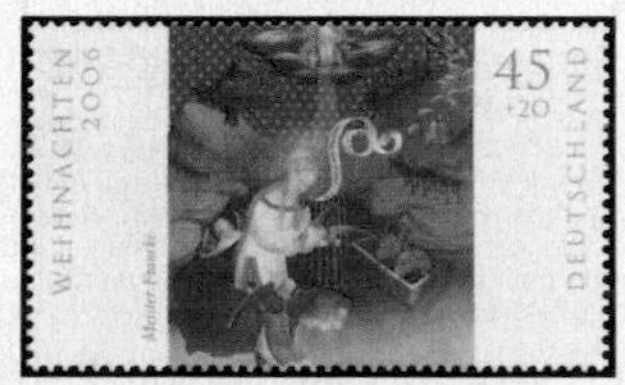

Christmas — SP454

15th Cent. altarpiece art by Meister Francke: 45c+20c, Nativity. 55c+25c, Adoration of the Magi.

2006, Nov. 9 Litho. *Perf. 14*

B982 SP454 45c +20c multi 1.40 1.40
B983 SP454 55c +25c multi 1.75 1.75

SP455

Designs: 45c+20c, Canoe World Championships. No. B985, Handball World Championships. No. B986, Gymnastics World Championships. 145c+55c, Modern Pentathlon World Championships.

2007 Litho. *Perf. 13x13½*

B984 SP455 45c +20c multi 1.75 1.75
B985 SP455 55c +25c multi 2.10 2.10
B986 SP455 55c +25c multi 2.00 2.00
B987 SP455 145c +55c multi 4.75 4.75
a. Souvenir sheet, #B984-B987 10.50 10.50
Nos. B984-B987 (4) 10.60 10.60

Issued: B985, 1/2. B984, B986-B987, 2/8. B987a, 5/3.

Souvenir Sheet

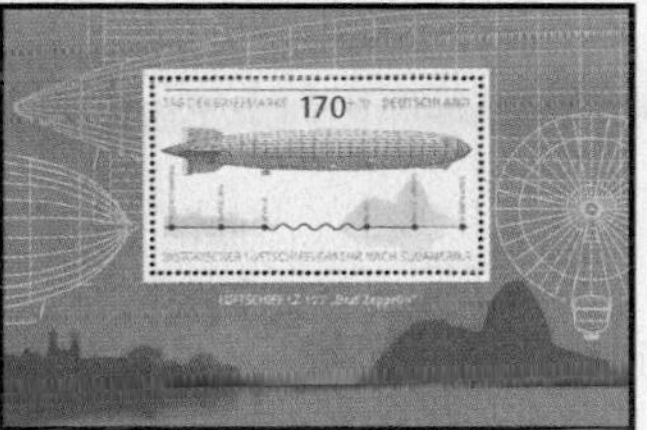

Graf Zeppelin and Itinerary of Flight to South America — SP456

Litho. & Engr.

2007, Mar. 1 *Perf. 14x14¼*

B988 SP456 170c +70c multi 6.50 6.50

Stamp Day.

Souvenir Sheet

Hans Huckelbein, der Unglücksrabe, by Wilhelm Busch — SP457

No. B989: a, Bird eating berry jam. b, Bird standing in jam. c, Bird tipping pan of jam. d, Bird dirtying clean laundry.

2007, June 14 Litho. *Perf. 13¼*

B989 SP457 Sheet of 4 10.00 10.00
a. 45c +20c multi 1.75 1.75
b.-c. 55c +25c either single 1.75 1.75
d. 145c +55c multi 1.75 1.75

Christmas SP458

Designs: 45c+20c, Magi. 55c+25c, Madonna and Child, donkey and bull.

2007, Nov. 8 Litho. *Perf. 13¼*

B990 SP458 45c +20c multi 1.60 1.60
B991 SP458 55c +25c multi 1.90 1.90

Adult and Juvenile Animals — SP459

Designs: 45c+20c, Guinea pigs. Nos. B993, B996, Horses. No. B994, Dogs. 145c+55c, Rabbits.

2007, Dec. 27 Photo. *Perf. 13¾x14*

B992 SP459 45c +20c multi 1.90 1.90
B993 SP459 55c +25c multi 1.90 1.90
B994 SP459 55c +25c multi 1.90 1.90
B995 SP459 145c +55c multi 5.25 5.25
Nos. B992-B995 (4) 10.95 10.95

Self-Adhesive

Die Cut Perf. 11

B996 SP459 55c +25c multi 2.25 2.10
a. Booklet pane of 10 21.00

Sports Championships — SP460

Designs: 45c+20c, World Gliding Championships, Berlin. No. B998, Chess Olympiad, Dresden. No. B999, European Soccer Championships, Austria and Switzerland. 145c+55c, 2008 Summer Olympics, Beijing.

Perf. 13¼x13½

2008, Mar. 13 Litho.

B997 SP460 45c +20c multi 1.75 1.75
B998 SP460 55c +25c multi 1.75 1.75
B999 SP460 55c +25c multi 1.75 1.75
B1000 SP460 145c +55c multi 4.25 4.25
Nos. B997-B1000 (4) 9.50 9.50

Knut, Polar Bear Cub in Berlin Zoo SP461

2008, Apr. 10 Litho. *Perf. 14*

B1001 SP461 55c +25c multi 2.10 2.10

Aircraft — SP462

Designs: 45c+20c, Dornier Do J Wal. No. B1003, Junkers Ju 52. Nos. B1004, B1006, Airbus A380. 145c+55c, Messerschmitt-Bölkow-Blohm BO 105 helicopter.

2008, June 12 Litho. *Perf. 14*

B1002 SP462 45c +20c multi 1.60 1.60
B1003 SP462 55c +25c multi 1.75 1.75
B1004 SP462 55c +25c multi 1.75 1.75
B1005 SP462 145c +55c multi 4.25 4.25
Nos. B1002-B1005 (4) 9.35 9.35

Self-Adhesive

Die Cut Perf. 11

B1006 SP462 55c +25c multi 2.25 2.10
a. Booklet pane of 10 21.00

Miniature Sheet

Dinosaurs — SP463

No. B1007: a, Triceratops. b, Diplodocus. c, Tyrannosaurus rex. d, Plateosaurus.

2008, Sept. 4 Litho. *Perf. 13x13½*

B1007 SP463 Sheet of 4 13.00 13.00
a. 45c +20c multi 2.50 2.50
b.-c. 55c +25c Eitner single 2.50 2.50
d. 145c +55c multi 5.25 5.25

Christmas SP464

Designs: 45c+20c, Nativity, by Albrecht Dürer. 55c+25c, Adoration of the Magi, by Raphael, horiz.

2008, Nov. 13 Litho. *Perf. 14*

B1008 SP464 45c +20c multi 1.45 1.45
B1009 SP464 55c +25c multi 1.75 1.75

See Vatican City Nos. 1399-1401.

Atmospheric Phenomena — SP465

Designs: 45c+20c, Rainbow. Nos. B1011, B1014, Clouds. No. B1012, Aurora borealis. 145c+55c, Lightning.

2009, Jan. 2 Litho. *Perf. 14*

B1010 SP465 45c +20c multi 1.75 1.75
B1011 SP465 55c +25c multi 1.90 1.90
B1012 SP465 55c +25c multi 1.90 1.90
B1013 SP465 145c +55c multi 4.75 4.75
Nos. B1010-B1013 (4) 10.30 10.30

Self-Adhesive

Die Cut Perf. 11

B1014 SP465 55c +25c multi 1.90 1.75
a. Booklet pane of 10 22.00

2009 World Track and Field Championships, Berlin — SP466

Designs: 45c+20c, Hurdles. No. B1016, Pole vault. No. B1017, Runners. 145c+55c, Discus.

2009, Apr. 9 *Perf. 13x13½*

B1015 SP466 45c +20c multi 1.90 1.90
B1016 SP466 55c +25c multi 1.90 1.90
a. Booklet pane of 8, 4 each #B1015-B1016 19.50 19.50
Complete booklet, #B1016a 224.00
B1017 SP466 55c +25c multi 1.90 1.90
B1018 SP466 145c +55c multi 4.75 4.75
Nos. B1015-B1018 (4) 10.45 10.45

Stamp Day — SP467

2009, May 7 *Perf. 13¾ Syncopated*

B1019 SP467 55c +25c multi 2.00 1.75

"Our Sandman" Children's Television Show, 50th Anniv. SP468

Sandman: 45c+20c, On beach with boy. No. B1021, In flying suitcase. No. B1022, On train. 145c+55c, In spaceship.

2009, Aug. 13 *Perf. 13¼*

B1020 SP468 45c +20c multi 1.90 1.90
B1021 SP468 55c +25c multi 1.90 1.90
B1022 SP468 55c +25c multi 1.90 1.90
B1023 SP468 145c +55c multi 4.75 4.75
Nos. B1020-B1023 (4) 10.45 10.45

Christmas — SP469

Illuminated manuscripts depicting: 45c+20c, Adoration of the Magi. 55c+25c, Nativity.

2009, Nov. 12 *Perf. 14*

B1024 SP469 45c +20c multi 1.45 1.45
B1025 SP469 55c +25c multi 1.75 1.75

Fruit — SP470

Blossom and fruit (whole and halved): 45c+20c, Apple (Malus domestica). No. B1027, Lemon (Citrus limon). Nos. B1028, B1030, Strawberry (Fragaria ananassa). 145c+55c, Blueberry (vaccinium myrtillus).

2010, Jan. 2 Litho. *Perf. 14*

B1026 SP470 45c +20c multi 1.90 1.90
B1027 SP470 55c +25c multi 1.90 1.90
B1028 SP470 55c +25c multi 1.90 1.90
B1029 SP470 145c +55c multi 1.90 1.90
Nos. B1026-B1029 (4) 7.60 7.60

Self-Adhesive

Die Cut Perf. 10¾

B1030 SP470 55c +25c multi 2.10 1.75
a. Booklet pane of 10 22.00

Nos. B1026-B1030 have a scratch-and sniff coating on the whole and halved fruit parts of the vignette having the scent of the fruit shown.

Athletes — SP471

Designs: 45c+20c, Skier at Winter Paralympics, Vancouver. No B1032, Skier at 2010 Winter Olympics, Vancouver. Designs: No. B1033, Soccer players, 2010 World Cup Soccer Championships, South Africa. 145c+55c, Ice hockey players, 2010 World Ice Hockey Championships, Germany.

2010 Litho. *Perf. 14*

B1031 SP471 45c +20c multi 1.75 1.45
B1032 SP471 55c +25c multi 1.90 1.75
B1033 SP471 55c +25c multi 1.75 1.75
B1034 SP471 145c+55c multi 5.00 4.50
Nos. B1031-B1034 (4) 10.40 9.45

Issued: Nos. B1031-B1032, 2/11. Nos. B1033-B1034, 4/8.

Protection of the Seas — SP472

2010, May 6 Litho. *Perf. 13x13½*

B1035 SP472 55c +25c multi 1.75 1.75

Steamers — SP473

Designs: 45c+20c, Deutschland. No. B1037, Aller. No. B1038, Imperator. 145c+55c, Columbus.

2010, Aug. 12 Litho. *Perf. 13x13¼*

B1036 SP473 45c +20c multi 1.90 1.90
B1037 SP473 55c +25c multi 1.90 1.90
B1038 SP473 55c +25c multi 1.90 1.90
B1039 SP473 145c +55c multi 4.75 4.75
Nos. B1036-B1039 (4) 10.45 10.45

Christmas — SP474

Creche figures: 45c+20c, Nativity. 55c+25c, Adoration of the Magi.

2010, Nov. 11 Litho. *Perf. 13x13½*

B1040 SP474 45c +20c multi 1.45 1.45
B1041 SP474 55c +25c multi 1.75 1.75

Cartoons by Loriot (Bernhard-Viktor von Bülow) — SP475

Designs: 45c+20c, Two men and talking dog. Nos. B1043, B1046, Two men at racetrack fence. No. B1044, Two naked men standing in bathtub. 145c+55c, Man and woman at breakfast table.

2011, Jan. 3 Litho. *Perf. 13¾x14*

B1042 SP475 45c +20c multi 1.90 1.90
B1043 SP475 55c +25c multi 1.90 1.90
B1044 SP475 55c +25c multi 1.90 1.90
B1045 SP475 145c +55c multi 4.75 4.75
Nos. B1042-B1045 (4) 11.75 11.75

Self-Adhesive

Die Cut Perf. 11

B1046 SP475 55c +25c multi 1.75 1.75
a. Booklet pane of 10 22.00

Athletes — SP476

Designs: 45c+20c, Goalie, 2011 Women's Soccer World Championships, Germany. No. B1048, Soccer players, 2011 Women's Soccer World Championships. No. B1049, Gymnasts, 2011 European Gymnastics Championships, Berlin. 145c+55c, Field hockey players, 2011 Men's European Field Hockey Championships, Mönchengladbach.

2011, Apr. 7 *Perf. 13¼x13½*

B1047 SP476 45c +20c multi 2.00 2.00
B1048 SP476 55c +25c multi 2.00 2.00
a. Booklet pane of 8, 4 each #B1047-B1048 16.00 —
Complete booklet, #B1048a 16.00
B1049 SP476 55c +25c multi 2.00 2.00
B1050 SP476 145c +55c multi 4.75 4.75
Nos. B1047-B1050 (4) 10.75 10.75

Issued: No. B1048a, 6/9.

Stamp Day, 75th Anniv. SP477

2011, Aug. 11 *Perf. 13½x13¾*

B1051 SP477 55c +25c multi 2.00 2.00

Astronomy — SP478

Designs: 45c+20c, Horeshead Nebula. No. B1053, Earth, Saturn, other planets, half of Sun. No. B1054, Jupiter, other planets, half of Sun. 145c+55c, Pleiades.

2011, Aug. 11 *Perf. 14*

B1052 SP478 45c +20c multi 2.00 2.00
B1053 SP478 55c +25c multi 2.00 2.00
B1054 SP478 55c +25c multi 2.00 2.00
a. Horiz. pair, #B1053-B1054 4.00 4.00
B1055 SP478 145c +55c multi 5.00 5.00
Nos. B1052-B1055 (4) 11.00 11.00

Christmas — SP479

Stained-glass windows depicting: 45c+20c, St. Martin. 55c+25c, St. Nicholas.

2011, Nov. 10 Litho. *Perf. 13x13½*

B1056 SP479 45c+20c multi 1.60 1.60
B1057 SP479 55c+25c multi 2.00 2.00

Gems — SP480

Designs: 55c+25c, Ruby. 90c+40c, Emerald. 145c+55c, Sapphire.

2012, Jan. 2 *Perf. 13¼x13½*

B1058 SP480 55c +25c multi 2.10 2.10
B1059 SP480 90c +40c multi 3.50 3.50
B1060 SP480 145c +55c multi 5.25 5.25
Nos. B1058-B1060 (3) 10.85 10.85

Self-Adhesive

Die Cut Perf. 11

B1061 SP480 55c +25c multi 2.10 2.10
a. Booklet pane of 10 21.00

Sports — SP481

Designs: 55c+25c, 2012 European Soccer Championships, Poland and Ukraine. 90c+40c, 2012 Summer Olympics, London. 145c+55c, 2012 World Team Table Tennis Championships, Dortmund.

2012, Apr. 12 *Perf. 13¼x13½*

B1062 SP481 55c +25c multi 2.00 2.00
B1063 SP481 90c +40c multi 3.25 3.25
B1064 SP481 145c +55c multi 5.00 5.00
Nos. B1062-B1064 (3) 10.25 10.25

"Waste is Raw Material" SP482

2012, May 2 Litho. *Perf. 13¾*
B1065 SP482 55c +25c multi 1.40 1.40

Historical Locomotives — SP483

Designs: 55c+25c, S3/6. 90c+40c, PTL 2/2. 145c+55c, Leopold Friedrich.

2012, Aug. 9 *Perf. 13¾x14*
B1066 SP483 55c +25c multi 2.00 2.00
B1067 SP483 90c +40c multi 3.25 3.25
B1068 SP483 145c +55c multi 5.00 5.00
Nos. B1066-B1068 (3) 10.25 10.25

Christmas — SP484

2012, Nov. 2 Litho. *Perf. 13x13½*
B1069 SP484 55c +25c multi 1.40 1.40

Booklet Stamp
Self-Adhesive
Die Cut Perf. 11
B1070 SP484 55c +25c multi 1.40 1.40
a. Booklet pane of 10 14.00

Trees — SP485

Designs: 58c+27c, Linden tree. 90c+40c, Wild cherry tree. 145c+55c, Horse chestnut tree.

2013, Feb. 7 *Perf. 13¾x14*
B1071 SP485 58c +27c multi 2.25 2.25
B1072 SP485 90c +40c multi 3.50 3.50
B1073 SP485 145c +55c multi 5.25 5.25
Nos. B1071-B1073 (3) 11.00 11.00

Booklet Stamp
Self-Adhesive
Die Cut Perf. 10¾
B1074 SP485 58c +27c multi 2.25 2.25
a. Booklet pane of 10 22.50

Sports SP486

Mouse: 58c+27c, In runner's starting blocks. 90c+40c, On sailboat with Swiss cheese sail. 145c+55c, On parallel bars.

2013, May 2 *Perf. 13¾*
B1075 SP486 58c +27c multi 2.10 2.10
B1076 SP486 90c +40c multi 3.25 3.25
B1077 SP486 145c +55c multi 5.00 5.00
Nos. B1075-B1077 (3) 10.35 10.35

Environmental Protection Type of 1998 Inscribed "Hochwasserhilfe 2013"

2013, July 18 *Perf. 13x13½*
B1078 SP411 58c +42c multi 2.50 2.50

Surtax for flood victims relief.

Birds — SP487

Designs: 58c+27c, Stieglitz (goldfinch). 90c+40c, Gimpel (bullfinch). 145c+55c, Blaumeise (blue tit).

2013, Aug. 8 *Perf. 13¾*
B1079 SP487 58c +27c multi 2.25 2.25
B1080 SP487 90c +40c multi 3.50 3.50
B1081 SP487 145c +55c multi 5.50 5.50
Nos. B1079-B1081 (3) 11.25 11.25

Saxonia Steam Locomotive, 175th Anniv. SP488

2013, Sept. 5 Litho. *Perf. 13¾*
B1082 SP488 58c+27c multi 2.25 2.25

Stamp Day.

Christmas SP489

2013, Nov. 2 Litho. *Perf. 13¾*
B1083 SP489 58c +27c multi 2.25 2.25

Booklet Stamp
Self-Adhesive
Die Cut Perf. 10½
B1084 SP489 58c +27c multi 2.25 2.25
a. Booklet pane of 10 22.50

Hansel and Gretel SP490

Designs: 60c+30c, Hansel and Gretel find witch's house. 90c+40c, Hansel imprisoned by witch. 145c+55c, Gretel riding on swan.

2014, Feb. 6 Litho. *Perf. 13¾*
B1085 SP490 60c +30c multi 2.50 2.50
B1086 SP490 90c +40c multi 3.75 3.75
B1087 SP490 145c +55c multi 5.50 5.50
Nos. B1085-B1087 (3) 11.75 11.75

Self-Adhesive
Die Cut Perf. 10¼
B1088 SP490 60c +30c multi 2.50 2.50
a. Booklet pane of 10 25.00

Surtax for Federal Association of Voluntary Welfare Work.

Protection of Water Resources SP491

2014, Apr. 3 Litho. *Perf. 13¾*
B1089 SP491 60c +30c multi 2.50 2.50

Cartoon Mouse by Uli Stein — SP492

Mouse: 60c+30c, Running with sports trophy. 90c+40c, Wearing shirt in colors of German flag. 145c+55c, Cheering on victory stand.

2014, May 8 Litho. *Perf. 13¾*
B1090 SP492 60c +30c multi 2.50 2.50
B1091 SP492 90c +40c multi 3.50 3.50
B1092 SP492 145c +55c multi 5.50 5.50
Nos. B1090-B1092 (3) 11.50 11.50

The Dream Eater, by Michael Ende (1929-95) SP493

Designs: 60c+30c, Princess Schlafittchen in bed. 90c+40c, Dream Eater. 145c+55c, Slumberland.

2014, Aug. 7 Litho. *Perf. 13¾*
B1093 SP493 60c +30c multi 2.40 2.40
B1094 SP493 90c +40c multi 3.50 3.50
B1095 SP493 145c +55c multi 5.25 5.25
Nos. B1093-B1095 (3) 11.15 11.15

Christmas — SP494

2014, Nov. 3 Litho. *Perf. 13½x13¾*
B1096 SP494 60c +30c multi 2.25 2.25

Booklet Stamp
Self-Adhesive
Size: 39x23mm
Die Cut Perf. 10
B1097 SP494 60c +30c multi 2.25 2.25
a. Booklet pane of 10 22.50

Sleeping Beauty SP495

Designs: 62c+30c, Sleeping Beauty, old woman and spinning wheel. 85c+40c, People at castle asleep. 145c+55c, Sleeping Beauty awakened by Prince's kiss.

2015, Feb. 5 Litho. *Perf. 13¾*
B1098 SP495 62c +30c multi 2.10 2.10
B1099 SP495 85c +40c multi 2.75 2.75
B1100 SP495 145c +55c multi 4.50 4.50
Nos. B1098-B1100 (3) 9.35 9.35

Self-Adhesive
Die Cut Perf. 10¼
B1101 SP495 62c +30c multi 2.10 2.10
a. Booklet pane of 10 21.00

Surtax for Federal Association of Voluntary Welfare Work.

Sports for the Handicapped — SP496

Designs: 62c+30c, Wheelchair tennis. 85c+40c, Runner with prosthetic legs. 145c+55c, Para-alpine skier.

2015, May 7 Litho. *Perf. 13½x13¾*
B1102 SP496 62c +30c multi 2.10 2.10
B1103 SP496 85c +40c multi 2.75 2.75
B1104 SP496 145c +55c multi 4.50 4.50
Nos. B1102-B1104 (3) 9.35 9.35

Fish SP497

Designs: 62c+30c, Äsche (grayling). 85c+40c, Barbe (barbel). 145c+55c, Stör (sturgeon)

2015, Aug. 6 Litho. *Perf. 13½x13¾*
B1105 SP497 62c +30c multi 2.10 2.10
B1106 SP497 85c +40c multi 3.00 3.00
B1107 SP497 145c +55c multi 4.50 4.50
a. Booklet pane of 6, #B1107, 5 #B1105 + 2 labels 15.00 —
Complete booklet, #B1107a 15.00
Nos. B1105-B1107 (3) 9.60 9.60

See Nos. B1119-B1121.

Penny Black, 175th Anniv. SP498

2015, Sept. 1 Litho. *Perf. 14*
B1108 SP498 62c +30c multi 2.10 2.10

Stamp Day.

Christmas SP499

2015, Nov. 2 Litho. *Perf. 13¾*
B1109 SP499 62c +30c multi 2.10 2.10

Booklet Stamp
Self-Adhesive
Die Cut Perf. 10½
B1110 SP499 62c +30c multi 2.10 2.10
a. Booklet pane of 10 21.00

Little Red Riding Hood SP500

Designs: 70c+30c, Little Red Riding Hood and wolf in forest. 85c+40c, Little Red Riding

Hood seeing wolf in grandmother's clothing. 145c+55c, Capture of wolf.

2016, Feb. 11 Litho. *Perf. 13¾*

B1111 SP500 70c +30c multi 2.25 2.25
B1112 SP500 85c +40c multi 2.75 2.75
B1113 SP500 145c +55c multi 4.50 4.50
Nos. B1111-B1113 (3) 9.50 9.50

Self-Adhesive

Die Cut Perf. 10¼

B1114 SP500 70c +30c multi 2.25 2.25
a. Booklet pane of 10 22.50

Surtax for Federal Association of Voluntary Welfare Work. No. B1114 was also issued in coils.

Balls — SP501

Designs: 70c+30c, Soccer ball. 85c+40c, Rugby football. 145c+55c, Golf ball.

2016, May 2 Litho. *Perf. 13¾*

B1115 SP501 70c +30c multi 2.40 2.40
B1116 SP501 85c +40c multi 3.00 3.00
B1117 SP501 145c +55c multi 4.75 4.75
Nos. B1115-B1117 (3) 10.15 10.15

Protection of the Alps SP502

2016, June 2 Litho. *Perf. 14*

B1118 SP502 70c +30c multi 2.25 2.25

Surtax for fund for Alpine protection projects.

Fish Type of 2015

Designs: 70c+30c, Hering (herring). 85c+40c, Kabeljau (cod). 145c+55c, Scholle (plaice).

2016, Aug. 4 Litho. *Perf. 13½x13¾*

B1119 SP497 70c +30c multi 2.25 2.25
B1120 SP497 85c +40c multi 2.75 2.75
B1121 SP497 145c +55c multi 4.50 4.50
Nos. B1119-B1121 (3) 9.50 9.50

Christmas — SP503

2016, Nov. 2 Litho. *Perf. 13½x13¾*

B1122 SP503 70c+30c multi 2.25 2.25

Booklet Stamp
Self-Adhesive
Size: 39x23mm

Die Cut Perf. 10

B1123 SP503 70c+30c multi 2.25 2.25
a. Booklet pane of 10 22.50

The Town Musicians of Bremen, Fairy Tale by the Brothers Grimm SP504

Designs: 70c+30c, Donkey, cat , dog, rooster and windmills (Meeting friend). 85c+40c, Animals making thieves leave house (The attack). 145c+55c, Animals and house (In the new home).

2017, Feb. 9 Litho. *Perf. 13¾*

B1124 SP504 70c +30c multi 2.10 2.10
B1125 SP504 85c +40c multi 2.75 2.75
B1126 SP504 145c +55c multi 4.25 4.25
Nos. B1124-B1126 (3) 9.10 9.10

Booklet Stamp
Self-Adhesive

Die Cut Perf. 10½

B1127 SP504 70c +30c multi 2.10 2.10
a. Booklet pane of 10 21.00

Surtax for Federal Association of Voluntary Welfare Work.

Athletes SP505

Designs: 70c+30c, Swimmer. 85c+40c, Fencers. 145c+55c, Rowers.

2017, May 11 Litho. *Perf. 13¾*

B1128 SP505 70c +30c multi 2.25 2.25
B1129 SP505 85c +40c multi 2.75 2.75
B1130 SP505 145c +55c multi 4.50 4.50
a. Booklet pane of 6, #B1129, B1130, 4 #B1128 + 2 labels 16.50 —
Complete booklet, #B1130a 16.50
Nos. B1128-B1130 (3) 9.50 9.50

German Sport Aid, 50th anniv.

Augsburger Puppenkiste Marionette Theater — SP506

Marionettes from : 70c+30c, *Urmel aus dem Eis.* 85c+40c, *Kleiner König Kalle Wirsch.* 145c+55c, *Kater Mikesch.*

Perf. 13½x13¾

2017, Aug. 10 Litho.

B1131 SP506 70c +30c multi 2.40 2.40
B1132 SP506 85c +40c multi 3.00 3.00
B1133 SP506 145c +55c multi 4.75 4.75
Nos. B1131-B1133 (3) 10.15 10.15

Fix and Foxi, Comic Strip Characters by Rolf Kauka (1917-2000) SP507

2017, Sept. 7 Litho. *Perf. 14*

B1134 SP507 70c +30c multi 2.40 2.40

Stamp Day.

Adoration of the Magi, by Stefan Lochner (c. 1410-51) — SP508

2017, Nov. 2 Litho. *Perf. 13½x13¾*

B1135 SP508 70c +30c multi 2.40 2.40

Booklet Stamp
Self-Adhesive
Size: 39x22mm

Die Cut Perf. 10

B1136 SP508 70c +30c multi 2.40 2.40
a. Booklet pane of 10 24.00

Christmas.

The Frog Prince, Fairy Tale by the Brothers Grimm SP509

Frog Prince: 70c+30c, Holding golden ball. 85c+40c, Holding knife, fork and spoon. 145c+55c, Sleeping.

2018, Feb. 1 Litho. *Perf. 13¾*

B1137 SP509 70c +30c multi 2.50 2.50
B1138 SP509 85c +40c multi 3.25 3.25
B1139 SP509 145c +55c multi 5.00 5.00
Nos. B1137-B1139 (3) 10.75 10.75

Self-Adhesive

Die Cut Perf. 10¼

B1140 SP509 70c +30c multi 2.50 2.50
a. Booklet pane of 10 + 2 stickers 25.00

Surtax for Federa; Association of Voluntary Welfare. No. B1140 was also issued in coils.

German Victories in the World Cup Soccer Championships — SP510

Broadcaster's quotes from covering championship of: 70c+30c, 1954. 85c+40c, 1974. 145c+55c, 1990.

2018, May 3 Litho. *Perf. 13½x13¾*

B1141 SP510 70c +30c multi 2.40 2.40
B1142 SP510 85c +40c multi 3.00 3.00
B1143 SP510 145c +55c multi 4.75 4.75
a. Booklet pane of 3, #B1141-B1143, + 5 labels 10.50 —
Complete booklet, #B1143a 10.50
Nos. B1141-B1143 (3) 10.15 10.15

Mushrooms SP511

Designs: 70c+30c, Echter pfifferling (chanterelle). 85c+40c, Echter steinpilz (porcini). 145c+55c, Maronen-Röhrling (chestnut pipe).

2018, Aug. 9 Litho. *Perf. 13¾*

B1144 SP511 70c +30c multi 2.40 2.40
B1145 SP511 85c +40c multi 3.00 3.00
B1146 SP511 145c +55c multi 4.75 4.75
Nos. B1144-B1146 (3) 10.15 10.15

A Large Piece of Turf, by Albrecht Dürer (1471-1528) SP512

2018, Sept. 13 Litho. *Perf. 14*

B1147 SP512 70c +30c multi 2.40 2.40

Biodiversity.

Stained-glass Window SP513

2018, Nov. 2 Litho. *Perf. 13¾*

B1148 SP513 70c +30c multi 2.25 2.25

Booklet Stamp
Self-Adhesive

Die Cut Perf. 10½x10¼

B1149 SP513 70c +30c multi 2.25 2.25
a. Booklet pane of 10 22.50

Christmas.

AIR POST STAMPS

Issues of the Republic

Post Horn with Wings — AP1

Biplane AP2

Perf. 15x14½

1919, Nov. 10 Typo. Unwmk.

C1 AP1 10pf orange .25 *2.60*
C2 AP2 40pf dark green .25 *3.00*
a. Imperf. 1,900.
Set, never hinged 1.35

No. C2a is ungummed.

Carrier Pigeon — AP3

1922-23 Wmk. 126 *Perf. 14, 14½*

Size: 19x23mm

C3 AP3 25(pf) chocolate .45 *18.00*
C4 AP3 40(pf) orange .40 *24.00*
C5 AP3 50(pf) violet .25 *8.25*
C6 AP3 60(pf) carmine .55 *19.50*
C7 AP3 80(pf) blue grn .40 *19.50*

Perf. 13x13½

Size: 22x28mm

C8 AP3 1m dk grn & pale grn .25 *3.75*
C9 AP3 2m lake & gray .25 *3.75*
C10 AP3 3m dk blue & gray .25 *4.50*
C11 AP3 5m red org & yel 2.60 *105.00*
C12 AP3 10m vio & rose ('23) .25 *9.00*
C13 AP3 25m brn & yel ('23) .25 *8.25*
C14 AP3 100m ol grn & rose ('23) .25 *6.75*
Nos. C3-C14 (12) 6.15 *230.25*
Set, never hinged 13.50

1923

C15 AP3 5m vermilion .25 *42.50*
C16 AP3 10m violet .25 *9.75*
C17 AP3 25m dark brown .25 *9.75*
C18 AP3 100m olive grn .25 *11.50*
C19 AP3 200m deep blue .25 *34.00*
a. Imperf. 60.00
Nos. C15-C19 (5) 1.25 107.50
Set, never hinged 1.90

Issued: Nos. C15-C18, 6/1. No. C19, 7/25.

Note following No. 160 applies to Nos. C1-C19.

1924, Jan. 11 *Perf. 14*

Size: 19x23mm

C20 AP3 5(pf) yellow grn 1.30 *2.25*
C21 AP3 10(pf) carmine 1.30 *2.25*
C22 AP3 20(pf) violet blue 6.75 5.25
C23 AP3 50(pf) orange 11.50 *26.00*
C24 AP3 100(pf) dull violet 30.00 *57.50*
C25 AP3 200(pf) grnsh bl 57.50 *75.00*
C26 AP3 300(pf) gray 97.50 105.00
a. Imperf. *900.00*
Nos. C20-C26 (7) 205.85 *273.25*
Set, never hinged 1,150.

German Eagle — AP4

1926-27

No.	Design	Description	Unused	Used
C27	AP4	5pf green	1.15	*1.15*
C28	AP4	10pf rose red	1.90	*1.15*
b.		Tête bêche pair	160.00	260.00
		Never hinged	260.00	
d.		Bklt. pane 10 (6 No. C28 + 4 No. C29)	225.00	340.00
		Never hinged	375.00	
C29	AP4	15pf lil rose ('27)	1.90	1.90
a.		Double impression	*1,375.*	
C30	AP4	20pf dull blue	1.90	*1.90*
a.		Tête bêche pair	160.00	260.00
		Never hinged	260.00	
b.		Bklt. pane 4 (4 No. C30 + 6 labels)	225.00	340.00
		Never hinged	375.00	
c.		Bklt. pane 5 (5 No. C30 + 5 labels)	450.00	975.00
		Never hinged	900.00	
C31	AP4	50pf brown org	18.00	5.25
C32	AP4	1m blk & sal	18.00	6.00
C33	AP4	2m black & blue	18.00	*22.50*
C34	AP4	3m blk & ol grn	52.50	*90.00*
		Nos. C27-C34 (8)	113.35	*129.85*
		Set, never hinged	900.00	

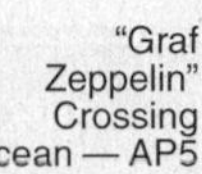

"Graf Zeppelin" Crossing Ocean — AP5

1928-31 **Photo.**

No.	Design	Description	Unused	Used
C35	AP5	1m carmine ('31)	24.00	*34.00*
C36	AP5	2m ultra	42.50	*50.00*
C37	AP5	4m black brown	26.00	*34.00*
		Nos. C35-C37 (3)	92.50	*118.00*
		Set, never hinged	425.00	

Issued: 2m, 4m, Sept. 20. 1m, May 8.

For overprints see Nos. C40-C45.

AP6

1930, Apr. 19 **Wmk. 126**

No.	Design	Description	Unused	Used
C38	AP6	2m ultra	250.00	*300.00*
C39	AP6	4m black brown	250.00	*300.00*
		Set, never hinged	2,600.	

First flight of Graf Zeppelin to South America. No. C38 is value with horizontal watermark. No. C39 is valued with vertical watermark. No. C38 with vertical watermark and No. C39 with horizontal watermark are worth 10%-20% more.

Counterfeits exist of Nos. C38-C45.

Nos. C35-C37 Overprinted in Brown

1931, July 15

No.	Design	Description	Unused	Used
C40	AP5	1m carmine	115.00	105.00
C41	AP5	2m ultra	170.00	*200.00*
C42	AP5	4m black brown	425.00	*675.00*
		Nos. C40-C42 (3)	710.00	*980.00*
		Set, never hinged	3,250.	

Polar flight of Graf Zeppelin.

Nos. C35-C37 Overprinted

1933, Sept. 25

No.	Design	Description	Unused	Used
C43	AP5	1m carmine	750.00	*375.00*
C44	AP5	2m ultra	75.00	*190.00*
C45	AP5	4m black brown	75.00	*190.00*
		Nos. C43-C45 (3)	900.00	*755.00*
		Set, never hinged	3,250.	

Graf Zeppelin flight to Century of Progress International Exhibition, Chicago.

Swastika Sun, Globe and Eagle — AP7

Otto Lilienthal — AP8

Design: 3m, Count Ferdinand von Zeppelin.

Perf. 14, 13½x13

1934, Jan. 21 **Typo.** **Wmk. 237**

No.	Design	Description	Unused	Used
C46	AP7	5(pf) brt green	1.15	.90
C47	AP7	10(pf) brt carmine	1.15	.90
C48	AP7	15(pf) ultra	1.75	1.25
C49	AP7	20(pf) dull blue	3.50	1.60
C50	AP7	25(pf) brown	4.50	1.90
C51	AP7	40(pf) red violet	6.75	1.15
C52	AP7	50(pf) dk green	12.00	.90
C53	AP7	80(pf) orange yel	3.75	3.75
C54	AP7	100(pf) black	7.50	2.60
C55	AP8	2m green & blk	16.50	*19.00*
C56	AP8	3m blue & blk	30.00	*42.50*
		Nos. C46-C56 (11)	88.55	76.45
		Set, never hinged	600.00	

"Hindenburg" — AP10

Perf. 14, 14½x14

1936, Mar. 16 **Engr.**

No.	Design	Description	Unused	Used
C57	AP10	50pf dark blue	18.00	.75
C58	AP10	75pf dull green	19.50	1.05

The note concerning gum after No. B68 also applies to Nos. C57-C58.

Unused values are for stamps without gum.

Count Zeppelin — AP11

Airship Gondola — AP12

1938, July 5 **Unwmk.** ***Perf. 13½***

No.	Design	Description	Unused	Used
C59	AP11	25pf dull blue	2.75	1.50
C60	AP12	50pf green	4.25	1.50
		Set, never hinged	42.50	

Count Ferdinand von Zeppelin (1838-1917), airship inventor and builder.

Catalogue values for unused stamps in this section, from this point to the end of the section, are for Never Hinged items.

Federal Republic

Lufthansa Emblem AP13

Perf. 13½x13

1955, Mar. 31 **Litho.** **Wmk. 295**

No.	Design	Description	Unused	Used
C61	AP13	5pf lilac rose & blk	.95	.70
C62	AP13	10pf green & blk	1.15	1.05
C63	AP13	15pf blue & blk	5.75	5.00
C64	AP13	20pf red & blk	15.50	5.75
		Nos. C61-C64 (4)	23.35	12.50

Re-opening of German air service, Apr. 1.

MILITARY AIR POST STAMP

Junkers 52 Transport MAP1

1942 **Unwmk.** **Typo.** ***Perf. 13½***

No.	Design	Description	Unused	Used
MC1	MAP1	ultramarine	.30	*.45*
		Never hinged	.70	
a.		Rouletted	.25	*.75*
		Never hinged	.45	

MILITARY PARCEL POST STAMPS

Nazi Emblem — MPP1

1942 **Unwmk.** **Typo.** ***Perf. 13½***

Size: 28x23mm

No.	Design	Description	Unused	Used
MQ1	MPP1	red brown	.30	*.30*
		Never hinged	.70	
a.		Rouletted	.25	*2.60*
		Never hinged	.45	

1944 **Size: 22½x18mm** ***Perf. 14***

No.	Design	Description	Unused	Used
MQ2	MPP1	bright green	.60	*1.90*
		Never hinged	1.30	

No. 520 Overprinted in Black

1944 **Engr.**

No.	Design	Description	Unused	Used
MQ3	A115	on 40pf brt red vio	.55	*3.00*
		Never hinged	1.15	

Forged surcharges exist.

Used values for Nos. MQ1-MQ3 are for CTO examples. Postally used stamps are scarce and sell for much more.

OFFICIAL STAMPS

Issues of the Republic

In 1920 the Official Stamps of Bavaria and Wurttemberg then current were overprinted "Deutsches Reich" and made available for official use in all parts of Germany. They were, however, used almost exclusively in the two states where they originated and we have listed them among the issues of those states.

O1 O2

O3 O4

O5 O6

O7 O8

O9 O10

O11 O12

1920-21 Typo. Wmk. 125 *Perf. 14*

O1 O1 5pf deep green .90 *13.50*
O2 O2 10pf car rose .25 1.60
O3 O2 10pf orange ('21) .60 *450.00*
O4 O3 15pf violet brn .25 2.25
a. Imperf. ('21) *750.00 750.00*
O5 O4 20pf deep ultra .25 1.90
O6 O5 30pf org, *buff* .25 1.90
O7 O6 40pf carmine .25 1.90
O8 O7 50pf violet, *buff* .25 1.90
O9 O8 60pf red brn ('21) .30 1.50
O10 O9 1m red, *buff* .25 1.90
O11 O10 1.25m dk bl, *yel* .25 3.75
O12 O11 2m dark blue 4.25 3.00
O13 O12 5m brown, *yel* .25 3.00
Nos. O1-O13 (13) 8.30 *488.10*
Set, never hinged 35.00

The value of No. O4a is for a stamp postmarked at Bautzen.

See No. O15. For surcharges see Nos. O29-O33, O35-O36, O38. For overprints see Upper Silesia Nos. O39-O51.

Postally Used vs. CTO

Values quoted for canceled examples of Nos. O1-O46 are for postally used stamps. See note after No. 160.

O13 O14

O15

Wmk. 126, 125 (#O16-O17)

1922-23

O14 O13 75pf dark blue .25 *7.50*
O15 O11 2m dark blue .25 *1.50*
a. Imperf. 97.50 —
O16 O14 3m brown, *rose* .25 *1.50*
O17 O15 10m dk grn, *rose* .25 *1.50*
O18 O15 10m dk grn, *rose* .25 *9.00*
O19 O15 20m dk bl, *rose* .25 *1.50*
O20 O15 50m vio, *rose* .25 *1.50*
a. Imperf 97.50 —
O21 O15 100m rose red, *rose* .25 *1.50*
a. Imperf 115.00 *750.00*
Nos. O14-O21 (8) 2.00 *25.50*
Set, never hinged 4.25

Issue date: Nos. O18-O21, 1923.
Nos. O20-O21 exist imperf.
For surcharges see Nos. O34, O37, O39.

Regular Issue of 1923 Overprinted — a

1923

O22 A34 20m red lilac .30 *7.50*
O23 A34 30m olive grn .25 *34.00*
O24 A29 40m green .30 *3.00*
O25 A35 200m car rose .25 *1.50*
O26 A35 300m green .25 *1.50*
O27 A35 400m dk brn .25 *1.50*
O28 A35 500m red orange .25 *1.50*
Nos. O22-O28 (7) 1.85 *50.50*
Set, never hinged 4.50

Official Stamps of 1920-23 Surcharged with New Values

Abbreviations:
Th=(Tausend) Thousand
Mil=(Million) Million
Mlrd=(Milliarde) Billion

1923 Wmk. 125

O29 O12 5th m on 5m .25 *3.00*
a. Inverted surcharge 50.00 *2,250.*
Never hinged 115.00
O30 O5 20th m on 30pf .25 *3.00*
a. Inverted surcharge 52.50 —
Never hinged 130.00
b. Imperf. 60.00 —
O31 O3 100th m on 15pf .25 *3.00*
a. Imperf. 60.00 —
Never hinged 150.00
b. Inverted surcharge 50.00 —
Never hinged 115.00
O32 O2 250th m on 10pf car rose .25 *3.00*
a. Double surcharge 37.50 —
Never hinged 90.00
O33 O5 800th m on 30pf .45 *300.00*

Official Stamps and Types of 1920-23 Surcharged with New Values

Wmk. 126

O34 O15 75th m on 50m .25 *3.00*
a. Inverted surcharge 50.00 —
Never hinged 115.00
O35 O3 400th m on 15pf brn .25 *27.00*
O36 O5 800th m on 30pf org, *buff* .30 *4.50*
O37 O13 1 mil m on 75pf .25 *37.50*
O38 O2 2 mil m on 10pf car rose .30 *3.75*
a. Imperf. 90.00 —
Never hinged 210.00
O39 O15 5 mil m on 100m .25 *5.75*
Nos. O29-O39 (11) 3.05 *393.50*
Set, never hinged 6.00

The 10, 15 and 30 pfennig are not known with this watermark and without surcharge.

Nos. 290-291, 295-299 Overprinted Type "a"

1923

O40 A39 100 mil m .25 *150.00*
O41 A39 200 mil m .30 *150.00*
O42 A39a 2 mlrd m .25 *115.00*
O43 A39a 5 mlrd m .25 *82.50*
O44 A39a 10 mlrd m 3.75 *135.00*
O45 A39a 20 mlrd m 3.75 *150.00*
O46 A39a 50 mlrd m 1.90 *200.00*
Nos. O40-O46 (7) 10.45 *982.50*
Set, never hinged 34.50

Same Overprint on Nos. 323-328, Values in Rentenpfennig

1923

O47 A40 3pf brown .25 *.75*
O48 A40 5pf dk green .25 *.75*
a. Inverted overprint 115.00 *750.00*
Never hinged 375.00
O49 A40 10pf carmine .25 *.75*
a. Inverted overprint 115.00 300.00
Never hinged 300.00
b. Imperf. 75.00 —
Never hinged 150.00
O50 A40 20pf dp ultra .60 *1.15*
O51 A40 50pf orange .60 *1.50*
O52 A40 100pf brown vio 3.75 *7.50*
Nos. O47-O52 (6) 5.70 *12.40*
Set, never hinged 22.50

Same Overprint On Issues of 1924

1924

O53 A41 3pf lt brown .70 *2.25*
a. Inverted overprint 60.00 —
Never hinged 300.00
O54 A41 5pf lt green .45 *.75*
a. Imperf. 75.00
Never hinged 225.00
b. Inverted overprint 105.00
Never hinged 300.00
O55 A41 10pf vermilion .30 *.75*
O56 A41 20pf blue .35 *.75*
O57 A41 30pf rose lilac 1.15 *.75*
O58 A41 40pf olive green 1.15 *.75*
O59 A41 50pf orange 5.75 3.75
O60 A47 60pf red brown 2.25 *3.75*
O61 A47 80pf slate 5.75 *35.00*
Nos. O53-O61 (9) 17.85 *48.50*
Set, never hinged 57.50

O16

1927-33 *Perf. 14*

O62 O16 3pf bister .30 *.75*
O63 O16 4pf lt bl ('31) .40 *.90*
O64 O16 4pf blue ('33) 14.50 *13.50*
O65 O16 5pf green .25 *.75*
O66 O16 6pf pale ol grn ('32) .70 *.90*
O67 O16 8pf dk grn .30 *.75*
O68 O16 10pf carmine 6.75 6.00
O69 O16 10pf ver ('29), wmk. upright 17.00 *26.00*
O70 O16 10pf red vio ('30) .40 *.90*
a. Imperf. 225.00
Never hinged 650.00
O71 O16 10pf choc ('33) 6.75 *9.00*
O72 O16 12pf org ('32) .40 *.90*
O73 O16 15pf vermilion 1.50 *.90*
O74 O16 15pf car ('29) .35 *.90*
O75 O16 20pf Prus grn, wmk. upright 7.50 3.00
O76 O16 20pf gray ('30), wmk. upright 1.90 1.15
O77 O16 30pf olive grn .85 .90
O78 O16 40pf violet, wmk upright .95 *.90*
O79 O16 60pf red brn ('28) 1.25 *1.90*
Nos. O62-O79 (18) 62.05 70.00
Set, never hinged 210.00

Swastika — O17

1934, Jan. 18 Wmk. 237

O80 O17 3pf bister .80 *1.10*
O81 O17 4pf dull blue .25 *.90*
O82 O17 5pf brt green .25 *1.10*
O83 O17 6pf dk green .25 *.90*
a. Imperf. 150.00 525.00
Never hinged 375.00
O84 O17 8pf vermilion 1.75 .90
O85 O17 10pf chocolate .40 *7.50*
O86 O17 12pf brt carmine 5.00 1.50
a. Unwmkd. .30 *4.50*
O87 O17 15pf claret 1.20 *9.00*
O88 O17 20pf light blue .45 *1.50*
O89 O17 30pf olive grn .70 *1.50*
O90 O17 40pf red violet .70 *1.50*
O91 O17 50pf orange yel 1.20 *3.75*
Nos. O80-O91 (12) 12.95 *31.15*
Set, never hinged 37.50

1942 Unwmk. *Perf. 14*

O92 O17 3pf bister brn .25 *1.15*
O93 O17 4pf dull blue .25 *3.00*
O94 O17 5pf deep olive .25 *15.00*
O95 O17 6pf deep violet .25 *1.15*
O96 O17 8pf vermilion .25 *1.15*
O97 O17 10pf chocolate .40 *11.50*
O98 O17 12pf rose car 1.60 *22.50*
a. Wmk. 237 3.00 *1.50*
O99 O17 15pf brown car 3.00 *52.50*
O100 O17 20pf light blue .25 *7.50*
O101 O17 30pf olive grn .25 *7.50*
O102 O17 40pf red violet .50 *19.00*
O103 O17 50pf dk green 4.00 *300.00*
Nos. O92-O103 (12) 11.25 *441.95*
Set, never hinged 42.50

LOCAL OFFICIAL STAMPS

For Use in Prussia

("Nr. 21" refers to the district of Prussia) — LO1

1903 Unwmk. Typo. *Perf. 14, 14½*

OL1 LO1 2pf slate 1.15 *4.50*
OL2 LO1 3pf bister brn 1.15 *4.50*
OL3 LO1 5pf green .25 *.55*
OL4 LO1 10pf carmine .25 *.55*
OL5 LO1 20pf ultra .25 *.55*
OL6 LO1 25pf org & blk, *yel* .75 *1.60*
OL7 LO1 40pf lake & blk .75 *2.00*
OL8 LO1 50pf pur & blk, *sal* .90 *1.90*
Nos. OL1-OL8 (8) 5.45 *16.15*
Set, never hinged 10.50

LO2 LO3

LO4 LO5

LO6 LO7

LO8

1920 Typo. Wmk. 125 *Perf. 14*

OL9 LO2 5pf green .25 *3.00*
OL10 LO3 10pf carmine .75 *1.50*
OL11 LO4 15pf vio brn .25 *2.25*
OL12 LO5 20pf dp ultra .25 *1.90*
OL13 LO6 30pf org, *buff* .25 *1.50*
OL14 LO7 50pf brn lil, *buff* .30 *1.50*
OL15 LO8 1m red, *buff* 8.25 *3.75*
Nos. OL9-OL15 (7) 10.30 *15.40*
Set, never hinged 35.00

For overprints see Upper Silesia Nos. O32-O38.

For Use in Baden

LO9

1905 Unwmk. Typo. *Perf. 14, 14½*

OL16 LO9 2pf gray blue 52.50 *75.00*
OL17 LO9 3pf brown 6.00 *10.50*
OL18 LO9 5pf green 4.25 *9.00*
OL19 LO9 10pf rose .75 *2.10*
OL20 LO9 20pf blue 1.50 *3.00*
OL21 LO9 25pf org & blk, *yel* 30.00 *52.50*
Nos. OL16-OL21 (6) 95.00 *152.10*
Set, never hinged 825.00

NEWSPAPER STAMPS

Newsboy and Globe — N1

Wmk. Swastikas (237)

1939, Nov. 1	**Photo.**		***Perf. 14***	
P1	N1	5pf green	.60	*5.25*
P2	N1	10pf red brown	.60	*5.25*
		Set, never hinged	4.50	

POSTAL TAX STAMPS

On November 28, 1948, the "Notopfer Berlin" ("Berlin emergency levy") was enacted by the West German authorities to raise funds to subsidize civilian operations in West Berlin. Part of this levy was a 2pf surtax on virtually all types of internal mail in West Germany, except that of the military governments and foreign consulates and surface mail to Berlin. Initially applied to the Bizone (American and British administration), this levy was later extended to the French zone of occupation, and was continued by the Federal Republic of Germany after its formation in Sept. 1949.

From Dec. 1, 1948, until the expiration of the levy on March 31, 1956, most mail was required to carry one of the "Notopfer" tax stamps.

PT1

1948 **Wmk. 286** **Typo.**

Imperf

RA1	PT1	2pf dk blue	.25	.25
		Never hinged	.75	

Compound Perf 12 and 14

RA2	PT1	2pf dk blue	.30	.25
		Never hinged	1.50	

No. RA2 also exists perf 9-10, 11, 11¼x11, 11½, compound 11½ and 12, 12x11½, 13½x11½ and rouletted, some of which were produced by local post offices or by private parties.

Issued: RA1, 12/1; RA2, 12/15.

Illustration PT1 actual size.

1948-50 **Wmk. 285** **Typo.**

Imperf

RA3	PT1	2pf dk blue	19.00	1.50
		Never hinged	45.00	

Compound Perf 12 and 14

RA4	PT1	2pf dk blue ('49)	15.00	.90
		Never hinged	60.00	

No. RA4 also exists perf 9½, 11, 11¼x11, 11½, 12, 12x11, 12x13½, 12¼ and rouletted, some of which were produced by local post offices or by private parties.

Wmk. 285

1950, June 10	**Litho.**		***Perf. 14***	
RA5	PT1	2pf dk blue	.25	.25
		Never hinged	1.15	

1955, Aug. 8			**Wmk. 295**	
RA6	PT1	2pf dk blue	.25	.25
		Never hinged	.55	

FRANCHISE STAMPS

For use by the National Socialist German Workers' Party

Party Emblem — F1

1938	**Typo.**	**Wmk. 237**	***Perf. 14***	
S1	F1	1pf black	.75	*3.00*
S2	F1	3pf bister	.75	*1.90*
S3	F1	4pf dull blue	.90	*1.50*
S4	F1	5pf brt green	.35	*1.50*
S5	F1	6pf dk green	.35	*1.50*
S6	F1	8pf vermilion	3.00	1.50
S7	F1	12pf brt car	5.50	1.50
S8	F1	16pf gray	.65	*9.00*
S9	F1	24pf citron	1.40	*5.00*
S10	F1	30pf olive	1.10	*7.50*
S11	F1	40pf red violet	1.30	*11.50*
		Nos. S1-S11 (11)	16.05	*45.40*
		Set, never hinged	127.00	

1942			**Unwmk.**	
S12	F1	1pf gray blk	.90	*30.00*
S13	F1	3pf bister brn	.25	*1.15*
S14	F1	4pf dk gray blue	.90	*3.00*
S15	F1	5pf gray green	.25	*22.50*
S16	F1	6pf violet	.25	*2.25*
S17	F1	8pf deep orange	.30	*2.25*
	a.	Imperf.	115.00	
		Never hinged	340.00	
S18	F1	12pf carmine	.30	*1.15*
S19	F1	16pf blue green	4.50	*75.00*
S20	F1	24pf yellow brn	.55	*30.00*
S21	F1	30pf dp olive grn	.70	*22.50*
S22	F1	40pf light rose vio	.70	*45.00*
		Nos. S12-S22 (11)	9.60	*234.80*
		Set, never hinged	37.50	

GERMAN OCCUPATION STAMPS

100 Centimes = 1 Franc
100 Pfennig = 1 Mark

Issued under Belgian Occupation

Belgian Stamps of 1915-1920 Overprinted

Perf. 11½, 14, 14½

1919-21				**Unwmk.**
1N1	A46	1c orange	.30	*.60*
1N2	A46	2c chocolate	.30	*.60*
1N3	A46	3c gray blk ('21)	.30	*2.25*
1N4	A46	5c green	.60	*1.10*
1N5	A46	10c carmine	1.10	*2.25*
1N6	A46	15c purple	.60	*1.10*
1N7	A46	20c red violet	.90	*1.10*
1N8	A46	25c blue	1.10	*1.90*
1N9	A54	25c dp blue ('21)	3.75	*11.00*

Belgian Stamps of 1915-1920 Overprinted

1N10	A47	35c brn org & blk	1.10	*1.10*
1N11	A48	40c green & blk	1.10	*2.25*
1N12	A49	50c car rose & blk	6.00	*10.50*
1N13	A56	65c cl & blk ('21)	3.00	*11.00*
1N14	A50	1fr violet	21.00	19.00
1N15	A51	2fr slate	35.00	*45.00*
1N16	A52	5fr deep blue	8.25	*11.00*
1N17	A53	10fr brown	45.00	60.00
		On cover		—
		Nos. 1N1-1N17 (17)	129.40	*181.75*
		Set, never hinged	450.00	

Nos. 1N1-1N17 were valid for postage until April 30, 1931, nearly one year after the Belgians and other occupation forces evacuated the Rhineland. Mixed frankings with Belgian stamps were permitted. The values for used stamps are for stamps with cancels from the Belgian military post offices in occupied Germany.

Nos. 1N14-1N17 exist with two overprint types: spacing between "Allemagne" and "Duitshland" 2mm (1919) and 1mm (1920).

Belgian Stamps of 1915 Surcharged

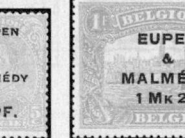

Nos. 1N18-1N22

Nos. 1N23-1N24

1920			**Black Surcharge**	
1N18	A46	5pf on 5c grn	.30	1.00
1N19	A46	10pf on 10c car	.30	1.10
1N20	A46	15pf on 15c pur	.50	1.50
1N21	A46	20pf on 20c red vio	.50	*1.90*
1N22	A46	30pf on 25c blue	.75	*1.90*

Red Surcharge

1N23	A49	75pf on 50c car rose & blk	15.00	19.00
1N24	A50	1m25pf on 1fr vio	21.00	20.00
		Nos. 1N18-1N24 (7)	38.35	*46.40*
		Set, never hinged	135.00	

EUPEN ISSUE

Belgian Stamps of 1915-20 Overprinted

Nos. 1N25-1N36

Nos. 1N37-1N41

1920-21			***Perf. 11½, 14, 14½***	
1N25	A46	1c orange	.35	*.90*
1N26	A46	2c chocolate	.35	*.90*
1N27	A46	3c gray blk ('21)	.60	*3.75*
1N28	A46	5c green	.60	*.90*
1N29	A46	10c carmine	.95	*1.25*
1N30	A46	15c purple	1.25	*1.25*
1N31	A46	20c red violet	1.50	*1.50*
1N32	A46	25c blue	1.25	*1.90*
1N33	A54	25c dp blue ('21)	4.50	*16.00*
1N34	A47	35c brn org & blk	1.90	*1.90*
1N35	A48	40c green & blk	2.25	*2.25*
1N36	49	50c car rose & blk	6.00	*7.50*
1N37	A56	65c cl & blk ('21)	3.25	*21.00*
1N38	A50	1fr violet	24.00	19.00
1N39	A51	2fr slate	40.00	30.00
1N40	A52	5fr deep blue	13.00	*11.00*
1N41	A53	10fr brown	60.00	*50.00*
		Nos. 1N25-1N41 (17)	161.75	*171.00*
		Set, never hinged	320.00	

MALMEDY ISSUE

Belgian Stamps of 1915-20 Overprinted

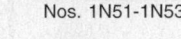

Nos. 1N42-1N50

Nos. 1N51-1N53

Nos. 1N54-1N58

1920-21				
1N42	A46	1c orange	.45	*.90*
1N43	A46	2c chocolate	.45	*.90*
1N44	A46	3c gray blk ('21)	.45	*3.75*
1N45	A46	5c green	.65	*.90*
1N46	A46	10c carmine	.95	*1.25*
1N47	A46	15c purple	1.50	*1.50*
1N48	A46	20c red violet	1.90	*1.90*
1N49	A46	25c blue	1.50	*1.90*
1N50	A54	25c dp blue ('21)	4.50	*16.00*
1N51	A47	35c brn org & blk	1.90	*1.90*
1N52	A48	40c green & blk	1.90	2.25
1N53	A49	50c car rose & blk	7.50	*7.50*
1N54	A56	65c cl & blk ('21)	3.25	*21.00*
1N55	A50	1fr violet	24.00	18.00
1N56	A51	2fr slate	40.00	30.00
1N57	A52	5fr deep blue	13.00	*16.00*
1N58	A53	10fr brown	60.00	*55.00*
		Nos. 1N42-1N58 (17)	163.90	*180.65*
		Set, never hinged	325.00	

OCCUPATION POSTAGE DUE STAMPS

Belgian Postage Due Stamps of 1919-20, Overprinted

1920		**Unwmk.**	***Perf. 14½***	
1NJ1	D3	5c green	.95	*1.10*
1NJ2	D3	10c carmine	1.90	*1.90*
1NJ3	D3	20c gray green	3.75	*4.50*
1NJ4	D3	30c bright blue	3.75	*4.50*
1NJ5	D3	50c gray	18.00	*15.00*
		Nos. 1NJ1-1NJ5 (5)	28.35	*27.00*
		Set, never hinged	57.50	

Belgian Postage Due Stamps of 1919-20, Overprinted

Unwmk.

1NJ6	D3	5c green	1.90	1.10
1NJ7	D3	10c carmine	3.75	1.90
	a.	Inverted overprint		—
1NJ8	D3	20c gray green	13.00	*11.00*
1NJ9	D3	30c bright blue	7.50	*8.00*
1NJ10	D3	50c gray	15.00	11.00
		Nos. 1NJ6-1NJ10 (5)	41.15	*33.00*
		Set, never hinged	82.50	

Nos. 1NJ1-1NJ10 were valid for postage until April 30, 1931, nearly one year after the Belgians and other occupation forces evacuated the Rhineland. Mixed frankings with Belgian stamps were permitted. The values for used stamps are for stamps with cancels from the Belgian military post offices in occupied Germany.

A. M. G. ISSUE

Issued jointly by the Allied Military Government of the US and Great Britain, for civilian use in areas under Allied occupation.

OS1

Type I. Thick paper, white gum.
Type II. Medium paper, yellow gum.
Type III. Medium paper, white gum.

Type III, Brunswick Printing

Perf. 11, 11½ and Compound

1945-46 **Litho.** **Unwmk.**

Size: 19-19½x22-22½mm

3N1	OS1	1pf slate gray	.25	*3.75*
3N2	OS1	3pf dull lilac	.25	*.90*
3N3	OS1	4pf lt gray	.25	*1.10*
3N4	OS1	5pf emerald	.25	*3.75*
3N5	OS1	6pf yellow	.25	*.90*
3N6	OS1	8pf orange	1.90	*30.00*
3N7	OS1	10pf yel brn	.25	*1.50*
3N8	OS1	12pf rose vio	.25	*.75*
3N9	OS1	15pf rose car	.25	*3.00*
3N10	OS1	16pf dp Prus grn	.25	*11.00*
3N11	OS1	20pf blue	.25	*3.75*
3N12	OS1	24pf choc	.25	*10.00*
3N13	OS1	25pf brt ultra	.25	*11.00*

Size: 21½x25mm

3N14	OS1	30pf olive	.25	*1.50*
3N15	OS1	40pf dp mag	.25	*3.75*
3N16	OS1	42pf green	.25	*1.50*
3N17	OS1	50pf slate grn	.25	*13.50*
3N18	OS1	60pf vio brn	.50	*15.00*
3N19	OS1	80pf bl blk	9.00	*225.00*

Size: 25x29½mm

3N20	OS1	1m dk ol grn ('46)	1.90	*400.00*
		Nos. 3N1-3N20 (20)	17.30	*741.65*
		Set, never hinged	40.00	

Most of Nos. 3N1-3N20 exist imperforate and part-perforate.

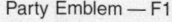

OS1a

Type I, Washington Printing
Size: 19-19½x22-22½mm

Perf. 11

3N2a	OS1a	3pf lilac	.25	*1.90*
3N3a	OS1a	4pf light gray	.25	*1.50*
3N4a	OS1a	5pf emerald	.25	*.35*
3N5a	OS1a	6pf yellow	.25	*.35*
3N6a	OS1a	8pf deep orange	.25	*.35*
3N7a	OS1a	10pf brown	.25	*.35*
3N8a	OS1a	12pf rose violet	.25	*.35*
3N9a	OS1a	15pf cerise	.25	*1.50*
3N13a	OS1a	25pf bright ultra	.25	*1.50*
	Nos. 3N2a-3N13a (9)			*8.15*
	Set, never hinged		2.00	

Type II, London Printing
Size: 19-19½x22-22½mm

Perf. 14, 14½ and Compound
Photo.

3N2b	OS1	3pf lilac	.25	*.60*
3N3b	OS1	4pf light gray	.25	*.60*
3N4b	OS1	5pf deep emerald	.25	*11.00*
3N5b	OS1	6pf orange yellow	.25	*.60*
3N6b	OS1	8pf dark orange	.25	*3.00*
3N8b	OS1	12pf rose violet	.25	*.60*
	Nos. 3N2b-3N8b (6)		1.50	*16.40*
	Set, never hinged		1.90	

ISSUED UNDER FRENCH OCCUPATION

Coats of Arms

Rhine Province OS3

Saarland OS5

Palatinate District OS4

Württemberg OS6

Baden OS7

Johann Wolfgang von Goethe OS8

Friedrich von Schiller — OS9

Heinrich Heine — OS10

Perf. 14x13½

1945-46		Unwmk.		Typo.
4N1	OS3	1pf blk, grn & lem	.25	.25
4N2	OS4	3pf dk red, blk & dl yel	.25	.25
4N3	OS6	5pf brn, blk & org yel	.25	.25
4N4	OS7	8pf brn, yel & red	.25	.25
4N5	OS3	10pf brn, grn & lem	6.50	*55.00*
4N6	OS4	12pf red, blk & org yel	.25	.25
4N7	OS5	15pf blk, ultra & red ('46)	.25	.25
4N8	OS6	20pf red, org yel & blk	.25	.25
4N9	OS5	24pf blk, dp ultra & red ('46)	.25	.25
4N10	OS7	30pf blk, org yel & red	.25	.25

Perf. 13
Engr.

4N11	OS8	1m lilac brn	.70	*18.00*
4N12	OS9	2m dp bl ('46)	.45	*52.50*
4N13	OS10	5m dl red brn ('46)	.55	*67.50*
	Nos. 4N1-4N13 (13)		10.45	*195.25*
	Set, never hinged		20.00	

Exist imperf. Value for set of 13, $475 mint never hinged.

BADEN

Johann Peter Hebel OS1

Girl of Constance OS2

Hans Baldung Grien — OS3

Rastatt Castle — OS4

Black Forest Scene OS5

Cathedral of Freiburg — OS6

1947		Unwmk.	Photo.	*Perf. 14*
5N1	OS1	2pf gray	.25	.30
5N2	OS2	3pf brown	.25	.30
5N3	OS3	10pf slate blue	.25	.30
5N4	OS1	12pf dk green	.25	.30
5N5	OS2	15pf purple	.25	.35
5N6	OS4	16pf olive green	.25	*1.50*
5N7	OS3	20pf blue	.25	.35
5N8	OS4	24pf crimson	.25	.30
5N9	OS2	45pf cerise	.25	*.90*
5N10	OS1	60pf deep orange	.25	.30
5N11	OS3	75pf brt blue	.25	*1.90*
5N12	OS5	84pf blue green	.25	*1.90*
5N13	OS6	1m dark brown	.25	*.75*
	Nos. 5N1-5N13 (13)			*9.45*
	Set, never hinged		2.25	

Festival Headdress OS7

Grand Duchess Stephanie OS8

1948				
5N14	OS1	2pf dp orange	.25	.30
5N15	OS2	6pf violet brn	.25	.30
5N16	OS7	8dpf blue green	.25	*1.10*
5N17	OS3	10pf dark brown	.25	.30
5N18	OS1	12pf crimson	.25	.30
5N19	OS2	15pf blue	.25	*.60*
5N20	OS4	16dpf violet	.35	*1.90*
5N21	OS3	20dpf brown	1.50	.95
5N22	OS4	24pf dark green	.25	.30
5N23	OS7	30pf cerise	.55	1.10
5N24	OS8	50pf brt blue	.55	.30
5N25	OS1	60dpf gray	1.90	.60
5N26	OS5	84dpf rose brn	2.75	*4.50*
5N27	OS6	1dm brt blue	2.75	*4.50*
	Nos. 5N14-5N27 (14)		12.10	*17.05*
	Set, never hinged		26.50	

1948-49		Without "PF"		
5N28	OS1	2(pf) dp orange	.50	*.50*
5N29	OS4	4(pf) violet	.30	*.45*
5N30	OS2	5(pf) blue	.35	*.60*
5N31	OS2	6(pf) violet brn	11.00	*13.50*
5N32	OS7	8(pf) rose brn	.35	*1.00*
5N33	OS3	10(pf) dark green	1.60	.50
5N37	OS3	20(pf) cerise	.65	.35
5N38	OS4	40(pf) brown	30.00	*75.00*
5N39	OS1	80(pf) red	3.75	*6.00*
5N40	OS5	90(pf) rose brn	29.00	*75.00*
	Nos. 5N28-5N40 (10)		77.50	*172.90*
	Set, never hinged		150.00	

Constance Cathedral and Insel Hotel — OS9

Type I. Frameline thick and straight. Inscriptions thick. Shading dark. Upper part of "B" narrow.

Type II. Frameline thin and zigzag. Inscriptions fine. Shading light. Upper part of "B" wide.

1949, June 22				
5N41	OS9	30pf dark blue (I)	9.00	*62.50*
		Never hinged	20.00	
	a.	Type II	*250.00*	*1,450.*
		Never hinged	475.00	

Issued to publicize the International Engineering Congress, Constance, 1949.

Conradin Kreutzer — OS10

1949, Aug. 27				
5N42	OS10	10pf dark green	1.50	*11.00*
		Never hinged	3.00	

Conradin Kreutzer (1780-1849), composer.

Stagecoach — OS11

Design: 20pf, Post bus, trailer and plane.

1949, Sept. 17				
5N43	OS11	10pf green	2.25	*10.50*
5N44	OS11	20pf red brown	2.25	*10.50*
	Set, never hinged		10.00	

Centenary of German postage stamps.

See Rhine Palatinate Nos. 6N39-6N40; Wurttemberg Nos. 8N38-8N39.

Globe, Olive Branch and Post Horn — OS12

1949, Oct. 4				
5N45	OS12	20pf dark red	2.75	*10.50*
5N46	OS12	30pf deep blue	2.75	*9.00*
	Set, never hinged		10.00	

75th anniv. of the UPU.

See Rhine Palatinate Nos. 6N41-6N42; Wurttemberg Nos. 8N40-8N41.

OCCUPATION SEMI-POSTAL STAMPS

Arms of Baden — OSP1

Perf. 13½x14

1949, Feb. 25		Photo.		Unwmk.
		Cross in Red		
5NB1	OSP1	10 + 20pf green	8.50	*75.00*
5NB2	OSP1	20 + 40pf lilac	8.50	*75.00*
5NB3	OSP1	30 + 60pf blue	8.50	*75.00*
5NB4	OSP1	40 + 80pf gray	8.50	*75.00*
	a.	Sheet of 4, #5NB1-5NB4, imperf.	110.00	*1,350.*
	Nos. 5NB1-5NB4 (4)		34.00	*300.00*
	Set, never hinged		75.00	

The surtax was for the Red Cross.

No. 5NB4a measures 90x101mm and has no gum.

See Rhine Palatinate Nos. 6NB3-6NB6; Wurttemberg Nos. 8NB1-8NB4.

Cornhouse, Freiburg — OSP2

10pf+20pf, Cathedral tower. 20pf+30pf, Trumpeting angel. 30pf+50pf, Fish pool.

1949, Feb. 24				*Perf. 14*
5NB5	OSP2	4 + 16pf dk vio	5.25	*35.00*
5NB6	OSP2	10 + 20pf dk grn	5.25	*35.00*
5NB7	OSP2	20 + 30pf car	5.25	*35.00*
5NB8	OSP2	30 + 50pf blue	6.75	*45.00*
	a.	Sheet of 4, #5NB5-5NB8	26.00	*210.00*
		Never hinged	52.50	
	b.	As "a," imperf.	26.00	*210.00*
		Never hinged	52.50	
	Nos. 5NB5-5NB8 (4)		22.50	*150.00*
	Set, never hinged		55.00	

The surtax was for the reconstruction of historical monuments in Freiburg.

Carl Schurz at Rastatt — OSP3

1949, Aug. 23				
5NB9	OSP3	10 + 5pf green	4.75	*29.00*
5NB10	OSP3	20 + 10pf cer	4.75	*29.00*
5NB11	OSP3	30 + 15pf blue	5.50	*29.00*
	Nos. 5NB9-5NB11 (3)		15.00	*87.00*
	Set, never hinged		29.00	

Centenary of the surrender of Rastatt.

Goethe — OSP4

Various Portraits.

1949, Aug. 12

No.	Type	Description	Unused	Used
5NB12	OSP4	10 + 5pf green	3.50	*19.00*
5NB13	OSP4	20 + 10pf cer	3.50	*19.00*
5NB14	OSP4	30 + 15pf blue	5.25	*45.00*
		Nos. 5NB12-5NB14 (3)	12.25	*83.00*
		Set, never hinged	26.00	

Johann Wolfgang von Goethe (1749-1832).

See Rhine Palatinate Nos. 6NB7-6NB9; Wurttemberg Nos. 8NB9-8NB11.

RHINE PALATINATE

Beethoven
OS1

Wilhelm E. F. von Ketteler
OS2

Girl Carrying Grapes
OS3

Porta Nigra, Trier
OS4

Karl Marx
OS5

"Devil's Table", Near Pirmasens
OS6

Street Corner, St. Martin
OS7

Cathedral of Worms
OS8

Cathedral of Mainz
OS9

Statue of Johann Gutenberg
OS10

Gutenfels and Pfalzgrafenstein Castles on Rhine — OS11

Statue of Charlemagne
OS12

1947-48 Unwmk. Photo. *Perf. 14*

No.	Type	Description	Unused	Used
6N1	OS1	2pf gray	.25	.30
6N2	OS2	3pf dk brown	.25	.30
6N3	OS3	10pf slate blue	.25	.30
6N4	OS4	12pf green	.25	.30
6N5	OS5	15pf purple	.25	.30
6N6	OS6	16pf lt ol grn	.25	*1.10*
6N7	OS7	20pf brt blue	.25	.30
6N8	OS8	24pf crimson	.25	.30
6N9	OS10	30pf cerise ('48)	.25	*2.25*
6N10	OS9	45pf cerise	.25	*.60*
6N11	OS9	50pf blue ('48)	.25	*2.25*
6N12	OS1	60pf dp orange	.25	.30
6N13	OS10	75pf blue	.25	*.60*
6N14	OS11	84pf green	.25	*1.40*
6N15	OS12	1m brown	.25	*.75*
		Nos. 6N1-6N15 (15)		*11.35*
		Set, never hinged	3.50	

Exist imperf. Value for set, $525 mint never hinged.

1948

No.	Type	Description	Unused	Used
6N16	OS1	2pf dp orange	.25	.30
6N17	OS2	6pf violet brn	.25	.30
6N18	OS4	8dpf blue green	.25	*1.10*
6N19	OS3	10pf dk brown	.25	.30
6N20	OS4	12pf crim rose	.25	.30
6N21	OS5	15pf blue	.60	*.60*
6N22	OS6	16dpf dk violet	.30	*1.40*
6N23	OS7	20dpf brown	1.40	.60
6N24	OS8	24pf green	.25	.30
6N25	OS9	30pf cerise	.45	.35
6N26	OS10	50pf brt blue	.75	.35
6N27	OS1	60dpf gray	3.75	.35
6N28	OS11	84dpf rose brown	1.90	*5.50*
6N29	OS12	1dm brt blue	3.00	*5.75*
		Nos. 6N16-6N29 (14)	13.65	*17.50*
		Set, never hinged	26.00	

Exist imperf. Value for set, $500 mint never hinged.

Types of 1947 Without "PF"

1948-49

No.	Type	Description	Unused	Used
6N30	OS1	2(pf) dp org	.30	.35
6N31	OS6	4(pf) vio ('49)	.30	.35
6N32	OS5	5(pf) blue ('49)	.35	*.60*
6N33	OS2	6(pf) vio brn	13.50	15.00
6N33A	OS4	8(pf) rose brn ('49)	30.00	*375.00*
6N34	OS3	10(pf) dk grn	.35	.35
a.		Imperf.	55.00	190.00
		Never hinged	110.00	
6N35	OS7	20(pf) cerise	.35	.35
6N36	OS8	40(pf) brn ('49)	1.40	*3.75*
6N37	OS4	80(pf) red ('49)	1.50	*5.00*
6N38	OS11	90(pf) rose brn ('49)	2.25	*15.00*
		Nos. 6N30-6N38 (10)	50.30	*415.75*
		Set, never hinged	110.00	

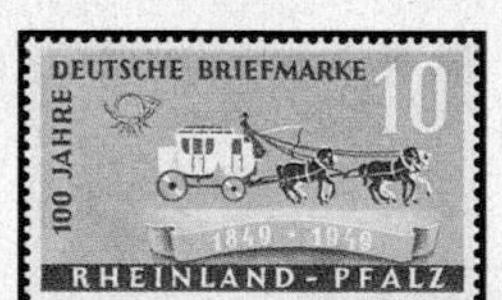
Stagecoach — OS13

1949, Sept. 17

No.	Type	Description	Unused	Used
6N39	OS13	10pf green	4.25	*19.00*
6N40	OS13	20pf red brown	4.25	*19.00*
		Set, never hinged	16.50	

Globe, Olive Branch and Post Horn — OS14

1949, Oct. 4

No.	Type	Description	Unused	Used
6N41	OS14	20pf dark red	3.00	*11.50*
6N42	OS14	30pf deep blue	3.00	*9.75*
		Set, never hinged	10.50	

OCCUPATION SEMI-POSTAL STAMPS

St. Martin — OSP1

Design: 30pf+50pf, St. Christopher.

1948 Unwmk. Photo. *Perf. 14*

No.	Type	Description	Unused	Used
6NB1	OSP1	20pf + 30pf dp cl	.60	*57.50*
6NB2	OSP1	30pf + 50pf dp bl	.60	*57.50*
		Set, never hinged	3.00	

The surtax was to aid victims of an explosion at Ludwigshafen.

Arms of Rhine Palatinate — OSP2

1949, Feb. 25 *Perf. 13½x14*

Cross in Red

No.	Type	Description	Unused	Used
6NB3	OSP2	10pf + 20pf grn	7.75	*82.50*
6NB4	OSP2	20pf + 40pf lil	7.75	*82.50*
6NB5	OSP2	30pf + 60pf bl	7.75	*82.50*
6NB6	OSP2	40pf + 80pf gray	7.75	*82.50*
a.		Sheet of 4, #6NB3-6NB6, imperf.	82.50	*1,050.*
		Nos. 6NB3-6NB6 (4)	31.00	*330.00*
		Set, never hinged	65.00	

The surtax was for the Red Cross.

No. 6NB6a measures 90x100mm and has no gum.

Goethe — OSP3

Various Portraits.

1949, Aug. 12

No.	Type	Description	Unused	Used
6NB7	OSP3	10pf + 5pf green	2.25	*18.00*
6NB8	OSP3	20pf + 10pf cerise	2.25	*18.00*
6NB9	OSP3	30pf + 15pf blue	4.50	*42.50*
		Nos. 6NB7-6NB9 (3)	9.00	*78.50*
		Set, never hinged	22.50	

WURTTEMBERG

Friedrich von Schiller
OS1

Castle of Bebenhausen
OS2

Friedrich Hölderlin
OS3

Town Gate of Wangen (Allgäu)
OS4

Lichtenstein Castle — OS5

Zwiefalten Church — OS6

1947-48 Unwmk. Photo. *Perf. 14*

No.	Type	Description	Unused	Used
8N1	OS1	2pf gray ('48)	.25	*.60*
8N2	OS3	3pf brown ('48)	.25	.30
8N3	OS4	10pf slate bl ('48)	.25	*.35*
8N4	OS1	12pf dk green	.25	.25
8N5	OS3	15pf purple ('48)	.25	*.45*
8N6	OS2	16pf ol grn ('48)	.25	*1.00*
8N7	OS4	20pf blue ('48)	.25	*1.00*
8N8	OS2	24pf crimson	.25	.30
8N9	OS3	45pf cerise	.25	*1.00*
8N10	OS1	60pf dp org ('48)	.25	.75
8N11	OS4	75pf brt blue	.25	*1.10*
8N12	OS5	84pf blue grn	.25	*1.40*
8N13	OS6	1m dk brown	.25	*1.10*
		Nos. 8N1-8N13 (13)		*9.60*
		Set, never hinged	2.25	

Nos. 8N4 and 8N10 exist imperf. Value, each $37.50, mint never hinged.

Waldsee
OS7

Ludwig Uhland
OS8

1948

No.	Type	Description	Unused	Used
8N14	OS1	2pf dp orange	.25	*.35*
8N15	OS3	6pf violet brn	.25	.30
8N16	OS7	8dpf blue grn	.35	*1.75*
8N17	OS4	10pf dk brown	.25	*.35*
8N18	OS1	12pf crimson	.25	.30
8N19	OS3	15pf blue	.30	*.35*
8N20	OS2	16dpf dk violet	.35	*1.60*
8N21	OS4	20dpf brown	.75	.75
8N22	OS2	24pf dk green	.45	*.60*
8N23	OS7	30pf cerise	.60	.60
8N24	OS8	50pf dull blue	.95	*.60*
8N25	OS1	60dpf gray	5.75	.60
8N26	OS5	84dpf rose brn	1.50	3.75
8N27	OS6	1dm brt blue	1.50	3.75
		Nos. 8N14-8N27 (14)	13.50	15.65
		Set, never hinged	26.00	

Nos. 8N14, 8N17, 8N22-8N23 exist imperf. Value, each $35, mint never hinged.

1948-49 Without "PF"

No.	Type	Description	Unused	Used
8N28	OS1	2(pf) dp orange	.35	*.60*
8N29	OS2	4(pf) violet	1.10	.35
8N30	OS3	5(pf) blue	3.00	2.25
8N31	OS3	6(pf) vio brown	3.00	*5.75*
8N32	OS7	8(pf) rose brn	3.00	2.25
8N33	OS4	10(pf) dk green	3.00	.35
8N34	OS4	20(pf) cerise	3.00	.35
8N35	OS2	40(pf) brown	9.75	*37.50*
8N36	OS1	80(pf) red	19.00	*37.50*
8N37	OS5	90(pf) rose brn	30.00	*97.50*
		Nos. 8N28-8N37 (10)	75.20	*184.40*
		Set, never hinged	150.00	

Nos. 8N29 and 8N31 exist imperf. Value, respectively $75 and $57.50, mint never hinged.

Stagecoach — OS9

1949, Sept. 17

No.	Type	Description	Unused	Used
8N38	OS9	10pf green	3.50	*12.00*
8N39	OS9	20pf red brown	3.50	*12.00*
		Set, never hinged	11.50	

Globe, Olive Branch and Post Horn — OS10

1949, Oct. 4

8N40	OS10	20pf dark red	2.25	*9.75*
8N41	OS10	30pf deep blue	2.25	*9.00*
		Set, never hinged	9.75	

OCCUPATION SEMI-POSTAL STAMPS

Arms of Württemberg — OSP1

Perf. 13½x14

1949, Feb. 25 Photo. Unwmk.

Cross in Red

8NB1	OSP1	10 + 20pf grn	16.00	*90.00*
8NB2	OSP1	20 + 40pf lilac	16.00	*90.00*
8NB3	OSP1	30 + 60pf blue	16.00	*90.00*
8NB4	OSP1	40 + 80pf gray	16.00	*90.00*
a.		Sheet of 4, imperf.	110.00	*1,350.*
		Nos. 8NB1-8NB4 (4)	64.00	*360.00*
		Set, never hinged	120.00	

The surtax was for the Red Cross.

No. 8NB4a measures 90x100mm and contains one each of Nos. 8NB1 to 8NB4, with red inscription in upper margin and no gum.

View of Isny OSP2

Design: 20pf+6pf, Skier and village.

Wmk. 116

1949, Feb. 11 Typo. *Perf. 14*

8NB5	OSP2	10 + 4pf dl grn	2.75	*22.50*
8NB6	OSP2	20 + 6pf red brn	2.75	*22.50*
		Set, never hinged	15.00	

Issued to commemorate the 1948-49 German Ski Championship at Isny im Allgau.

Gustav Werner — OSP3

1949, Sept. 4

8NB7	OSP3	10 + 5pf bl grn	2.25	*12.00*
8NB8	OSP3	20 + 10pf claret	2.25	*12.00*
		Set, never hinged	9.75	

Cent. of the founding of Gustav Werner's "Christianity in Action" and "House of Brotherhood."

Goethe — OSP4

Various Portraits.

1949, Aug. 12

8NB9	OSP4	10 + 5pf green	3.75	*19.00*
8NB10	OSP4	20 + 10pf cerise	5.50	*26.00*
8NB11	OSP4	30 + 15pf blue	5.50	*37.50*
		Nos. 8NB9-8NB11 (3)	14.75	*82.50*
		Set, never hinged	26.00	

OCCUPATION POSTAL TAX STAMPS

Wohnungsbau Issues

During July 1-December 31, 1949, a postal tax was levied on most categories of mail, with proceeds going to the 'Social Housing' (*Socialen Wohnungsbau*) program, which provided interest-free loans for housing construction and renovation intended to provide housing for economically-disadvantaged families.

Germany Nos. RA1, RA2, RA4 Overprinted in Red

Overprint 18.7mm wide

Wmk. 286

1949, July 1 Typo. *Imperf.*

8NRA1	PT1	2pf dk blue	225.00	*425.00*
		Never hinged	550.00	

Compound Perf 12, 14

8NRA2	PT1	2pf dk blue	15.00	2.75
		Never hinged	37.50	

Overprint 16.5 mm wide

1949, July 22 Wmk. 285 *Perf. 12¼*

8NRA3	PT1	2pf dk blue	3.75	1.75
		Never hinged	9.00	

OSPT1

1949 *Perf. 12¼*

8NRA4	OSPT1	2pf yellow	.25	*1.00*
		Never hinged	.50	
a.		2pf yellow orange	13.50	*15.00*
		Never hinged	30.00	
b.		2pf orange	.25	*1.00*
		Never hinged	.50	

Issued: No. 4a, 8/19; No. 4, 8/22. No. 4b, 8/25. No. 4c, 10/4.

Illustration OSPT1 actual size.

BERLIN

Issued for Use in the American, British and French Occupation Sectors of Berlin

Germany Nos. 557-569, 571-573 Overprinted Diagonally in Black — a

Wmk. 284

1948, Sept. 1 Typo. *Perf. 14*

9N1	A120	2pf brown blk	.90	*4.50*
9N2	A120	6pf purple	1.90	*4.50*
9N3	A121	8pf red	.75	*4.50*
9N4	A121	10pf yellow grn	.75	1.25
9N5	A122	12pf gray	.75	1.25
9N6	A120	15pf chocolate	4.00	*60.00*
9N7	A123	16pf dk blue grn	.90	*1.90*
9N8	A121	20pf blue	2.00	*6.75*
9N9	A123	24pf brown org	.60	*.45*
9N10	A120	25pf orange yel	4.50	*45.00*
9N11	A122	30pf red	1.75	*7.50*
9N12	A121	40pf red violet	2.25	*7.50*
9N13	A123	50pf ultra	2.50	*22.50*
9N14	A122	60pf red brown	1.10	.45
9N15	A122	80pf dark blue	3.00	*22.50*
9N16	A123	84pf emerald	3.75	*75.00*

Germany Nos. 574-577 Overprinted Diagonally in Black — b

Engr.

9N17	A124	1m olive	12.50	*120.00*
9N18	A124	2m dk brown vio	15.00	*375.00*
9N19	A124	3m copper red	19.00	*525.00*
9N20	A124	5m dark blue	26.00	*550.00*
		Nos. 9N1-9N20 (20)	103.90	1,836.
		Set, never hinged	270.00	

Forged overprints and cancellations are found on Nos. 9N1-9N20.

Stamps of Germany 1947-48 with "a" Overprint in Red

1948-49 Wmk. 284 Typo. *Perf. 14*

9N21	A120	2pf brn blk ('49)	.75	*2.25*
9N22	A120	6pf purple ('49)	6.00	2.25
9N23	A121	8pf red ('49)	13.00	4.50
9N24	A121	10pf yellow grn	1.50	1.25
9N25	A120	15pf chocolate	3.00	1.90
9N26	A121	20pf blue	1.10	1.10
9N27	A120	25pf org yel ('49)	30.00	40.00
9N28	A122	30pf red ('49)	25.00	4.75
9N29	A121	40pf red vio ('49)	25.00	13.50
9N30	A123	50pf ultra ('49)	25.00	7.50
9N31	A122	60pf red brown	3.75	.60
9N32	A122	80pf dk bl ('49)	40.00	7.50

With "b" Overprint in Red

Engr.

9N33	A124	1m olive	160.00	*400.00*
9N34	A124	2m dk brn vio	75.00	*210.00*
		Nos. 9N21-9N34 (14)	409.10	*697.10*
		Set, never hinged	1,000.	

Forgeries exist of the overprints on Nos. 9N21-9N34. No. 9N33 exists imperf.

A1

Statue of Heinrich von Stephan — A2

1949, Apr. 9 Litho. *Perf. 14*

9N35	A1	12pf gray	5.75	*7.50*
9N36	A1	16pf blue green	11.00	*15.00*
9N37	A1	24pf orange brn	7.50	.75
9N38	A1	50pf brown olive	50.00	37.50
9N39	A1	60pf brown red	50.00	30.00
9N40	A2	1m olive	26.00	*90.00*
9N41	A2	2m brown violet	35.00	*60.00*
		Nos. 9N35-9N41 (7)	185.25	*240.75*
		Set, never hinged	550.00	

75th anniv. of the UPU.

Brandenburg Gate, Berlin — A3

Tempelhof Airport — A4

Designs: 4pf, 8pf, 40pf, Schoeneberg, Rudolf Wilde Square. 5pf, 25pf, 5m, Tegel Castle. 6pf, 50pf, Reichstag Building. 10pf, 30pf, Cloisters, Kleist Park. 15pf, Tempelhof Airport. 20pf, 80pf, 90pf, Polytechnic College, Charlottenburg. 60pf, National Gallery. 2m, Gendarmen Square. 3m, Brandenburg Gate.

1949 Typo. Wmk. 284

Size: 22x18mm

9N42	A3	1pf black	.25	.35
a.		Bklt. pane 5 + label	9.00	*22.50*
		Never hinged	22.50	
b.		Tête bêche	.35	*1.25*
		Never hinged	1.00	
9N43	A3	4pf yellow brn	.25	.35
a.		Bklt. pane 5 + label	9.00	*22.50*
		Never hinged	22.50	
b.		Tête bêche	.95	*2.40*
		Never hinged	1.90	
9N44	A3	5pf blue green	.25	.35
9N45	A3	6pf red violet	.35	*1.10*
9N46	A3	8pf red orange	.35	*1.10*
9N47	A3	10pf yellow grn	.25	.35
a.		Bklt. pane 5 + label	65.00	*175.00*
		Never hinged	140.00	
9N48	A4	15pf chocolate	3.75	.90
9N49	A3	20pf red	1.25	.35
a.		Bklt. pane 5 + label	65.00	*175.00*
		Never hinged	140.00	
9N50	A3	25pf orange	6.00	.90
9N51	A3	30pf violet bl	3.00	.75
a.		Imperf.	*675.00*	
		Never hinged	1,350.	
9N52	A3	40pf lake	4.50	.75
9N53	A3	50pf olive	4.50	.35
9N54	A3	60pf red brown	15.00	.35
9N55	A3	80pf dark blue	3.00	.75
9N56	A3	90pf emerald	3.00	.90

Engr.

Size: 29¼-29¾x24-24½mm

9N57	A4	1m olive	5.50	1.10
9N58	A4	2m brown vio	15.00	1.50
9N59	A4	3m henna brn	67.50	15.00
9N60	A4	5m deep blue	32.50	15.00
		Nos. 9N42-9N60 (19)	166.20	42.20
		Set, never hinged	550.00	

See Nos. 9N101-9N102, 9N108-9N110.

Goethe and "Iphigenie" — A5

Designs (Goethe and scenes from his works): 20pf, "Reineke Fuchs." 30pf, "Faust."

1949, July 29 Litho. *Perf. 14*

9N61	A5	10pf green	30.00	*50.00*
9N62	A5	20pf carmine	32.50	*50.00*
9N63	A5	30pf ultra	7.50	*35.00*
		Nos. 9N61-9N63 (3)	70.00	*135.00*
		Set, never hinged	240.00	

Bicentenary of the birth of Johann Wolfgang von Goethe.

Germany Nos. 550, 565, 572 and 576 Surcharged in Dark Green

1949, Aug. 1 Typo.

9N64	A119	5pf on 45pf	1.10	.35
9N65	A123	10pf on 24pf	3.00	.35
9N66	A122	20pf on 80pf	15.00	12.50

Engr.

9N67	A124	1m on 3m	35.00	16.00
		Nos. 9N64-9N67 (4)	54.10	29.20
		Set, never hinged	190.00	

Statue of Atlas, New York — A6

1950, Oct. 1 Engr. Wmk. 116

9N68	A6	20pf dk carmine	30.00	30.00
		Never hinged	75.00	

European Recovery Plan.

Albert Lortzing — A7

1951, Apr. 22

9N69 A7 20pf red brown 16.00 *40.00*
Never hinged 45.00

Centenary of the death of Albert Lortzing, composer.

Freedom Bell, Berlin — A8

1951 ***Perf. 14***

9N70 A8 5pf brown .75 *6.00*
9N71 A8 10pf deep green 3.75 *18.00*
9N72 A8 20pf rose red 2.25 *18.00*
9N73 A8 30pf blue 15.00 *67.50*
9N74 A8 40pf rose violet 3.75 *45.00*
Nos. 9N70-9N74 (5) 25.50 *154.50*
Set, never hinged 75.00

Re-engraved

Bell clapper moved from left to right. Imprint "L. Schnell" in lower margin.

1951-52

9N75 A8 5pf olive bis ('52) .75 *1.90*
9N76 A8 10pf yellow grn 2.25 *3.75*
9N77 A8 20pf brt red 7.50 *15.00*
9N78 A8 30pf blue ('52) 21.00 *37.50*
9N79 A8 40pf dp car ('52) 7.50 *15.00*
Nos. 9N75-9N79 (5) 30.00 *73.15*
Set, never hinged 90.00

No. 9N76 exists imperf. Value, $575 unused, $1,100 mint never hinged.

See Nos. 9N94-9N98.

Ludwig van Beethoven — A9

1952, Mar. 26 **Engr.** **Unwmk.**

9N80 A9 30pf blue 12.50 *22.50*
Never hinged 32.50

125th anniversary of the death of Ludwig van Beethoven.

Olympic Symbols — A10

1952, June 20 **Litho.** **Wmk. 116**

9N81 A10 4pf yellow brown .35 *1.90*
9N82 A10 10pf green 3.75 *15.00*
9N83 A10 20pf rose red 6.75 *26.00*
Nos. 9N81-9N83 (3) 10.85 *42.90*
Set, never hinged 24.00

Pre-Olympic Festival Day, June 20, 1952.

Carl Friedrich Zelter — A11

Portraits: 5pf, Otto Lilienthal. 6pf, Walter Rathenau. 8pf, Theodor Fontane. 10pf, Adolph von Menzel. 15pf, Rudolf Virchow. 20pf, Werner von Siemens. 25pf, Karl Friedrich Schinkel. 30pf, Max Planck. 40pf, Wilhelm von Humboldt.

1952-53 **Engr.** **Wmk. 284**

9N84 A11 4pf brown .25 .55
9N85 A11 5pf dp blue ('53) .35 .55
9N86 A11 6pf choc ('53) 1.40 *7.00*
9N87 A11 8pf henna brn ('53) .75 *2.25*
9N88 A11 10pf deep green 1.10 .50
9N89 A11 15pf purple ('53) 4.25 *12.50*
9N90 A11 20pf brown red .75 .75
9N91 A11 25pf dp olive ('53) 14.00 5.00
9N92 A11 30pf brn vio ('53) 5.00 *7.00*
9N93 A11 40pf black ('53) 6.25 2.25
Nos. 9N84-9N93 (10) 34.10 38.35
Set, never hinged 100.00

Bell Type of 1951-1952

Second Re-engraving

Bell clapper hangs straight down. Marginal imprint omitted.

1953 **Wmk. 284** ***Perf. 14***

9N94 A8 5pf brown .35 *1.00*
9N95 A8 10pf deep green .90 *1.40*
9N96 A8 20pf brt red 2.10 2.75
9N97 A8 30pf blue 3.50 *8.50*
9N98 A8 40pf rose violet 15.00 *25.00*
Nos. 9N94-9N98 (5) 21.85 *38.65*
Set, never hinged 55.00

For overprint & surcharge see Nos. 9N106, 9NB17.

Arms Breaking Chains — A12

Design: 30pf, Brandenburg Gate.

1953, Aug. 17 **Typo.**

9N99 A12 20pf black 1.25 *1.50*
9N100 A12 30pf dp carmine 9.00 *25.00*
Set, never hinged 30.00

Strike of East German workers, 6/17/53.

Exposition Halls — A12a

Designs: 20pf, Olympic Stadium, Berlin.

1953-54 **Wmk. 284** ***Perf. 14***

9N101 A12a 4pf yellow brn ('54) 1.25 *3.50*
9N102 A12a 20pf red 15.00 2.25
Set, never hinged 55.00

Catalogue values for unused stamps in this section, from this point to the end of the section, are for Never Hinged items.

Allied Council Building — A13

1954, Jan. 25 **Litho.**

9N103 A13 20pf red 7.00 4.00

Four Power Conference, Berlin, 1954.

Prof. Ernst Reuter (1889-1953), Mayor of Berlin (1948-53) A14

1954, Jan. 18 **Engr.** **Wmk. 284**

9N104 A14 20pf chocolate 7.00 1.25

See No. 9N174.

Ottmar Mergenthaler and Linotype — A15

1954, May 11

9N105 A15 10pf dk blue grn 3.00 2.00

Cent. of the birth of Ottmar Mergenthaler.

No. 9N96 Overprinted in Black

1954, July 17 ***Perf. 13½x14***

9N106 A8 20pf bright red 4.00 *4.00*

Issued to publicize the West German presidential election held in Berlin July 17, 1954.

Germany in Bondage — A16

1954, July 20 **Typo.**

9N107 A16 20pf car & gray 4.00 4.00

10th anniv. of the attempted assassination of Adolf Hitler.

Exposition Halls — A16a

Designs: 40pf, Memorial library. 70pf, Hunting lodge, Grunewald.

1954 **Wmk. 284** ***Perf. 14***

9N108 A16a 7pf green blue 5.00 1.25
9N109 A16a 40pf rose lilac 9.00 2.75
9N110 A16a 70pf olive green 80.00 16.00
Nos. 9N108-9N110 (3) 94.00 20.00
Set, hinged 35.00

Richard Strauss — A17

1954, Sept. 18 **Engr.**

9N111 A17 40pf violet blue 9.00 3.00

5th anniv. of the death of Richard Strauss, composer.

Early Forge — A18

1954, Sept. 25

9N112 A18 20pf reddish brown 6.00 1.25

Centenary of the death of August Borsig, industrial leader.

M. S. Berlin and Arms of Berlin — A19

1955, Mar. 12 **Wmk. 284**

9N113 A19 10pf dp blue grn 1.00 .60
9N114 A19 25pf violet blue 6.00 3.00

Issued to publicize the resumption of shipping under West German ownership.

Wilhelm Furtwängler — A20

Perf. 13½x14

1955, Sept. 17 **Unwmk.**

9N115 A20 40pf ultra 14.00 14.00

Issued to honor the conductor Wilhelm Furtwangler and to publicize the Berlin Music Festival, September 1955.

Arms of Berlin — A21

1955, Oct. 17 **Litho.** **Wmk. 304**

9N116 A21 10pf red, org yel & blk .50 *.65*
9N117 A21 20pf red, org yel & blk 4.00 *7.50*

Meeting of the German Bundestag in Berlin, Oct. 17-22, 1955.

Arms of Berlin — A22

1956, Mar. 16

9N118 A22 10pf red, ocher & blk 1.20 .60
9N119 A22 25pf red, ocher & blk 4.00 4.00

Meeting of the German Bundesrat in Berlin Mar. 16, 1956.

Radio Station, Berlin
A23 A24

A23 has no top inscription.
A24 has top inscription.

Free University
A25

Monument of the Great Elector Frederick William
A26

Designs: 1pf, 3pf, Brandenburg Gate. 5pf, General Post Office. 8pf, City Hall, Neukölln. 10pf, Kaiser Wilhelm Memorial Church. 15pf, Airlift memorial. 25pf, Lilienthal Monument. 30pf, Pfaueninsel Castle. 40pf, Charlottenburg Castle. 50pf, Reuter power plant. 60pf, Chamber of Commerce and Industry and Stock Exchange. 70pf, Schiller Theater. 3m, Congress Hall.

Typo.; Litho. (3pf, #9N122)

1956-63 Wmk. 304 ***Perf. 14***

9N120	A25	1pf gray ('57)	.25	.25
9N120A	A25	3pf brt pur ('63)	.25	.25
9N121	A25	5pf rose lil ('57)	.25	.25
9N122	A23	7pf blue green	8.25	2.40
9N123	A24	7pf blue green	.25	.25
9N124	A24	8pf gray	.45	.35
9N125	A24	8pf red org ('59)	.30	.30
9N126	A24	10pf emerald	.25	.25
9N127	A24	15pf chlky blue	.40	.25
9N128	A25	20pf rose car	.40	.25
9N129	A24	25pf dull red brn	.40	.45

Engr.

9N130	A24	30pf gray grn ('57)	.85	.85
9N131	A25	40pf lt ultra ('57)	8.50	7.00
9N132	A24	50pf olive	.85	.85
9N133	A25	60pf lt brn ('57)	.85	.85
9N134	A25	70pf violet	21.00	12.00
9N135	A26	1m olive	1.75	2.00

Size: 29x24½mm

9N136	A25	3m rose cl ('58)	4.25	*16.00*
		Nos. 9N120-9N136 (18)	49.50	44.80

No. 9N120 exists on both ordinary and fluorescent paper; No. 9N120A on fluorescent paper only; others on ordinary paper.

Engineers' Society Emblem — A27

1956, May 12 Engr. ***Perf. 14***

9N140 A27 10pf dark green	1.75	1.75
9N141 A27 20pf dark red	3.25	*4.25*

Cent. of Soc. of German Civil Engineers.

Paul Lincke — A28

1956, Sept. 3

9N142 A28 20pf dark red	2.50	2.25

Death of Paul Lincke, composer, 10th anniv.

Radio Station, Berlin-Nikolassee
A29

1956, Sept. 15

9N143 A29 25pf brown	5.00	*7.00*

German Industrial Fair, Berlin, Sept. 15-30.

Spandau, 1850 — A30

1957, Mar. 7

9N144 A30 20pf gray ol & brn red	.60	.60

725th anniversary of Spandau.

Hansa Model Town and "B" — A31

Designs: 20pf, View of exposition grounds and "B." 40pf, Auditorium and "B."

1957 Engr.

9N145 A31 7pf violet brown	.25	.25
9N146 A31 20pf carmine	.65	.65
9N147 A31 40pf violet blue	1.50	2.00
Nos. 9N145-9N147 (3)	2.40	2.90

Intl. Building Show, Berlin, 7/6-9/29/57.

Friedrich Karl von Savigny, Law Teacher — A32

Portraits: 7pf, Theodor Mommsen, historian. 8pf, Heinrich Zille, painter. 10pf, Ernst Reuter, mayor of Berlin. 15pf, Fritz Haber, chemist. 20pf, Friedrich Schleiermacher, theologian. 25pf, Max Reinhardt, theatrical director. 40pf, Alexander von Humboldt, naturalist and geographer. 50pf, Christian Daniel Rauch, sculptor.

1957-59 Wmk. 304 ***Perf. 14***

Portraits in Brown

9N148 A32 7pf blue grn ('58)	.25	.25
9N149 A32 8pf gray ('58)	.25	.25
9N150 A32 10pf yel grn ('58)	.25	.25
9N151 A32 15pf dark blue	.35	.65
9N152 A32 20pf red ('58)	.25	.25
9N153 A32 25pf carmine	.65	.90
9N154 A32 30pf gray green	1.75	2.40
9N155 A32 40pf Prus blue ('59)	.70	.90
9N156 A32 50pf olive	3.50	*6.00*
Nos. 9N148-9N156 (9)	7.95	11.85

Issued to honor famous men of Berlin.
See No. 9NB19.

Uta Statue, Naumburg Cathedral — A33

1957, Aug. 6

9N157 A33 25pf brown red	.85	1.00

Issued to publicize the annual meeting of the East German Culture Society in Berlin.

"Unity and Justice and Liberty" — A34

1957, Oct. 15 Litho.

9N158 A34 10pf multicolored	.30	*.65*
9N159 A34 20pf multicolored	2.00	*3.00*

1st meeting of the 3rd German Bundesrat, Berlin, 10/15.

Postilion 1897-1925 — A35

1957, Oct. 23 Wmk. 304 ***Perf. 14***

9N160 A35 20pf multicolored	.85	.90

Issued for Stamp Day and BEPHILA stamp exhibition, Berlin, Oct. 23-27.

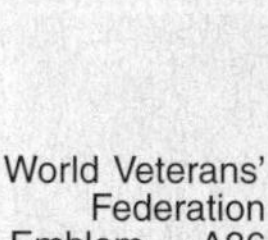

World Veterans' Federation Emblem — A36

1957, Oct. 28

9N161 A36 20pf bl grn, ol grn & yel	.90	.65

7th General Assembly of the World Veterans' Federation, Berlin, Oct. 24-Nov. 1.

Christ and the Cosmos — A37

1958, Aug. 13

9N162 A37 10pf lt bl grn & blk	.35	.50
9N163 A37 20pf rose lilac & blk	1.00	1.25

Issued in honor of the 78th German Catholics Meeting, Berlin, Aug. 13-17.

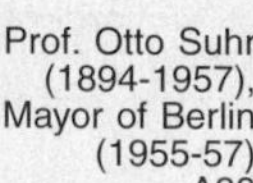

Prof. Otto Suhr (1894-1957), Mayor of Berlin (1955-57)
A38

1958, Aug. 30 Engr. ***Perf. 14***

9N164 A38 20pf rose red	1.10	1.25

Pres. Heuss — A38a

Litho., Engraved (40pf, 70pf)

1959

9N165 A38a 7pf blue green	.30	*.35*
9N166 A38a 10pf green	.30	*.35*
9N167 A38a 20pf dk car rose	.45	.35
9N168 A38a 40pf blue	2.00	*4.00*
9N169 A38a 70pf dull purple	7.00	*9.00*
Nos. 9N165-9N169 (5)	10.05	*14.05*

Nos. 9N168-9N169 were issued in sheets of 100 and in coils. Every fifth coil stamp has a control number on the back.

Aerial Bridge to Berlin — A39

1959, May 12 Engr.

9N170 A39 25pf maroon & blk	.60	.45

10th anniversary of Berlin Airlift.

Globe and Brandenburg Gate — A40

1959, June 18 Litho. ***Perf. 14***

9N171 A40 20pf lt blue & red	.80	.45

Issued to publicize the 14th International Municipal Congress, Berlin, June 18-23.

Friedrich von Schiller (1759-1805), Poet — A41

1959, Nov. 10 Engr. Wmk. 304

9N172 A41 20pf dull red & brn	.35	.45

Dr. Robert Koch (1843-1910), Bacteriologist
A42

1960, May 27 ***Perf. 14***

9N173 A42 20pf rose lake	.35	.45

A42a

Portrait: Dr. Walther Carl Rudolf Schreiber, Mayor of Berlin, 1953-54.

1960, June 30 Wmk. 304 ***Perf. 14***

9N174 A42a 20pf brown car	.50	.65

Hans Böckler (1875-1951), Labor Leader — A43

1961, Feb. 16 Litho. *Perf. 14*

9N175	A43	20pf dk brick red & blk	.30	.35

Hans Böckler (1875-1951), labor leader.

Fluorescent Paper was introduced for all stamps, starting with No. 9N176, and including Nos. 9N120 and 9N120A.

Albrecht Dürer — A44

Portraits: 5pf, Albertus Magnus. 7pf, St. Elizabeth of Thuringia. 8pf, Johann Gutenberg. 15pf, Martin Luther. 20pf, Johann Sebastian Bach. 25pf, Balthasar Neumann. 30pf, Immanuel Kant. 40pf, Gotthold Ephraim Lessing. 50pf, Johann Wolfgang von Goethe. 60pf, Friedrich von Schiller. 70pf, Ludwig van Beethoven. 80pf, Heinrich von Kleist. 1m, Annette von Droste-Hülshoff. 2m, Gerhart Hauptmann.

1961-62 Typo. Wmk. 304

9N176	A44	5pf olive	.25	.25
9N177	A44	7pf dk bistor	.25	.35
9N178	A44	8pf lilac	.25	.35
9N179	A44	10pf olive green	.25	.25
b.		Tête bêche pair	1.10	*2.25*
9N180	A44	15pf blue	.25	.35
9N181	A44	20pf dark red	.25	.25
9N182	A44	25pf orange brn	.25	.35

Engr.

9N183	A44	30pf gray	.25	*.50*
9N184	A44	40pf blue	.50	*.90*
9N185	A44	50pf red brown	.35	*.90*
9N186	A44	60pf dk car rose ('62)	.35	*1.10*
9N187	A44	70pf green	.50	*1.10*
9N188	A44	80pf brown	2.75	*7.00*
9N189	A44	1m violet blue	1.40	*3.25*
9N190	A44	2m yel grn ('62)	1.75	*4.50*
		Nos. 9N176-9N190 (15)	9.60	*21.40*

Nos. 9N176-9N182, 9N184 and 9N187 were issued in sheets and in coils. Every fifth coil stamp has a black control number on the back.

Louise Schroeder A45

1961, June 3 Engr. *Perf. 14*

9N192	A45	20pf dark brown	.50	.35

Issued to honor Louise Schroeder, acting mayor of Berlin (1947-1948).

A46

Design: 10pf, Emblem and St. Mary's Church. 20pf, Synod Emblem & Kaiser Wilhelm Memorial Church.

1961, July 19 Litho. Wmk. 304

9N193	A46	10pf green & vio	.25	.25
9N194	A46	20pf rose claret & vio	.25	.25

10th meeting of German Protestants (Evangelical Synod), Berlin, July 19-23.

Berlin Bear with Record, TV Set & Radio Tower — A47

1961, Aug. 3 Engr.

9N195	A47	20pf brn red & dk brn	.50	.45

German Radio, Television and Phonograph Exhibition, Berlin, Aug. 25-Sept. 3.

Berlin, 1650 — A48

Views of Old Berlin: 10pf, Spree and Waisenbrücke (Orphans' Bridge). 15pf, Mauer Street, 1780. 20pf, Berlin Palace, 1703. 25pf, Potsdam Square, 1825. 40pf, Bellevue Palace, 1800. 50pf, Fischer Bridge, 1830. 60pf, Halle Gate, 1880. 70pf, Parochial Church, 1780. 80pf, University, 1825. 90pf, Opera House, 1780. 1m, Grunewald Lake, 1790.

1962-63 Wmk. 304 *Perf. 14*

9N196	A48	7pf dk gray & gldn brn	.25	.25
9N197	A48	10pf grn & dk gray	.25	.25
9N198	A48	15pf bluish gray & dk bl ('63)	.25	.25
9N199	A48	20pf org brn & sep	.25	.25
9N200	A48	25pf ol & gray ('63)	.25	.25
9N201	A48	40pf bluish gray & ultra	.25	.35
9N202	A48	50pf gray & dk brn ('63)	.35	.35
9N203	A48	60pf gray & car rose ('63)	.40	.40
9N204	A48	70pf dk gray & lilac	.40	.40
9N205	A48	80pf dk gray & dk red ('63)	.40	.40
9N206	A48	90pf sep & brn org ('63)	.65	.65
9N207	A48	1m ol gray & dp grn	.80	.90
		Nos. 9N196-9N207 (12)	4.50	4.70

Gelber Hund, 1912, and Boeing 707 — A49

1962, Sept. 12 Litho.

9N208	A49	60pf brt blue & blk	.55	.55

50th anniv. of German airmail service.

Berlin Bear and Radio Tower — A50

1963, July 24 Unwmk. *Perf. 14*

9N209	A50	20pf bl, vio bl & gray	.50	.45

German Radio, Television and Phonograph Exhibition, Berlin, Aug. 30-Sept. 8.

Schöneberg City Hall, John F. Kennedy Place, Berlin — A51

1964, May 30 Engr. Wmk. 304

9N210	A51	20pf dk brn, *cr*	.50	.45

700th anniv. of the Schöneberg district of Berlin. The Senate and House of Representatives of West Berlin meet at Schöneberg City Hall.

Pres. Heinrich Lübke — A51a

1964, July 1 Litho. Unwmk.

9N211	A51a	20pf carmine	.25	.25
9N212	A51a	40pf ultra	.35	.35

See Nos. 9N263-9N264.

Reichstag Building, Berlin — A51b

1964, Sept. 14 Litho. *Perf. 14*

9N213	A51b	20pf lt blue, blk & grn	.50	.45

Kennedy — A51c

1964, Nov. 21 Engr. Wmk. 304

9N214	A51c	40pf dark blue	.50	.45

A52

A52a

Designs (German buildings through 12 centuries): 10pf, Wall pavilion, Zwinger, Dresden. 15pf, Tegel Castle, Berlin. 20pf, Portico, Lorsch. 40pf, Trifels Fortress, Palatinate. 50pf, Castle Gate, Ellwangen. 60pf, Treptow Gate, Neubrandenburg. 70pf, Osthofen Gate, Soest. 80pf, Elling Gate, Weissenburg.

1964-65 Typo. Unwmk.

9N215	A52	10pf brown ('65)	.25	.25
b.		Tête bêche pair	.45	*2.00*
9N216	A52	15pf dk green ('65)	.25	.25
9N217	A52a	20pf brn red ('65)	.25	.25

Engr

9N218	A52a	40pf vio bl ('65)	.60	*1.10*
9N219	A52a	50pf olive bis	1.40	*1.50*
9N220	A52a	60pf rose red	.95	*1.10*
9N221	A52a	70pf dk green ('65)	1.75	*3.50*
9N222	A52a	80pf chocolate	1.75	1.40
		Nos. 9N215-9N222 (8)	7.20	*9.35*

Nos. 9N215-9N218, 9N221 were issued in sheets of 100 and in coils. Every fifth coil stamp has a black control number on the back.

Kaiser Wilhelm Memorial Church — A53

The New Berlin: 15pf, German Opera House, horiz. 20pf, Philharmonic Hall, horiz. 30pf, Jewish Community Center, horiz. 40pf, Regina Martyrum Memorial, horiz. 50pf, Ernst Reuter Square, horiz. 60pf, Europa Center. 70pf, School of Engineering, horiz. 80pf, City Highway. 90pf, Planetarium and observatory, horiz. 1m, Schaeferberg radio tower, Wannsee. 1.10m, University clinic, Steglitz, horiz.

Engraved and Lithographed

1965-66 Unwmk. *Perf. 14*

9N223	A53	10pf multi	.25	.25
9N224	A53	15pf multi	.25	.25
9N225	A53	20pf multi	.25	.25
9N226	A53	30pf multi ('66)	.25	.25
9N227	A53	40pf multi ('66)	.25	.25
9N228	A53	50pf multi	.25	.30
9N229	A53	60pf multi ('66)	.30	.35
9N230	A53	70pf multi ('66)	.45	.45
9N231	A53	80pf multi	.45	.45
9N232	A53	90pf multi ('66)	.50	*.75*
9N233	A53	1m multi ('66)	.50	*.90*
9N234	A53	1.10m multi ('66)	.50	*.95*
		Nos. 9N223-9N234 (12)	4.20	5.40

Nordertor, Flensburg — A54

5pf, Berlin Gate, Stettin. 8pf, Castle, Kaub on the Rhine. 10pf, Wall Pavilion, Zwinger, Dresden. 20pf, Portico, Lorsch. 40pf, Trifels Fortress, Palatinate. 50pf, Castle Gate, Ellwangen. 60pf, Treptow Gate, Neubrandenburg. 70pf, Osthofen Gate, Soest. 80pf, Elling Gate, Weissenburg. 90pf, Zschocke Ladies' Home, Königsberg. 1m, Melanchthon House, Wittenberg. 1.10m, Trinity Hospital, Hildesheim. 1.30m, Tegel Castle, Berlin. 2m, Löwenberg Town Hall, interior view.

1966-69 Engr. *Perf. 14*

9N235	A54	5pf olive	.25	.25
9N236	A54	8pf car rose	.25	.25
9N237	A54	10pf dk brn ('67)	.25	.25
9N238	A54	20pf dk grn ('67)	.25	.25
9N239	A54	30pf yellow grn	.25	.25
9N240	A54	30pf red ('67)	.25	.25
9N241	A54	40pf ol bis ('67)	.55	*.75*
9N242	A54	50pf blue ('67)	.35	*.45*
9N243	A54	60pf dp org ('67)	1.50	*1.90*
9N244	A54	70pf sl grn ('67)	.75	.75
9N245	A54	80pf red brn ('67)	.95	*1.60*
9N246	A54	90pf black	.50	*.75*
9N247	A54	1m dull blue	.50	*.75*
9N248	A54	1.10m red brn	1.40	1.40
9N249	A54	1.30m green ('69)	2.25	2.25
9N250	A54	2m purple	2.25	1.90
		Nos. 9N235-9N250 (16)	12.50	14.00

Brandenburg Gate — A54a

1966-70 Typo. *Perf. 14*

9N251	A54a	10pf chocolate	.25	.25
a.		Bklt. pane of 10 (4 #9N251, 2 #9N252, 4 #9N253)	6.75	12.00
b.		Tête bêche pair	.90	1.10
c.		Bklt. pane of 6 (4 #9N251, 2 #9N253) ('70)	3.00	*4.50*
9N252	A54a	20pf dp green	.25	.25
a.		Bklt. pane of 4 (2 #9N252, 2 #9N253) ('70)	2.25	*3.00*
9N253	A54a	30pf red	.25	.25
a.		Tête bêche pair	1.10	2.40
9N254	A54a	50pf dk blue	.55	.35
9N255	A54a	100pf dk blue ('67)	4.25	4.25
		Nos. 9N251-9N255 (5)	5.55	5.35

Nos. 9N251-9N255 were issued in sheets of 100 and in coils. Every fifth coil stamp has a black control number on the back.

A55

Designs: 10pf, Young Man, by Conrat Meit, 1520. 20pf, The Great Elector Friedrich Wilhelm (1640-88), head from monument by Andreas Schlüter. 30pf, The Evangelist Mark, by Tilman Riemenschneider. 50pf, Head of "Victory" from Brandenburg Gate, by Gottfried Schadow, 1793. 1m, Madonna, by Joseph Anton Feuchtmayer. 1.10m, Jesus and John, wood sculpture, anonymous, c. 1320.

1967 Engr. *Perf. 14*

9N256	A55	10pf sepia & lemon	.25	.25
9N257	A55	20pf sl grn & bluish gray	.25	.25
9N258	A55	30pf brown & olive	.25	.25
9N259	A55	50pf black & gray	.35	.35
9N260	A55	1m blue & chlky blue	.75	.75

Size: 22x40mm

9N261	A55	1.10m brown & buff	1.10	*1.50*
		Nos. 9N256-9N261 (6)	2.95	3.35

Issued to publicize Berlin art treasures.

A56

Berlin Radio Tower and Television Screens

1967, July 19 Litho. and Engr.

9N262	A56	30pf multicolored	.30	.35

25th German Radio, Television and Phonograph Exhibition, Berlin, Aug. 25-Sept. 3.

Pres. Heinrich Lübke — A56a

1967, Oct. 14 Litho.

9N263	A56a	30pf carmine	.25	.25
9N264	A56a	50pf ultra	.35	.45

Old Court Building (Berlin Museum) — A57

1968, Mar. 16 Engr. *Perf. 14*

9N265	A57	30pf black	.30	.35

500th anniv. of the Berlin Court of Appeal.

Turners' Emblem — A58

1968, Apr. 29 Litho. *Perf. 14*

9N266	A58	20pf gray, blk & red	.30	.35

Issued to publicize the German Turner Festival, Berlin, May 28-June 3.

Newspaper Vendor by Christian Wilhelm Allers — A59

19th Century Berliners: 5pf, Hack, by Heinrich Zille, horiz. No. 9N269, Horse omnibus, coachman and passengers, 1890, by C. W. Allers. No. 9N270, Cobbler's apprentice, by Franz Kruger. No. 9N271, Cobbler, by Adolph von Menzel. No. 9N272, Blacksmiths, by Paul Meyerheim. No. 9N273, Three Ladies, by Franz Kruger. 50pf, Strollers at Brandenburg Gate, by Christian W. Allers.

1969 Engr. *Perf. 14*

9N267	A59	5pf black	.25	.25
9N268	A59	10pf dp brown	.25	.25
9N269	A59	10pf brown	.25	.25
9N270	A59	20pf dk olive grn	.25	.25
9N271	A59	20pf green	.25	.25
9N272	A59	30pf dk red brown	.50	.35
9N273	A59	30pf red brown	.50	.35
9N274	A59	50pf ultra	1.25	1.50
		Nos. 9N267-9N274 (8)	3.50	3.45

Souvenir Sheet

Berlin Zoo Animals — A60

Designs: 10pf, Orangutan family. 20pf, White pelicans. 30pf, Gaur and calf. 50pf, Zebra and foal.

Engraved and Lithographed

1969, June 4 *Perf. 14*

9N275	A60	Sheet of 4	1.90	1.90
	a.	10pf bister & black	.45	.45
	b.	20pf light green & black	.45	.45
	c.	30pf lilac rose & black	.45	.45
	d.	50pf blue & black	.45	.45

125th anniversary of the Berlin Zoo. The sheet was sold with a 20pf surtax for the benefit of the Zoo.

Australian Postman — A61

Designs: 20pf, African telephone operator. 30pf, Middle East telecommunications engineer. 50pf, Loading mail on plane.

1969, July 21 Litho. *Perf. 14*

9N276	A61	10pf ol & apple grn	.25	.25
9N277	A61	20pf dk brn, bis & brn	.25	.25
9N278	A61	30pf vio blk & bis	.50	.55
9N279	A61	50pf dk blue & blue	1.10	1.10
		Nos. 9N276-9N279 (4)	2.10	2.15

20th Congress of the Post Office Trade Union Federation, Berlin, July 7-11.

Joseph Joachim — A62

Design: 50pf, Alexander von Humboldt, painting by Joseph Stieler.

1969, Sept. 12 Photo. *Perf. 14*

9N280	A62	30pf multicolored	.50	.40
9N281	A62	50pf multicolored	.70	*1.00*

Cent. of the Berlin Music School and honoring its 1st director, Joseph Joachim (1831-1907), violinist, conductor and composer; Alexander von Humboldt (1769-1859), naturalist and explorer.

1970, Jan. 7

Theodor Fontane, painting by Hanns Fechner.

9N282	A62	20pf multicolored	.40	.30

150th anniv. of the birth of Theodor Fontane (1819-1898), poet and writer.

See No. 9N303.

Film Frame — A63

1970, June 18 Photo. *Perf. 14*

9N283	A63	30pf multicolored	.50	.55

20th International Film Festival.

President Heinemann — A63a

1970-73 Engr. *Perf. 14*

9N284	A63a	5pf dk gray	.25	.25
9N285	A63a	8pf olive bis	.70	.90
9N286	A63a	10pf brown	.25	.25
9N286A	A63a	15pf olive	.25	.25
9N287	A63a	20pf green	.25	.25
9N288	A63a	25pf dp yel grn	.90	.55
9N289	A63a	30pf red brown	.95	.55
9N290	A63a	40pf brown org	.55	.25
9N291	A63a	50pf dark blue	.55	.25
9N292	A63a	60pf blue	.90	.55
9N293	A63a	70pf dk brown	.70	.60
9N294	A63a	80pf slate grn	.90	.90
9N295	A63a	90pf magenta	1.75	2.25
9N296	A63a	1m olive	.90	.70
9N296A	A63a	110pf olive gray	1.10	1.10
9N297	A63a	120pf ocher	1.10	.90
9N298	A63a	130pf ocher	1.60	1.50
9N298A	A63a	140pf dk blue grn	1.60	1.50
9N299	A63a	150pf purple	1.60	.75
9N300	A63a	160pf orange	2.25	1.90
9N300A	A63a	170pf orange	1.60	1.60
9N300B	A63a	190pf dp claret	1.90	2.75
9N301	A63a	2m dp violet	1.90	1.40
		Nos. 9N284-9N301 (23)	24.45	21.90

Issued: 5pf, 1m, 7/23; 10, 20pf, 10/23; 30, 90pf, 2m, 1/7/71; 8, 40, 50, 70, 80pf, 4/8/71; 60pf, 6/25/71; 25pf, 8/27/71; 120, 160pf, 3/8/72; 15, 130pf, 6/20/72; 150pf, 7/5/72; 170pf, 9/11/72; 110, 140, 190pf, 1/16/73.

Symbols of Dance, Theater & Art — A64

1970, Sept. 4 Litho. *Perf. 13½x14*

9N302	A64	30pf gray & multi	.50	.50

20th Berlin Festival Weeks.

Portrait Type of 1969

30pf, Leopold von Ranke, by Julius Schrage.

1970, Oct. 23 Photo. *Perf. 13½x14*

9N303	A62	30pf multicolored	.40	.35

175th anniversary of the birth of Leopold von Ranke (1795-1886), historian.

Imperial Eagle — A64b

1971, Jan. 18 Litho. *Perf. 13½x14*

9N304	A64b	30pf org, red, gray & blk	.55	.55

Metropolitan Train, 1932 — A65

5pf, Suburban train, 1925. 10pf, Street cars, 1890. 20pf, Horsedrawn trolley. 50pf, Street car, 1950. 1m, Subway train, 1971.

1971 Litho. *Perf. 14*

9N305	A65	5pf multicolored	.25	.25
9N306	A65	10pf multicolored	.25	.25
9N307	A65	20pf multicolored	.25	.25
9N308	A65	30pf multicolored	.45	.35
9N309	A65	50pf multicolored	1.60	1.40
9N310	A65	1m multicolored	1.90	1.90
		Nos. 9N305-9N310 (6)	4.70	4.40

Issued: 30pf, 1m, Jan. 18; others, May 3.

Bagpipe Player, by Dürer — A66

1971, May 21 Engr. *Perf. 14*

9N311	A66	10pf black & brown	.45	.30

500th anniversary of the birth of Albrecht Dürer (1471-1528), painter and engraver.

Score from 2nd Brandenburg Concerto and Bach — A67

1971, July 14 Litho. *Perf. 14*

9N312	A67	30pf buff, brn & slate	.70	.60

250th anniv. of 1st performance of Johann Sebastian Bach's 2nd Brandenburg Concerto.

A68

Telecommunications tower, Berlin.

1971, July 14 Photo.

9N313	A68	30pf dk blue, blk & car	.75	.60

Intl. Broadcasting Exhibition, Berlin.

A69

1971, Aug. 27
9N314 A69 25pf multicolored .50 .35

Hermann von Helmholtz (1821-94), scientist. See Nos. 9N332-9N333, 9N341.

Souvenir Sheet

Racing Cars — A70

a, Opel racer. b, Auto Union racer. c, Mercedes-Benz SSKL, 1931. d, Mercedes and Auto Union cars racing on North embankment.

1971, Aug. 27 Litho. *Perf. 14*
9N315 A70 Sheet of 4 1.50 1.50
a. 10pf multi .25 .25
b. 25pf multi .25 .25
c. 30pf multi .35 .25
d. 60pf multi .60 .60

50th anniversary of Avus Race Track.

Accident Prevention — A70a

5pf, "Matches cause fires." 10pf, Broken ladder. 20pf, Hand & circular saw. 25pf, "Alcohol & automobile." 30pf, Safety helmets prevent injury. 40pf, Defective plug. 50pf, Nail sticking from board. 60pf, 70pf, Traffic safety (ball rolling before car). 100pf, Hoisted cargo. 150pf, Fenced-in open manhole.

1971-73 Typo. *Perf. 14*
9N316 A70a 5pf orange .25 .30
9N317 A70a 10pf dk brn .25 .25
a. Bklt. pane, 2 each #9N317-9N318, 9N320-9N321 ('74) 9.00 *9.00*
9N318 A70a 20pf purple .25 .25
9N319 A70a 25pf green .35 .60
9N320 A70a 30pf dk red .35 .30
9N321 A70a 40pf rose cl .35 .40
9N322 A70a 50pf Prus blue 1.90 1.10
9N323 A70a 60pf vio bl 1.90 2.25
9N323A A70a 70pf grn & vio bl 1.40 1.00
9N324 A70a 100pf olive 1.90 1.10
9N325 A70a 150pf red brn 5.75 6.75
Nos. 9N316-9N325 (11) 14.65 14.30

Issued in sheets of 100 and coils. Every fifth coil stamp has a control number on the back. Value, set $29.

Issued: 25pf, 60pf, 9/10; 5pf, 10/29; 10pf, 30pf, 3/8/72; 40pf, 6/20/72; 20pf, 100pf, 7/5/72; 150pf, 9/11/72; 50pf, 1/16/73; 70pf, 6/5/73.

Microscope and Metal Slide — A71

1971, Oct. 26 Photo. *Perf. 14*
9N326 A71 30pf multicolored .50 .35

Materials Testing Laboratory centenary.

Friedrich Gilly, by Gottfried Schadow — A72

1972, Feb. 4 Engr. *Perf. 14*
9N327 A72 30pf black & blue .50 .30

Friedrich Gilly (1772-1800), sculptor.

Grunewaldsee, by Alexander von Riesen — A73

Paintings of Berlin Lakes: 25pf, Wannsee, by Max Liebermann. 30pf, Schlachtensee, by Walter Leistikow.

1972, Apr. 14 Photo. *Perf. 14*
9N328 A73 10pf blue & multi .25 .25
9N329 A73 25pf green & multi .50 .55
9N330 A73 30pf black & multi .85 .60
Nos. 9N328-9N330 (3) 1.60 1.40

A74

1972, May 18
9N331 A74 60pf violet & blk 1.00 1.00

E. T. A. Hoffmann (1776-1822), writer and composer. (Portrait by Wilhelm Hensel.)

Portrait Type of 1971

Designs: No. 9N332, Max Liebermann (1847-1935), self-portrait. No. 9N333, Karl August, Duke of Hardenberg (1750-1822), Prussian statesman, by J. H. W. Tischbein.

1972 Photo. *Perf. 14*
9N332 A69 40pf multicolored .65 .45
9N333 A69 40pf multicolored .55 .45

Issued: No. 9N332, 7/18; No. 9N333, 11/10.

A75

1972, Oct. 20 Engr. & Litho.
9N334 A75 20pf Stamp-printing press .45 .30

Stamp Day 1972, and for the 5th National Youth Philatelic Exhib., Berlin, Oct. 26-29.

Streetcar, 1907 A76

No. 9N336, Double-decker bus, 1919. No. 9N337, Double-decker bus, 1925. No. 9N338, Electrobus, 1933. No. 9N339, Double-decker bus, 1970. No. 9N340, Elongated bus, 1973.

1973, Apr. 30 Litho. *Perf. 14*
9N335 A76 20pf gray & multi .35 .30
9N336 A76 30pf gray & multi .70 .40
9N337 A76 40pf gray & multi .90 .60

1973, Sept. 14
9N338 A76 20pf gray & multi .35 .30
9N339 A76 30pf gray & multi 1.00 .40
9N340 A76 40pf gray & multi .90 .60
Nos. 9N335-9N340 (6) 4.20 2.60

Public transportation in Berlin.

Portrait Type of 1971

Design: 40pf, Ludwig Tieck (1773-1853), poet and writer, by Carl Christian Vogel von Vogelstein.

1973, May 25 Photo. *Perf. 14*
9N341 A69 40pf multicolored .55 .40

Johann Joachim Quantz (1697-1773), Flutist and Composer — A77

1973, June 12 Engr. *Perf. 14*
9N342 A77 40pf black .75 .60

Souvenir Sheet

50 Years of Broadcasting — A78

a, Speaker, set, 1926. b, Hans Bredow. c, Girl, TV, tape recorder. d, TV camera.

1973, Aug. 23 Litho. *Perf. 14*
9N343 A78 Sheet of 4 3.75 3.75
a. A78 20pf multicolored .90 .60
b. A78 30pf multicolored .90 .90
c. A78 40pf multicolored .90 .90
d. A78 70pf multicolored .90 1.25

50 years of German broadcasting. Sold for 1.80m.

Georg W. von Knobelsdorff A79

1974, Feb. 15 Engr. *Perf. 14*
9N344 A79 20pf chocolate .35 .30

275th anniversary of the birth of Georg Wenzelslaus von Knobelsdorff (1699-1753), architect.

Gustav R. Kirchhoff — A80

1974, Feb. 15 Litho. & Engr.
9N345 A80 30pf gray & dk grn .35 .35

Sesquicentennial of the birth of Gustav Robert Kirchhoff (1824-1887), physicist.

Airlift Memorial, Allied Flags — A81

1974, Apr. 17 Photo. *Perf. 14*
9N346 A81 90pf multicolored 2.00 1.25

End of the Allied airlift into Berlin, 25th anniv.

Adolf Slaby and Waves — A82

1974, Apr. 17 Litho. *Perf. 14*
9N347 A82 40pf black & red .55 .40

125th anniversary of the birth of Adolf Slaby (1849-1913), radio pioneer.

School Seal Showing Athena and Hermes — A83

1974, July 13 Photo. *Perf. 14*
9N348 A83 50pf multicolored .70 .45

400th anniversary of the Gray Brothers' School, a secondary Franciscan school.

Berlin-Tegel Airport — A84

Lithographed and Engraved

1974, Oct. 15 *Perf. 14*
9N349 A84 50pf multicolored .80 .60

Opening of Berlin-Tegel Airport and Terminal, Nov. 1, 1974.

Venus, by F. E. Meyer, c. 1775 — A85

Berlin Porcelain: 40pf, "Astronomy," by W. C. Meyer, c. 1772. 50pf, "Justice," by J. G. Müller, c. 1785.

1974, Oct. 29 Litho. *Perf. 14*
9N350 A85 30pf carmine & multi .45 .45
9N351 A85 40pf carmine & multi .55 .55
9N352 A85 50pf carmine & multi .70 .70
Nos. 9N350-9N352 (3) 1.70 1.70

Gottfried Schadow — A86

1975, Jan. 15 Engr. *Perf. 14*
9N353 A86 50pf maroon .75 .55

Johann Gottfried Schadow (1764-1850), sculptor.

S.S. Princess Charlotte A87

Ships: 40pf, S.S. Siegfried. 50pf, S.S. Sperber. 60pf, M.S. Vaterland. 70pf, M.S. Moby Dick.

1975, Feb. 14 Litho. *Perf. 14*

9N354	A87	30pf gray & multi	.60	.30
9N355	A87	40pf olive & multi	.60	.30
9N356	A87	50pf ultra & multi	.80	.60
9N357	A87	60pf red brn & multi	.85	.60
9N358	A87	70pf dk blue & multi	1.10	1.00
		Nos. 9N354-9N358 (5)	3.95	2.80

Berlin passenger ships

Industry — A87a

5pf, Symphonie satellite. 10pf, Electric train. 20pf, Old Weser lighthouse. 30pf, Rescue helicopter. 40pf, Space shuttle. 50pf, Radar station. 60pf, X-ray machine. 70pf, Shipbuilding. 80pf, Tractor. 100pf, Coal excavator. 110pf, TV camera. 120pf, Chemical plant. 130pf, Brewery. 140pf, Heating plant. 150pf, Power shovel. 160pf, Blast furnace. 180pf, Payloader. 190pf, As #9N371. 200pf, Oil drill platform. 230pf, Frankfurt airport. 250pf, Airport. 300pf, Electric railroad. 500pf, Radio telescope.

1975-82 Engr. *Perf. 14*

9N359	A87a	5pf ol grn	.25	.25
9N360	A87a	10pf red lilac	.25	.25
9N361	A87a	20pf red org	.25	.25
9N362	A87a	30pf dp vio	.35	.25
9N363	A87a	40pf pck blue	.50	.25
9N364	A87a	50pf rose	.50	.25
9N365	A87a	60pf red	.80	.35
9N366	A87a	70pf blue	.90	.45
9N367	A87a	80pf blue grn	.90	.25
9N368	A87a	100pf brown	.90	.45
9N368A	A87a	110pf dp clar	1.40	1.10
9N369	A87a	120pf blue vio	1.25	.90
9N369A	A87a	130pf carmine	2.25	1.10
9N370	A87a	140pf red	1.25	1.25
9N371	A87a	150pf red brown	3.00	1.10
9N372	A87a	160pf dull green	2.90	1.25
9N373	A87a	180pf brown	3.00	1.90
9N373A	A87a	190pf org brn	3.00	2.10
9N374	A87a	200pf dp clar	1.60	.45
9N375	A87a	230pf lilac	2.40	1.90
9N375A	A87a	250pf green	4.00	2.10
9N375B	A87a	300pf bister	4.00	2.10
9N376	A87a	500pf dark blue	5.75	3.75
		Nos. 9N359-9N376 (23)	41.40	24.00

Issued: 40, 50, 100pf, 5/15; 10, 30, 70pf, 8/14; 80, 120, 160pf, 10/15; 5, 140, 200pf, 11/14; 20, 500pf, 2/17/76; 60pf, 11/16/78; 230pf, 5/17/79; 150, 180pf, 7/12/79; 110, 130, 300pf, 6/16/82; 190, 250pf, 7/15/82.

Ferdinand Sauerbruch — A88

Lithographed and Engraved

1975, May 15 *Perf. 13½x14*
9N379 A88 50pf dull red & dk brn .75 .55

Ferdinand Sauerbruch (1875-1951) surgeon, birth centenary.

Gymnasts' Emblem — A89

1975, May 15 Photo. *Perf. 14*
9N380 A89 40pf grn, gold & blk .55 .35

6th Gymnaestrada, Berlin, July 1-5.

Lovis Corinth (1858-1925), Self-portrait, 1900 — A90

1975, July 15 Photo. *Perf. 14*
9N381 A90 50pf multicolored .70 .50

Architecture — A91

Design: Houses, Naunynstrasse, Berlin-Kreuzberg.

1975, July 15 Litho. & Engr.
9N382 A91 50pf multicolored .75 .60

European Architectural Heritage Year.

Paul Löbe and Reichstag A92

1975, Nov. 14 Engr. *Perf. 14*
9N383 A92 50pf copper red .70 .50

Paul Löbe (1875-1967), president of German Parliament 1920-1932, birth centenary.

Grain — A93

1976, Jan. 5 Photo. *Perf. 14*
9N384 A93 70pf green & yellow .75 .60

Green Week International Agricultural Exhibition, Berlin, 50th anniversary.

Hockey A94

1976, May 13 Engr. *Perf. 14*
9N385 A94 30pf green .70 .35

Women's World Hockey Championships.

Treble Clef — A95

1976, May 13 Photo.
9N386 A95 40pf multicolored .75 .45

German Choir Festival.

Berlin Fire Brigade Emblem — A96

1976, May 13 Litho.
9N387 A96 50pf red & multi 1.10 .70

Berlin Fire Brigade, 125th anniversary.

Berlin Views — A97

Designs: 30pf, Sailboat on Havel River. 40pf, Spandau Castle. 50pf, Tiergarten.

1976, Nov. 16 Engr. *Perf. 14*

9N388	A97	30pf blue & blk	.45	.35
9N389	A97	40pf brown & blk	.65	.35
9N390	A97	50pf green & blk	.70	.35
		Nos. 9N388-9N390 (3)	1.80	1.05

See Nos. 9N422-9N424.

Castles — A97a

10pf, Glücksburg. 20pf, 190pf, Pfaueninsel. 25pf, Gemen. 30pf, Ludwigstein. 40pf, Eltz. 50pf, Neuschwanstein. 60pf, Marksburg. 70pf, Mespelbrunn. 90pf, Vischering. 200pf, Bürresheim. 210pf, Schwanenburg. 230pf, Lichtenberg.

1977-79 Typo. *Perf. 14*

9N391	A97a	10pf gray blue	.25	.25
a.		Bklt. pane, 4 #9N391, 2 each #9N394, 9N396	8.00	*10.50*
b.		Bklt. pane, 4 #9N391, 2 #9N394, 2 #9N440	4.00	*6.75*
c.		Bklt. pane, 4 #9N391, 2 #9N440, 2 #9N442	8.75	*15.00*
d.		Bklt. pane, 2 each #9N391, 9N394, 9N440-9N441	15.00	*22.50*
9N392	A97a	20pf orange	.25	.25
9N393	A97a	25pf crimson	.35	.35
9N394	A97a	30pf olive	.25	.25
9N395	A97a	40pf blue green	.30	.25
9N396	A97a	50pf rose car	.55	.25
9N397	A97a	60pf brown	.95	.45
9N398	A97a	70pf blue	.95	.45
9N399	A97a	90pf dark blue	.85	.75
9N400	A97a	190pf red brown	1.40	1.40
9N401	A97a	200pf green	1.40	1.40
9N402	A97a	210pf red brown	2.00	1.50
9N403	A97a	230pf dark green	2.00	1.50
		Nos. 9N391-9N403 (13)	11.50	9.05

Issued in sheets of 100 and coils. Every fifth coil stamp has a control number on the back.

Issued: 60pf, 200pf, 1/13; 40pf, 190pf, 2/16; 10pf, 20pf, 30pf, 4/14; 50pf, 70pf, 5/17; 230pf, 11/16/78; 25pf, 90pf, 1/11/79; 210pf, 2/14/79.

See Nos. 9N438-9N445.

Eugenie d'Alton, by Rausch — A98

1977, Jan. 13 Photo. *Perf. 14*
9N404 A98 50pf violet black .70 .50

Christian Daniel Rausch (1777-1857), sculptor, birth bicentenary.

Eduard Gaertner (1801-77), Painter — A99

1977, Feb. 16 Litho. & Engr.
9N405 A99 40pf lt grn, grn & blk .50 .30

Fountain, by Georg Kolbe — A100

1977, Apr. 14 Photo. *Perf. 14*
9N406 A100 30pf dark olive .45 .30

Georg Kolbe (1877-1947), sculptor.

"Bear each other's burdens" A101

1977, May 17 Litho. *Perf. 14*
9N407 A101 40pf green blk & yel .50 .30

17th meeting of German Protestants (Evangelical Synod), Berlin.

Patent Office, Berlin-Kreuzberg — A102

1977, July 13 Litho. & Engr.
9N408 A102 60pf gray & red 1.10 .65

Centenary of German patent laws.

Telephones, 1905 and 1977 — A103

1977, July 13 Litho.
9N409 A103 50pf multicolored 1.75 1.00

International Broadcasting Exhibition, Berlin, Aug. 26-Sept. 4, and centenary of telephone in Germany.

Painting by George Grosz (1893-1959) — A104

1977, July 13
9N410 A104 70pf multicolored .90 .90

15th European Art Exhibition, Berlin, Aug. 14-Oct. 16.

Rhinecanthus Aculeatus — A105

Designs: 30pf, Paddlefish. 40pf, Tortoise. 50pf, Rhinoceros iguana. Designs include statue of iguanodon from Aquarium entrance.

1977, Aug. 16 Photo. *Perf. 14*
9N411 A105 20pf multicolored .45 .45
9N412 A105 30pf multicolored .70 .60
9N413 A105 40pf multicolored .95 .75
9N414 A105 50pf multicolored 1.40 .90
Nos. 9N411-9N414 (4) 3.50 2.70

25th anniv. of the reopening of Berlin Aquarium.

Walter Kollo (1878-1940), Composer — A106

1978, Jan. 12 Engr. *Perf. 14*
9N415 A106 50pf brn, red & dk brn .85 .60

Chamber of Commerce Emblem — A107

1978, Apr. 13 Engr. *Perf. 14*
9N416 A107 90pf dk blue & red 1.25 1.25

American Chamber of Commerce in Germany, 75th anniversary.

Albrecht von Graefe — A108

1978, May 22 Engr. *Perf. 14*
9N417 A108 30pf red brn & blk .55 .35

Dr. von Graefe (1828-70) ophthalmologist.

Friedrich Ludwig Jahn — A109

1978, July 13 Engr. *Perf. 14*
9N418 A109 50pf dk carmine .75 .55

Friedrich Ludwig Jahn (1778-1852), founder of organized gymnastics.

Swimmers — A110

1978, Aug. 17 Litho. *Perf. 14*
9N419 A110 40pf multicolored 1.00 .80

3rd World Swimming Championships, Berlin, Aug. 18-28.

The Boat, by Karl Hofer — A111

1978, Oct. 12 Photo. *Perf. 14*
9N420 A111 50pf multicolored .70 .55

Karl Hofer (1878-1955), painter.

National Library A112

1978, Nov. 16 Engr. *Perf. 14*
9N421 A112 90pf red & olive 1.40 .95

Opening of new National Library building.

Berlin Views — A112a

Designs: 40pf, Belvedere, Charlottenburg Castle. 50pf, Shell House on Landwehr Canal. 60pf, Village Church, Alt-Lichtenrade.

1978, Nov. 16
9N422 A112a 40pf blue green & blk .60 .35
9N423 A112a 50pf lilac & blk .75 .60
9N424 A112a 60pf brown & blk .90 .70
Nos. 9N422-9N424 (3) 2.25 1.65

International Conference Center — A113

Photogravure and Engraved

1979, Feb. 14 *Perf. 14*
9N425 A113 60pf multicolored 1.10 .65

Opening of Intl. Conference Center in Berlin.

German Eagles — A114

1979, May 17 Litho. *Perf. 14*
9N426 A114 60pf multi 1.40 1.00

Cent. of German Natl. Printing Bureau.

TV Screen, Emblem — A115

1979, July 12 Photo. *Perf. 14*
9N427 A115 60pf multi 1.00 .75

Intl. Broadcasting Exhibition, Berlin.

Target and Arrows A116

1979, July 12
9N428 A116 50pf multicolored .70 .50

World Archery Championships, Berlin.

Moses Mendelssohn A117

1979, Aug. 9 Engr. *Perf. 14*
9N429 A117 90pf black 1.25 .75

Mendelssohn (1729-86), philosopher.

Gas Lamp — A118

Historic Street Lanterns: 40pf, Carbon arc lamp. 50pf, Hanging gas lamps. 60pf, 5-armed candelabra.

1979, Aug. 9 Litho.
9N430 A118 10pf multicolored .35 .25
9N431 A118 40pf multicolored .75 .60
9N432 A118 50pf multicolored 1.10 .60
9N433 A118 60pf multicolored 1.10 1.00
Nos. 9N430-9N433 (4) 3.30 2.45

300 years of street lighting in Berlin.

Orchid A119

1979, Aug. 9
9N434 A119 50pf multicolored .85 .55

Botanical Gardens, Berlin, 300th anniv.

Berlin Poster Columns, 125th Anniversary A120

Lithographed and Engraved

1979, Nov. 14 *Perf. 14*
9N435 A120 50pf multicolored 1.20 .65

Castles — A120a

35pf, Lichtenstein. 40pf, Wolfsburg. 50pf, Inzlingen. 60pf, Rheydt. 80pf, Wilhelmsthal. 120pf, Charlottenburg. 280pf, Ahrensburg. 300pf, Herrenhausen.

1979-82 Typo. *Perf. 14*
9N438 A120a 35pf red brn .30 .30
9N439 A120a 40pf brown .55 .30
9N440 A120a 50pf green .60 .30
9N441 A120a 60pf rose .90 .45
9N442 A120a 80pf olive .60 .30
9N443 A120a 120pf dk pur 1.00 .90
9N444 A120a 280pf blue 3.50 2.25
9N445 A120a 300pf orange 3.50 2.25
Nos. 9N438-9N445 (8) 10.95 7.05

Issued: 60pf, 11/14; 40pt, 50pf, 2/14/80; 35pf, 80pf, 30pf, 6/16/82; 120pf, 280pf, 7/15/82.

World Map Showing Continental Drift — A121

1980, Feb. 14 Litho. *Perf. 14*
9N451 A121 60pf multicolored 1.40 1.00

Alfred Wegener (1880-1930), geophysicist and meteorologist; founded theory of continental drift.

German Catholics Day — A122

Cardinal Count Preysing (1880-1950).

1980, May 8 Engr. *Perf. 14*
9N452 A122 50pf blk & car rose .70 .50

Prussian Museum, Berlin, 150th Anniv. A123

Designs: 40pf, Angel, enamel medallion, 12th cent. 60pf, Monks Reading, oak sculpture, by Ernest Barlach (1870-1938).

1980, July 10 Litho. *Perf. 14*
9N453 A123 40pf multicolored .60 .40
9N454 A123 60pf multicolored .90 .50

Von Steuben Leading Troops — A124

1980, Aug. 14 **Litho.** ***Perf. 14***
9N455 A124 40pf multicolored 1.00 .55

Friedrich Wilhelm von Steuben (1730-94).

Robert Stolz (1880-1975), Composer A125

1980, Aug. 14
9N456 A125 60pf dk blue & bis 1.00 .75

Lilienthal Memorial — A126

Designs: 50pf, Grosse Neugierde Memorial, 1835. 60pf, Lookout tower, Grunewald Memorial to Kaiser Wilhelm I.

1980, Nov. 13 **Engr.** ***Perf. 14***

9N457	A126 40pf dk green & blk	.75	.35
9N458	A126 50pf brown & blk	.80	.75
9N459	A126 60pf dk blue & blk	1.25	.75
	Nos. 9N457-9N459 (3)	2.80	1.85

Von Gontard and Kleist Park Colonnades, Berlin — A127

1981, Jan. 15 **Litho.** ***Perf. 14***
9N460 A127 50pf multicolored .90 .60

Karl Philipp von Gontard (1731-91), architect.

Achim von Arnim (1781-1831), Poet — A128

1981, Jan. 15 **Engr.**
9N461 A128 60pf dark green .80 .55

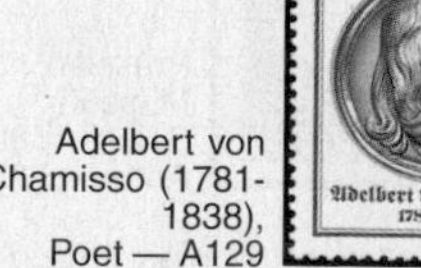
Adelbert von Chamisso (1781-1838), Poet — A129

1981, Jan. 15 **Litho.**
9N462 A129 60pf brn & gldn brn .80 .55

Berlin-Kreuzberg, Liberation Monument, 1813 — A130

1981, Feb. 12 **Engr.** ***Perf. 14***
9N463 A130 40pf brown 1.10 .75

Karl Friedrich Schinkel (1781-1841), architect, 400th anniversary of birth.

Arts and Science Medal, Awarded 1842-1933 — A131

1981, July 10 **Litho.** ***Perf. 14***
9N464 A131 40pf multicolored .75 .55

"Prussia — an attempt at a balance" exhibition.

Amor and Psyche, by Reinhold Begas (1831-1911) A132

1981, July 16 **Photo.**
9N465 A132 50pf multicolored .75 .55

Intl. Telecommunications Exhibition — A133

1981, July 16 **Litho.**
9N466 A133 60pf multicolored 1.25 .75

Peter Beuth (1781-1853), Constitutional Law Expert — A134

Lithographed and Engraved

1981, Nov. 12 ***Perf. 14***
9N467 A134 60pf gold & black .75 .60

Nijinsky, by Georg Kolbe, 1914 — A135

20th Century Sculptures: 60pf, Mother Earth II, by Ernst Barlach, 1920. 90pf, Flora Kneeling, by Richard Scheibe, 1930.

1981, Nov. 12 **Photo.**

9N468	A135 40pf multicolored	.55	.35
9N469	A135 60pf multicolored	.90	.60
9N470	A135 90pf multicolored	1.25	1.00
	Nos. 9N468-9N470 (3)	2.70	1.95

750th Anniv. of Spandau A136

Lithographed and Engraved

1982, Feb. 18 ***Perf. 14***
9N471 A136 60pf multicolored 1.25 .90

Berlin Philharmonic Centenary — A137

Lithographed and Embossed

1982, Apr. 15 ***Perf. 14***
9N472 A137 60pf multicolored 1.10 .60

Salzburg Emigration to Prussia, 250th Anniv. — A138

& 1982, May 5 **Litho.** **Engr.**
9N473 A138 50pf multicolored .75 .55

Italian Stone Carriers, by Max Pechstein — A139

80pf, Two Girls Bathing, by Otto Mueller.

1982, July 15 **Litho.** ***Perf. 14***

9N474	A139 50pf multicolored	.75	.55
9N475	A139 80pf multicolored	1.10	.80

Villa Borsig — A140

60pf, Sts. Peter and Paul Church. 80pf, Villa von der Heydt.

1982, Nov. 10 **Engr.** ***Perf. 14***

9N476	A140 50pf shown	1.10	.70
9N477	A140 60pf multicolored	1.10	.80
9N478	A140 80pf multicolored	1.50	.90
	Nos. 9N476-9N478 (3)	3.70	2.40

State Theater, Charlottenburg, 1790 — A141

1982, Nov. 10 **Litho. & Engr.**
9N479 A141 80pf multicolored 1.60 1.10

Carl Gotthard Langhans (1732-1808), architect.

A142

Various street pumps and fire hydrants, 1900.

1983, Jan. 13 **Litho.** ***Perf. 14***

9N480	A142 50pf multi	1.10	.75
9N481	A142 60pf multi	1.40	.75
9N482	A142 80pf multi	1.60	1.25
9N483	A142 120pf multi	2.25	2.00
	Nos. 9N480-9N483 (4)	6.35	4.75

A142a

1983, Feb. 8 **Engr.** ***Perf. 14***
9N484 A142a 80pf dark brown 1.75 1.40

Berlin-Koblenz Telegraph Service sesquicentennial.

Portrait of Barbara Campanini, 1745, by Antoine Pesne (1683-1757) A143

1983, May 5 **Photo.** ***Perf. 14***
9N485 A143 50pf multicolored .75 .60

Joachim Ringelnatz (1883-1934), Painter and Writer — A144

1983, July 14 **Litho.** ***Perf. 14***
9N486 A144 50pf Silhouette .85 .70

Intl. Radio Exhibition, Sept. 2-11 — A145

80pf, Nipkow's phototelegraphy diagram.

1983, July 14
9N487 A145 80pf multicolored 1.50 1.10

Ancient Artwork, Berlin Museum A146

30pf, Bust of Queen Cleopatra VII, 69-30 B.C. 50pf, Statue of Egyptian Couple, Giza, 2400 B.C. 60pf, Stone God with Beaded Turban, Mexico, 300 B.C. 80pf, Enamel Plate, 16th cent.

1984, Jan. 12 Litho. *Perf. 14*

9N488 A146 30pf multicolored .85 .70
9N489 A146 50pf multicolored 1.10 1.00
9N490 A146 60pf multicolored 1.40 1.25
9N491 A146 80pf multicolored 1.90 1.40
Nos. 9N488-9N491 (4) 5.25 4.35

Electricity Centenary — A147

Design: Allegorical figure holding light bulb (symbol of electric power).

1984, May 8 Litho. *Perf. 14*

9N492 A147 50pf black & org .90 .65

Conference Emblem — A148

1984, May 8

9N493 A148 60pf multicolored .85 .60

European Ministers of Culture, 4th Conf.

Erich Klausener (1885-1934), Chairman of Catholic Action — A149

1984, May 8 Engr. *Perf. 14x13½*

9N494 A149 80pf green 1.10 .75

Alfred Brehm (1829-1884), Zoologist — A150

Lithographed and Engraved

1984, Apr. 18 *Perf. 14*

9N495 A150 80pf Brehm, white stork 1.60 .95

Ernst Ludwig Heim (1747-1834), Botanist — A151

1984, Aug. 21 Engr. *Perf. 14*

9N496 A151 50pf lake & blk .85 .75

Sunflowers, by Karl Schmidt-Rottluff (1884-1976) A152

1984, Nov. 8 Litho. *Perf. 14*

9N497 A152 60pf multi .85 .70

Bettina von Arnim (1785-1859), Writer — A153

1985, Feb. 21 Litho. & Engr.

9N498 A153 50pf multicolored .85 .75

Wilhelm von Humboldt (1767-1835), Statesman A154

1985, Feb. 21 Engr.

9N499 A154 80pf blue, blk & red 1.25 1.10

1985 Berlin Horticultural Show — A155

1985, Apr. 16 Litho. *Perf. 14*

9N500 A155 80pf Symbolic flower 1.20 .85

Berlin Bourse, 300th Anniv. A156

1985, May 7 Litho. & Engr.

9N501 A156 50pf multicolored 1.10 .80

Otto Klemperer (1885-1973), Conductor — A157

1985, May 7 Engr.

9N502 A157 60pf dp blue violet 1.10 .85

Telefunken Camera, 1936 — A158

1985, July 16 Litho. *Perf. 14*

9N503 A158 80pf multicolored 1.60 1.50

German Television, 50th anniv., Intl. Telecommunications Exhibition, Berlin.

9th World Gynecological Congress — A159

Design: Emblem of the Intl. Federation for Gynecology and birth aid.

1985, July 16 Photo. *Perf. 13½x14*

9N504 A159 60pf pale yel, ap grn & dp grn .85 .85

Edict of Potsdam, 300th Anniv. A160

Lithographed and Engraved

1985, Oct. 15 *Perf. 14*

9N505 A160 50pf dk bluish lilac .75 .75

Kurt Tucholsky (1890-1935), Novelist, Journalist — A161

1985, Nov. 12 Litho. *Perf. 14*

9N506 A161 80pf multi 1.60 1.10

Wilhelm Furtwangler (1886-1954), Composer — A162

Score from Sonata in D Sharp.

Lithographed and Engraved

1986, Jan. 16 *Perf. 14*

9N507 A162 80pf multi 1.75 1.40

Ludwig Mies van der Rohe (1886-1969), Architect — A163

1986, Feb. 13

9N508 A163 50pf multi 1.10 .95

New Natl. Gallery, Berlin.

16th European Communities Day — A164

1986, Apr. 10 Litho. *Perf. 14*

9N509 A164 60pf Flags .95 .75

Leopold von Ranke (1795-1886), Historian — A165

Gottfried Benn (1886-1956), Writer and Physician — A166

1986, May 5 Litho.

9N510 A165 80pf brn blk & tan 1.50 .95

Engr.

9N511 A166 80pf brt blue 1.50 .95

Portals and Gateways A167

50pf, Charlotteburg Gate. 60pf, Gryphon Gate, Glienicke Castle. 80pf, Elephant Gate, Berlin Zoo.

1986, June 20 Litho. & Engr.

9N512 A167 50pf multicolored 1.20 1.20
9N513 A167 60pf multicolored 1.20 1.20
9N514 A167 80pf multicolored 1.40 1.40
Nos. 9N512-9N514 (3) 3.80 3.80

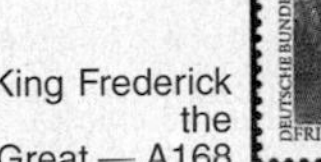

King Frederick the Great — A168

Painting: The Flute Concert (detail), by Adolph von Menzel.

1986, Aug. 14 Litho. *Perf. 14*

9N515 A168 80pf multicolored 1.50 1.20

Famous Women — A168a

Designs: 5pf, Emma Ihrer (1857-1911), politician, labor leader. 10pf, Paula Modersohn-Becker (1876-1907), painter. 20pf, Cilly Aussem (1909-63), tennis champion. 40pf, Maria Sibylla Merian. 50pf, Christine Teusch. 60pf, Dorothea Erxleben (1715-62), physician. 80pf, Clara Schumann. 100pf, Therese Giehse (1898-1975), actress. 130pf, Lise Meitner (1878-1968), physicist. 140pf, Cecile Vogt (1875-1962), neurologist. 170pf, Hannah Arendt (1906-75), American political scientist. 180pf, Lotte Lehmann (1888-1976), soprano. 240pf, Mathilde Franziska Anneke, (1817-84), American author. 250pf, Queen Louise of Prussia (1776-1810). 300pf, Fanny Hensel (1805-1847), composer-conductor. 350pf, Hedwig Dransfeld (1871-1925), women's rights activist. 500pf, Alice Salomon (1872-1948), feminist and social activist.

Type A168a

1986-89 Engr. *Perf. 14*

9N516	5pf bluish gray & org brn	.35	*2.00*
9N517	10pf vio & yel brn	.35	*1.40*
9N518	20pf lake & Prus bl	1.40	*3.50*
9N519	40pf dp bl & dk lil rose	1.10	*3.50*
9N520	50pf gray ol & Prus bl	1.75	*2.50*
9N521	60pf dp vio & grnsh blk	1.00	*3.50*
9N522	80pf dk grn & lt red brn	1.10	*2.50*
9N523	100pf dk red & grnsh blk	1.75	1.40
9N524	130pf Prus bl & dk vio	3.50	*11.00*
9N525	140pf blk & dk ol bis	4.25	*10.50*
9N526	170pf gray grn & dk brn	2.10	*8.50*
9N527	180pf bl & brn vio	3.25	*12.00*
9N528	240pf Prus bl & yel brn	2.75	*12.00*
9N529	250pf dp lil rose & dp bl	7.25	*20.00*
9N530	300pf dk vio & sage grn	7.00	*17.50*
9N531	350pf gray grn & lake	5.00	*14.00*
9N532	500pf slate grn & brt ver	7.75	*32.50*
	Nos. 9N516-9N532 (17)	51.65	*158.30*

Issued: 50pf, 80pf, 11/1/86; 40pf, 9/17/87; 10pf, 4/4/88; 20pf, 130pf, 5/5/88; 60pf, 100pf, 170pf, 240pf, 350pf, 11/10/88; 500pf, 1/12/89; 5pf, 2/9/89; 180pf, 250pf, 7/13/89; 140pf, 300pf, 8/10/89.

Berlin 750th Anniv. — A168b

Designs: a, Berlin, 1650, engraving by Caspar Merian. b, Charlottenburg Castle, c. 1830. c, AEG Company turbine construction building, by architect Walter Behrens, 1909. d, Philharmonic Concert Hall and Chamber Music Rooms on the Kemperplatz, 1987.

1987, Jan. 15 Litho. *Perf. 14*

9N536 A168b 80pf like #1496 1.90 1.50

Souvenir Sheet

Perf. 14x14½

9N537 Sheet of 4 4.25 4.25
- *a.* A168b 40pf multicolored .90 .75
- *b.* A168b 50pf multicolored .90 .75
- *c.* A168b 60pf multicolored .90 .90
- *d.* A168b 80pf multicolored 1.00 1.25

No. 9N537 contains four 43x25mm stamps.

Louise Schroeder (1887-1957), Politican — A169

1987, Feb. 12 Engr. *Perf. 14*

9N538 A169 50pf sep & red 1.10 1.10

Settlement of Bohemians at Rixdorf, 250th Anniv. — A170

Bohemian refugees, bas-relief detail from monument to King Friedrich Wilhelm I of Prussia, 1912.

1987, May 5 Litho. & Engr.

9N539 A170 50pf sep & pale gray grn .80 .90

1987 Intl. Architecture Exhibition — A171

1987, May 5 Litho. *Perf. 14x14½*

9N540 A171 80pf lt ultra, sil & blk 1.20 1.10

14th Int'l. Botanical Congress — A172

1987, July 16 Litho. *Perf. 14*

9N541 A172 60pf multicolored .85 .90

Int'l. Radio Exhibition A173

80pf, Gramophone, compact disc.

1987, Aug. 20

9N542 A173 80pf multi 1.10 .95

Historic Sites and Objects — A174

Designs: 5pf, Brunswick Lion. 10pf, Frankfurt Airport. 20pf, No. 9N550, Queen Nefertiti, bust, Egyptian Museum, Berlin. 30pf, Corner tower, Celle Castle, 14th cent. 40pf, Chile House, Hamburg. 50pf, Filigree tracery on spires, Freiburg Cathedral. 60pf, Bavaria Munich, bronze statue above the Theresienwiese, Hall of Fame. No. 9N551, Heligoland. 80pf, Entrance to Zollern II, coal mine, Dortmund. 100pf, Altotting Chapel, Bavaria. 120pf, Schleswig Cathedral. 140pf, Bronze flagon from Reinheim. 300pf, Hambach Castle. 350pf, Externsteine Bridge near Horn-Bad Meinberg.

Type A174

1987-90 Typo. *Perf. 14*

9N543 5pf Prus bl & gray .30 *.45*

9N544 10pf lt chalky bl & slate bl .35 .35

9N545 20pf dull blue & tan .35 *.75*

9N546 30pf aqua & org brn .05 .06

9N547 40pf ultra, dk red brn & org red 1.25 *2.10*

9N548 50pf ultra & yel brn 1.50 1.10

9N549 60pf cob & pale gray 1.50 1.10

9N550 70pf dull bl & fawn 1.50 *2.50*

9N551 70pf vio bl & henna brn 2.10 *4.50*

9N552 80pf cob & pale gray 1.50 1.10
- *a.* Bklt. pane of 8 (4 10pf, 2 50pf, 2 80pf) ('89) 22.50 *52.50*

9N553 100pf brt bluish grn & olive bis 1.10 *1.50*
- *a.* Bklt. pane of 8 (2 each 10pf, 60pf, 80pf, 100pf) 45.00 *90.00*

9N554 120pf brn org & lt grnsh bl 2.25 *3.50*

9N555 140pf tan & lt grn 2.25 *4.25*

9N556 300pf dk red brn & tan 4.50 4.50

9N557 350pf brt ultra & ol bis 4.50 *7.50*

Nos. 9N543-9N557 (15) 25.90 36.15

Issued: 30pf, 50pf, 60pf, 80pf, 11/6/87; 10pf, 300pf, 1/14/88; No. 9N550, 120pf, 7/14/88; 20pf, 140pf, 1/12/89; 100pf, 350pf, 2/9/89; 5pf, 2/15/90; No. 9N551, 6/21/90.

European Culture — A175

1988, Jan. 14 Litho. *Perf. 14*

9N568 A175 80pf Berlin Bear 1.50 1.25

Urania Science Museum, Cent. A176

1988, Feb. 18

9N569 A176 50pf multicolored 1.25 1.00

A177

Design: Thoroughbred Foal, bronze sculpture by Renee Sintenis (1888-1965).

1988, Feb. 18

9N570 A177 60pf multicolored .90 .90

A178

Design: The Great Elector with Family in Berlin Castle Gardens.

1988, May 5 Litho. & Engr.

9N571 A178 50pf multicolored 1.10 .95

The Great Elector of Brandenburg (d. 1688).

Intl. Monetary Fund and World Bank Congress, Berlin — A179

1988, Aug. 11 Litho.

9N572 A179 70pf multicolored 1.10 .85

Berlin-Potsdam Railway, 150th Anniv. — A180

1988, Oct. 13 Litho.

9N573 A180 10pf multicolored .65 .45

The Collector, 1913, by Ernst Barlach (1870-1938) A181

1988, Oct. 13

9N574 A181 40pf multicolored .70 .55

Berlin Airlift, 40th Anniv. — A182

1989, May 5 Photo. *Perf. 14*

9N575 A182 60pf multicolored 1.10 .95

13th Intl. Congress of the Supreme Audit Office, Berlin A183

1989, May 5 Litho.

9N576 A183 80pf multicolored 1.20 1.20

Ernst Reuter (1889-1953), Mayor of Berlin — A184

Litho. & Engr.

1989, July 13 *Perf. 14x14½*

9N577 A184 100pf multicolored 1.75 1.50

Intl. Radio Exhibition, Berlin — A185

1989, July 13 Litho.

9N578 A185 100pf multicolored 1.50 1.40

Plans of the Zoological Gardens, Berlin, and Designer Peter Joseph Lenne (1789-1866) — A186

Litho. & Engr.

1989, Aug. 10 *Perf. 14*

9N579 A186 60pf multicolored 1.50 1.10

Carl von Ossietzky (1889-1938), Awarded Nobel Peace Prize of 1935 — A187

1989, Aug. 10 Photo.

9N580 A187 100pf multicolored 1.60 1.40

450th Anniv. of the Reformation A188

Design: Nikolai Church, Spandau District.

1989, Oct. 12 Litho.

9N581 A188 60pf multicolored .95 .75

French Gymnasium, 300th Anniv. — A189

School from 1701 to 1873 and frontispiece of *Leges Gymnasie Gallici*, published in 1689.

1989, Oct. 12 Litho. & Engr.

9N582 A189 40pf multicolored .95 .85

Journalists, 1925, by Hannah Hoch (1889-1978) A190

1989, Oct. 12 Litho. *Perf. 13½*

9N583 A190 100pf multicolored 1.90 1.25

European Postal Service 500th Anniv. — A190a

Litho. & Engr.

1990, Jan. 12 ***Perf. 14***
9N584 A190a 100pf gray brn, blksh pur, beige 2.50 1.90

See Austria No. 1486, Belgium No. 1332, Germany No. 1592, and DDR No. 2791.

Public Transportation, 250th Anniv. — A191

1990, Jan. 12 **Litho.**
9N585 A191 60pf multicolored 1.90 1.20

Ernst Rudorff (1840-1916), Conservationist — A192

1990, Jan. 12
9N586 A192 60pf multicolored 1.90 1.40

People's Free Theater Organization, Cent. — A193

1990, Feb. 15 ***Perf. 13½***
9N587 A193 100pf multicolored 2.00 1.60

Parliament House, 40th Anniv. — A194

1990, Feb. 15 ***Perf. 14x14½***
9N588 A194 100pf multicolored 2.40 1.75

Bicent. of the Invention of the Barrel Organ — A195

1990, May 3 **Litho.** ***Perf. 14***
9N589 A195 100pf multicolored 2.00 1.50

90th German Catholics Day — A196

1990, May 3
9N590 A196 60pf multicolored 1.75 1.50

German Pharmaceutical Society, Cent. — A197

1990, Aug. 9 **Litho.** ***Perf. 14***
9N591 A197 100pf multicolored 3.50 2.00

Adolph Diesterweg (1790-1866), Educator — A198

1990, Sept. 27
9N592 A198 60pf multicolored 2.40 1.75

Stamps for Berlin were discontinued Oct. 3, 1990, when Germany and the German Democratic Republic merged. The stamps remained valid until Dec. 31, 1991.

OCCUPATION SEMI-POSTAL STAMPS

Offering Plate and Berlin Bear — SP1

Wmk. 284

1949, Dec. 1 **Litho.** ***Perf. 14***
9NB1 SP1 10 + 5pf grn 27.50 *125.00*
9NB2 SP1 20 + 5pf car 30.00 *125.00*
9NB3 SP1 30 + 5pf blue 30.00 *160.00*
a. Souv. sheet of 3, #9NB1-9NB3 350.00 *1,500.*
Never hinged 1,200.
Nos. 9NB1-9NB3 (3) 87.50 *410.00*
Set, never hinged 250.00

The surtax was for Berlin victims of currency devaluation.

Harp and Laurel Branch — SP2

"Singing Angels" — SP3

1950, Oct. 29 **Engr.** **Wmk. 116**
9NB4 SP2 10 + 5pf grn 14.00 *27.50*
9NB5 SP3 30 + 5pf dk sl bl 25.00 *12.50*
Set, never hinged 110.00

The surtax was to aid in reestablishing the Berlin Philharmonic Orchestra.

Young Stamp Collectors — SP4

1951, Oct. 7 ***Perf. 14***
9NB6 SP4 10 + 3pf grn 8.00 *21.00*
9NB7 SP4 20 + 2pf brn red 8.50 *27.50*
Set, never hinged 40.00

Stamp Day, Berlin, Oct. 7, 1951.

Kaiser Wilhelm Memorial Church — SP5

Design: 20pf+10pf, 30pf+15pf, Ruins of Kaiser Wilhelm Memorial Church.

1953, Aug. 9 **Wmk. 284**
9NB8 SP5 4 + 1pf choc .25 *14.00*
9NB9 SP5 10 + 5pf green .60 *40.00*
9NB10 SP5 20 + 10pf car 1.10 *40.00*
9NB11 SP5 30 + 15pf dp bl 7.00 *70.00*
Nos. 9NB8-9NB11 (4) 8.95 *164.00*
Set, never hinged 18.00

The surtax was to aid in reconstructing the church.

Catalogue values for unused stamps in this section, from this point to the end of the section, are for Never Hinged items.

Prussian Postilion — SP6

1954, Aug. 4 **Litho.** **Wmk. 284**
9NB12 SP6 20 + 10pf multi 12.00 *30.00*

National Stamp Exhibition, Berlin, Aug. 4-8.

Prussian Field Postilion — SP7

Perf. 13½x14

1955, Oct. 27 **Wmk. 304**
9NB13 SP7 25 + 10pf multi 5.00 *11.00*

The surtax was for the benefit of philately.

St. Otto, Bishop of Bamberg — SP8

Statues: 10pf+5pf, St. Hedwig, Duchess of Silesia. 20pf+10pf, St. Peter.

1955, Nov. 26 **Engr.** ***Perf. 14***
9NB14 SP8 7 + 3pf brown .70 *2.10*
9NB15 SP8 10 + 5pf gray grn 1.10 *2.50*
9NB16 SP8 20 + 10pf rose lil 1.75 *3.00*
Nos. 9NB14-9NB16 (3) 3.55 *7.60*

25th anniv. of the Bishopric of Berlin. The surtax was for the reconstruction of destroyed churches throughout the bishopric.

Bell Type of 1951 Surcharged

Perf. 13½x14

1956, Aug. 9 **Wmk. 284**
9NB17 OS8 20pf + 10pf citron 3.50 3.75

The surtax was for help for flood victims.

Postrider of Brandenburg, 1700 — SP9

Wmk. 304

1956, Oct. 26 **Litho.** ***Perf. 14***
9NB18 SP9 25pf + 10pf multi 2.50 3.50

The surtax was for the benefit of philately.

Ludwig Heck — SP10

1957, Sept. 7 **Engr.** ***Perf. 13½x14***
9NB19 SP10 20pf + 10pf red & dk brn .75 .90

Dr. Ludwig Heck, zoologist and long-time director of the Berlin Zoo. The surtax was for the Zoo.

Elly Heuss-Knapp and Relaxing Mothers SP11

1957, Nov. 30 ***Perf. 14***
9NB20 SP11 20pf + 10pf dk red 1.40 2.40

The surtax was for welfare work among mothers.

Boy at Window — SP12

Designs: 10pf+5pf, Girl going to school. 20pf+10pf, Girl with flower and mountains. 40pf+20pf, Boy at seashore.

1960, Sept. 15 **Litho.** **Wmk. 304**
9NB21 SP12 7pf + 3pf dk brn & brn .25 .30
9NB22 SP12 10pf + 5pf ol grn & slate grn .25 .30
9NB23 SP12 20pf + 10pf dk car & brn blk .50 .50
9NB24 SP12 40pf + 20pf bl & ind 1.20 3.25
Nos. 9NB21-9NB24 (4) 2.20 4.35

The surtax was for vacations for the children of Berlin.

Fluorescent Paper was introduced for semipostal stamps, starting with Nos. 9NB25-9NB28.

Sleeping Beauty — SP13

Various Scenes from Sleeping Beauty: No. 9NB25, The Curse Scene. No. 9NB26, Rose Pricks Her Finger. No. 9NB27, Prince Phillip standing above Sleeping Beauty. No. 9NB28, Cook, kid and black cat.

1964, Oct. 6 Unwmk. *Perf. 14*

9NB25	SP13	10pf + 5pf multi	.25	.25
9NB26	SP13	15pf + 5pf multi	.25	.25
9NB27	SP13	20pf + 10pf multi	.35	.30
9NB28	SP13	40pf + 20pf multi	.50	.85
		Nos. 9NB25-9NB28 (4)	1.35	1.65

The surtax was for independent welfare organizations.

Beginning with 9NB25-9NB28 semi-postals are types of Germany inscribed "Berlin" except Nos. 9NB129-9NB131.

Woodcock SP14

Birds: 15pf+5pf, Ring-necked pheasant. 20pf+10pf, Black grouse. 40pf+20pf, Capercaillie.

1965, Apr. 1 Litho. *Perf. 14*

9NB29	SP14	10pf + 5pf multi	.25	.25
9NB30	SP14	15pf + 5pf multi	.25	.25
9NB31	SP14	20pf + 10pf multi	.25	.25
9NB32	SP14	40pf + 20pf multi	.35	.70
		Nos. 9NB29-9NB32 (4)	1.10	1.45

Issued for the benefit of young people.

Cinderella SP15

Various Scenes from Cinderella: No. 9NB33, Cinderella feeding birds. No. 9NB34, Two birds holding yellow dress while flying and Cinderella. No. 9NB35, Cinderella without slipper, Prince holding slipper. No. 9NB36, Cinderella and Prince on horse.

1965, Oct. 6 Litho. *Perf. 14*

9NB33	SP15	10pf + 5pf multi	.25	.25
9NB34	SP15	15pf + 5pf multi	.25	.25
9NB35	SP15	20pf + 10pf multi	.35	.25
9NB36	SP15	40pf + 20pf multi	.35	.70
		Nos. 9NB33-9NB36 (4)	1.20	1.45

The surtax was for independent welfare organizations.

Roe Deer — SP16

20pf+10pf, Chamois. 30pf+15pf, Fallow deer. 50pf+25pf, Red deer.

1966, Apr. 22 Litho. *Perf. 14*

9NB37	SP16	10pf + 5pf multi	.25	.25
9NB38	SP16	20pf + 10pf multi	.25	.25
9NB39	SP16	30pf + 15pf multi	.35	.30
9NB40	SP16	50pf + 25pf multi	.55	.75
		Nos. 9NB37-9NB40 (4)	1.40	1.55

Issued for the benefit of young people.

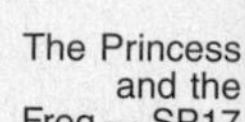

The Princess and the Frog — SP17

Various Scenes from The Princess and the Frog: No. 9NB41, The Princess and The Frog on edge of well. No. 9NB42, The Princess and The Frog at dining table. No. 9NB43, The Princess and The Prince. No. 9NB44, Princess and Prince in carriage.

1966, Oct. 5 Litho. *Perf. 14*

9NB41	SP17	10pf + 5pf multi	.25	.25
9NB42	SP17	20pf + 10pf multi	.25	.25
9NB43	SP17	30pf + 15pf multi	.25	.25
9NB44	SP17	50pf + 25pf multi	.45	.70
		Nos. 9NB41-9NB44 (4)	1.20	1.45

Surtax for independent welfare organizations.

Rabbit — SP18

20pf+10pf, Ermine. 30pf+15pf, Hamster. 50pf+25pf, Red fox.

1967, Apr. 4 Unwmk.

9NB45	SP18	10pf + 5pf multi	.25	.25
9NB46	SP18	20pf + 10pf multi	.25	.25
9NB47	SP18	30pf + 15pf multi	.35	.30
9NB48	SP18	50pf + 25pf multi	.85	1.25
		Nos. 9NB45-9NB48 (4)	1.70	2.05

Issued for the benefit of young people.

Frau Holle — SP19

Various Scenes from Frau Holle: No. 9NB49, Frau Holle at spinning wheel. No. 9NB50, Frau Holle making it snow by shaking her pillow. No. 9NB51, Girl under gold rain. No. 9NB52, Girl is showered in tar.

1967, Oct. 3 Litho. *Perf. 14*

9NB49	SP19	10pf + 5pf multi	.25	.25
9NB50	SP19	20pf + 10pf multi	.25	.25
9NB51	SP19	30pf + 15pf multi	.25	.35
9NB52	SP19	50pf + 25pf multi	.55	.75
		Nos. 9NB49-9NB52 (4)	1.30	1.60

The surtax was for independent welfare organizations.

Wildcat — SP20

Animals: 20pf+10pf, Otter. 30pf+15pf, Badger. 50pf+25pf, Beaver.

1968, Feb. 2 Photo. *Perf. 14*

9NB53	SP20	10pf + 5pf multi	.25	.45
9NB54	SP20	20pf + 10pf multi	.30	.45
9NB55	SP20	30pf + 15pf multi	.50	.85
9NB56	SP20	50pf + 25pf multi	1.60	2.10
		Nos. 9NB53-9NB56 (4)	2.65	3.85

Surtax for benefit of young people.

Dolls — SP21

Various 19th century dolls in sitting position: No. 9NB57, Doll wearing maroon dress. No. 9NB58, Doll wearing olive green dress. No. 9NB59, Doll wearing bright carmine dress. No. 9NB60, Doll wearing blue dress and yellow hat.

1968, Oct. 3 Litho. *Perf. 14*

9NB57	SP21	10pf + 5pf multi	.25	.25
9NB58	SP21	20pf + 10pf multi	.25	.25
9NB59	SP21	30pf + 15pf multi	.25	.35
9NB60	SP21	50pf + 25pf multi	.35	.70
		Nos. 9NB57-9NB60 (4)	1.10	1.55

The surtax was for independent welfare organizations.

Horses — SP22

10pf+5pf, Brown and white pony. 20pf+10pf, Brown work horse. 30pf+15pf, Black hotblood. 50pf+25pf, White thoroughbred.

1969, Feb. 6 Litho. *Perf. 14*

9NB61	SP22	10pf + 5pf multi	.25	.30
9NB62	SP22	20pf + 10pf multi	.30	.50
9NB63	SP22	30pf + 15pf multi	.45	.70
9NB64	SP22	50pf + 25pf multi	1.10	1.40
		Nos. 9NB61-9NB64 (4)	2.10	2.90

Surtax for benefit of young people.

Tin Toys — SP23

10pf+5pf, Coach. 20pf+10pf, Woman feeding chickens. 30pf+15pf, Woman grocer. 50pf+25pf, Postilion on horseback.

1969, Oct. 2 Litho. *Perf. 13½x14*

9NB65	SP23	10pf + 5pf multi	.25	.25
9NB66	SP23	20pf + 10pf multi	.25	.25
9NB67	SP23	30pf + 15pf multi	.35	.35
9NB68	SP23	50pf + 25pf multi	.90	.90
		Nos. 9NB65-9NB68 (4)	1.75	1.75

The surtax was for independent welfare organizations.

The Three Kings — SP24

1969, Nov. 13 Litho. *Perf. 13½x14*

9NB69	SP24	10pf + 5pf multi	.35	.30

Christmas.

Heinrich von Stretlingen — SP25

Minnesingers (and their Ladies): 20pf+10pf, Meinloh von Sevelingen. 30pf+15pf, Burkhart von Hohenfels. 50pf+25pf, Albrecht von Johansdorf.

1970, Feb. 5 Photo. *Perf. 13½x14*

9NB70	SP25	10pf + 5pf multi	.25	.25
9NB71	SP25	20pf + 10pf multi	.35	.40
9NB72	SP25	30pf + 15pf multi	.50	.55
9NB73	SP25	50pf + 25pf multi	1.10	1.25
		Nos. 9NB70-9NB73 (4)	2.20	2.45

Surtax for benefit of young people.

Puppets — SP26

10pf+5pf, "Kasperl." 20pf+10pf, Polichinelle. 30pf+5pf, Punch. 50pf+25pf, Pulcinella.

1970, Oct. 6 Litho. *Perf. 13½x14*

9NB74	SP26	10pf + 5pf multi	.25	.25
9NB75	SP26	20pf + 10pf multi	.25	.25
9NB76	SP26	30pf + 15pf multi	.50	.40
9NB77	SP26	50pf + 25pf multi	.85	.95
		Nos. 9NB74-9NB77 (4)	1.85	1.85

Surtax for independent welfare organizations.

Christmas — SP27

10pf+5pf, Rococo angel, from Ursuline Sisters' Convent, Innsbruck.

1970, Nov. 12

9NB78	SP27	10pf + 5pf multi	.30	.30

Children's Drawings SP28

10pf+5pf, Fly. 20pf+10pf, Fish. 30pf+15pf, Porcupine. 50pf+25pf, Cock. All stamps horizontal.

1971, Feb. 5 Litho. *Perf. 14*

9NB79	SP28	10pf + 5pf multi	.30	.30
9NB80	SP28	20pf + 10pf multi	.30	.30
9NB81	SP28	30pf + 15pf multi	.45	.50
9NB82	SP28	50pf + 25pf multi	1.10	1.20
		Nos. 9NB79-9NB82 (4)	2.15	2.30

Surtax for the benefit of young people.

Wooden Toys — SP29

10pf+5pf, Movable dolls in box. 25pf+10pf, Knight on horseback. 30pf+15pf, Jumping jack. 60pf+30pf, Nurse rocking babies.

1971, Oct. 5

9NB83	SP29	10pf + 5pf multi	.25	.25
9NB84	SP29	25pf + 10pf multi	.25	.35
9NB85	SP29	30pf + 15pf multi	.50	.50
9NB86	SP29	60pf + 30pf multi	.90	1.00
		Nos. 9NB83-9NB86 (4)	1.90	2.10

Christmas — SP30

10pf+5pf, Christmas angel with candles.

1971, Nov. 11

9NB87	SP30	10pf + 5pf multi	.35	.35

Animal Protection SP31

10pf+5pf, Boy trying to rob bird's nest. 25pf+10pf, Girl with kittens to be drowned. 30pf+15pf, Watch dog & man with whip. 60pf+30pf, Hedgehog & deer passing before car at night.

1972, Feb. 4

9NB88	SP31	10pf + 5pf multi	.25	.25
9NB89	SP31	25pf + 10pf multi	.30	.30
9NB90	SP31	30pf + 15pf multi	.50	.50
9NB91	SP31	60pf + 30pf multi	1.10	1.20
		Nos. 9NB88-9NB91 (4)	2.15	2.25

Surtax for the benefit of young people.

Chess — SP32

No. 9NB92, Knight. No. 9NB93, Rook. No. 9NB94, Queen. No. 9NB95, King.

1972, Oct. 5 Litho. *Perf. 14*

9NB92	SP32	20pf + 10pf	.30	.30
9NB93	SP32	30pf + 15pf	.45	.45
9NB94	SP32	40pf + 20pf	1.25	1.25
9NB95	SP32	70pf + 35pf	1.75	1.75
		Nos. 9NB92-9NB95 (4)	3.75	3.75

Surtax for independent welfare organizations.

Holy Family — SP33

1972, Nov. 10 Litho. *Perf. 14*

9NB96	SP33	20pf + 10pf multi	.50	.40

Christmas.

Birds of Prey — SP34

20pf+10pf, Goshawk. 30pf+15pf, Peregrine falcon. 40pf+20pf, Sparrow hawk. 70pf+35pf, Golden eagle.

1973, Feb. 6 Photo. *Perf. 14*

9NB97	SP34	20pf + 10pf multi	.40	.40
9NB98	SP34	30pf + 15pf multi	.55	.70
9NB99	SP34	40pf + 20pf multi	.85	.90
9NB100	SP34	70pf + 35pf multi	1.40	1.50
		Nos. 9NB97-9NB100 (4)	3.20	3.50

Surtax was for benefit of young people.

Musical Instruments SP35

20+10pf, Hurdygurdy, 17th cent. 30+15pf, Drum, 16th cent. 40+20pf, Archlute, 18th cent. 70+35pf, Organ, 16th cent.

1973, Oct. 5 Litho. *Perf. 14*

9NB101	SP35	20pf + 10pf multi	.35	.35
9NB102	SP35	30pf + 15pf multi	.70	.70
9NB103	SP35	40pf + 20pf multi	.70	.85
9NB104	SP35	70pf + 35pf multi	1.10	1.20
		Nos. 9NB101-9NB104 (4)	2.85	3.10

Surtax was for independent welfare organizations.

Christmas Star — SP36

1973, Nov. 9 Litho. & Engr.

9NB105	SP36	20pf + 10pf multi	.50	.50

International Youth Work — SP37

Designs: 20pf+10pf, Boy photographing. 30pf+15pf, Boy athlete. 40pf+20pf, Girl violinist. 70pf+35pf, Nurse's aid.

1974, Apr. 17 Photo. *Perf. 14*

9NB106	SP37	20pf + 10pf multi	.35	.40
9NB107	SP37	30pf + 15pf multi	.35	.40
9NB108	SP37	40pf + 20pf multi	.70	.90
9NB109	SP37	70pf + 35pf multi	1.10	1.25
		Nos. 9NB106-9NB109 (4)	2.50	2.95

Surtax was for benefit of young people.

Flowers — SP38

Designs: 30pf+15pf, Spring bouquet. 40pf+20pf, Autumn bouquet. 50pf+25pf, Roses. 70pf+35pf, Winter flowers. All horiz.

1974, Oct. 15 Litho. *Perf. 14*

9NB110	SP38	30pf + 15pf multi	.35	.35
9NB111	SP38	40pf + 20pf multi	.70	.70
9NB112	SP38	50pf + 25pf multi	.70	.70
9NB113	SP38	70pf + 35pf multi	.85	1.00
		Nos. 9NB110-9NB113 (4)	2.60	2.75

Surtax was for independent welfare organizations.

Christmas Bouquet SP39

1974, Oct. 29

9NB114	SP39	30pf + 15pf multi	.70	.75

Steam Locomotives — SP40

30pf+15pf, Dragon. 40pf+20pf, Class 89 (70-75). 50pf+25pf, Class O50. 70pf+35pf, Class O10.

1975, Apr. 15 Litho. *Perf. 14*

9NB115	SP40	30pf + 15pf multi	.70	.40
9NB116	SP40	40pf + 20pf multi	.70	.70
9NB117	SP40	50pf + 25pf multi	1.40	1.20
9NB118	SP40	70pf + 35pf multi	1.75	2.25
		Nos. 9NB115-9NB118 (4)	4.55	4.55

Surtax was for benefit of young people.

Alpine Flowers — SP41

30pf+15pf, Yellow gentian. 40pf+20pf, Arnica. 50pf+25pf, Cyclamen. 70pf+35pf, Blue gentian.

1975, Oct. 15 Litho. *Perf. 14*

9NB119	SP41	30pf + 15pf multi	.50	.50
9NB120	SP41	40pf + 20pf multi	.40	.40
9NB121	SP41	50pf + 25pf multi	.55	.55
9NB122	SP41	70pf + 35pf multi	1.00	1.00
		Nos. 9NB119-9NB122 (4)	2.45	2.45

Surtax was for independent welfare organizations.

Snow Heather — SP42

1975, Nov. 14

9NB123	SP42	30pf + 15pf multi	.70	.70

Christmas.

Sports — SP43

30+15pf, Shot put, women's. 40+20pf, Hockey. 50+25pf, Handball. 70+35pf, Swimming.

1976, Apr. 6 Litho. *Perf. 14*

9NB124	SP43	30pf + 15pf multi	.55	.60
9NB125	SP43	40pf + 20pf multi	.55	.60
9NB126	SP43	50pf + 25pf multi	.55	.70
9NB127	SP43	70pf + 35pf multi	1.25	1.40
		Nos. 9NB124-9NB127 (4)	2.90	3.30

Youth training for Olympic Games. The surtax was for the benefit of young people.

Iris — SP44

Flowers: 40pf+20pf, Wallflower. 50pf+25pf, Dahlia. 70pf+35pf, Larkspur.

1976, Oct. 14 Litho. *Perf. 14*

9NB128	SP44	30pf + 15pf	.35	.35
9NB129	SP44	40pf + 20pf	.35	.35
9NB130	SP44	50pf + 25pf	.55	.70
9NB131	SP44	70pf + 35pf	.85	1.00
		Nos. 9NB128-9NB131 (4)	2.10	2.40

Surtax was for independent welfare organizations.

Souvenir Sheet

Christmas — SP45

30pf+15pf, Annunciation to the Shepherds, stained-glass window, Frauenkirche, Esslingen.

1976, Nov. 16 Litho. & Engr.

9NB132	SP45	30pf + 15pf multi	.75	.65

Historic Ships SP46

30pf+15pf, Bremer Kogge, c. 1380. 40pf+20pf, Helena Sloman, 1850. 50pf+25pf, Passenger ship, Cap Polonio, 1914. 70pf+35pf, Freighter Widar, 1971.

1977, Apr. 14 Litho. *Perf. 14*

9NB133	SP46	30pf + 15pf	.35	.40
9NB134	SP46	40pf + 20pf	.40	.50
9NB135	SP46	50pf + 25pf	.70	.85
9NB136	SP46	70pf + 35pf	1.00	1.10
		Nos. 9NB133-9NB136 (4)	2.45	2.85

Surtax was for benefit of young people.

Meadow Flowers — SP47

30pf+15pf, Daisy. 40pf+20pf, Cowslip. 50pf+25pf, Sainfoin. 70pf+35pf, Forget-me-not.

1977, Oct. 13 Litho. *Perf. 14*

9NB137	SP47	30pf + 15pf	.30	.30
9NB138	SP47	40pf + 20pf	.50	.50
9NB139	SP47	50pf + 25pf	.55	.70
9NB140	SP47	70pf + 35pf	.85	1.00
		Nos. 9NB137-9NB140 (4)	2.20	2.50

Surtax was for independent welfare organizations.

See Nos. 9NB148-9NB151.

Souvenir Sheet

Christmas — SP48

30pf+15pf, Virgin and Child, stained-glass window, Sacristy of St. Gereon Basilica, Cologne.

1977, Nov. 10

9NB141	SP48	30pf + 15pf multi	.75	.75

Aviation SP49

Designs: 30pf+15pf, Montgolfier balloon, 1783. 40pf+20pf, Lilienthal's glider, 1891. 50pf+25pf, Wright brothers' plane, 1909. 70pf+35pf, Etrich/Rumpler Taube, 1910.

1978, Apr. 13 Litho. *Perf. 14*

9NB142	SP49	30pf + 15pf	.35	.40
9NB143	SP49	40pf + 20pf	.50	.55
9NB144	SP49	50pf + 25pf	.60	.70
9NB145	SP49	70pf + 35pf	1.10	1.20
		Nos. 9NB142-9NB145 (4)	2.55	2.85

Surtax was for benefit of young people.

Sports SP50

50+25pf, Bicycling. 70+35pf, Fencing.

1978, Apr. 13 Litho. *Perf. 14*

9NB146	SP50	50pf + 25pf	.85	.55
9NB147	SP50	70pf + 35pf	1.10	1.00

Surtax was for German Sports Foundation.

Woodland Flowers — SP51

30pf+15pf, Solomon's-seal. 40pf+20pf, Wood primrose. 50pf+25pf, Cephalanthera rubra (orchid). 70pf+35pf, Bugle.

1978, Oct. 12 Litho. *Perf. 14*

9NB148	SP51	30pf + 15pf	.40	.40
9NB149	SP51	40pf + 20pf	.50	.50
9NB150	SP51	50pf + 25pf	.70	.75
9NB151	SP51	70pf + 35pf	1.00	1.10
		Nos. 9NB148-9NB151 (4)	2.60	2.75

Surtax was for independent welfare organizations.

Souvenir Sheet

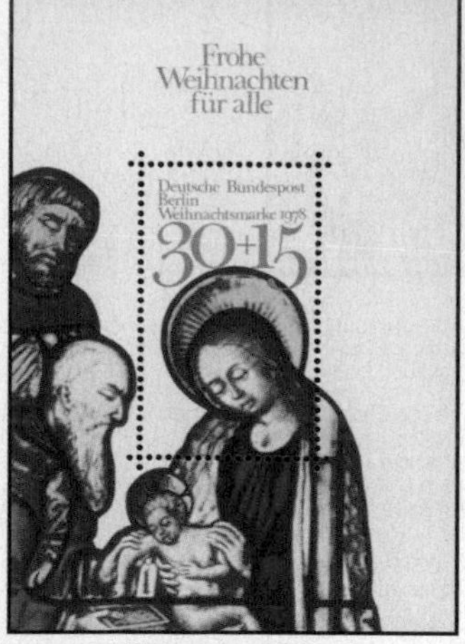

Christmas — SP52

30pf+15pf, Adoration of the Kings, stained glass window, Frauenkirche, Munich.

1978, Nov. 16 Litho. *Perf. 14*

9NB152	SP52	30pf + 15pf multi	.75	.75

Aviation SP53

Airplanes: 40pf+20pf, Vampyr, 1921. 50pf+25pf, Junkers JU52/3M, 1932. 60pf+30pf, Messerschmitt BF/ME 108, 1934. 90pf+45pf, Douglas DC3, 1935.

1979, Apr. 5 Litho. *Perf. 14*

9NB153	SP53	40pf + 20pf	.50	.50
9NB154	SP53	50pf + 25pf	.70	.70
9NB155	SP53	60pf + 30pf	.85	.90
9NB156	SP53	90pf + 45pf	1.00	1.40
		Nos. 9NB153-9NB156 (4)	3.05	3.50

Surtax was for benefit of young people.

Sports SP54

60pf+30pf, Runners. 90pf+45pf, Archers.

1979, Apr. 5

9NB157	SP54	60pf + 30pf	.85	.90
9NB158	SP54	90pf + 45pf	1.10	1.20

Surtax was for German Sports Foundation.

Woodland Plants SP55

40pf+20pf, Larch. 50pf+25pf, Hazelnut. 60pf+30pf, Horse chestnut. 90pf+45pf, Blackthorn.

1979, Oct. 11 Litho. *Perf. 14*

9NB159	SP55	40pf + 20pf	.40	.40
9NB160	SP55	50pf + 25pf	.70	.70
9NB161	SP55	60pf + 30pf	.90	.90
9NB162	SP55	90pf + 45pf	1.20	1.20
		Nos. 9NB159-9NB162 (4)	3.20	3.20

Surtax was for independent welfare organizations.

Christmas SP56

Design: Nativity, medieval manuscript, Cistercian Abby, Altenberg.

1979, Nov. 14 Litho. *Perf. 13½*

9NB163	SP56	40pf + 20pf multi	.85	.70

Aviation SP57

Designs: 40pf+20pf, Vickers Viscount, 1950. 50pf+25pf, Fokker 27 Friendship, 1955. 60pf+30pf, Sud Aviation Caravelle, 1955. 90pf+45pf, Sikorsky-55, 1949.

1980, Apr. 10 Litho. *Perf. 14*

9NB164	SP57	40 + 20pf multi	.60	.60
9NB165	SP57	50 + 25pf multi	.70	.70
9NB166	SP57	60 + 30pf multi	.90	.90
9NB167	SP57	90 + 45pf multi	1.25	1.25
		Nos. 9NB164-9NB167 (4)	3.45	3.45

Surtax was for benefit of young people.

Sports SP58

Designs: 50pf+25pf, Javelin. 60pf+30pf, Weight lifting. 90pf+45pf, Water polo.

1980, May 8 Photo. *Perf. 14*

9NB168	SP58	50 + 25pf multi	.70	.70
9NB169	SP58	60 + 30pf multi	.70	.70
9NB170	SP58	90 + 45pf multi	1.00	1.00
		Nos. 9NB168-9NB170 (3)	2.40	2.40

Surtax was for German Sports Foundation.

Wildflower SP59

Designs: 40pf+20pf, Orlaya. 50pf+25pf, Yellow gagea. 60pf+30pf, Summer pheasant's eye. 90pf+45pf, Small-flowered Venus' looking-glass.

1980, Oct. 9 Litho. *Perf. 14*

9NB171	SP59	40 + 20pf multi	.55	.60
9NB172	SP59	50 + 25pf multi	.70	.75
9NB173	SP59	60 + 30pf multi	.70	.75
9NB174	SP59	90 + 45pf multi	1.25	1.25
		Nos. 9NB171-9NB174 (4)	3.20	3.35

Surtax was for independent welfare organizations.

Christmas SP60

Design: 40pf+20pf, Annunciation to the Shepherds, from Altomunster manuscript, 12th century.

1980, Nov. 13 Litho. *Perf. 14x13½*

9NB175	SP60	40 + 20pf multi	.85	.80

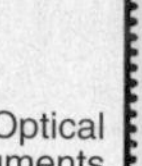

Optical Instruments SP61

40pf+20pf, Theodolite, 1810. 50pf+25pf, Equatorial telescope, 1820. 60pf +30pf, Microscope, 1790. 90pf+45pf, Sextant, 1830.

1981, Apr. 10 Litho. *Perf. 13½*

9NB176	SP61	40 + 20pf multi	.40	.50
9NB177	SP61	50 + 25pf multi	.60	.70
9NB178	SP61	60 + 30pf multi	.85	.90
9NB179	SP61	90 + 45pf multi	1.25	1.40
		Nos. 9NB176-9NB179 (4)	3.10	3.50

Surtax for benefit of young people.

Sports SP62

Designs: 60pf+30pf, Women's gymnastics. 90pf+45pf, Cross-county running.

1981, Apr. 10 *Perf. 14*

9NB180	SP62	60 + 30pf multi	.85	.80
9NB181	SP62	90 + 45pf multi	1.25	1.20

Surtax for the German Sports Foundation.

Endangered Species SP63

40pf+20pf, Common bistort. 50pf+25pf, Pedicularis sceptrum-carolinum. 60pf+30pf, Gladiolus palustris. 90pf+45pf, Iris sibirica.

1981, Oct. 8 Litho.

9NB182	SP63	40 + 20pf multi	.70	.70
9NB183	SP63	50 + 25pf multi	.70	.70
9NB184	SP63	60 + 30pf multi	.70	.70
9NB185	SP63	90 + 45pf multi	1.40	1.40
		Nos. 9NB182-9NB185 (4)	3.50	3.50

Surtax was for independent welfare organizations.

Christmas SP64

Adoration of the Kings, 19th cent. painting.

1981, Nov. 12 Litho.

9NB186	SP64	40 + 20pf multi	.85	.70

Antique Cars SP65

Designs: 40pf+20pf, Daimler, 1889. 50pf+25pf, Wanderer, 1911. 60pf+30pf, Adler limousine, 1913. 90pf+45pf, DKW-F, 1931.

1982, Apr. 15 Litho.

9NB187	SP65	40 + 20pf multi	.55	.60
9NB188	SP65	50 + 25pf multi	.60	.70
9NB189	SP65	60 + 30pf multi	.70	.85
9NB190	SP65	90 + 45pf multi	1.25	1.40
		Nos. 9NB187-9NB190 (4)	3.10	3.55

Surtax was for benefit of young people.

Sports SP66

60pf+30pf, Sprinting. 90pf+45pf, Volleyball.

1982, Apr. 15 **Litho.**
9NB191 SP66 60 + 30pf multi .85 .70
9NB192 SP66 90 + 45pf multi 1.40 1.00

Surtax was for the German Sports Foundation.

Endangered Species — SP67

Designs: 50pf+20pf, Floribunda grandiflora. 60pf+30pf, Tea-rose hybrid, diff. 80pf+40pf, Floribunda, diff. 120pf+60pf, Miniature rose.

1982, Oct. 14 **Litho.** ***Perf. 14***
9NB193 SP67 50 + 20pf multi .85 .85
9NB194 SP67 60 + 30pf multi .85 .85
9NB195 SP67 80 + 40pf multi 1.40 1.40
9NB196 SP67 120 + 60pf multi 2.25 2.25
Nos. 9NB193-9NB196 (4) 5.35 5.35

Surtax was for independent welfare organizations.

Christmas — SP68

Design: Adoration of the Kings, Oak altar, St. Peter's Church, Hamburg, 1380.

1982, Nov. 10
9NB197 SP68 50 + 20pf multi .85 .70

Motorcycles — SP69

Designs: 50pf+20pf, Hildebrand & Wolfmuller, 1894. 60pf+30pf, Wanderer, 1908. 80pf+40pf, DKW-Lomos, 1922. 120pf+60pf, Mars, 1925.

1983, Apr. 12 **Litho.** ***Perf. 14***
9NB198 SP69 50 + 20pf multi .70 .50
9NB199 SP69 60 + 30pf multi 1.00 .90
9NB200 SP69 80 + 40pf multi 1.20 .90
9NB201 SP69 120 + 60pf multi 2.60 2.40
Nos. 9NB198-9NB201 (4) 5.50 4.70

Surtax was for benefit of young people.

Sports SP70

Designs: 80pf+40pf, European Latin American Dance Championship. 120pf+60pf, World Hockey Championship.

1983, Apr. 12
9NB202 SP70 80 + 40pf multi 1.25 1.00
9NB203 SP70 120 + 60pf multi 1.90 1.75

Surtax was for German Sports Foundation.

Endangered Species — SP71

Designs: 50pf+20pf, Mountain wildflower 60pf+30pf, Alpine auricula. 80pf+40pf, Little primrose. 120pf+60pf, Einsele's aquilegia.

1983, Oct. 13 **Litho.** ***Perf. 14***
9NB204 SP71 50 + 20pf multi .50 .50
9NB205 SP71 60 + 30pf multi .85 .85
9NB206 SP71 80 + 40pf multi 1.50 1.50
9NB207 SP71 120 + 60pf multi 2.10 2.40
Nos. 9NB204-9NB207 (4) 4.95 5.25

Surtax was for welfare organizations.

Nativity — SP72

1983, Nov. 10 **Litho.**
9NB208 SP72 50 + 20pf multi .85 .75

Christmas.
Surtax was for free welfare work.

Insects — SP73

Designs: 50pf+20pf, Trichius fasciatus. 60pf+30pf, Agrumenia carniolioa. 80pf+40pf, Bombus terrestris. 120pf+60pf, Eristalis tenax.

1984, Apr. 12 **Litho.**
9NB209 SP73 50 + 20pf multi .90 .55
9NB210 SP73 60 + 30pf multi .90 .70
9NB211 SP73 80 + 40pf multi 1.40 1.25
9NB212 SP73 120 + 60pf multi 2.10 2.10
Nos. 9NB209-9NB212 (4) 5.30 4.60

Surtax was for German Youth Stamp Foundation.

Olympics SP74

Women's Events: 60pf+30pf, Hurdles. 80pf+40pf, Cycling. 120pf+60pf, Kayak.

1984, Apr. 12
9NB213 SP74 60 + 30pf multi 1.40 1.00
9NB214 SP74 80 + 40pf multi 1.40 1.00
9NB215 SP74 120 + 60pf multi 2.50 2.50
Nos. 9NB213-9NB215 (3) 5.30 4.50

Surtax was for German Sports Foundation.

Orchids SP75

50+20pf, Listera cordata. 60pf+30pf, Ophrys insectifera. 80pf+40pf, Epipactis palustris. 120pf+60pf, Ophrys coriophora.

1984, Oct. 18 **Litho.** ***Perf. 14***
9NB216 SP75 50 + 20pf multi 1.50 1.00
9NB217 SP75 60 + 30pf multi 1.50 1.00
9NB218 SP75 80 + 40pf multi 2.40 2.10
9NB219 SP75 120 + 60pf multi 3.75 3.50
Nos. 9NB216-9NB219 (4) 9.15 7.60

Surtax was for welfare organizations.

St. Nicholas SP76

1984, Nov. 8 **Litho.**
9NB220 SP76 50 + 20pf multi 1.00 1.00

Christmas.
Surtax was for welfare organizations.

Sports SP77

No. 9NB221, Basketball. No. 9NB222, Table Tennis.

1985, Feb. 21 **Photo.**
9NB221 SP77 80 + 40pf multi 1.25 1.25
9NB222 SP77 120 + 60pf multi 2.10 2.10

Surtax was for German Sport Foundation.

Bicycles SP78

50pf+20pf, Bussing bicycle, 1868. 60pf+30pf, Child's tricycle, 1885. 80pf+40pf, Jaray bicycle, 1925. 120pf+60pf, Opel racer, 1925.

1985, Apr. 16 **Litho.**
9NB223 SP78 50 + 20pf multi 1.00 1.00
9NB224 SP78 60 + 30pf multi 1.00 1.00
9NB225 SP78 80 + 40pf multi 1.40 1.50
9NB226 SP78 120 + 60pf multi 3.00 3.25
Nos. 9NB223-9NB226 (4) 6.40 6.75

Surtax was for benefit of young people. Each stamp also shows the International Youth Year emblem.

Prayer Books SP79

No. 9NB227, Red, blue and pink flowers, lady bugs. No. 9NB228, Red and blue flowers, bird and butterfly. No. 9NB229, Pink and blue flowers, butterfly and bee. No. 9NB230, Yellow and pink flowers, butterfly and snail.

1985, Oct. 15 **Litho.** ***Perf. 14***
9NB227 SP79 50 + 20pf multi 1.00 1.00
9NB228 SP79 60 + 30pf multi 1.40 1.40
9NB229 SP79 80 + 40pf multi 1.40 1.40
9NB230 SP79 120 + 60pf multi 1.75 2.10
Nos. 9NB227-9NB230 (4) 5.55 5.90

Surtax for welfare organizations.

Christmas SP80

Woodcut: Worship of the Kings, Epiphany Altar, Frieburg Cathedral, by Hans Baldung Grien (1485-1545).

1985, Nov. 12 **Litho.** ***Perf. 14***
9NB231 SP80 50 + 20pf multi 1.00 .90

Surtax for welfare organizations.

European Sports Championships — SP81

No. 9NB232, Swimming. No. 9NB233, Show jumping.

1986, Feb. 13 **Litho.** ***Perf. 14***
9NB232 SP81 80 + 40pf multi 1.50 1.75
9NB233 SP81 120 + 55pf multi 2.00 2.10

Surtax for the Natl. Sports Promotion Foundation.

Vocational Training — SP82

No. 9NB234, Glass worker. No. 9NB235, Metal Worker. No. 9NB236, Tailor. No. 9NB237, Carpenter.

1986, Apr. 10
9NB234 SP82 50 + 25pf multi 1.00 1.20
9NB235 SP82 60 + 30pf multi 1.40 1.60
9NB236 SP82 70 + 35pf multi 1.40 1.60
9NB237 SP82 80 + 40pf multi 1.75 1.90
Nos. 9NB234-9NB237 (4) 5.55 6.30

Surtax for German Youth Stamp Foundation.

Glassware — SP83

No. 9NB238, Cantharus, 1st cent. No. 9NB239, Tumbler, c. 200. No. 9NB240, Jug, 3rd cent. No. 9NB241, Diatreta, 4th cent.

1986, Oct. 16 **Litho.** ***Perf. 13x13½***
9NB238 SP83 50 + 25pf multi 1.00 1.00
9NB239 SP83 60 + 30pf multi 1.40 1.40
9NB240 SP83 70 + 35pf multi 1.40 1.40
9NB241 SP83 80 + 40pf multi 1.40 1.75
Nos. 9NB238-9NB241 (4) 5.20 5.55

Surtax for public welfare organizations.

Christmas SP84

Design: Adoration of the Magi, Ortenberg Altarpiece, c. 1420.

1986, Nov. 13 **Litho.** ***Perf. 14***
9NB242 SP84 50 + 25pf multi .85 .90

Surtax for public welfare organizations.

Sports Championships — SP85

No. 9NB243, Gymnastics. No. 9NB244, Judo.

1987, Feb. 12 **Litho.**
9NB243 SP85 80 + 40pf multi 1.40 1.40
9NB244 SP85 120 + 55pf multi 1.75 1.75

Surtax for the benefit of the national Sports Promotion Foundation.

Youth in Industry SP86

No. 9NB245, Cooper. No. 9NB246, Stonemason. No. 9NB247, Furrier. No. 9NB248, Painter.

1987, Apr. 9				**Litho.**
9NB245	SP86	50 + 25pf multi	.85	1.00
9NB246	SP86	60 + 30pf multi	.90	1.00
9NB247	SP86	70 + 35pf multi	1.40	1.75
9NB248	SP86	80 + 40pf multi	1.40	1.40
		Nos. 9NB245-9NB248 (4)	4.55	5.15

Surtax for youth organizations.

Gold and Silver Artifacts SP87

No. 9NB249, Bonnet ornament, 5th cent. No. 9NB250, Athena plate, 1st cent. B.C. No. 9NB251, Armilla armlet, c. 1180. No. 9NB252, Snake bracelet, 300 B.C.

1987, Oct. 15				
9NB249	SP87	50 + 25pf multi	.70	.90
9NB250	SP87	60 + 30pf multi	1.00	1.20
9NB251	SP87	70 + 35pf multi	1.25	1.50
9NB252	SP87	80 + 40pf multi	1.50	1.75
		Nos. 9NB249-9NB252 (4)	4.45	5.35

Surtax for welfare organizations sponsoring free museum exhibitions.

Christmas SP88

Illustration from Book of Psalms, 13th cent., Bavarian Natl. Museum: Adoration of the Magi.

1987, Nov. 6				
9NB253	SP88	50 + 25pf multi	.85	.85

Surtax for public welfare ogranizations.

Sports SP89

No. 9NB254, Trapshooting. No. 9NB255, Figure skating. No. 9NB256, Hammer throw.

1988, Feb. 18				**Litho.**
9NB254	SP89	60 + 30pf multi	1.25	1.25
9NB255	SP89	80 + 40pf multi	1.25	1.25
9NB256	SP89	120 + 55pf multi	1.75	1.75
		Nos. 9NB254-9NB256 (3)	4.25	4.25

Music SP90

No. 9NB257, Piano terzet. No. 9NB258, Wind quintet. No. 9NB259, Guitar, mandolin, recorder. No. 9NB260, Children's choir.

1988, Apr. 14		**Litho.**		***Perf. 14***
9NB257	SP90	50 +25pf multi	1.00	1.00
9NB258	SP90	60 +30pf multi	1.40	1.50
9NB259	SP90	70 +35pf multi	1.40	1.50
9NB260	SP90	80 +40pf multi	2.10	2.25
		Nos. 9NB257-9NB260 (4)	5.90	6.25

Surtax for German Youth Stamp Foundation.

Gold and Silver Artifacts SP91

No. 9NB261, Brooch, c. 1700, Schmuck Jewelry Museum, Pforzheim. No. 9NB262, Lion, 1540, Kunstgewerbe Museum, Berlin. No. 9NB263, Lidded goblet, 1536, Kunstgewerbe Museum. No. 9NB264, Cope clasp, c. 1400, Aachen cathedral.

1988, Oct. 13				**Litho.**
9NB261	SP91	50 +25pf multi	1.00	*1.10*
9NB262	SP91	60 +30pf multi	1.10	*1.20*
9NB263	SP91	70 +35pf multi	1.25	*1.25*
9NB264	SP91	80 +40pf multi	1.50	1.75
		Nos. 9NB261-9NB264 (4)	4.85	5.30

Surtax for welfare organizations.

Christmas SP92

Illumination from *The Gospel Book of Henry the Lion*, Helmarshausen, 1188, Prussian Cultural Museum, Bavaria: Angels announce the birth of Christ to the shepherds.

1988, Nov. 10				**Litho.**
9NB265	SP92	50 +25pf multi	1.10	1.10

Surtax for public welfare organizations.

Sports SP93

No. 9NB266, Volleyball. No. 9NB267, Hockey.

1989, Feb. 9				**Litho.**
9NB266	SP93	100 +50pf multi	2.10	2.10
9NB267	SP93	140 +60pf multi	2.75	3.25

Surtax for the Natl. Sports Promotion Foundation.

Circus SP94

No. 9NB268, Tamer and tigers. No. 9NB269, Trapeze artists. No. 9NB270, Seals. No. 9NB271, Jugglers.

1989, Apr. 20				**Litho.**
9NB268	SP94	60 +30pf multi	1.40	1.40
9NB269	SP94	70 +30pf multi	1.75	1.75
9NB270	SP94	80 +35pf multi	2.40	2.75
9NB271	SP94	100 +50pf multi	2.75	3.25
		Nos. 9NB268-9NB271 (4)	8.30	9.15

Surtax for natl. youth welfare organizations.

Mail Transport SP95

No. 9NB272, Messenger, 15th cent. No. 9NB273, Brandenburg mail wagon, c. 1700. No. 9NB274, Prussian postal workers, 19th cent.

1989, Oct. 12				**Litho.**
9NB272	SP95	60 +30pf multi	2.10	2.10
9NB273	SP95	80 +35pf multi	2.75	2.40
9NB274	SP95	100 +50pf multi	3.50	3.50
		Nos. 9NB272-9NB274 (3)	8.35	8.00

Surtax for the benefit of Free Welfare Work.

Christmas SP96

Designs: No. 9NB275, Angel. No. 9NB276, Nativity.

1989, Nov. 16				**Litho.**
9NB275	SP96	40 +20pf multi	1.00	1.00
9NB276	SP96	60 +30pf multi	1.75	.175

Surtax for the benefit of the Federal Working Assoc. of Free Welfare Work.

Sports SP97

Designs: No. 9NB277, Water polo. No. 9NB278, Wheelchair basketball.

1990, Feb. 15				**Litho.**
9NB277	SP97	100 +50pf multi	2.75	3.25
9NB278	SP97	140 +60pf multi	5.00	*6.00*

Surtax for the Natl. Sports Promotion Foundation.

Max and Moritz SP98

No. 9NB279, Moritz filling pipe with gunpowder. No. 9NB280, Max & Moritz get baked into dough and eat their way out. No. 9NB281, Max & Moritz cutting holes in sack. No. 9NB282, The uncle and the May bug.

1990, Apr. 19				**Litho.**
9NB279	SP98	60 +30pf multi	1.50	*1.75*
9NB280	SP98	70 +30pf multi	2.40	*2.50*
9NB281	SP98	80 +35pf multi	2.40	*2.50*
9NB282	SP98	100 +50pf multi	2.40	*2.50*
		Nos. 9NB279-9NB282 (4)	8.70	9.25

Surcharge for the German Youth Stamp Foundation.

Post and Telecommunications — SP99

Designs: 60pf + 30pf, Railway mail car, 1900. 80pf + 35pf, Telephone installation, 1900. 100pf + 50pf, Mail truck, 1900.

1990, Sept. 27		**Litho.**		***Perf. 13½x14***
9NB283	SP99	60 +30pf multi	1.75	2.10
9NB284	SP99	80 +35pf multi	2.40	2.75
9NB285	SP99	100 +50pf multi	3.50	3.50
		Nos. 9NB283-9NB285 (3)	7.65	8.35

Surtax for welfare organizations.

GERMANY OFFICES ABROAD

OFFICES IN CHINA

100 Pfennings = 1 Mark
100 Cents = 1 Dollar (1905)

Stamps of Germany, 1889-90, Overprinted in Black at 56 degree Angle

1898		**Unwmk.**		***Perf. 13½x14½***
1	A9	3pf dark brown	5.75	*6.00*
a.		3pf yellow brown	12.00	*12.00*
b.		3pf reddish ocher	37.50	*125.00*
2	A9	5pf green	3.25	3.25
3	A10	10pf carmine	5.75	*6.25*
4	A10	20pf ultramarine	17.00	16.50
5	A10	25pf orange	32.50	30.00
6	A10	50pf red brown	16.00	13.50
		Nos. 1-6 (6)	80.25	75.50

Overprinted at 45 degree Angle

1c	A9	3pf yellow brown	135.00	*23,000.*
1d	A9	3pf reddish ocher	375.00	
e.		3pf gray brown	*1,850.*	23,000.
2a	A9	5pf green	11.50	*13.00*
3a	A10	10pf carmine	32.50	10.50
4a	A10	20pf ultramarine	14.50	10.50
5a	A10	25pf orange	50.00	*65.00*
6a	A10	50pf red brown	21.00	17.50

Value for No. 1c used is for a stamp with small 1898 Shanghai cancel. Examples with other cancellations or later Shanghai cancels sell for about half the value quoted.

Foochow Issue

Nos. 3 and 3a Handstamp Surcharged

1900				
16	A10	5pf on 10pf, #3	550.00	*800.00*
a.		On No. 3a	650.00	*950.00*

For similar 5pf surcharges on 10pf carmine, see Tsingtau Issue, Kiauchau.

Tientsin Issue

German Stamps of 1900 Issue Handstamped

1900				
17	A11	3pf brown	600.00	800.00
18	A11	5pf green	400.00	360.00
19	A11	10pf carmine	950.00	875.00
20	A11	20pf ultra	800.00	*950.00*
21	A11	30pf org & blk, *sal*	*4,750.*	*4,750.*
22	A11	50pf pur & blk, *sal*	*16,000.*	*13,500.*
23	A11	80pf lake & blk, *rose*	*4,750.*	*4,750.*

This handstamp is known inverted and double on most values. Used values for Nos. 16-23 are for postally used items, CTO on philatelic usage is about half.

Excellent faked handstamps are plentiful.

Regular Issue

Germany No. 53 Overprinted

Germany No. 64 Ovptd.

Germany No. 65A Ovptd.

1901 *Perf. 14, 14½*

Overprinted Horizontally in Black

24	A11	3pf brown	1.50	2.10
a.		3pf light red brown	105.00	*45.00*
25	A11	5pf green	1.50	1.60
26	A11	10pf carmine	2.40	1.25
27	A11	20pf ultra	3.25	1.60
28	A11	25pf org & blk, *yel*	9.50	*16.00*
29	A11	30pf org & blk, *sal*	9.50	*13.00*
30	A11	40pf lake & blk	9.50	9.50
31	A11	50pf pur & blk, *sal*	9.50	9.50
32	A11	80pf lake & blk, *rose*	11.00	11.00

Overprinted in Black or Red

33	A12	1m car rose	27.50	*32.50*
34	A13	2m gray blue	27.50	*29.00*
35	A14	3m blk vio (R)	47.50	*65.00*
36	A15	5m slate & car, I	1,350.	*2,400.*
b.		Red and/or white retouched	210.00	*300.00*
36A	A15	5m slate & car, II	210.00	*325.00*
		Nos. 24-36A (14)	1,720.	*2,917.*

See note after Germany No. 65A for information on retouches on No. 36. For description of the 5m Type I and Type II, see note above Germany No. 62.

Surcharged on German Stamps of 1902 in Black or Red

a

b

c

1905 **Unwmk.**

37	A16(a)	1c on 3pf	3.00	*3.50*
38	A16(a)	2c on 5pf	3.00	1.60
39	A16(a)	4c on 10pf	5.50	1.60
40	A16(a)	10c on 20pf	3.00	1.75
41	A16(a)	20c on 40pf	19.00	7.25
42	A16(a)	40c on 80pf	30.00	13.50
43	A17(b)	½d on 1m (26x17 perf. holes)	16.00	*20.00*
44	A21(b)	1d on 2m	16.00	*22.50*
45a	A19(c)	1 ½d 1 ½d on 3m, 25x16 perf. holes	17.00	47.50
46	A20(b)	2 ½d on 5m	100.00	*300.00*
		Nos. 37-46 (10)	212.50	*419.20*

Surcharged on German Stamps of 1905 in Black or Red

1906-13 **Wmk. 125**

47	A16(a)	1c on 3pf	.65	*1.25*
48	A16(a)	2c on 5pf	.45	*1.25*
49	A16(a)	4c on 10pf	.80	*1.60*
50	A16(a)	10c on 20pf	.80	*7.00*
51	A16(a)	20c on 40pf	1.60	*3.50*
52	A16(a)	40c on 80pf	1.60	*52.50*
53	A17(b)	½d on 1m	6.50	*40.00*
54	A21(b)	1d on 2m	10.50	*40.00*
55	A19(c)	1 ½d on 3m (R)	8.00	*120.00*
56	A20(b)	2 ½d on 5m (26x17 perf. holes)	29.00	*80.00*
		Nos. 47-56 (10)	59.90	*347.10*

Forged cancellations exist.

OFFICES IN MOROCCO

100 Centimos = 1 Peseta

Stamps of Germany Surcharged in Black

1899 **Unwmk.** *Perf. 13½x14½*

1	A9	3c on 3pf dk brn	3.25	2.10
2	A9	5c on 5pf green	3.25	2.40
3	A10	10c on 10pf car	9.00	9.00
4	A10	25c on 20pf ultra	18.00	13.50
5	A10	30c on 25pf orange	27.50	*32.50*
6	A10	60c on 50pf red brn	22.50	*37.50*
		Nos. 1-6 (6)	83.50	97.00

Before Nos. 1-6 were issued, the same six basic stamps of Germany's 1889-1900 issue were overprinted "Marocco" diagonally without the currency-changing surcharge line, but were not issued. Value, set $750.

German Stamps of 1900 Surcharged in Black and Red

Germany No. 54 Srchd.

Germany No. 62 Srchd.

Germany No. 63 Srchd.

Germany No. 64 Srchd.

Germany No. 65A Srchd.

1900 *Perf. 14, 14½*

7	A11	3c on 3pf brn	1.25	*2.25*
8	A11	5c on 5pf grn	1.50	1.50
9	A11	10c on 10pf car	2.25	1.50
10	A11	25c on 20pf ultra	3.00	2.75
11	A11	30c on 25pf org & blk, *yel*	9.00	*15.00*
12	A11	35c on 30pf org & blk, *sal*	6.75	6.00
13	A11	50c on 40pf lake & blk	6.75	6.00
14	A11	60c on 50pf pur & blk, *sal*	13.50	*29.00*
15	A11	1p on 80pf lake & blk, *rose*	12.00	10.50
16	A12	1p25c on 1m car rose	30.00	*45.00*
17	A13	2p50c on 2m gray bl	37.50	*57.50*
18	A14	3p75c on 3m blk vio (R)	45.00	*65.00*
19	A15	6p25c on 5m sl & car, type I	975.00	*1,325.*
b.		Red and/or white retouched	165.00	*300.00*
19A	A15	6p25c on 5m sl & car, type II	1,500.	—
		Nos. 7-19A (14)	2,644.	*1,567.*

See note after Germany No. 65A for information on retouches on No. 19. For description of the 5m Type I and Type II, see note above Germany No. 62.

Germany No. 54 Srchd.

Germany No. 62 Srchd.

Germany No. 63 Srchd.

Germany No. 64 Srchd.

Germany No. 65A Srchd.

1903 **New Surcharge Plates**

8D	A11	5c on 5pf grn	70.00	11.00
16D	A12	1p25c on 1m car rose	350.00	180.00
17D	A13	2p50c on 2m gray bl	500.00	110.00
18D	A14	3p75c on 3m blk vio (R)	1,300.	240.00
19D	A15	6p25c on 5m sl & car, type II	200.00	260.00

The 1903 printing Nos. 8D, 16D-18D, 19D differs from Nos. 8, 16-18 and 19A in that the surcharge font is thicker, especially the "M" and "t".

German Stamps of 1902 Surcharged in Black or Red

a

b

c

1905 **Unwmk.**

20	A16(a)	3c on 3pf	2.60	3.50
21	A16(a)	5c on 5pf	4.50	1.10
22	A16(a)	10c on 10pf	8.25	1.10
23	A16(a)	25c on 20pf	18.00	3.25
24	A16(a)	30c on 25pf	6.00	6.00
25	A16(a)	35c on 30pf	9.00	5.50
26	A16(a)	50c on 40pf	9.00	7.50
27	A16(a)	60c on 50pf	20.00	*22.50*
28	A16(a)	1p on 80pf	20.00	18.00
29	A17(b)	1p25c on 1m	50.00	35.00
30	A21(b)	2p50c on 2m	95.00	*135.00*
31	A19(c)	3p75c on 3m (R)	42.50	*52.50*
32	A20(b)	6p25c on 5m	150.00	*200.00*
		Nos. 20-32 (13)	434.85	*490.95*

Surcharged on Germany No. 54

32A	A11(a)	5c on 5pf	7.50	*24.00*

German Stamps of 1905 Surcharged

1906-11 **Wmk. 125**

33	A16(a)	3c on 3pf	8.25	2.00
34	A16(a)	5c on 5pf	6.50	1.10
35	A16(a)	10c on 10pf	6.50	1.10
36	A16(a)	25c on 20pf	19.00	7.50
37	A16(a)	30c on 25pf	19.00	15.00
38	A16(a)	35c on 30pf	15.00	9.75
39	A16(a)	50c on 40pf	30.00	*135.00*
40	A16(a)	60c on 50pf	22.50	17.00
41	A16(a)	1p on 80pf	*110.00*	*260.00*
42	A17(b)	1p25c on 1m	60.00	*165.00*
43	A21(b)	2p50c on 2m	60.00	*165.00*
44	A20(b)	6p25c on 5m	110.00	*300.00*
		Nos. 33-44 (12)	466.75	*1,078.*

Excellent forgeries exist of No. 41.

Surcharge Spelled "Marokko" in Black or Red

1911

45	A16(a)	3c on 3pf	.55	*.75*
46	A16(a)	5c on 5pf	.55	*1.00*
47	A16(a)	10c on 10pf	.55	*1.10*
48	A16(a)	25c on 20pf	.65	*1.40*
49	A16(a)	30c on 25pf	1.50	*16.00*
50	A16(a)	35c on 30pf	1.50	*8.75*
51	A16(a)	50c on 40pf	*1.25*	5.25
52	A16(a)	60c on 50pf	*2.40*	*37.50*
53	A16(a)	1p on 80pf	1.60	*24.00*
54	A17(b)	1p25c on 1m	*4.50*	*65.00*
55	A21(b)	2p50c on 2m	*6.00*	*47.50*
56	A19(c)	3p75c on 3m (R)	10.50	*225.00*
57	A20(b)	6p25c on 5m	19.00	*325.00*
		Nos. 45-57 (13)	50.55	*758.25*

Forged cancellations exist.

OFFICES IN THE TURKISH EMPIRE

Unused values for Nos. 1-6 are for stamps with original gum. Stamps without gum sell for about one-third of the figures quoted.

---

40 Paras = 1 Piaster

German Stamps of 1880-83 Surcharged in Black or Blue

Germany No. 30 Surcharged

Germany No. 31 Surcharged

1884 **Unwmk.** *Perf. 13½x14½*

1	A6	10pa on 5pf dull vio	52.50	30.00
2	A7	20pa on 10pf rose	75.00	75.00
3	A7	1pi on 20pf ultra (Bk)	60.00	7.50
4	A7	1pi on 20pf ultra (Bl)	2,250.	72.50
5	A7	1 ¼pi on 25pf brn	120.00	*260.00*
6	A7	2 ½pi on 50pf gray grn	120.00	140.00
a.		2 ½pi on 50pf deep olive grn	275.00	210.00
		Nos. 1-6 (6)	2,678.	585.00

There are two types of the surcharge on the 1 ¼pi and 2 ½pi stamps, the difference being in the spacing between the figures and the word "PIASTER."

There are re-issues of these stamps which vary only slightly from the originals in overprint measurements.

German Stamps of 1880-1900 Surcharged in Black

Germany No. 47 Surcharged

Germany No. 48 Surcharged

Germany No. 50 Surcharged

1889

8	A9	10pa on 5pf grn	3.50	3.75
9	A10	20pa on 10pf car	9.00	3.25
10	A10	1pi on 20pf ultra	6.00	2.25
11	A10	1¼pi on 25pf org	22.50	20.00
12	A10	2½pi on 50pf choc	35.00	22.50
a.		2½pi on 50pf copper brown	190.00	110.00
		Nos. 8-12 (5)	76.00	51.75

German Stamps of 1900 Surcharged

Germany No. 55 Surcharged

Germany No. 62 Srchd.

Germany No. 63 Srchd.

Germany No. 64 Srchd.

Germany No. 65A Srchd.

1900 *Perf. 14, 14½*

Black or Red Surcharge

13	A11	10pa on 5pf grn	1.75	1.75
14	A11	20pa on 10pf car	2.75	2.25
15	A11	1pi on 20pf ultra	4.50	1.75
16	A11	1¼pi on 25pf org & blk, *yel*	6.00	4.50
17	A11	1½pi on 30pf org & blk, *sal*	6.00	4.50
18	A11	2pi on 40pf lake & blk	6.00	4.50
19	A11	2½pi on 50pf pur & blk, *sal*	12.00	*13.00*
20	A11	4pi on 80pf lake & blk, *rose*	13.50	13.00
21	A12	5pi on 1m car rose	35.00	37.50
22	A13	10pi on 2m gray bl	30.00	*42.50*
23	A14	15pi on 3m blk vio (R)	45.00	*110.00*
24	A15	25pi on 5m sl & car, type I	640.00	*1,250.*
a.		Double surcharge		*9,000.*
d.		Red and/or white retouched	175.00	*250.00*
e.		White only retouched	290.00	500.00
24B	A15	25pi on 5m sl & car, type II	290.00	*500.00*
c.		Double surcharge	*9,750.*	—
		Nos. 13-24B (13)	1,093.	1,985.

See note after Germany No. 65A for information on retouches on No. 24. For description of the 5m Type I & Type II, see note above Germany No. 62.

German Stamps of 1900 Surcharged in Black

1903-05

25	A11	10pa on 5pf green	9.00	*13.50*
26	A11	20pa on 10pf car	30.00	19.00
27	A11	1pi on 20pf ultra	8.25	7.25

German Stamps of 1900, 1905 Surcharged in Black

28	A12	5pi on 1m car rose	140.00	95.00
29	A13	10pi on 2m bl ('05)	150.00	*260.00*
30	A15	25pi on 5m sl & car	190.00	*525.00*
a.		Double surcharge	*4,500.*	
		Nos. 25-30 (6)	527.25	*919.75*

The 1903-05 surcharges may be easily distinguished from those of 1900 by the added bar at the top of the letter "A."

German Stamps of 1902 Surcharged in Black or Red

a

b

1905 **Unwmk.**

31	A16(a)	10pa on 5pf	3.50	2.50
32	A16(a)	20pa on 10pf	9.00	3.25
33	A16(a)	1pi on 20pf	19.00	2.00
34	A16(a)	1¼pi on 25pf	9.00	7.50
35	A16(a)	1½pi on 30pf	13.50	15.00
36	A16(a)	2pi on 40pf	22.50	15.00
37	A16(a)	2½pi on 50pf	9.00	*22.50*
38	A16(a)	4pi on 80pf	27.50	17.50
39	A17(b)	5pi on 1m	45.00	45.00
40	A21(b)	10pi on 2m	37.50	*45.00*
41	A19(b)	15pi on 3m (R)	45.00	*52.50*
42	A20(b)	25pi on 5m	225.00	*525.00*
		Nos. 31-42 (12)	465.50	*752.75*

German Stamps of 1905 Surcharged in Black or Red

1906-12 **Wmk. 125**

43	A16(a)	10pa on 5pf	2.25	.90
44	A16(a)	20pa on 10pf	4.50	.90
45	A16(a)	1pi on 20pf	6.00	.90
46	A16(a)	1¼pi on 25pf	12.00	12.00
47	A16(a)	1½pi on 30pf	12.00	10.00
48	A16(a)	2pi on 40pf	6.00	1.75
49	A16(a)	2½pi on 50pf	9.00	*16.50*
50	A16(a)	4pi on 80pf	15.00	*22.50*
51	A17(b)	5pi on 1m	35.00	30.00
52	A21(b)	10pi on 2m	35.00	*45.00*
53	A19(b)	15pi on 3m (R)	60.00	*450.00*
54	A20(b)	25pi on 5m	30.00	*75.00*
		Nos. 43-54 (12)	226.75	665.45

German Stamps of 1905 Surcharged Diagonally in Black

1908

55	A16	5c on 5pf	1.90	*2.75*
56	A16	10c on 10pf	2.75	*4.50*
57	A16	25c on 20pf	6.00	*22.50*
58	A16	50c on 40pf	30.00	*55.00*
59	A16	100c on 80pf	52.50	*60.00*
		Nos. 55-59 (5)	93.15	*144.75*

Forged cancellations exist on Nos. 37, 53-54, 57-59.

GERMAN DEMOCRATIC REPUBLIC

LOCATION — Eastern Germany
GOVT. — Republic
AREA — 41,659 sq. mi.
POP. — 16,701,500 (1983)
CAPITAL — Berlin (Soviet sector)

100 Pfennigs = 1 Deutsche Mark (East)

100 Pfennigs = 1 Mark of the Deutsche Notenbank (MDN) (1965)

100 Pfennigs = 1 Mark of the National Bank (M) (1969)

100 Pfennigs = 1 Deutsche Mark (West) (1990)

Catalogue values for unused stamps in this country are for Never Hinged items, beginning with Scott 48 in the regular postage section, Scott B14 in the semi-postal section, Scott C1 in the air-post section, and Scott O1 official section.

Watermarks

Watermark 292, see Germany.

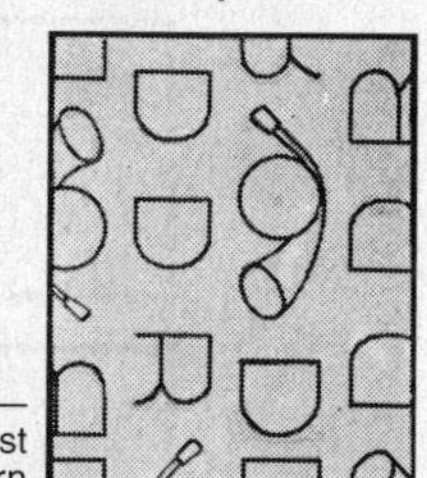

Wmk. 297 — DDR and Post Horn

Wmk. 313 — Quatrefoil and DDR

Wmk. 397

FOR USE IN ALL PROVINCES IN THE RUSSIAN ZONE

When the mark was revalued in June, 1948, a provisional overprint, consisting of various city and town names and post office or zone numerals, was applied by hand in black, violet or blue at innumerable post offices to their stocks.

Germany Nos. 557 to 573 Overprinted in Black

1948, July 3 **Wmk. 284** *Perf. 14*

10N1	A120	2pf	brn blk	.25	.25
10N2	A120	6pf	purple	.25	*.30*
10N3	A121	8pf	red	.25	*.30*
10N4	A121	10pf	yel grn	.25	*.30*
10N5	A122	12pf	gray	.25	*.30*
10N6	A120	15pf	choc	.25	*.30*
10N7	A123	16pf	dk blue grn	.25	*.50*
10N8	A121	20pf	blue	.25	*.30*
10N9	A123	24pf	brn org	.25	*.25*
10N10	A120	25pf	org yel	.25	.25
10N11	A122	30pf	red	.65	*.30*
10N12	A121	40pf	red violet	.25	*.30*
10N13	A123	50pf	ultra	.25	*.65*
10N14	A122	60pf	red brn	.25	*.65*
a.		60pf	brown red	30.00	*125.00*
10N15	A122	80pf	dark blue	.80	*.80*
10N16	A123	84pf	emerald	.80	*1.10*
			Nos. 10N1-10N16 (16)	5.50	6.85
			Set, never hinged	14.00	

Same Overprint on Numeral Stamps of Germany, 1946

1948, Sept.

10N17	A119	5pf	yellow grn	.25	*.70*
10N18	A119	30pf	olive	.40	*2.00*
10N19	A119	45pf	brt red	.25	*.80*
10N20	A119	75pf	deep ultra	.25	*.80*
10N21	A119	84pf	emerald	.40	*1.60*
			Nos. 10N17-10N21 (5)	1.55	5.90
			Set, never hinged	4.75	

Nos 10N1-10N21 all exist with inverted overprint, and majority with double overprint.

Same Overprint on Berlin-Brandenburg Nos. 11N1-11N7

Unwmk.

1948, Sept. **Litho.** *Perf. 14*

10N22	OS1	5pf	green	.25	.80
a.			Serrate roulette	.25	.80
10N23	OS1	6pf	violet	.25	.80
10N24	OS1	8pf	red	.25	.80
10N25	OS1	10pf	brown	.25	.80
10N26	OS1	12pf	rose	.25	*1.20*
10N27	OS1	20pf	blue	.25	*1.20*
10N28	OS1	30pf	olive	.25	*1.20*
			Nos. 10N22-10N28 (7)	1.75	6.80
			Set, never hinged	3.25	

The overprint made Nos. 10N22-10N28 valid for postage throughout the Russian Zone.

Gerhard Hauptmann — OS2

Designs: 2pf, 20pf, Käthe Kollwitz. 40pf, Gerhard Hauptmann. 8pf, 50pf, Karl Marx. 10pf, 84pf, August Bebel. 12pf, 30pf, Friedrich Engels. 15pf, 60pf, G. W. F. Hegel. 16pf, 25pf, Rudolf Virchow. 24pf, 80pf, Ernst Thälmann.

Perf. 13x12½

1948 **Typo.** **Wmk. 292**

10N29	OS2	2pf	gray	.25	*1.20*
10N30	OS2	6pf	violet	.25	*1.20*
10N31	OS2	8pf	red brn	.25	*1.20*
10N32	OS2	10pf	blue grn	.25	*1.00*
10N33	OS2	12pf	blue	.80	*.80*
10N34	OS2	15pf	brown	.30	*1.75*
10N35	OS2	16pf	turquoise	1.75	*1.75*
10N36	OS2	20pf	maroon	.30	*1.25*
10N37	OS2	24pf	carmine	.60	*1.20*
10N38	OS2	25pf	olive grn	.35	*2.00*
10N39	OS2	30pf	red	.60	*1.75*
10N40	OS2	40pf	red violet	4.00	*2.50*
10N41	OS2	50pf	dk ultra	.30	*1.60*
10N42	OS2	60pf	dull green	1.75	*2.00*
10N43	OS2	80pf	dark blue	.30	*1.75*
10N44	OS2	84pf	brown lake	.30	*3.50*
			Nos. 10N29-10N44 (16)	12.35	26.45
			Set, never hinged	40.00	

See German Democratic Republic Nos. 122-136.

Karl Liebknecht and Rosa Luxemburg OS3

Perf. 13½x13

1949, Jan. 15 Litho. Wmk. 292

10N45	OS3 24pf rose	.25	*.80*
	Never hinged	.65	

30th anniv. of the death of Karl Liebknecht and Rosa Luxemburg, German socialists.

Dove and Laurel — OS4

1949

10N46	OS4 24pf carmine rose	.45	*1.75*
	Never hinged	1.25	

Overprinted in Black: "3. Deutscher Volkskongress 29.-30. Mai 1949"

1949, May 29

10N47	OS4 24pf carmine rose	.50	*2.25*
	Never hinged	1.60	

Nos. 10N46 and 10N47 were issued for the 3rd German People's Congress.

GERMAN DEMOCRATIC REPUBLIC

Catalogue values for unused stamps in this section, from this point to the end of the section, are for Never Hinged items.

Canceled to Order

The government stamp agency started in 1949 to sell canceled sets of new issues.

Used values are for CTO's for Nos. 48-2831, except for souvenir sheets, which are valued as postally used.

Pigeon, Letter and Globe A5

Wmk. Flowers Multiple (292)

1949, Oct. 9 Litho. ***Perf. 13½***

48	A5 50pf lt blue & dk blue	8.50	8.50

75th anniv. of the UPU.

Letter Carriers — A6

1949, Oct. 27 ***Perf. 13***

49	A6 12pf blue	6.00	*6.00*
50	A6 30pf red	8.50	*12.00*

"Day of the International Postal Workers' Trade Union," October 27-29, 1949.

Skier — A7

1950, Mar. 2 ***Perf. 13***

51	A7 12pf shown	4.25	3.50
52	A7 24pf Skater	5.50	4.75

1st German Winter Sport Championship Matches, Schierke, 1950.

Globe and Sun — A8

1950, May 1 **Typo.**

53	A8 30pf deep carmine	12.00	11.00

60th anniv. of Labor Day.

A9

Pres. Wilhelm Pieck — A10

1950-51 Wmk. 292 ***Perf. 13x12½***

54	A9 12pf dark blue	15.00	1.50
55	A9 24pf red brown	21.00	.95
	Perf. 13x13½		
56	A10 1m olive green	21.00	4.75
	Litho.		
57	A10 2m red brown	12.00	4.75
	Engr.		
57A	A10 5m deep blue ('51)	6.00	1.20
	Nos. 54-57A (5)	75.00	13.15

See Nos. 113-117, 120-121.

Leonhard Euler — A11

Portraits: 5pf, Alexander von Humboldt. 6pf, Theodor Mommsen. 8pf, Wilhelm von Humboldt. 10pf, H. L. F. von Helmholtz. 12pf, Max Planck. 16pf, Jacob Grimm. 20pf, W. H. Nernst. 24pf, Gottfried von Leibnitz. 50pf, Adolf von Harnack.

Wmk. 292

1950, July 10 Litho. ***Perf. 12½***

58	A11 1pf gray	3.00	1.20
59	A11 5pf dp green	4.25	3.00
60	A11 6pf purple	8.50	3.00
61	A11 8pf orange brn	9.50	6.00
62	A11 10pf dk gray grn	8.50	6.00
63	A11 12pf dk blue	6.00	2.50
64	A11 16pf Prus blue	12.00	12.00
65	A11 20pf violet brn	11.00	9.50
66	A11 24pf red	11.00	3.25
67	A11 50pf dp ultra	15.00	12.00
	Nos. 58-67 (10)	88.75	58.45
	Set, hinged	25.00	

250th anniv. of the founding of the Academy of Science, Berlin.

See Nos. 352-354.

Miner — A12

Design: 24pf, Smelting copper.

1950, Sept. 1 ***Perf. 13***

68	A12 12pf blue	4.25	*4.75*
69	A12 24pf dark red	6.50	4.75

750th anniv. of the opening of the Mannsfeld copper mines.

Symbols of a Democratic Vote — A13

1950, Sept. 28

70	A13 24pf brown red	9.50	3.00

Publicizing the election of Oct. 15, 1950.

Hand Between Dove and Tank — A14

Designs show hand shielding dove from: 8pf, Exploding shell. 12pf, Atomic explosion. 24pf, Cemetery.

1950, Dec. 15 Litho. ***Perf. 13***

71	A14 6pf violet blue	3.00	2.00
72	A14 8pf brown	2.75	1.20
73	A14 12pf blue	3.25	2.75
74	A14 24pf red	3.50	1.75
	Nos. 71-74 (4)	12.50	7.70

Issued to publicize the "Fight for Peace."

Tobogganing A15

Design: 24pf, Ski jump.

1951, Feb. 3 Litho. ***Perf. 13***

76	A15 12pf blue	5.50	4.75
77	A15 24pf rose	7.25	6.00

Issued to publicize the second Winter Sports Championship Matches at Oberhof.

A16

1951, Mar. 4 Wmk. 292 ***Perf. 13***

78	A16 24pf rose carmine	9.50	10.00
79	A16 50pf violet blue	10.00	10.00

Issued to publicize the 1951 Leipzig Fair.

Pres. Wilhelm Pieck and Pres. Boleslaw Bierut Shaking Hands Across Oder-Neisse Frontier — A17

1951, Apr. 22 ***Perf. 13***

80	A17 24pf scarlet	13.00	11.00
81	A17 50pf blue	13.00	11.00

Visit of Pres. Boleslaw Bierut of Poland to the Russian Zone of Germany.

Mao Tse-tung A18

Redistribution of Chinese Land — A19

1951, June 27 ***Perf. 13***

82	A18 12pf dark green	60.00	17.50
83	A19 24pf deep carmine	85.00	22.50
84	A18 50pf violet blue	60.00	22.50
	Nos. 82-84 (3)	205.00	62.50
	Set, hinged	65.00	

Issued to publicize East Germany's friendship toward Communist China.

Boy Raising Flag — A20

Design: 24pf, 50pf, Girls dancing.

1951, Aug. 3

Grayish Paper, Except 30pf

85	A20 12pf choc & org brn	8.50	4.50
86	A20 24pf dk car & yel grn	8.50	2.50
87	A20 30pf dk bl grn & org brn, *cit*	9.75	5.00
88	A20 50pf vio bl & dk car	9.75	5.00
	Nos. 85-88 (4)	36.50	17.00

3rd World Youth Festival, Berlin, 1951.

5-Year Plan Symbolism — A21

1951, Sept. 2 Typo. Wmk. 292

89	A21 24pf multicolored	3.25	2.00

East Germany's Five-Year Plan.

Karl Liebknecht — A22

1951, Oct. 7 Litho. ***Perf. 13½x13***

90	A22 24pf red & blue gray	4.00	2.00

Karl Liebknecht, socialist, 80th birth anniv.

Father and Children with Stamp Collection A23

1951, Oct. 28 ***Perf. 13***

91	A23 12pf deep blue	4.50	2.00

Stamp Day, Oct. 28, 1951.

Stalin and Wilhelm Pieck A24

Design: 12pf, Pavel Bykov and Erich Wirth.

1951

92 A24 12pf deep blue 4.00 3.00
93 A24 24pf red 4.50 3.50

Month of East German-Soviet friendship. Issue dates: 12pf, Dec. 15, 24pf, Dec. 1.

Winter Sports Championship Matches, Oberhof, 1952 — A25

Design: 12pf, Skier. 24pf, Ski jump.

1952, Jan. 12 **Wmk. 292**

94 A25 12pf blue green 4.00 3.00
95 A25 24pf deep blue 4.00 3.00

Ludwig van Beethoven, 125th Death Anniv. — A26

Design: 12pf, Beethoven full face.

1952, Mar. 26 ***Perf. 13½***

96 A26 12pf bl gray & vio bl 2.00 .50
97 A26 24pf gray & red brn 2.25 .75

See Nos. 100-102.

Cyclists — A27

1952, May 5 **Photo.** ***Perf. 13x13½***

98 A27 12pf blue 3.00 1.25

5th International Bicycle Peace Race, Warsaw-Berlin-Prague.

Klement Gottwald — A28

1952, May 1

99 A28 24pf violet blue 2.25 1.40

Friendship between German Democratic Republic and Czechoslovakia.

Type of 1952

Portraits: 6pf, G. F. Handel. 8pf, Albert Lortzing. 50pf, C. M. von Weber.

1952, July 5 **Litho.** **Wmk. 297**

100 A26 6pf brn buff & choc 2.25 1.25
101 A26 8pf pink & dp rose pink 2.25 2.25
102 A26 50pf bl gray & dp bl 2.50 2.50
Nos. 100-102 (3) 7.00 6.00

Victor Hugo — A29

Portraits: 20pf, Leonardo da Vinci. 24pf, Nicolai Gogol. 35pf, Avicenna.

Wmk. 292

1952, Aug. 11 **Photo.** ***Perf. 13***

103 A29 12pf brown 2.50 *2.75*
104 A29 20pf green 2.50 *2.75*
105 A29 24pf rose 2.50 *2.75*
106 A29 35pf blue 4.00 *4.00*
Nos. 103-106 (4) 11.50 12.25

Machine, Globe and Dove — A30

1952, Sept. 7 **Wmk. 297** ***Perf. 13***

108 A30 24pf red 2.00 .75
109 A30 35pf deep blue 2.00 1.25

Issued to publicize the 1952 Leipzig Fair.

Friedrich Ludwig Jahn — A31

1952, Oct. 15 **Litho.**

110 A31 12pf blue 1.75 1.00

Jahn (1778-1852), introduced gymnastics to Germany, and was a politician.

Halle University — A32

1952, Oct. 18 **Photo.**

111 A32 24pf green 1.75 .75

450th anniv. of the founding of Halle University, Wittenberg.

Stamp, Flags, Wreath, Dove and Hammer — A33

1952, Oct. 26

112 A33 24pf red brown 2.25 .85

Stamp Day, Oct. 26, 1952.

Pieck Types of 1950

Perf. 13x12½

1952-53 **Wmk. 297** **Typo.**

113 A9 5pf blue green 6.50 2.75
114 A9 12pf dark blue 17.50 1.25
115 A9 24pf red brown 17.50 1.25

Perf. 13x13½

116 A10 1m olive green 22.50 13.00

Litho. ***Perf. 13***

117 A10 2m red brown ('53) 22.50 2.75
Nos. 113-117 (5) 86.50 21.00
Set, hinged 24.00

Globe, Dove and St. Stephen's Cathedral — A34

1952, Dec. 8 **Photo.** ***Perf. 13***

118 A34 24pf brt carmine 1.50 *1.60*
119 A34 35pf deep blue 1.50 *3.00*

Issued to publicize the Congress of Nations for Peace, Vienna, Dec. 12-19, 1952.

Pres. Wilhelm Pieck — A35

1953 ***Perf. 13x13½***

120 A35 1m olive 10.00 .50
a. 1m dark olive 10.00 .50
121 A35 2m red brown 7.00 .50

See Nos. 339-340, 532.

Portrait Types of Russian Occupation, 1948

Designs as before.

Perf. 13x12½

1953 **Typo.** **Wmk. 297**

122 OS2 2pf gray 2.50 *2.75*
123 OS2 6pf purple 2.50 1.75
124 OS2 8pf red brown 1.60 1.75
125 OS2 10pf blue grn 4.50 2.50
126 OS2 15pf brown 10.00 10.00
127 OS2 16pf turquoise 4.00 2.75
128 OS2 20pf maroon 6.50 1.75
129 OS2 25pf olive grn 130.00 *175.00*
130 OS2 30pf red 16.00 6.50
131 OS2 40pf red violet 3.25 3.25
132 OS2 50pf dk ultra 20.00 14.00
133 OS2 60pf dull green 4.00 2.75
134 OS2 80pf dark blue 4.00 1.75
a. Varnish coating, dark ultramarine 8.00 6.00
135 OS2 80pf crimson 10.00 6.50
136 OS2 84pf brown lake 52.50 *65.00*
Nos. 122-136 (15) 271.35 298.00
Set, hinged 85.00

"Industry" and Red Flag — A36

Karl Marx Speaking — A38

Marx and Engels — A37

Karl Marx Medallion — A39

Designs: 12pf, Spasski tower and communist flag. 16pf, Marching workers. 24pf, Portrait of Karl Marx. 35pf, Marx addressing audience. 48pf, Karl Marx and Friedrich Engels. 60pf. Red banner above heads and shoulders of workers.

1953 **Photo.** ***Perf. 13***

137 A36 6pf grnsh gray & red 1.00 .65
138 A37 10pf grnsh gray & dk brn 3.25 .65
139 A36 12pf grn, dp plum & dk grn .95 .65
140 A37 16pf vio bl & dk car 2.50 1.75
141 A38 20pf brown & buff 1.00 .65
142 A38 24pf brown & red 2.50 .65
143 A36 35pf dp pur & cr 2.50 1.75
144 A36 48pf dk ol grn & red brn 1.25 .65
a. Souvenir sheets of 6 perf. & imperf. 120.00 *200.00*
Hinged 45.00
145 A37 60pf vio brn & red 3.25 2.25
146 A39 84pf blue & brown 2.50 1.75
a. Souvenir sheets of 4 perf. & imperf. 120.00 *200.00*
Hinged 45.00
Nos. 137-146 (10) 20.70 11.40

No. 144a contains one each of the denominations in types A36 and A38. Perf. and imperf.

No. 146a contains one each of the denominations in types A37 and A39. Perf. and imperf.

Maxim Gorky — A40

1953, Mar. 28

147 A40 35pf brown .45 .40

Bicycle Racers — A41

24pf, 60pf, Different views of bicycle race.

1953, May 2 **Wmk. 297** ***Perf. 13***

148 A41 24pf bluish green 2.00 1.25
149 A41 35pf deep ultra 1.00 .80
150 A41 60pf chocolate 1.25 1.00
Nos. 148-150 (3) 4.25 3.05

6th International Bicycle Peace Race.

Heinrich von Kleist — A42

20pf, Evangelical Marienkirche. 24pf, Sailboat on Oder River. 35pf, City Hall, Frankfurt-on-Oder.

1953, July 6 **Litho.**

151 A42 16pf chocolate 1.10 *1.75*
152 A42 20pf blue green .80 *1.75*
153 A42 24pf rose red 1.10 *1.75*
154 A42 35pf violet blue 1.25 *2.25*
Nos. 151-154 (4) 4.25 7.50

700th anniversary of the founding of Frankfurt-on-Oder.

Woman Mariner — A43

Designs: 1pf, Coal miner. 6pf, German and Soviet workers. 8pf, Mother teaching Marxist principles. 10pf, Machinists. 12pf, Worker, peasant and intellectual. 15pf, Teletype operator. 16pf, Steel worker. 20pf, Bad Elster. 24pf, Stalin Boulevard. 25pf, Locomotive building. 30pf, Dancing couple. 35pf, Sports Hall, Berlin. 40pf, Laboratory worker. 48pf, Zwinger Castle, Dresden. 60pf, Launching ship. 80pf, Agricultural workers. 84pf, Dove and East German family.

1953 **Litho.** ***Perf. 13x12½***

155 A43 1pf black brown 1.25 .25
156 A43 5pf emerald 1.60 .25
157 A43 6pf violet 1.60 .25
158 A43 8pf orange brn 2.25 .25
159 A43 10pf blue green 1.60 .25
160 A43 12pf blue 1.60 .25
161 A43 15pf purple 2.60 .25
162 A43 16pf dk violet 5.00 .25
163 A43 20pf olive 3.75 .25
163A A43 24pf carmine 7.00 .25

164	A43	25pf dk green	5.00	.25
165	A43	30pf dp car	15.00	.25
166	A43	35pf violet bl	13.00	.25
167	A43	40pf rose red	10.00	.25
168	A43	48pf rose red	10.00	.25
169	A43	60pf deep blue	10.00	.25
170	A43	80pf aqua	12.00	.25
171	A43	84pf chocolate	10.00	.25
		Nos. 155-171 (18)	113.25	4.50
		Set, hinged	40.00	

See Nos. 187-204, 227-230A, 330-338, 476-482. For surcharges see Nos. 216-223A.

Used values of Nos. 155-171 are for cto reprints with printed cancellations, printed in 1957. The reprints differ slightly from originals in design and shade.

Power Shovel — A44

Design: 35pf, Road-building machine.

1953, Aug. 29 Photo. *Perf. 13*

172	A44	24pf red brown	2.00	2.00
173	A44	35pf deep green	2.00	2.00

The 1953 Leipzig Fair.

G. W. von Knobelsdorff and Berlin State Opera House — A45

Design: 35pf, Balthasar Neumann and Wurzburg bishop's palace.

1953, Sept. 16 *Perf. 13x12½*

174	A45	24pf cerise	1.60	.70
175	A45	35pf dk slate blue	1.60	1.10

200th anniv. of the deaths of G. W. von Knobelsdorff and Balthasar Neumann, architects.

Lucas Cranach — A46

1953, Oct. 16 *Perf. 13x13½*

176	A46	24pf brown	2.50	1.25

400th anniversary of the death of Lucas Cranach (1472-1553), painter.

Nurse Applying Bandage — A47

Perf. 13½x13

1953, Oct. 23 Wmk. 297

177	A47	24pf brown & red	2.10	1.25

Issued to honor the Red Cross.

Mail Delivery — A48

1953, Oct. 25 Photo.

178	A48	24pf blue gray	2.25	.60

Stamp Day, Oct. 24, 1953.

Lion and Lioness — A49

1953, Nov. 2 *Perf. 13x13½*

179	A49	24pf olive brown	2.00	.50

75th anniversary of Leipzig Zoo.

Thomas Muntzer and Attackers A50

16pf, H. F. K. vom Stein. 20pf, Ferdinand von Schill leading cavalry. 24pf, G. L. Blucher and battle scene. 35pf, Students fighting for National Unity. 48pf, Revolution of 1848.

1953, Nov. Photo. *Perf. 13x12½*

180	A50	12pf brown	1.20	.40
181	A50	16pf dp brown	1.20	.40
182	A50	20pf dk car rose	1.20	.30
183	A50	24pf deep blue	1.20	.30
184	A50	35pf dk green	2.00	1.25
185	A50	48pf dk brown	3.00	1.00
		Nos. 180-185 (6)	9.80	3.65

Issued to honor German patriots.

Franz Schubert — A51

1953, Nov. 13 *Perf. 13½x13*

186	A51	48pf brt orange brn	2.50	1.25

Death of Franz Schubert, 125th anniv.

Types of 1953 Redrawn

Designs as before.

1953-54 Typo. *Perf. 13x12½*

187	A43	1pf black brn	.60	.25
188	A43	5pf emerald	2.00	.25
a.		Bklt. pane, 3 #188 + 3 #227	24.00	28.00
b.		Bklt. pane, 3 #188 + 3 #228	24.00	28.00
189	A43	6pf purple	3.25	.25
190	A43	8pf orange brn	3.25	.25
191	A43	10pf blue grn	30.00	.25
192	A43	12pf grnsh blue	4.50	.25
193	A43	15pf brt vio ('54)	14.00	.25
194	A43	16pf dk purple	3.25	.25
195	A43	20pf olive ('54)	60.00	.25
196	A43	24pf carmine	4.00	.25
197	A43	25pf dk bl grn	3.25	.25
198	A43	30pf dp carmine	6.50	.25
199	A43	35pf dp vio bl	4.00	.25
200	A43	40pf rose red ('54)	8.00	.25
201	A43	48pf rose vio	8.00	.25
202	A43	60pf blue	14.00	.25
203	A43	80pf aqua	3.25	.25
204	A43	84pf chocolate	13.00	.25
		Nos. 187-204 (18)	184.85	4.50
		Set, hinged	50.00	

Nos. 155-171 were printed from screened halftones, and shading consists of dots. Shading in lines without screen on Nos. 187-204. Designers' and engravers' names added below design on all values except 6, 12, 16 and 35pf. There are many other minor differences.

See note on used values after No. 171.

Gotthold E. Lessing — A52

1954, Jan. 20 Photo. *Perf. 13*

205	A52	20pf dark green	2.00	.75

225th anniversary of the birth of G. E. Lessing, dramatist.

Dove Over Conference Table — A53

1954, Jan. 25 *Perf. 12½x13*

206	A53	12pf blue	1.40	.75

Four Power Conference, Berlin, 1954.

Joseph V. Stalin — A54

1954, Mar. 5 Typo. *Perf. 13x12½*

207	A54	20pf gray, dk brn & red org	2.50	.75

1st anniv. of the death of Joseph V. Stalin.

Cyclists A55

Design: 24pf, Cyclists passing farm.

1954, Apr. 30 Photo.

208	A55	12pf brown	1.20	.60
209	A55	24pf dull green	1.75	.85

7th International Bicycle Peace Race.

Dancers — A56

Design: 24pf, Boy, two girls and flag.

1954, June 3 *Perf. 13*

210	A56	12pf emerald	.95	.65
211	A56	24pf rose brown	.95	.65

Issued to publicize the 2nd German youth meeting for peace, unity and freedom.

Fritz Reuter — A57

1954, July 12

212	A57	24pf sepia	1.40	.75

Death of Fritz Reuter, writer, 80th anniv.

Ernst Thälmann — A58

1954, Aug. 18 *Perf. 13½x13*

213	A58	24pf red org & indigo	1.00	.60

10th anniv. of the death of Ernst Thälmann (1886-1944), Communist leader.

Hall of Commerce, Leipzig Fair — A59

1954, Sept. 4 *Perf. 13x13½*

214	A59	24pf dark red	.65	.50
215	A59	35pf gray blue	.65	.50

Issued to publicize the 1954 Leipzig Fair.

Redrawn Types of 1953-54 Surcharged with New Value and "X" in Black

1954 Typo. *Perf. 13x12½*

216	A43	5pf on 6pf purple	.90	.25
217	A43	5pf on 8pf org brn	1.10	.25
218	A43	10pf on 12pf grnsh bl	1.10	.25
219	A43	15pf on 16pf dk pur	.90	.25
220	A43	20pf on 24pf car	.90	.25
221	A43	40pf on 48pf rose vio	3.00	.25
222	A43	50pf on 60pf blue	3.00	.25
223	A43	70pf on 84pf choc	8.50	.25
		Nos. 216-223 (8)	19.40	2.00

See note on used values after No. 171.

No. 163A Surcharged with New Value and "X" in Black

1955 Litho.

223A	A43	20pf on 24pf car	.80	.45

Counterfeit surcharges exist on other values of the lithographed set (Nos. 155-171).

Pres. Wilhelm Pieck and Flags A60

1954, Oct. 6 Photo.

224	A60	20pf brown	2.00	.65
225	A60	35pf greenish blue	2.00	.85

5th anniv. of the founding of the German Democratic Republic.

Cologne Cathedral, Leipzig Monument and Unissued Stamp Design — A61

1954, Oct. 23 *Perf. 13x13½*

226	A61	20pf brt car rose	1.25	.60
a.		Souvenir sheet, imperf.	32.50	35.00

Stamp Day. No. 226a has frame and inscription in blue. Size: 60x80mm.

Redrawn Types of 1953-54

Designs: 10pf, Worker, peasant and intellectual. 15pf, Steelworker. 20pf, Stalin Boulevard. 40pf, Zwinger Castle, Dresden. 50pf, Launching ship. 70pf, Dove and East German family.

1955 Typo. *Perf. 13x12½*

227	A43	10pf blue	1.50	.25
a.		Bklt. pane, 4 #227 + 2 #228	28.00	28.00
227B	A43	15pf violet	2.75	.25
228	A43	20pf carmine	1.50	.25
229	A43	40pf rose violet	4.00	.25
230	A43	50pf deep blue	6.25	.25
230A	A43	70pf chocolate	7.50	.25
		Nos. 227-230A (6)	23.50	1.50

See note on used values after No. 171.

Soviet Pavilion, Leipzig Spring Fair — A62

Design: 35pf, Chinese pavilion.

Perf. 13x13½

1955, Feb. 21 Photo. Wmk. 297

231 A62	20pf rose violet	.90	.40
232 A62	35pf violet blue	1.10	.40

Issued to publicize the Leipzig Spring Fair.

Women of Three Nations — A63

1955, Mar. 1 *Perf. 13x13½*

233 A63	10pf green	.90	.30
234 A63	20pf red	.90	.30

International Women's Day, 45th year.

Workers' Demonstration — A64

1955, Mar. 15 *Perf. 13x12½*

235 A64	10pf black & red	.90	.70

Intl. Trade Union Conference, Apr., 1955.

A65

Monument to the Victims of Fascism.

1955, Apr. 9 *Perf. 13½x13*

236 A65	10pf violet blue	.70	.60
237 A65	20pf cerise	1.00	.90
a.	Souv. sheet of 2, #236-237, imperf.	15.00	15.00

No. 237a sold for 50pf.

A66

Russian War Memorial, Berlin.

1955, Apr. 15 *Perf. 12½x13*

238 A66	20pf lilac rose	1.30	.80

Nos. 236-238 issued for 10th anniv. of liberation, No. 237a for reconstruction of natl. memorial sites.

Cyclists — A67

1955 Wmk. 297 *Perf. 13½x13*

239 A67	10pf blue green	.80	.35
240 A67	20pf car rose	.80	.45

8th International Bicycle Peace Race, Prague-Berlin-Warsaw.

Starting with the 1955 issues, commemorative stamps which are valued in italics were sold on a restricted basis.

Friedrich von Schiller — A68

Various Portraits of Schiller.

1955, Apr. 30

241 A68	5pf dk gray grn	*2.00*	*1.75*
242 A68	10pf brt blue	.50	.25
243 A68	20pf chocolate	.50	.25
a.	Souv. sheet, #241-243, imperf.	*18.00*	*18.00*
	Nos. 241-243 (3)	*3.00*	*2.25*

150th anniv. of the death of Friedrich von Schiller, poet.

No. 243a sold for 50pf.

Karl Liebknecht — A69

Portraits: 10pf, August Bebel. 15pf, Franz Mehring. 20pf, Ernst Thalmann. 25pf, Clara Zetkin. 40pf, Wilhelm Liebknecht. 60pf, Rosa Luxemburg.

1955, June 20 Photo. *Perf. 13x12½*

244 A69	5pf blue green	.30	.30
245 A69	10pf deep blue	.30	.30
246 A69	15pf violet	*4.25*	*2.50*
247 A69	20pf red	.40	.30
248 A69	25pf slate	.40	.30
249 A69	40pf rose carmine	2.00	.30
250 A69	60pf dk brown	.40	.30
	Nos. 244-250 (7)	*8.05*	*4.30*

Issued to honor German communists.

Optical Goods — A70

Design: 20pf, Pottery and china.

1955, Aug. 29 Photo. *Perf. 13x13½*

253 A70	10pf dark blue	.60	.35
254 A70	20pf slate green	.60	.35

Issued to publicize the 1955 Leipzig Fair.

Farmer Receiving Deed — A71

Harvesters A72

10pf, Construction of new farm community.

1955, Sept. 3 *Perf. 13½x13, 13x13½*

255 A71	5pf dull green	*4.25*	*3.50*
256 A71	10pf ultra	.60	.25
257 A72	20pf lake	.60	.25
	Nos. 255-257 (3)	*5.45*	*4.00*

10th anniv. of the Land-Reform Program.

Man Holding Badge of Peoples' Solidarity — A73

Perf. 13½x13

1955, Oct. 10 Wmk. 297

258 A73	10pf dark blue	.60	.40

10th anniv. of the "Peoples' Solidarity."

Engels at "First International," 1864 — A74

Designs: 10pf, Marx and Engels writing the Communist Manifesto. 15pf, Engels as newspaper editor. 20pf, Friedrich Engels. 30pf, Friedrich Engels. 70pf, Engels on the barricades in 1848.

1955, Nov. 7 *Perf. 13½x13*

259 A74	5pf Prus blue & olive	.25	.25
260 A74	10pf dk blue & yel	.50	.25
261 A74	15pf dk green & ol	.50	.25
262 A74	20pf brn vio & org	1.00	.25
263 A74	30pf org brn & lt bl	*6.00*	*5.00*
264 A74	70pf gray grn & rose car	3.00	.25
a.	Souvenir sheet of 6, #259-264	*60.00*	*120.00*
	Nos. 259-264 (6)	*11.25*	*6.25*

Friedrich Engels, 135th birth anniv.

Cathedral at Magdeburg — A75

German Buildings: 10pf, German State Opera. 15pf, Old City Hall, Leipzig. 20pf, City Hall, Berlin. 30pf, Cathedral at Erfurt. 40pf, Zwinger at Dresden.

1955, Nov. 14

265 A75	5pf black brown	.65	.35
266 A75	10pf gray green	.65	.35
267 A75	15pf purple	.65	.35
268 A75	20pf carmine	.65	.65
269 A75	30pf dk red brown	*6.00*	*8.50*
270 A75	40pf indigo	1.25	.65
	Nos. 265-270 (6)	*9.85*	*10.85*

For surcharges see Nos. B29-B30.

Georgius Agricola — A76

1955, Nov. 21 Wmk. 297

271 A76	10pf brown	.60	.40

400th anniv. of the death of Georgius Agricola, mineralogist and scholar.

Paintings in Dresden Gallery — A77

Famous Paintings: 5pf, Portrait of a Young Man, by Dürer. 10pf, Chocolate Girl, by Liotard. 15pf, Portrait of a Boy, by Pinturicchio. 20pf, Self-portrait with Saskia, by Rembrandt. 40pf, Girl with Letter, by Vermeer. 70pf, Sistine Madonna, by Raphael.

1955, Dec. 15 *Perf. 13½x13*

272 A77	5pf dk red brown	.55	.25
273 A77	10pf chestnut	.55	.25
274 A77	15pf pale purple	*19.00*	*19.00*
275 A77	20pf brown	.55	.25
276 A77	40pf olive green	.55	.35
277 A77	70pf deep blue	1.25	.65
	Nos. 272-277 (6)	*22.45*	*20.75*

Issued to publicize the return of famous art works to the Dresden Art Gallery.

See Nos. 355-360, 439-443.

Mozart — A78

Designs: 20pf, Portrait facing left.

1956, Jan. 27 Photo.

278 A78	10pf gray green	*9.00*	*6.00*
279 A78	20pf copper brown	3.00	1.50

200th anniv. of the birth of Wolfgang Amadeus Mozart, composer.

Flag and Schoenefeld Airport, Berlin — A79

Lufthansa Plane A80

Designs: 15pf, Plane facing right. 20pf, Plane facing down and left.

1956, Feb. 1 *Perf. 13x12½*

280 A79	5pf multicolored	*11.00*	*8.00*
281 A80	10pf gray green	.65	.35
282 A80	15pf dull blue	.65	.35
283 A80	20pf brown red	.65	.35
	Nos. 280-283 (4)	*12.95*	*9.05*

Issued to commemorate the opening of passenger service of the German Lufthansa.

Heinrich Heine — A81

Design: 20pf, Heine (different portrait.)

1956, Feb. 17 *Perf. 13½x13*

284 A81	10pf Prus green	*9.00*	*5.00*
285 A81	20pf dark red	*2.00*	.50

Cent. of the death of Heinrich Heine, poet.

Railroad Cranes — A82

1956, Feb. 26 *Perf. 13x13½*

286 A82	20pf brown red	.60	.40
287 A82	35pf violet blue	.90	.75

Issued to publicize the Leipzig Spring Fair.

Ernst Thälmann
A83

1956, Apr. 16 Litho. *Perf. 13x13½*

288 A83 20pf blk ol & red .60 .35
a. Souvenir sheet of 1, imperf *8.00 22.50*

Birth of Ernst Thälmann, 70th anniv.

No. 288a was sold at double face value. The proceeds were used for national memorials at former concentration camps.

Wheel, Hand and Olive Branch — A84

Design: 20pf, Wheel and coats of arms of Warsaw, Berlin, Prague.

Perf. 13½x13

1956, Apr. 30 Wmk. 297

289 A84 10pf lt green .65 .25
290 A84 20pf brt carmine .65 .25

9th International Bicycle Peace Race, Warsaw-Berlin-Prague, May 1-15, 1956.

City Hall and Old Market — A85

Designs: 20pf, Hofkirche and Elbe Bridge. 40pf, Technical College.

1956, June 1

291 A85 10pf green .35 .25
292 A85 20pf carmine rose .35 .25
293 A85 40pf brt purple *1.25 1.60*
Nos. 291-293 (3) 1.95 2.10

750th anniversary of Dresden.

Worker Holding Cogwheel Emblem — A86

1956, June 30 *Perf. 13½x13*

294 A86 20pf rose red .45 .25

10th anniversary of nationalized industry.

Robert Schumann (Music by Schubert) A87

1956, July 20 *Perf. 13x13½*

295 A87 10pf brt green 1.00 .90
296 A87 20pf rose red 1.00 .25

Centenary of the death of Robert Schumann, composer. See Nos. 303-304.

Soccer Players — A88

Designs: 10pf, Javelin Thrower. 15pf, Women Hurdlers. 20pf, Gymnast.

1956, July 25 *Perf. 13½x13*

297 A88 5pf green .30 .25
298 A88 10pf dk vio blue .30 .25
299 A88 15pf red violet *1.75 1.10*
300 A88 20pf rose red .30 .25
Nos. 297-300 (4) 2.65 1.85

Second Sports Festival, Leipzig, Aug. 2-5.

Thomas Mann — A89

1956, Aug. 13 Wmk. 297

301 A89 20pf bluish black .85 .45

Death of Thomas Mann, novelist, 1st anniv.

Jakub Bart Cisinski — A90

1956, Aug. 20 Photo.

302 A90 50pf claret .85 .45

Birth centenary of Jakub Bart Cisinski, poet.

Robert Schumann (Music by Schumann) A91

1956, Oct. 8 *Perf. 13x13½*

303 A91 10pf brt green *4.75 1.25*
304 A91 20pf rose red 2.00 .25

See Nos. 295, 296.

Lace — A92

Design: 20pf, Sailboat.

1956, Sept. 1 Typo. *Perf. 13½x13*

305 A92 10pf green & blk .30 .30
306 A92 20pf rose red & blk .30 .30

Leipzig Fair, Sept. 2-9.

Olympic Rings, Laurel and Torch — A93

Design: 35pf, Classic javelin thrower.

1956, Sept. 28 Litho.

307 A93 20pf brown red .45 .35
308 A93 35pf slate blue .65 .45

16th Olympic Games at Melbourne, Nov. 22-Dec. 8, 1956.

Post Runner of 1450 — A94

1956, Oct. 27

309 A94 20pf red .50 .05

Issued to publicize the Day of the Stamp.

Greifswald University Seal — A95

1956, Oct. 17 *Perf. 13x13½*

310 A95 20pf magenta .55 .35

500th anniv. of Greifswald University.

Ernst Abbe — A96

Zeiss Works, Jena A97

Portrait: 25pf, Carl Zeiss.

Perf. 12½x13, 13x12½

1956, Nov. 9 Photo. Wmk. 297

311 A96 10pf dark green .25 .25
312 A97 20pf brown red .25 .25
313 A96 25pf bluish black .35 .30
Nos. 311-313 (3) .85 .80

Carl Zeiss Optical Works, Jena, 110th anniv.

Chinese Girl with Flowers — A98

Designs: 10pf, Negro woman and child. 25pf, European man and dove.

1956, Dec. 10 Litho. *Perf. 13*

314 A98 5pf ol, *pale lem* *1.10 .75*
315 A98 10pf brown, *pink* .25 .25
316 A98 25pf vio bl, *pale vio bl* .25 .25
Nos. 314-316 (3) 1.60 1.25

Issued for Human Rights Day.

Elephants A99

1956, Dec. 14 Photo. *Perf. 13x12½*

Design in Gray

317 A99 5pf shown .25 .25
318 A99 10pf Flamingoes .25 .25
319 A99 15pf White rhinoceros *4.50 3.00*
320 A99 20pf Mouflon .25 .25
321 A99 25pf Bison .25 .25
322 A99 30pf Polar bear .25 .25
Nos. 317-322 (6) 5.75 4.25

Issued to publicize the Berlin Zoo.

Freighter A100

Design: 25pf, Electric Locomotive.

1957, Mar. 1 Litho. Wmk. 313

323 A100 20pf rose red .25 .25
324 A100 25pf bright blue .25 .25

Leipzig Spring Fair.

Silver Thistle A101

10pf, Emerald lizard. 20pf, Lady's-slipper.

1957, Apr. 12 Photo. Wmk. 313

325 A101 5pf chocolate .25 .25
326 A101 10pf dk slate grn *2.00 1.75*
327 A101 20pf red brown .25 .25
Nos. 325-327 (3) 2.50 2.25

Nature Conservation Week, Apr. 14-20.

Children at Play — A102

20pf, Friedrich Froebel and Children.

1957, Apr. 18 Litho. *Perf. 13*

328 A102 10pf black & olive *1.00 .70*
329 A102 20pf black & brown red .25 .25

175th anniv. of the birth of Friedrich Froebel, educator.

Redrawn Types of 1953

Designs: 5pf, Woman mariner. 10pf, Worker, peasant and intellectual. 15pf, Steel worker. 20pf, Stalin Boulevard. 25pf, Locomotive building. 30pf, Dancing couple. 40pf, Zwinger Castle, Dresden. 50pf, Launching ship. 70pf, Dove and East German family.

Imprint: "E. Gruner K. Wolf"
No imprint on 10pf, 15pf

Perf. 13x12½, 14

1957-58 Typo. Wmk. 313

330 A43 5pf emerald .60 .25
a. Bklt. pane, 3 #330 + 3 #331b 27.50 27.50
b. Bklt. pane, 3 #330 + 3 #333 27.50 27.50
c. Booklet pane of 6 5.00 4.75
331 A43 10pf blue ('58) .25 .25
a. Bklt. pane, 4 #331b + 2 #333 40.00 40.00
b. Perf. 13x12½ 5.50 .25
332 A43 15pf violet ('58) .60 .25
a. Perf. 13x12½ .60 .25
333 A43 20pf carmine .25 .25
a. Bklt. pane, 5 #333 + 1 #477 4.00 8.00
334 A43 25pf bluish green .30 .25
335 A43 30pf dull red .25 .25
336 A43 40pf rose violet .25 .25
337 A43 50pf bright blue .25 .25
338 A43 70pf chocolate .25 .25

See Nos. 476-482.

Pieck Type of 1953

Photo. *Perf. 13x13½*

339 A35 1m dk olive grn ('58) 1.75 .30
340 A35 2m red brown ('58) 3.75 .30
Nos. 330-340 (11) 8.50 2.85

No. 334 comes only perf 13x12½. Nos 330-333 and 335-338 come both perf 13x12½ and perf 14. Values are for the cheaper perf 14 varieties.

Bicycle Race Route — A103

Perf. 13x13½

1957, Apr. 30 Litho. Wmk. 313

346 A103 5pf orange .35 .25

Issued to publicize the 10th International Bicycle Peace Race, Prague-Berlin-Warsaw.

Steam Shovel A104

Miner — A105

Design: 20pf, Coal conveyor.

Perf. 13x12½, 13½x13 (25pf)

1957, May 3

347 A104 10pf green .25 .25
348 A104 20pf redsh brown .25 .25
349 A105 25pf blue violet *2.00 1.00*
Nos. 347-349 (3) 2.50 1.50

Issued in honor of the coal mining industry.

Henri Dunant and Globe A106

25pf, Henri Dunant facing right and globe.

1957, May 7 Photo. ***Perf. 13x12½***

350 A106 10pf green, red & blk .25 .25
351 A106 25pf brt blue, red & blk .25 .25

Tenth Red Cross world conference.

Portrait Type of 1950, Redrawn

Portraits: 5pf, Joachim Jungius. 10pf, Leonhard Euler. 20pf, Heinrich Hertz.

1957, June 7 Litho.

352 A11 5pf brown *1.25* .75
353 A11 10pf green .25 .25
354 A11 20pf henna brown .25 .25
Nos. 352-354 (3) 1.75 1.25

Issued to honor famous German scientists.

Painting Type of 1955.

Famous Paintings: 5pf, Holy Family, by Mantegna. 10pf, The Dancer Campani, by Carriera. 15pf, Portrait of Morette, by Holbein. 20pf, The Tribute Money, by Titian. 25pf, Saskia with Red Flower, by Rembrandt. 40pf, Young Standard Bearer, by Piazetta.

Perf. 13½x13

1957, June 26 Photo. Wmk. 313

355 A77 5pf dk brown .30 .25
356 A77 10pf lt yellow grn .30 .25
357 A77 15pf brown olive .30 .25
358 A77 20pf rose brown .30 .25
359 A77 25pf deep claret .30 .25
360 A77 40pf dk blue gray *3.50 1.50*
Nos. 355-360 (6) 5.00 2.75

Clara Zetkin — A107

1957, July 5 ***Perf. 13x13½***

361 A107 10pf dk green & red .60 .25

Centenary of the birth of Clara Zetkin, politician and founder of the socialist women's movement.

Bertolt Brecht — A108

1957, Aug. 14 ***Perf. 13½x13***

362 A108 10pf dark green .30 .25
363 A108 25pf deep blue .40 .25

Brecht (1898-1956), playwright and poet.

Congress Emblem — A109

1957, Aug. 23 Litho.

364 A109 20pf brt red & black .55 .25

4th Intl. Trade Union Congress, Leipzig, Oct. 4-15.

Fair Emblem — A110

1957, Aug. 30 Wmk. 313

365 A110 20pf crimson & ver .30 .25
366 A110 25pf brt blue & lt blue .30 .25

Issued to publicize the 1957 Leipzig Fair.

Savings Book — A111

1957, Oct. 10 ***Perf. 13½x13***

367 A111 10pf grn & blk, *gray* .80 .50
368 A111 20pf rose car & blk, *gray* .30 .30

Issued to publicize "Savings Weeks."

Postrider, 1563 — A112

1957, Oct. 25 Wmk. 313

369 A112 5pf black, *pale sepia* .50 .25

Issued for the Day of the Stamp.

Sputnik I — A113

20pf, Stratospheric balloon above clouds. 25pf, Ship with plumb line exploring deep sea.

1957-58 ***Perf. 12½x13***

370 A113 10pf blue black .40 .25
371 A113 20pf car rose ('58) .50 .25
372 A113 25pf brt blue ('58) *1.60 1.10*
Nos. 370-372 (3) 2.50 1.60

IGY. The 10pf also for the launching of the 1st artificial satellite.

Storming of the Winter Palace — A114

1957, Nov. 7 Photo.

373 A114 10pf yellow grn & red .25 .25
374 A114 25pf brt blue & red .25 .25

40th anniv. of the Russian Revolution.

Guenther Ramin — A115

Portrait: 20pf, Hermann Abendroth.

Perf. 13½x13

1957, Nov. 22 Litho. Wmk. 313

375 A115 10pf yellow grn & blk *.85 .75*
376 A115 20pf red orange & blk .25 .25

Ramin (1898-1956) and Abendroth (1883-1956), musicians, on the 1st anniv. of their death.

Dove and Globe — A116

1958, Feb. 27 ***Perf. 13x13½***

377 A116 20pf rose red .30 .25
378 A116 25pf blue .30 .25

Issued to publicize the 1958 Leipzig Fair.

Radio Tower, Morse Code and Post Horn A117

Design: 20pf, Radio tower and small post horn.

1958, Mar. 6 ***Perf. 13x12½***

379 A117 5pf gray & blk *.75 .45*
380 A117 20pf crim rose & dk red .30 .25

Conf. of Postal Ministers of Communist countries, Moscow, Dec. 3-17, 1957.

Sketch by Zille — A118

Design: 20pf, Self-portrait of Zille.

1958, Mar. 20 ***Perf. 13½x13***

381 A118 10pf green & gray *2.10 1.10*
382 A118 20pf dp car & gray .55 .25

Centenary of the birth of Heinrich Zille, artist.

Symbolizing Quantum Theory — A119

Design: 20pf, Max Planck.

1958, Apr. 23 Litho.

383 A119 10pf gray green *1.00 .90*
384 A119 20pf magenta .35 .25

Centenary of the birth of Max Planck, physicist.

Prize Cow — A120

10pf, Mowing machine. 20pf, Beet harvester.

Perf. 13x13½

1958, June 4 Wmk. 313

Size: 28x23mm

385 A120 5pf gray & blk *1.75 1.00*

Size: 39x22mm

Perf. 13x12½

386 A120 10pf brt green .35 .25
387 A120 20pf rose red .35 .25
Nos. 385-387 (3) 2.45 1.50

6th Agricultural Show, Markkleeberg.

Charles Darwin — A121

Portrait: 20pf, Carl von Linné.

1958, June 19 ***Perf. 13x13½***

388 A121 10pf green & black *1.20 .85*
389 A121 20pf dk red & black .25 .25

Cent. of Darwin's theory of evolution and the bicent. of Linné's botanical system.

Seven Towers of Rostock and Ships — A122

10pf, Ship at pier. 25pf, Ships in harbor.

1958 ***Perf. 13½x13***

390 A122 10pf emerald .25 .25
391 A122 20pf red orange .50 .25
392 A122 25pf lt blue *.90 .90*
Nos. 390-392 (3) 1.65 1.40

Establishment of Rostock as a seaport.

Issue dates: 20pf, July 5; 10pf and 25pf, Nov. 24.

For overprint see No. 500.

Congress Emblem — A123

1958, June 25 ***Perf. 13x13½***

393 A123 10pf rose red .35 .30

5th congress of the Socialist Party of the German Democratic Republic (SED).

Mare and Foal A124

Designs: 10pf, Trotter. 20pf, Horse race.

1958, July 22 Photo. ***Perf. 13x12½***

394 A124 5pf black brown *1.90 1.50*
395 A124 10pf dk ol grn .25 .25
396 A124 20pf dark red brown .25 .25
Nos. 394-396 (3) 2.40 2.00

Grand Prize of the DDR, 1958.

Jan Amos Komensky (Comenius) A125

Design: 20pf, Teacher and pupils, 17th cent.

1958, Aug. 7 Litho. ***Perf. 13x13½***

397 A125 10pf brt bl grn & blk *1.25 .90*
398 A125 20pf org brn & blk .25 .25

University Seal A126

Design: 20pf, Schiller University, Jena.

1958, Aug. 19 ***Perf. 13x12½***

399 A126 5pf gray & black *1.20 .90*
400 A126 20pf dark red & gray .25 .25

Friedrich Schiller University in Jena, 400th anniv.

Soldier on Obstacle Course — A127

Design: 20pf, Spartacist emblem. 25pf, Marching athletes, map and flag.

Perf. 13½x13

1958, Sept. 19 Litho. Wmk. 313

401 A127 10pf emerald & brn *1.20 .75*
402 A127 20pf brown red & yel .25 .25
403 A127 25pf lt blue & red .25 .25
Nos. 401-403 (3) 1.70 1.25

1st Spartacist Sports Meet of Friendly Armies, Leipzig, Sept. 20-28.

Arms Breaking A-Bomb — A128

1958, Sept. 19 ***Perf. 13x13½***

404 A128 20pf rose red .25 .25
405 A128 25pf blue .40 .25

People's fight against atomic death.

Woman and Leipzig Railroad Station A129

Design: 25pf, Woman in Persian lamb coat and old City Hall, Leipzig.

1958, Aug. 29 ***Perf. 13x12½***

406 A129 10pf green, brn & blk .25 .25
407 A129 25pf blue & black .25 .25

Issued to publicize the 1958 Leipzig Fair.

Post Wagon, 17th Century A130

Design: 20pf, Mail train and plane.

1958, Oct. 23 Wmk. 313

408 A130 10pf green *1.60 1.00*
409 A130 20pf lake .35 .25

Issued for the Day of the Stamp.

Brandenburg Gate, Berlin — A131

1958, Nov. 29 ***Perf. 13x13½***

410 A131 20pf rose red .35 .25
411 A131 25pf dark blue *2.25 1.25*

Issued to commemorate 10 years of democratic city administration of Berlin.

Head from Greek Tomb — A132

20pf, Giant's head from Pergamum frieze.

1958, Dec. 2 ***Perf. 13½x13***

412 A132 10pf blue grn & blk *1.20 .85*
413 A132 20pf dp rose & black .25 .25

Return of art treasures from Russia. See Nos. 484-486.

Negro and Caucasian Men — A133

Design: 25pf, Chinese and Caucasian girls.

1958, Dec. 10 ***Perf. 13x12½***

414 A133 10pf brt blue grn & blk .25 .25
415 A133 25pf blue & black *1.60 .90*

10th anniv. of the signing of the Universal Declaration of Human Rights.

Worker and Soldier — A134

1958, Nov. 7 ***Perf. 12½x13***

416 A134 20pf blk, ver & dl pur *7.50 12.50*

40th anniv. of the Revolution of Nov. 7. (Stamp inscribed Nov. 9.) Withdrawn from sale on day of issue.

Otto Nuschke — A135

Perf. 13½x13

1958, Dec. 27 Wmk. 313

417 A135 20pf red .30 .25

First anniversary of the death of Otto Nuschke, vice president of the republic.

Communist Newspaper, "The Red Flag" — A136

1958, Dec. 30 ***Perf. 13x12½***

418 A136 20pf red .35 .25

German Communist Party, 40th anniv.

Rosa Luxemburg Addressing Crowd — A137

20pf, Karl Liebknecht addressing crowd.

Perf. 13x13½

1959, Jan. 15 Wmk. 313

419 A137 10pf blue green *1.75 1.10*
420 A137 20pf henna brn & blk .25 .25

40th anniversary of the death of Rosa Luxemburg and Karl Liebknecht.

Gewandhaus, Leipzig — A138

Design: 25pf, Opening theme of Mendelssohn's A Major symphony.

1959, Feb. 28 Engr. ***Perf. 14***

421 A138 10pf green, *grnsh* .35 .30
422 A138 25pf blue, *bluish* *1.25 2.25*

150th anniversary of the birth of Felix Mendelssohn-Bartholdy, composer.

President Wilhelm Pieck — A139

1959, Jan. 3 Photo. ***Perf. 13½x13***

423 A139 20pf henna brown .40 .25

83rd birthday of President Wilhelm Pieck. See No. 511

"Black Pump" Plant A140

Design: 25pf, Photographic equipment.

1959, Feb. 28 Litho. ***Perf. 13x12½***

424 A140 20pf carmine rose .25 .25
425 A140 25pf lt ultra .35 .25

1959 Leipzig Spring Fair.

Boy and Girl — A141

1959, Apr. 2 ***Perf. 13½x13***

426 A141 10pf blk, *lt grn* *1.25 .85*
427 A141 20pf blk, *salmon* .25 .25

5 years of the Youth Consecration ceremony.

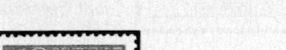

Statue of Handel, Halle — A142

20pf, Handel by Thomas Hudson, 1749.

1959, Apr. 27 Wmk. 313

428 A142 10pf bluish grn & blk *1.40 .90*
429 A142 20pf rose & blk .25 .25

Bicentenary of the death of George Frederick Handel, composer.

Alexander von Humboldt and Central American View — A143

Design: 20pf, Portrait and Siberian view.

1959, May 6

430 A143 10pf bluish grn *1.25 .90*
431 A143 20pf rose .30 .25

Centenary of the death of Alexander von Humboldt, naturalist and geographer.

Post Horn — A144

1959, May 30 ***Perf. 13½x13***

432 A144 20pf scar, yel & blk .30 .25
433 A144 25pf lt bl, yel & blk *.60 .60*

Conference of socialist postal ministers.

Gray Heron A145

10pf, Bittern. 20pf, Lily of the valley & butterfly. 25pf, Beaver. 40pf, Pussy willows and bee.

1959, June 26 ***Perf. 13x12½***

434 A145 5pf lt bl, blk & lil .25 .25
435 A145 10pf grnsh bl, dk brn & org .25 .25
436 A145 20pf org red, grn & vio .25 .25
437 A145 25pf lilac, yel & blk .35 .25
438 A145 40pf gray bl, yel & blk *4.75 3.00*
Nos. 434-438 (5) 5.85 4.00

Issued to publicize wildlife protection.

Painting Type of 1955.

Famous Paintings: 5pf, Portrait, by Angelica Kauffmann. 10pf, The Lady Lace Maker, by Gabriel Metsu. 20pf, Mademoiselle Lavergne, by Liotard. 25pf, Old Woman with Brazier, by Rubens. 40pf, Young Man in Black Coat, by Hals.

1959, June 29 Photo. ***Perf. 13½x13***

439 A77 5pf olive .25 .25
440 A77 10pf green .25 .25
441 A77 20pf dp org .25 .25
442 A77 25pf chestnut .35 .25
443 A77 40pf dp magenta *4.50 2.25*
Nos. 439-443 (5) 5.60 3.25

Great Cormorant A146

Birds: 10pf, Black Stork. 15pf, Eagle owl. 20pf, Black grouse. 25pf, Hoopoe. 40pf, Peregrine falcon.

Perf. 13x13½

1959, July 2 Litho. Wmk. 313

Designs in Black

444 A146 5pf yellow .25 .25
445 A146 10pf lt green .25 .25
446 A146 15pf pale violet *4.25 2.50*
447 A146 20pf deep pink .25 .25
448 A146 25pf blue .25 .25
449 A146 40pf vermilion .25 .25
Nos. 444-449 (6) 5.50 3.75

Protection of native birds.

Youths of Three Races — A147

25pf, Swedish girl kissing African girl, horiz.

1959, July 25 ***Perf. 12½x13, 13x12½***

450 A147 20pf crimson .30 .25
451 A147 25pf bright blue *.75 .60*

7th World Youth Festival, Vienna, 7/26-8/14.

Glass Tea Service A148

Design: 25pf, Distilling apparatus, vert.

1959, Sept. 1 ***Perf. 13x12½, 12½x13***

452 A148 10pf bluish green .25 .25
453 A148 25pf bright blue *1.60 1.00*

75 years of Jena glassware.

Lunik 2 Hitting Moon — A149

1959, Sept. 21 ***Perf. 13½x13***

454 A149 20pf rose red .50 .35

Landing of the Soviet rocket Lunik 2 on the moon, Sept. 13, 1959.

New Buildings, Leipzig, Globe and Fair Emblem A150

1959, Aug. 17 ***Perf. 13x12½***

455 A150 20pf gray & rose .35 .30

1959 Leipzig Fall Fair.

Flag and Harvester — A151

10pf, Fritz Heckert rest home. 15pf, Zwinger, Dresden. 20pf, Steelworker. 25pf, Chemist. 40pf, Central Stadium, Leipzig. 50pf, Woman tractor driver. 60pf, Airplane. 70pf, Merchant ship. 1m, 1st atomic reactor of the DDR.

1959, Oct. 6 ***Perf. 13½x13***

Flag in Black, Red & Orange Yellow Inscription and Design in Black & Red

456 A151 5pf yellow .25 .25
457 A151 10pf gray .25 .25
458 A151 15pf citron .25 .25
459 A151 20pf gray .25 .25
460 A151 25pf lt gray olive .25 .25
461 A151 40pf citron .25 .25
462 A151 50pf salmon .25 .25
463 A151 60pf pale bluish grn .25 .25
464 A151 70pf pale grnsh yel .25 .25
465 A151 1m bister brn .35 .40
Nos. 456-465 (10) 2.60 2.65

German Democratic Republic, 10th anniv.

Johannes R. Becher — A152

1959, Oct. 28 Litho. ***Perf. 13x13½***

466 A152 20pf red & slate 1.25 .25

1st anniversary of the death of Johannes R. Becher, writer.

Printed with alternating yellow labels. The label carries in blue a verse from the national anthem and Becher's signature.

Schiller's Home, Weimar — A153

Design: 20pf, Friedrich von Schiller.

1959, Nov. 10 Engr. ***Perf. 14***

467 A153 10pf dl grn, *grnsh* *1.25 .90*
468 A153 20pf lake, *pink* .45 .25

Birth of Friedrich von Schiller, 200th anniv.

Post Rider and Mile Stone, 18th Century — A154

Design: 20pf, Motorized mailman.

1959, Nov. 17 Litho. ***Perf. 13½x13***

469 A154 10pf green *1.20 .85*
470 A154 20pf dk car rose .25 .25

Issued for the Day of the Stamp.

Red Squirrels A155

1959, Nov. 27 ***Perf. 13x12½***

471 A155 5pf shown .35 .25
472 A155 10pf Hares .40 .25
473 A155 20pf Roe deer .40 .25
474 A155 25pf Red deer .45 .25
475 A155 40pf Lynx *9.50 3.00*
Nos. 471-475 (5) 11.10 4.00

Redrawn Types of 1953

Without Imprint

Perf. 14, 13x12½ (#477)

1959-60 Wmk. 313 Typo.

476 A43 5pf emerald .25 .25
477 A43 10pf lt bl grn *(Machinists)* .25 .25
a. Perf. 14 1.00 .40
b. Bklt. pane of 6 #477 6.00 4.75
478 A43 20pf carmine .25 .25
a. Se-tenant with DEBRIA label .95 .25
479 A43 30pf dull red .25 .25
480 A43 40pf rose violet .25 .25
481 A43 50pf brt blue .25 .25
482 A43 70pf choc ('60) .25 .25
Nos. 476-482 (7) 1.75 1.75

No. 478a was issued Sept. 3, 1959, to commemorate the 2nd German Stamp Exhibition, Berlin. Sheet contains 60 stamps, 40 labels.

Two other stamps without imprint are Nos. 331-332.

Type of 1958 and

Pergamum Altar of Zeus — A156

Designs: 5pf, Head of an Attic goddess, 580 B.C. 10pf, Head of a princess from Tell el Amarna, 1360 B.C. 20pf, Bronze figure from Toprak-Kale (Armenia), 7th century B.C.

1959, Dec. 29 Litho. ***Perf. 13½x13***

484 A132 5pf yellow & black .30 .25
485 A132 10pf bluish grn & blk .30 .25
486 A132 20pf rose & black .30 .25
487 A156 25pf lt blue & blk *.65 .65*
Nos. 484-487 (4) 1.55 1.40

Boxing — A157

10pf, Sprinters. 20pf, Ski jump. 25pf, Sailboat.

Perf. 13x13½

1960, Jan. 27 Wmk. 313

488 A157 5pf brown & ocher *4.00 2.00*
489 A157 10pf green & ocher .25 .25
490 A157 20pf car & ocher .25 .25
491 A157 25pf ultra & ocher .25 .25
Nos. 488-491 (4) 4.75 2.75

1960 Winter and Summer Olympic Games.

Technical Fair, North Entrance A158

Design: 25pf, "Ring" Fair building.

1960, Feb. 17 ***Perf. 13x12½***

492 A158 20pf red & gray .25 .25
493 A158 25pf lt blue & gray .25 .25

1960 Leipzig Spring Fair.

Purple Foxglove — A159

Medicinal Plants: 10pf, Camomile. 15pf, Peppermint. 20pf, Poppy. 40pf, Dog rose.

1960, Apr. 7 ***Perf. 12½x13***

494 A159 5pf grn, gray & car rose .25 .25
495 A159 10pf citron, gray & grn .25 .25
496 A159 15pf fawn, gray & grn .25 .25
497 A159 20pf grnsh bl, gray & vio .25 .25
498 A159 40pf brn, gray, grn & red *4.00 1.90*
Nos. 494-498 (5) 5.00 2.90

Lenin — A160

1960, Apr. 22 Engr. ***Perf. 14***

499 A160 20pf lake .35 .25

90th anniversary of the birth of Lenin.

No. 390 Overprinted: "Inbetriebnahme des Hochseehafens 1.Mai 1960"

1960, Apr. 28 Litho. ***Perf. 13½x13***

500 A122 10pf emerald .50 .35

Inauguration of the seaport Rostock.

Russian Soldier and Liberated Prisoner — A161

1960, May 5 Litho. ***Perf. 13x13½***

501 A161 20pf rose red .35 .25

15th anniv. of Germany's liberation from fascism.

Model of Vacation Ship — A162

Designs: 25pf, Ship before Leningrad.

Perf. 13½x13

1960, June 23 Wmk. 313

502 A162 5pf slate, cit & blk .25 .25
503 A162 25pf blk, yel & ultra *3.75 3.25*
Nos. 502-503,B58-B59 (4) 4.50 4.00

Launching of the trade union (FDGB) vacation ship, June 25, 1960.

Masked Dancer in Porcelain — A163

Meissen porcelain: 10pf, Plate with Meissen mark and date. 15pf, Otter. 20pf, Potter. 25pf, Coffee pot.

1960, July 28 ***Perf. 12½x13***

504 A163 5pf blue & orange .25 .25
505 A163 10pf blue & emerald .25 .25
506 A163 15pf blue & purple *3.00 3.00*
507 A163 20pf blue & orange red .25 .25
508 A163 25pf blue & apple grn .25 .25
Nos. 504-508 (5) 4.00 4.00

Meissen porcelain works, 250th anniv.

Lenin Monument, Eisleben A164

Design: 20pf, Thälmann monument, gift for Pushkin, USSR.

Perf. 13x13½

1960, July 2 **Wmk. 313**

509 A164 10pf dark green .25 .25
510 A164 20pf bright red .25 .25

Pieck Type of 1959

1960, Sept. 10 **Litho.** ***Perf. 13½x13***

511 A139 20pf black .40 .30
a. Souv. sheet of 1, imperf. 1.20 1.90

Pres. Wilhelm Pieck (1876-1960).

Modern Postal Trucks A165

Design: 25pf, Railroad mail car, 19th cent.

1960, Oct. 6 ***Perf. 13x12½***

512 A165 20pf car rose, blk & yel .25 .25
513 A165 25pf blue, gray & blk *2.50 1.25*

Issued for the Day of the Stamp, 1960.

New Opera House, Leipzig A166

Design: 25pf, Car, sailboat, tent, campers.

1960, Aug. 29 **Wmk. 313**

514 A166 20pf rose brn & gray .25 .25
515 A166 25pf blue & grysh brn .30 .30

1960 Leipzig Fall Fair.

Hans Burkmair Medal, 1518 — A167

25pf, Dancing Peasants by Albrecht Dürer.

1960, Oct. 20 **Litho.** ***Perf. 12½x13***

516 A167 20pf buff, grn & ocher .25 .25
517 A167 25pf lt blue & blk *1.25 1.50*

400th anniv. of the Dresden Art Gallery.

Neidhardt von Gneisenau — A168

20pf, Neidhardt von Gneisenau, horiz.

1960, Oct. 27 ***Perf. 13x12½, 12½x13***

518 A168 20pf dk car & blk .25 .25
519 A168 25pf ultra *1.10 1.10*

200th anniversary of the birth of Count August Neidhardt von Gneisenau, Prussian Field Marshal.

Rudolf Virchow A169

Humboldt University, Berlin — A170

10pf, Robert Koch. 25pf, Wilheim & Alexander von Humboldt medal. 40pf, Wilheim Griesinger.

1960, Nov. 4 **Litho.** ***Perf. 13x12½***

520 A169 5pf ocher & blk .25 .25
521 A169 10pf green & blk .25 .25
522 A170 20pf cop red, gray & blk .25 .25
523 A170 25pf brt blue & blk .25 .25
524 A169 40pf car rose & blk *2.00 1.20*
Nos. 520-524 (5) *3.00 2.20*

Nos. 520, 521, 524 for the 250th anniv. of the Charité (hospital), Berlin; Nos. 522-523 the 150th anniv. of Humboldt University, Berlin.

Nos. 520 and 523, and Nos. 521 and 522 are printed se-tenant.

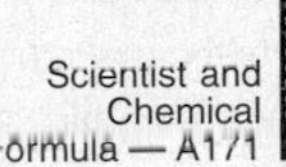

Scientist and Chemical Formula — A171

Designs: 10pf, Chemistry worker (fertilizer). 20pf, Woman worker (automobile). 25pf, Laboratory assistant (synthetic fabrics).

Perf. 13x13½

1960, Nov. 10 **Wmk. 313**

525 A171 5pf dk red & gray .25 .25
526 A171 10pf orange & brt grn .25 .25
527 A171 20pf blue & red .25 .25
528 A171 25pf yellow & ultra *1.50 1.75*
Nos. 525-528 (4) *2.25 2.50*

Day of the Chemistry Worker.

"Young Socialists' Express" A172

20pf, Sassnitz Harbor station & ferry. 25pf, Diesel locomotive & 1835 "Adler."

Perf. 13x13½; 13x12½ (20pf)

1960, Dec. 5

Sizes: 10pf, 25pf, 28x23mm; 20pf, 38½x22mm

529 A172 10pf emerald & blk .25 .25
530 A172 20pf red & blk .25 .25
531 A172 25pf blue & blk *4.00 3.50*
Nos. 529-531 (3) *4.50 4.00*

125th anniv. of German railroads. No. 530 exists imperf. Values: unused $4; used $1.25.

Pieck Type of 1953 with Dates Added

1961, Jan. 3 **Photo.** ***Perf. 13x13½***

532 A35 20pf henna brn & blk .40 .30

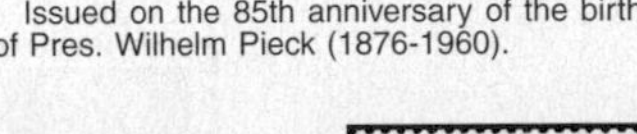

Issued on the 85th anniversary of the birth of Pres. Wilhelm Pieck (1876-1960).

380 Kilovolt Switch — A173

Design: 25pf, Leipzig Press Center.

1961, Mar. 3 **Litho.** ***Perf. 13½x13***

533 A173 10pf brt grn & dk gray .30 .25
534 A173 25pf vio blue & dk gray .30 .25

Leipzig Spring Fair of 1961.

Lilienstein — A174

Designs: 5pf, Rudelsburg on Saale. 10pf, Wartburg. No. 538, City Hall, Wernigerode. 25pf, Brocken, Harz Mts., horiz.

1961 **Typo.** ***Perf. 14***

535 A174 5pf gray .25 .25
536 A174 10pf blue green .25 .25
537 A174 20pf red brown .25 .25
538 A174 20pf dull red .25 .25
539 A174 25pf dark blue .25 .25
Nos. 535-539 (5) 1.25 1.25

Issued: No. 538, 25pf, 3/14; 5pf, 10pf, No. 537, 6/22.

Trawler — A176

Designs: 20pf, Fishermen. 25pf, S.S. Robert Koch. 40pf, Cannery worker.

1961, Apr. 4 **Engr.** **Wmk. 313**

545 A176 10pf gray green .25 .25
546 A176 20pf claret .25 .25
547 A176 25pf slate .25 .25
548 A176 40pf dull violet *1.90 1.40*
Nos. 545-548 (4) *2.65 2.15*

Deep-sea fishing industry.

Vostok 1 Leaving Earth A177

Designs: 20pf, Cosmonaut in capsule. 25pf, Parachute landing of capsule.

1961, Apr. **Litho.** ***Perf. 13x12½***

549 A177 10pf lt blue grn & red 1.00 .65
550 A177 20pf red 1.00 .65
551 A177 25pf lt blue *3.50 3.25*
Nos. 549-551 (3) *5.50 4.55*

1st man in space, Yuri A. Gagarin, 4/12/61. Issue dates: 10pf, Apr. 18; others, Apr. 20.

Zebra A178

Dresden Zoo cent.: 20pf, Black-and-white colobus monkeys.

1961, May 9

552 A178 10pf green & blk *4.00 4.00*
553 A178 20pf lilac rose & blk .65 .40

Engels, Marx, Lenin and Crowd — A179

1961, Apr. 20 **Litho.** ***Perf. 13½x13***

554 A179 20pf red .40 .30

15th anniversary of Socialist Unity Party of Germany (SED).

Stag Leap — A180

Designs: 20pf, Arabesque. 25pf, Exercise on parallel bars, horiz.

1961, June 3 ***Perf. 13½x13, 13x13½***

555 A180 10pf blue green .25 .25
556 A180 20pf rose pink .25 .25
557 A180 25pf brt blue *4.50 3.75*
Nos. 555-557 (3) *5.00 4.25*

3rd Europa Cup for Women's Gymnastics.

Salt Miners and Castle Giebichenstein — A181

20pf, Chemist and "Five Towers" of Halle.

1961, June 22 ***Perf. 13x12½***

558 A181 10pf blk, grn & yel *1.20 .65*
559 A181 20pf blk, dk red & yel 1.20 .65

1000th anniv. of the founding of Halle.

Kayak Slalom A182

10pf, Canoe. 20pf, Two seater canoe.

1961, July 6 **Litho.** **Wmk. 313**

560 A182 5pf gray & Prus bl *2.50 2.10*
561 A182 10pf gray & olive .25 .25
562 A182 20pf gray & car rose .25 .25
Nos. 560-562 (3) *3.00 2.60*

Canoe Slalom and Rapids World Championships.

Target Line Casting A183

Design: 20pf, River fishing.

1961, July 21
563 A183 10pf green & blue *2.50 2.00*
564 A183 20pf dk red brn & blue .30 .30

World Fishing Championships, Dresden.

Tulip — A184

1961, Sept. 13 Photo. *Perf. 14*
565 A184 10pf shown .35 .25
566 A184 20pf Dahlia .35 .25
567 A184 40pf Rose *7.00 7.00*
Nos. 565-567 (3) *7.70 7.50*

Intl. Horticulture Exhibition, Erfurt.

"Alte Waage," Historical Building, Leipzig — A185

Design: 25pf, Old Exchange Building.

Perf. 13½x13
1961, Aug. 23 Litho. Wmk. 313
568 A185 10pf citron & bl grn .25 .25
569 A185 25pf lt blue & ultra .85 .30

1961 Leipzig Fall Fair. See Nos. 595-597.

Liszt's Hand, French Sculpture — A186

Designs: 5pf, Liszt and Hector Berlioz. 20pf, Franz Liszt, medallion by Ernst Rietschel, 1852. 25pf, Liszt and Frederic Chopin.

1961, Oct.-Nov. Engr. *Perf. 14*
570 A186 5pf gray .25 .25
571 A186 10pf blue green *1.60 1.60*
572 A186 20pf dull red .25 .25
573 A186 25pf chalky blue *2.00 2.00*
Nos. 570-573 (4) *4.10 4.10*

150th anniversary of the birth of Franz Liszt, composer.

Television Camera and Screen — A187

Design: 20pf, Microphone and radio dial.

1961, Oct. 25 *Perf. 13x13½*
574 A187 10pf brt green & blk *1.40 1.40*
575 A187 20pf brick red & blk .25 .25

Issued for Stamp Day, 1961.

Maj. Gherman Titov and Young Pioneers — A188

10pf, Titov in Leipzig, vert. 15pf, Titov in spaceship. 20pf, Titov & Walter Ulbricht. 25pf, Spaceship Vostok 2. 40pf, Titov & Ulbricht in Berlin.

1961, Dec. 11 Litho. *Perf. 13½*
576 A188 5pf carmine & vio .25 .25
577 A188 10pf olive grn & car .25 .25
578 A188 15pf blue & lilac *6.50 6.50*
579 A188 20pf blue & car rose .25 .25
580 A188 25pf carmine & blue .25 .25
581 A188 40pf car & dk blue 1.20 .40
Nos. 576-581 (6) *8.70 7.90*

Visit of Russian Maj. Gherman Titov to the German Democratic Republic.

Chairman Walter Ulbricht — A189

1961-67 Wmk. 313 Typo. *Perf. 14*
Size: 17x21mm
582 A189 5pf slate .25 .25
a. Booklet pane of 8 24.00 32.50
583 A189 10pf brt green .25 .25
a. Booklet pane of 8 10.50 16.00
584 A189 15pf red lilac .25 .25
585 A189 20pf dark red .30 .25
586 A189 25pf dull bl ('63) .30 .25
587 A189 30pf car rose ('63) .25 .25
588 A189 40pf brt vio ('63) .25 .25
589 A189 50pf ultra ('63) .25 .25
589A A189 60pf dp yel grn ('64) .30 .25
590 A189 70pf red brn ('63) .30 .25
590A A189 80pf brt blue ('67) .40 .40
Engr.
Size: 24x28½mm
590B A189 1dm dull grn ('63) .75 .35
590C A189 2dm brown ('63) 1.50 .50
Nos. 582-590C (13) 5.35 3.75

See Nos. 751-752, 1112A-1114A, 1483. Currency abbreviation is "DM" on Nos. 590B-590C, "MDN" on Nos. 751-752, "M" on Nos. 1113-1114A.

Red Ants A190

1962, Feb. 16 Photo.
591 A190 5pf shown *3.25 5.00*
592 A190 10pf Weasels .25 .25
593 A190 20pf Shrews .25 .25
594 A190 40pf Bat .45 .40
Nos. 591-594 (4) *4.20 5.90*

See Nos. 663-667.

Type of 1961

Buildings: 10pf, "Coffee Tree House." 20pf, Gohlis Castle. 25pf, Romanus House.

1962, Feb. 22 Litho. *Perf. 13x13½*
595 A185 10pf olive grn & brn .25 .25
596 A185 20pf org red & blk .30 .25
597 A185 25pf brt blue & brn .65 .65
Nos. 595-597 (3) 1.20 1.15

Leipzig Spring Fair of 1962.

Air Defense A191

Designs: 10pf, Motorized infantry. 20pf, Soldier and worker as protectors. 25pf, Sailor and destroyer escort. 40pf, Tank and tankman.

1962, Mar. 1 *Perf. 13x12½*
598 A191 5pf light blue .25 .25
599 A191 10pf bright green .25 .25
600 A191 20pf red .25 .25
601 A191 25pf ultra .25 .25
602 A191 40pf brown *1.25 1.20*
Nos. 598-602 (5) *2.25 2.20*

National People's Army, 6th anniv.

Cyclists and Hradcany, Prague — A192

25pf, Cyclist, East Berlin City Hall and dove.

1962, Apr. 26 Litho. Wmk. 313
603 A192 10pf multicolored .25 .25
604 A192 25pf multicolored *1.10 1.10*
Nos. 603-604,B89 (3) *1.60 1.60*

15th International Bicycle Peace Race, Berlin-Warsaw-Prague.

Johann Gottlieb Fichte — A193

10pf, Fichte's birthplace in Rammenau.

1962, May 17 *Perf. 13x13½*
605 A193 10pf brt green & blk *1.20 1.50*
606 A193 20pf vermilion & blk .25 .25

Bicentenary of the birth of Johann Gottlieb Fichte, philosopher.

Cross, Crown of Thorns and Rose — A194

1962, June 7 *Perf. 12½x13*
607 A194 20pf red & black .25 .25
608 A194 25pf brt blue & blk *.80 1.00*

20th anniversary of the destruction of Lidice in Czechoslovakia by the Nazis.

George Dimitrov at Reichstag Trial, Leipzig — A195

20pf, Dimitrov as Premier of Bulgaria.

1962, June 18 Photo. *Perf. 14*
609 A195 5pf blue grn & blk *.45 .35*
610 A195 20pf car rose & blk .25 .25
a. Pair, #609-610, + label 4.50 *32.50*

George Dimitrov, (1882-1949), communist leader and premier of the Bulgarian Peoples' Republic.

Nos. 609-610 also printed se-tenant, divided by a label inscribed with a Dimitrov quotation.

Corn Planter A196

20pf, Milking machine. 40pf, Combine harvester.

1962, June 26 Litho. *Perf. 13x12½*
611 A196 10pf multicolored .25 .25
612 A196 20pf multicolored .25 .25
613 A196 40pf yel, grn & dk red *1.25 1.20*
Nos. 611-613 (3) *1.75 1.70*

10th Agricultural Exhibition, Markkleeberg.

Map of Baltic Sea and Emblem — A197

Designs: 20pf, Hotel, Rostock, vert. 25pf, Cargo ship "Frieden" in Rostock harbor.

Perf. 13x13½, 13½x13 (20pf)
1962, July 2 Wmk. 313
614 A197 10pf bluish grn & ultra .25 .25
615 A197 20pf dk red & yellow .25 .25
616 A197 25pf blue & bister *1.75 1.60*
Nos. 614-616 (3) *2.25 2.10*

5th Baltic Sea Week, Rostock, July 7-15.

Brandenburg Gate, Berlin — A198

No. 618 Heads of youths of three races. No. 619, Peace dove. No. 620, National Theater, Helsinki.

1962, July 17 *Perf. 13½x13*
617 A198 5pf multicolored *1.60 2.50*
618 A198 5pf multicolored *1.60 2.50*
619 A198 20pf multicolored *1.60 2.50*
620 A198 20pf multicolored *1.60 2.50*
a. Block of 4, #617-620 *8.50 13.00*
Nos. 617-620 (4) *6.40 10.00*

8th Youth Festival for Peace and Friendship, Helsinki, July 28-Aug. 6, 1962.

No. 620a forms the festival flower emblem.

Free Style Swimming A199

Designs: 10pf, Back stroke. 25pf, Butterfly stroke. 40pf, Breast stroke. 70pf, Water polo.

1962, Aug. 7 Litho. *Perf. 13x13½*
Design in Greenish Blue
621 A199 5pf orange .25 .25
622 A199 10pf grnsh blue .25 .25
623 A199 25pf ultra .25 .25
624 A199 40pf brt violet *1.00 1.00*
625 A199 70pf red brown .25 .25
a. Block of 6, #621-625, B92 2.00 2.00
Nos. 621-625,B92 (6) *2.25 2.25*

10th European Swimming Championships. Leipzig, Aug. 18-25.

Nos. 621-625, B92 each printed in sheets of 50, No. 625a in sheet of 60.

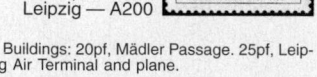

Municipal Store, Leipzig — A200

Buildings: 20pf, Mädler Passage. 25pf, Leipzig Air Terminal and plane.

Engr. & Photo.

1962, Aug. 28 Wmk. 313 *Perf. 14*

626 A200 10pf black & emerald .25 .25
627 A200 20pf black & red .30 .25
628 A200 25pf black & blue .65 .50
Nos. 626-628 (3) 1.20 1.00

Leipzig Fall Fair of 1962.

"Transportation and Communication" — A201

1962, Oct. 3 Litho. *Perf. 13½x13*

629 A201 5pf light blue & black .30 .25

10th anniv. of the Friedrich List Transportation College.

Souvenir Sheet

Pavel R. Popovich, Andrian G. Nikolayev and Space Capsules — A202

1962, Sept. 13 Wmk. 313 *Imperf.*

630 A202 70pf dk blue, lt grn & yel *2.75 5.00*

1st Russian group space flight of Vostoks III and IV, Aug. 11-13, 1962.

DDR Television Signal A203

Young Collectors and World Map — A204

1962, Oct. 25 *Perf. 13½x13*

631 A203 20pf green & gray .25 .25
632 A204 40pf brt pink & blk *1.25 1.25*

No. 631 for the 10th anniv. of television in the German Democratic Republic; No. 632 is for Stamp Day.

Gerhart Hauptmann A205

1962, Nov. 15 *Perf. 13x13½*

633 A205 20pf red & black .35 .25

Centenary of the birth of Gerhart Hauptmann, playwright.

Souvenir Sheet

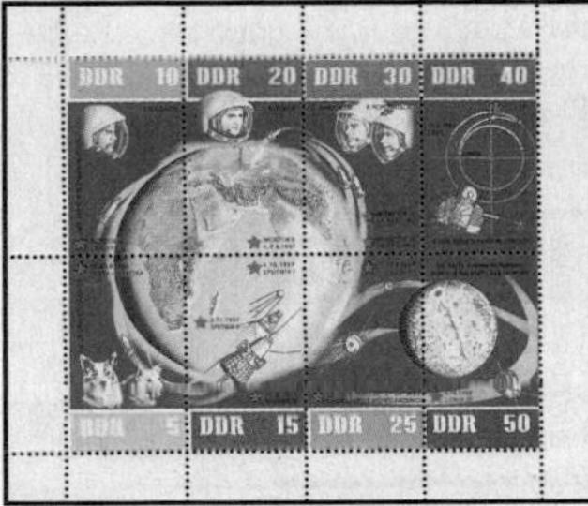

Russian Space Flights and Astronauts — A206

1962, Dec. 28 Litho. *Perf. 12½x13*

634 A206 Sheet of 8 *25.00 32.50*
a. 5pf yellow *1.00 1.00*
b. 10pf emerald *1.00 1.00*
c. 15pf magenta *2.25 2.25*
d. 20pf red *2.25 2.25*
e. 25pf greenish blue *2.25 2.25*
f. 30pf red brown *2.25 2.25*
g. 40pf crimson *1.00 1.00*
h. 50pf ultramarine *1.00 1.00*

Issued to show the development of Russian space flights from Sputnik 1 to Vostoks 3 and 4, and to honor the Russian astronauts Gagarin, Titov, Nikolayev and Popovich.

Pierre de Coubertin — A207

Design: 25pf, Stadium and Olympic rings.

1963, Jan. 2 *Perf. 13½x13*

635 A207 20pf carmine & gray .25 .25
636 A207 25pf blue & bister *1.25 1.75*

Baron Pierre de Coubertin, organizer of the modern Olympic Games, birth cent.

Congress Emblem, Flag with Marx, Engels and Lenin — A208

1963, Jan. 15 *Perf. 13x13½*

637 A208 10pf yel, org, red & blk .30 .25

6th congress of Socialist Unity Party of Germany (SED).

World Map and Exterminator — A209

Designs: 25pf, Map, cross and staff of Aesculapius. 50pf, Map, cross, mosquito.

1963, Feb. 6 *Perf. 13x12½*

638 A209 20pf dp org, dk red & blk .25 .25
639 A209 25pf multicolored .25 .25
640 A209 50pf multicolored *1.00 1.00*
Nos. 638-640 (3) 1.50 1.50

WHO drive to eradicate malaria.

Silver Fox A210

Design: 25pf, Karakul.

1963, Feb. 14 Photo. *Perf. 14*

641 A210 20pf rose & black .25 .25
642 A210 25pf blue & black *1.50 1.50*

Intl. Fur Auctions, Leipzig, 2/14-15, 4/21-24.

Barthels House, Leipzig — A211

Designs: 20pf, New Leipzig City Hall. 25pf, Belltower Building.

Engr. & Photo.

1963, Feb. 26 Wmk. 313 *Perf. 14*

643 A211 10pf black & citron .25 .25
644 A211 20pf black & red org .30 .25
645 A211 25pf black & blue 1.00 1.00
Nos. 643-645 (3) 1.55 1.50

1963 Leipzig Spring Fair.

Souvenir Sheet

On March 12, 1963, a souvenir sheet publicizing "Chemistry for Peace and Socialism" was issued. It contains two imperforate stamps, 50pf and 70pf, printed on ungummed synthetic tissue. Size: 105x74mm. Values: unused $4; used $20.

Richard Wagner and "The Flying Dutchman" — A213

Portrait & Scene from Play: 5pf, Johann Gottfried Seume (1763-1810). 10pf, Friedrich Hebbel (1813-63). 20pf, Georg Büchner (1813-37).

1963, Apr. 9 Litho. *Perf. 13x12½*

647 A213 5pf brt citron & blk .25 .25
648 A213 10pf brt green & blk .25 .25
649 A213 20pf orange & blk .25 .25
650 A213 25pf dull blue & blk *1.25 1.50*
Nos. 647-650 (4) 2.00 2.25

Anniversaries of German dramatists and the 150th anniv. of the birth of Richard Wagner, composer.

First Aid Station A214

Design: 20pf, Ambulance and hospital.

1963, May 14 Wmk. 313

651 A214 10pf multicolored *1.00 1.00*
652 A214 20pf red, blk & gray .25 .25

Centenary of International Red Cross.

Eugene Pottier, Writer — A215

25pf, Pierre-Chretien Degeyter, composer.

1963, June 18 *Perf. 13x13½*

653 A215 20pf vermilion & blk .25 .25
654 A215 25pf vio blue & blk *1.00 1.00*

75th anniv. of the communist song "The International."

A216

No. 655, Valentina Tereshkova, Vostok 6. No. 656, Valeri Bykovski, Vostok 5.

1963, July 18 Photo. *Perf. 13½*

655 20pf blue, blk & gray bl .65 .25
656 20pf blue, blk & gray bl .65 .25
a. A216 Pair, #655-656 1.50 .75

Space flights of Valeri Bykovski, June 14-19, and Valentina Tereshkova, 1st woman cosmonaut, June 16-19, 1963.

Motorcyclist in "Motocross" at Apolda — A217

20pf, Motorcyclist at Sachsenring, horiz. 25pf, 2 motorcyclists at Sachsenring, horiz.

Engr. & Photo.

1963, July 30 *Perf. 14*

Size: 23x28mm

657 A217 10pf lt grn & dk grn *2.50 3.00*

Size: 48½x21mm

658 A217 20pf rose & dk red .25 .25
659 A217 25pf lt blue & dk blue .25 .25
Nos. 657-659 (3) 3.00 3.50

Motorcycle World Championships.

Monument at Treblinka A218

Perf. 13x13½

1963, Aug. 20 Litho. Wmk. 313

660 A218 20pf brick red & dk blue .30 .25

Erection of a memorial at Treblinka (Poland) concentration camp.

A219

No. 661, Globe, car and train. No. 662, Globe, plane and bus.

1963, Aug. 27 *Perf. 13½x13*

661 10pf multicolored .60 .25
662 10pf multicolored .60 .25
a. A219 Pair, #661-662 1.90 .40

Issued to publicize the 1963 Leipzig Fall Fair.

Fauna Type of 1962

10pf, Stag beetle. 20pf, Fire salamander. 30pf, Pond turtle. 50pf, Green toad. 70pf, Hedgehogs.

1963, Sept. 10 Photo. *Perf. 14*

663 A190 10pf emer, brn & blk .25 .25
664 A190 20pf crimson, blk & yel .25 .25
665 A190 30pf multicolored .25 .25
666 A190 50pf multicolored *2.50 2.50*

667 A190 70pf claret brn, brn & bis .55 .55
Nos. 663-667 (5) 3.80 3.80

Neidhardt von Gneisenau and Gebhard Leberecht von Blücher — A220

Designs: 10pf, Cossacks and home guard, Berlin. 20pf, Ernst Moritz Arndt and Baron Heinrich vom Stein. 25pf, Lützow's volunteers before battle. 40pf, Gerhard von Scharnhorst and Prince Mikhail I. Kutuzov.

1963, Oct. 10 Litho. *Perf. 13½x13*
Center in Tan and Black

668 A220 5pf brt yellow .25 .25
669 A220 10pf emerald .25 .25
670 A220 20pf dp orange .25 .25
671 A220 25pf dp ultra .25 .25
672 A220 40pf dark red *1.75* 1.00
Nos. 668-672 (5) 2.75 2.00

150th anniversary of War of Liberation.

Valentina Tereshkova and Space Craft — A221

No. 674, Tereshkova and map of DDR, vert. No. 675, Yuri A. Gagarin and map of DDR, vert. 25pf, Tereshkova in space capsule.

Size: 28x28mm (10pf, 25pf); 28x37mm (20pf)

1963 *Perf. 13½x13, 13x13½*

673 A221 10pf ultra & green .25 .25
674 A221 20pf red, blk & ocher .25 .25
675 A221 20pf red, grn & ocher .25 .25
676 A221 25pf orange & blue *3.25* 2.00
Nos. 673-676 (4) 4.00 2.75

Visit of astronauts Valentina Tereshkova & Yuri A. Gagarin to the German Democratic Republic.

Burning Synagogue and Star of David in Chains — A222

Perf. 13½x13
1963, Nov. 8 Wmk. 313
677 A222 10pf multicolored .30 .25

25th anniv. of the "Crystal Night," the start of the systematic persecution of the Jews in Germany. Inscribed: "Never again Crystal Night."

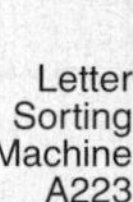

Letter Sorting Machine A223

Design: 20pf, Mechanized mail loading.

1963, Nov. 25 *Perf. 13x12½*
678 A223 10pf multicolored *1.40 1.40*
679 A223 20pf multicolored .25 .25

Issued for Stamp Day.

Ski Jump and Olympic Rings A224

1963, Dec. 16 Litho. *Perf. 13½x13*
680 A224 5pf shown .25 .25
681 A224 10pf Start .25 .25
682 A224 25pf Landing *1.75 1.75*
Nos. 680-682,B111 (4) 2.50 2.50

9th Winter Olympic Games, Innsbruck, Jan. 29-Feb. 9, 1964.

Admiral — A225

Butterflies: 15pf, Alpine Apollo. 20pf, Swallowtail. 25pf, Postilion. 40pf, Great fox.

Wmk. 313
1964, Jan. 15 Photo. *Perf. 14*
Butterflies in Natural Colors

683 A225 10pf citron & blk .35 .25
684 A225 15pf pale violet & blk .35 .25
685 A225 20pf lt brick red & blk .35 .25
686 A225 25pf lt blue & dk brn .35 .25
687 A225 40pf lt ultra & blk *5.00* 2.00
Nos. 683-687 (5) 6.40 3.00

William Shakespeare — A226

20pf, Quadriga, Brandenburg Gate, Berlin. 25pf, Keystone, History Museum (Zeughaus), Berlin.

1964, Feb. 6 Litho. *Perf. 13x12½*
688 A226 20pf rose & dk blue .25 .25
689 A226 25pf lt blue & mag .25 .25
690 A226 40pf lt vio & dk bl grn *1.10 1.00*
Nos. 688-690 (3) 1.60 1.50

200th anniv. of the birth of the sculptor Johann Gottfried Schadow (20pf); 300th anniv. of the birth of the sculptor Andreas Schlüter (25pf); 400th anniv. of the birth of William Shakespeare, dramatist (40pf).

Electrical Engineering Exhibit — A227

20pf, Bräunigkes Court, exhibition hall, 1700.

Perf. 13x13½
1964, Feb. 26 Wmk. 313
691 A227 10pf brt green & blk 2.00 .25
692 A227 20pf red & black 2.00 .25
a. Block, 1 each #691-692 + 2 labels 16.00 1.50

Leipzig Spring Fair, Mar. 1-10, 1964.

Khrushchev and Inventors — A228

40pf, Khrushchev, Tereshkova & Gagarin.

1964, May 15 *Perf. 13x13½*
693 A228 25pf blue .25 .25
694 A228 40pf lilac & grnsh blk *2.25 1.75*

Issued in honor of Premier Nikita S. Khrushchev of the Soviet Union.

Youth Training for Leadership A229

Designs: 20pf, Young athletes. 25pf, Accordion player and girl with flowers.

1964, May 13 Litho.
Center in Black

695 A229 10pf ultra, mag & emer .25 .25
696 A229 20pf emer, ultra & mag .25 .25
697 A229 25pf magenta, emer & ultra *1.25* .65
Nos. 695-697 (3) 1.75 1.15

German Youth Meeting, Berlin.

Television Antenna and Puppets — A230

Children's Day: Various characters from children's television programs.

1964, June 1 *Perf. 13x13½*
698 A230 5pf multicolored .25 .25
699 A230 10pf multicolored .25 .25
700 A230 15pf multicolored .25 .25
701 A230 20pf multicolored .25 .25
702 A230 40pf multicolored *1.20 1.40*
Nos. 698-702 (5) 2.20 2.40

Woman as Educator and Portrait of Jenny Marx — A231

Designs: 25pf, Women in industry and transistor diagram. 70pf, Women in agriculture.

Perf. 13½x13
1964, June 26 Litho. Wmk. 313
703 A231 20pf crimson, gray & yel .30 .25
704 A231 25pf lt blue, gray & red *.80* .65
705 A231 70pf emer, gray & yel .55 .25
Nos. 703-705 (3) 1.65 1.15

Congress of Women of the German Democratic Republic, June 25-27.

Bicycling A232

Diving — A233

Litho. & Engr.
1964, July 15 *Perf. 14*
706 A232 5pf shown .25 .25
707 A232 10pf Volleyball .25 .25
708 A232 20pf Judo .25 .25
709 A232 25pf Woman diver .25 .25
710 A232 70pf Equestrian *1.25 1.25*
Nos. 706-710,B118 (6) 2.50 2.50

Litho.
Perf. 13x13½
711 A233 10pf shown 2.25 2.25
712 A233 10pf Volleyball 2.25 2.25
713 A233 10pf Bicycling 2.25 2.25
714 A233 10pf Judo 2.25 2.25
a. Block of 6, #711-714, B119-B120 17.00 17.00

18th Olympic Games, Tokyo, Oct. 10-25, 1964. See Nos. B118-B120. No. 714a printed in 2 horiz. rows: (1st: #711, #B119, #712. 2nd: #713, #B120, #714). The Olympic rings extend over the 6 stamps.

Monument, Leningrad A234

1964, Aug. 8 Litho. *Perf. 13x13½*
715 A234 25pf brt blue, blk & yel .75 .25

Issued to honor the victims of the siege of Leningrad, Sept. 1941-Jan. 1943.

Bertha von Suttner — A235

Designs: 20pf, Frederic Joliot Curie. 50pf, Carl von Ossietzky.

1964, Sept. 1 *Perf. 14*
716 A235 20pf red & black .25 .25
717 A235 25pf ultra & black .25 .25
718 A235 50pf lilac & black *1.00* .65
Nos. 716-718 (3) 1.50 1.15

Issued to promote World Peace.

Medieval Glazier and Goblet — A236

15pf, Jena glass for chemical industry.

1964, Sept. 3 *Perf. 14*
719 A236 10pf lt ultra & multi .45 .25
720 A236 15pf red & multi .45 .25
a. Pair, #719-720 + label 2.00 .70

Issued for the Leipzig Fall Fair, 1964.

Handstamp of First Socialist International, 1864 — A237

1964, Sept. 16 Photo. Wmk. 313
721 A237 20pf orange red & blk .25 .25
722 A237 25pf dull blue & blk *.55 .55*

Centenary of First Socialist International.

Stamp of 1955 (Durer's Portrait of Young Man) — A238

1964, Sept. 23 Litho. *Perf. 13x13½*

723 A238 50pf gray & dk red brn 1.50 1.25
Nos. 723,B124-B125 (3) 2.05 1.75

Natl. Stamp Exhibition, Berlin, Oct. 3-18.

Coal Transport A239

No. 724, Navigation. No. 725, Flag & new Berlin buildings. No. 727, Chemist. No. 728, Soldier. No. 729, Farm woman & cows. No. 730, Steel worker. No. 731, Woman scientist & lecture hall. No. 732, Heavy industry. No. 733, Optical industry. No. 734, Consumer goods (woman examining cloth). No. 735, Foreign trade, Leipzig fair emblem. No. 736, Buildings industry. No. 737, Sculptor. No. 738, Woman skier.

Perf. 13½x13

1964, Oct. 6 Litho. Wmk. 313

724 A239 10pf blue & multi .30 .30
725 A239 10pf blue & multi .30 .30
726 A239 10pf gray & multi .30 .30
727 A239 10pf red & multi .30 .30
728 A239 10pf red & multi .30 .30
729 A239 10pf yel grn & multi .30 .30
730 A239 10pf red & multi .30 .30
731 A239 10pf red & multi .30 .30
732 A239 10pf gray & multi .30 .30
733 A239 10pf gray & multi .30 .30
734 A239 10pf blue & multi .30 .30
735 A239 10pf blue & multi .30 .30
736 A239 10pf yel grn & multi .30 .30
737 A239 10pf yel grn & multi .30 .30
738 A239 10pf blue & multi .30 .30
Nos. 724-738 (15) 4.50 4.50

German Democratic Republic, 15th anniv.
A souvenir sheet contains 15 imperf. stamps similar to Nos. 724-738. Size: 210x287mm. Values: $40 unused, $75 used.
For surcharge see No. B134.

Man from Mönchgut, Rügen — A240

Regional Costumes: No. 740, Woman from Mönchgut, Rügen. No. 741, Man from Spreewald. No. 742, Woman from Spreewald. No. 743, Man from Thuringia. No. 744, Woman from Thuringia.

1964, Nov. 25 Photo. *Perf. 14*

739 A240 5pf multicolored *5.00 4.25*
740 A240 5pf multicolored *5.00 4.25*
a. Pair, #739-740 *25.00 10.00*
741 A240 10pf multicolored 1.50 .90
742 A240 10pf multicolored 1.50 .90
a. Pair, #741-742 7.50 3.00
743 A240 20pf multicolored 1.50 .90
744 A240 20pf multicolored 1.50 .90
a. Pair, #739-740 7.50 3.00
Nos. 739-744 (6) 16.00 12.10

Printed in checkerboard arrangement.
See Nos. 859-864.

Souvenir Sheets

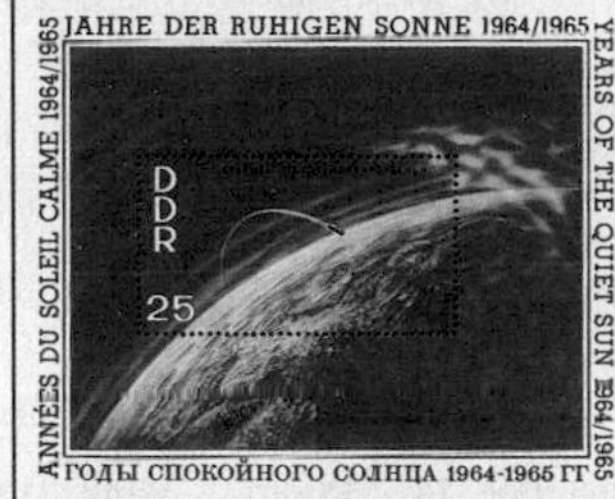

Exploration of Ionosphere — A241

Designs: 40pf, Exploration of sun activities. 70pf, Exploration of radiation belt.

1964, Dec. 29 Litho. *Perf. 13½x13*

745 A241 25pf vio bl & yel *4.50 8.00*
746 A241 40pf vio bl, yel & red *2.25 4.00*
747 A241 70pf dp grn, vio bl & yel *1.75 4.00*
Nos. 745-747 (3) 8.50 16.00

Intl. Quiet Sun Year, 1964-65.

Albert Schweitzer as Physician A242

Designs (Schweitzer): 20pf, As fighter against war and atom bomb. 25pf, At the organ with score of Organ Prelude by Bach.

Wmk. 313

1965, Jan. 14 Photo. *Perf. 14*

748 A242 10pf emerald, blk & bis .50 .25
749 A242 20pf crimson, blk & bis .50 .25
750 A242 25pf blue, blk & bis *3.00 1.75*
Nos. 748-750 (3) 4.00 2.25

90th birthday of Dr. Albert Schweitzer, medical missionary.

Ulbricht Type of 1961-63

Currency in "Mark of the Deutsche Notenbank" (MDN)

1965, Feb. 10 Engr.

Size: 24x28½mm

751 A189 1mdn dull green .40 1.00
752 A189 2mdn brown .50 1.50

See note below Nos. 590B-590C.

August Bebel — A243

10pf, Wilhelm Conrad Roentgen. No. 753A, Adolph von Menzel. 25pf, Wilhelm Külz. 40pf, Erich Weinert. 50pf, Dante Alighieri.

1965 Photo. *Perf. 14*

753 A243 10pf dk brn, yel & emer .35 .25
753A A243 10pf dk brn, yel & org .45 .25
754 A243 20pf ol brn, red & buff .35 .25
754A A243 25pf ol brn, yel & bl .75 .25
754B A243 40pf ol brn, buff & car rose .40 .25
755 A243 50pf dk brn, yel & org 1.25 .25
Nos. 753-755 (6) 3.55 1.50

Roentgen (1845-1923), physicist, discoverer of X-rays. Sesquicentennial of the birth of Adolph von Menzel, painter and graphic artist. Bebel, labor leader (1840-1913). 90th anniv. of the birth of Wilhelm Külz, politician. 75th anniv. of the birth of Erich Weinert, poet. Alighieri (1265-1321), Italian poet.
Issued: No. 753, 3/24; No. 753A, 12/8; 20pf, 2/22; 25pf, 7/5; 40pf, 7/28; 50pf, 4/15.

A244

Designs: 10pf, Gold Medal, Leipzig Fair. 15pf, Obverse of medal, arms of German Democratic Republic. 25pf, Chemical plant.

1965, Feb. 25 Wmk. 313

756 A244 10pf lilac rose & gold .25 .25
757 A244 15pf lilac rose & gold .25 .25
758 A244 25pf brt blue, yel & gold .50 .25
Nos. 756-758 (3) 1.00 .75

1965 Leipzig Spring Fair; 800th anniv. of the Fair.

A245

Designs: 10pf, Giraffe. 25pf, Common iguana, horiz. 30pf, White-tailed gnu.

1965, Mar. 24

759 A245 10pf green & gray .25 .25
760 A245 25pf dk vio bl & gray .25 .25
761 A245 30pf brown & gray *1.60 1.25*
Nos. 759-761 (3) 2.10 1.75

10th anniversary of Berlin Zoo.

Col. Pavel Belyayev and Lt. Col. Alexei Leonov A246

25pf, Lt. Col. Leonov floating in space.

Perf. 13½x13

1965, Apr. 15 Litho. Wmk. 313

762 A246 10pf red .30 .25
763 A246 25pf dk ultra *1.75 1.25*

Space flight of Voskhod 2 and the first man walking in space, Lt. Col. Alexei Leonov.

Boxing Glove and Laurel Wreath — A247

1965, Apr. 27 Photo. *Perf. 14*

764 A247 20pf blk, red & gold *.65 .65*

16th European Boxing Championship, Berlin, May, 1965. See No. B126.

Walter Ulbricht and Erich Weinert Distributing "Free Germany" Leaflets on the Eastern Front — A248

50pf, Liberation of concentration camps. 60pf, Russian soldiers raising flag on Reichstag, Berlin. 70pf, Political demonstration.

1965, May 5 Photo. *Perf. 14*

Flags in Red, Black & Yellow

765 A248 40pf blue grn & red .25 .25
766 A248 50pf dull blue & red .25 .25
767 A248 60pf brown & red *2.25 2.25*
768 A248 70pf vio blue & red .25 .25
Nos. 765-768,B127-B131 (9) 4.25 4.25

20th anniv. of liberation from fascism.

Radio Tower and Globe — A249

40pf, Workers & broadcasting equipment.

1965, May 12 Litho. *Perf. 12½x13*

769 A249 20pf dk car rose & blk .30 .25
770 A249 40pf vio bl & blk *1.20 .60*

20th anniv. of the German Democratic broadcasting system.

ITU Emblem and Frequency Diagram — A250

25pf, ITU emblem & telephone diagram.

1965, May 17

771 A250 20pf olive, yel & blk .35 .25
772 A250 25pf vio, pale vio & blk *1.60 .40*

Cent. of the ITU.

Emblem of Free German Trade Union — A251

Hemispheres with Crowd of Workers — A252

1965, June 10 Photo. *Perf. 14*

773 A251 20pf red & gold .35 .25
774 A252 25pf gold, blue & blk *1.10 .45*

20th anniv. of the Free German Trade Union (FDGB) and of the World Organization of Trade Unions.

Symbols of Industry — A253

Designs: 20pf, Red Tower. 25pf, City Hall.

1965, June 16

775 A253 10pf gold & emerald .25 .25
776 A253 20pf gold & crimson .25 .25
777 A253 25pf gold & brt blue *.75 .45*
Nos. 775-777 (3) 1.25 .95

800th anniv. of Chemnitz (Karl Marx City).

Marx and Lenin — A254

1965, June 21 Litho. ***Perf. 13½x13***

778 A254 20pf red, black & buff .45 .25

6th Conference of Postal Ministers of Communist Countries, Peking, June 21-July 15.

"Alte Waage" and New Building, Leipzig — A255

25pf, Old City Hall. 40pf, Opera House & General Post Office. 70pf, Hotel "Stadt Leipzig."

Unwmk.

1965, Aug. 25 Photo. ***Perf. 14***

781 A255 10pf gold, cl brn & ultra .25 .25
a. Souv. sheet of 2, #781, 784 *3.00 4.75*
782 A255 25pf gold, brn, & ocher .25 .25
a. Souv. sheet of 2, #782-783 *2.00 4.00*
783 A255 40pf gold, brn, ocher & yel grn .25 .25
784 A255 70pf gold & ultra *1.60 .70*
Nos. 781-784 (4) 2.35 1.45

800th anniv. of the City of Leipzig. No. 781a sold for 90pf; No. 782a for 80pf. The souvenir sheets were issued Sept. 4, 1965.

Cameras — A256

Leipzig Fall Fair: 15pf, Electric guitar and organ. 25pf, Microscope.

1965, Sept. 9 ***Perf. 14***

785 A256 10pf green, blk & gold .25 .25
786 A256 15pf multicolored .25 .25
787 A256 25pf multicolored .70 .25
Nos. 785-787 (3) 1.20 .75

Equestrian — A257

Perf. 13½x13

1965, Sept. 15 Litho. Unwmk.

789 A257 10pf shown .25 .25
790 A257 10pf Swimmer .25 .25
791 A257 10pf Runner *2.00 2.00*
Nos. 789-791,B135-B136 (5) 3.00 3.00

Intl. Modern Pentathlon Championships, Leipzig.

Alexei Leonov and Brandenburg Gate — A258

Designs: No. 793, Pavel Belyayev and Berlin City Hall. 25pf, Leonov floating in space and space ship.

Wmk. 313

1965, Oct. 1 Litho. ***Perf. 14***

Size: 23½x28½mm

792 A258 20pf blue, sil & red *.45 .55*
793 A258 20pf blue, sil & red *.45 .55*

Size: 51x28½mm

794 A258 25pf blue, sil & red *.45 .55*
a. Strip of 3, #792-794 *2.50 3.00*

Visit of the Russian astronauts to the German Democratic Republic.

Memorial Monument, Putten — A259

1965, Oct. 19 ***Perf. 13x13½***

795 A259 25pf brt bl, pale yel & blk .65 .25

Issued in memory of the victims of a Nazi attack on Putten, Netherlands, Sept. 30, 1944.

Furnace A260

After old woodcuts: 15pf, Ore miners. 20pf, Proustite crystals. 25pf, Sulphur crystals.

Perf. 13x12½

1965, Nov. 11 Litho. Unwmk.

796 A260 10pf black & multi .25 .25
797 A260 15pf black & multi *.55 .55*
798 A260 20pf black & multi .25 .25
799 A260 25pf black & multi .25 .25
Nos. 796-799 (4) 1.30 1.30

Mining Academy in Freiberg, bicent.

Red Kite — A261

Birds: 10pf, Lammergeier. 20pf, Buzzard. 25pf, Kestrel. 40pf, Northern goshawk. 70pf, Golden eagle.

1965, Dec. 8 Photo. ***Perf. 14***

Gold Frame

800 A261 5pf orange & blk .25 .25
801 A261 10pf emer, brn & blk .25 .25
802 A261 20pf car, red brn & blk .25 .25
803 A261 25pf blue, red brn & blk .25 .25
804 A261 40pf lilac, blk & dk red .35 .25
805 A261 70pf brn, blk & yel *3.00 1.75*
Nos. 800-805 (6) 4.35 3.00

Otto Grotewohl — A262

1965, Dec. 14 Photo. Wmk. 313

806 A262 20pf black .55 .25

Issued in memory of Otto Grotewohl (1894-1964), prime minister (1949-1964).

Souvenir Sheet

Spartacus Letter, Karl Liebknecht and Rosa Luxemburg — A263

1966, Jan. 3 Unwmk.

807 A263 Sheet of 2 1.75 *5.00*
a. 20pf red & black .35 .60
b. 50pf red & black .35 .60

50th anniv. of the natl. conf. of the Spartacus organization.

Tobogganing, Women's Singles A264

20pf, Men's doubles. 25pf, Men's singles.

Perf. 13½x13

1966, Jan. 25 Litho. Unwmk.

808 A264 10pf citron & dp grn .25 .25
809 A264 20pf car rose & dk vio bl .25 .25
810 A264 25pf blue & dk blue *1.00 .65*
Nos. 808-810 (3) 1.50 1.15

10th Intl. Tobogganing Championships, Friedrichroda, Feb. 8-13.

Electronic Computer A265

Design: 15pf, Drill and milling machine.

1966, Feb. 24 ***Perf. 13x12½***

811 A265 10pf multicolored .25 .25
812 A265 15pf multicolored .70 .25

Leipzig Spring Fair, 1966.

Jan Arnost Smoler and Linden Leaf — A266

25pf, House of the Sorbs, Bautzen, Saxony.

1966, Mar. 1 ***Perf. 13x13½***

813 A266 20pf brt bl, blk & brt red .25 .25
814 A266 25pf brt red, blk & brt bl *.55 .45*

Smoler (1816-84), philologist of the Sorbian language. The Sorbs are a small group of slavic people in Saxony.

Soldier and National Gallery, Berlin — A267

Designs (Soldier and): 10pf, Brandenburg Gate. 20pf, Factory. 25pf, Combine.

Wmk. 313

1966, Mar. 1 Photo. ***Perf. 14***

815 A267 5pf ol gray, blk & yel .25 .25
816 A267 10pf ol gray, blk & yel .25 .25
817 A267 20pf ol gray, blk & yel .25 .25
818 A267 25pf ol gray, blk & yel .85 .65
Nos. 815-818 (4) 1.60 1.40

National People's Army, 10th anniversary.

Luna 9 on Moon — A268

1966, Mar. 7 Unwmk.

819 A268 20pf multicolored 1.75 .35

1st soft landing on the moon by Luna 9, 2/3/66.

Medal for Scholarship — A269

1966, Mar. 7 Litho. ***Perf. 13½x13***

820 A269 20pf multicolored .45 .25

20th anniv. of the State Youth Organization.

Traffic Signs — A270

Traffic safety: 15pf, Automobile and child with scooter. 25pf, Bicyclist and signaling hand. 50pf, Motorcyclist, ambulance and glass of beer.

1966, Mar. 28 Litho. ***Perf. 13***

821 A270 10pf dk & lt bl, red & blk .25 .25
822 A270 15pf brt grn, citron & blk .25 .25
823 A270 25pf ol bis, brt bl & blk .25 .25
824 A270 50pf car, yel, gray & blk *.80 .45*
Nos. 821-824 (4) 1.55 1.20

Marx, Lenin and Crowd — A271

Designs: 5pf, Party emblem and crowd, vert. 15pf, Marx, Engels and title page of Communist Manifesto, vert. 20pf, Otto Grotewohl and

Wilhelm Pieck shaking hands, and Party emblem, vert. 25pf, Chairman Walter Ulbricht receiving flowers.

1966, Mar. 31 Photo. *Perf. 14*

825 A271 5pf multicolored .25 .25
826 A271 10pf multicolored .25 .25
827 A271 15pf green & blk .25 .25
828 A271 20pf dk carmine & blk .25 .25
829 A271 25pf multicolored *1.25 1.00*
Nos. 825-829 (5) 2.25 2.00

20th anniversary of Socialist Unity Party of Germany (SED).

WHO Headquarters, Geneva — A272

Perf. 13x12½

1966, Apr. 26 Litho. Unwmk.

830 A272 20pf multicolored .40 .30

Inauguration of WHO Headquarters, Geneva.

Rügen Island, Königsstuhl — A273

National Parks: 10pf, Spree River woodland. 20pf, Saxon Switzerland. 25pf, Dunes at Westdarss. 30pf, Thale in Harz, Devil's Wall. 50pf, Feldberg Lakes, Mecklenburg.

Perf. 13x12½

1966, May 17 Litho. Unwmk.

831 A273 10pf multicolored .25 .25
832 A273 15pf multicolored .25 .25
833 A273 20pf multicolored .25 .25
834 A273 25pf multicolored .25 .25
835 A273 30pf multicolored *1.60 .85*
836 A273 50pf multicolored .25 .25
Nos. 831-836 (6) 2.85 2.10

Plauen Lace — A274

Various Lace Designs.

1966, May 26 *Perf. 13x13½*

837 A274 10pf green & lt green .25 .25
838 A274 20pf dk blue & lt blue .25 .25
839 A274 25pf brown red & ver .25 .25
840 A274 50pf dk vio & bluish lil *1.90 1.00*
Nos. 837-840 (4) 2.65 1.75

Rhododendron A275

Flowers: 20pf, Lilies of the Valley. 40pf, Dahlias. 50pf, Cyclamen.

Photo. & Engr.

1966 Unwmk. *Perf. 14x13½*

841 A275 20pf multicolored .25 .25
842 A275 25pf multicolored .25 .25
843 A275 40pf multicolored .30 .25
844 A275 50pf multicolored *3.00 2.90*
Nos. 841-844 (4) 3.80 3.65

Intl. Flower Show, Erfurt.
Issued: 20pf, Aug. 16; others, June 28.

Parachutist Landing on Target — A276

15pf, Group parachute jump. 20pf, Free fall.

1966, July 12 Litho. *Perf. 12½x13*

845 A276 10pf blue, blk & ol .25 .25
846 A276 15pf multicolored *.45 .45*
847 A276 20pf sky blue, blk & ol .25 .25
Nos. 845-847 (3) .95 .95

8th Intl. Parachute Championships, Leipzig.

Hans Kahle, Song of German Fighters and Medal of Spanish Republic — A277

15pf, Hans Beimler and street fighting in Madrid.

1966, July 15 Photo. *Perf. 14*

848 A277 5pf multicolored .25 .25
849 A277 15pf multicolored .25 .25
Nos. 848-849,B137-B140 (6) 2.50 2.25

German fighters in the Spanish Civil War.

Television Set A278

Design: 15pf, Electric typewriter.

Perf. 13x12½

1966, Aug. 29 Litho. Unwmk.

850 A278 10pf brt grn, blk & gray .50 .25
851 A278 15pf red, blk & gray 1.20 .25

1966 Leipzig Fall Fair.

Women's Doubles Kayak Race — A279

1966, Aug. 16

852 A279 15pf brt blue & multi *.90 .75*

7th Canoe World Championships, Berlin. See No. B141.

Oradour sur Glane Memorial and French Flag — A280

Perf. 13x13½

1966, Sept. 9 Wmk. 313

853 A280 25pf ultra, blk & red .50 .25

Issued in memory of the victims of the Nazi attack on Oradour, France, June 10, 1944.

Emblem of the Committee for Health Education — A281

5pf, Symbolic blood donor & recipient, horiz.

1966, Sept. 13 *Perf. 14*

854 A281 5pf brt green & red .25 .25
855 A281 40pf brt blue & red *1.40 .45*
Nos. 854-855,B142 (3) 2.00 .95

Blood donations and health education.

Weight Lifter — A282

Perf. 13½x13

1966, Sept. 22 Litho. Unwmk.

856 A282 15pf lt brown & blk *1.20 1.20*

Intl. and European Weight Lifting Championships, Berlin. See No. B143.

Congress Hall — A283

Emblem — A284

1966, Oct. 10 *Perf. 13*

857 A283 10pf multicolored *.40 .35*
858 A284 20pf dk blue & yellow .25 .25

6th Cong. of the Intl. Organ. of Journalists, Berlin.

Costume Type of 1964

Regional Costumes: 5pf, Woman from Altenburg. No. 860, Man from Altenburg. No. 861, Woman from Mecklenburg. 15pf, Man from Mecklenburg. 20pf, Woman from Magdeburg area. 30pf, Man from Magdeburg area.

1966, Oct. 25 Photo. *Perf. 14*

859 A240 5pf multicolored .35 .25
860 A240 10pf multicolored .35 .25
a. Pair, #859-860 1.00 .75
861 A240 10pf lt green & multi .35 .25
862 A240 15pf lt green & multi .35 .25
a. Pair, #861-862 1.00 .75
863 A240 20pf yellow & multi *1.60 1.25*
864 A240 30pf yellow & multi *1.60 1.25*
a. Pair, #863-864 *4.00 3.25*
Nos. 859-864 (6) 4.60 3.50

Printed in checkerboard arrangement.

Megalamphodus Megalopterus — A285

Various Tropical Fish in Natural Colors.

1966, Nov. 8 Litho. *Perf. 13x12½*

865 A285 5pf lt blue & gray .25 .25
866 A285 10pf blue & indigo .25 .25
867 A285 15pf citron & blk *2.00 1.60*
868 A285 20pf green & blk .25 .25
869 A285 25pf ultra & blk .25 .25
870 A285 40pf emerald & blk .30 .25
Nos. 865-870 (6) 3.30 2.85

Map of Oil Pipeline and Oil Field — A286

Design: 25pf, Map of oil pipelines and "Walter Ulbricht" Leuna chemical factory.

1966, Nov. 8 *Perf. 13½x13*

871 A286 20pf red & black .25 .25
872 A286 25pf blue & black *.65 .35*

Chemical industry.

Detail from Ishtar Gate, Babylon, 580 B.C. — A287

Designs from Babylon c. 580 B.C.: 20pf, Mythological animal from Ishtar Gate. 25pf, Lion facing right and ornaments, vert. 50pf, Lion facing left and ornaments, vert.

Perf. 13½x14, 14x13½

1966, Nov. 23 Photo.

873 A287 10pf multicolored .25 .25
874 A287 20pf multicolored .25 .25
875 A287 25pf multicolored .25 .25
876 A287 50pf multicolored *.45 .90*
Nos. 873-876 (4) 1.20 1.65

Near East Museum, Berlin.

Wartburg, Thuringia A288

Design: 25pf, Wartburg, Palace.

1966, Nov. 23 Litho. *Perf. 13x13½*

877 A288 20pf olive .25 .25
878 A288 25pf violet brown *.65 .30*
Nos. 877-878,B145 (3) 1.25 .80

900th anniv. (in 1967) of the Wartburg (castle) near Eisenach, Thuringia.

Gentian — A289

Protected Flowers: 20pf, Cephalanthera rubra (orchid). 25pf, Mountain arnica.

Black Background

1966, Dec. 8 Litho. ***Perf. 12½x13***

879 A289 10pf yel, grn & bl .25 .25
880 A289 20pf yel, grn & red .25 .25
881 A289 25pf red, yel & grn *1.10 .65*
Nos. 879-881 (3) *1.60 1.15*

Son Leaving Home — A290

Various Scenes from Fairy Tale "The Table, the Ass and the Stick."

1966, Dec. 8 ***Perf. 13½x13***

882 A290 5pf multicolored .25 .30
883 A290 10pf multicolored .25 .30
884 A290 20pf multicolored .55 .60
885 A290 25pf multicolored .55 .60
886 A290 30pf multicolored .25 .30
887 A290 50pf multicolored .25 .30
a. Sheet of 6, #882-887 2.50 4.00

See Nos. 968-973, 1063-1068, 1087-1092, 1176-1181, 1339-1344.

City Hall, Stralsund — A291

Buildings: 5pf, Wörlitz Castle, horiz. 15pf, Chorin Convent. 20pf, Ribbeck House, Berlin, horiz. 25pf, Moritzburg, Zeitz. 40pf, Old City Hall, Potsdam.

Perf. 14x13½, 13½x14

1967, Jan. 24 Photo.

888 A291 5pf multicolored .25 .25
889 A291 10pf multicolored .25 .25
890 A291 15pf multicolored .25 .25
891 A291 20pf multicolored .25 .25
892 A291 25pf multicolored .25 .25
893 A291 40pf multicolored *1.00 .65*
Nos. 888-893 (6) *2.25 1.90*

See Nos. 1018, 1020, 1071-1076.

Rifle Shooting, Prone — A292

Designs: 20pf, Shooting on skis. 25pf, Relay race with rifles on skis.

1967, Feb. 15 Litho. ***Perf. 13x12½***

894 A292 10pf Prus bl gray & brt pink .25 .25
895 A292 20pf sl grn, brt bl & grn .25 .25
896 A292 25pf ol grn, ol & grnsh bl *.60 .40*
Nos. 894-896 (3) *1.10 .90*

World Biathlon Championships (skiing and shooting), Altenberg, Feb. 15-19.

Circular Knitting Machine — A293

Design: 15pf, Zeiss telescope and galaxy.

1967, Mar. 2 ***Perf. 13½x13***

897 A293 10pf dull mag & brt grn .25 .25
898 A293 15pf ultra & gray .65 .25

Leipzig Spring Fair of 1967.

Mother and Child — A294

Design: 25pf, Working women.

1967, Mar. 7 ***Perf. 13x13½***

899 A294 20pf rose brn, red & gray .25 .25
900 A294 25pf dk bl, brt bl & brn *.65 .60*

20th anniv. of the Democratic Women's Federation of Germany.

Marx, Engels, Lenin and Electronic Control Center — A295

Designs (Portraits and): 5pf, Farmer driving combine. No. 903, Students and teacher. 15pf, Family. No. 905, Soldier, sailor and aviator. No. 906, Ulbricht among workers. 25pf, Soldier, sailor, aviator and factories. 40pf, Farmers with modern equipment. Nos. 901, 903-905 are vertical.

1967 Photo. ***Perf. 14***

901 A295 5pf multicolored .25 .25
902 A295 10pf multicolored .25 .25
903 A295 10pf multicolored .25 .25
904 A295 15pf multicolored *.35 .40*
905 A295 20pf multicolored .25 .25
906 A295 20pf multicolored .25 .25
907 A295 25pf multicolored .25 .25
908 A295 40pf multicolored *.35 .60*
Nos. 901-908 (8) *2.20 2.50*

7th congress of Socialist Unity Party of Germany (SED), Apr. 17.

Issued: Nos. 902, 906-908 3/22; Nos. 901, 903-905, 4/6.

Tahitian Women, by Paul Gauguin — A296

Paintings from Dresden Gallery: 20pf, Young Woman, by Ferdinand Hodler. 25pf, Peter in the Zoo, by H. Hakenbeck. 30pf, Venetian Episode (woman feeding pigeons), by R. Bergander. 50pf, Grandmother and Granddaughter, by J. Scholtz. 70pf, Cairn in the Snow, by Caspar David Friedrich.

1967, Mar. 29

909 A296 20pf multi, vert. .25 .25
910 A296 25pf multi, vert. .25 .25
911 A296 30pf multi, vert. .25 .25
912 A296 40pf multi .25 .25
913 A296 50pf multi, vert. *1.25 1.00*
914 A296 70pf multi .30 .25
Nos. 909-914 (6) *2.55 2.25*

Barn Owl — A297

Protected Birds: 10pf, Eurasian crane. 20pf, Peregrine falcon. 25pf, Bullfinches. 30pf, European kingfisher. 40pf, European roller.

1967, Apr. 27 Photo. ***Perf. 14***

Birds in Natural Colors

915 A297 5pf gray blue .25 .25
916 A297 10pf gray blue .25 .25
917 A297 20pf gray blue .25 .25
918 A297 25pf gray blue .25 .25
919 A297 30pf gray blue *3.25 1.75*
920 A297 40pf gray blue .30 .25
Nos. 915-920 (6) *4.55 3.00*

Arms of Warsaw, Berlin and Prague A298

Design: 25pf, Bicyclists and doves.

Perf. 13x12½

1967, May 10 Litho. Wmk. 313

921 A298 10pf org, blk & lil .25 .25
922 A298 25pf lt bl & dk car *.40 .35*

20th Intl. Bicycle Peace Race, Berlin-Warsaw-Prague.

Cat A299

Children's Drawings: 10pf, Snow White and the Seven Dwarfs. 15pf, Fire truck. 20pf, Cock. 25pf, Flowers in vase. 30pf, Children playing ball.

1967, June 1 Unwmk.

923 A299 5pf multicolored .25 .25
924 A299 10pf black & multi .25 .25
925 A299 15pf dk blue & multi .25 .25
926 A299 20pf orange & multi .25 .25
927 A299 25pf multicolored .25 .25
928 A299 30pf multicolored *.85 .65*
Nos. 923-928 (6) *2.10 1.90*

Issued for International Children's Day.

Girl with Straw Hat, by Salomon Bray — A300

Paintings: 5pf, Three Horsemen, by Rubens, horiz. 10pf, Girl Gathering Grapes, by Gerard Dou. 20pf, Spring Idyl, by Hans Thoma, horiz. 25pf, Wilhelmine Schroder-Devrient, by Karl Begas. 50pf, The Four Evangelists, by Jacob Jordaens.

1967, June 7 Photo. ***Perf. 14***

929 A300 5pf lt & dk blue .25 .25
930 A300 10pf lt red brn & red brn .25 .25
931 A300 20pf lt & dp yel grn .25 .25
932 A300 25pf pale rose & rose lil .25 .25
933 A300 40pf pale grn & ol grn .25 .25
934 A300 50pf tan & sepia *1.25 .75*
Nos. 929-934 (6) *2.50 2.00*

Issued to publicize paintings missing from museums since World War II.

Exhibition Emblem and Map of DDR — A301

Perf. 12½x13

1967, June 14 Litho. Unwmk.

935 A301 20pf dk grn, ocher & red .35 .25

15th Agricultural Exhib., Markkleeberg.

Marie Curie — A302

Portraits: 5pf, Georg Herwegh, poet. 20pf, Käthe Kollwitz. 25pf, Johann J. Winckelmann, archaeologist. 40pf, Theodor Storm, writer.

1967 Engr. ***Perf. 14***

936 A302 5pf brown .25 .25
937 A302 10pf dark blue .25 .25
938 A302 20pf dull red .25 .25
939 A302 25pf gray .25 .25
940 A302 40pf slate green *.65 .45*
Nos. 936-940 (5) *1.65 1.45*

150th anniv. of the birth of Herwegh, Winckelmann and Storm, and the birth centenaries of Curie and Kollwitz.

German Playing Cards — A303

Designs: Various German playing cards.

1967, July 18 Photo.

941 A303 5pf red & multi .25 .25
942 A303 10pf green & multi .25 .25
943 A303 20pf multicolored .25 .25
944 A303 25pf multicolored *4.00 2.75*
Nos. 941-944 (4) *4.75 3.50*

Mare and Foal A304

Horses: 10pf, Stallion. 20pf, Horse race finish. 50pf, Colts, vert.

Perf. 13½x13, 13x13½

1967, Aug. 15 Litho. Unwmk.

945 A304 5pf multicolored .25 .25
946 A304 10pf org, blk & dk brn .25 .25
947 A304 20pf blue & multi .25 .25
948 A304 50pf multicolored *2.60 1.60*
Nos. 945-948 (4) *3.35 2.35*

Thoroughbred Horse Show of Socialist Countries, Hoppegarten, Berlin.

Small Electrical Appliances A305

Leipzig Fall Fair: 15pf, Woman's fur coat and furrier's trademark.

Perf. 14x13½

1967, Aug. 8 Photo. Unwmk.

949 A305 10pf brt bl, blk & yel .35 .25
950 A305 15pf yellow, brn & blk .70 .35

Max Reichpietsch and Warship — A306

15pf, Albin Köbis, warship. 20pf, Sailors marching with red flag, warship.

1967, Sept. 5 Litho. *Perf. 13½x13*
Bluish Paper

951 A306 10pf dk blue, gray & red .25 .25
952 A306 15pf dk blue, gray & red *.90 .45*
953 A306 20pf dk blue, gray & red .35 .25
Nos. 951-953 (3) 1.50 .95

50th anniv. of the sailors' uprising at Kiel.

Monument at Kragujevac A307

1967, Sept. 20 *Perf. 13x13½*
954 A307 25pf dk red, yel & blk .60 .30

Issued in memory of the victims of the Nazis at Kragujevac, Yugoslavia, Oct. 21, 1941.

Worker and Symbols of Electrification — A308

Communist Emblem and: 5pf, Worker, Communist newspaper masthead. 15pf, Russian War Memorial, Berlin-Treptow. 20pf, Russian and German soldiers, coat of arms. 40pf, Lenin, cruiser Aurora.

1967, Oct. 6 Photo. *Perf. 14x14½*
955 A308 5pf multicolored .25 .25
956 A308 10pf multicolored .25 .25
957 A308 15pf multicolored .25 .25
958 A308 20pf multicolored .30 .25
959 A308 40pf multicolored *2.00 1.60*
a. Souvenir sheet of 2 1.25 2.50
Nos. 955-959 (5) 3.05 2.60

50th anniv. of the Russian October Revolution. No. 959a contains 2 imperf. stamps similar to Nos. 958-959 with simulated perforations. It commemorates the Red October Jubilee Stamp Exhibition, Karl-Marx-Stadt, Oct. 6-15. Sold for 85pf.

Martin Luther, by Lucas Cranach — A309

Designs: 25pf, Luther's House, Wittenberg, horiz. 40pf, Castle Church, Wittenberg.

Engraved and Photogravure
1967, Oct. 17 *Perf. 14*
960 A309 20pf black & rose lilac .25 .25
961 A309 25pf black & blue .25 .25
962 A309 40pf black & lemon *1.75 .65*
Nos. 960-962 (3) 2.25 1.15

450th anniversary of the Reformation.

Young Inventors and Fair Emblem — A310

Designs: No. 964, Boy's and girl's heads and emblem of the Free German Youth Organization. 25pf, Young workers receiving awards, and medal.

Size: 23x28½mm

1967, Nov. 15 Unwmk. *Perf. 14*
963 A310 20pf multicolored .50 .40
964 A310 20pf multicolored .50 .40

Size: 51x28½mm

965 A310 25pf multicolored .50 .40
a. Strip of 3, #963-965 3.00 3.00

Issued to publicize the 10th Masters of Tomorrow Fair, Leipzig, Nov. 15-26.

Goethe House, Weimar A311

Design: 25pf, Schiller House, Weimar.

1967, Nov. 27 Litho. *Perf. 13x12½*
966 A311 20pf gray, blk & brn .25 .25
967 A311 25pf citron, dk grn & brn *1.25 .40*

Honoring German classical humanism.

Fairy Tale Type of 1966

Various Scenes from King Drosselbart.

1967, Nov. 27 *Perf. 13½x13*
968 A290 5pf multicolored .25 .25
969 A290 10pf multicolored .25 .25
970 A290 15pf multicolored .65 .80
971 A290 20pf multicolored .65 .80
972 A290 25pf multicolored .25 .25
973 A290 30pf multicolored .25 .25
a. Sheet of 6, #968-973 4.50 4.50

Farmers, Stables and Silos — A312

Perf. 13x12½
1967, Dec. 6 Litho. Unwmk.
974 A312 10pf multicolored .30 .25

1st agricultural co-operatives, 15th anniv.

Nutcracker and Figurines — A313

20pf, Candle holders: angel and miner.

1967, Dec. 6 Photo. *Perf. 13½x14*
975 A313 10pf green & multi *.65 .30*
976 A313 20pf red & multi .25 .25

Issued to publicize local handicrafts of the Erzgebirge in Saxony (Ore Mountains).

Speed Skating — A314

Sport and Olympic Rings: 15pf, Slalom. 20pf, Ice hockey. 25pf, Figure skating, pair. 30pf, Long-distance skiing.

Perf. 13½x13
1968, Jan. 17 Litho. Unwmk.
977 A314 5pf blue, dk bl & red .25 .25
978 A314 15pf multicolored .25 .25
979 A314 20pf grnsh bl, dk bl & red .25 .25
980 A314 25pf multicolored .25 .25
981 A314 30pf grnsh bl, vio bl & red *2.50 .90*
Nos. 977-981,B146 (6) 3.75 2.15

10th Winter Olympic Games, Grenoble, France, Feb. 6-18.

Actinometer, Sun and Potsdam Meteorological Observatory A315

Designs: 20pf, Antenna, Cloud Formation and Map of Europe. 25pf, Weather influence on farming (fields by day and night, produce).

1968, Jan. 24 *Perf. 13½x13*
Size: 23x28mm
982 A315 10pf brt mag, org & blk .40 .30
Size: 50x28mm
983 A315 20pf multicolored .40 .30
Size: 23x28mm
984 A315 25pf olive, blk & yel .40 .30
a. Strip of 3, #982-984 3.50 3.50

75th anniversary of the Meteorological Observatory in Potsdam.

Venera 4 Interplanetary Station — A316

Design: 25pf, Earth satellites Kosmos 186 and 188 orbiting earth.

1968, Jan. 24 Photo. *Perf. 14*
985 A316 20pf multicolored .25 .25
986 A316 25pf multicolored *.70 .30*

Russian space explorations.

Fighters of The Underground A317

20pf, "The Liberation." 25pf, "The Partisans."

1968, Feb. 21 Photo. *Perf. 14x13½*
987 A317 10pf black & multi .25 .25
988 A317 20pf black & multi .25 .25
989 A317 25pf black & multi .35 .25
Nos. 987-989 (3) .85 .75

The designs are from the stained glass window triptych by Walter Womacka in the Sachsenhausen Memorial Museum.

Diesel Locomotive — A318

Design: 15pf, Refrigerator fishing ship.

1968, Feb. 29 *Perf. 14*
990 A318 10pf multicolored .30 .25
991 A318 15pf multicolored .70 .35

The 1968 Leipzig Spring Fair.

Woman from Hoyerswerda A319

Sorbian Regional Costumes: 20pf, Woman from Schleife. 40pf, Woman from Crostwitz. 50pf, Woman from Spreewald.

1968, Mar. 14
992 A319 10pf citron & multi .25 .25
993 A319 20pf fawn & multi .25 .25
994 A319 40pf blue grn & multi .25 .25
995 A319 50pf green & multi *2.00 .75*
Nos. 992-995 (4) 2.75 1.50

Maxim Gorky and View of Gorky — A320

25pf, Stormy petrel and toppling towers.

1968, Mar. 14 Engr.
996 A320 20pf brown & rose car .25 .25
997 A320 25pf brown & rose car *.55 .30*

Maxim Gorky (1868-1936), Russian writer.

Ring-necked Pheasants A321

15pf, Gray partridges. 20pf, Mallards. 25pf, Graylag geese. 30pf, Wood pigeons. 40pf, Hares.

1968, Mar. 26 Litho. *Perf. 13½x13*
998 A321 10pf gray & multi .25 .25
999 A321 15pf gray & multi .25 .25
1000 A321 20pf gray & multi .25 .25
1001 A321 25pf gray & multi .25 .25
1002 A321 30pf gray & multi .30 .25
1003 A321 40pf gray & multi *2.25 4.25*
Nos. 998-1003 (6) 3.55 5.50

Karl Marx — A322

Designs: 10pf, Title page of the "Communist Manifesto." 25pf, Title page of "Das Kapital."

1968, Apr. 25 Photo. *Perf. 14*
1004 A322 10pf yel grn & blk .25 .25
1005 A322 20pf mag, yel & blk .25 .25
1006 A322 25pf lem, blk & red brn .25 .25
a. Strip of three 1.25 3.25
b. Souvenir sheet of 3 1.10 3.25

Karl Marx (1818-83). Nos. 1004-1006 are printed se-tenant. No. 1006a contains 3 imperf. stamps similar to Nos. 1004-1006 with simulated perforations.

Fritz Heckert — A323

Design: 20pf, Young workers, new apartment buildings and Congress emblem.

1968, Apr. 25

1007 A323 10pf multicolored .25 .25
1008 A323 20pf multicolored .25 .25

7th Congress of the Free German Trade Unions.

"Right to Work" — A324

Designs: 10pf, "Right to Live," tree and globe. 25pf, "Right for Peace," dove and sun.

1968, May 8 Litho. *Perf. 13½x13*

1009 A324 5pf maroon & pink .25 .25
1010 A324 10pf brn ol & ol bister .25 .25
1011 A324 25pf Prus bl & lt bl .65 .35
Nos. 1009-1011 (3) 1.15 .85

International Human Rights Year.

Angler A325

Designs: No. 1013, Rowing (woman). No. 1014, High jump (woman).

Unwmk.

1968, June 6 Photo. *Perf. 14*

1012 A325 20pf ol grn, sl bl & dk red .40 .35
1013 A325 20pf Prus bl, dk bl & ol .25 .25
1014 A325 20pf cop red, dp cl & bl .25 .25
Nos. 1012-1014 (3) .90 .85

World angling championships, Gustrow (No. 1012); European women's rowing championships, Berlin (No. 1013); 2nd European youth athletic competition, Leipzig (No. 1014).

Brandenburg Gate, Torch — A326

Design: 25pf, Stadium and torch.

1968, June 20 Litho. *Perf. 13½x13*

1015 A326 10pf multicolored .25 .25
1016 A326 25pf multicolored .70 .45

2nd Children's and Youths' Spartakiad, Berlin.

Youth Festival Emblem — A327

1968, June 20

1017 A327 25pf multicolored .60 .35

9th Youth Festival for Peace & Friendship, Sofia.

See No. B148.

Type of 1967 and

Moritzburg Castle, Dresden — A328

Buildings: 10pf, City Hall, Wernigerode, vert. 25pf, City Hall, Greifswald, vert. 30pf, Sanssouci Palace, Potsdam.

1968, June 25 Photo. *Perf. 13½x14*

1018 A291 10pf multicolored .25 .25
1019 A328 20pf multicolored .25 .25
1020 A291 25pf multicolored .25 .25
1021 A328 30pf multicolored .60 .60
Nos. 1018-1021 (4) 1.35 1.35

Walter Ulbricht and Arms of Republic A329

Photo. & Engr.

1968, June 27 *Perf. 14*

1022 A329 20pf org, dp car & blk .45 .25

75th birthday of Walter Ulbricht, chairman of the Council of State, Communist party secretary and deputy prime minister.

Old Rostock and Arms A330

Design: 25pf, Historic and modern buildings, 1968, and arms of Rostock.

1968, July 9 Photo.

1023 A330 20pf multicolored .25 .25
1024 A330 25pf multicolored .40 .35

750th anniv. of Rostock and to publicize the 11th Baltic Sea Week.

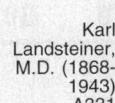

Karl Landsteiner, M.D. (1868-1943) A331

Portraits: 15pf, Emanuel Lasker (1868-1941), chess champion and writer. 20pf, Hanns Eisler (1898-1962), composer. 25pf, Ignaz Semmelweis, M.D. (1818-1865). 40pf, Max von Pettenkofer (1818-1901), hygienist.

1968, July 17 Engr. *Perf. 14*

1025 A331 10pf gray green .25 .25
1026 A331 15pf black .25 .25
1027 A331 20pf brown .25 .25
1028 A331 25pf gray blue .25 .25
1029 A331 40pf rose lake .60 .50
Nos. 1025-1029 (5) 1.60 1.50

"Trener" Stunt Plane — A332

25pf, 2 "Trener" stunt planes in parallel flight.

1968, Aug. 13 Litho. *Perf. 12½x13*

1030 A332 10pf multicolored .25 .25
1031 A332 25pf blue & multi .50 .35

Peasant Woman, by Wilhelm Leibl — A333

Paintings from Dresden Gallery: 10pf, "On the Beach," by Walter Womacka, horiz. 15pf, Mountain Farmers Mowing, by Albin Egger-Lienz, horiz. 40pf, The Artist's daughter, by Venturelli. 50pf, High School Girl, by Michaelis. 70pf, Girl with Guitar, by Castelli.

Perf. 14x13½, 13½x14

1968, Aug. 20 Photo.

1032 A333 10pf multicolored .25 .25
1033 A333 15pf multicolored .25 .25
1034 A333 20pf multicolored .25 .25
1035 A333 40pf multicolored .35 .25
1036 A333 50pf multicolored .35 .25
1037 A333 70pf multicolored 1.90 .85
Nos. 1032-1037 (6) 3.35 2.10

Model Trains — A334

1968, Aug. 29 *Perf. 14x13½*

1038 A334 10pf lt ultra, red & blk .30 .25

The 1968 Leipzig Fall Fair.

Spremberg Dam — A335

Designs: 10pf, Pöhl Dam, vert. 15pf, Ohra Dam, vert. 20pf, Rappbode Dam.

Perf. 13x12½, 12½x13

1968, Sept. 11 Litho.

1039 A335 5pf multicolored .25 .25
1040 A335 10pf multicolored .25 .25
1041 A335 15pf multicolored .35 .35
1042 A335 20pf multicolored .25 .25
Nos. 1039-1042 (4) 1.10 1.10

Issued to publicize dams built since 1945.

Runner A336

Designs: 25pf, Woman gymnast, vert. 40pf, Water polo, vert. 70pf, Sculling.

1968, Sept. 18 Photo. *Perf. 14*

1043 A336 5pf multicolored .25 .25
1044 A336 25pf multicolored .25 .25
1045 A336 40pf multicolored .25 .25
1046 A336 70pf blue & multi 1.25 1.00
Nos. 1043-1046,B149-B150 (6) 2.50 2.25

19th Olympic Games, Mexico City, 10/12-27.

Monument, Fort Breendonk, Belgium — A337

1968, Oct. 10 Litho. *Perf. 13x13½*

1047 A337 25pf multicolored .35 .25

Issued in memory of the victims of the Nazis at the Fort Breendonk Concentration Camp.

Tiger Beetle — A338

Insects: 15pf, Ground beetle (Cychrus caraboides). 20pf, Ladybug. 25pf, Ground beetle (Carabus arcensis hrbst.). 30pf, Hister beetle. 40pf, Checkered beetle.

1968, Oct. 16 *Perf. 13½x13*

1048 A338 10pf yellow & multi .25 .25
1049 A338 15pf bluish lil & blk .25 .25
1050 A338 20pf multicolored .25 .25
1051 A338 25pf lt lilac & blk 1.60 1.40
1052 A338 30pf lt grn, blk & red .25 .25
1053 A338 40pf pink & black .25 .25
Nos. 1048-1053 (6) 2.85 2.65

Lenin and Letter to Spartacists — A339

Designs: 20pf, Workers, soldiers and sailors with masthead and slogans. 25pf, Karl Liebknecht and Rosa Luxemburg.

1968, Oct. 29 Litho. *Perf. 13x12½*

1054 A339 10pf lemon, red & blk .25 .25
1055 A339 20pf lemon, red & blk .25 .25
1056 A339 25pf lemon, red & blk .40 .40
Nos. 1054-1056 (3) .90 .90

November Revolution in Germany, 50th anniv.

Cattleya — A340

Orchids: 10pf, Paphiopedilum albertianum. 15pf, Cattleya fabia. 20pf, Cattleya aclandiae. 40pf, Sobralia macrantha. 50pf, Dendrobium alpha.

1968, Nov. 12 Photo. *Perf. 13*

Flowers in Natural Colors

1057 A340 5pf bluish lilac .25 .25
1058 A340 10pf green .25 .25
1059 A340 15pf bister .25 .25
1060 A340 20pf green .25 .25
1061 A340 40pf light brown .25 .25
1062 A340 50pf gray 1.40 1.00
Nos. 1057-1062 (6) 2.65 2.25

Fairy Tale Type of 1966

Various Scenes from Puss in Boots.

1968, Nov. 27 Litho. ***Perf. 13½x13***

1063	A290	5pf multicolored	.25	.25
1064	A290	10pf multicolored	.25	.25
1065	A290	15pf multicolored	.80	.80
1066	A290	20pf multicolored	.80	.80
1067	A290	25pf multicolored	.25	.25
1068	A290	30pf multicolored	.25	.25
a.		Sheet of 6, #1063-1068	4.25	7.50

Young Pioneers A341

Design: 15pf, Five Young Pioneers.

1968, Dec. 3 ***Perf. 13x13½***

1069	A341	10pf blue & multi	.25	.25
1070	A341	15pf multicolored	*.50*	*.30*

20th anniv. of the founding of the Ernst Thalmann Young Pioneers' organization.

Buildings Type of 1967

Buildings: 5pf, City Hall, Tangermunde. 10pf, German State Opera, Berlin. 20pf, Wall Pavilion, Dresden. 25pf, Burgher's House, Luckau. 30pf, Rococo Palace, Dornburg. 40pf, "Stockfish" House, Erfurt.

1969, Jan. 1 Photo. ***Perf. 14***

1071	A291	5pf multi	.25	.25
1072	A291	10pf multi, horiz.	.25	.25
1073	A291	20pf multi	.25	.25
1074	A291	25pf multi	*.65*	*.45*
1075	A291	30pf multi, horiz.	.25	.25
1076	A291	40pf multi	.25	.25
		Nos. 1071-1076 (6)	*1.90*	*1.70*

Martin Andersen Nexö, Danish Writer — A342

Portraits: 20pf, Otto Nagel (1894-1967), painter. 25pf, Alexander von Humboldt (1769-1859), naturalist, traveler, statesman. 40pf, Theodor Fontane (1819-1898), writer.

1969, Feb. 5 Engr. ***Perf. 14***

1077	A342	10pf olive	.25	.25
1078	A342	20pf deep brown	.25	.25
1079	A342	25pf violet blue	*.65*	*.35*
1080	A342	40pf brown	.25	.25
		Nos. 1077-1080 (4)	*1.40*	*1.10*

Issued to honor famous men.

Be Attentive and Considerate! A343

10pf, Watch ahead! (car, truck & traffic signal). 20pf, Watch railroad crossings! (train & car at crossing). 25pf, If in doubt don't pass! (cars & truck).

1969, Feb. 18 Litho. ***Perf. 13x13½***

1081	A343	5pf lt blue & multi	.25	.25
1082	A343	10pf yellow & multi	.25	.25
1083	A343	20pf pink & multi	.25	.25
1084	A343	25pf multicolored	*.40*	*.35*
		Nos. 1081-1084 (4)	*1.15*	*1.10*

Traffic safety campaign.

Combine A344

Leipzig Spring Fair: 15pf, Planeta-Variant offset printing press.

1969, Feb. 26 Photo. ***Perf. 14***

1085	A344	10pf multicolored	.25	.25
1086	A344	15pf crimson, blk & bl	.25	.25

Jorinde and Joringel A345

Various Scenes from Fairy Tale "Jorinde and Joringel."

1969, Mar. 18 Litho. ***Perf. 13½x13***

1087	A345	5pf black & multi	.25	.25
1088	A345	10pf black & multi	.25	.25
1089	A345	15pf black & multi	.40	.45
1090	A345	20pf black & multi	.40	.45
1091	A345	25pf black & multi	.25	.25
1092	A345	30pf black & multi	.25	.25
a.		Sheet of 6, #1087-1092	2.25	2.75

See Nos. 1176-1181.

Spring Snowflake — A346

Protected Plants: 10pf, Adonis. 15pf, Globeflowers. 20pf, Garden Turk's-cap. 25pf, Button snakeroot. 30pf, Dactylorchis latifolia.

1969, Apr. 4 Photo. ***Perf. 14***

1093	A346	5pf green & multi	.25	.25
1094	A346	10pf green & multi	.25	.25
1095	A346	15pf green & multi	.25	.25
1096	A346	20pf green & multi	.25	.25
1097	A346	25pf green & multi	*2.10*	*1.25*
1098	A346	30pf green & multi	.30	.25
		Nos. 1093-1098 (6)	*3.40*	*2.50*

Red Cross, Crescent, Lion and Sun Emblems — A347

Design: 15pf, Large Red Cross, Red Crescent and Lion and Sun Emblems.

1969, Apr. 23 Litho. ***Perf. 12½x13***

1099	A347	10pf gray, red & yel	.25	.25
1100	A347	15pf multicolored	*.90*	*.40*

League of Red Cross Societies, 50th anniv.

Conifer Nursery — A348

10pf, Forests as natural resources (timber & resin). 20pf, Forests as regulators of climate. 25pf, Forests as recreation areas (tents along lake)

1969, Apr. 23

1101	A348	5pf multicolored	.25	.25
1102	A348	10pf multicolored	.25	.25
1103	A348	20pf multicolored	.25	.25
1104	A348	25pf multicolored	*1.40*	*.75*
		Nos. 1101-1104 (4)	*2.15*	*1.50*

Prevention of forest fires.

Erythrite from Schneeberg A349

Minerals: 10pf, Fluorite from Halsbrücke. 15pf, Galena from Neudorf. 20pf, Smoky quartz from Lichtenberg. 25pf, Calcite from Niederrabenstein. 50pf, Silver from Freiberg.

1969, May 21 Photo. ***Perf. 13½x14***

1105	A349	5pf tan & multi	.25	.25
1106	A349	10pf multicolored	.25	.25
1107	A349	15pf gray & multi	.25	.25
1108	A349	20pf lemon & multi	.25	.25
1109	A349	25pf multicolored	*.65*	*.45*
1110	A349	50pf lt blue & multi	.25	.25
		Nos. 1105-1110 (6)	*1.90*	*1.70*

Women and Symbols of Agriculture, Science and Industry — A350

Design: 25pf, Woman's head and symbols.

1969, May 28 Engr. ***Perf. 14***

1111	A350	20pf dk red & blue	.25	.25
1112	A350	25pf blue & dk red	*.70*	*.30*

2nd Women's Congress of the German Democratic Republic.

Ulbricht Type of 1961-67

1969-71 Wmk. 313 Typo. ***Perf. 14***

Size: 17x21mm

1112A	A189	35pf Prus blue ('71)	.45	.45

Unwmk.

Engr.

Size: 24x28½mm

1113	A189	1m dull green	.35	1.00
1114	A189	2m brown	.45	1.10
		Nos. 1112A-1114 (3)	1.25	2.55

See note below Nos. 590B-590C.

Coil Stamp

1970, Jan. 20 Typo. Wmk. 313

Size: 17x21mm

1114A	A189	1m olive	.65	4.00

Emblem of DDR Philatelic Society — A351

1969, June 4 Photo Unwmk.

1115	A351	10pf red, gold & ultra	.30	.25

National Philatelic Exhibition "20 Years DDR," Magdeburg, Oct. 31-Nov. 9.

Worker Protecting Children — A352

25pf, Workers of various races. 20pf+5pf, Berlin buildings: Brandenburg Gate, Council of State, Soviet Cenotaph, Town Hall Tower, Television Tower, Teachers' Building & Hall.

Size: 23x28mm

1969, June 4 Litho. ***Perf. 13***

1116	A352	10pf lemon & multi	.45	.65

Size: 50x28mm

1117	A352	20pf + 5pf multi	.45	.65

Size: 23x28mm

1118	A352	25pf lemon & multi	.45	.65
a.		Strip of 3, #1116-1118	3.00	3.25

Intl. Peace Meeting, Berlin. The surtax on No. 1117 was for the Peace Council of the German Democratic Republic.

Opening Ceremony before Battle of Leipzig Monument — A353

15pf, Parading athletes & stadium. 25pf, Running, hurdling, javelin & flag waving. 30pf, Presentation of colors before old Leipzig Town Hall.

Photo. & Engr.

1969, June 18 ***Perf. 14***

1119	A353	5pf multi & black	.25	.25
1120	A353	15pf multi & black	.25	.25
1121	A353	25pf multi & black	*1.00*	*.40*
1122	A353	30pf multi & black	.25	.25
		Nos. 1119-1122,B152-B153 (6)	*2.25*	*1.65*

5th German Gymnastic and Sports Festival, Leipzig.

Pierre de Coubertin, by Wieland Forster — A354

Design: 25pf, Coubertin column, Memorial Grove, Olympia.

1969, June 6 ***Perf. 14x13½***

1123	A354	10pf black & lt blue	.25	.25
1124	A354	25pf black & sal pink	*.70*	*.55*

Revival of the Olympic Games, 75th anniv.

Knight — A355

No. 1126, Bicycle wheel. No. 1127, Volleyball.

1969, July 29 Photo. ***Perf. 14***

1125	A355	20pf red, gold & dk brn	.25	.25
1126	A355	20pf green, gold & red	.25	.25
1127	A355	20pf multicolored	.25	.25
		Nos. 1125-1127 (3)	.75	.75

16th Students' Chess World Championships, Dresden (No. 1125); Indoor Bicycle World Championships, Erfurt (No. 1126); 2nd Volleyball World Cup (No. 1127).

Merchandise
A356

1969, Aug. 27 Litho. *Perf. 12½x13*
1128 A356 10pf multicolored .30 .25

Leipzig Fall Fair, Aug. 31-Sept. 7, 1969.

Arms of Republic and View of Rostock
A357

1m, DDR Arms, Town Hall, Marienkirche and Television Tower, Berlin, vert.

1969, Sept. 23 Photo. *Perf. 14*
1129 A357 10pf Rostock .25 .25
1130 A357 10pf Neubrandenburg .25 .25
1131 A357 10pf Potsdam .25 .25
1132 A357 10pf Eisenhüttenstadt .25 .25
1133 A357 10pf Hoyerswerda .25 .25
1134 A357 10pf Magdeburg .25 .25
1135 A357 10pf Halle-Neustadt .25 .25
1136 A357 10pf Suhl .25 .25
1137 A357 10pf Dresden .25 .25
1138 A357 10pf Leipzig .25 .25
1139 A357 10pf Karl-Marx-Stadt .25 .25
1140 A357 10pf Berlin .25 .25
Nos. 1129-1140 (12) 3.00 3.00

Souvenir Sheet

1141 A357 1m multicolored 1.25 3.75

Nos. 1129-1141, 1142-1145 for 20th anniv. of the German Democratic Republic.
No. 1141 contains one 29x52mm stamp.

Television Tower, Berlin — A358

People and Flags — A359

Designs: 20pf, Sphere of Television Tower and TV test picture. No. 1144, Television Tower and TV test picture.

1969, Oct. 6 *Perf. 14*
1142 A358 10pf multicolored .25 .25
1143 A358 20pf multicolored .25 .25

Souvenir Sheets

1144 A358 1m dk blue & multi 1.40 2.75

Perf. 13x12½

1145 A359 1m red & multi 1.10 3.25

No. 1144 contains one 21½x60mm stamp.

Cathedral, Otto von Guericke Monument and Hotel International, Magdeburg — A360

1969, Oct. 28 Litho. *Perf. 13x12½*
1146 A360 20pf multicolored .30 .25

Natl. Postage Stamp Exhibition in honor of the 20th anniv. of the German Democratic Republic, Magdeburg. Oct. 31-Nov. 9. See No. B154.

UFI Emblem — A361

1969, Oct. 28 *Perf. 13x13½*
1147 A361 10pf multicolored .25 .25
1148 A361 15pf multicolored *1.10 .35*

36th UFI Congress (Union des Foires Internationales), Leipzig, Oct. 28-30.

Memorial Monument, Copenhagen-Ryvangen — A362

1969, Oct. 28 *Perf. 13*
1149 A362 25pf multicolored .60 .25

Issued in memory of the victims of the Nazis in Denmark.

Rostock University Seal and Building — A363

Design: 15pf, Steam turbine, curve and Rostock University emblem.

1969, Nov. 12 *Perf. 12½x13*
1150 A363 10pf brt blue & multi .25 .25
1151 A363 15pf violet & multi *.80 .25*

550th anniversary of Rostock University.

ILO Emblem — A364

1969, Nov. 12 *Perf. 13½x14*
1152 A364 20pf dp green & silver .25 .25
1153 A364 25pf lil rose & silver *1.10 .30*

50th anniv. of the ILO.

Mold for Christmas Cookies — A365

50pf, Negro couple, shaped spice cookie.

1969, Nov. 25 Litho. *Perf. 13½x13*
1154 A365 10pf dull org, bl & red brn .80 .80
1155 A365 50pf lt blue & multi 1.25 1.25
a. Pair, #1154-1155 4.75 4.00
Nos. 1154-1155,B155 (3) 2.35 2.35

Folk art of Lusatia.

Antonov An-24
A366

Planes: 25pf, Ilyushin Il-18. 30pf, Tupolev Tu-134. 50pf, Mi-8 helicopter.

1969, Dec. 2 *Perf. 13x12½*
1156 A366 20pf blue, red & blk .25 .25
1157 A366 25pf vio, red & blk *.90 .75*
1158 A366 30pf ultra, red & blk .25 .25
1159 A366 50pf olive, red & blk .25 .25
Nos. 1156-1159 (4) *1.65 1.50*

Siberian Teacher, by D. K. Sveshnikov
A367

Russian Paintings from Dresden Gallery of Modern Masters: 10pf, Steelworker, by V. A. Serov. 20pf, Still Life, by E. A. Aslamasjan. 25pf, Hot Day (boats on river), by J. D. Romas. 40pf, Spring is Coming (young woman and snow-covered street), by L. V. Kabatchek. 50pf, Man on River Bank, by V. J. Makovskij.

1969, Dec. 10 Photo. *Perf. 13*
1160 A367 5pf gray & multi .25 .25
1161 A367 10pf gray & multi .25 .25
1162 A367 20pf gray & multi .25 .25
1163 A367 25pf gray & multi *.80 .80*
1164 A367 40pf gray & multi .25 .25
1165 A367 50pf gray & multi .25 .25
Nos. 1160-1165 (6) *2.05 2.05*

Ernst Barlach (1870-1938), Sculptor and Writer — A368

Portraits: 10pf, Johann Gutenberg (1400-68). 15pf, Kurt Tucholsky (1890-1935), writer. 20pf, Ludwig van Beethoven. 25pf, Friedrich Hölderlin (1770-1843), poet. 40pf, Georg Wilhelm Friedrich Hegel (1770-1831), philosopher.

1970, Jan. 20 Engr. *Perf. 14*
1166 A368 5pf blue violet .25 .25
1167 A368 10pf gray brown .25 .25
1168 A368 15pf violet blue .25 .25
1169 A368 20pf rose lilac .30 .25
1170 A368 25pf blue green *1.60 .60*
1171 A368 40pf rose claret .30 .25
Nos. 1166-1171 (6) *2.95 1.85*

Rabbit — A369

1970, Feb. 5 Photo. *Perf. 13½x14*
1172 A369 10pf shown .25 .25
1173 A369 20pf Red fox .25 .25
1174 A369 25pf Mink *2.10 2.00*
1175 A369 40pf Hamster .30 .25
Nos. 1172-1175 (4) *2.90 2.75*

525th International Fur Auctions, Leipzig.

Fairy Tale Type of 1969

Various Scenes from Fairy Tale "Little Brother and Sister."

1970, Feb. 17 Litho. *Perf. 13½x13*
1176 A345 5pf lilac & multi .25 .25
1177 A345 10pf lilac & multi .25 .25
1178 A345 15pf lilac & multi .45 .50
1179 A345 20pf lilac & multi .45 .50
1180 A345 25pf lilac & multi .25 .25
1181 A345 30pf lilac & multi .25 .25
a. Sheet of 6, #1176-1181 5.50 3.75

Telephone Coordinating Station — A370

15pf, High voltage testing transformer, vert.

1970, Feb. 24 *Perf. 13x12½, 12½x13*
1182 A370 10pf multicolored .25 .25
1183 A370 15pf multicolored .40 .25

Leipzig Spring Fair, Mar. 1-10, 1970.

Horseman's Tombstone (700 A.D.) — A371

Treasures from the Halle Museum: 20pf, Helmet (500 A.D.). 25pf, Bronze basin (1000 B.C.). 40pf, Clay drum (2500 B.C.).

1970, Mar. 3 Photo. *Perf. 13*
1184 A371 10pf dp grn, gray & dk brn .25 .25
1185 A371 20pf multicolored .25 .25
1186 A371 25pf yellow & multi *.50 .90*
1187 A371 40pf multicolored .25 .25
Nos. 1184-1187 (4) *1.25 1.65*

Lenin and Clara Zetkin — A372

Designs: 10pf, Lenin, "ISKRA" (newspaper's name), composing frame and printing press. 25pf, Lenin and title page of German edition of "State and Revolution." 40pf, Lenin statue, Eisleben. 70pf, Lenin monument and Lenin Square, Berlin. 1m, Lenin portrait, vert.

Photogravure and Engraved

1970, Apr. 16 *Perf. 14*
1188 A372 10pf multicolored .25 .25
1189 A372 20pf multicolored .25 .25
1190 A372 25pf multicolored *1.25 1.00*
1191 A372 40pf multicolored .25 .25
1192 A372 70pf multicolored .30 .25
Nos. 1188-1192 (5) *2.30 2.00*

Souvenir Sheet

1193 A372 1m dk car & multi 1.40 7.00

Sea Kale — A373

Protected Plants: 20pf, European pasqueflower. 25pf, Fringed gentian. 30pf, Galeate orchis. 40pf, Marsh tea. 70pf, Round-leaved wintergreen.

1970, Apr. 28 **Photo.**

1194 A373 10pf multicolored .25 .25
1195 A373 20pf violet & multi .25 .25
1196 A373 25pf multicolored *1.25 1.40*
1197 A373 30pf multicolored .25 .25
1198 A373 40pf multicolored .25 .25
1199 A373 70pf multicolored .30 .25
Nos. 1194-1199 (6) *2.55 2.65*

Red Army Soldier Raising Flag over Berlin Reichstag A374

20pf, Spasski Tower, Kremlin; State Council Building, Berlin; coats of arms of USSR and DDR, newspaper clipping about friendship treaty with USSR. 25pf, Mutual Economic Aid Building, Moscow, flags of member countries. 70pf, Memorial monument, Buchenwald.

1970, May 5 **Litho.** ***Perf. 13x13½***

1200 A374 10pf multi .25 .25
1201 A374 20pf multi .25 .25
1202 A374 25pf multi *.90 .60*
Nos. 1200-1202 (3) *1.40 1.10*

Souvenir Sheet

1203 A374 70pf multi, horiz. 1.25 4.50

25th anniv. of liberation from Fascism.

Shortwave Antenna, RBI Emblem and Globe — A375

15pf, Berlin Radio Station, emblems of Radio Berlin Intl. (RBI), Radio DDR & Radio Germany.

1970, May 13 **Litho.** ***Perf. 13½x13***

Size: 23x28mm

1204 A375 10pf ap grn, vio bl & bl .45 .45

Size: 50x28mm

1205 A375 15pf vio bl, dp rose & ap grn .65 .65
a. Pair, #1204-1205 3.00 1.75

DDR broadcasting system, 25th anniv.

Grain and Globe — A376

25pf, House of Culture, Dresden, and grain.

1970, May 19

1206 A376 20pf vio bl, yel & bl .60 .60
1207 A376 25pf vio bl, yel & bl .60 .60
a. Strip of 2, #1206-1207 + label 3.00 3.00

Issued to publicize the 5th World Cereal and Bread Congress, Dresden, May 24-29.

Fritz Heckert Medal A377

Design: 25pf, Globes and "FSM."

1970, June 9 ***Perf. 13x12½***

1208 A377 20pf red, yel & brn .25 .25
1209 A377 25pf red, bl & yel *.45 .40*

25th anniv. of the Free German Trade Union and of the World Organization of Trade Unions.

Traffic Policeman — A378

Designs: 10pf, Young Pioneers congratulating police woman. 15pf, Volga police car. 20pf, Railroad policeman with radio-telephone. 25pf, River police in Volga wing-type boat.

1970, June 23 **Litho.** ***Perf. 13x12½***

1210 A378 5pf ocher & multi .25 .25
1211 A378 10pf green & multi .25 .25
1212 A378 15pf ultra & multi .25 .25
1213 A378 20pf multicolored .25 .25
1214 A378 25pf multicolored *2.00 .30*
Nos. 1210-1214 (5) *3.00 1.30*

25th anniversary of the People's Police.

Gods Amon, Shu and Tefnut — A379

Designs from Lion Temple in Musawwarat: 15pf, Head of King Arnekhamani. 20pf, Cow from cattle frieze. 25pf, Head of Prince Arka. 30pf, Head of God Arensnuphis, vert. 40pf, Elephants and prisoners of war. 50pf, Lion God Apedemak.

Perf. 13½x14, 14x13½

1970, June 23 **Photo.**

1215 A379 10pf multicolored .25 .25
1216 A379 15pf multicolored .25 .25
1217 A379 20pf multicolored .25 .25
1218 A379 25pf multicolored *.60 .50*
1219 A379 30pf multicolored .25 .25
1220 A379 40pf multicolored .25 .25
1221 A379 50pf multicolored .25 .25
Nos. 1215-1221 (7) *2.10 2.00*

Archaeological work in the Sudan by the Humboldt University, Berlin.

Arms and Flags of DDR and Poland — A380

1970, July 1 **Litho.** ***Perf. 13x12½***

1222 A380 20pf multicolored .30 .25

20th anniversary of the Görlitz Agreement concerning the Oder-Neisse border.

25th Anniv. of the German Kulturbund. — A381

Design: 10pf, Culture Association Emblem. 25pf, Johannes R. Becher medal.

1970, July 1 **Photo.** ***Perf. 14***

1223 10pf ultra, sil & brn 1.40 1.40
1224 25pf ultra, gold & brn 1.40 1.40
a. A381 Strip of 2, #1223-1224 + label 7.00 8.50

Athlete on Pommel Horse — A382

1970, July 1 ***Perf. 14x13½***

1225 A382 10pf blk, yel & brn red .30 .25

Issued to publicize the 3rd Children's and Youths' Spartakiad. See No. B156.

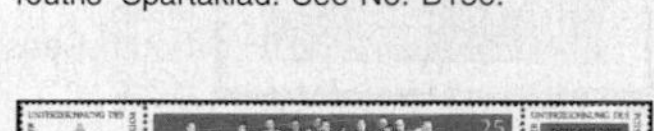

Meeting of the American, British and Russian Delegations — A383

10pf, Cecilienhof Castle. 20pf, "Potsdam Agreement" in German, English, French & Russian.

1970, July 28 **Litho.** ***Perf. 13***

Size: 23x28mm

1226 10pf blk, cit & red .25 .25
1227 20pf blk, cit & red .25 .25

Size: 77x28mm

1228 25pf red & blk .25 .25
a. A383 Strip of 3, #1226-1228 1.40 2.25

25th anniv. of the Potsdam Agreement among the Allies concerning Germany at the end of WWII.

Men's Pocket and Wrist Watches — A384

1970, Aug. 25 **Photo.** ***Perf. 13½x14***

1229 A384 10pf ultra, blk & gold .30 .25

Leipzig Fall Fair, 1970.

Theodor Neubauer and Magnus Poser — A385

"Homeland" from Soviet Cenotaph, Berlin-Treptow A386

1970, Sept. 2 ***Perf. 13x12½, 12½x13***

1230 A385 20pf dk bl, car & pale grn .25 .25
1231 A386 25pf dp car, pale bl .25 .25

Issued in memory of fighters against "fascism and imperialistic wars."

Competition Map and Compass — A387

Design: 25pf, Competition map and runner at 3 different stations.

1970, Sept. 15 **Litho.** ***Perf. 13x12½***

1232 A387 10pf yellow & multi .25 .25
1233 A387 25pf yellow & multi *.90 .30*

World Orienting Championships.

Mother and Child, by Käthe Kollwitz — A388

Works of Art: 10pf, Forest Worker Scharf's Birthday, by Otto Nagel. 20pf, Portrait of a Girl, by Otto Nagel. 25pf, No More War, (Woman with raised arm) by Käthe Kollwitz. 40pf, Head from Gustrow Memorial, by Ernst Barlach. 50pf, The Flutist, by Ernst Barlach.

Photo.; Litho. (25pf, 30pf)

1970, Sept. 22 ***Perf. 14x13½***

1234 A388 10pf multicolored .25 .25
1235 A388 20pf multicolored .25 .25
1236 A388 25pf pink & dk brn *.65 .75*
1237 A388 30pf sal & blk .25 .25
1238 A388 40pf yel & blk .25 .25
1239 A388 50pf yel & blk .25 .25
Nos. 1234-1239 (6) *1.90 2.00*

Issued in memory of the artists Otto Nagel, Käthe Kollwitz and Ernst Barlach.

The Little Trumpeter A389

1970, Oct. 1 **Photo.**

1240 A389 10pf dp ultra, brn & org .25 .30

2nd Natl. Youth Stamp Exhib., Karl Marx-Stadt, Oct. 4-11. The design shows the memorial in Halle for Fritz Weineck, trumpeter for the Red War Veterans' Organization. See No. B160.

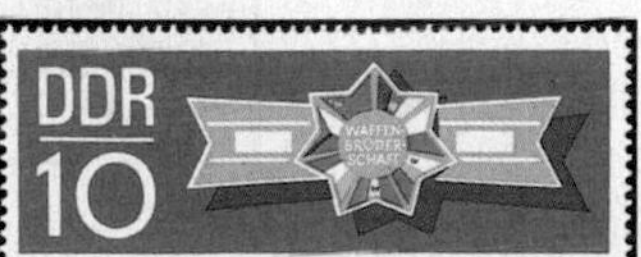

Emblem with Flags of East Block Nations — A390

1970, Oct. 1 Litho. ***Perf. 13x12½***
1241 A390 10pf carmine & multi .25 .25
1242 A390 20pf multicolored .25 .25

Issued to publicize the Brothers in Arms maneuvers of the East Bloc countries in the territory of the German Democratic Republic.

Musk Ox — A391

Berlin Zoo: 15pf, Shoebill. 20pf, Addax. 25pf, Malayan sun bear.

1970, Oct. 6 Photo. ***Perf. 14***
1243 A391 10pf blue & multi .30 .25
1244 A391 15pf green & multi .30 .25
1245 A391 20pf org & multi .45 .00
1246 A391 25pf multicolored *4.25 4.25*
Nos. 1243-1246 (4) 5.30 5.05

UN Headquarters and Emblem — A392

1970, Oct. 20 Photo. ***Perf. 13***
1247 A392 20pf ultra & multi .55 .25

25th anniversary of the United Nations.

Friedrich Engels — A393

20pf, Friedrich Engels and Karl Marx. 25pf, Engels and title page of his polemic against Dühring.

Photogravure and Engraved

1970, Nov. 24 ***Perf. 14***
1248 A393 10pf ver, gray & blk .25 .25
1249 A393 20pf ver, dk grn & blk .25 .25
1250 A393 25pf ver, dk car rose & blk *.80 .65*
Nos. 1248-1250 (3) 1.30 1.15

Friedrich Engels (1820-1895), socialist, collaborator with Karl Marx.

Epiphyllum — A394

Flowering Cactus Plants: 10pf, Astrophytum myriostigma. 15pf, Echinocereus salm-dyckianus. 20pf, Selenicereus grandiflorus. 25pf, Hamatocactus setispinus. 30pf, Mamillaria boolii.

1970, Dec. 2 Photo. ***Perf. 14***
1251 A394 5pf multicolored .25 .25
1252 A394 10pf dk blue & multi .25 .25
1253 A394 15pf multicolored .25 .25
1254 A394 20pf multicolored .25 .25
1255 A394 25pf dk blue & multi *1.25 1.20*
1256 A394 30pf purple & multi .25 .25
Nos. 1251-1256 (6) 2.50 2.45

Souvenir Sheet

Ludwig van Beethoven — A395

1970, Dec. 10 Engr. ***Perf. 14***
1257 A395 1m gray 1.40 2.75

Bicentenary of the birth of Ludwig van Beethoven (1770-1827), composer.

Dancer's Mask, South Seas A396

Works from Ethnological Museum, Leipzig: 20pf, Bronze head, Africa. 25pf, Tea pot, Asia. 40pf, Clay figure (jaguar), Mexico.

1971, Jan. 12 Photo. ***Perf. 13***
1258 A396 10pf multicolored .25 .25
1259 A396 20pf multicolored .25 .25
1260 A396 25pf multicolored *.50 .40*
1261 A396 40pf multicolored .25 .25
Nos. 1258-1261 (4) 1.25 1.15

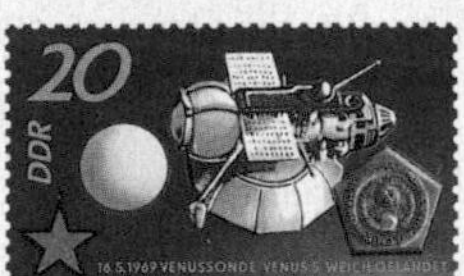

Venus 5, Soft-landing on Moon — A397

No. 1263, Model of space station. No. 1264, Luna 16 and Luna 10 satellites. No. 1265, Group flight of Sojuz 6, 7 and 8. No. 1266, Proton 1, radiation measuring satellite. No. 1267, Communications satellite Molniya 1. No. 1268, Yuri A. Gagarin, first flight of Vostok 1. No. 1269, Alexei Leonov walking in space, Voskhod 2.

1971, Feb. 11 Litho. ***Perf. 13x12½***
1262 A397 20pf dk blue & multi .25 .25
1263 A397 20pf dk blue & multi .25 .25
1264 A397 20pf dk blue & multi .40 .40
1265 A397 20pf dk blue & multi .40 .40
1266 A397 20pf dk blue & multi .40 .40
1267 A397 20pf dk blue & multi .40 .40
1268 A397 20pf dk blue & multi .25 .25
1269 A397 20pf dk blue & multi .25 .25
a. Sheet of 8, #1262-1269 4.25 4.25

Soviet space research.

Johannes R. Becher — A398

Portraits: 10pf, Heinrich Mann. 15pf, John Heartfield. 20pf, Willi Bredel. 25pf, Franz Mehring. 40pf, Rudolf Virchow. 50pf, Johannes Kepler.

1971 Engr. ***Perf. 14***
1270 A398 5pf brown .25 .25
1271 A398 10pf vio blue .25 .25
1272 A398 15pf black .25 .25
1273 A398 20pf rose lake .25 .25
1274 A398 25pf green *.40 .35*
1274A A398 40pf pale purple .40 .25
1275 A398 50pf dp black .25 .25
Nos. 1270-1275 (7) 2.05 1.85

Honoring prominent Germans. See Nos. 1349-1353.

Karl Liebknecht — A399

Design: 25pf, Rosa Luxemburg.

1971, Feb. 23 Photo.
1276 A399 20pf gold, mag & blk .35 .35
1277 A399 25pf gold, mag & blk .35 .35
a. Pair, #1276-1277 .85 1.10

Karl Liebknecht (1871-1919) and Rosa Luxemburg (1871-1919), leaders of Spartacist Movement.

Soldier and Army Emblem — A400

1971, Mar. 1 ***Perf. 13½x14***
1278 A400 20pf gray & multi .30 .25

15th anniv. of the National People's Army.

Crushing and Conveyor Plant, Magdeburg — A401

Leipzig Spring Fair: 15pf, Dredger for low temperature work.

1971, Mar. 9 Litho. ***Perf. 13x12½***
1279 A401 10pf green & multi .25 .25
1280 A401 15pf multicolored .25 .25

Proclamation of the Commune, Town Hall, Paris — A402

Designs: 20pf, Barricade at Place Blanche, defended by women. 25pf, Illustration by Theophile A. Steinlen for the International. 30pf, Title page for "The Civil War in France," by Karl Marx.

1971, Mar. 9 ***Perf. 13***
1281 A402 10pf red, bis & blk .25 .25
1282 A402 20pf red, bis & blk .25 .25
1283 A402 25pf red, buff & blk *.40 .35*
1284 A402 30pf red, gray & blk .25 .25
Nos. 1281-1284 (4) 1.15 1.10

Centenary of the Paris Commune.

Lunokhod 1 on Moon — A403

1971, Mar. 30 Photo. ***Perf. 14***
1285 A403 20pf multicolored .45 .30

Luna 17 unmanned, automated moon mission, Nov. 10-17, and the 24th Communist Party Congress of the Soviet Union.

Discobolus — A404

1971, Apr. 6 Litho. ***Perf. 13½x13***
1286 A404 20pf dull bl, lt bl & buff .55 .25

20th anniversary of the Olympic Committee of German Democratic Republic.

Köpenick Castle — A405

Berlin Buildings: 10pf, St. Mary's Church, vert. 20pf, Old Library. 25pf, Ermeler House, vert. 50pf, New Guard Memorial. 70pf, Natl. Gallery of Art.

Perf. 13½x14, 14x13½

1971, Apr. 6 Photo.
1287 A405 10pf multicolored .25 .25
1288 A405 15pf multicolored .25 .25
1289 A405 20pf multicolored .25 .25
1290 A405 25pf multicolored *2.10 1.75*
1291 A405 50pf multicolored .25 .25
1292 A405 70pf multicolored .30 .25
Nos. 1287-1292 (6) 3.40 3.00

Clasped Hands — A406

Lithographed and Embossed

1971, Apr. 20 ***Perf. 13x13½***
1293 A406 20pf red, blk & gold .30 .25

25th anniversary of Socialist Unity Party of Germany (SED).

Dance Costume, Schleife — A407

Sorbian Dance Costumes from: 20pf, Hoyerswerda. 25pf, Cottbus. 40pf, Kamenz.

1971, May 4 Litho. ***Perf. 13½x13***
Size: 33x42mm
1294 A407 10pf multicolored .25 .25
1295 A407 20pf green & multi .25 .25
1296 A407 25pf blue & multi *.45 .65*
1297 A407 40pf multicolored .25 .25
Nos. 1294-1297 (4) 1.20 1.40

1971, Nov. 23 ***Perf. 13½x13***

Booklet Stamps

Size: 23x28mm

No.	Type	Description		
1297A	A407	10pf multicolored	.25	.25
c.		Booklet pane of 4	1.40	1.10
d.		Booklet pane, 2 #1297A, 2 #1297B	3.25	2.50
1297B	A407	20pf multicolored	.55	.40

Self-Portrait, by Dürer — A408

Art Works by Dürer: 40pf, Three Peasants. 70pf, Portrait of Philipp Melanchthon.

1971, May 18 ***Perf. 12½x13***

No.	Type	Description		
1298	A408	10pf multicolored	.25	.25
1299	A408	40pf brown & multi	.25	.25
1300	A408	70pf gray & multi	*1.25*	*.65*
		Nos. 1298-1300 (3)	*1.75*	*1.15*

500th anniversary of the birth of Albrecht Dürer (1471-1528), painter and engraver.

Building Industry — A409

Congress Emblem — A410

Designs: 10pf, Science and technology. No. 1303, Farming. 25pf, Civilian defense.

1971, June 9 **Photo.** ***Perf. 14***

No.	Type	Description		
1301	A409	5pf cream, red & blk	.25	.25
1302	A409	10pf cream, red & blk	.25	.25
1303	A409	20pf cream, red, bl & blk	.25	.25
1304	A410	20pf gold, dp car & red	.25	.25
1305	A409	25pf cream, red & blk	*.30*	*.35*
		Nos. 1301-1305 (5)	*1.30*	*1.35*

8th Congress of Socialist Unity Party of Germany (SED).

Golden Fleece, 1730 A411

Treasures from the Green Vault, Dresden: 5pf, Cherry stone with 180 heads carved on it, 1590. 15pf, Tankard, Nuremberg, 1530. 20pf, Moor with drums on horseback, 1720. 25pf, Decorated writing box, 1562. 30pf, St. George pendant, 1570.

1971, June 22 ***Perf. 13***

No.	Type	Description		
1306	A411	5pf dp car & multi	.25	.25
1307	A411	10pf green & multi	.25	.25
1308	A411	15pf violet & multi	.25	.25
1309	A411	20pf multicolored	.25	.25
1310	A411	25pf multicolored	*.45*	*.45*
1311	A411	30pf multicolored	.25	.25
		Nos. 1306-1311 (6)	*1.70*	*1.70*

Prisoners, by Fritz Cremer A412

Design: 25pf, Brutality in Buchenwald Concentration Camp, by Fritz Cremer.

1971, June 22 **Litho.** ***Perf. 13***

No.	Type	Description		
1312	A412	20pf bister & blk	.40	.45
1313	A412	25pf lt blue & blk	.40	.45
a.		Pair, #1312-1313 with label between	1.20	1.60

Intl. Federation of Resistance Fighters (FIR), 20th anniv.

Coat of Arms of Mongolia — A413

1971, July 6 **Litho.** ***Perf. 13***

No.	Type	Description		
1314	A413	20pf dk red, yel & blk	.30	.25

50th anniv. of the Mongolian People's Revolution.

Child's Head, UNICEF Emblem A414

1971, July 13 **Photo.**

No.	Type	Description		
1315	A414	20pf multicolored	.35	.25

25th anniv. of UNICEF.

Militiaman, Soldier and Brandenburg Gate — A415

Design: 35pf, Brandenburg Gate and new buildings in East Berlin.

1971, Aug. 12

No.	Type	Description		
1316	A415	20pf red & multi	.50	.25
1317	A415	35pf yel & multi	1.25	.90

10 years of Berlin Wall.

Passenger Ship Iwan Franko — A416

Ships: 15pf, Freighter, type 17. 20pf, Freighter Rostock, type XD. 25pf, Fish processing ship "Junge Welt." 40pf, Container cargo ship. 50pf, Explorer ship Akademik Kurtschatow.

1971, Aug. 24 **Engr.**

No.	Type	Description		
1318	A416	10pf pale purple	.25	.25
1319	A416	15pf pale brn & ind	.25	.25
1320	A416	20pf gray green	.25	.25
1321	A416	25pf slate	*.85*	*.80*
1322	A416	40pf maroon	.25	.25
1323	A416	50pf grysh blue	.25	.25
		Nos. 1318-1323 (6)	*2.10*	*2.05*

Shipbuilding industry.

Butadiene Plant — A417

Leipzig Fall Fair: 25pf, Refinery.

1971, Sept. 2 **Photo.** ***Perf. 13***

No.	Type	Description		
1324	A417	10pf olive, vio & mag	.25	.25
1325	A417	25pf blue, vio & ol	.25	.25

Raised Fists, Photo Montage by John Heartfield, 1937 A418

1971, Sept. 23

No.	Type	Description		
1326	A418	35pf grnsh bl, blk & sil	.30	.25

Intl. Year Against Racial Discrimination.

Karl Marx Monument A419

1971, Oct. 5 **Photo.** ***Perf. 14x13½***

No.	Type	Description		
1327	A419	35pf vio brn, pink & buff	.35	.25

Unveiling of Karl Marx memorial at Karl-Marx-Stadt (Chemnitz).

Wiltz Memorial, Flag of Luxembourg A420

1971, Oct. 5

No.	Type	Description		
1328	A420	25pf multicolored	.25	.25

Memorial for Nazi victims, Wiltz, Luxembourg.

Postal Milestones, Saxony, and Zürner's Surveyor Carriage — A421

Photo. & Engr.

1971, Oct. 5 ***Perf. 14***

No.	Type	Description		
1329	A421	25pf blue, olive & lilac	.35	.35

Philatelists' Day 1971. See No. B162.

Darbuka, North Africa — A422

Musical Instruments: 15pf, Two morin chuur, Mongolia. 20pf, Violin, Germany. 25pf, Mandolin, Italy. 40pf, Bagpipes, Bohemia. 50pf, Kasso, Sudan.

1971, Oct. 26 **Photo.** ***Perf. 14x13½***

No.	Type	Description		
1330	A422	10pf multicolored	.25	.25
1331	A422	15pf multicolored	.25	.25
1332	A422	20pf ocher & multi	.25	.25
1333	A422	25pf blue & multi	.25	.25
1334	A422	40pf gray & multi	.25	.25
1335	A422	50pf multicolored	*.75*	*.65*
		Nos. 1330-1335 (6)	*2.00*	*1.90*

Instruments from the Music Museum in Markneukirchen.

Geodetic Apparatus — A423

20pf, Ergaval microscope. 25pf, Planetarium.

1971, Nov. 9 **Photo.** ***Perf. 13½x14***

Size: 23½x28½mm

No.	Type	Description		
1336	A423	10pf blue, blk & red	.35	.35
1337	A423	20pf blue, blk & red	.35	.35

Size: 50½x28½mm

No.	Type	Description		
1338	A423	25pf blue, vio bl & yel	.35	.35
a.		Strip of 3, #1336-1338	3.25	3.25

Carl Zeiss optical works in Jena, 125th anniv.

Fairy Tale Type of 1966

Designs: Various Scenes from Fairy Tale "The Bremen Town Musicians."

1971, Nov. 23 **Litho.** ***Perf. 13½x13***

No.	Type	Description		
1339	A290	5pf multicolored	.25	.25
1340	A290	10pf ocher & multi	.25	.25
1341	A290	15pf gray & multi	.45	.65
1342	A290	20pf ver & multi	.45	.65
1343	A290	25pf violet & multi	.25	.25
1344	A290	30pf yellow & multi	.25	.25
a.		Sheet of 6, #1339-1344	3.00	8.00

Olympic Rings and Sledding — A424

Olympic Rings and: 20pf, Long-distance skiing. 25pf, Biathlon. 70pf, Ski jump.

1971, Dec. 7 **Photo.** ***Perf. 13½x14***

No.	Type	Description		
1345	A424	5pf green, car & blk	.25	.25
1346	A424	20pf car rose, vio & blk	.25	.25
1347	A424	25pf vio, car & blk	*1.10*	*.90*
1348	A424	70pf vio bl, vio & blk	.25	.25
		Nos. 1345-1348,B163-B164 (6)	*2.35*	*2.15*

11th Winter Olympic Games, Sapporo, Japan, Feb. 3-13, 1972.

Portrait Type of 1971

Portraits: 10pf, Johannes Tralow (1882-1968), playwright. 20pf, Leonhard Frank (1882-1961), writer. 25pf, K. A. Kocor (1822-1904), composer. 35pf, Heinrich Schliemann (1822-1890), archaeologist. 50pf, F. Caroline Neuber (1697-1760), actress.

1972, Jan. 25 Engr. *Perf. 14*

1349 A398 10pf green .25 .25
1350 A398 20pf rose claret .25 .25
1351 A398 25pf dk blue .25 .25
1352 A398 35pf brown .25 .25
1353 A398 50pf rose violet *.65 1.00*
Nos. 1349-1353 (5) 1.65 2.00

Honoring famous personalities.

Gypsum, Eisleben A425

Minerals found in East Germany: 10pf, Zinnwaldite, Zinnwald. 20pf, Malachite, Ullersreuth. 25pf, Amethyst, Wiesenbad. 35pf, Halite, Merkers. 50pf, Proustite, Schneeberg.

1972, Feb. 22 Photo. *Perf. 13*

1354 A425 5pf grnsh bl & brn blk .25 .25
1355 A425 10pf citron, brn & blk .25 .25
1356 A425 20pf multicolored .25 .25
1357 A425 25pf multicolored .25 .25
1358 A425 35pf lt green, ind & blk .25 .25
1359 A425 50pf gray & multi *.80 .85*
Nos. 1354-1359 (6) 2.05 2.10

Russian Pavilion and Fair Emblem A426

Design: 25pf, Flags of East Germany and Russia, and Fair emblem.

1972, Mar. 3 Photo. *Perf. 14*

1360 A426 10pf vio blue & multi .25 .25
1361 A426 25pf claret & multi .25 .25

50 years of Russian participation in the Leipzig Fair.

Miniature Sheets

Anemometer, 1896, and Meteorological Chart, 1876 — A427

Designs: 35pf, Dipole and cloud photograph taken by satellite. 70pf, Meteor weather satellite and weather map.

1972, Mar. 23 Litho. *Perf. 13x12½*

1362 A427 20pf multicolored .60 1.00
1363 A427 35pf multicolored .60 1.00
1364 A427 70pf green & multi .60 1.00
Nos. 1362-1364 (3) 1.80 3.00

Intl. Meteorologists' Cent. Meeting, Leipzig.

World Health Organization Emblem — A428

1972, Apr. 4 Photo. *Perf. 13*

1365 A428 35pf lt bl, vio bl & sil .30 .25

World Health Day.

Kamov Helicopter A429

Aircraft: 10pf, Agricultural spray plane. 35pf, Ilyushin jet. 1m, Jet and tail with Interflug emblem.

1972, Apr. 25 *Perf. 14*

1366 A429 5pf blue & multi .25 .25
1367 A429 10pf multicolored .25 .25
1368 A429 35pf blue grn & multi .25 .25
1369 A429 1m multicolored *1.10 1.25*
Nos. 1366-1369 (4) 1.85 2.00

Wrestling and Olympic Rings — A430

Sport and Olympic Rings: 20pf, Pole vault. 35pf, Volleyball. 70pf, Women's gymnastics.

1972, May 16 Photo. *Perf. 13½x14*

1370 A430 5pf blue, gold & blk .25 .25
1371 A430 20pf mag, gold & blk .25 .25
1372 A430 35pf ol bis, gold & blk .25 .25
1373 A430 70pf yel grn, gold & blk *2.25 1.40*
Nos. 1370-1373,B166-B167 (6) 3.50 2.65

20th Olympic Games, Munich, 8/26-9/11.

Flags of USSR and German Democratic Republic — A431

20pf, Flags, Leonid Brezhnev & Erich Honecker.

1972, May 24 Engr. & Photo.

1374 A431 10pf red, yel & blk .85 .65
1375 A431 20pf red, yel & blk .85 .65

Soc. for German-Soviet Friendship, 25th anniv.

Workers — A432

Design: 35pf, Students.

1972, May 24 Litho. *Perf. 13*

1376 A432 10pf dull yel, org & mag .25 .25
1377 A432 35pf dull yel & ultra .25 .25
a. Strip of 2, #1376-1377 + label 1.00 .85

8th Congress of Free German Trade Unions, Berlin.

Karneol Rose A433

10pf, Berger's Erfurt Rose. 15pf, Charme. 20pf, Izetka Spree-Athens. 25pf, Kopenick summer. 35pf, Prof. Knoll.

1972, June 13 Photo. *Perf. 13*
Size: 36x36mm

1378 A433 5pf shown .25 .25
1379 A433 10pf multicolored .25 .25
1380 A433 15pf multicolored *1.10 1.10*
1381 A433 20pf multicolored .25 .25
1382 A433 25pf multicolored .25 .25
1383 A433 35pf multicolored .25 .25
Nos. 1378-1383 (6) 2.35 2.35

International Rose Exhibition.

Redrawn

1972, Aug. 22 *Perf. 13½x13*
Booklet Stamps
Size: 23x28mm

1383A A433 10pf multicolored .25 .25
d. Booklet pane of 4 1.25 .80
1383B A433 25pf multicolored .90 .35
e. Booklet pane of 4 (2 #1383B, 2 #1383C) 5.25 3.75
1383C A433 35pf multicolored .90 .35
Nos. 1383A-1383C (3) 2.05 .95

Young Mother and Child, by Cranach A434

Paintings by Lucas Cranach: 5pf, Young man. 35pf, Margarete Luther (Martin's mother). 70pf, Reclining nymph, horiz.

1972, July 4 *Perf. 14x13½, 13½x14*

1384 A434 5pf gold & multi .25 .25
1385 A434 20pf gold & multi .25 .25
1386 A434 35pf gold & multi .25 .25
1387 A434 70pf gold & multi *1.60 2.40*
Nos. 1384-1387 (4) 2.35 3.15

Lucas Cranach (1472-1553), painter.

Compass and Motorcyclist — A435

Designs: 10pf, Parachute and light plane. 20pf, Target and military obstacle race. 25pf, Amateur radio transmitter, Morse key and tape. 35pf, Propeller and sailing ship.

1972, Aug. 8 Photo. *Perf. 14*

1388 A435 5pf multicolored .25 .25
1389 A435 10pf multicolored .25 .25
1390 A435 20pf multicolored .25 .25
1391 A435 25pf multicolored *.45 .45*
1392 A435 35pf multicolored .25 .25
Nos. 1388-1392 (5) 1.45 1.45

Society for Sport and Technology.

Young Worker Reading, by Jutta Damme — A436

1972, Aug. 22 Photo. *Perf. 13½x14*

1393 A436 50pf multicolored .45 .30

International Book Year 1972.

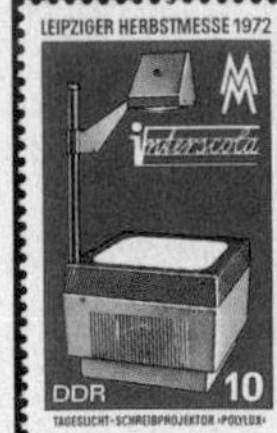

Polylux Writing Projector — A437

25pf, Pentacon-audiovision projector, horiz.

Perf. 12½x13, 13x12½

1972, Aug. 29 Litho.

1394 A437 10pf crimson & blk .25 .25
1395 A437 25pf brt green & blk .25 .25

Leipzig Fall Fair, 1972.

George Dimitrov — A438

1972, Sept. 19 *Perf. 13x13½*

1396 A438 20pf rose red & blk .35 .25

George Dimitrov (1882-1949), Bulgarian Communist party leader.

Bird Catchers, Egypt, c. 2400 B.C. — A439

Design: 20pf, Tapestry with animal design, Anatolia, c. 1400 A.D.

1972, Sept. 19 Photo. *Perf. 14*

1397 A439 10pf multicolored .25 .25
1398 A439 20pf multicolored .25 .25
Nos. 1397-1398,B168-B169 (4) 1.40 1.30

Interartes Philatelic Exhib., Berlin, Oct. 4-Nov. 11.

Red Cross Trainees and Red Cross — A440

Designs: 15pf, Red Cross rescue launch in the Baltic. 35pf, Red Cross with world map, ship, plane and vehicles.

1972, Oct. 3 Litho. *Perf. 13*
Size: 23x28mm

1399 A440 10pf grnsh bl, dk bl & red .30 .25
1400 A440 15pf grnsh bl, dk bl & red .30 .25

Size: 50x28mm

1401 A440 35pf grnsh bl, dk bl & red .30 .25
a. Strip of 3, #1399-1401 1.50 1.75

Red Cross at work in the DDR.

Arab Celestial Globe, 1279 — A441

10pf, Globe, by Joachim R. Praetorius, 1568. 15pf, Globe clock, by Reinhold & Roll, 1586. 20pf, Globe clock, by J. Bürgi, c. 1590. 25pf, Armillary sphere, by J. Moeller, 1687. 35pf, Heraldic celestial globe, 1690.

1972, Oct. 17 Photo. *Perf. 14x13½*

1402	A441	5pf	gray & multi	.25	.25
1403	A441	10pf	gray & multi	.25	.25
1404	A441	15pf	gray & multi	1.60	2.25
1405	A441	20pf	gray & multi	.25	.25
1406	A441	25pf	gray & multi	.25	.25
1407	A441	35pf	gray & multi	.25	.25
			Nos. 1402-1407 (6)	2.85	3.50

Celestial and terrestrial globes from the National Mathematical and Physics Collection, Dresden.

Anti-Fascists Monument — A442

1972, Oct. 24 Litho. *Perf. 12½x13*

1408	A442	25pf	multicolored	.35	.25

Monument for Polish soldiers and German anti-Fascists, unveiled in Berlin, May 14, 1972.

Young Workers Receiving Technical Education — A443

25pf, Workers with modern welding machine.

1972, Nov. 2 Photo. *Perf. 13½x14*

1409	A443	10pf	blue & multi	.25	.25
1410	A443	25pf	blue & multi	.25	.25
a.			Strip of 2, #1409-1410 + label	.80	1.25

15th Central Fair of Masters of Tomorrow.

Mauz and Hoppel A444

Children's television characters: 10pf, Fox and magpie. 15pf, Mr. Owl. 20pf, Mrs. Hedgehog and Borstel. 25pf, Schnuffel and Peips. 35pf, Paul from the Library.

1972, Nov. 28 Litho. *Perf. 13½x13*

1411	A444	5pf	shown	.25	.25
1412	A444	10pf	multicolored	.25	.25
1413	A444	15pf	multicolored	.60	.65
1414	A444	20pf	multicolored	.60	.65
1415	A444	25pf	multicolored	.25	.25
1416	A444	35pf	multicolored	.25	.25
a.			Sheet of 6, #1411-1416	2.40	2.60

Grandmother, Children, Magic Mirror — A445

Scenes from Hans Christian Andersen's "Snow Queen": 10pf, Kay and Snow Queen. 15pf, Gerda in magic garden. 20pf, Gerda and crows at palace. 25pf, Gerda and reindeer in Lapland. 35pf, Gerda and Kay at Snow Queen's palace.

1972, Nov. 28 *Perf. 13x13½*

1417	A445	5pf	multicolored	.25	.25
1418	A445	10pf	multicolored	.45	.65
1419	A445	15pf	multicolored	.25	.25
1420	A445	20pf	multicolored	.25	.25
1421	A445	25pf	multicolored	.45	.65
1422	A445	35pf	multicolored	.25	.25
a.			Sheet of 6, #1417-1422	4.00	8.50

See designs A469, A490.

Souvenir Sheet

Heinrich Heine — A446

1972, Dec. 5 *Perf. 12½x13*

1423	A446	1m	brn ol, blk & red	1.25	2.00

150th anniversary of the birth of Heinrich Heine (1797-1856), poet.

Coat of Arms of USSR — A447

1972, Dec. 5 Photo. *Perf. 13½x14*

1424	A447	20pf	red & multi	.35	.25

50th anniversary of the Soviet Union.

Michelangelo da Caravaggio — A448

1973 Litho. *Perf. 13½x13*

1425	A448	5pf	brown	.50	.50
1426	A448	10pf	dull green	.25	.25
1427	A448	20pf	rose lilac	.25	.25
1428	A448	25pf	blue	.25	.25
1429	A448	35pf	brown red	.25	.25
1429A	A448	40pf	rose claret	.25	.25
			Nos. 1425-1429A (6)	1.75	1.75

Michelangelo da Caravaggio (1565(?)-1609), Italian painter (5pf). Friedrich Wolf (1888-1953), writer (10pf). Max Reger (1873-1916), composer (20pf). Max Reinhardt (1873-1943), Austrian theatrical director (25pf). Johannes Dieckmann (1893-1969), member and president of People's Chamber (35pf). Hermann Matern (1893-1971), vice-president of DDR (40pf).

Lenin Square, Berlin — A449

Coat of Arms of DDR — A449a

Designs: 5pf, Pelican, Berlin Zoo. 10pf, Neptune Fountain, City Hall Street. 15pf, Fisherman's Island, Berlin. 25pf, World clock, Alexander Square, Berlin. 30pf, Workers' Memorial, Halle. 35pf, Marx monument, Karl-Marx-Stadt. 40pf, Brandenburg Gate, Berlin. 50pf, New Guardhouse, Berlin. 60pf, Zwinger, Dresden. 70pf, Old Town Hall, Office Building, Leipzig. 80pf, Old and new buildings, Rostock-Warnemunde. 1m, Soviet War Memorial, Treptow.

1973-74 Engr. *Perf. 14x13¾*
Size: 29x23½mm

1430	A449	5pf	blue green	.25	.25
1431	A449	10pf	emerald	.30	.25
1432	A449	15pf	rose lilac	.35	.25
1433	A449	20pf	rose mag	.65	.25
1434	A449	25pf	grnsh blue	.65	.25
1435	A449	30pf	orange	.35	.25
1436	A449	35pf	grnsh blue	.65	.30
1437	A449	40pf	dull violet	.35	.25
1438	A449	50pf	blue, *bluish*	.40	.25
1439	A449	60pf	lilac ('74)	.55	.30
1440	A449	70pf	redsh brn	.45	.35
1441	A449	80pf	vio blue ('74)	.65	.30
1442	A449	1m	olive	.75	.25
1443	A449a	2m	lake	1.00	.25
1443A	A449a	3m	rose lil ('74)	3.25	.80
			Nos. 1430-1443A (15)	10.60	4.55

See Nos. 1610-1617, 2071-2085.

Lebachia Speciosa (Oldest Conifer) A450

Fossils from Natural History Museum, Berlin: 15pf, Sphenopteris hollandica (carbon fern). 20pf, Pterodactylus kochi (flying reptile). 25pf, Botryopteris (permian fern). 35pf, Archaeopteryx lithographica (primitive reptile-like bird). 70pf, Odontopieura ovata (trilobite).

1973, Feb. 6 Photo. *Perf. 13*

1444	A450	10pf	multicolored	.25	.25
1445	A450	15pf	ultra, gray & blk	.25	.25
1446	A450	20pf	yellow & multi	.25	.25
1447	A450	25pf	emer, blk & brn	.25	.25
1448	A450	35pf	ocher & multi	.25	.25
1449	A450	70pf	ind, blk & yel	1.20	1.20
			Nos. 1444-1449 (6)	2.45	2.45

Bobsled Track, Oberhof — A451

1973, Feb. 13 Litho. *Perf. 12½x13*

1450	A451	35pf	dk bl, bl & org	.35	.30

15th Bobsledding Championships, Oberhof.

Combines A452

Leipzig Spring Fair: 25pf, Computerized threshing and silage producing machine.

1973, Mar. 6 Litho. *Perf. 13x12½*

1451	A452	10pf	olive & multi	.25	.25
1452	A452	25pf	blue & multi	.30	.30

Firecrests A453

Songbirds: 10pf, White-winged crossbill. 15pf, Waxwing. 20pf, White-spotted and red-spotted bluethroats. 25pf, Goldfinch. 35pf, Golden oriole. 40pf, Gray wagtail. 50pf, Wall creeper.

1973, Mar. 20 Photo. *Perf. 14x13½*

1453	A453	5pf	multicolored	.25	.25
1454	A453	10pf	multicolored	.25	.25
1455	A453	15pf	multicolored	.25	.25
1456	A453	20pf	multicolored	.25	.25
1457	A453	25pf	multicolored	.25	.25
1458	A453	35pf	multicolored	.25	.25
1459	A453	40pf	multicolored	.25	.25
1460	A453	50pf	ocher & multi	2.00	2.00
			Nos. 1453-1460 (8)	3.75	3.75

Copernicus and Title Page — A454

1973, Feb. 13 Litho. *Perf. 13½x13*

1461	A454	70pf	multicolored	.65	.35

500th anniversary of the birth of Nicolaus Copernicus (1473-1543), astronomer.

Electric Locomotive — A455

Railroad Cars Manufactured in DDR: 10pf, Refrigerator car. 20pf, Long-distance coach. 25pf, Multiple tank car with pneumatic filling device. 35pf, Two-story coach. 85pf, International coaches.

1973, May 22 Litho. *Perf. 13x12½*

1462	A455	5pf	gray & multi	.25	.25
1463	A455	10pf	brt blue & multi	.25	.25
1464	A455	20pf	dk blue & multi	.25	.25
1465	A455	25pf	gray & multi	.25	.25
1466	A455	35pf	multicolored	.25	.25
1467	A455	85pf	green & multi	1.60	1.60
			Nos. 1462-1467 (6)	2.85	2.85

King Lear, Staged by Wolfgang Langhoff A456

Great Theatrical Productions: 25pf, Midsummer Marriage, staged by Walter Felsenstein. 35pf, Mother Courage, staged by Bertolt Brecht.

1973, May 29 Photo. *Perf. 13*

1468 A456 10pf mar, rose & yel .25 .25
1469 A456 25pf vio bl, lt bl & rose .25 .25
1470 A456 35pf dk gray, bis & bl *.60 .55*
Nos. 1468-1470 (3) *1.10 1.05*

Goethe and his Home in Weimar — A457

Designs (Portraits and Houses): 15pf, Christoph Martin Wieland. 20pf, Friedrich von Schiller. 25pf, Johann Gottfried Herder. 35pf, Lucas Cranach, the Elder. 50pf, Franz Liszt.

1973, June 26 Litho. *Perf. 12½x13*

1471 A457 10pf blue & multi .25 .25
1472 A457 15pf multicolored .25 .25
1473 A457 20pf multicolored .25 .25
1474 A457 25pf multicolored .25 .25
1475 A457 35pf green & multi .25 .25
1476 A457 50pf multicolored *1.60 .80*
Nos. 1471-1476 (6) *2.85 2.05*

Famous men and their homes in Weimar.

Fireworks, TV Tower, World Clock — A458

Designs (Festival Emblem and): 15pf, Vietnamese and European men, book and girder. 20pf, Construction workers and valve. 30pf, Negro and European students, dam and retort. 35pf, Emblems of World Federation of Democratic Youth and International Students Union. 50pf, Brandenburg Gate.

1973

1477 A458 5pf vio blue & multi .25 .25
a. Booklet pane of 4 1.60 1.25
1478 A458 15pf olive & multi .25 .25
1479 A458 20pf multicolored .25 .25
a. Booklet pane of 4 1.60 1.25
1480 A458 30pf blue & multi *.70 .35*
1481 A458 35pf green & multi .25 .25
Nos. 1477-1481 (5) *1.70 1.35*

Souvenir Sheet

1482 A458 50pf aqua & multi 1.00 1.60

10th Festival of Youths and Students, Berlin, July 1973.

Issued: Nos. 1477-1481, 7/3; No. 1482, 7/26.

Ulbricht Type of 1961-67

1973, Aug. 8 Engr. *Perf. 14*
Size: 24x28½mm

1483 A189 20pf black .45 .30

In memory of Walter Ulbricht (1893-1973), chairman of Council of State.

Pylon, Map of Electric Power System — A459

1973, Aug. 14 Photo. *Perf. 14*

1484 A459 35pf mag, org & lt bl .35 .30

10th anniversary of the united East European electric power system "Peace."

Sports Equipment — A460

Design: 25pf, Sailboat, guitar, electric drill.

1973, Aug. 28 Photo. *Perf. 14*

1485 A460 10pf multicolored .25 .25
1486 A460 25pf multicolored .30 .25

Leipzig Fall Fair and EXPOVITA exhibition for leisure time equipment.

Militiaman and Emblem A461

Designs: 20pf, Militia guarding border at Brandenburg Gate. 50pf, Representatives of Red Veterans' League, International Brigade in Spain and Workers' Militia in DDR, vert.

1973, Sept. 11 Litho. *Perf. 13x12½*

1487 A461 10pf multicolored .25 .25
1488 A461 20pf tan, red & blk .30 .25

Souvenir Sheet
Perf. 12½x13

1489 A461 50pf multicolored .45 1.60

20th anniversary of Workers' Militia of the German Democratic Republic.

Globe and Red Flag Emblem A462

1973, Sept. 11 Photo. *Perf. 13½x14*

1490 A462 20pf gold & red .40 .25

15th anniversary of the review "Problems of Peace and Socialism," published in Prague in 28 languages.

Memorial, Langenstein-Zwieberge — A463

1973, Sept. 18 *Perf. 14x13½*

1491 A463 25pf multicolored .40 .25

In memory of the workers who perished in the subterranean munitions works at Langenstein-Zwieberge.

UN Headquarters, NY, UN and DDR Emblems — A464

1973, Sept. 21 *Perf. 13*

1492 A464 35pf multicolored .40 .25

Admission of the DDR to the UN.

Union Emblem A465

1973, Oct. 11 Photo. *Perf. 14x13½*

1493 A465 35pf silver & multi .35 .30

8th Congress of the World Federation of Trade Unions, Varna, Bulgaria.

Rocket Launching — A466

20pf, Emblem with map of Russia & hammer & sickle, horiz. 25pf, Oil refinery, Ryazan.

1973, Oct. 23 *Perf. 14*

1494 A466 10pf violet bl & multi .25 .25
1495 A466 20pf vio bl, red & sil .25 .25
1496 A466 25pf multicolored *.65 .55*
Nos. 1494-1496 (3) *1.15 1.05*

Soviet Science & Technology Days in DDR.

Madonna with the Rose, by Parmigianino A467

Paintings: 10pf Child with Doll, by Christian L. Vogel. 20pf, Woman with Plaited Blond Hair, by Rubens. 25pf, Lady in White, by Titian. 35pf, Archimedes, by Domenico Fetti. 70pf, Bouquet with Blue Iris, by Jan D. de Heem.

1973, Nov. 13 Photo. *Perf. 14*

1497 A467 10pf gold & multi .25 .25
1498 A467 15pf gold & multi .25 .25
1499 A467 20pf gold & multi .25 .25
1500 A467 25pf gold & multi .25 .25
1501 A467 35pf gold & multi .25 .25
1502 A467 70pf gold & multi *1.90 1.25*
Nos. 1497-1502 (6) *3.15 2.50*

Human Rights Flame A468

1973, Nov. 20 *Perf. 13*

1503 A468 35pf dp rose, dk car & sil .40 .30

25th anniv. of the Universal Declaration of Human Rights.

At the Bidding of the Pike — A469

Designs: Various scenes from Russian Folktale "At the Bidding of the Pike."

1973, Dec. 4 Litho. *Perf. 13x13½*

1504 5pf multicolored .25 .25
1505 10pf multicolored .65 1.00
1506 15pf multicolored .25 .25
1507 20pf multicolored .25 .25
1508 25pf multicolored .65 1.00
1509 35pf multicolored .25 .25
a. A469 Sheet of 6, #1504-1509 2.25 6.00

Edwin Hoernle — A470

No. 1511, Etkar Andre. No. 1512, Paul Merker. No. 1513, Hermann Duncker. No. 1514, Fritz Heckert. No. 1515, Otto Grotewohl. No. 1516, Wilhelm Florin. No. 1517, Georg Handke. No. 1518, Rudolf Breitscheid. No. 1519, Kurt Bürger. No. 1519A Carl Moltmann.

1974 Litho. *Perf. 13½x13*

1510 A470 10pf gray green .25 .25
1511 A470 10pf rose violet .25 .25
1512 A470 10pf dark blue .25 .25
1513 A470 10pf brown .25 .25
1514 A470 10pf dull green .25 .25
1515 A470 10pf red brown .25 .25
1516 A470 10pf vio blue .25 .25
1517 A470 10pf olive brown .25 .25
1518 A470 10pf slate green .25 .25
1519 A470 10pf dull violet .25 .25
1519A A470 10pf brown .25 .25
Nos. 1510-1519A (11) 2.75 2.75

Leaders of German labor movement.
Issued: Nos. 1510-1517, 1/8; others 7/9.

Flags of Comecon Members A471

1974, Jan. 22 Photo. *Perf. 13*

1520 A471 20pf red & multi .35 .25

25th anniversary of the Council of Mutual Economic Assistance (Comecon).

Pablo Neruda and Chilean Flag A472

1974, Jan. 22 *Perf. 14*

1521 A472 20pf multicolored .35 .25

Pablo Neruda (Neftali Ricardo Reyes, 1904-1973), Chilean poet.

Echinopsis Multiplex — A473

Various Flowering Cacti: 10pf, Lobivia haageana. 15pf, Parodia sanguiniflora. 20pf, Gymnocal. monvillei. 25pf, Neoporteria rapifera. 35pf, Notocactus concinnus.

1974, Feb. 12 Photo. *Perf. 14*

1522 A473 5pf multicolored .25 .25
1523 A473 10pf tan & multi .25 .25
1524 A473 15pf green & multi 1.60 1.60
1525 A473 20pf multicolored .25 .25
1526 A473 25pf violet & multi .25 .25
1527 A473 35pf multicolored .25 .25
Nos. 1522-1527 (6) 2.85 2.85

Fieldball — A474

Design: Various fieldball scenes.

1974, Feb. 26 Litho. *Perf. 13*

1528 A474 5pf green & multi .30 .30
1529 A474 10pf green & multi .30 .30
1530 A474 35pf green & multi .30 .30
a. Strip of 3, #1528-1530 1.00 1.10

8th World Fieldball Championships for Men.

Power Testing Station — A475

Leipzig Spring Fair: 25pf, Robotron EC 2040 data processer, horiz.

1974, Mar. 5 Photo. *Perf. 14*

1531 A475 10pf multicolored .25 .25
1532 A475 25pf multicolored .30 .25

Poisonous European Mushrooms A476

Designs: 5pf, Rhodophyllus Sinuatus. 10pf, Boletus satanas. 15pf, Amanita pantherina. 20pf, Amanita muscaria. 25pf, Gyromitra esculenta. 30pf, Inocybe patouillardii. 35pf, Amanita phalloides. 40pf, Clitocybe dealbata.

1974, Mar. 19 Litho. *Perf. 13x13½*

1533 A476 5pf buff & multi .25 .25
1534 A476 10pf buff & multi .25 .25
1535 A476 15pf buff & multi .25 .25
1536 A476 20pf buff & multi .25 .25
1537 A476 25pf buff & multi .25 .25
1538 A476 30pf buff & multi .25 .25
1539 A476 35pf buff & multi .25 .25
1540 A476 40pf buff & multi 1.25 .80
Nos. 1533-1540 (8) 3.00 2.55

Gustav Robert Kirchhoff — A477

Portraits: 10pf, Immanuel Kant. 20pf, Ehm Welk. 25pf, Johann Gottfried Herder. 35pf, Lion Feuchtwanger.

1974, Mar. 26 Litho. *Perf. 13½x13*

1541 A477 5pf black & gray .25 .25
1542 A477 10pf vio bl & dull bl .25 .25
1543 A477 20pf maroon & rose .25 .25
1544 A477 25pf slate grn & grn .25 .25
1545 A477 35pf brn & lt brn .55 .40
Nos. 1541-1545 (5) 1.55 1.40

"Peace" A477a

1974, Apr. 16 *Perf. 13*

1548 A477a 35pf silver & multi .35 .30

1st World Peace Congress, 25th anniv.

Oil Pipeline Operator and Arms of DDR A477b

1974, Apr. 30 Photo. *Perf. 13*

1549 A477b 10pf shown .25 .25
1550 A477b 20pf Students .25 .25
1551 A477b 25pf Woman worker .25 .25
1552 A477b 35pf Family .75 .65
Nos. 1549-1552 (4) 1.50 1.40

25th anniv. of the DDR.

Buk Lighthouse, 1878, and Map — A478

Lighthouses, Maps and Nautical Charts: 15pf, Warnemünde, 1898. 20pf, Darsser Ort, 1848. 35pf, Arkona, 1827 and 1902. 40pf, Greifswalder Oie, 1855.

1974, May 7 Litho. *Perf. 14*

1553 A478 10pf multicolored .25 .25
1554 A478 15pf multicolored .25 .25
1555 A478 20pf multicolored .25 .25
1556 A478 35pf multicolored .25 .25
1557 A478 40pf multicolored .00 .00
Nos. 1553-1557 (5) 1.90 1.80

Hydrographic Service of German Democratic Republic. See Nos. 1645-1649.

The Ages of Man, by C. D. Friedrich — A479

C. D. Friedrich, Self-portrait — A480

Paintings by Friedrich: 10pf, Two Men Observing Moon. 25pf, The Heath near Dresden. 35pf, View of Elbe Valley.

1974, May 21 Photo. *Perf. 13½*

1558 A479 10pf gold & multi .25 .25
1559 A479 20pf gold & multi .25 .25
1560 A479 25pf gold & multi 1.25 1.25
1561 A479 35pf gold & multi .25 .25
Nos. 1558-1561 (4) 2.00 2.00

Souvenir Sheet

Engr.

Perf. 14x13½

1562 A480 70pf sepia 1.10 2.00

Caspar David Friedrich (1774-1840), German Romantic painter.

Plauen Lace — A481

Designs: Various Plauen lace patterns.

1974, June 11 Litho. *Perf. 13*

1563 A481 10pf violet, lil & blk .25 .25
1564 A481 20pf brown ol & blk .25 .25
1565 A481 25pf bl, lt bl & blk 1.00 .85
1566 A481 35pf lil rose, rose & blk .25 .25
Nos. 1563-1566 (4) 1.75 1.60

Trotter — A482

Designs: 10pf, Thoroughbred hurdling, vert. 25pf, Haflinger breed horses. 35pf, British thoroughbred race horse.

Perf. 14x13½, 13½x14

1974, Aug. 13 Photo.

1570 A482 10pf olive & multi .25 .25
1571 A482 20pf multicolored .25 .25
1572 A482 25pf lt blue & multi 1.10 1.40
1573 A482 35pf ocher & multi .25 .25
Nos. 1570-1573 (4) 1.85 2.15

International Horse Breeders' of Socialist Countries Congress, Berlin.

Crane Lifting Diesel Locomotive — A483

Leipzig Fall Fair: 25pf, Sugar beet harvester, type KS6.

1974, Aug. 27 Litho. *Perf. 13x12½*

1574 A483 10pf multicolored .25 .25
1575 A483 25pf orange & multi .30 .25

Miniature China and Mirror Exhibits — A484

Scenes from 18th century Thuringia, Dolls' Village, Arnstadt Castle Museum: 10pf, Harlequin barker at Fair. 15pf, Wine tasters. 20pf, Cooper and apprentice. 25pf, Bagpiper. 35pf, Butcher and beggar, women.

1974, Sept. 10 Photo. *Perf. 14x13½*

1576 A484 5pf shown .25 .25
1577 A484 10pf multicolored .25 .25
1578 A484 15pf multicolored .25 .25
1579 A484 20pf multicolored .25 .25
1580 A484 25pf multicolored 1.00 1.00
1581 A484 35pf multicolored .25 .25
Nos. 1576-1581 (6) 2.25 2.25

Bound Guerrillas, Ardeatine Caves, Rome — A485

Design: No. 1583, Resistance Fighters, monument near Chateaubriant, France.

1974, Sept. 24 *Perf. 13½x14*

1582 A485 35pf green, blk & red .30 .30
1583 A485 35pf blue, blk & red .30 .30

International war memorials.

Souvenir Sheet

Family and Flag — A486

1974, Oct. 3 Photo. *Perf. 13*

1584 A486 1m multicolored 1.25 3.00

25th anniv. of the DDR.

Freighter and Paddle Steamer — A487

Cent. of the UPU: 20pf, Old steam locomotive and modern Diesel. 25pf, Bi-plane and jet. 35pf, Mail coach and truck.

1974, Oct. 9 ***Perf. 14***

1585 A487 10pf green & multi .25 .25
1586 A487 20pf multicolored .25 .25
1587 A487 25pf blue & multi .25 .25
1588 A487 35pf multicolored *.80 .65*
Nos. 1585-1588 (4) *1.55 1.40*

"In Praise of Dialectics" A488

Designs: 10pf+5pf, "Praise to the Revolutionaries." 25pf, "Praise to the Party." Designs are from bas-reliefs by Rossdeutscher, Jastram and Wetzel, illustrating poems by Bertholt Brecht.

1974, Oct. 24 **Litho.** ***Perf. 13x13½***

1589 A488 10pf + 5pf multi *.25 .25*
1590 A488 20pf multicolored *.25 .25*
1591 A488 25pf multicolored *.25 .25*
a. Strip of 3, #1589-1591 *1.00 .85*

DDR '74 Natl. Stamp Exhib., Karl-Marx-Stadt.

Souvenir Sheet

Drawings by Young Pioneers — A489

a, Sun shines on everybody. b, My Friend Sascha. c, Carsten, the Best Swimmer. d, Me at the Blackboard.

1974, Nov. 26 **Litho.** ***Perf. 14***

1592 A489 Sheet of 4 *1.25 2.00*
a. 20pf multicolored *.30 .30*
b. 20pf multicolored *.30 .30*
c. 20pf multicolored *.30 .30*
d. 20pf multicolored *.30 .30*

Young Pioneers' drawings (7-10 years old).

Man Cutting Tree, and Bird — A490

Designs: Various scenes from Russian folktale "Twittering To and Fro."

1974, Dec. 3 ***Perf. 13x13½***

1593 A490 10pf multicolored *.25 .25*
1594 A490 15pf multicolored *.75 .75*
1595 A490 20pf multicolored *.25 .25*
1596 A490 30pf multicolored *.25 .25*
1597 A490 35pf multicolored *.75 .75*
1598 A490 40pf multicolored *.25 .25*
a. Sheet of 6, #1593-1598 *2.50 4.00*

Meditating Girl, by Wilhelm Lachnit — A491

Paintings: 10pf, Still Life, by Ronald Paris, horiz. 20pf, Fisherman's House, Vitte, by Harald Hakenbeck. 35pf, Girl in Red, by Rudolf Bergander, horiz. 70pf, The Artist's Parents, by Willi Sitte.

1974, Dec. 10 ***Perf. 13½x14, 14x13½***

1599 A491 10pf multicolored .25 .25
1600 A491 15pf multicolored .25 .25
1601 A491 20pf multicolored .25 .25
1602 A491 35pf multicolored .25 .25
1603 A491 70pf multicolored *1.25 1.10*
Nos. 1599-1603 (5) *2.25 2.10*

Paintings in Berlin Museums.

Banded Jasper — A492

Minerals from the collection of the Mining Academy in Freiberg: 15pf, Smoky quartz. 20pf, Topaz. 25pf, Amethyst. 35pf, Aquamarine. 70pf, Agate.

1974, Dec. 17 **Photo.** ***Perf. 14***

1604 A492 10pf lt yellow & multi .25 .25
1605 A492 15pf lt yellow & multi .25 .25
1606 A492 20pf lt yellow & multi .25 .25
1607 A492 25pf lt yellow & multi .25 .25
1608 A492 35pf lt yellow & multi .25 .25
1609 A492 70pf lt yellow & multi *1.25 1.10*
Nos. 1604-1609 (6) *2.50 2.35*

Type of 1973
Coil Stamps

1974-75 **Photo.** ***Perf. 14***

Size: 21x17½mm

1610 A449 5pf blue grn ('74) .25 .25
1611 A449 10pf emerald .35 .35
1612 A449 20pf rose magenta .35 .35
1613 A449 25pf green ('75) .40 .35
1615 A449 50pf blue ('74) .60 .45
1617 A449 1m olive ('74) 1.25 1.25
Nos. 1610-1617 (6) *3.20 3.00*

Black control number on back of every fifth stamp.

The 20pf was issued in sheets of 100 in 1975.

Martha Arendsee (1885-1953), Communist Politician — A493

1975, Jan. 14 **Litho.** ***Perf. 13½x13***

1618 A493 10pf dull red .30 .25

Souvenir Sheet

Peasants' War, Contemporary Woodcuts — A494

1975, Feb. 11 ***Perf. 12½x13***

1619 A494 Sheet of 6 + label *3.50 3.00*
a. 5pf Forced labor *.30 .30*
b. 10pf Peasant paying tithe *.30 .30*
c. 20pf Thomas Munzer *.30 .30*
d. 25pf Armed peasants *.45 .45*
e. 35pf Peasant, "Liberty" flag *.45 .45*
f. 50pf Peasant on trial *.30 .30*

Peasants' War, 450th anniversary.

Black Women — A495

Designs: 20pf, Caucasian women. 25pf, Indian woman and child.

1975, Feb. 25 **Litho.** ***Perf. 13***

1620 A495 10pf red & multi *.25 .25*
1621 A495 20pf red & multi *.25 .25*
1622 A495 25pf red & multi *.25 .25*
a. Strip of 3, Nos. 1620-1622 *.90 .85*

International Women's Year 1975.

Microfilm Pentakta Camera A496

Leipzig Spring Fair: 25pf, Sket cement plant.

1975, Mar. 4 **Photo.** ***Perf. 14***

1623 A496 10pf ultra & multi .25 .25
1624 A496 25pf orange & multi .25 .25

A497

Portraits: 5pf, Hans Otto (1900-33), actor. 10pf, Thomas Mann (1875-1955), writer. 20pf, Albert Schweitzer (1875-1965), medical missionary. 25pf, Michelangelo (1475-1564), painter and sculptor. 35pf, André Marie Ampère (1775-1836), scientist.

1975, Mar. 18 **Litho.** ***Perf. 13½x13***

1625 A497 5pf dk blue .25 .25
1626 A497 10pf dk car rose .25 .25
1627 A497 20pf dk green .25 .25
1628 A497 25pf sepia .25 .25
1629 A497 35pf vio blue *.65 .40*
Nos. 1625-1629 (5) *1.65 1.40*

Famous men, birth anniversaries.

A498

German Zoological Gardens: 5pf, Blue and yellow macaws, Magdeburg Zoo. 10pf, Orangutan family, Dresden. 15pf, Siberian chamois, Halle. 20pf, Rhinoceros, Berlin. 25pf, Dwarf hippopotamus, Erfurt. 30pf, Baltic seal and pup, Rostock. 35pf, Siberian tiger, Leipzig. 50pf, Boehm's zebra, Cottbus. 20pf, 25pf, 30pf, 35pf are horiz.

1975, Mar. 25 ***Perf. 13½x13, 13x13½***

1630 A498 5pf multicolored .25 .25
1631 A498 10pf multicolored .25 .25
1632 A498 15pf multicolored .25 .25
1633 A498 20pf multicolored .25 .25
1634 A498 25pf multicolored .25 .25
1635 A498 30pf multicolored .25 .25
1636 A498 35pf multicolored .25 .25
1637 A498 50pf multicolored *1.25 1.25*
Nos. 1630-1637 (8) *3.00 3.00*

Soldiers, Industry and Agriculture — A499

1975, May 6 **Photo.** ***Perf. 13½x14***

1638 A499 20pf multicolored .85 .30

20th anniv. of the signing of the Warsaw Treaty (Bulgaria, Czechoslovakia, DDR, Hungary, Poland, Romania, USSR).

Soviet War Memorial, Berlin-Treptow A500

Designs (Arms of German Democratic Rep. and): 20pf, Buchenwald Memorial (detail). 25pf, Woman reconstruction worker. 35pf, Skyscraper and statue at Orenburg (economic integration). 50pf, Soldier raising Red Flag on Reichstag Building, Berlin.

1975, May 6 ***Perf. 14x13½***

1639 A500 10pf red & multi .25 .25
1640 A500 20pf red & multi .25 .25
1641 A500 25pf red & multi .25 .25
1642 A500 35pf red & multi *.55 .40*
Nos. 1639-1642 (4) *1.30 1.15*

Souvenir Sheet

Imperf

1643 A500 50pf red & multi .80 1.75

30th anniversary of liberation from fascism.

Ribbons, Youth Organization Emblems of DDR and USSR — A501

1975, May 13 ***Perf. 14***

1644 A501 10pf multicolored .35 .25

Third Friendship Festival of Russian and German Youths, Halle, 1975.

Lighthouse Type of 1974

Lighthouses, Maps and Nautical Charts: 5pf, Timmendorf, 1872. 10pf, Gellen, 1905. 20pf, Sassnitz, 1904. 25pf, Dornbush, 1888. 35pf, Peenemünde, 1954.

1975, May 13 **Litho.** ***Perf. 14***

1645 A478 5pf multicolored .25 .25
1646 A478 10pf multicolored .25 .25
1647 A478 20pf multicolored .25 .25
1648 A478 25pf multicolored .25 .25
1649 A478 35pf multicolored *.65 .55*
Nos. 1645-1649 (5) *1.65 1.55*

Hydrographic Service of the DDR.

Wilhelm Liebknecht, August Bebel — A502

20pf, Tivoli House & front page of Protocol of Gotha. 25pf, Karl Marx & Friedrich Engels.

1975, May 21 **Photo.**

1650 A502 10pf buff, brn & red *.25 .25*
1651 A502 20pf sal, brn & red *.25 .25*
1652 A502 25pf buff, brn & red *.25 .25*
a. Strip of 3, #1650-1652 *.85 .85*

Centenary of the Congress of Gotha, the beginning of German Socialist Workers' Party.

Construction Workers, Union Emblem — A503

1975, June 10 **Photo.** ***Perf. 14***

1653 A503 20pf red & multi .30 .25

Free German Association of Trade Unions (FDGB), 30th anniversary.

"Socialist Scientific Cooperation" Mosaic by Walter Womacka A504

1975, June 10 **Litho.** ***Perf. 13***

1654 A504 20pf multicolored .30 .25

Eisenhüttenstadt, first socialist city of DDR, 25th anniversary.

Automatic Clock by Paulus Schuster, 1585 — A505

Clocks, Dresden Museums: 10pf, Astronomical table clock, Augsburg, c. 1560. 15pf, Automatic clock, Hans Schlottheim, c. 1600. 20pf, Table clock, Johann Heinrich Köhler, c. 1720. 25pf, Table clock, Köhler, c. 1700. 35pf, Astronomical clock, Johannes Klein, 1738.

1975, June 24 **Photo.** ***Perf. 14***

1655 A505 5pf multicolored .25 .25
1656 A505 10pf ultra & multi .25 .25
1657 A505 15pf red & multi *1.00 1.00*
1658 A505 20pf olive & multi .25 .25
1659 A505 25pf multicolored .25 .25
1660 A505 35pf ocher & multi .25 .25
Nos. 1655-1660 (6) 2.25 2.25

Dictionary, Compiled by Jacob and Wilhelm Grimm — A506

20pf, Karl-Schwarzschild Observatory, Tautenburg near Jena. 25pf, Electron microscope & chemical plant (scientific & practical cooperation). 35pf, Intercosmos 10 satellite.

1975, July 2 **Litho.** ***Perf. 13½x13***

1661 A506 10pf plum, ol & blk .25 .25
1662 A506 20pf vio bl & blk .25 .25
1663 A506 25pf green, yel & blk .25 .25
1664 A506 35pf blue & multi *.65 .60*
Nos. 1661-1664 (4) 1.40 1.35

German Academy of Sciences, 275th anniv.

Torch Bearer — A507

1975, July 15 ***Perf. 13½x13***

1665 A507 10pf shown .25 .25
1666 A507 20pf Hurdling .25 .25
1667 A507 25pf Diving .25 .25
1668 A507 35pf Gymnast on bar *.65 .60*
Nos. 1665-1668 (4) 1.40 1.35

5th Children and Youths Spartakiad.

Map of Europe A508

1975, July 30 **Photo.** ***Perf. 13***

1669 A508 20pf multicolored .40 .25

European Security and Cooperation Conference, Helsinki, July 30-Aug. 1.

China Aster — A509

1975, Aug. 19 **Photo.** ***Perf. 13½x14***

1670 A509 5pf shown .25 .25
1671 A509 10pf Geranium .25 .25
1672 A509 20pf Transvaal daisies .25 .25
1673 A509 25pf Carnation .25 .25
1674 A509 35pf Chrysanthemum .25 .25
1675 A509 70pf Pansies *1.90 1.60*
Nos. 1670-1675 (6) 3.15 2.85

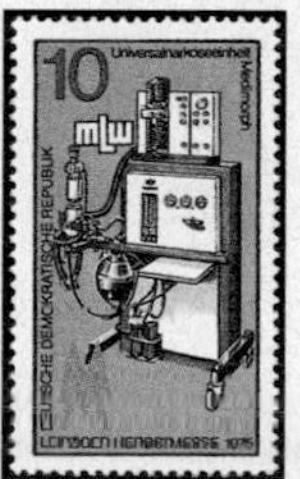

Medimorph Anesthesia Unit — A510

Leipzig Fall Fair: 25pf, Motorcycle, type MZ TS 250, horiz.

1975, Aug. 28 ***Perf. 14***

1676 A510 10pf multicolored .25 .25
1677 A510 25pf yellow & multi .25 .25

Children and Child Crossing Guard A511

Designs: 15pf, Traffic policewoman. 20pf, Policeman helping, motorist. 25pf, Motor vehicle inspection. 35pf, Volunteer instructor.

1975, Sept. 9 **Litho.** ***Perf. 13x12½***

1678 A511 10pf multicolored .25 .25
1679 A511 15pf green & multi *1.00 .50*
1680 A511 20pf brown & multi .25 .25
1681 A511 25pf violet & multi .25 .25
1682 A511 35pf multicolored .25 .25
Nos. 1678-1682 (5) 2.00 1.50

Traffic police serving and instructing the public.

Soyuz Take-off — A512

Designs: 20pf, Soyuz and Apollo in space. 70pf, Spacecraft after link-up, horiz., 79x28mm.

Perf. 14x13½, 13½x14

1975, Sept. 15 **Photo.**

1683 A512 10pf multicolored .25 .25
1684 A512 20pf multicolored .25 .25
1685 A512 70pf multicolored *1.25 1.20*
Nos. 1683-1685 (3) 1.75 1.70

Apollo Soyuz space test project (Russo-American space cooperation), launching July 15; link-up, July 17.

Weimar, 1630, after Merian — A513

Designs: 20pf, Buchenwald Liberation Monument, vert. 35pf, Composite view of old and new buildings in Weimar.

1975, Sept. 23 **Litho.** ***Perf. 13½x13***

1686 A513 10pf green, gray & blk .25 .25
1687 A513 20pf red & multi .25 .25
1688 A513 35pf ultra & multi *.40 .35*
Nos. 1686-1688 (3) .90 .85

Millennium of Weimar.

Monument, Vienna — A514

1975, Oct. 14 **Photo.** ***Perf. 14x13½***

1689 A514 35pf red & multi .35 .25

Memorial for the victims of the struggle for a free Austria, 1934-1945.

Louis Braille and Dots — A515

Designs: 35pf, Hands reading Braille. 50pf, Eyeball and protective glasses.

1975, Oct. 14

1690 A515 20pf gray & multi .25 .25
1691 A515 35pf multicolored .25 .25
1692 A515 50pf multicolored *1.00 .95*
Nos. 1690-1692 (3) 1.50 1.45

World Braille Year 1975. Sesquicentennial of the invention of Braille system of writing for the blind, by Louis Braille (1809-1852).

Post Office Bärenfels A516

1975, Oct. 21 **Photo.** ***Perf. 14***

1693 A516 20pf multicolored .35 .25

Philatelists' Day 1975. See No. B177.

Emperor Ordering Clothes — A517

Designs: Scenes from "The Emperor's New Clothes," by Hans Christian Andersen and Andersen portrait.

1975, Nov. 18 **Litho.** ***Perf. 14x13***

1694 A517 20pf ocher & multi *.35 .35*
1695 A517 35pf ocher & multi *.55 .55*
1696 A517 50pf ocher & multi *.35 .35*
a. Sheet of 3, #1694-1696 *1.75 1.75*

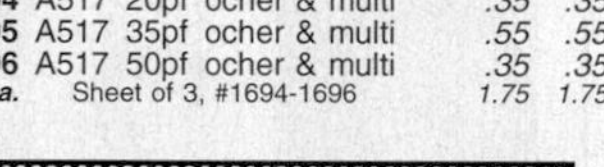

Tobogganing and Olympic Rings — A518

Olympic Rings and: 20pf, Speed-skating Rink, Berlin. 35pf, Figure-skating Hall, Karl-Marx Stadt. 70pf, Mass skiing at Schmiedefeld. 1m, Innsbruck & surrounding mountains.

1975, Dec. 2 **Photo.** ***Perf. 14***

1697 A518 5pf multicolored .25 .25
1698 A518 20pf olive & multi .25 .25
1699 A518 35pf multicolored .25 .25
1700 A518 70pf multicolored *1.40 1.20*
Nos. 1697-1700,B178-B179 (6) 2.65 2.45

Souvenir Sheet

1701 A518 1m ultra & multi *1.75 1.25*

12th Winter Olympic Games, Innsbruck, Austria, Feb. 4-15, 1976.
No. 1701 contains one 32x27mm stamp.

Pres. Wilhelm Pieck (1876-1960) A519

1975, Dec. 30 **Litho.** ***Perf. 13½x13***

1702 A519 10pf lt ultra & blk .25 .25

Ernst Thälmann (1886-1944) A520

Labor Leaders: No. 1704, Georg Schumann (1886-1945). No. 1705, Wilhelm Koenen (1886-1963). No. 1706, John Schehr (1896-1934).

1976, Jan. 13 *Perf. 13½x13*

1703	A520	10pf rose & blk		.25	.25
1704	A520	10pf emerald & blk		.25	.25
1705	A520	10pf ocher & blk		.25	.25
1706	A520	10pf violet & blk		.25	.25
		Nos. 1703-1706 (4)		*1.00*	*1.00*

See Nos. 1852-1854.

Silbermann Organ, Rötha — A521

Silbermann Organs: 20pf, Freiberg. 35pf, Fraureuth. 50pf, Dresden.

1976, Jan. 27 **Photo.** *Perf. 14*

1707	A521	10pf green & multi	.25	.25
1708	A521	20pf red & multi	.25	.25
1709	A521	35pf multicolored	.25	.25
1710	A521	50pf brown & multi	*1.00*	*.65*
		Nos. 1707-1710 (4)	*1.75*	*1.40*

Organs built by Gottfried Silbermann (1683-1753).

Souvenir Sheet

Richard Sorge — A522

1976, Feb. 3 **Litho.** *Imperf.*

1711	A522	1m multicolored	*1.50*	*3.25*

Dr. Richard Sorge (1895-1944), Soviet intelligence agent. No. 1711 contains one stamp with simulated perforations.

Military Flag, Sailor, Soldier, Aviator — A523

20pf, Military flag, ships, tanks, missile & planes.

1976, Feb. 24 **Litho.** *Perf. 13½x14*

1712	A523	10pf multicolored	.25	.25
1713	A523	20pf multicolored	.30	.25

National People's Army, 20th anniversary.

Telephone — A524

1976, Mar. 2 *Perf. 13*

1714	A524	20pf light blue	.30	.25

Centenary of first telephone call by Alexander Graham Bell, March 10, 1876.

Apartment House, Leipzig — A525

Design: 25pf, Ocean super trawler, horiz.

1976, Mar. 9 **Photo.** *Perf. 14*

1715	A525	10pf green & multi	.25	.25
1716	A525	25pf vio blue, blk & grn	.35	.25

Leipzig Spring Fair.

Palace of the Republic — A526

1976, Apr. 22 **Photo.** *Perf. 14*

1717	A526	10pf vio blue & multi	.60	.25

Inauguration of Palace of the Republic, Berlin. See No. 1721.

Post Office Radar Station — A527

1976, Apr. 27 **Photo.** *Perf. 13½x14*

1718	A527	20pf multicolored	.30	.25

Intersputnik 1976.

Marx, Engels, Lenin and Party Flag — A528

20pf, New factories & apartment houses, party flag, horiz. 1m, Palace of the Republic.

1976, May 11 *Perf. 14x13½, 13½x14*

1719	A528	10pf dp mag, gold & red	.25	.25
1720	A528	20pf multicolored	.25	.25

Souvenir Sheet

Perf. 14

1721	A526	1m multicolored	*1.25*	*2.50*

9th Congress of Unity Party (SED).

Peace Bicycle Race and Olympic Rings — A529

Designs: 20pf, Town and sport halls, Suhl. 25pf, Regatta course, Brandenburg. 70pf, 1500-meter race. 1m, Central Stadium, Leipzig.

1976, May 18 **Photo.** *Perf. 13½x14*

1722	A529	5pf green & multi	.25	.25
1723	A529	20pf blue & multi	.25	.25
1724	A529	25pf multicolored	.25	.25
1725	A529	70pf ultra & multi	*1.75*	*1.50*
		Nos. 1722-1725,B180-B181 (6)	*3.00*	*2.75*

Souvenir Sheet

Perf. 14

1726	A529	1m multicolored	*1.25*	*1.10*

21st Olympic Games, Montreal, Canada, July 17-Aug. 1. No. 1726 contains one stamp (32x27mm).

Ribbons and Emblem A530

Design: 20pf, Young man and woman, industrial installations.

1076, May 25 *Perf. 14*

1727	A530	10pf blue & multi	.25	.25
1728	A530	20pf multicolored	.25	.25

10th Parliamentary Meeting of the Free German Youth Organization.

European orchids — A531

10pf, Himantoglossum Hircinum. 20pf, Dactylorhiza incarnata. 25pf, Anacamptis pyramidalis. 35pf, Dactylorhiza sambucina. 40pf, Orchis coriophora. 50pf, Cypripedium calceolus.

1976, June 15 **Litho.** *Perf. 12½x13*

1729	A531	10pf multi	.25	.25
1730	A531	20pf multi	.25	.25
1731	A531	25pf multi	.25	.25
1732	A531	35pf multi	.25	.25
1733	A531	40pf multi	.25	.25
1734	A531	50pf multi	*1.90*	*1.25*
		Nos. 1729-1734 (6)	*3.15*	*2.50*

Dancer at Rest, by Walter Arnold — A532

Small Sculptures: 10pf, Shetland Pony, by Heinrich Drake, horiz. 25pf, "At the Beach," by Ludwig Engelhardt. 35pf, Hermann Duncker, by Walter Howard. 50pf, "The Conversation," by Gustav Weidanz.

1976, June 22 **Photo.** *Perf. 14*

1735	A532	10pf blk & bl grn	.25	.25
1736	A532	20pf ocher & blk	.25	.25
1737	A532	25pf ocher & blk	.25	.25
1738	A532	35pf yel grn & blk	.25	.25
1739	A532	50pf brick red & blk	*1.25*	*1.10*
		Nos. 1735-1739 (5)	*2.25*	*2.10*

Marx, Engels, Lenin, Red Flags, Berlin Buildings A533

1976, June 29 **Photo.** *Perf. 14*

1740	A533	20pf blue, red & dk red	.35	.25

European Communist Workers' Congress, Berlin.

Coronation Coach, 1790 — A534

Historic Coaches: 20pf, Open carriage, Russia, 1800. 25pf, Court landau, Saxony, 1840. 35pf, State carriage, Saxony, 1860. 40pf, Mail coach, 1850. 50pf, Town carriage, Saxony, 1889.

1976, July 27

1741	A534	10pf multicolored	.25	.25
1742	A534	20pf multicolored	.25	.25
1743	A534	25pf multicolored	.25	.25
1744	A534	35pf multicolored	.25	.25
1745	A534	40pf multicolored	.25	.25
1746	A534	50pf multicolored	*2.00*	*1.75*
		Nos. 1741-1746 (6)	*3.25*	*3.00*

View of Gera A535

Design: 10pf+5pf, View of Gera, c. 1652.

1976, Aug. 5 **Litho.** *Perf. 13*

1747	A535	10pf + 5pf multi	.25	.25
1748	A535	20pf multicolored	.25	.25
a.		Pair, #1747-1748 + label	.80	.65

4th German Youth Philatelic Exhib., Gera.

Boxer — A536

Dogs: 10pf, Airedale terrier. 20pf, German shepherd. 25pf, Collie. 35pf, Giant schnauzer. 70pf, Great Dane.

1976, Aug. 17 *Perf. 14*

1749	A536	5pf multicolored	.25	.25
1750	A536	10pf multicolored	.25	.25
1751	A536	20pf multicolored	.25	.25
1752	A536	25pf multicolored	.25	.25
1753	A536	35pf multicolored	.25	.25
1754	A536	70pf multicolored	*1.75*	*1.75*
		Nos. 1749-1754 (6)	*3.00*	*3.00*

Oil Distillery A537

Design: 25pf, German Library, Leipzig.

1976, Sept. 1 *Perf. 13x12½*

1755	A537	10pf multicolored	.25	.25
1756	A537	25pf multicolored	.30	.25

Leipzig Fall Fair.

Templin Lake Bridge — A538

Designs: 15pf, Overpass, Berlin-Adlergestell. 20pf, Elbe River Bridge, Rosslau. 25pf, Göltzschtal Viaduct. 35pf, Elbe River Bridge, Magdeburg. 50pf, Grosser Dreesch Overpass, Schwerin.

1976, Sept. 21 Photo. ***Perf. 14***

1757 A538 10pf multicolored .25 .25
1758 A538 15pf multicolored .25 .25
1759 A538 20pf multicolored .25 .25
1760 A538 25pf multicolored .25 .25
1761 A538 35pf multicolored .25 .25
1762 A538 50pf multicolored *1.25 1.25*
Nos. 1757-1762 (6) 2.50 2.50

Memorial Monument (detail), Budapest — A539

1976, Oct. 5 Photo. ***Perf. 14***

1763 A539 35pf tan & multi .35 .30

Memorial to World War II victims.

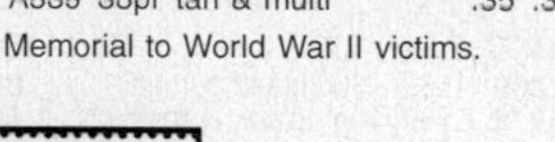

Brass Jug, c. 1500 — A540

Artistic Handicraft Works: 20pf, Faience vase with lid, c. 1710. 25pf, Porcelain centerpiece (woman carrying bowl), c. 1768. 35pf, Porter, gilded silver, c. 1700. 70pf, Art Nouveau glass vase, c. 1900.

1976, Oct. 19

1764 A540 10pf dk car & multi .25 .25
1765 A540 20pf ultra & multi .25 .25
1766 A540 25pf green & multi .25 .25
1767 A540 35pf vio blue & multi .25 .25
1768 A540 70pf red brn & multi *1.40 1.40*
Nos. 1764-1768 (5) 2.40 2.40

Guppy A541

Designs: Various guppies.

1976, Nov. 9 Litho. ***Perf. 13½x13***

1769 A541 10pf multicolored .25 .25
1770 A541 15pf multicolored .25 .25
1771 A541 20pf multicolored .25 .25
1772 A541 25pf multicolored .25 .25
1773 A541 35pf multicolored .25 .25
1774 A541 70pf multicolored *1.50 1.25*
Nos. 1769-1774 (6) 2.75 2.50

Vessels, c. 3000 B.C. — A542

20pf, Cult cart, c. 1300 B.C. 25pf, Roman gold coin, 270-273 A.D. 35pf, Gold pendant, 950 A.D. 70pf, Glass cup, 3rd cent. A.D.

1976, Nov. 23 Photo. ***Perf. 13***

1775 A542 10pf multicolored .25 .25
1776 A542 20pf multicolored .25 .25
1777 A542 25pf multicolored .25 .25
1778 A542 35pf multicolored .25 .25
1779 A542 70pf multicolored *1.40 1.40*
Nos. 1775-1779 (5) 2.40 2.40

Archaeological finds in DDR.

"Air," by Rosalba Carriera — A543

Paintings, Dresden Museum: 15pf, Virgin and Child, by Murillo. 20pf, Woman Viola da Gamba Player, by Bernardo Strozzi. 25pf, Ariadne Forsaken, by Angelica Kauffmann. 35pf, Old Man with Black Cap, by Bartolomeo Nazzari. 70pf, Officer Reading a Letter, by Gerard Terborch.

1976, Dec. 14 Photo. ***Perf. 13½x14***

1780 A543 10pf multicolored .25 .25
1781 A543 15pf multicolored .25 .25
1782 A543 20pf multicolored .25 .25
1783 A543 25pf multicolored .25 .25
1784 A543 35pf multicolored .25 .25
1785 A543 70pf multicolored *1.60 1.20*
Nos. 1780-1785 (6) 2.85 2.45

Rumpelstiltskin and King — A544

Scenes from fairy tale "Rumpel-stiltskin."

1976, Dec. 14 Litho. ***Perf. 13***

1786 A544 5pf multicolored .25 .25
1787 A544 10pf multicolored .45 .45
1788 A544 15pf multicolored .25 .25
1789 A544 20pf multicolored .25 .25
1790 A544 25pf multicolored .45 .45
1791 A544 30pf multicolored .25 .25
a. Sheet of 6, #1786-1791 2.10 2.10

Arnold Zweig and Quotation A545

Designs: 20pf, Otto von Guericke and Magdeburg hemispheres. 35pf, Albrecht D. Thaer, wheat, plow and sheep. 40pf, Gustav Hertz and diagram of separation of isotopes.

1977, Feb. 8 Litho. ***Perf. 13x12½***

1792 A545 10pf rose & blk .25 .25
1793 A545 20pf gray & blk .25 .25
1794 A545 35pf lt green & blk .25 .25
1795 A545 40pf blue & blk *.65 .65*
Nos. 1792-1795 (4) 1.40 1.40

Zweig (1887-1968), novelist; von Guericke (1602-86), physicist; Thaer (1752-1828), agronomist & physician; Hertz (1887-1975), physicist.

Spring near Plaue — A546

Natural Monuments: 20pf, Small Organ, Johnsdorf. 25pf, Ivenacker Oaks, Reuterstadt. 35pf, Stone Rose, Saalburg. 50pf, Rauenscher Stein (boulder), Furstenwalde.

1977, Feb. 24 Litho. ***Perf. 12½x13***

1796 A546 10pf multicolored .25 .25
1797 A546 20pf multicolored .25 .25
1798 A546 25pf multicolored .25 .25
1799 A546 35pf multicolored .25 .25
1800 A546 50pf multicolored *1.10 1.10*
Nos. 1796-1800 (5) 2.10 2.10

Fair Building, Book Fair A547

Leipzig Spring Fair: 25pf, Wide aluminum roll casting machine, Nachterstedt factory.

1977, Mar. 8 Photo. ***Perf. 14***

1801 A547 10pf multicolored .25 .25
1802 A547 25pf multicolored .25 .25

Costume Senftenberg — A548

Sorbian Costumes from: 20pf, Bautzen. 25pf, Klitten. 35pf, Nochten. 70pf, Muskau.

1977, Mar. 22

1803 A548 10pf multicolored .25 .25
1804 A548 20pf multicolored .25 .25
1805 A548 25pf multicolored .25 .25
1806 A548 35pf multicolored .25 .25
1807 A548 70pf multicolored *1.75 1.25*
Nos. 1803-1807 (5) 2.75 2.25

Start after Wheel Change — A549

Designs: 20pf, Sprint. 35pf, At finish line.

1977, Apr. 19 Photo. ***Perf. 14***

1808 A549 10pf multicolored *.25 .25*
1809 A549 20pf multicolored *.25 .25*
1810 A549 35pf multicolored *.25 .25*
a. Strip of 3. #1808-1810 *1.10 1.10*

30th International Peace Bicycling Race.

Carl Friedrich Gauss A550

1977, Apr. 19 Litho. ***Perf. 13x12½***

1811 A550 20pf lt ultra & blk .45 .25

Carl Friedrich Gauss (1777-1855), mathematician, 200th birth anniversary.

Flags and Handshake A551

1977, May 3 Photo. ***Perf. 13***

1812 A551 20pf vio bl & multi .30 .25

9th German Trade Union Congress, Berlin.

VKM Channel Converter, Filter and ITU Emblem — A552

1977, May 17 Litho. ***Perf. 14***

1813 A552 20pf multicolored .45 .25

International Telecommunications Day.

Pistol Shooting A553

Designs: 20pf, Deep-sea diver. 35pf, Radio controlled model boat.

1977, May 17 Photo.

1814 A553 10pf lt green & multi .25 .25
1815 A553 20pf lt blue & multi .25 .25
1816 A553 35pf salmon & multi *.60 .60*
Nos. 1814-1816 (3) 1.10 1.10

Organization for Physical and Technical Training.

Accordion, c. 1900 — A554

Designs: 20pf, Treble viola da gamba, 1747. 25pf, Oboe, 1785, Clarinet, 1830 and flute, 1817. 35pf, Concert zither, 1891. 70pf, Trumpet, 1860.

1977, June 14

1817 A554 10pf multicolored .25 .25
1818 A554 20pf multicolored .25 .25
1819 A554 25pf multicolored .25 .25
1820 A554 35pf multicolored .25 .25
1821 A554 70pf multicolored *1.60 1.50*
Nos. 1817-1821 (5) 2.60 2.50

Vogtland musical instruments from Markneukirchen Museum.

Mercury and Argus, by Rubens — A555

Rubens Paintings in Dresden Gallery: 10pf, Bath of Bathsheba, vert. 20pf, The Drunk Hercules, vert. 25pf, Diana Returning from the

Hunt. 35pf, Old Woman with Brazier, vert. 50pf, Leda and the Swan.

1977, June 28 Photo. *Perf. 14*

1822 A555 10pf multicolored .25 .25
1823 A555 15pf multicolored .25 .25
1824 A555 20pf multicolored .25 .25
1825 A555 25pf multicolored .25 .25
1826 A555 35pf multicolored .25 .25
1827 A555 50pf multicolored *2.60 1.75*
Nos. 1822-1827 (6) *3.85 3.00*

Peter Paul Rubens (1577-1640), Flemish painter, 400th birth anniversary.

Souvenir Sheet

Wreath, Flags of USSR and DDR — A556

1977, June 28

1828 A556 50pf multicolored *.75 1.60*

Soc. for German-Soviet Friendship, 30th anniv.

Tractor with Plow — A557

Designs: 20pf, Fertilizer-spreader. 25pf, Potato digger and loader. 35pf, High-pressure harvester. 50pf, Rotating milking machine.

1977, July 12 Litho. *Perf. 13x12½*

1829 A557 10pf multicolored .25 .25
1830 A557 20pf multicolored .25 .25
1831 A557 25pf multicolored .25 .25
1832 A557 35pf multicolored .25 .25
1833 A557 50pf multicolored *1.40 1.25*
Nos. 1829-1833 (5) *2.40 2.25*

Motorized modern agriculture.

High Jump A558

Designs: 20pf, Hurdles, girls. 35pf, Dancing. 40pf, Torch bearer and flags.

1977, July 19

1834 A558 5pf red & multi .25 .25
1835 A558 20pf lt green & multi .25 .25
1836 A558 35pf green & multi .25 .25
1837 A558 40pf blue & multi *1.25 1.25*
Nos. 1834-1837,B183-B184 (6) 2.50 2.50

6th Gymnastics and Sports Festival and 6th Children's and Youth Spartacist Games.

"Bread for all" by Wolfram Schubert — A559

Design: 25pf, "When Communists Dream," by Walter Womacka (detail) and Sozphilex emblem.

1977, Aug. 16 Photo. *Perf. 14*

1838 A559 10pf multicolored .25 .25
a. Souvenir sheet of 4 .90 1.25
1839 A559 25pf multicolored .40 .35
a. Souvenir sheet of 4 1.75 1.60

SOZPHILEX '77 Philatelic Exhibition, Berlin, Aug. 19-28. See No. B185.

Konsument Department Store, Leipzig — A560

Design: 25pf, Glasses and wooden plate.

1977, Aug. 30

1840 A560 10pf blue & multi .30 .25
1841 A560 25pf multicolored .30 .25

Leipzig Fall Fair.

Souvenir Sheet

Dzerzhinski and Quotation from Mayakovsky — A561

1977, Sept. 6 Litho. *Perf. 12½x13*

1842 A561 Sheet of 2 *1.00 2.60*
a. 20pf multicolored .40 .65
b. 35pf multicolored .40 .90

Feliks E. Dzerzhinski (1877-1926), organizer and head of Russian Secret Police (Cheka), birth centenary.

Muldenthal Locomotive, 1861 — A562

Designs: 10pf, Trolley car, Dresden, 1896. 20pf, First successful German plane, 1909. 25pf, 3-wheel car "Phäno-mobile," 1924. 35pf, Passenger steamship on the Elbe, 1837.

1977, Sept. 13 Photo. *Perf. 14*

1843 A562 5pf green & multi .25 .25
1844 A562 10pf green & multi .25 .25
1845 A562 20pf green & multi .25 .25
1846 A562 25pf green & multi .25 .25
1847 A562 35pf green & multi *2.00 1.60*
Nos. 1843-1847 (5) *3.00 2.60*

Transportation Museum, Dresden.

Cruiser "Aurora" A563

Designs: 25pf, Storming of the Winter Palace. 1m, Lenin, vert.

1977, Sept. 20

1848 A563 10pf multicolored *.30 .25*
1849 A563 25pf multicolored *.40 .35*

Souvenir Sheet

Perf. 12½x13

1850 A563 1m carmine & blk *1.60 2.60*

60th anniversary of the Russian Revolution.

Mother Russia and Obelisk — A564

1977, Sept. 20 Litho. *Perf. 14*

1851 A564 35pf multicolored .35 .25

Soviet soldiers' memorial, Berlin-Schönholz.

Labor Leaders Type of 1976

Portraits: No. 1852, Ernst Meyer (1887-1930). No. 1853, August Fröhlich (1877-1966). No. 1854, Gerhart Eisler (1897-1968).

1977, Oct. 18 Litho. *Perf. 14*

1852 A520 10pf olive & brown .25 .25
1853 A520 10pf rose & brown .25 .25
1854 A520 10pf lt blue & blk brn .25 .25
Nos. 1852-1854 (3) .75 .75

Souvenir Sheet

Heinrich von Kleist, by Peter Friedl, 1801 — A565

1977, Oct. 18

1855 A565 1m multicolored *2.10 2.60*

Heinrich von Kleist (1777-1811), poet and playwright, birth bicentenary.

Rocket A566

Design: 20pf, as 10pf, design reversed.

1977, Nov. 8 Photo. *Perf. 14*

1856 A566 10pf red, blk & sil *.25 .25*
1857 A566 20pf ultra, blk & gold *.25 .25*
a. Pair, #1856-1857 + label *.75 .75*

20th Central Young Craftsmen's Exhibition (Masters of Tomorrow).

A567

Hunting in East Germany: 10pf, Mouflons. 15pf, Red deer. 20pf, Retriever with pheasant, hunter. 25pf, Red fox, wild duck. 35pf, Tractor driver saving fawn. 70pf, Wild boars.

1977, Nov. 15

1858 A567 10pf multicolored .25 .25
1859 A567 15pf multicolored *1.60 1.60*
1860 A567 20pf multicolored .25 .25
1861 A567 25pf multicolored .25 .25
1862 A567 35pf multicolored .25 .25
1863 A567 70pf multicolored .30 .25
Nos. 1858-1863 (6) *2.90 2.85*

A568

Firemen's Activities: 10pf, Firemen racing with ladders. 20pf, Children Visiting Firehouse. 25pf, Fire engines fighting forest and brush fires. 35pf, Artificial respiration. 50pf, Fireboat alongside freighter.

1977, Nov. 22 Litho. *Perf. 14*

1864 A568 10pf multi, horiz. .25 .25
1865 A568 20pf multi .25 .25
1866 A568 25pf multi, horiz. .25 .25
1867 A568 35pf multi .25 .25
1868 A568 50pf multi, horiz. *1.60 1.40*
Nos. 1864-1868 (5) *2.60 2.40*

Knight and King — A569

Designs: Various scenes from fairytale: "Six Men Around the World."

1977, Nov. 22 *Perf. 13x13½*

1869 A569 5pf black & multi .25 .25
1870 A569 10pf black & multi .60 .60
1871 A569 20pf black & multi .25 .25
1872 A569 25pf black & multi .25 .25
1873 A569 35pf black & multi .60 .60
1874 A569 60pf black & multi .25 .25
a. Sheet of 6, #1869-1874 3.00 2.60

Hips and Dog Rose A570

Medicinal Plants: 15pf, Birch. 20pf, Chamomile. 25pf, Coltsfoot. 35pf, Linden. 50pf, Elder.

1978, Jan. 10 Photo. *Perf. 14*

1875 A570 10pf multicolored .25 .25
1876 A570 15pf multicolored .25 .25
1877 A570 20pf multicolored .25 .25
1878 A570 25pf multicolored .25 .25
1879 A570 35pf multicolored .25 .25
1880 A570 50pf multicolored *1.75 1.60*
Nos. 1875-1880 (6) *3.00 2.85*

Amilcar Cabral — A571

1978, Jan. 17 Litho. *Perf. 14*

1881 A571 20pf multicolored .35 .30

Amilcar Cabral (1924-1973), freedom movement leader from Guinea-Bissau.

Town Hall, Suhl-Heinrichs A572

Half-timbered Buildings, 17th-18th Centuries: 20pf, Farmhouse, Niederoderwitz. 25pf, Farmhouse, Strassen. 35pf, Townhouse, Quedlinburg. 40pf, Townhouse, Eisenach.

1978, Jan. 24 Photo. *Perf. 14*

1882 A572 10pf multicolored .25 .25
1883 A572 20pf multicolored .25 .25
1884 A572 25pf multicolored .25 .25

1885 A572 35pf multicolored .25 .25
1886 A572 40pf multicolored *1.60 1.50*
Nos. 1882-1886 (5) 2.60 2.50

Mail Truck, 1921 A573

Past and Present Mail Transport: 20pf, Mail truck, 1978. 25pf, Railroad mail car, 1896. 35pf, Railroad mail car, 1978.

1978, Feb. 9 Litho. *Perf. 13x12½*

1887 A573 10pf brown & multi .25 .25
1888 A573 20pf brown & multi .35 .35
1889 A573 25pf brown & multi .40 .40
1890 A573 35pf brown & multi .55 .55
a. Block of 4, #1887-1890 2.25 2.25

Earring, 11th Century — A574

Archaeological Artifacts: 20pf, Earring, 10th century. 25pf, Bronze sheath, 10th century. 35pf, Bronze horse, 12th century. 70pf, Arabian coin, 8th century.

1978, Feb. 21 Photo. *Perf. 14*

1891 A574 10pf multicolored .25 .25
1892 A574 20pf multicolored .25 .25
1893 A574 25pf multicolored .25 .25
1894 A574 35pf multicolored .25 .25
1895 A574 70pf multicolored *1.25 1.25*
Nos. 1891-1895 (5) 2.25 2.25

Treasures found on Slavic sites.

Royal House, Leipzig — A575

Leipzig Spring Fair: 25pf, Universal measuring instrument by Carl Zeiss.

1978, Mar. 7

1896 A575 10pf multicolored .25 .25
1897 A575 25pf multicolored .35 .30

M-100 Meteorological Rocket — A576

Designs: 20pf, Intercosmos I satellite. 35pf, Meteor satellite with spectometric complex. 1m, MFK-6 multi-spectral camera over city.

1978, Mar. 21 Photo. *Perf. 14x13½*

1898 A576 10pf multicolored .25 .25
1899 A576 20pf multicolored .25 .25
1900 A576 35pf multicolored *.80 .80*
Nos. 1898-1900 (3) 1.30 1.30

Souvenir Sheet

1901 A576 1m multicolored *2.00 1.60*

Achievements in atmospheric and space research.

Samuel Heinicke, Leipzig, c. 1800 A577

25pf, Deaf child learning sign language.

1978, Apr. 4 Litho. *Perf. 13x12½*

1902 A577 20pf multicolored .25 .25
1903 A577 25pf multicolored *.55 .55*

National Institute for the Education of the Deaf, established by Samuel Heinicke, 200th anniversary.

Radio Tower, Dequede, TV Truck — A578

Design: 20pf, TV equipment and tower, vert.

1978, Apr. 25 *Perf. 13½x14, 14x13½*

1904 A578 10pf multicolored .25 .25
1905 A578 20pf multicolored *.25 .25*

World Telecommunications Day.

Saxon Miner, 19th Century — A579

Dress Uniforms, 19th Century: 20pf, Foundry worker, Freiberg. 25pf, Mining Academy student. 35pf, Chief Inspector of Mines.

1978, May 9 *Perf. 12½x13*

1906 A579 10pf silver & multi .25 .25
1907 A579 20pf silver & multi .25 .25
1908 A579 25pf silver & multi .25 .25
1909 A579 35pf silver & multi *1.00 .65*
Nos. 1906-1909 (4) 1.75 1.40

Lion Cub — A580

Young Animals: 20pf, Leopard. 35pf, Tiger. 50pf, Snow leopard.

1978, May 23 Photo. *Perf. 14*

1910 A580 10pf multicolored .25 .25
1911 A580 20pf multicolored .25 .25
1912 A580 35pf multicolored .25 .25
1913 A580 50pf multicolored *1.00 1.00*
Nos. 1910-1913 (4) 1.75 1.75

Centenary of Leipzig Zoo.

Loading Container — A581

Designs: 20pf, Loading container on flatbed truck. 35pf, Container trains in terminal. 70pf, Loading container on ship.

1978, June 13 Litho. *Perf. 12½x13*

1914 A581 10pf multicolored .25 .25
1915 A581 20pf multicolored .25 .25
1916 A581 35pf multicolored .25 .25
1917 A581 70pf multicolored *1.40 1.10*
Nos. 1914-1917 (4) 2.15 1.85

Ceramic Bull — A582

Designs: 10pf, Woman's head, ceramic. 20pf, Gold armband, horiz. 25pf, Animal head, gold ring. 35pf, Seated family from signet ring. 40pf, Necklace, horiz.

Perf. 14x13½, 13½x14

1978, June 20 Photo.

1918 A582 5pf multicolored .25 .25
1919 A582 10pf multicolored .25 .25
1920 A582 20pf multicolored .25 .25
1921 A582 25pf multicolored .25 .25
1922 A582 35pf multicolored .25 .25
1923 A582 40pf multicolored *1.00 .85*
Nos. 1918-1923 (6) 2.25 2.10

African art from 1st and 2nd centuries in Berlin and Leipzig Egyptian museums.

Old and New Buildings, Cottbus — A583

Design: 10pf + 5pf, View of Cottbus, 1730.

1978, July 18 Litho. *Perf. 13x12½*

1924 10pf + 5pf multi *.25 .25*
1925 20pf multicolored *.25 .25*
a. A583 Pair, #1924-1925 + label *.55 .55*

5th Youth Philatelic Exhibition, Cottbus.

Justus von Liebig, Wheat and Retort A584

Famous Germans: 10pf, Joseph Dietzgen (1828-1888) and title page. 15pf, Alfred Döblin (1878-1957) and title page. 20pf, Hans Loch (1898-1960) and signature, president of Liberal Democratic Party. 25pf, Dr. Theodor Brugsch (1878-1963), and blood circulation. 35pf, Friedrich Ludwig Jahn (1778-1852) and gymnast. 70pf, Dr. Albrecht von Graefe (1828-1870) and ophthalmological instruments.

1978, July 18

1926 A584 5pf yellow & blk .25 .25
1927 A584 10pf gray & blk .25 .25
1928 A584 15pf yel grn & blk .25 .25
1929 A584 20pf ultra & blk .25 .25
1930 A584 25pf salmon & blk .25 .25
1931 A584 35pf lt green & blk .25 .25
1932 A584 70pf ol & blk *1.10 1.00*
Nos. 1926-1932 (7) 2.60 2.50

Festival Emblem and New Buildings, Havana — A585

35pf, Balloons and new buildings, Berlin.

1978, July 25 Litho. *Perf. 13x12½*

1933 20pf multicolored *.30 .30*
1934 35pf multicolored *.30 .30*
a. A585 Strip of 2, #1933-1934 + label *.90 .90*

11th World Youth Festival, Havana, 7/28-8/5.

Foot Soldier, by Hans Schäufelein — A586

Etchings: 20pf, Woman Reading Letter, by Jean Antoine Watteau. 25pf, Seated Boy, by Gabriel Metsu. 30pf, Seated Young Man, by Cornelis Saftleven. 35pf, St. Anthony, by Mathias Grunewald. 50pf, Seated Man, by Abraham van Diepenbeeck.

1978, July 25 *Perf. 13½x14*

1935 A586 10pf lemon & black .25 .25
1936 A586 20pf lemon & black .65 .65
1937 A586 25pf lemon & black .25 .25
1938 A586 30pf lemon & black .25 .25
1939 A586 35pf lemon & black .65 .65
1940 A586 50pf lemon & black .25 .25
a. Sheet of 6, #1935-1940 2.40 2.40

Etchings from Berlin Museums.

Fair Building "Three Kings," Leipzig — A587

Leipzig Fall Fair: 10pf, IFA Multicar 25 truck, horiz.

1978, Aug. 29 Photo. *Perf. 14*

1941 A587 10pf multicolored .25 .25
1942 A587 25pf multicolored .35 .30

Mauthausen Memorial — A588

1978, Sept. 5 *Perf. 13½x14*

1943 A588 35pf multicolored .35 .25

International war memorials.

Soyuz, Intercosmos and German-Soviet Space Flight Emblems — A589

Soyuz, Camera and Space Complex A590

Designs: 10pf, Soyuz and Albert Einstein. 20pf, Sigmund Jähn, 1st German cosmonaut, vert. 35pf, Salyut-Soyuz space station, Otto Lilienthal and his glider. 1m, Cosmonauts Bykovsky and Jähn and space ships.

1978, Sept. Photo. *Perf. 14*

1944 A589 20pf multicolored .35 .25

Litho.

Perf. 13½x13

1945 A590 5pf multicolored .25 .25
1946 A590 10pf multicolored .25 .25
1947 A590 20pf multicolored .25 .25
1948 A590 35pf multicolored *.65 .65*
Nos. 1944-1948 (5) 1.75 1.65

Souvenir Sheet

Perf. 13½x14

1949 A590 1m multicolored 1.60 3.25

1st German cosmonaut on Russian space mission. No. 1949 contains 1 54x33mm stamp.

Issued: No. 1944, 9/4; others, 9/21.

Marching Soldiers, Tractor, Factory A591

Design: 35pf, Russian and German Soldiers, Communist war veteran, 1933.

1978, Sept. 19 Photo. *Perf. 14*

1950 A591 20pf multicolored .35 .30
1951 A591 35pf multicolored .35 .30
a. Strip of 2, #1950-1951 + label 1.10 1.60

Workers' military units, 25th anniv.

Seven-person Pyramid — A592

10pf, Elephant on tricycle. 20pf, Dressage. 35pf, Polar bear kissing woman trainer.

1978, Sept. 26 Photo. *Perf. 14*

1952 A592 5pf black & multi .30 .50
1953 A592 10pf black & multi .55 .75
1954 A592 20pf black & multi .90 1.25
1955 A592 35pf black & multi 1.25 2.25
a. Block of 4, #1952-1955 *5.25 12.50*

Circus in German Democratic Republic.

Construction of Gas Pipe Line, Drushba Section — A593

1978, Oct. 3 Litho. *Perf. 13x12½*

1956 A593 20pf multicolored .35 .25

German youth helping to build gas pipe line from Orenburg to Russian border.

African Behind Barbed Wire — A594

1978, Oct. 3 Litho. *Perf. 12½x13*

1957 A594 20pf multicolored .35 .25

Anti-Apartheid Year.

Papilio Hahneli — A595

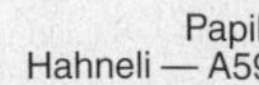

20pf, Agama lehmanni (lizards). 25pf, Agate from Wiederau. 35pf, Paleobatrachus diluvianus. 40pf, Clock, 1720. 50pf, Table telescope, 1750.

1978, Oct. 24 Photo. *Perf. 14*

1958 A595 10pf multicolored .25 .25
1959 A595 20pf multicolored .25 .25
1960 A595 25pf multicolored .25 .25
1961 A595 35pf multicolored .25 .25
1962 A595 40pf multicolored .25 .25
1963 A595 50pf multicolored *1.60 1.40*
Nos. 1958-1963 (6) 2.85 2.65

Dresden Museum of Natural History, 250th anniversary.

Wheel Lock Gun, 1630 — A596

Hunting Guns: 10pf, Double-barreled gun, 1978. 20pf, Spring cock gun, 1780. 25pf, Superimposed double-barreled gun, 1978. 35pf, Percussion gun, 1850. 70pf, Three-barreled gun, 1978.

1978, Nov. 21 Photo. *Perf. 14*

1964 A596 5pf silver & multi .25 .25
1965 A596 10pf silver & multi .25 .25
1966 A596 20pf silver & multi .25 .25
1967 A596 25pf silver & multi .30 .30
1968 A596 35pf silver & multi .35 .35
a. Vert. strip of 3, 5, 20, 35pf 1.10 1.10
1969 A596 70pf silver & multi .80 .80
a. Vert. strip of 3, 10, 25, 70pf 2.10 1.90
Nos. 1964-1969 (6) 2.20 2.20

Printed in sheets of 9.

Rapunzel's Father and Witch — A597

Designs: Scenes from fairy tale "Rapunzel."

1978, Nov. 21 Litho. *Perf. 13*

1970 A597 10pf multicolored .25 .25
1971 A597 15pf multicolored .70 .70
1972 A597 20pf multicolored .25 .25
1973 A597 25pf multicolored .25 .25
1974 A597 35pf multicolored .70 .70
1975 A597 50pf multicolored .25 .25
a. Sheet of 6, #1970-1975 2.50 2.50

Chaffinches A598

Song Birds: 10pf, Nuthatch. 20pf, Robin. 25pf, Bullfinches. 35pf, Blue tit. 50pf, Red linnets.

1979, Jan. 9 Photo. *Perf. 13½x14*

1976 A598 5pf multicolored .25 .25
1977 A598 10pf multicolored .25 .25
1978 A598 20pf multicolored .25 .25
1979 A598 25pf multicolored .25 .25
1980 A598 35pf multicolored .25 .25
1981 A598 50pf multicolored *1.90 .95*
Nos. 1976-1981 (6) 3.15 2.20

Chabo Cock — A599

German Cocks: 15pf, Kraienkopp. 20pf, Porcelain-colored bantam. 25pf, Saxonian. 35pf, Phoenix. 50pf, Striped Italian.

1979, Jan. 23 *Perf. 14x13½*

1982 A599 10pf multicolored .25 .25
1983 A599 15pf multicolored .25 .25
1984 A599 20pf multicolored .25 .25
1985 A599 25pf multicolored .25 .25
1986 A599 35pf multicolored .25 .25
1987 A599 50pf multicolored *1.60 1.25*
Nos. 1982-1987 (6) 2.85 2.50

Telephone Operators, 1900 and 1979 — A600

35pf, Telegraph operators, 1880 and 1979.

1979, Feb. 6 Photo. *Perf. 13½x14*

1988 A600 20pf multicolored .25 .25
1989 A600 35pf multicolored .80 .40

Development of German postal telephone and telegraph service.

Souvenir Sheet

Albert Einstein (1879-1955), Theoretical Physicist — A601

1979, Feb. 20 Litho. *Perf. 14*

1990 A601 1m multicolored *1.75 3.00*

Max Klinger House, Leipzig — A602

Leipzig Spring Fair: 25pf, Horizontal drilling and milling machine, horiz.

1979, Mar. 6 Litho. *Perf. 14*

1991 A602 10pf multicolored .25 .25
1992 A602 25pf multicolored .30 .25

Container Ship, Tug, World Map and IMCO Emblem — A603

1979, Mar. 20 Photo.

1993 A603 20pf multicolored .45 .25

World Navigation Day.

Otto Hahn and Equation of Nuclear Fission A604

Famous Germans: 10pf, Max von Laue (1879-1969) and diagram of sulphide zinc. 20pf, Arthur Scheunert (1879-1957), symbol of nutrition and health. 25pf, Friedrich August Kekulé (1829-1896), and benzene ring. 35pf, George Forster (1754-1794) and Capt. Cook's ship Resolution. 70pf, Gotthold Ephraim Lessing (1729-1781) and title page for Nathan the Wise.

1979, Mar. 20 Litho. *Perf. 13x12½*

1994 A604 5pf pale salmon & blk .25 .25
1995 A604 10pf blue gray & blk .25 .25
1996 A604 20pf lemon & blk .25 .25
1997 A604 25pf lt green & blk .25 .25
1998 A604 35pf lt blue & blk .25 .25
1999 A604 70pf pink & blk *1.60 1.00*
Nos. 1994-1999 (6) 2.85 2.25

See Nos. 2088-2093.

Miniature Sheet

A605

Design: 20pf, Horch 8, 1911. 35pf, Trabant 601S de luxe, 1978.

1979, Apr. 3 Litho. *Perf. 14*

2000 A605 Sheet of 2 + label *1.60 1.25*
a. 20pf multicolored *.30 .30*
b. 35pf multicolored *.45 .45*

Sachsenring automobile plant, Zwickau.

Self-Propelled Car — A606

DDR Railroad Cars: 10pf, Self-unloading freight car Us-y. 20pf, Diesel locomotive BR 110. 35pf, Laaes automobile carrier.

1979, Apr. 17 Litho. *Perf. 13*

2001 A606 5pf multicolored .25 .25
2002 A606 10pf multicolored .25 .25
2003 A606 20pf multicolored .25 .25
2004 A606 35pf multicolored *.65 .55*
Nos. 2001-2004 (4) 1.40 1.30

Durga, 18th Century — A607

Indian Miniatures in Berlin Museums: 35pf, Mahavira, 15th-16th cents. 50pf, Todi Ragini, 17th cent. 70pf, Asavari Ragini, 17th cent.

1979, May 8 Photo. *Perf. 14x13½*

2005 A607 20pf multicolored .25 .25
2006 A607 35pf multicolored .25 .25
2007 A607 50pf multicolored .25 .25
2008 A607 70pf multicolored *1.75 1.75*
Nos. 2005-2008 (4) 2.50 2.50

Youth Gathering — A608

Design: 10pf+5pf, Torchlight parade of German youth, Oct. 7, 1949.

1979, May 22 Photo. *Perf. 14*

2009	10pf + 5pf multi	.25	.25
2010	20pf multicolored	.25	.25
a.	A608 Strip of 2, #2009-2010 + label	.65	.65

National Youth Festival, Berlin.

Housing Project, Berlin A609

20pf, Berlin-Marzahn building site & surveyors.

1979, May 22 Litho. *Perf. 13x12½*

2011	A609 10pf multicolored	.25	.25
2012	A609 20pf multicolored	.30	.30

Berlin Project of Free German Youth.

Children Playing and Reading — A610

20pf, Doctor with black & white children.

1979, May 22 Photo. *Perf. 14*

2013	A610 10pf multicolored	.25	.25
2014	A610 20pf multicolored	.35	.35

International Year of the Child.

Exhibition Emblem — A611

1979, June 5

2015	A611 10pf multicolored	.35	.25

Agra '79 Agricultural Exhib., Markkleeberg.

Ferry Boats — A612

1979, June 26 Photo. *Perf. 14*

2016	20pf Rostock	.30	.30
2017	35pf Rugen	.30	.30
a.	A612 Strip of 2, #2016-2017 + label	1.20	.90

Railroad ferry from Sassnitz, DDR, to Trelleborg, Sweden, 70th anniversary.

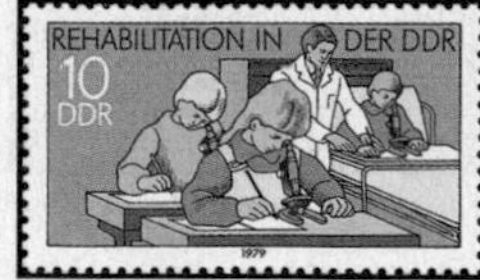
Hospital Classroom — A613

Design: 35pf, Handicapped workers.

1979, June 26 Litho. *Perf. 13x12½*

2018	A613 10pf multicolored	.25	.25
2019	A613 35pf multicolored	.40	.35

Rehabilitation in DDR.

Bicyclists A614

Design: 20pf, Roller skating.

1979, July 3

2020	A614 10pf multicolored	.25	.25
2021	A614 20pf multicolored	.40	.35

7th Children's and Youth Spartakiad, Berlin.

Dahlia "Rubens" A615

Dahlias: 20pf, Rosalie. 25pf, Corinna. 35pf, Enzett-Dolli. 50pf, Enzett-Carola. 70pf, Don Lorenzo.

1979, July 17 Photo. *Perf. 13*

2022	A615 10pf multicolored	.25	.25
2023	A615 20pf multicolored	.25	.25
2024	A615 25pf multicolored	.25	.25
2025	A615 35pf multicolored	.25	.25
2026	A615 50pf multicolored	.25	.25
2027	A615 70pf multicolored	2.00	1.75
	Nos. 2022-2027 (6)	3.25	3.00

Dahlias shown at International Garden Exhibition, Erfurt.

Russian Alphabet Around Congress Emblem A616

1979, Aug. 7 Photo. *Perf. 13*

2028	A616 20pf multicolored	.30	.25

4th International Congress of Teachers of Russian Language and Literature, Berlin.

Dandelion Fountain, Dresden — A617

1979, Aug. 7 *Perf. 14*

2029	A617 20pf multicolored	.25	.25

Souvenir Sheet

Composite of Dresden Buildings — A618

1979, Aug. 7 Litho. *Perf. 13x12½*

2030	A618 1m multicolored	1.60	1.40

DDR '79, Natl. Stamp Exhib., Dresden. See No. B187.

Italian Lira da Gamba, 1592 — A619

Musical Instruments, Leipzig Museum: 25pf, French "serpent," 17th-18th centuries. 40pf, French barrel lyre, 18th century. 85pf, German tenor trumpet, 19th century.

1979, Aug. 21 *Perf. 14*

2031	A619 20pf multicolored	.25	.25
2032	A619 25pf multicolored	.25	.25
2033	A619 40pf multicolored	.25	.25
2034	A619 85pf multicolored	1.90	1.40
	Nos. 2031-2034 (4)	2.65	2.15

Galloping — A620

1979, Aug. 21

2035	A620 10pf shown	.25	.25
2036	A620 25pf Dressage	.65	.60

30th International Horse-breeding Congress of Socialist Countries, Berlin.

Memorial Monument, Nordhausen A621

1979, Aug. 28 Photo. *Perf. 14*

2037	A621 35pf dull vio & blk	.40	.30

Memorial to World War II victims.

Teddy Bear — A622

Leipzig Autumn Fair: 25pf, Grosser Blumenberg (building), Leipzig, horiz.

1979, Aug. 28

2038	A622 10pf multicolored	.25	.25
2039	A622 25pf multicolored	.25	.25

Philipp Dengel (1888-1948) A623

Working-Class Movement Leaders: No. 2041, Heinrich Rau (1899-1961). No. 2042, Otto Buchwitz (1879-1964). No. 2043, Bernard Koenen (1889-1964).

1979, Sept. 11 Litho.

2040	A623 10pf multicolored	.25	.25
2041	A623 10pf multicolored	.25	.25
2042	A623 10pf multicolored	.25	.25
2043	A623 10pf multicolored	.25	.25
	Nos. 2040-2043 (4)	1.00	1.00

See Nos. 2166-2169, 2249-2253, 2314-2318, 2390-2392, 2452-2454.

DDR Arms and Flag, Worker A624

DDR Arms, Flag and: 10pf, Young man and woman. 15pf, Soldiers. 20pf, Workers.

1979, Oct. 2 Photo. *Perf. 13*

2044	A624 5pf multicolored	.25	.25
2045	A624 10pf multicolored	.25	.25
2046	A624 15pf multicolored	.35	.35
2047	A624 20pf multicolored	.25	.25
	Nos. 2044-2047 (4)	1.10	1.10

Souvenir Sheet

2048	A624 1m multicolored	1.25	2.10

DDR, 30th anniv. No. 2048 contains one stamp (33x55mm).

Woman Applying Make-Up, 1967 — A625

Meissen Porcelain and Hallmark, 18th-20th Centuries: 10pf, Altozier coffee pot. 15pf, "Grosser Ausschnitt" coffee pot, 1974. 20pf, Covered vase. 25pf, Parrot. 35pf, Harlequin drinking. 50pf, Woman selling flowers. 70pf, Sake bottle.

1979, Nov. 6 Photo. *Perf. 14*

2049	A625 5pf multicolored	.25	.25
2050	A625 10pf multicolored	.25	.25
2051	A625 15pf multicolored	.25	.25
2052	A625 20pf multicolored	.30	.30
a.	Block of 4, #2049-2052	2.60	2.00

2053 A625 25pf multicolored .35 .35
2054 A625 35pf multicolored .55 .55
2055 A625 50pf multicolored .75 .75
2056 A625 70pf multicolored 1.00 1.00
a. Block of 4, #2053-2056 5.25 5.00

Rag Doll, 1800 — A626

Historic Dolls: 15pf, Ceramic, 1960. 20pf, Wooden, 1780. 35pf, Straw, 1900. 50pf, Jointed, 1800. 70pf, Tumbler, 1820.

1979, Nov. 20 **Litho.**
2057 A626 10pf multicolored .25 .25
2058 A626 15pf multicolored .80 .80
2059 A626 20pf multicolored .25 .25
2060 A626 35pf multicolored .25 .25
2061 A626 50pf multicolored .80 .80
2062 A626 70pf multicolored .25 .25
a. Sheet of 6, #2057-2062 3.00 3.00

Bobsledding, by Gunter Rechn, Olympic Rings — A627

Olympic Rings and: 20pf, Figure Skating, by Johanna Stake, vert. 35pf, Speed Skating, by Axel Wunsch, vert. 1m, Cross-country Skiing, by Lothar Zitzmann.

1980, Jan. 15 **Photo.** ***Perf. 14***
2063 A627 10pf multicolored .25 .25
2064 A627 20pf multicolored .25 .25
2065 A627 35pf multicolored 1.10 1.00
Nos. 2063-2065,B189 (4) 1.85 1.75

Souvenir Sheet

2066 A627 1m multicolored 1.75 3.25

13th Winter Olympic Games, Lake Placid, NY, Feb. 12-24. No. 2066 contains one 29x23½mm stamp. See Nos. 2098-2099, 2119-2121, B189-B190, B192.

"Quiet Music," Grossedlitz — A628

Baroque Gardens: 20pf, Orange grove, Belvedere, Weimar. 50pf, Flower garden, Dornburg Castle. 70pf, Park, Rheinsberg Castle.

1980, Jan. 29
2067 A628 10pf multicolored .25 .25
2068 A628 20pf multicolored .25 .25
2069 A628 50pf multicolored .25 .25
2070 A628 70pf multicolored 1.20 1.20
Nos. 2067-2070 (4) 1.95 1.95

Type of 1973

Designs as before and: 10pf, Palace of the Republic, Berlin.

1980-81 **Engr.** ***Perf. 14***
Size: 22x17mm

2071 A449 5pf blue green .25 .25
2072 A449 10pf emerald .25 .25
2073 A449 15pf rose lilac .25 .25
2074 A449 20pf rose mag .40 .25
2075 A449 25pf grnsh bl .35 .30
2076 A449 30pf org ('81) .40 .30
2077 A449 35pf blue .40 .30
2078 A449 40pf dull vio .65 .50
2079 A449 50pf blue .45 .30
2080 A449 60pf lilac ('81) .55 .30
2081 A449 70pf redsh brn ('81) .60 .60
2082 A449 80pf vio bl ('81) .70 .50
2083 A449 1m olive .80 .45
2084 A449a 2m red 1.40 .55
2085 A449a 3m rose lil ('81) 2.25 .65
Nos. 2071-2085 (15) 9.70 5.75

Cable-Laying Vehicle, Dish Antenna — A629

20pf, Radio tower, television screen.

1980, Feb. 5 **Photo.**
2086 A629 10pf multicolored .25 .25
2087 A629 20pf multicolored .25 .25

Famous Germans Type of 1979

Designs: 5pf, Johann Wolfgang Dobereiner (1780-1849), chemist. 10pf, Frederic Joliot-Curie (1900-1958), French physicist. 20pf, Johann Friedrich Naumann (1780-1857), ornithologist. 25pf, Alfred Wegener (1880-1930), geophysicist and meteorologist. 35pf, Carl von Clausewitz (1780-1831), Prussian major general. 70pf, Helene Weigel (1900-1971), actress.

1980, Feb. 26 **Litho.** ***Perf. 13x12½***
2088 A604 5pf pale yel & blk .25 .25
2089 A604 10pf multicolored .25 .25
2090 A604 20pf lt yel grn & blk .25 .25
2091 A604 25pf multicolored .25 .25
2092 A604 35pf lt blue & blk .25 .25
2093 A604 70pf lt red brn & blk 1.10 .85
Nos. 2088-2093 (6) 2.35 2.10

Type ZT-303 Tractor A630

1980 Leipzig Spring Fair: 10pf, Karl Marx University, Leipzig, vert.

1980, Mar. 4 **Photo.** ***Perf. 14***
2094 A630 10pf multicolored .25 .25
2095 A630 25pf multicolored .30 .25

Werner Eggerath (1900-1977), Labor Leader — A631

1980, Mar. 18 **Litho.**
2096 A631 10pf brick red & blk .40 .30

Souvenir Sheet

Cosmonauts, Salyut 6 and Soyuz — A632

1980, Apr. 11 **Litho.** ***Perf. 14***
2097 A632 1m multicolored 1.60 2.60

Intercosmos cooperative space program.

Olympic Type of 1980

Designs: 10pf, On the Bars, by Erich Wurzer. 50pf, Scull's Crew, by Wilfried Falkenthal.

1980, Apr. 22 **Photo.** ***Perf. 14***
2098 A627 10pf multicolored .25 .25
2099 A627 50pf multicolored 1.10 .90
Nos. 2098-2099,B190 (3) 1.60 1.40

22nd Summer Olympic Games, Moscow, July 19-Aug. 3. See No. B190.

Flags of Member Countries — A633

1980, May 13 **Photo.**
2100 A633 20pf multicolored .40 .25

Signing of Warsaw Pact (Bulgaria, Czechoslovakia, DDR, Hungary, Poland, Romania, USSR), 25th anniv.

Bauhaus Cooperative Society Building, 1928, Gropius — A634

Bauhaus Architecture: 10pf, Socialists' Memorial, 1926, by Mies van der Rohe, horiz. 15pf, Monument, 1922, by William Gropius. 20pf, Steel building, 1926, by Muche and Paulick, horiz. 50pf, Trade-Union School, 1928, by Meyer. 70pf, Bauhaus Building, 1926, by Gropius, horiz.

1980, May 27
2101 A634 5pf multicolored .25 .25
2102 A634 10pf multicolored .25 .25
2103 A634 15pf multicolored .25 .25
2104 A634 20pf multicolored .25 .25
2105 A634 50pf multicolored .30 .25
2106 A634 70pf multicolored 1.60 1.40
Nos. 2101-2106 (6) 2.90 2.65

Rostock View A635

1980, June 10 **Photo.** ***Perf. 14***
2107 A635 10pf shown .25 .25
2108 A635 20pf Dancers .30 .25

18th Workers' Festival, Rostock, June 27-29.

Dish Antenna, Interflug Airlines A636

25pf, Jet. 35pf, Agricultural plane. 70pf, Aerial photography.

1980, June 10 **Litho.** ***Perf. 13x12½***
2109 A636 20pf shown .30 .30
2110 A636 25pf multi .30 .30
2111 A636 35pf multi .40 .40
2112 A636 70pf multi .80 .80
a. Block of 4, #2109-2112 2.25 2.25

Interflug Airlines. See No. B191

Okapi — A637

10pf, Red pandas. 15pf, Prairie wolf. 20pf, Arabian oryx. 25pf, White-eared pheasant. 35pf, Musk oxen.

1980, June 24 ***Perf. 14***
2113 A637 5pf shown .25 .25
2114 A637 10pf multi .25 .25
2115 A637 15pf multi .25 .25
2116 A637 20pf multi .25 .25
2117 A637 25pf multi .25 .25
2118 A637 35pf multi 1.60 1.60
Nos. 2113-2118 (6) 2.85 2.85

Olympic Type of 1980

Designs: 10pf, Judo, by Erhard Schmidt. 50pf, Final Spurt, by Siegfried Schreiber. 1m, Spinnaker Yachts, by Karl Raetsch.

1980, July 8 **Photo.** ***Perf. 14***
2119 A627 10pf multicolored .25 .25
2120 A627 50pf multicolored 1.10 .90
Nos. 2119-2120,B192 (3) 1.60 1.40

Souvenir Sheet

2121 A627 1m multicolored 1.60 2.60

22nd Summer Olympic Games, Moscow, 7/19-8/3. No. 2121 contains one 29x24mm stamp.

6th National Youth Philatelic Exhibition, Suhl — A638

Design: 10pf + 5pf, View of Suhl, 1700. 20pf, Old and New Buildings, Suhl.

1980, July 22 **Litho.** ***Perf. 13x12½***
2122 10pf + 5pf multi .30 .30
2123 20pf multicolored .30 .30
a. A638 Pair, #2122-2123 + label 1.00 .85

Surtax for East German Association of Philatelists.

Huntley Microscope, London, 1740 — A639

Optical Museum, Karl Zeiss Foundation, Jena: 25pf, Magny microscope, Paris, 1751. 35pf, Amici microscope, Modena, 1845. 70pf, Zeiss microscope, Jena, 1873.

1980, Aug. 12 **Photo.** ***Perf. 14***
2124 A639 20pf multicolored .30 .30
2125 A639 25pf multicolored .30 .30
2126 A639 35pf multicolored .45 .45
2127 A639 70pf multicolored .65 .65
a. Block of 4, #2124-2127 3.00 3.00

Maidenek Memorial — A640

1980, Aug. 26
2128 A640 35pf multicolored .40 .30

Leipzig 1980 Autumn Fair, Information Center — A641

1980, Aug. 26
2129 A641 10pf shown .25 .25
2130 A641 25pf Carpet loom .40 .25

67th Interparliamentary Conference, Berlin — A642

1980, Sept. 9 Photo. *Perf. 14*
2131 A642 20pf Republic Palace, Berlin .60 .25

Paintings by Frans Hals (1580-1666) A643

10pf, *Laughing Boy with Flute.* 20pf, *Man in Gray Coat.* 25pf, *The Mulatto.* 35pf, *Man in Black Coat.*
1m, *Self-portrait,* horiz.

1980, Sept. 23
2132 A643 10pf multicolored .25 .25
2133 A643 20pf multicolored .25 .25
2134 A643 25pf multicolored .25 .25
2135 A643 35pf multicolored *.80 .65*
Nos. 2132-2135 (4) 1.55 1.40

Souvenir Sheet

2136 A643 1m multicolored *1.60 3.25*

A644

Edible Mushrooms: 5pf, Leccinum Testaceo Scabrum. 10pf, Boletus erythropus. 15pf, Agaricus campester. 20pf, Xerocomus badius. 35pf, Boletus edulis. 70pf, Cantharellus cibarius.

1980, Oct. 28 Litho. *Perf. 13x13½*
2137 A644 5pf multicolored .25 .25
2138 A644 10pf multicolored .25 .25
2139 A644 15pf multicolored .25 .25
2140 A644 20pf multicolored .25 .25
2141 A644 35pf multicolored .25 .25
2142 A644 70pf multicolored 1.40 1.25
Nos. 2137-2142 (6) 2.65 2.50

Exploration of Lignite Deposits (Gravimetry) — A645

Geophysical Exploration: 25pf, Bore-hole measuring (water). 35pf, Seismic geology. (mineral oil, natural gas). 50pf, Seismology.

1980, Nov. 11 Litho. *Perf. 13*
2143 A645 20pf multicolored .30 .25
2144 A645 25pf multicolored .35 .30
2145 A645 35pf multicolored .40 .40
2146 A645 50pf multicolored .65 .65
a. Block of 4, #2143-2146 3.00 2.40

Radebeul-Radeburg Railroad Locomotive — A646

No. 1247 — b, Passenger car.
No. 1248 — a, Bad Doberan-Osteebad Kuhlungsborn Locomotive. b, Passenger car.

1980, Nov. 25 *Perf. 13x12½*
2147 Strip of 2 + label *1.25 1.25*
a. A646 20pf shown .30 .30
b. A646 25pf multi .30 .30
2148 Strip of 2 + label *1.25 1.25*
a. A646 20pf multi .30 .30
b. A646 35pf multi .30 .30

Labels show maps of routes and Moritzburg Castle (No. 2147), Bad Doberan Street (No. 2148).
See Nos. 2205-2206.

A647

1980, Dec. 9 *Perf. 14*
2149 A647 Sheet of 6 *2.60 2.50*
a. 10pf Toy Locomotive, 1850 *.30 .30*
b. 20pf Airplane, 1914 *.80 .80*
c. 25pf Steam roller, 1920 *.30 .30*
d. 35pf Ship, 1825 *.30 .30*
e. 40pf Car, 1900 *.80 .80*
f. 50pf Balloon, 1920 *.30 .30*

Souvenir Sheet

Wolfgang Amadeus Mozart, 225th Birth Anniv. — A648

1981, Jan. 13 Litho.
2150 A648 1m multicolored *2.00 3.00*

St. John's Apple — A649

10pf, Snow drop, horiz. 20pf, Bladder bush. 25pf, Paulownia tomentose. 35pf, German honeysuckle, horiz. 50pf, Genuine spice bush.

1981, Jan. 13 Photo.
2151 A649 5pf shown .25 .25
2152 A649 10pf multicolored .25 .25
2153 A649 20pf multicolored .25 .25
2154 A649 25pf multicolored .25 .25
2155 A649 35pf multicolored .25 .25
2156 A649 50pf multicolored *1.60 1.40*
Nos. 2151-2156 (6) 2.85 2.65

Heinrich von Stephan (1831-97), Founder of UPU — A650

1981, Jan. 20 Litho. *Perf. 13x13½*
2157 A650 10pf lt lemon & blk .45 .25

Dedication of National Commemorative Plaza, Sachsenhausen — A651

1981, Jan. 27 Photo. *Perf. 14*
2158 A651 10pf shown .25 .25
2159 A651 20pf Changing of guard .30 .25

National People's Forces, 25th anniversary.

Socialist Union Party, 10th Congress — A652

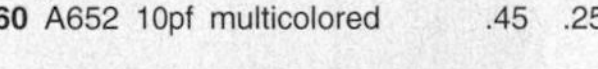

1981, Feb. 10
2160 A652 10pf multicolored .45 .25

Postal and Newspaper Apprentice Training — A653

10pf, Telephone and telex service. 15pf, Radio communications. 20pf, School of Engineering, Leipzig. 25pf, Communications Academy, Dresden.

1981, Feb. 10 Litho.
2161 A653 5pf shown .25 .25
2162 A653 10pf multicolored .25 .25
2163 A653 15pf multicolored .25 .25
2164 A653 20pf multicolored .25 .25
2165 A653 25pf multicolored *.90 .65*
Nos. 2161-2165 (5) 1.90 1.65

Working-class Leader Type of 1979

Designs: No. 2166, Erich Baron (1881-1933). No. 2167, Conrad Blenkle (1901-1943). No. 2168, Arthur Ewert (1890-1959). No. 2169, Walter Stoecker (1891-1939).

1981, Feb. 24 Litho. *Perf. 14*
2166 A623 10pf gray grn & blk .25 .25
2167 A623 10pf lemon & blk .25 .25
2168 A623 10pf bl vio & blk .25 .25
2169 A623 10pf lt red brn & blk .25 .25
Nos. 2166-2169 (4) 1.00 1.00

Merkur Hotel, Leipzig — A654

1981 Leipzig Spring Fair: 25pf, Takraf mining conveyor system, horiz.

1981, Mar. 10 Photo. *Perf. 14*
2170 A654 10pf multicolored .25 .25
2171 A654 25pf multicolored .35 .25

Ernst Thälmann, by Willi Sitte — A655

10th Communist Party Congress (Paintings): 20pf, Worker, by Bernhard Heising, 25pf, Festivities, by Rudolf Bergander. 35pf, Brotherhood in Arms, by Paul Michaelis. 1m, When Communists Dream, by Walter Womacka.

1981, Mar. 24
2172 A655 10pf multicolored .25 .25
2173 A655 20pf multicolored .25 .25
2174 A655 25pf multicolored *.65 .55*
2175 A655 35pf multicolored .25 .25
Nos. 2172-2175 (4) 1.40 1.30

Souvenir Sheet

2176 A655 1m multicolored *1.25 1.60*

Souvenir Sheet

Opening of Sport and Recreation Center, Berlin — A656

1981, Mar. 24 Litho.
2177 A656 1m multicolored *1.90 3.25*

Energy Conservation A657

1981, Apr. 21 Litho. *Perf. 12½x13*
2178 A657 10pf orange & blk .25 .25

Heinrich Barkhausen (1881-1956), Physicist — A658

Famous Men: 20pf, Johannes R. Becher (1891-1958), poet. 25pf, Richard Dedekind (1831-1916), mathematician. 35pf, Georg Philipp Telemann (1681-1767), composer. 50pf, Adelbert V. Chamisso (1781-1838), botanist. 70pf, Wilhelm Raabe (1831-1910), writer.

1981, May 5 *Perf. 13x12½*
2179 A658 10pf dull bl & blk .25 .25
2180 A658 20pf brick red & blk .25 .25
2181 A658 25pf dull brn & blk *1.90 1.25*
2182 A658 35pf lt vio & blk .25 .25
2183 A658 50pf yel grn & blk .30 .25
2184 A658 70pf ol bis & blk .40 .25
Nos. 2179-2184 (6) *3.35 2.50*

Free German Youth Members A659

1981, May 19

2185 A659 10pf shown .25 .25
2186 A659 20pf Youths, diff. .25 .25
a. Pair, #2185-2186 + label .70 .65

Free German Youth, 11th Parliament, Berlin.

View and Map of Worlitz Park — A660

1981, June 9 Litho. *Perf. 12½x13*

2187 A660 5pf shown .25 .25
2188 A660 10pf Tiefurt .25 .25
2189 A660 15pf Marxwalde .25 .25
2190 A660 20pf Branitz .25 .25
2191 A660 25pf Treptow 1.25 1.00
2192 A660 35pf Wiesenburg .25 .25
Nos. 2187-2192 (6) 2.50 2.25

Artistic Gymnastics — A661

8th Children's and Youth Spartacist Games: No. 2193, children and youths.

1981, June 23 Photo. *Perf. 14*

2193 A661 10pf + 5pf multi .45 .35
2194 A661 20pf multicolored .25 .25

Javelin Throwers A662

1981, June 23 Litho. *Perf. 13x12½*

2195 A662 5pf shown .25 .25
2196 A662 15pf Men at museum .25 .25
a. Pair, #2195-2196 + label .65 .50

Intl. Year of the Disabled.

Schinkel's Berlin Playhouse — A663

Karl Friedrich Schinkel, (1781-1841), Architect: 25pf, Old Museum, Berlin.

1981, June 23 Litho. & Engr.

2197 A663 10pf tan & blk .70 .25
2198 A663 25pf tan & blk 1.60 .70

Sugar Loaf House, Gross Zicker — A664

Frame Houses: 10pf, Zaulsdorf, 19th cent., vert. 25pf, Farmhouse, stable, Weckersdorf, vert. 35pf, Restaurant (former farmhouse), Pillgram. 50pf, Eschenbach, vert. 70pf, Farmhouse, Lüdersdorf.

1981, July 7 Photo.

2199 A664 10pf multicolored .25 .25
2200 A664 20pf multicolored .25 .25
2201 A664 25pf multicolored .25 .25
2202 A664 35pf multicolored .25 .25
2203 A664 50pf multicolored .30 .25
2204 A664 70pf multicolored 2.25 1.75
Nos. 2199-2204 (6) 3.55 3.00

Railroad Type of 1980

No. 2205 — a, Locomotive, Freital-Kurort-Kipsdorf line. b, Luggage car.
No. 2206 — a, Locomotive, Putbus-Gohren line. b, Passenger car.

1981, July 21 Litho. *Perf. 13x12½*

2205 Strip of 2 + label .70 .65
a. A646 5pf multi .25 .25
b. A646 15pf multi .25 .25
2206 Strip of 2 + label .70 .65
a. A646 5pf multi .25 .25
b. A646 20pf multi .25 .25

Labels show maps of train routes.

Ebers Papyrus (Egyptian Medical Text, 1600 B.C.), Leipzig — A665

Literary Treasures in DDR Libraries: 35pf, Maya manuscript, 12th cent., Dresden. 50pf, Petrarch sonnet illustration, 16th century French manuscript, Berlin.

1981, Aug. 18 Photo. *Perf. 14*

2207 A665 20pf multicolored .25 .25
2208 A665 35pf multicolored .25 .25
2209 A665 50pf multicolored 1.20 1.20
Nos. 2207-2209 (3) 1.70 1.70

Chemical Plant — A666

Leipzig 1981 Autumn Fair: 25pf, Concert Hall, Leipzig, horiz.

1981, Aug. 18

2210 A666 10pf multicolored .25 .25
2211 A666 25pf multicolored .35 .30

Anti-Fascist Resistance Monument, Sassnitz A667

1981, Sept. 8 Photo. *Perf. 14*

2212 A667 35pf multicolored .40 .30

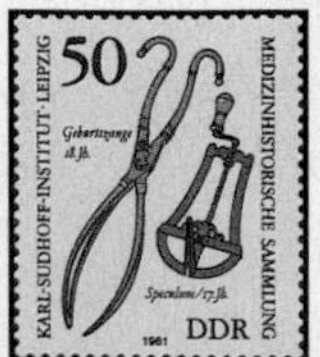

Forceps, 18th Cent., Speculum, 17th Cent. — A668

Historic Medical Instruments, Karl Sudhoff Institute, Leipzig: 10pf, Henbana, censer, 16th cent. 20pf, Pelican, dental elevator and extractors, 17th cent. 25pf, Seton forceps, 17th cent. 35pf, Lithotomy knife, 18th cent., hernia scissors, 17th cent. 85pf, Elevators, 17th cent. 10pf, 20pf, 25pf, 35pf horiz.

1981, Sept. 22

2213 A668 10pf multicolored .25 .25
2214 A668 20pf multicolored .25 .25
2215 A668 25pf multicolored .25 .25
2216 A668 35pf multicolored .25 .25
2217 A668 50pf multicolored 2.00 2.00
2218 A668 85pf multicolored .45 .30
Nos. 2213-2218 (6) 3.45 3.30

Philatelists' Day — A669

10pf, Letter by Engels, 1840. 20pf, Postcard by Marx, 1878.

1981, Oct. 6 Photo. *Perf. 14*

2219 A669 10pf + 5pf multi .65 .15
2220 A669 20pf multi .25 .25

River Boat A670

1981, Oct. 20

2221 A670 10pf Tugboat .25 .25
2222 A670 20pf Tugboat, diff. .25 .25
2223 A670 25pf Diesel paddle liner .25 .25
2224 A670 35pf Ice breaker .25 .25
2225 A670 50pf Motor freighter .30 .25
2226 A670 85pf Bucket dredger 2.10 2.00
Nos. 2221-2226 (6) 3.40 3.25

Windmill, Dabel — A671

1981, Nov. 10 Photo. *Perf. 14*

2227 A671 10pf shown .25 .25
2228 A671 20pf Pahrenz .25 .25
2229 A671 25pf Dresden-Gohlis .25 .25
2230 A671 70pf Ballstadt 1.25 1.20
Nos. 2227-2230 (4) 2.00 1.95

Toys — A672

1981, Nov. 24 Litho. *Perf. 13½*

2231 A672 Sheet of 6 3.00 3.25
a. 10pf Jointed snake, 1850 .30 .30
b. 20pf Teddy bear, 1910 .30 .30
c. 25pf Fish, 1935 .80 .80
d. 35pf Hobby horse, 1850 .80 .80
e. 40pf Cuckoo, 1800 .30 .30
f. 70pf Frog, 1930 .30 .30

Meissen Porcelain Teapot, 1715 — A673

20pf, Vase, 1715. 25pf, Oberon figurine, 1969. 35pf, Day and Night vase, 1979.

1982, Jan. 26 Photo. *Perf. 14*

2232 A673 10pf shown .25 .25
2233 A673 20pf multicolored .30 .30
2234 A673 25pf multicolored .40 .40
2235 A673 35pf multicolored .55 .55
a. Block of 4, #2232-2235 1.90 1.60

Souvenir Sheet

2236 Sheet of 2 2.10 3.25
a. A673 50pf Portrait .65 1.25
b. A673 50pf Emblem .65 1.25

Johann Friedrich Bottger (1682-1719), inventor of Dresden china. No. 2236 contains two 24x29mm stamps.

Post Offices — A674

1982, Feb. 9

2237 A674 20pf Liebenstein .25 .25
2238 A674 25pf Berlin .25 .25
2239 A674 35pf Erfurt .25 .25
2240 A674 50pf Dresden 1.60 1.10
Nos. 2237-2240 (4) 2.35 1.85

Intl. Fur Auction, Leipzig A675

1982, Feb. 23 Photo. *Perf. 14*

2241 A675 10pf Marmot, vert. .25 .25
2242 A675 20pf Polecat .25 .25
2243 A675 25pf Mink .25 .25
2244 A675 35pf Stone marten 1.00 .85
Nos. 2241-2244 (4) 1.75 1.60

Souvenir Sheet

Goethe-Schiller Awards, 1980-1984 — A676

1982, Mar. 9 Litho.

2245 A676 Sheet of 2 2.25 3.25
a. 50pf Goethe .85 1.25
b. 50pf Schiller .85 1.25

1982 Leipzig Spring Fair A677

1982, Mar. 9 *Perf. 13x12½*

2246 A677 10pf Entrance .25 .25
2247 A677 25pf Exhibit .30 .25

Souvenir Sheet

TB Bacillus Centenary — A678

1982, Mar. 23 ***Perf. 14***

2248 A678 1m multi *1.60 3.25*

Working-class Leader Type of 1979

No. 2249, Max Fechner (1892-1973). No. 2250, Ottomar Greschke (1882-1957). No. 2251, Helmut Lehmann (1882-1959). No. 2252, Herbert Warnke (1902-75). No. 2253, Otto Winzer (1902-75).

1982, Mar. 23 **Engr.**

2249 A623 10pf dk red brn .25 .25
2250 A623 10pf green .25 .25
2251 A623 10pf violet .25 .25
2252 A623 10pf dull blue .25 .25
2253 A623 10pf gray olive .25 .25
Nos. 2249-2253 (5) 1.25 1.25

Poisonous Plants — A679

1982, Apr. 6 **Litho.** ***Perf. 14***

2254 A679 10pf Meadow saffron .25 .25
2255 A679 15pf Water arum .25 .25
2256 A679 20pf Marsh tea .25 .25
2257 A679 25pf White bryony .25 .25
2258 A679 35pf Common monks-hood .25 .25
2259 A679 50pf Henbane *1.25 1.10*
Nos. 2254-2259 (6) *2.50 2.35*

Free Federation of German Trade Unions, 10th Congress A680

Paintings: 10pf, Mother and Child, by Walter Womacka. 20pf, Discussion at the Innovator Collective, by Willi Neubert, horiz. 25pf, Young Couple, by Karl-Heinz Jacob.

1982, Apr. 20 **Photo.**

2260 A680 10pf multi .25 .25
2261 A680 20pf multi .25 .25
2262 A680 25pf multi .45 .40
Nos. 2260-2262 (3) .95 .90

Intl. Book Art Exhibition, Leipzig — A681

1982, Apr. 20

2263 A681 15pf "I" *.35 .35*
2264 A681 35pf Emblem *.35 .35*
a. Pair, #2263-2264 + label *1.10 1.00*

A682

Protected species. 10pf, 25pf, 35pf vert.

Perf. 13½x14, 14x13½

1982, May 18 **Photo.**

2265 A682 10pf Fish hawk .30 .25
2266 A682 20pf Sea eagle .30 .25
2267 A682 25pf Tawny eagle .30 .25
2268 A682 35pf Eagle owl *1.10 1.00*
Nos. 2265-2268 (4) *2.00 1.75*

19th Workers' Festival, Neubrandenburg — A683

10pf, View of Neubrandenburg. 20pf, Traditional costumes.

1982, June 8 **Photo.** ***Perf. 14***

2269 A683 10pf multicolored .25 .25
2270 A683 20pf multicolored .35 .30

Souvenir Sheet

Dimitrov Memorial Medal — A684

1982, June 8

2271 A684 1m multi *2.25 3.25*

George Dimitrov (1882-1947), first prime minister of Bulgaria.

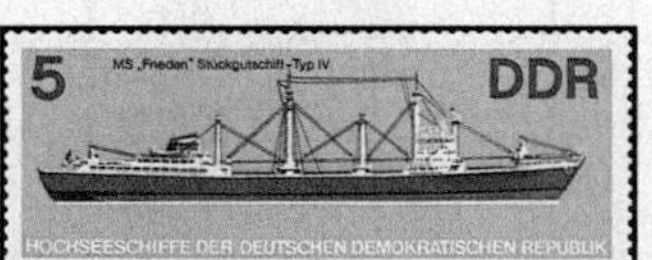

Cargo Ship Frieden — A685

1982, June 22

2272 A685 5pf shown .25 .25
2273 A685 10pf Fichtelberg .25 .25
2274 A685 15pf Brocken .25 .25
2275 A685 20pf Weimar .25 .25
2276 A685 25pf Vorwarts .25 .25
2277 A685 35pf Berlin *1.10 .90*
Nos. 2272-2277 (6) *2.35 2.15*

Society for Sport & Technology — A686

1982, June 22 **Litho.** ***Perf. 13x12½***

2278 A686 20pf multi .35 .25

Bird Wedding — A687

Sorbian Folklore: 20pf, Zampern masqueraders. 25pf, Easter egg game. 35pf, Painting Easter eggs. 40pf, St. John's Day parade. 50pf, Christmas celebration.

1982, July 6 **Litho.** ***Perf. 13x12½***

2279 A687 Block of 6 *3.25 3.00*
a. 10pf multi *.25 .25*
b. 20pf multi *.25 .25*
c. 25pf multi *.30 .30*
d. 35pf multi *.45 .45*
e. 40pf multi *.55 .55*
f. 50pf multi *.65 .65*

Views of Schwerin — A688

7th Youth Stamp Exhibition, Schwerin: No. 2280, View, 1640. No. 2281, Modern Schwerin.

1982, July 6

2280 10pf + 5pf multi *.30 .30*
2281 20pf multi *.30 .30*
a. A688 Pair, #2280-2281 + label *1.25 1.00*

7th Pioneer Meeting, Dresden A689

No. 2282, Pioneers, banner. No. 2283, Bugle, pennant.

1982, July 20 **Photo.** ***Perf. 14x13½***

2282 A689 10pf + 5pf multi *.40 .35*
2283 A689 20pf multi .25 .25

Seascape, by Ludolf Backhuysen (1631-1708) — A690

17th Cent. Paintings in Natl. Museum, Schwerin: 10pf, Music Making at Home, by Frans van Mieris (1635-1681), vert. 20pf, The Gate Guard, by Carel Fabritius (1622-1654), vert. 25pf, Farmers Company, by Adriaen Brouwer (1606-1638). 35pf, Breakfast Table with Ham, by Willem Claesz Heda (1593-1680). 70pf, River Landscape, by Jan van Goyen (1596-1656).

1982, Aug. 10 ***Perf. 14***

2284 A690 5pf multi .25 .25
2285 A690 10pf multi .25 .25
2286 A690 20pf multi .25 .25
2287 A690 25pf multi .25 .25
2288 A690 35pf multi .25 .25
2289 A690 70pf multi *1.60 1.20*
Nos. 2284-2289 (6) *2.85 2.45*

1982 Leipzig Autumn Fair A691

1982, Aug. 24 **Litho.** ***Perf. 13x12½***

2290 A691 10pf Exhibition Hall .25 .25
2291 A691 25pf Decorative box, ring .25 .25

Karl-Marx-Stadt Buildings and Monument — A692

1982, Aug. 24 **Photo.** ***Perf. 14***

2292 A692 10pf multi + label .30 .25

Org. for the Cooperation of Socialist Countries and Posts and Telecommunications Dept., 13th Conference, Karl-Marx-Stadt, Sept. 6-11.

Intl. Federation of Resistance Fighters, 9th Congress, Berlin — A693

1982, Sept. 7 **Litho.** ***Perf. 14***

2293 A693 10pf Emblem .35 .25

Auschwitz-Birkenau Intl. Memorial A694

1982, Sept. 7 **Photo.**

2294 A694 35pf multi .35 .30

Autumn Flowers — A695

5pf, Autumn anemones. 10pf, Student flowers. 15pf, Hybrid gazanias. 20pf, Sunflowers. 25pf, Chrysanthemums. 35pf, Cosmos bipinnatus.

1982, Sept. 21

2295 A695 5pf multicolored .25 .25
2296 A695 10pf multicolored .25 .25
2297 A695 15pf multicolored .25 .25
2298 A695 20pf multicolored .25 .25
2299 A695 25pf multicolored .25 .25
2300 A695 35pf multicolored *1.60 1.20*
Nos. 2295-2300 (6) *2.85 2.45*

Ambulance — A696

1982, Oct. 5 **Litho.** ***Perf. 13x12½***

2301 A696 5pf shown .25 .25
2302 A696 10pf Street cleaner .25 .25
2303 A696 20pf Bus .25 .25
2304 A696 25pf Platform truck .25 .25
2305 A696 35pf Platform truck, diff. .25 .25
2306 A696 85pf Milk truck *1.90 1.40*
Nos. 2301-2306 (6) *3.15 2.65*

25th Masters of Tomorrow Central Fair A697

1982, Oct. 19 ***Perf. 14***

2307 A697 20pf multicolored .30 .25

Martin Luther (1483-1546) A698

Designs: 10pf, Seal of Eisleben (town of birth and death). 20pf, Portrait, Eisenach, 1521. 35pf, Wittenberg seal, 1500. 85pf, Portrait, after Cranach, 1528.

1982, Nov. 23 Photo. *Perf. 14x13½*

2308 A698 10pf multi .25 .25
2309 A698 20pf multi .25 .25
a. Miniature sheet of 10 6.50 6.50
2310 A698 35pf multi .35 .25
2311 A698 85pf multi *2.60 1.90*
Nos. 2308-2311 (4) *3.45 2.65*

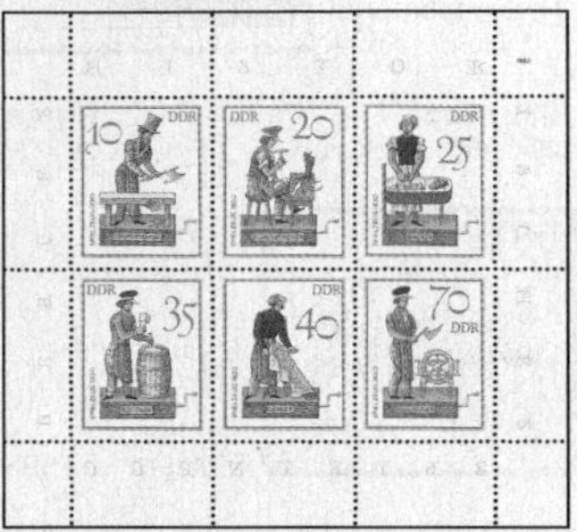

A699

1982, Nov. 23 Litho. *Perf. 14*

2312 A699 Sheet of 6 *3.00 3.00*
a. 10pf Toy Carpenter, 1830 *.25 .25*
b. 20pf Cobbler *.90 .90*
c. 25pf Baker *.25 .25*
d. 35pf Cooper *.25 .25*
e. 40pf Tanner *.90 .90*
f. 70pf Carter *.25 .25*

Souvenir Sheet

Johannes Brahms (1833-1897), Composer — A700

1983, Jan. 11 Litho. *Perf. 14*

2313 A700 1.15m multi *2.25 4.00*

Working-class Leader Type of 1979

No. 2314, Franz Dahlem (1892-1981). No. 2315, Karl Maron (1903-75). No. 2316, Josef Miller (1883-1964). No. 2317, Fred Oelssner (1903-77). No. 2318, Siegfried Radel (1893-1943).

1983, Jan. 25 Photo.

2314 A623 10pf dark brown .25 .25
2315 A623 10pf dark green .25 .25
2316 A623 10pf dark olive grn .25 .25
2317 A623 10pf deep plum .25 .25
2318 A623 10pf dark blue .25 .25
Nos. 2314-2318 (5) 1.25 1.25

World Communications Year — A701

5pf, Telephone receiver, buttons. 10pf, Rugen radio. 20pf, Surface and air mail. 35pf, Optical conductors.

1983, Feb. 8 Photo. *Perf. 14*

2319 A701 5pf multicolored .25 .25
2320 A701 10pf multicolored .25 .25
2321 A701 20pf multicolored .25 .25
2322 A701 35pf multicolored *1.10 .60*
Nos. 2319-2322 (4) *1.85 1.35*

Otto Nuschke (1883-1957), Statesman A702

1983, Feb. 8

2323 A702 20pf red brn, bl & blk .40 .25

Town Hall, Gera, 1576 — A703

10pf, Stolberg, 1482, horiz. 25pf, Possneck, 1486. 35pf, Berlin, 1869, horiz.

1983, Feb. 22 Photo. *Perf. 14*

2324 A703 10pf multi .25 .25
2325 A703 20pf shown .25 .25
2326 A703 25pf multi .25 .25
2327 A703 35pf multi *1.10 .85*
Nos. 2324-2327 (4) *1.85 1.60*

1983 Leipzig Spring Fair — A704

10pf, Fair building. 25pf, Robotron microcomputer.

1983, Mar. 8

2328 A704 10pf multi .25 .25
2329 A704 25pf multi .35 .25

Paul Robeson (1898-1976), Singer — A705

1983, Mar. 22 Litho. *Perf. 13x12½*

2330 A705 20pf multicolored .30 .25

Souvenir Sheet

Schulze-Boysen/Harnack Resistance Org. — A706

Arvid Harnack (1901-42), Harro Schulze-Boysen (1909-42), John Sieg (1903-42).

1983, Mar. 22

2331 A706 85pf multicolored 1.20 2.00

Karl Marx (1818-1883), and Newspaper Mastheads — A707

Portraits and: 20pf, Lyons silk weavers' revolt, 1831, French-German Yearbook. 35pf, Engels, Communist Manifesto. 50pf, Das Kapital titlepage. 70pf, Program of German Workers' Movement text. 85pf, Engels, Lenin, globe. 1.15m Portrait (24x29mm).

1983, Apr. 11 Photo. *Perf. 13x12½*

2332 A707 10pf multicolored .25 .25
2333 A707 20pf multicolored .25 .25
2334 A707 35pf multicolored .25 .25
2335 A707 50pf multicolored .25 .25
2336 A707 70pf multicolored .40 .25
2337 A707 85pf multicolored *2.00 2.00*
Nos. 2332-2337 (6) *3.40 3.25*

Souvenir Sheet

Litho. *Perf. 14*

2338 A707 1.15m multi *2.00 3.25*

Works of Art from Berlin State Museums — A708

1983, Apr. 19 Photo. *Perf. 14*

2339 A708 10pf Athena .25 .25
2340 A708 20pf Amazon, bronze, 430 BC .35 .25

Narrow-Gauge Railroads — A709

No. 2341, Wernigerode-Nordhausen line. No. 2342, Zittau-Oybin/Johnsdorf line.

1983, May 17 Litho. *Perf. 13x12½*

2341 Pair *1.25 1.00*
a. A709 15pf Locomotive *.35 .35*
b. A709 20pf Passenger car *.35 .35*
2342 Pair *1.25 1.00*
a. A709 20pf Locomotive *.35 .35*
b. A709 50pf Freight car *.35 .35*

Nos. 2341 and 2342 se-tenant with labels showing maps. See Nos. 2405-2406.

Sand Glasses and Sundials — A710

5pf, Sand glass, 1674. 10pf, Sand glass, 1700. 20pf, Sundial, 1611. 30pf, Sundial, 1750. 50pf, Sundial, 1760. 85pf, Sundial, 1800.

1983, June 7 Photo. *Perf. 14*

2343 A710 5pf multi .25 .25
2344 A710 10pf multi .25 .25
2345 A710 20pf multi .25 .25
a. Sheet of 8 *2.00 2.00*
2346 A710 30pf multi .25 .25
2347 A710 50pf multi .35 .25
2348 A710 85pf multi *2.10 2.00*
Nos. 2343-2348 (6) *3.45 3.25*

Cacti — A711

5pf, Coryphantha elephantidens. 10pf, Thelocactus schwarzii. 20pf, Leuchtenbergia principis. 25pf, Submatucana madisoniorum. 35pf, Oroya peruviana. 50pf, Copiapoa cinerea.

1983, June 21

2349 A711 5pf multicolored .25 .25
2350 A711 10pf multicolored .25 .25
2351 A711 20pf multicolored .25 .25
2352 A711 25pf multicolored .25 .25
2353 A711 35pf multicolored .25 .25
2354 A711 50pf multicolored *1.25 1.20*
Nos. 2349-2354 (6) *2.50 2.45*

Naumberg Cathedral Statues, 15th Cent. A712

20pf, Thimo and Wilhelm. 25pf, Gepa and Gerburg. 35pf, Hermann and Reglindis. 85pf, Eckehard and Uta.

1983, July 5 Photo. *Perf. 13*

2355 A712 20pf multicolored .35 .35
2356 A712 25pf multicolored .40 .40
2357 A712 35pf multicolored .45 .45
2358 A712 85pf multicolored 1.10 1.10
a. Block of 4, #2355-2358 3.00 2.25

Technical Training, by Harald Metzkes (b. 1929) A713

SOZPHILEX '83 Junior Stamp Exhibition, Berlin: 10pf+5pf, Glasewaldt and Zinna Defending the Barricade-18th March, 1848, by Theodor Hosemann, vert. Surtax was for exhibition.

1983, July 5 Litho. *Perf. 13x12½*

2359 A713 10pf + 5pf multi *.55 .45*
2360 A713 20pf multi .25 .25

Volleyball A714

1983, July 19 Photo. *Perf. 14*

2361 A714 10pf + 5pf Passing beach balls *.50 .40*
2362 A714 20pf shown .25 .25

7th Gymnastic and Sports Meeting; 9th Children's and Youth Spartikiade, Leipzig.

Simon Bolivar (1783-1830) — A715

35pf, Bolivar, Alexander von Humboldt.

1983, July 19

2363 A715 35pf multicolored .45 .30

A715a

A716

City Arms

1983, Aug. 9

2364 A715a 50pf Berlin *.65 .55*
2365 A716 50pf Cottbus *.65 .55*
2366 A716 50pf Dresden *.65 .55*
2367 A716 50pf Erfurt *.65 .55*
2368 A716 50pf Frankfurt *.65 .55*
Nos. 2364-2368 (5) 3.25 2.75

See Nos. 2398-2402, 2464-2468.

1983 Leipzig Autumn Fair — A717

10pf, Central Palace. 25pf, Microelectronic pattern.

1983, Aug. 30

2369 A717 10pf multicolored .25 .25
2370 A717 25pf multicolored .40 .25

Leonhard Euler (1707-1783), Mathematician — A718

1983, Sept. 6

2371 A718 20pf multi .40 .25

Souvenir Sheet

30th Anniv. of Working-Class Brigade Groups — A719

1983, Sept. 6 Litho. ***Perf. 12½x13***

2372 A719 1m multicolored *1.90 2.25*

Governmental Palaces, Potsdam Gardens — A720

10pf, Sanssouci Palace. 20pf, Chinese teahouse. 40pf, Charlottenhof Palace. 50pf, Royal Stables, Film Museum.

1983, Sept. 20 ***Perf. 13x12½***

2373 A720 10pf multicolored .25 .25
2374 A720 20pf multicolored .25 .25
2375 A720 40pf multicolored .35 .25
2376 A720 50pf multicolored *2.00 2.00*
Nos. 2373-2376 (4) 2.85 2.75

Monument, Mamajew-Kurgan Hill — A721

1983, Oct. 4 ***Perf. 14***

2377 A721 35pf Mother Home .40 .25

Souvenir Sheet

Martin Luther — A722

1983, Oct. 18 Litho. ***Perf. 14***

2378 A722 1m multi *2.25 4.00*

Margin shows title page from Luther Bible, 1541.

Thuringian Glass — A723

1983, Nov. 8 Photo. ***Perf. 13½x14***

2379 A723 10pf Cock .25 .25
2380 A723 20pf Cup .25 .25
2381 A723 25pf Vase .25 .25
2382 A723 70pf Ornamental Glass *1.60 1.25*
Nos. 2379-2382 (4) 2.35 2.00

Souvenir Sheet

New Year 1984 — A724

1983, Nov. 22 Litho. ***Perf. 14***

2383 A724 Sheet of 4 *1.50 3.25*
a. 10pf multi *.25 .25*
b. 20pf multi *.25 .35*
c. 25pf multi *.35 .65*
d. 35pf multi *.45 .80*

Winter Olympics 1984, Sarajevo A725

1983, Nov. 22 Photo. ***Perf. 14***

2384 A725 10pf + 5pf 2-man luge .25 .25
2385 A725 20pf + 10pf Ski jump .25 .25
2386 A725 25pf Skiing .25 .25
2387 A725 35pf Biathlon *1.25 .85*
Nos. 2384-2387 (4) 2.00 1.60

Souvenir Sheet

2388 A725 85pf Olympic Center *1.50* 3.00

Jena Glass Centenary — A726

1984, Jan. 10 Litho. ***Perf. 12½x13***

2389 A726 20pf Otto Schott .35 .25

Working-class Leader Type of 1979

Designs: No. 2390, Friedrich Ebert (1894-1979). No. 2391, Fritz Grosse (1904-1957). No. 2392, Albert Norden (1904-1982).

1984, Jan. 24 Engr. ***Perf. 14***

2390 A623 10pf black .25 .25
2391 A623 10pf dark green .25 .25
2392 A623 10pf dark blue .25 .25
Nos. 2390-2392 (3) .75 .75

Souvenir Sheet

Felix Mendelssohn (1809-1847), Composer — A727

1984, Jan. 24 Litho.

2393 A727 85pf multi .90 1.60

Margin shows Song Without Words score.

Postal Milestones — A728

Designs: 10pf, Muhlau, 1725; Oederan, 1722. 20pf, Johanngeorgenstadt, 1723; Schonbrunn, 1724. 35pf, Freiberg, 1723. 85pf, Pegau, 1723.

1984, Feb. 7 Photo. ***Perf. 14***

2394 A728 10pf multi .25 .25
2395 A728 20pf multi .30 .25
2396 A728 35pf multi .35 .30
2397 A728 85pf multi .65 .65
Nos. 2394-2397 (4) 1.55 1.45

City Arms Type of 1983

1984, Feb. 21

2398 A716 50pf Gera .40 .35
2399 A716 50pf Halle .40 .35
2400 A716 50pf Karl-Marx-Stadt .40 .35
2401 A716 50pf Leipzig .40 .35
2402 A716 50pf Magdeburg .40 .35
Nos. 2398-2402 (5) 2.00 1.75

1984 Leipzig Spring Fair A729

1984, Mar. 6 ***Perf. 14***

2403 A729 10pf Old Town Hall .25 .25
2404 A729 25pf Factory .30 .25

Railroad Type of 1983

No. 2405: Cranzahl Oberwiesenthal Line — a, Locomotive. b, Passenger car.

No. 2406: Selke Valley Line — a, Locomotive. b, Passenger car.

1984, Mar. 20 Litho. ***Perf. 13x12½***

2405 Pair 1.25 1.10
a. A709 30pf multi .25 .25
b. A709 80pf multi .55 .55
2406 Pair 1.25 .90
a. A709 40pf multi .30 .30
b. A709 60pf multi .35 .35

Labels show maps of routes.

Stone Door, Rostock — A730

Intl. Society of Monument Preservation 7th General Meeting: 10pf, Town Hall, Rostock. 15pf, Albrecht Castle, Meissen. 85pf, Stable Courtyard, Dresden. 10pf, 15pf, 85pf horiz.

1984, Apr. 24 Photo. ***Perf. 14***

2407 A730 10pf multi .25 .25
2408 A730 15pf multi .25 .25
2409 A730 40pf multi .40 .30
2410 A730 85pf multi 1.00 .85
Nos. 2407-2410 (4) 1.90 1.65

Council Building — A731

1984, May 8

2411 A731 70pf multi .70 .30

Standing Commission of Posts and Telecommunications of Council of Mutual Economic Aid, 25th meeting.

Cast-iron Bowl, 19th Cent. — A732

Cast-Iron, Lauchhammer: 85pf, Ascending Man, by Fritz Cremer, 1967.

1984, May 22

2412 A732 20pf multi .25 .25
2413 A732 85pf multi .70 .70

Marionette — A733

1984, June 5

2414	A733	50pf	shown	.45	.45
2415	A733	80pf	Puppet	.70	.70

Natl. Youth Festival — A734

10pf + 5pf, Demonstration. 20pf, Construction workers.

1984, June 5 Litho. *Perf. 13x12½*

2416	10pf + 5pf multi		.25	.25
2417	20pf multicolored		.25	.25
a.	A734 Pair, #2416-2417 + label		1.00	.55

20th Workers' Festival — A735

1984, June 19

2418	10pf View of Gera	.25	.25
2419	20pf Traditional costumes	.25	.25
a.	A735 Pair, #2418-2419 + label	.80	.55

Natl. Stamp Exhib., Halle — A736

1984, July 3 *Perf. 13½x14*

2420	A736	10pf + 5pf	Salt carrier	.25	.25
2421	A736	20pf	Wedding couple	.30	.25

Historic Seals, 1442 — A737

5pf, Baker, Berlin. 10pf, Wool weaver, Berlin. 20pf, Wool weaver, Cologne. 35pf, Shoemaker, Cologne.

1984, Aug. 7 Litho. *Perf. 14*

2422	A737	5pf	multi	*.30*	.25
2423	A737	10pf	multi	*.45*	.30
2424	A737	20pf	multi	*.85*	.35
2425	A737	35pf	multi	*1.40*	1.25
a.			Block of 4, #2422-2425	*4.25*	3.25

Building Renovation and Construction A738

Ironwork Collective Combine East — A739

No. 2428, Surface mining. No. 2429, Armed forces. No. 2430, Petro-chemical Collective Combine, Schwedt.

No. 2431, Privy Council Building. No. 2432, Family.

Litho., Photo. (#2427, 2429, 25pf)

1984 *Perf. 14x13½*

2426	A738	10pf	shown	.25	.25
2427	A739	10pf	shown	.25	.25
2428	A738	20pf	multicolored	.30	.30
2429	A739	20pf	multicolored	.25	.25
2430	A739	25pf	multicolored	.30	.30
			Nos. 2426-2430 (5)	1.35	1.35

Souvenir Sheets

2431	A738	1m	multicolored	1.00	2.00
2432	A739	1m	multicolored	1.00	2.00

DDR, 35th anniv. Issued: A738, 8/21; A739, 9/11.

1984 Leipzig Autumn Fair — A740

10pf, Frege House, Katharine St. 25pf, Crystal bowl, Olbernhau.

1984, Aug. 28 Photo. *Perf. 14*

2433	A740	10pf	multicolored	.25	.25
2434	A740	25pf	multicolored	.30	.25

Members of the Resistance, Sculpture by Arno Wittig — A741

1984, Sept. 18 Photo. *Perf. 14*

2435	A741	35pf	multi	.60	.30

A742

No. 2436, View of Magdeburg. No. 2437, Old & modern buildings.

1984, Oct. 4 Litho. *Perf. 13x12½*

2436	10pf + 5pf multi	.25	.25
2437	20pf multi	.25	.25
a.	A742 Pair, #2436-2437 + label	.90	.65

8th Youth Stamp Exhibition, Magdeburg.

35th Anniv. of Republic — A743

10pf, Construction. 20pf, Military. 25pf, Heavy industry. 35pf, Agriculture.
1m, Arms, dove, vert.

1984, Oct. 4 Photo. *Perf. 14*

2438	A743	10pf	multicolored	.25	.25
2439	A743	20pf	multicolored	.25	.25
2440	A743	25pf	multicolored	.30	.30
2441	A743	35pf	multicolored	.35	.35
			Nos. 2438-2441 (4)	1.15	1.15

Souvenir Sheet

2442	A743	1m	multicolored	.90	2.00

Figurines, Green Vault of Dresden — A744

1984, Oct. 23

2443	A744	10pf	Spring	.25	.25
2444	A744	20pf	Summer	.25	.25
a.			Miniature sheet of 8, litho., perf. 12½x13	2.10	2.10
2445	A744	35pf	Autumn	.30	.30
2446	A744	70pf	Winter	.65	.65
			Nos. 2443-2446 (4)	1.45	1.45

Falkenstein Castle — A745

1984, Nov. 6 Litho. *Perf. 14*

2447	A745	10pf	shown	.25	.25
2448	A745	20pf	Kriebstein	.25	.25
2449	A745	35pf	Ranis	.55	.40
2450	A745	80pf	Neuenburg	.80	.65
			Nos. 2447-2450 (4)	1.85	1.55

See Nos. 2504-2507.

Dead Tsar's Daughter and the Seven Warriors A746

Various scenes from the fairytale.

1984, Nov. 27 Litho. *Perf. 13*

2451	Sheet of 6	*8.50*	4.00
a.	A746 5pf multi	*.35*	.25
b.	A746 10pf multi	*.35*	.25
c.	A746 15pf multi	*2.25*	1.25
d.	A746 20pf multi	*2.25*	1.25
e.	A746 35pf multi	*.35*	.25
f.	A746 50pf multi	*.35*	.25

Working-class Leader Type of 1979

Designs: No. 2452, Anton Ackermann (1905-1973). No. 2453, Alfred Kurella (1895-1975). No. 2454, Otto Schon (1905-1968).

1985, Jan. 8 Engr. *Perf. 14*

2452	A623	10pf	blk brn	.25	.25
2453	A623	10pf	red brn	.25	.25
2454	A623	10pf	gray vio	.25	.25
			Nos. 2452-2454 (3)	.75	.75

24th World Luge Championship — A747

1985, Jan. 22 Photo.

2455	A747	10pf	Single seat luge	.30	.25

Antique Mailboxes — A748

1985, Feb. 5 Litho. *Perf. 14*

2456	A748	10pf	1850	.25	.25
2457	A748	20pf	1860	.25	.25
2458	A748	35pf	1900	.30	.30
2459	A748	50pf	1920	.40	.40
a.			Block of 4, Nos. 2456-2459	1.20	1.60

Souvenir Sheet

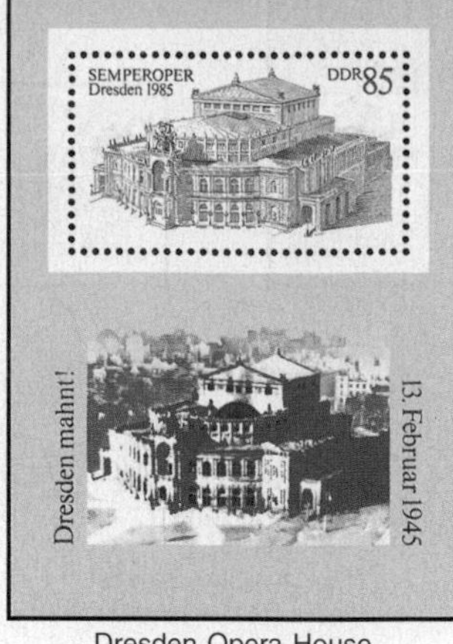

Dresden Opera House Heopening — A749

Litho. & Engr.

1985, Feb. 12 *Perf. 13*

2460	A749	85pf	multicolored	.85	1.50

1985 Leipzig Spring Fair — A750

10pf, Statue of Bach, Leipzig. 25pf, Porcelain pot, Meissen.

1985, Mar. 5 Photo. *Perf. 14*

2461	A750	10pf	multicolored	.25	.25
2462	A750	25pf	multicolored	.30	.25

Souvenir Sheet

Bach, Handel and Schutz Tribute — A751

a, Bach. b, Handel. c, Heinrich Schutz (1585-1672).

1985, Mar. 19 Litho.

2463	A751		Sheet of 3	2.00	3.00
a.			10pf multicolored	.50	.65
b.			20pf multicolored	.50	.65
c.			85pf multicolored	.65	1.25

City Arms Type of 1983

1985, Apr. 9 Photo. *Perf. 14*

2464	A716	50pf	Neubrandenburg	.40	.35
2465	A716	50pf	Potsdam	.40	.35
2466	A716	50pf	Rostock	.40	.35
2467	A716	50pf	Schwerin	.40	.35
2468	A716	50pf	Suhl	.65	.65
			Nos. 2464-2468 (5)	2.25	2.05

Seelow Heights Memorial — A752

1985, Apr. 16 Photo. *Perf. 14*
2469 A752 35pf multi .40 .30

Egon Erwin Kisch, Journalist (1885-1948) — A753

1985, Apr. 23 Photo. *Perf. 14*
2470 A753 35pf multi .30 .25

No. 2470 was printed se-tenant with label showing the house where Kisch was born. Value, single with attached label: unused 50c; used 40c.

Liberation from Fascism, 40th Anniv. — A754

Designs: 10pf, German and Soviet astronauts. 20pf, Coal miner Adolf Hennecke, symbols of industry and energy. 25pf, farm workers, symbols of socialist agriculture. 50pf, Technicians manufacturing microchips, science and technology.

1m, Berlin-Treptow Soviet Heroes Monument.

1985, May 7 Photo. *Perf. 14x13½*
2471 A754 10pf multi .25 .25
2472 A754 20pf multi .30 .30
2473 A754 25pf multi .30 .30
2474 A754 50pf multi .40 .40
Nos. 2471-2474 (4) 1.25 1.25

Souvenir Sheet

Perf. 12½x13

2475 A754 1m multi 1.00 2.00

Warsaw Treaty, 30th Anniv. — A755

20pf, Flags of pact nations.

1985, May 14 Litho. *Perf. 13x12½*
2476 A755 20pf multi .35 .25

Historical and Modern Buildings — A756

12th Youth Parliament, Berlin: 20pf, Ernst Thalmann, flags.

1985, May 21 Litho.
2477 A756 10pf + 5pf multi .25 .25
2478 A756 20pf multi .25 .25
a. Pair, #2477-2478 + label .55 .55

Intl. Olympic Committee 90th Meeting — A757

1985, May 28 Litho. *Perf. 14*
2479 A757 35pf Flag .45 .25

No. 2479 was printed setenant with label depicting Olympic Torches. Value of single with attached label: unused 85c; used 65c.

Free German Trade Unions, 40th Anniv. — A758

1985, June 11 Photo.
2480 A758 20pf Red flags .30 .25

Wildlife Preservation A759

5pf, Harpy eagle, vert. 10pf, Red-necked goose. 20pf, Spectacled bear. 50pf, Banteng (Javanese) buffalo. 85pf, Sunda Straits crocodile.

1985, June 25 Photo.
2481 A759 5pf multicolored .25 .25
2482 A759 10pf multicolored .25 .25
2483 A759 20pf multicolored .25 .25
2484 A759 50pf multicolored .40 .35
2485 A759 85pf multicolored .80 .80
Nos. 2481-2485 (5) 1.95 1.90

19th Century Steam Engines A760

10pf, Bock engine, vert. 85pf, Beam engine.

1985, July 9 Photo.
2486 A760 10pf multicolored .25 .25
2487 A760 85pf multicolored .70 .65

12th World Youth and Student Festival, Moscow — A761

20pf + 5pf, Students reading. 50pf, Student demonstration.

1985, July 23 Litho. *Perf. 13x12½*
2488 20pf + 5pf multi .25 .25
2489 50pf multicolored .35 .35
a. A761 Pair, #2488-2489 + label .85 .80

2nd World Orienteering and Deep-sea Diving Championship — A762

10pf, Diver at turning buoy. 70pf, Long-distance divers.

1985, Aug. 13 Photo. *Perf. 14*
2490 A762 10pf multicolored .25 .25
2491 A762 70pf multicolored .65 .65

Bose House Fair Building, St. Thomas Churchyard — A763

1985, Aug. 27 Photo.
2492 A763 10pf shown .25 .25
2493 A763 25pf Bach trumpet .35 .25

Leipzig Autumn Fair.

A764

SOZPHILEX '85: 19th century coach and team, 1878, bas-relief by Hermann Steinemann, in the court of the former Berlin Post Office.

1985, Sept. 10 Litho. *Perf. 13x12½*
2494 5pf multi .25 .25
2495 20pf + 5pf multi .25 .25
a. Miniature sheet of 4 #2495b .75 .75
b. A764 Pair, #2494-2495 .45 .45

No. 2495b has a continuous design.

German Railways 150th Anniv. — A765

Socialist Railway Org.: 20pf, GS II signal box, track diagram. 25pf, 1838 Saxonia, first German locomotive, designer Johann Andreas Schubert (1808-1870), Model 250 electric locomotive. 50pf, Helicopter lifting cable drum, section electrification. 85pf, Leipzig Central Station.

Litho.

Perf. 12½x13

1985, Sept. 24
2496 A765 20pf multi .25 .25
2497 A765 25pf multi .30 .25
2498 A765 50pf multi .55 .45
2499 A765 85pf multi .80 .80
Nos. 2496-2499 (4) 1.90 1.75

Bridges in East Berlin A766

Photo.; Litho. (#2501a)

1985, Oct. 8 *Perf. 14*
2500 A766 10pf Gertrauden .25 .25
2501 A766 20pf Jungfern .25 .25
a. Min. sheet of 8, perf. 13x12½ 2.60 2.60
2502 A766 35pf Weidendammer .35 .35
2503 A766 70pf Marx-Engels .55 .55
Nos. 2500-2503 (4) 1.40 1.40

Castles Type of 1984

1985, Oct. 15 Litho.
2504 A745 10pf Hohnstein .25 .25
2505 A745 20pf Rochsburg .25 .25
2506 A745 35pf Schwarzenberg .30 .30
2507 A745 80pf Stein .80 .80
Nos. 2504-2507 (4) 1.60 1.60

Humboldt University, 175th Anniv. — A767

20pf, Administration building. 85pf, Charité Hospital, Berlin, 275th anniv., buildings, 1897, 1982.

1985, Oct. 22 *Perf. 14*
2508 A767 20pf multicolored .30 .25
2509 A767 85pf multicolored .80 .80

Castle Cacilienhof, UN Emblem A768

1985, Oct. 22 Photo. *Perf. 13*
2510 A768 85pf multi .80 .40

UN, 40th Anniv.

Circus Art — A769

10pf, Elephant training. 20pf, Trapeze artist. 35pf, Acrobats on unicycles. 50pf, Tiger training.

1985, Nov. 12 *Perf. 14*
2511 A769 10pf multicolored .30 .30
2512 A769 20pf multicolored .40 .40
2513 A769 35pf multicolored .80 .80
2514 A769 50pf multicolored 1.10 1.10
a. Block of 4, #2511-2514 5.00 11.00

Souvenir Sheet

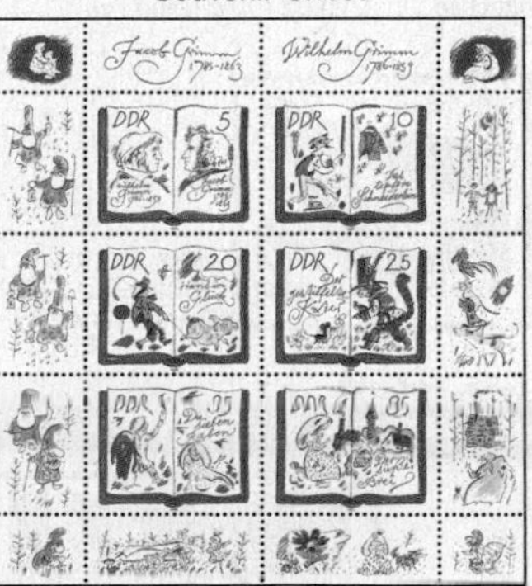

Brothers Grimm, Fabulists & Philologists — A770

Fairy tales compiled by Wilhelm (1786-1859) and Jacob (1785-1863) Grimm.

1985, Nov. 26 Litho. *Perf. 13½x13*
2515 A770 Sheet of 6 2.50 6.50
a. 5pf Wilhelm & Jacob Grimm .25 .25
b. 10pf Valiant Tailor .25 .25
c. 20pf Lucky John .45 1.25
d. 25pf Puss-in-Boots .45 1.25
e. 35pf Seven Ravens .25 .25
f. 85pf Sweet Porridge .25 .25

Monuments to Water Power — A772

Designs: 10pf, Cast iron hand pump, c. 1900. 35pf, Berlin-Altglienicke water tower, c. 1900. 50pf, Berlin-Friedrichshagen waterworks, 1893. 70pf, Rapphoden Hydro-electric Dam, 1959.

Engr., Photo. & Engr. (35pf)

1986, Jan. 21 *Perf. 14*

2516 A772 10pf dk grn & lake .25 .25
2517 A772 35pf buff, blk & dk grn .30 .30
2518 A772 50pf dk red brn & lt ol grn .45 .45
2519 A772 70pf dk bl & brn .60 .60
Nos. 2516-2519 (4) 1.60 1.60

Postal Uniforms, c. 1850 — A773

10pf, Saxon postillion. 20pf, Prussian postman. 85pf, Prussian P.O. clerk. 1m, Mecklenburg clerk.

1986, Feb. 4 **Photo.** *Perf. 14*

2520 A773 10pf multicolored .25 .25
a. Litho., perf. 12½x13 .25 .25
2521 A773 20pf multicolored .35 .25
a. Litho., perf. 12½x13 .30 .25
2522 A773 85pf multicolored .90 .85
a. Litho., perf. 12½x13 .90 .85
2523 A773 1m multicolored 1.20 1.20
a. Litho., perf. 12½x13 1.20 1.20

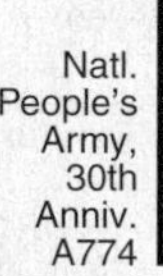

Natl. People's Army, 30th Anniv. A774

1986, Feb. 18 *Perf. 14*

2524 A774 20pf multi .45 .30

No. 2524 printed se-tenant with gold and red inscribed label. Value of single with attached label: unused 80c; used 45c.

Free German Youth Org., 40th Anniv. — A775

1986, Feb. 18

2525 A775 20pf multi .40 .30

Leipzig Spring Fair A776

35pf, Fair grounds entrance, 1946. 50pf, Trawler Atlantik 488.

1986, Mar. 11 **Litho.** *Perf. 13x12½*

2526 A776 35pf multicolored .30 .25
2527 A776 50pf multicolored .40 .35

Manned Space Flight, 25th Anniv. — A777

Designs: 40pf, Yuri Gagarin, Soviet cosomonaut, Vostok rocket, 1961. 50pf, Cosmonauts V. Bykowski, USSR, and S. Jahn, DDR, Vega probe, 1986, Intercosmos emblem. 70pf, Venera probe, Venus, spectrometer. 85pf, MKF-6 multi-spectral reconnaissance camera.

1986, Mar. 25 *Perf. 14*

2528 A777 40pf multi .30 .40
2529 A777 50pf multi .35 .40
2530 A777 70pf multi .45 .55
2531 A777 85pf multi .60 .65
a. Block of 4, #2528-2531 3.25 3.50

Socialist Unity 11th Party Day — A778

10pf, Marx, Engels & Lenin. 20pf, Ernst Thalmann. 50pf, Wilhelm Pieck & Otto Grotewohl, Uniting Party Day, 1946. 85pf,Family, motto. 1m, Construction worker, key to economic progress.

1986, Apr. 8 *Perf. 13½x13*

2532 A778 10pf multi .25 .25
2533 A778 20pf multi .25 .25
2534 A778 50pf multi .40 .40
2535 A778 85pf multi .80 .80
Nos. 2532-2535 (4) 1.70 1.70

Souvenir Sheet

Perf. 13x14

2536 A778 1m multi .90 2.00

Ernst Thalmann Park Opening, Berlin — A779

1986, Apr. 15 **Photo.** *Perf. 14*

2537 A779 20pf Memorial statue .35 .30

Trams and Streetcars — A780

Designs: 10pf, Dresden horse-drawn tram, 1886. 20pf, Leipzig streetcar, 1896. 40pf, Berlin streetcar, 1919. 70pf, Halle streetcar, 1928.

1986, May 20 **Photo.** *Perf. 14*

2538 A780 10pf multicolored .25 .25
2539 A780 20pf multicolored .25 .25
2540 A780 40pf multicolored .45 .45
2541 A780 70pf multicolored .65 .65
Nos. 2538-2541 (4) 1.60 1.60

Dresden Zoo, 125th Anniv. — A781

1986, May 27 **Litho.** *Perf. 14*

2542 A781 10pf Orangutan .25 .25
2543 A781 20pf Colobus monkey .35 .30
2544 A781 50pf Mandrill .65 .65
2545 A781 70pf Lemur .80 .80
Nos. 2542-2545 (4) 2.05 2.00

Berlin, 750th Anniv. — A782

Desigsn: 10pf, City seal, 1253. 20pf, Map, 1648, horiz. 50pf, City arms, 1253, horiz. 70pf, Nicholas Church, 1832.
1m, Cabinet Council House.

Litho. & Engr., Engr. (70pf, 1m)

1986, June 3 *Perf. 12½x13, 13x12½*

2546 A782 10pf multi .25 .25
2547 A782 20pf multi .40 .25
2548 A782 50pf multi .80 .55
2549 A782 70pf multi 1.25 .85
Nos. 2546-2549 (4) 2.70 1.90

Souvenir Sheet

2550 A782 1m multi 1.10 1.60

21st Workers' Games, Magdeburg — A783

20pf, Couple in folk dress, house construction. 50pf, Magdeburg Port, River Elbe.

1986, June 17 **Litho.** *Perf. 13x12½*

2551 20pf multicolored .30 .30
2552 50pf multicolored .30 .30
a. A783 Pair, #2551-2552 + label .85 .85

9th Youth Stamp Exhibition, Berlin — A784

10pf + 5pf, Berlin, c. 1652. 20pf, Art, architecture, 1986.

1986, July 22 **Litho.** *Perf. 13x12½*

2553 10pf + 5pf multicolored .25 .25
2554 20pf multicolored .25 .25
a. A784 Pair, #2553-2554 + label .55 .65

Castles A785

1986, July 29 *Perf. 13x12½*

2555 A785 10pf Schwerin .25 .25
a. Miniature sheet of 4 .55 .55
2556 A785 20pf Gustrow .25 .25
a. Miniature sheet of 4 .90 .90
2557 A785 85pf Rheinsberg .80 .80
2558 A785 1m Ludwigslust 1.00 1.00
Nos. 2555-2558 (4) 2.30 2.30

Intl. Peace Year A786

1986, Aug. 5 **Photo.** *Perf. 13*

2559 A786 35pf multi .45 .40

Berlin Wall, 25th Anniv. — A787

20pf, Soldiers, Brandenburg Gate.

1986, Aug. 5 **Litho.** *Perf. 14*

2560 A787 20pf multicolored .80 .40

Souvenir Sheet

Leipzig Autumn Fair — A788

1986, Aug. 19

2561 A788 Sheet of 2 1.10 2.00
a. 25pf Fair building .25 .40
b. 85pf Cloth merchants, 15th cent. .65 1.25

City Coins A789

10pf, Rostock, 1637. 35pf, Nordhausen, 1660. 50pf, Erfurt, 1633. 85pf, Magdeburg, 1638. 1m, Stralsund, 1622.

1986, Sept. 2 **Photo.** *Perf. 13*

2562 A789 10pf multi .25 .25
2563 A789 35pf multi .30 .30
2564 A789 50pf multi .40 .35
2565 A789 85pf multi .65 .65
2566 A789 1m multi .90 .90
Nos. 2562-2566 (5) 2.50 2.45

44th World Sports Shooting Championships, Suhl — A790

20pf, Rifle shooting. 70pf, Woman firing handgun. 85pf, Skeet-shooting.

1986, Sept. 2 *Perf. 14*

2567 A790 20pf multicolored .25 .25
2568 A790 70pf multicolored .65 .55
2569 A790 85pf multicolored .80 .70
Nos. 2567-2569 (3) 1.70 1.50

11th World Trade Unions Congress, Berlin — A791

1986, Sept. 9

2570 A791 70pf multi + label .45 .45

Border Guards, 40th Anniv. — A792

1986, Sept. 9

2571	A792	20pf multi	.65	.40

Intl. Brigades in Spain, 50th Anniv. — A793

20pf, Memorial, Friedrichshain.

1986, Sept. 11

2572	A793	20pf multicolored	.35	.25

Natl. Memorial for Concentration Camp Victims, Sachsenhausem, 25th Anniv. — A794

1986, Sept. 23

2573	A794	35pf multicolored	.40	.30

Mukran-Klaipeda Train-Ferry, Inauguration — A795

1986, Sept. 23

2574	50pf Pier, Mukran	.35	.35
2575	50pf Ferry	.35	.35
a.	A795 Pair, #2574-2575	.70	.70

Souvenir Sheet

Carl Maria von Weber (1786-1826), Composer — A796

1986, Nov. 4 **Litho.** ***Perf. 14***

2576	A796	85pf multi	1.00	1.60

Indira Gandhi (1917-1984), Prime Minister of India — A797

1986, Nov. 18 **Photo.**

2577	A797	10pf multi	.30	.25

Miniature Sheet

Chandeliers from the Ore Mountains — A798

Wrought iron candle-carrying chandeliers presented to Johann Georgenstadt miners annually by the mine blacksmith.

1986, Nov. 18 **Photo.** ***Perf. 14***

2578	A798	Sheet of 6	2.00	2.40
a.		10pf 1778	.25	.25
b.		20pf 1796	.25	.25
c.		25pf 1810	.45	.45
d.		35pf 1821	.45	.45
e.		40pf 1830	.25	.25
f.		85pf 1925	.25	.25

Statues of Roland, Medieval Hero — A799

10pf, Stendal, 1525. 20pf, Halle, 1719. 35pf, Brandenburg, 1474. 50pf, Quedlinburg, 1460.

1987, Jan. 20 **Photo.** ***Perf. 14½x14***

2579	A799	10pf multicolored	.25	.25
2580	A799	20pf multicolored	.25	.25
2581	A799	35pf multicolored	.30	.30
2582	A799	50pf multicolored	.45	.45
		Nos. 2579-2582 (4)	1.25	1.25

See Nos. 2782-2785.

Historic Post Offices A800

10pf, Freiberg, 1889. 20pf, Perleberg, 1897. 70pf, Weimar, 1889. 1.20m, Kirschau, 1926.

1987, Feb. 3 **Photo.** ***Perf. 14x14½***

2583	A800	10pf multi	.25	.25
2584	A800	20pf multi	.25	.25
2585	A800	70pf multi	.45	.45
2586	A800	1.20m multi	.90	.90
a.		Block of 4, #2583-2586	2.00	2.00

Nos. 2583-2586 printed in sheets of fifty and se-tenant in sheets of 40.

Berlin, 750th Anniv. A801

Architecture: 20pf, Reconstructed Palais Ephraim, Nikolai Quarter, demolished 1936, reopened 1987, vert. 35pf, Old Marzahn Village, modern housing. 70pf, Marx-Engels Forum, Central Berlin. 85pf, Reconstructed Friedrichstadt Palace Theater, reopened 1984.

Perf. 12½x13, 13x12½

1987, Feb. 17 **Engr.**

2587	A801	20pf vio brn & bluish grn	.25	.25
2588	A801	35pf sage grn & dk rose brn	.35	.25
2589	A801	70pf org & dk bl	.65	.60
2590	A801	85pf dk ol grn & yel grn	1.00	.85
		Nos. 2587-2590 (4)	2.25	1.95

See Nos. 2628-2631.

Democratic Women's Federation, 40th Anniv. — A802

1987, Mar. 3 **Litho.** ***Perf. 13½***

2591	A802	10pf sil, dk bl & brt red	.30	.25

Leipzig Spring Fair A803

35pf, New Fair Hall No. 20. 50pf, Traders at market, c. 1804.

1987, Mar. 10 ***Perf. 13x12½***

2592	A803	35pf multicolored	.30	.25
2593	A803	50pf multicolored	.55	.55

Leaders of the German Workers' Movement — A804

No. 2594, Fritz Gabler (1897-1974). No. 2595, Robert Siewert (1887-1973). No. 2596, Walter Vesper (1897-1978). No. 2597, Clara Zetkin (1857-1933).

1987, Mar. 24 **Engr.** ***Perf. 14***

2594	A804	10pf dark gray	.25	.25
2595	A804	10pf dark green	.25	.25
2596	A804	10pf black	.25	.25
2597	A804	10pf vio black	.25	.25
		Nos. 2594-2597 (4)	1.00	1.00

See Nos. 2721-2724.

K.A. Lingner (1861-1916), Museum A805

1987, Apr. 7 **Photo.** ***Perf. 14***

2598	A805	85pf multi	.70	.65

German Hygiene Museum, Dresden, 75th anniv.

Free German Trade Unions 11th Congress — A806

1987, Apr. 7 **Litho.** ***Perf. 13x12½***

2599	20pf Construction	.25	.25
2600	50pf Computer, ship	.40	.40
a.	A806 Pair, #2599-2600 + label	[illegible]	[illegible]

German Red Cross 10th Congress A807

1987, Apr. 7 **Photo.** ***Perf. 14***

2601	A807	35pf multi	.40	.30

Agricultural Cooperative, 35th Anniv. — A808

1907, Apr. 21 **Litho.** ***Perf 13x12½***

2602	A808	20pf multi	.35	.30

Famous Men A809

Designs: 10pf, Ludwig Uhland (1787-1862), poet, philologist. 20pf, Arnold Zweig (1887-1968), novelist. 35pf, Gerhart Hauptmann (1862-1946), 1912 Nobel laureate for literature, and scene from The Weavers. 50pf, Gustav Hertz (1887-1975), physicist, and atomic energy transmission diagram.

1987, May 5

2603	A809	10pf multi	.25	.25
2604	A809	20pf multi	.25	.25
2605	A809	35pf multi	.35	.35
2606	A809	50pf multi	.40	.40
		Nos. 2603-2606 (4)	1.25	1.25

Freshwater Fish — A810

5pf, Abramis brama. 10pf, Salmo trutta fario. 20pf, Silurus glanis. 35pf, Thymallus thymallus. 50pf, Barbus barbus. 70pf, Esox lucius.

1987, May 19 **Litho.** ***Perf. 13x12½***

2607	A810	5pf multi	.25	.25
2608	A810	10pf multi	.25	.25
2609	A810	20pf multi	.25	.25
2610	A810	35pf multi	.35	.35
2611	A810	50pf multi	.45	.35
2612	A810	70pf multi	.65	.65
		Nos. 2607-2612 (6)	2.20	2.10

Nos. 2608-2609 exist in sheets of 4.

Fire Engines A811

10pf, Hand-operated, 1756. 25pf, Steam, 1903. 40pf, LF 15, 1919. 70pf, LF 16-TS 8, 1971.

1987, June 16

2613	A811	10pf multi	.25	.25
2614	A811	25pf multi	.25	.25
2615	A811	40pf multi	.40	.40
2616	A811	70pf multi	.65	.65
a.		Block of 4, Nos. 2613-2616	2.25	2.25

Souvenir Sheet

Esperanto Movement, Cent. — A812

1987, July 7 Litho. *Perf. 14*

2617 A812 85pf L.L. Zamenhof, globe .80 1.60

World Wildlife Fund A813

1987, July 7 Photo.

2618	A813	10pf	Two otters	.25	.25
2619	A813	25pf	Otter swimming	.25	.25
2620	A813	35pf	Otter	.35	.30
2621	A813	60pf	Close-up of head	.80	.80
			Nos. 2618-2621 (4)	1.65	1.60

8th Sports Festival and 11th Youth Sports Championships, Leipzig — A814

1987, July 21

2622	A814	5pf	Tug-of-war	.25	.25
2623	A814	10pf	Handball	.25	.25
2624	A814	20pf	+ 5pf Girls' long jump	.25	.25
2625	A814	35pf	Table tennis	.30	.25
2626	A814	40pf	Bowling	.40	.35
2627	A814	70pf	Running	.60	.60
			Nos. 2622-2627 (6)	2.05	1.95

Berlin Anniversary Type of 1987

Perf. 12½x13, 13x12½

1987, Feb. 17 Engr.

2628	A801	10pf	like No. 2587	.25	.25
a.			Miniature sheet of 4	1.00	1.10
2629	A801	10pf	like No. 2588	.25	.25
a.			Miniature sheet of 4	1.00	1.10
2630	A801	20pf	like No. 2589	.25	.25
a.			Miniature sheet of 4	1.10	1.40
2631	A801	20pf	like No. 2590	.25	.25
a.			Miniature sheet of 4	1.00	1.40
			Nos. 2628-2631 (4)	1.00	1.00

Assoc. of Sports and Science, 35th Anniv. A815

1987, Aug. 4 Litho. *Perf. 13x12½*

2632 A815 10pf multi .30 .25

Stamp Day — A816

Designs: 10pf+5pf, Court Post Office, Berlin, 1760. 20pf, Wartenberg Palace, former Prussian General Post Office, 1770.

1987, Aug. 11 Photo. *Perf. 14*

2633	10pf +5pf multi		.25	.25
2634	20pf multi		.25	.25
a.	A816	Pair, #2633-2634 + label	.50	1.10

Souvenir Sheet

Leipzig Autumn Fair — A817

1987, Aug. 25 Litho. *Perf. 13½*

2635	A817	Sheet of 2	1.10	1.60
a.		40pf multi	.35	.45
b.		50pf multi	.45	.45

Intl. War Victims' Memorial, Budapest A818

35pf, Statue by József Somogyi.

1987, Sept. 8 Photo. *Perf. 14*

2636 A818 35pf multi .35 .25

Souvenir Sheet

Thalmann Memorial — A819

Litho. & Engr.

1987, Sept. 8 *Perf. 14*

2637 A819 1.35m buff, ver & blk 1.25 2.25

City of Berlin, 750th anniv.

10th Natl. Art Exhibition, Berlin — A820

Designs: 10pf, Weidendamm Bridge, Berlin, 1986, by Arno Mohr. 50pf, They Only Wanted to Learn How to Read and Write, Nicaragua, 1985-86, by Willi Sitte. 70pf, Large Figure of a Man in Mourning, 1983, scupture by Wieland Forster. 1m, Ceramic bowl, 1986, by Gerd Lucke. Nos. 2638-2640, vert.

1987, Sept. 28 Litho.

2638	A820	10pf	multi	.25	.25
2639	A820	50pf	multi	.40	.45
2640	A820	70pf	multi	.55	.60
2641	A820	1m	multi	.80	.90
			Nos. 2638-2641 (4)	2.00	2.20

Lenin, Flag, Smolny Institute, Cruiser Aurora A821

1987, Oct. 27 Photo. *Perf. 14*

2642	A821	10pf	shown	.25	.25
2643	A821	20pf	Spasski Tower	.25	.25

October Revolution, Russia, 70th anniv.

Robot ZIM 10-S Welding A822

10pf, Personal computer.

1987, Nov. 3 Litho. *Perf. 13x12½*

2644	A822	10pf	multicolored	.25	.25
2645	A822	20pf	shown	.25	.25

30th MMM Science Fair and 10th Central Industrial Fair for Students and Youth Scientists, Leipzig.

Miniature Sheet

Christmas Candle Carousels from the Ore Mountains — A823

Designs: 10pf, Annaberg, c. 1810. 20pf, Freiberg, c. 1830. 25pf, Neustadtel, c. 1870. 35pf, Schneeberg, c. 1870. 40pf, Lossnitz, c. 1880. 85pf, Seiffen, c. 1910.

1987, Nov. 3 Litho. *Perf. 12½x13*

2646	A823	Sheet of 6	2.25	2.60
a.		10pf multi	.25	.25
b.		20pf multi	.45	.55
c.		25pf multi	.25	.25
d.		35pf multi	.25	.25
e.		40pf multi	.45	.55
f.		85pf multi	.25	.25

1988 Winter Olympics, Calgary — A824

5pf, Ski jumping. 10pf, Speed skating. 20pf +10pf, 4-Man bobsled. 35pf, Biathlon. 1.20m, Single and double luge.

1988, Jan. 19 Photo. *Perf. 14½x14*

2647	A824	5pf	multi	.25	.25
2648	A824	10pf	multi	.25	.25
2649	A824	20pf	+10pf multi	.35	.30
2650	A824	35pf	multi	.40	.35
			Nos. 2647-2650 (4)	1.25	1.15

Souvenir Sheet

Perf. 13x12½

2651 A824 1.20m multi 1.25 2.00

No. 2649 surtaxed for the Olympic Promotion Society.

Postal Buildings, East Berlin A825

15pf, Berlin-Buch post office. 20pf, Natl. Postal Museum. 50pf, General post office, Berlin-Marzahn.

1988, Feb. 2 *Perf. 14*

2652	A825	15pf	multicolored	.25	.25
2653	A825	20pf	multicolored	.35	.25
2654	A825	50pf	multicolored	.80	.55
			Nos. 2652-2654 (3)	1.40	1.05

Souvenir Sheet

Bertolt Brecht (1898-1956), Playwright — A826

1988, Feb. 2 Litho. *Perf. 13x12½*

2655 A826 70pf multicolored .85 1.60

Flowering Plants — A827

10pf, Tillandsia macrochlamys. 25pf, Tillandsia bulbosa. 40pf, Tillandsia kalmbacheri. 70pf, Guzmania blassii.

1988, Feb. 16 Photo. *Perf. 14*

2656	A827	10pf	multicolored	.25	.25
2657	A827	25pf	multicolored	.25	.25
2658	A827	40pf	multicolored	.35	.35
2659	A827	70pf	multicolored	.55	.55
			Nos. 2656-2659 (4)	1.40	1.40

Leipzig Spring Fair — A828

20pf, Entrance #8. 70pf, Faust & Mephistopheles, bronze statue by Matthieu Molitor.

1988, Mar. 8 Litho. *Perf. 12½x13*

2660	A828	20pf	multi	.25	.25
2661	A828	70pf	multi	.80	.55

Madler Passage (arcade), 75th anniv.

Souvenir Sheet

A829

1988, Mar. 8 *Perf. 14*
2662 A829 70pf multi 1.10 1.60

Joseph von Eichendorff (1788-1857), poet.

Seals — A830

10pf, Muhlhausen saddler, 1565. 25pf, Dresden butcher, 1564. 35pf, Nauen smith, 16th cent. 50pf, Frankfurt-Oder clothier, 16th cent.

1988, Mar. 22 **Photo.** *Perf. 14*
2663 A830 10pf multicolored .25 .25
2664 A830 25pf multicolored .25 .25
2665 A830 35pf multicolored .30 .30
2666 A830 50pf multicolored .35 .35
a. Block of 4, #2663-2666 1.25 1.25

Georg Forster Antarctic Research Station A831

1988, Mar. 22 **Litho.** *Perf. 13x12½*
2667 A831 35pf multi .40 .30

District Capitals A832

5pf, Wismar. 10pf, Anklam. 25pf, Ribnitz-Damgarten. 60pf, Stralsund. 90pf, Bergen. 1.20m, Greifswald.

1988, Apr. 5 **Photo.** *Perf. 14*
2668 A832 5pf multi .25 .25
2669 A832 10pf multi .25 .25
2670 A832 25pf multi .25 .25
2671 A832 60pf multi .45 .40
2672 A832 90pf multi .65 .65
2673 A832 1.20m multi .85 .85
Nos. 2668-2673 (6) 2.70 2.65

Souvenir Sheet

Ulrich von Hutten (1488-1523), Promulgator of the Lutheran Movement — A833

1988, Apr. 5 **Litho.** *Perf. 12½x13*
2674 A833 70pf multi .90 1.25

USSR-DDR Manned Space Flight, 10th Anniv. — A834

Designs: 5pf, Cosmonauts S. Jahn and Valery Bykowski, Soyuz-29 landing, Sept. 3, 1978. 10pf, MKS-M multi-channel spectrometer. 20pf, MIR space station.

1988, June 21 **Litho.** *Perf. 14*
2675 A834 5pf multi .25 .25
2676 A834 10pf multi .25 .25
2677 A834 20pf multi .25 .25
Nos. 2675-2677 (3) .75 .75

See Nos. 2698-2700.

10th Youth Stamp Exhibitions in Erfurt and Karl-Marx-Stadt — A835

Designs: 10pf+5pf, Erfurt. c. 1520. 20+5pf, Chemnitz, c. 1620. 25pf, Historic and modern buildings of Erfurt. 50pf, Historic and modern buildings of Karl-Marx-Stadt.

1988, June 21 **Photo.**
2678 A835 10pf +5pf multi .25 .25
2679 A835 20pf +5pf multi .25 .25
2680 A835 25pf multi .25 .25
a. Pair, #2678, 2680 + label .60 1.00
2681 A835 50pf multi .45 .55
a. Pair, #2679, 2681 + label .80 1.60

Nos. 2678-2679 surtaxed to benefit the Philatelists' League of the DDR Cultural Union.

22nd Workers' Games, Frankfurt-on-Oder — A836

1988, June 7 **Litho.** *Perf. 13x12½*
2682 20pf multi .25 .25
2683 50pf multi, diff. .45 .45
a. A836 Pair, #2682-2683 + label .90 .80

Workers' Militia, 35th Anniv. — A837

5pf, Oath. 10pf, Ernst Thalmann tribute. 15pf, Roll call. 20pf, Weapons exchange.

1988, July 5 **Photo.** *Perf. 14*
2684 A837 5pf multicolored .25 .25
2685 A837 10pf multicolored .25 .25
2686 A837 15pf multicolored .25 .25
2687 A837 20pf multicolored .25 .25
Nos. 2684-2687 (4) 1.00 1.00

A838

No. 2688, 8th Young Pioneers' Congress, Karl-Marx-Stadt. No. 2689, Youths playing musical instruments.

1988, July 19 **Litho.** *Perf. 13x12½*
2688 10pf multi .25 .25
2689 10pf +5pf multi .25 .25
a. A838 Pair, #2688-2689 + label 1.00 1.00

Surtax financed the congress.

1988 Summer Olympics, Seoul A839

5pf, Swimming. 10pf, Handball. 20pf +10pf, Hurdles. 25pf, Rowing. 35pf, Boxing. 50pf, Cycling.
85pf, Relay race.

1988, Aug. 9 **Photo.** *Perf. 14*
2690 A839 5pf multi .25 .25
2691 A839 10pf multi .25 .25
2692 A839 20pf +10pf multi .30 .30
2693 A839 25pf multi .30 .30
2694 A839 35pf multi .30 .30
2695 A839 50pf +20pf multi .60 .60
Nos. 2690-2695 (6) 2.00 2.00

Souvenir Sheet
Litho.
Perf. 13x12½

2696 A839 85pf multi 1.60 3.00

Souvenir Sheet

Leipzig Autumn Fair — A840

1988, Aug. 30 **Litho.** *Perf. 14*
2697 A840 Sheet of 3 1.60 2.00
a. 5pf Fair, c. 1810 .25 .40
b. 15pf Battle of Leipzig Memorial .25 .40
c. 1m Fair, c. 1820 .80 .80

DDR-USSR Manned Space Flight Type

1988, Aug. 30 **Litho.** *Perf. 14*
2698 A834 10pf like No. 2675 .25 .25
a. Sheet of 4 .85 1.00
2699 A834 20pf like No. 2676 .30 .30
a. Sheet of 4 1.10 1.10
2700 A834 35pf like No. 2677 .40 .40
a. Sheet of 4 2.10 2.10
Nos. 2698-2700 (3) .95 .95

Fascism Resistance Memorial, Como, Italy — A841

1988, Sept. 13 **Photo.**
2701 A841 35pf multi .35 .30

Memorial at Buchenwald, 30th Anniv. — A842

1988, Sept. 13 *Perf. 14*
2702 A842 10pf multi .25 .25

Mariner's Soc., Stralsund, 500th Anniv. — A843

Paintings: 5pf, *Adolph Friedrich* at Stralsund, by C. Leplow. 10pf, *Die Gartenlaube* (built in 1872) at Stralsund, by J.F. Kruger. 70pf, Brigantine *Auguste Mathilde* (built in 1830) at Stralsund, by I.C. Grunwaldt. 1.20m, Brig *Hoffnung* at Cologne, by G.A. Luther.

1988, Sept. 20 **Litho.** *Perf. 13½x13*
2703 A843 5pf multi .30 .25
2704 A843 10pf multi .30 .25
2705 A843 70pf multi .65 .65
2706 A843 1.20m multi 1.00 1.00
Nos. 2703-2706 (4) 2.25 2.15

Ship Lifts and Bridges A844

5pf, Magdeburg. 10pf, Magdeburg-Rothensee. 35pf, Niederfinow. 70pf, Altfriesack. 90pf, Rugendamm.

1988, Oct. 18 **Photo.** *Perf. 14x14½*
2707 A844 5pf multi .25 .25
2708 A844 10pf multi .25 .25
2709 A844 35pf multi .30 .25
2710 A844 70pf multi .55 .55
2711 A844 90pf multi .65 .65
Nos. 2707-2711 (5) 2.00 1.95

1st Nazi Pogrom (Kristallnacht), Nov. 9, 1938 — A845

1988, Nov. 8 *Perf. 14*
2712 A845 35pf Menorah .40 .30

Paintings by Max Lingner (1888-1959) A846

5pf, *In the Boat*, 1931. 10pf, *Yvonne*, 1939. 20pf, *Free, Strong and Happy*, 1944. 85pf, *New Harvest*, 1951.

1988, Nov. 8

2713	A846	5pf multicolored	.30	.25
2714	A846	10pf multicolored	.30	.25
2715	A846	20pf multicolored	.30	.25
2716	A846	85pf multicolored	.85	.70
		Nos. 2713-2716 (4)	1.75	1.45

Souvenir Sheet

Friedrich Wolf (1888-1953), Playwright — A847

1988, Nov. 22 **Litho.**

2717	A847	1.10m multi	1.00	3.00

WHO, 40th Anniv. — A848

1988, Nov. 22 **Photo.**

2718	A848	85pf multi	.80	.40

Miniature Sheet

Council for Mutual Economic Aid, 40th Anniv. A850

1989, Jan. 10 **Photo.** ***Perf. 13***

2720	A850	20pf multi	.40	.25

Labor Leaders Type of 1987

Portraits: No. 2721, Edith Baumann (1909-1973). No. 2722, Otto Meier (1889-1962). No. 2723, Fritz Selbmann (1899-1975). No. 2724, Alfred Oelssner (1879-1962).

1989, Jan. 24 **Engr.** ***Perf. 14***

2721	A804	10pf dark vio brn	.25	.25
2722	A804	10pf dark grn	.25	.25
2723	A804	10pf dark blue	.25	.25
2724	A804	10pf brn blk	.25	.25
		Nos. 2721-2724 (4)	1.00	1.00

Telephones A851

Designs: 10pf, Philipp Reis, 1861. 20pf, Siemens & Halske wall model, 1882. 50pf, Wall model OB 03, 1903. 85pf, Table model OB 05, 1905.

1989, Feb. 7 **Litho.**

2725	A851	10pf shown	.25	.25
2726	A851	20pf multi	.35	.25
2727	A851	50pf multi	.40	.40
2728	A851	85pf multi	.65	.65
a.		Block of 4, #2725-2728	2.00	2.25

Famous Men A852

No. 2729, Ludwig Renn (1889-1979). No. 2730, Carl von Ossietzky (1889-1938). No. 2731, Adam Scharrer (1889-1948). No. 2732, Rudolf Mauersberger (1889-1971). No. 2733, Johann Beckmann (1739-1811).

1989, Feb. 28 **Photo.**

2729	A852	10pf multicolored	.25	.25
2730	A852	10pf multicolored	.25	.25
2731	A852	10pf multicolored	.25	.25
2732	A852	10pf multicolored	.25	.25
2733	A852	10pf multicolored	.25	.25
		Nos. 2729-2733 (5)	1.25	1.25

Leipzig Spring Fair — A853

1989, Mar. 7 **Litho.**

2734	A853	70pf shown	.60	.50
2735	A853	85pf Buildings, 1690	.70	.70

Handelshof, 80th anniv. (70pf).

Bone Lace from Erzgebirge — A849

Various lace designs.

1988, Nov. 22 **Litho.** ***Perf. 12½x13***

2719	A849	Sheet of 6	2.00	2.00
a.		20pf multi	.25	.25
b.		25pf multi	.45	.45
c.		35pf multi	.25	.25
d.		40pf multi	.25	.25
e.		50pf multi	.45	.45
f.		85pf multi	.25	.25

Souvenir Sheet

Thomas Muntzer (c. 1468-1525), Religious Reformer — A854

1989, Mar. 21 ***Perf. 13x12½***

2736	A854	1.10m multi	1.10	2.25

1st Long-distance German Railway, Leipzig-Dresden, Sesquicentennial — A855

15pf, Georg Friedrich List (1789-1846), industrialist, economist. 20pf, Dresden Station in Leipzig, 1839. 50pf, Leipzig Station in Dresden, 1839.

1989, Apr. 4 ***Perf. 14***

2737	A855	15pf multi	.30	.25
2738	A855	20pf multi	.30	.25
2739	A855	50pf multi	.45	.45
		Nos. 2737-2739 (3)	1.05	.95

A856

Designs: Meissen Onion-pattern Porcelain, 250th anniv., and sword emblem.

1989, Apr. 18 **Litho.** ***Perf. 12½x13***

2740	A856	10pf Tea caddy	.25	.25
2741	A856	20pf Vase	.25	.30
2742	A856	35pf Breadboard	.35	.45
2743	A856	70pf Teapot	.65	.80
		Nos. 2740-2743 (4)	1.50	1.80

Size: 33x56mm

Perf. 14

2744		Block of 4	1.60	2.25
a.		A856 10pf like No. 2740	.30	.30
b.		A856 20pf like No. 2741	.25	.25
c.		A856 35pf like No. 2742	.35	.35
d.		A856 70pf like No. 2743	.75	.75

A857

1989, May 2 **Photo.** ***Perf. 14½x14***

2745	A857	20pf "I"	.25	.25
2746	A857	50pf "B"	.40	.35
2747	A857	1.35m "A"	1.10	1.10
		Nos. 2745-2747 (3)	1.75	1.70

Intl. Book Fair (IBA), Leipzig.

Student Government — A858

No. 2748, 8th World Youth Festival, Pyongyang. No. 2749, Whitsun meeting of Free German Youth.

1989, May 9 **Litho.** ***Perf. 13½x12½***

2748		20pf multicolored	.30	.40
2749		20pf +5pf multi	.30	.40
a.		A858 Pair, #2748-2749 + label	.60	1.25

Princess Luise — A859

Sculptures by Johann Gottfried Schadow (1764-1850), Prussian Court Sculptor — No. 2751, Princess Friederike.

1989, May 16 **Photo.** ***Perf. 14½x14***

2750	A859	50pf shown	.55	.40
2751	A859	85pf multicolored	.90	.80

Carl Zeiss Foundation, Jena, Cent. — A860

Modern medical technology: 50pf, Interference microscope Jenaval. 85pf, Bicoordinate measuring instrument ZKM 01-250C.

1989, May 16

2752		50pf multi	.35	.35
2753		85pf multi	.65	.65
a.		A860 Pair, #2752-2753 + label	1.25	2.00

Label pictures founder Ernst Abbe (1840-1905).

Jena University Inaugural Address, Bicent. — A861

1989, May 23 **Photo.** ***Perf. 14***

2754		25pf Frontispiece	.25	.25
2755		85pf Excerpt	.60	.60
a.		A861 Pair, #2754-2755 + label	.90	.90

Label pictures bust of Friedrich Schiller, author of the address.

Souvenir Sheet

Zoologists — A862

Designs: a, Alfred Brehm (1829-1884). b, Christian Brehm (1787-1864).

1989, June 13 **Litho.**

2756	A862	Sheet of 2	1.60	10.00
a.		50pf multicolored	.40	3.25
b.		85pf multicolored	.80	5.25

French Revolution, Bicent. A863

5pf, Storming of the Bastille, July 14, 1789. 20pf, Revolutionaries, flag bearer. 90pf, Storming Tuileries Palace, Aug. 10, 1792.

1989, July 4 Photo. *Perf. 13*

2757 A863 5pf multi .25 .25
2758 A863 20pf multi .25 .25
2759 A863 90pf multi .65 1.10
Nos. 2757-2759 (3) 1.15 1.60

Intl. Congress of Horse Breeders from Socialist States — A864

10pf, Haflinger. 20pf, English thoroughbred. 70pf, Cold blood. 110pf, Noble warm blood.

1989, July 18 Litho. *Perf. 13½*

2760 A864 10pf multicolored .25 .25
2761 A864 20pf multicolored .25 .25
2762 A864 70pf multicolored .55 .55
2763 A864 110pf multicolored .85 .85
Nos. 2760-2763 (4) 1.90 1.90

Natl. Stamp Exhibition, Magdeburg — A865

20pf, Owlglass Fountain. 70pf +5pf, Demons Fountain.

1989, Aug. 8 Litho. *Perf. 13x12½*

2764 A865 20pf multicolored .25 .25
2765 A865 70pf +5pf multi .65 .60

No. 2765 surtaxed for the philatelic unit of the Kulturbund.

Souvenir Sheet

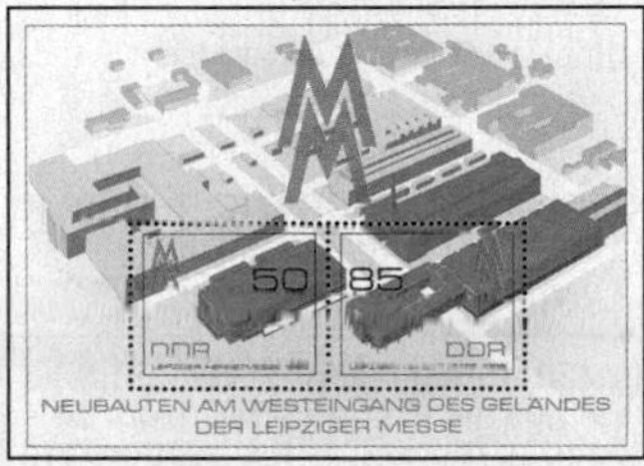

Leipzig Autumn Fair — A866

1989, Aug. 22 *Perf. 14*

2766 A866 Sheet of 2 1.25 2.50
a. 50pf Fairground .10 .70
b. 85pf Fairground, diff. .65 1.25

Thomas Muntzer (1489-1525), Religious Reformer A867

Various details of the painting *Early Bourgeois Revolution in Germany in 1525*, by W. Tubke.

1989, Aug. 22

2767 A867 5pf Globe .25 .25
2768 A867 10pf Fountain .25 .25
2769 A867 20pf Battle scene .25 .25
a. Souvenir sheet of 4 1.60 3.00
2770 A867 50pf Ark .40 .40
2771 A867 85pf Rainbow, battle .85 .85
Nos. 2767-2771 (5) 2.00 2.00

Muttergruppe, 1965, Bronze Statue in the Natl. Memorial, Ravensbruck A868

1989, Sept. 5 Photo. *Perf. 14*

2772 A868 35pf multi .35 .35

Natl. Memorial, Ravensbruck, 30th anniv.

Flowering Cacti *(Epiphyllum)* A869

1989, Sept. 19 Litho. *Perf. 13*

2773 A869 10m Adriana .25 .25
2774 A869 35m Feuerzauber .40 .30
2775 A869 50m Franzisko .55 .55
Nos. 2773-2775 (3) 1.20 1.10

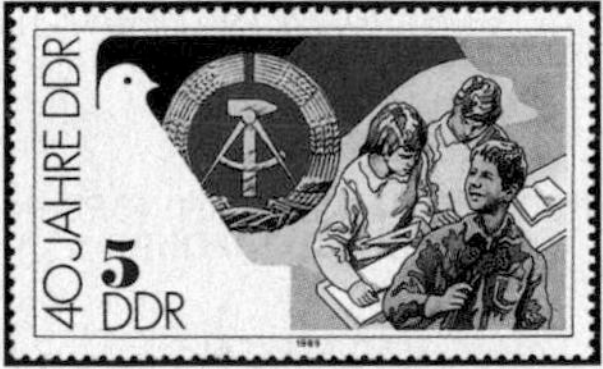

DDR, 40th Anniv. — A870

1989, Oct. 3 *Perf. 14*

2776 A870 5pf Education .25 .25
2777 A870 10pf Agriculture .25 .25
2778 A870 20pf Construction .30 .30
2779 A870 25pf Machinist, computer user .30 .30
Nos. 2776-2779 (4) 1.10 1.10

Souvenir Sheet

2780 A870 135pf Two workers 4.00 4.00

Jawaharlal Nehru, 1st Prime Minister of Independent India — A871

1989, Nov. 7 Photo. *Perf. 14*

2781 A871 35pf multicolored .35 .35

Statues of Roland Type of 1987

5pf, Zerbst, 1445. 10pf, Halberstadt, 1433. 20pf, Buch-Altmark, 1611. 50pf, Perleberg, 1546.

1989, Nov. 7 *Perf. 14½x14*

2782 A799 5pf multicolored .25 .25
2783 A799 10pf multicolored .25 .25
2784 A799 20pf multicolored .25 .25
2785 A799 50pf multicolored .40 .40
Nos. 2782-2785 (4) 1.15 1.15

Miniature Sheet

Chandeliers from Erzgebirge — A872

Designs: a, Schneeburg, circa 1860. b, Schwarzenberg, circa 1850. c, Annaberg, circa 1880. d, Seiffen, circa 1900. e, Seiffen, circa 1930. f, Annaberg, circa 1925.

Litho. & Engr.

1989, Nov. 28 *Perf. 14*

2786 A872 Sheet of 6 2.00 2.25
a. 10pf multicolored .25 .25
b. 20pf multicolored .45 .45
c. 25pf multicolored .25 .25
d. 35pf multicolored .25 .25
e. 50pf multicolored .45 .45
f. 70pf multicolored .25 .25

Bees Collecting Nectar — A873

5pf, Apple blossom. 10pf, Blooming heather. 20pf, Rape blossom. 50pf, Red clover.

1990, Jan. 9 Litho.

2787 A873 5pf multicolored .25 .25
2788 A873 10pf multicolored .25 .25
2789 A873 20pf multicolored .25 .25
2790 A873 50pf multicolored .55 .55
Nos. 2787-2790 (4) 1.30 1.30

The Young Post Rider, an Engraving by Albrecht Durer — A874

1990, Jan. 12 Litho. *Perf. 13*

2791 A874 35pf choc, gray brn, dark beige .40 .40

Postal communications in Europe, 500th anniv.

See Austria No. 1486, Belgium No. 1332, Germany No. 1592 and Berlin No. 9N584.

Labor Leaders — A875

Portraits: No. 2792, Bruno Leuschner (1910-65). No. 2793, Erich Weinert (1890-1953).

1990, Jan. 16 *Perf. 14*

2792 A875 10pf gray brown .25 .25
2793 A875 10pf deep blue .25 .25

Coats of Arms — A876

Early postal agency insignia: 10pf, Schwarzburg-Rudolstadt and Thurn & Taxis. 20pf, Royal Saxon letter collection. 50pf, Imperial Postal Agency. 1.10pf, Auxiliary post office.

1990, Feb. 6 Photo. *Perf. 14*

2794 A876 10pf multicolored .25 .25
2795 A876 20pf multicolored .25 .25
2796 A876 50pf multicolored .65 .55
2797 A876 110pf multicolored 1.25 1.20
Nos. 2794-2797 (4) 2.40 2.25

Size: 32x42mm

Perf. 13½

Litho.

2798 Block of 4 3.25 3.25
a. A876 10pf like No. 2794 .35 .25
b. A876 20pf like No. 2795 .35 .25
c. A876 50pf like No. 2796 .65 .55
d. A876 110pf like No. 2797 1.25 1.20

Posts & Telecommunications Workers' Day.

August Bebel (1840-1913), Co-founder of the Social Democratic Party — A877

1990, Feb. 20 Photo.

2799 A877 20pf multicolored .40 .40

Flying Machine Designed by Leonardo da Vinci — A878

No. 2801, Melchior Bauer. No. 2802, Albrecht Berblinger. No. 2803, Otto Lilienthal.

1990, Feb. 20 Litho. *Perf. 13½x13*

2800 A878 20pf shown .25 .25
2801 A878 35pf +5pf multi .40 .40
2802 A878 50pf multicolored .55 .45
2803 A878 90pf multicolored .90 .90
Nos. 2800-2803 (4) 2.10 2.00

LILIENTHAL '91 airmail exhibition. No. 2801 surtaxed for philatelic promotion.

Leipzig Spring Fair Seals — A879

1990, Mar. 6 *Perf. 12½x13*

2804 A879 70pf Seal, 1268 1.10 .60
2805 A879 85pf Seal, 1497 1.20 .70

City of Leipzig and the Leipzig Spring Fair, 825th annivs.

Dying Warriors — A880

Sculptures by Andreas Schluter.

1990, Mar. 6 Photo. *Perf. 13½x14*

2806 A880 40pf shown .45 .65
2807 A880 70pf multi, diff. .65 .80

Museum of German History in the Zeughaus of Berlin.

Famous Men A881

Portraits: No. 2808, Friedrich Diesterweg (1790-1866), educator. No. 2809, Kurt Tucholsky (1890-1935), novelist, journalist.

1990, Mar. 20 **Photo.** ***Perf. 14***

2808	A881	10pf multicolored	.30	.30
2809	A881	10pf multicolored	.30	.30

Labor Day, Cent. — A882

20pf, Flower, "1890/1990".

1990, Apr. 3

2810	A882	10pf shown	.40	.40
2811	A882	20pf red, sil & blk	.70	.70

Dicraeosaurus — A883

25pf, Kentrurosaurus. 35pf, Dysalotosaurus. 50pf, Brachiosaurus. 85pf, Brachiosaurus skull.

Perf. 13x12½, 12½x13

1990, Apr. 17 **Litho.**

2812	A883	10pf shown	.25	.25
2813	A883	25pf multicolored	.25	.25
a.		Miniature sheet of 4	1.25	1.25
2814	A883	35pf multicolored	.30	.30
2815	A883	50pf multicolored	.40	.40
2816	A883	85pf multicolored	.85	.85
		Nos. 2812-2816 (5)	2.05	2.05

Natural History Museum of Berlin, cent. Nos. 2815-2816 vert.

Penny Black, 150th Anniv. — A884

1990, May 8 ***Perf. 14***

2817	A884	20pf shown	.35	.35
2818	A884	35pf +15pf Saxony #1	.60	.60
2819	A884	110pf No. 48	1.60	1.60
		Nos. 2817-2819 (3)	2.55	2.55

A885

Intl. Telecommunications Union, 125th Anniv.: 10pf, David Edward Hughes (1831-1900), type-printing telegraph, 1855. 20pf, Distribution linkage, Berlin-Kopenick post office. 25pf, TV and microwave tower. 50pf, Molniya news satellite, globe. 70pf, Philipp Reis (1834-1874), physicist, designed sound transmission equipment.

1990, May 15

2820	A885	10pf multicolored	.30	.30
2821	A885	20pf multicolored	.30	.30
2822	A885	25pf multicolored	.30	.30
2823	A885	50pf multicolored	.80	.80
		Nos. 2820-2823 (4)	1.70	1.70

Souvenir Sheet

2824	A885	70pf multicolored	1.75	3.00

Pope John Paul II, 70th Birthday — A886

1990, May 15

2825	A886	35pf multicolored	.80	1.00

11th Youth Stamp Exhibition, Halle — A887

10pf +5pf, 18th cent. Halle. 20pf, 20th cent. Halle.

1990, June 5 ***Perf. 13x12½***

2826		10pf +5pf multi	.30	.30
2827		20pf multi	.30	.30
a.		A887 Pair, #2826-2827 + label	.65	.85

Treasures in the German State Library, Berlin A888

Designs: 20pf, Rules of an order, 1264. 25pf, Rudimentum novitiorum, 1475. 50pf, Chosrou wa Schirin, 18th cent. 110pf, Bookcover of Amalienbibliothek, 18th cent.

1990, June 19

2828	A888	20pf multicolored	.40	.25
2829	A888	25pf multicolored	.40	.25
2830	A888	50pf multicolored	1.10	.60
2831	A888	110pf multicolored	1.80	1.40
		Nos. 2828-2831 (4)	3.70	2.50

Castle Albrechtsburg and Cathedral, Meissen — A889

30pf, Goethe-Schiller Monument, Weimar. 50pf, Brandenburg Gate, Berlin. 60pf, Kyffhauser Monument. 70pf, Semper Opera, Dresden. 80pf, Castle Sanssouci, Potsdam. 100pf, Wartburg, Eisenach. 200pf, Magdeburg Cathedral. 500pf, Schwerin Castle.

1990, July 2 **Photo.** ***Perf. 14***

2832	A889	10pf ultramarine	.35	.30
2833	A889	30pf olive green	.65	.30
2834	A889	50pf bluish green	.65	.65
2835	A889	60pf violet brown	.65	.65
2836	A889	70pf dark brown	.65	.65
2837	A889	80pf red brown	.65	.65
2838	A889	100pf dark carmine	1.10	1.10
2839	A889	200pf dark violet	2.00	2.00
2840	A889	500pf green	4.00	4.00
		Nos. 2832-2840 (9)	10.70	10.30

Nos. 2832-2852 have face values based on the Federal Republic's Deutsche mark and were valid for postage in both countries.

Postal System, 500th Anniv. A890

30pf, 15th cent. postman. 50pf, 16th cent. postrider. 70pf, Post carriages c. 1595, 1750. 100pf, Railway mail carriages 1842, 1900.

1990, Aug. 28 **Litho.** ***Perf. 13x13½***

2841	A890	30pf multicolored	.35	.35
2842	A890	50pf multicolored	.45	.45
2843	A890	70pf multicolored	.60	.60
2844	A890	100pf multicolored	1.00	1.00
		Nos. 2841-2844 (4)	2.40	2.40

Louis Lewandowski (1821-94), Composer — A891

50pf+15pf, New Synagogue, Berlin.

1990, Sept. 18 ***Perf. 14***

2845	A891	30pf multicolored	.30	.30
2846	A891	50pf +15pf multi	.55	.55

Heinrich Schliemann (1822-1890), Archaeologist A892

Design: 30pf, shown. 50pf, Schliemann, double pot c. 2600-1900 B.C., horiz.

1990, Oct. 2 **Photo.**

2847	A892	30pf multicolored	.35	.35
2848	A892	50pf multicolored	.65	.65

Intl. Astronautics Federation, 41st Congress, Dresden A893

1990, Oct. 2

2849	A893	30pf Dresden skyline	.25	.25
2850	A893	50pf Globe	.40	.40
2851	A893	70pf Moon	.65	.85
2852	A893	100pf Mars	.90	.90
		Nos. 2849-2852 (4)	2.20	2.40

Stamps of the German Democratic Republic were replaced starting Oct. 3, 1990 by those of the Federal Republic of Germany. Nos. 2832-2852 remained valid until Dec. 31, 1991.

FOR USE IN ALL PROVINCES IN THE RUSSIAN ZONES

SEMI-POSTALS

Leipzig Fair Issue

Type of German Semi-Postal Stamps

16pf+9pf, 1st New Year's Fair, 1459. 50pf+25pf, Arrival of clothmakers from abroad, 1469.

Wmk. 292

1948, Aug. 29 **Litho.** ***Perf. 13½***

10NB1	SP252	16 + 9pf dk vio brn	.25	.55
10NB2	SP252	50 + 25pf dl vio bl	.25	.55
		Set, never hinged	1.20	

The 1948 Leipzig Autumn Fair.

Emblem of Philatelic Institute — OSP1

1948, Oct. 23 ***Perf. 13x13½***

10NB3	OSP1	12 + 3pf red	.25	.85
		Never hinged	.65	

Stamp Day, Oct. 24, 1948.

Type of German Semi-Postal Stamps of 1947

30pf+15pf, First fair in newly built Town Hall, 1556. 50pf+25pf, Italians at the Fair, 1536.

1949, Mar. 6 **Litho.** ***Perf. 13½***

10NB4	SP252	30 + 15pf red	1.00	3.50
10NB5	SP252	50 + 25pf blue	1.25	4.00
		Set, never hinged	6.50	

1949 Leipzig Spring Fair.

Goethe — OSP2

Designs: Different Goethe portraits.

1949, July 20 **Wmk. 292** ***Perf. 13***

10NB6	OSP2	6 + 4pf dl vio	.80	2.25
10NB7	OSP2	12 + 8pf dl brn	.80	2.25
10NB8	OSP2	24 + 16pf red brn	.65	2.00
10NB9	OSP2	50 + 25pf dk bl	.65	2.00
10NB10	OSP2	84 + 36pf ol gray	1.00	4.00
		Nos. 10NB6-10NB10 (5)	3.90	12.50
		Set, never hinged	9.00	

Johann Wolfgang von Goethe, birth bicent.

Souvenir Sheet

Profile of Goethe — OSP3

1949, Aug. 22 **Engr.** ***Perf. 14***

10NB11	OSP3	50pf + 4.50m blue	100.00	400.00
		Never hinged	140.00	

The sheet measures 106x105mm. The surtax was for the reconstruction of Weimar.

Type of German Semi-Postal Stamps

12pf+8pf, Russian merchants at the Fair, 1650. 24pf+16pf, Young Goethe at the Fair, 1765.

1949, Aug. 30 **Litho.** ***Perf. 13½***

10NB12	SP252	12 + 8pf gray	1.60	6.50
10NB13	SP252	24 + 16pf lake brn	2.00	8.00
		Set, never hinged	10.50	

1949 Leipzig Autumn Fair.

GERMAN DEMOCRATIC REPUBLIC SEMI-POSTAL STAMPS

Catalogue values for unused stamps in this section, from this point to the end of the section, are for Never Hinged items.

Canceled to Order

Used values are for CTO's from No. B14 to No. B203.

Some se-tenants include a semi-postal stamp. To avoid splitting the se-tenant piece the semi-postal is listed with the regular issue.

Bavaria No. 1 and Magnifier — SP4

Wmk. 292

1949, Oct. 30 Litho. *Perf. 14*
B14 SP4 12pf + 3pf gray blk 5.25 5.25

Stamp Day, 1949. See No. B21a.

Leipzig Fair Issue.
German Type of 1947
Inscribed: "Deutsche Demokratische Republik"

Leipzig Spring Fair: 24pf+12pf, First porcelain at Fair, 1710. 30pf+14pf, First Fair at Municipal Store, 1894.

1950, Mar. 5 *Perf. 13*
B15 SP252 24 + 12pf red vio 6.50 8.00
B16 SP252 30 + 14pf rose car 8.00 *8.00*

Shepherd Boy with Double Flute — SP5

"Bach Year": 24pf+6pf, Girl with hand organ. 30pf+8pf, Johann Sebastian Bach. 50pf+16pf, Chorus.

1950, June 14 *Perf. 14*
B17 SP5 12pf + 4pf bl grn 5.00 4.00
B18 SP5 24pf + 6pf olive 5.00 4.00
B19 SP5 30pf + 8pf dk red 6.50 6.50
B20 SP5 50pf + 16pf blue 13.00 12.00
Nos. B17-B20 (4) 29.50 26.50

Saxony No. 1, Globe and Dove — SP6

1950, July 1 Photo. Wmk. 292
B21 SP6 84 + 41pf brn red 32.50 9.00
a. Souv. sheet of 2, #B14, B21, imperf. *100.00* *110.00*
No. B21a hinged 25.00

German Stamp Exhib. (DEBRIA) held at Leipzig for the cent. of Saxony's 1st postage stamp.

Clearing Land — SP7

Reconstruction program: 24pf+6pf, Bricklaying. 30pf+10pf, Carpentry. 50pf+10pf, Inspecting plans.

1952, May 1 Litho.
B22 SP7 12pf + 3pf brt vio 2.25 .65
B23 SP7 24pf + 6pf henna brn 1.25 .65
B24 SP7 30pf + 10pf dp grn 2.25 .65
B25 SP7 50pf + 10pf vio bl 2.25 1.25
Nos. B22-B25 (4) 8.00 3.20

Dam — SP8

1954, Aug. 16 Unwmk.
B26 SP8 24pf + 6pf green .60 .65

The surtax was for flood victims.

Surcharged with New Value and "X"

1955, Feb. 25
B27 SP8 20 +5pf on 24+6pf .75 .45

The surtax was for flood victims.

Buchenwald Memorial — SP9

Perf. 13½x13

1956, Sept. 8 Wmk. 297
B28 SP9 20pf + 80pf rose red *.90* *3.25*

The surtax was for the erection of national memorials at the concentration camps of Buchenwald, Ravensbruck and Sachsenhausen. See No. B43.

Type of 1955 Surcharged "HELFT AGYPTEN +10" (#B29) or "HELFT DEM SOZIALISTISCHEN UNGARN +10" (#B30)

Perf. 13½x13

1956, Dec. 20 Wmk. 313
B29 A75 20pf + 10pf carmine .55 .35
B30 A75 20pf + 10pf carmine .55 .35

Monument to Ravensbrück SP10

Memorial Park and Lake — SP11

Perf. 13x13½, 13½x13

1957, Apr. 25 Litho.
B31 SP10 5pf + 5pf grn *.30* *.25*
B32 SP11 20pf + 10pf rose red *.35* *.35*

Intl. Day of Liberation. See Nos. B54, B70.

Ernst Thälmann — SP12

Portraits: 25pf+15pf, Rudolf Breitscheid. 40pf+20pf, Rev. Paul Schneider.

1957, Dec. 3 Photo. *Perf. 13*
Portraits in Gray
B33 SP12 20pf + 10pf dp plum .25 .25
B34 SP12 25pf + 15pf dk blue .25 .25
B35 SP12 40pf + 20pf violet .35 .35
a. Souv. sheet of 3, #B33-B35, imperf. 40.00 110.00
Nos. B33-B35 (3) .85 .85

No. B35a issued Sept. 15, 1958.

1958, July 11 Wmk. 313 *Perf. 13*

Portraits: 5pf+5pf, Albert Kuntz. 10pf+5pf, Rudi Arndt. 15pf+10pf, Kurt Adams. 20pf+10pf, Rudolf Renner. 25pf+15pf, Walter Stoecker.

Portraits in Gray
B36 SP12 5pf + 5pf brn blk .30 .65
B37 SP12 10pf + 5pf dk sl grn .30 .65
B38 SP12 15pf + 10pf dp vio .30 3.25
B39 SP12 20pf + 10pf dk red brn .30 .65
B40 SP12 25pf + 15pf bl blk *.90* *10.00*
Nos. B36-B40 (5) *2.10* *15.20*

Issued to honor the murdered victims of the Nazis at Buchenwald. The surtax was for the erection of national memorials.

See Nos. B49-B53, B55-B57, B60-B64, B71-B75, B79-B81.

Bugler, Flag and Camp — SP13

Design: 20pf+10pf, Pioneers and flag.

1958, Aug. 7 Litho. *Perf. 12½*
B41 SP13 10pf + 5pf green .35 .25
B42 SP13 20pf + 10pf red .35 .25

Pioneer organization, 10th anniversary.

Type of 1956 Overprinted in Black "14. September 1958"

Perf. 13½x13

1958, Sept. 15 Unwmk.
B43 SP9 20pf + 20pf rose red *.60* *.55*

Dedication of the memorial at Buchenwald concentration camp, Sept. 14, 1958.

Exercises with Hoops — SP14

Designs: 10pf+5pf, High jump. 20pf+10pf Vaulting. 25pf+10pf, Girl gymnasts. 40pf+20pf, Leipzig stadium and fireworks.

Perf. 13x13½

1959, Aug. 10 Litho. Wmk. 313
B44 SP14 5pf + 5pf org .25 .25
B45 SP14 10pf + 5pf grn .25 .25
B46 SP14 20pf + 10pf brt car .25 .25
B47 SP14 25pf + 10pf brt bl .25 .25
B48 SP14 40pf + 20pf red vio *1.40* *.45*
Nos. B44-B48 (5) 2.40 1.45

3rd German Sports Festival, Leipzig.

Portrait Type of 1957-58

Portraits: 5pf+5pf, Tilde Klose. 10pf+5pf, Kathe Niederkirchner. 15pf+10pf, Charlotte Eisenblatter. 20pf+10pf, Olga Benario-Prestes. 25pf+15pf, Maria Grollmuss.

1959, Sept. 3 Photo. *Perf. 13*
Portraits in Gray
B49 SP12 5pf + 5pf sep .25 .25
B50 SP12 10pf + 5pf dp grn .25 .25
B51 SP12 15pf + 10pf dp vio .25 .25
B52 SP12 20pf + 10pf mag .25 .25
B53 SP12 25pf + 15pf dk bl *.35* *.80*
Nos. B49-B53 (5) *1.35* *1.80*

Issued to honor women murdered by the Nazis at Buchenwald.

Ravensbrück Type of 1957 Dated: "12. September 1959"

Perf. 13½x13

1959, Sept. 11 Litho. Wmk. 313
B54 SP11 20pf + 10pf dp car & blk .45 .30

Portrait Type of 1957-58

5pf+5pf, Lothar Erdmann. 10pf+5pf, Ernst Schneller. 20pf+10pf, Lambert Horn.

1960, Feb. 25 Photo. *Perf. 13½x13*
Portraits in Gray
B55 SP12 5pf + 5pf ol bis .25 .25
B56 SP12 10pf + 5pf dk grn .25 .25
B57 SP12 20pf + 10pf dl mag .25 .25
Nos. B55-B57 (3) .75 .75

Issued to honor murdered victims of the Nazis at Sachsenhausen.

Type of Regular Issue, 1960

Designs: 10pf+5pf, Vacation ship under construction, Wismar. 20pf+10pf, Ship before Stubbenkammer and sailboat.

Wmk. 313

1960, June 23 Litho. *Perf. 13*
B58 A162 10pf + 5pf blk, yel & red .25 .25
B59 A162 20pf + 10pf blk, red & bl .25 .25

Portrait Type of 1957-58

Portraits: 10pf+5pf, Max Lademann. 15pf+5pf, Lorenz Breunig. 20pf+10pf, Mathias Thesen. 25pf+10pf, Gustl Sandtner. 40pf+20pf, Hans Rothbarth.

1960 Wmk. 313 *Perf. 13½x13*
Portraits in Gray
B60 SP12 10pf + 5pf grn .25 .25
B61 SP12 15pf + 5pf dp vio *.65* *.45*
B62 SP12 20pf + 10pf maroon .25 .25
B63 SP12 25pf + 10pf dk bl .25 .25
B64 SP12 40pf + 20pf lt red brn *1.40* *2.00*
Nos. B60-B64 (5) *2.80* *3.20*

Issued to honor the murdered victims of the Nazis at Sachsenhausen.

Bicyclist — SP15

25pf+10pf, Bicyclists and spectators.

1960, Aug. 3 *Perf. 13x13½, 13x12½*
Size: 28x23mm
B65 SP15 20pf + 10pf multi .25 .25
Size: 38½x21mm
B66 SP15 25pf + 10pf bl, gray & brn *1.20* *2.25*

Bicycling World Championships, Aug. 3-14.

Rook and Congress Emblem SP16

20pf+10pf, Knight. 25pf+10pf, Bishop.

Perf. 14x13½

1960, Sept. 19 Engr. Wmk. 313
B67 SP16 10pf + 5pf blue green .25 .25
B68 SP16 20pf + 10pf rose claret .25 .25
B69 SP16 25pf + 10pf blue *.65* *2.40*
Nos. B67-B69 (3) *1.15* *2.90*

14th Chess Championships, Leipzig.

Type of 1957

Design: Monument and memorial wall of Sachsenhausen National Memorial.

1960, Sept. 8 Litho. *Perf. 13x13½*
B70 SP10 20pf + 10pf dp car .35 .30

No. B70 was re-issued Apr. 20, 1961, with gray label adjoining each stamp in sheet, to commemorate the dedication of Sachsenhausen National Memorial. Values: unused 90c; used 40c.

Type of 1957

Portraits: 5pf+5pf, Werner Kube. 10pf+5pf, Hanno Gunther. 15pf+5pf, Elvira Eisenschneider. 20pf+10pf, Hertha Lindner. 25pf+10pf, Herbert Tschäpe.

1961, Feb. 6 *Perf. 13½x13*
Portraits in Black
B71 SP12 5pf + 5pf brt grn .25 .25
B72 SP12 10pf + 5pf bl grn .25 .25
B73 SP12 15pf + 5pf brt lilac *.90* *1.75*
B74 SP12 20pf + 10pf dp rose .25 .25
B75 SP12 25pf + 10pf brt bl .25 .25
Nos. B71-B75 (5) 1.90 2.75

Surtax for the erection of natl. memorials.

Pioneers Playing Volleyball SP17

Designs: 20pf+10pf, Folk dancing. 25pf+10pf, Building model airplanes.

1961, May 25 ***Perf. 13x12½***
B76 SP17 10pf + 5pf multi .25 .25
B77 SP17 20pf + 10pf multi .25 .25
B78 SP17 25pf + 10pf multi *2.50 2.00*
Nos. B76-B78 (3) 3.00 2.50

Young Pioneers' meeting, Erfurt.

Type of 1957 and

Sophie and Hans Scholl SP18

Portraits: 5pf+5pf, Carlo Schönhaar. 10pf+5pf, Herbert Baum. 20pf+10pf, Liselotte Herrmann. 40pf+20pf, Hilde and Hans Coppi.

Perf. 13½x13, 13x13½
1961, Sept. 7 Litho. Wmk. 313
Portraits in Black
B79 SP12 5pf + 5pf green .25 .25
B80 SP12 10pf + 5pf bl grn .25 .25
B81 SP12 20pf + 10pf rose car .25 .25
B82 SP18 25pf + 10pf blue .25 .25
B83 SP18 40pf + 20pf rose brn *1.60 4.25*
Nos. B79-B83 (5) 2.60 5.25

Surtax was the support of natl. memorials at Buchenwald, Ravensbrück & Sachsenhausen.

Danielle Casanova of France — SP19

Portraits: 10pf+5pf, Julius Fucik, Czechoslovakia. 20pf+10pf, Johanna Jannetje Schaft, Netherlands. 25pf+10pf, Pawel Finder, Poland. 40pf+20pf, Soya Anatolyevna Kosmodemyanskaya, Russia.

1962, Mar. 22 Engr. ***Perf. 13½***
B84 SP19 5pf + 5pf gray .25 .25
B85 SP19 10pf + 5pf green .25 .25
B86 SP19 20pf + 10pf maroon .25 .25
B87 SP19 25pf + 10pf deep blue .25 .25
B88 SP19 40pf + 20pf sepia *1.25 1.75*
Nos. B84-B88 (5) 2.25 2.75

Issued in memory of foreign victims of the Nazis.

Type of Regular Issue, 1962

Design: 20pf+10pf, Three cyclists and Warsaw Palace of Culture and Science.

Perf. 13x12½
1962, Apr. 26 Litho. Wmk. 313
B89 A192 20pf + 10pf ver, bl, blk & yel .25 .25

Folk Dance — SP20

15pf+5pf, Youths of three nations parading.

1962, July 17 Wmk. 313 ***Perf. 14***
B90 10pf + 5pf multi .30 .25
B91 15pf + 5pf multi .30 .25
a. SP20 Pair, #B90-B91 1.00 .90

Issued to publicize the 8th Youth Festival for Peace and Friendship, Helsinki, July 28-Aug. 6, 1962.

No. B91a forms the festival emblem.

Type of Regular Issue, 1962

Design: 20pf+10pf, Springboard diving.

1962, Aug. 7 Wmk. 313 ***Perf. 13***
B92 A199 20pf + 10pf lil rose & grnsh bl .25 .25

René Blieck of Belgium — SP21

Seven Cervi Brothers of Italy SP22

Portraits: 10pf+5pf, Dr. Alfred Klahr, Austria. 15pf+5pf, José Diaz, Spain. 20pf+10pf, Julius Alpari, Hungary.

1962, Oct. 4 Engr. ***Perf. 14***
B93 SP21 5pf + 5pf dk bl gray .25 .25
B94 SP21 10pf + 5pf green .25 .25
B95 SP21 15pf + 5pf brt vio .25 .25
B96 SP21 20pf + 10pf dl red brn .25 .25
B97 SP22 70pf + 30pf sepia *1.40 2.10*
Nos. B93-B97 (5) 2.40 3.10

Issued to commemorate foreign victims of the Nazis.

Walter Bohne, Runner — SP23

Portraits: 10pf+5pf, Werner Seelenbinder, wrestler. 15pf+5pf, Albert Richter, bicyclist. 20pf+10pf, Heinz Steyer, soccer player. 25pf+10pf, Kurt Schlosser, mountaineer.

Engr. & Photo.
1963, May 27 Wmk. 313 ***Perf. 14***
B98 SP23 5pf + 5pf yel & blk .25 .25
B99 SP23 10pf + 5pf pale yel grn & blk .25 .25
B100 SP23 15pf + 5pf rose lil & blk .25 .25
B101 SP23 20pf + 10pf pink & blk .25 .25
B102 SP23 25pf + 10pf pale bl & blk *1.60 4.00*
Nos. B98-B102 (5) 2.60 5.00

Issued to commemorate sportsmen victims of the Nazis. Each stamp printed with alternating label showing sporting events connected with each person honored. The surtax went for the maintenance of national memorials. See Nos. B106-B110.

Gymnasts — SP24

Designs: 20pf+10pf, Women gymnasts. 25pf+10pf, Relay race.

1963, June 13 Litho. ***Perf. 12½x13***
B103 SP24 10pf + 5pf blk, yel grn & lem .25 .25
B104 SP24 20pf + 10pf blk, red & vio .25 .25
B105 SP24 25pf + 10pf blk, bl, & gray *3.25 2.25*
Nos. B103-B105 (3) 3.75 2.75

4th German Gymnastic and Sports Festival, Leipzig. The surtax went to the festival committee.

Type of 1963

Portraits: 5pf+5pf, Hermann Tops, gymnastics instructor. 10pf+5pf, Käte Tucholla, field hockey players. 15pf+5pf, Rudolph Seiffert, long-distance swimmers. 20pf+10pf, Ernst Grube, sportsmen demonstrating for peace. 40pf+20pf, Kurt Biedermann, kayak in rapids.

Engraved and Photogravure
1963, Sept. 24 Wmk. 313 ***Perf. 14***
B106 SP23 5pf + 5pf yel & blk .25 .25
B107 SP23 10pf + 5pf grn & blk .25 .25
B108 SP23 15pf + 5pf lil & blk .25 .25
B109 SP23 20pf + 10pf pale pink & blk .25 .25
B110 SP23 40pf + 20pf lt bl & blk *1.90 2.40*
Nos. B106-B110 (5) 2.90 3.40

See note after No. B102.

Type of Regular Issue, 1963

Design: 20pf+10pf, Ski jumper in mid-air.

Perf. 13½x13
1963, Dec. 16 Litho. Wmk. 313
B111 A224 20pf + 10pf multi .25 .25

Surtax for the Natl. Olympic Committee.

Anton Saefkow SP25

Designs: 10pf+5pf, Franz Jacob. 15pf+5pf, Bernhard Bästlein. 20pf+5pf, Harro Schulze-Boysen. 25pf+10pf, Adam Kuckhoff. 40pf+10pf, Mildred and Arvid Harnack. Nos. B112-B114 show group posting anti-Hitler and pacifist posters. Nos. B115-B117 show production of anti-fascist pamphlets.

1964, Mar. 24 Wmk. 313 ***Perf. 13***
Size: 41x32mm
B112 SP25 5pf + 5pf .25 .25
B113 SP25 10pf + 5pf .25 .25
B114 SP25 15pf + 5pf .25 .25
B115 SP25 20pf + 5pf .25 .25
B116 SP25 25pf + 10pf .35 .25
Size: 48½x28mm
B117 SP25 40pf + 10pf *1.00 1.25*
Nos. B112-B117 (6) 2.35 2.50

The surtax was for the support of national memorials for victims of the Nazis.

Olympic Types of Regular Issues

Designs: 40pf+20pf, Two runners. No. B119, Equestrian. No. B120, Three runners.

Lithographed and Engraved
1964, July 15 Wmk. 313 ***Perf. 14***
B118 A232 40pf + 20pf multi .25 .25
Litho.
Perf. 13
B119 A233 10pf + 5pf multi 2.00 2.25
B120 A233 10pf + 5pf multi 2.00 2.25
Nos. B118-B120 (3) 4.25 4.75

See note after No. 714.

Pioneers Studying — SP26

Designs: 20pf+10pf, Pioneers planting tree. 25pf+10pf, Pioneers playing.

1964, July 29
B121 SP26 10pf + 5pf multi 1.60 .35
B122 SP26 20pf + 10pf multi 1.60 .35
B123 SP26 25pf + 10pf multi *3.25 3.25*
Nos. B121-B123 (3) 6.45 3.95

Fifth Young Pioneers Meeting, Karl-Marx-Stadt.

Stamp Exhibition Type of 1964

Designs: 10pf+5pf, Stamp of 1958 (No. 390). 20pf+10pf, Stamp of 1950 (No. 73).

Perf. 13x13½
1964, Sept. 23 Litho. Wmk. 313
B124 A238 10pf + 5pf org & emer .25 .25
B125 A238 20pf + 10pf brt pink & bl .30 .25

Boxing Type of Regular Issue

10pf+5pf, Two boxing gloves and laurel.

Perf. 13½x14
1965, Apr. 27 Photo. Wmk. 313
B126 A247 10pf + 5pf blk, gold, red & blue .25 .25

The surtax went to the German Turner and Sport Organization.

Type of Regular Issue, 1965

5pf+5pf, George Dimitrov at Leipzig trial & communist newspaper. 10pf+5pf, Anti-fascists clandestinely distributing leaflets. 15pf+5pf, Fighting in Spanish Civil War. 20pf+10pf, Ernst Thalman behind bars & demonstration for his release. 25pf+10pf, Founding of Natl. Committee for Free Germany & signatures.

Wmk. 313
1965, May 5 Photo. ***Perf. 14***
Flags in Red, Black and Yellow
B127 A248 5pf + 5pf blk, org & red .25 .25
B128 A248 10pf + 5pf grn & red .25 .25
B129 A248 15pf + 5pf lil, red & yel .25 .25
B130 A248 20pf + 10pf blk & red .25 .25
B131 A248 25pf + 10pf ol grn, yel & blk .25 .25
Nos. B127-B131 (5) 1.25 1.00

The surtax went for the maintenance of national memorials.

Doves, Globe and Finnish Flag — SP27

1965, July 5 Litho. ***Perf. 13x13½***
B132 SP27 10pf + 5pf vio bl & emer .25 .25
B133 SP27 20pf + 5pf red & vio bl *.40 .30*

World Peace Congress, Helsinki, July 10-17. The surtax went to the peace council of the DDR.

No. 725 Surcharged

Perf. 13½x13
1965, Aug. 23 Wmk. 313
B134 A239 10pf + 10pf multi .35 .25

Surtax was for North Viet Nam.

Sports Type of Regular Issue
Perf. 13½x13
1965, Sept. 15 Litho. Unwmk.
B135 A257 10pf + 5pf Fencer .25 .25
B136 A257 10pf + 5pf Pistol shooter .25 .25

International Modern Pentathlon Championships, Leipzig.

Type of Regular Issue

Designs: 10pf+5pf, Willi Bredel and instruction of International Brigade. 20pf+10pf, Heinrich Rau and parade after battle of Brunete. 25pf+10pf, Hans Marchwitza, international fighters and globe. 40pf+10pf, Artur Becker and battle on the Ebro.

1966, July 15 Photo. ***Perf. 14***
B137 A277 10pf + 5pf multi .25 .25
B138 A277 20pf + 10pf multi .25 .25
B139 A277 25pf + 10pf multi .25 .25
B140 A277 40pf + 10pf multi *1.25 1.00*
Nos. B137-B140 (4) 2.00 1.75

The surtax was for the maintenance of national memorials.

Canoe Type of Regular Issue

Design: 10pf+5pf, Men's single canoe race.

Perf. 13x12½

1966, Aug. 16 Litho. Unwmk.
B141 A279 10pf + 5pf multi .25 .25

Red Cross Type of Regular Issue

Design: ICY Red Crescent, Red Cross, and Red Lion and Sun emblems, horiz.

1966, Sept. 13 Wmk. 313 *Perf. 14*
B142 A281 20pf + 10pf vio & red .35 .25

International health cooperation. Surtax for German Red Cross.

Sports Type of Regular Issue

Design: 20pf+5pf, Weight lifter.

Perf. 13½x13

1966, Sept. 22 Litho. Unwmk.
B143 A282 20pf + 5pf ultra & blk .35 .25

Armed Woman Planting Flower — SP28

1966, Oct. 25 *Perf. 13½x13*
B144 SP28 20pf + 5pf blk & pink .50 .25

Surtax was for North Viet Nam.

Wartburg Type of Regular Issue

Design: Wartburg, view from the East.

1966, Nov. 23 *Perf. 13x13½*
B145 A288 10pf + 5pf slate .35 .25

See note after No. 878.

Olympic Type of Regular Issue

Design: 10pf+5pf, Tobogganing.

1968, Jan. 17 Litho. *Perf. 13½x13*
B146 A314 10pf + 5pf grnsh bl, vio bl & red .25 .25

The surtax was for the Olympic Committee of the German Democratic Republic.

Armed Mother and Child — SP29

1968, May 8 *Perf. 13½x13*
B147 SP29 10pf + 5pf yel & multi .25 .25

Surtax was for North Viet Nam.

Festival Type of Regular Issue

1968, June 20 Litho. *Perf. 13½x13*
B148 A327 20pf + 5pf multi .30 .25

Olympic Games Type of Regular Issue, 1968

Designs: 10pf+5pf, Pole vault, vert. 20pf+10pf, Soccer, vert.

1968, Sept. 18 Photo. *Perf. 14*
B149 A336 10pf + 5pf multi .25 .25
B150 A336 20pf + 10pf multi .25 .25

The surtax was for the Olympic Committee.

Armed Vietnamese Couple — SP30

1969, June 4
B151 SP30 10pf + 5pf multi .30 .25

Surtax was for North Viet Nam.

Sports Type of Regular Issue, 1969

Designs: 10pf+5pf, Gymnastics. 20pf+5pf, Art Exhibition with sports motifs.

Photo. & Engr.

1969, June 18 *Perf. 14*
B152 A353 10pf + 5pf multi .25 .25
B153 A353 20pf + 5pf multi .25 .25

The surtax was for the German Gymnastic and Sports League.

Otto von Guericke's Vacuum Test with Magdeburg Hemispheres — SP31

1969, Oct. 28 Litho. *Perf. 13x12½*
B154 SP31 40pf + 10pf multi *.85 .55*

See note after No. 1146.

Folk Art Type of Regular Issue

Design: 20pf+5pf, Decorative plate.

1969, Nov. 25 Litho. *Perf. 13½x13*
B155 A365 20pf + 5pf yel blk & ultra .30 .30

Sports Type of Regular Issue

Design: 20pf+5pf, Children hurdling.

1970, July 1 Photo. *Perf. 14x13½*
B156 A382 20pf + 5pf multi .35 .25

6th Youth Pioneer Meeting, Cottbus — SP32

Design: 10pf+5pf, Pioneer Waving Kerchief, and Pioneer Activities. 25pf+5pf, Girl Pioneer holding kerchief, and Pioneer activities.

1970, July 28 Litho. *Perf. 13x12½*
B157 10pf + 5pf multi .25 .25
B158 25pf + 5pf multi .25 .25
a. SP32 Pair, #B157-B158 .85 *2.00*

No. B158a has continuous design.

Ho Chi Minh — SP33

1970, Sept. 2 *Perf. 13x13½*
B159 SP33 20pf + 5pf rose, blk & red .35 .25

Surtax was for North Viet Nam.

German Democratic Republic No. 460 — SP34

1970, Oct. 1 Photo. *Perf. 14x13½*
B160 SP34 15pf + 5pf multi *.25 .30*

2nd National Youth Philatelic Exhibition, Karl-Marx-Stadt, Oct. 4-11.

Mother and Child — SP35

Photo. & Engr.

1971, Sept. 2 *Perf. 14*
B161 SP35 10pf + 5pf multi .30 .25

Surtax was for North Viet Nam.

Type of Regular Issue

10pf+5pf, Loading & unloading mail at airport.

Photo. & Engr.

1971, Oct. 5 *Perf. 14*
B162 A421 10pf + 5pf multi .25 .25

Olympic Games Type of Regular Issue

Olympic Rings and: 10pf+5pf, Figure skating, pairs. 15pf+5pf, Speed skating.

1971, Dec. 7 Photo. *Perf. 13½x14*
B163 A424 10pf + 5pf bl, car & blk .25 .25
B164 A424 15pf + 5pf grn, blk & bl .25 .25

Vietnamese Farm Woman — SP36

1972, Feb. 22 Litho. *Perf. 13½x13*
B165 SP36 10pf + 5pf multi .30 .25

Surtax was for North Viet Nam.

Olympic Games Type of Regular Issue

Sport and Olympic Rings: 10pf+5pf, Diving. 25pf+10pf, Rowing.

1972, May 16 Photo. *Perf. 13½x14*
B166 A430 10pf + 5pf grnsh bl, gold & blk .25 .25
B167 A430 25pf + 10pf multi .25 .25

Interartes Type of Regular Issue

Designs: 15pf+5pf, Spear carrier, Persia, 500 B.C. 35pf+5pf, Grape Sellers, by Max Lingner, 1949, horiz.

1972, Sept. 19 Photo. *Perf. 14*
B168 A439 15pf + 5pf multi *.65 .55*
B169 A439 35pf + 5pf multi .25 .25

Flags and World Time Clock — SP37

25pf+5pf, Youth group with guitar and dove.

1973, Feb. 13 Litho. *Perf. 12½x13*
B170 SP37 10pf + 5pf multi .25 .25
B171 SP37 25pf + 5pf multi .30 .25

10th World Youth Festival, Berlin.

Young Couple, by Günter Glombitza — SP38

1973, Oct. 4 Photo. *Perf. 13½x14*
B172 SP38 20pf + 5pf multi .30 .25

Philatelists' Day and for the 3rd National Youth Philatelic Exhibition, Halle.

Child, Symbols of Reconstruction SP39

1973, Oct. 11 *Perf. 14x13½*
B173 SP39 10pf + 5pf multi .30 .25

Surtax was for North Viet Nam.

Luis Corvalan, Red Flag — SP40

25pf+5pf, Salvador Allende, Chilean flag.

1973, Nov. 5 *Perf. 13½x14*
B174 SP40 10pf + 5pf multi *.25 .25*
B175 SP40 25pf + 5pf multi *.35 .35*

Solidarity with the people of Chile.

Raised Fist and Star — SP41

1975, Sept. 23 Litho. *Perf. 13x13½*
B176 SP41 10pf + 5pf multi .30 .25

Surtax was for the Solidarity Committee of the German Democratic Republic.

Restored Post Gate, Wurzen, 1734 — SP42

1975, Oct. 21 Photo. *Perf. 14*
B177 SP42 10pf + 5pf multi *.35 .35*

Philatelists' Day 1975.

Olympic Games Type of 1975

Designs: 10pf+5pf, Luge run, Oberhof. 25pf+5pf, Ski jump, Rennsteig at Oberhof.

1975, Dec. 2 Photo. *Perf. 14*
B178 A518 10pf + 5pf multi .25 .25
B179 A518 25pf + 5pf multi .25 .25

Olympic Games Type of 1976

Designs: 10pf+5pf, Swimming pool, High School for Physical Education, Leipzig. 35pf+10pf, Rifle range, Suhl.

1976, May 18 Photo. *Perf. 13½x14*
B180 A529 10pf + 5pf multi .25 .25
B181 A529 35pf + 10pf multi .25 .25

TV Tower, Berlin, and Perforations SP43

1976, Oct. 19 **Litho.** ***Perf. 13***
B182 SP43 10pf + 5pf org & bl .30 .25

Surtax was for Sozphilex 77, Philatelic Exhibition of Socialist Countries, in connection with 60th anniversary of October Revolution.

Sports Type of 1977

10pf+5pf, Young milers. 25pf+5pf, Girls artistic gymnastic performance.

1977, July 19 **Litho.** ***Perf. 13x12½***
B183 A558 10pf + 5pf multi .25 .25
B184 A558 25pf + 5pf multi .25 .25

Sozphilex Type of 1977
Souvenir Sheet

Design: 50pf+20pf, World Youth Song, by Lothar Zitzmann, horiz.

1977, Aug. 16 **Photo.** ***Perf. 13***
B185 A559 50pf + 20pf multi *1.10 2.60*

Hand Holding Torch — SP44

1977, Oct. 18 **Litho.** ***Perf. 14***
B186 SP44 10pf + 5pf multi .30 .25

Surtax was for East German Solidarity Committee.

Fountain Type of 1979

Design: 10pf+5pf, Goose Boy Fountain.

1979, Aug. 7 **Photo.** ***Perf. 14***
B187 A617 10pf + 5pf multi *.40 .35*

Vietnamese Soldier, Mother and Child — SP45

1979, Nov. 6 **Litho.** ***Perf. 14***
B188 SP45 10pf + 5pf red org & blk .35 .25

Surtax was for Vietnam.

Olympic Type of 1980

Ski Jump, sculpture by Gunther Schutz.

1980, Jan. 15 **Photo.**
B189 A627 25pf + 10pf multi .25 .25

1980, Apr. 22 **Photo.** ***Perf. 14***

Design: 20pf+5pf, Runners at the Finish, by Lothar Zitzmann.

B190 A627 20 + 5pf multi .25 .25

Interflug Type of 1980
Souvenir Sheet

1980, June 10 **Litho.** ***Perf. 13x12½***
B191 A636 1m + 10pf Jet, globe *1.90 4.00*

AEROSOZPHILEX 1980 International Airpost Exhibition, Berlin, Aug. 1-10.

Olympic Type of 1980

Design: Swimmer, by Willi Sitte, vert.

1980, July 8 **Photo.** ***Perf. 14***
B192 A627 20pf + 10pf multi .25 .25

22nd Summer Olympic Games, Moscow, July 19-Aug. 3.

International Solidarity — SP46

1980, Oct. 14 **Photo.** ***Perf. 14***
B193 SP46 10pf + 5pf multi .40 .25

International Solidarity — SP47

1981, Oct. 6 **Photo.** ***Perf. 14***
B194 SP47 10pf + 5pf multi .35 .25

Palestinian Solidarity — SP48

Palestinian family, Tree of Life.

1982, Sept. 21 **Litho.** ***Perf. 14***
B195 SP48 10pf + 5pf multi .35 .25

Nicaraguan Solidarity SP49

Literacy, home defense.

1983, Nov. 8 **Litho.** ***Perf. 14x13½***
B196 SP49 10pf + 5pf multi .30 .25

Solidarity — SP50

1984, Oct. 23 **Photo.** ***Perf. 14***
B197 SP50 10pf + 5pf Knot .35 .25

Solidarity SP51

10pf +5pf, Globe, peace dove.

1985, May 28 **Photo.**
B198 SP51 10pf + 5pf multi .25 .25

Surtax for the Solidarity Committee.

Technical Assistance to Developing Nations — SP52

1986, Nov. 4 **Photo.**
B199 SP52 10pf + 5pf multi .30 .25

Surtax for the Solidarity Committee.

Solidarity with South Africans Opposing Apartheid SP53

1987, June 16 **Litho.** ***Perf. 14***
B200 SP53 10pf +5pf multi .30 .25

Solidarity SP54

1988, Oct. 4 **Photo.** ***Perf. 14***
B201 SP54 10pf +5pf multi .40 .40

Surtax for the Solidarity Committee. No. B201 printed se-tenant with label containing a Wilhelm Pieck quote.

UNICEF Emblem and Children of Africa — SP55

1989, Sept. 5 **Photo.** ***Perf. 14½x14***
B202 SP55 10pf +5pf multi .30 .25

Surtax for the Solidarity Committee.

Leipzig Church, Municipal Arms SP56

1990, Feb. 28 **Photo.** ***Perf. 13***
B203 SP56 35pf +15pf multi .75 .55

We are the People.

Intl. Literacy Year — SP57

1990, July 24 **Photo.** ***Perf. 14***
B204 SP57 30pf+5pf on 10pf+5pf .80 .80

Not issued without surcharge.

AIR POST STAMPS

Catalogue values for all unused stamps in this section are for Never Hinged items.

Canceled to Order
Used values are for CTO's.

Stylized Plane
AP1 AP2

Perf. 13x12½, 13x13½ (AP2)

1957, Dec. 13 **Litho.** **Wmk. 313**
C1 AP1 5pf gray & blk 3.25 .25
C2 AP1 20pf brt car & blk .25 .25
C3 AP1 35pf violet & blk .25 .25
C4 AP1 50pf maroon & blk .30 .25
C5 AP2 1m olive & yel .90 .25
C6 AP2 3m choc & yel 1.40 .40
C7 AP2 5m dk bl & yel 3.25 .60
Nos. C1-C7 (7) 9.60 2.25

Plane and Envelope — AP3

1982-87 **Photo.** ***Perf. 14***
C8 AP3 5pf lt bl & blk .25 .25
C9 AP3 15pf brt rose lil & blk .25 .30
C10 AP3 20pf ocher & blk .25 .25
C11 AP3 25pf ol bis & blk .30 .30
C12 AP3 30pf brt grn & blk .25 .25
C13 AP3 40pf ol grn & blk .30 .25
C14 AP3 1m blue & blk .60 .40
C15 AP3 3m brown & blk 3.00 1.75
C16 AP3 5m dk red & blk 3.25 1.20
Nos. C8-C16 (9) 8.45 4.95

Issued: 30, 40pf, 1m, 10/26; 5, 20pf, 10/4/83; 3m, 4/10/84; 5m, 9/10/85; 15, 25pf, 10/6/87.

OFFICIAL STAMPS

While valid, these Official stamps were not sold to the public unused. After their period of use, some sets were sold abroad by the government stamp sales agency. Used values of Official stamps are for canceled-to-order examples. Reprints of type O1 stamps have printed cancellations.

Catalogue values for all unused stamps in this section are for Never Hinged items.

Arms of Republic — O1

Perf. 13x12½

1954 **Wmk. 297** **Litho.**
O1 O1 5pf emerald 13.50 .25
O2 O1 6pf violet 6.50 .25
O3 O1 8pf org brown 9.00 .25
O4 O1 10pf lt bl grn 20.00 .25
O5 O1 12pf blue 32.50 .25
O6 O1 15pf dark violet 32.50 .25
O7 O1 16pf dark violet 6.50 .25
O8 O1 20pf olive 13.00 .25
O9 O1 24pf brown red 6.50 .25
O10 O1 25pf sage green 6.50 .25
O11 O1 30pf brown red 6.50 .25
O12 O1 40pf red 9.75 .25
O13 O1 48pf rose lilac 4.50 .65
O14 O1 50pf rose lilac 4.50 .25
O15 O1 60pf bright blue 4.00 .25
O16 O1 70pf brown 4.00 .25
O17 O1 84pf brown 10.00 2.00
Nos. O1-O17 (17) 189.75 6.40

Type of 1954 Redrawn

Arc of compass projects at right except on No. O22.

1954-56			Typo.	
O18	O1	5pf emer ('54)	3.25	.25
O19	O1	10pf bl grn	2.50	.25
O20	O1	12pf dk bl ('54)	2.50	.25
O21	O1	15pf dk vio	2.50	.25
O22	O1	20pf ol, arc at left ('55)	*32.50*	.25
a.		Arc of compass projects at right ('56)	325.00	.25
O23	O1	25pf dark green	2.00	.35
O24	O1	30pf brown red	4.00	.35
O25	O1	40pf red	5.25	.25
O26	O1	50pf rose lilac	2.00	.25
O27	O1	70pf brown	2.00	.25
		Nos. O18-O27 (10)	58.50	2.70

Shaded background of emblem consists of vertical lines; on Nos. O1-O17 it consists of dots.

Granite paper was used for a 1956 printing of the 5pf, 10pf, 15pf, 20pf and 40pf. Value for set unused $1,800, used $5.50.

See Nos. O37-O43.

O2

1956		Wmk. 297	*Perf. 13x12½*	
O28	O2	5pf black	.25	.25
O29	O2	10pf black	.25	.25
O30	O2	20pf black	.30	.25
O31	O2	40pf black	.35	.25
O32	O2	70pf black	.40	.40
		Nos. O28-O32 (5)	1.55	1.40

O3

1956		Litho.	Wmk. 297	
O33	O3	10pf lilac & black	.80	.65
O34	O3	20pf lilac & black	*120.00*	.65
O35	O3	40pf lilac & black	1.25	.65
O36	O3	70pf lilac & black	2.00	2.25
		Nos. O33-O36 (4)	*124.05*	4.20

Nos. O33-O36 exist also with black or violet overprint of 4-digit control number.

See Nos. O44-O45.

No. O34 was reprinted with watermark sideways ("DDR" vertical). Value $4.

Redrawn Type of 1954-56

Perf. 13x12½, 14

1957-60		Typo.	Wmk. 313	
		Granite Paper		
O37	O1	5pf emerald	.35	.25
O38	O1	10pf blue green	.35	.25
O39	O1	15pf dark vio	.35	.25
O40	O1	20pf olive	.35	.25
O41	O1	30pf dark red ('58)	.40	.25
O42	O1	40pf red	.35	.25
O42A	O1	50pf rose lilac ('60)	1.10	1.60
O43	O1	70pf brown ('58)	1.10	1.60
		Nos. O37-O43 (8)	4.35	4.70

Nos. O37-O43 were all issued in perf. 13x12½. Nos. O37-O40 were also issued perf. 14. Values are the same. Postally used No. O42A is rare. Nos. O37-O41 are valued with Wmk. 313 reversed.

Nos. O37-O42 exist with Wmk. 313 normal, but overprinted cancel reprints value only slightly higher.

Type of 1956

1957		Litho.	*Perf. 13x12½*	
O44	O3	10pf lilac & black	.45	.35
O45	O3	20pf lilac & black	.40	.05

Nos. O44-O45 have black or violet overprint of four-digit control number.

Stamps similar to type O3 were issued later, with denomination expressed in dashes: one for 10pf, two for 20pf.

ISSUED UNDER RUSSIAN OCCUPATION

BERLIN-BRANDENBURG

Berlin Bear — OS1

6pf, Bear holding spade. 8pf, Bear on shield. 10pf, Bear holding brick. 12pf, Bear carrying board. 20pf, Bear on small shield. 30pf, Oak sapling, ruins.

1945		Litho.	*Perf. 14*	
11N1	OS1	5pf green	.25	*.45*
11N2	OS1	6pf violet	.25	*.35*
11N3	OS1	8pf org red	.25	*.35*
11N4	OS1	10pf brown	.25	*.45*
11N5	OS1	12pf red	.25	*.35*
11N6	OS1	20pf blue	.25	*.45*
11N7	OS1	30pf olive	.25	*.65*
		Nos. 11N1-11N7 (7)		*3.05*
		Set, never hinged	2.00	

Issued: 5pf, 8pf, 6/9; 12pf, 7/5; others, 7/18.

1945, Dec. 6			*Serrate Roulette 13½*	
11N1a	OS1	5pf	.25	*.55*
11N2a	OS1	6pf	3.75	*90.00*
11N3a	OS1	8pf	2.25	*90.00*
11N4a	OS1	10pf	3.75	*90.00*
11N5a	OS1	12pf	4.50	*125.00*
11N6a	OS1	20pf	3.00	*97.50*
11N7a	OS1	30pf	4.50	*125.00*
		Nos. 11N1a-11N7a (7)	22.00	*618.05*
		Set, never hinged	110.00	

No. 11N1a comes with two different roulettes. The roulette that matches Nos. 11N2a-11N7a is valued at $2. No. 11N5a in the second roulette is rare.

MECKLENBURG-VORPOMMERN

OS1

Plowman — OS2

OS2a

1945-46		Typo.	*Perf. 10½*	
12N1	OS1	6pf blk, *grn*	.25	*2.00*
12N2	OS1	6pf purple	1.00	*3.25*
12N3	OS1	8pf pur, *grn*	1.00	*3.25*
12N4	OS2	8pf red, *rose*	.30	*2.00*
a.		8pf red lilac, *rose*	.65	*19.00*
12N5	OS2	8pf blk, *rose*	1.60	*8.50*
12N6	OS2	8pf red lil, *grn*	.45	*4.00*
12N7	OS2	8pf blk, *grn*	2.60	*13.00*
12N8	OS2	8pf brown	.40	*4.00*
12N9	OS2a	12pf blk, *rose*	.25	*2.00*
12N10	OS2a	12pf brn lil	.30	*2.00*
12N11	OS2a	12pf red	1.60	*10.00*
12N12	OS2a	12pf red, *rose*	.30	*2.10*
		Nos. 12N1-12N12 (12)	10.05	*56.10*
		Set, never hinged	30.00	

Many shades.

Issued: Nos. 12N1, 12N9, 8/28; No. 12N4, 10/6; No. 12N5, 10/19; No. 12N7, 11/2; No. 12N6, 11/3; No. 12N10, 11/9; No. 12N2, 11/16; No. 12N11, 12/20; No. 12N8, 1/7/46; No. 12N3, 1/11/46; No. 12N12, 1/30/46.

Buildings — OS3

Designs: 4pf, Deer. 5pf, Fishing boats. 6pf, Harvesting grain. 8pf, Windmill. 10pf, Two-horse plow. 12pf, Bricklayer on scaffolding. 15pf, Tractor plowing field. 20pf, Ship, warehouse. 30pf, Factory. 40pf, Woman spinning.

1946		Typo.	*Imperf.*	
12N13	OS3	3pf brown	1.00	*37.50*
12N14	OS3	4pf blue	12.00	*52.50*
12N15	OS3	4pf red brown	1.00	*37.50*
12N16	OS3	5pf green	1.00	*37.50*
12N17	OS3	8pf orange	1.00	*37.50*
12N18	OS3	10pf brown	.80	*37.50*
		Perf. 10½		
12N19	OS3	6pf purple	.65	*6.00*
12N20	OS3	6pf blue	.65	*6.00*
12N21	OS3	12pf red	.55	*3.00*
12N22	OS3	15pf brown	.55	*6.50*
12N23	OS3	20pf blue	.80	*8.50*
12N24	OS3	30pf blue green	.65	*10.00*
12N25	OS3	40pf red violet	.65	*10.00*
		Nos. 12N13-12N25 (13)	21.30	*290.00*
		Set, never hinged	62.50	

Issued: 3pf, No. 12N14, 5pf, 6pf, 8pf, 1/17; 10pf, 12pf, 40pf, 1/22; 15pf, 1/24; 30pf, 1/26; 20pf, 1/29; No. 12N15, 2/25.

Nos. 12N13-12N21 exist on both white and toned paper.

MECKLENBURG-VORPOMMERN SEMI-POSTAL STAMPS

Rudolf Breitscheid (1874-1944), Politician OSP1

Designs: 8pf+22pf, Dr. Erich Klausener (1885-1934), theologian. 12pf+28pf, Ernst Thalmann (1886-1944), politician.

1945, Oct. 21		Typo.	*Perf. 10½x11*	
12NB1	OSP1	6 +14pf grn	9.00	*52.50*
12NB2	OSP1	8 +22pf pur	9.00	*52.50*
12NB3	OSP1	12 +28pf red	9.00	*52.50*
		Nos. 12NB1-12NB3 (3)	27.00	*157.50*
		Set, never hinged	75.00	

Sower — OSP2

6pf+14pf, Horsedrawn Plow. 12pf+28pf, Reaper.

1945				
12NB4	OSP2	6 +14pf bl grn	1.60	*35.00*
12NB5	OSP2	6 +14pf grn	2.00	*35.00*
12NB6	OSP2	8 +22pf brn	2.00	*35.00*
12NB7	OSP2	8 +22pf yel brn	2.00	*35.00*
12NB8	OSP2	12 +28pf red	2.00	*35.00*
12NB9	OSP2	12 +28pf org	2.00	*35.00*
		Nos. 12NB4-12NB9 (6)	11.60	*210.00*
		Set, never hinged	32.50	

Issued: Nos. 12NB4, 12NB6, 12NB8, 12/8; others 12/31.

Child Welfare — OSP3

No. 12NB10, Child in hand. No. 12NB11, Girl in winter. No. 12NB12, Boy.

1945, Dec. 31			*Perf. 11*	
12NB10	OSP3	6 +14pf org	2.25	*40.00*
12NB11	OSP3	8 +22pf ultra	.85	*40.00*
12NB12	OSP3	12 +28pf car	.85	*40.00*
		Nos. 12NB10-12NB12 (3)	3.95	*120.00*
		Set, never hinged	10.00	

SAXONY PROVINCE

Coat of Arms — OS1

Perf. 13x12½

1945-46		Typo.	Wmk. 48	
13N1	OS1	1pf slate	.25	*2.00*
a.		Imperf.	.25	*4.00*
		Never hinged	.55	
13N2	OS1	3pf yellow brown	.25	*2.00*
a.		Imperf.	.25	*2.60*
		Never hinged	.55	
13N3	OS1	5pf green	.25	*2.00*
a.		Imperf.	.45	*10.00*
		Never hinged	1.25	
13N4	OS1	6pf purple	.25	*2.25*
a.		Imperf.	.35	*2.00*
		Never hinged	.90	
13N5	OS1	8pf orange	.25	*2.25*
a.		Imperf.	.25	*2.60*
		Never hinged	.55	
13N6	OS1	10pf brown	.25	*2.00*
a.		Imperf.	4.50	*120.00*
		Never hinged	10.00	
13N7	OS1	12pf red	.25	*2.00*
a.		Imperf.	.25	*2.00*
		Never hinged	.55	
13N8	OS1	15pf red brown	.25	*20.00*
13N9	OS1	20pf blue	.25	*3.25*
13N10	OS1	24pf orange brown	.25	*3.25*
13N11	OS1	30pf olive green	.25	*3.25*
13N12	OS1	40pf lake	.55	*6.50*
		Nos. 13N1-13N12 (12)	3.30	*50.75*
		Set, never hinged	8.75	

Issued: Nos. 13N1-13N12, 12/1945; Nos. 13N1a-13N5a, 13N7a, 10/10/45; No. 13N6a, 1/1946.

Land Reform — OS2

1945-46		Unwmk.	*Imperf.*	
13N13	OS2	6pf green	.25	*1.90*
13N14	OS2	12pf red	.25	*1.90*

On Thin Transparent Paper

Wmk. 397

Perf. 13x13½

13N15	OS2	6pf green	.25	*1.90*
13N16	OS2	12pf red	.25	*1.90*
		Nos. 13N13-13N16 (4)		*7.60*
		Set, never hinged	1.00	

Issued: Nos. 13N13-13N14, 12/17/45; others 2/21/46.

SAXONY PROVINCE SEMI-POSTAL STAMPS

Reconstruction OSP1

Designs: 6+4pf, Housing construction. 12+8pf, Bridge repair. 42+28pf, Locomotives.

1946, Jan. 19		Typo.	*Perf. 13*	
13NB1	OSP1	6pf +4pf green	.25	*1.90*
a.		Imperf.	.25	*10.00*
13NB2	OSP1	12pf +8pf red	.25	*1.90*
a.		Imperf.	.25	*16.00*
13NB3	OSP1	42pf +28pf violet	.25	*1.90*
a.		Imperf.	.25	*16.00*
		Nos. 13NB1-13NB3 (3)		*5.70*
		Set, never hinged	.75	
		Set, 13NB1a-13NB3a, never hinged	1.25	

Nos. 13NB1a-13NB3a issued Feb. 21.

WEST SAXONY

OS1

1945 Typo. Wmk. 48 *Perf. 13x12½*

No.	Type	Description	Unused	Used
14N1	OS1	3pf brown	.25	2.00
14N2	OS1	4pf slate	.25	3.00
14N3	OS1	5pf green	.25	2.00
a.		Imperf.	.25	2.00
		Never hinged	.25	
14N4	OS1	6pf violet	.25	2.00
a.		Imperf.	.25	2.00
		Never hinged	.25	
14N5	OS1	8pf orange	.25	4.00
a.		Imperf.	.25	2.00
		Never hinged	.25	
14N6	OS1	10pf gray	.25	3.50
14N7	OS1	12pf red	.25	2.00
a.		Imperf.	.25	2.00
		Never hinged	.25	
14N8	OS1	15pf red brown	.30	3.50
14N9	OS1	20pf blue	.25	3.25
14N10	OS1	30pf olive green	.30	2.00
14N11	OS1	40pf red lilac	.50	4.00
14N12	OS1	60pf maroon	.30	16.00
		Nos. 14N1-14N12 (12)	3.40	47.25
		Set, never hinged	7.00	

Issued: 3-4, 20-30pf, 11/9; 5-8, 12pf, 11/12; 10, 15, 40-60pf, 11/15; imperfs., 9/28.

Leipzig Fair — OS2

1945, Oct. 18

No.	Type	Description	Unused	Used
14N13	OS2	6pf green	.30	2.50
14N14	OS2	12pf red	.30	2.50
		Set, never hinged	1.60	

Leipzig Arms — OS3

Designs: 5pf, 6pf, St. Nicholas Church. 8pf, 12pf, Leipzig Town Hall.

1946, Feb. 12

No.	Type	Description	Unused	Used
14N15	OS3	3pf brown	.25	5.00
a.		Unwatermarked	.25	7.50
14N16	OS3	4pf slate	.25	5.00
a.		Unwatermarked	.25	7.50
14N17	OS3	5pf green	.25	5.00
a.		Unwatermarked	.25	7.50
14N18	OS3	6pf violet	.25	5.00
a.		Unwatermarked	.25	7.50
14N19	OS3	8pf orange	.25	5.00
a.		Unwatermarked	.25	7.50
14N20	OS3	12pf red	.25	5.00
a.		Unwatermarked	.25	7.50
		Nos. 14N15-14N20 (6)		30.00
		Set, never hinged	2.40	
		Set, 14NB15a-14NB20a, never hinged	2.40	

Nos. 14N15a-14N20a issued Mar. 15.

WEST SAXONY SEMI-POSTAL STAMPS

OSP1

1946 Typo. Wmk. 48 *Perf. 13x12½*

No.	Type	Description	Unused	Used
14NB1	OSP1	3 +2pf yel brn	.25	2.60
14NB2	OSP1	4 +3pf slate	.25	2.60
14NB3	OSP1	5 +3pf grn	.25	2.60
14NB4	OSP1	6 +4pf violet	.25	2.60
14NB5	OSP1	8 +4pf org	.25	2.60
14NB6	OSP1	10 +5pf gray	.25	2.60
14NB7	OSP1	12 +6pf red	.25	2.60
14NB8	OSP1	15 +10pf red brn	.25	2.60
14NB9	OSP1	20 +10pf blue	.25	2.60
14NB10	OSP1	30 +20pf ol grn	.25	3.25
14NB11	OSP1	40 +30pf red lilac	.25	2.60
14NB12	OSP1	60 +40pf lake	.25	4.00
		Nos. 14NB1-14NB12 (12)	3.00	33.25
		Set, never hinged	5.75	

Issue dates: Nos. 14NB1, 14NB4, 14NB7, 14NB11, Jan. 7; others, Jan. 28.

Market, Old Town Hall — OSP2

1946, May 8 *Perf. 13*

No.	Type	Description	Unused	Used
14NB13	OSP2	6 +14pf vio	.25	2.25
a.		Imperf.	.35	12.00
b.		Unwatermarked	.35	3.00
14NB14	OSP2	12 +18pf bl gray	.25	4.00
a.		Imperf.	.35	12.00
b.		Unwatermarked	.25	5.25
14NB15	OSP2	24 +26pf org brn	.25	2.25
a.		Imperf.	.35	12.00
b.		Unwatermarked	.30	2.00
14NB16	OSP2	84 +66pf grn	.25	6.50
a.		Imperf.	.35	24.00
c.		Sheet of 4, #14NB13a-14NB16a	65.00	225.00
		Nos. 14NB13-14NB16 (4)	1.00	15.00
		Set, never hinged	1.25	
		Set, 14NB13a-14NB16a, never hinged	3.25	
		Set, 14NB13b-14NB15b, never hinged	2.40	

Issue date: Imperf., May 20.

EAST SAXONY

OS1

1945, June 23 Photo. *Imperf.*

No.	Type	Description	Unused	Used
15N1	OS1	12pf red	160.00	525.00
		Never hinged	400.00	

Withdrawn on day of issue.

OS2

Litho. (3pf, #15N9), Photo.

1945-46

No.	Type	Description	Unused	Used
15N2	OS2	3pf sepia	.30	2.25
15N3	OS2	4pf blue gray	.25	1.60
a.		4pf gray	.25	.95
15N4	OS2	5pf brown	.30	1.75
15N5	OS2	6pf green	2.25	8.00
15N6	OS2	6pf violet	.25	1.60
15N7	OS2	8pf dark violet	.35	1.75
15N8	OS2	10pf dark brown	.40	3.50
15N9	OS2	10pf gray	.30	2.25
15N10	OS2	12pf red	.30	1.75
15N11	OS2	15pf lemon	.40	2.25
15N12	OS2	20pf blue	.25	1.60
a.		20pf gray blue	.55	2.25
		Never hinged	1.10	
15N13	OS2	25pf blue	.40	2.25
15N14	OS2	30pf yellow	.25	1.60
15N15	OS2	40pf lilac	.40	2.25

Typo.

Perf. 13x12½

No.	Type	Description	Unused	Used
15N16	OS2	3pf brown	.25	1.60
15N17	OS2	5pf green	.25	1.60
15N18	OS2	6pf violet	.25	1.60
15N19	OS2	8pf orange	.25	1.60
15N20	OS2	12pf vermilion	.25	1.60
		Nos. 15N2-15N20 (19)	7.65	42.40
		Set, never hinged	20.00	

Issued: 12pf, 6/28; No. 15N5, 6/30; 8pf, No. 15N8, 7/3; 25pf, 7/5; 5pf, 6/6; 40pf, 7/7; 15pf, 7/10; No. 15N12a, 7/26; Nos. 15N9, 15N12, 15N17-15N20, 11/3; No. 15N3, 30pf, 11/5; 3pf, 12/5; No. 15N15, 12/21; No. 15N6, 1/22/46.

EAST SAXONY SEMI-POSTAL STAMPS

Zwinger, Dresden — OSP1

Design: 12pf+88pf, Rathaus, Dresden.

1946, Feb. 6 Photo. *Perf. 11*

No.	Type	Description	Unused	Used
15NB1	OSP1	6pf +44pf grn	.25	5.50
15NB2	OSP1	12pf +88pf red	.25	5.50
		Set, never hinged	1.75	

THURINGIA

Fir Trees — OS1

Designs: 6pf, 8pf, Posthorn. 12pf, Schiller. 20pf, 30pf, Goethe.

1945-46 Typo. *Perf. 11*

No.	Type	Description	Unused	Used
16N1	OS1	3pf brown	.25	2.60
16N2	OS1	4pf black	.25	2.60
16N3	OS1	5pf green	.25	3.25
a.		Souvenir sheet of 3, #16N1-16N3	140.00	725.00
		Never hinged	300.00	
16N4	OS1	6pf dark green	.25	2.00
16N5	OS1	8pf orange	.25	2.00
16N6	OS1	12pf red	.25	2.25
16N7	OS1	20pf blue	.25	2.00
a.		Imperf.	.25	3.00
		Never hinged	.35	
b.		Souv. sheet of 4, #16N2, 16N4, 16N6-16N7, rouletted x imperf. btwn.	525.00	2,150.
		Never hinged	1,150.	
16N8	OS1	30pf gray	.45	3.00
a.		Imperf.	2.25	26.00
		Never hinged	9.00	
		Nos. 16N1-16N8 (8)	2.20	19.70
		Set, never hinged	2.60	

No. 16N3a sold for 2m, No. 16N7b for 10m.

Issued: 6pf, 10/1; 12pf, 10/19; 5pf, 10/20; 8pf, 11/3; 20pf, 11/24; NOS. 16N3a, 16N7b, 12/18; 30pf, 12/22; 3pf, 4pf, 1/4/46.

Souvenir Sheet

Rebuilding of German Natl. Theater, Weimar — OS2

a, 6pf, Schiller. b, 10pf, Goethe. c, 12pf, Liszt. d, 16pf, Wieland. e, 40pf, Natl. Theater.

1946, Mar. 27 Wmk. 48 *Imperf.*

No.	Type	Description	Unused	Used
16N9	OS2	Sheet of 5, #a.-e.	13.00	52.50
f.		Sheet, unwatermarked, roulettted	23.00	140.00
		Never hinged	52.50	

No. 16N9 was issued without gum. Sold for 7.50 marks.

THURINGIA SEMI-POSTAL STAMPS

Bridge Reconstruction OSP1

Designs: 10pf+60pf, Saalburg Bridge. 12pf+68pf, Camsdorf Bridge, Jena. 16pf+74pf, Goschwitz Bridge. 24pf+76pf, Ilm Bridge, Mellingen.

1946, Mar. 30 Typo. *Imperf.*

No.	Type	Description	Unused	Used
16NB1	OSP1	10 +60pf red brn	.25	8.00
16NB2	OSP1	12 +68pf red	.25	8.00
16NB3	OSP1	16 +74pf dark grn	.25	8.00
16NB4	OSP1	24 +76pf brn	.25	8.00
a.		Souv. sheet of 4, #16NB1-16NB4	130.00	1,100.
		Never hinged	275.00	
		Nos. 16NB1-16NB4 (4)		32.00
		Set, never hinged	2.60	

GHANA

ˈgä-nə

LOCATION — West Africa between Togo and Ivory Coast
GOVT. — Republic
AREA — 92,010 sq. mi.
POP. — 18,101,000 (1997 est.)
CAPITAL — Accra

Ghana is the former British colony of Gold Coast, which achieved independence March 6, 1957. It includes the former trusteeship territory of British Togoland.

12 Pence = 1 Shilling
20 Shillings = 1 Pound
100 Pesewas = 1 Cedi (1965, 1972)
100 New Pesewas = 1 New Cedi (1967)

Used Values in Italics

In 1961 the government canceled all remainder stocks, using cancellations that closely resemble genuine postmarks. Catalogue values in italics for these stamps (Nos. 1-13, 61-65, 67-77) are for canceled-to-order stamps. Postally used stamps are worth more.

Catalogue values for all unused stamps in this country are for Never Hinged items.

Watermark

Wmk. 325 — Stars and G Multiple

Kwame Nkrumah, Map and Palm-nut Vulture — A1

Perf. 14x14½

1957, Mar. 6 Wmk. 4 Photo.

1 A1 2p rose red .25 *.25*
2 A1 2½p green .25 *.25*
3 A1 4p brown .25 *.25*
4 A1 1sh3p dark blue .35 *.25*
Nos. 1-4 (4) 1.10 *1.00*

Independence, Mar. 6, 1957.
For overprints see Nos. 28-31.

Stamps of Gold Coast, 1952-54, Overprinted in Black or Red

Perf. 11½x12, 12x11½

1957, Mar. 6 Engr.

5 A14 ½p yel brown & car .50 *.25*
6 A14 1p deep blue (R) .50 *.25*
7 A14 1½p green .50 *.25*
8 A14 3p rose .85 *.25*
9 A15 6p org & black (R) .50 *.25*
10 A14 1sh red org & black .50 *.25*
11 A14 2sh rose car & ol brn 1.25 *.25*
12 A14 5sh gray & red vio 2.00 *.25*
13 A15 10sh olive grn & black 2.25 *.50*
Nos. 5-13 (9) 8.85 *2.50*

Nos. 5-6 exist in vertical coils.
See Nos. 25-27.

Viking Ship and Angelfish A2

1sh3p, Medieval galleon and swordfish. 5sh, Modern cargo ship and flyingfish.

Perf. 12x11½

1957, Dec. 27 Engr. Unwmk.

14 A2 2½p emerald .25 .25
15 A2 1sh3p dark blue .30 *1.25*
16 A2 5sh red lilac .90 *3.00*
Nos. 14-16 (3) 1.45 4.50

Black Star Line inauguration.

Ambassador Hotel — A3

Coat of Arms — A4

Design: 2½p, Opening of Parliament. 1sh3p, National monument.

Perf. 14x14½, 14½x14

1958, Mar. 6 Photo. Wmk. 4

Flags in Original Colors

17 A3 ½p car rose & black .25 *.40*
18 A3 2½p org yel, red & blk .25 .25
19 A3 1sh3p blue & black .25 .25
20 A4 2sh multicolored .25 *.50*
Nos. 17-20 (4) 1.00 1.40

First anniversary of Independence.

Map of Africa — A5

Map and Torch — A6

1958, Apr. 15 *Perf. 13½x14½*

21 A5 2½p multicolored .25 .25
22 A5 3p multicolored .25 .25
23 A6 1sh multicolored .25 .25
24 A6 2sh6p multicolored .25 *.65*
Nos. 21-24 (4) 1.00 1.40

1st conf. of Independent African States, Accra, Apr. 15-22.

Gold Coast Nos. 151-152 and 154 Overprinted Like Nos. 5-13

Perf. 11½x12, 12x11½

1958, May 26 Engr. Wmk. 4

25 A15 2p chocolate .50 .35
26 A15 2½p red 1.25 *1.40*
27 A14 4p deep blue 6.00 *9.00*
Nos. 25-27 (3) 7.75 10.75

Nos. 25-27 were prepared in 1957 and some were sold without authorization. The set was officially released in 1958.

Nos. 1-4 Overprinted "Prime Minister's Visit U. S. A. and Canada"

1958, July 18 Photo. *Perf. 14x14½*

28 A1 2p rose red .25 *.40*
29 A1 2½p green .25 *.30*
30 A1 4p brown .25 *.50*
31 A1 1sh3p dark blue .25 *.25*
Nos. 28-31 (4) 1.00 *1.45*

Prime Minister Kwame Nkrumah's visit to the US and Canada, July, 1958.

Palm-nut Vulture over Globe — A7

"Britannia" Plane — A8

Designs: 2sh, Stratocruiser and albatross. 2sh6p, Palm-nut vulture and jet plane, horiz.

1958, July 15 *Perf. 14x14½, 14½x14*

32 A7 2½p multicolored .25 .25
33 A8 1sh3p multicolored .35 .25
34 A8 2sh multicolored .45 .45
35 A7 2sh6p olive bister & blk .70 .85
Nos. 32-35 (4) 1.75 1.80

Inauguration of Ghana Airways.

A9

Perf. 14x14½

1958, Oct. 24 Wmk. 4 Litho.

36 A9 2½p multicolored .25 .25
37 A9 1sh3p multicolored .25 .25
38 A9 2sh6p multicolored .25 .30
Nos. 36-38 (3) .75 .80

United Nations Day, Oct. 24.

A10

Lincoln Memorial and Kwame Nkrumah.

Perf. 14x14½

1959, Feb. 12 Photo. Wmk. 325

39 A10 2½p dp plum & brt pink .25 .25
40 A10 1sh3p dp blue & lt bl .25 .25
41 A10 2sh6p ol gray & org yel .25 .30
a. Souv. sheet of 3, #39-41, imperf. .80 1.50
Nos. 39-41 (3) .75 .80

Lincoln's birth sesquicentennial.

Kente Cloth with Traditional Symbols A11

Symbol of Greeting — A12

2½p, Talking drums and elephant hornblower. 2sh, Map of Africa, flag and palm tree.

Perf. 14½x14, 14x14½

1959, Mar. 6 Photo. Wmk. 325

42 A11 ½p multicolored .25 .25
43 A11 2½p multicolored .25 .25
44 A12 1sh3p multicolored .25 .25
45 A11 2sh multicolored .25 1.00
Nos. 42-45 (4) 1.00 1.75

Independence, 2nd anniversary.

Flags of Independent States of Africa and Globe — A13

1959, Apr. 15 *Perf. 14½x14*

46 A13 2½p multicolored .25 .25
47 A13 8½p multicolored .25 .25

Africa Freedom Day, Apr. 15.

Kente Cloth and "God's Omnipotence" Symbol — A13a

Nkrumah Statue, Accra — A14

Shell Ginger — A15

Cacao A16

"God's Omnipotence" Symbol — A16a

Blackwinged Red Bishop — A17

1½p, Ghana timber. 2p, Volta river. 4p, Diamond and mine. 11p, Golden spider lily. 2sh6p, Great blue turaco. 5sh, Tiger orchid. 10sh, Jewelfish (tropical African cichlid).

Perf. 11½x12, 12x11½, 14x14½, 14½x14

1959, Oct. 5 Photo. Wmk. 325

Size: 30½x21mm, 21x30½mm

48	A13a	½p multi *(God's Omnipotence)*	.25	.25
49	A14	1p multicolored	.30	.25

Size: 26½x37mm, 37x26½mm

50	A15	1½p multicolored	.25	.25
51	A16	2p multicolored	.25	.25
52	A16	2½p multicolored	1.00	.25
53	A16a	3p multi *(God's Omnipotence)*	.25	.25
54	A16	4p multicolored	3.50	.60
55	A17	6p multicolored	1.50	.25
a.		Booklet pane of 4	6.50	
56	A15	11p multicolored	.25	.25
57	A15	1sh multicolored	.25	.25
58	A17	2sh6p multicolored	1.50	.25
59	A15	5sh multicolored	2.25	.60

Size: 45x26mm

60	A16	10sh multicolored	2.00	.70
		Nos. 48-60,C1-C2 (15)	16.30	5.05

Nos. 48 and 53 inscribed "God's Omnipotence." Nos. 95-96 inscribed "Gye Nyame."

For surcharges see Nos. 216-217, 219-225, 277-283.

Map and Gold Cup — A18

1p, Soccer players, vert. 3p, Flags and goalkeeper in stadium. 8p, Soccer player at goal. 2sh6p, Kwame Nkrumah Gold Cup, vert.

1959, Oct. 15 *Perf. 14½x14, 14x14½*

61	A18	½p multicolored	.25	*.25*
62	A18	1p multicolored	.25	*.25*
63	A18	3p multicolored	.25	*.25*
64	A18	8p multicolored	.25	*.25*
65	A18	2sh6p multicolored	.25	*.30*
		Nos. 61-65 (5)	1.25	*1.30*

West African Soccer Competitions.

Prince Philip A19

Perf. 14½x14

1959, Nov. 24 Photo. Wmk. 325

66	A19	3p brt pink & black	.30	.25

Visit of Prince Philip.

Talking Drums A20

Designs: 6p, 1sh3p, Ghana flag and UN emblem, vert. 2sh6p, Pile of Ceremonial Stools and "UNTC," vert.

1959, Dec. 10 *Perf. 14½x14, 14x14½*

Flag in Original Colors

67	A20	3p violet & org yel	.25	*.25*
68	A20	6p Prus green & blk	.25	*.25*
69	A20	1sh3p grnsh bl, blk & vio	.25	*.25*
70	A20	2sh6p dark blue & black	.25	*.25*
		Nos. 67-70 (4)	1.00	*1.00*

United Nations Trusteeship Council.

Three Flying Eagles — A21

Designs: 3p, Three clusters of fireworks. 1sh3p, Ghana flag forming "3" and dove. 2sh, Ghana flag forming triple sail of symbolic ship.

Perf. 13½x14½

1960, Mar. 6 Wmk. 325

71	A21	½p multicolored	.25	*.25*
72	A21	3p multicolored	.25	*.25*
73	A21	1sh3p multicolored	.25	*.25*
74	A21	2sh multicolored	.25	*.25*
		Nos. 71-74 (4)	1.00	*1.00*

Independence, 3rd anniversary.

Flags Forming "A" and Map A22

Designs: 6p, Letter "F." 1sh, "D."

1960, Apr. 15 Photo. Wmk. 325

Flags in Original Colors

75	A22	3p green, red & black	.25	*.25*
76	A22	6p rose & black	.25	*.25*
77	A22	1sh blue, black & red	.25	*.25*
		Nos. 75-77 (3)	.75	*.75*

Africa Freedom Day, Apr. 15.

President Kwame Nkrumah — A23

Designs: 1sh3p, Flag and star. 2sh, Hand holding torch. 10sh, Coat of Arms and flag of Ghana, horiz.

Perf. 14x14½, 14½x14

1960, July 1 Litho.

78	A23	3p multicolored	.25	.25
79	A23	1sh3p multicolored	.25	.25
80	A23	2sh multicolored	.30	.30
81	A23	10sh multicolored	.70	.70
a.		Souv. sheet of 4, #78-81, imperf.	.50	1.00
		Nos. 78-81 (4)	1.50	1.50

Declaration of the Republic, July 1, 1960.

Map and Arch — A25

Designs: 3p, Flag and Kwame Nkrumah, horiz. 6p, Star and Nkrumah.

1960, Sept. 21 Photo.

86	A25	3p multicolored	.25	.25
87	A25	6p multicolored	.25	.25
88	A25	1sh3p multicolored	.25	.30
		Nos. 86-88 (3)	.75	.80

Founder's Day, Sept. 21, birthday of Dr. Kwame Nkrumah.

UN Emblem and Ghana Flag — A26

6p, Flame & emblem. 1sh3p, UN Emblem.

1960, Dec. 10 *Perf. 14x14½*

89	A26	3p multicolored	.25	.25
90	A26	6p multicolored	.25	.25
91	A26	1sh3p multicolored	.25	.45
		Nos. 89-91 (3)	.75	.95

Human Rights Day, Dec. 10, 1960.

Talking Drums and Map — A27

Designs: 6p, Map of Africa showing 25 independent states. 2sh, Map of Africa and flags of independent nations in 1958, horiz.

Perf. 14x14½, 14½x14

1961, Apr. 15 Wmk. 325

92	A27	3p multicolored	.25	.25
93	A27	6p multicolored	.25	.25
94	A27	2sh multicolored	.25	.35
		Nos. 92-94 (3)	.75	.85

Africa Freedom Day, Apr. 15, 1961.

Types of 1959 Redrawn and

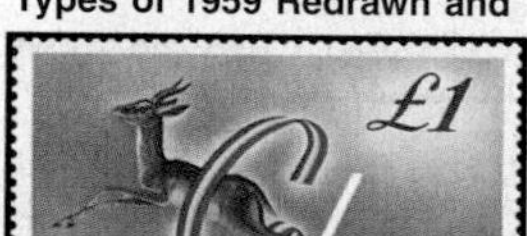

Red-fronted Gazelle — A28

Perf. 11½x12, 14½x14

1961, Apr. 29 Photo. Wmk. 325

95	A13a	½p "Gye Nyame"	.25	.25
96	A16a	3p "Gye Nyame"	.25	.25
a.		Booklet pane of 4	1.00	

Perf. 14x14½

97	A28	£1 multicolored	5.00	5.00
		Nos. 95-97 (3)	5.50	5.50

Nos. 95-96 are the same sizes as Nos. 48 and 53 which are inscribed "God's Omnipotence."

For surcharges see Nos. 218, 226, 284.

Column, Eagle and Star — A29

Designs: 1sh3p, Symbolic flower and star. 2sh, Star and 3 Ghana flags.

1961, July 1 *Perf. 14x14½*

98	A29	3p multicolored	.25	.25
99	A29	1sh3p multicolored	.25	.25
100	A29	2sh multicolored	.25	*1.00*
		Nos. 98-100 (3)	.75	1.50

First anniversary of the Republic.

Dove with Olive Branch — A30

World Map, Chain and Olive Branch A31

Design: 5sh, Rostrum and olive branch.

1961, Sept. 1 *Perf. 14x14½, 14½x14*

101	A30	3p green	.25	.25
102	A31	1sh3p dark blue	.25	.25
103	A31	5sh rose carmine	.25	*.90*
		Nos. 101-103 (3)	.75	1.40

Conference of Non-aligned Nations, Belgrade, Sept. 1961.

Kwame Nkrumah and Globe A32

Designs: 1sh3p, Kente cloth and Nkrumah, vert. 5sh, Kwame Nkrumah, vert.

Perf. 14½x14, 14x14½

1961, Sept. 21 Wmk. 325

104	A32	3p multicolored	.25	.25
a.		Souvenir sheet of 4, imperf.	1.00	*1.75*
105	A32	1sh3p multicolored	.25	.25
a.		Souvenir sheet of 4, imperf.	1.00	*2.50*
106	A32	5sh multicolored	.40	*2.00*
a.		Souvenir sheet of 4, imperf.	3.00	*6.00*
		Nos. 104-106 (3)	.90	2.50

Founder's Day.

The souvenir sheets contain four imperf. stamps each with simulated perforations.

Elizabeth II and Map of Africa A33

1961, Nov. 10 *Perf. 14½x14*

Gold Inscriptions: Design in Black, Red, Yellow & Green

107	A33	3p claret	.25	.25
108	A33	1sh3p Prussian blue	.25	.25
109	A33	5sh violet blue	1.00	1.00
a.		Souvenir sheet of 4	3.50	*7.00*
		Nos. 107-109 (3)	1.50	1.50

Visit of Queen Elizabeth II to Ghana, Nov. 10-22.

1960, Aug. 15 Photo. Wmk. 325

82	A24	3p multicolored	.25	.25
83	A24	6p multicolored	.25	.25
84	A24	1sh3p multicolored	.25	.25
85	A24	2sh6p multicolored	.35	.25
		Nos. 82-85 (4)	1.10	1.00

17th Olympic Games, Rome, Aug. 25-Sept. 11.

No. 109a contains four imperf. examples of No. 109 with simulated perforations.

Map of Tema Harbor and Ships
A34

Perf. 14x13

1962, Feb. 10 Litho. Unwmk.

110 A34 3p multicolored .25 .25
Nos. 110,C3-C4 (3) 1.45 1.45

Opening of Tema Harbor, as part of Volta River Project.

Dove Flying over Map of Africa — A35

1962, Mar. 6 ***Perf. 13x14***

111 A35 3p multicolored .25 .25
Nos. 111,C5-C6 (3) 1.15 1.15

Conference of African heads of state at Casablanca, 1st anniv.

"Freedom" Illuminating Africa — A36

Perf. 14x14½

1962, Apr. 15 Photo. Wmk. 325

112 A36 3p multicolored .25 .25
113 A36 6p multicolored .25 .25
114 A36 1sh3p multicolored .25 .25
Nos. 112-114 (3) .75 .75

Africa Freedom Day, Apr. 15.

"Five Continents at Peace" — A37

Designs: 6p, Atom bomb blast in shape of skull. 1sh3p, Peace dove and globe.

1962, June 21 Wmk. 325

115 A37 3p dp rose & blk .25 .25
116 A37 6p black & dk red .25 *.30*
117 A37 1sh3p greenish blue .30 *.50*
Nos. 115-117 (3) .80 1.05

Accra Assembly of Africans for a "World Without Bomb," June 21-28.

Patrice Lumumba
A38

1962, June 30 ***Perf. 14½x14***

118 A38 3p black & orange .25 .25
119 A38 6p mar, grn & blk .25 *.30*
120 A38 1sh3p dk grn, pink & blk .25 *.35*
Nos. 118-120 (3) .75 .90

1st anniv. (on Feb. 12) of the death of Patrice Lumumba, premier of Congo.

Arch and Star — A39

Designs: 6p, Torch in flag colors and globe. 1sh3p, Palm-nut vulture trailing flag, horiz.

Perf. 13x13½, 13½x13

1962, July 1 Unwmk.

121 A39 3p multicolored .25 .25
122 A39 6p multicolored .25 .25
123 A39 1sh3p multicolored .25 .35
Nos. 121-123 (3) .75 .85

Second anniversary of the republic.

Kwame Nkrumah — A40

3p, Nkrumah medal. 1sh3p, Nkrumah's head & stars. 2sh, Hands with trowel & building block.

1962, Sept. 21 Litho. ***Perf. 13x14***

124 A40 1p multicolored .25 .25
125 A40 3p multicolored .25 .25
126 A40 1sh3p ultra & black .25 .25
127 A40 2sh multicolored .25 *1.00*
Nos. 124-127 (4) 1.00 1.75

Founder's Day, Nkrumah's 53rd birthday.

Malaria Eradication Emblem — A41

Perf. 14x14½

1962, Dec. 1 Photo. Wmk. 325

128 A41 1p carmine rose .25 .25
129 A41 4p yellow green .25 *1.00*
130 A41 6p olive bister .25 *.30*
131 A41 1sh3p violet .25 *.80*
a. Souvenir sheet of 4, imperf. 1.00 *1.50*
Nos. 128-131 (4) 1.00 *2.35*

WHO drive to eradicate malaria.

No. 131a contains one each of Nos. 128-131, with simulated perforation.

Wheat Emblem and Globe — A42

Designs: 4p, Hands holding Wheat Emblem, horiz. 1sh3p, Globe, horiz.

Perf. 14x14½, 14½x14

1963, Mar. 21 Wmk. 325

132 A42 1p multicolored .30 .25
133 A42 4p multicolored .45 *1.00*
134 A42 1sh3p multicolored 1.75 1.50
Nos. 132-134 (3) 2.50 2.75

FAO "Freedom from Hunger" campaign.

Map of Africa in Sun — A43

Designs: 4p, Symbolic wood carving, horiz. 1sh3p, Map of Africa and ceremonial fire. 2sh6p, Gazelle and flag.

1963, Apr. 15 Photo.

135 A43 1p crimson & gold .25 .25
136 A43 4p orange, blk & red .25 .25
137 A43 1sh3p multicolored .25 .25
138 A43 2sh6p multicolored .25 *1.00*
Nos. 135-138 (4) 1.00 1.75

Africa Freedom Day, Apr. 15.

Cross, Flag and Centenary Emblem — A44

1½p, Centenary emblem, horiz. 4p, Family & emblem, horiz. 1sh3p, Emblem & globe.

Perf. 14x14½, 14½x14

1963, May 28 Wmk. 325

139 A44 1p multicolored .45 .25
140 A44 1½p multicolored .75 *1.75*
141 A44 4p multicolored 1.00 .25
142 A44 1sh3p multicolored 2.00 2.00
a. Souvenir sheet of 4, imperf. 4.25 *10.00*
Nos. 139-142 (4) 4.20 4.25

Cent. of the founding of the Intl. Red Cross.

No. 142a contains one each of Nos. 139-142, with simulated perforation.

A45

Designs: 4p, Three flags. 1sh3p, Map of Africa with Ghana, vert. 2sh6p, Torch, vert.

Perf. 14½x14, 14x14½

1963, July 1 Photo.

143 A45 1p multicolored .25 .25
144 A45 4p multicolored .25 .25
145 A45 1sh3p multicolored .25 .25
146 A45 2sh6p multicolored .25 *1.75*
Nos. 143-146 (4) 1.00 2.50

The 3rd anniversary of the republic.

Dancers, Fireworks and Nkrumah
A46

1p, Nkrumah & streamer. 4p, Nkrumah & flag. 5sh, Wisdom symbol.

Perf. 14x14½, 14½x14

1963, Sept. 21

147 A46 1p multi, vert. .25 .25
148 A46 4p multi, vert. .25 .25
149 A46 1sh3p multi .25 .25
150 A46 5sh multi .25 *.40*
Nos. 147-150 (4) 1.00 1.15

Founder's Day, Nkrumah's 54th birthday.

Ramses II at Abu Simbel — A47

Designs: 1½p, Rock painting, bird and fish, horiz. 2p, Queen Nefertari, horiz. 4p, Sphinx of Wadi es-Sebua. 1sh3p, Statues of Ramses II at Abu Simbel, horiz.

1963, Nov. 1 Unwmk. ***Perf. 11½x11***

151 A47 1p multicolored .25 .25
152 A47 1½p multicolored .25 *.50*
153 A47 2p multicolored .25 .25
154 A47 4p multicolored .50 .25
155 A47 1sh3p multicolored 1.50 1.00
Nos. 151-155 (5) 2.75 2.25

UNESCO world campaign to save historic monuments in Nubia.

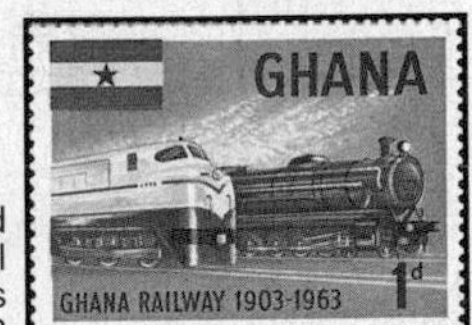

Steam and Diesel Engines
A48

Perf. 14½x14

1963, Nov. 1 Wmk. 325

156 A48 1p multicolored .25 .25
157 A48 6p multicolored .65 .25
158 A48 1sh3p multicolored 1.10 .50
159 A48 2sh6p multicolored 1.40 1.40
Nos. 156-159 (4) 3.40 2.40

The 60th anniversary of Ghana's railroads.

Eleanor Roosevelt and Flame — A49

6p, Mrs. Roosevelt & flag. 1sh3p, Mrs. Roosevelt, flag, flame & Ghanaian symbols, horiz.

Perf. 11½x11, 11x11½

1963, Dec. 10 Unwmk.

160 A49 1p multicolored .25 .25
161 A49 4p multicolored .25 .30
162 A49 6p multicolored .25 .25
163 A49 1sh3p multicolored .25 .25
Nos. 160-163 (4) 1.00 1.05

Eleanor Roosevelt; 15th anniv. of the Universal Declaration of Human Rights.

Imperforates
Starting in 1964, certain sets of Ghana exist imperf.

IQSY Emblem and Satellites — A50

1964, June 1 Photo. *Perf. 14*

164	A50	3p multicolored	.25	.25
165	A50	6p multicolored	.25	.25
166	A50	1sh3p multicolored	.25	.25
a.		Souvenir sheet of 4	.90	*2.00*
		Nos. 164-166 (3)	.75	.75

Intl. Quiet Sun Year, 1964-65. No. 166a contains 4 imperf. stamps similar to No. 166 with simulated perforations.

See Nos. 186-188.

Harvest on State Farm A51

Designs: 6p, Oil refinery, Tema. 1sh3p, Communal labor. 5sh, Ghana flag and people.

1964, July 1 *Perf. 13x14*

167	A51	3p multicolored	.25	.25
168	A51	6p multicolored	.25	.25
169	A51	1sh3p multicolored	.25	.25
170	A51	5sh multicolored	.25	.90
a.		Souvenir sheet of 4	.80	*1.60*
		Nos. 167-170 (4)	1.00	1.65

4th anniv. of the Republic. No. 170a contains four stamps similar to Nos. 167-170 with simulated perforations.

Dove, Globe, Olive Branch and Flag — A52

Designs: 6p, Map of Africa and quill pen, vert. 1sh3p, Knotted rope and map of Africa. 5sh, Hands planting symbolic tree, vert.

1964, July 6 *Perf. 14*

171	A52	3p multicolored	.25	.25
172	A52	6p black & red	.25	.25
173	A52	1sh3p blue & multi	.25	.25
174	A52	5sh yel & multi	.25	.60
		Nos. 171-174 (4)	1.00	1.35

Signing of the African Unity Charter, 1st anniv.

Nkrumah and Hibiscus — A53

Perf. 14x14½

1964, Sept. 21 Photo. Wmk. 325

Design in Brown, Green and Rose Red

175	A53	3p light blue	.25	.25
176	A53	6p yellow	.25	.25
177	A53	1sh3p gray	.25	.25
178	A53	2sh6p emerald	.25	.90
a.		Souvenir sheet of 4	1.10	*2.00*
		Nos. 175-178 (4)	1.00	1.65

Founder's Day, Nkrumah's 55th birthday.

No. 178a contains four of No. 178 with simulated perforation.

Boxing — A54

Sport: 1p, Hurdling, horiz. 2½p, Running, horiz. 4p, Broad jump. 6p, Soccer. 1sh3p, Athlete with Olympic torch. 5sh, Banners and Tokyo Olympic emblem, horiz.

1964, Oct. 25 *Perf. 14½x14*

179	A54	1p yellow & multi	.25	.25
180	A54	2½p multicolored	.25	1.00
181	A54	3p red & multi	.25	.25
182	A54	4p blue & multi	.25	.25
183	A54	6p multicolored	.25	.25
184	A54	1sh3p blue & multi	.25	.25
185	A54	5sh gray & multi	.25	*2.50*
a.		Souvenir sheet of 3	1.30	*2.25*
		Nos. 179-185 (7)	1.75	4.75

18th Olympic Games, Tokyo, Oct. 10-25.

No. 185a contains stamps similar to Nos. 183-185 with simulated perforation.

Quiet Sun Year Type of 1964

Unwmk.

1964, Oct. Photo. *Perf. 14*

186	A50	3p gray, bl, grn, yel & red	1.25	1.25
187	A50	6p pink, bl, grn, yel & red	2.25	2.25
188	A50	1sh3p tan, bl, grn, yel, & red	3.50	3.50
		Nos. 186-188 (3)	7.00	7.00

Each issued in sheets of 12, with star-strewn blue border inscribed "Ghana International Quiet Sun Year." Stamps arranged in square surrounding vignette of New York World's Fair Unisphere in blue.

G. W. Carver and Sweet Potato A55

Design: 1sh3p, Albert Einstein, theory of relativity formula and atom symbol.

1964, Dec. 7 Wmk. 325 *Perf. 14½*

189	A55	6p grn & dk blue	.30	.30
190	A55	1sh3p Prus bl & claret	.45	.40
191	A55	5sh org ver & brn blk	1.50	*3.00*
a.		Souvenir sheet of 3	3.00	2.00
		Nos. 189-191 (3)	2.25	3.70

Human Rights Day; Albert Einstein (1878-1955) and George Washington Carver (1864-1943), scientists.

No. 191a commemorates UNESCO Week and contains one each of Nos. 189-191 with simulated perforations.

Secretary Bird — A56

Designs: 1p, Elephant, vert. 2½p, Purple wreath, vert. 3p, Gray parrot, vert. 4p, Blue-naped mousebird. 6p, African tulip tree flowers. 1sh3p, Amethyst starling. 2sh6p, Hippopotamuses.

Perf. 11½x11, 11x11½

1964, Dec. 14 Photo. Unwmk.

192	A56	1p blue & multi	.45	.40
193	A56	1½p org & multi	.65	*1.40*
194	A56	2½p lt green & multi	.50	*.90*
a.		Souv. sheet of 3, #192-194, imperf.	2.75	2.75
195	A56	3p lt green & multi	1.10	.50
196	A56	4p multicolored	1.10	.70
197	A56	6p multicolored	.50	.30
198	A56	1sh3p multicolored	1.25	1.00
199	A56	2sh6p multicolored	1.25	3.50
a.		Souv. sheet of 5, #195-199, imperf.	6.25	*10.00*
		Nos. 192-199 (8)	6.80	8.70

ICY Emblem A57

1965, Feb. 15 Litho. *Perf. 14x13*

Design in Black, Red and Green

200	A57	1p gray	.35	.60
201	A57	4p bister	1.25	1.50
202	A57	6p tan	1.25	.45
203	A57	1sh3p light green	1.60	2.25
a.		Souvenir sheet of 4	4.75	4.75
		Nos. 200-203 (4)	4.45	4.80

Intl. Cooperation Year. No. 203a contains 4 imperf. stamps similar to No. 203.

ITU Emblem, Old and New Communication Equipment — A58

1965, Apr. 12 *Perf. 13½*

204	A58	1p multicolored	.25	.25
205	A58	6p multicolored	.25	.25
206	A58	1sh3p multicolored	.75	.25
207	A58	5sh multicolored	2.00	2.00
a.		Souvenir sheet of 4	10.00	10.00
		Nos. 204-207 (4)	3.25	2.75

Cent. of the ITU. No. 207a contains 4 imperf. stamps similar to Nos. 204-207 with simulated perforations.

Lincoln's Home, Springfield, Ill. — A59

1sh3p, Inaugural Address and Lincoln. 2sh, Lincoln and his signature. 5sh, Adaptation of 1869 US Lincoln stamp (No. 122).

Wmk. 325

1965, Apr. Photo. *Perf. 12½*

208	A59	6p multicolored	.25	.25
209	A59	1sh3p multicolored	.25	.25
210	A59	2sh multicolored	.25	.30
211	A59	5sh red & black	.30	1.25
a.		Souvenir sheet of 4	1.25	2.25
		Nos. 208-211 (4)	1.05	2.05

Centenary of death of Abraham Lincoln.

No. 211a contains one each of Nos. 208-211 with simulated perforation.

5-Pesewa Coin, Nkrumah's Head — A60

Coins: 10pa, 10 pesewas. 25pa, 25 pesewas. 50pa, 50 pesewas.

Perf. 11x13

1965, July 19 Unwmk. Litho.

Coin in Silver and Black

Size: 45x32mm

212	A60	5pa red, grn & lt grn	.25	.25
213	A60	10pa red, grn, & pink	.25	.25

Size: 62x39mm

214	A60	25pa red, grn, & pink	.60	.90

Size: 71x43½mm

215	A60	50pa red, grn & lt grn	1.25	2.00
		Nos. 212-215 (4)	2.35	3.40

Introduction of decimal currency.

Regular Issue of 1959-61 Surcharged in Red, Blue, Brown, Black or White with New Value and: "Ghana New Currency / 19th July, 1965"

Perf. 12x11½, 14½x14, 14x14½

1965, July 19 Photo. Wmk. 325

216	A14	1pa on 1p (R)	.25	.25
217	A16	2pa on 2p (Bl)	.25	.25
218	A16a	3pa on 3p (#96, Br)	1.00	*5.50*
219	A16	4pa on 4p (Bl)	4.50	.50
220	A17	6pa on 6p (Bk)	.50	.25
221	A15	11pa on 11p (W)	.25	.25
222	A15	12pa on 1sh (Bl)	.25	.25
223	A17	30pa on 2sh6p (Bl)	4.50	*8.00*
224	A15	60pa on 5sh (Bl)	4.00	.70
225	A16	1.20c on 10s (Bl)	.75	*2.00*
226	A28	2.40c on £1 (Bl)	1.00	*6.25*
		Nos. 216-226,C7-C8 (13)	21.25	25.25

The two lines of the overprint are diagonal on the 1pa, 11pa, 12pa, 60pa, 1.20c and 2.40c.

The surcharge exists double or inverted on six or more denominations.

Numerous inverted surcharges, double surcharges, sideways surcharges, and surcharges on back exist on Nos. 216-226. Values, $10 to $200 each.

Summit Conference, Accra — A61

Map of Africa and Flags A62

Designs: 2pa, "OAU" and three heads (triangle pointing up). 5pa, Symbol of African Unity. 15pa, Sunburst and map of Africa. 24pa, Map of Africa.

Perf. 14, 14½x14

1965, Oct. 21 Photo.

Ghana Flag in Red, Black & Green

227	A61	1pa multicolored	.25	.25
228	A61	2pa multicolored	.25	.25
229	A61	5pa multicolored	.25	.25
230	A62	6pa orange & black	.25	.25
231	A62	15pa light blue & blk	.25	.30
232	A62	24pa lt ultra & green	.25	.50
		Nos. 227-232 (6)	1.50	1.80

Summit Conference of the Organization for African Unity, Accra, Oct. 1965.

Soccer Goalkeeper — A63

Designs: 15pa, Soccer player and cup, vert. 24pa, Two soccer players and cup.

Perf. 14x13, 13x14

1965, Nov. 15 Unwmk.

233	A63	6pa ocher & multi	.25	.25
234	A63	15pa multicolored	.40	.30
235	A63	24pa lt blue & multi	.45	.60
		Nos. 233-235 (3)	1.10	1.15

African Soccer Cup competition.

For overprints see Nos. 244-246.

John F. Kennedy and Eternal Flame A64

Various Kennedy portraits.

1965, Dec. 15 Wmk. 325 *Perf. 12½*

236	A64	6pa blk, yel, gold & grn	.25	.25
237	A64	15pa vio, crim & brt grn	.25	.30
238	A64	24pa dp pur & blk	.25	.50
239	A64	30pa vio brn & blk	.25	.80
a.		Souvenir sheet of 4 ('66)	3.25	5.50
		Nos. 236-239 (4)	1.00	1.85

President John F. Kennedy (1917-1963).

No. 239a contains four imperf. stamps similar to Nos. 236-239.

Generators, Volta River Project A65

Designs: 15pa, Dam and Lake Volta. 24pa, "Ghana" forming dam. 30pa, Grain.

Perf. 11x11½

1966, Jan. 22 Unwmk.

240	A65	6pa	sepia & multi	.25	.25
241	A65	15pa	multicolored	.25	.25
242	A65	24pa	multicolored	.25	.25
243	A65	30pa	brt blue & blk	.30	.50
			Nos. 240-243 (4)	1.05	1.25

Opening of the Volta River dam and electric power station at Akosombo.

Nos. 233-235 Overprinted Diagonally: "Black Stars Retain Africa Cup / 21st Nov. 1965"

1966, Feb. 7 *Perf. 14x13, 13x14*

244	A63	6pa	ocher & multi	.25	.25
245	A63	15pa	multicolored	.30	.30
246	A63	24pa	lt bl & multi	.55	.65
			Nos. 244-246 (3)	1.10	1.20

Ghana's soccer victory, Nov. 21, 1965.

Varieties exist, including overprint in green on No. 244.

Inauguration of WHO Headquarters, Geneva — A66

Designs: 24pa, 30pa, WHO Headquarters from the west and WHO emblem.

Perf. 14x14½

1966, July 1 Photo. Wmk. 325

247	A66	6pa	multicolored	.55	.25
248	A66	15pa	multicolored	1.10	.50
249	A66	24pa	multicolored	1.30	1.30
250	A66	30pa	multicolored	1.50	3.00
a.			Souvenir sheet of 4	28.00	28.00
			Nos. 247-250 (4)	4.45	5.05

No. 250a contains 4 imperf. stamps similar to Nos. 247-250 with simulated perforations.

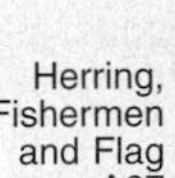

Herring, Fishermen and Flag A67

Designs: 15pa, Flatfish and canoes. 24pa, Spadefish and schooner. 30pa, Red snapper and fishing trawler "Shama." 60pa, Mackerel and steamer.

1966, Aug. 10 Unwmk. *Perf. 14x13*

251	A67	6pa	ocher & multi	.25	.25
252	A67	15pa	yel grn & multi	.40	.25
253	A67	24pa	ver & multi	.50	.30
254	A67	30pa	blue & multi	.70	.70
a.			Souvenir sheet of 4	11.00	11.00
255	A67	60pa	green & multi	1.00	3.00
			Nos. 251-255 (5)	2.85	4.50

1966 Freedom from Hunger campaign "Young World Against Hunger."

No. 254a contains 4 imperf. stamps similar to No. 254.

Flags of African Unity Charter Signers, Map and Diamond A68

Designs: 6p, Ghana flag and links enclosing map of Africa, vert. 24p, Ship's wheel enclosing map of Africa, and cacao pod.

1966, Sept. Unwmk. *Perf. 13x13½*

256	A68	6pa	brt blue & multi	.25	.25
257	A68	15pa	blue & multi	.25	.45
258	A68	24pa	dp green & multi	.25	.50
			Nos. 256-258 (3)	.75	1.20

Signing of the African Unity Charter, 3rd anniv.

Soccer Player and Rimet Cup — A69

Various Soccer Scenes.

Perf. 14½x14

1966, Nov. 14 Photo. Wmk. 325

259	A69	5pa	brown & multi	.25	.25
260	A69	15pa	blue & multi	.70	.30
261	A69	24pa	green & multi	.90	.50
262	A69	30pa	brt rose & multi	1.10	1.10
263	A69	60pa	lilac & multi	1.25	*4.00*
a.			Souvenir sheet of 4	26.00	26.00
			Nos. 259-263 (5)	4.20	6.15

World Cup Soccer Championship, Wembley, England, July 11-30.

No. 263a contains 4 imperf. stamps similar to No. 263 with simulated perforations.

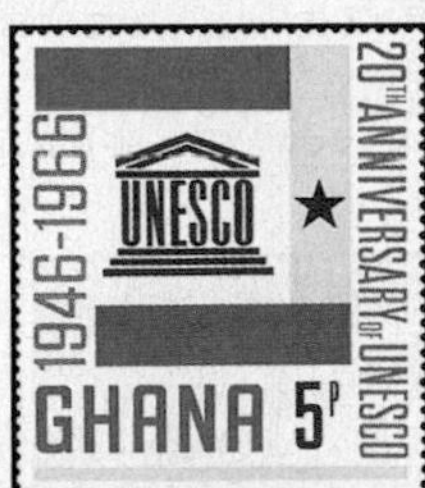

UNESCO Emblem A70

1966, Dec. 23 Wmk. 325 *Perf. 14½*

264	A70	5pa	multicolored	.25	.25
265	A70	15pa	multicolored	.75	.50
266	A70	24pa	multicolored	1.00	1.00
267	A70	30pa	multicolored	1.50	1.25
268	A70	60pa	multicolored	2.25	*5.00*
a.			Souvenir sheet of 5	27.50	27.50
			Nos. 264-268 (5)	5.75	8.00

UNESCO, 20th anniv. No. 268a contains 5 imperf. stamps similar to Nos. 264-268 with simulated perforations.

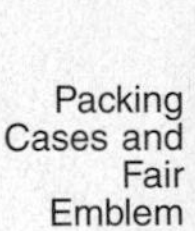

Packing Cases and Fair Emblem A71

Fair Emblem and: 15pa, World map and trade routes to Accra. 24pa, Freighters and loading crane, vert. 36pa, Hand holding cargo net.

1967, Feb. 1 *Perf. 14½x14, 14x14½*

269	A71	5pa	multicolored	.25	.25
270	A71	15pa	multicolored	.25	.25
271	A71	24pa	multicolored	.25	.30
272	A71	36pa	multicolored	.30	*1.50*
			Nos. 269-272 (4)	1.05	2.30

International Trade Fair, Accra, Feb. 1-19.

Eagle and Flag — A72

1967, Feb. 24 Photo. *Perf. 14x14½*

Flag in Red, Yellow, Black and Green

273	A72	1np	gray bl & dk brn	.25	*.75*
274	A72	4np	ocher & dk brn	.25	.25
275	A72	12½np	ol grn & dk brn	.30	.30
276	A72	25np	dl cl & dk brn	.50	*2.25*
a.			Souvenir sheet of 4, #273-276	6.50	8.00
			Nos. 273-276 (4)	1.30	3.55

1st anniv. of the revolution which overthrew the regime of Kwame Nkrumah.

No. 276a has dull claret marginal inscriptions. An imperf. sheet similar to No. 276a has solid margins of dull claret, colorless inscriptions. Value $10.

Nos. 51, 54-58, 60 and 97 Surcharged in Black, Red or White

Size: 30½x21mm, 21x30½mm

1967, Feb. 27 *Perf. 14½x14, 14x14½*

277	A16	1½np	on 2p (B)	2.00	*10.00*
278	A16	3½np	on 4p (R)	8.00	4.00
279	A17	5np	on 6p (R)	4.00	2.00
280	A15	9np	on 11p (W)	.30	1.00
281	A15	10np	on 1sh (W)	.35	*2.00*
282	A17	25np	on 2sh6p (R)	3.00	*8.00*

Size: 45x26mm

283	A16	1nc	on 10sh (R)	2.50	*16.00*
284	A28	2nc	on £1 (R)	4.00	*25.00*
			Nos. 277-284,C9-C10 (10)	33.15	75.00

Corn — A73

Forest Kingfisher — A74

Ghana Mace (golden staff) — A74a

Commelina Flower — A74b

African Lungfish A75

Adomi Bridge, Volta River — A75a

Chameleon — A75b

Quay No. 2, Tema Harbor — A75c

Cape Hare — A75d

Black-winged Stilt — A75e

Chief's Ceremonial Stool — A75f

Frangipani — A75g

State Chair — A75h

4np, Rufous-crowned roller, vert. 6np, Akosombo Dam, Volta River.

Perf. 11½x12, 12x11½ (A73), 14x14½, 14½x14 (A74-A75)

1967 Photo. Wmk. 325

286	A73	1np	multicolored	.25	.25
287	A74	1½np	multicolored	1.00	*2.75*
288	A74a	2np	multicolored	.25	.25
289	A74b	2½np	multicolored	.40	.25
290	A75	3np	multicolored	.25	*.45*
291	A74	4np	multicolored	1.50	.25
292	A75	6np	multicolored	.25	*1.75*
293	A75a	8np	multicolored	.25	*.75*
294	A75b	9np	multicolored	.75	.25
295	A75c	10np	multicolored	.25	.25
296	A75d	20np	blue	.05	.05
297	A75e	50np	multicolored	8.50	4.00
298	A75f	1nc	multicolored	2.00	1.00
299	A75g	2nc	multicolored	2.25	*3.50*
300	A75h	2.50nc	multicolored	2.50	*11.00*
			Nos. 286-300 (15)	20.65	*26.95*

For overprints & surcharges see Nos. 356-370, 858, 1091, 1092A-1092C, 1092E-1093, 1095, 1096B.

Kumasi Fort, 1896
A76

Castles on Ghana Coast: 12½np, Christiansborg Castle, 1659, and British galleon. 20np, Elmina Castle, 1482, and Portuguese galleon. 25np, Cape Coast Castle, 1664, and Spanish galleon.

1967, June 12 *Perf. 14½*

301 A76 4np grnsh bl & multi .25 .25
302 A76 12½np red org & multi .70 1.00
303 A76 20np brt grn & multi 1.00 2.25
304 A76 25np lt red brn & multi 1.25 3.00
Nos. 301-304 (4) 3.20 6.50

Orbiter 1 Landing on Moon — A77

Designs: 4np, Luna 10 on the moon, and globe. 12½np, Astronaut walking in space.

1967, Aug. 16 **Unwmk.** *Perf. 13½*

305 A77 4np multicolored .25 .25
306 A77 10np multicolored .25 *.30*
307 A77 12½np multicolored .25 *.60*
a. Souvenir sheet of 3 2.00 *3.75*
Nos. 305-307 (3) .75 *1.15*

Achievements in space. Issued in Ghana in sheets of 30. Sheets of 12 with ornamented, inscribed border also exist; these were sold in Ghana in 1968.

No. 307a contains 3 imperf. stamps similar to Nos. 305-307.

Boy Scouts at Campfire
A78

Designs: 10np, Hiking Boy Scout. 12½np, Lord Baden-Powell.

1967, Sept. 18 **Photo.** *Perf. 14x13½*

308 A78 4np multicolored .25 .25
309 A78 10np multicolored .35 .35
310 A78 12½np multicolored .45 *.95*
a. Souvenir sheet of 3 6.00 *8.50*
Nos. 308-310 (3) 1.05 1.55

50th anniv. of the Ghana (Gold Coast) Boy Scouts. Issued in Ghana in sheets of 30. Sheets of 12 with ornamented, inscribed border also exist; these were sold in Ghana in 1968.

No. 310a contains 3 imperf. stamps similar to Nos. 308-310 with simulated perforations.

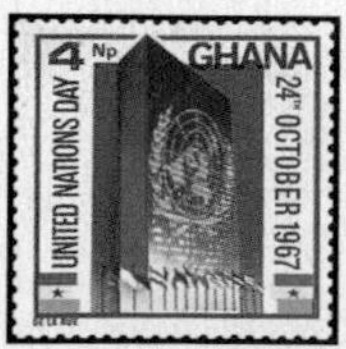

UN Secretariat Building — A79

Design: 50np, 2.50nc, UN Headquarters.

1967, Oct. 24 **Litho.** *Perf. 13½x13*

311 A79 4np multicolored .25 .25
312 A79 10np multicolored .25 .25
313 A79 50np multicolored .30 *.60*
314 A79 2.50nc multicolored .60 *3.00*
a. Souvenir sheet 4.00 *9.00*
Nos. 311-314 (4) 1.40 4.10

United Nations Day. No. 314a contains one imperf. stamp similar to No. 314 with simulated perforations.

Leopard — A80

Designs: 12½np, Christmas butterfly. 20np, Nubian carmine bee-eaters. 50np, Waterbuck.

Wmk. 325

1967, Dec. 28 **Photo.** *Perf. 12½*

315 A80 4np multicolored 1.25 .25
316 A80 12½np multicolored 3.00 1.75
317 A80 20np multicolored 3.50 3.50
318 A80 50np multicolored 4.00 *8.00*
a. Souvenir sheet of 3 [illegible] [illegible]
Nos. 315-318 (4) 11.75 13.50

Intl. Tourist Year. No. 318a contains 3 imperf. stamps similar to Nos. 316-318 with simulated perforations.

Convoy Entering Accra
A81

12½np, Victory parade. 20np, Waving crowd. 40np, Singing and dancing crowd.

Unwmk.

1968, Feb. 24 **Litho.** *Perf. 14*

319 A81 4np sal & multi .25 .25
320 A81 12½np multicolored .25 .25
321 A81 20np multicolored .30 .30
322 A81 40np yel & multi .65 *1.75*
Nos. 319-322 (4) 1.45 2.55

2nd anniversary of Feb. 24th Revolution.

Cacao Beans and Microscope
A82

4np, 25np, Cacao tree & beans, microscope.

Perf. 14½x14

1968, Mar. 18 **Photo.** **Wmk. 325**

323 A82 2½np grn & multi .25 *1.00*
324 A82 4np gray & multi .25 .25
325 A82 10np scar & multi .25 .25
326 A82 25np multicolored .40 *1.00*
a. Souvenir sheet of 4 3.25 3.25
Nos. 323-326 (4) 1.15 2.50

Issued to publicize Ghana's cocoa production. Sheets of 30.

No. 326a contains four imperf. stamps similar to Nos. 323-326 with simulated perforations.

Nos. 323-326 also exist in sheets of 12 believed not to have been on sale in Ghana.

Lt. Gen. E. K. Kotoka
A83

Various portraits of Lt. Gen. Kotoka. 40np vert.

1968, Apr. 17 **Unwmk.** *Perf. 14*

327 A83 4np pur & multi .25 .25
328 A83 12½np grn & multi .25 .25
329 A83 20np multicolored .35 *.60*
330 A83 40np gray & multi .50 *2.00*
Nos. 327-330 (4) 1.35 3.10

Lt. Gen. Emmanuel Kwasi Kotoka (1926-67), leader of the Revolution of 1966 against Nkrumah.

Tobacco — A84

Designs: 5np, Crested porcupine. 12½np, Tapped rubber tree. 20np, Cymothoe sangaris butterfly. 40np, Charaxes ameliae butterfly.

1968, Aug. **Photo.** *Perf. 14x14½*

331 A84 4np multicolored .25 .25
332 A84 5np multicolored .25 *1.00*
333 A84 12½np multicolored .75 .75
334 A84 20np multicolored 2.25 2.75
335 A84 40np multicolored 2.50 *5.00*
a. Souvenir sheet of 4 6.75 *8.00*
Nos. 331-335 (5) 6.00 9.75

No. 335a contains 4 stamps similar to Nos. 331, 332-335 with simulated perforations.

Nos. 331-335 exist imperf. Value, set $13.

Surgical Team
A85

1968, Nov. 11 *Perf. 14x13*

336 A85 4np grn & multi .25 .25
337 A85 12½np multicolored .55 .30
338 A85 20np pur & multi .90 *1.00*
339 A85 40np bl & multi 1.50 *2.50*
a. Souvenir sheet of 4 4.75 *7.00*
Nos. 336-339 (4) 3.20 *4.05*

WHO, 20th anniv. No. 339a contains 4 imperf. stamps similar to Nos. 336-339.

Hurdling — A86

12½np, Boxing. 20np, Torch bearer, flags & Olympic rings. 40np, Soccer.

1968, Dec. **Unwmk.** *Perf. 14x14½*

340 A86 4np gray & multi .25 .25
341 A86 12½np gray & multi .25 .25
342 A86 20np ultra & multi .40 *.70*
343 A86 40np gray & multi .60 *2.50*
a. Souvenir sheet of 4 4.50 *7.00*
Nos. 340-343 (4) 1.50 3.70

19th Olympic Games, Mexico City, Oct. 12-27, 1968. No. 343a contains 4 imperf. stamps with simulated perforations similar to Nos. 340-343.

UN Headquarters and Flags — A87

UN Day, 1968: 12np, UN emblem and Ghanaian staff and stool. 20np, UN Headquarters, New York, UN emblem and Ghana flag. 40np, UN emblem surrounded by flags.

1969, Feb. 1 **Litho.** *Perf. 13x13½*

344 A87 4np multicolored .25 .25
345 A87 12½np pink & multi .25 .25
346 A87 20np blk & multi .25 *.35*
347 A87 40np lt bl & multi .25 *1.75*
a. Souvenir sheet of 4 1.10 *3.25*
Nos. 344-347 (4) 1.00 2.60

No. 347a contains 4 imperf. stamps with simulated perforations similar to Nos. 344-347.

Nos. 344-347 exist imperf. Value, set $4.50.

Joseph Boakye Danquah
A88

12½np, 20np, Dr. Martin Luther King, Jr., Human Rights flame & flag of Ghana.

1969, Mar. 7 **Photo.** *Perf. 14½x14*

348 A88 4np gray & multi .25 .25
349 A88 12½np multicolored .25 .30
350 A88 20np blue & multi .50 *.75*
351 A88 40np grn & multi .60 *2.00*
a. Souvenir sheet of 4 1.50 *3.50*
Nos. 348-351 (4) 1.60 *3.30*

Intl. Human Rights Year, Rev. Martin Luther King, Jr. (1929-1968), American civil rights leader, and Joseph Boakye Danquah (1895-1965), lawyer, writer and Ghanaian political leader.

No. 351a contains 4 imperf. stamps with simulated perforations similar to Nos. 348-351.

Parliament
A89

Design: 12½np, 40np, Coat of Arms.

Perf. 14½x14

1969, Sept. **Wmk. 325**

352 A89 4np multicolored .25 .25
353 A89 12½p multicolored .25 .25
354 A89 20np multicolored .25 .25
355 A89 40np multicolored .25 *.60*
a. Souvenir sheet of 4 1.00 *2.50*
Nos. 352-355 (4) 1.00 1.35

3rd anniv. of the revolution. No. 355a contains 4 imperf. stamps with simulated perforations similar to Nos. 352-355.

Nos. 352-355 exist imperf. Value, set $5.

Nos. 286-300 Overprinted in Black, Yellow or Red

Perf. 11½x12, 12x11½ (A73), 14x14½, 14½x14 (A74-A75)

1969, Oct. 1 **Photo.** **Wmk. 325**

356 A73 1np multicolored .25 *2.25*
357 A74 1½np multicolored 1.75 *4.50*
358 A73 2np multicolored .25 *3.50*
359 A73 2½np multicolored .25 *2.25*
360 A75 3np multicolored .70 *2.50*
361 A73 4np multi (Y) 2.25 .75
362 A75 6np multicolored .25 *2.75*
363 A73 8np multicolored .25 *3.00*
364 A75 9np multicolored .25 *3.00*
365 A75 10np multicolored .25 *3.00*
366 A74 20np blue .65 *2.25*
367 A74 50np multicolored 5.00 *8.50*
368 A74 1nc multicolored 2.00 *11.00*
369 A74 2nc multi (R) 2.50 *12.00*
370 A74 2.50nc multicolored 2.50 *13.00*
Nos. 356-370 (15) 19.10 74.25

Overprint vertical on vertical stamps.

The 4np also exists with overprint in black and in red.

Map of Africa, Two Ghana Flags Rising from Ghana — A90

Designs: 12½np, "2" with laurel and star. 20np, Three hands and egg (symbol of rebirth) and Kente cloth. 40np, like 4np.

Unwmk.

1969, Dec. 4 Litho. *Perf. 14*

371	A90	4np	multicolored	.25	.25
372	A90	12½np	bl & multi	.30	.30
373	A90	20np	multicolored	.40	.40
374	A90	40np	bl & multi	.80	.80
			Nos. 371-374 (4)	1.75	1.75

Inauguration of the 2nd Republic, Oct. 1969.

Cogwheels and ILO Emblem A91

Perf. 14½x14

1970, Jan. 5 Photo. Wmk. 325

375	A91	4np	rose red & multi	.25	.25
376	A91	12½np	multicolored	.25	*.45*
377	A91	20np	multicolored	.30	*.90*
a.			Souvenir sheet of 3	1.40	*2.50*
			Nos. 375-377 (3)	.80	*1.60*

ILO, 50th anniv. No. 377a contains 3 imperf. stamps similar to Nos. 375-377 with simulated perforations.

Nos. 375-377 printed in sheets of 12.

Red Cross Helping Wounded A92

4np, Red Cross & globe, vert. 12½np, Henri Dunant, Red Cross, Red Crescent, Lion & Sun emblems. 40np, Red Cross and first aid.

1970, Feb. 2 *Perf. 14x14½, 14½x14*

378	A92	4np	gold & multi	.45	.45
379	A92	12½np	gold & multi	.55	.55
380	A92	20np	blue & multi	.65	*.85*
381	A92	40np	multicolored	.85	*2.50*
a.			Souvenir sheet of 4	3.75	*6.00*
			Nos. 378-381 (4)	2.50	4.35

League of Red Cross Societies, 50th anniv. No. 381a contains 4 imperf. stamps similar to Nos. 378-381 with simulated perforations.

Kotoka Airport, Gen. Kotoka and VC10 — A93

12½np, Control tower & tail section of VC10. 20np, Bird's eye view of airport and runway. 40np, Flags in front of Kotoka Airport.

Perf. 13x14

1970, Apr. Unwmk. Litho.

382	A93	4np	multicolored	.25	.25
383	A93	12½np	multicolored	.25	.25
384	A93	20np	multicolored	.40	.40
385	A93	40np	multicolored	.75	.75
			Nos. 382-385 (4)	1.65	1.65

Inauguration of Kotoka Airport.

Lunar Landing Module and Spacecraft — A94

Designs: 12½np, Neil A. Armstrong stepping onto the moon. 20np, Scientific experiments on the moon, horiz. 40np, Neil A. Armstrong, Michael Collins and Edwin E. Aldrin, Jr., after return to earth, horiz.

1970, June 15 Litho. *Perf. 12½*

386	A94	4np	multicolored	.25	.25
387	A94	12½np	multicolored	.85	.85
388	A94	20np	multicolored	1.10	1.10
389	A94	40np	multicolored	3.00	3.00
a.			Souvenir sheet of 4	6.25	*10.00*
			Nos. 386-389 (4)	5.20	5.20

See note after US No. C76. No. 389a contains 4 imperf. stamps similar to Nos. 386-389. Exists with and without simulated perfs.

Nos. 386-389 and 389a were overprinted "PHILYMPIA/LONDON 1970" in black or silver in Sept. 1970. They are believed not to have been regularly issued. Value, set $20.

Adult Education A95

Education Year Emblem and: 12½np, Children of various races studying together. 20np, "Ntesie" symbol of wisdom and knowledge. 40np, Nursery school children.

1970, Aug. 10 Litho. *Perf. 13x12½*

390	A95	4np	blue & multi	.25	.25
391	A95	12½np	blue & multi	.25	.25
392	A95	20np	blue & multi	.30	.30
393	A95	40np	blue & multi	.45	.45
			Nos. 390-393 (4)	1.25	1.25

Issued for International Education Year.

Inauguration of Second Republic A96

Designs: 12½np, Mace and words of proclamation by K. A. Busia. 20np, Mace and globe with doves. 40np, Opening of Parliament of Second Republic.

1970, Oct. 1 Litho. *Perf. 13*

398	A96	4np	multicolored	.25	.25
399	A96	12½np	multicolored	.25	.25
400	A96	20np	multicolored	.40	.40
401	A96	40np	lt bl & multi	.45	.45
			Nos. 398-401 (4)	1.35	1.35

First anniversary of the Second Republic.

Kuduo Brass Casket A98

Designs: 12½np, Akan traditional house, Danmum. 20np, Larabanga Mosque. 40np, Akan funerary clay head.

1970, Dec. 7 Litho. *Perf. 14½x14*

406	A98	4np	gray & multi	.25	.25
407	A98	12½np	blue & multi	.35	.30
408	A98	20np	multicolored	.55	.55
a.			Souvenir sheet of 4	7.00	*9.50*
409	A98	40np	blue & multi	1.50	1.60
			Nos. 406-409 (4)	2.65	2.70

No. 408a contains stamps similar to Nos. 406 and 408, a 12½np (Pompeii Basilica) and a 40np (Pompeii scene). Simulated perforation.

Fair Building and Emblem A99

Fair Emblem and: 12½np, Drugstore merchandise. 20np, Automotives and tools. 40np, Cranes and trucks. 50np, Cargo, ship and plane, vert.

Perf. 14½x14, 14x14½

1971, Feb. 5 Photo. Wmk. 325

410	A99	4np	multicolored	.25	.25
411	A99	12½np	lilac & multi	.35	.35
412	A99	20np	blue & multi	.60	.60
413	A99	40np	multicolored	1.25	1.25
414	A99	50np	multicolored	1.50	1.50
			Nos. 410-414 (5)	3.95	3.95

2nd Ghana International Trade Fair, Accra, Feb. 1-14, 1971.

Crucifixion A100

Easter: 12½np, Jesus and disciples. 20np, Resurrection.

Perf. 13½

1971, May 19 Litho. Unwmk.

415	A100	4np	multicolored	.25	.25
416	A100	12½np	multicolored	.40	.40
417	A100	20np	multicolored	.70	.70
			Nos. 415-417 (3)	1.35	1.35

Corn and FAO Emblem — A101

Perf. 14x14½

1971, June Wmk. 325 Photo.

418	A101	4np	lilac & multi	.25	.25
419	A101	12½np	lt bl & multi	.30	.30
420	A101	20np	multicolored	.55	*1.25*
			Nos. 418-420 (3)	1.10	1.80

Freedom from Hunger, second development decade, 1970-1980.

The overprint "In Memoriam / Lord Boyd ORR / 1880-1971" was applied to Nos. 418-420 in October, 1971. The 4np was also surcharged "60NP."

Girl Guide Emblem on Flag of Ghana A102

12½np, Mrs. Elsie Ofuatey-Kodjoe, national founder. 20np, Girl Guides at play. 40np, Campfire and tent. 50np, Girl Guides signalling.

Unwmk.

1971, July 22 Litho. *Perf. 14*

421	A102	4np	multicolored	.25	.25
422	A102	12½np	yel & multi	.70	.70
423	A102	20np	sal & multi	1.40	1.40
424	A102	40np	multicolored	2.25	2.25
425	A102	50np	lilac & multi	2.40	2.40
a.			Souvenir sheet of 5	12.00	12.00
			Nos. 421-425 (5)	7.00	7.00

50th anniversary of the Girl Guides of Ghana. No. 425a contains 5 imperf. stamps similar to Nos. 421-425.

Nos. 421-425 exist imperf. Value, set $24.

Child Care Center — A103

YWCA Emblem and: 12½np, World Council Meeting and map of Ghana. 20np, Typing class. 40np, Building fund day.

1971, Aug. 5 *Perf. 13*

426	A103	4np	multicolored	.25	.25
427	A103	12½np	ultra & multi	.25	.25
428	A103	20np	blue & multi	.25	.25
429	A103	40np	yel & multi	.40	*.80*
a.			Souvenir sheet of 4	1.10	1.10
			Nos. 426-429 (4)	1.15	1.55

World Council Meeting of Young Women's Christian Association, Accra, Aug. 5. No. 429a contains 4 stamps similar to Nos. 426-429 with simulated perforations.

Nos. 426-429 exist imperf. Value, set $5.

African Nativity Scene A104

Christmas: 1np, Fireworks, vert. 6np, Flight into Egypt.

Perf. 14x14½, 14½x14

1971, Nov. Photo. Wmk. 325

433	A104	1np	multicolored	.25	*.70*
434	A104	3np	orange & multi	.25	*.70*
435	A104	6np	blue & multi	.25	*.70*
			Nos. 433-435 (3)	.75	*2.10*

UNICEF Emblem, and Child A105

UNICEF Emblem and: 5np, Infant weighed in net scale, vert. 30np, Student midwife, vert. 50np, Boy in day care center.

Perf. 13½x13, 13x13½

1971, Dec. 20 Litho. Unwmk.

436	A105	5np	grn & multi	.25	.25
437	A105	15np	yel & multi	.25	*.30*
438	A105	30np	pink & multi	.35	*.70*
439	A105	50np	blue & multi	.50	*1.75*
a.			Souvenir sheet of 4	4.25	*6.50*
			Nos. 436-439 (4)	1.35	*3.00*

25th anniv. of UNICEF. No. 439a contains 4 stamps with simulated perforations similar to Nos. 436-439.

Fair Emblem, Map of Africa, Symbol of Unity A106

Fair Emblem and: 15np, Horn of Plenty. 30np, Fireworks over Africa. 60np, 1nc, Names of participating nations over map of Africa.

1972, Feb. 23 Litho. *Perf. 14*

440	A106	5np lt brn & multi	.25	.25
441	A106	15np lt bl & multi	.25	*.30*
442	A106	30np green & multi	.25	*.60*
443	A106	60np yel & multi	.25	*1.25*
444	A106	1nc lt bl & multi	.35	*1.75*
		Nos. 440-444 (5)	1.35	*4.15*

First All-Africa Trade Fair, Nairobi, Kenya, Feb. 23-Mar. 5.

Nos. 440-444 were overprinted "BELGICA 72" in red for release June 24, 1972. The regularity of this issue has been questioned. Value $7.50.

Nos. 440-444 exist imperf. Value, set $7.

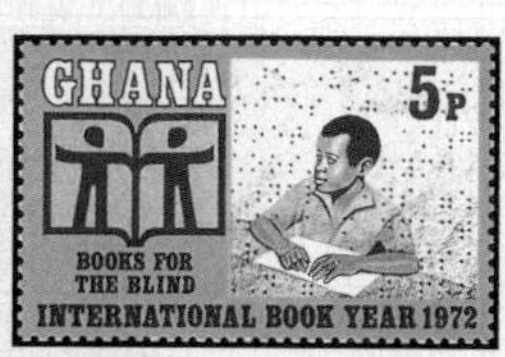

Books for the Blind A107

Book and Flame of Knowledge A108

Book Year Emblem and: 15p, Books for Children ("Anansi and Snake the Postman"). 30p, Books for Recreation (Accra Central Library). 50p, Books for Students (2 students).

1972, Apr. 21 *Perf. 13½*

445	A107	5p blue & multi	.25	.25
446	A107	15p yel & multi	.65	.50
447	A107	30p lilac & multi	.85	1.00
448	A107	50p green & multi	1.50	*2.25*
449	A108	1ce blue & multi	2.25	*4.25*
a.		Souvenir sheet of 5	9.00	*12.00*
		Nos. 445-449 (5)	5.50	*8.25*

Intl. Book Year. No. 449a contains one each of Nos. 445-449 with simulated perforations.

Star Grass A109

15p, Mona monkey. 30p, Amaryllis. 1ce, Side-striped squirrel.

1972, July 3 Litho. *Perf. 13½*

450	A109	5p shown	.25	.25
451	A109	15p multicolored	.65	.65
452	A109	30p multicolored	4.25	4.25
453	A109	1ce multicolored	4.75	4.75
		Nos. 450-453 (4)	9.90	9.90

Olympic Emblems, Soccer A110

1972, Sept. 5 Litho. *Perf. 13½x13*

454	A110	5p shown	.25	.25
455	A110	15p Running	.25	.25
456	A110	30p Boxing	.35	.45
457	A110	50p Long jump	.70	*1.75*
458	A110	1ce High jump	1.50	*3.00*
		Nos. 454-458 (5)	3.05	5.70

Souvenir Sheet

459		Sheet of 2	3.25	*6.00*
a.	A110	40p like 30p	1.25	*2.25*
b.	A110	60p like 5p	1.75	*3.00*

20th Olympic Games, Munich, 8/26-9/11.

Senior and Cub Scouts, Badge A111

Designs: 15p, Scout in front of tent. 30p, 40p, Sea Scouts in canoe. 50p, Cub Scouts with den mother. 60p, 1ce, Scouts studying.

1972, Oct. Litho. *Perf. 14*

460	A111	5p blue grn & multi	.25	.25
461	A111	15p ocher & multi	.45	.45
462	A111	30p lilac & multi	.85	.85
463	A111	50p rose & multi	1.50	1.50
464	A111	1ce blue & multi	3.00	3.00
		Nos. 460-464 (5)	6.05	6.05

Souvenir Sheet

Perf. 13½

465		Sheet of 2	4.00	4.00
a.		A111 40p brown & multi	1.35	1.35
b.		A111 60p green & multi	2.25	2.25

Boy Scout Movement, 65th anniversary. For overprints see Nos. 484-489.

Virgin and Child, by Holbein the Younger — A112

Paintings: 1p, Holy Night, by Correggio. 15p, Virgin and Child, by Andrea Rico. 30p, Melchior. 60p, Virgin and Child with Caspar. 1ce, Balthasar. 30p, 60p, 1ce, are from early 16th century stained glass windows.

1972, Dec. 2 *Perf. 14x13½*

466	A112	1p black & multi	.25	.25
467	A112	3p black & multi	.25	.25
468	A112	15p black & multi	.30	.30
469	A112	30p black & multi	.60	.60
470	A112	60p black & multi	1.40	1.40
471	A112	1ce black & multi	2.00	2.00
a.		Souvenir sheet of 3	7.25	7.25
		Nos. 466-471 (6)	4.80	4.80

Christmas. No. 471a contains one each of Nos. 469-471 with simulated perforations.

Market A113

Designs: 1p, Unity Declaration at Kumasi Durbar. 5p, Woman with child selling bananas, vert. 15p, Farmer at rest and produce, vert. 30p, Market. 40p, 1ce, Farmer cutting palm nuts with cutlass. 60p, Miners.

Perf. 14x13½, 13½x14

1973, Apr. Litho.

472	A113	1p multicolored	.25	.25
473	A113	3p multicolored	.25	.25
474	A113	5p multicolored	.25	.25
475	A113	15p multicolored	.25	.25
476	A113	30p multicolored	.25	*.40*
477	A113	1ce multicolored	.30	*1.25*
		Nos. 472-477 (6)	1.55	2.65

Souvenir Sheet

478		Sheet of 2	2.00	2.00
a.		A113 40p multicolored	.70	.70
b.		A113 60p multicolored	1.05	1.05

Operation "Feed Yourself" and for 1st anniv. of the Oct. 13 Revolution.

Nos. 472-477 exist imperf. Value, set $4.75.

Children's Clinic — A114

WHO Emblem and: 15p, Radiology. 30p, Immunization. 50p, Fight against malnutrition (starving child). 1ce, WHO Headquarters, Geneva.

1973, July *Perf. 14x13½*

479	A114	5p rose red & multi	.25	.25
480	A114	15p blue & multi	.25	.25
481	A114	30p bister & multi	.30	*.40*
482	A114	50p green & multi	.50	*.75*
483	A114	1ce multicolored	.95	*1.75*
		Nos. 479-483 (5)	2.25	3.40

WHO, 25th anniversary.

Nos. 460-465 Overprinted: "1st WORLD SCOUTING CONFERENCE IN AFRICA"

1973, July Litho. *Perf. 14*

484	A111	5p blue grn & multi	.25	.25
485	A111	15p ocher & multi	.25	*.50*
486	A111	30p lilac & multi	.50	*1.25*
487	A111	50p rose & multi	.85	*2.00*
488	A111	1ce blue & multi	1.60	*3.00*
		Nos. 484-488 (5)	3.45	*7.00*

Souvenir Sheet

Perf. 13½

489		Sheet of 2	3.50	*10.00*
a.		A111 40p brown & multi	1.25	*3.00*
b.		A111 60p green & multi	1.75	*6.00*

24th Boy Scout World Conference (1st in Africa), Nairobi, Kenya, July 16-21.

Poultry Farming A115

FAO/UN Emblem and: 15p, 40p, Tractor. 50p, Cacao harvest. 60p, 1ce, FAO Headquarters, Rome.

1973 Litho. *Perf. 14½x14*

490	A115	5p blue & multi	.25	.25
491	A115	15p blue & multi	.25	.25
492	A115	50p blue & multi	.30	*.80*
493	A115	1ce blue & multi	.45	*1.60*
		Nos. 490-493 (4)	1.25	2.90

Souvenir Sheet

494		Sheet of 2	1.00	*2.25*
a.		A115 40p blue & multi	.30	*.80*
b.		A115 60p blue & multi	.45	*1.10*

World Food Program, 10th anniversary.
Nos. 490-493 exist imperf. Value, set $4.75.

INTERPOL Emblem, Observer A116

INTERPOL Emblem and: 30p, Judge's wig, poison bottle, handcuffs. 50p, photograph and fingerprint. 1ce, Corpse and question mark.

1973 *Perf. 13x13½*

495	A116	5p emerald & multi	.25	.25
496	A116	30p rose red & multi	.75	.75
497	A116	50p ultra & multi	1.75	1.75
498	A116	1ce gray & multi	2.75	2.75
		Nos. 495-498 (4)	5.50	5.50

50th anniv. the Intl. Criminal Police Org. (INTERPOL). Nos. 495-498 exist imperf. Value, set $7.50.

Handclasp and "OAU" A117

"OAU" and: 30p, Africa Hall, Addis Ababa. 50p, OAU emblem (map of Africa). 1ce, "X" in Ghana flag colors.

1973, Oct. 22 Litho. *Perf. 14x14½*

499	A117	5p lt bl, blk & brn	.25	.25
500	A117	30p bluish grn, blk & brn	.25	*.30*
501	A117	50p pink, black & ol	.25	*.75*
502	A117	1ce multicolored	.30	*1.10*
		Nos. 499-502 (4)	1.05	*2.40*

Org. for African Unity, 10th anniv. Nos. 499-502 exist imperf. Value, set $5.00

Weather Balloon, WMO Emblem A118

WMO Emblem and: 15p, 40p, Tiros weather satellite. 30p, 60p, Computer weather map. 1ce, Radar cloud scanner.

1973, Nov. 16

503	A118	5p multicolored	.25	.25
504	A118	15p multicolored	.25	.25
505	A118	30p multicolored	.30	*.60*
506	A118	1ce multicolored	.55	*1.75*
		Nos. 503-506 (4)	1.35	2.85

Souvenir Sheet

507		Sheet of 2	1.50	*3.25*
a.		A118 40p multicolored	.45	*.90*
b.		A118 60p multicolored	.85	*1.60*

Intl. meteorological cooperation, cent. No. 507 exists imperf.

Adoration of the Kings — A119

Christmas: 3p, 40p, Madonna and Child (contemporary). Nos. 510, 511d, Madonna and Child, by Murillo. No. 511, 60p, Adoration of the Kings, by Tiepolo. No. 511b as 1p.

1973, Dec. 10 *Perf. 14*

508	A119	1p black & multi	.25	.25
509	A119	3p gray & multi	.25	.25
510	A119	30p multicolored	.35	.35
511	A119	50p multicolored	.75	.75
		Nos. 508-511 (4)	1.60	1.60

Souvenir Sheet

Imperf

511A		Sheet of 4	2.00	2.00
b.		A119 30p black & multi	.30	.30
c.		A119 40p gray & multi	.40	.40
d.		A119 50p multicolored	.50	.50
e.		A119 60p multicolored	.60	.60

No. 511A has simulated perforations. Nos. 508-511 exist imperf. Value, set $5.

Various Envelopes A120

UPU Emblem and: 9p, 30p, UPU Headquarters, Bern. 40p, 50p, Airmail envelope with Ghana No. 296. 60p, 1ce, Ghana No. 296.

1974, May **Litho.** ***Perf. 14½***
512 A120 5p blue, blk & org .25 .25
513 A120 9p blue, blk & org .25 .25
514 A120 50p blue, blk & org .25 *.80*
515 A120 1ce blue, blk & org .50 *1.50*
Nos. 512-515 (4) 1.25 2.80

Souvenir Sheet

515A Sheet of 4 .90 *1.40*
b. A120 20p blue, blk & org .25 *.35*
c. A120 30p blue, blk & org .25 *.35*
d. A120 40p blue, blk & org .25 *.35*
e. A120 60p blue, blk & org .25 *.35*

Centenary of Universal Postal Union.
Nos. 512-515 exist imperf. Value, set $7. No. 515A exists imperf. Value $20.
For overprints see Nos. 521-524A.

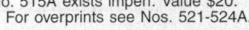

Jesus Carrying Cross — A121

The Betrayal — A121a

Designs: 5p, 15p, Jesus Carrying Cross, painting by Thomas de Coloswar, 1427. 20p, 30p, The Betrayal. 25p, 50p, The Deposition. 40p, 1ce, Risen Christ and Mary Magdalene. The designs (except 5p, 15p) are from 15th century English ivory carvings.

1974, Apr. **Litho.** ***Perf. 14***
516 A121 5p black & multi .25 .25
517 A121a 30p sil, ultra & brn .25 *.30*
518 A121a 50p sil, red & brn .25 *.50*
519 A121a 1ce silver, ol & brn .35 *.90*
Nos. 516-519 (4) 1.10 *1.95*

Souvenir Sheet
Imperf

520 Sheet of 4 1.00 *1.60*
a. A121 15p black & multi .25 *.40*
b. A121a 20p silver, ultra & brn .25 *.40*
c. A121a 25p silver, red & brn .25 *.40*
d. A121a 40p silver, olive & brn .25 *.40*

Easter. No. 520 contains 4 stamps with simulated perforations.
Nos. 516-519 exist imperf. Value, set $6.25.

Nos. 512-515A Overprinted "INTERNABA 1974"

1974, June 7 ***Perf. 14½***
521 A120 5p blue, blk & org .25 .25
522 A120 9p blue, blk & org .25 .25
523 A120 50p blue, blk & org .30 *.80*
524 A120 1ce blue, blk & org .45 *1.25*
Nos. 521-524 (4) 1.25 2.55

Souvenir Sheet

524A Sheet of 4 1.75 *3.50*
b. A120 20p blue, blk & org .25 *.35*
c. A120 30p blue, blk & org .25 *.35*
d. A120 40p blue, blk & org .25 *.50*
e. A120 60p blue, blk & org .30 *.60*

INTERNABA 1974 International Philatelic Exhibition, Basel, June 7-16.
Overprint is applied to individual stamps of No. 524A.

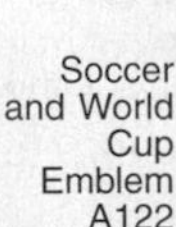

Soccer and World Cup Emblem A122

Designs: Various soccer scenes and world cup emblem.

1974, June 17 **Litho.** ***Perf. 14½, 13***
525 A122 5p multicolored .25 .25
526 A122 30p multicolored .25 *.50*
527 A122 50p multicolored .25 *.75*
528 A122 1ce multicolored .25 *1.00*
Nos. 525-528 (4) 1.00 2.50

Souvenir Sheet
Perf. 14½

529 Sheet of 4 1.75 *3.00*
a. A122 25p multicolored .25 *.30*
b. A122 40p multicolored .25 *.40*
c. A122 55p multicolored .25 *.45*
d. A122 60p multicolored .30 *.50*

World Cup Soccer Championship, June 13-July 7.
Nos. 525-528 were issued in sheets of 30, perf. 14½, and in sheets of 5 plus label, perf. 13.
For overprints, see Nos. 535-539, 549-553.

Traffic Diagram at Traffic Circle A123

Designs: 15p, Traffic sign "Two-way traffic." 30p, "Change to right hand drive!," vert. 50p, Warning hands sign, vert. 1ce, 2 hands and car symbolizing traffic change, vert.

1974, July 16 ***Perf. 13½***
Size: 35x28½mm
530 A123 5p yel grn, red & blk .25 .25
531 A123 15p lilac, red & blk .25 *.30*
Size: 28½x41mm
Perf. 14½
532 A123 30p multicolored .25 .25
533 A123 50p multicolored .60 .60
534 A123 1ce red, green & blk 1.25 1.25
Nos. 530-534 (5) 2.60 2.65

Publicity for change to right-hand driving, Aug. 4, 1974.

Nos. 525-529 Overprinted: "WEST GERMANY WINNERS"

1974, Aug. 30 **Litho.** ***Perf. 14½, 13***
535 A122 5p multicolored .25 .25
536 A122 30p multicolored .35 .35
537 A122 50p multicolored .55 .55
538 A122 1ce multicolored .90 .90
Nos. 535-538 (4) 2.05 2.05

Souvenir Sheet

539 Sheet of 4 1.75 1.75
a. A122 25p multicolored .25 .25
b. A122 40p multicolored .35 .35
c. A122 55p multicolored .40 .40
d. A122 60p multicolored .45 .45

World Cup Soccer Championship, 1974, victory of German Federal Republic. Overprint is applied to individual stamps of No. 539.

Family and WPY Emblem A124

30p, Clinic. 50p, Immunization of children. 1ce, Census.

1974, Sept. 27 ***Perf. 12½***
540 A124 5p shown .25 .25
541 A124 30p multicolored .25 .30
542 A124 50p multicolored .25 *.50*
543 A124 1ce multicolored .40 *1.25*
Nos. 540-543 (4) 1.15 2.30

World Population Year.

Angel — A125

Nativity — A127

Three Kings, Candles — A126

Design: 60p, 1ce, Annunciation.

Perf. 13½, 14 (7p)
1974, Dec. 19 **Litho.**
544 A125 5p red & multi .25 .25
545 A126 7p blue & multi .25 .25
546 A127 9p orange & multi .25 .25
547 A127 1ce orange & multi .40 *1.25*
Nos. 544-547 (4) 1.15 2.00

Souvenir Sheet
Imperf

548 Sheet of 4 1.15 *2.00*
a. A125 15p red & multi .25 *.50*
b. A126 30p blue & multi .25 *.50*
c. A127 45p orange & multi .25 *.50*
d. A127 60p orange & multi .25 *.50*

Christmas. No. 548 contains 4 stamps with simulated perforations.

Nos. 525-529 Overprinted "APOLLO / SOYUZ / JULY 15, 1975"

1975, Aug. 15 **Litho.** ***Perf. 14½, 13***
549 A122 5p multicolored .25 .25
550 A122 30p multicolored .25 .25
551 A122 50p multicolored .40 .40
552 A122 1ce multicolored .70 .70
Nos. 549-552 (4) 1.60 1.60

Souvenir Sheet
Perf. 14½

553 Sheet of 4 2.25 2.25
a. A122 25p multicolored .25 .25
b. A122 40p multicolored .30 .30
c. A122 55p multicolored .50 .50
d. A122 60p multicolored .55 .55

Apollo Soyuz space test project (Russo-American cooperation), launching July 15, link-up, July 17.
Overprint is applied to individual stamps of No. 553.
Nos. 549-552 with perf. 13 are from the sheets of 5 plus label.

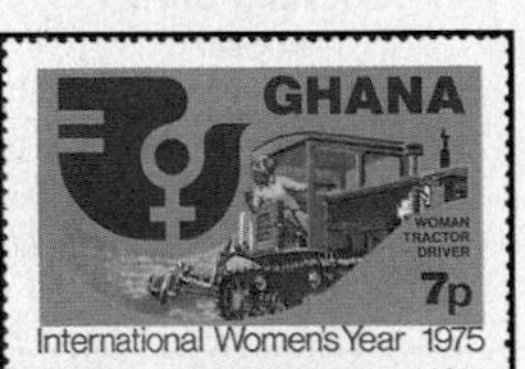

IWY Emblem, Woman Tractor Driver — A128

Intl. Women's Year Emblem and: 15p, like 7p. 30p, 40p, Automobile mechanic. 60p, 65p, Factory workers. 80p, 1ce, Cocoa research.

1975, Sept. 3 **Litho.** ***Perf. 14***
554 A128 7p multicolored .25 .25
555 A128 30p lt violet & multi .45 .45
556 A128 60p multicolored 1.10 1.10
557 A128 1ce lilac & multi 1.75 1.75
Nos. 554-557 (4) 3.55 3.55

Souvenir Sheet
Imperf

558 Sheet of 4 3.25 *5.00*
a. A128 15p Prus green & multi .25 *.40*
b. A128 40p light violet & multi .60 *.90*
c. A128 65p dull green & multi .85 *1.25*
d. A128 80p lilac & multi 1.00 *1.50*

Intl. Women's Year. No. 558 contains 4 stamps with simulated perforations.

Angel over Child in Crib A129

Angel with Harp A130

Designs: 7p, 40p, Angels with lute and bell. 30p, 65p, Angel with viol. 1ce, 80p, Angels with trumpets. 15p, like 5p.

1975, Dec. 31 **Litho.** ***Perf. 14x13½***
559 A129 2p org & multi .25 .25
560 A130 5p yel, brown & grn .25 .25
561 A130 7p yel, brown & grn .25 .25
562 A130 30p yel, brown & grn .30 .25
563 A130 1ce yel, brown & grn .40 .75
Nos. 559-563 (5) 1.45 1.75

Souvenir Sheet
Imperf

564 Sheet of 4 1.60 *2.50*
a. A130 15p yellow, green & brown .25 *.25*
b. A130 40p yellow, green & brown .25 *.25*
c. A130 65p yellow, green & brown .40 *.65*
d. A130 80p yellow, green & brown .50 *.75*

Christmas. No. 564 has simulated perforations.

Boy Scouts Reading Map — A131

30p, 40p, Sailing. 60p, 65p, Hiking. 80p, 1ce, Life saving (swimmers). 15p, like 7p.

1976, Jan. 5 ***Perf. 13½x14***
565 A131 7p ocher & multi .25 .25
566 A131 30p blue & multi .70 .70
567 A131 60p green & multi 1.45 1.45
568 A131 1ce multicolored 2.10 2.10
Nos. 565-568 (4) 4.50 4.50

Souvenir Sheet

569 Sheet of 4 4.00 *6.00*
a. A131 15p ocher & multi .30 *.50*
b. A131 40p blue & multi .70 *1.10*
c. A131 65p green & multi 1.00 *1.50*
d. A131 80p rose claret & multi 1.25 *1.75*

Nordjamb 75, 14th World Boy Scout Jamboree, Lillehammer, Norway, July 29-Aug. 7.
For overprints, see Nos. 578-582.

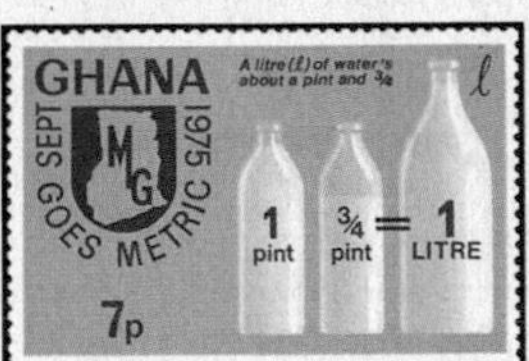

1 ¾ Pints Equal 1 Liter A132

Map of Ghana and: 30p, "2¼ lbs of jam a little more than a kilogram." 60p, "A meter of cloth will be a little more than 3 foot 3." 1ce, Thermometer, ice and boiling tea kettle.

1976, Jan. 5 **Litho.** ***Perf. 14x13½***
570 A132 7p bluish gray & blk .25 .25
571 A132 30p vio blue & multi .35 .35
572 A132 60p ocher & multi .70 .70
573 A132 1ce multicolored 1.25 1.25
Nos. 570-573 (4) 2.55 2.55

Introduction of metric system, Sept. 1975.

Fair Grounds — A133

Designs: Various exhibition halls.

1976, Apr. 6 Litho. *Perf. 14*

574 A133 7p multicolored .25 .25
575 A133 30p yellow & multi .25 .25
576 A133 60p multicolored .25 *.60*
577 A133 1ce salmon & multi .35 *1.00*
Nos. 574-577 (4) 1.10 2.10

International Trade Fair, Accra, Feb. 1-15.

Nos. 565-569 Overprinted in Violet Blue

1976, May 29 Litho. *Perf. 13½x14*

578 A131 7p ocher & multi .25 .25
579 A131 30p blue & multi .45 .45
580 A131 60p green & multi .90 .75
581 A131 1ce multicolored 1.25 1.25
Nos. 578-581 (4) 2.85 2.70

Souvenir Sheet

582 Sheet of 4 2.00 2.00
a. A131 15p ocher & multi .25 .25
b. A131 40p blue & multi .35 .35
c. A131 65p green & multi .45 .45
d. A131 80p rose claret & multi .45 .45

Interphil 76 International Philatelic Exhibition, Philadelphia, Pa., May 29-June 6. Overprint applied to individual stamps of No. 582.

Shot Put — A134

Olympic Rings, Map of Ghana and: 15p, like 7p. 30p, 40p, Soccer. 60p, 65p, Women's 1500 meters. 80p, 1ce, Boxing.

1976, Aug. 9 Litho. *Perf. 14x13½*

583 A134 7p lt blue & multi .25 .25
584 A134 30p yellow & multi .25 .25
585 A134 60p multicolored .55 .55
586 A134 1ce yellow & multi .75 .75
Nos. 583-586 (4) 1.80 1.80

Souvenir Sheet

587 Sheet of 4 1.50 1.50
a. A134 15p light blue & multi .25 .25
b. A134 40p yellow & multi .25 .25
c. A134 65p emerald & multi .25 .25
d. A134 80p yellow & multi .30 .30

21st Olympic Games, Montreal, Canada, July 17-Aug. 1.

For overprints see Nos. 606-610.

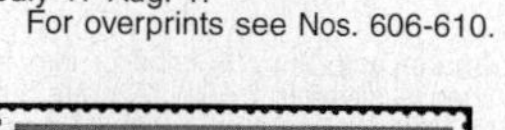

Supreme Court, Accra A135

Designs: Various views of Supreme Court Building, Scales of Justice, law book.

1976, Sept. 7 Litho. *Perf. 14*

588 A135 8p lilac & multi .25 .25
589 A135 30p blue & multi .25 .25
590 A135 60p ver & multi .30 *.50*
591 A135 1ce multicolored .55 *1.00*
Nos. 588-591 (4) 1.35 2.00

Ghana Supreme Court, centenary.

Examination for River Blindness — A136

Designs: 30p, Ghanaian entomologist with microscope. 60p, Flowers. 1ce, Boatmen checking effectiveness of black fly larvae insecticide.

1976, Oct. 28 Litho. *Perf. 14½x14*

592 A136 7p multicolored .70 .25
593 A136 30p multicolored 1.90 1.75
594 A136 60p multicolored 3.00 3.00
595 A136 1ce multicolored 5.00 5.00
Nos. 592-595 (4) 10.60 10.00

World Health Day. Prevention of blindness.

A137

A137a

Designs: 6p, 15p, Children with firecrackers. 30p, 65p, Family at Christmas dinner. 8p, 40p, 80p, 1ce, Children with Gifts and Christmas Tree.

1976, Dec. 15 Litho. *Perf. 13½*

596 A137 6p multicolored .25 .25
597 A137a 8p multicolored .25 .25
598 A137a 30p multicolored .50 .50
599 A137a 1ce multicolored 1.25 1.25
Nos. 596-599 (4) 2.25 2.25

Souvenir Sheet

Imperf

600 Sheet of 4 2.50 2.50
a. A137 15p multicolored .25 .25
b. A137a 40p multicolored .40 .40
c. A137a 65p multicolored .70 .70
d. A137a 80p multicolored 1.00 1.00

Christmas. No. 600 has simulated perfs.

1876 Gallows Frame Telephone and A. G. Bell — A138

A. G. Bell and: 15p, like 8p. 30p, 40p, 1895 telephone. 60p, 65p, 1929 telephone. 80p, 1ce, 1976 telephone.

1976, Dec. 17 *Perf. 14½*

601 A138 8p multicolored .25 .25
602 A138 30p multicolored .40 .40
603 A138 60p multicolored 1.15 1.15
604 A138 1ce multicolored 1.35 1.35
Nos. 601-604 (4) 3.15 3.15

Souvenir Sheet

Perf. 13

605 Sheet of 4 2.50 2.50
a. A138 15p multicolored .25 .25
b. A138 40p multicolored .45 .45
c. A138 65p multicolored .70 .70
d. A138 80p multicolored .80 .80

Centenary of first telephone call by Alexander Graham Bell, Mar. 10, 1876.

For overprints, see Nos. 616-620.

Nos. 583-587 Overprinted

a. EAST GERMANY / WINNERS
b. U.S.S.R. WINNERS
c. U.S.A. WINNERS

1977, Feb. 22 Litho. *Perf. 14x13½*

606 A134(a) 7p multicolored .25 .25
607 A134(a) 30p multicolored .30 .25
608 A134(b) 60p multicolored .65 .65
609 A134(c) 1ce multicolored 1.30 1.30
Nos. 606-609 (4) 2.50 2.45

Souvenir Sheet

610 Sheet of 4 3.00 3.00
a. A134(a) 15p multicolored .25 .25
b. A134(a) 40p multicolored .60 .60
c. A134(b) 65p multicolored .90 .90
d. A134(c) 80p multicolored .95 .95

1976 Montreal Olympic Games' winners.

Klama Dance, Dipo Tribe — A139

Festival Emblem and: 15p, like 8p. 30p, 40p, African artifacts. 60p, 65p, Acon dance. 80p, 1ce, Mud, straw and wooden huts.

1977, Mar. 24 Litho. *Perf. 14x13½*

611 A139 8p multicolored .25 .25
612 A139 30p multicolored .40 *.60*
613 A139 60p multicolored .65 *1.10*
614 A139 1ce multicolored 1.00 *1.75*
Nos. 611-614 (4) 2.30 3.70

Souvenir Sheet

615 Sheet of 4 3.00 3.00
a. A139 15p multicolored .30 .30
b. A139 40p multicolored .65 .65
c. A139 65p multicolored .85 .85
d. A139 80p multicolored 1.05 1.05

2nd World Black and African Festival of Arts and Culture, Lagos, Nigeria, Jan. 15-Feb. 12.

Nos. 601-605 Overprinted: "PRINCE CHARLES / VISITS GHANA / 17th TO 25th / MARCH, 1977"

1977, June 2 Litho. *Perf. 14½*

616 A138 8p multicolored .65 .65
617 A138 30p multicolored 1.60 1.60
618 A138 60p multicolored 2.50 2.50
619 A138 1ce multicolored 3.25 3.25
Nos. 616-619 (4) 8.00 8.00

Souvenir Sheet

Perf. 13

620 Sheet of 4 11.00 11.00
a. A138 15p multicolored 1.20 1.05
b. A138 40p multicolored 2.10 1.75
c. A138 65p multicolored 3.00 2.50
d. A138 80p multicolored 3.50 3.00

Visit of Prince Charles, Mar. 17-25. Overprint applied to individual stamps of No. 620.

Olive Colobus — A140

Wildlife Fund Emblem and: 15p, like 8p. 20p, 40p, Ebien palm squirrel. 30p, 65p, African wild dog. 60p, 80p, West African manatee.

1977, June 22 Litho. *Perf. 13½x14*

621 A140 8p multicolored *2.75* *1.50*
622 A140 20p multicolored *5.75* *1.75*
623 A140 30p multicolored *7.25* *4.50*
624 A140 60p multicolored *11.00* *6.50*
Nos. 621-624 (4) *26.75* *14.25*

Souvenir Sheet

625 Sheet of 4 18.00 18.00
a. A140 15p multicolored 2.00 2.00
b. A140 40p multicolored 3.75 3.75
c. A140 65p multicolored 4.50 4.50
d. A140 80p multicolored 5.50 5.50

Wildlife protection.

Nos. 621-624 exist imperf. Value, set $27.50.

Suzanne Fourment in Velvet Hat, by Rubens — A141

Paintings: 15p, like 8p. 30p, 40p, Isabella of Portugal, by Titian. 60p, 65p, Duke and Duchess of Cumberland, by Gainsborough. 80p, 1ce, Rubens and his wife Isabella, by Rubens.

1977, Sept. Litho. *Perf. 14x13½*

626 A141 8p lt blue & multi .25 .25
627 A141 30p lt blue & multi .50 .50
628 A141 60p lt blue & multi 1.10 1.10
629 A141 1ce lt blue & multi 2.00 2.00
Nos. 626-629 (4) 3.85 3.85

Souvenir Sheet

630 Sheet of 4 3.50 3.50
a. A141 15p light blue & multi .25 .25
b. A141 40p light blue & multi .70 .70
c. A141 65p light blue & multi 1.10 1.10
d. A141 80p light blue & multi 1.25 1.25

Painters, birth annivs.: Peter Paul Rubens (1577-1640); Titian (1477-1576); Thomas Gainsborough (1727-1788).

Adoration of the Kings — A142

Guild of the Good Shepherd, Abossey Okai — A143

Designs: 6p, 40p, Methodist Church, Wesley, Accra. 8p, Virgin and Child, and Star. 15p, like 2p. 30p, 65p, Holy Spirit Cathedral, Accra. 80p, 1ce, Ebenezer Presbyterian Church, Osu, Accra. Type A143 designs include score of "Hark the Herald Angels Sing."

Perf. 14x14½, 14

1977, Dec. 30 Litho.

631 A142 1p multicolored .25 .25
632 A143 2p multicolored .25 .25
633 A143 6p multicolored .25 .25
634 A142 8p multicolored .25 .25
635 A143 30p multicolored .50 .50
636 A143 1ce multicolored 1.50 1.50
Nos. 631-636 (6) 3.00 3.00

Souvenir Sheet

Imperf

637 Sheet of 4 4.00 4.00
a. A143 15p multicolored .25 .25
b. A143 40p multicolored .65 .65
c. A143 65p multicolored 1.05 1.05
d. A143 80p multicolored 1.25 1.25

Christmas. No. 637 has simulated perfs.

No. 631-637 Overprinted: "REFERENDUM 1978 VOTE EARLY"

Perf. 14x14½, 14

1978, Mar. 28 Litho.

638 A142 1p multicolored .25 .25
639 A143 2p multicolored .25 .25
640 A143 6p multicolored .25 .25
641 A142 8p multicolored .25 .25
642 A143 30p multicolored .50 .50
643 A143 1ce multicolored 1.75 1.75
Nos. 638-643 (6) 3.25 3.25

Souvenir Sheet

Imperf

644 Sheet of 4 *30.00* *25.00*
a. A143 15p multicolored *2.50* *2.00*
b. A143 40p multicolored *5.50* *3.50*
c. A143 65p multicolored *8.50* *6.25*
d. A143 80p multicolored *11.00* *7.25*

Banana Harvest — A144

Designs: 8p, Vegetable garden. 30p, Produce market. 60p, Fishing. 1ce, Tractor.

1978, May 15 ***Perf. 14***

No.	Description	Unused	Used
645	A144 2p multicolored	.25	.25
646	A144 8p multicolored	.25	.25
647	A144 30p multicolored	.40	.40
648	A144 60p multicolored	.95	.95
649	A144 1ce multicolored	1.60	1.60
	Nos. 645-649 (5)	3.45	3.45

Operation feed yourself.

Wright Biplane and Crowd — A145

Planes and Crowd: 15p, like 8p. 30p, 40p, Heracles, 1st practical airliner. 60p, 65p, D. H. Comet, 1st jet airliner. 80p, 1ce, Concorde, 1st supersonic airliner.

1978, June 6 Litho. ***Perf. 14x13½***

No.	Description	Unused	Used
650	A145 8p multicolored	.25	.25
651	A145 30p multicolored	.65	.55
652	A145 60p multicolored	1.25	1.10
653	A145 1ce multicolored	2.00	1.40
	Nos. 650-653 (4)	4.15	3.30

Souvenir Sheet

No.	Description	Unused	Used
654	Sheet of 4	6.00	3.25
a.	A145 15p multicolored	.35	.25
b.	A145 40p multicolored	1.10	.60
c.	A145 65p multicolored	1.90	1.00
d.	A145 80p multicolored	2.10	1.10

75th anniversary of first powered flight. The cheering crowd forms a continuing design on Nos. 650-654.

Nos. 650-653 exist imperf. Value, set $6.

Nos. 650-653, 654a-654d Overprinted: "CAPEX 78 / JUNE 9-18 1978"

1978, June 9

No.	Description	Unused	Used
655	A145 8p multicolored	.25	.25
656	A145 30p multicolored	.40	.25
657	A145 60p multicolored	.65	.50
658	A145 1ce multicolored	1.75	.80
	Nos. 655-658 (4)	3.05	1.80

Souvenir Sheet

No.	Description	Unused	Used
659	Sheet of 4	2.50	2.25
a.	A145 15p multicolored	.25	.25
b.	A145 40p multicolored	.45	.40
c.	A145 65p multicolored	.70	.65
d.	A145 80p multicolored	.90	.80

CAPEX, Canadian International Philatelic Exhibition, Toronto, Ont., June 9-18.

Soccer, Africa Cup Emblem and Ghana Flag — A146

15p, like 8p. 30p, 40p, Three soccer players, Africa Cup emblem, Ghana flag. 60p, 65p, Two soccer players. Argentina '78 emblem, Argentine flag. 80p, 1ce, Goalkeeper, Argentina '78 emblem and Argentine flag.

1978, July 1 Litho. ***Perf. 13½x14***

No.	Description	Unused	Used
660	A146 8p multicolored	.25	.25
661	A146 30p multicolored	.30	.30
662	A146 60p multicolored	.70	.70
663	A146 1ce multicolored	1.30	1.30
	Nos. 660-663 (4)	2.55	2.55

Souvenir Sheet

No.	Description	Unused	Used
664	Sheet of 4	1.75	1.75
a.	A146 15p multicolored	.25	.25
b.	A146 40p multicolored	.35	.35
c.	A146 65p multicolored	.55	.55
d.	A146 80p multicolored	.60	.60

11th African Cup of Nations, Ghana, Mar. 5-19, and 11th World Cup Soccer Championship, Argentina, June 1-25.

Nos. 660-663 exist imperf. Value, set $7.25.

Nos. 660-661, 664a-664b Overprinted: "GHANA WINNERS" Nos. 662-663, 664c-664d Overprinted: "ARGENTINA WINS"

1978, Aug. 21 Litho. ***Perf. 13½x14***

No.	Description	Unused	Used
665	A146 8p multicolored	.25	.25
666	A146 30p multicolored	.40	.40
667	A146 60p multicolored	.80	.80
668	A146 1ce multicolored	1.40	1.40
	Nos. 665-668 (4)	2.85	2.85

Souvenir Sheet

No.	Description	Unused	Used
669	Sheet of 4	1.50	1.50
a.	A146 15p multicolored	.25	.25
b.	A146 40p multicolored	.25	.25
c.	A146 65p multicolored	.35	.35
d.	A146 80p multicolored	.55	.55

Winners, 11th African Cup and 11th World Cup Soccer Championships.

Overprint on 60p and 65p is in two lines.

The Betrayal, by Dürer — A147

Etchings by Albrecht Dürer: 39p, The Crucifixion. 60p, The Deposition. 1ce, The Resurrection.

1978, Sept. 1 Litho. ***Perf. 14x13½***

No.	Description	Unused	Used
670	A147 11p lilac & black	.25	.25
671	A147 39p salmon & black	.30	.30
672	A147 60p orange & black	.45	.45
673	A147 1ce yel green & black	.75	.75
	Nos. 670-673 (4)	1.75	1.75

Easter.

Bauhinia Purpurea A148

Flowers: 39p, Cassia fistula. 60p, Frangipani. 1ce, Jacaranda mimosifolia.

1978, Nov. 20 Litho. ***Perf. 14x13½***

No.	Description	Unused	Used
674	A148 11p multicolored	.25	.25
675	A148 39p multicolored	.25	.25
676	A148 60p multicolored	.40	.40
677	A148 1ce multicolored	.60	.60

Nos. 674-677 exist imperf. Value, set $10.

	Nos. 674-677 (4)	1.50	1.60

Mail Railroad Car — A149

Ghana railroad, 75th Anniv.: 39p, Pay and bank car. 60p, Locomotive, 1922. 1ce, Diesel locomotive, 1960.

1978, Dec. 4 Litho. ***Perf. 13½***

No.	Description	Unused	Used
678	A149 11p multicolored	.25	.25
679	A149 39p multicolored	.45	*.65*
680	A149 60p multicolored	.75	*1.00*
681	A149 1ce multicolored	1.10	*1.50*
	Nos. 678-681 (4)	2.55	*3.40*

Pioneer Venus Space Project — A150

15p, like 11p. 39p, 40p, Multiprobe spacecraft. 60p, 65p, Orbiter and Multiprobe circling Venus. 2ce, 3ce, Radar chart of Venus.

1979, July 5 Litho. ***Perf. 14x13½***

No.	Description	Unused	Used
682	A150 11p multicolored	.25	.25
683	A150 39p multicolored	.25	.25
684	A150 60p multicolored	.35	.35
685	A150 3ce multicolored	.55	*1.10*
	Nos. 682-685 (4)	1.40	1.95

Souvenir Sheet
Imperf

No.	Description	Unused	Used
686	Sheet of 4	1.90	1.90
a.	A150 15p multicolored	.25	.25
b.	A150 40p multicolored	.25	.25
c.	A150 65p multicolored	.40	.40
d.	A150 2ce multicolored	.90	.90

O Come All Ye Faithful A152

Christmas Carols: 10p, O Little Town of Bethlehem. 15p, 65p, We Three Kings of Orient Are. 20p, I Saw Three Ships Come Sailing By. 25p, like 8p. No. 696, 1ce, Away in a Manger. 4ce, No. 698d, Ding Dong Merrily on High.

1979, Dec. 20 ***Perf. 14½***

No.	Description	Unused	Used
692	A152 8p multicolored	.25	.25
693	A152 10p multicolored	.25	.25
694	A152 15p multicolored	.25	.25
695	A152 20p multicolored	.25	.25
696	A152 2ce multicolored	.25	*.60*
697	A152 4ce multicolored	.25	*1.10*
	Nos. 692-697 (6)	1.50	2.70

Souvenir Sheet

No.	Description	Unused	Used
698	Sheet of 4	1.10	1.10
a.	A152 25p multicolored	.25	.25
b.	A152 65p multicolored	.25	.25
c.	A152 1ce multicolored	.25	.25
d.	A152 2ce multicolored	.50	.50

Christmas.

Nos. 692-697 exist imperf. Value, set $6.

J.B. Danquah (1895-1965) A153

National Leaders: 65p, John Mensah Sarbah (1864-1910). 80p, J.E.K. Aggrey (1875-1925). 2ce, Kwame Nkrumah (1909-1972). 4ce, G.E. Grant (1878-1956).

1980, Jan. 21 Litho. ***Perf. 13½x14***

No.	Description	Unused	Used
699	A153 20p multicolored	.25	.25
700	A153 65p multicolored	.25	.25
701	A153 80p multicolored	.25	.25
702	A153 2ce multicolored	.35	.35
703	A153 4ce multicolored	.65	.65
	Nos. 699-703 (5)	1.75	1.75

Man with Clack Bells, Hill A154

Hill and: 25p, Man with clack bells. 50p, 65p, Chief, elephant staff. 1ce, 2ce, Drummer. 4ce, 5ce, Chief, ivory staff.

1980, Mar. 12 Litho. ***Perf. 14½***

No.	Description	Unused	Used
704	A154 20p multicolored	.25	.25
705	A154 65p multicolored	.25	.25
706	A154 2ce multicolored	.45	.45
707	A154 4ce multicolored	.80	.80
	Nos. 704-707 (4)	1.75	1.75

Souvenir Sheet

No.	Description	Unused	Used
708	Sheet of 4	1.75	1.75
a.	A154 25p multicolored	.25	.25
b.	A154 50p multicolored	.25	.25
c.	A154 1ce multicolored	.30	.30
d.	A154 5ce multicolored	.85	.85

Sir Rowland Hill (1795-1879), originator of penny postage.

Nos. 708a-708d also exist perf 13½, issued in small individual sheetlets. Values slightly more than perf 14½.

For overprints see Nos. 714-718. Nos. 704-708 exist imperf. Value, set $14.

Students, IYC Emblem — A155

IYC Emblem and: 25p like 20p. 50p, 65p, Boys playing soccer. 1ce, 2ce, Boys in canoe. 3ce, 4ce, Mother and child.

1980, Apr. 2 Litho. ***Perf. 15***

No.	Description	Unused	Used
709	A155 20p multicolored	.25	.25
710	A155 65p multicolored	.25	*.30*
711	A155 2ce multicolored	.50	*.80*
712	A155 4ce multicolored	1.05	*1.60*
	Nos. 709-712 (4)	2.05	*2.95*

Souvenir Sheet

No.	Description	Unused	Used
713	Sheet of 4	2.25	2.25
a.	A155 25p multicolored	.25	.25
b.	A155 50p multicolored	.25	.25
c.	A155 1ce multicolored	.30	.30
d.	A155 3ce multicolored	.75	.75

Intl. Year of the Child (in 1979).

For overprints see Nos. 719-723. Nos. 709-712 exist imperf. Value, set $9.50.

Nos. 704-708 Overprinted: "LONDON 1980" / 6th-14th May 1980

1980, May 6 Litho. ***Perf. 14½***

No.	Description	Unused	Used
714	A154 20p multicolored	.25	.25
715	A154 65p multicolored	.30	.30
716	A154 2ce multicolored	.75	.75
717	A154 4ce multicolored	1.25	1.25
	Nos. 714-717 (4)	2.55	2.55

Souvenir Sheet

No.	Description	Unused	Used
718	Sheet of 4	3.00	3.00
a.	A154 25p multicolored	.25	.25
b.	A154 50p multicolored	.25	.25
c.	A154 1ce multicolored	.45	.45
d.	A154 5ce multicolored	1.90	1.90

London 1980 Intl. Stamp Exhib., May 6-14. Nos. 718a-718d also exist perf 13½, issued in small individual sheetlets. Value, unused or used, $15. Nos. 714-717 exist imperf. Value, set $8.50.

Nos. 709-713 Overprinted: "PAPAL VISIT" / 8th-9th May / 1980

1980, May 8 ***Perf. 15***

No.	Description	Unused	Used
719	A155 20p multicolored	.75	.25
720	A155 65p multicolored	1.40	.70
721	A155 2ce multicolored	2.25	1.40
722	A155 4ce multicolored	3.50	2.25
	Nos. 719-722 (4)	7.90	4.60

Souvenir Sheet

No.	Description	Unused	Used
723	Sheet of 4	15.00	15.00
a.	A155 25p multicolored	1.00	1.00
b.	A155 50p multicolored	2.10	2.10
c.	A155 1ce multicolored	3.25	3.25
d.	A155 3ce multicolored	7.75	7.75

Visit of Pope John Paul II to Ghana, May 8-9.

Nos. 719-722 exist imperf. Value, set $12.50.

Parliament House A156

1980, Aug. 4 Litho. *Perf. 14*
724 A156 20p shown .25 .25
725 A156 65p Supreme Court .25 .25
726 A156 2ce The Castle .25 *.60*
Nos. 724-726 (3) .75 1.10

Souvenir Sheet

727 Sheet of 3 .65 *1.00*
a. A156 25p like #724 .25 .25
b. A156 1ce like #725 .25 .25
c. A156 3ce like #726 .25 .30

Third Republic.
Nos. 724-726 exist imperf. Value, $1.75.

Map of West African Member Countries, Flag of Ghana, Jet — A157

1980, Nov. 5 Litho. *Perf. 14½*
728 A157 20p shown .25 .25
729 A157 65p Dish antenna .25 .25
730 A157 80p Cogwheels .25 .25
731 A157 2ce Corn .25 .25
Nos. 728-731 (4) 1.00 1.00

5th Anniversary of ECOWAS (Economic Community of West African States).

A158

20p, "OAU". 65p, OAU Banner, Maps. 80p, Waves on map of Africa. 2ce, Flag, banner, map.

1980, Nov. 26
732 A158 20p multicolored .25 .25
733 A158 65p multicolored .25 .25
734 A158 80p multicolored .25 .25
735 A158 2ce multicolored .25 .25
Nos. 732-735 (4) 1.00 1.00

Org. for African Unity summit conference, Lagos, Nigeria, Apr. 28-29. Nos. 732-735 exist imperf. Value, set $3.25.

A159

Christmas (Fra Angelico Paintings): 15p, 25p, Adoration of the Magi. 20p, 50p, Virgin and Child Enthroned with Four Angels. 1ce, 2ce, Virgin and Child Enthroned with Eight Angels. 3ce, 4ce, Annunciation.

1980, Dec. 10 *Perf. 14*
736 A159 15p multicolored .25 .25
737 A159 20p multicolored .25 .25
738 A159 2ce multicolored .35 *.60*
739 A159 4ce multicolored .65 *1.25*
Nos. 736-739 (4) 1.50 2.35

Souvenir Sheet

740 Sheet of 4 1.00 1.00
a. A159 25p multicolored .25 .25
b. A159 50p multicolored .25 .25
c. A159 1ce multicolored .25 .25
d. A159 3ce multicolored .30 .30

Nos. 736-739 exist imperf. Value, set $5.50.

Nurse Weighing Newborn, Rotary Emblem A160

65p, Map of Ghana and world. 2ce, Helping hands, world map. 4ce, Food distribution.

1980, Dec. 18
741 A160 20p shown .25 .25
742 A160 65p multicolored .25 .25
743 A160 2ce multicolored .45 *.75*
744 A160 4ce multicolored .85 *1.40*
Nos. 741-744 (4) 1.80 2.65

Souvenir Sheet

745 Sheet of 4 2.00 2.00
a. A160 25p like #741 .25 .25
b. A160 50p like #742 .25 .25
c. A160 1ce like #743 .25 .25
d. A160 3ce like #744 .80 .80

Rotary International, 75th anniv.
Nos. 741-745 exist imperf. Value, set $11.50.

Narina Trogon — A161

65p, White-crowned robin-chat. 2ce, Swallow-tailed bee-eater. 4ce, Long-tailed parakeet.

1981, Jan. 12 Litho. *Perf. 14*
746 A161 20p shown 1.25 .25
747 A161 65p multicolored 2.50 .60
748 A161 2ce multicolored 3.25 1.75
749 A161 4ce multicolored 4.50 3.25
Nos. 746-749 (4) 11.50 5.85

Souvenir Sheet

750 Sheet of 4 10.50 10.50
a. A161 25p like #746 .40 .30
b. A161 50p like #747 1.00 .45
c. A161 1ce like #748 1.75 .80
d. A161 3ce like #749 5.50 2.40

Nos. 746-749 exist imperf. Value, set $14.

Pope John Paul II, Pres. Limann, Archbishop of Canterbury — A162

1981, Mar. 3 Litho. *Perf. 14*
751 A162 20p multicolored .25 .25
752 A162 65p multicolored .60 .60
753 A162 80p multicolored .75 .75
754 A162 2ce multicolored 2.40 2.40
Nos. 751-754 (4) 4.00 4.00

Visit of Pope John Paul II, May 8-10, 1980.
Nos. 751-754 exist imperf. Value, set $14.

Earth Satellite Station — A163

65p, Satellites orbiting earth. 80p, Satellite. 4ce, Satellite, earth.

1981, Sept. 28 Litho. *Perf. 14*
755 A163 20p shown .25 .25
756 A163 65p multicolored .25 .25
757 A163 80p multicolored .25 .25
758 A163 4ce multicolored 1.10 1.10
Nos. 755-758 (4) 1.85 1.85

Souvenir Sheet

758A Sheet of 4 1.40 1.40
b. A163 25p like #755 .25 .25
c. A163 50p like #756 .25 .25
d. A163 1ce like #757 .25 .25
e. A163 3ce like #758 .60 .60

Earth Satellite Station commission.

Common Design Types pictured following the introduction.

Royal Wedding Issue
Common Design Type

1981 Litho. *Perf. 14*
759 CD331a 20p Couple .25 .25
759A CD331a 65p like 20p .25 .25
760 CD331a 80p Charles .25 .25
760A CD331a 1ce like 80p .25 .25
760B CD331a 3ce like 4ce .40 .40
761 CD331a 4ce Royal yacht Britannia .50 .50
Nos. 759-761 (6) 1.90 1.90

Souvenir Sheet

762 CD331 7ce St. Paul's Cathedral .80 .80

Booklet Stamps

763 CD331 2ce like 4ce 1.10 1.10
764 CD331 5ce like 20p 2.40 2.40
a. Bklt. pane, 2 each #763-764 7.25 7.25

Nos. 759-761 each printed se-tenant with label showing heraldic design. Nos. 763-764 issued only in booklets.
Issued: 20p, 80p, 4ce, 7ce, 7/8; 65p, 1ce, 2ce, 3ce, 5ce, 9/16.
For surcharges see Nos. 859, 866, 871, 880, 1168-1169, 1195-1197.

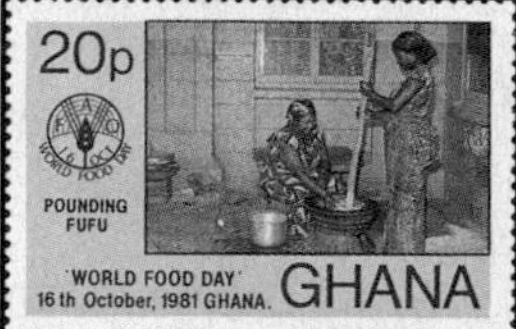

World Food Day A164

20p, Women pounding fufu. 65p, Plucking cocoa. 80p, Preparing banku. 2ce, Processing garri.

1981, Oct. 16 Litho. *Perf. 14*
765 A164 20p multicolored .25 .25
766 A164 65p multicolored .25 .25
767 A164 80p multicolored .40 .40
768 A164 2ce multicolored .75 .75
Nos. 765-768 (4) 1.65 1.65

Souvenir Sheet

769 Sheet of 4 1.50 1.50
a. A164 25p like #765 .25 .25
b. A164 50p like #766 .25 .25
c. A164 1ce like #767 .30 .30
d. A164 3ce like #768 .85 .85

Nos. 765-768 exist imperf. Value, set $5.50.

Angelic Musicians Play for Mary and Child, by Aachener Altares (1480-1520) A165

Christmas (Paintings): 15p, The Betrothal of St. Catherine of Alexandria, by Lucas Cranach (1472-1553). 65p, Child Jesus Embracing His Mother, by Gabriel Metsu (1629-1667). 80p, Virgin and Child, by Fra Filippo Lippi (1406-1469). $2, The Virgin with Infant Jesus, by Barnaba da Modena (1361-1383). $4, The Immaculate Conception, by Bartolome Murillo (1618-1682). $6, Virgin and Child, by Hans Memling (1430-1494).

1981, Nov. 26 *Perf. 14*
770 A165 15p multicolored .25 .25
771 A165 20p multicolored .25 .25
772 A165 65p multicolored .25 .25
773 A165 80p multicolored .25 .25
774 A165 $2 multicolored .50 .50
775 A165 $4 multicolored .65 .65
Nos. 770-775 (6) 2.15 2.15

Souvenir Sheet

776 A165 $6 multicolored 1.50 1.50

Intl. Year of the Disabled A166

1982, Feb. 8 Litho. *Perf. 14*
777 A166 20p Blind man .25 .25
778 A166 65p Woman, crutch .30 .30
779 A166 80p Girl reading Braille .40 .40
780 A166 4ce Couple 1.50 1.50
Nos. 777-780 (4) 2.45 2.45

Souvenir Sheet

781 A166 6ce Group 2.25 2.25

Clawless Otter — A167

1982, Feb. 22
782 A167 20p shown .25 .25
783 A167 65p Bushbuck .50 .50
784 A167 80p Aardvark .60 .60
785 A167 1ce Scarlet bell tree .80 .80
786 A167 2ce Glory lilies 1.35 1.35
787 A167 4ce Blue peas 3.00 3.00
Nos. 782-787 (6) 6.50 6.50

Souvenir Sheet

788 A167 5ce Chimpanzees 3.00 3.00

Nos. 782-787 exist imperf. Value, set $10.

Blue-spot Commodore A168

65p, Emperor swallowtail. 2ce, Orange admiral. 4ce, Giant charaxes.

1982, Apr. 27 Litho. *Perf. 14*
789 A168 20p shown .85 .85
790 A168 65p multicolored 1.40 1.40
791 A168 2ce multicolored 2.50 2.50
792 A168 4ce multicolored 4.25 4.25
Nos. 789-792 (4) 9.00 9.00

Souvenir Sheet
Perf. 14½

793 Sheet of 4 9.50 9.50
a. A168 25p like #789 .70 .70
b. A168 50p like #790 1.20 1.20
c. A168 1ce like #791 1.90 1.90
d. A168 3ce like #792 4.75 4.75

Nos. 789-792 exist imperf. Value, set $14.

Scouting Year A169

1982, June 1 Litho. *Perf. 15*
794 A169 20p Tree planting .25 .25
795 A169 65p Camping .75 .75
796 A169 80p Sailing .95 .95
797 A169 3ce Watching elephant 2.50 2.50
Nos. 794-797 (4) 4.45 4.45

Souvenir Sheet

798 A169 5ce Baden-Powell, vert. 4.25 4.25

For surcharges see Nos. 867, 870, 875, 877.

Kpong Hydroelectric Dam Opening — A170

1982, June 28 Litho. *Perf. 14*

799 A170 20p Cranes, lifts .50 .25
800 A170 65p Construction 1.00 .55
801 A170 80p Turbines 1.50 1.50
802 A170 2ce Aerial view 3.00 3.00
Nos. 799-802 (4) 6.00 5.30

Nos. 799-802 exist imperf. Value, set $6.

1982 World Cup A171

Perf. 15, 14½x15 (30p, No. 807, 1ce, 3ce)

1982, July 19 Litho.

803 A171 20p multi .25 .25
804 A171 30p multi, like 20p .25 .25
805 A171 65p multi .80 .80
806 A171 80p multi, like 65p 1.00 1.00
807 A171 80p multi, diff. .55 .55
808 A171 1ce multi, like #807 .70 .70
809 A171 3ce multi 1.60 1.60
810 A171 4ce multi, like 3ce 2.50 2.50
Nos. 803-810 (8) 7.65 7.65

Souvenir Sheet

811 A171 6ce multi 2.10 2.10

Nos. 804, 806, 808-809 in sheets of 5 plus label.

For overprints & surcharges see Nos. 826-834, 861-862, 864-865, 868-869, 872-873, 878-879, 912-917.

TB Bacillus Centenary A172

20p, Child immunization. 65p, Koch, Berlin. 80p, Koch, Africa. 1ce, Looking through microscope. 2ce, Koch, 1905 Nobel medal.

1982, Aug. 9 *Perf. 14*

812 A172 20p multicolored .50 .50
813 A172 65p multicolored 1.40 1.40
814 A172 80p multicolored 1.75 1.75
815 A172 1ce multicolored 2.10 2.10
816 A172 2ce multicolored 3.50 3.50
Nos. 812-816 (5) 9.25 9.25

Christmas — A173

1982, Dec. Litho. *Perf. 15*

817 A173 15p Nativity .25 .25
818 A173 20p Holy Family .25 .25
819 A173 65p Three Kings .00 .00
820 A173 4ce Angel with banner 1.10 1.10
Nos. 817-820 (4) 1.90 1.90

Souvenir Sheet

821 A173 6ce Nativity, diff. 2.00 2.00

Nos. 817-820 exist imperf. Value, set $3.75.

A173a

1983, Mar. 10 Litho. *Perf. 15*

822 A173a 20p Flags .25 .25
823 A173a 55p Aerial view .45 .45
824 A173a 80p Minerals 1.10 1.10
825 A173a 3ce Eagle 1.75 1.75
Nos. 822-825 (4) 3.55 3.55

Commonwealth Day. For surcharges see Nos. 860, 863, 874, 876.

Nos. 803-811 Overprinted in Gold: "WINNER ITALY / 3-1"

1983, June Litho.

826 A171 20p multicolored .25 .25
827 A171 30p multicolored .25 .25
828 A171 65p multicolored .40 .40
829 A171 80p multi, on #806 .40 .40
830 A171 80p multi, on #807 1.25 1.25
831 A171 1ce multicolored 1.40 1.40
832 A171 3ce multicolored 2.75 2.75
833 A171 4ce multicolored 2.50 2.50
Nos. 826-833 (8) 9.20 9.20

Souvenir Sheet

834 A171 6ce multicolored 3.50 3.50

Italy's victory in 1982 World Cup.

For surcharges see Nos. 862, 865, 869, 873, 879, 913, 915, 917.

World Communications Year — A173b

1.40ce, Dish antenna. 2.30ce, Cable ship. 3ce, Switchboard. 5ce, Control tower.
6ce, Satellite.

1983, Dec. 13 Litho. *Perf. 14*

835 A173b 1ce shown .25 .25
836 A173b 1.40ce multicolored .25 .25
837 A173b 2.30ce multicolored .55 .55
838 A173b 3ce multicolored .75 .75
839 A173b 5ce multicolored 1.10 1.10
Nos. 835-839 (5) 2.90 2.90

Souvenir Sheet

840 A173b 6ce multicolored .80 .80

For surcharges see Nos. 1107-1111.

Coastal Marine Mammals A173c

1ce, Short fin pilot whale. 1.40ce, Gray dolphin. 2.30ce, False killer whale. 3ce, Spinner dolphin. 5ce, Atlantic humpback dolphin.
6ce, White Alantic humpback dolphin.

1983, Nov. 15 Litho. *Perf. 15*

841 A173c 1ce multicolored 1.75 1.75
842 A173c 1.40ce multicolored 1.90 1.90
843 A173c 2.30ce multicolored 2.25 2.25
844 A173c 3ce multicolored 2.75 2.75
845 A173c 5ce multicolored 3.50 3.50
Nos. 841-845 (5) 12.15 12.15

Souvenir Sheet

846 A173c 6ce multicolored 5.25 5.25

For surcharges see Nos. 918-920.
Nos. 841-846 exist imperf. Value, set $22.

A174

Christmas A175

70p, Children receiving gifts. 1ce, Nativity. 1.40ce, Children playing. 2.30ce, Family praying. 3ce, Bongo drums, festivities.

1983, Dec. 28 *Perf. 14x13½, 14½x14*

852 A174 70p multicolored .25 .25
853 A175 1ce multicolored .25 .25
854 A175 1.40ce multicolored .40 .40
855 A175 2.30ce multicolored .45 .45
856 A174 3ce multicolored .50 .50
Nos. 852-856 (5) 1.85 1.85

Souvenir Sheet

857 A175 6ce like #855 .50 .50

For surcharge see No. 2676.

Surcharges

Many inverts, doubles, etc., exist on the surcharged stamps that follow.

Previous Issues Surcharged

1984, Feb. 8

858 A74 1ce on 20np #296 .40 .25
859 CD331 1ce on 20p #759 5.00 4.25
860 A173a 1ce on 20p #822 .40 .25
861 A171 1ce on 20p #803 .60 .40
862 A171 1ce on 20p #826 .40 .25
863 A173a 9ce on 55p #823 .90 .65
864 A171 9ce on 65p #805 1.60 1.00
865 A171 9ce on 65p #828 .90 .65
866 CD331 9ce on 80p #760 6.25 5.50
867 A169 10ce on 20p #794 .90 .65
868 A171 10ce on 80p #806 1.60 1.00
869 A171 10ce on 80p #830 .90 .65
870 A169 19ce on 65p #795 1.75 1.25
871 CD331 20ce on 4ce #761 8.00 *8.75*
872 A171 20ce on 4ce #810 3.50 2.40
873 A171 20ce on 4ce #833 1.75 1.25
874 A173a 30ce on 80p #824 3.50 2.40
875 A169 30ce on 3ce #797 3.50 2.40
876 A173a 50ce on 3ce #825 6.00 4.00
Nos. 858-876 (19) 47.85 37.95

Souvenir Sheets

877 A169 60ce on 5ce #798 2.50 *4.75*
878 A171 60ce on 6ce #811 2.50 *3.25*
879 A171 60ce on 6ce #834 2.50 *4.75*
880 CD331 60ce on 7ce #762 2.50 *2.50*

For surcharges ee Nos. 1092A-1092C.

Namibia Day — A176

50p, Soldiers raising rifles. 1ce, Soldiers, tank. 1.40ce, Machete cutting chains. 2.30ce, Namibian woman. 3ce, Soldiers in combat.

1984, Jan. 26 *Perf. 14*

881 A176 50p multicolored .25 .25
882 A176 1ce multicolored .25 .25
883 A176 1.40ce multicolored .25 .25
884 A176 2.30ce multicolored .25 .25
885 A176 3ce multicolored .25 .25
Nos. 881-885 (5) 1.25 1.25

Scorpion Weight — A177

5p, Hemichramis fasciatus, horiz. 10p, Hemichramis fasciatus, map, horiz. 20p, Haemanthus rupestris. 50p, Mounted warrior (gold statuette). 2ce, Jet, horiz. 3ce, Cercocebus torquatus. 4ce, Galagoides demidovii. 5ce, Kaempheria nigerica. 10ce, Camaroptera brevicaudata.

1983, Dec. 12 Litho. *Perf. 14*

886 A177 5p multicolored .35 .25
887 A177 10p multicolored .60 .25
888 A177 20p multicolored .70 .25
889 A177 50p multicolored .70 .30
890 A177 1ce shown .80 .25
891 A177 2ce multicolored .80 .30
892 A177 3ce multicolored 2.50 .30
893 A177 4ce multicolored .70 .40
894 A177 5ce multicolored .80 .45
895 A177 10ce multicolored 1.00 1.00
Nos. 886-895 (10) 8.95 3.75

For surcharges see Nos. 1089A-1090, 1092, 1092D, 1093A-1094A, 1096-1096A.

Easter — A178

1ce, Cross, crown of thorns. 1.40ce, Jesus praying. 2.30ce, Jesus going to Jerusalem. 3ce, Jesus entering Jerusalem. 50ce, Jesus with Disciples.
60ce, Cross, crown of thorns.

1984, Apr. Litho. *Perf. 14½*

906 A178 1ce multicolored .25 .25
907 A178 1.40ce multicolored .25 .25
908 A178 2.30ce multicolored .25 .25
909 A178 3ce multicolored .25 .25
910 A178 50ce multicolored .80 *2.50*
Nos. 906-910 (5) 1.80 3.50

Souvenir Sheet

911 A178 60ce multicolored 3.25 3.25

Nos. 804, 806, 809, 827, 829, 832 Surcharged

1984, Feb. 8 Litho.

912 A171 9ce on 3ce #809 .85 .85
913 A171 9ce on 3ce #832 .55 .55
914 A171 10ce on 30p #804 .85 .85
915 A171 10ce on 30p #827 .55 .55
916 A171 20ce on 80p #806 2.00 2.00
917 A171 20ce on 80p #829 1.00 1.00
Nos. 912-917 (6) 5.80 5.80

Nos. 844-846 Surcharged and Overprinted in Red with UPU Emblem and:"19th U.P.U. CONGRESS-HAMBURG"

1984 Litho. *Perf. 14½*

918 A173c 10ce on 3ce multi .50 .50
919 A173c 50ce on 5ce multi 2.50 2.50

Souvenir Sheet

920 A173c 60ce on 6ce multi 3.00 3.00

Local Flowers — A179

1ce, Amorphophallus johnsonii. 1.40ce, Pancratium trianthum. 2.30ce, Eulophia cucullata. 3ce, Amorphophallus abyssinicus. 50ce, Chlorophytum togoense.

1984, July Litho. *Perf. 14*

921 A179 1ce multicolored .25 .25
922 A179 1.40ce multicolored .25 .25
923 A179 2.30ce multicolored .25 .25
924 A179 3ce multicolored .25 .25
925 A179 50ce multicolored 2.50 *2.75*
Nos. 921-925 (5) 3.50 3.75

Souvenir Sheet

926 A179 60ce like 1ce 2.75 2.75

Endangered Species — A180

1ce, Bongo. 2.30ce, Males locking horns. 3ce, Family. 20ce, Herd.
No. 931, Kob. No. 932, Bushbuck.

1984, Aug. *Perf. 14*

927 A180 1ce multi .55 .55
928 A180 2.30ce multi 1.10 1.10
929 A180 3ce multi 1.35 1.35
930 A180 20ce multi 3.75 3.75
Nos. 927-930 (4) 6.75 6.75

Souvenir Sheets

931 A180 70ce multi 6.00 6.00
932 A180 70ce multi 6.00 6.00

Nos. 927-930 exist imperf. Value: set, $21.

1984 Summer Olympics — A181

1ce, Running. 1.40ce, Boxing. 2.30ce, Field hockey. 3ce, Hurdles. 50ce, Rhythmic gymnastics.
70ce, Soccer.

1984, Aug. *Perf. 15*

933 A181 1ce multi .25 .25
934 A181 1.40ce multi .25 .25
935 A181 2.30ce multi .25 .25
936 A181 3ce multi .25 .25
937 A181 50ce multi 2.75 *4.00*
Nos. 933-937 (5) 3.75 5.00

Souvenir Sheet

938 A181 70ce multi 2.50 2.50

For surcharges see Nos. 945-950, 1112-1116.

Native Dancers — A182

1984, Sept. *Perf. 14*

939 A182 1ce Dipo .30 .25
940 A182 1.40ce Adowa .30 .25
941 A182 2.30ce Agbadza .30 .25
942 A182 3ce Damba .30 .25
943 A182 50ce Dipo, diff. 2.00 *3.00*
Nos. 939-943 (5) 3.20 4.00

Souvenir Sheet

944 A182 70ce Mandolin player 4.00 4.00

Nos. 933-938 Ovptd. in Gold with Winner and Country

1ce, Valerie Brisco-Hooks, US. 1.40ce, US winners. 2.30ce, Pakistan, (field hockey). 3ce, Edwin Moses, US. 50ce, Lauri Fung, Canada.
70ce, France.

1984, Dec. 3 Litho. *Perf. 15*

945 A181 1ce multicolored .25 .25
946 A181 1.40ce multicolored .25 .25
947 A181 2.30ce multicolored .25 .25
948 A181 3ce multicolored .25 .25
949 A181 50ce multicolored 1.60 1.60
Nos. 945-949 (5) 2.60 2.60

Souvenir Sheet

950 A181 70ce multicolored 2.50 2.50

Christmas — A183

70p, Adoration of the Magi. 1ce, Chorus of angels. 1.40ce, Adoration of the shepherds. 2.30ce, Flight into Egypt. 3ce, King holding Christ. 50ce, Adoration of the angels.

1984, Nov. 19 *Perf. 12x12½*

951 A183 70p multicolored .25 .25
952 A183 1ce multicolored .25 .25
953 A183 1.40ce multicolored .25 .25
954 A183 2.30ce multicolored .25 .25
955 A183 3ce multicolored .25 .25
956 A183 50ce multicolored 1.35 1.35
Nos. 951-956 (6) 2.60 2.60

Souvenir Sheet

957 A183 70ce like 70p 2.60 2.60

Queen Mother, 85th Birthday — A184

Portraits.

1985 *Perf. 14*

958 A184 5ce multicolored .25 .25
959 A184 8ce like 5ce .25 .25
960 A184 12ce multicolored .25 .25
961 A184 20ce like 12ce .25 .25
962 A184 70ce multicolored .90 .90
963 A184 100ce like 70ce 1.10 1.10
Nos. 958-963 (6) 3.00 3.00

Souvenir Sheet

964 A184 110ce multicolored 3.00 3.00

Issue dates: 5ce, 12ce, 100ce, 110ce, July 29. 8ce, 20ce, 70ce, Dec.
Nos. 959, 961-962 issued in sheets of 5 + label.
For surcharges see Nos. 1117-1119A, 1198-1200, 1311-1317.

Id-El-Fitr Islamic Festival — A185

5ce, Entering mosque. 8ce, Prayer rug. 12ce, Mosque. 18ce, Public Koran reading. 50ce, Map, Banda Nkwanta Mosque.

1985, Aug. 1

965 A185 5ce multicolored .30 .30
966 A185 8ce multicolored .40 .40
967 A185 12ce multicolored .65 .65
968 A185 18ce multicolored 1.15 1.15
969 A185 50ce multicolored 3.00 3.00
Nos. 965-969 (5) 5.50 5.50

Intl. Youth Year — A186

1985, Aug. 9

970 A186 5ce Street clean-up .25 .25
971 A186 8ce Tree planting .25 .25
972 A186 12ce Food production .30 .30
973 A186 100ce Education 1.25 *2.50*
Nos. 970-973 (4) 2.05 3.30

Souvenir Sheet

974 A186 110ce like 8ce 2.00 2.00

Motorcycle Centenary — A187

5ce, 1984 Honda Interceptor. 8ce, 1938 DKW. 12ce, 1923 BMW R 32. 100ce, 1900 NSU.
110ce, 1973 Zundapp.

1985, Sept. 9

975 A187 5ce multicolored .50 .30
976 A187 8ce multicolored .70 .40
977 A187 12ce multicolored 1.10 .85
978 A187 100ce multicolored 6.00 6.00
Nos. 975-978 (4) 8.30 7.55

Souvenir Sheet

979 A187 110ce multicolored 5.25 5.25

Audubon Birth Bicent. — A188

5ce, York-tailed flycatcher. 8ce, Barred owl. 12ce, Black-throated mango. 100ce, White-crowned pigeon.
110ce, Downy woodpecker.

1985, Oct. 16

980 A188 5ce multicolored 1.40 1.40
981 A188 8ce multicolored 2.25 2.25
982 A188 12ce multicolored 2.25 2.25
983 A188 100ce multicolored 5.50 5.50
Nos. 980-983 (4) 11.40 11.40

Souvenir Sheet

984 A188 110ce multicolored 7.50 7.50

For surcharges see Nos. 1124-1127.

UN, 40th Anniv. A189

5ce, UN building. 8ce, UN building, diff. 12ce, Dove. 18ce, General Assembly. 100ce, Flags.
110ce, UN No. 36.

1985, Oct. 24 *Perf. 14½x14*

985 A189 5ce multicolored .25 .25
986 A189 8ce multicolored .25 .25
987 A189 12ce multicolored .25 *.30*
988 A189 18ce multicolored .25 *.40*
989 A189 100ce multicolored 1.75 *2.25*
Nos. 985-989 (5) 2.75 3.45

Souvenir Sheet

990 A189 110ce multicolored 1.75 1.75

UNCTAD, 20th Anniv. A190

1985, Nov. 4 *Perf. 14*

991 A190 5ce Coffee .25 .25
992 A190 8ce Cocoa .25 .25
993 A190 12ce Lumber .30 .30
994 A190 18ce Bauxite mining 1.00 1.00
995 A190 100ce Gold mining 6.25 6.25
Nos. 991-995 (5) 8.05 8.05

Souvenir Sheet

Perf. 15x14

996 A190 110ce Produce 2.50 2.50

UN Child Survival Campaign A191

5ce, Weighing. 8ce, Oral rehydration therapy. 12ce, Breast-feeding. 100ce, Immunization.
110ce, Emblem, pinwheel.

1985, Dec. 16 *Perf. 14*

997 A191 5ce multicolored .25 .25
998 A191 8ce multicolored .25 .25
999 A191 12ce multicolored .50 .50
1000 A191 100ce multicolored 3.75 3.75
Nos. 997-1000 (4) 4.75 4.75

Souvenir Sheet

Perf. 15x14

1001 A191 110ce multicolored 2.10 2.10

AMERIPEX '86 — A192

5ce, Young collectors. 25ce, Earth, jet. 100ce, Stewardess, vert.
150ce, Young collectors, diff.

Perf. 14½x14, 14x14½

1986, Oct. 27 Litho.

1002 A192 5ce multicolored .30 .30
1003 A192 25ce multicolored .85 .85
1004 A192 100ce multicolored 2.40 2.40
Nos. 1002-1004 (3) 3.55 3.55

Souvenir Sheet

1005 A192 150ce multicolored 3.50 3.50

INTER-TOURISM '86, Nov. 8-17 — A193

Designs: 5ce, Kejetia Roundabout, Kumasi. 15ce, Fort St. Jago, Elmina. 25ce, Warriors. 100ce, Chief, retinue. 150ce, Elephants.

1986, Nov. 10 *Perf. 14*

1006 A193 5ce multi .25 .25
1007 A193 15ce multi .50 .50
1008 A193 25ce multi .75 .75
1009 A193 100ce multi 2.75 2.75
Nos. 1006-1009 (4) 4.25 4.25

Souvenir Sheet

Perf. 15x14

1010 A193 150ce multi 4.75 4.75

1986 World Cup Soccer Championships, Mexico — A194

Various soccer plays.

1987, Jan. 16 Litho. *Perf. 14x14½*

1011 A194 5ce multi .30 .30
1012 A194 15ce multi .35 .35
1013 A194 25ce multi .55 .55
1014 A194 100ce multi 2.00 2.00
Nos. 1011-1014 (4) 3.20 3.20

Souvenir Sheet

1015 A194 150ce multi 2.40 2.40

For surcharges see Nos. 1120-1123D.

Fertility Dolls — A195

Various dolls.

1987, Jan. 22

1016	A195	5ce	multi	.30	.30
1017	A195	15ce	multi	.30	.30
1018	A195	25ce	multi	.50	.50
1019	A195	100ce	multi	2.00	2.00
			Nos. 1016-1019 (4)	3.10	3.10

Souvenir Sheet

1020	A195	150ce	like #1016	2.00	2.00

Intl. Peace Year A196

5ce, Children playing. 25ce, Plow. 100ce, Earth, doves, vert.
150ce, Dove, plow, vert.

Perf. 14½x14, 14x14½

1987, Mar. 2 **Litho.**

1021	A196	5ce	multicolored	.30	.30
1022	A196	25ce	multicolored	.85	.85
1023	A196	100ce	multicolored	3.00	3.00
			Nos. 1021-1023 (3)	4.15	4.15

Souvenir Sheet

1024	A196	150ce	multicolored	2.50	2.50

GIFEX '87 A197

5ce, Lumber, house construction. 15ce, Furniture. 25ce, Tree stumps. 200ce, Logs, art objects.

1987, Mar. 10 ***Perf. 14***

1025	A197	5ce	multicolored	.25	.25
1026	A197	15ce	multicolored	.25	.25
1027	A197	25ce	multicolored	.40	.40
1028	A197	200ce	multicolored	2.25	2.25
			Nos. 1025-1028 (4)	3.15	3.15

Ghana Intl. Forestry Exposition, Accra.

A198

Halley's Comet — A199

Designs: 5ce, Mikhail Vasilyevich Lomonosov (1711-1765), Russian scientist, and the Chamber of Curiosities. 25ce, Landing of the US probe Surveyor on the Moon's surface, 1966. 200ce, Wedgwood memorial to Sir Isaac Newton, the appearance of Halley's Comet in 1790 and US astronauts Armstrong and Aldrin landing Eagle on the Moon in 1969. 250ce, Comet over Fishermen near Christianborg Castle,

1987, Apr. 8 ***Perf. 14½x14***

1029	A198	5ce	multi	.30	.25
1030	A198	25ce	multi	.90	.90
1031	A198	200ce	multi	4.25	4.25
			Nos. 1029-1031 (3)	5.45	5.40

Souvenir Sheet

1032	A199	250ce	multi	5.00	5.00

For surcharges see Nos. 1128-1131,

Solidarity with South Africans for Abolition of Apartheid — A200

5ce, Liberated prisoner. 15ce, Miner, gold ingots. 25ce, Zulu warrior. 100ce, Nelson Mandela, shackles.
150ce, Mandela, map, star.

1987, May 18 ***Perf. 14x14½***

1033	A200	5ce	multicolored	.25	.25
1034	A200	15ce	multicolored	.30	.30
1035	A200	25ce	multicolored	.30	.30
1036	A200	100ce	multicolored	1.60	1.60
			Nos. 1033-1036 (4)	2.45	2.45

Souvenir Sheet

1037	A200	150ce	multicolored	2.40	2.40

Traditional Musical Instruments — A201

5ce, Horns. 15ce, Xylophone. 25ce, String instruments. 100ce, Drums.
200ce, Percussion instruments.

1987, July 13 ***Perf. 14½x14***

1038	A201	5ce	multicolored	.25	.25
1039	A201	15ce	multicolored	.30	.30
1040	A201	25ce	multicolored	.45	.45
1041	A201	100ce	multicolored	1.30	1.30
			Nos. 1038-1041 (4)	2.30	2.30

Souvenir Sheet

1042	A201	200ce	multicolored	2.75	2.75

Intl. Year of Shelter for the Homeless A202

5ce, Public well. 15ce, Home construction. 25ce, Village, bridge, car. 100ce, Village, electric power lines.

1987, Sept. 21 **Litho.** ***Perf. 14***

1043	A202	5ce	multicolored	.25	.25
1044	A202	15ce	multicolored	.25	.25
1045	A202	25ce	multicolored	.40	.40
1046	A202	100ce	multicolored	1.25	1.25
			Nos. 1043-1046 (4)	2.15	2.15

Festivals — A203

Designs: Preparation of Kpokpoi, Homowo Festival. 15ce, Hunters with catch, Aboakyir Festival. 25ce, Chief dancing, Odwira Festival. 100ce, Chief held aloft in a palanquin, Yam Festival.

1988, Jan. 6 **Litho.** ***Perf. 15***

1047	A203	5ce	multi	.25	.25
1048	A203	15ce	multi	.25	.25
1049	A203	25ce	multi	.35	.35
1050	A203	100ce	multi	1.15	1.15
			Nos. 1047-1050 (4)	2.00	2.00

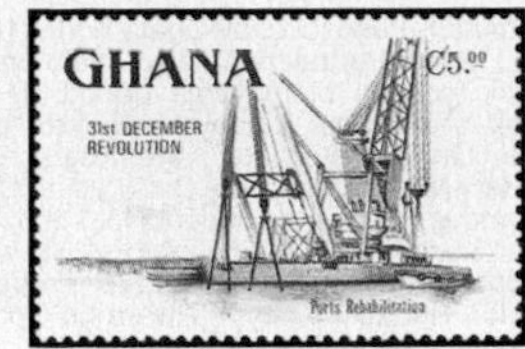

December 31, 1981 Revolution — A203a

5ce, Ports. 15ce, Railways. 25ce, Cocoa industry. 100ce, Mining industry.

1988, Jan. 26 **Litho.** ***Perf. 13***

1050A	A203a	5ce	multi	1.50	.50
1050B	A203a	15ce	multi	13.50	3.00
1050C	A203a	25ce	multi	2.75	.75
1050D	A203a	100ce	multi	16.00	16.00
			Nos. 1050A-1050D (4)	33.75	20.25

UN Universal Immunization Campaign — A204

Child Survival Campaign emblem and: 5ce, Nurse immunizing woman. 15ce, Child receiving intramuscular vaccine. 25ce, Youth crippled by polio. 100ce, Nurse handing infant to mother.

1988, Feb. 1 ***Perf. 15***

1051	A204	5ce	multi	.25	.25
1052	A204	15ce	multi	.25	.25
1053	A204	25ce	multi	.40	.40
1054	A204	100ce	multi	.90	.90
			Nos. 1051-1054 (4)	1.80	1.80

Intl. Fund for Agricultural Development — A204a

5ce, Fishing. 15ce, Harvesting. 25ce, Cattle. 100ce, Granary.

1988, Apr. 14 ***Perf. 13***

1054A	A204a	5ce	multi	*1.75*	*1.75*
1054B	A204a	15ce	multi	*3.00*	*3.00*
1054C	A204a	25ce	multi	*5.00*	*5.00*
1054D	A204a	100ce	multi	*11.00*	*11.00*
			Nos. 1054A-1054D (4)	*20.75*	*20.75*

Tribal Costumes — A205

1988, May 9 **Litho.** ***Perf. 14***

1055	A205	5ce	Akwadjan	.25	.25
1056	A205	75ce	Danaa	.50	.50
1057	A205	250ce	Agwasen	2.25	2.25
			Nos. 1055-1057 (3)	3.00	3.00

For surcharges, see Nos. 2677, 2682.

1988 Summer Olympics, Seoul A206

1988, Oct. 10

1058	A206	20ce	Boxing	.25	.25
1059	A206	60ce	Running	.55	.55
1060	A206	80ce	Discus	.70	.70
1061	A206	100ce	Javelin	.90	.90
1062	A206	350ce	Weight lifting	3.00	3.00
			Nos. 1058-1062 (5)	5.40	5.40

Souvenir Sheet

1063	A206	500ce	like 80ce	5.25	5.25

For overprints see Nos. 1084-1089.

Intl. Red Cross, 125th Anniv. — A207

20ce, Nutrition. 50ce, Voluntary service. 60ce, Disaster relief (flood). 200ce, Medical assistance.

1988, Dec. 14 **Litho.** ***Perf. 14***

1064	A207	20ce	multicolored	.55	.55
1065	A207	50ce	multicolored	1.15	1.15
1066	A207	60ce	multicolored	1.25	1.25
1067	A207	200ce	multicolored	3.25	3.25
			Nos. 1064-1067 (4)	6.20	6.20

Christmas Symbolism — A208

60ce, Mother and child, vert. 80ce, Mother, child, tree, vert. 100ce, Magi follow star. 350ce, Abstract, diff., vert.
500ce, Mother and child, diff., vert.

1988, Dec. 19 **Litho.** ***Perf. 14***

1068	A208	20ce	shown	.25	.25
1069	A208	60ce	multicolored	.45	.45
1070	A208	80ce	multicolored	.50	.50
1071	A208	100ce	multicolored	.65	.65
1072	A208	350ce	multicolored	2.75	2.75
			Nos. 1068-1072 (5)	4.60	4.60

Souvenir Sheet

1073	A208	500ce	multicolored	3.50	3.50

For surcharges see Nos. 2678, 2680-2681.

Organization of African Unity, 25th Anniv. — A209

20ce, Solidarity. 50ce, OAU, Addis Ababa. 60ce, Halle Selassie, Ethiopia. 200ce, Kwame Nkrumah, Ghana.

1989, Jan. 3

1074	A209	20ce	multicolored	.25	.25
1075	A209	50ce	multicolored	.25	.25
1076	A209	60ce	multicolored	.35	.35
1077	A209	200ce	multicolored	.55	.55
			Nos. 1074-1077 (4)	1.40	1.40

"Selassie" is spelled incorrectly on No. 1076. Nos. 1076-1077 horiz.

Titian, 500th Birth Anniv. (in 1988) — A210

20ce, Amor, 1515. 60ce, The Appeal. 80ce, Bacchus and Ariadne, c. 1523. 100ce, Portrait of a Musician, c. 1518. 350ce, Philip II Seated. 500ce, Portrait of a Gentleman, c. 1550.

1989, Jan. 16

1078 A210 20ce multicolored .45 .25
1079 A210 60ce multicolored .80 .80
1080 A210 80ce multicolored 1.10 1.10
1081 A210 100ce multicolored 1.25 1.25
1082 A210 350ce multicolored 3.25 3.25
Nos. 1078-1082 (5) 6.85 6.65

Souvenir Sheet

1083 A210 500ce multicolored 3.50 3.50

Nos. 1058-1063 Ovptd. with Winners' Names

20ce, "A. ZUELOW / DDR / 60 KG". 60ce, "G. BORDIN / ITALY / MARATHON". 80ce, "J. SCHULT / DDR". 100ce, "T. KORJUS / FINLAND". 350ce, "B. GUIDIKOV / BULGARIA / 75 KG".

1989, Jan. 23

1084 A206 20ce multicolored .40 .40
1085 A206 60ce multicolored .50 .50
1086 A206 80ce multicolored .60 .60
1087 A206 100ce multicolored .70 .70
1088 A206 350ce multicolored 1.00 1.00
Nos. 1084-1088 (5) 3.80 3.80

Souvenir Sheet

1089 A206 500ce multi 3.75 3.75

1988 Summer Olympics, Seoul. Margin of No. 1089 ovptd. "GOLD / J. SCHULT DDR / SILVER / R. OUBARTAS USSR / BRONZE / R. DANNEBERG W. GERMANY."

Stamps of 1967-1984 Surcharged

1988-91

1089A A177 20ce on 50p #889 .35 .30
1090 A177 20ce on 1ce #890 .35 .30
1091 A75 50ce on 10np #295 2.00 2.00
1092 A177 50ce on 10p #887 1.00 2.00
f. 50ce' on 10p Denomination below obliterator — —
1092A A74 50ce on 1ce #858 6.00 5.00
1092B A74 50ce on 1ce #858 10.00 10.00
1092C A74 50ce on 1ce #858 10.00 10.00
1092D A177 50ce on 1ce #890 6.00 .50
1092E A73 60ce on 1np #286 6.00 .50
1093 A73 60ce on 4np #291 6.00 .50
1093A A177 60ce on 3ce #892 1.00 .45
1094 A177 80ce on 5p #886 1.00 .45
1094A A177 80ce on 5ce #894 10.00 10.00
1094B A75 100ce on 3np #290 — —
1095 A74 100ce on 20np #296 10.00 10.00
1096 A177 100ce on 20p #888 1.00 1.00
1096A A177 100ce on 3ce #892 2.00 2.00
1096B A75 200ce on 6np #292 8.00 8.00

Surcharge has no decimal on No. 1092A, is vertical on No. 1092B and horizontal on No. 1092C.

No. 1090 also exists with 5mm spacing between block and $20.00.

Surcharge on No. 1093A has decimal point. Unauthorized surchages exist.

Issued: Nos. 1089A, 1096B, 7/1/88; Nos. 1092A, 1092B, 1092D, 1092E, 1094A, 1096A, 1990; No. 1092C, 1991; others, 1989.

Minamoto-no-Yoritomo, by Fujiwara-no-Takanobu (1142-1205) — A211

Paintings: 50ce, Takami Senseki, by Watanabe Kazan (1793-1841). 60ce, Ikkyu Sojum, by Bokusai, Muromachi period. 75ce, Nakamura Kuranosuke, by Ogata Korin (1658-1716). 125ce, Portrait of a Lady, Kyoto branch of Kano school, Momoyama period. 150ce, Portrait of Zemmui, anonymous, 12th cent. 200ce, Ono no Komachi, the Poetess, by Hokusai. No. 1104, Kobo Daisi as a Child, anonymous, Kamakura period. No. 1105, Portrait of Kodai-no-Kimi, attributed to Fujiwara-no-Nobuzane, 12th cent. No. 1106, Portrait of Emperor Hanazono, by Fujiwara-no-Goshin, 14th cent.

1989, Aug. 21 Litho. *Perf. 13½x14*

1097 A211 20ce shown .25 .25
1098 A211 50ce multi .40 .40
1099 A211 60ce multi .45 .45
1100 A211 75ce multi .65 .65
1101 A211 125ce multi 1.00 1.00
1102 A211 150ce multi 1.40 1.40
1103 A211 200ce multi 1.60 1.60
1104 A211 500ce multi 2.25 2.25
Nos. 1097-1104 (8) 8.00 8.00

Souvenir Sheets

1105 A211 500ce multi 6.00 6.00
1106 A211 500ce multi 6.00 6.00

Hirohito (1901-1989) and enthronement of Akihito as emperor of Japan.

Nos. 835-838 and 840 Surcharged

1989, July 3 Litho. *Perf. 14*

1107 A173b 60ce on 1ce .90 .60
1108 A173b 80ce on 1.40ce 1.10 .75
1109 A173b 200ce on 2.30ce 2.75 2.75
1110 A173b 300ce on 3ce 3.25 3.25
Nos. 1107-1110 (4) 8.00 7.35

Souvenir Sheet

1111 A173b 500ce on 6ce 6.50 6.50

Nos. 933-936 and 938 Surcharged

1989, July 3 *Perf. 15*

1112 A181 60ce on 1ce .40 .40
1113 A181 80ce on 1.40ce .60 .60
1114 A181 200ce on 2.30ce 1.40 1.40
1115 A181 300ce on 3ce 1.90 1.90
Nos. 1112-1115 (4) 4.30 4.30

Souvenir Sheet

1116 A181 600ce on 70ce 4.00 4.00

Nos. 958, 960 and 963-964 Surcharged

1989, Nov. 20 Litho. *Perf. 14*

1117 A184 80ce on 5ce #958 .60 .60
1118 A184 250ce on 12ce #960 1.90 1.90
1119 A184 300ce on 100ce #963 2.10 2.10
Nos. 1117-1119 (3) 4.60 4.60

Souvenir Sheet

1119A A184 500ce on 110ce #964 4.75 4.75

Nos. 1011-1013 and 1015 Surcharged

1989 Litho. *Perf. 14x14½*

1120 A194 60ce on 5ce #1011 .60 .60
1121 A194 200ce on 15ce #1012 1.90 1.90
1122 A194 300ce on 25ce #1013 2.50 2.50
Nos. 1120-1122 (3) 5.00 5.00

Souvenir Sheet

1123 A194 600ce on 150ce #1015 7.00 7.00

Nos. 1120-1123 Surcharged

1989 Litho. *Perf. 14x14½*

1123A A194 60ce on 5ce .90 .90
1123B A194 200ce on 15ce 3.00 3.00
1123C A194 300ce on 25ce 4.75 4.75
Nos. 1123A-1123C (3) 8.65 8.65

Souvenir Sheet

1123D A194 600ce on 150ce 10.00 10.00

Nos. 980-982 and 984 Surcharged

1989, Nov. 20 Litho. *Perf. 14*

1124 A188 80ce on 5ce #980 1.75 1.75
1125 A188 100ce on 8ce #981 3.25 3.25
1126 A188 300ce on 12ce #982 3.50 3.50
Nos. 1124-1126 (3) 8.50 8.50

Souvenir Sheet

1127 A188 500ce on 110ce #984 9.50 9.50

Nos. 1029-1032 Surcharged

1989, Nov. 20 *Perf. 14½x14*

1128 A198 60ce on 5ce #1029 1.00 1.00
a. With comet logo 1.00 1.00
1129 A198 80ce on 25ce #1030 1.25 1.25
a. With comet logo 1.25 1.25
1130 A198 500ce on 200ce #1031 4.25 4.25
a. With comet logo 4.25 4.25
Nos. 1128-1130 (3) 6.50 6.50
Nos. 1128a-1130a (3) 6.50 6.50

Souvenir Sheet

1131 A199 750ce on 250ce #1032 6.00 6.00
a. With comet logo 6.00 6.00

PHILEXFRANCE '89, French Revolution Bicent. — A212

Emblems, French arms and flags: 20ce, Tube-mounted field carriage, flag of 1643 to 1790. 60ce, Infantryman, flag of 1789. 80ce, Handgun, flag of 1789, diff. 350ce, Musket, flag of 1794 to 1814 and 1848 to present. 600ce, Map of Paris.

1989, Sept. 22 Litho. *Perf. 14*

1132 A212 20ce shown .70 .70
1133 A212 60ce multi 1.25 1.25
1134 A212 80ce multi 1.60 1.60
1135 A212 350ce multi 3.75 3.75
Nos. 1132-1135 (4) 7.30 7.30

Souvenir Sheet

1136 A212 600ce multi 4.25 4.25

Mushrooms
A213 A214

20ce, Collybia. 50ce, Lawyer's wig. 60ce, Xerocomus subtomentosus. 80ce, Wood belwits. 150ce, Suillus placidus. 200ce, Lepista nuda. 300ce, Fairy rings. 500ce, Field mushroom.

No. 1145, Three Amanita species. No. 1146, Three Boletus species.

1989, Oct. 2 Litho. *Perf. 14*

1137 A213 20ce multi .25 .25
1138 A213 50ce multi .35 .35
1139 A214 60ce multi .40 .40
1140 A213 80ce multi .60 .60
1141 A214 150ce multi 1.20 1.20
1142 A214 200ce multi 1.50 1.50
1143 A213 300ce multi 2.10 2.10
1144 A213 500ce multi 3.50 3.50
Nos. 1137-1144 (8) 9.90 9.90

Souvenir Sheets

1145 A213 600ce multi 4.25 4.25
1146 A214 600ce multi 4.25 4.25

Souvenir Sheet

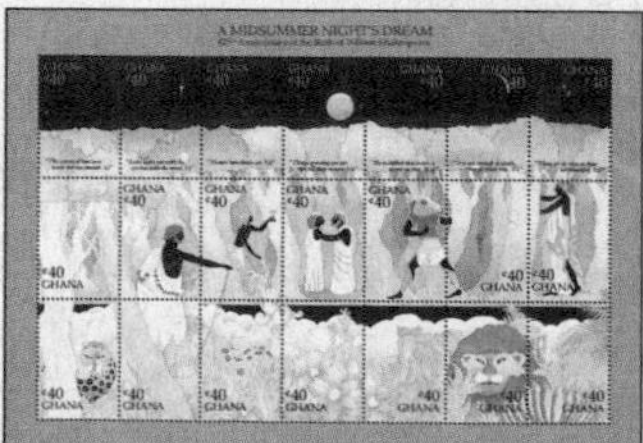

A Midsummer Night's Dream, by Shakespeare — A215

Designs: a, "The course of true love never did run smooth." b, "Love looks not with the eye but with the mind." c, "Nature here shows art." d, "Things growing are not ripe till their season." e, "He is defiled that draws a sword on thee." f, "It is not enough to speak but to speak true." g, "Thou art wise as thou art beautiful." h, Leopard behind trees. i, Theseus. j, Boy holding flower, trees. k, Oberon and Titania among trees. l, Bottom wearing head of a jackass. m, Bottom's leg, leopard behind trees. n, Hippolyta. o, Leopard, tree trunk. p, Tree trunk, foliage, lower portion of Theseus's robe. q, Wisps of fragrance, clouds, hills, foliage. r, Wisps of fragrance, flowering plants. s, Flowering plants. t, Lion, foliage. u, Lion's mane, foliage.

1989, Oct. 9 *Perf. 13½x13*

1147 A215 Sheet of 21 18.00 18.00
a.-u. 40ce any single .80 .80

425th Birth anniv. of William Shakespeare, playwright.

Birds A216

20ce, Spermestes cuculatus. 50ce, Motacilla aguimp. 60ce, Halcyon malimbicus. 80ce, Ispidina picta. 150ce, Striped kingfisher. 200ce, Shikra. 300ce, Gray parrot. 500ce, Black kite.

No. 1156, Four birds. No. 1157, Three birds.

1989, Oct. 16 *Perf. 14*

1148 A216 20ce multicolored .40 .25
1149 A216 50ce multicolored .60 .35
1150 A216 60ce multicolored 1.75 1.75
1151 A216 80ce multicolored 2.75 2.75
1152 A216 150ce multicolored 2.25 2.25
1153 A216 200ce multicolored 2.00 2.00
1154 A216 300ce multicolored 2.75 2.75
1155 A216 500ce multicolored 4.00 4.00
Nos. 1148-1155 (8) 16.50 16.10

Souvenir Sheets

1156 A216 600ce multicolored 8.25 8.25
1157 A216 600ce multicolored 8.25 8.25

Nos. 1152-1156 vert.

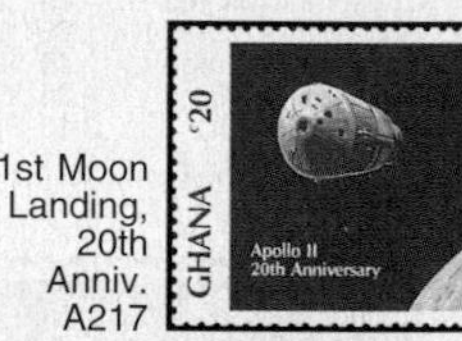

1st Moon Landing, 20th Anniv. A217

Highlights of the Apollo 11 mission.

1989, Nov. 6 *Perf. 14*

1158 A217 20ce Columbia .25 .25
1159 A217 80ce Footprint .75 .75
1160 A217 200ce Aldrin on Moon 1.50 1.50
1161 A217 300ce Splashdown 2.25 2.25
Nos. 1158-1161 (4) 4.75 4.75

Souvenir Sheets

1162 A217 500ce Liftoff, vert. 4.00 4.00
1163 A217 500ce Earth, vert. 4.00 4.00

World Environment Day — A218

20ce, Desertification. 60ce, Bush fires. 400ce, Industrial pollution. 500ce, Soil erosion.

1989, Nov. 20 Litho. *Perf. 14*

1164 A218 20ce multicolored .25 .25
1165 A218 60ce multicolored .60 .60
1166 A218 400ce multicolored 3.50 3.50
1167 A218 500ce multicolored 4.50 4.50
Nos. 1164-1167 (4) 8.85 8.85

Nos. 760 and 761 Surcharged

1989, Nov. 20 Litho. *Perf. 14*

1168 CD331 100ce on 80p .90 .90
1169 CD331 500ce on 4ce 4.75 4.75

French Revolution, Bicent. — A219

Designs: 20ce, Storming of the Bastille, vert. 60ce, Declaration of Human Rights and Citizenship, vert. 80ce, Storming of the Bastille, diff. 200ce, *Departure of the Volunteers in 1792*, high relief on the Arc de Triomphe, 1833-35, by Francis Rude. 350ce, Planting the Liberty Tree.

Perf. 14x13½, 13½x14

1989, Sept. 22

1170 A219 20ce multicolored .50 .50
1171 A219 60ce multicolored 1.10 1.10
1172 A219 80ce multicolored 1.35 1.35
1173 A219 200ce multicolored 2.50 2.50
1174 A219 350ce multicolored 3.25 3.25
Nos. 1170-1174 (5) 8.70 8.70

Butterflies A220

20ce, Bebearia arcadius. 60ce, Charaxes laodice. 80ce, Euryphura porphyrion. 100ce, Neptis nicomedes. 150ce, Citrinophila erastus. 200ce, Epitola honorius. 300ce, Precis westermanni. 500ce, Cymothoe hypatha.

No. 1183, Telipna bimacula. No. 1184, Pentila phidia.

1990, Feb. 15 Litho. *Perf. 14*

1175 A220 20ce multicolored .50 .50
1176 A220 60ce multicolored .65 .65
1177 A220 80ce multicolored .85 .85
1178 A220 100ce multicolored .95 .95
1179 A220 150ce multicolored 1.10 1.10
1180 A220 200ce multicolored 1.60 1.60
1181 A220 300ce multicolored 2.10 2.10
1182 A220 500ce multicolored 2.75 2.75
Nos. 1175-1182 (8) 10.50 10.50

Souvenir Sheets

1183 A220 600ce multicolored 5.75 5.75
1184 A220 600ce multicolored 5.75 5.75

Seashells — A221

20ce, Cymbium glans. 60ce, Cardium costatum. 80ce, Conus genuanus. 200ce, Ancilla tankervillei. 350ce, Tectarius coronatus.

1990, Feb. 20 *Perf. 14x14½*

1185 A221 20ce multicolored .70 .70
1186 A221 60ce multicolored 1.25 1.25
1187 A221 80ce multicolored 1.60 1.60
1188 A221 200ce multicolored 3.00 3.00
1189 A221 350ce multicolored 4.25 4.25
Nos. 1185-1189 (5) 10.80 10.80

Jawaharlal Nehru, 1st Prime Minister of Independent India — A222

Designs: 20ce, Greeting Pres. Kwame Nkrumah of Ghana. 60ce, Addressing Afro-Asian conference. 80ce, Return from tour of China, vert. 200ce, Releasing dove during a children's celebration in New Delhi, vert. 350ce, Portrait, vert.

Perf. 14½x14, 14x14½

1990, Mar. 27 Litho.

1190 A222 20ce shown .75 .75
1191 A222 60ce multicolored .90 .90
1192 A222 80ce multicolored 1.10 1.10
1193 A222 200ce multicolored 1.60 1.60
1194 A222 350ce multicolored 2.25 2.25
Nos. 1190-1194 (5) 6.60 6.60

Nos. 759A and 760A-760B Surcharged

1990 *Perf. 14*

1195 CD331 80ce on 65p 1.00 1.00
1196 CD331 100ce on 1ce 1.40 1.40
1197 CD331 300ce on 3ce 4.25 4.25
Nos. 1195-1197 (3) 6.65 6.65

Nos. 961, 959 and 962 Surcharged

1990

1198 A184 80ce on 20ce .75 .75
1199 A184 200ce on 8ce 1.90 1.90
1200 A184 250ce on 70ce 2.40 2.40
Nos. 1198-1200 (3) 5.05 5.05

Penny Black, 150th Anniv. A223

Great Britain No. 1 and: 20ce, City Medal containing portrait of Victoria by William Wyon adapted for use on the Penny Black. 60ce, No. 1208, Bath mail coach. 80ce, Leeds Mail coach. 200ce, Heath's engraving, based on the Wyon portrait. 350ce, Penny Black master die. 400ce, London mail coach. No. 1207, Printers and flat-bed presses of Perkins, Bacon & Petch, 1840.

1990, May 3 *Perf. 13½x14*

1201 A223 20ce shown .35 .35
1202 A223 60ce multicolored .65 .65
1203 A223 80ce multicolored .90 .90
1204 A223 200ce multicolored 1.75 1.75
1205 A223 350ce multicolored 2.40 2.40
1206 A223 400ce multicolored 2.40 2.40
Nos. 1201-1206 (6) 8.45 8.45

Souvenir Sheets

1207 A223 600ce multicolored 4.75 4.75
1208 A223 600ce multicolored 4.75 4.75

June 4, Revolution, 10th Anniv. (in 1989) — A224

60ce, Pineapple, lobsters. 80ce, Corn, cacao beans. 200ce, Mining. 350ce, Scales, sword.

1990, June 5 Litho. *Perf. 14½x14*

1209 A224 20ce shown .25 .25
1210 A224 60ce multicolored .50 .50
1211 A224 80ce multicolored .65 .65
1212 A224 200ce multicolored 1.60 1.60
1213 A224 350ce multicolored 2.50 2.50
Nos. 1209-1213 (5) 5.50 5.50

Intelsat, 25th Anniv. A225

Satellites over: 60ce, Pacific Ocean. 80ce, Pacific, diff. 200ce, South Atlantic. 350ce, Pacific, Indian Oceans.

1990, July 12 *Perf. 14x14½*

1214 A225 20ce multicolored .25 .25
1215 A225 60ce multicolored .50 .50
1216 A225 80ce multicolored .60 .60
1217 A225 200ce multicolored 1.40 1.40
1218 A225 350ce multicolored 2.00 2.00
Nos. 1214-1218 (5) 4.75 4.75

Introduction of Intl. Direct Dialing Service (in 1988) — A226

60ce, Man using telephone. 80ce, Man using pay telephone. 200ce, Telephone booths. 350ce, Satellite dish.

1990, July 16

1219 A226 20ce shown .25 .25
1220 A226 60ce multicolored .50 .50
1221 A226 80ce multicolored .60 .60
1222 A226 200ce multicolored 1.40 1.40
1223 A226 350ce multicolored 2.00 2.00
Nos. 1219-1223 (5) 4.75 4.75

Miniature Sheet

African Tropical Rain Forest — A227

Designs: No. 1224a, Blue fairy flycatcher. b, Boomslang. c, Superb sunbird. d, Bateleur eagle. e, Yellow-casqued hornbill. f, Salamis temora. g, Potto. h, Leopard. i, Bongo. j, Gray parrot. k, Okapi. l, Gorilla. m, Flap-necked chameleon. n, West African dwarf crocodile. o, Python. p, Giant pangolin. q, Pseudacraea boisduvali. r, African crested porcupine. s, Rosy-columned aerangis. t, Cymothoe sangaris.

No. 1225, Leopard, vert.

1990, Oct. 25 Litho. *Perf. 14x14½*

1224 A227 Sheet of 20 17.00 17.00
a.-t. 40ce any single .70 .70

Souvenir Sheet

1225 A227 600ce multicolored 7.25 7.25

Miniature Sheet

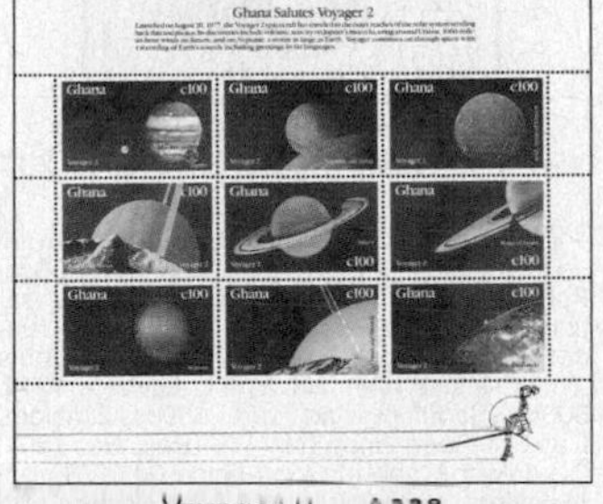

Voyager 2 — A228

Photographs from Voyager 2: No. 1226a, Jupiter. b, Neptune, Triton. c, Ariel, moon of Uranus. d, Saturn, Mimas. e, Saturn. f, Rings of Saturn. g, Neptune. h, Uranus, Miranda. i, Volcano on Io.

No. 1227, Voyager 2 liftoff, vert. No. 1228, Voyager 2, vert.

1990, Dec. 13 Litho. *Perf. 14*

1226 A228 100ce Sheet of 9, #1226a-1226i 8.50 8.50

Souvenir Sheets

1227 A228 600ce multi 3.50 3.50
1228 A228 600ce multi 3.50 3.50

Orchids — A229

Designs: 20ce, Eulophia guineensis. 40ce, Eurychone rothschildiana. 60ce, Bulbophyllum barbigerum. 80ce, Polystachya galeata. 200ce, Diaphananthe kamerunensis. 300ce, Podangis dactyloceras. 400ce, Ancistrochilus rothschildianus. 500ce, Rangaeris muscicola. No. 1237, Bolusiella imbricata. No. 1238, Diaphananthe rutila.

1990, Dec. 17

1229 A229 20ce multicolored .25 .25
1230 A229 40ce multicolored .30 .30
1231 A229 60ce multicolored .55 .55
1232 A229 80ce multicolored .70 .70
1233 A229 200ce multicolored 1.75 1.75
1234 A229 300ce multicolored 2.75 2.75
1235 A229 400ce multicolored 3.75 3.75
1236 A229 500ce multicolored 4.50 4.50
Nos. 1229-1236 (8) 14.55 14.55

Souvenir Sheets

1237 A229 600ce multicolored 7.25 7.25
1238 A229 600ce multicolored 7.25 7.25

Mushrooms — A230

Designs: 20ce, Coprinus atramentarius. 50ce, Marasmius oreades. 60ce, Oudamansiella radicata. 80ce, Cep. 150ce, Hebeloma crustuliniforme. 200ce, Coprinus micaceus. 300ce, Lepiota procera. 500ce, Amanita phalloides.

1990, Dec. 18

1239 A230 20ce multicolored .85 .55
1240 A230 50ce multicolored 1.10 .85
1241 A230 60ce multicolored 1.40 .85
1242 A230 80ce multicolored 1.75 1.25
1243 A230 150ce multicolored 2.25 1.75
1244 A230 200ce multicolored 3.25 2.50
1245 A230 300ce multicolored 3.25 3.25
a. Min. sheet of 4, #1240, 1243-1245 6.75 6.75
1246 A230 500ce multicolored 4.25 4.25
a. Min. sheet of 4, #1239, 1241-1242, 1246 6.75 6.75
Nos. 1239-1246 (8) 18.10 15.25

World Cup Soccer Championships, Italy — A231

Players from participating countries: 20ce, Italy. 50ce, Egypt. 60ce, Cameroun. 80ce, Romania. 100ce, Yugoslavia. 150ce, Cameroun, vert. 400ce, South Korea. 600ce, West Germany.

No. 1255, UAE. No. 1256, Colombia.

1990, Dec. 18 Litho. *Perf. 14*

1247 A231 20ce multi .50 .50
1248 A231 50ce multi .65 .65
1249 A231 60ce multi .70 .70
1250 A231 80ce multi .85 .85
1251 A231 100ce multi 1.00 1.00
1252 A231 150ce multi 1.60 1.60
1253 A231 400ce multi 2.60 2.60
1254 A231 600ce multi 3.00 3.00
Nos. 1247-1254 (8) 10.90 10.90

Souvenir Sheets

1255 A231 800ce multi 5.00 5.00
1256 A231 800ce multi 5.00 5.00

Peter Paul Rubens (1577-1640), Painter
A232

Portraits by Rubens: 20ce, Duke of Mantua. 50ce, Jan Brant. 60ce, Young man. 80ce, Michel Ophovius. 100ce, Caspar Gevaerts. 200ce, Head of a warrior (detail). 300ce, Bearded man. 400ce, Paracelsus. No. 1265. Archduke Ferdinand. No. 1266, Warrior with Two Pages.

1990, Dec. 24 Litho. *Perf. 14*

1257	A232	20ce multicolored	.25	.25
1258	A232	50ce multicolored	.40	.40
1259	A232	60ce multicolored	.50	.50
1260	A232	80ce multicolored	.60	.60
1261	A232	100ce multicolored	.75	.75
1262	A232	200ce multicolored	1.75	1.25
1263	A232	300ce multicolored	2.25	2.25
1264	A232	400ce multicolored	3.25	3.25
		Nos. 1257-1264 (8)	9.75	9.25

Souvenir Sheets

1265	A232	600ce multicolored	4.75	4.75
1266	A232	600ce multicolored	4.75	4.75

Minerals — A233

20ce, Manganese ore. 60ce, Iron ore. 80ce, Bauxite ore. 200ce, Gold ore. 350ce, Diamond.
600ce, Diamonds.

1991, May 2 Litho. *Perf. 14½x14*

1267	A233	20ce multi	.55	.55
1268	A233	60ce multi	.70	.70
1269	A233	80ce multi	1.25	1.25
1270	A233	200ce multi	3.00	3.00
1271	A233	350ce multi	4.00	4.00
		Nos. 1267-1271 (5)	9.50	9.50

Souvenir Sheet

1272	A233	600ce multi	9.00	9.00

Tribal Drums — A234

1991, May 9

1273	A234	20ce Damba	.45	.25
1274	A234	60ce Atumpan	.85	.55
1275	A234	80ce Kroboto	1.10	.70
1276	A234	200ce Asafo	1.60	1.60
1277	A234	350ce Obonu	2.50	2.50
		Nos. 1273-1277 (5)	6.50	5.60

Souvenir Sheet

1278	A234	600ce Single drum	6.50	6.50

Flowers — A235

20ce, Amorphophallus dracontioides. 60ce, Anchomanes difformis. 80ce, Kaemferia nigerica. 200ce, Aframomum sceptrum. 350ce, Amorphophallus flavovirens.
600ce, White flowers.

1991, May 15

1279	A235	20ce multicolored	.75	.35
1280	A235	60ce multicolored	1.10	.55
1281	A235	80ce multicolored	1.40	.70
1282	A235	200ce multicolored	2.25	2.25
1283	A235	350ce multicolored	2.50	2.50
		Nos. 1279-1283 (5)	8.00	6.35

Souvenir Sheet

1284	A235	600ce multicolored	6.00	6.00

1991, May 17 Litho. *Perf. 14½x14*

20ce, Urginea indica. 60ce, Hymenocallis littoralis. 80ce, Crinum jagus. 200ce, Dipcadi tacazzeanum. 350ce, Haemanthus rupestris.
600ce, Red flowers.

1285	A235	20ce multicolored	.55	.35
1286	A235	60ce multicolored	1.00	.55
1287	A235	80ce multicolored	1.40	.80
1288	A235	200ce multicolored	1.75	1.75
1289	A235	350ce multicolored	2.25	2.25
		Nos. 1285-1289 (5)	6.95	5.70

Souvenir Sheet

1290	A235	600ce multicolored	6.00	6.00

A236

Designs: 20ce, Satellite transmissions, airplane. 60ce, Scientific research, honey bee. 80ce, Literacy instruction. 200ce, Agricultural development. 350ce, Industry.

1991, June 21 Litho. *Perf. 13½x14*

1291	A236	20ce multicolored	.25	.25
1292	A236	60ce multicolored	.80	.55
1293	A236	80ce multicolored	.85	.70
1294	A236	200ce multicolored	1.40	1.40
1295	A236	350ce multicolored	2.25	2.25
		Nos. 1291-1295 (5)	5.55	5.15

UN Development Program, 40th anniv.

Lord Robert Baden-Powell (1857-1941), Founder of Boy Scouts — A237

Designs: 20ce, Sketch by Baden-Powell used in first scouting handbook, vert. 50ce, Portrait, vert. 80ce, Scout handbook illustration by Norman Rockwell. 100ce, Native runner, Cape of Good Hope #178. 200ce, Scouts aiding victims after V-1 attack, London, 1944. 500ce, Scout praying, vert. 600ce, Emblem, Cape of Good Hope No. 178 used. No. 1304, Cover with Cape of Good Hope No. 178 from Mafeking, 1900. No. 1305, Campsites, 17th World Scout Jamboree, Korea, 1991.

1991, July 16 Litho. *Perf. 14*

1296	A237	20ce buff & black	.60	.25
1297	A237	50ce multicolored	.75	.40
1298	A237	60ce multicolored	.75	.50
1299	A237	80ce black & buff	1.25	.65
1300	A237	100ce multicolored	1.50	1.00
1301	A237	200ce multicolored	1.90	1.90
1302	A237	500ce multicolored	4.00	4.00
1303	A237	600ce multicolored	4.50	4.50
		Nos. 1296-1303 (8)	15.25	13.20

Souvenir Sheets

1304	A237	800ce multicolored	4.75	4.75
1305	A237	800ce multicolored	4.75	4.75

For overprints see Nos. 1567-1572.

Chorkor Smoker
A238

Designs: 20ce, Placing fish on racks. 60ce, Preparing smokers. 80ce, Preparing fish. 200ce, Preparing racks for smoker. 350ce, Placing racks in smoker.

1991, July 22 Litho. *Perf. 14x14½*

1306	A238	20ce multicolored	.40	.25
1307	A238	60ce multicolored	.70	.45
1308	A238	80ce multicolored	.80	.65
1309	A238	200ce multicolored	1.75	1.75
1310	A238	350ce multicolored	2.25	2.25
		Nos. 1306-1310 (5)	5.90	5.35

Nos. 958-964 Overprinted "90th Birthday / 4th August 1990" and Surcharged

Perf. 14, 12½x12 (#1312-1313, 1315)

1991, July 22

1311	A184	20ce on 5ce #958	.50	.50
1312	A184	20ce on 8ce #959	.50	.50
1313	A184	40ce on 20ce #961	.80	.80
1314	A184	60ce on 12ce #960	1.50	1.50
1315	A184	80ce on 70ce #962	1.75	1.75
1316	A184	150ce on 100ce #963	3.50	3.50
		Nos. 1311-1316 (6)	8.55	8.55

Souvenir Sheet

1317	A184	200ce on 110ce #964	5.00	5.00

Nos. 1312-1313, 1315 issued in sheets of 5 + label. Overprint is vertical on stamp in No. 1317, horizontal on sheet margin.
The status of this issue is uncertain.

Fish
A239

20ce, Cephalopholis taeniops. 50ce, Synodontis sorex. 80ce, Balistes forcipatus. 100ce, Petrocephalus bane. 200ce, Syngnathus rastellatus. 300ce, Gymnarchus niloticus. 400ce, Hemichromis bimaculatus. 500ce, Sphyrna zygaena.
No. 1326, Bagrus bayad. No. 1327, Dactyloptena orientalis.

1991, July 29 Litho. *Perf. 14*

1318	A239	20ce multicolored	.25	.25
1319	A239	50ce multicolored	.35	.35
1320	A239	80ce multicolored	.35	.35
1321	A239	100ce multicolored	.45	.45
1322	A239	200ce multicolored	.85	.85
1323	A239	300ce multicolored	2.25	2.25
1324	A239	400ce multicolored	3.00	3.00
1325	A239	500ce multicolored	2.50	2.50
		Nos. 1318-1325 (8)	10.00	10.00

Souvenir Sheets

1326	A239	800ce multicolored	5.25	5.25
1327	A239	800ce multicolored	3.75	3.75

While Nos. 1320-1322, 1325, 1327 have the same issue date as Nos. 1318-1319, 1323-1324, 1326, the value of Nos. 1320-1322, 1325, 1327 was lower when they were released.
For overprints see Nos. 1573-1578.

Paintings by Vincent Van Gogh
A240

Designs: 20ce, Reaper with Sickle. 50ce, The Thresher. 60ce, The Sheaf Binder. 80ce, The Sheep Shearers. 100ce, Peasant Woman Cutting Straw. 200ce, The Sower. 500ce, The Plow and the Harrow, horiz. 600ce, The Woodcutter. No. 1336, Evening: The Watch. No. 1337, Evening: The End of the Day.

Perf. 13x13½, 13½x13

1991, Aug. 12 Litho.

1328	A240	20ce multicolored	.25	.25
1329	A240	50ce multicolored	.40	.40
1330	A240	60ce multicolored	.50	.50
1331	A240	80ce multicolored	.65	.65
1332	A240	100ce multicolored	.80	.80
1333	A240	200ce multicolored	1.60	1.60
1334	A240	500ce multicolored	3.25	3.25
1335	A240	600ce multicolored	4.00	4.00
		Nos. 1328-1335 (8)	11.45	11.45

Size: 106x80mm

Imperf

1336	A240	800ce multicolored	5.75	5.75
1337	A240	800ce multicolored	5.75	5.75

10th Non-aligned Ministers Conference, Accra — A241

Natl. Leaders: 20ce, Nasser, Egypt (1952-1970). 60ce, Tito, Yugoslavia (1945-1980). 80ce, Nehru, India (1947-1964). 200ce, Nkrumah, Ghana (1957-1966). 350ce, Sukarno, Indonesia (1945-1967).

1991, Sept. 2 *Perf. 13½x14*

1338	A241	20ce multicolored	.45	.35
1339	A241	60ce multicolored	.55	.50
1340	A241	80ce multicolored	3.50	1.50
1341	A241	200ce multicolored	2.00	2.00
1342	A241	350ce multicolored	2.50	2.50
		Nos. 1338-1342 (5)	9.00	6.85

Birds of Ghana — A242

Designs: No. 1343a, Melba finch. b, Orange-cheeked waxbill. c, Paradise flycatcher. d, Blue plantain-eater, e, Red bishop. f, Splendid glossy starling. g, Red-headed lovebird. h, Palm swift. i, Narina trogon. j, Tawny eagle. k, Bateleur eagle. l, Hoopoe. m, Secretary bird. n, White-backed vulture. o, Bare-headed rockfowl. p, Ground hornbill.
No. 1344a, Openbilled stork. b, African spoonbill. c, Pink-backed pelican. d, Little bittern. e, King reed-hen. f, Saddlebill stork. g, Glossy ibis. h, White-faced tree duck. i, Black-headed heron. j, Hammerkop. k, African darter. l, Woolly-necked stork. m, Yellow-billed stork. n, Black-winged stilt. o, Goliath heron. p, Lily trotter.
No. 1345a, Shikra. b, Abyssinian roller (c, g). c, Carmine bee-eater (g). d, Pintailed whydah (h). e, Purple glossy starling. f, Yellow-backed whydah (j). g, Pel's fishing owl. h, Verreaux's touraco (l). i, Red-cheeked cordon-bleu. j, Olive-bellied sunbird. k, Red-billed hornbill. l, Red-billed quelea. m, Crowned crane (i). n, Blue quail. o, Egyptian vulture (p). p, Helmeted guineafowl.
No. 1346, Marabou stork. No. 1347, Saddlebill stork, diff. No. 1348, African river eagle.

1991, Oct. 14 Litho. *Perf. 14½x14*

Sheets of 16

1343	A242	80ce #a.-p.	7.50	7.50
1344	A242	100ce #a.-p.	11.50	11.50
1345	A242	100ce #a.-p.	13.50	13.50
		Nos. 1343-1345 (3)	32.50	32.50

Souvenir Sheets

1346	A242	800ce multicolored	5.25	5.25
1347	A242	800ce multicolored	5.25	5.25
1348	A242	800ce multicolored	5.25	5.25

While No. 1344 has the same issue date as No. 1345, the value of No. 1344 was lower when it was released.

Insects
A243

20ce, Nularda. 50ce, Zonocrus. 60ce, Gryllotalpa africana. 80ce, Weevil. 100ce, Coenagrion. 150ce, Sahlbergella. 200ce, Anthia. 350ce, Megacephala.
600ce, Lacetus.

1991, Oct. 25 *Perf. 14x13½*

No.	Type	Value	Description	Unused	Used
1349	A243	20ce	multi	.75	.25
1350	A243	50ce	multi	.90	.40
1351	A243	60ce	multi	1.25	.50
1352	A243	80ce	multi	1.75	1.25
1353	A243	100ce	multi	2.25	2.00
1354	A243	150ce	multi	2.50	2.25
1355	A243	200ce	multi	3.00	3.00
1356	A243	350ce	multi	4.00	3.00
			Nos. 1349-1356 (8)	16.40	12.65

Souvenir Sheet

Perf. 13x12

No.	Type	Value	Description	Unused	Used
1357	A243	600ce	multi	13.50	13.50

Landmarks — A243a

Leucodon Cowrie — A243b

Achatina Achatina — A243c

Designs: 50ce, Boti Falls, vert. 60ce, Larabanga Mosque. 80ce, Fort Sebastian, Shama. 100ce, Cape Coast Castle.

100ce exists in four types:

Type I, "G" has angled curve, bars in "A"s slope down to left, "c" has straight line, bottom inscription 10mm.

Type II, "G" is rounded, bars in "A"s slope down to right, "c" has slanted line, bottom inscription 13mm.

Type III, "G" is rounded, bars in "A"s slope down to right, "c" has straight line, bottom inscription 10mm.

Type IV, "G" rounded, but cut off at top, bars in "A"s slope to right, "C" with slanted line, bottom inscription 10mm.

200ce, 400ce

Nos. 1357E, 1357Ej, 1357F, Type I: "G" has angled curve, bar in "A's" slope down to left.

Nos. 1357Ek, 1357Fl, Type II: "G" is rounded, bars in "A's" slope down to right.

Perf. 13¾x13½, 13½x13¾

1991 **Litho.**

No.	Type	Value	Description	Unused	Used
1357A	A243a	50ce	multi	—	—
o.			Perf. 13¾x14¼		—
1357B	A243a	60ce	multi	—	—
p.			Perf. 14¼x13¾	—	—
1357C	A243a	80ce	multi	—	—
1357D	A243a	100ce	multi (I)		—
g.			Type II		
h.			Type I, perf 14¼x13¾		
i.			Type III, perf 14¼x13¾		
m.			Type IV	—	—
1357E	A243b	200ce	multi (I)		—
j.			Type I, perf. 14¼x13¾	—	—
k.			Type II, perf. 14¼x13¾	—	—
1357F	A243c	400ce	multi (I)		—
l.			Type II, perf. 14¼x13¾	—	—
n.			Type I, perf. 11½		—

This set was printed locally. Shades exist.

Issue dates: 50ce, Nov. 21; others, Dec. 12. No. 1357Dm, 2004(?).

For surcharge, see No. 2687.

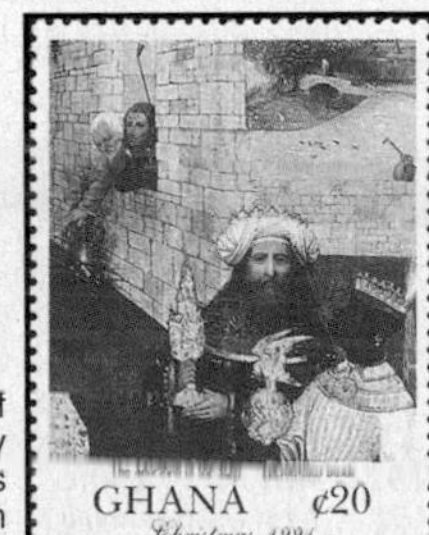

Adoration of the Magi by Hieronymus Bosch A244

Details or entire paintings: 50ce, The Annunciation by Robert Campin. 60ce, Virgin and Child by Dirk Bouts. 80ce, Presentation in the Temple by Hans Memling. 100ce, The Virgin and Child Enthroned with an Angel and a Donor by Memling. 200ce, The Virgin and Child with Saints and a Donor by Jan van Eyck. 400ce, St. Luke Painting the Virgin by Rogier van der Weyden. 700ce, Virgin and Child by Bouts, diff. No. 1366, The Annunciation by Memling. No. 1367, The Virgin and Child Standing in a Niche by van der Weyden.

1991, Dec. 23 *Perf. 12*

No.	Type	Value	Description	Unused	Used
1358	A244	20ce	multicolored	.25	.25
1359	A244	50ce	multicolored	.40	.40
1360	A244	60ce	multicolored	.50	.50
1361	A244	80ce	multicolored	.60	.60
1362	A244	100ce	multicolored	.80	.80
1363	A244	200ce	multicolored	1.50	1.50
1364	A244	400ce	multicolored	3.00	3.00
1365	A244	700ce	multicolored	5.25	5.25
			Nos. 1358-1365 (8)	12.30	12.30

Souvenir Sheets

Perf. 14½

No.	Type	Value	Description	Unused	Used
1366	A244	800ce	multicolored	5.50	5.50
1367	A244	800ce	multicolored	5.50	5.50

Christmas.

Reunification of Germany — A245

Designs: 20ce, Opening of German border, Nov. 9, 1989. 60ce, Signing of Two Plus Four Treaty, Sept. 12, 1990. 80ce, Opening of Brandenburg Gate, Dec. 22, 1989. 800ce, German leaders, Unity Day, Oct. 3, 1990. 1000ce, Currency union, July 1, 1990.

No. 1371Ab, USSR Pres. Mikhail Gorbachev, vert. c, Chancellor Helmut Kohl, vert. d, Map of West Germany, vert. e, Map of East Germany, vert.

No. 1371g, Doves. h, German Chancellor Helmut Kohl, Foreign Minister Hans-Dietrich Genscher.

1992, Feb. 17 **Litho.** *Perf. 14*

No.	Type	Value	Description	Unused	Used
1368	A245	20ce	multi	.30	.25
1369	A245	60ce	multi	.50	.50
1370	A245	80ce	multi	.70	.70
1371	A245	1000ce	multi	8.00	8.00
			Nos. 1368-1371 (4)	9.50	9.45

Souvenir Sheets

No.	Type	Value	Description	Unused	Used
1371A	A245	300ce	Sheet of 4, #b.-e.	6.75	6.75
1371F	A245	400ce	Sheet of 2, #g.-h.	2.00	2.00
1372	A245	800ce	multicolored	4.75	4.75

While No. 1371F has the same issue date as No. 1371A, the dollar value of No. 1371F was lower when it was released.

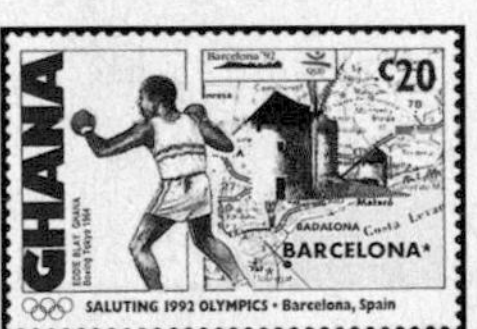

1992 Summer Olympics, Barcelona A246

Map and: 20ce, Eddie Blay, boxing, Ghana, 1964. 60ce, Mike Ahey, track, Ghana, 1964-1972. 80ce, T. Wilson, ski jumping, US, 1988. 100ce, East German 4-Man bobsled, 1988. 200ce, Greg Louganis, diving, US, 1984. 300ce, L. Visser, speed skating, Netherlands, 1988. 350ce, J. Passler, biathlon, Italy, 1988. 400ce, Mary Lou Retton, gymnastics, US, 1984. 500ce, Jurgen Hingsen, decathlon, Germany, 1984. 600ce, R. Neubert, heptathlon, West Germany, 1984. No. 1380, Jai alai player, vert. No. 1381, Windmill.

1992, Mar. 3 **Litho.** *Perf. 14*

No.	Type	Value	Description	Unused	Used
1373	A246	20ce	multi	.40	.25
1373A	A246	60ce	multi	.50	.45
1374	A246	80ce	multi	.70	.55
1375	A246	100ce	multi	1.00	.90
1376	A246	200ce	multi	1.75	1.60
1377	A246	300ce	multi	1.75	2.10
1378	A246	350ce	multi	1.75	2.10
1378A	A246	400ce	multi	2.40	2.75
1378B	A246	500ce	multi	2.40	2.75
1379	A246	600ce	multi	2.40	2.75
			Nos. 1373-1379 (10)	15.05	16.20

Souvenir Sheets

No.	Type	Value	Description	Unused	Used
1380	A246	800ce	multi	6.00	6.00
1381	A246	800ce	multi	6.00	6.00

While Nos. 1373A, 1378A-1378B have the same issue date as rest of the set the dollar value of Nos. 1373A, 1378A-1378B were lower when they were released.

Phila Nippon '91 A247

60ce, Torii of Itsukushima Jingu shrine. 80ce, Geisha. 100ce, Samurai residence. 200ce, Bonsai tree. 400ce, Olympic sports hall. 500ce, Great Buddha. 600ce, Nagoya castle.

No. 1390, Takamatsu castle. No. 1391, Heian shrine.

1992, Feb. 16 **Litho.** *Perf. 14*

No.	Type	Value	Description	Unused	Used
1382	A247	20ce	shown	.25	.25
1383	A247	60ce	multicolored	.35	.35
1384	A247	80ce	multicolored	.45	.45
1385	A247	100ce	multicolored	.60	.60
1386	A247	200ce	multicolored	1.40	1.40
1387	A247	400ce	multicolored	2.75	2.75
1388	A247	500ce	multicolored	3.25	3.25
1389	A247	600ce	multicolored	4.25	4.25
			Nos. 1382-1389 (8)	13.30	13.30

Souvenir Sheets

No.	Type	Value	Description	Unused	Used
1390	A247	800ce	multicolored	6.00	6.00
1391	A247	800ce	multicolored	6.00	6.00

Ghana Natl. Railways A248

Designs: 20c, Engine, 1903, Gold Coast Railway. 50c, Diesel passenger locomotive, Ghana Railways Corp. 60ce, First class coach, 1931 Gold Coast Railway. 80ce, Official inspection coach, Gold Coast Railway. 100ce, Engine No. 401 on turntable. 200c, Twin-bogie cocoa wagon, 1921, Gold Coast Railway. 500ce, Engine No. 223, "Prince of Wales." 600c, Twin-bogie cattle wagon, Gold Coast Railway. No. 1400, German-made locomotive, Gold Coast Railway. No. 1401, Beyer-Garratt #301, 1943, Gold Coast Railway.

1992, Mar. 2

No.	Type	Value	Description	Unused	Used
1392	A248	20ce	multicolored	.25	.25
1393	A248	50ce	multicolored	.25	.25
1394	A248	60ce	multicolored	.35	.35
1395	A248	80ce	multicolored	.45	.45
1396	A248	100ce	multicolored	.55	.55
1397	A248	200ce	multicolored	1.20	1.20
1398	A248	500ce	multicolored	3.00	3.00
1399	A248	600ce	multicolored	4.00	4.00
			Nos. 1392-1399 (8)	10.05	10.05

Souvenir Sheets

No.	Type	Value	Description	Unused	Used
1400	A248	800ce	multicolored	5.00	5.00
1401	A248	800ce	multicolored	5.00	5.00

Decade of Revolutionary Progress A249

20ce, Bore hole water. 50ce, Mining industry. 60ce, Small scale industry. 80ce, Timber industry. 200ce, Cocoa rehabilitation. 350ce, Rural electrification.

1992, Feb. 2 **Litho.** *Perf. 14x13½*

No.	Type	Value	Description	Unused	Used
1402	A249	20ce	multicolored	.25	.25
1403	A249	50ce	multicolored	.30	.30
1404	A249	60ce	multicolored	.40	.40
1405	A249	80ce	multicolored	.45	.45
1406	A249	200ce	multicolored	.80	.80
1407	A249	350ce	multicolored	1.00	1.00
			Nos. 1402-1407 (6)	3.20	3.20

Reptiles A251

20ce, Angides lugubris. 50ce, Kinixys erosa. 60ce, Agama agama. 80ce, Chameleo gracilis. 100ce, Naja melanleuca. 200ce, Crocodylus niloticus. 400ce, Chelonia mydas. 500ce, Varanus exanthematicus.

600ce, Snake & tortoise.

1992, Mar. 30 **Litho.** *Perf. 14*

No.	Type	Value	Description	Unused	Used
1414	A251	20ce	multicolored	.25	.25
1415	A251	50ce	multicolored	.35	.35
1416	A251	60ce	multicolored	.35	.35
1417	A251	80ce	multicolored	.45	.45
1418	A251	100ce	multicolored	.60	.60
1419	A251	200ce	multicolored	1.00	1.00
1420	A251	400ce	multicolored	2.00	2.00
1421	A251	500ce	multicolored	2.50	2.50
			Nos. 1414-1421 (8)	7.50	7.50

Souvenir Sheet

No.	Type	Value	Description	Unused	Used
1422	A251	600ce	multicolored	5.50	5.50

Numbers have been reserved for additional values in this set.

Easter A252

Details from paintings: 20ce, The Four Apostles: Sts. John, Peter, Paul & Mark, by Durer. 50ce, The Last Judgment, by Rubens. 60ce, The Four Apostles: Sts. John, Peter, Paul and Mark, diff. by Durer. 80ce, The Last Judgment, diff. by Rubens. 100ce, Crucifixion, by Rubens. 200ce, The Last Judgment, diff. by Rubens. 500ce, Christum Videre, by Rubens. 600ce, The Last Judgment, diff. by Rubens. No. 1432, Last Communion of St. Francis of Assisi, by Rubens. No. 1432A, Scourging the Money Changers from the Temple, by El Greco, horiz.

1992, Mar. 13 *Perf. 13½x14*

No.	Type	Value	Description	Unused	Used
1424	A252	20ce	multi	.25	.25
1425	A252	50ce	multi	.35	.35
1426	A252	60ce	multi	.45	.45
1427	A252	80ce	multi	.55	.55
1428	A252	100ce	multi	.65	.65
1429	A252	200ce	multi	1.00	1.00
1430	A252	500ce	multi	2.50	2.50
1431	A252	600ce	multi	2.75	2.75
			Nos. 1424-1431 (8)	8.50	8.50

Souvenir Sheets

No.	Type	Value	Description	Unused	Used
1432	A252	800ce	multi	5.25	5.25

Perf. 14x13½

No.	Type	Value	Description	Unused	Used
1432A	A252	800ce	multi	5.25	5.25

Spanish Art — A253

Paintings by Velazquez: 20ce, Two Men at Table. 60ce, Christ in the House of Mary and Martha (detail). 80ce, The Supper at Emmaus. 100ce, Three Muscians. 200ce, Old Woman Cooking Eggs, vert. 400ce, Old Woman Cooking Eggs (detail), vert. 500ce, The Surrender of Breda (detail) diff., vert. 700ce, The Surrender of Breda (detail), vert.

No. 1441, They Still Say that Fish is Expensive, by Joaquin Sorolla y Bastida. No. 1442, The Waterseller of Seville.

1992, May 4 *Perf. 13½*

No.	Type	Value	Description	Unused	Used
1433	A253	20ce	multicolored	.25	.25
1434	A253	60ce	multicolored	.30	.30
1435	A253	80ce	multicolored	.35	.35
1436	A253	100ce	multicolored	.50	.50
1437	A253	200ce	multicolored	1.10	1.10
1438	A253	400ce	multicolored	1.75	1.75
1439	A253	500ce	multicolored	2.25	2.25
1440	A253	700ce	multicolored	3.50	3.50

Size: 120x95mm

Imperf

No.	Type	Value	Description	Unused	Used
1441	A253	900ce	multicolored	5.00	5.00
1442	A253	900ce	multicolored	4.50	4.50
			Nos. 1433-1442 (10)	19.50	19.50

Granada '92. While Nos. 1434-1435, 1438-1439, 1442 have the same issue date as Nos. 1433, 1436-1437, 1440-1441, the value in relation to the dollar of Nos. 1434-1435, 1438-1439, 1442 was lower when they were released.

Butterflies — A254

20ce, African monarch. 60ce, Mocker swallowtail. 80ce, Painted lady. 100ce, Mountain beauty. 200ce, Blue temora. 400ce, Foxy charaxes. 500ce, Blue pansy. 700ce, Golden pansy.

No. 1451, Gaudy commodore. No. 1452, Christmas butterfly.

1992, May 25 Litho. *Perf. 14*

1443	A254	20ce multicolored	.25	.25
1444	A254	60ce multicolored	.40	.40
1445	A254	80ce multicolored	.55	.55
1446	A254	100ce multicolored	.65	.65
1447	A254	200ce multicolored	1.50	1.50
1448	A254	400ce multicolored	3.00	3.00
1449	A254	500ce multicolored	3.50	3.50
1450	A254	700ce multicolored	4.75	4.75
		Nos. 1443-1450 (8)	14.60	14.60

Souvenir Sheets

1451	A254	900ce multicolored	5.50	5.50
1452	A254	900ce multicolored	5.50	5.50

Genoa '92. For overprints see Nos. 1471-1480.

Dinosaurs — A255

20ce, Iguanodon. 50ce, Anchisaurus. 60ce, Heterodontosaurus. 80ce, Ouranosaurus. 100ce, Anatosaurus. 200ce, Elaphrosaurus. 500ce, Coelophysis. 600ce, Rhamphorynchus.

1992, June 1 Litho. *Perf. 14*

1453	A255	20ce multi	.45	.35
1454	A255	50ce multi	.65	.45
1455	A255	60ce multi	.70	.45
1456	A255	80ce multi	.75	.55
1457	A255	100ce multi	1.00	.65
1458	A255	200ce multi	1.60	1.60
1459	A255	500ce multi	2.75	2.75
1460	A255	600ce multi	3.25	3.25
		Nos. 1453-1460 (8)	11.15	10.05

Souvenir Sheets

1461	A255	1500ce like #1459	6.75	6.75
1462	A255	1500ce like #1458	6.75	6.75

While Nos. 1453, 1456, 1458-1459 and 1462 have the same issue date as Nos. 1454-1455, 1457, 1460-1461, their value in relation to the dollar was lower when they were released.

Discovery of America, 500th Anniv. — A256

No. 1463: a, Capt. Martin Alonzo Pinzon, Pinta. b, Capt. Vicente Yanez Pinzon, Nina. c, Columbus, Fr. Marchena in La Rabida, 1485. d, Columbus in cabin. e, Land sighted, Oct. 12, 1492. f, Columbus lands on Samana Cay. g, Shipwreck of Santa Maria. h, Columbus returns to Spanish Court, 1493.

No. 1464, Columbus, ship.

1992, July Litho. *Perf. 14*

1463	A256	200ce Sheet of 8, #a.-h.	9.50	9.50

Souvenir Sheet

1464	A256	500ce multicolored	3.75	3.75

World Columbian Stamp Expo '92, Chicago.

Shells — A257

No. 1465, Olivancillaria hiatula. No. 1465A, Tympanotonus fuscatus. No. 1466, Donax rugosus. No. 1466A, Murex cornutus. No. 1467, Sigaretus concavus. No. 1467A, Tivela tripla. No. 1468, Pila africana. No. 1468A, Cypraea stercoraria. No. 1469, Thais hiatula. No. 1469A, Cassis tesselata.

No. 1470, Natica favel. No. 1470A, Semifusos morio.

1992, Oct. 5 Litho. *Perf. 14*

1465	A257	20ce multicolored	.25	.25
1465A	A257	20ce multicolored	.25	.25
1466	A257	60ce multicolored	.35	.35
1466A	A257	60ce multicolored	.35	.35
1467	A257	80ce multicolored	.45	.45
1467A	A257	80ce multicolored	.45	.45
1468	A257	200ce multicolored	1.10	1.10
1468A	A257	200ce multicolored	1.10	1.10
1469	A257	350ce multicolored	1.75	1.75
1469A	A257	350ce multicolored	1.75	1.75
		Nos. 1465-1469A (10)	7.80	7.80

Souvenir Sheet

1470	A257	600ce multicolored	4.50	4.50
1470A	A257	600ce multicolored	4.50	4.50

Nos. 1443-1452 Ovptd. "40th / Anniversary / of the / Accession / of / HM Queen / Elizabeth II / 1952-1992" in Silver

1992, Aug. 10 Litho. *Perf. 14*

1471	A254	20ce on #1443	.25	.25
1472	A254	60ce on #1444	.30	.30
1473	A254	80ce on #1445	.40	.40
1474	A254	100ce on #1446	.50	.50
1475	A254	200ce on #1447	1.00	1.00
1476	A254	400ce on #1448	1.75	1.75
1477	A254	500ce on #1449	2.50	2.50
1478	A254	700ce on #1450	3.25	3.25
		Nos. 1471-1478 (8)	9.95	9.95

Souvenir Sheets

1479	A254	900ce on #1451	5.00	5.00
1480	A254	900ce on #1452	5.00	5.00

Christmas A259

Details or entire paintings: 20ce, Presentation in the Temple, by Master of Brunswick. 50ce, Presentation in the Temple, by Master of St. Severin. 60ce, The Visitation, by Sebastiano del Piombo. 80ce, The Visitation, by Giotto. 100ce, The Circumcision, by Studio of Giovanni Bellini. 200ce, The Circumcision, by Workshop of Benvenuto Garofalo. 500ce, The Visitation, by Workshop of Rogier van der Weyden. 800ce, The Visitation, by Workshop of Rogier Van der Weyden. No. 1491, The Visitation, by Giotto. No. 1492, The Presentation in the Temple, by Bartolo di Fredi.

1992 Litho. *Perf. 13½x14*

1483	A259	20ce multicolored	.25	.25
1484	A259	50ce multicolored	.30	.30
1485	A259	60ce multicolored	.35	.35
1486	A259	80ce multicolored	.40	.40
1487	A259	100ce multicolored	.50	.50
1488	A259	200ce multicolored	1.00	1.00
1489	A259	500ce multicolored	2.75	2.75
1490	A259	800ce multicolored	4.25	4.25
		Nos. 1483-1490 (8)	9.80	9.80

Souvenir Sheet

1491	A259	900ce multicolored	4.50	4.50
1492	A259	900ce multicolored	4.50	4.50

No. 1492 exists imperf.

Anniversaries and Events
A260 A261

Designs: 20ce, LZ3, floating hangar at Lake Constance, horiz. 100ce, Lift-off of Ariane 4 rocket, horiz. 200ce, Leopard in tree, horiz. 300ce, Roman Colosseum, fruits and vegetables, horiz. 400ce, Wolfgang Amadeus Mozart. 600ce, Lift-off of H-1 rocket, Japan. 800ce, LZ10, Schwaben, horiz. No. 1501, Scene from "The Marriage of Figaro." No. 1502, Space shuttle, US. No. 1503, Count Ferdinand von Zeppelin. No. 1504, Bongo, horiz.

1992, Dec. Litho. *Perf. 14*

1493	A260	20ce multicolored	.30	.30
1494	A260	100ce multicolored	.60	.60
1495	A260	200ce multicolored	1.15	1.15
1496	A260	300ce multicolored	1.75	1.75
1497	A261	400ce multicolored	2.60	2.60
1499	A260	600ce multicolored	4.00	4.00
1500	A260	800ce multicolored	5.25	5.25
		Nos. 1493-1500 (7)	15.65	15.65

Souvenir Sheets

1501	A261	900ce multicolored	5.00	5.00
1502	A260	900ce multicolored	5.00	5.00
1503	A260	900ce multicolored	5.00	5.00
1504	A260	900ce multicolored	5.00	5.00

Count Ferdinand von Zeppelin, 75th anniv. of death (Nos. 1493, 1500, 1503). Intl. Space Year (Nos. 1494, 1499, 1502). UN Earth Summit, Rio de Janeiro (Nos. 1495, 1504). WHO, Intl. Conference on Nutrition, Rome (No. 1496). Mozart, bicent. of death (in 1991) (Nos. 1497, 1501).

Flowers — A262

Designs: Nos. 1505, 1514d (100ce), Lagerstroemia flos-reginae. No. 1506, Clerodendrum thomsoniae. Nos. 1507, 1514c (50ce), Spathodea campanulata. No. 1508, Cassia fistula. Nos. 1509, 1514e (150ce), Mellitea ferrugenea. Nos. 1510, 1514j (300ce), Hildegardia barteri. Nos. 1511, 1514i (150ce), Ipomoea asarifolia. No. 1512, Petrea volubilis. Nos. 1513, 1514f (300ce), Ritchiea reflexa. Nos. 1514, 1514h (100ce), Bryphyllum pinnatum.

1993, Mar. 1 Litho. *Perf. 14*

1505	A262	20ce multicolored	.25	.25
1506	A262	20ce multicolored	.25	.25
1507	A262	60ce multicolored	.30	.30
1508	A262	60ce multicolored	.30	.30
1509	A262	80ce multicolored	.40	.40
1510	A262	80ce multicolored	.40	.40
1511	A262	200ce multicolored	.90	.90
1512	A262	200ce multicolored	.90	.90
1513	A262	350ce multicolored	1.40	1.40
1514	A262	350ce multicolored	1.40	1.40
		Nos. 1505-1514 (10)	6.50	6.50

Souvenir Sheets

1514A	A262	Sheet of 4, #c.-f.	3.50	3.50
1514B	A262	Sheet of 4, #g.-j.	3.50	3.50

Intl. Conference on Nutrition, Rome — A263

20ce, Energy foods. 60ce, Body-building foods. 80ce, Protective foods. 200ce, Disease prevention. 400ce, Food quality control, preservation.

1993, Jan. Litho. *Perf. 14*

1515	A263	20ce multicolored	.25	.25
1516	A263	60ce multicolored	.30	.30
1517	A263	80ce multicolored	.40	.40
1518	A263	200ce multicolored	1.00	1.00
1519	A263	400ce multicolored	1.75	1.75
		Nos. 1515-1519 (5)	3.70	3.70

Crabs A264

Designs: 20ce, Clappa rubroguttata. 60ce, Cardisoma amatum. 80ce, Maia squinado. 400ce, Ocypoda cursor. 800ce, Grapus grapsus.

1993, Feb. *Perf. 14x13½*

1520	A264	20ce multicolored	.25	.25
1521	A264	60ce multicolored	.35	.35
1522	A264	80ce multicolored	.45	.45
1523	A264	400ce multicolored	2.10	2.10
a.		Souv. sheet of 4, #1520-1523	7.50	7.50
1524	A264	800ce multicolored	4.25	4.25
		Nos. 1520-1524 (5)	7.40	7.40

Miniature Sheet of 8

Louvre Museum, Bicent. — A265

No. 1525 — Details or entire paintings, by Giovanni Domenico Tiepolo (1727-1804) (a-e) and Giovanni Battista Tiepolo (1696-1770) (f-h): a-c, Carnival Scene, (left, center, right). d-e, Tooth Puller, (left, right). f, Rebecca at the Well. g-h, Presenting Christ to the People, (left, right).

700ce, Chancellor Seguier, by Le Brun, horiz.

1993, Mar. 1 Litho. *Perf. 12*

1525	A265	200ce Sheet of 8, #a.-h. + label	9.00	9.00

Souvenir Sheet

Perf. 14½

1526	A265	700ce multicolored	4.00	4.00

No. 1526 contains one 55x88mm stamp.

Oil Palm Fruit — A265a

1993, Apr. Litho. *Perf. 13½*

1526A	A265a	20ce multi	—	—

Faberge Eggs — A266

Easter: 50ce, Resurrection Egg. 80ce, Imperial Red Cross Egg with Resurrection

Triptych. 100ce, Imperial Uspensky Cathedral Egg. 150ce, Imperial Red Cross Egg with portraits. 200ce, Orange Tree Egg. 250ce, Rabbit Egg. 400ce, Imperial Coronation Egg. 900ce, Silver-gilt enamel Easter Egg. No. 1535, Spring Flower Egg. No. 1536, Egg charms, horiz.

1993, Apr. 26 *Perf. 14*

1527	A266	50ce multi	.30	.30
1528	A266	80ce multi	.50	.50
1529	A266	100ce multi	.00	.00
1530	A266	150ce multi	.90	.90
1531	A266	200ce multi	1.25	1.25
1532	A266	250ce multi	1.75	1.75
1533	A266	400ce multi	3.50	3.50
1534	A266	900ce multi	7.50	7.50
		Nos. 1527-1534 (8)	16.30	16.30

Souvenir Sheets

1535	A266	1000ce multi	6.50	6.50
1536	A266	1000ce multi	6.50	6.50

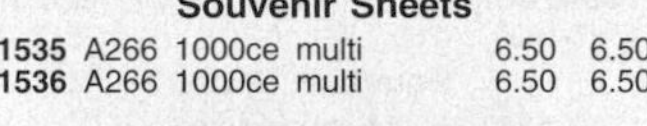

Wild Animals — A267

20ce, African buffalo. 50ce, Giant forest hog. 60ce, Potto. 80ce, Bay duiker. 100ce, Royal antelope. 200ce, Serval. 500ce, Golden cat. 800ce, Megaloglossus woermanni.

No. 1545, Dormouse. No. 1546, White collared mangabey.

1993, May 24 **Litho.** *Perf. 14*

1537	A267	20ce multi	.25	.25
1538	A267	50ce multi	.50	.50
1539	A267	60ce multi	.60	.60
1540	A267	80ce multi	.80	.80
1541	A267	100ce multi	1.00	1.00
1542	A267	200ce multi	2.00	2.00
1543	A267	500ce multi	5.00	5.00
1544	A267	800ce multi	8.00	8.00
		Nos. 1537-1544 (8)	18.15	18.15

Souvenir Sheets

1545	A267	900ce multi	6.50	6.50
1546	A267	900ce multi	6.50	6.50

4th Republic — A268

50ce, Kwame Nkrumah Mausoleum, horiz. 100ce, Kwame Nkrumah Conference Center, horiz. 200ce, Constitution book. 350ce, Independence Square. 400ce, Christiansborg Castle.

1993, May **Litho.** *Perf. 14*

1547	A268	50ce multicolored	.25	.25
1548	A268	100ce multicolored	.50	.50
1549	A268	200ce multicolored	1.05	1.05
1550	A268	350ce multicolored	1.90	1.90
1551	A268	400ce multicolored	2.25	2.25
		Nos. 1547-1551 (5)	5.95	5.95

A269

Aviation and Automotive Anniversaries — A270

50ce, Graf Zeppelin over Alps, vert. No. 1552, Mercedes Benz 300 SLR in 1955 Mille Miglia. No. 1553, LZ7 Deutschland. No. 1554, Vulcan bomber. No. 1555, Ford Tri-motor. No. 1556, 1920 Ford Depot Wagon. No. 1557, Nieuport 27, vert. No. 1558, Graf Zeppelin taking aboard letters, vert. No. 1559, 1970 Ford Mach 1 Mustang. No. 1560, LZ10 Schwaben. No. 1561, Mercedes wins 1937 Monaco Grand Prix.

No. 1562, Graf Zeppelin over Rome. No. 1563, 1955 Mercedes Benz Type 196. No. 1564, Early US air mail flight. No. 1565, S.E.5A, 1918. No. 1566, 1910 Ford Super T, 999.

1993 **Litho.** *Perf. 14*

1551A	A269	50ce multi	.35	.35
1552	A270	150ce multi	.90	.90
1553	A269	150ce multi	.90	.90
1554	A269	400ce multi	2.75	2.75
1555	A269	400ce multi	2.75	2.75
1556	A270	400ce multi	2.75	2.75
1557	A269	600ce multi	4.00	4.00
1558	A269	600ce multi	4.00	4.00
1559	A270	600ce multi	4.00	4.00
1560	A269	800ce multi	5.00	5.00
1561	A270	800ce multi	5.00	5.00
		Nos. 1551A-1561 (11)	32.40	32.40

Souvenir Sheets

1562	A269	1000ce multi	4.75	4.75
1563	A270	1000ce multi	4.75	4.75
1564	A269	1000ce multi	4.75	4.75
1565	A269	1000ce multi	4.75	4.75
1566	A270	1000ce multi	4.75	4.75

Capt. Hugo Eckener, 125th birth anniv. (Nos. 1551A, 1553-1554, 1562). Benz's first four-wheeled vehicle, cent. (Nos. 1552, 1561, 1563). Royal Air Force, 75th anniv. (Nos. 1554, 1557, 1564). Henry Ford's first gasoline powered engine, cent. (Nos. 1556, 1559, 1566).

No. 1564 contains one 57x42mm stamp. Nos. 1563, 1566 contains one 85x28mm stamp.

Issued: Nos. 1555-1556, 1558-1559, 1565-1566, May. Nos. 1551A-1554, 1557, 1560-1564, June.

Nos. 1300-1305 Ovptd.

1993 **Litho.** *Perf. 14*

1567	A237	100ce multicolored	.65	.65
1568	A237	200ce multicolored	1.60	1.60
1569	A237	500ce multicolored	3.25	3.25
1570	A237	600ce multicolored	4.50	4.50
		Nos. 1567-1570 (4)	10.00	10.00

Souvenir Sheet

1571	A237	800ce on #1304	5.50	5.50
1572	A237	800ce on #1305	5.50	5.50

Nos. 1321, 1323-1327 Ovptd.

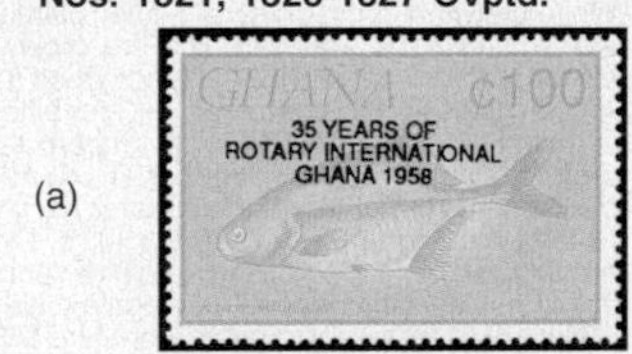

(a)

(b)

1993

1573	A239(a)	100ce multi	.75	.75
1574	A239(b)	300ce multi	1.75	1.75
1575	A239(b)	400ce multi	2.75	2.75
1576	A239(a)	500ce multi	3.25	3.25
		Nos. 1573-1576 (4)	8.50	8.50

Souvenir Sheets

1577	A239(a)	800ce on #1326	5.25	5.25
1578	A239(b)	800ce on #1327	5.25	5.25

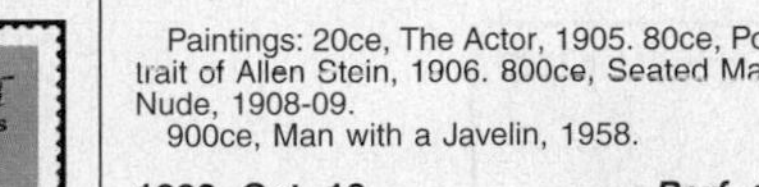

A271

Mushrooms A272

Designs: 20ce, Cantharellus cibarius. 50ce, Russula cyanoxantha. 60ce, Clitocybe rivulosa. No. 1581, Boletus chrysenteron. No. 1582, Cortinarius elatior. No. 1583, Mycena galericulata. No. 1584, Boletus edulis. No. 1585, Tricholoma gambosum. No. 1586, Lepista saeva. 250ce, Gyroporus castaneus. No. 1589, Nolanea sericea. No. 1590, Hygrophorus puiceus. 500ce, Gomphidius glutinosus. No. 1592, Russula olivacea. 1000ce, Russula aurata.

No. 1594a, 100ce, Cantharellus cibarius. b, 150ce, Cortinarius elatior. c, 300ce, Tricholoma gambosum. d, 600ce, Hygrophorus puiceus.

No. 1595: a, 50ce, like #1581. b, 100ce, like #1583. c, 150ce, like #1584. d, 1000ce, like #1589.

1993, July 30 **Litho.** *Perf. 14*

1579	A271	20ce multi	.25	.25
1580	A271	50ce multi	.25	.25
1581	A271	60ce multi	.25	.25
1582	A271	80ce multi	.35	.35
1583	A271	80ce multi	.35	.35
1584	A271	200ce multi	.85	.85
1585	A271	200ce multi	.85	.85
1586	A272	200ce multi	.85	.85
1587	A272	250ce multi	1.05	1.05
1588	A271	300ce multi	1.25	1.25
1589	A271	350ce multi	1.60	1.60
1590	A271	350ce multi	1.60	1.60
1591	A272	500ce multi	2.50	2.50
1592	A272	600ce multi	3.00	3.00
1593	A272	1000ce multi	5.00	5.00
		Nos. 1579-1593 (15)	20.00	20.00

Souvenir Sheets

1594	A271	Sheet of 4, #a.-d.	7.25	7.25
1595	A271	Sheet of 4, #a.-d.	7.25	7.25

Copernicus (1473-1543) A273

Designs: 20ce, Early astronomical instrument. 200ce, Telescope. No. 1598, Copernicus, long hair. No. 1599, Copernicus, shorter hair.

1993, Oct. 19 **Litho.** *Perf. 13½x14*

1596	A273	20ce multicolored	.50	.50
1597	A273	200ce multicolored	3.00	3.00

Souvenir Sheets

Perf. 13x13

1598	A273	1000ce multicolored	6.00	6.00
1599	A273	1000ce multicolored	6.00	6.00

Picasso (1881-1973) A274

Paintings: 20ce, The Actor, 1905. 80ce, Portrait of Allen Stein, 1906. 800ce, Seated Male Nude, 1908-09.

900ce, Man with a Javelin, 1958.

1993, Oct. 19 *Perf. 14*

1600-1602	A274	Set of 3	5.50	5.50

Souvenir Sheet

1603	A274	900ce multi	5.50	5.50

Polska '93 — A275

Paintings: 200ce, Tattoo, by Sobocki, 1978. 600ce, Prison, by Blonder, 1934. 1000ce, Fable of the Fortunate Man, by Michalak, 1925, horiz.

1993, Oct. 19

1604-1605	A275	Set of 2	5.00	5.00

Souvenir Sheet

1606	A275	1000ce multicolored	5.00	5.00

1994 World Cup Soccer, US — A276

Designs: 50ce, Abedi Pele, Ghana. 80ce, Pedro Troglio, Argentina. 100ce, Fernando Alvez, Uruguay. 200ce, Franco Baresi, Italy. 250ce, Gomez, Colombia; Katanec, Yugoslavia. 600ce, Diego Maradona, Argentina. 800ce, Hasek, Czech Republic; Wynalda, US. 1000ce, Lothar Matthaeus, Germany.

No. 1615, Giuseppe Giannini, Italy. No. 1616, Rabie Yassein, Egypt; Ruud Gullit, Holland.

1993, Dec. 1 *Perf. 13½x14*

1607	A276	50ce multi	.25	.25
1608	A276	80ce multi	.45	.45
1609	A276	100ce multi	.55	.55
1610	A276	200ce multi	1.10	1.10
1611	A276	250ce multi	1.50	1.50
1612	A276	600ce multi	3.25	3.25
1613	A276	800ce multi	4.25	4.25
1614	A276	1000ce multi	5.00	5.00
		Nos. 1607-1614 (8)	16.35	16.35

Souvenir Sheets

Perf. 13

1615	A276	1200ce multi	6.50	6.50
1616	A276	1200ce multi	6.50	6.50

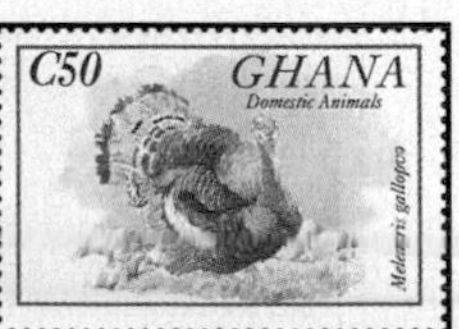

Domestic Animals A277

Designs: 50ce, Meleagris gallopvo. 100ce, Capra hircus. 150ce, Carina moschata. 200ce, Eguus asinus. 250ce, Male gallus gallus. 300ce, Sus vittatus. 400ce, Numida meleagris. 600ce, Canis domesticus. 800ce, Female gallus gallus. 1000ce, Ovis aries.

No. 1627: a, 100ce, Like #1618. b, 250ce, Like #1624. c, 350ce, Like #1622. d, 500ce, Like #1626.

No. 1628: a, 100ce, Like #1623. b, 250ce, Like #1621. c, 350ce, Like #1625. d, 500ce, Like #1617.

1993, Dec. 8 *Perf. 14*

1617-1626	A277	Set of 10	18.00	18.00

Souvenir Sheets

1627	A277	Sheet of 4, #a-d	7.00	7.00
1628	A277	Sheet of 4, #a-d	7.00	7.00

Arts and Crafts — A278

Designs: No. 1629, 50ce, Doll. No. 1630, 50ce, Pot and lid. No. 1631, 200ce, Beads. No. 1632, 200ce, Snake charmers. No. 1633, 250ce, Hoe. No. 1634, 250ce, Scabbard. No. 1635, 600ce, Pipe. No. 1636, 600ce, Deer. No. 1637, 1000ce, Mask. No. 1638, 1000ce, Doll with baby.

No. 1639: a, 100ce, Like #1629. b, 250ce, Like #1631. c, 350ce, Like #1633. d, 500ce, Like #1635.

No. 1640: a, 100ce, Like #1630. b, 250ce, Like #1632. c, 350ce, Like #1634. d, 500ce, Like #1636.

1994, Jan. 24 Litho. *Perf. 14*

1629-1638 A278 Set of 10 13.50 13.50

Souvenir Sheets

1639 A278 Sheet of 4, #a-d 4.00 4.00
1640 A278 Sheet of 4, #a-d 4.00 4.00

Christmas A279

Paintings and Woodcuts: 50ce, Adoration of the Magi. 100ce, The Virgin and Child with Saint John and an Angel, by Botticelli. 150ce, Mary as Queen of Heaven. 200ce, Saint Anne. 250ce, The Madonna of the Magnificat, by Botticelli. 400ce, The Madonna of the Goldfinch, by Tiepolo. 600ce, The Virgin and the Child with the Young St. John the Baptist, by Correggio. 1000ce, Adoration of the Shepherds.

No. 1649, Mystic Nativity (detail), by Botticelli, horiz. No. 1650, Madonna in a Circle, by Durer.

Woodcuts (50ce, 150ce, 200ce, 1000ce) are from Nuremberg Prayer Books, by Durer.

Perf. 13½x14, 14x13½

1993, Dec. 20 Litho.

1641-1648 A279 Set of 8 13.00 13.00

Souvenir Sheets

1649 A279 1000ce multicolored 6.00 6.00
1650 A279 1000ce multicolored 6.00 6.00

A280

Hong Kong '94 — A281

Stamps, tram from Kennedy Town to Shau Kei: No. 1651, Hong Kong #470, back of tram. No. 1652, Front of tram, #1392.

No. 1653 — Imperial Palace clocks: a, Windmill. b, Horse. c, Balloon. d, Zodiac. e, Shar-Pei dog. f, Cat.

1994, Feb. 18 Litho. *Perf. 14*

1651 200ce multicolored .90 .90
1652 200ce multicolored .90 .90
a. A280 Pair, #1651-1652 1.80 1.80

Miniature Sheet

1653 A281 100ce Sheet of 6, #a.-f. 6.00 6.00

Nos. 1651-1652 issued in sheets of 5 pairs. No. 1652a is a continuous design.

New Year 1994 (Year of the Dog) (No. 1653e).

Mickey Mouse, 65th Birthday A282

Mickey's films: 50ce, Steamboat Willie, 1928. 100ce, The Band Concert, 1937. 150ce, Moose Hunters, 1937. 200ce, Brave Little Taylor, 1938. 250ce, Fantasia, 1940. 400ce, The Nifty Nineties, 1941. 600ce, Canne Caddy, 1944. 1000ce, Mickey's Christmas Carol, 1983.

No. 1662, 1200ce, Mickey's Elephant, 1936. No. 1663, 1200ce, Mickey's Amateurs, 1937.

1994, Mar. 1 Litho. *Perf. 13½x14*

1654-1661 A282 Set of 8 11.50 11.50

Souvenir Sheets

1662-1663 A282 Set of 2 10.00 10.00

A283

Hummel Figurines: 50ce, Boy with backpack, walking stick. 100ce, Girl holding basket behind back. 150ce, Boy with rabbits. 200ce, Boy carrying chicks in basket. 250ce, Girl with chicks. 400ce, Girl petting lamb. 600ce, Lamb, girl waving handkerchief. 1000ce, Girl with basket, flowers.

No. 1672: a, 500ce, Like #1665; b, 150ce, Like #1671; c, 1200ce, Like #1667.

No. 1673: a, 300ce, Like #1668; b, 200ce, Like #1669; c, 500ce, Like #1670; d, 1000ce, Like #1666.

1994, Apr. 6 *Perf. 14*

1664-1671 A283 Set of 8 9.50 9.50

Souvenir Sheets

1672 A283 Sheet of 4, #a.-c., #1664 5.00 5.00
1673 A283 Sheet of 4, #a.-d. 5.00 5.00

World Wildlife Fund — A284

Diana Monkeys: 50ce, Adult, young. 200ce, Sitting in tree. 500ce, Holding food. 800ce, Close-up of face.

1994, May 16 Litho. *Perf. 14*

1674-1677 A284 Set of 4 7.50 7.50
1677a Sheet, 3 each #1674-1677 24.00 24.00

For surcharges see Nos. 2530-2533.

Wild Animals A285

Designs: 100ce, Bushbuck. 150ce, Spotted hyena. 1000ce, Aardvark. No. 1681, 2000ce, Leopard, vert. No. 1682, 2000ce, Waterbuck, vert.

1994, May 16

1678-1680 A285 Set of 3 6.50 6.50

Souvenir Sheets

1681-1682 A285 Set of 2 13.00 13.00

Cats A286

No. 1683, 200ce: a, Sorrel Abyssinian. b, Silver classic tabby. c, Chocolate-point Siamese. d, Brown tortie Burmese. e, Exotic shorthair. f, Havana brown. g, Devon rex. h, Black manx. i, British blue shorthair. j, Calico American wirehair. k, Spotted oriental Siamese. l, Red classic tabby.

No. 1684, 200ce: a, Norwegian forest cat. b, Blue longhair. c, Red self longhair. d, Black longhair. e, Chinchilla. f, Dilut calico longhair. g, Blue tabby-&-white longhair. h, Ruby somali. i, Blue smoke longhair. j, Calico longhair. k, Brown tabby longhair. l, Balinese.

No. 1685, 2000ce, Brown mackeral tabby Scottish fold. No. 1686, 2000ce, Seal-point colorpoint.

1994, June 6 Litho. *Perf. 14*

Sheets of 12, #a-l

1683-1684 A286 Set of 2 16.00 16.00

Souvenir Sheets

1685-1686 A286 Set of 2 11.00 11.00

Birds A287

No. 1687, 200ce: a, Red-bellied paradise flycatcher (b, e). b, Many-colored bush-shrike. c, Broad-tailed paradise whydah (b, e). d, White-crowned robin-chat. e, Violet plantain-eater. f, Village weaver. g, Fire-crowned bishop. h, Shoveler. i, Spur-winged goose (l). j, African crake. k, King reed-hen. l, Tiger bittern.

No. 1688, 200ce: a, Moho. b, Superb sunbird. c, Blue-breasted kingfisher. d, Blue cuckoo-shrike. e, Blue plantain-eater (d, g). f, Greater flamingo (i). g, Lily-trotter (j). h, Night heron. i, Black-winged stilt (l). j, White-spotted pigmy rail. k, Pigmy goose. k, Angola pitta.

No. 1689, 2000ce, Goliath heron. No. 1690, 2000ce, African spoonbill.

1994, June 13 Sheets of 12, #a-l

1687-1688 A287 Set of 2 19.00 19.00

Souvenir Sheets

1689-1690 A287 Set of 2 12.50 12.50

4th Republic, 1st Anniv. A288

Designs: 50ce, Rural water projects. 100ce, Honoring farmers. 200ce, Rural electrification. 600ce, Rural bridge construction. 800ce, Natl. Theater. 1000ce, Lighting Perpetual Flame.

1994, July 11 Litho. *Perf. 14*

1691-1696 A288 Set of 6 6.50 6.50

D-Day, 50th Anniv. A289

Designs: 60ce, 15-inch Monitor HMS Roberts fires on Houlgate Battery. 100ce, HMS Warspite hits Villerville. 200ce, Flagship USS Augusta.

1500ce, USS Nevada bombards Utah Beach.

1994, July 4 Litho. *Perf. 14*

1697-1699 A289 Set of 3 3.75 3.75

Souvenir Sheet

1700 A289 1500ce multicolored 7.00 7.00

First Manned Moon Landing, 25th Anniv. A290

No. 1701 — German, Japanese, scientist-astronauts: a, Sigmund Jahn. b, Ulf Merbold. c, Hans Wilhelm Schlegal. d, Ulrich Walter. e, Reinhard Furrer. f, Ernst Messerschmid. g, Mamoru Mohri. h, Klaus-Dietrich Flade. i, Chaiki Naito-Mukai.

2000ce, "Frau im Mond."

1994, July 4

1701 A290 300ce Sheet of 9, #a.-i. 8.75 8.75

Souvenir Sheet

1702 A290 2000ce multicolored 8.00 8.00

Duiker Antelopes A291

Designs: 50ce, Crowned. 100ce, Red-flanked. 200ce, Yellow-backed. 400ce, Ogilby's. 600ce, Bay. 800ce, Jentink's.

No. 1709, 2000ce, Cephalophus natalensis. No. 1710, 2000ce, Cephalophus niger.

1994, May 16 Litho. *Perf. 14*

1703-1708 A291 Set of 6 7.00 7.00

Souvenir Sheets

1709-1710 A291 Set of 2 10.00 10.00

For surcharges see Nos. 2539-2544.

A292

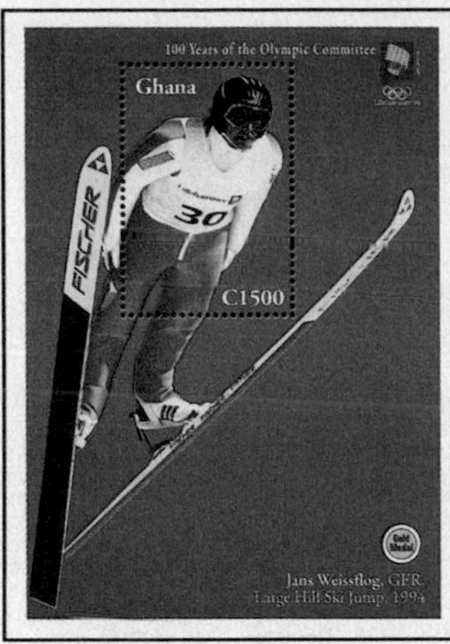

Intl. Olympic Committee, Cent. — A293

Designs: 300ce, Dieter Modenburg, Germany, high jump, 1984. 400ce, Ruth Fuchs, German Democratic Republic, javelin, 1972, 1976.

1500ce, Jans Weissflog, Germany, large hill ski jump, 1994.

1994, July 4 Litho. *Perf. 14*

1711 A292 300ce multicolored 1.10 1.10
1712 A292 400ce multicolored 1.40 1.40

Souvenir Sheet

1713 A293 1500ce multicolored 5.00 5.00

A294

PHILAKOREA '94 — A295

Designs: 20ce, Ch'unghak-dong village elder in traditional clothes. 150ce, Stone pagoda, Punhwangsa, Korea. 300ce, Traditional country house, Andong region.

No. 1717 — Letter pictures, eight-panel screen, Choson Dynasty, 20th cent: a, Shown. b, f, Birds. c, Rooster. d, Animal with antennae. e, g, Flowers. h, Fish.

1500ce, Temple judges determine final afterlife judgments, horiz.

1994, July 4 *Perf. 14, 13 (#1717)*

1714-1716 A294 Set of 3 2.00 2.00
1717 A295 250ce Sheet of 8, #a.-h. 7.25 7.25

Souvenir Sheet

1718 A294 1500ce multicolored 6.00 6.00

Miniature Sheet of 6

1994 World Cup Soccer Championships, US — A296

No. 1719: a, Dennis Bergkamp, Netherlands. b, Lothar Matthaus, Germany. c, Giuseppe Signori, Italy. d, Carlos Valderrama, Colombia. e, Jorge Campos, Mexico. f, Tony Meola, US.

No. 1720, 1200ce, Citrus Bowl, Orlando, FL, vert. No. 1721, 1200ce, Giants Stadium, Meadowlands, NJ, vert.

1994, July 25 *Perf. 14*

1719 A296 200ce Sheet of 6, #a.-f. 4.00 4.00

Souvenir Sheets

1720-1721 A296 Set of 2 7.00 7.00

Christmas A297

Italian art: 100ce, Madonna of the Annunciation, by Simone Martini. 200ce, Madonna and Child, by Niccolo di Pietro Gerini. 250ce, Virgin and Child on the Throne with Angels and Saints, by Raffaello Botticelli. 300ce, Madonna and Child with Saints, by Antonio Fiorentino. 400ce, Adoration of the Magi, by Bartolo di Fredi. 500ce, The Annunciation, by Cima da Congeliano. 600ce, Virgin and Child with the Young St. John the Baptist, by Workshop of Botticelli. 1000ce, The Holy Family, by Giorgione.

Details from Adoration of the Kings, by Giorgione: No. 1730, 2000ce, Presenting gifts. No. 1731, 20000ce, Madonna & Child.

1994, Dec. 5 Litho. *Perf. 13½x14*

1722-1729 A297 Set of 8 9.00 9.00

Souvenir Sheets

1730-1731 A297 Set of 2 10.00 10.00

Intl. Year of the Family — A298

Designs: 50ce, Family. 100ce, Technical training. 200ce, Child care. 400ce, Care for the aged. 600ce, Vocational training. 1000ce, Adult education.

1994, Dec. 20 *Perf. 14*

1732-1737 A298 Set of 6 6.00 6.00

Ghana Civil Aviation Authority, 50th Anniv. A299

Designs: 100ce, Control tower. 400ce, Insignia, marker light. 1000ce, Airplane leaving runway.

1994, Dec. 20

1738-1740 A299 Set of 3 4.50 4.50

See Nos. 1766-1768. For surcharges see Nos. 2548-2550.

Red Cross & Red Crescent Societies in Ghana, 75th Anniv. A300

Designs: 50ce, Transporting victim. 200ce, Aiding mother, children. 600ce, Erecting tents.

1994, Dec. 20 Litho. *Perf. 14*

1741-1743 A300 Set of 3 4.00 4.00

Souvenir Sheet

1744 Sheet of 3, #1741-1742, 1744a 6.50 6.50
a. A300 1000ce like #1743 6.50 6.50

For surcharges see Nos. 2545-2547.

Fertility Dolls — A301

Various carvingswith background colors of: 50ce, Green. 100ce, Yellow (red frame). 150ce, Blue (black doll). 200ce, Rose. 400ce, Dull orange. 600ce, Yellow green. 800ce, Yellow (green frame). 1000ce, Blue (white doll).

1994, Dec. 20

1745-1752 A301 Set of 8 9.00 9.00

Souvenir Sheet

1753 Sheet of 4, #1745, 1748-1749, 1753a 6.75 6.75
a. A301 250ce like #1752 1.60 1.60

For surcharges see Nos. 2551-2558.

Donald Duck, 60th Birthday (in 1994) — A302

Designs: 40ce, Pluto, Donald, Chip 'n Dale. 50ce, Mickey, pup. 60ce, Daisy. 100ce, Goofy. 150ce, Goofy, diff. 250ce, Donald, Goofy. 400ce, Ludwig Von Drake, Pluto. 500ce, Gramdma Duck, pups. 1000ce, Mickey, Minnie. 1500ce, Pluto.

No. 1764, 2000ce, Daisy, Donald, cake, Mickey, vert. No. 1765, 2000ce, Donald holding fork, spoon, vert.

1995, Feb. 2 Litho. *Perf. 14x13½*

1754-1763 A302 Set of 10 10.00 10.00

Souvenir Sheets

Perf. 13½x14

1764-1765 A302 Set of 2 10.50 10.50

Civil Aviation Authority Type of 1994 with ICAO Emblem and New Inscription

Designs: 100ce, Like #1738. 400ce, Like #1739. 1000ce, Like #1740.

1994, Dec. 20 Litho. *Perf. 14*

1766-1768 A299 Set of 3 9.00 9.00

Nos. 1766-1768 are inscribed "50th Anniversary of The International Civil Aviation Organization (ICAO)."

For surcharges see Nos. 2559-2561.

Panafest '94 — A303

Designs: 50ce, Northern region dancer. 100ce, Relics with landmark. 200ce, Chief sitting in state. 400ce, Royalist ceremonial dress. 600ce, Cape Coast Castle. 800ce, Clay figurines of West Africa.

1994, Dec. 9 Litho. *Perf. 13½*

1769-1774 A303 Set of 6 8.50 8.50

Pan African Historical Theatre Festival, Dec. 1994.

Forts A304

Castles A305

Forts: 50ce, Apolonia, Beyin. 200ce, Patience, Apam. 250ce, Amsterdam, Kormantin. 300ce, St. Jago, Elmina. 400ce, William, Anomabo. 600ce, Kumasi.

Castles: 150ce, Cochem, Germany. 600ce, Hohenzollern, Germany. 800ce, Uwajima, Japan. 100ce, Hohenschwangau, Germany.

Castles: No. 1785a, Windsor, England. b, Osaka, Japan. c, Vaj Dahunyad, Hungary. d, Karlstejn, Czech Republic. e, Kronborg, Denmark. f, Alcazar of Segovia, Spain. g, Chambourd, France. h, Linderhof, Bavaria. i, Red Fort, India.

No. 1786, 800ce, Elmira Castle. No. 1787, 1000ce, Fort St. Antonio, Axim. No. 1788, 2500ce, Himeji Castle, Japan. No. 1789, 2500ce, Neuschwanstein Castle, Germany.

1995, Apr. 3 *Perf. 14*

1775-1780 A304 Set of 6 5.50 5.50
1781-1784 A305 Set of 4 8.00 8.00
1785 A305 500ce Sheet of 9, #a.-i. 11.00 11.00

Souvenir Sheets

1786-1787 A304 Set of 2 4.50 4.50
1788-1789 A305 Set of 2 8.50 8.50

Water Birds A306

Designs: 200ce, Eurasian pochard. 500ce, Maccoa duck. 800ce, Cape shoveler. 1000ce, Red-crested pochard.

No. 1794: a, African pygmy goose. b, Southern pochard. c, Cape teal. d, Ruddy shelduck. e, Fulvous whistling duck. f, White-faced whistling geese. g, Ferruginous white-eye. h, Hottentot teal. i, African black duck. j, Yellow-billed duck. k, White-checked pintail duck. l, Hartlaub's duck.

No. 1795, 2500ce, Roseate tern. No. 1796, 2500ce, Northern shoveler.

1995, Apr. 28

1790-1793 A306 Set of 4 7.00 7.00
1794 A306 400ce Sheet of 12, #a.-l. 10.50 10.50

Souvenir Sheets

1795-1796 A306 Set of 2 11.00 11.00

Nos. 1794-1796 have a continuous design. Nos. 1790-1793 have a white border.

1996 Summer Olympics, Atlanta A307 A308

Athletes: 500ce, Carl Lewis. 800ce, Eric Liddell. 900ce, Runner. 1000ce, Jim Thorpe.

No. 1801: a, Cycling. b, Archery. c, Diving. d, Swimming. e, Gymnastics-Floor Exercise. f, Fencing. g, Boxing. h, Gymnastics-Rings. i, Javelin. j, Tennis. k, Soccer. l, Equestrian.

No. 1802, 1200ce, John Akii Bua. No. 1803, 1200ce, Pierre de Cobertin.

1995, May 2

1797-1800 A307 Set of 4 6.50 6.50

1801 A308 300ce Sheet of 12, #a.-l. 7.50 7.50

Souvenir Sheets

1802-1803 A308 Set of 2 5.00 5.00

UN, 50th Anniv. — A309

No. 1804 — Secretaries General: a, 200ce, Trygve Lie, Norway, 1946-52. b, 300ce, Dag Hammarskjold, Sweden, 1953-61. c, 400ce, U Thant, Burma, 1961-71. d, 500ce, Kurt Waldheim, Austria, 1972-81. e, 600ce, Javier Perez de Cuellar, Peru, 1982-91. f, 800ce, Boutros Boutros-Ghali, Egypt, 1992-.

No. 1805, UN flag, horiz.

1995, July 6 Litho. *Perf. 14*

1804 A309 Sheet of 6, #a.-f. 6.00 6.00

Souvenir Sheet

1805 A309 1200ce multicolored 3.00 3.00

Miniature Sheets

A310

End of World War II, 50th Anniv. — A311

No. 1806 — Military decorations: a, US Navy Cross, US Purple Heart. b, UK Air Force Cross, UK Distinguished Flying Cross. c, US Navy and Marine Corps Medal, US Distinguished Service Cross. d, UK Distinguished Service Medal, UK Distinguished Conduct Medal. e, UK Military Medal, UK Military Cross. f, UK Distinguished Service Cross, UK Distinguished Service Order.

No. 1807: a, Churchill. b, Eisenhower. c, Air Chief Marshall Sir Arthur Tedder. d, Montgomery. e, Bradley. f, de Gaulle. g, French Resistance Organization. h, Patton.

No. 1808, 1200ce, U.S. Medal of Honor. No. 1809, 1200ce, Fuhrer's promise.

1995, July 6 Litho. *Perf. 14*

1806 A310 500ce Sheet of 6, #a.-f. + label 7.50 7.50

1807 A311 400ce Sheet of 8, #a.-h. + label 7.50 7.50

Souvenir Sheets

1808-1809 A310 Set of 2 6.50 6.50

No. 1809 contains one 42x56mm stamp.

FAO, 50th Anniv. A312

Designs: 200ce, Fish preservation. 300ce, Fishing. 400ce, Ox-drawn plow. 600ce, Harvesting. 800ce, Aforestation.

2000ce, Boat, shoreline, oxen, fruit.

1995, July 6 Litho. *Perf. 14*

1810-1814 A312 Set of 5 4.75 4.75

Souvenir Sheet

1815 A312 2000ce multicolored 4.00 4.00

For surcharges see Nos. 2534-2538.

Rotary Intl., 90th Anniv. A313

Designs: 600ce, Natl. flag, Rotary emblem. 1200ce, Rotary emblem on banner, vert.

1995, July 6

1816 A313 600ce multicolored 1.75 1.75

Souvenir Sheet

1817 A313 1200ce multicolored 3.00 3.00

1995 Boy Scout Jamboree, Holland — A314

No. 1818: a, 400ce, Two boys. 800ce, Two boys, one wearing glasses. c, 1000ce, Two boys facing left.

1200ce, Boy with bamboo poles.

1995, July 6

1818 A314 Strip of 3, #a.-c. 4.50 4.50

Souvenir Sheet

1819 A314 1200ce multicolored 4.00 4.00

No. 1818 is a continuous design.

Queen Mother, 95th Birthday — A315

No. 1820: a, Drawing. b, Bright green blue hat. c, Formal portrait. d, Coral outfit.

2500ce, Pale blue outfit.

1995, July 6 *Perf. 13½x14*

1820 A315 600ce Strip or block of 4, #a.-d. 5.00 5.00

Souvenir Sheet

1821 A315 2500ce multicolored 4.50 4.50

No. 1820 was issued in sheets of 8 stamps.

For surcharges see Nos. 2333-2334.

Singapore '95 — A316

No. 1822, 400ce: a, Seismosaurus (d-f). b, Supersaurus (a, d). c, Ultrasaurus (f). d, Saurolophus (e). e, Lambeosaurus (d, g-h). f, Parasaurolophus (e, i). g, Triceratops (h). h, Styracosaurus (e, g i). i, Pachyrhinosaurus (h).

No. 1823, 400ce: a, Peteinosaurus (b, d-e). b, Quetzalcoatlus (a, c, e). c, Eudimorphodon (b). d, Allosaurus (e-f, h-i). e, Daspletosaurus (f). f, Tarbosaurus (i). g, Velociraptor (h-i). h, Herrerasaurus (i). i, Coelophysis.

No. 1824, 2500ce, Albertosaur. No. 1825, 2500ce, Tyrannosaurus rex.

1995, Aug. 8 Litho. *Perf. 14*

Sheets of 9, #a-i

1822-1823 A316 Set of 2 15.00 15.00

Souvenir Sheets

1824-1825 A316 Set of 2 10.00 10.00

Nobel Prize Recipients — A317

No. 1826: a, Nelson Mandela, peace, 1993. b, Albert Schweitzer, peace, 1952. c, Wole Soyinka, literature, 1986. d, Emil Fischer, chemistry, 1902. e, Rudolf Mossbauer, physics, 1961. f, Archbishop Desmond Tutu, peace, 1984. g, Max Born, physics, 1954. h, Max Planck, physics, 1918. i, Hermann Hesse, literature, 1946.

1200ce, Paul Ehrlich, medicine, 1908.

1995, Oct. 2 Litho. *Perf. 14*

1826 A317 400ce Sheet of 9, #a.-i. 9.00 9.00

Souvenir Sheet

1827 A317 1200ce multi 3.50 3.50

Asantehene, 25th Anniv. — A318

Designs: 50ce, Emblem. 100ce, Silver casket. 200ce, Golden stool. 400ce, Busummuru sword bearer. 600ce, 800ce, Diff. portraits of Otumfuo Opoku Ware II. 1000ce, Mponponsuo sword bearer.

1995 *Perf. 13½x13*

1828-1834 A318 Set of 7 7.00 7.00

A319

Fauna — A319a

Designs: 400ce, Cymothoe beckeri. 500ce, Graphium policene. 1000ce, Urotriorchis macrourus, vert. 2000ce, Xiphias gladius. 3000ce, Monodoctylus sabee. 5000ce, Ardea purpurea, vert.

400ce exists in two types:

Type I — Large flower bud under second "A" in "Ghana," the top of which is above cross line of "A" (shown in illustration).

Type II — Small flower bud under second "A" in "Ghana," the top of which is below cross line of "A."

Perf. 14¼x13¾, 13¾x14¼

1995, June 19 Litho.

1835 A319 400ce multi .80 .80

1835A A319 400ce multi, type II —

1836 A319 500ce multi 1.00 1.00

1837 A319 1000ce multi 2.00 2.00

a. Perf. 11½

1838 A319a 2000ce multi 4.25 4.25

1839 A319 3000ce multi 6.00 6.00

1840 A319 5000ce multi 10.00 10.00

Nos. 1835-1840 (7) 24.05 24.05

No. 1838 has denomination at left. Compare with type A503. No. 1840 has green frame and "A's" of "Ghana" with cross lines sloping down to right.

Christmas A320

Details or entire paintings: 50ce, The Infant Jesus and the Young St. John, by Murillo. 80ce, Rest on Flight to Egypt, by Memling. 300ce, Sacred Family, by Van Dyck. 600ce, The Virgin and the Infant, by Uccello. 800ce, The Virgin and the Infant, by Van Eyck. 1000ce, Head of Christ, by Rembrandt.

No. 1847, 2500ce, Madonna, by Montagna. No. 1848, 2500ce, The Holy Family, by Pulzone.

1995, Dec. 1 Litho. *Perf. 13½x14*

1841-1846 A320 Set of 6 6.00 6.00

Souvenir Sheets

1847-1848 A320 Set of 2 17.00 17.00

Motion Pictures, Cent. A321

No. 1849: a, 1903 H. Ernmann camera. b, Charles Chaplin. c, Rudolph Valentino. d, Will Rogers. e, Greta Garbo. f, Jackie Cooper. g, Bette Davis. h, John Barrymore. i, Shirley Temple.

No. 1850, Laurel and Hardy.

1995, Dec. 8

1849 A321 400ce Sheet of 9, #a.-i. 10.50 10.50

Souvenir Sheet

1850 A321 2500ce multi 7.00 7.00

A322

John Lennon (1940-80) A323

No. 1852: a-g, i, Various portraits. h, Like No. 1851.

2000ce, Lennon playing guitar, water in background.

1995, Dec. 8 *Perf. 14*

1851 A322 400ce shown 3.50 3.50

Miniature Sheet
Perf. 13½x14

1852 A323 400ce Sheet of 9, #a.-i. 12.00 12.00

Souvenir Sheet

1853 A323 2000ce multi 9.00 9.00

No. 1851 was issued in sheets of 16.

Louis Pasteur (1822-95) — A324

No. 1854: a, In laboratory. b, Discovery of rabies virus and vaccine. c, Pneumococcus discovery, 1880. d, Development of first vaccine with birds. e, Perfection of brewer's yeast culture.

1995, Dec. 13 *Perf. 14*

1854 A324 600ce Sheet of 5, #a.-e. 7.25 7.25

Paintings from the Metropolitan Museum of Art — A325

No. 1855, 400ce: a, Portrait of a Man, by Van Der Goes. b, Paradise, by Giovanni di Paolo. c, Portrait of a Young Man, by Antonello da Messina. d, Tommaso Portinari, by Memling. e, Wife Maria Portinari, by Memling. f, Portrait of a Lady, by Ghirlandaio. g, St. Christopher & Infant Christ, by Ghirlandaio. h, Francesco D'Este, by van der Weyden.

No. 1856, 400ce: a, The Interrupted Sleep, by Boucher. b, Diana and Cupid, by Batoni. c, Boy Blowing Bubbles, by Chardin. d, Ancient Rome, by Pannini. e, Modern Rome, by Pannini. f, The Calmady Children, by Lawrence. g, The Triumph of Marius, by G.B. Tiepolo. h, Garden at Vaucresson, by E. Vuillard.

No. 1857, 2500ce, The Epiphany, by Giotto. No. 1858, 2500ce, The Calling of Matthew, by Hemessen.

1996, Feb. 12 Litho. *Perf. 13½x14*

Sheets of 8, #a-h, + Label

1855-1856 A325 Set of 2 14.00 14.00

Souvenir Sheets
Perf. 14

1857-1858 A325 Set of 2 14.00 14.00

Nos. 1857-1858 each contain one 85x57mm stamp.

New Year 1996 (Year of the Rat) — A326

Nos. 1859-1860 — Stylized rats: a, With musical instruments, on horseback. b, Holding banners. c, Carrying rat in palanquin. d, Carrying box, holding fish.

1000ce, Four rats transporting rat in palanquin, horiz.

1996, Jan. 28 Litho. *Perf. 14*

Country Name in White

1859 A326 250ce Strip of 4, #a.-d. 4.50 4.50

Country Name in Red

1860 A326 250ce Sheet of 4, #a.-d. 4.50 4.50

Souvenir Sheet

1861 A326 1000ce red, pink & yellow 4.50 4.50

No. 1859 was issued in sheets of 12 stamps.

Fauna of the Rainforest — A327

No. 1862, 400ce: a, Ramphastos toco. b, Choloepus didactylus. c, Pongo pygmaeus. d, Spiaetus cirrhatus. e, Panthera tigris. f, Ibis leucocephallus. g, Ara chloroptera. h, Saimiri sciureus. i, Macaca fascicularis. j, Cithaerias menander, ithomiidae. k, Coryptophanes cristatus, gekkonidae. l, Boa caninus.

No. 1863, 400ce: a, Opisthoccomus hoazin. b, Tarsius bancanus. c, Leontopithecus rosalia. d, Pteropus gouldii. e, Rupicola rupicola. f, Pharomachrus mocino. g, Hyla boans, dendrobates leucomeles. h, Lemur catta. i, Iguana iguana. j, Heliconius burneyi. k, Mellisuga minima. l, Propithecus verreauxi.

No. 1864, 3000ce, Sarcoramphus papa. No. 1865, 3000ce, Pteridophora alberti.

1996, Apr. 15 **Sheets of 12, #a-l**

1862-1863 A327 Set of 2 20.00 20.00

Souvenir Sheets

1864-1865 A327 Set of 2 14.00 14.00

China '96 — A328

No. 1866: a, Kaiyuan Si Temple, Fujian. b, Kaiyuan Si Temple, Hebei. c, Fogong Si Temple, Shanxi. d, Xiangshan, Beijing.

No. 1867, Baima Si Temple, Henan.

1996, May 13 Litho. *Perf. 14*

1866 A328 400ce Strip of 4, #a.-d. 7.00 7.00

Souvenir Sheet

1867 A328 1000ce multicolored 5.50 5.50

No. 1866 was issued in sheets of 8 stamps. See No. 1913.

Queen Elizabeth II, 70th Birthday — A329

No. 1868: a, Portrait. b, Wearing blue hat, coat. c, Wearing printed dress, wide-brim hat.

2500ce, Riding in horse-drawn carriage, horiz.

1996, June 10 Litho. *Perf. 14¼x14*

1868 A329 1000ce Strip of 3, #a.-c. 7.00 7.00

Souvenir Sheet
Perf. 14x13½

1869 A329 2500ce multicolored 6.50 6.50

No. 1868 was issued in sheets of 9 stamps.

1996 Summer Olympics, Atlanta A330

Designs: 300ce, Two wrestlers, javelin thrower, Bas Relief, 500BC. 500ce, Wilma Rudolph, gold medalist in track and field, Rome, 1960, Olympic torch. 600ce, The Forum, St. Peter's Basilica, Colosseum, Olympic Stadium, Rome, 1960. 800ce, Soviet flag, ladies' kayak pairs gold medal winners, Rome, 1960.

No. 1874, 400ce — Medalists in swimming, diving: a, Aileen Riggin, springboard, 1920. b, Pat McCormick, platform, 1952. c, Dawn Fraser, 100m freestyle, 1956. d, Chris Von Saltza, 400m freestyle, 1960. e, Anita Lonsbrough, 200m breaststroke, 1960. f, Debbie Meyer, 400m freestyle, 1968. g, Shane Gould, 400m freestyle, 1972. h, Petra Thuemer, 800m freestyle, 1976. i, Marjorie Gestring, springboard, 1936.

No. 1875, 400ce, vert. — Soccer players: a, Abedi Pele, Ghana. b, Quico Navarez, Spain. c, Heino Hanson, Denmark. d, Mostafa Ismail, Egypt. e, Anthony Yeboah, Ghana. f, Jurgen Klinsmann, Germany. g, Cobi Jones, US. h, Franco Baresi, Italy. i, Igor Dobrovolski, Russia.

No. 1876, 2000ce, Kornella Ender, 200m freestyle gold medalist, 1976. No. 1877, 2000ce, Tracy Caulkins, 200m individual medlay gold medalist, 1984.

1996, June 27 *Perf. 14*

1870-1873 A330 Set of 4 4.50 4.50

Sheets of 9, #a-i

1874-1875 A330 Set of 2 17.00 17.00

Souvenir Sheets

1876-1877 A330 Set of 2 11.00 11.00

Intl. Amateur Boxing Assoc., 50th Anniv. — A331

Boxers: 300ce, Serafim Todorow, Bulgaria. 400ce, Oscar de La Hoya, US. 800ce, Ariel Hernandez, Cuba. 1500ce, Arnaldo Mesa, Cuba.

3000ce, Tadahiro Sasaki, Japan.

1996, July 31

1878-1881 A331 Set of 4 6.50 6.50

Souvenir Sheet

1882 A331 3000ce multicolored 6.50 6.50

UNESCO, 50th Anniv. — A332

Designs: 400ce, The Citadel, Haiti, vert. 800ce, Ait-Ben-Haddou (Fortified Village), Morocco, vert. 1000ce, Spissky Hrad (exterior of castle), Slovakia.

2000ce, Capo Coast, Ghana.

1996, July 31 Litho. *Perf. 14*

1883-1885 A332 Set of 3 6.50 6.50

Souvenir Sheet

1886 A332 2000ce multicolored 6.00 6.00

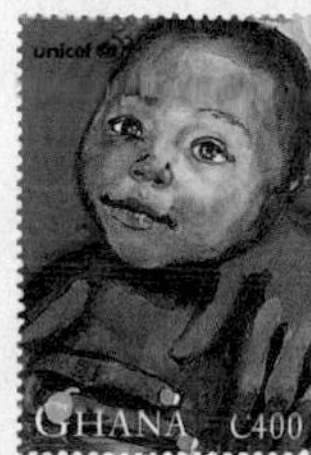

UNICEF, 50th Anniv. — A333

Designs: 400ce, Baby. 500ce, Mother, baby. 600ce, Mother, child drinking from glass.

1000ce, Child, diff.

1996, July 31

1887-1889 A333 Set of 3 3.00 3.00

Souvenir Sheet

1890 A333 1000ce multicolored 2.50 2.50

Jerusalem, 3000th Anniv. — A334

Landmark, flower: 400ce, St. Stephen's (Lion) Gate, Jasminum mesnyi. 600ce, Citadel and Tower of David, nerium oleander. 800ce, Chapel of the Ascension, romulea bulbocodium.

2000ce, Russian Church of St. Mary Magdalene.

1996, July 31

1891-1893 A334 Set of 3 4.50 4.50

Souvenir Sheet

1894 A334 2000ce multicolored 6.00 6.00

For overprints see Nos. 2032-2035.

Musical Instruments A335

No. 1895: a, Fiddles. b, Proverbial drum. c, Double clapless bell & castanet. d, Gourd rattle. e, Horns.

1996, Aug. 5

1895 A335 500ce Sheet of 5, #a.-e. 5.00 5.00

Disney's Best Friends — A336

No. 1896, 60ce, Ariel, Flounder, Sebastian. No. 1897, 60ce, Pinocchio, Jiminy Cricket. No. 1898, 60ce, Cogsworth, Lumiere. No. 1899, 60ce, Copper, Tod. No. 1900, 60ce, Pocahontas, Meeko, Flit. No. 1901, 60ce, Bambi, Flower, Thumper.

No. 1902: a, 450ce, Pocahontas, Meeko, Flit. b, 150ce, Pinocchio, Jiminy Cricket. c, 200ce, Copper, Tod. d, 600ce, Aladdin, Abu. e, 700ce, Penny, Rufus. f, 350ce, Cogsworth, Lumiere. g, 800ce, Mowgli, Baloo. h, 200ce, Ariel, Flounder, Sebastian. i, 300ce, Bambi, Flower, Thumper.

No. 1903, Winnie the Pooh, vert. No. 1904, Simba, Pumbaa.

Perf. 14x13½, 13½x14

1996, Aug. 25

1896-1901 A336 Set of 6 2.75 2.75

1902 A336 Sheet of 9, #a.-i. 8.50 8.50

Souvenir Sheets

1903 A336 3000ce multicolored 4.75 4.75

1904 A336 3000ce multicolored 4.75 4.75

Stampshow '96 (No. 1902).

E.W. Agyare (1937-72), Ghana Broadcasting Corp. Technician — A337

1996, July 31 ***Perf. 14***
1905 A337 100ce multicolored .50 .50

Radio, Cent. A338

Entertainers: 500ce, Frank Sinatra. No. 1907, 600ce, Judy Garland. No. 1908, 600ce, Bing Crosby. 800ce, Dean Martin, Jerry Lewis. 2000ce, Edgar Bergen, Charlie McCarthy.

1996, July 31 ***Perf. 13½x14***
1906-1909 A338 Set of 4 3.25 3.25

Souvenir Sheet

1910 A338 2000ce multicolored 3.25 3.25

Sylvester Stallone in Movie, "Rocky II" — A339

1996, Nov. 21 **Litho.** ***Perf. 14***
1911 A339 2000ce multi 2.40 2.40

Issued in sheets of 3.

New Year 1997 (Year of the Ox) — A340

Various scenes from Chinese story, "Herd Boy and Girl Weaver."

1997, Jan. 22 **Litho.** ***Perf. 14***
1912 A340 500ce Sheet of 9, #a.-i. 7.00 7.00

Souvenir Sheet

China '96 — A341

Statue of the Devil.

1996, May 13 **Litho.** ***Perf. 14***
1913 A341 1000ce multicolored 3.25 3.25

No. 1913 was not available until March 1997.

African Hair Styles — A342

No. 1914, 1000ce: a, Dipo. b, Oduku. c, Dansinkran. d, Mbobom. e, Oduku 2.
No. 1915, 1000ce: a, African corn row. b, Chinese raster. c, Chinese raster 2. d, Corn row. e, Mbakaa.

1997, Mar. 3 **Sheets of 5, #a-e**
1914-1915 A342 Set of 2 9.00 9.00

Dr. Hideyo Noguchi (1876-1928), Pathologist A343

No. 1916: a, Tomb. b, Portrait. c, Birth place. d, Noguchi Institute, Legon. e, Noguchi Gardens, Accra.
No. 1917, 3000ce, Dr. Noguchi in laboratory. No. 1918, 3000ce, Statue.

1997, Mar. 3
1916 A343 1000ce Sheet of 5, #a.-e. 6.50 6.50

Souvenir Sheets

1917-1918 A343 Set of 2 7.00 7.00

Independence, 40th Anniv. — A344

Designs: 200ce, Emblem. 550ce, Dr. Kwame Nkrumah, first president of Ghana, vert. 800ce, Achievement in education. 1100ce, Akosombo Dam.
2000ce, Declaration of independence, Old Polo Grounds, vert. 3000ce, Kofi Annan, UN Secretary General, vert.

1997, Mar. 6 **Litho.** ***Perf. 14***
1919-1922 A344 Set of 4 7.00 7.00

Souvenir Sheets

1923 A344 2000ce multicolored 2.75 2.75
1924 A344 3000ce multicolored 4.25 4.25

Deng Xiaoping (1904-97), Chinese Leader — A345

No. 1925: a, 300ce, Smiling. b, 600ce, Wearing glasses. c, 800ce, Like #1925b. d, 1000ce, Like #1925a.
No. 1926: a, 500ce, Lips pursed. b, 600ce, Teeth showing. c, 800ce, Like #1926b. d, 1000ce, Like #1926a.
No. 1927, Reading. No. 1928, Hand in air.

1997, Apr. 28 ***Perf. 14x13½***
1925 A345 Sheet of 4, #a.-d. 3.50 3.50
1926 A345 Sheet of 4, #a.-d. 3.50 3.50

Souvenir Sheets

Perf. 13½

1927 A345 3000ce multicolored 3.50 3.50
1928 A345 4000ce multicolored 4.00 4.00

Nos. 1927-1928 each contain one 51x38mm stamp.

Paintings by Hiroshige (1797-1858) A346

No. 1929: a, Nihonbashi Bridge and Edobashi Bridge. b, View of Nihonbashi Tori 1-chome. c, Open Garden at Fukagawa Hachiman Shrine. d, Inari Bridge and Minato Shrine, Teppozu. e, Bamboo Yards, Kyobashi Bridge. f, Hall of Thirty-Three Bays, Fukagawa.
No. 1930, 3000ce, Teppozu and Tsukiji Honganji Temple. No. 1931, 3000ce, Sumiyoshi Festival, Tsukudajima.

1997, May 29 **Litho.** ***Perf. 13½x14***
1929 A346 600ce Sheet of 6, #a.-f. 5.00 5.00

Souvenir Sheets

1930-1931 A346 Set of 2 7.00 7.00

Queen Elizabeth II, Prince Philip, 50th Wedding Anniv. A347

No. 1932: a, Queen. b, Royal Arms. c, Queen, Prince waving. d, Queen, Prince. e, Royal carriage. f, Portrait of Prince Philip.
3000ce, Portrait of Queen Elizabeth II.

1997, May 29 ***Perf. 14***
1932 A347 800ce Sheet of 6, #a.-f. 5.50 5.50

Souvenir Sheet

1933 A347 3000ce multicolored 2.00 2.00

Heinrich von Stephan (1831-97), Founder of UPU A348

No. 1934 — Portrait of Von Stephan and: a, Automobile used for postal delivery. b, UPU emblem. c, First airmail flight, Pierre Blanchard, 1784.
3000ce, African messenger with cleft stick.

1997, May 29 **Litho.** ***Perf. 14***
1934 A348 1000ce Sheet of 3, #a.-c. 3.50 3.50

Souvenir Sheet

1935 A348 3000ce multicolored 3.50 3.50

PACIFIC 97.

Paul P. Harris (1868-1947), Founder of Rotary Intl. — A349

Portrait of Harris, Rotary emblem and: 2000ce, PolioPlus oral vaccine administration, Egypt. 3000ce, Emblem for PolioPlus vaccine, "A world free of disease."

1997, May 29
1936 A349 2000ce multicolored 3.25 3.25

Souvenir Sheet

1937 A349 3000ce multicolored 3.25 3.25

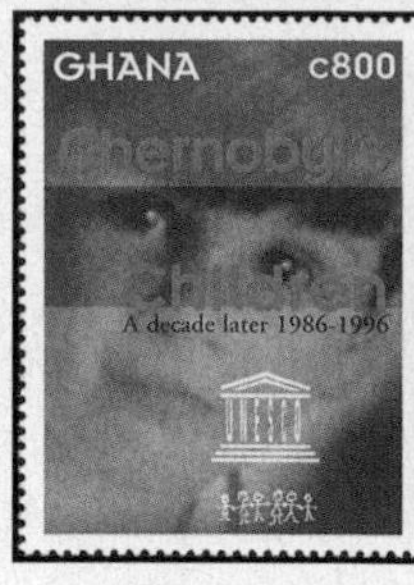

Chernobyl, 10th Anniv. A350

Designs: 800ce, UNESCO. 1000ce, Chabad's Children of Chernobyl.

1997, May 29 ***Perf. 13½x14***
1938 A350 800ce multicolored 2.25 2.25
1939 A350 1000ce multicolored 2.50 2.50

Ajumpan Drums — A350a

Cyrestes Camillus — A350b

Kente Cloth — A350c

Perf. 13½x14¼, 14¼x13½

1997 **Litho.**
1939A A350a 550ce multi — —
1939B A350b 800ce multi — —
1939C A350c 1100ce multi — —

Issued: 550ce, 5/30; 800ce, 6/4. 1100ce, 6/7.
For surcharges see Nos. 2360, 2360A, 2675.

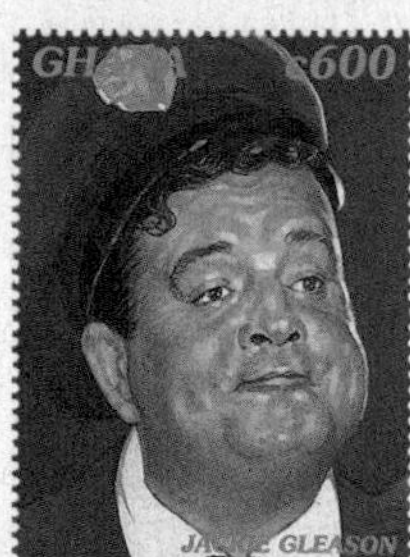

A351

Entertainers — A352

No. 1940: a, Jackie Gleason. b, Danny Kaye. c, John Cleese. d, Lucille Ball. e, Jerry Lewis. f, Sidney James. g, Louis de Fuenes. h, Mae West. i, Bob Hope.

No. 1941: a, Professor Ajax Bukana with fingers making "V." b, Bukana with arms spread.

3000ce, Groucho Marx.

1997, July 1 *Perf. 13½x14*

1940 A351 600ce Sheet of 9, #a.-i. 7.00 7.00

Souvenir Sheets

Perf. 14

1941 A352 2000ce Sheet of 2, #a-b 3.25 3.25

Perf. 13½x14

1942 A351 3000ce multicolored 2.25 2.25

Mushrooms A353

Designs: 200ce, Galerina calyptrata. 300ce, Lepiota ignivolvata. 400ce, Omphalotus olearius. 550ce, Amanita phalloides. 600ce, Entoloma conferendum. 800ce, Entoloma nitidum.

No. 1949: a, Coprinus picaceus. b, Stropharia aurantiaca. c, Cortinarius splendens. d, Gomphidius roseus. e, Russula sardonia. f, Geastrum schmidelia.

No. 1950, 3000ce, Mycena crocata. No. 1951, 3000ce, Craterellus cornucopioides.

1997, July 9 *Perf. 14*

1943-1948 A353 Set of 6 3.50 3.50

1949 A353 800ce Sheet of 6, #a.-f. 5.50 5.50

Souvenir Sheets

1950-1951 A353 Set of 2 6.50 6.50

Fish A354

Seabirds, Marine Life A355

Designs: 400ce, African pygmy angelfish. 600ce, Angelfish. 800ce, Broomtail wrasse. 1000ce, Indian butterfly fish.

No. 1956: a, Violet crested turaco. b, Pied avocet. c, Bottle-nosed dolphin. d, Bottle-nosed dolphin, long-toed lapwing. e, Longfined spadefish (i). f, Imperial angelfish, manta ray. g, Raccoon butterfly fish, African pompano (h, k). h, Silvertip shark (g, l). i, Longfin banner fish (e, j). j, Longfin banner fish, manta ray (f, i). k, Rusty parrot fish (j). l, Coral trout.

No. 1957, 3000ce, Crown butterfly fish. No. 1958, 3000ce, King angelfish.

1997, July 15

1952-1955 A354 Set of 4 3.50 3.50

1956 A355 500ce Sheet of 12, #a.-l. 7.00 7.00

Souvenir Sheets

1957-1958 A355 Set of 2 8.00 8.00

Flowers A356

Designs: 200ce, Eurychone rothschildiana. 550ce, Bulbophyllum lepidum. No. 1961, 800ce, Ansellia africana. 1100ce, Combretum grandiflorum.

No. 1963, vert: a, Strophanthus preusii. b, Ancistrochilus rothchildianus. c, Mussaendra arcuata. d, Microcoelia guyoniana. e, Gloriosa simplex. f, Brachycorythis kalbreyeri. g, Aframomum sceptrum. h, Thunbergia alata. i, Clerodendrum thomsoniae.

No. 1964, 3000ce, Kigelia africana. No. 1965, 3000ce, Spathodea campanulata.

1997, Aug. 1 **Litho.** *Perf. 14½*

1959-1962 A356 Set of 4 3.75 3.75

1963 A356 800ce Sheet of 9, #a.-i. 9.50 9.50

Souvenir Sheets

1964-1965 A356 Set of 2 7.50 7.50

1998 World Cup Soccer Championships, France — A357

Stadiums: 200ce, Azteca, Mexico, 1970, 1986. 300ce, Rose Bowl, US, 1994. 400ce, Giuseppe Meazza, Italy, 1990. 500ce, Olympic, Germany, 1974. 1000ce, Maracana, Brazil, 1950. 2000ce, Bernabeu, Spain, 1982.

No. 1972 — Soccer players: a, Patrick Kluivert, Holland. b, Roy Deane, Ireland. c, Abedi Pele Ayew, Ghana. d, Peter Schmeichel, Denmark. e, Roberto di Matteo, Italy. f, Bebeto, Brazil. g, Stevo McManaman, England. h, George Appong Weah, Liberia.

No. 1973, 3000ce, Juninho, Brazil. No. 1974, 3000ce, Seaman, England.

1997, July 12 *Perf. 14x13½*

1966-1971 A357 Set of 6 4.50 4.50

1972 A357 600ce Sheet of 8, #a.-h. + label 4.50 4.50

Souvenir Sheets

1973-1974 A357 Set of 2 7.00 7.00

Nos. 1966-1971 were issued in sheets of 10 each.

Birds — A358

Designs: 200ce, Eurasian goldfinch. 300ce, Cape batis. 400ce, Bearded barbet. 500ce, White-necked raven. 600ce, Purple grenadier. 1000ce, Zebra waxbill.

No. 1981: a, Black bustard. b, Northern lapwing. c, Sandgrouse. d, Red-crested turaco. e, White-browed coucal. f, Lilac-breasted roller. g, Golden pipet. h, Crimson breasted gonolek. i, Blackcap.

No. 1982, 3000ce, Nectarina famosa. No. 1983, 3000ce, Vidua regia.

1997, Oct. 20 **Litho.** *Perf. 14*

1975-1980 A358 Set of 6 3.50 3.50

1981 A358 800ce Sheet of 9, #a.-i. 8.00 8.00

Souvenir Sheets

1982-1983 A358 Set of 2 7.50 7.50

Cats and Dogs A359

Cats, Nos. 1984-1989: 20ce, Havana. 50ce, Singapura. 100ce, Sphinx. 150ce, British white. 300ce, Snowshoe. 600ce, Persian.

Dogs, Nos. 1989A-1989F: 80ce, Papillon. 200ce, Bulldog. 400ce, Shetland sheepdog. 500ce, Schnauzer. 800ce, Shih tzu. 2000ce, Chow chow.

No. 1990, 1000ce — Dogs and cats: a, Russian wolfhound. b, Birman. c, Basset hound. d, Silver tabby. e, Afghan. f, Burmilla.

No. 1991, 1000ce: a, Abyssinian. b, Border terrier. c, Scottish fold. d, Boston terrier. e, Oriental. f, Keeshond.

No. 1992, 3000ce, Ragdoll. No. 1992A, 3000ce, Alaskan malamute.

1997, Oct. 20

1984-1989 A359 Set of 6 2.75 2.75

1989A-1989F A359 Set of 6 8.00 8.00

Sheets of 6, #a-f

1990-1991 A359 Set of 2 17.50 17.50

Souvenir Sheets

1992-1992A A359 Set of 2 8.00 8.00

Return of Hong Kong to China — A360

No. 1993: a, Lin Tsi-Hsu (1785-1850). b, Gwan Tian-Pei.

1997, Nov. 10

1993 A360 1000ce Sheet of 4, 2 each #a.-b. 7.00 7.00

Huang Binhong (1865-1955) — A361

No. 1994 — Various details of "Color Landscape": a, 200ce. b, 300ce. c, 400ce. d, 500ce. e, 600ce. f, 800ce. g, 1000ce. h, 2000ce.

No. 1995: a, Detail with Chinese inscription. b, Detail without inscription.

1997, Nov. 10

1994 A361 Sheet of 8, #a.-h. 7.00 7.00

Souvenir Sheet

1995 A361 2000ce Sheet of 2, #a.-b. 5.50 5.50

Nos. 1994a-1994h are each 28x90mm.

Christmas A362

Entire paintings or details: 200ce, Cupid by Botticelli. 550ce, Zephyr and Chloris, by Botticelli. 800ce, Trumphant Cupid, by Caravaggio. 1100ce, The Seven Works of Mercy, by Caravaggio. 1500ce, The Toilet of Venus, by Diego Velazquez. 2000ce, Freeing of Saint Peter, by Raphael.

Sculptures: No. 2002, 5000ce, The Cavalcant Annunciation, by Donatello. No. 2003, 5000ce, Isis and Nepthys Protecting the Cartouches of Tutankhamen with their Wings.

1997, Dec. 8 **Litho.** *Perf. 14*

1996-2001 A362 Set of 6 6.00 6.00

Souvenir Sheets

2002-2003 A362 Set of 2 9.00 9.00

Diana, Princess of Wales (1961-97) — A363

Various portraits, background color of sheet margin: No. 2004, 1200ce, Pink. No. 2005, 1200ce, Blue.

Portraits with (in margin): No. 2006, 3000ce, Elizabeth Taylor. No. 2007, 3000ce, Henry Kissinger.

1997, Dec. 22 **Sheets of 6, #a-f**

2004-2005 A363 Set of 2 11.00 11.00

Souvenir Sheets

2006-2007 A363 Set of 2 7.00 7.00

Mickey and Friends A364

No. 2008, 1000ce — Characters, month: a, Mortie and Ferdie, Jan. b, Minnie, Feb. c, Goofy, Mar. d, Mickey, Minnie, & Pluto, Apr. e, Minnie, May. f, Daisy, June.

No. 2009, 1000ce: a, Donald, July. b, Donald and Daisy, Aug. c, Morty and Ferdie, Sept. d, Huey, Dewey, & Louie, Oct. e, Mickey, Nov. f, Mickey & Minnie, Dec.

Characters, season: No. 2010, 5000ce, Daisy, nephews, winter, horiz. No. 2011, 5000ce, Goofy, fall. No. 2012, 5000ce, Mickey, spring, horiz. No. 2013, 5000ce, Minnie, summer.

Perf. 13½x14, 14x13½

1998, Jan. 29 **Litho.**

Sheets of 6, #a-f

2008-2009 A364 Set of 2 16.00 16.00

Sheets of 6 With Added Marginal Inscription

2008g-2009g Set of 2 27.50 27.50

Souvenir Sheets

2010-2013 A364 Set of 4 28.00 28.00

Souvenir Sheets With Added Marginal Inscriptions

2012a-2013a Set of 2 57.50 57.50

Nos. 2008g, 2009g, 2012a, 2013a have added inscription in sheet margin showing "Happy Birthday," Mickey Mouse, and "1998" in emblem.

Issued: Nos. 2008g, 2009g, 2012a, 2013a, 8/4/98.

Trains A365

Designs: 300ce, Union Pacific SD60M, US. 500ce, ETR 450, Italy. No. 2018, 800ce, X200 Sweden. 1000ce, TGV Duplex, France. 2000ce, El Class Co-Co, Australia. 3000ce, Eurostar, Britain.

No. 2020, 800ce: a, SPS 4-4-0, Pakistan. b, Class WP 4-6-2, India. c, Class QI 2-10-2, China. d, Class 12 4-4-2, Belgium. e, Class P8 4-6-0, Germany. f, Castle Class 4-6-0, Britain. g, Tank engine 2-6-0, Austria. h, Class P36 4-8-4, Russia. i, William Mason 4-4-0, US.

No. 2021, 800ce: a, AVE, Spain. b, Class 1600, Luxembourg. c, Bullet train, Japan. d, GM F7 Warbonnet, US. e, Class E1500, Morocco. f, Deltic, Great Britain. g, XPT, Australia. h, Le Shuttle, France/Britain. i, Class 201, Ireland.

No. 2022, 5500ce, Duchess Class 4-6-2, Britain. No. 2023, 5500ce, TGV, France.

1998, Feb. 26 Litho. *Perf. 14*

2014-2019 A365 Set of 6 7.50 7.50

Sheets of 9, #a-i

2020-2021 A365 Set of 2 13.50 13.50

Souvenir Sheets

2022-2023 A365 Set of 2 10.00 10.00

Nos. 2022-2023 each contain one 57x42mm stamp.

Lunar New Year — A366

No. 2025 — Signs of Chinese zodiac: a, Horse. b, Monkey. c, Ram. d, Rooster. e, Dog. f, Ox. g, Rabbit. h, Boar. i, Snake. j, Dragon. k, Tiger. l, Rat.

1998 Litho. *Perf. 13½*

2025 A366 400ce Sheet of 12, #a.-l. 6.00 6.00

Numbers have been reserved for additional values in this set.

Great Black Writers of the 20th Century — A368

No. 2027: a, Maya Angelou. b, Alex Haley. c, Charles Johnson. d, Richard Wright. e, Toni Cade Bambara. f, Henry Louis Gates, Jr.

1998, Mar. 25 Litho. *Perf. 14*

2027 A368 350ce Sheet of 6, #a.-f. 5.00 5.00

Aircraft A369

No. 2028, 800ce: a, Messerschmitt Bf 109 E-7. b, Lockheed PV-2 Harpoon. c, Airspeed Oxford MK1. d, Junkers Ju87D-1. e, Yakovlev Yak-9D. f, North American P-51D Mustang. g, Douglas A-20 Havoc. h, Supermarine Attacker F1. i, Mikoyan-Gurevich MIG-15.

No. 2029, 800ce: a, Breguet 14 B2. b, Curtiss BF2C-1 Goshawk. c, Supermarine Spitfire MK IX. d, Fiat G.50. e, Douglas B-18A. f, Boeing FB-5. g, Bristol F.2B. h, Hawker Fury 1. i, Fiat CR42.

No. 2030, 3000ce, Mitsubishi AGM8 Reisen. No. 2031, 3000ce, Supermarine Spitfire MK XIV, Supermarine Spitfire MK 1.

1998, May 5 Sheets of 9, #a-i

2028-2029 A369 Set of 2 13.50 13.50

Souvenir Sheets

2030-2031 A369 Set of 2 5.50 5.50

Nos. 2030-2031 each contain one 57x42mm stamp.

Nos. 1891-1894 Overprinted

1998, May 13

2032 A334 400ce multi .90 .90
2033 A334 600ce multi 1.10 1.10
2034 A334 800ce multi 1.50 1.50

Souvenir Sheet

2035 A334 2000ce multi 4.50 4.50

No. 2035 contains additional inscription in sheet margin: "ISRAEL 98 — WORLD STAMP EXHIBITION / TEL-AVIV 13-21 MAY 1998." No. 2034 exists with an inverted surcharge.

Ships A370

No. 2036, 800ce — Ocean liners: a, Empress of Ireland. b, Transylvania. c, Mauritania. d, Reliance. e, Aquitania. f, Lapland. g, Cap Polonio. h, France. i, Imperator.

No. 2037, 800ce — Warships: a, HMS Rodney. b, USS Alabama. c, HMS Nelson. d, SS Ormonde. e, USS Radford. f, SS Empress of Russia. g, Type XIV, Germany. h, Type A Midget, Japan. i, Brin, Italy.

No. 2038, 5500ce, Titanic. No. 2039, 5500ce, Amistad.

1998, May 5 Litho. *Perf. 14*

Sheets of 9, #a-i

2036-2037 A370 Set of 2 14.00 14.00

Souvenir Sheets

2038-2039 A370 Set of 2 9.75 9.75

Nos. 2038-2039 each contain one 42x56mm stamp.

Orchids — A371

No. 2040, 800ce: a, Renanthera imschootiana. b, Arachnis flosaeris. c, Restrepia lansbergi. d, Paphiopedilum tonsum. e, Phalaenopsis ebauche. f, Pleione limprichti.

No. 2041, 800ce: a, Phragmipedium schroderae. b, Zygopetalum clayii. c, Vanda coerulea. d, Odontonia boussole. e, Disa uniflora. f, Dendrobium bigibbum.

No. 2042, 5500ce, Cypripedium calceolus. No. 2043, 5500ce, Sobralia candida.

1998, June 2 Sheets of 6, #a-f

2040-2041 A371 Set of 2 11.00 11.00

Souvenir Sheets

2042-2043 A371 Set of 2 12.00 12.00

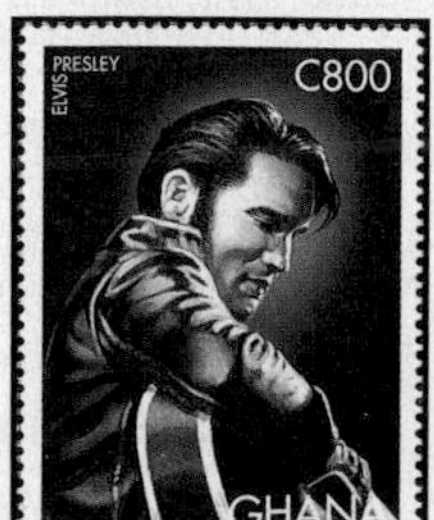

Elvis Presley (1935-77), Television Comeback Special, 30th Anniv. A372

Various portraits during performance.

1998, June 16 Litho. *Perf. 13½*

2044 A372 800ce Sheet of 6, #a.-f. 5.25 5.25

Japanese Flowers — A373

No. 2045, 2000ce — Predominant color of flowers, location of denomination : a, Green (bamboo), UR. b, Red, LR. c, Yellow, LR. d, Pale green & pink, UR.

No. 2046, 2000ce: a, Pale green, yellow & pink, LR. b, Red, UR. c, Pink, LR. d, White, LR.

No. 2047, 5500ce, Small pink & yellow, LR. No. 2048, 5500ce, Pink, UL.

1998, June 2 Litho. *Perf. 14*

Sheets of 4, #a-d

2045-2046 A373 Set of 2 13.50 13.50

Souvenir Sheets

2047-2048 A373 Set of 2 11.00 11.00

Ghana Cocoa Board, 50th Anniv. A374

Designs: 200ce, Tetteh Quarshie, pioneer of Ghana Cocoa industry. 550ce, Ripe hybrid cocoa pods. 800ce, Opening of cocoa pods. 1100ce, Fermenting cocoa beans. 1500ce, Shipment of cocoa.

1998, July 8 *Perf. 13x13½*

2049-2053 A374 Set of 5 5.00 5.00

Metropolitan Assembly, Cent. — A375

Designs: 200ce, AMA Centennial emblem. 550ce, King Tackie Tawiah I (1862-1902). 800ce, Achimota School, Accra. 1100ce, Korle Bu Hospital, Accra. 1500ce, Christianborg Castle, Accra.

1998, July 8

2054-2058 A375 Set of 5 4.50 4.50

Intl. Year of the Ocean A376

No. 2059: a, Dolphins. b, Dolphin (f). c, Seagull. d, Least tern, seagulls. e, Emperor angelfish (i). f, Whit ear. g, Blue shark, diver (k). h, Parrotfish. i, Dottyback. j, Blue-spotted stingray (m, n). k, Masked butterfly fish. l, Jack knife fish (h). m, Octopus (i). n, Turkeyfish (lionfish) (j, k, o). o, Seadragon. p, Rock cod.

No. 2060, 3000ce, Devil ray. No. 2061, 3000ce, Great white shark.

1998, Aug. 18 *Perf. 14*

2059 A376 500ce Sheet of 16, #a.-p. 17.50 17.50

Souvenir Sheets

2060-2061 A376 Set of 2 14.50 14.50

Inventors and Inventions — A377

No. 2062, 1000ce: a, Edison, light bulb. b, Peephole kinetoscope, Edison. c, Tesla coil, Tesla. d, Nikola Tesla (1856-1943). e, Gottlieb Wilhelm Daimler (1834-1900). f, Motorcycle, Daimler. g, Transmitter circuit for telescope, Marconi. h, Guglielmo Marconi.

No. 2063, 1000ce: a, Orville & Wright. b, 1st Flyer, Wright Brothers. c, Neon lighting and signs, Claude. d, Georges Claude (1870-1960). e, Alexander Graham Bell. f, The telephone, transmitter, Bell. g, Various uses of lasers, Townes. h, Charles Townes (b. 1915).

No. 2064, 5500ce, Robert Goddard (1882-1945), physicist. No. 2065, 5500ce, Paul Ehrlich (1854-1915), chemist, bacteriologist.

1998, Sept. 1 *Perf. 14*

Sheets of 8, #a-h

2062-2063 A377 Set of 2 15.00 15.00

Souenir Sheets

2064-2065 A377 Set of 2 10.00 10.00

Nos. 2062b-2062c, 2062f-2062g, 2063b-2063c, 2063f-2063g are each 53x38mm.

Christmas — A378

Cats and dogs in Christmas scenes: 500ce, British colorpoint. 600ce, American shorthair-Dilute calico. 800ce, Peke-faced Persian. 1000ce, Small German spitz. 2000ce, British shorthair blue. 3000ce, Persian Dilute calico.

No. 2072, 5500ce, English pointer. No. 2073, 5500ce, Rumpy max.

1998, Dec. 1 Litho. *Perf. 14*

2066-2071 A378 Set of 6 10.00 10.00

Souvenir Sheets

2072-2073 A378 Set of 2 13.00 13.00

Ferrari Automobiles — A378a

No. 2073A: c, Lampredi. d, 250 GT Cabriolet. e, 121 LM.

3000ce, 365 GTS/4 Spyder.

1998, Dec. 24 Litho. *Perf. 14*

2073A A378a 2000ce Sheet of 3, #c-e 5.00 5.00

Souvenir Sheet

Perf. 13¾x14¼

2073B A378a 3000ce multi 4.00 4.00

No. 2073A contains three 39x25mm stamps.

Diana, Princess of Wales (1961-97) — A379

No. 2074: a, Inscription panel at left. b, Panel at right.

1998, Dec. 24 Litho. *Perf. 14½*

2074 A379 1000ce Horiz. pair, #a-b 3.50 3.50

No. 2074 was issued in sheets of 3 pairs.

Gandhi — A380

No. 2075: a, After 8 month prison term in Poona, 1931. b, On Salt March, 1930. c, Picking up natural salt at end of Salt March, 1930. d, After graduating from high school in Rajkot, 1887.

5500ce, At age 61, 1931.

1998, Dec. 24

2075 A380 2000ce Sheet of 4, #a.-d. 10.00 10.00

Souvenir Sheet

2076 A380 5500ce multi 9.00 9.00

Nos. 2075b-2075c are each 53x38mm.

Pablo Picasso A381

Designs: No. 2077, 1000ce, Collage, Composition with Butterfly, 1932. No. 2078, 1000ce, Sculpture, Mandolin and Clarinet, 1913, vert. 2000ce, Painting, Ballplayers on the Beach, 1931.

5500ce, Tomato Plant, 1944, vert.

1998, Dec. 24 *Perf. 14x14½*

2077-2079 A381 Set of 3 3.75 3.75

Souenir Sheet

2080 A381 5500ce multicolored 5.25 5.25

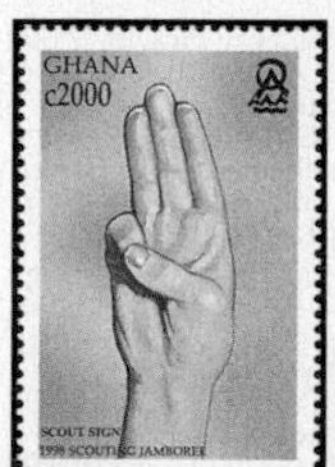

19th World Scouting Jamboree, Chile — A382

No. 2081: a, Scout sign. b, Camping. c, Tying a bowline.

5000ce, Robert Baden Powell

1998, Dec. 24 *Perf. 14*

2081 A382 2000ce Sheet of 3, #a.-c. 5.50 5.50

Souvenir Sheet

2082 A382 5000ce multicolored 4.75 4.75

Royal Air Force, 80th Anniv. A383

No. 2083: a, C130 Hercules. b, Chinook HC2. c, C130 Hercules W2. d, Panavia Tornado F3ADV.

No. 2084, 5500ce, Eurofighter 2000, Chipmunk. No. 2085, 5500ce, Hawk's head, biplane.

1998, Dec. 24

2083 A383 2000ce Sheet of 4, #a.-d. 7.25 7.25

Souvenir Sheets

2084-2085 A383 Set of 2 10.00 10.00

New Year 1999 (Year of the Rabbit) A384

No. 2086 — Scenes showing farmer from "Farmer and Rabbit," by Han Fei Tzu: a, Working in field. b, Watching rabbit run into tree. c, Holding rabbit. d, Dreaming of rabbit.

1999, Jan. 4

2086 A384 1400ce Sheet of 4, #a.-d. 5.50 5.50

Dinosaurs A385

Designs: 400ce, Corythosaurus. 600ce, Struthiomimus. 1000ce, Lambeosaurus. No. 2089A, 2000ce, Hesperosuchus.

No. 2090, 800ce: a, Ankylosaurus. b, Anatosaurus. c, Diplodocus. d, Monoclonius. e, Tyrannosaurus. f, Camptosaurus. g, Ornitholestes. h, Archaeopteryx. i, Allosaurus.

No. 2091, 800ce: a, Pterodactylus. b, Scelidosaurus. c, Pteranodon. d, Plateosaurus. e, Ornithosuchus. f, Kentrosaurus. g, Hypsognathus. h, Erythrosuchus. i, Stegoceros.

No. 2092, 5000ce, Dimorphodon, vert. No. 2093, 5000ce, Apatosaurus.

1999, Mar. 1 Litho. *Perf. 13½*

2087-2089A A385 Set of 4 4.00 4.00

Sheets of 9, #a-i

2090-2091 A385 800ce Set of 2 14.00 14.00

Souvenir Sheets

2092-2093 A385 5000ce Set of 2 9.00 9.00

Australia '99, World Stamp Expo A386

Butterflies: 300ce, California sister. 500ce, Red-splashed sulphur. 600ce, Checked white 800ce, Blue emperor.

No. 2098, 1000ce, vert: a, Red admiral. b, Buckeye. c, Desert checkered skipper. d, Orange sulphur. e, Tiger swallowtail. f, Orange-bordered blue. g, Agraulis vanillae. h, Monarch.

No. 2099, 1000ce, vert: a, Small tortoise-shell. b, Brimstone. c, Camberwell beauty. d, Marbled white. e, Purple emperor. f, Clouded yellow. g, Ladoga camilla. h, Marsh fritillary.

No. 2100, 5000ce, Papilio homerus, vert. No. 2101, 5000ce, Blue copper.

1999, Apr. 26 Litho. *Perf. 14*

2094-2097 A386 Set of 4 3.50 3.50

Sheets of 8, #a-h

2098-2099 A386 Set of 2 16.00 16.00

Souvenir Sheets

2100-2101 A386 Set of 2 10.00 10.00

Shirley Temple as "Curly Top" — A387

No. 2102, vert.: a, Saying prayers. b, Actor John Boles looking at portrait. c, Taking Boles' hand. d, Dressed as old woman.

No. 2103: a, Hugging older sister. b, Dressed as a man. c, Looking at stuffed animals. d, Pulling Boles' tie. e, With family. f, Looking at sister and Boles together.

5000ce, In pink dress, vert.

Perf. 13½x14, 14x13½

1999, Mar. 1 Litho.

2102 A387 1000ce Sheet of 4, #a.-d. 3.50 3.50

2103 A387 1000ce Sheet of 6, #a.-f. 5.50 5.50

Souvenir Sheet

2104 A387 5000ce multicolored 5.50 5.50

Amorphophallus Flavovirens — A387a

1999, May 6 Litho. *Perf. 14x14¼*

2104A A387a 200ce multi —

Trains A388

Designs: 400ce, ICE 2, Germany, 1966. 500ce, M41, Hungary, 1982, 600ce, DVR, Finland, 1963. 1000ce, AVE 100 class, Spain, 1982.

No. 2109, 1300ce: a, EMD GP7 Illinois Terminal RR, 1949-54. b, EMD SD 38-2, 1972-79. c, EMD SD 60M Soo Line, 1989-96. d, GE U25C, 1963-65. e, EMD GP 28, 1961-63. f, EMD SD 9, 1954-59.

No. 2110, 1300ce: a, Conrail EMD SD80, 1993-99. b, Columbus & Greenville RR EMD SDP35, 1964-66. c, Providence & Worcester RR, MLW M420 Loc. Works, 1973-77. d, Missouri Pacific C36-7, 1978-85. e, Alco C-420 Virginia & Maryland RR, 1963-68. f, Reading RR EMD GP30, 1961-63.

No. 2111, 5000ce, Swiss Federal RR Class RE 6/6 Co-Co, 1972. No. 2112, 5000ce, AGP44, ABB Traction, Inc. 1990-91.

1999, May 10 *Perf. 14*

2105-2108 A388 Set of 4 2.50 2.50

Sheets of 6, #a-f

2109-2110 A388 Set of 2 13.00 13.00

Souvenir Sheets

2111-2112 A388 Set of 2 9.00 9.00

Paintings by Hokusai (1760-1849) — A389

No. 2113: a, Girl Picking Plum Blossoms. b, Surveying a Region. c, Sumo Wrestlers (rear view). d, Sumo Wrestlers (front view). e, Landscape with Seaside Village. f, Courtiers Crossing a Bridge.

No. 2114: a, Climbing the Mountain. b, Nakahara in Sagami Province. c, Sumo Wrestlers (2 fighting). d, An Oiran and Maid by a Fence. e. Fujiwara Yoshitaka.

No. 2115, 5000ce, Palanquin Bearers on a Steep Hill, vert. No. 2116, 5000ce, Three Ladies by a Well, vert.

1999, Aug. 3 Litho. *Perf. 13¾*

2113 A389 1300ce Sheet of 6, #a.-f. 6.25 6.25

2114 A389 1300ce Sheet of 6, #a.-e., 2113c 6.25 6.25

Souvenir Sheets

2115-2116 A389 Set of 2 8.00 8.00

IBRA '99, World Philatelic Exhibition, Nuremberg — A390

Exhibition emblem, sailing ship Schomberg and: No. 2117, 500ce, Hanover #1. No. 2119, 1000ce, Lubeck #1.

Emblem, Class P8 4-6-0 locomotive and: No. 2118, 800ce, Hamburg #1. No. 2120, 2000ce, Heligoland #1A.

5000ce, Germany #66 tied to airmail label on cover, vert.

1999, Aug. 3 *Perf. 14x14½*

2117-2120 A390 Set of 4 4.00 4.00

Souvenir Sheet

Perf. 14½x14

2121 A390 5000ce multicolored 4.00 4.00

First Manned Moon Landing, 30th Anniv. — A391

No. 2122: a, Command Module. b, Lunar Module ascension. c, Giant moon rock. d, Lunar module signals home. e, Neil Armstrong. f, One small step.

5000ce, Earth rise, horiz.

1999, Aug. 3 *Perf. 14*

2122 A391 1300ce Sheet of 6, #a.-f. 8.00 8.00

Souvenir Sheet

2123 A391 5000ce multicolored 4.75 4.75

Queen Mother, 100th Birthday (in 2000) — A392

Queen Mother, 100th Birthday (in 2000) — No. 2124: a, Lady Elizabeth Bowles-Lyon with brother David, 1904. b, Queen Elizabeth, 1957. c, Queen Mother, 1970. d, Queen Mother, 1992.

5000ce, Queen Mother, 1970, diff.

1999, Aug. 4 **Gold Frames**

2124 A392 2000ce Sheet of 4, #a.-d. + label 7.25 7.25

Souvenir Sheet

2125 A392 5000ce multicolored 6.00 6.00

No. 2125 contains one 38x50mm stamp. Margins of sheets are embossed.

See Nos. 2273-2274.

Fauna A393

Designs: 200ce, Meles meles. 800ce, Vulpes vulpes.

No. 2128: a, Martes martes. b, Strix aluco. c, Sus scrofa. d, Accipiter gentilis. e, Eliomys quercinus. f, Lucanus cervus.

No. 2129: a, Merops apiaster. b, Upupa epops. c, Cervus elaphus. d, Circaetus gallicus. e, Lacerta ocellata. f, Lynx pardellus.

5000ce, Canis lupus, vert.

1999, Mar. 29 **Litho.** ***Perf. 14***

2126-2127 A393 Set of 2 2.00 2.00
2128 A393 1000ce Sheet of 6, #a.-f. 5.00 5.00
2129 A393 1000ce Sheet of 6, #a.-f. 5.00 5.00

Souvenir Sheet

2130 A393 5000ce multicolored 5.00 5.00

1999

Birds: 400ce, Cyanopica cyana. 600ce, Ciconia ciconia. 2000ce, Aegypius monachus, vert. 3000ce, Garrulus glandarius, vert. 5000ce, Aquila heliaca adalberti.

2131-2134 A393 Set of 4 5.50 5.50

Souvenir Sheet

2135 A393 5000ce multicolored 4.50 4.50

Rights of the Child — A394

No. 2136: a, Child, UN building. b, Dove, earth. c, Mother, child.

5000ce, Child.

1999, Aug. 3 **Litho.** ***Perf. 14***

2136 A394 3000ce Sheet of 3, #a.-c. 7.50 7.50

Souvenir Sheet

2137 A394 5000ce multicolored 5.00 5.00

Souvenir Sheets

PhilexFrance 99 — A395

Locomotives: No. 2138, 5000ce, 232-U1 Four cylinder compound 4-6-4. No. 2139, 5000ce, 0-6-0 Suburban tank engine.

1999, Aug. 3 ***Perf. 14x13¾***

2138-2139 A395 Set of 2 15.00 15.00

Johann Wolfgang von Goethe (1749-1832), German Poet — A396

No. 2140: a, Wagner entreats Faust in his study. b, Goethe and Friedrich von Schiller. c, Mephistopheles disguised as the fool.

5000ce, Faust attended by spirits.

1999, Aug. 3 **Litho.** ***Perf. 14***

2140 A396 2000ce Sheet of 3, #a.-c. 5.75 5.75

Souvenir Sheet

2141 A396 5000ce multicolored 5.00 5.00

Return of Macao to People's Republic of China — A397

1999, Aug. 20 **Litho.** ***Perf. 14x13¾***

2142 A397 1000ce multicolored 3.00 3.00

Issued in sheets of 4.

Save the Ozone Layer — A398

Designs: 200ce, Fish. 550ce, Earth surrounded by ozone layer, man. 800ce, Crying Earth. 1100ce, People holding up shield against sunlight. 1500ce, Objects with ozone-depleting and non-harmful chemicals.

1999 **Litho.** ***Perf. 13½x13***

2143-2147 A398 Set of 5 8.50 8.50

SOS Children's Villages, 50th Anniv. A399

Designs: 200ce, Grandma Alice. 550ce, Kindergarten. 800ce, SOS Children's Village founder Herrmann Gmeiner (1919-86), Asikawa SOS building. 1100ce, Food preparation.

1999 ***Perf. 13x13½***

2148-2151 A399 Set of 4 3.00 3.00

Dr. Ephraim Apu, Musician, Birth Cent. — A400

Designs: 200ce, Apu, clef, note. 800ce, Apu playing Odurugya flute. 1100ce, Apu, indiginous flutes.

1999 ***Perf. 13½x13***

2152-2154 A400 Set of 3 2.00 2.00

Millennium — A401

Designs: 300ce, Millennium emblem, vert. 700ce, Emblem, Kwame Nkrumah. 1200ce, Emblem, University of Ghana, vert.

1999, Dec. 28 **Litho.** ***Perf. 13¼***

2155-2157 A401 Set of 3 6.00 6.00

New Year 2000 — A402

Various scenes from Chinese story, "Daughter of the Dragon King." Stamps from the two sheets are numbered 1-12 in Chinese numeral characters. The numerals are at the bottom of the top group of Chinese characters. See Chinese numerals in Illustrated Identifier.

2000, Feb. 5 ***Perf. 14½x14¼***

2158 A402 1600ce Sheet of 6, #a.-f. 5.00 5.00
2159 A402 1700ce Sheet of 6, #a.-f. 5.50 5.50

Wildlife A403

Designs: 300ce, Black-faced impala. 500ce, Cheetah. 1000ce, Wildebeest. 3000ce, Hippopotamus.

No. 2164, vert.: a, Chimpanzee. b, Boomslang. c, Vulture. d, Leopard. e, Rhinoceros. f, Zebra. g, Crowned crane. h, Lesser kudu.

No. 2165, vert.: a, Purple roller. b, Pelicans. c, Egrets. d, Orange-breasted waxbill. e, Giraffe, f, African buffalo. g, African elephant. h, African lion.

No. 2166, 7000ce, Waterbuck. No. 2167, 7000ce, Ostrich.

2000, Feb. 28 **Litho.** ***Perf. 14***

2160-2163 A403 Set of 4 3.00 3.00
2164 A403 1100ce Sheet of 8, #a.-h. 6.25 6.25
2165 A403 1200ce Sheet of 8, #a.-h. 6.50 6.50

Souvenir Sheets

2166-2167 A403 each 8.00 8.00

Tourism A404

No. 2168: a, 300ce, Building, palm trees. b, 300ce, Mud building, natives. c, 300ce, Elephants. d, 1100ce, Natives. e, 1200ce, Natives carrying animal. f, 1800ce, Natives, diff.

2000 **Litho.** ***Perf. 13x13¼***

2168 A404 Booklet pane of 6, #a.-h. 5.00 5.00
Complete booklet, 4 #2168 20.00

There are 2 types of No. 2168, which differ only by the arrangement of the stamps on the pane. The booklet contains 2 of each type.

Wildlife A405

Designs: 500ce, Zebra duiker. 600ce, Leopard. 2000ce, Bush buck. 3000ce, African wood owl.

No. 2173, 1600ce: a, Blotted genet. b, Tree pangolin. c, Bongo. d, Elephant. e, Flap-necked chameleon. f, West African dwarf crocodile.

No. 2174, 1600ce: a, Lowe's monkey. b, Diana monkey. c, Potto. d, Moustached monkey. e, Thomas's galago. f, Chimpanzee.

No. 2175, 1600ce: a, Gray parrot. b, Hoopoe. c, European roller. d, European bee-eater. e, Blue-breasted kingfisher. f, White-throated bee-eater.

No. 2176, 6000ce, Hippopotamus, vert. No. 2177, 6000ce, Great blue turaco, vert.

2000, May 1 **Litho.** ***Perf. 14***

2169-2172 A405 Set of 4 3.50 3.50

Sheets of 6, #a.-f.

2173-2175 A405 Set of 3 13.00 13.00

Souvenir Sheets

2176-2177 A405 Set of 2 7.50 7.50

Mushrooms — A406

No. 2178, horiz.: a, Slippery jack. b, Violet deceiver. c, Fairy stool. d, Honey fungus. e, Shaggy parasol. f, Russula sp.

No. 2179, horiz.: a, Grisette. b, Common puffball. c, Fan. d, Gray chanterelle. e, Fairies' bonnets. f, Russula sp., diff.

5000ce, Great orange elf-cup. 8000ce, Bitter boletus.

2000, May 15

2178 A406 1500ce Sheet of 6, #a.-f. 6.00 6.00
2179 A406 2000ce Sheet of 6, #a.-f. 8.00 8.00

Souvenir Sheets

2180 A406 5000ce multi 3.00 3.00
2181 A406 8000ce multi 4.00 4.00

The Stamp Show 2000, London.

Eurasian Goldfinch — A406a

2000, June 1 **Litho.** ***Perf. 13¾x13¼***

2181A A406a 300ce multi — —

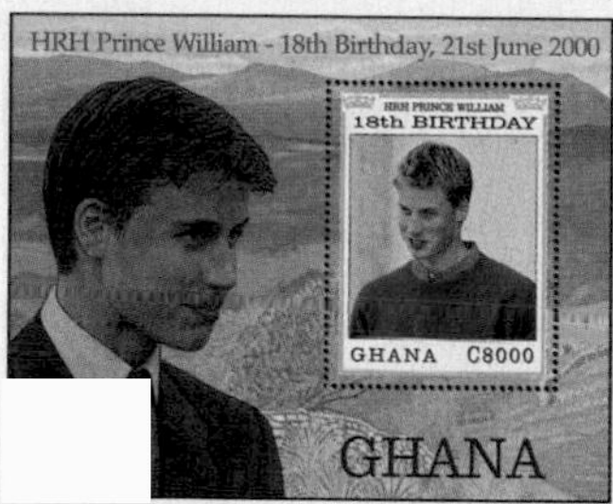

Prince William, 18th Birthday — A407

No. 2182: a, In ski gear. b, With ribbons wrapped around fingers. c, With jacket, no tie. d, Close-up.
8000ce, In sweater.

2000, June 26 Litho. *Perf. 14*

2182 A407 2000ce Sheet of 4, #a-d 5.50 5.50

Souvenir Sheet

Perf. 13¾

2183 A407 8000ce multi 5.50 5.50

No. 2182 contains four 28x42mm stamps.

First Zeppelin Flight, Cent. — A408

No. 2184: a, LZ-129. b, LZ-9. c, LZ-4.
5000ce, LZ-11.

2000, June 26 *Perf. 13¾*

2184 A408 1600ce Sheet of 3, #a-c 3.50 3.50

Souvenir Sheet

2185 A408 5000ce multi 4.25 4.25

Berlin Film Festival, 50th Anniv. — A409

No. 2186: a, Wetherby. b, Die Frau und der Fremde. c, Hong Gao Liang (Red Sorghum). d, Skrivánci na Niti. e, Music Box. f, Tema.
6000ce, Justice Est Faite.

2000, June 26 *Perf. 14*

2186 A409 2000ce Sheet of 6, #a-f 7.50 7.50

Souvenir Sheet

2187 A409 6000ce multi 4.00 4.00

Apollo-Soyuz Mission, 25th Anniv. — A410

No. 2188: a, Apollo 18. b, Docked spacecraft. c, Soyuz 19.
8000ce, Soyuz, Earth.

2000, June 26

2188 A410 4000ce Sheet of 3, #a-c 6.50 6.50

Souvenir Sheet

2189 A410 8000ce multi 5.00 5.00

Souvenir Sheets

2000 Summer Olympics, Sydney — A411

No. 2190: a, Gymnastics. b, Long jump. c, Los Angeles Coliseum, and US flag. d, Ancient Greek chariot racer.

2000, June 26

2190 A411 1300ce Sheet of 4, #a-d 4.50 4.50

Public Railways, 175th Anniv. — A412

No. 2191: a, Marc Seguin. b, Blenkinsop locomotive. c, Pumping station, Dawlish.

2000, June 26

2191 A412 4000ce Sheet of 3, #a-c 7.00 7.00

Albert Einstein (1879-1955) — A413

2000, June 26 *Perf. 13¾*

2192 A413 8000ce multi 10.00 10.00

Ghana Home Economics Assoc. — A414

Designs: 300ce, Women, cooking pots. 700ce, Woman with home economics textbook, vert. 1200ce, Emblem, Alberta Ollennu, Patience A. Adow. 1800ce, Emblems, vert.

2000 *Perf. 13x13¼, 13¼x13*

2193-2196 A414 Set of 4 3.75 3.75

Space — A415

No. 2197, horiz.: a, Mercury. b, Gemini. c, Apollo. d, Vostok. e, Voskhod 2. f, Soyuz.

2000, June 26 Litho. *Perf. 14*

2197 A415 2000ce Sheet of 6, #a-f 7.75 7.75

Souvenir Sheet

2198 A415 2000ce Challenger 51-L patch 6.00 6.00

World Stamp Expo 2000, Anaheim.

Cats and Dogs — A416

Designs: 1100ce, African shorthair. 1200ce, Russian Blue. 1800ce, Basenji. 2000ce, Basset hound.

No. 2203, horiz. a, 1600ce, Weimaraner. b, 1800ce, Keeshond. c, 1800ce, Fox terrier. d, 1800ce, Saluki. e, 1800ce, Dalmatian. f, 1800ce, English setter.

No. 2204, 1800ce, horiz.: a, Silver Persian. b, Creampoint Himalayan. c, British tortoiseshell shorthair. d, American shorthair tabby. e, Black Persian. f, Turkish Van.

No. 2205, 8000ce, Cocker spaniels. No. 2206, 8000ce, Lilac Persian.

2000, Aug. 21

2199-2202 A416 Set of 4 3.25 3.25

Sheets of 6, #a-f

2203-2204 A416 Set of 2 10.00 10.00

Souvenir Sheets

2205-2206 A416 Set of 2 8.00 8.00

Scenes from Tale of the White Snake — A417

No. 2207, 2500ce: a, Xu Xian offers umbrella to White Lady and maid. b, White Lady (with basket) helps husband Xu Xian with business. c, Monk Fa Hai (with necklace) talks to Xu Xian. d, Xu Xian gives wine to wife. e, White Lady becomes snake, Xu Xian has heart attack. f, White Lady (with swords) trying to get medicinal herbs.

No. 2208, 2500ce: a, White Lady and maid at Fa Hai's temple. b, Maid threatens to kill Xu Xian. c, Fa Hai captures White Lady in bowl. d, Maid, Xu Xian at pagoda. e, Maid with sword attacks Fa Hai. f, Maid turns Fa Hai into crab.

Illustration reduced.

2001, Jan. 2 Litho. *Perf. 14*

Sheets of 6, #a-f

2207-2208 A417 Set of 2 8.50 8.50

New Year 2001 (Year of the snake).

Edward G. Robinson — A418

Color of photograph: a, Gray green. b, Lilac. c, Red violet (with hat). d, Brown (with cigar). e, Orange brown (with pipe). f, Blue green.

2001, Apr. 16 Litho. *Perf. 14*

2209 A418 4000ce Sheet of 6, #a-f 6.00 6.00

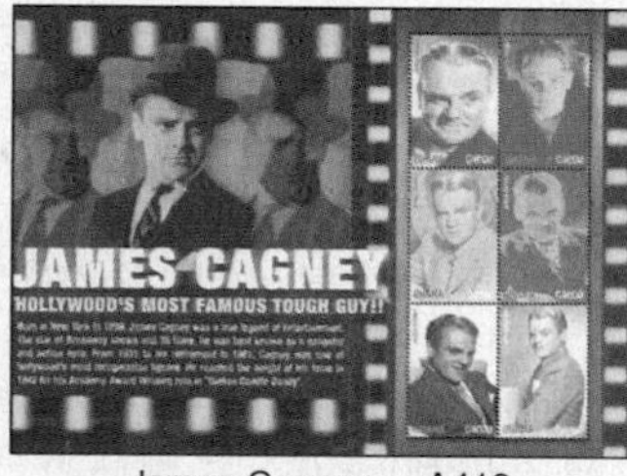

James Cagney — A419

Color of photograph: a, Olive green. b, Emerald. c, Blue. d, Brown. e, Red violet. f, Orange.

2001, Apr. 16

2210 A419 4000ce Sheet of 6, #a-f 6.50 6.50

Millennium — A420

No. 2211, 2500ce — Architects: a, Walter Gropius. b, Aldo Rossi. c, Le Corbusier. d, Antonio Gaudi. e, Paolo Soleri. f, Ludwig Mies van de Rohe.

No. 2212, 2500ce — Artists: a, Wassily Kandinsky. b, Henry Moore. c, Marc Chagall. d, Norman Rockwell. e, Antonio López García. f, Frida Kahlo.

No. 2213, 14,000ce, Frank Lloyd Wright. No. 2214, 14,000ce, Pablo Picasso. No. 2215, 14,000ce, Human Genome Project.

2001, Apr. 16 Sheets of 6, #a-f

2211-2212 A420 Set of 2 8.00 8.00

Souvenir Sheets

2213-2215 A420 Set of 3 11.00 11.00

Jazz Musicians — A421

No. 2216, 4000ce: a, Scott Joplin. b, Clarence Williams. c, Sidney Bechet. d, Willie "The Lion" Smith. e, Ferdinand "Jelly Roll" Morton. f, Coleman "Bean" Hawkins.

No. 2217, 4000ce: a, Kid Ory. b, Earl "Fatha" Hines. c, Lil Hardin Armstrong. d, John Philip Sousa. e, James P. Johnson. f, Johnny St. Cyr.

No. 2218, 14,000ce, Joe "King" Oliver. No. 2219, 14,000ce, Louis "Satchmo" Armstrong.

2001, Apr. 16 **Sheets of 6, #a-f**

2216-2217 A421 Set of 2 12.50 12.50

Souvenir Sheets

2218-2219 A421 Set of 2 7.50 7.50

Oriental Art A422

Designs: 500ce, Cranes, by Kano Eisenin Michinobu. 800ce, Flowers and Trees in Chen Chun's Style, by Tsubaki Chinzan. 1200ce, A Poetry Contest of 42 Matches, by unknown artist. 2000ce, Cranes, by Kano, diff. 5000ce, A Poetry Contest of 42 Matches, diff. 12,000ce, Plum Trees, by Tani Buncho.

No. 2226, 3000ce, vert. — The Tales of Ise, by Sumiyoshi Jokei: a, Chapter 1. b, Chapter 4. c, Chapter 6. d, Chapter 9 (Eastboud Trip, Mt. Utsu). e, Chapter 9, (Eastbound Trip, Mt. Fuji). f, Chapter 9, (Eastbound Trip, Black-headed Gulls). g, Chapter 23, (Crossing Kawachi). h, Chapter 23, (By the Well Wall).

No. 2227, 4000ce, vert. — The Story of Sakyamuni, by unknown artist: a, Siddhartha's Excursion Through the South Gate. b, Siddhartha's Excursion Through the East Gate. c, Siddhartha's Excursion Through the North Gate. d, Siddhartha's Excursion Through the West Gate. e, Sakyamuni Entering Nirvana. f, Untitled.

No. 2228, 14,000ce, Cranes, by Kano (red denomination), diff. No. 2229, 14,000ce, Cranes, by Kano (yellow denomination), diff. No. 2230, 14,000ce, Chapter 1, by Sumiyoshi. No. 2231, Chapter 12, by Sumiyoshi.

2001, Apr. 30

2220-2225 A422 Set of 6 5.75 5.75

2226 A422 3000ce Sheet of 8, #a-h 6.50 6.50

2227 A422 4000ce Sheet of 6, #a-f 6.50 6.50

Souvenir Sheets

2228-2231 A422 Set of 4 14.00 14.00

Phila Nippon '01, Japan.

Automobiles — A423

Designs: 2000ce, 1950 Bentley S Series convertible. 3000ce, 1948 Chrysler Town and Country. 5000ce, 1957 Lotus Elite. 6000ce, 1966 Chevrolet Corvette Sting Ray.

No. 2236, 4000ce: a, 1956-59 BMW 507. b, 1934 Bentley English Tourer. c, 1948 Morris Minor MM. d, 1954 Daimler SP-250 Dart. e, 1950 DeSoto custom convertible. f, 1955-60, Ford Thunderbird.

No. 2237, 4000ce: a,1959-63 Porshe 356B. b, 1962 Rolls-Royce Silver Cloud. c, 1958 Austin Healey Sprite MK-1. d, 1954-57 Mercedes 300SL. e, 1949 Citroen 2CV. f, 1949 Cadillac Series 62.

No. 2238, 14,000ce: a, 1933 Mercedes-Benz. No. 2239, 1953-55 Triumph TR-2.

2001, June 18

2232-2235 A423 Set of 4 4.50 4.50

Sheets of 6, #a-f

2236-2237 A423 Set of 2 12.50 12.50

Souvenir Sheets

2238-2239 A423 Set of 2 7.50 7.50

Belgica 2001 Intl. Stamp Exhibition, Brussels. No. 2238-2239 each contain one 85x28mm stamp.

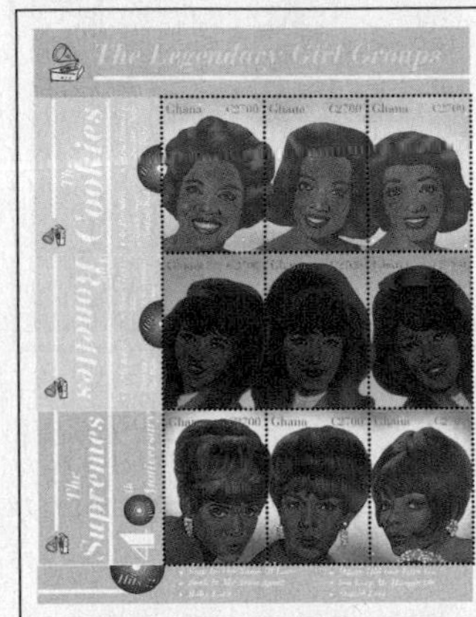

Female Recording Groups of the 1960s — A424

No. 2240 — Various members of: a-c, The Cookies. d-f, The Ronettes. g-i, The Supremes.

2001, Apr. 16 **Litho.** ***Perf. 14***

2240 A424 2700ce Sheet of 9, #a-i 6.50 6.50

Mao Zedong (1893-1976) — A425

No. 2241: a, With arm raised, orange and light orange background. b, Portrait. c, With arm raised, tan gray and blue background.

12,000ce, With flag.

2001, Aug. 27

2241 A425 7000ce Sheet of 3, #a-c 6.00 6.00

Souvenir Sheet

2242 A425 12,000ce multi 3.50 3.50

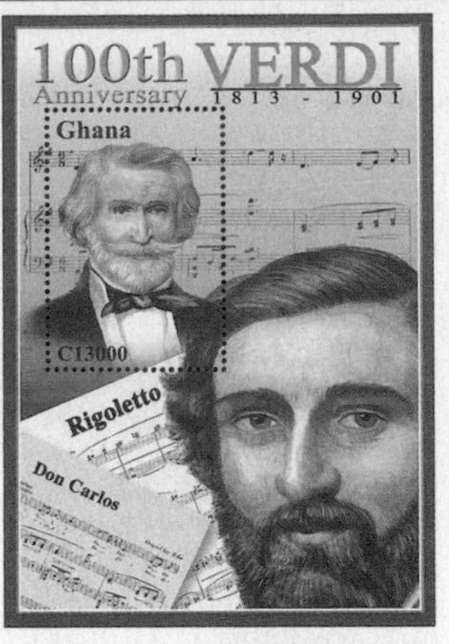

Giuseppe Verdi (1813-1901), Opera Composer — A426

No. 2243: a, Verdi. b, Scores for Aida and Rigoletto. c, Verdi's birthplace. d, Map of Italy.

13,000ce, Verdi and score.

2001, Aug. 27

2243 A426 5000ce Sheet of 4, #a-d 5.50 5.50

Souvenir Sheet

2244 A426 13,000ce multi 3.50 3.50

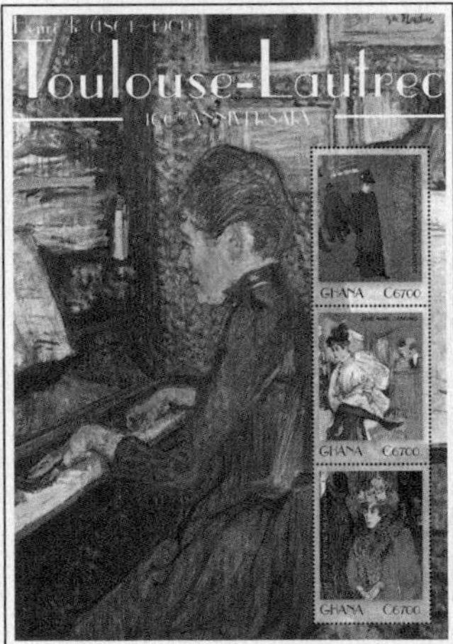

Toulouse-Lautrec Paintings — A427

No. 2245: a, Jane Avril Leaving the Moulin Rouge. b, Jane Avril Dancing. c, Jane Avril Entering the Moulin Rouge.

2001, Aug. 27 ***Perf. 13¾***

2245 A427 6700ce Sheet of 3, #a-c 5.50 5.50

Monet Paintings — A428

No. 2246, horiz.: a, Zaandam. b, On the Seine at Bennecourt. c, The Studio Boat. d, Houses on the Waterfront, Zaandam.

15,000ce, Madame Gaudibert.

2001, Aug. 27

2246 A428 5000ce Sheet of 4, #a-d 5.50 5.50

Souvenir Sheet

2247 A428 15,000ce multi 4.00 4.00

Queen Victoria (1819-1901) — A429

No. 2248: a, Victoria. b, Prince Albert. c, Albert and Victoria. d, Victoria and Albert on wedding day.

12,000ce, Victoria with green and white headpiece.

2001, Aug. 27 ***Perf. 14***

2248 A429 5000ce Sheet of 4, #a-d 5.50 5.50

Souvenir Sheet

2249 A429 12,000ce multi 3.25 3.25

Queen Elizabeth II, 75th Birthday — A430

No. 2250, vert.: a, Bright pink hat. b, White hat. c, Peach hat. d, Crown. e, Blue and pink hat. f, In uniform.

15,000ce, with Prince Philip.

2001, Aug. 27

2250 A430 4000ce Sheet of 6, #a-f 6.50 6.50

Souvenir Sheet

2251 A430 15,000ce multi 4.00 4.00

Whales A431

Designs: 1000ce, Killer whale. 3000ce, Narwhal. 5000ce, Beluga. 6000ce, Bowhead whale.

No. 2256, 4000ce: a, Blue whale. b, Killer whale, diff. c, Northern bottlenose whale. d, Sperm whale. e, Southern right whale. f, Pygmy right whale.

No. 2257, 4000ce: a, Humpback whale. b, Fin whale. c, Bowhead whale, diff. d, Gray whale. e, Narwhal, diff. f, Beluga, diff.

No. 2258, 14,000ce, Sperm whale. No. 2259, 14,000ce, Blue whales.

2001, Oct. 1

2252-2255 A431 Set of 4 6.00 6.00

Sheets of 6, #a-f

2256-2257 A431 Set of 2 19.00 19.00

Souvenir Sheets

2258-2259 A431 Set of 2 13.00 13.00

Rotary Intl. In Ghana, 40th Anniv. (in 1998) A432

Rotary Intl. emblem and: 300ce, Polio victim. 1100ce, Clean water. 1200ce, Founder Paul Harris. 1800ce, Blood donation.

2001 ? ***Perf. 13¼***

2260-2263 A432 Set of 4 2.25 2.25

Orchids — A433

Designs: 1100ce, Paphiopedilum hennisianum. 1200ce, Vuylstekeara cambria Plush. 1800ce, Cymbidium ormoulu. 2000ce, Phalaenopsis Barbara Moler.

No. 2268, 4500ce: a, Cattleya capra. b, Odontoglossum rossii. c, Epidendrum pseudepidendrum. d, Encyclia cochleata. e, Cymbidium baldoyle Melbury. f, Phalaenopsis asean.

No. 2269, 4500ce: a, Odontocidium Tigersun. b, Miltonia Emotion. c, Odontonia sappho Excul. d, Cymbidium Bulbarrow. e, Dendrobium nobile. f, Paphiopedilum insigne.

No. 2270, 15,000ce, Calanthe vestita. No. 2271, 15,000ce, Angraecum eburneum.

2001, Oct. 30 **Litho.** ***Perf. 14***

2264-2267 A433 Set of 4 2.75 2.75

Sheets of 6, #a-f

2268-2269 A433 Set of 2 16.00 16.00

Souvenir Sheets

2270-2271 A433 Set of 2 9.00 9.00

Musical Instruments — A434

No. 2272: a, Bamboo orchestra. b, Mmensuon. c, Fontomfrom. d, Pati.

2001, Dec. 3 ***Perf. 14¼***

2272 A434 4000ce Sheet of 4, #a-d 4.50 4.50

Queen Mother Type of 1999 Redrawn

No. 2273: a, Lady Elizabeth Bowles-Lyon with brother David, 1904. b, In Rhodesia, 1957. c, In 1970. d, In 1992.

5000ce, In 1970, diff.

2001, Dec. ***Perf. 14***

Yellow Orange Frames

2273 A392 2000ce Sheet of 4, #a-d, + label 4.50 4.50

Souvenir Sheet

Perf. 13¾

2274 A392 5000ce multi 3.00 3.00

Queen Mother's 101st birthday. No. 2274 contains one 38x50mm stamp with a darker background than on No. 2125. Sheet margins of Nos. 2273-2274 lack embossing and gold arms and frames found on Nos. 2124-2125.

Kwame Nkrumah University of Science and Technology, Kumasi, 50th Anniv. A435

Designs: 300ce, Emblem. No. 2276, 700ce, No. 2280a, 4000ce, Main gate. No. 2277, 1100ce, No. 2280b, 4000ce, Dairy production. No. 2278, 1200ce, No. 2280c, 4000ce, Pharmacy Department. No. 2279, 1800ce, No. 2280d, 4000ce, Residence hall.

2001 ***Perf. 13x13¼***

2275-2279 A435 Set of 5 2.00 2.00

Souvenir Sheet

2280 A435 4000ce Sheet of 4, #a-d 4.25 4.25

For surcharge, see No. 2683.

Nobel Prizes, Cent. (In 2001) — A436

No. 2281, 4000ce — Chemistry laureates: a, George A. Olah, 1994. b, Kary Mullis, 1993. c, Sir Harold W. Kroto, 1996. d, Richard R. Ernst, 1991. e, Ahmed H. Zewail, 1999. f, Paul Crutzen, 1995.

No. 2282, 4000ce — Chemistry laureates: a, John E. Walker, 1997. b, Jens C. Skou, 1997. c, Alan G. MacDiarmid, 2000. d, Thomas Robert Cech, 1989. e, John Pole, 1998. f, Rudolph A. Marcus, 1992.

No. 2283, 4000ce — Chemistry laureates: a, Walter Kohn, 1998. b, F. Sherwood Rowland, 1995. c, Mario Molina, 1995. d, Hideki Shirakawa, 2000. e, Paul D. Boyer, 1997. f, Richard Smalley, 1996.

No. 2284, 15,000ce, Svante Arrhenius, Chemistry, 1903. No. 2285, 15,000ce, Alfred Werner, Chemistry, 1913. No. 2286, 15,000ce, Peter Debye, Chemistry, 1936. No. 2287, 15,000ce, Wole Soyinka, Literature, 1986. No. 2288, 15,000ce, Nelson Mandela, Peace, 1993.

2002, Jan. 9 ***Perf. 14***

Sheets of 6, #a-f

2281-2283 A436 Set of 3 19.00 19.00

Souvenir Sheets

2284-2288 A436 Set of 5 20.00 20.00

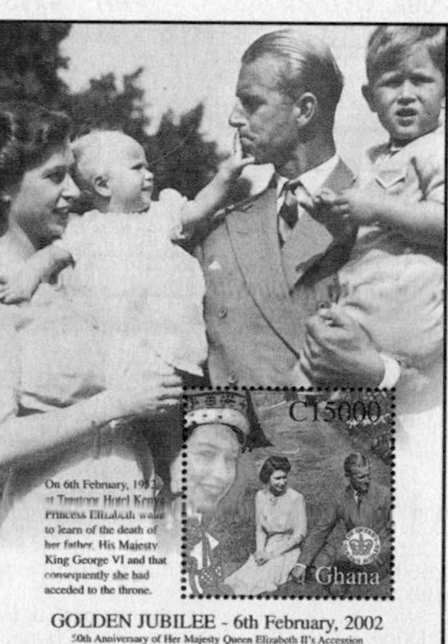

Reign of Queen Elizabeth II, 50th Anniv. — A437

No. 2289: a, Wearing pink dress. b, Sitting on horse. c. Looking at horses. d, In carriage with Prince Philip.

15,000ce, Sitting with Prince Philip (black and white photograph).

2002, Feb. 6 **Litho.** ***Perf. 14¼***

2289 A437 6500ce Sheet of 4, #a-d 7.00 7.00

Souvenir Sheet

2290 A437 15,000ce multi 4.25 4.25

Intl. Copyright Conference, Accra — A438

Designs: 300ce, Conference emblem, vert. 700ce, Person reading. 1100ce, Spider, web, map of Ghana. 1200ce, Map of Ghana, Kente cloth. 1800ce, Drummer.

2002, Feb. 20 ***Perf. 14¼x14, 14x14¼***

2291-2295 A438 Set of 5 1.75 1.75

2002 World Cup Soccer Championships, Japan and Korea — A439

World Cup trophy and: 100ce, Jay Jay Okacha, flag of Nigeria. 150ce, South African player and flag. 300ce, Pele, flag of Brazil. 400ce, Roger Milla, flag of Cameroun. 500ce, Bobby Charlton, flag of England. 800ce, Michel Platini, flag of France. 1000ce, Franz Beckenbauer, flag of West Germany. 1500ce, Ulsan Munsu Stadium, Korea, horiz. 2000ce, German player and flag. 3000ce, Brazilian player and flag. 4000ce, Korean player and flag. 5000ce, Yokohama Intl. Sports Stadium, Japan, horiz. 6000ce, Italian player and flag. 11,000ce, 1950 World Cup poster. 12,000ce, 1934 World Cup poster.

No. 2311, 15,000ce, Geoff Hurst's hat trick for England, 1966. No. 2312, 15,000ce, Gordon Banks making save on Pele, 1970.

2002, Mar. 4 ***Perf. 14***

2296-2310 A439 Set of 15 12.50 12.50

Souvenir Sheets

2311-2312 A439 Set of 2 8.50 8.50

Souvenir Sheet

New Year 2002 (Year of the Horse) — A440

No. 2313: a, Brown panel at L, country name at LR. b, Brown panel at R, country name at UR. c, Brown panel at L, country name at LL. d, Brown panel at R, country name at LR.

2002, Mar. 4 ***Perf. 13¾***

2313 A440 4000ce Sheet of 4, #a-d 4.75 4.75

Visit of Netherlands Prince Willem-Alexander and Princess Máxima to Ghana — A441

Couple: a, With Prince wearing sash. b, Holding hands, Prince wearing hat. c, With windmills and flags. d, At wedding ceremony, with another man. e, In crowd. f, Kissing.

2002 ***Perf. 14***

2314 A441 6000ce Sheet of 6, #a-f 8.50 8.50

Amphilex 2002 Intl. Stamp Show, Amsterdam.

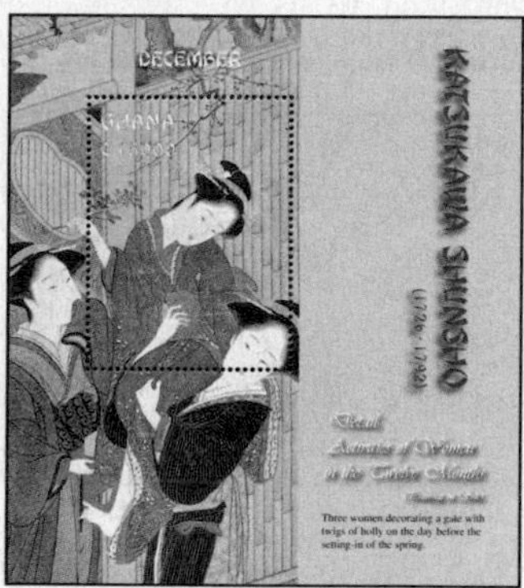

Paintings of Shunsho Katsukawa — A442

No. 2315, 9000ce — Activities of Women in the Twelve Months: a, Trying to retrieve a ball caught in a tree (March). b, Listening to a cuckoo in the bedroom (April). c, Holding a cage filled with fireflies for a woman to read a book (May).

No. 2316, 9000ce — Activities of Women in the Twelve Months: a, Mother and child taking a tub bath while woman holds a revolving lantern (June). b, Strips of paper with wishes and poems are tied on bamboo (July). c, Women enjoying the cool air on a boat (August).

No. 2317, 9000ce — Activities of Women in the Twelve Months: a, Celebrating Feast of the Chrysanthemum (September). b, Looking out for colored leaves (October). c, Mother reading picture book while sitting at a foot warmer (November).

No. 2318, 15,000ce, Three women decorating a gate (woman in blue kimono), from Activities of Women in the Twelve Months. No. 2319, 15,000ce, Part 1 (woman in red kimono) from Snow, Moonlight and Flowers. No. 2320, 15,000ce, Part 2 (woman in black kimono) from Snow, Moonlight and Flowers. No. 2321, 15,000ce, Part 3 (woman in gray kimono) from Snow, Moonlight and Flowers.

2002, July 29 **Litho.** ***Perf. 14¼***

Sheets of 3, #a-c

2315-2317 A442 Set of 3 19.00 19.00

Souvenir Sheets

2318-2321 A442 Set of 4 14.00 14.00

United We Stand — A443

2002, Aug. 15 ***Perf. 14***

2322 A443 7000ce multi 3.25 3.25

Printed in sheets of 4.

2002 Winter Olympics, Salt Lake City — A444

Designs: No. 2323, 7000ce, Figure skaters. No. 2324, 7000ce, Freestyle skier.

2002, Aug. 15

2323-2324 A444 Set of 2 3.50 3.50

2324a Souvenir sheet, #2323-2324 3.75 3.75

Intl. Year of Mountains — A445

No. 2325: a, Tateyama, Japan. b, Mt. Shivling, India. c, Wong Leng, Hong Kong. d, Mt. Blanc, France.

15,000ce, Mt. Fuji, Japan.

2002, Aug. 15

2325 A445 6000ce Sheet of 4, #a-d 6.00 6.00

Souvenir Sheet

2326 A445 15,000ce multi 3.75 3.75

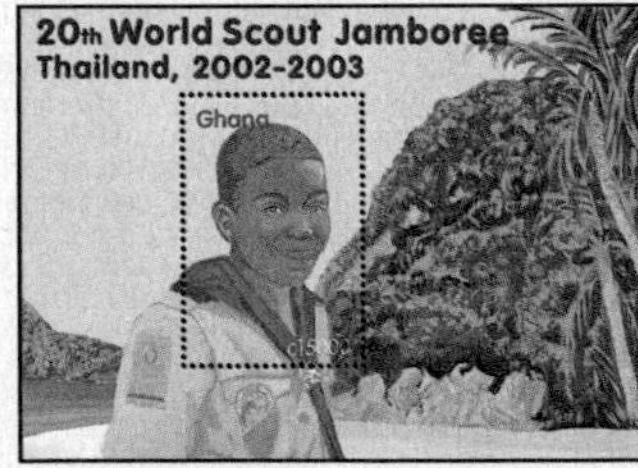

20th World Scout Jamboree, Thailand — A446

No. 2327, horiz.: a, Scout with walking stick. b, Scout with backpack. c, Tent and campfire. d, Tent and scout tying knots.

15,000ce, Scout with red neckerchief.

2002, Aug. 15

2327 A446 6500ce Sheet of 4, #a-d 6.00 6.00

Souvenir Sheet

2328 A446 15,000ce multi 4.25 4.25

First Solo Transatlantic Flight, 75th Anniv. — A447

No. 2329, 8500ce, horiz.: a, Charles Lindbergh and Spirit of St. Louis. b, Charles and Anne Morrow Lindbergh in airplane.

15,000ce, Lindbergh wearing flying gear.

2002, Aug. 15

2329 A447 8500ce Sheet of 2, #a-b 4.00 4.00

Souvenir Sheet

2330 A447 15,000ce multi 3.75 3.75

Intl. Year of Ecotourism — A448

No. 2331: a, Nectarinia venusta. b, Panthera pardus. c, Kobus kob. d, Syncerus caffer. e, Pan troglodytes. f, Galago.

12,000ce, Loxodonta africana.

2002, Aug. 15

2331 A448 4000ce Sheet of 6, #a-f 9.50 9.50

Souvenir Sheet

2332 A448 12,000ce multi 5.00 5.00

Nos. 1820-1821 Surcharged

2002, Aug. 15 ***Perf. 13½x14***

2333	Strip or block of 4	3.00	3.00
a.	A315 3000ce on 600ce #1820a	.75	.75
b.	A315 3000ce on 600ce #1820b	.75	.75
c.	A315 3000ce on 600ce #1820c	.75	.75
d.	A315 3000ce on 600ce #1820d	.75	.75

Souvenir Sheet

2334 A315 20,000ce on 2500ce #1821 5.00 5.00

No. 2334 and sheets of No. 2333 are additionally overprinted in margin with black border and inscription "In Memoriam / 1900-2002."

Butterflies, Moths, Insects and Birds — A449

No. 2335, 4500ce — Butterflies: a, Iolaus menas. b, Neptis melicerta. c, Cymothoe lucasi. d, Euphaedra francina. e, Lilac nymph. f, Mocker swallowtail.

No. 2336, 4500ce — Moths: a, Phiala cunina. b, Mazuca strigicincta. c, Steindachner's emperor. d, Amphicallia pactolicus. e, Verdant sphinx. f, Oleander hawkmoth.

No. 2337, 4500ce — Insects: a, Bush hopper. b, Ant lion. c, Digger bee. d, Stag beetle. e, Mantis. f, Longhorn beetle.

No. 2338, 4500ce — Birds: a, Malachite kingfisher. b, Brown harrier eagle. c, Heuglin's masked weaver. d, Egyptian plover. e, Swallow-tailed bee-eater. f, Black-faced fire finch.

No. 2339, 15,000ce, Giant blue swallowtail butterfly. No. 2340, 15,000ce, African moon moth. No. 2341, 15,000ce, Mantis nymph. No. 2342, 15,000ce, Rufous fishing owl.

2002, Aug. 26 ***Perf. 14***

Sheets of 6, #a-f

2335-2338 A449 Set of 4 25.00 25.00

Souvenir Sheets

2339-2342 A449 Set of 4 14.00 14.00

Edina Bakatue Festival A450

Designs: No. 2343, 1000ce, No. 2349e, 4000ce, Casting of net. No. 2344, 2000ce, No. 2349b, 4000ce, Chief in palanquin. No. 2345, 2500ce, No. 2349c, 4000ce, Regatta. No. 2346, 3000ce, No. 2349d, 4000ce, Festival boat. No. 2347, 4000ce, Opening ritual. No. 2348, 5000ce, No. 2349a, 4000ce, Priestesses.

2002, Oct. 21 ***Perf. 14x13½***

2343-2348 A450 Set of 6 4.00 4.00

2349 A450 Sheet of 6, #2347, 2349a-e 5.50 5.50

Japan Overseas Cooperation Volunteers, 25th Anniv. in Ghana — A451

Designs: No. 2350, 1000ce, Health. No. 2351, 1000ce, Education (Home economics). 2000ce, Education (Science and math). 2500ce, Education (Computer technology). 3000ce, Sports.

No. 2355 (without white inscriptions): a, Like 2000ce. b, Like No. 2350. c, Like 3000ce. d, Like 2500ce. e, Like No. 2351.

2002, Oct. 23 ***Perf. 14***

2350-2354 A451 Set of 5 2.40 2.40

2355 A451 4000ce Sheet of 5, #a-e 5.00 5.00

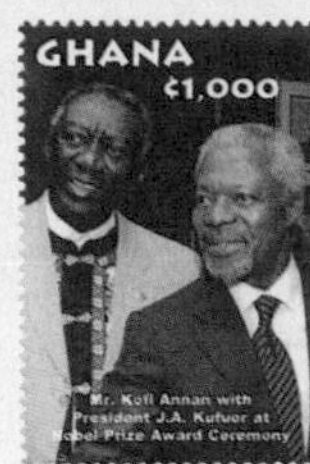

Awarding of Nobel Peace Prize to UN Secretary General Kofi Annan — A452

Designs: 1000ce, With Ghana Pres. J. A. Kufuor at award ceremony. 2000ce, With Nobel medal and citation. 2500ce, Portrait. 3000ce, In academic procession at Kwame Nkrumah University.

2002, Oct. 28

2356-2359 A452 Set of 4 3.50 3.50

No. 1939C Surcharged

No. 1939B Surcharged

Methods and Perfs As Before

2002, Mar. 7

2360	A350c 1000ce on 1100ce multi, 10½x6mm obliterator	—	—
b.	Obliterator 10½x4mm		—
2360A	A350b 2500ce on 800ce multi	—	—

Obliterator on No. 2360 is 10½x6mm.

Charlie Chaplin (1889-1977) — A453

No. 2361: a, In suit and tie. b, As "Little Tramp," wearing hat. c, Wearing overalls. d, Holding Academy Award.

2003, Jan. 14 **Litho.** ***Perf. 14***

2361 A453 6500ce Sheet of 4, #a-d 6.00 6.00

Marlene Dietrich (1901-92) — A454

No. 2362 — Background colors: a, Violet black (hair parted in middle, name at left). b, Gray (wearing scarf, name at right). c, Brown (name at left). d, Dark brown (wearing hat). e,

Blue gray (name at left). f, Brown black (name at right).
15,000ce, Holding cigarette.

2003, Jan. 14
2362 A454 4500ce Sheet of 6, #a-f 6.50 6.50

Souvenir Sheet

2363 A454 15,000ce multi 3.50 3.50

Popeye in Amsterdam — A455

No. 2364: a, Along the canal. b, Anne Frank House. c, Restaurant Row. d, Downtown. e, Central Station. f, Windmills.

2003, Jan. 14 ***Perf. 13¾***
2364 A455 4500ce Sheet of 6, #a-f 6.50 6.50

Souvenir Sheet

2365 A455 15,000ce shown 3.50 3.50

No. 2364 contains six 38x51mm stamps.

New Year 2003 (Year of the Ram) — A456

2003, Feb. 24 ***Perf. 14***
2366 A456 5000ce multi 3.00 3.00

Issued in sheets of 4.

Famous Women — A457

Designs: 1000ce, Nana Yaa Asantewaa (1822-1923), Asante warrior. 2000ce, Justice Annie Jiagge (1918-96). 2500ce, Dr. Esther Ocloo (1919-2002), industrialist. 3000ce, Dr. Efua T. Sutherland (1924-96), playwright. 5000ce, Rebecca Dedei Aryeetey (1924-60), activist.

2003, Apr. 23 ***Perf. 13½x14***
2367-2371 A457 Set of 5 3.00 3.00

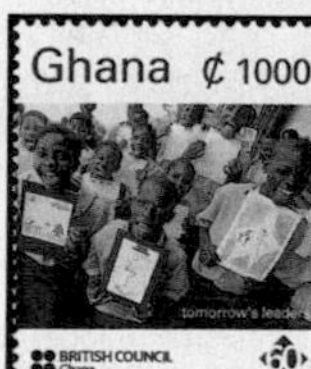

British Council, 60th Anniv. — A458

Designs: 1000ce, Tomorrow's leaders. 2000ce, Women reading Africawoman Newspaper. 2500ce, Partners in culture. 3000ce, Window on the world. 5000ce, Leadership through sport.

2003, June 12
2372-2376 A458 Set of 5 3.00 3.00

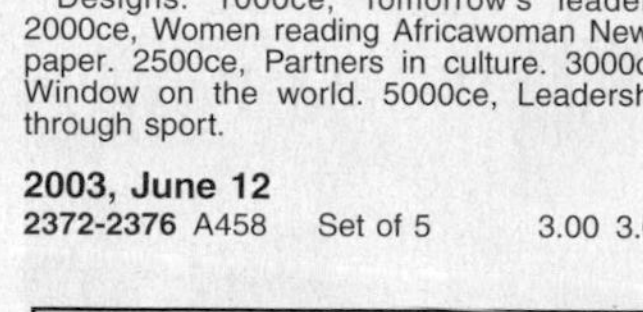

General Motors Automobiles — A459

No. 2377, 7000ce — Cadillacs: a, 1941 Sixty Special. b, 1953 Eldorado. c, 1957 Eldorado Brougham. d, 1959 Eldorado Convertible.
No. 2378, 7000ce — Corvettes: a, 1962. b, 1963 Sting Ray. c, 1964 Sting Ray. d, 1968.
No. 2379, 20,000ce, Cadillac. No. 2380, 20,000ce, 1966 Corvette Sting Ray.

2003, July 2 ***Perf. 13¾***

Sheets of 4, #a-d

2377-2378 A459 Set of 2 13.50 13.50

Souvenir Sheets

2379-2380 A459 Set of 2 8.50 8.50

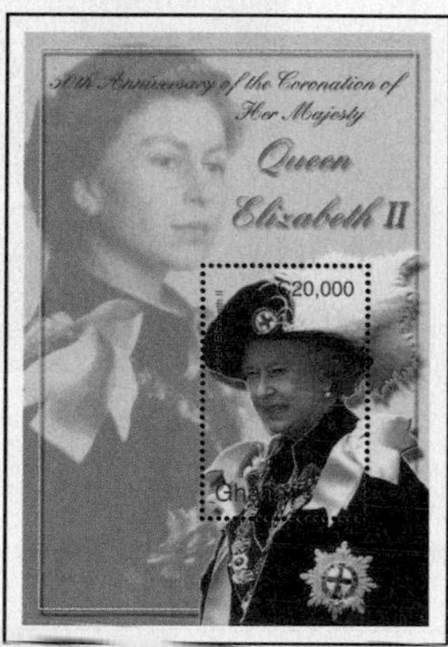

Coronation of Queen Elizabeth II, 50th Anniv. — A460

No. 2381: a, Wearing tiara. b, Wearing blue hat. c, Wearing black hat.
20,000ce, Wearing black hat, diff.

2003, July 2 ***Perf. 14***
2381 A460 10,000ce Sheet of 3, #a-c 7.00 7.00

Souvenir Sheet

2382 A460 20,000ce multi 4.50 4.50

Tour de France Bicycle Race, Cent. — A461

No. 2383: a, Romain Maes, 1935. b, Sylvére Maes, 1936. c, Roger Lapebie, 1937. d, Gino Bartali, 1938.
20,000ce, Henri Pelissier, 1923.

2003, July 2 ***Perf. 13½x13¼***
2383 A461 7000ce Sheet of 4, #a-d 6.50 6.50

Souvenir Sheet

2384 A461 20,000ce multi 4.50 4.50

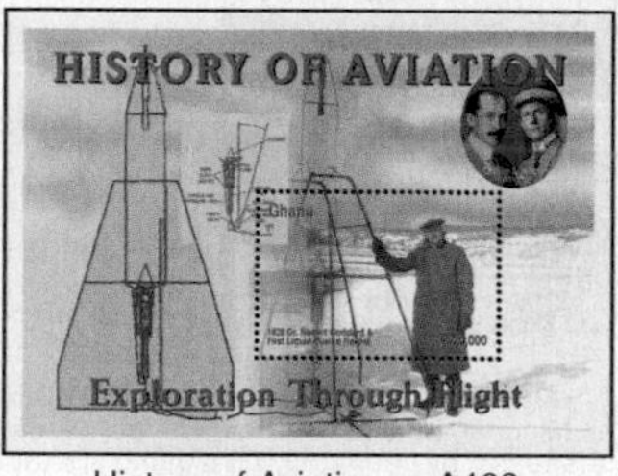

History of Aviation — A462

No. 2385: a, Charles Lindbergh makes first non-stop solo Atlantic crossing, 1927. b, Wiley Post makes first round-the-world solo flight, 1933. c, Heinkel He178, first turbojet powered aircraft, 1939. d, Chuck Yeager flies Bell X-1 to break sound barrier, 1947.
20,000ce, Dr. Robert Goddard and first liquid-fueled rocket, 1926.

2003, July 2 ***Perf. 14***
2385 A462 7000ce Sheet of 4, #a-d 6.50 6.50

Souvenir Sheet

2386 A462 20,000ce multi 4.50 4.50

Christmas A463

Children's art: 2000ce, Preparation for Christmas, by Kwame Owusu Aduomi. 4000ce, Typical Christmas Present, by Thomas Kyeremateng, vert. 4500ce, Making Merry at Christmas, by Samuel Baffoe Maison. 5000ce, Christmas is Here, by Patrick Annan-Noonoo.

Perf. 14x13¼, 13¼x14

2003, Dec. 1 **Litho.**
2387-2390 A463 Set of 4 3.75 3.75

Boletus Edulis — A463a

2003 **Litho.** ***Perf. 14x13½***
2390A A463a 1000ce multi — —

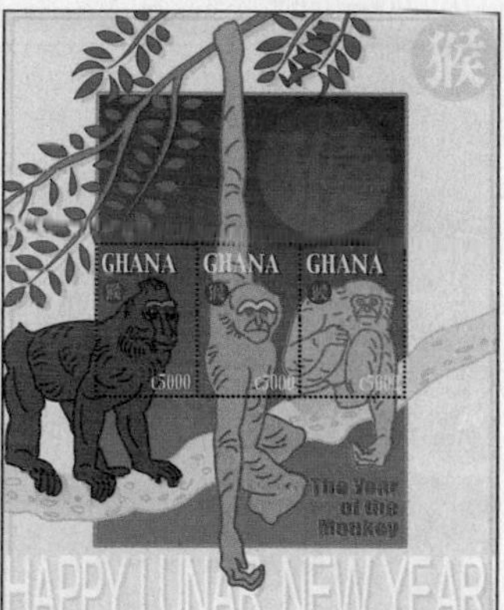

New Year 2004 (Year of the Monkey) — A464

No. 2391: a, Dark gray monkey. b, Light gray monkey. c, Buff monkey.

2004, Jan. 29 **Litho.** ***Perf. 14***
2391 A464 5000ce Sheet of 3, #a-c 5.00 5.00

Chinese Actors — A465

No. 2392, 5000ce — Richie Jen: a, With hair below ears, wearing black shirt. b, With hair above ears, wearing black shirt. c, Wearing helmet. d, With mustache. e, Wearing head covering. f, Wearing red jacket.
No. 2393, 5000ce — Ray Lui: a, Wearing suit and tie. b, With shaved head. c, Wearing black hood. d, Wearing polka dot shirt. e, Wearing costume. f, Wearing costume with red headpiece. g, Wearing costume with wound on forehead.
No. 2394, 5000ce — Jiang Wen: a, Wearing glasses, fingers showing at LR. b, Wearing costume with headpiece. c, Sepia photograph, wearing glasses. d, Wearing suit and tie. e, Sepia photograph, without glasses. f, Wearing striped shirt.

2004, Feb. 1 ***Perf. 13¾***

Sheets of 6, #a-f

2392-2394 A465 Set of 3 21.00 21.00

Kente Cloth Patterns A466

Designs: 2000ce, Edwene Asa. 4000ce, Fatia Fata Nkruma. 4500ce, Asam Takra. 5000ce, Toku Akra Ntoma. 6000ce, Sika Futuro.

2004, Feb. 27 ***Perf. 14x13¼***
2395-2399 A466 Set of 5 5.00 5.00

Hogbetsotso Festival — A467

Designs: 2000ce, Exodus from Notsie. 4000ce, Misego Dance. 4500ce, Royal stools. 5000ce, Pouring libation. 6000ce, King aloft.
No. 2405: a, Pouring libation, diff. b, Togbe Adeladza II, Awomefia of Anlo. c, Display of traditional symbols of wealth. d, Exodus from Notsie, diff. e, Procession of the royalty. f, Royalty at Durbar. g, Ewe cultural dance. h, Bountiful harvest. i, Royal stools, diff.

2004, Mar. 1
2400-2404 A467 Set of 5 5.00 5.00
2405 A467 3000ce Sheet of 9, #a-i 6.00 6.00

Paintings of Scouts by Norman Rockwell (1894-1978) — A468

No. 2406 — Paintings from 1974 Boy Scout Calendar: a, Female scout leader. b, Webelo (plaid neckerchief). c, Boy scout (green cap). d, Cub scout (blue and yellow neckerchief).
20,000ce, Good Friends.

2004, Mar. 18 ***Perf. 14***

2406 A468 7000ce Sheet of 4, #a-d 6.50 6.50

Souvenir Sheet

2407 A468 20,000ce multi 4.50 4.50

Paintings by Pablo Picasso (1881-1973) — A469

No. 2408: a, Jacqueline in a Black Scarf. b, Portrait of Olga. c, Woman in White (Sara Murphy). d, Portrait of Dora Maar.
16,000ce, Portrait of the Artist's Sister, Lola.

2004, Mar. 18 ***Perf. 14¼***

2408 A469 6500ce Sheet of 4, #a-d 7.50 7.50

Imperf

2409 A469 16,000ce multi 4.50 4.50

No. 22408 contains four 37x50mm stamps.

Paintings of James Abbott McNeill Whistler (1834-1903) A470

Designs: 2000ce, Head of a Peasant Woman. 4000ce, The Master Smith of Lyme Regis. 5000ce, The Little Rose of Lyme Regis. 6000ce, Arrangement in Gray: Portrait of a Painter (self-portrait).
No. 2414: a, Rose and Siver: La Princesse du Pays de la Porcelaine. b, Variations in Flesh Color and Green: The Balcony. c, Caprice in Purple and Gold: The Golden Screen. d, Purple and Rose: The Lange Lijzen of the Six Marks.
20,000ce, Harmony in Green and Rose: The Music Room, horiz.

2004, Mar. 18 ***Perf. 14¼***

2410-2413 A470 Set of 4 4.00 4.00

2414 A470 7500ce Sheet of 4, #a-d 6.75 6.75

Souvenir Sheet

2415 A470 20,000ce multi 4.50 4.50

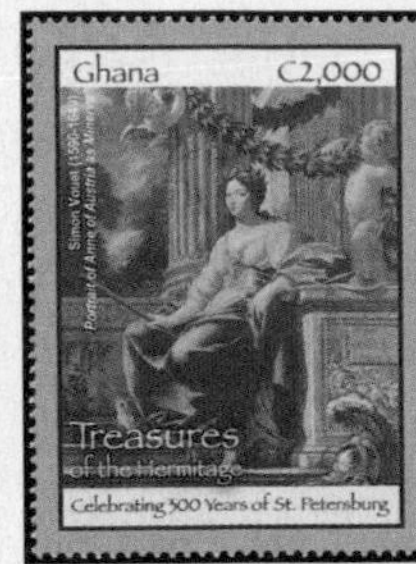

Paintings in the Hermitage, St. Petersburg, Russia A471

Designs: 2000ce, Portrait of Anne of Austria as Minerva, by Simon Vouet. 3000ce, Lasciviousness, by Pompeo Girolamo Batoni. 10,000ce, Allegory of Faith, by Moretto da Brescia.
No. 2419: a, Allegory of the Arts, by Bernardo Strozzi. b, Vulcan's Forge, by Luca Giordano. c, Daedalus and Icarus, by Charles Lebrun. d, The Infant Hercules Strangling Serpents in His Cradle, by Sir Joshua Reynolds.
No. 2420, Cupid Undoing Venus's Belt, by Reynolds. No. 2421, Perseus Liberating Andromeda, by Peter Paul Rubens, horiz.

2004, Mar. 18 ***Perf. 14¼***

2416-2418 A471 Set of 3 3.50 3.50

2419 A471 6500ce Sheet of 4, #a-d 6.00 6.00

Imperf

Size: 55x78mm

2420 A471 20,000ce multi 4.50 4.50

Size: 78x55mm

2421 A471 20,000ce multi 4.50 4.50

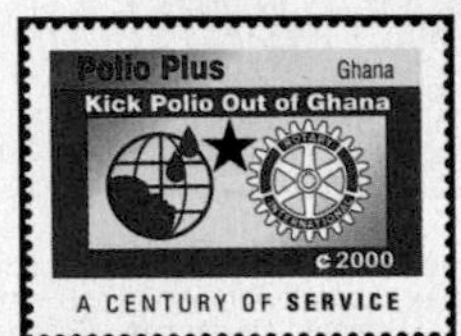

Rotary International, Cent. (in 2005) — A471a

Rotary International emblem and: 2000ce, Polio Plus emblem. 4000ce, Anopheles mosquito, flag of Ghana, vert. 4500ce, Paul P. Harris, flag of Ghana, vert. 5000ce, 2003-04 Rotary International President Jonathan B. Majiyagbe, flag of Ghana, vert. 6000ce, "100 Years," flag of Ghana, vert.
No. 2421F, vert.: g, Women filling water containers. h, Men building shelters. i, Women planting tree.

Perf. 13x13¼, 13¼x13

2004, Sept. 14 **Litho.**

2421A-2421E A471a Set of 5 4.75 4.75

Souvenir Sheet

2421F A471a 10,000ce Sheet of 3, #g-i 6.75 6.75

No. 2421F contains three 28x42mm stamps.

Souvenir Sheet

Deng Xiaoping (1904-97), Chinese Leader — A472

2004, Nov. 29 **Litho.** ***Perf. 14***

2422 A472 20,000ce multi 4.50 4.50

Souvenir Sheet

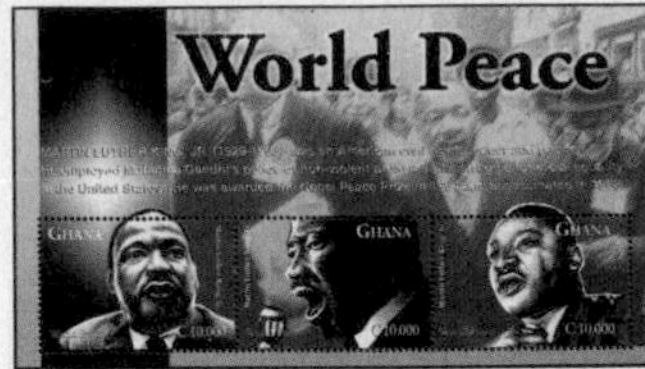

World Peace — A473

No. 2423 — Dr. Martin Luther King, Jr. with: a, Country name at UL. b, Microphone. c, Hands at tie.

2004, Nov. 29

2423 A473 10,000ce Sheet of 3, #a-c 9.25 9.25

Miniature Sheet

Election of Pope John Paul II, 25th Anniv. (in 2003) — A474

No. 2424 — Photos from: a, 1980. b, 1982. c, 1991. d, 2000. e, 2001.

2004, Nov. 29

2424 A474 6000ce Sheet of 5, #a-e 6.75 6.75

2004 Summer Olympics, Athens A475

Designs: 500ce, Intl. Olympic Committee President Jacques Rogge. 800ce, Soccer player Abedi Ayew Pele. 7000ce, Athlete Margaret Simpson. 10,000ce, Art depicting athletes of ancient Greece, horiz.

2004, Nov. 29 ***Perf. 14¼***

2425-2428 A475 Set of 4 4.00 4.00

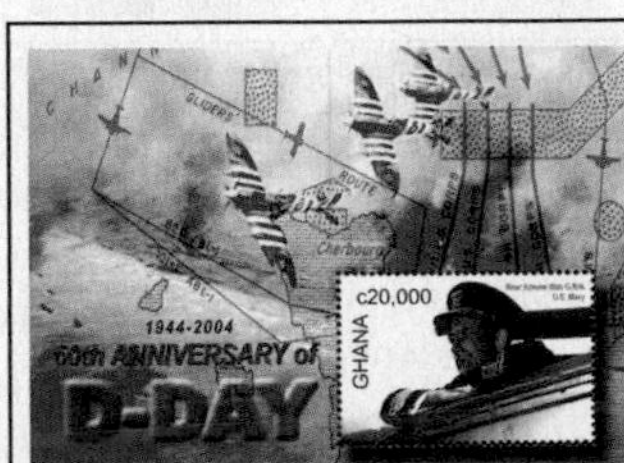

D-Day, 60th Anniv. — A476

No. 2429, vert.: a, Fleet Admiral Ernest J. King. b, Gen. William C. Lee. c, Lt. Commander John D. Bulkeley. d, Admiral Sir Bertram H. Ramsey.
20,000ce, Rear Admiral Alan G. Kirk.

2004, Nov. 29

2429 A476 8000ce Sheet of 4, #a-d 7.25 7.25

Souvenir Sheet

2430 A476 20,000ce multi 4.50 4.50

European Soccer Championships, Portugal — A477

No. 2431, vert.: a, Gerd Müller. b, Presentation of European Cup. c, Franz Beckenbauer. d, Heysel Stadium, Brussels.
20,000ce, 1972 German team.

2004, Nov. 29 ***Perf. 14***

2431 A477 7500ce Sheet of 4, #a-d 6.75 6.75

Souvenir Sheet

Perf. 14¼

2432 A477 20,000ce multi 4.50 4.50

No. 2431 contains four 28x42mm stamps.

Worldwide Fund for Nature (WWF) — A478

No. 2433 — African lions: a, Three cubs. b, Lions in water. c, Male lion. d, Female and cubs.

2004, Dec. 27 ***Perf. 14***

2433 A478 5000ce Block or strip of 4, #a-d 4.50 4.50

e. Miniature sheet, 2 each #2433a-2433d 9.00 9.00

Mushrooms — A479

Designs: 500ce, Boletus badius. 3000ce, Clitocybe nebularis. 5000ce, Amanita muscaria. 8000ce, Russula vesca.
No. 2438, vert.: a, Boletus parasiticus. b, Cortinarius armillatus. c, Gymnopilus spectabilis. d, Cortinarius flexipes.
20,000ce, Chlorosplenium aeruginosum, vert.

2004, Dec. 27

2434-2437 A479 Set of 4 5.00 5.00

2438 A479 7500ce Sheet of 4, #a-d 8.00 8.00

Souvenir Sheet

2439 A479 20,000ce multi 5.00 5.00

Orchids A480

Designs: 800ce, Oncidium desertorum. 3500ce, Oncidium variegatum. 4000ce, Anguloa uniflora, vert. 10,000ce, Oncidium gardneri, vert.
No. 2444: a, Vanda rothschildiana. b, Laelia cattleya. c, Laelia anceps. d, Odontioda dalmar.
20,000ce, Renanthera bella, vert.

2004, Dec. 27

2440-2443	A480	Set of 4	6.00	6.00
2444	A480	7500ce Sheet of 4, #a-d	7.50	7.50

Souvenir Sheet

2445	A480	20,000ce multi	5.00	5.00

Mammals — A481

Designs: 1000ce, Serval. 1200ce, Sable antelope. 2000ce, Cheetah. 3000ce, Bohor reedbuck.

No. 2450, horiz.: a, White rhinoceros. b, Leopard. c, Burchell's zebra. d, Red river hog. 20,000ce, Hippopotamus, horiz.

2004, Dec. 27

2446-2449	A481	Set of 4	2.50	2.50
2450	A481	7500ce Sheet of 4, #a-d	7.50	7.50

Souvenir Sheet

2451	A481	20,000ce multi	5.00	5.00

Sharks — A482

No. 2452: a, Zebra bullhead shark. b, Swell-shark. c, Port Jackson shark. d, Leopard shark.

20,000ce, California horn shark.

2004, Dec. 27

2452	A482	7500ce Sheet of 4, #a-d	7.50	7.50

Souvenir Sheet

2453	A482	20,000ce multi	5.00	5.00

New Juaben Akwantukese Afahye Festival — A483

Designs: 2000ce, State emblem Yiadom and Hwedie. No. 2455, 4000ce, Migrating to freedom. 4500ce, Crossing Suhyien River. 5000ce, Chief at State Durbar. 6000ce, Sacrificing at the cave.

No. 2459: a, Like 4500ce. b, Palace guards. c, Like 2000ce. d, Like 5000ce. e, Libation pouring. f, Parading the royal treasury.

2005, Mar. 1 *Perf. 13¼x13*

2454-2458	A483	Set of 5	4.75	4.75
2459	A483	4000ce Sheet of 6, #a-f	5.50	5.50

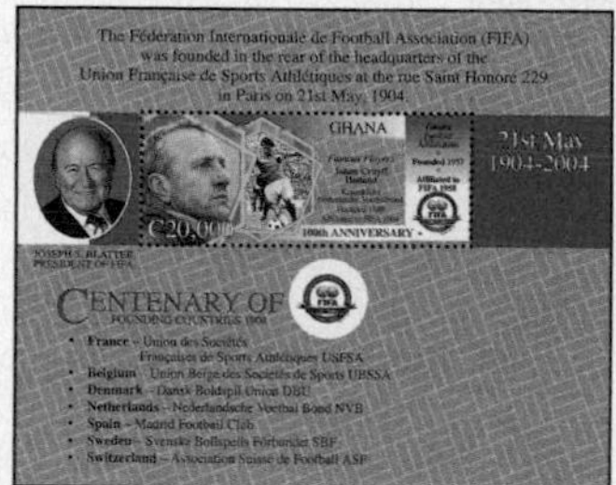

FIFA (Fédération Internationale de Football Association), Cent. — A484

No. 2460: a, Roberto Di Matteo. b, Marcel Desailly. c, Osei Kufuor. d, Eusebio.

20,000ce, Johan Cruyff.

2005, Mar. 14 *Perf. 13¼*

2460	A484	7500ce Sheet of 4, #a-d	7.25	7.25

Souvenir Sheet

2461	A484	20,000ce multi	4.75	4.75

Ipomoea Asarifolia — A485

2005 ? **Litho.** *Perf. 13¾x13½*

2462	A485	2000ce multi	—	—

Trains — A486

No. 2463, 5000ce: a, Stanier Class 5-4-6-0. b, Central Pacific Jupiter. c, Robe River RSC3 Class 9401. d, Bangkok BTS train. e, Streamlined tank locomotive. f, ETR450.

No. 2464, 5000ce: a, Talgo train, Spain. b, VIA Turbotrain, Canada. c, Southern Pacific 4-8-4 #4449. d, Union Pacific "City of Portland." e, Shinkansen, Japan (white denomination). f, Deltic Diesel-electric engine, Great Britain.

No. 2465, 5000ce: a, Mogul 2-6-0. b, Milwaukee Railroad 4-6-2. c, Shinkansen (red denomination). d, Former Reading #2101 4-8-4. e, HST Inter-city 125. f, Daylight train.

No. 2466: a, Baldwin 4-6-0 steam train. b, Atchison, Topeka & Santa Fe 4-4-0 "American" steam train. c, Baldwin 4-6-0 Engine #44. d, Baldwin 2-6-0 #3 Three-spot.

No. 2467, 20,000ce, Chicago Transit Authority train. No. 2468, 20,000ce, Santa Fe train. No. 2469, 20,000ce, Empire Builder. No. 2470, 20,000ce, LMS 5305 steam train.

2005, June 1 **Litho.** *Perf. 12¾*

Sheets of 6, #a-f

2463-2465	A486	Set of 3	20.00	20.00
2466	A486	8000ce Sheet of 4, #a-d	7.00	7.00

Souvenir Sheets

2467-2470	A486	Set of 4	18.00	18.00

Motor Vehicles A487

Designs: 2000ce, Setra State Transport bus. 4000ce, Albium double-decker bus. 4500ce, Bedford Mummy truck and trailer. 5000ce, 1925 Mail carrier. 6000ce, Morris truck.

2005, June 21 **Litho.** *Perf. 13x13¼*

2471-2475	A487	Set of 5	5.00	5.00

Friedrich von Schiller (1759-1805), Writer — A488

No. 2476: a, Schiller, with hand touching head. b, Schiller and birthplace. c, Brahms with beard.

20,000ce, Portraits of Schiller and Johannes Brahms.

2005 **Litho.** *Perf. 13¼*

2476	A488	11,000ce Sheet of 3, #a-c	7.25	7.25

Imperf

2477	A488	20,000ce shown	4.75	4.75

No. 2476 contains three 42x28mm stamps.

World Cup Soccer Championships, 75th Anniv. — A489

No. 2478: a, 1938 Italian team. b, Scene from 1938 Italy vs. Hungary match. c, Olympic Stadium. d, Silvio Piola.

20,000ce, Italian team with World Cup.

2005 *Perf. 13¼*

2478	A489	8000ce Sheet of 4, #a-d	7.25	7.25

Souvenir Sheet

2479	A489	20,000ce multi	4.75	4.75

Panafest 05 — A489a

Inscriptions: No. 2479A, Biribi wo soro (a symbol of hope). No. 2479B, A royal entry, horiz. No. 2479C, 4000ce, Let's hold hands together, horiz. No. 2479D, 4500ce, Clarion call for Black Unity, horiz. No. 2479E, Sankofa (back to your roots). No. 2479F, Bi-nnka-bi (bite not one another), horiz. No. 2479G, 6000ce, Nkyinkyim (changing oneself; playing many roles).

Perf. 13½x13¼, 13¼x13½

2005 ? **Litho.**

2479A	A489a	2000ce multi	—
2479B	A489a	2000ce multi	—
2479C	A489a	4000ce multi	—
2479D	A489a	4500ce multi	—
2479E	A489a	5000ce multi	—
2479F	A489a	5000ce multi	—
2479G	A489a	6000ce multi	—

The editors would like to examine any examples of any additional stamps that might exist in this set.

Disease Treatment and Prevention A490

Designs: No. 2480, 2000ce, Emaciated people on rugs. No. 2481, 2000ce, Map of Ghana, symbols of medicine, red ribbon. No. 2482, 2000ce, People holding signs, horiz. 3000ce, Red ribbon, head. 4000ce, Maps of Africa and Ghana, arms, stylized people. No. 2485, 4500ce, Diseases on ladder destroying human body of bricks. No. 2486, 4500ce, Hand holding egg depicting health care workers. No. 2487, 5000ce, Emaciated man carrying bags of diseases. No. 2488, 5000ce, Heart, man lifting stylized globe. 6000ce, Whistle, hands holding cards with slogans.

2006, Jan. 26 *Perf. 13¼x13, 13x13¼*

2480-2489	A490	Set of 10	8.50	8.50

National Basketball Association Players and Team Emblems — A491

No. 2490, 3500ce: a, Carlos Boozer. b, Utah Jazz emblem.

No. 2491, 3500ce: a, Carlos Arroyo. b, Detroit Pistons emblem.

No. 2492, 3500ce: a, Corey Magette. b, Los Angeles Clippers emblem.

No. 2493, 3500ce: a, David Wesley. b, Houston Rockets emblem.

No. 2494, 3500ce: a, Manu Ginobili. b, San Antonio Spurs emblem.

No. 2495, 3500ce: a, Al Harrington. b, Atlanta Hawks emblem.

2006, Mar. 15 *Perf. 13¼*

Sheets of 12, 10 each #a, 2 each #b

2490-2495	A491	Set of 6	55.00	55.00

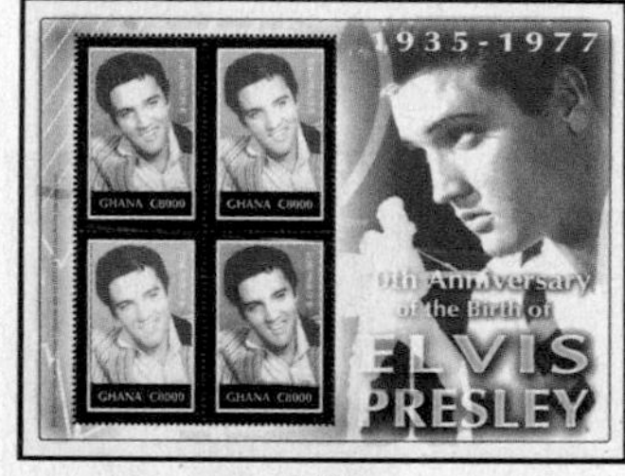

A492

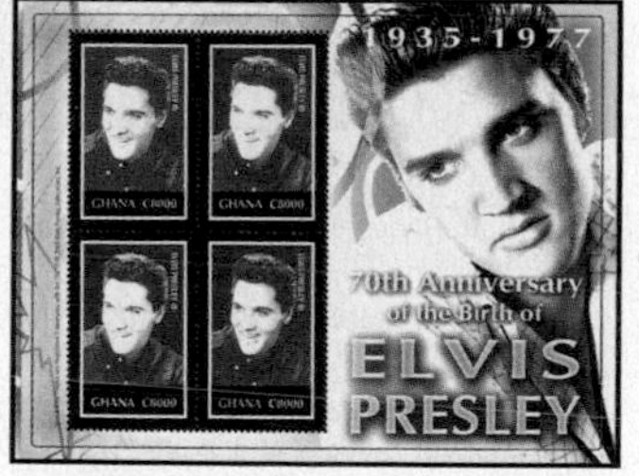

A493

Elvis Presley (1935-77) — A494

No. 2496 — Background color: a, Lilac. b, Green. c, Yellow green. d, Blue.

No. 2497 — Face color: a, Lilac. b, Green. c, Yellow green. d, Blue.

No. 2498: a, Blue background. b, Green background with dark red halo, ghost image at right. c, Yellow background with orange halo. d, Green background with orange red halo, ghost image above head. e, Yellow background, ghost image showing teeth at left. f, Yellow background, gray area at right. g, Green background, blue halo.

2006, Mar. 15 *Perf. 14*

2496	A492	8000ce	Sheet of 4, #a-d	7.00	7.00
2497	A493	8000ce	Sheet of 4, #a-d	7.00	7.00
2498	A494	3500ce	Sheet of 9, #a-f, 3 #g	7.00	7.00

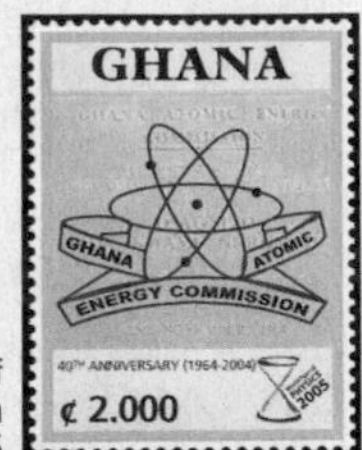

Intl. Year of Physics (in 2005) — A495

Designs: 2000ce, Emblem of Ghana Atomic Energy Commission. 4000ce, Ghana research reactor. 4500ce, Albert Einstein. 5000ce, Prof. Francis K. Allotey, physicist. 6000ce, Electricity experiment in physics laboratory.

2006, Mar. 29 *Perf. 13¼x14*

2499-2503	A495	Set of 5	7.25	7.25

Pope John Paul II (1920-2005) A496

2006, Apr. 7 *Perf. 13¼*

2504	A496	12,000ce multi	2.75	2.75

Printed in sheets of 4.

Battle of Trafalgar, Bicent. (in 2005) A497

Designs: 2000ce, Sir John Jervis. 3000ce, Chase and Race. 5000ce, Goliath fires at Guerrier, horiz. 10,000ce, Death of Adm. Horatio Nelson, horiz.

20,000ce, Napoleon's flagships, Agamemnon. Vanguard, Elephant and Captain, horiz.

2006, Apr. 7 *Perf. 13x13¼, 13¼x13*

2505-2508	A497	Set of 4	4.50	4.50

Souvenir Sheet

Perf. 12

2509	A497	20,000ce multi	4.50	4.50

Jules Verne (1828-1905), Writer — A498

No. 2510: a, Verne. b, Original book illustrations of balloons in flight. c, Montgolfier hot air balloon. d, Modern hot air balloon.

20,000ce, The Hindenburg.

2006, Apr. 7 *Perf. 12¾*

2510	A498	8000ce	Sheet of 4, #a-d	7.50	7.50

Souvenir Sheet

2511	A498	20,000ce multi	5.00	5.00

2006 World Cup Soccer Championships, Germany — A499

Designs: No. 2512, 2000ce, Line of Ghana Black Stars players. No. 2513, 2000ce, Captain Stephen Appiah and opposing player, vert. No. 2514, 4000ce, Exchange of pennants. No. 2515, 4000ce, Joy of success. No. 2516, 4500ce, Michael Essien. No. 2517, 4500ce, Franz Beckenbauer, FIFA World Cup Stadium, Hanover. No. 2518, 5000ce, Scene from Ghana vs. Burkina Faso match. No. 2519, 5000ce, Black Stars team photo. No. 2520, 6000ce, Scene from Ghana vs. South Africa match. No. 2521, 6000ce, Fans celebrating Black Stars victory.

No. 2522, 4000ce: a, Appiah. b, Issah Ahmed. c, John Paintsil. d, Laryea Kingston. e, Essien, diff. f, Sule Ali Muntari. g, Joe Tex Frimpong. h, Coach Ratomir Dujkovic.

No. 2523, 4000ce: a, Asamoah Gyan. b, Sammy Adjei. c, Matthew Amoah. d, John Mensah. e, Emmanuel Pappoe. f, Mark Caniel Edusei. g, Abubakari Yakubu. h, Godwin Attram.

2006, May 18 *Perf. 13½*

2512-2521	A499	Set of 10	9.50	9.50

Sheets of 8, #a-h

Perf. 13¼

2522-2523	A499	Set of 2	14.00	14.00

Nos. 2522-2523 each contain eight 42x28mm stamps.

Tympanotonus Fuscatus — A500

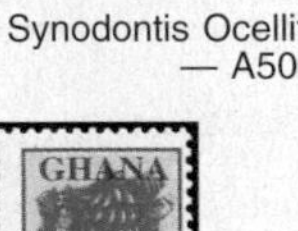

Synodontis Ocellifer — A500a

Musa Sapientum — A501

Gomphidius Glutinosus — A501a

Bebearia Arcadius — A502

Polemaetus Bellicosus — A502a

Xaphia Gladius (Denomination at Center) — A503

Euphaedra Francina — A504

Falco Tinnunculus — A504a

Lagerstroemia Flos-reginae — A504b

Ardea Purpurea (With Brown Frame and "A's" of "Ghana" With Horizontal Cross Lines — A504c

Spathodea Campanulata — A505

2003-07 **Litho.** *Perf. 13½*

2524	A500	500ce	multi		—
2524A	A500a	500ce	multi		—
2525	A501	800ce	multi	—	—
2525A	A501a	1000ce	multi		—
2526	A502	1500ce	multi		—
2526A	A502a	1500ce	multi	—	—
2527	A503	2000ce	multi		—
2528	A504	2000ce	multi	—	—
2528A	A504a	2500ce	multi	—	—
2528B	A504b	4000ce	multi		—
2528C	A504c	5000ce	multi		—
2529	A505	6000ce	multi	—	—

Issued: No. 2524, July 2003; Nos. 2524A, 2528B, Oct. 2005. No. 2525A, 2529, 2006; Nos. 2526A, 2528A, 2528C, 2007; No. 2527, 2005.

Compare No. 2527 with No. 1838.

For surcharge see No. 2679.

Nos. 1674-1677 Surcharged

2006, Aug. 28 **Litho.** *Perf. 14*

2530	A284	2000ce	on 50ce #1674	29.00	10.00
2531	A284	2000ce	on 200ce #1675	29.00	10.00
2532	A284	2000ce	on 500ce #1676	29.00	10.00
2533	A284	2000ce	on 800ce #1677	29.00	10.00
			Nos. 2530-2533 (4)	116.00	40.00

Nos. 1810-1814 Surcharged

2006, Aug. 28 **Litho.** *Perf. 14*

2534	A312	2000ce	on 200ce #1810	.45	.45
2535	A312	2000ce	on 300ce #1811	.45	.45
2536	A312	2000ce	on 400ce #1812	.45	.45
2537	A312	2000ce	on 600ce #1813	.45	.45
2538	A312	2000ce	on 800ce #1814	.45	.45
			Nos. 2534-2538 (5)	2.25	2.25

Nos. 1703-1708 Surcharged

2006, Aug. 28 **Litho.** *Perf. 14*

2539	A291	3000ce	on 50ce #1703	.65	.65
2540	A291	3000ce	on 100ce #1704	.65	.65
2541	A291	3000ce	on 200ce #1705	.65	.65
2542	A291	3000ce	on 400ce #1706	.65	.65
2543	A291	3000ce	on 600ce #1707	.65	.65
2544	A291	3000ce	on 800ce #1708	.65	.65
			Nos. 2539-2544 (6)	3.90	3.90

Nos. 1741-1743 Surcharged

2006, Aug. 28 **Litho.** *Perf. 14*

2545	A300	4000ce	on 50ce #1741	.90	.90
2546	A300	4000ce	on 200ce #1742	.90	.90
2547	A300	4000ce	on 600ce #1743	.90	.90
			Nos. 2545-2547 (3)	2.70	2.70

Nos. 1738-1740 Surcharged

2006, Aug. 28 **Litho.** *Perf. 14*

2548	A299	4500ce	on 100ce #1738	1.00	1.00
2549	A299	4500ce	on 400ce #1739	1.00	1.00
2550	A299	4500ce	on 1000ce #1740	1.00	1.00
			Nos. 2548-2550 (3)	3.00	3.00

Nos. 1745-1752 Surcharged

2006, Aug. 28 **Litho.** *Perf. 14*

2551	A301	5000ce	on 50ce #1745	1.10	1.10
2552	A301	5000ce	on 100ce #1746	1.10	1.10
2553	A301	5000ce	on 150ce #1747	1.10	1.10
2554	A301	5000ce	on 200ce #1748	1.10	1.10
2555	A301	5000ce	on 400ce #1749	1.10	1.10
2556	A301	5000ce	on 600ce #1750	1.10	1.10
2557	A301	5000ce	on 800ce #1751	1.10	1.10
2558	A301	5000ce	on 1000ce #1752	1.10	1.10
			Nos. 2551-2558 (8)	8.80	8.80

Nos. 1766-1768 Surcharged

2006, Aug. 28 Litho. *Perf. 14*

2559 A299 6000ce on 100ce #1766 1.25 1.25
2560 A299 6000ce on 400ce #1767 1.25 1.25
2561 A299 6000ce on 1000ce #1768 1.25 1.25
Nos. 2559-2561 (3) 3.75 3.75

Miniature Sheets

Ghana Soccer Players — A506

No. 2562, 4000ce: a, Asamoah Gyan. b, Sammy Adjei. c, Matthew Amoah. d, John Mensah. e, Emmanuel Pappoe. f, Mark Daniel Edusei. g, Abubakari Yakubu. h, Godwin Attram.

No. 2563, 4000ce: a, Stephen Appiah. b, Issah Ahmed. c, John Paintsil. d, Laryea Kingston. e, Michael Essien. f, Sule Ali Muntari. g, Joe Tex Frimpong. h, Ghana Team Coach Ratomir Dujkovic.

2007, Jan. 22 Litho. *Perf. 13½*
Sheets of 8, #a-h

2562-2563 A506 Set of 2 14.00 14.00

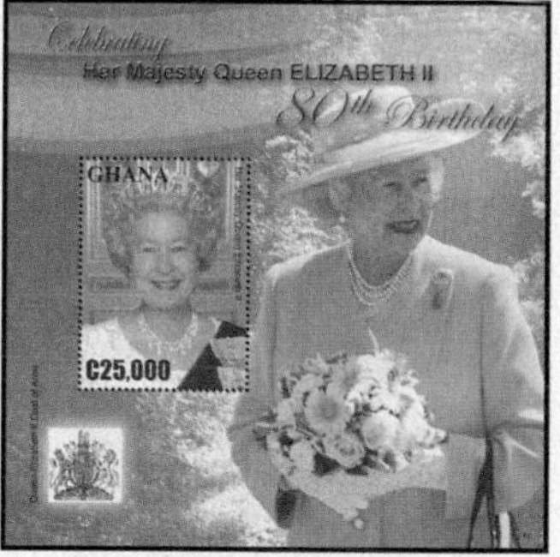

Queen Elizabeth II, 80th Birthday — A507

No. 2564: a, Holding flowers. b, Wearing purple hat. c, Wearing light green hat, denomination in purple. d, Wearing light green hat, denomination in white.

25,000ce, Wearing tiara.

2007, Jan. 22

2564 A507 6000ce Sheet of 4, #a-d 5.25 5.25

Souvenir Sheet

2565 A507 25,000ce multi 5.50 5.50

Marilyn Monroe (1926-62), Actress — A508

No. 2566: a, Wearing glasses. b, Wearing bathrobe. c, Looking left. d, Wearing red dress and earrings.

20,000ce, With eyes closed.

2007, Jan. 22

2566 A508 9000ce Sheet of 4, #a-d 8.00 8.00

Souvenir Sheet

2567 A508 20,000ce multi 4.50 4.50

Space Achievements — A509

No. 2568, horiz. — Luna 9: a, Distant view of spacecraft and moon, denomination in black. b, Spacecraft, denomination in white. c, Close-up view of spacecraft and moon, denomination in black. d, Spacecraft in frame, denomination in white.

No. 2569, 6500ce, horiz. — Apollo-Soyuz Test Project: a, Apollo and Soyuz spacecraft docked. b, Mission emblem. c, Astronaut Tom Stafford. d, Cosmonaut Aleksei Leonov. e, Astronaut Deke Slayton. f, Astronaut Vance Brand and Cosmonaut Valeri Kubasov.

No. 2570, 6500ce — Giotto Comet Probe: a, Probe in space, black background. b, Comet, probe in space, red text at bottom. c, Top of probe, white background. d, Comet, probe in space, purple background. e, Probe and schematic diagram. f, Bottom of probe.

No. 2571, 20,000ce, Astronaut Buzz Aldrin. No. 2572, 20,000ce, Apollo-Soyuz crew members shaking hands in space, horiz. No. 2573, 20,000ce, Viking 1, horiz.

2007, Jan. 22

2568 A509 10,000ce Sheet of 4, #a-d 8.75 8.75

Sheets of 6, #a-f

2569-2570 A509 Set of 2 17.00 17.00

Souvenir Sheets

2571-2573 A509 Set of 3 13.00 13.00

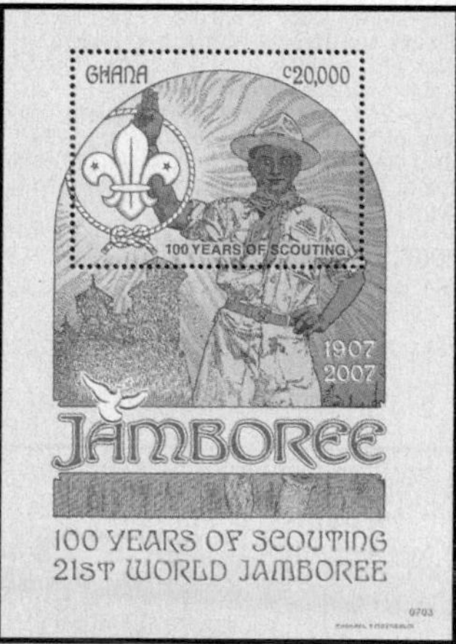

Scouting, Cent. — A510

No. 2574, vert. — Dove, Scout emblem and Scout: a, Giving Scout sign. b, Blowing bugle. c, Carrying injured boy.

20,000ce, Scout emblem, Scout giving Scout sign.

2007 *Perf. 13¼*

2574 A510 12,000ce Sheet of 3, #a-c 8.00 8.00

Souvenir Sheet

2575 A510 20,000ce multi 4.50 4.50

Independence, 50th Anniv — A511

2007, Sept. 15 Litho. *Perf. 13¼*

2576 A511 4000ce multi .90 .90

Kente Cloth Designs — A512

Designs: 4000ce, Sika ne Barima. 7300ce, Edwene Si So. 7500ce, Dakoro Yesore. No. 2580, 9000ce, Agyenegyne Nsu. No. 2581, 9000ce, Nkatoa Sa. 10,000ce, Edwene Asa.

2007, Sept. 15 *Perf. 13½x13¼*

2577-2582 A512 Set of 6 10.00 10.00

Aburi Botanical Gardens — A513

Designs: 4000ce, Bamboo groves. 7300ce, School of Horticulture. 7500ce, Silk cotton tree, vert. 9000ce, Royal Palm Walkway. 10,000ce, Famous ficus tree, vert.

No. 2588: a, Like 9000ce. b, Like 7300ce. c, Silk cotton tree. d, Famous ficus tree. e, Like 4000ce. f, Sanatorium.

Perf. 13¼x13½, 13½x13¼
2007, Sept. 15

2583-2587 A513 Set of 5 8.25 8.25
2588 A513 6000ce Sheet of 6, #a-f 7.75 7.75

Cocoa — A514

Designs: 4000ce, Cocoa beverages and spread. 7300ce, Cocoa Pebbles. 7500ce, Assorted chocolates. 9000ce, Man at cocoa processing plant. 10,000ce, Finished cocoa products.

No. 2594: a, Like 10,000ce. b, Cacao pods. c, Like 7500ce. d, Like 9000ce. e, Like 7300ce. f, Workers packaging cocoa products.

2007, Sept. 15 *Perf. 13¼x13½*

2589-2593 A514 Set of 5 8.25 8.25
2594 A514 6000ce Sheet of 6, #a-f 7.75 7.75

Cats and Dogs — A515

Designs: 6000ce, Chartreux cat. 7000ce, Blue-mitted ragdoll cat. 8000ce, Blue lynx point Birman cat, horiz. 9000ce, Norwegian Forest cat.

No. 2599, horiz.: a, American bulldog. b, Old English sheepdog. c, Shar-pei. d, Boston terrier.

No. 2600, 20,000ce, Cinnamon point Siamese cat. No. 2601, 20,000ce, Greyhound.

2007, Sept. 15 *Perf. 14*

2595-2598 A515 Set of 4 6.50 6.50
2599 A515 7500ce Sheet of 4, #a-d 6.50 6.50

Souvenir Sheets

2600-2601 A515 Set of 2 8.75 8.75

Orchids — A516

No. 2602: a, Epipactis atrorubens. b, Galeandra bicarinata. c, Platanthera tipuloides. d, Platanthera ciliaris.

20,000ce, Spathoglottis plicata.

2007, Sept. 15

2602 A516 7500ce Sheet of 4, #a-d 6.50 6.50

Souvenir Sheet

2603 A516 20,000ce multi 4.50 4.50

Birds — A517

No. 2604, horiz.: a, Red-billed hornbill. b, Bearded barbet. c, Hoopoe. d, Pygmy kingfisher.

20,000ce, Gray-crowned crane.

2007, Sept. 15

2604 A517 7500ce Sheet of 4, #a-d 6.50 6.50

Souvenir Sheet

2605 A517 20,000ce multi 4.50 4.50

Traditional Costumes A518

Designs: 4000ce, War dress, Northern Ghana. 7300ce, Woman. 7500ce, Mourning wear. 9000ce, Smock. 10,000ce, Wulomo costume.

Perf. 13½x13¼

2007, Sept. 15 **Litho.**
2606-2610 A518 Set of 5 8.25 8.25

Famous People — A519

Designs: No. 2611, 4000ce, Sir Arko Korsah, first Chief Justice. No. 2612, 4000ce, Amon Kotei, designer of national coat of arms. No. 2613, 4000ce, Philip Gbeho, composer of national anthem. 4500ce, F. K. Buah, historian. 6000ce, Prof. Albert Adu Boahene, historian and politician. 7300ce, Leticia Obeng, aquatic biologist. 7500ce, Peter Cardinal Appiah Turkson, first Ghanaian cardinal. 0000ce, Susanna Alhassan, first femal government minister.

2007, Sept. 15 *Perf. 13¼*
2611-2618 A519 Set of 8 10.00 10.00

On July 3, 2007, Ghana's currency was revalued at a rate of 10,000 old cedis to 1 new cedi. Old cedis continued to be valid until Dec. 31, 2007. Nos. 2576-2618 and 2641-2646 were issued after July 3, but have denominations expressed in old cedis.

Antrak Air A520

Airplane: 40p, On ground. 73p, In flight.

2007, Sept. 15 *Perf. 13¼*
2619-2620 A520 Set of 2 2.25 2.25

Accra Tourist Attractions — A521

Designs: 20p, Independence Arch. 40p, Independence Square. 73p, Supreme Court. 75p, National Theater. 90p, Intl. Conference Center.

2007, Sept. 15
2621-2625 A521 Set of 5 6.50 6.50

Agricultural Development Bank — A522

Designs: 40p, Emblem. 75p, Home Link Account, vert. 90p, Young Farmers Program, vert. 1ce, Gold Drive Motor Loan, vert.

2007, Sept. 15
2626-2629 A522 Set of 4 6.75 6.75

Ghana Commercial Bank — A523

Designs: 40p, Emblem. 73p, Eagle, world map. 75p, Ghana Commercial Bank Tower, vert. 90p, Xpress Money Transfer, vert.

2007, Sept. 15
2630-2633 A523 Set of 4 6.00 6.00

State Insurance Company A524

Designs: 40p, Emblem. 73p, Executives. 75p, New office building. 90p, Child pointing. 1ce, Three CIMG Awards, vert.

2007, Sept. 15
2634-2638 A524 Set of 5 8.25 8.25

Ghanaian Heads of State — A525

Dr. Kwame Nkrumah and Pres. J. A. Kufuor With State Sword — A526

No. 2639: a, Dr. Kwame Nkrumah. b, Lieutenant General J. A. Ankrah. c, General A. A. Afrifa. d, Dr. Kofi Abrefa Busia. e, General I. K. Acheampong. f, Lieutenant General W. A. Akuffo. g, Dr. Hilla Limann. h, Flight Lieutenant J. J. Rawlings. i, Pres. J. A. Kufuor.

2007, Sept. 15 *Perf. 13½x13¼*
2639 A525 60p Sheet of 9, #a-i 11.00 11.00

Souvenir Sheet

2640 A526 1ce multi 1.10 1.10

Pope Benedict XVI — A527

2007, Nov. 15 *Perf. 13¼*
2641 A527 4000ce multi .90 .90

Printed in sheets of 8.

Gold A528

Designs: 4000ce, Gold ore. 7300ce, Melting gold ore. 7500ce, Woman holding gold bar. 9000ce, Entrance of Obuasi Gold Mines, horiz. 10,000ce, Gold-plated chair.

2007 *Perf. 13½x13¼, 13¼x13½*
2642-2646 A528 Set of 5 8.25 8.25

24th UPU Congress, Nairobi A529

Designs: 40p, Dancers. 73p, Flags of Ghana and Kenya, warrior with shield, vert. 75p, UPU emblem in opened box. 90p, UPU emblem on map of Africa, vert.

No. 2651: a, Part of UPU emblem, folded map of world, denomination at LL. b, Part of UPU emblem, folded map of world, denomination at UR. c, Folded map of world, map and flag of Kenya.

2007, Dec. 3 *Perf. 12½*
2647-2650 A529 Set of 4 6.00 6.00

Souvenir Sheet

2651 A529 1ce Sheet of 3, #a-c 6.50 6.50

Miniature Sheet

Wedding of Queen Elizabeth II and Prince Philip, 60th Anniv. (in 2007) — A530

No. 2652: a, Queen, denomination in green. b, Couple, denomination in green. c, Couple, denomination in orange. d, Queen, denomination in orange. e, Queen, denomination in blue. f, Couple, denomination in blue.

2008, Jan. 31 **Litho.** *Perf. 13¼x13½*
2652 A530 60p Sheet of 6, #a-f 7.75 7.75

Paintings by Qi Baishi (1864-1957) — A531

No. 2653: a, Top half of Lotus and Mandarin Ducks (lotus). b, Top half of River Landscape with Boats (boats). c, Bottom half of Lotus and Mandarin Ducks (ducks). d, Bottom half of River Landscape with Boats (trees).
3ce, Peony in a Dragon Vase.

2008, Jan. 31 *Perf. 12x11½*
2653 A531 90p Sheet of 4, #a-d 7.75 7.75

Souvenir Sheet

Perf. 11½

2654 A531 3ce multi 6.50 6.50

No. 2653 contains four 30x40mm stamps.

Miniature Sheet

2008 Summer Olympics, Beijing — A532

No. 2655: a, Boxing. b, Relay race. c, Long jump. d, Soccer.

2008, May 8 *Perf. 12¾*
2655 A532 40p Sheet of 4, #a-d 3.25 3.25

Souvenir Sheet

Visit of US Pres. George W. Bush to Ghana — A533

No. 2656: a, US Pres. George W. Bush. b, Ghana Pres. John Agyekum Kufuor.

2008, Sept. 17 ***Perf. 13½***
2656 A533 1.25ce Sheet of 2, #a-b 4.50 4.50

Khilafat Ahmadiyya, Cent. — A533a

Designs: 40p, Flag, minaret, world map. 73p, T. I. Ahmadiyya Senior High School, Kumasi. 90p, Wheat. 1ce, Ahmadiuua Muslim Hospital, Daboase.

2008 **Litho.** ***Perf. 14½***
2656C-2656F A533a Set of 4 *9.50 9.50*

Coat of Arms — A534

2009, Mar. 31 **Litho.** ***Perf. 14x15***
2657 A534 1ce gray + label 1.40 1.40

Vegetables A535

Designs: 1ce, Tomatoes. 1.20ce, Tomatoes and white eggplants. 1.30ce, White eggplants.

2009, Mar. 31 **Litho.** ***Perf. 14¾x14***
2658-2660 A535 Set of 3 5.00 5.00

Korle Bu Teaching Hospital A536

Designs: 1ce, Medical block. No. 2662, 1.10ce, Cardiothoracic Center. No. 2663, 1.10ce, New administration block. 1.20ce, Prof. Frimpong Boateng, heart surgeon, vert.

2009, Mar. 31 ***Perf. 14¾x14, 14x14¾***
2661-2664 A536 Set of 4 6.25 6.25

Tweneboa Kodua High School A537

Designs: 1ce, Administration block. 1.10ce, Girls dormitory. 1.20ce, Students at ICT Center. 1.30ce, Students playing volleyball.

2009, Mar. 31 ***Perf. 14¾x14***
2665-2668 A537 Set of 4 6.50 6.50

Soccer Players — A538

Designs: No. 2669, 1ce, Edward Acquah. No. 2670, 1ce, Aggrey Fynn. No. 2671, 1ce, Nana Gyamfi II. No. 2672, 1ce, Robert Mensah. No. 2673, 1ce, Baba Yara.

2009, Mar. 31 ***Perf. 14x14¾***
2669-2673 A538 Set of 5 7.25 7.25

Peony A539

2009, Apr. 10 ***Perf. 13¼***
2674 A539 1ce multi 1.40 1.40

Printed in sheets of 8.

Pres. Kwame Nkrumah (1909-72) — A539a

Pres. Nkrumah: 1ce, At Afro-Asian Solidarity Conference. 1.10ce, And Africa Union emblem, horiz. 1.20ce, With Prince Philip at Balmoral Castle. 1.30ce, Signing Charter of African Unity. 1.40ce, With Mao Zedong.

2009, Dec. 8 **Litho.** ***Perf. 13¼x13***
2674A A539a 1ce multi —
2674B A539a 1.10ce multi —
2674C A539a 1.20ce multi —
2674D A539a 1.30ce multi —
2674E A539a 1.40ce multi —

A souvenir sheet was issued in this set. The editors would like to examine any examples.

Nos. 852, 1055, 1068, 1939B, and 2525 Surcharged

No. 2675

No. 2676

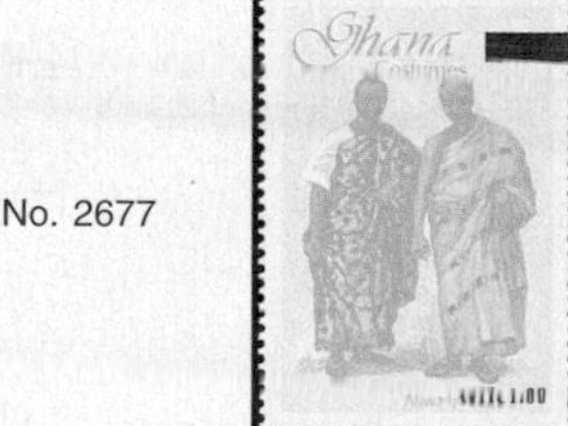

No. 2677

No. 2678

No. 2679

Methods and Perfs. As Before

2009 ?
2675 A350a 20p on 800ce #1939B — —
2676 A174 1ce on 70p #852 — —
2677 A205 1ce on 5ce #1055 — —
2678 A208 1ce on 20ce #1068 — —
2679 A501 1.20ce on 800ce #2525 —

The editors suspect more stamps may have been surcharged and would like to examine any examples.

No. 1057 Surcharged Like No. 2677, Nos. 1069-1070 Surcharged Like No. 2678 and

Methods and Perfs As Before

2009 ?
2680 A208 1ce on 60ce #1069 —
2681 A208 1ce on 80ce #1070 —
2682 A205 1ce on 250ce #1057 —
2683 A435 1.20ce on 1100ce #2277 —

The editors suspect more stamps may have been issued in this set and would like to examine any examples.

No. 2683 No. 1357Bp Surcharged

Methods and Perfs As Before

2009 ?
2687 A243a 1.30ce on 60ce #1357Bp — —
a. Double surcharge —

At least seven additional surcharges were issued in this set. The editors would like to examine any examples.

Volta River Authority — A539b

Designs: 1ce, Kwame Nkrumah switching on Akosombo Generating Station. 1.10ce, Takoradi Thermal Plant. 1.20ce, Kwame Nkrumah signing Akosombo Dam Agreement. 1.30ce, Akosombo Dam. 1.40ce, Akosombo Generating Station retrofit.

2010, Mar. 2 **Litho.** ***Perf. 13x13¼***
2689A A539b 1ce multi —
2689B A539b 1.10ce multi —
2689C A539b 1.20ce multi —
2689D A539b 1.30ce multi —
2689E A539b 1.40ce multi —

One additonal item was issued in this set. The editors would like to examine any examples. Numbers may change.

Friendship Between Ghana and People's Republic of China, 50th Anniv. — A539c

No. 2689F: g, Chinese symbol for friendship, Ghanaian unity symbol. h, National Theater, flags of People's Republic of China and Ghana. i, Kwame Nkrumah and Zhou Enlai, flags of People's Republic of China and Ghana. j, Great Wall of China.

2010, July 8 **Litho.** ***Perf. 12***
2689F Horiz. strip of 4 — —
g.-h. A539c 1ce Either single — —
i. A539c 1.30ce multi — —
j. A539c 1.40ce multi — —

A540

Wedding of Prince William and Catherine Middleton — A541

Designs: Nos. 2690, 2692, Couple. No. 2691: a, Prince William. b, Catherine Middleton. No. 2693, Couple, diff.

2011, June 15 **Litho.** ***Perf. 12***
2690 A540 3.50ce multi 4.75 4.75
2691 A541 3.50ce Horiz. pair, #a-b 9.25 9.25

Souvenir Sheets

2692 A540 12ce multi 16.00 16.00
2693 A541 12ce multi 16.00 16.00

No. 2690 was printed in sheets of 4. No. 2691 was printed in sheets containing 2 pairs.

2010 World Cup Soccer Championships, South Africa — A541a

Design: No. 2693A, Ghana Black Stars soccer team. No. 2693B, Michael Essien showing sportsmanship. No. 2693C, Goalkeeper Richard Kingson in action. No. 2693D, Asamoah Gyan and Nigerian players.

No. 2693E: f, Stephen Appiah. g, Agyeman Badu and Egyptian player Ahmed Hassan. h, Ghana soccer fans with flag of Ghana. i, Sulley Muntari and opponent. j, Samuel Inkoom and Didier Drogba. k, Anthony Annan and opponent. l, Kwadwo Asamoah, Andre Dede and opponent. m, Coach Milovan Rajevac.

2011, Sept. 14 **Litho.** ***Perf. 13x13¼***
2693A A541a 1ce multi — —
2693B A541a 1ce multi — —
2693C A541a 1.20ce multi — —
2693D A541a 1.40ce multi — —

Miniature Sheet

2693E Sheet of 8 — —
f.-m. A541a 50p Any single — —

2010 World Cup Soccer Championships, South Africa — A541b

Designs: No. 2693N, 1ce, Dominic Adiyiah celebrating goal. No. 2693O,Team Captain Andre Dede Ayew and opponent. No. 2693P, Coach Sellas Tetteh being congratulated by Brazilian coach. No. 2693Q, Players celebrating shootout with Brazil. No. 2693R: s, Dominic Adiyiah and Ransford Osei. t, Adiyiah and South African opponent. u, Players praying before penalty shootout against Brazil. v, Players dancing after win against Brazil. w, Goalkeeper Daniel Adjei. x, Players lifting Coach Tetteh. y, Players holding trophy behind chanpionship banner. z, Players holding trophy, diff.

2011, Sept. 14 Litho. *Perf. 13x13¼*

2693N	A541b	1ce multi	—	—
2693O	A541b	1ce multi	—	—
2693P	A541b	1.20ce multi	—	—
2693Q	A541b	1.40ce multi	—	—

Miniature Sheet

2693R	Sheet of 8	—	—
s.-z.	A541b 50p Any single	—	—

Drafting of the Emancipation Proclamation by Abraham Lincoln, 150th Anniv. — A542

No. 2694: a, 1863 *Harper's Weekly* illustration, by Thomas Nast. b, 1863 photograph of Lincoln, by Thomas Le Mere. c, Watercolor by Henry L. Stephens. d, First Reading of the Emancipation Proclamation of President Lincoln, painting by Francis B. Carpenter.

No. 2695, horiz.: a, 1861 photograph of Lincoln, by Alexander Gardner. b, Text of Emancipation Proclamation from the *National Republican.*

2012, July 9 *Perf. 14*

2694 A542 2ce Sheet of 4, #a-d 8.25 8.25

Souvenir Sheet

2695 A542 3ce Sheet of 2, #a-b 6.25 6.25

Sinking of the Titanic, Cent. — A543

No. 2696: a, Dollar bill recovered from the Titanic wreckage. b, Captain Edward J. Smith. c, Titanic at sea. d, Spoons recovered from the Titanic wreckage.

5ce, Titanic at sea, horiz.

2012, July 9 *Perf. 12*

2696 A543 2ce Sheet of 4, #a-d 8.25 8.25

Souvenir Sheet

2697 A543 5ce multi 5.25 5.25

Burning of the Hindenburg, 75th Anniv. — A544

Hindenburg and: 2ce, Map of Europe. 5ce, Spotlights, vert.

2012, July 9 *Perf. 12*

2698 A544 2ce multi 2.10 2.10

Souvenir Sheet

2699 A544 5ce multi 5.25 5.25

No. 2699 contains one 30x50mm rectangular stamp.

Butterflies — A545

No. 2700: a, Acraea hypoleuca. b, Desmolycaena mazoensis. c, Aphnaeus erikssoni. d, Lycaena gigantea. e, Mimacraea marshalli. f, Iolaus alienus.

No. 2701: a, Female Durbania pallida. b, Male Durbania pallida.

2012, July 9 *Perf. 13 Syncopated*

2700 A545 2ce Sheet of 6, #a-f 12.50 12.50

Souvenir Sheet

2701 A545 3ce Sheet of 2, #a-b 6.25 6.25

Birds — A546

No. 2702: a, Hoopoe. b, Long-tailed glossy starling. c, Northern carmine bee-eater. d, Double-collared sunbird.

5ce, Ostrich.

2012, July 9 *Perf. 12*

2702 A546 2ce Sheet of 4, #a-d 8.25 8.25

Souvenir Sheet

Perf. 12¾

2703 A546 5ce multi 5.25 5.25

No. 2703 contains one 38x51mm stamp.

Parrots — A547

No. 2704: a, Cape parrot. b, Red-bellied parrot. c, Meyer's parrot. d, Ruppell's parrot. e, African gray parrot. f, Brown-headed parrot.

5ce, Senegal parrot.

2012, July 9 *Perf. 14*

2704 A547 2ce Sheet of 6, #a-f 12.50 12.50

Souvenir Sheet

Perf. 12

2705 A547 5ce multi 5.25 5.25

Worldwide Fund for Nature (WWF) — A548

No. 2706 — Bohor reedbuck: a, Three animals. b, Two animals butting heads. c, Two animals running. d, One animal in water.

2012, Aug. 21 *Perf. 14*

2706 A548 1.50ce Block of 4, #a-d 6.50 6.50

e. Souvenir sheet of 8, 2 each #a-d 13.00 13.00

Souvenir Sheets

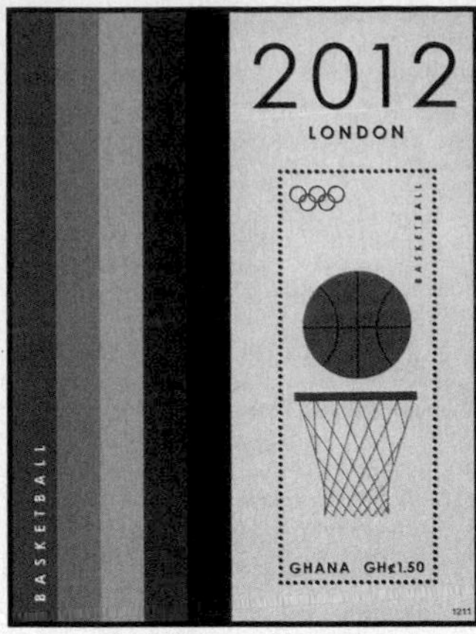

2012 Summer Olympics, London — A549

Designs: No. 2707, 1.50ce, Basketball. No. 2708, 1.50ce, Table tennis. No. 2709, 1.50ce, Synchronized swimming. No. 2710, 1.50ce, Cycling.

2012, Aug. 21 *Perf. 14*

2707-2710 A549 Set of 4 6.50 6.50

Miniature Sheet

Primates — A550

No. 2711: a, Mandrills. b, Chimpanzees. c, Gorillas. d, Orangutans. e, Vervet monkeys.

2012, Sept. 13 Litho.

2711 A550 2ce Sheet of 5, #a-e 10.50 10.50

Souvenir Sheet

2009 Visit of President Barack Obama to Ghana — A551

No. 2712: a, U.S. flag and President Barack Obama. b, Ghana flag and Pres. John Atta Mills.

2012, Oct. 1 *Perf. 12¾*

2712 A551 3ce Sheet of 2, #a-b 6.50 6.50

Souvenir Sheets

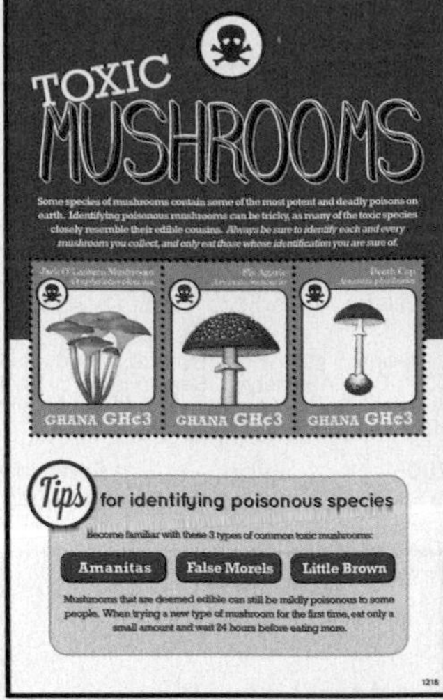

Mushrooms — A552

No. 2713, 3ce — Toxic mushrooms: a, Jack o'lantern mushrooms. b, Fly agaric. c, Death cap.

No. 2714, 3ce — Edible mushrooms: a, Oyster mushrooms. b, Almond mushrooms. c, Saffron milk caps.

2012, Dec. 12 *Perf. 12*

Sheets of 3, #a-c

2713-2714 A552 Set of 2 19.00 19.00

Aircraft Carriers — A553

No. 2715: a, Arromanches. b, Béarn. c, Commandant Teste. d, HMS Hermes.

6ce, HMS Ark Royal.

2012, Dec. 12 *Perf. 12*

2715 A553 2ce Sheet of 4, #a-d 8.50 8.50

Souvenir Sheet

Perf. 12¾

2716 A553 6ce multi 6.25 6.25

No. 2715 contains four 47x27mm stamps.

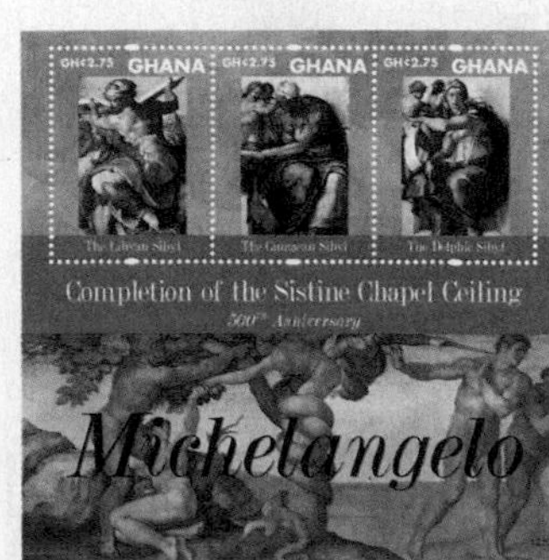

Completion of the Painting of the Sistine Chapel, 500th Anniv. — A554

No. 2717: a, Libyan Sibyl. b, Cumaean Sibyl. c, Delphic Sibyl.

7ce, First Day of Creation.

2012, Dec. 12 ***Perf. 13 Syncopated***
2717 A554 2.75ce Sheet of 3, #a-c 8.75 8.75

Souvenir Sheet

2718 A554 7ce multi 7.50 7.50

Miniature Sheet

Muhammad Ali and His Boxing Opponents — A554a

No. 2718A — Photographs from fights between Ali and: b, Doug Jones, 1963. c, Sonny Liston, 1965. d, Ernie Terrell, 1967. e, Joe Frazier, 1975.

2012 **Litho.** ***Perf. 13 Syncopated***
2718A A554a 2ce Sheet of 4, #b-e 8.50 8.50

Fruits and Vegetables — A555

Design: 10p, Pawpaws. 25p, Pineapples. 27p, Unripe oranges. 1ce, Shallot plants. 1.10ce, Tomatoes. 1.20ce, Shallots. 1.30ce, Carrots. 1.40ce, Mangoes. 3ce, Avocados. 5ce, Coconuts.

2012, Feb. 28 **Litho.** ***Perf. 13¼x14***
2719 A555 10p multi —
2720 A555 25p multi —
2721 A555 27p multi —
2722 A555 1ce multi —
2723 A555 1.10ce multi —
2724 A555 1.20ce multi —
2725 A555 1.30ce multi — —
2726 A555 1.40ce multi —
2727 A555 3ce multi — —
2728 A555 5ce multi —

Souvenir Sheet

Statue of Lao Tsu and Hanguguan Pass, Hanguguan, People's Republic of China — A556

2013, Jan. 1 **Litho.** ***Perf. 12***
2729 A556 10ce multi 10.50 10.50

Rat — A557

Ox — A558

Chinese Zodiac Animals — A559

No. 2732: a, Rat. b, Ox. c, Tiger. d, Rabbit. e, Dragon. f, Sanke. g, Horse. h, Sheep. i, Monkey. j, Rooster. k, Dog. l, Boar.

2013, Feb. 12 **Litho.** ***Perf. 13¼x13***
2730 A557 50p multi .55 .55
2731 A558 50p multi .55 .55

Perf. 14

2732 A559 50p Sheet of 12, #a-l 6.25 6.25

2013 Beijing Intl. Philatelic Exhibition (#2732).

World Environment Day — A560

No. 2733: a, Electical plug and socket. b, Recycling bucket. c, Lightbulb. d, Hand and faucet.
7ce, Wind generators.

2013, Feb. 12 **Litho.** ***Perf. 13¼***
2733 A560 2.25ce Sheet of 4, #a-d 9.50 9.50

Souvenir Sheet

2734 A560 7ce multi 7.50 7.50

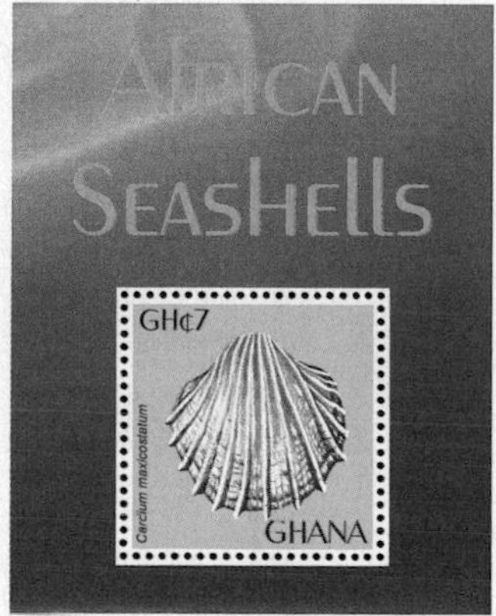

Shells — A561

No. 2735: a, Gymnobela abyssorum. b, Cypraea stercoraria minima. c, Euspira notabilis. d, Conus ateralbus.
7ce, Cardium maxicostatum.

2013, Feb. 12 **Litho.** ***Perf. 12½***
2735 A561 2.25ce Sheet of 4, #a-d 9.50 9.50

Souvenir Sheet

2736 A561 7ce multi 7.50 7.50

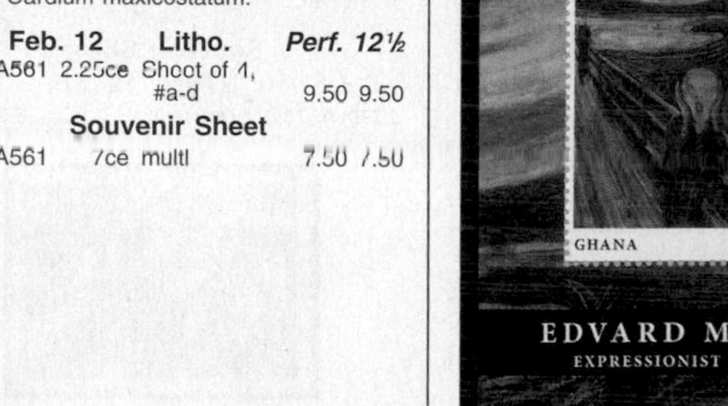

London Underground, 150th Anniv. — A562

No. 2737: a, Stockwell Staation, 1939. b, Cannon Street Station, 1866. c, Passenger drinking tea in train car, 1964. d, Bayswater Station, 1868. e, Oxford Circus Station, 2012. f, Escalators at Leicester Square Station, 1935.
7ce, Baker Street Station, 1863.

Perf. 12½x13¼

2013, Feb. 12 **Litho.**
2737 A562 2ce Sheet of 6, #a-f 12.50 12.50

Souvenir Sheet

Perf. 13¼

2738 A562 7ce multi 7.50 7.50

No. 2738 contains one 51x38mm stamp.

Minerals — A563

No. 2739 — Agate with: a, Brown, blue and orange rings. b, Purple rings with a dark center. c, Greenish blue and white rings, dark green blue center. d, Red violet and white rings, red violet center. e, Brown ring with gray blue crystals in center. f, Dark and light blue rings.
7ce, Amethyst, vert.

2013, May 1 **Litho.** ***Perf. 13¾***
2739 A563 2ce Sheet of 6, #a-f 12.50 12.50

Souvenir Sheet

Perf. 12½

2740 A563 7ce multi 7.25 7.25

No. 2740 contains one 38x51mm stamp.

Paintings by Edvard Munch (1863-1944) — A564

No. 2741: a, Death in the Sickroom. b, Portrait of Friedrich Nietzsche. c, The Vampire.
7ce, The Scream.

2013, May 1 **Litho.** ***Perf. 12½***
2741 A564 2.75ce Sheet of 3, #a-c 8.50 8.50

Souvenir Sheet

2742 A564 7ce multi 7.25 7.25

Souvenir Sheet

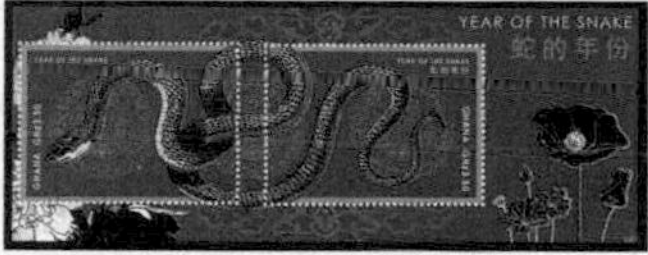

New Year 2013 (Year of the Snake) — A565

No. 2743: a, Head of snake. b, Tail of snake.

2013, May 15 **Litho.** ***Perf. 12½***
2743 A565 3.50ce Sheet of 2, #a-b 7.00 7.00

Lady Margaret Thatcher (1925-2013), British Prime Minister — A566

No. 2744 — Thatcher meeting with: a, Henry Kissinger, 1983. b, Pres. Ronald Reagan, 1984. c, Deng Xiaoping, 1982. d, Mikhail Gorbachev, 1990.
7ce, Thatcher, vert.

2013, June 24 **Litho.** ***Perf. 12***
2744 A566 2.25ce Sheet4 of 4, #a-d 9.00 9.00

Souvenir Sheet

Perf. 12½

2745 A566 7ce black 7.00 7.00

No. 2745 contains one 38x51mm stamp.

Reptiles — A567

No. 2746, 2.25ce: a, Desert monitor. b, Nile crocodile. c, African slender-snouted crocodile. d, Ground agama.
No. 2747, 2.25ce: a, African striped skink. b, Mwanza flat-headed agana. c, Red-headed rock agama. d, Rock monitor.
No. 2748, 7cc, Yellow-throated day gecko.
No. 2749, 7ce, Mozambique spitting cobra, vert.

2013, July 7 **Litho.** ***Perf. 14***

Sheets of 4, #a-d

2746-2747 A567 Set of 2 18.00 18.00

Souvenir Sheets

Perf. 12½

2748-2749 A567 Set of 2 14.00 14.00

No. 2748 contains one 51x38mm stamp.
No. 2749 contains one 38x51mm stamp.

History of Art — A568

No. 2750, 2.75ce — Byzantine art: a, St. Acathius of Melitene. b, Menologion of Basil II. c, Emperor Alexius I.

No. 2751, 2.75ce — Gothic art: a, Beata Umilta Transports Bricks to the Monastery, by Pietro Lorenzetti. b, Portrait of a Princess of the House of Este, by Pisanello. c, Cambridge Altarpiece, by Simone Martini.

No. 2752, 7ce, Book of Lindisfarne. No. 2753, 7ce, Illustration from Bury St. Edmunds Bible, by Master Hugo, horiz.

2013, July 7 Litho. *Perf. 12½*

Sheets of 3, #a-c

2750-2751 A568 Set of 2 16.50 16.50

Souvenir Sheets

2752-2753 A568 Set of 2 14.00 14.00

2006 Visit of Pope Benedict XVI to Bavaria, Germany — A569

2008 Visit of Pope Benedict XVI to the United States — A570

No. 2754 — Pope Benedict XVI: a, Waving. b, Wearing miter and holding crucifix. c, Kneeling at gravesite. d, Greeting children.

No. 2755 — Pope Benedict XVI: a, With New York City Mayor Michael Bloomberg. b, Standing behind candle between two priests. c, Holding censer. d, With arms extended.

No. 2756, Pope Benedict XVI and flower bushes. No. 2757, Pope Benedict XVI with Pres. George W. Bush.

Perf. 13 Syncopated

2013, July 19 Litho.

2754 A569 2.25ce Sheet of 4, #a-d 8.75 8.75

2755 A570 2.25ce Sheet of 4, #a-d 8.75 8.75

Souvenir Sheets

2756 A569 7ce multi 6.75 6.75

2757 A570 7ce multi 6.75 6.75

A571

African Animals — A572

No. 2758: a, Lion. b, Cheetah. c, Impala. d, African elephant.

No. 2759: a, African elephant (30x80mm). b, Impala (30x40mm). c, Lesser flamingo (30x40mm). d, Rhinoceros (30x40mm). e, Cheetah (30x40mm).

No. 2760: a, Chimpanzee. b, Giraffe. c, Southern ground hornbill. d, Southern ground hornbill, tree in background. e, Zebra. f, Lion.

7ce, Meerkats.

Perf. 12, 14 (A572)

2013, Aug. 28 Litho.

2758 A571 2.25ce Sheet of 4, #a-d 8.50 8.50

2759 A572 2.25ce Sheet of 5, #a-e 10.50 10.50

2760 A572 2.25ce Sheet of 6, #a-f 12.50 12.50

Souvenir Sheet

2761 A571 7ce multi 6.50 6.50

Miniature Sheet

Camellias — A573

No. 2762 — Camellia variety: a, Asmodee. b, Benaria Nova. c, Carlotta Nencini. d, Henry Clay. e, Imperatrice Eugenie. f, Isolina Corsi. g, L'Italia. h, Venetia la Bella. i, Brozzoni Nova.

2013, Sept. 10 Litho. *Perf. 13¾*

2762 A573 2ce Sheet of 9, #a-i 16.50 16.50

2013 China Intl. Collection Expo.

Pres. John F. Kennedy (1917-63) — A574

No. 2763 — Pres. Kennedy: a, Facing left, emblem at UR. b, Emblem at UL. c, Facing left, flag in background, emblem at UR. d, Facing Right, emblem at LL. e, Clapping, emblem at LR.

7ce, Pres. Kennedy in rocking chair.

2013, Sept. 10 Litho. *Perf. 14*

2763 A574 2ce Sheet of 5, #a-e 9.25 9.25

Souvenir Sheet

Perf. 12

2764 A574 7ce multi 6.50 6.50

UNESCO World Heritage Sites — A575

No. 2765: a, Mount Huangshan, People's Republic of China. b, Naeroyfjord, Norway. c, Thingvellir National Park, Iceland. d, Victoria Falls, Zambia and Zimbabwe.

No. 2766, 7ce, Cape Castle as seen from ocean, Ghana. No. 2767, 7ce, Larabanga Mosque, Ghana. No. 2768, 7ce, Cannons on Cape Castle.

2013, Sept. 10 Litho. *Perf. 12¾*

2765 A575 2.25ce Sheet of 4, #a-d 8.50 8.50

Souvenir Sheets

2766-2768 A575 Set of 3 19.50 19.50

Birth of Prince George of Cambridge — A576

No. 2769: a, Head of Duchess of Cambridge. b, Head of Duke of Cambridge. c, Duke of Cambridge holding Prince George of Cambridge. d, Duke and Duchess of Cambridge, Prince George.

7ce, Prince George of Cambridge.

2013, Oct. 1 Litho. *Perf. 14*

2769 A576 2.25ce Sheet of 4, #a-d 8.25 8.25

Souvenir Sheet

Perf. 12

2770 A576 7ce multi 6.50 6.50

John Atta Mills (1944-2012), President of Ghana — A576a

Design: 1.30ce, Mills meeting with United Nations Secretary-General Kofi Annan.

2013, Oct. 9 Litho. *Perf. 14*

2770A A576a 1.30ce multi — —

Two strips of stamps, three sheets of four stamps and a souvenir sheet were issued in this set. The editors would like to examine examples of the strips and sheets in their entirety.

Miniature Sheets

A577

Mao Zedong (1893-1976), Chinese Communist Leader — A578

No. 2771: a, Photograph of Mao Zedong and three other people, 1949. b, Photograph of Mao Zedong on chair with three children, 1951. c, Painting o f Mao Zedong with arches in background. d, Painting of Mao Zedong, in brown coat, leading people. e, Painting of Mao Zedong, in black coat, leading people. f, Painting of Mao Zedong with people and horses.

No. 2772: a, Photograph from 1937. b, Photograph from 1953. c, Photograph of Mao Zedong, red brown panel. d, As "c," green panel. e, As "c," dull purple panel. f, As "c," dull brown panel.

2013, Dec. 20 Litho. *Perf. 14*

2771 A577 50p Sheet of 6, #a-f 2.60 2.60

2772 A578 50p Sheet of 6, #a-f 2.60 2.60

Khon Masks — A579

No. 2773: a, Mask with three faces (35x70mm). b, Maske with green face (35x35mm). c, Mask with white face (35x35mm).

7ce, Mask, diff.

2013, Sept. 1 Litho. *Perf. 13¾*

2773 A579 2.75ce Sheet of 3, #a-c 7.75 7.75

Souvenir Sheet

2774 A579 7ce multi 6.50 6.50

Thailand 2013 World Stamp Exhibition, Bangkok. No. 2774 contains one 35x70mm stamp.

Souvenir Sheet

Election of Pope Francis — A580

No. 2775: a, Pope Francis. b, Arms of Pope Francis.

2013 Litho. *Imperf.*

2775 A580 10ce Sheet of 2, #a-b 17.00 17.00

Dogs — A581

No. 2776: a, English pointer. b, Polish hound. c, Westphalian Dachsbracke. d, Pharaoh hound.
12ce, Welsh Springer spaniel.

2014, Mar. 19 Litho. *Perf. 14*

2776 A581 4ce Sheet of 4, #a-d 13.00 13.00

Souvenir Sheet

Perf. 12¾

2777 A581 12ce multi 9.50 9.50

No. 2777 contains one 51x38mm stamp.

Miniature Sheets

Flowers — A582

No. 2778: a, Yellow disa. b, Blue disa. c, Flame lily. d, Sugarbush protea. e, Drip disa (large). f, Drip disa (small). g, Soprano lilac African spoon daisy.
No. 2779: a, Wood iris. b, Red disa. c, Comon sugarbush. d, Aloe. e, Ice plant.

2014, Mar. 19 Litho. *Perf. 14*

2778 A582 3.50ce Sheet of 7, #a-g 19.50 19.50
2779 A582 4ce Sheet of 5, #a-e 16.00 16.00

Orchids — A583

No. 2780, 4ce — Butterfly orchids of different colors with background color of: a, Dull green. b, Golden brown. c, Gray brown. d, Bright yellow green.
No. 2781, 4ce: a, Phalaenopsis. b, Cymbidium. c, Orchis mascula. d, Disa riette.
No. 2782, 12ce, Phalaenopsis, diff. No. 2783, 12ce, Butterfly orchid, diff., horiz.

2014, Mar. 19 Litho. *Perf. 14*

Sheets of 4, #a-d

2780-2781 A583 Set of 2 25.00 25.00

Souvenir Sheets

Perf. 12½

2782-2783 A583 Set of 2 19.00 19.00

No. 2782 contains one 38x51mm stamp. No. 2783 contains one 51x38mm stamp.

A584

A585

A586

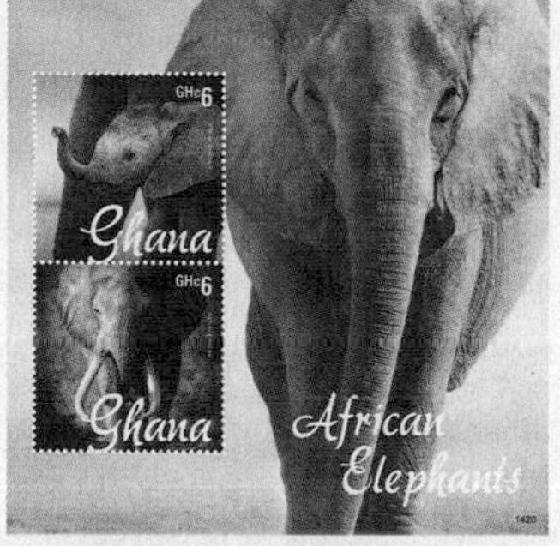

African Elephants — A587

No. 2784 — Elephants: a, Without tusks. b, With tusks.
No. 2785 — Elephant: a, Without tusks, b, With tusks.
No. 2786 — Elephant: a, With trunk raised. b, With trunk dangling.
No. 2787 — Elephants: a, Without tusks. b, With tusks.

2014, Mar. 19 Litho. *Perf. 13¾*

2784 A584 4ce Pair, #a-b 7.00 7.00
2785 A585 4ce Pair, #a-b 7.00 7.00

Souvenir Sheets

2786 A586 6ce Sheet of 2, #a-b 10.00 10.00
2787 A587 6ce Sheet of 2, #a-b 10.00 10.00

Nos. 2784 and 2785 each were printed in sheets containing two pairs.

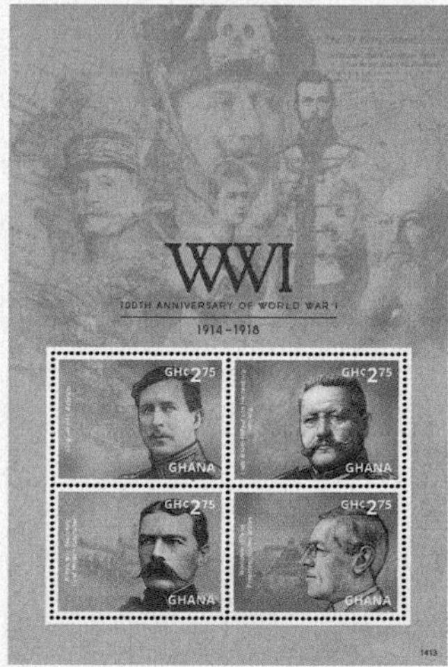

World War I, Cent. — A588

No. 2788, 2.75ce: a, King Albert I of Belgium. b, Field Marshal Paul von Hindenburg, Germany. c, Lord Horatio Kitchener, British War Secretary. d, Woodrow Wilson, U.S. President.
No. 2789, 2.75ce: a, U.S. soldiers in Renault FT-17 tank. b, British Mark IV Lodestar III tank. c, French Saint-Chomond tank. d, German A7V tank.
No. 2790, 4.50ce: a, Helmuth von Moltke, German Chief of Staff. b, Marshal Joseph Joffre, France.
No. 2791, 4.50ce: a, Hornsby chain track tractor. b, Mark V Hybrid Whippet tank.

2014, Mar. 19 Litho. *Perf. 14*

Sheets of 4, #a-d

2788-2789 A588 Set of 2 17.00 17.00

Souvenir Sheets of 2, #a-b

Perf. 12¼

2790-2791 A588 Set of 2 14.00 14.00

Nos. 2790-2791 each contain two 51x38mm stamps.

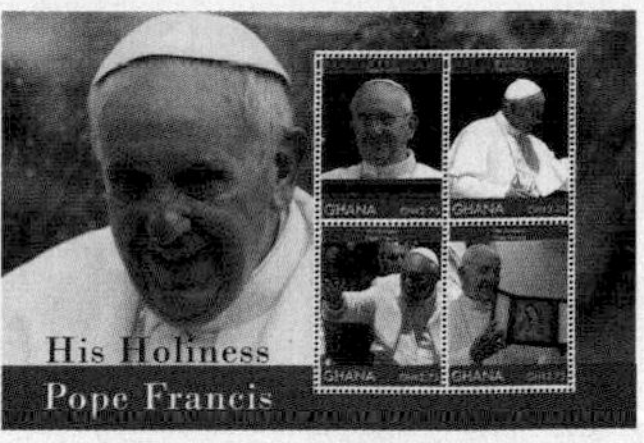

Pope Francis — A589

No. 2792, 2.75ce — Pope Francis: a, Wearing eyeglasses. b, Facing right. c, Waving. d, Holding icon.
No. 2793, 2.75ce — Pope Francis: a, With Italian Prime Minister Enrico Letta. b, Holding crucifix. c, Holding staff with crown. d, With Trinidad and Tobago President Anthony Carmona.
No. 2794, 4.50ce, horiz. — Pope Francis: a, With young boy. b, With Thailand Prime Minister Yingluck Shinawtra.
No. 2795, 4.50ce, horiz. — Pope Francis: a, Waving. b, With Lithuanian Prime Minister Algirdas Butkevicius.

2014, Mar. 19 Litho. *Perf. 14*

Sheets of 4, #a-d

2792-2793 A589 Set of 2 17.50 17.50

Souvenir Sheets of 2, #a-b

2794-2795 A589 Set of 2 14.50 14.50

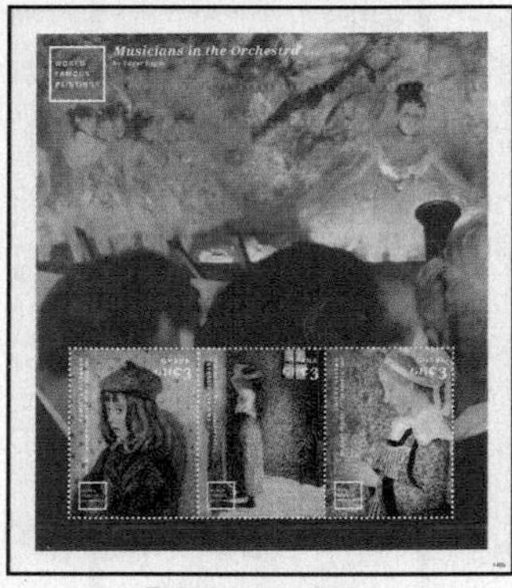

Paintings — A590

No. 2796, 3ce: a, Portrait of Félix Pissarro, by Camille Pissarro. b, Young Peasant at Her Toilette, by Pissarro. c, Brittany Peasant at the Pardon, by Childe Hassam.
No. 2797, 3ce: a, Marcella, by Ernst Ludwig Kirchner. b, The Arnolfini Portrait, by Jan van Eyck. c, Two Lovers, by Vincent van Gogh.
No. 2798, 9ce, Portrait of a Lute Player, by Francesco Salviati. No. 2799, 9ce, The Salon de la Rue des Moulins, by Henri de Toulouse-Lautrec.

2014, Mar. 19 Litho. *Perf. 12¾*

Sheets of 3, #a-c

2796-2797 A590 Set of 2 14.00 14.00

Size: 100x100mm

Imperf

2798-2799 A590 Set of 2 14.00 14.00

Paintings by Qi Baishi (1864-1957) — A591

No. 2800, 2.75ce: a, Mother Hen, Chicks and Banana Leaves. b, Loquats in a Basket. c, Crows Returning to Wintry Trees. d, Mother and Child.
No. 2801, 2.75ce: a, Pomegranates. b, Mynahs and Amaranthus. c, Begonias and Rock. d, Camellias.
No. 2802, 4.50ce: a, Lotus and Mandarin Ducks. b, Magpie and Plum Blossoms.
No. 2803, 4.50ce: a, Autumn Landscape with Cormorants. b, Sunrise Over Water.

2014, Mar. 19 Litho. *Perf. 14*

Sheets of 4, #a-d

2800-2801 A591 Set of 2 17.00 17.00

Souvenir Sheets of 2, #a-b

2802-2803 A591 Set of 2 14.00 14.00

Chinese Leaders — A592

Designs: No. 2804, Deng Xiaoping (1904-97), red brown background.

No. 2805: a, Deng Xiaoping, yellow orange background. b, Hu Jintao. c, Mao Zedong (1893-1976). d, Xi Jinping.

Perf. 13 Syncopated

2014, Sept. 4 Litho.

2804 A592 2.75ce multi 1.75 1.75

2805 A592 2.75ce Sheet of 4, #a-d 7.00 7.00

No. 2804 was printed in sheets of 4.

Mei Lanfang (1894-1961), Peking Opera Performer — A593

No. 2806: a, In costume with fan. b, In costume without fan.

9ce, Wearing suit and tie.

2014, Sept. 4 Litho. *Perf. 12½*

2806 A593 2.75ce Pair, #a-b 3.50 3.50

Souvenir Sheet

2807 A593 9ce multi 5.75 5.75

No. 2806 was printed in sheets containing 3 pairs.

Endangered Animals of Africa — A594

No. 2808, 2.75ce: a, Addax. b, Bonobo. c, Wattled crane. d, West African giraffe.

No. 2809, 2.75ce: a, Dorcas gazelle. b, Eastern lowland gorilla. c, African penguin. d, White rhinoceros.

No. 2810, 4.50ce: a, Hartmann's mountain zebra. b, Verreaux's sifaka.

No. 2811, 4.50ce: a, Cheetah. b, Forest elephant.

2014, Sept. 15 Litho. *Perf. 12*

Sheets of 4, #a-d

2808-2809 A594 Set of 2 14.50 14.50

Souvenir Sheets of 2, #a-b

2810-2811 A594 Set of 2 12.00 12.00

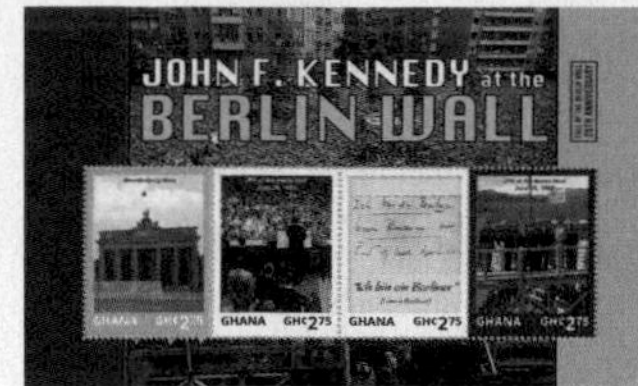

Fall of the Berlin Wall, 25th Anniv. — A595

No. 2812, 2.75ce: a, Brandenburg Gate. b, Pres. John F. Kennedy delivering speech at Berlin Wall, 1963. c, "Ich bin ein Berliner" quotation by Kennedy. d, Kennedy and others on platform with staircase.

No. 2813, 2.75ce: a, People on Berlin Wall, 1989. b, Pres. Ronald Reagan at podium in front of Berlin Wall, 1987. c, Quotation from Reagan's Berlin Wall speech. d, Reagan at podium in front of Brandenburg Gate, 1987.

No. 2814, 4.50ce, horiz.: a, Man waving German flag at fall of Berlin Wall, 1989. b, Sepia photograph of damaged segment of Berlin Wall.

No. 2815, 4.50ce, horiz.: a, People climbing on Berlin Wall, 1989. b, Color photograph of damaged segment of Berlin Wall.

2014, Sept. 15 Litho. *Perf. 14*

Sheets of 4, #a-d

2812-2813 A595 Set of 2 14.00 14.00

Souvenir Sheets of 2, #a-b

Perf. 12

2814-2815 A595 Set of 2 11.50 11.50

Dinosaurs — A596

No. 2816, 2.75ce: a, Dilophosaurus. b, Tyrannosaurus. c, Ornitholestes. d, Compsognathus.

No. 2817, 2.75ce: a, Kentrosaurus. b, Achelousaurus. c, Brachiosaurus. d, Camarasaurus.

No. 2818, 4.50ce: a, Majungosaurus. b, Ceratosaurus.

No. 2819, 4.50ce, horiz.: a, Aucasaurus, country name at LL. b, Aucasaurus, country name at LR.

2014, Sept. 15 Litho. *Perf. 14*

Sheets of 4, #a-d

2816-2817 A596 Set of 2 14.00 14.00

Souvenir Sheets of 2, #a-b

Perf. 12¾

2818-2819 A596 Set of 2 11.50 11.50

No. 2818 contains two 38x51mm stamps. No. 2819 contains two 51x38mm stamps.

Frogs — A597

No. 2820, 2.50ce: a, Nest tree frog. b, Mababe River frog. c, Banana frog. d, African bullfrog. e, Banded grass frog.

No. 2821, 2.50ce: a, Snoring puddle frog. b, Mascarene grass frog. c, Painted reed frog. d, Nest frog. e, Spiny reed frog.

No. 2822: a, Nosed grass frog. b, Water lily frog

2014, Sept. 15 Litho. *Perf. 13¾*

Sheets of 5, #a-e

2820-2821 A597 Set of 2 17.00 17.00

Souvenir Sheet

2822 A597 4.50ce Sheet of 2, #a-b 6.00 6.00

Statue of Four Sheep A598

Woman and Goat — A599

Paintings by Qi Baishi (1864-1957) — A600

No. 2825 — Painting with: a, White goat. b, Black goat.

2014, Nov. 24 Litho. *Perf. 12¾*

2823 A598 2.75ce multi 1.75 1.75

Perf. 13¾

2824 A599 3ce multi 1.90 1.90

Souvenir Sheet

Perf. 12

2825 A600 4.50ce Sheet of 2, #a-b 5.75 5.75

New Year 2015 (Year of the Goat). No. 2823 was printed in sheets of 4. No. 2824 was printed in sheets of 8 + 4 labels.

Lightning — A601

No. 2826 — Various lightning bolts, as shown.

9ce, Lightning, diff.

2015, Mar. 2 Litho. *Perf. 14*

2826 A601 3.50ce Sheet of 6, #a-f 12.00 12.00

Souvenir Sheet

Perf. 12

2827 A601 9ce multi 5.25 5.25

Snakes — A602

No. 2828, 4ce: a, Blotched snake. b, Caspian whipsnake. c, Grass snake. d, Long-nosed viper.

No. 2829, 4ce: a, Smooth snake. b, Mangrove snake. c, Corn snake. d, Common garter snake.

No. 2830, 9ce, Aesculapian snake. No. 2831, 9ce, Royal python, vert.

2015, Mar. 2 Litho. *Perf. 14*

Sheets of 4, #a-d

2828-2829 A602 Set of 2 18.50 18.50

Souvenir Sheets

Perf. 12

2830-2831 A602 Set of 2 10.50 10.50

Horses — A603

No. 2832, 4ce: a, Mustang, North America. b, Fjord horse, Norway. c, Fell pony, England. d, Icelandic horse, Iceland.

No. 2833, 4ce, horiz.: a, Friesian horse, Netherlands. b, Thoroughbred, England. c, Andalusian horse, Iberian Peninsula. d, Arabian horse, Arabian Peninsula.

No. 2834, 9ce, Shire horse, England. No. 2835, 9ce, Appaloosa, United States, horiz.

2015, Mar. 2 Litho. *Perf. 14*
Sheets of 4, #a-d
2832-2833 A603 Set of 2 18.50 18.50

Souvenir Sheets
Perf. 12
2834-2835 A603 Set of 2 10.50 10.50

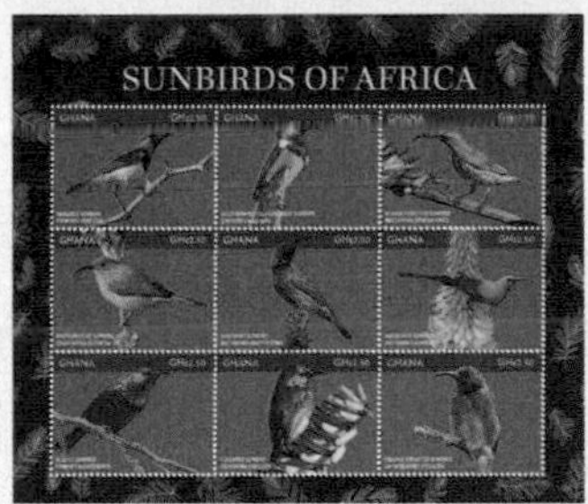

Sunbirds — A604

No. 2836: a, Variable sunbird. b, Southern double-collared sunbird. c, Scarlet-chested sunbird. d, Eastern olive sunbird. e, Amethyst sunbird. f, Malachite sunbird. g, Marico sunbird. h, Collared sunbird. i, Orange-breasted sunbird.
9ce, Splendid sunbird.

2015, Mar. 2 Litho. *Perf. 14*
2836 A604 2.50ce Sheet of 9, #a-i 13.00 13.00

Souvenir Sheet
2837 A604 9ce multi 5.25 5.25

Miniature Sheets

Characters From *Downton Abbey* Television Series — A605

No. 2838, 2ce: a, Earl of Grantham. b, Countess of Grantham. c, Lady Mary Crawley. d, Lady Edith Crawley. e, Lady Rose MacClare.
No. 2839, 2ce: a, Mr. Carson. b, Mrs. Hughes. c, Mr. Bates. d, Anna. e, Mrs. Patmore.
No. 2840, 2ce: a, Dowager Countess of Grantham. b, Mrs. Crawley. c, Mr. Barrow. d, Mr. Molesley. e, Daisy.

2015, Mar. 24 Litho. *Perf.*
Sheets of 5, #a-e
2838-2840 A605 Set of 3 16.00 16.00

Birds — A606

No. 2841: a, Secretary bird. b, Great white pelican. c, Lesser flamingo. d, Beautiful sunbird.
7ce, Saddlebilled stork, vert.

2015, June 5 Litho. *Perf. 14*
2841 A606 3ce Sheet of 4, #a-d 6.25 6.25

Souvenir Sheet
2842 A606 7ce multi 3.75 3.75

No. 2842 contains one 30x80mm stamp.

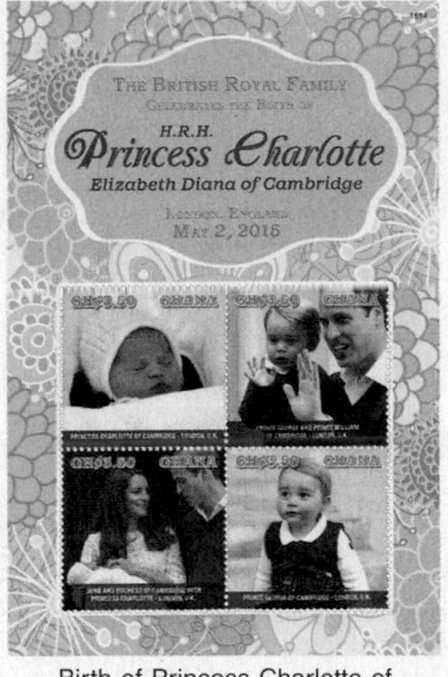

Birth of Princess Charlotte of Cambridge — A607

No. 2843: a, Princess Charlotte. b, Princes William and George. c, Duke and Duchess of Cambridge with Princess Charlotte. d. Prince George.
9ce, Duke and Duchess of Cambridge, Prince George, Princess Charlotte, horiz.

2015, June 5 Litho. *Perf. 13¾*
2843 A607 3.50ce Sheet of 4, #a-d 7.25 7.25

Souvenir Sheet
2844 A607 9ce multi 4.75 4.75

No. 2844 contains one 70x35mm stamp.

Palace Museum, Beijing, 50th Anniv. — A608

No. 2845: a, Buildings inside of walls of Forbidden City (1) (60x40mm). b, Painting of the Ming Dynasty Era Chinese official Xu Xianqing (2) (30x40mm). c, Sundial (3) (30x40mm). d, Portrait of Prince Zhu Youyuan (4) (30x40mm). e, Forbidden City Turret (5) (30x40mm). f, Neolithic era pot (6) (30x40mm). g, Painting of the Kangxi Emperor of the Qing Dynasty (7) (30x80mm). h, Forbidden City Main Gate Temple and Tiananmen Square (8) (60x40mm). i, Ornamented gate (9) (60x40mm). j, Lion-head handle on fire bowl (10) (30x40mm). k, Painting of the Ming Dynasty Era Chinese official Xu Xianqing (11) (30x40mm).
7ce, Portrait of the Qianlong Emperor in armor, horiz.

2015, June 5 Litho. *Perf. 14*
2845 A608 2ce Sheet of 11, #a-k 11.50 11.50

Souvenir Sheet
2846 A608 7ce multi 3.75 3.75

No. 2846 contains one 40x30mm stamp.

Swans — A609

No. 2847: a, Mute swan in flight. b, Mute swan standing. c, Black-necked swan.
9ce, Mute swan in flight, vert.

2015, Aug. 3 Litho. *Perf. 12*
2847 A609 4ce Sheet of 3, #a-c 6.25 6.25

Souvenir Sheet
2848 A609 9ce multi 4.75 4.75

Singapore 2015 Intl. Philatelic Exhibition.

Christmas
A610

Religious paintings by Sandro Botticelli: 2ce, Madonna and Child with Adoring Angel. 3ce, Madonna and Child. 4ce, Madonna of the Book. 5ce, The Adoration of the Magi.

2015, Sept. 2 Litho. *Perf. 12½*
2849-2852 A610 Set of 4 7.50 7.50

Butterflies — A611

No. 2853, 4ce: a, White morpho. b, Graphium. c, Thamyris morpho. d, Rice paper butterfly.
No. 2854, 4ce: a, Orange-barred sulphur. b, Leopard lacewing. c, Giant striped morpho. d, Orange albatross.
No. 2855, 12ce, Malachite. No. 2856, 12ce, Citrus swallowtail.

2015, Nov. 2 Litho. *Perf. 12*
Sheets of 4, #a-d
2853-2854 A611 Set of 2 16.50 16.50

Souvenir Sheets
2855-2856 A611 Set of 2 12.50 12.50

Wild Cats — A612

No. 2857 — Caracal: a, With both ears touching top of stamp. b, Facing left. c, Two juveniles. d, On tree branch. e, With mouth open. f, With one ear touching top of stamp.
No. 2858 — Lion: a, Female facing right with open mouth. b, Head of male. c, Male looking left. d, Female facing right with closed mouth.
No. 2859, 12ce, Jaguar. No. 2860, 12ce, Cheetah.

2015, Nov. 2 Litho. *Perf. 14*
2857 A612 3.50ce Sheet of 6, #a-f 11.00 11.00
2858 A612 4ce Sheet of 4, #a-d 8.25 8.25

Souvenir Sheets
Perf. 12
2859-2860 A612 Set of 2 12.50 12.50

No. 2860 contains one 50x30mm stamp.

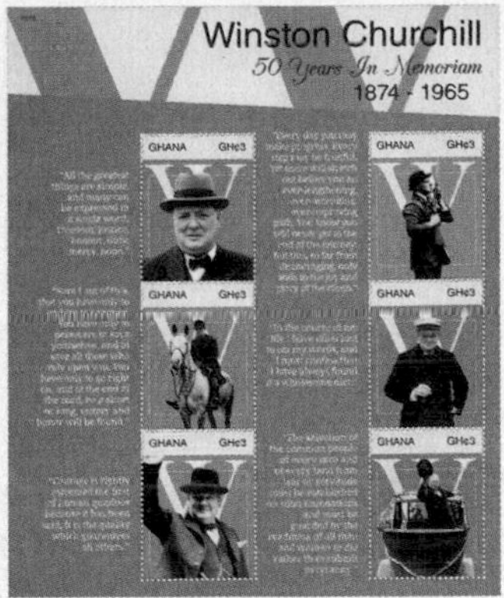

Sir Winston Churchill (1874-1965), British Prime Minister — A613

No. 2861 — Churchill: a, Wearing hat. b, Holding rifle. c, On horse. d, Holding cigar. e, Wearing hat, waving. f, In carriage, waving hat.
7ce, Churchill with cigar and cane.

2015, June 5 Litho. *Perf. 14*
2861 A613 3ce Sheet of 6, #a-f 9.25 9.25

Souvenir Sheet
2862 A613 7ce multi 3.75 3.75

Souvenir Sheet

New Year 2016 (Year of the Monkey) — A614

No. 2863: a, Monkey at left, with arm raised, Chinese characters at LL. b, Monkey with arm extended to left. c, Monkey with arm raised, Chinese characters at LR.

2015, Sept. 25 Litho. *Perf. 12*
2863 A614 4ce Sheet of 3, #a-c 6.50 6.50

Mushrooms — A615

No. 2864: a, Shiitake mushroom. b, Chanterelle mushroom. c, Russula mushroom. d, Button mushroom. e, Oyster mushroom. f, Porcini mushroom.
9ce, Morel.

2015, Nov. 2 Litho. *Perf. 14*
2864 A615 3.50ce Sheet of 6, #a-f 11.00 11.00

Souvenir Sheet
Perf. 12
2865 A615 9ce multi 4.75 4.75

No. 2865 contains one 50x30mm stamp. The mushroom on No. 2864c, Russula fellea, is inedible.

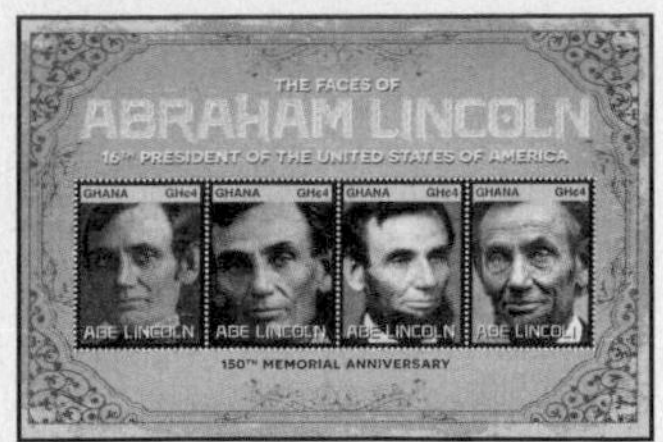

Pres. Abraham Lincoln (1809-65) — A616

No. 2866 — Various photographs of Lincoln, as shown.
9ce, Lincoln reading to son, Tad.

2015, Nov. 2 Litho. *Perf. 14*
2866 A616 4ce Sheet of 4, #a-d 8.25 8.25

Souvenir Sheet
Perf. 12

2867 A616 9ce multi 4.75 4.75

Sinking of the RMS Lusitania, Cent. — A617

No. 2868: a, Boat deck. b, First class dining room. c, Crowd on dock near Lusitania. d, Stern of Lusitania (no smokestacks). e, Midships of Lusitania. f, Bow of Lusitania (one smokestack).
9ce, Lusitania at sea.

2015, Nov. 2 Litho. *Perf. 14*
2868 A617 3.50ce Sheet of 6, #a-f 11.00 11.00

Souvenir Sheet
Perf. 12½

2869 A617 9ce multi 4.75 4.75
No. 2869 contains one 51x38mm stamp.

Queen Elizabeth II, Longest-Reigning British Monarch — A618

No. 2870 — Queen Elizabeth II wearing hat with colors: a, Ultramarine and white. b, Pale blue. c, Yellow. d, Peach.
9ce, Queen Elizabeth II wearing cerise hat and coat.

2015, Nov. 25 Litho. *Perf. 14*
2870 A618 4ce Sheet of 4, #a-d 8.25 8.25

Souvenir Sheet

2871 A618 9ce multi 4.75 4.75

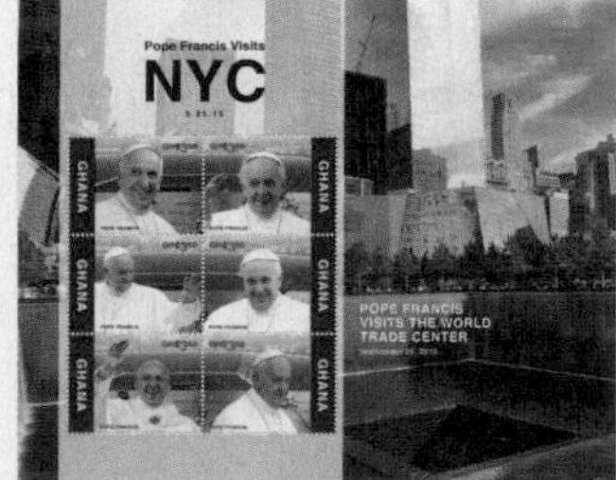

Visit of Pope Francis to New York City — A619

No. 2872 — World Trade Center Memorial and: a, Pope not waving, rose at LR. b, Pope waving, hand at left, 2 roses behind head. c, Pope waving, hand at right, rose at LR. d, Pope not waving, rose at LL and at right. e, Pope waving, hand at left, rose at left and LR. f, Pope not waving, rose stem at right.
9ce, Pope Francis waving, buildings.

2015, Nov. 25 Litho. *Perf. 14*
2872 A619 3.50ce Sheet of 6, #a-f 11.00 11.00

Souvenir Sheet
Perf. 12

2873 A619 9ce multi 4.75 4.75

Oct. 20, 2015 State Dinner at Buckingham Palace — A620

No. 2874: a, Duchess of Cambridge, hands not visible (35x35mm). b, Duchess of Cambridge holding glass (35x35mm). c, Duchess of Cambridge toasting Chinese President Xi Jinping (35x70mm).
9ce, Duchess of Cambridge, President Xi, Queen Elizabeth II, horiz.

2015, Dec. 7 Litho. *Perf. 13¾*
2874 A620 4ce Sheet of 3, #a-c 6.25 6.25

Souvenir Sheet
Perf. 14

2875 A620 9ce multi 4.75 4.75
No. 2875 contains one 80x30mm stamp.

Magna Carta, 800th Anniv. — A621

No. 2876: a, Seal of King John of England (seated). b, People near King John, seated on throne. c, Seal of King John (on horse). d, King John signing Magna Carta.
9ce, King John.

2015, Dec. 21 Litho. *Perf. 14*
2876 A621 4ce Sheet of 4, #a-d 8.50 8.50

Souvenir Sheet
Perf. 12

2877 A621 9ce multi 4.75 4.75

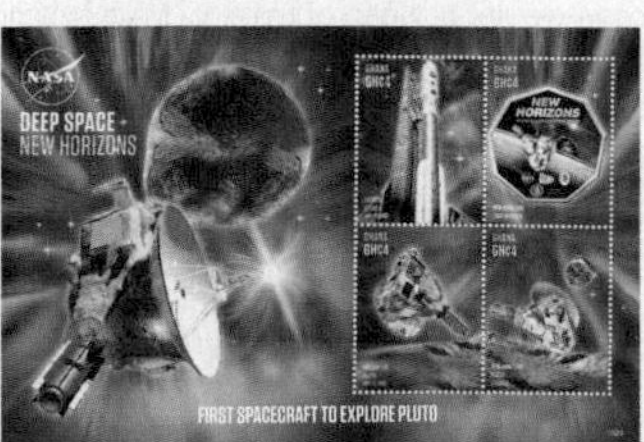

New Horizons Space Probe — A622

No. 2878: a, Atlas V on launchpad. b, Mission emblem. c, New Horizons over Pluto. d, New Horizons, Pluto and Charon.
9ce, New Horizons approaching Pluto.

2015, Dec. 21 Litho. *Perf. 14*
2878 A622 4ce Sheet of 4, #a-d 8.50 8.50

Souvenir Sheet
Perf. 12

2879 A622 9ce multi 4.75 4.75

Souvenir Sheets

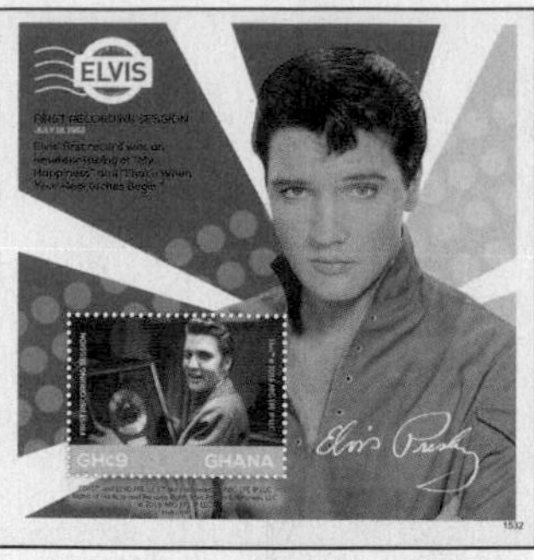

Elvis Presley (1935-77) — A623

Inscriptions: No. 2880, 9ce, First recording session. No. 2881, 9ce, Purchases Rising Sun. No. 2882, 9ce, Promoted to Private First Class, vert. No. 2883, 9ce, Waterskiing on McKellar Lake.

Perf. 12, 14 (#2883)
2015, Dec. 21 Litho.
2880-2883 A623 Set of 4 19.00 19.00

Paintings by Vincent van Gogh (1853-90) — A624

No. 2884: a, A Pair of Shoes, 1888 (40x30mm). b, Cypresses with Two Women, 1889 (40x60mm). c, Portrait of Patience Escalier, 1888 (40x30mm). d, Peasant Burning Weeds, 1883 (40x30mm). e, Country Churchyard and Old Church Tower, 1885 (40x30mm). f, Portrait of Eugene Boch, 1888 (40x60mm). g, Cottage with Decrepit Barn and Stooping Woman, 1885 (80x30mm). h, Still Life with Clogs and Pots, 1884 (40x30mm). i, Avenue of Poplars in Autumn, 1884 (40x60mm). j, Still Life with Absinthe, 1887 (40x30mm). k, Cows, 1890 (40x30mm).
9ce, Self-portrait with Gray Felt Hat, 1887.

2015, Dec. 31 Litho. *Perf. 14*
2884 A624 2ce Sheet of 11, #a-k 11.50 11.50

Souvenir Sheet
Perf. 12

2885 A624 9ce multi 4.75 4.75
No. 2885 contains one 40x60mm stamp. Inscription on No. 2884i is incorrect.

Gray-Crowned Crane — A625

No. 2886: a, Crane facing right, neck visible. b, Two cranes. c, Crane facing forward. d, Crane facing right, neck not visible.
12ce, Crane, diff.

2016, Feb. 20 Litho. *Perf. 14*
2886 A625 4ce Sheet of 4, #a-d 8.25 8.25

Souvenir Sheet
Perf. 12½

2887 A625 12ce multi 6.25 6.25
No. 2887 contains one 38x51mm stamp.

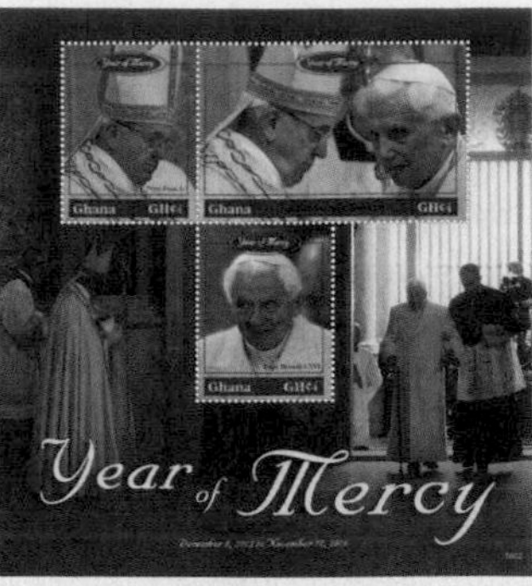

Extraordinary Jubilee of Mercy — A626

No. 2888: a, Pope Francis (30x40mm). b, Popes Francis and Benedict XVI (60x40mm). c, Pope Benedict XVI (30x40mm).
9ce, Popes Francis and Benedict XVI, vert.

2016, Feb. 20 Litho. *Perf. 14*
2888 A626 4ce Sheet of 3, #a-c 6.25 6.25

Souvenir Sheet
Perf. 12½

2889 A626 9ce multi 4.75 4.75
No. 2889 contains one 38x51mm stamp.

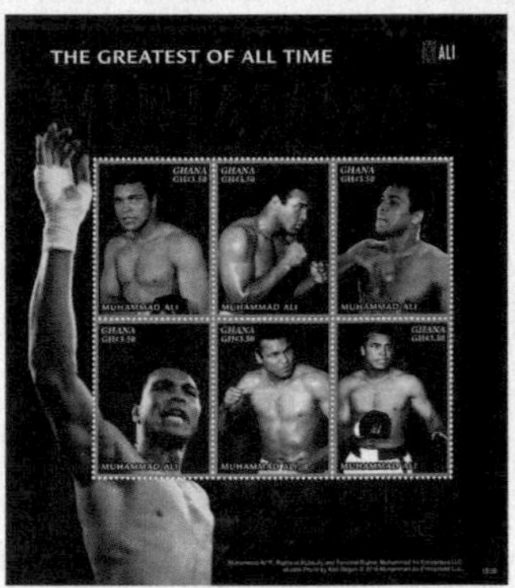

Muhammad Ali (1942-2016), Boxer — A627

No. 2890 — Various images of Ali, as shown.
9ce, Ali, horiz.

2016, Mar. 8 Litho. *Perf. 14*
2890 A627 3.50ce Sheet of 6, #a-f 11.00 11.00

Souvenir Sheet

2891 A627 9ce multi 4.75 4.75
No. 2891 contains one 80x30mm stamp.

New York City Landmarks — A628

No. 2892: a, Manhattan Bridge. b, Williamsburg Bridge. c, Brooklyn Bridge. d, Hell Gate Bridge.
20ce, New York City skyline.

2016, Apr. 8 Litho. *Perf. 12*
2892 A628 5ce Sheet of 4, #a-d 10.50 10.50

Souvenir Sheet
Perf. 14

2893 A628 20ce multi 10.50 10.50
No. 2893 contains one 160x60mm stamp. Inscription on No. 2892d is incorrect.

Worldwide Fund for Nature (WWF) — A629

No. 2894 — Various depictions of Slender-snouted crocodile: a, Denomination at UR. b, Denomination at UL, crocodile facing left. c, Denomination at LR. d, Denomination at UL, crocodile facing right.

2016, Apr. 8 Litho. *Perf. 14*

2894 A629 5ce Block of 4, #a-d 10.50 10.50
e. Souvenir sheet of 8, 2 each #2894a-2894d, perf. 12 21.00 21.00

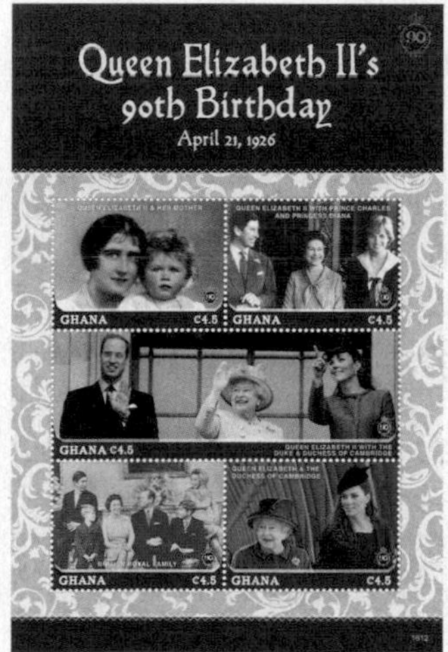

Queen Elizabeth II, 90th Birthday — A630

No. 2895 — Queen Elizabeth II: a, As child, with her mother (40x30mm). b, With Prince Charles and Princess Diana (40x30mm). c, With Duke and Duchess of Cambridge (80x30mm). d, With her family (40x30mm). e, With Duchess of Cambridge (40x30mm).
19ce, Queen Elizabeth II as infant, with parents.

2016, May 16 Litho. *Perf. 14*

2895 A630 4.50ce Sheet of 5, #a-e 11.50 11.50

Souvenir Sheet

Perf. 12½

2896 A630 19ce multi 9.75 9.75

No. 2896 contains one 51x38mm stamp.

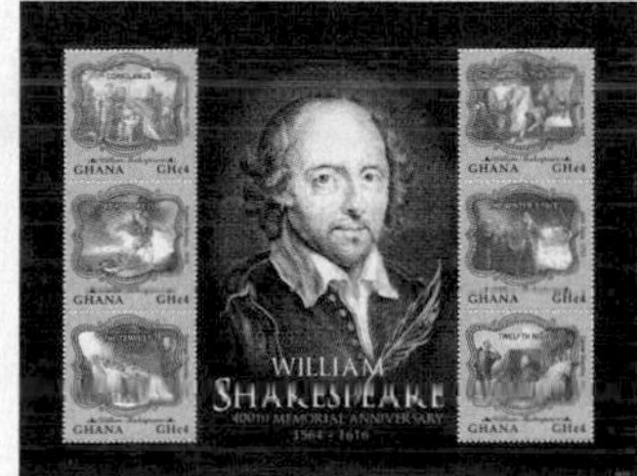

William Shakespeare (1564-1616), Writer — A631

No. 2897 — Scenes from: a, Coriolanus. b, The Taming of the Shrew. c, As You Like It. d, The Winter's Tale. e, The Tempest. f, Twelfth Night.
No. 2898 — Scenes from: a, Romeo and Juliet. b, Hamlet. c, Macbeth. d, King Lear.
19ce, First Folio, 1623, horiz.

2016, May 16 Litho. *Perf. 13¾*

2897 A631 4ce Sheet of 6, #a-f 12.50 12.50
2898 A631 5ce Sheet of 4, #a-d 10.50 10.50

Souvenir Sheet

Perf. 12½

2899 A631 19ce multi 9.75 9.75

No. 2899 contains one 38x51mm stamp.

African Mammals — A632

No. 2900: a, Giant forest hog. b, Hyena. c, Lion. d, Striped grass mouse. e, Spotted-necked otter. f, Old World porcupine.
No. 2901, horiz.: a, Bat-eared fox. b, Cape hare. c, Caracal. d, Desert hedgehog.
9ce, Wildebeest.

2016, May 16 Litho. *Perf. 14*

2900 A632 3.50ce Sheet of 6, #a-f 11.00 11.00
2901 A632 4ce Sheet of 4, #a-d 8.25 8.25

Souvenir Sheet

Perf. 12

2902 A632 9ce multi 4.75 4.75

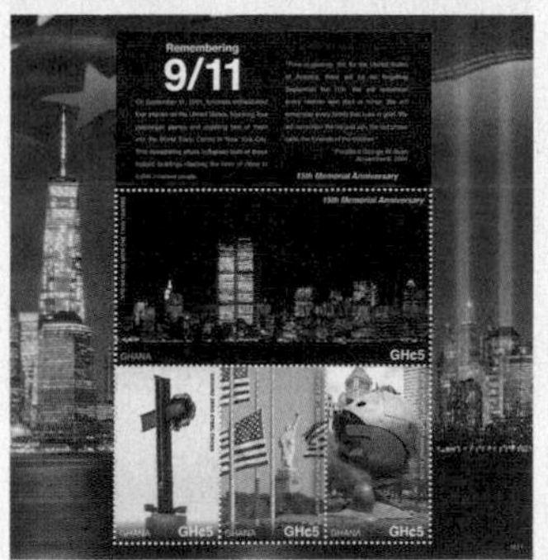

Sept. 11, 2001 Terrorist Attacks, 15th Anniv. — A633

No. 2903: a, Nighttime New York City skyline with World Trade Center (90x50mm). b, Ground Zero steel cross (30x50mm). c, Statue of Liberty, flags at half-staff (30x50mm). d, World Trade Center bronze globe (30x50mm).
19ce, Ground Zero Tribute in Light.

2016, May 16 Litho. *Perf. 12*

2903 A633 5ce Sheet of 4, #a-d 10.50 10.50

Souvenir Sheet

Perf. 12

2904 A633 19ce multi 9.75 9.75

No. 2904 contains one 60x50mm stamp.

Flowers — A634

No. 2905: a, Arum lily. b, Blue water lily. c, African violet. d, Impala lily.
9ce, Cape daisy, horiz.

2016, May 30 Litho. *Perf. 13¾*

2905 A634 4ce Sheet of 4, #a-d 8.25 8.25

Souvenir Sheet

Perf. 12½

2906 A634 9ce multi 4.75 4.75

No. 2906 contains one 51x38mm stamp.

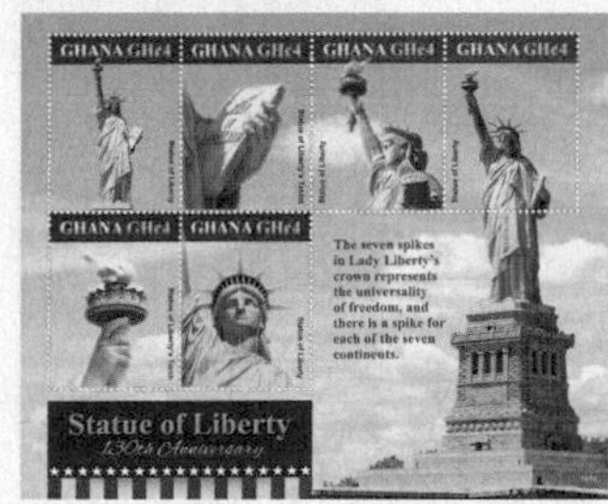

Statue of Liberty, 130th Anniv. — A635

No. 2907: a, Entire statue. b, Tablet. c, Top of statue, torch touching top panel. d, Top of statue, torch below top panel. e, Torch. f, Head of statue.
9ce, Statue of Liberty, diff.

2016, June 15 Litho. *Perf. 14*

2907 A635 4ce Sheet of 6, #a-f 12.50 12.50

Souvenir Sheet

Perf.

2908 A635 9ce multi 4.50 4.50

No. 2908 contains one 33x43mm oval stamp.

Funtunfunefu Symbol — A635a

2016, Aug. 17 Litho. *Perf. 14*

2908A A635a 2ce multi —

2016 National Elections. At least four additional stamps were issued in this set. The editors would like to examine any examples.

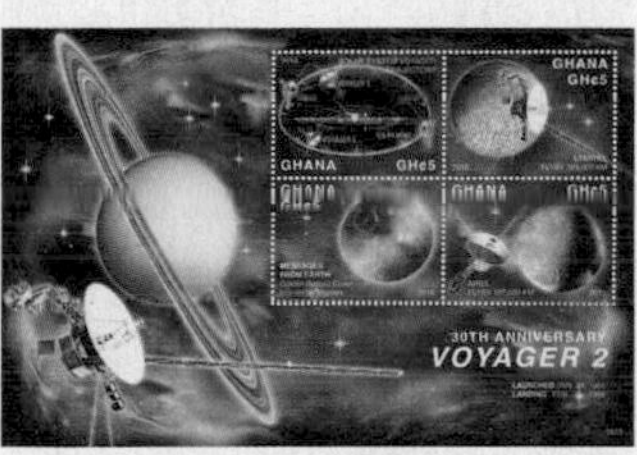

Voyager 2, 30th Anniv. (in 2017) — A636

No. 2909: a, Trajectories of Voyagers 1 and 2, Pioneers 10 and 11. b, Voyager 2 flyby of Umbriel. c, Cover of Golden Record. d, Voyager 2 flyby of Ariel.
19ce, Launch of Voyager 2, vert.

2016, Sept. 9 Litho. *Perf. 14*

2909 A636 5ce Sheet of 4, #a-d 10.00 10.00

Souvenir Sheet

2910 A636 19ce multi 9.50 9.50

Sheet margin of No. 2909 has incorrect information about launch date and a non-existent landing date.

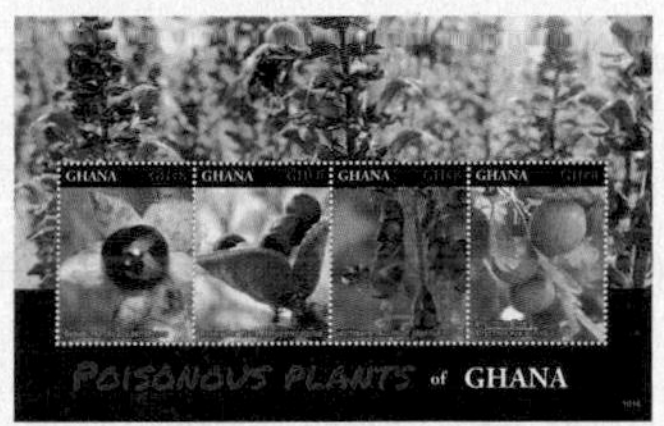

Poisonous Plants — A637

No. 2911: a, Belladonna. b, Rosary pea plant. c, Wolfsbane. d, Strychnine tree.
No. 2912, horiz.: a, Castor oil plant. b, Angel's trumpet.
16ce, Yew tree.

2016, Sept. 13 Litho. *Perf. 14*

2911 A637 8ce Sheet of 4, #a-d 16.00 16.00

Souvenir Sheets

Perf. 12

2912 A637 12ce Sheet of 2 12.00 12.00
2913 A637 16ce multi 8.00 8.00

Visit of Pres. Barack Obama to Japan — A638

No. 2914: a, 5ce, Pres. Obama, U.S. flag (40x30mm). b, 5ce, Japanese Prime Minister Shinzo Abe, Japanese flag (40x30mm). c, 5ce, Obama and Abe, flags (40x30mm). d, 10ce, Obama and Abe, flags, diff. (40x60mm).
No. 2915: a, Obama, Presidential Seal, U.S. flag. b, Abe, emblem of Prime Minister, Japanese flag.

2016, Oct. 10 Litho. *Perf. 14*

2914 A638 Sheet of 4, #a-d 12.50 12.50

Souvenir Sheets

Perf. 13¾

2915 A638 10ce Sheet of 2, #a-b 10.00 10.00

No. 2915 contains two 35x35mm stamps.

Visit to Bhutan of Duke and Duchess of Cambridge — A639

No. 2916: a, Duke and Duchess of Cambridge, person behind Duchess. b, Duke of Cambridge. c, Duchess of Cambridge. d, Duke and Duchess, people in background.
No. 2917: a, Duke and Duchess, Duke holding jacket. b, Duke and Duchess, no hands visible.

2016, Oct. 14 Litho. *Perf. 12*
2916 A639 8ce Sheet of 4, #a-d 16.00 16.00

Souvenir Sheet
Perf. 13¾

2917 A639 12ce Sheet of 2, #a-b 12.00 12.00

No. 2917 contains two 35x35mm stamps.

Patas Monkeys — A640

No. 2918 — Monkey: a, Eating foliage, hand at mouth. b, Facing left with mouth open. c, Facing left with mouth closed. d, With food in mouth and hand near mouth. e, Facing right with mouth closed. f, Holding food with both hands.
No. 2919: a, Monkey on all fours. b, Monkey sitting.

2016, Oct. 24 Litho. *Perf. 14*
2918 A640 3ce Sheet of 6, #a-f 9.00 9.00

Souvenir Sheet

2919 A640 8ce Sheet of 2, #a-b 8.00 8.00

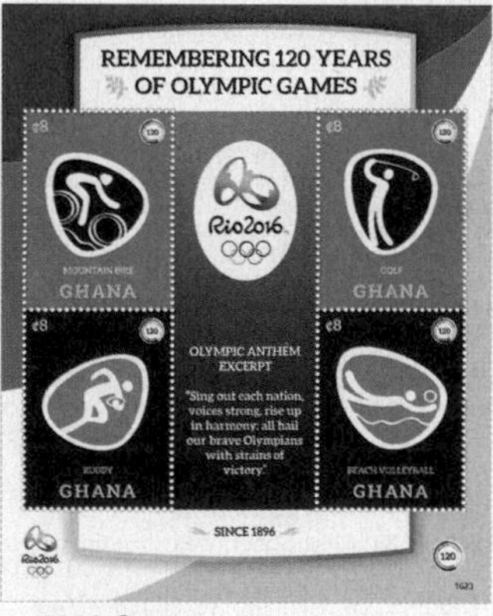

2016 Summer Olympics, Rio de Janeiro — A641

No. 2920, 8ce: a, Mountain biking. b, Golf. c, Rugby. d, Beach volleyball.
No. 2921, 8ce: a, Canoe sprint. b, Volleyball. c, Gymnastics. d, Equestrian eventing.
No. 2922: a, Greco-Roman wrestling. b, Kurt Leucht, Greco-Roman wrestler.

2016, Nov. 14 Litho. *Perf. 14*
Sheets of 4, #a-d

2920-2921 A641 Set of 2 30.00 30.00

Souvenir Sheet
Perf. 12½

2922 A641 12ce Sheet of 2, #a-b 11.50 11.50

No. 2922 contains two 38x51mm stamps.

Star Trek Television Series, 50th Anniv. — A642

No. 2923 — Scenes from episode entitled: a, Amok Time. b, Plato's Stepchildren. c, Errand of Mercy. d, The Devil in the Dark. e, The Doomsday Machine. f, Arena.
16ce, Where No Man Has Gone Before.

2016, Oct. 24 Litho. *Perf. 14*
2923 A642 4ce Sheet of 6, #a-f 12.00 12.00

Souvenir Sheet
Perf. 12¾

2924 A642 16ce multi 8.00 8.00

No. 2924 contains one 51x38mm stamp.

Christmas A643

Designs: No. 2925, 5ce, Christmas tree. No. 2926, 5ce, Christmas ornaments, gifts and holly. No. 2927, 8ce, Snowflake, Christmas ornaments and text. No. 2928, 8ce, Bell and text.

2016, Dec. 5 Litho. *Perf. 12½*
2925-2928 A643 Set of 4 12.50 12.50

A644

New Year 2017 (Year of the Rooster) — A645

No. 2929 — Rooster with: a, Head at left. b, Head at right. c, Hen and chicks.
No. 2930 — Rooster facing: a, Right, pale green background. b, Left, lavender gray background. c, Right, lavender gray background. d, Left, pale green background.

2016, Dec. 5 Litho. *Perf. 13¾*
2929 A644 8ce Sheet of 3, #a-c 11.50 11.50
2930 A645 8ce Sheet of 4, #a-d 15.50 15.50

Miniature Sheet

New Year Stamps of People's Republic of China — A646

No. 2931 — Stamps from People's Republic of China: a, #3338, Monkey. b, #3418, Rooster. c, #3466, Dog. d, #3557, Pig. e, #3647, Rat. f, #3714, Ox. g, #3798, Tiger. h, #3877, Rabbit. i, #3982, Dragon. j, #4061, Snake. k, #4171, Horse. l, #4252, Sheep.

2016, Dec. 28 Litho. *Perf. 12½*
2931 A646 2ce Sheet of 12, #a-l 11.50 11.50

Miniature Sheet

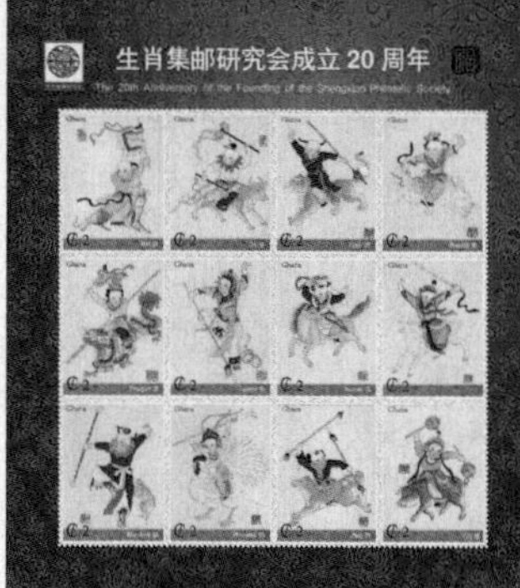

Shengxiao Philatelic Society, 20th Anniv. — A647

No. 2932 — Chinese person and: a, Rat. b, Ox. c, Tiger. d, Rabbit. e, Dragon. f, Snake. g, Horse. h, Sheep. i, Monkey. j, Rooster. k, Dog. l, Pig.

2016, Dec. 28 Litho. *Perf. 14*
2932 A647 2ce Sheet of 12, #a-l 11.50 11.50

On No. 2932h the word "Sheep" is pink.

Souvenir Sheet

Monkey King — A648

2016, Dec. 28 Litho. *Perf. 13¾*
2933 A648 16ce multi 7.75 7.75

A649

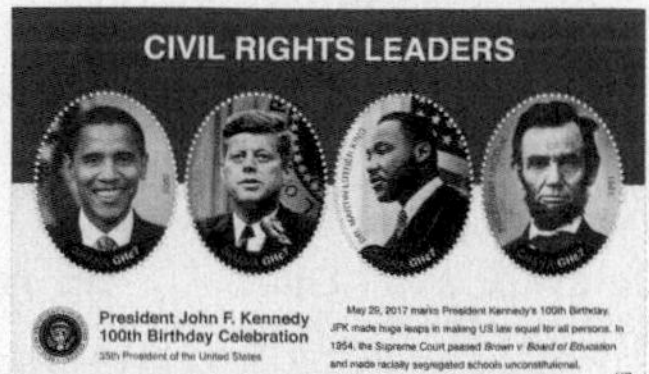

Pres. John F. Kennedy (1917-63) — A650

No. 2934: a, Pres. Kennedy with Dr. Martin Luther King, Jr. and other civil rights leaders (70x35mm). b, Pres. Kennedy and Nina Khrushchev (35x35mm). c, Jacqueline Kennedy and Nikita Khrushchev (35x35mm). d, Dr. King delivering "I Have a Dream" speech (35x35mm). e, Pres. Kennedy (35x35mm). f, Pres. Kennedy delivering speech in Berlin (70x35mm).
No. 2935 — Civil rights leaders: a, Pres. Barack Obama. b, Pres. Kennedy. c, Dr. King. d, Pres. Abraham Lincoln.
16ce, Pres. Kennedy and Presidential seal.

2017, Mar. 14 Litho. *Perf. 14x13¾*
2934 A649 5ce Sheet of 6, #a-f 14.00 14.00

Perf.

2935 A650 7ce Sheet of 4, #a-d 13.00 13.00

Souvenir Sheet

2936 A650 16ce multi 7.50 7.50

No. 2936 contains one 38mm diameter stamp.

Souvenir Sheets

A651

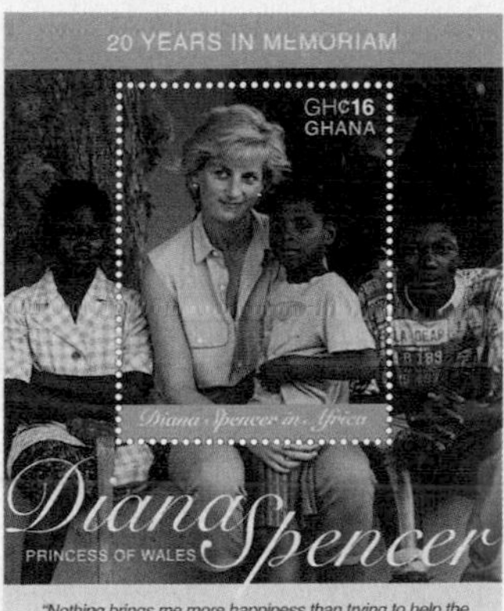

20 YEARS IN MEMORIAM
GH¢16 GHANA
Diana Spencer
PRINCESS OF WALES
"Nothing brings me more happiness than trying to help the most vulnerable people in society. It is a goal and an essential part of my life – a kind of destiny. Whoever is in distress can call on me. I will come running wherever they are."

A652

Princess Diana (1961-97) — A653

2017, Mar. 14 **Litho.** ***Perf. 14***

2937 A651 16ce multi 7.50 7.50

Perf. 12¾

2938 A652 16ce multi 7.50 7.50

Perf. 12

2939 A653 16ce multi 7.50 7.50
Nos. 2937-2939 (3) 22.50 22.50

Miniature Sheets

A654

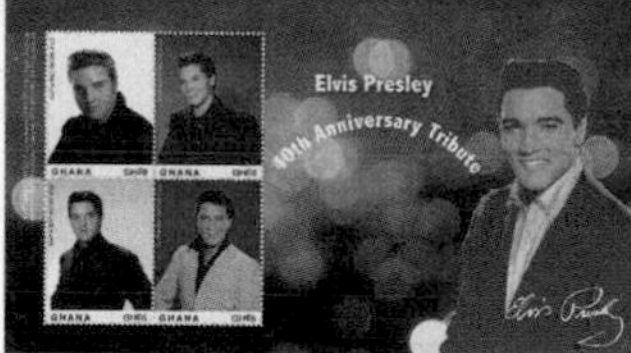

Elvis Presley (1935-77) — A655

No. 2940 — Presley wearing: a, Red shirt, Turquoise green background. b, Brown red shirt, dull scarlet background. c, Slate lilac shirt, brick wall background. d, Suit and tie. e, White shirt, red background with circles. f, Red shirt and gray jacket.

No. 2941 — Presley wearing: a, Maroon jacket, pale green background. b, Maroon shirt and jacket, red background. c, Maroon shirt and jacket, gray background. d, Maroon shirt and gray sweater, red background.

2017, June 3 **Litho.** ***Perf. 14***

2940 A654 5ce Sheet of 6, #a-f 14.00 14.00

2941 A655 8ce Sheet of 4, #a-d 15.00 15.00

Miniature Sheet

Birds — A656

No. 2942: a, Gouldian finch. b, Parrot finch. c, Purple grenadier. d, Red bishop. e, Red-crested cardinal. f, Spectacled monarch. g, Crimson chat. h, Greater necklaced laughing-thrush. i, Chestnut-backed jewel babbler.

Perf. 13½x12½

2017, June 14 **Litho.**

2942 A656 4ce Sheet of 9, #a-i 16.50 16.50

Animals — A657

No. 2943: a, 6ce, Ashy-faced owl. b, 8ce, Binturong. c, 12ce, Malachite green butterfly. d, 14ce, Vancouver Island marmot.
25ce, Giant panda, vert.

2017, July 21 **Litho.** ***Perf. 12½***

2943 A657 Sheet of 4, #a-d 18.50 18.50

Souvenir Sheet

2944 A657 25ce multi 11.50 11.50

New Year 2018 (Year of the Dog) — A658

No. 2945 — Dogs: a, Shar pei. b, Pekingese. c, Chinese crested dog. d, Chinese Chongqing dog.

No. 2946 — Dogs: a, Chow chow. b, Shih Tzu.

2017, Aug. 8 **Litho.** ***Perf. 13¾***

2945 A658 8ce Sheet of 4, #a-d 14.50 14.50

Souvenir Sheet

2946 A658 12ce Sheet of 2, #a-b 11.00 11.00

Whales — A659

No. 2947: a, Humpback whale breaching surface. b, Orca. c, Humpback whale underwater.
20ce, Humpback whale, vert.

2017, Sept. 11 **Litho.** ***Perf. 14***

2947 A659 12ce Sheet of 3, #a-c 16.50 16.50

Souvenir Sheet

Perf. 12

2948 A659 20ce multi 9.25 9.25

No. 2948 contains one 30x50mm stamp.

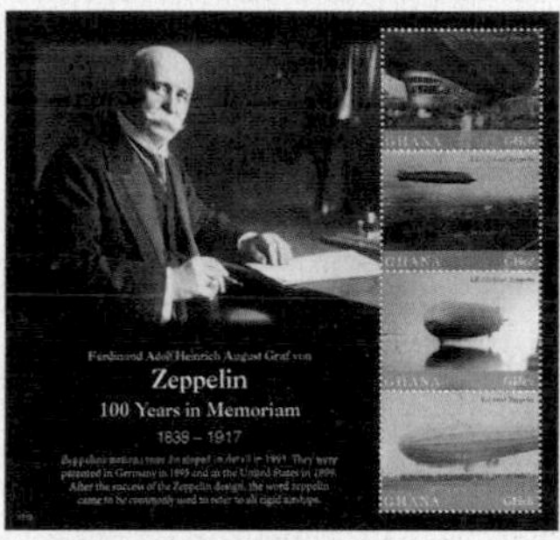

Zeppelins — A660

No. 2949: a, Workers holding tether ropes of LZ-127 Graf Zeppelin. b, LZ-127 Graf Zeppelin in flight. c, LZ-127 Graf Zeppelin on beach. d, L-2 Zeppelin.
16ce, Count Ferdinand von Zeppelin (1838-1917), vert.

2017, Oct. 26 **Litho.** ***Perf. 12***

2949 A660 8ce Sheet of 4, #a-d 14.50 14.50

Souvenir Sheet

Perf. 12½

2950 A660 16ce multi 7.25 7.25

No. 2950 contains one 38x51mm stamp.

Butterflies — A661

No. 2951: a, Euphaedra janetta. b, Aeropetes tulbaghia. c, Colotis antevippe. d, Graphium leonidas.
16ce, Neptis nysiades.

2017, Oct. 26 **Litho.** ***Perf. 14***

2951 A661 8ce Sheet of 4, #a-d 14.50 14.50

Souvenir Sheet

Perf. 12

2952 A661 16ce multi 7.25 7.25

Souvenir Sheets

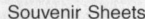

Elvis Presley (1935-77) — A662

Inscription: No. 2953, 16ce, Buys personal jet. No. 2954, 16ce, Made honorary Memphis Police Captain. No. 2955, 16ce, Wins third Grammy Award. No. 2956, 16ce, Performs biggest concert ever.

2017, Oct. 26 **Litho.** ***Perf. 12¾***

2953-2956 A662 Set of 4 29.00 29.00

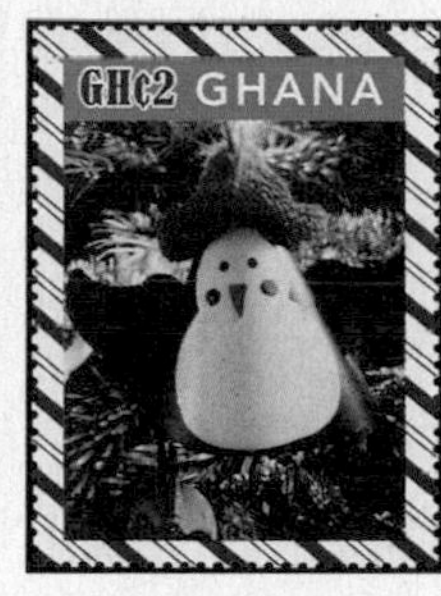

Christmas A663

Designs: 2ce, Penguin. 3ce, Round Christmas ornaments. 4ce, Teddy bear and Christmas ornament on tree. 5ce, Santa Claus Christmas ornament.
10ce, Gingerbread man and house, horiz.

2017, Dec. 25 **Litho.** ***Perf. 12½***

2957-2960 A663 Set of 4 6.25 6.25

Souvenir Sheet

2961 A663 10ce multi 4.50 4.50

SEMI-POSTAL STAMPS

Starlets, 1995 Under-17 World Soccer Champions — SP1

200ce+50ce, Holding gold cup won at Ecuador, vert. 550ce+50ce, Starlets '95 team photo. 800ce+50ce, Abu Idorisu, vert. 1100ce+50ce, Emmanuel Bentil, vert. 1600ce+50ce, Bashiru Gambo, vert.

Perf. 13½x13, 13x13½

1997, Aug. 12 **Litho.**

B1-B5 SP1 Set of 5 6.25 6.25

AIR POST STAMPS

Type of Regular Issue

Designs: 1sh3p, Pennant-winged nightjar. 2sh, Crowned cranes, vert.

Perf. 14½x14, 14x14½

1959, Oct. 5 **Photo.** **Wmk. 325**

C1 A17 1sh3p multicolored 1.50 .25
a. Booklet pane of 4 6.50

C2 A17 2sh multicolored 1.25 .40

For surcharges see Nos. C7-C10.

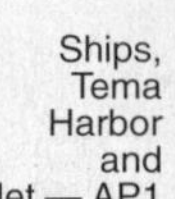

Ships, Tema Harbor and Jet — AP1

Perf. 14x13

1962, Feb. 10 Litho. Unwmk.

C3	AP1	1sh3p multicolored	.35	.35
C4	AP1	2sh6p multicolored	.85	.85
		Nos. C3-C4,110 (3)	1.60	1.60

Opening of Tema Harbor, as part of the Volta River Project.

Type of Regular Issue, 1962

1962, Mar. 6 ***Perf. 13x14***

C5	A35	1sh3p multicolored	.30	.30
C6	A35	2sh6p multicolored	.60	.60

Nos. C1-C2 Surcharged in White or Green with New Value and: "Ghana New Currency / 19th July, 1965"

Perf. 14½x14, 14x14½

1965, July 19 Photo. Wmk. 325

C7	A17	15pa on 1sh3p multi (W)	2.00	.70
C8	A17	24pa on 2sh multi (G)	2.00	.35

The two lines of the overprint are diagonal on No. C8.

Nos. C1, C8 Surcharged in White or Red

1967, Feb. 27 Photo. Wmk. 325

C9	A17	12½np on 1sh3p (W)	4.00	3.00
C10	A17	20np on 24pa on 2sh	5.00	4.00

POSTAGE DUE STAMPS

Gold Coast Nos. J2-J6 Overprinted "GHANA" and Bar in Red

Perf. 14

1958, June 25 Wmk. 4 Typo.

J1	D1	1p black	.25	*.45*
J2	D1	2p black	.25	*.45*
J3	D1	3p black	.25	*.45*
J4	D1	6p black	.25	*1.00*
J5	D1	1sh black	.25	*2.00*
		Nos. J1-J5 (5)	1.25	*4.35*

Type of Gold Coast Inscribed "Ghana"

1958, Dec. 1 ***Perf. 14***

J6	D1	1p carmine rose	.25	*.45*
J7	D1	2p green	.25	*.45*
J8	D1	3p orange	.25	*.45*
J9	D1	6p ultramarine	.25	*1.00*
J10	D1	1sh purple	.25	*2.00*
		Nos. J6-J10 (5)	1.25	4.35

Nos. J6-J10 Surcharged in Black, Blue or Red with New Value and "Ghana New Currency / 19th July, 1965."

1965, July 19

J11	D1	1pa on 1p car rose	.25	*.75*
J12	D1	2pa on 2p grn (Bl)	.25	*1.40*
J13	D1	3pa on 3p org (Bl)	.25	*1.40*
J14	D1	6pa on 6p ultra (R)	.35	*2.50*
J15	D1	12pa on 1sh pur (Bl)	.60	*2.75*
		Nos. J11-J15 (5)	1.70	8.80

Surcharge diagonal on Nos. J11 and J15.

No. J12 with additional surcharge, "1½Np" in red, was reported to have been used at one branch post office (Burma Camp) despite official intention. Four similar added surcharges were prepared: 1np on 1pa, 2½np on 3pa, 5np on 6pa, and 10np on 12pa.

D2

1970 Unwmk. Litho. ***Perf. 14½x14***

J16	D2	1np carmine rose	1.30	*5.00*
J17	D2	1½np green	1.50	*6.00*
J18	D2	2½np orange	1.90	*8.00*
J19	D2	5np ultramarine	2.40	*8.50*
J20	D2	10np dull purple	3.50	*9.50*
		Nos. J16-J20 (5)	10.60	*37.00*

1981 Litho. ***Perf. 14½x14***

J21	D2	2p red orange	1.50	*5.25*
J22	D2	3p brown	1.50	*5.25*

GIBRALTAR

jə-'brol-tər

LOCATION — A fortified promontory, including the Rock, extending from Spain's southeast coast at the entrance to the Mediterranean Sea
GOVT. — British Crown Colony
AREA — 2.5 sq. mi.
POP. — 29,165 (1999 est.)
CAPITAL — Gibraltar

12 Pence = 1 Shilling
20 Shillings = 1 Pound
100 Centimos = 1 Peseta (1889-95)
100 Pence = 1 Pound (1971)

Catalogue values for unused stamps in this country are for Never Hinged items, beginning with Scott 119 in the regular postage section and Scott J1 in the postage due section.

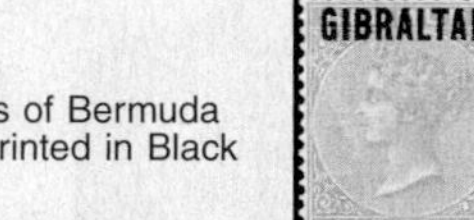

Types of Bermuda Overprinted in Black

1886, Jan. 1 Wmk. 2 ***Perf. 14***

1	A6	½p green	24.00	13.00
2	A1	1p rose	92.50	6.50
3	A2	2p violet brown	155.00	92.50
4	A8	2½p ultra	220.00	4.25
5	A7	4p orange brn	210.00	120.00
6	A4	6p violet	330.00	250.00
7	A5	1sh bister brn	500.00	400.00
		Nos. 1-7 (7)	1,532.	886.25

Forged overprints of No. 7 are plentiful.

Victoria
A6 A7

A8

A9

1886-98 Typo.

8	A6	½p dull green ('87)	18.50	4.50
9	A6	½p gray grn ('98)	14.50	2.00
10	A7	1p rose ('87)	52.50	5.00
11	A7	1p car rose ('98)	14.50	.55
12	A8	2p brn violet	35.00	36.00
13	A8	2p brn vio & ultra ('98)	30.00	2.25
14	A9	2½p brt ultra ('98)	47.50	.80
a.		2½p ultramarine	95.00	3.25
16	A8	4p orange brn	90.00	90.00
17	A8	4p org brn & grn ('98)	21.00	7.50
18	A8	6p violet	145.00	145.00
19	A8	6p vio & car rose ('98)	47.50	25.00
20	A8	1sh bister	275.00	250.00
21	A8	1sh bis & car rose ('98)	47.50	12.00
		Nos. 8-14,16-21 (13)	838.50	580.60

Stamps of 1886 Issue Surcharged in Black

1889, July

22	A6	5c on ½p green	14.00	*32.50*
23	A7	10c on 1p rose	15.00	*20.00*
24	A8	25c on 2p brn vio	6.00	*11.50*
a.		Small "I" in "CENTIMOS"	140.00	*190.00*
b.		Broken "N"	140.00	*190.00*
25	A9	25c on 2½p ultra	30.00	2.75
a.		Small "I" in "CENTIMOS"	400.00	125.00
b.		Broken "N"	400.00	125.00
26	A8	40c on 4p org brn	62.50	*87.50*
27	A8	50c on 6p violet	67.50	*87.50*
28	A8	75c on 1sh bister	67.50	*82.50*
		Nos. 22-28 (7)	262.50	*324.25*
		Set, ovptd. "SPECIMEN"	375.00	

There are two varieties of the figure "5" in the 5c, 25c, 50c and 75c.

A11

1889-95

29	A11	5c green	7.00	1.25
30	A11	10c rose	5.50	.60
a.		Value omitted	7,000.	
31	A11	20c ol green ('95)	19.00	*100.00*
31A	A11	20c ol grn & brn ('95)	30.00	25.00
32	A11	25c ultra	27.50	.90
33	A11	40c orange brn	4.50	*4.75*
34	A11	50c violet	3.75	2.75
35	A11	75c olive green	37.50	37.50
36	A11	1p bister	90.00	24.00
36A	A11	1p bis & bl ('95)	6.00	*8.50*
37	A11	2p blk & car rose ('95)	13.00	*35.00*
38	A11	5p steel blue	50.00	*120.00*
		Nos. 29-38 (12)	293.75	*360.25*

A12

King Edward VII — A13

1903, May 1

39	A12	½p grn & bl grn	14.50	11.00
40	A12	1p violet, *red*	37.50	.70
41	A12	2p grn & car rose	32.50	*45.00*
42	A12	2½p vio & blk, *bl*	8.75	.70
43	A12	6p violet & pur	40.00	26.00
44	A12	1sh blk & car rose	32.50	*42.50*
45	A13	2sh green & ultra	200.00	*275.00*
46	A13	4sh vio & green	150.00	*225.00*
47	A13	8sh vio & blk, *bl*	170.00	*200.00*
48	A13	£1 vio & blk, *red*	650.00	*750.00*

1904-12 Wmk. 3

Ordinary or Chalky Paper

49	A12	½p blue grn ('07)	16.00	2.00
49Ab	A12	½p dull grn & br grn ('04)	14.00	9.00
50b	A12	1p vio, *red* ('05)	8.50	1.00
a.		Bisected, used as ½p on card		1,800.
51	A12	1p car ('07)	6.50	.70
52a	A12	2p grn & car rose ('07)	10.00	*15.00*
53	A12	2p gray ('10)	10.00	*13.00*
54	A12	2½p vio & blk, *bl* ('07)	45.00	*110.00*
55	A12	2½p ultra ('07)	9.00	1.90
56b	A12	6p vio & pur ('08)	35.00	22.50
a.		6p vio & red violet ('12)	160.00	*450.00*
57a	A12	1sh blk & car rose ('06)	57.50	25.00
58	A12	1sh blk, *grn* ('10)	27.50	24.00
59a	A13	2sh grn & ultra ('07)	120.00	*150.00*
60	A13	2sh vio & bl, *bl* ('10)	67.50	*57.50*
61	A13	4sh vio & grn	350.00	425.00
62	A13	4sh blk & red ('10)	170.00	*190.00*
63	A13	8sh vio & grn ('11)	250.00	*250.00*
64	A13	£1 vio & blk, *red*	650.00	*700.00*
		Nos. 49-64 (17)	1,847.	1,997.

Nos. 51, 53, 55 are on ordinary paper. Nos. 54, 58, 60-64 are on chalky paper. Others come on both papers. The least expensive varieties are listed above. For detailed listings, see the *Scott Specialized Catalogue of Stamps and Covers.*

No. 56a, used, must have a 1912 cancellation. Stamps used later sell for about the same as unused.

A14

King George V — A15

1912, July 17 Ordinary Paper

66	A14	½p green	4.00	.80
67	A14	1p carmine	4.75	.90
a.		1p scarlet ('16)	10.00	1.60
68	A14	2p gray	21.00	1.75
69	A14	2½p ultra	11.00	3.00

Chalky Paper

70	A14	6p dl vio & red vio	11.00	*19.00*
71	A14	1sh black, *green*	19.50	4.00
a.		1sh black, *emerald* ('24)	32.50	*110.00*
b.		1sh blk, *bl grn,* ol back ('19)	29.00	27.50
c.		1sh blk, *emer,* ol back ('23)	32.50	*92.50*
72	A15	2sh vio & ultra, *bl*	30.00	4.50
73	A15	4sh black & scar	40.00	*65.00*
74	A15	8sh vio & green	110.00	*130.00*
75	A15	£1 vio & blk, *red*	160.00	*275.00*
		Nos. 66-75 (10)	411.25	*503.95*

1921-32 Ordinary Paper Wmk. 4

76	A14	½p grn ('26)	1.60	*1.60*
77	A14	1p rose red	2.10	1.25
78a	A14	1½p pale red brn ('22)	2.25	.60
79	A14	2p gray	1.60	1.60
80	A14	2½p ultra	22.50	*60.00*
81	A14	3p ultra	2.75	1.75

Chalky Paper

82	A14	6p dl vio & red vio ('26)	1.75	*4.00*
a.		6p gray lilac & red violet ('23)	7.00	6.50
83	A14	1sh blk, *emer*	12.00	*26.00*
84	A14	1sh ol grn & blk	17.50	*42.50*
a.		1sh brn olive & black ('32)	17.50	*21.00*
85a	A15	2sh red vio & ultra, *blue* ('25)	8.25	*47.50*
86	A15	2sh red brn & black	11.00	*40.00*
87	A15	2sh6p grn & blk	11.00	*30.00*
88	A15	4sh blk & scar	75.00	*130.00*
89	A15	5sh car & blk	19.00	*75.00*
90	A15	8sh vio & grn	325.00	*550.00*
91	A15	10sh ultra & blk	37.50	*80.00*
92	A15	£1 org & blk	190.00	*300.00*
93	A15	£5 dl vio & blk	1,750.	*6,000.*
		Nos. 76-92 (15)	730.30	*1,344.*

Years issued: Nos. 83, 85, 4sh, 8sh, 1924. 2sh6p, 5sh, 10sh, £5, 1925. £1, 1927. Nos. 84, 86, 1929.

No. 81 is inscribed "3 PENCE".

No. 81

No. 94

1930, Apr. 12 Ordinary Paper

94	A14	3p ultramarine	9.50	2.25

No. 94 is inscribed "THREE PENCE".

Rock of Gibraltar A16

1931-33 Engr. ***Perf. 14***

96	A16	1p red	2.75	*3.00*
a.		Perf. 13½x14	22.50	8.50
97	A16	1½p red brown	2.75	*3.00*
a.		Perf. 13½x14	18.00	5.00

98 A16 2p gray ('32) 13.50 2.00
a. Perf. 13½x14 25.00 4.25
99 A16 3p dk blue ('33) 11.00 3.50
a. Perf. 13½x14 45.00 42.50
Nos. 96-99 (4) 30.00 11.50
Set, never hinged 47.50
Nos. 96a-99a (4) 110.50 60.25
Set, never hinged 185.00

Common Design Types pictured following the introduction.

Silver Jubilee Issue
Common Design Type

1935, May 6 ***Perf. 11x12***
100 CD301 2p black & ultra 1.50 *2.25*
101 CD301 3p ultra & brown 3.25 4.50
102 CD301 6p indigo & grn 11.00 *16.00*
103 CD301 1sh brn vio & ind 13.00 *20.00*
Nos. 100-103 (4) 28.75 42.75
Set, never hinged 57.50

Coronation Issue
Common Design Type

1937, May 12 ***Perf. 11x11½***
104 CD302 ½p deep green .25 *.45*
105 CD302 2p gray black .75 *3.00*
106 CD302 3p deep ultra 1.25 *3.00*
Nos. 104-106 (3) 2.25 6.45
Set, never hinged 4.50

George VI — A17

Rock of Gibraltar A18

Designs: 2p, Rock from north side. 3p, 5p, Europa Point. 6p, Moorish Castle. 1sh, Southport Gate. 2sh, Eliott Memorial. 5sh, Government House. 10sh, Catalan Bay.

Perf. 13, 13½x14 (½p, No. 118), 14 (1½p)

1938-49 **Engr.** **Wmk. 4**
107 A17 ½p gray green .25 *.40*
108 A18 1p red brn ('42) .80 .60
a. 1p chestnut, perf. 14 *20.00* 2.75
b. 1p chestnut, perf. 13½ 20.00 2.50
c. Perf. 13½, wmk. sideways ('40) *4.50* *7.75*
109 A18 1½p car rose 20.00 .90
b. Perf. 13½ 190.00 30.00
109A A18 1½p gray vio ('43) .45 *1.60*
110 A18 2p dk gray ('43) 1.40 1.50
a. Perf. 14 22.00 .55
c. Perf. 13½ 4.00 .45
d. Perf. 13½, wmk. sideways ('41) 500.00 52.50
110B A18 2p car rose ('44) 1.00 .55
111 A18 3p blue ('42) 2.00 .35
a. Perf. 14 100.00 6.00
b. Perf. 13½ 22.50 1.10
112 A18 5p red org ('47) 1.00 1.25
113 A18 6p dl vio & car rose 6.00 1.90
a. Perf. 14 90.00 1.60
b. Perf. 13½ 30.00 4.00
114 A18 1sh grn & blk ('42) 2.25 *4.50*
a. Perf. 14 30.00 27.50
b. Perf. 13½ 45.00 8.25
115 A18 2sh org brn & blk ('42) 6.00 6.50
a. Perf. 14 40.00 30.00
b. Perf. 13½ 90.00 55.00
116 A18 5sh dk car & blk ('44) 12.50 *14.00*
a. Perf 14 ('38) 60.00 *175.00*
b. Perf. 13½ 35.00 16.00
117 A18 10sh bl & blk ('43) 22.50 22.50
a. Perf. 14 45.00 *150.00*
118 A17 £1 orange 30.00 *55.00*
Nos. 107-118 (14) 106.15 111.55
Set, never hinged 200.00

Nos. 108c and 110d were issued in coils.

No. 108 (1p, perf. 13) exists with watermark both normal and sideways. Nos. 110 and 110B (both 2p, perf. 13) have watermark sideways.

For overprints see Nos. 127-130.

Catalogue values for unused stamps in this section, from this point to the end of the section, are for Never Hinged items.

Peace Issue
Common Design Type

1946, Oct. 12 ***Perf. 13½x14***
119 CD303 ½p bright green .30 *.50*
120 CD303 3p bright ultra .45 *.50*

Silver Wedding Issue
Common Design Types

1948, Dec. 1 **Photo.** ***Perf. 14x14½***
121 CD304 ½p dark green 1.00 *3.00*

Engr.; Name Typo.

Perf. 11½x11

122 CD305 £1 brown orange 60.00 *75.00*
Set, hinged 40.00

UPU Issue
Common Design Types

Engr.; Name Typo. on 3p, 6p

Perf. 13½, 11x11½

1949, Oct. 10 **Wmk. 4**
123 CD306 2p rose carmine 1.25 1.25
124 CD307 3p indigo 2.00 1.50
125 CD308 6p rose violet 1.40 *2.00*
126 CD309 1sh blue green 1.25 *4.00*
Nos. 123-126 (4) 5.90 *8.75*

Nos. 110B, 111, 113-114 overprinted in Black or Carmine

1950, Aug. 1 ***Perf. 13x12½***
127 A18 2p carmine rose .40 *1.50*
128 A18 3p blue .85 *1.25*
129 A18 6p dl vio & car rose 1.00 *2.00*
a. Double overprint 1,000. *1,300.*
130 A18 1sh grn & blk (C) 1.25 *2.00*
Nos. 127-130 (4) 3.50 *6.75*

Adoption of Constitution of 1950.

Coronation Issue
Common Design Type

1953, June 2 **Engr.** ***Perf. 13½x13***
131 CD312 ½p olive green & black .50 .50

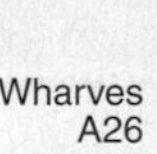

Wharves A26

Moorish Castle — A27

Designs: 1p, South view. 1½p, Tunny fishing industry. 2p, Southport Gate. 2½p, Sailing in the bay. 3p, Ocean liner. 4p, Coaling wharf. 5p, Airport. 6p, Europa Point. 1sh, Strait from Buena Vista. 2sh, Rosia Bay. 5sh, Government House. £1, Arms of Gibraltar.

1953, Oct. 19 ***Perf. 13***
132 A26 ½p dk grn & ind .25 .25
133 A26 1p blue green 1.60 .95
134 A26 1½p dark gray 1.00 *1.75*
135 A26 2p sepia 2.00 1.25
136 A26 2½p car lake 3.25 1.00
137 A26 3p grnsh blue 4.50 1.25
138 A26 4p ultra 7.25 3.50
139 A26 5p deep plum 1.75 1.50
140 A26 6p blue & black 4.25 2.00
141 A26 1sh red brn & bl .90 *1.25*
142 A26 2sh vio & org 32.50 6.00
143 A26 5sh dark brown 40.00 15.00
144 A27 10sh ultra & brn 47.50 45.00
145 A27 £1 yellow & red 57.50 55.00
Nos. 132-145 (14) 204.25 135.70
Set, hinged 100.00

See Nos. 1390-1403.

Inscribed: "ROYAL VISIT 1954"

1954, May 10
146 A26 3p greenish blue .50 .30

Candytuft — A28

Rock and Badge of Gibraltar Regiment — A30

Moorish Castle A29

Designs: 2p, St. George's Hall and cannons. 2½p, The keys. 3p, Rock by moonlight. 4p, Catalan Bay. 6p, Map. 7p, Air terminal. 9p, American war memorial. 1sh, Barbary ape. 2sh, Barbary partridge. 5sh, Blue rock thrush. 10sh, Narcissus.

Wmk. 314

1960, Oct. 29 **Photo.** ***Perf. 12½***
147 A28 ½p brt green & lil .25 *.50*
148 A29 1p black & yel grn .25 .25
149 A29 2p org brn & sl 1.00 .25
150 A28 2½p blue & black 1.25 .70
151 A29 3p dk blue & ver .30 .25
152 A29 4p choc & grnsh bl 3.00 .90
a. Wmkd. sideways ('66) .30 *1.00*
153 A28 6p brown & emer 1.00 .70
154 A28 7p gray & car 2.50 1.75
155 A28 9p grnsh blue & bluish gray 1.00 .95
156 A29 1sh brown & green 1.50 .70
157 A29 2sh dark red brn & ultra 18.00 3.00
158 A29 5sh ol & Prus grn 8.50 7.00
159 A28 10sh blue, yel & grn 24.00 17.50

Perf. 14

Engr.

160 A30 £1 org red & slate 20.00 17.50
Nos. 147-160 (14) 82.55 51.95

For overprints see Nos. 165-166.

Freedom from Hunger Issue
Common Design Type

1963, June 4 ***Perf. 14x14½***
161 CD314 9p sepia 4.00 2.25

Red Cross Centenary Issue
Common Design Type

1963, Sept. 2 **Litho.** ***Perf. 13***
162 CD315 1p black & red .75 *1.40*
163 CD315 9p ultra & red 5.50 4.00

Shakespeare Issue
Common Design Type

1964, Apr. 23 **Photo.** ***Perf. 14x14½***
164 CD316 7p brown .65 .55

Nos. 151 and 153 Overprinted

1964, Oct. 16 ***Perf. 12½***
165 A29 3p dk blue & ver .25 .25
166 A28 6p brown & emer .35 *.50*
a. No period in overprint 17.00 *27.50*

ITU Issue
Common Design Type

Perf. 11x11½

1965, May 17 **Litho.** **Wmk. 314**
167 CD317 4p emerald & yel 2.25 .45
168 CD317 2sh ap grn & dk bl 6.75 5.50

Intl. Cooperation Year Issue
Common Design Type

1965, Oct. 25 ***Perf. 14½***
169 CD318 ½p lt violet & grn .25 2.25
170 CD318 4p blue green & cl 1.00 .50

Churchill Memorial Issue
Common Design Type

1966, Jan. 24 **Photo.** ***Perf. 14***

Design in Black, Gold and Carmine Rose

171 CD319 ½p bright blue .25 *2.25*
172 CD319 1p green .35 .25
173 CD319 4p brown 1.35 .30
174 CD319 9p violet 1.10 *2.50*
Nos. 171-174 (4) 3.05 5.30

World Cup Soccer Issue
Common Design Type

1966, July 1 **Litho.** ***Perf. 14***
175 CD321 2½p multicolored .75 *1.25*
176 CD321 6p multicolored 1.10 .50

Sea Bream A30a

7p, Orange scorpionfish. 1sh, Stone bass, vert.

Perf. 14x13½, 13½x14

1966, Aug. 27 **Photo.** **Wmk. 314**
177 A30a 4p ultra, rose red & blk .30 .25
178 A30a 7p ol, rose red & blk .35 *.70*
a. Value omitted *1,800.*
179 A30a 1sh brt grn, brn & blk .55 .35
Nos. 177-179 (3) 1.20 1.30

European Sea Angling Championships, Gibraltar, Aug. 28-Sept. 3.

WHO Headquarters Issue
Common Design Type

1966, Sept. 20 **Litho.** ***Perf. 14***
180 CD322 6p multicolored 2.75 1.50
181 CD322 9p multicolored 3.75 3.00

"Our Lady of Europa" A31

Perf. 14x14½

1966, Nov. 15 **Photo.** **Wmk. 314**
182 A31 2sh ultra & black .50 *.90*

Enthronement of the recovered statue of the Madonna in its new shrine, cent.

UNESCO Anniversary Issue
Common Design Type

1966, Dec. 1 **Litho.** ***Perf. 14***
183 CD323 2p "Education" .50 .25
184 CD323 7p "Science" 2.00 .25
185 CD323 5sh "Culture" 4.00 2.75
Nos. 183-185 (3) 6.50 3.25

Cable Ship Mirror — A32

Ships and Arms of Gibraltar: ½p Victory, Nelson's flagship. 1p, S.S. Arab. 2p, H.M.S. Carmania. 2½p, M.V. Mons Calpe. 3p, S.S.

Canberra. 4p, H.M.S. Hood. 6p, Xebec, Moorish vessel. 7p, Amerigo Vespucci, Italian training ship (sails). 9p, Raffaello, Italian liner. 1sh, H.M.S. Royal Katherine, 17th century British warship. 2sh, H.M.S. Ark Royal, aircraft carrier. 5sh, H.M.S. Dreadnought, atomic submarine. 10sh, S.S. Neuralia, troopship. £1, Mary Celeste, 19th century mystery ship (sails).

Perf. 14x14½

1967-69 Photo. Wmk. 314

Design in Black, Red and Gold; Background as Indicated

186	A32	½p	deep rose	.25	.25
187	A32	1p	yellow	.25	.25
188	A32	2p	ultra	.25	.25
189	A32	2½p	orange	.40	.30
190	A32	3p	violet	.25	.25
191	A32	4p	rose	.35	.25
191A	A32	5p	brn & multi ('69)	2.50	.65
192	A32	6p	gray	.35	.60
193	A32	7p	yellow grn	.35	.50
194	A32	9p	green	.35	.95
195	A32	1sh	rose brown	.35	.35
196	A32	2sh	brt yellow	4.00	2.50
197	A32	5sh	brick red	3.50	*6.75*
198	A32	10sh	emerald	12.00	*18.50*
199	A32	£1	lt ultra	14.00	*18.50*
			Nos. 186-199 (15)	39.15	*50.85*

Cable Car and ITY Emblem — A33

ITY emblem and: 9p, Bull shark, horiz. 1sh, Skin diver, horiz.

Perf. 14½x14, 14x14½

1967, June 15 Photo. Wmk. 314

200 A33	7p	red brn, red & blk	.25	.25
201 A33	9p	brt blue, blk & slate	.25	.25
202 A33	1sh	emer, blk & org brn	.25	.25
		Nos. 200-202 (3)	.75	.75

International Tourist Year.

Holy Family A34

Christmas: 6p, Church window, vert.

1967, Nov. 1 *Perf. 14½*

203 A34	2p	dark red & multi	.25	.25
204 A34	6p	dark green & multi	.25	.25

General Eliott and Map of Europe and Great Britain A35

Designs: 9p, Eliott Memorial and tower. 1sh, Gen. Eliott and map of Gibraltar, vert. 2sh, Gen. Eliott directing rescue operations for enemy sailors during Great Siege 1779-83.

Perf. 14½x14, 14x14½

1967, Dec. 11 Photo. Wmk. 314

Size: 37x21mm, 21x37mm

205 A35	4p	multicolored	.25	.25
206 A35	9p	multicolored	.25	.25
207 A35	1sh	multicolored	.25	.25

Size: 58x21½mm

208 A35	2sh	multicolored	.30	.25
		Nos. 205-208 (4)	1.05	1.00

250th anniv. of the birth of General George Augustus Eliott (1717-1790), Governor of Gibraltar during Great Siege.

Lord Baden-Powell — A36

Designs: 7p, Scout flag, Rock of Gibraltar and globe with map of Europe. 9p, Symbolic tents, heads and Scout salute. 1sh, Three Scout badges.

Perf. 14x14½

1968, Mar. 27 Photo. Wmk. 314

209 A36	4p	dull yellow & pur	.25	.25
210 A36	7p	brn org, brn & grn	.25	.25
211 A36	9p	ultra, black & org	.25	*.30*
212 A36	1sh	yellow & emerald	.25	*.30*
		Nos. 209-212 (4)	1.00	1.10

60th anniv. of the Gibraltar Scout Assoc.

Nurse and WHO Emblem A37

20th anniv. of WHO: 4p, Physician with microscope and WHO emblem.

1968, July 1 Photo. Wmk. 314

213 A37	2p	yellow, ultra & blk	.25	.25
214 A37	4p	pink, black & slate	.25	.25

King John Signing Magna Carta — A38

Design: 2sh, Rock of Gibraltar, "Freedom" and Human Rights flame.

1968, Aug. 26 *Perf. 13½x14½*

215 A38	1sh	org, gold & dk brn	.25	.25
216 A38	2sh	brt green & gold	.40	.40

International Human Rights Year.

Shepherd, Lamb and Star — A39

Christmas: 9p, Mary, Jesus and lamb.

1968, Nov. 1 *Perf. 14x13½*

217 A39	4p	lt brown & multi	.25	.25
218 A39	9p	rose & multi	.25	.25

Government House, Gibraltar — A40

9p, Rock of Gibraltar, Commonwealth Parliamentary Association emblem. 2sh, Big Ben, London, arms of Gibraltar.

Perf. 14½x14, 14x14½

1969, May 26 Photo. Wmk. 314

219 A40	4p	green & gold	.25	.25
220 A40	9p	brt violet & gold	.25	.25
221 A40	2sh	lt ultra, gold & red	.25	.25
		Nos. 219-221 (3)	.75	.75

Meeting of the Executive Committee of the General Council of the Commonwealth Parliamentary Assoc., Gibraltar, May 1969.

Rock of Gibraltar A41

1969, July 30 *Perf. 14½x13½*

222 A41	½p	orange & gold	.25	.25
223 A41	5p	emerald & silver	.25	.25
224 A41	7p	brt rose lil & silver	.25	.25
225 A41	5sh	ultra & gold	.85	.85
		Nos. 222-225 (4)	1.60	1.60

Gibraltar's new constitution.

Nos. 222-225 are valued with surrounding selvage.

Royal Artillery Officer, 1758 — A42

Uniforms: 6p, Contemporary soldier of the Royal Anglian Regiment. 9p, Soldier, Royal Engineers, 1786. 2sh, Private of Fox's Marines, 1704.

1969, Nov. 6 Photo. *Perf. 14*

226 A42	1p	gold & multi	.25	.25
227 A42	6p	silver, gold & multi	.25	.25
228 A42	9p	silver, gold & multi	.35	.25
229 A42	2sh	gold & multi	.75	.75
		Nos. 226-229 (4)	1.60	1.50

Descriptions are printed on back on top of gum.

See Nos. 234-237, 276-279, 286-289, 299-302, 310-313, 318-321, 330-333.

Madonna della Seggiola, by Raphael — A43

Christmas (Paintings): 7p, Madonna and Child, by Luis Morales. 1sh, Virgin of the Rocks, by Leonardo da Vinci.

1969, Dec. 1 *Perf. 13½x Roulette 9*

230 A43	5p	gold & multi	.25	.25
231 A43	7p	gold & multi	.25	.25
232 A43	1sh	gold & multi	.25	.25
a.		Triptych, Nos. 230, 232, 231	1.10	1.10

Europa Issue

Europa Point — A44

1970, June 8 *Perf. 13½*

233 A44	2sh	multicolored	.45	.40

Uniform Type of 1969

Uniforms: 2p, Royal Scots officer, 1839. 5p, Private of South Wales Borderers. 7p, Private of Queen's Royal Regiment, 1742. 2sh, Piper of Royal Irish Rangers, 1969.

1970, Aug. 28 Photo. *Perf. 14*

234 A42	2p	gold & multi	.35	.25
235 A42	5p	gold & multi	.50	.25
236 A42	7p	gold & multi	.55	.35
237 A42	2sh	gold & multi	1.25	1.00
		Nos. 234-237 (4)	2.65	1.85

Descriptions are printed on back on top of gum.

No. 178a and Rock of Gibraltar A45

Design: 2sh, No. 30a and Moorish Castle.

1970, Sept. 18 *Perf. 13*

238 A45	1sh	red & olive	.25	.25
239 A45	2sh	ultra & rose	.40	.55

Philympia, London Phil. Exhib., Sept. 18-26.

Virgin Mary by Gabriel Loire A46

1970, Dec. 1 Photo. *Perf. 13x14*

240 A46	2sh	multicolored	.35	.35

Christmas. The design is after a stained glass window in the Church of Our Lady of Perpetual Succour, Glasgow.

Decimal Currency Issue

Prince George of Cambridge Quarters, and Trinity Church — A47

Designs show for each denomination a 19th century print and a contemporary photograph of the same view: ½p Battery Rosia. 1½p, Wellington Monument, Alameda Gardens. 2p, View from North Bastion. 2½p, Catalan Bay. 3p, Convent, seen from garden. 4p, The Exchange and Spanish Chapel. 5p, Commercial Square, Library and Main Guard. 7p, South Barracks and Rosia Magazine. 8p, Moorish Mosque and Castle. 9p, Europa Pass. 10p, South Barracks, from Rosia Bay. 12½p, Southport Gates. 25p, Guards on Alameda. 50p, Europa Pass Gorge, vert. £1 Prince Edward Gate, vert.

In the listing the 1st number is for the 19th cent. design, the 2nd for the 20th cent. design.

Wmk. 314 Sideways

1971, Feb. 15 Litho. *Perf. 14*

Multicolored and:

241		½p	brown red	.25	.25
242		½p	brown red	.25	.25
a.	A47		Pair, Nos. 241-242	.50	*.50*
243		1p	light blue	.80	.25
244		1p	light blue	.80	.25
b.	A47		Pair, Nos. 243-244	1.75	.60
245		1½p	emerald	.25	*.25*
246		1½p	emerald	.25	*.25*
a.	A47		Pair, Nos. 245-246	.50	*.90*
247		2p	dark brown	1.25	*2.25*
248		2p	dark brown	1.25	*2.25*
b.	A47		Pair, Nos. 247-248	3.00	*5.75*
249		2½p	vermilion	.25	*.35*
250		2½p	vermilion	.25	*.35*
a.	A47		Pair, Nos. 249-250	.50	*.75*
251		3p	pale green	.25	.25
252		3p	pale green	.25	.25
a.	A47		Pair, Nos. 251-252	.50	.40
253		4p	gray	1.40	*2.50*
254		4p	gray	1.40	*2.50*
b.	A47		Pair, Nos. 253-254	4.00	*6.50*
255		5p	dark green	.35	.35
256		5p	dark green	.35	.35
a.	A47		Pair, Nos. 255-256	.75	.90
257		7p	orange	.65	.65
258		7p	orange	.65	.65
a.	A47		Pair, Nos. 257-258	1.40	*1.50*
259		8p	dark blue	.70	.70
260		8p	dark blue	.70	.70
a.	A47		Pair, Nos. 259-260	1.50	*2.00*
261		9p	brick red	.70	.70
262		9p	brick red	.70	.70
a.	A47		Pair, Nos. 261-262	1.50	*2.00*

263 10p black .80 .80
264 10p black .80 .80
a. A47 Pair, Nos. 263-264 1.75 *2.00*
265 12½p bister 1.00 *1.75*
266 12½p bister 1.00 *1.75*
a. A47 Pair, Nos. 265-266 2.25 *4.25*
267 25p deep purple 1.00 *1.75*
268 25p deep purple 1.00 *1.75*
a. A47 Pair, Nos. 267-268 2.25 *4.75*
269 50p blue 1.25 *2.75*
270 50p blue 1.25 *2.75*
a. A47 Pair, Nos. 269-270 3.25 *6.50*
271 £1 sepia 2.25 *4.00*
272 £1 sepia 2.25 *4.00*
a. A47 Pair, Nos. 271-272 5.00 *10.00*
Nos. 241-272 (32) 26.30 *39.10*

Se-tenant both horizontally and vertically.

1973, Sept. 12 Wmk. 314 Upright

247a A47 2p dark brown & multi 1.50 *2.50*
248a A47 2p dark brown & multi 1.50 *2.50*
c. Pair, Nos. 247a-248a 4.00 *6.50*
253a A47 4p gray & multi 1.75 *2.50*
254a A47 4p gray & multi 1.75 *2.50*
c. Pair, Nos. 253a-254a 4.50 *6.50*
Nos. 247a-254a (4) 6.50 *10.00*

1975, July 9 Wmk. 373

243a A47 1p blue & multi 1.60 *2.50*
244a A47 1p blue & multi 1.60 *2.50*
c. Pair, Nos. 243a-244a 4.50 *7.00*

Elizabeth II — A48

Coil Stamps

Perf. 14½x14

1971, Feb. 15 Photo. Wmk. 314

273 A48 ½p red orange .25 *.25*
274 A48 1p bright blue .25 *.25*
275 A48 2p lt yellow green .50 *.80*
a. Strip of 5 (½p, ½p, 1p, 1p, 2p) 1.60 *5.00*
Nos. 273-275 (3) 1.00 *1.30*

Uniform Type of 1969

Uniforms: 1p, Soldier, Black Watch, 1845. 2p, Drum Major with antelope mascot, Royal Fusiliers, 1971. 4p, Soldier, Kings Own Royal Border Regiment, 1704. 10p, Soldier, Devonshire and Dorset Regiment, 1801.

1971, Sept. 6 Litho. *Perf. 14*

276 A42 1p silver & multi .35 .30
277 A42 2p gold & multi .60 .30
278 A42 4p gold & multi .75 .50
279 A42 10p sil, gold & multi 3.00 2.75
Nos. 276-279 (4) 4.70 3.85

Descriptions are printed on back on top of gum.

Regimental Coat of Arms — A49

1971, Sept. 25 *Perf. 13x12*

280 A49 3p red, bister & black .50 .35

Presentation of colors to Gibraltar Regiment, Sept. 25, 1971.

Nativity — A50

Christmas: 5p, Journey to Bethlehem.

1971, Dec. 1 Photo. *Perf. 13x13½*

281 A50 3p silver & multi .50 .50
282 A50 5p gold & multi .50 .50

Artificer, 1773 — A51

3p, Tunneler with drill, 1969. 5p, Royal Engineers, 1772 and 1972, and regimental crest, horiz.

1972, Mar. 6 *Perf. 14x13½, 13½x14*

283 A51 1p dk blue & multi .50 *.55*
284 A51 3p red & multi .60 *.80*
285 A51 5p green & multi .75 *.90*
Nos. 283-285 (3) 1.85 2.25

Bicent. of the Royal Engineers in Gibraltar.

Uniform Type of 1969

Uniforms: 1p, Soldier, Duke of Cornwall's Light Infantry, 1704. 3p, Officer, King's Royal Rifle Corps, 1830. 7p, Officer, 37th North Hampshire Regiment, 1825. 10p, Sailor, Royal Navy, 1972.

1972, July 19 Litho. *Perf. 14*

286 A42 1p silver & multi .55 .25
287 A42 3p slate & multi 1.25 .40
288 A42 7p silver & multi 2.10 .70
289 A42 10p gold & multi 2.50 1.60
Nos. 286-289 (4) 6.40 2.95

Design descriptions printed on back on top of gum.

"Our Lady of Europa" — A52

1972, Oct. 1 *Perf. 14½x14*

290 A52 3p brown & multi .25 .25
291 A52 5p green & multi .25 .35

Christmas. Design description printed on back.

Silver Wedding Issue, 1972

Common Design Type

Design: Queen Elizabeth II, Prince Philip, keys of Gibraltar and white narcissus.

1972, Nov. 20 Photo. *Perf. 14x14½*

292 CD324 5p car rose & multi .25 .25
293 CD324 7p slate green & multi .25 .25

Flags of EEC Members and EEC Emblem — A53

Perf. 14½x14

1973, Feb. 22 Litho. Unwmk.

294 A53 5p red & multi .55 .40
295 A53 10p ultra & multi .60 .60

Entry into European Economic Community.

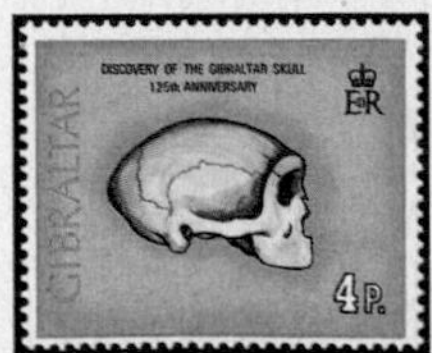

Gibraltar Skull — A54

Designs: 6p, Head of Neanderthal man. 10p, Neanderthal family.

1973, May 22 Wmk. 314 *Perf. 13½*

296 A54 4p lilac rose & multi 1.25 .60
297 A54 6p lt ultra & multi 1.50 1.25
298 A54 10p yel green & multi 2.25 2.25
Nos. 296-298 (3) 5.00 4.10

125th anniv. of the discovery of the Gibraltar skull.

Uniform Type of 1969

Uniforms: 1p, Fifer, King's Own Scottish Borderers, 1770. 4p, Officer, Royal Welsh Fusiliers, 1800. 6p, Soldier, Royal Northumberland Fusiliers, 1736. 10p, Private, Grenadier Guards, 1898.

1973, Aug. 22 Litho. *Perf. 14*

299 A42 1p multicolored .50 .35
300 A42 4p multicolored 1.25 .60
301 A42 6p multicolored 2.00 1.25
302 A42 10p multicolored 3.00 *2.50*
Nos. 299-302 (4) 6.75 *4.70*

Descriptions printed on back on top of gum.

Nativity, by Justus Danckerts — A55

1973, Oct. 17 Litho. *Perf. 12½x12*

303 A55 4p brown org & blue .45 .25
304 A55 6p green & claret .50 *.80*

Christmas.

Princess Anne's Wedding Issue

Common Design Type

1973, Nov. 14 *Perf. 14*

305 CD325 6p bl grn & multi .25 .25
306 CD325 14p brt grn & multi .30 .30

Wedding of Princess Anne and Capt. Mark Phillips, Nov. 14, 1973.

V.R. (Queen Victoria) Pillar Box — A56

Pillar Boxes: 6p, G.R. (King George). 14p, E.R. (Queen Elizabeth).

1974, May 2 Litho. *Perf. 14*

307 A56 2p yel green & multi .25 .25
308 A56 6p gray & multi .25 *.30*
309 A56 14p dull yel & multi .35 *.60*
a. Souvenir booklet 11.00
Nos. 307-309 (3) .85 *1.15*

UPU, cent.

No. 309a contains 2 self-adhesive panes printed on peelable paper backing with multicolored advertising on back. One pane of 6 contains 3 each similar to Nos. 307-308; the other pane of 3 contains one each similar to Nos. 307-309. Stamps are imperf. x roulette.

Uniform Type of 1969

Uniforms: 4p, Officer, East Lancashire Regiment, 1742. 6p, Sergeant, Somerset Light Infantry, 1833. 10p, Company man, Royal Sussex Regiment, 1790. 16p, Officer, Royal Air Force, 1974.

1974, Aug. 21 *Perf. 14*

310 A42 4p silver & multi .55 .45
311 A42 6p silver & multi .80 .60
312 A42 10p silver & multi 1.25 *1.25*
313 A42 16p silver & multi 3.00 *3.25*
Nos. 310-313 (4) 5.60 *5.55*

Descriptions are printed on back on top of gum.

Virgin with Green Cushion, Andrea Solario — A57

Christmas (Painting): 6p, Madonna of the Meadow, by Giovanni Bellini.

1974, Nov. 5 Litho.

314 A57 4p gold & multi .40 .30
315 A57 6p gold & multi .60 *.90*

Churchill, Parliament and Big Ben A58

20p, Churchill & George V-class battleship.

1974, Nov. 30 *Perf. 14x14½*

316 A58 6p violet & multi .25 .25
317 A58 20p multicolored .50 .50
a. Souvenir sheet of 2, #316-317 5.00 *5.50*

Sir Winston Churchill (1874-1965).

Uniform Type of 1969

Uniforms: 4p, Officer, East Surrey Regiment, 1846. 6p, Private, Highland Light Infantry, 1777. 10p, Officer, Coldstream Guards, 1704. 20p, Sergeant, Gibraltar Regiment, 1974.

1975, Mar. 14 Wmk. 373 *Perf. 14*

318 A42 4p multicolored .35 .25
319 A42 6p multicolored .55 .40
320 A42 10p multicolored .80 .80
321 A42 20p multicolored 1.50 *1.75*
Nos. 318-321 (4) 3.20 *3.20*

Descriptions are printed on back on top of gum.

Girl Guides Emblem A59

1975, Oct. 10 *Perf. 13½x13*

322 A59 5p violet, gold & blue .30 *.40*
323 A59 7p red brn, gold & blk .45 *.50*
324 A59 15p ocher, silver & blk .75 *.90*
Nos. 322-324 (3) 1.50 1.80

Girl Guides, 50th anniversary.

Child and Bird — A60

b, Angel playing lute. c, Singing boy. d, Mother & children. e, Praying child. f, Child & lamb.

1975, Nov. 25 *Perf. 14x14½*

325 Block of 6 2.75 *3.25*
a.-f. A60 6p any single .40 *.55*

Christmas. No. 325 printed in sheets of 60 containing 10 blocks of 6 (3x2) stamps with horizontal and vertical gutters between blocks.

Bruges Madonna, by Michelangelo
A61

Sculptures by Michelangelo: 9p, Traddei Madonna. 15p, Pietà.

1975, Dec. 17 Litho. *Perf. 14x13½*

326	A61	6p blue blk & multi	.25	.25
327	A61	9p black brn & multi	.25	*.40*
328	A61	15p dk purple & multi	.35	*.95*
a.		Souvenir booklet	5.50	
		Nos. 326-328 (3)	.85	*1.60*

500th birth anniv. of Michelangelo Buonarroti (1475-1564), Italian sculptor, painter and architect.

No. 328a contains 2 self-adhesive panes printed on peelable paper backing with stamp dealer's advertisements on back. One pane of 6 contains 2 each similar to Nos. 326-328; the other pane of 3 contains one each similar to Nos. 326-328. Stamps are imperf. x roulette.

American Bicentennial Emblem, Arms of Gibraltar — A62

1976, May 28 *Perf. 14x14½*

329	A62	25p multicolored	.70	.70
a.		Souvenir sheet of 4	4.75	*5.75*

American Bicentennial. No. 329a is rouletted all around.

Uniform Type of 1969

Uniforms: 1p, Suffolk Regiment, 1795. 6p, Northamptonshire Regiment, 1779. 12p, Lancashire Fusiliers, 1793. 25p, Royal Army Ordinance Corps. 1896.

1976, July 21 *Perf. 14*

330	A42	1p multicolored	.25	.25
331	A42	6p multicolored	.40	.25
332	A42	12p multicolored	.55	.50
333	A42	25p multicolored	.75	*1.25*
		Nos. 330-333 (4)	1.95	2.25

Descriptions printed on back on top of gum.

Holy Family — A63

Stained Glass Windows: 9p, St. Bernard of Clairvaux. 12p, St. John the Evangelist. 20p, Archangel Michael.

1976, Nov. 3 Litho. Wmk. 373

334	A63	6p ultra & multi	.25	.25
335	A63	9p brt green & multi	.30	.25
336	A63	12p orange & multi	.45	*.50*
337	A63	20p dk carmine & multi	.85	*1.10*
		Nos. 334-337 (4)	1.85	2.10

Christmas.

Elizabeth II and Royal Crest — A64

1977, Feb. 7 Litho. *Perf. 14x13½*

338	A64	6p multicolored	.25	.25
339	A64	£1 multicolored	1.40	*1.50*
a.		Souv. sheet of 2, #338-339, perf. 13	2.00	*2.50*

25th anniv. of the reign of Queen Elizabeth II. Nos. 338-339 issued in sheets of 9.

Red Mullet
A65

½p, Toothed orchid. 2p, Large blue. 2½p, Sardinian warbler. 3p, Giant squill. 4p, Gray wrasse. 5p, Red admiral. 6p, Black kite. 9p, Scorpion vetch. 10p, John Dory. 12p, Clouded yellow. 15p, Winged asparagus pea (inscr. "1980"). 20p, Andouin's gull. 25p, Barbary nut. 50p, Swordfish. £ 1, Swallowtail. £ 2, Hoopoe. £ 5, Coat of Arms (inscr. "1979").

½p, 3p, 9p, 15p, 25p, Flowers. 1p, 4p, 10p, 50p, Fish. 2p, 5p, 12p, £1, Butterflies. 2½p, 6p, 20p, £2, Birds. ½p, 2½p, 3p, 6p, 9p, 15p, 20p, 25p, £2, £5, vertical.

1977-80 *Perf. 14½x14, 14x14½*

Inscribed "1977," except as noted

340	A65	½p multi	.50	*2.00*
a.		Chalky paper, inscribed "1982"	5.00	4.00
341	A65	1p shown	.25	*.45*
342	A65	2p multi	.25	*1.00*
343	A65	2½p multi	1.00	*1.50*
344	A65	3p multi	.25	.25
345	A65	4p multi	.25	.25
346	A65	5p multi	.40	*.80*
347	A65	6p multi	1.50	.45
348	A65	9p multi	.50	.55
a.		Inscribed "1978"	.60	.60
349	A65	10p multi	.35	.25
350	A65	12p multi	.75	.35
350A	A65	15p multi	1.25	.45
351	A65	20p multi	1.50	*2.75*
352	A65	25p multi	1.00	*2.00*
353	A65	50p multi	1.50	.80
354	A65	£1 multi	3.50	*5.00*
355	A65	£2 multi	7.25	*11.00*
355A	A65	£5 multi	9.00	*12.00*
		Nos. 340-355A (18)	31.00	*41.85*

Issued: No. 348a, 2/1/78; £ 5, 5/16/79; 15p, 11/12/80; No. 340a, 2/22/82; others, 4/1/77.

Inscribed "1981"

1981, Apr. 21 Chalky Paper

345a	A65	4p multicolored	.50	*.70*
349a	A65	10p multicolored	1.00	*1.50*
350a	A65	12p multicolored	4.00	4.00
352a	A65	25p multicolored	5.00	*5.50*
353a	A65	50p multicolored	6.50	6.50
		Nos. 345a-353a (5)	17.00	*18.20*

Gibraltar No. 182 — A66

12p, Gibraltar #233. 25p, Gibraltar #294.

1977, May 27 Litho. *Perf. 14*

356	A66	6p multi	.25	.25
357	A66	12p multi, vert.	.25	*.35*
358	A66	25p multi, vert.	.30	*.50*
		Nos. 356-358 (3)	.80	1.10

Amphilex 77 Intl. Phil. Exhib., Amsterdam, May 26-June 5. Issued in sheets of 6.

Annunciation, by Rubens — A67

Rubens Paintings: 9p, Nativity. 12p, Adoration of the Kings. 15p, Holy Family under Apple Tree.

Perf. 14x13½, 13½x14

1977, Nov. 2 Litho.

359	A67	3p multi	.25	.25
360	A67	9p multi	.25	.25
361	A67	12p multi, horiz.	.25	.25
362	A67	15p multi	.35	.35
a.		Souvenir sheet of 4, #359-362	3.75	*3.75*
		Nos. 359-362 (4)	1.10	1.10

Christmas and 400th birth anniv. of Peter Paul Rubens

Gibraltar from Space
A68

Design: 25p, Strait of Gibraltar, aerial view.

1978, May 3 Litho. *Perf. 13½*

363	A68	12p multicolored	.35	*.50*

Souvenir Sheet

364	A68	25p multicolored	.90	.90

No. 363 issued in sheets of 10.

No. 364 contains one stamp.

Holyroodhouse — A69

Royal Houses: 9p, St. James Palace. 12p, Sandringham House. 18p, Balmoral.

1978, June 12 Litho. *Perf. 13½*

365	A69	6p multicolored	.25	.25
366	A69	9p multicolored	.25	.25
367	A69	12p multicolored	.35	.30
368	A69	18p multicolored	.40	.40
a.		Souvenir booklet	3.75	
		Nos. 365-368 (4)	1.25	1.20

25th anniv. of coronation of Queen Elizabeth II. No. 368a contains 2 panes printed on peelable paper backing with pictures of castles. One pane contains 6 rouletted stamps, 3 each similar to Nos. 367-368; the other pane contains one 25p (Windsor Castle) rouletted stamp.

Sunderland Seaplane Landing — A70

Gibraltar and: 9p, Two-tiered Caudron taking off, 1918. 12p, Shackleton, 1953-1966. 16p, Hunter warplane, 1954-1966. 18p, Nimrod, 1969-1978.

1978, Sept. 6 Litho. *Perf. 14*

369	A70	3p multicolored	.25	.25
370	A70	9p multicolored	.25	*.35*
371	A70	12p multicolored	.40	*.45*
372	A70	16p multicolored	.50	*.70*
373	A70	18p multicolored	.60	*.90*
		Nos. 369-373 (5)	2.00	*2.65*

Royal Air Force, 60th anniversary.

Madonna with Goldfinch, by Dürer — A71

Christmas (Paintings by Albrecht Dürer): 5p, Madonna with Animals. 9p, Nativity. 15p, Adoration of the Kings.

1978, Nov. 1 Litho. *Perf. 14*

374	A71	5p multicolored	.25	.25
375	A71	9p multicolored	.25	.25
376	A71	12p multicolored	.30	*.35*
377	A71	15p multicolored	.35	*.75*
		Nos. 374-377 (4)	1.15	1.60

Rowland Hill and Gibraltar No. 10 — A72

Sir Rowland Hill (1795-1879), originator of penny postage and: 9p, Gibraltar No. 274. 12p, Parchment scroll with early postal regulations. 25p, "Barred G" cancellation used on British stamps in Gibraltar.

1979, Feb. 7 Litho. *Perf. 13½*

378	A72	3p multicolored	.25	.25
379	A72	9p multicolored	.25	.25
380	A72	12p yellow grn & black	.25	.25
381	A72	25p yellow & black	.30	*.45*
		Nos. 378-381 (4)	1.05	1.20

Satellite Earth Station, Post Horn, Telephone — A73

1979, May 16 *Perf. 13½x14*

382	A73	3p lt green & green	.25	.25
383	A73	9p lt brown & brown	.25	*.55*
384	A73	12p gray & ultra	.30	*.95*
		Nos. 382-384 (3)	.80	*1.75*

European telecommunications system.

Children, IYC Emblem, Nativity — A74

a, African girl. b, Chinese girl. c, Pacific islands girl. d, American Indian girl. e, Shown. f, Scandinavian boy.

Litho.; Silver Embossed

1979, Nov. 14 *Perf. 14*

385		Block of 6	1.75	1.75
a.-f.		A74 12p any single	.25	.25

Christmas; IYC. No. 385 printed in sheets of 12 containing 2 No. 385 with vertical rouletted gutter between.

Officers, Exchange and Commercial Library, 1830 — A75

Gibraltar Police Force, 150th anniv.: 6p, Early and modern uniforms, Rock of Gibraltar. 12p, Traffic Officer, ambulance. 37p, Policeman and woman, Police Station, Irish Town.

Perf. 14x14½

1980, Feb. 5 Litho. Wmk. 373

386	A75	3p multicolored	.25	.25
387	A75	6p multicolored	.25	.25
388	A75	12p multicolored	.30	.35
389	A75	37p multicolored	.50	*.95*
		Nos. 386-389 (4)	1.30	1.80

Archbishop Peter Amigo (1864-1949) A76

Europa: No. 391, Gustavo Charles Bacarisas (1872-1971), artist. No. 392, John Mackintosh (1865-1940), philanthropist.

1980, May 6 Wmk. 373 *Perf. 14½*

390	A76	12p multicolored	.25	*.30*
391	A76	12p multicolored	.25	*.30*
392	A76	12p multicolored	.25	*.30*
		Nos. 390-392 (3)	.75	.90

Queen Mother Elizabeth Birthday Issue

Common Design Type

1980, Aug. 4 Litho. *Perf. 14*

393	CD330	15p multicolored	.35	.35

"Victory" and Rock of Gibraltar, by Monamy Swaine A77

Paintings: 3p, Lord Nelson, by John Francis Rigaud, 1781, vert. 15p, Lord Nelson, by William Beechey, vert. 40p, Victory Towed into Gibraltar by Clarkson Stanfield.

1980, Aug. 20 Litho. *Perf. 14*

394	A77	3p multicolored	.25	.25
395	A77	9p multicolored	.25	.25
396	A77	15p multicolored	.35	.35
a.		Souvenir sheet	1.00	*1.40*
397	A77	40p multicolored	.80	*1.00*
		Nos. 394-397 (4)	1.65	1.85

Horatio Nelson (1758-1805).

Holy Family A78

1980, Nov. 12

398	A78	15p shown	.25	.25
399	A78	15p Three kings	.25	*.25*
a.		Pair, #398-399	.80	*.80*

Christmas. No. 399a has continuous design.

Hercules Separating Africa and Europe — A79

Europa: 15p, Hercules standing on Rock of Gibraltar and Morocco.

Perf. 14x13½

1981, Feb. 24 Wmk. 373

400	A79	9p multicolored	.25	.25
401	A79	15p multicolored	.30	*.35*

Dining Room, The Convent — A80

1981, May 22 Litho. *Perf. 14½x14*

402	A80	4p shown	.25	.25
403	A80	14p King's Chapel	.25	.25
404	A80	15p Aerial view	.30	.25
405	A80	55p Cloister	.60	*.70*
		Nos. 402-405 (4)	1.40	1.45

450th anniv. of The Convent (Governor's residence, originally Franciscan monastery).

Prince Charles and Lady Diana A81

1981, July 27 Litho. *Perf. 14½*

406	A81	£1 multicolored	1.60	1.60

Royal wedding. Se-tenant with decorative label.

Queen Elizabeth II — A82

1981, Sept. 29 *Perf. 14½*

Booklet Stamps

407	A82	1p black	.45	.45
a.		Bklt. pane of 10 + 2 labels (2 #407, 2 #408, 6 #409)	4.50	
b.		Bklt. pane of 5 + label (#407, #408, 3 #409)	2.25	
408	A82	4p dark blue	.45	.45
409	A82	15p green	.45	.45
		Nos. 407-409 (3)	1.35	1.35

Airmail Service, 50th Anniv. A83

14p, Paper plane. 15p, Envelopes, aerogram. 55p, Airplane circling globe.

1981, Sept. 29 *Perf. 14½*

410	A83	14p multicolored	.25	.25
411	A83	15p multicolored	.25	.25
412	A83	55p multicolored	.80	.80
		Nos. 410-412 (3)	1.30	1.30

Intl. Year of the Disabled A84

1981, Nov. 19 Litho. Wmk. 373

413	A84	14p multicolored	.30	.30

Christmas A85

15p, Children singing carols. 55p, Decorated mailbox, vert.

1981, Nov. 19 *Perf. 14*

414	A85	15p multicolored	.30	.25
415	A85	55p multicolored	1.10	.75

Douglas DC-3 — A86

2p, Vickers Viking. 3p, Airspeed Ambassador. 4p, Vickers Viscount. 5p, Boeing 727. 10p, Vickers Vanguard. 14p, Short Solent. 15p, Fokker F-27 Friendship. 17p, Boeing 737. 20p, BAC One-eleven. 25p, Lockheed Constellation. 50p, De Havilland Comet 4B. £ 1, Saro Windhover. £ 2, Hawker Siddeley Trident 2. £ 5, DH-89A Dragon Rapide.

1982, Feb. 10 Litho. *Perf. 14*

416	A86	1p shown	.25	*1.00*
417	A86	2p multicolored	.25	*1.00*
a.		Wmk. 384, dated 1986 ('87)	2.75	*3.50*
418	A86	3p multicolored	.25	*.50*
419	A86	4p multicolored	.40	.25
420	A86	5p multicolored	.60	.30
a.		Wmk. 384, dated 1986 ('87)	2.75	*3.50*
421	A86	10p multicolored	1.10	.55
422	A86	14p multicolored	1.25	*2.00*
423	A86	15p multicolored	1.75	*2.25*
424	A86	17p multicolored	.85	.90
425	A86	20p multicolored	1.25	.65
a.		Inscribed "1985"	1.60	1.60
426	A86	25p multicolored	3.50	*4.25*
427	A86	50p multicolored	3.75	2.25
428	A86	£1 multicolored	5.25	2.25
429	A86	£2 multicolored	6.50	5.25
430	A86	£5 multicolored	9.00	*14.00*
		Nos. 416-430 (15)	35.95	37.40

Royal Navy Ship Crests — A87

1982, Apr. 14 Litho. *Perf. 14*

431	A87	½p Opossum	.25	.25
432	A87	15½p Norfolk	.45	*.50*
433	A87	17p Fearless	.55	*.60*
434	A87	60p Rooke	1.00	*2.25*
		Nos. 431-434 (4)	2.25	*3.60*

See Nos. 449-452, 465-468, 474-477, 492-495, 501-504, 528-531, 552-555, 574-577, 587-590.

Europa A88

14p, Planes preparing for takeoff. 17p, Generals Eisenhower and Giraud.

1982, June 11 Litho. *Perf. 14*

435	A88	14p multicolored	.25	*.60*
436	A88	17p multicolored	.35	*.75*

Operation Torch, 1943.

Chamber of Commerce Centenary — A89

Anniversaries: 15½p, British Forces Postal Service centenary. 60p, Scouting year.

1982, Sept. 22

437	A89	½p multicolored	.25	.25
438	A89	15½p multicolored	.45	.35
439	A89	60p multicolored	1.25	*1.50*
		Nos. 437-439 (3)	1.95	2.10

Intl. Direct Telephone Dialing System Inauguration — A90

1982, Oct. 1 *Perf. 14½*

440	A90	17p Map	.45	.45

Christmas A91

Perf. 14x14½

1982, Nov. 18 Litho. Wmk. 373

441	A91	14p Holly	.30	.25
442	A91	17p Mistletoe	.40	.30

A92

4p, Local street. 14p, Scouts on parade. 17p, Flag, vert. 60p, Queen Elizabeth II, vert.

1983, Mar. 14 Litho. *Perf. 14*

443	A92	4p multicolored	.25	.25
444	A92	14p multicolored	.25	.25
445	A92	17p multicolored	.35	.30
446	A92	60p multicolored	.95	*1.10*
		Nos. 443-446 (4)	1.80	*1.90*

Commonwealth Day.

Europa A93

1983, May 21 *Perf. 14x13½*

447	A93	16p St. George's Hall	.35	.35
448	A93	19p Water catchments	.40	.45

Royal Navy Crest Type of 1982

1983, July 1 Litho. *Perf. 14*

449	A87	4p Faulknor	.40	.25
450	A87	14p Renown	.60	.40
451	A87	17p Ark Royal	.80	.50
452	A87	60p Sheffield	1.75	1.75
		Nos. 449-452 (4)	3.55	2.90

Fortresses — A94

4p, Landport Gate, 1729. 17p, Koehler gun 1782. 77p, King's Bastion, 1799.

1983, Sept. 13 *Perf. 13½x14*

453	A94	4p multicolored	.25	.25
454	A94	17p multicolored	.35	.25
455	A94	77p multicolored	1.30	1.25
a.		Souvenir sheet of 3, #453-455	3.00	3.00
		Nos. 453-455 (3)	1.90	1.75

Christmas
A95

Raphael Paintings: 4p, Adoration of the Magi. 17p, Madonna of Foligno, vert. 60p, Sistine Madonna, vert.

1983, Nov. 17 Litho. *Perf. 14*
456 A95 4p multicolored .30 .25
457 A95 17p multicolored .75 .35
458 A95 60p multicolored 1.90 1.40
Nos. 456-458 (3) 2.95 2.00

Europa (1959-1984)
A96

Intl. Postal and Telecommunication Links — 17p, No. 98. 23p, Communications circuit.

1984, Mar. 6 Litho. *Perf. 14½*
459 A96 17p multicolored .40 *.50*
460 A96 23p multicolored .50 *.90*

Field Hockey
A97

1984, May 25 Litho. *Perf. 14*
461 A97 20p shown .65 *.70*
462 A97 21p Basketball .65 *.70*
463 A97 26p Rowing .65 *.90*
464 A97 29p Soccer .75 *1.25*
Nos. 461-464 (4) 2.70 *3.55*

Royal Navy Crest Type of 1982

1984, Sept. 21 Litho. *Perf. 13½x13*
465 A87 20p Active 1.60 *1.60*
466 A87 21p Foxhound 1.60 *1.60*
467 A87 26p Valiant 1.90 *1.90*
468 A87 29p Hood 2.00 *2.00*
Nos. 465-468 (4) 7.10 *7.10*

Christmas
A98

Perf. 14x14½
1984, Nov. 7 Litho. Wmk. 373
469 A98 20p Parade float .45 .45
470 A98 80p Float, diff. 2.00 2.00

Europa Issue

Musical
Symbols — A99

1985, Feb. 26 Photo. *Perf. 12½*
Granite Paper
471 A99 20p multi, diff. .35 .35
472 A99 29p shown .45 *1.40*

Save the
Children
Fund
A100

Globe and legend in various positions.

1985, May 3 Litho. *Perf. 13x13½*
473 Strip of 4 5.00 *5.00*
a.-d. A100 26p any single 1.00 *1.00*

Royal Navy Crest Type of 1982

1985, July 3 Litho. *Perf. 14*
474 A87 4p Duncan .75 .50
475 A87 9p Fury 1.00 1.40
476 A87 21p Firedrake 2.50 *2.75*
477 A87 80p Malaya 4.25 *5.00*
Nos. 474-477 (4) 8.50 *9.65*

Intl. Youth
Year — A101

4p, Emblem. 20p, Hands, diamond. 80p, Girl Guides anniv. emblem.

1985, Sept. 6 *Perf. 14½*
478 A101 4p multicolored .50 .25
479 A101 20p multicolored 1.50 1.25
480 A101 80p multicolored 4.00 *3.00*
Nos. 478-480 (3) 6.00 *4.50*

St. Joseph's
Parish Church,
Cent. — A102

Creche,
Detail — A103

Perf. 13½; Roulette 7 Between
1985, Oct. 25 Wmk. 373 Litho.
481 A102 Pair 2.00 *2.50*
a. 4p Centenary seal .75 .60
b. 4p Church .75 .60
c. No. 481a, perf. 13½ on 4 sides .80 .60

Perf. 13½
482 A103 80p multicolored 5.25 *5.25*

Christmas. Nos. 481a-481b rouletted between. Printed in sheets of 10 pairs with the bottom row containing 5 No. 481c. Strips of 3, Nos. 481a-481c exist.

Europa
A104

1986, Feb. 10 Litho. *Perf. 13x13½*
483 A104 22p Butterfly, house *.75 .45*
484 A104 29p Seagull, hotel *1.25 3.00*

Postage Stamp
Cent. — A105

1986, Mar. 25 *Perf. 13½x13*
485 A105 4p No. 18 .35 .25
486 A105 22p No. 42 1.10 1.10
487 A105 32p No. 67 1.75 *2.00*
488 A105 36p No. 118 2.00 *2.50*

Size: 32x48mm
Perf. 14
489 A105 44p No. 131 2.25 *3.00*
Nos. 485-489 (5) 7.45 *8.85*

Souvenir Sheet
490 A105 29p No. 2 3.75 3.75

Elizabeth II, 60th
Birthday — A106

1986, May 22 Litho. *Perf. 14*
491 A106 £1 multicolored 2.25 *3.00*

Royal Navy Crest Type of 1982

1986, Aug. 28 Litho. *Perf. 14*
492 A87 22p Lightning 2.00 1.00
493 A87 29p Hermione 2.25 1.75
494 A87 32p Laforey 2.50 *3.00*
495 A87 44p Nelson 3.25 *4.00*
Nos. 492-495 (4) 10.00 *9.75*

Christmas, Intl. Peace
Year — A107

18p, St. Mary the Crowned Cathedral. 32p, St. Andrew's Church.

1986, Oct. 14 Litho. *Perf. 14½x14*
496 A107 18p multicolored 1.00 .50
497 A107 32p multicolored 1.50 *2.75*

Souvenir Sheet

Wedding of Prince Andrew and Sarah
Ferguson — A108

1986, Aug. 28 Litho. *Perf. 15*
498 A108 44p multicolored 1.50 *2.00*

Europa — A109

1987, Feb. 17 Wmk. 384 *Perf. 15*
499 A109 22p Neptune House *1.25 .50*
500 A109 29p Ocean Heights *2.00 3.25*

Royal Navy Crest Type of 1982

1987, Apr. 2 *Perf. 13½x13*
501 A87 18p Wishart 1.75 .70
502 A87 22p Charybdis 2.00 1.10
503 A87 32p Antelope 2.75 *3.00*
504 A87 44p Eagle 3.00 *3.75*
Nos. 501-504 (4) 9.50 *8.55*

Warrant Granted to
the Royal
Engineers, 200th
Anniv. — A110

18p, Victoria Stadium. 32p, Casket, Freedom Scroll. 44p, Monogram.

1987, Apr. 25 Wmk. 373 *Perf. 14½*
505 A110 18p multicolored 1.50 .50
506 A110 32p multicolored 2.25 *3.00*
507 A110 44p multicolored 3.00 *4.00*
Nos. 505-507 (3) 6.75 *7.50*

Guns and
Artillery
A111

Designs: 1p, 13-inch mortar, 1783. 2p, 6-inch Coast, 1909. 3p, 8-inch Howitzer, 1783. 4p, Bofors L40/70, 1951. 5p, 100-ton RML, 1882. 10p, 5.25 HAA, 1953. 18p, 25-pounder Gun-howitzer, 1943. 19p, 64-pounder RML, 1873. 22p, 12-pounder, 1758. 50p, 10-inch RML, 1870. £1, Russian 24-pounder, 1854. £3, 9.2-inch Coast Mk. 10, 1935. £5, 24-pounder, 1779.

1987, June 1 Wmk. 373 *Perf. 12½*
508 A111 1p multicolored .25 *.60*
509 A111 2p multicolored .35 *.50*
510 A111 3p multicolored .35 *.95*
511 A111 4p multicolored .45 .25
512 A111 5p multicolored .45 .65
513 A111 10p multicolored .45 .50
514 A111 18p multicolored .70 *1.40*
515 A111 19p multicolored .70 *1.00*
516 A111 22p multicolored .70 .50
517 A111 50p multicolored 1.40 *2.25*
518 A111 £1 multicolored 2.50 2.50
519 A111 £3 multicolored 4.50 *6.00*
520 A111 £5 multicolored 8.00 *15.00*
Nos. 508-520 (13) 20.80 *32.10*

For surcharge see No. 595.

Christmas — A112

1987, Nov. 12 Wmk. 384 *Perf. 14½*
521 A112 4p Three Wise Men .25 .25
522 A112 22p Holy Family 1.00 .90
523 A112 44p Shepherds 1.90 *2.75*
Nos. 521-523 (3) 3.15 *3.90*

Europa — A113

Transport and communication: No. 524, Rock of Gibraltar, Cruise Ship. No. 525, Passenger jet, yacht, dish aerial. No. 526, Bus, buggy. No. 527, Rock of Gibraltar, automobile, telephone.

Perf. 14½x14 on 3 Sides; Rouletted Between

1988, Feb. 16 Litho. Wmk. 373

524	22p multicolored	*1.25*	*1.50*
525	22p multicolored	*1.25*	*1.50*
a.	A113 Pair, #524-525	*3.25*	*3.25*
526	32p multicolored	*1.75*	*2.00*
527	32p multicolored	*1.75*	*2.00*
a.	A113 Pair, #526-527	*4.25*	*4.25*
	Nos. 524-527 (4)	*6.00*	*7.00*

Nos. 525a, 527a have continuous design.

Royal Navy Crest Type of 1982

Perf. 13½x13

1988, Apr. 7 Wmk. 384

528	A87 18p Clyde	1.75	.65
529	A87 22p Foresight	2.25	1.25
530	A87 32p Severn	2.75	*3.00*
531	A87 44p Rodney	3.50	*4.50*
	Nos. 528-531 (4)	10.25	*9.40*

Birds
A114

1988, June 15 Wmk. 373 *Perf. 14*

532	A114 4p Bee eater	1.00	.25
533	A114 22p Common puffin	2.00	.85
534	A114 32p Honey buzzard	2.50	*2.25*
535	A114 44p Blue rock thrush	3.25	*4.00*
	Nos. 532-535 (4)	8.75	*7.35*

Operation Raleigh, 1984-88
A115

Designs: 19p, Square-rigger. 22p, Sir Walter Raleigh and expedition emblem. 32p, Maps and modern transport ship Sir Walter Raleigh. 44p, Ship Sir Walter Raleigh.

Perf. 13x13½

1988, Sept. 14 Litho. Wmk. 373

536	A115 19p multicolored	.75	.75
537	A115 22p multicolored	.90	.90
538	A115 32p multicolored	1.25	1.25
	Nos. 536-538 (3)	2.90	2.90

Souvenir Sheet

539	Sheet of 2, #537, 539a	5.25	5.25
a.	A115 44p multicolored	2.25	2.25

400th anniv. of Sir Walter Raleigh's voyage to the New World to establish the 1st English-speaking colony, in what is now North Carolina.

Christmas
A116

Children's drawings: 4p, Snowman, by Rebecca Falero. 22p, Nativity, by Dennis Penalver. 44p, Santa Claus, by Gavin Key.

1988, Nov. 2 Wmk. 384 *Perf. 14*

540	A116 4p multicolored	.25	.25
541	A116 22p multicolored	.55	.55

Size: 25x33mm

542	A116 44p multicolored	1.10	*1.75*
	Nos. 540-542 (3)	1.90	*2.55*

Europa
A117

Toys: 32p, Doll, doll house, puppy, ball, boat.

Perf. 13x13½

1989, Feb. 15 Wmk. 384

543	A117 25p shown	*1.10*	*.75*
544	A117 32p multicolored	*1.50*	*2.50*

Gibraltar Regiment, 50th Anniv. — A118

4p, The Port Sergeant. 22p, Regimental colors, Queen's colors. 32p, Drum Major.

Perf. 13½x13

1989, Apr. 28 Wmk. 373

545	A118 4p multicolored	.50	.25
546	A118 22p multicolored	1.50	1.00
547	A118 32p multicolored	2.00	*2.75*
	Nos. 545-547 (3)	4.00	4.00

Souvenir Sheet

548	Sheet of 2, Nos. 546, 548a	5.75	*5.75*
a.	A118 44p Regimental arms	2.50	2.50

Intl. Red Cross, 125th Anniv. — A119

25p, Mother and child. 32p, Malnourished children. 44p, Accident victims.

Perf. 15x14½

1989, July 7 Wmk. 384

549	A119 25p multicolored	1.10	.60
550	A119 32p multicolored	1.40	*1.50*
551	A119 44p multicolored	1.75	*2.50*
	Nos. 549-551 (3)	4.25	*4.60*

Royal Navy Crest Type of 1982

1989, Sept. 7 Litho. *Perf. 14*

552	A87 22p Blankney	1.75	.70
553	A87 25p Deptford	1.75	1.50
554	A87 32p Exmoor	2.50	2.50
555	A87 44p Stork	3.50	*4.25*
	Nos. 552-555 (4)	9.50	8.95

Souvenir Sheets

Coins — A120

No. 556: a, 1p Barbary Partridge. b, 2p Lighthouse at Europa Point. c, 10p Tower of Homage. d, 5p Barbary Ape.

No. 557: a, 50p Gibraltar Candytuft. b, £5 Pillars of Hercules. c, £2 Cannon from the Great Siege Period, 1779-1783. d, £1 Natl. coat of arms. e, Common obverse side of coins picturing Maklouf head of Queen Elizabeth II. f, 20p Our Lady of Europa.

1989, Oct. 10 *Perf. 14½x15*

556	A120 Sheet of 4	2.00	2.00
a.-d.	4p any single	.50	.50
557	A120 Sheet of 6	6.75	6.75
a.-f.	22p any single	1.25	1.25

Christmas
A121

4p, Santa's sleigh. 22p, Shepherds see star. 32p, Holy family. 44p, Adoration of the Magi.

Wmk. 384

1989, Oct. 11 Litho. *Perf. 14½*

558	A121 4p multicolored	.25	.25
559	A121 22p multicolored	1.10	.80
560	A121 32p multicolored	1.75	*1.90*
561	A121 44p multicolored	2.75	*3.25*
	Nos. 558-561 (4)	5.85	*6.20*

Europa 1990 — A122

Post offices: No. 562, G.P.O. exterior. No. 563, Carved crown and "VR" from p.o. archway and G.P.O. interior. No. 564, South District P.O. interior. No. 565, South District P.O. exterior.

Perf. 14½, Rouletted 9½ Between

1990, Mar. 6 Litho. Unwmk.

562	22p multicolored	*1.00*	*1.00*
563	22p multicolored	*1.00*	*1.00*
a.	A122 Pair, #562-563	*2.75*	*2.75*
564	32p multicolored	*1.25*	*1.25*
565	32p multicolored	*1.25*	*1.25*
a.	A122 Pair, #564-565	*3.75*	*3.75*
	Nos. 562-565 (4)	4.50	*4.50*

Pairs are rouletted between.

Early Fire Truck
A123

4p, Early firemen, hose, vert. 42p, Modern truck. 44p, Modern fireman, vert.

1990, Apr. 2 *Perf. 14½x14*

566	A123 4p multicolored	1.00	.25
567	A123 20p shown	2.50	1.00
568	A123 42p multicolored	3.00	3.00
569	A123 44p multicolored	3.25	3.25
	Nos. 566-569 (4)	9.75	7.50

Fire Service, 125th anniv.

Penny Black, 150th Anniv. — A124

19p, Henry Corbould, Great Britain No. 1. 22p, 1st Royal Mail coach, Bristol-London. 32p, Sir Rowland Hill, Great Britain No. 1. 44p, Great Britain No. 1, Maltese Cross cancel.

1990, May 3 *Perf. 13½x14*

570	A124 19p multicolored	1.00	.90
571	A124 22p multicolored	1.25	.95
572	A124 32p multicolored	2.50	2.50
	Nos. 570-572 (3)	4.75	4.35

Souvenir Sheet

573	A124 44p multicolored	6.25	6.25

Royal Navy Crest Type of 1982

1990, July 10 Litho. *Perf. 14*

574	A87 22p Calpe	2.00	.80
575	A87 25p Gallant	2.25	1.90
576	A87 32p Wrestler	2.75	*3.00*
577	A87 44p Greyhound	3.50	*4.00*
	Nos. 574-577 (4)	10.50	9.70

Europort Model
A125

23p, Building components. 25p, Land reclamation.

1990, Oct. 10 Litho. *Perf. 14½*

578	A125 22p shown	.90	.80
579	A125 23p multicolored	.90	*1.25*
580	A125 25p multicolored	1.00	*1.25*
	Nos. 578-580 (3)	2.80	*3.30*

Christmas — A126

1990, Oct. 10 *Perf. 13½*

581	A126 4p shown	.25	.25
582	A126 22p Santa Claus	.80	.50
583	A126 42p Christmas tree	1.75	*2.25*
584	A126 44p Creche	1.75	*2.25*
	Nos. 581-584 (4)	4.55	*5.25*

Europa
A127

25p, Spaceplane, satellite. 32p, ERS-1 satellite.

1991, Feb. 26 Litho. *Perf. 13½*

585	A127 25p multicolored	*.80*	*.60*
586	A127 32p multicolored	*1.10*	*1.50*

Royal Navy Crest Type of 1982

1991, Apr. 9 Litho. *Perf. 13½x13*

587	A87 4p Hesperus	.60	.25
588	A87 21p Forester	2.00	1.25
589	A87 22p Furious	2.00	1.25
590	A87 62p Scylla	4.50	*6.00*
	Nos. 587-590 (4)	9.10	*8.75*

Birds
A128

1991, May 30 Litho. *Perf. 13½*

591	A128 13p Black stork	1.25	1.25
592	A128 13p Egyptian vulture	1.25	1.25
593	A128 13p Barbary partridge	1.25	1.25
594	A128 13p Shag	1.25	1.25
a.	Block of 4, #591-594	6.50	*7.50*

World Wildlife Fund.

No. 519 Surcharged

Wmk. 373

1991, May 30 Litho. *Perf. 12½*
595 A111 £1.05 on £3 multi 5.75 2.75

Views of Gibraltar A129

Paintings: 22p, North View of Gibraltar, by Gustavo Bacarisas (1873-1971). 26p, Parson's Lodge, by Elena Mifsud (1906-1989). 32p, Governor's Parade, by Jacobo Azabury, OBE (1890-1980). 42p, Waterport Wharf, by Rudesindo Mannia (1899-1982), vert.

1991, Sept. 10 Litho. *Perf. 15x14*
596 A129 22p multicolored 1.00 .50
597 A129 26p multicolored 1.25 .90
598 A129 32p multicolored 1.75 *2.00*

Perf. 14x15

599 A129 42p multicolored 2.75 *3.50*
Nos. 596-599 (4) 6.75 *6.90*

Christmas A130

Christmas carols: 4p, Once in Royal David's City. 24p, Silent Night. 25p, Angels We Have Heard on High. 49p, O Come All Ye Faithful.

1991, Oct. 15 Litho. *Perf. 14½*
600 A130 4p multicolored .40 .25
601 A130 24p multicolored 1.50 .60
602 A130 25p multicolored 1.50 .90
603 A130 49p multicolored 3.00 *4.00*
Nos. 600-603 (4) 6.40 *5.75*

Souvenir Sheet

Phila Nippon '91 — A131

1991, Nov. 15
604 A131 £1.05 Plain tiger 4.75 4.75

Queen Elizabeth II's Accession to the Throne, 40th Anniv.
Common Design Type

Wmk. 373

1992, Feb. 6 Litho. *Perf. 14*
605 CD349 4p multicolored .25 .25
606 CD349 20p multicolored .75 .75
607 CD349 24p multicolored .90 *1.00*
608 CD349 44p multicolored 1.50 *1.50*
609 CD349 54p multicolored 1.75 *2.00*
Nos. 605-609 (5) 5.15 *5.50*

Discovery of America, 500th Anniv. — A132

No. 610, Columbus, Santa Maria. No. 611, Map, Nina. No. 612, Map, Pinta. No. 613, Map, sailor.

1992, Feb. 6 Unwmk. *Perf. 14½*
610 A132 24p multicolored 1.25 *1.50*
611 A132 24p multicolored 1.25 *1.50*
a. Pair, #610-611 3.50 *3.75*
612 A132 34p multicolored 1.75 *1.90*
613 A132 34p multicolored 1.75 *1.90*
a. Pair, #612-613 4.00 *4.00*
Nos. 610-613 (4) 6.00 *6.80*

Europa. Printed in sheets containing 4 pairs.

Around the World Yacht Rally, 1991-92 — A133

Compass rose, sail and maps of routes through: 21p, Atlantic Ocean, vert. 24p, Malay Archipelago. 25p, Indian Ocean. 49p, Mediterranean and Red Seas, vert.

1992, Apr. 15 Litho. *Perf. 13½*
614 A133 21p multicolored .90 .75
615 A133 24p multicolored 1.25 1.25
616 A133 25p multicolored 1.25 *1.50*
Nos. 614-616 (3) 3.40 *3.50*

Souvenir Sheet

617 A133 Sheet of 2, #614 & 617a 3.00 3.00
a. A133 49p multicolored 2.00 2.00

Anglican Diocese of Gibraltar, 150th Anniv. A134

4p, Holy Trinity Cathedral, vert. 24p, Crest and map. 44p, Construction work on Cathedral during 1800's. 54p, Bishop Tomlinson, first Bishop of Diocese (1842-1863), vert.

1992, Aug. 21 Litho. *Perf. 14*
618 A134 4p multicolored .40 .25
619 A134 24p multicolored 1.10 .60
620 A134 44p multicolored 2.00 *2.25*
621 A134 54p multicolored 2.25 *3.00*
Nos. 618-621 (4) 5.75 *6.10*

Christmas A135

Designs: 4p, Church of the Sacred Heart of Jesus. 24p, Cathedral of St. Mary the Crowned. 34p, St. Andrew's Church. 49p, St. Joseph's Church.

1992, Nov. 10 Litho. *Perf. 14*
622 A135 4p multicolored .35 .25
623 A135 24p multicolored 1.50 .50
624 A135 34p multicolored 2.00 2.00
625 A135 49p multicolored 2.50 *4.25*
Nos. 622-625 (4) 6.35 7.00

Contemporary Art — A136

Europa: No. 626, Masks of Comedy and Tragedy, record. No. 627, Painting, dancer, pottery. No. 628, Architecture, sculpture. No. 629, Video camera, 35mm film.

1993, Mar. 2 Litho. *Perf. 14½*
626 A136 24p multicolored 1.50 1.50
627 A136 24p multicolored 1.50 1.50
a. Pair, #626-627 3.50 *4.25*
628 A136 34p multicolored 1.75 .200
629 A136 34p multicolored 1.75 2.00
a. Pair, #628-629 4.50 *5.25*
Nos. 626-629 (4) 6.50 5.20

Souvenir Sheet

World War II Warships — A137

Designs: a, HMS Hood. b, HMS Ark Royal c, HMAS Waterhen. d, USS Gleaves.

1993, Apr. 27 Litho. *Perf. 14*
630 A137 24p Sheet of 4, #a.-d. 11.00 11.00

See Nos. 660, 684, 714, 732.

Architectural Heritage A138

1p, Landport Gate. 2p, St. Mary the Crowned. 3p, Parsons Lodge Battery. 4p, Moorish Castle. 5p, General Post Office. 10p, South Barracks. 21p, American War Memorial. 24p, Garrison Library. 25p, Southport Gates. 26p, Casemates Gate. 50p, Central Police Station. £ 1, Prince Edward's Gate. £ 3, Lighthouse. £ 5, Coat of arms, keys to fortress, vert.

1993-94 Litho. *Perf. 13*
631 A138 1p multicolored .25 *.75*
632 A138 2p multicolored .30 *.75*
633 A138 3p multicolored .30 .25
634 A138 4p multicolored .30 .25
635 A138 5p multicolored .40 .25
636 A138 10p multicolored .40 .25
637 A138 21p multicolored 1.00 .85
638 A138 24p multicolored 1.10 .95
639 A138 25p multicolored 1.10 .95
640 A138 26p multicolored 1.25 1.00
641 A138 50p multicolored 2.00 1.75
642 A138 £1 multicolored 3.00 3.00
643 A138 £3 multicolored 9.00 *10.00*
644 A138 £5 multicolored 13.00 13.00
Nos. 631-644 (14) 33.40 34.00

Nos. 631, 635, 637, 639, 642-643 are vert.
Portions of the design on No. 644 were applied by a thermographic process producing a shiny, raised effect.
Issued: £5, 6/6/94; others, 6/28/93.
See Nos. 686-693.

Anniversaries — A139

21p, Coins. 24p, Jet, biplane fighters. 34p, Garrison Library. 49p, Churchill, searchlights.

1993, Sept. 21 Litho. *Perf. 13*
645 A139 21p multicolored 1.25 .70
646 A139 24p multicolored 1.75 .90
647 A139 34p multicolored 1.75 2.25
648 A139 49p multicolored 4.00 4.00
Nos. 645-648 (4) 8.75 7.85

First decimal coins, 25th anniv. Royal Air Force, 75th anniv. Garrison Library, bicent. Churchill's visit to Gibraltar, 50th anniv.

Christmas A140

Mice and: 5p, Christmas tree. 24p, Christmas cracker. 44p, Singing carols. 49p, Snowman.

1993, Nov. 16 Litho. *Perf. 13½*
649 A140 5p multicolored .25 .25
650 A140 24p multicolored 1.00 .70
651 A140 44p multicolored 2.00 2.50
652 A140 49p multicolored 3.00 3.00
Nos. 649-652 (4) 6.25 6.45

European Discoveries — A141

Europa: No. 653, Atoms exploding, Lord Penney (1909-91). No. 654, Chemistry flasks, polonium, radium, Marie Curie. No. 655, Diesel engine, Rudolf Diesel. No. 656, Telescope, Galileo.

1994, Mar. 1 Litho. *Perf. 13½*
653 A141 24p multicolored 1.00 1.25
654 A141 24p multicolored 1.00 1.25
a. Pair, #653-654 3.00 3.00
655 A141 34p multicolored 1.40 1.50
656 A141 34p multicolored 1.40 1.50
a. Pair, #655-656 3.50 3.50
Nos. 653-656 (4) 4.80 5.50

1994 World Cup Soccer Championships, US — A142

26p, FIFA cup, US map, flag. 39p, Players, US map as playing field. 49p, Leg action.

1994, Apr. 19 Litho. *Perf. 13½*
657 A142 26p multi 1.00 .65
658 A142 39p multi 1.50 2.00
659 A142 49p multi, vert. 2.00 2.75
Nos. 657-659 (3) 4.50 5.40

World War II Warships Type of 1993
Souvenir Sheet

Designs: a, 5p, HMS Penelope. b, 25p, HMS Warspite. c, 44p, USS McLanahan. d, 49p, HNLMS Isaac Sweers.

1994, June 6 Litho. *Perf. 13½x13*
660 A137 Sheet of 4, #a.-d. 9.00 9.00

Souvenir Sheet

PHILAKOREA '94 — A143

1994, Aug. 16 Litho. *Perf. 13*
661 A143 £1.05 multicolored 4.00 4.00

Marine Life — A144

21p, Golden star coral. 24p, Star fish. 34p, Gorgonian sea fan. 49p, Turkish wrasse.

1994, Sept. 27 Litho. *Perf. 14*
662 A144 21p multicolored .90 .50
663 A144 24p multicolored 1.10 .60
664 A144 34p multicolored 1.75 1.50
665 A144 49p multicolored 2.50 2.50
Nos. 662-665 (4) 6.25 5.10

Intl. Olympic Committee, Cent. — A145

1994, Nov. 22 Litho. *Perf. 14*
666 A145 49p Discus 2.50 2.25
667 A145 54p Javelin 2.50 2.50

Christmas Songbirds A146

1994, Nov. 22 *Perf. 13½*
668 A146 5p Great tit, vert. .80 .25
669 A146 24p Robin 2.50 .75
670 A146 34p Blue tit 2.75 1.50
671 A146 54p Goldfinch, vert. 3.75 *4.25*
Nos. 668-671 (4) 9.80 6.75

New Members in European Union A147

Flags: 24p, Austria. 26p, Finland. 34p, Sweden. 49p, Sweden, Finland, Austria, emblem of European Union.

1995, Jan. 3 Litho. *Perf. 14*
672 A147 24p multicolored .80 .45
673 A147 26p multicolored .90 .55
674 A147 34p multicolored 1.10 1.00
675 A147 49p multicolored 1.75 *2.50*
Nos. 672-675 (4) 4.55 *4.50*

Peace & Freedom — A148

Europa: No. 676, Cross, barbed wire, text. No. 677, Rainbow, dove, hands. No. 678, Shackles, text. No. 679, Doves, hands.

1995, Feb. 28 Litho. *Perf. 13½*
676 24p multicolored 1.25 1.25
677 24p multicolored 1.25 1.25
a. A148 Pair, #676-677 3.25 3.00
678 34p multicolored 1.40 1.40
679 34p multicolored 1.40 1.40
a. A148 Pair, #678-679 4.00 4.00
Nos. 676-679 (4) 5.30 *5.30*

Island Games — A149

1995, May 8 Litho. *Perf. 14x13½*
680 A149 24p Sailing .80 .75
681 A149 44p Running 1.75 1.75
682 A149 49p Swimming 1.75 1.75
Nos. 680-682 (3) 4.30 4.25

680a Booklet pane of 3 3.75
681a Booklet pane of 3 6.50
682a Booklet pane of 3 8.00
682b Bklt. pane, 1 ea. #680-682 6.00
Commemorative booklet, 1 each #680a-682b 24.50

Souvenir Sheet

VE Day, 50th Anniv. — A150

1995, May 8
683 A150 £1.05 multicolored 5.00 5.00

World War II Warships Type of 1993

Designs: a, 5p, HMS Calpe. b, 24p, HMS Victorious. c, 44p, USS Weehawken. d, 49p, FFS Savorgnan de Brazza.

Souvenir Sheet

1995, June 6 Litho. *Perf. 13½x14*
684 A137 Sheet of 4, #a.-d. 10.00 10.00

Singapore '95 — A151

Orchids: a, 22p, Bee. b, 23p, Brown bee. c, 24p, Pyramidal. d, 25p, Mirror. e, 26p, Sawfly.

1995, Sept. 1 Litho. *Perf. 14x14½*
685 A151 Strip of 5, #a.-e. 8.25 6.25

Architectural Heritage Type of 1993

6p, House of Assembly. 7p, Bleak House. 8p, Bust of Gen. Elliott. 9p, Supreme Court Building. 20p, Convent. 30p, St. Bernard's Hospital. 40p, City Hall. £2, Church of Sacred Heart of Jesus.

1995, Sept. 1 Litho. *Perf. 13*
686 A138 6p multicolored .70 .40
687 A138 7p multicolored .70 .40
688 A138 8p multicolored .90 .40
689 A138 9p multicolored 1.10 .65
690 A138 20p multicolored 1.25 .70
691 A138 30p multicolored 1.40 1.50
692 A138 40p multicolored 1.60 2.00
693 A138 £2 multicolored 6.00 7.50
Nos. 686-693 (8) 13.65 13.55

Nos. 686, 688, 691, 693 are vert.

UN, 50th Anniv. A152

1995, Oct. 24 Litho. *Perf. 13½*
694 A152 34p shown 1.90 1.90
695 A152 49p Peace dove 2.00 2.00

Miniature Sheets of 4 + 4 Labels

Motion Pictures, Cent. — A153

Designs: No. 696: a, Ingrid Bergman. b, Vittorio De Sica. c, Marlene Dietrich. d, Laurence Olivier.

No. 697: a, 38p, Audrey Hepburn. b, 25p, Romy Schneider. c, 28p, Yves Montand. d, 5p, Marilyn Monroe.

1995, Nov. 13 Litho. *Perf. 14½x14*
696 A153 24p #a.-d. 3.50 3.50
697 A153 #a.-d. 3.50 3.50

Christmas A154

Designs: 5p, Santa Claus. 24p, Sack of toys. 34p, Reindeer. 54p, Santa with sleigh, reindeer flying over rooftops.

1995, Nov. 27 *Perf. 14*
698 A154 5p multicolored .45 .25
699 A154 24p multicolored 1.40 .55
700 A154 34p multicolored 2.00 1.50
701 A154 54p multicolored 3.00 *4.00*
Nos. 698-701 (4) 6.85 *6.30*

Miniature Sheet

Puppies — A155

No. 702: a, 5p, Shih tzu. b, 21p, Dalmatian. c, Cocker spaniel. d, 25p, West Highland white terrier. e, 34p, Labrador. f, 35p, Boxer.

1996, Jan. 24 Litho. *Perf. 14*
702 A155 Sheet of 6, #a.-f. 6.00 6.00

No. 702 is a continuous design.

Women of the British Royal Family A156

1996, Feb. 9 Litho. *Perf. 13½*
703 A156 24p Princess Anne 1.40 1.40
704 A156 24p Princess Diana 1.40 1.40
705 A156 34p Queen Mother 1.60 1.60
706 A156 34p Queen Elizabeth II 1.60 1.60
Nos. 703-706 (4) 6.00 6.00

Europa.

European Soccer — A157

Team members in action scenes: 21p, West Germany, 1980. 24p, France, 1964. 34p, Holland, 1988. £1.20, Denmark, 1992.

1996, Apr. 2 Litho. *Perf. 13*
707 A157 21p multicolored .60 .60
708 A157 24p multicolored .85 .85
709 A157 34p multicolored 1.25 1.25
710 A157 £1.20 multicolored 3.25 3.25
a. Souvenir sheet, Nos. 707-710 9.00 9.00
Nos. 707-710 (4) 5.95 5.95

Modern Olympic Games, Cent. A158

34p, Ancient athletes. 49p, Athletes, 1896. £1.05, Athletes, 1990s.

1996, May 2 Litho. *Perf. 13½*
711 A158 34p multi 1.10 1.10
712 A158 49p multi 1.60 1.60
713 A158 £1.05 multi 3.25 3.25
Nos. 711-713 (3) 5.95 5.95

World War II Warships Type of 1993
Souvenir Sheet

a, 5p, HMS Starling. b, 25p, HMS Royalist. c, 49p, USS Philadelphia. d, 54p, HMCS Prescott.

1996, June 8 Litho. *Perf. 13½x14*
714 A137 Sheet of 4, #a.-d. 7.50 7.50

UNICEF, 50th Anniv. A159

a, 21p, Girl, boy. b, 24p, Three children. c, 49p, Three children, diff. d, 54p, Girl, boy, diff.

1996, June 8 *Perf. 13½x13*
715 A159 Strip of 4, #a.-d. 5.00 5.00

World Wildlife Fund A160

Red kite. a, In flight. b, One adult. c, One on rock, one in flight. d, Adults, young in nest.

1996, July 12 Litho. *Perf. 14½*
716 A160 34p Block or strip of 4, #a.-d. 7.00 7.00

Christmas Images Formed with "Lego" Blocks — A161

1996, Nov. 27 Litho. *Perf. 14*
717 A161 5p Pudding .25 .25
718 A161 21p Snowman .65 .65
719 A161 24p Present .80 .80
720 A161 34p Santa Claus 1.00 1.00
721 A161 54p Candle 1.50 1.50
Nos. 717-721 (5) 4.20 4.20

Sailing Ship "Mary Celeste" — A162

Europa: No. 722, "Mary Celeste" in rough seas. No. 723, Men on board ship. No. 724, Boat approaching "Mary Celeste." No. 725, In full sail.

1997, Feb. 12 Litho. *Perf. 14*

722 A162 28p multicolored 1.00 1.00
723 A162 28p multicolored 1.00 1.00
724 A162 30p multicolored 1.10 1.10
725 A162 30p multicolored 1.10 1.10
Nos. 722-725 (4) 4.20 4.20

Kittens A163

Designs; a, 5p, Silver tabby American shorthair. b, 24p, "Rumpy" Manx red tabby. c, 26p, Blue point Birmans. d, 28p, Red self long-hair. e, 30p, British shorthair, tortoiseshell & white. f, 35p, British bicolor shorthairs.

1997, Feb. 12

726 A163 Sheet of 6, #a.-f. 7.75 7.75
g. Bklt. pane of 3, #726a, 726c, 726e 3.00 3.00
h. Bklt. pane of 3, #726b, 726c, 726d 4.00
i. Bklt. pane of 4, #726a, 726b, 726e, 726f 4.75
j. Bklt. pane of 4, #726c, 726d, 726e, 726f 5.50
k. Booklet pane, #726 7.00
Complete booklet, #726g-726k 24.00

Hong Kong '97. No. 726k is rouletted at left and does not have Hong Kong '97 emblem and inscription in bottom selvage.

Butterflies — A164

Designs: 23p, Anthocharis belia euphenoides. 26p, Charaxes jasius. 30p, Vanessa cardui. £1.20, Iphiclides podalirius.

1997, Apr. 7 Litho. *Perf. 14x13½*

728 A164 23p multicolored .75 .75
729 A164 26p multicolored .90 .90
730 A164 30p multicolored 1.10 1.10
731 A164 £1.20 multicolored 3.75 3.75
a. Souvenir sheet of 4, #728-731 8.00 8.00
Nos. 728-731 (4) 6.50 6.50

World War II Warships Type of 1993

Souvenir Sheet

a, 24p, HMS Enterprise. b, 26p, HMS Cleopatra. c, 38p, USS Iowa. d, 50p, Polish Warship Orkan.

1997, June 9 Litho. *Perf. 13½*

732 A137 Sheet of 4, #a.-d. 5.75 5.75

Queen Elizabeth II and Prince Philip, 50th Wedding Anniv. — A165

Designs: £1.20, Prince Philip driving a four-in-hand, Queen beside him. £1.40, Queen, Prince Philip at Royal Ascot, Queen "Trooping the Color."

1997, July 10 Litho. *Perf. 14x13½*

733 A165 £1.20 multicolored 4.75 4.75
734 A165 £1.40 multicolored 5.50 5.50
a. Pair, #733-734 11.00 11.00

1997 Dior Fashion Designs, by John Galliano — A166

30p, Long black dress, hat. 35p, Mini skirt, lace top. 50p, Formal gown. 62p, Suit, hat. £1.20, Formal gown, diff.

1997, Sept. 9 Litho. *Perf. 13½x13*

735 A166 30p multicolored .85 .85
736 A166 35p multicolored 1.00 1.00
737 A166 50p multicolored 1.25 1.25
a. Pair, #735, 737 3.00 3.00
738 A166 62p multicolored 1.75 1.75
a. Pair, #736, 738 4.00 4.00
Nos. 735-738 (4) 4.85 4.85

Souvenir Sheet

739 A166 £1.20 multicolored 4.00 4.00

Christmas A167

Stained glass windows: 5p, Our Lady and St. Bernard. 26p, The Epiphany of the Lord. 38p, St. Joseph holding Jesus. 50p, The Holy Family. 62p, The Miraculous Medal Madonna.

1997, Nov. 18 Litho. *Perf. 13½*

740 A167 5p multicolored .25 .25
741 A167 26p multicolored 1.00 1.00
742 A167 38p multicolored 1.25 1.25
743 A167 50p multicolored 1.75 1.75
744 A167 62p multicolored 2.00 *2.00*
Nos. 740-744 (5) 6.25 6.25

A168

1997, Dec. 15 Litho. *Perf. 13*

745 A168 26p multicolored 1.20 1.20

Sir Joshua Hassan (1915-97), government leader.

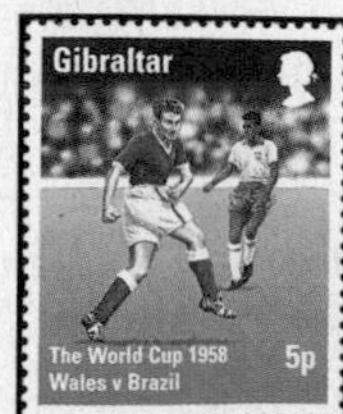

A169

Scenes from previous World Cup Championships: 5p, Wales v. Brazil, 1958. 26p, N. Ireland v. France, 1958. 38p, Scotland v. Holland, 1978. £1.20, England v. W. Germany, 1966.

1998, Jan. 23

746 A169 5p multicolored .35 .25
747 A169 26p multicolored 1.00 1.00
748 A169 38p multicolored 1.25 1.25
749 A169 £1.20 multicolored 3.50 3.50
a. Souvenir sheet, #746-749 6.50 6.50
Nos. 746-749 (4) 6.10 6.00

1998 World Cup Soccer Championships, France.

Diana, Princess of Wales (1961-97)

Common Design Type

Various portraits: a, 26p, Wearing black & white outfit. b, 26p, Wearing pink & white outfit. c, 38p, In black dress. d, 38p, In blue & gold jacket.

1998, Mar. 31 Litho. *Perf. 14½x14*

754 CD355 Sheet of 4, #a.-d. 4.75 4.75

The 20p surtax from international sales was donated to the Princess Diana Memorial Fund and the surtax from national sales was donated to a designated local charity.

Royal Air Force, 80th Anniv.

Common Design Type of 1993 Re-inscribed

Designs: 24p, Saro London. 26p, Fairey Fox. 38p, Handley Page Halifax GR.VI. 50p, Hawker Siddeley Buccaneer S.2B.

No. 759: a, 24p, Sopwith 1½ Strutter. b, 26p, Bristol M.1B. c, 38p, Supermarine Spitfire XII. d, 50p, Avro York.

1998, Apr. 1 *Perf. 14*

755 CD350 24p multicolored .80 .80
756 CD350 26p multicolored .90 .90
757 CD350 38p multicolored 1.25 1.25
758 CD350 50p multicolored 1.75 1.75
Nos. 755-758 (4) 4.70 4.70

Souvenir Sheet of 4

759 CD350 #a.-d. 5.00 5.00

Europa — A170

Costumes worn by Miss Gibraltar for National Day: No. 760, Military style. No. 761, Long skirt, long-sleeved top. No. 762, Short skirt, long cape. No. 763, Black lace scarf, ruffled petticoat.

1998, May 22 Litho. *Perf. 13*

760 A170 26p multicolored .90 .90
761 A170 26p multicolored .90 .90
762 A170 38p multicolored 1.30 1.30
763 A170 38p multicolored 1.30 1.30
Nos. 760-763 (4) 4.40 4.40

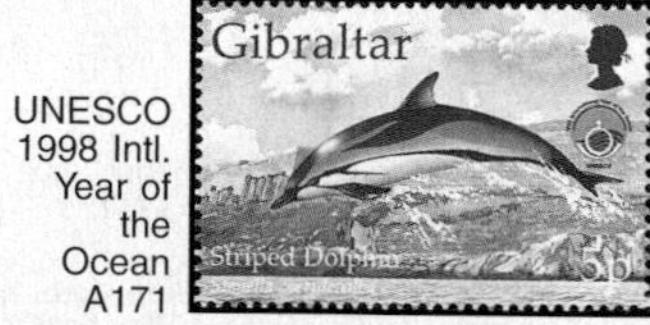

UNESCO 1998 Intl. Year of the Ocean A171

Marine life: a, 5p, Striped dolphin. b, 26p, Killer whale, vert. c, £1.20, Blue whale. d, 5p, Common dolphin, vert.

1998, May 22 *Perf. 14*

764 A171 Sheet of 4, #a.-d. 7.25 7.25

Italia '98 and Portugal '98.

Battle of the Nile — A172

1998, Aug. 1 Litho. *Perf. 13½*

765 A172 12p Nileus .85 .85
766 A172 26p Lord Nelson 1.10 1.10
a. Booklet pane of 1 1.50
767 A172 28p Frances Nisbet 1.25 1.25
a. Bklt. pane, #765-767 3.50
768 A172 35p HMS Vanguard 1.40 1.40

Size: 45x27mm

769 A172 50p Battle of the Nile 2.25 2.25
a. Bklt. pane, #768-769, 2 #766 7.25
b. Bklt. pane, #766, 768-769 5.75
c. Bklt. pane, #765-769 8.00
Complete booklet, #766a, 767a, 769a-769c 26.00
Nos. 765-769 (5) 6.85 6.85

Quotations From Famous People A173

No. 770, "Love comforts like sunshine after rain," Shakespeare. No. 771, "The price of greatness is responsibility," Churchill. No. 772, "Hate the sin, love the sinner," Gandhi. No. 773, "Imagination is more important than knowledge," Einstein.

1998, Oct. 6 Litho. *Perf. 14½*

770 A173 26p multicolored .90 .90
771 A173 26p multicolored .90 .90
772 A173 38p multicolored 1.50 1.50
773 A173 38p multicolored 1.50 1.50
Nos. 770-773 (4) 4.80 4.80

Nos. 770-773 were each printed in sheets of 6 with se-tenant labels.

A174

1998, Nov. 10 Litho. *Perf. 13*

774 A174 5p Nativity .45 .45
775 A174 26p Star over manger 1.10 1.10
776 A174 30p Balthasar 1.25 1.25
777 A174 35p Melchoir 1.40 1.40
778 A174 50p Caspar 1.75 1.75
Nos. 774-778 (5) 5.95 5.95

Christmas.

A175

1999, Mar. 4 Litho. *Perf. 13½*

779 A175 1p claret .25 .25
780 A175 2p brown .25 .25
781 A175 4p blue .25 .25
782 A175 5p green .25 .25
783 A175 10p brown orange .40 .40
784 A175 12p red .45 .45
785 A175 20p blue green .75 .75
786 A175 28p lilac rose 1.00 1.00
787 A175 30p vermilion 1.10 1.10
788 A175 40p gray olive 1.50 1.50
789 A175 42p slate 1.60 1.60

Size: 22½x28mm

Perf. 14½

790 A175 50p olive bister 1.90 1.90
791 A175 £1 black 3.75 3.75
792 A175 £3 ultramarine 9.00 9.00

Self-Adhesive

Die Cut Perf. 9x9½

793 A175 1st vermilion 1.10 1.10
Nos. 779-793 (15) 23.55 23.55

No. 793 was valued at 26p on day of issue. See Nos. 885-886.

Nature Reserves — A176

1999, Mar. 4 *Perf. 13½x13*

794	A176	30p Barbary macaque	1.50	1.50
795	A176	30p Dartford warbler	1.50	1.50
796	A176	42p Kingfisher	1.90	1.90
797	A176	42p Dusky perch	1.90	1.90
		Nos. 794-797 (4)	6.80	6.80

Europa.

Maritime Heritage — A177

Designs: 5p, Roman Anchorage. 30p, Medieval galley house. 42p, British relief ships. £1.20, HMS Berwick.

1999, Mar. 19 *Perf. 12½*

798	A177	5p multicolored	.40	.25
799	A177	30p multicolored	1.25	.75
800	A177	42p multicolored	2.00	2.00
801	A177	£1.20 multicolored	4.50	4.50
a.		Souvenir sheet, #798-801	8.75	8.75
		Nos. 798-801 (4)	8.15	7.50

John Lennon (1940-80) A178

Portraits: 20p, With flower over one eye. 30p, Black and white photo. 40p, Wearing glasses.

No. 805, Holding marriage license in front of Rock of Gibraltar. No. 806, Standing in front of airplane.

1999, Mar. 20 *Perf. 13*

802	A178	20p multicolored	1.00	.60
803	A178	30p multicolored	1.25	.90
804	A178	40p multicolored	1.50	1.50
		Nos. 802-804 (3)	3.75	3.00

Souvenir Sheets

805	A178	£1 multicolored	6.50	6.50
806	A178	£1 multicolored	6.50	6.50

UPU, 125th Anniv. — A179

1999, June 7 **Litho.** *Perf. 12½*

807	A179	5p Postal van	.25	.25
808	A179	30p Space station	1.25	1.25

Fighter Planes and Raptors A180

Designs: No. 809, RAF Eurofighter 2000 Typhoon. No. 810, RAF F3 Tornado. No. 811, RAF GR7 Harrier II. No. 812, Lesser kestrel. No. 813, Peregrine falcon. No. 814, Kestrel.

1999, June 7 *Perf. 13x13¼*

809	A180	30p multicolored	1.00	1.00
810	A180	30p multicolored	1.00	1.00
811	A180	30p multicolored	1.00	1.00
a.		Sheet of 3, #809-811	3.25	3.25
812	A180	42p multicolored	1.10	1.10
a.		Pair, #809, 812	3.00	3.00
813	A180	42p multicolored	1.10	1.10
a.		Pair, #810, 813	3.00	3.00
814	A180	42p multicolored	1.10	1.10
a.		Pair, #811, 814	3.00	3.00
b.		Sheet of 3, #812-814	6.25	6.25

See Nos. 851-853, 887-889.

Wedding of Prince Edward and Sophie Rhys-Jones A181

Perf. 13x13¼, 13¼x13

1999, June 19 **Litho.**

815	A181	30p shown	1.40	1.40
816	A181	42p Couple, vert.	1.60	1.60

Sports in Gibraltar, Cent. — A182

1999, July 2 *Perf. 13*

817	A182	30p Soccer	1.00	1.00
818	A182	42p Rowing	1.50	1.50
819	A182	£1.20 Cricket	3.50	3.50
		Nos. 817-819 (3)	6.00	6.00

Wedding of Prince Edward to Sophie Rhys-Jones A183

Perf. 13x13¼, 13¼x13

1999, Oct. 11 **Litho.**

820	A183	54p shown	1.75	1.75
821	A183	66p Couple standing, vert.	2.25	2.25

Christmas and New Year's Greetings A184

Designs: No. 822, "Happy Christmas," Santa, sleigh. No. 823, "Season's Greetings." No. 824, "Happy Millennium." No. 825, "Happy Christmas," Santa, reindeer. 42p, "Yo ho ho." 54p, Santa, tree, fireplace.

1999, Nov. 11 **Litho.** *Perf. 14*

822	A184	5p multicolored	.25	.25
823	A184	5p multicolored	.25	.25
824	A184	30p multicolored	1.00	1.00
825	A184	30p multicolored	1.00	1.00
826	A184	42p multicolored	1.50	1.50
827	A184	54p multicolored	1.75	1.75
		Nos. 822-827 (6)	5.75	5.75

Stampin' the Future Children's Stamp Design Contest Winners A185

Artwork by: 30p, Colin Green. 42p, Kim Barea. 54p, Stephan Williamson-Fa. 66p, Michael Podesta.

2000. Jan. 28 **Litho.** *Perf. 14½x14*

828	A185	30p multi	1.25	1.25
829	A185	42p multi	1.25	1.25
830	A185	54p multi	1.25	1.25
831	A185	66p multi	1.25	1.25
a.		Block or strip of 4, #828-831	7.25	7.25

European Soccer — A186

2000, Apr. 17 **Litho.** *Perf. 12½*

832	A186	30p France	.85	.85
833	A186	30p Holland	.95	.95
834	A186	42p Denmark	1.10	1.10
835	A186	42p Germany	1.25	1.25
a.		Souvenir sheet, #832-835	5.50	5.50
836	A186	54p England	1.50	1.50
a.		Souvenir sheet of 4	7.00	7.00
		Nos. 832-836 (5)	5.65	5.65

The Stamp Show 2000, London (No. 836a).

Europa — A187

2000, Apr. 17 *Perf. 13¼x13*

837	A187	30p Fountain	1.00	.80
838	A187	40p Hands	1.25	1.25
839	A187	42p Airplane	1.50	1.50
840	A187	54p Rainbow	1.75	1.75
		Nos. 837-840 (4)	5.50	5.30

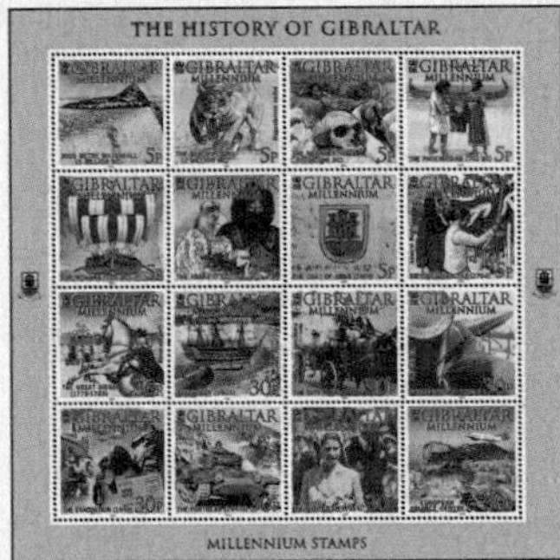

Millennium — A188

History of Gibraltar: a, 3000-meter waterfall. b, The sandy plains. c, The Neanderthals. d, The Phoenicians. e, The Romans. f, The Arabs. g, Coat of arms, 1502. h, British Gibraltar. i, The great siege. j, Trafalgar. k, The city. l, Fortifications. m, The evacuation. n, The fortress. o, Queen Elizabeth II. p, European finance center.

2000, May 9 *Perf. 14*

841	A188	Sheet of 16	12.00	12.00
a.-h.		5p Any single	.30	.30
i.-p.		30p Any single	1.25	1.25
q.		Souvenir booklet	27.50	

No. 841q contains a pane of 2 of each of Nos. 841a-841j and a pane of 3 of each of Nos. 841k-841p.

Prince William, 10th Birthday — A189

Designs: 30p, With Princess Diana. 42p, As child. 54p, With Prince Charles. 66p, In suit.

2000, June 21 **Litho.** *Perf. 12½*

842	A189	30p multi	.80	.70
843	A189	42p multi	1.25	.85
844	A189	54p multi	1.50	1.50
845	A189	66p multi	1.75	1.75
a.		Souvenir sheet, #842-845	7.25	7.25
		Nos. 842-845 (4)	5.30	4.80

Queen Mother, 100th Birthday — A190

Designs: 30p, As young woman. 42p, With King George VI. 54p, With blue hat. 66p, With orange hat.

2000, Aug. 4

846	A190	30p multi	.85	.75
847	A190	42p multi	1.25	1.00
848	A190	54p multi	1.50	1.50
849	A190	66p multi	1.75	1.75
a.		Souvenir sheet, #846-849	6.75	6.75
		Nos. 846-849 (4)	5.35	5.00

Moorish Castle A191

Photo. & Engr.

2000, Sept. 15 *Perf. 11½x11¾*

850	A191	£5 multi	15.00	15.00

Fighter Planes and Raptors Type

No. 851: a, RAF "Gibraltar" Supermarine Spitfire. b, Male merlin.

No. 852: a, RAF "City of Lincoln" Avro Lancaster B1-3. b, Bonelli's eagle.

No. 853: a, RAF Hawker Hurricane MK IIC. b, Female merlin.

2000, Sept. 15 **Litho.** *Perf. 14½x14*

851		Pair	4.00	4.00
a.		A180 30p multi	1.50	1.50
b.		A180 42p multi	1.75	1.75
852		Pair	4.00	4.00
a.		A180 30p multi	1.50	1.50
b.		A180 42p multi	1.75	1.75
853		Pair	4.00	4.00
a.		A180 30p multi	1.50	1.50
b.		A180 42p multi	1.75	1.75
c.		Souvenir sheet, #851a, 852a, 853a	5.00	5.00
d.		Souvenir sheet, #851b, 852b, 853b	7.25	7.25
		Nos. 851-853 (3)	12.00	12.00

Christmas A192

5p, Baby Jesus. No. 855, 30p, Joseph, Mary, donkey. No. 856, 30p, Mary, Jesus. 40p, Joseph, Mary, innkeeper. 42p, Holy Family, donkey. 54p, Holy Family, Magi.

2000, Nov. 13 *Perf. 14*

854-859	A192	Set of 6	6.50	6.50

Queen Victoria (1819-1901) A193

Designs: 30p, On wedding day. 42p, Portrait. 54p, In carriage. 66p, Jubilee portrait.

2001, Jan. 22 *Perf. 12¾*

860-863	A193	Set of 4	7.50	7.50

New Year 2001 (Year of the Snake) — A194

Snakes: No. 864, 5p, Grass. No. 865, 5p, Ladder. No. 866, 5p, Montpelier. No. 867, 30p, Viperine. No. 868, 30p, Southern smooth. No. 869, 30p, False smooth. 66p, Horseshoe whip.

2001, Feb. 1 Litho. *Perf. 13¾*

864-870	A194	Set of 7	6.00	6.00
870a		Souvenir sheet, #864-870	8.75	8.75

Size of No. 870: 31x62mm. Hong Kong 2001 Stamp Exhibition (No. 870a).

Europa — A195

Designs: 30p, Long-snouted seahorse. 40p, Snapdragon. 42p, Yellow-legged gull. 54p, Goldfish.

2001, Feb. 1 *Perf. 13¼x13*

871-874	A195	Set of 4	9.25	9.25

Queen Elizabeth II, 75th Birthday A196

Designs: No. 875, 30p, As child. No. 876, 30p, As young woman. No. 877, 42p, In wedding dress. No. 878, 42p, At coronation. 54p, Wearing hat.
£2, In blue dress.

2001, Apr. 21 Litho. *Perf. 14*

875-879	A196	Set of 5	6.75	6.75

Souvenir Sheet

Perf. 13¾

880	A196	£2 multi	7.00	7.00

No. 880 contains one 35x48mm stamp.

Gibraltar Chronicle, Bicent. — A197

Designs: 30p, Battle of Trafalgar. 42p, Invention of the telephone. 54p, The end of World War II. 66p, First man on the Moon.

2001, May 21 *Perf. 14x14½*

881-884	A197	Set of 4	8.00	8.00

Queen Type of 1999

2001, June 1 Litho. *Perf. 14x14¼*

Size: 22x28mm

885	A175	£1.20 carmine	4.50	4.50
886	A175	£1.40 blue	5.00	5.00

Fighter Planes and Raptors Type of 1999

No. 887: a, 40p, RAF Jaguar GR1B. b, 40p, Hobby.
No. 888: a, 40p, Royal Navy Sea Harrier FA MK 2. b, 40p, Marsh harrier.
No. 889: a, 40p, RAF Hawk T MK 1. b, 40p, Sparrowhawk.

2001, Sept. 3 Litho. *Perf. 14½x14*

Pairs, #a-b

887-889	A180	Set of 3	8.75	8.75
889c		Souvenir sheet, #887a, 888a, 889a	4.50	4.50
889d		Souvenir sheet, #887b, 888b, 889b	4.50	4.50

Christmas A198

Snoopy, from Peanuts comic strip: 5p, In Santa Claus suit ringing bell, Woodstock. 30p, Charlie Brown, Christmas tree. 40p, Wreath. 42p, In Santa Claus suit carrying cookies, Woodstock. 54p, On dog house.

2001, Nov. 12 *Perf. 14*

890-894	A198	Set of 5	6.50	6.50
894a		Souvenir sheet, #890-894	7.50	7.50

Souvenir Sheet

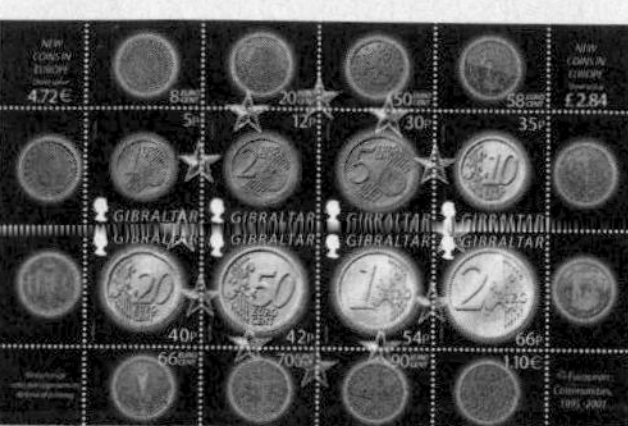

Introduction of Euro Coinage to Europe — A199

Coins in denominations of: a, 5p, 1 cent. b, 12p, 2 cents. c, 30p, 5 cents. d, 35p, 10 cents. e, 40p, 20 cents. f, 42p, 50 cents. g, 54p, 1 euro. h, 66p, 2 euro.

2002, Jan. 1 Litho. *Perf. 13¼x13*

895	A199	Sheet of 8, #a-h	10.00	10.00

A clear varnish was applied by a thermographic process producing a shiny, raised effect.

Reign Of Queen Elizabeth II, 50th Anniv. Issue

Common Design Type

Designs: No. 896, 30p, Princess Elizabeth in field, 1942. No. 897, 30p, Wearing tiara, 1961. No. 898, 30p, With Princess Margaret, microphones. No. 899, 30p, Wearing hat, 1993. 75p, 1955 portrait by Annigoni (38x50mm).

Perf. 14¼x14½, 13¾ (75p)

2002, Feb. 6 Litho. Wmk. 373

896	CD360	30p multicolored	1.10	1.10
897	CD360	30p multicolored	1.10	1.10
898	CD360	30p multicolored	1.10	1.10
899	CD360	30p multicolored	1.10	1.10
900	CD360	75p multicolored	2.25	2.25
900a		Souvenir sheet, #896-900	7.75	7.75

Europa — A200

Famous clowns: 30p, Joseph Grimaldi (1778-1831). 40p, Karl Adrien Wettach (1880-1959). 42p, Nicholai Polakovs (1900-74). 54p, Hubert Jean Charles Cairoli (1910-80).

Perf. 13¼x13

2002, Mar. 4 Litho. Unwmk.

901-904	A200	Set of 4	6.00	6.00

Bobby Moore, English Soccer Player — A201

Moore in 1966: 30p, Holding up World Cup. 42p, Kissing World Cup. 54p, With Queen Elizabeth II. 66p, In action.

Perf. 13¼x13

2002, May 1 Litho. Unwmk.

905-908	A201	Set of 4	7.00	7.00
908a		Souvenir sheet, #905-908	7.00	7.00

Wildlife A202

Designs: No. 909, 30p, Red fox. No. 910, 30p, Barbary macaque, vert. 40p, White tooth shrew. £1, Rabbit, vert.

Perf. 14¼x14, 14x14¼

2002, June 6 Litho. Unwmk.

909-912	A202	Set of 4	7.50	7.50
912a		Souvenir sheet, #909-912	7.50	7.50

Prince Harry, 18th Birthday — A203

Designs: 30p, As child in Princess Diana's arms. 42p, Waving. 54p, Wearing baseball cap. 66p, In suit and tie.

2002, Sept. 15 Litho. *Perf. 12½*

913-916	A203	Set of 4	6.75	6.75
916a		Souvenir sheet, #913-916	7.25	7.25

Rock of Gibraltar — A204

View of Rock from: a, North. b, South. c, East (46x38mm). d, West (46x38mm).

2002, Sept. 15 Litho. *Perf. 13¼x13*

917		Horiz. strip of 4	9.50	9.50
a.-b.		A204 30p Either single	.90	.90
c.-d.		A204 £1 Either single	2.75	2.75

Particles of the Rock of Gibraltar were applied to portions of the designs by a thermographic process.

Christmas — A205

Creche scenes from: 5p, Cathedral of St. Mary the Crowned. 30p, St. Joseph's Parish Church. 40p, St. Theresa's Parish Church. 42p, Our Lady of Sorrows Church, Catalan Bay. 52p, St. Bernard's Church. 54p, Cathedral of the Holy Trinity.

2002, Nov. 13 *Perf. 13*

918-923	A205	Set of 6	8.50	8.50

Coronation of Queen Elizabeth II, 50th Anniv. — A206

Designs: No. 924, 30p, Queen receiving crown. No. 925, 30p, Queen on throne. 40p, Queen holding orb. £1, Queen in profile.

Perf. 12½

2003, Feb. 20 Litho. Unwmk.

924-927	A206	Set of 4	6.75	6.75
927a		Souvenir sheet, #924-927	7.25	7.25

Europa — A207

Poster art for: 30p, Drama Festival. 40p, Spring Festival. 42p, Art Festival. 54p, Dance Festival.

2003, Mar. 3 *Perf. 14x14½*

928-931	A207	Set of 4	5.75	5.75

Powered Flight, Cent. A208

Designs: 30p, Wright Flyer, 1903. No. 933, 40p, Charles Lindbergh and Spirit of St. Louis, 1927. No. 934, 40p, Boeing 314 Yankee Clipper, 1939. 42p, Saunders Roe SARO-21 Windhover Amphibian, 1931 (77x27mm). 44p, Concorde, 1976 (77x27mm). 66p, Space Shuttle Columbia, 1981, vert. (37x57mm).

2003, Mar. 31 Litho. *Perf. 13x13¼*

932-937	A208	Set of 6	11.00	11.00
937a		Souvenir sheet, #932-937, perf. 12½	12.00	12.00

Martyrdom of St. George, 1700th Anniv. — A209

Designs: 30p, Cross of St. George. 40p, Constantinian Order of St. George. £1.20, Stained glass window depiction of St. George, vert. (31x63mm).

2003, Apr. 23 *Perf. 13¾*

938-940	A209	Set of 3	6.50	6.50
940a		Souvenir sheet, #938-940	7.00	7.00

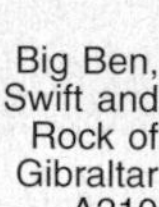

Big Ben, Swift and Rock of Gibraltar A210

Photo. & Engr.

2003, June 21 *Perf. 11½*

941	A210	(£3) multi	10.50	10.50

Prince William, 21st Birthday — A211

Prince William: No. 942, 30p, As a child, with Princess Diana. No. 943, 30p, With hands in pockets. 40p, Close-up, wearing suit. £1, Wearing sweatshirt.

2003, June 21 Litho. *Perf. 12½*

942-945	A211	Set of 4	10.00	10.00
945a		Souvenir sheet, #942-945	10.00	10.00

Enlargement of European Union — A212

National flowers of newly-added countries: 30p, Daisy (Latvia), Cornflower (Estonia), Rue (Lithuania). 40p, Rose (Cyprus), Maltese centaury (Malta). 42p, Tulip (Hungary), Carnation (Slovenia), Dog rose (Slovakia). 54p, Corn poppy (Poland), Scented thyme (Czech Republic).

2003, Sept. 15 Litho. *Perf. 13¾*
946-949 A212 Set of 4 6.50 6.50

Mushrooms A213

Designs: No. 950, 30p, Lepista nuda. No. 951, 30p, Clitocybe odora. No. 952, 30p, Hypholoma fasciculare. £1.20, Agaricus campestris.

2003, Sept. 15 *Perf. 14¼*
950-953 A213 Set of 4 8.75 8.75
953a Souvenir sheet, #950-953 9.25 9.25

A214

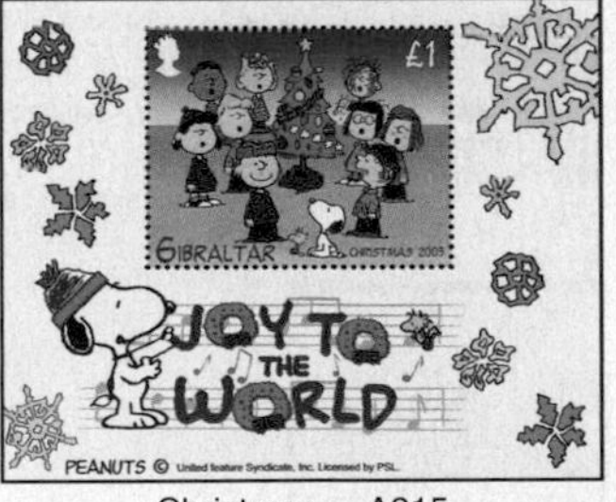

Christmas — A215

Designs: 5p, Baby Jesus crib, Our Lady of Sorrows Church. 30p, Building a traditional creche at home. 40p, Three Kings Cavalcade on January 5. 42p, Children's provisions for Santa and reindeer on Christmas Eve. 54p, Christmas Eve midnight mass at the Cathedral of St. Mary the Crowned.

2003, Nov. 17 Litho. *Perf. 14*
954-958 A214 Set of 5 6.00 6.00

Souvenir Sheet

Perf. 12¼x12
959 A215 £1 multi 4.75 4.75

Europa — A216

Designs: No. 960, 40p, Outdoor cafe. No. 961, 40p, St. Michael's Cave. No. 962, 54p, Seaside cafe. No. 963, 54p, Dolphin.

2004, Feb. 20 Litho. *Perf. 14x14½*
960-963 A216 Set of 4 7.00 7.00

British Gibraltar, 300th Anniv. A217

Designs: 8p, British flag, Gibraltar coat of arms.
No. 965: a, Ship with large flag. b, Ship, rowboat, cannons. c, Soldiers. d, Military uniform. e, Telephone booth, police hat. f, Mail box. g, Neckties, university documents, graduates in caps and gowns. h, Crowd waving flags. i. British flag.

2004 Litho. *Perf. 13x13¼*
964 A217 8p multi .70 .70
965 Sheet of 9 14.50 14.50
a.-h. A217 30p Any single 1.00 1.00
i. A217 £1.20 multi 4.00 4.00
j. Souvenir sheet, #965i 5.25 5.25

Issued: Nos. 964-965i, 4/26. No. 965j, 9/10.
Sir Elton John's Tercentenary Concert (No. 965j).
A perforated "black print" sheet of No. 965 exists with cancels.

Visit of Queen Elizabeth II to Gibraltar, 50th Anniv. — A218

Queen: 38p, Holding flowers. 40p, With arm extended. 47p, In limousine. £1, With children and soldiers.
£1.50, Standing in limousine with Prince Philip.

2004, May 4 *Perf. 12½*
966-969 A218 Set of 4 8.00 8.00

Souvenir Sheet

970 A218 £1.50 multi 6.00 6.00

European Soccer — A219

Designs: 30p, Goalie defending shot. No. 972, 40p, Players near side of goal. No. 973, 40p, Player making scissor kick. £1, Goalie playing ball near goal post.
£1.50, Player with arms extended, horiz.

2004, June 6
971-974 A219 Set of 4 7.50 7.50
974a Souvenir sheet, #971-974 7.50 7.50

Souvenir Sheet

975 A219 £1.50 multi 5.00 5.00

No. 975 contains one 48x37mm stamp.

D-Day, 60th Anniv. A220

Designs: 38p, Soldiers leaving landing craft. 40p, Tank approaching beach. 47p, Airplane. £1, Ships.

2004, June 6 *Perf. 13x13¼*
976-979 A220 Set of 4 8.25 8.25
979a Souvenir sheet, #976-979 8.25 8.25

Flowers — A221

Designs: 1p, Mallow-leaved bindweed. 2p, Gibraltar sea lavender. 5p, Gibraltar chickweed. G, Romulea. 10p, Common centaury. G1, Pyramidal orchid. S, Friar's cowl. UK, Corn poppy. E, Giant Tangier fennel. U, Snapdragon. 50p, Common gladiolus. £1, Yellow horned poppy. £3, Gibraltar candytuft.

2004, Sept. 10 Litho. *Perf. 13¼*
980 A221 1p multi .25 .25
a. Booklet pane of 1 .25 —
981 A221 2p multi .25 .25
a. Booklet pane of 1 .25 —
982 A221 5p multi .25 .25
a. Booklet pane of 1 .25 —
983 A221 G multi .25 .25
a. Booklet pane of 1 .25 —
984 A221 10p multi .40 .40
a. Booklet pane of 1 .40 —
985 A221 G1 multi .55 .55
a. Booklet pane of 1 .55 —
986 A221 S multi 1.00 1.00
a. Booklet pane of 1 1.00 —
987 A221 UK multi 1.50 1.50
a. Booklet pane of 1 1.50 —
988 A221 E multi 1.60 1.60
a. Booklet pane of 1 1.60 —
989 A221 U multi 1.75 1.75
a. Booklet pane of 1 1.75 —
990 A221 50p multi 2.00 2.00
a. Booklet pane of 1 2.00 —
991 A221 £1 multi 3.50 3.50
a. Booklet pane of 1 3.50 —
992 A221 £3 multi 11.00 11.00
a. Booklet pane of 1 11.00 —
Complete booklet, #980a-992a 28.00
Nos. 980-992 (13) 24.30 24.30

Nos. 983, 985, 986, 987, 988 and 989 sold for 7p, 12p, 28p, 38p, 40p and 47p respectively on day of issue.
See Nos. 1033B-1036.

Ferrari Race Cars A222

Designs: No. 993, 5p, F2003GA. No. 994, 5p, F2004. No. 995, 30p, F2001. No. 996, 30p, F2002. No. 997, 75p, F399. No. 998, 75p, F1-2000.

2004, Nov. 12 *Perf. 14¾x14¼*
993-998 A222 Set of 6 9.00 9.00
998a Souvenir sheet, #993-998 9.00 9.00

Christmas A223

Christmas tree ornaments: 7p, Santa Claus. 28p, Angel. 38p, Red star. 40p, Gold bell. 47p, Red ball. 53p, White star.

2004, Nov. 12 *Perf. 12½*
999-1004 A223 Set of 6 9.00 9.00

Battle of Trafalgar, Bicent. — A224

Designs: 38p, Soldier guarding wine cask containing Admiral Horatio Nelson's body. 40p, HMS Entrepenante. 47p, Admiral Nelson, vert. £1.60, HMS Victory.
£2, HMS Vctory being towed to Gibraltar.

2005, Jan. 29 Litho. *Perf. 13¼*
1005-1008 A224 Set of 4 14.50 14.50

Souvenir Sheet

Perf. 13¾
1009 A224 £2 multi 11.00 11.00

No. 1008 has particles of wood from the HMS Victory embedded in the areas covered by a thermographic process that produces a raised, shiny effect. No. 1009 contains one 44x44mm stamp.
See Nos. 1027-1028.

Europa — A225

Designs: No. 1010, 47p, Sherry trifle. No. 1011, 47p, Spinach pie. No. 1012, 47p, Veal birds. No. 1013, 47p, Grilled sea bass.

Perf. 14¼x14¾
2005, Mar. 31 Litho.
1010-1013 A225 Set of 4 8.25 8.25

V-E Day, 60th Anniv. — A226

Designs: 38p, Winston Churchill. 40p, Woman, children, British flags. 47p, Servicewomen in car waving flags. £1, People at dock.

2005, May 8
1014-1017 A226 Set of 4 9.00 9.00
1017a Souvenir sheet, #1014-1017 9.00 9.00

Anniversaries — A227

Designs: 38p, Royal Gibraltar Police, 175th anniv. 47p, Gibraltar Museum, 75th anniv. £1, Grant of Charter of Justice, 175th anniv.

2005, June 17 *Perf. 14¾x14¼*
1018-1020 A227 Set of 3 8.50 8.50

Cruise Ships A228

Designs: 38p, Circassia. 40p, Nevassa. 47p, Black Prince. £1, Arcadia.

2005, June 17 *Perf. 13x13¼*
1021-1024 A228 Set of 4 9.75 9.75
1024a Souvenir sheet, #1021-1024 9.75 9.75

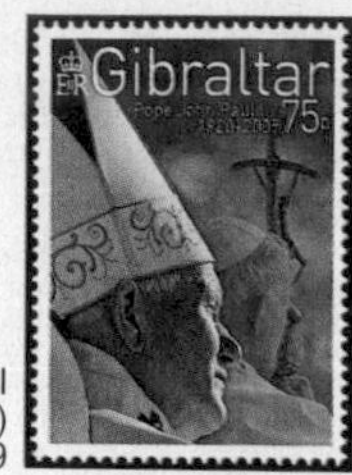

Pope John Paul II (1920-2005) A229

2005, July 15 ***Perf. 14¼x14¾***

1025 A229 75p multi 3.50 3.50

Printed in sheets of 6.

Europa Stamps, 50th Anniv. (in 2006) — A230

Litho. With Foil Application

2005, Sept. 30 ***Perf. 14¼***

1026 A230 £5 multi 18.00 18.00

Battle of Trafalgar Type of 2005

Souvenir Sheets

Designs: Nos. 1027, 1028a, Admiral Nelson mortally wounded.

2005, Oct. 21 **Litho.** ***Perf. 13¼***

1027 A224 £1 multi 4.25 4.25

1028 Sheet, #1028a, Isle of Man #1127a 8.75 8.75

a. A224 £1 multi, 47x30mm 4.25 4.25

No. 1028 has a Gibraltar Post emblem in sheet margin. See Isle of Man No. 1127.

Christmas A231

Various angels: 7p, 38p, 40p, 47p, 53p.

2005, Oct. 21 ***Perf. 13¼x13***

1029-1033 A231 Set of 5 8.00 8.00

1033a Souvenir sheet, #1029-1033 8.75 8.75

Flowers Type of 2004

Designs: 3p, Gibraltar restharrow. 15p, Paper-white narcissus. 53p, Gibraltar campion. £1.60, Sea daffodil.

2006, Jan. 31 **Litho.** ***Perf. 13¼***

1033B A221 3p multi .25 .25

1034 A221 15p multi .55 .55

1035 A221 53p multi 1.90 1.90

1036 A221 £1.60 multi 5.75 5.75

Nos. 1033B-1036 (4) 8.45 8.45

Worldwide Fund for Nature (WWF) A232

Various depictions of Giant devil ray.

2006, Feb. 20 ***Perf. 13x13¼***

1037 Strip of 4 11.00 11.00

a. A232 38p multi 1.25 1.25

b. A232 40p multi 1.50 1.50

c. A232 47p multi 1.75 1.75

d. A232 £1 multi 4.00 4.00

Queen Elizabeth II, 80th Birthday A233

Various photographs.

2006, Mar. 31 ***Perf. 14¾x14***

1038 Block of 4 10.50 10.50

a. A233 38p multi 1.50 1.50

b. A233 40p multi 1.75 1.75

c. A233 47p multi 2.00 2.00

d. A233 £1 multi 4.00 4.00

e. Souvenir sheet, #1038b, 1038c 4.00 4.00

f. Souvenir sheet, #1038a, 1038d 6.00 6.00

Miniature Sheet

2006 World Cup Soccer Championships, Germany — A234

No. 1039 — Children with faces painted as flags of World Cup champions: a, Uruguay. b, Italy. c, Germany. d, Brazil. e, England. f, Argentina. g, France.

2006, May 4 ***Perf. 15***

1039 A234 Sheet of 7 11.50 11.50

a.-g. 38p Any single 1.50 1.50

Europa A235

Children: No. 1040, 47p, Holding books and notebook paper. No. 1041, 47p, Playing musical instruments. No. 1042, 47p, Building birdhouse. No. 1043, 47p, Playing soccer.

2006, June 30 ***Perf. 13x13¼***

1040-1043 A235 Set of 4 8.00 8.00

Gibraltar Packet Agency, Bicent: A236

Ships: 8p, Cornwallis. 40p, Meteor. 42p, Carteret. 68p, Prince Regent.

Perf. 14¾x14¼

2006, Sept. 15 **Litho.**

1044-1047 A236 Set of 4 9.00 9.00

Airmail Service, 75th Anniv. A237

Airplanes: 8p, Saro A21 Windhover. 40p, Vickers Vanguard. 49p, Vickers Viscount. £1.60, Boeing 737.

2006, Sept. 15

1048-1051 A237 Set of 4 14.00 14.00

Cruise Ships A238

Designs: 40p, Coral. 42p, Legend of the Seas. 66p, Saga Ruby. 78p, Costa Concordia.

2006, Sept. 15 ***Perf. 13***

1052-1055 A238 Set of 4 12.00 12.00

1055a Souvenir sheet, #1052-1055 12.50 12.50

See Nos. 1076-1079, 1153-1156.

Christopher Columbus (1451-1506), Explorer — A239

Designs: 40p, Navigational equipment. 42p, Columbus on ship. 66p, Santa Maria. 78p, Columbus and Indian.

£1.60, Nina, Pinta and Santa Maria

2006, Nov. 1 **Litho.** ***Perf. 13x13¼***

1056-1059 A239 Set of 4 12.00 12.00

Souvenir Sheet

Perf. 13¼

1060 A239 £1.60 multi 8.00 8.00

No. 1060 contains one 48x48mm stamp.

Christmas A240

Various depictions of Santa Claus with panel colors of: 8p, Red brown. 40p, Prussian blue. 42p, Olive bister. 49p, Green. 55p, Gray blue.

2006, Nov. 1 ***Perf. 13¼x13***

1061-1065 A240 Set of 5 9.50 9.50

1065a Souvenir sheet, #1061-1065, perf. 13¼x12½ 9.50 9.50

Miniature Sheet

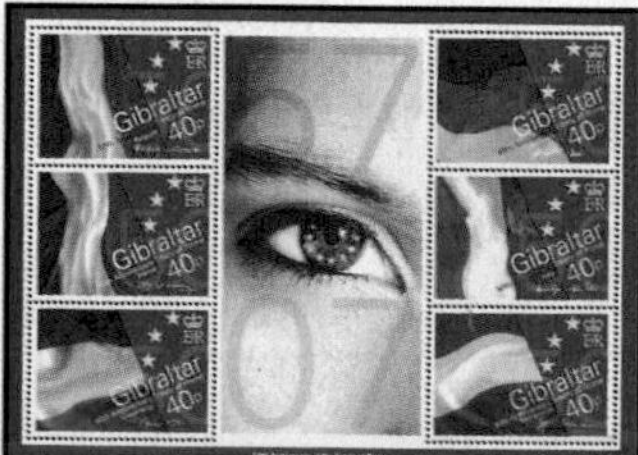

Treaty of Rome, 50th Anniv. — A241

No. 1066 — European Union flag and flag of: a, Belgium. b, Germany. c, France. d, Italy. e, Luxembourg. f, Netherlands.

Perf. 14½x14¼

2007, Feb. 28 **Litho.**

1066 A241 40p Sheet of 6, #a-f 10.50 10.50

Wedding of Queen Elizabeth II and Prince Philip, 60th Anniv. — A242

Designs: 40p, Royal engagement, 1947. 42p, Royal wedding, 1947. 66p, Silver anniversary, 1972. 78p, Ruby anniversary, 1987.

£1.60, Wedding party.

2007, Feb. 28 ***Perf. 13½***

1067-1070 A242 Set of 4 10.00 10.00

Souvenir Sheet

Perf. 13½x13

1071 A242 £1.60 multi 8.50 8.50

No. 1071 contains one 85x85mm diamond-shaped stamp.

Princess Diana (1961-97) A243

Various photographs: 8p, 40p, 42p, £1.60.

2007, Mar. 31 ***Perf. 13½***

1072-1075 A243 Set of 4 11.00 11.00

1075a Souvenir sheet, #1072-1075 11.00 11.00

Cruise Ships Type of 2006

Designs: 40p, Oriana. 42p, Oceana. 66p, Queen Elizabeth 2.78p, Queen Mary 2.

2007, May 15 **Litho.** ***Perf. 14¾x14***

1076-1079 A238 Set of 4 11.50 11.50

1079a Souvenir sheet, #1076-1079 11.50 11.50

Europa — A244

Designs: 8p, Scout from 1908. 40p, Scout from 1950s, 42p, Sea Scout from 1980s. £1, Scout from 2007.

2007, June 30 **Litho.** ***Perf. 13***

1080-1083 A244 Set of 4 10.00 10.00

Gibraltar Postal Anniversaries — A245

Designs: 8p, Last-day-of-validity postcard from Fez, Morocco (cessation of Gibraltar's responsibility for the British postal service in Morocco in 1907). 40p, Stampless cover with last Gibraltar datestamp of the Packet Agency (creation of Gibraltar Post Office in 1857). 42p, Cover franked with stamps of Great Britain (sale of British stamps in Gibraltar in 1857). £1, Cover to London from Morocco via Gibraltar (placement of British postal service in Morocco under control of Gibraltar in 1857).

2007, Sept. 26 ***Perf. 14¾x14***

1084-1087 A245 Set of 4 11.50 11.50

Stork Carrying Baby, Baby Bottle, Pacifier, Rubber Duck — A246

Diamond Ring and Heart — A247

Sheep, Lion, Dog at Party — A248

Lamb, Dolphins, Rock of Gibraltar — A249

Shell, Crab and Heart — A250

2007, Sept. 26 ***Perf. 12½x13***

1088 A246 G multi + label .40 .40
1089 A247 G multi + label .40 .40
1090 A248 G multi + label .40 .40
1091 A249 G multi + label .40 .40
1092 A250 G multi + label .40 .40
1093 A246 E multi + label 2.00 2.00
1094 A247 E multi + label 2.00 2.00
1095 A248 E multi + label 2.00 2.00
1096 A249 E multi + label 2.00 2.00
1097 A250 E multi + label 2.00 2.00
Nos. 1088-1097 (10) 12.00 12.00

On day of issue Nos. 1088-1092 each sold for 8p, and Nos. 1093-1097 each sold for 42p. Labels shown with each stamp are the generic labels for that stamp type. Labels could be personalized for an additional fee.

Prehistoric Wildlife of Gibraltar A251

Designs: 8p, Bears and dolphins. 40p, Eagle owl. 42p, Great auk and eagle. 55p, Red deer and bear. 78p, Wolf and vulture eating horse.
£2, Ibex.

2007, Sept. 26 ***Perf. 13***

1098-1102 A251 Set of 5 11.00 11.00
1098a Booklet pane of 1 .50 —
1099a Booklet pane of 1 2.00 —
1100a Booklet pane of 1 2.25 —
1101a Booklet pane of 1 2.75 —
1102a Booklet pane of 1 3.75 —
Complete booklet, #1098a-1103a, 1103b 34.00

Souvenir Sheet

1103 A251 £2 multi 11.00 11.00
a. Booklet pane of 1 11.00 —
b. Booklet pane of 6, #1098-1102 11.00 —

No. 1103a has text in margin not found on the margin of No. 1103.

Views of Gibraltar — A252

Trinity Lighthouse — A253

Various views: 40p, 42p, 55p, 78p.

2007, Nov. 2 **Litho.** ***Perf. 13¼***

1104-1107 A252 Set of 4 10.50 10.50

Souvenir Sheet
Perf. 13¼x13

1108 A253 £1.70 multi 8.00 8.00

Christmas A254

Porcelain Nativity figurines: No. 1109, 8p, Joseph. No. 1110, 8p, Baby Jesus. 40p, Mary. 42p, King Melchior. 49p, King Balthasar. 55p, King Gaspar.

2007, Nov. 2 ***Perf. 13¼x13***

1109-1114 A254 Set of 6 9.50 9.50
1114a Miniature sheet, #1109-1114 9.50 9.50

Perf. 12½x13
Size: 32x32mm

1114B A254 8p multi + label .75 .75
1114C A254 40p multi + label 2.75 2.75

Nos. 1114B and 1114C were available with generic labels. Labels could be personalized for an additional fee.

Birds — A255

Designs: 1p, Woodchat shrike. 2p, Balearic shearwater. 5p, Eagle owl. G, European bee-eater. 10p, Razorbill. S, Egyptian vulture. UK, Blue rock thrush. E, Hoopoe. U, Bonelli's eagle. 50p, Greater flamingo. 55p, Mediterranean shag. £1, Honey buzzard. £5, Lesser kestrel.

2008, Feb. 15 **Litho.** ***Perf. 13x12½***

1115 A255 1p multi .25 .25
1116 A255 2p multi .25 .25
1117 A255 5p multi .25 .25
1118 A255 G multi .35 .35
1119 A255 10p multi .40 .40
1120 A255 S multi 1.25 1.25
1121 A255 UK multi 1.60 1.60
1122 A255 E multi 1.75 1.75
1123 A255 U multi 1.90 1.90
1124 A255 50p multi 2.00 2.00
1125 A255 55p multi 2.25 2.25

Size: 32x45mm
Perf. 13x13¼

1126 A255 £1 multi 4.00 4.00
1127 A255 £5 multi 18.00 18.00
Nos. 1115-1127 (13) 34.25 34.25

On day of issue Nos. 1118, 1120, 1121, 1122 and 1123 sold for 8p, 30p, 40p, 42p and 49p, respectively.
See Nos. 1202-1204, 1244-1246, 1326-1328. For surcharge, see No. 1412.

Admiral Horatio Nelson (1758-1805) A256

Designs: No. 1128, 40p, HMS Agamemnon. No. 1129, 40p, HMS La Minerve. No. 1130, 42p, HMS Captain. No. 1131, 42p, HMS Vanguard. No. 1132, 49p, HMS Amphion. No. 1133, 49p, HMS Victory.
£2, Nelson's Birthplace, Burnham Thorpe, England, horiz.

Perf. 14¼x14¾

2008, Mar. 15 **Litho.**

1128-1133 A256 Set of 6 17.50 17.50

Souvenir Sheet
Perf. 14¾x14¼

1134 A256 £2 multi 13.50 13.50

Royal Air Force, 90th Anniv. — A257

Rock of Gibraltar and airplanes: No. 1135, 40p, Short 184, Saro London. No. 1136, 40p, Spitfire IV, Hurricane IIc. No. 1137, 42p, Beaufighter II, Lancaster TS III. No. 1138, 42p, Hunter Mk. 6, Shackleton MR2. No. 1139, 49p, Vulcan, Mosquito. No. 1140, 49p, Tornado GR4, Jaguar GR3.
£2, Felixstowe F3.

2008, Mar. 15 ***Perf. 14¼x14¾***

1135-1140 A257 Set of 6 17.50 17.50

Souvenir Sheet

1141 A257 £2 multi 13.50 13.50

Europa — A258

Famous letter writers: 10p, Sir Winston Churchill. 42p, Admiral Horatio Nelson. 44p, Pres. John F. Kennedy. £1, Mohandas K. Gandhi.

2008, June 1 **Litho.** ***Perf. 14x14¾***

1142-1145 A258 Set of 4 10.00 10.00

New Seven Wonders of the World — A259

Designs: No. 1146, 8p, Roman Colosseum. No. 1147, 8p, Christ the Redeemer Statue, Rio de Janeiro. No. 1148, 38p, Great Wall of China. No. 1149, 38p, Petra, Jordan. No. 1150, 40p, Chichen Itza Pyramid, Mexico. No. 1151, 40p, Machu Picchu, Peru. 66p, Taj Mahal, India.

2008, June 1

1146-1152 A259 Set of 7 13.50 13.50

Cruise Ships Type of 2006

Designs: 40p, Century. 42p, Grand Princess. 66p, Queen Victoria. 78p, Costa Mediterranea.

2008, Sept. 15 **Litho.** ***Perf. 13x13¼***

1153-1156 A238 Set of 4 13.50 13.50
1156a Souvenir sheet, #1153-1156 13.50 13.50

Miniature Sheet

National Aeronautics and Space Administration, 50th Anniv. — A260

No. 1157: a, Liftoff of Apollo 11. b, Earthrise from Moon. c, Lunar Module leaving Moon. d, US flag on Moon.

2008, Sept. 15 ***Perf. 13¼***

1157 A260 Sheet of 4 13.50 13.50
a. 10p multi .60 .60
b. 17p multi 1.00 1.00
c. 42p multi 2.00 2.00
d. £2 multi 9.50 9.50

Royal Gibraltar Regiment — A261

Designs: No. 1158, 10p, Gibraltar Volunteer Corps in World War I. No. 1159, 10p, Gibraltar Defense Force in World War II. No. 1160, 10p, National Service recruits at Buena Vista Barracks. No. 1161, 42p, Soldiers and large guns, Thomson's Battery of Gibraltar Regiment, 1958-91. No. 1162, 42p, Soldier from Infantry Company of Gibraltar Regiment, 1958-99. No. 1163, 44p, Soldier from Air Defense Troop of Gibraltar Regiment, 1958-91. No. 1164, 44p, Royal Gibraltar Regiment soldier guarding the rock. No. 1165, 51p, Royal Gibraltar Regiment soldier training African Peacekeepers. No. 1166, 51p, Royal Gibraltar Regiment soldier serving in operations in Iraq. £2, Royal Gibraltar Regiment soldier serving in operations in Afghanistan.

2008, Nov. 11 **Litho.** ***Perf. 15x14***

1158-1167 A261 Set of 10 22.50 22.50

Christmas A262

Songs: 10p, When Santa Got Stuck in a Chimney. 42p, Rudolph, the Red-nosed Reindeer. 44p, Oh, Christmas Tree. 51p, Away in a Manger. 59p, Jingle Bells.

2008, Nov. 11 ***Perf. 12½***

1168-1172 A262 Set of 5 10.00 10.00

King Henry VIII, 500th Anniv. of Accession to the Throne — A263

Designs: No. 1173, 10p, Catherine of Aragon (first wife). No. 1174, 10p, Anne Boleyn (second wife). No. 1175, 42p, Jane Seymour (third wife). No. 1176, 42p, Anne of Cleves (fourth wife). No. 1177, 44p, Catherine Howard (fifth wife). No. 1178, 44p, Catherine Parr (sixth wife). No. 1179, 51p, Henry VIII. No. 1180, 51p, The Mary Rose.
£2, King Henry VIII at Hampton Court.

2009, Jan. 10 Litho. *Perf. 12½*
1173-1180 A263 Set of 8 16.00 16.00

Souvenir Sheet

1181 A263 £2 multi 10.50 10.50

Gibraltar Shrine to Our Lady of Europe, 700th Anniv. — A264

2009, Feb. 10 *Perf. 14x14¾*
1182 A264 61p multi 4.50 4.50

Printed in sheets of 4. See Vatican City No. 1402.

Naval Aviation, Cent. — A265

Designs: No. 1183, 42p, Short 184. No. 1184, 42p, Short S27. No. 1185, 42p, SS Type non-rigid airship. No. 1186, 42p, Caudron G-III. No. 1187, 42p, Avro 504. No. 1188, 42p, Morane-Saulnier L and Zeppelin LZ-37.
£2, Short 184 and ships.

2009, Mar. 15
1183-1188 A265 Set of 6 16.00 16.00

Souvenir Sheet

1189 A265 £2 multi 12.00 12.00

Grandchildren of Queen Elizabeth II — A266

Designs: No. 1190, 42p, Prince William of Wales. No. 1191, 42p, Prince Henry of Wales. No. 1192, 42p, Princess Beatrice of York. No. 1193, 42p, Princess Eugenie of York. No. 1194, 42p, Viscount Severn. No. 1195, 42p, Lady Louise Windsor. No. 1196, 42p, Peter Phillips. No. 1197, 42p, Zara Phillips.

2009, May 1 *Perf. 12½*
1190-1197 A266 Set of 8 16.00 16.00

Europa — A267

Designs: 10p, Aristotle (384-322 B.C), philosopher. 42p, Galileo Galilei (1564-1642), astronomer and physicist. 44p, Nicolaus Copernicus (1473-1543), astronomer. £1.50, Sir Isaac Newton (1642-1727), physicist and mathematician.

2009, June 1 *Perf. 13x12½*
1198-1201 A267 Set of 4 11.00 11.00

Intl. Year of Astronomy.

Birds Type of 2008

Designs: 10p, Black stork. £2, Northern gannet. £3, Osprey.

2009, Sept. 16 Litho. *Perf. 13*
1202 A255 10p multi .35 .35

Size: 32x45mm
Perf. 13x13¼

1203 A255 £2 multi 6.50 6.50
1204 A255 £3 multi 9.50 9.50
Nos. 1202-1204 (3) 16.35 16.35

Old Views of Gibraltar — A268

Designs: No. 1205, 10p, Road to the frontier. No. 1206, 42p, Catalan Bay village. No. 1207, 44p, Rock of Gibraltar. 51p, Moorish Castle. 59p, South Barracks.
No. 1210: a, 10p, Garrison Library. b, 42p, Piazza. c, 44p, Piazza Casemates. d, £1, Main Street.

2009, Sept. 16 *Perf. 14x14¾*
1205-1209 A268 Set of 5 10.00 10.00

Souvenir Sheet

1210 A268 Sheet of 4, #a-d 9.75 9.75

Charles Darwin (1809-82), Naturalist — A269

Darwin and: 10p, HMS Beagle, bird and books. 42p, Books and pages with scientific drawings. 44p, Books and pages with drawings of horse and bone. £2, Book, page with drawing of bird, notebook.
£2.42, Darwin, book and house.

2009, Nov. 12 *Perf. 14x14¾*
1211-1214 A269 Set of 4 13.50 13.50

Souvenir Sheet

1215 A269 £2.42 multi 13.50 13.50

Christmas A270

Christmas tree ornaments: 10p, Santa Claus. 42p, Angel. 44p, Teddy bear. 51p, Christmas tree. £2, Bells.

2009, Nov. 12 *Perf. 13½x13*
1216-1220 A270 Set of 5 16.50 16.50

Miniature Sheet

100-Ton Guns of Gibraltar and Malta — A271

No. 1221 — 100-ton gun from: a, Napier of Magdala Battery, Gibraltar, 1880. b, Napier of Magdala Battery, 2010. c, Fort Rinella, Malta, 2010. d, Fort Rinella, 1882.

2010, Feb. 19 Litho. *Perf. 13¾*
1221 A271 75p Sheet of 4, #a-d 14.00 14.00

See Malta No. 1400.

Battle of Britain, 70th Anniv. A272

Airplanes: No. 1222, 50p, Boulton Paul Defiant. No. 1223, 50p, Bristol Blenheim. No. 1224, 50p, Gloster Gladiator. No. 1225, 50p, Hawker Hurricane. No. 1226, 50p, Miles Master. No. 1227, 50p, Supermarine Spitfire.
£2, Douglas Bader, British ace pilot, vert.

2010, Feb. 21 *Perf. 14*
1222-1227 A272 Set of 6 16.00 16.00

Souvenir Sheet

1228 A272 £2 multi 10.50 10.50

Accession to Throne of King George V, Cent. A273

King George V: 10p, As child, with family. 42p, Examining stamp collection. 44p, On horse, reviewing troops. £2, On deck of gunship.

2010, Mar. 26 *Perf. 13*
1229-1232 A273 Set of 4 15.00 15.00

Europa A274

Scenes from children's stories by Roald Dahl: 10p, Charlie and the Chocolate Factory. 42p, Matilda. 44p, The Twits. £1.50, The BFG.

2010, May 4 Litho. *Perf. 13*
1233-1236 A274 Set of 4 10.50 10.50

Miniature Sheet

Sites in San Marino and Gibraltar — A275

No. 1237: a, Second Tower, San Marino. b, Moorish Castle, Gibraltar. c, Mt. Titano, San Marino. d, Rock of Gibraltar.

2010, June 30 *Perf. 14¾x14*
1237 A275 75p Sheet of 4, #a-d 13.50 13.50

See San Marino No. 1822.

Souvenir Sheet

Emblem of Miss World Pageant and Name of 2009 Winner — A276

Litho. With Foil Application

2010, June 30 *Perf. 14x14¾*
1238 A276 £2 gold & black 9.00 9.00

Aviation Centenaries — A277

Designs: No. 1239, 10p, Airplane of Baroness Raymonde de Laroche, first woman to obtain pilot's license. No. 1240, 42p, LZ-7, first Zeppelin flight with fare-paying customers. No. 1241, 49p, Antoinette VII, airplane of Hubert Latham, setting altitude record of 4,541 feet. No. 1242, £2, Clément-Bayard No. 2, first airship to cross the English Channel.
No. 1243 — Seaplanes: a, 10p, Le Canard, seaplane of Henri Fabre, first seaplane to take off from water. b, 42p, Supermarine S.6B, first aircraft to surpass 400 miles per hour in speed. c, 49p, Short Sunderland of 204th Squadron. d, £2, Saunders-ROE Princess.

2010, Aug. 20 Litho. *Perf. 14¾x14*
1239-1242 A277 Set of 4 13.50 13.50

Souvenir Sheet

1243 A277 Sheet of 4, #a-d 16.00 16.00

Birds Type of 2008

Designs: 59p, Barbary partridge. 76p, Ortolan bunting. £2, Pallid swift.

2010, Oct. 20 Litho. *Perf. 13*
1244 A255 59p multi 1.90 1.90
1245 A255 76p multi 2.50 2.50
1246 A255 £2 multi 6.50 6.50
Nos. 1244-1246 (3) 10.90 10.90

Girl Guides, Cent. A278

Uniform of: 10p, Rainbow. 42p, Brownie. 44p, Guide. £2, Senior.

2010, Oct. 20 *Perf. 13½*
1247-1250 A278 Set of 4 13.50 13.50

Souvenir Sheet

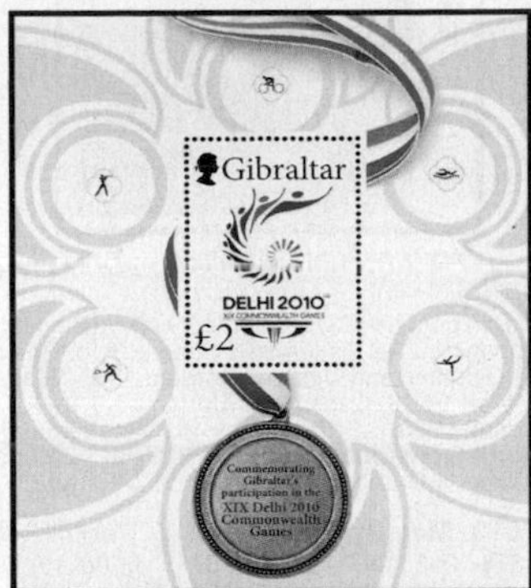

2010 Commonwealth Games, Delhi — A279

2010, Oct. 20 ***Perf. 14¼x14¾***
1251 A279 £2 multi 10.50 10.50

Souvenir Sheet

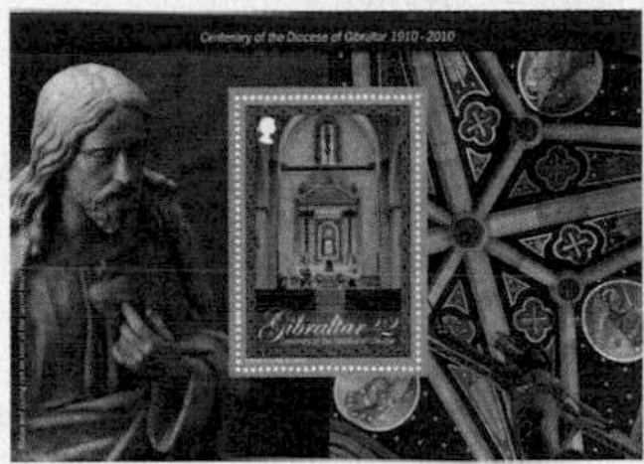

Dicoese of Gibraltar, Cent. — A280

2010, Nov. 16 Litho. ***Perf. 15x14***
1252 A280 £2 multi 9.00 9.00

Christmas A281

Designs: 10p, Christmas crackers, gifts, ornaments, stocking, candle, bell and candy cane. 42p, Stockings hung on mantle. 44p, Santa Claus and reindeer in flight. 51p, Three snowmen.

2010, Nov. 26 ***Perf. 13x13¼***
1253-1256 A281 Set of 4 6.75 6.75

Royal British Legion A282

British troops in action In: No. 1257, 50p, World War I. No. 1258, 50p, World War II. No. 1259, 50p, Northern Ireland. No. 1260, 50p, The Falkland Islands. No. 1261, 50p, The Gulf War. No. 1262, 50p, The Balkans. No. 1263, 50p, Afghanistan. No. 1264, 50p, Iraq.

£2, Statue, poppies, words from poem, "In Flanders Fields."

2011, Jan. 14 Litho ***Perf. 13***
1257-1264 A282 Set of 8 18.00 18.00

Souvenir Sheet

Perf. 13x13½

1265 A282 £2 multi 9.00 9.00

Nos. 1257-1264 each were printed in sheets of 6.

Souvenir Sheet

Engagement of Prince William and Catherine Middleton — A283

2011, Jan. 14 ***Perf. 14¾x14¼***
1266 A283 £2 multi 9.50 9.50

Service of Queen Elizabeth II and Prince Philip — A284

Designs: 10p, Queen Elizabeth II. 42p, Queen and Prince Philip. 44p, Queen and Prince Philip, diff. 51p, Queen and Prince Philip, diff. 55p, Queen and Prince Philip, diff. £2, Prince Philip.

£3, Queen and Prince Philip at wedding, diff.

Perf. 13¼

2011, Feb. 6 Litho. Unwmk.
1267-1272 A284 Set of 6 17.50 17.50
1272a Sheet of 6, #1267-1272, + 3 labels 17.50 17.50

Souvenir Sheet

1273 A284 £3 multi 18.00 18.00

Europa — A285

Designs: 10p, Alpine forest, Swiss National Forest, Switzerland. 42p, Amazon rainforest, Brazil. 44p, Forest and waterfall, Yosemite National Park, US. £1.50, Forest and waterfall, Plitvice Lakes National Park, Croatia.

2011, Apr. 4 ***Perf. 12½***
1274-1277 A285 Set of 4 8.25 8.25

Intl. Year of Forests.

Gibraltar Postage Stamps, 125th Anniv. — A286

Details from Gibraltar stamps: 10p, #7. 42p, #48. 44p, #93. 55p, #118. £1.50, #131.

2011, Apr. 15 ***Perf. 13¼***
1278-1282 A286 Set of 5 12.00 12.00

Souvenir Sheet

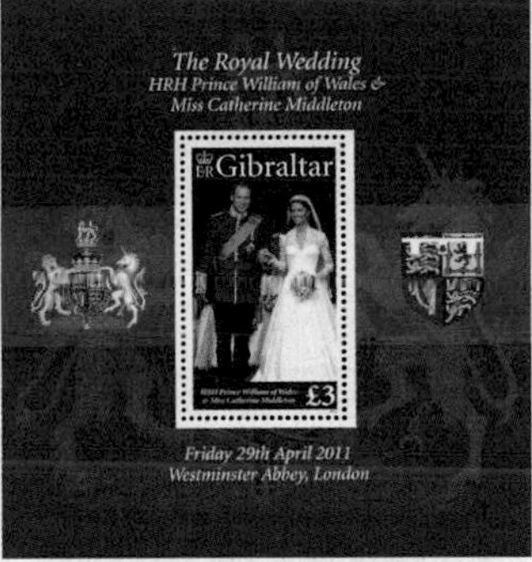

Wedding of Prince William and Catherine Middleton — A287

2011, July 15 Litho. ***Perf. 14¾x14¼***
1283 A287 £3 multi 12.00 12.00

Endangered Animals — A288

Designs: No. 1284, 42p, Asian elephant. No. 1285, 42p, Bengal tiger. No. 1286, 42p, Black rhinoceros. No. 1287, 42p, Giant panda. No. 1288, 42p, Polar bear. No. 1289, 42p, Sumatran orangutan.

2011, July 31 ***Perf. 14x14¾***
1284-1289 A288 Set of 6 10.00 10.00
1289a Souvenir sheet of 6, #1284-1289 10.00 10.00

See Nos. 1353-1358, 1405-1410.

Barbary Macaques — A289

Design: 10p, Macaque on tourist binoculars. 42p, Macaque on rock. 44p, Macaque on branch. 51p, Macaque on wall. 59p, Macaque on rock, diff. £1.50, Two macaques on rock.

2011, Sept. 28 ***Perf. 15x14***
1290-1295 A289 Set of 6 12.00 12.00

Supermarine Spitfire Airplanes, 75th Anniv. — A290

Designs: 10p, Spitfire K5054 modified to Mk 1 standard, in flight. 42p, Pilot in Spitfire on ground for first flight, Mar. 5, 1936. 49p, Ground crew testing Spitfire before first flight. No. 1299, £2, Spitfire prototype K5054 under construction.

No. 1300, £2, Pilot in Royal Air Force 92nd Squadron Spitfire Mk 1B.

2011, Sept. 28 ***Perf. 14¾x14***
1296-1299 A290 Set of 4 10.00 10.00

Souvenir Sheet

1300 A290 £2 multi 7.00 7.00

Tariq Ibn Ziyad, 8th Century Muslim General A291

Scenes from Tariq Ibn Ziyad's invasion of Gibraltar in 711: 42p, Soldiers rowing boat. 44p, Boats on shore. 66p, Soldiers on horses. £2, Battle scene.

2011, Nov. 7 ***Perf. 13¼***
1301-1304 A291 Set of 4 12.00 12.00

Christmas A292

Nativity paintings by: 10p, Charles Le Brun. 42p, Lorenzo Lotto, 44p, Il Bronzino. 51p, Gerard van Honthorst. £2, Giorgione da Castelfranco.

2011, Nov. 7 ***Perf. 14¼***
1305-1309 A292 Set of 5 12.00 12.00

Gibraltar Intl. Chess Festival, 10th Anniv. — A293

Chessboard positions in matches between: 2p, Viktor Bologan and Pia Cramling. 30p, Michael Adams and Natalia Zhukova. 75p, Fabiano Caruana and Viktor Korchnoi. £2, Vassily Ivanchuk and Nigel Short.

2012, Jan. 23 ***Perf. 13x13¼***
1310-1313 A293 Set of 4 10.00 10.00

Sinking of the Titanic, Cent. A294

Milestones in history of the Titanic: 10p, Fitting of Titanic completed Mar. 31, 1912. 42p, Titanic sets sail on maiden voyage, April 10, 1912. 44p, Iceberg strikes starboard bow, April 14, 1912. 54p, First lifeboats lowered to the sea, April 15, 1912. 66p, Stern rises and starts sinking, April 15, 1912.

2012, Jan. 30 ***Perf. 13¼***
1314-1318 A294 Set of 5 7.00 7.00

Reign of Queen Elizabeth II, 60th Anniv. — A295

Queen Elizabeth II wearing: 10p, Light green hat. 42p, Tiara. 44p, Flowered hat. 51p,

Large pendant earrings. 55p, Pearl necklace. £2, Red Cross hat.
£3, Queen Elizabeth II wearing sash and crown.

2012, Feb. 27

1319-1324 A295 Set of 6 13.00 13.00
1324a Souvenir sheet of 6, #1319-1324, + 3 labels 13.00 13.00

Souvenir Sheet

1325 A295 £3 multi 9.50 9.50

Birds Type of 2008

Designs: S, Red-necked nightjar. UK, Little owl. £3.44, Spotted flycatcher.

2012, Apr. 16 ***Perf. 13x13¼***

1326 A255 S multi 1.00 1.00
1327 A255 UK multi 1.40 1.40
1328 A255 £3.44 multi 11.00 11.00
Nos. 1326-1328 (3) 13.40 13.40

On day of issue, No. 1326 sold for 31p and No. 1327 sold for 41p. For surcharge, see No. 1411.

Royal Air Force Squadron Emblems and Aircraft A296

Royal Air Force Squadron Emblems — A297

Designs: No. 1329, 10p, Westland WS-61 Sea King helicopter, emblem of 22nd Squadron. No. 1330, 42p, Gloster Javelin FAW.7 Mk IV airplane, emblem of 89th Squadron. No. 1331, 76p, Panavia tornado airplane, emblem of 111th Squadron. No. 1332, £2, Bristol Type 156 Beaufighter airplane, emblem of 248th Squadron.
No. 1333 — Emblem of: a, 22nd Squadron. b, 89th Squadron. c, 111th Squadron. d, 248th Squadron.

2012, Apr. 16 ***Perf. 13¼***

1329-1332 A296 Set of 4 11.00 11.00
1333 A297 Sheet of 4 11.00 11.00
a. 10p multi .35 .35
b. 42p multi 1.40 1.40
c. 76p multi 2.50 2.50
d. £2 multi 6.50 6.50

See Nos. 1370-1374, 1477-1481, 1522-1526.

Tourism — A298

Designs: 10p, Aerial view of harbor, city and Rock of Gibraltar. 42p, Tower of Homage, Moorish Castle. 44p, Aerial view of city and Rock of Gibraltar. 51p, St. Michael's Cave. 54p, Trinity Lighthouse. 66p, Eliott's Column, Alameda Botanical Gardens.

2012, June 15 **Litho.** ***Perf. 13¼***

1334-1339 A298 Set of 6 8.25 8.25

Europa (42p, 44p).

Gibraltar Intl. Jazz Festival A299

2012, June 19 ***Perf. 13x13¼***

1340 A299 75p multi 2.40 2.40

Old Views of Gibraltar — A300

Designs: No. 1341, 10p, Moorish Castle. 30p, Grand Casemates. 61p, Landing Pier. 78p, Waterport. £1.75, Alameda Gardens.
No. 1346: a, 10p, Marching band on Sand Hill Road. b, 42p, South Port Gates. c, 50p, Victoria Monument. d, £1, Hargraves Barracks.

2012, Sept. 14 ***Perf. 13¼***

1341-1345 A300 Set of 5 11.50 11.50

Souvenir Sheet

1346 A300 Sheet of 4, #a-d 6.50 6.50

Charles Dickens (1812-70), Writer — A301

Photograph of Dickens and: 10p, Cover and illustration from *David Copperfield.* 42p, First page and illustration from *Oliver Twist.* 44p, Cover and first page from *A Tale of Two Cities.* No. 1350, £2, Cover and illustration from *A Christmas Carol.*
No. 1351, £2, Photograph of Dickens over book cover.

2012, Sept. 14 ***Perf. 14¼x15***

1347-1350 A301 Set of 4 9.50 9.50

Souvenir Sheet

1351 A301 £2 multi 6.50 6.50

Souvenir Sheet

Visit to Gibraltar of Earl and Countess of Wessex — A302

2012, Sept. 14 ***Perf. 13¼***

1352 A302 £1 Sheet of 3, #a-c 9.75 9.75

Endangered Animals Type of 2011

Designs: No. 1353, 42p, Arabian oryx. No. 1354, 42p, Asian one-horned rhinoceros. No. 1355, 42p, European wolf. No. 1356, 42p, Iberian lynx. No. 1357, 42p, Snow leopard. No. 1358, 42p, Western lowland gorilla.

2012, Nov. 2 ***Perf. 13¼x13***

1353-1358 A288 Set of 6 8.25 8.25
1358a Souvenir sheet of 6, #1353-1358 8.25 8.25

Christmas A303

Designs: 10p, Santa Claus, gifts and "Merry Christmas." 42p, Santa Claus with sack of gifts and lantern. 44p, Snowman, Christmas tree, gifts, flying sleigh and reindeer. 51p, Santa Claus in flying sleigh. £2, Reindeer, elf, Santa Claus holding bell.

2012, Nov. 2 ***Perf. 13x13¼***

1359-1363 A303 Set of 5 11.50 11.50

New Year 2013 (Year of the Snake) — A304

No. 1364: a, Head of snake. b, Entire snake.

Litho. & Embossed With Foil Application

2013, Jan. 30 ***Perf. 12¾***

1364 A304 Horiz. pair 4.75 4.75
a. 42p multi 1.40 1.40
b. £1 multi 3.25 3.25

Coronation of Queen Elizabeth II, 60th Anniv. — A305

Various black-and-white photographs of Queen Elizabeth II on day of coronation: 10p, 42p, 44p, £1.50.
£3, Color photograph of Queen Elizabeth II.

2013, Jan. 30 **Litho.** ***Perf. 13¼***

1365-1368 A305 Set of 4 7.75 7.75

Souvenir Sheet

1369 A305 £3 multi 9.50 9.50

Royal Air Force Squadrons Types of 2012

Designs: No. 1370, 10p, VS Spitfire 5C, emblem of 43rd Squadron. No. 1371, 42p, Hawker Hurricane, emblem of 87th Squadron. No. 1372, 76p, Consolidated PBY Catalina IV A, emblem of 210th Squadron. No. 1373, £2, Avro Shackleton MR2, emblem of 224th Squadron.
No. 1374 — Emblem of: a, 43rd Squadron. b, 87th Squadron. c, 210th Squadron. d, 224th Squadron.

2013, Mar. 25 ***Perf. 13x13¼***

1370-1373 A296 Set of 4 10.00 10.00

Perf. 13¼

1374 A297 Sheet of 4 10.00 10.00
a. 10p multi .30 .30
b. 42p multi 1.25 1.25
c. 76p multi 2.40 2.40
d. £2 multi 6.00 6.00

Gibraltar Literary Festival A306

Designs: 10p, Open books. 42p, Braille print. £2, Book and electronic tablet.

2013, May 3 ***Perf. 13x13¼***

1375-1377 A306 Set of 3 8.00 8.00

Old Views of Gibraltar — A307

Designs: No. 1378, 10p, Moorish Castle and Landport. 30p, Casemates Square. 61p, Rock of Gibraltar and Victoria Gardens. 78p, Main Street. £1.75, Casemates Barracks.
No. 1383: a, 10p, Rock of Gibraltar and North Front Camp. b, 42p, Rosia Bay. c, 50p, Alameda Gardens. d, £1, Gunner's Parade.

2013, May 3 ***Perf. 13¼***

1378-1382 A307 Set of 5 11.00 11.00

Souvenir Sheet

1383 A307 Sheet of 4, #a-d 6.25 6.25

Acceptance of Gibraltar to Union of European Football Associations (UEFA) — A308

2013, May 31 ***Perf. 14¾x14***

1384 A308 54p multi 1.75 1.75

Treaty of Utrecht, 300th Anniv. — A309

No. 1385: a, Union Jack. b, Text from treaty concerning permanence of transfer of control of Gibraltar from Spain to Great Britain.

2013, June 20 ***Perf. 12¾***

1385 A309 Horiz. pair 1.60 1.60
a. 10p multi .30 .30
b. 42p multi 1.25 1.25

Europa A310

Postal vehicles: 10p, 1911 Dennis mail van. 42p, Horse-drawn mail cart. 44p, 1914 Rover motorcycle and sidecar. £1.75, 1928 Electromobile mail van.

2013, June 20 ***Perf. 13x13¼***

1386-1389 A310 Set of 4 8.25 8.25

Types of 1953

Queen Elizabeth II and: 2p, Wharves. 10p, South view. 16p, Tunny fishing industry. 20p, Southport Gate. 22p, Sailing in the bay. 30p, Ocean liner. 42p, Airport. 44p, Coaling wharf. 50p, Europa Point. 58p, Strait from Buena Vista. 60p, Rosia Bay. £2, Government House. £3, Moorish Castle £5, Arms of Gibraltar.

2013, Aug. 1 ***Perf. 12¾***

1390 A26 2p dk grn & ind .25 .25
1391 A26 10p blk & bl grn .30 .30
1392 A26 16p brownish gray .50 .50
1393 A26 20p sepia .65 .65
1394 A26 22p car lake .70 .70
1395 A26 30p blue .95 .95
1396 A26 42p plum 1.25 1.25
1397 A26 44p ultra 1.40 1.40
1398 A26 50p blue & blk 1.60 1.60
1399 A26 58p red brn & bl 1.75 1.75
1400 A26 60p vio & org 1.90 1.90
1401 A26 £2 dk brown 6.25 6.25
1402 A27 £3 ultra & brn 9.25 9.25
1403 A27 £5 org & org red 15.50 15.50
Nos. 1390-1403 (14) 42.25 42.25

Birth of Prince George of Cambridge A311

2013, Aug. 16 ***Perf. 14x14¾***
1404 A311 £2 multi 6.50 6.50

Printed in sheets of 6.

Endangered Animals Type of 2011

Designs: No. 1405, 42p, African penguin. No. 1406, 42p, Atlantic bluefin tuna. No. 1407, 42p, Asiatic cheetah. No. 1408, 42p, Chinese alligator. No. 1409, 42p, Red-crowned crane. No. 1410, 42p, Leatherneck sea turtle.

2013, Sept. 14 ***Perf. 12½x13***
1405-1410 A288 Set of 6 8.00 8.00
1410a Souvenir sheet of 6, #1405-1410, perf. 13¼x13 8.00 8.00

Nos. 1117 and 1327 Surcharged in Gray or Black

Methods and Perfs As Before

2013, Nov. 2
1411 A255 14p on UK #1327 (G) .45 .45
1412 A255 28p on 5p #1117 .90 .90

Ceremony of the Keys — A312

2013, Nov. 2 **Litho.** ***Perf. 13¼***
1413 A312 £1 multi + 2 flanking labels 3.25 3.25

Christmas A313

"Merry Christmas" and: 12p, Holly. 50p, Christmas tree and gifts. 54p, Santa Claus in sleigh. 64p, Christmas gift. £2.50, Christmas ornaments.

2013, Nov. 2 **Litho.** ***Perf. 14x13¾***
1414-1418 A313 Set of 5 14.00 14.00
1418a Souvenir sheet of 5, #1414-1418 14.00 14.00

New Year 2014 (Year of the Horse) — A314

No. 1419: a, Horse's head. b, Horse.

2014, Jan. 31 **Litho.** ***Perf. 12¾***
1419 A314 Horiz. pair 5.00 5.00
a. 50p multi 1.60 1.60
b. £1 multi 3.25 3.25

Queen Elizabeth II
A315 A316

2014, Jan. 31 **Litho.** ***Perf. 14x13½***
Self-Adhesive

1420	A315	2p rose car	.25	.25
1421	A315	4p dp plum	.25	.25
1422	A315	6p dk vio	.25	.25
1423	A315	8p blk vio	.25	.25
1424	A315	10p dk green	.35	.35
1425	A316	G blue	.40	.40
1426	A315	14p red	.45	.45
1427	A315	20p sl green	.65	.65
1428	A315	28p dp plum	.90	.90
1429	A315	40p dk brn	1.40	1.40
1430	A315	50p blue grn	1.60	1.60
1431	A316	54p car rose	1.75	1.75
1432	A316	64p sepia	2.10	2.10
1433	A315	70p blk vio	2.25	2.25
1434	A315	£2 green	6.50	6.50
1435	A315	£2.50 claret	8.25	8.25
		Nos. 1420-1435 (16)	27.60	27.60

No. 1425 sold for 12p on day of issue. See Nos. 1509-1512.

World War I, Cent. A317

Inscriptions: 12p, Your Country Wants You. 40p, Joining up. 50p, Leaving family. 64p, Kit. 68p, Training. £1, Embarkation.

2014, Feb. 19 **Litho.** ***Perf. 14***
1436-1441 A317 Set of 6 11.50 11.50

Nos. 1436-1441 each were printed in sheets of 8 + central label. See Nos. 1498-1503.

Royal Air Force Red Arrows, 50th Anniv. — A318

Royal Air Force roundel and various Red Arrows airplanes: 50p, 54p, 64p, 70p, £2.

2014, Mar. 20 **Litho.** ***Perf. 13¼***
1442-1446 A318 Set of 5 14.50 14.50

Old Views of Gibraltar — A319

Designs: No. 1447, 12p, Waterport Wharf. No. 1448, 40p, Eliott's Monument. No. 1449, 50p, Town area. 64p, Sandpits. 70p, Alameda Gardens.

No. 1452: a, 12p, Main Street. b, 40p, The Wharfs. c, 50p, The Market. d, £1, The Cascade.

2014, Mar. 20 **Litho.** ***Perf. 13¼***
1447-1451 A319 Set of 5 8.00 8.00

Souvenir Sheet

1452 A319 Sheet of 4, #a-d 6.75 6.75

Europa — A320

Designs: 50p, Royal Gibraltar Regiment Band at Buckingham Palace. £1, Drum Corps.

2014, May 2 **Litho.** ***Perf. 13¼x13***
1453-1454 A320 Set of 2 5.00 5.00

Dolphins A321

Designs: 68p, Common dolphin. 84p, Striped dolphin. £2.50, Bottlenose dolphin.

2014, May 2 **Litho.** ***Perf. 13¼x13½***
1455-1457 A321 Set of 3 13.50 13.50

William Shakespeare (1564-1616), Writer — A322

Various depictions of Shakespeare, quote and opening page from: 12p, *Macbeth.* 40p, *Hamlet.* 64p, *A Midsummer Night's Dream.* No. 1461, £2, *Romeo and Juliet.*

No. 1462, £2, Statue of Shakespeare, quote from *Twelfth Night.*

2014, June 2 **Litho.** ***Perf. 12½***
1458-1461 A322 Set of 4 10.50 10.50

Souvenir Sheet

1462 A322 £2 multi 6.75 6.75

Flowers — A323

Designs: 10p, Gibraltar saxifrage. 12p, Gibraltar restharrow. 50p, Gibraltar chickweed. 54p, Gibraltar candytuft. 64p, Gibraltar campion. 70p, Gibraltar thyme. £2, Gibraltar sea lavender.

2014, July 15 **Litho.** ***Perf. 13½***
1463-1469 A323 Set of 7 15.50 15.50

Evacuation of Gibraltar, 75th Anniv. A324

Designs: 12p, People on gangplank. 50p, People hugging. 54p, People on ship waving. £1, People on gangplanks and stairs. £2, Family and text.

Perf. 13½x13¾

2014, Sept. 10 **Litho.**
1470-1474 A324 Set of 5 13.50 13.50

Gibraltar Sea Scouts, Cent. — A325

Designs: 40p, Sea Scout leaders. 64p, Sea Scouts marching.

2014, Sept. 13 **Litho.** ***Perf. 13¼x13***
1475-1476 A325 Set of 2 3.50 3.50

Royal Air Force Squadrons Types of 2012

Designs: No. 1477, 54p, British Aerospace Hawks, emblem of the 100th Squadron. No. 1478, 64p, Short/Saro London, emblem of the 202nd Squadron. No. 1479, 70p, Buccaneer S2s, emblem of 208th Squadron. No. 1480, £2, Lockheed Hudson V, emblem of 233rd Squadron.

No. 1481 — Emblem of: a, 100th Squadron. b, 202nd Squadron. c, 208th Squadron. d, 233rd Squadron.

Perf. 14¾x14¼

2014, Sept. 15 **Litho.**
1477-1480 A296 Set of 4 12.50 12.50

Perf. 13¼

1481 A297 Sheet of 4 12.50 12.50
a. 54p multi 1.75 1.75
b. 64p multi 2.00 2.00
c. 70p multi 2.25 2.25
d. £2 multi 6.50 6.50

Royal Marines, 350th Anniv. — A326

2014, Oct. 25 **Litho.** ***Perf. 13¼x13***
1482 A326 £2 multi 6.50 6.50

Christmas A327

Various details from artwork by disabled people at the St. Bernadette Resource Center: G, Santa Claus. 40p, Stars. 64p, Animals wearing stocking caps. 70p, Three people. 80p, Christmas tree,

£3, Center section of entire work of art.

2014, Nov. 3 **Litho.** ***Perf. 12¾***
1483-1487 A327 Set of 5 8.75 8.75

Souvenir Sheet

1488 A327 £3 multi 9.50 9.50

No. 1483 sold for 22p on day of issue.

New Year 2015 (Year of the Goat) — A328

No. 1489: a, Goat's head. b, Goat.

2015, Jan. 30 **Litho.** ***Perf. 12¾***
1489 A328 Horiz. pair 4.50 4.50
a. 50p multi 1.50 1.50
b. £1 multi 3.00 3.00

Gibraltar Fire and Rescue Service, 150th Anniv. — A329

Designs: 10p, Firemen spraying water. 12p, Firemen spraying foam. 40p, Rescue worker tending to injured man. 50p, Helmet and visor. 54p, Rescue diver. 64p, Rescue workers at automobile accident. 70p, Firemen in hazardous material protective wear. £2, Fireman spraying water on vehicle fire.

2015, Feb. 11 Litho. *Perf. 13¼x13*
1490-1497 A329 Set of 8 15.50 15.50

World War I, Cent. Type of 2014

Inscriptions: 22p, Machine guns. 40p, Ships. 64p, Gas. 70p, Aircraft. 80p, Bayonets. £1.20, Tanks.

2015, Feb. 18 Litho. *Perf. 13*
1498-1503 A317 Set of 6 12.00 12.00

Nos. 1498-1503 each were printed in sheets of 8 + central label.

Sir Winston Churchill (1874-1965), British Prime Minister — A330

Churchill: 22p, On ship's deck. 64p, Inspecting military vehicles. 70p, Wearing helmet. 80p, Inspecting bombed buildings.
£3, Churchill giving "V for Victory" sign.

2015, Mar. 20 Litho. *Perf. 12*
1504-1507 A330 Set of 4 7.00 7.00

Souvenir Sheet

1508 A330 £3 multi 7.00 7.00

Queen Elizabeth II Type of 2014 and

Queen Elizabeth II — A331

2015, Apr. 24 Litho. *Perf. 14x13½*

Self-Adhesive

1509 A315 12p green .40 .40
1510 A315 18p brown .55 .55
1511 A315 80p blue 2.50 2.50
1512 A315 £3 red brown 9.25 9.25

Die Cut

1513 A331 £1 black 3.00 3.00
Nos. 1509-1513 (5) 15.70 15.70

Souvenir Sheet

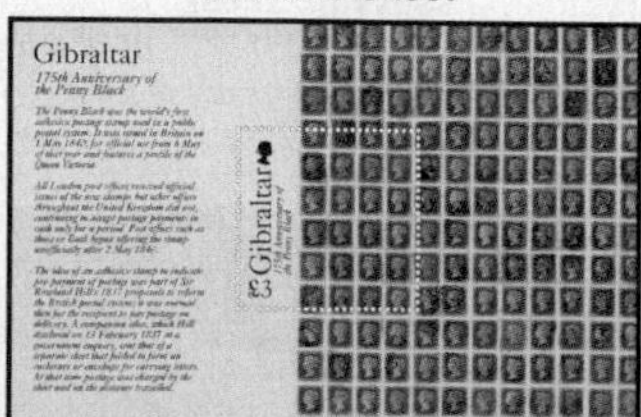

Penny Black, 175th Anniv. — A332

2015, Apr. 24 Litho. *Perf. 13½*
1514 A332 £3 multi 9.25 9.25

Toys — A333

Designs: 14p, Soldier. 22p, Carousel. 64p, Top. 70p, Teddy bear. 80p, Yo-yo. £1.20 Wooden train cars.

2015, May 5 Litho. *Perf. 14¼x14¾*
1515-1520 A333 Set of 6 11.50 11.50

Europa (Nos. 1517-1518).

Queen Elizabeth II — A334

Litho. With Foil Application

2015, May 30 *Perf. 13*
1521 A334 £10 multi 30.00 30.00

Royal Air Force Squadrons Type of 2012

Designs: 54p, Handley Page Halifax Mk. V, emblem of 520th Squadron. 64p, Vickers Wellington Mk. IV, emblem of 544th Squadron. 70p, Bristol Blenheim Mk. IV, emblem of 600th Squadron. £2, De Havilland Vampire Mk. V, emblem of 608th Squadron.

No. 1526 — Emblem of: a, 520th Squadron. b, 544th Squadron. c, 600th Squadron. d, 608th Squadron.

Perf. 14¾x14¼

2015, Aug. 31 Litho.
1522-1525 A296 Set of 4 12.00 12.00

Perf. 13¼

1526 A297 Sheet of 4 12.00 12.00
a. 54p multi 1.75 1.75
b. 64p multi 2.00 2.00
c. 70p multi 2.10 2.10
d. £2 multi 6.00 6.00

Rock of Gibraltar — A335

Moorish Castle — A336

Bouquet and Hands of Bride and Groom — A337

2015, Sept. 7 Litho. *Perf. 14¼*
1527 A335 G multi .70 .70
1528 A336 G multi .70 .70
1529 A337 G multi .70 .70
1530 A335 E multi 2.25 2.25
1531 A336 E multi 2.25 2.25
1532 A337 E multi 2.25 2.25
Nos. 1527-1532 (6) 8.85 8.85

Nos. 1527-1529 each sold for 22p and Nos. 1530-1532 each sold for 70p on day of issue. The stamps were available with adjacent labels that could be personalized for an additional fee.

A 50p stamp of Type A335 was printed in limited quantities in sheets of 4 having QR codes in sheet margin.

Opening of University of Gibraltar — A338

2015, Sept. 21 Litho. *Perf. 13¼*
1533 A338 80p multi 2.50 2.50

Christmas — A339

Designs: G, Christmas tree. 40p, Candy canes, bow and holly leaves. 64p, Gift box. 70p, Reindeer. 80p, "Merry Christmas & Happy New Year."

2015, Nov. 2 Litho. *Perf. 14¼*
1534-1538 A339 Set of 5 8.50 8.50

No. 1534 sold for 22p on day of issue.

Souvenir Sheet

Magna Carta, 800th Anniv. — A340

No. 1539 — Text of illuminated Magna Carta with panels at left in: a, Gray blue. b, Dull brown.

2015, Nov. 13 Litho. *Perf. 13x13¼*
1539 A340 £2 Sheet of 2, #a-b 12.00 12.00

New Year 2016 (Year of the Monkey) — A341

No. 1540: a, Head of monkey. b, Entire monkey.

2016, Jan. 30 Litho. *Perf. 12½*
1540 A341 Horiz. pair 11.50 11.50
a.-b. £2 Either single 5.75 5.75

Queen Elizabeth II, 90th Birthday — A342

Various photographs of Queen Elizabeth II.

2016, Feb. 19 Litho. *Perf. 12½*
1541 A342 12p multi .35 .35
1542 A342 18p multi .50 .50
1543 A342 22p multi .65 .65
1544 A342 40p multi 1.10 1.10
1545 A342 50p multi 1.40 1.40
1546 A342 64p multi 1.75 1.75
1547 A342 70p multi 2.00 2.00
1548 A342 80p multi 2.25 2.25
1549 A342 £1 multi 3.00 3.00

Size: 40x40mm

Perf. 13

1550 A342 £5 multi 14.00 14.00
Nos. 1541-1550 (10) 27.00 27.00

A343

Europa A344

2016, Mar. 30 Litho. *Perf. 14*
1551 A343 €1.50 multi 4.25 4.25
1552 A344 €1.50 multi 4.25 4.25

Think Green Issue.

Battle of the Somme, Cent. A345

Poppies and various soldiers in battle: 22p, 64p, 70p, 80p, £2.

2016, May 16 Litho. *Perf. 13¼x13½*
1553-1557 A345 Set of 5 12.50 12.50

Souvenir Sheet

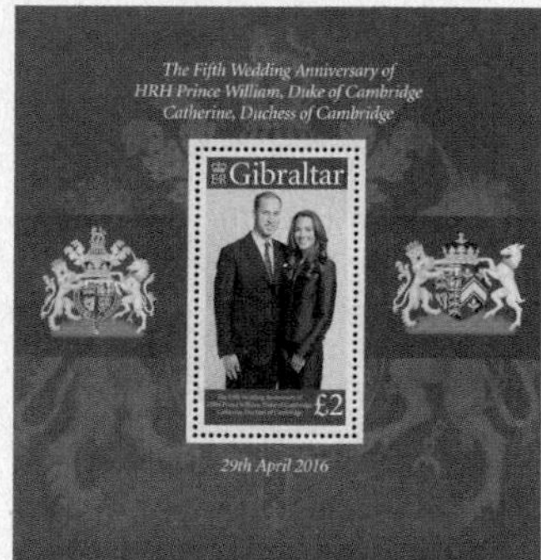

Duke and Duchess of Cambridge, 5th Wedding Anniversary — A346

2016, May 16 Litho. *Perf. 14¾x14*
1558 A346 £2 multi 5.75 5.75

Alameda Gardens, 200th Anniv. — A347

Designs: 64p, Gun at main entrance. 70p, Prince of Wales' Summer House bandstand, Aloe pseudorubroviolacea. 80p, Bridge, bust of Giuseppe Codali, landscape gardener. £1, Italian Garden. £2, Monument to General George Augustus Elliott.

2016, July 25 Litho. *Perf. 12½x13*
1559-1563 A347 Set of 5 13.50 13.50

Historic Gates
A348

Designs: 22p, Rugged Staff Gates. 64p, Prince Edward's Gate. 70p, Landport Gate. 80p, Grand Casemates Gates. £1, Old Waterport Gates. £2, Southport Gates.

2016, July 25 Litho. *Perf. 13x13¼*
1564-1569 A348 Set of 6 14.50 14.50

Gorham's Cave UNESCO World Heritage Site — A349

Designs: 22p, Sun and cave entrance. 64p, Archaeologists in cave. 70p, Rock of Gibraltar. 80p, Neanderthals. £2, Lines on cave wall.

2016, Sept. 20 Litho. *Perf. 14¼*
1570-1574 A349 Set of 5 11.50 11.50

Pillar Boxes — A350

Pillar box from reign of: 22p, Queen Victoria. 64p, King Edward VII. 70p, King George V. 80p, King George VI. £2, Queen Elizabeth II.

2016, Oct. 10 Litho. *Perf. 13¼*
1575-1579 A350 Set of 5 11.00 11.00

Historic Streets of Gibraltar — A351

Sign for: 22p, Cannon Lane. 40p, Castle Street. 50p, George's Lane. 54p, Cloister Ramp. 64p, Engineer Lane. 70p, Main Street. 80p, Flat Bastion Road. £2, Convent Place.

2016, Oct. 10 Litho. *Perf. 13¼*
1580-1587 A351 Set of 8 14.50 14.50

Christmas
A352

Cookies shaped like: G, Santa Claus. 40p, Reindeer. 64p, Bell. 70p, Christmas tree. 80p, Star of Bethlehem. £2, Snowman.

2016, Nov. 2 Litho. *Perf. 12½*
1588-1593 A352 Set of 6 12.00 12.00

No. 1588 sold for 22p on day of issue.

New Year 2017 (Year of the Rooster) — A353

No. 1594: a, Rooster's head. b, Rooster.

2017, Jan. 30 Litho. *Perf. 12¾*
1594 A353 £2 Horiz. pair, #a-b 10.00 10.00

A354

Moorish Castle
A355

2017, Feb. 6 Litho. *Perf. 12½*
1595 A354 £1.50 multi 3.75 3.75
1596 A355 £1.50 multi 3.75 3.75

Europa.

Accession of Queen Elizabeth II to the Throne, 65th Anniv.
A356

Black-and-white photographs of Queen Elizabeth II: 22p, Holding flowers. 64p, Bowing. 70p, Wearing robe. 80p, Seated, wearing crown. £2, Wearing crown, holding orb. No. 1602, £3, Waving.

No. 1603, £3, Color photograph of Queen Elizabeth II wearing sash.

2017, Feb. 6 Litho. *Perf. 13½*
1597-1602 A356 Set of 6 18.00 18.00

Souvenir Sheet

1603 A356 £3 multi 7.50 7.50

Ships Named HMS Gibraltar
A357

Inscriptions: 22p, Edgar-class cruiser, 1892. 54p, 101-gun screw first rate, 1860. 64p, 80-gun Fénix. 70p, 14-gun brig, 1779. 00p, 45,000-ton aircraft carrier, 1943. £1, 20-gun sixth rate, 1711. £3, 20-gun sixth rate, 1754.

2017, May 25 Litho. *Perf. 13¼x13½*
1604-1610 A357 Set of 7 18.00 18.00

70th Wedding Anniversary of Queen Elizabeth II and Prince Philip — A358

Various wedding photographs: 22p, 40p, 50p, 64p, 70p, 80p, £1.50, £2. £3, Couple in coach.

2017, May 25 Litho. *Perf. 13¼*
1611-1618 A358 Set of 8 17.50 17.50

Souvenir Sheet

1619 A358 £3 multi 7.75 7.75

A359

1967 Sovereignty Referendum, 50th Anniv. — A360

Designs: £5, Queen Elizabeth II. No. 1621 — Union Jack pennants and various depictions of Gibraltarians showing British heritage.

2017, June 19 Litho. *Perf. 13*
1620 A359 £5 multi 13.00 13.00

Miniature Sheet
Perf. 12½

1621 A360 Sheet of 4 9.50 9.50
a. 22p multi .60 .60
b. 64p multi 1.75 1.75
c. 70p multi 1.90 1.90
d. £2 multi 5.25 5.25

Miniature Sheet

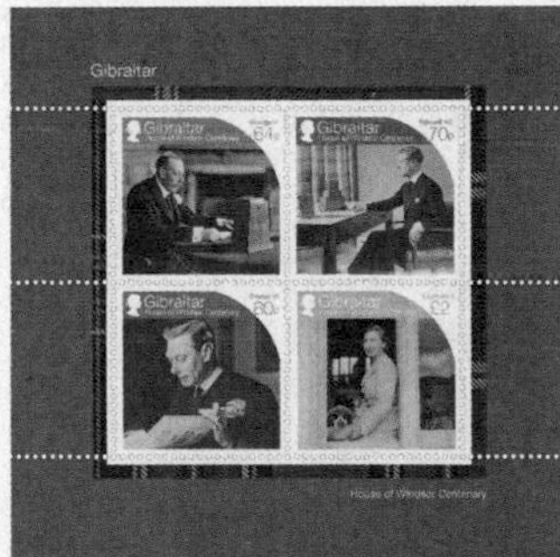

House of Windsor, Cent. — A361

No. 1622: a, King George V. b, King Edward VIII. c, King George VI. d, Queen Elizabeth II.

2017, June 19 Litho. *Perf. 12½*
1622 A361 Sheet of 4 11.00 11.00
a. 64p multi 1.75 1.75
b. 70p multi 1.90 1.90
c. 80p multi 2.10 2.10
d. £2 multi 5.75 5.75

Princess Diana (1961-97)
A363

Various photographs of Princess Diana: 64p, 70p, £1, £2.

2017, Aug. 31 Litho. *Perf. 12½*
1632-1635 A363 Set of 4 11.50 11.50

Upper Rock Nature Reserve — A364

Designs: 22p, Windsor Bridge. 50p, Great Siege tunnels. 64p, Apes den. 70p, Cable car. 80p, St. Michael's Cave. £1, Mediterranean Steps. £2, Moorish Castle.

2017, Sept. 30 Litho. *Perf. 12*
1636-1642 A364 Set of 7 15.50 15.50

Christmas
A365

Decorated cupcakes featuring: 22p, Barbary macaque. 40p, Pan dulce cake. 64p, Snowman. 70p, Rock of Gibraltar. 80p, Penguin. £2, Legs of Santa Claus.

2017, Nov. 2 Litho. *Perf. 13¼x13*
1643-1648 A365 Set of 6 13.00 13.00

Worldwide Fund for Nature (WWF)
A366

No. 1649: a, Schreiber's bent-winged bat. b, European free-tailed bat. c, Greater noctule bat. d, Isabelline serotine bat.

2017, Nov. 30 Litho. *Perf. 13x13¼*
1649 Strip of 4 12.50 12.50
a. A366 70p multi 1.90 1.90
b. A366 80p multi 2.25 2.25
c. A366 £1 multi 2.75 2.75
d. A366 £2 multi 5.50 5.50

New Year 2018 (Year of the Dog) — A367

No. 1650: a, Dog's head. b, Dog.

2018, Jan. 30 Litho. *Perf. 12¾*
1650 A367 £2 Horiz. pair, #a-b 11.50 11.50

Military Heritage of Gibraltar
A362

Designs: 18p, The Convent (home of Governor of Gibraltar). 22p, Cross of Sacrifice. 40p, 100-ton Victorian gun. 50p, Gibraltar War Memorial. 64p, Nelson's Anchorage. 70p, Parson's Lodge. 80p, Garrison Library. £1, Battle of Trafalgar Cemetery. £3, American War Memorial.

2017, July 25 Litho. *Perf. 13x13½*
1623-1631 A362 Set of 9 20.00 20.00

Europa
A368

Designs: No. 1651, 70p, Corral Road Bridge. No. 1652, 70p, Landport Bridge. No. 1653, £1.50, Montagu Curtain. No. 1654, £1.50, Windsor Bridge.

2018, Feb. 6 Litho. *Perf. 12*
1651-1654 A368 Set of 4 12.00 12.00

Cannons
A369

Designs: 10p, 5.25 heavy anti-aircraft gun, 1953. 12p, 6-inch coast cannon, 1909. 18p, 8-inch howitzer, 1783. 22p, 9.2-inch coast MK 10 cannon, 1935. 40p, 10-inch rifled muzzle-loading gun, 1870. 50p, 12-pounder, 1758. 64p, 24-pounder, 1779. 70p, 13-inch mortar, 1783. 80p, 25-pounder gun-howitzer, 1943. £1, 64-pounder rifled muzzle-loading gun, 1873. £2, Bofors L40-70, 1951. £3, Russian 24-pounder, 1854.

2018, Mar. 5 Litho. *Perf. 12*
1655-1666 A369 Set of 12 27.00 27.00

Souvenir Sheet

Engagement of Prince Harry and Meghan Markle — A370

2018, Mar. 5 Litho. *Perf. 13¼*
1667 A370 £3 multi 8.50 8.50

Coronation of Queen Elizabeth II, 65th Anniv. — A371

2018, May 10 Litho. *Perf. 12*
1668 A371 £4 multi 11.00 11.00

Souvenir Sheet

HMS Queen Elizabeth — A372

2018, May 10 Litho. *Perf. 12*
1669 A372 £3 multi 8.00 8.00

Royal Air Force, Cent. — A373

Designs: No. 1670, 22p, Supermarine Spitfire Mark V. No. 1671, 64p, Hawker Sea Hurricane Mark I in flight. No. 1672, 70p, Consolidated Catalina Mark I on water. No. 1673, 80p, Short Sunderland Mark I on water. £2, Vickers Wellington Mark IC. No. 1675, £3, Lockheed Hudson III (black-and-white photograph).

No. 1676: a, 64p, Eurofighter Typhoon T.1 on ground. b, 70p, Row of Hawker Siddeley Buccaneer S.2 on ground. c, 80p, Hawker Siddeley Nimrod MR in flight. d, £3, Two Boeing C-17A (color photograph).

2018, May 18 Litho. *Perf. 12*
1670-1675 A373 Set of 6 20.00 20.00

Souvenir Sheet

1676 Sheet of 4 14.00 14.00
a. A373 64p multi 1.75 1.75
b. A373 70p multi 1.90 1.90
c. A373 80p multi 2.25 2.25
d. A373 £3 multi 8.00 8.00

Rock of Gibraltar A374

Designs: 22p, Rock of Gibraltar and Moorish Castle. 64p, Southern view from top of Rock of Gibraltar. 70p, Eastern side of Rock of Gibraltar. 80p, Rock of Gibraltar and Catalan Bay Beach. £1, Western side of Rock of Gibraltar (80x30mm). £2, Trintiy Lighthouse at Europa Point (80x30mm).

2018, July 31 Litho. *Perf. 13x13¼*
1677-1682 A374 Set of 6 14.00 14.00
1682a Souvenir sheet of 6, #1677-1682 14.00 14.00

Prince Charles, 70th Birthday — A375

Various photographs of Prince Charles: 22p, 64p, 70p, 80p, £2, £3.

2018, Sept. 21 Litho. *Perf. 12½*
1683-1688 A375 Set of 6 19.50 19.50

End of World War I, Cent. — A376

No. 1689: a, Soldiers leaving trench. b, Ten soldiers marching. c, Six soldiers marching under clouds. d, Eleven soldiers standing.

No. 1690, Gibraltar Arboretum War Memorial.

2018, Sept. 21 Litho. *Perf. 12½*
1689 A376 Sheet of 4 14.50 14.50
a. 70p multi 1.90 1.90
b. 80p multi 2.10 2.10
c. £1 multi 2.60 2.60
d. £3 multi 7.75 7.75

Souvenir Sheet

1690 A376 £3 multi 7.75 7.75

Christmas — A377

Painting by: 22p, Bernardino Luini. 40p, Fra Angelico. 64p, Gentile da Fabriano. 70p, Luini, diff. 80p, Fabriano, diff. £2, Giotto. £3, Johann Martin.

2018, Nov. 2 Litho. *Perf. 12*
1691-1697 A377 Set of 7 20.00 20.00
1697a Souvenir sheet of 7, #1691-1697 20.00 20.00

SEMI-POSTAL STAMPS

Souvenir Sheet

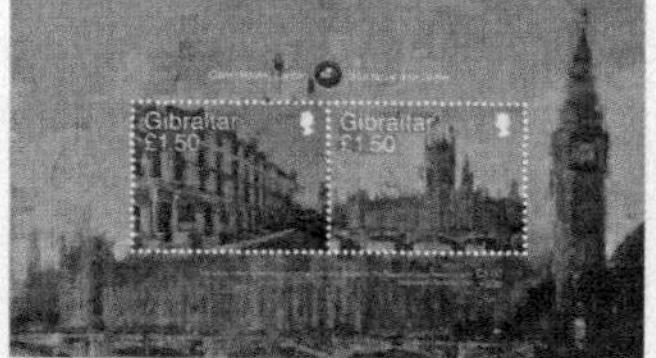

Calpe House, London — SP1

No B1: a, New Calpe House, London. b, Houses of Parliament and Westminster Bridge, London.

2018, Nov. 2 Litho. *Perf. 12*
B1 SP1 Sheet of 2 9.00 9.00
a.-b. £1.50 Either single 4.50 4.50

Calpe House, lodging for Gibraltar residents traveling to London for medical treatment. No. B1 sold for £3.50, with 50p going to the Friends of Calpe House Charity.

POSTAGE DUE STAMPS

Catalogue values for unused stamps in this section are for Never Hinged items.

D1

Perf. 14
1956, Dec. 1 Wmk. 4 Typo.
Chalky Paper
J1 D1 1p green 1.25 *1.75*
J2 D1 2p brown 2.00 *3.00*
J3 D1 4p ultramarine 2.50 *3.50*
Nos. J1-J3 (3) 5.75 *8.25*

"p" instead of "d"
Perf. 17½x18
1971, Feb. 15 Typo. Wmk. 314
Chalky Paper
J4 D1 ½p green .30 *.60*
J5 D1 1p dark brown .35 *.55*
J6 D1 2p dark blue .45 *.60*
Nos. J4-J6 (3) 1.10 *1.75*

D2

Perf. 14x13½
1976, Oct. 13 Litho. Wmk. 373
J7 D2 1p orange .25 *.50*
J8 D2 3p bright ultra .25 *.50*
J9 D2 5p vermilion .25 *.65*
J10 D2 7p bright red lilac .25 *.75*
J11 D2 10p gray .35 *1.50*
J12 D2 20p green .65 *2.25*
Nos. J7-J12 (6) 2.00 *6.15*

D3

1984, July 2 *Perf. 14½x14*
J13 D3 1p black .25 .25
J14 D3 3p red .25 .25
J15 D3 5p blue .25 .25
J16 D3 10p sky blue .40 *.40*
J17 D3 25p lilac 1.00 *1.25*
J18 D3 50p orange 1.75 *2.00*
J19 D3 £1 green 3.00 *4.00*
Nos. J13-J19 (7) 6.90 *8.40*

D4

Landmarks: 1p, Water Port Gates. 10p, HM Dockyard. 25p, Military Hospital. 50p, Governor's Cottage. £1, Laguna. £2, Catalan Bay.

1996, Sept. 30 Litho. *Perf. 14½x14*
J20 D4 1p multicolored .25 .25
J21 D4 10p multicolored .35 .35
J22 D4 25p multicolored .80 .80
J23 D4 50p multicolored 1.50 1.50
J24 D4 £1 multicolored 2.75 2.75
J25 D4 £2 multicolored 5.75 5.75
Nos. J20-J25 (6) 11.40 11.40

Finches — D5

Designs: 5p, Greenfinch. 10p, Serin. 20p, Siskin. 50p, Linnet. £1, Chaffinch. £2, Goldfinch.

Perf. 13x13¼
2002, June 6 Litho. Unwmk.
J26-J31 D5 Set of 6 14.00 14.00

WAR TAX STAMP

No. 66 Overprinted

1918, Apr. Wmk. 3 *Perf. 14*
MR1 A14 ½p green 1.75 *2.40*
a. Double overprint 900.00

GILBERT & ELLICE ISLANDS

'gil-bərt ən,d, 'e-ləs 'ī-lənds

LOCATION — Groups of islands in the Pacific Ocean northeast of Australia
GOVT. — British Crown Colony
AREA — 375 sq. mi.
POP. — 57,816 (est. 1973)
CAPITAL — Tarawa

The Gilbert group of which Butaritari, Tarawa and Tamana are the more important, is on the Equator. Ellice Islands, Phoenix Islands, Line Islands (Fanning, Washington and Christmas), and Ocean Island are included in the Colony. The islands were annexed by Great Britain in 1892 and formed into the Gilbert and Ellice Islands Colony in 1915 on request of the native governments.

The colony divided into the Gilbert Islands and Tuvalu, Jan. 1, 1976.

12 Pence = 1 Shilling
20 Shillings = 1 Pound
100 Cents = 1 Dollar (1966)

Catalogue values for unused stamps in this country are for Never Hinged items, beginning with Scott 52.

Stamps and Type of Fiji Overprinted in Black or Red

1911, Jan. 1 Wmk. 3 *Perf. 14*

Ordinary Paper

1 A22 ½p green 7.50 *52.50*
2 A22 1p carmine 52.50 30.00
a. Pair, one without overprint
3 A22 2p gray 22.50 *17.50*
4 A22 2½p ultramarine 18.50 *52.50*

Chalky Paper

5 A22 5p violet & ol grn 67.50 *97.50*
6 A22 6p violet 26.00 *52.50*
7 A22 1sh black, *green* 27.00 *72.50*
Nos. 1-7 (7) 221.50 *375.00*

Nos. 1-7 are known with a forged Ocean Island postmark dated "JY 15 11."

Pandanus — A2

1911, Mar. Engr. Ordinary Paper

8 A2 ½p green 5.00 *25.00*
9 A2 1p carmine 2.75 *12.50*
10 A2 2p gray 1.75 *7.00*
11 A2 2½p ultramarine 13.00 *17.50*
Nos. 8-11 (4) 22.50 *62.50*

King George V — A3

For description of Dies I and II, see front section of the Catalogue.

1912-24 Die I Typo.

14 A3 ½p deep green .60 *6.00*
15 A3 1p carmine 2.50 *15.50*
a. 1p scarlet ('15) 4.25 *15.00*
16 A3 2p gray ('16) 16.00 *27.00*
17 A3 2½p ultra ('16) 3.25 *11.50*

Chalky Paper

18 A3 3p vio, *yel* ('19) 2.75 *13.50*
19 A3 4p blk & red, *yel* .90 *6.50*
20 A3 5p vio & ol grn 2.00 *6.25*
21 A3 6p vio & red vio 1.50 *6.75*
22 A3 1sh black, *green* 1.50 *5.25*
23 A3 2sh vio & ultra, *bl* 15.00 *36.00*
24 A3 2sh6p blk & red, *bl* 23.00 *26.00*
25 A3 5sh grn & red, *yel* 37.50 *67.50*

Die II

26 A3 £1 vio & blk, *red* ('24) 600.00 *1,650.*
Nos. 14-26 (13) 706.50 *1,878.*

Die II

1921-27 Wmk. 4 Ordinary Paper

27 A3 ½p green 4.00 3.50
28 A3 1p deep vio ('27) 5.00 *8.75*
29 A3 1½p scarlet ('24) 8.50 3.75
30 A3 2p gray 8.00 *47.50*

Chalky Paper

31 A3 10sh green & red, *emer* ('24) 170.00 *400.00*
Nos. 27-31 (5) 195.50 *463.50*

Common Design Types pictured following the introduction.

Silver Jubilee Issue

Common Design Type

1935, May 6 Engr. *Perf. 11x12*

33 CD301 1p black & ultra 2.40 *17.50*
34 CD301 1½p car & blue 1.90 *3.50*
35 CD301 3p ultra & brn 6.50 *26.00*
36 CD301 1sh brn vio & indigo 26.00 *20.00*
Nos. 33-36 (4) 36.80 *67.00*
Set, never hinged 62.50

Coronation Issue

Common Design Type

1937, May 12 *Perf. 13½x14*

37 CD302 1p dark purple .25 *.70*
38 CD302 1½p carmine .25 *.70*
39 CD302 3p bright ultra .35 *.75*
Nos. 37-39 (3) .85 *2.15*
Set, never hinged 1.10

Great Frigate Bird — A4

Pandanus — A5

Designs: 1½p, Canoe crossing reef. 2p, Canoe and boat house. 2½p, Islander's house. 3p, Seascape. 5p, Ellice Islands canoe. 6p, Coconut trees. 1sh, Phosphate loading jetty, Ocean Island. 2sh, Cutter "Nimanoa." 2sh6p, Gilbert Islands canoe. 5sh, Coat of arms of colony.

Perf. 11½x11 (Nos. 40, 43, 50), 12½ (Type A5), 13½ (Nos. 42, 44, 45, 48)

1939, Jan. 14 Engr. Wmk. 4

40 A4 ½p dk grn & sl bl .35 *1.00*
41 A5 1p dk vio & brt bl green .25 *1.50*
42 A4 1½p car & black .25 *1.25*
43 A4 2p black & brn .75 *1.00*
44 A4 2½p dp olive & blk .55 *1.00*
45 A4 3p ultra & black .35 *1.00*
a. Perf. 12 ('55) .55 *3.50*
46 A5 5p dk brn & dp ultra 3.25 2.75
47 A5 6p dl vio & olive .40 *.60*
48 A4 1sh gray bl & blk 8.00 3.75
b. Perf. 12 ('51) 1.75 *20.00*
49 A5 2sh red org & ultra 4.75 11.00
50 A4 2sh6p brt bl grn & bl 4.75 *11.00*
51 A5 5sh dp blue & red 6.50 *16.00*
Nos. 40-51 (12) 30.15 *51.85*
Set, never hinged 57.50

Catalogue values for unused stamps in this section, from this point to the end of the section, are for Never Hinged items.

Peace Issue

Common Design Type

1946, Dec. 16 *Perf. 13½x14*

52 CD303 1p deep magenta .25 *.55*
53 CD303 3p deep blue .25 *.55*

Silver Wedding Issue

Common Design Types

1949, Aug. 29 Photo. *Perf. 14x14½*

54 CD304 1p violet .25 *1.25*

Engraved; Name Typographed

Perf. 11½x11

55 CD305 £1 red 14.00 *25.00*

UPU Issue

Common Design Types

Engr.; Name Typo. on 2p, 3p

1949, Oct. 1 *Perf. 13½, 11x11½*

56 CD306 1p rose violet .70 *2.50*
57 CD307 2p gray black 2.00 *4.00*
58 CD308 3p indigo .85 *4.00*
59 CD309 1sh blue .75 *2.50*
Nos. 56-59 (4) 4.30 *13.00*

Coronation Issue

Common Design Type

1953, June 2 Engr. *Perf. 13½x13*

60 CD312 2p gray & black .65 *2.25*

Types of 1939-42 with Portrait of Queen Elizabeth II, and

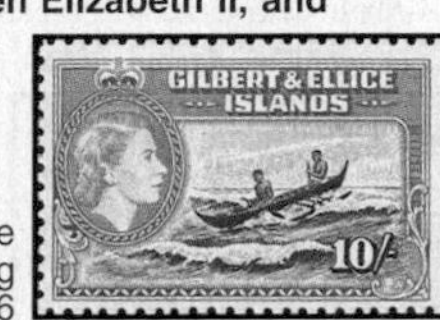

Canoe Crossing Reef — A6

Perf. 11½x11 (Nos. 61, 63, 70), 12½ (Type A5), 12 (Nos. 64-65, 68, 72)

1956, Aug. 1

61 A4 ½p brt ultra & blk .65 *1.25*
62 A5 1p violet & olive .60 *1.25*
63 A4 2p dull pur & brt green .90 *2.50*
64 A4 2½p green & black .50 *.65*
65 A4 3p dk car & black .50 *.65*
66 A5 5p red org & brt ultra 8.75 3.75
67 A5 6p dk gray & red brn .85 *2.75*
68 A4 1sh ol green & blk 3.00 1.25
69 A5 2sh dk brn & brt ultra 6.00 4.00
70 A4 2sh6p dp ultra & rose red 7.50 4.25
71 A5 5sh green & blue 8.50 6.00
72 A6 10sh turq blue & blk 29.00 10.00
Nos. 61-72 (12) 66.75 *38.30*

See Nos. 84-85.

Loading Phosphate on Freighter A7

2½p, Original lump of phosphate. 1sh, Loading phosphate on truck, Ocean Island.

Wmk. 314

1960, May 1 Photo. *Perf. 12*

73 A7 2p rose lilac & green .80 *.85*
74 A7 2½p olive & black .80 *.85*
75 A7 1sh grnsh blue & blk .80 *.85*
Nos. 73-75 (3) 2.40 2.55

60th anniversary of the discovery of phosphate deposits at Ocean Island.

Freedom from Hunger Issue

Common Design Type

1963, June 4 *Perf. 14x14½*

76 CD314 10p ultramarine 1.40 .40

Red Cross Centenary Issue

Common Design Type

1963, Sept. 2 Litho. *Perf. 13*

77 CD315 2p black & red .65 *1.00*
78 CD315 10p ultra & red 1.35 *2.50*

Plane and Fiji-Ellice-Gilbert Route — A8

Designs: 1sh, Eastern reef heron in flight, horiz. 3sh7p, Plane and Tarawa sailboat.

1964, July 20 *Perf. 11½x11, 11x11½*

79 A8 3p lt blue, bl & blk .75 .35
80 A8 1sh dk blue, bl & blk .90 .35
81 A8 3sh7p lt green, grn & blk 1.50 1.50
Nos. 79-81 (3) 3.15 2.20

Inauguration of air service between Fiji and Gilbert and Ellice Islands.

Queen Types of 1956

Perf. 11½x11, 12½

1964-65 Engr. Wmk. 314

84 A4 2p dull pur & brt green 1.10 *1.40*
85 A5 6p dk gray & red brown 1.50 1.50

Issue dates: 2p, Oct. 30. 6p, Apr. 1965.

ITU Issue

Common Design Type

1965, June 4 Litho. *Perf. 11x11½*

87 CD317 3p dp org & turq blue .25 .25
88 CD317 2sh6p grnsh bl & red lilac .60 .35

Village Elder Blowing Conch and Meeting House (Maneaba) — A9

Designs: 1p, Ellice Islanders torch fishing. 2p, Gilbertese girl weaving frangipani garland. 3p, Gilbertese woman dancing The Ruoia. 4p, Gilbertese man dancing. 5p, Gilbertese woman drawing water. 6p, Ellice kosu dance. 7p, Fatele taua dance, Ellice men. 1sh, Gilbertese woman harvesting taro roots (babai). 1sh6p, Ellice man and woman dancing fatele toka. 2sh, Ellice Islanders pounding taro roots. 3sh7p, Gilbertese sitting dance, ruoia, horiz. 5sh, Gilbertese boys playing stick game, horiz. 10sh, Ellice men beating box-drum, horiz. £1, Coat of arms, horiz.

Perf. 12x11, 11x12

1965, Aug. 16 Litho. Wmk. 314

89 A9 ½p blue grn & multi .25 .25
90 A9 1p vio bl & multi .25 .25
91 A9 2p lt olive & multi .25 .25
92 A9 3p red & multi .25 .25
93 A9 4p purple & multi .25 .25
94 A9 5p car rose & multi .25 .25
95 A9 6p multicolored .25 .25
96 A9 7p brown & multi .40 .25
97 A9 1sh bl vio & multi .70 .25
98 A9 1sh6p yel & multi 1.00 1.00
99 A9 2sh multicolored 1.15 *1.40*
100 A9 3sh7p ultra & multi 1.60 .70
101 A9 5sh multicolored 1.75 .90
102 A9 10sh green & multi 2.50 1.10
103 A9 £1 blue & multi 3.00 1.90
Nos. 89-103 (15) 13.85 9.25

See Nos. 135-149. For surcharges see Nos. 110-124.

Intl. Cooperation Year Issue

Common Design Type

1965, Oct. 25 Litho. *Perf. 14½*

104 CD318 ½p blue grn & cl .25 .25
105 CD318 3sh7p lt violet & grn .60 .35

Churchill Memorial Issue

Common Design Type

1966, Jan. 24 Photo. *Perf. 14*

Design in Black, Gold and Carmine Rose

106 CD319 ½p brt blue .25 .25
107 CD319 3p green .30 .25
108 CD319 3sh brown .45 .40
109 CD319 3sh7p violet .50 .40
Nos. 106-109 (4) 1.50 1.30

Nos. 89-103 Surcharged

Perf. 12x11, 11x12

1966, Feb. 14 Litho.

110	A9	1c on 1p multi	.25	.25
111	A9	2c on 2p multi	.25	.25
112	A9	3c on 3p multi	.25	.25
113	A9	4c on ½p multi	.25	.25
114	A9	5c on 6p multi	.25	.25
115	A9	6c on 4p multi	.25	.25
116	A9	8c on 5p multi	.25	.25
117	A9	10c on 1sh multi	.25	.25
118	A9	15c on 7p multi	.70	*1.00*
119	A9	20c on 1sh6p multi	.50	.40
120	A9	25c on 2sh multi	.50	.35
121	A9	35c on 3sh7p multi	1.10	.25
122	A9	50c on 5sh multi	.60	.45
123	A9	$1 on 10sh multi	.60	.50
124	A9	$2 on £1 multi	2.00	*3.25*
		Nos. 110-124 (15)	8.00	8.20

World Cup Soccer Issue
Common Design Type

1966, July 1 Litho. *Perf. 14*

125	CD321	3c multicolored	.25	.25
126	CD321	35c multicolored	.45	.35

WHO Headquarters Issue
Common Design Type

1966, Sept. 20 Litho. *Perf. 14*

127	CD322	3c multicolored	.25	.25
128	CD322	12c multicolored	.55	.45

UNESCO Anniversary Issue
Common Design Type

1966, Dec. 1 Litho. *Perf. 14*

129	CD323	5c "Education"	.50	*.80*
130	CD323	10c "Science"	.75	.25
131	CD323	20c "Culture"	1.25	*1.40*
		Nos. 129-131 (3)	2.50	*2.45*

H.M.S. Royalist, 1892, and Union Jack A10

10c, Cutter & canoe at trading post. 35c, Family.

Perf. 14½x14

1967, Sept. 1 Photo. Wmk. 314

132	A10	3c green, blue & red	.25	*.50*
133	A10	10c multicolored	.25	.25
134	A10	35c multicolored	.25	*.50*
		Nos. 132-134 (3)	.75	*1.25*

75th anniv. as a British Protectorate.

Type of 1965
Perf. 12x11, 11x12

1968, Jan. 1 Litho. Wmk. 314

135	A9	1c like 1p	.25	.25
136	A9	2c like 2p	.25	.25
137	A9	3c like 3p	.25	.25
138	A9	4c like ½p	.25	.25
139	A9	5c like 6p	.25	.25
140	A9	6c like 4p	.25	.25
141	A9	8c like 5p	.25	.25
142	A9	10c like 1sh	.25	.25
143	A9	15c like 7p	.50	.25
144	A9	20c like 1sh6p	.70	.25
145	A9	25c like 2sh	1.25	.25
146	A9	35c like 3sh7p	1.50	.25
147	A9	50c like 5sh	1.50	*2.50*
148	A9	$1 like 10sh	1.75	*3.75*
149	A9	$2 like £1	4.50	*5.50*
		Nos. 135-149 (15)	13.70	14.75

Map of Tarawa Atoll — A11

Designs: 10c, US Marines wading ashore at Betio. 15c, Battle scene on Betio. 35c, Raising US and British flags on Betio.

1968, Nov. 21 Photo. *Perf. 14*

150	A11	3c multicolored	.25	.25
151	A11	10c multicolored	.25	.25
152	A11	15c multicolored	.25	*.35*
153	A11	35c multicolored	.25	*.50*
		Nos. 150-153 (4)	1.00	1.35

Battle of Tarawa against Japan, 25th anniv.

School Boy and Map of Abemama Atoll A12

Designs: 10c, Secondary school boy and girl on map of Tarawa, with rest of Gilbert and Ellice Islands. 35c, Student in cap and gown on main Fiji island (Viti Levu) and map of South Pacific Islands.

1969, June 2 Litho. *Perf. 12½*

154	A12	3c dull org & multi	.25	.25
155	A12	10c black & multi	.25	.25
156	A12	35c dull grn & multi	.25	*.35*
		Nos. 154-156 (3)	.75	.85

1st anniv. of the University of the South Pacific in Fiji, and to show the progress of education in the area it serves.

Polynesian Madonna A13

1969, Oct. 20 *Perf. 11½*

157	A13	2c multicolored	.25	.25
158	A13	10c multicolored	.25	.25

Christmas.

Canceled to Order

The Philatelic Bureau of Gilbert and Ellice Islands began in 1970 to sell canceled sets of new issues. Values in the second ("used") column are for these canceled-to-order stamps.

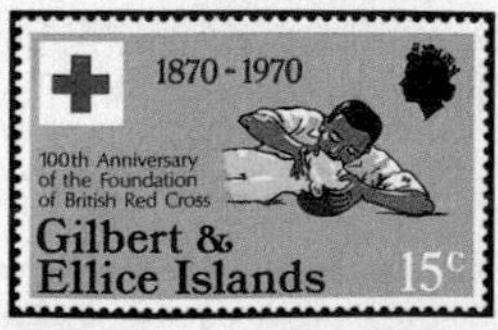

Mouth-to-Mouth Resuscitation — A14

1970, Mar. 9 Litho. *Perf. 14½*

159	A14	10c multi	.25	.25
160	A14	15c multi, diff.	.35	*.45*
161	A14	35c multi, diff.	.50	*.90*
		Nos. 159-161 (3)	1.10	1.60

Centenary of the British Red Cross.

Mother and Child Care A15

Designs: 10c, Woman physician and laboratory equipment. 15c, Chest X-ray and technician. 35c, Map of Gilbert and Ellice Islands and UN emblem.

Perf. 12½x13

1970, June 26 Litho. Wmk. 314

162	A15	5c lilac & multi	.25	.25
163	A15	10c black, gray & red	.25	.25
164	A15	15c yellow & multi	.25	.25
165	A15	35c blue grn, bl & blk	.30	*.45*
		Nos. 162-165 (4)	1.05	1.20

25th anniv. of the United Nations.

Map of Onotoa, Beru, Tamana and Arorae Islands A16

Designs: 10c, Sailing ship "John Williams III," vert. 25c, Rev. Samuel James Whitmee, vert. 35c, Map of Islands and steamship "John Williams VII."

Perf. 14x14½, 14½x14

1970, Sept. 1 Litho. Wmk. 314

166	A16	2c blue & multi	.25	.25
167	A16	10c brt green & black	.35	.25
168	A16	25c lt ultra & red brn	.25	.25
169	A16	35c ver, blk & lt gray	.55	*.65*
		Nos. 166-169 (4)	1.40	1.40

Centenary of the landing in the Southern Gilbert Islands by the first missionaries of the London Missionary Society.

Island Child with Halo on Pandanus Mat — A17

Christmas: 10c, Sanctuary of New Tarawa Cathedral. 35c, Three Gilbertese sailing canoes within Star of Bethlehem.

1970, Oct. 3 *Perf. 14½*

170	A17	2c ocher & multi	.25	.25
171	A17	10c ocher & multi	.25	.25
172	A17	35c pink & multi	.25	.25
		Nos. 170-172 (3)	.75	.75

Harvesting Copra — A18

Lagoon Fishing A19

3c, Women cleaning pandanus leaves. 4c, Fishermen casting nets. 5c, Gilbertese canoes. 6c, Dehusking coconuts. 8c, Woman weaving pandanus fronds. 10c, Basket weaving. 15c, Tiger shark. 20c, Beating rolled pandanus leaf. 25c, Loading copra. 35c, Night fishing. 50c, Local handicraft. $1, Woman weaving coconut screen. $2, Coat of arms.

Wmk. 314 Upright (A18), Sideways (A19)

1971, May 31 Litho. *Perf. 14*

173	A18	1c multicolored	.25	.25
174	A19	2c multicolored	.25	.25
175	A19	3c multicolored	.25	.25
176	A19	4c multicolored	.30	.25
177	A19	5c multicolored	.60	.25
178	A18	6c multicolored	.40	.35
179	A18	8c multicolored	.55	.35
180	A18	10c multicolored	.50	.45
181	A18	15c multicolored	3.00	.90
182	A19	20c multicolored	1.60	1.75
183	A19	25c multicolored	2.00	1.40
184	A19	35c multicolored	2.40	1.00
185	A18	50c multicolored	1.25	2.40
186	A18	$1 multicolored	1.75	*2.00*
187	A18	$2 multicolored	4.75	*8.00*
		Nos. 173-187 (15)	19.85	19.85

Wmk. 314 Upright (A19), Sideways (A18)

1972-73

174a	A19	2c multicolored	9.25	*16.00*
177a	A19	5c multicolored	3.50	*4.25*
178a	A18	6c multicolored	9.25	*16.50*
181a	A18	15c multicolored	3.75	*5.00*
182a	A19	20c multicolored	4.00	*6.00*
		Nos. 174a-182a (5)	29.75	*47.75*

Issue dates: 9/7/72, 5c, 15c, 20c; 6/13/73, 2c, 6c.

Legislative Council, 1971 (former House of Representatives) — A20

New Constitution: 10c, Meeting House.

1971, Aug. 1 Wmk. 314 *Perf. 14*

188	A20	3c orange & multi	.25	.25
189	A20	10c green & multi	.25	.25

Nativity Scene — A21

Christmas: 10c, Star of Bethlehem and palm fronds. 35c, Fishermen in outrigger canoe looking at Star.

1971, Oct. 1

190	A21	3c vio blue, blk & yel	.25	*.35*
191	A21	10c grnsh bl, blk & gold	.25	.25
192	A21	35c car rose, blk & rose	.25	*.35*
		Nos. 190-192 (3)	.75	*.95*

Children and UNICEF Emblem A22

25th Anniv. of UNICEF: 10c, Seated child. 35c, Child's head.

1971, Dec. 11

193	A22	3c brt pink & multi	.25	*.80*
194	A22	10c black & multi	.25	.25
195	A22	35c blue & multi	.55	*.80*
		Nos. 193-195 (3)	1.05	*1.85*

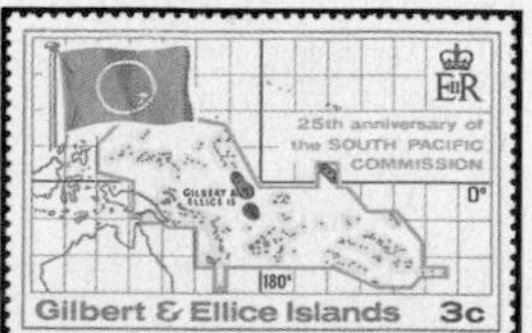

Commission Flag, Map of South Pacific — A23

South Pacific Commission, 25th Anniv.: 10c, Island boats. 35c, Flags of 8 member nations plus Tonga, a non-member.

1972, Feb. 21				*Perf. 13½x14*	
196	A23	3c	gray & multi	.25	*.30*
197	A23	10c	tan, ultra & brown	.25	.25
198	A23	35c	ultra & multi	.25	*.85*
			Nos. 196-198 (3)	.75	*1.40*

Corals A24

1972, May 26				*Perf. 14x14½*	
199	A24	3c	Alveopora	.25	*.40*
200	A24	10c	Euphyllia	.40	.25
201	A24	15c	Melithea	.55	.35
202	A24	35c	Spongodes	1.50	.90
			Nos. 199-202 (4)	2.70	1.90

"Peace" on Star of Bethlehem A25

Christmas: 10c, Holy Family, made of shells. 35c, Christ child sleeping in giant clam and covered with dawn cowrie, horiz.

1972, Sept. 15				*Perf. 13½*	
203	A25	3c	gold & multi	.25	.25
204	A25	10c	gold & multi	.25	.25
205	A25	35c	gold & multi	.25	.25
			Nos. 203-205 (3)	.75	.75

Silver Wedding Issue, 1972
Common Design Type

Design: Queen Elizabeth II, Prince Philip and kaue floral headdress.

1972, Nov. 20	**Photo.**		*Perf. 14x14½*	
206	CD324	3c olive & multi	.25	.25
207	CD324	35c rose brown & multi	.25	.25

Funafuti, Land of Bananas A26

Designs: 10c, Butaritari, the smell of the sea. 25c, Tarawa, the center of the world. 35c, Abemama, the land of the moon.

1973, Mar. 5			**Litho.**	*Perf. 14½x14*	
208	A26	3c	yellow & multi	.25	*.55*
209	A26	10c	brt green & multi	.30	.35
210	A26	25c	dull blue & multi	.40	*.60*
211	A26	35c	orange & multi	.45	*.70*
			Nos. 208-211 (4)	1.40	*2.20*

Legends of island names.

Ellice Dancer — A27

Christmas (Within Outline of Nautilus Shell): 10c, Outrigger canoe in lagoon. 35c, Evening on the lagoon. 50c, Map of Christmas Island, Pacific Ocean.

1973, Sept. 24				*Perf. 14*	
212	A27	3c	vio blue & multi	.25	.25
213	A27	10c	multicolored	.25	.25
214	A27	35c	multicolored	.25	.25
215	A27	50c	vio blue & multi	.30	*1.50*
			Nos. 212-215 (4)	1.05	2.25

Princess Anne's Wedding Issue
Common Design Type

1973, Nov. 14			*Perf. 14*	
216	CD325	3c brt green & multi	.25	.25
217	CD325	35c slate & multi	.25	.25

Meteorological Observation — A28

WMO Emblem and: 10c, Island observation station. 35c, Wind finding radar. 50c, Map of Gilbert and Ellice Islands world weather watch stations.

1973, Nov. 26			**Litho.**	*Perf. 14½*	
218	A28	3c	orange & multi	.75	.45
219	A28	10c	dp bister & multi	.80	.30
220	A28	35c	gray & multi	1.00	.45
221	A28	50c	dk blue & multi	1.50	1.50
			Nos. 218-221 (4)	4.05	2.70

Cent. of intl. meteorological cooperation.

Te-Mataaua Crest and Canoe — A29

Designs: Various family crests and canoes.

1974, Mar. 4			**Litho.**	*Perf. 13½*	
222	A29	3c	tan & multi	.25	.25
223	A29	10c	lt blue & multi	.25	.25
224	A29	35c	yellow & multi	.25	.25
225	A29	50c	pink & multi	.25	*1.50*
a.			Souvenir sheet of 4, #222-225	6.25	*7.50*
			Nos. 222-225 (4)	1.00	2.25

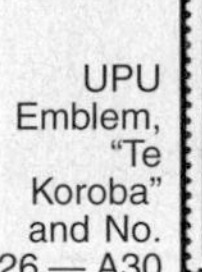

UPU Emblem, "Te Koroba" and No. 26 — A30

UPU cent.: 10c, Sailing ship "Kiakia" and No. 51. 25c, BAC 111 jet and No. 187. 35c, UPU emblem.

1974, June 10				*Perf. 14*	
226	A30	4c	blue green & multi	.25	*.35*
227	A30	10c	orange & multi	.25	.25
228	A30	25c	dp blue & multi	.25	.25
229	A30	35c	red orange & black	.35	*.45*
			Nos. 226-229 (4)	1.10	1.30

Toy Canoe, Star and Boat A31

Star of Bethlehem and: 10c, Pinwheel and boat. 25c, Coconut ball (crate) and boat. 35c, Three boats (Wise Men) and stars.

1974, Sept. 23					
230	A31	4c	yel green & multi	.25	.25
231	A31	10c	red brown & multi	.25	.25
232	A31	25c	multicolored	.25	*.45*
233	A31	35c	red brown & multi	.25	*.55*
			Nos. 230-233 (4)	1.00	1.50

Christmas.

Blenheim Palace, Entrance — A32

Churchill Painting — A33

Design: 35c, Churchill Statue, London.

1974, Nov. 30			**Litho.**	*Perf. 14*	
234	A32	4c	multicolored	.25	*.35*
235	A33	10c	ultra & black	.25	.25
236	A33	35c	blue, ocher & blk	.25	*.45*
			Nos. 234-236 (3)	.75	*1.05*

Sir Winston Churchill (1874-1965).

Carpilius Maculatus — A34

Crabs: 10c, Ranina ranina. 25c, Portunus pelagicus. 35c, Ocypode ceratophthalma.

1975, Jan. 27			**Litho.**	*Perf. 14*	
237	A34	4c	violet & multi	.25	*1.00*
238	A34	10c	green & multi	.50	.50
239	A34	25c	buff & multi	1.25	1.25
240	A34	35c	lt blue & multi	1.50	*1.75*
			Nos. 237-240 (4)	3.50	4.50

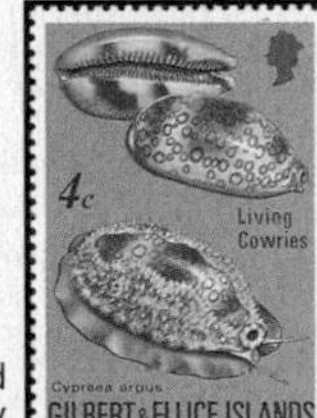

Living Cowries and Empty Shells — A35

1975, May 26			**Wmk. 314**	*Perf. 14*	
241	A35	4c	Cypraea argus	.55	*1.00*
242	A35	10c	Cypraea cribraria	.80	.50
243	A35	25c	Cypraea talpa	1.40	*1.60*
244	A35	35c	Cypraea mappa	2.25	*2.50*
a.			Souvenir sheet of 4, #241-244	16.00	*17.00*
			Nos. 241-244 (4)	5.00	*5.60*

Map of Beru (The Bud) A36

Designs: 10c, Map of Onotoa (Six Giants) 25c, Map of Abaiang (Land to the North). 35c, Map of Marakei (Floating fish trap).

Wmk. 314

1975, Aug. 1			**Litho.**	*Perf. 14*	
245	A36	4c	brt green & multi	.25	*.45*
246	A36	10c	brown & multi	.25	.25
247	A36	25c	vio blue & multi	.25	*.35*
248	A36	35c	org red & multi	.40	.50
			Nos. 245-248 (4)	1.15	*1.55*

Legends of island names.

Christ Child Within Coconut — A37

Christmas: 10c, Sadd Memorial Chapel (Protestant), Tarawa. 25c, R.C. Church, Ocean Island. 35c, Fishermen in outrigger canoes seeing star.

1975, Sept. 22				*Perf. 14*	
249	A37	4c	brown & multi	.25	*.75*
250	A37	10c	brt blue & multi	.25	.25
251	A37	25c	violet & multi	.35	*.90*
252	A37	35c	green & multi	.45	*1.50*
			Nos. 249-252 (4)	1.30	*3.40*

POSTAGE DUE STAMPS

D1

1940, Aug.	**Typo.**	**Wmk. 4**		*Perf. 12*	
J1	D1	1p	emerald	5.50	*25.00*
J2	D1	2p	dark red	6.00	*25.00*
J3	D1	3p	chocolate	8.25	*25.00*
J4	D1	4p	deep blue	10.00	*26.00*
J5	D1	5p	deep green	12.00	*35.00*
J6	D1	6p	brt red vio	12.00	*35.00*
J7	D1	1sh	dull violet	20.00	*47.50*
J8	D1	1sh6p	turq green	30.00	*90.00*
			Nos. J1-J8 (8)	103.75	*308.50*
			Set, never hinged	180.00	

WAR TAX STAMP

No. 15a Overprinted

1918		**Wmk. 3**	*Perf. 14*	
MR1	A3	1p scarlet	.70	*6.75*

GILBERT ISLANDS

'gil-bərt 'ī-ləndz

LOCATION — A group of islands in the Pacific Ocean northeast of Australia.
GOVT. — British Crown Colony
AREA — 270 sq. mi.
POP. — 52,000 (1973)
CAPITAL — Tarawa

The Gilbert Islands Colony consists of the Gilbert Islands, Phoenix, Ocean and Line Islands. They were part of the Gilbert and Ellice Islands colony until 1976. See Tuvalu.

Catalogue values for all unused stamps in this country are for Never Hinged items.

Stamps and Types of Gilbert and Ellice Islands 1971 Overprinted in Red, Black or Gold

Wmk. 373; 314 (2c, 4c)

1976, Jan. 2 Litho. *Perf. 14*

253 A18 1c multi (R) .25 *1.60*
a. Watermark 314 .25 *.90*
254 A19 2c multi (R) .45 *.30*
a. Watermark upright .55 2.40
255 A19 3c multi (R) .40 *2.50*
a. Watermark 314 12.00 21.00
256 A19 4c multi (R) .30 *1.10*
257 A19 5c multi (R) .50 *.90*
258 A18 6c multi (B) .50 *.90*
259 A18 8c multi (B) .50 *1.10*
260 A18 10c multi (B) .50 *1.10*
261 A18 15c multi (B) 2.75 1.40
262 A19 20c multi (R) 1.00 *2.25*
a. Watermark 314 sideways 6.25 3.25
b. Watermark 314 upright *125.00*
263 A19 25c multi (B) 1.50 1.40
a. Watermark 314 29.00 50.00
264 A19 35c multi (G) 2.00 1.75
a. Watermark 314 950.00 1,000.
265 A18 50c multi (B) 1.75 *2.25*
a. Watermark 314 850.00 *1,100.*
266 A18 $1 multi (R) 3.75 *7.75*
Nos. 253-266 (14) 16.15 26.30

Location of overprint varies.

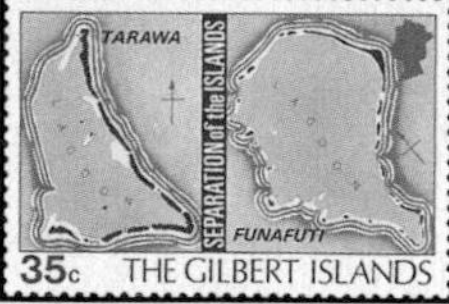

Maps of Tarawa and Funafuti A38

4c, Charts of Gilbert and Tuvalu Islands.

1976, Jan. 2 Wmk. 373

267 A38 4c multicolored .55 *1.00*
268 A38 35c multicolored .90 *1.50*

Separation of the Gilbert and Ellice Islands.

M.V. Teraaka A39

3c, M.V. Tautunu. 4c, Moorish idol. 5c, Hibiscus. 6c, Reef egret. 7c, Roman Catholic Cathedral, Tarawa. 8c, Frangipani. 10c, Maneaba meeting house. 12c, Betio Harbor. 15c, Sunset. 20c, Marakei Atoll. 35c, Chapel, Tangintebu. 40c, Flamboyant tree. 50c, Hypolimnas bolina elliciana (butterfly). $1, Landing craft, Tabakea. $2, Gilbert Islands flag.

1976, July 1 Litho. *Perf. 14*

269 A39 1c multicolored .40 *.65*
270 A39 3c multicolored .60 *.75*
271 A39 4c multicolored .35 *.65*
272 A39 5c multicolored .40 .30
273 A39 6c multicolored 1.50 .90
274 A39 7c multicolored .25 *.30*
275 A39 8c multicolored .25 *.30*
276 A39 10c multicolored .25 *.30*
277 A39 12c multicolored .45 .45
278 A39 15c multicolored .40 .45
279 A39 20c multicolored .25 .35
280 A39 35c multicolored .25 .40
281 A39 40c multicolored .50 .50
282 A39 50c multicolored 1.40 *1.75*
283 A39 $1 multicolored .90 *2.50*
284 A39 $2 multicolored 1.25 *2.50*
Nos. 269-284 (16) 9.40 13.05

Church A40

Children's Drawings: 15c, Feasting (vegetables, fish, pig, chicken), vert. 20c, Communal meeting house, vert. 35c, Children watching dancer.

1976, Sept. 15 Litho. *Perf. 14*

285 A40 5c blue & multi .25 .25
286 A40 15c green & multi .40 .25
287 A40 20c rose & multi .40 .35
288 A40 35c salmon & multi .40 *.50*
Nos. 285-288 (4) 1.45 1.35

Christmas.

Porcupine Fish Helmet — A41

Artifacts: 15c, Shark's teeth dagger. 20c, Fighting gauntlet. 35c, Coconut body armor.

1976, Dec. 6 Litho. *Perf. 13½x13*

289 A41 5c multicolored .25 .25
290 A41 15c multicolored .35 .25
291 A41 20c multicolored .35 .45
292 A41 35c multicolored .60 .55
a. Souvenir sheet of 4, #289-292 8.25 *11.00*
Nos. 289-292 (4) 1.55 1.50

Prince Charles, 1970 Visit — A42

Designs: 20c, Prince Philip, 1959 visit. 40c, Queen in coronation robes.

1977, Feb. 7 *Perf. 14*

293 A42 8c multicolored .25 .25
294 A42 20c multicolored .25 .25
295 A42 40c multicolored .25 *.35*
Nos. 293-295 (3) .75 .85

Reign of Queen Elizabeth II, 25th anniv.

Arrows, Tarawa and Abemama Islands, School Insignia A47

John Byron and Dolphin, 1765 A43

Explorers: 15c, Edmund Fanning, 1798, and "Betsey." 20c, Fabian Gottlieb von Bellingshausen, 1820, and "Vostok." 35c, Charles Wilkes, 1838-42, and "Vincennes."

1977, June 1 Wmk. 373 *Perf. 14*

296 A43 5c multicolored .55 *1.50*
297 A43 15c multicolored .65 *2.75*
298 A43 20c multicolored .65 *2.75*
299 A43 35c multicolored .90 *4.00*
Nos. 296-299 (4) 2.75 *11.00*

Resolution and Discovery off Christmas Island — A44

15c, Capt. Cook's logbook entry, 1777. 20c, Capt. Cook on board ship. 40c, Capt. Cook landing on Christmas Island.

1977, Sept. 12 Litho. *Perf. 14*

300 A44 8c multi .40 .25
301 A44 15c multi, horiz .40 .25
302 A44 20c multi .60 .30
303 A44 40c multi, horiz. .60 .65
a. Souvenir sheet of 4, #300-303 5.00 *7.50*
Nos. 300-303 (4) 2.00 1.45

Christmas; bicentenary of Capt. Cook's discovery of Christmas Island

Scout Emblem, Beach Scene — A45

15c, Patrol meeting. 20c, Scout weaving mat. 40c, Canoeing.

1977, Dec. 5 Litho. *Perf. 13*

304 A45 8c gold & multi .30 .25
305 A45 15c gold & multi, horiz. .40 .25
306 A45 20c gold & multi, horiz. .40 .30
307 A45 40c gold & multi .65 .65
Nos. 304-307 (4) 1.75 1.45

50th anniversary of Gilbert Islands Scouting.

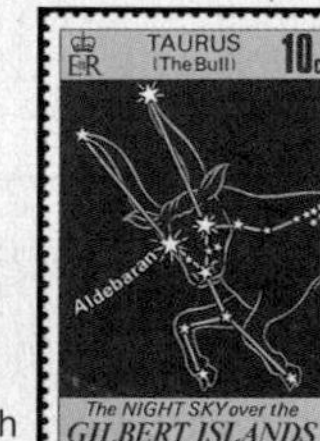

Taurus with Aldebaran — A46

Night Sky over Gilbert Islands: 20c, Canis Major with Sirius. 25c, Scorpio with Antares. 45c, Orion with Betelgeuse and Rigel.

1978, Feb. 20 Litho. *Perf. 14*

308 A46 10c blue & black .50 .35
309 A46 20c dp rose & black .55 .40
310 A46 25c olive grn & black .60 .60
311 A46 45c orange & black .80 *.90*
Nos. 308-311 (4) 2.45 2.25

Common Design Types pictured following the introduction.

Elizabeth II Coronation Anniversary
Common Design Types
Souvenir Sheet

1978, Apr. 21 Unwmk.

312 Sheet of 6 1.25 1.25
a. CD326 45c Unicorn of Scotland .25 .25
b. CD327 45c Elizabeth II .25 .25
c. CD328 45c Great frigate bird .25 .25

10c, Birds inscribed Bikenibeu, Abemama, Bairiki (school locations). 25c, Children greeting each other from maps of Islands. 45c, Abemama & Tarawa school buildings.

Perf. 14x13½

1978, June 5 Wmk. 373

313 A47 10c multicolored .25 .25
314 A47 20c multicolored .25 .25
315 A47 25c multicolored .25 .25
316 A47 45c multicolored .35 .35
Nos. 313-316 (4) 1.10 1.10

King George V School, 25th anniversary of return from Abemama to Tarawa.

Garland A48

Christmas: Various garlands.

1978, Sept. 4 Litho. *Perf. 14*

317 A48 10c multicolored .25 .25
318 A48 20c multicolored .25 .25
319 A48 25c multicolored .25 .25
320 A48 45c multicolored .25 .30
a. Souvenir sheet of 4, #317-320, perf. 13x13½ 1.75 *4.25*
Nos. 317-320 (4) 1.00 1.05

Endeavour A49

Designs: 20c, Green turtle. 25c, Quadrant. 45c, Capt. Cook after Flaxman/Wedgwood medallion.

1979, Jan. 15 Litho. *Perf. 11*

321 A49 10c multicolored .25 .25
322 A49 20c multicolored .30 .30
323 A49 25c multicolored .30 *.45*

Litho.; Embossed

324 A49 45c multicolored .35 *.80*
Nos. 321-324 (4) 1.20 1.80

Capt. Cook's voyages.

Gilbert Islands stamps were replaced in 1979 by those of Kiribati.

GOLD COAST

'gōld 'kōst

LOCATION — West Africa between Togo and Ivory Coast
GOVT. — Former British Crown Colony
AREA — 91,843 sq. mi.
POP. — 3,089,000 (1952)
CAPITAL — Accra

Attached to the colony were Ashanti and Northern Territories (protectorate). Togoland, under British mandate, was also included for administrative purposes.

Gold Coast became the independent state of Ghana in 1957.

See Ghana.

12 Pence = 1 Shilling
20 Shillings = 1 Pound

Catalogue values for unused stamps in this country are for Never Hinged items, beginning with Scott 128.

Queen Victoria — A1

Perf. 12½

1875, July Typo. Wmk. 1

1 A1 1p blue 550.00 100.00
2 A1 4p red violet 525.00 150.00
3 A1 6p orange 825.00 82.50
Nos. 1-3 (3) 1,900. 332.50

1876-79 ***Perf. 14***

4 A1 ½p bister ('79) 100.00 42.50
5 A1 1p blue 42.50 8.00
a. Half used as ½p on cover *4,500.*
6 A1 2p green ('79) 150.00 11.50
a. Half used as 1p on cover *4,250.*
b. Quarter used as ½p on cover *7,500.*
7 A1 4p red violet 275.00 7.25
a. Quarter used as 1p on cover *10,000.*
b. Half used as 2p on cover *8,000.*
8 A1 6p orange 325.00 28.00
a. One sixth used as 1p on cover *13,000.*
b. Half used as 3p on cover *10,000.*
Nos. 4-8 (5) 892.50 97.25

Handstamp Surcharged "1D" in Black

1883, May

9 A1 1p on 4p red violet

Some experts question the status of No. 9. One canceled example is in the British Museum. Another example is supposed to exist (Ferrari).

1883-91 Wmk. 2

10 A1 ½p bister ('83) 275.00 85.00
11 A1 ½p green ('84) 5.00 1.50
12 A1 1p blue ('83) 1,000. 85.00
13 A1 1p rose ('84) 6.25 .60
a. Half used as ½p on cover *5,000.*
14 A1 2p gray ('84) 50.00 7.00
b. Half used as 1p on cover *5,000.*
15 A1 2½p bl & org ('91) 14.00 .85
16 A1 3p ol green ('89) 27.50 15.00
a. 3p olive bister 27.50 13.00
17 A1 4p dull vio ('84) 29.00 4.25
a. 4p claret 65.00 8.00
b. Half used as 2p on cover —
18 A1 6p orange ('89) 27.50 6.50
a. One sixth used as 1p on cover —
19 A1 1sh purple ('88) 16.00 3.25
a. 1sh violet 50.00 15.00
20 A1 2sh brown ('84) 60.00 17.50
a. 2sh yellow brown ('88) 115.00 45.00

No. 18 Surcharged in Black

1889, Mar.

21 A1 1p on 6p orange 150.00 60.00
a. Double surcharge *4,750.*

The surcharge exists in two spacings between "PENNY" and bar: 7mm (normal) and 8mm.

No. 21a does not exist unused.

Queen Victoria — A3

1889

22 A3 5sh lilac & ultra 82.50 30.00
23 A3 10sh lilac & red 145.00 18.00
24 A3 20sh green & red 3,500.

1894

25 A3 20sh vio & blk, *red* 190.00 40.00

1898-1902

26 A3 ½p lilac & green 7.50 1.75
27 A3 1p lil & car rose 8.00 .60
28 A3 2p lil & rod ('02) 60.00 *175.00*
29 A3 2½p lilac & ultra 11.00 12.50
30 A3 3p lilac & yel 11.00 4.75
31 A3 6p lilac & purple 15.00 3.75
32 A3 1sh gray grn & blk 20.00 *45.00*
33 A3 2sh gray grn & car rose 37.50 *45.00*
34 A3 5sh grn & lil ('00) 110.00 65.00
35 A3 10sh grn & brn ('00) 225.00 72.50
Nos. 26-35 (10) 505.00 *425.85*

Numerals of 2p, 3p and 6p of type A3 are in color on colorless tablet.

Nos. 29 and 31 Surcharged in Black

1901, Oct. 6

36 A3 1p on 2½p lil & ultra 12.00 8.00
a. "ONE" omitted 1,200.
37 A3 1p on 6p lilac & pur 12.00 5.50
a. "ONE" omitted 325.00 *650.00*

Beware of copies offered as No. 37a that have part of "ONE" showing.

King Edward VII — A5

1902 Wmk. 2

38 A5 ½p violet & green 1.75 .50
39 A5 1p vio & car rose 1.75 .25
40 A5 2p vio & red org 47.50 8.50
41 A5 2½p vio & ultra 5.50 *11.00*
42 A5 3p vio & orange 7.50 3.00
43 A5 6p violet & pur 8.00 3.00
44 A5 1sh green & blk 25.00 4.50
45 A5 2sh grn & car rose 25.00 *40.00*
46 A5 5sh green & violet 67.50 *120.00*
47 A5 10sh green & brn 87.50 *160.00*
48 A5 20sh vio & blk, *red* 200.00 *210.00*
Nos. 38-48 (11) 477.00 *590.75*

Numerals of 2p, 3p, 6p and 2sh6p of type A5 are in color on colorless tablet.

1904-07 Wmk. 3

Chalky or Ordinary Paper

49 A5 ½p vio & grn ('07) 3.00 4.00
50 A5 1p vio & car rose 17.50 2.75
51 A5 2p vio & red org 16.00 2.50
52 A5 2½p vio & ultra ('06) 65.00 *80.00*
53a A5 3p vio & org ('06) 29.00 1.50
54 A5 6p vio & pur ('06) 90.00 9.00
55 A5 2sh6p grn & yel ('06) 35.00 *140.00*
Nos. 49-55 (7) 255.50 *244.25*

Nos. 50, 51 and 54 exist on both ordinary and chalky paper. No. 55 is on chalky paper only. No. 53a, is the chalky-paper variety of the more expensive No. 53. For detailed listings, see the *Scott Classic Specialized Catalogue of Stamps and Covers.*

1907-13 Ordinary Paper

56 A5 ½p green 12.00 .40
57 A5 1p carmine 20.00 .50
58 A5 2p gray ('09) 3.00 1.00
59 A5 2½p ultramarine 22.50 5.25

Chalky Paper

60 A5 3p vio, *yel* ('09) 9.50 1.25
61 A5 6p dull vio ('08) 42.50 2.25
a. 6p dull violet & red violet 8.50 8.00
62 A5 1sh blk, *grn* ('09) 28.00 1.50
63a A5 2sh Ordinary paper 9.50 19.00
64 A5 2sh6p blk & red, *blue* ('11) 42.50 *105.00*
65 A5 5sh grn & red, *yel* ('13) 65.00 *250.00*
Nos. 56-65 (9) 245.00 *367.15*

No. 63 is on both ordinary and chalky paper.

King Edward VII — A6

1908, Nov. Ordinary Paper

66 A6 1p carmine 9.50 .25

King George V
A7 A8

For description of Dies I and II, see front section of the Catalogue.

Die I

1913-21 Ordinary Paper

69 A7 ½p green 3.00 2.25
70 A8 1p carmine 2.25 .25
a. 1p scarlet 4.25 .60
71 A7 2p gray 12.50 3.00
72 A7 2½p ultramarine 16.00 2.75

Chalky Paper

73 A7 3p vio, *yel* ('15) 4.50 1.00
a. Die II ('19) 65.00 6.75
74 A7 6p dull vio & red vio 14.00 3.00
75 A7 1sh black, *green* 6.75 2.75
a. 1sh black, *emerald* 4.00 2.50
b. 1sh black, *bl grn*, ol back 18.00 .95
c. Die II ('21) 3.25 .60
76 A7 2sh vio & bl, *bl* 14.00 5.25
a. Die II ('21) 190.00 77.50
77 A7 2sh6p blk & red, *bl* 14.50 *16.00*
a. Die II ('21) 45.00 45.00
78 A7 5sh grn & red, *yel* 30.00 *70.00*
a. Die II ('21) 52.50 *180.00*
79 A7 10sh grn & red, *grn* ('16) 70.00 *120.00*
a. 10sh grn & red, *emer* 50.00 *200.00*
b. 10sh grn & red, *bl grn*, ol back 45.00 *100.00*
80 A7 20sh vio & blk, *red* ('16) 175.00 120.00

Surface-colored Paper

81 A7 3p violet, *yel* 2.10 1.00
82 A7 5sh grn & red, *yel* 30.00 *72.50*
Nos. 69-82 (14) 394.60 *419.75*

Numerals of 2p, 3p, 6p and 2sh6p of type A7 are in color on plain tablet.

Die II

1921-25 Ordinary Paper Wmk. 4

83 A7 ½p green ('22) 1.50 .75
84 A8 1p brown ('22) 1.00 .25
85 A7 1½p carmine ('22) 2.75 .25
86 A7 2p gray 2.00 .40
87 A7 2½p orange ('23) 3.25 *16.00*
88 A7 3p ultra ('22) 2.10 1.50

Chalky Paper

89 A7 6p dl vio & red vio ('22) 5.00 *3.50*
90 A7 1sh blk, *emer* ('25) 11.00 4.25
91 A7 2sh vio & bl, *bl* ('24) 4.50 4.00
92 A7 2sh6p blk & red, *bl* ('25) 14.00 *47.50*
93 A7 5sh grn & red, *yel* ('25) 28.00 *85.00*

Die I

94 A7 15sh dl vio & grn ('21) 200.00 *700.00*
a. Die II ('25) 140.00 *700.00*
95 A7 £2 grn & org 550.00 *2,000.*
Nos. 83-95 (13) 825.70 *2,863.*

Christiansborg Castle — A9

1928, Aug. 1 Photo. ***Perf. 13½x14½***

98 A9 ½p green 1.50 .50
99 A9 1p red brown 1.00 .25
100 A9 1½p scarlet 4.50 1.60
101 A9 2p slate 4.50 .25
102 A9 2½p yellow 4.75 3.50
103 A9 3p ultramarine 4.50 .50
104 A9 6p dull vio & blk 5.25 .50
105 A9 1sh red org & blk 8.00 1.90
106 A9 2sh purple & black 36.00 7.25
107 A9 5sh ol green & car 72.50 55.00
Nos. 98-107 (10) 142.50 71.25

Common Design Types pictured following the introduction.

Silver Jubilee Issue
Common Design Type

1935, May 6 Engr. ***Perf. 11x12***

108 CD301 1p black & ultra .75 .60
109 CD301 3p ultra & brown 3.00 *7.50*
110 CD301 6p indigo & grn 17.00 *30.00*
111 CD301 1sh brn vio & indigo 5.00 *40.00*
Nos. 108-111 (4) 25.75 *78.10*
Set, never hinged 40.00

Coronation Issue
Common Design Type

1937, May 12 ***Perf. 11x11½***

112 CD302 1p brown .85 *2.50*
113 CD302 2p dark gray 1.00 *4.75*
114 CD302 3p deep ultra 1.25 *2.75*
Nos. 112-114 (3) 3.10 *10.00*
Set, never hinged 6.00

A10

George VI and Christiansborg Castle — A11

Perf. 12x11½, 11½x12 (#123, 124, 125, 126, 127)

1938-41 Wmk. 4

115 A10 ½p green .35 *.50*
116 A10 1p red brown .35 .25
117 A10 1½p rose red .35 *.50*
118 A10 2p gray black .35 .25
119 A10 3p ultramarine .35 .35
120 A10 4p rose lilac .70 *1.25*
121 A10 6p rose violet .70 .25
122 A10 9p red orange 1.10 .55
123 A11 1sh gray grn & blk 1.40 .65
124 A11 1sh3p turq grn & red brown 1.75 .50
125 A11 2sh dk vio & dp bl 4.00 *21.00*
126 A11 5sh rose car & ol green 7.50 *24.00*
127 A11 10sh pur & blk 7.50 *32.50*
Nos. 115-127 (13) 26.40 *82.55*
Set, never hinged 40.00

Issued: 10sh, July, 1940; 1sh3p, Apr. 12, 1941; others, Apr. 1.

Perf. 12

115a A10 ½p green 7.50 4.00
116a A10 1p red brown 12.00 .30
117a A10 1½p rose red 12.50 8.00
118a A10 2p gray black 10.00 2.00
119a A10 3p ultramarine 6.50 1.50
120a A10 4p rose lilac 6.50 4.50
121a A10 6p rose violet 15.00 2.00
122a A10 9p red orange 6.50 3.25
123a A10 1sh gray grn & blk 17.50 2.25
125a A10 2sh dk vio & dp blue 45.00 20.00
126a A10 5sh rose car & ol grn 65.00 35.00
Nos. 115a-126a (11) 204.00 91.80

Catalogue values for unused stamps in this section, from this point to the end of the section, are for Never Hinged items.

Peace Issue
Common Design Type

1946, Oct. 14 ***Perf. 13½***

128 CD303 2p purple .25 .25
a. Perf. 13½x14 25.00 3.00
129 CD303 4p deep red violet 1.60 *3.50*
a. Perf. 13½x14 5.00 3.75
Nos. 128-129 (2) 1.85 *3.75*

A12

A13

½p, Mounted Constable. 1p, Christiansborg Castle. 1½p, Emblem of Joint Provincial Council. 2p, Talking Drums. 2½p, Map. 3p, Manganese mine. 4p, Lake Bosumtwi. 6p, Cacao farmer. 1sh, Breaking cacao pods. 2sh, Trooping the colors. 5sh, Surfboats. 10sh, Forest.

1948, July 1 Engr. *Perf. 12*

130 A12	½p emerald	.25	*.60*
131 A13	1p deep blue	.25	.25
132 A13	1½p red	1.50	1.50
133 A12	2p chocolate	.65	.25
134 A13	2½p lt brown & red	2.00	*5.50*
135 A13	3p blue	4.00	1.75
136 A13	4p dk car rose	4.75	6.00
137 A12	6p org & black	1.00	.40
138 A13	1sh red org & blk	3.25	.40
139 A13	2sh rose car & ol brn	11.00	4.75
140 A13	5sh gray & red vio	42.50	14.00
141 A12	10sh ol grn & black	22.00	17.00
	Nos. 130-141 (12)	93.15	52.40

Silver Wedding Issue

Common Design Types

1948, Dec. 20 Photo. *Perf. 14x14½*

142 CD304 1½p scarlet .25 *.70*

Engraved; Name Typographed

Perf. 11½x11

143 CD305 10sh dk brn olive 35.00 *47.50*

UPU Issue

Common Design Types

Engr.; Name Typo. on 2½p and 3p

1949, Oct. 10 *Perf. 13½, 11x11½*

144 CD306	2p red brown	.25	.25
145 CD307	2½p deep orange	1.60	*8.00*
146 CD308	3p indigo	.35	*1.75*
147 CD309	1sh blue green	.35	.35
	Nos. 144-147 (4)	2.55	*10.35*

Map of West Africa — A14

Mounted Constable — A15

Designs: 1p, Christiansborg Castle. 1½p, Emblem of Joint Provincial Council. 2p, Talking drums. 3p, Manganese mine. 4p, Lake Bosumtwi. 6p, Cacao farmer. 1sh, Breaking cacao pods. 2sh, Trooping the colors. 5sh, Surfboats. 10sh, Forest.

Perf. 11½x12, 12x11½

1952-54 Engr.

148 A14	½p yel brn & car	.25	.25
149 A14	1p deep blue	.40	.25
150 A14	1½p green	.40	*1.50*
151 A15	2p chocolate	.40	.25
152 A15	2½p red	.45	*1.50*
153 A14	3p rose	1.25	.25
154 A14	4p deep blue	.50	*.45*
155 A15	6p orange & black	1.00	.25
156 A14	1sh red org & black	3.25	.25
157 A14	2sh rose car & ol brn	16.00	1.00
158 A14	5sh gray & red vio	29.00	8.00
159 A15	10sh olive grn & blk	26.00	14.00
	Nos. 148-159 (12)	78.90	27.95

Nos. 148-149 exist in vertical coils.

Issued: 2½p, 12/19/52; ½p, 1½p, 3p, 4p, 4/1/53; 1p, 2p, 6p, 1sh-10sh, 3/1/54.

For overprints see Ghana #5-13, 25-27.

Coronation Issue

Common Design Type

1953, June 2 *Perf. 13½x13*

160 CD312	2p dk brown & black	1.00	.25
	Nos. 160 (1)	1.00	.25

POSTAGE DUE STAMPS

D1

1923 Typo. Wmk. 4 *Perf. 14*

Yellowish Toned Paper

J1 D1	½p black	20.00	*125.00*
J2 D1	1p black	.95	*1.50*
J3 D1	2p black	13.00	*3.00*
J4 D1	3p black	22.50	*2.50*
	Nos. J1-J4 (4)	56.45	*132.00*

1951-52 Typo. Wmk. 4 *Perf. 14*

Chalk-Surfaced Paper

J5 D1	2p black	4.00	*32.50*
a.	Wmk. 4a (error)	750.00	
b.	Wmk. 4, crown missing (error)	1,600.	
J6 D1	3p black	4.50	*30.00*
a.	Wmk. 4a (error)	700.00	
b.	Wmk. 4, crown missing (error)	1,500.	
J7 D1	6p black ('52)	2.10	*18.00*
a.	Wmk. 4a (error)	1,300.	
b.	Wmk. 4, crown missing (error)	2,250.	
J8 D1	1sh black ('52)	2.10	*80.00*
a.	Wmk. 4a (error)	1,700.	
	Nos. J5-J8 (4)	12.70	*160.50*

Issued: Nos. J7-J8, 10/1.

WAR TAX STAMP

Regular Issue of 1913 Surcharged

1918, June Wmk. 3 *Perf. 14*

MR1 A8 1p on 1p scarlet 4.00 1.00

GRAND COMORO

'grand 'kä-mə-ˌrō

LOCATION — One of the Comoro Islands in the Mozambique Channel between Madagascar and Mozambique.
GOVT. — French Colony
AREA — 385 sq. mi. (approx.)
POP. — 50,000 (approx.)
CAPITAL — Moroni

100 Centimes = 1 Franc

See Comoro Islands.

Navigation and Commerce — A1

Perf. 14x13½

1897-1907 Typo. Unwmk.

Name of Colony in Blue or Carmine

1 A1	1c blk, *lil bl*	1.25	1.25
2 A1	2c brn, *buff*	1.60	1.60
3 A1	4c claret, *lav*	2.25	2.25
4 A1	5c grn, *grnsh*	4.25	3.75
5 A1	10c blk, *lavender*	9.50	6.00
6 A1	10c red ('00)	11.00	11.00
7 A1	15c blue, quadrille paper	22.00	14.50
8 A1	15c gray, *lt gray* ('00)	11.00	11.00
9 A1	20c red, *grn*	12.50	12.50
10 A1	25c blk, *rose*	18.50	15.00
11 A1	25c blue ('00)	22.00	21.50
12 A1	30c brn, *bister*	23.00	20.00
13 A1	35c blk, *yel* ('06)	22.00	20.00
14 A1	40c red, *straw*	23.00	18.00
15 A1	45c blk, *gray grn* ('07)	80.00	70.00
16 A1	50c car, *rose*	40.00	24.00
17 A1	50c brn, *bluish* ('00)	45.00	40.00
18 A1	75c dp vio, *org*	60.00	40.00
19 A1	1fr brnz grn, *straw*	40.00	32.00
	Nos. 1-19 (19)	448.85	364.35

Perf. 13½x14 stamps are counterfeits.

Issues of 1897-1907 Surcharged in Black or Carmine

1912

20 A1	5c on 2c brn, *buff*	1.50	1.50
a.	Inverted surcharge	260.00	
21 A1	5c on 4c cl, *lav* (C)	1.25	1.25
22 A1	5c on 15c blue (C)	1.25	1.25
23 A1	5c on 20c red, *grn*	1.25	1.25
24 A1	5c on 25c blk, *rose* (C)	1.50	1.50
25 A1	5c on 30c brn, *bis* (C)	1.50	1.50
26 A1	10c on 40c red, *straw*	1.50	1.50
27 A1	10c on 45c blk, *gray grn* (C)	2.50	2.50
28 A1	10c on 50c car, *rose*	2.00	2.00
29 A1	10c on 75c dp vio, *org*	2.50	2.50
	Nos. 20-29 (10)	16.75	16.75

Two spacings between the surcharged numerals are found on Nos. 20-29. For detailed listings, see the *Scott Classic Specialized Catalogue of Stamps and Covers.*

Nos. 20-29 were available for use in Madagascar and the entire Comoro archipelago.

Stamps of Grand Comoro were superseded by those of Madagascar, and in 1950 by those of Comoro Islands.

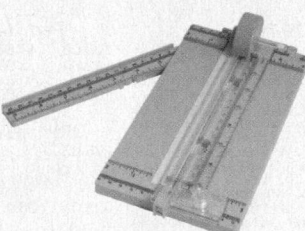

ScottMounts

Sign-up now to get weekly email exclusive online deals and the latest product updates. Visit AmosAdvantage.com/Newsletter and register today.

ITEM	W x H (mm)	DESCRIPTION	MOUNTS	RETAIL	AA*
PRE-CUT SINGLE MOUNTS					
901	40 x 25	U.S. Standard Comm. Hor. Water Activated	40	$3.50	**$2.39**
902	25 x 40	U.S. Standard Comm. Vert. Water Activated	40	$3.50	**$2.39**
903	25 x 22	U.S. Regular Issue – Hor. Water Activated	40	$3.50	**$2.39**
904	22 x 25	U.S. Regular Issue – Vert. Water Activated	40	$3.50	**$2.39**
905	41 x 31	U.S. Semi-Jumbo – Horizontal	40	$3.50	**$2.39**
906	31 x 41	U.S. Semi-Jumbo – Vertical	40	$3.50	**$2.39**
907	50 x 31	U.S. Jumbo – Horizontal	40	$3.50	**$2.39**
908	31 x 50	U.S. Jumbo – Vertical	40	$3.50	**$2.39**
909	25 x 27	U.S. Famous Americans/Champions Of Liberty	40	$3.50	**$2.39**
910	33 x 27	United Nations	40	$3.50	**$2.39**
911	40 x 27	United Nations	40	$3.50	**$2.39**
976	67 x 25	Plate Number Coils, Strips of Three	40	$6.25	**$3.99**
984	67 x 34	Pacific '97 Triangle	10	$3.50	**$2.39**
985	111 x 25	Plate Number Coils, Strips of Five	25	$6.25	**$3.99**
986	51 x 36	U.S. Hunting Permit/Express Mail	40	$6.25	**$3.99**
1045	40 x 26	U.S. Standard Comm. Hor. Self-Adhesive	40	$3.50	**$2.39**
1046	25 x 41	U.S. Standard Comm. Vert. Self-Adhesive	40	$3.50	**$2.39**
1047	22 x 26	U.S. Definitives Vert. Self Adhesive	40	$3.50	**$2.39**
966	Value Pack	(Assortment pre-cut sizes)	320	$23.25	**$15.25**
975	Best Pack	(Assortment pre-cut sizes - Black Only)	160	$14.75	**$9.99**
PRE-CUT PLATE BLOCK, FDC, POSTAL CARD MOUNTS					
912	57 x 55	Regular Issue Plate Block	25	$6.25	**$3.99**
913	73 x 63	Champions of Liberty	25	$6.25	**$3.99**
914	106 x 55	Rotary Press Standard Commemorative	20	$6.25	**$3.99**
915	105 x 57	Giori Press Standard Commemorative	20	$6.25	**$3.99**
916	127 x 70	Giori Press Jumbo Commemorative	10	$6.25	**$3.99**
917	165 x 94	First Day Cover	10	$6.25	**$3.99**
918	140 x 90	Postal Card Size/Submarine Booklet Pane	10	$6.25	**$3.99**
1048	152 x 107	Large Postal Cards	8	$10.25	**$6.99**
STRIPS 215MM LONG					
919	20	U.S. 19th Century, Horizontal Coil	22	$7.99	**$5.25**
920	22	U.S. Early Air Mail	22	$7.99	**$5.25**
921	24	U.S., Vertical Coils, Christmas (#2400, #2428 etc.)	22	$7.99	**$5.25**
922	25	U.S. Commemorative and Regular	22	$7.99	**$5.25**
1049	26	U.S. Commemorative and Regular	22	$7.99	**$5.25**
923	27	U.S. Famous Americans	22	$7.99	**$5.25**
924	28	U.S. 19th Century, Liechtenstein	22	$7.99	**$5.25**
1050	29	Virginia Dare, British Empire, etc.	22	$7.99	**$5.25**
925	30	U.S. 19th Century; Jamestown, etc; Foreign	22	$7.99	**$5.25**
926	31	U.S. Horizontal Jumbo and Semi-Jumbo	22	$7.99	**$5.25**
927	33	U.S. Stampin' Future, UN	22	$7.99	**$5.25**
1054	34	U.S. American Landmarks, Eclipse	22	$7.99	**$5.25**
928	36	U.S. Hunting Permit, Canada	15	$7.99	**$5.25**
1051	37	U.S., British Colonies	22	$7.99	**$5.25**
929	39	U.S. Early 20th Century	15	$7.99	**$5.25**
930	41	U.S. Vert. Semi-Jumbo ('77 Lafayette, Pottery, etc.)	15	$7.99	**$5.25**
931		Multiple Assortment: One strip of each size 22-41 above (SMKB) (2 x 25mm strips)	12	$7.99	**$5.25**
1052	42	U.S., British Colonies	22	$7.99	**$5.25**
1053	43	U.S., British Colonies	22	$7.99	**$5.25**
932	44	U.S. Vertical Coil Pair Garden Flowers Booklet Pane	15	$7.99	**$5.25**
933	48	U.S. Farley, Gutter Pair	15	$7.99	**$5.25**
934	50	U.S. Jumbo (Lyndon Johnson, '74 U.P.U., etc.)	15	$7.99	**$5.25**
935	52	U.S. Standard Commemorative Block (Butterflies)	15	$7.99	**$5.25**
936	55	U.S. Standard Plate Block - normal margins	15	$7.99	**$5.25**
937	57	U.S. Standard Plate Block - wider margins	15	$7.99	**$5.25**
938	61	U.S. Blocks, Israel Tabs, '99 Christmas Madonna Pane	15	$7.99	**$5.25**
STRIPS 240MM LONG					
939	63	U.S. Jumbo Commemorative Horizontal Block	10	$9.25	**$5.99**
940	66	U.S. CIPEX Souvenir Sheet, Self-Adhesive Booklet Pane (#2803a, 3012a)	10	$9.25	**$5.99**
941	68	U.S. ATM Booklet Pane, Farley Gutter Pair & Souvenir Sheet	10	$9.25	**$5.99**
942	74	U.S. TIPEX Souvenir Sheet	10	$9.25	**$5.99**
943	80	U.S. Standard Commemorative Vertical Block	10	$9.25	**$5.99**
944	82	U.S. Blocks of Four, U.N. Chagall	10	$9.25	**$5.99**
945	84	Israel Tab Block, Mars Pathfinder Sheetlet	10	$9.25	**$5.99**
946	89	Submarine Booklet, Souvenir Sheet World Cup, Rockwell	10	$9.25	**$5.99**
947	100	U.S. '74 U.P.U. Block, U.N. Margin Inscribed Block	7	$9.25	**$5.99**
948	120	Various Souvenir Sheets and Blocks	7	$9.25	**$5.99**
STRIPS 265MM LONG					
1035	25	U.S. Coils Strips of 11	12	$9.25	**$5.99**
949	40	U.S. Postal People Standard Standard & Semi-Jumbo Commemorative Strip	10	$9.25	**$5.99**
981	44	U.S. Long self-adhesive booklet panes	10	$9.25	**$5.99**
1030	45	Various (Canada Scott #1725-1734)	10	$9.25	**$5.99**
1036	46	U.S. Long self adhesive booklet panes of 15	10	$9.25	**$5.99**
950	55	U.S. Regular Plate Block or Strip of 20	10	$9.25	**$5.99**
951	59	U.S. Double Issue Strip	10	$9.25	**$5.99**
952	70	U.S. Jumbo Commemorative Plate Block	10	$12.50	**$8.50**
1031	72	Various (Canada Scott #1305a-1804a)	10	$12.50	**$8.50**
1032	75	Plate Blocks: Lance Armstrong, Prehistoric Animals, etc.	10	$12.50	**$8.50**
1060	76	U.S. 1994 Stamp Printing Centennial Souvenir Sheet, etc.	10	$12.50	**$8.50**
953	91	U.S. Self-Adhesive Booklet Pane '98 Wreath, '95 Santa	10	$12.50	**$8.50**
1033	95	Mini-Sheet Plate Blocks w/top header	10	$12.50	**$8.50**
1061	96	U.S., Foreign	10	$12.50	**$8.50**
954	105	U.S. Standard Semi-Jumbo Commemorative Plate Number Strip	10	$12.50	**$8.50**
955	107	Same as above–wide margin	10	$12.50	**$8.50**
956	111	U.S. Gravure-Intaglio Plate Number Strip	10	$14.75	**$9.99**
1062	115	Foreign Small Sheets	10	$17.50	**$11.99**
957	127	U.S. 2000 Space S/S, World War II S/S	10	$17.50	**$11.99**
1063	131	Looney Tunes sheets; World War II Souvenir Sheet Plate Block	10	$17.50	**$11.99**
1064	135	U.S., Japan Gifts of Friendship sheet	10	$17.50	**$11.99**
958	137	Great Britain Coronation	10	$17.50	**$11.99**
1065	139	Sheets: Soda Fountain, Lady Bird Johnson, Earthscapes, etc.	10	$17.50	**$11.99**
1066	143	Sheets: Merchant Marine Ships, 2013 Hanukkah, etc.	10	$17.50	**$11.99**
1067	147	Sheets: Pickup Trucks, Animal Rescue, Washington D.C., etc.	10	$17.50	**$11.99**
1068	151	Sheets: Go Green, Bicycling, Happy New Year, Ben Franklin, etc.	10	$17.50	**$11.99**

ITEM	W x H (mm)	DESCRIPTION	MOUNTS	RETAIL	AA*
STRIPS 265MM LONG, continued					
959	158	American Glass, U.S. Football Coaches Sheets	10	$17.99	**$12.50**
1077	160	Sheets: Pacific '97 Triangle Mini, Trans-Mississippi	5	$12.50	**$8.50**
1069	163	Sheets: Modern Architecture, UN Human Rights, etc	5	$12.50	**$8.50**
1070	167	Sheets: John F. Kennedy, Classics Forever, Made in America, etc.	5	$12.50	**$8.50**
1071	171	Film Directors, Foreign Souvenir Sheets	5	$12.50	**$8.50**
960	175	Large Block, Souvenir Sheet	5	$12.50	**$8.50**
1072	181	Sheets: Jimi Hendrix, Johnny Cash, American Photography, etc.	5	$17.50	**$11.99**
1073	185	Frank Sinatra, Ronald Reagan, Arthur Ashe, Creast Cancer, etc.	5	$17.50	**$11.99**
1074	188	Sheets: Yoda, 9/11 Heroes, Andy Warhol, Frida Kahlo, etc	5	$17.50	**$11.99**
1078	192	Olympic, etc.	5	$17.50	**$11.99**
1075	198	Sheets: Modern American Art, Super Heroes, Baseball Sluggers, etc.	5	$17.50	**$11.99**
1076	215	Celebrity Chefs sheets; Foreign sheets	5	$17.50	**$11.99**
961	231	U.S. Full Post Office Pane Regular and Commemorative	5	$17.99	**$12.50**
SOUVENIR SHEETS/SMALL PANES					
962	204 x 153	New Year 2000, U.S. Bicentennial S/S	4	$9.25	**$5.99**
963	187 x 144	55¢ Victorian Love Pane, U.N. Flag Sheet	9	$15.50	**$10.25**
964	160 x 200	U.N., Israel Sheet	10	$15.50	**$10.25**
965	120 x 207	U.S. AMERIPEX Presidential Sheet	4	$6.25	**$3.99**
968	229 x 131	World War II S/S Plate Block Only	5	$9.25	**$5.99**
970	111 x 91	Columbian Souvenir Sheet	6	$6.25	**$4.75**
972	148 x 196	Apollo Moon Landing/Carnivorous Plants	4	$7.99	**$5.25**
989	129 x 122	U.S. Definitive Sheet: Harte, Hopkins, etc.	8	$10.25	**$6.99**
990	189 x 151	Chinese New Year	5	$10.25	**$6.99**
991	150 x 185	Breast Cancer/Fermi/Soccer/'96 Folk Heroes	5	$10.25	**$6.99**
992	198 x 151	Cherokee Strip Sheet	5	$10.25	**$6.99**
993	185 x 151	Bernstein/NATO/Irish/Lunt/Gold Rush Sheets	5	$10.25	**$6.99**
994	198 x 187	Postal Museum	4	$10.25	**$6.99**
995	156 x 187	Sign Language/Statehood	5	$10.25	**$6.99**
996	188 x 197	Illustrators, '98 Music: Folk, Gospel; Country/Western	4	$10.25	**$6.99**
997	151 x 192	Olympic	5	$10.25	**$6.99**
998	174 x 185	Buffalo Soldiers	5	$10.25	**$6.99**
999	130 x 198	Silent Screen Stars	5	$10.25	**$6.99**
1000	190 x 199	Stars Stripes/Baseball/Insects & Spiders/Legends West/ Aircraft, Comics, '96 Olympics, Civil War	4	$10.25	**$6.99**
1001	178 x 181	Cranes	4	$10.25	**$6.99**
1002	183 x 212	Wonders of the Sea, We the People	3	$10.25	**$6.99**
1003	156 x 264	$14 Eagle	4	$10.25	**$6.99**
1004	159 x 270	$9.95 Moon Landing	4	$10.25	**$6.99**
1005	159 x 259	$2.90 Priority/$9.95 Express Mail	4	$10.25	**$6.99**
1006	223 x 187	Hubble, Hollywood Legends, O'Keefe Sheets	3	$10.25	**$6.99**
1007	185 x 181	Deep Sea Creatures, Olmsted Sheets	4	$10.25	**$6.99**
1008	152 x 228	Indian Dances/Antique Autos	5	$10.25	**$6.99**
1009	165 x 150	River Boat/Hanukkah	6	$10.25	**$6.99**
1010	275 x 200	Dinosaurs/Large Gutter Blocks	2	$10.25	**$6.99**
1011	161 x 160	Pacific '97 Triangle Mini Sheets	6	$10.25	**$6.99**
1012	174 x 130	Road Runner, Daffy, Bugs, Sylvester & Tweety	6	$10.25	**$6.99**
1013	196 x 158	Football Coaches	4	$10.25	**$6.99**
1014	184 x 184	American Dolls, Flowering Trees Sheets	4	$10.25	**$6.99**
1015	186 x 230	Classic Movie Monsters	3	$10.25	**$6.99**
1016	187 x 160	Trans-Mississippi Sheet	4	$10.25	**$6.99**
1017	192 x 230	Celebrate The Century	3	$10.25	**$6.99**
1018	156 x 204	Space Discovery	5	$10.25	**$6.99**
1019	182 x 209	American Ballet	5	$10.25	**$6.99**
1020	139 x 151	Christmas Wreaths	5	$10.25	**$6.99**
1021	129 x 126	Justin Morrill, Henry Luce	8	$10.25	**$6.99**
1022	184 x 165	Baseball Fields, Bright Eyes	4	$10.25	**$6.99**
1023	185 x 172	Shuttle Landing Pan Am Invert Sheets	4	$10.25	**$6.99**
1024	172 x 233	Sonoran Desert	3	$10.25	**$6.99**
1025	150 x 166	Prostate Cancer	5	$10.25	**$6.99**
1026	201 x 176	Famous Trains	4	$10.25	**$6.99**
1027	176 x 124	Canada - Historic Vehicles	5	$10.25	**$6.99**
1028	245 x 114	Canada - Provincial Leaders	5	$10.25	**$6.99**
1029	177 x 133	Canada - Year of the Family	5	$10.25	**$6.99**
1034	181 x 213	Arctic Animals	3	$10.25	**$6.99**
1037	179 x 242	Louise Nevelson	3	$10.25	**$6.99**
1038	179 x 217	Library Of Congress	3	$10.25	**$6.99**
1039	182 x 232	Youth Team Sports	3	$10.25	**$6.99**
1040	183 x 216	Lucille Ball Scott #3523	3	$10.25	**$6.99**
1041	182 x 244	American Photographers	3	$10.25	**$6.99**
1042	185 x 255	Andy Warhol	3	$10.25	**$6.99**
1043	165 x 190	American Film Making	4	$10.25	**$6.99**
1044	28 x 290	American Eagle PNC Strips of 11	12	$9.25	**$5.99**

Available in clear or black background. Please specify color choice when ordering.

2018 NATIONAL, MINUTEMAN OR ALL-AMERICAN SUPPLEMENT MOUNT PACKS

ITEM	*DESCRIPTION*	*RETAIL*	*AA**
2018 B	2017 National, Minuteman or All-American Supplement Mount Pack - BLACK	$49.99	**$39.99**
2018 C	2017 National, Minuteman or All-American Supplement Mount Pack - CLEAR	$49.99	**$39.99**

www.AmosAdvantage.com

Call 1-800-572-6885

Outside U.S. & Canada 937-498-0800

Mail to: P.O. Box 4129, Sidney OH 45365

ORDERING INFORMATION: *AA prices apply to paid subscribers of Amos Media titles, or orders placed online. Prices, terms and product availability subject to change. Taxes will apply in CA, OH, & IL. Shipping and handling rates will apply.
SHIPPING & HANDLING: United States: Order total $0-$10.00 charged $3.99 shipping; Order total $10.01-$79.99 charged $7.99 shipping; Order total $80.00 or more charged 10% of order total for shipping. Maximum Freight Charge $45.00. **Canada:** 20% of order total. Minimum charge $19.99; maximum charge $200.00. **Foreign:** Orders are shipped via FedEx Int'l. or USPS and billed actual freight.

GREAT BRITAIN

'grāt 'bri-tən

(United Kingdom)

LOCATION — Northwest of the continent of Europe and separated from it by the English Channel
GOVT. — Constitutional monarchy
AREA — 94,511 sq. mi.
POP. — 59,128,000 (1998 est.)
CAPITAL — London

12 Pence = 1 Shilling
20 Shillings = 1 Pound
100 Pence = 1 Pound (1970)

Catalogue values for unused stamps in this country are for Never Hinged items, beginning with Scott 264 in the regular postage section, Scott B1 in the semi-postal section, Scott J34 in the postage due section, and Scott 93, Scott 246 and Scott 521 in British Offices in Morocco. All of the listings in British Offices — Middle East Forces, for Use in Eritrea, for Use in Somalia and for Use in Tripolitania are valued as never-hinged.

The letters in the corners of the early postage issues indicate position in the horizontal and vertical rows in which that particular specimen was placed.

In the case of illustration A1, this stamp came from the 15th horizontal row (O) and was the second stamp (B) from the left in that row. The left corner refers to the horizontal row and the right corner to the vertical row. Thus no two stamps on the plate bore the same combination of letters.

When four corner letters are used (starting in 1858), the lower ones indicate the stamp's position in the sheet and the top ones are the same letters reversed.

Watermarks

Wmk. 18 — Small Crown

Wmk. 19 — V R

Wmk. 20 — Large Crown

Wmk. 21 — Small Garter

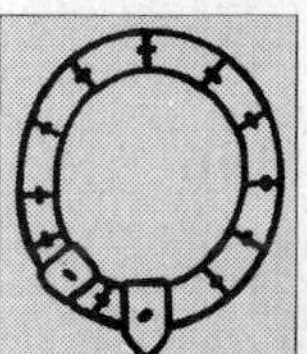

Wmk. 22 — Medium Garter

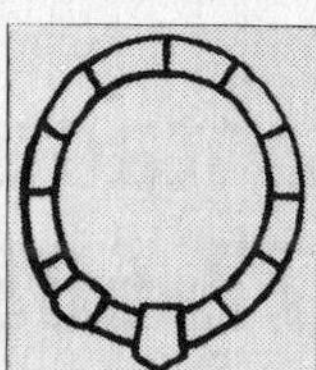

Wmk. 23 — Large Garter

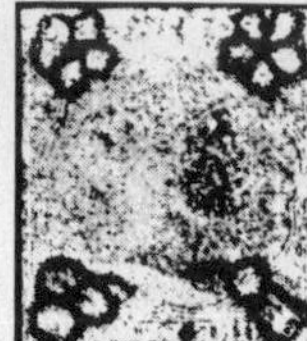

Wmk. 24 — Heraldic Emblems

Wmk. 25 — Spray of Rose

Wmk. 26 — Maltese Cross

Wmk. 27 — "Half Penny" in Script

Wmk. 28 — Anchor

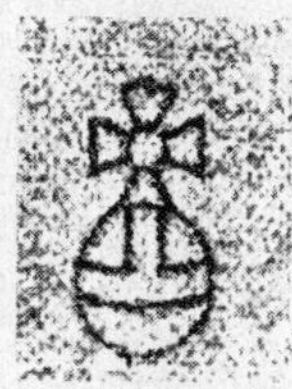

Wmk. 29 — Orb

Wmk. 30 — Imperial Crown

Wmk. 31 — Anchor

Wmk. 32 — Crown and GvR Multiple

Wmk. 33 — Crown and GvR

Wmk. 33 — In the normal watermark (sometimes termed the "repeated" watermark) the letters "GvR" are extended. The royal cyphers are placed one above the other and usually two appear on each stamp. In the multiple watermark the letters "GvR" are condensed, the cyphers are smaller and are so placed that those in each succeeding row are below the spaces between the cyphers in the row above.

Wmk. 34 — Large Crown and GvR

Wmk. 35 — Crown and Block GvR Multiple

Wmk. 219 — Large Crown and GvR

Wmk. 250 — Crown and E8R Multiple

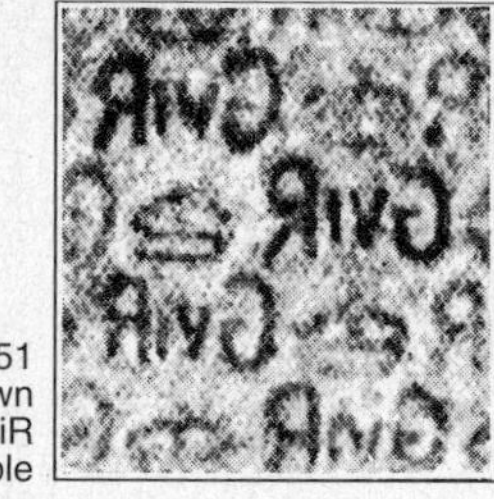

Wmk. 251 — Crown and GviR Multiple

Wmk. 259 — Crown and Large G VI R

Wmk. 298 — Tudor Crown and E 2 R Multiple

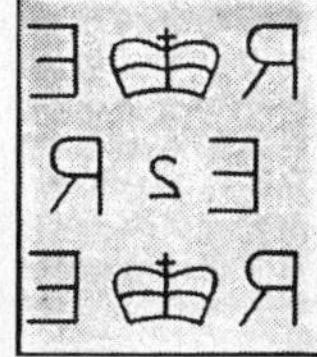

Wmk. 308 — St. Edward's Crown and E 2 R Multiple

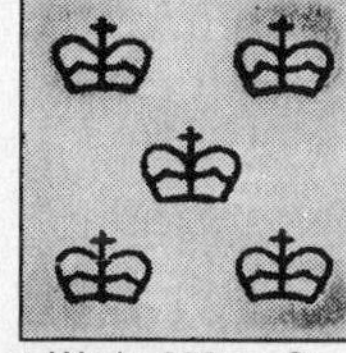

Wmk. 322 — St. Edward's Crown Multiple

Wmk. 401

Values for mint stamps of Great Britain are for stamps with original gum as defined in the catalogue introduction.

Values for unused and used stamps in this country are for examples with fresh color and all the attributes of fine-to-very fine condition (unless specified otherwise) through 1900 (Scott 126). All other stamps are for examples in the condition of very fine. Expect perforations to touch the design on one or two sides on all engraved stamps (Scott Nos. 8-21, 29-33 and 58) and early small format typographed stamps (Nos. 22-28, 34-56, 59-73, 78-89 and 94-95) because of the very narrow spacing between the stamps in the setting of the plates. Examples with margins clear of the design on all four sides range from scarce to very rare and command substantial premiums.

Cancellations on stamps from the 1847 issue to the 1900 issues, and in many cases beyond, are usually heavy. Values quoted are for stamps with better than average cancellations. **Poorly centered stamps and heavily canceled stamps may sell for 10 to 20 percent of the values listed here.**

Stamps with circular datestamps (especially those with a steel cds) range from scarce to very rare and command much higher prices. Premiums to be applied for fresh mint stamps with original gum and for used stamps that have both fine to very fine centering and circular datestamps can be found in footnotes for stamps from Scott 8 through Scott 126, including Official stamps for this period. For stamps that have both fine to very fine centering and circular datestamps, add the premiums together. Apply these premiums to covers, taking into account the overall condition of the cover and the stamps.

Queen Victoria — A1

1840, May Wmk. 18 Engr. *Imperf.*
White Paper

1	A1 1p black	11,000.	320.00
2	A1 2p blue	35,000.	700.00

No. 1 was printed from 11 plates; No. 2 from 2 plates. The 1p plates 1, 2, 5, 6, 8 and 9 can be found in two or more states. Stamp values are for the most common plates.

Issue dates: 1p, May 6; 2p, May 7.

See Nos. 3, 8-9, 11-12, 14, 16, 18, 20, O1.

Compare designs A1-A2 with A8, A10.

A1a

A2

1841 Bluish Paper

3	A1a 1p red brown	625.00	9.00
c.	Rouletted 12	*26,000.*	
d.	"A" missing in lower right corner (position BA, P77)	—	*25,000.*
f.	On deep blue paper	725.00	24.00
4	A2 2p blue	4,500.	50.00
c.	2p violet blue	*15,000.*	1,000.
e.	"Ivory Head"	6,500.	90.00

No. 3 exists on silk thread paper, but was not regularly issued.

No. 4 was printed from two plates.

See Nos. 10, 13, 15, 17, 19, 21.

For shades, see the *Scott Classic Specialized Catalogue of Stamps and Covers.*

During the reigns of Victoria and Edward VII, many color trials were produced on perfed, gummed and watermarked papers.

Nos. 5-7 were printed one stamp at a time on the sheet. Space between the stamps usually is very small. Impressions that touch, or even overlap, are numerous.

Stamps with margins ½mm beyond the outer frame are considered as having full margins.

Values for Nos. 5-6 are for examples with complete frames and clear white margins on all four sides. Values for No. 7 are for examples with complete design but not necessarily clear margins around the design.

A3

With Vertical Silk Threads

1847 Embossed Unwmk.

5 A3 1sh pale green 20,000. 900.00
a. 1sh green 20,000. 925.00
Cut to shape 15.00

Die numbers (on base of bust): 1 and 2.

A3a

1848

6 A3a 10p red brown 11,500. 1,500.
Cut to shape *500.00* 20.00

Die numbers (on base of bust): 1, 2, 3, 4; also without die number.

A4

"Thick"

"Thin"

1854 Wmk. 19

7 A4 6p red violet 18,000. 1,000.
a. 6p dull violet 18,000. 1,000.
b. 6p deep violet *26,000.* 4,250.
Cut to shape 10.00

1854-55 Wmk. 18 Engr. *Perf. 16*
Bluish Paper

8 A1 1p red brown 325.00 30.00
a. 1p yellow brown 375.00 45.00
9 A1 1p red brn, re-engraved ('55) 425.00 60.00
a. Imperf. —
10 A2 2p blue 4,000. 90.00
a. 2p pale blue 4,500. 100.00

In the re-engraved 1p stamps, the lines of the features are deeper and stronger, the fillet behind the ear more distinct, the shading about the eye heavier, the line of the nostril is turned downward at right and an indentation of color appears between lower lip and chin.

Perf. 14

11 A1 1p red brown ('55) 625.00 80.00
a. Imperf. —
12 A1 1p red brn, re-engraved ('55) 600.00 67.50
a. 1p org brn, re-engraved 1,700. 150.00
13 A2 2p blue ('55) 10,000. 210.00
a. Imperf. (P5) *10,000.*

Wmk. 20 exists in two types. The first includes two vertical prongs, rising from the top of the crown's headband and extending into each of the two balancing midsections. The second type (illustrated), introduced in 1861, omits these prongs.

1855 Wmk. 20 *Perf. 16*
Bluish Paper

14 A1 1p red brn, re-engraved 2,000. 110.00
15 A2 2p blue 14,000. 450.00
a. Imperf. (P5) *11,000.*

Some specialists regard No. 15a as a proof.

1855 Bluish Paper *Perf. 14*

16 A1 1p red brn, re-engraved 225.00 21.00
a. 1p orange brn, re-engraved 650.00 62.50
b. 1p brown rose, re-engraved 325.00 50.00
c. Imperf. 4,000. 3,500.
17 A2 2p blue 2,500. 72.50

Nos. 19, 21 With Lines Above and Below Head Thinner

1856-58 White Paper *Perf. 16*

18 A1 1p rose red, re-engraved ('57) 2,400. 72.50
19 A2 2p blue, thin lines ('58) 12,500. 375.00

Perf. 14

20 A1 1p rose red, re-engraved ('57) 55.00 11.50
a. Imperf. 4,500. 3,500.
b. 1p red brown, re-engraved 2,000. 375.00
21 A2 2p blue, thin lines ('57) 3,000. 70.00
a. Imperf. — *11,000.*
b. Vertical pair, imperf horiz. 20,000.

For examples of Nos. 8-21 with margins clear of the design on all four sides, add a 50 percent premium to the value listed. For stamps with clear circular datestamps, apply a 75 percent premium.

Queen Victoria — A5

1855 Typo. Wmk. 21

22 A5 4p rose, *bluish* 8,750. 440.00
23 A5 4p rose, *white* — 1,150.

Compare design A5 with A11, A16, A31.

1856 Wmk. 22

24 A5 4p rose, *bluish* *11,250.* 540.
25 A5 4p rose, *white* 8,800. 400.

1857 Wmk. 23

26 A5 4p rose, *white* 1,750. 125.00

A6 A7

1856 Wmk. 24

27 A6 6p lilac 1,400. 100.00
a. 6p deep lilac 1,850. 140.00
b. Wmk. 3 roses and shamrock — —
28 A7 1sh green 3,000. 300.00
a. 1sh pale green 3,000. 300.00
b. 1sh deep green 5,750. 450.00
e. Imperf —

Compare design A6 with A13, A18, A22. Compare A7 with A15, A21, A29.

A8

1858-69 Engr. Wmk. 20 *Perf. 14*

29 A8 2p deep blue (P9) 350.00 12.50
Plate 7 1,600. 55.00
Plate 8 1,450. 40.00
Plate 12 3,000. 135.00
b. Imperf. (P9) *12,500.*

Plate numbers are contained in the scroll work at the sides of the stamp.

Lines Above and Below Head Thinner

30 A8 2p blue ('69) (P13) 350.00 32.50
Plate 14 475.00 35.00
Plate 15 500.00 35.00
a. Imperf. (P13) *10,500.*

A9

1860-70

31 A9 1½p lil rose, *bluish* (P1) ('60) 8,750. *11,000.*
32 A9 1½p dull rose ('70) (P3) 500.00 65.00
a. 1½p lake red 600.00 65.00
Plate 1 725.00 90.00
c. Imperf (P13) *9,500.*

The 1½p stamps from Plate 1 carry no plate number. The Plate 3 number is in the border at each side above the lower corner letters.

No. 31 was prepared but not issued.

Queen Victoria — A10

1864

33 A10 1p rose red 25.00 2.75
a. 1p brick red 25.00 2.75
b. 1p lake red 25.00 2.75
c. Imperf. (P116, see footnote) *8,750.* *4,500.*

Plate numbers are contained in the scroll work at the sides of the stamp.

No. 33 was printed from 1864 to 1879.

Thirty-nine plate numbers besides Plate 116 (No. 33c) are also known imperforate and used. Values for used examples start at $450.

Stamps from plate 177 have been altered and offered as plate 77.

For examples of Nos. 29-33 with margins clear of the design on all four sides, add a 50 percent premium to the value listed. For stamps with clear circular datestamps, apply a 75 percent premium.

Plate Numbers

Plate 71	52.50	4.00
Plate 72	57.50	5.00
Plate 73	57.50	4.00
Plate 74	57.50	3.00
Plate 76	52.50	3.00
Plate 77	—	*500,000.*
Plate 78	125.00	3.00
Plate 79	45.00	3.00
Plate 80	62.50	3.00
Plate 81	62.50	3.00
Plate 82	125.00	5.00
Plate 83	150.00	9.00
Plate 84	77.50	3.00
Plate 85	57.50	4.00
Plate 86	67.50	5.00
Plate 87	45.00	3.00
Plate 88	180.00	10.00
Plate 89	57.50	3.00
Plate 90	57.50	3.00
Plate 91	72.50	7.25
Plate 92	52.50	3.00
Plate 93	67.50	3.00
Plate 94	62.50	6.00
Plate 95	57.50	3.00
Plate 96	62.50	3.00
Plate 97	57.50	4.50
Plate 98	67.50	7.00
Plate 99	72.50	6.00
Plate 100	77.50	3.00
Plate 101	77.50	11.50
Plate 102	62.50	3.00
Plate 103	67.50	5.00
Plate 104	100.00	6.25
Plate 105	125.00	9.50
Plate 106	72.50	3.00
Plate 107	77.50	9.00
Plate 108	105.00	3.00
Plate 109	115.00	4.50
Plate 110	77.50	11.50
Plate 111	67.50	3.00
Plate 112	87.50	3.00
Plate 113	67.50	16.00
Plate 114	325.00	16.00
Plate 115	125.00	3.00
Plate 116	100.00	11.50
Plate 117	62.50	3.00
Plate 118	67.50	3.00
Plate 119	62.50	3.00
Plate 120	26.00	3.00
Plate 121	57.50	11.50
Plate 122	26.00	3.00
Plate 123	57.50	3.00
Plate 124	42.50	3.00
Plate 125	57.50	3.00
Plate 127	72.50	3.00
Plate 129	57.50	11.00
Plate 130	72.50	3.00
Plate 131	82.50	21.00
Plate 132	180.00	28.00
Plate 133	155.00	11.50
Plate 134	26.00	3.00
Plate 135	125.00	30.00
Plate 136	125.00	25.00
Plate 137	42.50	3.00
Plate 138	32.50	3.00
Plate 139	77.50	21.00
Plate 140	32.50	3.00
Plate 141	155.00	11.50
Plate 142	92.50	30.00
Plate 143	77.50	17.50
Plate 144	125.00	26.00
Plate 145	47.50	3.00
Plate 146	57.50	7.00
Plate 147	67.50	4.00
Plate 148	57.50	4.00
Plate 149	57.50	7.00
Plate 150	26.00	3.00
Plate 151	77.50	11.50
Plate 152	77.50	7.50
Plate 153	135.00	11.50

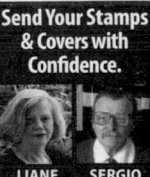

Plate	Unused	Used
Plate 154	67.50	3.00
Plate 155	67.50	3.00
Plate 156	62.50	3.00
Plate 157	67.50	3.00
Plate 158	47.50	3.00
Plate 159	47.50	3.00
Plate 160	47.50	3.00
Plate 161	77.50	9.00
Plate 162	67.50	9.00
Plate 163	67.50	9.00
Plate 164	67.50	9.00
Plate 165	62.50	3.00
Plate 166	62.50	7.25
Plate 167	62.50	3.00
Plate 168	67.50	11.00
Plate 169	77.50	9.25
Plate 170	52.50	3.00
Plate 171	26.00	3.00
Plate 172	47.50	3.00
Plate 173	92.50	11.50
Plate 174	47.50	3.00
Plate 175	77.50	4.50
Plate 176	77.50	3.00
Plate 177	57.50	3.00
Plate 178	77.50	4.50
Plate 179	67.50	3.00
Plate 180	77.50	6.75
Plate 181	62.50	3.00
Plate 182	125.00	6.75
Plate 183	72.50	4.00
Plate 184	47.50	3.00
Plate 185	67.50	4.00
Plate 186	87.50	3.00
Plate 187	67.50	3.00
Plate 188	92.50	12.50
Plate 189	92.50	12.50
Plate 190	67.50	7.50
Plate 191	47.50	9.25
Plate 192	67.50	3.00
Plate 193	47.50	3.00
Plates 194-195	67.50	11.00
Plate 196	67.50	11.00
Plate 197	67.50	11.50
Plate 198	57.50	7.25
Plate 199	72.50	7.25
Plate 200	77.50	3.00
Plate 201	47.50	6.25
Plate 202	77.50	11.00
Plate 203	47.50	21.00
Plate 204	72.50	3.00
Plate 205	72.50	4.00
Plate 206	72.50	11.50
Plate 207	77.50	11.50
Plate 208	72.50	18.50
Plate 209	62.50	10.50
Plate 210	87.50	16.00
Plate 211	92.50	26.00
Plate 212	77.50	13.50
Plate 213	77.50	13.50
Plate 214	87.50	24.00
Plate 215	87.50	24.00
Plate 216	92.50	24.00
Plate 217	92.50	9.25
Plate 218	87.50	11.00
Plate 219	125.00	87.50
Plate 220	57.50	9.25
Plate 221	92.50	21.00
Plate 222	105.00	52.50
Plate 223	125.00	77.50
Plate 224	155.00	57.50
Plate 225	3,300.	825.00

A11

1862 Typo. Wmk. 23

34 A11 4p vermilion 1,900. 75.00
- *b.* Hair lines (P4) 2,150. 65.00
- *d.* Imperf. (P4) 3,800.

Hair lines on No. 34b are fine colorless lines drawn diagonally across the corners of the stamp. For more detail, see *Scott Classic Specialized Catalogue of Stamps & Covers 1840-1940*.

A12

A13

A14 A15

1862 Wmk. 24

37 A12 3p pale rose 2,500. 300.00
- *a.* 3p deep rose 5,000. 525.00
- *b.* With white dots under side ornaments *40,000.* *16,000.*

39 A13 6p lilac (P3) 2,250. 105.00
- *c.* 6p lilac, wmk. 3 roses & thistle — *8,000.*
- *d.* 6p lilac, hair lines (P4) ('64) 2,900. 210.00
- *e.* As "d," imperf. 4,500.
- *h.* 6p deep lilac (P3) 2,600. 120.00

40 A14 9p straw (p2) 3,900. 400.00
- *c.* 9p straw, wmk. 3 roses & thistle —
- *d.* 9p bister (P2) 5,500. 525.00
- *e.* 9p bister, hair lines (P3) *35,000.* *14,000.*

42 A15 1sh green 3,100. 260.00
- *a.* 1sh deep green (P1) 4,750. 450.00
- *c.* 1sh deep green, with hair lines (P2) *35,000.*

Hair lines on Nos. 39d, 39e, 39f, 39g, 40e and 42c are fine colorless lines drawn diagonally across the corners of the stamp. For details, see *Scott Classic Specialized Catalogue of Stamps & Covers 1840-1940*.

Compare design A14 with A19.

Forgeries exist of Nos. 39a and 40a.

A16

1865 Wmk. 23

43 A16 4p vermilion (P12) 600.00 62.50

	Unused	Used
Plate 9	625.00	72.50
Plate 10	850.00	150.00
Plate 11	650.00	72.50
Plate 13	375.00	47.50
Plate 14	800.00	92.50

- *a.* 4p dull vermilion (P8) 550.00 90.00

	Unused	Used
Plate 7	600.00	100.00
Plate 8	625.00	72.50
Plates 9	625.00	72.50
Plate 10	850.00	150.00
Plate 11	650.00	72.50
Plate 12	600.00	62.50
Plate 14	800.00	92.50
Plate 13	375.00	47.50

- *b.* Imperf. (P11,12) 7,750.

A17

(Hyphen after SIX) — A18

A19

A20

A21

1865 Wmk. 24

44 A17 3p rose (P4) 2,350. 215.00
- *a.* Wmk. error, 3 roses & shamrock 6,250. 1,250.

45 A18 6p lilac (P5) 1,125. 100.00
- *a.* 6p deep lilac 1,875. 180.00
  - Plate 6 3,700. 190.00
- *b.* Double impression (P6) *16,500.*
- *c.* Wmk. error, 3 roses & shamrock (P5) *1,400.*
  - As "c," Plate 6 *2,400.*

46 A19 9p straw (P4) 4,500. 575.00
- Plate 5 *20,000.*
- *a.* Wmk. error, 3 roses & shamrock (P4) — *2,250.*

47 A20 10p red brn (P1) *55,000.*

48 A21 1sh grn (P4) 2,500. 225.00
- *b.* Wmk. error, 3 roses & shamrock 1,500.
- *c.* Vert. pair, imperf. btwn. *16,500.*

No. 46, plate 5 is from a proof sheet.

See Nos.49-50, 52-54. Compare design A17 with A27.

For examples of Nos. 43-48 with margins clear of the design on all four sides, add a 40 percent premium to the value listed. For stamps with clear circular datestamps, apply a 60 percent premium.

(No hyphen after SIX) — A22

A23

1867-80 Wmk. 25

49 A17 3p rose (P5) 525.00 62.50
- *a.* 3p deep rose 825.00 92.50

	Unused	Used
Plate 4	1,850.	300.00
Plate 6	550.00	62.50
Plate 7	400.00	67.50
Plate 8	600.00	62.50
Plate 9	600.00	67.50
Plate 10	900.00	145.00

- *b.* Imperf. (P5,6,8,9) 10,000.

50 A18 6p dl vio (P6) 1,850. 92.50
- *a.* 6p bright violet (P6) 1,750. 100.00
- *b.* Imperf. (P6) *5,000.*

51 A22 6p red vio ('69) (P9) 650.00 90.00
- *a.* 6p violet (P9) 675.00 92.50
  - Plate 8 675.00 135.00
  - Plate 10 *35,000.*
- *b.* Imperf. (P8, 9) 10,000. 4,500.

52 A19 9p bis (P4) ('67) 2,400. 300.00
- *a.* Imperf. (P4) 15,000.

53 A20 10p red brn (P1) 3,500. 350.00
- Plate 2 *50,000.* *15,000.*
- *a.* 10p deep red brown 5,000. 600.00
- *b.* Imperf. (P1) 12,000.

54 A21 1sh grn (P4) 1,200. 40.00

	Unused	Used
Plate 5	825.00	40.00
Plate 6	1,200.	40.00
Plate 7	1,400.	82.50

- *a.* 1sh deep green 1,250. 70.00
- *b.* Imperf. (P4) *8,750.* *5,500.*

55 A20 2sh blue (P1) 0,750. 200.00
- *a.* 2sh pale blue 4,750. 240.00
  - Plate 3 *14,000.*
- *b.* Imperf. (P1) 20,000.

56 A23 2sh pale brn (P1) ('80) *27,500.* 3,750.
- *a.* Imperf. *27,500.*

No. 51, plate 10 and No. 53, plate 2, are from proof sheets.

For examples of Nos. 49-56 with margins clear of the design on all four sides, add a 35 percent premium to the value listed. For stamps with clear circular datestamps, apply a 40 percent premium.

A24

1867 Wmk. 26 *Perf. 15½x15*

57 A24 5sh rose (P1) 11,000. 600.00
- Plate 2 17,500. 1,200.
- *a.* 5sh pale rose 11,000. 600.00
  - Plate 2 17,500. 1,200.
- *b.* Imperf. (P1) *19,000.* *19,000.*

See No. 90. Compare design A24 with A51.

For examples of No. 57 with margins clear of the design on all four sides, add a 50 percent premium to the value listed. For stamps with clear circular datestamps, apply a 50 percent premium.

A25

1870 Engr. Wmk. 27 *Perf. 14*

58 A25 ½p rose (P5) 110.00 22.00

	Unused	Used
Plate 1	325.00	90.00
Plate 3	225.00	50.00
Plate 4	150.00	37.50
Plate 5	110.00	22.50
Plate 6	125.00	22.00
Plate 8	575.00	210.00
Plate 9	6,000.	850.00
Plate 10	125.00	22.00
Plate 11, 13	125.00	22.00
Plate 12, 14	125.00	22.00
Plate 15	180.00	40.00
Plate 19	300.00	60.00
Plate 20	350.00	80.00

- *a.* Imperf (see footnote) — —
- *b.* Watermark inverted & reversed 310.00 100.00

Plates 1, 4-6, 8, 13 and 14 are known imperf. Values: from $3,750 unused, $3,250 used.

For examples of No. 58 with margins clear of the design on all four sides, add a 125 percent premium to the value listed. For stamps with clear circular datestamps, apply a 75 percent premium.

A26

1872-73 Wmk. 25 Typo.

59 A26 6p brown (P11) 800.00 55.00
- Plate 12 *4,000.*
- *a.* 6p deep brown (P11) 1,300. 110.00
  - Plate 12 *3,500.*
- *b.* 6p pale buff (P11) 1,000. 100.00
  - Plate 12 3,300. 300.00

60 A26 6p gray (P12) ('73) 1,900. 250.00
- *a.* Imperf. *10,000.*

For examples of Nos. 59-60 with margins clear of the design on all four sides, add a 25 percent premium to the value listed. For stamps with clear circular datestamps, apply a 25 percent premium.

A27

A28

A29

Type A28 has a lined background.

1873-80

61 A27 3p rose (shades) (P11) 400.00 50.00

	Unused	Used
Plates 12	500.00	50.00
Plate 14	525.00	50.00
Plates 15-16	400.00	50.00
Plates 17-18	500.00	50.00
Plate 19	425.00	50.00
Plate 20	800.00	110.00

62 A28 6p gray (P13-16) 500.00 70.00
- Plate 17 1,000. 165.00

63 A28 6p buff (P13) *25,000.*

64 A29 1sh pale green (P12, 13) 600.00 120.00

	Unused	Used
Plate 10	750.00	160.00
Plate 11	750.00	140.00
Plate 14		*40,000.*

- *a.* 1sh deep green (P8, 9) 1,000. 180.00

65 A29 1sh sal (P13) ('80) 4,750. 700.00

No. 63, plate 13, and No. 64, plate 14, are from proof sheets.

See Nos. 83, 86-87. For surcharges see Nos. 94-95. For overprints see Nos. O6, O30.

For examples of Nos. 61-65 with margins clear of the design on all four sides, add a 40 percent premium to the value listed. For stamps with clear circular datestamps, apply a 60 percent premium.

A30

1875 Wmk. 28

66 A30 2½p claret (P1, 2) 600.00 90.00
- Plate 3 900.00 135.00
- *a.* Bluish paper (P1) 900.00 140.00
  - Plate 2 *8,250.* 1,500.
  - Plate 3 *5,500.*
- *b.* Lettered "LH-FL" *29,000.* 2,500.

Forgeries exist of 66a.

1876-80 Wmk. 29

67 A30 2½p claret (P4-9, 11-16) 500.00 60.00

	Unused	Used
Plate 3	1,300.	125.00
Plate 10	550.00	75.00
Plate 17	1,750.	275.00

68 A30 2½p ultra ('80) (P19, 20) 550.00 65.00

	Unused	Used
Plate 17	550.00	65.00
Plate 18	550.00	45.00

See No. 82.

A31

A32

1876-80 Wmk. 23

69 A31 4p vermilion (P15) 2,750. 500.00
- Plate 16 *35,000.*

70 A31 4p pale ol grn ('77) (P16) 1,350. 325.00
Plate 15 1,350. 325.00
Plate 17 20,000.
a. Imperf (P15) *1,400.*
71 A31 4p gray brn (P17) ('80) 2,750. 500.00
72 A32 8p brn lilac (P1) ('76) 11,750.
73 A32 8p org (P1) ('76) 1,750. 350.00

Some specialists consider No. 70a a proof.
No. 72 was never placed in use.
No. 69, plate 16, is from proof sheets.
See No. 84.
For examples of Nos. 66-73 with margins clear of the design on all four sides, add a 50 percent premium to the value listed. For stamps with clear circular datestamps, apply a 50 percent premium. Add the two premiums together for covers with stamps having these attributes.

A33

A34

1878 Wmk. 26 *Perf. 15½x15*
74 A33 10sh grnsh gray (P1) 60,000. 3,250.
75 A34 £1 brn lilac (P1) 90,000. 4,500.

See Nos. 91-92. Compare design A34 with A52.
For examples of Nos. 74-75 with margins clear of the design on all four sides, add a 40 percent premium to the value listed. For stamps with clear circular datestamps, apply a 60 percent premium.

A35

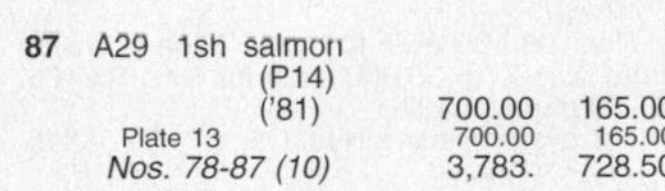
A36

A37

A38

A39

1880-81 Wmk. 30 *Perf. 14*
78 A35 ½p deep green 50.00 13.50
a. Imperf. 4,400.
b. No watermark *9,000.*
79 A36 1p red brown 27.50 12.50
a. Imperf. 5,000.
b. Wmk. 29, error 25,000.
80 A37 1½p red brown 240.00 50.00
81 A38 2p lilac rose 300.00 100.00
82 A30 2½p ultra ('81) (P23) 425.00 32.50
Plate 21 475.00 40.00
Plate 22 425.00 40.00
a. Imperf. (P23) *750.00*
83 A27 3p rose ('81) (P21) 500.00 90.00
Plate 20 900.00 155.00
84 A31 4p gray brown (P17, 18) 440.00 67.50
85 A39 5p dp indigo ('81) 725.00 125.00
a. Imperf. *6,750.* *4,500.*
86 A28 6p gray (P18) 375.00 72.50
Plate 17 440.00 72.50

87 A29 1sh salmon (P14) ('81) 700.00 165.00
Plate 13 700.00 165.00
Nos. 78-87 (10) 3,783. 728.50

Some specialists consider No. 82a a proof.
The 1sh in purple was not issued. Value, unused, $8,750.
See No. 98. For overprints, see Nos. O2-O3.
Compare design A35 with A54.
For examples of Nos. 78-87 with margins clear of the design on all four sides, add a 50 percent premium to the value listed. For stamps with clear circular datestamps, apply a 25 percent premium.

A40

Die I

Die II

1881
88 A40 1p lilac (14 dots in each angle) 225.00 32.50
89 A40 1p lilac (16 dots in each angle) 2.75 2.00
a. Printed on both sides 900.
b. Imperf., pair 7,250.
c. Unwmkd. 7,750.
d. Bluish paper 4,750.
e. Printed on the gummed side 925.

For overprints, see Nos. O4, O37, O45 and O55.
For examples of Nos. 88-89 with margins clear of the design on all four sides, add a 25 percent premium to the value listed. For stamps with clear circular datestamps, apply a 25 percent premium.

1882-83 Wmk. 31
90 A24 5sh rose, *bluish* (P4) 35,000. 5,000.
a. White paper 32,500. 5,000.
91 A33 10sh slate, *bluish* (P1) 135,000. 5,500.
a. White paper 155,000. 4,750.
92 A34 £1 brown lilac, *bluish* (P1) 155,000. 10,000.
a. White paper 180,000. 9,250.

A41

1882 Wmk. Two Anchors (31)
93 A41 £5 brt org (P1) 14,000. 5,000.
a. £5 pale dull org, *bluish* *72,500.* *15,500.*
b. £5 bright org, *bluish* *72,500.* *15,500.*

The paper of No. 93b is less bluish than that of No. 93a, and it is a later printing.
For examples of Nos. 90-93 with margins clear of the design on all four sides, add a 25 percent premium to the value listed. For stamps with clear circular datestamps, apply a 50 percent premium.

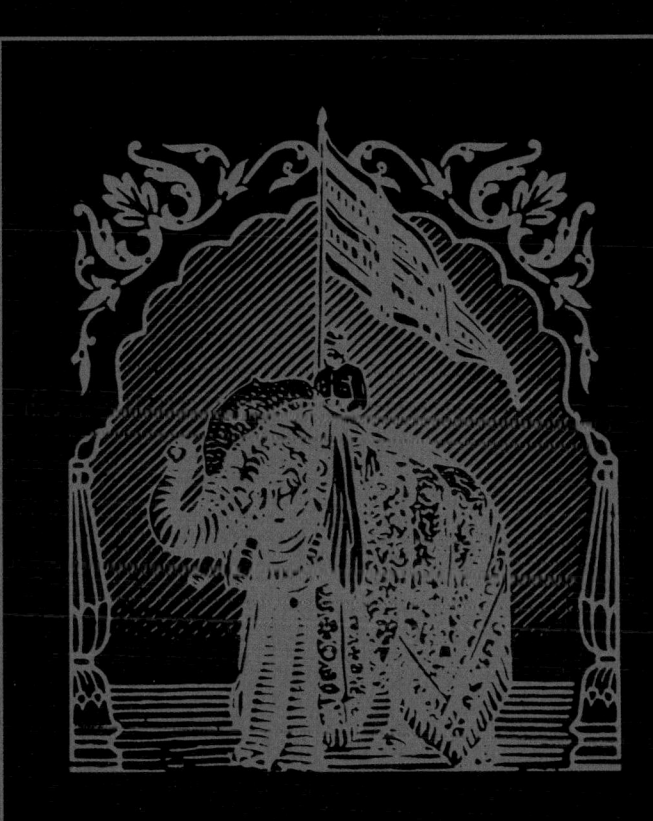

Types of 1873-80 Surcharged in Carmine

1883 **Wmk. 30**

94 A27 3p on 3p violet 625.00 150.00
95 A28 6p on 6p violet 675.00 150.00
a. Double surcharge *12,500.*

For examples of Nos. 94-95 with margins clear of the design on all four sides, add a 40 percent premium to the value listed. For stamps with clear circular datestamps, apply a 50 percent premium.

A44

1883 **Wmk. 31**

96 A44 2sh6p lilac 625.00 165.00
a. Bluish paper *9,250.* *3,750.*

For examples of No. 96 with margins clear of the design on all four sides, add a 25 percent premium to the value listed. For stamps with clear circular datestamps, apply a 25 percent premium.

See British Offices Abroad for overprints on types A44-A133.
These overprints include "M.E.F.," "B.A.," "B.M.A.," "E.A.F.," "CHINA," "Morocco Agencies," "TANGIER," "LEVANT," "PARAS," and "PIASTRE(S)."

A45 A46

A47 A48

A49 A50

1883-84 **Wmk. 30**

98 A35 ½p slate bl ('84) 29.00 9.00
99 A45 1½p lilac ('84) 120.00 42.50
100 A46 2p lilac ('84) 225.00 77.50
101 A47 2½p lilac ('84) 90.00 18.00
102 A48 3p lilac ('84) 275.00 100.00
103 A49 4p green ('84) 575.00 210.00
104 A45 5p green ('84) 575.00 210.00
105 A46 6p green ('84) 600.00 240.00
106 A50 9p green 1,250. 475.00
107 A48 1sh green ('84) 1,450. 300.00

For examples of Nos. 98-107 with margins clear of the design on all four sides, add a 50 percent premium to the value listed. For stamps with clear circular datestamps, apply a 50 percent premium.

Nos. 99-107 were printed by De La Rue in a newly invented doubly fugitive ink that was only available in lilac and green. The stamps were unpopular with the public and postal clerks because they were unattractive and the different denominations were difficult to distinguish from one another.

Values are for stamps of good color. Faded stamps sell for much less. Soaking stamps will cause the color to run.

No. 104 with line instead of period under "d" was not regularly issued. Value, $27,500.

Nos. 98-105 and 107 exist imperf. Values from $3,500 to $5,000 each for Nos. 98-105, $7,500 for No. 107.

For overprints see Nos. O5, O7, O27-O29.

A51 A52

1884 **Wmk. 31**

108 A51 5sh car rose 1,100. 250.00
a. Bluish paper 18,750. 4,000.
109 A52 10sh ultra 2,250. 550.00
a. 10sh cobalt *40,000.* 8,500.
b. Bluish paper *40,000.* *8,500.*
c. As "a," bluish paper *65,000.* *14,000.*

For overprints see Nos. O8-O9.

For examples of Nos. 108-109 with margins clear of the design on all four sides, add a 25 percent premium to the value listed. For stamps with clear circular datestamps, apply a 25 percent premium.

A53

1884 **Wmk. 30**

110 A53 £1 brn violet 32,500. 3,000.

See Nos. 123-124. For overprints see Nos. O10, O13, O15.

For examples of No. 110 with margins clear of the design on all four sides, add a 25 percent premium to the value listed. For stamps with clear circular datestamps, apply a 25 percent premium.

Queen Victoria Jubilee Issue

A54 A55

A56 A57

A58 A59

A60 A61

A62 A63

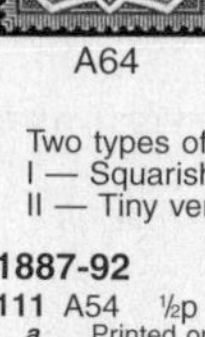

A64 A65

Two types of 5p:
I — Squarish dots beside "d."
II — Tiny vertical dashes beside "d."

1887-92 **Wmk. 30**

111 A54 ½p vermilion 1.80 1.10
a. Printed on both sides
b. Double impression *29,000.*
112 A55 1½p violet & grn 18.00 8.25
113 A56 2p grn & car rose 35.00 13.50
a. 2p green & vermilion 440.00 250.00
114 A57 2½p violet, *blue* 25.00 3.50
115 A58 3p violet, *yel* 25.00 3.50
a. 3p violet, *orange* 825.00 175.00
116 A59 4p brn & grn 40.00 15.00
117 A60 4½p car rose & grn ('92) 11.00 45.00
118 A61 5p lilac & bl, II 42.50 12.50
a. Type I 825.00 125.00
119 A62 6p violet, *rose* 40.00 12.50
120 A63 9p blue & lilac 77.50 45.00
121 A64 10p car rose & lilac ('90) 62.50 42.50
122 A65 1sh green 275.00 72.50
Nos. 111-122 (12) 653.30 274.85

The unpopular green and lilac issue (Nos. 98-107) were replaced by these stamps in colored inks and papers that made it easier to distinguish the different denominations.

Soaking these stamps will cause the color to run.

See Nos. 125-126. For overprints see Nos. O11-O12, O14, O16-O18, O31-O36, O38, O44, O46-O48, O54, O56-O58, O65-O66.

1888 **Wmk. Three Orbs (29)**

123 A53 £1 brown violet 75,000. 4,400.

1891 **Wmk. 30**

124 A53 £1 green 4,000. 800.00

1900 **Wmk. 30**

125 A54 ½p blue green 2.00 *2.25*
a. Imperf *7,250.*
126 A65 1sh car rose & grn 67.50 *145.00*

No. 125 in bright blue is a color changeling.

For examples of Nos. 111-126 with margins clear of the design on all four sides, add a 25 percent premium to the value listed. For stamps with clear circular datestamps, apply a 25 percent premium.

King Edward VII
A66 A67

A68 A69

A70 A71

A72 A73

A74 A75

A76 A77

A78

1902-11 **Wmk. 30** ***Perf. 14***

Ordinary Paper

127 A66 ½p gray green 2.00 1.75
128 A66 1p scarlet 2.25 1.60
c. 1p aniline rose ('11) 225.00 145.00
e. Booklet pane of 6 60.00
f. No watermark ('11) 47.50 *90.00*
g. Imperf., pair *29,000.*
129 A67 1½p vio & green 45.00 22.50
130 A68 2p yel grn & car 52.50 22.50
b. 2p deep grn & red ('11) 27.50 20.00
131 A66 2½p ultra 22.50 11.50
132 A69 3p dull pur, *org yel* 45.00 19.00
133 A70 4p gray brn & grn 57.50 35.00
134 A71 5p dull pur & ultra 67.50 22.50
135 A66 6p pale dull vio 45.00 22.50
a. 6p slate purple 45.00 22.50
b. 6p red violet 45.00 26.00
c. 6p dark violet 45.00 30.00
136 A72 9p ultra & dull vio 100.00 70.00
137 A73 10p car & dull pur 100.00 70.00
a. 10p scarlet & dull pur 92.50 85.00
138 A74 1sh car & dull grn 92.50 40.00
a. 1sh scar & dark green ('11) 125.00 70.00

Wmk. 31

139 A75 2sh6p lilac 260.00 150.00
a. 2sh6p dark violet ('11) 300.00 200.00
140 A76 5sh car rose 400.00 225.00
b. 5sh carmine 425.00 225.00
141 A77 10sh ultra 875.00 525.00

Wmk. Three Imperial Crowns (30)

142 A78 £1 blue green 2,000. 825.00
Nos. 127-138 (12) 631.75 338.85

Nos. 129, 130 and 132 to 139 inclusive exist on both ordinary and chalky paper.

See Nos. 143, 144, 146-150. For overprints see Nos. O19-O26, O39-O43, O49-O53, O59-O64, O67-O83.

See British Offices Abroad for overprints on types A44-A133.
These overprints include "M.E.F.," "B.A.," "B.M.A.," "E.A.F.," "CHINA," "Morocco Agencies," "TANGIER," "LEVANT," "PARAS," and "PIASTRE(S)."

Type of 1902-11 Issue

1904 **Wmk. 30**

143 A66 ½p pale yel grn 2.00 1.75
b. Booklet pane of 5 + label 525.00
c. Booklet pane of 6 190.00
d. Double impression *29,000.*
e. Imperf., pair *37,500.*

Edward VII — A79

1909-10

144 A70 4p pale orange ('10) 20.00 16.00
145 A79 7p gray ('10) 42.50 *22.50*

Type of 1902-11 Issue

1911 *Perf. 15x14*

146 A66 ½p dull yel green 45.00 *50.00*
147 A66 1p carmine rose 17.50 17.50
148 A66 2½p brt ultra 25.00 17.50
149 A69 3p violet, *yellow* 52.50 17.50
a. 3p gray, *lemon* 3,400.
150 A70 4p orange 35.00 17.50
Nos. 146-150 (5) 175.00 120.00

King George V
A80 A81

Perf. 15x14

1911, June 22 **Wmk. 30**

151 A80 ½p yellow green 5.75 4.50
a. Booklet pane of 6 175.00
b. Perf. 14 (error) *18,500.* 1,050.
152 A81 1p carmine 5.25 3.00
a. Booklet pane of 6 175.00
b. Perf. 14 (error) — —
c. 1p pale carmine 16.00 3.50
d. As "c," booklet pane of 6 *125.00*

1912, Jan. 1 **Re-engraved**

153 A80 ½p yellow green 10.00 4.50
154 A81 1p scarlet 7.50 3.50
b. 1p aniline scarlet 180.00 100.00

In the re-engraved stamps the lines of the hair and beard are clearer. The re-engraved ½p has 3 lines of shading instead of 4 between the point of neck and frame; in the 1p the body of the lion is nearly covered by lines of shading.

1912, Aug. **Wmk. 33** *Perf. 15x14*

Die I (Before Re-engraving)

155 A80 ½p yellow green 45.00 45.00
a. Booklet pane of 6 270.00
156 A81 1p scarlet 30.00 30.00
a. Booklet pane of 6 210.00

Die II (Re-engraved)

157 A80 ½p yellow green 8.00 3.50
158 A81 1p scarlet 9.25 4.75

1912, Sept.-Oct. **Wmk. 32**

158A A80 ½p yellow green 15.50 9.25
e. Imperf., pair 300.00
158B A81 1p scarlet 20.00 11.50
e. Imperf., pair 300.00

A82 A83

A84 A85

A86 A87

A88 A89

King George V — A90

TWO PENCE:
Die I — Four horizontal lines above the head. Heavy colored lines above and below the bottom tablet. The inner frame line is closer to the central design than it is to the outer frame line.
Die II — Three lines above the head. Thinner lines above and below the bottom tablet. The inner frame line is midway between the central design and the outer frame line.

1912-13 **Wmk. 33** *Perf. 15x14*

159 A82 ½p green ('13) 1.10 1.10
a. Double impression *26,000.*
b. Booklet pane of 6 110.00
160 A83 1p scarlet 1.10 1.10
a. Booklet pane of 6 110.00
b. Tete beche pair *77,500.*
161 A84 1½p red brown 4.50 1.75
a. "PENCF" 350.00 260.00
b. 1½p orange brown 21.00 17.50
e. 1½p chocolate brown 11.50 2.25
f. As "e," Unwmkd. 235.00 235.00
g. Booklet pane of 6 425.00
h. Booklet pane of 4 + 2 labels 675.00
162 A85 2p deep org (I) 5.00 3.50
a. 2p deep orange (II) ('21) 5.75 4.25
b. Booklet pane of 6 (I) 500.00
c. Booklet pane of 6 (II) 600.00
163 A86 2½p ultramarine 14.00 4.50
164 A87 3p bluish vio ('13) 9.25 3.25
165 A88 4p slate green 17.50 2.25
166 A89 5p yellow brown 17.50 5.75
a. Unwmkd. 1,250.
167 A89 6p rose lilac 17.50 8.00
a. 6p dull violet ('13) 30.00 11.50
b. Perf. 14 92.50 *115.00*
168 A89 7p ol grn ('13) 22.50 10.50
169 A89 8p blk, *yel* ('13) 37.50 12.50
170 A90 9p blk brn ('13) 22.50 6.75
171 A90 10p light blue ('13) 25.00 22.50
172 A90 1sh bister ('13) 24.00 4.50
Nos. 159-172 (14) 218.95 87.95

No. 167 is on chalky paper.
Nos. 159-172 were printed in a variety of shades.
See Nos. 177-178, 183, 187-200, 210, 212-220.
For overprints see Ireland Nos. 1-11, 15-35, 39-55, 59-62.
Compare design A82 with A97.

See British Offices Abroad for overprints on types A44-A133. These overprints include "M.E.F.," "B.A.," "B.M.A.," "E.A.F.," "CHINA," "Morocco Agencies," "TANGIER," "LEVANT," "PARAS," and "PIASTRE(S)."

Waterlow Brothers & Layton Printing (1913)

"Britannia Rule the Waves" A91

Measure 22mm vertically. Perforation holes are larger and evenly spaced.

1913 **Engr.** **Wmk. 34** *Perf. 11x12*

173 A91 2sh6p dk brn 250.00 160.00
174 A91 5sh rose car 475.00 340.00
175 A91 10sh indigo blue 900.00 425.00
176 A91 £1 green 3,000. 1,400.
Nos. 173-176 (4) 4,625. 2,325.

De La Rue & Co. Printing (1915)

Measure 22mm vertically. Gum tends to be yellowish and patchy. The top right and top left perf teeth are wider than the others. Perforation holes are smaller.

1915 **Engr.** **Wmk. 34** *Perf. 11x12*

173a A91 2sh6p lt brn (worn plate) 325.00 260.00
174a A91 5sh br car 425.00 340.00
175a A91 10sh light blue 2,700. 750.00

See Nos. 179-181, 222-224.
For overprints see Ireland Nos. 12-14, 36-38, 56-58, 77-79.

1913 **Wmk. 32** **Typo.** *Perf. 15x14*

Coil Stamps

177 A82 ½p green 160.00 *190.00*
178 A83 1p scarlet 240.00 *240.00*

Bradbury, Wilkinson & Co. Printing (1918-19)

Seahorses Types of 1913-15 Retouched

1919 **Engr.** **Wmk. 34** *Perf. 11x12*

179 A91 2sh6p olive brown 110.00 70.00
180 A91 5sh car rose 275.00 115.00
181 A91 10sh blue 340.00 150.00
Nos. 179-181 (3) 725.00 335.00

The retouched stamps usually have a dot above the middle of the top frame. They are 22¾mm high, whereas Nos. 173-176 are 22mm high.

Type of 1912-13

1922 **Typo.** **Wmk. 33** *Perf. 15x14*

183 A90 9p olive green 110.00 32.00

British Empire Exhibition Issue

British Lion and George V
A92

Wmk. 35

1924, Apr. 23 **Engr.** *Perf. 14*

185 A92 1p vermilion 5.00 5.50
Never hinged 8.50
186 A92 1½p dark brown 8.00 8.00
Never hinged 13.50

See Nos. 203-204.

Types of 1912-13 Issue

1924 **Typo.** *Perf. 15x14*

187 A82 ½p green .60 .60
Never hinged .90
a. Wmk. sideways 8.00 4.00
Never hinged 16.00
b. Booklet pane of 6 65.00
Never hinged 95.00
c. Double impression *12,500.*
188 A83 1p scarlet .50 .50
Never hinged 1.00
a. Wmk. sideways 15.00 10.00
Never hinged 30.00
b. Booklet pane of 6 70.00
Never hinged 105.00
189 A84 1½p red brown .50 .50
Never hinged 1.00
a. Tête bêche pair 550.00 *875.00*
Never hinged 775.00
b. Wmk. sideways 14.00 4.00
Never hinged 27.50
c. Booklet pane of 6 70.00
Never hinged 105.00
d. Bklt. pane of 4 + 2 labels 110.00
Never hinged 160.00
e. Double impression *19,000.*
190 A85 2p dp org (II) 1.00 1.00
Never hinged 2.25
a. Wmk. sideways 110.00 *110.00*
Never hinged 225.00
b. Unwatermarked 2,000.
Never hinged 2,400.
191 A86 2½p ultra 3.50 3.00
Never hinged 10.00
a. Unwatermarked 3,000.
Never hinged 4,000.
192 A87 3p violet 6.50 2.25
Never hinged 15.00
193 A88 4p slate green 7.50 2.25
Never hinged 29.00
194 A89 5p yel brown 12.50 3.00
Never hinged 42.50
195 A89 6p dull violet 2.00 1.50
Never hinged 4.25
198 A90 9p olive green 7.00 3.00
Never hinged 20.00
199 A90 10p dull blue 30.00 30.00
Never hinged 90.00
200 A90 1sh bister 19.00 2.75
Never hinged 47.50
Nos. 187-200 (12) 90.60 50.35

Nos. 187a, 188a, 189b, 190a issued in coils.
Inverted watermarks on the three lowest values are usually from booklet panes.
Nos. 188-189 were issued also on experimental paper with variety of Wmk. 35: closer spacing; letters shorter, rounder.

British Empire Exhibition Issue

Type of 1924, Dated "1925"

1925, May 9 **Engr.** *Perf. 14*

203 A92 1p vermilion 11.50 8.25
Never hinged 20.00
204 A92 1½p brown 28.00 37.50
Never hinged 50.00

A93 A94 A95

1929, May 10 **Typo.** *Perf. 15x14*

205 A93 ½p green 1.40 1.40
Never hinged 3.75
a. Wmk. sideways 25.00 25.00
Never hinged 37.50
b. Booklet pane of 6 90.00
206 A94 1p scarlet 1.40 1.40
Never hinged 3.75
a. Wmk. sideways 45.00 45.00
Never hinged 70.00
b. Booklet pane of 6 90.00
207 A94 1½p dark brown 1.40 1.10
Never hinged 3.75
a. Wmk sideways 25.00 25.00
Never hinged 37.50
b. Booklet pane of 6 60.00
c. Booklet pane of 4 + 2 labels 400.00
208 A95 2½p deep blue 6.50 6.50
Never hinged 17.50
Nos. 205-208 (4) 10.70 10.40
Set, never hinged 28.75

Inverted watermarks on the three lowest values are usually from booklet panes.
Nos. 205a, 206a and 207a were issued in coils.

St. George Slaying the Dragon A96

Wmk. 219

1929, May 10 Engr. *Perf. 12*

209 A96 £1 black 750. 675.
Never hinged 1,100.

Universal Postal Union, 9th Congress.

A97

Type A97 designs are re-engraved versions of the types of the 1912-13 issue, with the most obvious difference being the solid appearance of the central field. The backgrounds appear to be solid, although the photoengraving screen can be seen under magnification.

Perf. 14½x14

1934-36 Photo. Wmk. 35

210 A97 ½p dark green .25 .25
Never hinged .35
a. Wmk. sideways 6.50 3.25
Never hinged 13.00
b. Booklet pane of 6 30.00
211 A97 1p carmine .25 .25
Never hinged .75
a. Wmk. sideways 13.00 13.00
Never hinged 35.00
b. Booklet pane of 6 60.00
c. Imperf., pair *7,500.* 5,250.
d. Pair, imperf. btwn. 13,000. *9,000.*
212 A97 1½p red brown .25 .25
Never hinged .75
a. Imperf., pair 1,800. *1,400.*
b. Wmk. sideways 7.50 3.50
Never hinged 15.00
c. Booklet pane of 6 50.00
d. Booklet pane of 4 + 2 labels 45.00
213 A97 2p red org ('35) .60 .60
Never hinged 1.40
a. Imperf., pair *7,500.* *6,000.*
b. Wmk. sideways 90.00 70.00
Never hinged 275.00
214 A97 2½p ultra ('35) .65 .50
Never hinged 1.50
215 A97 3p dk violet ('35) .75 .65
Never hinged 2.25
216 A97 4p dk sl grn ('35) 1.00 .90
Never hinged 3.50
217 A97 5p yel brown ('36) 5.00 1.75
Never hinged 12.50
218 A97 9p dk ol grn ('35) 7.00 2.25
Never hinged 17.00
219 A97 10p Prus blue ('36) 12.00 8.00
Never hinged 29.00
220 A97 1sh bister brn ('36) 13.00 1.25
Never hinged 37.50
Nos. 210-220 (11) 40.75 16.65
Set, never hinged 106.50

The designs in this set are slightly smaller than the 1912-13 issue.

Inverted watermarks on the three lowest values are usually from booklet panes.

Nos. 210a, 211a, 212b and 213b were issued in coils.

Britannia Type of 1913-19 Reengraved

1934 Engr. Wmk. 34 *Perf. 11x12*

222 A91 2sh6p brown 80.00 25.00
Never hinged 150.00
223 A91 5sh carmine 175.00 60.00
Never hinged 375.00
224 A91 10sh dark blue 375.00 65.00
Never hinged 750.00
Nos. 222-224 (3) 630.00 150.00

Printed by Waterlow & Sons. Can be distinguished by the crossed lines in background of portrait. Previous issues have horizontal lines only.

For overprints see Ireland Nos. 93-95.

Silver Jubilee Issue

A98

Perf. 14½x14

1935, May 7 Photo. Wmk. 35

226 A98 ½p dark green .40 .25
Never hinged .75
a. Booklet pane of 4 9.50
227 A98 1p carmine .75 *.40*
Never hinged 1.50
a. Booklet pane of 4 18.00
228 A98 1½p red brown .50 .25
Never hinged 1.00
a. Booklet pane of 4 12.50
229 A98 2½p ultra 3.50 *3.50*
Never hinged 6.25
a. 2½p Prussian blue *13,500.* *15,000.*
Never hinged *18,500.*
Nos. 226-229 (4) 5.15 *4.40*
Set, never hinged 9.50

25th anniv. of the reign of George V. Device at right differs on 1½p and 2½p.

Inverted watermarks on the three lowest values are usually from booklet panes.

Edward VIII — A99

1936 Wmk. 250

230 A99 ½p dark green .25 .25
Never hinged .25
a. Booklet pane of 6 16.00
Never hinged 20.00
231 A99 1p crimson .25 .25
Never hinged .30
a. Booklet pane of 6 20.00
Never hinged 30.00
232 A99 1½p red brown .25 .25
Never hinged .25
a. Booklet pane of 6 16.00
Never hinged 20.00
b. Booklet pane of 4 + 2 labels 20.00
Never hinged 25.00
c. Booklet pane of 2 20.00
Never hinged 25.00
233 A99 2½p bright ultra .25 *.75*
Never hinged .30
Nos. 230-233 (4) 1.00 *1.50*
Set, never hinged 1.10

Inverted watermarks on the three lowest values are usually from booklet panes.

King George VI and Queen Elizabeth A100

Perf. 14½x14

1937, May 13 Wmk. 251

234 A100 1½p purple brown .25 .25
Never hinged .30

Coronation of George VI and Elizabeth.

See British Offices Abroad for overprints on types A44-A133.
These overprints include "M.E.F.," "B.A.," "B.M.A.," "E.A.F.," "CHINA," "Morocco Agencies," "TANGIER," "LEVANT," "PARAS," and "PIASTRE(S)."

A101

A102

King George VI — A103

Nos. 235-240 show face and neck highlighted, background solid.

1937-39

235 A101 ½p deep green .25 .25
Never hinged .25
a. Wmk. sideways .35 .30
Never hinged .75
b. Booklet pane of 6 65.00
Never hinged 90.00
c. Booklet pane of 4 50.00 25.00
Never hinged 75.00
d. Booklet pane of 2 75.00
Never hinged 105.00
236 A101 1p scarlet .25 .25
Never hinged .25
a. Wmk. sideways 9.50 9.00
Never hinged 20.00
b. Booklet pane of 6 160.00
Never hinged 210.00
c. Booklet pane of 4 50.00 *50.00*
Never hinged 75.00
d. Booklet pane of 2 75.00
Never hinged 105.00
237 A101 1½p red brown .25 .25
Never hinged .25
a. Wmk. sideways .80 *1.25*
Never hinged 1.25
b. Booklet pane of 6 160.00
Never hinged 210.00
c. Booklet pane of 4 + 2 labels 100.00
Never hinged 140.00
d. Booklet pane of 2 27.00
Never hinged 37.50
238 A101 2p org ('38) .70 .40
Never hinged 1.40
a. Wmk. sideways 28.00 32.50
Never hinged 60.00
b. Booklet pane of 6 85.00
Never hinged 110.00
239 A101 2½p bright ultra .25 .25
Never hinged .25
a. Wmk. sideways 33.00 32.50
Never hinged 77.50
b. Booklet pane of 6 65.00
Never hinged 90.00
c. Tête bêche pair *22,000.*
240 A101 3p dk pur ('38) 2.25 .80
Never hinged 4.50
241 A102 4p gray grn ('38) .25 *.55*
Never hinged .40
a. Imperf., pair *7,500.*
Never hinged *9,500.*
b. Horiz. pair, imperf. on 3 sides *8,000.*
Never hinged *10,000.*
242 A102 5p lt brn ('38) 1.25 .70
Never hinged 2.50
a. Imperf., pair *7,000.*
Never hinged *9,000.*
b. Horiz. pair, imperf. on 3 sides *7,500.*
Never hinged *9,500.*
243 A102 6p rose lil ('39) .65 .50
Never hinged 1.25
244 A103 7p emer ('39) 2.00 .50
Never hinged 5.00
a. Horiz. pair, imperf. on 3 sides *7,500.*
Never hinged *9,500.*
245 A103 8p brt rose ('39) 3.00 .75
Never hinged 7.75
246 A103 9p dp ol grn ('39) 2.75 .75
Never hinged 5.75
247 A103 10p royal bl ('39) 2.75 .75
Never hinged 5.50
a. Imperf., pair *5,700.*
Never hinged *7,000.*
248 A103 1sh brown ('39) 2.75 .70
Never hinged 6.25
Nos. 235-248 (14) 19.35 7.40
Set, never hinged 40.90

Nos. 235a, 236a, 237a, 238a and 239a were issued in coils.

Nos. 235c and 236c are watermarked sideways.

The ½p, 1p, 1½p, 2p and 2½p with watermark inverted are from booklet panes.

No. 238 bisects were used in Guernsey from 12/27/40 to 2/24/41. Value, on cover $32.50.

See Nos. 258-263, 266, 280-285.

Oman Surcharges

Various definitive and commemorative stamps between Nos. 243 and 372 were surcharged in annas (a), new paisa (np) and rupees (r) for use in Oman. The surcharges do not indicate where the stamps were used.

King George VI and Royal Arms — A104

King George VI — A105

1939-42 Engr. Wmk. 259 *Perf. 14*

249 A104 2sh6p chestnut 45.00 9.00
Never hinged 110.00
249A A104 2sh6p yel grn ('42) 6.50 1.50
Never hinged 14.50
250 A104 5sh dull red 9.50 2.00
Never hinged 20.00
251 A105 10sh indigo 135.00 22.50
Never hinged 275.00
251A A105 10sh ultra ('42) 15.00 4.50
Never hinged 42.50
Nos. 249-251A (5) 211.00 39.50
Set, never hinged 462.00

See No. 275.

Victoria and George VI A106

Perf. 14½x14

1940, May 6 Photo. Wmk. 251

252 A106 ½p deep green .25 .25
Never hinged .25
253 A106 1p scarlet .25 .25
Never hinged .35
254 A106 1½p red brown .25 .25
Never hinged .30
255 A106 2p orange .40 .25
Never hinged .55
256 A106 2½p brt ultra .90 .25
Never hinged 1.35
257 A106 3p dark purple 2.00 *3.00*
Never hinged 3.00
Nos. 252-257 (6) 4.05 4.25
Set, never hinged 5.80

Centenary of the postage stamp.

No. 255 bisects were used in Guernsey from 12/27/40 to 2/24/41. Value, on cover, $40.

Type of 1937-39, with Background Lightened

1941-42

258 A101 ½p green .25 .25
Never hinged .25
a. Booklet pane of 6 16.00
Never hinged 22.00
b. Booklet pane of 2 2.50
Never hinged 3.00
c. Imperf., pair *6,500.*
Never hinged *8,500.*
d. Tete beche pair *8,000.*
Never hinged *18,500.*
e. Booklet pane of 4 *1,500.*
259 A101 1p vermilion .25 .25
Never hinged .25
a. Wmk. sideways ('42) 2.50 *3.50*
Never hinged 3.75
b. Booklet pane of 2 2.50
Never hinged 3.00
c. Imperf., pair *6,000.*
Never hinged *8,000.*
d. Booklet pane of 4 *1,500.*
e. Horiz. pair, imperf on 3 sides *6,000.*
Never hinged *8,500.*
260 A101 1½p lt red brn ('42) .40 *.75*
Never hinged .45
a. Booklet pane of 2 4.50
Never hinged 6.25
b. Booklet pane of 4 *3,900.*
261 A101 2p light orange .30 *.35*
Never hinged .35
a. Wmk. sideways ('42) 12.50 12.50
Never hinged 16.00
b. Booklet pane of 6 28.00
Never hinged 40.00
c. Imperf., pair *5,500.*
Never hinged *7,500.*
d. Tete beche pair *16,000.*
Never hinged *18,500.*
262 A101 2½p ultra .25 .25
Never hinged .25
a. Wmk. sideways ('42) 9.00 *10.00*
Never hinged 12.00
b. Booklet pane of 6 16.50
Never hinged 23.00
c. Imperf., pair *3,500.*
Never hinged *5,000.*
d. Tete beche pair *12,000.*
Never hinged *18,500.*
263 A101 3p violet .80 .80
Never hinged 1.25
Nos. 258-263 (6) 2.25 2.65
Set, never hinged 2.80

The ½p, 2p and 2½p with inverted watermarks are from booklets.

Nos. 259a, 261a and 262a were issued in coils.

Nos. 258b, 258e, 259b, 259d, 260a-260b are made from sheets.

Catalogue values for unused stamps in this section, from this point to the end of the section, are for Never Hinged items.

Peace Issue

A107

King George VI and Symbols of Peace and Industry A108

Perf. 14½x14

1946, June 11 Photo. Wmk. 251

No.	Type	Description	Unused	Used
264	A107	2½p bright ultra	.25	.25
265	A108	3p violet	.25	.25

Return to peace at the close of WW II.

George VI Type of 1939

1947, Dec. 29

No.	Type	Description	Unused	Used
266	A103	11p violet brown	2.50	2.00

A109

King George VI and Queen Elizabeth A110

1948, Apr. 26 *Perf. 14½x14, 14x14½*

No.	Type	Description	Unused	Used
267	A109	2½p brt ultra	.40	.25
268	A110	£1 dp chalky blue	30.00	25.00

25th anniv. of the marriage of King George VI and Queen Elizabeth.

A111

Vraicking (Gathering Seaweed) A112

1948, May 10 *Perf. 14½x14*

No.	Type	Description	Unused	Used
269	A111	1p red	.25	.25
270	A112	2½p bright ultra	.25	.25

3rd anniversary of the liberation of the Channel Islands from German occupation.

Sold at post offices in the Channel Islands and at major philatelic windows in the United Kingdom, and valid for postage throughout Great Britain.

A113

A114

A115

A116

1948, July 29

No.	Type	Description	Unused	Used
271	A113	2½p bright ultra	.25	.25
272	A114	3p deep violet	.35	.25
273	A115	6p red violet	2.75	.90
274	A116	1sh dark brown	3.75	1.20
		Nos. 271-274 (4)	7.10	2.60

1948 Olympic Games held at Wembley during July and August.

George VI Type of 1939

Wmk. 259

1948, Oct. 1 Engr. *Perf. 14*

No.	Type	Description	Unused	Used
275	A105	£1 red brown	25.00	20.00

A117

A118

A119

A120

Perf. 14½x14

1949, Oct. 10 Photo. Wmk. 251

No.	Type	Description	Unused	Used
276	A117	2½p bright ultra	.25	.25
277	A118	3p brt violet	.25	.25
278	A119	6p red violet	.35	.25
279	A120	1sh brown	.50	.25
		Nos. 276-279 (4)	1.35	1.00

UPU, 75th anniversary.

Types of 1937

1950-51 Wmk. 251 *Perf. 14½x14*

No.	Type	Description	Unused	Used
280	A101	½p light orange	.25	.25
a.		Booklet pane of 2	4.00	
b.		Booklet pane of 4	6.00	
c.		Booklet pane of 6	6.00	
d.		Imperf., pair	*7,500.*	
e.		Tete beche pair	*18,000.*	
281	A101	1p ultramarine	.25	.25
a.		Wmk. sideways	.35	*.50*
b.		Booklet pane of 2	5.25	
c.		Booklet pane of 4	11.00	
d.		Booklet pane of 6	10.00	
e.		Booklet pane of 3 + 3 labels	7.50	
f.		Imperf., pair	*5,000.*	
g.		Horiz. pair, imperf on 3 sides	*6,500.*	
282	A101	1½p green	.25	.25
a.		Wmk. sideways	1.25	*2.50*
b.		Booklet pane of 2	3.00	
c.		Booklet pane of 4	6.00	
d.		Booklet pane of 6	8.25	
283	A101	2p lt red brown	.40	.35
a.		Wmk. sideways	.75	*1.00*
b.		Booklet pane of 6	12.00	
c.		Tete beche pair	*18,000.*	
d.		Horiz. pair, imperf on 3 sides	*8,000.*	
284	A101	2½p vermilion	.25	.25
a.		Wmk. sideways	.75	.75
b.		Booklet pane of 6	8.25	
c.		Tete beche pair		
285	A102	4p ultra ('50)	1.50	1.50
a.		Double impression		*8,250.*
		Nos. 280-285 (6)	2.90	2.85

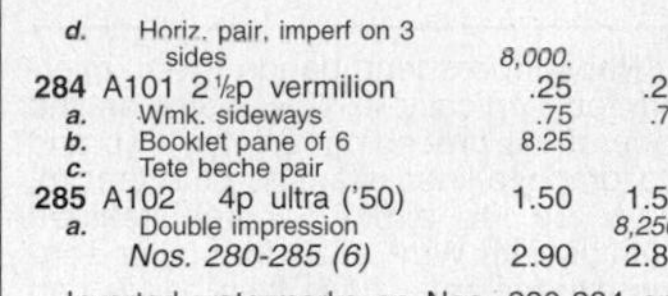

Inverted watermarks on Nos. 280-284 are usually from booklets.

Nos. 281a, 282a, 283a and 284a were issued in coils.

H.M.S. Victory A121

St. George Slaying the Dragon A122

Royal Arms A123

Design: 5sh, White Cliffs, Dover.

Perf. 11x12

1951, May 3 Engr. Wmk. 259

No.	Type	Description	Unused	Used
286	A121	2sh6p green	7.50	1.00
287	A121	5sh dull red	16.00	1.00
288	A122	10sh ultra	22.50	8.00
289	A123	£1 lt red brown	34.00	15.00
		Nos. 286-289 (4)	80.00	25.00

Britannia, Symbols of Commerce and Prosperity, King George VI — A124

Festival Symbol A125

Perf. 14½x14

1951, May 3 Photo. Wmk. 251

No.	Type	Description	Unused	Used
290	A124	2½p scarlet	.25	.25
291	A125	4p bright ultra	.25	.25

Festival of Britain, 1951.

Queen Elizabeth

A126 A127

A128

A129

A130

A131

A132

The 2½d exists in two types: Type I, in the front cross of the diadem, the top line extends half the width of the cross; Type II, the top line extends across the full width of the top of the cross.

Perf. 14½x14

1952-54 Photo. Wmk. 298

No.	Type	Description	Unused	Used
292	A126	½p red orange ('53)	.25	.25
a.		Booklet pane of 2	1.00	
b.		Booklet pane of 4	2.50	
c.		Booklet pane of 6	15.00	
293	A126	1p ultra ('53)	.25	.25
a.		Booklet pane of 2	1.10	
b.		Booklet pane of 4	2.50	
c.		Booklet pane of 6	17.00	
d.		Booklet pane 3 + 3 labels	7.50	
294	A126	1½p green ('52)	.25	.25
a.		Booklet pane of 2	1.10	
b.		Booklet pane of 4	2.40	
c.		Booklet pane of 6 ('53)	8.50	
d.		Wmk. sideways	.40	*.40*
e.		As "c," imperf. (error)	*750.00*	
295	A126	2p red brn ('53)	.25	.25
a.		Booklet pane of 6	17.00	
b.		Wmk. sideways	.75	*2.25*
296	A127	2½p scarlet, Type I ('52)	.25	.25
a.		Booklet pane of 6, Type II ('53)	6.00	
b.		Wmk. sideways, Type I ('54)	5.00	*5.00*
c.		Type II	1.00	1.00
297	A127	3p dk purple	.70	.65
298	A128	4p ultra ('53)	2.50	1.10
299	A129	5p lt brn ('53)	.65	*1.50*
300	A129	6p lilac rose	3.50	.75
301	A129	7p emerald	8.00	4.50
302	A130	8p brt rose ('53)	.60	.60
303	A130	9p dp ol grn	17.50	4.25
304	A130	10p royal blue	15.00	4.00
305	A130	11p vio brown	27.50	11.50
306	A131	1sh brown ('53)	.60	.45
307	A132	1sh3p dk grn ('53)	4.25	2.50
308	A131	1sh6p dk bl ('53)	19.00	3.75
		Nos. 292-308 (17)	101.05	36.80

Nos. 294d, 295b, 296b issued in coils.

Nos. 292-296 with watermark inverted are from booklets.

Type II stamps of No. 296 come only from booklet panes.

See Nos. 317-333, 353-369, 1801-1803, 2022-2023, 2086, 2125.

Compare design A128 with A139.

See regional issues, Guernsey, Jersey and Isle of Man for other stamps showing this portrait of the Queen, which have different frames or devices added to the design.

See British Offices Abroad for overprints on types A44-A133. These overprints include "M.E.F.," "B.A.," "B.M.A.," "E.A.F.," "CHINA," "Morocco Agencies," "TANGIER," "LEVANT," "PARAS," and "PIASTRE(S)."

Windsor, England A133

Castles: 2sh6p, Carrickfergus, Ireland. 5sh, Caernarfon Castle, Wales. 10sh, Edinburgh, Scotland.

1955 Engr. Wmk. 308 *Perf. 11x12*

No.	Type	Description	Unused	Used
309	A133	2sh6p dark brown	12.50	1.50
310	A133	5sh crimson	37.50	4.25
311	A133	10sh brt ultra	80.00	9.00
312	A133	£1 intense blk	110.00	37.50
		Nos. 309-312 (4)	240.00	52.25

See Nos. 371-374, 525-528, 2278.

A134

A135

A136

A137

Perf. 14½x14

1953, June 3 Photo. Wmk. 298

313 A134 2½p scarlet	.35	.25
314 A135 4p ultra	1.25	.35
315 A136 1sh3p dark green	4.75	1.60
316 A137 1sh6p dark blue	10.00	3.75
Nos. 313-316 (4)	16.35	5.95

See Nos. 1942, 2126.

Types of 1952-54

1955-57 Wmk. 308 *Perf. 14½x14*

317 A126 ½p red org ('56)	.25	.25
a. Booklet pane of 6	3.25	
b. Booklet pane of 4	1.40	
d. Booklet pane of 2	6.75	
318 A126 1p ultra ('56)	.34	.25
a. Bklt. pane of 3 + 3 labels	5.00	
b. Booklet pane of 6	6.00	
c. Booklet pane of 4	2.50	
e. Tete Beche pair	—	
f. Booklet pane of 2	11.00	
319 A126 1½p green ('56)	.25	.25
a. Booklet pane of 6	4.50	
b. Booklet pane of 4	1.50	
c. Wmk. sideways ('56)	.30	*.65*
e. Tete beche pair	*3,000.*	
f. Booklet pane of 2	6.50	
320 A126 2p red brown	.30	.25
a. Wmk. sideways	.40	*.65*
b. Booklet pane of 6	3.00	
d. Tete beche pair	*2,000.*	
e. Vert. pair, imperf. between	*4,500.*	
f. As "a," horiz. pair, imperf. between	*4,500.*	
h. Imperf., pair	*350.00*	
321 A127 2½p scar, Type I ('56)	.25	.25
a. Booklet pane of 6, Type II	5.50	
b. Wmk. sideways, Type I ('56)	1.25	*1.40*
d. Type II	.55	.40
e. Tete beche pair	*3,000.*	
f. Imperf., pair	*300.00*	
322 A127 3p dk pur ('56)	.30	.25
a. Booklet pane of 6	4.75	
b. Booklet pane of 4	2.25	
c. Wmk. sideways	15.00	12.00
e. Tete beche pair	*3,000.*	
323 A128 4p ultra	1.35	.45
324 A129 5p lt brn ('56)	5.25	5.25
325 A129 6p lil rose ('56)	5.00	1.25
326 A129 7p emerald	45.00	10.00
327 A130 8p brt rose ('56)	6.50	1.10
328 A130 9p dp ol grn ('56)	18.00	2.75
329 A130 10p royal bl ('56)	18.00	2.75
330 A130 11p vio brown	.75	*.85*
331 A131 1sh brown	21.00	.60
332 A132 1sh3p dk grn ('56)	25.00	1.50
333 A131 1sh6p dark blue	30.00	1.50
Nos. 317-333 (17)	177.54	29.50

Nos. 319c, 320a, 321b, 322c issued in coils.

Nos. 317-322 with watermark inverted are from booklets. See Nos. 353-369.

Black Graphite Lines on Back

1957-59 Wmk. 308

317c A126 ½p red orange	.25	.25
p. Phosphor. ('59)	3.00	3.00
318d A126 1p ultra	.25	.25
p. Phosphor. ('59)	12.00	8.50
319d A126 1½p green	1.00	*1.50*
p. Phosphor. ('59)	3.25	3.25
320c A126 2p red brown	1.10	*1.40*
p. Phosphor. ('59)	160.00	125.00
321c A127 2½p scarlet (II)	5.25	5.25
322d A127 3p dark purple	.50	.45
Nos. 317c-322d (6)	8.35	9.10

The vertical black graphite lines were applied to facilitate mail sorting by an electronic machine. The 2p has one line (at right, seen from back), the others two.

No. 321c exists with phosphor bands. This variety likely was not officially issued.

Phosphorescent bands were overprinted vertically in Nov. 1959 on the face of the preceding ½p, 1p, 1½p and 2p graphite-lined stamps, plus the 2p, 2½p, 3p, 4p and 4½p graphite-lined stamps with Wmk. 322, in a letter-sorting experiment. These faint bands can be seen best with an ultraviolet lamp; without it they can be seen best on unused stamps.

Scout Emblem and Rolling Hitch Knot A138

4p, Swallows. 1sh3p, Globe encircled by compass.

Perf. 14½x14

1957, Aug. 1 Wmk. 308

334 A138 2½p scarlet	.40	.35
335 A138 4p ultra	.60	*.60*
336 A138 1sh3p dk green	4.25	3.50
Nos. 334-336 (3)	5.25	4.45

50th anniv. of the Boy Scout movement and the World Scout Jubilee Jamboree, Sutton Coldfield, Aug. 1-12.

A139

1957, Sept. 12 Photo.

337 A139 4p ultra	.65	*.70*

46th Conf. of the Inter-Parliamentary Union, London, Sept. 12-19.

Welsh Dragon A140

Designs: 6p, Flag with British Empire and Commonwealth Games Emblem. 1sh3p, Welsh dragon holding laurel.

1958, July 18 *Perf. 14½x14*

338 A140 3p dk purple	.25	.25
339 A140 6p red lilac	.25	.25
340 A140 1sh3p green	1.75	1.15
Nos. 338-340 (3)	2.25	1.65

6th British Empire and Commonwealth Games, Cardiff, July 18-26.

Regional Issues of Great Britain for Guernsey, Jersey, Isle of Man, Northern Ireland, Scotland and Wales-Monmouthshire are listed in separate sections following Great Britain Envelopes.

Types of 1952-55

Perf. 14½x14

1958-65 Photo. Wmk. 322

353 A126 ½p red orange	.25	.25
a. Booklet pane of 6	3.50	
b. Booklet pane of 4	1.50	
e. Booklet pane of 4 (3 No. 353 + No. 357) ('63)	2.00	2.00
f. Tete beche pair	*2,250.*	
g. Booklet pane of 4 (2 Nos. 353 + 2 No. 357) ('64)	.80	.80
h. Wmk. sideways	.25	.35
354 A126 1p ultra ('59)	.25	.25
a. Booklet pane of 6 ('59)	3.50	
b. Booklet pane of 4	1.50	
e. Imperf., pair	—	
f. Bklt. pane, #2 #354, 2 #358 ('65)	2.50	2.50
g. Têtê-beche pair		
h. Wmk. sideways	.80	.75
355 A126 1½p green	.25	.25
a. Booklet pane of 6	6.00	
b. Booklet pane of 4	1.50	
e. Têtê-beche pair		
f. Wmk. sideways	8.00	6.50
g. As "f," booklet pane of 4	35.00	
356 A126 2p red brown	.25	.25
a. Wmk. sideways	.60	*.80*
b. Booklet pane of 6	7.25	
357 A127 2½p scarlet, type II ('59)	.25	.25
a. Type I ('61)	3.25	.65
b. Wmk. sideways, type I	.50	.40
c. Booklet pane of 6, Type II ('59)	6.25	
f. Tete beche pair, type II	*5,000.*	
g. Booklet pane of 4, type II ('64)	2.00	
h. Imperf., pair	—	
i. Wmk. sideways, type II ('59)	.60	.75
358 A127 3p dark purple	.25	.25
a. Booklet pane of 6	9.00	
b. Booklet pane of 4	4.00	
e. Imperf., pair	250.00	
g. Wmk. sideways	.25	.35
359 A128 4p ultra	.25	.25
b. Booklet pane of 6 ('65)	3.50	
c. Booklet pane of 4 ('65)	2.10	
d. Wmk. sideways	1.25	.55
360 A128 4½p henna brn	.25	.25
361 A129 5p light brown	.30	.40
362 A129 6p lil rose ('59)	.25	.25
363 A129 7p emerald	.45	.45
364 A130 8p brt rose ('60)	.45	.40
365 A130 9p dp ol grn ('59)	.45	.40
366 A130 10p royal blue	.80	.65
367 A131 1sh brown	.45	.35
368 A132 1sh3p dk grn ('59)	.45	.35
369 A131 1sh6p dark blue	5.25	.60
Nos. 353-369 (17)	10.85	5.85

Nos. 356a and 357b were issued in coils. The 3p and 4p watermarked sideways may be from a coil or booklet pane of 4.

Booklet panes of this issue have watermarks upright, inverted or sideways.

Part perf. booklet panes exist of No. 353a and No. 354a.

Black Graphite Lines on Back

1958-59 Wmk. 322

353c A126 ½p red orange ('59)	7.75	7.75
d. Booklet pane of 6	45.00	
354c A126 1p ultra	2.00	1.50
d. Booklet pane of 6	12.00	
355c A126 1½p green ('59)	85.00	75.00
d. Booklet pane of 6	510.00	
356c A126 2p red brown	8.00	2.75
cp. Phosphor. ('59)	5.25	4.75
357d A127 2½p scarlet (II) ('59)	8.75	7.50
dp. Phosphor. ('59)	19.00	15.00
e. Booklet pane of 6	55.00	
358c A127 3p dark purple	.35	.30
cp. Phosphor. ('59)	8.50	7.75
d. Booklet pane of 6	2.75	
359a A128 4p ultra ('59)	6.00	5.00
ap. Phosphor. ('59)	17.00	14.00
360a A128 4½p henna brn ('59)	6.00	5.00
ap. Phosphor. ('59)	25.00	17.50
Nos. 353c-360a (8)	123.85	104.80

The vertical black graphite lines were applied to facilitate mail sorting by an electronic machine. The 2p has one line; the others two. Missing or misplaced lines occur on 1p, 3p and 4p.

Nos. 353c and 354c were issued only in booklets or coils; No. 355c only in booklets.

Booklet pane values are for panes with untrimmed perforations on all sides.

Phosphorescent Stamps of 1958-65

1960-67 Wmk. 322

353p A126 ½p red orange	.25	.25
ap. Booklet pane of 6	2.10	
bp. Booklet pane of 4	11.50	
hp. Wmk. sideways ('61)	8.00	8.00
354p A126 1p ultra	.25	.25
ap. Booklet pane of 6	1.00	
bp. Booklet pane of 4	9.00	
fp. Booklet pane of 2 each #354p, 358p	40.00	
hp. Wmk. sideways ('61)	.45	.45
355p A126 1½p green	.25	.25
ap. Booklet pane of 6	7.00	
bp. Booklet pane of 4	12.00	
fp. Wmk. sideways ('61)	8.00	7.50
356p A126 2p red brown	.25	.25
ap. Watermark sideways	.40	*.40*
357p A127 2½p scarlet (II)	.25	*.30*
ap. Type I ('61)	47.50	40.00
cp. Booklet pane of 6	60.00	
358p A127 3p dark purple	.45	*.50*
ap. Booklet pane of 6	3.00	
bp. Booklet pane of 4	25.00	
gp. Watermark sideways	.90	.90
359p A128 4p ultramarine	.25	.25
bp. Booklet pane of 6	1.25	
cp. Booklet pane of 4	5.00	
dp. Watermark sideways	.30	*.50*
360p A128 4½p henna brown ('61)	.25	.25
361p A129 5p lt brown ('67)	.25	.25
362p A129 6p lilac rose	.35	.30
363p A129 7p emerald ('67)	.45	.40
364p A130 8p brt rose ('67)	.40	.40
365p A130 9p dp ol grn ('67)	.50	.45
366p A130 10p royal blue ('67)	.65	.65
367p A131 1sh brown ('67)	.45	.35
368p A132 1sh3p dark green	1.90	*2.50*
369p A131 1sh6p dark blue ('66)	3.00	3.00
Nos. 353p-369p (17)	10.15	10.60

The 2p, 2½p (II) and 3p were issued with both one and two phosphorescent bands. The less expensive is valued here.

Watermarked sideways, the 2p is from a coil; the 3p and 4p from booklet pane or coil; the ½p, 1p and 1½p from booklet panes.

Booklet panes of 4 with phosphorescent bands;

No 354fp exists with 3p having one or two phosphorescent bands. No. 357cp exists with either one or two phosphorescent bands.

Castle Type of 1955

Perf. 11x12

1959-68 Engr. Wmk. 322

371 A133 2sh6p dark brown	.40	.40
372 A133 5sh crimson	1.40	.50
373 A133 10sh bright ultra	3.00	2.00
374 A133 £1 intense blk	11.00	6.00
Nos. 371-374 (4)	15.80	8.90

See Nos 525-528.

Postboy on Horseback A147

Queen Elizabeth II, Oak Leaves and 1660 Post Horn — A148

Perf. 14½x14, 14x14½

1960, July 7 Photo. Wmk. 322

375 A147 3p bright violet	.25	.25
376 A148 1sh3p dark green	2.40	*2.40*

Tercentenary of the act establishing the General Letter Office (General Post Office).

Symbolic Wheel CD3

Perf. 14½x14

1960, Sept. 19 Wmk. 322

377 CD3 6p red lilac & grn	.50	.50
378 CD3 1sh6p dk bl & red brn	7.50	4.50

1st anniv. of the establishment of CEPT.

Symbolic Thrift Plant — A150

Nut Tree, Nest, Squirrel, Owl A151

Thrift Plant A152

Perf. 14x14½, 14½x14

1961, Aug. 28 Photo. Wmk. 322

379 A150 2½p scar & blk	.25	.25
a. Black omitted	*27,500.*	
380 A151 3p pur & org	.25	.25
a. Orange omitted	1,800.	—
381 A152 1sh6p dk bl & ver	.95	.95
Nos. 379-381 (3)	1.45	1.45

Centenary of Post Office Savings Bank.

CEPT Emblem A153

Nineteen Doves Flying as One CD4

Design: 10p, Queen at right.

1961, Sept. 18 *Perf. 14½x14*

382 A153 2p red brn, yel & rose .25 .25
a. Orange omitted *19,000.*
383 CD4 4p ultra, pink & buff .25 .25
384 CD4 10p dk bl, yel grn & Prus blue .25 .25
a. Yellow green omitted *28,000.*
b. Dark blue omitted *8,500.*
Nos. 382-384 (3) .75 .75

Hammer Beam Roof of Westminster Hall — A155

Parliament — A156

Perf. 14½x14, 14x14½

1961, Sept. 25 **Wmk. 322**

385 A155 6p red lil & gold .25 .25
a. Gold omitted *2,800.*
386 A156 1sh3p grn & slate 1.25 1.25
a. Slate (Queen's head) omitted *45,000.*

7th Commonwealth Parliamentary Conf.

National Productivity Symbol — A157

Designs: 3p, Two arrows and map of the British Isles. 1sh3p, Five arrows pointing up.

Perf. 14½x14

1902, Nov. 14 **Photo.** **Wmk. 322**

387 A157 2½p car rose & dk grn .25 .25
388 A157 3p violet & blue .25 .25
a. Queen's head omitted *6,750.*
389 A157 1sh3p dk grn, car rose & bl 1.40 *1.40*
a. Queen's head omitted *18,000.*
Nos. 387-389 (3) 1.90 1.90

Phosphorescent

387p A157 2½p car rose & dk grn .30 .35
388p A157 3p violet & blue .50 .60
389p A157 1sh3p dk grn, car rose & bl 19.50 13.00
Nos. 387p-389p (3) 20.30 13.95

National Productivity Year. The watermark on Nos. 387-388 is inverted.

Phosphorescent Commemorative stamps between Nos. 387-493 were issued both with and without phosphorescence on the front unless otherwise noted with the issue.

Starting with No. 514, commemorative stamps were issued only with phosphorescence on the front unless otherwise noted.

Phosphorescent Regulars: Starting in 1967, all small stamps (lower values) of the regular series were issued only with phosphorescence.

Wheat Emblem and People A158

1sh3p, Children of different races.

1963, Mar. 21 **Wmk. 322**

390 A158 2½p pink & dp car .25 .25
p. Phosphor. 1.00 1.00
391 A158 1sh3p yellow & brn 1.50 1.00
p. Phosphor. 19.00 14.00

FAO "Freedom from Hunger" campaign.

Paris Postal Conference A159

1963, May 7 **Wmk. 322**

392 A159 6p purple & green .35 .35
a. Green omitted *6,500.*
p. Phosphor. 5.25 4.25

Cent. of the 1st Intl. Postal Conf., Paris, 1863, and Paris Postal Conf., May 7-9, 1963.

Buttercups, Daisies and Bee A160

Design: 4½p, Badger, Fawn, woodpecker, lark, titmouse, butterfly, mouse and wild plants.

1963, May 16 *Perf. 14½x14*

393 A160 3p multicolored .25 .25
p. Phosphor. .50 .50
394 A160 4½p multicolored .25 .25
p. Phosphor. 2.00 2.00

Natl. Nature Week, May 18-25, and the importance of wildlife conservation.

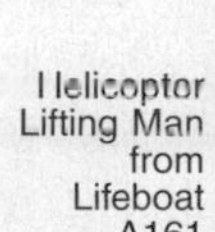
Helicopter Lifting Man from Lifeboat A161

Lifeboat Men A162

Design: 4p, 19th cent. lifeboat under sail.

1963, May 31 **Photo.**

395 A161 2½p multicolored .25 .25
396 A161 4p multicolored .30 .35
397 A162 1sh6p multicolored 2.00 2.10
Nos. 395-397 (3) 2.55 2.70

Phosphorescent

395p A161 2½p multicolored .50 .30
396p A161 4p multicolored .40 *.50*
397p A162 1sh6p multicolored 32.50 19.00
Nos. 395p-397p (3) 33.40 19.80

9th Intl. Life-Boat Conf., Edinburgh, 6/3-5.

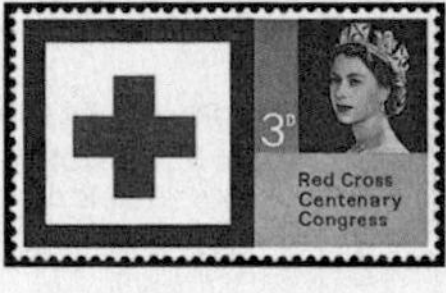

Red Cross and Elizabeth II — A163

1sh3p, Cross at UL. 1sh6p, Cross in center.

1963, Aug. 15 **Wmk. 322**

Cross in Red

398 A163 3p purple .25 .25
a. Red cross omitted *19,000.*
399 A163 1sh3p gray & blue 1.90 1.90
400 A163 1sh6p dl bl & ol bister 1.90 1.90
Nos. 398-400 (3) 4.05 4.05

Phosphorescent

398p A163 3p purple .50 .50
a. Red cross omitted 50,000.
399p A163 1sh3p gray & blue 27.50 24.00
400p A163 1sh6p dull blue & ol bister 20.00 12.00
Nos. 398p-400p (3) 48.00 36.50

Red Cross Cent. Cong., Geneva, Sept. 2.

Cable Around World and Under Sea A164

1963, Dec. 3 *Perf. 14½x14*

401 A164 1sh6p blue & blk 1.75 *1.75*
a. Black omitted *9,000.*
p. Phosphor. 10.50 10.50

Opening of the Commonwealth Pacific (telephone) cable service, COMPAC.

Puck and Bottom from "A Midsummer Night's Dream," Shakespeare — A165

Hamlet Holding Yorick's Skull A166

First Folio Portrait of Shakespeare and: 6p, Feste the Clown, from "Twelfth Night." 1sh3p, Romeo and Juliet. 1sh6p, Henry V praying at Agincourt.

Perf. 14½x14

1964, Apr. 23 **Photo.** **Wmk. 322**

402 A165 3p multicolored .25 .25
403 A165 6p multicolored .25 .25
404 A165 1sh3p multicolored .45 *.50*
405 A165 1sh6p multicolored .55 .45

Perf. 11x12

Engr.

406 A166 2sh6p dark gray 1.40 1.40
Nos. 402-406 (5) 2.90 2.85

Phosphorescent

402p A165 3p multicolored .25 *.25*
403p A165 6p multicolored .40 *.80*
404p A165 1sh3p multicolored 3.50 *3.50*
405p A165 1sh6p multicolored 4.25 3.50
Nos. 402p-405p (4) 8.40 8.05

400th anniv. of the birth of William Shakespeare. No. 406 was not issued with phosphorescence.

Apartment Buildings, London A170

Designs: 4p, Shipyards, Belfast. 8p, Bedgelert Forest Park, Snowdonia. 1sh6p, Dounreay nuclear reactor and sheaves of wheat.

1964, July 1 **Photo.** *Perf. 14½x14*

410 A170 2½p multicolored .25 .25
411 A170 4p multicolored .25 .25
a. Violet ("4d") omitted *300.00*
b. Ocher omitted *475.00*
c. Violet & ocher omitted *550.00*
412 A170 8p multicolored .50 .50
a. Green omitted *25,000.*
413 A170 1sh6p multicolored 2.00 2.00
Nos. 410-413 (4) 3.00 3.00

Phosphorescent

410p A170 2½p multicolored .25 .35
411p A170 4p multicolored .65 .90
412p A170 8p multicolored 1.60 2.75
413p A170 1sh6p multicolored 17.50 12.00
Nos. 410p-413p (4) 20.00 16.00

20th Intl. Geographical Cong., London, July 20-28.

Spring Gentian A171

6p, Dog rose. 9p, Honeysuckle. 1sh3p, Fringed water lily.

1964, Aug. 5 **Wmk. 322**

414 A171 3p shown .25 .25
a. Blue omitted *25,000.*
b. Sage green omitted *29,000.*
415 A171 6p multi .25 .25
416 A171 9p multi 1.10 *1.25*
a. Light green omitted *26,500.*
417 A171 1sh3p multi 1.35 1.25
a. Yellow omitted 50,000.
Nos. 414-417 (4) 2.95 3.00

Phosphorescent

414p A171 3p Spring Gentian .25 .25
415p A171 6p Dog rose 1.00 1.25
416p A171 9p Honeysuckle 3.75 3.25
417p A171 1sh3p Fringed water lily 14.00 9.50
Nos. 414p-417p (4) 19.00 14.25

10th Intl. Botanical Cong., Edinburgh, Aug. 3-12.

Forth Road Bridge A172

Design: 6p, Bridge and railroad bridge.

1964, Sept. 4 *Perf. 14½x14*

418 A172 3p blk, lil & blue .25 .25
p. Phosphor. .50 .50
419 A172 6p vio blk, grnsh bl & car lake .25 .25
a. Greenish blue omitted *8,000.* *2,000.*
p. Phosphor. 4.00 4.00

Opening of Forth Road Bridge, Scotland.

Winston Churchill A173

Design: 1sh3p, Large portrait.

1965, July 8 **Photo.** **Wmk. 322**

420 A173 4p dk brown & blk .25 .25
p. Phosphor. .25 .25
421 A173 1sh3p gray & black .30 .25
p. Phosphor. 1.75 *2.00*

Sir Winston Spencer Churchill (1874-1965), statesman and WWII leader.

Seal of Simon de Montfort A174

St. Stephen's Hall, Westminster Hall and Abbey, Engraving by Wenceslaus Hollar, 1647 — A175

1965, July 19 *Perf. 14½x14*
422 A174 6p dark olive .25 .25
p. Phosphor. .60 .75
423 A175 2sh6p brown black .55 .60

700th anniv. of Parliament. No. 423 was not issued with phosphorescence; size: 58x21mm.

Salvation Army Band and "Blood and Fire" Flag A176

1sh6p, Salvation Army officers and flag.

1965, Aug. 9
424 A176 3p dk bl, yel & brt car .25 .25
p. Phosphor. .25 .35
425 A176 1sh6p red, yel & brt bl .50 .50
p. Phosphor. 1.60 1.90

Centenary of the Salvation Army.

Lister's Carbolic Spray A177

1sh, Joseph Lister & carbolic acid formula.

1965, Sept. 1
426 A177 4p gray, bluish blk & red brn .25 .25
a. Red brown (tubing) omitted 700.00
b. Bluish black omitted 7,000.
p. Phosphor. .25 .25
427 A177 1sh blk, blue & pur .50 .60
p. Phosphor. 1.75 2.00

Introduction of antiseptic surgery by Joseph Lister, cent.

Trinidad Folk Dancers, Shrove Monday Carnival A178

Design: 1sh6p, French Canadian folk dancers, Les Feux Follets.

Perf. 14½x14
1965, Sept. 1 Photo. Wmk. 322
428 A178 6p orange & blk .25 .25
p. Phosphor. .30 .40
429 A178 1sh6p brt vio & blk .50 .70
p. Phosphor. 2.40 2.60

1st Commonwealth Arts Festival, 9/16-10/2.

Supermarine Spitfire Fighters — A179

Anti-Aircraft Gun Battery in Action A180

Designs: No. 431, Pilot in cockpit of Hawker Hurricane fighter. No. 432, Wing tips of Messerschmitt ME-109 and Spitfire. No. 433, Two Spitfires attacking Heinkel HE-111 bomber. No. 434, Spitfire attacking Junkers JU-187B Stuka dive bomber. No. 435, Hurricanes returning over wreckage of Dornier DO-17 Z bomber. 1sh3p, Vapor trails over St. Paul's Cathedral, London.

Perf. 14½x14
1965, Sept. 13 Photo. Wmk. 322
430 A179 4p slate & dk ol .40 .45
431 A179 4p slate & dk ol .40 .45
432 A179 4p sl, dk ol, brt bl & red .40 .45
433 A179 4p slate & dk ol .40 .45
434 A179 4p slate & dk ol .40 .45
435 A179 4p sl, dk ol & brt blue .40 .45
a. Bright blue omitted 6,500.
b. Block of 6, #430-435 4.50 5.00
436 A180 9p vio bl, org & vio black 1.75 1.75
437 A180 1sh3p brt bl, sl & grnsh gray 1.75 1.75
Nos. 430-437 (8) 5.90 6.20

Phosphorescent

430p A179 4p slate & dark ol .90 1.00
431p A179 4p slate & dark ol .90 1.00
432p A179 4p sl, dk ol, brt bl & red .90 1.00
433p A179 4p slate & dark ol .90 1.00
434p A179 4p slate & dark ol .90 1.00
435p A179 4p sl, dk ol & brt bl .90 1.00
a. Block of 6, #430p-435p 9.50 12.00
436p A180 9p vio bl, org & vio black 1.90 2.00
437p A180 1sh3p brt bl, slate & grnsh gray 1.90 2.00
Nos. 430p-437p (8) 9.20 10.00

25th anniv. of the Battle of Britain. Nos. 430-435 printed in blocks of 6 (3x2) in sheets of 120.

Post Office Tower and Georgian Buildings — A181

Design: 1sh3p, Post Office Tower and Nash Terrace, Regents Park, horiz.

1965, Oct. 8 *Perf. 14x14½, 14½x14*
438 A181 3p brt bl, ocher & ol green .25 .25
a. Lemon omitted 7,000. 2,500.
p. Phosphor. .25 .25
439 A181 1sh3p grn, ol grn & bl .25 .25
p. Phosphor. .25 .25

Opening of the Post Office Tower, London.

UN Emblem A182

ICY Emblem A183

1965, Oct. 25 *Perf. 14½x14*
440 A182 3p multicolored .25 .25
p. Phosphor. .25 .25
441 A183 1sh6p multicolored .45 .50
p. Phosphor. 1.90 2.00

20th anniv. of the UN and Intl. Cooperation Year, 1965.

"World Telecommunication Stations" — A184

ITU Cent.: 1sh6p, "Radio waves & switchboard."

1965, Nov. 15 Photo. Wmk. 322
442 A184 9p multicolored .25 .25
p. Phosphor. .50 .50
443 A184 1sh6p bl, red, blk, ind & pink .60 .70
a. Pink omitted 4,750. 2,750.
p. Phosphor. 3.75 4.00

Robert Burns and Saltier Cross of St. Andrew A185

Design: 1sh3p, Alexander Nasmyth portrait of Burns, his signature and symbols of his life. Portrait of Burns on 4p stamp is adaptation of Archibald Skirvings', chalk drawing, 1798.

1966, Jan. 25 *Perf. 14½x14*
444 A185 4p blue, blk & dk sl .25 .25
p. Phosphor. .30 .35
445 A185 1sh3p org, blk & Prus blue .30 .40
p. Phosphor. 1.10 1.25

Robert Burns (1759-1796), Scottish national poet.

Westminster Abbey — A186

Fan Vaulting, Chapel of Henry VII A187

1966, Feb. 28 Photo. *Perf. 14½x14*
452 A186 3p blue, blk, & red brn .25 .25
p. Phosphor. .25 .25

Perf. 11x12
Engr.
453 A187 2sh6p black .40 .45

900th anniv. of Westminster Abbey. No. 453 issued only without phosphor.

Landscape near Hassock, Sussex A188

Views: 6p, Antrim, Northern Ireland. 1sh3p, Harlech Castle, Wales. 1sh6p, The Cairngorms (mountains), Scotland.

Perf. 14½x14
1966, May 2 Photo. Wmk. 322
454 A188 4p multicolored .25 .25
455 A188 6p multicolored .25 .25
456 A188 1sh3p multicolored .25 .25
457 A188 1sh6p multicolored .25 .25
Nos. 454-457 (4) 1.00 1.00

Phosphorescent

454p A188 4p multicolored .25 .25
455p A188 6p multicolored .25 .25
456p A188 1sh3p multicolored .25 .25
457p A188 1sh6p multicolored .25 .25
Nos. 454p-457p (4) 1.00 1.00

Soccer Players — A189

Players and Crowd A190

1sh3p, Goalkeeper and two players.

Perf. 14x14½, 14½x14
1966, June 1 Photo. Wmk. 322
458 A189 4p multicolored .25 .25
459 A190 6p multicolored .25 .25
a. Black omitted 250.00
b. Yellow green omitted 7,500.
c. Red omitted 13,000.
460 A190 1sh3p multicolored .25 .25
a. Blue omitted 400.00
Nos. 458-460 (3) .75 .75

Phosphorescent

458p A189 4p multicolored .25 .25
459p A190 6p multicolored .25 .25
d. Black omitted 3,500.
460p A190 1sh3p multicolored .25 .25
Nos. 458p-460p (3) .75 .75

Final games of the 1965-66 World Soccer Championship for the Jules Rimet Cup, Wembley, July 11-30.

See No. 465.

Black-headed Gull — A191

Perf. 14½x14
1966, Aug. 8 Photo. Wmk. 322
Birds in Natural Colors
461 A191 4p shown .25 .25
p. Phosphor. .25 .25
462 A191 4p Blue tit .25 .25
p. Phosphor. .25 .25
463 A191 4p European robin .25 .25
p. Phosphor. .25 .25
464 A191 4p European blackbird .25 .25
p. Phosphor. .25 .25
a. Block of 4, #461-464 1.00 1.00
b. Block of 4, #461p-464p 1.00 1.00

Seven colors have been found omitted (singly or in combinations) on Nos. 461-464; green, red, ultramarine, brown, red brown, yellow and black. Values range from $125 to $20,000.

No. 458 Inscribed: "ENGLAND WINNERS"

1966, Aug. 18 *Perf. 14x14½*
465 A189 4p multicolored .25 .25

England's victory in the World Soccer Cup Championship.

Jodrell Bank Radio Telescope A192

Designs: 6p, Automobiles (Jaguar and 3 Mini-Minors). 1sh3p, SR N6 Hovercraft. 1sh6p, Windscale atomic reactor.

1966, Sept. 19 *Perf. 14½x14*
466 A192 4p yellow & blk .25 .25
467 A192 6p org, red & dk bl .25 .25
a. Red (Mini-Minors) omitted 23,000. —
b. Dark blue (Jaguar & imprint) omitted 19,000.
468 A192 1sh3p sl, blk, org & bl .25 .25
469 A192 1sh6p multicolored .25 .25
Nos. 466-469 (4) 1.00 1.00

Phosphorescent

466p A192 4p yellow & black .25 .25
467p A192 6p org, red & dk bl .25 .25
468p A192 1sh3p slate, blk, org & bl .25 .25
469p A192 1sh6p multicolored .25 .25
Nos. 466p-469p (4) 1.00 1.00

British technology.

Battle of Hastings A193

Battle of Hastings from Bayeux Tapestry: No. 471, Two knights on horseback, one killed, one attacking. No. 472, Slain Harold on horseback and knight with shield. No. 473, Knight with shield and axe fighting horseman. No. 474, Knight on foot killing man, and horseman attacking with lance. No. 475, Four knights and two horses in battle scene. 6p, Norman ship. 1sh3p, King Harold's housecarls (body guard) battling Normans.

Photo.; Gold Impressed on 6p, 1sh3p

Perf. 14½x14

1966, Oct. 14 **Wmk. 322**

Size: 38½x22mm

470 A193 4p multicolored .25 .25
471 A193 4p multicolored .25 .25
472 A193 4p multicolored .25 .25
473 A193 4p multicolored .25 .25
474 A193 4p multicolored .25 .25
475 A193 4p multicolored .25 .25
a. Strip of 6, #470-475 1.75 1.75
476 A193 6p multi & gold .25 .25

Size: 58x22mm

477 A193 1sh3p multi & gold .25 .25
Nos. 470-477 (8) 2.00 2.00

Phosphorescent

470p A193 4p multicolored .25 .25
471p A193 4p multicolored .25 .25
472p A193 4p multicolored .25 .25
473p A193 4p multicolored .25 .25
474p A193 4p multicolored .25 .25
475p A193 4p multicolored .25 .25
b. Strip of 6, #470p-475p 1.75 1.75
476p A193 6p multi & gold .25 .25
477p A193 1sh3p multi & gold .25 .25
Nos. 470p-477p (8) 2.00 2.00

900th anniv. of the Battle of Hastings.

Eight colors have been found omitted (singly or in pair) on Nos. 470-475 and 470p-477p: gray, orange, blue, dark blue, bright green, olive green, brown and magenta. Also violet on 1sh3p. Values for various color-omitted examples of Nos. 470-475 and 470p-475p, $65-$75. Values for color-omitted examples of No. 477, $5,000.; No. 477p, $1,250.

Gold Omitted

The variety "Gold (Queen's head) omitted" can be forged by chemically removing the gold.

Christmas — A194

Photo.; Gold Impressed

1966, Dec. 1 ***Perf. 14x14½***

478 A194 3p King .25 .25
b. Green omitted — 4,500.
p. Phosphor. .25 .25
479 A194 1sh6p Snowman .25 .25
b. Pink omitted 4,750.
p. Phosphor. .25 .25

Loading Ship at Dock and Train A195

Design: 1sh6p, Loading plane from trucks and flags of EFTA members.

Perf. 14½x14

1967, Feb. 20 **Photo.** **Wmk. 322**

480 A195 9p blue & multi .25 .25
p. Phosphor. .25 .25
481 A195 1sh6p vio & multi .25 .25
p. Phosphor. .25 .25

European Free Trade Assoc. Tariffs were abolished Dec. 31, 1966, among EFTA members (Austria, Denmark, Finland, Great Britain, Norway, Portugal, Sweden, Switzerland).

Colors omitted include: 9p — yellow, brown, light blue, light violet and green singly; black, brown, light blue and yellow simultaneously. 1sh6p — dark blue, bister, yellow, red, ultramarine and gray. 9p, value range for one-color omissions, $75 to $200. 1sh6p, value for red omitted $5,000 (used), dark blue omitted $500, value for other color-omitted errors $75 to $125 each.

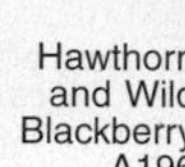

Hawthorn and Wild Blackberry A196

Flowers: No. 489, Morning glory and viper's bugloss. No. 490, Ox-eye daisy, coltsfoot and buttercup. No. 491, Bluebell, red campion and wood anemone. 9p, Dog violet. 1sh9p, Primrose.

Perf. 14½x14

1967, Apr. 24 **Photo.** **Wmk. 322**

488 A196 4p multicolored .25 .25
489 A196 4p multicolored .25 .25
490 A196 4p multicolored .25 .25
491 A196 4p multicolored .25 .25
492 A196 9p multicolored .25 .25
493 A196 1sh9p multicolored .25 .25
Nos. 488-493 (6) 1.50 1.50

Phosphorescent

488p A196 4p multicolored .25 .25
489p A196 4p multicolored .25 .25
490p A196 4p multicolored .25 .25
491p A196 4p multicolored .25 .25
492p A196 9p multicolored .25 .25
493p A196 1sh9p multicolored .25 .25
Nos. 488p-493p (6) 1.50 1.50

Four colors have been found omitted on Nos. 488-491 and three on 488p-491p: dark brown, red, violet and dull purple. Values range from $500 to $5,000.

For QEII Machin definitives, see listings following Regional Issues and preceding Booklets.

Master Lambton, by Thomas Lawrence — A198

Mares and Foals, by George Stubbs A199

Design: 1sh6p, Children Coming out of School, by Laurence Stephen Lowry.

Photo.; Gold Impressed on 4p, 1sh6p

Perf. 14x14½, 14½x14

1967, July 10 **Unwmk.**

514 A198 4p multi .25 .25
a. Gold (Queen's head & value) omitted 350.00
b. Blue omitted 22,500.
515 A199 9p multi .25 .25
a. Black (Queen's head & value) omitted 1,250.
b. Black (Queen's head only) omitted 2,600.
516 A199 1sh6p multi .25 .25
a. Blue omitted 375.00
b. Gray omitted 190.00
c. Gold (Queen's head) omitted 13,500.
Nos. 514-516 (3) .75 .75

See Nos. 568-571.

Gipsy Moth IV — A200

1967, July 24 **Photo.** ***Perf. 14½x14***

517 A200 1sh9p multicolored .25 .25

Sir Francis Chichester's one-man voyage around the world, Aug. 27, 1966-May 28, 1967.

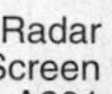

Radar Screen A201

British Discoveries: 1sh, Penicillin mold. 1sh6p, Vickers 10 twin jet engines. 1sh9p, Television camera, vert.

Perf. 14½x14, 14x14½

1967, Sept. 19 **Photo.** **Wmk. 322**

518 A201 4p multi .25 .25
519 A201 1sh multi .25 .25
520 A201 1sh6p multi .25 .25
521 A201 1sh9p multi .25 .25
a. Gray omitted 4,500.
b. Orange (queen's head) omitted 32,500.
Nos. 518-521 (4) 1.00 1.00

Adoration of the Shepherds, Ascribed to School of Seville — A202

Adoration of the Shepherds, by Le Nain A203

Christmas 1967: 4p, Madonna and Child, by Murillo.

Photo.; Gold Impressed

Perf. 14x14½, 14½x14

1967 **Unwmk.**

522 A202 3p multi .25 .25
a. Gold (Queen's head & value) omitted 110.00
b. Pink omitted 3,750.
523 A202 4p multi .25 .25
a. Gold (Queen's head & value) omitted 80.00
b. Gold ("4d" only) omitted 3,000.
c. Yellow omitted 7,500.
d. Greenish yellow & gold omitted 15,000.
524 A203 1sh6p multi .25 .25
a. Gold (Queen's head & value) omitted 18,500.
b. Blue omitted 900.00
c. Yellow omitted 20,000.
d. Gold (Queen's head only) omitted 3,000.
Nos. 522-524 (3) .75 .75

Issue dates: 4p, Oct. 18; 3p, 1sh6p, Nov. 27.

Castle Type of 1955

Perf. 11x12

1967-68 **Engr.** **Unwmk.**

525 A133 2sh6p dk brown ('68) .40 .40
526 A133 5sh crimson ('68) .95 .65
527 A133 10sh brt ultra ('68) 4.75 3.75
528 A133 £1 intense black 6.00 4.00
Nos. 525-528 (4) 12.10 8.80

Aberfeldy Bridge, Perthshire A204

Designs: 4p, Prehistoric Tarr Steps, Exmoor. 1sh6p, Menai Bridge, North Wales, 1826. 1sh9p, Viaduct, Highway M4.

Perf. 14½x14

1968, Apr. 29 **Photo.** **Unwmk.**

560 A204 4p gold & multi .25 .25
561 A204 9p gold & multi .25 .25
a. Blue omitted 7,000.
b. Gold (Queen's head) omitted 300.00
562 A204 1sh6p gold & multi .25 .25
a. Gold (Queen's head) omitted 450.00
b. Red omitted 475.00
563 A204 1sh9p gold & multi .25 .25
a. Gold (Queen's head) omitted 450.00
Nos. 560-563 (4) 1.00 1.00

Emmeline Pankhurst Statue A205

Designs: 4p, Letters "TUC" and faces. 1sh, Sopwith Camel 1914-1918 fighter plane and formation of Lightning jets. 1sh9p, Capt. Cook's "Endeavour" and signature.

1968, May 29

564 A205 4p brt grn, blk, ol & bl .25 .25
565 A205 9p gray, violet & blk .25 .25
566 A205 1sh gray, ol, red, bl & blk .25 .25
567 A205 1sh9p blk & bister .25 .25
Nos. 564-567 (4) 1.00 1.00

Cent. of Trades Union Congress (4p); 50th anniv. of women's suffrage (9p); 50th anniv. of the Royal Air Force (1sh); bicent. of Captain Cook's first discovery voyage (1sh9p).

Paintings Types of 1967

Paintings: 4p, Elizabeth I, c. 1575, artist unknown. 1sh, Pinkie (Miss Sarah Moulton-Barrett) by Sir Thomas Lawrence. 1sh6p, St. Mary le Port, by John Piper. 1sh9p, The Hay Wain (landscape), by John Constable.

Photo.; Gold Impressed

Perf. 14x14½, 14½x14

1968, Aug. 12

568 A198 4p multi .25 .25
a. Gold (Queen's head & value) omitted 350.00
b. Vermilion omitted 700.00
569 A198 1sh multi .25 .25
a. Gold (Queen's head & value) omitted 8,000.
570 A198 1sh6p multi .25 .25
a. Gold (Queen's head & value) omitted 375.00
571 A199 1sh9p multi .25 .25
a. Gold (Queen's head & value) omitted 1,100.
b. Red omitted 15,000.
Nos. 568-571 (4) 1.00 1.00

Sizes: 4p, 27x37½mm; 1sh, 25½x37½mm; 1sh6p, 31x37½mm; 1sh9p, 38x28mm.

Boy and Girl with Rocking Horse A206

Girl Playing with Dolls and Dollhouse — A207

Christmas: 1sh6p, Boy with toy train and building blocks.

Perf. 14½x14, 14x14½

1968, Nov. 25 **Photo.**

572 A206 4p gold & multi .25 .25
a. Gold omitted 9,000.
b. Vermilion omitted 700.00
c. Ultramarine omitted 600.00
573 A207 9p gold & multi .25 .25
a. Yellow omitted 190.00
574 A207 1sh6p gold & multi .25 .25
a. Turquoise-green omitted 22,500.
Nos. 572-574 (3) .75 .75

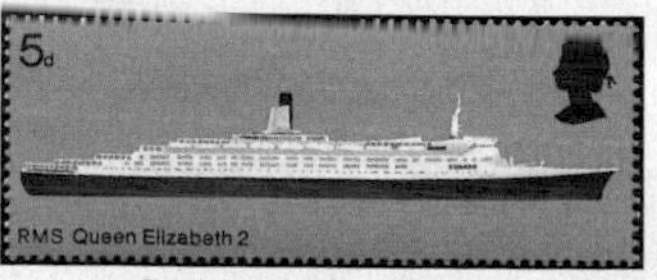

British Ships — A208

Designs: 5p, R.M.S. Queen Elizabeth 2. No. 576, Elizabethan Galleon. No. 577, East Indiaman. No. 578, Cutty Sark. No. 579, S.S. Great Britain. No. 580, R.M.S. Mauretania.

1969, Jan. 15 ***Perf. 14½x14***

Size: 58x22mm

575 A208 5p multicolored .25 .25
- *a.* Black omitted 3,750.
- *b.* Gray omitted 290.00
- *c.* Red omitted 325.00

Size: 38½x22mm

576 A208 9p multicolored .25 .25
- *a.* Red & blue omitted 4,000.
- *b.* Blue omitted 4,000.

577 A208 9p multicolored .25 .25
578 A208 9p multicolored .25 .25
- *a.* Strip of 3, #576-578 .75

Size: 58x22mm

579 A208 1sh multicolored .25 .25
- *a.* Greenish yellow omitted 5,000.

580 A208 1sh multicolored .25 .25
- *a.* Pair, #579-580 .50
- *b.* Carmine (hull overlay) omitted 40,000.
- *c.* Red (funnels) omitted 30,000.
- *d.* Carmine and red omitted 30,000.

Nos. 575-580 (6) 1.50 1.50

British seamen and shipbuilders.

Concorde over Great Britain and France A209

Designs: 9p, Concorde seen from above and from side, flags of France and Great Britain. 1sh6p, Outlines of plane's nose and tail superimposed.

1969, Mar. 3 **Photo.** ***Perf. 14½x14***

581 A209 4p multicolored .25 .25
- *a.* Violet omitted 900.00
- *b.* Orange omitted 900.00

582 A209 9p multicolored .25 .25
583 A209 1sh6p multicolored .25 .25
- *a.* Silver omitted 900.00

Nos. 581-583 (3) .75 .75

First flight of the prototype Concorde plane at Toulouse, France, Mar. 1, 1969.

Alcock, Brown, Daily Mail and Vickers Vimy Plane A210

"EUROPA" and "CEPT" CD12

Hand Holding Wrench A212

Flags of NATO Nations Forming one Flag A213

Vickers-Vimy Plane and Globe — A214

1969, Apr. 2

584 A210 5p multi .25 .25
585 CD12 9p multi .25 .25
586 A212 1sh multi .25 .25
587 A213 1sh6p multi .25 .25
- *a.* Black omitted 120.00
- *b.* Green omitted 90.00
- *c.* Yellow omitted 4,500.

588 A214 1sh9p multi .25 .25

Nos. 584-588 (5) 1.25 1.25

50th anniv. of the 1st non-stop Atlantic flight from Newfoundland to Ireland of Capt. John Alcock and Lt. Arthur Whitten Brown; 10th anniv. of the Conference of European Postal and Telecommunications Administrations; 50th anniv. of the ILO (1sh); 20th anniv. of NATO; 50th anniv. of the first England to Australia flight (1sh9p).

Durham Cathedral A215

British Cathedrals: No. 590, York Minster. No. 591, St. Giles', Edinburgh. No. 592, Canterbury. 9p, St. Paul's. 1sh6p, Liverpool Metropolitan.

Perf. 14½x14

1969, May 28 **Photo.** **Unwmk.**

589 A215 5p multi .25 .25
- *a.* Bluish violet omitted 25,000.

590 A215 5p multi .25 .25
- *a.* Bluish violet omitted 25,000.

591 A215 5p multi .25 .25
- *a.* Green omitted 100.00

592 A215 5p multi .25 .25
- *a.* Block of 4, #589-592 1.10 1.10

593 A215 9p multi .25 .25
- *a.* Black (denomination) omitted 325.00

594 A215 1sh6p multi .25 .25
- *a.* Black (denomination) omitted 5,000.

Nos. 589-594 (6) 1.50 1.50

King's Gate, Caernarvon Castle, Wales — A216

Celtic Cross, Margam Abbey, Glamorgan A217

Prince of Wales — A218

Designs: No. 596, Eagle Tower, Caernarvon Castle (2 flags). No. 597, Queen Eleanor's Gate, Caernarvon Castle.

Perf. 14x14½

1969, July 1 **Photo.** **Unwmk.**

595 A216 5p silver & multi .25 .25
596 A216 5p silver & multi .25 .25
597 A216 5p silver & multi .25 .25
- *a.* Strip of 3, #595-597 .40 .40

598 A217 9p gold, gray & black .25 .25
599 A218 1sh black & gold .25 .25

Nos. 595-599 (5) 1.25 1.25

Investiture of Prince Charles as Prince of Wales, July 1.

Mahatma Gandhi and Flag of India A219

1969, Aug. 13 ***Perf. 14½x14***

600 A219 1sh6p orange, blk & grn .30 .25

Mohandas K. Gandhi (1869-1948), leader in India's fight for independence.

Emblem of Post Office Bank A220

International Subscriber Dialing — A221

Automatic Letter Sorting A222

Design: 1sh, Telecommunications (pulse code modulation graph).

Perf. 13½x14

1969, Oct. 1 **Litho.** **Unwmk.**

601 A220 5p blue & multi .25 .25
602 A221 9p ultra & multi .25 .25
603 A221 1sh green & multi .25 .25
604 A222 1sh6p multicolored .25 .25

Nos. 601-604 (4) 1.00 1.00

Technological advancements of the British Post Office, transfer of responsibility from the government to the Post Office Corporation.

Angel A223

Christmas: 5p, Three shepherds. 1sh6p, The Three Kings.

Photo.; Gold Embossed

1969, Nov. 26 ***Perf. 14x15***

605 A223 4p multicolored .25 .25
606 A223 5p multicolored .25 .25
607 A223 1sh6p multicolored .25 .25

Nos. 605-607 (3) .75 .75

Fife Harling House, Scotland A224

British Rural Architecture: 9p, Cotswold limestone house, Gloucestershire, England. 1sh, Aberaeron town house, Wales ("Stwco Cymreig Welsh Stucco"). 1sh6p, Irish cottage with Ulster thatching.

Perf. 14x15

1970, Feb. 11 **Photo.** **Unwmk.**

Size: 38½x22mm

608 A224 5p multicolored .25 .25
609 A224 9p multicolored .25 .25

Size: 38½x27mm

610 A224 1sh multicolored .25 .25
611 A224 1sh6p multicolored .25 .25

Nos. 608-611 (4) 1.00 1.00

Mayflower Leaving Plymouth, England A225

Designs: 5p, Signing of the Declaration of Arbroath. 9p, Florence Nightingale and soldiers in Scutari Hospital. 1sh, Earl Grey, Great Britain; Charles Robert, France; Victor Bohmert, Germany; De Keussler, Russia, and document in 4 languages. 1sh9p, Sir William Herschel, Francis Bailey, Sir John Herschel and telescope.

Photo.; Gold Embossed

1970, Apr. 1 ***Perf. 14x15***

612 A225 5p red & multi .25 .25
613 A225 9p blue & multi .25 .25
614 A225 1sh lt blue & multi .25 .25
615 A225 1sh6p olive & multi .25 .25
616 A225 1sh9p brt pink & multi .25 .25

Nos. 612-616 (5) 1.25 1.25

650th anniv. of the Declaration of Arbroath (5p); Florence Nightingale (1820-1910), nurse and hospital reformer (9p); Intl.Cooperative Alliance, 75th anniv. (1sh); 350th anniv. of Mayflower sailing (1sh6p); sesquicentennial of the Royal Astronomical Soc. (1sh9p).

Missing colors or embossing occur on each denomination.

"The Pickwick Papers," by Dickens A226

Wordsworth's Grasmere, Lake District A227

Designs: No. 618, Mr. and Mrs. Micawber ("David Copperfield"). No. 619, David Copperfield and Betsy Trotwood ("David Copperfield"). No. 620, "Oliver Twist."

Perf. 14x14½

1970, June 3 **Photo.** **Unwmk.**

617 A226 5p orange & multi .25 .25
618 A226 5p lil rose & multi .25 .25
619 A226 5p grnsh blue & multi .25 .25
620 A226 5p lemon & multi .25 .25
- *a.* Block of 4, #617-620 1.00 1.00

621 A227 1sh6p citron & multi .25 .25

Nos. 617-621 (5) 1.25 1.25

Charles Dickens (1812-70), novelist. William Wordsworth (1770-1850), poet, No. 621.

No. 620a exists imperf. Value $2,250.

Athletics A228

1970, July 15 **Litho.** ***Perf. 14x14½***

639 A228 5p shown .25 .25
640 A228 1sh6p Swimming .25 .25
641 A228 1sh9p Bicycling .25 .25

Nos. 639-641 (3) .75 .75

9th British Commonwealth Games, Edinburgh, July 16-25.

Philympia, London Phil. Exhib., Sept. 18-26 — A229

5p, Penny black. 9p, 1847 1-shilling stamp, #5. 1sh6p, 1855 4-pence stamp, #22.

1970, Sept. 18 **Photo.** ***Perf. 14x14½***

642 A229 5p multicolored .25 .25
643 A229 9p multicolored .25 .25
644 A229 1sh6p multicolored .25 .75

Nos. 642-644 (3) .75 1.25

Christmas (Illuminations from 14th Century de Lisle Psalter) — A230

Designs: 4p, Angel and Shepherds. 5p, Nativity. 1sh6p, Adoration of the Kings.

1970, Nov. 25 Photo. *Perf. 14x14½*

645	A230	4p red & multi	.25	.25
646	A230	5p violet & multi	.25	.25
a.		Imperf., pair	500.00	
647	A230	1sh6p olive & multi	.25	.25
		Nos. 645-647 (3)	.75	.75

Decimal Currency Issue

Mountain Road, by T.P. Flanagan A231

Paintings from Northern Ireland: 7½p, Deer's Meadow, by Thomas Carr. 9p, Tollymore Forest Park, by Colin Middleton.

"P" instead of "D"

1971, June 16 Photo. *Perf. 14½x14*

648	A231	3p multicolored	.25	.25
649	A231	7½p multicolored	.25	.25
650	A231	9p multicolored	.25	.25
		Nos. 648-650 (3)	.75	.75

Ulster '71 Festival, Belfast, May-Oct.

John Keats (1795-1821) — A232

Writers and their signatures: 5p, Thomas Gray (1716-71). 7½p, Sir Walter Scott (1771-1832).

1971, July 28 Photo. *Perf. 14½x14*

651	A232	3p dull bl, blk & gold	.25	.25
652	A232	5p olive, blk & gold	.25	.25
653	A232	7½p yel brn, blk & gold	.25	.25
		Nos. 651-653 (3)	.75	.75

Soldier, Sailor, Airman, Nurse, 1921, and Poppy A233

Designs: 7½p, Roman centurion on horseback, York Castle and coat of arms. 9p, Rugby players 100 years ago, and rose.

1971, Aug. 25

654	A233	3p ultra & multi	.25	.25
655	A233	7½p ocher & multi	.25	.25
656	A233	9p olive & multi	.25	.25
		Nos. 654-656 (3)	.75	.75

50th anniv. of the British Legion (3p); 1900th anniv. of the founding of York (7½p); cent. of the Rugby Football Union (9p).

Physical Sciences Building, University College of Wales, Aberystwyth — A234

Modern University Buildings: 5p, Faraday Building, Engineering Faculty, University of Southampton. 7½p, Engineering Building, University of Leicester. 9p, Hexagon Restaurant, University of Essex.

1971, Sept. 22 Photo. *Perf. 14½x14*

657	A234	3p citron & multi	.25	.25
658	A234	5p rose vio & multi	.25	.25
659	A234	7½p dp brn & multi	.25	.25
660	A234	9p dk blue & multi	.25	.25
		Nos. 657-660 (4)	1.00	1.00

No. 658 exists with large "p" in "5p." These are from plate combination 1A1B1C1D and were not officially issued.

Dream of the Kings A235

Christmas (from Stained Glass Windows, Canterbury Cathedral): 3p, Adoration of the Kings. 7½p, Journey of the Kings.

1971, Oct. 13

661	A235	2½p scarlet & multi	.25	.25
662	A235	3p ultra & multi	.25	.25
663	A235	7½p green & multi	.25	.25
		Nos. 661-663 (3)	.75	.75

James Clark Ross (1800-1862) and Map of South Polar Sea — A236

British Polar Explorers: 5p, Martin Frobisher (1535-1594), and Desceliers map, 1550. 7½p, Henry Hudson (c. 1560-1611) and Petrus Plancius map, 1592. 9p, Robert Falcon Scott (1868-1912) and map of Antarctica.

1972, Feb. 16 *Perf. 14x14½*

664	A236	3p dp bister & multi	.25	.25
665	A236	5p brick red & multi	.25	.25
666	A236	7½p violet & multi	.25	.25
667	A236	9p blue & multi	.25	.25
		Nos. 664-667 (4)	1.00	1.00

See Nos. 689-693.

Head of Tutankhamen as Fisherman — A237

Coast Guard A238

Ralph Vaughan Williams and "Sea Symphony" A239

1972, Apr. 26 Photo. *Perf. 14½x14*

668	A237	3p gold & multi	.25	.25

Photo.; Queen's Head Gold Embossed

669	A238	7½p blue & multi	.25	.25
670	A239	9p multicolored	.25	.25
		Nos. 668-670 (3)	.75	.75

50th anniv. of the discovery of the tomb of Tutankhamen by Howard Carter and Lord Carnarvon; sesquicentennial of the British Coast guard; Ralph Vaughan Williams (1872-1958), composer.

St. Andrew's, Greensted-Juxta-Ongar — A240

Old Village Churches: 4p, All Saints, Earls Barton. 5p, St. Andrew's, Letheringsett. 7½p, St. Andrew's, Helpringham. 9p, St. Mary the Virgin, Huish Episcopi.

Photo.; Queen's Head Gold Embossed

1972, June 21 *Perf. 14x14½*

671	A240	3p dull blue & multi	.25	.25
672	A240	4p olive & multi	.25	.25
673	A240	5p dp grn & multi	.25	.25
674	A240	7½p red & multi	.25	.25
675	A240	9p blue & multi	.25	.25
		Nos. 671-675 (5)	1.25	1.25

Various BBC Microphones — A241

Designs: 5p, Wooden horn loudspeaker 1925. 7½p, Color TV camera, 1972. 9p, Marconi's oscillator and spark transmitter, 1897.

1972, Sept. 13 Photo. *Perf. 14½x14*

676	A241	3p black, brn & yel	.25	.25
677	A241	5p henna brn & blk	.25	.25
678	A241	7½p black & magenta	.25	.25
679	A241	9p black & yel	.25	.25
		Nos. 676-679 (4)	1.00	1.00

Daily broadcasting in the United Kingdom, 50th anniv. (British Broadcasting Corp., Nos. 676-678), Marconi-Kemp experiments resulting in the 1st radio transmission across water, 75th anniv. (No. 679).

Angel with Trumpet — A242

Photo.; Gold Embossed

1972, Oct. 18 *Perf. 14x14½*

680	A242	2½p shown	.25	.25
681	A242	3p Angel with lute	.25	.25
682	A242	7½p Angel with harp	.25	.25
		Nos. 680-682 (3)	.75	.75

Christmas.

Queen Elizabeth II, Prince Philip — A243

1972, Nov. 20 Photo. *Perf. 14x14½*

683	A243	3p dk bl, sep & sil	.25	.25
684	A243	20p dk pur, sepia & sil	.70	.75

25th anniv. of the marriage of Queen Elizabeth II and Prince Philip. No. 684 is without phosphor.

Britain as Part of European Community A244

1973, Jan. 3

685	A244	3p brown org & multi	.25	.25
686	A244	5p blue & multi	.25	.25
687	A244	5p emerald & multi	.25	.25
a.		Pair, #686-687	.65	.70
		Nos. 685-687 (3)	.75	.75

Britain's entry into the European Community.

Oak A245

1973, Feb. 28 Photo. *Perf. 14½x14*

688	A245	9p multicolored	.25	.25

Tree Planting Year.

Explorer Type of 1972

British Explorers: No. 689, David Livingstone and map of Africa. No. 690, Henry Stanley and map of Africa. 5p, Sir Francis Drake and world map. 7½p, Sir Walter Raleigh and world map. 9p, Charles Sturt and map of Australia.

1973, Apr. 8 Photo. *Perf. 14x14½*

689	A236	3p multicolored	.25	.25
690	A236	3p multicolored	.25	.25
a.		Pair, #689-690	.50	.50
691	A236	5p multicolored	.25	.25
692	A236	7½p multicolored	.25	.25
693	A236	9p multicolored	.25	.25
		Nos. 689-693 (5)	1.25	1.25

William Gilbert Grace — A246

Designs: Caricatures of William Gilbert Grace, the Great Cricketer, by Harry Furniss.

1973, May 16 Photo. *Perf. 14x14½*

694	A246	3p brown & black	.25	.25
695	A246	7½p green & black	.40	.40
696	A246	9p blue & black	.55	.60
		Nos. 694-696 (3)	1.20	1.25

Centenary of British County Cricket.

Sir Joshua Reynolds, Self-portrait A247

Paintings: 5p, Sir Henry Raeburn (1756-1823), self-portrait. 7½p, Nelly O'Brien, by Reynolds (1723-92). 9p, Rev. R. Walker (The Skater), by Raeburn.

1973, July 4 Photo. *Perf. 14x14½*

697	A247	3p multicolored	.25	.25
698	A247	5p multicolored	.25	.25
699	A247	7½p multicolored	.25	.25
700	A247	9p gray & multi	.25	.25
		Nos. 697-700 (4)	1.00	1.00

Tuscan Portico, St. Paul's Church, Covent Garden
A248

Designs: No. 701, Costumes for Oberon and Titania. No. 703, Prince's Lodging, Newmarket. No. 704, Stage scenery for Oberon.

Litho. and Typo.

1973, Aug. 15 ***Perf. 14½x14***

701 A248 3p black, pur & gold .25 .25
702 A248 3p gold, brn & blk .25 .25
a. Pair, #701-702 .50 .50
703 A248 5p black, blue & gold .25 .25
704 A248 5p gold, olive & blk .25 .25
a. Pair, #703-704 .50 .50
Nos. 701-704 (4) 1.00 1.00

400th birth anniv. of Inigo Jones (1573-1652), architect and designer.

Parliament, from Millbank
A249

Design: 8p, Parliament, from Whitehall.

1973, Sept. 12 **Engr. and Typo.**

705 A249 8p buff, gray & blk .25 .25
706 A249 10p black & gold .25 .25

Opening by the Queen of the 19th Commonwealth Parliamentary Assoc. Conf., Westminster Hall.

Princess Anne and Mark Phillips
A250

1973, Nov. 14 **Photo.** ***Perf. 14½x14***

707 A250 3½p violet & silver .25 .25
708 A250 20p brown & silver .35 .35

Wedding of Princess Anne and Captain Mark Phillips, Nov. 14, 1973.

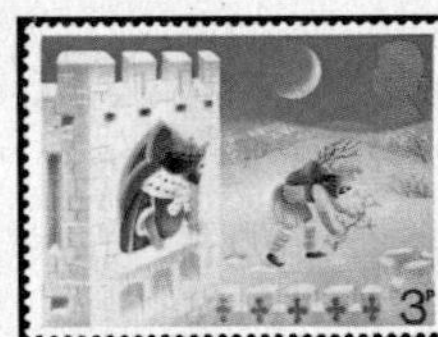

Good King Wenceslas
A251

Illustrations for Christmas carol "Good King Wenceslas" showing king and page: No. 710, Page looking out of window. No. 711, Page leaving castle. No. 712, Page in storm. No. 713, Page bringing gifts. No. 714, Page and peasant.

1973, Nov. 28

709 A251 3p shown .30 .30
710 A251 3p multicolored .30 .30
711 A251 3p multicolored .30 .30
712 A251 3p multicolored .30 .30
713 A251 3p multicolored .30 .30
a. Strip of 5, #709-713 1.50 1.50
714 A251 3½p multicolored .30 .30
Nos. 709-714 (6) 1.80 1.80

Horse Chestnut
A252

1974, Feb. 27 **Photo.** ***Perf. 14½x14***

715 A252 10p green & multi .30 .25

Fire Engine, 1766
A253

Designs: 3½p, First motorized fire engine, 1904. 5½p, Prize winning Sutherland fire engine, 1863. 8p, First steam engine, 1830.

1974, Apr. 24

716 A253 3½p multicolored .25 .25
717 A253 5½p multicolored .25 .25
718 A253 8p multicolored .25 .25
719 A253 10p multicolored .25 .25
Nos. 716-719 (4) 1.00 1.00

Fire Prevention (Metropolis) Act, bicent.

Packet "Peninsular," 1888, and "Southampton Packet Letter" Postmark — A254

Development of Overseas Mail Transport: 5½p, Farnham Biplane and "Aerial Post" postmark. 8p, Truck and pillar box for airmail and "London F.S. Air Mail" postmark. 10p, Imperial Airways flying boat and "Southampton Airport" postmark.

1974, June 12 ***Perf. 14½x14***

720 A254 3½p multicolored .25 .25
721 A254 5½p multicolored .25 .25
722 A254 8p multicolored .25 .25
723 A254 10p multicolored .25 .25
Nos. 720-723 (4) 1.00 1.00

UPU, Cent.

Robert the Bruce
A255

"Great Britons" on caparisoned chargers.

1974, July 10 ***Perf. 14½x14***

724 A255 4½p shown .25 .25
725 A255 5½p Owain Glyndwr .25 .25
726 A255 8p King Henry V .25 .25
727 A255 10p Black Prince .25 .25
Nos. 724-727 (4) 1.00 1.00

Churchill, Lord Warden of the Cinque Ports, 1942 — A256

Designs (Churchill): 5½p, with bowler and cigar, 1940. 8p, with top hat, as Secretary of War and Air, 1919. 10p, in uniform of South African Light Horse Regiment, 1899.

1974, Oct. 9 **Photo.** ***Perf. 14x14½***

728 A256 4½p silver & multi .25 .25
729 A256 5½p silver & multi .25 .25
730 A256 8p silver & multi .30 .25
731 A256 10p silver & multi .35 .25
Nos. 728-731 (4) 1.15 1.00

Sir Winston Spencer Churchill (1874-1965).

Adoration of the Kings, York Minster, c. 1355
A257

Christmas (Roof Bosses): 4½p, Nativity, St. Helen's, Norwich, c. 1480. 8p, Virgin and Child, Church of Ottery St. Mary, Devonshire, c. 1350. 10p, Virgin and Child, Lady Chapel, Worcester Cathedral, c. 1224.

1974, Nov. 27 ***Perf. 14½x14***

732 A257 3½p gold & multi .25 .25
733 A257 4½p gold & multi .25 .25
734 A257 8p gold & multi .25 .25
735 A257 10p gold & multi .25 .25
Nos. 732-735 (4) 1.00 1.00

"Peace-Burial at Sea," by Turner — A258

Paintings: 5½p, "Snowstorm-Steamer off a Harbour's Mouth." 8p, "Arsenal, Venice." 10p, "View of St. Laurent."

1975, Feb. 19 **Photo.** ***Perf. 14½x14***

736 A258 4½p multicolored .25 .25
737 A258 5½p multicolored .25 .25
738 A258 8p multicolored .25 .25
739 A258 10p multicolored .25 .25
Nos. 736-739 (4) 1.00 1.00

Birth bicent. of Joseph Mallord William Turner (1775-1851), painter.

Charlotte Square, Edinburgh
A259

National Theater, London
A260

Designs: No. 740, The Rows, Chester (double-storied medieval shopping streets). 8p, Sir Christopher Wren's Flamsteed House, Royal Observatory, Greenwich. 10p, St. George's Chapel, Windsor.

1975, Apr. 23 ***Perf. 14½x14***

740 A259 7p multicolored .25 .25
741 A259 7p multicolored .25 .25
a. Pair, #740-741 .50 .50
742 A259 8p multicolored .25 .25
743 A259 10p multicolored .25 .25
744 A260 12p multicolored .25 .25
Nos. 740-744 (5) 1.25 1.25

European Architectural Heritage Year 1975. Nos. 740-741 printed se-tenant in sheets of 100. 300th anniv. of Royal Observatory, (No. 742) and 500th anniv. of St. George's Chapel (No. 743).

Dinghies
A261

1975, June 11 **Photo. & Engr.**

745 A261 7p shown .25 .25
746 A261 8p Racing keelboats .25 .25
747 A261 10p Cruising yachts .25 .25
748 A261 12p Multihulls .25 .25
Nos. 745-748 (4) 1.00 1.00

Royal Thames Yacht Club bicent. and other sailing club anniversaries.

Stephenson's Locomotion, 1825 — A262

Locomotives: 8p, Abbotsford, Waverley Class, 1876. 10p, Caerphilly Castle, 1923. 12p, High-speed train, 1975.

1975, Aug. 13 **Photo.** ***Perf. 14½x14***

749 A262 7p multicolored .25 .25
750 A262 8p multicolored .25 .25
751 A262 10p multicolored .25 .25
752 A262 12p multicolored .35 .35
Nos. 749-752 (4) 1.10 1.10

Sesquicentennial of public railroads in Great Britain.

Parliament
A263

1975, Sept. 3

753 A263 12p multicolored .30 .30

62nd Inter-Parliamentary Conference, London, Sept. 1975.

Emma and Mr. Woodhouse from "Emma" — A264

Designs (Illustrations by Barbara Brown of Characters from Jane Austen's Novels): 10p, Catherine Morland from "Northanger Abbey." 11p, Mr. Darcy from "Pride and Prejudice." 13p, Mary and Henry Crawford from "Mansfield Park."

1975, Oct. 22 **Photo.** ***Perf. 14x14½***

754 A264 8½p multicolored .25 .25
755 A264 10p multicolored .25 .25
756 A264 11p multicolored .25 .25
757 A264 13p multicolored .25 .25
Nos. 754-757 (4) 1.00 1.00

Jane Austen (1775-1817), novelist.

Angels with Lute and Harp
A265

Christmas: 8½p, Angel with mandolin. 11p, Angel with horn. 13p, Angel with trumpet.

1975, Nov. 26 **Photo.** ***Perf. 14½x14***

758 A265 6½p violet & multi .25 .25
759 A265 8½p multicolored .25 .25
760 A265 11p multicolored .25 .25
761 A265 13p ocher & multi .25 .25
Nos. 758-761 (4) 1.00 1.00

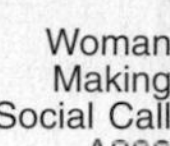

Woman Making Social Call A266

Designs: 10p, Policeman making emergency call. 11p, District nurse making social welfare call. 13p, Refinery worker making field call.

1976, Mar. 10 Photo. ***Perf. 14½x14***

777 A266 8½p multicolored .25 .25
778 A266 10p multicolored .25 .25
779 A266 11p multicolored .25 .25
780 A266 13p multicolored .25 .25
Nos. 777-780 (4) 1.00 1.00

1st telephone call by Alexander Graham Bell, Mar. 10, 1876.

Coal Miner's Hands (Thomas Hepburn) A267

Designs: 10p, Child's hands, textile mill (Robert Owen). 11p, Boy's hand sweeping chimney (Lord Shaftesbury). 13p, Woman's hands holding prison bars (Elizabeth Frey).

1976, Apr. 28 Photo. ***Perf. 14½x14***

781 A267 8½p gray & black .25 .25
782 A267 10p multicolored .25 .25
783 A267 11p multicolored .25 .25
784 A267 13p multicolored .25 .25
Nos. 781-784 (4) 1.00 1.00

19th cent. industrial & social reformers: Hepburn formed 1st miners' union in 1831; Owen, improved working conditions in his mill and established schools; Lord Shaftesbury, philanthropist and sponsor of reform work laws; Frey, pioneer of women's prison reforms.

Benjamin Franklin, by Jean-Jacques Caffieri — A268

1976, June 2 ***Perf. 14x14½***

785 A268 11p multicolored .30 .30

American Bicentennial.

Royal National Rose Society, Centenary A269

Roses Painted by Kristin Rosenberg — 8½p, Elizabeth of Glamis Rose. 10p, Grandpa Dickson. 11p, Rosa Mundi. 13p, Sweet Briar.

1976, June 30 Photo. ***Perf. 14x14½***

786 A269 8½p multicolored .25 .25
787 A269 10p multicolored .25 .25
788 A269 11p multicolored .25 .25
789 A269 13p multicolored .25 .25
Nos. 786-789 (4) 1.00 1.00

Archdruid, Eisteddfod A270

Morris Dancing — A271

British Cultural Traditions: 11p, Piper and dancers, Highland gathering. 13p, Woman playing Welsh harp (telyn), Eisteddfod.

1976, Aug. 4 Photo. ***Perf. 14x14½***

790 A270 8½p multicolored .25 .25
791 A271 10p multicolored .25 .25
792 A271 11p multicolored .25 .25
793 A270 13p multicolored .25 .25
Nos. 790-793 (4) 1.00 1.00

Squire, from Canterbury Tales — A272

Designs: 10p, Page from Tretyse of Love, c. 1493, set in Caxton typetace. 11p, Philosopher, from The Game and Playe of Chesse, c. 1483. 13p, Printing press and printers, early 16th century woodcut.

Photo.; Queen's Head Gold Embossed

1976, Sept. 29 ***Perf. 14x14½***

794 A272 8½p blue & indigo .25 .25
795 A272 10p olive & dk grn .25 .25
796 A272 11p gray & black .25 .25
797 A272 13p ocher & red brn .25 .25
Nos. 794-797 (4) 1.00 1.00

500 years of British printing, introduced by William Caxton (1422-1491).

Virgin and Child, Clare Chasuble A273

Christmas (English medieval embroideries): 8½p, Angel with crown. 11p, Angel appearing to the shepherds. 13p, Three Kings bringing gifts, Butler-Bowden cope.

1976, Nov. 24 Photo. ***Perf. 14½x14***

798 A273 6½p multicolored .25 .25
799 A273 8½p multicolored .25 .25
800 A273 11p multicolored .25 .25
801 A273 13p multicolored .25 .25
Nos. 798-801 (4) 1.00 1.00

Racket Sports A274

1977, Jan. 12 Photo. ***Perf. 14½x14***

802 A274 8½p Tennis .25 .25
803 A274 10p Table tennis .25 .25
804 A274 11p Squash .25 .25
805 A274 13p Badminton .25 .25
Nos. 802-805 (4) 1.00 1.00

Wimbledon Tennis Championships, cent. and 1977 World Table Tennis Championships, Birmingham.

Steroids Conformational Analysis — A275

Designs: 10p, Vitamin C synthesis (formula and orange). 11p, Starch chromatography. 13p, Salt crystallography.

1977, Mar. 2 Photo. ***Perf. 14½x14***

806 A275 8½p multicolored .25 .25
807 A275 10p multicolored .25 .25
808 A275 11p multicolored .25 .25
809 A275 13p multicolored .25 .25
Nos. 806-809 (4) 1.00 1.00

British chemists who won Nobel prize. Derek Barton, 1969 (8½p); Walter Norman Haworth, 1937 (10p); Archer J. P. Martin and Richard L. M. Synge, 1952 (11p); William and Lawrence Bragg, 1915 (13p).

Queen Elizabeth II — A276

1977 Photo. ***Perf. 14½x14***

810 A276 8½p silver & multi .25 .25
811 A276 9p silver & multi .30 .30
812 A276 10p silver & multi .25 .25
813 A276 11p silver & multi .25 .25
814 A276 13p silver & multi .25 .25
Nos. 810-814 (5) 1.30 1.30

25th anniv. of the reign of Elizabeth II. Issue dates: 9p, June 15; others, May 11.

Pentagons, Symbolic of Continents and Nations — A277

1977, June 8 Photo. ***Perf. 14x14½***

815 A277 13p multicolored .30 .30

Summit Conference of Commonwealth Heads of Government, London, June 1977.

Wildlife Protection — A278

1977, Oct. 5 Photo. ***Perf. 14x14½***

816 A278 9p Hedgehog .25 .25
817 A278 9p Brown hare .25 .25
818 A278 9p Red squirrel .25 .25
819 A278 9p Otter .25 .25
820 A278 9p Badger .25 .25
a. Strip of 5, #816-820 1.25

"Two Turtle Doves, Three French Hens. . ." A279

The Twelve Days of Christmas: No. 822, 4 colly birds, 5 gold rings, 6 geese a-laying. No. 823, 7 swans a-swimming, 8 maids a-milking. No. 824, 9 drummers drumming, 10 pipers piping. No. 825, 11 ladies dancing, 12 lords a-leaping. 9p, A partridge in a pear tree.

1977, Nov. 23 Photo. ***Perf. 14½x14***

821 A279 7p multicolored .25 .25
822 A279 7p multicolored .25 .25
823 A279 7p multicolored .25 .25
824 A279 7p multicolored .25 .25
825 A279 7p multicolored .25 .25
a. Strip of 5, #821-825 1.25
826 A279 9p multicolored .25 .25
Nos. 821-826 (6) 1.50 1.50

Oil Production Platform, North Sea — A280

Designs: 10½p, Coal, pithead. 11p, Natural gas, flame. 13p, Electricity-producing nuclear power plant and uranium atom diagram.

1978, Jan. 25 Photo. ***Perf. 14x14½***

827 A280 9p multicolored .25 .25
828 A280 10½p multicolored .25 .25
829 A280 11p multicolored .25 .25
830 A280 13p multicolored .25 .25
Nos. 827-830 (4) 1.00 1.00

Great Britain's wealth of energy resources.

Tower of London A281

British Architecture: 10½p, Abbey and Palace, Holyrood House, Edinburgh. 11p, Caernarvon Castle, Wales. 13p, Hampton Court Palace, London.

1978, Mar. 1 Photo. ***Perf. 14½x14***

831 A281 9p multicolored .25 .25
832 A281 10½p multicolored .25 .25
833 A281 11p multicolored .25 .25
834 A281 13p multicolored .25 .25
a. Souv. sheet of 4, #831-834 1.10 1.10
Nos. 831-834 (4) 1.00 1.00

No. 834a issued to publicize London 1980 Intl. Stamp Exhib. and sold for 53½p. The surtax went to exhibition fund.

Gold State Coach — A282

Designs: 10½p, St. Edward's crown. 11p, Orb. 13p, Imperial State crown.

1978, May 31 Photo. ***Perf. 14x14½***

835 A282 9p vio blue & gold .25 .25
836 A282 10½p car lake & gold .25 .25
837 A282 11p dp green & gold .25 .25
838 A282 13p purple & gold .25 .25
Nos. 835-838 (4) 1.00 1.00

25th anniv. of coronation of Elizabeth II.

Shire Horse
A283

British Horses: 10½p, Shetland pony. 11p, Merlyn Cymreig Welsh pony. 13p, Thoroughbred.

1978, July 5 Photo. ***Perf. 14½x14***

839 A283 9p multicolored .25 .25
840 A283 10½p multicolored .25 .25
841 A283 11p multicolored .25 .25
842 A283 13p multicolored .25 .25
Nos. 839-842 (4) 1.00 1.00

"Penny-farthing," 19th Century — A284

British bicycles: 10½p, 1920 touring bicycles. 11p, Modern small-wheel bicycles. 13p, Road racers.

1978, Aug. 2 Photo. ***Perf. 14½x14***

843 A284 9p multicolored .25 .25
844 A284 10½p multicolored .25 .25
845 A284 11p multicolored .25 .25
846 A284 13p multicolored .25 .25
Nos. 843-846 (4) 1.00 1.00

Cent. of 1st natl. cycling organizations: British Cycling Fed. and Cyclists Touring Club.

Carolers Around Christmas Tree
A285

Christmas: 9p, Christmas waits (watchmen). 11p, 18th century carolers. 13p, Boar's head carol.

1978, Nov. 22 Photo. ***Perf. 14½x14***

847 A285 7p multicolored .25 .25
848 A285 9p multicolored .25 .25
849 A285 11p multicolored .25 .25
850 A285 13p multicolored .25 .25
Nos. 847-850 (4) 1.00 1.00

Old English Sheepdog
A286

British dogs: 10½p, Welsh springer spaniel. 11p, West Highland white terrier. 13p, Irish setter.

1979, Feb. 7 Photo. ***Perf. 14½x14***

851 A286 9p multicolored .25 .25
852 A286 10½p multicolored .25 .25
853 A286 11p multicolored .25 .25
854 A286 13p multicolored .25 .25
Nos. 851-854 (4) 1.00 1.00

British Wild Flowers — A287

1979, Mar. 21 Photo. ***Perf. 14x14½***

855 A287 9p Primroses .25 .25
856 A287 10½p Daffodils .25 .25
857 A287 11p Bluebells .25 .25
858 A287 13p Snowdrops .25 .25
Nos. 855-858 (4) 1.00 1.00

Flags of Member Nations as Ballots
A288

Flags of European Community Members: United Kingdom, Italy, Denmark, Belgium, Fed. Rep. of Germany, France, Netherlands, Ireland, Luxembourg. Positions of hands and flags different on each denomination.

1979, May 9 Photo. ***Perf. 14½x14***

859 A288 9p multicolored .25 .25
860 A288 10½p multicolored .25 .25
861 A288 11p multicolored .25 .25
862 A288 13p multicolored .25 .25
Nos. 859-862 (4) 1.00 1.00

European Parliament, 1st direct elections, 6/7-10.

Saddling of Mahmoud, 1936 Derby, by Alfred Munnings
A289

200th Anniv. of the Derby: 10½p, Liverpool Great National Steeple Chase, 1839, aquatint by F. C. Turner. 11p, First Spring Meeting, Newmarket, 1793, by J. N. Sartorius. 13p, Charles II watching racing at Dorsett Ferry, Windsor, 1684, by Francis Barlow.

1979, June 6 Photo. ***Perf. 14½x14***

863 A289 9p multicolored .25 .25
864 A289 10½p multicolored .25 .25
865 A289 11p multicolored .25 .25
866 A289 13p multicolored .25 .25
Nos. 863-866 (4) 1.00 1.00

Peter Rabbit — A290

Children's books: 10½p, The Wind in the Willows. 11p, Winnie the Pooh. 13p, Alice's Adventures in Wonderland.

1979, July 11 Photo. ***Perf. 14x14½***

867 A290 9p multicolored .25 .25
868 A290 10½p multicolored .30 .25
869 A290 11p multicolored .30 .25
870 A290 13p multicolored .40 .25
Nos. 867-870 (4) 1.25 1.00

International Year of the Child.

Rowland Hill — A291

Designs: 11½p, Bellman, early 19th cent. 13p, London post office and mailman, early 19th cent. 15p, Victorian woman and child mailing letter.

1979, Aug. 22 Photo. ***Perf. 14x14½***

871 A291 10p multicolored .25 .25
872 A291 11½p multicolored .25 .25
873 A291 13p multicolored .25 .25
874 A291 15p multicolored .30 .25
a. Souvenir sheet of 4, #871-874 1.05 1.00
Nos. 871-874 (4) 1.05 1.00

Sir Rowland Hill (1795-1879), originator of penny postage.

No. 874a issued 10/24/79 to publicize London 1980 Intl. Stamp Exhib. and sold for 59½p. The surtax went to exhibition fund.

Police Constable and Children
A292

Designs: 11½p, Police constable directing traffic. 13p, Police woman on horseback. 15p, River patrol boat.

1979, Sept. 26 Photo. ***Perf. 14½x14***

875 A292 10p multicolored .25 .25
876 A292 11½p multicolored .25 .25
877 A292 13p multicolored .30 .25
878 A292 15p multicolored .35 .25
Nos. 875-878 (4) 1.15 1.00

London Metropolitan Police, 150th anniv.

Three Kings Following Star
A293

Christmas: 10p, Angel appearing before the shepherds. 11½p, Nativity. 13p, Joseph and Mary traveling to Bethlehem. 15p, Annunciation.

1979, Nov. 21 Photo. ***Perf. 14½x14***

879 A293 8p multicolored .25 .25
880 A293 10p multicolored .25 .25
881 A293 11½p multicolored .25 .25
882 A293 13p multicolored .25 .25
883 A293 15p multicolored .25 .25
Nos. 879-883 (5) 1.25 1.25

Kingfisher — A294

1980, Jan. 16 Photo. ***Perf. 14x14½***

884 A294 10p shown .25 .25
885 A294 11½p Dipper .25 .25
886 A294 13p Moorhen .25 .25
887 A294 15p Yellow wagtail .35 .25
Nos. 884-887 (4) 1.10 1.00

"Rocket" Locomotive
A295

No. 905, 1st, 2nd class cars. No. 906, 3rd class and sheep cars. No. 907, Flat cars. No. 908, Flat car, mail coach.

1980, Mar. 12 Photo. ***Perf. 14½x14***

904 A295 12p shown .25 .25
905 A295 12p multicolored .25 .25
906 A295 12p multicolored .25 .25
907 A295 12p multicolored .25 .25
908 A295 12p multicolored .25 .25
a. Strip of 5, #904-908 1.35 1.35

Liverpool-Manchester Railroad, 150th anniv. No. 908a has a continuous design.

London View
A296

1980, Apr. 9 Engr. ***Perf. 14½***

909 A296 50p brown 1.10 1.00
a. Souvenir sheet 1.25 1.00

London 1980, Intl. Stamp Exhib., May 6-14. No. 909a, issued May 7, sold for 75p.

Buckingham Palace — A297

12p, Albert Memorial. 13½p, Royal Opera House. 15p, Hampton Court. 17½p, Kensington Palace.

1980, May 7 Photo. ***Perf. 14x14½***

910 A297 10½p shown .25 .25
911 A297 12p multicolored .25 .25
912 A297 13½p multicolored .25 .25
913 A297 15p multicolored .25 .25
914 A297 17½p multicolored .30 .25
Nos. 910-914 (5) 1.30 1.25

Emily Bronte and "Wuthering Heights"
A298

Victorian novelists and scenes from their novels: 12p, Charlotte Bronte, "Jane Eyre." 13½p, George Eliot, "The Mill on the Floss." 17½p, Mrs. Gaskell, "North and South." 12p and 13½p show CEPT (Europa) emblem.

1980, July 9 Photo. ***Perf. 15x14***

915 A298 12p multicolored .25 .25
916 A298 13½p multicolored .30 .25
917 A298 15p multicolored .35 .30
918 A298 17½p multicolored .40 .35
Nos. 915-918 (4) 1.30 1.15

Queen Mother Elizabeth, 80th Birthday — A299

1980, Aug. 4 Photo. ***Perf. 14x14½***

919 A299 12p multicolored .40 .25

English Conductors
A300

Designs: 12p, Henry Wood (1869-1944). 13½p, Thomas Beecham (1879-1961). 15p, Malcolm Sargent (1895-1967). 17½p, John Barbirolli (1899-1970).

1980, Sept. 10

920	A300	12p multicolored	.25	.25
921	A300	13½p multicolored	.30	.25
922	A300	15p multicolored	.35	.25
923	A300	17½p multicolored	.40	.30
		Nos. 920-923 (4)	1.30	1.05

Running — A301

1980, Oct. 10 Litho. *Perf. 14x14½*

924	A301	12p shown	.25	.25
925	A301	13½p Rugby	.30	.25
926	A301	15p Boxing	.35	.30
927	A301	17½p Cricket	.40	.30
		Nos. 924-927 (4)	1.30	1.10

Centenaries: Amateur Athletics Assoc.; Welsh Rugby Union; Amateur Boxing Assoc.; 1st cricket test match against Australia.

Christmas Tree with Candles A302

Christmas (Traditional Decorations): 12p, Candles, ivy, ribbons. 13½p, Mistletoe, apples. 15p, Paper chain and bell. 17½p, Holly wreath.

1980, Nov. 19 Photo. *Perf. 14½x14*

928	A302	10p multicolored	.25	.25
929	A302	12p multicolored	.25	.25
930	A302	13½p multicolored	.25	.25
931	A302	15p multicolored	.30	.25
932	A302	17½ multicolored	.40	.30
		Nos. 928-932 (5)	1.45	1.30

Lovebirds, Angels and Heart (Valentine's Day) A303

Folklore: 18p, Morris Dancers, 16th century window, Shropshire. 22p, Wheat, fruit, farm couple dancing (Lammastide). 25p, Medieval mummers, 14th century manuscript illustration. 14p and 18p show CEPT (Europa) emblem.

1981, Feb. 6 Photo. *Perf. 14½x14*

933	A303	14p multicolored	.30	.30
934	A303	18p multicolored	.40	.35
935	A303	22p multicolored	.50	.40
936	A303	25p multicolored	.50	.40
		Nos. 933-936 (4)	1.70	1.45

Guide Dog Leading Blind Man A304

1981, Mar. 25 Photo.

937	A304	14p shown	.30	.25
938	A304	18p Sign language	.35	.25
939	A304	22p Man in wheelchair	.50	.40
940	A304	25p Foot painting	.55	.45
		Nos. 937-940 (4)	1.70	1.35

International Year of the Disabled.

Small Tortoiseshell A305

1981, May 13 *Perf. 14x14½*

941	A305	14p shown	.30	.25
942	A305	18p Large blue	.35	.30
943	A305	22p Peacock	.50	.40
944	A305	25p Checkered skipper	.55	.45
		Nos. 941-944 (4)	1.70	1.40

Glenfinnan, Highlands, Scotland A306

50th anniv. of National Trust for Scotland: 18p, Derwentwater, Lake District, England. 20p, Stackpole Head, Dyfed, Wales. 22p, Giant's Causeway, County Antrim, Northern Ireland. 25p, St. Kilda, Scotland.

1981, June 24 Photo. *Perf. 14½x14*

945	A306	14p multicolored	.25	.25
946	A306	18p multicolored	.35	.35
947	A306	20p multicolored	.40	.30
948	A306	22p multicolored	.45	.40
949	A306	25p multicolored	.50	.45
		Nos. 945-949 (5)	1.95	1.75

Prince Charles and Lady Diana — A307

1981, July 22 Photo. *Perf. 14x14½*

950	A307	14p multicolored	.25	.25
951	A307	25p multicolored	.75	.50

Wedding of Charles, Prince of Wales, and Lady Diana Spencer, St. Paul's Cathedral, July 29.

Hikers Reading Map A308

18p, Girl at potter's wheel. 22p, Woman administering artificial respiration. 25p, Hurdler.

1981, Aug. 12 Litho. *Perf. 14*

952	A308	14p shown	.25	.25
953	A308	18p multicolored	.35	.30
954	A308	22p multicolored	.45	.35
955	A308	25p multicolored	.55	.45
		Nos. 952-955 (4)	1.60	1.35

The Duke of Edinburgh's Awards (expeditions, skills, service, recreation), 25th anniv.

Cockle Dredging A309

1981, Sept. 23 Photo. *Perf. 14½x14*

956	A309	14p shown	.25	.25
957	A309	18p Hauling trawl net	.35	.30
958	A309	22p Lobster potting	.45	.35
959	A309	25p Hauling seine net	.55	.45
		Nos. 956-959 (4)	1.60	1.35

Fishermen's Year and Royal Natl. Mission to Deep Sea Fishermen centenary.

Santa Claus — A309a

Joseph and Mary Arriving at Bethlehem A310

Christmas: Children's Drawings.

1981, Nov. 18 Photo.

960	A309a	11½p Santa Claus	.25	.25
961	A310	14p Jesus	.25	.25
962	A309a	18p Angel	.35	.30
963	A310	22p shown	.50	.45
964	A309a	25p Three Kings	.55	.50
		Nos. 960-964 (5)	1.90	1.75

Death Centenary of Charles Darwin (1809-1882) — A311

1982, Feb. 10 Photo.

965	A311	15½p Giant tortoises	.30	.30
966	A311	19½p Iguanas	.40	.40
967	A311	26p Darwin's finches	.60	.50
968	A311	29p Skulls	.65	.60
		Nos. 965-968 (4)	1.95	1.80

Youth Organizations A312

1982, Mar. 24 Photo. *Perf. 14x14½*

983	A312	15½p Boy's Brigade	.30	.35
984	A312	19½p Girl's Brigade	.40	.40
985	A312	26p Boy Scouts	.60	.50
986	A312	29p Girl Guides	.65	.60
		Nos. 983-986 (4)	1.95	1.85

75th anniv. of scouting and 125th birth anniv. of founder Robert Baden-Powell (26p).

Performing Arts — A313

15½p, Ballet. 19½p, Pantomime. 26p, Shakespearean drama. 29p, Opera.

1982, Apr. 28 Photo. *Perf. 14x14½*

987	A313	15½p multicolored	*.25*	*.25*
988	A313	19½p multicolored	*.35*	*.35*
989	A313	26p multicolored	*.60*	*.50*
990	A313	29p multicolored	*.85*	*.70*
		Nos. 987-990 (4)	*2.05*	*1.80*

Nos. 987-990 show CEPT (Europa) emblem.

King Henry VIII and the Mary Rose A314

19½p, Admiral Blake, Triumph. 24p, Lord Nelson, Victory. 26p, Lord Fisher, Dreadnought. 29p, Viscount Cunningham, Warspite.

1982, June 16 *Perf. 14½x14*

991	A314	15½p shown	.35	.25
992	A314	19½p multicolored	.45	.35
993	A314	24p multicolored	.45	.40
994	A314	26p multicolored	.50	.50
995	A314	29p multicolored	.65	.60
		Nos. 991-995 (5)	2.40	2.10

Textile Designs — A315

15½p, Strawberry Thief, 1883. 19½p, Tulips, 1906. 26p, Cherry Orchard, 1930. 29p, Chevron, 1973.

1982, July 23 Photo. *Perf. 14x14½*

996	A315	15½p multicolored	.30	.25
997	A315	19½p multicolored	.45	.35
998	A315	26p multicolored	.55	.45
999	A315	29p multicolored	.60	.55
		Nos. 996-999 (4)	1.90	1.60

Information Technology — A316

15½p, Hieroglyphics, library, word processor. 26p, Viewdata set, satellite, laser pen.

1982, Sept. 8 Photo.

1000	A316	15½p multicolored	.30	.30
1001	A316	26p multicolored	.55	.50

Austin's Seven (1922) and Metro A317

Cars: 19½p, Ford Model T (1913) and Escort. 26p, Jaguar SS (1931) and XJ6 (1967). 29p, Rolls-Royce Silver Ghost (1907) and Silver Spirit (1982).

1982, Oct. 13 Litho. *Perf. 14½x14*

1002	A317	15½p multicolored	.30	.25
1003	A317	19½p multicolored	.50	.40
1004	A317	26p multicolored	.55	.45
1005	A317	29p multicolored	.65	.55
		Nos. 1002-1005 (4)	2.00	1.65

Christmas 1982 A318

Christmas carols — No. 1006, While Shepherds Watched. No. 1007, The Holly and the Ivy. No. 1008, I Saw Three Ships. No. 1009, We Three Kings. No. 1010, Good King Wenceslas.

1982, Nov. 17 Photo.

1006	A318	12½p multi	.25	.25
1007	A318	15½p multi	.30	.25
1008	A318	19½p multi	.40	.35
1009	A318	26p multi	.50	.40
1010	A318	29p multi	.55	.50
		Nos. 1006-1010 (5)	2.00	1.75

River Fish A319

1983, Jan. 26 Photo. Perf. 15x14

1011 A319 15½p Salmon .30 .25
1012 A319 19½p Pike .40 .45
1013 A319 26p Trout .60 .45
1014 A319 29p Perch .65 .50
Nos. 1011-1014 (4) 1.95 1.65

Commonwealth Day — A320

Landscapes by Donald Hamilton Fraser.

1983, Mar. 9 Photo. Perf. 14x14½

1015 A320 15½p Tropical island .30 .30
1016 A320 19½p Desert .40 *.45*
1017 A320 26p Farmland .55 .55
1018 A320 29p Mountains .60 .60
Nos. 1015-1018 (4) 1.85 1.90

Engineering Achievements (Europa) — A321

16p, Humber Bridge. 20½p, Thames Flood Barrier. 28p, Emergency oil rig support vessel Lolair.

1983, May 25 Photo. Perf. 15x14

1019 A321 16p multicolored *.40 .25*
1020 A321 20½p multicolored *.50 .50*
1021 A321 28p multicolored *.70 .70*
Nos. 1019-1021 (3) *1.60 1.45*

A322

Designs: 16p, The Royal Scots (Royal Regiment). 20½p, Royal Welsh Fusiliers. 26p, Royal Green Jackets. 28p, Irish Guards. 31p, Parachute Regiment.

1983, July 6 Perf. 14x14½

1022 A322 16p multicolored .30 .30
1023 A322 20½p multicolored .45 .45
1024 A322 26p multicolored .50 .50
1025 A322 28p multicolored .55 .55
1026 A322 31p multicolored .65 .65
Nos. 1022-1026 (5) 2.45 2.45

A323

Designs: 16p, 20th cent. garden, Sissinghurst. 20½p, Biddulph Grange, 19th cent. 28p, Blenheim, 18th cent. 31p, Pitmeeden, 17th cent.

1983, Aug. 24 Litho. Perf. 14

1027 A323 16p multicolored .35 .25
1028 A323 20½p multicolored .45 .40
1029 A323 28p multicolored .60 .45
1030 A323 31p multicolored .65 .50
Nos. 1027-1030 (4) 2.05 1.60

British Fairs A324

16p, Merry-go-round. 20½p, Animals, rides. 28p, Games. 31p, Ancient market fair.

1983, Oct. 5 Photo. Perf. 14½x14

1031 A324 16p multicolored .35 .25
1032 A324 20½p multicolored .45 .40
1033 A324 28p multicolored .60 .45
1034 A324 31p multicolored .65 .50
Nos. 1031-1034 (4) 2.05 1.60

850th anniv. of St. Bartholomew's Fair.

Christmas A325

12½p, Birds mailing cards. 16p, Three Kings chimney pots. 20½p, Birds under umbrella. 28p, Birds under street lamp. 31p, Topiary dove.

1983, Nov. 16 Photo.

1035 A325 12½p multicolored .25 .25
1036 A325 16p multicolored .30 .25
1037 A325 20½p multicolored .45 .35
1038 A325 28p multicolored .55 .50
1039 A325 31p multicolored .55 .50
Nos. 1035-1039 (5) 2.10 1.85

Heraldry A326

Designs: 16p, Arms of The College of Arms. 20½p, Arms of Richard III, founder. 28p, Arms of The Earl Marshal. 31p, Arms of The City of London.

1984, Jan. 17 Photo. Perf. 14½

1040 A326 16p multicolored .30 .25
1041 A326 20½p multicolored .40 .35
1042 A326 28p multicolored .60 .45
1043 A326 31p multicolored .65 .50
Nos. 1040-1043 (4) 1.95 1.55

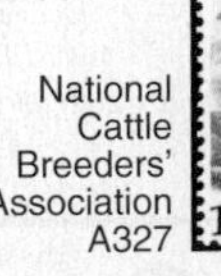

National Cattle Breeders' Association A327

16p, Highland Cow. 20½p, Chillingham Wild Bull. 26p, Hereford Bull. 28p, Welsh Black Bull. 31p, Irish Moiled Cow.

1984, Mar. 6 Litho. Perf. 15x14½

1044 A327 16p multicolored .25 .25
1045 A327 20½p multicolored .40 .35
1046 A327 26p multicolored .55 .40
1047 A327 28p multicolored .60 .45
1048 A327 31p multicolored .60 .45
Nos. 1044-1048 (5) 2.40 1.90

Royal Institute of British Architects Sesquicentennial — A328

Urban renewal projects and plans.

1984, Apr. 3 Photo.

1049 A328 16p Liverpool .30 .25
1050 A328 20½p Durham .45 .40
1051 A328 28p Bristol .55 .50
1052 A328 31p Perth .65 .55
Nos. 1049-1052 (4) 1.95 1.70

Europa (1959-1984) — A329

No. 1053, No. 1055, Bridge. No. 1054, No. 1056, Abduction of Europa.

1984, May 9 Photo. Perf. 14½x14

1053 A329 16p gray, dk bl, blk *.45 .25*
1054 A329 16p gray, dk bl, blk *.45 .25*
a. Pair, #1053-1054 *1.00 .75*
1055 A329 20½p brn rose, dp car, blk *.55 .40*
1056 A329 20½p brn rose, dp car, blk *.55 .40*
a. Pair, #1055-1056 *1.25 1.25*
Nos. 1053-1056 (4) *2.00 1.30*

Nos. 1054, 1056 also for 2nd Election of the European Parliament.

London Economic Summit, June 7-9 — A330

1984, June 5 Photo. Perf. 14x15

1057 A330 31p Lancaster House .70 *.75*

Greenwich Meridian, Cent. — A331

16p, View from Apollo 11. 20½p, English Channel map. 28p, Greenwich Observatory. 31p, Airy's transit telescope, 1850.

1984, June 26 Litho. Perf. 14x14½

1058 A331 16p multicolored .30 .30
1059 A331 20½p multicolored .45 *.50*
1060 A331 28p multicolored .60 .50
1061 A331 31p multicolored .70 .60
Nos. 1058-1061 (4) 2.05 1.90

Bath-Bristol-London Mail Coach Bicentenary — A332

18th century drawings by James Pollard — No. 1062, Bath, 1784. No. 1063, Exeter, 1816. No. 1064, Norwich, 1827. No. 1065, Holyhead & Liverpool. No. 1066, Edinburgh, 1831.

Photo. & Engr.

1984, July 31 Perf. 14½x14

1062 A332 16p multicolored .35 .35
1063 A332 16p multicolored .35 .35
1064 A332 16p multicolored .35 .35
1065 A332 16p multicolored .35 .35
1066 A332 16p multicolored .35 .35
a. Strip of 5, #1062-1066 1.90 1.85

50th Anniv. of British Council A333

17p, Education for development. 22p, Promoting the arts. 31p, Technical training. 34p, Language & libraries.

1984, Sept. 25 Photo.

1067 A333 17p multicolored .30 .30
1068 A333 22p multicolored .40 .40
1069 A333 31p multicolored .55 .55
1070 A333 34p multicolored .80 .80
Nos. 1067-1070 (4) 2.05 2.05

Christmas 1984 A334

Crayon Sketches by Yvonne Gilbert: 13p, Holy Family. 17p, Arrival in Bethlehem. 22p, Shephard and Lamb. 31p, Virgin and child. 34p, Offering Frankincense.

1984, Nov. 20 Photo. Perf. 15x14

1088 A334 13p multicolored .25 .25
a. Booklet pane of 20 (BK770) 7.00
1089 A334 17p multicolored .35 .30
1090 A334 22p multicolored .40 .50
1091 A334 31p multicolored .65 .55
1092 A334 34p multicolored .75 .70
Nos. 1088-1092 (5) 2.40 2.30

Bklt. of 20 13p sold at 30p discount. Stamps have blue stars printed on the back.

Great Western Railway Sesquicentennial — A335

1985, Jan. 22 Photo. Perf. 15x14

1093 A335 17p Flying Scotsman .35 .35
1094 A335 22p Golden Arrow .55 .50
1095 A335 29p Cheltenham Flyer .60 .60
1096 A335 31p Royal Scot .80 .75
1097 A335 34p Cornish Riviera .80 .80
Nos. 1093-1097 (5) 3.10 3.00

Insects — A336

17p, Buff tailed bumble bee. 22p, Seven spotted ladybird. 29p, Wart-biter bush-cricket. 31p, Stag beetle. 34p, Emperor dragonfly.

1985, Mar. 12 Photo. Perf. 15x14½

1098 A336 17p multicolored .30 .25
1099 A336 22p multicolored .45 .50
1100 A336 29p multicolored .55 .60
1101 A336 31p multicolored .70 .70
1102 A336 34p multicolored .75 .75
Nos. 1098-1102 (5) 2.75 2.80

Music Year (Europa) A337

British Composers: 17p, Water Music, by George Frideric Handel. 22p, The Planets Suite, by Gustav Holst. 31p, The First Cuckoo, by Frederick Delius. 34p, Sea Pictures, by Edward Elgar.

1985, May 14 *Perf. 14½*

1103	A337	17p	Reflections in pool	*.40*	*.35*
1104	A337	22p	View of planets	*.85*	*.65*
1105	A337	31p	Roosting cuckoo	*1.00*	*1.00*
1106	A337	34p	Waves, wing	*1.00*	*1.05*
			Nos. 1103-1106 (4)	*3.25*	*3.05*

Safety at Sea A338

17p, Lifeboat. 22p, Beachy Head Lighthouse, chart. 31p, Marecs-A satellite. 34p, Signal buoy, yacht.

1985, June 18 **Litho.** *Perf. 14*

1107	A338	17p	multicolored	.30	*.35*
1108	A338	22p	multicolored	.45	*.50*
1109	A338	31p	multicolored	.75	.70
1110	A338	34p	multicolored	.75	.70
			Nos. 1107-1110 (4)	2.25	2.25

Royal Mail Service, 350th Anniv. — A339

Designs: 17p, Royal Mail Datapost motorcyclist and plane. 22p, Postbus on country road. 31p, Parcel service delivery. 34p, Postman delivering mail.

1985, July 30 **Photo.** *Perf. 14x14½*

1111	A339	17p	multicolored	.30	*.35*
a.			Booklet pane of 10 (BK631)	6.00	
1112	A339	22p	multicolored	.50	.50
1113	A339	31p	multicolored	.65	.60
1114	A339	34p	multicolored	.75	.75
			Nos. 1111-1114 (4)	2.20	2.20

Arthurian Legends A340

Designs: 17p, Arthur consulting with Merlin. 22p, The Lady of the Lake with the sword "Excalibur." 31p, Guinevere and Lancelot fleeing from Camelot. 34p, Sir Galahad praying during his quest for the Holy Grail.

1985, Sept. 3 **Photo.** *Perf. 15x14*

1115	A340	17p	multicolored	.35	.35
1116	A340	22p	multicolored	.45	*.50*
1117	A340	31p	multicolored	.70	.70
1118	A340	34p	multicolored	.70	.70
			Nos. 1115-1118 (4)	2.20	2.25

500th anniv. of William Caxton's edition of Le Morte D'Arthur, by Sir Thomas Mallory.

20th Cent. Stars and Directors of Film — A341

Photographs: 17p, Peter Sellers (1925-80). 22p, David Niven (1910-83). 29p, Charlie Chaplin (1889-1977). 31p, Vivien Leigh (1913-67). 34p, Sir Alfred Hitchcock (1899-1980), director.

1985, Oct. 8 **Photo.** *Perf. 14½*

1119	A341	17p	multicolored	.30	.30
1120	A341	22p	multicolored	.40	*.45*
1121	A341	29p	multicolored	.75	.70
1122	A341	31p	multicolored	.75	.70
1123	A341	34p	multicolored	.80	.80
			Nos. 1119-1123 (5)	3.00	2.95

Christmas Pantomime A342

1985, Nov. 19 **Photo.** *Perf. 15x14½*

1124	A342	12p	Principal boy	.25	.25
a.			Booklet pane of 20 (BK 780)	6.50	
1125	A342	17p	Genie	.30	.30
1126	A342	22p	Grande dame	.45	.45
1127	A342	31p	Good fairy	.65	.60
1128	A342	34p	Cat	.70	.65
			Nos. 1124-1128 (5)	2.35	2.25

No. 1124a has random star design printed on back.

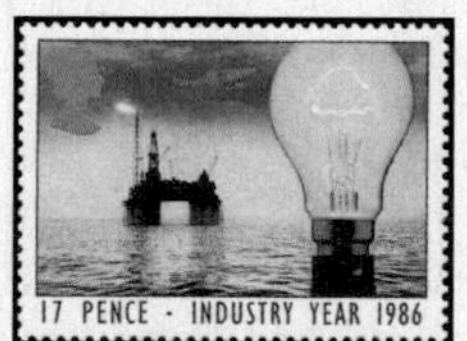

Industry Year A343

17p, North Sea oil rig, light bulb. 22p, Medical research lab, thermometer. 31p, Steel mill, garden hoe. 34p, Cornfield, bread.

1986, Jan. 14 **Litho.** *Perf. 15x14*

1129	A343	17p	multicolored	.30	.30
1130	A343	22p	multicolored	.45	.50
1131	A343	31p	multicolored	.70	.55
1132	A343	34p	multicolored	.80	.65
			Nos. 1129-1132 (4)	2.25	2.00

Halley's Comet A344

Designs: 17p, Caricature, Edmond Halley (1656 1742), astronomer. 22p, European Space Agency Giotto spacecraft pursuing comet. 31p, Comet and legend, Maybe Twice in a Lifetime. 34p, Comet orbiting sun.

1986, Feb. 18 **Photo.**

1133	A344	17p	multicolored	.30	.30
1134	A344	22p	multicolored	.50	.45
1135	A344	31p	multicolored	.70	.65
1136	A344	34p	multicolored	.80	.70
			Nos. 1133-1136 (4)	2.30	2.10

A345

Queen Elizabeth II, 60th Birthday A346

1986, Apr. 21 **Photo.**

1137	A345	17p	multicolored	.35	.35
1138	A346	17p	multicolored	.35	.35
a.			Pair, #1137-1138	.80	.80
1139	A345	34p	multicolored	.95	.95
1140	A346	34p	multicolored	.95	.95
a.			Pair, #1139-1140	2.10	2.10

Europa A347

1986, May 20 **Photo.** *Perf. 14½*

1141	A347	17p	Barn owl	*.35*	*.35*
1142	A347	22p	Pine marten	*.50*	*.50*
1143	A347	31p	Wild cat	*.75*	*.75*
1144	A347	34p	Natterjack toad	*.80*	*.75*
			Nos. 1141-1144 (4)	*2.40*	*2.35*

Domesday Book, 900th Anniv. A348

1986, June 17 **Photo.**

1145	A348	17p	Peasant	.35	.35
1146	A348	22p	Freeman	.50	.50
1147	A348	31p	Knight	.70	.70
1148	A348	34p	Lord	.75	.75
			Nos. 1145-1148 (4)	2.30	2.30

Domesday Book, first nationwide survey in British history.

Sports A349

1986, July 15 **Photo.** *Perf. 15x14*

1149	A349	17p	Track and field	.30	.30
1150	A349	22p	Rowing	.40	.55
1151	A349	29p	Weight lifting	.60	.55
1152	A349	31p	Shooting	.70	.55
1153	A349	34p	Field hockey	.70	.70
			Nos. 1149-1153 (5)	2.70	2.65

1986 Commonwealth Games, Edinburgh. World Hockey Cup, London.

Wedding of Prince Andrew and Sarah Ferguson — A350

1986, July 22 *Perf. 14x15*

1154	A350	12p	multicolored	.40	.35
1155	A350	17p	multicolored	.50	*.55*

Commonwealth Parliamentary Assoc. Conf., London — A351

1986, Aug. 19 **Litho.** *Perf. 14x14½*

1156	A351	34p	multicolored	.80	*.85*

Royal Air Force Commanders and Aircraft A352

Designs: 17p, Lord Dowding (1882-1970), Hurricane. 22p, Lord Tedder (1890-1967), Hawker Typhoon. 29p, Lord Trenchard (1873-1956), De Havilland 9A World War I bomber. 31p, Sir Arthur Harris (1892-1984), Avro Lancaster. 34p, Lord Portal (1893-1971), De Havilland Mosquito.

1986, Sept. 16 **Photo.** *Perf. 14½*

1157	A352	17p	multicolored	.30	.30
1158	A352	22p	multicolored	.50	.55
1159	A352	29p	multicolored	.65	.60
1160	A352	31p	multicolored	.75	.70
1161	A352	34p	multicolored	.80	.85
			Nos. 1157-1161 (5)	3.00	3.00

Christmas A353

Customs: 12p, 13p, Glastonbury Thorn. 18p, Tanad Valley Plygain. 22p, Hebrides Tribute. 31p, Dewsbury Church Knell. 34p, Hereford Boy Bishop.

1986, Nov. 18 **Photo.** *Perf. 15x14½*

1162	A353	12p	multicolored	.25	.25
1163	A353	13p	multicolored	.25	.25
a.			Pane of 36	12.50	
1164	A353	18p	multicolored	.35	.35
1165	A353	22p	multicolored	.55	.45
1166	A353	31p	multicolored	.65	.55
1167	A353	34p	multicolored	.65	.60
			Nos. 1162-1167 (6)	2.70	2.45

No. 1163a printed in two panes of 18 with gutter between, stars on back; folded and sold in discount booklet for £4.30.

Flora — A354

Photographs by Alfred Lammer.

1987, Jan. 20 **Photo.** *Perf. 14½*

1168	A354	18p	Gaillardia	.30	.30
1169	A354	22p	Echinops	.50	.50
1170	A354	31p	Echeveria	.65	.65
1171	A354	34p	Colchicum	.80	.80
			Nos. 1168-1171 (4)	2.25	2.25

Sir Isaac Newton (1642-1727), Physicist, Mathematician A355

Manuscripts and principles: 18p, Philosophiae Naturalis Principia Mathematica, 1687. 22p, Motion of bodies in ellipses. 31p, Opticks Treatise of the Refraction, Reflections and Colors of Light. 34p, The System of the World.

1987, Mar. 24 Photo. *Perf. 14*

1172 A355 18p multicolored .35 .35
1173 A355 22p multicolored .50 .50
1174 A355 31p multicolored .65 .65
1175 A355 34p multicolored .75 .75
Nos. 1172-1175 (4) 2.25 2.25

Europa
A356

Modern architecture: 18p, Willis Faber & Dumas Building, Ipswich, designed by Norman Foster. 22p, Pompidou Centre, Paris, designed by Richard Rogers and Renzo Piano. 31p, Staatsgalerie, Stuttgart, designed by James Stirling and Michael Wilford. 34p, European Investment Bank, Luxembourg, designed by Sir Denys Lasdun.

1987, May 12 Photo. *Perf. 15x14*

1176 A356 18p multicolored *.30 .30*
1177 A356 22p multicolored *.55 .55*
1178 A356 31p multicolored *.65 .65*
1179 A356 34p multicolored *.85 .85*
Nos. 1176-1179 (4) *2.35 2.35*

St. John
Ambulance,
Cent. — A357

First aid: 18p, Ambulance, 1887. 22p, War victims, 1940. 31p, Public event, 1965. 34p, Transplant organ flight, 1987.

1987, June 16 Litho. *Perf. 14x14½*

1180 A357 18p multicolored .35 .35
1181 A357 22p multicolored .50 .50
1182 A357 31p multicolored .65 .65
1183 A357 34p multicolored .75 .75
Nos. 1180-1183 (4) 2.25 2.25

Order of the
Thistle,
Scotland,
300th Anniv. of
Revival
A358

Coats of arms: 18p, Lord Lyon, King of Arms, 1687. 22p, Duke of Rothesay, bestowed on Prince Charles in 1974. 31p, Royal Scottish Academy of Painting, Sculpture & Architecture, 1826. 34p, The Royal Society of Edinburgh, 1783.

1987, July 21 Photo. *Perf. 14½*

1184 A358 18p multicolored .35 .35
1185 A358 22p multicolored .50 .50
1186 A358 31p multicolored .65 .65
1187 A358 34p multicolored .75 .75
Nos. 1184-1187 (4) 2.25 2.25

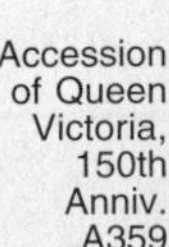

Accession
of Queen
Victoria,
150th
Anniv.
A359

Portraits of Victoria and: 18p, Great Exhibition (1851) at the Crystal Palace, Grace Darling's rescue (1838) of the Forfashire's survivors, and Monarch of the Glen, by Sir Edwin Henry Landseer. 22p, Launching of Brunel's ship Great Eastern, portrait of Prince Consort Albert, Mrs. Beeton's Book of Household Management (1889). 31p, The Albert Memorial, Prime Minister Disraeli and 1st ballot box. 34p, The Boer War, Guglielmo Marconi's wireless telegraph communications linking Paris and London (1898), and diamond jubilee emblem.

Photo. & Engr.

1987, Sept. 8 *Perf. 15x14*

1188 A359 18p multicolored .35 .35
1189 A359 22p multicolored .50 .50
1190 A359 31p multicolored .65 .65
1191 A359 34p multicolored .80 .75
Nos. 1188-1191 (4) 2.30 2.25

Studio Pottery
A360

1987, Oct. 13 Photo. *Perf. 14½*

1192 A360 18p Bernard Leach .35 .35
1193 A360 26p Elizabeth Fritsch .60 .60
1194 A360 31p Lucie Rie .65 .65
1195 A360 34p Hans Coper .70 .70
Nos. 1192-1195 (4) 2.30 2.30

Christmas
A361

Childhood memories: 13p, Decorating tree. 18p, Looking out window, Christmas eve. 26p, Sweet dreams. 31p, Reading new book to toys, Christmas morning. 34p, Playing horn, snowman.

1987, Nov. 17 Photo. *Perf. 15x14*

1196 A361 13p multicolored .25 .25
a. Pane of 36 12.50
1197 A361 18p multicolored .35 .35
1198 A361 26p multicolored .50 .50
1199 A361 31p multicolored .60 .55
1200 A361 34p multicolored .70 .70
Nos. 1196-1200 (5) 2.40 2.35

No. 1196a printed in two panes of 18 with gutter between, stars on back; folded and sold in discount booklets for £4.30.

Linnean
Society of
London,
200th
Anniv.
A362

1988, Jan. 19 *Perf. 15x14½*

1201 A362 18p Bull-rout fish .35 .35
1202 A362 26p Yellow waterlily .50 .50
1203 A362 31p Bewick's swan .65 .65
1204 A362 34p Morel .70 .70
Nos. 1201-1204 (4) 2.20 2.20

Linnaeus (Carl von Linne, 1707-78), inventor of system of taxonomic nomenclature.

Welsh Bible,
400th
Anniv. — A363

1988, Mar. 1 Photo. *Perf. 14½*

1205 A363 18p William Morgan .35 .35
1206 A363 26p William Salesbury .55 .50
1207 A363 31p Richard Davies .65 .60
1208 A363 34p Richard Parry .65 *.70*
Nos. 1205-1208 (4) 2.20 2.15

Sports — A364

1988, Mar. 22 Photo. *Perf. 14½*

1209 A364 18p Balance beam .30 .30
1210 A364 26p Downhill skiing .55 .50
1211 A364 31p Tennis .65 .65
1212 A364 34p Soccer .70 .70
Nos. 1209-1212 (4) 2.20 2.15

Ski Club of Great Britain and centenaries of the British Amateur Gymnastics Assoc., Lawn Tennis Assoc. and the Soccer League.

Europa
1988
A365

Transportation and communication, 1938: 18p, Mallard locomotive. 26p, Queen Elizabeth ocean liner. 31p, Tram No. 1173, Glasgow. 34p, Handley Page aircraft, Croydon Airport.

1988, May 10 *Perf. 15x14*

1213 A365 18p multicolored *.30 .35*
1214 A365 26p multicolored *.55 .50*
1215 A365 31p multicolored *.65 .65*
1216 A365 34p multicolored *.80 .80*
Nos. 1213-1216 (4) *2.30 2.30*

A366

Designs: No. 1217, Armada approaching The Lizard, July 19, 1588. No. 1218, Royal Navy vessels sailing from Plymouth to engage Spaniards in battle, July 21. No. 1219, Battle scene off the Isle of Wight, July 25. No. 1220, Battle scene off Calais, France, July 28-29. No. 1221, Spanish ships foundering in the North Sea storms, July 30-Aug. 2. Printed in a continuous design.

1988, July 19

1217 A366 18p multicolored .40 *.55*
1218 A366 18p multicolored .40 *.55*
1219 A366 18p multicolored .40 *.55*
1220 A366 18p multicolored .40 *.55*
1221 A366 18p multicolored .40 *.55*
a. Strip of 5, Nos. 1217-1221 2.00 *2.20*

Defeat of the Spanish Armada by the Royal Navy, 400th Anniv.

Australia
Bicentennial
A367

Designs: No. 1222, Colonist, First Fleet vessel. No. 1223, British and Australian parliaments, Queen Elizabeth II. No. 1224, Cricketer W.G. Grace. No. 1225, John Lennon (1940-1980), William Shakespeare (1564-1616) and Sydney Opera House. Flag of Australia appears on Nos. 1223a, 1225a.

1988, June 21 Litho. *Perf. 14½*

1222 A367 18p multicolored .35 .35
1223 A367 18p multicolored .35 .35
a. Pair, #1222-1223 .75 .75
1224 A367 34p multicolored .75 .75
1225 A367 34p multicolored .75 .75
a. Pair, #1224-1225 1.60 1.60
Nos. 1222-1225 (4) 2.20 2.20

See Australia Nos. 1082-1085.

Nonsensical Drawings by Edward Lear (1812-1888) — A368

Illustrations and text: 19p, *The Owl and the Pussycat*, 1867. 27p, Self-portrait as a bird, pen-and-ink sketch from a letter. 32p, "C" is for Cat, alphabet book character. 35p, Girl, birds and part of a limerick.

1988, Sept. 6 Photo. *Perf. 15x14*

1226 A368 19p multicolored .30 .30
1227 A368 27p multicolored .55 .50
1228 A368 32p multicolored .75 .70
1229 A368 35p multicolored .80 .75
a. Souv. sheet of 4, #1226-1229 3.75 *4.00*
Nos. 1226-1229 (4) 2.40 2.25

No. 1229a sold for £1.35. The surtax benefited Stamp World London '90.

Photographs of Castles by Prince Andrew — A369

£1, Carrickfergus. £1.50, Caernarfon. £2, Edinburgh. £5, Windsor.

1988, Oct 18 Engr.

1230 A369 £1 green 2.60 .50
1231 A369 £1.50 maroon 4.00 .90
1232 A369 £2 blue 5.50 1.00
1233 A369 £5 brown 13.50 3.50
Nos. 1230-1233 (4) 25.60 5.90

See Nos. 1445-1448.

Christmas
Cards
A370

14p, Journey to Bethlehem. 19p, Shepherds see star. 27p, Magi follow star. 32p, Nativity. 35p, The Annunciation.

1988, Nov. 15 Photo. *Perf. 15x14½*

1234 A370 14p multicolored .25 .25
1235 A370 19p multicolored .40 .30
1236 A370 27p multicolored .50 .50
1237 A370 32p multicolored .65 .60
1238 A370 35p multicolored .80 *.85*
Nos. 1234-1238 (5) 2.60 2.50

Birds — A371

1989, Jan. 17 *Perf. 14x15*

1239 A371 19p Puffin .35 .35
1240 A371 27p Avocet .50 *.55*
1241 A371 32p Oystercatcher .70 .70
1242 A371 35p Gannet .80 .75
Nos. 1239-1242 (4) 2.35 2.35

Special
Occasions
A372

1989, Jan. 31 Photo. *Perf. 15x14*

Booklet Stamps

1243 A372 19p Rose 2.75 2.40
1244 A372 19p Cupid 2.75 2.40
1245 A372 19p Ships 2.75 2.40
1246 A372 19p Fruit bowl 2.75 2.40
1247 A372 19p Teddy Bear 2.75 2.40
a. Bklt. pane of 10 (2 each #1243-1247) +12 labels (BK733) 34.00
Nos. 1243-1247 (5) 13.75 12.00

Labels inscribed "CONGRATULATIONS," "BEST WISHES," "HAPPY BIRTHDAY," "HAPPY ANNIVERSARY," "WITH LOVE," or "THANK YOU."

No. 1247a is valued with perfs guillotined. Full perfs sell for more.

Food and Farming Year — A373

Foods and tile mosaics in agricultural motifs.

1989, Mar. 7 Photo. *Perf. 14½*

1248 A373 19p Fruit and vegetables .35 *.40*
1249 A373 27p Meat, fish, fruit .65 .60
1250 A373 32p Dairy products .70 .65
1251 A373 35p Breads, cake, cereal .70 *.75*
Nos. 1248-1251 (4) 2.40 2.40

Fireworks — A374

1989, Apr. 11 Photo. *Perf. 14x14½*

1252 A374 19p Mortarboard .55 .25
1253 A374 19p "X" on ballot .55 .25
a. Pair, #1252-1253 1.25 1.25
1254 A374 35p Posthorn 1.00 .50
1255 A374 35p Globe 1.00 .50
a. Pair, #1254-1255 2.25 2.25
Nos. 1252-1255 (4) 3.10 1.50

Public education in England and Wales, 150th anniv. (No. 1252); European Parliament 3rd elections (No. 1253); 26th world congress of Postal Telegraph and Telephone Intl., Brighton, Sept. 18-23 (No. 1254); Interparliamentary Union Cent. Conf., 82nd session, Sept. 4-9 (No. 1255).

Europa 1989 — A375

Children's toys: 19p, Airplane, locomotive. 27p, Building-block tower. 32p, Checkerboard, die, ladder, chips. 35p, Doll house, boat, robot.

1989, May 16 *Perf. 14x15*

1256 A375 19p multicolored *.40 .40*
1257 A375 27p multicolored *.55 .55*
1258 A375 32p multicolored *.80 .80*
1259 A375 35p multicolored *1.00 1.00*
Nos. 1256-1259 (4) *2.75 2.75*

Industrial Archaeology A376

1989, July 4 Photo. *Perf. 14x15*

1280 A376 19p Ironbridge .40 .40
1281 A376 27p Tin Mine .60 .60
1282 A376 32p Mills .65 .65
1283 A376 35p Pontcysyllte Aqueduct .70 *.80*
Nos. 1280-1283 (4) 2.35 2.45

1989, July 25 Souvenir Sheet

1284 Sheet of 4 3.75 *4.00*
a. A376 19p like #1280, horiz. .50 .50
b. A376 27p like #1281, horiz. .75 .75
c. A376 32p like #1282, horiz. 1.00 .95
d. A376 35p like #1283, horiz. 1.20 1.00

No. 1284 sold for £1.40.

Microscopy A377

Specimens under magnification: 19p, Snowflake, the soc. emblem. 27p, Blue fly. 32p, Blood cells. 35p, Microchip.

1989, Sept. 5 Litho. *Perf. 14½x14*

1285 A377 19p multicolored .40 .40
1286 A377 27p multicolored .60 .60
1287 A377 32p multicolored .65 .65
1288 A377 35p multicolored .75 .75
Nos. 1285-1288 (4) 2.40 2.40

Royal Microscopical Soc., 150th anniv.

The Lord Mayor's Show, London — A378

Procession of the Lord Mayor's coach from Guildhall to the Law Courts in the Strand: No. 1289, Royal mail coach and The Guildhall. No. 1290, Drummer, cavalrymen and Mansion House. No. 1291, Gold coach, 1757, and The Royal Exchange. No. 1292, Coachman and St. Paul's Cathedral. No. 1293, Drummer, cavalryman and the Law Courts.

1989, Oct. 17 Litho. *Perf. 14x15*

1289 A378 20p multicolored .40 *.45*
a. Perf. 14x14¼ 1.50 1.50
b. Booklet pane of 4 #1289a (BK189) 6.00 —
1290 A378 20p multicolored .40 *.45*
1291 A378 20p multicolored .40 *.45*
1292 A378 20p multicolored .40 *.45*
1293 A378 20p multicolored .40 *.45*
a. Strip of 5, #1289-1293 2.10 *2.25*

Issued. Nos. 1289a, 1289b, 8/19/09.

Ely Cathedral, Cambridgeshire, 800th Anniv. — A379

1989, Nov. 14 Photo. *Perf. 15x14*

1294 A379 15p Gothic arches, 4 peasants .30 .25
Nos. 1294,B2-B5 (5) 2.50 2.50

Christmas.

For stamps and souvenir sheets with the design shown above, see Nos. MH190-MH198A in the Machins section.

Royal Soc. for the Prevention of Cruelty to Animals, 150th Anniv. — A381

1990, Jan. 23 Litho. *Perf. 14x15*

1300 A381 20p Kitten .40 .40
1301 A381 29p Rabbit .65 .65
1302 A381 34p Duckling .80 .80
1303 A381 37p Puppy 1.00 1.00
Nos. 1300-1303 (4) 2.85 2.85

A382

A382a

A382b

A382c

A382d

A382e

A382f

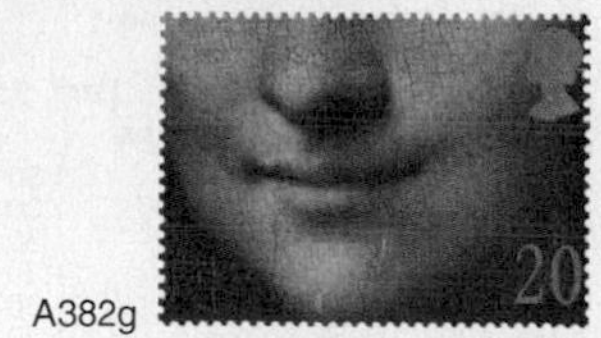
A382g

A382h

Famous Smiles — A382i

No. 1304, Teddy bear. No. 1305, Dennis the Menace. No. 1306, Mr. Punch. No. 1307, Cheshire Cat. No. 1308, Man in the Moon. No. 1309, The Laughing Policeman. No. 1310, Clown. No. 1311, Mona Lisa. No. 1312, Queen of Hearts. No. 1313, Stan Laurel.

1990, Feb. 6 Photo. *Perf. 15x14*

1304 A382 20p multi 1.60 1.45
1305 A382a 20p multi 1.60 1.45
1306 A382b 20p multi 1.60 1.45
1307 A382c 20p multi 1.60 1.45
1308 A382d 20p multi 1.60 1.45
1309 A382e 20p multi 1.60 1.45
1310 A382f 20p multi 1.60 1.45
1311 A382g 20p multi 1.60 1.45
1312 A382h 20p multi 1.60 1.45
1313 A382i 20p multi 1.60 1.45
a. Pane of 10, #1304-1313 16.00 14.50
Nos. 1304-1313 (10) 16.00 14.50

No. 1313a sold folded and unattached in booklet cover.

See Nos. 1364-1373.

A383

Europa 1990: No. 1314, Alexandra Palace. No. 1315, School of Art, Glasgow. 29p, British Philatelic Bureau, Edinburgh. 37p, Templeton Carpet Factory, Glasgow.

1990, Mar. 6 Photo. *Perf. 14x15*

1314 A383 20p multicolored .45 .45
a. Bklt. pane of 4 + printed margin 2.25
1315 A383 20p multicolored .45 .45
1316 A383 29p multicolored .70 .75
1317 A383 37p multicolored .95 1.00
Nos. 1314-1317 (4) 2.55 2.65

Stamp World '90, London (No. 1314); Glasgow, European City of Culture (Nos. 1315, 1317).

For Prestige booklet containing pane No. 1314a, see listings in the Booklets section.

Queen's Awards for Export and Technological Achievement, 25th Anniv. — A384

No. 1318, No. 1320, Export. No. 1319, No. 1321, Technology.

1990, Apr. 10 Litho.

1318 A384 20p yel & blue, sil .40 .40
1319 A384 20p yel & blue, sil .40 .40
a. Pair, #1318-1319 1.00 1.00
1320 A384 37p blue, yel, sil .90 .80
1321 A384 37p blue, yel, sil .90 .80
a. Pair, #1320-1321 2.00 2.00
Nos. 1318-1321 (4) 2.60 2.40

Se-tenant pairs have continuous designs.

Kew Gardens, 150th Anniv. — A385

1990, June 5 **Photo.**

1322	A385	20p Cycad	.40	.35
1323	A385	29p Stone pine	.60	.60
1324	A385	34p Willow tree	.70	.70
1325	A385	37p Cedar	.75	.75
		Nos. 1322-1325 (4)	2.45	2.40

Thomas Hardy (1840-1928), Writer and Clyffe Clump, Dorset — A386

1990, July 10 **Photo.** ***Perf. 14x15***

1326	A386	20p multicolored	.45	.45

Queen Mother, 90th Birthday — A387

Portraits of Queen Elizabeth, The Queen Mother: 20p, Recent portrait. 29p, As Queen Consort, 1937. 34p, As Duchess of York. 37p, As Lady Elizabeth Bowes-Lyon.

1990, Aug. 2 ***Perf. 14x15, 14½***

1327	A387	20p multicolored	.60	*.65*
1328	A387	29p multicolored	.90	.90
1329	A387	34p multicolored	1.05	1.05
1330	A387	37p multicolored	1.25	1.20
		Nos. 1327-1330 (4)	3.80	3.80

Gallantry Awards — A388

Designs: No. 1331, Victoria Cross. No. 1332, George Cross. No. 1333, Military Cross, Military Medal. No. 1334, Distinguished Flying Cross, Distinguished Flying Medal. No. 1335, Distinguished Service Cross, Distinguished Service Medal. Nos. 1333-1335 horiz.

1990, Sept. 11 ***Perf. 14x15, 15x14***

1331	A388	20p multicolored	.50	.50
a.		Litho., perf. 14x14¼, black denomination ('06)	5.75	5.00
b.		Booklet pane of 4 #1331a (BK180)	23.00	—
1332	A388	20p multicolored	.50	.50
1333	A388	20p multicolored	.50	.50
1334	A388	20p multicolored	.50	.50
1335	A388	20p multicolored	.50	.50
		Nos. 1331-1335 (5)	2.50	2.50

Denomination on No. 1331 is gray. Nos. 1331a, 1331b issued 9/21/2006.

Astronomy A389

Designs: 22p, Armagh Observatory, Jodrell Bank and La Palma telescopes. 26p, Early telescope, celestial diagram. 31p, Greenwich Old Observatory, sextant, chronometer. 37p, Stonehenge, celestial navigation.

1990, Oct. 16 ***Perf. 14***

1336	A389	22p multicolored	.40	*.50*
1337	A389	26p multicolored	.50	.50
1338	A389	31p multicolored	.70	.70
1339	A389	37p multicolored	.80	.70
		Nos. 1336-1339 (4)	2.40	2.40

Christmas A390

17p, Building snowman. 22p, Carrying Christmas tree. 26p, Caroling. 31p, Sledding. 37p, Ice skating.

1990, Nov. 13 **Litho.** ***Perf. 15x14***

1340	A390	17p multicolored	.30	.30
a.		Booklet pane of 20	8.25	
1341	A390	22p multicolored	.40	.40
1342	A390	26p multicolored	.55	.50
1343	A390	31p multicolored	.65	.60
1344	A390	37p multicolored	.75	.70
		Nos. 1340-1344 (5)	2.65	2.50

Dogs — A391

Paintings by George Stubbs: 22p, King Charles Spaniel. 26p, A Pointer. 31p, Two Hounds in a Landscape. 33p, A Rough Dog. 37p, Fino and Tiny.

1991, Jan. 8 **Photo.** ***Perf. 14x14½***

1345	A391	22p multicolored	.40	.40
1346	A391	26p multicolored	.50	.45
1347	A391	31p multicolored	.65	.65
1348	A391	33p multicolored	.65	.65
1349	A391	37p multicolored	.70	.70
		Nos. 1345-1349 (5)	2.90	2.85

Royal Veterinary College bicentennial, National Canine Defense League and Cruft's Dog Show, centennial.

Symbols of Good Luck A392

No. 1351, Shooting star, rainbow. No. 1352, Bird, charm bracelet. No. 1353, Black cat. No. 1354, Bluebird, key. No. 1355, Duck, frog. No. 1356, Black boot, shamrocks. No. 1357, Rainbow, pot of gold. No. 1358, Peacock moths. No. 1359, Wishing well, sixpence.

1991, Feb. 5 **Photo.** ***Perf. 15x14***

Booklet Stamps

1350	A392	1st shown	1.30	1.20
1351	A392	1st multicolored	1.30	1.20
1352	A392	1st multicolored	1.30	1.20
1353	A392	1st multicolored	1.30	1.20
1354	A392	1st multicolored	1.30	1.20
1355	A392	1st multicolored	1.30	1.20
1356	A392	1st multicolored	1.30	1.20
1357	A392	1st multicolored	1.30	1.20
1358	A392	1st multicolored	1.30	1.20
1359	A392	1st multicolored	1.30	1.20
a.		Bklt. pane of 10, #1350-1359 (BK1160)	13.25	

No. 1359a printed se-tenant with 12 greetings labels. No. 1359a sold for £2.20 at date of issue.

Scientists & Their Technology A393

Designs: No. 1360, Michael Faraday, electricity. No. 1361, Charles Babbage, computers. 31p, Radar, developed by Robert Watson-Watt. 37p, Jet engine developed by Frank Whittle.

1991, Mar. 5 ***Perf. 14x15***

1360	A393	22p multicolored	.45	.45
1361	A393	22p multicolored	.45	.45
1362	A393	31p multicolored	.70	.70
1363	A393	37p multicolored	.80	.80
		Nos. 1360-1363 (4)	2.40	2.40

Famous Smiles Type of 1990

No. 1364, Teddy bear. No. 1365, Dennis the Menace. No. 1366, Mr. Punch. No. 1367, Cheshire Cat. No. 1368, Man in the Moon. No. 1369, The Laughing Policeman. No. 1370, Clown. No. 1371, Mona Lisa. No. 1372, Queen of Hearts. No. 1373, Stan Laurel.

1991, Mar. 26 **Photo.** ***Perf. 15x14***

Booklet Stamps

1364	A382	1st multicolored	1.35	1.20
a.		Sheet of 20 + 20 labels, litho., perf. 14¼x14	37.50	—
1365	A382a	1st multicolored	1.35	1.20
a.		Sheet, 10 each #1364-1365 + 20 labels	32.50	
b.		Sheet of 20 + 20 labels, litho., perf. 14¼x14	37.50	—
1366	A382b	1st multicolored	1.35	1.20
1367	A382c	1st multicolored	1.35	1.20
1368	A382d	1st multicolored	1.35	1.20
1369	A382e	1st multicolored	1.35	1.20
1370	A382f	1st multicolored	1.35	1.20
1371	A382g	1st multicolored	1.35	1.20
1372	A382h	1st multicolored	1.35	1.20
1373	A382i	1st multicolored	1.35	1.20
a.		Booklet pane of 10	13.50	—
b.		Sheet, #1364-1373 + 10 labels	22.00	

No. 1373a sold for £2.20 at date of issue. No. 1373a was affixed to booklet cover and was printed se-tenant with 12 greetings labels.

No. 1373b issued 5/22/00. Labels depict ribbons and are inscribed "The Stamp Show / 2000". The sheet with ribbon labels sold for £2.95, while the sheet with personalized labels sold for £5.95.

A sheet similar to No. 1373b with labels inscribed "Collect British Stamps" was specially produced for stamp dealers. Value, $225.

No. 1365a issued 2002. It sold for £5.95 and had labels that could be personalized.

Nos. 1364a, 1365b issued 2002. Each sold for £14.95 and has labels that can be personalized.

A394

Europa — A395

1991, Apr. 23 **Photo.** ***Perf. 14x15***

1374	A394	22p Planets	*.50*	*.40*
1375	A394	22p Stars	*.50*	*.40*
a.		Pair, #1374-1375	*1.10*	*1.10*
1376	A395	37p shown	*.85*	*.60*
1377	A395	37p Crescent eye	*1.00*	*.60*
a.		Pair, #1376-1377	*2.00*	*2.00*
		Nos. 1374-1377 (4)	*2.85*	*2.00*

Sports — A396

1991, June 11 **Photo.** ***Perf. 14½x14***

1378	A396	22p Fencing	.45	.50
1379	A396	26p Hurdling	.60	.55
1380	A396	31p Diving	.75	.70
1381	A396	37p Rugby	.80	.85
		Nos. 1378-1381 (4)	2.60	2.60

World Student Games, Nos. 1378-1380. Rugby World Cup, No. 1381.

Roses — A397

22p, Silver Jubilee. 26p, Mme. Alfred Carriere. 31p, Rosa moyesii. 33p, Harvest Fayre. 37p, Mutabilis.

1991, July 16 **Litho.** ***Perf. 14½x14***

1382	A397	22p multicolored	.40	.40
1383	A397	26p multicolored	.75	.75
1384	A397	31p multicolored	.60	.60
1385	A397	33p multicolored	.60	.60
1386	A397	37p multicolored	.70	.70
		Nos. 1382-1386 (5)	3.05	3.05

Dinosaurs A398

1991, Aug. 20 **Photo.** ***Perf. 14½x14***

1387	A398	22p Iguanodon	.50	.50
1388	A398	26p Stegosaurus	.60	.60
1389	A398	31p Tyrannosaurus	.70	.70
1390	A398	33p Protoceratops	.75	.75
1391	A398	37p Triceratops	.85	.85
		Nos. 1387-1391 (5)	3.40	3.40

First use of word "dinosaur" by Sir Richard Owen, 150th anniv.

Ordnance Survey Maps, Bicent. — A399

Maps of village of Hamstreet, Kent.

1991, Sept. 17 **Litho. & Engr.**

1392	A399	24p 1816	.50	.50

Litho.

1393	A399	28p 1906	.60	.60
1394	A399	33p 1959	.75	.75
1395	A399	39p 1991	.90	.90
		Nos. 1392-1395 (4)	2.75	2.75

Christmas
A400

Illuminated letters from Venetian manuscript "Acts of Mary and Jesus": 18p, "P," Adoration of the Magi. 24p, "M," Mary placing Jesus in manger. 28p, "A," Angel warning Joseph. 33p, "Q," The Annunciation. 39p, "N," Flight into Egypt.

1991, Nov. 12 Photo. *Perf. 15x14*

1416 A400 18p multicolored .35 .30
a. Booklet pane of 20 8.00
1417 A400 24p multicolored .50 .45
1418 A400 28p multicolored .55 .50
1419 A400 33p multicolored .70 .70
1420 A400 39p multicolored .75 *.80*
Nos. 1416-1420 (5) 2.85 2.75

Animals in Winter
A401

18p, Fallow deer. 24p, Brown hare. 28p, Fox. 33p, Redwing. 39p, Welsh mountain sheep.

1992, Jan. 14 Photo. *Perf. 15x14*

1421 A401 18p multicolored .40 *.35*
1422 A401 24p multicolored .50 .50
1423 A401 28p multicolored .60 .55
1424 A401 33p multicolored .75 .75
1425 A401 39p multicolored .80 *.90*
a. Booklet pane of 4 3.25
Nos. 1421-1425 (5) 3.05 3.05

For Prestige booklet containing pane No. 1425a, see BK156.
Issue date: No. 1425a, Mar. 1.

Memories
A402

No. 1426, Flowers. No. 1427, Locket. No. 1428, Key. No. 1429, Model car. No. 1430, Compass, 4-leaf clover. No. 1431, Pocket watch. No. 1432, Envelope, fountain pen. No. 1433, Buttons, pearls. No. 1434, Marbles. No. 1435, Starfish, shovel and bucket.

1992, Jan. 28 Litho. *Perf. 15x14*
Booklet Stamps

1426 A402 1st multicolored 1.35 1.20
1427 A402 1st multicolored 1.35 1.20
1428 A402 1st multicolored 1.35 1.20
1429 A402 1st multicolored 1.35 1.20
1430 A402 1st multicolored 1.35 1.20
1431 A402 1st multicolored 1.35 1.20
1432 A402 1st multicolored 1.35 1.20
1433 A402 1st multicolored 1.35 1.20
1434 A402 1st multicolored 1.35 1.20
1435 A402 1st multicolored 1.35 1.20
a. Bklt. pane of 10, #1426-1435 (BK1171) 13.50 —

No. 1435a printed se-tenant with 12 greeting labels and sold for £2.40 at date of issue.

Queen Elizabeth II's Accession to the Throne, 40th Anniv.
A403

Queen Elizabeth II: No. 1436, In coronation regalia. No. 1437, Facing right, wearing garter robes as head of Church of England. No. 1438, Holding infant Prince Andrew. No. 1439, Wearing military uniform at Trooping of the Color. No. 1440, Wearing purple hat.

1992, Feb. 6 Litho. *Perf. 14½x14*

1436 A403 24p multicolored .75 .75
1437 A403 24p multicolored .75 .75
1438 A403 24p multicolored .75 .75
1439 A403 24p multicolored .75 .75
1440 A403 24p multicolored .75 .75
a. Strip of 5, #1436-1440 4.00 *4.00*

Alfred, Lord Tennyson, Death Cent. — A404

Portraits and illustrations for poems: 24p, The Beguiling of Merlin by Sir Edward Burne-Jones. 28p, April Love by Arthur Hughes. 33p, The Lady of Shalott by John William Waterhouse. 39p, Mariana by Dante Gabriel Rossetti.

1992, Mar. 10 Photo.

1441 A404 24p multicolored .50 .50
1442 A404 28p multicolored .65 .60
1443 A404 33p multicolored .75 *.80*
1444 A404 39p multicolored .90 .90
Nos. 1441-1444 (4) 2.80 2.80

Castle Type of 1988

Nos. 1445-1448 have been re-engraved to show greater detail than on Nos. 1230-1233. The silhouette of the Queen's head on Nos. 1445-1448 is printed in a special ink that changes color from green to gold.

Perf. 15x14 Syncopated

1992-95 Engr.

1445 A369 £1 like #1230 3.25 .80
1446 A369 £1.50 like #1231 5.00 1.00
1447 A369 £2 like #1232 6.75 .95
1447A A369 £3 like #1230 12.00 1.75
1448 A369 £5 like #1233 14.00 2.25
Nos. 1445-1448 (5) 41.00 6.75

Nos. 1445-1447, 1448 were re-issued 12/6/94 with lines strengthened. Castles appear darker than on original issue. Etching in queen's head is square shaped instead of diamond shaped. Values, set: unused $39, used $8.
Issued: £3, 8/22/95; others, 3/24/92.

Castle Type Re-engraved

1997, July 29

1446a A369 £1.50 Caernarfon 9.75 5.75
1447b A369 £2 Edinburgh 12.00 1.50
1447Ac A369 £3 Carrickfergus 25.00 1.90
1448a A369 £5 Windsor 30.00 6.00

Queen's head is silkscreened and feels smooth on Nos. 1446a, 1447b, 1447Ac, 1448a. Letters "C" and "S" in Castle do not have serifs. Letters in castle names also differ from the 1992 and 1995 printings. The elliptical perforation begins one perf hole higher than on the earlier printings.

Discovery of America, 500th Anniv.
A405

Design: 39p, Sailing ship, Operation Raleigh Grand Regatta.

Litho. & Engr.

1992, Apr. 7 *Perf. 14½*

1449 A405 24p multicolored *1.25* .40
1450 A405 39p multicolored *1.75* .90

Europa.

Events
A406

Designs: No. 1451, British Olympic Assoc. flag. No. 1452, Flying torch flag of British Paralympic Assoc. No. 1453, British pavilion.

1992, Apr. 7 Litho.

1451 A406 24p multicolored .50 .40
1452 A406 24p multicolored .50 .40
a. Pair, #1451-1452 1.40 1.50
1453 A406 39p multicolored 1.25 1.00
Nos. 1451-1453 (3) 2.25 1.80

1992 Summer Olympics (No. 1451) and Paralympics (No. 1452), Barcelona. Expo '92, Seville (No. 1453).

English Civil War, 350th Anniv. — A407

1992, June 16 Photo. *Perf. 14½*

1454 A407 24p Pikeman .50 .50
1455 A407 28p Drummer .65 .60
1456 A407 33p Musketeer .75 .75
1457 A407 39p Standard bearer .85 *.90*
Nos. 1454-1457 (4) 2.75 2.75

Yeoman of the Guard, by Gilbert & Sullivan
A408

Scenes from comic operas: 24p, The Gondoliers. 28p, The Mikado. 33p, The Pirates of Penzance. 39p, Iolanthe.

1992, July 21 Photo. *Perf. 14½x14*

1458 A408 18p multicolored .35 .35
1459 A408 24p multicolored .50 .50
1460 A408 28p multicolored .65 .65
1461 A408 33p multicolored .70 .70
1462 A408 39p multicolored .80 .80
Nos. 1458-1462 (5) 3.00 3.00

Sir Arthur Sullivan, 150th anniv. of birth.

Protect the Environment
A409

Children's drawings: 24p, Acid rain kills. 28p, Ozone layer. 33p, Greenhouse effect. 39p, Bird of hope.

1992, Sept. 15 Photo *Perf. 14½*

1463 A409 24p multicolored .45 .45
1464 A409 28p multicolored .60 .60
1465 A409 33p multicolored .75 .70
1466 A409 39p multicolored .90 .85
Nos. 1463-1466 (4) 2.70 2.60

Single European Market
A410

1992, Oct. 13 Photo. *Perf. 15x14*

1467 A410 24p multicolored .55 .55

Christmas
A411

Stained glass windows. 18p, Angel Gabriel. 24p, Madonna and Child. 28p, King offering gold crown. 33p, Shepherds. 39p, Kings offering frankincense and myrrh.

1992, Nov. 10 Photo. *Perf. 15x14*

1468 A411 18p multicolored .40 .30
a. Booklet pane of 20 8.00
1469 A411 24p multicolored .50 .50
1470 A411 28p multicolored .60 .60
1471 A411 33p multicolored .75 .75
1472 A411 39p multicolored .80 *.90*
Nos. 1468-1472 (5) 3.05 3.05

Mute Swans — A412

Designs: 18p, Male, St. Catherine's Chapel, Abbotsbury. 24p, Cygnet, reed bed, Abbotsbury Swannery. 28p, Pair, cygnet. 33p, Eggs in nest, Tithe Barn. 39p, Head of young swan.

1993, Jan. 19 Photo. *Perf. 14x15*

1473 A412 18p multicolored .60 .50
1474 A412 24p multicolored .90 .80
1475 A412 28p multicolored 1.00 .95
1476 A412 33p multicolored 1.25 1.20
1477 A412 39p multicolored 1.40 1.40
Nos. 1473-1477 (5) 5.15 4.85

Abbotsbury Swannery, 600th anniv.

Britannia — A413

Litho., Typo. and Embossed
Perf. 14x14½ Syncopated

1993, Mar. 2 Granite Paper

1478 A413 £10 multicolored 27.50 10.00
a. Silver (Queen's head, security crosses) omitted *6,750.*

Soaking may damage these stamps.

Greetings Stamps
A414

Children's Characters: No. 1479, Long John Silver, parrot. No. 1480, Tweedledum, Tweedledee. No. 1481, Just William, Violet Elizabeth. No. 1482, Toad, Mole. No. 1483, Bash Street Kids, teacher. No. 1484, Peter Rabbit, Mrs. Rabbit. No. 1485, Father Christmas, Snowman. No. 1486, Big Friendly Giant, Sophie. No. 1487, Rupert Bear, Bill Badger. No. 1488, Aladdin, Genie.

Perf. 15x14 Syncopated

1993, Feb. 2 Litho.

1479 A414 (1st) multicolored 1.35 1.20
1480 A414 (1st) multicolored 1.35 1.20
1481 A414 (1st) multicolored 1.35 1.20
1482 A414 (1st) multicolored 1.35 1.20
1483 A414 (1st) multicolored 1.35 1.20
1484 A414 (1st) multicolored 1.35 1.20
a. Booklet pane of 4 (BK158) 8.00 —
1485 A414 (1st) multicolored 1.35 1.20
1486 A414 (1st) multicolored 1.35 1.20
1487 A414 (1st) multicolored 1.35 1.20

1488 A414 (1st) multicolored 1.35 1.20
a. Booklet pane of 10, #1479-1488 (BK1172) 13.50

No. 1479-1488 sold for 24p on day of issue. No. 1488a printed se-tenant with 20 greetings labels. See note above No. 1445.

Issue date: No. 1484a, Aug. 10.

For booklets containing panes of No. 1484a and No. 1488a, see BK158 and BK1172, respectively.

Marine Chronometer No. 4 — A415

Designs: 24p, Face. 28p, Escapement, remontoire and fusee. 33p, Balance spring, temperature compensator. 39p, Back of movement.

1993, Feb. 16 Litho. *Perf. 14½*
1489 A415 24p multicolored .50 .50
1490 A415 28p multicolored .60 .60
1491 A415 33p multicolored .70 .70
1492 A415 39p multicolored .80 .80
Nos. 1489-1492 (4) 2.60 2.60

John Harrison (1693-1776), inventor of marine chronometer.

Orchids A416

14th World Orchid Conf., Glasgow: 18p, Dendrobium hellwigianum. 24p, Paphiopedilum Maudiae "Magnificum." 28p, Cymbidium lowianum. 33p, Vanda Rothschildiana. 39p, Dendrobium vexillarius.

1993, Mar. 16 Litho. *Perf. 15x14*
1493 A416 18p multicolored .35 .35
1494 A416 24p multicolored .50 .50
1495 A416 28p multicolored .60 .55
1496 A416 33p multicolored .75 .70
1497 A416 39p multicolored .80 *.85*
Nos. 1493-1497 (5) 3.00 2.95

Contemporary Art — A417

Europa: 24p, Sculpture, Family Group, by Henry Moore. 28p, Print, Kew Gardens, by Edward Bawden. 33p, Painting, St. Francis and the Birds, by Stanley Spencer. 39p, Painting, Still Life, Odyssey 1, by Ben Nicholson.

1993, May 11 Photo. *Perf. 14x14½*
1498 A417 24p multicolored *.55* *.50*
1499 A417 28p multicolored *.60* *.60*
1500 A417 33p multicolored *.75* *.70*
1501 A417 39p multicolored *.90* *.90*
Nos. 1498-1501 (4) *2.80* *2.70*

Roman Artifacts A418

24p, Gold aureus of Claudius. 28p, Bronze bust of Hadrian. 33p, Gemstone carved with head of Roma. 39p, Mosaic of Christ.

1993, June 15 Photo. *Perf. 14½x14*
1502 A418 24p multicolored .50 .50
1503 A418 28p multicolored .60 .55
1504 A418 33p multicolored .75 .70
1505 A418 39p multicolored .90 *1.00*
Nos. 1502-1505 (4) 2.75 2.75

British Canals, Bicent. A419

Designs: 24p, Grand Junction Canal boats. 28p, Stainforth and Keadby Canal. 33p, Brecknock and Abergavenny Canal boats, horse. 39p, Crinan Canal, steamers and fishing boats.

1993, July 20 Litho. *Perf. 14½x14*
1506 A419 24p multicolored .50 .50
1507 A419 28p multicolored .60 .55
1508 A419 33p multicolored .75 .70
1509 A419 39p multicolored .90 *1.00*
Nos. 1506-1509 (4) 2.75 2.75

Autumn Fruits A420

1993, Sept. 14 Photo. *Perf. 15x14*
1510 A420 18p Horse chestnut .35 .30
1511 A420 24p Blackberries .50 .50
1512 A420 28p Filbert .65 .65
1513 A420 33p Rowanberries .70 .70
1514 A420 39p Pears .85 *.90*
Nos. 1510-1514 (5) 3.05 3.05

Sherlock Holmes — A421

Holmes and: No. 1515, Dr. Watson, The Reigate Squire. No. 1516, Sir Henry, The Hound of the Baskervilles. No. 1517, Lestrade, The Six Napoleons. No. 1518, Mycroft, The Greek Interpreter. No. 1519, Moriarty, The Final Problem.

1993, Oct. 12 Litho. *Perf. 14x14½*
1515 A421 24p multicolored .60 .60
1516 A421 24p multicolored .60 .60
1517 A421 24p multicolored .60 .60
1518 A421 24p multicolored .60 .60
1519 A421 24p multicolored .60 .60
a. Strip of 5, #1515-1519 3.00 3.00

"A Christmas Carol," by Charles Dickens, 150th Anniv. A423

Designs: 19p, Tiny Tim, Bob Cratchit. 25p, Mr. & Mrs. Fezziwig. 30p, Scrooge. 35p, Prize Turkey. 41p, Mr. Scrooge's Nephew.

1993, Nov. 9 Photo. *Perf. 15x14*
1528 A423 19p multicolored .40 .30
a. Booklet pane of 20 8.75
1529 A423 25p multicolored .50 .50
1530 A423 30p multicolored .65 .65
1531 A423 35p multicolored .75 .70
1532 A423 41p multicolored .90 .85
Nos. 1528-1532 (5) 3.20 3.00

For booklet containing No. 1528a, see BK857.

No. BK803 contains No. 1529.

Age of Steam — A424

Designs: 19p, Tandem locomotives, West Highland Line, North British Railway. 25p, Locomotive No. 60149, Kings Cross Station, London. 30p, Locomotive No. 43000 on turntable, Blyth North engine shed. 35p, Locomotive entering station. 41p, Locomotive on bridge over Worcester & Birmingham Canal.

1994, Jan. 18 Photo. *Perf. 14½*
1533 A424 19p black & green .45 .40
1534 A424 25p black & purple .60 .60
1535 A424 30p black & red brn .75 .75
1536 A424 35p black & red violet .80 .80
1537 A424 41p black & dark blue .95 .95
Nos. 1533-1537 (5) 3.55 3.50

Dan Dare A425

The Three Bears A426

Rupert the Bear A427

Alice in Wonderland — A428

Noggin the Nog A429

Peter Rabbit A430

Little Red Riding Hood A431

Orlando, the Marmalade Cat A432

Biggles A433

Paddington A434

Perf. 15x14 Syncopated
1994, Feb. 1 Photo.
Booklet Stamps
1538 A425 (1st) multicolored 1.45 1.25
1539 A426 (1st) multicolored 1.45 1.25
1540 A427 (1st) multicolored 1.45 1.25
1541 A428 (1st) multicolored 1.45 1.25
1542 A429 (1st) multicolored 1.45 1.25
1543 A430 (1st) multicolored 1.45 1.25
1544 A431 (1st) multicolored 1.45 1.25
1545 A432 (1st) multicolored 1.45 1.25
1546 A433 (1st) multicolored 1.45 1.25
1547 A434 (1st) multicolored 1.45 1.25
a. Bklt. pane of 10, #1538-1547 14.50

Nos. 1538-1547 sold for 25p on day of issue. No. 1547a was printed se-tenant with 20 greetings labels.

For booklet containing No. 1547a, see BK1182.

Investiture of Prince of Wales, 25th Anniv. A435

Watercolor landscapes, by Prince Charles: 19p, Chirk Castle, Clwyd, Wales. 25p, Ben Arkle, Sutherland, Scotland. 30p, Mourne Mountains, County Down, Northern Ireland. 35p, Dersingham, Norfolk, England. 41p, Dolwyddelan, Gwynedd, Wales.

1994, Mar. 1 Photo. *Perf. 15x14*
1548 A435 19p multicolored .35 .35
1549 A435 25p multicolored .50 .55
1550 A435 30p multicolored .65 .70
a. Booklet pane of 4 2.75
1551 A435 35p multicolored .80 .80
1552 A435 41p multicolored .90 .90
Nos. 1548-1552 (5) 3.20 3.30

For booklet containing pane No. 1550a, see No. BK159.

British Picture Postcards, Cent. — A436

Seaside characters: 19p, "Bather at Blackpool." 25p, "Where's my Little Lad." 30p, "Wish You Were Here." 35p, "Punch and Judy Show." 41p, "The Tower Crane."

1994, Apr. 12 Litho. *Perf. 14x14½*
1553 A436 19p multicolored .35 .35
1554 A436 25p multicolored .50 .55
1555 A436 30p multicolored .65 .70
1556 A436 35p multicolored .80 .80
1557 A436 41p multicolored .90 .90
Nos. 1553-1557 (5) 3.20 3.30

Blackpool Tower, cent. (No. 1553). Tower Bridge, cent. (No. 1557).

Opening of Channel Tunnel — A437

Nos. 1558, 1560, British lion, French rooster, meeting over Channel. Nos. 1559, 1561, Joined hands above speeding train.

1994, May 3	**Photo.**	***Perf. 14x14½***	
1558	25p dk blue & multi	.35	.35
1559	25p dk blue & multi	.50	*.55*
a.	A437 Pair, #1558-1559	1.00	1.00
1560	41p lt blue & multi	.65	.65
1561	41p multicolored	.80	.75
a.	A437 Pair, #1560-1561	1.50	1.50
	Nos. 1558-1561 (4)	2.30	2.30

See France Nos. 2421-2424.

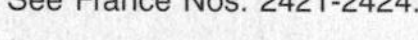

D-Day, 50th Anniv. — A438

Photographs from Imperial War Museum's archives: No. 1562, Ground crew reloading FAF Bostons. No. 1563, Coastal bombardment by HMS Warspite. No. 1564, Commandos landing on Gold Beach. No. 1565, Infantry regrouping on Sword Beach. No. 1566, Advancing inland from Ouistreham.

1994, June 6	**Litho.**	***Perf. 14***	
1562	A438 25p multicolored	.65	.65
1563	A438 25p multicolored	.65	.65
1564	A438 25p multicolored	.65	.65
1565	A438 25p multicolored	.65	.65
1566	A438 25p multicolored	.65	.65
a.	Strip of 5, #1562-1566	3.50	3.60

Honorable Company of Edinburgh Golfers, 250th Anniv. — A439

Golf courses: 19p, St. Andrews, old course. 25p, Muirfield, 18th hole. 30p, Carnoustie, 15th hole. 35p, Royal Troon, "postage stamp" 8th hole. 41p, Turnberry, 9th hole.

1994, July 5	**Photo.**	***Perf. 14***	
1567	A439 19p multicolored	.35	.35
1568	A439 25p multicolored	.50	.55
1569	A439 30p multicolored	.70	.70
1570	A439 35p multicolored	.80	.75
1571	A439 41p multicolored	.90	.90
	Nos. 1567-1571 (5)	3.25	3.25

Summertime Events — A440

Designs: 19p, Royal Welsh Agricultural Show, Llanelwedd. 25p, Wimbledon. 30p, Yachts on Solent during Cowes Week. 35p, Cricket at Lord's. 41p, Scottish Highland Games, Braemar.

1994, Aug. 2		***Perf. 14½x14***	
1572	A440 19p multicolored	.35	.35
1573	A440 25p multicolored	.50	.50
1574	A440 30p multicolored	.65	.65
1575	A440 35p multicolored	.75	.75
1576	A440 41p multicolored	.85	.85
	Nos. 1572-1576 (5)	3.10	3.10

Medical Discoveries — A441

Europa: 25p, Ultrasonic imaging. 30p, Scanning electron microscopy. 35p, Magnetic resonance imaging. 41p, Computed tomography.

1994, Sept. 27	**Photo.**	***Perf. 14x14½***	
1577	A441 25p multicolored	*.50*	*.60*
1578	A441 30p multicolored	*.75*	*.70*
1579	A441 35p multicolored	*.80*	*.80*
1580	A441 41p multicolored	*1.00*	*1.00*
	Nos. 1577-1580 (4)	*3.05*	*3.10*

Christmas A442

School children portraying: 19p, Mary, Joseph, with infant Jesus. 25p, Magi. 30p, Mary holding Jesus. 35p, Shepherds. 41p, Angels.

1994, Nov. 1	**Photo.**	***Perf. 15x14***	
1581	A442 19p multicolored	.35	.35
a.	Booklet pane of 20	8.00	
1582	A442 25p multicolored	.50	.50
1583	A442 30p multicolored	.65	.65
1584	A442 35p multicolored	.70	.70
1585	A442 41p multicolored	.90	.90
	Nos. 1581-1585 (5)	3.10	3.10

For booklet containing No. 1581a, see No. BK858.

No. BK804 contains No. 1582.

Cats A443

Designs: 19p, Black cat. 25p, Siamese, tabby cats. 30p, Yellow cat. 35p, Calico, Abyssinian cats. 41p, Black & white cat.

1995, Jan. 17	**Litho.**	***Perf. 15x14***	
1586	A443 19p multicolored	.35	.35
1587	A443 25p multicolored	.50	.50
1588	A443 30p multicolored	.70	.70
1589	A443 35p multicolored	.80	.80
1590	A443 41p multicolored	.90	.90
	Nos. 1586-1590 (5)	3.25	3.25

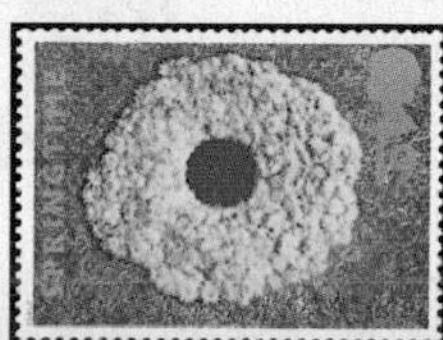

Springtime A444

Sculptures from natural materials, by Andy Goldsworthy: 19p, Dandelions. 25p, Chestnut leaves. 30p, Garlic leaves. 35p, Hazel leaves. 41p, Spring grass.

1995, Mar. 14	**Photo.**	***Perf. 15x14***	
1591	A444 19p multicolored	.35	.30
1592	A444 25p multicolored	.50	.50
1593	A444 30p multicolored	.70	.70
1594	A444 35p multicolored	.75	.75
1595	A444 41p multicolored	.90	.90
	Nos. 1591-1595 (5)	3.20	3.15

La Danse a'la Campagne, by Renoir A445

Troilus and Criseyde, by Peter Brookes A446

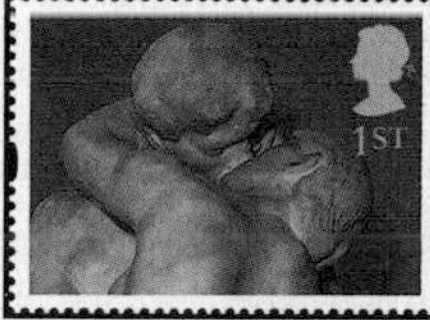

The Kiss, by Rodin A447

Girls on the Town, by Beryl Cook A448

Jazz, by Andrew Mockett A449

Girls Performing aKathal Dance (Aurangzeb Period) A450

Alice Keppel with her Daughter, by Alice Hughes A451

Children Playing, by L.S. Lowry A452

Circus Clowns, by Emily Firmin and Justin Mitchell A453

Decoration from All the Love Poems of Shakespeare, by Eric Gill — A454

Perf. 14 Syncopated

1995, Mar. 21		**Litho.**	
1596	A445 1st multicolored	1.35	1.20
1597	A446 1st multicolored	1.35	1.20
1598	A447 1st multicolored	1.35	1.20
1599	A448 1st multicolored	1.35	1.20
1600	A449 1st multicolored	1.35	1.20
1601	A450 1st multicolored	1.35	1.20
1602	A451 1st multicolored	1.35	1.20
1603	A452 1st multicolored	1.35	1.20
1604	A453 1st multicolored	1.35	1.20
1605	A454 1st multicolored	1.35	1.20
a.	Bklt. pane of 10, #1596-1605	13.50	

Complete booklet sold for £2.50 on day of issue.

For booklet containing No. 1605a, see No. BK1183.

National Trust, Cent. — A455

Designs: 19p, Celebrating 100 years. 25p, Protecting land. 30p, Conserving art. 35p, Saving coast. 41p, Repairing buildings.

1995, Apr. 11	**Photo.**	***Perf. 14x15***	
1606	A455 19p multicolored	.35	.30
1607	A455 25p multicolored	.50	.50
a.	Booklet pane of 6	3.00	
1608	A455 30p multicolored	.65	.70
1609	A455 35p multicolored	.75	.75
1610	A455 41p multicolored	.90	.90
	Nos. 1606-1610 (5)	3.15	3.15

For booklet containing panes No. 1607a, see No. BK160.

Issued: No. 1607a, 4/25/95.

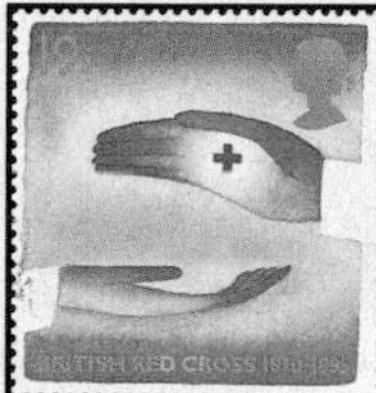

Peace & Freedom A456

Designs: No. 1611, Hands, British Red Cross 1870-1995. No. 1612, British troops, people celebrating liberation of Paris. No. 1613, Dove, outstretched hand, UN, 1945-95. No. 1614, St. Paul's Cathedral, floodlights forming Victory V. 30p, Hands above earth, UN 1945-95.

1995, May 2	**Photo.**	***Perf. 14½x14***	
1611	A456 19p multicolored	.45	.45
1612	A456 19p multicolored	.45	.45
1613	A456 25p multicolored	.70	.70
1614	A456 25p multicolored	.70	.70
1615	A456 30p multicolored	.85	.85
	Nos. 1611-1615 (5)	3.15	3.15

End of World War II, 50th anniv. (Nos. 1612, 1614), Europa (Nos. 1613, 1615).

See No. 2294a.

H. G. Wells (1866-1946), Science Fiction Writer — A457

Novels: 25p, The Time Machine. 30p, The First Men on the Moon. 35p, The War of the Worlds. 41p, The Shape of Things to Come.

1995, June 6	**Litho.**	***Perf. 14½x14***	
1616	A457 25p multicolored	.55	.60
1617	A457 30p multicolored	.70	.70
1618	A457 35p multicolored	.80	.75
1619	A457 41p multicolored	.95	.95
	Nos. 1616-1619 (4)	3.00	3.00

Opening of Shakespeare's New Globe Theatre A458

Bankside theatres: No. 1620, Swan, 1595. No. 1621, The Rose, 1595. No. 1622, The

Globe, 1599. No. 1623, The Hope, 1613. No. 1624, The Globe, 1614.

1995, Aug. 8 Litho. *Perf. 14½x14*

1620 A458 25p multicolored .60 *.65*
1621 A458 25p multicolored .60 *.65*
1622 A458 25p multicolored .60 *.65*
1623 A458 25p multicolored .60 *.65*
1624 A458 25p multicolored .60 *.65*
a. Strip of 5, #1620-1624 3.00 *3.25*

Pioneers of Communication — A459

Designs: 19p, Sir Rowland Hill, introduction of uniform penny postage. 25p, Hill as older man, design A1. 41p, Guglielmo Marconi, early wireless equipment. 60p, Marconi as older man using radiophone, sinking *Titanic*.

Litho. & Engr.

1995, Sept. 5 *Perf. 14½*

1625 A459 19p multicolored .35 .35
1626 A459 25p multicolored .55 .55
1627 A459 41p multicolored .90 .90
1628 A459 60p multicolored 1.20 1.20
Nos. 1625-1628 (4) 3.00 3.00

Rugby League, Cent. — A460

1995, Oct. 3 Photo. *Perf. 14x14½*

1629 A460 19p Harold Wagstaff .35 .35
1630 A460 25p Gus Risman .50 .55
1631 A460 30p Jim Sullivan .65 .65
1632 A460 35p Billy Batten .70 .65
1633 A460 41p Brian Bevan .85 .85
Nos. 1629-1633 (5) 3.05 3.05

Christmas — A461

Designs showing robin in winter scene: 19p, In pillar box. 25p, On fence rail, holly bush. 30p, Standing on snow covered milk bottle. 41p, Sitting on snow covered road sign, blue fence. 60p, Sitting on door knob, Christmas decoration on door.

1995, Oct. 30 Photo. *Perf. 14¾x14*

1634 A461 19p multicolored .35 .35
a. Booklet pane of 20 8.50
b. Sheet of 20 + 20 labels *225.00*
1635 A461 25p multicolored .50 .50
1636 A461 30p multicolored .65 .65
1637 A461 41p multicolored .90 .90
1638 A461 60p multicolored 1.20 1.20
a. Booklet pane of 4 7.25
Nos. 1634-1638 (5) 3.60 3.60

No. 1634b was issued 10/3/00. It sold for £3.99 and has labels that read "Seasons Greetings" and "Glad Tidings." Sheets with personalized labels were made available only to select Royal Post customers via mail order purchases, and sold for more.

For booklets containing Nos. 1634a and 1638a, see Nos. BK859 and BK792, respectively.

No. BK805 contains No. 1635.

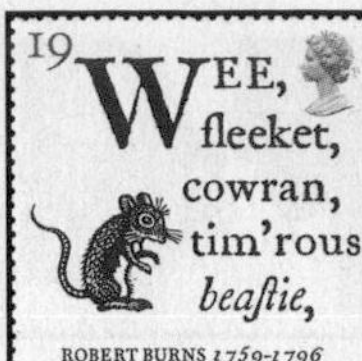

Robert Burns (1759-1796), Poet — A462

Lines from poems: 19p, "Wee sleeket, cowran, tim'rous beastie." 25p, "O my luve's like a red, red rose." 41p, "Scots, wha hae wi Wallace bled." 60p, "Should auld acquaintance be forgot."

1996, Jan. 25 Litho. *Perf. 14½*

1639 A462 19p multicolored .40 .40
1640 A462 25p multicolored .55 .60
1641 A462 41p multicolored 1.00 1.00
1642 A462 60p multicolored 1.30 1.25
Nos. 1639-1642 (4) 3.25 3.25

Greetings Cartoons A463

No. 1643, More Love. No. 1644, Sincerely. No. 1645, Human condition. No. 1646, Mental Floss. No. 1647, Don't ring. No. 1648, Dear lottery prize winner. No. 1649, I'm writing to you... No. 1650, Fetch this... No. 1651, My day starts... No. 1652, The check in the post.

Perf. 14½ Syncopated

1996-2001 Litho.

1643 A463 1st black & lilac 1.35 1.20
1644 A463 1st black & green 1.35 1.20
1645 A463 1st black & blue 1.35 1.20
1646 A463 1st black & purple 1.35 1.20
1647 A463 1st black & red 1.35 1.20
1648 A463 1st black & blue 1.35 1.20
1649 A463 1st black & red 1.35 1.20
1650 A463 1st black & purple 1.35 1.20
1651 A463 1st black & green 1.35 1.20
1652 A463 1st black & lilac 1.35 1.20
a. Booklet pane, #1643-1652+20 labels 13.50
b. Sheet of 10, #1643-1652, + 10 labels, perf. 14½x14 12.50 —
c. Sheet of 20, 2 each #1643-1652, + 20 labels, perf. 14¼ — —

Issued: No. 1652b, 12/18/01. 1652a, 2/26/96. 1652c, 7/29/03.

No. 1652b lacks perforation syncopation. Labels could be personalized for an additional amount.

Nos. 1643-1652 sold for 25p on day of issue.

No. 1652c sold for £6.15.

For booklet containing No. 1652a, see No. BK1184.

No. 1652a was issued on phosphored paper. Booklet panes with two phosphor bands exist. Value, $37.50.

Wildfowl and Wetlands Trust, 50th Anniv. A464

Paintings by Charles Tunnicliffe RA (1901-79): 19p, Muscovy duck. 25p, Lapwing. 30p, White-fronted goose. 35p, Bittern. 41p, Whooper swan.

1996, Mar. 12 Photo. *Perf. 14x14½*

1653 A464 19p multicolored .35 .35
1654 A464 25p multicolored .50 .50
1655 A464 30p multicolored .65 .65
1656 A464 35p multicolored .75 .75
1657 A464 41p multicolored .90 .90
Nos. 1653-1657 (5) 3.15 3.15

Motion Pictures, Cent. — A465

Designs: 19p, Exterior of Odeon at Harrogate, 1930s theater. 25p, Laurance Olivier, Vivien Leigh in scene from "That Hamilton Woman." 30p, Cinema ticket from "The Picture House." 35p, Rooster emblem of Pathe News, motion picture newsreels. 41p, Theater marquee.

1996, Apr. 16 Photo. *Perf. 14x14½*

1658 A465 19p multicolored .40 .40
1659 A465 25p multicolored .55 .55
1660 A465 30p multicolored .70 .70
1661 A465 35p multicolored .75 .75
1662 A465 41p multicolored .85 .85
Nos. 1658-1662 (5) 3.25 3.25

1996 European Soccer Championships — A466

Lengendary players: 19p, Dixie Dean (1907-80). 25p, Bobby Moore (1941-93). 35p, Duncan Edwards (1936-58). 41p, Billy Wright (1924-94). 60p, Danny Blanchflower (1926-93).

1996, May 14 Litho. *Perf. 15x14*

1663 A466 19p gray, red & blk .40 .35
a. Bklt. pane of 4 + printed margin (BK161) 1.60
1664 A466 25p gray, grn & blk .55 .55
a. Bklt. pane of 4 + printed margin (BK161) 2.25
1665 A466 35p gray, yel & blk .75 .75
1666 A466 41p blk, blue & gray .90 .90
1667 A466 60p gray, org & blk 1.20 1.20
a. Bklt. pane, 2 ea #1665-1667 (BK161) 5.75
Nos. 1663-1667 (5) 3.80 3.75

1996 Summer Olympic, Paralympic Games, Atlanta A467

1996, July 9 Litho. *Perf. 15x14*

1688 A467 26p Sprinting .60 .55
1689 A467 26p Javelin .60 .55
1690 A467 26p Basketball .60 .55
1691 A467 26p Swimming .60 .55
1692 A467 26p Victorious athlete .60 .55
a. Strip of 5, #1688-1692 3.25 3.00

Compare with Type A588.

20th Century Women of Achievement A468

Designs: 20p, Dorothy Hodgkin (1910-94), chemist. 26p, Margot Fonteyn (1919-91), ballerina. 31p, Elisabeth Frink (1930-93), sculptor. 37p, Daphne du Maurier (1907-89), novelist. 43p, Marea Hartman (1920-94), sports administrator.

1996, Aug. 6 Photo. *Perf. 14½*

1693 A468 20p multicolored *.50 .50*
1694 A468 26p multicolored *.55 .55*
1695 A468 31p multicolored *.70 .70*
1696 A468 37p multicolored *.80 .80*
1697 A468 43p multicolored *.95 .95*
Nos. 1693-1697 (5) *3.50 3.50*

Europa, Nos. 1694-1695.

British Television Programs for Children, 50th Anniv. A469

Designs: 20p, Annette Mills, "Muffin the Mule." 26p, Sooty. 31p, String puppets Troy Tempest and Lord Titan. 37p, The Clangers. 43p, Dangermouse.

1996, Sept. 3 *Perf. 14½x14*

1698 A469 20p multicolored .45 .45
a. Pane of 4 #1698b + printed margin 5.00
b. Perf. 15x14 1.20 *1.40*
1699 A469 26p multicolored .50 *.55*
1700 A469 31p multicolored .65 *.70*
1701 A469 37p multicolored .70 *.75*
1702 A469 43p multicolored .95 *1.00*
Nos. 1698-1702 (5) 3.25 *3.45*

For Prestige booklet containing pane No. 1698a, see BK162.

Issued: No. 1698a, 9/23/97.

Classic British Sports Cars — A470

Designs: 20p, 1955 Triumph TR3. 26p, MG TD. 37p, Austin-Healy 100. 43p, 1948 Jaguar XK 120. 63p, Morgan Plus Four.

1996, Oct. 1 Photo. *Perf. 14½*

1703 A470 20p multicolored .45 .35
1704 A470 26p multicolored .55 .55
1705 A470 37p multicolored .75 .75
1706 A470 43p multicolored .90 *1.00*
1707 A470 63p multicolored 1.30 1.30
Nos. 1703-1707 (5) 3.95 3.95

Christmas A471

Designs: 2nd, Three kings, star. 1st, The Annunciation. 31p, Mary, Joseph on journey to Bethlehem. 43p, Madonna and Child. 63p, Angel telling shepherds of Christ's birth.

1996, Oct. 28 Photo. *Perf. 14½x14*

1708 A471 2nd multicolored .85 .65
a. Booklet pane of 20 20.00
1709 A471 1st multicolored 1.05 .95
1710 A471 31p multicolored .65 .70
1711 A471 43p multicolored .90 .95
1712 A471 63p multicolored 1.20 1.20
Nos. 1708-1712 (5) 4.65 4.45

Nos. 1708-1709 sold for 20p and 26p respectively on day of issue.

For booklet containing No. 1708a, see No. BK1220.

No. BK1194 contains No. 1709.

Gentiana Acaulis A472

Magnolia Altissima A473

Camellia Japonica A474

Tulip
A475

Fuchsia
"Princess
of Wales"
A476

Le
Perroquet
Rouge
A477

Gazania
Splendens
A478

Iris Latifolia
A479

Amaryllis
Bresiliensis
A480

Granadilla
A481

Perf. 14½x14 Syncopated

1997, Jan. 6 **Litho.**

Booklet Stamps

1713 A472 1st multicolored 1.30 1.20
a. Perf 15x14 4.75 4.75
1714 A473 1st multicolored 1.30 1.20
1715 A474 1st multicolored 1.30 1.20
1716 A475 1st multicolored 1.30 1.20
a. Perf 15x14 2.50 2.50
1717 A476 1st multicolored 1.30 1.20
1718 A477 1st multicolored 1.30 1.20
1719 A478 1st multicolored 1.30 1.20
1720 A479 1st multicolored 1.30 1.20
a. Perf 15x14 4.75 4.75
b. Booklet pane, #1713a, 1720a, 2 #1716a (BK176) 15.00
1721 A480 1st multicolored 1.30 1.20
1722 A481 1st multicolored 1.00 1.00
a. Bklt. pane of 10, #1713-1722 13.00
b. Sheet, 2 each #1713-1722, + 20 labels, perf. 14¼ 37.50

Nos. 1713-1722, 1722a issued 1/9/97. 1722a sold for £2.50 on day of issue, but stamps each had 26p of franking value.

No. 1722b issued 2003. It sold for £14.95 and had labels that could be personalized.

No. 1720a issued 5/25/04. 1720a sold for £1.12 on day of issue.

For booklet containing No. 1722a, see No. BK1195.

See Nos. 2671-2672.

King Henry
VIII and
His Six
Wives
A482

1997, Jan. 21 **Photo.** ***Perf. 15***

1723 A482 26p shown .70 .70

Size: 27x38mm

Perf. 14x15

1724 A482 26p Catherine of Aragon .70 .70
1725 A482 26p Anne Boleyn .70 .70
1726 A482 26p Jane Seymour .70 .70
1727 A482 26p Anne of Cleves .70 .70
1728 A482 26p Catherine Howard .70 .70
1729 A482 26p Catherine Parr .70 .70
a. Strip of 6, #1724-1729 4.25 4.25
Nos. 1723-1729 (7) 4.90 4.90

St. Augustine
of Canterbury
& St. Columba
of
Iona — A483

Designs: 26p, St. Columba's journey across Irish Sea to Iona. 37p, St. Columba at work, Ionian Sea. 43p, St. Augustine baptizing King Ethelbert. 63p, St. Augustine outside Cathedral at Canterbury, Kent coastline.

1997, Mar. 11 **Photo.** ***Perf. 14½x14***

1730 A483 26p multicolored .60 .60
1731 A483 37p multicolored .80 .80
1732 A483 43p multicolored 1.05 1.05
1733 A483 63p multicolored 1.30 1.30
Nos. 1730-1733 (4) 3.75 3.75

Stories and
Legends — A484

Europa: 26p, Dracula. 31p, Frankenstein. 37p, Dr. Jekyll and Mr. Hyde. 43p, The Hound of the Baskervilles.

1997, May 13 **Photo.** ***Perf. 14x15***

1754 A484 26p multicolored *.60 .60*
1755 A484 31p multicolored *.75 .75*
1756 A484 37p multicolored *.90 .90*
1757 A484 43p multicolored *1.25 1.25*
Nos. 1754-1757 (4) *3.50 3.50*

Aircraft,
Designers
A485

20p, Supermarine Spitfire, R.J. Mitchell. 26p, Avro Lancaster, Roy Chadwick. 37p, DeHavilland Mosquito, R.E. Bishop. 43p, Gloster Meteor, George Carter. 63p, Hawker Hunter, Sidney Camm.

1997, June 10 **Photo.** ***Perf. 15x14***

1758 A485 20p multicolored .45 .35
a. Litho., perf. 14¼x14 (#2587b) ('08) 2.50 2.50
1759 A485 26p multicolored .55 .55
1760 A485 37p multicolored .75 .80
1761 A485 43p multicolored 1.05 1.00
1762 A485 63p multicolored 1.45 1.40
Nos. 1758-1762 (5) 4.25 4.10

Issued: No. 1758a, 9/18/08.

On Nos. 1758-1762 the face of the aircraft designer was hidden in the clouds.

All the
Queen's
Horses
A486

20p, 43p, Carriage horses from Royal Mews. 26p, 63p, Mount horses from Household Cavalry.

1997, July 9 **Litho.** ***Perf. 14x14½***

1763 A486 20p multicolored .50 .40
1764 A486 26p multicolored .60 .65
1765 A486 43p multicolored 1.05 1.10
1766 A486 63p multicolored 1.45 1.45
Nos. 1763-1766 (4) 3.60 3.60

British Horse Society, 50th anniv.

Post Offices
A487

Designs: 20p, Haroldswick, Shetland Islands, Scotland. 26p, Painswick, Gloucestershire, England. 43p, Beddgelert, Gwynedd, Wales. 63p, Ballyroney, County Down, Northern Ireland.

1997, Aug. 12 **Litho.** ***Perf. 14½x14***

1767 A487 20p multicolored .45 .35
1768 A487 26p multicolored .60 .60
1769 A487 43p multicolored 1.05 1.10
1770 A487 63p multicolored 1.40 1.40
Nos. 1767-1770 (4) 3.50 3.45

Enid Blyton,
Author of
Children's
Stories, Birth
Cent. — A488

Characters from books: 20p, "Noddy." 26p, "Famous Five." 37p, "Secret Seven." 43p, "Faraway Tree." 63p, "Malory Towers."

1997, Sept. 9 **Litho.** ***Perf. 14x14½***

1771 A488 20p multicolored .45 .40
1772 A488 26p multicolored .50 *.60*
1773 A488 37p multicolored .75 *.85*
1774 A488 43p multicolored 1.00 *1.05*
1775 A488 63p multicolored 1.30 *1.35*
Nos. 1771-1775 (5) 4.00 *4.25*

Christmas
Crackers
A489

Designs: 2nd, Santa as Man in Moon sharing cracker with two children. 1st, Santa bursting through wrapping paper with cracker. 31p, Santa riding across sky on giant cracker. 43p, Santa on giant snowball holding cracker. 63p, Santa climbing into chimney with sack full of crackers.

1997, Oct. 27 **Photo.** ***Perf. 15x14***

1776 A489 2nd multicolored .85 .65
a. Booklet pane of 20 17.50
1777 A489 1st multicolored 1.00 .90
b. Sheet of 10 + 10 labels *200.00*
c. Sheet of 20 + 20 labels, litho., perf 14½x14 40.00
1778 A489 31p multicolored .65 *.70*
1779 A489 43p multicolored 1.00 1.00
1780 A489 63p multicolored 1.15 1.25
Nos. 1776-1780 (5) 4.65 4.50

Nos. 1776-1777 were sold for 20p and 26p, respectively, on day of issue.

No. 1777b issued 10/3/00. It sold for £2.95 and has labels that read "Seasons Greetings" and "Ho Ho Ho." Sheets with personalized labels were made available only to select Royal Post customers via mail order purchases, and sold for more.

No. 1777c issued 2003. It sold for £5.95 and had labels that could be personalized.

For booklet containing No. 1776a, see No. BK1221.

No. BK1198 contains No. 1777.

Queen
Elizabeth
II, Prince
Philip, 50th
Wedding
Anniv.
A490

Designs: 20p, 43p, Wedding portrait, 1947. 26p, 63p, Anniversary portrait, 1997.

1997, Nov. 13 **Photo.** ***Perf. 15***

1781 A490 20p multicolored .65 .50
1782 A490 26p multicolored .75 .75
1783 A490 43p multicolored 1.50 1.45
1784 A490 63p multicolored 2.00 1.75
Nos. 1781-1784 (4) 4.90 4.45

Endangered
Species — A491

Designs: 20p, Common dormouse. 26p, Lady's slipper orchid. 31p, Song thrush. 37p, Shining ram's horn snail. 43p, Mole cricket. 63p, Devil's bolete.

1998, Jan. 20 **Litho.** ***Perf. 14x14½***

1785 A491 20p multicolored .50 .40
1786 A491 26p multicolored .65 .65
1787 A491 31p multicolored .80 .80
1788 A491 37p multicolored .90 .85
1789 A491 43p multicolored 1.15 1.10
1790 A491 63p multicolored 1.45 1.45
Nos. 1785-1790 (6) 5.45 5.25

Diana, Princess of
Wales (1961-
97) — A492

Portraits of Diana wearing: No. 1791, Choker. No. 1792, Blue dress. No. 1793, Tiara. No. 1794, Checked dress. No. 1795, Black dress.

1998, Feb. 3 **Photo.** ***Perf. 14x15***

1791 A492 26p multicolored .60 .60
1792 A492 26p multicolored .60 .60
1793 A492 26p multicolored .60 .60
1794 A492 26p multicolored .60 .60
1795 A492 26p multicolored .60 .60
a. Strip of 5, #1791-1795 3.00 3.00
b. As "a," imperf. 26,000.

Order of
the Garter,
650th
Anniv.
A493

Queen's Beasts (supporters of Royal Arms created for Queen Elizabeth II's coronation in 1953): No. 1796, Lion of England, Griffin of Edward III. No. 1797, Falcon of Plantagenet, Bull of Clarence. No. 1798, Lion of Mortimer, Yale of Beaufort. No. 1799, Greyhound of Richmond, Dragon of Wales. No. 1800, Unicorn of Scotland, Horse of Hanover.

Litho. & Engr.

1998, Feb. 24 *Perf. 15x14*
1796 A493 26p multicolored .60 .60
1797 A493 26p multicolored .60 .60
1798 A493 26p multicolored .60 .60
1799 A493 26p multicolored .60 .60
1800 A493 26p multicolored .60 .60
a. Strip of 5, #1796-1800 3.75 3.75

Queen Type of 1952 with Face Values in Decimal Currency

Perf. 14 Syncopated

1998, Mar. 10 **Litho.**
1801 A129 20p dk grn & lt grn .70 .50
a. Booklet pane of 6 + printed margin (BK163) 4.25
1802 A129 26p dk brn & lt brn .90 .80
a. Booklet pane of 9 + printed margin (BK163) 8.25
1803 A129 37p dk red lil & lt lil 2.50 2.00
a. Booklet pane 3 each #1802-1803 + printed margin (BK163) 10.50
b. Booklet pane, 4 #1801, 2 ea #1802-1803 + printed margin (BK163) 9.75

Lighthouses A494

1998, Mar. 24 *Perf. 14x14½*
1804 A494 20p St. John's Point .50 .40
1805 A494 26p The Smalls .60 .60
1806 A494 37p Needles Rocks .80 *.85*
1807 A494 43p Bell Rock 1.15 *1.20*
1808 A494 63p Eddystone 1.50 1.50
Nos. 1804-1808 (5) 4.55 4.55

Comedians A495

20p, Tommy Cooper (1922-84). 26p, Eric Morecambe (1926-84). 37p, Joyce Grenfell (1910-79). 43p, Les Dawson (1933-93). 63p, Peter Cook (1937-95).

1998, Apr. 23 **Litho.** *Perf. 14½x14*
1809 A495 20p multicolored .50 .40
1810 A495 26p multicolored .60 .60
1811 A495 37p multicolored .80 .80
1812 A495 43p multicolored 1.15 1.15
1813 A495 63p multicolored 1.50 1.50
Nos. 1809-1813 (5) 4.55 4.45

National Health Service, 50th Anniv. — A496

Designs: 20p, Hands forming heart, "10,000 donors give blood every day." 26p, Adult hand clasping child's, "1,700,000 prescriptions dispensed every day." 43p, Hands forming cradle, "2,000 babies delivered every day." 63p, Taking pulse, "130,000 hospital outpatients seen every day."

1998, June 23 **Litho.** *Perf. 14x14½*
1814 A496 20p multicolored .50 .40
1815 A496 26p multicolored .60 .60
1816 A496 43p multicolored 1.20 1.20
1817 A496 63p multicolored 1.50 1.50
Nos. 1814-1817 (4) 3.80 3.70

Magical World of Children's Literature A496a

Stories depicted: 20p, "The Hobbit," by J.R.R. Tolkien. 26p, "The Lion, The Witch and the Wardrobe," by C.S. Lewis. 37p, "The Phoenix and the Carpet," by E. Nesbit. 43p, "The Borrowers," by Mary Norton. 63p, "Through the Looking Glass," by Lewis Carroll.

1998, July 21 **Photo.** *Perf. 15x14*
1820 A496a 20p multicolored .50 .40
1821 A496a 26p multicolored .60 .60
1822 A496a 37p multicolored .85 .85
1823 A496a 43p multicolored 1.10 1.10
1824 A496a 63p multicolored 1.40 1.40
Nos. 1820-1824 (5) 4.45 4.35

Notting Hill Carnival A497

Expressionist photographic images of dancers, color of costumes: 20p, Yellow. 26p, Blue. 43p, Gold and white. 63p, Green.

1998, Aug. 25 *Perf. 14x14½*
1825 A497 20p multicolored *.55* *.40*
1826 A497 26p multicolored *.60* *.55*
1827 A497 43p multicolored 1.25 1.25
1828 A497 63p multicolored 1.60 1.60
Nos. 1825-1828 (4) *4.00* *3.80*

Europa (Nos. 1825-1826).

Land Speed Records A498

Car, driver, year, record speed: 20p, Bluebird, Sir Malcolm Campbell, 1925, 151 mph. 26p, Red Sunbeam, Sir Henry Segrave, 1926, 152 mph. 30p, Babs, John G. Parry Thomas, 1926, 171 mph. 43p, Railton Mobil Special, John R. Cobb, 1947, 394 mph. 63p, Bluebird CN7, Donald Campbell, 1964, 403 mph.

1998, Sept. 29 **Photo.** *Perf. 15x14*
1829 A498 20p multicolored .45 .35
a. Perf. 14½x13½ 1.40 1.40
b. As "a," booklet pane of 4 + printed margin (BK164) 5.75
1830 A498 26p multicolored .55 .55
1831 A498 30p multicolored .65 .65
1832 A498 43p multicolored 1.05 1.05
1833 A498 63p multicolored 1.35 1.35
Nos. 1829-1833 (5) 4.05 3.95

Christmas Angels A499

1998, Nov. 2 **Photo.** *Perf. 15x14*
1834 A499 20p shown .55 .40
a. Booklet pane of 20 14.00
1835 A499 26p Praying .60 .65
1836 A499 30p Playing flute .70 .75
1837 A499 43p Playing lute 1.25 1.25
1838 A499 63p Praying, diff. 1.60 1.60
Nos. 1834-1838 (5) 4.70 4.65

No. BK1199 contains No. 1835.

British Achievements During Past 1000 Years — A500

Inventions: 20p, Timekeeping, John Harrison's chronometer. 26p, Development of steam power. 43p, William Henry Fox Talbot's use of negatives to create photographs. 63p, Development of computers.

Transportation: 20p, Jet travel. 26p, Development of bicycle. 43p, Isambard Kingdom Brunel's Clifton Suspension Bridge, Great Western Railway. 63p, Capt. Cook's expeditions.

Health care: 20p, First smallpox vaccination, by Edward Jenner. 26p, Development of nursing care. 43p, Discovery of penicillin, by Alexander Fleming. 63p, First "test tube" baby (in-vitro fertilization), pioneered by Patrick Steptoe and Robert Edwards.

Emigration: 20p, Migration to Scotland. 26p, Pilgrim fathers. 43p, Destination Australia. 63p, Migration to UK.

Workers: 19p, Weavers. 26p, Mill towns. 44p, Ship building. 64p, City finance.

Entertainment and sports: 19p, Freddie Mercury, lead singer of Queen. 26p, Bobby Moore, 1966 World Cup Soccer Champions. 44p, Dalek from "Dr. Who" television series. 64p, Charlie Chaplin.

Citizens' Rights: 19p, Equal rights. 26p, Right to health. 44p, Right to learn. 64p, First rights.

Scientists: 19p, Decoding DNA. 26p, Darwin's theory. 44p, Faraday's electricity. 64p, Newton, Hubble Telescope.

Farmers: 19p, Strip farming (Europa). 26p, Mechanical farming. 44p, Food from afar. 64p, Satellite agriculture.

Soldiers: 19p, Battle of Bannockburn. 26p, Civil War. 44p, World Wars, cemetery. 64p, Peace keeping.

Christians: 19p, John Wesley (1703-91), founder of Methodism, and "Hark, The Herald Angels Sing," hymn by brother Charles (1707-88). 26p, King James Bible. 44p, St. Andrews Pilgrimage. 64p, First Christmas.

Artists: 19p, World of the stage. 26p, World of music. 44p, World of literature. 64p, New worlds.

1999 **Photo.** *Perf. 14¼x14½*

Inventions

1839 A500 20p multi (48) .55 .45
1840 A500 26p multi (47) .60 .60
1841 A500 43p multi (46) 1.10 1.10
1842 A500 63p multi (45) 1.50 *1.50*
a. Perf. 13¾ 3.00 3.00
b. Booklet pane, 4 #1842a (BK166) 12.00

Transportation

1843 A500 20p multi (44) .55 .45
1844 A500 26p multi (43) .60 .60
1845 A500 43p multi (42) 1.10 1.10
1846 A500 63p multi (41) 1.50 *1.60*

Health Care

Perf. 13¾x14

1847 A500 20p multi (40) .55 .45
a. Booklet pane of 4 (BK166) 2.25
1848 A500 26p multi (39) .60 .60
1849 A500 43p multi (38) 1.10 1.10
1850 A500 63p multi (37) 1.50 *1.60*

Emigration

Perf. 14¼x14½

1851 A500 20p multi (36) .55 .45
1852 A500 26p multi (35) .60 .60
1853 A500 43p multi (34) 1.10 1.10
1854 A500 63p multi (33) 1.50 *1.60*

Workers

Perf. 14¼x14½

1855 A500 19p multi (32) .55 .45
1856 A500 26p multi (31) .60 .60
a. Booklet pane #1852, 1856 (BK1141) 1.25
1857 A500 44p multi (30) 1.10 1.10
1858 A500 64p multi (29) 1.50 *1.60*

Entertainment & Sports

Perf. 14¼x14½

1859 A500 19p multi (28) .55 .45
1860 A500 26p multi (27) .60 .60
1861 A500 44p multi (26) 1.10 1.10
1862 A500 64p multi (25) 1.50 *1.50*

Citizen's Rights

Perf. 14¼x14½

1863 A500 19p multi (24) .55 .45
1864 A500 26p multi (23) .60 .60
1865 A500 44p multi (22) 1.10 1.10
1866 A500 64p multi (21) 1.50 *1.60*

Scientists

Perf. 14¼ (#1868-1869), 13¾ (#1867, 1870)

1867 A500 19p multi (20) .55 .45
1868 A500 26p multi (19) .60 .60
a. Perf. 14¼x14 2.25 2.25
b. Booklet pane, 4 #1868a (BK166) 9.00
1869 A500 44p multi (18) 1.10 1.10
a. Perf. 14¼x14 2.75 2.75
b. Booklet pane, 4 #1869a (BK166) 11.00
1870 A500 64p multi (17) 1.50 *1.60*
a. Perf. 14¼ 4.50 4.50
b. Souvenir sheet, 4 #1870a 13.75 *14.50*

Farmers

Perf. 14¼x14½

1871 A500 19p multi (16) *.55* *.45*
1872 A500 26p multi (15) .60 .60
a. Booklet pane of 2 (BK1142) 1.25
1873 A500 44p multi (14) 1.10 1.10
1874 A500 64p multi (13) 1.50 *1.60*

Europa, No. 1871.

Soldiers

Perf. 14¼x14½

1875 A500 19p multi (12) .55 .45
1876 A500 26p multi (11) .60 .60
1877 A500 44p multi (10) 1.10 1.10
1878 A500 64p multi (9) 1.50 *1.60*

Christians

1879 A500 19p multi (8) .55 .45
a. Booklet pane of 20 11.00
1880 A500 26p multi (7) .60 .60
1881 A500 44p multi (6) 1.10 1.10
1882 A500 64p multi (5) 1.50 *1.60*

Artists

Perf. 14¼x14½

1883 A500 19p multi (4) .55 .45
1884 A500 26p multi (3) .60 .60
1885 A500 44p multi (2) 1.10 1.10
1886 A500 64p multi (1) 1.50 *1.60*
Nos. 1839-1886 (48) 45.00 44.80

Issued: Nos. 1839-1842, 1/12; Nos. 1843-1846, 2/2; Nos. 1847-1850, 3/2; Nos. 1851-1854, 4/6; Nos. 1855-1858, 5/4; Nos. 1859-1862, 6/1; Nos. 1863-1866, 7/6; Nos. 1867-1870, 8/3; Nos. 1871-1874, 9/7; Nos. 1870b, 8/11; Nos. 1875-1878, 10/5; Nos. 1879-1882, 11/2; Nos. 1883-1886, 12/7.

See Nos. 1889, 1890-1937, 1938.

No. BK1200 contains No. 1880.

Marriage of Prince Edward and Sophie Rhys-Jones — A501

1999, June 15 **Photo.** *Perf. 15x14*
1887 A501 26p shown .60 *.75*
1888 A501 64p Profile portrait 1.50 1.50

Souvenir Sheet

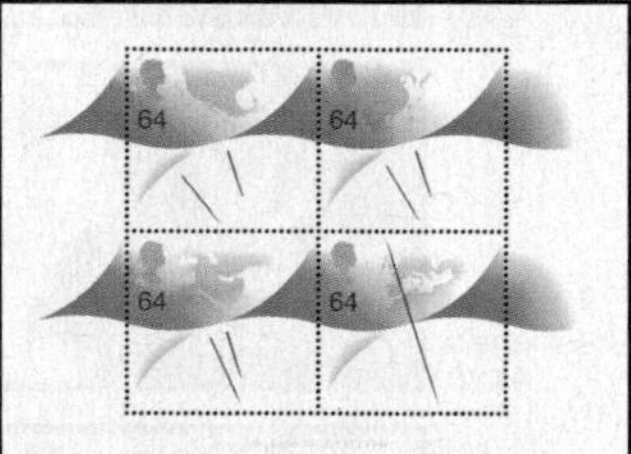

Millennium — A502

Clock and globe showing: a, North America. b, Southeast Asia. c, Middle East. d, Europe.

Perf. 14¼x14½

1999, Dec. 14 **Photo.**
1889 A502 Sheet of 4 14.50 14.50
a.-d. 64p any single 3.50 3.50

No. 1889 exists overprinted "EARLS COURT, LONDON...STAMP SHOW 2000." It was sold at a substantial premium as part of a premium entrance fee. Value, $24.

Millennium Projects A503

Above and Beyond: 19p, Barn owl's head, 3rd Millennium conservation projects, Muncaster. 26p, Night sky, National Space Center, Leicester. 44p, Buildings and waterfall, Torrs Walkway project, Derbyshire. 64p, Sea birds, Scottish Sea Bird Center.

Fire & Light: 19p, Beacon, Beacon Millennium project. 26p, Rheilffordd Eryri / Snowdonia, Welsh Highland Railway rebuilding project. 44p, Lightning bolt, Dynamic Earth project. 64p, Lights, Croydon Skyline project.

Water & Coast: 19p, Stones, Durham Coast restoration project. 26p, Frog, flowers, National Pondlife Center, conservation project. 44p, Parc Arfordirol project. 64p, Portsmouth Harbor project.

Life & Earth: 2nd, Wetlands, ECOS/Ballymena Project. 1st, Ants, Web of Life Exhibition at London Zoo. 44p, Solar cells,

Earth Center, Doncaster. 64p, Plant leaves in water, Project SUZY, Teeside.

Art & Craft: 2nd, Ceramica project, Stoke-on-Trent. 1st, Tate Gallery of Modern Art, London. 45p, Cycle Network Artworks Project. 65p, The Lowry Arts Complex, Balford.

People & Place: 2nd, Millennium Greens project. 1st, Gateshead Millennium Bridge, Newcastle. 45p, Mile End Park, London. 65p, On the Line project.

Stone & Soil: 2nd, Raising of Strangford Stone, Killyleagh, Northern Ireland. 1st, Trans Pennine Trail project. 45p, Kingdom of Fife Cycle Ways project, Scotland. 65p, Changing Places project of Groundwork Foundation.

Tree & Leaf: 2nd, Yews for the Millennium project. 1st, Eden Project, St. Austell. 45p, Millennium Seed Bank project, Ardingly. 65p, Forest for Scotland project.

Mind & Matter: 2nd, Ant's head, Wildscreen at Bristol Project. 1st, People in rowboat, Norfolk and Norwich Project, Newport. 45p, X-ray image of hand and computer mouse, Millennium Point Project, Birmingham. 65p, Plaid globe, Scottish Cultural Resources Access Network.

Body & Bone: 2nd, Dancers, Millennium Dome project, Greenwich. 1st, Soccer players, Hampden Park project, Glasgow. 45p, Bath Spa project. 65p, Center for Life, Newcastle.

Spirit & Faith: 2nd, Stained glass window, St. Edmundsbury Cathedral project. 1st, Church floodlighting project. 45p, St. Patrick Center project, Downpatrick. 65p, York mystery plays.

Sound & Vision: 2nd, Bells, Ringing in the Millennium project. 1st, Eye, Year of the Artist. 45p, Harp, Camofym Millennium Center, Cardiff. 65p, TS2K Talent and Skills project.

Above & Beyond

Photo., Litho. (#1892, 1900, 1911, 1913)

Perf. 13¾x14, 14¼x14½ (#1892)

2000

1890 A503 19p multi (1) .50 .50
1891 A503 26p multi (2) .60 .60
1892 A503 44p multi (3) 1.15 1.15
1893 A503 64p multi (4) 1.60 1.60

Perf. 14¼x14½

Fire & Light

1894 A503 19p multi (5) .50 .50
1895 A503 26p multi (6) .60 .60
1896 A503 44p multi (7) 1.15 1.15
1897 A503 64p multi (8) 1.60 1.60

Water & Coast

1898 A503 19p multi (9) .50 .50
1899 A503 26p multi (10) .60 .60
1900 A503 44p multi (11) 1.15 1.15
1901 A503 64p multi (12) 1.60 1.60

Life & Earth

1902 A503 2nd multi (13) .85 .75
1903 A503 1st multi (14) 1.00 1.05
1904 A503 44p multi (15) 1.10 1.10
1905 A503 64p multi (16) 1.60 1.60

Art & Craft

1906 A503 2nd multi (17) .85 .75
1907 A503 1st multi (18) 1.00 1.05
1908 A503 45p multi (19) 1.10 1.10
1909 A503 65p multi (20) 1.60 1.60

People & Place

1910 A503 2nd multi (21) .85 .75
1911 A503 1st multi (22) 1.00 1.05
1912 A503 45p multi (23) 1.10 1.10
1913 A503 65p multi (24) 1.60 1.60

Stone & Soil

1914 A503 2nd multi (25) .85 .75
1915 A503 1st multi (26) 1.00 1.05
1916 A503 45p multi (27) 1.10 1.10
1917 A503 65p multi (28) 1.60 1.60
a. Booklet pane of 2 (BK169) 3.25

Tree & Leaf

1918 A503 2nd multi (29) .85 .75
a. Bklt. pane of 4 (BK169) 1.75
1919 A503 1st multi (30) 1.00 1.05
a. Bklt. pane, #1915, 1919 (BK1202) 2.00
1920 A503 45p multi (31) 1.10 1.10
a. Bklt. pane of 4 (BK169) 4.50
1921 A503 65p multi (32) 1.60 1.60
a. Bklt. pane of 2 (BK169) 3.25

Mind & Matter

Litho.

1922 A503 2nd multi (33) .85 .80
1923 A503 1st multi (34) 1.10 1.10
1924 A503 45p multi (35) 1.15 1.15
1925 A503 65p multi (36) 1.60 1.60

Body & Bone

1926 A503 2nd multi (37) .80 .80

Photo.

Perf. 13¾

1927 A503 1st multi (38) 1.00 1.00
1928 A503 45p multi (39) 1.10 1.10
1929 A503 65p multi (40) 1.60 1.60

Perf. 14¼

Spirit & Faith

1930 A503 2nd multi (41) .85 .80
a. Bklt. pane of 20 (BK1211) 16.00
1931 A503 1st multi (42) 1.00 1.00
1932 A503 45p multi (43) 1.10 1.10
1933 A503 65p multi (44) 1.60 1.60

Sound & Vision

1934 A503 2nd multi (45) .85 .80
1935 A503 1st multi (46) 1.00 1.00
1936 A503 45p multi (47) 1.10 1.10
1937 A503 65p multi (48) 1.60 1.60
Nos. 1890-1937 (48) 52.60 52.20

Nos. 1902, 1906, 1910, 1914, 1918, 1922, 1926, 1930, 1934 sold for 19p; No. 1903, sold for 26p; Nos. 1907, 1911, 1915, 1919, 1923, 1927, 1931, 1935 sold for 27p on day of issue.

Issued: Nos. 1890-1893, 1/18; Nos. 1894-1897, 2/1; Nos. 1898-1901, 3/7; Nos. 1902-1905, 4/4; Nos. 1906-1909, 5/2; Nos. 1910-1913, 6/6; Nos. 1914-1917, 7/4; Nos. 1918-1921, 8/1; Nos. 1917a-1921a, 9/18; Nos. 1922-1925, 9/5; Nos. 1926-1929, 10/3; Nos. 1930-1933, 11/7; Nos. 1934-1937, 12/5.

No. BK1203 contains No. 1931.

2000-02 Photo. *Perf. 14¼x14½*

1938 A503 (1st) Like #1891 4.00 4.00
a. Booklet pane, #1903, 1938 (BK1201) 8.75
b. Booklet pane of 4 (BK172) 16.00

Issued: No. 1938, 5/26. No. 1938b, 9/24/02.

Nos. 1938 sold for 27p on day of issue, and was issued only in booklets.

Souvenir Sheet

Types of 1953 and 2000

Stamp Show 2000, London — A503a

2000, May 23 Photo. *Perf. 14¾x14*

1942 A136 Sheet, #1942a, 4 #MH335 13.00 13.00
a. £1 dark green 12.00 12.00

Souvenir Sheet

Queen Mother's 100th Birthday — A504

Designs: a, Queen Elizabeth II. b, Prince William. c, Queen Mother. d, Prince Charles.

2000, Aug. 4 Photo. *Perf. 14½*

1943 A504 Sheet of 4 8.00 9.50
a.-d. 27p Any single 1.75 1.65
e. Booklet pane, #1943 with silver border (BK168) 8.25 8.25
f. Booklet pane, 4 #1943c (BK168) 7.00

Millennium 2001 A505

Painted faces of children: 2nd, Flower. 1st, Tiger. 45p, Owl. 65p, Butterfly.

Perf. 14¼x14½

2001, Jan. 16 Photo.

1944 A505 2nd multi .85 .75
1945 A505 1st multi 1.10 1.10
1946 A505 45p multi 1.15 1.15
1947 A505 65p multi 1.60 1.60
Nos. 1944-1947 (4) 4.70 4.60

Stamps inscribed "2nd" and "1st" sold for 19p and 27p respectively on day of issue.

Greetings A506

2001, Feb. 6 Photo. *Perf. 14¼*

1948 A506 1st shown 1.20 1.20
1949 A506 1st Cheers 1.20 1.20
1950 A506 1st Love 1.20 1.20
1951 A506 1st Thanks 1.20 1.20
1952 A506 1st Welcome 1.20 1.20
a. Sheet, 4 vert. strips #1948-1952 + 20 labels, litho. 200.00 25.00
Nos. 1948-1952 (5) 6.00 6.00

Nos. 1948-1952 each sold for 27p on day of issue.

No. 1952a issued 6/5/01. No. 1952a sold for £5.95.

A sheet containing 7 No. 1949 and 3 No. 1951 + 10 labels depicting Spiderman was specially produced for stamp dealers.

Dogs and Cats A507

Designs: No. 1953, Dog and man on park bench. No. 1954, Dog in bathtub. No. 1955, Dog looking over carrel. No. 1956, Cat in handbag. No. 1957, Cat on fence. No. 1958, Dog in automobile. No. 1959, Cat in curtained window. No. 1960, Dog looking over fence. No. 1961, Cat looking at bird through window. No. 1962, Cat in sink.

2001, Feb. 13 *Die Cut Perf. 14½x14*

Self- Adhesive

Booklet Stamps

1953 A507 1st blk & sil 1.45 1.20
1954 A507 1st blk & sil 1.45 1.20
1955 A507 1st blk & sil 1.45 1.20
1956 A507 1st blk & sil 1.45 1.20
1957 A507 1st blk & sil 1.45 1.20
1958 A507 1st blk & sil 1.45 1.20
1959 A507 1st blk & sil 1.45 1.20
1960 A507 1st blk & sil 1.45 1.20
1961 A507 1st blk & sil 1.45 1.20
1962 A507 1st blk & sil 1.45 1.20
a. Booklet, #1953-1962 14.50
b. Booklet, #1953-1962, 2 #MH297 18.50
Nos. 1953-1962 (10) 14.50 12.00

Nos. 1953-1962 each sold for 27p on day of issue.

The Weather A508

Designs: 19p, Rain. 27p, Fair. 45p, Much rain, storms. 65p, Very dry, set fair.

Perf. 14¼x14½

2001, Mar. 13 Photo.

1963 A508 19p multi .50 .50
1964 A508 27p multi .65 .65
1965 A508 45p multi 1.40 1.40
1966 A508 65p multi 2.25 2.25
a. Souvenir sheet, #1963-1966 14.00 14.00
Nos. 1963-1966 (4) 4.80 4.80

Purple cloud at bottom of No. 1964 is printed with thermochromic ink and changes color to blue when warmed.

Submarines — A509

Designs: 2nd, Vanguard Class, 1992. 1st, Swiftsure Class, 1973. 45p, Unity Class, 1939. 65p, Holland Class, 1901.

2001 Photo. *Perf. 14¾x14*

1967 A509 2nd multi 1.15 .50
a. Perf. 15¼x14¾ 3.25 3.25
1968 A509 1st multi 1.35 .65
a. Perf. 15¼x14¾ 2.25 2.25
1969 A509 45p multi .95 *1.40*
a. Perf. 15¼x14¾ 3.25 3.25
b. Booklet pane, 2 each #1967a, 1969a (BK170) 13.00
1970 A509 65p multi 1.35 *2.25*
a. Perf. 15¼x14¾ 3.25 3.25
b. Booklet pane, 2 each #1968a, 1970a (BK170) 11.00
Nos. 1967-1970 (4) 4.80 4.80

Self-Adhesive

Die Cut Perf. 15½x14¼

1971 A509 1st multi 45.00 40.00
a. Booklet, 2 #1971, 4 #MH298 95.00

Issued: Nos. 1967-1970, 4/10; No. 1971, 4/17; Nos. 1967a, 1968a, 1969a, 1970a, 10/22/01.

On day of issue No. 1967 sold for 19p and Nos. 1968 and 1971 sold for 27p.

Buses A510

Designs: No. 1972, Blue and red Leyland X-type (half), London General (No. 11), yellow green and orange Leyland Titan, dark green and yellow AEC Regent I (half). No. 1973, AEC Regent I (half), Daimler COG5 (No. 8), Guy Arab Mk II (No. 51), green and yellow AEC Regent (half). No. 1974, AEC Regent (half), Bristol KSW 5G (No. 68), AEC Routemaster (No. 21), red and yellow Bristol Lodekka (half). No. 1975, Bristol Lodekka (half), Leyland Titan (No. 12B), Leyland Atlantean (No. 53X), red and yellow Daimler Fleetline (half). No. 1976, Daimler Fleetline (half), MCW Metrobus (No. 770), Leyland Olympian (No. 12), red and blue Dennis Trident (half).

2001, May 15 Photo. *Perf. 14¼x14*

1972 A510 1st multi 1.20 1.20
1973 A510 1st multi 1.20 1.20
1974 A510 1st multi 1.20 1.20
1975 A510 1st multi 1.20 1.20
1976 A510 1st multi 1.20 1.20
a. Horiz. strip, #1972-1976 5.75 5.75
b. Souvenir sheet, #1972-1976 9.00 9.00

Nos. 1972-1976 each sold for 27p on day of issue.

Women's Hats — A511

Hats designed by: 1st, Pip Hackett. E, Dai Rees. 45p, Stephen Jones. 65p, Philip Treacy.

Perf. 14½x14¼

2001, June 19 Litho.

1977 A511 1st multi 1.25 1.25
1978 A511 E multi 1.75 1.50
1979 A511 45p multi 1.15 1.25
1980 A511 65p multi 1.60 1.75
Nos. 1977-1980 (4) 5.75 5.75

Nos. 1977 and 1978 sold for 27p and 36p respectively on day of issue.

Europa
A512

2001, July 10 Photo. *Perf. 14¾x14*

1981 A512 1st Frog 1.25 1.25
1982 A512 E Great diving beetle 1.60 1.45
1983 A512 45p Stickleback 1.25 1.25
1984 A512 65p Dragonfly 1.90 1.90
Nos. 1981-1984 (4) 6.00 5.85

Nos. 1981 and 1982 sold for 27p and 36p respectively on day of issue.

Puppets — A513

2001, Sept. 4 Photo. *Perf. 14x15*

1985 A513 1st Policeman 1.20 1.10
1986 A513 1st Clown 1.20 1.10
1987 A513 1st Punch 1.20 1.10
1988 A513 1st Judy 1.20 1.10
1989 A513 1st Beadle 1.20 1.10
1990 A513 1st Crocodile 1.20 1.10
a. Horiz. strip of 6, #1985-1990 7.50 6.75
Nos. 1985-1990 (6) 7.20 6.60

Booklet Stamps
Self-Adhesive
Die Cut Perf. 14x15½

1991 A513 1st Punch 20.00 18.00
1992 A513 1st Judy 20.00 18.00
a. Booklet, Nos. 1991-1992, 4 #MH298 47.50

Nos. 1985-1992 sold for 27p on day of issue.

Nobel Prizes, Cent. — A514

Items symbolic of prize categories: 2nd, Carbon 60 molecule (Chemistry). 1st, Globe (Economics). E, Dove (Peace). 40p, Crosses (Physiology or Medicine). 45p, The Addressing of Cats, by T.S. Eliot (Literature). 65p, Boron atom (Physics)

2001, Oct. 2 Photo. *Perf. 14½x14¼*

1993 A514 2nd multi 1.50 1.10

Photo. & Engr.

1994 A514 1st multi 1.90 1.35

Photo. & Embossed

1995 A514 E multi 2.40 1.75

Photo.

1996 A514 40p multi 1.90 1.45
1997 A514 45p multi 2.25 1.60

Photo. With Hologram Affixed

1998 A514 65p multi 3.00 2.25
Nos. 1993-1998 (6) 12.95 9.50

Nos. 1993-1995 each sold for 19p, 27p and 37p respectively on day of issue. Molecule on No. 1993 is covered with a thermochromic film that changes color when warmed. No. 1996 has a scrach and sniff coating with a eucalyptus odor. Soaking in water may affect holographic images.

Flags — A515

Designs: Nos. 1999a, 2001, White ensign. No. 1999b, Union flag. Nos. 1999c, 2000, Jolly Roger. No. 1999d, Flag of the Chief of the Defense Staff.

2001, Oct. 22 Photo. *Perf. 14¾*
Miniature Sheet

1999 A515 Sheet of 4 8.00 8.00
a.-d. 1st Any single 1.90 1.25
e. Booklet pane, #1999 + selvage at L (BK170) 8.25
f. Sheet of 20 #1999b + 20 labels, litho. 50.00 —
g. Sheet of 20 #1999a + 20 labels, litho. 27.50 —
h. Booklet pane of 3 #1999a, litho. (BK178) 5.75 —
i. Booklet pane of 4, 2 each #1999a, 1999b, litho. (BK184) 7.75 —
j. Booklet pane of 4, 2 each #1999a, 1999b, litho. (BK190) 12.00 —

Booklet Stamps
Self-Adhesive
Die Cut Perf. 14¾

2000 A515 1st multi 20.00 20.00
2001 A515 1st multi 20.00 20.00
a. Booklet, #2000-2001, 4 #MH298 47.50

Nos. 1999a-1999d, 2000-2001 each sold for 27p on day of issue. The left edge of No. 1999 is straight while rouletting separates the selvage from the sheet on No. 1999e.

No. 1999f issued 2004. It sold for £14.95 and has labels that can be personalized.

No. 1999h issued 10/18/2005. No. 1999i issued 1/8/2008. No. 1999j issued 9/17/2009.

Christmas
A516

Robins and: 2nd, Snowman. 1st, Birdhouse. E, Birdbath. 45p, Suet ball. 65b, Nest.

Die Cut Perf. 14¼x14½
2001, Nov. 6 Photo.
Self-Adhesive

2002 A516 2nd multi 1.05 .90
a. Booklet of 24 26.00
b. Sheet of 20 + 20 labels, litho. 24.00 —
2003 A516 1st multi 1.25 1.15
a. Booklet of 12 15.00
b. Sheet of 20 + 20 labels, litho. 26.00
c. Sheet, 10 each #2002-2003 +20 labels, litho. 14.00 —
2004 A516 E multi 2.25 1.45
2005 A516 45p multi .85 1.15
2006 A516 65p multi 1.25 1.75
Nos. 2002-2006 (5) 6.65 6.40

Nos. 2002-2004 each sold for 19p, 27p, and 37p respectively on day of issue.

Issued: No. 2003b, 9/30/03. No. 2003b sold for £6.15 and had labels that could be personalized.

Issued: No. 2202b, 2203c, 2005. No. 2002b sold for £9.95 and had labels that could be personalized. No. 2003c sold for £5.60.

Just So Stories, by Rudyard Kipling, Cent.
A517

Designs: No. 2007, How the Whale Got His Throat (whale in bed). No. 2008, How the Camel Got His Hump (genie, camel). No. 2009, How the Rhinoceros Got His Skin (man in palm tree, rhinoceros). No. 2010, How the Leopard Got His Spots (man putting spots on leopard). No. 2011, The Elephant's Child (crocodile, elephant, snake). No. 2012, The Sing-song of Old Man Kangaroo (dog chasing kangaroo). No. 2013, The Beginning of the Armadilloes (jaguar, armadillo). No. 2014, The Crab That Played With the Sea (people in boat, giant crab). No. 2015, The Cat That Walked by Himself (people, dog, cat and shadow in cave). No. 2016, The Butterfly That Stamped (castle, giant butterfly).

Serpentine Die Cut 14½x14
2002, Jan. 15 Photo.
Booklet Stamps
Self-Adhesive

2007 A517 1st multi 1.30 1.00
2008 A517 1st multi 1.30 1.00
2009 A517 1st multi 1.30 1.00
2010 A517 1st multi 1.30 1.00
2011 A517 1st multi 1.30 1.00
2012 A517 1st multi 1.30 1.00
2013 A517 1st multi 1.30 1.00
2014 A517 1st multi 1.30 1.00
2015 A517 1st multi 1.30 1.00
2016 A517 1st multi 1.30 1.00
a. Booklet, #2007-2016 13.00

Nos. 2007-2016 each sold for 27p on day of issue. Titles of stories are not on stamps, but in margin.

Reign of Queen Elizabeth II, 50th Anniv. — A518

Photographs of Queen by: 2nd, Dorothy Wilding, 1952. 1st, Cecil Beaton, 1968. E, Lord Snowdon, 1978, 45p, Yousuf Karsh, 1984. 65p, Tim Graham, 1996.

Perf. 14½x14¼
2002, Feb. 6 Photo. Wmk. 401

2017 A518 2nd blk & sil 1.20 .90
2018 A518 1st blk & sil 1.35 1.10
2019 A518 E blk & sil 2.50 1.35
2020 A518 45p blk & sil 1.00 *1.20*
a. Booklet pane, #2017-2020 (BK171) 13.50 13.50
2021 A518 65p blk & sil 1.35 *2.25*
a. Booklet pane, #2018-2021 (BK171) 14.00 14.00
Nos. 2017-2021 (5) 7.40 6.80

Nos. 2017-2019 each sold for 19p, 27p, and 37p respectively on day of issue.

Stamps in Nos. 2020a and 2021a have an upright watermark.

Queen Types of 1952
Tan Surface-colored Paper
Perf. 14¾x14 Syncopated
2002, Feb. 6 Photo. Wmk. 401

2022 A127 2nd red 2.00 1.00
2023 A126 1st green 2.50 1.50
a. Booklet pane, 5 #2022, 4 #2023, + label (BK171) 25.00 —

Nos. 2022 and 2023 sold for 19p and 27p respectively on day of issue.

A New Baby
A519

Hello
A520

Moving
A521

Best Wishes
A522

Love
A523

Perf. 14¾x14
2002-3 Litho. Unwmk.

2024 A519 1st multi 1.30 1.20
a. Perf. 14¼ + label 2.50 2.50
2025 A520 1st multi 1.30 1.20
a. Perf. 14¼ + label 2.50 2.50
2026 A521 1st multi 1.30 1.20
a. Perf. 14¼ + label 2.50 2.50
2027 A522 1st multi 1.30 1.20
a. Perf. 14¼ + label 2.50 2.50
2028 A523 1st multi 1.30 1.20
a. Perf. 14¼ + label 2.50 2.50
c. Sheet of 20, 4 each #2024-2028, + 20 labels, perf. 14¼ 50.00 —
Nos. 2024-2028 (5) 6.50 6.00

Self-Adhesive
Booklet Stamp
Die Cut Perf. 14¾x14

2028A A520 1st multi 5.75 5.00
b. Booklet pane, 2 #2028A, 4 #MH300 19.00

Nos. 2024-2028A each sold for 27p on day of issue.

Nos. 2024a-2028a each sold for £14.95 and have labels that can be personalized. No. 2028c sold for £5.95.

Sheets of No. 2025a with a Washington 2006 World Philatelic Exhibition margin and labels sold for £6.95. Value $27.50. Sheets with other margins exist.

Issued, Nos. 2024-2028, 3/5/02; No. 2028c, 4/23/02; Nos. 2024a-2028a, 2002; No. 2028A, 3/4/03.

Aerial Photographs of Coastline
A524

2002, Mar. 19 *Perf. 14¼x14½*

2029 A524 27p Studland Bay .80 .80
2030 A524 27p Luskentyre .80 .80
2031 A524 27p Dover .80 .80
2032 A524 27p Padstow .80 .80
2033 A524 27p Broadstairs .80 .80
2034 A524 27p St. Abb's Head .80 .80
2035 A524 27p Dunster Beach .80 .80
2036 A524 27p Newquay .80 .80
2037 A524 27p Portrush .80 .80
2038 A524 27p Conwy .80 .80
a. Block of 10, #2029-2038 8.00 8.00

Circus — A525

Designs: 2nd, High wire performer. 1st, Lion tamer. E, Trick tricyclists. 45p, Krazy kar. 65p, Equestrienne.

2002, Apr. 9 Photo. *Perf. 14¼x14½*

2039 A525 2nd multi 1.00 1.00
2040 A525 1st multi 1.20 1.20
2041 A525 E multi 1.50 1.50

2042 A525 45p multi 1.30 1.30
2043 A525 65p multi 1.75 1.75
Nos. 2039-2043 (5) 6.75 6.75

Europa (Nos. 2040-2041). Nos. 2039-2041 sold for 19p, 27p and 37p respectively on day of issue.

First day covers of Nos. 2039-2043 bear an April 9, 2001, date, but the issue of the stamps was delayed until April 10 due to the funeral of the Queen Mother.

Queen Mother (1900-2002) A526

2002, Apr. 25 ***Perf. 14x14¾***

2044 A526 1st 1990 photo 1.25 .90
2045 A526 E 1948 photo 2.25 1.40
2046 A526 45p 1930 photo .90 *1.40*
2047 A526 65p 1907 photo 1.30 *1.40*
Nos. 2044-2047 (4) 5.70 5.10

Nos. 2044-2045 sold for 27p and 37p respectively on day of issue. Compare with Type A387.

Jet Aircraft — A527

Designs: 2nd, Airbus A340-600, 2002. 1st, Concorde, 1976. E, Trident, 1964. 45p, VC10, 1964. 65p, Comet, 1952.

2002, May 2 ***Perf. 14½***

2048 A527 2nd multi 1.10 1.10
2049 A527 1st multi 1.35 1.35
a. Litho. (#2619a) ('09) 9.50 9.50
2050 A527 E multi 1.60 1.60
2051 A527 45p multi 1.50 1.50
2052 A527 65p multi 2.50 2.50
a. Souvenir sheet, #2048-2052 10.00 9.50
Nos. 2048-2052 (5) 8.05 8.05

Booklet Stamp
Self-Adhesive
Die Cut Perf. 14½

2053 A527 1st multi 5.75 6.00
a. Booklet, 2 #2053, 4 #MH297 19.00

Nos. 2048-2052 sold for 19p, 27p and 37p respectively on day of issue.

No. 2049a issued 1/13/09. No. 2049a sold for 36p on day of issue.

A528

2002 World Cup Soccer Championships, Japan and Korea — A529

Soccer ball and: Nos. 2056a, 2057, Upper left portion of English flag. Nos. 2056b, 2058, Upper right portion of English flag. No. 2056c, Lower left portion of English flag. Nos. 2055, 2056d, Lower right portion of English flag.

Photo., Litho. (#2055)

2002, May 21 ***Perf. 14¼***

2054 A528 1st multi 1.75 1.75
2055 A529 1st dull blue & multi 1.75 1.75

Souvenir Sheet

2056 Sheet, #2054, #2056a-2056d 7.25 6.50
a.-d. A529 1st deep blue & multi, perf. 14¾x14, any single 1.50 1.50

Booklet Stamps
Die Cut Perf. 14¾x14
Self-Adhesive

2057 A529 1st dp blue & multi 4.25 4.25
2058 A529 1st dp blue & multi 4.25 .425
a. Booklet, #2057, 2058, 4 #MH298 16.00

Nos. 2054, 2056a-2056d, 2057-2058 sold for 27p on day of sale. No. 2055 was issued only in sheets of 20 stamps + 16 labels that sold for £5.95, and which could have the labels personalized for an additional fee.

17th Commonwealth Games, Manchester — A530

Designs: 2nd, Swimming. 1st, Running. E, Cycling. 47p, Long jump. 68p, Wheelchair racing.

Perf. 14¾x14¼

2002, July 16 **Photo.**

2059 A530 2nd multi 1.10 .80
2060 A530 1st multi 1.25 1.00
2061 A530 E multi 2.25 1.20
2062 A530 47p multi 1.00 *1.35*
2063 A530 68p multi 1.40 *2.10*
Nos. 2059-2063 (5) 7.00 6.45

Nos. 2059-2061 each sold for 19p, 27p and 37p respectively on day of issue.

Peter Pan, by J. M. Barrie, 150th Anniv. A531

Designs: 2nd, Tinkerbell. 1st, Darling children. E, Crocodile and clock. 47p, Captain Hook. 68p, Peter Pan.

Perf. 14¾x14¼

2002, Aug. 20 **Photo.**

2064 A531 2nd multi 1.15 .90
2065 A531 1st multi 1.45 1.15
2066 A531 E multi 1.75 1.40
2067 A531 47p multi 1.45 1.40
2068 A531 68p multi 2.10 1.75
Nos. 2064-2068 (5) 7.90 6.60

Nos. 2064-2066 each sold for 19p, 27p and 37p respectively on day of issue.

Thames River Bridges in London A532

2002, Sept. 10 **Litho.** ***Perf. 14¾x14***

2069 A532 2nd Millennium 1.00 .75
2070 A532 1st Tower 1.25 1.25
2071 A532 E Westminster 2.00 2.00
2072 A532 47p Blackfriars 2.25 2.25
2073 A532 68p London 2.75 2.75
Nos. 2069-2073 (5) 9.25 9.00

Booklet Stamp
Serpentine Die Cut 14¾x14

2074 A532 1st Tower 4.75 4.75
a. Booklet, 2 #2074, 4 #MH300 17.00

Nos. 2070 and 2074 sold for 27p; Nos. 2069, 2071 sold for 19p and 37p respectively on day of sale.

Souvenir Sheet

Astronomy — A533

No. 2075: a, Planetary nebula in Aquila. b, Seyfert 2 galaxy in Pegasus. c, Planetary nebula in Norma. d, Seyfert 2 galaxy in Circinus.

Perf. 14¾x14¼

2002, Sept. 24 **Photo.**

2075 A533 Sheet of 4 5.00 *6.00*
a.-d. (1st) Any single 1.20 1.20
e. Booklet pane, #2075, rouletted at left (BK172) 5.25

Nos. 2075a-2075d each sold for 27p on day of issue.

Pillar Boxes, 150th Anniv. — A534

Designs: 2nd, Decorative box, 1857. 1st, Mainland box, 1874. E, Airmail box, 1934. 47p, Oval dual-aperture box, 1939. 68p, Modern box, 1980.

Litho. & Engr.

2002, Oct. 8 ***Perf. 14x14¼***

2076 A534 2nd multi 1.10 .90
2077 A534 1st multi 1.25 1.15
2078 A534 E multi 2.40 1.40
2079 A534 47p multi 1.00 *1.40*
2080 A534 68p multi 1.40 *1.75*
Nos. 2076-2080 (5) 7.15 6.60

Nos. 2076-2078 each sold for 19p, 27p and 37p on day of issue.

Christmas A535

Die Cut Perf. 14½x14

2002, Nov. 5 **Photo.**

Self-Adhesive

2081 A535 2nd Spruce branches 1.25 1.00
a. Booklet pane of 24 30.00
2082 A535 1st Holly 1.45 1.20
a. Booklet pane of 12 17.50
2083 A535 E Ivy 2.60 1.45
2084 A535 47p Mistletoe 1.05 *1.45*
2085 A535 68p Pine cone 1.50 *1.75*
Nos. 2081-2085 (5) 7.85 6.85

Nos. 2081-2085 each sold for 19p, 27p and 37p on day of issue.

Types of 1952-54
Souvenir Sheet
Tan Surface-colored Paper

Perf. 14¾x14 Syncopated

2002, Dec. 5 **Photo.** **Wmk. 401**

2086 Sheet of 9, #2022-2023, 2086a-2086g + label 10.00 8.50
a. A126 1p red orange .30 .25
b. A126 2p ultramarine .30 .25
c. A126 5p brown .30 .25
d. A129 33p light brown 1.60 .90
e. A130 37p bright rose 2.00 1.00
f. A131 47p brown 2.40 1.10
g. A132 50p dark green 2.75 1.25

Barn Owl in Flight — A536

Barn Owl in Flight — A537

Barn Owl in Flight — A538

Barn Owl in Flight — A539

Barn Owl in Flight — A540

Kestrel in Flight — A541

Kestrel in Flight — A542

Kestrel in Flight — A543

Kestrel in Flight — A544

Kestrel in Flight — A545

2003, Jan. 14 Litho. *Perf. 14¼x14½*

2087 A536 1st multi 1.35 1.20
2088 A537 1st multi 1.35 1.20
2089 A538 1st multi 1.35 1.20
2090 A539 1st multi 1.35 1.20
2091 A540 1st multi 1.35 1.20
2092 A541 1st multi 1.35 1.20
2093 A542 1st multi 1.35 1.20
2094 A543 1st multi 1.35 1.20
2095 A544 1st multi 1.35 1.20
2096 A545 1st multi 1.35 1.20
a. Block of 10, #2087-2096 13.50 13.50

Nos. 2087-2096 each sold for 27p on day of issue.

Check-off Slogans A546

Designs: No. 2097, Gold star, See me, Playtime. No. 2098, I love you, XXXX, S.W.A.L.K. No. 2099, Angel, Poppet, Little terror. No. 2100, Yes, No, Maybe. No. 2101, Oops!, Sorry, Will try harder. No. 2102, I did it!, You did it!, We did it!

2003, Feb. 4 Litho. *Perf. 14¼x14*

2097 A546 1st multi 1.35 1.15
2098 A546 1st multi 1.35 1.15
2099 A546 1st multi 1.35 1.15
2100 A546 1st multi 1.35 1.15
2101 A546 1st multi 1.35 1.15
2102 A546 1st multi 1.35 1.15
a. Block of 6, #2097-2102 8.00 7.00
b. Sheet, 3 each #2097, 2099, 2101-2102, 4 each #2098, 2100 + 20 labels 30.00

No. 2102b sold for £5.95 and had labels that could be personalized.

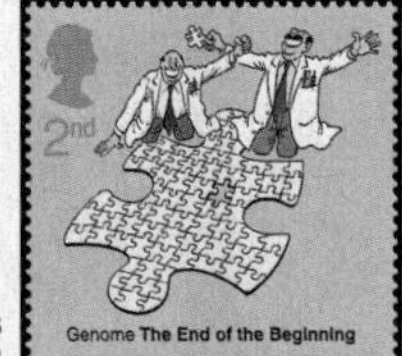

Genetics A548

Designs: 2nd, Scientists with jigsaw puzzle. 1st, Chimpanzee and scientist. E, Scientist, DNA double helix, snake. 47p, Scientists with animals. 68p, Scientist with doctor's satchel, crystal ball.

Perf. 14¼x14½

2003, Feb. 25 Litho.

2103 A548 2nd multi 1.10 .90
2104 A548 1st multi 1.25 1.15
a. Booklet pane, 2 each #2103-2104 (BK173) 4.75
2105 A548 E multi 2.25 1.40
a. Booklet pane of 4 (BK173) 9.00
2106 A548 47p multi 1.00 1.40
2107 A548 68p multi 1.35 *1.75*
Nos. 2103-2107 (5) 6.95 6.60

Nos. 2103-2105 sold for 19p, 27p and 37p respectively on day of issue.

Fruit and Vegetables A549

Die Cut Perf. 14¼x14

2003, Mar. 25 Photo.

Self-Adhesive

Booklet Stamps

2108 A549 1st Strawberry 1.25 1.00
2109 A549 1st Potato 1.25 1.00
2110 A549 1st Apple 1.25 1.00
2111 A549 1st Pepper 1.25 1.00
2112 A549 1st Pear 1.25 1.00
2113 A549 1st Orange 1.25 1.00
2114 A549 1st Tomato 1.25 1.00
2115 A549 1st Lemon 1.25 1.00
2116 A549 1st Brussels sprout 1.25 1.00
2117 A549 1st Eggplant 1.25 1.00
a. Pane, #2108-2117 + 76 stickers 12.50
b. Sheet, 2 each #2108-2117, litho., + 20 labels +93 stickers ('06) 26.00

Nos. 2108-2117 each sold for 27p on day of issue.

No. 2117b issued 3/7/06. No. 2117b sold for £6.55.

Adventurers — A550

Designs: 2nd, Amy Johnson (1903-41), first woman to fly to Australia. 1st, British Mount Everest expedition of 1953. E, Freya Stark (1893-1993), Middle East traveler and writer. 42p, Ernest Shackleton (1874-1922), Antarctic explorer. 47p, Francis Chichester (1901-72), sailor. 68p, Robert Falcon Scott (1868-1912), Antarctic explorer.

Perf. 14¾x14¼

2003, Apr. 29 Photo. Unwmk.

2118 A550 2nd multi 1.30 1.10
2119 A550 1st multi 1.50 1.35
2120 A550 E multi 2.75 1.60
2121 A550 42p multi 1.00 *1.50*
2122 A550 47p multi 1.10 1.60
2123 A550 68p multi 1.60 2.00
Nos. 2118-2123 (6) 9.25 9.15

Booklet Stamp

Self-Adhesive

Die Cut Perf. 14¾x14¼

2124 A550 1st multi 4.25 4.25
a. Booklet pane, 2 #2124, 4 #MH300 16.00

Nos. 2118-2120 each sold for 19p, 27p and 38p respectively on day of issue.

Types of 1952-54

A550a

Perf. 14¾x14 Syncopated

2003, May 20 Photo. Wmk. 401

Tan Surface-colored Paper

Souvenir Sheet

2125 A550a Sheet of 9 + label 9.50 11.00
a. A127 4p purple .25 .25
b. A128 8p ultramarine .30 .25
c. A128 10p lilac rose .35 .25
d. A129 20p emerald .65 .40
e. A130 28p deep olive green .90 .50
f. A130 34p violet brown 1.10 .65
g. A128 E henna brown 1.50 .80
h. A130 42p royal blue 1.45 .75
i. A131 68p dark blue 2.50 1.25

Booklet Stamp

Perf. 14¾x14

2126 A136 £1 dark green 42.50 42.50
a. Booklet pane, #2126, 2 each #2086f, 2125i (BK174) 52.50 52.50

No. 2125g sold for 38p on day of issue.

Coronation of Queen Elizabeth II, 50th Anniv. — A551

Designs: No. 2127, Aerial view of parade entering circle. No. 2128, Children reading coronation party sign. No. 2129, Queen at coronation. No. 2130, Children at wall of pictures. No. 2131, Queen holding orb and scepter. No. 2132, Children running in street. No. 2133, Royal carriage under arch. No. 2134, Children standing in front of house. No. 2135, Royal carriage. No. 2136, Children at party.

Perf. 14½x14¼

2003, June 2 Photo. Wmk. 401

2127 A551 1st multi 1.45 1.20
2128 A551 1st multi 1.45 1.20
2129 A551 1st multi 1.45 1.20
2130 A551 1st multi 1.45 1.20
2131 A551 1st multi 1.45 1.20
2132 A551 1st multi 1.45 1.20
2133 A551 1st multi 1.45 1.20
2134 A551 1st multi 1.45 1.20
a. Booklet pane, #2127, 2129, 2132, 2134 (BK174) 8.00
2135 A551 1st multi 1.45 1.20
2136 A551 1st multi 1.45 1.20
a. Block of 10, #2127-2136 14.50 12.00
b. Booklet pane, #2128, 2131, 2133, 2136 (BK174) 8.00

Nos. 2127-2136 each sold for 28p on day of issue.

Prince William, 21st Birthday A552

Various portraits.

2003, June 17 Photo. *Perf. 14¼*

Background Color

2137 A552 28p silver 1.45 .95
2138 A552 E brown 2.75 2.25
2139 A552 47p green 2.60 2.10
2140 A552 68p olive green 3.25 2.60
Nos. 2137-2140 (4) 10.05 7.90

No. 2138 sold for 38p on day of issue. Background colors are printed with Iriodin ink, giving the stamp a three dimensional appearance.

Scottish Scenery A553

Designs: 2nd: Loch Assynt, Sutherland. 1st, Ben More, Isle of Mull. E, Rothiemurchus, Cairngorms. 42p, Dalveen Pass, Lowther Hills. 47p, Glenfinnan Viaduct, Lochaber. 68p, Papa Little, Shetland Islands.

2003, July 15 Photo. *Perf. 14½*

2141 A553 2nd multi 1.10 .90
2142 A553 1st multi 1.30 1.15
2143 A553 E multi 2.25 1.40
2144 A553 42p multi .85 *1.25*
2145 A553 47p multi .95 *1.40*
2146 A553 68p multi 1.40 *1.75*
Nos. 2141-2146 (6) 7.85 7.85

Booklet Stamp

Self-Adhesive

Die Cut Perf. 14½

2147 A553 1st multi 5.00 *5.25*
a. Booklet pane, 2 #2147, 4 #MH300 17.50

Nos. 2141 and 2143 each sold for 20p and 38p respectively on day of issue, while Nos. 2142 and 2147 sold for 28p on day of issue.

Pub Signs — A554

Designs: 1st, The Station, Thurnscoe. E, Black Swan, Lincoln. 42p, The Cross Keys, London. 47p, The Mayflower, Southsea. 68p, The Barley Sheaf, Bodmin.

2003, Aug. 12 Photo. *Perf. 14x14¼*

2148 A554 1st multi 1.50 1.15
a. Booklet pane of 4 (BK175) 6.00 —
2149 A554 E multi 2.75 1.45
2150 A554 42p multi 1.00 *1.60*
2151 A554 47p multi 1.10 *1.70*
2152 A554 68p multi 1.60 *2.10*
Nos. 2148-2152 (5) 7.95 *8.00*

Europa (Nos. 2148-2149).

Nos. 2148 and 2149 each sold for 28p and 38p, respectively, on day of issue.

Toys A555

Designs: 1st, Meccano Constructor Biplane, c. 1931. E, Wells-Brimtoy Clockwork Double-decker Omnibus, c. 1938. 42p, Hornby M1 Clockwork Locomotive and Tender, c. 1948. 47p, Dinky Toys Ford Zephyr, c. 1956. 68p, Mettoy Friction drive Space Ship Eagle c. 1960.

2003, Sept. 18 Photo. *Perf. 14¼x14*

2153 A555 1st multi 1.10 1.05
2154 A555 E multi 2.00 1.30
2155 A555 42p multi .75 *1.50*
2156 A555 47p multi 1.00 *1.60*
2157 A555 68p multi 1.25 *1.90*
a. Souvenir sheet, #2153-2157 7.50 7.50
Nos. 2153-2157 (5) 6.10 7.35

Booklet Stamp

Self-Adhesive

Die Cut Perf. 14¼x14

2158 A555 1st multi 4.50 4.50
a. Booklet, 2 #2158, 4 #MH300 16.50

Nos. 2153 and 2158 each sold for 28p on day of issue. No. 2154 sold for 38p on day of issue.

British Museum, 250th Anniv. — A556

Museum Exhibits: 2nd, Coffin of Denytenamun, c. 900 B.C. 1st, Bust of Alexander the Great, c. 200 B.C. E, Sutton Hoo Helmet, c. 600. 42p, Sculpture of Indian Goddess Parvati, c. 1500. 47p, Mask of Xiuhtecuhtli, c. 1500. 68p, Hoa Hakananai'a Easter Island moai, c. 1000.

2003, Oct. 7 *Perf. 14x14¼*

2159 A556 2nd multi .85 .85
2160 A556 1st multi 1.30 1.30
2161 A556 E multi 1.75 1.50
2162 A556 42p multi 1.40 1.40
2163 A556 47p multi 1.50 1.50
2164 A556 68p multi 2.00 2.00
Nos. 2159-2164 (6) 8.80 8.55

Nos. 2159-2161 each sold for 20p, 28p and 38p respectively on day of issue.

Christmas
A557

Ice and snow sculptures by Andy Goldsworthy: 2nd, Ice Spiral. 1st, Icicle Star. E, Wall of Frozen Snow. 53p, Ice Ball. 68p, Ice Hole. £1.12, Snow Pyramids.

Die Cut Perf. 14¼x14

2003, Nov. 4 **Photo.**

Self-Adhesive

2165 A557 2nd multi .85 .85
a. Booklet pane of 24 25.00
b. Sheet of 20 + 20 labels, litho. 17.50
2166 A557 1st multi 1.30 1.30
a. Booklet pane of 12 16.00
b. Sheet of 20 + 20 labels, litho. 26.00
2167 A557 E multi 1.75 1.50
2168 A557 53p multi 1.50 1.50
2169 A557 68p multi 1.90 1.60
2170 A557 £1.12 multi 3.00 2.75
Nos. 2165-2170 (6) 10.30 9.50

Nos. 2165-2167 sold for 20p, 28p and 38p respectively on day of issue.
Nos. 2165b and 2166b sold for £4.20 and £6.15 respectively and had labels that could be personalized.

Souvenir Sheet

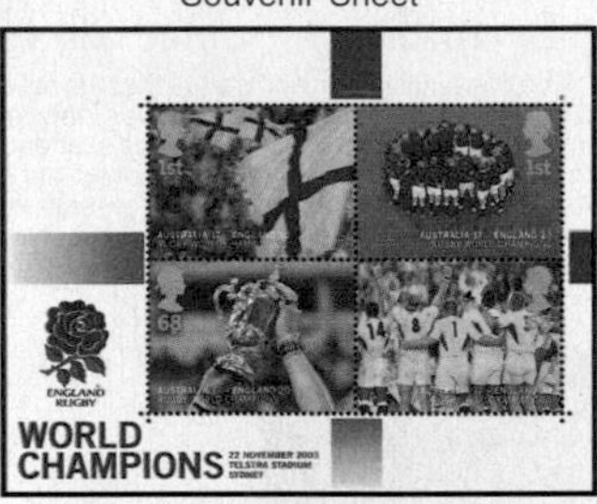

England, Winners of 2003 Rugby World Cup Championships — A558

No. 2171: a, English flags. b, Players with red shirts in huddle. c, World Cup. d, Players in white jerseys, celebrating.

2003, Dec. 19 **Litho.** ***Perf. 13¾x14***
2171 A558 Sheet of 4 12.00 12.00
a.-b. 1st Either single 2.00 2.00
c.-d. 68p Either single 4.00 4.00

Nos. 2171a-2171b sold for 28p on day of issue.

Locomotives — A559

Designs: 20p, Dolgoch 0-4-0T. 28p, CR 439 0-4-4T. E, GCR 8K 2-8-0. 42p, GWR Manor 4-6-0. 47p, SR West Country 4-6-2. 68p, BR Standard 4 2-6-4T.

2004, Jan. 13 **Litho.** ***Perf. 14¾x14¼***
2172 A559 20p multi .70 .60
2173 A559 28p multi .90 .90
2174 A559 E multi 1.75 1.75
2175 A559 42p multi 1.50 1.50
a. Booklet pane, #2173-2175 (BK175) 3.75 —
2176 A559 47p multi 1.75 1.75
2177 A559 68p multi 2.25 2.25
a. Souvenir sheet, #2172-2177 18.50 18.50
Nos. 2172-2177 (6) [illegible] [illegible]

First steam locomotive, bicent. No. 2174 sold for 38p on day of issue.

Special Occasions
A560

2004, Feb. 3 **Litho.** ***Perf. 14¼x14***
2178 A560 1st Postman 1.20 1.05
2179 A560 1st Face 1.20 1.05
2180 A560 1st Duck 1.20 1.05
2181 A560 1st Baby 1.20 1.05
2182 A560 1st Airplane 1.20 1.05
a. Horiz. strip of 5, #2178-2182 6.00 5.25
c. Sheet, 4 each #2178-2182, + 20 labels 24.00 —

Nos. 2178-2182 each sold for 28p on day of issue. No. 2182c sold for £6.15 and had labels that could not be personalized.

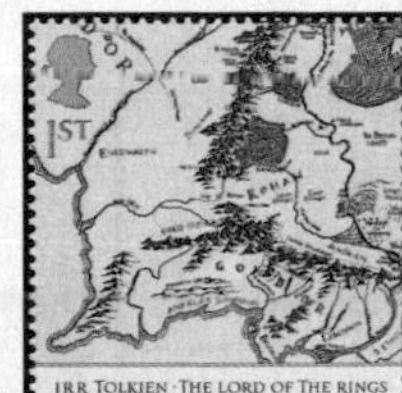

Map — A561

Forest of Lothlórien
A562

The Fellowship of the Ring — A563

Rivendell
A564

Hall at Bag-End
A565

Orthanc
A566

Doors of Durin — A567

Barad-Dur
A568

Minas Tirith — A569

Fangorn Forest
A570

2004, Feb. 26 ***Perf. 14½x14¼***
2183 A561 1st multi 1.20 1.10
2184 A562 1st multi 1.20 1.10
2185 A563 1st multi 1.20 1.10
2186 A564 1st multi 1.20 1.10
2187 A565 1st multi 1.20 1.10
2188 A566 1st multi 1.20 1.10
2189 A567 1st multi 1.20 1.10
2190 A568 1st multi 1.20 1.10
2191 A569 1st multi 1.20 1.10
2192 A570 1st multi 1.20 1.10
a. Block of 10, #2183-2192 12.00 11.00

Publication of *The Lord of the Rings*, by J.R.R. Tolkein, 50th anniv. Nos. 2183-2192 each sold for 28p on day of issue.

Northern Ireland Scenery
A571

Designs: 2nd, Ely, Island, Lower Lough Erne. 1st, Giant's Causeway, Antrim Coast. E, Slemish, Antrim Mountains. 42p, Banns Road, Mourne Mountain. 47p, Glenelly Valley, Sperrins. 68p, Islandmore, Strangford Lough.

2004, Mar. 16 **Photo.** ***Perf. 14½***
2193 A571 2nd multi 1.00 .70
2194 A571 1st multi 1.20 .90
2195 A571 E multi 2.10 1.25
2196 A571 42p multi .80 1.10
2197 A571 47p multi .90 1.25
2198 A571 68p multi 1.25 1.50
Nos. 2193-2198 (6) 7.25 6.70

Booklet Stamp

Self-Adhesive

Die Cut Perf. 14½

2199 A571 1st multi 5.25 5.25
a. Booklet, 2 #2199, 4 #MH300 18.00

Nos. 2193-2195 each sold for 20p, 28p and 38p respectively on day of issue.

Entente Cordiale, Cent. — A572

Designs: 28p, Lace 1 (trial proof) 1968, by Sir Terry Frost. 57p, Coccinelle, by Sonia Delaunay.

2004, Apr. 6 **Photo.** ***Perf. 14x14¼***
2200 A572 28p multi .80 .80
2201 A572 57p multi 1.60 1.60

See France Nos. 3009-3010.

Ocean Liners
A573

Designs: 1st, RMS Queen Mary 2, 2004. E, SS Canberra, 1961. 42p, RMS Queen Mary, 1936. 47p, RMS Mauretania, 1907. 57p, SS City of New York, 1888. 68p, PS Great Western, 1838.

2004, Apr. 13 ***Perf. 14¼x14***
2202 A573 1st multi 1.00 .85
2203 A573 E multi 1.90 1.05
2204 A573 42p multi 1.15 1.15
2205 A573 47p multi 1.15 1.15
2206 A573 57p multi 1.30 1.30
2207 A573 68p multi 1.60 1.60
a. Souvenir sheet, #2202-2207 11.00 9.50
b. Litho. (from #2356a) 5.50 5.50
Nos. 2202-2207 (6) 8.10 7.10

Booklet Stamp

Self-Adhesive

Serpentine Die Cut 14¼x14

2208 A573 1st multi 5.00 5.00
a. Booklet pane, 2 #2208, 4 #MH300 17.50

Nos. 2202 and 2203 sold for 28p and 40p respectively on day of issue.
No. 2207b is contained in the booklet pane No. 2356a, issued 2/23/06.

Royal Horticultural Society, Bicent.
A574

Designs: 2nd, Dianthus Allwoodii Group. 1st, Dahlia "Garden Princess." E, Clematis "Arabella." 42p, Miltonia "French Lake." 47p, Lilium "Lemon Pixie." 68p, Delphinium "Clifford Sky."

2004, May 25 **Photo.** ***Perf. 14½***
2209 A574 2nd multi .95 .90
2210 A574 1st multi 1.20 1.10
a. Perf. 14¼ + label, litho. 3.50 3.25
2211 A574 E multi 1.75 1.40
2212 A574 42p multi 1.25 1.20
2213 A574 47p multi 1.40 1.30
a. Booklet pane, 2 each #2210, 2213 (BK176) 5.50 —
2214 A574 68p multi 1.75 1.60
a. Souvenir sheet, #2209-2214 9.75 9.75
b. Booklet pane, #2209, 2211, 2212, 2214 (BK176) 6.00 —
Nos. 2209-2214 (6) 8.30 7.50

Nos. 2209-2211 each sold for 21p, 28p and 40p respectively on day of issue.
No. 2210a was printed in sheets of 20 stamps + 20 labels that sold for £6.15.

Wales Scenery
A575

Designs: 2nd, Barmouth Bridge. 1st, Hyddgen, Plynlimon. 40p, Brecon Beacons National Park. 43p, Pen-pych, Rhondda Valley. 47p, Rhewl, Dee Valley. 68p, Marloes Sands.

2004, June 15 **Photo.** ***Perf. 14½***
2215 A575 2nd multi .90 .80
2216 A575 1st multi 1.10 1.00
2217 A575 40p multi 1.00 .95
2218 A575 43p multi 1.20 1.10
2219 A575 47p multi 1.30 1.20
2220 A575 68p multi 1.60 1.50
Nos. 2215-2220 (6) 7.10 6.55

Booklet Stamp
Self-Adhesive
Die Cut Perf. 14½

2221 A575 1st multi 5.75 5.75
a. Booklet pane, 2 #2221, 4 #MH300 19.00

Europa (Nos. 2216, 2217, 2221). Nos. 2215-2216 each sold for 21p and 28p respectively on day of issue.

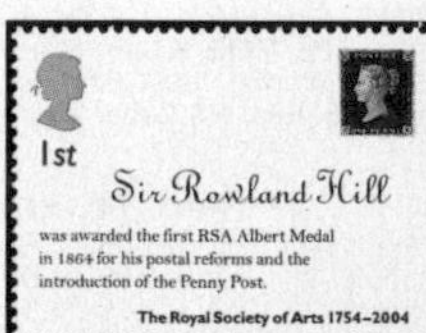

Royal Society of Arts, 250th Anniv. A576

Designs: 1st, Great Britain #1. 40p, William Shipley, Society founder. 43p, Stylized typewriter keys, shorthand. 47p, Apparatus for sweeping chimneys invented by George Smart. 57p, Typeface designed by Eric Gill. 68p, Zero waste.

Perf. 13¾x14¼

2004, Aug. 10 Litho.

2222 A576 1st multi 1.20 1.20
2223 A576 40p multi 1.60 1.60
2224 A576 43p multi 1.50 1.50
2225 A576 47p multi 1.60 1.60
2226 A576 57p multi 1.75 1.75
2227 A576 68p multi 2.00 2.00
Nos. 2222-2227 (6) 9.65 9.65

No. 2222 sold for 28p on day of issue.

Mammals A577

Perf. 14½x14¼

2004, Sept. 16 Photo.

2228 A577 1st Pine marten 1.35 1.30
2229 A577 1st Roe deer 1.35 1.30
2230 A577 1st Badger 1.35 1.30
2231 A577 1st Yellow-necked mouse 1.35 1.30
2232 A577 1st Wild cat 1.35 1.30
2233 A577 1st Red squirrel 1.35 1.30
2234 A577 1st Stoat 1.35 1.30
2235 A577 1st Natterer's bat 1.35 1.30
2236 A577 1st Mole 1.35 1.30
2237 A577 1st Fox 1.35 1.30
a. Block of 10, #2228-2237 13.50 13.50

Nos. 2228-2237 each sold for 28p on day of issue.

Crimean War, 150th Anniv. — A578

Photographs of Crimean War heroes: 2nd, Private Michael MacNamara. 1st, Piper David Muir. 40p, Sergeant Major Edward Edwards. 57p, Sergeant William Powell. 68p, Sergeant Major John Poole. £1.12, Sergeant Robert Glasgow.

2004, Oct. 12 Litho. ***Perf. 14x13¾***

2238 A578 2nd multi 1.00 .80
2239 A578 1st multi 1.25 1.00
2240 A578 40p multi 1.20 .95
2241 A578 57p multi 1.60 1.30
2242 A578 68p multi 1.80 1.50
2243 A578 £1.12 multi 3.00 2.50
Nos. 2238-2243 (6) 9.85 8.05

Nos. 2238-2239 each sold for 21p and 28p respectively on day of issue.

Christmas A579

Santa Claus: Nos. 2244a, 2245, Walking toward chimney in snow. Nos. 2244b, 2246, Looking at rising sun. Nos. 2244c, 2247, In wind. Nos. 2244d, 2248, With umbrella in rain storm. Nos. 2244e, 2249, With flashlight in fog. Nos. 2244f, 2250, Taking protection from hail storm.

2004, Nov. 2 Photo. ***Perf. 14½x14***

2244 Sheet of 6 10.00 10.00
a. A579 (2nd) multi 1.30 1.30
b. A579 (1st) multi 1.60 1.60
c. A579 40p multi 1.15 1.15
d. A579 57p multi 1.45 1.45
e. A579 68p multi 1.60 1.60
f. A579 £1.12 multi 3.00 3.00

Self-Adhesive
Die Cut Perf. 14½x14

2245 A579 (2nd) multi 1.00 1.00
a. Booklet pane of 24 25.00
b. Sheet of 20 + 20 personalized labels, litho. 30.00
2246 A579 (1st) multi 1.25 1.25
a. Booklet pane of 12 15.00 .25
b. Sheet, 10 each #2245-2246, + 20 labels, litho. 23.00
c. Sheet of 20 + 20 personalized labels, litho. 40.00
2247 A579 40p multi 1.20 1.05
2248 A579 57p multi 1.60 1.60
2249 A579 68p multi 2.25 1.60
2250 A579 £1.12 multi 2.75 2.40
Nos. 2245-2250 (6) 10.05 8.90

Nos. 2244a and 2245 each sold for 21p and Nos. 2244b and 2246 each sold for 28p on day of issue.

No. 2245b sold for £9.95; No. 2246b sold for £5.40; No. 2246c sold for £14.95.

Farm Animals A580

Designs: No. 2251, British Saddleback pigs. No. 2252, Two Khaki Campbell ducks. No. 2253, Clydesdale horses. No. 2254, Shorthorn cattle. No. 2255, Border collie. No. 2256, Chicks. No. 2257, Suffolk sheep. No. 2258, Bagot goat. No. 2259, Norfolk Black turkeys. No. 2260, Three Embden geese.

2005, Jan. 11 Photo. ***Perf. 14½***

2251 A580 1st multi 1.45 1.30
2252 A580 1st multi 1.45 1.30
2253 A580 1st multi 1.45 1.30
2254 A580 1st multi 1.45 1.30
2255 A580 1st multi 1.45 1.30
2256 A580 1st multi 1.45 1.30
2257 A580 1st multi 1.45 1.30
2258 A580 1st multi 1.45 1.30
2259 A580 1st multi 1.45 1.30
2260 A580 1st multi 1.45 1.30
a. Block of 10, #2251-2260 14.50 13.50
b. Sheet, 2 each #2251-2260 + 20 labels, litho. 30.00 —

Nos. 2251-2260 each sold for 28p on day of issue. No. 2260b sold for £6.15.

Southwestern England Scenery A581

Designs: 2nd, Old Harry Rocks, Studland Bay. 1st, Wheal Coates mine, St. Agnes. 40p, Start Point and Start Bay. 43p, Norton Down, Wiltshire. 57p, Chiselcombe, Exmoor. 68p, St. James Stone, Lundy.

2005, Feb. 8 Photo. ***Perf. 14½***

2261 A581 2nd multi 1.00 1.00
2262 A581 1st multi 1.25 1.25
2263 A581 40p multi 1.20 1.20
2264 A581 43p multi 1.35 1.35
2265 A581 57p multi 1.60 1.60
2266 A581 68p multi 1.90 1.90
Nos. 2261-2266 (6) 8.30 8.30

Nos. 2261 and 2262 sold for 21p and 28p respectively on day of issue.

Jane Eyre, by Charlotte Bronte (1816-55) — A582

Various characters.

2005, Feb. 24 Litho. ***Perf. 14¼***

2267 A582 2nd multi 1.00 1.00
2268 A582 1st multi 1.25 1.25
a. Booklet pane, 2 each #2267-2268 (BK177) 6.00 —
2269 A582 40p multi 1.20 1.20
2270 A582 57p multi 1.60 1.60
2271 A582 68p multi 1.80 1.80
2272 A582 £1.12 multi 3.00 3.00
a. Souvenir sheet, #2267-2272 9.50 9.50
b. Booklet pane, #2269-2272 (BK177) 10.00 —
Nos. 2267-2272 (6) 9.85 9.85

Nos. 2267 and 2268 sold for 21p and 28p respectively on day of issue.

Magic Tricks A583

Designs: 1st, Magician, "heads or tails" coin. 40p, Rabbit and hat. 47p, Popper. 68p, Ace of Hearts. £1.12, Pyramids and fezzes.

2005, Mar. 15 Photo. ***Perf. 14¼x14***

2273 A583 1st multi, unscratched coin 1.10 1.05
a. Scratched coin, heads 1.10 1.05
b. Scratched coin, tails 1.10 1.05
c. Vert. pair, unscratched 2.25 2.10
d. Sheet of 20 + 20 labels, unscratched, litho. 40.00 —
2274 A583 40p multi 1.30 1.20
2275 A583 47p multi 1.60 1.50
2276 A583 68p multi 2.00 1.90
2277 A583 £1.12 multi 3.00 2.75
Nos. 2273-2277 (5) 9.00 8.40

No. 2273 sold for 28p on day of issue. No. 2273 has a chalky covering over the coin that can be scratched away with a coin or other metal object to reveal a "heads" picture, showing a face composed of a planet, star and a crescent, or a "tails" picture, showing a shooting star. The chalky covering may, like earlier British chalky paper stamps, dissolve in any fluid.

No. 2273c will have both versions of the stamp. Vertical or horizontal pairs from No. 2273d will have both versions of the stamp. No. 2273d sold for £6.15.

Portions of the designs of Nos. 2275 and 2277 are printed with a thermochromic ink that changes color when warmed.

Castles Type of 1955
Miniature Sheet
Litho. & Engr.

2005, Mar. 22 ***Perf. 11x11¾***

On Cream-Colored Paper

2278 Sheet of 4 7.00 *7.75*
a. A133 50p Carrickfergus (brown) .85 *1.00*
b. A133 50p Windsor (black) 2.75 2.00
c. A133 £1 Caernarfon (red) 1.75 *2.00*
d. A133 £1 Edinburgh (blue) 1.75 *2.00*
e. Booklet pane of 4 #2278b (BK197) 11.00 —

Issued: No. 2278e, 9/9/11. Stamps from No. 2278e have a pale yellow background.

Miniature Sheet

Wedding of Prince Charles and Camilla Parker Bowles — A584

No. 2279 — Couple: a, 30p, Prince wearing blue, red and green tie. b, 68p, Prince wearing vest.

2005, Apr. 8 Litho. ***Perf. 13½x14***

2279 A584 Sheet, 2 each #a-b 6.75 *7.25*
a. 30p multi 1.75 1.75
b. 68p multi 2.75 2.75

The marginal inscription states that the wedding took place on Apr. 8, but it was delayed until Apr. 9, due to Prince Charles's attendance at the Apr. 8 funeral of Pope John Paul II. Post offices were requested not to sell the stamps until Apr. 9, but first day covers have Apr. 8 cancels.

UNESCO World Heritage Sites in Great Britain and Australia A585

Designs: No. 2280, Hadrian's Wall, England. No. 2281, Ayers Rock, Uluru-Kata Tjuta National Park, Australia. No. 2282, Stonehenge, England No. 2283, Wet Tropics of Queensland, Australia. No. 2284, Blenheim Palace, England. No. 2285, Greater Blue Mountains Area, Australia. No. 2286, Heart of Neolithic Orkney, Scotland. No. 2287, Purnululu National Park, Australia.

2005, Apr. 21 ***Perf. 14½***

2280 A585 2nd multi .85 .80
2281 A585 2nd multi .85 .80
a. Horiz. pair, #2280-2281 1.75 1.60
2282 A585 1st multi 1.05 1.00
2283 A585 1st multi 1.05 1.00
a. Horiz. pair, #2282-2283 2.10 2.00
2284 A585 47p multi 1.30 1.20
2285 A585 47p multi 1.30 1.20
a. Horiz. pair, #2284-2285 2.60 2.40
2286 A585 68p multi 1.60 1.50
2287 A585 68p multi 1.60 1.50
a. Horiz. pair, #2286-2287 3.25 3.00
Nos. 2280-2287 (8) 9.60 9.00

Nos. 2280 and 2281 each sold for 21p, and Nos. 2282 and 2283 each sold for 30p on day of issue.

See Australia Nos. 2369-2376.

Trooping the Color Ceremony A586

Designs: 2nd, Soldier holding regimental flag. 1st, Queen Elizabeth II saluting. 42p, Bugler on horseback. 60p, Soldier holding scabbard. 68p, Queen on horseback. £1.12, Queen and soldier in phaeton.

2005, June 7 Litho. ***Perf. 14½***

2288 A586 2nd multi 1.00 .95
2289 A586 1st multi 1.25 1.20
2290 A586 42p multi 1.25 1.20
2291 A586 60p multi 1.75 1.60
2292 A586 68p multi 1.90 1.75

2293 A586 £1.12 multi 2.75 2.50
a. Souvenir sheet, #2288-2293 9.75 9.75
Nos. 2288-2293 (6) 9.90 9.20

Nos. 2288 and 2289 sold for 21p and 30p respectively on day of issue.

St. Paul's Cathedral Type of 1995

Souvenir Sheet

2005, July 5 Photo. *Perf. 14½*

2294 Sheet of 6, #2294a, 5 #MH287 7.75 7.75
a. A456 (1st) deep blue & silver 1.60 1.60

No. 2294a issued 6/21/2005 and sold for 30p on day of issue. End of World War II, 60th anniv.

Motorcycles — A587

Designs: 1st, 1991 Norton F.1. 40p, 1969 BSA Rocket 3. 42p, 1949 Vincent Black Shadow. 47p, 1938 Triumph Speed Twin. 60p, 1930 Brough Superior. 68p, 1914 Royal Enfield.

2005, July 19 Litho. *Perf. 13¾x14*

2295 A587 1st multi 1.15 1.15
2296 A587 40p multi 1.10 1.05
2297 A587 42p multi 1.15 1.15
2298 A587 47p multi 1.40 1.35
2299 A587 60p multi 1.50 1.50
2300 A587 68p multi 1.75 1.75
Nos. 2295-2300 (6) 8.05 7.95

No. 2295 sold for 30p on day of issue.

Miniature Sheet

Selection of London as Host of 2012 Summer Olympics — A588

No. 2301: a, Javelin. b, Swimming. c, Sprinting. d, Basketball. e, Victorious athlete.

2005, Aug. 5 *Perf. 14¼*

2301 A588 Sheet of 6, #a-d, 2 #e 8.00 8.00
a.-e. 1st Any single 1.25 1.25

Nos. 2301a-2301e each sold for 30p on day of issue. Compare with Type A467.

Changing Tastes in Britain — A589

Designs: 2nd, Woman with rice bowl and chopsticks. 1st, Woman with mug of tea. 42p, Man eating sushi. 47p, Woman with pasta bowl and wine glass. 60p, Woman with bag of French fries. 68p, Man with bowl of fruit.

2005, Aug. 23 Photo. *Perf. 14½*

2302 A589 2nd multi .90 .90
2303 A589 1st multi 1.15 1.15
2304 A589 42p multi 1.15 1.15
2305 A589 47p multi 1.50 1.50
2306 A589 60p multi 1.50 1.50
2307 A589 68p multi 1.75 1.75
Nos. 2302-2307 (6) 7.95 7.95

Europa (Nos. 2303, 2304). Nos. 2302 and 2303 sold for 21p and 30p respectively on day of issue.

Television Shows A590

Designs: 2nd, Inspector Morse. 1st, Emmerdale. 42p, Rising Damp. 47p, The Avengers. 60p, The South Bank Show. 68p, Who Wants To Be a Millionaire?

2005, Sept. 15 Litho. *Perf. 14¼x14*

2308 A590 2nd multi .85 .80
2309 A590 1st multi 1.05 1.00
a. Sheet of 20 + 20 labels 21.00 —
2310 A590 42p multi 1.30 1.20
2311 A590 47p multi 1.30 1.20
2312 A590 60p multi 1.45 1.35
2313 A590 68p multi 1.60 1.50
Nos. 2308-2313 (6) 7.55 7.05

Independent Television, 50th anniv. Nos. 2308 and 2309 sold for 21p and 30p respectively on day of issue. No. 2309a sold for £6.65.

Labels on No. 2309a could be personalized for a fee.

Flower A591

Hello A592

Love — A593

Teddy Bear — A595

Flag — A594

Bird — A596

Serpentine Die Cut 14¾x14

2005, Oct. 4 Photo.

Self-Adhesive

Booklet Stamps

2314 A591 1st multi 2.75 2.75
a. Sheet of 20 + 20 labels, litho. 57.50 —
2315 A592 1st multi 2.75 2.75
a. Sheet of 20 + 20 labels, litho. 57.50 —
2316 A593 1st multi 2.75 2.75
a. Sheet of 20 + 20 labels, litho. 57.50 —
2317 A594 1st multi 2.75 2.75
a. Sheet of 20 + 20 labels, litho. 57.50 —
2318 A595 1st multi 2.75 2.75
a. Sheet of 20 + 20 labels, litho. 57.50 —
2319 A596 1st multi 2.75 2.75
a. Booklet pane, #2314-2319 16.50
b. Sheet of 20 + 20 labels, litho. 57.50 —
c. Sheet, 4 each #2315-2316, 3 each #2314, 2317-2319, + 20 labels, litho. ('06) 55.00

Each stamp sold for 30p on day of issue.

Nos. 2314a-2318a, 2319b each sold for £14.95 and had labels that could be personalized.

No. 2319 issued 7/4/06. No. 2319c sold for £6.95.

See Nos. 2427, 2537-2538a, 2545, 2793, 3452.

Souvenir Sheet

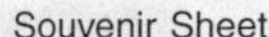

THE ASHES ENGLAND WINNERS 2005

Great Britain's Victory Over Australia in Ashes Cricket Test Match Series — A597

No. 2320: a, Players celebrating with trophy. b, Players celebrating. c, Batsman. d, Players in action.

2005, Oct. 6 Litho. *Perf. 14¼x14*

2320 A597 Sheet of 4 6.75 6.75
a.-b. 1st Either single 1.40 1.40
c.-d. 68p Either single 1.90 1.90

Nos. 2320a and 2320b each sold for 30p on day of issue.

Battle of Trafalgar, Bicent. — A598

Designs: No. 2321, Ships in battle. No. 2322, Wounded Admiral Horatio Nelson on deck of HMS Victory. No. 2323, Ship on fire. No. 2324, Ships in battle, diff. No. 2325, Columns of British ships. No. 2326, French and Spanish ships.

2005, Oct. 18 Litho. *Perf. 14¾x14¼*

2321 A598 1st multi 1.00 .90
2322 A598 1st multi 1.00 .90
a. Horiz. pair, #2321-2322 2.00 1.90
2323 A598 42p multi 1.20 1.15
2324 A598 42p multi 1.20 1.15
a. Horiz. pair, #2323-2324 2.40 2.30
2325 A598 68p multi 2.00 1.90
a. Booklet pane, #2321, 2323, 2325 (BK178) 4.25 —
2326 A598 68p multi 2.00 1.90
a. Horiz. pair, #2325-2326 4.00 4.00
b. Booklet pane, #2322, 2324, 2326 (BK178) 4.25 —
c. Souvenir sheet, #2321-2326 9.00 9.00
Nos. 2321-2326 (6) 8.40 7.90

Nos. 2321-2322 each sold for 30p on day of issue.

Christmas A599

Madonna and Child in artistic style of: 2nd, Haiti. 1st, Europe. 42p, Europe. 60p, Native Americans. 68p, India. £1.12, Australian Aborigines.

2005, Nov. 1 Photo. *Perf. 14½x14*

2327 Sheet of 6 10.00 10.00
a. A599 2nd multi 1.40 1.40
b. A599 1st multi 1.75 1.75
c. A599 42p multi 1.05 1.05
d. A599 60p multi 1.40 1.40
e. A599 68p multi 1.60 1.60
f. A599 £1.12 multi 2.90 2.90

Self-Adhesive

Die Cut Perf. 14¼x14

2328 A599 2nd multi .95 .85
a. Booklet pane of 24 25.00
2329 A599 1st multi 1.25 1.05
a. Booklet pane of 12 15.00
2330 A599 42p multi 1.25 1.05
2331 A599 60p multi 1.60 1.40
2332 A599 68p multi 1.75 1.60
2333 A599 £1.12 multi 3.00 2.50
Nos. 2328-2333 (6) 9.80 8.45

Nos. 2327a and 2328 each sold for 21p and Nos. 2327b and 2329 each sold for 30p on day of issue.

Animals From Children's Books — A600

Designs: No. 2334, Jeremy Fisher, from *The Tale of Mr. Jeremy Fisher,* by Beatrix Potter. No. 2335, Kipper, from *Kipper,* by Mick Inkpen. No. 2336, The Enormous Crocodile, from *The Enormous Crocodile,* by Roald Dahl. No. 2337, Paddington Bear, from *More About Paddington,* by Michael Bond. No. 2338, Boots, from *The Comic Adventures of Boots,* by Satoshi Kitamura. No. 2339, White Rabbit, from *Alice's Adventures in Wonderland,* by Lewis Carroll. No. 2340, The Very Hungry Caterpillar, from *The Very Hungry Caterpillar,* by Eric Carle. No. 2341, Maisy, from *Maisy's ABC,* by Lucy Cousins.

No. 2342, Like #2337.

2006, Jan. 10 Litho. *Perf. 14½*

2334 A600 2nd multi .85 .75
2335 A600 2nd multi .85 .75
a. Horiz. pair, #2334-2335 1.75 1.50
2336 A600 1st multi 1.00 .95
2337 A600 1st multi 1.00 .95
a. Horiz. pair, #2336-2337 2.00 1.90
2338 A600 42p multi 1.25 1.20
2339 A600 42p multi 1.25 1.20
a. Horiz. pair, #2338-2339 2.50 2.40
2340 A600 68p multi 2.00 1.90
2341 A600 68p multi 2.00 1.90
a. Horiz. pair, #2340-2341 4.00 4.00
Nos. 2334-2341 (8) 10.20 9.60

Self-Adhesive

Serpentine Die Cut 14½

2342 A600 1st multi + label 2.75 2.75

Nos. 2334-2335 each sold for 21p, and Nos. 2336-2337 each sold for 30p on day of issue. No. 2340 has two die cut holes repesenting holes eaten by the caterpillar.

See United States Nos. 3987, 3990.

No. 2342 had a franking value of 30p on the day of issue, and was issued in sheets of 20 stamps + 20 different labels that sold for £6.55.

English Scenery A601

Designs: No. 2343, Carding Mill Valley, Shropshire. No. 2344, Beachy Head, Sussex coast. No. 2345, St. Paul's Cathedral, London. No. 2346, Brancastle, Norfolk coast. No. 2347, Derwent Edge, Peak District. No. 2348, Robin Hood's Bay, Yorkshire coast. No. 2349, Buttermere, Lake District. No. 2350, Chipping Campden, Cotswolds. No. 2351, St. Boniface Down, Isle of Wight. No. 2352, Chamberlain Square, Birmingham.

2006, Feb. 7 Photo. *Perf. 14½*

2343 A601 1st multi 1.25 1.15
2344 A601 1st multi 1.25 1.15
2345 A601 1st multi 1.25 1.15
2346 A601 1st multi 1.25 1.15
2347 A601 1st multi 1.25 1.15
2348 A601 1st multi 1.25 1.15
2349 A601 1st multi 1.25 1.15
2350 A601 1st multi 1.25 1.15
2351 A601 1st multi 1.25 1.15
2352 A601 1st multi 1.25 1.15
a. Block of 10, #2343-2352 13.00 12.00
Nos. 2343-2352 (10) 12.50 11.50

Nos. 2343-2352 each sold for 30p on day of issue.

Isambard Kingdom Brunel (1806-1859), Engineer — A602

Engineering projects of Brunel: 1st, Royal Albert Bridge. 40p, Box Tunnel. 42p, Paddington Station. 47p, PSS Great Eastern. 60p, Clifton Suspension Bridge design. 68p, Maidenhead Bridge.

2006, Feb. 23 Litho. ***Perf. 14x13¼***

2353	A602 1st multi	1.00	.85
2354	A602 40p multi	1.15	1.15
2355	A602 42p multi	1.15	1.15
2356	A602 47p multi	1.40	1.40
a.	Booklet pane, #2356, 2 #2207b (BK179)	12.50	—
2357	A602 60p multi	1.60	1.60
a.	Booklet pane, #2354, 2356, 2357 (BK179)	4.25	—
2358	A602 68p multi	1.90	1.90
a.	Souvenir sheet, #2353-2358	8.50	8.50
b.	Booklet pane, #2353, 2355, 2358 (BK179)	4.00	—
	Nos. 2353-2358 (6)	8.20	8.05

No. 2353 sold for 30p on day of issue.

Ice Age Animals A603

Designs: 1st, Saber-tooth cat. 42p, Giant deer. 47p, Woolly rhinoceros. 68p, Woolly mammoth. £1.12, Cave bear.

Perf. 14¼x14½

2006, Mar. 21 Litho.

2359	A603 1st gray & blk	1.30	1.15
2360	A603 42p gray & blk	1.30	1.15
2361	A603 47p gray & blk	1.60	1.40
2362	A603 68p gray & blk	2.00	1.75
2363	A603 £1.12 gray & blk	3.50	2.90
	Nos. 2359-2363 (5)	9.70	8.35

No. 2359 sold for 30p on day of issue.

Queen Elizabeth II, 80th Birthday A604

Queen: No. 2364, Wearing sunglasses, 1972. No. 2365, With horse, 1985. No. 2366, Wearing hat, 2001. No. 2367, As child, with mother, 1931. No. 2368, Wearing tiara, 1951. No. 2369, Wearing hat, 1960. No. 2370, As teenager, 1940. No. 2371, With Prince Philip, 1950.

2006, Apr. 18 Photo. ***Perf. 14¼x14***

2364	A604 2nd gray & blk	.90	.80
2365	A604 2nd gray & blk	.90	.80
a.	Horiz. pair, #2364-2365	2.00	1.60
2366	A604 1st gray & blk	1.10	1.00
2367	A604 1st gray & blk	1.10	1.00
a.	Horiz. pair, #2366-2367	2.25	2.00
2368	A604 44p gray & blk	1.25	1.15
2369	A604 44p gray & blk	1.25	1.15
a.	Horiz. pair, #2368-2369	2.60	2.40
2370	A604 72p gray & blk	1.90	1.75
2371	A604 72p gray & blk	1.90	1.75
a.	Horiz. pair, #2370-2371	4.00	3.50
	Nos. 2364-2371 (8)	10.30	9.40

On day of issue, Nos. 2364-2365 each sold of 23p; Nos. 2366-2367 each sold for 32p.

2006 World Cup Soccer Championships, Germany — A605

Globe, soccer player and flag from: 1st, England. 42p, Italy. 44p, Argentina. 50p, Germany. 64p, France. 72p, Brazil.

2006, June 6 Litho. ***Perf. 14½***

2372	A605 1st multi	1.05	1.00
a.	Sheet of 20 + 20 labels	40.00	—
2373	A605 42p multi	1.30	1.20
2374	A605 44p multi	1.35	1.25
2375	A605 50p multi	1.60	1.50
2376	A605 64p multi	1.90	1.75
2377	A605 72p multi	2.40	2.25
	Nos. 2372-2377 (6)	9.60	8.95

No. 2372 sold for 32p on day of issue. No.2372a sold for £6.95.

Modern Architecture A606

Designs: 1st, 30 St. Mary Axe, London, designed by Sir Norman Foster. 42p, Maggie's Center, Dundee, designed by Frank Gehry. 44p, Selfridges, Birmingham, designed by Future Systems. 50p, Downland Gridshell, Chichester, by Edward Cullinan. 64p, An Turas, Isle of Tiree, by Sutherland Hussey Architects. 72p, The Deep Hull, by Terry Farrell and Partners.

2006, June 20 Photo.

2378	A606 1st multi	1.00	.95
2379	A606 42p multi	1.15	1.15
2380	A606 44p multi	1.40	1.40
2381	A606 50p multi	1.50	1.50
2382	A606 64p multi	1.75	*1.90*
2383	A606 72p multi	1.75	*1.00*
	Nos. 2378-2383 (6)	8.55	8.80

No. 2378 sold for 32p on day of issue.

National Portrait Gallery, 150th Anniv. — A607

Famous Britons in art from National Portrait Gallery: No. 2384, Sir Winston Churchill, by Walter Sickert. No. 2385, Self-portrait of Sir Joshua Reynolds. No. 2386, T. S. Eliot, by Patrick Heron. No. 2387, Emmeline Pankhurst, by Georgina Brakenbury. No. 2388, Virginia Woolf, photograph by George Beresford. No. 2389, Sir Walter Scott, bust by Sir Francis Chantry. No. 2390, Mary Seacole, by Albert Challen. No. 2391, William Shakespeare, by John Taylor. No. 2392, Dame Cicely Saunders, by Catherine Goodman. No. 2393, Charles Darwin, by John Collier.

2006, July 18 ***Perf. 14¼***

2384	A607 1st multi	1.35	1.25
2385	A607 1st multi	1.35	1.25
2386	A607 1st multi	1.35	1.25
2387	A607 1st multi	1.35	1.25
2388	A607 1st multi	1.35	1.25
2389	A607 1st multi	1.35	1.25
2390	A607 1st multi	1.35	1.25
2391	A607 1st multi	1.35	1.25
2392	A607 1st multi	1.35	1.25
2393	A607 1st multi	1.35	1.25
a.	Block of 10, #2384-2393	13.50	12.50
	Nos. 2384-2393 (10)	13.50	12.50

Nos. 2384-2393 each sold for 32p on day of issue.

Recipients of Victoria Cross A608

Designs: No. 2394, Corporal Agansing Rai. No. 2395, Boy Seaman First Class Jack Cornwell. No. 2396, Midshipman Charles Lucas. No. 2397, Captain Noel Chavasse. No. 2398, Captain Albert Ball. No. 2399, Captain Charles Upham.

2006, Sept. 21 Litho. ***Perf. 14¼x14***

2394	A608 1st multi	1.10	.90
2395	A608 1st multi	1.10	.90
a.	Horiz. pair, #2394-2395	2.25	1.90
2396	A608 64p multi	1.75	1.60
2397	A608 64p multi	1.75	1.60
a.	Horiz. pair, #2396-2397	3.50	3.25
2398	A608 72p multi	2.10	2.00
a.	Booklet pane, #2394, 2396, 2398 (BK180)	5.00	—
2399	A608 72p multi	2.60	2.40
a.	Horiz. pair, #2398-2399	4.75	4.50
b.	Booklet pane #2395, 2397, 2399 (BK180)	5.50	—
c.	Souvenir sheet, #1331a, 2394-2399	11.00	10.50
	Nos. 2394-2399 (6)	10.40	9.40

Nos. 2394-2395 each sold for 32p on day of issue.

Musicians and Dancers A609

Designs: 1st, Sitar player and dancer. 42p, Guitarist and drummer. 50p, Violinist and harpist. 72p, Saxophone player and guitarist. £1.19, Maracas player and dancers.

2006, Oct. 3 ***Perf. 14¼x14½***

2400	A609 1st multi	1.10	.95
2401	A609 42p multi	1.35	1.25
2402	A609 50p multi	*1.90*	*1.60*
2403	A609 72p multi	2.20	1.90
2404	A609 £1.19 multi	2.75	2.50
	Nos. 2400-2404 (5)	9.30	8.20

Europa (No. 2402).

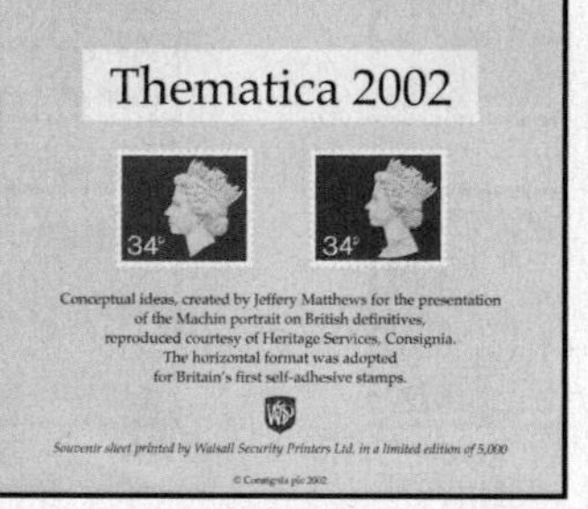

The gummed souvenir sheets shown above, created for the 2002 and 2006 Thematica stamp shows, contain invalid imperforate stamps with simulated perforations that were never issued by Royal Mail. The stamps on these sheets have no obliterators.

The gummed 2005 Thematica sheet reproduces reduced versions of Nos. 440, 441, 683, 1040 and 1796. These reproduced images lack obliterators, and are also invalid for postage.

Gummed Thematica sheets for other years exist, each showing reproductions of other stamps with obliterations to invalidate the images.

"New Baby" A610

"Best Wishes" A611

"Thank You" A612

Balloons A613

Fireworks A614

Flowers, Butterflies and Champagne Bottle A615

Die Cut Perf. 14¾x14¼

2006, Oct. 17 Photo.

Self-Adhesive

2405	A610 1st multi	2.25	1.15
2406	A611 1st multi	2.25	1.15
2407	A612 1st multi	2.25	1.15
2408	A613 1st multi	2.25	1.15
2409	A614 1st multi	2.25	1.15
2410	A615 1st multi	2.25	1.15
a.	Booklet pane, #2405-2410	13.50	
b.	Sheet, 3 each #2406-2409, 4 each #2405, 2410 + 20 labels, litho.	45.00	
	Nos. 2405-2410 (6)	13.50	6.90

Nos. 2405-2410 each sold for 32p on day of issue. No. 2410b sold for £6.95.

See Nos. 2546-2548, 2794.

Christmas

A616 A617

Designs: Nos. 2411a, 2411c, 2412, 2414, Snowman. Nos. 2411b, 2411d, 2413, 2415, Santa Claus. Nos. 2411e, 2416, Reindeer. Nos. 2411f, 2417, Christmas tree.

2006, Nov. 7 Photo. ***Perf. 14¾x14***

2411	Sheet of 6	10.00	9.75
a.	A616 2nd multi	.95	.95
b.	A616 1st multi	1.20	1.20
c.	A617 2nd Large multi	1.35	1.35
d.	A617 1st Large multi	1.90	1.75
e.	A616 72p multi	1.75	1.90
f.	A616 £1.19 multi	2.75	2.60

Self-Adhesive

Die Cut Perf. 14¾x14

2412	A616 2nd multi	.95	.95
a.	Booklet pane of 12	15.00	
2413	A616 1st multi	1.20	1.15
a.	Booklet pane of 12	15.00	
b.	Sheet, 10 each #2412-2413, + 20 labels, litho.	29.00	—
2414	A617 2nd Large multi	1.35	1.30
2415	A617 1st Large multi	1.75	1.75
2416	A616 72p multi	1.75	1.75
2417	A616 £1.19 multi	2.90	2.75
	Nos. 2412-2417 (6)	9.90	9.65

On day of issue, Nos. 2411a and 2412 each sold for 23p, Nos. 2411b and 2413 each sold for 32p, Nos. 2411c and 2414 each sold for 37p, and Nos. 2411d and 2415 each sold for 44p. No. 2413b sold for £6.

Souvenir Sheet

Battle of the Somme, 90th Anniv. — A618

Perf. 14½x14¼ (#2418a), 14¾x14 Syncopated

2006, Nov. 9 Photo.

2418	A618 Sheet of 5	11.00	11.00
a.	1st Poppies	2.75	2.75
b.	Sheet of 20 #2418a + 20 labels, litho.	55.00	—
c.	Single stamp, litho. (#2614b) ('08)	1.90	1.90

No. 2418 contains #2418a, England #13, Northern Ireland #24, Scotland #27 and Wales & Monmouthshire #27. No. 2418a sold for 32p on day of issue. No. 2418b sold for £6.95.

No. 2418c issued 11/6/08. It sold for 36p on day of issue.

Souvenir Sheet

Heritage of Scotland — A619

No. 2419: a, National flag (Scotland type A5). b, St. Andrew (58x22mm). c, Edinburgh Castle (58x22mm).

Perf. 14¾x14 Syncopated, 14¾x14 (#2419b, 2419c)

2006, Nov. 30 — Photo.

2419	A619	Sheet of 4, #2419a-2419c, Scotland #21	8.00	7.25
a.		1st multi	1.75	1.50
b.-c.		72p Either single	2.75	2.00
e.		As "a," litho. (2744k, MH440a)	2.00	2.00

No. 2419a sold for 32p on day of issue.
Issued: No. 2419e, 5/9/13.

Beatles Memorabilia — A620

Beatles Album Covers A621

No. 2420: a, Toy guitar, button. b, Lunch box, buttons. c, 45RPM record of "Love Me Do." d, Tray picturing the Beatles, buttons.
No. 2421, "With The Beatles." No. 2422, "Sgt. Pepper's Lonely Hearts Club Band." No. 2423, "Help!" No. 2424, "Abbey Road." No. 2425, "Let It Be." No. 2426, "Revolver."

2007, Jan. 9 — Litho. — *Perf. 14*

2420	A620	Sheet of 4	5.25	5.25
a.-d.		1st Any single	1.25	1.25

Self-Adhesive

Photo.

Die Cut Perf. 13x13¾

2421	A621	1st multi	1.25	1.25
2422	A621	1st multi	1.25	1.25
2423	A621	64p multi	1.90	1.90
2424	A621	64p multi	1.90	1.90
2425	A621	72p multi	2.00	2.00
2426	A621	72p multi	2.00	2.00
		Nos. 2421-2426 (6)	10.30	10.30

Nos. 2420a 2420d, 2421-2422 each sold for 32p on day of issue.

Love Type of 2005

Serpentine Die Cut 14¾x14 Syncopated

2007-08 — Photo. — Self-Adhesive

Booklet Stamp

2427	A593	1st multi	8.00	7.50
a.		Booklet pane, #2427, 5 #MH380	22.00	
b.		Booklet pane, 2 #2427, 4 #MH300 + 3 labels	23.50	
c.		As #2427, litho. (from 2538a)	11.00	11.00

No. 2427 sold for 32p on day of issue. Compare with No. 2316 which is not syncopated.
Issued: Nos. 2427, 2427a, 1/16/07. Nos. 2427b, 2427c, 1/15/08.
No. 2427c had a franking value of 34p on day of issue.

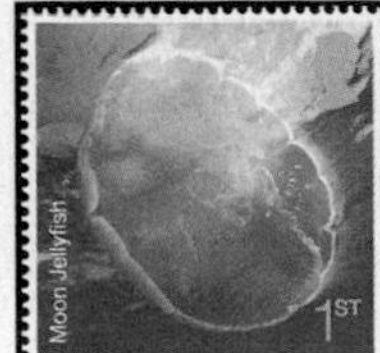

Marine Life — A622

Designs: No. 2428, Moon jellyfish. No. 2429, Common starfish. No. 2430, Beadlet anemone. No. 2431, Bass. No. 2432, Thornback ray. No. 2433, Lesser octopus. No. 2434, Common mussels. No. 2435, Gray seal. No. 2436, Shore crab. No. 2437, Common sun star.

2007, Feb. 1 — Litho. — *Perf. 14½*

2428	A622	1st multi	1.30	1.20
2429	A622	1st multi	1.30	1.20
2430	A622	1st multi	1.30	1.20
2431	A622	1st multi	1.30	1.20
2432	A622	1st multi	1.30	1.20
2433	A622	1st multi	1.30	1.20
2434	A622	1st multi	1.30	1.20
2435	A622	1st multi	1.30	1.20
2436	A622	1st multi	1.30	1.20
2437	A622	1st multi	1.30	1.20
a.		Block of 10, #2428-2437	13.00	12.00

Nos. 2428-2437 each sold for 32p on day of issue.

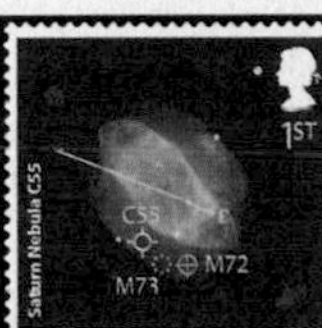

Astronomical Objects — A623

Designs: No. 2438, Saturn Nebula (C55). No. 2439, Eskimo Nebula (C39). No. 2440, Cat's Eye Nebula (C6). No. 2441, Helix Nebula (C63). No. 2442, Flaming Star Nebula (C31). No. 2443, Spindle Galaxy (C53).

Serpentine Die Cut 14¼x14

2007, Feb. 13 — Photo.

2438	A623	1st multi	1.45	1.30
2439	A623	1st multi	1.45	1.30
2440	A623	50p multi	1.75	1.60
2441	A623	50p multi	1.75	1.60
2442	A623	72p multi	2.25	2.10
2443	A623	72p multi	2.25	2.10
		Nos. 2438-2443 (6)	10.90	10.00

Nos. 2438-2439 each sold for 32p on day of issue.

World of Invention A624

Designs: Nos. 2444, 2450, Man thinking about bridge. Nos. 2445, 2451, Locomotive and tracks. Nos. 2446, 2452, People using telephones, maps of Great Britain, Ireland and Australia. Nos. 2447, 2453, Television camera, man with microphone, man watching television. Nos. 2448, 2454, Man at computer with cord in large ball. Nos. 2449, 2455, Man and woman travelers on cratered planet.

2007, Mar. 1 — Photo. — *Perf. 14½x14*

2444	A624	1st multi	1.30	.90
2445	A624	1st multi	1.30	.90
2446	A624	64p multi	2.50	2.50
2447	A624	64p multi	2.50	2.50
a.		Booklet pane, #2444-2447 (BK181)	9.00	—
2448	A624	72p multi	4.50	4.50
2449	A624	72p multi	4.50	4.50
a.		Souvenir sheet, #2444-2449	15.50	15.00
b.		Booklet pane, #2444-2445, 2448-2449	13.50	—
		Nos. 2444-2449 (6)	16.60	15.80

Self-Adhesive

Die Cut Perf. 14½x14

2450	A624	1st multi	1.30	.90
2451	A624	1st multi	1.90	1.75
2452	A624	64p multi	1.90	1.75
2453	A624	64p multi	1.30	1.25
2454	A624	72p multi	2.10	2.10
2455	A624	72p multi	2.10	2.10
		Nos. 2450-2455 (6)	10.60	9.85

Nos. 2444-2445, 2450-2451 each sold for 32p on day of issue.

Abolition of the Slave Trade, Bicent. — A625

Designs: No. 2456, William Wilberforce (1759-1833), abolitionist leader in Parliament, and poster. No. 2457, Olaudah Equiano (c. 1750-97), freed slave and abolitionist writer, and map. No. 2458, Granville Sharp (1735-1813), abolitionist, and ship. No. 2459, Thomas Clarkson (1760-1846), abolitionist and diagram of slaves in slave ship. No. 2460, Hannah More (1745-1833), religious writer, and illustration from Cheap Repository Tracts. No. 2461, Ignatius Sancho (c. 1729-80), abolitionist and actor, poster for performance by Sancho.

2007, Mar. 22 — Litho. — *Perf. 14¼*

2456	A625	1st multi	1.20	1.20
2457	A625	1st multi	1.20	1.20
a.		Horiz. pair, #2456-2457	2.50	2.50
2458	A625	50p multi	1.40	1.40
2459	A625	50p multi	1.40	1.40
a.		Horiz. pair, #2458-2459	3.00	3.00
2460	A625	72p multi	1.90	1.90
2461	A625	72p multi	1.90	1.90
a.		Horiz. pair, #2460-2461	4.00	4.00
		Nos. 2456-2461 (6)	9.00	9.00

Nos. 2456-2457 each sold for 32p on day of issue.

Souvenir Sheet

Heritage of England — A626

No. 2462: a, English flag (18x22mm). b, St. George slaying dragon (59x22mm). c, Parliament (59x22mm).

Perf. 14 Syncopated, 14¾x14 (#2462b, 2462c)

2007, Apr. 23 — Photo.

2462	A626	Sheet of 4, #2462a-2462c, England #7	8.00	7.50
a.		1st multi	1.75	1.50
b.-c.		78p Either single	2.25	1.50
e.		As "a," litho. (MH440a)	2.00	2.00

On day of issue, No. 2462a and England No. 7 sold for 34p.
Issued: No. 2462e, 5/9/13.

Seaside Resort Scenes A627

Designs: 1st, Giant ice cream cone. 46p, Sand castle. 48p, Carousel horses. 54p, Beach cabins. 69p, Beach chairs. 78p, Hitched donkeys.

2007, May 15 — Photo. — *Perf. 14½*

2463	A627	1st multi	1.20	1.20
2464	A627	46p multi	1.35	1.35
2465	A627	48p multi	1.35	1.35
2466	A627	54p multi	1.50	1.50
2467	A627	69p multi	1.90	1.90
2468	A627	78p multi	2.10	2.10
		Nos. 2463-2468 (6)	9.40	9.40

No. 2463 sold for 34p on day of issue.
See No. 2573.

Crowned Lion of England — A628

2007, May 17 — Litho. — *Perf. 14½x14¼*

2469	A628	1st gray bl & dk red + label	2.75	2.75

Souvenir Sheet

Photo.

2470		Sheet, #2470a, 2 each England #6, 15 + label	8.50	8.50
a.	A628	1st bl grn & brt red	2.00	.70

No. 2469 was issued in sheets of 20 stamps + 20 labels that sold for £7.35. No. 2470 sold for £2.38 on day of issue. Nos. 2469 and 2470 each had a franking value of 34p on day of issue.

Souvenir Sheet

Definitive Stamps Designed by Arnold Machin, 40th Anniv. — A629

Design: No. 2472, Arnold Machin.

Perf. 14½x14¼ (#2471a-2471b, 2472)

Photo. & Embossed (#2471a-2471b)

2007, June 5

2471	A629	Sheet, #2471a, 2471b, MH237, MH373	8.00	8.00
a.		1st Arnold Machin	2.50	2.50
b.		1st #MH6	2.50	2.50
c.		Booklet pane, 2 each #2471a, 2471b (BK182)	10.00	—

Photo.

2472	A629	1st multi + label	2.75	2.75

Nos. 2471a and 2471b each sold for 34p on day of issue and were only issued in the souvenir sheet and the booklet pane.
No. 2472, having a franking value of 34p on day of issue, was issued only in sheets of 20 stamps + 20 labels. The sheets sold for £7.35.

Grand Prix Race Cars and Drivers A630

Designs: No. 2473, 1957 Vanwall 2.5-liter, Stirling Moss. No. 2474, 1962 BRM P57, Graham Hill. No. 2475, 1963 Lotus 25 Climax, Jim Clark. No. 2476, 1973 Tyrrell 006/2, Jackie Stewart. No. 2477, 1976 McLaren M23, James Hunt. No. 2478, 1986 Williams FW11, Nigel Mansell.

2007, July 3 — Litho. — *Perf. 14¼x14*

2473	A630	1st multi	1.15	1.15
2474	A630	1st multi	1.15	1.15
2475	A630	54p multi	1.50	1.50
2476	A630	54p multi	1.50	1.50
2477	A630	78p multi	2.10	2.10
2478	A630	78p multi	2.10	2.10
		Nos. 2473-2478 (6)	9.50	9.50

Nos. 2473 and 2474 each sold for 34p on day of issue.

Publication of Last Harry Potter Novel by J. K. Rowling
A631

Coats of Arms From Harry Potter Novels
A632

Novels: No. 2479, Harry Potter and the Philosopher's Stone. No. 2480, Harry Potter and the Chamber of Secrets. No. 2481, Harry Potter and the Prisoner of Azkaban. No. 2482, Harry Potter and the Goblet of Fire. No. 2483, Harry Potter and the Order of the Phoenix. No. 2484, Harry Potter and the Half-Blood Prince. No. 2485, Harry Potter and the Deathly Hallows.

Arms of: Nos. 2486a, 2487, Gryffindor. Nos. 2486b, 2488, Hufflepuff. Nos. 2486c, 2489, Hogwarts. Nos. 2486d, 2490, Ravenclaw. Nos. 2486e, 2491, Slytherin.

2007, July 17 ***Perf. 14x14¼***

2479 A631 1st multi 1.40 1.50
2480 A631 1st multi 1.40 1.50
2481 A631 1st multi 1.40 1.50
2482 A631 1st multi 1.40 1.50
2483 A631 1st multi 1.40 1.50
2484 A631 1st multi 1.40 1.50
2485 A631 1st multi 1.40 1.50
a. Horiz. strip of 7, #2479-2485 10.00 10.50

Souvenir Sheet

Perf. 14¾x14

2486 Sheet of 5 7.25 6.75
a.-e. A632 1st Any single 1.45 1.25

Self-Adhesive

Die Cut Perf. 14¾x14

2487 A632 1st multi + label 1.90 1.90
2488 A632 1st multi + label 1.90 1.90
2489 A632 1st multi + label 1.90 1.90
2490 A632 1st multi + label 1.90 1.90
2491 A632 1st multi + label 1.90 1.90
a. Vert. strip of 5, #2487-2491, + 5 labels 10.00
Nos. 2487-2491 (5) 9.50 9.50

Nos. 2479-2485, 2486a-2486e, each sold for 34p on day of issue. Nos. 2487-2491, having a franking value of 34p on day of issue, were sold in a sheet of 20 stamps + 20 labels that sold for £7.35. Labels could be personalized for an extra fee.

Scouting, Cent.
A633

Designs: 1st, Scouts around campfire, Scout looking at sky. 46p, Scouts climbing rocks. 48p, Scout planting tree. 54p, Scout learning archery from volunteer. 69p, Scouts and glider. 78p, Nine Scouts.

2007, July 26 ***Perf. 14¼x14***

2492 A633 1st multi 1.20 1.20
2493 A633 46p multi 1.30 1.30
2494 A633 48p multi 1.30 1.30
2495 A633 54p multi 1.50 1.50
2496 A633 69p multi 1.90 1.90
2497 A633 78p multi 3.00 3.00
Nos. 2492-2497 (6) 10.20 10.20

Europa (Nos. 2492, 2494). No. 2492 sold for 34p on day of issue.

Endangered Birds — A634

2007, Sept. 4 Litho. ***Perf. 14½***

2498 A634 1st White-tailed eagle 1.30 1.25
2499 A634 1st Bearded tit 1.30 1.25
2500 A634 1st Red kite 1.30 1.25
2501 A634 1st Cirl bunting 1.30 1.25
2502 A634 1st Marsh harrier 1.30 1.25
2503 A634 1st Avocet 1.30 1.25
2504 A634 1st Bittern 1.30 1.25
2505 A634 1st Dartford warbler 1.30 1.25
2506 A634 1st Corncrake 1.30 1.25
2507 A634 1st Peregrine falcon 1.30 1.25
a. Block of 10, #2498-2507 13.00 13.00

Nos. 2498-2507 each sold for 34p on day of issue.

British Army Uniforms — A635

Designs: No. 2508, Non-commissioned officer, Royal Military Police, 1999. No. 2509, Tank commander, 5th Royal Tank Regiment, 1944. No. 2510, Observer, Royal Field Artillery, 1917. No. 2511, Rifleman, 95th Rifles, 1813. No. 2512, Grenadier, Royal Regiment of Foot of Ireland, 1704. No. 2513, Trooper, Earl of Oxford's Horse, 1661.

2007, Sept. 20 Litho. ***Perf. 14¼***

2508 A635 1st multi 1.30 1.30
2509 A635 1st multi 1.30 1.30
2510 A635 1st multi 1.30 1.30
a. Horiz. strip of 3, #2508-2510 4.00 4.00
b. Booklet pane of 3, #2508-2510 (BK183) 4.00 —
c. Booklet pane of 4 (BK208) 5.25 —
2511 A635 78p multi 2.00 2.00
2512 A635 78p multi 2.00 2.00
2513 A635 78p multi 1.75 1.75
a. Horiz. strip of 3, #2511-2513 6.00 6.00
b. Booklet pane of 3, #2511-2513 (BK183) 5.75 —
Nos. 2508-2513 (6) 9.65 9.65

Issued: No. 2510c, 5/14/15. Nos. 2508-2510 each sold for 34p on day of sale.

Wedding of Queen Elizabeth II and Prince Philip, 60th Anniv.
A636

Royal Family — A637

Various photographs of couple from: No. 2514, 2006. No. 2515, 1997. No. 2516, 1980. No. 2517, 1969. No. 2518, 1961. No. 2519, 1947.

No. 2520: a, Royal family, log and flowers (35x35mm). b, Queen Elizabeth II and Prince Philip (40x30mm). c, Royal family, baby carriage (41x30mm). d, Queen Elizabeth II, Prince Philip, Princess Anne and Prince Charles (27x38mm).

2007, Oct. 26 Litho. ***Perf. 14¼x14***

2514 A636 1st black 1.20 1.10
2515 A636 1st black 1.20 1.10
a. Horiz. pair, #2514-2515 2.50 2.25
2516 A636 54p black 1.50 1.40
2517 A636 54p black 1.50 1.40
a. Horiz. pair, #2516-2517 3.00 2.90
2518 A636 78p black 2.25 2.00
2519 A636 78p black 2.25 2.00
a. Horiz. pair, #2518-2519 4.50 4.00
Nos. 2514-2519 (6) 9.90 9.00

Souvenir Sheet

Self-Adhesive

2520 A637 Sheet of 4 7.00 7.00
a. 1st multi, die cut perf. 14½ 1.40 1.40
b. 1st multi, die cut perf. 14½x14¼ 1.40 1.40
c. 69p multi, die cut perf. 14¼x14 1.90 1.90
d. 78p multi, die cut perf. 14¼ 2.25 2.25

Nos. 2514-2515, 2520a and 2520b each sold for 34p on day of sale.

Madonna and Child, by William Dyce
A638

Madonna of Humility, by Lippo di Dalmasio
A639

Die Cut Perf. 14¾x14 Syncopated

2007, Nov. 6 Photo.

Self-Adhesive

2521 A638 2nd multi 1.60 .50
2522 A639 1st multi 2.00 .75

On day of issue, No. 2521 sold for 24p; No. 2522 for 34p.

Christmas
A640 A641

Angels with banners inscribed: Nos. 2523a, 2523c, 2524, 2526, Peace. Nos. 2523b, 2523d, 2525, 2527, Goodwill. Nos. 2523e, 2528, Joy. Nos. 2523f, 2529, Glory.

2007, Nov. 6 Photo. ***Perf. 14¾x14***

2523 Sheet of 6 10.75 10.75
a. A640 2nd multi 1.00 1.00
b. A640 1st multi 1.25 1.25
c. A641 2nd Large multi 1.40 1.40
d. A641 1st Large multi 1.90 1.90
e. A640 78p multi 2.00 2.00
f. A640 £1.24 multi 3.25 3.25

Self-Adhesive

Die Cut Perf. 14¾x14

2524 A640 2nd multi .90 .90
a. Booklet pane of 12 12.50
b. Sheet of 20 + 20 labels, litho. 20.00
2525 A640 1st multi 1.10 1.10
a. Booklet pane of 12 15.00
b. Sheet of 20 + 20 labels, litho. 25.00
2526 A641 2nd Large multi 1.35 1.35
2527 A641 1st Large multi 1.75 1.75
2528 A640 78p multi 2.00 2.00
a. Sheet, 8 each #2524-2525, 4 #2528, + 20 labels, litho. 25.00
b. Sheet of 10 + 10 labels, litho. 30.00
2529 A640 £1.24 multi 3.50 3.50
Nos. 2524-2529 (6) 10.60 10.60

On day of issue, Nos. 2523a and 2524 sold for 24p, Nos. 2523b and 2425 sold for 34p, Nos. 2523c and 2426 sold for 40p, and Nos. 2523d and 2427 sold for 48p. No. 2528a sold for £8.30. No. 2524b sold for £8.50, Nos. 2525b and 2528b each sold for £13.50. Labels on Nos. 2524b, 2525b, and 2528b were personalizable.

Poppy and Soldiers
A642

2007, Nov. 8 Litho. ***Perf. 14½x14¼***

2530 A642 1st multi 2.75 2.75
a. Souvenir sheet of 5 10.50 10.50

Battle of Passchendaele, 90th anniv. No. 2530a contains #2530, England #15, Northern Ireland #26, Scotland #29, and Wales & Monmouthshire #30. No. 2530 was also printed in a sheet of 20 + 5 labels that sold for £7.35, and a limited-quantity privately-contracted sheet of 10 + 10 labels, that sold for £28.50.

Book Covers of James Bond Novels by Ian Fleming — A643

Designs: No. 2531, Casino Royale. No. 2532, Doctor No. No. 2533, Goldfinger. No. 2534, Diamonds Are Forever. No. 2535, For Your Eyes Only. No. 2536, From Russia, with Love.

2008, Jan. 8 Litho. ***Perf. 14¾x14¼***

2531 A643 1st multi 1.25 1.25
2532 A643 1st multi 1.25 1.25
2533 A643 54p multi 1.60 1.60
2534 A643 54p multi 1.40 1.40
2535 A643 78p multi 2.25 2.25
a. Booklet pane of 3, #2531, 2533, 2535 (BK184) 5.25 —
2536 A643 78p multi 1.90 1.90
a. Miniature sheet of 6, #2531-2536 14.50 13.50
b. Booklet pane of 3, #2532, 2534, 2536 (BK184) 4.50 —
Nos. 2531-2536 (6) 9.65 9.65

On day of issue, Nos. 2531-2532 each sold for 34p.

Hello and Flag Types of 2005

Die Cut Perf 14¾x14 Syncopated

2008, Jan. 15 Litho.

Self-Adhesive

2537 A592 1st Hello 2.75 2.50
a. Sheet of 20 + 20 labels 55.00
2538 A594 1st Flag 2.75 2.50
a. Sheet, 8 #2427c, 6 each #2537-2538, + 20 labels 55.00

Issued: No. 2537a, 5/8/10. No. 2537a sold for £8.50. Labels could not be personalized.

No. 2538a sold for £7.35. Nos. 2537-2538 each had a franking value of 34p on day of issue.

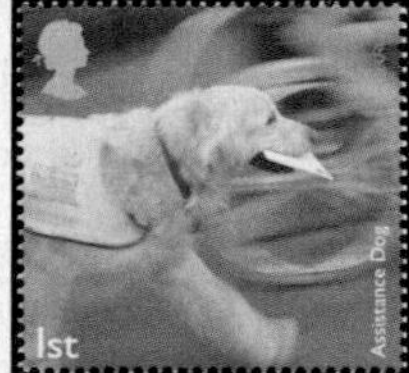

Working Dogs — A644

Designs: 1st, Assistance dog. 46p, Mountain rescue dog. 48p, Police dog. 54p, Customs dog. 69p, Sheepdog. 78p, Guide dog.

2008, Feb. 5 Litho. ***Perf. 14¼x14½***

2539 A644 1st multi 1.30 .95
2540 A644 46p multi 1.25 1.25
2541 A644 48p multi 1.25 1.25
2542 A644 54p multi 1.50 1.50
2543 A644 69p multi 1.90 1.90
2544 A644 78p multi 2.10 2.10
Nos. 2539-2544 (6) 9.30 8.95

No. 2539 sold for 34p on day of issue. Europa (No. 2539).

Types of 2005-06

Die Cut Perf. 14¾x14 Syncopated

2008, Feb. 28 Litho.

Booklet Stamps

Self-Adhesive

2545 A591 1st multi 7.50 7.50
2546 A613 1st multi 7.50 7.50
2547 A614 1st multi 7.50 7.50
a. Sheet of 20 + 20 labels 150.00
2548 A615 1st multi 7.50 7.50
a. Booklet pane of 6, #2537-2538, 2545-2548 40.00

On day of issue, Nos. 2545-2548 each sold for 34p.

Issued: No. 2547a, 1/20/12. No. 2547a sold for £11.47. Labels could not be personalized.

British Royalty and History — A645

Designs: No. 2549, King Henry IV. No. 2550, King Henry V. No. 2551, King Henry VI. No. 2552, King Edward IV. No. 2553, King Edward V. No. 2554, King Richard III.

No. 2555: a, Owen Glendower (Owain Glyn Dwr), Welsh rebel. b, Battle of Agincourt. c, Battle of Tewkesbury. d, William Caxton, first English printer.

2008, Feb. 28 Litho. ***Perf. 14¼***

2549 A645 1st multi 1.00 .95
2550 A645 1st multi 1.00 .95
2551 A645 54p multi 1.50 1.50

2552 A645 54p multi 1.50 1.50
2553 A645 69p multi 1.90 *2.00*
2554 A645 69p multi 1.90 *2.00*
Nos. 2549-2554 (6) 8.80 8.90

Souvenir Sheet

2555 Sheet of 4 6.25 6.25
a.-b. A645 1st Either single 1.00 .90
c.-d. A645 78p Either single 2.25 2.00

On day of issue, Nos. 2549, 2550, 2555a and 2555b each sold for 34p.

See Nos. 2653-2659, 2767-2774, 2807-2814, 2940-2946, 2990-2995.

Souvenir Sheet

Heritage of Northern Ireland — A646

No. 2556: a, Carrickfergus Castle (18x21mm). b, Giant's Causeway, ocean and sky (18x21mm). c, St. Patrick (57x21mm). d, Queen's Bridge and Friendship Beacon, Belfast (57x21mm).

Perf. 14¾x14¼ Syncopated, 14¾x14¼ (78p)

2008, Mar. 11 Litho.

2556 A646 Sheet of 4 7.25 7.25
a.-b. 1st Either single 1.10 1.00
c.-d. 78p Either single 2.50 2.40

On day of issue Nos. 2556a-2556b each sold for 34p.

Rescue at Sea
A647

Sea rescuers in action near: 1st, Barra. 46p, Appledore. 48p, Portland. 54p, St. Ives. 69p, Lee-on-Solent. 78p, Tenby.

Perf. 14¼x14 Syncopated

2008, Mar. 13

2557 A647 1st multi 1.00 .95
2558 A647 46p multi 1.30 1.30
2559 A647 48p multi 1.35 1.35
2560 A647 54p multi 1.50 1.50
2561 A647 69p multi 2.00 2.00
2562 A647 78p multi 2.25 2.25
Nos. 2557-2562 (6) 9.40 9.35

No. 2557 sold for 34p on day of issue.

Endangered Insects
A648

Designs: No. 2563, Adonis blue butterfly. No. 2564, Southern damselfly. No. 2565, Red-barbed ant. No. 2566, Barberry carpet moth. No. 2567, Stag beetle. No. 2568, Hazel pot beetle. No. 2569, Field cricket. No. 2570, Silver-spotted skipper. No. 2571, Purbeck mason wasp. No. 2572, Noble chafer.

2008, Apr. 15 Litho. *Perf. 14½*

2563 A648 1st multi 1.30 1.10
2564 A648 1st multi 1.30 1.10
2565 A648 1st multi 1.30 1.10
2566 A648 1st multi 1.30 1.10
2567 A648 1st multi 1.30 1.10
2568 A648 1st multi 1.30 1.10
2569 A648 1st multi 1.30 1.10
2570 A648 1st multi 1.30 1.10
2571 A648 1st multi 1.30 1.10
2572 A648 1st multi 1.30 1.10
a. Block of 10, #2563-2572 13.50 12.00

Nos. 2563-2572 each sold for 36p on day of issue.

Seaside Resorts Type of 2007

Die Cut Perf. 14½

2008, May 13 Photo.

Booklet Stamp

Self-Adhesive

2573 A627 1st Like #2463 3.75 3.75
a. Booklet pane, 2 #2573, 4 #MH300 15.00

No. 2573 sold for 36p on day of issue.

A649

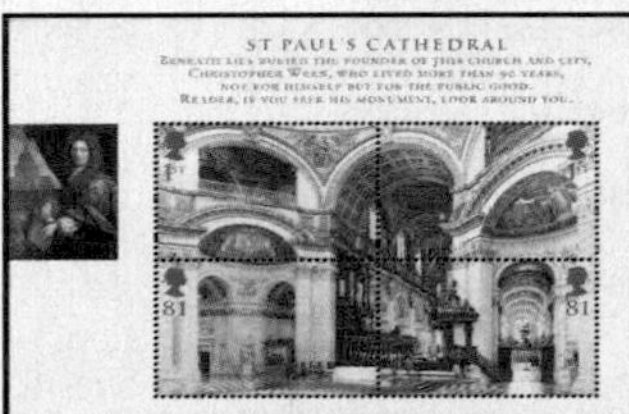

Cathedrals — A650

Designs: No. 2574, Lichfield Cathedral. 48p, Belfast Cathedral. 50p, Gloucester Cathedral. 56p, St. David's Cathedral, Wales. 72p, Westminster Cathedral. 81p, St. Magnus Cathedral, Orkney.

No. 2580 — St. Paul's Cathedral: a, Ceiling, denomination at UL. b, Ceiling, denomination at UR. c, Floor, denomination at UL. d, Floor, denomination at UR.

2008, May 13 Litho. *Perf. 14¼*

2574 A649 1st black 1.25 1.10
2575 A649 48p black 1.50 1.40
2576 A649 50p black 1.60 1.40
2577 A649 56p black 1.75 1.60
2578 A649 72p black 2.25 2.00
2579 A649 81p black 2.60 2.25
Nos. 2574-2579 (6) 10.95 9.75

Souvenir Sheet

2580 A650 Sheet of 4 7.00 7.00
a.-b. 1st Either single 1.10 1.00
c.-d. 81p Either single 2.40 2.25

Nos. 2574, 2580a-2580b each sold for 36p on day of issue.

Posters of British Comedy and Horror Films
A651

Poster for: 1st, Carry On Sergeant. 48p, Dracula. 50p, Carry On Cleo. 56p, The Curse of Frankenstein. 72p, Carry On Screaming. 81p, The Mummy.

2008, June 10 Litho. *Perf. 13¾x14*

2581 A651 1st multi 1.00 .85
2582 A651 48p multi 1.35 1.20
2583 A651 50p multi 1.40 1.25
2584 A651 56p multi 1.50 1.40
2585 A651 72p multi 2.00 1.75
2586 A651 81p multi 2.25 2.00
Nos. 2581-2586 (6) 9.50 8.45

No. 2581 sold for 36p on day of issue.

First Powered Flight in Great Britain, Cent.
A652

Air displays: 1st, Red Arrow aerobatic team. 48p, Royal Air Force Falcons parachuting squad. 50p, Boy watching airplanes in formation. 56p, Avro Vulcans and Avro 707s in flight. 72p, Parachutist Robert Wyndham on wing of Avro 504 biplane. 81p, Blériot airplane and air race tower.

2008, July 17 Photo. *Perf. 14¼x14*

2587 A652 1st multi 1.00 .90
a. Sheet of 20 + 17 labels, litho. 22.00 —
b. Litho. 3.60 3.60
c. Booklet pane of 4, 2 each #1758a, 2587b (BK185) 12.00 —
2588 A652 48p multi 1.35 1.20
2589 A652 50p multi 1.40 1.25
2590 A652 56p multi 1.50 1.40
2591 A652 72p multi 2.00 1.75
2592 A652 81p multi 2.25 2.00
Nos. 2587-2592 (6) 9.50 8.50

No. 2587 sold for 36p on day of issue. No. 2587a sold for £7.75. Labels could not be personalized.

No. 2587c issued 9/18.

Souvenir Sheet

2008 Olympic Games, Beijing and 2012 Olympic Games, London — A653

No. 2593: a, National Stadium, Beijing. b, London Eye. c, Tower of London. d, Corner Tower, Forbidden City, Beijing.

Litho. & Silk Screened

2008, Aug. 22 *Perf. 14½*

2593 A653 Sheet of 4 6.50 6.50
a.-d. 1st Any single 1.60 1.50

On day of issue Nos. 2593a-2593d each sold for 36p.

Royal Air Force Uniforms — A654

Designs: No. 2594, Drum major, Royal Air Force Central Band, 2007. No. 2595, Helicopter rescue winchman, 1984. No. 2596, Hawker Hunter pilot, 1951. No. 2597, Lancaster air gunner, 1944. No. 2598, Plotter, Women's Army Air Force, 1940. No. 2599, Pilot, 1918.

2008, Sept. 18 Litho. *Perf. 14¼*

2594 A654 1st multi 1.00 .95
2595 A654 1st multi 1.00 .95
2596 A654 1st multi 1.00 .95
a. Horiz. strip of 3, #2594-2596 3.25 3.00
b. Booklet pane of 3, #2594-2596 (BK185) 3.25 —
2597 A654 81p multi 2.25 2.10
2598 A654 81p multi 2.25 2.10
2599 A654 81p multi 2.25 2.10
a. Horiz. strip of 3, #2597-2599 7.00 6.50
b. Booklet pane of 3, #2597-2599 (BK185) 7.00 —
Nos. 2594-2599 (6) 9.75 9.15

Nos. 2594-2596 each sold for 36p on day of issue.

Miniature Sheet

Country Definitive Stamps, 50th Anniv. — A655

Perf. 14¾x14 Syncopated

2008, Sept. 29 Photo.

Buff Paper

2600 A655 Sheet of 9 + label 14.50 14.00
a. 1st Wales & Monmouthshire Type A1 1.50 1.50
b. 1st Scotland Type A1 1.50 1.50
c. 1st Wales & Monmouthshire Type A3 1.50 1.50
d. 1st Scotland Type A3 1.50 1.50
e. 1st Northern Ireland Type A1 1.50 1.50
f. 1st Wales & Monmouthshire Typo A2 1.50 1.50
g. 1st Scotland Type A2 1.50 1.50
h. 1st Northern Ireland Type A2 1.50 1.50
i. 1st Northern Ireland Type A3 1.50 1.50
j. As #2600e, litho., white paper 1.60 1.60
k. As #2600i, litho., white paper 1.60 1.60
l. As #2600h, litho., white paper 1.60 1.60
m. As #2600a, litho., white paper 1.60 1.60
n. As #2600c, litho., white paper 1.60 1.60
o. As #2600f, litho., white paper 1.60 1.60
p. As #2600b, litho., white paper 1.60 1.60
q. As #2600d, litho., white paper 1.60 1.60
r. As #2600g, litho., white paper 1.60 1.60
s. Booklet pane of 9, #2600j-2600r (BK186) 16.00
t. Booklet pane of 6, #2600p-2600r, 3 Scotland #21a (BK186) 11.00
u. Booklet pane of 6, #2600j-2600l, 3 Northern Ireland #18a (BK186) 9.75
v. Booklet pane of 6, #2600m-2600o, 3 Wales & Monmouthshire #21b (BK186) 14.00

Nos. 2600a-2600r each sold for 36p on day of issue.

Famous Women
A656

Designs: 1st, Millicent Garrett Fawcett (1847-1929), suffragist. 48p, Elizabeth Garrett Anderson (1836-1917), first female physician in Britain. 50p, Marie Stopes (1880-1958), birth control advocate. 56p, Eleanor Rathbone (1872-1946), politician and advocate for family allowance. 72p, Claudia Jones (1915-64), civil rights activist. 81p, Barbara Castle (1910-2002), politician and advocate for equal pay for women.

Perf. 14¼x14½

2008, Oct. 14 Photo.

2601 A656 1st multi 1.00 .95
2602 A656 48p multi 1.35 1.25
2603 A656 50p multi 1.40 1.30
2604 A656 56p multi 1.60 1.50
2605 A656 72p multi 2.00 1.90
2606 A656 81p multi 2.25 2.10
Nos. 2601-2606 (6) 9.60 9.00

On day of issue, No. 2601 sold for 36p.

Christmas
A657 A658

Pantomime actors: Nos. 2607a, 2607c, 2608, 2610, Ugly sisters from Cinderella. Nos. 2607b, 2607e, 2609, 2612, Genie from Aladdin. 50p, Captain Hook from Peter Pan. 81p, Wicked queen from Snow White.

2008, Nov. 4 Photo. *Perf. 14¾x14*

2607 Sheet of 6 9.25 9.25
a. A657 2nd multi .90 .75
b. A657 1st multi 1.15 1.15
c. A658 2nd Large multi 1.35 1.35
d. A657 50p multi 1.60 1.60
e. A658 1st Large multi 1.60 1.60
f. A657 81p multi 2.60 2.60

Self-Adhesive

Die Cut Perf. 14¾x14 Syncopated

2608 A657 2nd multi .90 .75
a. Booklet pane of 12 12.50
b. Litho. + label .85 .75
2609 A657 1st multi 1.15 1.15
a. Booklet pane of 12 15.00
b. Litho. + label 1.00 1.00
2610 A658 2nd Large multi 1.35 1.35
2611 A657 50p multi 1.60 1.60
2612 A658 1st Large multi 1.60 1.60
2613 A657 81p multi 2.60 2.60
a. Litho. + label 2.25 *2.50*
b. Sheet of 20, 8 each #2608b, 2609b, 4 #2613a + 20 labels 24.00 —
Nos. 2608-2613 (6) 9.20 9.05

On day of issue, the franking value of Nos. 2607a, 2608, and 2608b was 27p, and that of Nos. 2607b, 2609 and 2609b was 36p. On day of issue, Nos. 2607c and 2610 sold for 42p, and Nos. 2607e and 2612 sold for 52p. No. 2613b sold for £8.85. Labels could not be personalized.

No. 2608 was also printed in sheets of 20 stamps + 20 labels that could be personalized. No. 2609b was also printed in sheets of 10 stamps + 10 labels and 20 stamps + 20 labels that could be personalized. No. 2613a was also available in a sheet of 10 stamps + 10 labels that could be personalized.

Poppy With Soldier's Face — A659

2008, Nov. 6 Litho. ***Perf. 14½x14¼***

2614	A659	1st multi	2.50	1.00
	a.	Souvenir sheet of 5	10.50	10.50
	b.	Horiz. strip, #2418c, 2530, 2614	5.00	4.00
	c.	Booklet pane of 4, #2418c, 2614, 2 #2530 (BK217)	7.50	—

End of World War I, 90th anniv. On day of issue, No. 2614 sold for 36p. No. 2614a contains #2614, England #18, Northern Ireland #29, Scotland #32, and Wales and Monmouthshire #32. No. 2614 also was printed in a sheet of 20 + 5 labels that sold for £7.75, and in a series of limited-quantity privately contracted sheets of 10 + 10 labels that sold for various prices.

Issued: No. 2614c, 7/31/17.

British Design A660

Designs: No. 2615, Supermarine Spitfire, designed by R. J. Mitchell. No. 2616, Miniskirt, designed by Mary Quant. No. 2617, Mini Cooper, designed by Sir Alec Issigonis. No. 2618, Anglepoise lamp, designed by George Carwardine. No. 2619, Concorde, designed by Aérospatiale-BAC. No. 2620, K2 telephone kiosk, designed by Sir Giles Gilbert Scott. No. 2621, Polypropylene chair, designed by Robin Day. No. 2622, Penguin books, designed by Edward Young. No. 2623, London Underground map, designed by Harry Beck. No. 2624, Routemaster Bus, designed by AAM Durrant.

2009, Jan. 13 Litho. ***Perf. 14½***

2615	A660	1st multi	1.40	1.20
	a.	Sheet of 20 + 20 labels	30.00	—
2616	A660	1st multi	1.40	1.20
2617	A660	1st multi	1.40	1.20
	a.	Sheet of 20 + 20 labels	30.00	—
2618	A660	1st multi	1.40	1.20
2619	A660	1st multi	1.40	1.20
	a.	Booklet pane of 4, 2 each #2049a, 2619 (BK187)	21.00	—
	b.	Sheet of 20 + 20 labels	30.00	—
2620	A660	1st multi	1.40	1.20
2621	A660	1st multi	1.40	1.20
2622	A660	1st multi	1.40	1.20
2623	A660	1st multi	1.40	1.20
	a.	Booklet pane of 6, #2616, 2618, 2620-2623 (BK187)	8.50	—
2624	A660	1st multi	1.40	1.20
	a.	Block of 10, #2615-2624	14.00	14.00
	b.	Booklet pane of 4, #2615, 2617, 2 #2624 (BK187)	5.75	—

On day of issue, Nos. 2615-2624 each sold for 36p. Nos. 2617a, 2619b sold for £7.74. Labels on No. 2617a, No. 2619b could not be personalized.

Issued: No. 2619b, 3/2/09. No. 2615a, 9/15/10. No. 2615a sold for £8.50 and labels could not be personalized.

See Nos. 2640-2644, 2833.

Miniature Sheet

Robert Burns (1759-96), Poet — A661

No. 2625: a, Man with plow, text, "A Man's a Man for a' that". b, Portrait of Burns by Alexander Naysmith.

Perf. 14½ (#2625a, 2625b), 14¾x14 Syncopated

2009, Jan. 22 Photo.

2625	A661	Sheet of 6, #2625a, 2625b, Scotland #20, 21, 31, 32	8.00	8.00
	a.-b.	1st Either single	1.25	1.25

On day of issue, Nos. 2625a and 2625b each sold for 36p.

Miniature Sheet

Wildlife and HMS Beagle Map of Galapagos Islands — A662

No. 2626: a, Flightless cormorant. b, Giant tortoise, cactus finch. c, Marine iguana. d, Floreana mockingbird.

2009, Feb. 12 ***Perf. 14¼***

2626	A662	Sheet of 4	7.00	7.00
	a.-b.	1st Either single	1.10	1.00
	c.-d.	81p Either single	2.40	1.25
	e.	Booklet pane, #2626, litho. (BK188)	7.25	—

On day of issue, Nos. 2626a and 2626b each sold for 36p. No. 2626e has a rouletted label to the left of the sheet.

Charles Darwin (1809-82), Naturalist A663

Designs: Nos. 2627, 2633, Photograph of Darwin. Nos. 2628, 2634, Head of marine iguana (zoology). Nos. 2629, 2635, Heads of finches (ornithology). Nos. 2630, 2636, Island (geology). Nos. 2631, 2637, Bee orchid (botany). Nos. 2632, 2638, Orangutan (anthropology).

2009, Feb. 12 ***Perf. 14 Syncopated***

Booklet Stamps (#2627-2632)

2627	A663	1st multi (2632a)	5.50	5.00
2628	A663	48p multi (2630a)	6.50	6.00
2629	A663	50p multi (2630a)	7.00	6.50
2630	A663	56p multi (2630a)	7.50	7.00
	a.	Booklet pane of 3, #2628-2630 (BK188)	21.00	—
2631	A663	72p multi (2632a)	8.00	7.50
2632	A663	81p multi (2632a)	8.75	8.50
	a.	Booklet pane of 3, #2627, 2631, 2632 (BK188)	22.50	—
		Nos. 2627-2632 (6)	43.25	40.50

Self-Adhesive

Die Cut Perf. 14 Syncopated

2633	A663	1st multi	1.40	1.40
2634	A663	48p multi	1.35	1.35
2635	A663	50p multi	1.45	1.45
2636	A663	56p multi	1.60	1.60
2637	A663	72p multi	2.00	2.00
2638	A663	81p multi	2.25	2.25
		Nos. 2633-2638 (6)	10.05	10.05

On day of issue, Nos. 2627 and 2633 each sold for 36p.

Miniature Sheet

Heritage of Wales — A664

No. 2639: a, Flag of Wales (18x22mm). b, Red dragon (18x21mm). c, St. David (58x22mm). d, Welsh Assembly, Cardiff (58x22mm).

Perf. 14¾x14 Syncopated (#2639a), 14¾x14 (#2639b, 2639c)

2009, Feb. 26 Litho.

2639	A664	Sheet of 4	7.50	7.50
	a.-b.	1st Either single	1.00	1.00
	c.-d.	81p Either single	2.50	2.25

On day of issue, Nos. 2639a and 2639b each sold for 36p.

British Design Types of 2009

Designs: No. 2640, K2 telephone kiosk. No. 2641, Routemaster Bus. No. 2642, Mini Cooper automobile. No. 2643, Concorde. No. 2644, Miniskirt.

2009 Photo. ***Die Cut Perf. 14½***

Booklet Stamps

Self-Adhesive

2640	A660	1st multi	3.00	3.00
2641	A660	1st multi	3.00	3.00
	a.	Booklet pane, #2640-2641, 4 #MH004	13.50	
2642	A660	1st multi	3.00	3.00
	a.	Booklet pane, 2 #2642, 4 #MH384	13.50	
2643	A660	1st multi	3.00	3.00
	a.	Booklet pane of 6, 2 #2643, 4 #MH384	13.50	
2644	A660	1st multi	3.00	3.00
	a.	Booklet pane of 6, 2 #2644, 4 #MH384	13.50	

Issued: Nos. 2640, 2641, 2641a, 3/10; Nos. 2642, 2642a, 4/21; Nos. 2643, 2643a, 8/18; Nos. 2644, 2644a, 9/17. On day of issue, Nos. 2640-2641 each sold for 36p; Nos. 2642, 2643, 2644 sold for 39p.

Pioneers of the Industrial Revolution A665

Designs: No. 2645, Matthew Boulton (1728-1809), steam engine manufacturer. No. 2646, James Watt (1736-1819), steam engine pioneer and inventor. No. 2647, Richard Arkwright (1732-92), inventor of textile machines. No. 2648, Josiah Wedgwood (1730-95), manufacturer of decorative ceramics. No. 2649, George Stephenson (1781-1848), steam locomotive inventor. No. 2650, Henry Maudslay (1771-1831), engineer and machine tool inventor. No. 2651, James Brindley (1716-72), canal engineer. No. 2652, John McAdam (1756-1836), engineer, road builder.

Perf. 14¼x14½

2009, Mar. 10 Litho.

2645	A665	1st multi	1.00	1.00
2646	A665	1st multi	1.00	1.00
	a.	Horiz. pair, #2645-2646	2.00	2.00
2647	A665	50p multi	1.40	1.40
2648	A665	50p multi	1.40	1.40
	a.	Horiz. pair, #2647-2648	3.00	3.00
2649	A665	56p multi	1.60	1.60
2650	A665	56p multi	1.60	1.60
	a.	Horiz. pair, #2649-2650	3.25	3.25
2651	A665	72p multi	2.00	2.00
2652	A665	72p multi	2.00	2.00
	a.	Horiz. pair, #2651-2652	4.00	4.00
		Nos. 2645-2652 (8)	12.00	12.00

On day of issue, Nos. 2645-2646 each sold for 36p.

British Royalty and History Type of 2008

Designs: No. 2653, King Henry VII. No. 2654, King Henry VIII. No. 2655, King Edward VI. No. 2656, Lady Jane Grey. No. 2657, Queen Mary I. No. 2658, Queen Elizabeth I.

No. 2659: a, Warship Mary Rose. b, Field of Cloth of Gold Royal Conference. c, Royal Exchange. d, Sir Francis Drake, first English circumnavigator.

2009, Apr. 21 ***Perf. 14¼***

2653	A645	1st multi	1.00	.90
2654	A645	1st multi	1.00	.90
2655	A645	62p multi	1.75	1.50
2656	A645	62p multi	1.75	1.50
2657	A645	81p multi	2.25	2.00
2658	A645	81p multi	2.25	2.00
		Nos. 2653-2658 (6)	10.00	8.80

Souvenir Sheet

2659		Sheet of 4	7.25	6.50
	a.-b.	A645 1st Either single	1.10	1.00
	c.-d.	A645 90p Either single	2.60	2.25

On day of issue, Nos. 2653, 2654, 2659a and 2659b sold for 39p.

Endangered Plants A666

Designs: No. 2660, Round-headed leek. No. 2661, Floating water plantain. No. 2662, Lady's slipper orchid. No. 2663, Dwarf milkwort. No. 2664, Marsh saxifrage. No. 2665, Downy woundwort. No. 2666, Upright spurge. No. 2667, Plymouth pear. No. 2668, Sea knotgrass. No. 2669, Deptford pink.

2009, May 19 ***Perf. 14½***

2660	A666	1st multi	1.40	1.25
2661	A666	1st multi	1.40	1.25
2662	A666	1st multi	1.40	1.25
2663	A666	1st multi	1.40	1.25
2664	A666	1st multi	1.40	1.25
2665	A666	1st multi	1.40	1.25
2666	A666	1st multi	1.40	1.25
2667	A666	1st multi	1.40	1.25
2668	A666	1st multi	1.40	1.25
2669	A666	1st multi	1.40	1.25
	a.	Block of 10, #2660-2669	14.00	12.50

On day of issue, Nos. 2660-2669 each sold for 39p.

Miniature Sheet

Royal Botanic Gardens, Kew — A667

No. 2670: a, Palm House. b, Millennium Seed Bank, Wakehurst Place. c, Pagoda. d, Sackler Crossing.

2009, May 19 ***Perf. 14¼x14½***

2670	A667	Sheet of 4	7.50	6.75
	a.-b.	1st Either single	1.10	1.00
	c.-d.	90p Either single	2.60	2.25

On day of issue, Nos. 2670a and 2670b each sold for 39p.

Flowers Type of 1997

Die Cut Perf. 14½x14 Syncopated

2009, May 21 Photo.

Booklet Stamps

Self-Adhesive

2671	A475	1st multi	3.50	3.25
2672	A479	1st multi	3.60	3.25
	a.	Booklet pane, #2671-2672, 4 #MH384	14.50	

On day of issue Nos. 2671-2672 each sold for 39p.

Mythical Creatures A668

2009, June 16 Photo. ***Perf. 14½***

2673	A668	1st Dragon	1.10	.95
2674	A668	1st Unicorn	1.10	.95
2675	A668	62p Giant	1.75	1.50
2676	A668	62p Pixie	1.75	1.50
2677	A668	90p Mermaid	2.50	2.25
2678	A668	90p Fairy	2.50	2.25
		Nos. 2673-2678 (6)	10.70	9.40

On day of issue, Nos. 2673-2674 each sold for 39p.

Miniature Sheet

Post Boxes — A669

No. 2679: a, George V type B wall box. b, Edward VII Ludlow box. c, Victorian lamp box. d, Elizabeth II type A wall box.

2009, Aug. 18 Litho. *Perf. 14¼*

2679	A669	Sheet of 4	10.00	9.00
a.		1st multi	1.50	1.25
b.		56p multi	2.10	1.90
c.		81p multi	3.00	2.75
d.		90p multi	3.40	3.00
e.		Booklet pane of 4, #2679a-2679d (BK189)	10.00	—
f.		Sheet of 20 #2679a + 20 labels	30.00	—

No. 2679 sold for 39p on day of issue. No. 2679f sold for £8.35 on day of issue and its labels could not be personalized.

Fire and Rescue Service A670

Designs: 1st, Firefighting. 54p, Chemical fire. 56p, Emergency rescue. 62p, Flood rescue. 81p, Search and rescue. 90p, Fire safety.

Perf. 14¼x14½

2009, Sept. 1 Photo.

2680	A670	1st multi	1.10	1.00
2681	A670	54p multi	1.50	1.40
2682	A670	56p multi	1.60	1.45
2683	A670	62p multi	1.80	1.60
2684	A670	81p multi	2.25	2.10
2685	A670	90p multi	2.60	2.25
		Nos. 2680-2685 (6)	10.85	9.80

No. 2680 sold for 39p on day of issue.

Royal Navy Uniforms — A671

Designs: No. 2686, Flight deck officer, 2009. No. 2687, Captain, 1941. No. 2688, Second officer WRNS, 1918. No. 2689, Able seaman, 1880. No. 2690, Royal Marine, 1805. No. 2691, Admiral, 1795.

2009, Sept. 17 Litho. *Perf. 14¼*

2686	A671	1st multi	1.10	.95
2687	A671	1st multi	1.10	.95
2688	A671	1st multi	1.10	.95
a.		Horiz. strip of 3, #2686-2688	3.50	3.00
b.		Booklet pane of 3, #2686-2688 (BK190)	3.50	—
2689	A671	90p multi	2.40	2.25
2690	A671	90p multi	2.40	2.25
2691	A671	90p multi	2.40	2.25
a.		Horiz. strip of 3, #2689-2691	7.50	7.00
b.		Booklet pane of 3, #2689-2691 (BK190)	7.50	—
		Nos. 2686-2691 (6)	10.50	9.60

Nos. 2686-2688 each sold for 39p on day of issue.

Famous People A672

Designs: No. 2692, Fred Perry (1909-95), tennis player. No. 2693, Henry Purcell (1659-95), composer and musician. No. 2694, Sir Matt Busby (1909-94), soccer player and manager. No. 2695, William Gladstone (1809-98), prime minister. No. 2696, Mary Wollstonecraft (1759-97), writer on feminist themes. No. 2697, Sir Arthur Conan Doyle (1859-1930), writer and creator of Sherlock Holmes stories. No. 2698, Donald Campbell (1921-67), breaker of land and water speed records. No. 2699, Judy Fryd (1909-2000), founder of Royal Society for Mentally Handicapped Children. No. 2700, Samuel Johnson (1709-84), lexicographer, critic and poet. No. 2701, Sir Martin Ryle (1918-84), radio astronomer.

2009, Oct. 8 Litho. *Perf. 14½*

2692	A672	1st multi	1.30	1.25
2693	A672	1st multi	1.30	1.25
2694	A672	1st multi	1.30	1.25
2695	A672	1st multi	1.30	1.25
2696	A672	1st multi	1.30	1.25
a.		Horiz. strip of 5, #2692-2696	6.75	6.25
2697	A672	1st multi	1.30	1.25
2698	A672	1st multi	1.30	1.25
2699	A672	1st multi	1.30	1.25
2700	A672	1st multi	1.30	1.25
2701	A672	1st multi	1.30	1.25
a.		Horiz. strip of 5, #2697-2701	6.75	6.25
		Nos. 2692-2701 (10)	13.00	12.50

On day of issue, Nos. 2692-2701 each sold for 39p. Europa (No. 2701).

Sports of the 2012 Summer Olympics and Paralympics, London A673

Olympics or Paralympics emblem and: No. 2702, Canoe slalom. Nos. 2703, 2713, Archery (Paralympics). Nos. 2704, 2714, Track. No. 2705, Aquatics. No. 2706, Boccie (Paralympics). Nos. 2707, 2712, Judo. No. 2708, Equestrian (Paralympics). No. 2709, Badminton. No. 2710, Weight lifting. Nos. 2711, 2715, Basketball.

2009-10 Litho. *Perf. 14½*

2702	A673	1st multi	1.35	1.25
2703	A673	1st multi	1.35	1.25
2704	A673	1st multi	1.35	1.25
2705	A673	1st multi	1.35	1.25
2706	A673	1st multi	1.35	1.25
a.		Horiz. strip of 5, #2702-2706	6.75	6.25
2707	A673	1st multi	1.35	1.25
2708	A673	1st multi	1.35	1.25
a.		Booklet pane of 2, #2703, 2708 (BK200)	2.75	—
2709	A673	1st multi	1.35	1.25
2710	A673	1st multi	1.35	1.25
2711	A673	1st multi	1.35	1.25
a.		Horiz. strip of 5, #2707-2711	6.75	6.25
		Nos. 2702-2711 (10)	13.50	12.50

Booklet Stamps

Self-Adhesive

Photo.

Die Cut Perf. 14½

2712	A673	1st multi (2713a)	1.40	1.35
2713	A673	1st multi (2713a)	1.40	1.35
a.		Booklet pane of 6, #2712, 2713, 4 #MH384	10.50	
2714	A673	1st multi	1.40	1.35
2715	A673	1st multi	1.40	1.35
a.		Booklet pane of 6, #2714-2715, 4 #MH384	10.50	

On day of issue, Nos. 2702-2715 each sold for 39p. Issued: Nos. 2702-2711, 10/22; Nos. 2712-2713, 1/7/10; Nos. 2714-2715, 2/25/10. No. 2708a, 7/27/12.

See Nos. 2815-2826, 2840-2841, 2916-2927.

Christmas

A674 A675

Stained-glass windows. Nos. 2716a, 2716c, 2717, 2719, Angel, Church of St. James, Staveley. Nos. 2716b, 2716e, 2718, 2721, Madonna and Child, Church of Ormesby St. Michael, Great Yarmouth. 56p, Joseph, Church of St. Michael, Minehead. 90p, Wise Man, Church of St. Mary the Virgin, Rye. £1.35, Shepherd, Church of St. Mary's, Upavon.

Perf. 14¾x14 Syncopated

2009, Nov. 3 Photo.

2716		Sheet of 7	13.00	11.50
a.		A674 2nd multi	.85	.75
b.		A674 1st multi	1.05	.95
c.		A675 2nd Large multi	1.30	1.15
d.		A674 56p multi	1.50	1.40
e.		A675 1st Large multi	1.60	1.50
f.		A674 90p multi	2.50	2.25
g.		A674 £1.35 multi	3.75	3.25
h.		As "a," litho. (2716i)	1.90	1.90
i.		Booklet pane of 4 #2716h + label (BK196)	7.75	—

Self-Adhesive

Die Cut Perf. 14¾x14 Syncopated

2717	A674	2nd multi	.85	.80
a.		Booklet pane of 12	12.50	
b.		Litho., serpentine die cut 14¾x14 + label	.85	.75
2718	A674	1st multi	1.15	1.00
a.		Booklet pane of 12	15.00	
b.		Litho., serpentine die cut 14¾x14 + label	1.10	1.00
2719	A675	2nd Large multi	2.25	.75
2720	A674	56p multi	1.60	1.45
a.		Litho., serpentine die cut 14¾x14 + label	1.50	1.45
2721	A675	1st Large multi	1.75	1.60
2722	A674	90p multi	2.60	2.40
a.		Litho., serpentine die cut 14¾x14 + label	2.50	2.40
b.		Sheet of 20, 8 each #2717b, 2718b, 2 each #2720a, 2722a, + 20 labels	25.00	
2723	A674	£1.35 multi	4.00	3.50
		Nos. 2717-2723 (7)	14.20	11.50

On day of issue, Nos. 2716a and 2717 each sold for 30p; Nos. 2716b and 2718, 39p; Nos. 2716c and 2719, 47p; Nos. 2716e and 2721, 61p. No. 2722b sold for £9, and contains 20 labels that could not be personalized. No. 2717b was additionally sold in a sheet of 20 + 20 labels that could be personalized that sold for £9.50. No. 2718b was additionally sold in a sheet of 20 + 20 labels that could be personalized that sold for £13.50. No. 2720a was additionally sold in a sheet of 10 + 10 labels that could be personalized that sold for £9.50. No. 2722b was additionally sold in a sheet of 10 + 10 labels that could be personalized that sold for £13.50.

Issued: Nos. 2716h, 2716i, 5/5/11.

Let It Bleed, by The Rolling Stones A676

Led Zeppelin IV, by Led Zeppelin A677

The Rise and Fall of Ziggy Stardust and the Spiders from Mars, by David Bowie A678

Power, Corruption and Lies, by New Order — A679

Screamadelica, by Primal Scream — A680

The Division Bell, by Pink Floyd — A681

Tubular Bells, by Mike Oldfield A682

London Calling, by The Clash — A683

Parklife, by Blur — A684

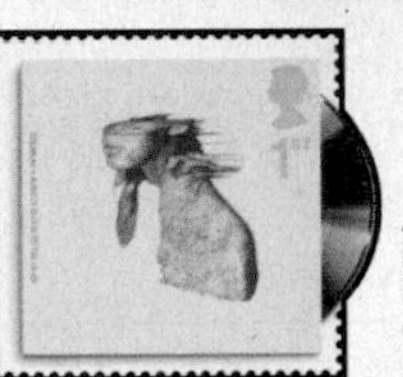

A Rush of Blood to the Head, by Coldplay A685

Perf. 14¾ Syncopated

2010, Jan. 7 Litho.

2724	A676	1st multi	2.50	1.90
2725	A677	1st multi	2.50	1.90
2726	A678	1st multi	2.50	1.90
2727	A679	1st multi	2.50	1.90
2728	A680	1st multi	2.50	1.90
2729	A681	1st multi	2.50	1.90
a.		Booklet pane of 6, #2724-2729 (BK191)	15.00	—
b.		Souvenir sheet of 10 #2729	25.00	—

No. 2729b sold for £4.75.

2730	A682	1st multi	2.50	1.90
2731	A683	1st multi	2.50	1.90
2732	A684	1st multi	2.50	1.90
2733	A685	1st multi	2.50	1.90
a.		Booklet pane of 4, #2730-2733 (BK191)	10.00	—
b.		Souvenir sheet, #2724-2733	37.50	35.00

No. 2733b has simulated creases and toning at the sides and corners of the album cover sheet margin.

Self-Adhesive

Photo.

Die Cut Perf. 14¾

2734	A681	1st multi	1.60	1.35
2735	A685	1st multi	1.60	1.35
2736	A684	1st multi	1.60	1.35
2737	A679	1st multi	1.60	1.35
2738	A676	1st multi	1.60	1.35
a.		Horiz. strip of 5, #2734-2738	8.25	6.75
2739	A683	1st multi	1.60	1.35
2740	A682	1st multi	1.60	1.35
2741	A677	1st multi	1.60	1.35
2742	A680	1st multi	1.60	1.35
2743	A678	1st multi	1.60	1.35
a.		Horiz. strip of 5, #2739-2743	8.25	6.75

On day of issue, Nos. 2724-2743 each sold for 39p.

Miniature Sheet

A686

Nos. 2744 and 2745: a, Airplane with propellers. b, Automobile. c, Sealing wax with crown impression. d, Birthday cake. e, Steam locomotive. f, Ocean liner. g, Poppies. h, Gift box. i, Bird carrying airmail letter. j, "Hello" in airplane's contrail.

Perf. 14¾x14 Syncopated

2010, Jan. 26 **Litho.**

2744 A686 Sheet of 10 17.00 15.00
a.-h. 1st Any single 1.50 1.25
i. (56p) multi 1.90 1.75
j. (90p) multi 3.00 2.75
k. Booklet pane of 8, #2419e, 2462a, 2639a, Northern Ireland #18, 4 #2744g (BK213) 12.50 —
l. Booklet pane of 8 #2744g + central label (BK217) 14.50 —
m. Booklet pane of 8, 4 each #2744g, MH440 (BK221) 15.00 —

Self-Adhesive

Die Cut Perf. 14¾x14 Syncopated

2745 A686 Sheet of 20, 2 each #a-j, + 20 labels 42.50
a.-h. 1st Any single + label 2.00 1.40
i. (56p) multi + label 2.00 2.00
j. (90p) multi + label 3.25 3.25
k. Sheet of 20 #2745d + 20 labels 44.00
l. Sheet of 20 #2745g + 20 labels 44.00
m. Sheet of 10 #2745h + 10 labels 31.00
n. Sheet of 10 #2745i + 10 labels 44.00
o. Sheet of 20 #2745c + 20 labels 40.00

On day of issue, Nos. 2744a-2744h sold for 39p. No. 2745 sold for £9.70, and Nos. 2745a-2745h had a franking value of 39p. Labels could not be personalized.

Nos. 2745k and 2745l each sold for £13.63; No. 2745m for £9.58; and No. 2745n for £13.60. Labels could be personalized on Nos. 2745k-2745n.

Issued: No. 2744k, 6/21/16; No. 2744l, 7/31/17; No. 2744m, 9/13/18; No. 2745o, 9/15/11. No. 2745o sold for £9.50. Labels could not be personalized.

No. 2745g has value and Queen's head in grayish black, die cut perfs at the left side of the stamp are incomplete to keep the label attached. Compare with No. 3118A.

Miniature Sheet

Girl Guides, Cent. — A687

No. 2746 — Girl Guides and: a, Kite, handprint, drawing of flower. b, Cupcake, magnifying glass, leaves, colored pencils. c, Archery target, climber's rope. d, Photographs, swimming goggles, map of Manchester.

2010, Feb. 2 ***Perf. 14¼x14½***

2746 A687 Sheet of 4 7.75 7.00
a. 1st multi 1.15 1.00
b. 56p multi 1.60 1.50
c. 81p multi 2.40 2.10
d. 90p multi 2.60 2.40

No. 2746a sold for 39p on day of issue.

Royal Society, 350th Anniv. A688

Scientists: No. 2747, Robert Boyle (1627-91), air pump. No. 2748, Sir Isaac Newton (1642-1727), color spectrum and optics diagram. No. 2749, Benjamin Franklin (1706-90), lightning. No. 2750, Edward Jenner (1749-1823), smallpox virus. No. 2751, Charles Babbage (1792-1871), gear diagram. No. 2752, Alfred Russel Wallace (1823-1913), oak tree. No. 2753, Sir Joseph Lister (1827-1912), spray. No. 2754, Ernest Rutherford (1871-1937), atom. No. 2755, Dorothy Hodgkin (1910-94), crystal diagram. No. 2756, Sir Nicholas Shackleton (1937-2006), microfossils.

2010, Feb. 25 **Litho.** ***Perf. 14½***

2747 A688 1st multi 1.60 1.50
2748 A688 1st multi 1.60 1.50
2749 A688 1st multi 1.60 1.50
2750 A688 1st multi 1.60 1.50
2751 A688 1st multi 1.60 1.50
2752 A688 1st multi 1.60 1.50
2753 A688 1st multi 1.60 1.50
2754 A688 1st multi 1.60 1.50
a. Booklet pane of 4, #2748, 2749, 2 #2754 (BK192) 6.50 —
2755 A688 1st multi 1.60 1.50
a. Booklet pane of 4, #2753, 2755, 2 #2750 (BK192) 6.50 —
2756 A688 1st multi 1.60 1.50
a. Block of 10, #2747-2756 16.00 15.00
b. Booklet pane of 4, #2747, 2751, 2752, 2756 (BK192) 6.50 —
Nos. 2747-2756 (10) 16.00 15.00

On day of issue, Nos. 2747-2756 each sold for 39p.

Battersea Dogs and Cats Home, 150th Anniv. A689

Designs: No. 2757, Pixie (dog). No. 2758, Button (cat). No. 2759, Herbie (dog). No. 2760, Mr. Tumnus (cat). No. 2761, Tafka (dog). No. 2762, Boris (dog). No. 2763, Casey (dog). No. 2764, Tigger (cat). No. 2765, Leonard (dog). No. 2766, Tia (dog).

2010, Mar. 11 ***Perf. 14½***

2757 A689 1st multi 1.50 1.40
2758 A689 1st multi 1.50 1.40
2759 A689 1st multi 1.50 1.40
2760 A689 1st multi 1.50 1.40
2761 A689 1st multi 1.50 1.40
2762 A689 1st multi 1.50 1.40
2763 A689 1st multi 1.50 1.40
2764 A689 1st multi 1.50 1.40
2765 A689 1st multi 1.50 1.40
2766 A689 1st multi 1.50 1.40
a. Block of 10, #2757-2766 15.00 14.00
Nos. 2757-2766 (10) 15.00 14.00

On day of issue, Nos. 2757-2766 each sold for 39p.

British Royalty and History Type of 2008

Designs: No. 2767, King James I of Scotland (1406-37). No. 2768, King James II of Scotland (1437-60). No. 2769, King James III. No. 2770, King James IV. No. 2771, King James V. No. 2772, Mary, Queen of Scots. No. 2773, King James VI.

No. 2774: a, Founding of St. Andrew's University, 1413. b, College of Surgeons, Edinburgh, 1505. c, Court of Session, 1532. d, John Knox, religious reformer.

2010, Mar. 23 ***Perf. 14¼***

2767 A645 1st multi 1.10 1.00
2768 A645 1st multi 1.10 1.00
2769 A645 1st multi 1.10 1.00
2770 A645 62p multi 1.75 1.60
2771 A645 62p multi 1.75 1.60
2772 A645 81p multi 2.40 2.10
2773 A645 81p multi 2.40 2.10
Nos. 2767-2773 (7) 11.60 10.40

Souvenir Sheet

2774 Sheet of 4 7.50 7.00
a.-b. A645 1st Either single 1.25 1.10
c.-d. A645 81p Either single 2.50 2.25

On day of issue, Nos. 2767-2769, 2774a-2774b each sold for 39p.

Land and Sea Mammals A690

Designs: No. 2775, Humpback whale. No. 2776, Wildcat. No. 2777, Brown long-eared bat. No. 2778, Polecat. No. 2779, Sperm whale. No. 2780, Water vole. No. 2781, Greater horseshoe bat. Nos. 2782, 2785, Otter. No. 2783, Dormouse. Nos. 2784, 2786, Hedgehog.

2010 ***Perf. 14½***

2775 A690 1st multi 1.50 1.40
2776 A690 1st multi 1.50 1.40
2777 A690 1st multi 1.50 1.40
2778 A690 1st multi 1.50 1.40
2779 A690 1st multi 1.50 1.40
2780 A690 1st multi 1.50 1.40
2781 A690 1st multi 1.50 1.40
2782 A690 1st multi 1.50 1.40
2783 A690 1st multi 1.50 1.40
2784 A690 1st multi 1.50 1.40
a. Block of 10, #2775-2784 15.50 14.00
Nos. 2775-2784 (10) 15.00 14.00

Photo.

Booklet Stamps

Self-Adhesive

Die Cut Perf. 14½

2785 A690 1st multi 3.50 3.00
2786 A690 1st multi 3.50 3.00
a. Booklet pane of 6, #2785-2786, 4 #MH384 14.50

Issued: Nos. 2775-2784, 4/13; Nos. 2785-2786, 6/15. On day of issue, Nos. 2775-2786 each sold for 41p.

King George V and Queen Elizabeth II — A691

British Empire Exhibition Stamps of 1924 — A692

"Britannia Rules the Waves" Stamps of 1913 — A693

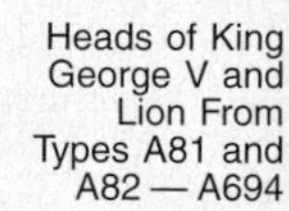

Heads of King George V and Lion From Types A81 and A82 — A694

Designs: No. 2788, Great Britain #185. No. 2789, Great Britain #186. No. 2790, Great Britain #176. No. 2791, Great Britain #175.

Perf. 14½x14 (#2787, 2792), 14¾x14¼

Litho. (#2787, 2792), Litho. & Engr.

2010

2787 A691 1st red 2.00 1.00
2788 A692 1st multi 2.00 1.00
2789 A692 1st multi 2.00 1.00
a. Booklet pane of 4, 2 each #2788-2789 (BK193) 8.00 —
2790 A693 £1 multi 4.50 2.60
2791 A693 £1 multi 4.50 2.60
a. Souvenir sheet of 4, #2788-2791 10.00 9.00
b. Booklet pane of 2, #2790-2791 (BK193) 9.00 —
2792 A694 £1 brown & silver 4.50 2.60
a. Souvenir sheet of 2, #2787, 2792 5.75 5.00
b. Booklet pane of 6, 3 each #2787, 2792 (BK193) 19.50 —
Nos. 2787-2792 (6) 19.50 10.80

Issued: No. 2787, 5/6; others, 5/8. London 2010 Festival of Stamps. Nos. 2787-2789 each sold for 41p on day of issue.

Bird and Thank You Types of 2005-06

Die Cut Perf. 14¾x14 Syncopated

2010, May 8 **Litho.**

Self-Adhesive

2793 A596 1st multi + label (2794a) 17.50 5.00
2794 A612 1st multi + label (2794a) 17.50 5.00
a. Sheet of 20, #2427, 2546, 2547, 2793, 2794, 2 each #2745i, 2745j, 3 #2538, 4 each #2745d, 2745g + 20 labels 32.50

No. 2794a sold for £10. Labels could not be personalized. Nos. 2793 and 2794 each had a franking value of 41p on day of issue.

Britain in World War II — A695

Designs: No. 2795, Prime Minister Winston Churchill reviewing troops. No. 2796, Girl on tractor. No. 2797, Home Guard. No. 2798, Evacuees. No. 2799, Air raid warden. No. 2800, Woman in factory. No. 2801, Firemen at fire. No. 2802, Royal broadcast.

No. 2803, Soldiers in water. No. 2804, Flotilla of small boats. No. 2805, Soldiers in boat. No. 2806, Soldiers on two boats.

2010, May 13 ***Perf. 14½***

2795 A695 1st multi 1.75 1.25
2796 A695 1st multi 1.75 1.25
2797 A695 60p multi 1.75 1.35
2798 A695 60p multi 1.75 1.35
2799 A695 67p multi 2.00 1.50
2800 A695 67p multi 2.00 1.50
2801 A695 97p multi 2.90 2.10
a. Booklet pane of 4, #2797-2799, 2801 (BK194) 8.50 —
2802 A695 97p multi 2.90 2.10
a. Booklet pane of 4, #2795-2796, 2800, 2802 (BK194) 8.50 —

Inscribed "Dunkirk"

2803 A695 1st multi 1.75 1.25
2804 A695 60p multi 1.75 .85
2805 A695 88p multi 2.60 1.25
2806 A695 97p multi 2.90 2.10
a. Souvenir sheet of 4, #2803-2806 8.50 8.25
b. Booklet pane of 4, #2803-2806 (BK194) 9.00 —
Nos. 2795-2806 (12) 25.80 17.85

Nos. 2795, 2796 and 2803 each sold for 41p on day of issue.

British Royalty and History Type of 2008

Designs: No. 2807, King James I of Great Britain (1603-25). No. 2808, King Charles I. No. 2809, King Charles II. No. 2810, King James II of Great Britain (1685-88). No. 2811, King William III. No. 2812, Queen Mary II. No. 2813, Queen Anne.

No. 2814: a, William Harvey, discoverer of blood circulation, 1628. b, Civil War Battle of Naseby, 1645. c, John Milton, author of Paradise Lost, 1667. d, Castle Howard, designed by John Vanbrugh.

2010, June 15 ***Perf. 14¼***

2807 A645 1st multi 1.50 .90
2808 A645 1st multi 1.50 .90
2809 A645 60p multi 1.75 1.35
2810 A645 60p multi 1.75 1.35
2811 A645 67p multi 2.00 1.50
2812 A645 67p multi 2.00 1.50
2813 A645 88p multi 2.60 2.00
Nos. 2807-2813 (7) 13.10 9.50

Souvenir Sheet

2814 Sheet of 4 8.75 8.75
a. A645 1st multi 1.50 .90
b. A645 60p multi 1.80 1.35
c. A645 88p multi 2.60 2.00
d. A645 97p multi 2.90 2.25

On day of issue, Nos. 2807, 2808 and 2814a each sold for 41p.

Sports of the 2012 Olympics and Paralympics Type of 2009-10

Olympics or Paralympics emblem and: Nos. 2815, 2825, Rowing (Paralympics). No. 2816, Shooting. Nos. 2817, Modern pentathlon. No. 2818, Taekwondo. No. 2819, Cycling. Nos. 2820, 2826, Table tennis (Paralympics). No. 2821, Field hockey. No. 2822, Soccer. No. 2823, Goalball (Paralympics). No. 2824, Boxing.

2010, July 27 **Litho.** ***Perf. 14½***

2815 A673 1st multi 1.30 .95
2816 A673 1st multi 1.30 .95
2817 A673 1st multi 1.30 .95
2818 A673 1st multi 1.30 .95
2819 A673 1st multi 1.30 .95
a. Horiz. strip of 5, #2815-2819 6.50 4.75
2820 A673 1st multi 1.30 .95
2821 A673 1st multi 1.30 .95
2822 A673 1st multi 1.30 .95
a. Booklet pane of 2, #2704, 2822 (BK200) 2.75 —
2823 A673 1st multi 1.30 .95
2824 A673 1st multi 1.30 .95
a. Horiz. strip of 5, #2820-2824 6.50 4.75
Nos. 2815-2824 (10) 13.00 9.50

Booklet Stamps
Self-Adhesive
Photo.
Die Cut Perf. 14½

2825	A673	1st multi (2826a)	3.50	1.00
2826	A673	1st multi (2826a)	3.50	1.00
a.		Booklet pane of 6, #2825, 2826, 4 #MH384	14.50	

Nos. 2815-2826 each sold for 41p on day of issue. See Nos. 2840-2841.
Issued: No. 2822a, 7/27/12.

Locomotives — A696

Designs: No. 2827, London Midland and Scottish Railway Coronation Class. No. 2828, British Rail Class 9F. No. 2829, Great Western Railway King Class. No. 2830, London North Eastern Railway Class A1. No. 2831, London Midland and Scottish Railway Northern Counties Committee Class WT. No. 2832, Southern Railway King Arthur Class.

2010, Aug. 19 Photo. *Perf. 14¼x14*

2827	A696	1st multi	1.30	.95
2828	A696	1st multi	1.30	.95
2829	A696	67p multi	2.00	1.50
2830	A696	67p multi	2.00	1.50
2831	A696	97p multi	2.90	2.25
2832	A696	97p multi	2.90	2.25
		Nos. 2827-2832 (6)	12.40	9.40

Nos. 2827-2828 each sold for 41p on day of issue.

British Design Type of 2009

Design: Supermarine Spitfire.

Die Cut Perf. 14½
2010, Sept. 15 Photo.
Booklet Stamp
Self-Adhesive

2833	A660	1st multi	4.25	1.00
a.		Booklet pane of 6, 2 #2833, 4 #MH384	16.00	

No. 2833 sold for 41p on day of issue.

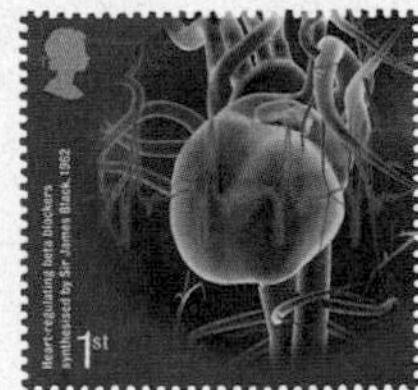

Medical Breakthroughs — A697

Designs: 1st, Heart-regulating beta blockers synthesized by Sir James Black, 1962. 58p, Antibiotic properties of penicillin discovered by Sir Alexander Fleming, 1928. 60p, Total hip replacement operation pioneered by Sir John Charnley, 1962. 67p, Artificial lens implant surgery pioneered by Sir Harold Ridley, 1949. 88p, Malaria parasite transmitted by mosquitoes proved by Sir Ronald Ross, 1897. 97p, Computed tomography scanner invented by Sir Godfrey Hounsfield, 1971.

Perf. 14¼x14½
2010, Sept. 16 Litho.

2834	A697	1st multi	1.30	.95
2835	A697	58p multi	1.75	1.30
2836	A697	60p multi	1.80	1.35
2837	A697	67p multi	2.00	1.50
2838	A697	88p multi	2.60	2.00
2839	A697	97p multi	2.90	2.25
		Nos. 2834-2839 (6)	12.35	9.35

No. 2834 sold for 41p on day of issue. See No. 2866.

Sports of the 2012 Olympics and Paralympics Type of 2009-10

Designs: No. 2840, Soccer. No. 2841, Cycling.

Die Cut Perf. 14½
2010, Oct. 12 Photo.
Booklet Stamps
Self-Adhesive

2840	A673	1st multi (2841a)	3.75	1.00
2841	A673	1st multi (2841a)	3.75	1.00
a.		Booklet pane of 6, #2840, 2841, 4 #MH384	15.00	

Nos. 2840-2841 each sold for 41p on day of issue.

Characters From Winnie-the-Pooh Stories by A. A. Milne — A698

Winnie-the-Pooh and: No. 2842, Christopher Robin. 58p, Piglet. No. 2844, Rabbit. 67p, Eeyore. No. 2846, Friends. No. 2847, Tigger.

No. 2848 — Winnie-the-Pooh and Christopher Robin with inscriptions: a, Wherever I am, there's always Pooh. b, There's always Pooh and Me, Whatever I do, he wants to do. c, "Where are you going to-day?" says Pooh: "Well, that's very odd 'cos I was too." d, "Let's go together," says Pooh, says he. "Let's go together," says Pooh.

2010, Oct. 12 Litho. *Perf. 14¼x14½*

2842	A698	1st multi	1.30	.95
2843	A698	58p multi	1.75	1.30
2844	A698	60p multi	1.80	1.35
2845	A698	67p multi	2.00	1.50
2846	A698	88p multi	2.60	2.00
2847	A698	97p multi	2.90	2.25
		Nos. 2842-2847 (6)	12.35	9.35

Souvenir Sheet
Perf. 14½

2848		Sheet of 4	8.75	8.25
a.		A698 1st multi	1.30	.95
b.		A698 60p multi	1.80	1.35
c.		A698 88p multi	2.60	2.00
d.		A698 97p multi	2.90	2.25

Europa (Nos. 2842, 2848a). Nos. 2842 and 2848a each sold for 41p on day of issue.

Christmas
A699 A700

Designs: 2nd, Wallace and Gromit singing Christmas carols. 1st, Gromit mailing Christmas cards. 2nd Large, Wallace and Gromit singing Christmas carols, Christmas tree at left. 60p, Wallace and Gromit decorating Christmas tree. 1st Large, Gromit mailing Christmas cards, Feathers McGraw at left. 97p, Gromit carrying Christmas pudding. £1.46, Gromit wearing large sweater.

Perf. 14¾x14 Syncopated
2010, Nov. 2 Photo.

2849		Sheet of 7	15.00	11.00
a.		A699 2nd multi	1.00	.75
b.		A699 1st multi	1.30	.95
c.		A700 2nd Large multi	1.60	1.15
d.		A699 60p multi	1.80	1.35
e.		A700 1st Large multi	2.00	1.50
f.		A699 97p multi	2.90	2.25
g.		A699 £1.46 multi	4.75	2.40

Self-Adhesive
Die Cut Perf. 14¾x14 Syncopated

2850	A699	2nd multi	1.00	.75
a.		Booklet pane of 12	20.00	
b.		Litho., serpentine die cut 14¾x14 syncopated, + label (2855b)	1.00	1.00
c.		Sheet of 20 #2850b	20.00	—
2851	A699	1st multi	1.30	.95
a.		Booklet pane of 12	15.50	
b.		Litho., serpentine die cut 14¾x14 syncopated, + label (2855b)	2.00	1.40
c.		Sheet of 20 #2851b	42.50	—
2852	A700	2nd Large multi	1.60	1.15
2853	A699	60p multi	1.80	1.35
a.		Litho., serpentine die cut 14¾x14 syncopated, + label (2855b)	1.80	1.80
b.		Sheet of 10 #2853a	30.00	—
2854	A700	1st Large multi	2.00	1.50
2855	A699	97p multi	2.90	2.25
a.		Litho., serpentine die cut 14¾x14 syncopated, + label (2855b)	2.90	2.90
b.		Sheet of 20, 8 each #2850b, 2851b, 2 each #2853a, 2855a, + 20 labels	30.00	—
c.		Sheet of 10 #2855a	45.00	—
2856	A699	£1.46 multi	4.50	3.25
		Nos. 2850-2856 (7)	15.10	11.20

On day of issue, Nos. 2849a and 2850 each sold for 32p, Nos. 2849b and 2851 each sold for 41p, Nos. 2849c and 2852 each sold for 51p, and Nos. 2849e and 2854 each sold for 66p. No. 2855b sold for £9.30 and contained 20 labels that could not be personalized.

Nos. 2850c, 2851c, 2853b and 2855c had labels that could be personalized. Nos. 2850a and 2853b each sold for £9.95; No. 2851c sold for £13.95; No. 2855c sold for £14.50. Sheets of 10 No. 2850b were also sold but these were halves of No. 2850c torn along the sheet's central row of rouletting. Nos. 2853b and 2855c have rouletting along the left or right side of the sheet, but these stamps were not sold in sheets of 20.

Television Shows Created By Gerry Anderson A701

Designs: No. 2857, Joe 90. No. 2858, Captain Scarlet. Nos. 2859, 2864, Thunderbirds. No. 2860, Stingray. No. 2861, Fireball XL5. No. 2862, Supercar.

No. 2863 — Opening sequence of show depicting Thunderbird: a, "4." b, "3." c, "2." d, "1."

2011, Jan. 11 Litho. *Perf. 14¼*

2857	A701	1st multi	1.30	.95
2858	A701	1st multi	1.30	.95
2859	A701	1st multi	1.30	.95
a.		Horiz. strip of 3, #2857-2859	4.00	2.90
2860	A701	97p multi	2.90	2.25
2861	A701	97p multi	2.90	2.25
2862	A701	97p multi	2.90	2.25
a.		Horiz. strip of 3, #2860-2862	8.75	6.75
		Nos. 2857-2862 (6)	13.95	6.90

Souvenir Sheet
Litho. With Three-Dimensional Plastic Affixed

2863		Sheet of 4	8.75	8.75
a.		A701 41p multi	1.30	1.30
b.		A701 60p multi	1.80	1.80
c.		A701 88p multi	2.00	2.00
d.		A701 97p multi	2.90	2.90

Booklet Stamp
Self-Adhesive
Die Cut Perf. 14¼x14

2864	A701	1st multi	4.00	1.00
a.		Booklet pane of 6, 2 #2864, 4 #MH384	15.50	

On day of issue, Nos. 2857-2859, 2864 each sold for 41p.

Miniature Sheet

Locomotives — A702

No. 2865: a, British Railways Dean Goods No. 2532. b, Peckett R2 Thor. c, Lancashire & Yorkshire Railway 1093 No. 1100. d, British Railways WD No. 90662.

2011, Feb. 1 Litho. *Perf. 14¼*

2865	A702	Sheet of 4	8.75	8.25
a.		1st multi	1.30	1.00
b.		60p multi	1.80	1.75
c.		88p multi	2.00	1.50
d.		97p multi	2.90	2.75
e.		Booklet pane of 4, 2 each #2865a, 2865d (BK204)	6.25	

No. 2865a sold for 41p on day of issue. Issued: No. 2865e, 2/20/14. See No. 2930.

Medical Breakthroughs Type of 2010

Design: Heart-regulating beta blockers, synthesized by Sir James Black, 1962.

Die Cut Perf. 14¼x14½
2011, Feb. 24 Photo.
Booklet Stamp
Self-Adhesive

2866	A697	1st multi	4.00	1.00
a.		Booklet pane of 6, 2 #2866, 4 #MH384	15.60	

No. 2866 sold for 41p on day of issue.

Musicals — A703

Designs: No. 2867, Oliver! No. 2868, Blood Brothers. No. 2869, We Will Rock You. No. 2870, Monty Python's Spamalot. No. 2871, Rocky Horror Show. No. 2872, Me and My Girl. No. 2873, Return to the Forbidden Planet. No. 2874, Billy Elliot.

2011, Feb. 24 Litho. *Perf. 14¼*

2867	A703	1st multi	1.30	.95
2868	A703	1st multi	1.30	.95
2869	A703	1st multi	1.30	.95
2870	A703	1st multi	1.30	.95
2871	A703	97p multi	2.90	2.25
2872	A703	97p multi	2.90	2.25
2873	A703	97p multi	2.90	2.25
2874	A703	97p multi	2.90	2.25
		Nos. 2867-2874 (8)	16.80	12.80

On day of issue, Nos. 2867-2870 each sold for 41p.

Fictional Wizards and Magicians A704

Designs: No. 2875, Rincewind, from Discworld, by Terry Pratchett. No. 2876, Nanny Ogg, from Discworld. No. 2877, Dumbledore, from Harry Potter stories, by J.K. Rowling. No. 2878, Lord Voldemort, from Harry Potter stories. No. 2879, Merlin, from Arthurian legend. No. 2880, Morgan Le Fay, from Arthurian legend. No. 2881, Aslan, from Narnia, by C. S. Lewis. No. 2882, The White Witch, from Narnia.

2011, Mar. 8 Photo. *Perf. 14½*

2875	A704	1st multi	1.30	.95
2876	A704	1st multi	1.30	.95
a.		Vert. pair, #2875-2876	2.60	1.90
2877	A704	1st multi	1.30	.95
2878	A704	1st multi	1.30	.95
a.		Vert. pair, #2877-2878	2.60	1.90
2879	A704	60p multi	1.80	1.35
2880	A704	60p multi	1.80	1.35
a.		Vert. pair, #2879-2880	2.75	2.75
2881	A704	97p multi	2.90	2.25
2882	A704	97p multi	2.90	2.25
a.		Vert. pair, #2881-2882	6.00	4.50
		Nos. 2875-2882 (8)	14.60	11.00

On day of issue, Nos. 2875-2878 each sold for 41p.

A705

Worldwide Fund for Nature (WWF), 50th Anniv. — A706

Designs: No. 2883, African elephant. No. 2884, Mountain gorilla. No. 2885, Siberian tiger. No. 2886, Polar bear. No. 2887, Amur leopard. No. 2888, Iberian lynx. No. 2889, Red panda. No. 2890. Black rhinoceros. No. 2891, African wild dog. No. 2892, Golden lion tamarin.

No. 2893, a, Spider monkey. b, Hyacinth macaw. c, Poison dart frog. d, Jaguar.

2011, Mar. 22 Litho. *Perf. 14½*

2883 A705 1st multi 1.30 .95
2884 A705 1st multi 1.30 .95
2885 A705 1st multi 1.30 .95
2886 A705 1st multi 1.30 .95
2887 A705 1st multi 1.30 .95
a. Horiz. strip of 5, #2883-2887 6.50 4.75
2888 A705 1st multi 1.30 .95
2889 A705 1st multi 1.30 .95
2890 A705 1st multi 1.30 .95
a. Booklet pane of 6, #2885-2890 (BK195) 8.00 —
2891 A705 1st multi 1.30 .95
2892 A705 1st multi 1.30 .95
a. Horiz. strip of 5, #2888-2892 6.50 4.75
b. Booklet pane of 4, #2883-2884, 2891-2892 (BK195) 5.25 —
Nos. 2883-2892 (10) 13.00 9.50

Perf. 14¼

2893 A706 Sheet of 4 8.75 8.25
a. 1st multi 1.30 .95
b. 60p multi 1.80 1.35
c. 88p multi 2.00 1.50
d. 97p multi 2.90 2.25
e. Booklet pane of 4, #2893a-2893d (BK195) 8.75 —

Europa (nos. 2893a, 2893e). On day of issue, Nos. 2883-2892 and 2893a each sold for 41p. No. 2893e is 150x96mm, and has additional printing in booklet pane margin beyond that shown in illustration A706.

A707

Royal Shakespeare Company, Stratford-on-Avon, 50th Anniv. — A708

Line from play by William Shakespeare and: No. 2894, David Tennant in *Hamlet.* 66p, Anthony Sher in *The Tempest.* No. 2896, Chuk Iwuji in *Henry VI.* No. 2897, Paul Schofield in *King Lear.* No. 2898, Sarah Kestelman in *A Midsummer Night's Dream.* £1.10, Ian McKellen and Francesca Annis in *Romeo and Juliet.*

No. 2900: a, Janet Suzman in *Hamlet* at Royal Shakespeare Theater. b, Patrick Stewart in *Antony and Cleopatra* at Swan Theater. c, Geoffrey Streatfeild in *Henry V* at the Courtyard Theater. d, Dame Judi Dench in *Macbeth* at the Other Place.

2011, Apr. 12 Photo. *Perf. 14½*

2894 A707 1st red & black 1.50 1.05
2895 A707 66p black & red 2.00 1.50
2896 A707 68p red & black 2.00 1.50
2897 A707 76p black & red 2.25 1.75
2898 A707 £1 red & black 3.00 2.25
2899 A707 £1.10 black & red 3.25 2.50
Nos. 2894-2899 (6) 14.00 10.55

Litho.

Perf. 14¼

2900 A708 Sheet of 4 8.75 8.50
a. 1st multi 1.50 1.05
b. 68p multi 2.00 1.50
c. 76p multi 2.25 1.75
d. £1 multi 3.00 2.25

On day of issue, Nos. 2894 and 2900 sold for 46p.

Souvenir Sheet

Wedding of Prince William and Catherine Middleton — A709

Perf. 14½x14¼

2011, Apr. 21 Photo.

2901 A709 Sheet of 4, 2 each #a-b 9.50 9.50
a. 1st Couple 1.50 1.00
b. £1.10 Couple, diff. 3.25 2.50

No. 2901a sold for 46p on day of issue.

William Morris & Company, 150th Anniv. A710

Designs: No. 2902, Floral fabric design, by William Morris, 1884. No. 2903, Cherry tree wall panel design, by Philip Webb, 1867. No. 2904, Floral wallpaper design, by John Henry Dearle, 1901. No. 2905, Floral ceramic tile design, by Kate Faulkner. No. 2906, Floral glazed tile design, by Morris and William De Morgan, 1876. No. 2907, The Merchant's Daughter, stained-glass by Edward Burne-Jones, c. 1864.

2011, May 5 Litho. *Perf. 14¼*

2902 A710 1st multi 1.50 1.00
2903 A710 1st multi 1.50 1.00
2904 A710 76p multi 2.25 1.75
2905 A710 76p multi 2.25 1.75
2906 A710 £1.10 multi 3.25 2.50
a. Booklet pane of 4, #2902, 2904, 2905, 2906 (BK196) 9.25 —
2907 A710 £1.10 multi 3.25 2.50
a. Booklet pane of 4, 2 each #2903, 2907 (BK196) 9.50 —
Nos. 2902-2907 (6) 14.00 10.50

No. 2902 sold for 46p on day of issue.

A711

Thomas the Tank Engine Children's Book Characters, by Rev. Wilbert Awdry (1911-97) — A712

Designs: No. 2908, Thomas. 66p, James. No. 2910, Percy. No. 2911, Daisy. No. 2912, Toby. £1.10, Gordon.

No. 2914 — Inscriptions: a, "Goodbye, Bertie," called Thomas. b, James was more dirty than hurt. c, "Yes, Sir," Percy shivered miserably. d, They told Henry, "We shall leave you there for always."

No. 2915, Like No. 2914a.

2011, June 14 *Perf. 14¾x14¼*

2908 A711 1st multi 1.50 1.00
2909 A711 66p multi 2.00 1.50
2910 A711 68p multi 2.00 1.50
2911 A711 76p multi 2.25 1.75
2912 A711 £1 multi 3.00 2.25
2913 A711 £1.10 multi 3.25 2.50
Nos. 2908-2913 (6) 14.00 10.50

Perf. 14¼

2914 A712 Sheet of 4 8.75 8.25
a. 1st multi 1.40 1.00
b. 68p multi 2.00 1.50
c. 76p multi 2.25 1.75
d. £1 multi 3.00 2.25

Booklet Stamp Self-Adhesive

Photo.

Die Cut Perf. 14¼

2915 A712 1st multi 3.00 1.25
a. Booklet pane of 6, 2 #2915, 4 #MH384 13.50

On day of issue, Nos. 2908, 2914a and 2915 each sold for 46p.

Sports of the 2012 Summer Olympics and Paralympics Type of 2009-10

Olympics or Paralympics emblem and: Nos. 2916, 2927, Sailing (Paralympics). No. 2917, High jump. No. 2918, Volleyball. Nos. 2919, 2926, Wheelchair rugby (Paralympics). No. 2920, Wrestling. No. 2921, Wheelchair tennis (Paralympics). Nos. 2922, 2929, Fencing. Nos. 2923, 2928, Gymnastics. No. 2924, Triathlon. No. 2925, Handball.

2011 Litho. *Perf. 14½*

2916 A673 1st multi 1.50 1.00
2917 A673 1st multi 1.50 1.00
a. Booklet pane of 2, #2705, 2917 (BK200) 3.00 —
2918 A673 1st multi 1.50 1.00
2919 A673 1st multi 1.50 1.00
2920 A673 1st multi 1.50 1.00
a. Horiz. strip of 5, #2916-2920 7.50 5.00
2921 A673 1st multi 1.50 1.00
2922 A673 1st multi 1.50 1.00
2923 A673 1st multi 1.50 1.00
2924 A673 1st multi 1.50 1.00
2925 A673 1st multi 1.50 1.00
a. Horiz. strip of 5, #2921-2925 7.50 5.00
b. Sheet of 30, #2702-2711, 2815-2824, 2916-2925 42.50 —
Nos. 2916-2925 (10) 15.00 10.00

Booklet Stamps Self-Adhesive

Photo.

Die Cut Perf. 14½

2926 A673 1st multi 3.75 1.00
2927 A673 1st multi 3.75 1.00
a. Booklet pane of 6, #2926-2927, 4 #MH384 15.50
2928 A673 1st multi 3.75 1.00
2929 A673 1st multi 3.75 1.00
a. Booklet pane of 6, #2928-2929, + 4 #MH384 15.50

Issued: Nos. 2916-2927, 7/27. Nos. 2928-2929, 9/15. No. 2917a, 7/27/12. No. 2925b, 7/27. Nos. 2916-2929 each sold for 46p on day of issue. No. 2925b sold for £13.80.

Locomotives Type of 2011

Design: British Railways Dean Goods No. 2532.

Die Cut Perf. 14¼

2011, Aug. 23 Photo.

Booklet Stamp Self-Adhesive

2930 A702 1st multi 3.75 1.00
a. Booklet pane of 6, 2 #2930, 4 #MH384 15.50

No. 2930 sold for 46p on day of issue.

British Crown Jewels A713

Designs: No. 2931, Sovereign's scepter with cross. No. 2932, St. Edward's crown. No. 2933, Rod and scepter with doves. No. 2934, Queen Mary's crown. No. 2935, Sovereign's orb. No. 2936, Jeweled sword of offering. No. 2937, Imperial state crown. No. 2938, Coronation spoon.

Perf. 14¼x14½

2011, Aug. 23 Litho.

2931 A713 1st multi 1.50 1.00
2932 A713 1st multi 1.50 1.00
2933 A713 68p multi 2.00 1.50
2934 A713 68p multi 2.00 1.50
2935 A713 76p multi 2.25 1.75
2936 A713 76p multi 2.25 1.75
2937 A713 £1.10 multi 3.25 2.50
2938 A713 £1.10 multi 3.25 2.50
Nos. 2931-2938 (8) 18.00 13.50

On day of issue Nos. 2931-2932 each sold for 46p.

Miniature Sheet

First Air Mail Flight in Great Britain, Cent. — A714

No. 2939: a, Pilot Gustav Hamel receives first mail bag. b, Hamel in plane ready to leave Hendon Aerodrome. c, Clement Greswell near his Blériot airplane at Windsor Castle. d, Air mail delivered at Windsor Castle.

2011, Sept. 9 Litho. *Perf. 14¼x14*

2939 A714 Sheet of 4 9.75 9.75
a. 1st multi 1.50 1.00
b. 68p multi 2.00 1.50
c. £1 multi 3.00 2.25
d. £1.10 multi 3.25 2.50
e. Booklet pane of 3, #2939c, 2 #2939b (BK197) 12.00 —
f. Booklet pane of 3, #2939d, 2 #2939a (BK197) 12.75 —

No. 2939a sold for 46p on day of issue.

British Royalty and History Type of 2008

Designs: No. 2940, King George I. No. 2941, King George II. No. 2942, King George III. No. 2943, King George IV. No. 2944, King William IV. No. 2945, Queen Victoria.

No. 2946: a, Robert Walpole, first Prime Minister. b, Interior of Kedleston Hall, designed by architect Robert Adam. c, Great Britain #1. d, Queen Victoria in 1897.

2011, Sept. 15 *Perf. 14¼*

2940 A645 1st multi 1.50 1.00
2941 A645 1st multi 1.50 1.00
2942 A645 76p multi 2.25 1.75
2943 A645 76p multi 2.25 1.75
2944 A645 £1.10 multi 3.25 2.50
2945 A645 £1.10 multi 3.25 2.50
Nos. 2940-2945 (6) 14.00 10.50
2946 Sheet of 4 8.75 8.50
a. A645 1st multi 1.50 1.00
b. A645 68p multi 2.00 1.50
c. A645 76p multi 2.25 1.75
d. A645 £1 multi 3.00 3.25

On day of issue, Nos. 2940, 2941 and 2946a each sold for 46p.

Great Britain Landmarks in Alphabetical Order — A715

Designs: No. 2947, Angel of the North sculpture, Gateshead. No. 2948, Blackpool Tower. No. 2949, Carrick-a-Rede rope bridge, near Ballintoy, Northern Ireland. No. 2950, 10 Downing Street (Prime Minister's residence, London). No. 2951, Edinburgh Castle. No. 2952, Forth Railway Bridge. No. 2953, Glastonbury Tor. No. 2954, Harlech Castle. No. 2955, Ironbridge. No. 2956, Jodrell Bank radio telescope. No. 2957, Kursaal, Southend. No. 2958, Lindisfarne Priory, Lindisfarne Island. No. 2959, Manchester Town Hall. No. 2960, Narrow Water Castle, near Warrenpoint, Northern Ireland. No. 2961, Old Bailey Courthouse, London. No. 2962, Portmeirion, Wales. No. 2963, Queen's College, Oxford University. No. 2964, Roman Baths, Bath. No. 2965, Stirling Castle, Stirling, Scotland. No. 2966, Tyne Bridge, Newcastle. No. 2967, Urquhart Castle, near Drumnadrochit, Scotland. No. 2968, Victoria and Albert Museum, London. No. 2969, White Cliffs of Dover. No. 2970, Station X, Bletchley Park. No. 2971, York Minster. No. 2972, ZSL London Zoo.

2011 *Perf. 14½*

2947 A715 1st multi 1.50 1.00
2948 A715 1st multi 1.50 1.00
2949 A715 1st multi 1.50 1.00
2950 A715 1st multi 1.50 1.00
2951 A715 1st multi 1.50 1.00
2952 A715 1st multi 1.50 1.00
a. Horiz. strip of 6, #2947-2952 9.00 6.25

2953 A715 1st multi 1.50 1.00
2954 A715 1st multi 1.50 1.00
2955 A715 1st multi 1.50 1.00
2956 A715 1st multi 1.50 1.00
2957 A715 1st multi 1.50 1.00
2958 A715 1st multi 1.50 1.00
a. Horiz. strip of 6, #2953-2958 9.00 6.25
Nos. 2947-2958 (12) 18.00 12.00
2959 A715 1st multi 1.50 1.00
2960 A715 1st multi 1.50 1.00
2961 A715 1st multi 1.50 1.00
2962 A715 1st multi 1.50 1.00
2963 A715 1st multi 1.50 1.00
2964 A715 1st multi 1.50 1.00
a. Horiz. strip of 6, #2959-2964 9.00 6.25
2965 A715 1st multi 1.50 1.00
2966 A715 1st multi 1.50 1.00
2967 A715 1st multi 1.50 1.00
2968 A715 1st multi 1.50 1.00
2969 A715 1st multi 1.50 1.00
2970 A715 1st multi 1.50 1.00
a. Horiz. strip of 6, #2965-2970 9.00 6.25
2971 A715 1st multi 1.50 1.00
2972 A715 1st multi 1.50 1.00
a. Horiz. pair, #2971-2972 3.00 2.00
b. Sheet of 26, #2947-2972, + 4 labels 90.00 90.00
Nos. 2959-2972 (14) 21.00 14.00
Nos. 2947-2972 (26) 39.00 26.00

Europa (No. 2968).

Issued: Nos. 2947-2958, 10/13. Nos. 2959-2972, 4/10/12. On day of issue, Nos. 2947-2972 each sold for 46p.

A716

A717

Designs: Nos. 2973a, 2973c, 2974, 2976, Angel visiting Joseph. Nos. 2973b, 2975, Madonna and Child, Nos. 2973e, 2978, Madonna and Child, livestock, dove. 68p, Baby Jesus in manger, livestock. £1.10, Angel visiting shepherds. £1.65, Magi and Star of Bethlehem.

Perf. 14¾x14 Syncopated

2011, Nov. 8 **Photo.**

2973 Sheet of 7 17.00 12.50
a. A716 2nd multi 1.20 .80
b. A716 1st multi 1.50 1.00
c. A717 2nd Large multi 1.75 1.30
d. A716 68p multi 2.00 1.50
e. A717 1st Large multi 2.25 1.75
f. A716 £1.10 multi 3.25 2.50
g. A716 £1.65 multi 5.00 3.75

Self-Adhesive
Die Cut Perf. 14¾x14 Syncopated

2974 A716 2nd multi 1.20 .80
a. Booklet pane of 12 14.50
b. Sheet of 20 #2974 + 20 labels, litho. 33.00
2975 A716 1st multi 1.50 1.00
a. Booklet pane of 12 18.00
b. Sheet of 10 #2975 + 10 labels, litho. 25.00
2976 A717 2nd Large multi 1.75 1.30
2977 A716 68p multi 2.00 1.50
a. Sheet of 10 #2977 + 10 labels, litho. 34.00
2978 A717 1st Large multi 2.25 1.75
2979 A716 £1.10 multi 3.25 2.50
a. Sheet of 20, 8 each #2974-2975, 2 each #2977, 2979, + 20 labels, litho. 32.50
b. Sheet of 10 #2979 + 10 labels, litho. 47.50
2980 A716 £1.65 multi 5.00 3.75
Nos. 2974-2980 (7) 16.95 12.60

On day of issue, Nos. 2973a and 2974 each sold for 36p; Nos. 2973b and 2975 for 46p; Nos. 2973c and 2976 for 58p; Nos. 2973e and 2978 for 75p. No. 2979a sold for £10.45. Labels on No. 2979a could not be personalized.

Nos. 2974b, 2975b, 2977a and 2979b had labels that could be personalized. No. 2974b sold for £10.95; No. 2975b, for £8.30; No. 2977a, for £10.75; and No. 2979b, for £15.80. No. 2975b was half of a larger sheet of 20 stamps and 20 labels that sold for £14.95, which was torn along central row of rouletting. Nos. 2977a and 2979b have rouletting along the left or right side of the sheet, but these stamps were not sold in sheets of 20.

Emblem of 2012 Summer Olympics
A718

Emblem of 2012 Paralympics
A719

Die Cut Perf. 14¾x14 Syncopated

2012, Jan. 5 **Photo.**

Self-Adhesive

2981 A718 1st gray, org & blk 1.50 1.00
2982 A719 1st gray, org & blk 1.50 1.00
a. Booklet pane of 6, 3 each #2981-2982, #2981 at UL 12.00
b. As "a," #2982 at UL 12.00 12.00

Nos. 2981 and 2982 each sold for 46p on day of issue.

See Nos. 3044-3045, C6-C9.

Illustratrions From Children's Books by Roald Dahl (1916-90) — A720

Designs: 1st, Charlie and the Chocolate Factory. 66p, Fantastic Mr. Fox. 68p, James and the Giant Peach. 76p, Matilda. £1, The Twits. £1.10, The Witches.

No. 2989 — Scenes from The BFG (Big Friendly Giant): a, Giant holding Sophie in hand. b, Big Friendly Giant and Sophie awakening other Giants. c, Sophie on Queen's window sill. d, Giant and Sophie at desk.

2012, Jan. 10 **Litho.** ***Perf. 14¼***

2983 A720 1st multi 1.50 1.00
2984 A720 66p multi 2.00 1.50
2985 A720 68p multi 2.00 1.50
2986 A720 76p multi 2.25 1.75
a. Booklet pane of 3, #2983, 2985, 2986 (BK198) 5.75 —
2987 A720 £1 multi 3.00 2.25
2988 A720 £1.10 multi 3.25 2.40
a. Booklet pane of 3, #2984, 2987, 2988 (BK198) 8.25 —
Nos. 2983-2988 (6) 14.00 10.40

Souvenir Sheet
Perf. 14¼x14½

2989 Sheet of 4 8.75 8.50
a. A720 1st multi 1.50 1.00
b. A720 68p multi 2.00 1.50
c. A720 76p multi 2.25 1.75
d. A720 £1 multi 3.00 2.25
e. Booklet pane of 4, #2989a-2989d (BK198) 8.75 —

On day of issue, Nos. 2983 and 2989a sold for 46p. No. 2989 contains four 36x35mm stamps.

British Royalty and History Type of 2008

Designs: No. 2990, King Edward VII. No. 2991, King George V. No. 2992, King Edward VIII. No. 2993, King George VI. £1.10, Queen Elizabeth II.

No. 2995: a, 1912 Scott Expedition to the South Pole. b, King George VI and Queen Mary talking with man amidst World War II damage. c, Victory of 1966 English World Cup soccer team. d, Opening of Channel Tunnel, 1994.

2012, Feb. 2 **Litho.** ***Perf. 14¼***

2990 A645 1st multi 1.50 1.00
2991 A645 68p multi 2.00 1.50
2992 A645 76p multi 2.25 1.75
2993 A645 £1 multi 3.00 2.25
2994 A645 £1.10 multi 3.25 2.50
Nos. 2990-2994 (5) 12.00 9.00

Souvenir Sheet

2995 Sheet of 4 8.75 8.75
a. A645 1st multi 1.50 1.00
b. A645 68p multi 2.00 1.50
c. A645 76p multi 2.25 1.75
d. A645 £1 multi 3.00 2.25

On day of issue, Nos. 2990 and 2995a each sold for 46p.

Miniature Sheet

Reign of Queen Elizabeth II, 60th Anniv. — A721

No. 2996 — Image of Queen Elizabeth II: a, Great Britain Type A131 redrawn. b, From 1960 one-pound banknote ("ND" at upper left). c, From 1971 five-pound banknote. d, From coin, without tiara. e, From coin, with tiara. f, Great Britain Type MH2 with iridescent overprint of "Diamond Jubilee" in wavy lines.

Perf. 14¾x14 Syncopated

2012, Feb. 6 **Photo.**

2996 A721 Sheet of 6 9.00 6.50
a.-f. 1st Any single 1.50 1.00
2996G A721 1st As #2996a, litho. (2996Gh) 3.75 2.00
h. Booklet pane of 8, 4 each #2996G, MH419, + central label (BK199) 30.00 —

Nos. 2996a-2996f each sold for 46p on day of issue.

Issued: No. 2996G, 2996Gh, 5/31. No. 2996G sold for 60p on day of issue.

Britons of Distinction
A722

Designs: No. 2997, New Coventry Cathedral, designed by Sir Basil Spence (1907-76). No. 2998, Frederick Delius (1862-1934), composer. No. 2999, Orange Tree embroidery by Mary "May" Morris (1862-1938), designer and textile artist. No. 3000, Odette Hallowes (1912-95), Special Operations Executive agent in World War II. No. 3001, Atmospheric steam engine invented by Thomas Newcomen (1664-1729). No. 3002, Kathleen Ferrier (1912-53), opera singer. No. 3003, Interior of Palace of Westminster, designed by Augustus Pugin (1812-53). No. 3004, Montague Rhodes James (1862-1936), medieval scholar and writer of ghost stories. No. 3005, Bombe code-breaking machine designed by Alan Turing (1912-54), mathematician and cryptanalyst. No. 3006, Joan Mary Fry (1862-1955), relief worker and social reformer.

2012, Feb. 23 **Litho.** ***Perf. 14½***

2997 A722 1st multi 1.50 1.00
2998 A722 1st multi 1.50 1.00
2999 A722 1st multi 1.50 1.00
3000 A722 1st multi 1.50 1.00
3001 A722 1st multi 1.50 1.00
a. Horiz. strip of 5, #2997-3001 7.50 5.00
3002 A722 1st multi 1.50 1.00
3003 A722 1st multi 1.50 1.00
3004 A722 1st multi 1.50 1.00
3005 A722 1st multi 1.50 1.00
3006 A722 1st multi 1.50 1.00
a. Horiz. strip of 5, #3002-3006 7.50 5.00
Nos. 2997-3006 (10) 15.00 10.00

Nos. 2997-3006 each sold for 46p on day of issue.

Miniature Sheet

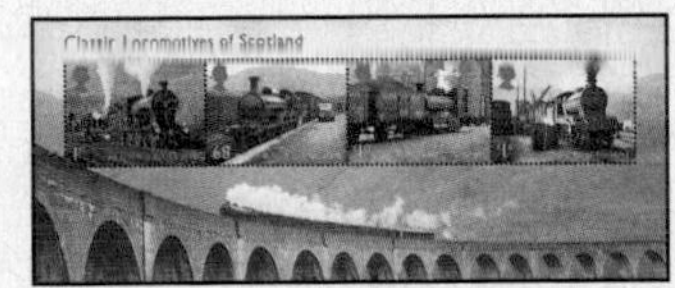

Scottish Locomotives — A723

No. 3007: a, British Railways D34 Nos. 62471 and 62496. b, British Railways D40 No. 62276. c, Andrew Barclay No. 807. d, British Railways 4P No. 54767.

2012, Mar. 8 ***Perf. 14¼***

3007 A723 Sheet of 4 9.75 7.50
a. 1st multi 1.50 1.00
b. 68p multi 2.00 1.50
c. £1 multi 3.00 2.25
d. £1.10 multi 3.25 2.50
e. Booklet pane of 4, 2 each #3007a, 3007b (BK204) 7.25 —

No. 3007a sold for 46p on day of issue.

Issued: No. 3007e, 2/20/14. See No. 3111.

Comic Book Covers and Characters
A724

Designs: No. 3008, The Dandy. No. 3009, The Beano. No. 3010, Eagle. No. 3011, The Topper. No. 3012, Tiger. No. 3013, Bunty. No. 3014, Buster. No. 3015, Valiant. No. 3016, Twinkle. No. 3017, 2000 A.D.

2012, Mar. 20 ***Perf. 14½***

3008 A724 1st multi 1.50 1.00
3009 A724 1st multi 1.50 1.00
3010 A724 1st multi 1.50 1.00
3011 A724 1st multi 1.50 1.00
3012 A724 1st multi 1.50 1.00
a. Horiz. strip of 5, #3008-3012 7.50 5.00
3013 A724 1st multi 1.50 1.00
3014 A724 1st multi 1.50 1.00
3015 A724 1st multi 1.50 1.00
3016 A724 1st multi 1.50 1.00
3017 A724 1st multi 1.50 1.00
a. Horiz. strip of 5, #3013-3017 7.50 5.00
Nos. 3008-3017 (10) 15.00 10.00

Nos. 3008-3017 each sold for 46p on day of issue.

Fashion
A725

Clothing designed by: No. 3018, Hardy Amies. No. 3019, Norman Hartnell. No. 3020, Granny Takes a Trip. No. 3021, Ossie Clark. No. 3022, Tommy Nutter. No. 3023, Jean Muir. No. 3024, Zandra Rhodes. No. 3025, Vivienne Westwood. No. 3025, Paul Smith. No. 3026, Alexander McQueen.

2012, May 15 **Litho.** ***Perf. 14½***

3018 A725 1st multi 1.90 1.35
3019 A725 1st multi 1.90 1.35
3020 A725 1st multi 1.90 1.35
3021 A725 1st multi 1.90 1.35
3022 A725 1st multi 1.90 1.35
a. Horiz. strip of 5, #3018-3022 9.50 6.75
3023 A725 1st multi 1.90 1.35
3024 A725 1st multi 1.90 1.35
3025 A725 1st multi 1.90 1.35
3026 A725 1st multi 1.90 1.35
3027 A725 1st multi 1.90 1.35
a. Horiz. strip of 5, #3023-3027 9.50 6.75
Nos. 3018-3027 (10) 19.00 13.50

Nos. 3018-3027 each sold for 60p on day of issue.

Reign of Queen Elizabeth II, 60th Anniv.
A726

Photographs of Queen Elizabeth II at: Nos. 3028, 3036, Golden Jubilee, 2002. No. 3029, Trooping the Color, 1967. No. 3030, The Royal Welsh, 2007. No. 3031, First Christmas TV Broadcast, 1957. No. 3032, Silver Jubilee Walkabout, 1977. No. 3033, Garter Ceremony, 1997. No. 3034, United Nations Address, 1957. No. 3035, Commonwealth Games, 1982.

Perf. 14¼x14½

2012, May 31 **Photo.**

3028 A726 1st multi 1.90 1.35
a. Litho. (3034b) 2.10 2.10

3029 A726 1st black 1.90 1.35
a. Litho. (3030b) 2.10 2.10
b. Horiz. pair, #3028-3029 4.00 2.75
3030 A726 77p multi 2.40 1.75
a. Litho. (3030b) 2.60 2.60
b. Booklet pane of 2, #3029a, 3030a (BK199) 4.75 —
3031 A726 77p black 2.40 1.75
a. Litho. (3035c) 2.60 2.60
b. Horiz. pair, #3030-3031 5.00 3.50
3032 A726 87p black 2.60 2.00
a. Litho. (3034b) 2.60 2.60
3033 A726 87p multi 2.60 2.00
a. Litho. (3034b) 2.60 2.60
b. Horiz. pair, #3032-3033 5.25 4.00
3034 A726 £1.28 black 4.00 2.90
a. Litho. (3034b) 4.50 4.50
b. Booklet pane of 4, #3028a, 3032a, 3033a, 3034a (BK199) 12.00 —
3035 A726 £1.28 multi 4.00 2.90
a. Litho. (3035c) 4.50 4.50
b. Horiz. pair, #3034-3035 8.00 6.00
c. Booklet pane of 2, #3031a, 3035a (BK199) 7.25 —
Nos. 3028-3035 (8) 21.80 16.00

Booklet Stamp
Self-Adhesive

Die Cut Perf. 14¾x14½

3036 A726 1st multi 4.50 1.35
a. Booklet pane of 6, 2 #3036, 4 #MH414 17.50

On day of issue, Nos. 3028, 3029 and 3036 each sold for 60p.

A727

Characters and Scenes From Novels by Charles Dickens (1812-70) — A728

Designs: 2nd, Mr. Bumble from *Oliver Twist.* No. 3038, Mr. Pickwick from *The Pickwick Papers.* 77p, The Marchioness from *The Old Curiosity Shop.* 87p, Mrs. Gamp from *Martin Chuzzlewit.* £1.28, Captain Cuttle from *Dombey and Son.* £1.90, Mr. Micawber from *David Copperfield.*

No. 3043 — Scenes from: a, *Nicholas Nickleby.* b, *Bleak House.* c, *Little Dorrit.* d, *A Tale of Two Cities.*

2012, June 19 Litho. *Perf. 14¼*

3037 A727 2nd multi 1.60 1.15
3038 A727 1st multi 1.90 1.35
3039 A727 77p multi 2.25 1.75
3040 A727 87p multi 2.60 2.00
3041 A727 £1.28 multi 4.00 2.90
3042 A727 £1.90 multi 5.75 4.25
Nos. 3037-3042 (6) 18.10 13.40

Miniature Sheet

3043 Sheet of 4 7.25 7.25
a.-d. A728 1st Any single 1.90 .95

On day of issue No. 3037 sold for 50p, and Nos. 3038, 3043a-3043d each sold for 60p.

Olympics and Paralympics Emblems Type of 2012

Perf. 14¾x14 Syncopated

2012, July 27 Litho.

Booklet Stamps

3044 A718 1st gray, org & blk (C9a) 5.25 5.25
3045 A719 1st gray, org & blk (C9a) 5.25 5.25

On day of issue Nos. 3044-3045 each sold for 60p.

Miniature Sheet

Welcome to the Summer Olympics — A729

No. 3046: a, Fencing, Tower Bridge. b, Runners, Olympic Stadium. c, Diver, Tate Modern Museum. d, Cyclist at left, London Eye.

2012, July 27 Litho. *Perf. 14¾*

3046 A729 Sheet of 4 11.50 11.50
a.-b. 1st Either single 1.75 1.35
c.-d. £1.28 Either single 3.75 2.90

On day of issue Nos. 3046a-3046b each sold for 60p.

Britsh Gold Medalists at 2012 Summer Olympics — A730

Photographs of gold medalists and inscription: No. 3047, Team GB, Rowing, Women's Pairs. No. 3048, Bradley Wiggins, Cycling: Road, Men's Time Trial. No. 3049, Team GB, Canoe Slalom: Men's, Canoe Double (C2). No. 3050, Peter Wilson, Shooting: Shotgun, Men's Double Trap. No. 3051, Team GB, Cycling: Track, Men's Team Sprint. No. 3052, Team GB, Rowing, Women's Double Sculls. No. 3053, Team GB, Cycling: Track, Men's Team Pursuit. No. 3054, Victoria Pendleton, Cycling: Track, Women's Keirin. No. 3055, Team GB, Rowing, Men's Fours. No. 3056, Team GB, Rowing: Lightweight Women's Double Sculls. No. 3057, Team GB, Cycling: Track Women's Team Pursuit. No. 3058, Jessica Ennis, Athletics: Combined Women's Heptathlon. No. 3059, Greg Rutherford, Athletics: Field, Men's Long Jump. No. 3060, Mo Farah, Athletics: Track, Men's 10,000m. No. 3061, Ben Ainslie, Sailing: Finn, Men's Heavyweight Dinghy. No. 3062, Andy Murray, Tennis, Men's Singles. No. 3063, Team GB, Equestrian: Jumping, Team. No. 3064, Jason Kenny, Cycling: Track, Men's Sprint. No. 3065, Alistair Brownlee, Triathlon, Men's. No. 3066, Team GB, Equestrian: Dressage, Team. No. 3067, Laura Trott, Cycling: Track, Women's Omnium. No. 3068, Chris Hoy, Cycling: Track, Men's Keirin. No. 3069, Charlotte Dujardin, Equestrian: Dressage, Individual. No. 3070, Nicola Adams, Boxing, Women's Flyweight. No. 3071, Jade Jones, Taekwondo, Women's Under 57kg. No. 3072, Ed McKeever, Canoe Sprint: Men's, Kayak Single (K1) 200m. No. 3073, Mo Farah, Athletics: Track, Men's 5000m. No. 3074, Luke Campbell, Boxing, Men's Bantamweight. No. 3075, Anthony Joshua, boxing, Men's Super Heavyweight.

Litho. With Digital Printing

2012 *Die Cut Perf. 14¾x14½*

Self-Adhesive

3047 A730 1st multi 1.75 1.35
3048 A730 1st multi 1.75 1.35
3049 A730 1st multi 1.75 1.35
3050 A730 1st multi 1.75 1.35
3051 A730 1st multi 1.75 1.35
3052 A730 1st multi 1.75 1.35
3053 A730 1st multi 1.75 1.35
3054 A730 1st multi 1.75 1.35
3055 A730 1st multi 1.75 1.35
3056 A730 1st multi 1.75 1.35
3057 A730 1st multi 1.75 1.35
3058 A730 1st multi 1.75 1.35
3059 A730 1st multi 1.75 1.35
3060 A730 1st multi 1.75 1.35
3061 A730 1st multi 1.75 1.35
3062 A730 1st multi 1.75 1.35
3063 A730 1st multi 1.75 1.35
3064 A730 1st multi 1.75 1.35
3065 A730 1st multi 1.75 1.35
3066 A730 1st multi 1.75 1.35
3067 A730 1st multi 1.75 1.35
3068 A730 1st multi 1.75 1.35
3069 A730 1st multi 1.75 1.35
3070 A730 1st multi 1.75 1.35
3071 A730 1st multi 1.75 1.35
3072 A730 1st multi 1.75 1.35
3073 A730 1st multi 1.75 1.35
3074 A730 1st multi 1.75 1.35
3075 A730 1st multi 1.75 1.35
Nos. 3047-3075 (29) 50.75 39.15

Issued: Nos. 3047-3048, 8/2; Nos. 3049-3051, 8/3; Nos. 3052-3055, 8/4; Nos. 3056-3060, 8/5; Nos. 3061-3062, 8/6; Nos. 3063-3064, 8/7; Nos. 3065-3068, 8/8; Nos. 3069-3071, 8/10; Nos. 3072-3075, 8/12.

Nos. 3047-3075 were each issued in sheets of six. Each stamp sold for 60p on day of issue

Miniature Sheet

Welcome to the Paralympics — A731

No. 3076: a, Runner with artificial leg, Olympic Stadium. b, Wheelchair basketball player, Palace of Westminster. c, Weight lifter, St. Paul's Cathedral and Millennium Bridge. d, London Eye, cyclist on right.

2012, Aug. 29 Litho. *Perf. 14¾*

3076 A731 Sheet of 4 11.50 11.50
a.-b. 1st Either single 1.75 1.35
c.-d. £1.28 Either single 3.75 2.90

On day of issue Nos. 3076a-3076b each sold for 60p.

British Gold Medalists at 2012 Summer Paralympics — A732

Photograph of gold medalist and inscription: No. 3077, Sarah Storey, Cycling: Track, Women's C5 Pursuit. No. 3078, Jonathan Fox, Swimming: Men's, 100m Backstroke, S7. No. 3079, Mark Colbourne, Cycling: Track, Men's C1 Pursuit. No. 3080, Hannah Cockroft, Athletics: Track, Women's 100m, T34. No. 3081, Paralympics GB, Cycling: Track, Men's B 1km Time Trial. No. 3082, Richard Whitehead, Athletics: Track, Men's 200m, T42. No. 3083, Natasha Baker, Equestrian: Individual, Championship Test, Grade II. No. 3084, Sarah Storey, Cycling: Track, Women's C4-5 500m Time Trial. No. 3085, Ellie Simmonds, Swimming: Women's, 400m Freestyle, S6. No. 3086, Paralympics GB, Rowing: Mixed, Coxed Four, LTA Mix 4+. No. 3087, Aled Davies, Athletics: Field, Men's Discus, F42. No. 3088, Paralympics GB, Cycling: Track, Men's B Sprint. No. 3089, Jessica-Jane Applegate, Swimming: Women's, 200m Freestyle, S14. No. 3090, Sophie Christiansen, Equestrian: Individual, Championship Test, Grade Ia. No. 3091, David Weir, Athletics: Track, Men's 5000m, T54. No. 3092, Natasha Baker, Equestrian: Individual, Freestyle Test, Grade II. No. 3093, Ellie Simmonds, Swimming: Women's, 200m Individual Medley, SM6. No. 3094, Mickey Bushell, Atheltics: Track, Men's 100m, T53. No. 3095, Danielle Brown, Archery: Women's, Individual Compound, Open. No. 3096, Heather Frederiksen, Swimming: Women's, 100m Backstroke, S8. No. 3097, Sophie Christiansen, Equestrian: Individual, Freestyle Test, Grade Ia. No. 3098, David Weir, Athletics: Track, Men's 1500m, T54. No. 3099, Sarah Storey, Cycling: Road, Women's C5 Time Trial. No. 3100, Ollie Hynd, Swimming: Men's, 200m Individual Medley, SM8. No. 3101, Paralympics GB, Equestrian, Team, Open. No. 3102, Helena Lucas, Sailing: Single-person, Keelboat 2.4mR. No. 3103, Sarah Storey, Cycling: Road, Women's C4-5 Road Race. No. 3104, Josef Craig, Swimming: Men's, 400m Freestyle, S7. No. 3105, Hannah Cockroft, Athletics: Track, Women's 200m, T34. No. 3106, David Weir, Atheltics: Track, Men's 800m, T54. No. 3107, Jonnie Peacock, Athletics: Track, Men's 100m, T44. No. 3108, Josie Pearson, Athletics: Field, Women's Discus, F51/52/53. No. 3109, David Stone, Cycling: Road, Mixed T1-2 Road Race. No. 3110, David Weir, Athletics: Road, Men's Marathon, T54.

Litho. With Digital Printing

2012 *Die Cut Perf. 14¾x14½*

Self-Adhesive

3077 A732 1st multi 1.75 1.35
3078 A732 1st multi 1.75 1.35
3079 A732 1st multi 1.75 1.35
3080 A732 1st multi 1.75 1.35
3081 A732 1st multi 1.75 1.35
3082 A732 1st multi 1.75 1.35
3083 A732 1st multi 1.75 1.35
3084 A732 1st multi 1.75 1.35
3085 A732 1st multi 1.75 1.35
3086 A732 1st multi 1.75 1.35
3087 A732 1st multi 1.75 1.35
3088 A732 1st multi 1.75 1.35
3089 A732 1st multi 1.75 1.35
3090 A732 1st multi 1.75 1.35
3091 A732 1st multi 1.75 1.35
3092 A732 1st multi 1.75 1.35
3093 A732 1st multi 1.75 1.35
3094 A732 1st multi 1.75 1.35
3095 A732 1st multi 1.75 1.35
3096 A732 1st multi 1.75 1.35
3097 A732 1st multi 1.75 1.35
3098 A732 1st multi 1.75 1.35
3099 A732 1st multi 1.75 1.35
3100 A732 1st multi 1.75 1.35
3101 A732 1st multi 1.75 1.35
3102 A732 1st multi 1.75 1.35
3103 A732 1st multi 1.75 1.35
3104 A732 1st multi 1.75 1.35
3105 A732 1st multi 1.75 1.35
3106 A732 1st multi 1.75 1.35
3107 A732 1st multi 1.75 1.35
3108 A732 1st multi 1.75 1.35
3109 A732 1st multi 1.75 1.35
3110 A732 1st multi 1.75 1.35
Nos. 3077-3110 (34) 59.50 45.90

Issued: No. 3077, 8/31; No. 3078, 9/1; Nos. 3079-3085, 9/3; Nos. 3086-3093, 9/4; Nos. 3094-3097, 9/5; Nos. 3098-3101, 9/7. Nos. 3102-3105, 9/8; Nos. 3106-3110, 9/10.

Nos. 3077-3110 were each issued in sheets of two. Each stamp sold for 60p on day of issue

Scottish Locomotives Type of 2012

Design: British Railways D34 Nos. 62471 and 62496.

Die Cut Perf. 14¼

2012, Sept. 27 Photo.

Booklet Stamp
Self-Adhesive

3111 A723 1st multi 3.75 1.35
a. Booklet pane of 6, 2 #3111, 4 #MH414 15.50

No. 3111 sold for 60p on day of issue.

Miniature Sheet

Scenes From 2012 Summer Olympics and Paralympics — A733

No. 3112: a, British Paralympics Team in procession. b, Athletes walking near stadium. c, Paralympic Games Opening Ceremonies. d, Olympic Closing Ceremony.

2012, Sept. 27 Litho. *Perf. 14¾*

3112 A733 Sheet of 4 11.50 11.50
a.-b. 1st Either single 1.75 1.35
c.-d. £1.28 Either single 3.75 2.90

On day of issue Nos. 3112a-3112b each sold for 60p.

Astronomical Bodies — A734

Designs: No. 3113, Sun. No. 3114, Venus. No. 3115, Mars. No. 3116, Asteroid Lutetia. No. 3117, Saturn. No. 3118, Titan, moon of Saturn.

2012, Oct. 10 *Perf. 14¼x14*

3113 A734 1st multi 1.75 1.35
3114 A734 1st multi 1.75 1.35
3115 A734 77p multi 2.40 1.75
3116 A734 77p multi 2.40 1.75
3117 A734 £1.28 multi 3.75 2.90
3118 A734 £1.28 multi 3.75 2.90
Nos. 3113-3118 (6) 15.80 12.00

First British satellite, 50th anniv. On day of issue, Nos. 3113-3114 each sold for 60p.

Poppy Type of 2010

Die Cut Perf14¾x14 Syncopated

2012, Dec. 23 Litho.

3118A A686 1st multi 2.25 2.25

No. 3118A has value and Queen's head in silver, die cuts are complete. There is no attached label.

Christmas
A735 A736

Designs: 2nd, Reindeer with Christmas ornaments on antlers. 1st, Bird on hand of Santa Claus. 2nd Large, Reindeer with Christmas ornaments on antlers, trees. 87p, Penguin and snowman. 1st Large, Bird on hand of Santa Claus, tree. £1.28, Bird carrying star Christmas ornament on holly branch. £1.90, Cat, mouse and Christmas tree.

Perf. 14¾x14 Syncopated

2012, Nov. 6 **Photo.**

3119		Sheet of 7	20.00	20.00
a.	A735 2nd multi		1.50	1.15
b.	A735 1st multi		1.75	1.35
c.	A736 2nd Large multi		2.10	1.60
d.	A735 87p multi		2.60	2.00
e.	A736 1st Large multi		2.75	2.00
f.	A735 £1.28 multi		3.75	2.90
g.	A735 £1.90 multi		5.75	4.25

Self-Adhesive

Die Cut Perf. 14¾x14 Syncopated

3120	A735	2nd multi	1.50	1.15
a.		Booklet pane of 12	18.00	
b.		Litho., + label (3125b)	1.60	1.60
3121	A735	1st multi	1.75	1.35
a.		Booklet pane of 12	21.00	
b.		Litho., + label (3125b)	1.90	1.90
3122	A736	2nd Large multi	2.10	1.60
3123	A735	87p multi	2.60	2.00
a.		Litho., + label (3125b)	2.75	2.75
3124	A736	1st Large multi	2.75	2.00
3125	A735	£1.28 multi	3.75	2.90
a.		Litho., + label (3125b)	4.00	4.00
b.		Sheet of 20, 8 each #3120b, 3121b, 2 each #3123a, 3125a, + 20 labels	42.50	
3126	A735	£1.90 multi	5.75	4.25
		Nos. 3120-3126 (7)	20.20	15.25

On day of issue, Nos. 3119a and 3120 each sold for 50p, Nos. 3119b and 3121 each sold for 60p, Nos. 3119c and 3122 each sold for 69p, and Nos. 3119e and 3124 each sold for 90p. No. 3125b sold for £13.60. Labels could not be personalized.

London Underground, 150th Anniv. — A737

Advertisements in London Underground — A738

Designs: No. 3127, Train and cars in tunnel, 1863. No. 3128, Workers tunneling under London streets, 1898. No. 3129, Suburban commuters in train car, 1911. Nos. 3130, 3134, Boston Manor Art Deco station exterior, 1934. No. 3131, Train cars, 1938. No. 3132, Escalators at Canary Wharf Jubilee Line Station, 1999.

No. 3133 — Underground emblem and various advertising posters promoting travel on the Underground.

2013, Jan. 9 **Litho.** ***Perf. 14¼***

3127	A737	2nd multi	1.50	1.15
3128	A737	2nd multi	1.50	1.15
3129	A737	1st multi	1.75	1.35
3130	A737	1st multi	1.75	1.35
3131	A737	£1.28 multi	3.75	2.90
3132	A737	£1.28 multi	3.75	2.90
		Nos. 3127-3132 (6)	14.00	10.80

Miniature Sheet

Perf. 14¾

3133	A738	Sheet of 4	10.50	10.50
a.		1st multi	1.75	1.35
b.		77p multi	2.40	1.75
c.		87p multi	2.60	2.00
d.		£1.28 multi	3.75	2.90

Booklet Stamp
Self-Adhesive

Die Cut Perf. 14¼

3134	A737	1st multi	3.00	1.75
a.		Booklet pane of 6, 2 #3134, 4 #MH426	14.00	

On day of issue, Nos.3127-3128 each sold for 50p, and Nos, 3129-3130, 3133a and 3134 each sold for 60p.

Scenes From Novels by Jane Austen — A739

Scene from: No. 3135, Sense and Sensibility. No. 3136, Pride and Prejudice. No. 3137, Mansfield Park. No. 3138, Emma. No. 3139, Northanger Abbey. No. 3140, Persuasion.

2013, Feb. 21 ***Perf. 14¼***

3135	A739	1st multi	1.75	1.35
3136	A739	1st multi	1.75	1.35
3137	A739	77p multi	2.40	1.75
3138	A739	77p multi	2.40	1.75
3139	A739	£1.28 multi	4.00	2.90
3140	A739	£1.28 multi	4.00	2.90
		Nos. 3135-3140 (6)	16.60	8.40

On day of issue, Nos. 3135-3136 each sold for 60p.

Matt Smith, Eleventh Doctor Who A740

David Tennant, Tenth Doctor Who A741

Christopher Eccleston, Ninth Doctor Who A742

Paul McGann, Eighth Doctor Who A743

Sylvester McCoy, Seventh Doctor Who A744

Colin Baker, Sixth Doctor Who A745

Peter Davison, Fifth Doctor Who A746

Tom Baker, Fourth Doctor Who A747

Jon Pertwee, Third Doctor Who A748

Patrick Troughton, Second Doctor Who A749

William Hartnell, First Doctor Who A750

Doctor Who Props and Characters — A751

Designs: Nos. 3152, 3153e, 3156, TARDIS (police call box). No. 3153a, Dalek. No. 3153b, Ood. No. 3153c, Weeping Angel. No. 3153d, Cyberman.

2013, Mar. 26 ***Perf. 14¼x14***

3141	A740	1st multi	1.75	1.35
3142	A741	1st multi	1.75	1.35
3143	A742	1st multi	1.75	1.35
a.		Horiz. strip of 3, #3141-3143	5.50	4.25
b.		Booklet pane of 3, #3141-3143 (BK201)	5.50	—
3144	A743	1st multi	1.75	1.35
3145	A744	1st multi	1.75	1.35
3146	A745	1st multi	1.75	1.35
3147	A746	1st multi	1.75	1.35
a.		Horiz. strip of 4, #3144-3147	7.25	5.50
b.		Booklet pane of 4, #3144-3147 (BK201)	7.25	—
3148	A747	1st multi	1.75	1.35
3149	A748	1st multi	1.75	1.35
3150	A749	1st black	1.75	1.35
3151	A750	1st black	1.75	1.35
a.		Horiz. strip of 4, #3148-3151	7.25	5.50
b.		Booklet pane of 4, #3148-3151 (BK201)	7.25	—
		Nos. 3141-3151 (11)	19.25	14.85

Booklet Stamp

Perf. 14¾x14 Syncopated

3152	A751	1st multi (3152a)	2.40	2.40
a.		Booklet pane of 8, #MH429-MH432, 4 #3152, + label (BK201)	21.50	

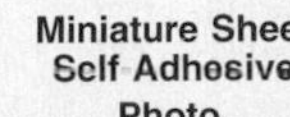

Miniature Sheet
Self Adhesive
Photo.

Die Cut Perf. 14½ Syncopated (#3153a-3153d), Die Cut Perf. 14¾x14 Syncopated (#3153e)

3153	A751	Sheet of 5	8.00	8.00
a.-d.		2nd Any single	1.50	1.15
e.		1st multi	1.75	1.35
f.-i.		2nd As #3153a-3153d, any single, litho. (3153k)	1.60	1.60
j.		1st As #3153e, litho., die cut perf. 14¾ syncopated (3153k)	1.90	1.90
k.		Booklet pane of 5, #3153f-3153j (BK201)	8.75	
l.		Sheet of 20 #3153e + 20 labels	36.00	

Booklet Stamps
Photo.

Die Cut Perf. 14¼

3154	A740	1st multi	6.00	1.75
3155	A750	1st multi	6.00	1.75

Die Cut Perf. 14¾x14 Syncopated

3156	A751	1st multi	6.00	1.75
a.		Booklet pane of 6, #3154-3155, 4 #3156	36.00	
		Nos. 3154-3156 (3)	18.00	5.25

Doctor Who television show, 50th anniv. On day of issue, Nos. 3153a-3153d, 3153f-3153i each had a franking value of 50p, and Nos. 3141-3152, 3153e, 3153j, 3154-3156 each had a franking value of 60p. No. 3153l sold for £12.50 and labels could be personalized for an additional fee.

Famous People — A752

Designs: No. 3157, Norman Parkinson (1913-90), photographer. No. 3158, Vivien Leigh (1913-67), actress. No. 3159, Peter Cushing (1913-94), actor. No. 3160, David Lloyd George (1863-1945), prime minister. No. 3161, Elizabeth David (1913-92), cookbook writer. No. 3162, John Archer (1863-1932), politician. No. 3163, Benjamin Britten (1913-76), composer. No. 3164, Mary Leakey (1913-96), anthropologist. No. 3165, Bill Shankly (1913-81), soccer player and manager. No. 3166, Richard Dimbleby (1913-65), broadcast journalist.

2013, Apr. 16 **Litho.** ***Perf. 14½***

3157	A752	1st multi	1.75	1.35
3158	A752	1st multi	1.75	1.35
3159	A752	1st multi	1.75	1.35
3160	A752	1st multi	1.75	1.35
3161	A752	1st multi	1.75	1.35
a.		Horiz. strip of 5, #3157-3161	9.00	6.75
3162	A752	1st multi	1.75	1.35
3163	A752	1st multi	1.75	1.35
3164	A752	1st multi	1.75	1.35
3165	A752	1st multi	1.75	1.35
3166	A752	1st multi	1.75	1.35
a.		Horiz. strip of 5, #3162-3166	9.00	6.75
		Nos. 3157-3166 (10)	17.50	13.50

On day of issue, Nos. 3157-3166 each sold for 60p.

Soccer Players — A753

Designs: Nos. 3167, 3178, Jimmy Greaves, England. Nos. 3168, 3179, John Charles (1931-2004), Wales. Nos. 3169, 3183, Gordon Banks, England. Nos. 3170, 3184, 3189, George Best (1946-2005), Northern Ireland. Nos. 3171, 3185, John Barnes, England. Nos. 3172, 3180, Kevin Keegan, England. No. 3173, 3181, Denis Law, Scotland. Nos. 3174, 3182, 3190, Bobby Moore (1941-93), England. Nos. 3175, 3186, Bryan Robson, England. Nos. 3176, 3187, Dave Mackay, Scotland. Nos. 3177, 3188, Bobby Charlton, England.

2013, May 9 **Litho.** ***Perf. 14¾x14½***

3167	A753	1st multi	1.90	1.40
3168	A753	1st multi	1.90	1.40
3169	A753	1st multi	1.90	1.40
3170	A753	1st multi	1.90	1.40

3171 A753 1st multi 1.90 1.40
a. Horiz. strip of 5, #3167-3171 9.50 7.00
3172 A753 1st multi 1.90 1.40
3173 A753 1st multi 1.90 1.40
3174 A753 1st multi 1.90 1.40
3175 A753 1st multi 1.90 1.40
3176 A753 1st multi 1.90 1.40
3177 A753 1st multi 1.90 1.40
a. Horiz. strip of 6, #3172-3177 11.50 8.50
b. Souvenir sheet of 11, #3167-3177 21.00 16.00
Nos. 3167-3177 (11) 20.90 15.40

Booklet Stamps
Self-Adhesive

Die Cut Perf. 14¾x14½

3178 A753 1st multi 2.75 2.75
3179 A753 1st multi 2.75 2.75
3180 A753 1st multi 2.75 2.75
3181 A753 1st multi 2.75 2.75
3182 A753 1st multi 2.75 2.75
a. Booklet pane of 5, #3178-3182 (BK202) 14.00
3183 A753 1st multi 2.75 2.75
3184 A753 1st multi 2.75 2.75
3185 A753 1st multi 2.75 2.75
3186 A753 1st multi 2.75 2.75
3187 A753 1st multi 2.75 2.75
3188 A753 1st multi 2.75 2.75
a. Booklet pane of 6, #3183-3188 (BK202) 17.00

Photo.

Die Cut Perf. 14¾x14

3189 A753 1st multi 5.00 2.00
3190 A753 1st multi 5.00 2.00
a. Booklet pane of 6, #3189-3190, 4 #MH426 17.50
Nos. 3178-3190 (13) 40.25 34.25

On day of issue, Nos. 3172-3190 each had a franking value of 60p. See Nos. 3266-3267.

Portraits of Queen Elizabeth II — A754

Portrait by: 2nd, Terence Cuneo, 1953. 1st, Nicky Philipps, 2013. 78p, Andrew Festing, 1999. 88p, Pietro Annigoni, 1955. £1.28, Sergei Pavlenko, 2000. £1.88, Richard Stone, 1992.

2013, May 30 Photo. *Perf. 14¼*

3191 A754 2nd multi 1.50 1.15
3192 A754 1st multi 1.75 1.35
3193 A754 78p multi 2.40 1.75
3194 A754 88p multi 2.60 2.00
3195 A754 £1.28 multi 4.00 2.90
3196 A754 £1.88 multi 5.75 4.25
Nos. 3191-3196 (6) 18.00 13.40

On day of issue, No. 3191 sold for 50p, and No. 3192 sold for 60p.

Northern Ireland Steam Locomotives — A755

Designs: 1st, Ulster Transport Authority W No. 103. 78p, Ulster Transport Authority SG3 No. 35. 88p, Peckett No. 2. £1.28, County Donegal Railways Joint Commission Class 5 No. 4.

2013, June 18 Litho. *Perf. 14¼*

3197 A755 Sheet of 4 11.00 8.00
a. 1st multi 1.75 1.35
b. 78p multi 2.40 1.75
c. 88p multi 2.60 2.00
d. £1.28 multi 4.00 2.90
e. Booklet pane of 4, 2 each #3197a, 3197b (BK204) 8.25 —

Booklet Stamp
Self-Adhesive
Photo.

Die Cut Perf. 14¼

3198 A755 1st multi 3.75 1.75
a. Booklet pane of 6, 2 #3198, 4 #MH426 15.50

On day of issue Nos. 3197a and 3198 each sold for 60p. Issued: No. 3197e, 2/20/14.

Butterflies A756

Designs: Nos. 3199, 3210, Comma butterfly. No. 3200, Orange-tip butterfly. No. 3201, Small copper butterfly. Nos. 3202, 3209, Chalkhill blue butterfly. No. 3203, Swallowtail butterfly. No. 3204, Purple emperor butterfly. No. 3205, Marsh fritillary butterfly. No. 3206, Brimstone butterfly. No. 3207, Red admiral butterfly. No. 3208, Marbled white butterfly.

2013, July 11 Litho. *Perf. 14¼*

3199 A756 1st multi 1.75 1.35
3200 A756 1st multi 1.75 1.35
3201 A756 1st multi 1.75 1.35
3202 A756 1st multi 1.75 1.35
3203 A756 1st multi 1.75 1.35
a. Horiz. strip of 5, #3199-3203 9.00 6.75
3204 A756 1st multi 1.75 1.35
3205 A756 1st multi 1.75 1.35
3206 A756 1st multi 1.75 1.35
3207 A756 1st multi 1.75 1.35
3208 A756 1st multi 1.75 1.35
a. Horiz. strip of 5, #3204-3208 9.00 6.75
Nos. 3199-3208 (10) 17.50 13.50

Booklet Stamps
Self-Adhesive

Die Cut Perf. 14¼

3209 A756 1st multi 3.75 1.75
3210 A756 1st multi 3.75 1.75
a. Booklet pane of 6, #3209-3210, 4 #MH426 15.50

Nos. 3199-3210 each sold for 60p on day of issue.

Miniature Sheet

Victory of Andy Murray in 2013 Wimbledon Men's Singles Tennis Final — A757

No. 3211 — Murray: a, Kissing trophy. b, Serving. c, Chasing shot. d, Holding trophy.

2013, Aug. 8 Litho. *Perf. 14¾*

3211 A757 Sheet of 4 11.50 8.50
a.-b. 1st Either single 1.75 1.35
c.-d. £1.28 Either single 4.00 2.90

On day of issue, Nos. 3211a-3211b each sold for 60p.

A758

Motor Vehicles — A759

Designs: No. 3212, 1961 Jaguar E-Type. No. 3213, 1965 Rolls-Royce Silver Shadow. No. 3214, 1963, Aston Martin DB5. No. 3215, 1962 MG MGB. No. 3216, 1968 Morgan Plus 8. No. 3217, 1976 Lotus Esprit.

No. 3218: a, 1953-71 Morris Minor Van. b, 1958-97 Austin FX4. c, 1959-67 Ford Anglia 105E. d, 1990-2013 Land Rover Defender 110.

2013, Aug. 13 Litho. *Perf. 13¼*

3212 A758 1st multi 1.75 1.35
3213 A758 1st multi 1.75 1.35
3214 A758 1st multi 1.75 1.35
a. Horiz. strip of 3, #3212-3214 5.50 4.25
3215 A758 £1.28 multi 4.00 2.90
3216 A758 £1.28 multi 4.00 2.90
3217 A758 £1.28 multi 4.00 2.90
a. Horiz. strip of 3, #3215-3217 12.00 8.75
Nos. 3212-3217 (6) 17.25 12.75

Miniature Sheet

Perf. 14¼x14

3218 A759 Sheet of 4 7.25 5.50
a.-d. 1st Any single 1.75 1.35

Europa (#3218a). On day of issue, Nos. 3212-3214 and 3218a-3218d each sold for 60p.
See No. 3226.

Merchant Navy Ships A760

World War II Atlantic and Arctic Convoys — A761

Ships: No. 3219, Atlas, 1813. No. 3220, Britannia, 1840. No. 3221, Cutty Sark, 1870. No. 3222, Clan Matheson, 1919. No. 3223, Queen Elizabeth. No. 3224, Lord Hinton.

No. 3225: a, Ships in convoy, flag flying on ship at UL. b, Sailor signaling another ship with semaphore flag. c, Sailors removing snow from deck of ship. d, Convoy of ships.

2013, Sept. 19 Litho. *Perf. 14¼x14*

3219 A760 1st multi 1.75 1.35
3220 A760 1st multi 1.75 1.35
3221 A760 1st multi 1.75 1.35
a. Booklet pane of 3, #3219-3221 (BK203) 5.25 —
3222 A760 £1.28 multi 4.00 2.90
3223 A760 £1.28 multi 4.00 2.90
3224 A760 £1.28 multi 4.00 2.90
a. Booklet pane of 3, #3222-3224 (BK203) 12.00 —
Nos. 3219-3224 (6) 17.25 12.75

Souvenir Sheet

3225 A761 Sheet of 4 7.25 5.50
a.-d. 1st Any single 1.75 1.35
e. Booklet pane of 4, #3225a-3225d (BK203) 7.25 —

On day of issue Nos. 3219-3221, 3225a-3225d each sold for 60p. Margin on No. 3225e differs from that on No. 3225.
See No. 3227.

Motor Vehicles and Merchant Navy Types of 2013

Designs: No. 3226, Morris Minor Van. No. 3227, Britannia.

Die Cut Perf. 14¼x14

2013, Sept. 19 Photo.

Booklet Stamps
Self-Adhesive

3226 A759 1st multi 4.50 2.25
3227 A760 1st multi 4.50 2.25
a. Booklet pane of 6, #3226-3227, 4 #MH426 17.00

On day of issue, Nos. 3226-3227 each sold for 60p. Europa (#3226).

Dinosaurs A762

Designs: No. 3228, Polacanthus. No. 3229, Ichthyosaurus. No. 3230, Iguanaodon. No. 3231, Ornithocheirus. No. 3232, Baryonyx. No. 3233, Dimorphodon. No. 3234, Hypsilophodon. No. 3235, Cetiosaurus. No. 3236, Megalosaurus. No. 3237, Pleisiosaurus.

Die Cut Perf. 13½x14

2013, Oct. 10 Photo.

Self-Adhesive

3228 A762 1st multi 1.75 1.35
3229 A762 1st multi 1.75 1.35
3230 A762 1st multi 1.75 1.35
3231 A762 1st multi 1.75 1.35
3232 A762 1st multi 1.75 1.35
a. Horiz. strip of 5, #3228-3232 9.00 6.75
3233 A762 1st multi 1.75 1.35
3234 A762 1st multi 1.75 1.35
3235 A762 1st multi 1.75 1.35
3236 A762 1st multi 1.75 1.35
3237 A762 1st multi 1.75 1.35
a. Horiz. strip of 5, #3233-3237 9.00 6.75
Nos. 3228-3237 (10) 17.50 13.50

On day of issue, Nos. 3228-3237 each sold for 60p.

A763

Christmas — A764

Details from paintings: Nos. 3238a, 3238c, 3239, 3241, Virgin and Child with the Young St. John the Baptist, by Antoniazzo Romano. Nos. 3238b, 3238e, 3240, 3243, Madonna and Child, by Francesco Granacci. 88p, St. Roch Praying to the Virgin for an End to the Plague, by Jacques-Louis David. £1.28, La Vierge au Lys, by William-Adolphe Bouguereau. £1.88, Theotokos, Mother of God, by Fadi Mikhail.

2013, Nov. 5 Photo. *Perf. 14½x15*

3238 Sheet of 7 20.00 20.00
a. A763 2nd multi 1.50 1.15
b. A763 1st multi 1.75 1.35
c. A764 2nd Large multi 2.10 1.60
d. A763 88p multi 2.60 2.00
e. A764 1st Large multi 2.75 2.00
f. A763 £1.28 multi 4.00 2.90
g. A763 £1.88 multi 5.75 4.25

Self-Adhesive

Die Cut Perf. 14½x15

3239 A763 2nd multi 1.50 1.15
a. Booklet pane of 12 18.00
b. Litho., die cut perf. 14½x15 syncopated, + label (#3245b) 1.50 1.50
3240 A763 1st multi 1.75 1.35
a. Booklet pane of 12 21.00
b. Litho., die cut perf. 14½x15 syncopated, + label (#3245b) 1.75 1.75
3241 A764 2nd Large multi 2.10 1.60
3242 A763 88p multi 2.60 2.00
a. Litho., die cut perf. 14½x15 syncopated, + label (#3245b) 3.00 3.00
3243 A764 1st Large multi 2.75 2.00
3244 A763 £1.28 multi 4.00 2.90
a. Litho., die cut perf. 14½x15 syncopated, + label (#3245b) 5.75 5.75
3245 A763 £1.88 multi 5.75 4.25
a. Litho., die cut perf. 14½x15 syncopated, + label (#3245b) 8.50 8.50
b. Sheet of 20 + 20 labels, #3244a, 3245a, 2 #3242a, 8 each #3239b, 3240b 50.00
Nos. 3239-3245 (7) 20.45 15.25

On day of issue, Nos. 3238a and 3239 each sold for 50p, Nos. 3238b and 3240 each sold for 60p, Nos. 3238c and 3241 each sold for 69p, and Nos. 3238e and 3241 each sold for 90p. No. 3245b sold for £14.22. Labels could not be personalized.

Christmas — A765

Winning art in children's Christmas stamp design contest: 2nd, Angels, by Rosie Hargreaves. 1st, Santa Claus, by Molly Robson.

Die Cut Perf. 14¾

2013, Nov. 5 **Photo.**

3246	A765	2nd multi	2.50	1.50
3247	A765	1st multi	3.00	1.75

On day of issue, No. 3246 sold for 50p and No. 3247 sold for 60p.

Children's Television Characters — A766

Designs: No. 3248, Andy Pandy and Teddy. No. 3249, Ivor the Engine. No. 3250, Dougal from *The Magic Roundabout*. No. 3251, Windy Miller from *Camberwick Green*. No. 3252, Mr. Benn. No. 3253, Great Uncle Bulgaria from *The Wombles*. No. 3254, Bagpuss. No. 3255, Paddington Bear. No. 3256, Postman Pat and cat, Jess. No. 3257, Bob the Builder. No. 3258, Peppa Pig. No. 3259, Shaun the Sheep.

Die Cut Perf. 15

2014, Jan. 17 **Photo.**

Self-Adhesive

3248	A766	1st black	1.75	1.35
3249	A766	1st multi	1.75	1.35
3250	A766	1st multi	1.75	1.35
3251	A766	1st multi	1.75	1.35
3252	A766	1st multi	1.75	1.35
3253	A766	1st multi	1.75	1.35
a.		Horiz. strip of 6, #3248-3253	11.00	8.25
3254	A766	1st multi	1.75	1.35
3255	A766	1st multi	1.75	1.35
3256	A766	1st multi	1.75	1.35
3257	A766	1st multi	1.75	1.35
3258	A766	1st multi	1.75	1.35
3259	A766	1st multi	1.75	1.35
a.		Horiz. strip of 6, #3254-3259	11.00	8.25
		Nos. 3248-3259 (12)	21.00	16.20

On day of issue, Nos. 3248-3259 each sold for 60p.

Horses A767

Inscriptions: No. 3260, Riding for the Disabled Association. No. 3261, The King's Troop Ceremonial Horses. No. 3262, Dray Horses. No. 3263, Royal Mews Carriage Horses. No. 3264, Police Horses. No. 3265, Forestry Horse.

2014, Feb. 4 **Litho.** ***Perf. 14¼x14***

3260	A767	1st multi	1.75	1.35
3261	A767	1st multi	1.75	1.35
3262	A767	88p multi	2.75	2.00
3263	A767	88p multi	2.75	2.00
3264	A767	£1.28 multi	4.00	2.90
3265	A767	£1.28 multi	4.00	2.90
		Nos. 3260-3265 (6)	17.00	12.50

On day of issue Nos. 3260 and 3261 each sold for 60p.

Soccer Players Type of 2013

Designs: No. 3266, John Charles (1931-2004), Wales. No. 3267, Dave Mackay, Scotland.

Die Cut Perf. 14¾x14

2014, Feb. 20 **Photo.**

Booklet Stamps
Self-Adhesive

3266	A753	1st multi	4.50	1.90
3267	A753	1st multi	4.50	1.90
a.		Booklet pane of 6, #3266-3267, 4 #MH426	17.00	

On day of issue, Nos. 3266-3267 each sold for 60p.

Miniature Sheet

Locomotives of Wales — A768

No. 3268: a, LMS No. 7720. b, Hunslet No. 589 Blanche. c, Welshpool & Llanfair Light Railway No. 822 The Earl. d, British Railways 5600 No. 5652.

2014, Feb. 20 **Litho.** ***Perf. 14¼***

3268	A768	Sheet of 4	11.00	8.00
a.		1st multi	1.75	1.35
b.		78p multi	2.40	1.75
c.		88p multi	2.75	2.00
d.		£1.28 multi	4.00	2.90
e.		Booklet pane of 4, 2 each #3268a, 3268b (BK204)	8.50	—

On day of issue No. 3268a sold for 60p. See No. 3320.

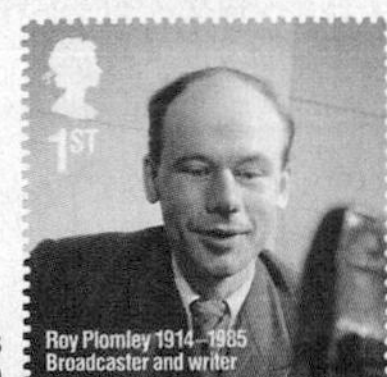

Famous People — A769

Designs: No. 3269, Roy Plomley (1914-84), broadcaster, writer. No. 3270, Barbara Ward (1914-81), economist, broadcaster. No. 3271, Joe Mercer (1914-90), Soccer player, team manager. No. 3272, Kenneth More (1914-82), actor. No. 3273, Dylan Thomas (1914-53), poet, writer. No. 3274, Sir Alec Guinness (1914-2000), actor. No. 3275, Noorunissa Inayat Khan (1914-44), Special Operations Executive agent. No. 3276, Max Perutz (1914-2002), molecular biologist, 1962 Nobel laureate in Chemistry. No. 3277, Joan Littlewood (1914-2002), theater director, writer. No. 3278, Abram Games (1914-96), graphic designer.

2014, Mar. 25 **Litho.** ***Perf. 14½***

3269	A769	1st black	1.75	1.35
3270	A769	1st black	1.75	1.00
3271	A769	1st black	1.75	1.00
3272	A769	1st black	1.75	1.00
3273	A769	1st black	1.75	1.00
a.		Horiz. strip of 5, #3269-3273	9.00	6.75
3274	A769	1st black	1.75	1.35
3275	A769	1st black	1.75	1.35
3276	A769	1st black	1.75	1.35
3277	A769	1st black	1.75	1.35
3278	A769	1st black	1.75	1.35
a.		Horiz. strip of 5, #3274-3278	9.00	6.75
		Nos. 3269-3278 (10)	17.50	12.10

Nos. 3269-3278 each sold for 60p on day of issue.

Historic Views of Exterior of Buckingham Palace — A770

Rooms in Buckingham Palace — A771

Image of Buckingham Palace from: No. 3279, 2014. No. 3280, Circa 1862. No. 3281, 1846. No. 3282, 1819 (Buckingham House). No. 3283, 1714 (Buckingham House). No. 3284, Circa 1700 (Buckingham House).

No. 3285: a, Throne Room. b, Grand Staircase. c, Blue Drawing Room. d, Green Drawing Room.

No. 3286, Like #3285b. No. 3287, Like #3285a.

2014, Apr. 15 **Litho.** ***Perf. 14¾***

3279	A770	1st multi	1.90	1.40
a.		Perf. 14x13¼ (#3280b)	2.00	2.00
3280	A770	1st multi	1.90	1.40
a.		Perf. 14x13¼ (#3280b)	2.00	2.00
b.		Booklet pane of 4, 2 each #3279a-3280a (BK205)	8.00	—
3281	A770	1st multi	1.90	1.40
a.		Perf. 14x13¼ (#3284c)	2.00	2.00
b.		Horiz. strip of 3, #3279-3281	5.75	4.25
3282	A770	1st multi	1.90	1.40
a.		Perf. 14x13¼ (#3284c)	2.00	2.00
3283	A770	1st multi	1.90	1.40
a.		Perf. 14x13¼ (#3284c)	2.00	2.00
3284	A770	1st multi	1.90	1.40
a.		Perf. 14x13¼ (#3284c)	2.00	2.00
b.		Horiz. strip of 3, #3282-3284	5.75	4.25
c.		Booklet pane of 4, #3281a, 3282a, 3283a, 3284a (BK205)	8.00	—
		Nos. 3279-3284 (6)	11.40	8.40

Perf. 14¼x14

3285		Sheet of 4	7.50	5.75
a.-d.	A771	1st Any single	1.90	1.40
e.		Booklet pane of 4, #3285a-3285d (BK205)	7.50	—

Photo.

Booklet Stamps
Self-Adhesive

Die Cut Perf. 14¼x14

3286	A771	1st multi	4.00	1.90
3287	A771	1st multi	4.00	1.90
a.		Booklet pane of 6, #3286-3287, 4 #MH426	16.00	

Nos. 3279-3284, 325a-3285d, 3286-3287 each sold for 62p on day of issue.

Scenes From British Films — A772

Scenes From Films Made by General Post Office Film Unit — A773

Scene from: No. 3288, *A Matter of Life and Death*. No. 3289, *Lawrence of Arabia*. No. 3290, *2001: A Space Odyssey*. No. 3291, *Chariots of Fire*. No. 3292, *Secrets & Lies*. No. 3293, *Bend It Like Beckham*.

No. 3294 — Scenes from: a, *Night Mail*. b, *Love on the Wing*. c, *A Colour Box*. d, *Spare Time*.

2014, May 13 **Litho.** ***Perf. 14¾***

3288	A772	1st multi	1.90	1.40
3289	A772	1st multi	1.90	1.40
3290	A772	1st multi	1.90	1.40
a.		Horiz. strip of 3, #3288-3290	5.75	4.25
3291	A772	£1.28 multi	4.00	2.90
3292	A772	£1.28 multi	4.00	2.90
3293	A772	£1.28 multi	4.00	2.90
a.		Horiz. strip of 3, #3291-3293	12.00	8.75
		Nos. 3288-3293 (6)	17.70	12.90

Miniature Sheet

Perf. 14¼x14

3294	A773	Sheet of 4	7.50	5.75
a.-d.		1st Any single	1.90	1.40

Nos. 3288-3290 and 3294a-3294d each sold for 62p on day of issue.

Fish — A774

Designs: No. 3295, Herrings. No. 3296, Red gurnard. No. 3297, Dab. No. 3298, Poutings. No. 3299, Cornish sardines. No. 3300, Common skate. No. 3301, Spiny dogfish. No. 3302, Wolffish. No. 3303, Sturgeon. No. 3304, Conger eel.

2014, June 5 **Litho.** ***Perf. 14¼***

3295	A774	1st multi	1.90	1.40
3296	A774	1st multi	1.90	1.40
3297	A774	1st multi	1.90	1.40
3298	A774	1st multi	1.90	1.40
3299	A774	1st multi	1.90	1.40
a.		Horiz. strip of 5, #3295-3299	9.50	7.00
3300	A774	1st multi	1.90	1.40
3301	A774	1st multi	1.90	1.40
3302	A774	1st multi	1.90	1.40
3303	A774	1st multi	1.90	1.40
3304	A774	1st multi	1.90	1.40
a.		Horiz. strip of 5, #3300-3304	9.50	7.00
		Nos. 3295-3304 (10)	19.00	14.00

Nos. 3295-3304 each sold for 62p on day of issue. See Nos. 3318-3319.

20th Commonwealth Games, Glasgow — A775

Designs: 2nd, Judo. 1st, Swimming. 97p, Track. £1.28, Squash. £1.47, Netball. £2.15, Cycling.

2014, July 17 **Litho.** ***Perf. 14¼***

3305	A775	2nd multi	1.60	1.20
3306	A775	1st multi	1.90	1.40
3307	A775	97p multi	2.90	2.25
3308	A775	£1.28 multi	4.00	2.90
3309	A775	£1.47 multi	4.50	3.25
3310	A775	£2.15 multi	6.50	4.75
		Nos. 3305-3310 (6)	21.40	15.75

Photo.

Booklet Stamp
Self-Adhesive

Die Cut Perf. 14¼

3311	A775	1st multi	4.00	1.90
a.		Booklet pane of 6, 2 #3311, 4 #MH420	16.00	

No. 3305 sold for 53p and Nos. 3306 and 3311 each sold for 62p on day of issue.

Poppy, Painting by Fiona Strickland A776

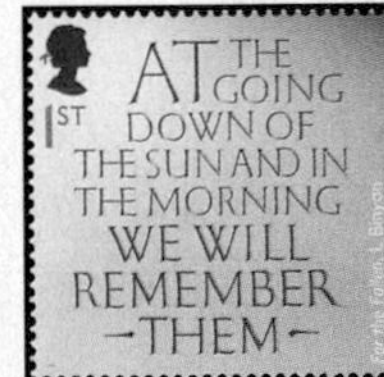

Line From *For the Fallen*, Poem by Laurence Binyon — A777

Private William Cecil Tickle — A778

A Star Shell, Painting by Christopher Richard Wynne Nevinson A779

The Response, Sculpture by William Goscombe John — A780

Princess Mary's Gift Fund Box — A781

2014, July 28 Litho. *Perf. 14¼*

No.	Type	Description	Unused	Used
3312	A776	1st multi	1.90	1.40
3313	A777	1st multi	1.90	1.40
3314	A778	1st multi	1.90	1.40
a.		Booklet pane of 3, #3312-3314 (BK206)	5.75	—
3315	A779	£1.47 multi	4.50	3.25
3316	A780	£1.47 multi	4.50	3.25
3317	A781	£1.47 multi	4.50	3.25
a.		Booklet pane of 3, #3315-3317 (BK206)	13.50	—
		Nos. 3312-3317 (6)	19.20	13.95

World War I, cent. Nos. 3312-3314 each sold for 62p on day of issue. See No. 3778.

Fish Type of 2014

Designs: No. 3318, Common skate. No. 3319, Cornish sardines.

Die Cut Perf. 14¼

2014, Aug. 18 Photo.

Booklet Stamps Self-Adhesive

No.	Type	Description	Unused	Used
3318	A774	1st multi	4.50	1.90
3319	A774	1st multi	4.50	1.90
a.		Booklet pane of 6, #3318-3319, 4 #MH426	17.00	

Nos. 3318-3319 each sold for 62p on day of issue.

Locomotives of Wales Type of 2014

Design: No. 3320, LMS No. 7720.

Die Cut Perf. 14¼

2014, Sept. 18 Photo.

Booklet Stamp Self-Adhesive

No.	Type	Description	Unused	Used
3320	A768	1st multi	5.00	2.00
a.		Booklet pane of 6, 2 #3320, 4 #MH426	18.00	

No. 3320 sold for 62p on day of issue.

Seaside Architecture A782

Designs: No. 3321, Eastbourne Bandstand. No. 3322, Tinside Lido, Plymouth. No. 3323, Bangor Pier. No. 3324, Southwold Lighthouse. No. 3325, Casino, Blackpool Pleasure Beach. No. 3326, Shelter, Bexhill-on-Sea.

No. 3327: a, Llandudno Pier. b, Worthing Pier. c, Dunoon Pier. d, Brighton Pier.

2014, Sept. 18 Litho. *Perf. 14¼*

No.	Type	Description	Unused	Used
3321	A782	1st multi	1.90	1.40
3322	A782	1st multi	1.90	1.40
3323	A782	97p multi	2.90	2.25
3324	A782	97p multi	2.90	2.25
3325	A782	£1.28 multi	4.00	2.90
3326	A782	£1.28 multi	4.00	2.90
		Nos. 3321-3326 (6)	17.60	13.10
3327		Sheet of 4	11.50	8.75
a.-b.		A782 1st Either single	1.90	1.40
c.-d.		A782 £1.28 Either single	4.00	2.90

Europa (No. 3321). Nos. 3321, 3322, 3327a and 3327b each sold for 62p on day of issue.

Prime Ministers A783

Designs: No. 3328, Lady Margaret Thatcher (1925-2013). No. 3329, Harold Wilson (1916-95). No. 3330, Clement Attlee (1883-1967). No. 3331, Sir Winston Churchill (1874-1965). No. 3332, William Gladstone (1809-98). No. 3333, Sir Robert Peel (1788-1850). No. 3334, Charles Grey, 2nd Earl Grey (1764-1845). No. 3335, William Pitt, the Younger (1759-1806).

2014, Oct. 14 Litho. *Perf. 14½*

No.	Type	Description	Unused	Used
3328	A783	1st multi	1.90	1.40
3329	A783	1st multi	1.90	1.40
3330	A783	1st multi	1.90	1.40
3331	A783	1st multi	1.90	1.40
a.		Horiz. strip of 4, #3328-3331	7.75	5.75
3332	A783	97p multi	2.90	2.25
3333	A783	97p multi	2.90	2.25
3334	A783	97p multi	2.90	2.25
3335	A783	97p multi	2.90	2.25
a.		Horiz. strip of 4, #3332-3335	12.00	9.00
		Nos. 3328-3335 (8)	19.20	14.60

Nos. 3328-3331 each sold for 62p on day of issue.

A784

Christmas — A785

Designs: Nos. 3336a, 3336c, 3337, 3339, Collecting a Christmas tree. Nos. 3336b, 3336d, 3338, 3340, Posting Christmas cards. £1.28, Building a snowman. £1.47, Carolers. £2.15, Ice skaters.

2014, Nov. 4 Photo. *Perf. 14½x15*

No.	Type	Description	Unused	Used
3336		Sheet of 7	23.00	23.00
a.		A784 2nd multi	1.60	1.20
b.		A784 1st multi	1.90	1.40
c.		A785 2nd Large multi	2.25	1.60
d.		A785 1st Large multi	2.75	2.10
e.		A784 £1.28 multi	4.00	2.90
f.		A784 £1.47 multi	4.50	3.25
g.		A784 £2.15 multi	6.50	5.00

Self-Adhesive

Die Cut Perf. 14½x15

No.	Type	Description	Unused	Used
3337	A784	2nd multi	1.60	1.20
a.		Booklet pane of 12	19.50	
b.		Litho., die cut perf. 14½x15 syncopated, + label (3342b)	1.75	1.75
3338	A784	1st multi	1.90	1.40
a.		Booklet pane of 12	23.00	
b.		Litho., die cut perf. 14½x15 syncopated, + label (3342b)	2.00	2.00
3339	A785	2nd Large multi	2.25	1.60
3340	A785	1st Large multi	2.75	2.10
3341	A784	£1.28 multi	4.00	2.90
a.		Litho., die cut perf. 14½x15 syncopated, + label (3342b)	4.25	4.25
3342	A784	£1.47 multi	4.50	3.25
a.		Litho., die cut perf. 14½x15 syncopated, + label (3342b)	4.75	4.75
b.		Sheet of 20, 8 each #3337b, 3338b, 2 each #3341a, 3342a, + 20 labels	48.00	
3343	A784	£2.15 multi	6.50	5.00
		Nos. 3337-3343 (7)	23.50	17.45

On day of issue, Nos. 3336a and 3337 each sold for 53p, Nos. 3336b and 3338 each sold for 62p, Nos. 3336c and 3339 each sold for 73p, and Nos. 3336d and 3340 each sold for 93p. No. 3342b sold for £15.20 and labels could not be personalized.

Publication of *Alice's Adventures in Wonderland,* by Lewis Carroll, 150th Anniv. — A786

Designs: No. 3344, Alice and the White Rabbit. No. 3345, Alice falling down the Rabbit Hole. Nos. 3346, 3353B, Alice holding bottle with tag inscribed "Drink Me." Nos. 3347, 3353C, Alice bent over in the White Rabbit's house. No. 3348, Alice and the Cheshire Cat. No. 3349, Alice, March Hare, Dormouse and the Hatter at the Tea Party. No. 3350, Queen of Hearts. No. 3351, Alice and flamingo at the Queen's Croquet Ground. No. 3352, Alice giving evidence at the trial of the Knave of Hearts. No. 3353, Alice and playing cards.

2015, Jan. 6 Litho. *Perf. 14½*

No.	Type	Description	Unused	Used
3344	A786	2nd multi	1.60	1.20
3345	A786	2nd multi	1.60	1.20
a.		Vert. pair, #3344-3345	3.20	2.40
3346	A786	1st multi	1.90	1.40
3347	A786	1st multi	1.90	1.40
a.		Vert. pair, #3346-3347	3.80	2.90
3348	A786	81p multi	2.50	1.90
3349	A786	81p multi	2.50	1.90
a.		Vert. pair, #3348-3349	5.00	4.00
3350	A786	£1.28 multi	4.00	3.00
3351	A786	£1.28 multi	4.00	3.00
a.		Vert. pair, #3350-3351	8.00	6.00
3352	A786	£1.47 multi	4.50	3.25
3353	A786	£1.47 multi	4.50	3.25
a.		Vert. pair, #3352-3353	9.00	6.75
		Nos. 3344-3353 (10)	29.00	21.50

Photo.

Booklet Stamps Self-Adhesive

Die Cut Perf. 14½

No.	Type	Description	Unused	Used
3353B	A786	1st multi	6.50	4.00
3353C	A786	1st multi	6.50	4.00
d.		Booklet pane of 6, #3353B-3353C, 4 #MH426	22.50	

On day of issue, Nos. 3344 and 3345 each sold for 53p and Nos. 3346, 3347, 3353B and 2253C each sold for 62p.

A787

A788

A789

A790

A791

A792

A793

A794

Perf. 14¾x14 Syncopated

2015, Jan. 20 Litho.

No.	Type	Description	Unused	Used
3354		Sheet of 8	15.50	11.50
a.		A787 1st multi	1.90	1.40
b.		A788 1st multi	1.90	1.40
c.		A789 1st multi	1.90	1.40
d.		A790 1st multi	1.90	1.40
e.		A791 1st multi	1.90	1.40
f.		A792 1st multi	1.90	1.40
g.		A793 1st multi	1.90	1.40
h.		A794 1st multi	1.90	1.40

Photo.

Booklet Stamps Self-Adhesive

Die Cut Perf. 14¾x14

No.	Type	Description	Unused	Used
3355	A791	1st multi	2.50	1.90
3356	A787	1st multi	2.50	1.90
3357	A790	1st multi	2.50	1.90
3358	A794	1st multi	2.50	1.90
3359	A788	1st multi	2.50	1.90
3360	A789	1st multi	2.50	1.90
3361	A793	1st multi	2.50	1.90
3362	A792	1st multi	2.50	1.90
a.		Booklet pane of 12, #3356, 3359, 3361, 3362, 2 each #3355, 3357, 3358, 3360	30.00	
b.		Sheet of 20, 3 each #3355, 3357, 3358, 3360, 2 each #3356, 3359, 3361, 3362, + 20 labels, litho.	60.00	
		Nos. 3355-3362 (8)	20.00	15.20

On day of issue, Nos. 3354a-3354h, 3355-3362 each sold for 62p. No. 3362b sold for £12.90. Labels could not be personalized.

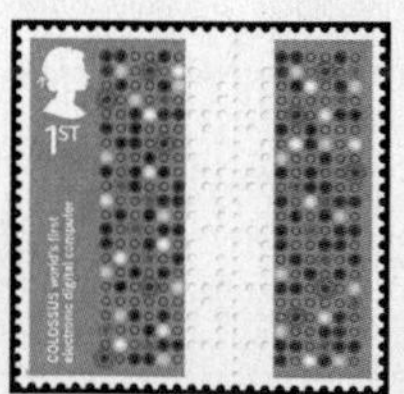

Inventions A795

Designs: No. 3363, Colossus computer. No. 3364, World Wide Web. No. 3365, Catseye reflectors. No. 3366, Fiber optics. No. 3367, Stainless steel. No. 3368, Carbon fiber. No. 3369, DNA sequencing. No. 3370, I-limb bionic hand.

2015, Feb. 19 Litho. *Perf. 14½*

No.	Type	Description	Unused	Used
3363	A795	1st multi	1.90	1.40
a.		Booklet pane of 4, #2970, 3363, 2 #3005 (BK207)	6.50	—
3364	A795	1st multi	1.90	1.40
a.		Horiz. pair, #3363-3364	3.80	2.90
3365	A795	81p multi	2.50	1.90
3366	A795	81p multi	2.50	1.90
a.		Horiz. pair, #3365-3366	5.00	4.00
3367	A795	£1.28 multi	4.00	3.00
3368	A795	£1.28 multi	4.00	3.00
a.		Horiz. pair, #3367-3368	8.00	6.00
3369	A795	£1.47 multi	4.50	3.50
a.		Booklet pane of 4, #3365, 3366, 3368, 3369 (BK207)	14.50	—
3370	A795	£1.47 multi	4.50	3.50
a.		Horiz. pair, #3369-3370	9.00	7.00
b.		Booklet pane of 4, #3363, 3364, 3367, 3370 (BK207)	13.00	—
		Nos. 3363-3370 (8)	25.80	19.60

Nos. 3363-3364 each sold for 62p on day of issue.

Bridges A796

Designs: No. 3371, Tarr Steps Bridge over Barle River. No. 3372, Row Bridge over Mosedale Beck. No. 3373, Pulteney Bridge over Avon River. No. 3374, Craigellachie Bridge over Spey River. No. 3375, Menai Suspension Bridge over Menai Strait. No. 3376, High Level Bridge over Tyne River. No. 3377, Royal Border Bridge over Tweed River. No. 3378, Tees Transporter Bridge over Tees River. No. 3379, Humber Bridge over Humber River. No. 3380, Peace Bridge over Foyle River.

2015, Mar. 5 Litho. *Perf. 14½x14¼*

No.	Type	Description	Unused	Used
3371	A796	1st multi	1.90	1.40
3372	A796	1st multi	1.90	1.40
3373	A796	1st multi	1.90	1.40
3374	A796	1st multi	1.90	1.40
3375	A796	1st multi	1.90	1.40
a.		Horiz. strip of 5, #3371-3375	9.50	7.00
3376	A796	1st multi	1.90	1.40
3377	A796	1st multi	1.90	1.40
3378	A796	1st multi	1.90	1.40
3379	A796	1st multi	1.90	1.40
3380	A796	1st multi	1.90	1.40
a.		Horiz. strip of 5, #3376-3380	9.50	7.00
		Nos. 3371-3380 (10)	19.00	14.00

Nos. 3371-3380 each sold for 62p on day of issue.

Comedians A797

Designs: No. 3381, Spike Milligan (1918-2002). No. 3382, Ronnie Corbett and Ronnie Barker (1929-2005) (The Two Ronnies). No. 3383, Billy Connolly. No. 3384, 3392, Eric Morecambe (1926-84) and Ernie Wise (1925-99). Nos. 3385, 3391, Norman Wisdom (1915-2010). No. 3386, Lenny Henry. No. 3387, Peter Cook (1937-95) and Dudley Moore (1935-2002). No. 3388, Monty Python. No. 3389, Dawn French and Jennifer Saunders. No. 3390, Victoria Wood.

2015, Apr. 1 Litho. *Perf. 14¼*

No.	Type	Description	Unused	Used
3381	A797	1st multi	1.90	1.40
3382	A797	1st multi	1.90	1.40
3383	A797	1st multi	1.90	1.40
3384	A797	1st multi	1.90	1.40
3385	A797	1st multi	1.90	1.40
a.		Horiz. strip of 5, #3381-3385	9.50	7.00
3386	A797	1st multi	1.90	1.40
3387	A797	1st multi	1.90	1.40
3388	A797	1st multi	1.90	1.40
3389	A797	1st multi	1.90	1.40
3390	A797	1st multi	1.90	1.40
a.		Horiz. strip of 5, #3386-3390	9.50	7.00
		Nos. 3381-3390 (10)	19.00	14.00

Photo.
Booklet Stamps
Self-Adhesive
Die Cut Perf. 14¼x14

3391	A797	1st multi	4.00	3.00
3392	A797	1st multi	4.00	3.00
a.		Booklet pane of 6, #3391, 3392, 4 #MH426	16.00	

Nos. 3381-3392 each sold for 63p on day of issue.

Penny Black, 175th Anniv. — A798

Designs: Nos. 3393a, 3394, 3396, Great Britain #1. Nos. 3393b, 3395, Great Britain #2.

Perf. 14¾x14 Syncopated

2015, May 6 **Litho.**

3393	A798	Sheet of 4, 2 each #3393a-3393b	7.75	6.00
a.-b.		1st Either single	1.90	1.40

Self-Adhesive
Die Cut Perf. 14¾x14

3394	A798	1st multi + label	4.00	4.00
3395	A798	1st multi + label	4.00	4.00

Photo.
Booklet Stamp

3396	A798	1st multi	2.50	1.90
a.		Booklet pane of 6	15.00	

Nos. 3393a, 3393b, 3394-3396 each had a franking value of 63p on day of issue. Nos. 3394 and 3395 were printed together in sheets containing 10 of each stamp + 20 labels that could not be personalized. The sheet sold for £13.10. No. 3394 was also printed in sheets of 10 + 10 labels that could be personalized that sold for £10.20, and sheets of 20 + 20 labels that could be personalized that sold for £18.65.

World War I, Cent. — A799

Designs: No. 3397, *Poppies,* painting by Howard Hodgkin. No. 3398, Line from poem, *All the Hills and Vales Along,* by Charles Sorley. No. 3399, Kulbir Thapa, Nepalese Gurkha rifleman. No. 3400, *The Kensingtons at Laventie,* painting by Eric Kennington. No. 3401, Soldier at grave, Cape Helles, Gallipoli, Turkey. No. 3402, London Irish Rifles' soccer ball from Battle of Loos.

2015, May 14 **Litho.** ***Perf. 14¼***

3397	A799	1st multi	1.90	1.40
3398	A799	1st multi	1.90	1.40
3399	A799	1st multi	1.90	1.40
a.		Booklet pane of 3, #3397-3399 (BK208)	5.75	—
3400	A799	£1.52 multi	4.50	3.50
3401	A799	£1.52 multi	4.50	3.50
3402	A799	£1.52 multi	4.50	3.50
a.		Booklet pane of 3, #3400-3402 (BK208)	13.50	—
		Nos. 3397-3402 (6)	19.20	14.70

On day of issue, Nos, 3397-3399 each sold for 63p.

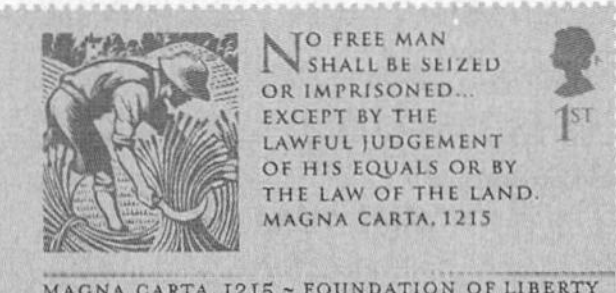

Magna Carta, 800th Anniv. — A800

Designs: No. 3403, Farmer, quotation from Magna Carta. No. 3404, King and nobleman, quotation from Simon de Montfort's Parliament. No. 3405, Man and woman, quotation from British Bill of Rights. No. 3406, Man and jail cell, quotation from American Bill of Rights. No. 3407, Dove, quotation from Universal Declaration of Human Rights. No. 3408, Women, quotation from Charter of the Commonwealth.

2015, June 2 **Litho.** ***Perf. 14¾***

3403	A800	1st multi	1.90	1.40
3404	A800	1st multi	1.90	1.40
3405	A800	£1.33 multi	4.00	3.00
3406	A800	£1.33 multi	4.00	3.00
3407	A800	£1.52 multi	4.50	3.50
3408	A800	£1.52 multi	4.50	3.50
		Nos. 3403-3408 (6)	20.80	15.80

On day of issue, Nos. 3403 and 3404 each sold for 63p.

A801

Battle of Waterloo, 200th Anniv. — A802

Paintings: No. 3409, The Defense of Hougoumont. No. 3410, The Scots Greys During the Charge of the Union Brigade. No. 3411, The French Cavalry's Assault on Allied Defensive Squares. No. 3412, The Defense of La Haye Sainte by the King's German Legion. No. 3413, The Capture of Plancenoit by the Prussians. No. 3414, The French Imperial Guard's Final Assault.

No. 3415 — Soldier from: a, Prussian Army 15th Infantry Regiment, IV Corps. b, Anglo-Allied Army King's German Legion Light Infantry. c, Anglo-Allied Army 92nd Gordon Highlanders. d, French Army Imperial Guard Grenadiers.

2015, June 18 **Litho.** ***Perf. 14¾***

3409	A801	1st multi	1.90	1.40
3410	A801	1st multi	1.90	1.40
3411	A801	£1 multi	3.00	2.25
3412	A801	£1 multi	3.00	2.25
3413	A801	£1.52 multi	4.50	3.50
a.		Booklet pane of 4, #3410-3413 (BK209)	12.50	—
3414	A801	£1.52 multi	4.50	3.50
a.		Booklet pane of 2, #3409, 3414 (BK209)	6.50	—
		Nos. 3409-3414 (6)	18.80	14.30

Miniature Sheet
Perf. 14¼

3415	A802	Sheet of 4	12.00	9.00
a.-b.		1st Either single	1.90	1.40
c.-d.		£1.33 Either single	4.00	3.00
e.		Booklet pane of 4, #3415a-3415d (BK209)	12.00	—

On day of issue, Nos. 3409-3410, 3415a-3415b each sold for 63p.

Miniature Sheet

Battle of Britain, 75th Anniv. — A803

No. 3416: a, Pilots scramble to their Hurricanes. b, Supermarine Spitfires on patrol. c, Armorer replaces ammunition boxes. d, Spotters of the Auxiliary Territorial Service. e, Operations Room at Bentley Priory. f, Pilots of 32 Squadron await orders.

2015, July 16 **Litho.** ***Perf. 14¼***

3416	A803	Sheet of 6	18.00	13.50
a.-c.		1st Any single	1.90	1.40
d.-f.		£1.33 Any single	4.00	3.00
g.		Booklet pane of 4, #3416a, 3416c, 2 #3416b (BK220)	7.50	—

On day of Issue, Nos. 3416a-3416c each sold for 63p.

Issued: No. 3416g, 3/20/18.

A804

Bees — A805

Designs: 2nd, Scabious bee on field scabious. Nos. 3418, 3424, Great yellow bumblebee on bird's foot trefoil. £1, Northern Colletes bee on wild carrot. No. 3420, Bilberry bumblebee on bilberry. £1.52, Large mason bee on horseshoe vetch. £2.25, Potter flower bee on ground ivy.

No. 3423: a, Waggle dance. b, Pollination. c, Making honey. d,Tending young.

Perf. 14¼x14½

2015, Aug. 18 **Litho.**

3417	A804	2nd multi	1.60	1.20
3418	A804	1st multi	1.90	1.40
3419	A804	£1 multi	3.00	2.25
3420	A804	£1.33 multi	4.00	3.00
3421	A804	£1.52 multi	4.50	3.50
3422	A804	£2.25 multi	6.75	5.00
		Nos. 3417-3422 (6)	21.75	16.35

Miniature Sheet

3423	A805	Sheet of 4	12.00	9.00
a.-b.		1st Either single	1.90	1.40
c.-d.		£1.33 Either single	4.00	3.00

Photo.
Booklet Stamp
Self-Adhesive
Die Cut Perf. 14¼x14½

3424	A804	1st multi	3.00	2.00
a.		Booklet pane of 6, 2 #3424, 4 #MH426	12.00	

On day of issue, No. 3417 sold for 54p; Nos. 3418, 3423a, 3423b and 3424, for 63p each.

2015 Rugby World Cup, Great Britain A806

Designs: No. 3425, Tackle. No. 3426, Scrum. Nos. 3427, 3433, Try. No. 3428, 3434, Conversion attempt. No. 3429, Pass. No. 3430, Drop goal. No. 3431, Ruck. No. 3432, Line-out.

2015, Sept. 18 **Litho.** ***Perf. 14¼***

3425	A806	2nd multi	1.60	1.20
3426	A806	2nd multi	1.60	1.20
a.		Horiz. pair, #3425-3426	3.25	2.50
3427	A806	1st multi	1.90	1.40
3428	A806	1st multi	1.90	1.40
a.		Horiz. pair, #3427-3428	4.00	2.90
3429	A806	£1 multi	3.00	2.25
3430	A806	£1 multi	3.00	2.25
a.		Horiz. pair, #3429-3430	6.00	4.50
3431	A806	£1.52 multi	4.50	3.50
3432	A806	£1.52 multi	4.50	3.50
a.		Horiz. pair, #3431-3432	9.00	7.00
		Nos. 3425-3432 (8)	22.00	16.70

Photo.
Booklet Stamps
Self-Adhesive
Die Cut Perf 14¼

3433	A806	1st multi	3.50	2.00
3434	A806	1st multi	3.50	2.00
a.		Booklet pane of 6, #3433, 3434, 4 #MH457	12.00	

On day of issue, Nos. 3425-3426 each sold for 54p and Nos. 3427-3428, 3433-3434 each sold for 63p.

A807

Premiere of Movie *Star Wars: The Force Awakens* — A808

Designs: Nos. 3435, 3448, Darth Vader. Nos. 3436, 3447, Yoda. No. 3437, Obi-Wan Kenobi. Nos. 3438, 3450, Stormtrooper. Nos. 3439, 3449, Han Solo. No. 3440, Rey. No. 3441, Princess Leia. No. 3442, The Emperor. No. 3443, Luke Skywalker. No. 3444, Boba Fett. No. 3445, Finn. No. 3446, Kylo Ren.

No. 3451: a, X-Wing Starfighter with red stripe (60x21mm). b, AT-AT walkers (41x30mm). c, TIE Fighters (27x36mm). d, TIE Fighters and Death Star (35x36mm). e, X-Wing Starfighter and planet (60x21mm). f, Millennium Falcon (60x30mm).

2015, Oct. 20 **Litho.** ***Perf. 14½***

3435	A807	1st multi	1.90	1.40
3436	A807	1st multi	1.90	1.40
3437	A807	1st multi	1.90	1.40
3438	A807	1st multi	1.90	1.40
3439	A807	1st multi	1.90	1.40
3440	A807	1st multi	1.90	1.40
a.		Horiz. strip of 6, #3435-3440	11.50	8.50
3441	A807	1st multi	1.90	1.40
3442	A807	1st multi	1.90	1.40
3443	A807	1st multi	1.90	1.40
a.		Booklet pane of 6, #3436, 3438, 3439, 3441, 3442, 3443 (BK210)	11.50	—
3444	A807	1st multi	1.90	1.40
3445	A807	1st multi	1.90	1.40
3446	A807	1st multi	1.90	1.40
a.		Horiz. strip of 6, #3441-3446	11.50	8.50
b.		Booklet pane of 6, #3435, 3437, 3440, 3444, 3445, 3446 (BK210)	11.50	—
		Nos. 3435-3446 (12)	22.80	16.80

Self-Adhesive
Die Cut Perf. 14½

3447	A807	1st multi + label	2.00	2.00
3448	A807	1st multi + label	2.00	2.00
3449	A807	1st multi + label	2.00	2.00
3450	A807	1st multi + label	2.00	2.00
a.		Sheet of 10, 3 each #3447-3448, 2 each #3449-3450, + 10 labels	20.00	
		Nos. 3447-3450 (4)	8.00	8.00

Miniature Sheet
Die Cut Perf. 14¼, 14½ (#3451a-3451e), 14¾ (#3451f)

3451	A808	Sheet of 6	11.50	11.50
a.-f.		1st Any single	1.90	1.40
g.		Booklet pane of 3, #3451a-3451c (BK210)	5.75	
h.		Booklet pane of 3, #3451d-3451f (BK210)	5.75	

Issued: Nos. 3443a, 3446b, 3451g, 12/17.

On day of issue, Nos. 3435-3436, 3451a-3451f each sold for 63p. Nos. 3447-3450 each had a franking value of 63p on day of issue. No. 3450a sold for £6.80 and labels could not be personalized.

Flag Type of 2005
Perf. 14¾x14 Syncopated

2015, Dec. 17 **Litho.**

Booklet Stamp

3452	A594	1st multi	2.40	2.00
a.		Booklet pane of 8, 4 #3452, 2 each #MH401Cf, MH440, + label (BK210)	25.00	—

No. 3452 had a franking value of 63p on day of issue.

A809

Christmas
A810

Designs: Nos. 3453a, 3453c, 3454, 3456, Journey to Bethlehem. Nos. 3453b, 3453d, 3455, 3457, Nativity. £1, Animals and palm tree. £1.33, Shepherds and angel. £1.52, Magi and Star of Bethlehem. £2.25, Annunciation.

2015, Nov. 3 Photo. *Perf. 14½x15*

Miniature Sheet

3453		Sheet of 8	27.50	21.00
a.	A809 2nd multi		1.60	1.20
b.	A809 1st multi		1.90	1.40
c.	A810 2nd Large multi		2.25	1.65
d.	A810 1st Large multi		2.90	2.10
e.	A809 £1 multi		3.00	2.25
f.	A809 £1.33 multi		4.00	3.00
g.	A809 £1.52 multi		4.50	3.50
h.	A809 £2.25 multi		6.75	5.00

Self-Adhesive

Die Cut Perf. 14½x15

3454	A809	2nd multi	1.60	1.20
a.		Booklet pane of 12	21.00	
b.		Litho., die cut perf. 14½x15 syncopated + label (3461b)	1.60	1.60
3455	A809	1st multi	1.90	1.40
a.		Booklet pane of 12	23.00	
b.		Litho., die cut perf. 14½x15 syncopated + label (3461b)	1.90	1.90
3456	A810	2nd Large multi	2.25	1.65
3457	A810	1st Large multi	2.90	2.10
3458	A809	£1 multi	3.00	2.25
a.		Litho., die cut perf. 14½x15 syncopated + label (3461b)	4.50	4.50
3459	A809	£1.33 multi	4.00	3.00
a.		Litho., die cut perf. 14½x15 syncopated + label (3461b)	6.00	6.00
3460	A809	£1.52 multi	4.50	3.50
a.		Litho., die cut perf. 14½x15 syncopated + label (3461b)	6.75	6.75
3461	A809	£2.25 multi	6.75	5.00
a.		Litho., die cut perf. 14½x15 syncopated + label (3461b)	10.00	10.00
b.		Sheet of 20, #3458a, 3459a, 3460a, 3461a, 8 each #3454b, 3455b, + 20 labels	55.00	
		Nos. 3454-3461 (8)	26.90	20.10

On day of issue, Nos. 3453a and 3454 each sold for 54p; Nos. 3453b and 3455, for 63p; Nos. 3453c and 3456, for 74p; and Nos. 3453d and 3457, for 95p. No. 3461b sold for £15.96 and labels could not be personalized.

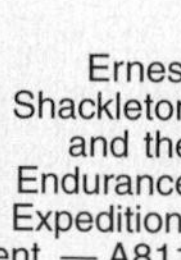

Ernest Shackleton and the Endurance Expedition, Cent. — A811

Designs: No. 3462, Entering the Antarctic ice, December 1914. No. 3463, Endurance frozen in pack ice, January 1915. No. 3464, Striving to free Endurance, February 1915. No. 3465, Trapped in a pressure crack, October 1915. No. 3466, Patience Camp, December 1915-April 1916. No. 3467, Safe arrival at Elephant Island, April 1916. No. 3468, Setting out for South Georgia, April 1916. No. 3469, Rescue of Endurance crew, August 1916.

2016, Jan. 7 Litho. *Perf. 14¼x14½*

3462	A811	1st multi	1.90	1.40
3463	A811	1st multi	1.90	1.40
a.		Horiz. pair, #3462-3463	3.80	2.90
3464	A811	£1 multi	3.00	2.25
3465	A811	£1 multi	3.00	2.25
a.		Horiz. pair, #3464-3465	6.00	4.50
3466	A811	£1.33 multi	4.00	3.00
3467	A811	£1.33 multi	4.00	3.00
a.		Horiz. pair, #3466-3467	8.00	6.00
3468	A811	£1.52 multi	4.50	3.50
3469	A811	£1.52 multi	4.50	3.50
a.		Horiz. pair, #3468-3469	9.00	7.00
		Nos. 3462-3469 (8)	26.80	20.30

On day of issue, Nos. 3462-3463 each sold for 63p.

Royal Mail, 500th Anniv. — A812

Post Office Posters — A813

Designs: No. 3470, Sir Brian Tuke, 16th Century Master of the Posts. No. 3471, Packet ship. No. 3472, Penfold pillar box. No. 3473, River post. No. 3474, Mail coach. No. 3475, Medway Mail Center.

No. 3476 — Inscriptions: a, "Quickest way by air mail." b, "Adderss your letters plainly." c, "Pack your parcels carefully." d, "Stamps in books save time."

Perf. 14½x14¼

2016, Feb. 17 Litho.

3470	A812	1st multi	1.75	1.40
3471	A812	1st multi	1.75	1.40
3472	A812	1st multi	1.75	1.40
3473	A812	£1.52 multi	4.25	3.50
a.		Booklet pane of 3, #3470, 3472, 3473 (BK211)	9.25	—
3474	A812	£1.52 multi	4.25	3.50
3475	A812	£1.52 multi	4.25	3.50
a.		Booklet pane of 3, #3471, 3474, 3475 (BK211)	12.00	—
		Nos. 3470-3475 (6)	18.00	14.70

Miniature Sheet

3476	A813	Sheet of 4	11.00	11.00
a.-b.		1st Either single	1.75	1.40
c.-d.		£1.33 Either single	3.75	2.90
e.		Booklet pane of 4, #3476a-3476d (BK211)	13.00	—

On day of issue, Nos. 3470-3472, 3476a and 3476b each sold for 63p.

Penny Red (Great Britain No. 3), 175th Anniv. — A814

Perf. 14¾x14 Syncopated

2016, Feb. 18 Litho.

Booklet Stamps

3477	A814	1st multi	2.50	2.50
a.		Booklet pane of 8, 2 #3393a, 3 each #3393b, 3477, + central label (BK211)	20.00	—

Self-Adhesive

Photo.

Die Cut Perf. 14¾x14 Syncopated

3478	A814	1st multi	2.50	2.00
a.		Booklet pane of 6	9.00	
b.		Litho., pane of 20 + 20 labels	37.00	

Nos. 3477-3478 had a franking value of 63p on day of issue. No. 3478b sold for £13.10, and labels could not be personalized.

Humanitarians
A815

Designs: No. 3479, Sir Nicholas Winton (1909-2015), rescuer of children in World War II. No. 3480, Sue Ryder (1924-2000), charity founder. No. 3481, John Boyd Orr (1880-1971), Director General of United Nations Food and Agriculture Organization. No. 3482, Eglantyne Jebb (1876-1928), founder of Save the Children Fund. No. 3483, Joseph Rowntree (1836-1925), philanthropist. No. 3484, Josephine Butler (1828-1906), social reformer and feminist.

Perf. 14½x14¼

2016, Mar. 15 Litho.

3479	A815	1st black	1.90	1.40
3480	A815	1st black	1.90	1.40
3481	A815	1st black	1.90	1.40
a.		Horiz. strip of 3, #3479-3481	5.75	4.25
3482	A815	£1.33 black	3.75	2.90
3483	A815	£1.33 black	3.75	2.90
3484	A815	£1.33 black	3.75	2.90
a.		Horiz. strip of 3, #3482-3484	11.50	8.75
		Nos. 3479-3484 (6)	16.95	12.90

On day of issue, Nos. 3479-3481 each sold for 63p.

Quotations From Works by William Shakespeare (1564-1616) A816

Quotation from: No. 3485, Hamlet. No. 3486, Julius Caesar. No. 3487, Romeo and Juliet. No. 3488, As You Like It. No. 3489, Much Ado About Nothing. No. 3490, Sonnet 30. No. 3491, Venus and Adonis. No. 3492, The Tempest. No. 3493, Macbeth. No. 3494, Richard II.

2016, Apr. 5 Litho. *Perf. 14½x14¼*

3485	A816	1st multi	1.90	1.40
3486	A816	1st multi	1.90	1.40
3487	A816	1st multi	1.90	1.40
3488	A816	1st multi	1.90	1.40
3489	A816	1st multi	1.90	1.40
a.		Horiz. strip of 5, #3485-3489	9.50	7.00
3490	A816	1st multi	1.90	1.40
3491	A816	1st multi	1.90	1.40
3492	A816	1st multi	1.90	1.40
3493	A816	1st multi	1.90	1.40
3494	A816	1st multi	1.90	1.40
a.		Horiz. strip of 5, #3490-3494	9.50	7.00
		Nos. 3485-3494 (10)	19.00	14.00

On day of issue, Nos. 3485-3494 each sold for 64p.

Princess Elizabeth and King George VI, c. 1930 — A817

Queen Elizabeth II at State Opening of Parliament, 2012 — A818

Queen Elizabeth II, Princess Anne, Prince Charles, 1952 — A819

Queen Elizabeth II Visiting New Zealand, 1977 — A820

Queen Elizabeth II and Prince Philip, 1957 — A821

Queen Elizabeth II and Nelson Mandela, 1996 — A822

Queen Elizabeth II and Heirs to the Throne — A823

Designs: Nos. 3501a, 3502, Prince Charles. Nos. 3501b, 3503, Queen Elizabeth II. Nos. 3501c, 3504, Prince George of Cambridge. Nos. 3501d, 3505, Prince William of Cambridge.

2016 Litho. *Perf. 14¼x14½*

3495	A817	1st multi	1.90	1.40
3496	A818	1st multi	1.90	1.40
3497	A819	1st multi	1.90	1.40
a.		Horiz. strip of 3, #3495-3497	5.75	4.25
3498	A820	£1.52 multi	4.50	3.50
3499	A821	£1.52 multi	4.50	3.50
a.		Booklet pane of 2, #3498-3499 (BK212)	9.50	—
3500	A822	£1.52 multi	4.50	3.50
a.		Horiz. strip of 3, #3498-3500	13.50	10.50
b.		Booklet pane of 4, #3495, 3496, 3497, 3500 (BK212)	10.50	—
		Nos. 3495-3500 (6)	19.20	14.70

Miniature Sheet

Perf. 14¼

3501	A823	Sheet of 4	7.75	7.75
a.-d.		1st Any single	1.90	1.40
e.		Booklet pane of 4, #3501a-3501d (BK212)	7.75	—

Booklet Stamps

Self-Adhesive

Photo.

Die Cut Perf. 14¼

3502	A823	1st multi	3.00	1.40
3503	A823	1st multi	3.00	1.40
a.		Booklet pane of 6, #3502, 3503, 4 #MH457	11.50	
3504	A823	1st multi	3.00	1.40
3505	A823	1st multi	3.00	1.40
a.		Booklet pane of 6, #3504, 3505, 4 #MH457	10.50	
		Nos. 3502-3505 (4)	12.00	5.60

90th birthday of Queen Elizabeth II.

Issued: Nos. 3495-3503, 4/21; Nos. 3504-3505, 6/9.

On day of issue, Nos. 3495-3497, 3501a-3501d, 3502-2505 each sold for 64p.

Miniature Sheet

Animals — A824

No. 3506: a, Woodpecker (36x40mm). b, Snake (31x49mm). c, Chimpanzee (39x50mm). d, Bat (26x49mm). e, Orangutan (29x50mm). f, Koalas (41x35mm).

Die Cut Perf. 14¾x14¼ Syncopated

2016, May 17 Litho.

Self-Adhesive

3506	A824	Sheet of 6	18.00	
a.-b.		1st Either single	1.90	1.40
c.-d.		£1.05 Either single	3.00	2.25
e.-f.		£1.33 Either single	4.00	3.00

On day of issue, Nos. 3506a-3506b each sold for 64p.

World War I, Cont. — A825

Post Office at War, 1914-18 — A826

Designs: No. 3507, Munitions worker Lottie Meade. No. 3508, Quotation from "To My Brother," by Vera Brittain. No. 3509, Battlefield Poppy, by Giles Revell. No. 3510, Battle of Jutland commemorative medal. No. 3511, Thiepval Memorial, Somme, France. No. 3512, Travoys Arriving with Wounded, by Sir Stanley Spencer.

No. 3513: a, Post Office Rifles. b, Soldier writing a letter from the Western Front. c, Delivering the mail on the home front. d, Home Depot at Regent's Park, London.

2016, June 21 Litho. *Perf. 14¼*

3507	A825	1st multi	1.75	1.35
3508	A825	1st multi	1.75	1.35
3509	A825	1st multi	1.75	1.35
a.		Booklet pane of 3, #3507-3509 (BK213)	5.50	—
3510	A825	£1.52 multi	4.00	3.00
3511	A825	£1.52 multi	4.00	3.00
3512	A825	£1.52 multi	4.00	3.00
a.		Booklet pane of 3, #3510-3512 (BK213)	12.50	—

Miniature Sheet

Perf. 14¼x14

3513	A826	Sheet of 4	10.50	10.50
a.-b.		1st Either single	1.75	1.35
c.-d.		£1.33 Either single	3.50	2.60
e.		Booklet pane of 4, #3513a-3513d (BK213)	11.00	—

On day of issue, Nos. 3507-3509, 3513a, 3513b each sold for 64p.

Pink Floyd Concerts — A827

The Piper at the Gates of Dawn, by Pink Floyd, 1967 — A828

Atom Heart Mother, by Pink Floyd, 1970 — A829

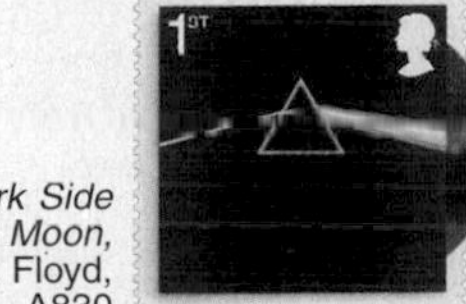

The Dark Side of the Moon, by Pink Floyd, 1973 — A830

Wish You Were Here, by Pink Floyd, 1975 — A831

Animals, by Pink Floyd, 1977 — A832

The Endless River, by Pink Floyd, 2014 — A833

No. 3514: a, UFO Club concert, 1966. b, The Dark Side of the Moon tour, 1973. c, The Wall tour, 1981. d, The Division Bell tour, 1994.

2016, July 7 Litho. *Perf. 14¾x14½*

3514	A827	Sheet of 4	11.50	11.50
a.-b.		1st Either single	1.75	1.35
c.-d.		£1.52 Either single	4.00	3.00

Self-Adhesive

Photo.

Die Cut Perf. 14¾ Syncopated

3515	A828	1st multi	1.75	1.35
3516	A829	1st multi	1.75	1.35
3517	A830	1st multi	1.75	1.35
3518	A831	£1.52 multi	4.00	3.00
3519	A832	£1.52 multi	4.00	3.00
3520	A833	£1.52 multi	4.00	3.00
		Nos. 3515-3520 (6)	17.25	13.05

On day of issue, Nos. 3514a-3514b, 3515-3517 each sold for 64p. A sheet of ten perf. 14¾x14½ stamps with water-activated gum of type A830 sold for £12.95.

Characters From Stories by Beatrix Potter (1866-1943) A834

Designs: Nos. 3521, 3528, Peter Rabbit. Nos. 3522, 3529, Mrs. Tiggy-Winkle. No. 3523, Squirrel Nutkin. No. 3524, Jemima Puddle-Duck. No. 3525, Tom Kitten. No. 3526, Benjamin Bunny.

No. 3527 — Scenes from *The Tale of Peter Rabbit*: a, Mother Rabbit adjusting coat on Peter Rabbit. b, Peter Rabbit and potted plants. c, Peter Rabbit crawling under fence. d, Farmer chasing Peter Rabbit.

2016, July 28 Litho. *Perf. 14½x14¼*

3521	A834	1st multi	1.75	1.35
3522	A834	1st multi	1.75	1.35
a.		Horiz. pair, #3521-3522	3.50	2.75
3523	A834	£1.33 multi	3.50	2.60
3524	A834	£1.33 multi	3.50	2.60
a.		Horiz. pair, #3523-3524	7.00	5.25
3525	A834	£1.52 multi	4.00	3.00
a.		Booklet pane of 3, #3522, 3524, 3525 (BK214)	10.00	—
3526	A834	£1.52 multi	4.00	3.00
a.		Horiz. pair, #3525-3526	8.00	6.00
b.		Booklet pane of 3, #3521, 3523, 3526 (BK214)	10.00	—
		Nos. 3521-3526 (6)	18.50	13.90

Miniature Sheet

3527		Sheet of 4	10.50	10.50
a.-b.		A834 1st Either single	1.75	1.35
c.-d.		A834 £1.33 Either single	3.50	2.60
e.		Booklet pane of 4, #3527a-3527d (BK214)	11.00	—

Booklet Stamps
Self-Adhesive

Photo.

Die Cut Perf. 14½x14¼

3528	A834	1st multi	3.50	1.75
3529	A834	1st multi	3.50	1.75
a.		Booklet pane of 6, #3528, 3529, 4 #MH457	10.50	

On day of issue, Nos. 3521-3522, 3527a-3527b, 3528-3529 each sold for 64p.

Landscape Gardens Designed by Lancelot "Capability" Brown (c. 1716-83) A835

Designs: No. 3530, Blenheim Palace. No. 3531, Longleat. Nos. 3532, 3538, Compton Verney. Nos. 3533, 3539, Highclere Castle. No. 3534, Alnwick Castle. No. 3535, Berrington Hall. No. 3536, Stowe. No. 3537, Croome Park.

2016, Aug. 16 Litho. *Perf. 14¼x14*

3530	A835	2nd multi	1.50	1.10
3531	A835	2nd multi	1.50	1.10
a.		Horiz. pair, #3530-3531	3.00	2.25
3532	A835	1st multi	1.75	1.35
3533	A835	1st multi	1.75	1.35
a.		Horiz. pair, #3532-3533	3.50	2.75
3534	A835	£1.05 multi	2.75	2.00
3535	A835	£1.05 multi	2.75	2.00
a.		Horiz. pair, #3534-3535	5.50	4.00
3536	A835	£1.33 multi	3.50	2.60
3537	A835	£1.33 multi	3.50	2.60
a.		Horiz. pair, #3536-3537	7.00	5.25
		Nos. 3530-3537 (8)	19.00	14.10

Booklet Stamps
Self-Adhesive

Photo.

Die Cut Perf. 14¼x14

3538	A835	1st multi	3.50	1.75
3539	A835	1st multi	3.50	1.75
a.		Booklet pane of 6, #3538, 3539, 4 #MH457	10.50	

Nos. 3530-3531 each sold for 55p and Nos. 3532-3533 and 3538-3539 each sold for 64p on day of issue.

Great Fire of London, 350th Anniv. — A836

Cartoon depictions of fire events with map features: No. 3540, Pudding Lane and Thames Street. No. 3541, River Thames. No. 3542, Finch Lane, Birchin Lane, Cornhill. No. 3543, Paternoster Row. No. 3544, Moorfields. No. 3545, Whitehall.

2016, Sept. 2 Litho. *Perf. 14½x14¼*

3540	A836	1st multi	1.75	1.35
3541	A836	1st multi	1.75	1.35
a.		Horiz. pair, #3540-3541	3.50	2.75
3542	A836	£1.05 multi	2.75	2.00
3543	A836	£1.05 multi	2.75	2.00
a.		Horiz. pair, #3542-3543	5.50	4.00
3544	A836	£1.52 multi	4.00	3.00
3545	A836	£1.52 multi	4.00	3.00
a.		Horiz. pair, #3544-3545	8.00	6.00
		Nos. 3540-3545 (6)	17.00	12.70

On day of issue, Nos. 3540-3541 each sold for 64p.

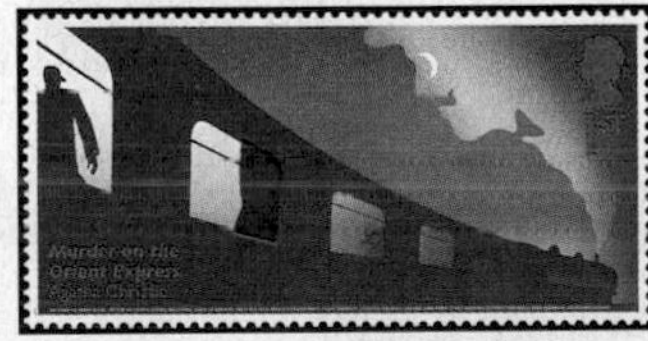

Scenes From Novels by Agatha Christie (1890-1976) — A837

Scene from: No. 3546, *Murder on the Orient Express*. No. 3547, *And Then There Were None*. No. 3548, *The Mysterious Affair at Styles*. No. 3549, *The Murder of Roger Ackroyd*. No. 3550, *The Body in the Library*. No. 3551, *A Murder is Announced*.

Perf. 14¾x14½

2016, Sept. 15 Litho.

3546	A837	1st multi	1.75	1.35
3547	A837	1st multi	1.75	1.35
a.		Vert. pair, #3546-3547	3.50	2.75
3548	A837	£1.33 multi	3.50	2.00
3549	A837	£1.33 multi	3.50	2.00
a.		Vert. pair, #3548-3549	7.00	4.00
3550	A837	£1.52 multi	4.00	3.00
3551	A837	£1.52 multi	4.00	3.00
a.		Vert. pair, #3550-3551	8.00	6.00
		Nos. 3546-3551 (6)	18.50	12.70

On day of issue, Nos. 3546-3547 each sold for 64p.

Children's Book Characters by Roger Hargreaves A838

Designs: Nos. 3552, 3562a, 3563, Mr. Happy. Nos. 3553, 3562b, Little Miss Naughty. Nos. 3554, 3562c, Mr. Bump. Nos. 3555, 3562d, Little Miss Sunshine. Nos. 3556, 3562e, 3564, Mr. Tickle. Nos. 3557, 3562f, Mr. Grumpy. Nos. 3558, 3562g, Little Miss Princess. Nos. 3559, 3562h, Mr. Strong. Nos. 3560, 3562i, Little Miss Christmas. Nos. 3561, 3562j, Mr. Messy.

2016, Oct. 20 Litho. *Perf. 14½*

3552	A838	1st multi	1.75	1.35
3553	A838	1st multi	1.75	1.35
3554	A838	1st multi	1.75	1.35
3555	A838	1st multi	1.75	1.35
3556	A838	1st multi	1.75	1.35
a.		Horiz. strip of 5, #3552-3556	8.75	6.75
3557	A838	1st multi	1.75	1.35
3558	A838	1st multi	1.75	1.35
3559	A838	1st multi	1.75	1.35
3560	A838	1st multi	1.75	1.35
3561	A838	1st multi	1.75	1.35
a.		Horiz. strip of 5, #3557-3561	8.75	1.35
		Nos. 3552-3561 (10)	17.50	13.50

Self-Adhesive

Litho.

Die Cut Perf. 14½

3562		Sheet of 10 + 10 labels	17.50	
a.-j.		A838 1st Any single + label	1.75	1.75

Booklet Stamps

Photo.

3563	A838	1st multi	3.75	2.50
3564	A838	1st multi	3.75	2.50
a.		Booklet pane of 6, #3563-3564, 4 #MH426	15.50	

On day of issue, Nos. 3552-3561 and 3563-3564 each sold for 64p. No. 3562 sold for £6.90, and Nos. 3562a-3562j each have a franking value of 64p. Nos. 3563 and 3564 each have a fuzzy dot structure most visible on the thin black lines of the Hargreaves signature.

A839

Christmas — A840

Designs: Nos. 3565a, 3565c, 3566, 3568, Snowman. Nos. 3565b, 3565d, 3567, 3569, Robin. £1.05, Christmas tree, £1.33, Christmas lantern. £1.52, Christmas stocking. £2.25, Christmas pudding.

2016, Nov. 8 Photo. *Perf. 14½x15*

Miniature Sheet

3565		Sheet of 8	23.50	12.00
a.		A839 2nd multi	1.60	1.20
b.		A839 1st multi	1.75	1.35
c.		A840 2nd Large multi	2.10	1.60
d.		A840 1st Large multi	2.60	2.00
e.		A839 £1.05 multi	3.00	2.10
f.		A839 £1.33 multi	3.75	2.90
g.		A839 £1.52 multi	4.25	3.25
h.		A839 £2.25 multi	6.25	4.75

Self-Adhesive

Die Cut Perf. 14½x15

3566	A839	2nd multi	1.60	1.60
a.		Booklet pane of 12	17.00	
b.		Litho., die cut perf. 14½x15 syncopated + label (3567c)	1.75	1.75
3567	A839	1st multi	1.75	1.00
a.		Booklet pane of 12	19.50	
b.		Litho., die cut perf. 14½x15 syncopated + label (3567c)	1.75	1.75
c.		Sheet of 20, 10 each #3566b, 3567b + 20 labels, litho.	35.00	
3568	A840	2nd Large multi	2.10	1.60
3569	A840	1st Large multi	2.60	2.00
3570	A839	£1.05 multi	3.00	2.10
a.		Litho., die cut perf. 14½x15 syncopated + label (3573b)	4.75	4.75
3571	A839	£1.33 multi	3.75	2.90
a.		Litho., die cut perf. 14½x15 syncopated + label (3573b)	6.00	6.00
3572	A839	£1.52 multi	4.25	3.25
a.		Litho., die cut perf. 14½x15 syncopated + label (3573b)	6.75	6.75

3573 A839 £2.25 multi 6.25 4.75
a. Litho., die cut perf. 14½x15 syncopated + label (3573b) 10.00 10.00
b. Sheet of 20, #3570a, 3571a, 3572a, 3573a, 8 each #3566b, 3567b + 20 labels 55.00
Nos. 3566-3573 (8) 25.30 19.55

On day of issue, Nos. 3565a and 3566 each sold for 55p; Nos. 3565b and 3567, for 64p; Nos. 3565c and 3568, for 76p; and Nos. 3565d and 3569, for 95p. No. 3567c sold for £12.40 and labels could not be personalized. No. 3573b sold for £16.21 and labels could not be personalized.

Ancient Britain
A841

Designs: No. 3574, Battersea shield, London, 350-50 B.C. No. 3575, Skara Brae village, Orkney Islands, 3100-2500 B.C. No. 3576, Star Carr headdress, Yorkshire, 9000 B.C. No. 3577, Maiden Castle hill fort, Dorset, 400 B.C. No. 3578, Avebury stone circles, Wiltshire, 2500 B.C. No. 3579, Drumbest horns, County Antrim, 800 B.C. No. 3580, Grime's Graves flint mines, Norfolk, 2500 B.C. No. 3581, Mantell yr Wyddgrug Mold cape, Flintshire, 1900-1600 B.C.

2017, Jan. 17 Litho. *Perf. 14¼*
3574 A841 1st multi 1.75 1.35
3575 A841 1st multi 1.75 1.35
a. Horiz. pair, #3574-3575 3.50 2.75
3576 A841 £1.05 multi 3.00 2.25
3577 A841 £1.05 multi 3.00 2.25
a. Horiz. pair, #3576-3577 6.00 4.50
3578 A841 £1.33 multi 3.75 2.90
3579 A841 £1.33 multi 3.75 2.90
a. Horiz. pair, #3578-3579 7.50 6.00
3580 A841 £1.52 multi 4.25 3.25
3581 A841 £1.52 multi 4.25 3.25
a. Horiz. pair, #3580-3581 8.50 6.50
Nos. 3574-3581 (8) 25.50 19.50

On day of issue, Nos. 3574-3575 each sold for 64p.

Windsor Castle — A842

St. George's Chapel, Windsor Castle — A843

Designs: No. 3582, Long Walk. No. 3583, Round Tower. No. 3584, Norman Gate.
No. 3585, St. George's Hall. No. 3586, Queen's Ballroom. No. 3587, Waterloo Chamber.
No. 3588: a, Sir Reginald Bray roof boss. b, Fan-vaulted roof. c, Garter banners. d, St. George's Cross roof boss.
No. 3589, Like #3588a. No. 3590, Like #3588b.

2017, Feb. 15 Litho. *Perf. 14¾*
3582 A842 1st multi 1.60 1.20
3583 A842 1st multi 1.60 1.20
3584 A842 1st multi 1.60 1.20
a. Horiz. strip of 3, #3582-3584 4.80 3.60
3585 A842 £1.52 multi 3.75 2.75
a. Booklet pane of 2, #3582, 3585 (BK215) 5.75 —
3586 A842 £1.52 multi 3.75 2.75
3587 A842 £1.52 multi 3.75 2.75
a. Horiz. strip of 3, #3585-3587 11.50 8.25
b. Booklet pane of 4, #3583-3584, 3586-3587 (BK215) 11.50 —
Nos. 3582-3587 (6) 16.05 11.85

Miniature Sheet
Perf. 14¼
3588 A843 Sheet of 4 9.75 9.75
a.-b. 1st Either single 1.60 1.20
c.-d. £1.33 Either single 3.25 2.50
e. Booklet pane of 4, #3588a-3588d (BK215) 10.50 —

Booklet Stamps
Self-Adhesive
Photo.
Die Cut Perf. 14¼
3589 A843 1st multi 3.00 1.50
3590 A843 1st multi 3.00 1.50
a. Booklet pane of 6, #3589-3590, 4 #M426 14.00

Europa (No. 3584). On day of issue, Nos. 3582-3584, 3588a-3588b, 3589-3590 each sold for 64p. Complete booklet sold for £14.58.

David Bowie (1947-2016), Rock Musician — A844

Hunky Dory, by Bowie, 1971 — A845

Aladdin Sane, by Bowie, 1973 — A846

"Heroes," by Bowie, 1977 — A847

Let's Dance, by Bowie, 1983 — A848

Earthling, by Bowie, 1997 — A849

Blackstar, by Bowie, 2016 — A850

No. 3591: a, Ziggy Stardust tour, 1973. b, Serious Moonlight tour, 1983. c, Stage tour, 1978. d, A Reality tour, 2004.

2017, Mar. 14 Litho. *Perf. 14½*
3591 A844 Sheet of 4 11.00 8.25
a.-b. 1st Either single 1.60 1.20
c.-d. £1.52 Either single 3.75 2.75

Perf. 14½ Syncopated
3591E Sheet of 6 *85.00* —
f. A845 1st multi *8.75 8.75*
g. A846 1st multi *8.75 8.75*
h. A847 1st multi *17.50 17.50*
i. A848 £1.52 multi *17.50 17.50*
j. A849 £1.52 multi *17.50 17.50*
k. A850 £1.52 multi *17.50 17.50*

No. 3591E sold for £12.95. The franking value of Nos. 3591Ef-3591Eh was 64p. Sheets containing five examples of Nos. 3591Ef-3591Eh each sold for £7.50.

Photo.
Self-Adhesive
Die Cut Perf. 14¾ Syncopated
3592 A845 1st multi 1.60 1.20
3593 A846 1st multi 1.60 1.20
3594 A847 1st multi 1.60 1.20
a. Booklet pane of 6, #3593-3594, 4 #MH426 9.75
3595 A848 £1.52 multi 3.75 2.75
3596 A849 £1.52 multi 3.75 2.75
3597 A850 £1.52 multi 3.75 2.75
Nos. 3592-3597 (6) 16.05 11.85

On day of issue, Nos. 3591a-3591b, 3592-3594 each sold for 64p.

Famous Race Horses
A851

Designs: No. 3598, Frankel. No. 3599, Red Rum. No. 3600, Shergar. No. 3601, Kauto Star. No. 3602, Desert Orchid. No. 3603, Brigadier Gerard. No. 3604, Arkle. No. 3605, Estimate.

2017, Apr. 6 Litho. *Perf. 14¼*
3598 A851 1st multi 1.75 1.30
3599 A851 1st multi 1.75 1.30
3600 A851 £1.17 multi 3.00 2.25
3601 A851 £1.17 multi 3.00 2.25
3602 A851 £1.40 multi 3.75 2.75
3603 A851 £1.40 multi 3.75 2.75
3604 A851 £1.57 multi 4.25 3.25
3605 A851 £1.57 multi 4.25 3.25
Nos. 3598-3605 (8) 25.50 19.10

On day of issue, Nos. 3598-3599 each sold for 65p.

Songbirds
A852

Designs: No. 3606, Great tit. No. 3607, Wren. No. 3608, Willow warbler. No. 3609, Goldcrest. No. 3610, Skylark. No. 3611, Blackcap. No. 3612, Song thrush. No. 3613, Nightingale. No. 3614, Cuckoo. No. 3615, Yellowhammer.

2017, May 4 Litho. *Perf. 14½*
3606 A852 1st multi 1.75 1.30
3607 A852 1st multi 1.75 1.30
3608 A852 1st multi 1.75 1.30
3609 A852 1st multi 1.75 1.30
3610 A852 1st multi 1.75 1.30
a. Horiz. strip of 5, #3606-3610 8.75 6.50
3611 A852 1st multi 1.75 1.30
3612 A852 1st multi 1.75 1.30
3613 A852 1st multi 1.75 1.30
3614 A852 1st multi 1.75 1.30
3615 A852 1st multi 1.75 1.30
a. Horiz. strip of 5, #3611-3615 8.75 6.50
Nos. 3606-3615 (10) 17.50 13.00

On day of issue, Nos. 3606-3615 each sold for 65p.

Mills — A853

Designs: No. 3616, Nutley Windmill, East Sussex. No. 3617, New Abbey Corn Mill, Dumfries and Galloway. No. 3618, Ballycopeland Windmill, County Down. No. 3619, Cheddleton Flint Mill, Staffordshire. No. 3620, Woodchurch Windmill, Kent. No. 3621, Felin Cochwillan Mill, Gwynedd.

Perf. 14½x14¼
2017, June 20 Litho.
3616 A853 1st multi 1.75 1.30
3617 A853 1st multi 1.75 1.30
a. Vert. pair, #3616-3617 3.50 2.60
3618 A853 £1.40 multi 3.75 2.75
3619 A853 £1.40 multi 3.75 2.75
a. Vert. pair, #3618-3619 7.50 5.50
3620 A853 £1.57 multi 4.25 3.25
3621 A853 £1.57 multi 4.25 3.25
a. Vert. pair, #3620-3621 8.50 6.50
Nos. 3616-3621 (6) 19.50 14.60

On day of issue, Nos. 3616-3617 each sold for 65p.

Contemporary Architecture
A854

Designs: No. 3622, London Aquatics Center. No. 3623, Library of Birmingham. No. 3624, SEC Armadillo, Glasgow. No. 3625, Scottish Parliament, Edinburgh. No. 3626, Giant's Causeway Visitor Center, Northern Ireland. No. 3627, National Assembly for Wales, Cardiff. No. 3628, Eden Project, St. Austell. No. 3629, Everyman Theater, Liverpool. No. 3630, IWM (Imperial War Museum) North, Manchester. No. 3631, Switch House, Tate Modern Art Gallery, London.

2017, July 13 Litho. *Perf. 14½*
3622 A854 1st multi 1.75 1.30
3623 A854 1st multi 1.75 1.30
3624 A854 1st multi 1.75 1.30
3625 A854 1st multi 1.75 1.30
3626 A854 1st multi 1.75 1.30
a. Horiz. strip of 5, #3622-3626 8.75 6.50
3627 A854 1st multi 1.75 1.30
3628 A854 1st multi 1.75 1.30
3629 A854 1st multi 1.75 1.30
3630 A854 1st multi 1.75 1.30
3631 A854 1st multi 1.75 1.30
a. Horiz. strip of 5, #3627-3631 8.75 6.50
Nos. 3622-3631 (10) 17.50 13.00

On day of issue, Nos. 3622-3631 each sold for 65p.

World War I, Cent. — A855

Designs: No. 3632, Shattered Poppy, by J. Ross. No. 3633, Dead Man's Dump, by I. Rosenberg. No. 3634, Nurses Elsie Knocker and Mairi Chisholm. No. 3635, Dry Docked for Scaling and Painting, by E. Wadsworth. No. 3636, Tyne Cot Cemetery, Belgium. No. 3637, Private Lemuel Thomas Rees's life-saving Bible.

2017, July 31 Litho. *Perf. 14½*
3632 A855 1st multi 1.75 1.30
3633 A855 1st multi 1.75 1.30
a. Booklet pane of 4, #3313, 3398, 3508, 3633 (BK221) 7.50 —
3634 A855 1st multi 1.75 1.30
a. Booklet pane of 3, #3632-3634 (BK217) 5.50 —
3635 A855 £1.57 multi 4.25 3.25
3636 A855 £1.57 multi 4.25 3.25
3637 A855 £1.57 multi 4.25 3.25
a. Booklet pane of 3, #3635-3637 (BK217) 13.50 —
Nos. 3632-3637 (6) 18.00 13.65

Issued: No. 3633a, 9/13/18. On day of issue, Nos. 3632-3634 each sold for 65p.

Toys — A856

Designs: No. 3638, Merrythought teddy bear. No. 3639, Sindy Weekender doll. No. 3640, Spirograph. No. 3641, Stickle Bricks. No. 3642, Herald Trojan warriors. No. 3643, Spacehopper. No. 3644, Fuzzy-Felt farm set. No. 3645, Meccano Ferris wheel. No. 3646, Action Man Red Devil parachutist. No. 3647, Hornby Dublo electric trains.

2017, Aug. 22 Litho. Perf. 14½

3638 A856 1st multi 1.75 1.30
3639 A856 1st multi 1.75 1.30
3640 A856 1st multi 1.75 1.30
3641 A856 1st multi 1.75 1.30
3642 A856 1st multi 1.75 1.30
a. Horiz. strip of 5, #3638-3642 8.75 6.50
3643 A856 1st multi 1.75 1.30
3644 A856 1st multi 1.75 1.30
3645 A856 1st multi 1.75 1.30
3646 A856 1st multi 1.75 1.30
3647 A856 1st multi 1.75 1.30
a. Horiz. strip of 5, #3643-3647 8.75 6.50
Nos. 3638-3647 (10) 17.50 13.00

On day of issue, Nos. 3638-3647 each sold for 65p.

Ladybird Books A857

Various children's books, with book series inscription at lower left of: No. 3648, Adventures from History. No. 3649, Well-loved Tales. No. 3650, Key Words Reading Scheme. No. 3651, Early Tales and Rhymes. No. 3652, Hobbies and How It Works. No. 3653, People at Work. No. 3654, Nature and Conservation. No. 3655, Achievements.

2017, Sept. 14 Litho. Perf. 14¼

3648 A857 2nd multi 1.50 1.15
3649 A857 2nd multi 1.50 1.15
a. Horiz. pair, #3648-3649 3.00 2.30
3650 A857 1st multi 1.75 1.30
3651 A857 1st multi 1.75 1.30
a. Horiz. pair, #3650-3651 3.50 2.60
3652 A857 £1.40 multi 3.75 2.75
3653 A857 £1.40 multi 3.75 2.75
a. Horiz. pair, #3652-3653 7.50 5.50
3654 A857 £1.57 multi 4.25 3.25
3655 A857 £1.57 multi 4.25 3.25
a. Horiz. pair, #3654-3655 8.50 6.50
Nos. 3648-3655 (8) 22.50 16.90

On day of issue, Nos. 3648-3649 each sold for 56p; Nos. 3650-3651, for 65p.

Droids and Aliens From *Star Wars* Movies A858

Designs: Nos. 3656, 3664a, BB-8. Nos. 3657, 3664g, R2-D2. Nos. 3658, 3664h, C-3PO. Nos. 3659, 3664b, K-2SO. Nos. 3660, 3664c, Maz Kanata. Nos. 3661, 3664d, Chewbacca. Nos. 3662, 3664e, Supreme Leader Snoke. Nos. 3663, 3664f, Porg.

2017, Oct. 12 Litho. Perf. 14½

3656 A858 1st multi 1.75 1.30
3657 A858 1st multi 1.75 1.30
3658 A858 1st multi 1.75 1.30
a. Booklet pane of 4, #3439, 3441, 3657, 3658 (BK218) 7.75 —
3659 A858 1st multi 1.75 1.30
a. Horiz. strip of 4, #3656-3659 7.00 5.25
3660 A858 1st multi 1.75 1.30
3661 A858 1st multi 1.75 1.30
3662 A858 1st multi 1.75 1.30
a. Booklet pane of 4, #3436, 3440, 3660, 3662 (BK218) 7.75 —
3663 A858 1st multi 1.75 1.30
a. Horiz. strip of 4, #3660-3663 7.00 5.25
b. Sheet of 20, #3435 3448, 3656-3663 35.00 35.00
c. Booklet pane of 4, #3656, 3659, 3661, 3663 (BK218) 7.75 —
Nos. 3656-3663 (8) 14.00 10.40

Self-Adhesive

Litho.

Die Cut Perf. 14½

3664 Sheet of 10, #3664c-3664h, 2 each #3664a-3664b, + 10 labels 19.00
a.-h. A858 1st Any single 1.90 1.90
i. Like #3664a, photo. (3664k) 2.50 2.00
j. Like #3664g, photo. (3664k) 2.50 2.00
k. Booklet pane of 6, #3664i, 3664j, 4 #MH426 12.00
l. Like #3664c, photo. (3664n) 2.50 2.00
m. Like #3664d, photo. (3664n) 2.50 2.00
n. Booklet pane of 6, #3664l, 3664m, 4 #MH426 12.00

On day of issue, Nos. 3646-3663, 3664a-3664j, 3664m-3664n had a franking value of 65p. No. 3664 has 10 labels that could not be personalized, and sold for £7. The lithogrpahed stamps, Nos. 3664a-3664h, have a smaller dot size than photogravue stamps, 3664i-3664j, 3664l-3664m.

Virgin and Child, Attributed to Gerard David — A859

Madonna and Child, by William Dyce — A860

Virgin and Child, Attributed to Gerard David — A861

Madonna and Child, by William Dyce — A862

Virgin Mary and Child, Attributed to Quentin Massys A863

Small Cowper Madonna, by Raphael A864

Madonna and Child, by Il Sassoferrato A865

Virgin and Child, by Jakob von Steinle A866

2017, Nov. 7 Photo. Perf. 14½x15

3665 Sheet of 8 26.00 26.00
a. A859 2nd multi 1.50 1.15
b. A860 1st multi 1.75 1.30
c. A861 2nd Large multi 2.10 1.60
d. A862 1st Large multi 2.75 2.10
e. A863 £1.17 multi 3.25 2.50
f. A864 £1.40 multi 3.75 2.75
g. A865 £1.57 multi 4.25 3.25
h. A866 £2.27 multi 6.25 4.75

Self-Adhesive

Die Cut Perf. 14½x15

3666 A859 2nd multi 1.50 1.10
a. Booklet pane of 12 18.00
b. Litho. die cut perf. 14½x15 syncopated + label (3673b) 1.60 1.60
3667 A860 1st multi 1.75 1.30
a. Booklet pane of 12 21.00
b. Litho. die cut perf. 14½x15 syncopated + label (3673b) 1.75 1.75
3668 A861 2nd Large multi 2.10 1.60
3669 A862 1st Large multi 2.75 2.10
3670 A863 £1.17 multi 3.25 2.50
a. Litho. die cut perf. 14½x15 syncopated + label (3673b) 5.25 5.25
3671 A864 £1.40 multi 3.75 2.75
a. Litho. die cut perf. 14½x15 syncopated + label (3673b) 6.25 6.25
3672 A865 £1.57 multi 4.25 3.25
a. Litho. die cut perf. 14½x15 syncopated + label (3673b) 7.00 7.00
3673 A866 £2.27 multi 6.25 4.75
a. Litho. die cut perf. 14½x15 syncopated + label (3673b) 10.50 10.50
b. Sheet of 20, #3670a, 3671a, 3672a, 3673a, 8 each #3666b, 3667b, + 20 labels 57.50
Nos. 3666-3673 (8) 25.60 19.35

Christmas. On day of issue, Nos. 3665a and 3666 each sold for 56p; Nos. 3665b and 3667, for 65p; Nos. 3665c and 3668, for 76p; Nos. 3665d and 3669, for 98p.

No. 3673b sold for £16.40 and labels could not be personalized.

Family of Snowmen, by Arwen Wilson A867

Santa Claus, by Ted Lewis-Clark A868

Family of Snowmen, by Arwen Wilson — A869

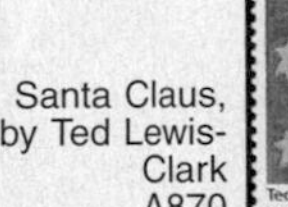
Santa Claus, by Ted Lewis-Clark A870

Die Cut Perf. 14½x15

2017, Nov. 7 Photo.

Self-Adhesive

3674 A867 2nd multi 1.50 1.10
a. Booklet pane of 12, 6 each #3666, 3674 18.00
b. Litho. die cut perf. 14½x15 syncopated + label (3675c) 1.60 1.60
3675 A868 1st multi 1.75 1.30
a. Booklet pane of 12, 6 each #3667, 3675 21.00
b. Litho. die cut perf. 14½x15 syncopated + label (3675c) 1.75 1.75
c. Sheet of 20, 10 each #3674b, 3675b, + 20 labels 33.50
3676 A869 2nd Large multi 2.10 1.60
3677 A870 1st Large multi 2.75 2.10
Nos. 3674-3677 (4) 8.10 6.10

Christmas. On day of issue, No. 3674 sold for 56p; No. 3675, for 65p; No. 3676, for 76p; No. 3677, for 98p.

No. 3675c sold for £12.60 and labels could not be personalized.

Miniature Sheet

70th Wedding Anniversary of Queen Elizabeth II and Prince Philip — A871

No. 3678: a, Princess Elizabeth and Duke of Edinburgh walking. b, Wedding procession. c, Princess Elizabeth and Duke of Edinburgh on bench on honeymoon. d, Engagement of Princess Elizabeth and Duke of Edinburgh seated, diff. e, Princess Elizabeth in wedding dress with Duke of Ediburgh. f, Princess Elizabeth holding arm of Duke of Edinbugh on honeymoon.

2017, Nov. 20 Litho. Perf. 14¼

3678 A871 Sheet of 6 18.00 18.00
a.-c. 1st Any single 1.75 1.30
d.-f. £1.57 Any single 4.25 3.25

On day of issue, Nos. 3678a-3678c each sold for 65p.

Characters From *Game of Thrones* Television Series A872

Iron Throne — A873

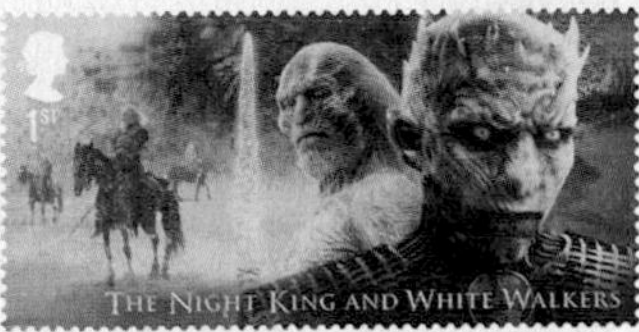

Characters From *Game of Thrones* Television Series — A874

Designs: No. 3679, Sansa Stark. No. 3680, Jon Snow. No. 3681, Eddard Stark. No. 3682, Olenna Tyrell. No. 3683, Tywin Lannister. No. 3684, Tyrion Lannister. No. 3685, Cersei Lannister. No. 3686, Arya Stark. No. 3687, Jaime Lannister. No. 3688, Daenerys Targaryen.

Nos. 3690, 3695a, Night King and White Walkers. Nos. 3691, 3695b, Giants. Nos. 3692, 3695c, Direwolves. Nos. 3693, 3695d, Dragons.

No. 3694: a, Sansa Stark. b, Jon Snow. c, Eddard Stark. d, Olenna Tyrell. e, Tywin Lannister. f, Tyrion Lannister. g, Cersei Lannister. h, Arya Stark. i, Jaime Lannister. j, Daenerys Targaryen.

2018, Jan. 23 Litho. Perf. 14¼x14

3679 A872 1st multi 1.90 1.40
3680 A872 1st multi 1.90 1.40
3681 A872 1st multi 1.90 1.40
3682 A872 1st multi 1.90 1.40
3683 A872 1st multi 1.90 1.40
a. Horiz. strip of 5, #3679-3683 9.50 7.00
3684 A872 1st multi 1.90 1.40
3685 A872 1st multi 1.90 1.40
3686 A872 1st multi 1.90 1.40
a. Booklet pane of 6, #3679-3681, 3684-3686 (BK219) 12.00 —
3687 A872 1st multi 1.90 1.40
3688 A872 1st multi 1.90 1.40
a. Horiz. strip of 5, #3684-3688 9.50 7.00
b. Booklet pane of 4, #3682-3683, 3687-3688 (BK219) 8.00 —
Nos. 3679-3688 (10) 19.00 14.00

Booklet Stamps

Perf. 14¾x14 Syncopated

3689 A873 1st multi 2.00 1.50
a. Booklet pane of 8, #MH255a, MH471, 2 each #3689, MH429, Northern Ireland 17, + central label (BK219) 13.00 —

Perf. 14¾

3690 A874 1st multi 1.90 1.40
3691 A874 1st multi 1.90 1.40
3692 A874 1st multi 1.90 1.40
3693 A874 1st multi 1.90 1.40
a. Booklet pane of 4, #3690-3693 (BK219) 8.00 —
Nos. 3689-3693 (5) 9.60 7.10

Die Cut Perf. 14¼x14½

3694 Sheet of 10 + 10 labels 21.00
a.-j. A872 1st Any single + label 2.10 2.10

Self-Adhesive

Die Cut Perf. 14¾, Die Cut Perf. 14¾x14 Syncopated (#3695e)

3695 Sheet of 5 9.50
a.-d. A874 1st Any single 1.90 1.40
e. A873 1st multi 1.90 1.40
f. As "e," photo. 1.90 1.40
g. Booklet pane of 6 #3695f 11.50

On day of issue, Nos. 3679-3688, 3695a-3695f each sold for 65p, and Nos. 3689-3693 each had a franking value of 65p.

No. 3694 sold for £7.50. Nos. 3694a-3694j each had a franking value of 65p on day of issue.

No. 3695f has larger dots than No. 3695e.

Woman Suffrage, Cent.
A875

Designs: No. 3696, Lone suffragette in Whitehall, c. 1908. No. 3697, The Great Pilgrimage of Suffragists, 1913. No. 3698, Suffragette leaders at Earl's Court, 1908. No. 3699, Women's Freedom League Poster Parade, c. 1907. No. 3700, Welsh suffragettes in Coronation procession, 1911. No. 3701, Mary Leigh (1885-1978) and Edith New (1877-1951) released from prison, 1908. No. 3702, Sophia Duleep Singh (1876-1948) sells *The Suffragette,* 1913. No. 3703, Suffragette Prisoners' Pageant, 1911.

2018, Feb. 15 Litho. *Perf. 14¼x14*

3696	A875	2nd multi		1.60	1.20
3697	A875	2nd multi		1.60	1.20
a.	Horiz. pair, #3696-3697			3.20	2.40
3698	A875	1st multi		1.75	1.30
3699	A875	1st multi		1.75	1.30
a.	Horiz. pair, #3698-3699			3.50	2.60
3700	A875	£1.40 multi		4.00	3.00
3701	A875	£1.40 multi		4.00	3.00
a.	Horiz. pair, #3700-3701			8.00	6.00
3702	A875	£1.57 multi		4.50	3.50
3703	A875	£1.57 multi		4.50	3.50
a.	Horiz. pair, #3702-3703			9.00	7.00
	Nos. 3696-3703 (8)			23.70	18.00

On day of issue Nos. 3696-3697 each sold for 56p; Nos. 3698-3699, for 65p.

Royal Air Force, Cent.
A876

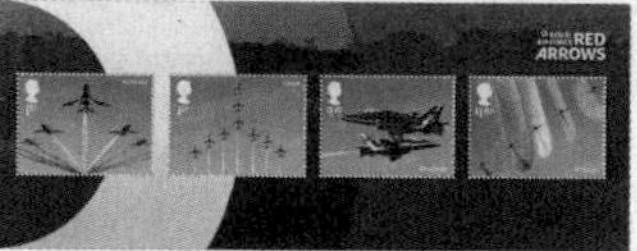

Royal Air Force Red Arrows Aerobatic Team — A877

Designs: Nos. 3704, 3712, Lightning F6. Nos, 3705, 3711, Hurricane MK I. No. 3706, Vulcan B2. No. 3707, Typhoon FGR4. No. 3708, Sopwith Camel F1. No. 3709, Nimrod MR2.

Nos. 3710a, 3713, Flypast. Nos. 3710b, 3714, Swan. No. 3710c, Synchro. No. 3710d, Python.

2018 Litho. *Perf. 14¼x14*

3704	A876	1st multi	1.90	1.40
3705	A876	1st multi	1.90	1.40
a.	Horiz. pair, #3704-3705		3.80	2.80
3706	A876	£1.40 multi	4.00	3.00
3707	A876	£1.40 multi	4.00	3.00
a.	Horiz. pair, #3706-3707		8.00	6.00
b.	Booklet pane of 4, 2 each #3704, 3707 (BK220)		11.50	—
3708	A876	£1.57 multi	4.50	3.50
3709	A876	£1.57 multi	4.50	3.50
a.	Horiz. pair, #3708-3709		9.00	7.00
b.	Booklet pane of 4, #3705, 3706, 3708, 3709 (BK220)		15.00	—
	Nos. 3704-3709 (6)		20.80	15.80

Miniature Sheet

3710	A877	Sheet of 4	12.00	12.00
a.-b.	1st Either single		1.90	1.40
c.-d.	£1.40 Either single		4.00	3.00
e.	Booklet pane of 4, #3710a-3710d (BK220)		11.50	—

Booklet Stamps Self-Adhesive

Die Cut Perf. 14¼x14

3711	A876	1st multi	2.50	2.00
3712	A876	1st multi	2.50	2.00
a.	Booklet pane of 6, #3711, 3712, 4 #MH426		12.00	
3713	A877	1st multi	2.50	2.00
3714	A877	1st multi	2.50	2.00
a.	Booklet pane of 6, #3713, 3714, 4 #MH426		12.00	
	Nos. 3711-3714 (4)		10.00	8.00

Issued: Nos. 3704-3712, 3/20; Nos. 3713-3714, 5/11. Nos. 3704, 3705, 3710a, 3710b, 3711, 3712 each sold for 65p on day of issue. Nos. 3713, 3714 each sold for 67p on day of issue.

Reintroduced Species
A878

Designs: No. 3715, Osprey. No. 3716, Large blue butterfly. No. 3717, Eurasian beaver. No. 3718, Pool frog. No. 3719, Stinking hawk's beard. No. 3720, Sand lizard.

2018, Apr. 17 Litho. *Perf. 14¼*

3715	A878	1st multi	1.90	1.40
3716	A878	1st multi	1.90	1.40
a.	Horiz. pair, #3715-3716		3.80	2.80
3717	A878	£1.45 multi	4.00	3.00
3718	A878	£1.45 multi	4.00	3.00
a.	Horiz. pair, #3717-3718		8.00	6.00
3719	A878	£1.55 multi	4.25	3.25
3720	A878	£1.55 multi	4.25	3.25
a.	Horiz. pair, #3719-3720		8.50	6.50
	Nos. 3715-3720 (6)		20.30	15.30

On day of issue, Nos. 3715-3716 each sold for 67p.

Adult Barn Owl — A879

Adult Little Owl — A880

Adult Tawny Owl — A881

Adult Short-eared Owl — A882

Adult Long-eared Owl — A883

Juvenile Barn Owls — A884

Juvenile Little Owls — A885

Juvenile Tawny Owl — A886

Juvenile Short-eared Owl — A887

Juvenile Long-eared Owl — A888

2018, May 11 Litho. *Perf. 14¼*

3721	A879	1st multi	1.90	1.40
3722	A880	1st multi	1.90	1.40
3723	A881	1st multi	1.90	1.40
3724	A882	1st multi	1.90	1.40
3725	A883	1st multi	1.90	1.40
a.	Horiz. strip of 5, #3721-3725		9.50	7.00
3726	A884	1st multi	1.90	1.40
3727	A885	1st multi	1.90	1.40
3728	A886	1st multi	1.90	1.40
3729	A887	1st multi	1.90	1.40
3730	A888	1st multi	1.90	1.40
a.	Horiz. strip of 5, #3726-3730		9.50	7.00
	Nos. 3721-3730 (10)		19.00	14.00

On day of issue, Nos. 3721-3730 each sold for 67p.

Miniature Sheet

Wedding of Prince Harry and Meghan Markle — A889

No. 3731 — Photograph of couple in: a, Color. b, Black-and-white.

2018, May 19 Litho. *Perf. 14¼*

3731	A889	Sheet of 4, 2 each #a-b	12.50	12.50
a.	1st multi		1.90	1.40
b.	£1.55 multi		4.25	3.25

On day of issue, No. 3731a sold for 67p.

Royal Academy of Arts, 250th Anniv.
A890

Designs: No. 3732, Summer Exhibition, by Grayson Perry. No. 3733, Queen of the Sky, by Fiona Rae. No. 3734, St. Kilda: The Great Sea Stacs, by Norman Ackroyd. No. 3735, Inverleith Allotments and Edinburgh Castle, by Barbara Rae. No. 3736, Queuing at the RA, by Yinka Shonibare. No. 3737, Saying Goodbye, by Tracey Emin.

2018, June 5 Litho. *Perf. 14¼*

3732	A890	1st multi	1.75	1.40
3733	A890	1st multi	1.75	1.40
a.	Vert. pair, #3732-3733		3.50	2.80
3734	A890	£1.25 multi	3.25	2.50
3735	A890	£1.25 multi	3.25	2.50
a.	Vert. pair, #3734-3735		6.50	5.00
3736	A890	£1.55 multi	4.25	3.25
3737	A890	£1.55 multi	4.25	3.25
a.	Vert. pair, #3736-3737		8.50	6.50
	Nos. 3732-3737 (6)		18.50	14.30

On day of issue, Nos. 3732-3733 each sold for 67p.

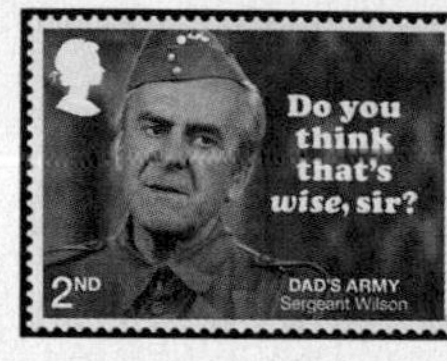

Dad's Army Television Series, 50th Anniv.
A891

Characters: No. 3738, Sergeant Wilson. No. 3739, Private Pike. Nos. 3740, 3746, Captain Mainwaring. Nos. 3741, 3747, Lance Corporal Jones. No. 3742, Private Walker. No. 3743, Private Frazer. No. 3744, Private Godfrey. No. 3745, Chief Warden Hodges.

2018, June 26 Litho. *Perf. 14¼x14*

3738	A891	2nd multi	1.60	1.20
3739	A891	2nd multi	1.60	1.20
a.	Horiz. pair, #3738-3739		3.20	2.40
3740	A891	1st multi	1.75	1.30
3741	A891	1st multi	1.75	1.30
a.	Horiz. pair, #3740-3741		3.50	2.60
3742	A891	£1.45 multi	3.75	2.75
3743	A891	£1.45 multi	3.75	2.75
a.	Horiz. pair, #3742-3743		7.50	5.50
3744	A891	£1.55 multi	4.25	3.25
3745	A891	£1.55 multi	4.25	3.25
a.	Horiz. pair, #3744-3745		8.50	6.50
	Nos. 3738-3745 (8)		22.70	17.00

Self-Adhesive

Photo.

Die Cut Perf. 14¼x14

3746	A891	1st multi (3747c)	2.25	2.00
a.	Litho., die cut perf. 14¼x14¾ + label		2.00	2.00
3747	A891	1st multi (3747c)	2.25	2.00
a.	Litho., die cut perf. 14¼x14¾ + label		2.00	2.00
b.	Sheet of 10, 5 each #3746a, 3747a + 10 labels		20.00	
c.	Booklet pane, #3746, 3747, 4 #MH426		10.50	

No. 3747b sold for £7.50. Labels on No. 3746a and 3747a could not be personalized. On day of issue, Nos. 3738-3739 each sold for 58p, and Nos. 3740-3741, 3746-3747 each sold for 67p.

A892

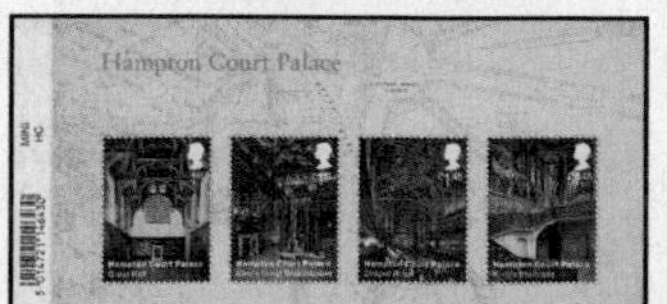

Hampton Court Palace — A893

Designs: No. 3748, South Front. No. 3749, West Front. No. 3750, East Front. No. 3751, Pond Gardens. No. 3752, Palace Maze. No. 3753, Great Fountain Garden.

Nos. 3754a, 3755, Great Hall. No. 3754b, 3756, King's Great Bedchamber. No. 3754c, Chapel Royal. No. 3754d, King's Staircase.

2018, July 31 Litho. *Perf. 14½x14¾*

3748	A892	1st multi	1.75	.90
3749	A892	1st multi	1.75	.90
3750	A892	1st multi	1.75	.90
a.	Horiz. strip of 3, #3748-3750		5.25	2.75

3751 A892 £1.55 multi 4.25 2.10
3752 A892 £1.55 multi 4.25 2.10
3753 A892 £1.55 multi 4.25 2.10
a. Horiz. strip of 3, #3751-3753 12.75 6.50
Nos. 3748-3753 (6) 18.00 9.00

Miniature Sheet

Perf. 14¼

3754 A893 Sheet of 4 11.50 6.00
a.-b. 1st Either single 1.75 .90
c.-d. £1.45 Either single 4.00 2.00

Booklet Stamps
Self-Adhesive

Photo.

Die Cut Perf. 14¼

3755 A893 1st multi 1.75 .90
3756 A893 1st multi 1.75 .90
a. Booklet pane of 6, #3755-3756, 4 #MH426 10.50

On day of issue, Nos. 3748-3750, 3754a, 3754b, 3755-3756 each sold for 67p.

A894

Voyage of the Endeavour, 250th Anniv. — A895

Designs: No. 3757, Painting of Joseph Banks (1743-1820), naturalist, by Sir Joshua Reynolds, red-tailed tropicbird, red passion flowers. No. 3758, Chief mourner of Tahiti and canoe. No. 3759, Painting of Captain James Cook (1728-79), by Nathaniel Dance, and Triumph of the Navigators, by Robin Brooks. No. 3760, Sextant and drawings of the transit of Venus. No. 3761, Drawings of Scarlet clianthus and Maori Chief by Sydney Parkinson. No. 3762, Blue-black grassquit and self-portrait by Parkinson.

No. 3763: a, Map of Endeavour's voyage around Australia and New Zealand. b, Raiatea boathouse and canoes. c, Maori fort on rock arch. d, Repairing of the Endeavour on the Endeavour River, Australia.

2018, Aug. 16 Litho. *Perf. 14¼*

3757 A894 2nd multi 1.50 .75
3758 A894 2nd multi 1.50 .75
a. Horiz. pair, #3757-3758 3.00 1.50
3759 A894 1st multi 1.75 .85
3760 A894 1st multi 1.75 .85
a. Horiz. pair, #3759-3760 3.50 1.75
3761 A894 £1.45 multi 3.75 1.90
3762 A894 £1.45 multi 3.75 1.90
a. Horiz. pair, #3761-3762 7.50 3.80
Nos. 3757-3762 (6) 14.00 7.00

Miniature Sheet

3763 A895 Sheet of 4 11.00 5.50
a.-b. 1st Either single 1.75 .85
c.-d. £1.45 Either single 3.75 1.90

On day of issue, Nos. 3757-3758 each sold for 58p, and Nos. 3759-3760 and 3763a-3763b each sold for 67p.

Old Vic Theater, London, 200th Anniv. — A896

Designs: No. 3764, Laurence Olivier in 1967 production of *The Dance of Death*. No. 3765, Glenda Jackson in 2016 production of *King Lear*. No. 3766, Albert Finney in 1975 production of *Hamlet*. No. 3767, Maggie Smith in 1970 production of *Hedda Gabler*. No. 3768, John Gielgud and Ralph Richardson in 1975 production of *No Man's Land*. No. 3769, Sharon Benson in 1991 production of *Carmen Jones*. No. 3770, Judi Dench and John Stride in 1960 production of *Romeo and Juliet*. No. 3771, Richard Burton in 1955 production of *Henry V*.

2018, Aug. 30 Litho. *Perf. 14¼*

3764 A896 1st multi 1.75 .85
3765 A896 1st multi 1.75 .85
a. Horiz. pair, #3764-3765 3.50 1.75
3766 A896 £1.25 multi 3.25 1.60
3767 A896 £1.25 multi 3.25 1.60
a. Horiz. pair, #3766-3767 6.50 3.25
3768 A896 £1.45 multi 3.75 1.90
3769 A896 £1.45 multi 3.75 1.90
a. Horiz. pair, #3768-3769 7.50 3.80
3770 A896 £1.55 multi 4.00 2.00
3771 A896 £1.55 multi 4.00 2.00
a. Horiz. pair, #3770-3771 8.00 4.00
Nos. 3764-3771 (8) 25.50 12.70

On day of issue, No. 3764-3765 each sold for 67p.

World War I, Cent. Type of 2014 and

World War I, Cent. — A897

Designs: Nos. 3772, 3779. Image from *100 Poppies*, photograph by Zafer and Barbara Baran. No. 3773, Line from poem, "Anthem for Doomed Youth," by Wilfred Owen. No. 3774, Second Lieutenanat Walter Tull. No. 3775, *We Are Making a New World*, painting by Paul Nash. No. 3776, Grave of the Unknown Warrior, Westmister Abbey. No. 3777, Goggles of pilot Lieutenant Francis Hopgood.

2018, Sept. 13 Litho. *Perf. 14¼*

3772 A897 1st multi 1.75 .85
3773 A897 1st multi 1.75 .85
3774 A897 1st multi 1.75 .85
a. Booklet pane of 3, #3772-3774 (BK221) 5.50 —
3775 A897 £1.55 multi 4.00 2.00
3776 A897 £1.55 multi 4.00 2.00
3777 A897 £1.55 multi 4.00 2.00
a. Booklet pane of 3, #3775-3777 (BK221) 13.00 —
b. Sheet of 30, #3312-3317, 3397-3402, 3507-3512, 3632-3637, 3772-3777 87.50 87.50
Nos. 3772-3777 (6) 17.25 8.55

Booklet Stamps
Self-Adhesive

Photo.

Die Cut Perf. 14¼

3778 A776 1st multi 1.75 .85
3779 A897 1st multi 1.75 .85
a. Booklet pane of 6, #3778-3779, 4 #MH426 10.50

On day of issue, Nos. 3772-3774, 3778-3779 each sold for 67p.

A898

Characters from *Harry Potter* Movies — A899

Designs: Nos. 3780, 3791a, 3791k, Hermione Granger. Nos. 3781, 3791c, Hogwarts Express. Nos. 3782, 3791e, 3791l, Harry Potter. Nos. 3783, 3791g, Flying Ford Anglia. Nos. 3784, 3791i, Ron Weasley. Nos. 3785, 3791b, Hagrid's Motorbike. Nos. 3786, 3791d, Ginny Weasley. Nos. 3787, 3791f, Triwizard Cup. Nos. 3788, 3791h, Neville Longbottom. Nos. 3789, 3791j, Knight Bus.

No. 3790: a, Pomona Sprout. b, Horace Slughorn. c, Sybill Trelawney. d, Remus Lupin. e, Severus Snape.

2018 Litho. *Perf. 14¼*

3780 A898 1st multi 1.75 .85
3781 A898 1st multi 1.75 .85
3782 A898 1st multi 1.75 .85
3783 A898 1st multi 1.75 .85
3784 A898 1st multi 1.75 .85
a. Horiz. strip of 5, #3780-3784 8.75 4.25
3785 A898 1st multi 1.75 .85
3786 A898 1st multi 1.75 .85
3787 A898 1st multi 1.75 .85
3788 A898 1st multi 1.75 .85
a. Booklet pane of 5, #3780, 3782, 3784, 3786, 3788 (BK222) 9.50 —
3789 A898 1st multi 1.75 .85
a. Horiz. strip of 5, #3785-3789 8.75 4.25
b. Booklet pane of 5, #3781, 3783, 3785, 3787, 37898 (BK222) 9.50 —
Nos. 3780-3789 (10) 17.50 8.50

Miniature Sheets
Self-Adhesive

Die Cut Perf. 14¼

3790 A899 Sheet of 5 8.75
a.-e. 1st Any single 1.75 .85
f. Booklet pane of 3, #3790a-3790c (BK222) 5.75
g. Booklet pane of 3, #3790d-3790e (BK222) 3.75
3791 Sheet of 10 + 10 labels 20.00
a.-j. A898 1st Any single 2.00 2.00
k. As #3791a, photo. (#3791m) 1.75 .85
l. As #3791e, photo. (#3791m) 1.75 .85
m. Booklet pane of 6, #3791k, 3791l, 4 #MH426 10.50

Issued: Nos. 3788a, 3789a, 3790f, 3790g, 12/4; others, 10/16. Nos. 3780-3790, 3790a-3790e, 3791k-3791l each sold for 67p on day of issue. No. 3791 sold for £7.70.

A900

Christmas A901

People in winter near mailboxes from: Nos. 3792a, 3792c, 3793, 3795, King Edward VII era. Nos. 3792b, 3792d, 3794, 3796, Queen Elizabeth II era. £1.25, King George VI era. £1.45, Queen Victoria era. £1.55, King Edward VIII era. £2.25, King George V era.

2018, Nov. 1 Litho. *Perf. 14½x15*

3792 Sheet of 8 25.00 25.00
a. A900 2nd multi 1.50 .75
b. A900 1st multi 1.75 .85
c. A901 2nd Large multi 2.10 1.10
d. A901 1st Large multi 2.60 1.40
e. A900 £1.25 multi 3.25 1.60
f. A900 £1.45 multi 3.75 1.90
g. A900 £1.55 multi 4.00 2.00
h. A900 £2.25 multi 6.00 3.00

Photo.
Self-Adhesive

Die Cut Perf. 14½x15

3793 A900 2nd multi 1.50 .75
a. Booklet pane of 12 18.00
b. Litho., die cut perf. 14½x15 syncopated + label (#3800b) 1.60 1.60
3794 A900 1st multi 1.75 .85
a. Booklet pane of 12 21.00
b. Litho., die cut perf. 14½x15 syncopated + label (#3800b) 1.90 1.90
3795 A901 2nd Large multi 2.10 1.10
3796 A901 1st Large multi 2.60 1.40
3797 A900 £1.25 multi 3.25 1.60
a. Litho., die cut perf. 14½x15 syncopated + label (#3800b) 3.50 3.50
3798 A900 £1.45 multi 3.75 1.90
a. Litho., die cut perf. 14½x15 syncopated + label (#3800b) 4.00 4.00
3799 A900 £1.55 multi 4.00 2.00
a. Litho., die cut perf. 14½x15 syncopated + label (#3800b) 4.25 4.25
3800 A900 £2.25 multi 6.00 3.00
a. Litho., die cut perf. 14½x15 syncopated + label (#3800b) 6.25 6.25
b. Sheet of 20, #3797a, 3798a, 3799a, 3800a, 8 each #3793b, 3794b + 20 labels 46.00
Nos. 3793-3800 (8) 24.95 12.60

On day of issue, Nos. 3792a and 3793 each sold for 58p; Nos. 3792b and 3794, for 67p; Nos. 3792c and 3795, for 79p; Nos. 3792d and 3796, for £1.01. No. 3800b sold for £17.50 and labels could not be personalized.

Miniature Sheet

Prince Charles, 70th Birthday — A902

No. 3801: a, Prince Charles wearing blue suit. b, Prince Charles with wife, the Duchess of Cornwall. c, Prince Charles with sons, Princes William and Harry, in military uniforms. d, Prince Charles with sons in sports shirts. e, Prince Charles at Castle of Mey. f, Prince Charles and children waving Welsh flags.

Die Cut Perf. 14¼x14

2018, Nov. 14 Litho.

Self-Adhesive

3801 A902 Sheet of 6 17.50
a.-c. 1st Any single 1.75 .85
d.-f £1.55 Any single 4.00 2.00

On day of issue, Nos. 3801a-3801c each sold for 67p.

Miniature Sheet

Classic British Stamps — A903

No. 3802: a, Great Britain #124 (73x30mm). b, Unissued 2p stamp depicting King Edward VII prepared in 1910 (31x30mm). c, Great Britain #173 (52x30mm). d, Great Britain #232 (33x30mm). e, Great Britain #252 (42x30mm). f, Great Britain #313 (52x30mm).

2019, Jan. 15 Litho. *Perf. 14x13½*

3802 A903 Sheet of 6 + label 17.50 17.50
a.-c. 1st Any single 1.75 1.40
d.-f. £1.55 Any single 4.00 3.00

On day of issue, Nos. 3802a-3802c each sold for 67p.

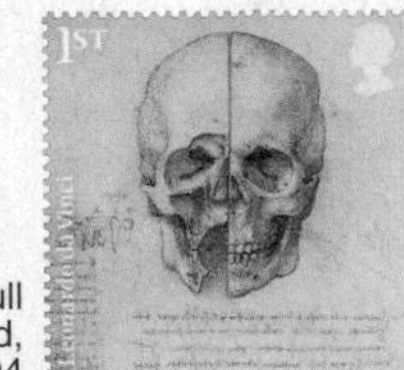

The Skull Sectioned, 1489 — A904

A Sprig of Guelder-Rose, c. 1506-12 A905

Studies of Cats, c. 1517- 18 A906

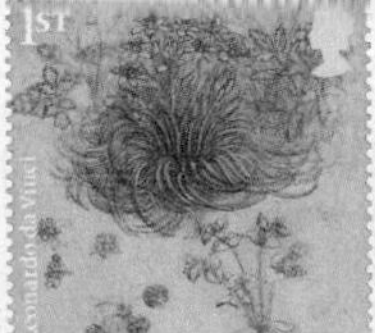

A Star of Bethlehem and Other Plants, c. 1506-12 A907

The Anatomy of the Shoulder and Foot, c. 1510-11
A908

The Head of Leda, c. 1505-08
A909

The Head of a Bearded Man, c. 1517-18
A910

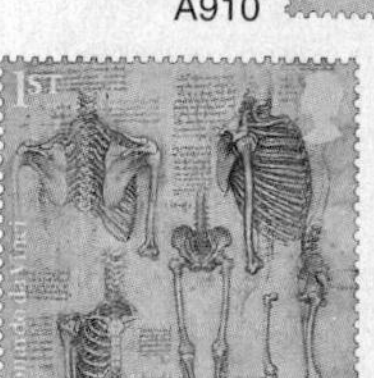

The Skeleton, c. 1510-11
A911

The Head of St. Philip, c. 1495 — A912

A Woman in a Landscape, c. 1517-18
A913

A Design for an Equestrian Monument, c. 1485-88
A914

The Fall of Light on a Face, c. 1488 — A915

2019, Feb. 13 Litho. *Perf. 14½*

3803 A904 1st multi 1.75 1.40
3804 A905 1st multi 1.75 1.40
3805 A906 1st multi 1.75 1.40
3806 A907 1st multi 1.75 1.40
3807 A908 1st multi 1.75 1.40
3808 A909 1st multi 1.75 1.40
a. Horiz. strip of 6, #3803-3808 10.50 8.50
3809 A910 1st multi 1.75 1.40
3810 A911 1st multi 1.75 1.40
3811 A912 1st multi 1.75 1.40
3812 A913 1st multi 1.75 1.40
a. Booklet pane of 4, #3808-3809, 3811-3812 (BK223) 7.75 —
3813 A914 1st multi 1.75 1.40
a. Booklet pane of 4, #3804-3806, 3813 (BK223) 7.75 —
3814 A915 1st multi 1.75 1.40
a. Horiz. strip of 6, #3809-3814 10.50 8.50
b. Booklet pane of 4, #3803, 3807, 3810, 3814 (BK223) 7.75 —
Nos. 3803-3814 (12) 21.00 16.80

Drawings by Leonardo da Vinci (1452-1519) in the Royal Collection. Nos. 3803-3814 each sold for 67p on day of issue.

SEMI-POSTAL STAMPS

Catalogue values for unused stamps in this section are for Never Hinged items.

Handicapped Person — SP1

Perf. 14½x14

1975, Jan. 22 Photo. Unwmk.

B1 SP1 4½p +1½p blue & lt blue .25 .25

For the benefit of health and handicap charities. No. B1 is phosphorescent.

Christmas Type of 1989

Ely Cathedral, Cambridgeshire: No. B2, Romanesque arches, west front. No. B3, Central tower. No. B4, Interlocking arches, Romanesque arcades, west transept. No. B5, Peasant, stained-glass window in triple arch, west front.

1989, Nov. 14 Photo. *Perf. 15x14*

B2 A379 15p +1p multicolored .30 .30
B3 A379 20p +1p multicolored .45 .45
B4 A379 34p +1p multicolored .70 .70
B5 A379 37p +1p multicolored .75 *.80*
Nos. B2-B5 (4) 2.20 2.25

AIR POST STAMPS

Queen Elizabeth II
AP1 AP2

Serpentine Die Cut 14¾x14 Syncopated

2003, Mar. 27 Photo.

Self-Adhesive

Booklet Stamps

C1 AP1 (52p) blue & red 4.50 4.50
a. Booklet pane of 4 18.00
C2 AP2 (£1.12) red & blue 6.50 6.00
a. Booklet pane of 4 26.00

Queen Elizabeth II — AP3

Die Cut Perf. 14¾x14 Syncopated

2004, Apr. 1 Photo.

Self-Adhesive

C3 AP3 (43p) blk, red & blue 4.00 1.75
a. Booklet of 4 + 4 etiquettes 16.00

Nos. C1-C3 were sold for 52p, £1.12 and 43p, respectively, when issued.

Queen Elizabeth II
AP4 AP5

Die Cut Perf. 14¾x14 Syncopated

2010, Mar. 30 Photo.

Booklet Stamps

Self-Adhesive

C4 AP4 (60p) grn, red & blue 4.00 1.90
a. Booklet pane of 4 16.00
C5 AP5 (97p) pur, red & blue 5.50 3.00
a. Booklet pane of 4 22.00

Emblem of 2012 Olympics
AP6

Emblem of 2012 Paralympics
AP7

Die Cut Perf. 14¾x14 Syncopated

2012, Jan. 5 Photo.

Self-Adhesive

C6 AP6 (£1.10) multi 6.00 4.00
C7 AP7 (£1.10) multi 6.00 4.00
a. Sheet of 20, 8 each #2981-2982, 2 each #C6-C7, + 20 labels, litho. 47.50

Issued: No. C7a, 7/27/12. No. C7a sold for £15.22. Labels on No. C7a could not be personalized.

Olympic and Paralympic Emblems Type of 2012

Perf. 14¾x14 Syncopated

2012, July 27 Litho.

Booklet Stamps

C8 AP6 (£1.28) multi 17.50 17.50
C9 AP7 (£1.28) multi 17.50 17.50
a. Booklet pane of 8, #C8, C9, 3 each #3044-3045 (BK200) 45.00 —

On day of issue Nos. C8-C9 each had a franking value of £1.28.

SPECIAL DELIVERY STAMPS

Queen Elizabeth II
SD1 SD2

Die Cut Perf. 14¾x14 Syncopated

2010, Oct. 26 Photo.

Self-Adhesive

E1 SD1 (£5.05) dk bl & gray 15.00 10.00
E2 SD2 (£5.50) gray & dk bl 17.00 12.00

POSTAGE DUE STAMPS

The watermarks on Nos. J1-J67 are sideways.

D1

Perf. 14x14½

1914-24 Typo. Wmk. 33

J1 D1 ½p emerald .90 .30
Never hinged 3.00
J2 D1 1p rose .90 .25
Never hinged 3.00
J3 D1 1½p red brown ('22) 50.00 20.00
Never hinged 160.00
J4 D1 2p brown black .85 .25
Never hinged 3.00
J5 D1 3p violet ('18) 11.00 2.00
Never hinged 30.00
J6 D1 4p gray green ('21) 50.00 3.00
Never hinged 160.00
J7 D1 5p org brown 7.00 2.00
Never hinged 19.00
J8 D1 1sh blue ('15) 50.00 4.50
Never hinged 170.00
Nos. J1-J8 (8) 170.65 32.30

Values for No. J6 are for stamps with sideways inverted watermark. No. J6 also exists on paper with sideways watermark. Values thus: $150 unused, $50 used.

From the front of the stamp the sideways watermark reads up in normal type. From the back, the watermark still reads up, but the letters are reversed. The sideways inverted watermark reads down.

D2

1924-30 Wmk. 35

J9 D1 ½p emerald .75 .60
Never hinged 3.00
J10 D1 1p car rose .65 .30
Never hinged 3.00
J11 D1 1½p red brown 52.50 22.50
Never hinged 175.00
J12 D1 2p black brown 1.60 .30
Never hinged 9.50
J13 D1 3p violet 1.75 .30
Never hinged 9.50
a. Experimental wmk. 95.00 95.00
Never hinged 160.00
b. Printed on the gummed side 135.00
Never hinged 190.00
J14 D1 4p deep green 15.00 2.75
Never hinged 65.00
J15 D1 5p org brown ('30) 55.00 37.50
Never hinged 175.00
J16 D1 1sh blue 9.50 .75
Never hinged 37.50
J17 D2 2sh6p brown, *yellow* 75.00 1.90
Never hinged 275.00
Nos. J9-J17 (9) 211.75 66.90

The experimental watermark of No. J13a resembles Wmk. 35 but is spaced more closely, with letters short and rounded, crown with flat arch and sides high, lines thicker.

1936-37 Wmk. 250

J18 D1 ½p emerald ('37) 9.75 *10.00*
Never hinged 20.00
J19 D1 1p car rose ('37) 1.15 *1.75*
Never hinged 2.25
J20 D1 2p blk brn ('37) 9.00 *9.50*
Never hinged 16.00
J21 D1 3p violet ('37) 1.10 *1.40*
Never hinged 2.00
J22 D1 4p slate green 21.00 *30.00*
Never hinged 35.00
J23 D1 5p bister ('37) 20.00 *26.00*
Never hinged 34.00
a. 5p orange brown 37.50 30.00
Never hinged 72.50
J24 D1 1sh blue ('36) 6.25 *8.50*
Never hinged 10.00
J25 D2 2sh6p brn, *yel* ('37) 100.00 15.50
Never hinged 400.00
Nos. J18-J25 (8) 168.25 *102.65*

1938-39 Wmk. 251

J26 D1 ½p emerald 8.75 5.50
Never hinged 11.00
J27 D1 1p carmine rose 1.50 .40
Never hinged 3.00
J28 D1 2p black brown 1.15 .40
Never hinged 2.25
J29 D1 3p violet 6.00 .45
Never hinged 10.50
J30 D1 4p slate green 30.00 8.50
Never hinged 85.00
J31 D1 5p bister ('39) 6.75 1.60
Never hinged 11.50
J32 D1 1sh blue 20.00 1.00
Never hinged 57.50
J33 D2 2sh6p brown, *yel* ('39) 40.00 1.75
Never hinged 90.00
Nos. J26-J33 (8) 114.15 19.60

Catalogue values for unused stamps in this section, from this point to the end of the section, are for Never Hinged items.

1951-52

J34 D1 ½p orange 2.90 2.90
J35 D1 1p violet blue 1.25 .60
J36 D1 1½p green ('52) 2.00 *2.50*
J37 D1 4p bright blue 40.00 15.00
J38 D1 1sh olive bister 32.50 5.50
Nos. J34-J38 (5) 78.65 26.50

1954-55 Wmk. 298

J39 D1 ½p orange ('55) 8.75 *9.75*
J40 D1 2p brn blk ('55) 37.50 26.00
J41 D1 3p purple ('55) 60.00 40.00
J42 D1 4p brt blue ('55) 30.00 23.00
a. Imperf., pair 250.00

J43 D1 5p bis brn ('55) 20.00 12.00
J44 D2 2sh6p dk pur brn, *yel* 110.00 7.75
Nos. J39-J44 (6) 266.25 118.50

1955-57 Wmk. 308 *Perf. 14x14½*

J45 D1 ½p orange ('56) 5.25 3.25
J46 D1 1p ultra ('56) 5.25 .90
J47 D1 1½p green ('56) 13.50 12.00
J48 D1 2p brown blk ('56) 34.00 4.50
J49 D1 3p purple ('56) 4.50 2.25
J50 D1 4p brt blue ('56) 25.00 4.00
J51 D1 5p bister brn ('56) 19.00 3.00
J52 D1 1sh dp olive bister 52.50 1.75
J53 D2 2sh6p dk red brn, *yel* ('57) 165.00 6.00
J54 D2 5sh red, *yellow* 75.00 23.00
Nos. J45-J54 (10) 399.00 60.65

1959-63 Wmk. 322 *Perf. 14x14½*

J55 D1 ½p orange ('61) .25 .25
J56 D1 1p ultra ('60) .25 .25
J57 D1 1½p green ('60) 2.60 *2.90*
J58 D1 2p brown black 1.10 .40
J59 D1 3p purple .25 .25
J60 D1 4p brt blue ('60) .30 *.35*
J61 D1 5p bister brn ('62) .40 *.45*
J62 D1 6p dp mag ('62) .45 .35
J63 D1 1sh dp ol bis ('60) .75 .25
J64 D2 2sh6p dk red brn, *yel* ('61) 3.00 .55
J65 D2 5sh red, *yellow* ('61) 5.75 .85
J66 D2 10sh ultra, *yel* ('63) 15.00 3.50
J67 D2 £1 blk, *yellow* ('63) 34.00 8.50
Nos. J55-J67 (13) 64.10 18.85

Nos. J1-J67 are watermarked sideways.

Perf. 14x14½

1968-69 Unwmk. Typo.

J68 D1 2p greenish black .25 *.40*
J69 D1 3p purple .40 *.45*
J70 D1 4p bright blue .30 *.35*
J71 D1 5p brown org ('69) 4.50 *4.75*
J72 D1 6p deep magenta .50 *.70*
J73 D1 1sh bister ('69) 1.75 .95
Nos. J68-J73 (6) 7.70 *7.60*

1968-69 Photo.

J74 D1 4p bright blue ('69) 5.75 5.75
J75 D1 8p bright red .45 *.65*

D3

D4

Perf. 14x14½

1970-75 Photo. Unwmk.

J79 D3 ½p grnsh blue ('71) .25 .60
J80 D3 1p magenta ('71) .25 .25
J81 D3 2p green ('71) .25 .25
J82 D3 3p ultra ('71) .25 .25
J83 D3 4p olive bister ('71) .25 .25
J84 D3 5p bluish lilac ('71) .25 .25
J85 D3 7p brown red ('74) .35 .40
J86 D4 10p carmine rose .35 .25
J87 D4 11p slate ('75) .60 .60
J88 D4 20p olive .50 .35
J89 D4 50p ultramarine 1.40 .75
J90 D4 £1 black 2.50 .75
J91 D4 £5 org & black ('73) 20.00 3.25
Nos. J79-J91 (13) 27.20 8.20

D5

1982, June 9 Photo. *Perf. 14x14½*

J92 D5 1p rose carmine .25 .25
J93 D5 2p ultramarine .25 .25
J94 D5 3p deep rose lilac .25 .25
J95 D5 4p dark blue .25 .25
J96 D5 5p sepia .25 .25
J97 D5 10p brown .25 .25
J98 D5 20p dark ol green .45 .40
J99 D5 25p slate blue .70 .70
J100 D5 50p black 1.25 1.20
J101 D5 £1 vermilion 1.90 1.00
J102 D5 £2 greenish blue 4.00 3.25
J103 D5 £5 yellow bister 9.50 1.50
Nos. J92-J103 (12) 19.30 9.55

D6

Perf. 15x14 Syncopated, Type C (2 Sides)

1994, Feb. 15 Photo. & Embossed

J104 D6 1p ver & org .25 *.60*
J105 D6 2p red lilac & red .25 *.60*
J106 D6 5p yel & brn .40 *.75*
J107 D6 10p yel & grn .50 *.75*
J108 D6 20p green & blue 1.10 *2.50*
J109 D6 25p red 2.40 *3.00*
J110 D6 £1 vio & red lilac 6.00 *6.50*
J111 D6 £1.20 blue & green 7.00 *7.00*
J112 D6 £5 green & black 20.00 7.50
Nos. J104-J112 (9) 37.90 *29.20*

OFFICIAL STAMPS

Type of Regular Issue of 1840 "V R" in Upper Corners

O1

1840 Wmk. 18 *Imperf.*

O1 O1 1p black *35,000. 35,000.*

No. O1 was never placed in use but examples are known used and on covers that passed through the mails by oversight. The stamp also was used experimentally to test cancellations.

Postage stamps perforated with a crown and initials "H.M.O.W.," "O.W.," "B.T." or "S.O.," or with only the initials "H.M.S.O." or "D.S.I.R.," were used for official purposes.

Counterfeits exist of Nos. O2-O83.

Inland Revenue

Regular Issues Overprinted in Black

a

b

Type "a" is overprinted on the stamps of ½ penny to 1 shilling inclusive, type "b" on the higher values.

1882-85 Wmk. 30 *Perf. 14*

O2 A35 ½p pale green 135.00 52.50
O3 A35 ½p slate bl ('85) 87.50 30.00
O4 A40 1p lilac 7.75 5.25
a. "OFFICIAL" omitted *10,000.*
b. Ovpt. lines transposed
O5 A47 2½p lilac ('85) 520.00 190.00
O6 A48 6p gray 600.00 140.00
O7 A48 1sh green ('85) *6,250.* 1,900.

Wmk. 31

O8 A51 5sh car rose ('85) 10,000. 2,500.
a. Bluish paper ('85) *17,500.* *6,250.*
O9 A52 10sh ultra *11,500.* 3,600.
a. 10sh cobalt *37,500.* 10,000.
b. Bluish paper *24,000.* 7,250.

Wmk. Three Imperial Crowns (30)

O10 A53 £1 brown vio *80,000. 31,500.*

1888-89 Wmk. 30

O11 A54 ½p vermilion 12.50 5.25
a. "I.R." omitted *5,750.*
O12 A65 1sh green ('89) 950.00 350.00

1890 Wmk. Three Orbs (29)

O13 A53 £1 brown vio *100,000. 42,500.*

1891 Wmk. 30

O14 A57 2½p violet, *blue* 150.00 21.00

Wmk. Three Imperial Crowns (30)

1892

O15 A53 £1 green *12,500.* 2,600.
a. No period after "R" — *4,250.*

For examples of Nos. O2-O15 with margins clear of the design on all four sides, add a 20 percent premium to the value listed. For stamps with clear circular datestamps, apply a 20 percent premium. Add the two premiums together for covers with stamps having these attributes.

1901 Wmk. 30

O16 A54 ½p blue green 19.00 12.50
O17 A62 6p violet, *rose* 400.00 115.00
O18 A65 1sh car rose & green 4,400. 1,900.

1902-04

O19 A66 ½p gray grn 32.50 3.25
O20 A66 1p carmine 21.00 2.50
O21 A66 2½p ultra 950.00 260.00
O22 A66 6p dull vio ('04) *400,000. 190,000.*
O23 A74 1sh car rose & grn 3,750. 725.00

Wmk. 31

O24 A76 5sh car rose *36,500. 10,500.*
O25 A77 10sh ultra *110,000. 47,500.*

Wmk. Three Imperial Crowns (30)

O26 A78 £1 green *62,500. 25,000.*

Nos. O4, O8, O9 and O13 also exist with overprint in blue black.

Government Parcels

Overprinted

1883-86 Wmk. 30

O27 A45 1½p lilac ('86) 400.00 92.50
O28 A46 6p green ('86) 3,150. 1,250.
O29 A50 9p green 2,600. 1,050.
O30 A29 1sh sal (P13) 1,675. 290.00
Plate 14 3,500. 525.00
Nos. O27-O30 (4) 7,825. 2,683.

1887-92

O31 A55 1½p vio & grn 145.00 18.50
O32 A56 2p grn & car rose ('91) 235.00 40.00
O33 A60 4½p car rose & grn ('92) 375.00 260.00
O34 A62 6p violet, *rose* 260.00 62.50
O35 A63 9p blue & lil ('88) 400.00 92.50
O36 A65 1sh green 675.00 260.00
Nos. O31-O36 (6) 2,090. 733.50

1897

O37 A40 1p lilac 92.50 22.50
a. Inverted overprint 7,250. 3,400.

1900

O38 A65 1sh car rose & grn 625.00 260.00
a. Inverted overprint *17,500.*

For examples of Nos. O27-38 with margins clear of the design on all four sides, add a 25 percent premium to the value listed. For stamps with clear circular datestamps, apply a 100 percent premium. Add the two premiums together for covers with stamps having these attributes.

1902

O39 A66 1p carmine 32.50 14.00
O40 A68 2p green & car 160.00 40.00
O41 A66 6p dull violet 260.00 40.00
O42 A72 9p ultra & violet 625.00 175.00
O43 A74 1sh car rose & grn 1,350. 300.00
Nos. O39-O43 (5) 2,428. 569.00

Office of Works

Overprinted

1896

O44 A54 ½p vermilion 300.00 135.00
O45 A40 1p lilac 500.00 135.00

For examples of Nos. O44-O45 with margins clear of the design on all four sides, add a 20 percent premium to the value listed. For stamps with clear circular datestamps, apply a 15 percent premium. Add the two premiums together for covers with stamps having these attributes.

1901-02

O46 A54 ½p blue green 450.00 200.00
O47 A61 5p lilac & ultra 3,650. 1,250.
O48 A64 10p car rose & lil 6,250. 2,100.

1902

O49 A66 ½p gray grn 575.00 160.00
O50 A66 1p carmine 575.00 160.00
O51 A68 2p grn & car 2,000. 425.00
O52 A66 2½p ultra 3,400. 625.00
O53 A73 10p car rose & vio *40,000.* 7,000.

Army

Overprinted

a

b

1896

O54 A54(a) ½p vermilion 6.25 2.75
a. "OFFICIAI" 290.00 125.00
O55 A40(a) 1p lilac 6.25 6.00
a. "OFFICIAI" 225.00 140.00
O56 A57(b) 2½p violet, *blue* 45.00 30.00
Nos. O54-O56 (3) 57.50 38.75

1900

O57 A54(a) ½p blue green 6.25 *12.50*

For examples of Nos. O54-O57 with margins clear of the design on all four sides, add a 20 percent premium to the value listed. For stamps with clear circular datestamps, apply a 15 percent premium. Add the two premiums together for covers with stamps having these attributes.

1901

O58 A62(b) 6p violet, *rose* 100.00 52.50

1902

O59 A66(a) ½p gray green 6.00 2.40
O60 A66(a) 1p carmine 6.00 2.40
a. "ARMY" omitted —
O61 A66(a) 6p dull violet 175.00 80.00
Nos. O59-O61 (3) 187.00 84.80

Overprinted

1903

O62 A66 6p dull violet 3,250. 1,550.

Royal Household

Overprinted
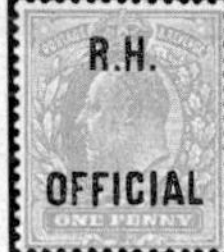

1902

O63 A66 ½p gray green 400.00 220.00
O64 A66 1p carmine 350.00 190.00

Board of Education

Overprinted

1902

O65 A61 5p lilac & ultra 4,650. 1,150.
O66 A65 1sh car rose & grn 10,500. 5,750.

1902-04

O67 A66 ½p gray green 160.00 40.00
O68 A66 1p carmine 160.00 40.00
O69 A66 2½p ultramarine 5,000. 410.00
O70 A71 5p lilac & ultra ('04) 31,500. 10,000.
O71 A74 1sh car rose & grn *180,000.* —

Admiralty

Overprinted

1903

O72 A66 ½p gray green 28.00 13.50
O73 A66 1p carmine 17.00 6.75
O74 A67 1½p vio & green 310.00 145.00
O75 A68 2p green & car 340.00 160.00
O76 A66 2½p ultra 475.00 145.00
O77 A69 3p violet, *yel* 425.00 160.00
Nos. O72-O77 (6) 1,595. 630.25

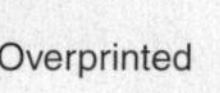

Overprinted

1903

O78 A66 ½p gray green 57.50 22.50
O79 A66 1p carmine 57.50 22.50
O80 A67 1½p vio & grn 1,150. 625.00
O81 A68 2p grn & car 2,750. 840.00
O82 A66 2½p ultramarine 2,850. 890.00
O83 A69 3p violet, *yel* 2,500. 375.00

The two types of the "Admiralty Official" overprint differ principally in the shape of the letter "M."

ENVELOPES

Britannia Sending Letters to World (William Mulready, Designer) — E1

1840

U1 E1 1p black 360.00 *525.00*
U2 E1 2p blue 450.00 *2,000.*

LETTER SHEETS

U3 E1 1p black 335.00 *500.00*
U4 E1 2p blue 440.00 *2,000.*

REGIONAL ISSUES

Sold only at post offices within the respective regions, but valid for postage throughout Great Britain. Issues for Guernsey, Jersey and Isle of Man are listed with the Bailiwick issues that follow.

Starting in 1967, all Regional stamps were issued only with phosphorescence.

Catalogue values for unused stamps in this section are for Never Hinged items.

ENGLAND

Three Lions — A1

Perf. 15x14 Syncopated

2001-02 **Photo.**

1 A1 2nd shown 1.40 1.40
2 A1 1st Crowned Lion 1.75 1.75
3 A1 E Oak tree 2.75 2.90
4 A1 65p Tudor rose 2.90 2.90
5 A1 68p Tudor rose 2.90 2.90
Nos. 1-5 (5) 11.70 11.85

Issued: Nos. 1-4, 4/23/01. No. 5, 7/4/02.
Nos. 1-3 sold for 19p, 27p and 36p respectively on day of issue.

Three Lions — A2

Crowned Lion — A3

Oak Tree — A4

Tudor Rose — A5

Perf. 14¾x14 Syncopated

2003, Oct. 14

6 A2 2nd multi 1.40 1.40
7 A3 1st multi 1.75 1.75
a. Litho. (Wales #21a) 3.00 3.00
8 A4 E multi 2.75 2.75
9 A5 68p multi 2.75 2.25
Nos. 6-9 (4) 8.65 8.15

Nos. 6-8 each sold for 20p, 28p and 38p respectively on day of issue.

2004, May 11

10 A4 40p multi 1.60 1.50
a. Booklet pane, 2 each #6, 10 + label (BK177) 8.00 —

No. 10a issued 2/24/05.

2005, Apr. 5

11 A4 42p multi 1.75 1.75

2006, Mar. 28

12 A4 44p multi 1.90 1.90
13 A5 72p multi 2.50 2.50

2007

14 A4 48p multi 1.75 *1.90*
15 A5 78p multi 2.50 2.50

Litho.
Self-Adhesive
Die Cut Perf. 14¾x14
Stamp + Label

16 A3 1st multi 2.25 2.00

Issued: Nos. 14, 15, 3/27; No. 16, 4/23. No. 16 was issued in sheets of 20 stamps + 20 labels that sold for £7.35 and had a franking value of 34p on day of issue.

Perf. 14¾x14 Syncopated

2008, Apr. 1 **Photo.**

17 A4 50p multi 1.90 1.75
18 A5 81p multi 2.75 2.50

Litho.
Self-Adhesive
Stamp + Label
Die Cut Perf. 14¾x14 Syncopated

18A A3 1st multi 3.50 3.50

Issued: No. 18A, 9/29/08. See Wales & Monmouthshire No. 32Ab.

2009, Mar. 31

19 A4 56p multi 1.75 1.75
20 A5 90p multi 2.75 2.75

Heritage of England Type of 2007

Design: English flag (like #2462a).

Self-Adhesive

Die Cut Perf. 14¾x14

2009, Apr. 21 **Litho.**

21 A626 1st multi + label 2.50 2.50

No. 21 was issued in a sheet of 20 stamps + 20 labels that sold for £8.35, and had a franking value of 39p on day of issue.

Types of 2003

Perf. 14¾x14 Syncopated

2010, Mar. 30 **Photo.**

22 A4 60p multi 1.90 1.75
23 A5 97p multi 3.00 2.75

2011, Mar. 29 **Litho.**

24 A4 68p multi 2.25 2.00
25 A5 £1.10 multi 3.50 3.50

2012, Apr. 25

26 A4 87p multi 4.25 3.75
27 A5 £1.28 multi 3.90 3.50

2013, Mar. 27

28 A4 88p multi 2.75 2.10

2014, Mar. 26

29 A4 97p multi 3.25 2.50

Types of 2003

Perf. 14¾x14 Syncopated

2015, Mar. 24 **Litho.**

30 A4 £1 multi 2.60 2.60
31 A5 £1.33 multi 3.50 3.50

Oak Tree Type of 2003

Perf. 14¾x14 Syncopated

2016, Mar. 22 **Litho.**

32 A4 £1.05 multi 2.75 2.75

Types of 2003

Perf. 14¾x14 Syncopated

2017, Mar. 21 **Litho.**

33 A4 £1.17 multi 3.00 1.50
34 A5 £1.40 multi 3.50 1.75

Three Lions — A6

Crowned Lion — A7

Oak Tree — A8

Tudor Rose — A9

Perf. 14¾x14 Syncopated

2018, Mar. 20 **Litho.**

35 A6 2nd multi 1.60 .80
36 A7 1st multi 1.90 .95
37 A8 £1.25 multi 3.50 1.75
38 A9 £1.45 multi 4.25 2.10
Nos. 35-38 (4) 11.25 5.60

On day of issue, No. 35 sold for 56p and No. 36 sold for 65p.

NORTHERN IRELAND

A1

A2

Flax and Red Hand of Ulster — A3

Perf. 15x14

1958-67 **Photo.** **Wmk. 322**

1 A1 3p dark purple .25 .25
p. Phosphor. ('67) .25 .25
2 A1 4p ultra ('66) .25 .25
p. Phosphor. ('67) .25 .25
3 A2 6p rose lilac .30 .30
4 A2 9p dk green ('67) .25 .35
5 A3 1sh3p dark green .35 .45
6 A3 1sh6p dark blue ('67) .25 .35
Nos. 1-6 (6) 1.65 1.95

Nos. 4, 6 and following are phosphorescent. For stamps with denomination of "1st" see No. 2600.

1968-69 **Unwmk.**

Design: 1sh6p, Flax plant, Red Right Hand of Ulster and Ulster field gate.

7 A1 4p ultramarine .25 .25
8 A1 4p olive brown .25 .25
9 A1 4p bright red ('69) .25 .25
10 A1 5p dark blue .25 .25
11 A3 1sh6p dark blue ('69) 2.00 *2.10*
Nos. 7-11 (5) 3.00 3.10

Giant's Causeway — A4

Perf. 14¾x14 Syncopated

2001-02 **Litho.**

12 A4 2nd shown 1.45 1.45
13 A4 1st Farm fields 1.75 1.75
a. Booklet pane, 5 #12, 4 #13 (BK173) 14.50
14 A4 E Linen 2.40 2.40
15 A4 65p Parian China 3.00 3.00
16 A4 68p Parian China 3.25 3.25
Nos. 12-16 (5) 11.85 11.85

Issued: Nos. 12-15, 3/6/01; No. 16, 7/4/02; No. 13a, 2/25/03.
Nos. 12-14 sold for 19p, 27p and 36p respectively on day of issue.

Giant's Causeway A5

Farm Fields A6

Linen — A7

Parian China — A8

2003, Oct. 14

17 A5 2nd multi 1.45 1.45
a. Photo. 1.45 1.45
18 A6 1st multi 1.75 1.75
a. Photo. ('07) 1.60 1.60
19 A7 E multi 2.75 2.75
20 A8 68p multi 2.75 2.75
Nos. 17-20 (4) 8.70 8.70

Nos. 17-19 each sold for 20p, 28p and 38p respectively on day of issue.

2004, May 11

21 A7 40p multi 1.90 1.90

2005, Apr. 5

22 A7 42p multi 2.60 2.60

2006, Mar. 28

23 A7 44p multi 1.75 1.75
24 A8 72p multi 3.25 3.25

2007, Mar. 27 **Photo.**

25 A7 48p multi 1.50 1.50
26 A8 78p multi 2.50 2.50

Self-Adhesive
Stamp + Label
Die Cut Perf. 14¾x14

2008, Mar. 11 **Litho.**
27 A6 1st multi 2.75 2.75

No. 27 was issued in sheets of 20 stamps + 20 labels that sold for £7.35, and had a franking value of 34p on day of issue.

Perf. 14¾x14 Syncopated

2008, Apr. 1 **Photo.**
28 A7 50p multi 1.60 1.60
29 A8 81p multi 2.60 2.60

2009
30 A7 56p multi 1.75 1.75
31 A8 90p multi 2.75 2.75

Litho.
Self-Adhesive
Stamp + Label
Die Cut Perf. 14¾x14 Syncopated
32 A6 1st multi 2.25 2.25

Issued: Nos. 30-31, 3/31; No. 32, 4/21. No. 32 was issued in a sheet of 20 stamps + 20 labels that sold for £8.35, and had a franking value of 39p on day of issue.

Perf. 14¾x14 Syncopated

2010, Mar. 30 **Photo.**
33 A7 60p multi 1.90 1.90
34 A8 97p multi 2.75 2.75

2011, Mar. 29 **Litho.**
35 A7 68p multi 2.25 1.90
36 A8 £1.10 multi 3.50 3.50

2012, Apr. 25
37 A7 87p multi 4.00 4.00
38 A8 £1.28 multi 3.75 3.75

2013, Mar. 27
39 A7 88p multi 3.25 3.25

2014, Mar. 26 **Litho.**
40 A7 97p multi 3.50 3.50

Types of 2003
Perf. 14¾x14 Syncopated

2015, Mar. 24 **Litho.**
41 A7 £1 multi 3.00 2.60
42 A8 £1.33 multi 3.75 3.25

Linen Type of 2003
Perf. 14¾x14 Syncopated

2016, Mar. 22 **Litho.**
43 A7 £1.05 multi 3.00 2.60

Types of 2003
Perf. 14¾x14 Syncopated

2017, Mar. 21 **Litho.**
44 A7 £1.17 multi 3.00 1.50
45 A8 £1.40 multi 3.50 1.75

Giant's Causeway A9

Farm Fields A10

Linen — A11

Parian China — A12

Perf. 14¾x14 Syncopated

2018, Mar. 20 **Litho.**
46 A9 2nd multi 1.60 .80
47 A10 1st multi 1.90 .95
48 A11 £1.25 multi 3.50 1.75
49 A12 £1.45 multi 4.25 2.10
Nos. 46-49 (4) 11.25 5.60

On day of issue, No. 46 sold for 50p and No. 47 sold for 65p.

SCOTLAND

St. Andrew's Cross and Thistle — A1

A2

A3

Perf. 15x14

1958-67 **Photo.** **Wmk. 322**
1 A1 3p dark purple .25 .25
p. Phosphor. .25 .25
2 A1 4p ultra ('66) .25 .25
p. Phosphor. ('67) .25 .25
3 A2 6p rose lilac .25 .25
p. Phosphor. ('63) .25 .25
4 A2 9p dark green ('67) .40 .40
5 A3 1sh3p dark green .40 .40
p. Phosphor. ('63) .40 .40
6 A3 1sh6p dark blue ('67) .45 .45
Nos. 1-6 (6) 2.00 2.00

The 3p with two phosphorescent bands was issued in 1963; with one side band in 1965, and one center band in 1967. The value of No. 1p is for one center band. Nos. 4, 6 and following are phosphorescent. For stamps with denomination of "1st" see No. 2600.

1967-70 **Unwmk.**
7 A1 3p purple ('68) .25 .25
8 A1 4p ultramarine .25 .25
9 A1 4p olive brown ('68) .25 .25
10 A1 4p brt red ('69) .25 .25
11 A1 5p dark blue ('68) .25 .25
12 A2 9p dark green ('70) 3.75 3.75
13 A3 1sh6p dark blue ('68) 1.10 1.10
Nos. 7-13 (7) 6.10 6.10

Natl. Flag (St. Andrew's Cross) — A4

Perf. 14¾x14 Syncopated

1999-2002 **Photo.**
14 A4 (2nd) shown 1.45 1.45
15 A4 (1st) Lion Rampant 1.75 1.60
a. Booklet pane, #15, 4 England #1, 4 England #2 (BK172) 14.50
16 A4 (E) Thistle 2.25 2.25
a. Booklet pane, 4 each #15-16, + label (BK170) 16.00
17 A4 64p Tartan 8.00 8.00
18 A4 65p As #17 2.60 2.60
a. Booklet pane, 6 #14, 2 #18 + label (BK168) 14.00
19 A4 68p Tartan 3.25 3.25
Nos. 14-19 (6) 19.30 19.15

nos. 14-16 sold for 19p, 26p, & 30p, respectively, on day of issue.
Issued: Nos. 14-17, 6/8; No. 18, 4/25/00; No. 18a, 8/4/00; No. 16a, 10/22/01. No. 19, 7/4/02. No. 15a, 9/24/02.

Natl. Flag (St. Andrew's Cross) A5

Lion Rampant A6

Thistle — A7

Tartan — A8

2003, Oct. 14
20 A5 2nd multi 1.45 1.45
a. Booklet pane, 3 each England #9, Scotland #20 (BK175) 12.50 —
21 A6 1st multi 1.75 1.75
a. Litho. (Wales #21a, GB 2600t) 2.00 2.00
22 A7 E multi 2.90 2.90
23 A8 68p multi 2.10 1.75
Nos. 20-23 (4) 9.00 9.00

Nos. 20-22 each sold for 20p, 28p and 38p respectively on day of issue.
No. 20a issued 3/18/04. No. 21a issued 9/28/08.
See Great Britain No. 2419a for National Flag stamp inscribed "1st."

2004, May 11
24 A7 40p multi 1.75 1.35
a. Souvenir sheet, #20, 2 each #21, 24 6.00 6.00

No. 24a issued 10/5/04.

2005, Apr. 5
25 A7 42p multi 1.90 1.40

2006, Mar. 28
26 A7 44p multi 1.75 1.75
27 A8 72p multi 2.90 2.90

2007, Mar. 27
28 A7 48p multi 1.75 1.75
29 A8 78p multi 2.75 2.75

Self-Adhesive
Stamp + Label
Die Cut Perf. 14¾x14

2007, Nov. 30 **Litho.**
30 A6 1st multi 2.75 2.75

No. 30 was issued in sheets of 20 stamps + 20 labels that sold for £8.50, and had a franking value of 34p on day of issue.

Perf. 14¾x14 Syncopated

2008, Apr. 1 **Photo.**
31 A7 50p multi 1.90 1.75
32 A8 81p multi 2.75 2.25

Litho.
Self-Adhesive
Stamp + Label
Die Cut Perf. 14¾x14 Syncopated
32A A6 1st multi 3.75 2.90

Issued: No. 32A, 9/29/08. See Wales & Monmouthshire No. 32Ab.

2009, Mar. 31
33 A7 56p multi 1.90 1.90
34 A8 90p multi 2.75 2.75

Flag of Scotland — A9

35 A9 1st multi + label 2.00 2.00

No. 35 was printed in a sheet of 20 + 20 labels that could not be personalizd that sold for £8.35. See No. 2419a for similar stamp with water-activated gum.

Types of 2003

2010, Mar. 30 **Photo.**
36 A7 60p multi 2.40 1.90
37 A8 97p multi 3.75 2.90

2011, Mar. 29 **Litho.**
38 A7 68p multi 2.40 2.40
39 A8 £1.10 multi 3.50 3.50

2012, Apr. 25
40 A7 87p multi 4.25 3.25
41 A8 £1.28 multi 3.75 2.60

2013, Mar. 27
42 A7 88p multi 2.75 2.00

2014, Mar. 26
43 A7 97p multi 3.25 2.25

Types of 2003
Perf. 14¾x14 Syncopated

2015, Mar. 24 **Litho.**
44 A7 £1 multi 3.00 2.25
45 A8 £1.33 multi 4.00 3.00

Thistle Type of 2003
Perf. 14¾x14 Syncopated

2016, Mar. 22 **Litho.**
46 A7 £1.05 multi 3.00 2.25

Types of 2003
Perf. 14¾x14 Syncopated

2017, Mar. 21 **Litho.**
47 A7 £1.17 multi 3.00 1.50
48 A8 £1.40 multi 3.50 1.75

National Flag (St. Andrew's Cross) A10

Lion Rampant A11

Thistle A12

Tartan A13

Perf. 14¾x14 Syncopated

2018, Mar. 20 **Litho.**
49 A10 2nd multi 1.60 .80
50 A11 1st multi 1.90 .95
51 A12 £1.25 multi 3.50 1.75
52 A13 £1.45 multi 4.25 2.10
Nos. 49-52 (4) 11.25 5.60

On day of issue, No. 49 sold for 56p and No. 50 sold for 65p.

WALES & MONMOUTHSHIRE

A1

A2

Welsh Dragon — A3

Designs: 6p, 9p, Dragon in rectangular panel at bottom. 1sh3p, 1sh6p, Dragon and leek.

Perf. 15x14

1958-67 **Photo.** **Wmk. 322**
1 A1 3p dark purple .25 .25
p. Phosphor. band ('67) .25 .25
2 A1 4p ultra ('66) .25 .25
p. Phosphor. bands ('67) .25 .25
3 A2 6p rose lilac .40 .35
4 A2 9p dark green ('67) .40 .40
5 A3 1sh3p dark green .50 .50
6 A3 1sh6p dark blue ('67) .40 .40
Nos. 1-6 (6) 2.20 2.15

Nos. 4, 6 and following are phosphorescent. For stamps with denomination of "1st" see No. 2600.

1967-69 **Unwmk.**
7 A1 3p dark purple .25 .25
8 A1 4p ultra ('68) .25 .25
9 A1 4p olive brown ('68) .25 .25
10 A1 4p brt red ('69) .25 .25
11 A1 5p dark blue ('68) .25 .25
12 A3 1sh6p dark blue ('69) 3.50 3.50
Nos. 7-12 (6) 4.75 4.75

Leek — A4

Perf. 15x14 Syncopated

1999-2002 Photo.

13 A4 2nd shown 1.40 1.40
14 A4 1st Dragon 1.75 1.75
15 A4 E Daffodil 2.25 2.25
16 A4 64p Prince of Wales feathers 8.00 7.50
17 A4 65p Prince of Wales feathers 3.00 3.00
Nos. 13-17 (5) 16.40 15.90
18 A2 2nd Leek, perf 13¾x14¼ 3.75 3.00
a. Booklet pane, 4 each #18, MH336 + label (BK169) 23.00
19 A4 68p Prince of Wales Feathers 3.00 3.00

Nos. 13, 18 sold for 19p; No. 14, 26p; & No. 15, 30p, on day of issue.

Issued: Nos. 13-16, 6/8; No. 17, 4/25/00; No. 19, 7/4/02.

No. 18 is a booklet stamp.

Leek — A5

Dragon — A6

Daffodil A7

Prince of Wales Feathers A8

Perf. 14¾x14 Syncopated

2003, Oct. 14

20 A5 2nd multi 1.45 1.45
21 A6 1st multi 1.90 1.75
a. Booklet pane, litho., England #7a, Northern Ireland #18, Scotland, #21a, Wales & Monmouthshire #21b, + 5 labels (BK183) ('07) 9.75
b. Litho. (#21a, GB #2600v) ('07) 3.00 3.00
22 A7 E multi 2.90 2.90
23 A8 68p multi 2.25 2.00
a. Souvenir sheet, #20, 2 each #21, 23 ('06) 7.00 7.00
Nos. 20-23 (4) 8.50 8.10

Nos. 20-22 each sold for 20p, 28p and 38p respectively on day of issue.

No. 23a issued 3/1/06. No. 21b issued 9/28/08

2004, May 11

24 A7 40p multi 1.75 1.75

2005, Apr. 5

25 A7 42p multi 2.25 2.25

2006-07

26 A7 44p multi 1.75 1.75
a. Booklet pane, 3 each Scotland #20, Wales & Monmouthshire #26 (BK181) ('07) 11.50 —
27 A8 72p multi 2.50 2.25

Self-Adhesive

Litho.

Stamp + Label

Die Cut Perf. 14¾x14

28 A6 1st multi 2.75 2.25

No. 28 was issued in a sheet of 20 stamps + 20 different se-tenant labels that sold for £6.95. The franking value of No. 28 was 32p on day of issue.

Issued: Nos. 26, 27, 3/28; Nos. 26a, 28 issued 3/1/07.

Perf. 14¾x14 Syncopated

2007, Mar. 27 Photo.

29 A7 48p multi 1.90 1.75
30 A8 78p multi 2.50 2.50

2008, Apr. 1

31 A7 50p multi 1.90 1.75
32 A8 81p multi 3.25 2.40

Litho.

Self-Adhesive

Stamp + Label

Die Cut Perf. 14¾x14 Syncopated

32A A6 1st multi 3.25 3.25
b. Sheet, 5 each #32A, England #18A, Northern Ireland #32, Scotland #32A, + 20 labels 27.50 —

Issued: No. 32A, 9/29/08.

No. 32Ab sold for £7.74. Labels could not be personalized.

2009, Mar. 31

33 A7 56p multi 1.75 1.75
34 A8 90p multi 2.75 2.75

Flag of Wales — A9

Die Cut Perf. 14¾x14 Syncopated

2010, Mar. 1 Self-Adhesive Litho.

35 A9 1st multi + label 2.25 1.75

Issued: No. 32A, 9/29/08. No. 35 was printed in a sheet of 20 + 20 labels that could not be personalizd that sold for £8.35. See No. 2639a for similar stamp with water-activated gum.

Types of 2003

Perf. 14¾x14 Syncopated

2010, Mar. 30 Photo.

36 A7 60p multi 1.90 1.40
37 A8 97p multi 3.00 2.25

2011, Mar. 29 Litho.

38 A7 68p multi 2.40 1.90
39 A8 £1.10 multi 3.50 2.60

2012, Apr. 25

40 A7 87p multi 4.25 3.25
41 A8 £1.28 multi 3.75 2.90

2013, Mar. 27

42 A7 88p multi 2.75 2.10

2014, Mar. 26

43 A7 97p multi 3.50 2.60

Types of 2003

Perf. 14¾x14 Syncopated

2015, Mar. 24 Litho.

44 A7 £1 multi 3.00 2.25
45 A8 £1.33 multi 4.00 3.25

Daffodil Type of 2003

Perf. 14¾x14 Syncopated

2016, Mar. 22 Litho.

46 A7 £1.05 multi 3.00 2.25

Types of 2003

Perf. 14¾x14 Syncopated

2017, Mar. 21 Litho.

47 A7 £1.17 multi 3.00 1.50
48 A8 £1.40 multi 3.50 1.75

Leek A10

Dragon A11

Daffodil A12

Prince of Wales Feathers A13

Perf. 14¾x14 Syncopated

2018, Mar. 20 Litho.

49 A10 2nd multi 1.60 .80
50 A11 1st multi 1.90 .95
51 A12 £1.25 multi 3.50 1.75
52 A13 £1.45 multi 4.25 2.10
Nos. 49-52 (4) 11.25 5.60

On day of issue, No. 49 sold for 56p and No. 50 sold for 65p.

MACHINS

MACHIN DEFINITIVE STAMPS

Sterling Currency Issue

MA1

Type I Type II

Two types of 2p:

Type I — Head off-center to right. Foot of "2" 1mm from left margin.

Type II — Head centered. Foot of "2" ½mm from left margin.

MH21

MH168

Two types of "£" symbol:

No. MH21 has a loop at the bottom and the numeral is a figure "1."

No. MH168 has no loop and numeral is like a capital "I."

Perf. 15x14

1967-69 Photo. Unwmk.

Size: 17½x21½mm

MH1 ½ brown orange .25 .25
MH2 1p olive .25 .25
a. Booklet pane of 6 (BK101-BK104, BK121) 1.00
MH3 2p maroon (I) .25 .25
MH4 2p maroon (II) .25 .25
MH5 3p dark violet .25 .25
a. Booklet pane of 6 (BK121) 1.25
b. Booklet pane, 2 ea #MH2, MH5 (BK83) .80
c. imperf, pair 850.00
MH6 4p brown black .25 .25
a. Bklt. pane of 2 + 2 labels (BK84) .50
b. Bklt. pane of 4 (BK83-BK84) 1.00
c. Booklet pane of 6 (BK101-BK102, BK114-BK115, BK121-BK122) 1.25
d. Booklet pane, 4 #MH2, 2 #MH6 (BK122) 1.50
MH7 4p bright red .25 .25
a. Bklt. pane of 2 + 2 labels (BK85) .50
b. Booklet pane of 4 (BK85) 1.00
c. Booklet pane of 6 (BK103-BK104, BK116-BK117, BK123-BK124) 1.50
d. Booklet pane of 15 + recipe (BK125-BK126) 3.00
e. Booklet pane, 4 #MH2, 2 #MH7 (BK123-BK124) 1.50
f. Coil strip of 5, #MH2, #MH5, #MH7, 2 #MH4 1.25
MH8 5p dark blue .25 .25
a. Booklet pane of 6 (BK110-BK112, BK122-BK124) 1.50
b. Booklet pane, 6 each #MH2, #MH7, 3 #MH8 + recipe (BK125-BK126) 3.00
c. Booklet pane of 15 + recipe (BK125-BK126) 3.00
MH9 6p magenta .25 .25
MH10 7p bright green .35 .35
MH11 8p scarlet .25 .50
MH12 8p lt greenish blue .40 .50
MH13 9p dark green .40 .30
MH14 10p gray .75 .75
MH15 1sh light violet .45 .30
MH16 1sh6p indigo & grnsh bl .50 .50
a. Greenish blue omitted 150.00
MH17 1sh9p blk & org .60 .50

Perf. 12

Engr.

Size: 27x31mm

MH18 2sh6p brown .45 .25
MH19 5sh dark carmine 1.40 .70
MH20 10sh ultramarine 4.75 4.75
MH21 £1 bluish black 2.90 1.75
Nos. MH1-MH21 (21) 15.45 13.40

Nos. MH10-MH13 have denomination at right. Many of Nos. MH1-MH17 exist with phosphor bands omitted in error.

Issued: ½p, 1p, No. MH3, 6p, 2/5/68; No. MH4, 8/27/69; 3p, 4/6/68; No. MH6, 1sh, 1sh9p, 6/5/67; Nos. MH7, MH12, 1/6/69; 5p, 7p, No. MH11, 10p, 7/1/68; 9p, 1sh6p, 8/8/67; Nos. MH18-MH21, 3/5/69.

Decimal Currency Issues

(P Instead of D)

MA2

Original

Type MA2: Upper lip not defined by sharp line, nostril is incomplete, hairlines not sharply defined, upper corners of cross formeé are widely separated.

Nos. MH22-MH189, MH199-MH243 are Type MA2.

Redrawn portrait: Upper lip sharply outlined, nostril is complete and defined by two lines, hairlines are sharply defined, upper corners of cross formeé are close together so they nearly complete a square.

See listings begining with No. MH245 for Type MA2 Redrawn.

Specialized illustrations are shown for identification purposes.

Two types of 1p: Type I: Thick numeral and "p," which are 2½mm from bottom of design. Type II: Thinner numeral and "p," which are 3mm from bottom of design.

Perf. 15x14

1970-95 Photo. Unwmk.

Size: 17½x21½mm

MH22 ½p greenish blue .25 .25
a. Booklet pane of 5 + label (BK129-BK130, BK132, BK138, BK143) 1.25
MH23 1p magenta, Type I .25 .25
MH23A 1p magenta, Type II .45 .45
MH24 1½p black .25 .25
a. Booklet pane, 2 each #MH23-MH24 (BK127-BK128) 1.00

Issued: ½p, No. MH23, 1½p, 2/15/71. No. MH23A, 8/4/80.

a

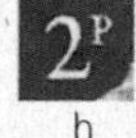

b

c

Three types of 2p:
a, Wide "2," thick at bottom of curve.
b, Wide "2," thin at bottom of curve.
c, Narrow "2."

MH25 2p light green (a) .25 .25
a. Coil strip, 2 ea #MH22-MH23, 1 #MH25 .90
MH26 2p light green (b) .55 .25
a. Booklet pane, 2 each #MH22, MH26(BK127-BK128) 1.50
b. Booklet pane of 6 + printed margin (BK145) 3.50
MH27 2p dark green (c) .35 .25
MH28 2p light green (c) 6.75 3.25

Litho.

MH29 2p dk grn, perf 14 (a) .30 .25
MH30 2p dark green (a) .40 .25
MH31 2p dark green (c) .75 .65
MH31A 2p dk grn, perf 14 (c) 2.00 .25

Nos. MH24a, MH26a exist with with stamps se-tenant vertically or horizontally.

Issued: No. MH25, 12/12/79; No. MH26, 2/15/71; No. MH27, 9/5/88; No. MH28, 7/26/88; No. MH29, 5/21/80; No. MH30, 7/10/84; No. MH31, 2/23/88; No. MH31A, 2/9/93.

No. MH31A comes from No. MH128a (BK420) only.

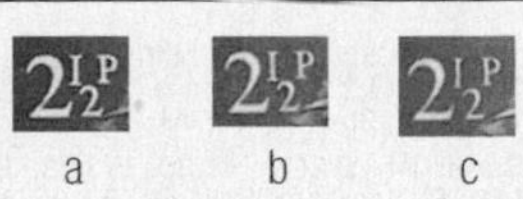

a b c

Three types of 2½p:
a, Thick numerals & "P," end of curve of small "2" is thick.
b, Thinner numerals & "P," end of curve of small "2" is thin.
c, Very thin numerals & "P," end of curve of small "2" is pointy.

MH32 2½p pink (a) .40 .40
- *a.* Booklet pane of 4 + 2 labels (BK129-BK130, BK132) 1.75
- *b.* Booklet pane of 5 + label (BK129-BK130, BK132, BK138, BK143) 2.00

MH33 2½p pink (b) .30 *.60*
MH34 2½p pink (c) 1.25 *1.75*
- *a.* Booklet pane, 3 #MH22, 9 #MH34 + printed margin (BK144) 27.50
- *b.* Booklet pane, 4 #MH22, 2 #MH34 + printed margin (BK144) 8.00

Nos. MH34a, MH34b valued in F-VF condition.

MH35 2½p vermilion (b) .25 *.40*

Issued: No. MH32 2/15/71; No. MH33, 5/21/75; No. MH34, 5/24/72; No. MH35, 1/14/81.
No. MH34 issued only in booklets.

a b

Two types of 3p:
a, Thick numeral with top serif.
b, Thin numeral without serif.

MH36 3p ultramarine (a) .25 .25
- *a.* Booklet pane, 2 #MH32, 4 #MH36 (BK138, BK143) 2.50
- *b.* Booklet pane, 5 + label (BK131, BK133-BK136, BK139) 2.00
- *c.* Bklt. pane of 6 (BK138, BK143) 1.50
- *d.* Booklet pane of 12, 6 each #MH34, #MH36 + printed margin (BK144) 20.00
- *e.* Booklet pane of 12 + printed margin (BK144) 5.50

MH37 3p deep lilac rose (a) .25 .25
- *a.* Coil strip, #MH35, 3 #MH37 .90 .90

MH38 3p deep lilac rose (b) 1.75 .75

Issued: No. MH36, 9/10/73; No. MH37, 10/22/80; No. MH38, 1/21/92.

a b

Two types of 3½p:
a, Numerals in fraction aligned diagonally.
b, Numerals in fraction aligned vertically.

MH39 3½p gray green (a) .40 .40
- *a.* Booklet pane of 5 + label (BK137, BK139-BK141) 2.25

MH40 3½p violet brown (b) .45 *.55*

Issued: No. MH39, 6/24/74; No. MH40, 3/30/83.

4P 4P 4P

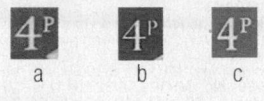

a b c

Three types of 4p:
a, Wide "4" with large serif and thick crossbar.
b, Wide "4" with small serif and thin crossbar.
c, Narrow "4."

MH41 4p olive bister (a) .30 .25
- *a.* Imperf., pair

MH42 4p greenish blue (a) .60 *.75*
- *a.* Coil strip, #MH22, 3 MH42 1.25 *2.50*

MH43 4p brt greenish bl (a) .50 *.60*
- *a.* Coil strip, #MH23, 3 MH43 1.50
- *b.* Coil strip, #MH28, 3 MH43 8.25

MH44 4p greenish blue (b) 1.60 *1.90*
MH45 4p brt greenish bl (c) 1.50 *1.90*
MH46 4p bright blue (c) .40 .25
- *a.* Coil strip, #MH38, 3 MH46 4.00

MH47 4p Prussian blue, litho., perf 13½x14 (b) .30 .30
MH48 4p Prus blue, litho. (c) .35 .30
MH49 4½p grayish blue .25 .25
- *a.* Booklet pane of 5 + label (BK140, BK142) 9.75

Issued: No. MH41, 2/15/71; Nos. MH42-MH42a, 12/30/81; Nos. MH43-MH43a, 8/14/84; No. MH43b, 9/5/88. No. MH44, 8/26/81; No. MH45, 9/3/84; No. MH46, 7/26/88; No. MH46a, 9/19/89. No. MH47, 1/30/80; No. MH48, 5/13/86; 4 1/2p, 10/24/73.
No. MH43 issued only in strips.

a b

Two types of 5p:
a, 5p is 3.25mm wide.
b, 5p is 2.75mm wide.

MH50 5p bluish lilac (a) .25 .25
MH51 5p lilac, litho., perf 13½x14 (a) .45 .45
MH52 5p red brown, litho., perf 13½x14 (a) .60 .60
MH53 5p red brown, litho. (a) .70 .60
MH54 5p red brown (b) 2.25 2.25
MH55 5p brown (b) .45 .35
- *a.* Coil strip, #MH55, 3 #MH46 2.00
- *b.* Coil strip, 2 ea #MH46, MH55 2.00
- *c.* Coil strip, #MH46, 3 MH55 2.00

MH56 5½p dark violet .35 .35

Issued: No. MH50, 2/15/71; No. MH51, 5/21/80; No. MH52, 1/27/82; No. MH53, 2/21/84; No. MH54, 10/20/86; No. MH55, 7/26/88; No. MH55a, 11/27/90; No. MH55b, 10/1/91. No. MH55c, 1/31/95. 5 1/2p, 10/24/73.

a b c

Three types of 6p:
a, Thick numeral and "P."
b, Thinner numeral and "P," numeral is pointed at top and very thin where loop joins.
c, Narrow numeral.

MH57 6p light emerald (a) .35 .25
MH58 6p light emerald (b) .75 .25
- *a.* Booklet pane, #MH58, 2 MH22, 3 MH23 (BK225) 1.75
- *b.* Coil strip, #MH23, MH26, MH58, 2 #MH22 1.50

MH59 6p brt olive green (c) .40 .25
MH60 6½p Prussian blue .35 *.40*

Issued: No. MH57, 2/15/71; No. MH58, 6/9/76; No. MH58b, 12/3/75. No. MH59, 9/10/91; 6 1/2p, 9/4/74.
No. MH58 issued only in booklets and strips.

 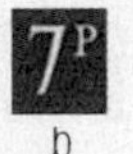

a b

Two types of 7p:
a, Wide numeral.
b, Narrow numeral.

MH61 7p dark red brown (a) .25 *.30*
- *a.* Coil strip, #MH61, 2 ea MH22-MH23 .95
- *b.* Booklet pane, #MH61, 2 ea MH22-MH23 + label (BK226) .75

MH62 7p henna brown (b) .85 *1.50*
MH63 7½p lt red brown .35 *.40*
MH64 8p red .25 .25
- *a.* Coil strip, #MH64, 2 MH23 + 2 labels .75
- *b.* Booklet pane, #MH64, 2 MH23 + label (BK227) .75

MH65 8½p yellow green .35 .25
- *a.* Bklt. pane, 2 ea #MH22-MH23, MH60, 4 MH65 (BK228) 2.60

No. MH65a exists with the four 8 1/2p stamps se-tenant on either the left or right side of the pane.

MH66 9p black & ocher .50 .25
MH67 9p violet blue .35 .25
- *a.* Booklet pane, 2 #MH23, 3 ea MH61, MH67 (BK229-BK230) 2.25
- *b.* Booklet pane, 10 ea #MH61, MH67 (BK672) 5.50

No. MH67a exists with the three 9p stamps se-tenant on either the left or right side of the pane.

MH68 9½p bright lilac .40 *.50*

Issued: No. MH61, 1/15/75; No. MH61a, 12/14/77. No. MH62, 10/29/85; 7 1/2p, 2/15/71; 8p, 10/24/73; No. MH64a, 1/16/80. 8½p, 9/24/75; No. MH66, 2/15/71; No. MH67, 9 1/2p, 2/25/76.

a b c

Three types of 10p:
a, Round "0."
b, Thin part of "0" at upper left, lower right.
c, Thin part of "0" at top, bottom.

MH69 10p org brn & lt org (a) .50 .35
MH70 10p light org brn (b) .40 .30
- *a.* Bklt. pane of 9 + printed margin (BK145) 3.75
- *b.* Booklet pane, 2 ea #MH26, MH64, 3 #MH70 + label (BK231-BK232) 2.25
- *c.* Booklet pane, 10 ea #MH64, MH70 (BK709) 6.00

MH70D 10p light org brn (c) 29.00 20.00

No. MH70b exists with the three 10p stamps se-tenant on either the left or right side of the pane.

MH71 10p brn orange (c) .55 .50
MH72 10½p yellow .50 .50
MH73 10½p steel blue .65 .60
MH74 11p pink .50 .25

Issued: No. MH69, 8/11/71; Nos. MH70, MH72, 11p, 2/25/76; No. MH71, 9/4/90; No. MH73, 4/26/78; No. MH70D, 9/4/84.

a b

Two types of 11½p:
a, Thin numerals in fraction.
b, Thick numerals in fraction.

MH75 11½p olive bister (a) .55 .55
MH76 11½p gray brown (a) .45 .40
- *a.* Booklet pane, 2 #MH44, 3 each MH35, MH76 (BK236) 5.00

No. MH76a exists with the three 11½p stamps se-tenant on either the left or right side of the pane.

MH77 11½p gray brown (b) 1.00 .25

No. MH77 comes from No. MH86c (BK826), only.
Issued: No. MH75, 8/15/79; No. MH76, 1/14/81; No. MH77, 11/11/81;

a b

Two types of 12p:
a, Wide numerals.
b, Narrow, thin numerals.

MH78 12p yellow green (a) .55 .50
- *a.* Booklet pane of 9 + printed margin (BK145) 5.00
- *b.* Booklet pane of 9 (#MH26, 4 each #MH70, MH78) + printed margin (BK145) 4.50
- *c.* Booklet pane of 10 each #MH70, MH78 (BK759) 9.50
- *d.* Booklet pane, 3 #MH26, 2 each MH70, MH78 + label (BK233) 3.50

No. MH78d exists with the three 2p stamps se-tenant on either the left or right side of the pane.

MH79 12p bright green (b) .55 .35
- *a.* Booklet pane of 9 + printed margin (BK140) 5.00
- *b.* Booklet pane, 2 #MH23, 4 MH79 (BK245) 9.50

Issued: No. MH78, 1/30/80; No. MH79, 10/29/85.

a b

Two types of 12½p:
a, Thin, narrow numerals.
b, Thick, wider numerals.

MH80 12½p light emerald (a) .55 .25
- *a.* Booklet pane of 6 + printed margin (BK146-BK147) 3.50
- *b.* Booklet pane of 9, #MH25, MH37, 7 MH80 + printed margin (BK146) 4.25
- *c.* Booklet pane, #MH22, 4 MH37, 3 MH80 (BK237-BK238) 2.75
- *e.* Booklet pane of 20 (BK760) *11.00*

No. MH80c exists with the three 12½p stamps se-tenant on either the left or right side of the pane. Booklets with 20 No. MH80 were sold at a discount. Stamps in these booklets had 5-point double-lined stars printed on the reverse.

MH81 12½p green (b) .60 .25
- *a.* Booklet pane, 2 #MH23, 3 each MH40, MH81 (BK239+) 5.00

No. MH81 comes from Nos. BK239, BK513-BK514 and from No. MH93d (BK572-BK574).
Issued: No. MH80, 1/27/82; No. MH81, 2/1/82.

a b

Two types of 13p:
a, "3" with serif.
b, "3" without serif.

MH82 13p gray green (a) .65 .55
MH83 13p lt red brown (b) .50 .25
- *a.* Booklet pane of 6 + printed margin (BK148, BK151) 3.00
- *b.* Booklet pane of 9 + printed margin (BK149, BK151) 4.50
- *c.* Booklet pane, 2 #MH45, 3 each MH23, MH83 (BK240) 5.00
- *d.* Booklet pane, #MH23, 2 MH54, 3 MH83 (BK244, BK248) 6.25
- *e.* Booklet pane of 4, margins all around (BK285) 2.00
- *f.* Booklet pane of 10, margins all around (BK534) 5.00
- *g.* As "d," imperf edges (BK248A, BK250-BK251) 5.25

Panes of No. MH83 with stars printed on the reverse were sold at a discount.

MH84 13p lt red brn, litho. (b) .75 *.85*
- *a.* Booklet pane of 6 + printed margin (BK152) 4.50

MH85 13½p brown purple .70 .70

Issued: No. MH82, 8/15/79; No. MH83, 8/28/84; No. MH84, 2/9/88; 13½p, 1/30/80.

a b

Two types of 14p:
a, Wide "4."
b, Narrow "4."

MH86 14p gray blue (a) .60 .60
- *a.* Bklt. pane, #MH22-MH23, MH86, 3 MH76 (BK234-BK235) 2.40
- *b.* Booklet pane, 4 #MH76, 6 MH86 (BK524) 5.50
- *c.* Booklet pane, 10 each #MH77, MH86 (BK826) 16.00

No. MH86a exists with the three 11½p stamps se-tenant on either the left or right side of the pane.

MH87 14p dark blue (b) .60 .40
- *a.* Booklet pane of 4, margins all around (BK295) *4.75*
- *b.* Booklet pane of 4, imperf on T, B (BK296) *5.75*
- *c.* Booklet pane of 4, imperf on T, B, R (BK297) *27.00*
- *d.* Boolet pane of 10, margins all around (BK558) 12.00
- *e.* Booklet pane of 10, imperf on T, B (BK560) 7.50

MH88 14p dark blue, litho. (b) 2.25 2.00
MH89 14p dark blue, litho., perf 14 (b) 6.75 1.00

No. MH89 comes from No. MH108a (BK412), only.

MH90 15p deep ultramarine .65 .65
MH91 15p bright blue .80 .80

Issued: No. MH86, 1/14/81; No. MH87, 9/5/88; No. MH88, 10/11/88; No. MH89, 4/25/89; No. MH90, 8/15/79; No. MH91, 9/26/89.

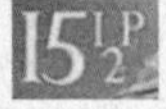 

a b

Two types of 15½p:
a, Thin numerals in fraction, top bar of "5" thin.
b, Thick numerals in fraction, top bar of "5" thick.

MH92 15½p light violet (a) .60 .50
- *a.* Booklet pane of 6 + printed margin (BK146) 3.75
- *b.* Booklet pane of 9 + printed margin (BK146) 5.50

MH93 15½p light violet (b) .65 *.75*
d. Booklet pane, 4 #MH81, 6 MH93 (BK572-BK574) 6.50
e. Booklet pane, 10 each #MH80, MH93 (BK802) 12.00

No. MH93e was printed with 10-point single-line blue stars on the reverse over the gum.

MH94 16p brownish gray .65 .65
a. Booklet pane, #MH37, 2 MH40 6 MH94 + printed margin (BK147) 5.00
b. Booklet pane of 9 + printed margin (BK147) 5.75
c. Booklet pane, 4 #MH80, 6 MH94 (BK594) 6.75

Panes of No. MH94 with double-line D printed on reverse were sold at a discount in BK584.

MH95 16½p fawn .80 *.85*

Issued: No. MH92, 1/14/81; No. MH93, 2/1/82; 16p, 3/30/83; 16½p, 1/27/82.
No. MH93 issued only in booklets.

a

b

Two types of 17p:
a, Wide "7."
b, Narrow "7."

MH96 17p light green (a) .75 *.80*
MH97 17p blue gray (b) .50 .50
a. Booklet pane of 3 + label (star printed on reverse-BK241-BK242) 2.75
b. Booklet pane of 9 + printed margin (BK149-BK150) 4.50
c. Booklet pane of 6 + printed margin (BK148-BK150) 3.00
d. Booklet pane, #MH70D, MH83, 7 MH97 + printed margin (BK148) 33.00
e. Booklet pane, 4 #MH79, 6 MH97 (BK616-BK618) 5.25
f. Booklet pane, 4 #MH83, 6 MH97 (BK641) 5.00
g. Booklet pane of 10 (double-lined "D" printed on reverse-BK652) 5.00
MH98 17p dark blue (b) 1.10 1.00
a. Bklt. pane of 3 + label (BK256) 7.00
MH99 17p dk bl, litho. (b) .95 .95
a. Booklet pane of 6 + printed margin (BK155) 5.75
MH100 17½p lt red brown 1.00 1.00
MH101 18p violet blue .80 .80
MH102 18p olive green .60 .50
a. Booklet pane of 9 + printed margin (BK151) 5.50
b. Booklet pane, #MH23, MH83, 2 MH102 (BK246-BK247, BK249) 3.00
c. Booklet pane of 4, margins all around (BK328) 3.00
d. Booklet pane, #MH83, 5 MH102 (BK406-BK407) 4.00
e. Booklet pane of 10, margins all around (BK714) 6.00
f. As "d," imperf edges (BK408-BK410) 6.00
MH103 18p ol grn, litho. .80 *.90*
a. Booklet pane of 6 + printed margin (BK152) 5.00
b. Booklet pane of 9 + printed margin (BK152) 7.25
MH104 18p brt yel grn .85 .85
MH105 18p brt yel grn, litho. .95 *1.00*
a. Booklet pane of 6 + printed margin (BK157) 5.75
MH106 19p brt orange .75 .50
a. Bklt. pane, #MH87, 2 #MH106 + label (BK252-BK253) 6.25
b. Booklet pane, 2 #MH87, 4 MH106 (BK411, BK413) 5.25
c. Booklet pane of 4, margins all around (BK348) *5.25*
d. Booklet pane of 4, imperf on T, B (BK349) *6.50*
e. Booklet pane of 4, imperf on T, B, R (BK350) *26.00*
f. Booklet pane of 10, margins all around (BK729) 8.50
g. Booklet pane of 10, imperf on T, B (BK730) *9.25*
MH107 19p red org, litho. 2.00 2.00
MH108 19p red org, litho., perf 14 3.25 3.25
a. Booklet pane, 2#MH89, 4 #MH108 (BK412) 26.50
MH110 19½p olive gray 1.75 1.50

Issued: No. MH96, 1/30/80; No. MH97, 3/30/80; No. MH98, 9/4/90; No. MH99, 3/19/91; 17½p, 1/30/80; No. MH101, 1/14/81; No. MH102, 8/28/84; No. MH103, 2/9/88; No. MH104, 9/10/91; No. MH105, 10/27/92; No. MH106, 8/3/88; No. MH107, 10/11/88; No. MH108, 4/25/89; 19½p, 1/27/82.
Nos. MH99, MH103, MH105, MH108 issued only in booklets.

a

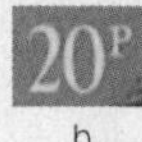
b

Two types of 20p:
a, Thin part of "0" at upper left, lower right.
b, Thin part of "0" at top, bottom.

MH111 20p dp pur brn (a) .95 .95
MH112 20p dp pur brn, litho., perf 13¾x14 (a) 1.40 1.40
MH113 20p dp pur brn, litho., perf 15x14 (b) 2.00 1.75
MH114 20p greenish bl (b) .85 .80
MH115 20p brown black (b) .90 .90
a. Booklet pane, 2 #MH91, MH115 + label (BK254) 13.00
b. Booklet pane of 5 + label (BK414) 6.25
MH116 20½p ultramarine 1.20 1.20
MH117 22p dark blue .85 .85
MH118 22p yellow green .90 .90
MH119 22p yel grn, litho. (MH150a) 13.00 9.00
MH120 22p orange red .95 .90
a. Booklet pane, 2 #MH98, 3 MH120 + 3 labels (BK417) 5.25
MH121 22p org red, litho. 1.00 1.00
a. Booklet pane of 9 + printed margin (BK155) 9.00
MH122 23p rose pink 1.25 1.10
MH123 23p brt yel grn 1.25 1.25
MH124 24p violet 1.40 1.40
MH125 24p brown red 2.00 2.00
MH126 24p brown .95 .90
a. Booklet pane, 2 each #MH23, MH126 (BK257-BK259) 2.25
b. Booklet pane, 2 #MH27, 4 MH126 + 2 labels (BK418-BK419) 4.50
MH127 24p brown, litho. 1.00 1.00
a. Booklet pane of 6 + printed margin (BK157) 6.00
MH128 24p brn, litho. perf 14 1.25 1.25
a. Booklet pane, 2 #MH31A, 4 MH128 + 2 labels (BK420) 9.00
MH129 25p lilac 1.00 *1.10*
MH129A 25p salmon 14.50 14.00

Issued: No. MH111, 2/25/76; No. MH112, 5/21/80; No. MH113, 5/13/86; No. MH114, 8/23/88; No. MH115, 9/26/89; 20½p, 3/30/83; No. MH117, 10/22/80; No. MH118, 8/28/84; No. MH119, 2/9/88; No. MH120, 9/4/90; No. MH121, 3/19/91; No. MH122, 3/30/83; No. MH123, 8/3/88; No. MH124, 8/28/84; No. MH125, 9/26/89; No. MH126, 9/10/91; No. MH127, 10/27/92; No. MH128, 2/9/93; 25p, 1/14/81.
Nos. MH119, MH121, MH127 issued only in booklets.
No. MH129A was issued 2/6/96 only in coils.

26P a

26P b

Two types of 26p:
a, Wide numerals.
b, Narrow numerals.

MH130 26p red (a) .95 .70
a. Booklet pane, #MH23, MH130, 2 MH83, 5 MH102 + printed margin (BK151) 5.50
MH131 26p red (b) 3.75 3.75
a. Booklet pane of 4, margins all around (BK446) 15.00
MH132 26p olive gray (b) 1.10 1.00
MH133 27p brown 1.10 1.10
a. Booklet pane of 4, margins all around (BK456) 8.25
b. Booklet pane of 4, horiz. edges imperf (BK457) 25.00
MH134 27p violet 1.10 1.00
MH135 28p deep violet blue .95 .95
MH136 28p dk olive bister 1.10 1.00
MH137 28p dull blue green 1.10 1.10

Issued: No. MH130, 1/27/82; No. MH131, 8/4/87; No. MH132, 9/4/90; No. MH133, 8/3/88; No. MH134, 9/4/90; No. MH135, 3/30/83; No. MH136, 8/23/88; No. MH137, 9/10/91.
No. MH131 issued only in booklets.

a

b

Two types of 29p:
a, Wide numerals.
b, Narrow numerals.

MH138 29p brown olive (a) 1.25 1.25
MH139 29p dp rose lilac (b) 1.75 1.75
MH140 29p dp rose lilac, litho., perf 14 (b) 3.00 3.00
a. Booklet pane of 4, imperf edges (BK478) 12.50
MH141 30p dk olive green 1.15 1.15
MH142 31p brt rose lilac 1.15 1.15
a. Bklt. pane, #MH142, 6 MH79, 2 MH97 + printed margin (BK150) 5.50
MH143 31p ultramarine 1.60 1.60
MH144 31p ultra, litho., perf 14 1.90 1.90
a. Booklet pane of 4, imperf on T, B (BK503) 7.75
MH145 32p Prussian blue 1.40 1.20
MH146 33p emerald 1.40 1.20
MH147 33p emerald, litho. 2.00 2.00
a. Bklt. pane, 6 #MH121, 2 MH147 + label, printed margin (BK155) 10.00
MH148 33p emer, litho. perf 14 2.10 2.10
a. Booklet pane of 4, imperf. on T, B (BK544) 8.50
MH149 34p dark brown 1.35 1.35
a. Bklt. pane, #MH149, 2 MH45, 4 MH83, 2 MH97 + printed margin (BK149) 7.50
MH150 34p dark brn, litho. 11.50 9.00
a. Bklt. pane, 6 #MH84, 1 ea MH103, MH119, MH150 + printed margin (BK152) 30.00
MH151 34p dull blue green 2.00 2.00
MH152 34p brt rose lilac 1.75 1.75
MH153 35p dark brown 1.75 1.75
MH154 35p orange yellow 1.75 1.75
MH155 37p scarlet 1.75 1.50
MH156 39p brt rose lilac 1.90 1.90
MH157 39p brt rose lil, litho. perf 14 2.25 2.25
a. Booklet pane of 4, imperf on T, B (BK662) 9.00
MH158 39p brt rose lil, litho. (MH178a, MH187b) 2.00 2.00

Issued: No. MH138, 1/27/82; No. MH139, 9/26/89; No. MH140, 10/2/89; No. MH141, 9/26/89; No. MH142, 3/30/83; No. MH143, 9/4/90; No. MH144, 9/17/90; No. MH145, 8/23/88; No. MH146, 9/4/90; No. MH147, 3/19/91; No. MN148, 9/16/91; No. MH149, 8/28/84; No. MH150, 2/9/88; No. MH151, 9/26/89; No. MH152, 9/10/91; No. MH153, 8/23/88; No. MH154, 9/10/91; No. MH155, 9/26/89; No. MH156, 9/10/91; No. MH157, 9/16/91; No. MH158, 10/27/92.
Nos. MH144, MH147-MH148, MH150 issued only in booklets.

a

b

Two types of 50p:
a, Wide numerals.
b, Narrow numerals.

MH159 50p bister brown (a) 2.00 .75
MH160 50p ocher (b) 4.00 1.60

Issued: No. MH159, 2/2/77; No. MH160, 5/21/80.

a

b

Two types of 75p:
a, Wide numerals.
b, Narrow numerals.

MH161 75p black, litho., perf 13½x14 (a) 3.00 1.50
MH162 75p black, litho. (a) 3.25 2.00
MH163 75p black, litho. (b) 9.50 9.50
MH164 75p black (b) 7.00 2.00

Issued: No. MH161, 3/1/80; No. MH162, 2/21/84; No. MH163, 2/23/88; No. MH164, 7/26/88.

Engr.
Perf. 12
Size: 27x31mm

MH165 10p carmine rose .75 *1.00*
MH166 20p olive .80 .25
MH167 50p ultramarine 1.60 .60
p. Phosphor 2.00 .60
MH168 £1 bluish black 3.75 1.00

For illustration of £1, see above No. MH1.
No. MH168, imperf, are from printers' waste.
Issued: Nos. MH165-MH167, 6/17/70; £1, 12/6/72.

Photo.
Perf. 14x15
Size: 27x38mm

MH169 £1 olive grn & yel 2.75 .25
MH170 £1.30 slate bl & buff 4.50 *6.00*
MH171 £1.33 black & pale rose lilac 6.75 *7.25*
MH172 £1.41 indigo & buff 7.75 7.75
MH173 £1.50 blk & lt pink 5.75 5.00
MH174 £1.60 indigo & buff 5.75 *6.25*
MH175 £2 mar & lt grn 5.50 .75
MH176 £5 dk bl & pink 13.50 2.75

Issued: £1, 2/2/77; £1.30, 8/3/83; £1.33, 8/28/84; £1.41, 9/17/85; £1.50, 9/2/86; £1.60, 9/15/87; £2, £5, 2/2/77.

2nd or 1st Class (Non-Denominated)

2nd and 1st class stamps sell for the current rates and remain valid indefinitely for the indicated service

1989-90
Perf. 15x14

MH177 2nd bright blue 1.45 1.45
a. Booklet pane of 4, imperf on T, B, R (BK961) 32.50
b. Booklet pane of 10, imperf on T, B (BK1028, BK1037) 14.50
MH178 2nd bright blue, litho. 1.60 1.60
a. Booklet pane, 2 each #MH105, MH147, MH158, MH178 + label, printed margin (BK158) 13.00
MH179 2nd bright blue, litho., perf 14 1.40 1.40
a. Booklet pane of 4, imperf on T, B, R (BK960) 5.75
b. Booklet pane of 4, imperf on T, B (BK963-BK964) 5.75
c. Booklet pane of 10, imperf on T, B (BK1034-BK1035) 14.00

Nos. MH177-MH179 each sold for 14p on day of issue.

MH180 2nd dark blue 1.75 1.75
a. Booklet pane of 10, imperf on T, B (BK1030) 17.50
MH181 2nd dark blue, litho. 2.75 2.75
MH182 2nd dark blue, litho., perf 14 1.35 1.00
a. Booklet pane of 4, imperf on T, B (BK962) 5.50
b. Booklet pane of 10, imperf on T, B (BK1032) 13.50

Nos. MH180-MH182 each sold for 15p on day of issue.

MH183 1st brown black 2.00 1.60
a. Booklet pane of 4, imperf on T, B, R (BK995) 35.00
b. Booklet pane of 10, imperf on T, B (BK1041) 16.00
MH184 1st brown black, litho., perf 14 2.75 2.75
a. Booklet pane of 4, imperf on T, B, R (BK994) 11.00
MH185 1st brown black, litho. 2.25 2.25

Nos. MH183-MH185 each sold for 19p on day of issue.
Issued: No. MH183c, 6/5/17.

MH186 1st orange red 1.60 1.60
a. Booklet pane of 10, imperf on T, B (BK1068, BK1091) 16.00
MH187 1st orange red, litho. 1.60 1.00
a. Booklet pane, 3 each #MH178, MH187 + printed margin (BK158) 9.75
b. Booklet pane, #MH178, MH187, 2 ea MH105, MH127, MH158 + label, printed margin (BK157) *15.00*
c. Booklet pane of 8+ label, printed margin (BK156) 11.50
d. Booklet pane of 10, imperf on T, B (BK1092-BK1093) 16.00

No. MH187c contains Nos. MH178, MH187, 2 each Nos. MH147, WMMH34, WMMH45.

MH188 1st orange red, litho., perf 14 1.60 1.60
a. Booklet pane of 4, imperf on T, B (BK996-BK997) 6.50
b. Booklet pane of 10, imperf on T, B (BK1070) 16.00
MH189 1st orange red, litho., perf 13x13½ 5.00 5.00
a. Booklet pane of 4, imperf. on T, B (BK996A) 20.00 —

Nos. MH186-MH189 each sold for 20p on day of issue.
Distance of denomination to the margin and bust may vary on different printings of the same stamp.
Issued: No. MH177, 8/22/89; No. MH178, 9/18/89; No. MH179, 8/22/89; Nos. MH180-MH182, 8/7/90; Nos. MH183-MH184, 8/22/89; No. MH185, 9/19/89; Nos. MH186-MH188, 8/7/90; No. MH189, 10/90.
Nos. MH177-MH189 issued only in booklets.

Victoria and Elizabeth II — MA3

1990-2000 Photo. *Perf. 15x14*

MH190 15p bright blue .85 .85
a. Booklet pane of 10, imperf on T, B (BK619) 8.50
MH191 15p brt bl, litho., perf 14 1.50 *1.75*
a. Booklet pane of 4 with imperf on T, B, R (BK307) 6.00

b. Booklet pane of 10 with imperf on T, B, R (BK620) 15.00
MH192 15p bright blue, litho. 2.25 *2.50*
a. Booklet pane of 10 (BK621) 22.50
MH193 20p black & brown black .90 .90
a. Booklet pane, #MH193, 2 MH190 + label (BK255) 10.50
b. Booklet pane of 4 with imperf on T, B, R (BK371) 7.00
c. Bklt. pane of 5 + label (BK415) 8.50
d. Booklet pane of 6 + printed margin (BK154) 6.75
e. Booklet pane of 10 with imperf on T, B (BK743) 9.00
f. Souvenir sheet of 1 3.75 3.75
MH194 20p black & brn blk, litho., perf 14 1.50 *1.75*
a. Booklet pane of 4 with imperf on T, B, R (BK372) 6.50
b. Bklt. pane of 5 + label (BK416) 14.00
c. Booklet pane of 10 with imperf on T, B, R (BK744) 17.50
MH195 20p black & brn blk, litho. 2.50 *2.60*
a. Booklet pane of 10 (BK745) 25.00
MH196 29p deep rose lilac 1.60 1.60
a. Booklet pane, #MH91, MH115, MH160, MH177, MH183, MH190, MH193, MH196 + label, printed margin (BK154) 15.50
MH197 34p dull blue green 1.90 1.90
MH198 37p scarlet 2.00 2.00

Perf. 13¾x14¼ Syncopated

MH198A 1st blk & yel 2.75 2.75
b. Booklet pane of 6 (BK167) 16.50

Nos. MH191-MH192, MH194-MH195, MH198A were issued only in booklets.

No. MH198A sold for 26p on day of issue. No. MH198A is redrawn.

Issued: Nos. MH190, MH193, MH196-MH198, 1/10; Nos. MH191, MH194, 1/30; Nos. MH192, MH195, 4/17; No. MH198A, 2/15/00; No. MH193c, 6/5/17.

Syncopated Perf. 15x14

1993-97 **Type MA2**

MH199 1p magenta .25 .25
MH200 1p mag, litho. (MH216b) .90 .90
MH201 2p dark green .25 .25
MH202 4p Prussian blue .45 .45
MH203 5p rose brown .35 .35
MH204 6p bright olive green .45 .45
MH205 6p bright olive green, litho. (MH214a) 14.00 14.00
MH206 10p brown orange .45 .45
MH207 10p brown orange, litho. (MH231a) 7.00 7.00
MH208 19p olive green .70 .70
MH209 19p ol grn, litho. (MH214a, MH231a) 1.25 1.25
a. Booklet pane of 6 + printed margin (BK160) 7.50
MH210 20p greenish blue .95 .95
MH211 20p bright yel grn 1.75 1.75
MH212 20p brt yel grn, litho. (MH216a-MH216b) 3.75 3.50
MH213 25p salmon .90 .90
a. Booklet pane of 2 + 2 labels (BK260-BK262) 1.90
MH214 25p sal, litho. (MH231a) .95 .95
a. Bklt. pane, #MH205, MH209, 4 MH214 + printed margin (BK159) 19.50
b. Booklet pane of 8 + label, printed margin (see footnote) (BK161) 7.75

No. MH214b contains 2 each Nos. MH214, NIMH59, SMH65, WMMH60.

MH215 26p brown 1.60 1.60
MH216 26p brown, litho. 1.25 1.25
a. Bklt. pane, #MH212, 7 MH216 (BK749) 12.50
b. Bklt. pane, #MH212, 2 MH200, 3 MH216 + 2 labels (BK426) 9.25
MH218 29p gray 1.25 1.25
MH219 30p olive green 1.25 1.25
MH220 30p olive green, litho. (MH231a) 7.00 7.00
MH221 31p deep rose lilac 1.75 1.75
MH222 35p orange yellow 1.75 1.75
MH223 35p org yel, litho. 1.90 1.90
a. Booklet pane of 4 (BK562-BK563) 7.75
MH224 36p blue 1.75 1.75
MH225 37p bright rose lilac 2.00 2.00
MH226 37p brt rose lilac, litho. 4.25 4.25
a. Booklet pane of 4 (BK605) 17.00
MH227 38p red 1.90 1.90
MH228 39p bright pink 2.00 2.00
MH230 41p drab 2.00 2.00
MH231 41p drab, litho. 2.25 2.25
a. Booklet pane, #MH207, MH220, MH223, MH231, 2 each MH209, MH214 + label, printed margin (BK160) 22.50
b. Booklet pane of 4 (BK685-BK686) 9.00
MH232 43p dark brown 2.50 2.50
MH233 50p ocher 2.60 2.60
MH234 60p slate blue, litho. 2.75 2.75
a. Booklet pane of 4 (BK790-BK791) 11.00
MH235 63p bright green 3.25 3.25
MH236 63p brt grn, litho. 4.50 4.50
a. Bklt. pane of 4 (BK815) 18.00
MH237 £1 violet 5.00 4.75

No. MH237 is printed with Iriodin ink, giving stamp design a three dimensional appearance.

MH238 2nd bright blue 1.35 1.35
MH239 2nd bright blue, litho. 1.35 1.35
MH240 1st orange red 1.60 1.60
MH241 1st orange red, litho. 1.60 1.60
a. Miniature sheet of 1 7.00 7.00
b. Booklet pane of 4 + label (BK1000, BK1002, BK1004) 6.50
c. Booklet pane of 9 + printed margin (BK165) 14.50

No. MH241a was sold for £1 on day of issue in pre-packaged greeting cards at Boots pharmacy. Unfolded examples were later sold by British Philatelic Bureau. Value indicated is for unfolded example.

MH243

MH309

Size: 21½x17½mm

Self-Adhesive

Die Cut 14x15 Syncopated

Litho.

MH243 1st orange red 1.75 1.75
a. Booklet pane of 20 35.00

Nos. MH238-MH239 each sold for 18p on day of issue; Nos. MH240-MH241, MH243 each for 24p.

Issued: No. MH201, 4/11/95; No. MH204, 4/27/93; No. MH219, 7/27/93; No. MH222, 8/17/93; No. MH234, 8/9/94; No. MH237, 8/22/95; No. MH238, 9/7/93; No. MH241, 9/6/93. No. MH241c, 2/16/99.

Nos. MH239, MH240, 4/6/93.

Nos. MH199, MH203, MH212, MH206, 6/8/93.

No. MH243, 10/19/93.

Nos. MH208, MH213, MH218, MH224, MH227, MH230, 10/26/93.

Nos. MH214, MH223, MH223, 11/1/93.

Nos. MH202, MH210, MH233, 12/14/93.

Nos. MH205, MH209, 7/26/94.

Nos. MH207, MH220, 4/25/95.

Nos. MH215, MH221, MH225, MH228, MH232, MH235, 6/25/96.

Nos. MH200, MH216, MH226, MH236, 7/8/96.

Nos. MH200, MH205, MH207, MH209, MH212, MH216, MH219, MH226, MH231, MH236 issued only in booklets.

No. MH243a is a complete booklet.

Stamps similar to those shown above are listed in the Great Britain Air Post and Special Delivery sections.

Queen Type of 1970 with Redrawn Portrait

Redrawn

Redrawn portrait: Upper lip sharply outlined, nostril is complete and defined by two lines, hairlines are sharply defined, upper corners of cross formeé are close together so they nearly complete a square.

5p Type c — The top line of the 5 has a curved top edge.

Type MA2: Upper lip not defined by sharp line, nostril is incomplete, hairlines not sharply defined, upper corners of cross formeé are widely separated.

See Nos. MH22-MH189, MH199-MH243 for Type MA2.

Perf. 15x14 Syncopated, 13¾x14¼ Syncopated (#MH251, MH254A, MH264B, MH269, MH285, MH289)

1996-2010 **Photo.**

MH245 1p magenta .25 .25
a. Litho. (MH372c) 3.50 3.50
MH246 2p dark green .25 .25
a. Litho. (MH401b) 4.00 4.00
MH247 4p Prussian blue .60 .60
MH248 5p rose brown (b) .25 .25
a. Litho. (b) (MH363c) .95 .95
c. Booklet pane of 8, #2419e, 2462e, 2639a, Northern Ireland 18, 2 each #MH246a, MH248a, + central label (BK204) 17.00 —

Issued: No. MH248c, 2/20/14.

MH248B 5p red brown, litho. (c) (MH350Ad) 6.25 6.25
MH249 6p bright olive green .95 .95
MH249A 7p gray 4.50 4.25
MH249B 8p dk olive bister .75 .75
MH250 10p brown orange .35 .35
a. Litho. (MH363c) 1.75 1.25
MH251 10p brn org, perf 13¾x14¼ 3.75 3.75
MH254 19p bister 2.40 2.40
MH254A 19p bister (MH264c), perf 13¾x14¼ 1.90 1.90
MH255 20p bright yellow green .75 .75
a. Litho. (MH368c) 1.25 1.25
MH256 26p gold 1.50 1.60
MH257 26p brown 1.40 1.40
a. Booklet pane, 3 each #MH255, MH257 + printed margin (BK162) 6.50
b. Bklt. pane, #MH255, 2 MH245, 3 MH257 + 2 labels (BK427) 27.50
c. Booklet pane, #MH255, 7 MH257 (BK751) 27.50
d. Booklet pane, #MH245-MH246, MH254, 3 #MH257 + 2 labels (BK428) 7.00
e. Booklet pane, #MH254, 7 #MH257 (BK752) 12.50
f. Booklet pane, 4 #MH245, 3 #MH254, 1 #MH257 + label 9.50
MH259 30p olive green 1.75 1.75
MH260 31p deep rose lil 2.00 2.00
MH261 33p dk blue green 1.75 1.75
MH261A 34p olive green 7.75 7.75
MH262 37p brt rose lilac 2.25 2.25
MH263 37p black 1.90 1.75
MH264 38p dark blue 2.25 2.25
MH264B 38p dk blue, perf 13¾x14¼ 6.00 6.00
c. Booklet pane, 4 #MH254A, 2 #MH264B (BK167) 20.00
MH265 39p brt pink 2.25 2.25
MH266 40p chalky blue 1.90 1.90
a. Booklet pane of 4 (BK676) 7.75
MH267 41p carmine rose 2.00 2.00
MH267A 42p olive 1.90 1.90
MH268 43p dark brown 2.75 2.75
MH269 43p dk brn, perf 13¾x14¼ 2.25 2.25
a. Booklet pane, #NIMH70, SMH76, WMMH71, 3 MH269 + printed margin (BK164) 25.00
MH270 44p brown 6.50 6.50
MH270A 45p brt rose lilac 2.40 2.40
MH270B 47p blue green 2.10 2.10
MH271 50p ocher 2.00 2.00
MH275 63p bright green 3.50 3.50
MH276 64p greenish blue 3.50 3.50
MH277 65p Prussian blue 3.25 3.25
a. Booklet pane of 4 (BK830) 13.00
MH278 68p drab 3.00 3.00
MH279 £1 violet 4.50 4.50
a. Souv. sheet, see footnote 22.50 22.50

No. MH279 is printed with Iriodin ink, giving stamp design a three dimensional appearance.

No. MH279a contains Nos. MH247-MH249, MH250, MH260, MH265, MH276, MH279 + 2 labels.

Issued: No. MH246a, 5/8/10.

MH280 £1.50 red, engr. 6.00 2.25
MH281 £2 slate blue, engr. 7.50 3.25
MH282 £3 purple, engr. 10.50 4.75
MH283 £5 brown, engr. 17.00 8.00
MH284 2nd bright blue 1.35 1.00
a. Litho. (#MH287h) ('08) 3.50 2.00
MH285 2nd bright blue, perf 13¾x14¼ 1.60 1.30
a. Booklet pane, #NIMH74, SMH80, WMMH75, 3 MH285 + printed margin (BK164) 22.50
b. Booklet pane, 2 #MH251, 3 each MH269, MH285 + label, printed margin (BK164) 19.00
MH287 1st gold 1.60 1.60
a. Bklt. pane, 4 ea #MH256, MH287 + label, printed margin (BK162) 12.50
b. Booklet pane, 4 each #MH284, MH287 + label (BK174) 12.00
c. Booklet pane, 4 each #MH263, MH287 + label 14.00 —
d. Booklet pane, 2 each #MH267A, MH270B, 4 #MH287, + label (BK176) 14.50
e. Booklet pane, 2 each #MH271, MH278, 4 #MH287 + label (BK178) 16.50 —
f. Booklet pane of 8 + central label, litho. (BK184) 18.00 —
g. Litho. (#MH287f) ('08) 2.25 2.25
h. Booklet pane of 8, 4 each #MH284a, MH287g + label (BK185) ('08) 23.00 —
MH288 1st orange red (BK1005, BK1140) 1.60 1.60
a. Booklet pane of 8, label + printed margin (BK165) 13.00
b. Booklet pane of 8 (BK1141-BK1142) 13.00
c. Booklet pane of 4 + label (BK1006) 10.00
d. Booklet pane, #MH284, 3 #MH288 + 4 labels (BK429) 8.50
e. Bklt. pane, 2 #MH284, 4 #MH288 (BK753) 9.25
f. Miniature sheet of 1 5.00
MH289 1st org red, perf 13¾x14¼ 3.00 2.50
a. Booklet pane of 10 (BK1139A) 30.00
MH289B 1st blk, perf 14¾x14 Syncopated (MH440d) 2.00 2.00
MH290 E dark blue 2.40 1.75
a. Booklet pane of 4 (BK1010) 9.75
b. Booklet pane, 4 each #MH284, MH290, + label (BK171) 34.00 —
c. Booklet pane, 4 #MH287, 4 #MH290 + label (BK172, BK173) 16.00

Nos. MH284-MH285 sold for 20p on day of issue; Nos. MH287-MH289 for 26p; No. MH290 for 30p. Nos. MH284-MH285 were later sold for 19p. Selling prices for booklets containing these stamps will be considered to have 20p stamps.

Queen Type of 1970 with Redrawn Portrait

MH292 MH294

MH297 MH299

MH300

MH301

On Nos. MH292 and MH297, the numeral and letters are thinner, and perf tips are flat with distinct corners, while on MH294 and MH299, numeral and letters are thicker and bolder, and perf tips have a slight arc and are rounded at the corners.

On No. MH300 the numeral and letters are thick and bold and perf tips have a slight arc and are rounded at the corners, while on No. MH301, the numeral and letters are thin and perf tips are distinctly serpentine with little flatness on the peaks or valleys.

Die Cut Perf. 14¾x14 Sync., Die Cut Perf. 15x14¼ Sync. (MH 293, MH298)

Self-Adhesive

Booklet Stamps (MH293, MH298)

MH292 2nd bright blue 1.60 1.00
a. Booklet pane of 6 9.75
b. Booklet pane of 12 19.50
MH293 2nd bright blue 1.60 1.00
a. Booklet pane of 10 16.00
b. Booklet pane of 12 19.25
MH294 2nd bright blue 2.25 1.00
a. Booklet of 12 27.00
MH297 1st vermilion 1.90 1.75
a. Booklet pane of 6 11.50
b. Booklet pane of 12 23.00
MH298 1st vermilion 1.90 1.75
a. Booklet pane of 10 19.00
b. Booklet pane of 12 23.00
MH299 1st vermilion 2.75 1.75
a. Booklet of 6 16.50
MH300 1st gold 1.90 1.25
a. Booklet of 6 11.50
MH301 1st gold 1.90 1.25
a. Booklet of 6 11.50
b. Booklet of 12 23.00
MH302 E dark blue 4.50 4.50
a. Booklet of 6 27.00
MH304 42p olive 7.00 7.00
a. Booklet of 6 42.50
MH306 68p drab 7.00 7.00
a. Booklet of 6 42.50

Nos. MH292, MH297 and MH301 were also issued as coils, which have no selvage surrounding stamps.

No. MH293 & single stamps from No. MH292a sold for 19p on day of issue; No. MH292, 20p; No. MH297, 26p; No. MH298 & single stamps from Nos. MH297a, MH297b, 27p.

Nos. MH292a, MH293a, MH293b, MH297a, MH297b, MH298a, and MH298b are complete booklets.

No. MH297a exists with self-adhesive label depicting Queen Victoria.

Die Cut Perf. 14x15 Syncopated

Self-Adhesive Coil Stamps

Size: 21x17mm

MH308 2nd bright blue 3.25 3.25
MH309 1st orange red 3.25 3.25

Size: 30x40mm

Perf. 14x14½

MH310 1st black, engr. 3.25 2.75
a. Booklet pane of 4 + printed margin (BK165) 13.00
MH311 1st black, typo. 3.00 2.75
a. Booklet pane of 4 + printed margin (BK165) 12.00

Self-Adhesive

Die Cut Perf. 14x14½

MH312 1st gray, litho. & embossed 3.00 2.75
a. Booklet pane of 4 + printed margin (BK165) 12.00

No. MH312 is valued in used condition on piece. Soaking and pressing No. MH312 removes the embossed image of the Queen.

No. MH300 sold for 20p on day of issue. Nos. MH305, MH310-MH312 sold for 26p on day of issue.

Issued: No. MH268, 7/8/96. Nos. MH245, MH249, MH268, MH271, MH279, 4/1/97; Nos. MH256, MH287, 4/21/97. Nos. MH255, MH284, MH308, MH309, 4/29/97; Nos. MH246-MH248, MH250, MH259, MH265, 5/27/97; Nos. MH260, MH262, MH275, MH288, 8/26/97; No. MH257, 11/18/97; Nos. MH292, MH297, 4/6/98; Nos. MH251, MH269, MH285, 10/13/98; No. MH289, 12/1/98; No. MH290, 1/12/99; No. MH288c, 5/12/99; Nos. MH280-MH283, 3/9/99; Nos. MH310-MH312, 2/16/99; Nos. MH249A, MH254, MH264, MH270, MH276, 4/20/99; Nos. MH254A, MH264B, 2/15/00; Nos. MH249B, MH261, MH266, MH267, MH270A, MH277, MH288d, MH288e, 4/25/00; No. MH279a, 5/22/00; Nos. MH292a, MH293, MH293c, MH297a, MH297b, MH298, MH298c, 1/29/01; Nos. MH300-MH301, 6/5/02; Nos. MH263, MH267A, MH278, MH270B, MH294, MH299, MH302, MH304, MH306, 7/4/02; No. MH290c, 9/24/02; No. MH261A, 5/6/03; No. MH287b, 6/2/03. Nos. MH284a, MH287h, 9/18/08; No. MH287g, 1/8/08. Nos. MH248a, MH250a, 2/12/09. Nos. MH249B, MH255a, 1/7/10.

Nos. MH251, MH254A, MH264B, MH269, MH285 (BK164), MH289 (BK1139A), MH290 (BK1010) issued only in booklets.

No. MH290b issued 2/6/02. E stamps from MH 290b sold for 37p on day of issue. No. MH294 sold for 19p, Nos. MH299, MH300 and MH301 sold for 27p, and No. MH302 sold for 37p on day of issue.

Queen Type of 1970 With Redrawn Portraits

Printed in Iriodin Ink

Perf. 14¾x14 Syncopated

2003, July 1 Photo.

MH321 £1.50 rose 5.00 5.00
MH322 £2 grnsh blue 7.00 7.00
a. Pound symbol missing in denomination *200.00* —
MH323 £3 violet 10.50 10.50
a. Souvenir sheet of 1 ('06) 10.50 10.50
MH324 £5 light blue 17.50 17.50
Nos. MH321-MH324 (4) 40.00 40.00

Issued: £1.50, £2, £3, £5, 7/1. No. MH323a, 8/31/06.

No. MH323a has margin depicting invalid imperforate examples of Nos. 211, 231, and 236.

Queen Elizabeth II (No Frame, Perforations Touch Vignette) — MA4

Perf. 14¾x14 Syncopated

2000 Photo. Design MA4

MH335 1st olive green 1.90 1.10
a. Bklt. pane of 8 (BK1201) 15.00
b. Bklt. pane of 9 (BK168) 17.00
c. Bklt. pane of 4 + label (BK1007) 7.50

Perf. 13¾x14¼ Syncopated

MH336 1st olive green 2.00 1.40
a. Booklet pane of 10 (BK1144) 20.00
b. Booklet pane of 8 + label (BK167) 16.00

Issued: Nos. MH335, MH336, 1/6; No. MH336b, 2/15; No. MH335a, 5/26; No. MH335b, 8/4.

No. MH335c comes in two versions (as does No. BK1007): with Postman Pat on label and with Botanical Garden of Wales on label.

No. MH336 issued only in booklets. Perforations are Syncopated.

No. MH335 and MH336 sold for 26p on day of issue.

Queen Type of 1970 With Redrawn Portraits

Type a

Type b

54p Type a — "5" has thick straight top line, "4" has thick cross line.

Type b — "5" has thinner, slightly curved top line, "4" has thin cross line.

Perf. 14¾x14 Syncopated

2004-10 Type MA2 Photo.

MH344 7p bright pink .75 .75
MH346 9p brt orange .45 .25
a. Litho. (MH401b) 4.00 .25
MH347 12p blue green .90 .90
MH348 14p vermilion .75 .75
MH348A 15p brt pink .75 .75
MH349 16p lilac rose .75 .75
a. Litho. (MH365b) ('09) 4.25 4.25
MH350 17p olive green 1.30 1.30
b. Litho. (MH368b) 2.75 2.75
MH350A 22p brown 1.35 1.35
c. Litho. (MH368b) 3.00 3.00
d. Booklet pane of 9, 5 #MH250a, 2 each #MH248B, MH350Ac (BK191) 27.50 —
MH351 35p brown 1.90 1.90
MH352 35p olive green 1.90 1.90
MH353 37p olive green 1.90 1.90
MH354 39p gray 2.25 2.25
a. Booklet pane, 4 #MH284, 2 each #MH267A, MH354 + label (BK177) 18.00 —
MH355 40p Prussian blue 2.00 2.00
a. Booklet pane, 4 #MH287, 2 each #MH352, MH355 + central label (BK179) 14.50 —
MH358 43p emerald 2.25 2.25
MH359 44p bright blue 2.25 2.25
MH361 46p dk ol bister 2.00 2.00
MH363 48p brt rose lil 2.75 2.75
a. Booklet pane, 4 #MH246, 2 each #MH361, MH363, + label (BK182) 10.50 —
b. Litho. (MH363c) 5.50 5.50
c. Booklet pane, 2 each #MH248a, MH250a, MH287g, MH363b + label (BK188) 21.00 —
MH364 49p brown 2.50 2.50
MH365 50p gray 2.25 2.25
a. Litho. (MH365b) ('09) 5.75 5.75
b. Booklet pane, 4 each #MH349a, MH365a, + central label (BK187) ('09) 37.50 —
MH366 54p brown (a) 2.25 2.25
a. Booklet pane, 2 each #MH245, MH366, 4 #MH361, + label (BK183) 13.00
MH366B 54p brown, litho. (b) (MH368c) 6.00 6.00
c. Booklet pane of 8, 4#MH350Ac, 4 #MH366B, + label (BK192) 36.00 —
MH367 56p lt olive grn 2.25 2.25
MH368 62p carmine 2.25 2.25
a. Litho. (MH368b) 3.75 3.75
b. Booklet pane of 8, 4 #MH350b, 2 each #MH350Ac, MH368a + central label (BK189) 25.00 —
c. Booklet pane of 8, 4 #MH255a, 2 each #MH366B, MH368a + label (BK191) 25.00 —
MH370 72p carmine rose 2.90 2.90
MH371 78p emerald 3.50 3.50
MH372 81p greenish blue 3.25 3.25
MH372A 90p dark blue 3.50 3.50
b. Litho. (MH372c) 6.75 6.75
c. Booklet pane of 8, 4 #MH350b, 2 each #MH245a, MH372Ab + central label (BK190) 31.00 —
MH373 £1 cerise 4.75 4.75
a. Booklet pane of 2 + label (BK182) 9.50 —
Nos. MH344-MH373 (28) 61.60 61.40

Issued: 7p, 35p, 39p, 40p, 43p, 4/1. MH354a, 2/24/05. 9p, No. MH352, 46p, 4/5/05. No. MH355a, 2/23/06. 37p, 44p, 49p, 72p, 3/28/06. 12p, 14p, 8/1/06. 16p, 48p, 50p, 54p, 78p, 3/27/07. Nos. MH363a, MH373, 6/5/07. MH366a, 9/20/07. 15p, 56p, 81p, 4/1/08. Nos. MH349a, MH365a, MH365b, 1/13/09. Nos. MH363b, MH363c, 2/17/09. Nos. MH350, MH350A, MH368, MH372A, 3/31/09. Nos. MH350b, MH350Ac, MH368a, MH368b, 8/18/09. Nos. MH350Ad, MH366Bb, MH368c, 1/7/10. No. MH366Bc, 2/25/10. MH356a, 5/8/10.

Queen Elizabeth II
MA5 MA6

Perf. 14¾x14 Syncopated

2006 Photo.

MH375 MA5 2nd bright blue 1.75 1.25
MH376 MA5 1st gold 1.90 1.50
a. Booklet pane, 4 each #MH271, MH376 + central label (BK180) 15.50 —
b. Booklet pane, 4 each #MH248, MH376, + central label (BK181) 10.00 —

Inscribed "Large"

MH377 MA6 2nd bright blue 2.25 1.60
MH378 MA6 1st gold 2.90 2.00
a. Booklet pane, #MH375, MH376, 2 each #MH377-MH378, + label (BK182) 14.00 —
Nos. MH375-MH378 (4) 8.80 6.35

Booklet Stamps

Self-Adhesive

Serpentine Die Cut 14¾x14 Syncopated

MH379 MA5 2nd bright blue 2.00 .60
a. Booklet pane of 12 24.00
MH380 MA5 1st gold 2.10 .70
a. Booklet pane of 6 12.50
b. Booklet pane of 12 26.00

Inscribed "Large"

MH381 MA6 2nd bright blue 2.60 1.00
a. Booklet pane of 4 10.50
MH382 MA6 1st gold 3.00 1.00
a. Booklet pane of 4 12.00
Nos. MH379-MH382 (4) 9.70 3.30

Issued: Nos. MH375-MH378, 8/1; Nos. MH379-MH380, 9/12; Nos. MH381-MH382, 8/15. No. MH376a, 9/21. No. MH376b, 3/1/07. No. MH378a, 6/5/07.

On day of issue, Nos. MH375 and MH379 each sold for 23p, Nos. MH376 and MH380 each sold for 32p, Nos. MH377 and MH381 each sold for 37p, and Nos. MH378 and MH382 each sold for 44p.

Beginning with No. MH383, an iridescent "ROYAL MAIL" overprint was added to the design of many Machinhead stamps. These are identified in the listings below as having an "Iridescent Overprint of Royal Mail in Wavy Lines". Subsequent to the initial release of stamps with the overprint, both source and date codes were worked into the overprint as shown in the illustration.

The source codes currently in use are: MAIL (no code letter)—from counter sheets; ROYBL—from business sheets; MCIL—from "custom" booklets, including special stamps; MFIL—from booklets of four; MPIL—from prestige booklets; MRIL—from coil rolls; MSIL—from booklets of six; MTIL—from booklets of twelve.

Date codes were first used in 2010 and have a variety of forms: MA10—for 2010; MA11 or MIIL—for 2011; M12L—for 2012; MA13 or M13L—for 2013; M14L—for 2014.

Diamond Jubilee definitives have an iridescent "DIAMOND JUBILEE" wavy line overprint. On these stamps the source code replaces a letter at the end of "DIAMOND": DIAMBND—from business sheets; DIAMTND—from booklets of 12; DIAMMND—from miniature sheet.

New codes, when they appear, will be included in the above list.

Queen Type of 1970 With Redrawn Portraits and Type of 2006 With Two Die Cut Slits on Stamp and Iridescent Overprint of "Royal Mail" in Wavy Lines

Self-Adhesive

Die Cut Perf. 14¾x14 Syncopated

2009 Type MA2 Photo.

MH383 2nd bright blue 2.25 2.25
b. Booklet pane of 12 #MH383 27.00
MH384 1st gold 1.90 1.90
b. Booklet pane of 6 #MH384 11.50
c. Booklet pane of 12 #MH384 23.00
MH385 50p pale slate 2.00 2.00
a. Booklet pane of 8, 4 #MH384, 2 each #MH383, MH385, + central label (BK193) 16.50
MH386 £1 cerise 7.00 7.00
MH387 £1.50 brown red 4.25 4.25
MH388 £2 greenish blue 5.75 5.75
MH389 £3 violet 8.75 8.75
MH390 £5 light blue 14.00 14.00

Type MA6

MH391 2nd Large bright blue 2.90 2.90
b. Booklet pane of 4 #MH391 11.50
MH392 1st Large gold 3.50 3.50
b. Booklet pane of 4 #MH392 14.00
Nos. MH383-MH392 (10) 52.30 52.30

Issued: Nos. MH383-MH392, 2/17; Nos. MH383b, MH384b, MH384c, MH391b, MH392b, 3/31. MH385a, 5/8/10. On day of issue, No. MH383 sold for 27p; No. MH384, 36p; No. MH391, 42p; No. MH392, 52p.

No. MH383 was also issued in coils in 2012.

Victoria and Elizabeth II Type of 1990

Booklet Stamps

Perf. 14¾x14 Syncopated

2009 Type MA3 Litho.

MH393 20p blk & brn blk (MH394a) 2.75 2.75
a. photo. (MH440d) .90 .90
MH394 1st blk & brn blk (MH394a) 4.25 4.25
a. Booklet pane of 8, 4 each #MH393-MH394 + central label (BK189) 28.00 —

No. MH394 sold for 39p on day of issue.

MA7

MA8

With Two Die Cut Slits
Self-Adhesive

Die Cut Perf. 14¾x14 Syncopated

2009, Nov. 17 **Photo.**

MH395 MA7 1st yel & org 5.25 5.25

Die Cut Perf. 14½x14 Syncopated

MH396 MA8 1st Large yel & org 7.50 7.50

On day of issue, No. MH395 sold for £1.14; No. MH396, £1.36.

See Nos. MH436-MH437.

Queen Type of 1970 With Redrawn Portraits

Perf. 14¾x14 Syncopated

2010, Mar. 30 **Type MA2** **Photo.**

MH397 60p emerald 2.50 2.50
a. Litho. (MH397b) 5.00 5.00
b. Booklet pane of 8, 4 #MH248a, 2 each #MH250a, MH397a, + central label (BK194) 17.50 —

MH398 67p red violet 2.75 2.75
a. Litho. (MH401b) 7.75 7.75

MH399 88p cerise 3.50 3.50
a. Litho. (MH401b) 7.25 7.25

MH400 97p violet 4.00 4.00
a. Litho. (MH401b) 8.00 8.00
b. Booklet pane of 8, #MH398a, MH400a, 3 each # MH248a, MH250a + label (BK195) 23.00 —

MH401 £1.46 Prussian blue 5.25 5.25
a. Litho. (MH401b) 11.00 11.00
b. Sheet of 11 + label (see contents below) 40.00 40.00

Nos. MH397-MH401 (5) 18.00 18.00

Issued: Nos. MH397a, MH397b, 5/13/10. London 2010 Festival of Stamps (No. MH401b). Issued: Nos. MH398a, MH399a, MH400a, MH401a, MH401b, 5/8/10; No. MH400b, 3/22/11. No. MH401b contains Nos. MH245a, MH246a, MH248a, MH250a, MH255a, MH346a, MH397a, MH398a, MH399a, MH400a, MH401a + label.

Queen Type of 1970 With Redrawn Portrait With Iridescent Overprint of "Royal Mail" in Wavy Lines

Perf. 14¾x14 Syncopated

2010, May 13 **Type MA2** **Photo.**

MH401C 2nd bright blue 4.25 4.25
f. Litho., booklet stamp (3452a) 4.50 4.50

MH401D 1st gold 2.40 2.40
e. Miniature sheet of 10 24.00 24.00

On day of issue, No. MH401C sold for 32p, and No. MH401D sold for 41p.

Issued. No. MH401Cf, 10/20/15; No. MH401De, 9/14/11.

Queen Type of 1970 With Redrawn Portrait

Die Cut Perf. 14¾x14 Syncopated

2011 **Type MA2** **Photo.**

Self-Adhesive
With Two Oval Slits

MH402 1p magenta .70 .70
MH403 2p dark green .45 .45
MH404 5p red brown .50 .50
MH405 10p brn orange .70 .70
a. Booklet pane of 8, 2 each #MH385, MH405, 4 #MH404 + label (BK196) 7.50 —
MH406 20p brt yel grn .95 .95

With Iridescent Overprint of "Royal Mail" in Wavy Lines

MH407 68p greenish blue 2.50 2.50
MH408 76p pink 2.60 2.60
MH409 £1.10 olive green 3.75 3.75
MH410 £1.65 dk olive green 5.00 5.00
Nos. MH402-MH410 (9) 17.15 17.15

Issued: Nos. MH402, MH403, MH404, MH405, MH406, 3/8; Nos. MH407-MH410, 3/29; Nos. MH404a, MH405a, MH405b, 5/5.

See Nos. MH420-MH424 for stamps with iridescent overprint that are similar to Nos. MH402-MH406.

Queen Type of 1970 with Redrawn Portrait and Iridescent Overprint of "Royal Mail" in Wavy Lines

Perf. 14¾x14 Syncopated

2011, Sept. 9 **Type MA2** **Litho.**

MH411 1st gold (MH412a) 4.75 4.75
MH412 76p pink (MH412a) 7.25 7.25
a. Booklet pane of 8, 4 #MH248a, 2 each #MH411, MH412 (BK197) 28.00 —

No. MH411 sold for 46p on day of issue.

Queen Type of 1970 with Redrawn Portrait and Iridescent Overprint of "Royal Mail" in Wavy Lines

Perf. 14¾x14 Syncopated

2012, Jan. 5 **Type MA2** **Litho.**

MH413 68p greenish blue (MH413a) 4.75 4.75
a. Booklet pane of 8, 4 #MH413, 2 each #MH246a, MH250a + central label (BK198) 30.00 —

Queen Type of 1970 With Redrawn Portrait and Iridescent Overprint of "Diamond Jubilee" in Wavy Lines
Booklet Stamp
Self-Adhesive
With Two Oval Slits

Die Cut Perf. 14¾x14 Syncopated

2012, Feb. 6 **Type MA2** **Photo.**

MH414 1st gray blue 2.10 2.10
a. Booklet pane of 12 25.00
b. Booklet pane of 6 12.50

No. MH414 sold for 46p on day of issue. See No. 2996f for photogravure stamp with water-activated gum.

Issued: No. MH414b, 10/1.

Queen Type of 2006 With Redrawn Portrait and Iridescent Overprint of "Diamond Jubilee" in Wavy Lines
Self-Adhesive
With Two Oval Slits

Die Cut Perf. 14¾x14 Syncopated

2012, Apr. 25 **Type MA6** **Photo.**

MH415 1st Large gray blue 3.50 3.50
a. Booklet pane of 4 14.00

No. MH415 sold for 75p on day of issue.

Queen Type of 1970 With Redrawn Portrait and Iridescent Overprint of "Royal Mail" in Wavy Lines
Self-Adhesive
With Two Oval Slits

Die Cut Perf. 14¾x14 Syncopated

2012, Apr. 25 **Type MA2** **Photo.**

MH416 87p orange 4.75 4.75
MH417 £1.28 green 5.50 5.50
MH418 £1.90 red violet 6.50 6.50
Nos. MH416-MH418 (3) 16.75 16.75

Queen Type of 1970 With Redrawn Portrait and Iridescent Overprint of "Diamond Jubilee" in Wavy Lines
Booklet Stamp

Perf. 14¾x14 Syncopated

2012, May 31 **Type MA2** **Litho.**

MH419 1st gray blue (2996Gh) 5.00 5.00

No. MH419 sold for 60p on day of issue. See No. 2996f for photogravure stamp with water-activated gum.

Queen Type of 1970 With Redrawn Portrait and Type of 2006 With Iridescent Overprint of "Royal Mail" in Wavy Lines
Self-Adhesive With Two Oval Slits

Die Cut Perf. 14¾x14 Syncopated

2013, Jan. 3 **Type MA2** **Photo.**

MH420 1p magenta .25 .25
MH421 2p dark green .25 .25
MH422 5p red brown .25 .25
MH423 10p brn orange .35 .25
MH424 20p brt yel grn .65 .35
MH425 50p dark gray 1.75 .85
MH426 1st bright red 1.75 1.00
a. Booklet pane of 6 12.00
b. Booklet pane of 12 24.00
MH427 £1 brown 3.25 1.60

Type MA6

MH428 1st Large brt red 3.00 1.50
a. Booklet pane of 4 12.00
Nos. MH420-MH428 (9) 11.50 6.30

On day of issue, No. MH426 sold for 60p, and No. MH428 sold for 90p. For stamps similar to Nos. MH420-MH424 but without the iridescent overprint, see Nos. MH402-MH406.

Queen Type of 1970 With Redrawn Portrait and Iridescent Overprint of "Royal Mail" in Wavy Lines

Perf. 14¾x14 Syncopated

2013, Mar. 26 **Litho.**

Type MA2
Booklet Stamps

MH429 5p red brown (3152a) 1.00 .35
MH430 10p brn org (3152a) 1.00 .25
MH431 20p brt yel grn (3152a) 4.00 1.00
a. Booklet pane of 8, England #7a, Northern Ireland #18, Scotland #21a, Wales & Monmouthshire #21b, 2 each #MH430-MH431, + label (BK206) 20.00 —
MH432 87p orange (3152a) 6.00 6.00
Nos. MH429-MH432 (4) 12.00 7.60

Issued: No. MH431a, 7/28/14.

Queen Type of 1970 With Redrawn Portrait and Iridescent Overprint of "Royal Mail" in Wavy Lines

Die Cut Perf. 14¾x14 Syncopated

2013, Mar. 27 **Photo.**

Type MA2
Self-Adhesive
With Two Oval Slits

MH433 78p red lilac 2.40 1.25
MH434 88p org yel 2.75 1.40
MH435 £1.88 dk blue 5.75 3.00
Nos. MH433-MH435 (3) 10.90 5.65

Types of 2009 Inscribed "Royal Mail Signed For" With Iridescent Overprint of "Royal Mail" in Wavy Lines

Die Cut Perf. 14¾x14 Syncopated

2013, Mar. 27 **Photo.**

Self-Adhesive
With Two Oval Slits

MH436 MA7 1st yel & org 4.75 2.40

Die Cut Perf. 14½x14 Syncopated

MH437 MA8 1st Large yel & org 5.50 2.75

On day of issue, No. MH436 sold for £1.55; No. MH437, £1.85.

Queen Type of 1970 With Redrawn Portrait and Iridescent Overprint of "Royal Mail" in Wavy Lines

Perf. 14¾x14 Syncopated

2013, May 9 **Litho.**

Type MA2

MH438 1p magenta (MH440a) 1.00 .35
MH439 2p dk grn (MH439a) 1.00 .35
a. Booklet pane of 6, 2 each #MH429, MH430, MH439 (BK202) 9.50 —
MH440 1st brt red (MH440a) 3.50 3.50
a. Booklet pane of 8, #2419e, 2462e, 2639a, Northern Ireland #18, 2 each #MH438, MH440, + label (BK202) 25.00 —
c. Photo. (MH440d) 3.50 3.50
d. Booklet pane of 8, #MH289B, MH240, MH287, MH335, MH376, MH440c, 2 #MH393a + central label (BK216) 12.00 —
Nos. MH438-MH440 (3) 5.50 4.20

No. MH440 sold for 60p on day of issue.

Issued: Nos. MH440c, MH440d, 6/5/17.

Queen Type of 1970 With Redrawn Portrait and Iridescent Overprint of "Royal Mail" in Wavy Lines

Perf. 14¾x14 Syncopated

2013, Sept. 19 **Litho.**

Type MA2

MH441 50p dark gray 5.25 5.25
a. Booklet pane of 8, 4 each #MH429, MH441, + central label (BK203) 25.00 —

Queen Type of 1970 With Redrawn Portrait and Iridescent Overprint of "Royal Mail" in Wavy Lines

Die Cut Perf. 14¾x14 Syncopated

2014, Mar. 26 **Photo.**

Self-Adhesive
With Two Oval Slits
Type MA2

MH442 81p emerald 2.75 1.40
MH443 97p dull gray vio 3.25 1.60
MH444 £1.47 bluish lilac 5.00 2.50
MH445 £2.15 Prus blue 7.25 3.75
Nos. MH442-MH445 (4) 18.25 9.25

Queen Type of 1970 With Redrawn Portrait and Iridescent Overprint of "Royal Mail" in Wavy Lines

Perf. 14¾x14 Syncopated

2014 **Litho.**

Type MA2
Booklet Stamp

MH446 £1 dull brown (MH446a) 6.00 6.00
a. Booklet pane of 8, 2 each #MH430, MH446, 4 #MH431 + label (BK205) 30.00 —
b. Booklet pane of 1 (BK206) 6.00 —
c. Booklet pane of 8, 2 each #MH429, MH430, MH441, MH446 + central label (BK209) 26.00 —

Issued: Nos. MH446, MH446a, 4/15; No. MH446b, 7/28; No. MH446c, 6/18/15.

Queen Type of 1970 With Redrawn Portrait and Iridescent Overprint of "Royal Mail" in Wavy Lines

Perf 14¾x14 Syncopated

2015, Feb. 19 **Litho.**

Type MA2
Booklet Stamps

MH447 81p blue green (MH448a) *12.00 10.00*
MH448 97p dull gray vio (MH448a) 5.00 5.00
a. Booklet pane of 8, #MH447, 2 each #MH438, MH448, 3 #MH439, + label (BK207) 29.00 —

Queen Type of 1970 With Redrawn Portrait and Iridescent Overprint of "Royal Mail" in Wavy Lines

Die Cut Perf. 14¾x14 Syncopated

2015, Mar. 24 **Photo.**

Self-Adhesive
With Two Oval Slits
Type MA2

MH449 £1.33 org yellow 4.00 2.00
MH450 £1.52 red lilac 4.50 2.25
MH451 £2.25 dark vio 6.75 3.50
MH452 £2.45 brt bl grn 7.50 3.75
MH453 £3.15 turq grn 9.50 4.75
MH454 £3.30 magenta 10.00 5.00
Nos. MH449-MH454 (6) 42.25 21.25

Queen Type of 1970 With Redrawn Portrait and Iridescent Overprint of "Royal Mail" in Wavy Lines

Perf. 14¾x14 Syncopated

2015, May 14 **Litho.**

Booklet Stamp
Type MA2

MH455 £1.33 org yellow 8.50 8.50
a. Booklet pane of 8, 2 each #2744g, MH429, MH438, MH455, + central label (BK208) 24.00 —

Queen Type of 1970 With Redrawn Portrait and Iridescent Overprint of "Long to Reign Over Us" in Wavy Lines and

Queen Elizabeth II and William Wyon's City Medal — MA9

Queen Elizabeth II and Photograph by Dorothy Wilding MA10

Queen Elizabeth II and Badge of the House of Windsor MA11

Queen Elizabeth II and Device From Queen's Personal Flag — MA12

Perf. 14¼, 14¾x14 Syncopated (#MH456c)

Engr., Photo. (#MH456c, MH457)

2015, Sept. 9

Miniature Sheet

MH456 Sheet of 5 15.50 8.00
a. MA9 1st rose carmine 2.00 1.00
b. MA10 1st rose carmine 2.00 1.00
c. MA2 1st lilac 2.00 1.00
d. MA11 £1.52 purple 4.75 2.40
e. MA12 £1.52 purple 4.75 2.40

Booklet Stamp
Self-Adhesive
Type MA2

Die Cut Perf. 14¾x14 Syncopated

MH457 1st lilac 2.00 1.00
a. Booklet pane of 6 12.00

Queen Elizabeth II, longest-reigning British monarch. On day of issue, Nos. MH456a-MH456c, MH457 each sold for 63p.

Queen Type of 1970 With Redrawn Portrait and Iridescent Overprint of "Royal Mail" in Wavy Lines

Die Cut Perf. 14¾x14 Syncopated

2016, Mar. 22 **Photo.**

Self-Adhesive
With Two Oval Slits
Type MA2

MH458 £1.05 olive green 3.00 1.50

Queen Type of 1970 With Redrawn Portrait and Iridescent Overprint of "Long to Reign Over Us" in Wavy Lines

Perf. 14¾x14 Syncopated

2016, Apr. 21 **Litho.**

Type MA2
Booklet Stamp

MH459 1st lilac (MH459a) 5.00 5.00
a. Booklet pane of 8, England #7a, Northern Ireland #18, Scotland #21a, Wales & Monmouthshire #21b, 2 each #MH440, MH459 + central label (BK212) 27.00 —

Queen Type of 1970 With Redrawn Portrait and Iridescent Overprint of "Royal Mail" in Wavy Lines

Perf. 14¾x14 Syncopated

2016, July 28 **Litho.**

Type MA2
Booklet Stamp

MH460 £1.05 ol grn (MH460a) 4.50 4.50
a. Booklet pane of 8, 2 #MH430, 3 each #MH429, MH460 + central label (BK214) 21.00 —
b. Booklet pane of 8, #MH460, 2 each #MH430, MH439, 3 #MH440 (BK215) 8.50 —

Issued: No. MH460b, 2/15/2017.

Queen Type of 1970 With Redrawn Portrait and Iridescent Overprint of "65th Anniversary of Accession"

2017, Feb. 6 **Photo.** ***Perf. 14x15***

Type MA2
Size: 27x38mm

MH461 £5 brt ultra 12.50 6.25

Queen Type of 1970 With Redrawn Portrait and Iridescent Overprint of "Royal Mail" in Wavy Lines

Die Cut Perf. 14¾x14 Syncopated

2017, Mar. 21 **Photo.**

Self-Adhesive
With Two Oval Slits
Type MA2

MH462 £1.17 brt org 3.00 1.50
MH463 £1.40 gray grn 3.50 1.75
MH464 £1.57 lt olive grn 4.00 2.00
MH465 £2.27 lt bister 5.75 3.00
MH466 £2.55 car ver 6.50 3.25
Nos. MH462-MH466 (5) 22.75 11.50

Queen Type of 1970 With Redrawn Portrait and Iridescent Overprint of "Royal Mail" in Wavy Lines

Perf. 14¾x14 Syncopated

2017, June 5 **Photo.**

Type MA2
Booklet Stamp

MH467 £1 scarlet (MH467a) 2.60 2.60
a. Booklet pane of 8, #MH238, MH245, MH246, MH248, MH250, MH255, MH365, MH467 + central label (BK216) 6.75 —

Miniature Sheet

Machin Definitives, 50th Anniv. — MA13

No. MH468 — Machin portrait of Queen Elizabeth II and: a, January 1966 preliminary sketch of black 5p stamp with "Postage Revenue" inscription. b, February 1966 preliminary work using coinage head photograph and Machin's coin mold. c, April-May 1966 essay of pink 6p stamp with coinage head and "Postage Revenue" inscription. d, October 1966 essay of green 6p stamp with coinage head. e, August 1966 photograph of Queen Elizabeth II wearing diadem. f, October 1966 essay of plaster cast of Diadem head.

Photo. & Embossed

2017, June 5 ***Perf. 14¼x14***

MH468 MA13 Sheet of 6 10.50 5.25
a.-f. 1st Any single 1.75 .85
g. Booklet pane of 3, #MH468a-MH468c (BK216) 5.50 —
h. Booklet pane of 3, #MH468d-MH468f (BK216) 5.50 —

On day of issue, Nos. MH468a-MH468f each sold for 65p.

Queen Elizabeth II — MA14

Photo., Embossed With Foil Application (#MH469b)

Perf. 15x14, 14¾x14 Syncopated

2017, June 5

MH469 Sheet of 7, #MH50, MH193, MH335, MH376, MH440, MH469a, MH469b 10.00 5.00
a. 1st Like #MH243, perf. 14x15 syncopated 1.75 .85
b. MA14 £1 gold, perf. 14x14¾ 2.60 1.40
c. Booklet pane of 4 #MH469b (BK216) 11.00 —

Queen Type of 1970 With Redrawn Portrait and Iridescent Overprint of "Royal Mail" in Wavy Lines

Perf. 14¾x14 Syncopated

2017, Oct. 12 **Photo.**

Type MA2
Booklet Stamp

MH470 £1.40 gray grn 8.50 8.50
a. Booklet pane of 8, 2 each #MH401C, MH470, 4 #MH440 + central label (BK218) 39.50 —

Queen Type of 1970 With Redrawn Portrait and Iridescent Overprint of "Royal Mail" in Wavy Lines

Perf. 14¾x14 Syncopated

2018, Jan. 23 **Litho.**

Type MA2
Booklet Stamp

MH471 £1.17 brt orange (3689a) 3.50 3.50
a. Booklet pane of 8, 3 each #MH429, MH439, 2 #MH471, + central label (BK220) 7.25 —

Queen Type of 1970 With Redrawn Portrait and Iridescent Overprint of "Royal Mail" in Wavy Lines

Die Cut Perf. 14¾x14 Syncopated

2018, Mar. 20 **Photo.**

Self-Adhesive
With Two Oval Slits
Type MA2

MH472 £1.25 dark green 3.50 1.75
MH473 £1.45 gray 4.25 2.10
MH474 £1.55 greeninsh blue 4.50 2.25
MH475 £2.65 gray violet 7.50 3.75
Nos. MH472-MH475 (4) 19.75 9.85

Queen Type of 1970 With Redrawn Portrait and Iridescent Overprint of "Royal Mail" in Wavy Lines

Perf. 14¾x14 Syncopated

2018, Dec. 4 **Litho.**

Booklet Stamp
Type MA2

MH476 £1.25 dark green 3.50 3.50
a. Booklet pane of 8, 2 each # MH431, MH438, MH441, MH476, + central label (BK222) 11.50 —

Queen Type of 1970 With Redrawn Portrait and Iridescent Overprint of "Royal Mail" in Wavy Lines

Perf. 14¾x14 Syncopated

2019, Feb. 13 **Litho.**

Booklet Stamp
Type MA2

MH477 £1.55 greenish blue 4.50 4.50
a. Booklet pane of 8, 2 each # MH429, MH477, 4 #MH430, + central label (BK223) 10.50 —

MACHINS REGIONAL ISSUES

NORTHERN IRELAND

All stamps are Design MA2 unless noted.

Type I

Type II

Two types of crown (1981-91):
Type I: All pearls individually drawn.
Type II: Large pearls with strong white line below them.
First three pearls at left joined together.

Photogravure stamps in this section have a mottled background that is neither solid nor composed of distinct dots. The outside edges of the numerals have a jagged appearance. Some lithographed stamps, specifically Nos. NIMH16, NIMH19, NIMH21a, NIMH23, NIMH27-28, NIMH30, NIMH32, NIMH37, NIMH40, NIMH50, have a background composed of fine dots giving the impression of a phtogravure printing. The images on these stamps, however, are more finely detailed than those on a photogravure printing. The outside edges of the numerals are smooth. All other lithographed stamps in this section have a solid background.

1971-93 **Photo.** ***Perf. 15x14***

NIMH1 2½p bright pink .45 .40
NIMH2 3p ultramarine .40 .30
NIMH3 3½p slate .25 .25
NIMH4 4½p dark blue .25 .25
NIMH5 5p bright violet .60 .60
NIMH6 5½p dark violet .25 .25
NIMH7 6½p Prussian blue .25 .25
NIMH8 7p dark red brn .25 .25
NIMH9 7½p chestnut 1.00 1.00
NIMH10 8p red .30 .30
NIMH11 8½p yellow green .30 .30
NIMH12 9p violet blue .30 .30
NIMH13 10p orange brown .35 *.45*
NIMH14 10½p steel blue .45 .55
NIMH15 11p red .45 .45
NIMH16 11½p gray brn, litho, perf 13½x14 (I) .85 .85
NIMH17 12p yellow green .55 .55
NIMH18 12p brt grn, litho. (II) .95 .95
NIMH19 12½p lt emer, litho., perf 13½x14 (I) .55 .55
NIMH20 12½p lt emer, litho. (II) 3.50 3.50
NIMH21 13p lt red brown, litho., (II) 1.50 1.00
a. Type I .70 .65
NIMH22 13½p brown purple .65 .65
NIMH23 14p gray bl, litho., perf 13½x14 (I) .70 .70
NIMH24 14p dark bl, litho. (II) .70 .55
NIMH25 15p deep ultra .65 .65

Litho.

NIMH26 15p bright blue (II) .75 .50
NIMH27 15½p light violet, perf 13½x14 (I) .75 .75
NIMH28 16p brownish gray, perf 13½x14 (I) 1.00 1.00
NIMH29 16p brownish gray (II) 6.00 6.00
NIMH30 17p blue gray, (I) .90 *.95*
a. Type II 200.00
NIMH31 17p dark blue (II) .75 .55
NIMH32 18p violet blue, perf 13½x14 (I) .95 .95
NIMH33 18p olive green (II) .90 .80
NIMH34 18p bright yel grn (II) .95 .90
NIMH35 18p bright yel grn, perf 13½x14 (II) 9.75 9.75
NIMH36 19p red orange (II) .90 .90
NIMH37 19½p olive gray, perf 13½x14 (I) 1.00 1.00
NIMH38 20p brown black (II) .95 .75
NIMH39 20½p ultramarine, perf 13½x14 (I) 2.50 2.25
NIMH40 22p dark blue, perf 13½x14 (I) .90 .90
NIMH41 22p yellow green (I) .95 .95
NIMH42 22p red orange (II) .95 .70
NIMH43 23p bright yel grn (II) 1.00 .80
NIMH44 24p brown red (II) 1.30 1.10
NIMH45 24p brown (II) .95 .80
a. Bklt. pane, see footnote (BK158) 5.50

No. NIMH45a contains Nos. NIMH34, NIMH45, SMH35, SMH47, WMMH34, WMMH45.

NIMH46 26p red, perf 13½x14 (I) 1.00 1.00
NIMH47 26p red (II) 2.50 2.50
NIMH48 26p olive gray (II) 1.90 1.90
NIMH49 28p deep viol bl, perf 13½x14 (I) 1.10 1.10
NIMH50 28p deep viol bl (II) 1.60 1.60
NIMH51 28p dull blue green (II) 1.10 .90
NIMH52 31p brt rose lil (I) 1.60 *1.75*
a. Type II 2.25 2.00
NIMH53 32p Prussian blue (II) 1.50 1.50
NIMH54 34p dull blue green (II) 1.75 1.75
NIMH55 37p scarlet (II) 2.00 2.00
NIMH56 39p brt rose lilac (II) 2.00 2.00

Issued: Nos. NIMH1, NIMH9, 3p, 5p, 7/7/71; Nos. NIMH3, NIMH6, 8p, 1/23/74; No. NIMH4, 11/6/74;

Nos. NIMH7, NIMH11, 1/14/76; 10p, 11p, 10/20/76; 7p, 9p, NIMH14, 1/18/78.

Nos. NIMH17, NIMH22, NIMH25, 7/23/80; Nos. NIMH16, NIMH23, NIMH32, NIMH40, 4/8/81; No. NIMH19, 1/24/82; Nos. NIMH27, NIMH28, NIMH37, NIMH46, 2/24/82; Nos. NIMH39, NIMH49, 4/27/83;

Nos. NIMH20, NIMH29, 2/28/84; 13p, Nos. NIMH30, NIMH41, 31p, 10/23/84; No. NIMH18, 1/7/86; No. NIMH33, 1/6/87; No. NIMH50, 1/27/87; No. NIMH24, 19p, 23p, 32p, 11/8/88; Nos. NIMH26, NIHM44, 20p, 34p, 11/28/89; Nos. NIMH31, NIMH42, NIMH48, 37p, 12/4/90; Nos. NIMH34, NIMH45, NIMH51, 39p, 12/3/91; Nos. NIMH35, NIMH45a, 8/10/93; No. NIMH47, 12/7/93.

Perf. 15x14 Syncopated

1993-96 **Litho.**

NIMH57	19p	olive green	1.10	1.00
NIMH58	20p	brt yel green	1.75	1.75
NIMH59	25p	salmon	.90	.90
		a. Bklt. pane, see footnote (BK160)	6.00	

No. NIMH59a contains Nos. NIMH57, NIMH59, SMH63, SMH65, WMMH58, WMMH60 + label, printed margin.

NIMH60	26p	brown	1.90	1.90
NIMH61	30p	olive green	1.45	1.45
NIMH62	37p	bright rose lilac	3.25	3.00
NIMH63	41p	drab	1.75	1.75
		a. Bklt. pane, #NIMH61, NIMH63, 2 #NIMH57, 4 #NIMH59 + label, printed margin (BK159)	9.00	
		b. Bklt. pane, #NIMH57, NIMH59, NIMH61, NIMH63 + printed margin (BK159)	5.25	
NIMH64	63p	bright green	5.25	5.25

Issued: 19p, 25p, 30p, 41p, 12/7/93; No. NIMH59a, 4/25/95; 20p, 26, 37p, 63p, 7/23/96.

Queen Design of 1970 with Redrawn Portrait

Perf. 15x14 Syncopated

1997-2000 **Photo.**

NIMH68	19p	olive green	4.75	4.75
NIMH69	20p	brt yel grn	4.00	1.50
NIMH70	20p	brt yel grn, perf 14	6.00	6.00
NIMH73	26p	brown	2.60	2.25
NIMH74	26p	brown, perf 14	6.00	6.00
NIMH81	37p	bright rose lilac	3.25	3.00
		a. Bklt. pane, see footnote (BK162)	16.00	

No. NIMH81a contains Nos. NIMH73, NIMH81, SMH79, SMH87, WMMH74, WMMH82 + printed margin.

NIMH82	38p	dark blue	9.25	9.25
NIMH83	40p	chalky blue	5.50	5.50
NIMH91	63p	bright green	6.50	6.50
NIMH92	64p	greenish blue	10.00	10.00
NIMH93	65p	Prussian blue	5.00	4.75

Issued: Nos. NIMH69, NIMH73, 37p, 63p, 7/1/97; No. NIMH81a, 9/24/97; Nos. NIMH70, NIMH74, 10/13/98; Nos. NIMH68, NIMH82, NIMH92, 6/8/99; 40p, 65p, 4/25/00.

Nos. NIMH70, NIMH74 issued only in booklets (BK164).

Perf. 13¾x14¼ Syncopated

2000 **Photo.**

NIMH96	1st	orange red (WM-MH96a)	3.50	3.50

Perf. 15x14 Syncopated

NIMH99	1st	org red	11.00	10.00

Nos. NIMH96, NIMH99 sold for 26p on day of issue. No. NIMH96 issued only in booklets.

Issued: No. NIMH96, 2/15/00; No. NIMH99, 4/25/00.

SCOTLAND

All stamps are Design MA2 unless noted.

Type I

Type II

Two types of lion (1983-93)

Type I: Thin tongue, no line across bridge of nose, three "feathers" on left of tail are widely separated.

Type II: Thick tongue where it enters mouth, eye connected to background by solid line, three "feathers" on left of tail are close together.

Photogravure stamps in this section have a mottled background that is neither solid nor composed of distinct dots. The outside edges of the numerals have a jagged appearance. Some lithographed stamps, specifically Nos. SMH20-21a, SMH28-30, SMH38, SMH52-53, SMH56-57, have a background composed of fine dots giving the impression of a photogravure printing. The images on these stamps, however, are more finely detailed than those on a photogravure printing. The outside edges of the numerals are smooth. All other lithographed stamps in this section have a solid background.

1971-93 **Photo.** *Perf. 15x14*

SMH1	2½p	bright pink	.30	.25
SMH2	3p	ultramarine	.30	.25
SMH3	3½p	slate	.25	.25
SMH4	4½p	dark blue	.25	.25
SMH5	5p	brt violet	.55	.55
SMH6	5½p	dark violet	.25	.25
SMH7	6½p	Prussian blue	.25	.25
SMH8	7p	dark red brn	.25	*.30*
SMH9	7½p	chestnut	.75	*1.00*
SMH10	8p	red	.30	.25
SMH11	8½p	yellow green	.35	.35
SMH12	9p	violet blue	.35	*.40*
SMH13	10p	orange brown	.35	*.40*
SMH14	10½p	steel blue	.50	*.55*
SMH15	11p	red	.50	*.55*
SMH16	11½p	gray brn, litho., perf 13½x14 (I)	.65	.65
SMH17	12p	yellow green	.50	*.55*
SMH18	12p	brt green, litho., perf 13½x14 (II)	1.10	1.10
SMH19	12p	green, litho. (II)	1.50	*1.60*
SMH20	12½p	lt emer, litho., perf 13½x14 (I)	.65	*.75*
SMH21	13p	lt red brown, litho., perf 13½x14 (I)	.90	.80
		a. Type II	11.00	11.00
SMH22	13p	lt red brn, litho. (II)	.95	*1.00*
SMH23	13½p	brown purple	.70	*.80*
SMH24	14p	gray blue, litho., perf 13½x14 (I)	.55	.55
SMH25	14p	dk bl, litho. (II)	.55	.55
		a. Booklet pane of 6 + printed margin (BK153)	3.50	
SMH26	15p	deep ultra	.55	*.65*

Litho.

SMH27	15p	bright blue (II)	.70	.70

Perf. 13½x14

SMH28	15½p	light violet (I)	.70	.75
SMH29	16p	brownish gray (II)	.70	.75
SMH30	17p	blue gray (II)	2.00	2.00
		a. Type I	2.00	2.00

Perf. 15x14

SMH31	17p	blue gray (II)	2.25	2.25
SMH32	17p	dark blue (II)	.90	.90
SMH33	18p	violet blue, perf 13½x14 (I)	.90	.90
SMH34	18p	olive green (II)	.85	.65
SMH35	18p	bright yel grn (II)	.85	.60
SMH36	18p	brt yel grn, perf 13½x14 (II)	1.25	1.25
SMH37	19p	red orange (II)	.75	.75
		a. Booklet pane of 6 + printed margin (BK153)	4.50	
		b. Booklet pane of 9 + printed margin (BK153)	6.75	
SMH38	19½p	olive gray, perf 13½x14 (I)	.95	.95
SMH39	20p	brown black (II)	.90	.90

Perf. 13½x14

SMH40	20½p	ultra (II)	2.75	2.75
SMH41	22p	dk blue (I)	.90	.90
SMH42	22p	yel grn (I)	3.10	3.10
		a. Type II	30.00	20.00

Perf. 15x14

SMH43	22p	yellow green (II)	1.90	1.90
SMH44	22p	red orange (II)	.85	.65
SMH45	23p	bright yel grn (II)	1.00	.85
		a. Booklet pane #SMH45, 2 #SMH37, 5 #SMH25 + printed margin (BK153)	4.50	
SMH46	24p	brown red (II)	1.25	1.25
SMH47	24p	brown (II)	.95	.95
SMH48	24p	chestnut, perf 13½x14 (II)	2.75	2.75
SMH49	26p	red, perf 13½x14 (I)	1.00	1.00
SMH50	26p	red (II)	3.00	*3.25*
SMH51	26p	olive gray (II)	1.30	1.30
SMH52	28p	dp vio bl, perf 13½x14 (II)	1.10	1.10
SMH53	28p	deep violet blue (II)	1.60	1.60
SMH54	28p	dull bl grn (II)	1.35	*1.60*
SMH55	28p	dull bl grn, perf 13½x14 (II)	11.00	11.00
SMH56	31p	brt rose lilac, perf 13½x14 (I)	2.25	2.25
		a. Type II	*200.00*	*175.00*
SMH57	31p	brt rose lilac (II)	2.25	2.25
SMH58	32p	Prussian blue (II)	1.75	1.75
SMH59	34p	dull bl grn (II)	1.75	1.75
SMH60	37p	scarlet (II)	1.90	1.90
SMH61	39p	brt rose lilac (II)	2.00	2.00
SMH62	39p	brt rose lilac, perf 13½x14 (II)	19.00	19.00

Issued: Nos. SMH1, SMH9, 3p, 5p, 7/7/71; Nos. SMH3, SMH6, 8p, 1/23/74; No. SMH4, 11/6/74; Nos. SMH7, SMH11, 1/14/76; 10p, 11p, 10/20/76;

7p, 9p, No. SMH14, 1/18/78; Nos. SMH17, SMH23, SMH26, 7/23/80.

Nos. SMH16, SMH24, SMH33, SMH41, 4/8/81; Nos. SMH20, SMH28, SMH38, No. SMH49, 2/24/82;

16p, Nos. SMH40, SMH52, 4/27/83; Nos. SMH21, SMH30, SMH42, SMH56, 10/23/84; No. SMH18, 1/7/86; No. SMH19, 1/24/86; Nos. SMH31, SMH57, 4/29/86; No. SMH22, 11/4/86; No. SMH34, 1/6/87.

Nos. SMH43, SMH50, SMH53, 1/27/87; No. SMH25, 19p, 23p, 32p, 11/8/88; Nos. SMH27, SMH46, 20p, 34p, 11/28/89; Nos. SMH32, SMH44, SMH51, 37p, 12/4/90;

Nos. SMH35, SMH47, SMH54, SMH61, 12/3/91; No. SMH36, 9/26/92; No. SMH48, 10/92; No. SMH62, 11/92; No. SMH55, 2/18/93.

Perf. 15x14 Syncopated

1993-96 **Litho.**

SMH63	19p	olive green	1.10	1.00
SMH64	20p	brt yel green	1.75	1.75
SMH65	25p	salmon	.95	.85
SMH66	26p	brown	2.25	2.25
SMH67	30p	olive green	2.00	2.00
SMH68	37p	bright rose lilac	3.25	3.25
SMH69	41p	drab	2.25	2.25
SMH70	63p	bright green	4.75	4.75

Issued: 19p, 20p, 30p, 41p, 12/7/93; 20p, 26p, 37p, 63p, 7/23/96.

Queen Design of 1970 with Redrawn Portrait

Perf. 15x14 Syncopated

1997-98 **Photo.**

SMH75	20p	brt yel green	1.50	1.10
SMH76	20p	brt yel grn, perf 14	6.00	6.00
SMH79	26p	brown	2.25	1.90
SMH80	26p	brown, perf 14	6.00	6.00
SMH87	37p	bright rose lilac	3.00	3.00
SMH97	63p	bright green	6.00	6.00

Issued: Nos. SMH75, SMH79, 37p, 63p, 7/1/97; Nos. SMH76, SMH80, 10/13/98.

Nos. SMH76, SMH80 issued only in booklets (BK164).

Perf. 13¾x14¼ Syncopated

2000 **Photo.**

SMH101	1st	org red (WM-MH96a)	3.50	3.50

Issued: No. SMH96, 2/15/00. No. SMH96 sold for 26p on day of issue and was issued only in booklets.

WALES & MONMOUTHSHIRE

All stamps are Design MA2 unless noted.

Type I

Type II

Two types of dragon (1981-91):

Type I: Eye is complete with white dot in center. Wing tips, tail and tongue are thin.

Type II: Eye is joined to nose by solid line. Wing tips, tail and tongue are thick.

Photogravure stamps in this section have a mottled background that is neither solid nor composed of distinct dots. The outside edges of the numerals have a jagged appearance. Some lithographed stamps, specifically Nos. WMMH16, WMMH19, WMMH21, WMMH23, WMMH27-30, WMMH32, WMMH37, WMMH40, WMMH50, have a background composed of fine dots giving the impression of a photogravure printing. The images on these stamps, however, are more finely detailed than those on a photogravure printing. The outside edges of the numerals are smooth. All other lithographed stamps in this section have a solid background.

1971-93 **Photo.** *Perf. 15x14*

WMMH1	2½p	bright pink	.25	.25
WMMH2	3p	ultra	.30	.25
WMMH3	3½p	slate	.25	*.30*
WMMH4	4½p	dark blue	.00	.00
WMMH5	5p	brt violet	.70	.70
WMMH6	5½p	dark violet	.25	*.30*
WMMH7	6½p	Prussian blue	.25	.25
WMMH8	7p	dark red brn	.25	.25
WMMH9	7½p	chestnut	1.00	1.00
WMMH10	8p	red	.30	*.35*
WMMH11	8½p	yel grn	.35	*.35*
WMMH12	9p	violet blue	.30	.30
WMMH13	10p	orange brn	.35	*.45*
WMMH14	10½p	steel blue	.50	*.60*
WMMH15	11p	red	.50	*.60*
WMMH16	11½p	gray brn, litho., perf 13½x14 (I)	.85	*.90*
WMMH17	12p	yel grn	.50	*.60*

Litho.

WMMH18	12p	brt grn (I)	.95	.95
WMMH19	12½p	lt emer, perf 13½x14 (I)	.55	.55
WMMH20	12½p	lt emer (I)	4.50	4.00
WMMH21	13p	lt red brn (I)	.60	.60
		a. Type II	2.25	2.00

Photo.

WMMH22	13½p	brown pur	.70	*.80*
WMMH23	14p	gray blue, litho., perf 13½x14 (I)	.70	.70
WMMH24	14p	dark blue, litho. (II)	.70	.70
WMMH25	15p	deep ultra	.70	*.80*

Litho.

WMMH26	15p	bright blue (II)	.75	.65
WMMH27	15½p	light violet, perf. 13½x14 (I)	.75	.75
WMMH28	16p	brownish gray, perf 13½x14 (I)	1.10	1.10
WMMH29	16p	brownish gray (I)	1.10	1.10
WMMH30	17p	blue gray (I)	.85	*.95*
		a. Type II	67.50	55.00
WMMH31	17p	dark blue (II)	.80	.70
WMMH32	18p	vio bl, perf 13½x14 (I)	1.00	.95
WMMH33	18p	olive green (II)	.90	.85
WMMH34	18p	brt yel grn (II)	.90	.90
		a. Booklet pane of 6 + printed margin (BK156)	5.50	
WMMH35	18p	brt yel grn, perf 13½x14 (II)	2.30	2.30
WMMH36	19p	red orange (II)	.85	*.95*
WMMH37	19½p	ol gray, perf 13½x14 (I)	1.00	*1.25*
WMMH38	20p	brown black (II)	.95	.95
WMMH39	20½p	ultra (I)	2.50	2.50
WMMH40	22p	dk bl, perf 13½x14 (I)	1.10	*1.25*
WMMH41	22p	yel grn (I)	1.10	*1.25*
WMMH42	22p	orange red (II)	.90	*1.00*
WMMH43	23p	brt yel grn (II)	1.00	*1.10*
WMMH44	24p	brown red (II)	1.45	1.45
WMMH45	24p	brown (II)	.90	.90
		a. Booklet pane of 6 + printed margin (BK156)	5.50	
WMMH46	24p	brown, perf 13½x14 (II)	1.25	1.25
WMMH47	26p	red, perf 13½x14 (I)	1.00	1.00
WMMH48	26p	red (II)	4.25	*4.50*
WMMH49	26p	olive gray (II)	1.75	1.75
WMMH50	28p	dp vio bl, perf 13½x14 (I)	1.50	1.50
WMMH51	28p	dp vio bl (II)	1.90	1.90
WMMH52	28p	dull bl grn (II)	1.25	1.25
WMMH53	31p	brt rose lil (I)	1.35	1.35
WMMH54	32p	Prus blue (II)	1.60	1.60
WMMH55	34p	dull bl grn (II)	1.75	1.75
WMMH56	37p	scarlet (II)	2.00	2.00
WMMH57	39p	brt rose lil (II)	2.00	2.00

Issued: Nos. WMMH1, WMMH9, 3p, 5p, 7/7/71; Nos. WMMH3, WMMH6, 8p, 1/23/74; No. WMMH4, 11/6/74; Nos. WMMH7, WMMH11, 1/14/76; 10p, 11p, 10/20/76.

7p, 9p, No. WMMH14, 1/18/78; Nos. WMMH17, WMMH22, WMMH25, 7/23/80; Nos. WMMH16, WMMH23, WMMH32, WMMH40, 4/8/81;

Nos. WMMH19, WMMH27, WMMH37, WMMH47, 2/24/82; Nos. WMMH28, WMMH39, WMMH50, 4/27/83; Nos. WMMH20, WMMH29, 1/10/84.

Nos. WMMH30, WMMH41, 31p, 10/23/84; No. WMMH18, 1/7/86; No. WMMH33, 1/6/87.

Nos. WMMH48, WMMH51, 1/27/87; No. WMMH24, 19p, 23p, 32p, 8/11/88; Nos. WMMH26, 20p, WMMH44, 34p, 11/28/89.

Nos. WMMH31, WMMH42, WMMH49, 37p, 12/4/90; Nos. WMMH34, WMMH45, WMMH52, 39p, 12/3/91; No. WMMH46, 9/14/92; No. WMMH35, 1/12/93.

Perf. 15x14 Syncopated

1993-96 **Litho.**

WMMH58	19p olive green	1.10	1.00
WMMH59	20p brt yel grn	1.75	1.75
WMMH60	25p salmon	.95	.75
WMMH61	26p brown	2.25	2.25
WMMH62	30p olive green	2.00	2.00
WMMH63	37p bright rose lilac	3.25	3.25
WMMH64	41p drab	2.25	2.25
WMMH65	63p bright green	5.00	5.00

Issued: 19p, 25p, 30p, 41p, 12/7/93. 20p, 26p, 37p, 63p, 7/23/96.

Queen Design of 1970 with Redrawn Portrait

"P" Removed

Perf. 15x14 Syncopated

1997-98 **Photo.**

WMMH70	20p brt yel grn	1.75	1.75
WMMH71	20p brt yel grn, perf 14	6.00	6.00
WMMH74	26p brown	2.00	2.00
WMMH75	26p brown, perf 14	6.00	6.00
WMMH82	37p bright rose lilac	2.75	2.75
WMMH92	63p brt yel grn	6.00	6.00

Issued: Nos. WMMH70, WMMH74, 37p, 63p, 7/1/97; Nos. WMMH71, WMMH75, 10/13/98.

Nos. WMMH71, WMMH75 issued only in booklets (BK164).

Perf. 13¾x14¼ Syncopated

2000 **Photo.**

WMMH96	1st orange red	3.50	3.00
a.	Bklt. pane, 3 ea #NIMH96, SMH101, WMMH96 (BK167)	32.00	

Issued: No. WMMH96, 2/15/00. No. WMMH96 sold for 26p on day of issue and was issued only in booklets.

See Isle of Man Nos. 8-11 for additional Machin Head definitives.

GREAT BRITAIN BOOKLETS

Booklets are listed in denomination sequence by reign. Numbers in parenthesis following each listing reflect the number of cover varieties or edition numbers that apply to each cover style.

Values shown for complete booklets are for examples containing most panes having full perforations on two edges of the pane only. Booklets containing most or all panes with very fine, full perforations on all sides are scarce and will sell for more. Also, in booklets where most of the value is contained in only one pane of several, it is assumed that this pane has full perforations on two sides only. If this pane is very fine, the booklet will be worth a considerable premium over the value given.

Beginning with No. BK128, values for complete booklets are sometimes less than the sum of the individual panes. This is primarily due to market demand for a particular pane in the booklet or, in some cases, a single stamp found only in the booklet. Under these conditions, the value for the intact booklet reflects the market value for the key stamp or pane in the booklet.

This section does not contain complete booklets consisting solely of self-adhesive stamps. These are catalogued as minors under stamp listings.

Sterling Currency

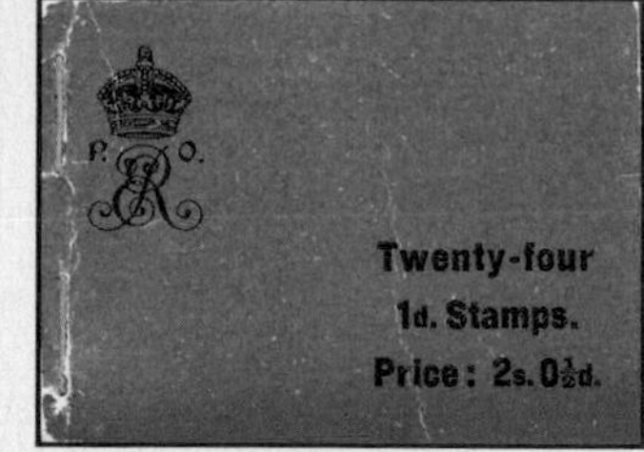

BC1

1904

BK1 BC1 2sh½p *red,* 4 #128e 450.00

1906-11

BK2 BC1 2sh *red,* 2 #128e, 3 #143c, #143b 2,000.

BK3 BC1 2sh *red,* 3 #128e, 1 each #143b-143c (4) 2,300.

Cover inscription on Nos. BK2-BK3 revised to reflect changed contents.

1911

BK4 BC1 2sh *red,* 2#151a, 3 #152a 1,400.

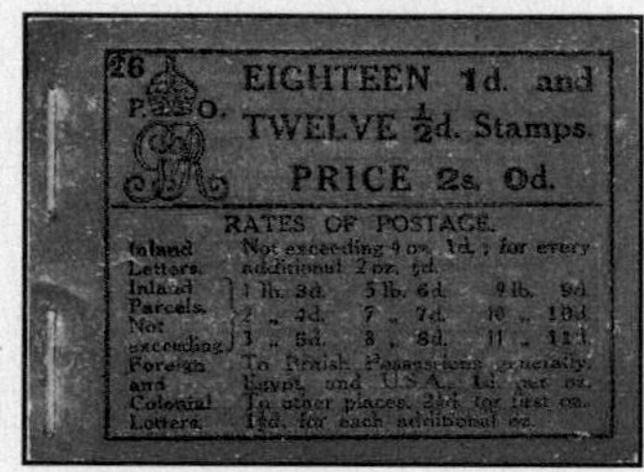

BC2

1912-13

BK5 BC2 2sh *red,* 2 #151a, 3 #152a 1,600.

BK6 BC2 2sh *red,* 2 #155a, 3 #156a (4) 1,250.

Cover inscription on Nos. BK5-BK6 shows only Inland Postage Rates.

1913

BK7 BC2 2sh *red,* 2 #159b, 3 #160a (35) 1,400.

BK8 BC2 2sh *org,* 2 #159b,3 #160a (20) 1,250.

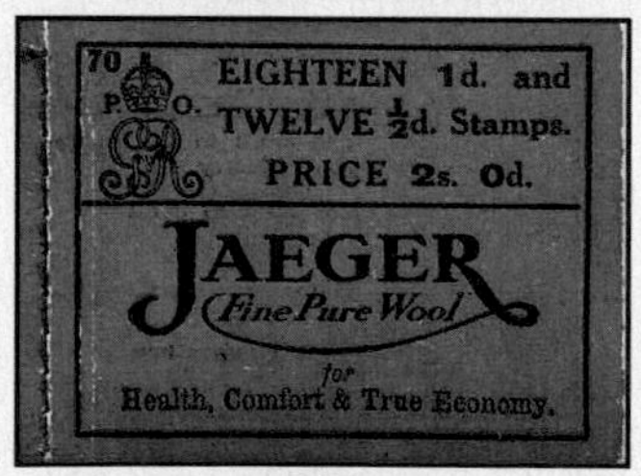

BC3

1917

BK9 BC3 2sh *org,* 2 #159b, 3 #160a (17) 1,150.

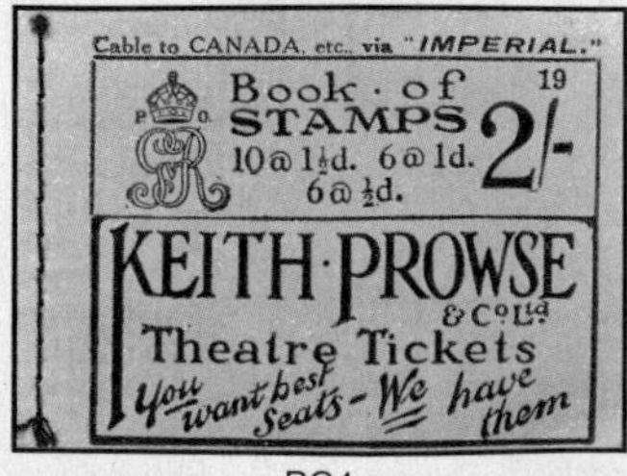

BC4

1924-34

BK10 BC4 2sh *blue,* #159b, 160a, 161g-161h (2) 2,200.

BK11 BC4 2sh *blue,* #187b, 188b, 189c-189d (277) 775.00

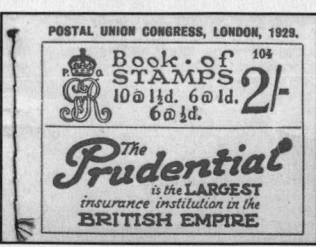

BC5

1929

BK12 BC5 2sh blue, *buff,* #205b-207b, 207c 550.00

1935

BK13 BC4 2sh *blue,* #210b-211b, 212c-212d (58) 550.00

BC6

1935

BK14 BC6 2sh blue, *buff,* #226a-227a, 3 #228a 90.00

1918-19

BK15 BC4 3sh *org,* 2 each #159b, 160a, 161g (11) 1,600.

BK16 BC4 3sh *org,* #159b, 160a, 3 #161g (15) 1,600.

Cover used for Nos. BK15-BK16 does not have inscription above top line.

1921

BK17 BC4 3sh *blue,* 3 #162b (3) 2,000.

BK18 BC4 3sh *blue,* 3 #162c (3) 2,000.

1922

BK19 BC4 3sh *scar,* #159b, 160a, 3 #161g (33) 850.00

BK20 BC4 3sh *blue,* 4 #161g (2) 900.00

1924-34

BK21 BC4 3sh *scar,* #187b-188b, 3 #189c (237) 525.00

1929

BK22 BC5 3sh blue, *buff,* #205b-206b, 3 #207b (5) 450.00

1935

BK23 BC4 3sh *scar,* #210b-211b, 3 #212c (27) 500.00

BK24 BC6 3sh red, *buff,* #226a-227a, 5 #228a (4) *90.00*

1920

BK25 BC4 3sh6p *org,* #160a, 3 #162b (6) 1,900.

Cover used for No. BK25 does not have inscription above top line.

1921

BK26 BC4 3sh6p *org red,* #159b, 160a, 161g, 2 #162b (7) 1,900.

BK27 BC4 3sh6p *org red,* #159b, 160a, 161g, 2 #162c (13) 2,450.

1931-35

BK28 BC4 5sh *grn,* #187b-188b, 189d, 5 #189c 5,250.

BK29 BC4 5sh *buff,* #187b-188b, 189d, 5 #189c (7) 1,900.

BK30 BC4 5sh *buff,* #210b-211b, 212d, 5 #212c (7) 450.00

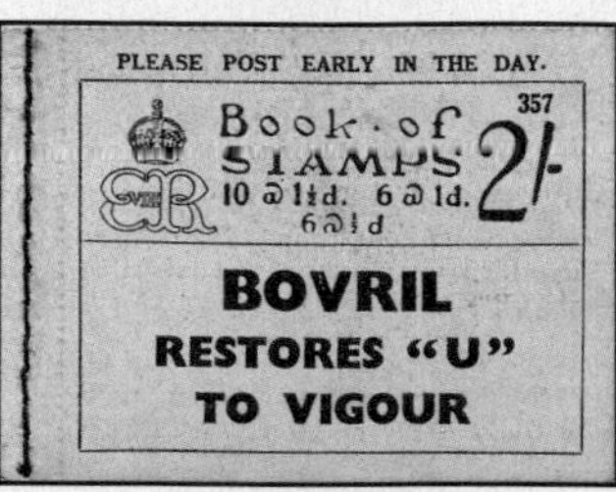

BC7

1936

BK31 BC7 6p *buff,* 2 #232c 40.00

BC8

BK32 BC8 2sh *blue,* #230a-231a, #232a-232b (31) 115.00

BK33 BC8 3sh *scar,* #230a-231a, 3 #232a (12) 100.00

BK34 BC8 5sh *buff,* #230a-231a, 6 #232a (2) 325.00

1938-40

BK35 BC7 6p *buff,* 2 #237d 75.00

BK36 BC7 6p *pink,* #235d-237d 325.00

BK37 BC7 6p *pale grn,* #235c-236c 150.00

No. BK37 is 53x41mm.

1947-51

BK38 BC7 1sh *buff,* 2 each #258b-259b, 260a 23.00

BK39 BC7 1sh *buff,* 2 each #280a, 281b-282b 22.00

BK40 BC7 1sh *buff,* #258e, 259d, 260b 7,500.

BK41 BC7 1sh *buff,* #280b-282b 34.00

Nos. BK40-BK41 are 53x41mm.

Round GPO Emblem — BC9

1952-53

BK42 BC9 1sh *buff,* #280b, 281c-282c 22.50

a. Inland postage rate corrected in ink on inside booklet cover 25.00

Oval GPO Emblem — BC10

1954

BK43 BC10 1sh *buff,* #280b, 281c-282c 22.00

1937

BK44 BC8 2sh *blue,* #235b-236b, #237b-237c (26) 950.00

BC11

1938

BK45 BC11 2sh *blue,* #235b-236b, #237b-237c (95) 950.00

1940-42 2sh6p Booklets

BK46 BC11 *scar,* #235b, #238b-239b (7) 1,400.

BK47 BC11 *blue,* #235b, #238b-239b (6) 1,400.

Denomination part of cover of Nos. BK46-BK47 is printed in white on black background.

BK48 BC11 *grn,* #235b, #238b-239b (80) 825.00

BK49 BC11 *grn,* #258a, #261b-262b (120) 825.00

BC12

1943

BK50 BC12 *grn,* #258a, #261b-262b (90) 85.00

With booklets issued in August and September 1943, commercial advertising on British booklets was discontinued. Covers and interleaving were used for Post Office slogans. Booklets were no longer numbered, but carried the month and year of issue.

1951-52

BK51 BC12 *grn,* #280c, #283b-284b (10) 50.00

BK52 BC12 *grn,* #280c, 281e, #282d, 284b (15) 40.00

1937-38 3sh Booklets

BK53 BC8 *scar,* #235b-236b, 3 #237b (10) 1,600.

BK54 BC11 *scar,* #235b-236b, 3 #237b (34) 1,600.

1937-43 5sh Booklets

BK55 BC8 *buff,* #235b-236b, 237c, 5 #237b (3) 1,700.

BK56 BC11 *buff,* #235b-236b, 237c, 5 #237b (9) 1,700.

BK57 BC11 *buff,* #235b, 238b, 3 #239b (16) 1,700.

BK58 BC11 *buff,* #258a, 261b, 3 #262b (20) 1,700.

1943-53

BK59 BC12 *tan,* #258a, 261b, 3 #262b (49) 140.00

BK60 BC12 *tan,* #258a, 261b, 3 #262b (20) 4,500.

Cover on No. BK60 has thick horizontal lines separating the GPO emblem and the various inscriptions.

BK61 BC12 *tan,* #280a, 283b, 3 #284b (5) 62.50

BK62 BC12 *tan,* #280c, 281e, 282d, 3 #284b (5) 50.00

BK63 BC12 *tan,* #280c, 281d-282d, 283b, 2 #284b (2) 62.50

BC13

1953-54 2sh6p Booklets

BK64 BC12 *grn,* #280c, 281e, 294c, #296a (6) 32.50

BK65 BC13 *grn,* #280c, 281e, 294c, 296a (7) 55.00

BK66 BC13 *grn,* #281e, 292c, 294c, 296a 550.00

5sh Booklets

BK67 BC12 *brn,* #280c, 281d, 283b, 294c, 2 #296a (3) 40.00

BK68 BC13 *brn,* #280c, 281d, 283b, 294c, 2 #296a (2) 50.00

BK69 BC13 *brn,* #281d, 283b, 292c, 294c, 2 #296a 300.00

BK70 BC13 *brn,* #283b, 292c-294c, 2 #296a 165.00

1953-57

1sh Booklets

BK71 BC7 *buff,* 2 each #292a-294a 6.50

BK72 BC7 *buff,* 2 each #317d, 318f, 319f 50.00

1954-59

BK73 BC10 *buff,* #292b-294b (2) 7.25

BK74 BC10 *buff,* #317b, 318c, 319b (3) 6.00

BK75 BC10 *buff,* #353b-355b (2) 6.00

1959

2sh Booklets

BK76 BC10 *salmon,* #317b, 318c, 319b, 322b 7.50

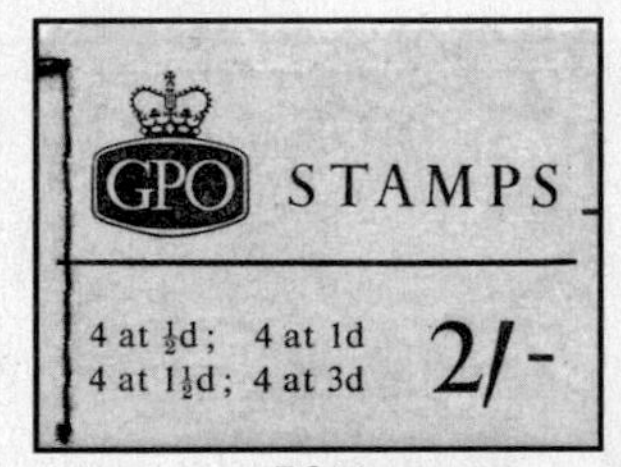

BC14

1960-65 2sh Booklets

BK77 BC14 *sal,* #353b-355b, 358b 9.00

BK77A BC14 *pale yel,* 353b-355b, 358b 9.00

BK78 BC14 red, *pale yel,* #353e, 2 #357g 6.00
a. White stiching 6.00

BK79 BC14 *pale yel,* #353b-355b, 358b (17) 32.50
a. #353bp-355bp, 358bp (13) 60.00

BK80 BC14 red, *pale yel,* 4 #353g 2.25

BK81 BC14 *org yel,* #354f, 359c (7) 4.75
a. #354fp, 359cp (12) 3.25

BK82 BC14 red, *org yel,* 2 #358b 8.00

No. BK77A has an upright watermark, No. BK79 a sideways watermark.

1968-69

BK83 BC14 *org yel,* #MH5b, MH6b (3) 1.45

BK84 BC14 *gray,* #MH6a-MH6b (5) .90

BK85 BC14 *gray,* #MH7a-MH7b (12) 1.40

1954, Mar. 2sh6p Booklets

BK86 BC13 *grn,* #292c, 293d, 294c, 296a (19) 52.50

No. BK86 inscribed Apr. 1954 through Aug. 1955 are valued. Booklet inscribed Mar. 1954 is valued at $325.

No. BK86 inscribed Aug. 1955 through Nov. 1955, may contain one or more panes watermarked 308 substituted for those listed. Value $57.50.

1955, Dec.

BK87 BC13 *grn,* #317a, 318b, 319a, 321a (16) 30.00

No. BK87 inscribed Dec. 1955 through June 1956 may contain one or more panes watermarked 298 substituted for those listed. Value $15.

1957

BK88 BC13 *grn,* #317a, 320b, 321a (9) 30.00

1958, Jan. 3sh Booklets

BK89 BC13 *red,* #317a, 318b, 319a, 322a (9) 25.00

No. BK89 inscribed Nov. 1958, may contain one or more panes watermarked 322 substituted for those listed. Value $13.

1958, Dec.-59

BK90 BC13 *red,* #353a-355a, 358a (5) 34.00
a. #353d, 354d, 355d, 358d (2) 250.00

No. BK90 dated Dec. 1958, may contain one or more panes watermarked 308 substituted for those listed. Value $14.

BK91 BC13 *brick red,* #353a-355a, 358a (14) 37.50
a. #353d, 354d, 355d, 358d (4) 310.00
b. #353ap, 354ap, 355ap, 358ap (2) 80.00

BC15

1960

BK92 BC15 *brick red,* #353a-355a, 358a (46) 42.50
a. #353ap-355ap, 358ap (35) 67.50

1953, Nov. 3sh9p Booklets

BK93 BC13 *red,* 3 #296a (10) 40.00

No. BK93 inscribed Oct. or Dec. 1955 may contain one or more panes watermarked 308 substituted for those listed. Value $16.

1956, Feb.

BK94 BC13 *red,* 3 #321a (10) 17.50

4sh6p Booklets

1957, Oct.-Dec. 1960

BK95 BC13 *dull mauve,* 3 #322a (7) 27.50

BK96 BC13 *dull mauve,* 3 #358a 120.00

BK97 BC14 *dull mauve,* 3 #358a (4) 28.00
a. 3 #358d 40.00

BK98 BC14 *pale reddish lil,* 3 #358a (9) 31.00
a. 3 #358d (4) 25.00
b. 3 #358ap 52.50

BK99 BC15 *pale reddish lil,* 3 #358a (36) 40.00
a. 3 #358ap (31) 40.00

1965

BK100 BC15 *slate bl,* #354a, 2 #359b (7) 27.50
a. #354ap, 2 #359bp (13) 10.50

1968

BK101 BC15 *slate bl,* #MH2a, 2 #MH6c 5.50

Ship with GPO Emblem — BC16

1968-70 4sh6p Booklets

BK102 BC16 *blue,* #MH2a, 2 #MH6c (3) 1.20

BK103 BC16 *blue,* #MH2a, 2 #MH7c (9) 1.20

Ship Type with St. Edward's Crown instead of GPO emblem

BK104 BC16 *blue,* #MH2a, 2 #MH7c (2) 3.25

1954, Mar 5sh Booklets

BK105 BC13 *brn,* #292c-294c, 295a-296a (10) 85.00

No. BK105 inscribed Sept. 1955 may contain one or more panes watermarked 308 substituted for those listed. Value $16.

1955, Nov.

BK106 BC13 *brn,* #317a, 318b, 319a, 320b, 321a (14) 35.00

No. BK106 inscribed Nov. 1955, Jan. 1956 or May 1956 may contain one or more panes watermarked 298 substituted for those listed. Value $17.

1958

BK107 BC13 *brn,* #317a, 318b, 321a, 2 #322a (5) 28.00

No. BK107 inscribed July or Nov. 1958 may contain one or more panes watermarked 322 substituted for those listed. Value $15.

1959, Jan.

BK108 BC14 *bl,* #353a-354a, 357c, 2 #358a (11) 32.50
a. #353d-354d, 357e, 2 #358d (3) 125.00
b. #353ap-354ap, 357cp, 2 #358ap 125.00

No. BK108 inscribed Jan. 1959 may contain one or more panes watermarked 308 substituted for those listed. Value $15.

1961, Jan.

BK109 BC15 *bl,* #353a-354a, 357c, 2 #358a (27) 57.50
a. #353ap-354ap, 357cp, 2 #358ap (24) 120.00

House with GPO Emblem — BC17

1968-70

BK110 BC17 *org brn,* 2 #MH8a (5) 2.75

House Type with St. Edward's Crown instead of GPO Emblem

BK111 BC17 5sh *org brn,* 2 #MH8a (7) 2.75

BC18

1970

BK112 BC18 *org brn,* 2 #MH8a 2.50

1965 6sh Booklets

BK113 BC15 *claret,* 3 #359b (23) 37.50
a. 3 #359bp (27) 37.50

1967

BK114 BC15 *claret,* 3 #MH6c (10) 25.00

Bird with GPO Emblem — BC19

1968-70

BK115 BC19 *org,* 3 #MH6c (8) 2.10
BK116 BC19 *org,* 3 #MH7c (5) 3.75

Bird Type with St. Edward's Crown instead of GPO Emblem

BK117 BC19 *org,* 3 #MH7c (5) 4.25

1961-67 10sh Booklets

BK118 BC15 *grn,* #353a-355a, 356b, 5 #358a (2) 140.00
BK119 BC15 *gray grn,* #354a-355a, 357c, 5 #358a (7) 120.00
BK120 BC15 *tan,* #354a, 358a, 4 #359b (5) 32.50
a. #354ap, 358ap, 4 #359bp (3) 8.25

Explorers with GPO Emblem — BC20

1968-70

BK121 BC20 *pur,* #MH2a, MH5a, 4 #MH6c (2) 5.75

Explorer Type with clear GPO Emblem

BK122 BC20 *yel grn,* #MH6d, 2 ea #MH6c, #MH8a 4.25
BK123 BC20 *yel grn,* #MH7c, MH7e, MH8a (4) 3.50

Explorer Type with St. Edward's Crown instead of GPO Emblem

BK124 BC20 *yel grn,* #MH7e, 2 ea #MH7c, MH8a (2) 7.50

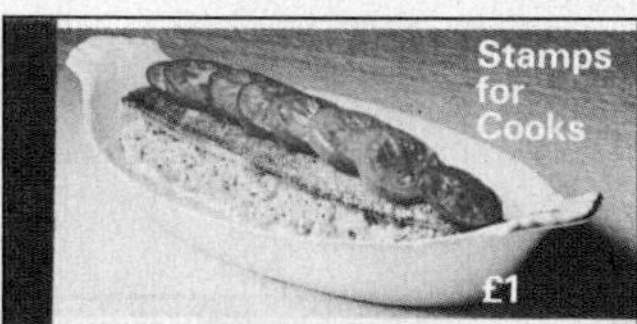

BC21

1969 £1 Booklets

BK125 BC21 multi, 2 #MH7d, MH8b-MH8c 9.00
BK126 BC21 2 #MH7d, MH8b-MH8c, stapled 450.00

Decimal Currency Booklets (Stitched)

BC22

1971-74

BK127 BC22 10p *org yel,* #MH24a, MH26a (21) 1.35

BC23

1974-76

BK128 BC23 10p *org yel,* #MH24a, MH26a (9) 1.50

BC24

1971-73

BK129 BC24 25p *dull purple* (12) 3.75
Contents: Nos. MH22a, MH32a-MH32b.

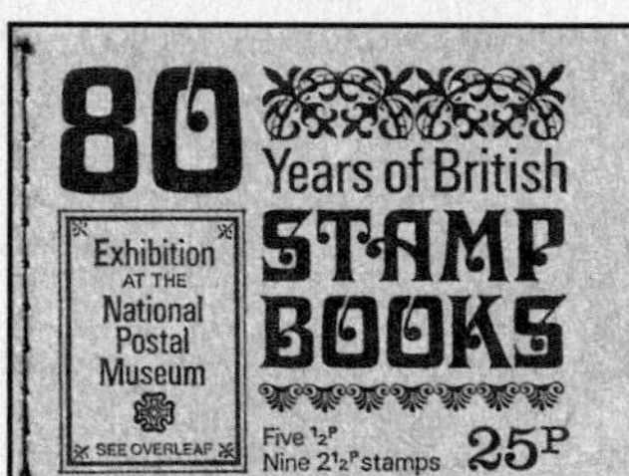

BC25

1971

BK130 BC25 25p *dull purple* 4.50
Contents: Nos. MH22a, MH32a-MH32b.
BK131 BC25 30p *bright pur,* 2 #MH36b 5.00

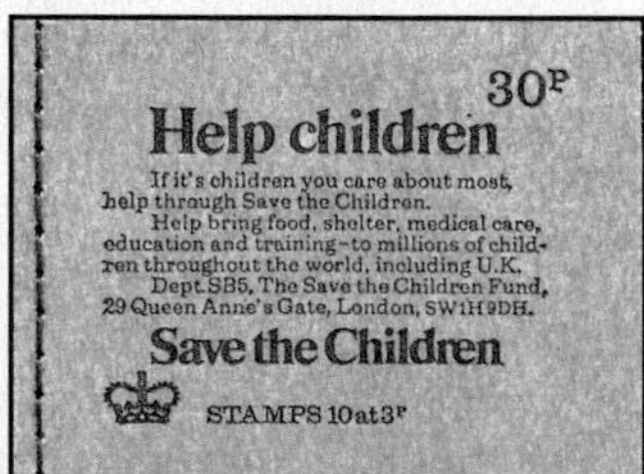

BC26

1973-74

BK132 BC26 25p *dull mauve* 8.00
Contents: Nos. MH22a, MH32a-MH32b.
BK133 BC26 30p *vermilion,* 2 #MH36b 3.75

Bird Type with St. Edward's Crown instead of GPO Emblem

1971-73

BK134 BC19 30p *pur,* 2 #MH36b (16) 3.75
BK135 BC19 30p *buff,* 2 #MH36b 7.75

BC27

1973-74

BK136 BC27 30p *red,* 2 #MH36b 4.75
BK137 BC27 35p *blue,* 2 #MH39a 3.50
BK138 BC27 50p *pale bluish grn* 7.75
Contents: Nos. MH22a, MH32b, MH36a, MH36c (4).
BK139 BC27 50p *pale grn,* MH36b, 2 #MH39a (2) 5.50
BK140 BC27 85p *purple,* #MH39a, 3 #MH49a 9.00

BC28

1973-74

BK141 BC28 35p *bl,* 2 #MH39a (3) 3.00
BK142 BC28 45p *yel brn,* 2 #MH49a (3) 4.50
a. 45p org brn, MH49a (1) 19.50

BC29

1971-72

BK143 BC29 50p *pale bluish green* 6.50
Contents: Nos. MH22a, MH32b, MH36a, MH36c (8).

Prestige Booklets

BC30

1972, May 24

BK144 BC30 £1 *Wedgwood* 60.00
Contents: Nos. MH34a-MH34b, #MH36d-MH36e. Valued with full perforations on the ½p stamps.

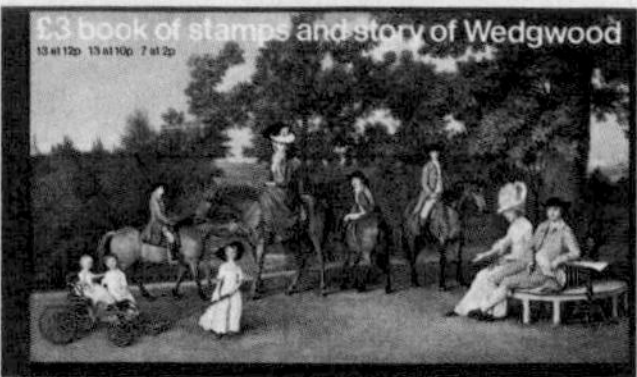

BC31

1980, Apr. 16

BK145 BC31 £3 *Wedgwood* 5.75
Contents: Nos. MH26b, MH70a, MH78a-MH78b.

1982, May 19

BK146 £4 *Stanley Gibbons* 7.00
Contents: Nos. MH80a-MH80b, MH92a-MH92b.

1983, Sept. 14

BK147 £4 *Royal Mint* 7.00
Contents: Nos. MH94a-MH94b, 2 #MH80a.

1984, Sept. 4

BK148 £4 *Christian Heritage* 33.00
Contents: Nos. MH97c-MH97d, 2 No. MH83a.

1985, Jan. 8

BK149 £5 *The Times* 15.00
Contents: Nos. MH83b, MH97b-MH97c, MH149a.

1986, Mar. 18

BK150 £5 *British Rail* 18.00
Contents: Nos. MH79a, MH97b-MH97c, MH142a.

1987, Mar. 3

BK151 £5 *P & O* 17.50
Contents: Nos. MH83a-MH83b, MH102a, MH130a.

1988, Feb. 9

BK152 £5 *The Financial Times* 32.50
Contents: Nos. MH84a, MH103a-MH103b, MH150a.

1989, Mar. 21

BK153 £5 *Scots Connection* 18.00
Contents: Nos. SMH25a, SMH37a-SMH37b, SMH45a.

1990, Mar. 20

BK154 £5 *London Life* 17.50
Contents: Nos. 1314a, MH196a, 2 No. MH193d.

1991, Mar. 19

BK155 £6 *Agatha Christie* 15.00
Contents: Nos. MH121a, MH147a, 2 No. MH99a.

1992, Feb. 25

BK156 £6 *Cymru-Wales* 15.00
Contents: Nos. 1425a, MH187c, WMMH34a, WMMH45a.

1992, Oct. 27

BK157 £6 *J.R.R. Tolkien* 15.50
Contents: Nos. MH105a, MH187b, 2 No. MH127a.

1993, Aug. 10

BK158 £5.64 *Beatrix Potter* 17.50
Although inscribed £6 on the cover, No. BK158 was sold for £5.64, the face value of its

contents, which were Nos. 1484a, MH178a, MH187a, NIMH45a.

1994, July 26
BK159 £6.04 *N. Ireland* 21.50

Contents: Nos. 1550a, MH214a, NIMH63a-NIMH63b, 2 postal cards.

1995, Apr. 25
BK160 £6 *National Trust* 21.50

Contents: Nos. 1607a, MH209a, MH231a, NIMH59a.

1996, May 14
BK161 £6.48 *European Soccer Championships* 13.00

Contents: Nos. 1663a, 1664a, 1667a, MH214b.

1997, Sept. 23
BK162 £6.15 *75th Anniv. of BBC* 16.00

Contents: Nos. 1698a, MH287a, MH257a, NIMH81a.

1998, Mar. 10
BK163 £7.49 *Definitive Portrait* 17.50

Contents: Nos. 1801a, 1802a, 1803a-1803b.

1998, Oct. 13
BK164 £6.16 *Breaking Barriers* 32.50

Contents: Nos. 1829b, MH269a, MH285a-MH285b.

1999, Feb. 16
BK165 (£7.54) *Profile on Print* 30.00

Contents: Nos. MH241c, MH288a, MH310a-MH312a.

1999, Sept. 21
BK166 (£6.99) *World Changers* 23.00

Contents: Nos. 1842b, 1847a, 1868b, 1869b, MH257f.

2000, Feb. 15
BK167 (£7.50) *Special by Design* 32.00

Contents: Nos. MH198Ab, MH264Bc, MH336b, WMMH96a.

2000, Aug. 4
BK168 (£7.03) *The Life of the Century* 22.50

Contents: Nos. 1943e, 1943f, Scotland 18a, MH335b.

2000, Sept. 18
BK169 (£7) *A Treasury of Trees* 22.50

Contents: Nos. 1917a, 1918a, 1920a, 1921a, Wales and Monmouthshire 18a.

2001, Oct. 22
BK170 (£6.76) *Unseen and Unheard* 32.00

Contents: Nos. 1969b, 1970b, 1999e, Scotland 16a.

2002, Feb. 6
BK171 (£7.23) *A Gracious Accession* 27.50

Contents: Nos. 2020a, 2021a, 2023a, MH200b

2002, Sept. 24
BK172 (£6.83) *Across the Universe* 27.00

Contents: 1938b, 2075e, Scotland 15a, MH290c.

2003, Feb. 25
BK173 (£6.99) *Microcosmos* 27.00

Contents: Nos. 2104a, 2105a, Northern Ireland 13a, MH290c.

2003, June 2
BK174 (£7.46) *A Perfect Coronation* 62.50

Contents: Nos. 2126a, 2134a, 2136b, MH287b.

2004, Mar. 16
BK175 (£7.44) *Letters by Night* 23.50

Contents: Nos. 2148a, 2175a, Scotland 20a, MH287c.

2004, May 25
BK176 (£7.23) *The Glory of the Garden* 26.00

Contents: Nos. 1720b, 2213a, 2214b, MH287d.

2005, Feb. 24
BK177 (£7.43) *The Bronte Sisters* 24.00

Contents: Nos. 2268a, 2272b, England 10a, MH354a.

2005, Oct. 18
BK178 (£7.26) *Battle of Trafalgar* 24.00

Contents: Nos. 1999h, 2325a, 2326b, MH287e.

2006, Feb. 23
BK179 (£7.40) *Isambard Kingdom Brunel* 21.00

Contents: Nos. 2356a, 2357a, 2358b, MH355a.

2006, Sept. 21
BK180 (£7.44) *Victoria Cross* 24.00

Contents: Nos. 1331b, 2398a, 2399b, MH376a.

2007, Mar. 1
BK181 (£7.49) *World of Invention* 22.50

Contents: Nos. 2447a, 2449b, Wales & Monmouthshire 26a, MH376b.

2007, June 5
BK182 (£7.66) *The Machin* 26.00

Contents: Nos. 2471c, MH363a, MH373a, MH378a.

2007, Sept. 20
BK183 (£7.66) *British Army Uniforms* 26.00

Contents: Nos. 2510b, 2513b, MH366a, Wales & Monmouthshire 21a.

2008, Jan. 8
BK184 (£7.40) *Ian Fleming's James Bond* 26.00

Contents: Nos. 1999i, 2535a, 2536b, MH287f.

2008, Sept. 18
BK185 (£7.15) *RAF Uniforms* 26.00

Contents: Nos. 2587c, 2596b, 2599b, MH287h.

2008, Sept. 29
BK186 (£9.72) *The Regional Definitives: Heraldry and Symbol* 34.00

Contents: Nos. 2600s, 2600t, 2600u, 2600v.

2009, Jan. 13
BK187 (£7.68) *British Design Classics* 40.00

Contents: Nos. 2619a, 2623a, 2624b, MH365b.

2009, Feb. 12
BK188 (£7.75) *Charles Darwin* 57.50

Contents: Nos. 2626e, 2630a, 2632a, MH363c.

2009, Aug. 18
BK189 (£8.18) *Treasures of the Archive* 28.00

Contents: Nos. 1289b, 2679e, MH368b, MH394a.

2009, Sept. 17
BK190 (£7.93) *Royal Navy Uniforms* 32.00

Contents: Nos. 1000j, 2688b, 2691b, MH372Ac.

2010, Jan. 7
BK191 (£8.06) *Classic Album Covers* 40.00

Contents: Nos. 2729a, 2733a, MH350Ad, MH368c.

2010, Feb. 25
BK192 (£7.72) *The Royal Society* 36.00

Contents: Nos. 2754a, 2755a, 2756b, MH366Bc.

2010, May 8
BK193 (£11.15) *King George V* 31.00

Contents: Nos. 2792b, 2791b, 2789a, MH385a.

2010, May 13
BK194 (£9.76) *Britain Alone* 29.00

Contents: Nos. MH397b, 2802a, 2801a, 2806b.

2011, Mar. 11
BK195 (£9.05) *WWF For a Living Planet* 28.00

Contents: Nos. 2890a, 2892b, 2893e, MH400b.

2011, May 5
BK196 (£9.44) *Morris & Co.* 28.00

No. BK196 sold for £9.99. Contents: Nos. 2716i, 2906a, 2907a, MH405a.

2011, Sept. 9
BK197 (£9.02) *First United Kingdom Aerial Post* 50.00

No. BK197 sold for £9.97. Contents: Nos, 2278e, 2939e, 2939f, MH412a.

2012, Jan. 10
BK198 (£10.52) *Roald Dahl: Master Stroyteller* 36.00

No. BK198 sold for £11.47. Contents: Nos. 2986a, 2988a, 2989e, MH413a.

2012, May 31
BK199 (£11.84) *The Diamond Jubilee* 36.00

No. BK199 sold for £12.77. Contents: Nos. 2996Gh, 3030b, 3034b, 3035c.

2012, July 27
BK200 (£9.76) *Keeping the Flame Alive* 60.00

No. BK200 sold for £10.71. Contents: Nos. 2708a, 2822a, 2917a, C9a.

2013, Mar. 26
BK201 (£12.82) *50 Years of Doctor Who* 37.50

No. BK201 sold for £13.77. Contents: Nos. 3143b, 3147b, 3151b, 3152a, 3153k.

2013, May 9
BK202 (£10.56) *Football Heroes* 35.00

No. BK202 sold for £11.11. Contents: Nos. 3182a, 3188a, MH439a, MH440a.

2013, Sept. 19
BK203 (£10.24) *Merchant Navy* 32.00

No. BK203 sold for £11.19. Contents: Nos. 3221a, 3224a, 3225e, MH441a.

2014, Feb. 20
BK204 (£13.02) *Classic Locomotives of the United Kingdom* 30.00

No. BK204 sold for £13.97. Contents: Nos. 2865e, 3007e, 3197e, 3268e, MH248c.

2014, Apr. 15
BK205 (£10.44) *Buckingham Palace* [illegible]

No. BK205 sold for £11.39. Contents: Nos. 3280b, 3284c, 3285e, MH446a.

2014, July 28
BK206 (£10.35) *The Great War 1914* 32.50

No. BK206 sold for £11.30. Contents: Nos. 3314a, 3317a, MH431a, MH446b.

2015, Feb. 19
BK207 (£13.67) *Inventive Britain* 34.00

No. BK207 sold for £14.60. Contents: Nos. 3363a, 3369a, 3370b, MH448a.

2015, May 14
BK208 (£13.01) *The Great War 1915* 35.00

No. BK208 sold for £13.96. Contents: Nos. 2510c, 3399a, 3402a, MH455a.

2015, June 18
BK209 (£12.12) *The Battle of Waterloo 1815* 37.50

No. BK209 sold for £14.47. Contents: Nos. 3513a, 3514a, 3515e, MH446c.

2015, Dec. 17
BK210 (£16.20) *The Making of Star Wars The British Story* 40.00

No. BK210 sold for £16.99. Contents: Nos. 3443a, 3446b, 3451g, 3451h, 3452a.

2016, Feb. 18
BK211 (£15.41) *500 Years of Royal Mail* 35.00

No. BK211 sold for £16.36. Contents: Nos. 3473a, 3475a, 3476e, 3477a.

2016, Apr. 21
BK212 (£14.16) *HM The Queen's 90th Birthday* 40.00

No. BK212 sold for £15.11. Contents: Nos. 3499a, 3500b, 3501e, MH459a.

2016, June 21
BK213 (£15.54) *The Great War 1916* 40.00

No. BK213 sold for £16.49. Contents: Nos. 2744k, 3509a, 3512a, 3513e.

2016, July 28
BK214 (£14.42) *The Tale of Beatrix Potter* 32.50

No. BK214 sold for £15.37. Contents: Nos. 3525a, 3526b, 3527e, MH460a.

2017, Feb. 15
BK215 (£13.63) *Windsor Castle* 36.50

No. BK215 sold for £14.68. Contents: Nos 3585a, 3587b, 3588e, MH460b.

2017, June 5
BK216 (£14.64) *The Machin Definitive: 50th Anniversary* 41.00

No. BK216 sold for £15.59. Contents: Nos. MH440d, MH467a MH468g, MH468h, MH469c.

2017, July 31
BK217 (£14.46) *The Great War 1917* 41.00

No. BK217 sold for £15.41. Contents: Nos. 2614c, 2744l, 3634a, 3637a.

2017, Oct. 12
BK218 (£14.22) *Star Wars: The Making of the Droids, Aliens and Creatures* 43.00

No. BK218 sold for £15.95. Contents: Nos. 3658a, 3662a, 3663c, MH470a.

2018, Jan. 23
BK219 (£12.99) *Game of Thrones* 40.00

No. BK219 sold for £13.95. Contents: Nos. 3686a, 3688b, 3689a, 3693a.

2018, Mar. 20
BK220 (£18.54) *The RAF Centenary* 53.00

No. BK220 sold for £18.69. Contents: Nos. 3416g, 3707b, 3709b, 3710e, MH471a.

2018, Sept. 13
BK221 (£14.70) *The Great War 1918* 41.00

No. BK221 sold for £15.65. Contents: Nos. 2744m, 3633a, 3774a, 3777a

2018, Dec. 4
BK222 (£13.97) *The Marauder's Map* 40.00

No. BK222 sold for £15.50. Contents: Nos. 3788a, 3789b, 3790f, 3790g, MH476a.

2019, Feb. 13
BK223 (£11.64) *Leonardo da Vinci 500 Years* 34.00

No. BK223 sold for £13.10. Contents: Nos. 3812a, 3813a, 3814b, MH477a.

Numbers have been reserved for future prestige booklets.

Decimal Currency Booklets (Folded)

Booklets are listed in denomination sequence in chronological order in this section.

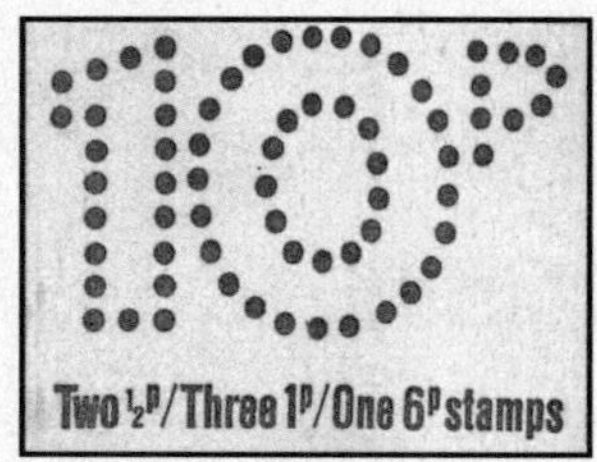

BC32

1976-77
BK225 BC32 10p red, *gray*, #MH58a (3) .80

BC33

1978
BK226 BC33 10p brn, *bl*, #MH61b (6) .55

1979-80
BK227 BC33 10p *London '80*, #MH64b (2) .45

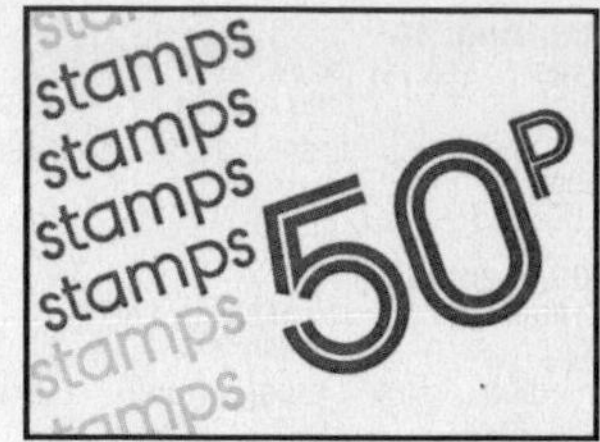

BC34

1977
BK228 BC34 50p #MH65a 2.00
BK229 BC34 50p #MH67a 2.25

Nos. BK228-BK238 exist with either version of Nos. MH65a, MH67a, MH70b, MH76a, MH78d, MH80c, MH86a. See the notes following the listings for these panes.

Commercial Vehicles — BC35

50p Booklets, Cover BC35

1978-95
BK230 *Commercial Vehicles*, #MH67a (6) 2.25
BK231 *Commercial Vehicles*, #MH70b 2.25
BK232 *Veteran Cars*, #MH70b 2.25
BK233 *Veteran Cars*, #MH78d (3) 2.25
BK234 *Veteran Cars*, #MH86a (2) 2.25
BK235 *Follies*, #MH86a 2.25
BK236 *Follies*, #MH76a (2) 5.00
BK237 *Follies*, #MH80c (4) 2.25
BK238 *Rare Farm Animals*, #MH80c 2.75
BK239 *Rare Farm Animals*, #MH81a (4) 5.00
BK240 *Orchids*, #MH83c (4) 5.00
BK241 *Pillar Box*, #MH97a 3.50
BK242 *Pond Life*, #MH97a (2) 2.75

Nos. BK241-BK242 sold for a 1p discount. Some panes have stars on reverse.

BK244 *Pond Life*, #MH83d (2) 3.25
BK245 *Roman Britain*, #MH79b 9.50
BK246 *Roman Britain*, #MH102b (2) 3.50
BK247 *Marylebone Cricket Club*, #MH102b (4) 6.25
BK248 *Botanical Gardens*, #MH83d (2) 5.25
BK248A *Botanical Gardens*, #MH83g (2) 3.00
BK249 *London Zoo*, #MH102b (2) 3.00
BK250 *London Zoo*, #MH83g 5.00
BK251 *Marine Life*, #MH83g 5.00
BK252 *Marine Life*, #MH106a 6.25
BK253 *Gilbert & Sullivan Operas*, #MH106a (3) 6.75
BK254 *Aircraft*, #MH115a 13.00
BK255 *Aircraft*, #MH193a 10.50
BK256 *Aircraft*, #MH98a (2) 7.00
BK257 *Archaeology*, #MH126a (4) 2.00
BK258 *Sheriff's Millennium*, #MH126a 2.40
BK259 *Postal History*, #MH126a (3) 2.00
BK260 *Postal History*, #MH213a 2.10
BK261 *Coaching Inns*, #MH213a (4) 2.10
BK262 *Sea Charts*, #MH213a (4) 2.10

With Window — BC36

Without Window — BC37

1987
BK285 BC36 52p #MH83e 2.00

1988-89
BK295 BC36 56p #MH87a (2) 4.75
BK296 BC37 56p #MH87b 5.75
BK297 BC37 56p #MH87c 27.00

1990
BK307 BC37 60p #MH191a 5.50

1976-77
BK317 BC34 65p 10 #MH60 7.50
BK325 BC34 70p 10 #MH61 5.75

Nos. BK317, BK325-BK327, BK370, BK394, BK404-BK405, BK467-BK468, BK488-BK492, BK513-BK514, BK524-BK533, BK554-BK557, BK573-BK574, BK584, BK594, BK616-BK618, BK631, BK641, BK651-BK652, BK673-BK675, BK696-BK699, BK709-BK713, BK715-BK718, BK728, BK732-BK733 exist with stamps affixed to cover by selvage at either right or left edges of block or pane of stamps.

BC38

1978-79 **70p Booklets**
BK326 BC38 *Country Crafts*, 10 #MH61 (6) 4.00
BK327 BC38 *Derby Mechanized Letter Office*, 10 #MH61 7.50

1987
BK338 BC36 72p red, yel & blk, #MH102c 3.00

1988-89
BK348 BC36 76p #MH106c (2) 5.25
BK349 BC37 76p #MH106d 6.50
BK350 BC37 76p #MH106e 26.00

BC39

1992
BK360 BC39 78p 2 #MH157 3.25

Cover of No. BK360 does not show the numeral four. Contents of Nos. BK360 is 1/2 of Nos. MH157a, the right hand vertical pair of stamps being removed.

1979
BK370 BC38 80p *Military Aircraft*, 10 #MH64 3.25

1990
BK371 BC37 80p red, yel & blk, #MH193b 7.00
BK372 BC37 80p red, yel & blk, #MH194a 6.50

1976-79
BK382 BC34 85p gray & ol grn, 10 #MH65 8.25
BK392 BC34 90p lt & dk bl, 10 #MH67 5.50
BK393 BC38 90p *British Canals*, 10 #MH67 (6) 4.50
BK394 BC38 90p *Derby Letter Office*, 10 #MH67 9.50

1979-95 **£1 Booklets**
BK403 BC38 *Industrial Archaeology*, 10 #MH70 4.00
BK404 BC38 *Military Aircraft*, 10 #MH70 (3) 1.00
BK405 BC35 *Violin*, 6 #MH97 4.00
BK406 BC35 *Musical Instruments*, #MH102d (2) 4.50
BK407 BC35 *Sherlock Holmes*, #MH102d (2) 4.00
BK408 BC35 *Sherlock Holmes*, #MH102f (2) 6.00
BK409 BC35 *London Zoo*, #MH102f 6.00
BK410 BC35 *Oliver Twist*, #MH102f 6.00
BK411 BC35 *Nicholas Nickleby*, #MH106b (2) 6.00
BK412 BC35 *Great Expectations*, #MH108a 26.50
BK413 BC35 *Marine Life*, #MH106b 5.50
BK414 BC35 *Wicken Fen*, #MH115b 6.25
BK415 BC35 *Click Mill*, #MH193c 8.50
BK416 BC35 *Wicken Fen*, #MH194b 14.00
BK417 BC35 *Jack & Jill Mills*, #MH120a (2) 5.25
BK418 BC35 *Punch Magazine*, #MH126b (4) 4.50
BK419 BC35 *Sheriff's Millennium*, #MH126b 4.50
BK420 BC35 *Educational Institutions*, #MH128a (3) 9.00
BK421 BC35 *Educational Institutions*, 4 #MH214 5.25
BK422 BC35 *Prime Ministers*, 4 #MH214 2.90
BK423 BC35 *Prime Ministers*, 4 #MH213 (3) 2.90
BK424 BC35 *End of World War II*, 4 #MH213 (4) 2.90

BC40

1996-2000

BK425 BC40 £1 multi, 4 #MH214 6.00
BK426 BC40 £1 multi, #MH216b 9.25
BK427 BC40 £1 multi, #MH257b 27.50
BK428 BC40 £1 multi, #MH257d 7.00
BK429 BC40 £1 #MH288d 8.50

1987-88 £1.04 Booklet

BK446 BC36 #MH131a 15.00

£1.08 Booklets

BK456 BC36 #MH133a 8.25
BK457 BC37 #MH133b 25.00

1981 £1.15 Booklets

BK467 BC38 *Military Aircraft,* 10 #MH76 (2) 4.50
BK468 BC38 *Museums,* 10 #MH76 (2) 4.50

1989 £1.16 Booklet

BK478 BC37 multi, #MH140a 12.50

1980-86 £1.20 Booklets

BK488 BC38 *Industrial Archaeology,* 10 #MH78 (3) 4.75
BK489 BC38 *Pillar Box,* 10 #MH79 6.25
BK490 BC38 *National Gallery,* 10 #MH79 6.00
BK491 BC38 *Handwriting,* 10 #MH79 6.00
BK492 BC38 *Christmas,* 10 #MH83 8.00

No. BK492 was sold at a discount. Each stamp has a blue double-line star printed on reverse.

BC41

1998 £1.20 Booklet

BK493 BC41 multi, 4 #MH259 6.75

1990 £1.24 Booklet

BK503 BC39 multi, #MH144a 7.75

1982-83 £1.25 Booklets

BK513 BC38 *Museums,* 10 #MH81 (4) 4.50
BK514 BC38 *Railway Engines,* 10 #MH81 (5) 6.00

1981-88 £1.30 Booklets

BK524 BC38 *Postal History,* #MH86b (2) 5.50
BK525 BC38 *Trams,* 10 #MH83 (4) 5.00
BK526 BC38 *Books for Children,* 10 #MH83 5.00
BK527 BC38 *Keep in Touch,* 10 #MH83 5.00
BK528 BC38 *Ideas for your Garden,* 10 #MH83 5.00
BK529 BC38 *Brighter Writer,* 10 #MH83 5.00
BK530 BC38 *Jolly Postman,* 10 #MH83 5.00
BK531 BC38 *Linnean Society,* 10 #MH83 5.00
BK532 BC38 *Recipe Cards,* 10 #MH83 5.00
BK533 BC38 *Party Pack,* 10 #MH83 5.00
BK534 BC36 red, yel & blk, #MH83f 5.00

1991 £1.32 Booklet

BK544 BC39 multi, #MH148a 8.50

1981-89 £1.40 Booklets

BK554 BC38 *Industrial Archaeology,* 10 #MH86 (2) 5.00
BK555 BC38 *Women's Costumes,* 10 #MH86 (2) 5.00
BK556 BC38 *Pocket Planner,* 10 #MH87 5.00
BK557 BC38 *William Henry Fox Talbot,* 10 #MH87 5.00

1988-95 £1.40 Booklets

BK558 BC36 #MH87d 12.00
BK559 BC36 10 #MH88 19.50
BK560 BC37 #MH87e 7.50
BK561 BC37 10 #MH88 19.50
BK562 BC39 #MH223a 7.50
BK563 BC41 #MH223a (2) 7.50

1982 £1.43 Booklets

BK573 BC38 *Postal History,* #MH93d (5) 4.50
BK574 BC38 *Holiday Postcard Stamp Book,* #MH93d 4.50

No. BK574 contains a postcard voucher on the back cover.

1983 £1.45 Booklet

BK584 BC38 *Britain's Countryside,* 10 #MH94 6.75

Stamps in No. BK584 have double-lined D printed on reverse.
No. BK584 had a face value of £1.60.

1983 £1.46 Booklet

BK594 BC38 *Postal History,* #MH94c (4) 6.75

BC42

1996-97 £1.48 Booklets

BK605 BC41 #MH226a (2) 14.00
BK606 BC42 4 #MH262 8.00

1986-90 £1.50 Booklets

BK616 BC38 *Pillar Box,* #MH97e 5.25
BK617 BC38 *National Gallery,* #MH97e 5.25
BK618 BC38 *Handwriting,* #MH97e 5.25
BK619 BC37 #MH190a 8.50
BK620 BC37 #MH191b 15.00
BK621 BC37 #MH192a 22.50

1999 £1.52 Booklet

BK630 BC41 4 #MH264 8.00

1985 £1.53 Booklet

BK631 BC38 *Royal Mail, 350th Anniv.,* #1111a 6.00

1984 £1.54 Booklet

BK641 BC38 *Postal History,* #MH97f (4) 5.00

1982-85 £1.55 Booklets

BK651 BC38 *Women's Costumes,* 10 #MH93 (4) 4.50
BK652 BC38 *Social Letter Writing,* 10 #MH97g 5.25

No. BK652 sold for a 15p discount. Panes have double-lined "D" printed on reverse.

1991 £1.56 Booklet

BK662 BC39 #MH157a 9.00

1978-2000 £1.60 Booklets

BK672 BC38 *Christmas,* #MH67b 3.75
BK673 BC38 *Birthday Box,* 10 #MH97 (2) 5.00
BK674 BC38 *Britain's Countryside,* 10 #MH94 6.50
BK675 BC38 *Write It,* 10 #MH97 5.00
BK676 BC41 #MH266a 7.25

1993-96 £1.64 Booklets

BK685 BC39 #MH231b 9.00
BK686 BC41 #MH231b (2) 8.00

1984-86 £1.70 Booklets

BK696 BC38 *Love Letters,* 10 #MH97 (2) 5.00
BK697 BC38 *Pillar Box,* 10 #MH97 (2) 5.00
BK698 BC38 *National Gallery,* 10 #MH97 5.00
BK699 BC38 *Handwriting,* 10 #MH97 5.00

1979-88 £1.80 Booklets

BK709 BC38 *Christmas,* #MH70c 6.00
BK710 BC38 *Books for Children,* 10 #MH102 6.00
BK711 BC38 *Keep in Touch,* 10 #MH102 6.00
BK712 BC38 *Ideas for your Garden,* 10 #MH102 6.00
BK713 BC38 *Brighter Writer,* 10 #MH102 6.00
BK714 BC36 red, yel & blk, #MH102e 6.00
BK715 BC38 *Jolly Postman,* 10 #MH102 6.00
BK716 BC38 *Linnean Society,* 10 #MH102 6.00
BK717 BC38 *Recipe Cards,* 10 #MH102 6.00
BK718 BC38 *Party Pack,* 10 #MH102 6.00

1988-89 £1.90 Booklets

BK728 BC38 *Pocket Planner,* 10 #MH106 7.50
BK729 BC36 red, yel & blk, #MH106f 8.50
BK730 BC37 #MH106g 9.25
BK731 BC37 10 #MH107 20.00
BK732 BC38 *William Henry Fox Talbot,* 10 #MH106 7.50

BC43

1989 £1.90 Booklet

BK733 BC43 *Greetings,* #1247a 34.00

Artwork for No. BC43 spanned six booklet covers. Only portions of the design appear on each cover.

Value is for pane with perfs guillotined. Value for booklet with pane having full perfs is approximately 60% more.

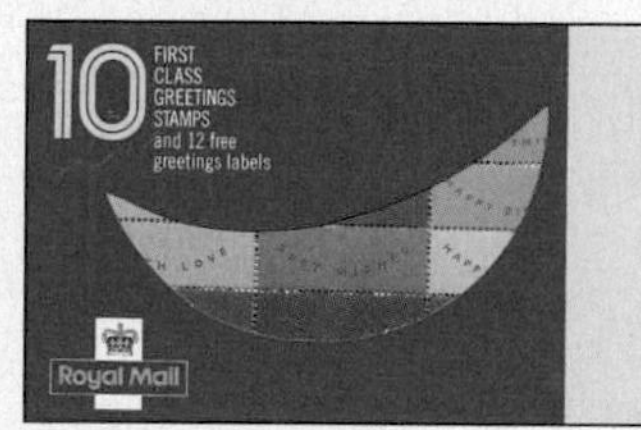

BC44

1990 £2 Booklets

BK742 BC44 #1313a 20.00
BK743 BC37 #MH193e 9.00
BK744 BC37 #MH194c 17.50
BK745 BC37 #MH195a 25.00
BK746 BC35 *Postal Vehicles,* 8 #MH213 (3) 5.00
BK747 BC35 *Rowland Hill,* 8 #MH213 (4) 5.00
BK748 BC40 8 #MH214 5.50
BK749 BC40 #MH216a 12.50

1998-2000

BK751 BC40 #MH257c 27.50
BK752 BC40 #MH257e 12.50
BK753 BC40 #MH288e 9.25

1980-93 £2.20 Booklets

BK759 BC38 *Christmas,* #MH78c 9.50
BK760 BC38 *Christmas,* #MH80e 11.00

£2.30 Booklet

BK770 BC38 *Christmas,* #1088a 7.00

£2.40 Booklet

BK780 BC38 *Christmas,* #1124a 6.50

Stamps in Nos. BK760, BK770, BK780 have double-line star printed on reverse over gum.

BC45

1994-95 £2.40 Booklets

BK790 BC39 #MH234a (2) 11.00
BK791 BC41 #MH234a (2) 11.00
BK792 BC45 #1638a 5.50

1981-94 £2.50 Booklets

BK802 BC38 *Christmas,* #MH93e 12.00

No. BK802 was sold for a 30p discount. Stamps in No. BK802 have a 10-point single-line blue star printed on reverse over gum.

BK803 BC45 *Santa, Reindeer,* 10 #1529 7.25
BK804 BC45 *Christmas Play Props,* 10 #1582 5.75
BK805 BC45 *Christmas Robin,* 10 #1635 5.50

1996-97 £2.52 Booklet

BK815 BC41 #MH236a (3) 18.00

1981 £2.55 Booklet

BK826 BC38 *Christmas,* #MH86c 16.00

1999 £2.56 Booklet

BK827 BC41 4 #MH276 8.25

2000 £2.60 Booklet

BK830 BC41 #MH277a 13.00

1990-95 £3.40 Booklet

BK836 BC45 *Snowman,* #1340a 8.25

£3.60 Booklets

BK846 BC45 *Holly,* #1416a 8.00
BK847 BC45 *Santa, Reindeer,* #1468a 8.00

£3.80 Booklets

BK857 BC45 *Santa, Reindeer,* #1528a 8.75
BK858 BC45 *Christmas Play Props,* #1581a 8.00
BK859 BC45 *Christmas Robin,* #1634a 8.50

No-Value Indicated Booklets

BC46

1989-2000

BK960 BC37 (56p) #MH179a 5.75
BK961 BC37 (60p) #MH177a 32.50
BK962 BC39 (60p) #MH182a 5.50
BK963 BC39 (68p) #MH179b 5.50
BK964 BC46 (72p) #MH179b 5.75
BK965 BC39 (72p) 4 #MH238 4.25
BK966 BC39 (72p) 4 #MH239 4.25
BK967 BC41 (76p) 4 #MH238 4.25
BK968 BC41 (76p) 4 #MH239 (2) 4.25
BK969 BC41 (80p) 4 #MH284 (4) 4.25
BK994 BC37 (76p) #MH184a 11.00
BK995 BC37 (80p) #MH183a 37.50
BK996 BC39 (80p) #MH188a (2) 6.50
BK996A BC39 (80p) #MH189a 20.00
BK997 BC46 (96p) #MH188a 6.50
BK998 BC39 (96p) 4 #MH240 5.50
BK999 BC39 (96p) 4 #MH241 5.00
BK1000 BC39 (£1) #MH241b 7.50
BK1001 BC41 (£1) 4 #MH241 (4) 5.00
BK1002 BC41 (£1) #MH241b (4) 6.50

(£1.04) Booklets

BK1003	BC41	4 #MH241	6.00
BK1004	BC41	#MH241b	6.50
BK1005	BC41	4 #MH288	5.00
BK1006	BC41	4 #MH288+label	6.00
BK1007	BC41	#MH335c	7.50

(£1.20) Booklet

BK1010	BC41	#MH290a	9.50

(£1.40) Booklets

BK1028	BC37	#MH177b	14.00
BK1029	BC37	10 #MH178	11.00

(£1.50) Booklets

BK1030	BC39	#MH180a	17.50
BK1031	BC39	10 #MH181	14.00
BK1032	BC39	#MH182b	13.50

(£1.70) Booklets

BK1033	BC39	10 #MH178	10.50
BK1034	BC39	#MH179c	14.00

(£1.80) Booklets

BK1035	BC46	#MH179c	14.00
BK1036	BC46	10 #MH178	10.50
BK1037	BC39	#MH177b	14.50
BK1038	BC39	10 #MH239 (3)	10.25

(£1.90) Booklets

BK1039	BC41	10 #MH239 (5)	10.25
BK1040	BC41	10 #MH238 (4)	10.25
BK1041	BC37	#MH183b	16.00

(£2) Booklets

BK1068	BC39	#MH186a (2)	16.00
BK1069	BC39	10 #MH187 (3)	12.50
BK1070	BC39	#MH188b (3)	16.00
BK1071	BC41	10 #MH284	12.50
BK1072	BC41	10 #MH285	12.50

(£2.40) Booklets

BK1091	BC46	#MH186a	16.00
BK1092	BC46	#MH187d	16.00
BK1093	BC39	#MH187d	16.00
BK1094	BC39	10 #MH240	13.00
BK1095	BC39	10 #MH241 (11)	13.00

(£2.50) Booklets

BK1116	BC41	10 #MH240 (11)	13.00
BK1117	BC41	10 #MH241 (12)	13.00

(£2.60) Booklets

BK1137	BC41	10 #MH287 (3)	13.00
BK1139	BC41	10 #MH288	13.00
BK1139A	BC41	#MH289a	30.00
BK1140	BC41	10 #MH288	13.00
BK1141	BC41	#1856a, MH288b	13.00
BK1142	BC41	#1872a, MH288b	13.00
BK1143	BC41	10 #MH335	13.00
BK1144	BC41	#MH336a	20.00

BC47

1991-2000 (£2.20) Booklets

BK1160	BC47	#1359a	13.50
BK1161	BC47	*Laughing Pillar Box*, #1373a	13.50

(£2.40) Booklets

BK1171	BC47	*Memories*, #1435a	13.50
BK1172	BC47	*Rupert Bear*, #1488a (3)	13.50

(£2.50) Booklets

BK1182	BC47	*Rupert Bear, Paddington Bear*, #1547a	14.50
BK1183	BC47	*Clown*, #1605a	13.50
BK1184	BC47	*More Love*, #1652a	13.50

(£2.60) Booklets

BK1194	BC47	*Christmas*, 10 #1709	13.00
BK1195	BC47	*Flower*, #1722a (4)	13.00
BK1196	BC47	*Chocolates*, #1722a	13.00
BK1197	BC47	*Memorable Post*, #1722a	13.00
BK1198	BC47	*Santa Claus*, 10 #1777	13.00
BK1199	BC47	*Christmas*, 10 #1835	6.25
BK1200	BC47	10 #1880	6.25

(£2.70) Booklets

BK1201	BC41	#1938a, MH335a	12.00
BK1202	BC47	#1919a, MH335a	15.00
BK1203	BC47	10 #1931	13.00

(£3.80) Booklet

BK1210	BC47	#1879a	11.00
BK1211	BC47	#1930a	21.00

(£4) Booklets

BK1220	BC47	*Magi*, #1708a	21.00
BK1221	BC47	*Santa Claus, Children*, #1776a	20.00
BK1222	BC47	*Christmas*, #1834a	15.00

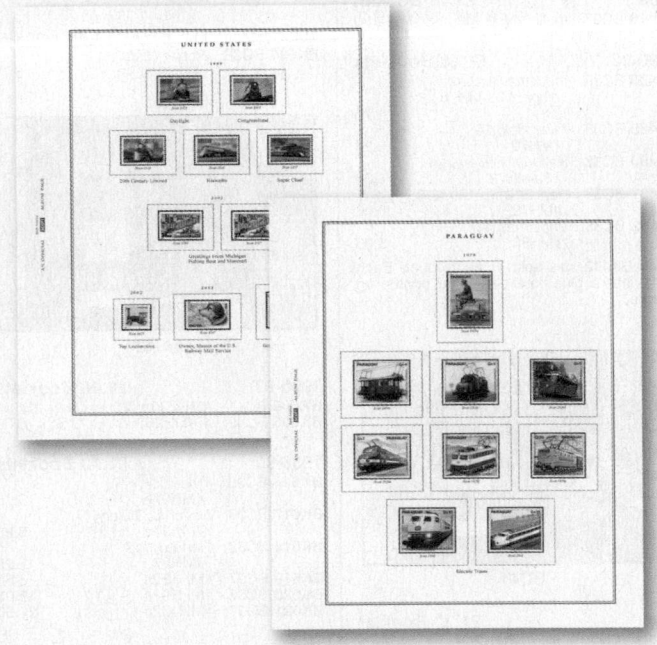

GREAT BRITAIN OFFICES ABROAD

OFFICES IN AFRICA

Catalogue values for unused stamps in this section are for Never Hinged stamps.

MIDDLE EAST FORCES

For use in Ethiopia, Cyrenaica, Eritrea, the Dodecanese and Somalia

Stamps of Great Britain, 1937-42 Overprinted in Black or Blue Black

London Printing — ovpt. 14mm long, square dots

1942-43 Wmk. 251 *Perf. 14½x14*

No.	Type	Description	Unused	Used
1	A101	1p scarlet	3.50	*4.75*
2	A101	2p orange	3.00	*6.00*
3	A101	2½p bright ultra	3.00	*2.00*
4	A101	3p dark purple	2.75	.35
a.		Double overprint		*6,400.*
5	A102	5p lt brn (Blk)	2.75	1.00
a.		Blue black overprint ('43)	4.25	.25
6	A102	6p rose lilac ('43)	.65	.25
7	A103	9p dp olive grn ('43)	1.00	.25
8	A103	1sh brown ('43)	.55	.25

Wmk. 259
Perf. 14

No.	Type	Description	Unused	Used
9	A104	2sh6p yel green ('43)	8.00	1.10
		Nos. 1-9 (9)	25.20	15.95

Same Overprint in Blue Black on Nos. 259, 261, 262 and 263

1943, Jan. 1 Wmk. 251

No.	Type	Description	Unused	Used
10	A101	1p vermilion	1.75	.25
11	A101	2p light orange	1.75	1.40
12	A101	2½p ultramarine	.55	.25
13	A101	3p violet	1.75	.25
		Nos. 10-13 (4)	5.80	2.15

There were two printings of Nos. 1-5, both issued Mar. 2, 1942, and both black. Nos. 5a and 6-13 compose a third printing, also made in London. On these stamps, issued Jan. 1, 1943, the overprint is 13½mm wide. The 2sh6p overprint is black, the others blue black.

Same Ovpt. in Black on #250, 251A

1947 Wmk. 259 *Perf. 14*

No.	Type	Description	Unused	Used
14	A104	5sh dull red	15.00	*20.00*
15	A105	10sh ultramarine	17.50	11.50

In 1950 Nos. 1-15 were declared valid for use in Great Britain. Used values are for stamps postmarked in territory of issue. Others sell for about 25 percent less.

POSTAGE DUE STAMPS

Catalogue values for unused stamps in this section are for Never Hinged items.

Postage Due Stamps of Great Britain Overprinted in Blue

1942 Wmk. 251 *Perf. 14x14½*

No.	Type	Description	Unused	Used
J1	D1	½p emerald	.40	*14.00*
J2	D1	1p carmine rose	.40	*2.00*
J3	D1	2p black brown	3.00	1.40
J4	D1	3p violet	.55	*4.75*
J5	D1	1sh blue	4.25	*14.00*
		Nos. J1-J5 (5)	8.60	*36.15*

No. J1-J5 were used in Eritrea.

FOR USE IN ERITREA

Catalogue values for unused stamps in this section are for Never Hinged items.

100 Cents = 1 Shilling

Stamps of Great Britain 1937-42 Surcharged — a

Perf. 14½x14

1948, June -49 Wmk. 251

No.	Type	Description	Unused	Used
1	A101	5c on ½p green (II)	2.75	.75
2	A101	10c on 1p vermilion (II)	2.00	*2.75*
3	A101	20c on 2p light org (II)	3.00	*2.50*
4	A101	25c on 2½p ultra (II)	2.00	.70
5	A101	30c on 3p violet (II)	2.50	*5.00*
6	A101	40c on 5p light brn	2.75	*4.75*
7	A101	50c on 6p rose lilac	2.25	*1.10*
8	A103	75c on 9p dp ol grn	3.75	*.85*
9	A103	1sh on 1sh brown	2.50	.55

Great Britain Nos. 249A, 250 and 251A Surcharged

Wmk. 259
Perf. 14

No.	Type	Description	Unused	Used
10	A104	2sh50c on 2sh6p yel grn	13.00	*11.50*
11	A104	5sh on 5sh dl red	14.00	*25.00*
12	A105	10sh on 10sh ultra	30.00	25.00

Great Britain No. 245 Surcharged Type "a"
Wmk. 251
Perf. 14½x14

No.	Type	Description	Unused	Used
13	A103	65c on 8p brt rose ('49)	8.00	2.25
		Nos. 1-13 (13)	88.50	*82.70*

"B. M. A." stands for British Military Administration.

Stamps of Great Britain 1937-42 Surcharged — c

1950, Feb. 6

No.	Type	Description	Unused	Used
14	A101	5c on ½p green (II)	1.50	*9.25*
15	A101	10c on 1p ver (II)	.45	*3.50*
16	A101	20c on 2p lt org (II)	1.50	*.90*
17	A101	25c on 2½p ultra (II)	1.00	.70
18	A101	30c on 3p violet (II)	.45	*2.50*
19	A102	40c on 5p light brown	3.00	*2.00*
20	A102	50c on 6p rose lilac	.45	.25
21	A103	65c on 8p bright rose	6.50	1.75
22	A103	75c on 9p dp ol grn	2.00	.30
23	A103	1sh on 1sh brown	.45	.25

Great Britain Nos 249A, 250, 251A Surcharged

Wmk. 259 *Perf. 14*

No.	Type	Description	Unused	Used
24	A104	2sh50c on 2sh6p yel grn	9.75	5.50
25	A104	5sh on 5sh dl red	9.75	*14.00*
26	A105	10sh on 10sh ultra	80.00	70.00
		Nos. 14-26 (13)	*116.80*	*110.90*

Great Britain Nos. 280, 281, 283 and 284 Surcharged Type "c"
Perf. 14½x14

1951, May 3 Wmk. 251

No.	Type	Description	Unused	Used
27	A101	5c on ½p lt orange	3.25	*4.25*
28	A101	10c on 1p ultra	2.75	*.85*
29	A101	20c on 2p lt red brown	3.25	.35
30	A101	25c on 2½p vermilion	3.25	.35

Great Britain Nos. 286-288 Surcharged

Perf. 11x12

1951, May 31 Wmk. 259

No.	Type	Description	Unused	Used
31	A121	2sh50c on 2sh6p grn	21.00	*30.00*
32	A121	5sh on 5sh dl red	24.00	*35.00*
33	A122	10sh on 10sh ultra	30.00	*35.00*
		Nos. 27-33 (7)	87.50	*105.80*

Surcharge arranged to fit the design on No. 33.

POSTAGE DUE STAMPS

Catalogue values for unused stamps in this section are for Never Hinged items.

Great Britain Nos. J26-J29, J32 Surcharged

1948 Wmk. 251 *Perf. 14x14½*

No.	Type	Description	Unused	Used
J1	D1	5c on ½p emer	11.00	*25.00*
J2	D1	10c on 1p car rose	11.00	*27.50*
J3	D1	20c on 2p blk brn	16.50	*18.00*
J4	D1	30c on 3p violet	13.00	*16.50*
J5	D1	1sh on 1sh blue	20.00	*35.00*
		Nos. J1-J5 (5)	71.50	*122.00*

Great Britain Nos. J26 to J29 and J32 Surcharged

1950, Feb. 6

No.	Type	Description	Unused	Used
J6	D1	5c on ½p emer	15.50	*65.00*
J7	D1	10c on 1p car rose	15.50	*21.00*
a.		"C" of CENTS omitted	*5,000.*	
		Lightly hinged	*3,000.*	
J8	D1	20c on 2p blk brn	16.00	*17.50*
J9	D1	30c on 3p violet	19.50	*26.00*
J10	D1	1sh on 1sh blue	21.00	*26.00*
		Nos. J6-J10 (5)	87.50	*155.50*

EAST AFRICAN FORCES

FOR USE IN SOMALIA (ITALIAN SOMALILAND)

Catalogue values for unused stamps in this section are for Never Hinged items.

12 Pence = 1 Shilling
100 Cents = 1 Shilling

Stamps of Great Britain 1938-42 Overprinted in Blue

Perf. 14½x14

1943, Jan. 15 Wmk. 251

No.	Type	Description	Unused	Used
1	A101	1p vermilion	.80	.65
2	A101	2p light orange	1.75	1.35
3	A101	2½p ultramarine	.80	*3.75*
4	A101	3p violet	1.10	.25
5	A101	5p light brown	1.90	.45
6	A101	6p rose lilac	1.10	*1.40*
7	A103	9p dp olive green	1.60	*2.40*
8	A103	1sh brown	2.75	.25

On Great Britain No. 249A

1946 Wmk. 259 *Perf. 14*

No.	Type	Description	Unused	Used
9	A104	2sh6p yellow green	16.00	8.00
		Nos. 1-9 (9)	27.80	*18.50*

Stamps of Great Britain, 1937-42 Surcharged

Perf. 14½x14

1948, May 27 Wmk. 251

No.	Type	Description	Unused	Used
10	A101	5c on ½p grn (II)	1.40	*2.15*
11	A101	15c on 1½p lt red brn (II)	2.00	*17.50*
12	A101	20c on 2p lt org (II)	3.50	*6.50*
13	A101	25c on 2½p ultra (II)	2.50	*5.00*
14	A101	30c on 3p vio (II)	2.50	*10.50*
15	A102	40c on 5p lt brown	1.40	.25
16	A102	50c on 6p rose lilac	.55	*2.25*
17	A103	75c on 9p dp ol grn	2.25	*27.50*
18	A103	1sh on 1sh brown	1.40	.25

Great Britain Nos. 249A and 250 Surcharged

Wmk. 259 *Perf. 14*

No.	Type	Description	Unused	Used
19	A104	2sh50c on 2sh6p yel grn	9.75	*29.00*
20	A104	5sh on 5sh dl red	21.00	*65.00*
		Nos. 10-20 (11)	48.25	*165.90*

Stamps of Great Britain 1937-42 Surcharged

Perf. 14½x14

1950, Jan. 2 Wmk. 251

No.	Type	Description	Unused	Used
21	A101	5c on ½p grn (II)	.25	*3.50*
22	A101	15c on 1½p lt red brn (II)	.85	*19.00*
23	A101	20c on 2p lt org (II)	.85	*8.50*
24	A101	25c on 2½p ultra (II)	.55	*13.50*
25	A101	30c on 3p violet (II)	1.40	*9.75*
26	A102	40c on 5p light brn	.65	*2.50*
27	A102	50c on 6p rose lilac	.55	*1.10*
28	A103	75c on 9p deep ol grn	2.25	*13.00*
29	A103	1sh on 1sh brown	.70	*1.75*

Great Britain Nos. 249A and 250 Surcharged

Wmk. 259 *Perf. 14*

No.	Type	Description	Unused	Used
30	A104	2sh50c on 2sh 6p yel grn	8.50	*37.50*
31	A104	5sh on 5sh dull red	22.00	*55.00*
		Nos. 21-31 (11)	38.55	*165.10*

FOR USE IN TRIPOLITANIA

Catalogue values for unused stamps in this section are for Never Hinged items.

Stamps of Great Britain, 1937-42, Surcharged

M.A.L. = Military Authority Lire

Perf. 14½x14

1948, July 1 **Wmk. 251**

1 A101 1 l on ½p green (II) 1.00 *4.50*
2 A101 2 l on 1p ver (II) .50 .25
3 A101 3 l on 1½p lt red brn (II) .50 *.50*
4 A101 4 l on 2p lt org (II) .50 *.75*
5 A101 5 l on 2½p ultra (II) .50 .25
6 A101 6 l on 3p violet (II) .50 *.45*
7 A102 10 l on 5p lt brown .50 .25
8 A102 12 l on 6p rose lilac .50 .25
9 A103 18 l on 9p dp ol grn 1.50 *1.75*
10 A103 24 l on 1sh brown 2.50 *3.00*

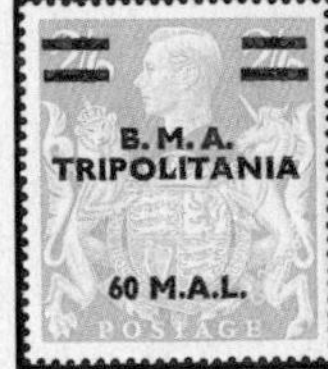

Great Britain Nos. 249A, 250 and 251A Surcharged

Wmk. 259 ***Perf. 14***

11 A104 60 l on 2sh6p yel grn 9.25 *16.50*
12 A104 120 l on 5sh dl red 28.00 *30.00*
13 A105 240 l on 10sh ultra 32.50 *150.00*
Nos. 1-13 (13) 78.25 *208.45*

Stamps of Great Britain 1937-42 Surcharged

Perf. 14½x14

1950, Feb. 6 **Wmk. 251**

14 A101 1 l on ½p green (II) 6.00 *13.00*
15 A101 2 l on 1p ver (II) 5.00 *.45*
16 A101 3 l on 1½p lt red brn (II) 4.00 *13.00*
17 A101 4 l on 2p lt org (II) 4.25 *4.40*
18 A101 5 l on 2½p ultra (II) 2.25 *.75*
19 A101 6 l on 3p violet (II) 3.75 *3.25*
20 A102 10 l on 5p lt brown 3.75 *4.00*
21 A102 12 l on 6p rose lilac 5.00 .50
22 A103 18 l on 9p dp ol grn 7.75 *2.75*
23 A103 24 l on 1sh brown 7.25 *3.75*

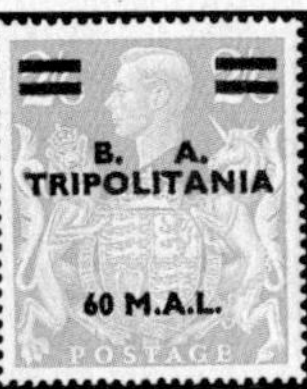

Great Britain Nos. 249A, 250 and 251A Surcharged

Wmk. 259 ***Perf. 14***

24 A104 60 l on 2sh6p yel grn 18.50 *40.00*
25 A104 120 l on 5sh dl red 40.00 *87.50*
26 A105 240 l on 10sh ultra 55.00 *165.00*
Nos. 14-26 (13) 162.50 *338.35*

Great Britain Nos. 280-284 Surcharged like Nos. 14-23

Perf. 14½x14

1951, May 3 **Wmk. 251**

27 A101 1 l on ½p lt org .55 *10.00*
28 A101 2 l on 1p ultra .55 *1.10*
29 A101 3 l on 1½p green .55 *9.25*
30 A101 4 l on 2p lt red brown .55 *1.40*
31 A101 5 l on 2½p ver .65 *8.50*

Great Britain Nos. 286-288 Surcharged

1951, May 3 **Wmk. 259** ***Perf. 11x12***

32 A121 60 l on 2sh6p grn 20.00 *40.00*
33 A121 120 l on 5sh dl red 20.00 *40.00*
34 A122 240 l on 10sh ultra 50.00 *82.50*
Nos. 27-34 (8) 92.85 *192.75*

Surcharge arranged to fit the design on No. 34.

POSTAGE DUE STAMPS

Catalogue values for unused stamps in this section are for Never Hinged items.

Great Britain Nos. J26-J29, J32 Surcharged

1948 **Wmk. 251** ***Perf. 14x14½***

J1 D1 1 l on ½p emer 7.50 *65.00*
J2 D1 2 l on 1p car rose 2.50 *57.50*
J3 D1 4 l on 2p blk brn 13.50 *52.50*
J4 D1 6 l on 3p violet 8.00 *30.00*
J5 D1 24 l on 1sh blue 30.00 *115.00*
Nos. J1-J5 (5) 61.50 *320.00*

Great Britain Nos. J26-J29, J32 Surcharged

1950, Feb. 6

J6 D1 1 l on ½p emer 15.00 *115.00*
J7 D1 2 l on 1p car rose 10.00 *35.00*
J8 D1 4 l on 2p blk brn 12.00 *50.00*
J9 D1 6 l on 3p violet 20.00 *80.00*
J10 D1 24 l on 1sh blue 57.50 *185.00*
Nos. J6-J10 (5) 114.50 *465.00*

CHINA

100 Cents = 1 Dollar

Stamps of Hong Kong, 1912-14, Overprinted

1917 **Wmk. 3** ***Perf. 14***

Ordinary Paper

1 A11 1c brown 4.50 3.00
2 A11 2c deep green 8.00 .35
3 A12 4c scarlet 6.25 .35
4 A13 6c orange 6.25 .70
5 A12 8c gray 14.00 1.40
6 A11 10c ultramarine 14.00 .35

Chalky Paper

7 A14 12c violet, *yel* 12.50 5.00
8 A14 20c olive grn & vio 14.00 .70
9 A15 25c red vio & dl vio (on #117) 9.25 *17.50*
10 A13 30c orange & violet 40.00 6.25
11 A14 50c black, *emerald* 40.00 6.50
a. 50c blk, *blue green*, ol back 75.00 1.75
b. 50c blk, *emerald*, ol back 50.00 9.75
12 A11 $1 blue & vio, *bl* 80.00 2.90
13 A14 $2 black & red 260.00 62.50
14 A13 $3 violet & grn 625.00 210.00
15 A14 $5 red & grn, *bl grn*, ol back 400.00 290.00
16 A13 $10 blk & vio, *red* 1,000. 550.00
Nos. 1-16 (16) 2,534. 1,158.

Stamps of Hong Kong, 1921-26, Overprinted

1922-27 **Ordinary Paper** **Wmk. 4**

17 A11 1c brown 2.60 *4.25*
18 A11 2c green 4.00 2.60
19 A12 4c scarlet 7.00 2.60
20 A13 6c orange 5.00 4.75
21 A12 8c gray 9.25 *17.50*
22 A11 10c ultramarine 10.00 4.00

Chalky Paper

23 A14 20c ol grn & vio 16.00 5.75
24 A15 25c red violet & dull vio 26.00 *80.00*
25 A14 50c blk, *emerald* ('27) 70.00 *210.00*
26 A11 $1 ultra & vio, *bl* 85.00 *70.00*
27 A14 $2 black & red 225.00 *290.00*
Nos. 17-27 (11) 459.85 *691.45*

MOROCCO

100 Centimos = 1 Peseta
12 Pence = 1 Shilling
20 Shillings = 1 Pound
100 Centimes = 1 Franc

These stamps were issued for various purposes:

a — For general use at the British Post Offices throughout Morocco.

b — For use in the Spanish Zone of Northern Morocco.

c — For use in the French Zone of Southern Morocco.

d — For use in the International Zone of Tangier.

For convenience these stamps are listed in four groups according to the coinage expressed or surcharged on the stamps, namely:

#1-108: Value expressed in Spanish currency.
#201-280: Value in British currency.
#401-440: Value in French currency.
#501-611: Stamps overprinted "Tangier."

Spanish Currency

Gibraltar Stamps of 1889-95 Overprinted

1898 **Wmk. 2** ***Perf. 14***

Black Overprint

1 A11 5c green 3.00 *3.00*
2 A11 10c carmine rose 5.00 .85
b. Double overprint 625.00
3 A11 20c olive green 11.00 6.25
4 A11 25c ultramarine 4.50 .70
5 A11 40c orange brown 7.00 3.75
6 A11 50c violet 20.00 *26.00*
7 A11 1pe bister & blue 20.00 *30.00*
8 A11 2pe blk & car rose 25.00 *30.00*
Nos. 1-8 (8) 95.50 *100.55*

Dark Blue Overprint

9 A11 40c orange brown *50.00* *35.00*
10 A11 50c violet 14.00 14.00
11 A11 1pe bister & blue *175.00* *210.00*

Inverted "V" for "A"

1a A11 5c 40.00 *50.00*
2a A11 10c 260.00 310.00
3a A11 20c 85.00 *95.00*
4a A11 25c 140.00 *150.00*
5a A11 40c 190.00 210.00
6a A11 50c 290.00 *375.00*
7a A11 1pe 275.00 *400.00*
8a A11 2pe 350.00 *400.00*

Overprinted in Black

(Narrower "M," ear of "g" horiz.)

1899

12 A11 5c green .55 *1.10*
13 A11 10c carmine rose 2.90 .35
14 A11 20c olive green 8.00 .80
15 A11 25c ultramarine 12.50 1.00
16 A11 40c orange brown 47.50 35.00
17 A11 50c violet 11.00 4.00
18 A11 1pe bister & blue 32.50 *50.00*
19 A11 2pe blk & car rose 62.50 *55.00*
Nos. 12-19 (8) 177.45 *147.25*

"M" with long serif

12a A11 5c 10.00 *15.00*
13a A11 10c 11.50 *13.50*
14a A11 20c 40.00 *42.50*
15a A11 25c 50.00 *55.00*
16a A11 40c 260.00 *290.00*
17a A11 50c 125.00 *140.00*
18a A11 1pe *175.00* *290.00*
19a A11 2pe 375.00 *400.00*

Type of Gibraltar, 1903, with Value in Spanish Currency, Overprinted

1903-05

20 A12 5c gray grn & bl grn 11.00 4.00
21 A12 10c violet, *red* 9.75 .45
22 A12 20c gray grn & car rose ('04) 20.00 *52.50*
23 A12 25c vio & blk, *bl* 9.25 .35
24 A12 50c violet 100.00 *190.00*
25 A12 1pe blk & car rose 47.50 *175.00*
26 A12 2pe black & ultra 57.50 *140.00*
Nos. 20-26 (7) 255.00 *562.30*

"M" with long serif

20a A12 5c 57.50 *62.50*
21a A12 10c 50.00 45.00
22a A12 20c 110.00 *210.00*
23a A12 25c 57.50 50.00
24a A12 50c 400.00 *700.00*
25a A12 1pe 260.00 *575.00*
26a A12 2pe 300.00 *550.00*

1905-06 **Wmk. 3** **Chalky Paper**

27 A12 5c gray grn & bl grn 11.00 *3.50*
28 A12 10c violet, *red* 12.50 3.25
29 A12 20c gray grn & car rose ('06) 6.25 *35.00*
30 A12 25c vio & blk, *bl* ('06) 45.00 9.75
31 A12 50c violet 8.50 *50.00*
32 A12 1pe blk & car rose 32.50 *92.50*
33 A12 2pe black & ultra 18.00 *40.00*
Nos. 27-33 (7) 133.75 *233.00*

No. 29 is on ordinary paper. Nos. 27 and 28 are on both ordinary and chalky paper.

"M" with long serif

27a A12 5c 62.50 50.00
28a A12 10c 62.50 42.50
29a A12 20c 57.50 *175.00*
30a A12 25c 350.00 175.00
31a A12 50c 175.00 *290.00*
32a A12 1pe 225.00 *375.00*
33a A12 2pe 210.00 *290.00*

Numerous other minor overprint varieties exist of Nos. 1-33.

British Stamps of 1902-10 Surcharged in Spanish Currency

a b

1907-10 **Wmk. 30**

34(a) A66 5c on ½p pale grn 9.25 .25
35(a) A66 10c on 1p car 13.50 .25
36(a) A67 15c on 1½p vio & grn 3.50 .25
a. "1" of "15" omitted 5,400.
37(a) A68 20c on 2p grn & car 3.00 .25
38(a) A66 25c on 2½p ultra 2.00 .25
39(a) A70 40c on 4p brn & grn 1.40 *3.50*
40(a) A70 40c on 4p org ('10) 1.10 .70
41(a) A71 50c on 5p lil & ultra 2.25 *3.75*
42(a) A73 1pe on 10p car rose & vio 25.00 *14.00*

Wmk. 31

43(b) A75 3pe on 2sh6p vio 24.00 *29.00*
44(b) A76 6pe on 5sh car rose 40.00 *52.50*
45(b) A77 12pe on 10sh ultra 85.00 85.00
Nos. 34-45 (12) 210.00 *189.70*

Nos. 36-37, 39-43 are on chalky paper.

Great Britain Nos. 153, 154 and 148 Surcharged

1912 **Wmk. 30** ***Perf. 15x14***

46(a) A80 5c on ½p yel grn 3.50 .25
47(a) A81 10c on 1p scarlet 1.10 .25
48(a) A66 25c on 2½p ultra 42.50 30.00
Nos. 46-48 (3) 47.10 30.50

British Stamps of 1912-18 Surcharged in Black or Carmine

c

d

e

1914-18 **Wmk. 33**
49 A82(a) 5c on ½p grn .85 .25
50 A83(d) 10c on 1p scar 1.75 .25
51 A84(c) 15c on 1½p red brn ('15) 1.10 .25
52 A85(d) 20c on 2p org (I) 1.10 .25
53 A86(d) 25c on 2½p ultra 2.00 .25
54 A90(d) 1pe on 10p lt bl 4.00 *8.00*

Wmk. 34
Perf. 11x12
55 A91(e) 3pe on 2sh6p lt brn 35.00 *160.00*
a. 3pe on 2sh6p dark brown 45.00 *125.00*
56 A91(e) 6pe on 5sh car 32.50 *55.00*
a. 6pe on 5sh light carmine 150.00 *210.00*
57 A91(e) 12pe on 10sh dk bl (C) 110.00 *190.00*
a. 12pe on 10sh blue 100.00 *190.00*
Nos. 49-57 (9) 188.30 *414.25*

Great Britain Nos. 159, 165 Surcharged in Spanish Currency

f

g

1917-23 **Wmk. 33** ***Perf. 15x14***
58 A82(f) 3c on ½p green 1.40 *5.00*
59 A88(g) 40c on 4p sl green 3.50 *4.50*

Great Britain Nos. 189, 191, 179 Surcharged in Spanish Currency

1926 **Wmk. 35**
60 A84(c) 15c on 1½p red brn 8.50 *26.00*
61 A86(d) 25c on 2½p ultra 2.90 *2.90*

Wmk. 34
Perf. 11x12
62 A91(e) 3pe on 2sh6p brn 26.00 *85.00*
Nos. 60-62 (3) 37.40 *113.90*

British Stamps of 1924 Surcharged in Spanish Currency

1929-31 **Wmk. 35** ***Perf. 15x14***
63 A82(a) 5c on ½p grn ('31) 3.00 *17.50*
64 A83(d) 10c on 1p scar 21.00 *30.00*
65 A85(d) 20c on 2p org (II) ('31) 3.50 *10.00*
66 A88(g) 40c on 4p sl grn ('30) 2.90 2.90
Nos. 63-66 (4) 30.40 *60.40*

Silver Jubilee Issue

Great Britain Nos. 220-229 Srchd. in Blue or Red

1935, May 8 ***Perf. 14½x14***
67 A98 5c on ½p dk grn 1.10 1.10
68 A98 10c on 1p car 3.00 2.50
a. Pair, one reading "CEN-TIMES" 1,600. 1,800.
69 A98 15c on 1½p red brn 6.25 *20.00*
70 A98 25c on 2½p ultra (R) 4.00 2.50
Nos. 67-70 (4) 14.35 *26.10*

25th anniv. of the reign of King George V.

Catalogue values for unused stamps in this section, from this point to the end of the section, are for Never Hinged items.

Great Britain Nos. 210-214, 216, 219 Surcharged in Spanish Currency

1935-37 **Photo.**
71 A97(a) 5c on ½p dk grn ('36) 1.25 *21.00*
72 A97(d) 10c on 1p car 3.25 *11.00*
73 A97(c) 15c on 1½p red brn 7.00 3.75
74 A97(d) 20c on 2p red org ('00) .75 .30
75 A97(d) 25c on 2½p ultra ('36) 1.75 *5.00*
76 A97(d) 40c on 4p dk sl grn ('37) .75 *3.50*
77 A97(d) 1pe on 10p Prus bl ('37) 7.00 .35
Nos. 71-77 (7) 21.75 *44.90*

Great Britain Nos. 230-233 Surcharged

"MOROCCO" 14mm

1936 **Wmk. 250**
78 A99 5c on ½p dk green .25 .25
79 A99 10c on 1p crimson .55 *2.25*
a. "Morocco" 15mm long 4.00 *16.00*
80 A99 15c on 1½p red brown .25 .25
81 A99 25c on 2½p brt ultra .25 .25
Nos. 78-81 (4) 1.30 *3.00*

Great Britain #234 Surcharged in Blue

Perf. 14½x14
1937, May 13 **Wmk. 251**
82 A100 15c on 1½p purple brn .80 .80

Coronation of George VI and Elizabeth.

Great Britain Nos. 235-237, 239, 241, 244 Surcharged in Blue or Black

h

1937-40
83 A101 5c on ½p dp grn (Bl) 1.40 .35
84 A101 10c on 1p scarlet 1.10 .25
85 A101 15c on 1½p red brown (Bl) 1.40 .30
86 A101 25c on 2½p brt ultra 2.25 1.40
87 A102 40c on 4p gray grn ('40) 35.00 15.00
88 A103 70c on 7p emer ('40) 2.00 *16.00*
Nos. 83-88 (6) 43.15 *33.30*

Great Britain Nos. 252-254, 256 Surcharged in Blue or Black

1940, May 6
89 A106 5c on ½p dp grn (Bl) .35 *3.00*
90 A106 10c on 1p scarlet 4.25 *2.90*
91 A106 15c on 1½p red brn (Bl) .80 *2.90*
92 A106 25c on 2½p brt ultra .90 *1.10*
Nos. 89-92 (4) 6.30 *9.90*

Centenary of the postage stamp.

Great Britain Nos. 267 and 268 Surcharged in Black

i

j

Perf. 14½x14, 14x14½
1948, Apr. 26 **Wmk. 251**
93 A109(i) 25c on 2½p 1.10 .35
94 A110(j) 45pe on £1 19.00 *25.00*

25th anniv. of the marriage of King George VI and Queen Elizabeth.

Great Britain Nos. 271-274 Surcharged "MOROCCO AGENCIES" and New Value

1948, July 29 ***Perf. 14½x14***
95 A113 25c on 2½p brt ultra .55 *1.40*
96 A114 30c on 3p dp vio .55 *1.40*
97 A115 60c on 6p red vio .55 *1.40*
98 A116 1.20pe on 1sh dk brn .70 *1.40*
a. Double surcharge 925.00
Nos. 95-98 (4) 2.35 *5.60*

1948 Olympic Games, Wembley, July-Aug. A square of dots obliterates the original denomination on No. 98.

Great Britain Nos. 280-282, 284-285, 247 Surcharged Type "h"

1951-52 **Wmk. 251** ***Perf. 14½x14***
99 A101 5c on ½p lt org 2.25 *5.00*
100 A101 10c on 1p ultra 3.75 *8.50*
101 A101 15c on 1½p green 2.00 *19.00*
102 A101 25c on 2½p ver 2.00 *11.00*
103 A102 40c on 4p ultra ('52) .70 *11.50*
104 A103 1pe on 10p ryl bl ('52) 2.50 *4.00*
Nos. 99-104 (6) 13.20 *59.00*

Great Britain Nos. 292-293 Surcharged Type "h"

1954-55 **Wmk. 298**
105 A126 5c on ½c red org .25 *2.00*
106 A126 10c on 1p ultra ('55) .50 *3.00*

Great Britain Nos. 317 and 323 Surcharged type "h"

1956 **Wmk. 308** ***Perf. 14x14½***
107 A126 5c on ½p red org .25 *2.00*
108 A128 40c on 4p ultra 1.10 *3.00*

BRITISH CURRENCY

Stamps of Morocco Agencies were accepted for postage in Great Britain, starting in mid-1950. Examples with contemporaneous Morocco cancellations sell for more.

British Stamps of 1902-11 Overprinted

a

b

Overprint "a" 14½mm long

1907-12 **Wmk. 30** ***Perf. 14***
Ordinary Paper
201 A66 ½p pale yel grn 2.50 *9.75*
202 A66 1p carmine 11.00 6.25

Chalky Paper
203 A68 2p green & car 11.50 6.25
204 A70 4p brown & grn 4.25 *4.50*
205 A70 4p orange ('12) 11.50 *12.50*
a. Perf. 15x14 25.00 *27.50*
206 A66 6p dull vio 17.00 *21.00*
207 A74 1sh car rose & grn 30.00 *19.00*

Overprinted Type "b"
Wmk. 31
208 A75 2sh6p violet 92.50 *140.00*
Nos. 201-208 (8) 180.25 *219.25*

British Stamps of 1912-18 Overprinted Type "a"
Perf. 14½x14, 15x14
1914-21 **Wmk. 33**
209 A82 ½p green ('18) 4.00 .55
210 A83 1p scarlet ('17) 1.00 .25
211 A84 1½p red brn ('21) 3.75 *14.00*
212 A85 2p orange ('18) 4.50 .70
213 A87 3p violet ('21) 1.40 .40
214 A88 4p slate grn ('21) 3.75 1.40
215 A89 6p dull vio ('21) 5.50 *17.50*
216 A90 1sh bister ('17) 6.25 1.40

c

Wmk. 34 ***Perf. 11x12***
217 A91 2sh6p lt brown 42.50 *57.50*
a. 2sh6p brown 55.00 35.00
b. 2sh6p black brown 52.50 *62.50*
c. Double overprint 1,900. 1,350.
Nos. 209-217 (9) 72.65 *93.70*

Same Overprint on Great Britain Nos. 179-180

1925-31
218 A91 2sh6p gray brown 42.50 29.00
219 A91 5sh car rose ('31) 62.50 *100.00*

British Stamps of 1924 Overprinted Type "a" (14½mm long)

1925-31 **Wmk. 35** ***Perf. 15x14***
220 A82 ½p green 2.25 .55
221 A84 1½p red brn ('31) 13.50 *15.00*
222 A85 2p dp org (Die II) 2.50 1.10
223 A86 2½p ultra 2.50 *5.75*
224 A89 6p red vio ('31) 2.25 *9.50*
225 A90 1sh bister 19.00 5.75
Nos. 220-225 (6) 42.00 *37.65*

Silver Jubilee Issue

Great Britain Nos. 226-229 Overprinted in Blue or Red

1935, May 8 ***Perf. 14½x14***
226 A98 ½p dark green (Bl) 1.40 *7.50*
227 A98 1p carmine (Bl) 1.40 *7.50*
228 A98 1½p red brown (Bl) 2.50 *11.00*
229 A98 2½p ultramarine (R) 2.90 2.90
Nos. 226-229 (4) 8.20 *28.90*

25th anniversary of the reign of King George V.

British Stamps of 1924 Overprinted Type "a" (15½mm long)

1935-36
230 A82 ½p green 9.50 *45.00*
231 A86 2½p ultra *110.00* 35.00
232 A88 4p slate green 8.00 *40.00*
233 A89 6p red violet 1.10 .70
234 A90 1sh bister 62.50 57.50
Nos. 230-234 (5) 191.10 *178.20*

British Stamps of 1934-36 Overprinted "MOROCCO AGENCIES"

1935-36
235 A97 1p carmine 3.50 *16.00*
236 A97 1½p red brn ('36) 3.50 *19.00*
237 A97 2p red org ('36) 1.40 *9.00*
238 A97 2½p ultra ('36) 2.00 *4.75*
239 A97 3p dk vio ('36) .55 .35
240 A97 4p dk sl grn ('36) .55 .35
241 A97 1sh bis brn ('36) .90 *4.00*

Overprinted Type "c"

Wmk. 34

Perf. 11x12

242 A91 2sh6p brown 45.00 *70.00*
243 A91 5sh car ('37) 27.50 *110.00*
Nos. 235-243 (9) 84.90 *233.45*

Catalogue values for unused stamps in this section, from this point to the end of the section, are for Never Hinged items.

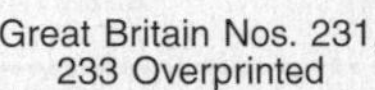
Great Britain Nos. 231, 233 Overprinted

"MOROCCO" 14mm

1936 Wmk. 250 *Perf. 14½x14*

244 A99 1p crimson .25 .25
a. "Morocco" 15mm long 7.00 *19.00*
245 A99 2½p bright ultra .25 .25
a. "Morocco" 15mm long 1.10 4.75

Great Britain Nos. 258-263, 241-248, 266, 249A-250 Overprinted "MOROCCO AGENCIES" (14½mm long)

1949, Aug. 16 Wmk. 251

246 A101 ½p green 2.00 *8.00*
247 A101 1p vermilion 3.00 *10.00*
248 A101 1½p lt red brown 3.00 *9.50*
249 A101 2p lt orange 3.50 *10.00*
250 A101 2½p ultra 3.75 *11.50*
251 A101 3p violet 1.75 *2.00*
252 A102 4p gray green .55 *1.40*
253 A102 5p lt brown 3.50 *17.00*
254 A102 6p rose lilac 1.75 1.75
255 A103 7p emerald .55 *18.00*
256 A103 8p brt rose 3.50 *7.50*
257 A103 9p dp olive grn .55 *12.50*
258 A103 10p royal blue .55 *7.50*
259 A103 11p violet brn .80 *8.50*
260 A103 1sh brown 3.00 *7.00*

"MOROCCO AGENCIES"

17½mm long

Wmk. 259

Perf. 14

261 A104 2sh6p yellow grn 18.00 *40.00*
262 A104 5sh dull red 32.50 *70.00*
Nos. 246-262 (17) 82.25 *242.15*

Great Britain Nos. 280-284, 286-287 Overprinted "MOROCCO AGENCIES" (14½mm long)

Perf. 14½x14

1951, May 3 Wmk. 251

263 A101 ½p lt orange 2.25 1.10
264 A101 1p ultra 2.25 1.60
265 A101 1½p green 2.25 *3.00*
266 A101 2p lt red brown 2.50 *4.50*
267 A101 2½p vermilion 2.25 *4.75*

"MOROCCO AGENCIES"

17½mm long

Wmk. 259

Perf. 11x12

268 A121 2sh6p green 15.00 *24.00*
269 A121 5sh dull red 15.00 *26.00*
Nos. 263-269 (7) 41.50 *64.95*

Great Britain Nos. 292-296, 298-300, 302 and 306 Overprinted "MOROCCO AGENCIES" (14½mm long)

1952-55 Wmk. 298 *Perf. 14½x14*

270 A126 ½p red orange .25 .25
271 A126 1p ultramarine .25 *2.00*
272 A126 1½p green ('52) .25 .25
273 A126 2p red brown .30 *2.25*
274 A127 2½p scarlet ('52) .25 *1.40*
275 A128 4p ultra ('55) 1.75 *4.00*
276 A129 5p light brown .75 .70
277 A129 6p lilac rose ('55) 1.00 *4.00*
278 A130 8p bright rose .80 .80
279 A131 1sh brown .80 .70
Nos. 270-279 (10) 6.40 *16.35*

Same Ovpt. on Great Britain No. 321

1956 Wmk. 308

280 A127 2½p scarlet 1.00 *3.75*

French Currency

British Stamps of 1912-22 Surcharged in French Currency in Red or Black

h

i

Perf. 14½x14, 15x14

1917-24 Wmk. 33

401 A82(h) 3c on ½p grn (R) 1.10 *2.90*
402 A82(h) 5c on ½p green .45 1.75
403 A83(h) 10c on 1p scarlet 3.75 .45
404 A84(h) 15c on 1½p red brn 2.90 .25
405 A86(h) 25c on 2½p ultra 2.25 .25
406 A88(h) 40c on 4p slate grn 2.90 1.75
407 A89(h) 50c on 5p yel brn ('23) .90 *3.00*
408 A90(h) 75c on 9p ol grn ('24) 1.10 .85
409 A90(i) 1fr on 10p lt blue 8.00 3.50
Nos. 401-409 (9) 23.35 *14.70*

Great Britain No. 179 Surcharged

k

1924 Wmk. 34 *Perf. 11x12*

410 A91(k) 3fr on 2sh6p brn 8.50 1.75

British Stamps of 1924 Surcharged in French Currency as in 1917-24

1925-26 Wmk. 35 *Perf. 15x14*

411 A82(h) 5c on ½p green .35 *7.50*
412 A83(h) 10c on 1p scarlet .35 *2.25*
413 A84(h) 15c on 1½p red brn 1.10 *2.00*
414 A86(h) 25c on 2½p ultra 1.75 .55
415 A88(h) 40c on 4p sl green .70 *.90*
416 A89(h) 50c on 5p yel brn 1.75 .25
417 A90(h) 75c on 9p ol green 4.00 .25
418 A90(i) 1fr on 10p dl blue 1.40 .25
Nos. 411-418 (8) 11.40 *13.95*

Great Britain Nos. 180, 198 and 200 Surcharged type "k"

1932 Wmk. 34 *Perf. 11x12*

419 A91 6fr on 5sh car rose 42.50 *47.50*

1934 Wmk. 35 *Perf. 14½x14*

420 A90 90c on 9p ol green 18.00 8.50
421 A90 1.50fr on 1sh bister 11.50 2.50

Silver Jubilee Issue

Great Britain Nos. 226-229 Surcharged in Blue or Red

1935, May 8 *Perf. 14½x14*

422 A98 5c on ½p dk green .25 .25
423 A98 10c on 1p carmine 3.00 .85
424 A98 15c on 1½p red brn .40 *.55*
425 A98 25c on 2½p ultra (R) .25 *.35*
Nos. 422-425 (4) 3.90 2.00

25th anniv. of the reign of King George V.

British Stamps of 1934-36 Surcharged Types "h" or "k"

Perf. 14½x14

1935-37 Photo. Wmk. 35

426 A97(h) 5c on ½p dk grn .55 *5.75*
427 A97(h) 10c on 1p car ('36) .40 .35
428 A97(h) 15c on 1½p red brn 5.50 *6.25*
429 A97(h) 25c on 2½p ultra .35 .25
430 A97(h) 40c on 4p dk sl grn .35 .25
431 A97(h) 50c on 5p yel brn .35 .25
432 A97(h) 90c on 9p dk ol grn .40 *2.00*
433 A97(k) 1fr on 10p Prus bl .35 .35
434 A97(h) 1.50fr on 1sh bister brn ('37) .85 *3.75*

Waterlow Printing

Wmk. 34 *Perf. 11x12*

435 A91(k) 3fr on 2sh6p brn 5.50 *14.00*
436 A91(k) 6fr on 5sh car ('36) 7.00 *24.00*
Nos. 426-436 (11) 21.60 *57.20*

Great Britain Nos. 230, 232 Surcharged

1936 Wmk. 250 *Perf. 14½x14*

437 A99 5c on ½p dark green .25 .25
438 A99 15c on 1½p red brown .25 .25

Great Britain No. 234 Surcharged in Blue

1937, May 13 Wmk. 251

439 A100 15c on 1½p pur brn .35 .25

Coronation of George VI and Elizabeth.

Great Britain No. 235 Surcharged in Blue

1937

440 A101 5c on ½p deep green 2.50 *2.90*

For Use in the International Zone of Tangier

Great Britain Nos. 187-190 Overprinted in Black — a

1927 Wmk. 35 *Perf. 15x14*

501 A82 ½p green 3.50 .25
502 A83 1p scarlet 3.50 .30
503 A84 1½p red brown 7.00 4.25
504 A85 2p orange (II) 3.75 .25
Nos. 501-504 (4) 17.75 5.05

Same Overprint on Great Britain Nos. 210-212

1934-35 Photo. *Perf. 14½x14*

505 A97 ½p dark green 1.40 *1.75*
506 A97 1p carmine 4.75 2.75
507 A97 1½p red brown .55 .25
Nos. 505-507 (3) 6.70 *4.75*

Silver Jubilee Issue

Great Britain Nos. 226-228 Overprinted in Blue

b

1935, May 8

508 A98 ½p dark green 1.40 *5.75*
509 A98 1p carmine 16.00 *17.00*
510 A98 1½p red brown 1.40 1.10
Nos. 508-510 (3) 18.80 *23.85*

25th anniv. of the reign of King George V.

Great Britain Nos. 230-232 Overprinted Type "a"

1936 Wmk. 250

511 A99 ½p dark green .25 .25
512 A99 1p crimson .25 .25
513 A99 1½p red brown .25 .25
Nos. 511-513 (3) .75 .75

Great Britain No. 234 Overprinted Type "b" in Blue

1937, May 13 Wmk. 251

514 A100 1½p purple brown .55 .55

Coronation of George VI and Elizabeth.

Great Britain Nos. 235-237 Overprinted in Blue or Black — c

1937 *Perf. 14½x14*

515 A101 ½p deep green (Bl) 2.75 1.75
516 A101 1p scarlet (Bk) 8.00 1.75
517 A101 1½p red brown (Bl) 2.75 .30
Nos. 515-517 (3) 13.50 3.80

Great Britain Nos. 252-254 Ovptd. Type "a" in Blue or Black

1940, May 6

518 A106 ½p deep green (Bl) .35 *5.50*
519 A106 1p scarlet (Bk) .50 *.60*
520 A106 1½p red brown (Bl) 2.25 *5.75*
Nos. 518-520 (3) 3.10 *11.85*

Centenary of the postage stamp.

Great Britain Nos. 258 and 259 Overprinted Type "c" in Blue or Black

1944-45

521 A101 ½p green (Bl) 12.50 5.00
522 A101 1p ver (Bk) ('45) 12.50 3.50

Catalogue values for unused stamps in this section, from this point to the end of the section, are for Never Hinged items.

Great Britain Nos. 264-265 Overprinted

d

e

1946, June 11

523 A107(d) 2½p bright ultra .75 .75
524 A108(e) 3p violet .75 *2.25*

Return to peace at close of World War II.

Great Britain Nos. 267 and 268 Overprinted Type "a"

1948, Apr. 26 *Perf. 14½x14, 14x14½*

525 A109 2½p bright ultra .60 .25
a. Pair, one without overprint *5,400.*
526 A110 £1 dp chalky bl 22.50 29.00

25th anniv. of the marriage of King George VI and Queen Elizabeth.

Great Britain Nos. 271 to 274 Overprinted Type "a"

1948, July 29 *Perf. 14½x14*

527 A113 2½p bright ultra 1.10 *2.25*
528 A114 3p deep violet 1.10 *2.25*
529 A115 6p red violet 1.10 *2.25*
530 A116 1sh dark brown 1.10 *1.40*
Nos. 527-530 (4) 4.40 *8.15*

1948 Olympic Games, Wembley, July-Aug.

Stamps of Great Britain, 1937-47, and Nos. 249A, 250 and 251A Overprinted Type "c"

1949, Jan. 1

531 A101 2p lt org (II) 5.75 *7.00*
532 A101 2½p ultra (II) 2.00 *7.00*
533 A101 3p violet (II) .80 *1.40*
534 A102 4p gray green 12.50 11.50
535 A102 5p light brown 4.25 *22.50*
536 A102 6p rose lilac .80 .35
537 A103 7p emerald 1.40 *15.00*
538 A103 8p bright rose 4.25 *12.50*
539 A103 9p deep ol grn 1.40 *13.50*
540 A103 10p royal blue 1.40 *15.00*

541 A103 11p violet brn 1.75 12.50
542 A103 1sh brown 1.40 3.00

Wmk. 259

Perf. 14

543 A104 2sh6p yellow grn 5.00 13.50
544 A104 5sh dull red 15.00 42.50
545 A105 10sh ultra 50.00 110.00
Nos. 531-545 (15) 107.70 287.25

Great Britain Nos. 276 to 279 Overprinted Type "a"

Perf. 14½x14

1949, Oct. 10 **Wmk. 251**

546 A117 2½p bright ultra .80 3.00
547 A118 3p bright violet .80 2.00
548 A119 6p red violet .80 1.40
549 A120 1sh brown .80 3.75
Nos. 546-549 (4) 3.20 10.15

Great Britain Nos. 280-288 Overprinted Type "c" or "a" (Shilling Values)

1950-51

550 A101 ½p lt orange 1.00 1.75
551 A101 1p ultra 1.10 3.50
552 A101 1½p green 1.10 16.00
553 A101 2p lt red brn 1.10 2.90
554 A101 2½p vermilion 1.10 5.75
555 A102 4p ultra ('50) 3.50 3.50

Wmk. 259

Perf. 11x12

556 A121 2sh6p green 11.00 5.75
557 A121 5sh dull red 17.50 19.00
558 A122 10sh ultra 22.50 19.00
Nos. 550-558 (9) 59.90 77.15

Great Britain Nos. 292-308 Overprinted Type c

1952-54 **Wmk. 298** ***Perf. 14½x14***

559 A126 ½p red org ('53) .25 .35
560 A126 1p ultra ('53) .25 .45
561 A126 1½p green ('52) .25 .35
562 A126 2p red brn ('53) .25 .90
563 A127 2½p scarlet ('52) .25 1.10
564 A127 3p dk pur (Dk Bl) .25 1.40
565 A128 4p ultra ('53) .70 2.25
566 A129 5p lt brown ('53) .70 2.25
567 A129 6p lilac rose .50 .25
568 A129 7p emerald .90 3.00
569 A130 8p brt rose ('53) .70 1.75
570 A130 9p dp olive grn 1.60 .85
571 A130 10p royal blue 1.60 3.00
572 A130 11p violet brn 1.60 3.75
573 A131 1sh brown ('53) .55 .80
574 A132 1sh3p dk grn ('53) .75 4.75
575 A131 1sh6p dk blue ('53) 1.10 2.00
Nos. 559-575 (17) 12.20 29.20

Stamp and Type of Great Britain 1955 Overprinted Type a

Perf. 11x12

1955, Sept. 23 **Engr.** **Wmk. 308**

576 A133 2sh6p dark brown 4.00 10.00
577 A133 5sh crimson 5.00 18.00
578 A133 10sh brt ultra 18.00 24.00
Nos. 576-578 (3) 27.00 52.00

Coronation Issue
Great Britain Nos. 313-316 Overprinted Type a

1953, June 3 **Photo.** **Wmk. 298**

579 A134 2½p scarlet .50 .40
580 A135 4p brt ultra .90 .65
581 A136 1sh3p dark green 2.75 1.90
582 A137 1sh6p dark blue 3.25 2.25
Nos. 579-582 (4) 7.40 5.20

Great Britain Nos. 317-323, 325 and 332 Overprinted Type c

1956 **Wmk. 308** ***Perf. 14½x14***

583 A126 ½p red orange .25 .55
584 A126 1p ultramarine .35 .55
585 A126 1½p green .65 1.40
586 A126 2p red brown 1.10 .55
587 A127 2½p scarlet .75 .55
588 A127 3p dark purple .85 1.00
589 A128 4p ultra 1.75 4.00
590 A129 6p lilac rose 1.10 1.00
591 A132 1sh3p dark green 1.25 15.00
Nos. 583-591 (9) 8.05 24.60

Great Britain Nos. 317-333 and 309-311 Overprinted 1857-1957 TANGIER

1957, Apr. 1 **Photo.** **Wmk. 308**

592 A126 ½p red orange .25 .25
593 A126 1p ultramarine .25 .25
594 A126 1½p green .25 .25
595 A126 2p red brown .25 .25
596 A127 2½p scarlet .25 1.40
597 A127 3p dark purple .25 .45
598 A128 4p ultramarine .35 .25
599 A129 5p lt brown .35 .40
600 A129 6p lilac rose .35 .40
601 A129 7p emerald .35 .40
602 A130 8p brt rose .35 1.10
603 A130 9p dp olive grn .35 .35
a. "TANGIER" omitted 5,500.
604 A130 10p royal blue .35 .35
605 A130 11p violet brown .35 .35
606 A131 1sh brown .35 .35
607 A132 1sh3p dark green .50 5.50
608 A131 1sh6p dark blue .55 1.75

Engr.

Perf. 11x12

609 A133 2sh6p dark brown 2.25 4.25
610 A133 5sh crimson 3.00 7.00
611 A133 10sh ultramarine 4.25 8.50
Nos. 592-611 (20) 15.20 33.80

Centenary of British P.O. in Tangier.

Nos. 609-611 are found with hyphen omitted (one stamp in sheet of 40).

British stamps overprinted "Tangier" were discontinued Apr. 30, 1957.

TURKISH EMPIRE

40 Paras = 1 Piaster
12 Pence = 1 Shilling (1905)

a

b

c

Surcharged on Great Britain Nos. 101, 104, 96

1885, Apr. 1 **Wmk. 30** ***Perf. 14***

1 A47(a) 40pa on 2½p lil 110.00 1.50
2 A45(b) 80pa on 5p grn 210.00 12.50

Wmk. 31

3 A44(c) 12pi on 2sh6p lil 52.50 27.50
a. Bluish paper 400.00 260.00
Nos. 1-3 (3) 372.50 41.50

Great Britain Nos. 114, 118 Surcharged

1887 **Wmk. 30**

4 A57(a) 40pa on 2½p vio, *bl* 4.75 .25
a. Double surcharge 2,250. 2,900.
5 A61(b) 80pa on 5p lil & bl 17.50 .35
a. Small "0" in "80" 225.00 100.00

Great Britain No. 111 Handstamp Surcharged — d

1893, Feb. 25

6 A54(d) 40pa on ½p ver 500.00 125.00

No. 6 was a provisional, made and used at Constantinople for five days. Excellent forgeries are known.

Great Britain No. 121 Surcharged — e

1896

7 A64(e) 4pi on 10p car rose & lil 47.50 9.25

British Stamps of 1902 Surcharged

1902-05 **Wmk. 30**

8 A66(a) 40pa on 2½p ultra 17.50 .25
9 A71(b) 80pa on 5p lil & bl 9.00 2.90
a. Small "0" in "80" 250.00 210.00
10 A73(e) 4pi on 10p car rose & vio 13.50 4.50

Wmk. 31

11 A75(c) 12pi on 2sh6p vio ('03) 40.00 40.00
12 A76(c) 24pi on 5sh car rose ('05) 35.00 47.50
Nos. 8-12 (5) 115.00 95.15

Great Britain Nos. 131, 134 Surcharged — f

1906 **Wmk. 30**

13 A66(f) 1pi on 2½p ultra 17.50 .25
14 A71(f) 2pi on 5p lil & ultra 32.50 2.75

Nos. 10, 11, 14 are on both ordinary and chalky paper.

Great Britain Nos. 127-135, 138 Overprinted — g

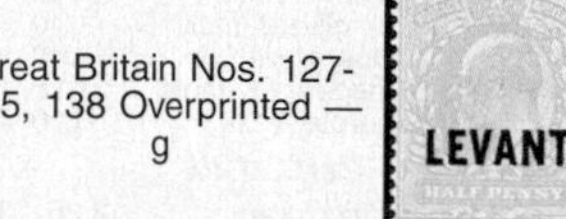

1905

15 A66 ½p pale green 10.00 .25
16 A66 1p carmine 9.50 .25
17 A67 1½p violet & grn 6.25 2.00
18 A68 2p green & car 3.50 8.00
19 A66 2½p ultra 10.00 22.50
20 A69 3p violet, *yel* 7.25 13.50
21 A70 4p brown & grn 10.00 50.00
22 A71 5p lilac & ultra 19.00 32.50
23 A66 6p dull violet 15.00 29.00
24 A74 1sh car rose & grn 42.50 57.50
Nos. 15-24 (10) 133.00 215.50

Nos. 17, 18 and 24 are on both ordinary and chalky paper.

No. 18 Surcharged

1906, July 2

25 A68 1pi on 2p grn & car 1,500. 700.00

British Stamps of 1902-09 Surcharged

j

k

1909

26 A67 30pa on 1½p vio & grn 11.50 1.40
27 A69 1pi10pa on 3p vio, *yel* 13.50 40.00
28 A70 1pi30pa on 4p brn & grn 5.75 19.00
29 A70 1pi30pa on 4p org 20.00 70.00
30 A66 2pi20pa on 6p dl vio 22.50 70.00
31 A74 5pi on 1sh car rose & grn 5.00 11.00
Nos. 26-31 (6) 78.25 211.40

No. 29 is on ordinary paper, the others are on chalky paper.

Great Britain Nos. 132, 144, 135 Surcharged

m

n

1910

32 A69(m) 1¼pi on 3p vio, *yel* .60 1.25
33 A70(m) 1¾pi on 4p orange .60 .75
34 A66(n) 2½pi on 6p dl vio 1.60 .80
Nos. 32-34 (3) 2.80 2.80

There are three different varieties of "4" in the fraction of the 1¾ piastre.

Great Britain Nos. 151-154 Overprinted Type g

1911-12 ***Perf. 15x14***

35 A80 ½p yellow green 2.25 1.75
36 A81 1p carmine .55 7.00

Re-engraved

37 A80 ½p yel grn ('12) .90 .25
38 A81 1p scarlet ('12) .90 1.75

Great Britain No. 148 Surcharged — o

39 A66(o) 1pi on 2½p ultra 15.00 3.00
Nos. 35-39 (5) 19.60 13.75

The surcharge on No. 39 exists in two types with the letters 2½ and 3mm high respectively. The stamp also differs from No. 13 in the perforation.

British Stamps of 1912-13 Surcharged with New Values

1913-14 **Wmk. 33**

40 A84(j) 30pa on 1½p red brn 4.00 16.00
41 A86(o) 1pi on 2½p ultra 8.50 .25
42 A87(m) 1¼pi on 3p vio 5.50 4.75
43 A88(m) 1¾pi on 4p sl grn 3.50 7.00
44 A90(o) 4pi on 10p lt bl 9.00 22.50
45 A90(o) 5pi on 1sh bis 45.00 70.00
Nos. 40-45 (6) 75.50 120.50

British Stamps of 1912-19 Overprinted Type "g"

1913-21

46 A82 ½p green .45 1.40
47 A83 1p scarlet .35 5.75
48 A85 2p orange ('21) 1.40 32.50
49 A87 3p violet ('21) 8.50 11.50
50 A88 4p sl grn ('21) 5.75 16.00
51 A89 5p yel brn ('21) 13.50 32.50
52 A89 6p dl vio ('21) 30.00 10.00
53 A90 1sh bister ('21) 15.00 10.00

Wmk. 34

Perf. 11x12

54 A91 2sh6p brn ('21) 42.50 100.00
Nos. 46-54 (9) 117.45 219.65

British Stamps of 1912-19 Surcharged as in 1909-10 and

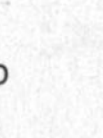
p

q

1921 **Wmk. 33** ***Perf. 14½x14***

55 A82(j) 30pa on ½p grn .90 13.50
a. Inverted surcharge 100.00
56 A83(p) 1½pi on 1p scar 1.75 1.40
57 A86(p) 3¾pi on 2½p ultra 1.50 .35
58 A87(p) 4½pi on 3p vio 2.25 4.25
59 A89(p) 7½pi on 5p yel brn .60 .25
60 A90(p) 15pi on 10p lt bl .85 .25
61 A90(p) 18¾pi on 1sh bis 5.00 5.00

Wmk. 34

Perf. 11x12

62 A91(q) 45pi on 2sh6p brown 22.50 52.50
63 A91(q) 90pi on 5sh car rose 30.00 35.00
64 A91(q) 180pi on 10sh blue 52.50 45.00
Nos. 55-64 (10) 117.85 157.50

GUERNSEY

'gərn-zē

LOCATION — A group of islands in the English Channel
GOVT. — Dependent territory (bailiwick) of the British Crown
AREA — 30 sq. mi.
POP. — 58,681 (1996)
CAPITAL — St. Peter Port

The bailiwick includes the islands of Guernsey, Alderney, Sark, Herm, Jethou and Lithou.

Following the establishment of the British General Post Office as a public corporation on October 1, 1969, the post office of the Bailiwick of Guernsey became a separate entity and British postage stamps ceased to be valid.

Catalogue values for unused stamps in this country are for Never Hinged items.

Watermark

Wmk. 396 — Link Fence

British Regional Issue

Guernsey Lily and Crown of William the Conqueror
A1 A2

Perf. 15x14

1958-69 Photo. Wmk. 322

1 A1 2½p rose red ('64) .35 .35
2 A2 3p light purple .30 .25
p. Phoshor. ('67) .25 .25
3 A2 4p ultra ('66) .30 .25
p. Phosphor. ('67) .25 .25

Unwmk.

4 A2 4p ultra ('68) .25 .25
5 A2 4p olive brown ('68) .25 .25
6 A2 4p bright red ('69) .25 .25
7 A2 5p dark blue ('68) .25 .25
Nos. 1-7 (7) 1.95 1.85

Nos. 4-7 are phosphorescent.

Sold to the general public only at post offices within Guernsey; Philatelic Bureau, Edinburgh; and Philatelic Centre, London, but valid for postage throughout Great Britain.

See also Great Britain Nos. 269-270, which were sold only in the Channel Islands and at a few philatelic windows in Great Britain, and may be considered to be precursors to the regional issues.

Bailiwick Issues

William the Conqueror, Queen Elizabeth II and Map of Bailiwick — A3

Creux Harbor, Sark — A4

Designs (Queen Elizabeth II and): ½p, Castle Cornet and Edward the Confessor. 1½p, Martello Tower and Henry II. 2p, Arms of Sark and King John. 3p, Arms of Alderney and Edward III. 4p, Guernsey lily and Henry V. 5p, Arms of Guernsey and Queen Elizabeth I. 6p, Arms of Alderney and Charles II. 9p, Arms of Sark and George III. 1sh, Arms of Guernsey and Queen Victoria. 1sh6p, Map of Bailiwick and William I. 1sh9p, Guernsey lily and Queen Elizabeth I. 2sh6p, Martello Tower and King John. 10sh, Braye Harbor, Alderney. £1, St. Peter Port, Guernsey.

Perf. 14½x14

1969-70 Photo. Unwmk.

8 A3 ½p magenta & blk .25 .25
9 A3 1p ultra & black .25 .25
10 A3 1½p bister & blk .25 .25
11 A3 2p dk blue & multi .25 .25
12 A3 3p deep org & multi .30 .25
13 A3 4p yel green & multi .30 .30
a. Booklet pane of 1 .60 .60
14 A3 5p vio blue & multi .30 .25
a. Booklet pane of 1 .75 .75
15 A3 6p ol green & multi .40 *.50*
16 A3 9p plum & multi .40 *.50*
17 A3 1sh dk olive & multi .40 *.50*
18 A3 1sh6p blue grn & blk .40 *.50*
19 A3 1sh9p magenta & multi 1.25 1.25
20 A3 2sh6p purple & blk 5.00 4.25

Perf. 12½

21 A4 5sh multicolored 3.25 3.00
22 A4 10sh multicolored 16.00 16.00
a. Perf. 13½x13 45.00 40.00

Perf. 13½x13

23 A4 £1 multicolored 3.00 2.50
a. Perf. 12½ 4.00 3.50
Nos. 8-23 (16) 32.00 30.80

Issued: Nos. 22a, 23, 3/4/70; others, 10/1/69.

Nos. 9 and 18 are inscribed "40o 30' N."

See Nos. 28-29, 41-55, 749.

Col. Isaac Brock — A5

Designs: 5p, Sir Isaac Brock as major general. 1sh9p, as ensign, flags of 1789 and 1969. 2sh6p, Regimental coat of arms and flags, horiz.

Perf. 14x13½, 13½x14

1969, Dec. 1 Litho. Unwmk.

24 A5 4p multicolored .25 .25
25 A5 5p black & multi .25 .25
26 A5 1sh9p dp blue & multi .90 .75
27 A5 2sh6p purple & multi .90 .75
Nos. 24-27 (4) 2.30 2.00

Sir Isaac Brock (1769-1812), born on Guernsey, commander of Quebec garrison.

Map Type of 1969 Redrawn

1969-70 Photo. *Perf. 14½x14*

28 A3 1p "49o 30'N" .35 .35
a. Booklet pane of 1 .45 .45
Complete booklet, 3 #13a, 2 #14a, 2 #28a 4.25
Complete booklet, 6 #13a, 4 #14a, 4 #28a 8.50
Complete booklet, 9 #13a, 6 #14a, 6 #28a 13.00
29 A3 1sh6p "49o 30'N" 2.50 2.00

Issued: No. 28a, 12/12/69; Nos. 28-29, 2/4/70.

Nos. 9 and 18 are inscribed "40o 30' N."

Booklets issued in 1970 have different covers from those issued in 1969.

Destroyer "Bulldog" near Castle Cornet — A6

Designs: 5p, Liberation fleet in roadsteads between Guernsey, Herm and Jethou. 1sh6p, Brigadier A. E. Snow reading proclamation of King George VI on steps of Elizabeth College in Guernsey, vert.

1970, May 9 Photo. *Perf. 11½*

30 A6 4p vio blue & lt blue .25 .25
31 A6 5p dp plum & gray .35 .25
32 A6 1sh6p dk brown & bis 1.25 1.25
Nos. 30-32 (3) 1.85 1.75

25th anniv. of Guernsey's liberation from the Germans.

Guernsey Cow — A7

1970, Aug. 12 Photo. *Perf. 11½*

33 A7 4p Tomatoes .50 .45
34 A7 5p shown .75 .45
35 A7 9p Guernsey bull 2.75 1.25
36 A7 1sh6p Freesias 3.00 2.50
Nos. 33-36 (4) 7.00 4.65

For similar design see No. 68.

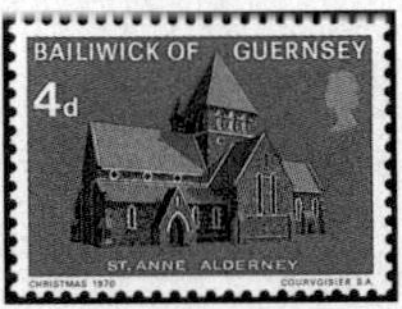

St. Anne, Alderney A8

Christmas (Churches): 5p, St. Peter, Town Church, Guernsey. 9p, St. Peter, Sark, vert. 1sh6p, St. Tugual Chapel, Herm, vert.

1970, Nov. 11 Photo. *Perf. 11½*

37 A8 4p blue, gold & brn .25 .25
38 A8 5p brt grn, gold & brn .35 .25
39 A8 9p rose red, gold & brown 1.10 1.00
40 A8 1sh6p brt pur, gold & brn 1.50 1.25
Nos. 37-40 (4) 3.20 2.75

Decimal Currency Issue Types of 1969 "p" instead of "d"

Designs: ½p, Castle Cornet and Edward the Confessor. 1p, 5p, Map of Bailiwick and William the Conqueror. 1½p, Martello Tower and Henry II. 2p, Guernsey lily and Henry V. 2½p, Arms of Guernsey and Elizabeth I. 3p, Arms of Alderney and Edward III. 3½p, Guernsey lily and Elizabeth I. 4p, Arms of Sark and King John. 6p, Arms of Alderney and Charles II. 7½p, Arms of Guernsey and Queen Victoria. 9p, Arms of Sark and George III. 10p, Martello Tower and King John. 20p, Creux Harbor. 50p, Braye Harbor.

1971 Photo. *Perf. 14½x14*

41 A3 ½p magenta & blk .25 .25
a. Booklet pane of 1 .20
42 A3 1p ultra & black .25 .25
43 A3 1½p bister & blk .25 .25
44 A3 2p yel green & multi .25 .25
a. Booklet pane of 1 .35
45 A3 2½p vio blue & multi .25 .25
a. Booklet pane of 1 .35
Complete booklet, 2 each #41a, 44a, 45a .60
Complete booklet, 4 each #41a, 44a, 45a 1.20
Complete booklet, 6 each #41a, 44a, 45a 1.80
46 A3 3p dp orange & multi .30 .30
47 A3 3½p magenta & multi .30 .30
48 A3 4p dk blue & multi .30 .30
49 A3 5p brt green & multi .30 .30
50 A3 6p dk green & multi .30 .30
51 A3 7½p brn olive & multi .40 .40
52 A3 9p plum & multi 1.00 .80
53 A3 10p purple & black 1.60 1.60

Perf. 13

54 A4 20p dk red & multi .80 1.00
55 A4 50p multicolored 1.75 1.75
Nos. 41-55 (15) 8.30 8.30

Issued: Nos. 53-55, 1/6; others 2/15.

Stamps from the booklets reprinted in 1973 are printed on whiter, chalk-surfaced paper, with different covers.

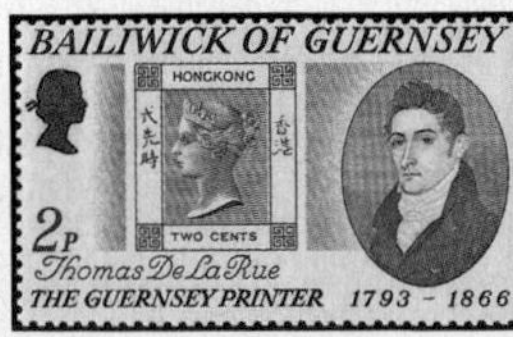

Thomas de la Rue, Hong Kong No. 1 — A9

Thomas de la Rue and: 2½p, GB No. 22. 4p, Italy No. 26. 7½p, US Confederate States No. 6.

1971, June 2 Engr. *Perf. 14x13½*

56 A9 2p brown .40 .25
57 A9 2½p carmine .40 .25
58 A9 4p dark green 1.25 1.10
59 A9 7½p violet blue 1.50 1.40
Nos. 56-59 (4) 3.55 3.00

Thomas de la Rue (1793-1866), founder of Thomas de la Rue & Co., Ltd., security printers.

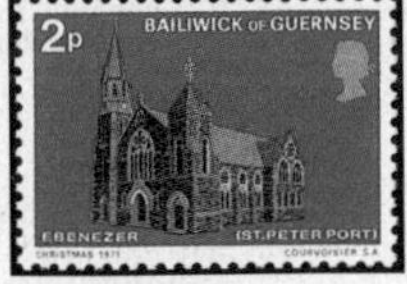

Ebenezer Methodist Church — A10

Historic Churches of Guernsey: 2½p, St. Pierre du Bois. 5p, St. Joseph's, vert. 7½p, St. Philippe de Torteval, vert.

1971, Oct. 27 Photo. *Perf. 11½*

60 A10 2p green, sil & blk .25 .25
61 A10 2½p blue, sil & blk .30 .25
62 A10 5p pur, silver & blk 1.10 1.10
63 A10 7½p red, silver & blk 1.50 1.40
Nos. 60-63 (4) 3.15 3.00

Christmas 1971.

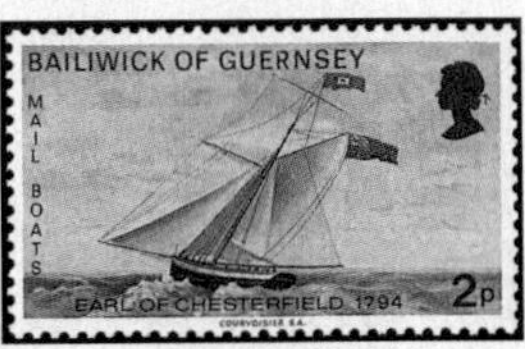

Earl of Chesterfield, 1794 — A11

Mail Boats — 2½p, Dasher, 1827. 7½p, Ibex, 1891. 9p, Alberta, 1900.

1972, Feb. 10 Photo. *Perf. 11½*

64 A11 2p shown .25 .25
65 A11 2½p multicolored .25 .25
66 A11 7½p multicolored .30 .30
67 A11 9p multicolored .50 .50
Nos. 64-67 (4) 1.30 1.30

See Nos. 77-80.

Guernsey Bull — A12

1972, May 22 Photo. *Perf. 11½*

68 A12 5p brown & multi .45 .45

Guernsey Breeders, 2nd World Conf. For similar designs see Nos. 33-36.

Wild Flowers A13

2p, Sorrel (Oxalis pes-caprae). 2½p, heath spotted orchid (Orchis maculata), vert. 7½p, kafir fig (Carpobrotus edulis). 9p, scarlet pimpernel (Anagallis arvensi), vert.

1972, May 24

69 A13 2p multicolored .25 .25
70 A13 2½p multicolored .25 .25
71 A13 7½p multicolored .35 .35
72 A13 9p multicolored .40 .40
Nos. 69-72 (4) 1.25 1.25

Angels, St. Martin's Church — A14

Stained Glass Windows from Guernsey Churches: 2½p, Virgin and Child, St. André's. 7½p, Virgin Mary, St. Sampson's. 9p, Christ Victorious, St. Pierre's.

1972, Nov. 20 Photo. *Perf. 11½*

73 A14 2p brick red & multi .25 .25
74 A14 2½p lt violet & multi .25 .25
75 A14 7½p yellow & multi .25 .25
76 A14 9p lt green & multi .30 .30
Nos. 73-76 (4) 1.05 1.05

Christmas 1972 and for the 25th anniv. of the marriage of Queen Elizabeth II and Prince Philip.

Mail Boat Type of 1972

2½p, St. Julien, 1925. 3p, Isle of Guernsey, 1932. 7½p, St. Patrick, 1947. 9p, Sarnia, 1961.

1973, Mar. 9 Photo. *Perf. 11½*

77 A11 2½p multicolored .25 .25
78 A11 3p multicolored .25 .25
79 A11 7½p multicolored .30 .30
80 A11 9p multicolored .35 .35
Nos. 77-80 (4) 1.15 1.15

No. 78 is incorrectly inscribed "Isle of Guernsey 1930."

Supermarine Sea Eagle — A15

Airplanes: 3p, Westland Wessex. 5p, De Havilland Rapide. 7½p, Douglas Dakota. 9p, Vickers Viscount.

1973, July 4 Photo. *Perf. 11½*

81 A15 2½p multicolored .25 .25
82 A15 3p multicolored .25 .25
83 A15 5p multicolored .25 .25
84 A15 7½p multicolored .35 .35
85 A15 9p multicolored .45 .45
Nos. 81-85 (5) 1.55 1.55

50th anniversary of air service to Guernsey.

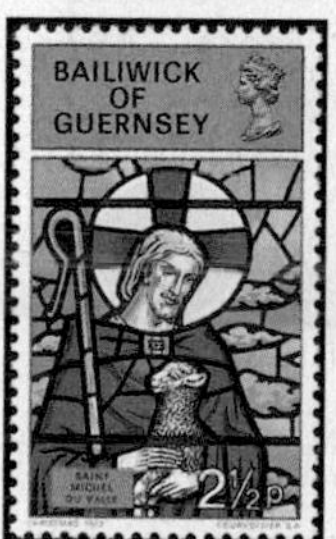

The Good Shepherd, St. Michel du Valle — A16

Stained-glass Windows from Guernsey Churches: 3p, Jesus preaching, St. Marie du Castel. 7½p, St. Dominic, Notre Dame du Rosaire. 20p, Virgin and Child, St. Sauveur.

1973, Oct. 24 Photo. *Perf. 11½*

86 A16 2½p salmon & multi .25 .25
87 A16 3p blue & multi .25 .25
88 A16 7½p yellow & multi .25 .25
89 A16 20p multicolored .40 .40
Nos. 86-89 (4) 1.15 1.15

Christmas 1973.

Princess Anne and Mark Phillips — A17

1973, Nov. 14

90 A17 25p blue & multi .50 .50

Wedding of Princess Anne and Capt. Mark Phillips, Nov. 14, 1973.

"John Lockett," 1875 — A18

Guernsey Lifeboats: 3p, "Arthur Lionel," 1875. 8p, "Euphrosyne Kendal," 1954. 10p, "Arun," 1972.

1974, Jan. 15 Photo. *Perf. 11½*
Granite Paper

91 A18 2½p multicolored .25 .25
92 A18 3p multicolored .25 .25
93 A18 8p multicolored .25 .25
94 A18 10p multicolored .25 .25
Nos. 91-94 (4) 1.00 1.00

Sesqui. of Royal Natl. Lifeboat Institution.

A19

Militia — A20

1974-78 Photo. *Perf. 11½*
Granite Paper (Nos. 95-107)

95 A19 ½p 1815 .25 .25
96 A19 1p 1825 .25 .25
97 A19 1½p 1787 .25 .25
98 A19 2p 1815 .25 .25
99 A19 2½p Royal, 1868 .25 .25
Complete booklet, pane of 8 (5 #95, 3 #99) ('74) .35
100 A19 3p Royal, 1895 .25 .25
Complete booklet, pane of 16 (4 #95, 6 #99 and 6 #100) ('74) 1.10
101 A19 3½p Royal, 1867 .25 .25
102 A19 4p 1822 .25 .25
102A A19 5p Royal, 1895 .25 .25
Complete booklet, pane of 8 (4 #96, #100, 2 #102, #102A) ('77) .85
Complete booklet, pane of 4 (#96, 2 #98, #102A) ('77) .55
103 A19 5½p Royal. 1833 .25 .25
104 A19 6p Royal. 1832 .25 .25
104A A19 7p 1822 .35 .35
105 A19 8p Royal, 1868 .25 .25
106 A19 9p 1785 .25 .25
107 A19 10p 1824 .25 .25

Perf. 13x13½, 13½x13

108 A20 20p Royal, 1848, vert. .60 .50
109 A20 50p Royal, 1868, vert. 1.50 1.40
110 A20 £1 1814 2.50 2.00
Nos. 95-110 (18) 8.45 7.75

Issued: Nos. 95-107, 4/2/74; Nos. 108-110, 4/1/75; No. 102A, 104A, 5/29/76; No. 96a, 2/8/77; No. 96b, 2/7/78.

Stamps in booklet panes are from special sheets of 80 (two 8x5 panes) which were sold separately. The booklets following Nos. 99 and 100 come from panes of 88 with no gutter.

Bailiwick Seal and UPU Emblem — A21

UPU Cent.: 3p, Map of Guernsey. 8p, UPU Headquarters, Bern, flag of Guernsey. 10p, Legislative Chamber, Parliament.

1974, June 11 Photo. *Perf. 11½*
Granite Paper

111 A21 2½p multicolored .25 .25
112 A21 3p ultra & multi .25 .25
113 A21 8p multicolored .25 .25
114 A21 10p multicolored .25 .25
Nos. 111-114 (4) 1.00 1.00

Cradle Rock, by Renoir A22

Paintings by Renoir: 5½p, Moulin-Huet Bay. 8p, Woman at the Shore, vert. 10p, Self-portrait, vert.

1974, Sept. 21 Photo. *Perf. 13¼*

115 A22 3p multicolored .25 .25
116 A22 5½p multicolored .25 .25
117 A22 8p multicolored .25 .25
118 A22 10p multicolored .25 .25
Nos. 115-118 (4) 1.00 1.00

Pierre Auguste Renoir (1841-1919), who painted pictures shown on Nos. 115-117 while visiting Guernsey.

Guernsey Spleenwort — A23

Designs: Guernsey ferns.

1975, Jan. 7 Photo. *Perf. 11½*

119 A23 3½p shown .25 .25
120 A23 4p Sand quillwort .25 .25
121 A23 8p Guernsey fern .25 .25
122 A23 10p Least adder's tongue .25 .25
Nos. 119-122 (4) 1.00 1.00

Hauteville, Hugo's House A24

Victor Hugo Statue, Candie Gardens — A25

Designs: 8p, United Europe Oak, Hauteville (planted by Hugo). 10p, Departure for the Hunt, Aubusson tapestry, Hauteville.

1975, June 6 Photo. *Perf. 11½*
Granite Paper

123 A24 3½p dull yel & multi .25 .25
124 A25 4p lt blue & multi .25 .25
125 A25 8p yel green & multi .25 .25
126 A24 10p multicolored .25 .25
a. Souvenir sheet of 4, #123-126 .80 .80
Nos. 123-126 (4) 1.00 1.00

Victor Hugo (1802-85), French writer, political exile in Guernsey (1855-70).
No. 126a is on thicker paper.

Arms and Map of Guernsey — A26

Designs (Globe with Map of Bailiwick): 6p, Flag of Guernsey. 10p, Flag of Guernsey and arms of Alderney, horiz. 12p, Flag of Guernsey and arms of Sark, horiz.

1975, Oct. 7 Photo. *Perf. 13½*

127 A26 4p olive green & multi .25 .25
128 A26 6p rose lilac & multi .25 .25
129 A26 10p brt green & multi .25 .25
130 A26 12p orange & multi .25 .25
Nos. 127-130 (4) 1.00 1.00

Christmas 1975.

Lighthouses — A27

1976, Feb. 10 Photo. *Perf. 11½*
Granite Paper

131 A27 4p Les Hanois .25 .25
132 A27 6p Les Casquets .25 .25
133 A27 11p Quesnard, Alderney .25 .25
134 A27 13p Point Robert, Sark .30 .30
Nos. 131-134 (4) 1.05 1.05

Guernsey Milk Can — A28

Europa: 25p, Silver christening cup.

1976, May 29 Photo. *Perf. 11½*
Granite Paper

135 A28 10p multicolored .30 .30
136 A28 25p multicolored .60 .50

Sheets of 9.

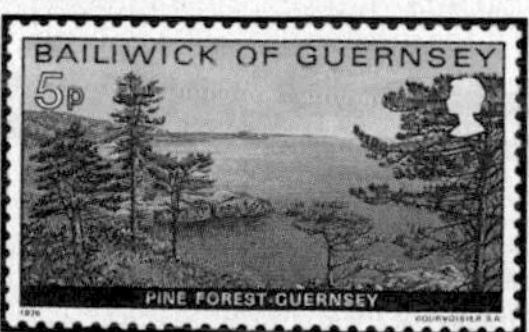

Pine Forest, Guernsey — A29

Guernsey Views: 7p, Herm Harbor and Jethou. 11p, Grande Grave Bay, Sark Cliffs, vert. 13p, Trois Vaux Bay, Alderney Cliffs, vert.

1976, Aug. 3 Photo. *Perf. 11½*
Granite Paper

137 A29 5p multicolored .25 .25
138 A29 7p multicolored .25 .25
139 A29 11p multicolored .25 .25
140 A29 13p multicolored .25 .25
Nos. 137-140 (4) 1.00 1.00

Royal Court House, Guernsey — A30

Christmas (Buildings in the Bailiwick): 7p, Elizabeth College, Guernsey. 11p, La Seigneurie, Sark. 13p, Island Hall, Alderney.

1976, Oct. 14 Photo. *Perf. 11½*
Granite Paper

141 A30 5p multicolored .25 .25
142 A30 7p multicolored .25 .25
143 A30 11p multicolored .25 .25
144 A30 13p multicolored .25 .25
Nos. 141-144 (4) 1.00 1.00

Elizabeth II with Order of the Garter — A31

Design: 7p, Queen Elizabeth II.

1977, Feb. 8 Photo. *Perf. 12x11½*

145 A31 7p blue & multi .25 .25
146 A31 35p purple & multi .60 .60

25th anniv. of the reign of Elizabeth II.

Talbots Valley — A32

Europa: 25p, Fields and hedges, Talbots Valley.

1977, May 17 Photo. *Perf. 11½*
Granite Paper

147 A32 7p multicolored .25 .25
148 A32 25p multicolored *.60 .60*

Megalithic Tomb, Le Catioroc — A33

Prehistoric monuments: 5p, Menhir (statue), Castel, vert. 11p, Roc à l'Epine Tourgis. 13p, Gràn'mère du Chim'quière, vert.

1977, Aug. 2 Photo. *Perf. 11½*

149 A33 5p multicolored .25 .25
150 A33 7p multicolored .25 .25
151 A33 11p multicolored .30 .30
152 A33 13p multicolored .30 .30
Nos. 149-152 (4) 1.10 1.10

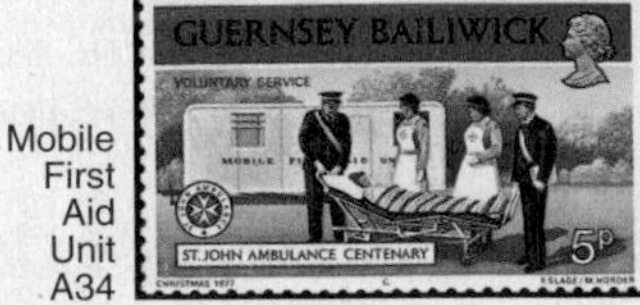

Mobile First Aid Unit A34

7p, Mobile radar & rescue coordination unit, for ships in distress. 11p, Marine ambulance "Flying Christine II," vert. 13p, Cliff rescue, vert.

1977, Oct. 25 Photo. *Perf. 11½*

153 A34 5p multicolored .25 .25
154 A34 7p multicolored .25 .25
155 A34 11p multicolored .30 .30
156 A34 13p multicolored .30 .30
Nos. 153-156 (4) 1.10 1.10

St. John Ambulance Assoc. cent. (in GB).

View from Clifton, c. 1830 — A35

19th Century Prints, Guernsey: 7p, Market Square, c. 1838. 11p, Petit-Bo Bay, c. 1839. 13p, The Quay, c. 1830.

1978, Feb. 7 Litho. *Perf. 14x13½*

157 A35 5p pale green & black .25 .25
158 A35 7p buff & black .25 .25
159 A35 11p pink & black .30 .30
160 A35 13p lt violet & black .30 .30
Nos. 157-160 (4) 1.10 1.10

See Nos. 236-239.

Memorial to Seamen of Ship Prosperity; Sank in 1974 — A36

Europa: 7p, Victoria monument, vert.

1978, May 2 Litho. *Perf. 14½*

161 A36 5p multicolored .25 .25
162 A36 7p multicolored *.25 .25*

Elizabeth II — A37

1978, May 2 Photo. *Perf. 11½*

163 A37 20p ultra & black .55 .55

25th anniv. of coronation of Elizabeth II.

Text at top and above GUERNSEY is different from No. 163 — A37a

1978, June 28

164 A37a 7p emerald & black .25 .25

Gannet A38

Birds: 7p, Firecrest. 11p, Dartford warbler. 13p, Spotted redshank.

1978, Aug. 29 Photo. *Perf. 11½*

165 A38 5p multicolored .25 .25
166 A38 7p multicolored .25 .25
167 A38 11p multicolored .25 .25
168 A38 13p multicolored .30 .30
Nos. 165-168 (4) 1.05 1.05

Solanum — A39

Christmas: 7p, Christmas rose. 11p, Holly, vert. 13p, Mistletoe, vert.

1978, Oct. 31 Photo. *Perf. 11½*

169 A39 5p multicolored .25 .25
170 A39 7p multicolored .25 .25
171 A39 11p multicolored .30 .30
172 A39 13p multicolored .30 .30
Nos. 169-172 (4) 1.10 1.10

1 Double, 1930 — A40

1979, Feb. 13 Granite Paper

173 A40 ½p 1 double, 1930 .25 .25
174 A40 1p 2 doubles, 1899 .25 .25
175 A40 2p 4 doubles, 1902 .25 .25
176 A40 4p 8 doubles, 1959 .25 .25
177 A40 5p 3 pence, 1956 .25 .25
178 A40 6p 5 new pence, 1968 .25 .25
a. Horiz. strip of 4, #178, 175, 2 #174 1.00
179 A40 7p 50 new pence, 1969 .25 .25
180 A40 8p 10 new pence, 1970 .25 .25
a. Horiz. strip of 5, #175, 2 each #178, 180 1.25
Complete booklet of 10, 5 each #176, 180 2.25
181 A40 9p ½ new penny, 1971 .25 .25
182 A40 10p 1 new penny, 1971 .25 .25
183 A40 11p 2 new pence, 1971 .25 .25
184 A40 12p 1 penny, 1977 .30 .25
Complete booklet of 15, 5 each #176, 180, 184 3.50
185 A40 13p 2 pence, 1977 .30 .25
Complete booklet of 10, 2 #176, 3 #181, 5 #185 2.25
Complete booklet of 15, 5 each #176, 181, 185 3.50
186 A40 14p 5 pence, 1977 .30 .25
187 A40 15p 10 pence, 1977 .20 .25
188 A40 20p 25 pence, 1977 .45 .25
Nos. 173-188 (16) 4.30 4.00

No. 177 is dark brown, No. 182, green & bronze. See Nos. 198B-203A.

Booklets were produced from sheets of 40, 30 and 20. These sheets were sold both as complete sheets and as strips, folded and affixed by the sheet selvage or inserted unattached into booklet covers. These booklet panes exist in two to four different arrangements.

Oldest Pillar Box, 1853 Cancel, Truck — A41

Europa: 8p, Telephone, 1897, telex machine.

1979, May 8 Photo. *Perf. 11½*

189 A41 6p multicolored .25 .25
190 A41 8p multicolored .25 .25

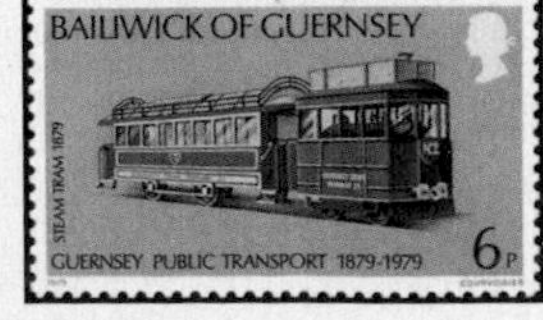

Steam Tram, 1879 A42

Public Transportation: 8p, Electric tram, 1896. 11p, Autobus, 1911. 13p, Autobus, 1979.

1979, Aug. 7 Photo. *Perf. 11½*

191 A42 6p multicolored .25 .25
192 A42 8p multicolored .25 .25
193 A42 11p multicolored .30 .30
194 A42 13p multicolored .30 .30
Nos. 191-194 (4) 1.10 1.10

Centenary of public transportation.

Postal Bureau and Headquarters — A43

Designs: 8p, Mail and telegram deliverymen. 13p, Parcel trucks. 15p, Post Office philatelic room.

1979, Oct. 1 Photo. *Perf. 11½*

195 A43 6p multicolored .25 .25
196 A43 8p multicolored .25 .25
197 A43 13p multicolored .30 .30
198 A43 15p multicolored .35 .35
a. Souvenir sheet of 4, Nos. 195-198 1.10 1.10
Nos. 195-198 (4) 1.15 1.15

Guernsey PO, 10th anniv.; Christmas 1979.

Coin Type of 1979

Designs: 10p, like No. 182. 11½p, ½ pence, 1979. 50p, Battle of Hastings coin, 1966. £1, Queen Elizabeth II 25th anniv., 1977, horiz. £2, Queen Elizabeth II 25th wedding anniv., 1972, horiz. £5, Official seal.

1980-81 Photo. *Perf. 11½*

198B A40 5p orange brown & multi .45 .45
Complete booklet of 15, 5 each #180, 185, 198B 2.00
Complete booklet of 10, #185, 4 #180, 5 #198B 3.50
199 A40 10p orange & bronze .25 .25
Complete booklet of 10, #177, 179, 199, 2 each #173, 175, 3 each #174 2.00
Complete booklet of 10, #174, 2 each #173, 175, 179, 3 #199 2.50
200 A40 11½p red & bronze .30 .25

Size: 26x45, 45x26mm

201 A40 50p red org & sil 1.75 1.25
202 A40 £1 green & sil 2.50 1.50
203 A40 £2 blue & silver 5.50 3.00
203A A40 £5 multi ('81) 10.00 9.00
Nos. 198B-203A (7) 20.75 15.70

No. 177 is dark brown.
For booklets, see note following No. 188.
Issue dates: £5, May 22, others, Feb. 5.

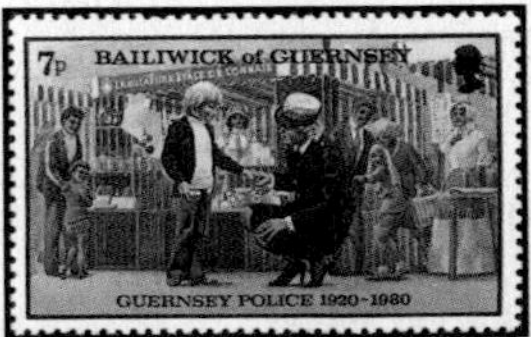

Policewoman Helping Child — A44

Guernsey Police Force, 60th Anniv.: 15p, Policeman on motorcycle. 17½p, Police dog and officer.

1980, May 6 Litho. *Perf. 14*

204 A44 7p multicolored .25 .25
205 A44 15p multicolored .35 .35
206 A44 17½p multicolored .40 .40
Nos. 204-206 (3) 1.00 1.00

Major Gen. John Gaspard Le Marchant — A45

Europa: 13½p, Admiral James Lord de Saumarez (1757-1836).

1980, May 6 Photo. *Perf. 11½*

Granite Paper

207 A45 10p multicolored *.25 .25*
208 A45 13½p multicolored *.35 .35*

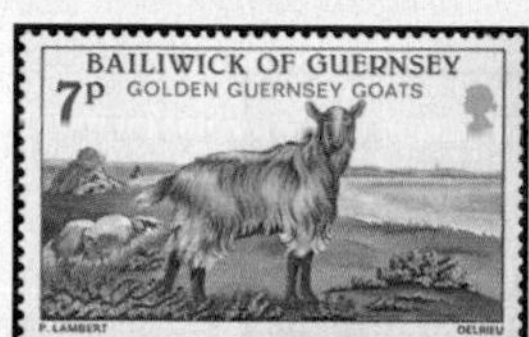

Guernsey Golden Goat — A46

Designs: Various Guernsey golden goats.

1980, Aug. 5 Photo. *Perf. 13*

209 A46 7p multicolored .25 .25
210 A46 10p multicolored .25 .25
211 A46 15p multicolored .35 .35
212 A46 17½p multicolored .45 .45
Nos. 209-212 (4) 1.30 1.30

Sark Cottage, by Peter Le Lievre, 1847 — A47

Christmas 1980 (Le Lievre Paintings): 10p, Moulin Huet, 1850. 13½p, Boats at Sea, 1850. 15p, Cow Lane, 1852, vert. 17½p, Portrait, by Le Lievre's sister, vert.

1980, Nov. 15 Photo. *Perf. 12*

Granite Paper

213 A47 7p multicolored .25 .25
214 A47 10p multicolored .25 .25
215 A47 13½p multicolored .35 .35
216 A47 15p multicolored .35 .35
217 A47 17½p multicolored .40 .40
Nos. 213-217 (5) 1.60 1.60

Common Blue A48

1981, Feb. 24 Photo. *Perf. 14½*

218 A48 8p shown .25 .25
219 A48 12p Red Admiral .25 .25
220 A48 22p Small Tortoiseshell .50 .50
221 A48 25p Wall Brown .60 .60
Nos. 218-221 (4) 1.60 1.60

Le Petit Bonhomme Andriou (Head-shaped Rock) — A49

1981, May 22 Litho. *Perf. 14½*

222 A49 12p shown *.35 .35*
223 A49 18p Guernsey lily *.45 .45*

Europa.

Royal Wedding — A50

a, Charles. b, Prince Charles and Lady Diana. c, Diana.

1981, July 29 Litho. *Perf. 14½x15*

224 A50 Strip of 3 .85 .85
a.-c. 8p any single .25 .25

225 A50 Strip of 3 1.00 1.00
a.-c. 12p any single .30 .30

Size: 49x32mm

226 A50 25p Royal family .75 .75
a. Souv. sheet, #224-226, perf. 14x14½ 2.75 2.75
Nos. 224-226 (3) 2.60 2.60

Sark Launch — A51

Designs: Interisland transportation.

1981, Aug. 25 Photo. *Perf. 11½*

Granite Paper

227 A51 8p shown .25 .25
228 A51 12p Trislander plane .35 .35
229 A51 18p Hydrofoil .50 .50
230 A51 22p Herm catamaran .60 .60
231 A51 25p Alderney coaster .75 .75
Nos. 227-231 (5) 2.45 2.45

Rifle-shooting Competition A52

1981, Nov. 17 Litho. *Perf. 14¾*

232 A52 8p shown .25 .25
233 A52 12p Riding .30 .30
234 A52 22p Swimming .55 .55
235 A52 25p Electronics workers .70 .70
Nos. 232-235 (4) 1.80 1.80

Intl. Year of the Disabled.

Print Type of 1978

1982, Feb. 2 Litho. & Engr.

236 A35 8p Jethou .25 .25
237 A35 12p Fermain Bay .30 .30
238 A35 22p The Terres .55 .55
239 A35 25p St. Pierre Port .60 .60
Nos. 236-239 (4) 1.70 1.70

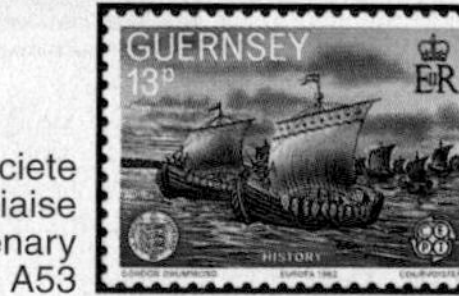

La Societe Guernesiaise Centenary A53

Society Emblem and Activities: 8p, Sir Edgar MacCulloch, founding president. 13p, William the Conqueror's fleet, Battle at Hastings (history). 20p, Sir James Saumarez's Crescent rescued from French fleet (history). 24p, Dragonfly (entomology). 26p, Vale Parish Church bird sanctuary (ornithology). 29p, Samian bowl, King's Road excavation (archaeology). 13p and 20p show CEPT (Europa) emblem.

1982, Apr. 28 Photo. *Perf. 11½*

Granite Paper

240 A53 8p multicolored .30 .30
241 A53 13p multicolored .40 .40
242 A53 20p multicolored .60 .60
243 A53 24p multicolored .65 .65
244 A53 26p multicolored .75 .75
245 A53 29p multicolored .80 .80
Nos. 240-245 (6) 3.50 3.50

Scouting Year — A54

8p, Sea scouts, Castle Cornet, St. Peter Port. 13p, Boy scouts building bridge. 26p, Cub scouts parading. 29p, Air scouts reading chart.

1982, July 13 Litho. *Perf. 14½*

246 A54 8p multicolored .25 .25
247 A54 13p multicolored .30 .30
248 A54 26p multicolored .65 .65
249 A54 29p multicolored .75 .75
Nos. 246-249 (4) 1.95 1.95

Christmas 1982 — A55

8p, Midnight mass, St. Peter Port Church. 13p, Exchanging presents. 24p, Dinner. 26p, Exchanging cards. 29p, Watching Queen's TV greeting.

1982, Oct. 12 Photo. *Perf. 14½*

250 A55 8p multicolored .25 .25
251 A55 13p multicolored .35 .35
252 A55 24p multicolored .55 .55
253 A55 26p multicolored .60 .60
254 A55 29p multicolored .75 .75
Nos. 250-254 (5) 2.50 2.50

Centenary of Boys' Brigade — A56

Designs: Various brigade activities.

1983, Jan. 18 *Perf. 14*

255 A56 8p multicolored .25 .25
256 A56 13p multicolored .40 .40
257 A56 24p multicolored .60 .60
258 A56 26p multicolored .65 .65
259 A56 29p multicolored .75 .75
Nos. 255-259 (5) 2.65 2.65

Europa 1983 — A57

Views of the development of St. Peter Port Harbor — No. 260, Construction of St. Peter Port Harbor. No. 261, Buildings on Harbor. No. 262, Ships and mountains on right. No. 263, Harbor waterways, mountains in distance.

1983, Mar. 14 Photo. *Perf. 11½*

Granite Paper

260 A57 13p gray frame *.35 .25*
261 A57 13p gray frame *.35 .25*
a. Pair, #260-261 *.75 .75*
262 A57 20p orange frame *.50 .50*
263 A57 20p orange frame *.50 .50*
a. Pair, #262-263 *1.25 1.25*

View at Guernsey, by Renoir — A58

Centenary of Renoir's Visit: 13p, Children at the Seashore (26x30mm). 26p, Marine Guernsey. 28p, Moulin Huet Bay through the Trees. 31p, Fog in Guernsey.

Perf. 12, 11½x12 (13p)

1983, Sept. 6 Photo.

Granite Paper

264 A58 9p multicolored .25 .25
265 A58 13p multicolored .35 .35
266 A58 26p multicolored .70 .70
267 A58 28p multicolored .80 .80
268 A58 31p multicolored .85 .85
Nos. 264-268 (5) 2.95 2.95

Star of the West, 1869 Merchant Ship, Capt. J.G. Lenfestey — A59

9p, Launching. 13p, Leaving St. Peter Port. 26p, Rio Grande Bar. 28p, St. Lucia. 31p, Voyage Map.

1983, Nov. 15 Photo. *Perf. 14½*

269 A59 9p multicolored .25 .25
270 A59 13p multicolored .35 .35
271 A59 26p multicolored .70 .70
272 A59 28p multicolored .80 .80
273 A59 31p multicolored .90 .90
Nos. 269-273 (5) 3.00 3.00

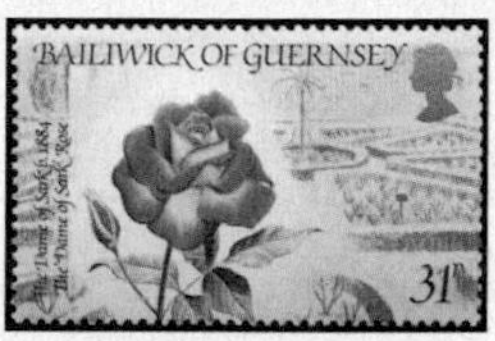

Dame of Sark (Sibyl Hathaway, 1884-1974) — A60

Biographical Scenes: 9p, Portrait, La Seigneurie (residence). 13p, German occupation, 1940-45. 26p, Royal visit, 1957. 28p, Chief Pleas (parliament). 31p, Dame of Sark rose.

1984, Feb. 7 Litho. *Perf. 14½*

274 A60 9p multicolored .25 .25
275 A60 13p multicolored .35 .35
276 A60 26p multicolored .70 .70
277 A60 28p multicolored .75 .75
278 A60 31p multicolored .80 .80
Nos. 274-278 (5) 2.85 2.85

Links with the Commonwealth — A61

Designs: 9p, Flag of Guernsey, Royal Court. 31p, Union Jack, Castle Cornet.

1984, Apr. 10 Litho. *Perf. 14½*

279 A61 9p multicolored .25 .25
280 A61 31p multicolored 1.00 1.00

Europa (1959-84) — A62

1984, Apr. 10 *Perf. 15*

281 A62 13p multicolored *.30 .30*
282 A62 20½p multicolored *.70 .70*

Petit Port — A63

1p, Little Chapel, vert. 2p, Ft. Grey. 3p, St. Apolline Chapel, vert. 5p, Little Russel. 6p, The Harbour, Herm. 7p, Saints. 8p, St. Saviour, vert. 9p, Cambridge Berth. 10p, Belvoir, Herm. 11p, La Seigneurie, Sark. 13p, St. Saviour's Reservoir. 14p, St. Peter Port, vert. 15p, Havelet, vert. 20p, La Coupee, Sark. 30p, Grandes Rocques. 40p, St. Torteval Church, vert. 50p, Bordeaux. £ 1, Albecq. £ 2, L'Ancresse.

Perf. 15x14½, 14½x15

1984-85 **Litho.**

No.	Type	Denom.	Description	Unused	Used
283	A63	1p	multi ('85)	.25	.25
284	A63	2p	multi ('85)	.25	.25
285	A63	3p	multi	.25	.25
286	A63	4p	shown	.25	.25
287	A63	5p	multi ('85)	.25	.25
288	A63	6p	multi ('85)	.25	.25
289	A63	7p	multi ('85)	.25	.25
290	A63	8p	multi ('85)	.25	.25
291	A63	9p	multi	.25	.25
292	A63	10p	multi	.35	.25
a.			Min. sheet, 2 2p, 4 4p, 2 5p, 2 10p	2.50	
293	A63	11p	multi ('85)	.25	.25
294	A63	13p	multi	.35	.35
a.			Min. sheet, 2 4p, 3 9p, 5 13p	3.00	
b.			Min. sheet, 5 each 4p, 9p, 13p	5.00	
295	A63	14p	multi	.25	.25
a.			Min. sheet, 4 9p, 6 14p	4.50	
b.			Min. sheet, 2 9p, 8 14p	4.75	
c.			Min. sheet, 5 10p, 5 14p	4.50	
296	A63	15p	multi ('85)	.35	.25
a.			Min. sheet, 3p, 2 4p, 4 11p, 3 15p	3.75	
b.			Min. sheet, 5 each 11p, 15p	4.50	
297	A63	20p	multi	.60	.25
a.			Booklet pane, 4 6p, 4 14p, 2 20p	3.00	
			Complete booklet, #297a	3.00	
b.			Booklet pane, 5 14p, 5 20p	3.50	
			Complete booklet, #297b	0.00	
298	A63	30p	multi ('85)	1.00	1.00
299	A63	40p	multi	1.10	1.10
300	A63	50p	multi	1.40	1.40
301	A63	£1	multi	2.50	2.50
302	A63	£2	multi ('85)	5.50	5.50
			Nos. 283-302 (20)	15.90	15.35

Issued: 1p, 2p, 5p, 6p, 7p, 8p, 11p, 15p, 30p, £2, 7/23/84; 3p, 4p, 9p, 10p, 13p, 14p, 20p, 40p, 50p, £1, 9/18/84; No. 292a, 12/2/85; Nos. 294a-294b, 9/18/84; Nos. 295a-295b, 3/19/85; No. 295c, 4/1/86; Nos. 296a-296b, 3/30/87; Nos. 297a-297b, 12/27/89.

Miniature sheets have surrounding selvage and were sold folded and unattached in booklet covers. Nos. 297a, 297b have straight edges around stamps and attached to booklet covers by tabs.

See Nos. 372-378, 453-454.

Lieutenant-General John Doyle (1756-1834) — A64

Designs: 13p, Portrait by James Ramsey, 1817. 29p, American War of Independence battle. 31p, Land fill, Grand Havre Bay. 34p, Ship approaching Casquets Reef, 1811. 29p, 31p, 34p horiz.

1984, Nov. 20 **Photo.** ***Perf. 11¾***

No.	Type	Denom.	Description	Unused	Used
303	A64	13p	multicolored	.30	.30
304	A64	29p	multicolored	.75	.75
305	A64	31p	multicolored	.80	.80
306	A64	34p	multicolored	1.00	1.00
			Nos. 303-306 (4)	2.85	2.85

Christmas 1984 — A65

Twelve Days of Christmas: a, Partridge in a Pear Tree. b, 2 Turtle Doves. c, 3 French Hens. d, 4 Colly Birds. e, 5 Golden Rings. f, 6 Geese-a-Laying. g, 7 Swans a-Swimming. h, 8 Maids a-Milking. i, 9 Drummers Drumming. j, 10 Pipers Piping. k, 11 Ladies Dancing. l, 12 Lords a-Leaping.

1984, Nov. 20 **Litho.** ***Perf. 14½***

No.	Type	Description	Unused	Used
307	A65	Sheet of 12	2.25	2.25
a.-l.		5p any single	.25	.25

Indigenous Fish — A66

1985, Jan. 22 **Photo.** ***Perf. 11¾***

No.	Type	Denom.	Description	Unused	Used
308	A66	9p	Cockoo Wrasse	.35	.35
309	A66	13p	Red Gurnard	.45	.45
310	A66	29p	Red Mullet	.90	.90
311	A66	31p	Mackerel	1.00	1.00
312	A66	34p	Sunfish	1.25	1.25
			Nos. 308-312 (5)	3.95	3.95

Liberation from German Forces, 40th Anniv. A67

1985, May 9 **Litho.** ***Perf. 14x14½***

No.	Type	Denom.	Description	Unused	Used
313	A67	22p	Peace dove	.80	.80

Celebrating the end of the war in Europe (VE-Day).

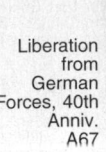

Europa 1985 — A68

Designs: 14p, Musical staff, flags of Great Britain, Netherlands, Germany, Italy, Cross of St. George. 22p, Music, cello, French horn.

1985, May 14 **Litho.** ***Perf. 14½***

No.	Type	Denom.	Description	Unused	Used
314	A68	14p	multicolored	*.45*	*.45*
315	A68	22p	multicolored	*.80*	*.80*

Intl. Youth Year — A69

9p, IYY emblem, circle of children. 13p, Girl Guides in camp.

1985, May 14 **Litho.** ***Perf. 14***

No.	Type	Denom.	Description	Unused	Used
316	A69	9p	multicolored	.25	.25
317	A69	31p	multicolored	1.00	1.00

Children's drawings.

Girl Guides, 75th Anniv. — A70

Child's drawing of leader, guide and brownie.

1985, May 14 **Litho.** ***Perf. 14***

No.	Type	Denom.	Description	Unused	Used
318	A70	34p	multicolored	1.10	1.10

Christmas 1985 — A71

Religious and folk figures: a, Santa Claus. b, Lussibruden. c, Balthasar. d, St. Nicholas. e, La Befana. f, Julenisse. g, Christkind. h, King Wenceslas. i, Shepherd of Les Baux. j, Caspar. k, Baboushka. l, Melchior.

1985, Nov. 19 **Litho.** ***Perf. 12½***

Granite Paper

No.	Type	Description	Unused	Used
319	A71	Sheet of 12	*4.00*	*4.00*
a.-l.		5p any single	.30	.30

Watercolors by Paul Jacob Naftel — A72

1985, Nov. 19 ***Perf. 15x14½***

No.	Type	Denom.	Description	Unused	Used
320	A72	9p	Vraicing	.30	.30
321	A72	14p	Castle Cornet	.45	.45
322	A72	22p	Rocquaine Bay	.70	.70
323	A72	31p	Little Russel	1.10	1.10
324	A72	34p	Seaweed Gatherers	1.40	1.40
			Nos. 320-324 (5)	3.95	3.95

Adm. Lord De Saumarez, 150th Death Anniv. — A73

Designs: 9p, Squadron off Nargue Is., 1809. 14p, Battle of the Nile, 1798. 29p, Battle of St. Vincent, 1797. 31p, HMS Crescent off Cherbourg, 1793. 34p, Battle of the Saints, 1782.

1986, Feb. 4 **Litho.** ***Perf. 11¾***

Granite Paper

No.	Type	Denom.	Description	Unused	Used
325	A73	9p	multicolored	.30	.30
326	A73	14p	multicolored	.40	.40
327	A73	29p	multicolored	.80	.80
328	A73	31p	multicolored	1.20	1.20
329	A73	34p	multicolored	1.25	1.25
			Nos. 325-329 (5)	3.95	3.95

Queen Elizabeth II, 60th Birthday — A74

1986, Apr. 21 ***Perf. 14***

No.	Type	Denom.	Description	Unused	Used
330	A74	60p	multicolored	1.90	1.90

Europa 1986 — A75

1986, May 22 ***Perf. 11½***

Granite Paper

No.	Type	Denom.	Description	Unused	Used
331	A75	10p	Operation Gannet	*.35*	*.35*
332	A75	14p	Whitsun orchid	*.40*	*.40*
333	A75	22p	Guernsey elm	*.75*	*.75*
			Nos. 331-333 (3)	1.50	1.50

Wedding of Prince Andrew and Sarah Ferguson — A76

1986, July 23 **Litho.** ***Perf. 14***

No.	Type	Denom.	Description	Unused	Used
334	A76	14p	Couple	.45	.45

Size: 48x32mm

No.	Type	Denom.	Description	Unused	Used
335	A76	34p	Couple, diff.	1.35	1.35

Sports A77

1986, July 24 ***Perf. 14½***

No.	Type	Denom.	Description	Unused	Used
336	A77	10p	Lawn bowling, vert.	.25	.25
337	A77	14p	Cricket, vert.	.35	.35
338	A77	22p	Badminton, vert.	.45	.45
339	A77	29p	Field hockey, vert.	.90	.90
340	A77	31p	Swimming	1.00	1.00
341	A77	34p	Rifle shooting	1.10	1.10
			Nos. 336-341 (6)	4.05	4.05

Museums A78

14p, Guernsey Museum and Art Gallery. 29p, Ft. Grey Maritime Museum. 31p, Castle Cornet. 34p, Natl. Trust of Guernsey Folk Museum.

1986, Nov. 18 **Litho.** ***Perf. 14½***

No.	Type	Denom.	Description	Unused	Used
342	A78	14p	multicolored	.35	.35
343	A78	29p	multicolored	.85	.85
344	A78	31p	multicolored	.90	.90
345	A78	34p	multicolored	1.00	1.00
			Nos. 342-345 (4)	3.10	3.10

Miniature Sheet

Christmas — A79

Carols: a, "While Shepherds Watched Their Flocks by Night." b, "In the Bleak Mid-Winter." c, "O Little Town of Bethlehem." d, "The Holly and the Ivy." e, "O Little Christmas Tree." f, "Away in a Manger." g, "Good King Wenceslas." h, "We Three Kings of Orient Are." i, "Hark the Herald Angels Sing." j, "I Saw Three Ships." k, "Little Donkey." l, "Jingle Bells."

1986, Nov. 18 ***Perf. 12½***

No.	Type	Description	Unused	Used
346	A79	Sheet of 12	2.75	2.75
a.-l.		6p any single	.25	.25

Souvenir Sheet

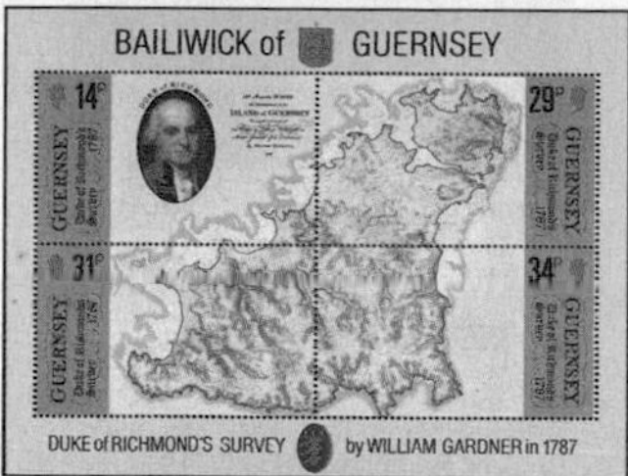

Duke of Richmond, 18th Century Map Detail — A80

14p, Duke of Richmond, part of map in bottom right corner. 29p, North. 31p, Southwest. 34p, Southeast.

1987, Feb. 10 Litho. *Perf. 14½*

347	A80	Sheet of 4	3.75	3.75
a.		14p multicolored	.40	.40
b.		29p multicolored	.85	.85
c.		31p multicolored	.95	.95
d.		34p multicolored	1.10	1.10

Duke of Richmond's survey of Guernsey, bicent.

Europa 1987 — A81

Modern architecture: No. 348, Postal headquarters. No. 349, Headquarters, schematic view. No. 350, Grammar school entrance. No. 351, School, schematic view.

1987, May 5 Litho. *Perf. 13x13½*

348	A81	15p multicolored	.35	.35
349	A81	15p multicolored	.35	.35
a.		Pair, #348-349	.85	.85
350	A81	22p multicolored	.60	.60
351	A81	22p multicolored	.60	.60
a.		Pair, #350-351	1.40	1.40

Andros and La Plaiderie Court House, Guernsey A82

Andros and: 29p, Governor's Palace, Virginia. 31p, "Governor Andros and the Boston People," print from Harper's New Monthly Magazine. 34p, Map of New Amsterdam (New York City).

1987, July 7 Granite Paper *Perf. 12*

352	A82	15p multicolored	.30	.30
353	A82	29p multicolored	.80	.80
354	A82	31p multicolored	1.00	1.00
355	A82	34p multicolored	1.10	1.10
		Nos. 352-355 (4)	3.20	3.20

Sir Edmund Andros (1637-1714), lieutenant-governor of Guernsey (1704-1706) and statesman of Colonial America (1672-1710).

William the Conqueror (c. 1028-1087), King of England (1066-1087) — A83

11p, Jester warning young William of a plot to murder him. No. 357, Battle of Hastings. No. 358, King William, his banner at the Battle of Hastings. No. 359, William the Conqueror. No. 360, Abbey at Caen & Queen Matilda of Flanders (d. 1083). 34p, Halley's Comet & regalia of William I.

1987, Sept. 9 *Perf. 13½x14*

356	A83	11p multicolored	.30	.30
357	A83	15p multicolored	.40	.40
358	A83	15p multicolored	.40	.40
a.		Pair, #357-358	1.10	1.10
359	A83	22p multicolored	.80	.80
360	A83	22p multicolored	.80	.80
a.		Pair, #359-360	1.75	1.75
361	A83	34p multicolored	1.00	1.00
		Nos. 356-361 (6)	3.70	3.70

Visit of John Wesley (1703-1791), Religious Reformer, Bicent. — A84

Designs: 7p, Preaching at the quay, Alderney. 15p, Preaching at Mon Plaisir. 29p, Preaching at Assembly Rooms, St. Peter Port. 31p, Wesley and La Ville Baudu, an early Methodist meeting place, Vale Parish. 34p, Wesley and Ebenezer Methodist Church, first Methodist chapel, Union Street, 1816.

1987, Nov. 17 Litho. *Perf. 14½*

362	A84	7p multicolored	.30	.30
363	A84	15p multicolored	.40	.40
364	A84	29p multicolored	.85	.85
365	A84	31p multicolored	.90	.90
366	A84	34p multicolored	1.00	1.00
		Nos. 362-366 (5)	3.45	3.45

Voyage of the Golden Spur, Apr. 12, 1872-Jan. 4, 1874 — A85

Designs: 11p, Off St. Sampson's Harbor. 15p, Entering Hong Kong Harbor. 29p, Anchored off Macao. 31p, In China Tea Race. 34p, Golden Spur, map of voyage.

1988, Feb. 9 Litho. *Perf. 13½x14*

367	A85	11p multicolored	.35	.35
368	A85	15p multicolored	.45	.45
369	A85	29p multicolored	.90	.90
370	A85	31p multicolored	1.00	1.00
371	A85	34p multicolored	1.10	1.10
		Nos. 367-371 (5)	3.80	3.80

Guernsey's Golden Age of Shipping: largest vessel built on Guernsey, the Golden Spur, launched Oct. 15, 1864, wrecked at Haiphong on Feb. 27, 1879.

Landscape Type of 1984

12p, Petit Bot beach, vert. 16p, St. John's Hostel for the Aged. 18p, Le Variouf, vert.

Perf. 14½x15, 15x14½

1987-89 Litho.

372	A63	12p multicolored	.45	.45
373	A63	16p multicolored	.55	.55
a.		Min. sheet, 5 each 12p, 16p	6.00	
b.		Min. sheet, 4 4p, 3 12p, 3 16p	4.75	
374	A63	18p multicolored	.60	.60
a.		Booklet pane, 4p, 6p, 3 12p, 3 18p	4.00	
		Complete booklet, #374a	4.00	
b.		Booklet pane, 4 12p, 4 18p	3.50	
		Complete booklet, #374b	4.00	
		Nos. 372-374 (3)	1.60	1.60

Nos. 373a-373b have surrounding selvage and were sold unattached in booklet covers. Nos. 374a, 374b with straight edges around stamps and attached to booklet covers by tabs.

Issued: Nos. 372-373b, 3/28/88; Nos. 374-374b, 2/28/89.

Coil Stamps

11p, La Seigneurie, Sark. 12p, Petit Bot beach, vert. 15p, Havelet, vert. 16p, St. John's Hostel for the Aged.

Sizes: 21½x17½mm, 17½x21½mm

Perf. 14x14½, 14½x14

375	A63	11p multicolored	.45	.45
376	A63	12p multicolored	.50	.50
377	A63	15p multicolored	.60	.60
378	A63	16p multicolored	.65	.65
		Nos. 375-378 (4)	2.20	2.20

Issued: 11p, 15p, 5/15/87; 12p, 16p, 3/28/88.

Waves, Map — A85a

Perf. 14½x14

1989, Apr. 3 Photo. Coil Stamp

380	A85a	(18p) green	1.00	1.00

Inscribed "MINIMUM FIRST CLASS POSTAGE TO UK PAID." See No. 431.

Europa 1988 A86

Communication and transportation: No. 381, Bedford Rascal postal van, Lihou Is. rowboat. No. 382, Rowboat, Viscount plane. No. 383, Horse and buggy, front wheel of bicycle. No. 384, Back wheel of bicycle, No. 4 coach.

1988, May 10 Litho. *Perf. 14½*

381	A86	16p multicolored	.40	.40
382	A86	16p multicolored	.40	.40
a.		Pair, #381-382	1.25	1.25
383	A86	22p multicolored	.70	.70
384	A86	22p multicolored	.70	.70
a.		Pair, #383-384	1.75	1.75
		Nos. 381-384 (4)	2.20	2.20

Nos. 382a, 384a have continuous designs.

Frederick Corbin Lukis (1788-1871), Archaeologist A87

Designs: 12p, Entrance to Lukis House, St. Peter Port, and portrait. 16p, Bound manuscript containing illustrations painted by Lukis's daughter Mary Anne (born 1822). 29p, Lukis supervising excavation of Le Creux es Faies dolmen at L'Eree, Guernsey. 31p, Rear of Lukis House and garden. 34p, Artifacts recovered by Lukis and preserved as part of the museum collection.

1988, July 12 Photo. *Perf. 12½*

Granite Paper

385	A87	12p multicolored	.30	.30
386	A87	16p multicolored	.35	.35
387	A87	29p multicolored	.80	.80
388	A87	31p multicolored	.90	.90
389	A87	34p multicolored	1.00	1.00
		Nos. 385-389 (5)	3.35	3.35

1988 World Offshore Powerboat Championships — A88

Designs: 16p, Racing boats, Royal Navy helicopter. 30p, Boats racing through Gouliot Passage (separating Sark from Brecqhou). 32p, Boats, helicopter, St. John's Ambulance rescue ship, vert. 35p, Race course marked in red on Admiralty Chart, vert.

1988, Sept. 6 *Perf. 12*

Granite Paper

390	A88	16p multicolored	.30	.30
391	A88	30p multicolored	.90	.90
392	A88	32p multicolored	1.10	1.10
393	A88	35p multicolored	1.25	1.25
		Nos. 390-393 (4)	3.55	3.55

Publication of *Flora Sarniensis,* Bicent. — A89

Designs: 12p, Joshua Gosselin (1739-1813), botanist, and herbarium made by Rollo Sherwill in 1976. No. 395, *Lagurus ovatus* (pressed specimen). No. 396, *Lagurus ovatus,* diff. No. 397, *Silene gallica quinquevulnera* (pressed specimen). No. 398, *Silene gallica quinquevulnera,* diff. 35p, *Limonium binervosum sarniense serquense.*

1988, Nov. 15 Litho. *Perf. 14*

394	A89	12p shown	.25	.25
395	A89	16p multicolored	.35	.35
396	A89	16p multicolored	.35	.35
a.		Pair, #395-396	1.00	1.00
397	A89	23p multicolored	.60	.60
398	A89	23p multicolored	.60	.60
a.		Pair, #397-398	1.50	1.50
399	A89	35p multicolored	1.25	1.25
		Nos. 394-399 (6)	3.40	3.40

Miniature Sheet

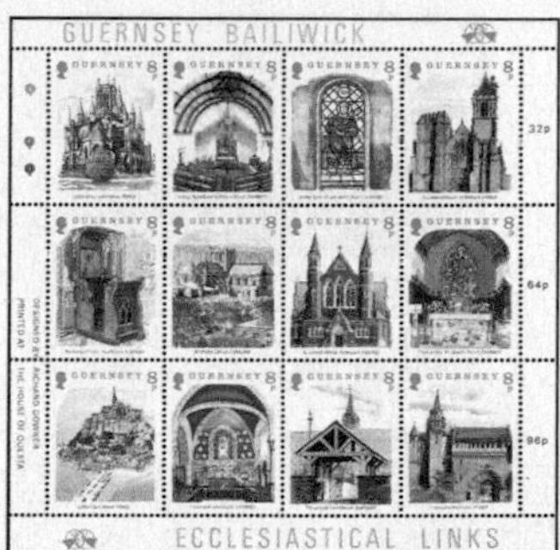

Ecclesiastical Links to France and Great Britain — A90

Church interiors, exteriors and artifacts: a, Coutances Cathedral, France. b, Notre Dame du Rosaire Church interior, Guernsey. c, Stained-glass window, St. Sampson's Church, Guernsey. d, Dol-de-Bretagne Cathedral, France. e, Bishop's Throne, Town Church, Guernsey. f, Winchester Cathedral, England. g, St. John's Cathedral, Portsmouth, England. h, High Altar, St. Joseph's Church, Guernsey. i, Mont Saint-Michel, France. j, Chancel, Vale Church, Guernsey. k, The Lychgate, Forest Church, Guernsey. l, Marmoutier Abbey, France.

1988, Nov. 15 *Perf. 14½x15*

400	A90	Sheet of 12	3.25	3.25
a.-l.		8p any single	.25	.25

Christmas 1988.

Europa 1989 — A91

Traditional children's toys and games.

1989, Feb. 28 Litho. *Perf. 13½*

401	A91	12p Tip cat (Le Cat)	.30	.30
402	A91	16p Girl, Cobo Alice doll	.45	.45
403	A91	23p Hopscotch (Le Colimachaon)	.75	.75
		Nos. 401-403 (3)	1.50	1.50

Aircraft A92

1989, May 5

404	A92	12p DH86 Express	.35	.35
a.		Booklet pane of 6	3.00	

405 A92 12p Southampton .35 .35
406 A92 18p DH89 Rapide .50 .50
a. Booklet pane of 6 4.50
407 A92 18p Sunderland .50 .50
408 A92 35p BAe 146 1.10 1.10
a. Booklet pane of 6 9.50
Complete booklet, #404a, 406a, 408a 17.50
409 A92 35p Shackleton 1.10 1.10
Nos. 404-409 (6) 3.90 3.90

Guernsey Airport, 50th anniv. (Nos. 404, 406, 408); others, 201st Squadron Affiliation, 50th anniv.

Visit of Queen Elizabeth II, May 20-24 — A93

30p, Portrait by June Mendoza.

1989, May 23 ***Perf. 15x14***
410 A93 30p multicolored .90 .90

Great Western Railway Steamer Service Between Weymouth and the Channel Isls., Cent. — A94

12p, S.S. Ibex, 1891. 18p, P.S. Great Western, 1872. 29p, S.S. St. Julien, 1925. 34p, S.S. Roebuck, 1925. 37p, S.S. Antelope, 1889.

1989, Sept. 5 **Litho.** ***Perf. 13½***
411 A94 12p multicolored .30 .30
412 A94 18p multicolored .40 .40
413 A94 29p multicolored .80 .80
414 A94 34p multicolored 1.10 1.10
415 A94 37p multicolored 1.25 1.25
a. Souvenir sheet of 5, #411-415 4.25 4.25
Nos. 411-415 (5) 3.85 3.85

Zoological Trust of Guernsey — A95

18p, Two-toed sloth. 29p, Capuchin monkey. 32p, White-lipped tamarin. 34p, Squirrel monkey. 37p, Lar gibbon.

1989, Nov. 17 **Litho.** ***Perf. 14x13½***
416 A95 18p multicolored .75 .75
417 A95 29p multicolored .75 .75
418 A95 32p multicolored .75 .75
419 A95 34p multicolored .75 .75
420 A95 37p multicolored .75 .75
a. Strip of 5, #416-420 5.25 5.25

Animals of the rainforest.

Miniature Sheet

Christmas — A96

Ornaments on tree: a, Star. b, Angel. c, Candles. d, Robin red breast. e, Presents on sled. f, Caroler. g, Santa Claus pictured on Christmas cracker. h, Herald and stars pictured on glass ball. i, Presents in stocking. j, Bell. k, Reindeer. l, Chapel.

1989, Nov. 17 ***Perf. 13***
421 A96 Sheet of 12 3.75 3.75
a.-l. 10p any single .25 .25

Europa 1990 — A97

Post offices.

1990, Feb. 27 **Litho.** ***Perf. 13½x14***
422 A97 20p Sark, c. 1890 *.50 .50*
423 A97 20p Sark, 1990 *.50 .50*
424 A97 24p Arcade, c. 1840 *.65 .65*
425 A97 24p Arcade, 1990 *.65 .65*
Nos. 422-425 (4) 2.30 2.30

Penny Black, 150th Anniv. A98

Designs: 14p, Great Britain No. 1, Maltese Cross cancellation in red, mail steamer in St. Peter Port Harbor. 20p, Great Britain No. 3, Maltese Cross cancellation in black, pedestrians, mailbox at Elm Grove and Union Street in 1853. 32p, Great Britain No. 255 bisected, 1940, and military band. 34p, Guernsey No. 2, crown of William the Conqueror, Guernsey lily. 37p, Guernsey No. 10, crowd in line outside Guernsey P.O.

1990, May 3 ***Perf. 14***
426 A98 14p multicolored .45 .45
427 A98 20p multicolored .65 .65
428 A98 32p multicolored .90 .90
429 A98 34p multicolored 1.00 1.00
430 A98 37p multicolored 1.25 1.25
a. Souvenir sheet of 5, #426-430 4.75 4.75
b. No. 430a ovptd. "NZ 1990" emblem, "FROM LONDON 90 TO NEW ZEALAND 90" 16.00 16.00
Nos. 426-430 (5) 4.25 4.25

Map and Waves Type of 1989

1989, Dec. 27 **Photo.** ***Perf. 14½x14***
Coil Stamp
431 A85a (14p) ultra & lt ultra .85 .85

Inscribed "MINIMUM BAILIWICK POSTAGE PAID."

Lord Anson's Circumnavigation of the World, 250th Anniv. — A99

Designs: 14p, Philip Saumarez writing ship's log. 20p, *Centurion, Gloucester, Severn, Pearle, Wager* and *Tryal* departing from Portsmouth. 29p, Landfall at St. Catherine's Is. off Brazil, 1740. 34p, *Tryal* rounding Cape Horn, 1741. 37p, Camp at Juan Fernandez, 1741.

1990, July 24 **Litho.** ***Perf. 13½x14***
436 A99 14p multicolored .35 .35
437 A99 20p multicolored .50 .50
438 A99 29p multicolored .90 .90
439 A99 34p multicolored 1.00 1.00
440 A99 37p multicolored 1.10 1.10
Nos. 436-440 (5) 3.85 3.85

Gray Seal A100

26p, Bottlenose dolphin. 31p, Basking shark. 37p, Harbor porpoise.

1990, Oct. 16 **Litho.** ***Perf. 14½***
441 A100 20p shown *.75* .55
442 A100 26p multicolored *1.25* 1.10
443 A100 31p multicolored *1.50* 1.25
444 A100 37p multicolored *2.00* 1.40
Nos. 441-444 (4) *5.50* 4.30

World Wildlife Fund.

Miniature Sheet

Christmas — A101

Winter birds: a, Blue and Great Tits. b, Snow Bunting. c, Kestrel. d, Starling. e, Greenfinch. f, Robin. g, Wren. h, Barn owl. i, Mistle Thrush. j, Heron. k, Chaffinch. l, Kingfisher.

1990, Oct. 16 ***Perf. 13½***
445 A101 Sheet of 12 4.00 4.00
a.-l. 10p any single .30 .30

Occupation Stamp No. N1, 50th Anniv. — A102

1991, Feb. 18 **Litho.** ***Perf. 13½***
446 A102 37p shown 1.25 1.25
447 A102 53p No. N2 1.50 1.50
448 A102 57p No. N3 1.75 1.75
a. Booklet pane of 3, #446-448 5.00
Complete booklet, 3 #448a 16.50
Nos. 446-448 (3) 4.50 4.50

No. 448a printed in three formats with Nos. 446-448 in different order.

Europa — A103

Designs: No. 449, Royal Visit to Guernsey, discovery of Neptune, 1846. No. 450, Royal Visit to Sark, launch of Sputnik, 1957. No. 451, Maiden voyage of ferry Sarnia, first manned space flight, 1961. No. 452, Independence of Guernsey Post Office, first man on moon, 1969.

1991, Apr. 30 **Litho.** ***Perf. 13½x14***
449 A103 21p multicolored *.60 .60*
450 A103 21p multicolored *.60 .60*
451 A103 26p multicolored *.80 .80*
452 A103 26p multicolored *.80 .80*
Nos. 449-452 (4) 2.80 2.80

Landscape Type of 1984

21p, King's Mills, St. Saviours. 26p, Town Church, St. Peter Port, vert.

1991 **Litho.** ***Perf. 15x14½, 14½x15***
453 A63 21p multicolored .80 .80
a. Booklet pane, 3 each #453, #296, 2 each #287, #288) 3.50
Complete booklet, #453a 3.00
b. Booklet pane, 5 each #453, #296) 6.00
Complete booklet, #453b 3.00
454 A63 26p multicolored .90 .90

Issued: 21p, 26p, 4/1; Nos. 453a, 453b, 4/2.

Nos. 453a, 453b with straight edges around stamps and attached to booklet covers by tabs.

Guernsey Yacht Club, Cent. — A104

15p, Guernsey Sailing Trust. 21p, Guernsey Regatta. 26p, Channel Islands Challenge. 31p, Rolex Swan Regatta. 37p, Old Gaffers Assoc.

1991, July 2 **Litho.** ***Perf. 14***
459 A104 15p multicolored .45 .45
460 A104 21p multicolored .70 .70
461 A104 26p multicolored .80 .80
462 A104 31p multicolored .90 .90
463 A104 37p multicolored 1.00 1.00
a. Souvenir sheet of 5, #459-463 4.75 4.75
Nos. 459-463 (5) 3.85 3.85

"Guernsey" and denomination in white on sheet stamps, yellow on souvenir sheet stamps.

Miniature Sheet

Christmas — A105

Children's Paintings: a, Reindeer by Melanie Sharpe. b, Christmas pudding by James Quinn. c, Snowman by Lisa Marie Guille. d, Snowman by Jessica Ede-Golightly. e, Birds by Sharon Le Page. f, Shepherds, sheep, angels by Anna Coquelin. g, Manger scene by Claudine Lihou. h, Three kings by Jonathan Le

Noury. i, Children, angels, Star of Bethlehem by Marcia Mahy. j, Christmas tree, presents by Laurel Garfield. k, Santa Claus by Rebecca Driscoll. l, Snowman by Ian Lowe.

1991, Oct. 15 Litho. *Perf. 13*
464 A105 Sheet of 12 4.25 4.25
a.-l. 12p any single .30 .30

Nature Conservation A106

Birds and plants: No. 465: a, Two oyster catchers. b, Three turnstones. c, Two dunlins, two turnstones. d, Curlew, two turnstones. e, Ringed plover, chicks.

No. 466: a, Violet and white flowers. b, Yellow flowers. c, Small yellow flowers. d, Violet, yellow and white flowers. e, Long-stemmed yellow flowers.

1991, Oct. 15 *Perf. 14½*
465 Strip of 5 2.50 2.50
a.-e. A106 15p any single .45 .45
466 Strip of 5 3.00 3.00
a.-e. A106 21p any single .55 .55

Discovery of America, 500th Anniv. — A107

No. 467, Columbus. No. 468, Columbus' signatures. No. 469, Map of 1st voyage. No. 470, Santa Maria.

1992, Feb. 6 Litho. *Perf. 13½x14*
467 A107 23p multicolored *.80 .80*
468 A107 23p multicolored *.80 .80*
469 A107 28p multicolored *1.10 1.10*
470 A107 28p multicolored *1.10 1.10*
a. Souvenir sheet, #467-470 *6.50 6.50*
b. No. 470a overprinted in brown in sheet margin *7.75 7.75*
Nos. 467-470 (4) 3.80 3.80

Europa. No. 470b overprint shows emblem of World Columbian Stamp Expo '92.
Issue date: No. 470b, May 22.

Queen Elizabeth II's Accession to Throne, 40th Anniv. — A108

Various portraits of Queen Elizabeth II from 1952, 1977, 1986 and 1992.

1992, Feb. 6 Litho. *Perf. 14*
471 A108 23p multicolored .60 .60
472 A108 28p multicolored .75 .75
473 A108 33p multicolored 1.00 1.00
474 A108 39p multicolored 1.25 1.25
Nos. 471-474 (4) 3.60 3.60

Souvenir Sheet

Guernsey Cows — A109

1992, May 22 Litho. *Perf. 14*
475 A109 75p multicolored 2.50 2.50

Royal Guernsey Agricultural and Horticultural Society, 150th anniv.

Flowers — A110

1p, Stephanotis floribunda. 2p, Potted hydrangea. 3p, Stock. 4p, Anemones. 5p, Gladiolus. 6p, Gypsophila paniculata, asparagus plumosus. 7p, Guernsey lily. 8p, Enchantment lily. 9p, Clematis freckles. 10p, Alstroemeria. 16p, Standard carnation, horiz. 20p, Spray rose. 23p, Mixed freesia, horiz. 24p, Standard rose, horiz. 25p, Iris ideal, horiz. 28p, Lisianthus, horiz. 30p, Spray chrysanthemum, horiz. 40p, Spray carnation. 50p, Single freesia, horiz. £ 1, Bouquet, horiz., inscribed "1992". £ 2, Chelsea flower show, horiz. £ 3, Floral fantasia, horiz.

1992-96 *Perf. 13*
476 A110 1p multicolored .25 .25
477 A110 2p multicolored .25 .25
478 A110 3p multicolored .25 .25
479 A110 4p multicolored .25 .25
480 A110 5p multicolored .25 .25
481 A110 6p multicolored .25 .25
482 A110 7p multicolored .25 .25
483 A110 8p multicolored .30 .30
484 A110 9p multicolored .30 .30
485 A110 10p multicolored .35 .35
486 A110 16p multicolored .55 .55
a. Perf. 14 on 3 sides, inscribed "1993" .65 .55
b. Booklet pane of 8 #486a 5.00
Complete booklet, 1 #486b 5.00
c. Inscribed "1992" .65 .55
487 A110 20p multicolored .75 .65
488 A110 23p multicolored .80 .80
a. Perf. 14 on 3 sides .85 .80
b. Bklt. pane of 5 #486c, 3 #488a 6.50 6.50
Complete booklet, 1 #488b 6.50
c. Booklet pane of 8, #488a 8.00 8.00
Complete booklet, 1 #488c 8.00
489 A110 24p multicolored .85 .65
a. Perf. 14 on 3 sides 1.00 .80
b. Booklet pane of 8 #489a 8.00
Complete booklet, 1 #489b 8.00
490 A110 25p multicolored .90 .65
a. Perf. 14½ on 3 sides 1.00 .80
b. As "a," booklet pane of 4 4.50
Complete booklet, 1 #490b 4.50
491 A110 28p multicolored .90 .70
a. Perf. 14 on 3 sides 1.25 .80
b. Booklet pane of 4 #491a 5.00
Complete booklet, 1 #491b 5.00
492 A110 30p multicolored 1.00 .90
493 A110 40p multicolored 1.25 1.25
494 A110 50p multicolored 1.50 1.25

Size: 39x30mm
Perf. 13¾
495 A110 £1 multicolored 3.00 2.50
a. Souv. sheet of 1 + label, perf. 13, inscribed "1994" 4.25 4.25
b. Souv. sheet of 1 + label, perf. 13, inscribed "1995" 4.25 4.25
496 A110 £2 multicolored 6.50 5.00

Size: 39x31mm
Perf. 13¼
497 A110 £3 multicolored 8.50 7.00
Nos. 476-497 (22) 29.20 24.60

PHILAKOREA '94 (No. 495a). Singapore '95 (No. 495b).

Issued: 3p, 4p, 5p, 10p, 16p, 20p, 23p, 40p, 50p, £1, 5/22/92; 1p, 2p, 6p, 7p, 8p, 9p, 24p, 28p, 30p, £2, No. 486a, 3/2/93; Nos. 486b, 489b, 491b, 3/3/93: Nos. 488a, 488b, 5/22/92; 25p, 2/18/94; No. 490b, 2/18/94; No. 495a, 8/94; No. 495b, 9/1/95; £3, 1/24/96.

Perf 14 or 14½ stamps issued only in booklets.

See Nos. 584-585.

Operation Asterix A111

1992, Sept. 18 Litho. *Perf. 13*
498 A111 16p Ship construction .45 .45
499 A111 23p Loading cargo .60 .60
500 A111 28p Ship at sea .85 .85
501 A111 33p Ship on fire 1.00 1.00
502 A111 39p Ship sinking 1.25 1.25
a. Bklt. pane of #498-502 + label 5.50
Complete booklet, 4 #502a 22.50
Nos. 498-502 (5) 4.15 4.15

No. 502a exists with four different labels: Great Britain, France, Italy, Germany. Booklet contains one of each type.

Historic Trams A112

Designs: 16p, Tram No. 10 decorated for Battle of Flowers. 23p, No. 10 passing Hougue a la Perre. 28p, Tram No. 1 at St. Sampsons. 33p, First steam tram, St. Peter Port, 1879. 39p, Last electric tram, 1934.

1992, Nov. 17 Litho. *Perf. 13½x14*
503 A112 16p multicolored .60 .60
504 A112 23p multicolored .75 .75
505 A112 28p multicolored .90 .90
506 A112 33p multicolored 1.00 1.00
507 A112 39p multicolored 1.25 1.25
Nos. 503-507 (5) 4.50 4.50

Christmas — A113

a, Father dressed as Santa. b, Girl pulling end of cracker. c, Mother. d, Champagne, mince pies. e, Turkey. f, Plum pudding. g, Cake. h, Cookies. i, Wine, blue cheese. j, Nuts. k, Ham. l, Cake roll.

1992, Nov. 17 *Perf. 13½*
508 A113 Sheet of 12 4.75 4.75
a.-l. 13p any single .35 .35

A114

Rupert Bear and friends, created by Mary Tourtel: No. 509: Rupert Bear, Bingo, and dog. No. 510a, 24p, Bill Badger, Willie Mouse, Reggie Rabbit, and Podgy Pig with snowman. No. 510b, 16p, Airplane above castle tower. No. 510c, 24p, Balloonist leaping away from Gregory on sled. No. 510d, 16p, Professor's servant and Autumn Elf. No. 510e, 16p, Algy Pug. No. 510f, 16p, Baby Badger on sled. No. 510g, 24p, Tiger Lily and Edward Trunk.

1993, Feb. 2 Litho. *Perf. 13½x13*
509 A114 24p multicolored .75 .75
510 A114 Sheet of 8, #a.-g. & #509 5.00 5.00

No. 510 printed in continuous design. Nos. 510b, 510d-510f are 25x26mm.

Nos. 509-510 were a joint issue with Great Britain No. BK1172. Within the booklet, Great Britain No. 1487 shows Rupert Bear, as does Guernsey No. 509.

Contemporary Art — A115

Europa: No. 511, Tapestry, by Kelly Fletcher. No. 512, The Fish Market, by Sally Reed. No. 513, Dress Shop, King's Road, by Damon Bell. No. 514, Red Abstract, by Molly Harris.

1993, May 7 Litho. *Perf. 13½x14*
Size: 45x30mm (#512, 513)
511 A115 24p multicolored *.70 .70*
512 A115 24p multicolored *.70 .70*
513 A115 28p multicolored *.85 .85*
514 A115 28p multicolored *.85 .85*
Nos. 511-514 (4) 3.10 3.10

Siege of Castle Cornet, 1643-51 — A116

16p, Shipboard arrest of Parliamentarian officials. 24p, Parliamentarian warships firing on castle. 28p, Captured officials fleeing from castle. 33p, Cannon firing from castle into St. Peter Port. 39p, Surrender of castle.

1993, May 7 *Perf. 15x14*
515 A116 16p multicolored .45 .45
516 A116 24p multicolored .70 .70
517 A116 28p multicolored .85 .85
518 A116 33p multicolored 1.00 1.00
519 A116 39p multicolored 1.10 1.10
a. Souvenir sheet of 5, #515-519 4.50 4.50
Nos. 515-519 (5) 4.10 4.10

Thomas de la Rue, Printer, Birth Bicent. — A117

Designs: 16p, Playing card king, queen and jack. 24p, Swift reservoir fountain pens. 28p, Envelope folding machine. 33p, Great Britain type A5. 39p, £1 Mauritius bank note, portrait of de la Rue.

1993, July 27 Litho. *Perf. 13½*
520 A117 16p multicolored .40 .40
521 A117 24p multicolored .75 .75
522 A117 28p multicolored .90 .90

Engr.
523 A117 33p rose carmine 1.00 1.00
524 A117 39p green 1.25 1.25
Nos. 520-524 (5) 4.30 4.30

520a Booklet pane of 4 3.00
521a Booklet pane of 4 4.25
522a Booklet pane of 4 4.75
523a Booklet pane of 4 5.50
524a Booklet pane of 4 6.50
Complete booklet, #520a-524a 24.00

Miniature Sheet

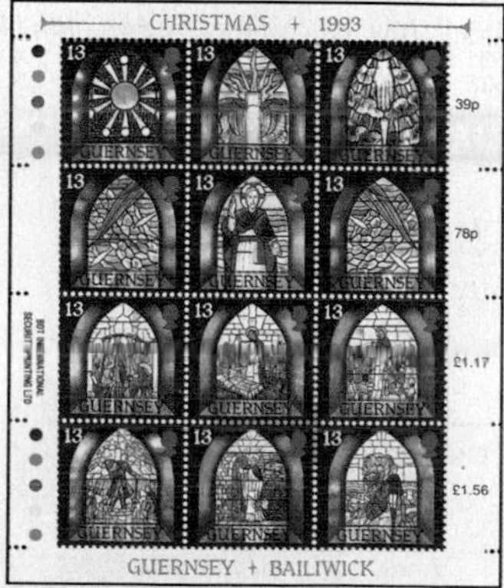

Christmas — A118

Stained glass windows, Chapel of Christ the Healer: a, Sunburst. b, Light from sun. c, Hand of God. d, Doves descending left. e, Christ raising hand. f, Doves descending right. g, Christ Child sitting in temple. h, Christ raising daughter of Jairus from dead. i, "Suffer little children to come unto me." j, Scene from Pilgrim's Progress. k, The Light of the World. l, Archangel of Healing.

1993, Nov. 2 Litho. *Perf. 13x13½*

525	A118	Sheet of 12	4.75	4.75
a.-l.		13p any single	.35	.25

Archaeological Discoveries — A119

Europa: No. 526, Warrior on horseback. No. 527, Burial site, Les Fouaillages. No. 528, Sword, scabbard, spear. No. 529, Cerny-style pots, arrowheads, axe.

1994, Feb. 18 Litho. *Perf. 13½*

526	A119	24p multicolored	*.65*	*.65*
a.		Sheet of 10 with added inscription	10.00	10.00
527	A119	24p multicolored	*.65*	*.65*
528	A119	30p multicolored	*.95*	*.95*
529	A119	30p multicolored	*.95*	*.95*
		Nos. 526-529 (4)	*3.20*	*3.20*

No. 526a inscribed in sheet margin with Hong Kong '94 emblem and "PHILATELIC EXHIBITION / 18-21 FEBRUARY 1994" in English and Chinese.

Souvenir Sheet

D-Day, 50th Anniv. — A120

£2, Canadian Wing Spitfires flying over Normandy coastline.

1994, June 6 Litho. *Perf. 14*

530	A120	£2 multicolored	6.00	5.00

Classic Cars A121

Designs: 16p, 1894 Peugeot Type 3. 24p, 1903 Mercedes Simplex. 35p, 1906 Humber 14.4hp. 41p, 1936 Bentley 4¼ L. 60p, 1948 MG TC.

1994, July 19 Litho. *Perf. 15x14*

531	A121	16p multicolored	.40	.40
532	A121	24p multicolored	.55	.55
533	A121	35p multicolored	1.00	1.00
534	A121	41p multicolored	1.25	1.25
535	A121	60p multicolored	1.75	1.75
		Nos. 531-535 (5)	4.95	4.95
531a		Booklet pane of 4	3.00	
532a		Booklet pane of 4	4.25	
533a		Booklet pane of 4	6.00	
534a		Booklet pane of 4	6.50	
535a		Booklet pane of 4	9.75	
		Complete booklet, #531a-535a	29.50	

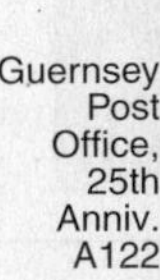

Guernsey Post Office, 25th Anniv. A122

Designs: 16p, Trident ferry. 24p, Handley Page Super Dart Herald of Channel Express. 35p, Aurigny Air Services' JOEY. 41p, Bon Marin de Serk ferry. 60p, Map of Guernsey, Herm, Alderney, Sark.

1994, Oct. 1 Litho. *Perf. 14*

536	A122	16p multicolored	.50	.50
537	A122	24p multicolored	.65	.65
538	A122	35p multicolored	1.10	1.10
539	A122	41p multicolored	1.50	1.50
540	A122	60p multicolored	2.00	2.00
a.		Souvenir sheet, #536-540	6.50	6.50
		Nos. 536-540 (5)	5.75	5.75

See Jersey Nos. 685-689a.

Miniature Sheets

Christmas — A123

Antique toys — No. 541: a, Doll house. b, Doll. c, Small teddy bear in carriage. d, Cards, post boxes with candy. e, Top. f, Picture puzzle blocks.

No. 542: a, Rocking horse. b, Large teddy bear. c, Tricycle. d, Wooden pull duck. e, Tin plate locomotive. f, Ludo game.

1994, Oct. 1 *Perf. 13*

541	A123	Sheet of 6	2.75	2.75
a.-f.		13p any single	.40	.40
542	A123	Sheet of 6	4.25	4.25
a.-f.		24p any single	.65	.65

Greetings — A124

Faces formed by: No. 543, Shrimp, oyster, lobster, fish. No. 544, Sand buckets, shovel, sand. No. 545, Flowers. No. 546, Lettuce, tomatoes, mushroom, squash. No. 547, Seaweed, shells. No. 548, Anchor, life preservers. No. 549, Wine, cork, knife, fork. No. 550, Butterflies, caterpillars.

1995, Feb. 2 Litho. *Perf. 14*

543	A124	24p multicolored	.70	.65
544	A124	24p multicolored	.70	.65
545	A124	24p multicolored	.70	.65
546	A124	24p multicolored	.70	.65
547	A124	24p multicolored	.70	.65
548	A124	24p multicolored	.70	.65
549	A124	24p multicolored	.70	.65
550	A124	24p multicolored	.70	.65
a.		Miniature sheet of 8, #543-550	5.75	5.25
		Complete booklet, #550a	6.00	
		Nos. 543-550 (8)	5.60	5.20

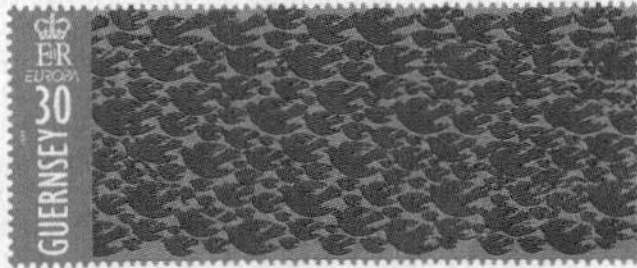

Doves — A125

Europa: 25p, Doves standing. 30p, Doves in flight.

1995, May 9 Litho. *Perf. 14*

551	A125	25p green	*.75*	*.75*
552	A125	30p blue	*.90*	*.90*

Nos. 551-552 contain a three-dimensional image hidden in the patterns composed of doves.

Liberation of Guernsey, 50th Anniv. — A126

Designs: 16p, Churchill making broadcast, crowd. 24p, St. Peter Port harbor. 35p, Military band. 41p, Red Cross ship Vega. 60p, Soldier kissing civilian woman.

1995, May 9 *Perf. 13½x14*

553	A126	16p multicolored	.45	.45
554	A126	24p multicolored	.70	.70
555	A126	35p multicolored	1.10	1.10
556	A126	41p multicolored	1.25	1.25
557	A126	60p multicolored	2.00	2.00
a.		Souvenir sheet of 5, #553-557	6.00	6.00
		Nos. 553-557 (5)	5.50	5.50

Visit by Prince of Wales A127

1995, May 9 *Perf. 14*

558	A127	£1.50 multicolored	4.75	4.75

UN, 50th Anniv. — A128

Portion of UN emblem, denomination: a, UL. b, UR. c, LL. d, LR.

Litho. & Embossed

1995, Oct. 24 *Perf. 14x13½*

559	A128	Block of 4	6.00	6.00
a.-d.		50p any single	1.25	1.25

Christmas — A129

Designs, with denomination at:

Shops in the city, children playing in snow — No. 560: a, LL. b, LR.

Homes in winter, children playing in snow — No. 561: a, LL. b, LR.

Children playing instruments, singing — No. 562: a, LL. b, LR.

Children of many nations — No. 563: a, LL. b, LR.

1995, Nov. 16 Litho. *Perf. 13½x13*

560	A129	Pair	.90	.90
a.-b.		13p any single	.45	.45
561	A129	Pair	.90	.90
a.-b.		13p +1p, any single	.45	.45
562	A129	Pair	1.50	1.50
a.-b.		24p any single	.75	.75
563	A129	Pair	1.50	1.50
a.-b.		24p +2p, any single	.75	.75
		Nos. 560-563 (4)	4.80	4.80

Nos. 560-563 are each continuous designs. UNICEF, 50th anniv.

Women of Achievement — A130

Europa: 25p, Princess Anne, children of different nations. 30p, Queen Elizabeth II, people of different nations.

1996, Apr. 21 Litho. *Perf. 14*

564	A130	25p multicolored	*.70*	*.70*
565	A130	30p multicolored	*.90*	*.90*

Queen Elizabeth II, 70th birthday (No. 565). See Isle of Man Nos. 679-680.

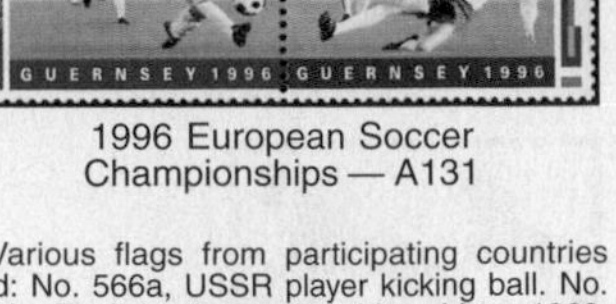

1996 European Soccer Championships — A131

Various flags from participating countries and: No. 566a, USSR player kicking ball. No. 566b, English players in white shirts, 1968. No. 567a, Italian player in blue shirt with ball. No. 567b, Belgium player in red, Italian players, 1972. No. 568a, Irish player in green kicking. No. 568b, Dutch player in blue, 1988. No. 569a, German player in white with ball. No. 569b, Danish player in red, 1992.

1996, Apr. 25 *Perf. 14x13½*

566	A131	Pair	1.10	1.10
a.-b.		16p any single	.55	.55
567	A131	Pair	1.60	1.60
a.-b.		24p any single	.80	.80
568	A131	Pair	2.25	2.25
a.-b.		35p any single	1.10	1.10
569	A131	Pair	2.50	2.50
a.-b.		41p any single	1.25	1.25
		Nos. 566-569 (4)	7.45	7.45

Souvenir Sheet

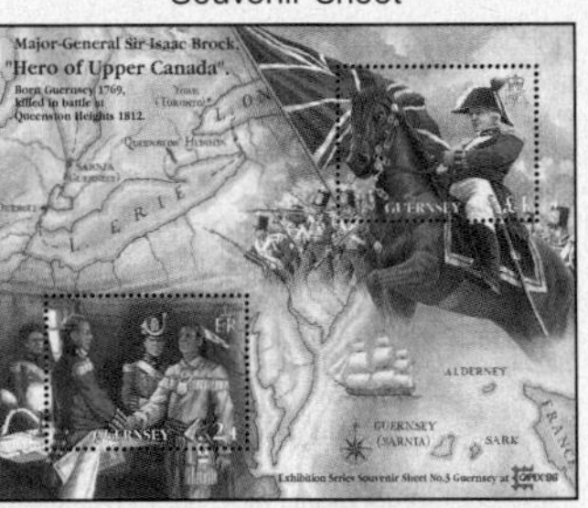

Sir Isaac Brock (1769-1812), British Commander in Upper Canada — A132

Designs: a, 24p, Brock shaking hands with Tecumseh. b, £1, Brock on horse.

1996, June 8 Litho. *Perf. 14x13½*

570	A132	Sheet of 2, #a.-b.	4.00	4.00

CAPEX '96.

Modern Olympic Games, Cent. — A133

The original pentathlon.

1996, July 19 Litho. *Perf. 14*

571	A133	16p Running	.50	.50
572	A133	24p Javelin	.90	.90
573	A133	41p Discus	1.25	1.25
574	A133	55p Wrestling	1.50	1.50
575	A133	60p Jumping	1.75	1.75
a.		Souvenir sheet, #571-575	6.75	6.75
		Nos. 571-575 (5)	5.90	5.90

No. 574 is 53x31mm. Olymphilex'96 (No.574).

Motion Pictures, Cent. A134

Classic Movie Detectives: 16p, Humphrey Bogart as Philip Marlowe. 24p, Peter Sellers as Inspector Clouseau. 35p, Basil Rathbone as Sherlock Holmes. 41p, Margaret Rutherford as Miss Marple. 60p, Warner Oland as Charlie Chan.

1996, Nov. 6 Litho. *Perf. 15x14*

576	A134	16p multicolored	.60	.60
577	A134	24p multicolored	.75	.75
578	A134	35p multicolored	.90	.90

579 A134 41p multicolored 1.00 1.00
580 A134 60p multicolored 1.50 1.50
Nos. 576-580 (5) 4.75 4.75

576a Booklet pane of 3 2.00
577a Booklet pane of 3 3.00
578a Booklet pane of 3 4.25
579a Booklet pane of 3 5.00
580a Booklet pane of 3 7.25
580b Bklt. pane of 5, #576-580 7.50
Complete booklet, #576a-580b 30.00

Christmas A135

Scenes depicting the Christmas story: 24p, Madonna and Child. 25p, Nativity.

No. 583, vert: a, Annuniciation by Angel Gabriel. b, Mary, Joseph on way to Bethlehem. c, Inn keeper turning them away. d, Angel appearing before shepherds. e, Holy Family in stable. f, Adoration of the shepherds. g, Magi following star. h, Magi presenting gifts. i, Prophet's warning to Mary, Joseph. j, Madonna and Child. k, Angel appearing in Joseph's dream. l, Flight into Egypt.

1996, Nov. 6 ***Perf. 13***
581 A135 24p multicolored .75 .75
582 A135 25p multicolored .80 .80

Miniature Sheet

583 Sheet of 12 4.75 4.75
a.-l. A135 13p Any single .35 .35

Flower Type of 1992

1997 Litho. ***Perf. 13***
584 A110 18p Standard rose .60 .50
a. Perf. 14 on 3 Sides .70 .00
b. As "a," booklet pane of 8 7.50
Complete booklet, #584b 7.50
585 A110 26p Freesia pink glow, horiz. .90 .65
a. Perf. 14 on 3 Sides 1.00 .65
b. As "a," booklet pane of 4 5.25
Complete booklet, #585b 5.25

Butterflies and Moths A136

Designs: 18p, Holly blue. 25p, Hummingbird hawk-moth. 26p, Emperor moth. 37p, Brimstone.

£1, Painted lady.

1997, Feb. 12 Litho. ***Perf. 14***
586 A136 18p multicolored .55 .55
587 A136 25p multicolored .90 .90
588 A136 26p multicolored 1.00 1.00
589 A136 37p multicolored 1.50 1.50
Nos. 586-589 (4) 3.95 3.95

Souvenir Sheet
Perf. 13½

590 A136 £1 multicolored 3.25 3.25

World Wildlife Fund (Nos. 586-589), Hong Kong '97 (No. 590).

Stories and Legends — A137

The Toilers of the Sea, by Victor Hugo: 26p, Man fighting sea monster, face in sea, ship. 31p, Ship, man seated on rock visualizing woman.

1997, Apr. 24 Litho. ***Perf. 13½***
591 A137 26p multicolored *.65 .65*
592 A137 31p multicolored *1.00 1.00*

Nos. 591-592 each issued in sheets of 10. Europa.

Island Scenes — A138

18p, Shell Beach, Herm. 25p, La Seigneurie, Sark, vert. 26p, Castle Comet, Guernsey.

Die Cut Perf. 9½x9, 9x9½

1997, Apr. 24 **Self-Adhesive**
593 A138 18p multicolored .65 .65
a. Booklet pane of 8 6.50
Complete booklet, #593a 6.50
594 A138 25p multicolored .90 .90
a. Booklet pane of 8 9.00
Complete booklet, #594a 9.00
595 A138 26p multicolored .90 .90
a. Booklet pane of 4 4.50
Complete booklet, #595a 4.50
Nos. 593-595 (3) 2.45 2.45

See Nos. 625-628.

Souvenir Sheet

PACIFIC 97 — A139

a, 30p, St. Peter Port, 1868. b, £1, Sailing ships.

1997, May 29 Litho. ***Perf. 14***
596 A139 Sheet of 2, #a.-b. 4.25 4.25

Communications — A140

1997, Aug. 21 Litho. ***Perf. 13½x13***
597 A140 18p Radio .50 .50
598 A140 25p Television .85 .85
599 A140 26p Telephone .85 .85
600 A140 37p Newspaper 1.25 1.25
601 A140 43p Post system 1.50 1.50
602 A140 63p Computer network 2.00 2.00
Nos. 597-602 (6) 6.95 6.95

Queen Elizabeth II and Prince Philip, 50th Wedding Anniv. — A141

Designs: 18p, At St. George's Hall, Guernsey, 1957. 25p, Queen being saluted by guardsman, 1953. 26p, Queen, family on horseback, 1957. 37p, Prince, Queen in casual attire, 1970. 43p, Queen saluting, at Trooping of the Color, 1987. 63p, Portrait, 1997.

1997, Nov. 20 Litho. ***Perf. 14***
603 A141 18p multicolored .50 .50
604 A141 25p multicolored .85 .85
a. Bklt. pane, 3 each #603-604 5.75
605 A141 26p multicolored .90 .90
606 A141 37p multicolored 1.25 1.25
a. Bklt. pane, 3 each #605-606 8.50
607 A141 43p multicolored 1.50 1.50
608 A141 63p multicolored 2.00 2.00
a. Bklt. pane, 3 each #607-608 13.50
b. Booklet pane, #603-608 9.00
Complete booklet, #604a, 606a, 608a, 608b 37.50
Nos. 603-608 (6) 7.00 7.00

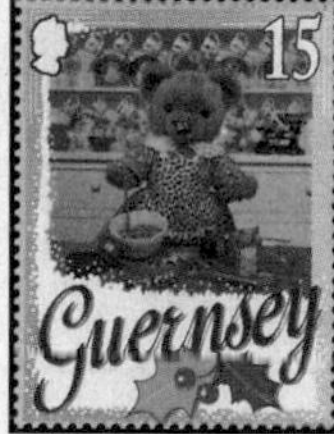

A142

Teddy Bears celebrating Christmas: 15p, Baking in kitchen. 25p, Beside Christmas tree. 26p, Seated in chair reading story. 37p, As Santa Claus. 43p, With presents. 63p, Seated at Christmas dinner.

1997, Nov. 6
609 A142 15p multicolored .55 .55
610 A142 25p multicolored .80 .80
611 A142 26p multicolored .80 .80
612 A142 37p multicolored 1.25 1.25
613 A142 43p multicolored 1.50 1.50
614 A142 63p multicolored 2.00 2.00
a. Souvenir sheet, #609-614 7.75 7.75
Nos. 609-614 (6) 6.90 6.90

A143

Millennium Tapestries: Embroidered panels showing images of Guernsey during last ten centuries, Guernsey-French inscriptions.

1998, Feb. 10 Litho. ***Perf. 14½***
615 A143 25p 11th century .80 .80
616 A143 25p 12th century .80 .80
617 A143 25p 13th century .80 .80
618 A143 25p 14th century .80 .80
a. Bklt. pane, 2 each #615-616, 1 each #617-618 6.50
619 A143 25p 15th century .80 .80
620 A143 25p 16th century .80 .80
a. Bklt. pane, 2 each #617-618, 1 each #619-620 6.50
621 A143 25p 17th century .80 .80
622 A143 25p 18th century .80 .80
a. Bklt. pane, 2 each #619-620, 1 each #621-622 6.50
623 A143 25p 19th century .80 .80
624 A143 25p 20th century .80 .80
a. Bklt. pane, 2 each #621-622, 1 each #623-624 6.50
b. Bklt. pane, 2 each #623-624, 1 each #615-616 6.50
Complete booklet, #618a, 620a, 622a, 624a-624b 35.00
c. Strip of 10, #615-624 8.50 8.50

Island Scenes Type of 1997
Die Cut Perf. 9½x9

1998, Mar. 25 Litho.
Self-Adhesive

625 A138 (20p) Fort Grey .70 .70
626 A138 (20p) Grand Havre .70 .70
a. Booklet pane, 4 each #625-626 7.00
Complete booklet, #626a 7.00
627 A138 (25p) Little Chapel .80 .80
628 A138 (25p) Guernsey cow .80 .80
a. Booklet pane, 4 each #627-628 8.00
Complete booklet, #628a 8.00
Nos. 625-628 (4) 3.00 3.00

Nos. 625-626 are inscribed "Bailwick Minimum Postage Paid" and were valued at 20p on day of issue. Nos. 627-628 are inscribed "UK Minimum Postage Paid" and were valued at 25p on day of issue.

Aircraft A144

Designs: 20p, Fairey IIIC, Balloon, Sopwith Camel, Avro 504. 25p, Fairey Swordfish, Tiger Moth, Supermarine Walrus, Gloster Gladiator. 30p, Hawker Hurricane, Supermarine Spitfire, Vickers Wellington, Short Sunderland, Westland Lysander, Bristol Blenheim. 37p, De Havilland Mosquito, Avro Lancaster, Auster III, Gloster Meteor, Horsa glider. 43p, Canberra, Hawker Sea Fury, Bristol Sycamore, Hawker Hunter, Handley Page Victor, BAe Lightning. 63p, Pavania Tornado GRI, BAe Hawk, BAe Sea Harrier, Westland Lynx, Hawker Siddeley Nimrod.

1998, May 7 ***Perf. 13½x13***
629 A144 20p multicolored .50 .50
630 A144 25p multicolored .60 .60
631 A144 30p multicolored .80 .80
632 A144 37p multicolored 1.25 1.25
633 A144 43p multicolored 1.50 1.50
634 A144 63p multicolored 2.00 2.00
Nos. 629-634 (6) 6.65 6.65

Royal Air Force, 80th anniv.

Souvenir Sheet

Cambridge Rules for Soccer, 150th Anniv. — A145

a, 30p, Jules Rimet, first president of FIFA. b, £1.75, Bobby Moore, Queen Elizabeth II.

1998, May 7 ***Perf. 13½x14***
635 A145 Sheet of 2, #a.-b. 6.00 6.00

Natl. Holidays and Festivals — A146

Europa: 20p, People in traditional costumes watching animals, West Show. 25p, Band in parade, Battle of Flowers, North Show. 30p, Prince Charles, Liberation Monument under Guernsey flag, tank, Liberation Day. 37p, Goat, equestrian event, flowers, South Show.

1998, Aug. 11 Litho. ***Perf. 13½***
636 A146 20p multicolored *.65 .65*
637 A146 25p multicolored *.75 .75*
638 A146 30p multicolored *.90 .90*
639 A146 37p multicolored *1.00 1.00*
Nos. 636-639 (4) 3.30 3.30

A147

Royal Yacht Britannia — A148

Designs: 1p, Small fishing boat. 2p, St. John Ambulance Inshore Rescue inflatable dinghy. 3p, Pilot boat. 4p, St. John Ambulance boat, Flying Christine III. 5p, Crab boat. 6p, Herm Island Ferry. 7p, St. Peter Port Harbor Authority launch, Sarnia. 8p, Fisheries Protecton vessel, Leopardess. 9p, Trawler. 10p, Powerboat. 20p, Dart 18 racing catamaran. 30p, Bermudan rigged sloop. 40p, Motor cruiser. 50p, Ocean-going yacht. 75p, Motor cruiser anchored. £1, Ocean liner, Queen Elizabeth II. £3, Cruise ship Oriana

1998-2000 Litho. ***Perf. 14***
640 A147 1p multicolored .25 .25
641 A147 2p multicolored .25 .25
642 A147 3p multicolored .25 .25
643 A147 4p multicolored .25 .25
644 A147 5p multicolored .25 .25

645 A147 6p multicolored .25 .25
646 A147 7p multicolored .25 .25
647 A147 8p multicolored .30 .30
648 A147 9p multicolored .35 .35

Size: 27x27mm

Perf. 14½x14¼

649 A147 10p multicolored .40 .40
650 A147 20p multicolored .80 .80
651 A147 30p multicolored 1.25 1.25
652 A147 40p multicolored 1.60 1.60
654 A147 50p multicolored 2.00 2.00
656 A147 75p multicolored 3.00 3.00

Size: 34x26mm

Litho. & Embossed

Perf. 14¼x14½

658 A148 £1 multicolored 4.00 4.00
660 A148 £3 multicolored 10.00 10.00

Size: 48x36mm

Perf. 14¾x14½

663 A148 £5 gold & multi 14.00 11.00
Nos. 640-663 (18) 39.45 36.45

Issued: £5, 8/11; 1p, 2p, 3p, 4p, 5p, 6p, 7p, 8p, 10p, 40p, 50p, 75p, £1, 7/27/99; 20p, 30p, £3, 8/4/00.

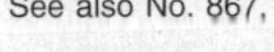
See also No. 867.

Introduction of Christmas Tree to Britain, 150th Anniv. — A149

Christmas tree and toys from past 150 years: 17p, Teletubby "Po," video game machine, 1998. 25p, Doll, double decker bus, c. 1968. 30p, Stuffed panda, toy army tank, c. 1938. 37p, Model of Bluebird race car, doll, c. 1928. 43p, Teddy bear, train pull toy, c. 1908. 63p, Spinning top, wooden doll, c. 1850.

1998, Nov. 10 Litho. ***Perf. 13½***

664 A149 17p multicolored .75 .75
665 A149 25p multicolored .90 .90
666 A149 30p multicolored 1.00 1.00
667 A149 37p multicolored 1.10 1.10
668 A149 43p multicolored 1.25 1.25
669 A149 63p multicolored 1.50 1.50
a. Souvenir sheet, #664-669 7.75 7.75
Nos. 664-669 (6) 6.50 6.50

Queen Elizabeth, the Queen Mother — A150

Three strings of pearls and photographs: No. 670, As a child, 1907. No. 671, At wedding, 1923. No. 672, Holding newly-born Princess Elizabeth, 1926. No. 673, Wearing crown at coronation of King George VI, 1937. No. 674, In green hat, 1940. No. 675, Holding fishing pole, 1966. No. 676, Wearing tiara, 1963. No. 677, Holding flowers, 1992. No. 678, Presenting trophy, 1989. No. 679, In blue hat, 1990.

1999, Feb. 4 Litho. ***Perf. 13***

Color of LL Corner

670 A150 25p pink .80 .80
671 A150 25p blue .80 .80
672 A150 25p red brown .80 .80
673 A150 25p purple .80 .80
a. Bklt. pane, 2 each #670-671, 1 each #672-673 6.50
674 A150 25p green .80 .80
675 A150 25p green .80 .80
a. Bklt. pane, 2 each #672-673, 1 each #673-674 6.50
676 A150 25p purple .80 .80
677 A150 25p red brown .80 .80
678 A150 25p blue .80 .80
a. Bklt. pane, 2 each #674-675, 1 each #676-677 6.50
679 A150 25p pink .80 .80
a. Bklt. pane, 2 each #676-677, 1 each #678-679 6.50
b. Bklt. pane, 2 each #678-679, 1 each #670-671 6.50
Complete booklet, #673a, 675a, 678a, 679a, 679b 35.00
c. Strip of 10, #670-679 8.50 8.50

Herm Island — A151

Local Carriage Labels and: 20p, Burnet roses, Shell Beach. 25p, Puffins, Belvoir Bay. 30p, Small Heath butterfly. 38p, Various shells, Shell Beach.

1999, Apr. 27 Litho. ***Perf. 13½x13***

680 A151 20p multicolored *.50 .50*
681 A151 25p multicolored *.85 .85*
682 A151 30p multicolored *.90 .90*
683 A151 38p multicolored *1.40 1.40*
Nos. 680-683 (4) 3.65 3.65

Europa.

Royal Lifeboat Assoc., 175th Anniv. A152

20p, Spirit of Guernsey, 1995. 25p, Sir William Arnold, 1973. 30p, Euphrosyne Kendal, 1954. 38p, Queen Victoria, 1929. 44p, Arthur Lionel, 1912. 64p, Vincent Kirk Ella, 1888.

1999, Apr. 27

684 A152 20p multicolored .50 .50
685 A152 25p multicolored .60 .60
686 A152 30p multicolored .75 .75
687 A152 38p multicolored 1.00 1.00
688 A152 44p multicolored 1.25 1.25
689 A152 64p multicolored 1.50 1.50
Nos. 684-689 (6) 5.60 5.60

Souvenir Sheet

Wedding of Prince Edward and Sophie Rhys-Jones — A153

1999, June 19 Litho. ***Perf. 13½***

690 A153 £1 multicolored 3.75 3.75

Royal Military Academy, Sandhurst, Bicent. — A154

20p, Major General Le Marchant, founder, 1799. 25p, Duke of York, sponsor, 1802. 30p, Field Marshal Earl Haig, 1884-85. 38p, Field Marshal Montgomery, 1907-08. 44p, Major David Niven, actor, 1928-30. 64p, Sir Winston Churchill, 1893-95.

1999, July 27 Litho. ***Perf. 14***

691 A154 20p multicolored .60 .60
692 A154 25p multicolored .65 .65
693 A154 30p multicolored .90 .90
694 A154 38p multicolored 1.25 1.25
695 A154 44p multicolored 1.50 1.50
696 A154 64p multicolored 1.90 1.90
Nos. 691-696 (6) 6.80 6.80

Christmas A155

Creche figures around manger: 17p, Magus, shepherd, Mary, Joseph, donkey. 25p, Mary. 30p, Joseph, Mary. 38p, Donkey, Mary, cow. 44p, Mary, two shepherds. 64p, Three Magi.

1999, Oct. 19 Litho. ***Perf. 13¾x14¼***

697 A155 17p multicolored .45 .45
698 A155 25p multicolored .65 .65
699 A155 30p multicolored 1.00 1.00
700 A155 38p multicolored 1.10 1.10
701 A155 44p multicolored 1.50 1.50
702 A155 64p multicolored 1.75 1.75
a. Souvenir sheet, #697-702 6.75 6.75
Nos. 697-702 (6) 6.45 6.45

Millennium A156

Children's drawings by: 20p, Fallon Ephgrave. 25p, Abigail Downing. 30p, Laura Martin. 38p, Sarah Haddow. 44p, Sophie Medland. 64p, Danielle McIver.

2000, Jan. 1 Litho. ***Perf. 14¼x14½***

703 A156 20p multi .65 .65
704 A156 25p multi .85 .85
705 A156 30p multi 1.00 1.00
706 A156 38p multi 1.25 1.25
707 A156 44p multi 1.50 1.50
708 A156 64p multi 2.00 2.00
Nos. 703-708 (6) 7.25 7.25

Nos. 703-708 depict the winning designs in the Future Children's Stamp Design Contest.

Europa Issue

Common Design Type and

A157

Designs: 21p, Kite. 26p, Yacht sails. 65p, Rainbow and doves.

2000, May 9 Litho. ***Perf. 13¼***

709 A157 21p multi *.75 .75*
710 A157 26p multi *1.00 1.00*
711 CD17 36p multi *1.25 1.25*
712 A157 65p multi *2.00 2.00*
Nos. 709-712 (4) 5.00 5.00

Battle of Britain, 60th Anniv. A158

Designs: 21p, Bristol Blenheim. 26p, Hawker Hurricane. 36p, Boulton Paul Defiant II. 40p, Gloster Gladiator. 45p, Bristol Beaufighter IF. 65p, Supermarine Spitfire IIc.

2000, April 28 Litho. ***Perf. 13¼x13***

713 A158 21p multi .65 .65
714 A158 26p multi .70 .70
715 A158 36p multi 1.25 1.25
716 A158 40p multi 1.40 1.40
717 A158 45p multi 1.50 1.50
a. Booklet pane, #713-715, 717 5.50
b. Booklet pane, #713, 715-717 6.00
c. Booklet pane, #714-717 6.00
718 A158 65p multi 2.00 2.00
a. Booklet pane of 2 5.50
b. Bklt. pane, #713-714, 716, 718 6.25
Complete booklet, #717a-717c, 718a-718b 30.00
Nos. 713-718 (6) 7.50 7.50

The Stamp Show 2000, London (Nos. 717a-717c, 718a-718b).

Flowers in Candie Gardens — A159

No. 719: a, Long styled iris. b, Watsonia. c, Arum lily. d, Hoop petticoat daffodil. e, Triteleia laxa. f, Peacock flower. g, African blue lily. h, Corn lily. i, Sea lily. j, Guernsey lily.

2000, Aug. 4 Litho. ***Perf. 13½x13***

719 Horiz. strip of 10 8.75 8.75
a.-j. A159 26p Any single .80 .80

Christmas A160

Snow-covered churches: 18p, Town Church, St. Peter's Port. 26p, St. Sampson's Church. 36p, Vale Church. 40p, St. Pierre du Bois Church. 45p, St. Martin's Church. 65p, St. John's Church, St. Peter's Port.

2000, Oct. 19 Litho. ***Perf. 14¼x13¾***

720 A160 18p multi .50 .50
721 A160 26p multi .80 .80
722 A160 36p multi 1.10 1.10
723 A160 40p multi 1.25 1.25
724 A160 45p multi 1.50 1.50
725 A160 65p multi 2.00 2.00
a. Souvenir sheet, #720-725 8.25 8.25
Nos. 720-725 (6) 7.15 7.15

Queen Victoria (1819-1901) — A161

Various portraits and: 21p, Statue of Victoria. 26p, Document. 36p, Statues of Victoria and Prince Albert. 40p, Commemoration stone, St. Peter's Port. 45p, Statue of Prince Albert. 65p, Victoria Tower.

2001, Jan. 22 ***Perf. 14¾***

726 A161 21p multi .60 .60
727 A161 26p multi .80 .80
728 A161 36p multi 1.10 1.10
729 A161 40p multi 1.25 1.25
730 A161 45p multi 1.50 1.50
731 A161 65p multi 2.00 2.00
a. Souvenir sheet, #726-731 8.25 8.25
Nos. 726-731 (6) 7.25 7.25

Hong Kong 2001 Stamp Exhibition (No. 731a).

Birds A162

2001, Feb. 1 Litho. ***Perf. 14x14¾***

732 A162 21p Kingfisher *.85 .85*
733 A162 26p Garganey *1.00 1.00*
734 A162 36p Little egret *1.40 1.40*
735 A162 65p Little ringed plover *2.50 2.50*
Nos. 732-735 (4) *5.75 5.75*

Europa (26p, 36p).

Guernsey Dog Club, Cent. — A163

Designs: 22p, Cavalier King Charles spaniel. 27p, Miniature schnauzer. 36p, German shepherd. 40p, Cocker spaniel. 45p, West Highland terrier. 65p, Dachshund.

2001, Apr. 26 Litho. *Perf. 13x13¼*

736 A163 22p multi .60 .60
737 A163 27p multi .75 .75
738 A163 36p multi 1.25 1.25
739 A163 40p multi 1.40 1.40
740 A163 45p multi 1.60 1.60
741 A163 65p multi 2.00 2.00
Nos. 736-741 (6) 7.60 7.60

Island Views — A164

No. 742: a, La Corbière sunset. b, Rue des Hougues. c, St. Saviour's Reservoir. d, Shell Beach, Herm. e, Telegraph Bay, Alderney. f, Alderney Railway. g, Vazon Bay. h, La Coupée, Sark. i, Les Hanois. j, Albecq,

Self-Adhesive

Serpentine Die Cut 14¼x14

2001, Apr. 26 Litho.

742 Sheet of 10 12.00
a.-e. A164 GY Any single 1.00 1.00
f.-j. A164 UK Any single 1.10 1.10
k. Booklet, 2 each #742a-742e 10.00
l. Booklet, 2 each #742f-742j 11.00
m.-q. As "a-e," photo., any single 2.25 2.25
r. Strip, #742m-742q 11.50
s.-w. As "f-j," photo., any single 2.50 2.50
x. Strip, #742s-742w 12.50

The photogravure stamps have a fuzzier appearance overall than the lithographed stamps. This is most noticeable in the crown where under magnification the bumps on the crown's outline are clearly distinct and well-defined as semicircles on the lithographed stamps, while ragged and ill-defined with a pointy appearance, on the photogravure stamps.

Nos. 742a-742e each sold for 22p, and Nos. 742f-742j each sold for 27p on day of issue.

No. 742 itself was available only from the Philatelic Bureau.

Type of 1969 and

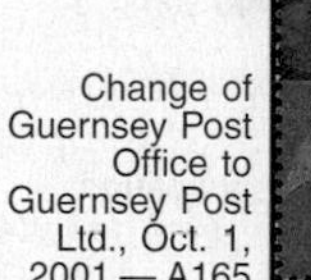

Change of Guernsey Post Office to Guernsey Post Ltd., Oct. 1, 2001 — A165

Designs: 22p, Vision (water droplet on leaf). 27p, Understanding (hummingbird and flower). 36p, Individuality (butterfly's wing). 40p, Strength (nautilus shell cross-section). 45p, Community (honeycomb). 65p, Maturity (Dandelion gone to seed). £1, Like No. 23.

2001, Aug. 1 Litho. *Perf. 13¼x13*

743 A165 22p multi .85 .85
a. Booklet pane of 3 3.00
744 A165 27p multi 1.00 1.00
a. Booklet pane of 3 3.25 —
745 A165 36p multi 1.10 1.10
a. Booklet pane of 3 4.00 —
746 A165 40p multi 1.25 1.25
a. Booklet pane of 3 5.00 —
747 A165 45p multi 1.50 1.50
a. Booklet pane of 3 5.50 —
748 A165 65p multi 2.00 2.00
a. Booklet pane of 3 7.50 —

Perf. 14x14¼

749 A4 £1 Booklet pane of 1 8.50 8.50
Booklet, #743a, 744a, 745a, 746a, 747a, 748a, 749 37.50
Nos. 743-749 (7) 16.20 16.20

Panels on the at top and bottom of No. 749 are dark blue and clouds in silver margin are distinct. Never-bound examples (without stitching holes) of No. 749 with Prussian blue panels and less distinct clouds in the silver margin were given to standing order subscribers at no charge.

Christmas A166

Decorations: 19p, Tree of Joy, St. Peter Port. 27p, Cross, Les Cotils Christian Center. 36p, Les Ruettes Cottage, St. Saviour's. 40p, 17th cent. farmhouse. 45p, Sark Post Office. 65p, High Street, St. Peter Port.

2001, Oct. 16 *Perf. 14¼x14½*

750 A166 19p multi .65 .65
751 A166 27p multi 1.00 1.00
752 A166 36p multi 1.10 1.10
753 A166 40p multi 1.25 1.25
754 A166 45p multi 1.50 1.50
755 A166 65p multi 2.00 2.00
a. Souvenir sheet, #750-755 8.75 8.75
Nos. 750-755 (6) 7.50 7.50

Hafnia 01 Philatelic Exhibition, Copenhagen (No. 755a).

Circus — A167

Designs: 22p, Juggler. 27p, Clowns. 36p, Trapeze artists. 40p, Knife thrower. 45p, Acrobat. 65p, High-wire cyclist.

2002, Feb. 6 Litho. *Perf. 14¾x14½*

756 A167 22p multi .85 .85
757 A167 27p multi *1.10 1.10*
758 A167 36p multi *1.25 1.25*
759 A167 40p multi 1.40 1.40
760 A167 45p multi 1.50 1.50
761 A167 65p multi 2.00 2.00
Nos. 756-761 (6) 8.10 8.10

Europa (27p, 36p).

Victor Hugo (1802-85), Writer — A168

Designs: 22p, Hugo and St. Peter Port. 27p, Cosette from Les Misérables. 36p, Valjean from Les Misérables. 40p, Javert from Les Misérables. 45p, Cosette and Marius from Les Misérables. 65p, Les Misérables, score from play based on book.

2002, Feb. 6 *Perf. 13¼x13*

762 A168 22p multi .75 .75
763 A168 27p multi 1.00 1.00
764 A168 36p multi 1.25 1.25
765 A168 40p multi 1.40 1.40
766 A168 45p multi 1.50 1.50
767 A168 65p multi 2.00 2.00
a. Souvenir sheet of 6, #762-767 8.00 8.00
Nos. 762-767 (6) 7.90 7.90

Souvenir Sheet

Pillar Boxes, 150th Anniv. — A169

2002, Apr. 30 *Perf. 14½x14¼*

768 A169 £1.75 multi 5.25 5.25

Reign of Queen Elizabeth II, 50th Anniv. — A170

Various views of Queen.

2002, Apr. 30 *Perf. 13½*

769 A170 22p multi .85 .85
770 A170 27p multi .90 .90
771 A170 36p multi 1.25 1.25
772 A170 40p multi 1.40 1.40
773 A170 45p multi 1.50 1.50
a. Booklet pane, #770 773 5.50
774 A170 65p multi 2.00 2.00
a. Booklet pane, #769, 772-774 6.25
b. Booklet pane, #769-771, 774 5.50
c. Booklet pane, #769-774 8.25
Nos. 769-774 (6) 7.90 7.90

For complete booklet, see Alderney No. 184a.

Vacations in Sark — A171

No. 775: a, Family on dock, boat near dock. b, Family disembarking tractor-pulled transport. c, Family at campground. d, Family with bicycles at La Coupée. e, Swimming at Venus Pool. f, Family at La Seigneurie Gardens. g, Family at village pillar box. h, Family in horse-drawn cart. i, Family dining outdoors. j, Family at beach.

2002, July 30 *Perf. 13¼*

775 A171 Block of 10 9.00 9.00
a.-j. 27p Any single .90 .90

A172

Designs: 22p, Parade of Elizabeth College Combined Cadet Corps, 1934. 27p, In battle, Tunisia, 1942. 36p, As repatriated prisoner of war, 1943. 40p, Presentation of Victoria Cross ribbon, 1943. 45p, Return to Guernsey, 1948. 65p, Carrying King's Colors, 1968.

2002, July 30 *Perf. 13¼x13*

777 A172 22p multi .85 .85
778 A172 27p multi 1.00 1.00
779 A172 36p multi 1.25 1.25
780 A172 40p multi 1.40 1.40
781 A172 45p multi 1.50 1.50
782 A172 65p multi 2.00 2.00
Nos. 777-782 (6) 8.00 8.00

Awarding of Victoria Cross to Major Herbert Wallace Le Patourel, 60th Anniv.

Souvenir Sheet

Queen Mother Elizabeth (1900-2002) — A173

Litho. With Foil Application

2002, Aug. 4 *Perf. 13¼*

783 A173 £2 multi 7.00 7.00

Christmas A174

Designs: 22p, Madonna and Child. 27p, Holy Family. 36p, Angel announcing birth to shepherds. 40p, Adoration of the shepherds. 45p, Three Kings. 65p, Star of Bethlehem.

2002, Oct. 17 Litho. *Perf. 13¼x13*

784 A174 22p multi .85 .85
785 A174 27p multi 1.10 1.10
786 A174 36p multi 1.40 1.40
787 A174 40p multi 1.50 1.50
788 A174 45p multi 1.60 1.60
789 A174 65p multi 2.25 2.25
a. Souvenir sheet, #784-789 9.25 9.25
Nos. 784-789 (6) 8.70 8.70

World War II — A175

Designs: 22p, Pilots and airplanes. 27p, Airplanes over shoreline. 36p, Airplanes and searchlights. 40p, Airplanes dropping bombs. £1.50, HMS Charybdis and HMS Limbourne.

2003, Jan. 30 *Perf. 14*

790 A175 22p multi .65 .65
791 A175 27p multi .85 .85
792 A175 36p multi 1.10 1.10
793 A175 40p multi 1.25 1.25

Size: 40x31mm

Perf. 14¼x14½

794 A175 £1.50 multi 5.50 5.50
Nos. 790-794 (5) 9.35 9.35

Dambusters Raid (Nos. 790-793), Operation Tunnel (No. 794), 60th anniv. See Nos. 827-831, 855-859.

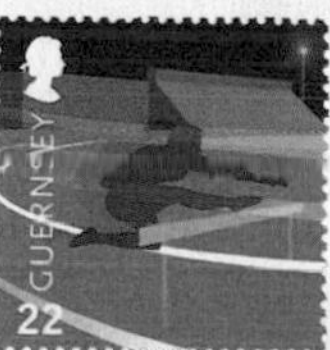

Island Games — A176

Designs: 22c, Hurdles. 27p, Cycling. 36p, Gymnastics. 40p, Windsurfing. 45p, Golf. 65p, Triathlon.

2003, Jan. 30 *Perf. 12½*

795 A176 22p multi .80 .80
796 A176 27p multi .90 .90
797 A176 36p multi 1.25 1.25
798 A176 40p multi 1.40 1.40
799 A176 45p multi 1.50 1.50
800 A176 65p multi 2.00 2.00
a. Souvenir sheet, #795-800 8.75 8.75
Nos. 795-800 (6) 7.85 7.85

Poster Art — A177

Poster art from: 22p, 2003. 27p, 1995. 36p, 1988. 40p, 1978. 45p, 1968. 65p, 1956.

2003, Apr. 10 *Perf. 14¾x14½*

801 A177 22p multi .70 .70
802 A177 27p multi *.85 .85*
803 A177 36p multi *1.10 1.10*
804 A177 40p multi 1.25 1.25
805 A177 45p multi 1.50 1.50
806 A177 65p multi 2.00 2.00
Nos. 801-806 (6) 7.40 7.40

Europa (Nos. 802, 803).

Souvenir Sheet

Decommissioning of HMS Guernsey — A178

2003, Apr. 10 *Perf. 13¾x14¼*

807 A178 £1.50 multi 4.75 4.75

Prince William, 21st Birthday — A179

No. 808: a, With Princess Diana, 1983. b, With Princes Charles and Harry, 1985. c, At play in military uniform, 1986. d, In school uniform, with Prince Harry, 1989. e, Holding hand of Prince Charles, 1990. f, In ski jacket, with Princess Diana, 1991. g, In suit, 1995. h, With Princes Charles and Harry, 1997. i, Wearing helmet, 2000. j, Playing polo, 2002.

2003, June 21 *Perf. 13½x13*

808 Horiz. strip of 10 9.00 9.00
a.-j. A179 27p Any single .90 .90
k. As #808a, perf. 13½x14 1.25 1.25
l. As #808b, perf. 13½x14 1.25 1.25
m. As #808c, perf. 13½x14 1.25 1.25
n. As #808d, perf. 13½x14 1.25 1.25
o. As #808e, perf. 13½x14 1.25 1.25
p. As #808f, perf. 13½x14 1.25 1.25
q. As #808g, perf. 13½x14 1.25 1.25
r. As #808h, perf. 13½x14 1.25 1.25
s. As #808i, perf. 13½x14 1.25 1.25
t. As #808j, perf. 13½x14 1.25 1.25
u. Booklet pane, #808k, 808m, 808p, 808q, 808s, 808t 7.50 —
v. Booklet pane, #808l, 808m, 808np, 808o, 808r, 808s 7.50 —
w. Booklet pane, #808k, 808n, 808p, 808q, 808r, 808t 7.50 —
x. Booklet pane, #808k, 808l, 808m, 808o, 808r, 808t 7.50 —
y. Booklet pane, #808l, 808n, 808o, 808p, 808q, 808s 7.50 —
Complete booklet, #808u-808y 37.50

Nos. 808k-808t come only from Nos. 808u-808y.

Letters A180

Litho. With Foil Application

2003, July 3 *Perf. 13¼*

809 A180 £5 multi 15.00 15.00

No. 809 is printed with thermochromatic ink that changes color when warmed.

Christmas A181

Scenes from *'Twas the Night Before Christmas*: 10p, Boy in bed, Christmas tree. 27p, Arrival of St. Nicholas. 36p, St. Nicholas near chimney. 40p, St. Nicholas carrying gifts. 45p, St. Nicholas placing gifts near tree. 65p, Departure of St. Nicholas.

2003, Oct. 16 **Litho.** *Perf. 14¼*

810 A181 10p multi .40 .40
811 A181 27p multi 1.00 1.00
812 A181 36p multi 1.25 1.25
813 A181 40p multi 1.40 1.40
814 A181 45p multi 1.50 1.50
815 A181 65p multi 2.00 2.00
a. Souvenir sheet, #810-815 7.75 7.75
Nos. 810-815 (6) 7.55 7.55

Souvenir Sheet

Golden Snub-nosed Monkey — A182

2004, Jan. 29 **Litho.** *Perf. 13¾x14¼*

816 A182 £2 multi 7.75 7.75

Clematis Flower Varieties — A183

Serpentine Die Cut 12½

2004, Jan. 29 **Litho.**

Self-Adhesive

Inscribed "GY"

817 A183 (22p) Rosemoor .95 .95
818 A183 (22p) Arctic Queen .95 .95
819 A183 (22p) Harlow Carr .95 .95
820 A183 (22p) Guernsey Cream .95 .95
821 A183 (22p) Josephine .95 .95
a. Booklet pane, 2 each #817-821 9.50
Complete booklet, No. 821a 9.50
b. Booklet pane, 2 each #817-821 (see note) 9.50
Complete booklet, 10 No. 821b 95.00

Inscribed "UK"

822 A183 (27p) Blue Moon 1.25 1.25
823 A183 (27p) Wisley 1.25 1.25
824 A183 (27p) Liberation 1.25 1.25
825 A183 (27p) Royal Velvet 1.25 1.25
826 A183 (27p) Hyde Hall 1.25 1.25
a. Sheetlet, #817-826 11.00
b. Booklet pane, 2 each #822-826 12.50
Complete booklet, #826b 12.50
c. Booklet pane, 2 each #822-826 (see note) 12.50
Complete booklet, 10 #826c 125.00
Nos. 817-826 (10) 11.00 11.00

Booklet panes Nos. 821a and 826b have blocks of 6 and 4 separated by a space with text. Nos. 821b and 826c do not have a space between stamps.

World War II Type of 2003

Scenes of D-Day: 26p, Royal Air Force Spitfire. 32p, Arrival of landing craft. 36p, Soldiers approaching Gold Beach, open door of landing craft. 40p, Soldiers seeking shelter behind obstacles. £1.50, SS Vega.

2004, May 12 *Perf. 14¼*

827 A175 26p multi 1.00 1.00
828 A175 32p multi 1.25 1.25
829 A175 36p multi 1.50 1.50
830 A175 40p multi 1.75 1.75

Perf. 14¾x14¼

Size: 40x30mm

831 A175 £1.50 multi 6.25 6.25
Nos. 827-831 (5) 11.75 11.75

Vacations — A184

Inscriptions: 26p, Sand, Beaches, Sunshine. 32p, Views, Walking, Cliff top trails. 36p, Marina, Yachts, Cruisers. 40p, Dining, Seafood, A la carte. 45p, Churches, History, Monuments. 65p, Fauna, Flora, Colors.

2004, May 12 *Perf. 13½*

832 A184 26p multi 1.00 1.00
833 A184 32p multi *1.25 1.25*
834 A184 36p multi *1.40 1.40*
835 A184 40p multi 1.60 1.60
836 A184 45p multi 1.75 1.75
837 A184 65p multi 2.25 2.25
Nos. 832-837 (6) 9.25 9.25

Europa (32p, 36p).

Loyalty to the British Crown, 800th Anniv. — A185

2004, June 24 *Perf. 13¼x14*

838 A185 26p Loyalty .95 .95
839 A185 32p Trade 1.10 1.10
840 A185 36p Unity 1.40 1.40
841 A185 40p Protection 1.50 1.50
842 A185 45p Justice 1.60 1.60
843 A185 65p Industry 2.25 2.25
a. Souvenir sheet, #838-843, perf. 14x13¼ 9.25 9.25
Nos. 838-843 (6) 8.80 8.80

2004 Summer Olympics, Athens — A186

2004, July 29 *Perf. 13½*

844 A186 32p Discus .90 .90
845 A186 36p Javelin 1.40 1.40
846 A186 45p Runners 1.50 1.50
a. Booklet pane, #845, 846, 2 #844 4.75 —
847 A186 65p Wrestlers 2.00 2.00
a. Booklet pane, #846, 847, 2 #845 6.50 —
b. Booklet pane, #844, 847, 2 #846 6.00 —
c. Booklet pane, #844, 845, 2 #847 6.50 —
d. Booklet pane, #844-847 6.00 —
Nos. 844-847 (4) 5.80 5.80

Nos. 846a, 847a-847d are perf 14¾x14.

Souvenir Sheet

Perf. 14¾x14

848 A186 £1 Athletes, horiz. 4.00 4.00
a. Booklet pane, #848 4.00 —
Complete booklet, Nos. 846a, 847a-847d, 848a 30.00

No. 848 contains one 40x30mm stamp. No. 848a has binding stub at left.

Christmas A187

Designs: No. 849a, Little Donkey. No. 849b, While Shepherds Watched. No. 849c, Away in a Manger. No. 849d, Unto Us a Child is Born. No. 849e, We Three Kings.

32p, Angel wings. 36p, Christmas tree ornament. 40p, Holly leaf and berries. 45p, Snowman's scarf and buttons. 65p, Christmas tree star.

2004, Oct. 28 **Litho.** *Perf. 13*

849 Horiz. strip of 5 3.75 3.75
a.-e. A187 20p Any single .75 .75
850 A187 32p multi 1.25 1.25
851 A187 36p multi 1.40 1.40
852 A187 40p multi 1.50 1.50
853 A187 45p multi 1.60 1.60
854 A187 65p multi 2.25 2.25
Nos. 849-854 (6) 11.75 11.75

World War II Type of 2003

Designs: 26p, Soldiers on Army Landrover greet Guernsey residents. 32p, Woman celebrating liberation from German rule. 36p, Parents reunite with children. 40p, Soldiers return home. £1.50, Winston Churchill.

2005, Feb. 3 **Litho.** *Perf. 14¼*

855 A175 26p multi .00 .00
856 A175 32p multi 1.00 1.00
857 A175 36p multi 1.10 1.10
858 A175 40p multi 1.25 1.25

Size: 40x30mm

Perf. 14¾x14¼

859 A175 £1.50 multi 4.75 4.75
Nos. 855-859 (5) 9.00 9.00

Paintings of Flowers by William John Caparne — A188

Designs: 26p, Iris "Dorothea" and "Royal." 32p, Nerine fothergilli "Major." 36p, Iris "Garnet." 40p, Narcissus "Sir Watkin." 45p, Narcissus "Rip Van Winkle." 65p, Narcissus "Sulphur Phoenix."

2005, Feb. 3 *Perf. 13¼*

860 A188 26p multi .85 .85
861 A188 32p multi 1.00 1.00
862 A188 36p multi 1.25 1.25
863 A188 40p multi 1.40 1.40
864 A188 45p multi 1.50 1.50
865 A188 65p multi 2.00 2.00
a. Souvenir sheet, #860-865 8.00 8.00
Nos. 860-865 (6) 8.00 8.00

Liberation of Guernsey, 60th Anniv. A189

No. 866: a, King George VI. b, Queen Elizabeth II.

Litho. With Foil Application

2005, May 9 *Perf. 14¾x14*

866 Horiz. pair 6.75 6.75
a.-b. A189 £1 Either single 3.25 3.25

Queen Mary 2 Ocean Liner — A190

Litho. & Embossed With Foil Application

2005, May 9 *Perf. 13¼*

867 A190 £4 multi 13.00 13.00

Gastronomy
A191

Dishes: 26p, Spider crab. 32p, Red mullet and crab cake. 36p, Lobster salad. 40p, Brill on spinach with mussels. 45p, Prawn salad. 65p, Salmon wrapped in spinach with mussels.

2005, May 9 Litho. *Perf. 14x13¼*

868 A191 26p multi .75 1.00
869 A191 32p multi .90 1.25
870 A191 36p multi 1.25 1.40
871 A191 40p multi 1.50 1.60
872 A191 45p multi 1.60 1.75
873 A191 65p multi 2.00 2.50
Nos. 868-873 (6) 8.00 9.50

Europa (32p, 36p).

Souvenir Sheet

Basking Shark — A192

2005, July 21 *Perf. 13¼*

874 A192 £2 multi 7.00 7.00

SeaGuernsey 2005 — A193

Designs: 26p, Fishing boat and gulls. 32p, Sailboat. 36p, Windsurfer. 40p, Fisherman. 65p, Horse and rider on beach.

2005, July 21 *Perf. 13¼x13¾*

875 A193 26p multi .80 .80
876 A193 32p multi 1.00 1.00
a. Booklet pane, 2 each #875-876 4.00 —
877 A193 36p multi 1.25 1.25
a. Booklet pane, 2 each #876-877 5.00 —
878 A193 40p multi 1.50 1.50
a. Booklet pane, 2 each #877-878 5.75 —
879 A193 65p multi 2.00 2.00
a. Booklet pane, 2 each #878-879 7.50 —
b. Booklet pane, 2 each #875, 879 6.00 —
c. Booklet pane, #876-879 6.75 —
Complete booklet, #876a, 877a, 878a, 879a, 879b, 879c 35.00
Nos. 875-879 (5) 6.55 6.55

Christmas — A194

No. 880 — Stained glass windows from: a, St. Pierre du Bois Church. b, St. Saviour's Church. c, St. Martin's Church. d, Torteval Church. e, St. Sampson's Church.

32p, Vale Church. 36p, Castel Church. 40p, St. Anne's Church, Alderney. 45p, St. Andrew's Church. 65p, Forest Church.

2005, Oct. 27 *Perf. 14x14¼*

880 Horiz. strip of 5 3.50 3.50
a.-e. A194 20p Any single .70 .70
881 A194 32p multi 1.10 1.10
882 A194 36p multi 1.25 1.25
883 A194 40p multi 1.40 1.40
884 A194 45p multi 1.50 1.50
885 A194 65p multi 2.00 2.00
Nos. 880-885 (6) 10.75 10.75

Victoria Cross, 150th Anniv. A195

Battle scenes and medals from: 29p, Iraq Conflict, 2004. 34p, Falklands Conflict, 1982. 38p, Battle of El Alamein, World War II, 1942. 42p, Battle of Gallipoli, World War I, 1915. 47p, Battle of Rorke's Drift, Zulu War, 1879. 68p, Charge of the Light Brigade, Crimean War, 1854.

Perf. 13¾x13½

2006, Feb. 10 Litho.

886 A195 29p multi 1.10 1.10
887 A195 34p multi 1.25 1.25
888 A195 38p multi 1.40 1.40
889 A195 42p multi 1.50 1.50
890 A195 47p multi 1.60 1.60
891 A195 68p multi 2.00 2.00
Nos. 886-891 (6) 8.85 8.85

Souvenir Sheet

Endangered Species of the Florida Everglades — A196

No. 892: a, £1, Leatherback turtle. b, £1.50, Wood stork.

2006, Feb. 16 *Perf. 14x14¾*

892 A196 Sheet of 2, #a-b 8.75 8.75

International Tourist Attractions — A197

Designs: 29p, Eiffel Tower, Paris. 34p, Sphinx, Egypt. 42p, Great Wall of China. 45p, Uluru (Ayers Rock), Australia. 47p, Statue of Liberty, New York. 68p, Taj Mahal, India.

2006, May 20 *Perf. 13¼x13½*

893 A197 29p multi 1.10 1.10
894 A197 34p multi 1.25 1.25
895 A197 42p multi 1.40 1.40
896 A197 45p multi 1.50 1.50
897 A197 47p multi 1.60 1.60
898 A197 68p multi 2.00 2.00
Nos. 893-898 (6) 8.85 8.85

Europa (34p, 42p).

Isambard Kingdom Brunel (1806-59) — A198

Designs: 29p, Brunel, mailbags for Guernsey at Paddington Station, London. 34p, Mail train leaving Paddington Station. 42p, Train on Wharncliffe Viaduct. 45p, Mail train and ship at harbor, Weymouth. 47p, Mailboat Ibex in English Channel. 68p, Ibex at St. Peter Port.

2006, May 20 *Perf. 13¼x13*

899 A198 29p multi 1.10 1.10
900 A198 34p multi 1.25 1.25
901 A198 42p multi 1.40 1.40
902 A198 45p multi 1.50 1.50
a. Booklet pane, #899-902 5.50 —
903 A198 47p multi 1.60 1.60
a. Booklet pane, #900-903 6.00 —
904 A198 68p multi 2.00 2.00
a. Booklet pane, #901-904 6.75 —
b. Booklet pane, #899, 902-904 6.50 —
c. Booklet pane, #899-900, 903-904 6.25 —
d. Booklet pane, #899-901, 904 6.00 —
Complete booklet, #902a, 903a, 904a-904d 34.00
Nos. 899-904 (6) 8.85 8.85

Andy Priaulx, Race Car Driver A199

Priaulx, car and events: 29p, British Speed Hill Climb Championship, 1995. 34p, Renault Spider Cup, 1999. 42p, British Formula 3, 2001. 45p, FIA European Touring Car Championship, 2004. 47p, Nürburgring, Germany, 2005. 68p, FIA World Touring Car Championship, 2005.

2006, May 20 *Perf. 13½*

905 A199 29p multi 1.10 1.10
906 A199 34p multi 1.25 1.25
907 A199 42p multi 1.40 1.40
908 A199 45p multi 1.50 1.50
909 A199 47p multi 1.60 1.60
910 A199 68p multi 2.00 2.00
a. Souvenir sheet, #905-910 9.00 9.00
Nos. 905-910 (6) 8.85 8.85

Queen Elizabeth II, 80th Birthday A200

Litho. & Embossed with Foil Application

2006, June 17 *Perf. 14¾x14¼*

911 A200 £10 multi 30.00 30.00

L'Erée Wetlands A201

Designs: 29p, Gray seal. 34p, Ormer. 42p, Common blenny. 45p, Le Creux ès Faies. 47p, Yellow-horned poppy. 68p, Oyster catchers.

2006, July 27 Litho. *Perf. 14x13¼*

912 A201 29p multi 1.10 1.10
913 A201 34p multi 1.25 1.25
914 A201 42p multi 1.40 1.40
915 A201 45p multi 1.50 1.50
916 A201 47p multi 1.60 1.60
917 A201 68p multi 2.00 2.00
a. Souvenir sheet, #912-917 9.00 9.00
Nos. 912-917 (6) 8.85 8.85

Addition of L'Erée Wetlands to Ramsar Convention Protected Wetlands List. See Nos. 972-977.

The Twelve Days of Christmas — A202

No. 918: a, A partridge in a pear tree. b, Two turtle doves. c, Three French hens. d, Four calling birds. e, Five gold rings. f, Six geese a-laying.

29p, Seven swans a-swimming. 34p, Eight maids a-milking. 42p, Nine ladies dancing. 45p, Ten lords a-leaping. 47p, Eleven pipers piping. 68p, Twelve drummers drumming.

2006, Nov. 2 Litho. *Perf. 14¾x15*

918 Horiz. strip of 6 4.25 4.25
a.-f. A202 22p Any single .75 .75
919 A202 29p multi 1.10 1.10
920 A202 34p multi 1.25 1.25
921 A202 42p multi 1.40 1.40
922 A202 45p multi 1.50 1.50
923 A202 47p multi 1.60 1.60
924 A202 68p multi 2.00 2.00
Nos. 918-924 (7) 13.10 13.10

La Société Guernesiaise, 125th Anniv. — A203

No. 925: a, Rocks, Albecq. b, Ivy bee. c, Vale Church. d, Common frog. e, Parasol mushroom. f, Southern marsh orchid. g, Shore crab. h, Alderney blonde hedgehog. i, Barn owl. j, Le Trépied dolmen.

Serpentine Die Cut 12½

2007, Mar. 8 Self-Adhesive

925 Sheet of 10 12.00 *12.00*
a.-e. A203 (32p) Any single 1.10 1.10
f.-j. A203 (37p) Any single 1.30 1.30
k. Booklet pane of 10, 2 each #925a-925e 11.00
Complete booklet, 1 #925k 11.00
l. Booklet pane of 10, 2 each #925f-925j 13.00
Complete booklet, 1 #925l 13.00
m. Booklet pane of 10, 2 each #925a-925e (see note) 11.00
Complete booklet, 10 #925m 110.00
n. Booklet pane of 10, 2 each #925f-925j (see note) 13.00
Complete booklet, 10 #925n 130.00

Nos. 925a-925e are inscribed "GY"; Nos. 925f-925j, "UK."

Booklet panes Nos. 925k and 925l have blocks of 6 and 4 separated by a space between stamps. Booklet panes Nos. 925m and 925n do not have a space between stamps.

See No. 997.

Falkland Islands War, 25th Anniv. A204

Designs: 32p, Troops leaving for war. 37p, Landing at San Carlos Bay. 45p, Harriers flying over SS Canberra. 48p, Lieutenant Colonel H. Jones firing gun. 50p, Helicopter evacuating men from ship. 71p, Troops marching toward Port Stanley.

2007, Mar. 8 *Perf. 13½*

926 A204 32p multi 1.10 1.10
927 A204 37p multi 1.40 1.40
928 A204 45p multi 1.50 1.50
929 A204 48p multi 1.60 1.60
930 A204 50p multi 1.75 1.75
931 A204 71p multi 2.25 2.25
a. Souvenir sheet, #926-931 9.75 9.75
Nos. 926-931 (6) 9.60 9.60

Scouting, Cent. — A205

Designs: 32p, 1907 Scout camping. 37p, 1924 Scout sailing. 45p, 1947 Scouts fishing. 48p, 1968 Scouts making model airplanes. 50p, 1990 Scouts exploring cave. 71p, 2007 Scouts on rollerblades.

2007, May 24 Litho. *Perf. 13¼x13*

932 A205 32p multi 1.20 1.20
933 A205 37p multi 1.40 1.40
934 A205 45p multi 1.50 1.50
935 A205 48p multi 1.60 1.60
936 A205 50p multi 1.75 1.75
937 A205 71p multi 2.50 2.50
Nos. 932-937 (6) 9.95 9.95

Europa (37p, 45p).

British Formula 1 World Championship Cars and Drivers — A206

Driver and championship year: No. 938, Mike Hawthorn, 1958. No. 939, Jackie Stewart, 1971. No. 940, Graham Hill, 1962. No.

941, James Hunt, 1976. 45p, Jim Clark, 1963. 48p, Nigel Mansell, 1992. 50p, John Surtees, 1964. 71p, Damon Hill, 1996.

2007, May 24 *Perf. 14x13¾*

938 A206 32p multi 1.00 1.00
939 A206 32p multi 1.00 1.00
940 A206 37p multi 1.40 1.40
941 A206 37p multi 1.40 1.40
942 A206 45p multi 1.50 1.50
943 A206 48p multi 1.60 1.60
944 A206 50p multi 1.75 1.75
945 A206 71p multi 2.50 2.50
Nos. 938-945 (8) 12.15 12.15

See Nos. 1142-1145.

Wedding of Queen Elizabeth II and Prince Philip, 60th Anniv. — A207

Designs: 32p, Princess Elizabeth and Prince Philip, c. 1947. 37p, With baby Princess Anne. 45p, Off duty, wearing casual clothes. 48p, On tour, Queen in jacket and hat. 50p, With grandchildren Princes William and Henry. 71p, Recent photo.

2007, Aug. 2 *Perf. 13¼x13¾*

Background Color

946 A207 32p red brown 1.20 1.20
947 A207 37p tan 1.40 1.40
a. Booklet pane, 2 each #946-947 5.50 —
948 A207 45p light blue 1.50 1.50
a. Booklet pane, 2 each #947-948 6.00 —
949 A207 48p light green 1.60 1.60
a. Booklet pane, 2 each #948-949 6.50 —
950 A207 50p orange 1.75 1.75
a. Booklet pane, 2 each #949-950 7.00 —
951 A207 71p lilac 2.50 2.50
a. Booklet pane, 2 each #950-951 8.75 —
b. Booklet pane, 2 each #946, 951 7.75 —
Complete booklet, #947a, 948a, 949a, 950a, 951a, 951b 42.00
Nos. 946-951 (6) 9.95 9.95

Souvenir Sheet

Mountain Gorilla — A208

2007, Aug. 2 *Perf. 14*

952 A208 £2.50 multi 8.75 8.75

Seaside Views A209

Designs: 32p, St. Peter Port Harbor. 37p, Fort Grey, Rocquaine. 45p, Point Robert Lighthouse, Sark. 48p, Brecqhou Island as seen from Sark. 50p, Vazon Bay. 71p, Fontenelle Bay.

2007, Oct. 1 Litho. *Perf. 13¾x13½*

953 A209 32p multi 1.10 1.10
954 A209 37p multi 1.40 1.40
955 A209 45p multi 1.60 1.60
956 A209 48p multi 1.75 1.75
957 A209 50p multi 1.90 1.90
958 A209 71p multi 2.50 2.50
Nos. 953-958 (6) 10.25 10.25

See Nos. 1057-1062, 1098, 1136-1141.

Christmas — A210

Decorations: No. 959, Crystal snowflake in snow. No. 960, Crystal snowflake pendant. No. 961, Angel candle accent. No. 962, Crystal angel pendant. No. 963, Pine cone in snow. No. 964, Spherical ornament with leaf pattern. 32p, Spherical ornament with spiral pattern. 37p, Candles. 45p, Bell. 48p, Ribbon bow. 50p, Christmas tree star. 71p, Porcelain angel.

2007, Oct. 25 *Perf. 14½x15*

959 A210 27p multi .95 .95
960 A210 27p multi .95 .95
961 A210 27p multi .95 .95
962 A210 27p multi .95 .95
963 A210 27p multi .95 .95
964 A210 27p multi .95 .95
965 A210 32p multi 1.25 1.25
966 A210 37p multi 1.40 1.40
967 A210 45p multi 1.50 1.50
968 A210 48p multi 1.60 1.60
969 A210 50p multi 1.75 1.75
970 A210 71p multi 2.25 2.25
Nos. 959-970 (12) 15.45 15.45

Souvenir Sheet

Race Cars Used by World Touring Car Champion Andy Priaulx — A211

Race cars used by Priaulx in: a, 2005 (40x30mm). b, 2006 (40x30mm). c, 2007 (60x48mm).

2008, Jan. 18 Litho. *Perf. 13¾x14¼*

971 A211 Sheet of 3 10.00 10.00
a.-c. £1 Any single 3.25 3.25

Wetlands Type of 2006

Designs: 34p, Beadlet anemones. 40p, Sand crocus. 48p, Fulmars. 51p, Sheep's bit. 53p, Thick-lipped gray mullets. 74p, Light bulb sea squirts.

2008, Feb. 28 *Perf. 13x13¼*

972 A201 34p multi 1.00 1.00
973 A201 40p multi 1.25 1.25
974 A201 48p multi 1.60 1.60
975 A201 51p multi 1.75 1.75
976 A201 53p multi 1.90 1.90
977 A201 74p multi 2.50 2.50
a. Miniature sheet, #972-977 10.00 10.00
Nos. 972-977 (6) 10.00 10.00

Addition of Gouliot Headland and Caves, Sark to Ramsar Convention Protected Wetlands List.

Flowers — A212

Designs: 10p, Red campion. 20p, Great bindweed. 30p, Spear thistle. 40p, Greater bird's foot trefoil. 50p, Sheep's bit. £1, Marguerite (daisy), vert. £2, Sea campion, vert.

2008, Feb. 28 Litho. *Perf. 14*

978 A212 10p multi .30 .30
979 A212 20p multi .60 .60
980 A212 30p multi 1.00 1.00
981 A212 40p multi 1.40 1.40
982 A212 50p multi 1.75 1.75

Litho. & Embossed

983 A212 £1 multi 3.25 3.25
984 A212 £2 multi 6.50 6.50
Nos. 978-984 (7) 14.80 14.80

See Nos. 1029-1038.

Mr. Men and Little Miss Children's Book Characters A213

Designs: 34p, Mr. Happy. 40p, Mr. Bump. 48p, Little Miss Naughty. 51p, Mr. Greedy. 53p, Mr. Strong. 74p, Mr. Tickle.

2008, May 15 Litho. *Perf. 14x13½*

985 A213 34p multi 1.10 1.10
986 A213 40p multi 1.40 1.40
987 A213 48p multi 1.60 1.60
988 A213 51p multi 1.75 1.75
989 A213 53p multi 1.90 1.90
990 A213 74p multi 2.50 2.50
Nos. 985-990 (6) 10.25 10.25

Guernesiais Phrases — A214

Guernesias phrases for: 34p, Till the next time. 40p, Hello. 48p, Oh! There you are. 51p, Good gracious. 53p, Cor blimey. 74p, How are things?

2008, May 15 *Perf. 13¼x13*

991 A214 34p multi 1.10 1.10
992 A214 40p multi 1.40 1.40
993 A214 48p multi 1.60 1.60
994 A214 51p multi 1.75 1.75
995 A214 53p multi 1.90 1.90
996 A214 74p multi 2.50 2.50
Nos. 991-996 (6) 10.25 10.25

Europa (40p, 48p).

La Société Guernsiaise Type of 2007

No. 997 — Photographs of Guernsey: a, Pleimont Point. b, Saint's Harbor. c, Rocks at Albecq. d, Groins at Vazon Bay. e, La Bette Bay. f, Bordeaux Harbor. g, St. Saviour's Reservoir. h, Vazon Bay. i, St. Peter Port Lighthouse. j, Petit Port.

Serpentine Die Cut 12½

2008, June 9 **Litho.**

Self-Adhesive

997 Sheet of 10 12.50 *12.50*
a.-e. A203 (34p) Any single 1.10 1.10
f.-j. A203 (40p) Any single 1.40 1.40
k. Booklet pane of 10, 2 each #997a-997e 11.00
l. Booklet pane of 10, 2 each #997f-997j 14.00

Nos. 997a-997e are inscribed "GY"; Nos. 997f-997j, "UK."

Nos. 997k and 997l each contain blocks of 6 and 4 stamps separated by a gutter. Booklet panes of 10 stamps without gutters come from booklets of 100 stamps with plain paper backing.

Ford Model T, Cent. A215

Model T: 34p, And house. 40p, Converted to truck. 48p, Converted to pickup truck. 51p, On tree-lined street. 53p, Converted to World War I army ambulance. 74p, Red 1912 Roadster.

2008, July 31 *Perf. 13¼*

998 A215 34p multi 1.10 1.10
999 A215 40p multi 1.40 1.40
1000 A215 48p multi 1.60 1.60
1001 A215 51p multi 1.75 1.75
a. Booklet pane of 4, #998-1001 6.00 —
1002 A215 53p multi 1.90 1.90
a. Booklet pane of 4, #998-999, 1001-1002 7.00 —
1003 A215 74p multi 2.50 2.50
a. Booklet pane of 4, #1000-1003 8.00 —
b. Booklet pane of 4, #998-999, 1002-1003 7.25 —
c. Booklet pane of 4, #999-1000, 1002-1003 7.75 —
d. Booklet pane of 4, #998, 1000-1001, 1003 7.25 —
Complete booklet, #1001a, 1002a, 1003a, 1003b, 1003c, 1003d 44.00
Nos. 998-1003 (6) 10.25 10.25

St. Paul's Cathedral, London, 300th Anniv. — A216

Blocks of granite from Guernsey and various depictions of cathedral.

2008, Oct. 30 *Perf. 13¼*

1004 A216 34p multi 1.10 1.10
1005 A216 40p multi 1.40 1.40
1006 A216 48p multi 1.60 1.60
1007 A216 51p multi 1.75 1.75
1008 A216 53p multi 1.90 1.90
1009 A216 74p multi 2.50 2.50
Nos. 1004-1009 (6) 10.25 10.25

Particles of granite were applied to parts of the designs by a thermographic process.

Christmas — A217

No. 1010, Spruce. No. 1011, Butchers broom. No. 1012, Mistletoe. No. 1013, Ivy. No. 1014, Christmas cactus. No. 1015, Cyclamen. No. 1016, Holly. No. 1017, Poinsettia. No. 1018, Bracken. No. 1019, Hawthorn. No. 1020, Clematis peppermint. No. 1021, Pyracantha.

2008, Oct. 30 *Perf. 13¾x13¼*

1010 A217 29p multicolored .70 .70
1011 A217 29p multicolored .70 .70
1012 A217 29p multicolored .70 .70
1013 A217 29p multicolored .70 .70
1014 A217 29p multicolored .70 .70
1015 A217 29p multicolored .70 .70
1016 A217 34p multicolored 1.10 1.10
1017 A217 40p multicolored 1.40 1.40
1018 A217 48p multicolored 1.50 1.50
1019 A217 51p multicolored 1.60 1.60
1020 A217 53p multicolored 1.75 1.75
1021 A217 74p multicolored 2.40 2.40
Nos. 1010-1021 (12) 13.95 13.95

Animals Encountered on Charles Darwin's Scientific Expeditions A218

Designs: 36p, Land iguana. 43p, Wallaby. 51p, Giant tortoise. 54p, Marine iguana. 56p, Guanaco. 77p, Komodo dragon.

2009, Feb. 26 Litho. *Perf. 14*

1022 A218 36p multi 1.10 1.10
1023 A218 43p multi 1.25 1.25
1024 A218 51p multi 1.50 1.50
1025 A218 54p multi 1.60 1.60
1026 A218 56p multi 1.60 1.60
1027 A218 77p multi 2.25 2.25
a. Miniature sheet of 6, #1022-1027 9.50 9.50
Nos. 1022-1027 (6) 9.30 9.30

Souvenir Sheet

Amur Leopard — A219

2009, Feb. 26 *Perf. 13¼x14*
1028 A219 £3 multi 8.50 8.50

Flowers Type of 2008

Designs: 1p, Stinking onion. 2p, Common mallow. 3p, Primrose. 4p, Loose-flowered orchid. 5p, Common centaury. 6p, Yellow horned poppy. 7p, Sea kale. 8p, Bluebell. 9p, Sea bindweed. £3, Common poppy, vert.

2009, May 28 **Litho.** *Perf. 13¼*
1029 A212 1p multi .25 .25
1030 A212 2p multi .25 .25
1031 A212 3p multi .25 .25
1032 A212 4p multi .25 .25
1033 A212 5p multi .25 .25
1034 A212 6p multi .25 .25
1035 A212 7p multi .25 .25
1036 A212 8p multi .25 .25
1037 A212 9p multi .30 .30

Litho. & Embossed

1038 A212 £3 multi 8.00 8.00
Nos. 1029-1038 (10) 10.30 10.30

Invention of Telescope, 400th Anniv. A220

Designs: 36p, Quasar. 43p, Asteroid. 51p, Sun and Earth. 54p, Sun and Jupiter. 56p, Total solar eclipse. 77p, Solar eruption.

2009, May 28 **Litho.** *Perf. 13¼*
1039 A220 36p multi 1.10 1.10
1040 A220 43p multi 1.25 1.25
1041 A220 51p multi 1.50 1.50
1042 A220 54p multi 1.60 1.60
1043 A220 56p multi 1.75 1.75
1044 A220 77p multi 2.25 2.25
Nos. 1039-1044 (6) 9.45 9.45

Europa (43p, 51p).

Coronation of King Henry VIII, 500th Anniv. A221

King Henry VIII: 36p, With hawk. 43p, On throne beside Catherine of Aragon. 51p, Meeting Francis I of France. 54p, With Cardinal Wolsey. 56p, With Anne Boleyn. 77p, And ships.

2009, July 30 **Litho.** *Perf. 13½*
1045 A221 36p multi 1.10 1.10
a. Booklet pane of 4 4.50 4.50
1046 A221 43p multi 1.25 1.25
a. Booklet pane of 4 5.25 5.25
1047 A221 51p multi 1.50 1.50
a. Booklet pane of 4 6.25 6.25
1048 A221 54p multi 1.60 1.60
a. Booklet pane of 4 6.50 6.50
1049 A221 56p multi 1.75 1.75
a. Booklet pane of 4 7.25 7.25
1050 A221 77p multi 2.25 2.25
a. Booklet pane of 4 9.25 9.25
Complete booklet, #1045a-1050a 39.00
Nos. 1045-1050 (6) 9.45 9.45

Postal Independence, 40th Anniv. — A222

"1969" and "2009" with inscription: 36p, The Psychedelic 60's. 43p, God Save the 70's. 51p, The POPular 80's. 54p, The Urban 90's. 56p, The Seductive 00's. 77p, Looking to the Future.

2009, July 30 **Litho.** *Perf. 14x13¾*
1051 A222 36p multi 1.10 1.10
1052 A222 43p multi 1.25 1.25
1053 A222 51p multi 1.50 1.50
1054 A222 54p multi 1.60 1.60
1055 A222 56p multi 1.75 1.75
1056 A222 77p multi 2.25 2.25
Nos. 1051-1056 (6) 9.45 9.45

Seaside Views Type of 2007

Designs: 36p, Jerbourg Point. 43p, Vazon Bay. 51p, Saints Bay Moorings. 54p, Le Jaonnet Bay. 56p, Rocquaine Bay. 77p, Bordeaux Harbor.

2009, Sept. 16 **Litho.** *Perf. 13½*
1057 A209 36p multi 1.10 1.10
1058 A209 43p multi 1.25 1.25
1059 A209 51p multi 1.50 1.50
1060 A209 54p multi 1.60 1.60
1061 A209 56p multi 1.75 1.75
1062 A209 77p multi 2.25 2.25
Nos. 1057-1062 (6) 9.45 9.45

Christmas — A223

Designs: No. 1063, St. Martin's Church. No. 1064, Castel Church. No. 1065, Torteval Church. No. 1066, St. John's Church. No. 1067, St. Peter Port Church. No. 1068, St. Sampson's Church. 36p, St. Matthew's Church. 43p, St. Saviour's Church. 51p, Forest Church. 54p, St. Andrew's Church. 56p, Vale Church. 77p, St. Peter's Church.

2009, Oct. 29
1063 A223 31p multi .95 .95
1064 A223 31p multi .95 .95
1065 A223 31p multi .95 .95
1066 A223 31p multi .95 .95
1067 A223 31p multi .95 .95
1068 A223 31p multi .95 .95
1069 A223 36p multi 1.10 1.10
1070 A223 43p multi 1.25 1.25
1071 A223 51p multi 1.50 1.50
1072 A223 54p multi 1.60 1.60
1073 A223 56p multi 1.75 1.75
1074 A223 77p multi 2.25 2.25
Nos. 1063-1074 (12) 15.15 15.15

Souvenir Sheet

Asian Elephant — A224

2010, Feb. 25 **Litho.** *Perf. 14*
1075 A224 £3.07 multi 8.75 8.75

Views of Guernsey A225

Designs: Nos. 1076, 1082a, Port à la Jument, Sark. Nos. 1077, 1082b, Dog and Lion Rocks. Nos. 1078, 1082c, Fort Grey. Nos. 1079, 1082d, West coast of Guernsey. Nos. 1080, 1082e, Slipway, Havelet Bay. Nos. 1081, 1082f, Castle Cornet.

2010, Mar. 18 *Perf. 13¼*
1076 A225 (48p) multi 1.50 1.50
1077 A225 (48p) multi 1.50 1.50
a. Vert. pair, #1076-1077 3.00 3.00
1078 A225 (50p) multi 1.60 1.60
1079 A225 (58p) multi 1.75 1.75
1080 A225 (58p) multi 1.75 1.75
a. Vert. pair, #1079-1080 3.50 3.50
1081 A225 (80p) multi 2.50 2.50
Nos. 1076-1081 (6) 10.60 10.60

Self-Adhesive

Serpentine Die Cut 12½

1082 Sheet of 6 11.00
a.-b. A225 (48p) Either single 1.50 1.50
c. A225 (50p) multi 1.60 1.60
d.-e. A225 (58p) Either single 1.75 1.75
f. A225 (80p) multi 2.50 2.50
g. Booklet pane of 4, 2 each #1082a-1082b 6.00
h. Booklet pane of 4, 2 each #1082d-1082e 7.00

Nos. 1076-1077, 1082a-1082b are inscribed "GY LARGE"; Nos. 1078, 1082c, "EUR"; Nos. 1079-1080, 1082d-1082e, "UK LARGE"; Nos. 1081, 1082f, "ROW."

Nos. 1082a-1082b, 1082d-1082e were issued in complete booklets of 50 consisting of 5 panes of 10 stamps. Each pane contained 5 of each denomination.

The Adventures of Penny the Postie A226

Children on treasure chest with sail and: 45p, Volcano. 50p, Map. £2, Pirate and ship.

2010, May 4 **Litho.** *Perf. 13¼*
1083 A226 45p multi 1.25 1.25

Size: 38x51mm

Perf. 14¼

1084 A226 50p multi 1.40 1.40
1085 A226 £2 multi 5.75 5.75
a. Souvenir sheet, #1083-1085 8.50 8.50
Nos. 1083-1085 (3) 8.40 8.40

Europa (Nos. 1083-1084).

Girl Guides, Cent. — A227

Designs: 36p, Outdoor activities. 45p, Help during World Wars I and II. 48p, Crystal Palace Maze. 50p, Agnes Baden-Powell. 58p, Mount Everest. 80p, Queen's Guide award.

2010, May 27 **Litho.** *Perf. 13¼*
1086 A227 36p multi 1.00 1.00
1087 A227 45p multi 1.10 1.10
1088 A227 48p multi 1.25 1.25
1089 A227 50p multi 1.50 1.50
1090 A227 58p multi 1.60 1.60
1091 A227 80p multi 2.25 2.25
Nos. 1086-1091 (6) 8.70 8.70

National Trust of Guernsey, 50th Anniv. — A228

Designs: 36p, Victorian Shop, 26 Cornet Street, St. Peter Port. 45p, Field, Jerbourg. 48p, Martello Tower, Fermain Bay. 50p, Ivy Gates. 58p, Pleinmont Headland. 80p, Moulin de Quanteraine.

2010, July 5 **Litho.** *Perf. 13½*
1092 A228 36p multi 1.00 1.00
1093 A228 45p multi 1.10 1.10
1094 A228 48p multi 1.25 1.25
1095 A228 50p multi 1.50 1.50
1096 A228 58p multi 1.60 1.60
1097 A228 80p multi 2.25 2.25
Nos. 1092-1097 (6) 8.70 8.70

Seaside Views Type of 2007

Design: Point Robert Lighthouse, Sark.

2010, June 18 *Perf. 13¾x13½*
1098 A209 55p multi 1.50 1.50

Evacuation of Guernsey, 70th Anniv. A229

Designs: 36p, Gas masks being loaded onto a truck, 1939. 45p, Guernsey children waiting to leave, 1940. 48p, German soldiers leaving Guernsey, 1945. 50p, Evacuees arriving back in Guernsey, 1945. 58p, Royal visit to Guernsey, June 1945. 80p, Liberation Day, 1946.

2010, July 29 *Perf. 13¾*
1099 A229 36p multi 1.10 1.10
1100 A229 45p multi 1.25 1.25
1101 A229 48p multi 1.40 1.40
1102 A229 50p multi 1.50 1.50
1103 A229 58p multi 1.75 1.75
1104 A229 80p multi 2.25 2.25
Nos. 1099-1104 (6) 9.25 9.25

2010 Commonwealth Games, Delhi — A230

Designs: 36p, Tennis. 45p, Lawn bowling. 48p, Shooting. 50p, Swimming. 58p, Track. 80p, Cycling.

2010, Sept. 23 *Perf. 13½*
1105 A230 36p multi .95 .95
a. Booklet pane of 4 4.00 —
1106 A230 45p multi 1.25 1.25
a. Booklet pane of 4 5.25 —
1107 A230 48p multi 1.40 1.40
a. Booklet pane of 4 5.75 —
1108 A230 50p multi 1.50 1.50
a. Booklet pane of 4 6.25 —
1109 A230 58p multi 1.60 1.60
a. Booklet pane of 4 6.50 —
1110 A230 80p multi 2.25 2.25
a. Booklet pane of 4 9.25 —
Complete booklet, #1005a, 1106a, 1107a, 1108a, 1109a, 1110a 37.50
Nos. 1105-1110 (6) 8.95 8.95

Christmas Carols A231

Designs: 31p, The Holly and the Ivy. 36p, Little Donkey. 45p, Silent Night. 48p, I Saw

Three Ships. 50p, Joy to the World. 58p, Ding Dong Merrily on High. 80p, We Three Kings.

2010, Nov. 4 Litho. *Perf. 13¼x14*

1111	A231	31p multi	1.00	1.00
1112	A231	36p multi	1.10	1.10
1113	A231	45p multi	1.25	1.25
1114	A231	48p multi	1.40	1.40
1115	A231	50p multi	1.50	1.50
1116	A231	58p multi	1.60	1.60
1117	A231	80p multi	2.00	2.00
		Nos. 1111-1117 (7)	11.45	11.45

Royal British Legion, 90th Anniv. — A232

Emblem, soldiers or veterans and word: 36p, Hope. 45p, Reflection. 52p, Comradeship. 58p, Selflessness. 65p, Service. 70p, Dedication.

2011, Feb. 23 Litho. *Perf. 13¼x13*

1118	A232	36p multi	1.10	1.10
1119	A232	45p multi	1.25	1.25
1120	A232	52p multi	1.40	1.40
1121	A232	58p multi	1.50	1.50
1122	A232	65p multi	1.75	1.75
1123	A232	70p multi	2.00	2.00
a.		Souvenir sheet of 6, #1118-1123	9.00	9.00
		Nos. 1118-1123 (6)	9.00	9.00

Souvenir Sheet

Blue Whale — A233

2011, Feb. 23 *Perf. 13¼*

1124	A233	£3 multi	9.00	9.00

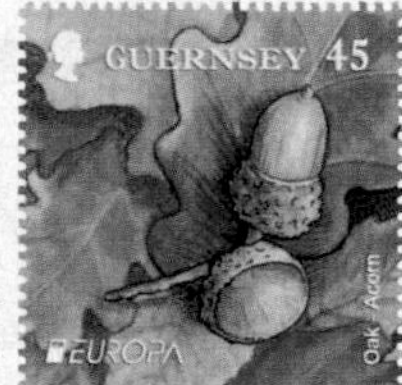

Intl. Year of Forests A234

Designs: 45p, Oak leaves, acorn. 52p, Hazel leaves, hazel nut. £2, Horse chestnut leaves and horse chestnut.

2011, May 4 *Perf. 13¾*

1125	A234	45p multi	1.25	1.25
1126	A234	52p multi	1.75	1.75
1127	A234	£2 multi	5.75	5.75
a.		Souvenir sheet of 3, #1125-1127	8.50	8.50
		Nos. 1125-1127 (3)	8.75	8.75

Europa (Nos. 1125-1126).

Souvenir Sheets

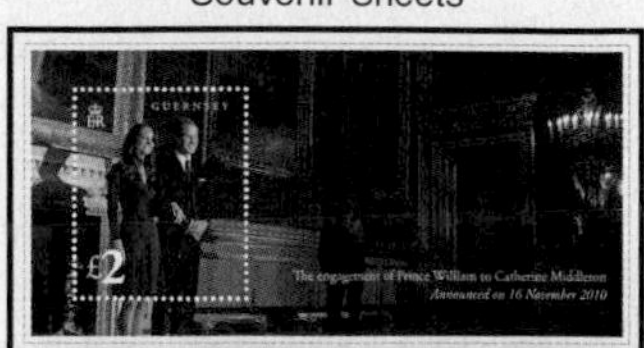

Wedding of Prince William and Catherine Middleton — A235

Designs: No. 1128, Engagement photo. No. 1129, Bride and groom on wedding day.

2011, June 2 *Perf. 14*

1128	A235	£2 multi	5.75	5.75
1129	A235	£2 multi	5.75	5.75

The Guernsey Literary and Potato Peel Pie Society, Book by Mary Ann Shaffer and Annie Barrows A236

Depictions of scenes from book: 36p, How to roast your pig. 47p, The books enjoyed by the Guernsey Literary and Potato Peel Pie Society. 48p, Juliet arrives at St. Peter Port weaing her red cloak. 52p, The view through Elizabeth's cottage window. 61p, Juliet and Dawsey's pivotal moment on the cliffs. 65p, Isola's legendary parrot, Zenobia.

2011, July 28 *Perf. 13¼*

1130	A236	36p multi	1.00	1.00
1131	A236	47p multi	1.10	1.10
1132	A236	48p multi	1.40	1.40
1133	A236	52p multi	1.50	1.50
1134	A236	61p multi	1.75	1.75
1135	A236	65p multi	2.00	2.00
		Nos. 1130-1135 (6)	8.75	8.75

Seaside Views Type of 2007

Designs: 36p, Victoria Marina, St. Peter Port. 45p, L'Ancresse Bay. 52p, Bordeaux Harbor Slipway. 58p, South Coast sunset. 65p, Salerie Harbor. 70p, Petit Port.

2011, Sept. 28 Litho. *Perf. 14¼*

1136	A209	36p multi	1.00	1.00
1137	A209	45p multi	1.25	1.25
1138	A209	52p multi	1.40	1.40
1139	A209	58p multi	1.50	1.50
1140	A209	65p multi	1.75	1.75
1141	A209	70p multi	2.00	2.00
		Nos. 1136-1141 (6)	8.90	8.90

British Formula 1 World Championship Cars and Drivers Type of 2007

Driver and championship year: 36p, Lewis Hamilton, 2008 (red background). 47p, Jenson Button, 2009 (purple background). 61p, Hamilton, 2008 (blue background). 65p, Button, 2009 (orange background).

2011, Oct. 27 *Perf. 13¼x13*

1142	A206	36p multi	1.00	1.00
1143	A206	47p multi	1.25	1.25
1144	A206	61p multi	1.75	1.75
1145	A206	65p multi	2.00	2.00
a.		Souvenir sheet of 4, #1142-1145	6.00	6.00
		Nos. 1142-1145 (4)	6.00	6.00

Guernsey in Winter A237

Winning entries in "Guernsey in Winter" photography contest: 31p, Forest Church, by John Shakerley. 36p, L'Ancresse Common, by Nigel Byrom. 47p, Guernsey Cows, by Sarah Plumley. 48p, St. Peter Port, by Karen Millard. 52p, La Coupée, by Sue Daly. 61p, St. Peter's Church, by Jason Bishop. 65p, Cobo Bay, by Eric Ferbrache.

2011, Oct. 27 *Perf. 13½x13¼*

1146	A237	31p multi	1.00	1.00
1147	A237	36p multi	1.10	1.10
1148	A237	47p multi	1.25	1.25
1149	A237	48p multi	1.40	1.40
1150	A237	52p multi	1.50	1.50
1151	A237	61p multi	1.60	1.60
1152	A237	65p multi	2.00	2.00
		Nos. 1146-1152 (7)	9.85	9.85

Souvenir Sheet

Bengal Tiger — A238

2012, Feb. 22 *Perf. 13¾*

1153	A238	£3 multi	8.50	8.50

Reign of Queen Elizabeth II, 60th Anniv. — A239

Gem and: 36p, Queen at coronation, birth of Prince Andrew. 47p, Queen presenting Jules Rimet trophy to captain of British soccer team, ocean liner Queen Elizabeth 2. 48p, Queen, Sydney Opera House, emblem of 1976 Montreal Summer Olympics. 52p, Queen riding horse, Princes William and Harry in school uniforms, 1989. 61p, Queen, Queen Mother, Nelson Mandela. 65p, Queen at Guernsey Liberation Day, Queen with Pres. Barack Obama.

2012, Feb. 22 *Perf. 12½*

1154	A239	36p multi	1.00	1.00
1155	A239	47p multi	1.25	1.25
1156	A239	48p multi	1.40	1.40
1157	A239	52p multi	1.50	1.50
1158	A239	61p multi	1.75	1.75
1159	A239	65p multi	2.00	2.00
a.		Souvenir sheet of 6, #1154-1159	9.00	9.00
		Nos. 1154-1159 (6)	8.90	8.90

Tourist Attractions A240

Designs: (39p), Surfer, Vazon Bay. (52p), Shell Beach, Herm. (53p), Grande Greve Beach, Sark. (59p), Bluestone Bay, Alderney. (69p), Sailboat off the coast of Herm. (74p), La Coupée, Sark.

2012, May 1 *Perf. 13x13¼*

1160	A240	(39p) multi	1.10	1.10
1161	A240	(52p) multi	1.25	1.25
1162	A240	(53p) multi	1.40	1.40
1163	A240	(59p) multi	1.50	1.50
1164	A240	(69p) multi	1.75	1.75
1165	A240	(74p) multi	2.00	2.00
a.		Souvenir sheet of 6, #1160-1165	10.00	10.00
		Nos. 1160-1165 (6)	9.00	9.00

Europa (53p, 59p). Inscriptions on: No. 1160, "GY Letter"; No. 1161, "GY Large"; No. 1162, "UK Letter"; No. 1163, "INT Letter 20G"; No. 1164, "UK Large"; No. 1165, "INT Letter 40G."

Duke of Cambridge, 30th Birthday — A241

Prince William: 36p, Carrying log, Chile, 2006. 47p, At St. Andrews University graduation ceremonies, 2005. 48p, Playing soccer, 2006. 52p, Climbing mountain, 2007. 67p, Riding motorcycle at Endura Africa Charity Motorcycle Ride, 2008. 65p, As rescue pilot, 2010.

2012, May 8 *Perf. 13½*

1166	A241	36p multi	1.00	1.00
a.		Booklet pane of 4	4.25	—
1167	A241	47p multi	1.10	1.10
a.		Booklet pane of 4	4.50	—
1168	A241	48p multi	1.50	1.50
a.		Booklet pane of 4	6.00	—
1169	A241	52p multi	1.60	1.60
a.		Booklet pane of 4	6.50	—
1170	A241	61p multi	1.75	1.75
a.		Booklet pane of 4	7.25	—
1171	A241	65p multi	2.00	2.00
a.		Booklet pane of 4	8.00	—
		Complete booklet, #1166a, 1167a, 1168a, 1169a, 1170a, 1171a	39.00	
		Nos. 1166-1171 (6)	8.95	8.95

War of 1812 — A242

No. 1172: a, Sir Isaac Brock (1769-1812), British Major General. b, Tecumseh (1768-1813), leader of Indian confederacy.

2012, June 15 *Perf. 13¼x12½*

1172	A242	Horiz. pair	5.50	5.50
a.-b.		£1 Either single	2.75	2.75

See Canada Nos. 2554-2555.

Royal Channel Islands Yacht Club, 150th Anniv. — A243

Various sailors on yachts.

2012, July 25 *Perf. 13¼x13½*

Denomination Color

1173	A243	39p purple	1.25	1.25
1174	A243	52p blue gray	1.40	1.40
1175	A243	53p blue	1.50	1.50
1176	A243	59p blue	1.75	1.75
1177	A243	69p olive green	1.90	1.90
1178	A243	74p orange brown	2.00	2.00
		Nos. 1173-1178 (6)	9.80	9.80

A244

Floral Guernsey, 20th Anniv. — A245

Designs: 39p, Flowers in wheelbarrow. 52p, Flowers and Seigneurie, home of Lord of Sark. 53p, Flower display and rope. 59p, Flowers and sea. 69p, Potted flowers in and near shelf. 74p, Flowers and building, diff.

£3, Floral Guernsey daffodil.

2012, Sept. 27 *Perf. 13½*

1179	A244	39p multi	1.25	1.25
1180	A244	52p multi	1.40	1.40
1181	A244	53p multi	1.50	1.50
1182	A244	59p multi	1.75	1.75

1183 A244 69p multi 1.90 1.90
1184 A244 74p multi 2.00 2.00
Nos. 1179-1184 (6) 9.80 9.80

Souvenir Sheet

Perf. 14

1185 A245 £3 multi 8.50 8.50

Christmas A246

Designs: 34p, Annunciation. 39p, Innkeeper shows Mary and Joseph to the stable. 52p, Jesus is born in a stable. 53p, Angels come down amongst the shepherds. 59p, The Three Kings. 69p, Mary and baby Jesus with Angels. 74p, Flight to Egypt.

2012, Oct. 31 ***Perf. 13¼x13***

1186 A246 34p multi 1.00 1.00
1187 A246 39p multi 1.10 1.10
1188 A246 52p multi 1.40 1.40
1189 A246 53p multi 1.50 1.50
1190 A246 59p multi 1.60 1.60
1191 A246 69p multi 1.75 1.75
1192 A246 74p multi 2.00 2.00
Nos. 1186-1192 (7) 10.35 10.35

Souvenir Sheet

Giant Panda — A247

2013, Feb. 20 ***Perf. 14x14¼***

1193 A247 £3 multi 8.50 8.50

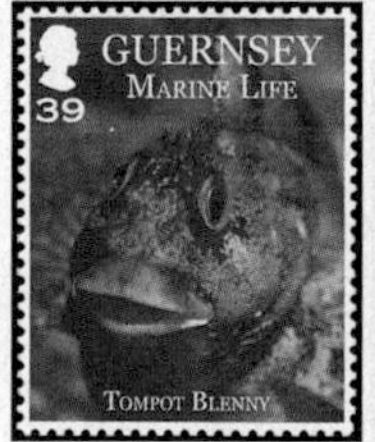

Fish — A248

Designs: 39p, Tompot blenny. 52p, Leopard-spotted goby. 53p, Red gurnard. 59p, Female cuckoo wrasse. 69p, Male cuckoo wrasse. 74p, John Dory.
£5, Black-face blenny.

2013, Feb. 20 ***Perf. 12½***

1194 A248 39p multi 1.25 1.25
1195 A248 52p multi 1.60 1.60
1196 A248 53p multi 1.60 1.60
1197 A248 59p multi 1.75 1.75
1198 A248 69p multi 1.90 1.90
1199 A248 74p multi 2.10 2.10
Nos. 1194-1199 (6) 10.55 10.55

Souvenir Sheet

Perf. 13¼x13½

1200 A248 £5 multi 14.00 14.00

No. 1200 contains one 48x66mm stamp.

Souvenir Sheet

Mailbox on Sark Painted Gold to Commemorate Olympic Gold Medalist Carl Hester — A249

2013, Mar. 20 ***Perf. 14¾x14¼***

1201 A249 £1 multi 3.00 3.00

No. 1201 was sent free of charge to Guernsey Post standing order customers in February 2013. It was offered for sale starting March 20 through online sales only.

Postal Vehicles A250

Designs: (40p), Guernsey Post Daihatsu Hijet van, GY Letter. (53p), La Poste Citroen 2CV van, France, GY Large Letter. (55p), Royal Mail Morris 6cwt O Type van, Great Britain, UK Letter. (63p), Deutsche Post Volkswagen Beetle van, Germany, Int Letter 20g. (71p), Posten AB Kalmar Tjorven van, Sweden, UK Large Letter. (79p), United States Post Office Studebaker Zip van, Int Letter 40g.

2013, May 8 ***Perf. 13¼x13***

1202 A250 (40p) multi 1.25 1.25
1203 A250 (53p) multi 1.75 1.75
1204 A250 (55p) multi 1.75 1.75
1205 A250 (63p) multi 2.00 2.00
1206 A250 (71p) multi 2.25 2.25
1207 A250 (79p) multi 2.50 2.50
a. Souvenir sheet of 6, #1202-1207 11.50 11.50
Nos. 1202-1207 (6) 11.50 11.50

Europa (Nos. 1204-1205).

Herm Island — A251

Designs: 40p, Mermaid Tavern sign. 53p, Shell Beach. 55p, Belvoir Bay. 63p, Harbor moorings. 71p, Fishermans Beach. 79p, Gift shop.

2013, May 29 ***Perf. 13x12½***

1208 A251 40p multi 1.25 1.25
1209 A251 53p multi 1.75 1.75
1210 A251 55p multi 1.75 1.75
1211 A251 63p multi 2.00 2.00
1212 A251 71p multi 2.25 2.25
1213 A251 79p multi 2.50 2.50
Nos. 1208-1213 (6) 11.50 11.50

Guernsey Newspapers, Bicent. A252

Designs: 40p, Text from first edition of *The Star,* 1813. 53p, Text and illustration from *The Star* announcing Diamond Jubilee of Queen Victoria. 55p, Guernsey #N1, Text from *The Evening Press* announcing occupation of Guernsey. 63p, Text from *The Guernsey Press* announcing bicentennial of newspaper. 71p, Text and illustration from *Guernsey Evening Press* announcing coronation of Queen Elizabeth II. 79p, Text and illustration from *Guernsey Evening Press* announcing end of World War II in Europe.

2013, July 31 **Litho.** ***Perf. 13***

1214 A252 40p gray & blk 1.25 1.25
1215 A252 53p gray & blk 1.75 1.75
1216 A252 55p multi 1.75 1.75
1217 A252 63p multi 2.00 2.00
1218 A252 71p gray & blk 2.25 2.25
1219 A252 79p gray & blk 2.50 2.50
Nos. 1214-1219 (6) 11.50 11.50

West Show, Cent. A253

Designs: 40p, Farmers looking at tractors and hay-kicker. 53p, Prize-winning produce. 55p, Brewery dray and shire horses. 63p, Guernsey cows. 71p, Steam tractor engine. 79p, Haymaking.

2013, Sept. 24 **Litho.** ***Perf. 13***

1220 A253 40p multi 1.25 1.25
1221 A253 53p multi 1.75 1.75
1222 A253 55p multi 1.75 1.75
1223 A253 63p multi 2.00 2.00
1224 A253 71p multi 2.25 2.25
1225 A253 79p multi 2.50 2.50
Nos. 1220-1225 (6) 11.50 11.50

Souvenir Sheet

Birth of Prince George of Cambridge — A254

2013, Sept. 24 **Litho.** ***Perf. 12½***

1226 A254 £3 multi 9.75 9.75

Clematis Varieties Developed by Raymond Evison A255

Clematis variety: 40p, Samaritan Jo. 53p, Anna Louise. 55p, Chelsea. 63p, Edda. 71p, The Countess of Wessex. 79p, Giselle.

2013, Nov. 13 **Litho.** ***Perf. 13¾***

1227 A255 40p multi 1.40 1.40
a. Booklet pane of 4 5.75 —
1228 A255 53p multi 1.75 1.75
a. Booklet pane of 4 7.00 —
1229 A255 55p multi 1.90 1.90
a. Booklet pane of 4 7.75 —
1230 A255 63p multi 2.10 2.10
a. Booklet pane of 4 8.50 —
1231 A255 71p multi 2.40 2.40
a. Booklet pane of 4 9.75 —
1232 A255 79p multi 2.60 2.60
a. Booklet pane of 4 10.50 —
Complete booklet, #1227a, 1228a, 1229a, 1230a, 1231a, 1232a 50.00
Nos. 1227-1232 (6) 12.15 12.15

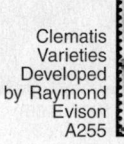

Christmas A256

Santa Claus: 35p, Outside of sleeping child's bedroom window. 40p, On roof. 53p, Stuck in chimney. 55p, Being pulled out of chimney by children. 63p, Sneezing. 71p, Placing gifts under Christmas tree. 79p, Above houses in flying sleigh.

2013, Nov. 13 **Litho.** ***Perf. 13x13½***

1233 A256 35p multi 1.25 1.25
1234 A256 40p multi 1.40 1.40
1235 A256 53p multi 1.75 1.75
1236 A256 55p multi 1.90 1.90
1237 A256 63p multi 2.10 2.10
1238 A256 71p multi 2.40 2.40
1239 A256 79p multi 2.60 2.60
Nos. 1233-1239 (7) 13.40 13.40

New Year 2014 (Year of the Horse) A257

Chinese character for "horse" and various depictions of horses.

2014, Jan. 8 **Litho.** ***Perf. 13***

1240 A257 40p multi 1.40 1.40
1241 A257 53p multi 1.75 1.75
1242 A257 55p multi 1.90 1.90
1243 A257 63p multi 2.10 2.10
1244 A257 71p multi 2.40 2.40
1245 A257 79p multi 2.60 2.60
a. Souvenir sheet of 6, #1240-1245 12.50 12.50
Nos. 1240-1245 (6) 12.15 12.15

Souvenir Sheet

Sumatran Orangutan — A258

2014, Feb. 12 **Litho.** ***Perf. 14x14¼***

1246 A258 £3 multi 9.75 9.75

Chifournie A259

Designs: 40p, Chifournie keys. 53p, Chifournie wooden pegs and turning handle. 55p, Chifournie rotating wheel. 63p, Chifournie wheel and strings. 71p, Chifournie turning handle and wheel. 79p, Entire chifournie.

2014, May 8 **Litho.** ***Perf. 13x13¼***

1247 A259 40p multi 1.40 1.40
1248 A259 53p multi 1.75 1.75
1249 A259 55p multi 1.90 1.90
1250 A259 63p multi 2.10 2.10
1251 A259 71p multi 2.40 2.40
1252 A259 79p multi 2.75 2.75
a. Souvenir sheet of 6, #1247-1252 12.50 12.50
Nos. 1247-1252 (6) 12.30 12.30

Europa (55p, 63p).

Postcrossing A260

2014, May 28 **Litho.** ***Perf. 13¼***

1253 A260 (66p) multi 2.25 2.25

Britain in Bloom Horticultural Campaign, 50th Anniv. — A261

Designs: (41p), St. Peter Port Marina. (54p), White House view, Herm. (55p), Mermaid Tavern, Herm. (66p), St. Pierre du Bois. (74p), St. Martin's Church. (83p), Albion Tavern, St. Peter Port.

2014, May 28 Litho. *Perf. 13½*

1254 A261 (41p) multi 1.40 1.40
1255 A261 (54p) multi 1.90 1.90
1256 A261 (55p) multi 1.90 1.90
1257 A261 (66p) multi 2.25 2.25
1258 A261 (74p) multi 2.50 2.50
1259 A261 (83p) multi 2.75 2.75
Nos. 1254-1259 (6) 12.70 12.70

Inscriptions: No. 1254, "GY Letter." No. 1255, "GY Large Letter." No. 1256, "UK Letter." No. 1257, "Int Letter 20g." No. 1258, "UK Large Letter." No. 1259, "Int Letter 40g."

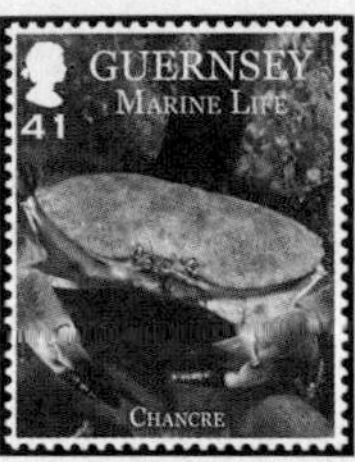

Crustaceans A262

Designs: 41p, Chancre (brown crab). 54p, Lobster. 55p, Velvet swimming crab. 66p, Hermit crab. 74p, Squat lobster. 83p, Spider crab. £3, Anemone shrimp.

2014, July 30 Litho. *Perf. 12½*

1260 A262 41p multi 1.40 1.40
1261 A262 54p multi 1.90 1.90
1262 A262 55p multi 1.90 1.90
1263 A262 66p multi 2.25 2.25
1264 A262 74p multi 2.50 2.50
1265 A262 83p multi 2.75 2.75
Nos. 1260-1265 (6) 12.70 12.70

Souvenir Sheet

Perf. 13¼x13¾

1266 A262 £3 multi 10.00 10.00

No. 1266 contains one 48x66mm stamp.

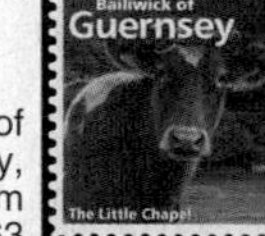

Views of Guernsey, Alderney, Herm and Sark — A263

No. 1267: a, Little Chapel and cow. b, Bec du Néz. c, Torteval Church. d, Moulin Huet. e, St. Peter Port Harbor. f, Fisherman's Beach, Herm. g, Creux Harbor, Sark. h, Fort Essex, Alderney. i, Vazon Bay, Guernsey. j, Petit Bot, Guernsey.

Serpentine Die Cut 12½

2014, July 30 Litho.

Self-Adhesive

1267 Sheet of 10 16.50
a.-e. A263 (41p) Any single 1.40 1.40
f.-j. A263 (55p) Any single 1.90 1.90
k. Booklet pane of 10, 2 each #1267a-1267e 14.00
l. Booklet pane of 10, 2 each #1267f-1267j 19.00

Nos. 1267a-1267e are inscribed "GY"; Nos. 1267f-1267j, "UK."

Christmas A264

Children's art depicting: 36p, Rudolph, the Red-nosed Reindeer and stars, by Katka Devon. 41p, Robins in tree, by Patience Ogler. 54p, Rudolph and candy canes, by Georgia Winstanley. 55p,Santa Claus, by Mali Chatterton. 66p, Robin in stocking cap, by Ruby Parker. 74p, Snowman and candy canes, by Giselle Fuller. 83p, Robin on chimney, by Keone Hardy.

Serpentine Die Cut

2014, Nov. 6 Litho.

Self-Adhesive

1268 A264 36p multi 1.25 1.25
1269 A264 41p multi 1.40 1.40
1270 A264 54p multi 1.75 1.75
1271 A264 55p multi 1.75 1.75
1272 A264 66p multi 2.10 2.10
1273 A264 74p multi 2.40 2.40
1274 A264 83p multi 2.60 2.60
Nos. 1268-1274 (7) 13.25 13.25

World War I, Cent. A265

Designs: 41p, Private Yves Cataroche. 54p, Major George Le Page. 55p, Munitions worker Dorothy Nicolls. 66p, Lieutenant Frank Lainé. 74p, Salvation Army worker Ada Le Poidevin. 83p, Private Latimer Le Poidevin.

2014, Nov. 11 Litho. *Perf. 14x14¾*

1275 A265 41p multi 1.25 1.25
a. Booklet pane of 4 5.00 —
1276 A265 54p multi 1.75 1.75
a. Booklet pane of 4 7.00 —
1277 A265 55p multi 1.75 1.75
a. Booklet pane of 4 7.00 —
1278 A265 66p multi 2.10 2.10
a. Booklet pane of 4 8.50 —
1279 A265 74p multi 2.40 2.40
a. Booklet pane of 4 9.75 —
1280 A265 83p multi 2.60 2.60
a. Booklet pane of 4 10.50 —
Complete booklet, #1275a, 1276a, 1277a, 1278a, 1279a, 1280a 48.00
Nos. 1275-1280 (6) 11.85 11.85

See Nos. 1320-1325, 1367-1372, 1409-1414, 1455-1460.

Souvenir Sheet

Sir Winston Churchill (1874-1965), British Prime Minister — A266

No. 1281 — Churchill: a, Walking in garden (40x30mm). b, Painting picture (40x30mm). c, Wearing military cap (60x48mm).

2015, Jan. 22 Litho. *Perf. 13x13¼*

1281 A266 Sheet of 3 9.00 9.00
a.-c. £1 Any single 3.00 3.00

New Year 2015 (Year of the Goat) A267

Various depictions of goats.

2015, Jan. 28 Litho. *Perf. 13x13¼*

1282 A267 41p red & gold 1.25 1.25
1283 A267 54p red & gold 1.60 1.60
1284 A267 55p red & gold 1.75 1.75
1285 A267 66p red & gold 2.00 2.00
1286 A267 74p red & gold 2.25 2.25
1287 A267 83p red & gold 2.50 2.50
a. Souvenir sheet of 6, #1282-1287 11.50 11.50
Nos. 1282-1287 (6) 11.35 11.35

Toys of the Royal Family A268

Designs: 41p, Prince George's rocking horse, c. 2013. 54p, Princess Victoria's wooden dolls, c. 1831. 55p, Prince Charles's toy car, c. 1950. 66p, Teddy bear from Royal Nursery. 74p, Princess Elizabeth's toy baker's wagon, c. 1930. 83p, Silver rattles, c. 1774, 1763 and 2003.

2015, May 1 Litho. *Perf. 13¾*

1288 A268 41p multi 1.25 1.25
1289 A268 54p multi 1.60 1.60
1290 A268 55p multi 1.75 1.75
1291 A268 66p multi 2.00 2.00
1292 A268 74p multi 2.25 2.25
1293 A268 83p multi 2.50 2.50
a. Souvenir sheet of 6, #1288-1293 11.50 11.50
Nos. 1288-1293 (6) 11.35 11.35

Europa (Nos. 1290-1291).

Liberation of Guernsey, 70th Anniv. — A269

Designs: (41p), Two boys enjoying chocolate for first time. (54p), Duke of Cornwall's Light Infantry Band. (55p), Col. H. R. Power tours St. Peter Port seafront. (66p), Petty Officer J. D. Langlois enjoying the moment. (74p), US 516 docks in St. Peter Port harbor. (83p), King George VI and Queen Elizabeth.

2015, May 1 Litho. *Perf. 13¼x13½*

1294 A269 (41p) multi 1.25 1.25
a. Booklet pane of 4 5.00 —
1295 A269 (54p) multi 1.60 1.60
a. Booklet pane of 4 6.50 —
1296 A269 (55p) multi 1.75 1.75
a. Booklet pane of 4 7.00 —
1297 A269 (66p) multi 2.00 2.00
a. Booklet pane of 4 8.00 —
1298 A269 (74p) multi 2.25 2.25
a. Booklet pane of 4 9.00 —
1299 A269 (83p) multi 2.50 2.50
a. Booklet pane of 4 10.00 —
Complete booklet, #1294a, 1295a, 1296a, 1297a, 1298a, 1299a 46.00
Nos. 1294-1299 (6) 11.35 11.35

Inscriptions on: No. 1294, "GY Letter." No. 1295, "GY Large Letter." No. 1296, "UK Letter." No. 1297, "EUR Letter." No. 1298, "UK Large Letter." No. 1299, "ROW Letter."

Souvenir Sheet

Penny Black, 175th Anniv. — A270

2015, May 1 Litho. *Perf. 12½*

1300 A270 £2 multi 6.25 6.25

Paintings A271

Designs: 42p, Moulin Huet Bay, by John Paul Jacob Naftel. 56p, La Moye Harbor, Le Gouffre, by Peter Le Lievre. 57p, Cradle Rock & Pea Stacks, by William John Caparne. 62p, La Saignée, Sark, by William A. Toplis. 68p, Grand Rocques Old Fort, by Ethel Cheeswright. 77p, Moulin Huet Bay, by Pierre-Auguste Renoir.

2015, July 22 Litho. *Perf. 14*

1301 A271 42p multi 1.40 1.40
1302 A271 56p multi 1.75 1.75
1303 A271 57p multi 1.75 1.75
1304 A271 62p multi 2.00 2.00
1305 A271 68p multi 2.10 2.10
1306 A271 77p multi 2.40 2.40
Nos. 1301-1306 (6) 11.40 11.40

A272

Sark as a Fief of the Crown, 450th Anniv. — A273

Designs: 42p, St. Magloire, patron saint of Sark. 57p, Sark in the 15th century. 62p, French invasion of Sark. 68p, Le Manoir, home of first seigneur of Sark. 77p, Silver and copper mine on Little Sark.

No. 1312: a, Bronze cannon, c. 1572 (40x26mm). b, Queen Elizabeth I (32x40mm).

2015, July 22 Litho. *Perf. 13x13¼*

1307 A272 42p multi 1.40 1.40
1308 A272 57p multi 1.75 1.75
1309 A272 62p multi 2.00 2.00
1310 A272 68p multi 2.10 2.10
1311 A272 77p multi 2.40 2.40
Nos. 1307-1311 (5) 9.65 9.65

Souvenir Sheet

Perf. 13 (#1312a), 12½ (#1312b)

1312 A273 Sheet of 2 9.50 9.50
a. £1 multi 3.25 3.25
b. £2 multi 6.25 6.25

Christmas — A274

St. Stephen's Church stained-glass windows by William Morris: 37p, Annunciation. 42p, Adoration of the Magi. 56p, Angels with harps. 57p, Angels and crucified Christ. 62p, Saint and angel. 68p, Church. 77p, Christ the King and angels.

Serpentine Die Cut 14¼

2015, Nov. 6 Litho.

Self-Adhesive

1313 A274 37p multi 1.10 1.10
1314 A274 42p multi 1.25 1.25
1315 A274 56p multi 1.75 1.75
1316 A274 57p multi 1.75 1.75
1317 A274 62p multi 1.90 1.90
1318 A274 68p multi 2.10 2.10
1319 A274 77p multi 2.40 2.40
Nos. 1313-1319 (7) 12.25 12.25

World War I, Cent. Type of 2014

Map, poppy and: 42p, Private Philip Carré, Christmas greetings from postmaster. 56p, Mailboat SS Vera. 57p, Christmas card from Lieutenant Peter Le Page, embroidered sampler. 62p, Post Office Rifles. 68p, Field service postcard noting status of Private Yves Cataroche. 77p, Robert and Ethel Bynam, Great Britain #128.

2015, Nov. 11 Litho. *Perf. 14x14¾*

1320 A265 42p multi 1.25 1.25
a. Booklet pane of 4 5.00 —
1321 A265 56p multi 1.75 1.75
a. Booklet pane of 4 7.00 —
1322 A265 57p multi 1.75 1.75
a. Booklet pane of 4 7.00 —
1323 A265 62p multi 1.90 1.90
a. Booklet pane of 4 7.75 —
1324 A265 68p multi 2.10 2.10
a. Booklet pane of 4 8.50 —

1325 A265 77p multi 2.40 2.40
a. Booklet pane of 4 9.75 —
Complete booklet, #1320a, 1321a, 1322a, 1323a, 1324a, 1325a 45.00
Nos. 1320-1325 (6) 11.15 11.15

New Year 2016 (Year of the Monkey) A275

Designs: 42p, Three Plenties Monkey. 56p, Fire Monkey. 57p, Aristocratic Monkey. 62p, Noble and Successful Monkey. 68p, Mother and Baby Monkey. 77p, Three Wealthy Monkeys.

2016, Jan. 20 Litho. *Perf. 13*

1326 A275 42p red & gold 1.25 1.25
1327 A275 56p red & gold 1.60 1.60
1328 A275 57p red & gold 1.75 1.75
1329 A275 62p red & gold 1.90 1.90
1330 A275 68p red & gold 2.00 2.00
1331 A275 77p red & gold 2.25 2.25
a. Souvenir sheet of 6, #1326-1331 11.00 11.00
Nos. 1326-1331 (6) 10.75 10.75

Souvenir Sheet

Philippine Eagle — A276

2016, Feb. 17 Litho. *Perf. 14x14¼*

1332 A276 £3 multi 8.50 8.50

Scenes from *Toilers of the Sea,* by Victor Hugo — A277

Designs: 43p, Gilliatt the Fisherman. 57p, Durande wrecked. 58p, Great Douvres. 64p, Great storm. 70p, Devilish octopus. 78p, Déruchette sails away.

2016, May 6 Litho. *Perf. 13¾x13½*

1333 A277 43p multi 1.25 1.25
a. Booklet pane of 4 5.00 —
1334 A277 57p multi 1.75 1.75
a. Booklet pane of 4 7.00 —
1335 A277 58p multi 1.75 1.75
a. Booklet pane of 4 7.00 —
1336 A277 64p multi 1.90 1.90
a. Booklet pane of 4 7.75 —
1337 A277 70p multi 2.00 2.00
a. Booklet pane of 4 8.00 —
1338 A277 78p multi 2.25 2.25
a. Booklet pane of 4 9.00 —
Complete booklet, #1333a, 1334a, 1335a, 1336a, 1337a, 1338a 44.00
Nos. 1333-1338 (6) 10.90 10.90

Europa A278

2016, May 6 Litho. *Perf. 13¼x13½*

1339 A278 64p multi 1.90 1.90

Think Green Issue.

Four Seasons A279

Designs: 43p, Bluebell Woods in spring. 57p, Petit Port Bay in summer. 64p, Sausmarez Park in autumn. 70p, St. Peter Port Lighthouse in winter.

2016, May 25 Litho. *Perf. 12½x13¼*

1340 A279 43p multi 1.25 1.25
1341 A279 57p multi 1.75 1.75
1342 A279 64p multi 1.90 1.90
1343 A279 70p multi 2.00 2.00
Nos. 1340-1343 (4) 6.90 6.90

Souvenir Sheet

Guernsey Cow — A280

2016, May 25 Litho. *Perf. 14¾*

1344 A280 £2 multi 5.75 5.75

World Stamp Show 2016, New York.

Postcrossing A281

Designs: (64p), Bird and fish. (70p), Butterfly, bee and bird.

2016, July 14 Litho. *Perf. 13¼*

1345 A281 (64p) multi 1.75 1.75
1346 A281 (70p) multi 1.90 1.90

No. 1345 is inscribed "EUR;" No. 1346, "ROW."

Island of Herm A282

Designs: 43p, Oysters. 57p, Mint sauce worms. 58p, Cowrie shells. 64p, Burial chamber. 70p, Common tern. 78p, Burnet roses.

2016, July 27 Litho. *Perf. 12½x13*

1347 A282 43p multi 1.25 1.25
1348 A282 57p multi 1.50 1.50
1349 A282 58p multi 1.50 1.50
1350 A282 64p multi 1.75 1.75
1351 A282 70p multi 1.90 1.90
1352 A282 78p multi 2.10 2.10
a. Souvenir sheet of 6, #1347-1352, perf. 13 10.00 10.00
Nos. 1347-1352 (6) 10.00 10.00

Royal Mail, 500th Anniv. A283

Designs: 43p, Royal Mail coach, 1784. 57p, Royal Mail steamboat Ariadne, 1824. 58p, Smith Street Post Office, St. Peter Port, 1883. 64p, Royal Mail underground train, 1927. 70p, Post Office Tower, London, 1965. 78p, Heathrow Distribution Center, 2003.
£2, Union Street pillar box installed in 1853, St. Peter Port, vert.

2016, July 27 Litho. *Perf. 13¼*

1353 A283 43p multi 1.25 1.25
1354 A283 57p multi 1.50 1.50
1355 A283 58p multi 1.50 1.50
1356 A283 64p multi 1.75 1.75
1357 A283 70p multi 1.90 1.90
1358 A283 78p multi 2.10 2.10
Nos. 1353-1358 (6) 10.00 10.00

Souvenir Sheet

1359 A283 £2 multi 5.25 5.25

No. 1359 contains one 52x52mm stamp.

Christmas A284

Bells and: 38p, Holly. 43p, Christmas tree. 57p, Gift. 58p, Santa Claus. 64p, Reindeer. 70p, Snowman. 78p, Stars.

Litho. With Foil Application
Serpentine Die Cut 7¼

2016, Nov. 8 Self-Adhesive

1360 A284 38p gold & green 1.00 1.00
1361 A284 43p green & gold 1.10 1.10
1362 A284 57p gold & green 1.50 1.50
1363 A284 58p green & gold 1.50 1.50
1364 A284 64p gold & green 1.60 1.60
1365 A284 70p green & gold 1.75 1.75
1366 A284 78p gold & green 2.00 2.00
Nos. 1360-1366 (7) 10.45 10.45

World War I, Cent. Type of 2014

Semaphore flag and men from Guernsey in British Navy: 43p, Seaman James Gale. 57p, Stoker First Class George Arthur Hicks. 58p, Sailors T. Gibson and H. Broadbent and other submariners. 64p, Seaman Wilfred Cochrane. 70p, First Class Petty Officer Harold de Putron Taylor and Lord Kitchener. 78p, Seaman John Helman.

2016, Nov. 11 Litho. *Perf. 14x14¾*

1367 A265 43p multi 1.10 1.10
a. Booklet pane of 4 4.50 —
1368 A265 57p multi 1.50 1.50
a. Booklet pane of 4 6.00 —
1369 A265 58p multi 1.50 1.50
a. Booklet pane of 4 6.00 —
1370 A265 64p multi 1.60 1.60
a. Booklet pane of 4 6.50 —
1371 A265 70p multi 1.75 1.75
a. Booklet pane of 4 7.00 —
1372 A265 78p multi 2.00 2.00
a. Booklet pane of 4 8.00 —
Complete booklet, #1367a, 1368a, 1369a, 1370a, 1371a, 1372a 38.00
Nos. 1367-1372 (6) 9.45 9.45

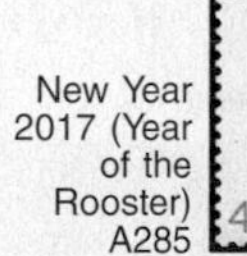

New Year 2017 (Year of the Rooster) A285

Various depictions of roosters.

2017, Jan. 18 Litho. *Perf. 13*

1373 A285 43p gold & scar 1.10 1.10
1374 A285 57p gold & scar 1.50 1.50
1375 A285 58p gold & scar 1.50 1.50
1376 A285 64p gold & scar 1.60 1.60
1377 A285 70p gold & scar 1.75 1.75
1378 A285 78p gold & scar 2.00 2.00
a. Souvenir sheet of 6, #1373-1378 9.50 9.50
Nos. 1373-1378 (6) 9.45 9.45

Worldwide Fund for Nature (WWF) — A286

Meadow Pipit:43p, Chick. 57p, On branch. 64p, In flight. 70p, Head with mouth open.

Perf. 13¼x13½

2017, Feb. 15 Litho.

1379 A286 43p multi 1.10 1.10
1380 A286 57p multi 1.40 1.40
1381 A286 64p multi 1.60 1.60
1382 A286 70p multi 1.75 1.75
a. Souvenir sheet of 4, #1379-1382 6.00 6.00
Nos. 1379-1382 (4) 5.85 5.85

A sheet of 8 containing 2 imperforate examples of each of Nos. 1379-1382 was produced in limited quantities.

Castle Cornet A287

Designs: 44p, Soldiers and cannon. 59p, Shrubs in garden. 60p, Dancers in circle. 73p, Audience watching historical presentation. 80p, Garden. 90p, Actors in historical presentation.
£3, Castle at night.

2017, May 4 Litho. *Perf. 13¾*

1383 A287 44p multi 1.10 1.10
1384 A287 59p multi 1.50 1.50
1385 A287 60p multi 1.60 1.60
1386 A287 73p multi 1.90 1.90
1387 A287 80p multi 2.10 2.10
1388 A287 90p multi 2.40 2.40
Nos. 1383-1388 (6) 10.60 10.60

Souvenir Sheet

Perf. 13½

1389 A287 £3 multi 7.75 7.75

Europa (Nos. 1384, 1386). No. 1389 contains one 45x45mm stamp.

Guernsey and Flag — A288

Sweater, measuring tape and flag of: 44p, Guernsey. 59p, Australia. 73p, United States. 80p, Japan.

2017, May 17 Litho. *Perf. 13½*

1390 A288 44p multi 1.10 1.10
1391 A288 59p multi 1.50 1.50
1392 A288 73p multi 1.90 1.90
1393 A288 80p multi 2.10 2.10
Nos. 1390-1393 (4) 6.60 6.60

Values are for stamps with side selvage.

Folklore — A289

Designs: 44p, The De Garis Family and the Pouques. 59p, The Fairies' Bat. 60p, The Fairy Invasion of Guernsey. 73p, The Fairies' Gallows. 80p, Pierre Dumont and Le P'tit Colin. 90p, The Devil's Hoofprint.
£3, The Corner of the Goat, horiz.

2017, July 19 Litho. *Perf. 13x13¼*

1394 A289 44p multi 1.25 1.25
1395 A289 59p multi 1.60 1.60
1396 A289 60p multi 1.60 1.60
1397 A289 73p multi 2.00 2.00
1398 A289 80p multi 2.10 2.10
1399 A289 90p multi 2.40 2.40
Nos. 1394-1399 (6) 10.95 10.95

Souvenir Sheet

Perf. 13¼

1400 A289 £3 multi 8.00 8.00

No. 1400 contains one 36x30mm stamp.

Coastal Scenes — A290

No. 1401: a, Rocquaine Bay, two boats at LL. b, Rocquaine Bay, one boat at LL. c, Rocquaine Bay, three boats at LL. d, Rocquaine Bay, two boats and boat ramp at LL. e, Fort Grey. f, Albert Marina. g, Victoria Marina, one boat and two gangways. h, Victoria Marina, sailboat and motorboat. h, Victoria Marina, sailboat and two gangways. i, Careening Hard.

Serpentine Die Cut 11

2017, Sept. 1 Litho.

Booklet Stamps Self-Adhesive

1401	Booklet pane of 10	13.50	
a.-e.	A290 GY Any single	1.10	1.10
f.-j.	A290 UK Any single	1.60	1.60
k.	Booklet pane of 10, 2 each #1401a-1401e	11.00	
l.	Booklet pane of 10, 2 each #1401f-1401j	16.00	

On day of issue, Nos. 1401a-1401e each sold for 44p; Nos. 1401f-1401j, 59p.

Princess of Wales's Royal Regiment, 25th Anniv. — A291

Designs: 44p, Carol service in Canterbury Cathedral. 59p, Presentation of colors. 60p, Flying Tigers Parachute Display Team. 73p, Homecoming. 80p, Formal parade. 90p, Infantry exercise.

£3, Princess Diana (1961-97).

2017, Sept. 1 Litho. *Perf. 13x12½*

1402	A291	44p multi	1.10	1.10
1403	A291	59p multi	1.60	1.60
1404	A291	60p multi	1.60	1.60
1405	A291	73p multi	1.90	1.90
1406	A291	80p multi	2.10	2.10
1407	A291	90p multi	2.40	2.40
		Nos. 1402-1407 (6)	10.70	10.70

Souvenir Sheet

Perf. 13¼x13½

1408	A291	£3 multi	7.75	7.75

No. 1408 contains one 36x44mm stamp.

World War I, Cent. Type of 2014

Designs: 44p, Captain Wilfred Picton-Warlow. 59p, Picture of Flight Lieutenant Charles Collet in aiplane from *Navy and Army Illustrated.* 60p, Alfred, Harold and Frederick Crespin and drawing of airplane. 73p, Captain Adrian Le Patourel Jones. 80p, Pilot and seaplane. 90p, Sergeant Frederick Fieldhouse Smith.

2017, Nov. 8 Litho. *Perf. 14x14¼*

1409	A265	44p multi	1.25	1.25
a.		Booklet pane of 4	5.00	—
1410	A265	59p multi	1.60	1.60
a.		Booklet pane of 4	6.50	—
1411	A265	60p multi	1.60	1.60
a.		Booklet pane of 4	6.50	—
1412	A265	73p multi	2.00	2.00
a.		Booklet pane of 4	8.00	—
1413	A265	80p multi	2.25	2.25
a.		Booklet pane of 4	9.00	—
1414	A265	90p multi	2.50	2.50
a.		Booklet pane of 4	10.00	—
		Complete booklet, #1409a, 1410a, 1411a, 1412a, 1413a, 1414a	45.00	
		Nos. 1409-1414 (6)	11.20	11.20

70th Wedding Anniversary of Queen Elizabeth II and Prince Philip — A292

Photograph of Queen Elizabeth II and Prince Philip from: 44p, 1951. 59p, 1965. 60p, 1976. 73p, 1977. 80p, 2010. 90p, 2016.

Litho. With Foil Application

2017, Nov. 8 *Perf. 14x13½*

1415	A292	44p sil & multi	1.25	1.25
1416	A292	59p sil & multi	1.60	1.60
1417	A292	60p sil & multi	1.60	1.60
1418	A292	73p sil & multi	2.00	2.00
1419	A292	80p sil & multi	2.25	2.25
1420	A292	90p sil & multi	2.50	2.50
		Nos. 1415-1420 (6)	11.20	11.20

Christmas A293

Lyrics from "Good King Wenceslas" and: 39p, King Wenceslas. 44p, Man carrying wood in snow. 59p, King Wenceslas and page. 60p, Page and King Wenceslas carrying wood near castle. 73p, Page and King Wenceslas carrying wood in forest. 80p, King Wenceslas, page, bird in tree. 90p, King Wenceslas and page bringing wood to man's house.

Serpentine Die Cut 10x9½

2017, Nov. 8 Litho.

Self-Adhesive

1421	A293	39p multi	1.10	1.10
1422	A293	44p multi	1.25	1.25
1423	A293	59p multi	1.60	1.60
1424	A293	60p multi	1.60	1.60
1425	A293	73p multi	2.00	2.00
1426	A293	80p multi	2.25	2.25
1427	A293	90p multi	2.50	2.50
		Nos. 1421-1427 (7)	12.30	12.30

New Year 2018 (Year of the Dog) A294

Various depictions of dogs.

2018, Feb. 1 Litho. *Perf. 13*

1428	A294	44p red & gold	1.25	1.25
1429	A294	59p red & gold	1.75	1.75
1430	A294	60p red & gold	1.75	1.75
1431	A294	73p red & gold	2.10	2.10
1432	A294	80p red & gold	2.25	2.25
1433	A294	90p red & gold	2.60	2.60
a.		Souvenir sheet of 6, #1428-1433	12.00	12.00
		Nos. 1428-1433 (6)	11.70	11.70

Souvenir Sheet

Black Rhinoceros — A295

2018, Feb. 14 Litho. *Perf. 14*

1434	A295	£3 multi	8.50	8.50

Royal Air Force, Cent. A296

Designs: 46p, Nimrod MR2P providing search and rescue. 62p, Sunderland attack on U-boat, 1943. 63p, London Flying Boat on first affiliation visit, 1939. 76p, Major William Barker's Victoria Cross action, 1918. 85p, First Squadron RNAS trench strafing, 1917. 94p, Flight Sub-Lieutenant Warneford attacking Zeppelin, 1915.

£3, Cargo airplane over Guernsey.

2018, Apr. 3 Litho. *Perf. 13¾*

1435	A296	46p multi	1.25	1.25
1436	A296	62p multi	1.75	1.75
1437	A296	63p multi	1.75	1.75
1438	A296	76p multi	2.10	2.10
1439	A296	85p multi	2.40	2.40
1440	A296	94p multi	2.60	2.60
		Nos. 1435-1440 (6)	11.85	11.85

Souvenir Sheet

1441	A296	£3 multi	8.25	8.25

Causeways and Bridges A297

Designs: 46p, Lihou Causeway. 62p, Castle Cornet. 63p, Fort Clonque Causeway. 76p, Reservoir Bridge. 85p, Fort Grey Causeway. 94p, Sark Coupée.

2018, May 2 Litho. *Perf. 13x13¼*

1442	A297	46p multi	1.25	1.25
1443	A297	62p multi	1.75	1.75
1444	A297	63p multi	1.75	1.75
1445	A297	76p multi	2.00	2.00
1446	A297	85p multi	2.25	2.25
1447	A297	94p multi	2.50	2.50
a.		Souvenir sheet of 6, #1442-1447	11.50	11.50
		Nos. 1442-1447 (6)	11.50	11.50

Europa (62p, 76p).

Souvenir Sheet

Wedding of Prince Harry and Meghan Markle — A298

No. 1448 — Couple looking at: a, Each other. b, Camera.

2018, May 2 Litho. *Perf. 14½*

1448	A298	Sheet of 2	11.00	11.00
a.-b.		£2 Either single	5.50	5.50

Aerial Views — A299

Designs: 46p, Vale Castle. 62p, Rousse. 63p, Torteval Church. 76p, Reservoir. 85p, Pembroke. 94p, Beaucette Marina.

2018, Aug. 1 Litho. *Perf. 13¼x13*

1449	A299	46p multi	1.25	1.25
1450	A299	62p multi	1.60	1.60
1451	A299	63p multi	1.75	1.75
1452	A299	76p multi	2.00	2.00
1453	A299	85p multi	2.25	2.25
1454	A299	94p multi	2.50	2.50
		Nos. 1449-1454 (6)	11.35	11.35

World War I, Cent. Type of 2014

"Lest we forget" and details of war memorials: 46p, Royal Guernsey Light Infantry Memorial, St. Peter Port. 62p, Guernsey Post Office Roll of Honor. 63p, Elizabeth College Roll of Honor. 76p, Alderney Stone. 85p, Guernsey War Memorial. 94p, Memorial Window, St. Peter's Church, Sark.

2018, Nov. 8 Litho. *Perf. 14x14¼*

1455	A265	46p multi	1.25	1.25
a.		Booklet pane of 4	5.00	—
1456	A265	62p multi	1.60	1.60
a.		Booklet pane of 4	6.50	—
1457	A265	63p multi	1.75	1.75
a.		Booklet pane of 4	7.00	—
1458	A265	76p multi	2.00	2.00
a.		Booklet pane of 4	8.00	—
1459	A265	85p multi	2.25	2.25
a.		Booklet pane of 4	9.00	—
1460	A265	94p multi	2.50	2.50
a.		Booklet pane of 4	10.00	—
		Complete booklet, #1455a, 1456a, 1457a, 1458a, 1459a, 1460a	46.00	
		Nos. 1455-1460 (6)	11.35	11.35

Prince Charles, 70th Birthday A300

Photograph of Prince Charles from: 46p, 2012. 62p, 1998. 63p, 1986. 76p, 1987. 85p, 1980. 94p, 2005.

2018, Nov. 8 Litho. *Perf. 13¼*

1461	A300	46p gold & multi	1.25	1.25
1462	A300	62p gold & multi	1.60	1.60
1463	A300	63p gold & multi	1.75	1.75
1464	A300	76p gold & multi	2.00	2.00
1465	A300	85p gold & multi	2.25	2.25
1466	A300	94p gold & multi	2.50	2.50
		Nos. 1461-1466 (6)	11.35	11.35

Scenes From *The Nutcracker and the Mouse King,* by E. T. A. Hoffmann (1776-1822) — A301

Designs: 41p, Fritz breaks the Nutcracker. 46p, The battle. 62p, Nutcracker repaired. 63p, The Mouse Queen and Pirlipat. 76p, Breaking the spell. 85p, Mouse King visits Marie. 94p, Drosselmeier's nephew and Marie.

Serpentine Die Cut 9½x10

2018, Nov. 8 Litho.

Self-Adhesive

1467	A301	41p multi	1.10	1.10
1468	A301	46p multi	1.25	1.25
1469	A301	62p multi	1.60	1.60
1470	A301	63p multi	1.75	1.75
1471	A301	76p multi	2.00	2.00
1472	A301	85p multi	2.25	2.25
1473	A301	94p multi	2.50	2.50
		Nos. 1467-1473 (7)	12.45	12.45

Christmas.

POSTAGE DUE STAMPS

Castle Cornet and St. Peter Port — D1

Perf. 12½x12

1969, Oct. 1 Photo. Unwmk.

Black Numeral

J1	D1	1p deep magenta	1.75	1.50
J2	D1	2p yellow green	2.00	1.50
J3	D1	3p red	3.00	3.00
J4	D1	4p ultra	4.00	4.00
J5	D1	5p yellow bister	5.50	5.00
J6	D1	6p greenish blue	6.00	5.50
J7	D1	1sh red brown	12.00	10.00
		Nos. J1-J7 (7)	34.25	30.50

Type of 1969

"p" instead of "d"

1971-76 Black Numeral

J8	D1	½p deep magenta	.25	.25
J9	D1	1p yellow green	.25	.25
J10	D1	2p red	.25	.25
J11	D1	3p ultra	.25	.25
J12	D1	4p yellow bister	.25	.25
J13	D1	5p greenish blue	.25	.25
J14	D1	6p purple ('76)	.25	.25
J15	D1	8p orange ('75)	.25	.25
J16	D1	10p red brown	.50	.50
J17	D1	15p gray ('76)	.50	.50
		Nos. J8-J17 (10)	3.00	3.00

Town Church, St. Peter Port — D2

1977-80 Photo *Perf. 13½x13*

Arms and Denomination in Black

J18 D2 ½p red brown .25 .25
J19 D2 1p lilac rose .25 .25
J20 D2 2p orange .25 .25
J21 D2 3p red .25 .25
J22 D2 4p greenish blue .25 .25
J23 D2 5p olive green .25 .25
J24 D2 6p greenish blue .25 .25
J25 D2 8p ocher .25 .25
J26 D2 10p dark blue .30 .30
J27 D2 14p green ('80) .40 .40
J28 D2 15p purple .40 .40
J29 D2 16p salmon rose ('80) .50 .50
Nos. J18-J29 (12) 3.60 3.60

Woman Milking Cow — D3

2p, Vale Mill. 3p, Sark cottage. 4p, St. Peter Port. 5p, Well, Moulin Huet. 16p, Seaweed gathering. 18p, Upper Walk, White Rock. 20p, Cobo Bay. 25p, Saints' Bay. 30p, La Coupee, Sark. 50p, Old Harbor, St. Peter Port. £1, Greenhouses, Victoria Tower.

1982, July 13 Litho. *Perf. 14½*

J30 D3 1p shown .25 .25
J31 D3 2p multicolored .25 .25
J32 D3 3p multicolored .25 .25
J33 D3 4p multicolored .25 .25
J34 D3 5p multicolored .25 .25
J35 D3 16p multicolored .40 .40
J36 D3 18p multicolored .45 .45
J37 D3 20p multicolored .50 .50
J38 D3 25p multicolored .55 .55
J39 D3 30p multicolored .75 .75
J40 D3 50p multicolored 1.10 1.10
J41 D3 £1 multicolored 2.50 2.50
Nos. J30-J41 (12) 7.50 7.50

OCCUPATION STAMPS

Issued Under German Occupation

Bisects of Great Britain Nos. 238 and 255 were used in Guernsey from 12/27/40 to 2./24/41. Values, on cover or postcard: No. 238, $45; No. 255, $40.

OS1

Rouletted 14x7

1941-44 Typo. Unwmk.

N1 OS1 ½p light green 3.50 3.50
N2 OS1 1p red 3.00 2.00
N3 OS1 2½p ultramarine 8.00 12.00
Nos. N1-N3 (3) 14.50 17.50

Issued: No. N1, from 7/43; No. N2, 2/18/41; No. N3, 4/12/44.

Additional shades and papers exist. The rouletting is very crude and may not be measurable. This is not a defect.

For detailed listings, see the Scott Classic Specialized catalogue.

Bluish French Bank Note Paper

Wmk. 396 Chain Link Fence

1942 *Rouletted 14x7*

N4 OS1 ½p green 22.50 22.50
N5 OS1 1p red 14.50 *21.00*

Issue dates: ½p, Mar. 11; 1p, Apr. 9.
Nos. N1-N5 remained valid until 4/13/46.

ALDERNEY

'ol-dər-nē

LOCATION — Northernmost of the Channel Islands in the Guernsey Bailiwick
GOVT. — Dependent territory under Bailiwick of Guernsey.
AREA — 3 sq. mi.
POP. — 2,373 (1994 est.)
CAPITAL — St. Anne's

Part of the Bailiwick of Guernsey, this island began issuing its own stamps.

Catalogue values for unused stamps in this section are for Never Hinged items.

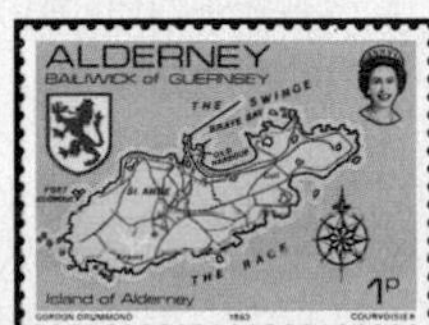

Map of Alderney, Arms — A1

1983, June 14 Litho. *Perf. 11¾*

1 A1 1p shown .25 .25
2 A1 4p Hanging Rock .25 .25
3 A1 9p States Building .25 .25
4 A1 10p St. Anne's Church .30 .30
5 A1 11p Yachts, Braye Bay .40 .40
6 A1 12p Victoria St., St. Anne .40 .40
7 A1 13p Map, arms .40 .40
8 A1 14p Ft. Clonque .45 .45
9 A1 15p Corblets Bay Port .45 .45
10 A1 16p Old Tower, St. Anne .45 .45
11 A1 17p Essex Castle Golf Course .50 .50
12 A1 18p Ships in Old Harbor .50 .50
Nos. 1-12 (12) 4.60 4.60

See Nos. 42-46, which is considered to be the higher-denomination continuation of this definitive set.

Oystercatcher, Telegraph Bay — A2

13p, Turnstone, Corblets Bay. 26p, Ringed plover, Corblets Bay. 28p, Dunlin, Arch Bay. 31p, Curlew, Old Harbor.

1984, June 12 *Perf. 14½*

13 A2 9p shown *1.10 1.10*
14 A2 13p multicolored *1.10 1.10*
15 A2 26p multicolored *2.25 2.25*
16 A2 28p multicolored *2.25 2.25*
17 A2 31p multicolored *2.25 2.25*
Nos. 13-17 (5) 8.95 8.95

Alderney Airport, 50th Anniv. A3

Aircraft: 9p, Wessex helicopter of the Queen's Flight, 1984. 13p, Aurigny Air loey Britten-Norman Trislander, 1981. 29p, Morton Air Services DeHavilland Heron, 1946. 31p, DeHavilland Dragon Rapide, c. 1930. 34p, Saunders-Roe Saro Windhover, 1935.

1985, Mar. 19 *Perf. 12x11½*

18 A3 9p multicolored *1.40 1.40*
19 A3 13p multicolored *1.75 1.75*
20 A3 29p multicolored *3.00 3.00*
21 A3 31p multicolored *3.25 3.25*
22 A3 34p multicolored *3.25 3.25*
Nos. 18-22 (5) 12.65 12.65

Regimental Uniforms, Alderney Garrison — A4

9p, Royal Engineers, 1890. 14p, Duke of Albany's Own Highlanders, 1856. 29p, Royal Artillery, 1855. 31p, South Hampshire Regiment, 1810. 34p, Royal Irish Regiment, 1782.

1985, Sept. 24 *Perf. 14½*

23 A4 9p multicolored .30 .30
24 A4 14p multicolored .90 .90
25 A4 29p multicolored .90 .90
26 A4 31p multicolored 1.25 1.25
27 A4 34p multicolored 1.50 1.50
Nos. 23-27 (5) 4.85 4.85

Forts — A5

1986, Sept. 23 Litho. *Perf. 13x13½*

28 A5 10p Grosnez 1.00 1.00
29 A5 14p Tourgis 1.00 1.00
30 A5 31p Clonque 2.00 2.00
31 A5 34p Albert 2.00 2.00
Nos. 28-31 (4) 6.00 6.00

Shipwrecks A6

11p, Liverpool, 1902. 15p, Petit Raymond, 1906. 29p, Maina, 1910. 31p, Burton, 1911. 34p, Point Law, 1975.

1987, May 5 Litho. *Perf. 14½*

32 A6 11p multicolored 1.50 1.50
33 A6 15p multicolored 1.60 1.60
34 A6 29p multicolored 3.00 3.00
35 A6 31p multicolored 3.25 3.25
36 A6 34p multicolored 3.50 3.50
Nos. 32-36 (5) 12.85 12.85

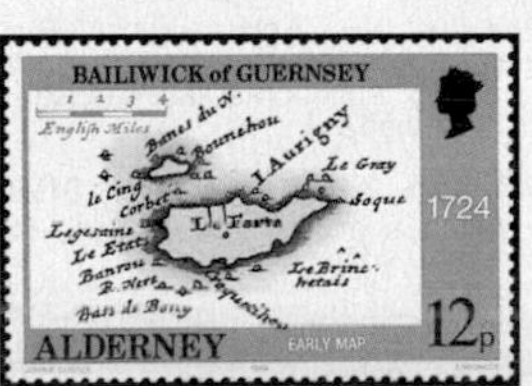

18th-20th Cent. Maps — A7

Designs: 12p, Herman Moll map, 1724. 18p, Survey by J.H. Bastide, 1739. 27p, Land survey by M.P. Goodwin, 1831. 32p, Wartime occupation map, 1943. 35p, Ordnance survey, 1988.

1989, July 7 Litho. *Perf. 13½x14*

37 A7 12p multicolored .40 .40
38 A7 18p multicolored .55 .55
39 A7 27p multicolored 1.00 1.00
40 A7 32p multicolored 1.10 1.10
41 A7 35p multicolored 1.40 1.40
Nos. 37-41 (5) 4.45 4.45

Quesnard Lighthouse A8

Designs: 21p, Inner Harbor, Braye. 23p, The Island Hall, Alderney. 24p, Alderney Railway locomotive, J. T. Daly. 28p, Lifeboat, Louis Marchesi of Round Table.

1989-93 Litho. *Perf. 15x14*

42 A8 20p multicolored 1.00 1.00
43 A8 21p multicolored 1.00 1.00
44 A8 23p multicolored .80 .80
45 A8 24p multicolored 1.75 1.75
46 A8 28p multicolored 2.25 2.25
Nos. 42-46 (5) 6.80 6.80

Issued: 20p, 12/27; 21p, 4/2/91; 23p, 2/6/92; 24p, 28p, 3/3/93.

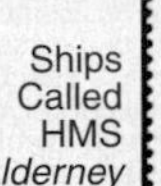

Ships Called HMS *Alderney* A9

14p, Bomb ketch, 1738. 20p, Sixth-rate, 1742. 29p, Sloop, 1755. 34p, A-Class submarine, 1945. 37p, Fishery protection vessel, 1979.

1990, May 3 Litho. *Perf. 13½*

55 A9 14p multicolored .40 .25
56 A9 20p multicolored .55 .40
57 A9 29p multicolored 1.00 1.00
58 A9 34p multicolored 1.25 1.25
59 A9 37p multicolored 1.40 1.40
Nos. 55-59 (5) 4.60 4.30

Automation of Casquets Lighthouse — A10

21p, Wreck of HMS Victory, 1744. 26p, Returning by rowboat. 31p, Helicopter relief. 37p, Lighthouse, birds. 50p, MV Patricia.

1991, Apr. 30 Litho. *Perf. 14x13½*

60 A10 21p multicolored 1.10 .65
61 A10 26p multicolored 1.90 1.60
62 A10 31p multicolored 2.25 2.25
63 A10 37p multicolored 2.25 2.25
64 A10 50p multicolored 2.50 2.50
Nos. 60-64 (5) 10.00 9.25

Battle of La Hogue, 300th Anniv. — A11

23p, 28p, and 33p, Various details from painting by unknown artist. 50p, Entire painting.

1992, Sept. 18 Litho. *Perf. 13½*

65 A11 23p multicolored 1.25 1.25
66 A11 28p multicolored 2.25 2.25
67 A11 33p multicolored 2.50 2.50

Size: 45x30mm

Perf. 14x14½

68 A11 50p multicolored 3.25 3.25
Nos. 65-68 (4) 9.25 9.25

Marine Life — A12

Designs: a, 24p, Palinurus elephas. b, 28p, Metridium senile. c, 33p, Luidia ciliaris. d, 39p, Psammechinus miliaris.

1993, Nov. 2 Litho. *Perf. 15x14½*

69 A12 Strip of 4, #a.-d. *6.00 6.00*

Flora and Fauna — A13

Designs: 1p, Ischnura elegans, ranunculus trichophyllus, sparganium erectum. 2p, Crocidura russula, hypericum linarifolium. 3p, Fulmarus glacialis, carpobrotus edulis. 4p, Colias croceus, trifolium pratense. 5p, Bombus lucorum, orobanche rapum-genistae, cytisus scoparius. 6p, Sylvia undata, cuscuta epithymum, ulex europaeus. 7p, Inachis io, cirsium acaule. 8p, Talpa europaea, endymion non-scripta. 9p, Tettigonia viridissima, ulex europaeus. 10p, Zygaena filipendulae, echium vulgare. 16p, Polyommatus icarus, anacamptis pyramidalis. 20p, Oryctolagus cuniculus, rannunculus repens, pteridium aquilinum. 24p, Larus marinus, romulea columnae. 30p, Fratercula arctica, sedum anglicum. 40p, Saturnia pavonia, rubus fruticosus. 50p, Erinaceus europaeus, oxalis articulata. £1, Sterna hirundo, cynodon dactylon, horiz. £2, Morus bassanus, fucus vesiculosus.

1994-95 Litho. *Perf. 14½x14¼*

70 A13 1p multicolored .25 .25
71 A13 2p multicolored .25 .25
72 A13 3p multicolored .25 .25
73 A13 4p multicolored .25 .25
74 A13 5p multicolored .25 .25
75 A13 6p multicolored .25 .25
76 A13 7p multicolored .25 .25
77 A13 8p multicolored .30 .30
78 A13 9p multicolored .35 .35
79 A13 10p multicolored .30 .30
80 A13 16p multicolored .50 .50
a. Perf. 14x15 on three sides .65 .65
b. As "a," booklet pane of 8 5.75
Complete booklet, #80b 5.75
81 A13 20p multicolored .40 .40
a. Perf. 14x15 on three sides .65 .65
b. As "a," booklet pane of 8 5.25
Complete booklet, #81b 5.25
82 A13 24p multicolored .55 .55
a. Perf. 14x15 on three sides .70 .70
b. As "a," booklet pane of 8 5.75
Complete booklet, #82b 5.75
83 A13 30p multicolored .75 .75
84 A13 40p multicolored .90 .90
85 A13 50p multicolored 1.50 1.50
86 A13 £1 multicolored 2.50 2.50

Perf. 14x15

87 A13 £2 multicolored 6.00 6.00
Nos. 70-87 (18) 15.80 15.80

No. 81 is dated "1994." Nos. 81a-81b are dated "1998."
Issued: £2, 2/28/95; others, 5/5/94.
See Nos. 98-100.

Career of Flt. Lt. Tommy Rose DFC (1895-1968) — A14

No. 88: a, 1917-18 Royal Flying Corps. b, 1939-45 Chief Test Pilot. c, Phillips & Powis (Miles) Aircraft.
No. 89: a, Winner, 1935 King's Cup Air Race. b, Winner, 1947 Manx Air Derby. c, UK-Cape-UK Speed Record, 1936.

1995, Sept. 1 Litho. *Perf. 14x15*

88 A14 35p Strip of 3, #a.-c. 3.50 3.50
89 A14 41p Strip of 3, #a.-c. 4.25 4.25

Nos. 88-89 printed in sheets of 12 stamps + 3 labels.

Souvenir Sheet

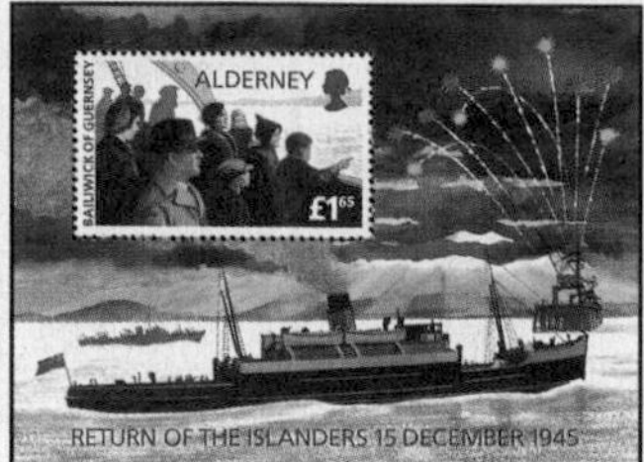

Return of Islanders, 50th Anniv. — A15

1995, Nov. 16 Litho. *Perf. 13½*

90 A15 £1.65 multicolored 5.25 5.25

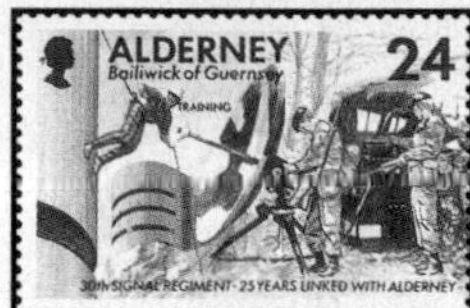

A16

a, 24p, Training. b, 41p, Natl. contingencies overseas. c, 60p, Strategic communications. d, 75p, UN operations.

1996, Jan. 24 Litho. *Perf. 14*

91 A16 Strip of 4, #a.-d. 5.75 5.75

30th Signal Regiment Activities in Alderney, 25th Anniv.

Domestic Cats — A17

16p, Butterfly, brown & white cat. 24p, Gray cat on table. 25p, Two cats on chair. 35p, Cat pulling on table cloth. 41p, Calico cat in toy cart, white cat. 60p, Siamese cat with yarn.

1996, July 19 Litho. *Perf. 13½*

92 A17 16p multicolored .60 .60
93 A17 24p multicolored .95 .95
94 A17 25p multicolored 1.00 1.00
95 A17 35p multicolored 1.25 1.25
96 A17 41p multicolored 1.50 1.50
97 A17 60p multicolored 2.00 2.00
a. Souvenir sheet, #92-97 7.50 7.50
Nos. 92-97 (6) 7.30 7.30

No. 97a is a continuous design.

Fauna and Flora Type of 1994

Designs: 18p, Aglais urticae, Buddleja davidii. 25p, Anthus petrosus, matthiola incana. 26p, Ammophila sabulosa, calystegia soldanella, horiz.

1997, Jan. 2 Litho. *Perf. 14½x14¼*

98 A13 18p multicolored .50 .50
a. Perf. 14x15 on 3 sides .90
b. As "a," booklet pane of 8 7.25
Complete booklet, #98b 7.25
99 A13 25p multicolored .80 .80
a. Perf. 14x15 on 3 sides .90
b. As "a," booklet pane of 8 7.25
Complete booklet, #99b 7.25
100 A13 26p multicolored .80 .80
Nos. 98-100 (3) 2.10 2.10

Alderney Cricket Club, 150th Anniv. — A18

1997, Aug. 21 Litho. *Perf. 13½*

101 A18 18p Harold Larwood .50 .50
102 A18 25p John Arlott .65 .65
103 A18 37p Pelham J. Warner 1.25 1.25
104 A18 43p W.G. Grace 1.50 1.50
105 A18 63p John Wisden 2.00 2.00
a. Souvenir sheet, #101-105 + label 8.00 8.00
Nos. 101-105 (5) 5.90 5.90

Garrison Island — A19

No. 106, Founding of the harbor. No. 107, Ariadne at anchor. No. 108, Quarrying at Mannez. No. 109, Earliest train ferrying stone. No. 110, Queen Victoria arrives ashore. No. 111, Royal yacht at anchor. No. 112, Railway and quarry workers greet the Queen. No. 113, Queen Victoria tours the island.

1997, Nov. 20 Litho. *Perf. 14½x14*

106 A19 18p multicolored .60 .60
107 A19 18p multicolored .60 .60
a. Pair, #106-107 1.25 1.25
108 A19 25p multicolored .70 .70
109 A19 25p multicolored .70 .70
a. Pair, #108-109 1.50 1.50
b. Booklet pane, #107a, 109a ('98) 3.00 3.00
110 A19 26p multicolored .80 .80
111 A19 26p multicolored .80 .80
a. Pair, #110-111 1.75 1.75
b. Booklet pane, #107a, 111a ('98) 3.50 3.50
112 A19 31p multicolored .90 .90
113 A19 31p multicolored .90 .90
a. Pair, #112-113 2.00 2.00
b. Booklet pane, #111a, 113a ('98) 3.75 3.75
c. Booklet pane, #109a, 113a ('98) 3.50 3.50
Nos. 106-113 (8) 6.00 6.00

Nos. 109b, 111b, 113b, 113c issued 11/10/98.
See Nos. 119-126, 134-141, 155-162, 176-183.

Alderney Diving Club, 21st Anniv. — A20

20p, Modern superlite helmet. 30p, Cousteau-Gagnan demand valve, 1943. 37p, Heinke closed helmet, 1845. 43p, Siebe closed helmet, 1840. 63p, Deane open helmet, 1829.

1998, Feb. 10 Litho. *Perf. 13*

114 A20 20p multicolored .60 .60
115 A20 30p multicolored .85 .85
116 A20 37p multicolored 1.25 1.25
117 A20 43p multicolored 1.60 1.60
118 A20 63p multicolored 2.00 2.00
a. Souvenir sheet, #114-118 + label 7.50 7.50
Nos. 114-118 (5) 6.30 6.30

Garrison Island Type of 1997

No. 119, Alderney Post Office. No. 120, Traders in Victoria Street. No. 121, Court House. No. 122, Police Station and Fire Service. No. 123, St. Anne's Church. No. 124, Wedding Party at The Albert Gate. No. 125, SS Courier unloading. No. 126, Fishermen at quay.

1998, Nov. 10 Litho. *Perf. 14½x14*

119 A19 20p multicolored .60 .60
120 A19 20p multicolored .60 .60
a. Pair, #119-120 1.40 1.40
121 A19 25p multicolored .70 .70
122 A19 25p multicolored .70 .70
a. Pair, #121-122 1.50 1.50
b. Booklet pane, #120a, 122a 3.00 *3.00*
123 A19 30p multicolored .80 .80
124 A19 30p multicolored .80 .80
a. Pair, #123-124 1.75 1.75
b. Booklet pane, #120a, 124a 3.50 *3.50*
125 A19 37p multicolored .90 .90
126 A19 37p multicolored .90 .90
a. Pair, #125-126 2.00 2.00
b. Booklet pane, #124a, 126a 3.75 *3.75*
c. Booklet pane, #122a, 126a 3.50 *3.50*
Complete booklet, #109b, 111b, 113b, 113c, 122b, 124b, 126b, 126c 27.50
Nos. 119-126 (8) 6.00 6.00

Booklet sold for £8.48.

Souvenir Sheet

The Wreck of the SS Stella, Cent. — A21

a, 25p, Stained glass window, Anglican Cathedral, Liverpool, dedicated to Mary Rogers, chief stewardess. b, £1.75, Ship leaving Southampton.

1999, Feb. 4 Litho. *Perf. 14*

127 A21 Sheet of 2, #a.-b. 7.50 7.50

UPU, 125th Anniv.

Total Solar Eclipse — A22

Stages of eclipse on 8/11/99: 20p, 10:15. 25p, 10:51. 30p, 11:14. 38p, 11:16. 44p, 11:17. 64p, 11:36.

1999, Apr. 27 Litho. *Perf. 13½x13*

128 A22 20p multicolored .45 .45
129 A22 25p multicolored .60 .60
130 A22 30p multicolored 1.00 1.00
131 A22 38p multicolored 1.25 1.25
132 A22 44p multicolored 1.40 1.40
133 A22 64p multicolored 1.75 1.75
a. Souvenir sheet, #128-133 + label 6.75 6.75
Nos. 128-133 (6) 6.45 6.45

IBRA '99, Nuremberg; Philex '99, Paris (No. 133a).

Garrison Island Type of 1997

Designs: No. 134, Fort Grosnez, c. 1855. No. 135, Ninth Battalion, Royal Garrison Artillery. No. 136, Arsenal, Fort Albert. No. 137, Royal Engineer Unit. No. 138, Fort Tourgis, c. 1865. No. 139, Second Battalion, Royal Scots Regiment. No. 140, Fort Houmet Herbé, c. 1870. No. 141, Royal Alderney Artillery Militia.

1999, Oct. 19 Litho. *Perf. 14¼x13¾*

134 A19 20p multicolored .60 .60
135 A19 20p multicolored .60 .60
a. Pair, #134-135 1.40 1.40
136 A19 25p multicolored .70 .70
137 A19 25p multicolored .70 .70
a. Pair, #136-137 1.50 1.50
b. Booklet pane, #135a, 137a 3.00 3.00
138 A19 30p multicolored .80 .80
139 A19 30p multicolored .80 .80
a. Pair, #138-139 1.75 1.75
b. Booklet pane, #135a, 139a 3.50 3.50
c. Booklet pane, #137a, 139a 3.25 3.25
140 A19 38p multicolored .90 .90
141 A19 38p multicolored .90 .90
a. Pair, #140-141 2.00 2.00
b. Booklet pane, #135a, 141a 3.75 3.75
c. Booklet pane, #137a, 141a 3.50 3.50
d. Booklet pane, #139a, 141a 3.75 3.75
Complete booklet, #137b, 139b, 139c, 141b, 141c, 141d 21.00
Nos. 134-141 (8) 6.00 6.00

Booklet sold for £6.78.

Peregrine Falcon — A23

Falcons: 21p, Attacking turnstone near lighthouse. 26p, With prey. 34p, With eggs. 38p, With chicks. 44p, With young near Fort Clonque. 64p, Preparing to fly.

2000, Feb. 4 Litho. *Perf. 14½x14*

142 A23 21p multi .55 .55
a. Booklet pane of 10 5.50
Complete booklet 6.00

143 A23 26p multi .65 .65
a. Booklet pane of 10 6.50
Complete booklet 7.00
144 A23 34p multi 1.00 1.00
145 A23 38p multi 1.20 1.20
146 A23 44p multi 1.75 1.75
147 A23 64p multi 2.25 2.25
Nos. 142-147 (6) 7.40 7.40

Worldwide Fund for Nature, Nos. 144-147.

The Wombles on Vacation A24

Wombles: 21p, With map. 26p, On beach. 36p, At lighthouse. 40p, Picnicking. 45p, On golf course. 65p, At airport.

2000, Apr. 28 Litho. *Perf. 14¼x13¾*
148 A24 21p multi .75 .75
149 A24 26p multi .90 .90
150 A24 36p multi 1.00 1.00
151 A24 40p multi 1.25 1.25
152 A24 45p multi 1.60 1.60
153 A24 65p multi 2.00 2.00
a. Souvenir sheet, #148-153 8.00 8.00
Nos. 148-153 (6) 7.50 7.50

The Stamp Show 2000, London (No. 153a).

Souvenir Sheet

Queen Mother, 100th Birthday — A25

Litho. with Foil Application

2000, Aug. 4 *Perf. 13¼*
154 A25 £1.50 multi 5.50 5.50

Garrison Island Type of 1997

No. 155, Regimental boxing tournament. No. 156, Sports Day of Alderney Gala Week, 1924. No. 157, Regimenal Band of 15th entertains. No. 158, Garrison Ball, 1873, Fort Albert mess room. No. 159, Garrison assembly for Queen's birthday celebrations, 1859. No. 160, Demonstration of field guns on the Butes. No. 161, Inspection of honor guard, 1863. No. 162, Arrival of Lt. Gov. Major Gen. Marcus Slade.

2000, Oct. 19 Litho. *Perf. 13¼x13*
155 A19 21p multi .60 .60
156 A19 21p multi .60 .60
a. Pair, #155-156 1.25 1.25
157 A19 26p multi .70 .70
158 A19 26p multi .70 .70
a. Pair, #157-158 1.50 1.50
b. Booklet pane, #156a, 158a 3.00 3.00
159 A19 36p multi .80 .80
160 A19 36p multi .80 .80
a. Pair, #159-160 1.75 1.75
b. Booklet pane, #158a, 160a 3.50 3.50
161 A19 40p multi .90 .90
162 A19 40p multi .90 .90
a. Pair, #161-162 2.00 2.00
b. Booklet pane, #156a, 162a 3.25 3.25
c. Booklet pane, #160a, 162a 3.75 3.75
Booklet, #158b, 162c, 2 each #160b, 162b 21.00
Nos. 155-162 (8) 6.00 6.00

Booklet sold for £7.38. Each of the two panes of Nos. 160b and 162b in the booklet have different selvages.

Souvenir Sheet

Queen Elizabeth, 75th Birthday — A26

2001, Feb. 1 Litho. *Perf. 14¼*
163 A26 £1.75 multi 5.75 5.75

Community Health Services A27

Health care workers and: 22p, Hospital x-ray department. 27p, Mignot Memorial Hospital in 1980s. 36p, Princess Anne visiting hospital, 1972. 40p, Nurse with infant, 1960s. 45p, Queen Elizabeth II laying hospital cornerstone, 1957. 65p, Opening of original hospital, 1920s.

2001-02 Litho. *Perf. 14¼x14½*
164 A27 22p multi .80 .80
a. Perf. 13¼x13 1.50 1.50
165 A27 27p multi .90 .90
a. Perf. 13¼x13 1.25 1.25
166 A27 36p multi 1.10 1.10
a. Perf. 13¼x13 1.25 1.25
167 A27 40p multi 1.40 1.40
a. Perf. 13¼x13 2.00 2.00
b. Booklet pane, #164a, 165a, 166a, 167a 6.00 —
168 A27 45p multi 1.60 1.60
a. Perf. 13¼x13 2.00 2.00
169 A27 65p multi 2.00 2.00
a. Perf. 13¼x13 3.00 3.00
b. Booklet pane, #166a, 167a, 168a, 169a 8.25 —
c. Booklet pane, #164a, 165a, 168a, 169a 6.75 —
Nos. 164-169 (6) 7.80 7.80

Issued: Nos. 164-169, 4/26/01; Nos. 164a-169a, 10/17/02.

See Nos. 196-201, 215-220, 239-244.

Alderney Golf Club — A28

Designs: 22p, Golf ball with core of feathers, 1901. 27p, Golfing fashions, 1920s. 36p, Player and ball on Alderney Golf Club green, 1970s. 40p, Modern putter. 45p, Golf accessories. 65p, Modern lofted wood.

2001, Aug. 1 Litho. *Perf. 14¾*
170 A28 22p multi .70 .70
171 A28 27p multi .90 .90
172 A28 36p multi 1.10 1.10
173 A28 40p multi 1.40 1.40
174 A28 45p multi 1.60 1.60
175 A28 65p multi 2.00 2.00
a. Souvenir sheet, #170-175 8.00 8.00
Nos. 170-175 (6) 7.70 7.70

Phila Nippon '01 (No. 175a).

Garrison Island Type of 1997

Designs: No. 176, Work continues at the breakwater. No. 177, Officials observe work in progress. No. 178, Steam frigate Emerald grounded. No. 179, Soldiers disembarking Emerald. No. 180, Torpedo boats moored at breakwater. No. 181, Railway provides mobile artillery. No. 182, HMS Majestic at anchor, 1901. No. 183, Torpedo boats maneuver at speed.

2001, Oct. 16 Litho. *Perf. 13¼x13*
176 A19 22p multi .65 .65
177 A19 22p multi .65 .65
a. Pair, #176-177 1.40 1.40
178 A19 27p multi .75 .75
179 A19 27p multi .75 .75
a. Pair, #178-179 1.60 1.60
b. Booklet pane, #177a, 179a 3.25 —
180 A19 36p multi .90 .90
181 A19 36p multi .90 .90
a. Pair, #180-181 2.00 2.00
b. Booklet pane, #179a, 181a 3.75 —
182 A19 40p multi 1.00 1.00
183 A19 40p multi 1.00 1.00
a. Pair, #182-183 2.25 2.25
b. Booklet pane, #177a, 183a 3.75 —
c. Booklet pane, #179a, 183a 4.00 —
d. Booklet pane, #181a, 183a 4.25 —
Booklet, #179b, 181b, 183c, 183d, 2 #183b 23.00
Nos. 176-183 (8) 6.60 6.60

Booklet sold for £7.50. Each of the two panes of No. 183b in the booklet have different selvages.

Souvenir Sheet

Reign of Queen Elizabeth II, 50th Anniv. — A29

2002, Feb. 6 Litho. *Perf. 13¾x13½*
184 A29 £2 multi 6.75 6.75
a. Booklet pane of 1 6.75
Complete booklet, #184a, Guernsey #773a, 774a, 774b, 774c 29.50

No. 184a is sewn into booklets, but is otherwise identical to No. 184.

Issued: No. 184: 2/6; No. 184a, 4/30.

Birds — A30

2002, Apr. 30 *Perf. 13¾*
185 A30 22p Hobby .50 .50
186 A30 27p Black kite .75 .75
187 A30 36p Merlin 1.00 1.00
188 A30 40p Honey buzzard 1.10 1.10
189 A30 45p Osprey 1.40 1.40
190 A30 65p Marsh harrier 2.00 2.00
a. Souvenir sheet, #185-190 9.00 9.00
Nos. 185-190 (6) 6.75 6.75

See Nos. 209-214, 233-238, 256-261.

Lighting at Les Casquets Lighthouse — A31

Designs: 22p, Coal fire, 1725. 27p, Oil lantern, 1779. 36p, Argand lamp, 1790. 45p, Revolving apparatus, 1818. 65p, Electrification, 1952.

2002, July 30 *Perf. 12¾x13¼*
191 A31 22p multi .80 .80
192 A31 27p multi .95 .95
193 A31 36p multi 1.40 1.40
194 A31 45p multi 1.60 1.60
195 A31 65p multi 2.25 2.25
Nos. 191-195 (5) 7.00 7.00

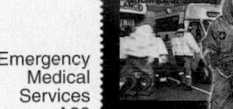

Emergency Medical Services A32

Designs: 22p, Ambulance technician, crew running to ambulance. 27p, Emergency medical technician on radio, ambulance on road. 36p, Doctor, transfer of patient to airplane. 40p, Pilot, Aurigny Trislander airplane. 45p, Emergency dispatch operator, transfer of patient to lifeboat. 65p, Lifeboat crewman, speeding lifeboat.

2002, Oct. 17 Litho. *Perf. 14x14½*
196 A32 22p multi .85 .85
a. Perf. 13¼x13 .85 .85
197 A32 27p multi 1.00 1.00
a. Perf. 13¼x13 1.00 1.00
198 A32 36p multi 1.40 1.40
a. Perf. 13¼x13 1.40 1.40
199 A32 40p multi 1.60 1.60
a. Perf. 13¼x13 1.60 1.60
b. Booklet pane, #196a, 197a, 198a, 199a 5.00 —
200 A32 45p multi 1.75 1.75
a. Perf. 13¼x13 1.75 1.75
201 A32 65p multi 2.50 2.50
a. Perf. 13¼x13 2.50 2.50
b. Booklet pane, #198a, 199a, 200a, 201a 6.25 —
c. Booklet pane, #196a, 197a, 200a, 201a 5.50 —
Complete booklet, #167b, 169b, 169c, 199b, 201b, 201c 35.00
Nos. 196-201 (6) 9.10 9.10

Souvenir Sheet

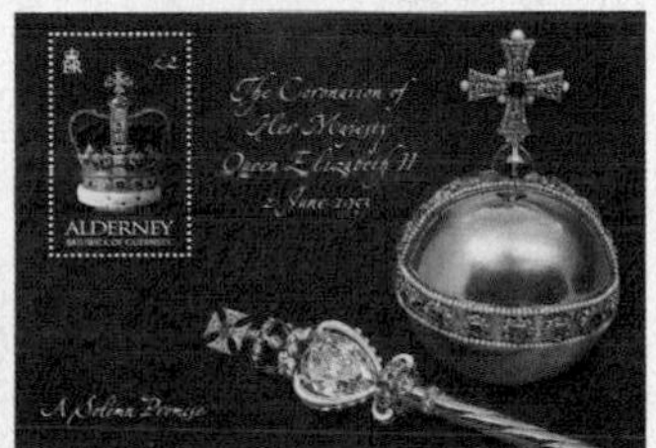

Coronation of Queen Elizabeth II, 50th Anniv. — A33

Litho. & Embossed

2003, Jan. 30 *Perf. 13½*
202 A33 £2 multi 7.00 7.00

Powered Flight, Cent. A34

Designs: 22p, Wright Flyer, 1903. 27p, Vickers Vimy, 1919. 36p, Douglas DC-3, 1936. 40p, Comet, 1946. 45p, Concorde, 1969. 65p, Airbus A380.

2003, Apr. 10 Litho.
203 A34 22p multi .75 .75
204 A34 27p multi .90 .90
205 A34 36p multi 1.25 1.25
206 A34 40p multi 1.40 1.40
207 A34 45p multi 1.50 1.50
208 A34 65p multi 2.25 2.25
Nos. 203-208 (6) 8.05 8.05

Bird Type of 2002

2003, July 3 *Perf. 13¾*
209 A30 22p Arctic tern .85 .85
210 A30 27p Great skua 1.00 1.00
211 A30 36p Sandwich tern 1.40 1.40
212 A30 40p Sooty shearwater 1.60 1.60
213 A30 45p Arctic skua 1.75 1.75
214 A30 65p Manx shearwater 2.50 2.50
a. Souvenir sheet, #209-214 9.25 9.25
Nos. 209-214 (6) 9.10 9.10

Island Police — A35

Police officer and: 22p, Policemen patrolling streets. 27p, Police vehicle. 36p, Member of forensics team. 40p, Policeman assisting child on bicycle. 45p, Police at car accident. 65p, Policeman working with customs officer.

2003, Oct. 16 Litho. *Perf. 13¼x13*
215 A35 22p multi .80 .80
216 A35 27p multi .90 .90
217 A35 36p multi 1.30 1.30
218 A35 40p multi 1.50 1.50
a. Booklet pane, #215-218 4.50 —
219 A35 45p multi 1.60 1.60
a. Booklet pane, #215-217, 219 4.75 —
220 A35 65p multi 2.25 2.25
a. Booklet pane, #215-216, 219-220 5.75 —
b. Booklet pane, #217-220 6.75 —

c. Booklet pane, #215-216, 218, 220 — 5.50 —
Complete booklet, #218a, 219a, 220a, 220c, 2 #220b — 34.00
Nos. 215-220 (6) — 8.35 8.35

The two examples of No. 220b in the booklet have different margins.

Fungi — A36

Designs: 22p, Sulphur tuft. 27p, Orange peel fungus. 36p, Shining ink-cap. 40p, Giant puffball. 45p, Parasol. 65p, Candle snuff fungus.

2004, Jan. 29 Litho. *Perf. 13¼*

221 A36 22p multi .85 .85
222 A36 27p multi 1.00 1.00
223 A36 36p multi 1.40 1.40
224 A36 40p multi 1.60 1.60
225 A36 45p multi 1.75 1.75
226 A36 65p multi 2.50 2.50
Nos. 221-226 (6) 9.10 9.10

FIFA (Fédération Internationale de Football Association), Cent. — A37

Designs: 26p, Challenge on Tourgis Close. 32p, Soccer on the beach. 36p, Playground school soccer. 40p, Friendly kickabout. 45p, Turning the defender. 65p, Tackling Dad at Arch Bay.

2004, May 12 Litho. *Perf. 13¼*

227 A37 26p multi 1.00 1.00
228 A37 32p multi 1.25 1.25
229 A37 36p multi 1.40 1.40
230 A37 40p multi 1.60 1.60
231 A37 45p multi 1.75 1.75
232 A37 65p multi 2.50 2.50
Nos. 227-232 (6) 9.50 9.50

Values are for stamps with surrounding selvage.

Birds Type of 2002

2004, July 29 Litho. *Perf. 13¼*

233 A30 26p Wheatear 1.00 1.00
234 A30 32p Redstart 1.25 1.25
235 A30 36p Yellow wagtail 1.40 1.40
236 A30 40p Hoopoe 1.60 1.60
237 A30 45p Ring ouzel 1.75 1.75
238 A30 65p Sand martin 2.50 2.50
a. Souvenir sheet, #233-238 9.50 9.50
Nos. 233-238 (6) 9.50 9.50

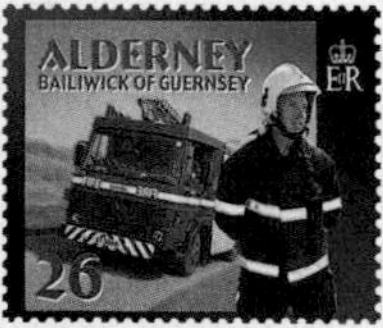

Fire Services A38

Designs: 26p, Fireman and fire truck. 32p, Firemen and fire truck. 36p, Fireman and airport fire truck. 40p, Fire chief, fire truck at station. 45p, Training grounds at airport. 65p, Road accicent training exercise.

2004, Oct. 28 Litho. *Perf. 13¼x13*

239 A38 26p multi .90 .90
240 A38 32p multi 1.10 1.10
241 A38 36p multi 1.25 1.25
242 A38 40p multi 1.40 1.40
a. Booklet pane, #239-242 4.75 —
243 A38 45p multi 1.60 1.60
a. Booklet pane, #239-241, 243 5.00 —
244 A38 65p multi 2.25 2.25
a. Booklet pane, #239-240, 243-244 6.00 —
b. Booklet pane, #241-244 6.50 —
c. Booklet pane, #239-240, 242, 244 5.75 —
Complete booklet, #242a, 243a, 244a, 244c, 2 #244b 35.00
Nos. 239-244 (6) 8.50 8.50

The two examples of No. 244b in the complete booklet have different margins.

Hans Christian Andersen (1805-75), Author — A39

Scenes from "The Little Mermaid": 26p, Mermaid, fish, castle. 32p, Mermaid rescues prince. 36p, Mermaid and sea witch. 40p, Mermaid and prince on land. 65p, Dead mermaid and angels.

2005, Feb. 3 Litho. *Perf. 13½*

245 A39 26p multi 1.00 1.00
246 A39 32p multi 1.25 1.25
247 A39 36p multi 1.40 1.40
248 A39 40p multi 1.60 1.60
249 A39 65p multi 2.50 2.50
Nos. 245-249 (5) 7.75 7.75

Battle of Trafalgar, Bicent. — A40

Designs: 26p, Admiral Horatio Nelson. 32p, HMS Victory. 36p, Enemy in sight. 40p, Fall of Nelson. 45p, Breaking the line. 65p, Admiral James de Saumarez.

2005, May 9 Litho. *Perf. 14x13¼*

250 A40 26p multi .90 .90
251 A40 32p multi 1.10 1.10
252 A40 36p multi 1.25 1.25
253 A40 40p multi 1.40 1.40
a. Booklet pane, #250-253 4.75 —
254 A40 45p multi 1.60 1.60
255 A40 65p multi 2.25 2.25
a. Booklet pane, #250-251, 254-255 6.00 —
b. Booklet pane, #252-255 6.50
c. Booklet pane, #251-252, 254-255 6.50
d. Booklet pane, #250, 253-255 5.75
Complete booklet, #255a, 255b, 255c, 255d, 2 #253a 35.00
Nos. 250-255 (6) 8.50 8.50

The two examples of No. 253a in the complete booklet have different pane margins.

Bird Type of 2002

26p, Little stint. 32p, Greenshank. 36p, Golden plover. 40p, Bar-tailed godwit. 45p, Green sandpiper. 65p, Sanderling.

2005, July 21 *Perf. 13¼*

256 A30 26p multicolored 1.10 1.10
257 A30 32p multicolored 1.40 1.40
258 A30 36p multicolored 1.50 1.50
259 A30 40p multicolored 1.75 1.75
260 A30 45p multicolored 2.00 2.00
261 A30 65p multicolored 2.75 2.75
a. Souvenir sheet, #256-261 12.00 12.00
Nos. 256-261 (6) 10.50 10.50

Souvenir Sheet

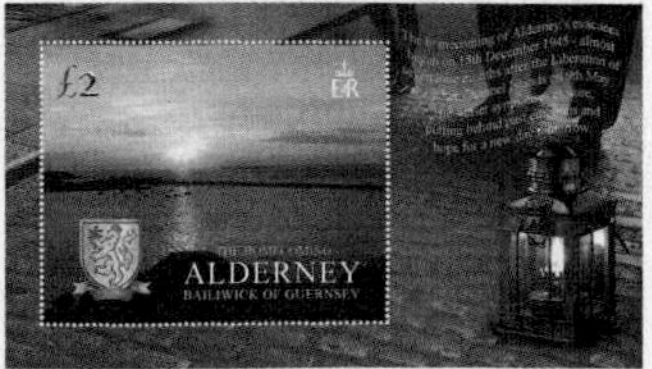

Homecoming of World War II Evacuees, 60th Anniv. — A41

2005, Oct. 27 *Perf. 13¾*

262 A41 £2 multi 7.50 7.50

T.H. White, Author of *The Once and Future King*, Birth Centenary — A42

Authorian legends: 29p, King Arthur. 34p, Merlyn. 38p, Morgause. 42p, Queen Guenever. 47p, Lancelot. 68p, Mordred.

2006, Feb. 16 Litho. *Perf. 13½x14*

263 A42 29p multi 1.10 1.10
264 A42 34p multi 1.40 1.40
265 A42 38p multi 1.50 1.50
266 A42 42p multi 1.60 1.60
267 A42 47p multi 1.90 1.90
268 A42 68p multi 2.75 2.75
a. Souvenir sheet, #263-268 10.00 10.00
Nos. 263-268 (6) 10.25 10.25

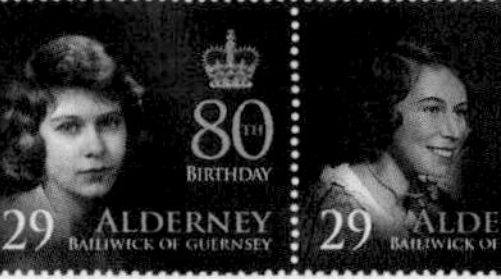

Queen Elizabeth II, 80th Birthday — A43

Various photographs of Queen with predominant background colors of:
No. 269: a, Blue violet. b, Red violet.
No. 270: a, Green. b, Orange brown.
No. 271: a, Yellow brown. b, Bright red.
No. 272: a, Red. b, Violet.

2006, Apr. 21 *Perf. 13¾*

269 A43 Horiz. pair 2.25 2.25
a.-b. 29p Either single 1.10 1.10
270 A43 Horiz. pair 3.00 3.00
a.-b. 34p Either single 1.50 1.50
271 A43 Horiz. pair 3.25 3.25
a.-b. 42p Either single 1.60 1.60
272 A43 Horiz. pair 3.50 3.50
a.-b. 45p Either single 1.75 1.75
Nos. 269-272 (4) 12.00 12.00

Birds — A44

Designs: 29p, Fulmar. 34p, Gannet. 42p, Lesser black-backed gull. 45p, Storm petrel. 47p, Kittiwake. 68p, Puffin.

2006, July 27 Litho. *Perf. 13¾*

273 A44 29p multi 1.00 1.00
a. Booklet pane of 4 4.00 —
274 A44 34p multi 1.30 1.30
a. Booklet pane of 4 5.25 —
275 A44 42p multi 1.40 1.40
a. Booklet pane of 4 5.75 —
276 A44 45p multi 1.60 1.60
a. Booklet pane of 4 6.50 —
277 A44 47p multi 1.75 1.75
a. Booklet pane of 4 7.00 —
278 A44 68p multi 2.50 2.50
a. Booklet pane of 4 10.00 —
Complete booklet, #273a, 274a, 275a, 276a, 277a, 278a 32.50
Nos. 273-278 (6) 9.55 9.55

See Nos. 297-302, 319-324, 344-349.

Corals and Anemones — A45

Designs: 1p, Burrowing anemone. 2p, Colonial anemone. 3p, Jewel anemone. 4p, Sagartia elegans. 5p, Red fingers. 6p, Plumose anemone. 7p, Fan coral. 8p, Jewel anemone, diff. 9p, Actinothoe sphyrodeta. 10p, Snakelocks anemone. £1, Beadlet anemone. £2, Sunset cup coral.

2006, Nov. 2 Litho. *Perf. 13x13½*

279 A45 1p multi .25 .25
280 A45 2p multi .25 .25
281 A45 3p multi .25 .25
282 A45 4p multi .25 .25
283 A45 5p multi .25 .25
284 A45 6p multi .25 .25
285 A45 7p multi .25 .25
286 A45 8p multi .30 .30
287 A45 9p multi .35 .35
288 A45 10p multi .40 .40

Litho. & Embossed
Size: 22x27mm
Perf. 12¾x13¼

289 A45 £1 multi 3.75 3.75
290 A45 £2 multi 7.75 7.75
Nos. 279-290 (12) 14.30 14.30

See Nos. 303-306.

Alderney Wetlands A46

Designs: 32p, Cushion starfish. 37p, Gannet. 45p, Spiny squat lobster. 48p, Gray seal. 50p, Golden samphire. 71p, Little egret.

2007, Mar. 8 Litho. *Perf. 13¼*

291 A46 32p multi 1.25 1.25
292 A46 37p multi 1.50 1.50
293 A46 45p multi 1.75 1.75
294 A46 48p multi 1.90 1.90
295 A46 50p multi 2.00 2.00
296 A46 71p multi 2.75 2.75
a. Souvenir sheet, #291-296 11.00 11.00
Nos. 291-296 (6) 11.15 11.15

Addition of Alderney Wetlands and Burhou Islands to Ramsar Convention Protected Wetlands List.

Birds Type of 2006

Designs: 32p, Blackbird. 37p, Dartford warbler. 45p, Blue tit. 48p, Wren. 50p, House sparrow. 71p, Jackdaw.

2007, May 24 Litho. *Perf. 13¾*

297 A44 32p multi 1.10 1.10
a. Booklet pane of 4 4.50 —
298 A44 37p multi 1.35 1.35
a. Booklet pane of 4 5.50 —
299 A44 45p multi 1.60 1.60
a. Booklet pane of 4 6.50 —
300 A44 48p multi 1.75 1.75
a. Booklet pane of 4 7.00 —
301 A44 50p multi 1.75 1.75
a. Booklet pane of 4 7.00 —
302 A44 71p multi 2.75 2.75
a. Booklet pane of 4 11.00 —
Complete booklet, #297a-302a 42.50
Nos. 297-302 (6) 10.30 10.30

Corals and Anemones Type of 2006

Designs: 20p. Devonshire cup coral. 40p, Fried egg anemone. 50p, Parasitic anemone. £4, Strawberry anemone.

2007, Aug. 2 Litho. *Perf. 14*
Size: 27x23mm

303 A45 20p multi .75 .75
304 A45 40p multi 1.50 1.50
305 A45 50p multi 1.90 1.90

Litho. & Embossed
Size: 27x28mm

306 A45 £4 multi 14.50 14.50
Nos. 303-306 (4) 18.65 18.65

Just So Stories, by Rudyard Kipling — A47

Designs: 32p, How the Camel Got His Hump. 37p, How the Whale Got His Throat. 45p, The Elephant's Child. 48p, How the Leopard Got His Spots. 50p, The Cat That Walked by Himself. 71p, How the Rhinoceros Got His Skin.

2007, Oct. 25 Litho. *Perf. 13x13¼*

307 A47 32p multi 1.25 1.25
308 A47 37p multi 1.35 1.35
309 A47 45p multi 1.75 1.75
310 A47 48p multi 1.75 1.75
311 A47 50p multi 1.90 1.90
312 A47 71p multi 2.75 2.75
a. Miniature sheet, #307-312 10.50 10.50
Nos. 307-312 (6) 10.75 10.75

Butterflies
A48

Butterflies: 34p, Painted lady. 40p, Grayling. 48p, Green hairstreak. 51p, Speckled wood. 53c, Common blue. 74p, Glanville fritillary.

2008, Feb. 28 Litho. *Perf. 13¾*
313 A48 34p multi 1.25 1.25
314 A48 40p multi 1.45 1.45
315 A48 48p multi 1.75 1.75
316 A48 51p multi 1.75 1.75
317 A48 53p multi 1.90 1.90
318 A48 74p multi 2.75 2.75
a. Miniature sheet, #313-318 10.50 10.50
Nos. 313-318 (6) 10.85 10.85

Birds Type of 2006

Designs: 34p, Common buzzard. 40p, Peregrine falcon. 48p, Kestrel. 51p, Barn owl. 53p, Long-eared owl. 74p, Sparrowhawk.

2008, May 15 Litho. *Perf. 13¾*
319 A44 34p multi 1.25 1.25
a. Booklet pane of 4 5.00 —
320 A44 40p multi 1.40 1.40
a. Booklet pane of 4 5.75 —
321 A44 48p multi 1.60 1.60
a. Booklet pane of 4 6.50 —
322 A44 51p multi 1.75 1.75
a. Booklet pane of 4 7.00 —
323 A44 53p multi 1.90 1.90
a. Booklet pane of 4 7.75 —
324 A44 74p multi 2.75 2.75
a. Booklet pane of 4 11.00 —
Complete booklet, #319a-324a 43.00
Nos. 319-324 (6) 10.65 10.65

Alderney Postage Stamps, 25th Anniv. — A49

Flag and tourist sites: 34p, Old Harbor. 40p, Breakwater. 48p, Fort Clonque Causeway. 51p, Golf course. 53p, Hanging Rock. 74p, Fort Clonque.

2008, June 14 Litho. *Perf. 14x13¾*
325 A49 34p multi 1.25 1.25
326 A49 40p multi 1.45 1.45
327 A49 48p multi 1.75 1.75
328 A49 51p multi 1.75 1.75
329 A49 53p multi 1.90 1.90
330 A49 74p multi 2.75 2.75
Nos. 325-330 (6) 10.85 10.85

See No. 376.

Heraldic Lion — A50

Litho. & Embossed With Foil Application

2008, June 14 *Perf. 14¼x13½*
331 A50 £5 multi 16.00 16.00

Aurigny Air Services, 40th Anniv. — A51

Airplanes: 34p, Britten-Norman Islander. 40p, Britten-Norman Trislander. 48p, DHC-6 Twin Otter. 51p, Short 360. 53p, Saab 340. 74p, ATR 72.

2008, Oct. 30 Litho. *Perf. 13½*
332 A51 34p multi 1.00 1.00
333 A51 40p multi 1.10 1.10
334 A51 48p multi 1.40 1.40
335 A51 51p multi 1.60 1.60
336 A51 53p multi 1.60 1.60
337 A51 74p multi 2.10 2.10
a. Souvenir sheet, #332-337 9.00 9.00
Nos. 332-337 (6) 8.80 8.80

Bees — A52

Flowers and: 36p, Tawny mining bee. 43p, Early bumblebee. 51p, Bug mining bee. 54p, Cuckoo bee. 56p, Solitary bee. 77p, Honey bee.

2009, Feb. 26 Litho. *Perf. 13¾*
338 A52 36p multi 1.10 1.10
339 A52 43p multi 1.25 1.25
340 A52 51p multi 1.50 1.50
341 A52 54p multi 1.60 1.60
342 A52 56p multi 1.60 1.60
343 A52 77p multi 2.25 2.25
a. Miniature sheet of 6, #338-343 9.50 9.50
Nos. 338-343 (6) 9.30 9.30

Birds Type of 2006

Designs: 36p, Turnstone. 43p, Curlew. 51p, Oystercatcher. 54p, Snipe. 56p, Dunlin. 77p, Ringed plover.

2009, May 28 Litho. *Perf. 13¾*
344 A44 36p multi 1.10 1.10
a. Booklet pane of 4 4.50 —
345 A44 43p multi 1.25 1.25
a. Booklet pane of 4 5.00 —
346 A44 51p multi 1.40 1.40
a. Booklet pane of 4 5.75 —
347 A44 54p multi 1.60 1.60
a. Booklet pane of 4 6.50 —
348 A44 56p multi 1.75 1.75
a. Booklet pane of 4 7.00 —
349 A44 77p multi 2.25 2.25
a. Booklet pane of 4 9.00 —
Complete booklet, #344a-349a 38.00
Nos. 344-349 (6) 10.40 10.40

Naval Aviation, Cent. — A53

Designs: 36p, Flying Boat over Castle Cornet. 43p, Fairey Swordfish attacking U-boat. 51p, Skuas divebombing Scharnhorst. 54p, Sea Fury over Alderney. 56p, Sea Hawk and Sea Fury. 77p, Merlin helicopter landing on HMS Daring.

2009, July 30 *Perf. 14¼x13¾*
350 A53 36p multi 1.05 1.05
351 A53 43p multi 1.30 1.30
352 A53 51p multi 1.50 1.50
353 A53 54p multi 1.60 1.60
354 A53 56p multi 1.60 1.60
355 A53 77p multi 2.25 2.25
Nos. 350-355 (6) 10.90 10.90

Scenes From Sherlock Holmes and the Curious Case of the Alderney Bull, by Sir Arthur Conan Doyle (1859-1930) — A54

Designs: 36p, Alice West reporting theft to Holmes. 43p, Holmes and policeman studying message, arrest of suspect. 51p, Holmes looking for clues with magnifying glass. 54p, Holmes with two men outside building. 56p, Holmes pointing to partially-built lighthouse. 77p, Holmes pointing to thief.

2009, Oct. 29 Litho. *Perf. 13¼x13*
356 A54 36p multi 1.05 1.05
357 A54 43p multi 1.30 1.30
358 A54 51p multi 1.50 1.50
359 A54 54p multi 1.60 1.60
360 A54 56p multi 1.60 1.60
361 A54 77p multi 2.25 2.25
Nos. 356-361 (6) 10.90 10.90

A miniature sheet of six containing one of each stamp was sold together with a special lens and a DVD for £9.99. The sheet was not available separately. Value, sheet $35.

Dragonflies
A55

Designs: 36p, Common darter. 45p, Emperor dragonfly. 56p, Blue-tailed damselfly. 66p, Brown hawker. 75p, Black-tailed skimmer. 83p, Red-veined darter.

2010, Feb. 25 Litho. *Perf. 13¾*
362 A55 36p multi 1.10 1.10
363 A55 45p multi 1.40 1.40
364 A55 56p multi 1.75 1.75
365 A55 66p multi 2.00 2.00
366 A55 75p multi 2.40 2.40
367 A55 83p multi 2.60 2.60
a. Souvenir sheet, #362-367 11.50 11.50
Nos. 362-367 (6) 11.25 11.25

Battle of Britain, 70th Anniv.
A56

Designs: 36p, Pilot Keith Gilman. 45p, Hawker Hurricanes in flight. 48p, Pilots scrambling to planes. 50p, Spitfire sortie. 58p, Air raid warden. 80p, Evacuees.
£2, Sir Douglas Bader, vert.

2010, May 4 *Perf. 14*
369 A56 36p blk & gray 1.10 1.10
370 A56 45p blk & gray 1.40 1.40
371 A56 48p blk & gray 1.50 1.50
372 A56 50p blk & gray 1.50 1.50
373 A56 58p blk & gray 1.75 1.75
374 A56 80p blk & gray 2.40 2.40
Nos. 369-374 (6) 9.65 9.65

Souvenir Sheet

375 A56 £2 blk & gray 6.50 6.50

Alderney Postage Stamps, 25th Anniv. Type of 2008

Design: Hanging Rock.

2010, June 18 *Perf. 14x13¾*
376 A49 55p multi 2.00 2.00

Florence Nightingale (1820-1910), Nurse — A57

Various quotes of Nightingale and: 36p, Hand carrying lantern. 45p, Hand reaching out. 48p, Hand holding bucket. 50p, Hands unwrapping gauze bandage. 58p, Hand writing. 80p, Hands in prayer.

2010, July 29 *Perf. 14½x14*
377 A57 36p multi 1.10 1.10
378 A57 45p multi 1.40 1.40
379 A57 48p multi 1.50 1.50
380 A57 50p multi 1.60 1.60
381 A57 58p multi 1.90 1.90
382 A57 80p multi 2.50 2.50
Nos. 377-382 (6) 10.00 10.00

Peter Pan, by Sir James M. Barrie (1860-1937) — A58

Designs: 36p, Children flying above London. 45p, Captain Hook and crocodile. 48p, Peter Pan visits Captain Hook's ship. 50p, Peter Pan waving a rainbow. 58p, Children on Neverpeak. 80p, Bonfire.
£3, Peter Pan, vert.

2010, Nov. 4 Litho. *Perf. 13¼x13½*
383 A58 36p multi 1.25 1.25
384 A58 45p multi 1.50 1.50
385 A58 48p multi 1.60 1.60
386 A58 50p multi 1.60 1.60
387 A58 58p multi 1.90 1.90
388 A58 80p multi 2.60 2.60
Nos. 383-388 (6) 10.45 10.45

Souvenir Sheet
Perf. 13½x13¼

389 A58 £3 multi 10.00 10.00

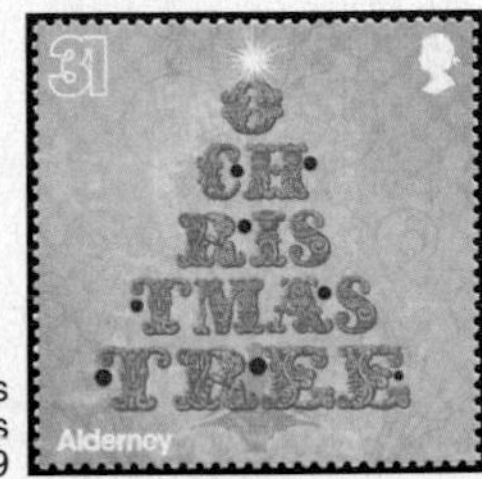

Christmas Carols
A59

Designs: 31p, O Christmas Tree. 36p, Away in a Manger. 45p, While Shepherds Watched Their Flocks By Night. 48p, Hark the Herald Angels Sing. 50p, O Holy Night. 58p, O Little Town of Bethlehem. 80p, Good King Wenceslas.

2010, Nov. 4 Litho. *Perf. 13¼x14*
390 A59 31p multi 1.00 1.00
391 A59 36p multi 1.25 1.25
392 A59 45p multi 1.50 1.50
393 A59 48p multi 1.60 1.60
394 A59 50p multi 1.60 1.60
395 A59 58p multi 1.90 1.90
396 A59 80p multi 2.60 2.60
Nos. 390-396 (7) 11.45 11.45

Hawk Moths
A60

Designs: 36p, Elephant hawkmoth. 45p, Hummingbird hawkmoth. 52p, Convolvulus hawkmoth. 58p, Poplar hawkmoth. 65p, Striped hawkmoth. 70p, Privet hawkmoth.

2011, Feb. 23 Litho. *Perf. 13¾*
397 A60 36p multi 1.25 1.25
398 A60 45p multi 1.50 1.50
399 A60 52p multi 1.75 1.75
400 A60 58p multi 1.90 1.90
401 A60 65p multi 2.10 2.10
402 A60 70p multi 2.25 2.25
a. Souvenir sheet of 6, #397-402 11.00 11.00
Nos. 397-402 (6) 10.75 10.75

See Nos. 440-445.

Birds — A61

Designs: 36p, Mediterranean gull. 45p, Shelduck. 48p, Firecrest. 52p, Balearic shearwater. 58p, Woodcock, 65p, Little grebe.

2011, May 4

403 A61 36p multi 1.25 1.25
404 A61 45p multi 1.50 1.50
405 A61 48p multi 1.60 1.60
406 A61 52p multi 1.75 1.75
407 A61 58p multi 1.90 1.90
408 A61 65p multi 2.10 2.10
a. Souvenir sheet of 6, #403-408 10.50 10.50
Nos. 403-408 (6) 10.10 10.10

Queen Elizabeth II, 85th Birthday, Prince Philip, 90th Birthday — A62

Various photographs of Queen and Prince.

2011, June 2 ***Perf. 13¾x13¼***

409 A62 36p silver & sepia 1.25 1.25
a. Booklet pane of 4 5.00 —
410 A62 45p silver & sepia 1.50 1.50
a. Booklet pane of 4 6.00 —
411 A62 48p silver & sepia 1.60 1.60
a. Booklet pane of 4 6.50 —
412 A62 52p silver & sepia 1.75 1.75
a. Booklet pane of 4 7.00 —
413 A62 58p silver & sepia 1.90 1.90
a. Booklet pane of 4 7.75 —
414 A62 65p silver & sepia 2.10 2.10
a. Booklet pane of 4 8.50 —
Complete booket, #409a, 410a, 411a, 412a, 413a, 414a 41.00
Nos. 409-414 (6) 10.10 10.10

Red Cross Uniforms, Cent. — A63

Designs: 36p, Women's Voluntary Aid Detachment uniform, c. 1915. 47p, Men's Voluntary Aid Detachment uniform, 1915. 48p, Nurse's uniform, c. 1966-78. 52p, Women's uniform, 1981-2001. 61p, Man's uniform, c. 2001. 65p, Women's uniform, c. 2011.

2011, July 28 ***Perf. 14¼x13¾***

415 A63 36p multi 1.25 1.25
416 A63 47p multi 1.50 1.50
417 A63 48p multi 1.60 1.60
418 A63 52p multi 1.75 1.75
419 A63 61p multi 2.00 2.00
420 A63 65p multi 2.10 2.10
Nos. 415-420 (6) 10.20 10.20

Alderney in Winter A64

Designs: 31p, Victoria Street. 36p, St. Anne's Church. 47p, Les Estacs Gannet Colonies, reindeer in flight. 48p, Reindeer pulling Santa's sleigh, Mannez Lighthouse. 52p, Alderney train. 61p, Children playing in snow, snowman. 65p, Boat in harbor.

2011, Oct. 27 Litho. ***Perf. 13½x14¼***

421 A64 31p multi 1.00 1.00
422 A64 36p multi 1.25 1.25
423 A64 47p multi 1.50 1.50
424 A64 48p multi 1.60 1.60
425 A64 52p multi 1.75 1.75
426 A64 61p multi 2.00 2.00
427 A64 65p multi 2.10 2.10
Nos. 421-427 (7) 11.20 11.20

Sinking of the Titanic, Cent. A65

Designs: 36p, Titanic leaving port. 47p, Rocket exploding over Titanic. 48p, Grand staricase. 52p, Musicians. 61p, Capt. Edward J. Smith. 65p, Lifeboat near sinking Titanic.

2012, Feb. 22 ***Perf. 13¼x13¾***

428 A65 36p multi 1.25 1.25
a. Booklet pane of 4 5.00 —
429 A65 47p multi 1.50 1.50
a. Booklet pane of 4 6.00 —
430 A65 48p multi 1.60 1.60
a. Booklet pane of 4 6.50 —
431 A65 52p multi 1.75 1.75
a. Booklet pane of 4 7.00 —
432 A65 61p multi 2.00 2.00
a. Booklet pane of 4 8.00 —
433 A65 65p multi 2.10 2.10
a. Booklet pane of 4 8.50 —
Complete booklet, #428a, 429a, 430a, 431a, 432a, 433a 41.00
Nos. 428-433 (6) 10.20 10.20

Charles Dickens (1812-70), Writer — A66

Various illustrations by George Cruikshank for original printing of Oliver Twist.

2012, May 8 ***Perf. 14***

434 A66 36p blk & ol brn 1.10 1.10
435 A66 47p blk & ol brn 1.50 1.50
436 A66 48p blk & ol brn 1.50 1.50
437 A66 52p blk & ol brn 1.60 1.60
438 A66 61p blk & ol brn 1.90 1.90
439 A66 65p blk & ol brn 2.00 2.00
Nos. 434-439 (6) 9.60 9.60

Moths Type of 2011

Designs: 39p, Garden tiger moth. 52p, Cream spot tiger moth. 53p, Buff ermine. 59p, Ruby tiger moth. 69p, Jersey tiger moth. 74p, Cinnabar.

2012, July 25 ***Perf. 13¾***

440 A60 39p multi 1.25 1.25
441 A60 52p multi 1.60 1.60
442 A60 53p multi 1.75 1.75
443 A60 59p multi 1.90 1.90
444 A60 69p multi 2.25 2.25
445 A60 74p multi 2.40 2.40
a. Souvenir sheet of 6, #440-445 11.50 11.50
Nos. 440-445 (6) 11.15 11.15

Alderney Harbor A67

Designs: 39p, Douglas Quay, Braye Harbor, c.1800. 52p, Breakwater completed, 1856. 53p, SS Courier, c. 1926. 59p, Little Crabby Harbor, 1985. 69p, RNLI Lifeboat Roy Baker I, c. 1995. 74p, Commercial Quay, 2011.

2012, Oct. 31

446 A67 39p multi 1.25 1.25
447 A67 52p multi 1.75 1.75
448 A67 53p multi 1.75 1.75
449 A67 59p multi 1.90 1.90
450 A67 69p multi 2.25 2.25
451 A67 74p multi 2.40 2.40
a. Souvenir sheet of 6, #446-451 11.50 11.50
Nos. 446-451 (6) 11.30 11.30

Christmas A68

Designs: 34p, Annunciation. 39p, No room at the inn. 52p, Birth of Jesus. 53p, Whilst shepherds watch their flocks. 59p, The Three Kings. 69p, Children of Bethlehem visiting baby Jesus. 74p, Flight to Egypt.

2012, Oct. 31 ***Perf. 13¼x12½***

452 A68 34p multi 1.10 1.10
453 A68 39p multi 1.25 1.25
454 A68 52p multi 1.75 1.75
455 A68 53p multi 1.75 1.75
456 A68 59p multi 1.90 1.90
457 A68 69p multi 2.25 2.25
458 A68 74p multi 2.40 2.40
Nos. 452-458 (7) 12.40 12.40

Beetles A69

Designs: 39p, Rose chafer. 52p, Burying beetle. 53p, Green tiger beetle. 59p, May bug. 69p, Netocia moria. 74p, Oil beetle.

2013, Feb. 20 ***Perf. 13¾***

459 A69 39p multi 1.25 1.25
460 A69 52p multi 1.60 1.60
461 A69 53p multi 1.60 1.60
462 A69 59p multi 1.75 1.75
463 A69 69p multi 2.10 2.10
464 A69 74p multi 2.25 2.25
a. Souvenir sheet of 6, #459-464 11.00 11.00
Nos. 459-464 (6) 10.55 10.55

Coronation of Queen Elizabeth II, 60th Anniv. — A70

Designs: 40p, Queen Elizabeth II wearing crown. 53p, Silversmith working on regalia. 55p, Queen Eliabeth II wearing George IV diadem. 63p, Queen Elizabeth II and clergymen. 71p, Administration of oath. 79p, Queen Elizabeth II holding orb and scepter.

2013, May 29 ***Perf. 13½***

465 A70 40p multi 1.25 1.25
a. Booklet pane of 4 5.00 —
466 A70 53p multi 1.75 1.75
a. Booklet pane of 4 7.00 —
467 A70 55p multi 1.75 1.75
a. Booklet pane of 4 7.00 —
468 A70 63p multi 2.00 2.00
a. Booklet pane of 4 8.00 —
469 A70 71p multi 2.25 2.25
a. Booklet pane of 4 9.00 —
470 A70 79p multi 2.50 2.50
a. Booklet pane of 4 10.00 —
Complete booklet, #465a-470a 44.00
Nos. 465-470 (6) 11.50 11.50

Beatrix Potter (1866-1943), Children's Book Author — A71

Potter and: 40p, Rabbit and signpost. 53p, Duck. 55p, Mouse and onions. 63p, Dog. 71p, Cat. 79p, Chicken.

2013, July 31

471 A71 40p multi 1.25 1.25
472 A71 53p multi 1.75 1.75
473 A71 55p multi 1.75 1.75
474 A71 63p multi 2.00 2.00
475 A71 71p multi 2.25 2.25
476 A71 79p multi 2.50 2.50
a. Souvenir sheet of 6, #471-476 11.50 11.50
Nos. 471-476 (6) 11.50 11.50

Christmas A72

Scenes from "Rudolph the Red-Nosed Reindeer": 35p, Santa Claus tending to Rudolph.. 40p, Elf comforting Rudolph. 53p, Rudolph and snowmen. 55p, Reindeer mocking Rudolph. 63p, Santa Claus surveying fog. 71p, Santa looking at Rudolph's nose. 79p, Rudolph leading reindeer in flight.

Perf. 13½x13¼

2013, Nov. 13 **Litho.**

477 A72 35p multi 1.25 1.25
478 A72 40p multi 1.40 1.40
479 A72 53p multi 1.75 1.75
480 A72 55p multi 1.90 1.90
481 A72 63p multi 2.10 2.10
482 A72 71p multi 2.40 2.40
483 A72 79p multi 2.60 2.60
Nos. 477-483 (7) 13.40 13.40

Ladybugs A73

Designs: 40p, Seven-spot ladybug. 53p, Newly-hatched seven-spot ladybug. 55p, Two-spot ladybug. 63p, Orange ladybug. 71p, Harlequin ladybugs. 79p, Harlequin ladybugs, diff.

2014, Feb. 12 **Litho.** ***Perf. 13¾***

484 A73 40p multi 1.40 1.40
485 A73 53p multi 1.75 1.75
486 A73 55p multi 1.90 1.90
487 A73 63p multi 2.10 2.10
488 A73 71p multi 2.40 2.40
489 A73 79p multi 2.60 2.60
a. Souvenir sheet of 6, #484-489 12.50 12.50
Nos. 484-489 (6) 12.15 12.15

Final Panel of the Bayeux Tapestry, Fabric Art by Kate Russell and Pauline Black — A74

Details from tapestry: 40p, William the Conqueror dining with family after Battle of Hastings victory. 53p, William the Conqueror and knights. 55p, London nobles submitting to William's rule. 63p, Blessing at coronation. 71p, Coronation of William. 79p, People acclaiming William as King.

£3, People acclaiming William as King, vert.

2014, May 28 **Litho.** ***Perf. 13¼x13***

490 A74 40p multi 1.40 1.40
a. Booklet pane of 4 5.75 —
491 A74 53p multi 1.75 1.75
a. Booklet pane of 4 7.00 —
492 A74 55p multi 1.90 1.90
a. Booklet pane of 4 7.75 —
493 A74 63p multi 2.10 2.10
a. Booklet pane of 4 8.50 —
494 A74 71p multi 2.40 2.40
a. Booklet pane of 4 9.75 —
495 A74 79p multi 2.75 2.75
a. Booklet pane of 4 11.00 —
Complete booklet, #490a, 491a, 492a, 493a, 494a, 495a 50.00
Nos. 490-495 (6) 12.30 12.30

Souvenir Sheet
On Cotton-Faced Paper

Perf. 14x14¼

496 A74 £3 multi 10.00 10.00

No. 496 contains one 30x41mm stamp.

First Birthday of Prince George of Cambridge — A75

No. 497: a, Prince George, Prince William, Prince Charles and Queen Elizabeth II. b, Prince George, Prince William and Duchess of Cambridge.

2014, July 22 **Litho.** ***Perf. 14¼***

497 A75 Horiz. pair 3.80 3.80
a.-b. 55p Either single 1.90 1.90

Ian Fleming (1908-64), Writer — A76

Photograph of Fleming and inscription: 41p, Commander in Naval Intelligence during World War II. 54p, Well traveled, he wrote vividly about the places he visited. 55p, In Jamaica, where all of the James Bond novels were written. 66p, Holding his son, Caspar, in 1952. 74p, Journalist and writer at his desk in London. 83p, As a journalist abroad.
£3, Fleming driving Bentley convertible.

Litho. With Foil Application

2014, July 30 *Perf. 13¼*

498 A76 41p blk & gold 1.40 1.40
499 A76 54p blk & gold 1.90 1.90
500 A76 55p blk & gold 1.90 1.90
501 A76 66p blk & gold 2.25 2.25
502 A76 74p blk & gold 2.50 2.50
503 A76 83p blk & gold 2.75 2.75
Nos. 498-503 (6) 12.70 12.70

Souvenir Sheet

Perf. 14¼

504 A76 £3 blk & gold 10.00 10.00

No. 504 contains one 43x43mm stamp. The stamp also was sold as an imperf. press sheet for £26 and a gold foil replica of the sheet for £95.

Christmas A77

Children's art depicting: 36p, North Pole, by Alexandra Campbell, Joe Blackham and Ian Adamson. 41p, Santa and snowman on a starry night, by Louis Smart, Danielle Allen, and Lydia Jenkins. 54p, Snowman and house, by Holly Neil, Libby Needham, Rosie Williams and Kamil Olbrycht. 55p, Snowmen and trees, by Sian Craig, Amber Shaw, Grace Millan, Cameron Tugby-Maloy, Keira Scott, and Harvey Olliver. 66p, Elves' Workshop, by Jasmine Sayer, Frankie Jenkins, Matthew Burke, Cameron Bunrham, Florence Carpenter, Scarlett Oldfield, Carl Evans, Andrew Page, and Chloe Faulkner. 74p, Alderney Lighthouse and children at mailbox, by Katie Shaw ans Kiri Winder. 83p, Bright Lights and Decorations, by Amelie Carpenter, Erin Atkinson, Bennett Blackham, and Owen Carré.

2014, Nov. 6 Litho. *Perf. 13¼x12¾*

Self-Adhesive

505 A77 36p multi 1.25 1.25
506 A77 41p multi 1.40 1.40
507 A77 54p multi 1.75 1.75
508 A77 55p multi 1.75 1.75
509 A77 66p multi 2.10 2.10
510 A77 74p multi 2.40 2.40
511 A77 83p multi 2.60 2.60
Nos. 505-511 (7) 13.25 13.25

Alice's Adventures in Wonderland, by Lewis Carroll, 150th Anniv. — A78

Designs: 41p, Alice and flamingo. 54p, White Rabbit. 55p, Caterpillar. 66p, Cheshire Cat. 74p, Mad Hatter. 83p, Queen of Hearts.
£3, Alice at tea party.

2015, Feb. 22 Litho. *Perf. 13¼x13*

512 A78 41p multi 1.25 1.25
513 A78 54p multi 1.60 1.60
514 A78 55p multi 1.75 1.75
515 A78 66p multi 2.00 2.00
516 A78 74p multi 2.25 2.25
517 A78 83p multi 2.60 2.60
Nos. 512-517 (6) 11.45 11.45

Souvenir Sheet

Perf. 13½x13¼

518 A78 £3 multi 9.25 9.25

No. 518 contains one 28x42mm stamp.

Flora and Fauna A79

Designs: (41p), Alderney sea lavender. (54p), Blonde hedgehog. (55p), Dwarf thistle. (66p), Black rabbit. (74p), Spotted rock rose. (83p), Mole.

2015, May 1 Litho. *Perf. 13¾*

519 A79 (41p) multi 1.25 1.25
520 A79 (54p) multi 1.60 1.60
521 A79 (55p) multi 1.75 1.75
522 A79 (66p) multi 2.00 2.00
523 A79 (74p) multi 2.25 2.25
524 A79 (83p) multi 2.50 2.50
a. Souvenir sheet of 6, #519-524 11.50 11.50
Nos. 519-524 (6) 11.35 11.35

Inscriptions on: No. 519, "Local Letter." No. 520, "Local Large Letter." No. 521, "UK Letter." No. 522, "EUR Letter." No. 523, "UK Large Letter." No. 524, "ROW Letter."

Forts A80

Designs: 42p, Fort Tourgis. 56p, Fort Clonque. 57p, Fort Grosnez. 62p, Fort Houmet Herbé. 68p, Fort Château à l'Etoc. 77p, Nunnery Roman Fort.

2015, July 22 Litho. *Perf. 14¾x14¼*

525 A80 42p multi 1.40 1.40
526 A80 56p multi 1.75 1.75
527 A80 57p multi 1.75 1.75
528 A80 62p multi 2.00 2.00
529 A80 68p multi 2.10 2.10
530 A80 77p multi 2.40 2.40
Nos. 525-530 (6) 11.40 11.40

Queen Elizabeth II, Longest-Reigning British Monarch — A81

Litho. With Foil Application

2015, Sept. 9 *Perf. 12½*

531 A81 £10 multi 30.00 30.00

Christmas — A82

Various stained-glass windows in St. Anne's Church dedicated to Anne French.

2015, Nov. 6 Litho. *Perf. 14¾*

532 A82 37p multi 1.10 1.10
533 A82 42p multi 1.25 1.25
534 A82 56p multi 1.75 1.75
535 A82 57p multi 1.75 1.75
536 A82 62p multi 1.90 1.90
537 A82 68p multi 2.10 2.10
538 A82 77p multi 2.40 2.40
Nos. 532-538 (7) 12.25 12.25

Souvenir Sheet

Alderney Homecoming, 70th Anniv. — A83

2015, Nov. 10 Litho. *Perf. 13¼*

539 A83 £3 multi 9.00 9.00

Flora and Fauna of Longis Nature Reserve — A84

Designs: 42p, Eelgrass. 56p, Glanville fritillary. 57p, Yarrow broomrape. 62p, Meadow pipit. 68p, Sand crocus. 77c, Greater white-toothed shrew.

2016, Feb. 17 Litho. *Perf. 13¼*

540 A84 42p multi 1.25 1.25
541 A84 56p multi 1.60 1.60
542 A84 57p multi 1.60 1.60
543 A84 62p multi 1.75 1.75
544 A84 68p multi 1.90 1.90
545 A84 77p multi 2.25 2.25
a. Souvenir sheet of 6, #540-545 10.50 10.50
Nos. 540-545 (6) 10.35 10.35

Queen Elizabeth II, 90th Birthday A85

Photographs of Queen Elizabeth II from: 43p, Trooping the Color, 2011. 57p, Birthday Parade, 2012. 58p, Birthday Parade, 2013. 64p, Trooping the Color, 2014. 70p, Birthday Parade, 2015. 78p, Sept. 9, 2015 (day she became longest-reigning British monarch).

2016, May 25 Litho. *Perf. 14¼x14*

546 A85 43p sil & multi 1.25 1.25
a. Booklet pane of 4 5.00 —
547 A85 57p sil & multi 1.75 1.75
a. Booklet pane of 4 7.00 —
548 A85 58p sil & multi 1.75 1.75
a. Booklet pane of 4 7.00 —
549 A85 64p sil & multi 1.90 1.90
a. Booklet pane of 4 7.75 —
550 A85 70p sil & multi 2.00 2.00
a. Booklet pane of 4 8.00 —
551 A85 78p sil & multi 2.25 2.25
a. Booklet pane of 4 9.00 —
Complete booklet, #546a, 547a, 548a, 549a, 550a, 551a 44.00
Nos. 546-551 (6) 10.90 10.90

Battle of Hastings, 950th Anniv. A86

Designs: 43p, William the Conqueror lands in England at Pevensey. 57p, King Harold II rides south from the Stamford Bridge. 58p, Norman knights charge the Saxon shield wall. 64p, Saxon fyrd shield breaks to attack fleeing Bretons. 70p, William lifts helmet to show he's still alive. 78p, Harold hard-pressed in shield wall.

2016, Sept. 14 Litho. *Perf. 13x13½*

552 A86 43p multi 1.10 1.10
553 A86 57p multi 1.50 1.50
554 A86 58p multi 1.50 1.50
555 A86 64p multi 1.75 1.75
556 A86 70p multi 1.90 1.90
557 A86 78p multi 2.00 2.00
a. Souvenir sheet of 6, #552-557 9.75 9.75

Christmas — A87

Snowflake and: 38p, Holly. 43p, Christmas tree. 57p, Gifts. 58p, Santa Claus. 64p, Reindeer and Christmas ornaments. 70p, Snowman. 78p, Stars.

Litho. With Foil Application

2016, Nov. 8 *Perf. 13¼*

Self-Adhesive

558 A87 38p sil & dp blue 1.00 1.00
559 A87 43p dp blue & sil 1.10 1.10
560 A87 57p sil & dp blue 1.50 1.50
561 A87 58p dp blue & sil 1.50 1.50
562 A87 64p sil & dp blue 1.60 1.60
563 A87 70p dp blue & sil 1.75 1.75
564 A87 78p sil & dp blue 2.00 2.00
Nos. 558-564 (7) 10.45 10.45

Map of Alderney and Burhou, by Addison Warren A88

Designs: 43p, Braye Bay area. 57p, Alderney Aerodrome area. 58p, St. Anne area. 64p, Northeastern area. 70p, Burhou and other islands. 78p, Entire map.
£3, Area south of Braye Bay and east of St. Anne, vert.

2017, Feb. 1 Litho. *Perf. 13½*

565 A88 43p brz & multi 1.10 1.10
566 A88 57p brz & multi 1.50 1.50
567 A88 58p brz & multi 1.50 1.50
568 A88 64p brz & multi 1.60 1.60
569 A88 70p brz & multi 1.75 1.75
570 A88 78p brz & multi 2.00 2.00
Nos. 565-570 (6) 9.45 9.45

Souvenir Sheet

Perf. 14

571 A88 £3 brz & multi 7.75 7.75

No. 571 contains one 29x43mm stamp.

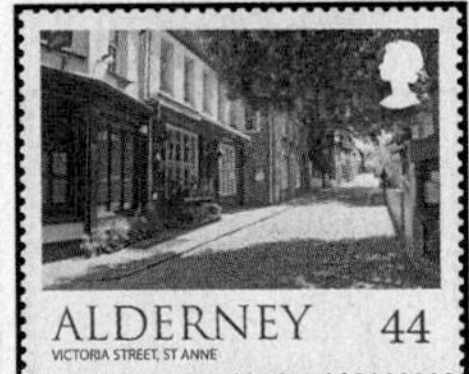

Tourist Attractions A89

Designs: 44p, Victoria Street, St. Anne. 59p, Château à l'Etoc and Saye Beach. 60p, Alderney Week, St. Anne. 73p, Pepperpot, Essex Castle. 80p, Alderney Railway, Mannez Quarry. 90p, Mannez Lighthouse, Quesnard Point.

2017, May 17 Litho. *Perf. 14x14¼*

572 A89 44p multi 1.10 1.10
a. Booklet pane of 4 4.50 —
573 A89 59p multi 1.50 1.50
a. Booklet pane of 4 6.00 —
574 A89 60p multi 1.60 1.60
a. Booklet pane of 4 6.50 —
575 A89 73p multi 1.90 1.90
a. Booklet pane of 4 7.75 —
576 A89 80p multi 2.10 2.10
a. Booklet pane of 4 8.50 —
577 A89 90p multi 2.40 2.40
a. Booklet pane of 4 9.75 —
Complete booklet, #572a, 573a, 574a, 575a, 576a, 577a 43.00
Nos. 572-577 (6) 10.60 10.60

Views of August 21, 2017 Solar Eclipse From Various Cities — A90

View of eclipse from: 44p, Vancouver, B.C., Canada. 59p, Miami, Florida. 60p, Hamilton, Bermuda. 73p, Dakar, Senegal. 80p, St. Anne, Alderney. 90p, Anadyr, Russia.

2017, July 19 Litho. *Perf. 13¾x13¼*

No.	Type	Description	Unused	Used
578	A90	44p multi	1.25	1.25
579	A90	59p multi	1.60	1.60
580	A90	60p multi	1.60	1.60
581	A90	73p multi	2.00	2.00
582	A90	80p multi	2.10	2.10
583	A90	90p multi	2.40	2.40
a.		Souvenir sheet of 6, #578-583	11.00	11.00
		Nos. 578-583 (6)	10.95	10.95

Portions of the vignettes of Nos. 578-573 were printed with a circle of thermochromic ink, which when warmed, allows the moon to be seen.

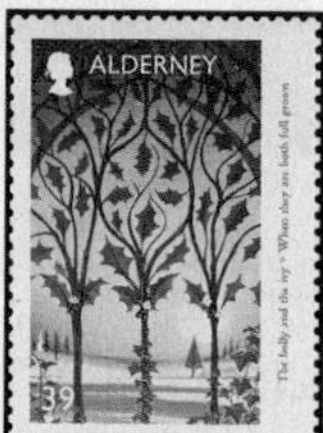

Christmas — A91

Lyrics from "The Holly and the Ivy" and: 39p, Holly on trees. 44p, Bird, holly on tree. 59p, Deers standing in forest. 60p, Deers running in forest. 73p, Pipe organ. 80p, Choir holding candles. 90p, Madonna and Child.

2017, Nov. 8 Litho. *Perf. 13¼x13*

No.	Type	Description	Unused	Used
584	A91	39p multi	1.10	1.10
585	A91	44p multi	1.25	1.25
586	A91	59p multi	1.60	1.60
587	A91	60p multi	1.60	1.60
588	A91	73p multi	2.00	2.00
589	A91	80p multi	2.25	2.25
590	A91	90p multi	2.50	2.50
		Nos. 584-590 (7)	12.30	12.30

Wombles, Characters From Children's Books by Elizabeth Beresford A92

Design and inscription: (44p), Uncle Bulgaria (Local Letter). (59p), Bungo and Orinoco (UK Letter). (60p), Madame Cholet (Local Large Letter). (73p), Uncle Bulgaria and Cousin Yellowstone (EUR Letter). (80p), Tobermoy and Bungo (ROW Letter). (90p), Tomsk (UK Large Letter).

Perf. 13¾x13¼

2018, Feb. 14 Litho.

No.	Type	Description	Unused	Used
591	A92	(44p) multi	1.25	1.25
592	A92	(59p) multi	1.75	1.75
593	A92	(60p) multi	1.75	1.75
594	A92	(73p) multi	2.10	2.10
595	A92	(80p) multi	2.25	2.25
596	A92	(90p) multi	2.60	2.60
a.		Souvenir sheet of 6, #591-596	12.00	12.00
		Nos. 591-596 (6)	11.70	11.70

Souvenir Sheet

View From the Lover's Chair — A93

No. 597 — Rocks, hearts and inscription: a, "à jomais dàns m'n tchoeur." b, "de mé à té."

2018, Feb. 14 Litho. *Perf. 13¾*

No.	Type	Description	Unused	Used
597	A93	Sheet of 2	3.50	3.50
a.-b.		59p Either single	1.75	1.75

Spring 2018 Stampex Philatelic Exhibition, London.

Coronation of Queen Elizabeth II, 65th Anniv. — A94

Photograph of Queen Elizabeth II from: 46p, 2001. 62p, 1954. 63p, 2012. 76p, 1971. 85p, 2002. 94p, 2006.

2018, May 23 Litho. *Perf. 13¼x13¾*

No.	Type	Description	Unused	Used
598	A94	46p multi	1.25	1.25
599	A94	62p multi	1.75	1.75
600	A94	63p multi	1.75	1.75
601	A94	76p multi	2.00	2.00
602	A94	85p multi	2.25	2.25
603	A94	94p multi	2.50	2.50
		Nos. 598-603 (6)	11.50	11.50

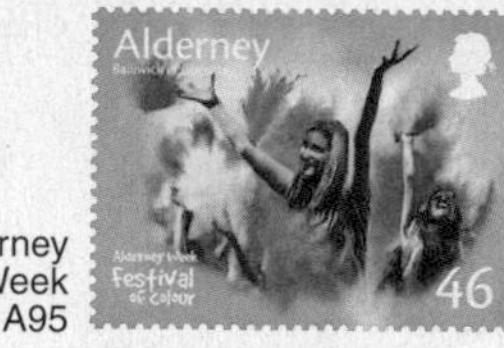

Alderney Week A95

Designs: 46p, Festival of Color. 62p, Cavalcade. 63p, Man-powered flight. 76p, Decorated float. 85p, Daft rafts. 94p, Torchlight parade.

2018, Aug. 1 Litho. *Perf. 13½x13¼*

No.	Type	Description	Unused	Used
604	A95	46p multi	1.25	1.25
a.		Booklet pane of 4	5.00	—
605	A95	62p multi	1.60	1.60
a.		Booklet pane of 4	6.50	—
606	A95	63p multi	1.75	1.75
a.		Booklet pane of 4	7.00	—
607	A95	76p multi	2.00	2.00
a.		Booklet pane of 4	8.00	—
608	A95	85p multi	2.25	2.25
a.		Booklet pane of 4	9.00	—
609	A95	94p multi	2.50	2.50
a.		Booklet pane of 4	10.00	—
		Complete booklet, #604a, 605a, 606a, 607a, 608a, 609a	46.00	
		Nos. 604-609 (6)	11.35	11.35

Scenes From *A Christmas Carol*, by Charles Dickens (1812-70) A96

Designs: 41p, Bob Cratchit and Tiny Tim. 46p, Bob Cratchit and Ebenezer Scrooge. 62p, Visit of Marley's ghost. 63p, Ghost of Christmas Past. 76p, Ghost of Christmas Present. 85p, Ghost of Christmas Future. 94p, Christmas celebration.

2018, Nov. 8 Litho. *Perf. 13¼*

No.	Type	Description	Unused	Used
610	A96	41p multi	1.10	1.10
611	A96	46p multi	1.25	1.25
612	A96	62p multi	1.60	1.60
613	A96	63p multi	1.75	1.75
614	A96	76p multi	2.00	2.00
615	A96	85p multi	2.25	2.25
616	A96	94p multi	2.50	2.50
		Nos. 610-616 (7)	12.45	12.45

Christmas.

JERSEY

jər-zē

LOCATION — Island in the English Channel

GOVT. — Dependent territory (bailiwick) of the British Crown

AREA — 45 sq. mi.

POP. — 89,721 (1999 est.)

CAPITAL — St. Helier

Following the establishment of the British General Post Office as a public corporation on October 1, 1969, the post office of the Bailiwick of Jersey became a separate entity and British postage stamps ceased to be valid.

Catalogue values for unused stamps in this country are for Never Hinged items.

British Regional Issue

A1

Royal Mace and Arms of Jersey — A2

Perf. 15x14

1958-69 Photo. Wmk. 322

No.	Type	Description	Unused	Used
1	A1	2½p rose red ('64)	.35	.25
2	A2	3p light purple	.35	.25
p.		Phosphor. ('67)	.25	.25
3	A2	4p ultra ('66)	.35	.25
p.		Phosphor. ('67)	.25	.25

Unwmk.

No.	Type	Description	Unused	Used
4	A2	4p olive brown ('68)	.25	.25
5	A2	4p brt red ('69)	.25	.25
6	A2	5p dark blue ('68)	.25	.25
		Nos. 1-6 (6)	1.80	1.50

Nos. 4-6 are phosphorescent.

Sold to the general public only at post offices within Jersey, but valid for postage throughout Great Britain.

See also Great Britain Nos. 269-270, which were sold only in the Channel Islands and at a few philatelic windows in Great Britain, and may be considered to be precursors to the regional issues.

Bailiwick Issues

Elizabeth Castle and Queen Elizabeth II — A3

Queen Elizabeth II — A4

Designs (Queen Elizabeth II and): 1p, La Hougue Bie (prehistoric tomb). 2p, Portelet Bay. 3p, La Corbière Lighthouse. 4p, Mont Orgueil by night. 5p, Arms of Jersey and Royal Mace. 6p, Jersey cow. 9p, 1sh6p, Map of English Channel with Jersey. 1sh, Mont Orgueil. 2sh6p, Airport. 5sh, Legislative Chamber. 10sh, Royal Court. £1, Queen Elizabeth II, photograph by Cecil Beaton.

Perf. 14½

1969, Oct. 1 Photo. Unwmk.

No.	Type	Description	Unused	Used
7	A3	½p ocher & multi	.25	.25
8	A3	1p brown & multi	.25	.25
a.		Booklet pane of 1	.35	
b.		Booklet pane of 2	.90	
9	A3	2p multicolored	.25	.25
10	A3	3p dp blue & multi	.25	.25
11	A3	4p multicolored	.25	.25
a.		Booklet pane of 1	.60	
		Complete booklet, 4 #8a, 5 #11a	2.00	
b.		Booklet pane of 2	1.10	
12	A3	5p multicolored	.25	.25
a.		Booklet pane of 2	1.75	
		Complete booklet, 3 each #8b & 12a, 6 #11b	17.50	
		Complete booklet, 2 #8b, 7 #11b, 6 #12a	12.50	
13	A3	6p multicolored	.25	.25
14	A3	9p multicolored	.25	*.25*
15	A3	1sh lilac & multi	.25	.25
16	A3	1sh6p green & multi	.85	.85
17	A4	1sh9p multicolored	1.20	1.20

Perf. 12

No.	Type	Description	Unused	Used
18	A3	2sh6p multicolored	1.75	1.75
19	A3	5sh multicolored	7.00	7.00
20	A3	10sh gray & multi	15.00	15.00
a.		10sh green & multi (error)	*5,500.*	
21	A4	£1 tan & multi	2.00	2.00
		Nos. 7-21 (15)	30.05	30.05

A second post-1971 printing of No. 21 shows the background drapery less purple and more blue. Value, $3.

See Nos. 34-48, 107-109.

Jersey Post Office First Day Cover A5

1969, Oct. 1 *Perf. 14¼*

No.	Type	Description	Unused	Used
22	A5	4p multicolored	.25	.25
23	A5	5p blue & multi	.25	.25
24	A5	1sh6p brown & multi	.50	*.75*
25	A5	1sh9p emerald & multi	.80	*1.00*
		Nos. 22-25 (4)	1.80	2.25

Inauguration of independent postal service.

Jersey Woman Reaching for Royal Mace, Flags of USSR, US and Great Britain — A6

4p, Lord Coutanche, Bailiff of Jersey, by James Gunn, vert. 5p, Sir Winston Churchill, by D. Van Praag, vert. 1sh9p, Swedish Red Cross ship "Vega."

1970, May 9 Photo. *Perf. 11½*

No.	Type	Description	Unused	Used
26	A6	4p gold & multi	.25	.25
27	A6	5p gold & multi	.25	.25
28	A6	1sh6p gold & multi	.65	.65
29	A6	1sh9p gold & multi	.65	.65
		Nos. 26-29 (4)	1.80	1.80

25th anniv. of Jersey's liberation from the Germans.

"Rags to Riches" Cinderella — A7

Designs (Parade Floats Made of Flowers): 4p, "A Tribute to Enid Blyton," author of children's books. 1sh6p, "Gourmet's Delight." 1sh9p, "We're the Greatest" (ostriches and trees).

1970, July 28 Photo. *Perf. 11½*

No.	Type	Description	Unused	Used
30	A7	4p gold & multi	.25	.25
31	A7	5p gold & multi	.25	.25
32	A7	1sh6p gold & multi	2.50	1.75
33	A7	1sh9p gold & multi	2.50	2.00
		Nos. 30-33 (4)	5.50	4.25

"Battle of Flowers" annual parade.

Decimal Currency Issue Types of 1969 "p" instead of "d"

Designs: ½p, Elizabeth Castle. 1p, La Corbiere Lighthouse. 1½p, Jersey cow. 2p, Mont Orgueil by night. 2½p, Arms of Jersey and Royal Mace. 3p, La Hougue Bie. 3½p, Portelet Bay. 4p, 7½p, Map of English Channel and Jersey. 5p, Mont Orgueil by day. 6p, Martello Tower at Archirondel. 9p, Queen Elizabeth II, by Cecil Beaton. 10p, Airport. 20p, Legislative Chamber. 50p, Royal Court.

1970-75 Photo. *Perf. 14½*

No.	Type	Description	Unused	Used
34	A3	½p ocher & multi ('71)	.25	.25
a.		Booklet pane of 1	.25	
35	A3	1p multicolored ('71)	.25	.25
a.		Booklet pane of 2 ('75)	.25	
b.		Booklet pane of 4 ('75)	.35	

36 A3 1½p multicolored ('71) .25 .25
37 A3 2p multicolored ('71) .25 .25
a. Booklet pane of 1 .25
b. Booklet pane of 2 .35
38 A3 2½p multicolored ('71) .25 .25
a. Booklet pane of 1 .35
Complete booklet, 2 each #34a, 37a, 38a 1.25
b. Booklet pane of 2 .45
Complete booklet,5 #37b, 3 #38b 1.75
Complete booklet,5 #37b, 6 #38b 3.75
Complete booklet, 4 #38b 4.00
39 A3 3p brn & multicolored ('71) .25 .25
a. Booklet pane of 1 ('72) .35
Complete booklet, 3 #34a, 1 #38a, 2 #39a 1.00
b. Booklet pane of 2 ('72) .45
Complete booklet, 5 #39b 4.00
Complete booklet, 4 #38b, 5 #39b 4.00
40 A3 3½p multicolored ('71) .25 .25
a. Booklet pane of 1 ('74) .35
Complete booklet, #39a, 2 #40a 1.00
Complete booklet, #34a, #40a, 2 #39a .60
Complete booklet, 2 #39a, 4 #40a .90
b. Booklet pane of 2 ('74) .50
Complete booklet, 3 #39b, 6 #40b 3.00
41 A3 4p multicolored ('71) .25 .25
a. Booklet pane of 2 ('75) .50
b. Booklet pane of 4 ('75) .75
42 A3 5p lilac & multi ('71) .25 .25
a. Booklet pane of 2 ('75) .55
Complete booklet, 3 each #35a, #41a, 2 #42a 2.75
b. Booklet pane of 4 ('75) .95
Complete booklet, 2 each #35b, 41b, 3 #42b 5.00
43 A3 6p green & multi ('71) .25 .25
44 A3 7½p multicolored ('71) .25 .25
45 A4 9p multicolored ('71) .35 .35

Perf. 12

46 A3 10p multicolored .40 .40
47 A3 20p multicolored .75 .75
48 A3 50p multicolored 1.50 1.50
Nos. 34-48 (15) 5.75 5.75

See also Nos. 107-109.

White-eared Pheasant — A8

2½p, Thick-billed parrots, vert. 7½p, Ursine colobus monkeys, vert. 9p, Ring-tailed lemurs.

1971, Mar. 9 Photo. *Perf. 11½*

49 A8 2p deep plum & multi .25 .25
50 A8 2½p dark gray & multi .25 .25
51 A8 7½p olive & multi 1.75 1.75
52 A8 9p vio blue & multi 4.00 4.00
Nos. 49-52 (4) 6.25 6.25

Jersey Wildlife Preservation Trust.
See Nos. 65-68.

British Legion Emblem A9

2½p, Poppy field & poppy emblem. 7½p, Jack Counter (1899-1970) & Victoria Cross. 9p, Flags of France & Great Britain.

1971, June 15 Litho. *Perf. 14½*

53 A9 2p multicolored .25 .25
54 A9 2½p multicolored .25 .25
55 A9 7½p multicolored 1.10 1.10
56 A9 9p multicolored 1.10 1.10
Nos. 53-56 (4) 2.70 2.70

50th anniversary of the British Legion.

English Fleet in Channel, by Peter Monamy A10

Paintings by Jersey Artists: 2p, Tante Elizabeth (women in farm kitchen), by Edmund Blampied, vert. 7½p, Boyhood of Raleigh (man and boys at seashore), by Sir John Millais. 9p, The Blind Beggar (old man and girl), by W. W. Ouless, vert.

1971, Oct. 5 Photo. *Perf. 11½*

57 A10 2p gold & multi .25 .25
58 A10 2½p gold & multi .25 .25
59 A10 7½p gold & multi .95 .95
60 A10 9p gold & multi 1.25 1.25
Nos. 57-60 (4) 2.70 2.70

Jersey Fern — A11

Jersey Wild Flowers: 5p, Thrift. 7½p, Orchid (laxiflora). 9p, Viper's bugloss.

1972, Jan. 18
Flowers in Natural Colors

61 A11 3p brown & blk .25 .25
62 A11 5p lt blue & blk .30 .25
63 A11 7½p lilac & blk 1.00 1.00
64 A11 9p green & blk 1.10 1.10
Nos. 61-64 (4) 2.65 2.60

Wildlife Type of 1971

2½p, Cheetahs. 3p, Rothschild's mynahs, vert. 7½p, Spectacled bear. 9p, Tuatara reptiles.

1972, Mar. 17 Photo. *Perf. 11½*
Queen's Head in Gold

65 A8 2½p Prus blue & multi .30 .25
66 A8 3p dk pur & multi .25 .25
67 A8 7½p yel bis & multi .50 .50
68 A8 9p multicolored .85 1.75
Nos. 65-68 (4) 1.00 2.75

Jersey Wildlife Preservation Trust.

Jersey Royal Artillery Shako — A12

3p, 2nd North Regiment. 7½p, South West Regiment. 9p, 3rd (South) Light Infantry.

1972, June 27

69 A12 2½p shown .25 .25
70 A12 3p multicolored .25 .25
71 A12 7½p multicolored .30 .30
72 A12 9p multicolored .50 .50
Nos. 69-72 (4) 1.30 1.30

Royal Jersey Militia shakos of 19th century.

Princess Anne — A13

Designs: 3p, Queen Elizabeth II and Prince Philip, horiz. 7½p, Prince Charles. 20p, Queen Elizabeth II and family, horiz.

1972, Nov. 1 Photo. Perf. 11½

73	A13	2½p citron & multi	.25	.25
74	A13	3p rose & multi	.25	.25
75	A13	7½p blue & multi	.25	.25
76	A13	20p gray & multi	.25	.25
		Nos. 73-76 (4)	1.00	1.00

25th anniversary of the marriage of Queen Elizabeth II and Prince Philip.

Silver Wine and Christening Cups, 18th Century A14

Designs: 3p, Gold torque, Bronze Age, vert. 7½p, Seal of Charles II, 1659, vert. 9p, Armorican (Brittany) coins, c. 55 B.C.

1973, Jan. 23 Photo. Perf. 11½

77	A14	2½p ultra & multi	.25	.25
78	A14	3p dp car & multi	.25	.25
79	A14	7½p org & multi	.25	.25
80	A14	9p blue & multi	.25	.25
		Nos. 77-80 (4)	1.00	1.00

Cent. of the Jersey Soc. Designs are from exhibits in the Soc. museum in St. Helier.

Balloon, Letter to Jersey from Siege of Paris, 1870 — A15

5p, Astra seaplane, 1912. 7½p, Supermarine Sea Eagle, 1923. 9p, De Havilland DH86, 1933.

1973, May 16 Photo. Perf. 11½

81	A15	3p brt blue & multi	.25	.25
82	A15	5p blue grn & multi	.25	.25
83	A15	7½p ultra & multi	.25	.25
84	A15	9p vio blue & multi	.35	.35
		Nos. 81-84 (4)	1.10	1.10

Aviation history connected with Jersey before 1939.

19th Century Locomotives A16

1973, Aug. 6 Photo. Perf. 11½

85	A16	2½p North Western	.25	.25
86	A16	3p Calvados	.25	.25
87	A16	7½p Carteret	.30	.30
88	A16	9p Caesarea	.35	.35
		Nos. 85-88 (4)	1.15	1.15

Centenary of Jersey Eastern Railroad.

Princess Anne and Mark Phillips A17

1973, Nov. 14 Photo. Perf. 11½

89	A17	3p lt blue & multi	.25	.25
90	A17	20p pink & multi	.60	*.80*

Wedding of Princess Anne and Capt. Mark Phillips, Nov. 14, 1973.

Spider Crab A18

1973, Nov. 15 Photo. Perf. 11½

91	A18	2½p shown	.25	.25
92	A18	3p Conger eel	.25	.25
93	A18	7½p Lobster	.25	.25
94	A18	20p Ormer	.25	.25
		Nos. 91-94 (4)	1.00	1.00

Jersey Spring Flowers — A19

1974, Feb. 13 Photo. Perf. 12x11½

95	A19	3p Freesias	.25	.25
96	A19	5½p Anemones	.25	.25
97	A19	8p Carnations & gladioli	.25	.25
98	A19	10p Daffodils & iris	.25	.25
		Nos. 95-98 (4)	1.00	1.00

First Letter Box, Letter with 1852 Cancel A20

UPU Cent.: 3p, Postmen, 1862 and 1969. 5½p, Contemporary pillar box and first day cover of No. 101. 20p, BAC 111 and paddle steamer "Aquila," 1874.

1974, June 7 Photo. Perf. 11½

99	A20	2½p multicolored	.25	.25
100	A20	3p ultra & multi	.25	.25
101	A20	5½p olive & multi	.25	.25
102	A20	20p gray & multi	.25	.25
		Nos. 99-102 (4)	1.00	1.00

John Wesley — A21

Lithographed and Engraved

1974, July 31 Perf. 13½x14

103	A21	3p shown	.25	.25
104	A21	3½p Hillary	.25	.25
105	A21	8p Wace	.25	.25
106	A21	20p Churchill	.25	.25
		Nos. 103-106 (4)	1.00	1.00

Anniversaries: Methodism in Jersey, bicen.; John Wesley, theologian, founder of Methodism. Sesquicentennial of Royal Natl. Lifeboat Institution, Lt. Col. Sir William Hillary, founder. 800th death anniv. of Canon Wace, poet and chronicler. Sir Winston Churchill, birth centenary.

Type of 1969

4½p, Arms of Jersey and Royal Mace. 5½p, Jersey cow. 8p, Mont Orgueil by night.

1974, Oct. 31 Photo. Perf. 14½

107	A3	4½p olive & multi	.25	.25
108	A3	5½p magenta & multi	.25	.25
109	A3	8p yellow & multi	.25	.25
		Nos. 107-109 (3)	.75	.75

English Yacht, 1660, by Peter Monamy A22

Marine paintings by Peter Monamy (d. 1749): 5½p, French ship. 8p, Dutch ship, horiz. 25p, Naval battle, 1662.

1974, Nov. 22 Photo. Perf. 11½

Size: 31x38, 38x31mm

116	A22	3½p gold & multi	.25	.25
117	A22	5½p gold & multi	.25	.25
118	A22	8p gold & multi	.25	.25

Size: 54x25mm

119	A22	25p gold & multi	.50	.50
		Nos. 116-119 (4)	1.25	1.25

Potato Digger — A23

19th cent. farming tools: 3½p, Cider apple crusher. 8p, Six-horse plow. 10p, Hay cart.

1975, Feb. 25 Photo. Perf. 11½

120	A23	3p multicolored	.25	.25
121	A23	3½p multicolored	.25	.25
122	A23	8p multicolored	.25	.25
123	A23	10p multicolored	.25	.25
		Nos. 120-123 (4)	1.00	1.00

Shell Design as Letter "J" — A24

Posters: 8p, Beach umbrella. 10p, Beach chair. 12p, Sand castle with Union Jacks & Jersey flag.

1975, June 8 Photo. Perf. 11½

124	A24	5p multicolored	.25	.25
125	A24	8p multicolored	.25	.25
126	A24	10p multicolored	.25	.25
127	A24	12p multicolored	.25	.25
a.		Souvenir sheet of 4	1.10	1.10
		Nos. 124-127 (4)	1.00	1.00

Tourist publicity. No. 127a contains Nos. 124-127 in continuous design extending into margin.

Queen Mother Elizabeth A25

1975, May 30 Photo. Perf. 11½

128	A25	20p multicolored	.75	.50

Visit of Queen Mother Elizabeth to Jersey.

Common Tern — A26

1975, July 28 Photo. Perf. 11½

129	A26	4p shown	.25	.25
130	A26	5p Storm petrel	.25	.25
131	A26	8p Brent geese	.25	.25
132	A26	25p Shag	.35	.35
		Nos. 129-132 (4)	1.10	1.10

Siskin 3A, 1925 — A27

R.A.F. Planes: 5p, Southampton 1, 1925. 10p, Spitfire 1, 1931. 25p, Gnat T.1, 1962.

1975, Oct. 30 Photo. Perf. 11½

133	A27	4p blue & multi	.25	.25
134	A27	5p lt green & multi	.25	.25
135	A27	10p yellow & multi	.25	.35
136	A27	25p ultra & multi	.35	.35
		Nos. 133-136 (4)	1.10	1.20

Royal Air Force Assoc., Jersey Branch, 50th anniv.

Map of Jersey with 12 Parishes A28

Arms of Trinity and Zoo — A29

Queen Elizabeth II — A30

Arms and scene: 5p, Church of St. Mary. 6p, Grouville, Seymour Tower. 7p, St. Brelade, La Corbière Lighthouse. 8p, Church of St. Saviour. 9p, St. Helier, Elizabeth Castle. 10p, St. Martin, Gorey Harbor. 11p, St. Peter, Jersey Airport. 12p, St. Ouen, Grosnez Castle. 13p, St. John, Bonne Nuit Harbor. 14p, St. Clement and Le Hocq Tower. 15p, St. Lawrence, Morel Farm. 20p, 12 Parishes, view of harbor. 30p, Jersey flag, map of Island. 40p, Postal Administration emblem, PO Headquarters. 50p, Jersey, Parliament and Royal Court. £1, Flag of Lt.-Governor, Government House.

1976-77 Litho. Perf. 14½

Size: 33x23mm

137	A28	½p lt blue & multi	.25	.25
138	A29	1p bister & multi	.25	.25
a.		Bklt. pane of 2 + 2 labels	.80	
b.		Booklet pane of 4	.80	
139	A29	5p rose & multi	.25	.25
a.		Booklet pane of 4	.80	
140	A29	6p vio blue & multi	.25	.25
a.		Booklet pane of 4 ('78)	1.00	
		Complete booklet, #138b, 4 #140a	3.75	
141	A29	7p fawn & multi	.25	.25
a.		Booklet pane of 4	1.10	
		Complete booklet, #138a, 139a, 141a	2.25	
		Complete booklet, #138b, 2 each #139a, 141a	4.00	
142	A29	8p yel grn & multi	.25	.25
a.		Booklet pane of 4 ('78)	1.10	
		Complete booklet, #138b, 3 #142a	3.75	
		Complete booklet, 2 each #138b, 140a, 142a	5.00	
143	A29	9p lil rose & multi	.25	.25
a.		Booklet pane of 4 ('80)	1.25	
		Complete booklet, 3 #138b, 2 each #141a, 143a	5.50	
144	A29	10p ol bis & multi	.25	.25
145	A29	11p bl grn & multi	.25	.25
146	A29	12p org & multi	.25	.25
147	A29	13p blue & multi	.25	.25
148	A29	14p yel org & multi	.40	.40
149	A29	15p vio & multi	.40	.40

Photo.
Perf. 12
Size: 41x26mm, 26x41mm

150 A29 20p gold & multi .45 .45
151 A28 30p gold & multi .55 .55
152 A29 40p gold & multi .80 .80
153 A29 50p gold & multi 1.00 1.00
154 A29 £1 gold & multi 2.75 2.75
155 A30 £2 multicolored ('77) 4.00 4.00
Nos. 137-155 (19) 13.10 13.10

Issue dates: Nos. 137-149, Jan. 29; Nos. 150-154, Aug. 20. No. 155, Nov. 16.
Booklet panes Nos. 138a, 138b, 140a, 142a exist with no date in the bottom selvage, while panes Nos. 138b, 143a and 146a have "May 1980" at bottom.

Sir Walter Raleigh and Old Map of Virginia — A31

US Bicentennial: 7p, Sir George Carteret and old map of New Jersey. 11p, Philippe Dauvergne and ships landing on Long Island. 13p, John Singleton Copley and his "Death of Major Pierson."

1976, May 29 **Photo.** ***Perf. 11½***
160 A31 5p multicolored .25 .25
161 A31 7p multicolored .25 .25
162 A31 11p multicolored .25 .25
163 A31 13p multicolored .35 .35
Nos. 160-163 (4) 1.10 1.10

Dr. Grandin, Central and Southern China Map A32

7p, Yangtze River journey. 11p, On horseback to Chaotung. 13p, Dr. Grandin holding infant.

1976, Nov. 25 **Photo.** ***Perf. 11½***
164 A32 5p multicolored .25 .25
165 A32 7p multicolored .25 .25
166 A32 11p multicolored .25 .25
167 A32 13p multicolored .35 .35
Nos. 164-167 (4) 1.10 1.10

Lilian Mary Grandin (1876-1924), Jersey-born missionary doctor in China.

Queen Wearing St. Edward's Crown — A33

7p, Queen with Jersey Bailiff Sir Alexander Coutanche, 1957. 25p, Portrait, 1976.

1977, Feb. 7 **Photo.** ***Perf. 11½***
168 A33 5p multicolored .25 .25
169 A33 7p multicolored .30 .30
170 A33 25p multicolored .50 .50
Nos. 168-170 (3) 1.05 1.05

25th anniv. of the reign of Elizabeth II.

⅓th sh, 1871 and ⅟₁₂th sh, 1877 A34

Coins: 7p, ⅟₁₂th sh, 1949. 11p, Silver crown, 1966. 13p, Silver £2, 1972.

1977, Mar. 25 **Litho.** ***Perf. 14***
171 A34 5p multicolored .25 .25
172 A34 7p multicolored .25 .25
173 A34 11p multicolored .25 .25
174 A34 13p multicolored .30 .30
Nos. 171-174 (4) 1.05 1.05

Centenary of Jersey's currency reform.

Sir William Weston and Santa Anna, 1530 A35

Designs: 7p, Sir William Drogo and horse-drawn ambulance, 1877. 11p, Duke of Connaught and Jersey ambulance, 1917. 13p, Richard, Duke of Gloucester and ambulance team, 1977.

1977, June 24 **Litho.** ***Perf. 14x13½***
175 A35 5p multicolored .25 .25
176 A35 7p multicolored .25 .25
177 A35 11p multicolored .25 .25
178 A35 13p multicolored .35 .35
Nos. 175-178 (4) 1.10 1.10

St. John Ambulance Assoc. cent. (in GB).

Victoria and Albert Arriving in Jersey, 1846 A36

Designs: 10½p, Victoria College, 1852. 11p, Statue of Sir Galahad near college gate, vert. 13p, College Hall, interior, vert.

1977, Sept. 29 **Litho.** ***Perf. 14½***
179 A36 7p multicolored .25 .25
180 A36 10½p multicolored .25 .25
181 A36 11p multicolored .25 .25
182 A36 13p multicolored .35 .35
Nos. 179-182 (4) 1.10 1.10

Jersey Victoria College, 125th anniv.

Harry Vardon Statuette, Layout of Golf Course A37

Designs: 8p, Golf grip and swing perfected by Vardon. 11p, Vardon's putting grip and stance. 13p, Vardon's British and US Open Golf trophies, his book "The Complete Golfer" and biography.

1978, Feb. 28 **Litho.** ***Perf. 14***
183 A37 6p multicolored .25 .25
184 A37 8p multicolored .25 .25
185 A37 11p multicolored .25 .25
186 A37 13p multicolored .35 .35
Nos. 183-186 (4) 1.10 1.10

Cent. of Royal Jersey Golf Club and to honor Vardon (1870-1937), Jersey-born golfer.

Mont Orgueil — A38

Europa: 8p, St. Aubin's Fort. 10½p, Elizabeth Castle.

1978, May 1 **Photo.** ***Perf. 11½***
187 A38 6p multicolored .25 .25
188 A38 8p multicolored .25 .25
189 A38 10½p multicolored .25 .25
Nos. 187-189 (3) .75 .75

Gaspe Basin, by P. J. Ouless — A39

8p, Early map of Gaspe Peninsula, after Capt. Cook. 10½p, Sailing ship Century. 11p, Early map of Jersey. 13p, St. Aubin's Bay Town & Harbor.

1978, June 9 **Litho.** ***Perf. 14x15***
190 A39 6p multicolored .25 .25
191 A39 8p multicolored .25 .25
192 A39 10½p multicolored .25 .25
193 A39 11p multicolored .25 .25
194 A39 13p multicolored .35 .35
Nos. 190-194 (5) 1.35 1.25

Jersey's links with Canada and for CAPEX, Canadian Intl. Phil. Exhib., Toronto, Ont., June 9-18.

Elizabeth II, Hallmarks of the reign,1953 and 1977 — A40

Design: 8p, Elizabeth II and Prince Philip.

1978, June 27 **Photo.** ***Perf. 11½***
195 A40 8p car, sil & black .25 .25
196 A40 25p blue, sil & black .75 .70

25th anniv. of coronation of Queen Elizabeth II and for Royal visit, June 27.

Mail Cutter — A41

Packets: 8p, Flamer, paddle vessel. 10½p, Diana, screw steamer. 11p, Ibex, steamer. 13p, Caesarea, mini-liner.

1978, Oct. 18 **Litho.** ***Perf. 14½x14***
197 A41 6p multicolored .25 .25
198 A41 8p multicolored .25 .25
199 A41 10½p multicolored .25 .25
200 A41 11p multicolored .25 .25
201 A41 13p multicolored .35 .35
Nos. 197-201 (5) 1.35 1.25

First Government packet between Britain and Jersey, bicentenary.

Jersey Pillar Box, 1860 — A42

Europa: No. 203, Mailman emptying 1979 mailbox. No. 204, Telephone switchboard, c. 1900. No. 205, Technician working on contemporary telecommunications system.

Perf. 14, 14½x15
1979, Mar. 1 **Litho.**
202 A42 8p yellow & blk .25 .25
203 A42 8p carmine & blk .25 .25
a. Pair, #202-203 .50 .50
204 A42 10½p violet & blk .25 .25
205 A42 10½p blue & blk .25 .25
a. Pair, #204-205 .75 .75
Nos. 202-205 (4) 1.00 1.00

Nos. 203a, 205a have continuous design. Both exist perf. 14 and 14½x15.

Soft-colored Jersey Heifer — A43

25p, Milk-laden Jersey cow with 1st Prize ribbon.

Perf. 14 (#206), 13¾ (#207)
1979, Mar. 1
206 A43 6p multicolored .25 .25
Size: 48x31mm
207 A43 25p multicolored .75 .75

30th anniv. of 1st Intl. Conf. of Jersey Breed Societies and 9th Conf. of the World Jersey Cattle Bureau.

Percival Mew Gull — A44

Planes: 8p, De Havilland Chipmunk. 10½p, Druine D-31 Turbulent. 11p, De Havilland Tiger Moth. 13p, North American Harvard Mk. 4.

1979, Apr. 24 **Photo.** ***Perf. 11½***
208 A44 6p multicolored .25 .25
209 A44 8p multicolored .25 .25
210 A44 10½p multicolored .25 .25
211 A44 11p multicolored .25 .25
212 A44 13p multicolored .35 .35
Nos. 208-212 (5) 1.35 1.35

25th International Air Rally.

My First Sermon, by Millais — A45

Paintings by Millais: 10½p, Orphan. 11p, The Princes in the Tower. 25p, Jesus in the Home of His Parents, horiz.

1979, Aug. 13 **Photo.** ***Perf. 11½***
Size: 25x35mm
213 A45 8p multicolored .25 .25
214 A45 10½p multicolored .25 .25
215 A45 11p multicolored .25 .25
Size: 49x30mm
Perf. 12x12½
216 A45 25p multicolored .60 .60
Nos. 213-216 (4) 1.35 1.35

IYC and for John Everett Millais (1829-96).

Waldrapp Ibis — A46

6p, Pink pigeons. 8p, Orangutans. 13p, Lowland gorillas. 15p, Rodrigues fruit bats.

1979, Nov. 8 **Photo.** ***Perf. 11½***
217 A46 6p multicolored .25 .25
218 A46 8p multicolored .25 .25
219 A46 11½p shown .25 .25
220 A46 13p multicolored .35 .35
221 A46 15p multicolored .40 .40
Nos. 217-221 (5) 1.50 1.50

Nos. 217-218, 220-221 vertical.

Mont Orgueil Fortress A47

Fortresses, 300th Anniversary: 11½p, St. Aubin Tower. 13p, Elizabeth. 25p, Map of Jersey showing fortress locations.

1980, Feb. 5 Litho. *Perf. 14½x13½*

222 A47 8p multicolored .25 .25
223 A47 11½p multicolored .25 .25
224 A47 13p multicolored .35 .35

Perf. 13½x14

Size: 37½x26mm

225 A47 25p multicolored .60 .60
Nos. 222-225 (4) 1.45 1.45

Potato Harvest — A48

Royal Jersey Potato Cent.: 7p, Planting potatoes. 17½p, Loading dock, Weighbridge.

1980, May 6 Litho. *Perf. 14*

226 A48 7p multicolored .25 .25
227 A48 15p multicolored .30 .30
228 A48 17½p multicolored .35 .35
Nos. 226-228 (3) .90 .90

A49

Europa (Wax Figures from Mont Orgueil and Elizabeth Castles): No. 229a, Sir Walter Raleigh; 229b, Paul Ivy. No. 230a, Charles II and Sir George Carteret; 230b, Lady Carteret. Pairs in continuous design.

1980, May 6

229 A49 Pair .50 .50
a.-b. 9p any single .25 .25
230 A49 Pair .60 .60
a.-b. 13½p any single .30 .30

Three-lap Motorcycle Race — A51

9p, Intl. road race. 13½p, Motorcycle scrambling. 15p, Sand racing, saloon cars. 17½p, Natl. Hill climb.

1980, July 24 Litho. *Perf. 12*

Granite Paper

231 A51 7p shown .25 .25
232 A51 9p multicolored .25 .25
233 A51 13½p multicolored .25 .25
234 A51 15p multicolored .30 .30
235 A51 17½p multicolored .35 .35
Nos. 231-235 (5) 1.40 1.40

Jersey Motorcycle and Light Car Club, 60th anniv.

"Eye of the Wind" Leaving St. Helier — A52

Designs: 9p, Medical research, Cuna Indians, Panama. 13½p, Exploration, Papua New Guinea. 14p, Capt. Scott's ship, Antarctica. 15p, Conservation, Sulawesi. 17½p, Marine studies.

1980, Oct. 1 Litho. *Perf. 14½*

236 A52 7p multicolored .25 .25
237 A52 9p multicolored .25 .25
238 A52 13½p multicolored .25 .25
239 A52 14p multicolored .30 .30
240 A52 15p multicolored .30 .30
241 A52 17½p multicolored .40 .40
Nos. 236-241 (6) 1.75 1.75

Operation Drake, a two-year, round-the-world scientific expedition in tribute to Royal Geographic Society sesquicentennial.

Armed Soldiers and Wounded Drummer A53

Designs: Details from The Death of Major Peirson, by John Singleton Copley.

1981, Jan. 6 Photo. *Perf. 12½*

Granite Paper

242 A53 7p multicolored .25 .25
243 A53 10p multicolored .25 .25
244 A53 15p multicolored .35 .35
245 A53 17½p multicolored .45 .45
a. Souvenir sheet of 4, #242-245 1.50 1.50
Nos. 242-245 (4) 1.30 1.30

Battle of Jersey bicentenary. No. 245a has continuous design.

De Bagot Family Arms — A54

Jersey, Channel Map A54a

Queen Elizabeth II, by Norman Hepple — A54b

1981-83 Litho. *Perf. 14*

246 A54 ½p shown .25 .25
247 A54 1p De Carteret .25 .25
a. Booklet pane of 6 .35
248 A54 2p La Cloche .25 .25
a. Booklet pane of 6 .55
249 A54 3p Dumaresq .25 .25
a. Booklet pane of 6 .65
250 A54 4p Payn .25 .25
251 A54 5p Janvrin .25 .25
252 A54 6p Poingdestre .25 .25
253 A54 7p Pipon .25 .25
a. Booklet pane of 6 1.90
254 A54 8p Marett .25 .25
a. Booklet pane of 6 ('83) 2.40
255 A54 9p Le Breton .25 .25
256 A54 10p Le Maistre .35 .25
a. Booklet pane of 6 2.75
Complete booklet, 2 #247a, 1 each #249a, 253a, 256a 6.00
Complete booklet, #247a, 248a, 253a, 256a 6.00
257 A54 11p Bisson .35 .25
b. Booklet pane of 6 ('83) 3.25
Complete booklet, #247a, #248a, 254a, 257b 6.00
258 A54 12p Robin .35 .25
259 A54 13p Herault .40 .25
260 A54 14p Messervy .45 .25
261 A54 15p Fiott .50 .30
262 A54 20p Badier .65 .30
263 A54 25p L'Arbalestier .80 .30
264 A54 30p Journeaulx 1.00 .35
265 A54 40p Lempriere 1.10 .50
266 A54 50p D'Auvergne 1.25 .60
267 A54a £1 shown 2.50 1.25

Photo.

Perf. 12½x12

268 A54b £5 multi 12.00 8.00
Nos. 246-268 (23) 24.20 15.35

Issued: Nos. 246-256, 2/24; No. 248a, 12/1; Nos. 257-262, 7/28; Nos. 263-267, 2/23/82; Nos. 254a, 257a, 4/19/83; £5, 11/17/83.

1984-88 *Perf. 15x14*

247b A54 1p ('88) .30 .30
248b A54 2p Bklt. pane of 6 ('86) .65
248c A54 2p ('84) .25 .25
249b A54 3p Bklt. pane of 6 ('84) .75
249c A54 3p ('84) .25 .25
250a A54 4p Bklt. pane of 6 ('87) 1.00
250b A54 4p ('86) .25 .25
251a A54 5p ('86) .30 .25
252a A54 6p ('86) .35 .35
255a A54 9p Bklt. pane of 6 ('84) 2.50
255b A54 9p ('84) .40 .40
256b A54 10p Bklt. pane of 6 ('86) 1.50
256c A54 10p ('86) .40 .30
257a A54 11p Bklt. pane of 6 ('87) 2.00
257c A54 11p ('87) .45 .45
258a A54 12p Bklt. pane of 6 ('84) 3.00
Complete booklet, 2 each #249b, 255a, 1 #258a 14.50
258b A54 12p ('84) .50 .50
259a A54 13p ('84) .50 .25
260a A54 14p Bklt. pane of 6 ('86) 2.50
Complete booklet, 2 each #248b, 256b, 1 #260a 9.50
260b A54 14p ('84) .40 .25
261a A54 15p ('87) .45 .45
261b A54 15p Bklt. pane of 6 ('87) 2.50
Complete booklet, 2 each #250a, 257a, 1 #261b 11.00
262a A54 20p ('86) .85 .60
264a A54 30p ('86) 1.00 1.00
265a A54 40p ('87) 1.50 1.50
266a A54 50p ('87) 2.00 2.00

Issued: Nos. 251a, 252a, 262a, 264a, 3/4.

No. 247a dated "February 1981," "December 1981" or "April 1983"; No. 248a dated "December 1981" or "April 1983"; Nos. 253a, 256a dated "February 1981" or "December 1981;" No. 250a dated "April 1987" or "May 1988." No. 258a dated "April 1984" or "May 1988."

See Nos. 381-388.

Knight of Hamby Killing the Dragon A55

Europa (Legends): 10p, La Hougue Bie. 18p, Easter Voyage of St. Brelade. No. 272, Servant killing Knight of Hamby. No. 273, Shipwreck of St. Brelade. No. 274, Whale, ships' departure.

1981, Apr. 7 *Perf. 14½*

271 A55 10p multicolored .25 .25
272 A55 10p multicolored .25 .25
a. Pair, #271-272 .60 .60
273 A55 18p multicolored .30 .30
274 A55 18p multicolored .30 .30
a. Pair, #273-274 1.00 1.00
Nos. 271-274 (4) 1.10 1.10

Royal Square by Gaslight A56

1981, May 22 Photo. *Perf. 12*

Granite Paper

275 A56 7p The Harbor .25 .25
276 A56 10p The Quay .25 .25
277 A56 18p shown .40 .40
278 A56 22p Halkett Place .45 .45
279 A56 25p Central Market .65 .65
Nos. 275-279 (5) 2.00 2.00

Gas light sesquicentennial.

Prince Charles and Lady Diana A57

1981, July 28 Photo. *Perf. 12*

Granite Paper

280 A57 10p multicolored .25 .25
281 A57 25p multicolored 1.00 1.00

Royal Wedding.

Christmas Tree, Royal Square, St. Helier — A58

10p, East window, St. Helier's Church, choir. 18p, Boxing Day, Jersey Drag Hunt.

1981, Sept. 29 Litho. *Perf. 14½*

282 A58 7p shown .25 .25
283 A58 10p multicolored .25 .25
284 A58 18p multicolored .45 .45
Nos. 282-284 (3) .95 .95

Christmas 1981.

Europa 1982 — A59

Designs: Maps showing formation of Channel Islands resulting from rise in sea level.

1982, Apr. 20 Litho. *Perf. 14½*

285 A59 11p 16,000 BC .25 .25
286 A59 11p 10,000 BC, vert. .25 .25
287 A59 19½p 7,000 BC, vert. .50 .50
288 A59 19½p 4,000 BC .50 .50
Nos. 285-288 (4) 1.50 1.50

Rollon Duke of Normandy, William the Conqueror, Clameur de Haro (Plea of Injunction) — A60

Links with France: No. 290, Kings John and Philippe Auguste, Siege of Rouen. No. 291, Jean Martell (1694-1753), brandy merchant. No. 292, Victor Hugo. No. 293, Pierre Teilhard de Chardin (1881-1955), theologian. No. 294, Charles Rey (1897-1981), meteorologist.

1982, June 11 Litho. *Perf. 14*

289 A60 8p multicolored .25 .25
290 A60 8p multicolored .25 .25
a. Bklt. pane of 4+label, 2 each #289-290 1.00 1.00
b. Pair, #289-290 .50 .50
291 A60 11p multicolored .30 .25
292 A60 11p multicolored .30 .25
a. Bklt. pane of 4+label, 2 each #291-292 1.50 1.50
b. Pair, #291-292 .70 .70
293 A60 19½p multicolored .45 .30
294 A60 19½p multicolored .45 .30
a. Bklt. pane of 4+label, 2 each #293-294 2.25 2.25
b. Pair, #293-294 1.00 1.00
Complete booklet, 2 each #290a, 292a, 294a 10.00
Nos. 289-294 (6) 2.00 1.60

Issue date: Nos. 290a-294a, Sept. 7. Two versions of Nos. 290a, 292a and 294a exist: the label is inscribed in English or French.

Scouting Year A61

Designs: 8p, Sir William Smith (Boys Brigade founder). 11p, Liberation parade, 1945, vert. 24p, Boys Brigade annual display, 1903. 26p, The Baden-Powells, 1924, vert. 29p, Scouts.

1982, Nov. 18 Photo. Perf. 12
Granite Paper

295 A61 8p multicolored .25 .25
296 A61 11p multicolored .25 .25
297 A61 24p multicolored .50 .50
298 A61 26p multicolored .65 .65
299 A61 29p multicolored .85 .85
Nos. 295-299 (5) 2.50 2.50

Port Egmont A62

250th Birth Anniv. of Capt. Philippe de Carteret (1733-97): 18th cent. engravings — 11p, Dolphin, Swallow. 19½p, Discovering Pitcairn Island. 24p, English Cove, New Ireland. 26p, Sinking pirate ship. 29p, Endymion.

1983, Feb. 15 Litho. Perf. 14¼

300 A62 8p shown .25 .25
301 A62 11p multicolored .30 .25
302 A62 19½p multicolored .50 .40
303 A62 24p multicolored .55 .50
304 A62 26p multicolored .65 .50
305 A62 29p multicolored .80 .65
Nos. 300-305 (6) 3.05 2.55

No. 19 — A63

Royal Mace — A64

1983, Apr. 19 Litho.

306 A63 11p shown .30 .30
307 A64 11p shown .30 .30
a. Pair, #306-307 1.00 1.00
308 A63 19½p No. 20a .40 .40
309 A64 19½p Bailiff's seal .40 .40
a. Pair, #308-309 1.10 1.10
Nos. 306-309 (4) 1.40 1.40

Europa.

World Communications Year — A65

1st Postmaster Charles William LeGeyt (1733-1827): 8p, Commanding Grenadier Co., 25th Foot, Battle of Minden, 1759. 11p, London-Weymouth mail coach. 24p, PO Mail Packet attacked by French privateer. 26p, Hue St. PO. 29p, St. Helier Harbor.

1983, June 21 Litho. Perf. 14

310 A65 8p multicolored .25 .25
311 A65 11p multicolored .30 .30
312 A65 24p multicolored .55 .55
313 A65 26p multicolored .65 .65
314 A65 29p multicolored .80 .80
Nos. 310-314 (5) 2.55 2.55

Intl. Assoc. of French-Speaking Parliamentarians 1983 General Assembly — A66

1983, June 21 Perf. 15

315 A66 19½p multicolored .70 .70

Cardinal Newman, by Walter William Ouless (1848-1933) A67

11p, M. De Cazotte and his Daughter. 20½p, Thomas Hardy. 31p, David with the Head of Goliath.

1983, Sept. 20 Photo. Perf. 11½

316 A67 8p shown .25 .25
317 A67 11p multicolored .40 .40
318 A67 20½p multicolored .60 .60

Size: 41x34mm

319 A67 31p multicolored .80 .80
Nos. 316-319 (4) 2.05 2.05

Jersey Wildlife Preservation Trust — A68

9p, Golden Lion Tamarin. 12p, Snow Leopard. 20½p, Jamaican Boa. 26p, Round Island Gecko. 28p, Coscoroba Swan. 31p, St. Lucia Parrot.

1984, Jan. 17 Litho. Perf. 14

320 A68 9p multicolored .25 .25
321 A68 12p multicolored .25 .25
322 A68 20½p multicolored .60 .60
323 A68 26p multicolored .75 .75
324 A68 28p multicolored .80 .80
325 A68 31p multicolored 1.00 1.00
Nos. 320-325 (6) 3.65 3.65

Europa 1984 (25th Anniv.) — A69

1984, Mar. 12 Perf. 14½x15

326 A69 9p multicolored .30 .30
327 A69 12p multicolored .35 .35
328 A69 20½p multicolored .55 .55
Nos. 326-328 (3) 1.20 1.20

Souvenir Sheet

Jersey Links with the Commonwealth — A70

1984, Mar. 12 Perf. 15x14½

329 A70 75p multicolored 2.50 2.50

Commonwealth Postal Administrations Conf.

Royal Natl. Lifeboat Institution Centenary A71

Rescue Scenes (Lifeboats and Ships): No. 330, Sarah Brooshoft, Demie de Pas Light. No. 331, Hearts of Oak, Maurice Georges. No. 332, Elizabeth Rippon, Hanna. No. 333, Elizabeth Rippon, Santa Maria. No. 334, Elizabeth Rippon, Bacchus. No. 335, Thomas James King, Cythara.

1984, June 1 Litho. Perf. 14½

330 A71 9p multicolored .25 .25
331 A71 9p multicolored .25 .25
332 A71 12p multicolored .35 .35
333 A71 12p multicolored .35 .35
334 A71 20½p multicolored .60 .60
335 A71 20½p multicolored .60 .60
Nos. 330-335 (6) 2.40 2.40

40th Anniv. of Intl. Civil Aviation Org. A72

9p, Bristol Type 170. 12p, Airspeed AS-57 Ambassador 2. 26p, De Havilland Heron 1B, De Havilland DH89A Dragon Rapide, 31p,

1984, July 24 Litho. Perf. 14
Granite Paper

336 A72 9p multicolored .25 .25
337 A72 12p multicolored .35 .35
338 A72 26p multicolored .75 .75
339 A72 31p multicolored 1.00 1.00
Nos. 336-339 (4) 2.35 2.35

Robinson Crusoe, by John Alexander Gilfillan (1793-1864) — A73

"Links with Australia" paintings by J.A. Gilfillan: 12p, Edinburgh Castle. 20½p, Maori Village. 26p, Australian Landscape. 28p, Waterhouse's Corner, Adelaide. 31p, Capt. Cook at Botany Bay

1984, Sept. 21 Photo. Perf. 11½

340 A73 9p shown .25 .25
341 A73 12p multicolored .30 .25
342 A73 20½p multicolored .60 .60
343 A73 26p multicolored .75 .75
344 A73 28p multicolored .85 .85
345 A73 31p multicolored .85 .85
Nos. 340-345 (6) 3.60 3.55

Christmas 1984 — A74

1984, Nov. 15 Photo. Perf. 12x11½

346 A74 9p St. Helier orchid .30 .30
347 A74 12p Mt. Bingham orchid .60 .60

Ship Paintings by Philip John Ouless (1817-85) — A75

1985, Feb. 26 Photo. Perf. 14x14½

348 A75 9p Hebe, 1874 .25 .25
349 A75 12p Gaspe .30 .30
350 A75 22p London, 1856 .60 .60
351 A75 31p Rambler .90 .90
352 A75 34p Elizabeth Castle 1.10 1.10
Nos. 348-352 (5) 3.15 3.15

Europa 1985 A76

Performing Arts: 10p, John Ireland, composer (1879-1962). 13p, Ivy St. Helier, actress (1886-1971). 22p, Claude Debussy, composer.

1985, Apr. 23 Litho. Perf. 14

353 A76 10p multicolored .35 .35
354 A76 13p multicolored .45 .45
355 A76 22p multicolored .80 .80
Nos. 353-355 (3) 1.60 1.60

Intl. Youth Year — A77

10p, Girls' Brigade. 13p, Girl Guides. 29p, Jersey Youth Service. 31p, Sea Cadet Corps. 34p, Air Training Corps.

1985, May 30 Litho. Perf. 14½

356 A77 10p multicolored .35 .35
357 A77 13p multicolored .40 .40
358 A77 29p multicolored .80 .80
359 A77 31p multicolored .90 .90
360 A77 34p multicolored 1.10 1.10
Nos. 356-360 (5) 3.55 3.55

Railway History A78

10p, Duke of Normandy, Cheapside. 13p, Saddletank, First Tower. 22p, La Moye, Millbrook. 29p, St. Helier's, St. Aubin. 34p, St. Aubyns, Corbiere.

1985, July 16 Photo. Perf. 12x11½

361 A78 10p multicolored .35 .35
362 A78 13p multicolored .45 .45
363 A78 22p multicolored .80 .80
364 A78 29p multicolored 1.00 1.00
365 A78 34p multicolored 1.10 1.10
Nos. 361-365 (5) 3.70 3.70

Centenary of Jersey's first train from St. Helier to Corbiere.

Huguenot Heritage A79

300th anniv. of revocation of the Edict of Nantes (religious tolerance) by King Louis XIV of France: No. 366, James Hemery (1814-1849), Dean of Jersey, Rector of St. Helier, Memorial window, St. Helier Town Church. No. 367, Francis Henry Jeune, Baron St. Helier, law lord and junior counsel in the Tichbourne case, houses of Parliament, Westminster. No. 368, Francois Voisin, merchant, Great Fair, Nijni-Novgorod, Russia. No. 369, Pierre Amiraux, silversmith, silver coffee pot, pitcher. No. 370, George Henry Ingouville, Victoria Cross recipient, Naval Battle of Viborg. No. 371, Robert Brohier, co-founder of Schweppes soft-drink company, glass bottles, carbonated water commercial patent.

1985, Sept. 10 Litho. *Perf. 14*

366 A79 10p multicolored .35 .35
a. Booklet pane of 4 1.40
367 A79 10p multicolored .35 .35
a. Booklet pane of 4 1.40
368 A79 13p multicolored .40 .40
a. Booklet pane of 4 1.60
369 A79 13p multicolored .40 .40
a. Booklet pane of 4 1.60
370 A79 22p multicolored .60 .60
a. Booklet pane of 4 2.50
371 A79 22p multicolored .60 .60
a. Booklet pane of 4 2.50
Complete booklet, #366a-371a 11.00
Nos. 366-371 (6) 2.70 2.70

Thomas Benjamin Frederick Davis (1867-1942), Shipping Magnate, Philanthropist — A80

Portrait and endowments: 10p, Howard Davis Hall, Victoria College. 13p, Yacht, racing schooner Westward. 31p, Howard Davis Park, St. Helier. 34p, Howard Davis Agricultural Development Farm, Trinity.

1985, Oct. 25 *Perf. 13½*

372 A80 10p multicolored .35 .35
373 A80 13p multicolored .40 .40
374 A80 31p multicolored .95 .95
375 A80 34p multicolored 1.10 1.10
Nos. 372-375 (4) 2.80 2.80

50th anniv. of Howard Davis Hall, Victoria College, donated by Davis in memory of his son.

Arms Type of 1981-82 and

Elizabeth II, 60th Birthday — A80a

16p, Malet. 17p, Mabon. 18p, De St. Martin. 19p, Hamptonne. 26p, De Bagot. 75p, Remon.

1985-91 Litho. *Perf. 15x14*

381 A54 16p multicolored .55 .35
a. Booklet pane of 6 ('88) 3.50
Complete booklet, 2 each #250a, 258a, 381a 15.00
382 A54 17p multicolored .55 .45
383 A54 18p multi ('88) .80 .75
384 A54 19p multi ('88) .95 .80
386 A54 26p multi ('88) .80 .65
388 A54 75p multi ('87) 2.40 1.75

Perf. 11½x12

389 A80a £1 multicolored 3.50 3.25

Photo.

Granite Paper

390 A80a £2 multicolored 6.00 4.00
Nos. 381-390 (8) 15.55 12.00

Issued: 16, 17p, 10/25; £1, 4/21/86; 75p, 4/23/87; 18, 19, 26p, 4/26/88; £2, 3/19/91.
No. 381a inscribed "May 1988."

Jersey Lily — A81

Lillie Langtry, by Sir John Millais — A82

1986, Jan. 28 Litho. *Perf. 15x14½*

391 A81 13p multicolored .45 .45
392 A82 34p multicolored 1.00 1.00
a. Souvenir sheet of 5 (4 13p, 34p) 3.50 3.50

Intl. Flower Gala, June 10-14.

Halley's Comet Sightings A83

Comet and coinciding historic events: 10p, Conquest of England, Bayeux Tapestry, A.D. 912 and 1066 sightings. 22p, Lady Carteret signing New Jersey over to William Penn, Edmond Halley observing comet, comets of 1301 & 1682. 31p, Giotto spacecraft and technology developed in 1910, 1986. Caesarea maiden voyage.

1986, Mar. 4 *Perf. 13½x13*

393 A83 10p multicolored .35 .35
394 A83 22p multicolored .80 .80
395 A83 31p multicolored 1.00 1.00
Nos. 393-395 (3) 2.15 2.15

Europa 1986 — A84

1986, Apr. 21 *Perf. 14½*

396 A84 10p Dwarf pansy .35 .35
397 A84 14p Sea stock .45 .45
398 A84 22p Sand crocus .75 .75
Nos. 396-398 (3) 1.55 1.55

Environmental conservation.

Jersey Natl. Trust, 50th Anniv. A85

10p, Le Rat cottage. 14p, The Elms, headquarters. 22p, Morel Farm entrance. 29p, Quetivel Mill. 31p, La Vallette.

1986, June 17 Litho. *Perf. 13½x13*

399 A85 10p multicolored .30 .30
400 A85 14p multicolored .40 .30
401 A85 22p multicolored .70 .70
402 A85 29p multicolored .85 .85
403 A85 31p multicolored 1.00 1.00
Nos. 399-403 (5) 3.25 3.15

Wedding of Prince Andrew and Sarah Ferguson — A86

1986, July 23 *Perf. 13½*

404 A86 14p multicolored .40 .40
405 A86 40p multicolored 1.20 1.20

Paintings by Edmund Blampied (1886-1966), Artist — A87

10p, Gathering Vraic. 14p, Driving Home in the Rain. 29p, The Miller. 31p, The Joy Ride. 34p, Tante Elizabeth.

1986, Aug. 28 Litho. *Perf. 14*

406 A87 10p multicolored .25 .25
407 A87 14p multicolored .40 .40
408 A87 29p multicolored .75 .75
409 A87 31p multicolored .90 .90
410 A87 34p multicolored 1.00 1.00
Nos. 406-410 (5) 3.30 3.30

Christmas, Intl. Peace Year — A88

1986, Nov. 4 *Perf. 14½*

411 A88 10p Dove, map, flower .30 .25
412 A88 14p Lovebirds .50 .40
413 A88 34p Dove, noise-maker 1.10 .90
Nos. 411-413 (3) 1.90 1.55

Racing Schooner Westward A89

10p, Under full sail. 14p, T.B. Davis, owner. 31p, Overhauling Britannia. 34p, Dry dock, St. Helier.

1987, Jan. 15 Litho. *Perf. 13½*

414 A89 10p multicolored .40 .40
415 A89 14p multicolored .55 .55
416 A89 31p multicolored 1.10 1.10
417 A89 34p multicolored 1.25 1.25
Nos. 414-417 (4) 3.30 3.30

Jersey Airport, 50th Anniv. A90

10p, DH86 Belcroute Bay. 14p, Boeing 757, Douglas DC-9. 22p, Britten Norman Trislander, Islander. 29p, Short SD330, Vickers Viscount. 31p, BAC1-11, HPR.7 Dart Herald.

1987, Mar. 3 Litho. *Perf. 14*

418 A90 10p multicolored .35 .35
419 A90 14p multicolored .50 .50
420 A90 22p multicolored .60 .60
421 A90 29p multicolored 1.00 1.00
422 A90 31p multicolored 1.10 1.10
Nos. 418-422 (5) 3.55 3.55

Europa 1987 A91

Modern architecture: 11p, St. Mary and St. Peter's Church. 15p, Villa Devereux. 22p, Fort Regent, St. Helier.

1987, Apr. 23 *Perf. 15x14*

423 A91 11p multicolored .45 .45
424 A91 15p multicolored .55 .55

Size: 61x31mm

425 A91 22p multicolored .75 .75
Nos. 423-425 (3) 1.75 1.75

Adm. Philippe D'Auvergne (1754-1816) — A92

Ships: 11p, Racehorse trapped in the Arctic. 15p, Alarm burned at Rhode Island. 29p, Arethusa wrecked off Ushant, France. 31p, Rattlesnake stranded on Trinidad. 34p, Mont Orgueil Castle.

1987, July 9 *Perf. 14*

426 A92 11p multicolored .35 .35
427 A92 15p multicolored .45 .45
428 A92 29p multicolored .75 .75
429 A92 31p multicolored .90 .90
430 A92 34p multicolored .95 .95
Nos. 426-430 (5) 3.40 3.40

William the Conqueror (c. 1028-87), King of England (1066-87) — A93

Designs in the style of the Bayeux Tapestry: 11p, King Charles negotiating peace with the Vikings, 911, and cession of Jersey to Rollo's son William, 933. 15p, Duke Robert I and King Edward ashore Jersey after storm, 1030; Edward's succession to the throne of England, 1042. 22p, William the Conqueror's coronation, 1066, and succession of William II, 1087. 29p, Death of King William Rufus, and Henry defeating Duke Robert to unite England and Normandy, 1106. 31p, Death of Henry, battle for the throne and succession of King Stephen, 1135. 34p, Successions of Henry II, 1154, and John Lackland, 1189.

1987 *Perf. 13½*

431 A93 11p multicolored .35 .35
a. Booklet pane of 4 + label 1.40
432 A93 15p multicolored .40 .40
a. Booklet pane of 4 + label 1.60
433 A93 22p multicolored .80 .65
a. Booklet pane of 4 + label 3.25
434 A93 29p multicolored .85 .85
a. Booklet pane of 4 + label 3.50
435 A93 31p multicolored .95 .95
a. Booklet pane of 4 + label 4.00
436 A93 34p multicolored 1.10 1.10
a. Booklet pane of 4 + label 4.50
Complete booklet, #431a-436a 22.00
Nos. 431-436 (6) 4.45 4.30

Paintings by John Le Capelain (1812-1848) — A94

11p, Grosnez Castle. 15p, St. Aubin's Bay. 22p, Mt. Orgueil Castle. 31p, Town Fort and Harbor, St. Helier. 34p, The Hermitage.

1987, Nov. 3 Photo. *Perf. 12x11½*
437 A94 11p multicolored .40 .40
438 A94 15p multicolored .60 .60
439 A94 22p multicolored .75 .75
440 A94 31p multicolored 1.00 1.00
441 A94 34p multicolored 1.20 1.20
Nos. 437-441 (5) 3.95 3.95

Christmas.

Hybrids, Eric Young Orchid Foundation, Trinity — A95

11p, Cymbidium pontac. 15p, Odontioda Eric Young, vert. 29p, Lycaste auburn Seaford and Ditchling. 31p, Odontoglossum St. Brelade, vert. 34p, Cymbidium mavourneen Jester.

1988, Jan. 12 Litho. *Perf. 14*
442 A95 11p multicolored .45 .45
443 A95 15p multicolored .55 .55
444 A95 29p multicolored .95 .95
445 A95 31p multicolored 1.00 1.00
446 A95 34p multicolored 1.20 1.20
Nos. 442-446 (5) 4.15 4.15

Jersey Dog Club, Cent. A96

11p, Labrador retriever. 15p, Wire-haired dachshund. 22p, Pekingese. 31p, Cavalier King Charles spaniel. 34p, Dalmatian.

1988, Mar. 2
447 A96 11p multicolored .45 .45
448 A96 15p multicolored .55 .55
449 A96 22p multicolored .85 .85
450 A96 31p multicolored 1.10 1.10
451 A96 34p multicolored 1.20 1.20
Nos. 447-451 (5) 4.15 4.15

Europa 1988 A97

Nos. 453 and 455 vert.

Perf. 14x13½, 13½x14
1988, Apr. 26 Litho.
452 A97 16p De Havilland DHC 7 .45 .45
453 A97 16p Weather radar and unstrument landing system .45 .45
454 A97 22p Hydrofoil .85 .85
455 A97 22p Port control tower .85 .85
Nos. 452-455 (4) 2.60 2.60

Wildlife Preservation Trust, 25th Anniv. — A98

12p, Rodrigues fody, vert. 16p, Volcano rabbit. 29p, White-faced marmoset, vert. 31p, Ploughshare tortoise. 34p, Mauritius kestrel, vert.

1988, July 6 Litho.
456 A98 12p multicolored .45 .45
457 A98 16p multicolored .60 .60
458 A98 29p multicolored 1.10 1.10
459 A98 31p multicolored 1.10 1.10
460 A98 34p multicolored 1.20 1.20
Nos. 456-460 (5) 4.45 4.45

Operation Raleigh A99

Activities: 12p, Rain Forest Leaf Frog, Costa Rica. 16p, Archaeological Survey, Peru. 22p, Glacier Climbing, Chile. 29p, Medical Assistance, Solomon Isls. 31p, Underwater Exploration, Australia. 34p, *Zebu* returns to St. Helier, Jersey.

1988, Sept. 27 Photo. *Perf. 12*
461 A99 12p multicolored .45 .45
462 A99 16p multicolored .50 .50
463 A99 22p multicolored .75 .75
464 A99 29p multicolored .90 .90
465 A99 31p multicolored .95 .95
466 A99 34p multicolored 1.20 1.20
Nos. 461-466 (6) 4.75 4.75

Operation Raleigh: voyage of the *Zebu*, on which youths were trained with the aim of remotivating them and helping them to earn new self-respect.
WHO 40th anniv. (29p).

Parish Churches A100

1988, Nov. 15 Litho. *Perf. 14*
467 A100 12p St. Clement .45 .45
468 A100 16p St. Ouen .55 .55
469 A100 31p St. Brelade 1.00 1.00
470 A100 34p St. Lawrence 1.10 1.10
Nos. 467-470 (4) 3.10 3.10

Christmas. See Nos. 549-552, 610-613.

Classic Cars A101

Designs: 12p, 1912 Talbot Tourer, seaweed harvest at Le Hocq. 16p, 1920 De Dion Bouton, Grosnez Castle ruins. 23p, 1926 Austin Chummy, brick kiln at Mont a l'Abbe. 30p, 1926 Ford Model T, harvest of the Jersey royal potato crop. 32p, 1930 Bentley 8-Litre, Guard House and Gate at Government House. 35p, 1931 Cadillac V16 Fleetwood Sports Phaeton, St. Ouen's Manor.

1989, Jan. 31
471 A101 12p multicolored .45 .45
472 A101 16p multicolored .55 .45
473 A101 23p multicolored .70 .55
474 A101 30p multicolored 1.00 .80
475 A101 32p multicolored 1.00 1.00
476 A101 35p multicolored 1.10 1.10
Nos. 471-476 (6) 4.80 4.35

See Nos. 604-609, 903-908.

Scenic Views — A102

Coronation of Queen Elizabeth II, 40th Anniv. — A102a

Royal Arms A102b

1p, Belcroute Bay. 2p, High St., St. Aubin. 4p, Royal Jersey Golf Course. 5p, Portelet Bay. 10p, Les Charrieres D'Anneport. 13p, St. Helier Marina. 14p, St. Ouen's Bay. 15p, Rozel Harbor. 16p, St. Aubin's Harbor. 17p, Jersey Airport. 18p, Corbiere Lighthouse. 19p, Val de la Mare. 20p, Elizabeth Castle. 21p, Greve de Lecq. 22p, Samares Manor. 23p, Bonne Nuit Harbor. 24p, Grosnez Castle. 25p, Augres Manor. 26p, Central Market. 27p, St. Brelade's Bay. 30p, St. Ouen's Manor. 40p, La Hougue Bie. 50p, Mont Orgueil Castle. 75p, Royal Square.

1989-95 Litho. *Perf. 13½*
477 A102 1p multicolored .25 .25
478 A102 2p multicolored .25 .25
480 A102 4p multicolored .25 .25
a. Booklet pane of 6 .80
481 A102 5p multicolored .25 .25
a. Booklet pane of 6 1.40
485 A102 10p multicolored .35 .35
486 A102 13p multicolored .45 .45
487 A102 14p multicolored .45 .45
a. Booklet pane of 6 3.00 3.00
b. Booklet pane of 8 3.75 3.75
Complete booklet, #487b ('92) 3.75
488 A102 15p multicolored .50 .50
a. Booklet pane of 6 3.25 3.25
489 A102 16p multicolored .55 .55
a. Booklet pane of 8 5.00 5.00
Complete booklet, #489a ('92) 5.00
490 A102 17p multicolored .55 .55
491 A102 18p multicolored .60 .60
a. Booklet pane of 6 4.25 4.25
Complete booklet, 2 each #480a, 487a, 491a ('90) 17.50
492 A102 19p multicolored .60 .60
493 A102 20p multicolored .50 .50
a. Booklet pane of 6 3.25 3.25
Complete booklet, 2 each #481a, 488a, 493a ('91) 20.00
494 A102 21p multicolored .55 .55
495 A102 22p multicolored .50 .50
a. Booklet pane of 8 4.50 4.50
Complete booklet, #495a ('92) 4.50
496 A102 23p multicolored .85 .85
497 A102 24p multicolored .70 .70
498 A102 25p multicolored .80 .80
499 A102 26p multicolored .90 .90
500 A102 27p multicolored .90 .90
501 A102 30p multicolored 1.00 1.00
502 A102 40p multicolored 1.20 1.20
503 A102 50p multicolored 1.60 1.60
504 A102 75p multicolored 2.50 2.50

Perf. 14½
505 A102a £1 multicolored 4.50 4.50

Perf. 15x14
506 A102b £4 multicolored 8.50 8.50
Nos. 477-506 (26) 30.05 30.05

Pane Nos. 480a, 487a and 491a issued for Stamp World London '90 and are inscribed "May 1990."
Issued: 1p-20p, 3/21/89; 21p-27p, 1/16/90; 30p-75p, 3/13/90; Nos. 481a, 488a, 493a, 2/12/91; £1, 6/2/93; £4, 1/2/95. Nos. 487b, 489a, 495a were released on May 22, but were not readily available until September 1992. Other booklet panes, 1990.

World Wildlife Fund — A103

No. 507, Large checkered skipper. No. 508, Agile frog, horiz. No. 509, Green lizard, horiz. No. 510, Barn owl.

1989, Apr. 25 Litho. *Perf. 13x13¼*
507 A103 13p multicolored *1.25 1.25*

Perf. 13¼x13
508 A103 13p multicolored *1.25 1.25*
509 A103 17p multicolored *1.25 1.25*

Perf. 13½x13¾
510 A103 17p multicolored *1.25 1.25*
Nos. 507-510 (4) *5.00 5.00*

Europa 1989 — A104

Children's games — No. 511, Playpen. No. 512, Playground. No. 513, Magician, games. No. 514, Cricket, rugby, tennis.

1989, Apr. 25 *Perf. 14*
511 A104 17p multicolored .55 .55
512 A104 17p multicolored .55 .55
513 A104 23p multicolored .80 .80
514 A104 23p multicolored .80 .80
Nos. 511-514 (4) 2.70 2.70

Visit of Queen Elizabeth II — A105

£1, Ferry Terminal, St. Helier.

1989, May 24 Litho. *Perf. 14½*
515 A105 £1 multicolored 3.00 3.00

French Revolution, Bicent. A106

Designs: 13p, D'Auvergne meets Louis XVI, 1786. 17p, Storming the Bastille, 1789. 23p, Marie de Bouillon at the Chateau de Navarre, 1790. 30p, Mission from Mont Orgueil, 1795. 32p, Support for the Chouans, 1796. 35p, The last Chouannerie, 1799.

1989, July 7 *Perf. 13½*
516 A106 13p multicolored .40 .30
a. Booklet pane of 4 1.60
517 A106 17p multicolored .50 .40
a. Booklet pane of 4 2.00
518 A106 23p multicolored .60 .50
a. Booklet pane of 4 2.50
519 A106 30p multicolored .95 .95
a. Booklet pane of 4 4.00
520 A106 32p multicolored 1.00 1.00
a. Booklet pane of 4 4.00
521 A106 35p multicolored 1.25 1.25
a. Booklet pane of 4 5.00
Complete booklet, #516a-521a 20.00
Nos. 516-521 (6) 4.70 4.40

Great Western Railway Steamer Service Between Weymouth and the Channel Isls., Cent. — A107

Steamers: 13p, St. Helier, 1925. 17p, Caesarea II, 1910. 27p, Reindeer, 1897. 32p, Ibex & Frederica, 1891. 35p, Lynx, 1889.

1989, Sept. 5 Litho. *Perf. 13½x14*
522 A107 13p multicolored .40 .30
523 A107 17p multicolored .35 .35
524 A107 27p multicolored .80 .80
525 A107 32p multicolored 1.00 1.00
526 A107 35p multicolored 1.20 1.20
Nos. 522-526 (5) 3.75 3.65

Paintings by Sarah Louisa Kilpack (1839-1909) — A108

1989, Oct. 24 Litho. ***Perf. 13x12½***
527 A108 13p Gorey Harbour .30 .30
528 A108 17p La Corbiere .35 .35
529 A108 23p Greve de Lecq .80 .80
530 A108 32p Bouley Bay 1.00 1.00
531 A108 35p Mont Orgueil 1.10 1.10
Nos. 527-531 (5) 3.55 3.55

Europa 1990 A109

Post offices — No. 532, Broad Street, 1969, vert. No. 533, Mont Millais, 1990, vert. No. 534, Hue Street, 1815. No. 535, Halkett Place, 1890.

Perf. 13½x14, 14x13½
1990, Mar. 13 Litho.
532 A109 18p multicolored .55 .55
533 A109 18p multicolored .55 .55
534 A109 24p multicolored .65 .65
535 A109 24p multicolored .65 .65
Nos. 532-535 (4) 2.40 2.40

Festival of Tourism — A110

1990, May 3 Litho. ***Perf. 14x13½***
536 A110 18p Battle of Flowers .65 .65
537 A110 24p Recreation .80 .80
538 A110 29p History .95 .95
539 A110 32p Salon Culinaire 1.00 1.00
a. Souvenir sheet of 4, #536-539 3.50 3.50
Nos. 536-539 (4) 3.40 3.40

News Media A111

14p, Print (newspapers), 1784-1889. 18p, The Evening Post, 1890. 34p, BBC Radio Jersey, 1982. 37p, Channel Television, 1962.

1990, June 26 Litho. ***Perf. 13½***
540 A111 14p multicolored .55 .55
541 A111 18p multicolored .55 .55
542 A111 34p multicolored 1.10 1.10
543 A111 37p multicolored 1.20 1.20
Nos. 540-543 (4) 3.40 3.40

UNESCO World Literacy Year.

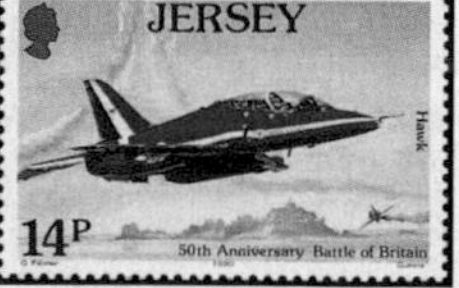

Battle of Britain, 50th Anniv. A112

1990, Sept. 4 ***Perf. 14***
544 A112 14p Hawk .45 .45
545 A112 18p Spitfire .60 .60
546 A112 24p Hurricane .95 .95
547 A112 34p Wellington 1.50 1.50
548 A112 37p Lancaster 1.60 1.60
Nos. 544-548 (5) 5.10 5.10

Parish Churches Type of 1988

1990, Nov. 13 Litho. ***Perf. 13½x14***
549 A100 14p St. Helier .55 .40
550 A100 18p Grouville .55 .40
551 A100 34p St. Saviour 1.20 1.20
552 A100 37p St. John 1.50 1.50
Nos. 549-552 (4) 3.80 3.50

Christmas.

Prince's Tower, La Hougue Bie, 1801 A113

Philippe d'Auvergne: 20p, Arrested in Paris, 1802. 26p, Plotting against Napoleon, 1803. 31p, Execution of Cadoudal, 1804. 37p, H.M. Cutter Surly, 1809. 44p, Prince de Bouillon, 1816.

1991, Jan. 22 Litho ***Perf. 13½***
553 A113 15p multicolored .50 .40
554 A113 20p multicolored .60 .60
555 A113 26p multicolored .80 .80
556 A113 31p multicolored 1.00 1.00
557 A113 37p multicolored 1.25 1.25
558 A113 44p multicolored 1.40 1.40
Nos. 553-558 (6) 5.55 5.45

A114

Europa (Satellites and their functions): No. 559, ERS-1, oceanography. No. 560, Landsat, Earth resources. No. 561, Meteosat, meteorology. No. 562, Olympus, communications.

1991, Mar. 19 Litho. ***Perf. 14½x13***
559 A114 20p multicolored .60 .60
560 A114 20p multicolored .60 .60
561 A114 26p multicolored .80 .80
562 A114 26p multicolored .80 .80
Nos. 559-562 (4) 2.80 2.80

A115

15p, German Occupation Stamps for Jersey, 50th anniv. 20p, Eastern Railway extension to Gorey Pier, 100th anniv. 26p, Jersey Herd Book, 125th anniv. 31p, Victoria Harbor, 150th anniv. 53p, Hospital bequest of Marie Bartlett, 250th anniv.

1991, May 16 Litho. ***Perf. 13½***
563 A115 15p multicolored .35 .35
564 A115 20p multicolored .60 .60
565 A115 26p multicolored .75 .75
566 A115 31p multicolored .90 .90
567 A115 53p multicolored 1.50 1.50
Nos. 563-567 (5) 4.10 4.10

Butterflies & Moths A116

15p, Glanville fritillary. 20p, Jersey tiger. 37p, Small elephant hawk-moth. 57p, Peacock.

1991, July 9 Litho. ***Perf. 13x12½***
568 A116 15p multicolored .45 .45
569 A116 20p multicolored .55 .35
570 A116 37p multicolored 1.75 1.75
571 A116 57p multicolored 2.00 2.00
Nos. 568-571 (4) 4.75 4.55

See Nos. 727-731.

Overseas Aid — A117

Designs: 15p, Water drilling rig, Ethiopia. 20p, Construction work, Rwanda. 26p, Technical school, Kenya. 31p, Leprosy and eye care, Tanzania. 37p, Agriculture and cultivation aid, Zambia. 44p, Health care and immunization, Lesotho.

1991, Sept. 3 Litho. ***Perf. 13½***
572 A117 15p multicolored .55 .45
573 A117 20p multicolored .60 .50
574 A117 26p multicolored .85 .85
575 A117 31p multicolored 1.00 1.00
576 A117 37p multicolored 1.25 1.25
577 A117 44p multicolored 1.40 1.40
Nos. 572-577 (6) 5.65 5.45

Christmas — A118

Illustrations by Edmund Blampied from Peter Pan: 15p, This is the place for me. 20p, The Island Come True. 37p, The Never Bird. 53p, The Great White Father.

1991, Nov. 5 Litho. ***Perf. 14***
578 A118 15p multicolored .45 .45
579 A118 20p multicolored .80 .80
580 A118 37p multicolored 1.40 1.40
581 A118 53p multicolored 1.90 1.90
Nos. 578-581 (4) 4.55 4.55

Winter Birds — A119

1992, Jan. 7 Litho. ***Perf. 13½x14***
582 A119 16p Pied wagtail .55 .55
583 A119 22p Firecrest .75 .75
584 A119 28p Snipe .95 .95
585 A119 39p Lapwing 1.40 1.40
586 A119 57p Fieldfare 2.00 2.00
Nos. 582-586 (5) 5.65 5.65

Shanghai Harbor, 1860 A120

William Mesny, 150th birth anniv: No. 588, Running the Taiping blockade, 1862. No. 589, General Mesny, River Gate, 1874. No. 590, Mesny accompanying Gill to Burma, 1877. No. 591, Mesny advises Governor Chang, 1882. No. 592, Mesny, Mandarin First Class, 1886.

1992, Feb. 25 Litho. ***Perf. 13½***
587 A120 16p multicolored .50 .50
588 A120 16p multicolored .50 .50
589 A120 22p multicolored .80 .80
590 A120 22p multicolored .80 .80
591 A120 33p multicolored 1.10 1.10
592 A120 33p multicolored 1.10 1.10
Nos. 587-592 (6) 4.80 4.80

587a Booklet pane of 4 2.00 2.00
588a Booklet pane of 4 2.00 2.00
589a Booklet pane of 4 3.25 3.25
590a Booklet pane of 4 3.25 3.25
591a Booklet pane of 4 4.50 4.50
592a Booklet pane of 4 4.50 4.50
Complete booklet, #587a-592a 23.00

Discovery of America, 500th Anniv. A121

Columbus, ship and: 22p, John Bertram (1796-1882). 28p, Sir George Carteret (1610-1680). 39p, Sir Walter Raleigh (1554-1618).

1992, Apr. 14 Litho. ***Perf. 14½***
593 A121 22p multicolored .80 .80
594 A121 28p multicolored .90 .90
595 A121 39p multicolored 1.40 1.40
Nos. 593-595 (3) 3.10 3.10

Europa.

Jersey-Built Sailing Ships — A122

1992, Apr. 14 Litho. ***Perf. 14***
596 A122 16p Tickler .55 .55
597 A122 22p Hebe .85 .85
598 A122 50p Gemini 1.60 1.60
599 A122 57p Percy Douglas 1.90 1.90
a. Souvenir sheet of 4, #596-599 4.50 4.50
Nos. 596-599 (4) 4.90 4.90

Batik — A123

16p, Snow leopards. 22p, Three elements. 39p, Three men in a tub. 57p, Cockatoos.

1992, June 23 Litho. ***Perf. 14½***
600 A123 16p multicolored .55 .55
601 A123 22p multicolored .80 .80
602 A123 39p multicolored 1.40 1.40
603 A123 57p multicolored 1.75 1.75
Nos. 600-603 (4) 4.50 4.50

Classic Car Type of 1989

Designs: 16p, 1925 Morris Cowley "Bullnose." 22p, 1932 Rolls Royce 20/25. 28p, 1924 Chenard & Walcker T5. 33p, 1932 Packard 900 Series Light Eight. 39p, 1927 Lanchester 21. 50p, 1913 Buick 30 Roadster.

1992, Sept. 8 Litho. ***Perf. 13x12½***
604 A101 16p multicolored .35 .35
605 A101 22p multicolored .55 .55
606 A101 28p multicolored .85 .85
607 A101 33p multicolored 1.10 1.10
608 A101 39p multicolored 1.25 1.25
609 A101 50p multicolored 1.60 1.60
Nos. 604-609 (6) 5.70 5.70

Parish Church Type of 1988

1992, Nov. 3 Litho. ***Perf. 13½x14***
610 A100 16p Trinity .50 .50
611 A100 22p St. Mary .70 .65
612 A100 39p St. Martin 1.25 1.25
613 A100 57p St. Peter 1.75 1.75
Nos. 610-613 (4) 4.20 4.15

Christmas.

Non-Value Indicator Stamps — A124

Scenic views: No. 614, Building with arches. No. 615, Cemetery, Trinity Church. No. 616, Daffodils, cattle. No. 617, Cattle in pasture.
Beach scenes: No. 618, People lying on beach with umbrella. No. 619, Man with windsurfer. No. 620, Crab facing right. No. 621, Crab, facing left.
Parade floats: No. 622, Smiling face, rainbow. No. 623, Dragon head, Oriental theme. No. 624, Umbrellas, Asian theme. No. 625, Elephant's tusks, African theme.

1993, Jan. 26 Litho. *Perf. 13½*
614 A124 (17p) Bailiwick .55 .55
615 A124 (17p) Bailiwick .55 .55
616 A124 (17p) Bailiwick .55 .55
617 A124 (17p) Bailiwick .55 .55
a. Block of 4, #614-617 2.25 2.25
b. Booklet pane of 8, 2 each #614-617 4.50
Complete booklet, #617b 5.00
618 A124 (23p) UK .70 .70
619 A124 (23p) UK .70 .70
620 A124 (23p) UK .70 .70
621 A124 (23p) UK .70 .70
a. Block of 4, #618-621 3.00 3.00
b. Booklet pane of 8, 2 each #618-621 6.00
Complete booklet, #621b 6.75
622 A124 (28p) European .85 .85
623 A124 (28p) European .85 .85
624 A124 (28p) European .85 .85
625 A124 (28p) European .85 .85
a. Block of 4, #622-625 3.25 3.25
b. Booklet pane of 8, 2 each #622-625 7.00 7.00
Complete booklet, #625b 7.75
Nos. 614-625 (12) 8.40 8.40

The minimum postage rate is represented for each area where mail is delivered.

Orchids — A125

17p, Phragmipedium Eric Young "Jersey." 23p, Odontoglossum Augres "Trinity." 28p, Miltonia Saint Helier "Colomberie." 39p, Phragmipedium pearcei. 57p, Calanthe Grouville "Gorey."

1993, Jan. 26 Litho. *Perf. 14½x13*
626 A125 17p multicolored .55 .55
627 A125 23p multicolored .80 .80
628 A125 28p multicolored .95 .95
629 A125 39p multicolored 1.40 1.40
630 A125 57p multicolored 2.00 2.00
Nos. 626-630 (5) 5.70 5.70

Europa — A126

Contemporary Art: 23p, Jersey Opera House, by Ian Rolls. 28p, The Ham and Tomato Bap, by Jonathan Hubbard. 39p, Vase of Flowers, by Neil MacKenzie.

1993, Apr. 1 Litho. *Perf. 13½x14*
631 A126 23p multicolored .75 .75
632 A126 28p multicolored .85 .85
633 A126 39p multicolored 1.40 1.40
Nos. 631-633 (3) 3.00 3.00

Royal Air Force, 75th Anniv. A127

Designs: 17p, Douglas Dakota. 23p, Wight Seaplane. 28p, Avro Shakleton AEW2. 33p, Gloster Meteor, DeHavilland Vampire. 39p, BAe Harrier GR1A. 57p, Panavia Tornado F3.

1993, Apr. 1 *Perf. 14*
634 A127 17p multicolored .55 .55
635 A127 23p multicolored .70 .70
636 A127 28p multicolored .85 .85
637 A127 33p multicolored .95 .95
638 A127 39p multicolored 1.20 1.20
639 A127 57p multicolored 1.90 1.90
a. Souvenir sheet of 2, #635, 639 6.00 6.00
Nos. 634-639 (6) 6.15 6.15

Stamps from No. 639a do not have white border.

German Occupation Stamps by Edmund Blampied, 50th Anniv. A128

1993, June 2 Litho. *Perf. 13½*
640 A128 17p No. N3 .40 .40
641 A128 23p No. N4 .60 .60
642 A128 28p No. N5 .80 .80
643 A128 33p No. N6 1.00 1.00
644 A128 39p No. N7 1.40 1.40
645 A128 50p No. N8 1.60 1.60
Nos. 640-645 (6) 5.80 5.80

Birds — A129

17p, Short-toed treecreeper. 23p, Dartford warbler. 28p, Wheatear. 39p, Cirl bunting. 57p, Jay.

1993, Sept. 7 Litho. *Perf. 13½x14*
646 A129 17p multicolored .50 .50
647 A129 23p multicolored .75 .75
648 A129 28p multicolored .90 .90
649 A129 39p multicolored 1.25 1.25
650 A129 57p multicolored 2.00 2.00
Nos. 646-650 (5) 5.40 5.40

Christmas — A130

Stained glass windows by Henry Bosdet, from St. Aubin on the Hill.

1993, Nov. 2 Litho. *Perf. 14½x13*
651 A130 17p multicolored .50 .50
652 A130 23p multicolored .75 .75
653 A130 39p multicolored 1.25 1.25
654 A130 57p multicolored 2.00 2.00
Nos. 651-654 (4) 4.50 4.50

Mushrooms A131

1994, Jan. 11 Litho. *Perf. 14½*
655 A131 18p Shaggy ink cap .55 .55
656 A131 23p Fly agaric .75 .75
657 A131 30p Chanterelle 1.00 1.00
658 A131 41p Parasol mushroom 1.40 1.40
659 A131 60p Latticed stinkhorn 1.90 1.90
Nos. 655-659 (5) 5.60 5.60

Souvenir Sheet

New Year 1994 (Year of the Dog) — A132

1994, Feb. 18 Litho. *Perf. 15x14½*
660 A132 £1 multicolored 3.50 3.50

Hong Kong '94.

Cats — A133

18p, Maine coon, vert. 23p, British shorthair. 35p, Persian, vert. 41p, Siamese. 60p, Non-pedigree, vert.

1994, Apr. 5 Litho. *Perf. 13½*
661 A133 18p multicolored .50 .50
662 A133 23p multicolored .75 .75
663 A133 35p multicolored .95 .95
664 A133 41p multicolored 1.40 1.40
665 A133 60p multicolored 1.40 1.40
Nos. 661-665 (5) 5.00 5.00

Jersey Cat Club, 21st anniv., and 4th Championship Show.

Europa — A134

Designs: No. 666, Mammoths on cliff, c. 250,000 B.C. No. 667, Paleolithic hunters dragging mammoth by tusks. No. 668, Neolithic dolmen, "La Hougue Bie," c. 4,000 B.C. No. 669, Exterior of "La Hougue Bie," during construction.

1994, Apr. 5 Litho. *Perf. 13½x14*
666 23p multicolored .60 .60
667 23p multicolored .60 .60
a. A134 Pair, #666-667 1.20 1.20
668 30p multicolored .90 .90
669 30p multicolored .90 .90
a. A134 Pair, #668-669 1.80 1.80
Nos. 666-669 (4) 3.00 3.00

D-Day, 50th Anniv. A135

No. 670, Airborne Forces enroute to drop zones. No. 671, Allied Fleet off Normandy Coast. No. 672, Coming ashore, Gold Beach. No. 673, Coming ashore, Sword Beach. No. 674, Spitfires on beachead patrol. No. 675, Normandy invasion map.

1994, June 6 Litho. *Perf. 13½*
670 A135 18p multicolored .65 .60
671 A135 18p multicolored .65 .60
a. Bklt. pane, 3 each #670-671 3.50
672 A135 23p multicolored .90 .90
673 A135 23p multicolored .90 .90
a. Bklt. pane, 3 each #672-673 5.60
674 A135 30p multicolored 1.00 1.00
675 A135 30p multicolored 1.00 1.00
a. Bklt. pane, 3 each #674-675 6.00
b. Bklt. pane of 6, #670-675 6.00
Complete booklet, #671a, 673a, 675a, 675b 20.00
Nos. 670-675 (6) 5.10 5.00

No. 675b also sold by the Philatelic Bureau separate from the booklet. without stitching, as a souvenir sheet.

Intl. Olympic Committee, Cent. — A136

1994, June 6 *Perf. 14*
676 A136 18p Sailing .45 .45
677 A136 23p Rifle shooting .65 .65
678 A136 30p Hurdles .85 .85
679 A136 41p Swimming 1.25 1.25
680 A136 60p Field hockey 1.75 1.75
Nos. 676-680 (5) 4.95 4.95

Marine Life A137

Designs: 18p, Strawberry anemone. 23p, Hermit crab, parasitic anemone. 41p, Velvet swimming crab. 60p, Common jellyfish.

1994, Aug. 2 Litho. *Perf. 13½x13*
681 A137 18p multicolored .45 .45
682 A137 23p multicolored .70 .70
683 A137 41p multicolored 1.40 1.40
684 A137 60p multicolored 1.90 1.90
Nos. 681-684 (4) 4.45 4.45

Postal Independence, 25th Anniv. — A138

Designs: 18p, Condor 10 Wavepiercer. 23p, Map of Jersey, postbox. 35p, BEA "Vanguard" aircraft. 41p, Aurigny "Short 360" aircraft. 60p, Sealink vessel "Caesarea."

1994, Oct. 1 Litho. *Perf. 14*
685 A138 18p multicolored .60 .60
686 A138 23p multicolored .70 .70
687 A138 35p multicolored 1.00 1.00
688 A138 41p multicolored 1.25 1.25
689 A138 60p multicolored 2.00 2.00
a. Souvenir sheet, #685-689 + label 5.75 5.75
Nos. 685-689 (5) 5.55 5.55

See Guernsey Nos. 536-540a.

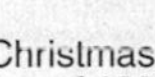

Christmas A139

Christmas carols: 18p, "Away in the manger..." 23p, "Hark! the herald angels sing..." 41p, "While shepherds watched..." 60p, "We three kings of Orient are..."

1994, Nov. 8
690 A139 18p multicolored .45 .45
691 A139 23p multicolored .60 .60
692 A139 41p multicolored 1.40 1.40
693 A139 60p multicolored 1.75 1.75
Nos. 690-693 (4) 4.20 4.20

Greetings Stamps — A140

Designs: No. 694, Dog, "Good Luck." No. 695, Rose, "With Love." No. 696, Chick, "Congratulations." No. 697, Bouquet of flowers, "Thank You."

No. 698, Dove, "With love." No. 699, Cat, "Good Luck." No. 700, Carnations, "Thank You." No. 701, Parrot, "Congratulations."
60p, Boar, "Happy New Year."

1995, Jan. 24 Litho. *Perf. 13½x13*

694 A140 18p multicolored .35 .25
695 A140 18p multicolored .35 .25
696 A140 18p multicolored .35 .25
697 A140 18p multicolored .35 .25
a. Strip of 4, #694-697 2.25 2.25
698 A140 23p multicolored .55 .30
699 A140 23p multicolored .55 .30
700 A140 23p multicolored .55 .30
701 A140 23p multicolored .55 .30
a. Strip of 4, #698-701 2.25 2.25

Size: 25x64mm

702 A140 60p multicolored .55 .30
a. Booklet pane, #697a, #701a, #702 7.00
Complete booklet, #702a 7.00
Nos. 694-702 (9) 4.15 2.50

New Year 1995 (Year of the Boar) (No. 702).

Camellias A141

18p, Captain Rawes. 23p, Brigadoon. 30p, Elsie Jury. 35p, Augusto L'Gouveia Pinto. 41p, Bella Romana.

1995, Mar. 21 Litho. *Perf. 14*

703 A141 18p multicolored .60 .50
704 A141 23p multicolored .90 .70
705 A141 30p multicolored 1.00 .85
706 A141 35p multicolored 1.20 1.20
707 A141 41p multicolored 1.30 1.30
Nos. 703-707 (5) 5.00 4.55

International Camellia Society conference, Jersey, Mar. 30-Apr. 4, 1995.

Liberation, by Philip Jackson A142

1995, May 9 Litho. *Perf. 13½*

708 A142 23p gray & black .65 .65
709 A142 30p pink & black .85 .85

Europa.

Liberation, 50th Anniv. A143

No. 710, Bailiff, Crown Officers taken to HMS Beagle. No. 711, Red Cross ship SS Vega. No. 712, Germans surrender on board HMS Beagle. No. 713, First troops of task force 135, Ordinance Yard, St. Helier. No. 714, Royal visitors, June 1945. No. 715, Supplies come ashore from LSTs, Operation Nestegg.
£1, Princess Elizabeth, Queen Elizabeth, Winston Churchill, King George VI, Princess Margaret at Buckingham Palace, VE Day.

1995, May 9 Litho. *Perf. 14½x14*

710 A143 18p multicolored .50 .50
711 A143 18p multicolored .50 .50
a. Bklt. pane, 3 each #710-711 3.00
712 A143 23p multicolored .70 .70
713 A143 23p multicolored .70 .70
a. Bklt. pane, 3 each #712-713 4.25
714 A143 60p multicolored 1.75 1.75
715 A143 60p multicolored 1.75 1.75
a. Bklt. pane, 3 each #714-715 11.00
Nos. 710-715 (6) 5.90 5.90

Souvenir Sheet

716 A143 £1 multicolored 3.25 3.25
a. Booklet pane, #716 3.00
Complete booklet, #711a, #713a, #715a, #716a 22.00

No. 716 contains one 81x29mm stamp.

Wild Flowers — A144

No. 717, Bell heather. No. 718, Sea campion. No. 719, Spotted rock-rose. No. 720, Thrift. No. 721, Sheep's-bit scabious. No. 722, Field bind-weed. No. 723, Common bird's-foot trefoil. No. 724, Sea holly. No. 725, Common centaury. No. 726, Dwarf pansy.

1995, July 4 Litho. *Perf. 13½*

717 A144 19p multicolored .45 .25
718 A144 19p multicolored .45 .25
719 A144 19p multicolored .45 .25
720 A144 19p multicolored .45 .25
721 A144 19p multicolored .45 .25
a. Strip of 5, #717-721 3.50 3.50
722 A144 23p multicolored .60 .25
723 A144 23p multicolored .60 .25
724 A144 23p multicolored .60 .25
725 A144 23p multicolored .60 .25
726 A144 23p multicolored .60 .25
a. Strip of 5, #722-726 4.00 4.00
Nos. 717-726 (10) 5.25 2.50

Butterfly & Moth Type of 1991

19p, Peacock pansy. 23p, Green-barred swallowtail. 30p, Orange emigrant. 41p, Scarlet mormon. 60p, Common birdwing.

1995, Sept. 1 Litho. *Perf. 14*

727 A116 19p multicolored .60 .60
728 A116 23p multicolored .65 .65
729 A116 30p multicolored .90 .90
730 A116 41p multicolored 1.20 1.20
731 A116 60p multicolored 1.90 1.90
a. Souvenir sheet of 2, #730-731 3.25 3.25
Nos. 727-731 (5) 5.25 5.25

Singapore '95 (No. 731a).
Stamps from No. 731a do not have border around the designs or inscriptions at bottom.

Christmas Pantomimes — A145

Childrens' stories: 19p, Puss in Boots. 23p, Cinderella. 41p, Sleeping Beauty. 60p, Aladdin.

1995, Oct. 24 Litho. *Perf. 13½*

732 A145 19p multicolored .70 .70
733 A145 23p multicolored .80 .80
734 A145 41p multicolored 1.40 1.40
735 A145 60p multicolored 1.75 1.75
Nos. 732-735 (4) 4.65 4.65

UN, 50th Anniv. A146

Nos. 736, 739, Doves, emblem. Nos 737, 738, Wheat ear, emblem.

1995, Oct. 24 Litho. *Perf. 13x14*

736 A146 19p dk blue, lt blue .70 .70
737 A146 23p emer, turq grn .80 .80
738 A146 41p turq grn, emer 1.40 1.40
739 A146 60p lt blue, dk blue 1.75 1.75
Nos. 736-739 (4) 4.65 4.65

UNICEF, 50th Anniv. A147

Children, map areas of UNICEF activities: 19p, Africa. 23p, Globe. 30p, Europe, Balkans. 35p, South America, Caribbean. 41p, South Asia. 60p, Australasia, South Pacific.

1996, Feb. 19 Litho. *Perf. 14½*

740 A147 19p multicolored .55 .50
741 A147 23p multicolored .65 .50
742 A147 30p multicolored .85 .75
743 A147 35p multicolored 1.10 1.10
744 A147 41p multicolored 1.20 1.20
745 A147 60p multicolored 1.75 1.75
Nos. 740-745 (6) 6.10 5.80

Souvenir Sheet

New Year 1996 (Year of the Rat) — A148

1996, Feb. 19 *Perf. 14*

746 A148 £1 multicolored 3.00 3.00

Queen Elizabeth II, 70th Birthday — A149

1996, Apr. 21 Litho. *Perf. 14x15*

747 A149 £5 multicolored 11.00 11.00

Women of Achievement A150

Europa: 23p, Elizabeth Garrett, first British woman physician. 30p, Emmeline Pankhurst (1858-1928), suffragist.

1996, Apr. 25 *Perf. 14*

748 A150 23p multicolored .65 .65
749 A150 30p multicolored 1.00 1.00

1996 European Soccer Chamionships — A151

Various soccer plays.

1996, Apr. 25

750 A151 19p multicolored .50 .40
751 A151 23p multicolored .60 .50
752 A151 35p multicolored 1.00 .90
753 A151 41p multicolored 1.00 1.00
754 A151 60p multicolored 1.60 1.60
Nos. 750-754 (5) 4.70 4.40

Modern Olympic Games, Cent. A152

1996, June 8 Litho. *Perf. 14*

755 A152 19p Rowing .50 .40
756 A152 23p Judo .60 .50
757 A152 35p Fencing 1.00 .90
758 A152 41p Boxing 1.00 1.00
759 A152 60p Basketball 1.60 1.60
Nos. 755-759 (5) 4.70 4.40

Souvenir Sheet

760 A152 £1 Olympic torch, flame 3.50 3.50

Intl. Amateur Boxing Assoc., 50th anniv. (No. 758). CAPEX '96 (No. 760). No. 760 contains one 50x38mm stamp.

Tourism A153

19p, North Coast. 23p, Portelet Bay. 30p, Greve de Lecq Bay. 35p, Beauport Beach. 41p, Plemont Bay. 60p, St. Brelade's Bay.

1996, June 8 Litho. *Perf. 14*

761 A153 19p multi .50 .50
762 A153 23p multi .60 .60
a. Bklt. pane, 3 each #761-762 3.50
763 A153 30p multi .80 .80
764 A153 35p multi .95 .95
a. Bklt. pane, 3 each #763-764 5.25
765 A153 41p multi 1.10 1.10
766 A153 60p multi 1.60 1.60
a. Bklt. pane, 1 each #761-766 5.75
b. Bklt. pane, 3 each #765-766 8.25
Complete booklet, #762a, 764a, 766a, 766b 23.00
Nos. 761-766 (6) 5.55 5.55

Horses A154

1996, Sept. 13 Litho. *Perf. 13½x14*

767 A154 19p Drag hunt .55 .55
768 A154 23p Horse driving .65 .65
769 A154 30p Race training .90 .90
770 A154 35p Show jumping 1.10 1.10
771 A154 41p Pony club 1.20 1.20
772 A154 60p Shire horses 1.75 1.75
Nos. 767-772 (6) 6.15 6.15

Christmas A155

19p, Journey to Bethlehem. 23p, Archangel Gabriel visits shepherds. 30p, Nativity. 60p, Magi.

1996, Nov. 12 *Perf. 13x13½*

773 A155 19p multicolored .55 .55
774 A155 23p multicolored .65 .65
775 A155 30p multicolored 1.00 1.00
776 A155 60p multicolored 1.60 1.60
Nos. 773-776 (4) 3.80 3.80

Souvenir Sheet

New Year 1997 (Year of the Ox) — A156

1997, Feb. 7 Litho. *Perf. 13½*

777 A156 £1 multicolored 3.50 3.50
a. With added inscription in sheet margin 4.00 4.00

No. 777a inscribed in sheet margin with "JERSEY AT HONG KONG '97" in red and Hong Kong '97 emblem in black.

Birds — A157

1p, Red-breasted merganser. 10p, Common tern. 15p, Black headed gull. 20p, Dunlin. 24p, Puffin. 37p, Oystercatcher. 75p, Redshank. £2, Shag.

Inscribed "1997"

1997, Feb. 12 *Perf. 14½*

778 A157 1p multicolored .25 .25
779 A157 10p multicolored .25 .25
780 A157 15p multicolored .35 .35
781 A157 20p multicolored .65 .50
782 A157 24p multicolored .75 .55
783 A157 37p multicolored .85 .85
784 A157 75p multicolored 2.25 2.25
785 A157 £2 multicolored 5.50 5.50
a. Souv. sheet of 8, #778-785 13.00 13.00
b. As "a," with added inscription in sheet margin 13.50 13.50

No. 785b contains PACIFIC '97 World Philatelic Exhibition emblem in sheet margin. Issued: 5/29.

See Nos. 825-832, 864-871, 909-916.

1998, Apr. 2 **Inscribed "1998"**

781a A157 20p Dunlin .75 .80
782a A157 24p Puffin .75 .80

Lillie the Cow — A158

Designs: No. 786, Building sand castle. No. 787, Taking photographs. No. 788, Lying on beach. No. 789, In restaurant.

1997, Feb. 12 ***Die Cut Perf 9½x9***

Self-Adhesive

Inscribed "1997"

786 A158 (23p) multicolored .80 .80
787 A158 (23p) multicolored .80 .80
788 A158 (23p) multicolored .80 .80
789 A158 (23p) multicolored .80 .80
b. Strip of 4, #786-789 3.25

Peelable backing is rouletted 9 between stamps.

1999, Apr. 16 **Inscribed "1999 ©"**

786d (25p) multi 7.00 7.00
787d (25p) multi 7.00 7.00
788d (25p) multi 7.00 7.00
789d (25p) multi 7.00 7.00
789e Strip of 4, #786d-789d 28.00

2000, Dec. 9 **Coil Stamps**

Inscribed "2000 ©"

786f (26p) Die cut perf. 8¾x9 6.00 6.00
787f (26p) Die cut perf. 8¾x9 6.00 6.00
788f (26p) Die cut perf. 8¾x9 6.00 6.00
789f (26p) Die cut perf. 8¾x9 6.00 6.00
789g Strip of 4, #786f-789f 25.00

Nos. 786-789 are inscribed "U.K. MINIMUM POSTAGE PAID."

Jersey Airport, 60th Anniv. A159

1997, Mar. 10 **Litho.** ***Perf. 13½x14***

790 A159 20p DH95 Flamingo .45 .40
791 A159 24p HPR1 Marathon .55 .40
792 A159 31p DH114 Heron .65 .65
793 A159 37p Boeing 737-236 .95 .95
794 A159 43p BN Trislander 1.10 1.10
795 A159 63p BAe 146-200 1.75 1.75
Nos. 790-795 (6) 5.45 5.25

Stories and Legends A160

Europa: 20p, Bull of St. Clement. 24p, Black Horse of St. Ouen. 31p, Black Dog of Bouley Bay. 63p, Les Fontaines des Mittes.

1997, Apr. 15 **Litho.** ***Perf. 14½x14***

796 A160 20p multicolored .70 .65
797 A160 24p multicolored .85 .75
798 A160 31p multicolored 1.10 1.10
799 A160 63p multicolored 1.40 1.40
Nos. 796-799 (4) 4.05 3.90

1997 Jersey Island Games A161

1997, June 28 **Litho.** ***Perf. 13½x14***

800 A161 20p Cycling .55 .55
801 A161 24p Archery .65 .65
a. Booklet pane, 3 each #800-801 3.75 —
802 A161 31p Windsurfing .80 .80
803 A161 37p Gymnastics 1.00 1.00
a. Booklet pane, 3 each #802-803 5.50 —
804 A161 43p Volleyball 1.10 1.10
805 A161 63p Running 1.75 1.75
a. Booklet pane, 3 each #804-805 9.00 —
b. Booklet pane, #800-805 6.00 —
Complete booklet, #801a, 803a, 805a-805b 25.00
Nos. 800-805 (6) 5.85 5.85

Jesey Wildlife Preservation Trust A162

Endangered species: 20p, Mallorcan midwife toad. 24p, Aye-aye. 31p, Echo parakeet. 37p, Pigmy hog. 43p, St. Lucia whip-tail. 63p, Madagascar teal.

1997, Sept. 2 **Litho.** ***Perf. 13***

806 A162 20p multicolored .55 .50
807 A162 24p multicolored .65 .55
808 A162 31p multicolored 1.00 1.00
809 A162 37p multicolored 1.10 1.10
810 A162 43p multicolored 1.25 1.25
811 A162 63p multicolored 1.90 1.90
Nos. 806-811 (6) 6.45 6.30

Trees — A163

1997, Sept. 2 ***Perf. 14½***

812 A163 20p Ash .55 .50
813 A163 24p Elder .65 .55
814 A163 31p Beech 1.00 1.00
815 A163 37p Sweet chestnut 1.10 1.10
816 A163 43p Hawthorn 1.25 1.25
817 A163 63p Common oak 1.90 1.90
Nos. 812-817 (6) 6.45 6.30

Christmas A164

Santa Claus at various Jersey landmarks: 20p, Jersey Airport. 24p, St. Aubin's Harbor. 31p, Mont Orgueil Castle. 63p, Royal Square, St. Helier.

1997, Nov. 11 **Litho.** ***Perf. 14***

818 A164 20p multicolored .60 .60
819 A164 24p multicolored .70 .70
820 A164 31p multicolored 1.00 1.00
821 A164 63p multicolored 1.90 1.90
Nos. 818-821 (4) 4.20 4.20

Queen Elizabeth II and Prince Philip, 50th Wedding Anniv. A165

Designs: No. 822, Wedding portrait. No. 823, Anniversary portrait.
£1.50, Full length wedding portrait, vert.

1997, Nov. 20 **Litho.** ***Perf. 14½***

822 A165 50p multicolored 1.25 1.25
823 A165 50p multicolored 1.25 1.25
a. Pair, #822-823 3.00 3.00

Souvenir Sheet

Perf. 13½x14

824 A165 £1.50 multicolored 4.00 4.00

No. 824 contains one 38x51mm stamp.

Bird Type of 1997

2p, Sanderling. 5p, Great crested grebe. 21p, Sandwich tern. 25p, Brent goose. 30p, Fulmar. 40p, Turnstone. 60p, Avocet. £1, Razorbill.

1998, Jan. 28 **Litho.** ***Perf. 14½***

825 A157 2p multicolored .25 .25
826 A157 5p multicolored .25 .25
827 A157 21p multicolored .45 .45
828 A157 25p multicolored .60 .60
829 A157 30p multicolored .70 .70
830 A157 40p multicolored .95 .95
831 A157 60p multicolored 1.40 1.40
832 A157 £1 multicolored 3.00 3.00
a. Souvenir sheet of 8, #825-832 8.00 8.00
Nos. 825-832 (8) 7.60 7.60

Souvenir Sheet

New Year 1998 (Year of the Tiger) — A166

1998, Jan. 28 ***Perf. 14***

833 A166 £1 multicolored 3.50 3.50

Buses A167

Designs: 20p, JMT Bristol 4 Tonner, 1923. 24p, SCS Regent Double Decker, 1934. 31p, Slade's Dennis Lancet, 1936. 37p, Tantivy Leyland PLSC Lion, 1947. 43p, JBS Morris Bus, 1958. 63p, JMT Leyland Titan TD4 Double Decker, 1961.

1998, Apr. 2 **Litho.** ***Perf. 14***

834 A167 20p multicolored .65 .55
835 A167 24p multicolored .75 .60
a. Bklt. pane, 3 each #834-835 5.25
836 A167 31p multicolored .85 .80
837 A167 37p multicolored 1.20 1.20
a. Bklt. pane, 3 each #836-837 6.25
838 A167 43p multicolored 1.25 1.25
839 A167 63p multicolored 1.75 1.75
a. Bklt. pane, 3 each #838-839 8.00
b. Bklt. pane, 1 each, #834-839 5.75
Complete booklet, #835a, 837a, 839a, 839b 27.50
Nos. 834-839 (6) 6.45 6.15

National Festivals — A168

Europa: 20p, Creative Arts Festival. 24p, Jazz Festival. 31p, Good Food Festival. 63p, Floral Festival.

1998, Apr. 2 ***Perf. 14x13½***

840 A168 20p multicolored .65 .45
841 A168 24p multicolored .70 .55
842 A168 31p multicolored .90 .90
843 A168 63p multicolored 1.75 1.75
Nos. 840-843 (4) 4.00 3.65

Yachting — A169

Nos. 844-848: Various Hobie Cats sailing in St. Aubin's Bay.

Nos. 849-853: Various yachts racing in annual "Lombard Challenge."

1998, May 18 **Litho.** ***Perf. 13***

844 A169 20p multicolored .50 .50
845 A169 20p multicolored .50 .50
846 A169 20p multicolored .50 .50
847 A169 20p multicolored .50 .50
848 A169 20p multicolored .50 .50
a. Strip of 5, #844-848 3.00 3.00
849 A169 24p multicolored .55 .55
850 A169 24p multicolored .55 .55
851 A169 24p multicolored .55 .55
852 A169 24p multicolored .55 .55
853 A169 24p multicolored .55 .55
a. Strip of 5, #849-853 3.25 3.25

"Days Gone By" — A170

Jersey lily and: No. 854, Cider making. No. 855, Potato barrels transported by horse and cart. No. 856, Gathering seaweed for fertilizer. No. 857, Milking Jersey cows by hand.

Serpentine Die Cut Perf. 11¼

1998, Aug. 11 **Litho.**

Self-Adhesive

Inscribed "1998"

854 A170 (20p) multicolored .90 .90
855 A170 (20p) multicolored .90 .90
856 A170 (20p) multicolored .90 .90
857 A170 (20p) multicolored .90 .90
a. Strip of 4, #854-857 4.00

Inscribed "1999"

854b (20p) multi 7.50 7.50
855b (20p) multi 7.50 7.50
856b (20p) multi 7.50 7.50
857b (20p) multi 7.50 7.50
857c Strip of 4, #854b-857b 30.00

Issued: 7/16/99.

Inscribed "2000"

854d (20p) multi 6.50 6.50
855d (20p) multi 6.50 6.50
856d (20p) multi 6.50 6.50
857d (20p) multi 6.50 6.50
857e Strip of 4, #854d-857d 26.00

Issued: 11/3/00.

Inscribed "2001"

854f (20p) multi 5.00 5.00
855f (20p) multi 5.00 5.00
856f (20p) multi 5.00 5.00
857f (20p) multi 5.00 5.00
857g Strip of 4, #854f-857f 22.50

Issued: 11/19/01.

Inscribed "2003"

854h (20p) multi 2.25 2.25
855h (20p) multi 2.25 2.25
856h (20p) multi 2.25 2.25
857h (20p) multi 2.25 2.25
857i Strip of 4, #854h-857h 10.00

Nos. 854-857h are inscribed "Bailiwick / Minimum Postage Paid."
Issued: 4/4/03.

Marine Life A171

1998, Aug. 11 Litho. *Perf. 15x14½*

No.	Type	Description	Unused	Used
858	A171	20p Bass	.45	.45
859	A171	24p Red gurnard	.70	.70
860	A171	31p Skate	.90	.90
861	A171	37p Mackerel	1.10	1.10
862	A171	43p Tope	1.20	1.20
863	A171	63p Cuckoo wrasse	1.75	1.75
		Nos. 858-863 (6)	6.10	6.10

Intl. Year of the Ocean.

Bird Type of 1997

4p, Gannet. 22p, Ringed plover. 26p, Grey plover. 31p, Golden plover. 32p, Greenshank. 35p, Curlew. 44p, Herring gull. 50p, Great black-backed gull.

1998, Aug. 11 *Perf. 14½*

No.	Type	Description	Unused	Used
864	A157	4p multicolored	.25	.25
865	A157	22p multicolored	.45	.45
866	A157	26p multicolored	.60	.60
867	A157	31p multicolored	.80	.80
868	A157	32p multicolored	.80	.80
869	A157	35p multicolored	.85	.85
870	A157	44p multicolored	1.10	1.10
871	A157	50p multicolored	1.20	1.20
a.		Souvenir sheet of 8, #864-871	7.00	7.00
		Nos. 864-871 (8)	6.05	6.05

Jersey Autumn Flowers A172

20p, Iris. 24p, Carnations. 31p, Chrysanthemums. 37p, Pinks. 43p, Roses. 63p, Lilies. £1.50, Lilium star gazer.

1998, Oct. 23 Litho. *Perf. 14½*

No.	Type	Description	Unused	Used
872	A172	20p multi	.60	.45
873	A172	24p multi	.70	.60
874	A172	31p multi	.90	.80
875	A172	37p multi	1.10	1.10
876	A172	43p multi	1.25	1.25
877	A172	63p multi	1.75	1.75
		Nos. 872-877 (6)	6.30	5.95

Souvenir Sheet

Perf. 14

No.	Type	Description	Unused	Used
878	A172	£1.50 multi	4.50	4.50

No. 878 contains one 50x38mm stamp. Italia '98 (No. 878).

Christmas A173

Island manger (crib), service club sponsor: 20p, Central Market, Jersey Round Table. 24p, St. Thomas' Church, Soroptimist Intl. of Jersey. 31p, Trinity Parish Church, Rotary Club of Jersey. 63p, Royal Square, Lions Club of Jersey.

1998, Nov. 10 *Perf. 13x13½*

No.	Type	Description	Unused	Used
879	A173	20p multicolored	.45	.45
880	A173	24p multicolored	.60	.60
881	A173	31p multicolored	.80	.80
882	A173	63p multicolored	1.90	1.90
		Nos. 879-882 (4)	3.75	3.75

Souvenir Sheet

New Year 1999 (Year of the Rabbit) — A174

1999, Feb. 16 Litho. *Perf. 13½*

No.	Type	Description	Unused	Used
883	A174	£1 multicolored	4.00	4.00

UPU, 125th Anniv. A175

Jersey mail transport: 20p, Eastern Railway train. 24p, Mail steamer, "Brighton." 43p, DH 86A, first airmail arrival. 63p, Morris Minor P.O. van.

1999, Feb. 16 *Perf. 14*

No.	Type	Description	Unused	Used
884	A175	20p multicolored	.60	.55
885	A175	24p multicolored	.70	.65
886	A175	43p multicolored	1.10	1.10
887	A175	63p multicolored	1.75	1.75
		Nos. 884-887 (4)	4.15	4.05

Royal Natl. Lifeboat Institution, 175th Anniv. A176

75p, Jessica Eliza, St. Catherine. £ 1, Alexander Coutanche, St. Helier.

1999, Feb. 16 *Perf. 14½*

No.	Type	Description	Unused	Used
888	A176	75p multicolored	2.25	1.00
889	A176	£1 multicolored	3.00	1.25
a.		Pair, #888-889	5.50	5.50

Orchids — A177

Designs: 21p, Cymbidium Maufant "Jersey." 25p, Miltonia Millbrook "Jersey." 31p, Paphiopedilum Transvaal. 37p, Paphiopedilum Elizabeth Castle. 43p, Calanthe Five Oaks. 63p, Cymbidium Icho Tower "Trinity."
£1.50, Miltonia Portelet.

Perf. 14¼x13¼

1999, Mar. 19 Litho.

No.	Type	Description	Unused	Used
890	A177	21p multicolored	.65	.50
891	A177	25p multicolored	.65	.50
892	A177	31p multicolored	.90	.70
893	A177	37p multicolored	1.00	.80
894	A177	43p multicolored	1.10	.90
895	A177	63p multicolored	2.50	2.00
		Nos. 890-895 (6)	6.80	5.40

Souvenir Sheet

Perf. 13½

No.	Type	Description	Unused	Used
896	A177	£1.50 multicolored	5.25	5.25

Australia '99 World Stamp Expo (No. 896).

IBRA'99 Intl. Philatelic Exhibition, Nuremberg A178

National Parks: 21p, Howard Davis Park. 25p, Sir Winston Churchill Memorial Park. 31p, Coronation Park. 63p, La Collette Gardens.

1999, Apr. 27 *Perf. 13x13½*

No.	Type	Description	Unused	Used
897	A178	21p multicolored	.60	.50
898	A178	25p multicolored	.85	.70
899	A178	31p multicolored	1.25	1.00
900	A178	63p multicolored	2.25	2.00
		Nos. 897-900 (4)	4.95	4.20

Europa (Nos. 898-899).

Wedding of Prince Edward and Sophie Rhys-Jones — A179

1999, June 19 Litho. *Perf. 14½*

No.	Type	Description	Unused	Used
901	A179	35p yellow & multi	1.25	1.25
902	A179	35p blue & multi	1.25	1.25
a.		Pair, #901-902	2.50	2.50

Classic Car Type of 1989

Designs: 21p, 1899 Jersey-built Benz. 25p, 1910 Star Tourer. 31p, 1938 Citroen "Traction Avant." 37p, 1937 Talbot BG110 Tourer. 43p, 1934 Morris Cowley Six Special Coupé. 63p, 1946 Ford Anglia E04A Saloon.

1999, July 2 Litho. *Perf. 14*

No.	Type	Description	Unused	Used
903	A101	21p multicolored	.55	.45
904	A101	25p multicolored	.65	.65
a.		Bklt. pane, 3 each #903-904	3.75	
905	A101	31p multicolored	.80	.65
906	A101	37p multicolored	1.25	1.00
a.		Bklt. pane, 3 each #905-906	6.25	
907	A101	43p multicolored	1.50	1.25
908	A101	63p multicolored	1.75	1.50
a.		Bklt. pane, 3 each #907-908	10.00	
b.		Booklet pane, #903-908	6.50	
		Complete booklet, #904a, 906a, 908a, 908b	27.50	
		Nos. 903-908 (6)	6.50	5.50

PhilexFrance '99 (Nos. 904a, 906a, 908a-908b).

Bird Type of 1997

23p, Bar-tailed godwit. 27p, Common scoter. 28p, Lesser black-backed gull. 29p, Little egret. 33p, Little grebe. 34p, Cormorant. 45p, Rock pipit. 65p, Gray heron.

1999, Aug. 21 Litho. *Perf. 14¾*

No.	Type	Description	Unused	Used
909	A157	23p multicolored	.55	.50
910	A157	27p multicolored	.65	.60
911	A157	28p multicolored	.75	.65
912	A157	29p multicolored	.75	.65
913	A157	33p multicolored	.80	.70
914	A157	34p multicolored	.80	.70
915	A157	45p multicolored	1.20	1.10
916	A157	65p multicolored	1.50	1.40
a.		Souvenir sheet of 8, #909-916	8.00	8.00
		Nos. 909-916 (8)	7.00	6.30

Small Mammals A180

Designs: 21p, Hedgehog. 25p, Red squirrel. 31p, Nathusius pipestrelle. 37p, Jersey bank vole. 43p, Lesser white-toothed shrew. 63p, Common mole.

1999, Aug. 21 Litho. *Perf. 13¼x13*

No.	Type	Description	Unused	Used
917	A180	21p multicolored	.55	.45
918	A180	25p multicolored	.65	.55
919	A180	31p multicolored	1.80	.65
920	A180	37p multicolored	1.25	1.10
921	A180	43p multicolored	1.25	1.10
922	A180	63p multicolored	2.50	2.25
		Nos. 917-922 (6)	8.00	6.10

Lighthouses A181

1999, Oct. 5 Litho. *Perf. 14*

No.	Type	Description	Unused	Used
923	A181	21p Gorey Pierhead	.55	.45
924	A181	25p La Corbiere	.65	.55
925	A181	34p Noirmont Point	.90	.75
926	A181	38p Demie de Pas	1.25	1.00
927	A181	44p Greve d'Azette	1.50	1.25
928	A181	64p Sorel Point	2.50	2.00
		Nos. 923-928 (6)	7.35	6.00

Christmas A182

Poinsettias and: 21p, Mistletoe. 25p, Holly. 34p, Ivy. 64p, Christmas rose.

1999, Nov. 9 Litho. *Perf. 13¾*

No.	Type	Description	Unused	Used
929	A182	21p multi	.55	.45
930	A182	25p multi	.65	.55
931	A182	34p multi	1.40	.75
932	A182	64p multi	2.00	2.00
		Nos. 929-932 (4)	4.60	3.75

Coat of Arms A183

Litho. & Embossed with Foil Application

2000, Jan. 1 *Perf. 13¼*

No.	Type	Description	Unused	Used
933	A183	£10 gold & multi	25.00	22.00

Millennium.

Souvenir Sheet

New Year 2000 (Year of the Dragon) — A184

2000, Feb. 5 Litho. *Perf. 13¾*

No.	Type	Description	Unused	Used
934	A184	£1 multi	3.50	3.50

Europa Issue

Common Design Type and

A185

2000, May 9 ***Perf. 13¼x13***

935 A185 26p multi 1.00 1.00
936 CD17 34p multi 1.40 1.40

Stampin' the Future — A186

Children's Stamp Design Contest Winners: No. 937, Ocean Adventure, by Gemma Carré. No. 938, Solar Power, by Chantal Varley-Best. No. 939, Floating City and Space Cars, by Nicola Singleton. No. 940, Conservation, by Carly Logan.

2000, May 9 **Litho.** ***Perf. 14***

937 A186 22p multi .75 .65
938 A186 22p multi .75 .65
939 A186 22p multi .75 .65
940 A186 22p multi .75 .65
a. Souvenir sheet, #937-940 3.00 3.00
Nos. 937-940 (4) 3.00 2.60

Ships — A187

No. 941, Roman merchant ship. No. 942, Viking long boat. No. 943, Warship, 13th cent. No. 944, Merchant ship, 14th-15th cent. No. 945, Tudor warship, 16th cent.

No. 946, Warship, 17th cent. No. 947, Navy cutter, 18th cent. #948, Barque, 19th cent. No. 949, Oyster cutter, 19th cent. No. 950, Ketch, 20th cent.

2000, May 22 ***Perf. 13¾***

941 A187 22p multi .55 .25
942 A187 22p multi .55 .25
943 A187 22p multi .55 .25
944 A187 22p multi .55 .25
945 A187 22p multi .55 .25
a. Strip of 5, #941-945 2.75 2.75
946 A187 26p multi .60 .25
947 A187 26p multi .60 .25
948 A187 26p multi .60 .25
949 A187 26p multi .60 .25
a. Booklet pane, #941-944, 946-949 4.75
950 A187 26p multi .60 .25
a. Strip of 5, #946-950 5.00 5.00
b. Souvenir sheet, #941-950 7.50 7.50
c. Booklet pane, #941-942, 944-946, 948-950 4.00
d. Booklet pane, #941, 943-947, 949-950 5.00 5.00
e. Booklet pane, #941-943, 945-948, 950 4.00
f. Bklt. pane, #942-945, 947-950 5.00
Booklet, #949a, 950c-950f 23.00
g. As "b," with London Stamp Show 2000 emblem added in sheet margin 7.50 7.50

London 2000 Stamp Show.

Marine Mammals A188

Designs: 22p, Bottle-nosed dolphin. 26p, Long-finned pilot whale. 34p, Harbor porpoise. 38p, Atlantic gray seal. 44p, Risso's dolphin. 64p, White-beaked dolphin.
£1.50, Common dolphin.

2000, June 5 ***Perf. 14¾x14***

951 A188 22p multi .60 .55
952 A188 26p multi .65 .60
953 A188 34p multi .95 .85
954 A188 38p multi 1.25 1.10
955 A188 44p multi 1.40 1.25
956 A188 64p multi 1.75 1.75
Nos. 951-956 (6) 6.60 6.10

Souvenir Sheet

957 A188 £1.50 multi 5.00 5.00
a. As #957, with World Stamp Expo 2000 emblem in margin 6.00 6.00

No. 957 contains one 81x29mm stamp.
Issued: No. 957a, 7/7/00.

Prince William, 18th Birthday A189

William &: No. 958, Mountain. No. 959, Polo player. No. 960, Fireworks. No. 961, Beaumarais Castle.

2000, June 21 ***Perf. 14¼x14½***

958 A189 75p multi 2.25 1.50
959 A189 75p multi 2.25 1.50
960 A189 75p multi 2.25 1.50
961 A189 75p multi 2.25 1.50
Nos. 958-961 (4) 9.00 6.00

Queen Mother, 100th Birthday A190

Litho. with Foil Application

2000, Aug. 4 ***Perf. 14½x14¼***

962 A190 50p Purple hat 1.50 1.25
963 A190 50p Pink hat 1.50 1.25
a. Souvenir sheet, #962-963 3.00 3.00

Battle of Britain, 60th Anniv. A191

Designs: 22p, Supermarine Spitfire Mk. Ia. 26p, Hawker Hurricane Mk. I. 36p, Bristol Blenheim Mk. IV. 40p, Vickers Wellington Mk. Ic. 45p, Boulton Paul Defiant Mk. I. 65p, Short Sunderland Mk. I.

2000, Sept. 15 **Litho.** ***Perf. 14¼x14***

964 A191 22p multi .65 .55
965 A191 26p multi .75 .65
966 A191 36p multi 1.00 .85
967 A191 40p multi 1.10 .95
968 A191 45p multi 1.25 1.10
969 A191 65p multi 1.90 1.60
Nos. 964-969 (6) 6.65 5.70

Christmas A192

2000, Nov. 7 ***Perf. 13***

970 A192 22p Virgin Mary .70 .55
971 A192 26p Shepherd .80 .65
972 A192 36p Angel 1.25 1.00
973 A192 65p Magus 2.00 1.60
Nos. 970-973 (4) 4.75 3.80

Souvenir Sheet

New Year 2001 (Year of the Snake) — A193

2001, Jan. 24 **Litho.** ***Perf. 13¾***

974 A193 £1 multi 3.25 3.25

Steamships on Jersey-France Route — A194

2001, Jan. 24 ***Perf. 13x13¼***

975 A194 22p Rose .60 .55
976 A194 26p Comete .75 .65
977 A194 36p Cygne .95 .85
978 A194 40p Victoria 1.10 .95
979 A194 45p Attala 1.40 1.25
980 A194 65p Brittany 2.00 1.60
Nos. 975-980 (6) 6.80 5.85

Agricultural Products — A195

No. 981: a, Jersey cows. b, Royal potatoes. c, Tomatoes. d, Cauliflower and purple broccoli. e, Zucchini and peppers.

Serpentine Die Cut 11¼

2001, Apr. 3 **Self-Adhesive**

Inscribed "2001"

981 Strip of 5 20.00
a.-e. A195 (26p) Any single 1.75 1.75
f. As No. 981, inscribed "2002" 14.00
g. As No. 981, inscribed "2003" 9.00
h. As No. 981, inscribed "2005" 8.00

Issued: No. 981f, 10/4/02; No. 981g, 4/4/03; No. 981h, 10/21/05.

Navy Ships Named Jersey A196

Ships in service from: 23p, 1654-91. 26p, 1694-98. 37p, 1698-1731. 41p, 1736-83. 46p, 1860-73. 66p, 1938-41.

2001, Apr. 3 ***Perf. 14***

982 A196 23p multi .60 .55
983 A196 26p multi .75 .65
984 A196 37p multi .95 .85
985 A196 41p multi 1.25 .95
986 A196 46p multi 1.40 1.25
987 A196 66p multi 2.00 1.60
Nos. 982-987 (6) 6.95 5.85

Queen Elizabeth II, 75th Birthday — A197

2001, Apr. 21 ***Perf. 14x14¾***

988 A197 £3 multi 7.50 7.50

Pond Life A198

Designs: 23p, Agile frog. 26p, Trout. 37p, White water lily. 41p, Common blue damselfly. 46p, Palmate newt. 66p, Tufted duck.
£1.50, Kingfisher.

2001, May 22 ***Perf. 14¾x14***

989 A198 23p multi .75 .65
990 A198 26p multi .85 .75
991 A198 37p multi 1.25 1.10
992 A198 41p multi 1.40 1.20
993 A198 46p multi 1.40 1.40
994 A198 66p multi 2.50 2.25
Nos. 989-994 (6) 8.15 7.35

Souvenir Sheet

Perf. 14¼

995 A198 £1.50 multi 6.00 6.00
a. As #995, with Belgica 2001 emblem in margin 7.00 7.00

Europa (Nos. 990-991). No. 995 contains one 38x50mm stamp.
Issued: No. 995a, 6/9/01.

Birds of Prey — A199

Designs: 23p, Long-eared owl. 26p, Peregrine falcon. 37p, Short-eared owl. 41p, Marsh harrier. 46p, Sparrowhawk. 66p, Tawny owl.
£1.50, Barn owl.

2001, July 3 **Litho.** ***Perf. 13½***

996 A199 23p multi .65 .55
997 A199 26p multi .75 .65
998 A199 37p multi 1.00 .85
999 A199 41p multi 1.25 .95
1000 A199 46p multi 1.50 1.10
a. Booklet pane, #997, 998, 2 each #996, 1000 7.50 —
1001 A199 66p multi 1.90 1.60
a. Booklet pane, #996-1001 7.50 —
b. Booklet pane, 2 each #996, 998, 1001 7.50 —
c. Booklet pane, #996-998, 1001, 2 #999 7.00 —
Nos. 996-1001 (6) 7.05 5.70
1002 A199 £1.50 Booklet pane of 1 12.00
Booklet, #1000a, 1001a, 1001b, 1001c, 1002 42.50

Souvenir Sheet

1003 A199 £1.50 multi 6.00 6.00
a. Like #1003, with Hafnia 01 emblem 6.00 6.00

Issued: No. 1003a, 10/16/01.

On No. 1002, "Tyto" is 4mm from the owl's head (owl is in center of stamp), while on No. 1003, it is 9mm from the head (owl is at right of stamp). The size of No. 1002 is 154x100mm, while the size of No. 1003 is 110x75.

Souvenir Sheet

Racing Yacht Jersey Clipper — A200

2001, Sept. 17 ***Perf. 13¾***
1004 A200 £1.50 multi 6.00 6.00

Fire Engines — A201

Designs: 23p, Tilley 26 manual, c. 1845. 26p, Albion Merryweather, c. 1935. 37p, Dennis Ace, c. 1940. 41p, Dennis F8 pump escape, c. 1952. 46p, Land Rover Merryweather, c. 1968. 66p, Dennis Carmichael, c. 1989.

2001, Sept. 25 ***Perf. 13x13¼***
1005 A201 23p multi .65 .55
1006 A201 26p multi .75 .65
1007 A201 37p multi 1.00 .85
1008 A201 41p multi 1.10 .95
1009 A201 46p multi 1.25 1.10
1010 A201 66p multi 1.90 1.60
Nos. 1005-1010 (6) 6.65 5.70

Christmas — A202

No. 1011: a, Nativity. b, Street decorations. c, Carolers. d, Santa Claus. e, Bells and other ornaments on Christmas tree.

No. 1012: a, Adoration of the Shepherds. b, Carolers, Santa Claus, reindeer. c, Bell ornament, Christmas tree with candles. d, Church bells. e, Cracker with bells on wrapper.

Serpentine Die Cut 11x11¼
2001, Nov. 6 **Self-Adhesive**
Coil Stamps
Inscribed "2001"

1011 Horiz. strip of 5 5.00
a.-e. A202 (23p) green & multi, any single 1.00 .75
1012 Horiz. strip of 5 6.00 —
a.-e. A202 (29p) red & multi, any single 1.20 .75
f. Booklet pane of 16, 2 each #1011a, 1011c-1011e, 1012a-1012b, 1012d-1012e 18.00

On Nos. 1011-1012, the matrix was stripped from around the stamps; on the booklets, the matrix remains surrounding the stamps.

2002, Nov. 23 **Inscribed "2002"**
1011f Horiz. strip of 5 9.00
g.-k. A202 (23p) any single 1.75 .75
1012g Horiz. strip of 5 11.00
h.-l. A202 (29p) any single 2.00 .75

2003, Nov. 10 **Inscribed "2003"**
1011l Horiz. strip of 5 12.00
m.-q. A202 (23p) any single 2.00 .75

Jersey State Vessels — A203

Designs: 23p, Launch "Duchess of Normandy." 29p, Tugboat "Duke of Normandy." 38p, Customs patrol boat "Challenger." 47p, Pilot boat "Le Fret." 68p, Sea fisheries protection boat "Norman Le Brocq."

2002, Jan. 22 **Litho.** ***Perf. 13x13¼***
1013 A203 23p multi .60 .55
1014 A203 29p multi .80 .70
1015 A203 38p multi .95 .85
1016 A203 47p multi 1.40 1.25
1017 A203 68p multi 2.00 1.90
Nos. 1013-1017 (5) 5.75 5.25

Reign of Queen Elizabeth II, 50th Anniv. — A204

Litho. & Embossed With Foil Application

2002, Feb. 6 ***Perf. 13¼***
1018 A204 £3 multi 8.00 8.00

Souvenir Sheet

New Year 2002 (Year of the Horse) — A205

2002, Feb. 12 **Litho.** ***Perf. 13¾***
1019 A205 £1 multi 3.00 3.00

Battle of Flowers Depictions of Circus Figures — A206

2002, Mar. 12 **Litho.** ***Perf. 13¾***
1020 A206 23p Elephant, cats .70 .55
1021 A206 29p Clown .90 .70
1022 A206 38p Clown, diff. 1.40 1.10
1023 A206 68p Seal 2.40 2.00
Nos. 1020-1023 (4) 5.40 4.35

Europa (Nos. 1021-1022).

La Moye Golf Club, Cent. — A207

Designs: 23p, Aubrey Boomer. 29p, Harry Vardon. 38p, Sir Henry Cotton. 47p, Golfer's swing. 68p, Golfer addressing ball.

2002, Apr. 16 ***Perf. 14***
1024 A207 23p multi .65 .55
1025 A207 29p multi .85 .70
1026 A207 38p multi 1.00 .85
1027 A207 47p multi 1.40 1.10
1028 A207 68p multi 2.10 1.75
Nos. 1024-1028 (5) 6.00 4.95

Police Vehicles — A208

Designs: 23p, Vauxhall 12, c. 1952. 29p, 1959-60 Jaguar 2.4 MkII. 38p, 1972-73 Austin 1800. 40p, Ford Cortina MkIV, c. 1978. 47p, 1995-2000 Honda motorcycle. 68p, 1998-2000 Vauxhall Vectra.

2002, May 24 **Litho.** ***Perf. 13x13¼***
1029 A208 23p multi .65 .55
1030 A208 29p multi .85 .70
1031 A208 38p multi 1.00 .85
1032 A208 40p multi 1.20 .80
1033 A208 47p multi 1.40 1.10
1034 A208 68p multi 2.00 1.75
Nos. 1029-1034 (6) 7.10 5.75

Insects — A209

Designs: 23p, Honeybee. 29p, Seven-spot ladybug. 38p, Great green bush cricket. 40p, Greater horntail. 47p, Emperor dragonfly. 68p, Hawthorn shield bug.

2002, June 18 ***Perf. 14¾x14***
1035 A209 23p multi .65 .55
1036 A209 29p multi .85 .70
1037 A209 38p multi 1.00 .85
1038 A209 40p multi 1.20 .80
1039 A209 47p multi 1.40 1.10
1040 A209 68p multi 2.00 1.75
Nos. 1035-1040 (6) 7.10 5.75

Queen Mother Elizabeth (1900-2002) — A210

Litho. with Foil Application
2002, Aug. 4 ***Perf. 14x14¾***
1041 A210 £2 multi 6.00 6.00

Battle of Flowers, Cent. — A211

Designs: 23p, Hydrangeas. 29p, Chrysanthemums. 38p, Hare's tails, pampas grass. 40p, Asters. 47p, Carnations. 68p, Gladioli.

£2, Float "Zanzibar."

2002, Aug. 8 **Litho.** ***Perf. 13x13¼***
1042 A211 23p multi .65 .55
1043 A211 29p multi .85 .70
1044 A211 38p multi 1.00 .85
1045 A211 40p multi 1.20 .80
1046 A211 47p multi 1.40 1.10
1047 A211 68p multi 2.00 1.75
a. Booklet pane, #1042-1047 9.75
Nos. 1042-1047 (6) 7.10 5.75

Souvenir Sheet
Perf. 13

1048 A211 £2 multi 6.00 6.00
a. Booklet pane of 1 6.00
Booklet, #1048a, 3 #1047a 27.50

No. 1047a has three different layouts of stamps on pane. No. 1048 contains one 76x39mm stamp. No. 1048a is larger than No. 1048, having extra selvage at left, with rouletting separating the selvage from the rest of the sheet.

Cats — A212

Designs: 23p, British dilute tortoiseshell. 29p, Cream Persian. 38p, Blue exotic shorthair. 40p, Black smoke Devon Rex. 47p, British silver tabby. 68p, Usual Abyssinian.

£2, British cream and white bi-color, vert.

2002, Oct. 12 ***Perf. 14¾x14¼***
1049 A212 23p multi .60 .55
1050 A212 29p multi .75 .70
1051 A212 38p multi 1.00 .85
1052 A212 40p multi 1.10 .90
1053 A212 47p multi 1.25 1.10
1054 A212 68p multi 1.90 1.75
Nos. 1049-1054 (6) 6.60 5.85

Souvenir Sheet
Perf. 14¼

1055 A212 £2 multi 6.00 6.00

No. 1055 contains one 38x50mm stamp.

Letter Boxes, 150th Anniv. — A213

Designs: 23p, Pillar box, Central Market. 29p, Wall box, Colomberie. 38p, Wall box, St. Clement's Inner Road. 40p, Ship box. 47p, Pillar box, Parade, 1952. 68p, Pillar box, La Collette, 2000.

£2, First letter box, David Place, 1852.

2002, Nov. 23 ***Perf. 14½x14¼***
1056 A213 23p multi .60 .55
1057 A213 29p multi .75 .70
1058 A213 38p multi 1.00 .85
1059 A213 40p multi 1.10 .90
1060 A213 47p multi 1.25 1.10
1061 A213 68p multi 1.90 1.75
Nos. 1056-1061 (6) 6.60 5.85

Souvenir Sheet
Perf. 14¾

1062 A213 £2 multi 6.00 6.00

No. 1062 contains one 39x76mm stamp.

Airplanes — A214

Designs: 23p, Sanchez-Besa Hydroplane. 29p, Supermarine S.6B. 38p, De Havilland DH84 Dragon. 40p, De Havilland DH89a Rapide. 47p, Vickers 701 Viscount. 68p, BAC One-Eleven.

£2, 1906 Biplane of Jacob Christian Hansen Ellehammer.

2003, Jan. 21 **Litho.** ***Perf. 13x13¼***
1063 A214 23p multi .60 .55
1064 A214 29p multi .80 .70
1065 A214 38p multi 1.10 .85
1066 A214 40p multi 1.10 .90
1067 A214 47p multi 1.20 1.10
1068 A214 68p multi 1.90 1.60
a. Booklet pane, #1063-1068 7.00 —
Nos. 1063-1068 (6) 6.70 5.70

Souvenir Sheet
Perf. 13¼x13

1069 A214 £2 multi 6.00 6.00
a. Booklet pane, #1069 8.00 —
Complete booklet, #1069a, 3 #1068a 30.00

No. 1069 contains one 60x40mm stamp.

The booklet contains three examples of No. 1068a, each with different margins. No. 1069a has a larger margin than No. 1069, which contains additional text and illustrations. The £2 stamp from the booklet pane No. 1069a has the date under the second "e" of "Ellehammer," while the date on the stamp from the souvenir sheet No. 1069 has the date under the first "m" of "Ellehammer."

Souvenir Sheet

New Year 2003 (Year of the Ram) — A215

2003, Feb. 1 *Perf. 13¾*
1070 A215 £1 multi 3.75 3.75

Poster Art A216

Designs: 23p, Portelet, c. 1935. 29p, Southern British Railways, c. 1952, vert. 38p, Chemins de Fer de l'Ouest, c. 1910, vert. 68p, Jersey, the Sunny Channel Island, c. 1947.

2003, Mar. 11 *Perf. 13½*
1071 A216 23p multi .55 .50
1072 A216 29p multi .90 .80
1073 A216 38p multi 1.40 1.25
1074 A216 68p multi 1.90 1.90
Nos. 1071-1074 (4) 4.75 4.45

Europa (29p, 38p).

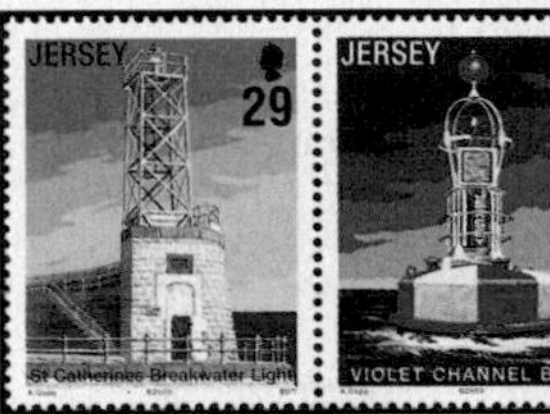

Lighthouses and Buoys — A217

No. 1075: a, St. Catherine's Breakwater Light. b, Violet Channel Buoy.
No. 1076: a, Mont Ubé Lighthouse. b, Frouquie Aubert Buoy.
No. 1077: a, Gronez Point Lighthouse. b, Banc des Ormes Buoy.

2003, Apr. 15 *Perf. 13¾*
1075 A217 Horiz. pair 1.50 1.50
a.-b. 29p Either single .60 .60
1076 A217 Horiz. pair 1.50 1.50
a.-b. 30p Either single .60 .60
1077 A217 Horiz. pair 2.50 2.50
a.-b. 48p Either single 1.00 1.00
Nos. 1075-1077 (3) 5.50 5.50

Wild Orchids — A218

Designs: 29p, Southern-marsh orchid. 30p, Loose-flowered orchid. 38p, Spotted orchid. 50p, Autumn Ladies Tresses. 53p, Green-winged orchid. 69p, Pyramidal orchid.
£2, Loose-flowered orchid, diff.

2003, May 13 *Perf. 13¼x13*
1078 A218 29p multi .80 .65
1079 A218 30p multi .85 .65
1080 A218 39p multi 1.10 .85
1081 A218 50p multi 1.40 1.10
1082 A218 53p multi 1.40 1.25
1083 A218 69p multi 1.90 1.50
Nos. 1078-1083 (6) 7.45 6.00

Souvenir Sheet

1084 A218 £2 multi 6.00 6.00
a. As #1084, with added marginal inscription 6.00 6.00

No. 1084a has Bangkok 2003 Philatelic Exhibition emblem and text, "Jersey at Bangkok 2003," added in margin. Issued, 10/4.

Coronation of Queen Elizabeth II, 50th Anniv. A219

Designs: 29p, Sovereign's orb. 30p, St. Edward's Crown. 39p, Scepter with Cross. 50p, Ampulla and Spoon. 53p, Sovereign's Ring. 69p, Armills.

Litho. With Foil Application

2003, June 2 *Perf. 14¾x14*
1085 A219 29p multi .80 .65
1086 A219 30p multi .85 .65
1087 A219 39p multi 1.10 .85
1088 A219 50p multi 1.40 1.10
1089 A219 53p multi 1.40 1.25
1090 A219 69p multi 1.90 1.50
a. Souvenir sheet, #1085-1090 7.50 7.50
Nos. 1085-1090 (6) 7.45 6.00

Souvenir Sheet

Prince William, Prince Charles and Queen Elizabeth II — A220

2003, June 21 **Litho.** *Perf. 13¾*
1091 A220 £2 multi 5.50 5.50

Prince William, 21st birthday.

Offshore Reefs and Flowers — A221

No. 1092: a, Les Ecrehous Reef, tree mallow. b, Les Minquiers Reef, smooth sow-thistle. c, Les Minquiers Reef, thrift. d, Paternosters Reef, rock samphire. e, Les Ecrehous Reef, bluebells.
Nos. 1092g, 1092m, Like No. 1092a. Nos. 1092h, 1092n, Like No. 1092b. Nos. 1092i, 1092o, Like No. 1092c. Nos. 1092j, 1092p, Like No. 1092d. Nos. 1092k, 1092q, Like No. 1092e.

Serpentine Die Cut 11
2003, Aug. 5 **Photo.** **Coil Stamps**
Self-Adhesive

1092 Horiz. strip of 5 7.00 7.00
a.-e. A221 (29p) Any single 1.25 1.25
f. Like #1092, serp. die cut 11¼, inscribed "2004" 8.00
g.-k. A221 (32p) Any single, serp. die cut 11¼ 1.40 1.40
l. Like #1092, serp. die cut 11¼, inscribed "2006" 7.00
m.-q. A221 (32p) Any single, serp. die cut 11¼, inscribed "2006" 1.40 1.40

Nos. 1092f-1092k issued 11/3/04. Nos. 1092l-1092q issued 11/16/06.

Pets — A222

Designs: 29p, Albino Rex rabbit. 30p, Labrador retriever. 38p, Canary and budgerigar. 53p, Hamster. 69p, Guinea pig.
£2, Border collie.

2003, Sept. 9 **Litho.** *Perf. 13¾*
1093 A222 29p multi .95 .95
1094 A222 30p multi .95 .95
1095 A222 38p multi 1.20 1.20
1096 A222 53p multi 1.75 1.75
1097 A222 69p multi 2.25 2.25
Nos. 1093-1097 (5) 7.10 7.10

Souvenir Sheet
Perf. 13¼

1098 A222 £2 multi 6.00 6.00

No. 1098 contains one 39x51mm stamp.

Winter Flowers A223

Designs: 29p, Japanese quince. 30p, Winter jasmine. 39p, Snowdrop. 48p, Winter heath. 53p, Chinese witch hazel. 69p, Winter daphne.

2003, Nov. 10 *Perf. 14¼*
1099 A223 29p multi .75 .65
1100 A223 30p multi .80 .65
1101 A223 39p multi 1.10 .85
1102 A223 48p multi 1.20 1.00
1103 A223 53p multi 1.40 1.10
1104 A223 69p multi 1.90 1.50
Nos. 1099-1104 (6) 7.15 5.75

Souvenir Sheet

New Year 2004 (Year of the Monkey) — A224

2004, Jan. 22 **Litho.** *Perf. 13¾*
1105 A224 £1 multi 3.75 3.75

British Chess Federation, Cent. — A225

2004, Jan. 22
1106 A225 29p Rook .95 .95
1107 A225 30p Knight .95 .95
1108 A225 39p Bishop 1.25 1.25
1109 A225 48p Pawn 1.50 1.50
1110 A225 53p Queen 1.75 1.75
1111 A225 69p King 2.00 2.00
Nos. 1106-1111 (6) 8.40 8.40

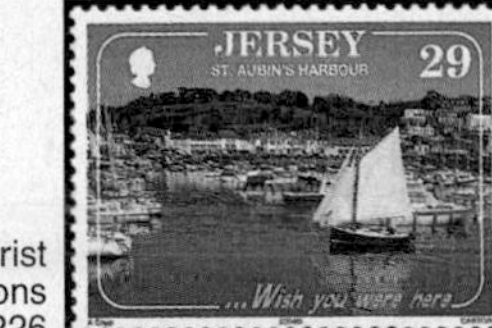

Tourist Attractions A226

Designs: 29p, St. Aubin's Harbor. 30p, Mont Orgueil Castle. 39p, Corbiere Lighthouse. 69p, Rozel Harbor.

2004, Mar. 9 *Perf. 13x13¼*
1112 A226 29p multi .95 .95
1113 A226 30p multi .95 .95
1114 A226 39p multi 1.25 1.25
1115 A226 69p multi 2.50 2.50
Nos. 1112-1115 (4) 5.65 5.65

Europa (Nos. 1113, 1114).

Waterfowl A227

Designs: 32p, Eurasian teal. 33p, Mute swan. 40p, Northern shoveler. 49p, Common pochard. 62p, Black swan. 70p, Eurasian wigeon.
£2, Mallard, vert.

2004, Apr. 6 *Perf. 14¾x14*
1116 A227 32p multi 1.00 1.00
1117 A227 33p multi 1.10 1.10
1118 A227 40p multi 1.25 1.25
1119 A227 49p multi 1.60 1.60
1120 A227 62p multi 2.00 2.00
1121 A227 70p multi 2.25 2.25
Nos. 1116-1121 (6) 9.20 9.20

Souvenir Sheet
Perf. 14¼

1122 A227 £2 multi 7.00 7.00

No. 1122 contains one 38x50mm stamp.

Orchids A228

Designs: 32p, Cymbidium lowianum "Concolor." 33p, Phragmipedium besseae var. flavum. 40p, Peristeria elata. 54p, Cymbidium tracyanum. 62p, Paphiopedilum "Victoria Village Isle of Jersey." 70p, Paphiopedilum hirsutissimum.
£2, Phragmipedium "Jason Fischer."

2004, May 25 *Perf. 13x13¼*
1123 A228 32p multi 1.00 1.00
1124 A228 33p multi 1.10 1.10
1125 A228 40p multi 1.25 1.25
1126 A228 54p multi 1.75 1.75
1127 A228 62p multi 2.00 2.00
1128 A228 70p multi 2.25 2.25
a. Booklet pane, #1123-1128 9.50 —
Nos. 1123-1128 (6) 9.35 9.35

Souvenir Sheet

1129 A228 £2 multi 6.50 6.50
a. Booklet pane #1129 6.50 —
Complete booklet, #1129a, 3 #1128a 35.00
b. Like #1129, with added marginal inscription 6.50 6.50

The booklet contains three examples of No. 1128a each with different arrangements of the stamps. No. 1129a has a larger margin than No. 1129.
No. 1129b issued 6/26. It is inscribed "Jersey at / Le Salon du Timbre 2004" in margin.

Souvenir Sheet

D-Day, 60th Anniv. — A229

2004, June 4 *Perf. 13*
1130 A229 £2 multi 6.50 6.50

Mont Orgueil Castle and Monarchs — A230

No. 1131: a, Castle in 13th century (49x32mm). b, King John, vert. (29x32mm).
No. 1132: a, Castle in 17th century (49x32mm). b, King Charles II, vert. (29x32mm).
No. 1133: a, Castle in 21st century (49x32mm). b, Queen Elizabeth II, vert. (29x32mm).

2004, June 25 *Perf. 14¾*
1131 A230 Horiz. pair 2.00 2.00
a.-b. 32p Either single 1.00 .40
1132 A230 Horiz. pair 2.00 2.00
a.-b. 33p Either single 1.00 .40

1133 A230 Horiz. pair 2.75 2.75
a.-b. 40p Either single 1.00 .50
Nos. 1131-1133 (3) 6.75 6.75

Worldwide Fund for Nature (WWF) A231

Designs: 32p, Wall lizard. 33p, Ant lion. 49p, Field cricket. 70p, Dartford warbler.

2004, July 27 ***Perf. 14¾x14***

1134 A231 32p multi 1.25 1.25
1135 A231 33p multi 1.25 1.25
1136 A231 49p multi 2.00 2.00
1137 A231 70p multi 2.75 2.75
a. Miniature sheet, 2 each #1134-1137 14.50 14.50
Nos. 1134-1137 (4) 7.25 7.25

Corals A232

Designs: 32p, Dead man's fingers. 33p, Devonshire cup. 40p, White sea fan. 54p, Pink sea fan. 62p, Sunset cup. 70p, Red fingers.

2004, Sept. 28 Litho. ***Perf. 13x13¼***

1138 A232 32p multi 1.25 1.25
1139 A232 33p multi 1.25 1.25
1140 A232 40p multi 1.60 1.60
1141 A232 54p multi 2.10 2.10
1142 A232 62p multi 2.50 2.50
1143 A232 70p multi 2.75 2.75
a. Souvenir sheet, #1141-1143 7.50 7.50
Nos. 1138-1143 (6) 11.45 11.45

Christmas A233

No. 1144: a, Nativity. b, Street with Christmas decorations. c, Santa Claus, children, Christmas tree. d, Church interior. e, Candles and holly. Each inscribed "Jersey Minimum Postage Paid."

No. 1145: a, Madonna and Child, lilies. b, Christmas stocking on mantle. c, Candles and flowers. d, Angel and candle. e, Candles in window. Each inscribed "U.K. Minimum Postage Paid."

Serpentine Die Cut 11¼x11½
2004, Nov. 2 Litho. Self-Adhesive
Coil Stamps

1144 Horiz. strip of 5 6.00
a.-e. A233 (32p) Any single 1.25 1.25
f. Like #1144, inscribed "2005" 6.00
g.-k. A233 (32p) Any single 1.25 1.25
l. Like #1144, inscribed "2006" 6.00
m.-q. A233 (32p) Any single 1.25 1.25
1145 Horiz. strip of 5 6.25
a.-e. A233 (33p) Any single 1.25 1.25
f. Like #1145, inscribed "2005" 6.25
g.-k. A233 (33p) Any single 1.25 1.25
l. Like #1145, inscribed "2006" 6.25
m.-q. A233 (33p) Any single 1.25 1.25

Nos. 1144f-1144k, 1145f-1145k issued 10/21/05. Nos. 1144l-1144q, 1145l-1145q issued 10/31/06.

Rescue Craft A234

Designs: 32p, Channel Islands Air Search airplane. 33p, Burby helicopter. 40p, Beach Lifeguard Service Surf Rescue boat. 49p, Fire Rescue inflatable boat. 70p, Royal Air Force Sea King helicopter.

2005, Jan. 18 Litho. ***Perf. 13x13¼***

1146 A234 32p multi .70 .70
1147 A234 33p multi .70 .70
1148 A234 40p multi .90 .85
1149 A234 49p multi 1.60 1.50
1150 A234 70p multi 1.90 1.75
Nos. 1146-1150 (5) 5.80 5.50

Souvenir Sheet

New Year 2005 (Year of the Rooster) — A235

2005, Feb. 9 ***Perf. 14¼***

1151 A235 £1 multi 3.75 3.75

Gastronomy A236

Designs: 32p, Conger eel soup. 33p, Oysters. 40p, Bean crock. 70p, Bourdélots with black butter.

2005, Mar. 8 Litho. ***Perf. 13¾***

1152 A236 32p multi .90 .70
1153 A236 33p multi .90 .70
1154 A236 40p multi 1.20 .85
1155 A236 70p multi 2.00 1.50
Nos. 1152-1155 (4) 5.00 3.75

Europa (33p, 40p).

Fairy Tales A237

Designs: 33p, Little Red Riding Hood. 34p, The Little Mermaid. 41p, Beauty and the Beast. 50p, Rumpelstiltskin. 73p, The Goose That Laid the Golden Egg.

£2, The Ugly Duckling.

2005, Apr. 2 ***Perf. 13x13¼***

1156 A237 33p multi .70 .70
1157 A237 34p multi .75 .75
1158 A237 41p multi .85 .85
1159 A237 50p multi 1.60 1.60
1160 A237 73p multi 2.10 2.10
Nos. 1156-1160 (5) 6.00 6.00

Souvenir Sheet
Perf. 13¼

1161 A237 £2 multi 6.00 6.00
a. As No. 1161, with Nordia 2005 emblem in sheet margin 6.00 6.00

No. 1161 contains one 49x35mm stamp, and has a hologram applied in the sheet margin. Hans Christian Andersen, birth bicentennial.

No. 1161a issued 5/26.

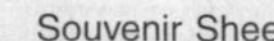
Souvenir Sheet

Jersey Soccer Association and Muratti Vase Soccer Competition, Cent. — A238

2005, Apr. 27 ***Perf.***

1162 A238 £2 multi 6.00 6.00

Souvenir Sheet

End of World War II, 60th Anniv. — A239

2005, May 9 Litho. ***Perf. 14¼***

1163 A239 £2 multi 6.00 6.00

Jersey Motor Festival A240

Automobiles: 33p, MGB GT. 34p, Mini Cooper. 41p, Citroen DS. 50p, Jaguar E Type. 56p, Volkswagen Beetle. 73p, Aston Martin DB5.

2005, June 6 ***Perf. 13x13¼***

1164 A240 33p multi 1.10 .70
1165 A240 34p multi 1.00 .75
1166 A240 41p multi 1.25 .85
1167 A240 50p multi 1.50 1.50
1168 A240 56p multi 1.75 1.75
1169 A240 73p multi 2.25 2.25
a. Booklet pane, #1164-1169 9.00 —
Complete booklet, 3 #1169a 27.50
Nos. 1164-1169 (6) 8.85 7.80

Complete booklet contains three examples of No. 1169a, each with a different margin and layout of the stamps.

Flowers — A241

Designs: 2p, Scarlet pimpernel. 4p, Common knapweed. 20p, Greater stitchwort. 30p, Common mallow. 40p, White campion. 50p, Common dog-violet. 65p, Herb Robert. £1, Three-cornered garlic.

2005, July 19 ***Perf. 13¼***

1170 A241 2p multi .25 .25
1171 A241 4p multi .25 .25
1172 A241 20p multi .60 .60
1173 A241 30p multi .90 .75
1174 A241 40p multi 1.20 .85
1175 A241 50p multi 2.75 1.75
1176 A241 65p multi 1.90 1.40
1177 A241 £1 multi 3.00 2.00
a. Souvenir sheet, #1170-1177 11.00 11.00
Nos. 1170-1177 (8) 10.85 7.85

See Nos. 1228-1235a, 1267-1274a.

Martello Towers — A242

2005, Aug. 9 ***Perf. 13¾***

1178 A242 33p Le Hocq 1.00 .70
1179 A242 34p Seymour 1.00 .75
1180 A242 41p Archirondel 1.25 .85
1181 A242 56p Kempt 1.75 1.75
1182 A242 73p Le Rocco 2.25 2.25
Nos. 1178-1182 (5) 7.25 6.30

Mushrooms A243

Designs: 33p, Pink waxcap. 34p, Boletus erythropus. 41p, Inocybe godeyi. 50p, Pepper-pot earthstar. 56p, White elfin saddle. 73p, Red waxy cap.

£2, Fairy ring mushrooms, horiz.

2005, Sept. 13 ***Perf. 13¾***

1183 A243 33p multi 1.00 .70
1184 A243 34p multi 1.00 .75
1185 A243 41p multi 1.25 .85
1186 A243 50p multi 1.50 1.10
1187 A243 56p multi 1.75 1.20
1188 A243 73p multi 2.25 1.60
Nos. 1183-1188 (6) 8.75 6.20

Souvenir Sheet
Perf. 14¼

1189 A243 £2 multi 6.00 6.00

No. 1189 contains one 50x38mm stamp.

Battle of Trafalgar, Bicent. A244

Designs: 33p, HMS Belleisle. 34p, HMS Royal Sovereign. 41p, HMS Neptune. 50p, HMS Euryalus. 73p, HMS Mars.

£2, HMS Victory.

2005, Oct. 21 ***Perf. 14***

1190 A244 33p multi 1.00 .70
1191 A244 34p multi 1.00 .75
1192 A244 41p multi 1.25 .95
1193 A244 50p multi 1.75 1.50
1194 A244 73p multi 2.25 2.00
Nos. 1190-1194 (5) 7.25 5.90

Souvenir Sheet
Perf. 14¼

1195 A244 £2 multi 6.00 6.00

No. 1195 contains one 50x38mm stamp.

Royal Jersey Militia Uniforms and Badges A245

Uniforms and badges from: 33p, Royal Jersey Regiment, ca. 1830. 34p, Royal Jersey Regiment, ca. 1844. 41p, Royal Jersey Artillery, ca. 1881. 50p, Royal Jersey Light Infantry ca. 1890. 73p, Royal Engineers, present day.

2006, Jan. 6 Litho. ***Perf. 13¼***

1196 A245 33p multi 1.00 .70
1197 A245 34p multi 1.00 .75
1198 A245 41p multi 1.25 .85
1199 A245 50p multi 1.75 1.50
1200 A245 73p multi 2.25 2.00
Nos. 1196-1200 (5) 7.25 5.80

Souvenir Sheet

New Year 2006 (Year of the Dog) — A246

2006, Jan. 29 **Litho.** ***Perf. 14¼***
1201 A246 £1 multi 3.00 3.00

Souvenir Sheet

Victoria Cross, 150th Anniv. — A247

2006, Jan. 29 ***Perf. 13¼x14***
1202 A247 £2 multi 6.00 6.00

Multiculturalism — A248

Designs: 33p, Chinese costumes. 34p, Portuguese Fado Music Festival. 41p, Polish Pisanki Easter egg tradition. 73p, Indian costumes.

2006, Mar. 7 ***Perf. 14***
1203 A248 33p multi 1.00 .70
1204 A248 34p multi 1.00 .75
1205 A248 41p multi 1.25 .85
1206 A248 73p multi 2.25 2.00
Nos. 1203-1206 (4) 5.50 4.30

Europa (34p, 41p).

Shells A249

Designs: 34p, Flat periwinkle. 37p, Painted top shell. 42p, Dog cockle. 51p, Variegated scallop. 57p, Blue-rayed limpet. 74p, European cowrie.
£2, Ormer shell.

2006, Apr. 4 **Litho.** ***Perf. 13x13¼***
1207 A249 34p multi 1.00 .75
1208 A249 37p multi 1.10 .80
1209 A249 42p multi 1.25 .90
1210 A249 51p multi 1.50 1.10
1211 A249 57p multi 1.75 1.20
1212 A249 74p multi 2.25 1.60
Nos. 1207-1212 (6) 8.85 6.35

Souvenir Sheet

Litho. & Embossed With Hologram Affixed

Perf.

1213 A249 £2 multi 6.00 6.00
a. Like #1213, with Belgica '06 emblem added in sheet margin 7.00 7.00

Portions of the designs of Nos. 1207-1212 were applied by a thermographic process producing a shiny, raised effect. No. 1213 contains one 46x30 oval stamp.
Issued: No. 1213a, 11/16.

Wedding of Prince Charles and Camilla Parker-Bowles, 1st Anniv. — A250

2006, Apr. 9 **Litho.** ***Perf. 13¼***
1214 A250 £2 multi 6.00 6.00

Queen Elizabeth II, 80th Birthday A251

Litho. & Embossed With Foil Application

2006, Apr. 21 ***Perf. 13½***
1215 A251 £5 dk bl & multi 15.00 15.00
a. Prussian blue & multi 15.00 15.00
b. Souvenir sheet, #1215a, New Zealand #2068a 20.00 20.00

See New Zealand No. 2068. No. 1215b sold for £7.

Souvenir Sheet

2006 World Cup Soccer Championships, Germany — A252

2006, June 9 **Litho.** ***Perf. 14¼***
1216 A252 £2 multi 6.00 6.00

Island Views — A253

Serpentine Die Cut 11¼

2006, July 11 **Self-Adhesive**

Coil Stamps

Inscribed "2006"

1217 A253 (37p) Greve de Lecq 1.75 1.75
a. Inscribed "2009" 1.75 1.75
1218 A253 (37p) La Rocque 1.75 1.75
a. Inscribed "2009" 1.75 1.75
1219 A253 (37p) Portelet 1.75 1.75
a. Inscribed "2009" 1.75 1.75
1220 A253 (37p) St. Brelade's Bay 1.75 1.75
a. Inscribed "2009" 1.75 1.75
b. Horiz. strip of 4, #1217-1220 7.50
c. Horiz. strip of 4, #1217a-1220a 7.50

Issued: Nos. 1217a-1220a, 1220c, 3/10/09.

Butterflies & Moths A254

Designs: 34p, Red underwing moth. 37p, Comma buttterfly. 42p, Black arches moth. 51p, Small copper butterfly. 57p, Holly blue butterfly. 74p, Orange-tip butterfly.

2006, Aug. 1 ***Perf. 14¾x14***

Stamps With White Margin

1221 A254 34p multi 1.00 .75
1222 A254 37p multi 1.10 .80
1223 A254 42p multi 1.25 .90
1224 A254 51p multi 1.50 1.10
1225 A254 57p multi 1.75 1.20
1226 A254 74p multi 2.25 1.60
Nos. 1221-1226 (6) 8.85 6.35

Souvenir Sheet

Stamps Without White Margin

1227 Sheet of 3 6.00 6.00
a. A254 51p multi 2.00 1.10
b. A254 57p multi 1.75 1.20
c. A254 74p multi 2.25 1.60

Flowers Type of 2005

Designs: 1p, Yellow bartsia. 3p, Wild angelica. 5p, Marsh St. John's wort. 15p, Bog pimpernel. 70p, Ragged robin. 75p, Brooklime. 85p, Cuckoo flower. 90p, Yellow iris.

2006, Sept. 26 **Litho.** ***Perf. 13¼***
1228 A241 1p multi .25 .25
1229 A241 3p multi .25 .25
1230 A241 5p multi .25 .25
1231 A241 15p multi .45 .35
1232 A241 70p multi 2.10 1.50
1233 A241 75p multi 2.25 1.60
1234 A241 85p multi 2.50 1.75
1235 A241 90p multi 2.75 2.00
a. Souvenir sheet, #1228-1235 11.00 11.00
Nos. 1228-1235 (8) 10.80 7.95

Jersey Post Vehicles A255

Designs: 34p, 2004 LDV Luton Van. 37p, 1999-2004 Renault Kangaroo. 42p, 1994-2004 LDV Pilot. 51p, 1988-96 Ford Transit Luton Body. 57p, Morris Marina 440/575, c. 1978. 74p, Morris Minor, c. 1969.

2006, Oct. 31 ***Perf. 13x13¼***
1236 A255 34p multi 1.00 .75
1237 A255 37p multi 1.10 .80
1238 A255 42p multi 1.25 .90
1239 A255 51p multi 1.50 1.10
1240 A255 57p multi 1.75 1.20
1241 A255 74p multi 2.25 1.60
a. Booklet pane, #1236-1241 9.50 —
b. Booklet pane, #1239-1241 + binding stub 6.00 —
Complete booklet, #1241b, 3 #1241a 35.00
c. Souvenir sheet, #1239-1241 6.00 6.00

No. 1241a has three different layouts of stamps on pane and three different margins. No. 1241c has a straight edge at left, while No. 1241b is separated from binding stub by a row of rouletting.

Minerals A256

Designs: 34p, Molybdenite. 37p, Muscovite in pegmatite vein, feldspar and quartz. 42p, Orthoclase and plagioclase. 51p, Quartz coated with manganese oxide. 74p, Smoky quartz.

2007, Jan. 23 **Litho.** ***Perf. 13x13¼***
1242 A256 34p multi 1.00 1.00
1243 A256 37p multi 1.10 1.10
1244 A256 42p multi 1.25 1.25
1245 A256 51p multi 1.50 1.50
1246 A256 74p multi 2.25 2.25
Nos. 1242-1246 (5) 7.10 7.10

Souvenir Sheet

New Year 2007 (Year of the Pig) — A257

2007, Feb. 18 ***Perf. 14¼***
1247 A257 £1 multi 3.75 3.75

Scouting, Cent. A258

Lord Robert Baden-Powell and Scouts: 34p, With kayak, sailboard and kite-propelled vehicle. 37p, With musical instruments and flags. 42p, In go-carts and wagons, scouts climbing. 74p, With uniform patches.

2007, Mar. 6 ***Perf. 14***
1248 A258 34p multi 1.00 1.00
1249 A258 37p multi 1.10 1.10
1250 A258 42p multi 1.25 1.25
1251 A258 74p multi 2.25 2.25
Nos. 1248-1251 (4) 5.60 5.60

Europa (37p, 42p).

Mammals A259

Designs: 34p, Long-tailed field mouse. 37p, Rabbits. 42p, Polecat. 51p, Common shrew. 57p, Stoat. 74p, Brown rat.

2007, Apr. 10 ***Perf. 14¾x14***

Stamps With White Frames

1252 A259 34p multi 1.00 1.00
1253 A259 37p multi 1.10 1.10
1254 A259 42p multi 1.25 1.25
1255 A259 51p multi 1.50 1.50
1256 A259 57p multi 1.75 1.75
1257 A259 74p multi 2.25 2.25
Nos. 1252-1257 (6) 8.85 8.85

Souvenir Sheet

Stamps Without White Frames

1258 Sheet of 3 6.00 6.00
a. A259 51p multi 1.50 1.50
b. A259 57p multi 1.75 1.75
c. A259 74p multi 2.25 2.25

Birds A260

Designs: 34p, House sparrow. 37p, Chaffinch. 42p, Blue tit. 51p, Blackbird. 57p, Magpie. 74p, Great tit.

2007, June 19 **Litho.** ***Perf. 13x13½***

Stamps With White Frames

1259 A260 34p multi 1.00 1.00
1260 A260 37p multi 1.10 1.10
1261 A260 42p multi 1.25 1.25
1262 A260 51p multi 1.50 1.50
1263 A260 57p multi 1.75 1.75
1264 A260 74p multi 2.25 2.25
a. Miniature sheet, #1259-1264 10.00 10.00
Nos. 1259-1264 (6) 8.85 8.85

Souvenir Sheet
Stamps Without White Frames

1265 Sheet of 3 6.00 6.00
a. A260 51p multi 1.50 1.50
b. A260 57p multi 1.75 1.75
c. A260 74p multi 2.25 2.25

See Nos. 1342-1348, 1389-1395, 1429-1435.

Souvenir Sheet

Gorey Regatta — A261

2007, June 22 ***Perf. 12¾x13½***
1266 A261 £2 multi 6.00 6.00

Flowers Type of 2005

Designs: 10p, Black bryony. 25p, Horseshoe vetch. 35p, English stonecrop. 45p, Tutsan. 55p, Ox-eye daisy. 60p, Rock sea-spurrey. 80p, Mouse-ear hawkweed. £1.50, Devil's-bit scabious.

2007, July 25 ***Perf. 13¼***
1267 A241 10p multi .30 .30
1268 A241 25p multi .75 .75
1269 A241 35p multi 1.00 1.00
1270 A241 45p multi 1.40 1.40
a. Dated "2011" 1.40 1.40
1271 A241 55p multi 1.75 1.60
1272 A241 60p multi 1.75 1.40
1273 A241 80p multi 2.40 2.25
1274 A241 £1.50 multi 4.50 4.50
a. Miniature sheet, #1267-1274 15.00 15.00
Nos. 1267-1274 (8) 13.85 13.20

Issued: No. 1270a, 6/16/11.

Summer Flowers A262

Designs: 34p, Clematis. 37p, Roses. 42p, Honeysuckles. 51p, Fuchsias. 57p, Sweet peas. 74p, Lilacs.

2007, July 25 ***Perf. 13½***
1275 A262 34p multi 1.00 1.00
1276 A262 37p multi 1.10 1.10
1277 A262 42p multi 1.25 1.25
1278 A262 51p multi 1.60 1.50
1279 A262 57p multi 2.00 1.75
1280 A262 74p multi 2.25 2.25
Nos. 1275-1280 (6) 9.20 8.85

Airplanes A263

Designs: 34p, Dornier Do 24 ATT. 37p, Avro Vulcan B-2. 42p, Junkers Ju-52. 51p, Sukhoi Su-27 Flanker. 57p, Boeing B-52 Stratofortress. 74p, Concorde.
£2.50, Red Arrows in formation.

2007, Sept. 13 ***Perf. 13x13¼***
1281 A263 34p multi 1.00 1.00
1282 A263 37p multi 1.10 1.10
1283 A263 42p multi 1.25 1.25
1284 A263 51p multi 1.60 1.50
1285 A263 57p multi 2.00 1.75
1286 A263 74p multi 2.25 2.25
a. Booklet pane, #1281-1286 9.50 —
Complete booklet, #1287a, 3 #1286a 29.00
Nos. 1281-1286 (6) 9.20 8.85

Souvenir Sheet
Perf. 13¼x13

1287 A263 £2.50 multi 7.50 7.50
a. Booklet pane, #1287 7.50

No. 1287 contains one 60x40mm stamp. Size of No. 1287a: 150x100mm. The complete booklet contains three examples of No. 1286a, each of which has a different arrangement of the stamps.

Jersey Attractions — A264

Designs: 34p, Queen's Valley Reservoir. 37p, Mont Orgueil Castle. 42p, Bonne Nuit Harbor. 51, La Hogue Bie. 57p, Bouley Bay. 74p, Le Corbiere Lighthouse.

2007, Oct. 1 ***Perf. 14x13½***
1288 A264 34p multi 1.00 1.00
1289 A264 37p multi 1.10 1.10
1290 A264 42p multi 1.25 1.25
1291 A264 51p multi 1.60 1.50
1292 A264 57p multi 2.00 1.75
1293 A264 74p multi 2.25 2.25
Nos. 1288-1293 (6) 9.20 8.85

No. 1290 inscribed "sepac". See Nos. 1396-1401, 1541-1546.

Christmas Songs A265

No. 1294: a, Minuit Chrétiens. b, While Shepherds Watched. c, O Come, All Ye Faithful. d, O Christmas Tree. e, Jingle Bells.

No. 1295: a, Hark! The Herald Angels Sing. b, We Three Kings. c, Ding Dong! Merrily On High. d, Holly and the Ivy. e, Good King Wenceslas.

Serpentine Die Cut 11¼
2007, Nov. 7 Litho. Self-Adhesive
Coil Stamps
Inscribed "2007"

1294 Horiz. strip of 5 5.50
a.-e. A265 (35p) Any single 1.00 1.00
g. As #1294, inscribed "2008" 6.00
h.-l. A265 (35p) As #1294a-1294e, any single, inscribed "2008" 1.10 1.10
m. As #1294, inscribed "2009" 6.00
n.-r. A265 (39p) As #1294a-1294e, any single, inscribed "2009" 1.10 1.10
1295 Horiz. strip of 5 6.50
a.-e. A265 (39p) Any single 1.25 1.25
g. As #1295, inscribed "2008" 7.00
h.-l. A265 (39p) As #1295a-1295e, any single, inscribed "2008" 1.25 1.25
m. As #1295, inscribed "2009" 7.00
n.-r. A265 (42p) As #1295a-1295e, any single, inscribed "2009" 1.25 1.25

Issued: Nos. 1294g, 1295g, 11/14/08; Nos. 1294m, 1295m, 11/10/09.

Wedding of Queen Elizabeth II and Prince Philip, 60th Anniv. — A266

2007, Nov. 20 ***Perf. 13¼***
1296 A266 £3 multi 9.00 9.00

Jersey Signal Station, 300th Anniv. A267

Designs: 35p, Sun, sunshine recorder, clouds. 39p, Clouds, weather symbols for wind speed, weather vane. 43p, Clouds, raindrops, weather symbols and barometer. 58p, Sun, thermometer and weather station. 76p, Tide measuring device, French flag, Moon.

2008, Jan. 15 Litho. ***Perf. 14***
1297 A267 35p multi 1.10 1.00
1298 A267 39p multi 1.25 1.25
1299 A267 43p multi 1.40 1.25
1300 A267 58p multi 1.75 1.75
1301 A267 76p multi 2.40 2.25
Nos. 1297-1301 (5) 7.90 7.50

Letters A268

Designs: 35p, Thank-you letter. 39p, Love letter. 43p, Letter to Santa Claus. 76p, Family letter.

2008, Feb. 14 ***Perf. 13½x14***
1302 A268 35p multi 1.10 1.00
1303 A268 39p multi 1.25 1.25
1304 A268 43p multi 1.40 1.25
1305 A268 76p multi 2.40 2.25
Nos. 1302-1305 (4) 6.15 5.75

Europa (39p, 43p).

Jersey Eisteddfod, Cent. A269

Designs: 35p, Arts and crafts. 39p, Dance and drama. 43p, Speech. 58p, Films and photography. 76p, Music.

2008, Mar. 3 ***Perf. 14***
1306 A269 35p multi 1.10 1.00
1307 A269 39p multi 1.25 1.25
1308 A269 43p multi 1.40 1.25
1309 A269 58p multi 1.75 1.75
1310 A269 76p multi 2.40 2.25
Nos. 1306-1310 (5) 7.90 7.50

Buses A270

Designs: 35p, Grey Bus Services Daimler CB bus. 39p, Safety Coach Service Ex LGOC K single decker bus. 43p, Jersey Motor Transport horse-drawn town bus. 52p, Jersey Motor Transport Leyland Lion Charcoal Burner bus. 58p, Jersey Bus Service Bedford WLB bus. 76p, Jersey Motor Transport Commer Commando bus.
£2.50, Jersey Motor Transport Ford Willowbrook bus.

2008, Apr. 8 ***Perf. 14¼x14***
1311 A270 35p multi 1.10 1.00
1312 A270 39p multi 1.25 1.25
1313 A270 43p multi 1.40 1.25
1314 A270 52p multi 1.60 1.40
1315 A270 58p multi 1.75 1.40
1316 A270 76p multi 2.40 1.75
Nos. 1311-1316 (6) 9.50 8.05

Souvenir Sheet
Perf. 13½x13¾

1317 A270 £2.50 multi 8.00 8.00
a. As #1317, with WIPA 08 emblem in sheet margin 8.00 8.00

No. 1317 contains one 75x30mm stamp.
No. 1317a issued 9/18.

Souvenir Sheet

World Jersey Cattle Bureau Conference — A271

2008, May 18 ***Perf. 13***
1318 A271 £2 multi 6.00 6.00

Orchids A272

Designs: 35p, Cymbidium Avranches "Victoria Village." 39p, Miltonia "Tesson Mill." 43p, Anguloa Victoire "Trinity." 52p, Phragmipedium La Hougette. 58p, Phragmipedium Havre des Pas "Jersey." 76p, Paphiopedilum Rolfei "Trinity."
£2.50, Paphiopedilum Rocco Tower.

2008, May 20 ***Perf. 13x13¼***
1319 A272 35p multi 1.10 1.00
1320 A272 39p multi 1.25 1.25
1321 A272 43p multi 1.40 1.25
1322 A272 52p multi 1.60 1.40
1323 A272 58p multi 1.75 1.40
1324 A272 76p multi 2.40 1.75
Nos. 1319-1324 (6) 9.50 8.05

Souvenir Sheet

1325 A272 £2.50 multi 8.00 8.00

Souvenir Sheet

2008 World Cricket League Division 5 Tournament, Jersey — A273

2008, May 23 Litho. ***Perf. 12¾x13¼***
1326 A273 £2 multi 6.50 6.50

Royal Navy Vessels A274

Designs: 35p, HMS Roebuck. 39p, HMS Monmouth. 43p, HMS Edinburgh. 52p, HMS Express. 58p, HMS Severn. 76p, HMS Cottesmore.
£2.50, HMY Britannia.

2008, June 24 Litho. ***Perf. 13x13¼***
1327 A274 35p multi 1.10 1.00
1328 A274 39p multi 1.25 1.25
1329 A274 43p multi 1.40 1.25
1330 A274 52p multi 1.60 1.40
1331 A274 58p multi 1.75 1.40
1332 A274 76p multi 2.40 1.75
a. Booklet pane, #1327-1332 9.50 9.50
Nos. 1327-1332 (6) 9.50 8.05

Souvenir Sheet
Perf. 13¼x13

1333 A274 £2.50 multi 8.00 8.00
a. Booklet pane of 1 #1333 8.00 8.00
Complete booklet, #1333a, 3 #1332a 37.50

No. 1333 contains one 60x40mm stamp.

No. 1333a has a binding stub at left. Complete booklet contains 3 examples of No. 1332a, each with a different margin and different arrangement of the stamps.

Souvenir Sheet

Jersey Festival of Speed — A275

2008, Aug. 23 Litho. *Perf. 13x13¼*
1334 A275 £2.50 multi 8.00 8.00

Farm Animals and Their Young — A276

No. 1335: a, Rooster, hen and chicks. b, Sheep and lambs. c, Sow and piglets. d, Ducks and ducklings. e, Cows and calf.

Serpentine Die Cut 11¼

2008, Aug. 26 Self-Adhesive

Coil Stamps

1335 Horiz. strip of 5 6.00
a.-e. A276 (35p) Any single 1.10 1.10
f. Horiz. strip of 5, dated "2010" 5.00
g.-k. (36p) As #1335a-1335e, dated "2010," any single .90 .90

Issued: No. 1335f, 4/2/10.

Insects A277

Designs: 35p, Carpenter bee. 39p, Buff-tailed bumblebee. 43p, Clown-faced bug. 52p, Large migrant hoverfly. 58p, Ruby-tailed wasp. 76p, 22-spot ladybug.

2008, Sept. 8 *Perf. 13x13¼*
1336 A277 35p multi 1.10 1.00
1337 A277 39p multi 1.25 1.25
1338 A277 43p multi 1.40 1.25
1339 A277 52p multi 1.60 1.50
1340 A277 58p multi 1.75 1.75
1341 A277 76p multi 2.25 2.25
Nos. 1336-1341 (6) 9.35 9.00

Birds Type of 2007

Designs: 35p, Northern wheatear. 39p, Whinchat. 43p, Pied flycatcher. 52p, Yellow wagtail. 58p, Ring ouzel. 76p, Common redstart.

2008, Oct. 21 Litho.

Stamps With White Frames

1342 A260 35p multi 1.10 1.10
1343 A260 39p multi 1.25 1.25
1344 A260 43p multi 1.40 1.40
1345 A260 52p multi 1.75 1.75
1346 A260 58p multi 1.90 1.90
1347 A260 76p multi 2.50 2.50
a. Souvenir sheet, #1342-1347 10.00 10.00
Nos. 1342-1347 (6) 9.90 9.90

Souvenir Sheet

Stamps Without White Frames

1348 Sheet of 3 6.00 6.00
a. A260 52p multi 1.75 1.75
b. A260 58p multi 1.90 1.90
c. A260 76p multi 2.50 2.50

Prince Charles, 60th Birthday A278

2008, Nov. 14 *Perf. 13¼*
1349 A278 £4 multi 12.00 12.00
a. Souvenir sheet of 1 12.00 12.00

Airplanes A279

Designs: 35p, Douglas C-47 Dakota 3 Pionair. 39p, Vickers Viscount 833. 43p, Handley Page HPR7 Dart-Herald. 52p, Bristol Superfreighter 32. 58p, Fokker F-27 Friendship. 76p, Bombardier Q400 Dash 8.
£3, De Havilland D.H. 84 Dragon 2.

2009, Jan. 13 Litho. *Perf. 14*
1350 A279 35p multi 1.00 1.00
1351 A279 39p multi 1.10 1.10
1352 A279 43p multi 1.25 1.25
1353 A279 52p multi 1.50 1.50
1354 A279 58p multi 1.60 1.60
1355 A279 76p multi 2.10 2.10
Nos. 1350-1355 (6) 8.55 8.55

Souvenir Sheet

1356 A279 £3 multi 8.25 8.25

First flight from Jersey to Southampton, 75th anniv. (No. 1356).

Intl. Year of Astronomy A280

Galileo Galilei, one quarter of Jupiter and: 35p, Jupiter's moon Io, Ursa Major and Cassiopeia constellations. 39p, Jupiter's moon Europa, Boötes and Corona Borealis constellations. 43p, Jupiter's moon Ganymede, Cygnus and Pegasus constellations. 76p, Jupiter's moon Callisto, Perseus and Orion constellations.

Litho. & Embossed With Foil Application

2009, Feb. 10 *Perf. 13x13¼*
1357 A280 35p multi 1.00 1.00
1358 A280 39p multi 1.10 1.10
1359 A280 43p multi 1.25 1.25
1360 A280 76p multi 2.25 2.25
Nos. 1357-1360 (4) 5.60 5.60

Europa (39p, 43p).

Endangered Species — A281

Designs: 35p, Blue iguana. 39p, Madagascar giant jumping rat. 43p, Mountain chicken frog. 52p, Livingstone's fruit bat. 58p, Andean bear. 76p, Western lowland gorilla.

2009, Mar. 10 Litho. *Perf. 14¾x14*
1361 A281 35p multi 1.10 1.10
1362 A281 39p multi 1.25 1.25
1363 A281 43p multi 1.25 1.25
1364 A281 52p multi 1.60 1.60
1365 A281 58p multi 1.75 1.75
1366 A281 76p multi 2.25 2.25
Nos. 1361-1366 (6) 9.20 9.20

Durrell Wildlife Conservation Trust, 50th anniv.

Spring Flowers A282

Designs: 35p, Crocus and grape hyacinth. 39p, Daffodils. 43p, Anemones de Caen. 52p, Tulips. 58p, Hyacinths. 76p, Polyanthus and primulas.

2009, Apr. 1 *Perf. 13¼*
1367 A282 35p multi 1.10 1.10
1368 A282 39p multi 1.25 1.25
1369 A282 43p multi 1.25 1.25
1370 A282 52p multi 1.60 1.60
1371 A282 58p multi 1.75 1.75
1372 A282 76p multi 2.25 2.25
Nos. 1367-1372 (6) 9.20 9.20

Locomotives and Rail Cars — A283

Designs: 37p, 0-4-2T Mont Orgueil locomotive. 42p, 2-4-0T Corbière locomotive. 45p, 0-4-2T Carteret locomotive. 55p, Pioneer rail car. 61p, 2-4-0T La Moye locomotive. 80p, 2-4-0T St. Brelades locomotive.
£3, 2-4-0T Corbière locomotive, diff.

2009, May 6 *Perf. 13x13¼*
1373 A283 37p multi 1.25 1.25
1374 A283 42p multi 1.40 1.40
1375 A283 45p multi 1.50 1.50
1376 A283 55p multi 1.75 1.75
1377 A283 61p multi 2.00 2.00
1378 A283 80p multi 2.60 2.60
a. Booklet pane of 6, #1373-1378 10.50 10.50
Nos. 1373-1378 (6) 10.50 10.50

Souvenir Sheet

Perf. 13¼x13

1379 A283 £3 multi 9.75 9.75
a. Booklet pane of 1 #1379 9.75 9.75
Complete booklet, #1379a, 3 #1378a 42.00
b. As #1379, with IBRA emblem in sheet margin 9.75 9.75

No. 1379 contains one 60x40mm stamp.
No. 1379a has a binding stub at left.
Complete booklet contains three examples of No. 1378a, each with a different margin and different arrangement of the stamps.

Souvenir Sheet

Surfing — A284

2009, June 2 *Perf. 13¼*
1380 A284 £3 multi 9.75 9.75

Jersey Surfboard Club, 50th anniv.

Souvenir Sheet

St. Helier Broad Street Post Office, Cent. — A285

2009, June 21 *Perf. 14*
1381 A285 £3 multi 9.75 9.75

Souvenir Sheet

Investiture of Prince Charles as Prince of Wales, 40th Anniv. — A286

2009, July 1 *Perf. 13¼*
1382 A286 £3 multi 9.75 9.75

Seaweed A287

Designs: 37p, Egg wrack. 42p, Gutweed. 45p, Red rags. 55p, Sea lettuce. 61p, Laminaria hyperborea. 80p, Velvet horn.

2009, July 7 *Perf. 13x13¼*
1383 A287 37p multi 1.25 1.25
1384 A287 42p multi 1.40 1.40
1385 A287 45p multi 1.50 1.50
1386 A287 55p multi 1.90 1.90
1387 A287 61p multi 2.00 2.00
1388 A287 80p multi 2.60 2.60
Nos. 1383-1388 (6) 10.65 10.65

Birds Type of 2007

Designs: 37p, Dunnock. 42p, Song thrush. 45p, Wren. 55p, Blackcap. 61p, Mistle thrush. 80p, Robin.

2009, Aug. 4 Litho. *Perf. 13x13¼*

Stamps With White Frames

1389 A260 37p multi 1.25 1.25
1390 A260 42p multi 1.40 1.40
1391 A260 45p multi 1.50 1.50
1392 A260 55p multi 1.90 1.90
1393 A260 61p multi 2.10 2.10
1394 A260 80p multi 2.75 2.75
a. Souvenir sheet, #1389-1394 11.00 11.00
Nos. 1389-1394 (6) 10.90 10.90

Souvenir Sheet

Stamps Without White Frames

1395 Sheet of 3 6.75 6.75
a. A260 55p multi 1.90 1.90
b. A260 61p multi 2.10 2.10
c. A260 80p multi 2.75 2.75

Jersey Attractions Type of 2007

Designs: 37p, Green Island. 42p, Gorey Castle. 45p, St. Aubin's Harbor. 55p, St. Peter's Valley. 61p, La Rocque Harbor. 80p, Greve de Lecq.

2009, Sept. 16 Litho. *Perf. 14x13½*
1396 A264 37p multi 1.25 1.25
1397 A264 42p multi 1.40 1.40
1398 A264 45p multi 1.50 1.50
1399 A264 55p multi 1.75 1.75
1400 A264 61p multi 2.00 2.00
1401 A264 80p multi 2.60 2.60
Nos. 1396-1401 (6) 10.50 10.50

Mushrooms A288

Designs: 37p, Parrot wax-cap. 42p, Russula sardonia. 45p, Velvet foot. 55p, Honey fungus. 61p, Orange peel fungus. 80p, Jewelled deathcap.

2009, Oct. 15 Litho. *Perf. 13¼x13*
1402 A288 37p multi 1.25 1.25
1403 A288 42p multi 1.40 1.40
1404 A288 45p multi 1.50 1.50
1405 A288 55p multi 1.90 1.90
1406 A288 61p multi 2.10 2.10
1407 A288 80p multi 2.75 2.75
Nos. 1402-1407 (6) 10.90 10.90

Ships on Which Sir George Carteret Sailed A289

Designs: 37p, HMS Garland. 42p, HMS Eighth Lion's Whelp. 45p, HMS Unicorn. 55p, HMS Mary Rose. 61p, HMS Antelope. 80p, HMS Rainbow.

2009, Oct. 15 Litho. *Perf. 13¼x13*

1408 A289 37p multi 1.25 1.25
1409 A289 42p multi 1.40 1.40
1410 A289 45p multi 1.50 1.50
1411 A289 55p multi 1.90 1.90
1412 A289 61p multi 2.10 2.10
1413 A289 80p multi 2.75 2.75
Nos. 1408-1413 (6) 10.90 10.90

Girl Guides, Cent. A290

Inscriptions: 37p, Healthy lifestyles. 42p, Global awareness. 45p, Skills & relationships. 61p, Celebrating diversity. 80p, Discovery.

2010, Jan. 12 Litho. *Perf. 14*

1414 A290 37p multi 1.25 1.25
1415 A290 42p multi 1.40 1.40
1416 A290 45p multi 1.50 1.50
1417 A290 61p multi 2.00 2.00
1418 A290 80p multi 2.60 2.60
Nos. 1414-1418 (5) 8.75 8.75

Maps of Jersey — A291

No. 1419 — Map: a, Circa 1685. b, Circa 1844. c, Circa 1980s. d, Circa 2000. e, Satellite view.

Serpentine Die Cut 11¼
2010, Feb. 9 Self-Adhesive
Coil Stamps

1419 Horiz. strip of 5 6.50
a.-e. A291 (42p) Any single 1.25 1.25

Children's Book Characters A292

Designs: 37p, Pushmi-pullyu from *Dr. Doolittle,* by Hugh Lofting. 42p, Elephant from *How the Elephant Got His Trunk,* by Rudyard Kipling. 45p, Mad Hatter from *Alice in Wonderland,* by Lewis Carroll. 80p, *The Dong with a Luminous Nose,* by Edward Lear.

2010, Feb. 9 *Perf. 13x13¼*

1420 A292 37p multi 1.10 1.10
1421 A292 42p multi 1.25 1.25
1422 A292 45p multi 1.40 1.40
1423 A292 80p multi 2.50 2.50
Nos. 1420-1423 (4) 6.25 6.25

Europa (42p, 45p).

Rocks A293

Designs: 37p, Brecciated pegmatite, orthoclase feldspar crystals re-cemented with chalcedony. 42p, Diorite with incipient orbicular structure. 45p, Granite. 61p, Jasper in andesite. 80p, Pebbles of granite, andesite and shale in Rozel conglomerate.

2010, Mar. 9 *Perf. 13x13¼*

1424 A293 37p multi 1.10 1.10
1425 A293 42p multi 1.25 1.25
1426 A293 45p multi 1.40 1.40
1427 A293 61p multi 1.90 1.90
1428 A293 80p multi 2.50 2.50
Nos. 1424-1428 (5) 8.15 8.15

Birds Type of 2007

Designs: 37p, Jay. 42p, Great spotted woodpecker. 45p, Short-toed treecreeper. 55p, Chiffchaff. 61p, Long-tailed tit. 80p, Turtle dove.

2010, Apr. 1
Stamps With White Frames

1429 A260 37p multi 1.10 1.10
1430 A260 42p multi 1.25 1.25
1431 A260 45p multi 1.40 1.40
1432 A260 55p multi 1.75 1.75
1433 A260 61p multi 1.90 1.90
1434 A260 80p multi 2.50 2.50
a. Souvenir sheet, #1429-1434 10.00 10.00
Nos. 1429-1434 (6) 9.90 9.90

Souvenir Sheet
Stamps Without White Frames

1435 Sheet of 3 6.25 6.25
a. A260 55p multi 1.75 1.75
b. A260 61p multi 1.90 1.90
c. A260 80p multi 2.50 2.50

British Regional Stamps of 1958-69 A294

Designs: 36p, Jersey #2. 39p, Jersey #1. 45p, Jersey #3. 55p, Jersey #4. 60p, Jersey #6. 72p, Jersey #5.

2010, May 8 *Perf. 13x13¼*

1436 A294 36p multi 1.10 1.10
1437 A294 39p multi 1.10 1.10
1438 A294 45p multi 1.40 1.40
1439 A294 55p multi 1.60 1.60
1440 A294 60p multi 1.75 1.75
1441 A294 72p multi 2.10 2.10
a. Souvenir sheet, #1436-1441 9.25 9.25
Nos. 1436-1441 (6) 9.05 9.05

Mail Ships A295

Designs: 39p, Royal Charlotte. 45p, Dispatch. 55p, Diana. 60p, Reindeer. 72p, Caesarea (II). 80p, St. Patrick (III).
£3, Watersprite.

2010, May 8 *Perf. 13x13¼*

1442 A295 39p multi 1.10 1.10
1443 A295 45p multi 1.40 1.40
1444 A295 55p multi 1.60 1.60
1445 A295 60p multi 1.75 1.75
1446 A295 72p multi 2.10 2.10
1447 A295 80p multi 2.40 2.40
a. Booklet pane, #1442-1447 10.50 —
b. Souvenir sheet, #1442-1447 10.50 10.50
Nos. 1442-1447 (6) 10.35 10.35

Souvenir Sheet
Perf. 13¼x13

1448 A295 £3 multi 8.75 8.75
a. Booklet pane of 1 + binding stub 8.75 —
Complete booklet, #1448a, 3 #1447a 41.00

No. 1448 contains one 60x40mm stamp. Complete booklet contains three examples of No. 1447a, each with a different margin and different arrangement of the stamps.

Roses A296

Rose varieties: 36p, Nostalgia. 39p, Mountbatten. 45p, Royal William. 55p, Elina. 60p, New Dawn. 72p, Lovers Meeting.
£3, Pride of England.

2010, June 8 *Perf. 13x13¼*

1449 A296 36p multi 1.10 1.10
1450 A296 39p multi 1.10 1.10
1451 A296 45p multi 1.40 1.40
1452 A296 55p multi 1.60 1.60
1453 A296 60p multi 1.75 1.75
1454 A296 72p multi 2.10 2.10
Nos. 1449-1454 (6) 9.05 9.05

Souvenir Sheet

1455 A296 £3 multi 8.75 8.75
a. As #1455, with Salon du Timbre emblem in sheet margin 9.25 9.25

Issued: No. 1455a, 6/12.

Sea Anemones A297

Designs: 36p, Strawberry anemone. 39p, Snakelock anemone. 45p, Jewel anemone. 55p, Parasitic anemone. 60p, Tube anemone. 72p, Beadlet anemone.
£3, Dahlia anemone.

2010, July 6 Litho.

1456 A297 36p multi 1.10 1.10
1457 A297 39p multi 1.25 1.25
1458 A297 45p multi 1.40 1.40
1459 A297 55p multi 1.75 1.75
1460 A297 60p multi 1.90 1.90
1461 A297 72p multi 2.25 2.25
Nos. 1456-1461 (6) 9.65 9.65

Souvenir Sheet

1462 A297 £3 multi 9.00 9.00

Automobiles — A298

Designs: 39p, 1912 Rolls Royce Silver Ghost. 45p, 1926 Bugatti Type 37. 55p, 1933 Austin Seven. 60p, 1938 Citroen Light 15. 72p, 1946 Morris 10. 80p, 1949 Rover 75 Sports Saloon.

2010, Aug. 3 *Perf. 14¼x14*

1463 A298 39p multi 1.25 1.25
1464 A298 45p multi 1.50 1.50
1465 A298 55p multi 1.75 1.75
1466 A298 60p multi 1.90 1.90
1467 A298 72p multi 2.40 2.40
1468 A298 80p multi 2.60 2.60
Nos. 1463-1468 (6) 11.40 11.40

Fish A299

Designs: 36p, Perch. 39p, Tench. 45p, Roach. 55p, Rudd. 60p, Mirror carp. 72p, Common bream.
£3, Brown trout.

2010, Sept. 7 Litho. *Perf. 14¾x14*

1469 A299 36p multi 1.10 1.10
1470 A299 39p multi 1.25 1.25
1471 A299 45p multi 1.40 1.40
1472 A299 55p multi 1.75 1.75
1473 A299 60p multi 1.90 1.90
1474 A299 72p multi 2.25 2.25
Nos. 1469-1474 (6) 9.65 9.65

Souvenir Sheet

1475 A299 £3 multi 9.25 9.25

La Cotte de St. Brelade Archaeological Site — A300

Designs: 39p, Human teeth, models of head of Neanderthal man. 45p, Skull of Woolly rhinoceros. 55p, Tooth and tusks of Woolly mammoth. 60p, Flint tools and timeline. 80p, Antler of Giant deer.

2010, Oct. 12 *Perf. 14*

1476 A300 39p multi 1.25 1.25
1477 A300 45p multi 1.50 1.50
1478 A300 55p multi 1.90 1.90
1479 A300 60p multi 2.00 2.00
1480 A300 80p multi 2.60 2.60
Nos. 1476-1480 (5) 9.25 9.25

Map of Jersey and Heraldic Lions — A301

Inscriptions: (36p), Standard Letter. (39p), Priority Letter. (45p), UK Letter.

Serpentine Die Cut 11½x11¼
2010, Nov. 1 Self-Adhesive
Coil Stamps
Background Color

1481 A301 (36p) dark red 1.25 1.25
1482 A301 (39p) blue 1.25 1.25
1483 A301 (45p) green 1.50 1.50
Nos. 1481-1483 (3) 4.00 4.00

Buses A302

Designs: 36p, Paragon C10 AEC B, c. 1926. 45p, Ramblers Tours Chevrolet, c. 1935. 55p, JMT Leyland Lioness, c. 1938. 60p, JMT Leyland PLSC1 Lion, c. 1939. 72p, Mascot Motors Morris C/F 13/5, c. 1948. 80p, Mascot Motors AEC Regal 4, c. 1961.

2011, Jan. 11 Litho. *Perf. 14*

1484 A302 36p multi 1.25 1.25
1485 A302 45p multi 1.50 1.50
1486 A302 55p multi 1.75 1.75
1487 A302 60p multi 1.90 1.90
1488 A302 72p multi 2.40 2.40
1489 A302 80p multi 2.60 2.60
Nos. 1484-1489 (6) 11.40 11.40

Intl. Year of Forests A303

Tree branches: 39p, Silver birch. 45p, English oak. 55p, Beech. 80p, Linden (Lime).

2011, Feb. 8 Litho. *Perf. 13¼*

1490 A303 39p multi 1.25 1.25
1491 A303 45p multi 1.50 1.50
1492 A303 55p multi 1.75 1.75
1493 A303 80p multi 2.60 2.60
Nos. 1490-1493 (4) 7.10 7.10

Europa (45p, 55p).

Famous Women A304

Designs: 36p, Dame Margot Fonteyn (1919-91), ballerina. 45p, Florence Nightingale (1820-1910), nurse. 60p, Marie Curie (1867-1934), chemist. 72p, Mother Teresa (1910-97), humanitarian.

2011, Mar. 8

1494 A304 36p multi 1.25 1.25
1495 A304 45p multi 1.50 1.50
1496 A304 60p multi 2.00 2.00
1497 A304 72p multi 2.40 2.40
Nos. 1494-1497 (4) 7.15 7.15

Marine Life A305

Designs: (36p), Gooseberry sea squirt. (39p), Finger sponge. (45p), Purse sponge. 60p, Star squirt. 72p, Light bulb sea squirt. 80p, Red sea squirt.

2011, Apr. 7 ***Perf. 14¾x14***

Stamps With White Frames

1498 A305 (36p) multi 1.25 1.25
1499 A305 (39p) multi 1.25 1.25
1500 A305 (45p) multi 1.50 1.50
1501 A305 60p multi 2.00 2.00
1502 A305 72p multi 2.40 2.40
1503 A305 80p multi 2.60 2.60
Nos. 1498-1503 (6) 11.00 11.00

Souvenir Sheet

Stamps Without White Frames

1504 Sheet of 3 7.00 7.00
a. A305 60p multi 2.00 2.00
b. A305 72p multi 2.40 2.40
c. A305 80p multi 2.60 2.60

Queen Elizabeth II, 85th Birthday A306

2011, Apr. 21 ***Perf. 13¼x13½***

1505 A306 £3 multi 10.00 10.00
a. Souvenir sheet of 1 10.00 10.00

Wedding of Prince William and Catherine Middleton — A307

2011, Apr. 29 ***Perf. 13½x13¼***

1506 A307 £3.50 multi 11.50 11.50

Printed in sheets of 4.

Orchids A308

Designs: (36p), Paphiopedilum La Garenne "Saint John." (39p), Odontioda Les Brayes "Pontac." (45p), Phragmipedium Don Wimber. 55p, Kriegerara Kemp Tower "Trinity." 60p, Angulocaste Noirmont "Isle of Jersey." 72p, Calanthe Beresford "Victoria Village."
£3, Miltonia Poinde des Pas "Jersey."

2011, May 17 ***Perf. 13x13¼***

1507 A308 (36p) multi 1.25 1.25
1508 A308 (39p) multi 1.25 1.25
1509 A308 (45p) multi 1.50 1.50
1510 A308 55p multi 1.90 1.90
1511 A308 60p multi 2.00 2.00
1512 A308 72p multi 2.40 2.40
Nos. 1507-1512 (6) 10.30 10.30

Souvenir Sheet

1513 A308 £3 multi 10.00 10.00

Birds Type of 2007

Designs: 42p, Barn swallow. 50p, Spotted flycatcher. 59p, Cuckoo. 64, Whitethroat. 79p, Linnet. 86p, Swift.

2011, June 16 **Litho.**

Stamps With White Frames

1514 A260 42p multi 1.40 1.40
1515 A260 50p multi 1.60 1.60
1516 A260 59p multi 1.90 1.90
1517 A260 64p multi 2.10 2.10
1518 A260 79p multi 2.60 2.60
1519 A260 86p multi 2.75 2.75
a. Souvenri sheet of 6, #1514-1519 12.50 12.50
Nos. 1514-1519 (6) 12.35 12.35

Souvenir Sheet

Stamps Without White Frames

1520 Sheet of 3 7.50 7.50
a. A260 64p multi 2.10 2.10
b. A260 79p multi 2.60 2.60
c. A260 86p multi 2.75 2.75

Shipwrecks — A309

Designs: 37p, TSS Princess Ena, 1935. 49p, SS Caledonia, 1881. 59p, TSS Ibex, 1897. 64p, SS Schokland, 1943. 79p, PT509, 1944. 86p, PS Superb, 1950.
£3, TSS Roebuck, 1911

2011, July 12 ***Perf. 13x13¼***

1521 A309 37p multi 1.25 1.25
1522 A309 49p multi 1.60 1.60
1523 A309 59p multi 2.00 2.00
1524 A309 64p multi 2.10 2.10
1525 A309 79p multi 2.60 2.60
1526 A309 86p multi 2.75 2.75
a. Booklet pane of 6, #1521-1526 12.50 —
Nos. 1521-1526 (6) 12.30 12.30

Souvenir Sheet

1527 A309 £3 multi 10.00 10.00
a. Booklet pane of 1 10.00 —
Complete booklet, #1527a, 3 #1526a 47.50

No. 1527 is 110x75mm; No. 1527a, 150x100mm. No. 1526ahas three different layouts of stamps on pane and three different margins.

National Trust for Jersey, 75th Anniv. A310

Designs: 42p, Marsh harrier, La Caumine à Marie Best, painted white. 50p, Swallowtail butterfly, Victoria Tower. 59p, Dartford warbler, La Cotte Battery. 64p, Red squirrel, Le Moulin de Quétivel. 75p, Marsh harrier, La Caumine à Marie Best, painted green. 79p, Puffins, North Coast sea cliffs.

2011, Aug. 3 ***Perf. 14¾x14***

1528 A310 42p multi 1.40 1.40
1529 A310 50p multi 1.60 1.60
1530 A310 59p multi 2.00 2.00
1531 A310 64p multi 2.10 2.10
1532 A310 75p multi 2.50 2.50
1533 A310 79p multi 2.60 2.60
Nos. 1528-1533 (6) 12.20 12.20

Ancient Celtic Coins Found Buried on Jersey A311

Obverse and reverse of: 37p, Billon stater of XN series. 49p, Durotriges base gold quarter stater. 59p, Baiocasses gold stater. 64p, Gold chute type stater. 79p, Southern British silver unit. 86p, Billon stater Coriosolite Tribe coin.

2011, Aug. 30

1534 A311 37p multi 1.25 1.25
1535 A311 49p multi 1.60 1.60
1536 A311 59p multi 1.90 1.90
1537 A311 64p multi 2.10 2.10
1538 A311 79p multi 2.50 2.50
1539 A311 86p multi 2.75 2.75
Nos. 1534-1539 (6) 12.10 12.10

Souvenir Sheet

Jersey's Finance Industry, 50th Anniv. — A312

Litho. & Embossed

2011, Sept. 12 ***Perf. 13x13¼***

1540 A312 £3 multi 9.50 9.50

Jersey Attractions Type of 2007

Designs: 42p, Beauport. 49p, St. Ouen's Bay. 50p, Ouaisné. 64p, St. Brelade's Bay. 79p, Mont Orgueil. 86p, Portelet Bay.

2011, Sept. 28 **Litho.** ***Perf. 13½***

1541 A264 42p multi 1.40 1.40
1542 A264 49p multi 1.60 1.60
1543 A264 50p multi 1.60 1.60
1544 A264 64p multi 2.00 2.00
1545 A264 79p multi 2.50 2.50
1546 A264 86p multi 2.75 2.75
Nos. 1541-1546 (6) 11.85 11.85

Mills A313

Designs: 37p, Rozel Windmill. 42p, Tesson Mill. 49p, St. Peter's Windmill. 50p, Ponterrin Mill. 59p, Quétivel Mill. 79p, Greve de Lecq Mill.

2011, Oct. 11 ***Perf. 14***

1547 A313 37p multi 1.25 1.25
1548 A313 42p multi 1.40 1.40
1549 A313 49p multi 1.60 1.60
1550 A313 50p multi 1.60 1.60
1551 A313 59p multi 1.90 1.90
1552 A313 79p multi 2.60 2.60
Nos. 1547-1552 (6) 10.35 10.35

Christmas A314

Various Christmas tree ornaments and decorations.

2011, Nov. 8 ***Perf. 13x13¼***

1553 A314 37p multi 1.25 1.25
1554 A314 42p multi 1.40 1.40
1555 A314 49p multi 1.60 1.60
1556 A314 50p multi 1.60 1.60
1557 A314 79p multi 2.50 2.50
1558 A314 86p multi 2.75 2.75
Nos. 1553-1558 (6) 11.10 11.10

Jersey Symphony Orchestra, 25th Anniv. — A315

Various musical scores and: 37p, Violin. 50p, Trumpets. 59p, Harp. 64p, Timpani. 79p, Bassoons. 86p, French horn.

2011, Nov. 15 ***Perf. 14***

1559 A315 37p multi 1.25 1.25
1560 A315 50p multi 1.60 1.60
1561 A315 59p multi 1.90 1.90
1562 A315 64p multi 2.00 2.00
1563 A315 79p multi 2.50 2.50
1564 A315 86p multi 2.75 2.75
Nos. 1559-1564 (6) 12.00 12.00

Tourism — A316

Designs: 42p, Food and wine bottle. 49p, Surfer, sailboats, land yachts. 59p, Cyclist, people on pathways. 86p, Military reenactment.

2012, Jan. 10 ***Perf. 13¼***

1565 A316 42p multi 1.40 1.40
1566 A316 49p multi 1.60 1.60
1567 A316 59p multi 1.90 1.90
1568 A316 86p multi 2.75 2.75
Nos. 1565-1568 (4) 7.65 7.65

Europa (49p, 59p).

Reign of Queen Elizabeth II, 60th Anniv. — A317

Nos. 1569 and 1570: a, Queen Elizabeth II. b, King George VI.

2012, Feb. 6 **Litho.** ***Perf. 13½***

Stamps With White Frames

1569 A317 Horiz. pair 13.00 13.00
a.-b. £2 Either single 6.50 6.50

Souvenir Sheet

Stamps Without White Frames

1570 A317 Sheet of 2 13.00 13.00
a.-b. £2 Either single 6.50 6.50

A sheet similar to No. 1570 having a diamond attached to the crown in the sheet margin was produced in limited quantities and sold for £131.95.

Jersey Airport, 75th Anniv. A318

Aircraft at Jersey Airport: 37p, DeHavilland DH86. 49p, Bristol 170 Wayfarer. 50p, Airspeed Ambassador. 64p, Hawker Siddeley Trident. 79p, Britten-Norman Trislander. 86p, Vickers VC10.
£3, Fairchild Dornier 328-110.

2012, Mar. 10 ***Perf. 13x13¼***

1571 A318 37p multi 1.25 1.25
1572 A318 49p multi 1.60 1.60
1573 A318 50p multi 1.60 1.60
1574 A318 64p multi 2.10 2.10
1575 A318 79p multi 2.50 2.50

1576 A318 86p multi 2.75 2.75
a. Booklet pane of 6, #1571-1576 12.00 —
Nos. 1571-1576 (6) 11.80 11.80

Souvenir Sheet

Perf. 13¼x13

1577 A318 £3 multi 9.50 9.50
a. Booklet pane of 1, 163x100mm 9.50 9.50
Complete booklet, #1577a, 3 #1576a 46.00

No. 1577 contains one 60x40mm stamp. Sheet size of No. 1577: 110x75mm. Complete booklet contains three examples of No. 1576a, each with different arrangements of the stamps.

Souvenir Sheet

Sinking of the Titanic, Cent. — A319

2012, Apr. 14 ***Perf. 14¼***
1578 A319 £3 multi 9.75 9.75

Butterflies and Moths A320

Designs: (45p), Broad-bordered yellow underwing moth. (55p), Painted lady butterfly. (60p), Merveille du jour moth. (68p), Queen of Spain fritillary butterfly. (72p), Large emerald moth. (86p), Red admiral butterfly.

2012, May 8 ***Perf. 13x13¼***

Stamps With White Frames

1579 A320 (45p) multi 1.40 1.40
1580 A320 (55p) multi 1.75 1.75
1581 A320 (60p) multi 1.90 1.90
1582 A320 (68p) multi 2.10 2.10
1583 A320 (72p) multi 2.25 2.25
1584 A320 (86p) multi 2.75 2.75
Nos. 1579-1584 (6) 12.15 12.15

Souvenir Sheet

Stamps Without White Frame

1585 Sheet of 3 7.25 7.25
a. A320 (68p) multi 2.10 2.10
b. A320 (72p) multi 2.25 2.25
c. A320 (86p) multi 2.75 2.75

Inscriptions: No. 1579, "Local Letter." No. 1580, "UK Letter." No. 1581, "Europe." Nos. 1582, 1585a, "Local Large." Nos. 1583, 1585b, "UK Large." Nos. 1584, 1585c, "International."

Mont Orgueil Castle A321

Archirondel Tower A322

La Corbière Lighthouse A323

Clasped Hands Sculpture A324

Serpentine Die Cut 13½

2012, May 8 **Litho.**

Self-Adhesive

1586 A321 (45p) multi 1.40 1.40
a. Serpentine die cut 12½x12¾ 1.40 1.40
1587 A322 (45p) multi 1.40 1.40
a. Booklet pane of 10 14.00
b. Serpentine die cut 12½x12¾ 1.40 1.40
1588 A323 (55p) multi 1.75 1.75
a. Serpentine die cut 12½x12¾ 1.75 1.75
1589 A324 (55p) multi 1.75 1.75
a. Booklet pane of 10 17.50
b. Serpentine die cut 12½x12¾ 1.75 1.75
c. Miniature sheet of 4, #1586a, 1587b, 1588a, 1589b 6.50
Nos. 1586-1589 (4) 6.30 6.30

Reign of Queen Elizabeth II, 60th Anniv. A325

Litho. with Hologram Affixed

2012, June 1 ***Perf. 13¼***
1590 A325 £10 blk & sil 31.00 31.00

Duke of Cambridge, 30th Birthday — A326

Prince William wearing various military uniforms. 68p, 70p, horiz.

2012, June 21 **Litho.** ***Perf. 14***
1591 A326 45p multi 1.40 1.40
1592 A326 68p multi 2.10 2.10
1593 A326 70p multi 2.25 2.25
1594 A326 88p multi 2.75 2.75
Nos. 1591-1594 (4) 8.50 8.50

Trees — A327

Designs: 45p, Magnolia. 55p, Swamp cypress. 60p, Flowering cherry. 68p, Maidenhair. 70p, Hill cherry. 88p, London plane.

2012, July 3 ***Perf. 13¼x14***
1595 A327 45p multi 1.40 1.40
1596 A327 55p multi 1.75 1.75
1597 A327 60p multi 1.90 1.90
1598 A327 68p multi 2.10 2.10
1599 A327 70p multi 2.25 2.25
1600 A327 88p multi 2.75 2.75
Nos. 1595-1600 (6) 12.15 12.15

Celebrations — A328

Designs: No. 1601, Champagne flutes. No. 1602, Flower. No. 1603, Curled ribbons. No. 1604, Teddy bear. No. 1605, Balloons. No. 1606, Birthday candles on cake. No. 1607, Ribbon bow. No. 1608, Ribbon in shape of heart.

Serpentine Die Cut 12½x12

2012, Aug. 2 **Self-Adhesive**

Inscribed "Local Letter"

1601 A328 (45p) multi 1.50 1.50
1602 A328 (45p) multi 1.50 1.50
1603 A328 (45p) multi 1.50 1.50
1604 A328 (45p) multi 1.50 1.50

Inscribed "UK Letter"

1605 A328 (55p) multi 1.75 1.75
1606 A328 (55p) multi 1.75 1.75
1607 A328 (55p) multi 1.75 1.75
1608 A328 (55p) multi 1.75 1.75
a. Miniature sheet of 8, #1601-1608 13.00
Nos. 1601-1608 (8) 13.00 13.00

Nos. 1601-1608 were each available in sheets of 20 stamps + 20 labels that could be personalized.

Birds Type of 2007

Designs: 45p, Lesser spotted woodpecker. 55p, Stonechat. 60p, Yellowhammer. 68p, Serin. 70p, Bullfinch. 88p, Cirl bunting.

Stamps With White Frames

2012, Aug. 14 ***Perf. 13x13½***
1609 A260 45p multi 1.50 1.50
1610 A260 55p multi 1.75 1.75
1611 A260 60p multi 2.00 2.00
1612 A260 68p multi 2.25 2.25
1613 A260 70p multi 2.25 2.25
1614 A260 88p multi 3.00 3.00
a. Souvenir sheet of 6, #1609-1614 13.00 13.00
Nos. 1609-1614 (6) 12.75 12.75

Souvenir Sheet

Stamps Without White Frames

1615 Sheet of 3 7.50 7.50
a. A260 68p multi 2.25 2.25
b. A260 70p multi 2.25 2.25
c. A260 88p multi 3.00 3.00

Jambo the Gorilla (1972-92), First Male Gorilla Born in Captivity A329

Jambo: 45p, With bushes in background. 60p, Amidst trees. 80p, With two other gorillas. 88p, Head.

£1, Jambo facing right, vert.

2012, Sept. 15 **Litho.** ***Perf. 14¾x14***
1616 A329 45p multi 1.50 1.50
1617 A329 60p multi 2.00 2.00
1618 A329 80p multi 2.60 2.60
1619 A329 88p multi 3.00 3.00
Nos. 1616-1619 (4) 9.10 9.10

Souvenir Sheet

Perf. 14x14¾

1620 A329 £1 multi 3.25 3.25

Towers A330

Designs: 45p, Flicquet Tower. 55p, Portelet Tower. 60p, Ouaisné Tower. 68p, Lewis Tower. 70p, Noirmont Tower. 80p, St. Catherine's Tower.

2012, Oct. 12 ***Perf. 14***
1621 A330 45p multi 1.50 1.50
1622 A330 55p multi 1.75 1.75
1623 A330 60p multi 1.90 1.90
1624 A330 68p multi 2.25 2.25
1625 A330 70p multi 2.25 2.25
1626 A330 80p multi 2.60 2.60
Nos. 1621-1626 (6) 12.25 12.25

Dolmens A331

Dolmens at: 45p, Mont Ubé. 55p, Le Couperon. 60p, Ville-és-Nouaux. 68p, Les Mont Grantez. 88p, La Pouquelaye de Faldouet.

2012, Nov. 2 **Litho.** ***Perf. 13***
1627 A331 45p multi 1.50 1.50
1628 A331 55p multi 1.75 1.75
1629 A331 60p multi 1.90 1.90
1630 A331 68p multi 2.25 2.25
1631 A331 88p multi 3.00 3.00
Nos. 1627-1631 (5) 10.40 10.40

Christmas A332

Scenes from *A Christmas Carol*, by Charles Dickens, with inscriptions of: 40p, A Merry Christmas one and all! 45p, Bah Humbug! 50p, The End of It. 55p, Scrooge with Marley's ghost. 60p, The Ghost of Christmas Past. 68p, The Ghost of Christmas Present. 80p, The Ghost of Christmas Future. 88p, Bob Cratchit and Tiny Tim.

2012, Nov. 15 **Litho.** ***Perf. 13x13½***
1632 A332 40p multi 1.25 1.25
1633 A332 45p multi 1.50 1.50
1634 A332 50p multi 1.60 1.60
1635 A332 55p multi 1.75 1.75
1636 A332 60p multi 2.00 2.00
1637 A332 68p multi 2.25 2.25
1638 A332 80p multi 2.60 2.60
1639 A332 88p multi 3.00 3.00
Nos. 1632-1639 (8) 15.95 15.95

Flora A333

Designs: 45p, Camellia sasonqua "Paradise Belinda." 55p, Butcher's broom. 60p, Snowdrop. 68p, Mistletoe. 80p, Bramble. 88p, Hawthorn.

2013, Jan. 8
1640 A333 45p multi 1.50 1.50
1641 A333 55p multi 1.90 1.90
1642 A333 60p multi 2.00 2.00
1643 A333 68p multi 2.25 2.25
1644 A333 80p multi 2.60 2.60
1645 A333 88p multi 3.00 3.00
Nos. 1640-1645 (6) 13.25 13.25

Statues of King Edward VII — A334

Statue in: 45p, Liverpool. 55p, Aberdeen, Scotland. 60p, Birmingham. 68p, Reading. 80p, Bristol. 88p, London.

£2, Queen's Park, Toronto, Ontario, Canada.

2013, Feb. 5 ***Perf. 13x13¼***
1646 A334 45p multi 1.40 1.40
1647 A334 55p multi 1.75 1.75
1648 A334 60p multi 1.75 1.75
1649 A334 68p multi 2.10 2.10
1650 A334 80p multi 2.40 2.40
1651 A334 88p multi 2.60 2.60
Nos. 1646-1651 (6) 12.00 12.00

Souvenir Sheet

1652 A334 £2 multi 6.00 6.00

Kennel Club of Jersey, 125th Anniv. A335

Dogs: 45p, Boxer. 55p, Lhasa Apso. 60p, Irish setter. 68p, Kerry blue terrier. 80p, Pomeranian. 88p, Afghan hound.

2013, Mar. 8 ***Perf. 13¼***
1653 A335 45p multi 1.40 1.40
1654 A335 55p multi 1.75 1.75
1655 A335 60p multi 1.75 1.75
1656 A335 68p multi 2.10 2.10
1657 A335 80p multi 2.40 2.40
1658 A335 88p multi 2.60 2.60
Nos. 1653-1658 (6) 12.00 12.00

Postal Vehicles — A336

Designs: 45p, Bicycles and mail cart. 55p, Vans. 60p, Van, truck, ferry. 80p, Airplanes and cargo bins.

2013, Mar. 19 *Perf. 13¼x13*

1659	A336 45p multi		1.40	1.40
1660	A336 55p multi		1.75	1.75
1661	A336 60p multi		1.90	1.90
1662	A336 80p multi		2.40	2.40
	Nos. 1659-1662 (4)		7.45	7.45

Europa (#1660, 1662).

Jersey Motor Transport Buses A337

Designs: 45p, Leyland bus, La Hogue Bie, c. 1948. 55p, Leyland bus, Mont Orgueil Castle, c. 1955. 60p, Karrier Bantam bus, West Park Pavilion, c. 1960. 68p, Leyland Tiger Cub bus, La Corbière Lighthouse, c. 1962. 80p, Leyland bus, Rozel Harbor, c. 1963. 88p, Leyland Triton bus, Odeon Cinema, St. Helier, c. 1963.

2013, Apr. 2 *Perf. 14¾x14*

1663	A337 45p multi	1.40	1.40
1664	A337 55p multi	1.75	1.75
1665	A337 60p multi	1.90	1.90
1666	A337 68p multi	2.10	2.10
1667	A337 80p multi	2.40	2.40
1668	A337 88p multi	2.75	2.75
	Nos. 1663-1668 (6)	12.30	12.30

Corbiere, Winner of 1983 Grand National Steeplechase — A338

Designs: 55p, Horses at start. 60p, Horses running. 68p, Corbiere jumping over fence. 80p, Horses near rail.

£2, Corbiere, jockey, La Corbière Lighthouse.

2013, Apr. 11 *Perf. 14x13¼*

1669	A338 55p multi	1.75	1.75
1670	A338 60p multi	1.90	1.90
1671	A338 68p multi	2.10	2.10
1672	A338 80p multi	2.50	2.50
	Nos. 1669-1672 (4)	8.25	8.25

Souvenir Sheet

1673	A338 £2 multi	6.25	6.25

No. 1673 contains one 80x51mm stamp.

International Red Cross, 150th Anniv. — A339

Designs: (45p), Tracing and messaging (volunteer at reuniting of family members). (55p), Red Cross staff and volunteers (distribution of supplies from trucks). (60p), Water, shelter and food (volunteer near water source). (68p), First aid training. (80p), Emergency response (helicopter). (88p), Protecting people in armed conflict (Princess Diana visting minefield).

£2, Red Cross ship SS Vega.

2013, May 8 **Litho.** *Perf. 14*

Inscription at Lower Left

1674	A339 (45p) Local Letter		1.40	1.40
1675	A339 (55p) UK Letter		1.75	1.75
1676	A339 (60p) Europe		1.90	1.90
1677	A339 (68p) Local Large		2.10	2.10
1678	A339 (80p) International		2.50	2.50
1679	A339 (88p) UK Large		2.75	2.75
	Nos. 1674-1679 (6)		12.40	12.40

Souvenir Sheet

1680	A339 £2 multi	6.25	6.25

No. 1680 contains one 85x43mm stamp.

Coronation of Queen Elizabeth II, 60th Anniv. — A340

No. 1681: a, Queen Elizabeth II. b, Jersey #14.

2013, June 2 *Perf. 13½*

1681	A340 Horiz. pair	12.50	12.50
a.-b.	£2 Either single	6.25	6.25
c.	Souvenir sheet of 2, #1681a-1681b	12.50	12.50

A341

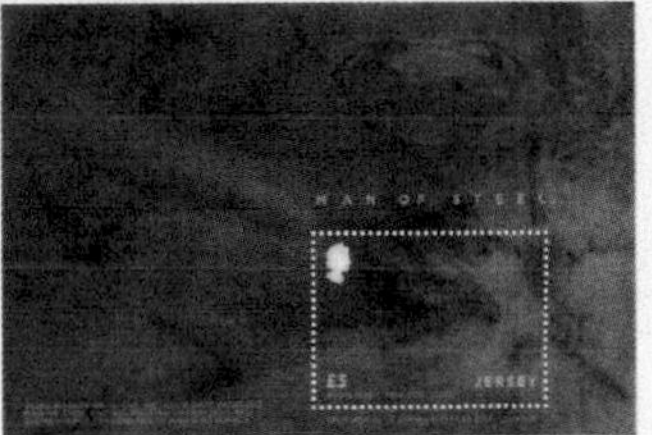

Scenes From Movie *Man of Steel* — A342

Various images of Henry Cavill portraying Superman.

Litho., Litho With Foil Application (60p), Litho. & Silk-Screened (80p, 88p)

2013, June 7 *Perf. 12½*

1682	A341 45p multi	1.40	1.40
1683	A341 60p multi	1.90	1.90
1684	A341 68p multi	2.10	2.10
1685	A341 80p multi	2.50	2.50
1686	A341 88p multi	2.75	2.75
	Nos. 1682-1686 (5)	10.65	10.65

Litho. With Three-Dimensional Plastic Affixed

Perf. 14¼

Souvenir Sheet

1687	A342 £3 multi	9.50	9.50

Litho. On Plastic Foil

Serpentine Die Cut 13

Self-Adhesive

1688	A341 55p multi	1.75	1.75

Portions of the design on No. 1684 are printed with thermochromic ink, which changes color when heated. Granite grit is embedded in the ink used on portions of the deagn on No. 1685. Portions of the design on No. 1686 are printed with glow-in-the-dark ink.

Dragonflies and Damselflies A343

Designs: 45p, Beautiful demoiselle. 55p, Golden-ringed dragonfly. 60p, Dainty damselfly. 68p, Large red damselfly. 80p, Willow emerald damselfly. 88p, Scarlet darter.

2013, July 4 **Litho.** *Perf. 14x13½*

1689	A343 45p multi	1.40	1.40
1690	A343 55p multi	1.75	1.75
1691	A343 60p multi	1.90	1.90
1692	A343 68p multi	2.10	2.10
1693	A343 80p multi	2.40	2.40
1694	A343 88p multi	2.75	2.75
	Nos. 1689-1694 (6)	12.30	12.30

Tall Ships A344

Designs: 45p, Stavros S. Niarchos. 55p, H.M. Bark Endeavour. 60p, STS Tenacious. 68p, Eye of the Wind. 80p, Prince William. 88p, Sk/S Christian Radich.

2013, Aug. 8 **Litho.** *Perf. 13x13½*

1695	A344 45p multi	1.50	1.50
1696	A344 55p multi	1.75	1.75
1697	A344 60p multi	1.90	1.90
1698	A344 68p multi	2.25	2.25
1699	A344 80p multi	2.60	2.60
1700	A344 88p multi	2.75	2.75
a.	Souvenir sheet of 6, #1695-1700	13.00	13.00
	Nos. 1695-1700 (6)	12.75	12.75

Military Vehicles A345

Designs: 45p, Stoewer R200. 55p, Kettenkrad NSU HK 101. 60p, HMMWV M998. 68p, Kubelwagen Type 82. 80p, Sd. Kfz 251 Ausf C Half Track. 88p, Ford Willys Jeep GPW.

2013, Aug. 30 **Litho.** *Perf. 14x13½*

1701	A345 45p multi	1.50	1.50
1702	A345 55p multi	1.75	1.75
1703	A345 60p multi	1.90	1.90
1704	A345 68p multi	2.25	2.25
1705	A345 80p multi	2.60	2.60
1706	A345 88p multi	2.75	2.75
a.	Booklet pane of 6, #1701-1706	13.00	—
	Complete booklet, 4 #1706a	52.00	
	Nos. 1701-1706 (6)	12.75	12.75

Complete booklet contains four examples of No. 1706a, each with different arrangements of the stamps and different pane margins.

Paintings of Jersey Cows by Kathy Rondel — A346

Cows named: (45p), Clover. (55p), Daisy. (60p), Butterfly. (68p), Florence. (80p), Dolly Maud. (88p), Buttercup.

Perf. 14¼x14¾

2013, Sept. 20 **Litho.**

Inscription at Lower Left

1707	A346 (45p) Local Letter	1.50	1.50
1708	A346 (55p) UK Letter	1.75	1.75
1709	A346 (60p) Europe	1.90	1.90
1710	A346 (68p) Local Large	2.25	2.25
1711	A346 (80p) International	2.60	2.60
1712	A346 (88p) UK Large	3.00	3.00
	Nos. 1707-1712 (6)	13.00	13.00

Formula 1 Race Cars of Nigel Mansell — A347

Designs: 45p, Lotus, 1984 US Grand Prix. 55p, Williams Honda, 1985 European Grand Prix. 60p, Ferrari, 1989 Brazilian Grand Prix. 68p, Williams Renault, 1992 Hungarian Grand Prix. 80p, Newman/Haas Lola Ford, 1993 Nazareth Speedway. 88p, Mansell with Ayrton Senna at Silverstone, 1991.

2013, Oct. 15 **Litho.** *Perf. 13¼x13¾*

1713	A347 45p multi	1.50	1.50
1714	A347 55p multi	1.75	1.75
1715	A347 60p multi	1.90	1.90
1716	A347 68p multi	2.25	2.25
1717	A347 80p multi	2.60	2.60
1718	A347 88p multi	3.00	3.00
a.	Souvenir sheet of 6, #1713-1718	13.00	13.00
	Nos. 1713-1718 (6)	13.00	13.00

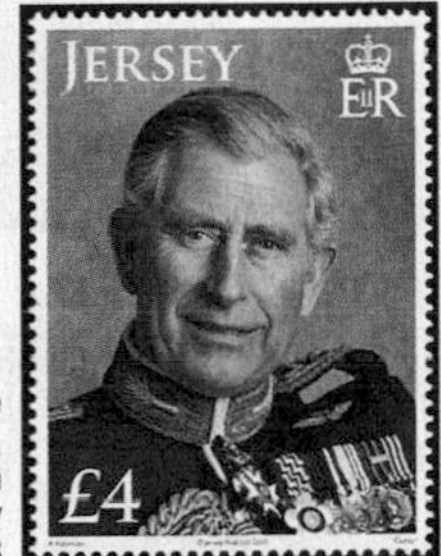

Prince Charles, 65th Birthday A348

2013, Nov. 14 **Litho.** *Perf. 13¼*

Stamp With White Frame

1719	A348 £4 multi	13.00	13.00

Souvenir Sheet

Stamp Without White Frame

1720	A348 £4 multi	13.00	13.00

Souvenir Sheet

Jersey Royal Mace, 350th Anniv. — A349

2013, Nov. 14 **Litho.** *Perf. 13¾*

1721	A349 £1 multi	3.25	3.25

Christmas A350

Traditional food and drink: 40p, Christmas pudding. 45p, Mulled wine. 50p, Gingerbread men and hearts. 55p, Christmas cake. 60p, Stollen. 68p, Mixed nuts. 88p, Gingerbread house. 95p, Chocolate Yule log.

2013, Nov. 27 Litho. *Perf. 14x13¼*

1722 A350 40p multi 1.40 1.40
1723 A350 45p multi 1.50 1.50
1724 A350 50p multi 1.60 1.60
1725 A350 55p multi 1.75 1.75
1726 A350 60p multi 2.00 2.00
1727 A350 68p multi 2.25 2.25
1728 A350 88p multi 3.00 3.00
1729 A350 95p multi 3.25 3.25
Nos. 1722-1729 (8) 16.75 16.75

Manor Houses A351

Designs: 45p, Trinity Manor. 55p, Longueville Manor. 60p, Rosel Manor. 68p, St. John's Manor. 80p, St. Ouen's Manor. 88p, Millbrook Manor.

2014, Jan. 7 Litho. *Perf. 13x13¼*

1730 A351 45p multi 1.50 1.50
1731 A351 55p multi 1.75 1.75
1732 A351 60p multi 2.00 2.00
1733 A351 68p multi 2.25 2.25
1734 A351 80p multi 2.60 2.60
1735 A351 88p multi 3.00 3.00
Nos. 1730-1735 (6) 13.10 13.10

Musical Instruments A352

Designs: 45p, Electric guitar. 55p, Piano. 60p, Saxophone. 80p, Banjo.

2014, Mar. 25 Litho. *Perf. 14*

1736 A352 45p multi 1.50 1.50
1737 A352 55p multi 1.90 1.90
1738 A352 60p multi 2.00 2.00
1739 A352 80p multi 2.75 2.75
Nos. 1736-1739 (4) 8.15 8.15

Europa (60p, 80p).

William Shakespeare (1564-1616), Writer — A353

Designs: 46p, Heart and dagger (Romeo and Juliet). 56p, Skull with crown (Hamlet). 62p, King chess piece (Macbeth). 70p, Raised fist (Othello). 82p, Guitar (Twelfth Night). 91p, Butterfly (A Midsummer Night's Dream).
£3, Shakespeare, horiz.

2014, Apr. 23 Litho. *Perf. 14x14¾*

1740 A353 46p multi 1.60 1.60
1741 A353 56p multi 1.90 1.90
1742 A353 62p multi 2.10 2.10
1743 A353 70p multi 2.40 2.40
1744 A353 82p multi 2.75 2.75
1745 A353 91p multi 3.25 3.25
Nos. 1740-1745 (6) 14.00 14.00

Souvenir Sheet

1746 A353 £3 multi 10.00 10.00

No. 1746 contains one 48x32mm stamp.

World War I, Cent. — A354

Designs: 46p, Poppies and group of soldiers. 56p, Poppy. 62p, Poppy and torch. 70p, Poppy and soldier with rifle. 82p, Poppy and military medal. 91p, Poppy and three soldiers.
£3, Poppies.

2014, May 6 Litho. *Perf. 13¼*

1747 A354 46p multi 1.60 1.60
1748 A354 56p multi 1.90 1.90
1749 A354 62p multi 2.10 2.10
1750 A354 70p multi 2.40 2.40
1751 A354 82p multi 2.75 2.75
1752 A354 91p multi 3.00 3.00
Nos. 1747-1752 (6) 13.75 13.75

Souvenir Sheet
Perf. 13½

1753 A354 £3 multi 10.00 10.00

Poppy seeds are found under a gummed circle of plastic affixed to Nos. 1747 and 1748. No. 1753 contains one 40x40mm stamp.

D-Day, 70th Anniv. A355

Invasion forces: 46p, Mine clearers at Sword Beach. 56p, Paratroopers jumping over Sainte-Mère-Eglise. 62p, Minesweepers at Gold Beach. 70p, Soldiers at Pegasus Bridge. 82p, Soldiers approaching Carentan. 91p, Soldiers off Gold Beach.
£2, Piper Bill and troops at Pegasus Bridge.

2014, June 6 Litho. *Perf. 13¼x13*

1754 A355 46p multi 1.60 1.60
1755 A355 56p multi 1.90 1.90
1756 A355 62p multi 2.10 2.10
1757 A355 70p multi 2.40 2.40
1758 A355 82p multi 2.75 2.75
1759 A355 91p multi 3.25 3.25
Nos. 1754-1759 (6) 14.00 14.00

Souvenir Sheet

1760 A355 £2 multi 7.00 7.00

Jersey in Summer A356

Photographs by Andy Le Gresley: 46p, Boat at Belcroute Bay. 56p, Seymour Tower at High Tide. 62p, Summer Calm at Beauport. 69p, Fisherman's Chapel, St. Brelade's Bay. 70p, The White House at Sunrise. 82p, South Coast Rocks. 91p, Reflections of Archirondel Tower. £1.20, A View Underwater at Les Ecréhous.

2014, June 30 Litho. *Perf. 13¼x14*

1761 A356 46p multi 1.60 1.60
1762 A356 56p multi 1.90 1.90
1763 A356 62p multi 2.10 2.10
1764 A356 69p multi 2.40 2.40
1765 A356 70p multi 2.40 2.40
1766 A356 82p multi 2.75 2.75
1767 A356 91p multi 3.25 3.25
1768 A356 £1.20 multi 4.25 4.25
Nos. 1761-1768 (8) 20.65 20.65

Royal Air Force Red Arrows 50th Display Season — A357

Designs: 46p, One airplane. 56p, Four airplanes. 62p, Seven airplanes. 70p, Seven airplanes, diff. 82p, One airplane, diff. 91p, Two airplanes.

2014, July 11 Litho. *Perf. 13x13¼*

1769 A357 46p multi 1.60 1.60
1770 A357 56p multi 1.90 1.90
1771 A357 62p multi 2.10 2.10
1772 A357 70p multi 2.40 2.40
1773 A357 82p multi 2.75 2.75
1774 A357 91p multi 3.25 3.25
a. Souvenir sheet of 6, #1769-1774 14.00 14.00
Nos. 1769-1774 (6) 14.00 14.00

World War I, Cent. — A358

Designs: 46p, Jersey militiaman. 56p, Volunteer Aid Detachment nurse. 62p, French reservist. 70p, Land worker. 82p, Flag seller. 91p, Royal Navy officer.
£1, Soldiers, cannon, nurse, Union Jack, horiz.

2014, Aug. 4 Litho. *Perf. 13¼*

1775 A358 46p multi 1.60 1.60
1776 A358 56p multi 1.90 1.90
1777 A358 62p multi 2.10 2.10
1778 A358 70p multi 2.40 2.40
1779 A358 82p multi 2.75 2.75
1780 A358 91p multi 3.25 3.25
a. Souvenir sheet of 6, #1775-1780 14.00 14.00
Nos. 1775-1780 (6) 14.00 14.00

Souvenir Sheet
Perf. 13½x13¼

1781 A358 £1 multi 3.50 3.50

No. 1781 contains one 50x36mm stamp.

Roman Connections of Jersey — A359

Various depictions of military and everyday life in Jersey under Roman rule and: 46p, Julius Caesar. 56p, Governor Gnaeus Julius Agricola. 62p, Emperor Hadrian. 70p, Emperor Constantine. 82p, Emperor Honorius. 91p, Emperor Nero.
£2, Elephant in battle.

2014, Aug. 27 Litho. *Perf. 13¼x14*

1782 A359 46p multi 1.60 1.60
1783 A359 56p multi 1.90 1.90
1784 A359 62p multi 2.10 2.10
1785 A359 70p multi 2.40 2.40
1786 A359 82p multi 2.75 2.75
1787 A359 91p multi 3.00 3.00
Nos. 1782-1787 (6) 13.75 13.75

Souvenir Sheet

1788 A359 £2 multi 6.75 6.75

New Jersey, 350th Anniv. — A360

Map and: 46p, Barnegat Lighthouse, New Jersey. 56p, Elizabeth Castle, Jersey. 62p, Corbière Lighthouse, Jersey. 70p, Seymour Tower, Jersey. 82p, Statue of Liberty, New Jersey and New York. 91p, George Washington Bridge, New Jersey and New York.

2014, Sept. 15 Litho. *Perf. 12½x13*

1789 A360 46p multi 1.50 1.50
1790 A360 56p multi 1.90 1.90
1791 A360 62p multi 2.00 2.00
1792 A360 70p multi 2.25 2.25
1793 A360 82p multi 2.60 2.60
1794 A360 91p multi 3.00 3.00
a. Souvenir sheet of 6, #1789-1794, perf. 12½ 13.50 13.50
Nos. 1789-1794 (6) 13.25 13.25

Oyster Fishing A361

Designs: 46p, Ships, 19th cent. 56p, Women hauling oyster baskets off ship, 19th cent. 62p, Oystermen bringing up catch, 19th cent. 70p, Oystermen tending to farmed oysters, 20th-21st cent. 82p, Loading farmed oysters on trailer, 20th-21st cent. 91p, Oyster boat, 20th cent.
£2, Oysters and basket.

2014, Oct. 9 Litho. *Perf. 13x13¼*

1795 A361 46p multi 1.50 1.50
1796 A361 56p multi 1.75 1.75
1797 A361 62p multi 2.00 2.00
1798 A361 70p multi 2.25 2.25
1799 A361 82p multi 2.60 2.60
1800 A361 91p multi 3.00 3.00
a. Booklet pane of 6, #1795-1800 13.50 —
Nos. 1795-1800 (6) 13.10 13.10

Souvenir Sheet

1801 A361 £2 multi 6.50 6.50
a. Booklet pane of 1 6.50 —
Complete booklet, #1801, 3 #1800a 47.00

The three examples of No. 1800a in the complete booklet have different pane margins and orders of component stamps. No. 1801a has a vertical row or rouletting at the left.

Pirates and Privateering — A362

Designs: 46p, The Vulture attacking French ship. 56p, Pirates on board a French ship. 69p, Crew of French ship escaping pirates in rowboat. £1.20, Ships Charming Nancy and Le Heron.

2014, Oct. 30 Litho. *Perf. 13¼x13¾*

1802 A362 46p multi 1.50 1.50
1803 A362 56p multi 1.75 1.75
1804 A362 69p multi 2.25 2.25
1805 A362 £1.20 multi 4.00 4.00
a. Souvenir sheet of 4, #1802-1805 9.50 9.50
Nos. 1802-1805 (4) 9.50 9.50

My Moments — A363

No. 1806: a, Teddy bear, blue background. b, Balloons. c, Hands making heart, island. d, Gift box. e, Arms of Jersey. f, Fireworks.
No. 1807: a, Teddy bear, red background. b, "Hello" written in beach sand. c, Heart-shaped rock with ribbon. d, Champagne flutes and bottle. e, Flag of Jersey. f, Map of Europe with lines coming from Jersey.

Die Cut Perf. 14¼x14 Syncopated
2014, Nov. 12 Litho.
Self-Adhesive
Inscribed "Local Letter"

1806 Horiz. strip of 6 9.00
a.-f. A363 (46p) Any single 1.50 1.50

Inscribed "UK Letter"

1807 Horiz. strip of 6 10.50
a.-f. A363 (56p) Any single 1.75 1.75

Christmas — A364

Santa Claus: 41p, With girl sitting on lap. 46p, Walking in snow. 51p, Wrapping gifts. 56p, At chimney. 62p, Holding cookie and drink. 70p, Holding list. 91p, Standing in snow with girl. £1.10, Leaving gifts under Christmas tree.

2014, Nov. 27 Litho. *Perf. 14x14¾*

1808 A364 41p multi 1.25 1.25
1809 A364 46p multi 1.50 1.50
1810 A364 51p multi 1.60 1.60
1811 A364 56p multi 1.75 1.75
1812 A364 62p multi 2.00 2.00
1813 A364 70p multi 2.25 2.25
1814 A364 91p multi 3.00 3.00
1815 A364 £1.10 multi 3.50 3.50
Nos. 1808-1815 (8) 16.85 16.85

Dragons A365

Designs: 46p, Beowulf dragon. 56p, St. George and the dragon. 62p, Bakunawa. 70p, Colchian dragon. 82p, Chinese dragons. 91p, Welsh dragon.

2015, Jan. 6 Litho. *Perf. 13x13¼*

1816 A365 46p multi 1.40 1.40
1817 A365 56p multi 1.75 1.75
1818 A365 62p multi 1.90 1.90
1819 A365 70p multi 2.10 2.10
1820 A365 82p multi 2.50 2.50
1821 A365 91p multi 2.75 2.75
a. Souvenir sheet of 6, #1816-1821 12.50 12.50
Nos. 1816-1821 (6) 12.40 12.40

Arms of Jersey — A366

2015, Feb. 18 Litho. *Perf. 14x13¾*

Denomination Color

1822 A366 1p purple .25 .25
1823 A366 2p bister .25 .25
1824 A366 3p dark blue .25 .25
1825 A366 4p dark green .25 .25
1826 A366 5p brown lake .25 .25
1827 A366 10p hot pink .30 .30
1828 A366 20p orange .60 .60
1829 A366 40p turq blue 1.25 1.25
1830 A366 50p yellow green 1.60 1.60
1831 A366 £1 red 3.00 3.00

Litho. With Hologram Affixed

Perf. 13½

Size: 38x51mm

1832 A366 £5 silver 15.50 15.50
Nos. 1822-1832 (11) 23.50 23.50

See Nos. 2017-2022.

Hornby Toy Trains — A367

Designs: 46p, British Pullman. 56p, GWR Passenger Freight train. 62p, Flying Scotsman. 70p, Cornishman. 82p, Mixed Freight train. 91p, Caledonian Belle.

Perf. 13¼x13¾

2015, Mar. 24 Litho.

1833 A367 46p multi 1.40 1.40
1834 A367 56p multi 1.75 1.75
1835 A367 62p multi 1.90 1.90
1836 A367 70p multi 2.10 2.10
1837 A367 82p multi 2.50 2.50
1838 A367 91p multi 2.75 2.75
Nos. 1833-1838 (6) 12.40 12.40

Europa (62p, 82p).

Hubble Space Telescope, 25th Anniv. — A368

Images from Hubble Space Telescope: 47p, Light echo of V838 Moncerotis. 57p, M74 (NGC 628) spiral galaxy. 64p, "Mystic Mountain" dust and gas clouds of Carina Nebula. 71p, New Red Spot on Jupiter. 73p, Cat's Eye Nebula (NGC 6543). 85p, Mars. 95p, Rose of Galaxies (Interacting galaxies UGC1810 and UGC1813). £1.25, Pistol Star.

£2, Hubble Space Telescope above Earth, vert.

2015, Apr. 24 Litho. *Perf. 13¼*

1839 A368 47p multi 1.50 1.50
1840 A368 57p multi 1.75 1.75
1841 A368 64p multi 2.00 2.00
1842 A368 71p multi 2.25 2.25
1843 A368 73p multi 2.25 2.25
1844 A368 85p multi 2.60 2.60
1845 A368 95p multi 3.00 3.00
1846 A368 £1.25 multi 3.75 3.75
Nos. 1839-1846 (8) 19.10 19.10

Souvenir Sheet

Perf. 13

1847 A368 £2 multi 6.25 6.25

No. 1847 contains one 36x42mm stamp.

Victory in World War II, 70th Anniv. A369

"V" and: 47p, Pennants, date of liberation. 57p, HMS Beagle, 64p, Arms and map of Jersey. 73p, International Red Cross ship SS Vega, map of Europe. 85p, Buildings and paving stones in Royal Square, St. Helier. 95p, Microphone.

£3, Sir Winston Churchill, vert.

2015, May 9 Litho. *Perf. 13x13¼*

1848 A369 47p multi 1.50 1.50
1849 A369 57p multi 1.75 1.75
1850 A369 64p multi 2.00 2.00
1851 A369 73p multi 2.25 2.25
1852 A369 85p multi 2.60 2.60
1853 A369 95p multi 3.00 3.00
a. Souvenir sheet of 6, #1848-1853 13.50 13.50
Nos. 1848-1853 (6) 13.10 13.10

Souvenir Sheet

Litho. & Engr.

1854 A369 £3 org & multi 9.25 9.25

No. 1854 contains one 58x72mm stamp.

Magna Carta, 800th Anniv. A370

Designs: 47p, Balance (Justice). 57p, Key (Freedom). 64p, Fist (Human rights). 73p, Dove (Liberty). 85p, Map of Jersey (Citizenship). 95p, Saltire (Democracy).

£1.50, Text.

2015, June 15 Litho. *Perf. 13¼*

1855 A370 47p multi 1.50 1.50
1856 A370 57p multi 1.75 1.75
1857 A370 64p multi 2.00 2.00
1858 A370 73p multi 2.25 2.25
1859 A370 85p multi 2.75 2.75
1860 A370 95p multi 3.00 3.00
Nos. 1855-1860 (6) 13.25 13.25

Souvenir Sheet

Perf. 14¼

1861 A370 £1.50 multi 4.75 4.75

No. 1861 contains one 43x43mm stamp.

16th Island Games A371

2015, June 27 Litho. *Perf. 13¼x14*

1862 A371 (62p) Beach volleyball 2.00 2.00
a. Perf. 13¼ 2.00 2.00
1863 A371 (62p) Basketball 2.00 2.00
a. Perf. 13¼ 2.00 2.00
1864 A371 (62p) Soccer 2.00 2.00
a. Perf. 13¼ 2.00 2.00
b. Booklet pane of 6, 2 each #1862a, 1863a, 1864a 12.00 —
1865 A371 (62p) Sailing 2.00 2.00
a. Perf. 13¼ 2.00 2.00
1866 A371 (62p) Swimming 2.00 2.00
a. Perf. 13¼ 2.00 2.00
1867 A371 (62p) Triathlon 2.00 2.00
a. Perf. 13¼ 2.00 2.00
b. Booklet pane of 6, 2 each #1865a, 1866a, 1867a 12.00 —
1868 A371 (62p) Badminton 2.00 2.00
a. Perf. 13¼ 2.00 2.00
1869 A371 (62p) Table tennis 2.00 2.00
a. Perf. 13¼ 2.00 2.00
1870 A371 (62p) Tennis 2.00 2.00
a. Perf. 13¼ 2.00 2.00
b. Booklet pane of 6, 2 each #1868a, 1869a, 1870a 12.00 —
1871 A371 (62p) Cycling 2.00 2.00
a. Perf. 13¼ 2.00 2.00
1872 A371 (62p) Track 2.00 2.00
a. Perf. 13¼ 2.00 2.00
1873 A371 (62p) Golf 2.00 2.00
a. Perf. 13¼ 2.00 2.00
b. Booklet pane of 6, 2 each #1871a, 1872a, 1873a 12.00 —
1874 A371 (62p) Shooting 2.00 2.00
a. Perf. 13¼ 2.00 2.00
1875 A371 (62p) Archery 2.00 2.00
a. Perf. 13¼ 2.00 2.00
b. Booklet pane of 4, 2 each #1874a, 1875a 8.00 —
Complete booklet, #1864b, 1867b, 1870b, 1873b, 1875b 56.00
Nos. 1862-1875 (14) 28.00 28.00

Nos. 1862-1875 are each inscribed "Postcard."

Battle of Britain, 75th Anniv. A372

Designs: 47p, Mk I Spitfire. 57p, Radar installation and airplanes. 64p, Royal Air Force emblem. 73p, Royal Air Force and Luftwaffe airplane insignia. 85p, Barrage balloons. 95p, Hawker Hurricanes, map of English Channel.

£3, Sir Winston Churchill.

2015, July 10 Litho. *Perf. 13x13¼*

1876 A372 47p multi 1.50 1.50
1877 A372 57p multi 1.75 1.75
1878 A372 64p multi 2.00 2.00
1879 A372 73p multi 2.25 2.25
1880 A372 85p multi 2.75 2.75
1881 A372 95p multi 3.00 3.00
a. Souvenir sheet of 6, #1876-1881 13.50 13.50
Nos. 1876-1881 (6) 13.25 13.25

Litho. & Engr.

Souvenir Sheet

1882 A372 £3 gray, blk lil & blk 9.50 9.50

No. 1882 contains one 58x72mm stamp.

World War I, Cent. A373

Inscriptions: 47p, Mechanization. 57p, Communication. 64p, Camouflage and deception. 73p, Uniforms. 85p, Observation. 95p, Tactics of war.

£1, Wight Seaplane of Flight Lieutenant Charles Stanley Mossop.

2015, Aug. 4 Litho. *Perf. 13½x13¼*

1883 A373 47p multi 1.50 1.50
1884 A373 57p multi 1.75 1.75
1885 A373 64p multi 2.00 2.00
1886 A373 73p multi 2.25 2.25
1887 A373 85p multi 2.60 2.60
1888 A373 95p multi 3.00 3.00
a. Souvenir sheet of 6, #1883-1888 13.50 13.50
Nos. 1883-1888 (6) 13.10 13.10

Souvenir Sheet

1889 A373 £1 multi 3.25 3.25

Souvenir Sheet

Sark as a Fief to the Crown, 450th Anniv. — A374

2015, Aug. 6 Litho. *Perf. 14x14¾*

1890 A374 £1.50 multi 4.75 4.75

Queen Elizabeth II, Longest-Reigning British Monarch — A375

Photographic portrait of Queen Elizabeth II for: 47p, 1953 Coronation, by Cecil Beaton. 57p, 1977 Silver Jubilee, by Peter Grugeon. 71p, 2002 Golden Jubilee, by John Swannell. £1.25, 2012 Diamond Jubilee, by Swannell.

£3, The Coronation Theater, Westminster Abbey: A Portrait of Her Majesty Queen Elizabeth II, painting by Ralph Heimans.

2015, Sept. 9 Litho. *Perf. 13¼x13*

1891 A375 47p multi 1.50 1.50
1892 A375 57p multi 1.75 1.75
1893 A375 71p multi 2.25 2.25
1894 A375 £1.25 multi 3.75 3.75
a. Souvenir sheet of 4, #1891-1894 9.25 9.25
Nos. 1891-1894 (4) 9.25 9.25

Souvenir Sheet

Silk-Faced Paper

Perf. 13¾x13¼

1895 A375 £3 multi 9.25 9.25

No. 1895 contains one 28x45mm stamp.

Flowers A376

2015, Sept. 22 Litho. *Perf. 13x13¼*

1896 A376 47p Magnolia 1.50 1.50
1897 A376 47p Camellia 1.50 1.50
1898 A376 47p Azalea 1.50 1.50
1899 A376 47p Hydrangea 1.50 1.50
1900 A376 47p Chrysanthemum 1.50 1.50
1901 A376 47p Peony 1.50 1.50
a. Souvenir sheet of 2, #1900-1901 3.00 3.00
Nos. 1896-1901 (6) 9.00 9.00

Jersey in Autumn A377

Photographs by Andy Le Gresley: 47p, Country Lane Near St. John's Village. 57p, Sun Through the Clouds at Corbière. 64p, Autumn in the Sand Dunes. 71p, Stormy Day at Noirmont Point. 73p, High Tide Shore Break at St. Catherine's Bay. 85p, Sunset at the Radio Tower, St. Brelade. 95p, Woodland Path Through St. Peter's Valley. £1.25, Kempt Tower Through the Beach Grass, St. Ouen.

2015, Oct. 15 Litho. *Perf. 13¼x13¾*

1902	A377	47p multi	1.50	1.50
1903	A377	57p multi	1.75	1.75
1904	A377	64p multi	2.00	2.00
1905	A377	71p multi	2.25	2.25
1906	A377	73p multi	2.25	2.25
1907	A377	85p multi	2.60	2.60
1908	A377	95p multi	3.00	3.00
1909	A377	£1.25 multi	4.00	4.00
		Nos. 1902-1909 (8)	19.35	19.35

Winning Children's Art in Stamp Design Contest — A378

No. 1910: a, Cow and flowers, by Millie Foley. b, House and flowers, by Jennifer Crocker. c, Surfboard, sailboat and Sun, by Matthew Brown. d, Children at beach, by Leah O'Brien. e, Tower, by Anna Le Moine Gray.

No. 1911: a, Puffin, by Sophie Dixon. b, Jersey Royal Potatoes, by Ciaran Britton. c, Cow and calf at beach, by Allan Giles McCartney. d, Lighthouse, by Skye Leather. e, Jersey Arms, by Claudia Dixon.

Serpentine Die Cut 12¼x13

2015, Nov. 9 Litho.

Self-Adhesive

Inscribed "Local Letter"

1910	Horiz. strip of 5	7.00	
a.-e.	A378 (47p) Any single	1.40	1.40

Inscribed "UK Priority Letter"

1911	Horiz. strip of 5	8.75	
a.-e.	A378 (57p) Any single	1.75	1.75

Christmas — A379

Stained-glass windows by Henry Thomas Bosdet depicting: 42p, Virgin Mary looking right. 47p, Archangel Gabriel looking left. 52p, Gabriel looking right. 57p, Mary hands clasped. 64p, Gabriel both hands shown. 73p, Mary's hands unclasped. 95p, Gabriel left hand down, right hand up. £1.15, Mary, hand over heart.

Perf. 13¾x13½

2015, Nov. 27 Litho.

1912	A379	42p multi	1.25	1.25
1913	A379	47p multi	1.40	1.40
1914	A379	52p multi	1.60	1.60
1915	A379	57p multi	1.75	1.75
1916	A379	64p multi	2.00	2.00
1917	A379	73p multi	2.25	2.25
1918	A379	95p multi	3.00	3.00
1919	A379	£1.15 multi	3.50	3.50
		Nos. 1912-1919 (8)	16.75	16.75

New Year 2016 (Year of the Monkey) A380

Monkey facing: 47p, Left. £1, Right.

2016, Jan. 5 Litho. *Perf. 13¼*

1920	A380 47p multi	1.40	1.40

Souvenir Sheet

1921	A380 £1 multi	3.00	3.00

No. 1921 contains one 60x60mm stamp.

Royal Air Force Search and Rescue Service, 75th Anniv. A381

Designs: 47p, Lockheed Hudson search plane over man in life raft. 57p, Rescue boat. 71p, Supermarine Walrus seaplane approaching men in life raft. 73p, Westland Whirlwind helicopter winching sinking boat. 95p, Westland Whirlwind helicopter near oil rig. £1.25, Westland Sea King helicopter making mountain rescue.

2016, Feb. 6 Litho. *Perf. 13x13¼*

1922	A381	47p multi	1.40	1.40
1923	A381	57p multi	1.60	1.60
1924	A381	71p multi	2.00	2.00
1925	A381	73p multi	2.10	2.10
1926	A381	95p multi	2.75	2.75
1927	A381	£1.25 multi	3.50	3.50
a.		Souvenir sheet of 6, #1922-1927	13.50	13.50
		Nos. 1922-1927 (6)	13.35	13.35

King George V (1865-1936) A382

King George V in: 47p, 1911. 57p, 1914. 64p, 1922. 73p, 1926. 85p, 1933. 95p, 1934. £2, King George V in 1934, horiz.

2016, Mar. 9 Litho. *Perf. 13½x14*

1928	A382 47p multi	1.40	1.40
1929	A382 57p multi	1.60	1.60
1930	A382 64p multi	1.90	1.90
1931	A382 73p multi	2.10	2.10
1932	A382 85p multi	2.40	2.40
1933	A382 95p multi	2.75	2.75
	Nos. 1928-1933 (6)	12.15	12.15

Souvenir Sheet

1934	A382 £2 multi	5.75	5.75

No. 1934 contains one 54x40mm stamp.

Queen Elizabeth II, 90th Birthday A383

Designs: No. 1935, Princess Elizabeth, 1928. No. 1936, Princess' Elizabeth and Margaret with parents, 1931. No. 1937, Princess Elizabeth with her fiancée, Lt. Philip Mountbatten, 1947. No. 1938, Princess Elizabeth, Princes Philip and Charles, Princess Anne, 1951. 66p, Queen Elizabeth II and Princes Andrew and Edward, 1964. 74p, Queen Elizabeth II, Prince Philip, their children, and grandson, Peter Phillips, 1979. 76p, Queen Elizabeth II, her mother, and her sister, Princess Margaret, 1980. 88p, Queen Elizabeth II and her mother, 1997. £1, Queen Elizabeth II and Prince Philip, 2005. £1.29, Queen Elizabeth II, Duke and Duchess of Cambridge, Princes Harry and George, 2015.

2016, Apr. 21 Litho. *Perf. 13¼*

1935	A383	48p blk & pink	1.40	1.40
1936	A383	48p blk & ol bister	1.40	1.40
1937	A383	60p blk & pale blue	1.75	1.75
a.		Booklet pane of 6, 2 each #1935-1937	9.25	—
1938	A383	60p blk & flesh	1.75	1.75
1939	A383	66p blk & azure	2.00	2.00
a.		Booklet pane of 4, 2 each #1938-1939	7.50	—
1940	A383	74p multi	2.25	2.25
1941	A383	76p multi	2.25	2.25
1942	A383	88p multi	2.60	2.60
a.		Booklet pane of 6, 2 each #1940-1942	14.50	—
1943	A383	£1 multi	3.00	3.00
1944	A383	£1.29 multi	3.75	3.75
a.		Booklet pane of 4, 2 each #1943-1944	13.50	—
		Complete booklet, #1937a, 1939a, 1942a, 1944a	45.00	
		Nos. 1935-1944 (10)	22.15	22.15

Duke and Duchess of Cambridge, 5th Wedding Anniversay A384

Duke and Duchess of Cambridge: 48p, On wedding day. 2011. 60p, Touring Tuvalu, 2012. 74p, With infant Prince George, 2013. £1, With Prince George on his first birthday, 2014. £1.29, With infant Princess Charlotte, 2015.

£2, Duke and Duchess of Cambridge, Prince George and Princess Charlotte.

2016, Apr. 29 Litho. *Perf. 13x13¼*

1945	A384	48p multi	1.75	1.75
1946	A384	60p multi	1.75	1.75
1947	A384	74p multi	2.25	2.25
1948	A384	£1 multi	3.00	3.00
1949	A384	£1.29 multi	3.75	3.75
		Nos. 1945-1949 (5)	12.50	12.50

Souvenir Sheet

Perf. 13¼x13

1950	A384	£2 multi	6.00	6.00

No. 1950 contains one 52x40mm stamp.

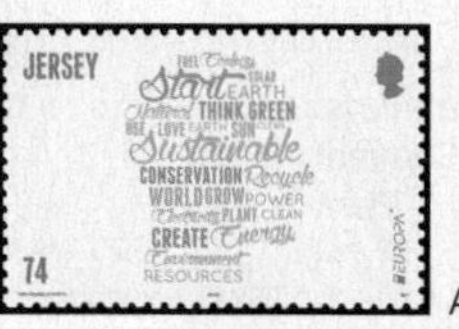

A385

"Think Green" A386

Ecology-related words in: 74p, Head. 76p, Map of Jersey. £1, Globe.

2016, May 3 Litho. *Perf. 13¼*

1951	A385	74p green	2.10	2.10
1952	A385	76p green	2.25	2.25
1953	A385	£1 green	3.00	3.00
1954	A386	£1.29 multi	3.75	3.75
		Nos. 1951-1954 (4)	11.10	11.10

Europa (#1951, 1954).

Publication of Albert Einstein's Theory of General Relativity, Cent. — A387

Einstein and: 48p, Gyroscope. 60p, Mercury and map of planetary orbits. 66p, Einstein field equations. 76p, Electromagnetic wave. 88p, Diagram of bending of light rays, space telescope. £1, Radio telescope.

£2, Einstein, Einstein field equation, diagram of space-time curvature.

2016, May 11 Litho. *Perf. 13¼*

1955	A387	48p multi	1.40	1.40
1956	A387	60p multi	1.75	1.75
1957	A387	66p multi	1.90	1.90
1958	A387	76p multi	2.25	2.25
1959	A387	88p multi	2.60	2.60
1960	A387	£1 multi	3.00	3.00
a.		Souvenir sheet of 6, #1955-1960	13.00	13.00
		Nos. 1955-1960 (6)	12.90	12.90

Souvenir Sheet

1961	A387	£2 multi	5.75	5.75
a.		As No. 1961, with World Stamp Show 2016, New York emblem in sheet margin	5.75	5.75

No. 1961 contains one 72x72mm stamp.

Jersey Old Motor Club, 50th Anniv. A388

Designs: 48p, 1948 MG TC. 60p, 1928 Rolls-Royce 20. 66p, 1903 60hp Mercedes. 74p, 1934 Daimler 15. 76p, 1929 Morgan Aero Three Wheeler. 88p, 1934 3½ liter Bentley. £1, 1929 Austin 7 Chummy. £1.29, 1902 Gladiator Tonneau.

£2, 1912 Talbot.

2016, June 7 Litho. *Perf. 14x13½*

1962	A388	48p multi	1.25	1.25
1963	A388	60p multi	1.60	1.60
1964	A388	66p multi	1.75	1.75
1965	A388	74p multi	2.00	2.00
1966	A388	76p multi	2.10	2.10
1967	A388	88p multi	2.40	2.40
1968	A388	£1 multi	2.75	2.75
1969	A388	£1.29 multi	3.50	3.50
		Nos. 1962-1969 (8)	17.35	17.35

Souvenir Sheet

1970	A388	£2 multi	5.50	5.50

No. 1970 contains one 42x34mm stamp.

Popular Culture of the 1950's A389

Designs: 48p, "Daddy-o." 68p, Dancers, records and juke box. 66p, Woman's full skirt. 76p, People watching coronation of Queen Elizabeth II on television 88p, Woman, child, molded gelatin. £1, Boy with model cars.

£2, Shops and restaurant.

2016, July 5 Litho. *Perf. 13¼*

1971	A389 48p multi	1.25	1.25
1972	A389 60p multi	1.60	1.60
1973	A389 66p multi	1.75	1.75
1974	A389 76p multi	2.00	2.00
1975	A389 88p multi	2.40	2.40
1976	A389 £1 multi	2.75	2.75
a.	Souvenir sheet of 6, #1971-1976	12.00	12.00
	Nos. 1971-1976 (6)	11.75	11.75

Souvenir Sheet

1977	A389 £2 multi	5.25	5.25

No. 1977 contains one 72x72mm stamp.

World War I, Cent. A390

Designs: 48p, First Battle of Ypres, 1914. 60p, Battle of Gallipoli, 1915-16. 66p, Battle of Jutland, 1916. 76p, Somme Offensive, 1916. 88p, Battle of Aqaba, 1917. £1, Battle of Passchendaele, 1917.

£2, Tank and soldiers at Battle of Cambrai, 1917.

2016, Aug. 4 Litho. *Perf. 13½*

1978	A390 48p multi	1.25	1.25
1979	A390 60p multi	1.60	1.60
1980	A390 66p multi	1.75	1.75
1981	A390 76p multi	2.00	2.00
1982	A390 88p multi	2.40	2.40
1983	A390 £1 multi	2.75	2.75
a.	Souvenir sheet of 6, #1978-1983	12.00	12.00
	Nos. 1978-1983 (6)	11.75	11.75

Souvenir Sheet

1984	A390 £2 multi	5.50	5.50

No. 1984 contains one 51x30mm stamp.

Waterfowl A391

Designs: No. 1985, Tufted duck. No. 1986, Mallard. No. 1987, Smew. No. 1988, Northern pintail. No. 1989, Common shelduck. No. 1990, Mandarins.

2016, Sept. 22 Litho. *Perf. 13¼*

No.	Type	Value	Color	Unused	Used
1985	A391	48p	multi	1.25	1.25
1986	A391	48p	multi	1.25	1.25
1987	A391	48p	multi	1.25	1.25
1988	A391	48p	multi	1.25	1.25
1989	A391	48p	multi	1.25	1.25
1990	A391	48p	multi	1.25	1.25
a.	Souvenir sheet of 2, #1989-1990			2.50	2.50
	Nos. 1985-1990 (6)			7.50	7.50

Myths and Legends A392

Designs: 48p, Fairies of St. Brelade's Church. 60p, William and the Sea Sprite. 74p, Witches of Rocqueberg. 76p, Dragon of St. Lawrence. £1, Black Dog of Bouley Bay. £1.29, Ghostly Bride of Waterworks Valley.

2016, Oct. 6 Litho. *Perf. 13x13¼*

No.	Type	Value	Color	Unused	Used
1991	A392	48p	multi	1.25	1.25
1992	A392	60p	multi	1.50	1.50
1993	A392	74p	multi	1.90	1.90
1994	A392	76p	multi	1.90	1.90
1995	A392	£1	multi	2.50	2.50
1996	A392	£1.29	multi	3.25	3.25
a.	Souvenir sheet of 6, #1991-1996			12.50	12.50
	Nos. 1991-1996 (6)			12.30	12.30

Jersey in Winter A393

Photographs by Andy Le Gresley: 48p, Corbière Lighthouse Surrounded by Stormy Winter Seas. 60p, A Winter Wonderland at St. Catherine's Woods. 66p, Cold Water at Noirmont Tower. 74p, Snow at Mont Orgueil Castle. 76p, Night Skies at Les Ecréhous. 88p, Hail Showers Passing by La Moye Golf Course. £1, Winter Woodland at Noirmont. £1.29, Gales Blow Into the Headland at Corbière.

2016, Nov. 4 Litho. *Perf. 13¼x14*

No.	Type	Value	Color	Unused	Used
1997	A393	48p	multi	1.25	1.25
1998	A393	60p	multi	1.50	1.50
1999	A393	66p	multi	1.75	1.75
2000	A393	74p	multi	1.90	1.90
2001	A393	76p	multi	2.00	2.00
2002	A393	88p	multi	2.25	2.25
2003	A393	£1	multi	2.60	2.60
2004	A393	£1.29	multi	3.25	3.25
	Nos. 1997-2004 (8)			16.50	16.50

Christmas A394

Designs: 43p, Father Christmas, flying sleigh, Corbière Lighthouse. 48p, Father Christmas' sleigh beginning flight, St. Ouen's Manor. 55p, Father Christmas at open mailbox, Royal Square. 60p, Flying sleigh above Trinity Church. 66p, Flying sleigh near Elizabeth Castle. 76p, Father Christmas, reindeer at Jersey Post Headquarters. £1, Father Christmas at Samarès Farmhouse. £1.19, Father Christmas in chimney, St. Thomas' Church.

£2.92, Father Christmas in house.

2016, Nov. 21 Litho. *Perf. 13x13¼*

No.	Type	Value	Color	Unused	Used
2005	A394	43p	multi	1.10	1.10
2006	A394	48p	multi	1.25	1.25
2007	A394	55p	multi	1.40	1.40
2008	A394	60p	multi	1.50	1.50
2009	A394	66p	multi	1.75	1.75
2010	A394	76p	multi	2.00	2.00
2011	A394	£1	multi	2.60	2.60
2012	A394	£1.19	multi	3.00	3.00
	Nos. 2005-2012 (8)			14.60	14.60

Souvenir Sheet

Perf. 13¼

No.	Type	Value	Color	Unused	Used
2013	A394	£2.92	multi	7.50	7.50

No. 2013 contains one 72x72mm stamp.

New Year 2017 (Year of the Rooster) A395

Designs: 48p, Rooster. £1, Hen and chicks.

2017, Jan. 5 Litho. *Perf. 13¼*

No.	Type	Value	Color	Unused	Used
2014	A395	48p	gold & multi	1.25	1.25

Souvenir Sheet

No.	Type	Value	Color	Unused	Used
2015	A395	£1	gold & multi	2.60	2.60

No. 2015 contains one 60x60mm stamp.

Souvenir Sheet

King Edward VIII (1894-1972) — A396

2017, Jan. 20 Litho. *Perf. 14¼x14*

No.	Type	Value	Color	Unused	Used
2016	A396	£2	multi	5.25	5.25

Arms Type of 2015

2017, Feb. 2 Litho. *Perf. 14x13¾*

Denomination Color

No.	Type	Value	Color	Unused	Used
2017	A366	48p	rose	1.25	1.25
2018	A366	60p	lavender	1.50	1.50
2019	A366	66p	aquamarine	1.75	1.75
2020	A366	76p	brt lilac	1.90	1.90
2021	A366	88p	org yellow	2.25	2.25
2022	A366	£1	dull claret	2.50	2.50
	Nos. 2017-2022 (6)			11.15	11.15

Castles A397

Designs: 74p, Grosnez Castle. 76p, Elizabeth Castle. £1, St. Aubin's Fort. £1.29, Mont Orgueil Castle.

2017, Mar. 2 Litho. *Perf. 13¼*

No.	Type	Value	Color	Unused	Used
2023	A397	74p	multi	1.90	1.90
2024	A397	76p	multi	1.90	1.90
2025	A397	£1	multi	2.50	2.50
2026	A397	£1.29	multi	3.25	3.25
a.	Souvenir sheet of 2, #2023, 2026			5.25	5.25
	Nos. 2023-2026 (4)			9.55	9.55

Europa (Nos. 2023, 2026).

Archaeological Artifacts — A398

Designs: 49p, Golden torque, 1st cent. B.C. 63p, Rotary quern, 1st cent. B.C. 73p, St. Lawrence Parish Church pillar, 800 A.D. 79p, Bronze dagger, 1st cent. B.C. 90p, Flint arrowhead, 2850-2250 B.C. £1.07, Silver and gilt brooch, 14th cent. £1.32, Bronze statue, 2nd cent. B.C. £2.52, Bronze Age axe head, 1500-800 B.C.

2017, Apr. 11 Litho. *Perf. 13½*

No.	Type	Value	Color	Unused	Used
2027	A398	49p	multi	1.25	1.25
2028	A398	63p	multi	1.60	1.60
2029	A398	73p	multi	1.90	1.90
2030	A398	79p	multi	2.10	2.10
2031	A398	90p	multi	2.40	2.40
2032	A398	£1.07	multi	2.75	2.75
a.	Booklet pane of 4, #2028, 2030-2032			9.00	—
2033	A398	£1.32	multi	3.50	3.50
2034	A398	£2.52	multi	6.50	6.50
a.	Booklet pane of 4, #2027, 2029, 2033-2034			13.50	—
	Complete booklet, 2 each #2032a, 2034a			45.00	
	Nos. 2027-2034 (8)			22.00	22.00

Complete booklet contains two examples of Nos. 2032a and 2034a, each with different pane margins.

King George VI (1895-1952) A399

Photograph of King George VI taken in: 49p, 1937. 63p, 1938. 73p, 1941. 79p, 1943. 90p, 1944. £1.07, 1948.

£2, 1939, horiz.

2017, May 12 Litho. *Perf. 13½x14*

No.	Type	Value	Color	Unused	Used
2035	A399	49p	multi	1.25	1.25
2036	A399	63p	multi	1.60	1.60
2037	A399	73p	multi	1.90	1.90
2038	A399	79p	multi	2.10	2.10
2039	A399	90p	multi	2.40	2.40
2040	A399	£1.07	multi	2.75	2.75
	Nos. 2035-2040 (6)			12.00	12.00

Souvenir Sheet

Perf. 14¼

No.	Type	Value	Color	Unused	Used
2041	A399	£2	multi	5.25	5.25

No. 2041 contains one 56x40mm stamp.

Lions Clubs International, Cent. — A400

Designs: 49p, Swimmers raising funds in Jersey Swimarathon. 63p, Treating eye diseases and recycled glasses. 73p, Worldwide disaster relief. 79p, Tackling environmental issues. 90p, Hearing tests and recycled hearing aids. £1.07, Holidays for the disabled.

£2, Worldwide disaster relief, diff.

2017, June 7 Litho. *Perf. 13x13¼*

No.	Type	Value	Color	Unused	Used
2042	A400	49p	multi	1.25	1.25
2043	A400	63p	multi	1.60	1.60
2044	A400	73p	multi	1.90	1.90
2045	A400	79p	multi	2.10	2.10
2046	A400	90p	multi	2.40	2.40
2047	A400	£1.07	multi	2.75	2.75
	Nos. 2042-2047 (6)			12.00	12.00

Souvenir Sheet

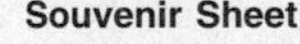

No.	Type	Value	Color	Unused	Used
2048	A400	£2	multi	5.25	5.25

Fauna A401

Charles Darwin (1809-82), Naturalist — A402

Designs: 49p, Mangrove finch. 63p, Livingstone's fruit bat. 73p, Telfair's skink. 79p, Mountain chicken. 90p, Hispaniolan solenodon. £1.07, Pygmy hog.

2017, June 14 Litho. *Perf. 13x13¼*

No.	Type	Value	Color	Unused	Used
2049	A401	49p	multi	1.25	1.25
2050	A401	63p	multi	1.60	1.60
2051	A401	73p	multi	1.90	1.90
2052	A401	79p	multi	2.10	2.10
2053	A401	90p	multi	2.40	2.40
2054	A401	£1.07	multi	2.75	2.75
	Nos. 2049-2054 (6)			12.00	12.00

Souvenir Sheet
On Sycamore Veneer
Self-Adhesive

Die Cut Perf. 7¼x6¾

No.	Type	Value	Color	Unused	Used
2055	A402	£3	multi	7.75	7.75

Darwin Initiative, 25th anniv.

Kaleidoscope, 200th Anniv. — A403

Kaleidoscopic images of: 49p, Shells and anemones. 63p, Feathers and eggs. 73p, Flowers. 79p, Mammals and birds. 90p, Insects. £1.07, Fish and crabs.

2017, July 10 Litho. *Perf. 13¾x13½*

No.	Type	Value	Color	Unused	Used
2056	A403	49p	multi	1.40	1.40
2057	A403	63p	multi	1.75	1.75
2058	A403	73p	multi	2.00	2.00
2059	A403	79p	multi	2.10	2.10
2060	A403	90p	multi	2.40	2.40
2061	A403	£1.07	multi	3.00	3.00
a.	Souvenir sheet of 6, #2056-2061			13.00	13.00
	Nos. 2056-2061 (6)			12.65	12.65

Airplanes of World War I — A404

Designs: 49p, Sopwith Camel. 63p, Airco DH.2 and Albatros D.II. 73p, Nieuport 16 and Fokker Eindecker. 79p, Fokker DR.I. 90p, Sopwith Triplane. £1.07, Nieuport 28.

£2, Airco DH.2.

2017, Aug. 4 Litho. *Perf. 13¼x13¾*

No.	Type	Value	Color	Unused	Used
2062	A404	49p	multi	1.25	1.25
2063	A404	63p	multi	1.60	1.60
2064	A404	73p	multi	1.90	1.90
2065	A404	79p	multi	2.10	2.10
2066	A404	90p	multi	2.40	2.40
2067	A404	£1.07	multi	2.75	2.75
a.	Souvenir sheet of 6, #2062-2067			12.00	12.00
	Nos. 2062-2067 (6)			12.00	12.00

Souvenir Sheet

Perf. 14

2068	A404	£2 multi	5.25	5.25

World War I, cent. No. 2068 contains one 70x42mm stamp.

Butterflies Found in Jersey and China — A405

Designs: No. 2069, Black-veined white butterfly. No. 2070, Small tortoiseshell butterfly. No. 2071, Swallowtail butterfly. No. 2072, Purple emperor butterfly. No. 2073, White admiral butterfly. No. 2074, Camberwell beauty butterfly.

2017, Sept. 1 Litho. *Perf. 13¼*

2069	A405	49p multi	1.25	1.25
2070	A405	49p multi	1.25	1.25
2071	A405	49p multi	1.25	1.25
a.		Souvenir sheet of 2, #2069, 2071	2.50	2.50
2072	A405	49p multi	1.25	1.25
2073	A405	49p multi	1.25	1.25
2074	A405	49p multi	1.25	1.25
a.		Souvenir sheet of 6, #2069-2074	7.50	7.50
		Nos. 2069-2074 (6)	7.50	7.50

A406

Lillie Langtry (1853-1929), Actress — A407

Langtry as: No. 2075, Kate Hardcastle in *She Stoops to Conquer.* No. 2076, Blanche Hays in *Ours.* No. 2077, Rosalind in *As You Like It.* No. 2078, Hester Grazebrook in *An Unequal Match.* 73p, Mademoiselle Mars in *Mademoiselle Mars.* 79p, Lena Despard in *As in a Looking Glass.* 90p, Lady Macbeth in *Macbeth.* £1.07, Pauline in *The Lady of Lyons.*

£2, Langry as Cleopatra in *Antony and Cleopatra.*

2017, Sept. 22 Litho. *Perf. 13¼x13*

Frame Color

2075	A406	49p pink	1.40	1.40
2076	A406	49p lilac	1.40	1.40
2077	A406	63p pale grnsh yel	1.75	1.75
2078	A406	63p cinnamon	1.75	1.75
2079	A406	73p sage green	2.00	2.00
2080	A406	79p light blue	2.10	2.10
2081	A406	90p lt tan	2.40	2.40
2082	A406	£1.07 lt rose	3.00	3.00
		Nos. 2075-2082 (8)	15.80	15.80

Souvenir Sheet
Self-Adhesive

Die Cut Perf. 7¾

2083	A407	£2 shown	5.50	5.50

Jersey Beekeepers Association, Cent. A408

Designs: 49p, Bee on flower. 63p, Bees on honeycomb. 73p, Apiarist with smoker near hives. 79p, Apiarist holding hive frame. 90p, Removing wax from frame. £1.07, Jar of honey and dipper.

£2, Bee on honeycomb.

2017, Oct. 3 Litho. *Perf. 13x13¼*

2084	A408	49p multi	1.40	1.40
2085	A408	63p multi	1.75	1.75
2086	A408	73p multi	2.00	2.00
2087	A408	79p multi	2.10	2.10
2088	A408	90p multi	2.40	2.40
2089	A408	£1.07 multi	3.00	3.00
		Nos. 2084-2089 (6)	12.65	12.65

Souvenir Sheet

Perf. 13

2090	A408	£2 multi	5.50	5.50

Nos. 2084-2090 are impregnated with a honey scent. No. 2090 contains one 40x35mm hexagonal stamp.

70th Wedding Anniversary of Queen Elizabeth II and Prince Philip — A409

Designs: 49p, Engagement photograph. 63p, Wedding day photograph. 73p, Honeymoon photograph 79p, Silver wedding anniversary photograph. 90p, Golden wedding anniversary photograph. £1.07, Diamond wedding anniversary photograph.

£2, 2016 photograph, horiz.

2017, Nov. 3 Litho. *Perf. 13¼x13*

2091	A409	49p multi	1.40	1.40
2092	A409	63p multi	1.75	1.75
2093	A409	73p multi	2.00	2.00
2094	A409	79p multi	2.10	2.10
2095	A409	90p multi	2.50	2.50
2096	A409	£1.07 multi	3.00	3.00
a.		Souvenir sheet of 6, #2091-2096	13.00	13.00
		Nos. 2091-2096 (6)	12.75	12.75

Souvenir Sheet

Perf. 13¼x14

2097	A409	£2 multi	5.50	5.50

No. 2097 contains one 51x40mm stamp.

Christmas A410

Designs: 43p, Family looking for Christmas tree. 49p, Christmas tree decorating. 55p, Children hanging stockings on fireplace mantle. 63p, Singing Christmas carols. 73p, Making a Christmas cake. 79p, Building a snowman. 90p, Exchanging gifts. £1.07, Nativity play.

2017, Nov. 20 Litho. *Perf. 13x13¼*

2098	A410	43p multi	1.25	1.25
2099	A410	49p multi	1.40	1.40
2100	A410	55p multi	1.50	1.50
2101	A410	63p multi	1.75	1.75
2102	A410	73p multi	2.00	2.00
2103	A410	79p multi	2.10	2.10
2104	A410	90p multi	2.50	2.50
2105	A410	£1.07 multi	3.00	3.00
		Nos. 2098-2105 (8)	15.50	15.50

New Year 2018 (Year of the Dog) — A411

Designs: 49p, Dog. £1, Dogs.

2018, Jan. 5 Litho. *Perf. 13¼*

2106	A411	49p gold & multi	1.40	1.40

Souvenir Sheet

2107	A411	£1 gold & multi	3.00	3.00

No. 2107 contains one 60x60mm stamp.

Popular Culture of the 1960s — A412

Designs: 49p, Flower Power. 63p, Rock guitarist. 73p, Women wearing miniskirts. 79p, Landing of men on the Moon. 90p, Cheese and pineapple sticks. £1.07, Girl and doll house.

£2, Shops in 1960s Jersey.

2018, Jan. 26 Litho. *Perf. 13¼*

2108	A412	49p multi	1.40	1.40
2109	A412	63p multi	1.75	1.75
2110	A412	73p multi	2.10	2.10
2111	A412	79p multi	2.25	2.25
2112	A412	90p multi	2.50	2.50
2113	A412	£1.07 multi	3.00	3.00
a.		Souvenir sheet of 6, #2108-2113	13.00	13.00
		Nos. 2108-2113 (6)	13.00	13.00

Souvenir Sheet

2114	A412	£2 multi	5.75	5.75

No. 2114 contains one 72x72mm stamps

Jersey in Spring A413

Photographs by Andy Le Gresley: No. 2115, Sunset from the Walkway at Devil's Hole. No. 2116, Waves Breaking at Ouaisné. 63p, Daffodils in Rozel Woods. 73p, Calm Seas at Portelet Bay. 79p, Grosnez Castle at Dusk. 90p, A St. Lawrence Valley View in Springtime. £1.07, The Headland Overlooking St. Brelade's Bay. £1.32, Sun Shining Through the Trees at Grantez.

Perf. 13¼x13½

2018, Feb. 14 Litho.

2115	A413	49p multi	1.40	1.40
2116	A413	49p multi	1.40	1.40
2117	A413	63p multi	1.75	1.75
2118	A413	73p multi	2.00	2.00
2119	A413	79p multi	2.25	2.25
2120	A413	90p multi	2.50	2.50
2121	A413	£1.07 multi	3.00	3.00
2122	A413	£1.32 multi	3.75	3.75
		Nos. 2115-2122 (8)	18.05	18.05

Bridges and Causeways A414

Designs: 73p, Havre de Pas Bridge. 79p, La Corbiere Causeway. 90p, Queen's Valley Reservoir. £1.07, Elizabeth Castle Causeway.

2018, Mar. 9 Litho. *Perf. 13½x13¼*

2123	A414	73p multi	2.10	2.10
2124	A414	79p multi	2.25	2.25
2125	A414	90p multi	2.60	2.60
a.		Souvenir sheet of 2, #2123, 2125	4.75	4.75
2126	A414	£1.07 multi	3.00	3.00
		Nos. 2123-2126 (4)	9.95	9.95

Europa (73p, 90p).

Royal Air Force, Cent. A415

Designs: 50p, Royal Aircraft Factory SE5a. 65p, Hawker Fury Mk. I. 76p, Short Stirling B.III. 82p, Supermarine Spitfire PR.XIX. 94p, English Electric Lightning F.6. £1.12, Eurofighter Typhoon.

Perf. 13¼x13½

2018, Mar. 31 Litho.

2127	A415	50p multi	1.40	1.40
2128	A415	65p multi	1.90	1.90
2129	A415	76p multi	2.10	2.10
2130	A415	82p multi	2.40	2.40
a.		Booklet pane of 3, #2127, 2129, 2130	6.00	—
2131	A415	94p multi	2.75	2.75
a.		Souvenir sheet of 2, #2128, 2131	4.75	4.75
b.		Booklet pane of 4, #2127, 2128, 2129, 2131	8.25	—
2132	A415	£1.12 multi	3.25	3.25
a.		Booklet pane of 3, #2127, 2130, 2132	7.25	—
b.		Booklet pane of 4, #2128, 2129, 2131, 2132	10.00	—
c.		Booklet pane of 4, #2128, 2130, 2131, 2132	10.50	—
		Complete booklet, #2130a, 2131b, 2132a, 2132b, 2132c	42.00	
		Nos. 2127-2132 (6)	13.80	13.80

Dam Busters Raid, 75th Anniv. A416

Designs: 50p, Airmen and airplane in flight. 65p, Pilot, airplane, anti-aircraft fire. 76p, Bombardier, airplane over reservoir. 82p, Bomb hitting water. 94p, Airplane over bomb hitting dam, Operation Chastise leaders looking at map, £1.12, Sir Barnes Wallis (1887-1979), inventor of bouncing bomb.

£2, Wing Commander Guy Gibson (1918-44).

2018, May 16 Litho. *Perf. 14x13¼*

2133	A416	50p multi	1.40	1.40
2134	A416	65p multi	1.75	1.75
2135	A416	76p multi	2.00	2.00
2136	A416	82p multi	2.25	2.25
2137	A416	94p multi	2.50	2.50
2138	A416	£1.12 multi	3.00	3.00
		Nos. 2133-2138 (6)	12.90	12.90

Souvenir Sheet

Perf. 13½

2139	A416	£2 multi	5.50	5.50

No. 2139 contains one 44x44mm stamp.

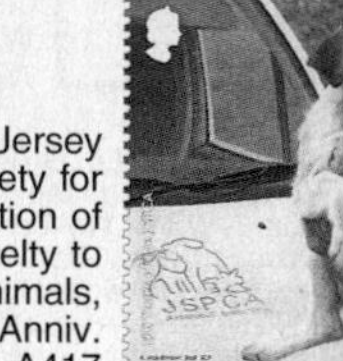

Jersey Society for Prevention of Cruelty to Animals, 150th Anniv. A417

Designs: 50p, Puppy, JSPCA vehicle. 65p, Dog in hands of veterinarian. 76p, Snake. 82p, Sleeping cat. 94p, Dog in shelter. £1.12, Dog on leash. £1.38, Rabbit. £2.64, Owl.

2018, May 25 Litho. *Perf. 14½*

2140	A417	50p multi	1.40	1.40
2141	A417	65p multi	1.75	1.75
2142	A417	76p multi	2.00	2.00
2143	A417	82p multi	2.25	2.25
2144	A417	94p multi	2.50	2.50
a.		Souvenir sheet of 2, #2143, 2144	4.75	4.75
2145	A417	£1.12 multi	3.00	3.00
2146	A417	£1.38 multi	3.75	3.75
2147	A417	£2.64 multi	7.00	7.00
		Nos. 2140-2147 (8)	23.65	23.65

"Frankenstein," by Mary Shelley, 200th Anniv. — A418

Quotations: 50p, "I began the creation of a human being." 65p, "I beheld the accomplishment of my toils." 76p, "His eyes, if eyes they may be called, were fixed on me." 82p, "I was a poor, helpless, miserable, wretch." 94p, "My heart yearned to be known and loved by these amiable creatures." £1.12, "Remember, that I am thy creature." £1.38, "You are my creator, but I am your master; - obey!" £2.64, "Where can I find rest but in death?"

£3, "I beheld the wretch - the miserable monster whom I had created."

2018, June 18 Litho. *Perf. 13x13¼*

2148 A418 50p sil & multi 1.40 1.40
2149 A418 65p sil & multi 1.75 1.75
2150 A418 76p sil & multi 2.00 2.00
2151 A418 82p sil & multi 2.25 2.25
2152 A418 94p sil & multi 2.50 2.50
2153 A418 £1.12 sil & multi 3.00 3.00
2154 A418 £1.38 sil & multi 3.75 3.75
2155 A418 £2.64 sil & multi 7.00 7.00
a. Souvenir sheet of 8, #2148-2155 24.00 24.00
Nos. 2148-2155 (8) 23.65 23.65

Souvenir Sheet

Litho. With Lenticular Lens Affixed

Perf. 14¼x14

2156 A418 £3 multi 8.00 8.00

Jersey Overseas Aid, 50th Anniv. A419

Projects: 50p, Jersey cow program, Rwanda. 65p, Famine relief, South Sudan. 76p, Tropical diseases, Uganda. 82p, Economic development, Nepal. 94p, Rural livelihoods, Madagascar. £1.12, Sand dam construction, Kenya.

2018, July 12 Litho. *Perf. 13¼x13*

2157 A419 50p multi 1.40 1.40
2158 A419 65p multi 1.75 1.75
2159 A419 76p multi 2.00 2.00
2160 A419 82p multi 2.25 2.25
2161 A419 94p multi 2.50 2.50
2162 A419 £1.12 multi 3.00 3.00
Nos. 2157-2162 (6) 12.90 12.90

End of World War I, Cent. — A420

Jersey residents taking part in World War I: 50p, Private Charles William Moody. 65p, Second Lieutenant Kenneth Strickland Dunlop. 76p, Petty Officer George Alfred Jeune. 82p, Private Clifford Helier Brée. 94p, Lieutenant William McCrae Bruce. £1.12, Nurse Madeleine Louise Norman.

£2, Corporal Robert Leonard Norman, horiz.

2018, Aug. 4 Litho. *Perf. 13¼x14*

2163 A420 50p multi 1.25 1.25
2164 A420 65p multi 1.75 1.75
2165 A420 76p multi 2.00 2.00
2166 A420 82p multi 2.10 2.10
2167 A420 94p multi 2.40 2.40
2168 A420 £1.12 multi 3.00 3.00
a. Souvenir sheet of 6, #2163-2168 12.50 12.50
Nos. 2163-2168 (6) 12.50 12.50

Souvenir Sheet

Perf. 13¾x13¼

2169 A420 £2 multi 5.25 5.25

No. 2169 contains one 55x42mm stamp.

Birds — A421

Designs: No. 2170, Red-billed chough. No. 2171, Yellowhammer. No. 2172, Barn swallow. No. 2173, Stonechat. No. 2174, Goldfinch. No. 2175, Linnet.

2018, Sept. 3 Litho. *Perf. 13¼*

2170 A421 50p multi 1.25 1.25
2171 A421 50p multi 1.25 1.25
2172 A421 50p multi 1.25 1.25
2173 A421 50p multi 1.25 1.25
a. Souvenir sheet of 2, #2170, 2173 2.50 2.50
2174 A421 50p multi 1.25 1.25
2175 A421 50p multi 1.25 1.25
a. Souvenir sheet of 6, #2170-2175 7.50 7.50
Nos. 2170-2175 (6) 7.50 7.50

Woman Suffrage, Cent. — A422

Suffragette holding sign or banner inscribed: 50p, "National Union of Women's Suffrage Societies." 65p, "Deeds Not Words." 76p, "Women's War Work." 82p, "Votes for Women." 94p, "First Vote for Women in Jersey." £1.12, "First Female MP in Parliament."

£2, "Votes for Women" sign.

2018, Oct. 2 Litho. *Perf. 13*

2176 A422 50p multi 1.25 1.25
2177 A422 65p multi 1.75 1.75
2178 A422 76p multi 2.00 2.00
2179 A422 82p multi 2.10 2.10
2180 A422 94p multi 2.40 2.40
2181 A422 £1.12 multi 3.00 3.00
a. Souvenir sheet of 6, #2176-2181 12.50 12.50
Nos. 2176-2181 (6) 12.50 12.50

Souvenir Sheet

Perf. 13¼x13¾

2182 A422 £2 multi 5.25 5.25

No. 2182 contains one 42x55mm stamp.

A423

A424

Prince Charles, 70th Birthday — A425

Photograph of Prince Charles taken in: 50p, 1957. 65p, 1966. 76p, 1975. 82p, c. 1977. 94p, 1998. £1.12, 2012. £3, 2006.

£2, 2017.

Litho., Litho. With Foil Application (£3)

2018, Nov. 14 *Perf. 13½x13¼*

2183 A423 50p sil & multi 1.25 1.25
2184 A423 65p sil & multi 1.75 1.75
2185 A423 76p sil & multi 2.00 2.00
2186 A423 82p sil & multi 2.10 2.10
2187 A423 94p sil & multi 2.40 2.40
2188 A423 £1.12 sil & multi 3.00 3.00

Perf. 13¼x13½

2189 A424 £3 sil & multi 7.75 7.75
Nos. 2183-2189 (7) 20.25 20.25

Souvenir Sheet

Perf. 11¾

2190 A425 £2 sil & multi 5.25 5.25

Christmas A426

Sweaters showing: 44p, Snowflakes. 50p, Angel playing horn. 57p, Santa Claus suit. 65p, Snowman. 76p, Christmas tree and gifts. 82p, Holly. 94p, Reindeer wearing snow cap. £1.12, Magi.

Serpentine Die Cut 14 Syncopated

2018, Nov. 19 Litho.

Self-Adhesive

2191 A426 44p multi 1.10 1.10
2192 A426 50p multi 1.25 1.25
2193 A426 57p multi 1.50 1.50
2194 A426 65p multi 1.75 1.75
2195 A426 76p multi 2.00 2.00
2196 A426 82p multi 2.10 2.10
2197 A426 94p multi 2.40 2.40
2198 A426 £1.12 multi 3.00 3.00
Nos. 2191-2198 (8) 15.10 15.10

New Year 2019 (Year of the Pig) — A427

Designs: 50p, Pig, bird and flowers.
£1, Pig, piglets, birds and flowers.

2019, Jan. 4 Litho. *Perf. 13¼*

2199 A427 50p gold & multi 1.25 1.25

Souvenir Sheet

2200 A427 £1 gold & multi 2.60 2.60

No. 2200 contains one 60x60mm stamp.

Popular Culture of the 1970s A428

Designs: 50p, "Boogie." 65p, "Punk" and safety pin. 76p, Flared pants. 82p, Cassette for video cassette recorder. 94p, Man and woman eating fondue. £1.12, Roller skate.

£2, Shops in 1970s Jersey.

2019, Jan. 18 Litho. *Perf. 13¼*

2201 A428 50p multi 1.25 1.25
2202 A428 65p multi 1.75 1.75
2203 A428 76p multi 2.00 2.00
2204 A428 82p multi 2.10 2.10
2205 A428 94p multi 2.40 2.40
2206 A428 £1.12 multi 3.00 3.00
a. Souvenir sheet of 6, #2201-2206 12.50 12.50
Nos. 2201-2206 (6) 12.50 12.50

Souvenir Sheet

2207 A428 £2 multi 5.25 5.25

No. 2207 contains one 72x72mm stamp.

Sir Walter Raleigh (c. 1552-1618), Governor of Jersey and New World Expedition Leader — A429

Designs: 50p, Fort Isabella Bellissima (Elizabeth Castle). 65p, Hand holding quill pen, and text, "Soldier, Sailor, Author, Poet & Adventurer." 76p, Ship and text, " Whosoever commands the sea commands the trade." 82p, Ship, map, monument and text, "When we have wandered all our ways. . ." 94p, Castle and text, "Twere pity to cast it down." £1.12, Raleigh and text, "To my verie loving friends the bailiffe and Justices of Jersey."

£2, Raleigh, ship and map.

2019, Feb. 5 Litho. *Perf. 14x13¼*

2208 A429 50p brnz & multi 1.40 1.40
2209 A429 65p brnz & multi 1.75 1.75
2210 A429 76p brnz & multi 2.00 2.00
2211 A429 82p brnz & multi 2.10 2.10
2212 A429 94p brnz & multi 2.50 2.50
2213 A429 £1.12 brnz & multi 3.00 3.00
Nos. 2208-2213 (6) 12.75 12.75

Souvenir Sheet

Perf. 14¼x14

2214 A429 £2 brnz & multi 5.25 5.25

No. 2214 contains one 56x40mm stamp.

POSTAGE DUE STAMPS

Numeral — D1

Map of Jersey — D2

Unwmk.

1969, Oct. 1 Litho. *Perf. 14*

J1 D1 1p violet blue 1.00 1.10
J2 D1 2p sepia 1.25 1.10
J3 D1 3p brt carmine 1.40 1.10
J4 D2 1sh emerald 8.00 5.00
J5 D2 2sh6p gray green 18.00 *14.00*
J6 D2 5sh red orange 21.00 16.00
Nos. J1-J6 (6) 50.65 38.30

Type of 1969

Decimal Currency

1971-75 Litho. *Perf. 14*

J7 D2 ½p black .25 .25
J8 D2 1p pale violet .25 .25
J9 D2 2p brown .25 .25
J10 D2 3p bright pink .25 .25
J11 D2 4p orange .25 .25
J12 D2 5p emerald .25 .25
J13 D2 6p orange ('74) .25 .25
J14 D2 7p brt yellow ('74) .25 .25
J15 D2 8p grnsh blue ('75) .25 .25
J16 D2 10p gray .25 .25
J17 D2 11p bister ('75) .40 .40
J18 D2 14p lilac .50 .50
J19 D2 25p dull green ('74) .75 .75
J20 D2 50p plum ('75) 1.40 1.40
Nos. J7-J20 (14) 5.55 5.55

St. Clement Arms, Dovecote, Samares — D3

Arms and Scenes from Jersey Parishes: 2p, St. Lawrence and Handois Reservoir. 3p, St. John and Sorel Point. 4p, St. Ouen and Pinnacle Rock. 5p, St. Peter and Quetivel Mill. 10p, St. Martin and St. Catherine's Breakwater. 12p, St. Helier and St. Helier Harbor. 14p, St. Saviour and Highlands College. 15p, St. Brelade and Beauport Bay. 20p, Grouville and La Hougue Bie. 50p, St. Mary and Perry Farm. £1, Trinity and Bouley Bay.

1978, Jan. 17 Litho. *Perf. 14*

J21 D3 1p brt green & blk .25 .25
J22 D3 2p orange & blk .25 .25
J23 D3 3p maroon & blk .25 .25
J24 D3 4p vermilion & blk .25 .25
J25 D3 5p dp ultra & blk .25 .25
J26 D3 10p olive & blk .25 .25

J27	D3	12p blue & blk	.25	.25
J28	D3	14p red org & blk	.25	.25
J29	D3	15p lilac rose & blk	.30	.30
J30	D3	20p yel green & blk	.35	.35
J31	D3	50p brown & blk	.80	.80
J32	D3	£1 violet & blk	1.25	1.25
		Nos. J21-J32 (12)	4.70	4.70

St. Brelade — D4

1982, Sept. 4 Litho. *Perf. 13½x14*

J33	D4	1p shown	.25	.25
J34	D4	2p St. Aubin	.25	.25
J35	D4	3p Rozel	.25	.25
J36	D4	4p Greve de Lecq	.25	.25
J37	D4	5p Bouley Bay	.25	.25
J38	D4	6p St. Catherine	.25	.25
J39	D4	7p Gorey	.25	.25
J40	D4	8p Bonne Nuit	.25	.25
J41	D4	9p La Rocque	.25	.25
J42	D4	10p St. Helier	.25	.25
J43	D4	20p Ronez	.40	.40
J44	D4	30p La Collette	.50	.50
J45	D4	40p Elizabeth Castle	.75	.75
J46	D4	£1 Upper Harbor Marina	2.00	2.00
		Nos. J33-J46 (14)	6.15	6.15

OCCUPATION STAMPS

Issued Under German Occupation

OS1

1941-42 Typo. Unwmk. *Perf. 11*

N1	OS1	½p bright green	7.00	6.00
N2	OS1	1p vermilion	7.00	5.00

Issue dates: No. N1, 1/29/42; No. N2, 4/1/41.

Jersey Views — OS2

Designs: ½p, Old Jersey farm; 1p, Portelet Bay; 1½p, Corbiere Lighthouse; 2p, Elizabeth Castle; 2½, Mont Orgueil Castle; 3p, Gathering seaweed.

1943-44 *Perf. 13½*

N3	OS2	½p dark green	7.25	12.00
a.		On rough, gray paper	9.00	14.00
N4	OS2	1p scarlet	1.75	.80
a.		On newsprint	2.10	1.50
N5	OS2	1½p brown	7.25	5.75
N6	OS2	2p orange	6.75	2.00
N7	OS2	2½p blue	2.00	1.40
a.		On newsprint	.90	1.75
N8	OS2	3p red violet	2.00	2.75
		Nos. N3-N8 (6)	27.00	24.70

Issued: ½p, 1p, 6/1/43; 1½p, 2p, 6/8/43; 2½p, 3p, 6/29/43; No. N4a, 2/28/44; No. N7a, 2/25/44.

Nos. N1-N8 remained valid until 4/13/46.

ISLE OF MAN

'ī(ə)l əv 'man

LOCATION — In the Irish Sea, off Northwest coast of England
GOVT. — Semi-autonomous within the British Commonwealth
AREA — 221 sq. mi.
POP. — 75,686 (1999 est.)
CAPITAL — Douglas

Catalogue values for unused stamps in this section are for Never Hinged items, beginning with Scott 1 in the regular postage section and Scott J1 in the postage due section.

British Regional Issues

A1

Manx Emblem — A2

Perf. 15x14

1958-69 Photo. Wmk. 322

1	A1	2½p rose red ('64)	.50	*1.10*
2	A2	3p purple	.50	.25
p.		Phosphor. ('68)	.25	.25
3	A2	4p ultra ('66)	1.50	*.50*
p.		Phosphor. ('67)	.25	1.50

Unwmk.

4	A2	4p ultra ('68)	.25	.25
5	A2	4p olive brown ('68)	.25	.25
6	A2	4p bright red ('69)	.45	*.75*
7	A2	5p dark blue ('68)	.45	*.75*
		Nos. 1-7 (7)	3.90	3.85

Nos. 4-7 are phosphorescent.

A 1963 printing of No. 2 is on chalky paper.

Manx Emblem — A3

1971, July 7 Photo. Unwmk.

8	A3	2½p bright pink	.30	.25
9	A3	3p ultramarine	.30	.25
10	A3	5p bluish lilac	.70	.70
11	A3	7½p light red brown	.70	.70
		Nos. 8-11 (4)	2.00	1.90

Sold to the general public only at post offices within the Isle of Man, but valid for postage throughout Great Britain.

Bailiwick Issues

Castletown and Manx Emblem A4

Manx Cat — A5

1p, Port Erin. 1½p, Mt. Snaefell. 2p, Laxey Village. 2½p, Tynwald Hill. 3p, Douglas Promenade. 3½p, Port St. Mary. 4p, Fairy Bridge. 5p, Peel, Castle and shore. 6p, Cregneish Village. 7½p, Ramsey Bay. 9p, Douglas Bay. 20p, Manx ram. 50p, Manx shearwaters. £1, Viking longship.

Perf. 11½

1973, July 5 Photo. Unwmk.

12	A4	½p shown	.25	.25
a.		Booklet pane of 2	*2.75*	
b.		Booklet pane of 4 ('74)	*.90*	
13	A4	1p multicolored	.25	.25
14	A4	1½p multicolored	.25	.25
15	A4	2p multicolored	.25	.25
a.		Booklet pane of 2	*2.75*	
16	A4	2½p multicolored	.25	.25
a.		Booklet pane of 2	*.75*	
		Complete booklet, #12a, 15a, 16a	*12.00*	
		Complete booklet, 5 #16a	*3.75*	
17	A4	3p multicolored	.25	.25
a.		Booklet pane of 2	*.70*	
		Complete booklet, 5 #17a	*22.50*	
		Complete booklet, 4 #16a, 5 #17a	*10.00*	
b.		Booklet pane of 4 ('74)	*.90*	
18	A4	3½p multicolored	.25	.25
a.		Booklet pane of 4 ('74)	*5.00*	
		Complete booklet, 2 #12b, 1 each #17b, 18a	*5.00*	
		Complete booklet, 2 #17b, 1 each #12b, 18a	*5.00*	
		Complete booklet, 3 #17b, 1 #18a	*5.00*	
19	A4	4p multicolored	.25	.25
20	A4	5p multicolored	.25	.25
21	A4	6p multicolored	.35	.35
22	A4	7½p multicolored	.35	.35
23	A4	9p multicolored	.35	.35
24	A5	10p shown	.45	.45
25	A5	20p multicolored	.75	.75
26	A5	50p multicolored	1.75	1.75
27	A5	£1 multicolored	3.50	3.50
		Nos. 12-27 (16)	9.75	9.75

See Nos. 52-59.

Vikings Landing on Man, 938 — A6

1973, July 5 *Perf. 14*

28	A6	15p multicolored	.50	.50

Inauguration of postal independence.

Compare with No. 251. Inscription under "Isle of Man" reads "Post Office Decennium" on No. 251.

Engine No. 1, Sutherland, 1873 — A7

1973, Aug. 4 *Perf. 14½x14*

29	A7	2½p shown	.25	.25
30	A7	3p Caledonia, 1885	.25	.25
31	A7	7½p Kissack, 1910	.35	.35
32	A7	9p Pender, 1873	.35	.35
		Nos. 29-32 (4)	1.20	1.20

Centenary of Manx steam railroad.

Leslie Randles, 1923 Winner A8

3½p, Alan Holmes, 1957 double winner.

1973, Sept. 4 Litho. *Perf. 14*

33	A8	3p multicolored	.25	.25
34	A8	3½p multicolored	.25	.25

Manx Grand Prix Motorcycle Race, 50th anniversary.

Princess Anne and Mark Phillips — A9

Litho. & Engr.

1973 Nov. 14 *Perf. 14x13½*

35	A9	25p lt blue & multi	.70	.70

Wedding of Princess Anne and Capt. Mark Phillips, Nov. 14, 1973.

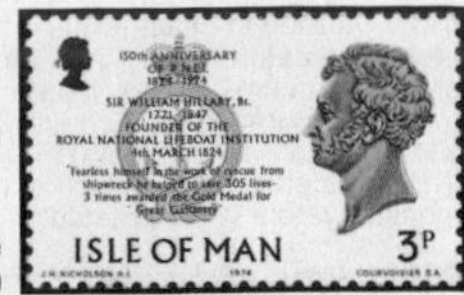

William Hillary, R.N.L.I. Badge A10

Wreck of "St. George" A11

Designs: 8p, Tower of Refuge and lifeboat "Manchester & Salford." 10p, "Osman Gabriel" at Port Erin. 3½p and 8p are from paintings.

1974, Mar. 4 Photo. *Perf. 11½*

36	A10	3p black & multi	.25	.25
37	A11	3½ black & multi	.25	.25
38	A11	8p black & multi	.25	.25
39	A11	10p black & multi	.30	.30
		Nos. 36-39 (4)	1.05	1.05

Sesqui. of the founding of the Royal Natl. Lifeboat Institution by Sir William Hillary.

Stanley Woods on Moto Guzzi Motorcycle — A12

Designs: 3½p, Freddie Frith on Norton. 8p, Max Deubel on BMW with sidecar. 10p, Mike Hailwood on Honda.

1974, May 29 Litho. *Perf. 13*

40	A12	3p yellow grn & multi	.25	.25
41	A12	3½p crimson & multi	.25	.25
a.		Perf. 14 (#1425b)	.25	.25
42	A12	8p yellow & multi	.25	.25
43	A12	10p ultra & multi	.25	*.35*
		Nos. 40-43 (4)	1.00	1.10

Tourist Trophy Motorcycle Races on the Isle of Man.

Issued: No. 41a, 2015.

Arms and Ruins of Rushen Abbey A13

Designs: 4½p, King Edgar of England visiting Chester in boat rowed by 8 kings including King Magnus Haraldson. 8p, Fleet under King Magnus' command and arms he gave to Isle of Man. 10p, Bridge at Avignon, Bishop's mitre and Three Legs of Man.

1974, Sept. 18 Litho. *Perf. 14*

44	A13	3½p multicolored	.25	.25
45	A13	4½p multicolored	.25	.25
46	A13	8p multicolored	.25	.25
47	A13	10p multicolored	.25	.25
		Nos. 44-47 (4)	1.00	1.00

1,000th death anniv. of Magnus Haraldson, King of Many Islands (Nos. 45-46), and 600th death anniv. of William Russell, Bishop of Sodor and Mann (Nos. 44, 47).

Churchill and "Bugler Dunne at Colenso, 1899" — A14

Sir Winston Churchill: 4½p, Government Buildings, Douglas, and Warrant of Appointment. 8p, Manx A.A. Regiment in action. 20p, Freedom of Douglas Scroll, and scroll casket.

1974, Nov. 22 Photo. *Perf. 11½*

48	A14	3½p	multicolored	.25	.25
49	A14	4½p	multicolored	.25	.25
50	A14	8p	multicolored	.25	.25
51	A14	20p	multicolored	.25	.25
a.			Souvenir sheet of 4, #48-51	1.10	1.10
			Nos. 48-51 (4)	1.00	1.00

Type of 1973

1975 Unwmk. *Perf. 11½*

52	A4	4½p	Tynwald Hill	.25	.25
53	A4	5½p	Douglas Promenade	.25	.25
54	A4	7p	Laxey Village	.30	.30
55	A4	8p	Ramsey Bay	.30	.30
58	A4	11p	Monk's Bridge	.35	.35
59	A4	13p	Derbyhaven	.50	.50
			Nos. 52-59 (6)	1.95	1.95

Issued: Nos. 52, 55, 1/8; Nos. 53-54, 5/28; Nos. 58-59, 10/29.

Log Cabin School, Cleveland Medal, Names of Settlers A15

Designs: 5½p, Terminal Tower Building, Cleveland, John Gill and Robert Carran. 8p, Clague House Museum, Margaret and Robert Clague. 10p, Thomas Quayle and S. S. William T. Graves.

1975, Mar. 14 Photo. *Perf. 11½*

62	A15	4½p	multicolored	.25	.25
63	A15	5½p	multicolored	.25	.25
64	A15	8p	multicolored	.25	.25
65	A15	10p	multicolored	.25	.35
			Nos. 62-65 (4)	1.00	1.10

Sesquicentennial of arrival of Manx settlers in Cleveland, Ohio area.

Tom Sheard and "Douglas" — A16

Designs: 7p, Walter L. Handley and "Rex-Acme." 10p, Geoffrey Duke and "Gilera." 12p, Peter Williams and "Norton."

1975, May 28 Litho. *Perf. 13½*

66	A16	5½p	bister & multi	.25	.25
67	A16	7p	salmon & multi	.25	.25
68	A16	10p	lt green & multi	.25	.25
69	A16	12p	ultra & multi	.25	.25
a.			Perf. 14 (#1425b)	.25	.25
			Nos. 66-69 (4)	1.00	1.00

Tourist Trophy Motorcycle races on Isle of Man.

Issued: No. 69a, 2015.

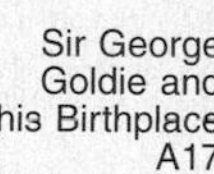

Sir George Goldie and his Birthplace A17

Designs (Sir George Goldie and): 7p, Map of Africa with Niger River basin, vert. 10p, Goldie as president of Royal Geographical Society and Society emblem, vert. 12p, River boats: trading hulk, native canoe, sternwheeler.

1975, Sept. 9 Photo. *Perf. 11½*

70	A17	5½p	multicolored	.25	.25
71	A17	7p	multicolored	.25	.25
72	A17	10p	multicolored	.25	.25
73	A17	12p	multicolored	.25	.25
			Nos. 70-73 (4)	1.00	1.00

Sir George Dashwood Goldie-Taubman (1846-1925), founder of Royal Niger Company.

Manx Bible — A18

Bicentenary of Manx Bible and Christmas 1975: 7p, Rev. Philip Moore and Old Ballaugh Church. 11p, Bishop Mark Hildesley and Bishops Court. 13p, Shipwreck off Cumberland Coast with John Kelly holding manuscript above water.

1975, Oct. 29 Litho. *Perf. 14*

74	A18	5½p	multicolored	.25	.25
75	A18	7p	multicolored	.25	.25
76	A18	11p	multicolored	.25	.25
77	A18	13p	multicolored	.25	.25
			Nos. 74-77 (4)	1.00	1.00

William Christian Listening to Patrick Henry — A19

Designs: 7p, Christian carrying Fincastle Resolutions to Williamsburg. 13p, Col. Patrick Henry and Lt. Col. William Christian of 1st Virginia Regiment. 20p, Christian as frontiersman and Indians.

1976, Mar. 12 Litho. *Perf. 13½*

78	A19	5½p	multicolored	.25	.25
79	A19	7p	multicolored	.25	.25
80	A19	13p	multicolored	.30	.30
81	A19	20p	multicolored	.35	.45
a.			Souv. sheet of 4, #78-81, perf. 14	1.25	1.25
			Nos. 78-81 (4)	1.15	1.25

American Bicentennial. William Christian (1743-1786), patriot, son of a Manx-man and Patrick Henry's brother-in-law.

First Double-decker Tram Car — A20

Designs: 7p, Toast-rack tram, 1890. 11p, Horse bus, 1895. 13p, Decorated tram with Queen Elizabeth II and Prince Philip.

1976, May 26 Photo. *Perf. 11½*

82	A20	5½p	multicolored	.25	.25
83	A20	7p	multicolored	.25	.25
84	A20	11p	multicolored	.30	.30
85	A20	13p	multicolored	.30	.30
			Nos. 82-85 (4)	1.10	1.10

Douglas horse trams, centenary.

Barroose Beaker, Bronze Age — A21

Europa (Manx Ceramic Art): No. 87, Souvenir teapot (3-legged man), 19th cent. No. 88, Laxey jug, 1854. No. 89, Cronk Aust food vessel, early Bronze Age. No. 90, Sansbury bowl, 1851. No. 91, Knox urn, 20th cent. Nos. 89-91, horiz.

1976, July 28 Photo. *Perf. 11½*

86	A21	5p	multicolored	.25	.25
87	A21	5p	multicolored	.25	.25
88	A21	5p	multicolored	.25	.25
a.			Strip of 3, #86-88	.75	.75
89	A21	10p	multicolored	.25	.25
90	A21	10p	multicolored	.25	.25
91	A21	10p	multicolored	.25	.25
a.			Strip of 3, #89-91	.75	.75
			Nos. 86-91 (6)	1.50	1.50

Printed in sheets of 9 (3x3).

Virgin and Child, on Sodor and Man Banner A22

Virgin and Child on Embroidered Church Banners: 7p, St. Peter's, Onchan, Mothers' Union. 11p, Castletown. 13p, St. Olav's, Ramsey.

1976, Oct. 14 Litho. *Perf. 14¾x14½*

92	A22	6p	multicolored	.25	.25
93	A22	7p	multicolored	.25	.25
94	A22	11p	multicolored	.25	.25
95	A22	13p	multicolored	.35	.35
			Nos. 92-95 (4)	1.10	1.10

Christmas 1976 & cent. of Mothers' Union.

Elizabeth II and Arms of Man A23

Designs: 7p, Queen Elizabeth II and Prince Philip, vert. 25p, Queen, 1976 portrait.

Perf. 13½x14, 14x13½

1977, Mar. 1 Litho. & Engr.

96	A23	6p	multicolored	.25	.25
97	A23	7p	multicolored	.25	.25
98	A23	25p	multicolored	.50	.50
			Nos. 96-98 (3)	1.00	1.00

25th anniv. of the reign of Elizabeth II.

Carrick Bay from Tom-the-Dipper's — A24

Europa: 10p, Looking south from Mooragh Park, Ramsey.

1977, May 25 Litho. *Perf. 14*

99	A24	6p	multicolored	.25	.25
100	A24	10p	multicolored	.35	.35

"Pa" Applebee at Ballig Bridge, 1912 — A25

Designs: 7p, Hairpin curve at Governor's Bridge and ambulance attendants. 11p, Boy Scouts tending casualties. 13p, John Williams at Windy Corner on Snaefell Mountain, winner of 1976 Open Classic Race.

1977, May 25 *Perf. 13½*

101	A25	6p	multicolored	.25	.25
102	A25	7p	multicolored	.25	.25
103	A25	11p	multicolored	.25	.25
104	A25	13p	multicolored	.25	.25
			Nos. 101-104 (4)	1.00	1.00

Tourist Trophy Motorcycle Races, and Boy Scouts, 70th anniv.; St. John Ambulance Assoc. cent. (in GB).

Meeting House, Mt. Morrison — A26

Designs: 7p, John Wesley preaching at Castletown, 1777. 11p, Wesley preaching outside Braddan Church. 13p, Methodist Church on Douglas Promenade, 1976.

1977, Oct. 19 Photo. *Perf. 11½*

Size: 30x24mm

105	A26	6p	multicolored	.25	.25

Size: 37½x24mm

106	A26	7p	multicolored	.25	.25
107	A26	11p	multicolored	.25	.25

Size: 30x24mm

108	A26	13p	multicolored	.25	.25
			Nos. 105-108 (4)	1.00	1.00

Bicentenary of John Wesley's first visit to the Isle of Man.

Seaplane and Carrier Ben My Chree — A27

Royal Air Force, 60th Anniv.: 7p, Bristol Scout and carrier Vindex, 1915. 11p, Boulton Paul Defiant over Douglas Bay, 1941. 13p, RAF Jaguar over Ramsey, 1977.

1978, Feb. 28 Litho. *Perf. 13½x14*

109	A27	6p	multicolored	.25	.25
110	A27	7p	multicolored	.25	.25
111	A27	11p	multicolored	.25	.25
112	A27	13p	multicolored	.25	.25
			Nos. 109-112 (4)	1.00	1.00

Watch Tower, Langness — A28

Jurby Church — A29

Fuchsia — A30

Landmarks: 6p, Government buildings. 7p, Tynwald Hill. 8p, Milner's Tower. 9p, Laxey Wheel. 10p, Castle Rushen. 11p, St. Ninian's Church. 12p, Tower of Refuge. 13p, St. German's Cathedral. 14p, Point of Ayre Lighthouse. 15p, Corrin's Tower. 16p, Douglas Head Lighthouse. 25p, Manx cat. 50p, Chough (crows). £1, Viking warrior.

1078 Litho. *Perf. 14*

113	A28	½p	multicolored	.25	.25
114	A29	1p	multicolored	.25	.25
115	A28	6p	multicolored	.25	.25
116	A29	7p	multicolored	.25	.25
117	A28	8p	multicolored	.25	.25
118	A28	9p	multicolored	.30	.30
119	A29	10p	multicolored	.45	.45
120	A28	11p	multicolored	.45	.45
121	A29	12p	multicolored	.50	.50
122	A28	13p	multicolored	.70	.70
123	A29	14p	multicolored	.70	.70
124	A29	15p	multicolored	.85	.85
125	A29	16p	multicolored	.60	.60

Photo.

Perf. 11½

126	A30	20p	multicolored	.60	.60
127	A30	25p	multicolored	.90	.90
128	A30	50p	multicolored	1.60	1.60
129	A30	£1	multicolored	3.50	3.50
			Nos. 113-129 (17)	12.40	12.40

Issued: Nos. 113-125, 2/28; Nos. 126-129, 10/18.

Perf. 14½

113a	A28	½p	multicolored	.25	.25
114a	A29	1p	multicolored	.25	.25
116a	A29	7p	multicolored	*9.00*	*7.00*
117a	A28	8p	multicolored	.40	.40
118a	A28	9p	multicolored	.30	.30

119a A29 10p multicolored .40 .40
120a A28 11p multicolored .45 .45
121a A29 12p multicolored .60 .60
122a A29 13p multicolored .35 .35
123a A29 14p multicolored .35 .35
124a A29 15p multicolored .35 .35
125a A29 16p multicolored 30.00 25.00
Nos. 113a-125a (12) 42.70 35.70

Elizabeth II — A31

1978, May 24 Litho. *Perf. 14½x14¼*

130 A31 25p blue & multi .75 .75

25th anniv. of coronation of Elizabeth II.

Keeil Chiggyrt Stone — A32

Europa (Carved Gravestones): No. 132, Wheel-headed cross slab. No. 133, Celtic Wheel cross. No. 134, Thor cross. No. 135, Olaf Liotulfson cross. No. 136, Odd's and Thorleif's crosses.

1978, May 24 *Perf. 11½*

131 A32 6p multicolored .25 .25
132 A32 6p multicolored .25 .25
133 A32 6p multicolored .25 .25
a. Strip of 3, #131-133 .40 *.45*
134 A32 11p multicolored .30 .30
135 A32 11p multicolored .30 .30
136 A32 11p multicolored .30 .30
a. Strip of 3, #134-136 1.00 *1.10*
Nos. 131-136 (6) 1.65 1.65

Printed se-tenant in sheets of 9 (3x3).

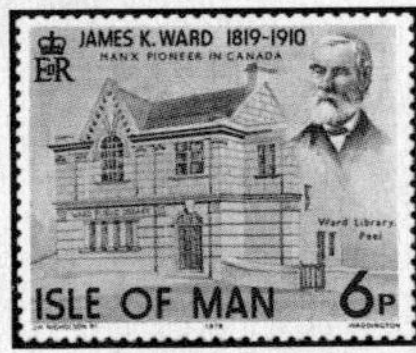

J. K. Ward, Ward Library, Peel — A33

13p, Lumber camp at Three Rivers & J. K. Ward.

1978, June 10 Litho. *Perf. 13½*

137 A33 6p multicolored .25 .25
138 A33 13p multicolored .25 .25

James K. Ward (1819-1910), Manx pioneer in Canada.

Athletes, Games' Emblem and Manx Arms A34

"Hunt the Wren" — A36

Eagle, Manx Arms, Maple Leaf A35

1978, June 10

139 A34 7p multicolored .25 .25
140 A35 11p multicolored .25 .25

11th Commonwealth Games, Edmonton, Aug. 3-12 (7p); North American Manx Soc., 50th anniv. (11p).

1978, Oct. 18 Litho. *Perf. 13*

141 A36 5p multicolored .25 .25

Christmas 1978.

Philip M. C. Kermode and Nassa Kermodei A37

7p, Peregrine falcons. 11p, Fulmars. 13p, Asilid fly.

1979, Feb. 27 Litho. *Perf. 14*

142 A37 6p multicolored .25 .25
143 A37 7p multicolored .25 .25
144 A37 11p multicolored .30 .30
145 A37 13p multicolored .40 .40
Nos. 142-145 (4) 1.20 1.20

Isle of Man Natural History and Antiquarian Society.

Viking Ship — A38

A39

Viking Raid at Garwick A40

Designs (Tynwald Emblem and): 7p, 10th century meeting at Tynwald. 11p, Tynwald Hill and St. John's Church. 13p, Contemporary Tynwald Day parade.

Perf. 14½x14 (#146-147), 13¼ (#148-151)

1979, May 16 Litho.

146 A38 3p *Insularem* .25 .25
a. Bklt. pane, 4 #146, 2 #147 .60
Complete booklet, #146a 1.00
Complete booklet, 2 #146a 1.50
Complete booklet, 3 #146a 2.00
b. *Insularum* (inscribed "1980") .25 .25
c. Bklt. pane, 4 #146b, 2 #147a 1.25
147 A39 4p multicolored .25 .25
a. Inscribed "1980" .25 .25
148 A40 6p multicolored .25 .25
149 A40 7p multicolored .25 .25
150 A40 11p multicolored .25 .25
151 A40 13p multicolored .25 .25
Nos. 146-151 (6) 1.50 1.50

Millennium of Tynwald, Legislative Council. Nos. 146-147 printed se-tenant in sheets of 80.

No. 146a comes in two arrangements.

The booklet panes were printed in strips of three panes: No. 146a (4p stamps in the middle); separated by a gutter from No. 146a (4p stamps on top); and separated by another gutter, from a pane of four 4p. The unsevered strips were available from the Philatelic Bureau.

See No. 190a.

19th Century Mailman — A41

Europa: 11p, Contemporary mailman.

1979, May 16 *Perf. 14½*

152 A41 6p multicolored .25 .25
153 A41 11p multicolored .35 .35

Ceremony on Tynwald Hill — A42

Design: 13p, Procession from St. John's Church to Tynwald Hill.

1979, July 5 Litho. *Perf. 14½*

154 A42 7p multicolored .25 .25
155 A42 13p multicolored .40 .40

Visit of Queen Elizabeth II for the celebration of millennium of Tynwald.

Girl Holding Teddy Bear — A43

Christmas and IYC: 7p, Children with Santa.

1979, Oct. 19 Litho. *Perf. 13¼x13½*

156 A43 5p multicolored .25 .25
157 A43 7p multicolored .25 .25

Capt. John Quilliam and Spencer A44

Capt. Quilliam: 6p, Seized by press gang. 8p, Battle of Trafalgar. 15p, Castle Rushen.

1979, Oct. 19 *Perf. 14*

158 A44 6p multicolored .25 .25
159 A44 8p multicolored .25 .25
160 A44 13p multicolored .30 .30
161 A44 15p multicolored .40 .40
Nos. 158-161 (4) 1.20 1.20

Capt. John Quilliam (1771-1829), British naval hero and member of House of Keys.

"Odin's Raven" A45

1979, Oct. 19 *Perf. 14x14½*

162 A45 15p multicolored .60 .60

Voyage of replica Viking longboat across North Sea (Trondheim to Peel), May 27-July 4.

See No. 176a.

Conglomerate Arch, Langness, and Emblem — A46

Royal Geographical Society Emblem and: 8p, Braaid Circle. 12p, Cashtal yn Ard (Neolithic burial ground). 13p, Volcanic rocks, Scarlett. 15p, Sugar-loaf Rock.

1980, Feb. 5 Litho. *Perf. 14½*

163 A46 7p multicolored .25 .25
164 A46 8p multicolored .25 .25
165 A46 12p multicolored .35 .35
166 A46 13p multicolored .35 .35
167 A46 15p multicolored .35 .35
Nos. 163-167 (5) 1.55 1.55

Royal Geographical Society, 150th anniv.

"Mona's Isle I" A47

8p, Douglas I. 11½p, Mona's Queen II, sinking U-boat. 12p, King Orry III. 13p, Ben-My-Chree IV. 15p, Lady of Mann II.

1980, May 6 Photo. *Perf. 11½*

Granite Paper

168 A47 7p shown .25 .25
169 A47 8p multicolored .25 .25
170 A47 11½p multicolored .30 .30
171 A47 12p multicolored .30 .30
172 A47 13p multicolored .35 .35
173 A47 15p multicolored .45 .45
a. Souvenir sheet of 6, #168-173 2.00 2.00
Nos. 168-173 (6) 1.90 1.90

Isle of Man Steam Packet Co. sesqui.; London 80 Intl. Stamp Exhib., May 6-14.

Thomas Edward Brown and Characters from his Poems — A48

Europa (Brown (1830-1897), Poet and Scholar): 13½p, Cricket game, Clifton College Bristol.

1980, May 6

174 A48 7p multicolored .25 .25
175 A48 13½p multicolored .35 .35

Visit of King Olav V of Norway A49

1980, June 13 Litho. *Perf. 14½*

176 A49 12p multicolored .60 .60
a. Souv. sheet of 2, #162, 176 1.00 1.00

Visit of King Olav V of Norway, Aug. 2-7, 1979, and NORWEX 80 stamp exhibition, Oslo, June 13-22.

William Kermode and "Robert Quayle" A50

Kermode Family (First Manx Pioneers in Tasmania): 9p, First homestead, Mona Vale, Merino sheep, 1834. 13½p, Ross Bridge, W. Kermode. 15p, Mona Vale (Calendar House), 1868. 17½p, Parliament Buildings, Hobart, Robert Quayle Kermode.

1980, Sept. 29 Litho.

177 A50 7p multicolored .25 .25
178 A50 9p multicolored .25 .25
179 A50 13½p multicolored .30 .30
180 A50 15p multicolored .35 .35
181 A50 17½p multicolored .40 .40
Nos. 177-181 (5) 1.55 1.55

Wren A51

1980, Sept. 29 Litho. *Perf. 13½x14*
182 A51 6p shown .25 .25
183 A51 8p Robin .25 .25

Wildlife conservation and Christmas 1980.

Luggers, Red Pier, Douglas A52

9p, Wanderer saving Lusitania Survivors. 18p, Nickey, Port St. Mary. 20p, Nobby, Ramsey Harbor. 22p, Sunbeam and Zebra, Port Erin.

1981, Feb. 24 Litho. *Perf. 14*
184 A52 8p shown .25 .25
185 A52 9p multicolored .25 .25
186 A52 18p multicolored .35 .35
187 A52 20p multicolored .45 .45
188 A52 22p multicolored .50 .50
Nos. 184-188 (5) 1.80 1.80

Royal National Mission to Deep Sea Fishermen centenary.

Peregrine Falcon — A53

1980, Sept. 29 Litho. *Perf. 14½x14*
Booklet Stamps
189 A53 1p shown .35 .35
190 A53 5p Loaghtyn ram .35 .35
a. Bklt. pane, 2 each #147a, 189, 190 1.25
Complete booklet, #146c, 190a 2.50
Complete booklet, 2 each #146c, 190a 5.00

Crosh Cuirn (Cross of Mountain Ash Twigs, Harvest Charm) — A54

Europa: 18p, Bollan fish cross-bone (fishermen's charm).

1981, May 22 Litho. *Perf. 14½*
191 A54 8p multicolored .25 .25
192 A54 18p multicolored .50 .50

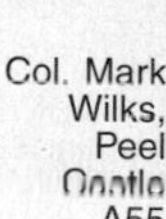

Col. Mark Wilks, Peel Castle A55

20p, Wilks, Fort. St. George, Madras. 22p, Wilks, Napoleon. 25p, Wilks at Kirby estate.

1981, May 22 *Perf. 14*
193 A55 8p shown .25 .25
194 A55 20p multicolored .45 .45
195 A55 22p multicolored .50 .50
196 A55 25p multicolored .60 .60
Nos. 193-196 (4) 1.80 1.80

Wilks (d. 1831), governor of St. Helena.

Suffragettes Emmeline Goulden Pankhurst and Sophia Jane Goulden — A56

1981, May 22 *Perf. 14*
197 A56 9p multicolored .35 .35

Centenary of women's suffrage and of House of Keys Election Act (granting widows and unmarried women voting rights).

Prince Charles and Lady Diana A57

1981, July 29 Litho. *Perf. 14*
198 A57 9p multicolored .25 .25
199 A57 25p multicolored .85 .85
a. Souv. sheet, 2 each #198-199 2.25 2.25

Royal Wedding.

Queen Elizabeth II — A58

1981, Sept. 29 Photo. *Perf. 11½*
Granite paper
200 A58 £2 multicolored 5.00 5.00

Douglas War Memorial, Poppies, Quote from Laurence Binyon's For the Fallen — A59

10p, Maj. R.H. Cain, Battle of Arnhem, 1944. 18p, Festival of Remembrance. 20p, Tynwald and Spitfire, Dunkirk, 1940.

1981, Sept. 29 Granite Paper
201 A59 8p shown .25 .25
202 A59 10p multicolored .25 .25
203 A59 18p multicolored .45 .45
204 A59 20p multicolored .55 .55
Nos. 201-204 (4) 1.50 1.50

Royal British Legion, 60th anniv.

Nativity Stained-glass Window, 1865, St. George's Church, Douglas — A60

9p: Christmas pageant, Glencrutchery Special School, Douglas.

1981, Sept. 29 Litho. *Perf. 14½x14*
205 A60 7p multicolored .25 .25
Size: 47x28mm
206 A60 9p multicolored .30 .30

Christmas and St. George's Church bicen. (7p), IYD (9p).

Scouting Year — A61

Designs: 9p, Cunningham House (Man Scout Headquarters). 10p, Baden-Powell's visit, 1911. 19½p, Portrait (32x41mm., Perf. 14½). 24p, Baden-Powell with scouts, message. 29p, Sign, handshake, globe, emblem.

1982, Feb. 23 Litho. *Perf. 13½x14*
207 A61 9p multicolored .25 .25
208 A61 10p multicolored .25 .25
209 A61 19½p multicolored .55 .55
210 A61 24p multicolored .70 .70
211 A61 29p multicolored .85 .85
Nos. 207-211 (5) 2.60 2.60

Europa 1982 — A62

Designs: 9p, Bishop Thomas Wilson (1663-1755) and his "The Principles and Duties of Christianity," first book printed in Manx, 1707. 19½p, Visit of Thomas, 2nd Earl of Derby, 1507.

1982, June 1 Photo. *Perf. 12½*
Granite Paper
212 A62 9p multicolored .25 .25
213 A62 19½p multicolored .50 .50

75th Anniv. of Tourist Trophy Motorcycle Races — A63

Designs: Winners on their bikes: 9p, Charlie Collier, 431 Matchless, 1907. 10p, Freddie Dixon, Douglas, 1923. 24p, Jimmie Simpson, Norton, 1932. 26p, Mike Hailwood, Norton, 1961. 29p, Jock Taylor, 700 Fowler Yamaha, '80.

1982, June 1 Litho. *Perf. 14*
214 A63 9p multicolored .25 .25
215 A63 10p multicolored .25 .25
216 A63 24p multicolored .70 .70
217 A63 26p multicolored .70 .70
218 A63 29p multicolored .70 .70
Nos. 214-218 (5) 2.60 2.60

Isle of Man Steam Packet Co. Mail Contract Sesquicentennial — A64

1982, Oct. 5 Litho. *Perf. 13½x14*
219 A64 12p Mona I .45 .45
220 A64 19½p Manx Maid II .60 .60

Christmas 1982 A65

8p, Three Kings. 11p, Robin, Christmas tree, vert.

Perf. 13¼x13½, 13½x13¼
1982, Oct. 5
221 A65 8p multicolored .25 .25
222 A65 11p multicolored .45 .45

Souvenir Sheet

Princess Diana and Prince William — A66

1982, Oct. 12 *Perf. 14½x14¼*
223 A66 50p multicolored 2.00 2.00

Birth of Prince William of Wales (June 21) and 21st birthday of Princess Diana (July 1).

Marine Birds A67

1p, Puffins, Cranstal. 2p, Gannets, Point of Ayre. 5p, Lesser black-backed gulls, Santon. 8p, Cormorants, Maughold Head. 10p, Kittiwakes, White Strand. 11p, Shags, Calf of Man. 12p, Herons, Douglas Foreshore. 13p, Herring gulls, Peel. 14p, Razorbills, Calf of Man. 15p, Great black-backed gulls, Calf of Man. 16p, Shelducks, Poyll Vaaish. 18p, Oystercatchers, Langness.

1983, Feb. 15 Litho. *Perf. 14½*
224 A67 1p multicolored .25 .25
225 A67 2p multicolored .25 .25
226 A67 5p multicolored .25 .25
227 A67 8p multicolored .35 .35
228 A67 10p multicolored .45 .45
229 A67 11p multicolored .50 .50
230 A67 12p multicolored .55 .55
231 A67 13p multicolored .60 .60
232 A67 14p multicolored .60 .60
233 A67 15p multicolored .70 .70
234 A67 16p multicolored .75 .75
235 A67 18p multicolored .80 .80

Size: 39x25mm
1983, Sept. 14 *Perf. 14*

20p, Arctic terns, Blue Point. 25p, Guillemots, Calf of Man. 50p, Redshanks, Langness. £1, Mute swans, Port St. Mary Bay.

236 A67 20p multicolored .90 .90
237 A67 25p multicolored 1.10 1.10
238 A67 50p multicolored 2.00 2.00
239 A67 £1 multicolored 4.00 4.00
Nos. 224-239 (16) 14.05 14.05

Centenary of Salvation Army in Isle of Man — A68

Designs: 10p, Citadel opening ceremony, 1932, T.H. Cannell. 12p, Founder William Booth, early meeting place (former Unitarian Church, Douglas). 19½p, Band, Bandmaster Gordon Cowley, 1981. 26p, Lt.-Col. Thomas Bridson, treating lepers in Dutch East Indies.

1983, Feb. 15 Photo. *Perf. 11½*
Granite Paper

240	A68	10p multicolored	.30	.30
241	A68	12p multicolored	.40	.40
242	A68	19½ multicolored	.55	.55
243	A68	26p multicolored	.75	.75
		Nos. 240-243 (4)	2.00	2.00

Europa 1983 — A69

10p, Laxey Wheel. 20½p, Designer Robert Casement.

1983, May 18 *Perf. 14*

244	A69	10p multicolored	.40	.40
245	A69	20½p multicolored	.70	.70

King William's College Sesquicentennial — A70

Graduates: 10p, Nick Keig, Yachtsman. 12p, College, arms. 28p, William Bragg, 1915 Nobel Prize winner in physics, ionization spectrometer. 31p, Gen. George Stuart White, Defense of Ladysmith, Boer War.

1983, May 18 Photo. *Perf. 11½*
Granite Paper

246	A70	10p multicolored	.25	.25
247	A70	12p multicolored	.30	.30
248	A70	28p multicolored	.90	.90
249	A70	31p multicolored	1.00	1.00
		Nos. 246-249 (4)	2.45	2.45

World Communications Year and 10th Anniv. of Post Office — A71

10p, New P.O. Headquarters. 15p, Viking landing, 938.

1983, July 5 Litho. *Perf. 15*

250	A71	10p multicolored	.35	.35
251	A6	15p multicolored	.60	.60

Compare No. 251 with No. 28.

Christmas 1983 A72

1983, Sept. 14 Litho. *Perf. 13x13½*

252	A72	9p Shepherds	.30	.30
253	A72	12p Three Kings	.40	.40

Karran Fleet A73

Links with Falkland Islands — A74

10p, Manx King, 1884. 13p, Hope, 1858. 20½p, Rio Grande, 1868. 28p, Lady Elizabeth, 1879. 31p, Sumatra, 1858.

1984, Feb. 14 Litho. *Perf. 14*

254	A73	10p multicolored	.25	.25
255	A73	13p multicolored	.35	.35
256	A73	20½p multicolored	.55	.55
257	A73	28p multicolored	.90	.90
258	A73	31p multicolored	1.00	1.00
		Nos. 254-258 (5)	3.05	3.05

1984, Feb. 14

259	A74	Sheet of 2, #257, 259a	2.75	2.75
a.		31p multicolored	1.25	1.25

Europa (1959-1984) A75

1984, Apr. 27 Photo. *Perf. 11½*

260	A75	10p dk yel org, dk brn & buff	.35	.35
261	A75	20½p blue, dk bl & lt bl	.65	.65

DH-48, Ronaldsway Airport — A76

13p, DH-86, Calf of Man. 26p, DC-3, Ronaldsway Airport. 28p, Vickers Viscount, Douglas. 31p, Islander, Ronaldsway Airport.

1984, Apr. 27 Litho. *Perf. 14*

262	A76	11p shown	.40	.40
263	A76	13p multicolored	.45	.45
264	A76	26p multicolored	.80	.80
265	A76	28p multicolored	.80	.80
266	A76	31p multicolored	.80	.80
		Nos. 262-266 (5)	3.25	3.25

50th Anniv. of official airmail service and 40th anniv. of Intl. Civil Aviation Org.

William Cain as Mayor of Melbourne, 1886-87 — A77

11p, Ballasalla (birthplace). 22p, Voyage to Australia. 28p, Railway, Victoria. 33p, Royal Exhibition Buildings, Melbourne.

1984, Sept. 21 Litho. *Perf. 14½*

267	A77	11p multicolored	.35	.35
268	A77	22p multicolored	.65	.65
269	A77	28p multicolored	.80	.80
270	A77	30p shown	.90	.90
271	A77	33p multicolored	.90	.90
		Nos. 267-271 (5)	3.60	3.60

William Cain (1831-1914), building contractor and public servant in Australia.

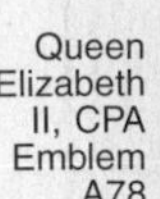

Queen Elizabeth II, CPA Emblem A78

1984, Sept. 21 *Perf. 14*

272	A78	14p shown	.40	.40
273	A78	33p Arms, Elizabeth II	1.00	1.00

30th Conference of Commonwealth Parliamentary Assoc., Sept. 28-Oct. 5.

Christmas — A79

Stained-glass windows: 10p, Birds, Glencrutchery House. 13p, Arms, Lonan Old Church.

1984, Sept. 21

274	A79	10p multicolored	.40	.40
275	A79	13p multicolored	.60	.60

75th Anniv. of Girl Guides — A80

Designs: 11p, Cunningham House (headquarters), Mrs. W. and J. Cunningham (early Island Commissioners). 14p, Princess Margaret (president), color guard. 29p, Lady Olave Baden-Powell, headquarters opening. 31p, Uniforms, 1910-85. 34p, Sign, handclasp, trefoil.

1985, Jan. 31 Photo. *Perf. 12*

276	A80	11p multicolored	.40	.40
277	A80	14p multicolored	.50	.50
278	A80	29p multicolored	.90	.90
279	A80	31p multicolored	1.00	1.00
280	A80	34p multicolored	1.20	1.20
		Nos. 276-280 (5)	4.00	4.00

Elizabeth II A81

1985, Jan. 31 Litho. *Perf. 14*

281	A81	£5 multicolored	12.00	12.00

Europa 1985 — A82

Manx composers: No. 282a, "O'Land of our Birth." No. 282b, William H. Gill (1839-1922). No. 283a, Hymn "Crofton;" No. 283b, Dr. John Clague (1842-1908).

1985, Apr. 24 Photo. *Perf. 12*

282	A82	Pair	1.20	1.20
a.-b.		22p any single	.60	.60
283	A82	Pair	1.40	1.40
a.-b.		22p any single	.70	.70

Motoring — A83

Motor races and winning vehicles: No. 284a, 1906 Tourist Trophy Race. No. 284b, 1922 Tourist Trophy Race. No. 285a, 1950 British Empire Trophy Race. No. 285b, 1934 Manin Moar Race. No. 286a, 1984 Tourist Trophy Motorcycle Race (official car). No. 286b, 1981 Rothmans Manx Intl. Rally.

1985, May 25 Litho. *Perf. 14*

284	A83	Pair	.80	.80
a.-b.		12p any single	.35	.35
285	A83	Pair	1.00	1.00
a.-b.		14p any single	.45	.45
286	A83	Pair	2.00	2.00
a.-b.		31p any single	.80	.80
		Nos. 284-286 (3)	3.80	3.80

H.R.H. Alexandra (1885-1925), Princess of Wales — A84

SSA presidents: 15p, Queen Mary (1925-1953). 29p, Earl Mountbatten of Burma (1953-1979). 34p, Prince Michael of Kent (1982-).

1985, Sept. 4 Litho. *Perf. 14*

287	A84	12p multicolored	.40	.40
288	A84	15p multicolored	.50	.50
289	A84	29p multicolored	.95	.95
290	A84	34p multicolored	1.20	1.20
		Nos. 287-290 (4)	3.05	3.05

Soldier's, Sailors' & Airmen's Families Assoc., cent.

Lt.-Gen. Sir Mark Cubbon, K.C.B. (1785-1861), Commissioner of Mysore — A85

12p, Kirk Maughold Parish Church, 14th century. 22p, Portrait, vert. 45p, Equestrian monument, 1866 Bangalore, India, vert.

1985, Oct. 2 Litho. *Perf. 14*

291	A85	12p multicolored	.45	.45
292	A85	22p multicolored	.75	.75
293	A85	45p multicolored	1.50	1.50
		Nos. 291-293 (3)	2.70	2.70

Christmas 1985 A86

11p, Onchan Parish Church, 1833. 14p, St. John's Church. 31p, Bride Parish Church, 1876.

1985, Oct. 2 Litho. *Perf. 13½*

294	A86	11p multicolored	.35	.35
295	A86	14p multicolored	.60	.60
296	A86	31p multicolored	1.10	1.10
		Nos. 294-296 (3)	2.05	2.05

1986 Commonwealth Games, Edinburgh — A87

1986, Feb. 5 Litho. *Perf. 14*

297 A87 12p Women's swimming .40 .40
298 A87 15p Walking .55 .55
299 A87 31p Rifle shooting .90 .90
300 A87 34p Bicycling 1.20 1.20
Nos. 297-300 (4) 3.05 3.05

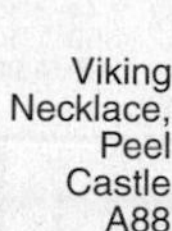

Viking Necklace, Peel Castle A88

Artifacts, architecture: 15p, Meayll Circle burial ground, Rushen. 22p, Prehistoric Cervus giganteus skeleton, Glose-y-Garey, vert. 26p, Norwegian viking longship, vert. 29p, Open-air Museum, Cregneash.

1986, Feb. 5 *Perf. 14½x14, 14x14½*

301 A88 12p multicolored .40 .40
302 A88 15p multicolored .50 .50
303 A88 22p multicolored .70 .70
304 A88 26p multicolored .80 .80
305 A88 29p multicolored 1.00 1.00
Nos. 301-305 (5) 3.40 3.40

Centenaries of Manx Museum and Ancient Monuments Act.
Nos. 303 and 304 are vert.

Europa 1986, Manx National Trust — A89

Designs: No. 306a, Bride hills and the Ayres. No. 306b, Calf of Man. No. 307a, Eary Cushlin. No. 307b, St. Michael's Isle.

1986, Apr. 10 Litho. *Perf. 12*

306 A89 Pair .90 .90
a.-b. 12p any single .45 .45
307 A89 Pair 1.60 1.60
a.-b. 22p any single .80 .80

Settling of Plymouth — A90

Designs: 12p, Ellanbane, Isle of Man, Myles Standish's home. 15p, The Mayflower. 31p, Pilgrims landing, 1620. 34p, Capt. Myles Standish (c. 1584-1656).

1986, May 22 *Perf. 13½*

308 A90 12p multicolored .40 .40
309 A90 15p multicolored .50 .50
310 A90 31p multicolored 1.00 1.00
311 A90 34p multicolored 1.25 1.25
a. Souvenir sheet of 2, #310-311, perf. 13x12½ 2.75 2.75
Nos. 308-311 (4) 3.15 3.15

AMERIPEX '86, Chicago, May 22-June 1.

Heritage Year — A91

2p, Viking longship bow. 10p, Celtic cross.

Booklet Stamps

1986, Apr. 10 Litho. *Perf. 15x14*

312 A91 2p multicolored .25 .25
a. Bklt. pane of 6, 2 #312, 4 #313 4.50
313 A91 10p multicolored .90 .90
a. Bklt. pane of 3 + 3 labels 2.75
Complete booklet, #190a, 313a 4.50
Complete booklet, #146c, 190a, 312a, 313a 10.00

Wedding of Prince Andrew and Sarah Ferguson A92

1986, July 23

314 A92 15p Wedding date .65 .65
315 A92 40p Engagement date 1.45 1.45

Royal Birthdays — A93

No. 316: a, Prince Philip, 65. b, Elizabeth II, 60. No. 317 is the same size as No. 316.

1986, Aug. 28 *Perf. 11½*

316 A93 Pair 1.20 1.20
a.-b. 15p any single .60 .60
317 A93 34p Royal couple 1.20 1.20

STOCKHOLMIA '86, Swedish Post Office 350th anniv. Stamps issued in sheets of 6.

Intl. Peace Year — A94

11p, Robins, globe, Braille. 14p, Hands, dove. 31p, Hand-holding, sign language.

1986, Sept. 25 Litho. *Perf. 14*

318 A94 11p multicolored .40 .40
319 A94 14p multicolored .45 .45
320 A94 31p multicolored 1.05 1.05
Nos. 318-320 (3) 1.90 1.90

Accession of Queen Victoria to the British Throne, 150th Anniv. A95

Photographs of Victorian Douglas, by John Miller Nicholson: 2p, North Quay. 3p, The Old Fish Market. 10p, Breakwater. 15p, Jubilee Clock. 31p, Loch Promenade. 34p, Beach.

1987, Jan. 21 Litho. *Perf. 14½*

321 A95 2p multicolored .25 .25
322 A95 3p multicolored .25 .25
323 A95 10p multicolored .40 .40
a. Bklt. pane of 8 (2 2p, 2 3p, 4 10p) ('87) 2.10
Complete booklet, #323a 2.10
324 A95 15p multicolored .60 .60
a. Bklt. pane of 8 (2 2p, 2 3p, 2 10p, 2 15p) ('87) 2.40
Complete booklet, #323a, #324a 4.50
325 A95 31p multicolored 1.10 1.10
326 A95 34p multicolored 1.20 1.20
Nos. 321-326 (6) 3.80 3.80

No. 323a comes in two arrangements.

19th Century Paintings by John Miller Nicholson (1840-1913) — A96

Harbor scenes: 12p, The Old Fish Market and Harbor, Douglas. 26p, Red Sails at Douglas. 29p, The Double Corner. 34p, Peel Harbor.

1987, Feb. 18 *Perf. 13½*

327 A96 12p multicolored .40 .40
328 A96 26p multicolored .80 .80
329 A96 29p multicolored .90 .90
330 A96 34p multicolored 1.10 1.10
Nos. 327-330 (4) 3.20 3.20

Promenade, Douglas — A97

No. 331, Sea Terminal, 1965. No. 332, Tower of Refuge, 1832. No. 333, Gaiety Theater, c. 1900. No. 334, Villa Marina.

1987, Apr. 29 Litho. *Perf. 13½*

331 12p multicolored .60 .60
332 12p multicolored .60 .60
a. A97 Pair, #331-332 1.20 1.20
333 22p multicolored .90 .90
334 22p multicolored .90 .90
a. A97 Pair, #333-334 2.00 2.00
Nos. 331-334 (4) 3.00 3.00

Europa 1987.

Tourist Trophy Motorcycle Races, 80th Anniv. — A98

12p, 1939 Supercharged BMW 500CC. 15p, 1953 Manx "Kneeler" Norton 350CC. 29p, 1956 MV Agusta 500CC 4. 31p, 1957 Guzzi 500CC V8. 34p, 1967 Honda 250CC 6.

1987, May 27 *Perf. 13½x13*

335 A98 12p multicolored .40 .40
336 A98 15p multicolored .50 .50
a. Perf. 14 (#1425b) .45 .45
337 A98 29p multicolored .90 .90
338 A98 31p multicolored 1.00 1.00
339 A98 34p multicolored 1.15 1.15
a. Souv. sheet of 5, #335-339 + 7 labels, perf 14x13½ 4.25 4.25
Nos. 335-339 (5) 3.95 3.95

Issued: No. 336a, 2015.

Wildflowers — A99

16p, Fuchsia, wild roses. 29p, Field scabius, ragwort. 31p, Wood anemone, celandine. 34p, Violets, primroses.

1987, Sept. 9 Litho. *Perf. 14½x13½*

340 A99 16p multicolored .50 .40
341 A99 29p multicolored .90 .90
342 A99 31p multicolored 1.00 1.00
343 A99 34p multicolored 1.20 1.20
Nos. 340-343 (4) 3.60 3.50

Christmas — A100

Victorian family scenes based on drawings by Alfred Hunt for The Illustrated London News, c. 1870-1890: 12p, Stirring the pudding. 15p, Christmas tree selection. 31p, Decorating tree.

1987, Oct. 16 *Perf. 14*

344 A100 12p multicolored .45 .45
345 A100 15p multicolored .55 .55
346 A100 31p multicolored 1.25 1.25
Nos. 344-346 (3) 2.25 2.25

Railways & Tramways A101

Designs: 1p, Horse-drawn "Toast Rack" tram, Douglas Bay, 1884. 2p, No. 5 electric tram, Snaefell Mountain Railway, 1895. 3p, No. 3 open-top double-deck electric tram, Marine Drive-Port Soderick line, Douglas Southern Electric Tramway, 1896. 5p, Tower of Refuge and open tram, Douglas Head Incline Railway. 10p, Electric tram at Maughold Head, 1893, Douglas and Laxey Coast Electric Tramway. 13p, Douglas Cable Car No. 72, 1896. 14p, Manx Northern Railway No. 4 Caledonia, a Dubs 0-6-0T, 1885, at Gob-y-Deigan. 15p, Great Laxey Mine Railway Lewin steam engine Ant pulling coal cars. 16p, Henry B. Loch, first locomotive on the island, Port Erin Breakwater Railway, 1864. 17p, Locomotive No. 1, Ramsey Harbor Tramway. 18p, Engine No. 7 Tynwald, 1880, Foxdale Railway. 19p, Douglas Corp. engine, Baldwin Reservoir Railway. 20p, "Kissack" leaving St. John's for Peel. 25p, "Hutchinson" leaving Douglas Station. 50p, "Polar Bear" of Groudle Glen Railway. £1, The Royal Train.

Inscribed 1988

1988 Litho. *Perf. 13½*

347 A101 1p multicolored .25 .25
348 A101 2p multicolored .25 .25
349 A101 3p multicolored .25 .25
a. Inscribed "1989" .25 .25
350 A101 5p multicolored .25 .25
351 A101 10p multicolored .40 .40
352 A101 13p multicolored .50 .50
353 A101 14p multicolored .55 .55
a. Inscribed "1989" .55 .55
354 A101 15p multicolored .60 .60
a. Inscribed "1990" .60 .60
355 A101 16p multicolored .65 .65
b. Bklt. pane, 2 #349, #352, 2 #355 2.25
Complete booklet #355b 3.00
c. Bklt. pane, 4 #352, 6 #355 6.00
Complete booklet #355b, 355c 11.50
356 A101 17p multicolored .70 .70
a. Bklt. pane, 2 #349a, 2 #353a, #356c 2.25
Complete booklet, #356a 3.00
b. Booklet pane, 4 #353a, 6 #356c 6.50
Complete booklet #356a, 356b 9.50
c. Inscribed "1989" .70 .70
d. Inscribed "1991" .70 .70
357 A101 18p multicolored .70 .70
358 A101 19p multicolored .75 .75
e. Inscribed "1990" .75 .75
f. Bklt. pane, 4 #354a, 6 #358e 7.00
Complete booklet, 4 #354a, 6 #358e 7.50
g. Bklt. pane, 1 #354a, 2 #358e 2.10
Complete booklet, #354a, 358e 2.50

Perf. 15

358A A101 20p multicolored .80 .80
358B A101 25p multicolored 1.00 1.00
358C A101 50p multicolored 2.00 2.00
a. Inscribed "1992" 4.00 4.00
358D A101 £1 multicolored 4.00 4.00
a. Inscribed "1992" 8.50 8.50
Nos. 347-358D (16) 13.65 13.65

Nos. 356a and 356b also exist in special booklet sheets of 50 stamps containing either 10 No. 356a or 5 No. 356b.

Issued: 1p-19p, 2/10; Nos. 355b-355c, 3/16; 20p-£1, 9/21; Nos. 356a, 356b, 10/16/89; No. 358f, 2/14/90.

See Nos. 448-459.

Car Racing — A102

Winning automobiles, drivers: 13p, Vauxhall Opel, Russell Brookes, 1985. 26p, Ford Escort, Ari Vatanen of Finland, 1976. 31p, Repco March 761, Terry Smith, 1980. 34p, Williams/Honda Nigel Mansell, 1986-87.

1988, Feb. 10 *Perf. 13½x14½*

359 A102 13p multicolored .55 .55
360 A102 26p multicolored 1.10 1.10
361 A102 31p multicolored 1.25 1.25
362 A102 34p multicolored 1.35 1.35
Nos. 359-362 (4) 4.25 4.25

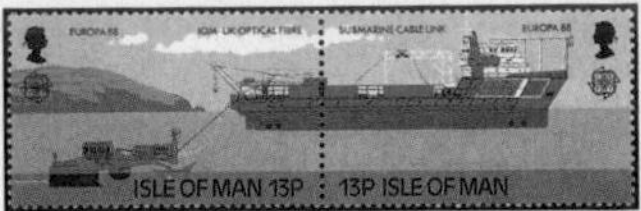

Europa 1988 — A103

Telecommunications: No. 363, IOM-UK optical fiber cable-laying plow. No. 364, Cable-laying ship. No. 365, 1st IOM Earth station, Braddan, established by Manx Telecom. No. 366, Intelsat V satellite.

1988, Apr. 14 Litho. *Perf. 14x13½*

363 13p multicolored .60 .60
364 13p multicolored .60 .60
a. A103 Pair, #363-364 1.25 1.25
365 22p multicolored 1.00 1.00
366 22p multicolored 1.00 1.00
a. A103 Pair, #365-366 2.00 2.00
Nos. 363-366 (4) 3.20 3.20

Submarine cable linking the Isle of Man and Silecroft in Cumbria, 1987 (13p). Nos. 364a, 366a have continuous designs.

Historic Ships Built on the Isle A104

Isle of Man flag, Australia bicen. emblem or US flag and: 16p, Euterpe, 1863, built in Ramsey. 29p, Vixen leaving Peel for Australia, 1853. 31p, Ramsey, an immigrant ship in Brisbane, 1870. 34p, Star of India (renamed in 1906, was the Euterpe), restored 1960-1976, Maritime Museum at San Diego.

1988, May 11 Litho. *Perf. 14*

367 A104 16p multicolored .55 .55
368 A104 29p multicolored 1.05 1.05
369 A104 31p multicolored 1.05 1.05
370 A104 34p multicolored 1.10 1.10
a. Souvenir sheet of 2 (16p, 34p) 2.50 2.50
Nos. 367-370 (4) 3.75 3.75

Fuchsia Blossoms — A105

1988, Sept. 21 Litho. *Perf. 13½x14*

371 A105 13p Magellanica .40 .30
372 A105 16p Pink cloud .45 .35
373 A105 22p Leonora .70 .65
374 A105 29p Satellite .95 .95
375 A105 31p Preston Guild 1.05 1.05
376 A105 34p Thalia 1.20 1.20
Nos. 371-376 (6) 4.75 4.50

British Fuchsia Society, 50th anniv.

Christmas A106

1988, Oct. 12 *Perf. 14*

377 A106 12p Long-earred owl .60 .60
378 A106 15p Robin .75 .75
379 A106 31p Partridge 1.40 1.40
Nos. 377-379 (3) 2.75 2.75

Manx Cats A107

Designs: 16p, Ginger. 27p, Black and white. 30p, Tortoiseshell and white. 40p, Tortoiseshell.

1989, Feb. 8

380 A107 16p multicolored .55 .55
381 A107 27p multicolored .95 .95
382 A107 30p multicolored 1.30 1.30
383 A107 40p multicolored 1.35 1.35
Nos. 380-383 (4) 4.15 4.15

Celtic Works of Art by Archibald Knox (1864-1933) — A108

Designs: 13p, Tudric pewter and enamel clock, 1903, vert. 16p, Cross, a watercolor, vert. 23p, Silver tankard, 1902, vert. 32p, Liberty silver and Cymric gold brooches. 35p, Silver jewel box with inlaid turquoise, mother-of-pearl and enamel, 1900.

1989, Feb. 8 Litho. *Perf. 13*

384 A108 13p multicolored .40 .40
385 A108 16p multicolored .50 .50
386 A108 23p multicolored .70 .70
387 A108 32p multicolored .90 .90
388 A108 35p multicolored 1.20 1.20
Nos. 384-388 (5) 3.70 3.70

Mutiny on the *Bounty* A109

Designs: 13p, William Bligh, Old Onchan Church. 16p, Bligh and crewmen cast adrift. 30p, Peter Heywood on Tahiti, 1770. 32p, *Bounty* off Pitcairn. 35p, Fletcher Christian on Pitcairn.

1989, Apr. 28 Litho. *Perf. 14*

389 A109 13p multicolored .35 .35
390 A109 16p multicolored .50 .50
391 A109 30p multicolored .80 .80
392 A109 32p multicolored .90 .90
393 A109 35p multicolored 1.00 1.00
Nos. 389-393 (5) 3.55 3.55

Souvenir Sheet

394 Sheet of 3 + label 3.50 3.50
a. A109 23p Pitcairn Isls. No. 321d .65 .65
b. A109 27p Norfolk Is. No. 453 .75 .75
c. Booklet pane, #394 3.50
d. Booklet pane, 1 each #389-393, 394a 4.50
e. Bklt. pane of 6, #389-393, #394b 4.50
f. Booklet pane, 3 each #394a, #394b 4.25
Complete booklet, #394c, 394d, 394e, 394f 17.50

See Norfolk Is. Nos. 452-456 and Pitcairn Isls. Nos. 320-322.

No. 394 contains Nos. 393, 394a-394b.

No. 394c is 145x101mm and is rouletted at left.

Europa 1989 A110

Children's games: No. 395, Jumping rope, hopscotch, London Bridge is falling down. No. 396, Running, wheelbarrow race, leap frog, piggyback ride. No. 397, Boy building fort, girl blowing soap bubbles, puzzle. No. 398, Doll house, blocks, girl playing with rag doll and puzzle.

1989, May 17 *Perf. 13½*

395 A110 13p multicolored .45 .45
396 A110 13p multicolored .45 .45
a. Pair, #395-396 .90 .90
397 A110 23p multicolored .95 .95
398 A110 23p multicolored .95 .95
a. Pair, #397-398 1.90 1.90
Nos. 395-398 (4) 2.80 2.80

Nos. 396a, 398a have continuous designs.

World Wildlife Fund — A111

1989, Sept. 20 Litho. *Perf. 14*

399 A111 13p Puffin 1.25 1.25
400 A111 13p Black guillemot 1.25 1.25
401 A111 13p Cormorant 1.25 1.25
402 A111 13p Kittiwake 1.25 1.25
a. Block or strip of 4, #399-402 6.25 6.25
Nos. 399-402 (4) 5.00 5.00

Exists as sheetlet of 16 with "World Stamp Expo '89" printed in selvage.

Intl. Red Cross, 125th Anniv. A112

14p, Training youths. 17p, Emblems. 23p, Signing 1st Geneva convention, 1864. 30p, Ambulance services. 35p, Henri Dunant, founder.

1989, Oct. 16 Litho. *Perf. 14*

403 A112 14p multicolored .45 .45
404 A112 17p multicolored .55 .55
405 A112 23p multicolored .75 .75
406 A112 30p multicolored 1.05 1.05
407 A112 35p multicolored 1.20 1.20
Nos. 403-407 (5) 4.00 4.00

Noble's Hospital, Douglas, cent.

Christmas — A113

13p, Maternity home. 16p, Mother and child. 34p, Madonna and child, scripture. 37p, Church, baptismal ceremony.

1989, Oct. 16 *Perf. 14½x15*

408 A113 13p multicolored .40 .40
409 A113 16p multicolored .50 .50
410 A113 34p multicolored 1.10 1.10
411 A113 37p multicolored 1.25 1.25
Nos. 408-411 (4) 3.25 3.25

Jane Crookall Maternity Home 50th anniv. (13p) and 75th anniv. of the consecration of St. Ninian's Church (37p).

Queen Elizabeth II, Lord of Man, Trooping the Colors — A114

1990, Feb. 14 Litho. *Perf. 14½*

412 A114 £2 multicolored 5.50 5.00

Humorous Edwardian Postcards — A115

15p, The Isle of Man Express Going Up a Gradient. 19p, A Way We Have in the Isle of Man. 32p, Douglas — Waiting for the Male Boat. 34p, The Last Toast Rack Home Douglas Parade. 37p, The Last Isle of Man Boat.

1990, Feb. 14 *Perf. 14*

413 A115 15p multicolored .45 .45
414 A115 19p multicolored .65 .65
415 A115 32p multicolored 1.05 1.05
416 A115 34p multicolored 1.25 1.25
417 A115 37p multicolored 1.50 1.50
Nos. 413-417 (5) 4.90 4.90

Europa 1990 — A116

Mailmen and post offices: No. 418, Mailman, 1990. No. 419, Ramsey P.O., 1990. No. 420, Mailman, c. 1890. No. 421, Douglas P.O., c. 1890.

1990, Apr. 18 Litho. *Perf. 13½*

Size of Nos. 419, 421: 42x28mm

418 15p multicolored .65 .65
419 15p multicolored .65 .65
a. A116 Pair, #418-419 1.30 1.30
420 24p multicolored 1.10 1.10
421 24p multicolored 1.10 1.10
a. A116 Pair, #420-421 2.25 2.25
Nos. 418-421 (4) 3.50 3.50

Great Britain No. 1 — A117

Designs: 19p, Wyon Medal. 32p, William Wyon's essay. 34p, Perkins Bacon engine-turned essay of 1839. 37p, Great Britain No. 2.

No. 423 (various Penny Blacks and text): a.-e. Positions AA-AE. f.-j. Positions BA-BE. k.-n. Positions CA-CE. p.-t. Positions DA-DE. u.-y. Positions EA-EE.

Note that A-A top of square on No. 423a, centered on No. 422a.

1990, May 3 Litho. *Perf. 14x13½*

422 Pane of 5 4.50 4.50
a. A117 1p shown .25 .25
b. A117 19p multicolored .65 .65
c. A117 32p multicolored 1.10 1.10
d. A117 34p multicolored 1.20 1.20
e. A117 37p multicolored 1.30 1.30
g. Bklt. pane, 2 each #422b-422e 8.50
h. No. 422 ovptd. "From STAMP WORLD LONDON '90 / To NEW ZEALAND '90" *17.00 17.00*

Miniature Sheet

423 Sheet of 25 2.25 2.25
a.-y. A117 1p like #422a, any single .25 .25
z. Pane of 8, #a.-d., f.-i. .50

Souvenir Sheet

Litho. & Engr.

424 A117 £1 4 Great Britain #1 4.00 4.00
a. Booklet pane of 1 4.00 4.00
Complete booklet, #422g, 423z, 424a 13.00

Left margin of Nos. 422g, 423z and 424a rouletted.

Queen Mother, 90th Birthday — A118

1990, Aug. 4 Litho. *Perf. 13x13½*

425 A118 90p multicolored 3.25 3.25

Sheets of 10 alternating with 10 labels.

Battle of Britain, 50th Anniv. A119

No. 426, Home defense. No. 427, Air sea rescue. No. 428, Rearming fighters. No. 429, Height of battle. No. 430, Civil defense. No. 431, Anti-aircraft defense.

1990, Sept. 5 Litho. *Perf. 14*

426	A119	15p multicolored	.65	.65
427	A119	15p multicolored	.65	.65
a.		Pair, #426-427	1.30	1.30
428	A119	24p multicolored	.95	.95
429	A119	24p multicolored	.95	.95
a.		Pair, #428-429	1.90	1.90
430	A119	29p multicolored	1.20	1.20
431	A119	29p multicolored	1.20	1.20
a.		Pair, #430-431	2.40	2.40
		Nos. 426-431 (6)	5.60	5.60

Sir Winston Churchill (1874-1965) — A120

1990, Sept. 5 *Perf. 13½*

432	A120	19p multicolored	.60	.60
433	A120	32p multicolored	1.00	1.00
434	A120	34p multicolored	1.10	1.10
435	A120	37p multicolored	1.20	1.20
		Nos. 432-435 (4)	3.90	3.90

Christmas — A121

1990, Oct. 10 *Perf. 13x13½*

436	A121	14p Mailing letters	.45	.45
437	A121	18p Sledding, skating	.55	.55
438	A121	34p Snowman	1.25	1.25
439	A121	37p Throwing snowball	1.40	1.40
a.		Souvenir sheet of 4, #436-439	3.75	3.75
		Nos. 436-439 (4)	3.65	3.65

Denominations on stamps in No. 439a are black.

Manx Photographers A122

Designs: 17p, Henry Bloom Noble, by Marshall Wane. 21p, Douglas, by Frederic Frith & Co. 26p, Studio Portrait, by Hilda Newby. 31p, Cashtal yn Ard, by Christopher Killip. 40p, Peel, by Colleen Corlett.

1991, Jan. 6 Litho. *Perf. 14x14½*

440	A122	17p black, gray	.50	.50
441	A122	21p brown	.60	.60
442	A122	26p sepia	.75	.75
443	A122	31p black, gray	1.05	1.05
444	A122	40p multicolored	1.35	1.35
		Nos. 440-444 (5)	4.25	4.25

Railways and Tramways Type of 1988 with Queen's Head in White (#448, 458)

Designs: 18p, TPO Special leaving Douglas Station, 1991. 23p, Double decker horse tram.

1991-92 Litho. *Perf. 13½*

448	A101	4p like No. 352	.25	.25
456	A101	18p multicolored	.70	.70
458	A101	21p like No. 353	.85	.85
a.		Souv. sheet, 2 each #448, #458	2.75	2.75
b.		Bklt. pane, #458, 3 #448, 4 #356d	3.75	
		Complete booklet, #458b	4.00	
c.		Bklt. pane, 3 #448, 1 each #356d, #458	1.90	
		Complete booklet, #458c	2.00	
459	A101	23p multicolored	.90	.90
a.		Bklt. pane, 6 #456, 4 #459	9.00	
		Complete booklet, #459a	2.00	
b.		Bklt. pane, 3 #456, 2 #459	5.00	
		Complete booklet, #459b	2.00	
		Nos. 448-459 (4)	2.70	2.70

No. 458a for Ninth Conf. of Commonwealth Postal Administrations, Douglas, Isle of Man.

Issued: 4p, 21p, Nos. 458b, 458c, 1/9; No. 458a, 7/1; 18p, 23p, No. 459a, 1/8/92.

No. 458b exists in special booklet sheets containing 5 No. 458b and 5 each Nos. 440, 458.

No. 458b dated 1991.

Manx Lifeboats A123

17p, Sir William Hillary. 21p, Osman Gabriel. 26p, James & Ann Ritchie. 31p, The Gough Ritchie. 37p, John Batstone.

1991, Feb. 13 *Perf. 14*

463	A123	17p multicolored	.55	.55
464	A123	21p multicolored	.75	.75
465	A123	26p multicolored	.85	.85
466	A123	31p multicolored	1.05	1.05
467	A123	37p multicolored	1.20	1.20
		Nos. 463-467 (5)	4.40	4.40

Europa — A124

1991, Apr. 24 Litho. *Perf. 14*

468		17p Satellites	.80	.80
469		17p Boats, Ariane rocket	.80	.80
a.	A124	Vert. pair, #468-469	1.60	1.60
470		26p Satellites, diff.	1.25	1.25
471		26p Space shuttle, jet	1.25	1.25
a.	A124	Vert. pair, #470-471	2.50	2.50
		Nos. 468-471 (4)	4.10	4.10

Tourist Trophy Mountain Course, 80th Anniv. A125

Designs: 17p, Oliver Godfrey, Indian 500cc, Bray Hill, 1911. 21p, Freddie Dixon, Douglas banking sidecar, Ballacraine, 1923. 26p, Bill Ivy, Yamaha 125cc, Waterworks, 1968. 31p, Giacomo Agostini, MV Agusta 500cc, Creg-ny-Baa, 1972. 37p, Joey Dunlop, RVF Honda 750cc, Ballaugh Bridge, 1985.

1991, May 30 Litho. *Perf. 14½x13*

472	A125	17p multicolored	.65	.65
473	A125	21p multicolored	.80	.80
474	A125	26p multicolored	.90	.90
475	A125	31p multicolored	1.15	1.15
476	A125	37p multicolored	1.40	1.40
a.		Souv. sheet of 5, #472-476 + 7 labels	5.25	5.25
b.		As "a," ovptd. in black & red in sheet margin	15.00	15.00
		Nos. 472-476 (5)	4.90	4.90

No. 476b overprint includes show emblem and "PHILA / NIPPON '91."

Issue date: No. 476b, Nov. 16.

Fire Engines A126

Designs: 17p, Laxey hand cart. 21p, Douglas horse drawn steamer. 30p, Merryweather Hatfield pump. 33p, Dennis F8 pumping appliance. 37p, Volvo turntable ladder.

1991, Sept. 18 Litho. *Perf. 14½*

477	A126	17p multicolored	.55	.55
478	A126	21p multicolored	.70	.70
479	A126	30p multicolored	.95	.95
480	A126	33p multicolored	1.10	1.10
481	A126	37p multicolored	1.25	1.25
		Nos. 477-481 (5)	4.55	4.55

Swans — A127

Designs: No. 482, Mute swans, Douglas Harbor. No. 483, Black swans, Curraghs Wildlife Park. No. 484, Whooper swans, Bishops Dub, Ballaugh. No. 485, Bewick's swans, Eairy Dam, Foxdale. No. 486, Coscoroba swans, Curraghs Wildlife Park. No. 487, Trumpeter swans, Corraghs Wildlife Park.

1991, Sept. 18 *Perf. 13*

482		17p multicolored	.70	.70
483		17p multicolored	.70	.70
a.	A127	Pair, #482-483	1.40	1.40
484		26p multicolored	1.20	1.20
485		26p multicolored	1.20	1.20
a.	A127	Pair, #484-485	2.40	2.40
486		37p multicolored	1.50	1.50
487		37p multicolored	1.50	1.50
a.	A127	Pair, #486-487	3.00	3.00
		Nos. 482-487 (6)	6.80	6.80

Pairs have continuous designs.

Christmas — A128

16p, Three kings. 20p, Jesus in manger, Mary. 26p, Shepherds. 37p, Angels.

1991, Oct. 14 *Perf. 14x14½*

488	A128	16p multicolored	.50	.50
489	A128	20p multicolored	.60	.60
490	A128	26p multicolored	.80	.80
491	A128	37p multicolored	1.10	1.10
		Nos. 488-491 (4)	3.00	3.00

Litho.

Die Cut

Self-Adhesive Booklet Stamps

492	A128	16p like #488	.90	.90
493	A128	20p like #489	1.10	1.10
a.		Bklt. pane, 8 #492, 4 #493	12.00	12.00
		Complete booklet, 2 #493a	24.00	

Queen Elizabeth II's Accession to the Throne, 40th Anniv. — A129

Various portraits of Queen Elizabeth II.

1992, Feb. 6 Litho. *Perf. 14*

494	A129	18p multicolored	.50	.50
495	A129	23p multicolored	.65	.65
496	A129	28p multicolored	.80	.80
497	A129	33p multicolored	.90	.90
498	A129	39p multicolored	1.20	1.20
		Nos. 494-498 (5)	4.05	4.05

Parachute Regiment, 50th Anniv. — A130

Designs: No. 499, North Africa & Italy, 1942-43. No. 500, Operation Overlord, Normandy, 1944. No. 501, Operation Market Garden, Arnhem, 1944. No. 502, Operation Varsity, Rhine, 1945. No. 503, Near, Middle and Far East, 1945-68. No. 504, Operation Corporate, Falkland Islands, 1982, and Utrinque Paratus, 1992.

1992, Feb. 6 *Perf. 14*

499		23p multicolored	.65	.65
500		23p multicolored	.65	.65
a.	A130	Pair, #499-500	1.30	1.30
501		28p multicolored	.80	.80
502		28p multicolored	.80	.80
a.	A130	Pair, #501-502	1.60	1.60
503		39p multicolored	1.25	1.25
504		39p multicolored	1.25	1.25
a.	A130	Pair, #503-504	2.50	2.50
		Nos. 499-504 (6)	5.40	5.40

Printed in sheets of 8.

Pilgrims' Voyage to America, 1620 — A131

Europa: No. 505, Pilgrims in longboats. No. 506, Speedwell, Delfshaven, Holland. No. 507, Mayflower. No. 508, Speedwell, Dartmouth, England.

1992, Apr. 16 Litho. *Perf. 14x13½*

505	A131	18p multicolored	.80	.80
506	A131	18p multicolored	.80	.80
a.		Pair, #505-506	1.60	1.60
507	A131	28p multicolored	1.75	1.75
508	A131	28p multicolored	1.75	1.75
a.		Pair, #507-508	3.50	3.50
		Nos. 505-508 (4)	5.10	5.10

Nos. 506a, 508a have continuous design.

Port Erin Marine Laboratory, Cent. A132

1992, Apr. 16 *Perf. 14½*

509	A132	18p Brittle stars	.55	.55
510	A132	23p Phytoplankton	.75	.75
511	A132	28p Herring	.85	.85
512	A132	33p Great scallop	.95	.95
513	A132	39p Dahlia anemone, delesseria	1.20	1.20
		Nos. 509-513 (5)	4.30	4.30

Union Pacific, First Transcontinental Railroad — A133

No. 514, "Jupiter," 1869. No. 515, "#119," 1869. No. 516, "#844," 1992. No. 517, "#3985," 1992. £1.50, Golden Spike Ceremony, Union Pacific and Central Pacific Railroads, 1869.

1992, May 22 Litho. *Perf. 13½x14*

514		33p multicolored	1.00	1.00
515		33p multicolored	1.00	1.00
a.	A133	Pair, #514-515 + label	2.10	2.10
516		39p multicolored	1.25	1.25
517		39p multicolored	1.25	1.25
a.	A133	Pair, #516-517 + label	2.75	2.75
b.		Bklt. pane, 1 ea #515a, 517a	4.75	4.75

Souvenir Sheet

518	A133	£1.50 multicolored	5.50	5.50
a.		Booklet pane, #518	5.50	
b.		Bklt. pane, #518a, 2 #517b	15.00	
		Complete booklet, #518b	15.00	

World Columbian Stamp Expo '92. No. 518 contains one 60x50mm stamp.

Nos. 514-515 and 516-517 issued in sheets of 10.

Nos. 515a, 517a have 3 different labels. No. 517b exists with two different pairs of labels. No. 518a has a rouletted white border at left and right.

Manx Harbors — A134

No. 519, King Orry V, Douglas Harbor. 23p, Castletown Harbor. 37p, Port St. Mary Harbor. 40p, Ramsey Harbor. a, King Orry. b, St. Eloi.

1992, Sept. 18 Litho. *Perf. 14½x14*

519	A134 18p multicolored		.55	.55
520	A134 23p multicolored		.70	.70
521	A134 37p multicolored		1.25	1.25
522	A134 40p multicolored		1.50	1.50
	Nos. 519-522 (4)		4.00	4.00

Souvenir Sheet

523	Sheet of 2	4.00	4.00
a.	A134 18p multicolored	.65	.65
b.	A134 £1 multicolored	3.25	3.25

Genoa '92. No. 523 contains 30x24mm stamps.

Christmas — A135

Designs: 17p, Nativity window, St. German's Cathedral, Peel. 22p, Adoration of the Magi panel, St. Matthew's Church, Douglas. 28p, Nativity window, St. George's Church, Douglas. 37p, Reredos of The Annunciation, St. Mary of the Isle, Douglas. 40p, Good Shepherd window, Trinity Methodist Church, Douglas.

1992, Oct. 13 Litho. *Perf. 14½*

524	A135 17p multicolored	.50	.50
525	A135 22p multicolored	.75	.75
526	A135 28p multicolored	1.00	1.00
527	A135 37p multicolored	1.00	1.00
528	A135 40p multicolored	1.40	1.40
	Nos. 524-528 (5)	4.65	4.65

Nigel Mansell, Formula I World Champion, 1992 A136

Williams Renault FW 14B at: 20p, British Grand Prix, 1992. 24p, French Grand Prix, 1992.

1992, Nov. 8 *Perf. 13½*

529	A136 20p multicolored	.75	.75
530	A136 24p multicolored	1.00	1.00

Ships A137

Royal Ensign of the Isle of Man — A137a

Queen Elizabeth II — A137b

1p, HMS Amazon. 2p, Fingal. 4p, Sir Winston Churchill. 5p, Dar Mlodziezy. 20p, Tynwald I. 21p, Ben Veg. 22p, Waverley. 23p, HMY Britannia. 24p, Francis Drake. 25p, Royal Viking Sky. 26p, Lord Nelson. 27p, Europa. 30p, Snaefell V. 35p, Sea Cat. 40p, Lady of Mann I. 50p, Mona's Queen II. £1, QE2, Mona's Queen V.

1993-96 Litho. *Perf. 13½*

531	A137	1p multi		.25	.25
532	A137	2p multi		.25	.25
533	A137	4p multi		.25	.25
a.		Inscribed "1997"		.25	.25
534	A137	5p multi		.25	.25
543	A137	20p multi		.45	.45
a.		Inscribed "1995"		.45	.45
544	A137	21p multi		.55	.55
a.		Inscribed "1997"		.55	.55
545	A137	22p multi		.55	.55
546	A137	23p multi		.60	.60
a.		Souv. sheet of 1, Perf. 13		1.00	1.00
547	A137	24p multi		.55	.55
a.		Bklt. pane, 4 #543, 6 #547		5.50	
		Complete booklet, #547a		5.50	
b.		Bklt. pane, 2 #543, 3 #547		2.75	
		Complete booklet, #547b		2.75	
c.		Inscribed "1995"		.55	.55
548	A137	25p multi		.65	.65
a.		Booklet pane, 2 #533a, 2 #544a, 2 #548b		4.25	
		Complete booklet, #548a		4.25	
b.		Inscribed "1997"		.65	.65
549	A137	26p multi		.70	.70
550	A137	27p multi		.70	.70
551	A137	30p multi		.80	.80
551A	A137	35p multi		.95	.95
552	A137	40p multi		1.10	1.10
553	A137	50p multi		1.40	1.40
553A	A137	£1 multi		3.50	3.50
a.		Inscribed "1997"		3.50	3.50

Perf. 14½

553B	A137a	£2 multi	5.00	5.00
553C	A137b	£5 multi	15.00	15.00
		Nos. 531-553C (19)	33.50	33.50

No. 546a, for return of Hong Kong to China, is wmk. 373. Stamp in No. 546a is dated "1997".

No. 553C has a holographic image. Soaking in water may affect the hologram.

Issued: 1p-5p, 20p-27p, 1/4/93; 30p, 40p-£1, 9/15/93; £2, 1/24/94; £5, 7/5/94; 35p, 1/11/96; No. 546a, 7/1/97; No. 548a, 1997.

See Nos. 683-697.

Manx Electric Railway, Cent. — A138

20p, #13 trailer, #1 motor car. 24p, #19 trailer, #9 tunnel car. 28p, #59 Royal trailer special saloon car, #19 motor car. 39p, #33 motor car, #45 trailer, #13 small van.

1993, Feb. 3 *Perf. 14*

554	A138 20p multicolored	.65	.65
555	A138 24p multicolored	.75	.75
556	A138 28p multicolored	1.00	1.00
557	A138 39p multicolored	1.10	1.10
a.	Booklet pane of #554-557	3.50	3.50
	Complete booklet, 4 #557a	14.00	
	Nos. 554-557 (4)	3.50	3.50

No. 557a exists with four different marginal inscriptions and in four different arrangements.

Contemporary Art by Bryan Kneale — A139

Europa: No. 558, Statue of Sir Hall Caine. No. 559, Painting, The Brass Bedstead. No. 560, Abstract bronze. No. 561, Drawing of polar bear skeleton.

1993, Apr. 14 Litho. *Perf. 14*

558	A139 20p multicolored	.65	.65
559	A139 20p multicolored	.65	.65
a.	Pair, #558-559	1.30	1.30
560	A139 28p multicolored	.85	.85
561	A139 28p multicolored	.85	.85
a.	Pair, #560-561	1.75	1.75
	Nos. 558-561 (4)	3.00	3.00

Motorcycling Events — A140

Riders and events: 20p, Gold Medalists Graham Oates, Bill Marshall, Intl. Six-Day Trial, 1933, Ariel Square Four. 24p, Geoff Duke, Team Sergeant, Royal Signals Display Team, 1947, Triumph Twin. 28p, Denis Parkinson, winner of Senior Manx Grand Prix, 1953, Manx Norton. 33p, Richard Swallow, winner of Junior Classic Manx Grand Prix, 1991, Aermacchi. 39p, Steve Colley, winner of Scottish Six-Day Trial, 1992, Beta Zero.

1993, June 3 Litho. *Perf. 13½x14*

562	A140 20p multicolored	.70	.70
563	A140 24p multicolored	.75	.75
564	A140 28p multicolored	.90	.90
565	A140 33p multicolored	1.10	1.10
566	A140 39p multicolored	1.25	1.25
a.	Souv. sheet of 5, #562-566 + 4 labels	4.75	4.75
	Nos. 562-566 (5)	4.70	4.70

Butterflies A141

1993, Sept. 15 Litho. *Perf. 14½*

567	A141 24p Dark green fritillary	.80	.80
568	A141 24p Painted lady	.80	.80
569	A141 24p Holly blue	.80	.80
570	A141 24p Red admiral	.80	.80
571	A141 24p Peacock	.80	.80
a.	Strip of 5, #567-571	4.00	4.00

Christmas — A142

Designs: 19p, Children decorating Christmas tree. 23p, Snowman, girl. 28p, Boy unwrapping presents. 39p, Girl, teddy bear. 40p, Girl with holly basket, boy on sled.

1993, Oct. 12 *Perf. 14*

572	A142 19p multicolored	.60	.60
	Complete booklet, 10 #572	6.00	
573	A142 23p multicolored	.70	.70
	Complete booklet, 10 #573	7.00	
574	A142 28p multicolored	.85	.85
575	A142 39p multicolored	1.20	1.20
576	A142 40p multicolored	1.20	1.20
	Nos. 572-576 (5)	4.55	4.55

Tourism A143

No. 577, Gaiety Theatre, Douglas. No. 578, Field hockey, golf, soccer (#577). No. 579, Yacht racing, artist's hand painting picture of castle (#580). No. 580, TT Motorcycle Races, Red Arrows demonstration squadron. (#581). No. 581, Musical instruments. No. 582, Laxey Wheel, Manx cat. No. 583, Tower of Refuge, beach, sand bucket (#584). No. 584, Cyclist. No. 585, Tynwald Day, classic racing car (#579, 580, 584, 586). No. 586, Santa Claus riding Mince Pie Train, Groudle Glen.

Booklet Stamps

1994, Feb, 18 Litho. *Perf. 13½*

577	A143 24p multicolored	.80	.80
578	A143 24p multicolored	.80	.80
579	A143 24p multicolored	.80	.80
580	A143 24p multicolored	.80	.80
581	A143 24p multicolored	.80	.80
582	A143 24p multicolored	.80	.80
583	A143 24p multicolored	.80	.80
584	A143 24p multicolored	.80	.80
585	A143 24p multicolored	.80	.80
586	A143 24p multicolored	.80	.80
a.	Booklet pane of 10, #577-586	8.25	
	Complete booklet, #586a + pane of 12 labels	8.25	

Birds A144

Magpie, Calf of Man Bird Observatory — A145

No. 587, White-throated robin. No. 588, Black-eared wheatear. No. 589, Goldcrest. No. 590, Northern oriole. No. 591, Kingfisher. No. 592, Hoopoe.

1994, Feb. 18 *Perf. 14*

587	A144 20p multicolored	.60	.60
588	A144 20p multicolored	.60	.60
a.	Pair, #587-588	1.20	1.20
589	A144 24p multicolored	.95	.95
590	A144 24p multicolored	.95	.95
a.	Pair, #589-590	1.90	1.90
591	A144 30p multicolored	1.25	1.25
592	A144 30p multicolored	1.25	1.25
a.	Pair, #591-592	2.50	2.50
	Nos. 587-592 (6)	5.60	5.60

Souvenir Sheet

Perf. 13½x13

593	A145	£1 shown	3.50	3.50

Hong Kong '94 (No. 593).

Europa A146

Designs, Forbes and Discoveries: No. 594, Eubranchus tricolor. No. 595, Loligo forbesii. No. 596, Edward Forbes (1815-54), naturalist. No. 597, Solaster moretonis. No. 598, Adamsia carciniopados on hermit crab. No. 599, Solaster endeca.

1994, May 5 Litho. *Perf. 13¼x14½*

594	A146 20p multicolored	.75	.75
595	A146 20p multicolored	.75	.75
596	A146 20p multicolored	.75	.75
a.	Strip of 3, #594-596	2.25	2.25
597	A146 30p multicolored	1.15	1.15
598	A146 30p multicolored	1.15	1.15
599	A146 30p multicolored	1.15	1.15
a.	Strip of 3, #597-599	3.50	3.50

D-Day, 50th Anniv. A147

Designs: No. 600, Transport Ben-My-Chree IV, landing ships, US Maj. Gen. Walter Bedell Smith. No. 601, Transports Victoria, Lady of Mann I, Adm. Sir Bertram Ramsay, RN, Naval Commander. No. 602, Infantry, tanks on Gold, Juno, Sword Beaches, Gen. Montgomery,

Commander, 21st Army Group. No. 603, Tanks, landing craft on Gold, Juno, Sword Beaches, Lt. Gen. Sir Miles C. Dempsey, Commander, British 2nd Army. No. 604, US 8th, 9th Air Forces, Air Chief Marshal Sir Trafford Leigh-Mallory, RAF, Air Force Commander. No. 605, Air Chief Marshall Sir Arthur Tedder, RAF, Deputy Supreme Allied Commander, RAF 2nd Tactical Air Force & Bomber Command. No. 606, Landing craft, Omaha, Utah Beaches, Lt. Gen. Omar N. Bradley, Commander, US 1st Army. No. 607, Infantry, tanks on Omaha, Utah Beaches, Gen. Eisenhower, Supreme Allied Commander.

1994, June 6 Litho. *Perf. 14*

600 A147 4p multicolored .25 .25
601 A147 4p multicolored .25 .25
a. Pair, #600-601 .25 .25
602 A147 20p multicolored .60 .60
a. Dated "2014" (#1658a) .55 .55
603 A147 20p multicolored .60 .60
a. Pair, #602-603 1.20 1.20
b. Dated "2014" (#1658a) .55 .55
604 A147 30p multicolored .95 .95
605 A147 30p multicolored .95 .95
a. Pair, #604-605 1.90 1.90
606 A147 41p multicolored 1.25 1.25
a. Dated "2014" (#1658a) 1.10 1.10
607 A147 41p multicolored 1.25 1.25
a. Pair, #606-607 2.50 2.50
b. Dated "2014" (#1658a) 1.10 1.10
Nos. 600-607 (8) 6.10 6.10

Nos. 601a, 603a, 605a, 607a are continuous designs.

Issued: Nos. 602a, 603b, 606a, 607b, 5/8/14.

Postman Pat A148

Postman Pat at: 1p, Sea Terminal, Douglas. 20p, Laxey Wheel. 24p, Cregneash. 30p, Manx Electric Railway. 36p, Peel Harbor. 41p, Tourist office, Douglas Promenade.

£1, Postman Pat.

1994, Sept. 14 Litho. *Perf. 14½x14*

608 A148 1p multicolored .25 .25
a. Booklet pane of 2 .25
609 A148 20p multicolored .65 .65
a. Booklet pane of 2 1.40
610 A148 24p multicolored .80 .80
a. Booklet pane of 2 1.60
611 A148 30p multicolored 1.00 1.00
a. Booklet pane of 2 2.10
612 A148 36p multicolored 1.25 1.25
a. Booklet pane of 2 2.50
613 A148 41p multicolored 1.40 1.40
a. Booklet pane of 2 3.00
Nos. 608-613 (6) 5.35 5.35

Souvenir Sheet

Perf. 13

614 A148 £1 multicolored 4.00 4.00
a. Booklet pane of 1 4.00 4.00
Complete booklet, #608a-614a 16.00

No. 614a is rouletted 9 at left.

Intl. Olympic Committee, Cent. — A149

1994, Oct. 11 *Perf. 14*

615 A149 10p Cycling .35 .35
616 A149 20p Alpine skiing .70 .70
617 A149 24p Swimming .80 .80
618 A149 35p Steeplechase 1.25 .125
619 A149 48p Emblem 1.40 1.40
Nos. 615-619 (5) 4.50 3.38

A150

Christmas: 19p, Santa, Mrs. Claus greeting children on Santa Train to Santon, horiz. 23p, Santa Claus on tractor, Postman Pat. 60p, Santa Claus arriving by boat, Port St. Mary, horiz.

1994, Oct. 11

620 A150 19p multicolored .65 .65
621 A150 23p multicolored .85 .85
622 A150 60p multicolored 1.75 1.75
Nos. 620-622 (3) 3.25 3.25

Snaefell Mountain Electric Railway, Cent. — A151

Designs: 20p, Opening day, Car No. 2. 24p, Car 3 ascending Laxey Valley, Car 4 in green livery. 35p, Car 5, Car 6. 42p, Caledonia on construction duty, Goods Car 7.

£1, Bungalow Hotel & Station, Snaefell.

1995, Feb. 8 Litho. *Perf. 14*

623 A151 20p multicolored .70 .70
624 A151 24p multicolored .85 .85
625 A151 35p multicolored 1.25 1.25
626 A151 42p multicolored 1.40 1.40
a. Bklt. pane, #623-626 4.25
Nos. 623-626 (4) 4.20 4.20

Souvenir Sheet

Perf. 14x13½

627 A151 £1 multicolored 3.25 3.25
a. Sheet from souvenir booklet 3.25 3.25
Complete booklet, 3 #626a, #627a 16.00

No. 627 contains one 61x38mm stamp.

No. 626a comes with three different arrangements of the stamps. Value the same for each.

No. 627a is rouletted in margin at left with additional vertical sheet margin inscriptions. At left is a description of the design. At right is "1895-Centenary Snaefell Mountain Railway-1995."

Steam-Powered Vehicles — A152

Designs: 20p, Foden Wagon, 5 ton. 24p, Clayton & Shuttleworth, 7hp, Fowler, 6hp. 30p, Wallis & Steevens, 6hp. 35p, Marshall, 6hp. 41p, Marshall Convertible, 5hp.

1995, Feb. 8 *Perf. 13½*

628 A152 20p multicolored .60 .60
629 A152 24p multicolored .80 .80
630 A152 30p multicolored 1.00 1.00
631 A152 35p multicolored 1.25 1.25
632 A152 41p multicolored 1.35 1.35
Nos. 628-632 (5) 5.00 5.00

Peace & Freedom — A153

Europa: 20p, Flight of doves forming tidal wave, Tower of Refuge, Douglas Bay. 30p, Dove with olive branch breaking barbed wire.

1995, Apr. 28 Litho. *Perf. 13½*

633 A153 20p multicolored .75 .75
634 A153 30p multicolored 1.00 1.00

VE Day, 50th Anniv. A154

Designs: No. 635, Spitfire, tank, 1939-45 Star, African Star. No. 636, France and Germany Star, Italy Star, Hawker Typhoon, artillery. No. 637, Lancaster bomber, aircraft carrier, Air Crew Europe Star, Atlantic Star. No. 638, Pacific Star, Burma Star, Avenger torpedo bomber, soldiers. No. 639, Parliament, Manx flag. No. 640, British flag, crowd celebrating. No. 641, Children celebrating at street party, Manx flag. No. 642, British flag, visit of Queen Elizabeth, King George VI, 1945.

1995, May 8 *Perf. 14*

635 A154 10p multicolored .35 .35
636 A154 10p multicolored .35 .35
a. Pair, #635-636 .70 .70
637 A154 20p multicolored .70 .70
638 A154 20p multicolored .70 .70
a. Pair, #637-638 1.40 1.40
639 A154 24p multicolored .75 .75
640 A154 24p multicolored .75 .75
a. Pair, #639-640 1.50 1.50
641 A154 40p multicolored 1.25 1.25
642 A154 40p multicolored 1.25 1.25
a. Pair, #641-642 2.50 2.50
Nos. 635-642 (8) 6.10 6.10

British Motor Car Racing, 90th Anniv. A155

Tourist Trophy Race drivers, cars: 20p, R. Parnell, 1951 Maserati 4 CLT. 24p, S. Moss, 1951 Frazer Nash. 30p, R.J.B. Seaman, 1936 Delage. 36p, Prince Bira, 1937 ERA R2B Romulus. 41p, K. Lee Guinness, 1914 Sunbeam 1. 42p, F. Dixon, 1934 Riley.

£1, John S. Napier, 1905 Arrol Johnston.

1995, May 8

643 A155 20p multicolored .70 .70
644 A155 24p multicolored .80 .80
645 A155 30p multicolored 1.00 1.00
646 A155 36p multicolored 1.25 1.25
647 A155 41p multicolored 1.35 1.35
648 A155 42p multicolored 1.45 1.45
Nos. 643-648 (6) 6.55 6.55

Souvenir Sheet

649 A155 £1 multicolored 3.75 3.75

No. 649 contains one 47x58mm stamp.

Mushrooms A156

Designs: 20p, Amanita muscaria. 24p, Boletus edulis. 30p, Coprinus disseminatus. 35p, Pleurotus ostreatus. 45p, Geastrum triplex.

£1, Shaggy ink cap, bee orchid.

1995, Sept. 1 Litho. *Perf. 13½x14*

650 A156 20p multicolored .70 .70
651 A156 24p multicolored .80 .80
652 A156 30p multicolored 1.05 1.05
653 A156 35p multicolored 1.20 1.20
654 A156 45p multicolored 1.50 1.50
Nos. 650-654 (5) 5.25 5.25

Souvenir Sheet

Perf. 14x13½

655 A156 £1 multicolored 3.25 3.25

No. 655 contains one 51x60mm stamp. Singapore '95 (No. 655).

Thomas the Tank Engine A157

Designs: 20p, Bertie arrives on the quayside. 24p, Mail train and Thomas. 30p, Bertie and trains at Ballasalla. 36p, Viking and Thomas at Port Erin. 41p, The mail gets through. 45p, Race at Laxey Wheel.

1995, Sept. 1 *Perf. 14*

656 A157 20p multicolored .60 .60
657 A157 24p multicolored .70 .70
a. Booklet pane of 2, #656-657 1.30
658 A157 30p multicolored .90 .90
a. Booklet pane of 2, #657-658 1.60
659 A157 36p multicolored 1.10 1.10
a. Booklet pane of 2, #658-659 2.00
660 A157 41p multicolored 1.30 1.30
a. Booklet pane of 2, #659-660 2.40
661 A157 45p multicolored 1.30 1.30
a. Booklet pane of 2, #656, 661 1.90
b. Booklet pane of 2, #660-661 2.75
Complete booklet, #657a, 658a, 659a, 660a, 661a-661b 13.00
Nos. 656-661 (6) 5.90 5.90

Christmas A158

Designs: 19p, Church, holly. 23p, Bird on holly branch. 42p, Snow crocuses, church. 50p, snowdrops, antique farming equipment in snow.

1995, Oct. 10 Litho. *Perf. 14x14½*

662 A158 19p multicolored .60 .60
663 A158 23p multicolored .70 .70
664 A158 42p multicolored 1.30 1.30
665 A158 50p multicolored 1.50 1.50
Nos. 662-665 (4) 4.10 4.10

Lighthouses — A159

Location, year opened: 20p, Langness, 1880, vert. 24p, Point of Ayre, 1818. 30p, Chicken Rock, 1873, vert. 36p, Calf of Man, 1818. 41p, Douglas Head, 1832. vert. 42p, Maughold Head, 1914.

1996, Feb. 27 Litho. *Perf. 14*

666 A159 20p multicolored .60 .60
a. Booklet pane of 4 + 4 labels 2.60
667 A159 24p multicolored .70 .70
a. Booklet pane of 4 3.00
668 A159 30p multicolored .95 .95
669 A159 36p multicolored 1.05 1.05
670 A159 41p multicolored 1.30 1.30
a. Booklet pane, 2 each #668, 670 + 4 labels 4.50
671 A159 42p multicolored 1.30 1.30
a. Bklt. pane, 2 ea #669, 671 4.75
Complete booklet, #666a, 667a, 670a, 671a 15.00
Nos. 666-671 (6) 5.90 5.90

Manx Cats A160

Various cats and: 20p, Arms of Man. 24p, British Union Flag as of ball yarn. 36p, Brandenburg Gate. 42p, US flag, Statue of Liberty. 48p, Australian flag, map.

£1.50, Gray adult cat, gray and yellow kittens.

1996, Mar. 14

672 A160 20p multicolored .55 .55
673 A160 24p multicolored .65 .65
674 A160 36p multicolored 1.00 1.00
675 A160 42p multicolored 1.20 1.20
676 A160 48p multicolored 1.40 1.40
Nos. 672-676 (5) 4.80 4.80

Souvenir Sheet

677 A160 £1.50 multicolored 4.50 4.50
a. With additional inscription 10.00 10.00

No. 677 contains one 51x60mm stamp. No. 677a contains CAPEX '96 exhibition emblem in sheet margin. Issued 6/8/96.

Douglas Borough, Cent. — A161

Die Cut Perf. 9x9½
1996, Mar. 14 **Litho.**
Self-Adhesive
678 A161 (40p) multicolored 1.20 1.20

The backing of No. 678 is rouletted 13.

Women of Achievement — A162

Europa: 24p, Princess Anne, children of different nations. 30p, Queen Elizabeth II, people of different nations.

1996 ***Perf. 14***
679 A162 24p multicolored .65 .65
680 A162 30p multicolored .95 .95

Queen Elizabeth II, 70th birthday (No. 680).
See Guernsey Nos. 564-565.

Ship Type of 1993
1996 **Litho.** ***Perf. 14***
Size: 21x19mm
683 A137 4p like #533 .65 .65
693 A137 20p like #543 .70 .70
697 A137 24p like #547 .90 .90
Nos. 683-697 (3) 2.25 2.25
a. Bklt. pane, 2 ea 4p, 20p, 24p *7.00*
Complete booklet, No. 697a *7.00*

Irish Winners of Tourist Trophy Motorcycle Races — A163

20p, Alec Bennett. 24p, Stanley Woods. 45p, Artie Bell. 60p, Robert & Joey Dunlop.
£1, Demonstration squadron Hawks flying over motorcycles, vert.

1996, May 30 **Litho.** ***Perf. 14***
701 A163 20p multicolored .65 .65
702 A163 24p multicolored .70 .70
703 A163 45p multicolored 1.35 1.35
704 A163 60p multicolored 1.75 1.75
Nos. 701-704 (4) 4.45 4.45

Souvenir Sheet
705 A163 £1 multicolored 3.25 3.25

See Ireland Nos. 1010-1014.

Royal British Legion, 75th Anniv. — A164

Poppies and: 20p, National poppy appeal trophy. 24p, Manx war memorial. 42p, Poppy appeal. 75p, Crest.

1996, June 8
706 A164 20p multicolored .55 .55
707 A164 24p multicolored .65 .65
708 A164 42p multicolored 1.20 1.20
709 A164 75p multicolored 2.10 2.10
Nos. 706-709 (4) 4.50 4.50

UNICEF, 50th Anniv. A165

Children receiving aid, map of country: No. 710, Mexico. No. 711, Sri Lanka. No. 712, Colombia. No. 713, Zambia. No. 714, Afghanistan. No. 715, Viet Nam.

1996, Sept. 18 **Litho.** ***Perf. 13½x14***
710 A165 24p multicolored .65 .65
711 A165 24p multicolored .65 .65
a. Pair, #710-711 1.30 1.30
712 A165 30p multicolored .85 .85
713 A165 30p multicolored .85 .85
a. Pair, #712-713 1.75 1.75
714 A165 42p multicolored 1.25 1.25
715 A165 42p multicolored 1.25 1.25
a. Pair, #714-715 2.50 2.50
Nos. 710-715 (6) 5.50 5.50

Dogs — A166

20p, Labrador. 24p, Border collie. 31p, Dalmatian. 38p, Mongrel. 43p, English setter. 63p, Alsatian.
£1.20, Border collie, labrador.

1996, Sept. 18 ***Perf. 14½***
716 A166 20p multi .60 .60
a. Booklet pane of 4 2.40
717 A166 24p multi .65 .65
a. Booklet pane of 4 2.60
718 A166 31p multi .90 .90
719 A166 38p multi 1.15 1.15
720 A166 43p multi 1.30 1.30
721 A166 63p multi 1.90 1.90
a. Booklet pane, 1 each #718-721 5.25
Nos. 716-721 (6) 6.50 6.50

Souvenir Sheet
Perf. 13½x14
722 A166 £1.20 multi 3.75 3.75
a. Booklet pane of 1 3.75
Complete booklet, #716a, 717a, 721a, 722a 15.00

Nos. 716-721 are each printed with se-tenant label. No. 722 contains one 38x50mm stamp. No. 722a is rouletted around margin of sheet.

Christmas A167

Children's drawings: 19p, Snowman. 23p, Santa, "Happy Christmas" in Manx. 50p, Family, Christmas tree, presents. 75p, Santa in sleigh flying over rooftops.

1996, Nov. 2 **Litho.** ***Perf. 14x14½***
723 A167 19p multicolored .55 .55
724 A167 23p multicolored .65 .65
725 A167 50p multicolored 1.30 1.30
726 A167 75p multicolored 2.25 2.25
Nos. 723-726 (4) 4.75 4.75

Owls — A168

20p, Barn owl. 24p, Short-eared owl. 31p, Long-eared owl. 36p, Little owl. 43p, Snowy owl. 56p, Tawny owl.
£1.20, Long-eared owl.

1997, Feb. 12 **Litho.** ***Perf. 14***
727 A168 20p multicolored .60 .60
a. Booklet pane of 4 2.40
728 A168 24p multicolored .75 .75
a. Booklet pane of 4 3.00
729 A168 31p multicolored 1.00 1.00
730 A168 36p multicolored 1.15 1.15
731 A168 43p multicolored 1.45 1.45
732 A168 56p multicolored 1.75 1.75
a. Booklet pane of 4, #729-732 5.50
Nos. 727-732 (6) 6.70 6.70

Souvenir Sheet
Perf. 13
733 A168 £1.20 multi 4.00 4.00
a. Booklet pane of 1 4.00
Complete booklet, #727a, 728a, 732a, 733a 15.00

No. 733, 733a each contain one 56x60mm stamp. No. 733a is rouletted at left. Hong Kong '97 (Nos. 733, 733a).

Springtime A169

1997, Feb. 12 ***Perf. 14***
734 A169 20p Spring flowers .55 .55
735 A169 24p Sheep .65 .65
736 A169 43p Waterfowl 1.30 1.30
737 A169 63p Frog, ducks 1.90 1.90
Nos. 734-737 (4) 4.40 4.40

Stories and Legends A170

21p, Moddey Dhoo. 25p, The Trammen Tree. 31p, Fairy Bridge. 36p, Fin Macooil. 37p, The Buggane of St. Trinian's. 43p, Fynoderee.

1997, Apr. 24 **Litho.** ***Perf. 13½x14***
738 A170 21p multicolored .55 .55
739 A170 25p multicolored .70 .70
740 A170 31p multicolored .90 .90
741 A170 36p multicolored 1.00 1.00
742 A170 37p multicolored 1.00 1.00
743 A170 43p multicolored 1.30 1.30
Nos. 738-743 (6) 5.45 5.45

Europa (Nos. 739-740).

Aircraft A171

Designs: No. 744, Sopwith Tabloid. No. 745, Grumman Tiger. No. 746, Manx Airlines BAe ATP. No. 747, Manx Airlines BAe 146-200. No. 748 Boeing 757-200. No. 749, Farman biplane. No. 750, Spitfire. No. 751, Hurricane.

1997, Apr. 24 ***Perf. 14***
744 A171 21p multicolored .55 .55
745 A171 21p multicolored .55 .55
a. Pair, #744-745 1.10 1.10
746 A171 25p multicolored .70 .70
747 A171 25p multicolored .70 .70
a. Pair, #746-747 1.40 1.40
748 A171 31p multicolored .95 .95
749 A171 31p multicolored .95 .95
a. Pair, #748-749 1.90 1.90
750 A171 36p multicolored 1.00 1.00
751 A171 36p multicolored 1.00 1.00
a. Pair, #750-751 2.00 2.00
Nos. 744-751 (8) 6.40 6.40

See No. 1671.

Golf Courses A172

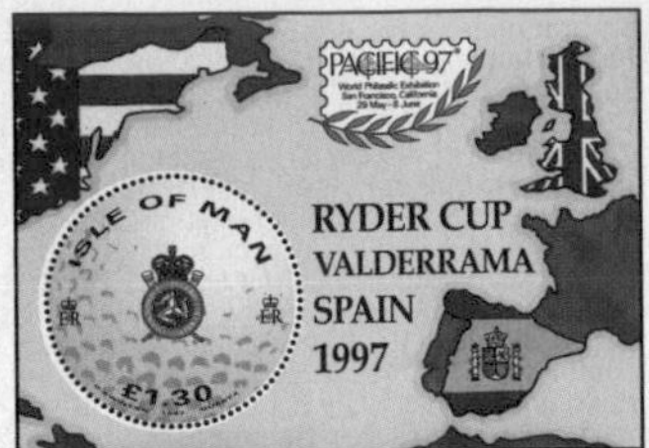

1997 Ryder Cup, Valderrama, Spain — A173

21p, 14th Hole, Ramsey Golf Club. 25p, 15th Hole, King Edward Bay Golf and Country Club. 43p, 17th Hole, Rowany Golf Club. 50p, 8th Hole, Castletown Golf Links.

1997, May 29 **Litho.** ***Perf. 14***
752 A172 21p multicolored .70 .70
a. Booklet pane of 3 2.10
753 A172 25p multicolored .90 .90
a. Booklet pane of 3 2.75
754 A172 43p multicolored 1.40 1.40
755 A172 50p multicolored 1.50 1.50
a. Bklt. pane, 2 ea #754-755 5.75
Nos. 752-755 (4) 4.50 4.50

Souvenir Sheet
756 A173 £1.30 multicolored 4.75 4.75
a. Booklet pane of 1 4.75
Complete booklet, #752a, 753a, 755a, 756a 15.50

PACIFIC 97 (No. 756). No. 756 contains one 40mm diameter stamp.
No. 756a has a large white border, is 155x96mm and is sewn into booklet.

Trial of Nations Motorcycle Competition — A174

Various motorcyclists: 21p, Steve Colley. 25p, Steve Saunders. 37p, Sammy Miller. 44p, Don Smith.

1997, Sept. 29 **Litho.** ***Perf. 13½***
757 A174 21p multicolored .60 .60
758 A174 25p multi, vert. .75 .75
759 A174 37p multi, vert. 1.25 1.25
760 A174 44p multicolored 1.40 1.40
Nos. 757-760 (4) 4.00 4.00

Queen Elizabeth II and Prince Philip, 50th Wedding Anniv. — A175

Designs: a, Early drawing of couple. b, Wedding portrait. c, Drawing of Queen waving, Prince in top hat. d, Portrait, 1997.
£1, Queen, Prince touring Isle of Man, 1989.

1997, Nov. 3 **Litho.** ***Perf. 14x14½***
761 A175 50p Strip of 4, #a.-d. 6.00 6.00

Souvenir Sheet
Perf. 14
762 A175 £1 multicolored 3.25 3.25

No. 761 was issued in sheets of 16 stamps. No. 762 contains one 48x58mm stamp.

Christmas — A176

20p, Angel, shepherd. 24p, Wise man, angel. 63p, Shepherd, Holy Family, two kings.

1997, Nov. 3 ***Perf. 14***
763 A176 20p multicolored .70 .70
764 A176 24p multicolored .75 .75

Size: 54x39mm

765 A176 63p multicolored 2.10 2.10
Nos. 763-765 (3) 3.55 3.55

Flowers — A177

4p, Shamrocks. 21p, Cushag. 25p, Princess of Wales Rose. 50p, Daffodil. £1, Spear thistle.

1998, Feb. 12 Litho. ***Perf. 13x13½***

766 A177 4p multi .25 .25
a. Inscribed "1999" *2.00 2.00*
767 A177 21p multi .70 .70
768 A177 25p multi .90 .90
a. Booklet pane, 2 ea #766-768 3.75
Complete booklet, #768a 3.75
769 A177 50p multi 1.75 1.75
770 A177 £1 multi 3.50 3.50
Nos. 766-770 (5) 7.10 7.10

Nos. 766-768 also exist in special booklet sheets containing 10 of each denomination. Booklet panes made from these sheets contain 2 each Nos. 766-768.

See Nos. 794-801.

A178

Viking Longships: 21p, Dragon's head figurehead. 25p, Ship under full sail. 31p, Ship with sail furled. 75p Ship's stern.

£1, Man on ship pointing, Peel Castle.

1998, Feb. 14 ***Perf. 14***

771 A178 21p multicolored .65 .65
772 A178 25p multicolored .85 .85
773 A178 31p multicolored 1.05 1.05
774 A178 75p multicolored 2.50 2.50
Nos. 771-774 (4) 5.05 5.05

Souvenir Sheet

775 A178 £1 multicolored 3.75 3.75

Marine Life A179

Designs: 10p, Bottle-nosed dolphin. 21p, Basking shark swimming right. 25p, Basking shark swimming forward. 31p, Minke whale. 63p, Killer whale.

1998, Mar. 14 Litho. ***Perf. 14***

776 A179 10p multicolored .35 .35
777 A179 21p multicolored .70 .70
a. Booklet pane of 6, 3 each #776-777 + 3 labels 3.25
778 A179 25p multicolored .90 .90
779 A179 31p multicolored 1.15 1.15
780 A179 63p multicolored 2.10 2.10
a. Bklt. pane of 8, #776-777, 2 ea #778-780 + label 9.50
Souvenir booklet, #777a, 780a 13.00
Nos. 776-780 (5) 5.20 5.20

Trains A180

Designs: 21p, Hutchinson 2-4-0. 25p, G.H. Wood 2-4-0. 31p, Maitland 2-4-0. 63p, Loch 2-4-0.

1998, May 2 Litho. ***Perf. 14½x14***

781 A180 21p multicolored .70 .70
782 A180 25p multicolored .85 .85
783 A180 31p multicolored 1.10 1.10
784 A180 63p multicolored 2.10 2.10
a. Bklt. pane of 4, #781-784 4.75 4.75
Nos. 781-784 (4) 4.75 4.75

Souvenir Sheet

785 A180 Sheet of 2 4.25 4.25
a. £1 Engine 3.50 3.50
b. 25p Passenger cars .75 .75
c. Booklet pane of 1 4.25 4.25
Complete bklt., #785c, 2 #784a 14.00
d. As #785, inscribed in sheet margin *15.00 15.00*

No. 784a exists with two different backgrounds and stamps in different order. Complete booklets contain one of each pane.

No. 785d is inscribed in sheet margin with PhilexFrance '99, World Philatelic Exhibition emblem and was issued 7/2/99.

Europa A181

National Days celebration: 25p, People under tent, seated in stand, watching ceremony. 30p, Women dancing in traditional costumes.

1998, July 2 ***Perf. 13x13½***

786 A181 25p multicolored .90 .90
787 A181 30p multicolored 1.10 1.10

1998 Tourist Trophy Motorcycle Races — A182

Designs: 21p, Eight-man pyramid. 25p, Joey Dunlop rounding curve. 31p, Dave Molyneux with side car. 43p, Naomi Taniguchi racing. 63p, Mike Hailwood racing.

1998, June 1 Litho. ***Perf. 14***

788 A182 21p multicolored .65 .65
789 A182 25p multicolored .85 .85
790 A182 31p multicolored 1.05 1.05
791 A182 43p multicolored 1.35 1.35
792 A182 63p multicolored 2.10 2.10
Nos. 788-792 (5) 6.00 6.00

A183

Diana, Princess of Wales (1961-97): a, In black evening dress. b, Accepting flowers. c, Holding hand to face. d, In protective clothing.

1998, June 19 ***Perf. 13***

793 A183 25p Strip of 4, #a.-d. 3.50 3.50
e. As "a," dated "2017," perf. 13½x13 .65 .65
f. As "b," dated "2017," perf. 13½x13 .65 .65
g. As "c," dated "2017," perf. 13½x13 .65 .65
h. As "d," dated "2017," perf. 13½x13 .65 .65
i. Horiz. strip of 4, #793e-793h 2.60 2.60

Issued: Nos. 793e-793i, 9/6/17.

Flower Type

Perf. 13, 13x13½ (5p, 22p, 26p)

1998-99 Litho.

Flowers: 1p, Bearded iris. 2p, Daisy. 5p, Silver jubilee rose. 10p, Oriental poppy. 20p, Heath spotted orchid. 22p, Gorse. 26p, Dog rose. 30p, Fuchsia - lady thumb.

794 A177 1p multicolored .25 .25
795 A177 2p multicolored .25 .25
796 A177 5p multicolored .25 .25
797 A177 10p multicolored .40 .40
798 A177 20p multicolored .80 .80
799 A177 22p multicolored .85 .85
800 A177 26p multicolored 1.00 1.00
a. Bklt. pane, #800, 2 #766, 3 #799 4.00
Complete booklet, #800a 4.00
801 A177 30p multicolored 1.25 1.25
Nos. 794-801 (8) 5.05 5.05

Issued: 5p, 22p, 26p, 4/26/99; others, 7/2/98.

Queen Mother and Queen Elizabeth II A185

1998, July 2 Litho. ***Perf. 13***

802 A185 £2.50 multicolored 8.50 8.50

Christmas A186

Santa Claus: 20p, Loading sleigh at North Pole. 24p, With list, reindeer standing in clouds, Isle of Man below. 30p, Going over Spring Valley Sorting Office. 43p, Passing through Baldrine. 63p, Leaving presents, children inside house.

1998, Sept. 25 Litho. ***Perf. 14½x14***

803 A186 20p multicolored .60 .60
804 A186 24p multicolored .70 .70
805 A186 30p multicolored 1.05 1.05
806 A186 43p multicolored 1.35 1.35
807 A186 63p multicolored 2.10 2.10
Nos. 803-807 (5) 5.80 5.80

Manx Nature Reserve and Parks (Europa) — A187

Designs: 25p, Cottage, Ballaglass Glen. 30p, Glen Maye Waterfall.

1999, Mar. 4 Litho. ***Perf. 14***

808 A187 25p multicolored 1.00 1.00
809 A187 30p multicolored 1.25 1.25

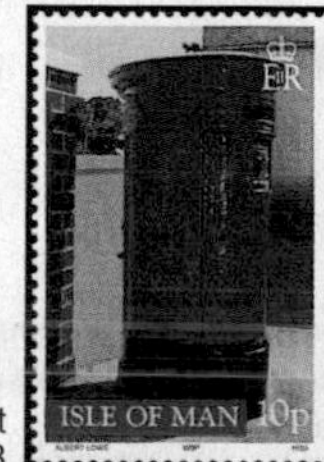

Post Boxes — A188

10p, Oval box, Kirk Onchan Post Office. 20p, Wall box, Ballaterson, Ballaugh. 21p, Cylindrical box, Laxey Station. 25p, Wall box, Spaldrick, Port Erin. 44p, Oval box, Derby Road, Douglas. 63p, Wall box, Baldrine Station.

1999, Mar. 4

810 A188 10p multicolored .35 .35
811 A188 20p multicolored .70 .70
812 A188 21p multicolored .70 .70
813 A188 25p multicolored .80 .80
814 A188 44p multicolored 1.35 1.35
815 A188 63p multicolored 2.00 2.00
Nos. 810-815 (6) 5.90 5.90

Royal Natl. Lifeboat Institution, 175th Anniv. — A189

21p, Ramsey lifeboat. 25p, Douglas lifeboat. 37p, Peel lifeboat. 43p, Port Erin lifeboat. 56p, Port St. Mary lifeboat. £1, William Hillary (1771-1847).

1999, Mar. 4

816 A189 21p multicolored .80 .80
817 A189 25p multicolored 1.00 1.00
818 A189 37p multicolored 1.50 1.50
819 A189 43p multicolored 1.60 1.60
820 A189 56p multicolored 3.00 2.00
a. Bklt. pane, #816-820 + 4 labels 7.00
Nos. 816-820 (5) 7.90 6.90

Booklet Stamps

821 A189 43p #38 5.00 5.00
822 A189 56p #464 7.00 7.00
a. Booklet pane, #816-818, #821-822 + 4 labels 16.00

Souvenir Sheet

823 A189 £1 multicolored 4.00 4.00
a. Booklet pane of 1 4.00
Complete booklet, #820a, #822a, #823a 27.00

IBRA '99 (No. 822a), Australia '99, World Stamp Expo. (No. 823). No. 823 contains one 38x50mm stamp.

An unstitched booklet pane containing 1 each of Nos. 816-818, 821-822 exists, just as No. 822a, but without the stitching.

Celtic Jewelry Depicting Seasons — A190

1999, May 11 ***Perf. 14½x14***

824 A190 22p Winter .70 .70
825 A190 26p Spring .80 .80
826 A190 50p Summer 1.50 1.50
827 A190 63p Autumn 2.00 2.00
Nos. 824-827 (4) 5.00 5.00

Manx Gaelic Society, Centennial.

20th Century British Monarchs A191

Monarch and Lord of Man: a, Victoria. b, Edward VII. c, George V. d, Edward VIII. e, George VI. f, Elizabeth II.

1999, June 2 Litho. ***Perf. 14***

828 A191 26p Sheet of 6, #a.-f. 5.50 5.50

Manx Buses A192

22p, 1922 Tilling Stevens 46 double-decker. 26p, 1928 Thornycroft BC 28-seat. 28p, 1927 ADC 416 28-seat. 37p, 1914 Staker Squire 25-seat. 38p, 1927 Thornycroft A2 20-seat. 40p, 1938 Leyland Lion LT9 34-seat.

1999, June 18

829 A192 22p multicolored .70 .70
830 A192 26p multicolored .80 .80
831 A192 28p multicolored .90 .90
832 A192 37p multicolored 1.20 1.20

833 A192 38p multicolored 1.20 1.20
834 A192 40p multicolored 1.30 1.30
Nos. 829-834 (6) 6.10 6.10

831a Bklt. pane, #829-830, 2 #831 3.50
832a Bklt. pane, #829-830, 2 #832 4.00
833a Bklt. pane, #829-830, 2 #833 4.00
834a Bklt. pane, #829-830, 2 #834 4.25
Complete booklet, #831a-834a 16.00

Wedding of Prince Edward and Sophie Rhys-Jones — A193

22p, Sophie, vert. 39p, Prince Edward, vert. 44p, Couple.

1999, June 19
835 A193 22p multicolored .70 .70
836 A193 30p multicolored 1.20 1.20
837 A193 44p multicolored 1.35 1.35
Nos. 835-837 (3) 3.25 3.25

Royal Wedding Photos — A193a

Designs: 26p, Couple standing. 53p, Couple seated in carriage, horiz.

1999, Sept. 1 Litho. *Perf. 14¼*
837A A193a 26p multi .85 .85
837B A193a 53p multi 1.75 1.75

Churches — A194

21p, St. Luke, Baldwin. 25p, St. Mark's, Malew. 30p, St. Germain Parish Church and Cathedral, Peel. 64p, Kirk Christ Church, Rushan.

Perf. 13¼x13½
1999, Sept. 22 Litho.
838 A194 21p multicolored .65 .65
839 A194 25p multicolored .75 .75
840 A194 30p multicolored .90 .90
841 A194 64p multicolored 2.00 2.00
Nos. 838-841 (4) 4.30 4.30

Bee Gees Songs A195

Designs: 22p, "Massachusetts." 26p, "Words." 29p, "I've Gotta Get a Message to You." 37p, "Ellan Vannin." 38p, "You Win Again." 66p, "Night Fever."
60p, "Immortality." 90p, "Stayin' Alive."

1999, Oct. 12 Litho. *Perf. 13¼x13½*
842 A195 22p multicolored .70 .70
843 A195 26p multicolored .80 .80
844 A195 29p multicolored .90 .90
845 A195 37p multicolored 1.10 1.10
846 A195 38p multicolored 1.10 1.10
847 A195 66p multicolored 2.00 2.00
Nos. 842-847 (6) 6.60 6.60

Souvenir Sheets
848 A195 60p multicolored 4.00 4.00
849 A195 90p multicolored 6.00 6.00

Nos. 848-849 each contain one 40mm diameter stamp. Nos. 842-847 each issued in sheets of 9 stamps and 3 labels.

Souvenir Sheet

Millennium — A196

Objects in the night sky: a, 50p, Mars, stars Deneb, Altair, Vega. b, £2, Constellations Lynx, Draco, Ursa Minor, Ursa Major. c, 50p, Mercury, Venus, Deneb, Vega, Altair, orbit of International Space Station (ISS).

Perf. 14¼x14½
1999, Dec. 31 Litho.
850 A196 Sheet of 3, #a.-c. 10.00 10.00

History of Time — A197

Clock escapements of: 22p, 1735 by John Harrison. 26p, 2000 by George Daniels. 29p, 1767 by Harrison. 34p, 1769 by Thomas Mudge. 38p, 1779 by John Arnold. 44p, 1780 by Thomas Earnshaw.

2000, Jan. 24 Litho. *Perf. 13x13½*
851 A197 22p multi .80 .80
852 A197 26p multi .90 .90
853 A197 29p multi 1.00 1.00
854 A197 34p multi 1.20 1.20
855 A197 38p multi 1.40 1.40
856 A197 44p multi 1.60 1.60
Nos. 851-856 (6) 6.90 6.90

Queen Mother (b. 1900) — A198

Pictures of Queen Mother from — No. 857: a, 1923. b, 1940. c, 1944.
No. 858: a, 1954. b, 1985. c, 1988.
No. 859, 1984.
£1, Queen Mother on Isle of Man.

2000, Feb. 29 Litho. *Perf. 14*
857 Strip of 3 2.50 2.50
a. A198 22p multi .65 .65
b. A198 26p multi .85 .85
c. A198 30p multi .90 .90
858 Strip of 3 5.00 5.00
a. A198 44p multi 1.35 1.35
b. A198 52p multi 1.60 1.60
c. A198 64p multi 2.00 2.00

Souvenir Sheet
Perf. 14¼
859 A198 £1 multi 3.75 3.75
a. With emblem of The Stamp Show 2000 in margin 8.50 8.50

Size of Nos. 857a-857c, 858a-858c, 42x28mm.
Issued: No. 859a, 5/22/00.

Song Birds — A199

2000, May 5 *Perf. 14½x14¼*
860 Strip of 4 6.75 6.75
a. A199 22p Swallow .80 .80
b. A199 26p Spotted flycatcher .90 .90
c. A199 64p Skylark 2.25 2.25
d. A199 77p Yellowhammer 2.60 2.60

World Wildlife Fund.

Military Leaders and Isle of Man Military Personnel A200

Battle of Britain, 60th Anniv. — A201

No. 861: a, John Quilliam (1771-1829), Admiral Lord Nelson (1758-1805). b, Caesar Bacon (1791-1876), Duke of Wellington (1769-1852).
No. 862: a, Thomas Leigh Goldie (1807-54), Earl of Cardigan (1797-1868). b, John Dunne (1884-1950), Sir Robert Baden-Powell (1857-1941).
No. 863: a, George Kneale (1896-1917), Viscount Kitchener (1850-1916). b, Alan Watterson (1910-42), Sir Winston Churchill (1874-1965).
No. 864: a, 60p, Planes in air. b, 60p, Plane on ground.

2000, May 22 Litho. *Perf. 13¼*
861 Pair, #a-b, + central label 1.60 1.60
a. A200 22p multi .70 .70
b. A200 26p multi .85 .85
862 Pair, #a-b, + central label 2.75 2.75
a. A200 36p multi 1.20 1.20
b. A200 48p multi 1.50 1.50
863 Pair, #a-b, + central label 4.00 4.00
a. A200 50p multi 1.60 1.60
b. A200 77p multi 2.40 2.40
c. Booklet pane, #861a, 861b, 862a, 862b, 863a 6.00
d. Booklet pane, #861a, 862b, 863a, 863b 5.75
Nos. 861-863 (3) 8.35 8.35

Souvenir Sheet
Perf. 14¾x14¼
864 A201 Sheet of 2, #a-b 5.25 5.25
c. Booklet pane, #864 5.25
Booklet, #863c, 863d, 864c 17.00

No. 864c has stitched margin at left.

Souvenir Sheet

Prince William, 18th Birthday — A202

2000, June 21 Litho. *Perf. 14*
865 A202 Sheet of 5 6.50 6.50
a. 22p As toddler .80 .80
b. 26p With Queen Mother 1.00 1.00
c. 45p In checked shirt 1.75 1.75
d. 52p With Princes Charles, Harry 1.90 1.90
e. 56p In ski gear 2.00 2.00

Gaiety Theater, Cent. A203

2000, July 16
866 A203 22p Ballet .70 .70
867 A203 26p Comedy .85 .85
868 A203 36p Drama 1.20 1.20
869 A203 45p Pantomime 1.50 1.50
870 A203 52p Opera 1.60 1.60
871 A203 65p Musicals 2.00 2.00
Nos. 866-871 (6) 7.85 7.85

Global Challenge Yacht Race — A204

Sail from yacht "Isle of Man," and ports of call: 22p, Southampton. 26p, Sydney. 36p, Wellington. 40p, Buenos Aires. 44p, Boston. 65p, Cape Town.

Perf. 13¼x13¾
2000, Sept. 10 Litho.
872 A204 22p multi .65 .65
873 A204 26p multi .85 .85
874 A204 36p multi 1.20 1.20
875 A204 40p multi 1.25 1.25
876 A204 44p multi 1.35 1.35
877 A204 65p multi 2.00 2.00
Nos. 872-877 (6) 7.30 7.30

Travel Poster Art of Isle of Man Steam Packet Co. — A205

Designs: 22p, Three legs of Man, ship. 26p, Cliffs and sailboats. 36p, Woman and Isle of Man. 45p, Woman, ship, flag. 65p, Ship.

2000, Oct. 6 *Perf. 13½x13¼*
878 A205 22p multi .65 .65
879 A205 26p multi .80 .80
880 A205 36p multi 1.10 1.10
881 A205 45p multi 1.40 1.40
882 A205 65p multi 1.90 1.90
Nos. 878-882 (5) 5.85 5.85

Europa, 2000
Common Design Type

2000, Nov. 7 *Perf. 14*
883 CD17 36p multi 1.75 1.75

Christmas A206

2000, Nov. 7
884 A206 21p Peace .75 .75
885 A206 25p Hope .85 .85
886 A206 45p Love 1.60 1.60
887 A206 65p Faith 2.25 2.25
Nos. 884-887 (4) 5.45 5.45

Souvenir Sheet

New Year 2001 (Year of the Snake) — A207

Litho. with Foil Application
2001, Jan. 22 *Perf. 13¾*
888 A207 £1 St. Patrick 4.00 4.00

Hong Kong 2001 Stamp Exhibition.

Queen Victoria (1819-1901) — A208

Designs: 22p, Wyon medal, Queen Victoria, Great Britain Type A1. 26p, Great Exhibition medal, Albert Tower. 34p, Coin, Steamship Great Britain. 39p, Coin, scene from Oliver Twist, St. Thomas' Church, Douglas. 40p, Coin, first train to arrive in Vancouver, Canada and Jubilee streetlamp standard. 52p, Coin,

Foxdale Clock Tower, family of diamond magnate Joe Mylchreest.

2001, Jan. 22 Litho. *Perf. 13½*

889	A208	22p multi	.70	.70
890	A208	26p multi	.80	.80
891	A208	34p multi	1.10	1.10
892	A208	39p multi	1.20	1.20
893	A208	40p multi	1.30	1.30
894	A208	52p multi	1.60	1.60
		Nos. 889-894 (6)	6.70	6.70

Insects
A209

Designs: 22p, White-tailed bumblebee. 26p, Seven-spot ladybug. 29p, Lesser mottled grasshopper. 58p, Manx robber fly. 66p, Elephant hawkmoth.

2001, Feb. 1 *Perf. 14½*

895	A209	22p multi	.70	.70
896	A209	26p multi	.85	.85
897	A209	29p multi	.95	.95
898	A209	58p multi	1.90	1.90
899	A209	66p multi	2.10	2.10
		Nos. 895-899 (5)	6.50	6.50

Souvenir Sheet

Queen Elizabeth II, 75th Birthday — A210

Stamps: 29p, Great Britain #MH1. 34p, Great Britain #300. 37p, Isle of Man #8. 50p, Isle of Man #3.

2001, Apr. 18 Litho. *Perf. 14*

900	A210	Sheet of 4, #a-d	5.50	5.50
e.		As #900, with Hafnia 01 emblem added in sheet margin	*10.50*	*10.50*

No. 900e issued 10/29.

Manx Postmen and Cancels — A211

2001, Apr. 18

901	A211	22p 1805	.70	.70
902	A211	26p 1859	.85	.85
903	A211	30p 1910	1.20	1.20
904	A211	39p 1933	1.30	1.30
905	A211	40p 1983	1.35	1.35
906	A211	66p 2001	2.10	2.10
		Nos. 901-906 (6)	7.50	7.50

William Joseph Dunlop (1952-2000), Motorcycle Racer — A212

Various photographs.

2001, May 17

907	A212	22p multi	.70	.70
908	A212	26p multi	.85	.85
909	A212	36p multi	1.20	1.20
910	A212	45p multi	1.50	1.50
911	A212	65p multi	2.10	2.10
912	A212	77p multi	2.40	2.40
a.		Sheet of 12, 6 each #911-912, + 6 labels	27.00	27.00
		Nos. 907-912 (6)	8.75	8.75

Issued: No. 912a, 5/15/13. No. 912a sold for £9.97.

Horse Racing A213

Designs: 22p, Manx Derby. 26p, Post Haste. 36p, Red Rum. 52p, Hyperion. 63p, Isle of Man.

2001, May 18 *Perf. 13¼x13½*

913	A213	22p multi	.75	.75
914	A213	26p multi	.90	.90
915	A213	36p multi	1.25	1.25
916	A213	52p multi	1.75	1.75
917	A213	63p multi	2.10	2.10
		Nos. 913-917 (5)	6.75	6.75

Gourmet Food — A214

2001, Aug. 10 Litho. *Perf. 14¼*

918	A214	22p Beef	.70	.70
919	A214	26p Queenies	.75	.75
a.		Sheet of 10	7.50	—
920	A214	36p Seafood	1.05	1.05
a.		Sheet of 10	10.50	—
921	A214	45p Lamb	1.35	1.35
922	A214	50p Kippers	1.60	1.60
923	A214	66p Lemon tart	2.00	2.00
		Nos. 918-923 (6)	7.45	7.45

Europa (Nos. 919, 920).

Architecture of Mackay Hugh Baillie Scott — A215

Designs: 22p, Castletown Police Station, 1901. 26p, Leafield/Braeside, 1897. 37p, Red House, 1893. 40p, Ivydene, 1893. 80p, Onchan Village Hall, 1898.

2001, Sept. 3 *Perf. 13¼x13½*

924	A215	22p multi	.75	.75
925	A215	26p multi	.85	.85
926	A215	37p multi	1.20	1.20
927	A215	40p multi	1.35	1.35
928	A215	80p multi	2.60	2.60
		Nos. 924-928 (5)	6.75	6.75

Reign of Queen Elizabeth II, 50th Anniv. (in 2002) — A216

Drawings of Queen: 22p, At dining table. 26p, With crowd, holding flower bouquet. 39p, With dogs. 40p, With men wearing hats. 45p, With correspondence. 65p, Alone, holding flower bouquet.

Litho. With Foil Application

2001-02 *Perf. 14¼*

929	A216	22p multi	.70	.70
930	A216	26p multi	.80	.80
931	A216	39p multi	1.30	1.30
a.		Booklet pane of 3, #929-931	3.00	—
932	A216	40p multi	1.30	1.30
933	A216	45p multi	1.40	1.40
934	A216	65p multi	2.00	2.00
a.		Booklet pane of 3, #932-934	5.00	—
		Nos. 929-934 (6)	7.50	7.50

Issued: Nos. 929-934, 10/29/01. Nos. 931a, 934a, 2/6/02.

Christmas A217

Floral arrangements: 21p, Holly on Christmas tree-shaped frame. 25p, Wreath. 37p, Table decoration with candles. 45p, Topiary tree. 65p, Wreath, diff.

Stamp + Label

2001, Nov. 5 Litho. *Perf. 14x14½*

Background Color

935	A217	21p green	.70	.70
936	A217	25p red	.85	.85
937	A217	37p gold	1.20	1.20
938	A217	45p silver	1.50	1.50
939	A217	65p violet	2.00	2.00
		Nos. 935-939 (5)	6.25	6.25

Reign of Queen Elizabeth II, 50th Anniv. — A218

No. 940 — Paintings: a, The Coronation, by Terence Cuneo. b, Her Majesty the Queen as Colonel in Chief, Grenadier Guards on Imperial, by Cuneo (Queen on horse). c, Her Majesty in Evening Dress, by June Mendoza. d, Her Majesty the Queen, by Chen Yan Ning. e, The Royal Family, by John Wonnacott.

£1, Her Majesty Queen Elizabeth II Lord of Mann, sculpture by David Cregeen.

Litho. with Foil Application

2002, Feb. 6 *Perf. 14*

940		Vert. strip of 5	8.50	8.50
a.-e.		A218 50p Any single	1.75	1.75
f.		Booklet pane of 3, #940a-940c	5.50	—
g.		Booklet pane of 2, #940d-940e	3.75	—

Souvenir Sheet

Perf. 14½x14

941	A218	£1 multi	3.50	3.50
a.		Booklet pane of 1 with larger margin	3.50	—
		Complete booklet, #931a, 934a, 940f, 940g, 941a	21.00	
b.		As 941, inscribed in sheet margin in purple The Isle of Man Celebrates The Jubilee / 4th June 2002	0.00	0.00

No. 941 contains one 60x40mm stamp.

17th Commonwealth Games, Manchester, England — A219

Designs: 22p, Cycling. 26p, Running. 29p, Javelin, women's high jump. 34p, Swimming. 40p, Hurdles, pole vault. 45p, Wheelchair racing.

2002, Mar. 11 Litho. *Perf. 14*

942	A219	22p multi	.75	.75
943	A219	26p multi	.85	.85
944	A219	29p multi	1.05	1.05
945	A219	34p multi	1.20	1.20
946	A219	40p multi	1.40	1.40
947	A219	45p multi	1.50	1.50
		Nos. 942-947 (6)	6.75	6.75

Queen Mother Elizabeth (1900-2002) A220

2002, Apr. 23 *Perf. 13x13¼*

948	A220	£3 multi	10.00	10.00

Paintings by Toni Onley A221

Designs: 22p, Monks' Bridge, Ballasalla. 26p, Laxey. 37p, Langness Lighthouse. 45p, King William's College. 65p, The Mull Circle & Bradda Head.

2002, May 1 *Perf. 13¼x13½*

949	A221	22p multi	.75	.75
950	A221	26p multi	.85	.85
951	A221	37p multi	1.30	1.30
952	A221	45p multi	1.50	1.50
953	A221	65p multi	2.10	2.10
		Nos. 949-953 (5)	6.50	6.50

2002 World Cup Soccer Championships, Japan and Korea — A222

Various players.

2002, May 1 *Perf. 13½*

954	A222	22p multi	.75	.75
955	A222	26p multi	.85	.85
956	A222	39p multi	1.35	1.35
957	A222	40p multi	1.35	1.35
958	A222	66p multi	2.10	2.10
959	A222	68p multi	2.40	2.40
		Nos. 954-959 (6)	8.80	8.80

Flower Sketches by Sir Paul McCartney A223

Various sketches.

2002, July 1 Litho. *Perf. 13¼x12¾*

960	A223	22p multi	.75	.75
961	A223	26p multi	.90	.90
962	A223	29p multi	1.00	1.00
963	A223	52p multi	1.75	1.75
964	A223	63p multi	2.25	2.25
965	A223	77p multi	2.75	2.75
		Nos. 960-965 (6)	9.40	9.40

Photographs of Local Scenes — A224

Nos. 966-967: a, Laxey Wheel, by Kathy Brown. b, Sheep at Druidale, by John Hall. c, Carousel at Silverdale, by Colin Edwards. d, Grandma, by Stephanie Corkill. e, Manx Rock, by Ruth Nicholls. f, TT Riders at Signpost, by Neil Brew. g, Groudle Railway, by Albert Lowe. h, Royal Cascade, by Brian Speedie. i, St. Johns, by John Hall. j, Niarbyl Cottages with Poppies, by Cathy Galbraith.

2002 Litho. *Perf. 14*

966 Block of 10 9.50 9.50
a.-j. A224 27p Any single .95 .95

Self-Adhesive

Serpentine Die Cut 6¼

967 Booklet of 10 16.00
a.-j. A224 27p Any single 1.60 1.60

Designs: a, Manx Milestone, by Mrs. B. J. Trimble. b, Plow Horses, by Miss D. Flint. c, Manx Emblem, by Ruth Nicholls. d, Loaghtan Sheep, by Diana Buford. e, Fishing Fleet at Port St. Mary, by Phil Thomas. f, Peel, by Michael Thompson. g, Daffodils, by Michael Thompson. h, Millennium Sword, by Mr. F. K. Smith. i, Peel Castle, by Kathy Brown. j, Snaefell Railway, by Joan Burgess.

Litho

Perf. 14

968 Block of 10 9.00 9.00
a.-j. A224 23p Any single .90 .90

Self-Adhesive

Serpentine Die Cut 6¼

969 Booklet of 10 16.00
a.-j. A224 23p Any single 1.60 1.60

Issued: Nos. 966-967, 8/30; Nos. 968-969, 10/1.

Christmas and Europa — A225

Designs: 22p, Santa Claus. 26p, Madonna and Child. 37p, Clown. 47p, Cymbal player. 68p, Fairy.
£1.30, "Christmas."

2002, Nov. 5 *Perf. 14x14½*

970 A225 22p multi .80 .80
971 A225 26p multi .95 .95
972 A225 37p multi 1.50 1.50
a. Sheet of 10 + 10 labels 15.00 15.00
973 A225 47p multi 1.50 1.50
974 A225 68p multi 2.50 2.50
Nos. 970-974 (5) 7.25 7.25

Miniature Sheet

Perf. 14¾

975 A225 £1.30 multi 5.00 5.00

Europa (No. 972). No. 975 contains one 99x38mm stamp.

Post Office Vehicles A226

Designs: 23p, Handcart. 27p, Morris Z van. 37p, Morris LD van. 42p, DI BSA Bantam motorcycle. 89p, Ford Escort 55 delivery van.

2003, Feb. 14 *Perf. 14¼*

976 A226 23p multi .90 .90
977 A226 27p multi 1.10 1.10
978 A226 37p multi 1.35 1.35
979 A226 42p multi 1.60 1.60
980 A226 89p multi 3.25 3.25
Nos. 976-980 (5) 8.20 8.20

Space Exploration — A227

No. 981: a, Tromode Teleport. b, Satellite earth station.

No. 982: a, Pioneering the space frontier (denomination at left). b, Pioneering the space frontier (denomination at right).

No. 983: a, Sea Launch Odyssey launch platform. b, Sea Launch Commander.

No. 984: a, Loral Skynet Telstar 1. b, Loral Skynet Telstar 8.

No. 985: a, Space station, Phobos. b, Astronauts, Mars.

2003, Feb. 14 *Perf. 13¼x13½*

981 A227 Horiz. pair 1.50 1.50
a.-b. 23p Either single .75 .75
982 A227 Horiz. pair 1.90 1.90
a.-b. 27p Either single .95 .95
983 A227 Horiz. pair 2.60 2.60
a.-b. 37p Either single 1.30 1.30
984 A227 Horiz. pair 2.75 2.75
a.-b. 42p Either single 1.35 1.35
Nos. 981-984 (4) 8.75 8.75

Souvenir Sheet

Perf. 13¼x13

985 A227 Horiz. pair 6.00 6.00
a.-b. 75p Either single 3.00 3.00

No. 985 contains two 29x38mm stamps.

Coronation of Queen Elizabeth II, 50th Anniv. — A228

No. 986: a, Queen wearing St. Edward's Crown (brown background, 29x59mm). b, Queen wearing Sovereign's ring and armills (29x29mm). c, Sovereign's orb (29x29mm). d, Scepter with Cross, Rod with Dove (29x29mm). e, Queen wearing Imperial State Crown (blue green background, 29x59mm) f, Queen in State Coach (89x29mm).

Litho. With Foil Application

2003, Apr. 12 *Perf. 13¼*

986 A228 Block of 6 10.00 10.00
a.-f. 50p Any single 1.60 1.60

Powered Flight, Cent. — A229

No. 987: a, DH 83 Fox Moth, Saro Cloud. b, DH 61 Giant Moth, DH Puss Moth. c, Avro Anson, B-17 Flying Fortress.

No. 988: a, Eurofighter Typhoon, Avro Vulcan. b, Handley Page Herald, Bristol Wayfarer. c, Concorde, A380 Airbus.

2003, May 9 Litho. *Perf. 13¼*

987 Strip of 3 3.00 3.00
a. A229 23p multi .75 .75
b. A229 27p multi .95 .95
c. A229 37p multi 1.30 1.30
988 Strip of 3 7.00 7.00
a. A229 40p multi 1.40 1.40
b. A229 67p multi 2.40 2.40
c. A229 89p multi 3.00 3.00

Souvenir Sheet

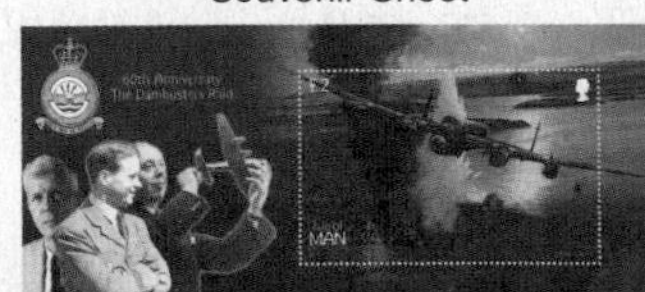

Dambuster's Raid, 60th Anniv. — A230

2003

989 A230 £2 multi 7.00 7.00
a. With "Ticino 2003" emblem in margin 8.50 8.50

Issued: No. 989, 5/9; No. 989a, 6/18.

Prince William, 21st Birthday A231

Various photographs.

2003, June 9 *Perf. 13¼x13½*

990 A231 42p black 1.50 1.50
991 A231 47p black 1.75 1.75
992 A231 52p black 1.75 1.75
993 A231 68p black 2.25 2.25
Nos. 990-993 (4) 7.25 7.25

Literature With Manx Connections — A232

Designs: 23p, Manx Gold, by Agatha Christie. 27p, Quartermass and the Pit, by Nigel Kneale. 30p, Flashman at the Charge, by George MacDonald Fraser. 38p, The Eternal City, by Hall Caine. 40p, Islanders, by Mona Douglas. 53p, Emma's Secret, by Barbara Taylor Bradford.

2003, July 9 *Perf. 13¼*

Stamp + Label

994 A232 23p multi .80 .80
995 A232 27p multi 1.00 1.00
996 A232 30p multi 1.10 1.10
997 A232 38p multi 1.50 1.50
a. Sheet of 10 + 10 labels 15.00 15.00
998 A232 40p multi 1.45 1.45
999 A232 53p multi 1.75 1.75
Nos. 994-999 (6) 7.60 7.60

Europa (No. 997).

End of Tudor Reign, 400th Anniv. A233

Designs: 23p, Crowning of King Henry VII at Bosworth. 27p, King Henry VIII, Dissolution of the Monasteries. 38p, Queen Elizabeth I, Sir Francis Drake circumnavigates the globe. 40p, King Henry VIII, Hampton Court. 47p, Queen Mary I, Tudor rose. 67p, Queen Elizabeth I, Spanish Armada.

2003, Sept. 15 *Perf. 14*

1000 A233 23p multi .75 .75
1001 A233 27p multi .95 .95
1002 A233 38p multi 1.30 1.30
1003 A233 40p multi 1.35 1.35
1004 A233 47p multi 1.60 1.60
1005 A233 67p multi 2.10 2.10
Nos. 1000-1005 (6) 8.05 8.05

Henry Bloom Noble Trust, Cent. — A234

No. 1006: a, Boys' Orphanage. b, Ramsey Cottage Hospital. c, Children's Home. d, Noble's Baths. e, Scout Headquarters.

No. 1007: a, Noble's Hospital. b, Villa Marina. c, Noble's Park. d, St. Ninian's Church. e, Noble's Library.

2003, Oct. 1

1006 Horiz. strip of 5 3.75 3.75
a.-e. A234 23p Any single .75 .75
1007 Horiz. strip of 5 4.75 4.75
a.-e. A234 27p Any single .95 .95

Booklet Stamps

Self-Adhesive

Serpentine Die Cut 6¼

1007F A234 23p Like #1006a 1.25 1.25
1007G A234 23p Like #1006b 1.25 1.25
1007H A234 23p Like #1006c 1.25 1.25
1007I A234 23p Like #1006d 1.25 1.25
1007J A234 23p Like #1006e 1.25 1.25
p. Booklet pane, 2 each #1007F-1007J 12.50 12.50
1007K A234 27p Like #1007a 1.50 1.50
1007L A234 27p Like #1007b 1.50 1.50
1007M A234 27p Like #1007c 1.50 1.50
1007N A234 27p Like #1007d 1.50 1.50
1007O A234 27p Like #1007e 1.50 1.50
q. Booklet pane, 2 each #1007K-1007O 15.00
Nos. 1007F-1007O (10) 13.75 13.75

Nos. 1007Jp and 1007Oq are complete booklets, the backing serving as the booklet covers.

Christmas A235

Various snowmen, based on Raymond Briggs' children's story *The Snowman*.

Litho. With Foil Application

2003, Nov. 5 *Perf. 14¼*

Background Color

1008 A235 22p red .80 .80
1009 A235 26p deep blue .90 .90
1010 A235 38p blue green 1.35 1.35
1011 A235 47p orange 1.75 1.75
1012 A235 68p yellow 2.25 2.25
Nos. 1008-1012 (5) 7.05 7.05

Debut of Movie *The Lord of the Rings: The Return of the King* — A236

Designs: 23p, Aragorn. 27p, Gimli. 30p, Gandalf the White. 38p, Legolas on horseback. 42p, Gollum. 47p, Frodo Baggins and Samwise Gamgee. 68p, Legolas with bow and arrow. 85p, Aragorn on horseback.
£2, Ring.

2003, Dec. 17 Litho. *Perf. 13¼*

1013 A236 23p multi .75 .75
1014 A236 27p multi .95 .95
1015 A236 30p multi 1.10 1.10
1016 A236 38p multi 1.30 1.30
1017 A236 42p multi 1.35 1.35
1018 A236 47p multi 1.60 1.60
1019 A236 68p multi 2.40 2.40
1020 A236 85p multi 3.00 3.00
Nos. 1013-1020 (8) 12.45 12.45

Souvenir Sheet

Perf. 13½

1021 A236 £2 multi 7.50 7.50

No. 1021 contains one 44x39mm stamp. Nos. 1013-1020 were each printed in sheets of six.

Steam Locomotives — A237

Designs: 23p, Maitland. 27p, Evening Star. 40p, Penydarren Tramroad locomotive. 57p, Duchess of Hamilton. 61p, City of Truro. 90p, Mallard.

2004, Feb. 21 Litho. *Perf. 13x13½*

1022 A237 23p multi .85 .85
1023 A237 27p multi 1.10 1.10
1024 A237 40p multi 1.50 1.50
1025 A237 57p multi 1.90 1.90
1026 A237 61p multi 2.25 2.25
1027 A237 90p multi 3.00 3.00
Nos. 1022-1027 (6) 10.60 10.60

D-Day, 60th Anniv. — A238

No. 1028: a, Two soldiers near walkways, tanks on beach. b, Soldiers in water, tanks on beach.

No. 1029: a, Soldiers in water between two boats. b, Soldiers in water, landing craft with gangway open.

No. 1030: a, Lady of Mann, two blimps. b, Ben-my-Chree, three landing craft, five blimps.

No. 1031: a, Two US B-24 Liberators, RAF Horsa glider. b, Three RAF Horsa gliders.

No. 1032: a, Sir Winston Churchill. b, Soldiers near airplane propeller. c, Military vehicles on street in residential area. d, Soldiers reading book.

Illustration reduced.

2004, Apr. 6 ***Perf. 14***

1028	A238 Horiz. pair	1.60	1.60
a.-b.	23p Either single	.80	.80
c.	As "a," dated "2014" (#1658a)	.70	.70
d.	As "b," dated "2014" (#1658a)	.70	.70
1029	A238 Horiz. pair	1.90	1.90
a.-b.	27p Either single	.95	.95
c.	As "a," dated "2014" (#1658a)	.80	.80
d.	As "b," dated "2014" (#1658a)	.80	.80
1030	A238 Horiz. pair	3.25	3.25
a.-b.	47p Either single	1.60	1.60
c.	As "a," dated "2014" (#1658a)	1.35	1.35
d.	As "b," dated "2014" (#1658a)	1.35	1.35
1031	A238 Horiz. pair	4.50	4.50
a.-b.	68p Either single	2.25	2.25
c.	As "a," dated "2014" (#1658a)	1.90	1.90
d.	As "b," dated "2014" (#1658a)	1.90	1.90
	Nos. 1028-1031 (4)	11.25	11.25

Souvenir Sheet

Perf. 13¼x13¾

1032	A238 Sheet of 4	8.00	8.00
a.-d.	50p Any single	2.00	2.00
e.	As "a," perf. 14, dated "2014" (#1658a)	1.75	1.75
f.	As "d," perf. 14, dated "2014" (#1658a)	1.75	1.75

Issued: Nos. 1028c, 1028d, 1029c, 1029d, 1030c, 1030d, 1031c, 1031d, 1032e, 1032f, 5/8/14.

Flowers A239

Designs: 25p, Lesser celandine. 28p, Red campion. 37p, Devil's bit scabious. 40p, Northern harebell. 68p, Wood anemone. 85p, Common spotted orchid.

2004, May 3 ***Perf. 13½***

1033	A239 25p multi	.85	.85
1034	A239 28p multi	.95	.95
1035	A239 37p multi	1.30	1.30
1036	A239 40p multi	1.35	1.35
1037	A239 68p multi	2.40	2.40
1038	A239 85p multi	3.00	3.00
	Nos. 1033-1038 (6)	9.85	9.85

George Formby (1904-61), Movie Actor — A240

Various scenes from film *No Limit* and text: 25p, No Limit. 28p, George. 40p, Speed Demon. 43p, Florence. 50p, Shuttleworth. 74p, Formby.

2004, May 26 ***Perf. 13¼***

1039	A240 25p multi	.85	.85
1040	A240 28p multi	.95	.95
1041	A240 40p multi	1.35	1.35
1042	A240 43p multi	1.50	1.50
1043	A240 50p multi	1.75	1.75
1044	A240 74p multi	2.60	2.60
	Nos. 1039-1044 (6)	9.00	9.00

2004 Summer Olympics, Athens A241

Designs: 25p, Johnny Weismuller, Paris Olympics, 1924. 28p, Jesse Owens, runners, Berlin Olympics, 1936. 43p, John Mark, torch bearer, London Olympics, 1948. 55p, Fanny Blankers-Koen, runners, London Olympics, 1948. 91p, Sir Steve Redgrave, rowers, Sydney Olympics, 2000.

2004, July 1 **Litho.** ***Perf. 14***

1045	A241 25p multi	.85	.85
1046	A241 28p multi	1.05	1.05
1047	A241 43p multi	1.50	1.50
1048	A241 55p multi	1.90	1.90
1049	A241 91p multi	3.25	3.25
	Nos. 1045-1049 (5)	8.55	8.55

Manx History — A242

Designs: Nos. 1050a, 1052, Celtic islander and Viking invaders. Nos. 1050b, 1053, Ships and the sea. Nos. 1050c, 1054, Laxey miners. Nos. 1050d, 1055, Kings and Lords of Mann. Nos. 1050e, 1056, Farmers and crofters. Nos. 1051a, 1057, Calf of Man. Nos. 1051b, 1058, Peel Castle. Nos. 1051c, 1059, Laxey Wheel. Nos. 1051d, 1060, Castle Rushen. Nos. 1051e, 1061, Cregneash.

2004, Aug. 3 ***Perf. 14¼***

1050	Horiz. strip of 5	5.00	5.00
a.-e.	A242 (25p) Any single	1.00	1.00
1051	Horiz. strip of 5	5.50	5.50
a.-e.	A242 (28p) Any single	1.10	1.10

Booklet Stamps

Self-Adhesive

Serpentine Die Cut 12½

1052	A242 (25p) multi	1.10	1.10
1053	A242 (25p) multi	1.10	1.10
1054	A242 (25p) multi	1.10	1.10
1055	A242 (25p) multi	1.10	1.10
1056	A242 (25p) multi	1.10	1.10
a.	Booklet pane, 2 each #1052-1056	11.00	
1057	A242 (28p) multi	1.20	1.20
1058	A242 (28p) multi	1.20	1.20
1059	A242 (28p) multi	1.20	1.20
1060	A242 (28p) multi	1.20	1.20
1061	A242 (28p) multi	1.20	1.20
a.	Booklet pane, 2 each #1057-1061	12.00	
	Nos. 1050-1061 (12)	22.00	22.00

Nos. 1056a and 1061a are complete booklets, the backing serving as the booklet covers.

Souvenir Sheet

Laxey Wheel, 150th Anniv. — A243

2004, Aug. 3 ***Perf. 14¼***

1062	A243 £2 multi	7.75	7.75
a.	With Sindelfingen 2004 emblem added in sheet margin	13.00	13.00

No. 1062a issued 10/29.

Watercolors by Alfred Heaton Cooper (1864-1929) A244

Designs: 25p, Maughold Church. 28p, Port St. Mary. 40p, Ballaugh Old Church. 41p, Douglas Bay (A Midsummer's Night). 43p, Point of Ayre. 74p, Peel Harbor and Castle.

2004, Oct. 21 **Litho.** ***Perf. 13¼x12¾***

1063	A244 25p multi	1.00	1.00
1064	A244 28p multi	1.10	1.10
a.	Sheet of 10 + 10 labels	11.00	11.00
1065	A244 40p multi	1.60	1.60
a.	Sheet of 10 + 10 labels	16.00	16.00
1066	A244 41p multi	1.60	1.60
1067	A244 43p multi	1.75	1.75
1068	A244 74p multi	3.00	3.00
	Nos. 1063-1068 (6)	10.05	10.05

Europa (Nos. 1064-1065).

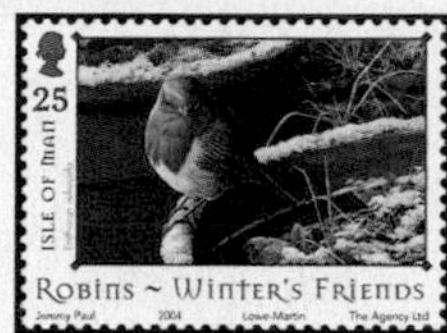

Robins A245

Robin on: 25p, Flowerpot. 28p, Rock. 40p, Branch. 47p, Window sill. 68p, Log.

2004, Nov. 9 ***Perf. 12½x13***

1069	A245 25p multi	.90	.90
1070	A245 28p multi	1.10	1.10
1071	A245 40p multi	1.60	1.60
1072	A245 47p multi	1.75	1.75
1073	A245 68p multi	2.50	2.50
a.	Miniature sheet, 2 each #1069-1073	24.00	24.00
	Nos. 1069-1073 (5)	7.85	7.85

Scenes from *Harry Potter and the Prisoner of Azkaban* A246

Designs: 25p, Harry Potter, Ron Weasley and Hermione Granger. 28p, Owl Post. 39p, Harry and Petronus. 40p, Hogwarts Express. 49p, Hagrid. 55p, Knight Bus. 57p, Harry and Dementor. 68p, Harry and Buckbeak.

2004, Dec. 7 ***Perf. 13¼***

1074	A246 25p multi	.90	.90
1075	A246 28p multi	1.10	1.10
1076	A246 39p multi	1.60	1.60
1077	A246 40p multi	1.75	1.75
1078	A246 49p multi	1.75	1.75
1079	A246 55p multi	2.00	2.00
1080	A246 57p multi	2.25	2.25
1081	A246 68p multi	2.50	2.50
	Nos. 1074-1081 (8)	13.85	13.85

Each printed in sheets of 5.

Battle of Trafalgar, Bicent. — A247

No. 1082: a, Nile Campaign. b, Battle of Copenhagen.

No. 1083: a, Emma Horatia Nelson. b, Band of brothers.

No. 1084: a, Prepare for battle. b, Victory in sight.

No. 1085: a, Fall of Nelson. b, Death of Nelson.

No. 1086: a, #861a. b, #159.

2005, Jan. 0 ***Perf. 12½x13***

1082	A247 Horiz. pair	1.90	1.90
a.-b.	25p Either single	.95	.95
1083	A247 Horiz. pair	2.10	2.10
a.-b.	28p Either single	1.05	1.05
1084	A247 Horiz. pair	3.50	3.50
a.-b.	50p Either single	1.75	1.75
1085	A247 Horiz. pair	4.50	4.50
a.-b.	65p Either single	2.25	2.25
	Nos. 1082-1085 (4)	12.00	12.00

Souvenir Sheet

Perf. 13¼x13

1086	A247 Sheet of 2	8.00	8.00
a.-b.	£1 Either single	4.00	4.00

Victory in World War II, 60th Anniv. — A248

No. 1087: a, Women and sailors. b, Soldiers and women marching together.

No. 1088: a, Soldier trying on hat. b, Servicewomen.

No. 1089: a, Winston Churchill and Royal family waving. b, Royal family in carriage.

No. 1090: a, Servicemen without shirts. b, Cemetery.

No. 1091: a, Manx Regiment. b, Royal visit, 1945.

2005, Apr. 15 **Litho.** ***Perf. 13¼x13¾***

1087	A248 Horiz. pair	1.90	1.90
a.-b.	26p Either single	.95	.95
1088	A248 Horiz. pair	2.10	2.10
a.-b.	29p Either single	1.05	1.05
1089	A248 Horiz. pair	4.25	4.25
a.-b.	60p Either single	2.10	2.10
1090	A248 Horiz. pair	5.00	5.00
a.-b.	65p Either single	2.50	2.50
	Nos. 1087-1090 (4)	13.25	13.25

Souvenir Sheet

1091	A248 Sheet of 2	8.50	8.50
a.-b.	£1 Either single	4.25	4.25

Paintings of Isle of Man Steam Packet Company Ships — A249

No. 1092: a, Mona's Isle, by Samuel Walters. b, Viking, by Norman Wilkinson.

No. 1093: a, King Orry, by Robert Lloyd. b, Mona's Queen, by Arthur Burgess.

No. 1094: a, Ben-my-Chree, by John Nicholson. b, King Orry, by Robert Lloyd, diff.

No. 1095: a, Ben-my-Chree, by Robert Lloyd. b, Lady of Mann, by Robert Lloyd.

2005, May 6 ***Perf. 14***

1092	A249 Horiz. pair	1.75	1.75
a.-b.	26p Either single	.85	.85
1093	A249 Horiz. pair	2.00	2.00
a.-b.	29p Either single	1.00	1.00
c.	Booklet pane, #1092, 1093	3.75	—
1094	A249 Horiz. pair	2.75	2.75
a.-b.	40p Either single	1.35	1.35
c.	Booklet pane, #1092, 1094	4.50	—
1095	A249 Horiz. pair	4.50	4.50
a.-b.	66p Either single	2.25	2.25
c.	Booklet pane, #1093, 1095	6.50	—
d.	Booklet pane, #1094, 1095	7.25	—
e.	Booklet pane, #1095	4.50	—
	Complete booklet, #1093c, 1094c, 1095c, 1095d, 1095e	26.50	
	Nos. 1092-1095 (4)	11.00	11.00

Complete booklet sold for £7.80.

Motorcycle Racers — A250

Designs: 26p, Bill Ivy, Phil Read. 29p, Joey Dunlop, Ray McCullough. 40p, Steve Hislop. 42p, Carl Fogarty. 68p, David Jefferies. 78p, John McGuinness.

2005, May 17

1096	A250 26p multi	.85	.85
1097	A250 29p multi	.95	.95
1098	A250 40p multi	1.35	1.35
1099	A250 42p multi	1.50	1.50
1100	A250 68p multi	2.40	2.40
1101	A250 78p multi	2.60	2.60
a.	Miniature sheet, 2 each #1096-1101	22.50	22.50
	Nos. 1096-1101 (6)	9.65	9.65

Yamaha motorcycles, 50th anniv.

Rotary International, Cent. — A251

Rotary International emblem, various photos and inscription: 26p, Paul Harris, The Man Behind The Movement. 29p, Rotary's Dreams For The Future. 40p, Polioplus: Rotary's Finest Hour. 42p, Youth Programme: Junior Masterchef. 64p, A Day In The Life of Rotary International. 68p, Serving The World Community.

Perf. 13¼x13½

2005, June 15 **Litho.**

1102 A251 26p multi .80 .80
1103 A251 29p multi .90 .90
1104 A251 40p multi 1.30 1.30
1105 A251 42p multi 1.40 1.40
a. Sheet of 10 + 10 labels 14.00 14.00
1106 A251 64p multi 2.00 2.00
1107 A251 68p multi 2.25 2.25
Nos. 1102-1107 (6) 8.65 8.65

No. 1105 is inscribed "Europa 2005."

Photographs of Everyday Life — A252

Inscriptions: Nos. 1108a, 1110, Guttin' Herrin'. Nos. 1108b, 1111, Pickin' Spuds. Nos. 1108c, 1112, Master Butcher. Nos. 1108d, 1113, Winckles: Foxdale. Nos. 1108e, 1114, Palace Ballroom. Nos. 1109a, 1115, Land Army. Nos. 1109b, 1116, Farmyard Glen Maye. Nos. 1109c, 1117, Summer Season Stars. Nos. 1109d, 1118, Donkey Rides. Nos. 1109e, 1119, Give us a go Mister!

2005, Aug. 12 ***Perf. 12½x13***

1108 Horiz. strip of 5 4.25 4.25
a.-e. A252 26p Any single .85 .85
1109 Horiz. strip of 5 4.75 4.75
a.-e. A252 29p Any single .95 .95

Booklet Stamps

Self-Adhesive

Serpentine Die Cut 10½x10¼

1110 A252 26p multi 1.00 1.00
a. Die cut perf 12½x13 1.25 1.25
1111 A252 26p multi 1.00 1.00
a. Die cut perf 12½x13 1.25 1.25
1112 A252 26p multi 1.00 1.00
a. Die cut perf 12½x13 1.25 1.25
1113 A252 26p multi 1.00 1.00
a. Die cut perf 12½x13 1.25 1.25
1114 A252 26p multi 1.00 1.00
a. Booklet pane, 2 each #1110-1114 10.00
Complete booklet, #1114a 10.00
b. Die cut perf 12½x13 1.25 1.25
c. Strip of 5, #1110a-1113a, 1114b 6.25
1115 A252 29p multi 1.10 1.10
a. Die cut perf 12½x13 1.25 1.25
1116 A252 29p multi 1.10 1.10
a. Die cut perf 12½x13 1.25 1.25
1117 A252 29p multi 1.10 1.10
a. Die cut perf 12½x13 1.25 1.25
1118 A252 29p multi 1.10 1.10
a. Die cut perf 12½x13 1.25 1.25
1119 A252 29p multi 1.10 1.10
a. Booklet pane, 2 each #1115-1119 11.00
Complete booklet, #1119a 11.00
b. Die cut perf 12½x13 1.25 1.25
c. Strip of 5, #1115a-1118a, 1119b 6.25
Nos. 1110-1119 (10) 10.50 10.50

Nos. 1114a and 1119a are complete booklets, the backing serving as booklet covers. The die-cut 12½x13 stamps are from sheets of 50.

Souvenir Sheet

20th World Youth Day, Cologne, Germany — A253

Perf. 14x14¾ on 3 Sides

2005, Aug. 15

1120 A253 Sheet of 2 + 2 labels 7.25 7.25
a. 42p Apostolic Palace 1.50 1.50
b. £1.50 St. Peter's Basilica 5.50 5.50

Scenes From *Harry Potter and the Goblet of Fire* — A254

Designs: 26p, Harry Potter. 29p, Harry, Ron Weasley, Hermione Granger, Goblet of Fire. 33p, Triwizard Cup. 64p, Hungarian Horntail. 68p, Hogwarts coat of arms. 75p, Murcus.

2005, Oct. 21 ***Perf. 13¼***

1121 A254 26p multi .85 .85
1122 A254 29p multi .95 .95
1123 A254 33p multi 1.20 1.20
1124 A254 64p multi 2.10 2.10
1125 A254 68p multi 2.40 2.40
1126 A254 75p multi 2.60 2.60
Nos. 1121-1126 (6) 10.10 10.10

Souvenir Sheet

Battle of Trafalgar, Bicent. — A255

2005, Oct. 21 **Litho.** ***Perf. 13¼***

1127 A255 Sheet, #1127a, Gibraltar #1028a 7.75 7.75
a. £1 Funeral of Admiral Nelson 3.75 3.75

See Gibraltar No. 1028. No. 1127 has an Isle of Man Post emblem in the margin.

Christmas — A256

Stained glass windows: 26p, Madonna and Child, St. German's Cathedral, Peel. 29p, Angel with Crown of Glory; St. German's Cathedral. 42p, Adoration of the Shepherds, St. German's Cathedral. 60p, Nativity, Kirk Church, Rushen. 68p, Adoration of the Magi, Kirk Church.

2005, Nov. 7 **Litho.** ***Perf. 13½x13***

1128 A256 26p multi .85 .85
1129 A256 29p multi .95 .95
1130 A256 42p multi 1.50 1.50
1131 A256 60p multi 2.00 2.00
1132 A256 68p multi 2.40 2.40
Nos. 1128-1132 (5) 7.70 7.70

Queen Elizabeth II, 80th Birthday A257

No. 1133: a, At age 5 with family, 1931. b, In uniform, 1944. c, Wearing tiara, 1952. d, With husband and children, 1972.

No. 1134: a, With Prince Philip, 1972. b, Seated in Throne Room, 2001. c, With Prince William. d, With crowd, 2002.

2006, Jan. 16 ***Perf. 13¾***

1133 Horiz. strip of 4 2.50 2.50
a.-d. A257 20p Any single .60 .60
1134 Horiz. strip of 4 10.00 10.00
a.-d. A257 80p Any single 2.50 2.50

Isle of Man Natural History and Antiquarian Society — A258

Designs: 26p, Jurby Church, chalice. 29p, Peel Castle, Viking pinhead. 64p, Meayll Hill, Neolithic potsherd. 68p, Cronk Sumark, Manx stoat. 78p, South Barrule Hill, hen harrier. 97p, Scarlett Point, ammonite fossil.

2006, Feb. 15 **Litho.** ***Perf. 14***

1135 A258 26p multi .80 .80
1136 A258 29p multi .90 .90
1137 A258 64p multi 2.00 2.00
1138 A258 68p multi 2.25 2.25
1139 A258 78p multi 2.40 2.40
1140 A258 97p multi 3.00 3.00
Nos. 1135-1140 (6) 11.35 11.35

Birds — A259

No. 1141: a, Peregrine falcon. b, Puffin. c, Manx shearwater. d, Chough. e, Guillemot.

No. 1142: a, Whinchat. b, Hen harrier. c, Goldcrest. d, Gray wagtail. e, Wren.

No. 1142G: i, Peregrine falcon. j, Puffin. k, Manx shearwater. l, Chough. m, Guillemot.

No. 1142H: n, Whinchat. o, Hen harrier. p, Goldcrest. q, Gray wagtail. r, Wren.

2006, Apr. 17 ***Perf. 12½***

1141 Horiz. strip of 5 5.50 5.50
a.-e. A259 28p multi 1.10 1.10
1142 Horiz. strip of 5 6.25 6.25
a.-e. A259 31p multi 1.25 1.25
f. Miniature sheet, #1141a-1141e, 1142a-1142e 12.00 12.00

Self-Adhesive

1142G Horiz. strip of 5 10.50 10.50
i.-m. A259 28p Any single 2.00 2.00
1142H Horiz. strip of 5 11.50 11.50
n.-r. A259 31p Any single 2.25 2.25

No. 1142f issued 10/11, for Belgica '06 Intl. Philatelic Exhibition.

Souvenir Sheet

Queen Elizabeth II, 80th Birthday — A260

No. 1143: a, Queen, swordbearer, Manx flag, 2003. b, Queen, crowd, cross, 1972.

2006, Apr. 21 ***Perf. 14***

1143 A260 Sheet of 2 7.50 7.50
a.-b. £1 Either single 3.75 3.75
c. As #1143a, perf. 12¾, dated "2017" 3.50 3.50
d. As #1143b, perf. 12¾, dated "2017" 3.50 3.50
e. Vert. pair, #1143c-1143d 7.00 7.00

Issued: Nos. 1143c, 1143d, 7/5/17. Nos. 1143c and 1143d were printed together in sheets of 10 (5 of each stamp) that sold for £12.50.

Souvenir Sheet

Europa Stamps, 50th Anniv. — A261

No. 1144: a, #100. b, #419a.

2006, May 2 ***Perf. 13¼x13¾***

1144 A261 Sheet of 2 5.00 5.00
a. 42p multi 1.75 1.75
b. 83p multi 3.25 3.25

2006 World Cup Soccer Championships, Germany — A262

Various photographs of English team's 1966 World Cup championship match and celebrations.

2006, May 2 ***Perf. 12½***

1145 A262 28p multi 1.00 1.00
1146 A262 31p multi 1.15 1.15
1147 A262 44p multi 1.60 1.60
1148 A262 72p multi 2.50 2.50
1149 A262 83p multi 3.00 3.00
1150 A262 94p multi 3.50 3.50
Nos. 1145-1150 (6) 12.75 12.75

Manx Ties to Washington, D.C. A263

Designs: 28p, Letitia Tyler, wife of Pres. John Tyler, White House. 31p, Speaker of the House Joseph G. Cannon, Cannon House Office Building. 45p, Matthew Quay, Medal of Honor recipient, battle scene. 50p, Mary Clemmer, journalist, inkwell and U.S. Constitution. 76p, Ewan Clague, economist, Castletown. 83p, Henry "Marse" Watterson, newspaper publisher, Pres. Theodore Roosevelt.

2006, May 23 ***Perf. 13¾***

1151 A263 28p multi 1.10 1.10
1152 A263 31p multi 1.25 1.25
1153 A263 45p multi 1.75 1.75
1154 A263 50p multi 2.00 2.00
1155 A263 76p multi 3.00 3.00
1156 A263 83p multi 3.25 3.25
Nos. 1151-1156 (6) 12.35 12.35

Peel Cars — A264

Designs: 28p, Peel P50. 31p, Trident. 38p, Viking Sport. 41p, BMC GRP Mini. 54p, Manxcar. 94p, P1000.

2006, July 23 ***Perf. 13¼***

1157 A264 28p multi 1.00 1.00
1158 A264 31p multi 1.15 1.15
1159 A264 38p multi 1.35 1.35
1160 A264 41p multi 1.45 1.45
1161 A264 54p multi 1.90 1.90
1162 A264 94p multi 3.50 3.50
Nos. 1157-1162 (6) 10.35 10.35

National Portrait Gallery, London, 150th Anniv. A265

Portraits: 28p, Ewan Christian, by unknown artist. 31p, Dame Agatha Christie, by John Gay. 38p, Sir Hall Caine, by Harry Furniss. 41p, William Bligh, by John Condé. 44p, Lady Maria Callcott, by Sir Thomas Lawrence. 54p, John Martin, by Henry Warren. 64p, Sir John

Betjeman, by Stephen Hyde. 96p, Sir Edward Elgar, by Herbert Lambert.

2006, Aug. 25 Litho. *Perf. 13½*

1163 A265 28p multi	1.00	1.00
1164 A265 31p multi	1.15	1.15
1165 A265 38p multi	1.35	1.35
1166 A265 41p multi	1.40	1.40
1167 A265 44p multi	1.60	1.60
1168 A265 54p multi	1.90	1.90
1169 A265 64p multi	2.25	2.25
1170 A265 96p multi	3.50	3.50
Nos. 1163-1170 (8)	14.15	14.15

Souvenir Sheet

Tales of Beatrix Potter — A266

No. 1171: a, Benjamin Bunny. b, Jemima Puddle-duck, horiz. c, Peter Rabbit, horiz. d, Jeremy Fisher.

2006, Oct. 11 *Perf. 13*

1171 A266 Sheet of 4	8.00	8.00
a. 28p multi	1.00	1.00
b. 50p multi	1.75	1.75
c. 72p multi	2.50	2.50
d. 75p multi	2.75	2.75

Christmas — A267

Various Christmas trees with panel colors of: 28p, Red. 31p, Dark violet. 41p, Green. 44p, Light blue. 72p, Purple. 94p, Orange.

Litho. with Foil Application

2006, Oct. 11 *Perf. 14¼*

1172 A267 28p multi	1.00	1.00
1173 A267 31p multi	1.15	1.15
a. Sheet of 10	11.50	
1174 A267 41p multi	1.35	1.35
1175 A267 44p multi	1.60	1.60
a. Sheet of 10	16.00	
1176 A267 72p multi	2.50	2.50
1177 A267 94p multi	3.50	3.50
Nos. 1172-1177 (6)	11.10	11.10

Self-Adhesive

Booklet Stamps

Die Cut Perf. 9x9½

1178 A267 28p multi	1.50	1.50
a. Booklet pane of 10	15.00	
1179 A267 31p multi	2.00	2.00
a. Booklet pane of 10	20.00	

Europa (31p, 44p).

Nos. 1178a and 1179a are complete booklets, the backing serving as the booklet covers.

TT Motorcycle Races, Cent. — A268

No. 1180 — Various racers with panel color of: a, Pink. b, Light blue. c, Purple. d, Indigo. e, Orange.

No. 1181: a, Red violet. b, Green. c, Gray blue. d, Red. e, Red brown.

2007, Jan. 1 Litho. *Perf. 14¼*

1180 Horiz. strip of 5	6.25	6.25
a.-e. A268 UK Any single	1.25	1.25
f. As "e," perf. 14¾, dated "2014" (#1324b)	1.40	1.40
1181 Horiz. strip of 5	8.75	8.75
a.-e. A268 E Any single	1.75	1.75
f. Sheet of 10, #1180a-1180e, 1181a-1181e, + 10 labels	*35.00*	*35.00*
g. Sheet of 12 #1181b + 13 labels	27.00	27.00

On day of issue Nos. 1180a-1180e each sold for 31p, Nos. 1181a-1181e each sold for 44p.

Issued: No. 1181f, 7/9. No. 1181g, 5/15/13. No. 11.81g sold for £8.52.

Issued: No. 1180f, 2014. No. 1180f sold for 42p on day of issue.

A269

Scouting, Cent. — A270

Designs: 28p, Hiking expedition near South Barrule. 31p, Scout investiture on Douglas Beach. 44p, Backpacking below Cronk-ny-Arrey-Laa. 72p, Manx Scouts on parade at St. Johns. 83p, Sea kayaking off Laxey Beach. £1, Manx Scouts operating the TT scoreboard.

No. 1188: a, Scouts and table (43x29mm). b, Scouts, tent and campfire (43x57mm).

2007, Feb. 22 Litho. *Perf. 14*

1182 A269 28p multi	1.00	1.00
1183 A269 31p multi	1.10	1.10
a. Sheet of 10	11.50	
1184 A269 44p multi	1.60	1.60
a. Booklet pane, #1182-1184	3.75	—
b. Sheet of 10	16.00	
1185 A269 72p multi	2.50	2.50
1186 A269 83p multi	3.00	3.00
a. Booklet pane, #1182, 1184, 1186	5.75	—
1187 A269 £1 multi	3.50	3.50
a. Booklet pane, #1185-1187	9.00	—
b. Booklet pane, #1183, 1185, 1187	7.25	—
Nos. 1182-1187 (6)	12.70	12.70

Souvenir Sheet

1188 A270 Sheet of 2	7.75	7.75
a. 50p multi	2.00	2.00
b. £1.50 multi	5.75	5.75
c. Booklet pane, #1188 (154x96mm)	7.75	—
Complete booklet, #1184a, 1186a, 1187a, 1187b, 1188c	33.50	
d. As No. 1188, with 2007 Intl. Scout Jamboree emblem in margin	12.00	12.00

Europa (31p, 44p).

No. 1188d issued 7/26.

Wedding of Queen Elizabeth II and Prince Philip, 60th Anniv. — A271

Various photos of Queen and Prince with denomination colors of: a, Dark blue. b, Lilac. c, Rose pink. d, Light blue. e, Dark green. f, Yellow bister.

2007, Feb. 22 *Perf. 14*

1189 Horiz. strip of 6	12.50	12.50
a.-f. A271 60p Any single	2.00	2.00

Paintings by Norman Sayle A272

Designs: Nos. 1190, 1198, Headland, Cornaa. Nos. 1191, 1199, Headland, Sound. Nos. 1192, 1200, St. Mark's Church. Nos. 1193, 1201, Castletown Harbour Moonlight. 42p, Bridge House, Castletown. 44p, Winter Sun. 65p, In Ancient Times. 75p, Bracken Mountain.

2007, Apr. 12 *Perf. 12½x13*

1190 A272 28p multi	1.00	1.00
1191 A272 28p multi	1.00	1.00
1192 A272 31p multi	1.10	1.10
1193 A272 31p multi	1.10	1.10
1194 A272 42p multi	1.60	1.60
1195 A272 44p multi	1.60	1.60
1196 A272 65p multi	2.40	2.40
1197 A272 75p multi	2.75	2.75
Nos. 1190-1197 (8)	12.55	12.55

Booklet Stamps

Self-Adhesive

Serpentine Die Cut 10x9½

1198 A272 28p multi	1.10	1.10
1199 A272 28p multi	1.10	1.10
a. Booklet pane, 5 each #1198-1199	11.00	
1200 A272 31p multi	1.25	1.25
1201 A272 31p multi	1.25	1.25
a. Booklet pane, 5 each #1200-1201	12.50	
Nos. 1198-1201 (4)	4.70	4.70

Nos. 1199a and 1201a are complete booklets, the backing serving as the booklet covers.

Settlement of Jamestown, Virginia, 400th Anniv. — A273

Designs: 28p, Map. 31p, Capt. John Smith and ships. 44p, Aerial view of settlement. 54p, Indians and colonists. 78p, Settlement buildings. 90p, Indian village.

2007, Apr. 26 *Perf. 13½*

1202 A273 28p multi	1.00	1.00
1203 A273 31p multi	1.10	1.10
1204 A273 44p multi	1.60	1.60
1205 A273 54p multi	2.00	2.00
1206 A273 78p multi	3.00	3.00
1207 A273 90p multi	3.50	3.50
Nos. 1202-1207 (6)	12.20	12.20

Royal Charter of Liverpool, 800th Anniv. A274

Designs: 31p, King John and Royal Charter. 48p, The spiritual heart of Liverpool. 54p, Liverpool war heroes. 74p, Liverpool heritage (St. George's Hall). 80p, Port of Liverpool. £1, Wall of Fame.

No. 1214: a, James Brown, Manx election pioneer. b, Joseph Cunningham, philantropist. c, William Gill, ship captain. d, Dalrymple Maitland, industrialist.

2007, Apr. 26 *Perf. 14*

1208 A274 31p multi	1.10	1.10
1209 A274 48p multi	1.75	1.75
1210 A274 54p multi	2.00	2.00
1211 A274 74p multi	2.75	2.75
1212 A274 80p multi	3.00	3.00
1213 A274 £1 multi	3.50	3.50
Nos. 1208-1213 (6)	14.10	14.10

2007, May 10 Souvenir Sheet

1214 Sheet of 4	9.00	9.00
a. A274 25p multi	1.00	1.00
b. A274 40p multi	1.50	1.50
c.-d. A274 80p Either single	3.25	3.25

Historical Maps of Isle of Man A275

Designs: 28p, Map by John Speed, 1605. 31p, Map by Capt. Greenville Collins, 1693. 44p, Map by John Drinkwater, 1826. 48p, Ordnance Survey County Series map, 1870. 75p, Six-inch Series map, 1975. 88p, 1:100,000 map by Isle of Man Government Mapping Office, 2006.

2007, Aug. 1 Litho. *Perf. 12½x13*

1215 A275 28p multi	1.00	1.00
1216 A275 31p multi	1.10	1.10
1217 A275 44p multi	1.60	1.60
1218 A275 48p multi	1.75	1.75
1219 A275 75p multi	2.75	2.75
1220 A275 88p multi	3.50	3.50
Nos. 1215-1220 (6)	11.70	11.70

Intl. Polar Year A276

Designs: 28p, Capt. John Ross, ship Victory trapped in ice. 31p, Flares shot from Victory. 55p, Victory crewmen hunting with Inuit. 75p, Musk ox hunted by Victory crewmen. 90p, Victory crewmen pulling sled after abandoning ship. 117p, Whaler Isabella rescuing Victory crewmen.

2007, Aug. 20

1221 A276 28p multi	1.00	1.00
1222 A276 31p multi	1.10	1.10
1223 A276 55p multi	2.00	2.00
1224 A276 75p multi	2.75	2.75
1225 A276 90p multi	3.50	3.50
1226 A276 117p multi	4.25	4.25
Nos. 1221-1226 (6)	14.60	14.60

Souvenir Sheet

Manx Connections With Northern Canada — A277

No. 1227: a, Ben-My-Chree Cabin, British Columbia. b, Graham "Jimmy" Oates, first man to reach Hudson Bay on rubber-tired vehicle, vert. c, Kermode bear, vert. d, Hudson Bay Post Office and dog team.

2007, Aug. 20 *Perf. 13*

1227 A277 Sheet of 4	10.00	10.00
a.-b. 50p Either single	2.00	2.00
c.-d. 75p Either single	3.00	3.00

Intl. Polar Year.

Europen Vintage Plowing Championships — A278

Designs: 28p, Manx-style plowing. 31p, Vintage plowing. 48p, Horse and digger plow. 71p, Swing plow. 90p, World-style plowing. £1.27, Jean Burns, first woman to compete in Manx plowing contest, on tractor.

2007, Sept. 1 *Perf. 13¼*

1228 A278 28p multi	1.00	1.00
1229 A278 31p multi	1.10	1.10
1230 A278 48p multi	1.75	1.75
1231 A278 71p multi	2.75	2.75
1232 A278 90p multi	3.50	3.50
1233 A278 £1.27 multi	4.75	4.75
Nos. 1228-1233 (6)	14.85	14.85

Christmas — A279

Various angels with panel color of: 28p, Blue. 31p, Pink. 69p, Orange. 78p, Green. £1.24, Dark blue.

Serpentine Die Cut 13x13¼

2007, Oct. 19

Self-Adhesive

1234	A279	28p multi	1.10	1.10
1235	A279	31p multi	1.25	1.25
1236	A279	69p multi	2.75	2.75
1237	A279	78p multi	3.00	3.00
1238	A279	£1.24 multi	4.75	4.75
		Nos. 1234-1238 (5)	12.85	12.85

Souvenir Sheet

Cunard Ocean Liners — A280

No. 1239: a, Queen Elizabeth 2. b, Queen Mary 2. c, Queen Victoria.

2008, Jan. 13 Litho. *Perf. 14x13¼*

1239	A280	Sheet of 3	11.00	11.00
a.-c.		£1 Any single	3.50	3.50
d.		Sheet of 10 #1239a + 10 labels	35.00	—
e.		Sheet of 10 #1239b + 10 labels	35.00	—
f.		Sheet of 10 #1239c + 10 labels	35.00	—

Royal Air Force, 90th Anniv. A281

Aircraft: No. 1240, H.P. 0/400, Bristol F2B fighter. No. 1241, Avro 504N, Westland Wapiti. No. 1242, Hawker Hurricane, Short Sunderland. No. 1243, Gloster Meteor, Westland Whirlwind. No. 1244, Hawker Hunter, E.E. Canberra. No. 1245, BAE Harrier, Lockheed Hercules.

2008, Jan. 15 *Perf. 13¼*

1240	A281	31p multi	1.15	1.15
1241	A281	31p multi	1.15	1.15
1242	A281	31p multi	1.15	1.15
a.		Horiz. strip, #1240-1242	3.50	3.50
1243	A281	90p multi	3.50	3.50
a.		Booklet pane, #1240-1243	7.00	—
1244	A281	90p multi	3.50	3.50
a.		Booklet pane, #1240-1241, 1243-1244	9.50	—
1245	A281	90p multi	3.50	3.50
a.		Horiz. strip, #1243-1245	10.50	10.50
b.		Booklet pane, #1242-1245	11.75	—
c.		Booklet pane, #1240-1241, 1244-1245	9.50	—
		Complete booklet, #1243a, 1244a, 1245b, 1245c	38.00	
		Nos. 1240-1245 (6)	13.95	13.95

Vikings on Isle of Man — A282

Designs: 28p, Pagan Lady of Peel. 31p, Ship burial. 44p, Godred Crovan (King Orry). 54p, Gautr Bjornsson the Sculptor. 69p, Sigurd the Dragon Slayer. £1.24, Coming of Christianity.

2008, Feb. 18 Litho. *Perf. 13¼*

1246	A282	28p multi	1.00	1.00
1247	A282	31p multi	1.15	1.15
1248	A282	44p multi	1.60	1.60
1249	A282	54p multi	2.00	2.00
1250	A282	69p multi	2.50	2.50
1251	A282	£1.24 multi	4.50	4.50
		Nos. 1246-1251 (6)	12.75	12.75

Manx Bank Notes A283

Designs: 30p, 1956 Isle of Man Bank one-pound note. 31p, 1972 Isle of Man Government ten-pound note. 44p, 1882 Manx Bank one-pound note. 56p, 1969 Isle of Man Government fifty-pence note. 85p, 1983 Isle of Man Government fifty-pound note. 114p, 1918 Parr's Bank one-pound note.

2008, Apr. 7 *Perf. 14*

1252	A283	30p multi	1.15	1.15
1253	A283	31p multi	1.15	1.15
1254	A283	44p multi	1.60	1.60
1255	A283	56p multi	2.00	2.00
1256	A283	85p multi	3.25	3.25
1257	A283	114p multi	4.00	4.00
		Nos. 1252-1257 (6)	13.15	13.15

Booklet Stamp

Self-Adhesive

Die Cut Perf. 12x12¼

1258	A283	30p multi	1.50	1.50
a.		Booklet pane of 10	15.00	
		Complete booklet, #1258a	15.00	

Miniature Sheet

2008 Summer Olympics, Beijing — A284

2008, Apr. 21 *Perf. 13¼*

1259	A284	Sheet of 4	4.50	4.50
a.		1p Archery	.25	.25
b.		2p Equestrian	.25	.25
c.		3p Cycling	.25	.25
d.		94p Olympic torch	4.25	4.25
e.		As No. 1259, with Olympex inscription in sheet margin	7.50	7.50
f.		Souvenir sheet, #1259c, #1259d	7.50	7.50

Issued: No. 1259e, 8/8; No. 1259f, 8/9.

Interceltic Music Festival, Lorient, France A285

Flags of regions with Celtic language heritage: 20p, Cornwall. 30p, Isle of Man. 31p, Scotland. 48p, Brittany. 50p, Ireland. 56p, Asturias. 72p, Wales. £1.13, Galicia.

2008, May 12 *Perf. 13¼*

1260	A285	20p multi	.70	.70
1261	A285	30p multi	1.15	1.15
1262	A285	31p multi	1.15	1.15
a.		Sheet of 10	11.50	11.50
1263	A285	48p multi	1.75	1.75
1264	A285	50p multi	1.75	1.75
a.		Sheet of 10	17.50	17.50
1265	A285	56p multi	2.00	2.00
1266	A285	72p multi	2.75	2.75
1267	A285	£1.13 multi	4.00	4.00
a.		Sheet of 8, #1260-1267 (Aug. 1)	20.00	—
		Nos. 1260-1267 (8)	15.25	15.25

Europa (31p, 50p).

Famous Race Drivers and Their Cars A286

Designs: 20p, Reg Parnell. 30p, Mike Hawthorn. 70p, Tony Brooks. 81p, Roy Salvadori. 94p, Stirling Moss. £1.22, Jim Clark.

2008, July 10 Litho. *Perf. 14*

1268	A286	20p multi	.70	.70
1269	A286	30p multi	1.15	1.15
1270	A286	70p multi	2.50	2.50
1271	A286	81p multi	3.00	3.00
1272	A286	94p multi	3.50	3.50
1273	A286	£1.22 multi	4.50	4.50
		Nos. 1268-1273 (6)	15.35	15.35

Miniature Sheet

Race Cars — A287

No. 1274: a, 1961 Aston Martin DB4 GT Zagato. b, 1965 Ferrari 250 LM. c, 1962 Ferrari 250 GTO. d, 1965 Ford GT40. e, 1955 Mercedes-Benz 300 SLR. f, 1964 Shelby Cobra.

2008, July 10 *Perf. 14¾x14*

1274	A287	Sheet of 6	11.50	11.50
a.-f.		50p Any single	1.90	1.90

Famous People — A288

No. 1275: a, Mary Louisa Wood (1839-1925), founder of Isle of Man Fine Arts and Industrial Guild. b, Harry Kelly (1852-1935), last native Manx speaker. c, Sir Frank Gill (1866-1950), telephone and communications engineer. d, Ramsey Gelling Johnson (1889-1972), judge, president of Royal Manx Agricultural Society. e, John Nicholson (1911-88), stamp designer.

No. 1276: a, Dr. Dorothy Pantin (1896-1985), first female doctor. b, Richard Costain (1839-1902), construction business entrepreneur. c, Sir William Percy Cowley (1886-1958), judge. d, Rev. Fred Cubbon (1902-80), philanthropist. e, William Henry Gill (1839-1922), author, musician.

2008, Aug. 1 *Perf. 13¼*

1275		Horiz. strip of 5	5.75	5.75
a.-e.		A288 31p Any single	1.15	1.15
1276		Horiz. strip of 5	9.00	9.00
a.-e.		A288 50p Any single	1.75	1.75

End of World War I, 90th Anniv. — A289

Poppy and letter from soldier: 30p, Second Lieutenant Roy F. Corlett. 31p, Second Lieutenant John W. Lewis. 44p, Private Joseph Killey. 56p, Lieutenant Colonel W. A. W. Crellin. 81p, Lance Corporal Tom Quilliam. 94p, Private Robert Oates.

£2, National War Memorial, St. John's.

2008, Oct. 1 Litho. *Perf. 14*

1277	A289	30p multi	1.10	1.10
1278	A289	31p multi	1.10	1.10
1279	A289	44p multi	1.60	1.60
1280	A289	56p multi	2.00	2.00
1281	A289	81p multi	3.00	3.00
1282	A289	94p multi	3.25	3.25
		Nos. 1277-1282 (6)	12.05	12.05

Souvenir Sheet

1283	A289	£2 multi	7.00	7.00

Flora and Fauna of Ballaugh Curragh A290

Designs: 30p, Orange-tip butterfly. 31p, Curlew. 50p, Birch bracket fungus. 70p, Large red damselfly. 82p, Marsh cinquefoil. £1.38, Royal fern.

2008, Oct. 1 *Perf. 13¼*

1284	A290	30p multi	1.00	1.00
1285	A290	31p multi	1.00	1.00
1286	A290	50p multi	1.60	1.60
1287	A290	70p multi	2.25	2.25
1288	A290	82p multi	2.75	2.75
1289	A290	£1.38 multi	4.50	4.50
		Nos. 1284-1289 (6)	13.10	13.10

Christmas A291

Postman from *The Jolly Christmas Postman,* by Janet and Allen Ahlberg: 28p, On bicycle, letters. 31p, And mouse in cracker box. 48p, And bear family. 50p, And Toy Town. 56p, On bicycle, with truck and horsecart on winding road. £1.56, At home.

2008, Oct. 20 *Perf. 14x14¼*

1290	A291	28p multi	.90	.90
1291	A291	31p multi	1.00	1.00
1292	A291	48p multi	1.60	1.60
1293	A291	50p multi	1.60	1.60
1294	A291	56p multi	1.90	1.90
1295	A291	£1.56 multi	4.50	4.50
		Nos. 1290-1295 (6)	11.50	11.50

Lewis Hamilton, Formula 1 Race Car Driver A292

No. 1296: a, Hamilton driving race car. b, Hamilton celebrating victory with champagne spray.

No. 1297: a, Hamilton driving past finish line. b, Hamilton in race car cockpit.

No. 1298: a, Hamilton driving race car, diff. b, Hamilton in helmet with arms extended.

2009, Jan. 15 Litho. *Perf. 14*

1296		Horiz. pair	1.75	1.75
a.		A292 30p multi	.85	.85
b.		A292 31p multi	.90	.90
1297		Horiz. pair	4.00	4.00
a.		A292 56p multi	1.60	1.60
b.		A292 85p multi	2.40	2.40
1298		Horiz. pair	6.75	6.75
a.		A292 98p multi	2.75	2.75
b.		A292 £1.42 multi	4.00	4.00
		Nos. 1296-1298 (3)	12.50	12.50

Naval Aviation, Cent. A293

No. 1299: a, Fairey Barracuda II. b, Blackburn Buccaneer S.2. c, Fairey Flycatcher.

No. 1300: a, EH101 Merlin helicopter. b, BAe Sea Harrier FRS.1. c, Sea Scout SS.24 airship.

2009, Jan. 15

1299		Horiz. strip of 3	3.75	3.75
a.		A293 30p multi	.85	.85
b.		A293 31p multi	.90	.90
c.		A293 72p multi	2.00	2.00
d.		Booklet pane of 4, 2 each #1299a, 1299b	3.50	—
1300		Horiz. strip of 3	9.00	9.00
a.		A293 85p multi	2.40	2.40
b.		A293 98p multi	2.75	2.75
c.		A293 £1.36 multi	3.75	3.75
d.		Booklet pane of 4, #1299a, 1299b, 1299c, 1300a	6.25	—
e.		Booklet pane of 4, #1299a, 1299b, 1300b, 1300c	8.25	—
f.		Booklet pane of 4, #1299c, 1300a, 1300b, 1300c	11.00	—
		Complete booklet, #1299d, 1300d, 1300e, 1300f	29.00	

Accession to the Throne of Henry VIII, 500th Anniv. A294

No. 1301: a, King Henry VIII. b, Catherine of Aragon (first wife). c, Anne Boleyn (second wife). d, Jane Seymour (third wife).

No. 1302: a, Anne of Cleves (fourth wife). b, Catherine Howard (fifth wife). c, Catherine Parr (sixth wife). d, Hampton Court.

2009, Feb. 18 *Perf. 13¼*

1301 Horiz. strip of 4 5.50 5.50
a.-d. A294 50p Any single 1.35 1.35
1302 Horiz. strip of 4 5.50 5.50
a.-d. A294 50p Any single 1.35 1.35

Photographs of Mills and Millers by Chris Killip — A295

No. 1303: a, Ballakilley Farm. b, Grenaby Farm.

No. 1304: a, Mr. Cubbon. b, Glenmoar Mill.

No. 1305: a, Golden Meadow Mill. b, Bernie Mylcraine.

No. 1306: a, Golden Meadow Mill, diff. b, Loughtan Farm.

No. 1307, Like #1303a. No. 1308, Like #1303b. No. 1309, Like #1304b. No. 1310, Like #1304a.

2009, Apr. 1 *Perf. 13¼*

1303 Pair 1.75 1.75
a.-b. A295 32p Either single .85 .85
1304 Pair 1.90 1.90
a.-b. A295 33p Either single .95 .95
1305 Pair 2.75 2.75
a.-b. A295 50p Either single 1.35 1.35
1306 Pair 4.50 4.50
a.-b. A295 78p Either single 2.25 2.25
Nos. 1303-1306 (4) 10.90 10.90

Booklet Stamps
Self-Adhesive
Serpentine Die Cut 12½

1307 A295 32p black .95 .95
1308 A295 32p black .95 .95
a. Booklet pane of 10, 5 each #1307-1308 9.00
Complete booklet, #1308a 9.00
1309 A295 33p black 1.00 1.00
1310 A295 33p black 1.00 1.00
a. Booklet pane of 10, 5 each #1309-1310 10.00
Complete booklet, #1310a 10.00
Nos. 1307-1310 (4) 3.90 3.90

Miniature Sheet

Peonies — A296

No. 1311 — Denomination color: a, Yellow. b, Light green. c, Pink. d, Blue. e, Violet. f, Red. g, Blue green. h, Olive green.

2009, Apr. 10 *Perf. 13¼*

1311 A296 Sheet of 8 2.40 2.40
a.-h. 10p Any single .30 .30

First Man on the Moon, 40th Anniv. A297

Paintings by Astronaut Alan Bean: 33p, First Boot Print, Sunrise Over Antares. 50p, Clan MacBean Arrives on the Moon, Documenting the Sample. 56p, Pete and Me. 81p, Headed for the Last Parking Lot. 105p, The Eagle is Headed Home, In the Beginning. 135p, Ceremony on the Plain at Hadley, The Hoer. £2.50, On the Rim, vert.

2009, Apr. 12 *Perf. 12½*

1312 A297 33p multi 1.00 1.00
a. Sheet of 10 10.00 10.00
1313 A297 50p multi 1.50 1.50
1314 A297 56p multi 1.75 1.75
a. Sheet of 10 17.50 17.50
1315 A297 81p multi 2.40 2.40
1316 A297 105p multi 3.25 3.25
1317 A297 135p multi 3.75 3.75
Nos. 1312-1317 (6) 13.65 13.65

Souvenir Sheet

1318 A297 £2.50 multi 7.25 7.25
1318a As #1318, with 40th anniversary emblem in sheet margin, perf. 12 12.50 12.50

Europa (33p, 56p).

Issued: No. 1318a, 7/20.

Honda Racing Motorcycles — A298

Motorcycle from the: 32p, 1950s. 33p, 1960s. 56p, 1970s. 62p, 1980s. 90p, 1990s. £1.77, 2000s.

2009, May 11 *Perf. 14*

1319 A298 32p multi .90 .90
1320 A298 33p multi 1.00 1.00
1321 A298 56p multi 1.60 1.60
1322 A298 62p multi 1.75 1.75
1323 A298 90p multi 2.75 2.75
1324 A298 £1.77 multi 5.25 5.25
a. Dated "2014" 5.25 5.25
b. Souvenir sheet of 8, 3 #1180f, 5 #1324a, + 4 labels 30.00 30.00
Nos. 1319-1324 (6) 13.25 13.25

Issued: Nos. 1324a, 1324b, 2014.

Souvenir Sheet

2009 England Vs. Australia The Ashes Cricket Test Match — A299

No. 1325: a, W. G. Grace at Lord's Cricket Ground (42x28mm). b, Marylebone Cricket Club Ashes trophy and urn (30x40mm). c, England vs. Australia, Lord's Cricket Ground, 2005 (42x28mm).

Perf. 14 (#1325a, 1325c), 14x14¾
2009, June 20

1325 A299 Sheet of 3 9.25 9.25
a.-c. £1 Any single 3.00 3.00

The Bee Gees, 50th Anniv. — A300

No. 1326: a, Barry, Robin and Maurice Gibb as children. b, "Children of the World" album cover. c, "Spirits Having Flown" album cover. d, "Still Waters" album cover.

No. 1327: a, "One Night Only" album cover. b, "This Is Where I Came In" album cover. c, "Number Ones" album cover. d, "The Studio Albums 1967-1968" album cover.

2009, July 1 *Perf. 13x12½*

1326 Horiz. strip of 4 + central label 5.00 5.00
a. A300 32p multi .90 .90
b. A300 33p multi 1.00 1.00
c. A300 50p multi 1.40 1.40
d. A300 54p multi 1.50 1.50
1327 Horiz. strip of 4 + central label 10.00 10.00
a. A300 56p multi 1.75 1.75
b. A300 62p multi 1.90 1.90
c. A300 78p multi 2.40 2.40
d. A300 £1.28 multi 3.75 3.75

Paintings of Wildlife by Jeremy Paul A301

Paintings: 32p, Brown Hare. 33p, Hedgehogs. 54p, Pheasants. 90p, Barn Owl. 92p, Cockerel. £1.58, On the Hill.

2009, Sept. 1 **Litho.** *Perf. 12½*

1328 A301 32p multi 1.00 1.00
1329 A301 33p multi 1.00 1.00
1330 A301 54p multi 1.60 1.60
1331 A301 90p multi 2.75 2.75
1332 A301 92p multi 2.75 2.75
1333 A301 £1.58 multi 4.75 4.75
a. Sheet of 6, #1328-1333 14.00 14.00
Nos. 1328-1333 (6) 13.85 13.85

Watercolors by Archibald Knox A302

Watercolors: 32p, Bridge Possibly at Laxey. 33p, Willows and Blue Mountain Possibly Greeba. 56p, Kew. 62p, Eairy Beg Glen Helen. 81p, Leaning Trees. 182p, Old Laxey.

2009, Sept. 16 *Perf. 12½*

1334 A302 32p multi .90 .90
1335 A302 33p multi 1.00 1.00
1336 A302 56p multi 1.60 1.60
1337 A302 62p multi 1.75 1.75
1338 A302 81p multi 2.40 2.40
1339 A302 182p multi 5.25 5.25
Nos. 1334-1339 (6) 12.90 12.90

Souvenir Sheet

Sinking of the Ellan Vannin, Cent. — A303

No. 1340: a, Captain James Teare and Ellan Vannan at sea. b, Ellan Vannan in harbor.

2009, Oct. 1 *Perf. 14*

1340 A303 Sheet of 2 8.50 8.50
a.-b. £1.50 Either single 4.25 4.25

Christmas — A304

Santa Claus: 30p, Filling stocking. 33p, Making a list. 56p, Holding bag of toys. 62p, Near chimney, holding gift. 81p, Holding staff and bag. 90p, Holding chalice.

2009, Oct. 20 *Perf. 14*

1341 A304 30p multi .90 .90
1342 A304 33p multi 1.00 1.00
1343 A304 56p multi 1.75 1.75
1344 A304 62p multi 1.90 1.90
1345 A304 81p multi 2.50 2.50
1346 A304 90p multi 2.75 2.75
Nos. 1341-1346 (6) 10.80 10.80

Size: 23x34mm
Self-Adhesive
Die Cut Perf. 13x13½

1347 A304 30p multi 1.25 1.25
1348 A304 33p multi 1.50 1.50

A305

A306

A307

A308

A309

A310

A311

A312

A313

Island Life — A314

2010, Jan. 12 *Perf. 12½*

1349 Horiz. strip of 4 4.25 4.25
a. A305 (32p) multi 1.00 1.00
b. A306 (32p) multi 1.00 1.00
c. A307 (32p) multi 1.00 1.00
d. A308 (32p) multi 1.00 1.00
1350 Horiz. strip of 4 4.50 4.50
a. A309 (33p) multi 1.10 1.10
b. A310 (33p) multi 1.10 1.10

c. A311 (33p) multi 1.10 1.10
d. A312 (33p) multi 1.10 1.10
1351 A313 56p multi 1.75 1.75
1352 A314 90p multi 3.00 3.00
Nos. 1349-1352 (4) 13.50 13.50

Booklet Stamps
Self-Adhesive
Serpentine Die Cut 13¾x13

1353 A305 (32p) multi 1.20 1.20
1354 A306 (32p) multi 1.20 1.20
1355 A307 (32p) multi 1.20 1.20
1356 A308 (32p) multi 1.20 1.20
a. Booklet pane of 12, 3 each #1353-1356 14.50
1357 A309 (33p) multi 1.30 1.30
1358 A310 (33p) multi 1.30 1.30
1359 A311 (33p) multi 1.30 1.30
1360 A312 (33p) multi 1.30 1.30
a. Booklet pane of 12, 3 each #1357-1360 16.00
Nos. 1353-1360 (8) 10.00 10.00

Nos. 1356a and 1360a are complete booklets, the backing serving as the booklet covers.

Girl Guides, Cent. — A315

No. 1361 — Rainbows with denomination in: a, Red. b, Blue.
No. 1362 — Brownies with denomination in: a, Red. b, Blue.
No. 1363 — Girl Guides with denomination in: a, Red. b, Blue.
No. 1364 — Senior Section members with denomination in: a, Red. b, Blue.
No. 1365 — Adult volunteers with denomination in: a, Red. b, Blue.

2010 ***Perf. 14***

1361 A315 Horiz. pair 1.75 1.75
a.-b. 32p Either single .85 .85
1362 A315 Horiz. pair 1.75 1.75
a.-b. 33p Either single .85 .85
c. Sheet of 10 #1362a 8.50 8.50
1363 A315 Horiz. pair 3.25 3.25
a.-b. 56p Either single 1.60 1.60
c. Sheet of 10 #1363a 16.00 16.00
1364 A315 Horiz. pair 5.50 5.50
a.-b. £1 Either single 2.75 2.75
Nos. 1361-1364 (4) 12.25 12.25

Souvenir Sheet

1365 A315 Sheet of 2 8.50 8.50
a.-b. £1.50 Either single 4.25 4.25
c. As #1365, with Centenary Camp emblem added in sheet margin 12.00 12.00

Issued: Nos. 1361-1365, 2/18; No. 1365c, 7/31. Europa (Nos. 1362a, 1363a).

A316

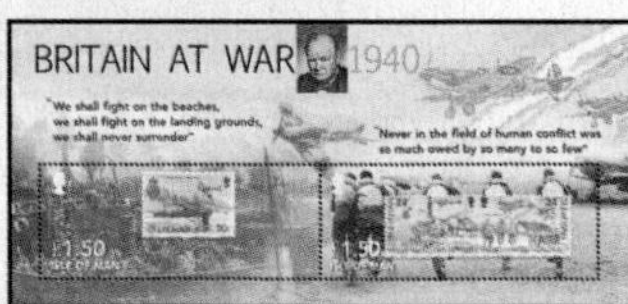

Battle of Britain, 70th Anniv. — A317

No. 1366: a, Messerschmitt BF110 and Hurricane. b, Blenheim I and Junkers 88. c, Heinkel III and Spitfire.
No. 1367: a, Messerschmitt BF109 and Defiant. b, Spitfire and Messerschmitt BF109. c, Junkers JU-87 and Hurricane.
No. 1368: a, Ben My Chree arriving at Folkstone with troops evacuated from Dunkirk, Isle of Man #204. b, Airmen running to planes, Isle of Man #429a.

2010, Apr. 20 ***Perf. 13¼***

1366 Horiz. strip of 3 6.50 6.50
a.-c. A316 70p Any single 2.10 2.10
d. As "a," dated "2015" 2.25 2.25
e. As "b," dated "2015" 2.25 2.25
f. As "c," dated "2015" 2.25 2.25
1367 Horiz. strip of 3 6.50 6.50
a.-c. A316 70p Any single 2.10 2.10
d. As "a," dated "2015" 2.25 2.25
e. As "b," dated "2015" 2.25 2.25
f. As "c," dated "2015" 2.25 2.25
g. Sheet of 12, 2 each #1366d-1366f, 1367d-1367f, + 8 labels 27.00 27.00

Souvenir Sheet
Perf. 13¾

1368 A317 Sheet of 2 9.25 9.25
a.-b. £1.50 Either single 4.50 4.50

Issued: Nos. 1366d-1366f, 1367d-1367f, 7/17/15.

Accession to Throne of King George V, Cent. A318

Photographs of 1920 royal visit to Isle of Man and items from Royal Philatelic Collection: 55p, Royal party at Bishops Court, Ballaugh, cast of proposed 1913 stamp depicting King George V. 60p, King George V and Queen Mary on Tynwald Hill, two used pairs of Cape of Good Hope 1p triangle stamps. 67p, Queen's Pier, Ramsey, unissued 2p plum stamp of Great Britain. 96p, Visit to war disabled at Ramsey Cottage Hospital, Niger Coast Protectorates #35. 97p, Tree planting at Bishops Court, Great Britain #151. £1.10, Royal party at Castletown, Mauritius #2.

2010, May 6 ***Perf. 14***

1369 A318 55p multi 1.45 1.45
1370 A318 60p multi 1.60 1.60
1371 A318 67p multi 1.75 1.75
1372 A318 96p multi 2.75 2.75
1373 A318 97p multi 2.75 2.75
1374 A318 £1.10 multi 3.00 3.00
Nos. 1369-1374 (6) 13.30 13.30

Model T Fords — A319

Designs: 35p, 1915 Speedster. 36p, 1926 Coupe. 60p, 1923 Van. 74p, 1912 Town Car. 97p, 1922 Charabanc. 172p, 1912 Tourer.

2010, May 7 ***Perf. 13¼***

1375 A319 35p multi 1.00 1.00
1376 A319 36p multi 1.00 1.00
1377 A319 60p multi 1.60 1.60
1378 A319 74p multi 2.00 2.00
1379 A319 97p multi 2.75 2.75
1380 A319 172p multi 4.75 4.75
Nos. 1375-1380 (6) 13.10 13.10

Railways A320

Designs: 35p, Caledonia at summit of Snaefell Mountain. 36p, Isle of Man Railways steam locomotive No. 1 and Manx Electric Railway car No. 1 at Laxey. 55p, Caledonia at Bulgham. 88p, Isle of Man Railways Loch locomotive at Skinscoe Curve. £1.32, Manx Electric Railway car No. 33 approaching Keristal. £1.46, Loch and Maitland locomotives near White Hoe.

2010, June 24 ***Perf. 14***

1381 A320 35p multi 1.00 1.00
1382 A320 36p multi 1.00 1.00
1383 A320 55p multi 1.60 1.60
1384 A320 88p multi 2.50 2.50
1385 A320 £1.32 multi 3.50 3.50
1386 A320 £1.46 multi 4.00 4.00
a. Sheet of 6, #1381-1386 + 3 labels 17.50 17.50
Nos. 1381-1386 (6) 13.60 13.60

History of Manx Coinage A321

Designs: 35p, 1709 Lord Derby halfpenny, Castle Rushen. 36p, 1798 Cartwheel penny, Soho Mint, Birmingham. 55p, 1839 Queen Victoria Farthing, Douglas. 60p, 1965 gold coin, Castle Rushen. 67p, 1971 Decimal currency 5p coin, Tower of Refuge. £1.87, 2010 £5 Laxey Wheel coin, Laxey Wheel.

2010, June 24 ***Perf. 12¾***

1387 A321 35p multi 1.00 1.00
1388 A321 36p multi 1.00 1.00
1389 A321 55p multi 1.60 1.60
1390 A321 60p multi 1.75 1.75
1391 A321 67p multi 1.90 1.90
1392 A321 £1.87 multi 5.25 5.25
Nos. 1387-1392 (6) 12.50 12.50

Souvenir Sheet

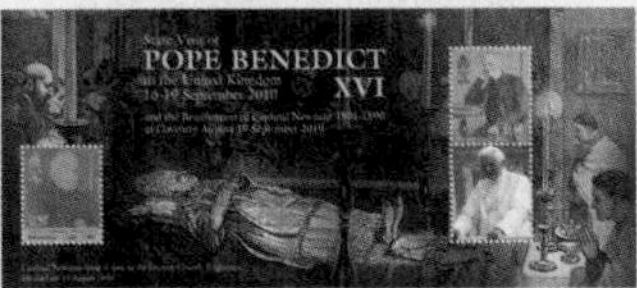

Beatification of Cardinal John Henry Newman (1801-90) — A322

No. 1393: a, Newman, table and book. b, Newman.

2010, Aug. 11 ***Perf. 13¼***

1393 A322 Sheet of 2 + label 8.50 8.50
a.-b. £1.50 Either single 4.25 4.25

State visit of Pope Benedict XVI.

Artwork by Internees in Isle of Man World War II Internment Camps A323

Designs: 35p, Three-legged Postman, by Bertram. 36p, Peveril Camp, Peel, by Herbert Kaden. 55p, Life at Palace Camp, Douglas, by Imre Goth. 67p, Douglas, Isle of Man, by Hermann Fechenbach. 132p, Violinist at Onchan Camp, by Ernst Eisenmayer. 172p, Portrait of Klaus E. Hinrichsen, by Kurt Schwitters.

2010, Sept. 24 **Litho.**

1394 A323 35p multi 1.00 1.00
1395 A323 36p multi 1.00 1.00
1396 A323 55p multi 1.60 1.60
1397 A323 67p multi 1.90 1.90
1398 A323 132p multi 3.50 3.50
1399 A323 172p multi 4.75 4.75
Nos. 1394-1399 (6) 13.75 13.75

Souvenir Sheet

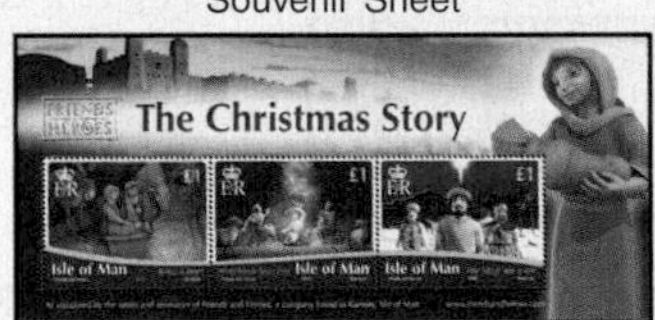

The Christmas Story — A324

No. 1400 — Characters from Friends and Heroes animated TV show depicting the Nativity: a, Jesus is born. b, Shepherds hear first. c, The Magi see a star.

2010, Oct. 1 Litho. ***Perf. 13¼x13¾***

1400 A324 Sheet of 3 9.00 9.00
a.-c. £1 Any single 3.00 3.00

Photographs of Snowfall of 2009-10 Winter — A325

Photographs of: 35p, Old Braddan Church, by Bill Dale. 36p, The Braaid, by Seamus Whelan. 60p, Dhoon Glen, by Simon Park. 88p, Dhoon Beach, by Park. 97p, Cronk ny Aree Laa, by Dale. £1.46, St. Patrick's Isle in Snow, by Victoria Harrop.

2010, Oct. 20 ***Perf. 13x13¼***

1401 A325 35p multi 1.10 1.10
1402 A325 36p multi 1.10 1.10
1403 A325 60p multi 1.75 1.75
1404 A325 88p multi 2.75 2.75
1405 A325 97p multi 3.00 3.00
1406 A325 £1.46 multi 4.25 4.25
Nos. 1401-1406 (6) 15.50 15.50

Souvenir Sheet

Engagement of Prince William of Wales and Catherine Middleton — A326

No. 1407 — Prince William: a, Close-up, no shirt visible. b, Shirt visible.

2010, Nov. 26 Litho. ***Perf. 14¾x14***

1407 A326 Sheet of 2 9.00 9.00
a.-b. £1.50 Either single 4.50 4.50

Service of Queen Elizabeth II and Prince Philip — A327

Designs: 35p, Queen Elizabeth II, 1953 coronation photograph. 36p, Queen and Prince Philip, 2007. 55p, Queen and Prince Philip as newlyweds. 60p, Queen and Prince Philip in uniforms, 1971. £1.14, Queen and Prince Philip, 2002. £1.46, Prince Philip at 1953 coronation.
£3, Queen and Prince Philip, 1970s.

2011, Feb. 6 ***Perf. 13¼***

1408 A327 35p multi 1.00 1.00
1409 A327 36p multi 1.10 1.10
1410 A327 55p multi 1.60 1.60
1411 A327 60p multi 1.75 1.75
1412 A327 £1.14 multi 3.50 3.50
1413 A327 £1.46 multi 4.25 4.25
a. Souvenir sheet of 6, #1408-1413, + 3 labels 13.50 13.50
Nos. 1408-1413 (6) 14.50 14.50

Souvenir Sheet

1414 A327 £3 multi 9.75 9.75
a. Sheet of 13, #1413, 1414, 3 #1411, 2 each #1408-1410, 1412, + 16 labels 36.00 36.00

Issued: No. 1414a, 6/4/12.
Stamps in No. 1413a have dull purple borders, while Nos. 1408-1413 have darker black purple borders.

Genealogy A328

Inscription in frame at UL: No. 1415, Baptisms. No. 1416, School Days. No. 1417, Working Life. No. 1418, Weddings. No. 1419, Family Album. No. 1420, Emigration. No. 1421, Memorials. No. 1422, Family Tree.

2011, Feb. 18 Litho. ***Perf. 13½***
Frame Color

1415 A328 35p org brown 1.00 1.00
1416 A328 35p deep claret 1.00 1.00
1417 A328 36p car rose 1.10 1.10
1418 A328 36p Prus blue 1.10 1.10
1419 A328 67p slate grn 2.00 2.00
1420 A328 67p emerald 2.00 2.00
1421 A328 £1.10 ol green 3.25 3.25
1422 A328 £1.10 brown 3.25 3.25
Nos. 1415-1422 (8) 16.20 16.20

Greatest TT Motorcycle Races — A329

No. 1423: a, Stanley Woods v. Jimmy Guthrie, 1935 Senior race. b, Mike Hailwood v. Giacomo Agostini, 1967 Senior race. c, John Williams v. Tom Herron, 1976 Senior race. d, George O'Dell and Kenny Arthur v. Dick Greasley and Mick Skeels, 1977 Sidecar A race. e, Alex George v. Mike Hailwood, 1979 Classic race.

No. 1424: a, Steve Hislop v. Carl Fogarty, 1992 Senior race. b, Joey Dunlop v. David Jefferies, 2000 Formula 1 race. c, John McGuiness v. Cameron Donald, 2008 Senior race. d, Klaus Klaffenbock and Dan Sayle v. John Holden and Andy Winkle, 2010 Sidecar 2 race. e, Ian Hutchinson v. Ryan Farquhar, 2010 Superstock race.

£3, Hislop v. Fogarty, 1992 Senior race, horiz..

2011, Apr. 1 Litho. *Perf. 14¼*

1423 Horiz. strip of 5 5.50 5.50
a.-e. A329 38p Any single 1.10 1.10
f. As "a," perf. 14¾ (#1425b) 1.25 1.25
1424 Horiz. strip of 5 10.00 10.00
a.-e. A329 68p Any single 2.00 2.00
f. As "a," perf. 14¾ (#1425b) 2.25 2.25

Souvenir Sheet

Perf. 14¼x15

1425 A329 £3 multi 9.00 9.00
a. Perf. 14 (#1425b) 10.00 10.00
b. Sheet of 8, #41a, 69a, 217, 336a, 703, 1423f, 1424f, 1425a, + 5 labels 18.50 18.50

No. 1425 contains one 45x30mm stamp.
Issued: Nos. 1423f, 1424f, 1425a, 2015. No. 1425b sold for £6.

Butterflies A330

Designs: No. 1426, Wall butterfly. No. 1427, Dark green fritillary. No. 1428, Comma butterfly. No. 1429, Red admiral. Nos. 1430, 1434, Small tortoiseshell butterfly. No. 1431, Common blue butterfly. No. 1432, Green-veined white butterfly. No. 1433, Speckled wood butterfly.

2011, Apr. 1 *Perf. 13¼*

With WWF Emblem at Lower Left

1426 A330 37p multi 1.25 1.25
1427 A330 38p multi 1.25 1.25
1428 A330 58p multi 1.90 1.90
1429 A330 115p multi 3.75 3.75
a. Sheet of 16, 4 each #1426-1429 33.00 33.00

Without WWF Emblem

1430 A330 37p multi 1.25 1.25
1431 A330 38p multi 1.25 1.25
1432 A330 58p multi 1.90 1.90
1433 A330 115p multi 3.75 3.75
Nos. 1426-1433 (8) 16.30 16.30

Booklet Stamp
Self-Adhesive

Serpentine Die Cut 13¼

1434 A330 37p multi 1.50 1.50
a. Booklet pane of 12 18.00

No. 1434a is a complete booklet, the backing serving as the booklet cover.

Souvenir Sheet

Wedding of Prince William and Catherine Middleton — A331

No. 1435: a, Middleton. b, Prince William.

2011, Apr. 15 *Perf. 14¾x14*

1435 A331 Sheet of 2 6.00 6.00
a.-b. £1 Either single, dated 2011 3.00 3.00
c. Sheet of 10, 5 each #1435a-1435b, + 10 labels 30.00 30.00
d.-e. £1 Either single, dated 2013 3.00 3.00
f. Sheet of 8, 4 each #1435d-1435e, + 4 labels 24.00 24.00
g.-h. £1 Either single, dated 2015 3.00 3.00
i. Sheet of 8, 4 each #1435g-1435h, + 4 labels 24.00 24.00

No. 1435f, was issued 7/31/13. Birth of Prince George of Cambridge (No. 1435f). No. 1435i has different labels noting the birth of Princess Charlotte: issued 5/11/15.

Political Cartoons by Harold "Dusty" Miller (1898-1964) A332

Designs: 37p, The Southern Hundred. 38p, I'm Staking My Claim On the Sands at Douglas. 68p, Over the Water - I Must Get Me a Bigger Horse. 76p, Will Uncle Sam Provide the Third Leg? 110p, Bob a Job Week. 165p, Well, Councilor - Did You Vote For Evening Meetings?

2011, May 10 *Perf. 13¼*

Color of Panel and Frame

1436 A332 37p red 1.00 1.00
1437 A332 38p purple 1.00 1.00
1438 A332 68p green 1.75 1.75
1439 A332 76p red violet 2.00 2.00
1440 A332 110p Prussian blue 3.00 3.00
1441 A332 165p bister 4.50 4.50
Nos. 1436-1441 (6) 13.25 13.25

Picture Post Cards Depicting Manx Cats A333

Various post cards depicting cats and arms of Isle of Man.

2011, June 23 *Perf. 13¼x13½*

Panel Color

1442 A333 37p dark blue 1.00 1.00
1443 A333 38p bister 1.00 1.00
1444 A333 58p light blue 1.50 1.50
1445 A333 76p red violet 2.00 2.00
1446 A333 115p red 3.00 3.00
1447 A333 165p brown 4.25 4.25
Nos. 1442-1447 (6) 12.75 12.75

Postal History of Knockaloe Internment Camp — A334

No. 1448: a, Post card depicting troops marching, half of 1908 Camp Knockaloe cancel. b, Address side of post card, Great Britain #143 with 1908 Camp Knockaloe cancel.

No. 1449: Post card depicting camp, part of 1914 Peel cancel. b, Address side of post card, pair of Great Britain #159 with 1914 Peel cancel.

No. 1450: a, Easter post card from 1915-19, half of registry label. b, Half of registry label, registered mail envelope with camp cancel.

No. 1451: a, Post card depicting camp, Knockaloe cancel. b, Internee-produced local stamp, local stamp on cover.

No. 1452: a, Post card depicting camp huts, Camp Knockaloe censor marking. b, Great Britain #160 with 1915 Camp Knockaloe cancel, prisoner-of-war cover. c, 1917 Easter post card, 1915 Camp Knockaloe cancel. d, Great Britain envelope stamp with 1915 Camp Knockaloe cancel, registered mail envelope.

2011, Aug. 8 *Perf. 13¼x13½*

1448 A334 Horiz. pair 2.25 2.25
a.-b. 37p Either single 1.10 1.10
1449 A334 Horiz. pair 2.25 2.25
a.-b. 38p Either single 1.10 1.10
1450 A334 Horiz. pair 3.50 3.50
a.-b. 58p Either single 1.75 1.75
1451 A334 Horiz. pair 7.00 7.00
a.-b. £1.15 Either single 3.50 3.50
Nos. 1448-1451 (4) 15.00 15.00

Souvenir Sheet

1452 A334 Sheet of 4 9.25 9.25
a.-b. 50p Either single 1.60 1.60
c.-d. £1 Either single 3.00 3.00

Miniature Sheet

Narcissi — A335

No. 1453: a, c, and e, Flowers, flower to right of "Man." b, d, and f, Flowers, diff, leaf to right of "Man."

2011, Sept. 1 Litho. *Perf. 13¾x13½*

1453 A335 Sheet of 6 3.25 3.25
a.-b. 5p Either single .20 .20
c.-d. 10p Either single .30 .30
e.-f. 35p Either single 1.10 1.10

Miniature Sheet

2011 Commonwealth Youth Games, Isle of Man — A336

No. 1454 — Mascot: a, Running (48x32mm). b, Playing badminton (24x26mm). c, Boxing (24x26mm). d, Playing rugby (24x26mm). e, Cycling (24x26mm). f, On gymnastics horse (24x26mm). g, Crossing finish line (24x26mm). h, Swimming (24x26mm).

Perf. 14x14¾ on 3 or 4 Sides

2011, Sept. 1

1454 A336 Sheet of 8 8.50 8.50
a.-h. 38p Any single 1.05 1.05

Birds in Winter — A337

Designs: (37p), Robin. (38p), Redwing. 58p, Goldfinch. 68p, Siskin. 76p, Waxwing. £2, Long-tailed tit.

2011, Sept. 28 *Perf. 13¼x13*

Panel Color

1455 A337 (37p) bright red 1.05 1.05
1456 A337 (38p) olive brown 1.05 1.05
1457 A337 58p bluish black 1.60 1.60
1458 A337 68p dark green 1.90 1.90
a. Perf. 12½x12 1.90 1.90
1459 A337 76p maroon 2.10 2.10
1460 A337 £2 gray blue 5.25 5.25
Nos. 1455-1460 (6) 12.95 12.95

Self-Adhesive
Panel Color

Rouletted 14

1461 A337 (37p) bright red 1.25 1.25
1462 A337 (38p) olive brown 1.25 1.25

Europa (No. 1458). No. 1458a was printed in sheets of 10.

Transportation Created on *Top Gear* Television Show — A338

Designs: 37p, Triumph Herald Sailboat. 38p, Citroen Grand Design. 58p, Polar Hilux. 68p, Hammerhead Eagle I-thrust. £1.10, Robin Reliant Space Shuttle. £1.82, Caravan Airship.

2011, Nov. 5 Litho. *Perf. 13*

1463 A338 37p multi + label 1.05 1.05
1464 A338 38p multi + label 1.05 1.05
1465 A338 58p multi + label 1.60 1.60
1466 A338 68p multi + label 1.90 1.90
1467 A338 £1.10 multi + label 3.00 3.00
1468 A338 £1.82 multi + label 5.25 5.25
Nos. 1463-1468 (6) 13.85 13.85

Self-Adhesive

Die Cut

1469 A338 £1.10 multi + label 3.25 3.25
1470 A338 £1.82 multi + label 5.75 5.75

Nos. 1469 and 1470 each were printed in sheets of 5.

2012 Summer Olympics, London A339

Designs: 37p, Sailing. 38p, Cycling. 58p, Swimming. 68p, Tennis. 76p, Rowing. £1, Track. £1.15, Archery.
£3, Cycling, diff.

2012, Jan. 1 *Perf. 13½*

1471 A339 37p multi 1.05 1.05
1472 A339 38p multi 1.05 1.05
1473 A339 58p multi 1.60 1.60
1474 A339 68p multi 1.75 1.75
1475 A339 76p multi 2.10 2.10
1476 A339 £1 multi 2.75 2.75
1477 A339 £1.15 multi 3.25 3.25
a. Souvenir sheet of 14, 2 each #1471-1477 30.00 30.00
Nos. 1471-1477 (7) 13.55 13.55

Souvenir Sheet

Perf. 13

1478 A339 £3 multi 8.25 8.25
a. Sheet of 6, 3 each #1472, 1478, + 6 labels 30.00 30.00

No. 1478 contains one 52x40mm stamp. No. 1478a sold for £10.

Reign of Queen Elizabeth II, 60th Anniv. — A340

Photographs of Queen Elizabeth II: 37p, Wearing tiara, 1990. 38p, Trooping the colors, 1979. 58p, Wearing tiara, 1955. 68p, Wearing blue hat, 1982. £1.10, Without hat, 1968. £1.82, Wearing red hat, 2008.
£3, Queen Elizabeth II wearing crown, 2005.

2012 *Perf. 13¼*

1479 A340 37p multi 1.05 1.05
1480 A340 38p multi 1.05 1.05
1481 A340 58p multi 1.60 1.60
1482 A340 68p multi 1.90 1.90
1483 A340 £1.10 multi 3.00 3.00

1484 A340 £1.82 multi 5.00 5.00
a. Souvenir sheet of 6, #1478-1484, + 3 labels 14.50 14.50
Nos. 1479-1484 (6) 13.60 13.60

Souvenir Sheet

1485 A340 £3 multi 8.75 8.75
a. Sheet of 11, #1483-1485, 2 each #1479-1482, + 18 labels 30.00 30.00

Issued: Nos. 1479-1484, 2/6; No. 1485, 4/21; No. 1484a, 2/6; No. 1485a, 6/5.

Frost Arbory, by William Hoggatt (1879-1961) — A341

A Colby Mill, by Hoggatt A342

Landing the Catch, Port St. Mary, by Hoggatt A343

Early Spring, by Hoggatt A344

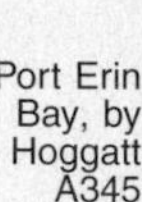

Port Erin Bay, by Hoggatt A345

2012, Feb. 20 *Perf. 14*

1486 A341 38p multi 1.05 1.05
1487 A342 38p multi 1.05 1.05
1488 A343 38p multi 1.05 1.05
1489 A344 38p multi 1.05 1.05
1490 A345 38p multi 1.05 1.05
a. Horiz. strip of 5, #1486-1490 5.25 5.25
Nos. 1486-1490 (5) 5.25 5.25

Sinking of the Titanic, Cent. A346

No. 1491: a, Titanic at dock and at sea, breakfast menu. b, Male passenger, dining room. c, Capt. Edward J. Smith, White Star Line stationery, life preserver.

No. 1492: a, Titanic sinking, life preserver. b, Lifeboats, newspaper boy with newspaper announcing sinking. c, Newspaper, Titanic, passengers.

2012, Apr. 2 **Litho.**

1491 Horiz. strip of 3 4.00 4.00
a. A346 37p multi 1.05 1.05
b. A346 38p multi 1.05 1.05
c. A346 68p multi 1.90 1.90
1492 Horiz. strip of 3 9.75 9.75
a. A346 76p multi 2.10 2.10
b. A346 £1.15 multi 3.25 3.25
c. A346 £1.65 multi 4.50 4.50
d. Souvenir sheet of 9, #1491a-1491c, 2 each #1492a-1492c, + 9 labels 26.50 26.50

Lighthouses A347

Designs: 1p, Castletown Harbor Lighthouse. 68p, Douglas Harbor Lighthouse. 75p, Peel Harbor Lighthouse. £1, Laxey Harbor Lighthouse. £1.30, Ramsey Harbor Lighthouse. £1.60, Port St. Mary Harbor Lighthouse.

2012, Apr. 2 *Perf. 13¾*

1493 A347 1p multi .25 .25
1494 A347 68p multi 1.90 1.90
a. Sheet of 10 19.00 19.00
1495 A347 75p multi 2.10 2.10
1496 A347 £1 multi 2.75 2.75
1497 A347 £1.30 multi 3.75 3.75
1498 A347 £1.60 multi 4.50 4.50
Nos. 1493-1498 (6) 15.25 15.25

Europa (No. 1494).

Manx Tourist Memorabilia — A348

Designs: (38p), Goss China Manx cottage. (41p), Crown Devon Manx race car. 58p, Royal Doulton Postman at Maughold spittoon. 68p, Willow Art China Manx dog. £1.10, Kettlespring Kilns commemorative plate depicting Ginger the Manx cat. £1.82, Archibald Knox Jewel.

2012, May 8 *Perf. 14¾x14¼*

1499 A348 (38p) multi 1.10 1.10
1500 A348 (41p) multi 1.10 1.10
1501 A348 58p multi 1.75 1.75
1502 A348 68p multi 1.90 1.90
1503 A348 £1.10 multi 3.25 3.25
1504 A348 £1.82 multi 5.25 5.25
Nos. 1499-1504 (6) 14.35 14.35

Inscriptions: No. 1499, "IOM." No. 1500, "UK."

Miniature Sheet

Thames Diamond Jubilee Pageant — A349

No. 1505: a, Eighteen-oarsman barge Gloriana (42x28mm). b, Lady of Mann near London Eye (42x28mm). c, Viking longboat Vital Spark (42x28mm). d, Royal barge Spirit of Chartwell (85x28mm).

2012, June 3 *Perf. 14*

1505 A349 Sheet of 4 8.50 8.50
a.-c. 50p Any single 1.40 1.40
d. £1.50 multi 4.25 4.25
e. Souvenir sheet of 12, 3 each #1505a-1505d, + 9 labels 26.00 26.00

Mark Cavendish, Cyclist A350

Cavendish: 38p, Holding Manx flag after winning 2006 Commonwealth Games Scratch race. 41p, Cycling in 2007 Scheldeprijs Vlaanderen. 65p, Cycling in 2009 Milan-San Remo Classic. 71p, Cycling in 2011 Tour de France. 80p, Celebrating victory in 2011 World Road Race Championships. 105p, Wearing rainbow jersey and medal. 116p, Cycling with rainbow jersey.

2012, June 19 *Perf. 13*

1506 A350 38p multi 1.05 1.05
1507 A350 41p multi 1.05 1.05
1508 A350 65p multi 1.75 1.75
1509 A350 71p multi 1.90 1.90
1510 A350 80p multi 2.10 2.10
1511 A350 105p multi 2.75 2.75
1512 A350 116p multi 3.25 3.25
a. Sheet of 13, #1510, 2 each #1506-1509, 1511-1512, + 7 labels 26.00 26.00
Nos. 1506-1512 (7) 13.85 13.85

Bees — A351

Designs: 38p, Colletes succinctus. 41p, Epeolus variegatus. £1, Osmia rufa. £1.05, Halictus rubicundus. £1.30, Bombus monticola. £1.47, Apis mellifera.

2012, Aug. 8 *Perf. 13*

1513 A351 38p multi 1.15 1.15
1514 A351 41p multi 1.15 1.15
1515 A351 £1 multi 3.00 3.00
1516 A351 £1.05 multi 3.00 3.00
1517 A351 £1.30 multi 3.75 3.75
1518 A351 £1.47 multi 4.25 4.25
Nos. 1513-1518 (6) 16.30 16.30

Booklet Stamps Self-Adhesive

Die Cut Perf. 13¼x12¾

1519 A351 38p multi 1.40 1.40
a. Booklet pane of 10 14.00
1520 A351 41p multi 1.40 1.40
a. Booklet pane of 10 14.00

Nos. 1513-1518 were impregnated with a honey scent.

Nos. 1519a and 1520a are complete booklets, the backing service as booklet covers.

Royal Flying Corps, Cent. A352

Military aircraft: 38p, AW FK.8 B5773, 1918. 41p, MS Type L 3253, 1915. 65p, DH.2 5964, 1916. 80p, Sopwith Camel B5648, 1918. £1.37, RAF BE.2C, 4359, 1917. £1.91, Short S.32 402, 1912.

2012, Sept. 20 *Perf. 13¼x13½*

1521 A352 38p multi 1.05 1.05
1522 A352 41p multi 1.20 1.20
1523 A352 65p multi 1.75 1.75
1524 A352 80p multi 2.25 2.25
1525 A352 £1.37 multi 3.75 3.75
1526 A352 £1.91 multi 5.25 5.25
Nos. 1521-1526 (6) 15.25 15.25

Souvenir Sheet

Antarctic Expedition of Robert Falcon Scott, Cent. — A353

No. 1527: a, Expedition ship, Dicovery, and ice. b, Memorial cairn.

2012, Oct. 2 *Perf. 13¼x13*

1527 A353 Sheet of 2 9.00 9.00
a.-b. £1.50 Either single 4.50 4.50

Christmas A354

Designs: 38p, Ramsey Christmas lights. 41p, Mail carrier delivering mail in Glen Auldyn. 71p, Castletown Police Station. £1.05, Sulby Glen. £1.16, Martin's Sweet Shop, Ramsey. £1.73, Lake Lane, Peel.

2012, Oct. 20 *Perf. 13*

1528 A354 38p multi 1.05 1.05
1529 A354 41p multi 1.20 1.20
1530 A354 71p multi 1.90 1.90
1531 A354 £1.05 multi 3.00 3.00
1532 A354 £1.16 multi 3.25 3.25
1533 A354 £1.73 multi 4.75 4.75
Nos. 1528-1533 (6) 15.15 15.15

Self-Adhesive

Serpentine Die Cut 11¼

1534 A354 38p multi 1.25 1.25
1535 A354 41p multi 1.40 1.40

Chronicles of Man and Lewis Chessmen A355

Various chessmen and segments of text from Chronicles with panel color of: 38p, Gray. 41p, Red violet. 71p, Bister. 80p, Purple. 130p, Green. 191p, Brown.

2013, Jan. 11 *Perf. 13½*

1536 A355 38p multi 1.05 1.05
1537 A355 41p multi 1.20 1.20
1538 A355 71p multi 2.10 2.10
1539 A355 80p multi 2.25 2.25
1540 A355 130p multi 3.75 3.75
1541 A355 191p multi 5.25 5.25
Nos. 1536-1541 (6) 15.60 15.60

Items Produced to Commemorate Coronations — A356

Items depicting: 38p, Queen Victoria. 41p, King Edward VII. 65p, King George V. £1.05, King George VI. £1.37, Queen Elizabeth II. £1.73, Queen Elizabeth II, diff.

2013, Feb. 6 *Perf. 14*

1542 A356 38p multi 1.05 1.05
1543 A356 41p multi 1.20 1.20
1544 A356 65p multi 1.75 1.75
1545 A356 £1.05 multi 3.00 3.00
1546 A356 £1.37 multi 3.75 3.75
1547 A356 £1.73 multi 4.75 4.75
a. Dated "2015" 5.25 5.25
b. Sheet of 26 57.50 57.50
Nos. 1542-1547 (6) 18.25 18.25

Issued: No. 1547a, 11/27/15. No. 1547a was issued in a sheet containing 26 stamps depicting Queen Elizabeth II from various countries. Twenty-four of the stamps in the sheet have the same designs as previously-issued stamps, though perforations may differ (Antigua No. 3182b, Ascension No. 1142, Bahamas No. 1438, Barbados No. 1198, British Antarctic Territory No. 486, Cook Islands No. 1542a, Falkland Islands No. 1147, Grenada No. 3912, Kenya No. 88, Nevis No. 1521a, New Zealand No. 2602. Niue No. 876, St. Kitts No. 696a, Samoa No. 1220c, Sierra Leone No. 2007, South Georgia and South Sandwich Islands No. 539, Tanzania No. 1595, Tokelau No. 404, Tonga No. 1282d, Tristan da Cunha No. 1047, Turks and Caicos Islands No. 1454b, Tuvalu No. 1234a, Uganda No. 1493 and Zambia No. 685a). The sheet also contains a stamp that is an altered version of St. Vincent No. 3820 and a Papua New Guinea stamp that is unlike any previous Papua New Guinea issue. The foreign stamps on the sheet may be recognized as valid in those countries, but the entire sheet was sold only by Isle of Man postal authorities for £20.

Miniature Sheet

New Year 2013 (Year of the Snake) — A357

No. 1548: a, Snake. b, Chinese character with fish, flowers and butterfly. c, Chinese character with cranes and peaches. d, Chinese character with deer. e, Chinese character with birds and flowers. f, Snake coiled in spiral.

2013, Feb. 8			***Perf. 12***	
1548	A357	Sheet of 6, #a-f	8.00	8.00
a.		5p multi	.25	.25
b.-e.		20p Any single	.45	.45
f.		£2.15 multi	5.50	5.50
g.		Sheet of 20, #1548b-1548e, 16 #1548a	4.00	4.00

Also exists as perf. 15 with same values.

Isle of Man Constabulary, 150th Anniv. — A358

Designs: 38p, Uniforms. 41p, Vehicles. 71p, Dogs. 80p, Communications. £1.47, Community. £1.82, Stations.

2013, Feb. 20			***Perf. 14***	
1549	A358	38p multi	1.05	1.05
1550	A358	41p multi	1.05	1.05
1551	A358	71p multi	1.90	1.90
1552	A358	80p multi	2.10	2.10
1553	A358	£1.47 multi	3.75	3.75
1554	A358	£1.82 multi	4.75	4.75
		Nos. 1549-1554 (6)	17.25	17.25

Souvenir Sheet

Isle of Man Fire and Rescue Services — A359

2013, Feb. 20			***Perf. 13¾x14***	
1555	A359	£3 multi	8.00	8.00

Manx Triskelion — A360

Various depictions of Manx triskelion (national symbol).

2013, Apr. 13			***Perf. 13¼***	
1556	A360	5p multi	.25	.25
1557	A360	10p multi	.25	.25
1558	A360	40p multi	1.05	1.05
1559	A360	42p multi	1.05	1.05
1560	A360	69p multi	1.75	1.75
1561	A360	73p multi	1.90	1.90
1562	A360	£1.19 multi	3.25	3.25
1563	A360	£2 multi	5.00	5.00
		Nos. 1556-1563 (8)	14.50	14.50

Booklet Stamps
Self-Adhesive

Die Cut Perf. 12¾x13¼

1564	A360	40p Like #1558	1.25	1.25
a.		Booklet pane of 10	12.50	
1565	A360	42p Like #1559	1.25	1.25
a.		Booklet pane of 10	12.50	

Nos. 1564a and 1565a are complete booklets, the backing serving as the booklet covers.

Souvenir Sheet

Coronation of Queen Elizabeth II, 60th Anniv. — A361

2013, Apr. 21			***Perf. 14¾x14***	
1566	A361	£3 multi	8.00	8.00

Robin Gibb (1949-2012), Singer A362

Record covers: 2p, Robin's Reign, 1970. 40p, How Old Are You, 1983. 42p, Secret Agent, 1984. 50p, Walls Have Eyes, 1985. 69p, Magnet, 2003. 73p, Robin Gibb Live with the Neue Philharmonie Orchestra, 2005. 120p, The Titanic Requiem, 2012. 178p, 50 St. Catherine's Drive, 2013.

2013, Apr. 24			***Perf. 13¼***	
1567	A362	2p multi	.25	.25
1568	A362	40p multi	1.05	1.05
1569	A362	42p multi	1.20	1.20
1570	A362	50p multi	1.35	1.35
1571	A362	69p multi	1.90	1.90
1572	A362	73p multi	1.90	1.90
1573	A362	120p multi	3.25	3.25
1574	A362	178p multi	4.75	4.75
a.		Sheet of 12, #1567-1570, 2 each #1571-1574, + 3 labels	32.00	32.00
		Nos. 1567-1574 (8)	15.65	15.65

Railways — A363

Rolling stock, company emblems and slogan: 40p, The Best Way to the Beauty Spots. 42p, The Perfect Resort So Near to Home. 69p, Breezy and Invigorating. 119p, Isle of Man for Happy Holidays. 160p, Port Erin Southern Beauty Spot. 161p, The Finest Glens and Mountain Views.

2013, May 17		**Litho.**	***Perf. 14***	
1575	A363	40p multi	1.05	1.05
1576	A363	42p multi	1.20	1.20
1577	A363	69p multi	1.90	1.90
1578	A363	119p multi	3.25	3.25
1579	A363	160p multi	4.25	4.25
1580	A363	161p multi	4.25	4.25
		Nos. 1575-1580 (6)	15.90	15.90

100th Tour de France Bicycle Race — A364

Cyclists: 1p, Eugène Christophe (1885-1970). 40p, Mark Cavendish. 42p, Brian Robinson. 69p, Miguel Indurain. 73p, Jacques Anquetil (1934-87). 108p, Eddy Merckx. 119p, Bernard Hinault. 120p, Bradley Wiggins.

2013, June 19			***Perf. 13¼***	
1581	A364	1p multi	.25	.25
a.		Dated "2014"	.25	.25
1582	A364	40p multi	1.05	1.05
a.		Dated "2014"	1.05	1.05
b.		Souvenir sheet of 2 #1582a + 3 labels	2.10	2.10
1583	A364	42p multi	1.05	1.05
a.		Dated "2014"	1.20	1.20
b.		Souvenir sheet of 2 #1583a + 3 labels	2.25	2.25
1584	A364	69p multi	1.75	1.75
a.		Dated "2014"	1.90	1.90
1585	A364	73p multi	1.90	1.90
a.		Dated "2014"	2.00	2.00
b.		Souvenir sheet of 2, #1584a, 1585a, + 3 labels	4.00	4.00
1586	A364	108p multi	2.75	2.75
a.		Dated "2014"	3.00	3.00
b.		Souvenir sheet of 2 #1586a + 3 labels	6.00	6.00
1587	A364	119p multi	3.25	3.25
a.		Dated "2014"	3.25	3.25
b.		Souvenir sheet of 2, #1581a, 1587a, + 3 labels	3.50	3.50
1588	A364	120p multi	3.25	3.25
a.		Dated "2014"	3.25	3.25
b.		Souvenir sheet of 2 #1588a + 3 labels	6.50	6.50
		Nos. 1581-1588 (8)	15.25	15.25

Issued: Nos. 1581a-1588a, 2014.

The Times Newspaper, 225th Anniv. — A365

News stories: 40p, Last flight of the Concorde, 2003. 42p, England wins the World Cup, 1966. 73p, Isle of Man postal independence, 1973. 108p, State visit of Queen Elizabeth II to the People's Republic of China, 1986. 141p, Assassination of Pres. John F. Kennedy in Dallas, 1963. 179p, Man lands on the Moon, 1969.

2013, July 4			***Perf. 14¾x14***	
1589	A365	40p multi + label	1.05	1.05
1590	A365	42p multi + label	1.05	1.05
1591	A365	73p multi + label	1.90	1.90
a.		Miniature sheet of 10 + 10 labels	19.00	19.00
1592	A365	108p multi + label	2.75	2.75
1593	A365	141p multi + label	3.75	3.75
1594	A365	179p multi + label	4.75	4.75
		Nos. 1589-1594 (6)	15.25	15.25

Europa (No. 1591).

Souvenir Sheet

St. Thomas' Church Murals by John Miller Nicholson (1840-1913) — A366

No. 1595: a, Angels with banner. b, Saints.

2013, Aug. 8			***Perf. 13x13¼***	
1595	A366	Sheet of 2	8.00	8.00
a.		£1 multi	2.75	2.75
b.		£2 multi	5.25	5.25

A367

Paintings of Wildlife by Jeremy Paul — A368

Designs: 40p, Lion. 42p, Snow leopard. 69p, Tiger. 120p, Cheetah. 160p, Leopard. 161p, Jaguar.

No. 1602: a, Baboon. b, Rhinoceros, horiz. c, Giraffes, horiz. d, Kudu.

2013, Sept. 13		**Litho.**	***Perf. 13¼***	
1596	A367	40p multi	1.05	1.05
1597	A367	42p multi	1.20	1.20
1598	A367	69p multi	1.90	1.90
1599	A367	120p multi	3.25	3.25
1600	A367	160p multi	4.25	4.25
1601	A367	161p multi	4.50	4.50
		Nos. 1596-1601 (6)	16.15	16.15

Souvenir Sheet

1602	A368	Sheet of 4	8.25	8.25
a.-d.		75p Any single	2.00	2.00

Christmas — A369

Details of vignettes from past Isle of Man Christmas stamps: 40p, Mailing letters, 1990 (#436). 42p, Three Kings, 1991 (#488). 73p, Angel with Crown of Glory, 2005 (#1129). 108p, Robin, 1988 (#378). 119p, Church and holly, 1995 (#662). 178p, Christmas tree, 2006 (#1172).

2013, Oct. 17		**Litho.**	***Perf. 13¼***	
1603	A369	40p multi	1.05	1.05
1604	A369	42p multi	1.20	1.20
1605	A369	73p multi	2.10	2.10
1606	A369	108p multi	3.00	3.00
1607	A369	119p multi	3.25	3.25
1608	A369	178p multi	5.00	5.00
		Nos. 1603-1608 (6)	15.60	15.60

Self-Adhesive

Serpentine Die Cut 11x11¼

1609	A369	40p multi	1.10	1.10
1610	A369	42p multi	1.25	1.25

Isle of Man, Island of Culture A370

Designs: No. 1611, Visual arts. No. 1612, Drama. No. 1613, Literaure. No. 1614, Film. No. 1615, Music. No. 1616, Craft. No. 1617, Dance. No. 1618, Design.

2014, Jan. 6		**Litho.**	***Perf. 13***	
1611	A370	IOM multi	1.20	1.20
1612	A370	IOM multi	1.20	1.20
1613	A370	UK multi	1.20	1.20
1614	A370	UK multi	1.20	1.20
1615	A370	EU multi	2.10	2.10
a.		Miniature sheet of 10	21.00	21.00
1616	A370	RoW multi	2.10	2.10
1617	A370	RoW multi	3.50	3.50
1618	A370	RoW multi	3.50	3.50
		Nos. 1611-1618 (8)	16.00	16.00

Europa (No. 1615). On day of issue, Nos. 1611-1612 each sold for 40p, Nos. 1613-1614 each sold for 42p, Nos. 1615 sold for 73p, and Nos. 1616-1618 each sold for £1.19.

Miniature Sheet

Winter Flora — A371

No. 1619: a, Ivy berries (denomination at UR). b, Teasels (denomination at UL). c, Hellebore flowers (denomination at UR). d, Rose hips (denomination at UL).

2014, Jan. 6		**Litho.**	***Perf. 13***	
1619	A371	Sheet of 4, #a-d	8.50	8.50
a.-d.		75p Any single	2.10	2.10

Compare No. 1619c with No. 1659.

World War I, Cent. A372

Photographs of soldiers, memorial poppies, and inscription: 40p, Communications. 42p, Sappers. 69p, Trenches. £1.08, Horses. £1.41, Christmas truce. £1.60, Officers' dugout.

2014, Feb. 19 Litho. *Perf. 14*

1620	A372	40p multi	1.20	1.20
1621	A372	42p multi	1.20	1.20
1622	A372	69p multi	1.90	1.90
1623	A372	£1.08 multi	3.00	3.00
1624	A372	£1.41 multi	4.00	4.00
1625	A372	£1.60 multi	4.50	4.50
		Nos. 1620-1625 (6)	15.80	15.80

See Nos. 1698-1703.

Souvenir Sheet

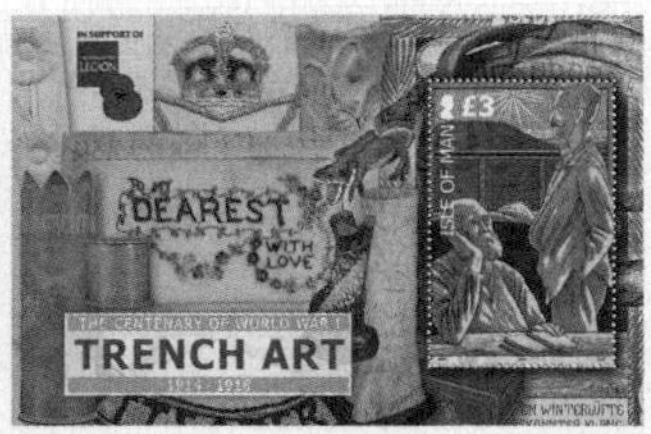

World War I Trench Art — A373

2014, Feb. 19 Litho. *Perf. 15x14¼*

1626	A373	£3 multi	8.50	8.50

Royal Air Force Red Arrows Aerobatic Team — A374

Various photographs of Red Arrows in flight.

2014, Feb. 19 Litho. *Perf. 13¼*

1627	A374	40p multi	1.20	1.20
1628	A374	42p multi	1.20	1.20
1629	A374	69p multi	1.90	1.90
1630	A374	73p multi	2.10	2.10
1631	A374	108p multi	3.00	3.00
1632	A374	265p multi	7.50	7.50
		Nos. 1627-1632 (6)	16.90	16.90

Red Arrows Type of 2014

Designs as before.

Serpentine Die Cut 13¾

2014 Self-Adhesive Litho.

Booklet Stamps

1633	A374	40p multi	1.40	1.40
1634	A374	42p multi	1.40	1.40
1635	A374	69p multi	2.25	2.25
a.		Booklet pane of 3, #1633-1635	5.25	
1636	A374	73p multi	2.40	2.40
1637	A374	108p multi	3.50	3.50
1638	A374	265p multi	8.75	8.75
a.		Booklet pane of 3, #1636-1638	15.00	
b.		Booklet pane of 6, #1633-1638	20.00	
		Complete booklet, #1635a, 1638a, 1638b	41.00	

No. 1638b was also sold separately from complete booklet.

Deer's Cry — A375

To the Virtue of His Crucifixion With — A376

In Splendor of Fire — A377

God's Wisdom to Guide Me — A378

In Compactness of Rock — A379

God's Shield to Protect Me — A380

His Ascension A381

In the Creator of the Universe A382

God's Way to Lie Before Me — A383

I Bind Myself Today To — A384

2014, Apr. 4 Litho. *Perf. 13¼x12½*

1639		Horiz. strip of 5	6.00	6.00
a.	A375	42p multi	1.20	1.20
b.	A376	42p multi	1.20	1.20
c.	A377	42p multi	1.20	1.20
d.	A378	42p multi	1.20	1.20
e.	A379	42p multi	1.20	1.20
1640		Horiz. strip of 5	11.00	11.00
a.	A380	75p multi	2.20	2.20
b.	A381	75p multi	2.20	2.20
c.	A382	75p multi	2.20	2.20
d.	A383	75p multi	2.20	2.20
e.	A384	75p multi	2.20	2.20

Booklet Stamps Self-Adhesive

Serpentine Die Cut 13½

1641	A375	42p multi	1.40	1.40
1642	A376	42p multi	1.40	1.40
1643	A377	42p multi	1.40	1.40
1644	A378	42p multi	1.40	1.40
1645	A379	42p multi	1.40	1.40
a.		Booklet pane of 12, 3 each #1641, 1645, 2 each #1642-1644	17.00	
		Nos. 1641-1645 (5)	7.00	7.00

Manuscript illuminations by Archibald Knox (1864-1933).

Battle of Clontarf, 1000th Anniv. — A385

Designs: 2p, Brodir the Warrior. 42p, Battle of Clontarf. 90p, Eithne weaves the raven banner. £1, Clontarf warrior. £1.60, King Brian Boru. £2.30, Fight for the raven banner.

2014, Apr. 15 Litho. *Perf. 14*

1646	A385	2p multi	.25	.25
1647	A385	42p multi	1.15	1.15
1648	A385	90p multi	2.40	2.40
1649	A385	£1 multi	2.75	2.75
1650	A385	£1.60 multi	4.50	4.50
1651	A385	£2.30 multi	6.25	6.25
		Nos. 1646-1651 (6)	17.30	17.30

Miniature Sheet

Rare Farm Animal Breeds — A386

No. 1652: a, Manx Loaghtan ram. b, Northern dairy shorthorn cattle. c, Cotswold sheep. d, Exmoor ponies. e, Gloucester old spot pig. f, Irish moiled cattle.

2014, Apr. 16 Litho. *Perf. 13¼x13½*

1652	A386	Sheet of 6	6.00	6.00
a.-f.		38p Any single	1.00	1.00

Southern District Agricultural Society, cent.; Rare Breeds Survival Trust, 40th anniv.

D-Day, 70th Anniv. A387

Various photographs of invading troops in action.

2014, May 8 Litho. *Perf. 14*

1653	A387	42p blk & red	1.15	1.15
1654	A387	75p blk & red	2.00	2.00
1655	A387	90p blk & red	2.40	2.40
1656	A387	110p multi	3.00	3.00
1657	A387	144p blk & red	4.00	4.00
1658	A387	182p blk & red	4.75	4.75
a.		Sheet of 16, #602a, 603b, 606a, 607b, 1028c, 1028d, 1029c, 1029d, 1030c, 1030d, 1031c, 1031d, 1032e, 1032f, 1657-1658	24.00	24.00
		Nos. 1653-1658 (6)	17.30	17.30

Winter Flowers A388

2014, July 16 Litho. *Perf. 12¾*

1659	A388	75p multi	2.10	2.10

Compare No. 1659 with No. 1619c.

Manx Playing Cards — A389

Designs: 42p, Ace of clubs with Peel Castle and Douglas Lighthouse. 75p, Ace of diamonds with Douglas and Douglas Iron Pier. 90p, Ace of spades with Webb's Louvre. 110p, Ace of hearts with Bradda Head and Douglas Lighthouse. 121p, Ace of spades with Laxey Wheel and Fort Anne Hotel. 182p, Ace of diamonds with Groudle Wheel and Peel Castle.

2014, Aug. 8 Litho. *Perf. 13x12½*

1660	A389	42p multi	1.15	1.15
1661	A389	75p multi	2.00	2.00
1662	A389	90p multi	2.40	2.40
1663	A389	110p multi	3.00	3.00
1664	A389	121p multi	3.25	3.25
1665	A389	182p multi	4.75	4.75
		Nos. 1660-1665 (6)	16.55	16.55

Souvenir Sheet

MS Queen Elizabeth and Map of Panama — A390

2014, Aug. 8 Litho. *Perf. 14¼*

1666	A390	£3.50 multi	9.25	9.25

Panama Canal, cent.

Constellations — A391

Designs: 42p, Orion. 164p, Leo. 182p, Cygnus. 230p, Andromeda.

2014, Sept. 1 Litho. *Perf. 14¼*

1667	A391	42p multi	1.15	1.15
1668	A391	164p multi	4.50	4.50
1669	A391	182p multi	4.75	4.75
1670	A391	230p multi	6.25	6.25
		Nos. 1667-1670 (4)	16.65	16.65

Aircraft Type of 1997

2014 Litho. *Perf. 14*

1671	A171	75p Sopwith Tabloid	2.00	2.00

No. 1671 was printed in sheets of 5 + 4 labels. Imperforate sheets of 5 + 4 labels sold for £7.50.

Manx Radio, 50th Anniv. A392

Designs: No. 1672, Mannin Line. No. 1673, Countryside. No. 1674, Weather reports. No. 1675, Jackson's Jollybodys. No. 1676, Mandate. No. 1677, Jazz Hour. No. 1678, Radio TT. No. 1679, Outside broadcasts.

2014, Oct. 1 Litho. *Perf. 13½*

1672	A392	42p multi	1.15	1.15
1673	A392	42p multi	1.15	1.15
1674	A392	50p multi	1.30	1.30
1675	A392	50p multi	1.30	1.30
1676	A392	75p multi	1.90	1.90
1677	A392	75p multi	1.90	1.90

1678 A392 £1.20 multi 3.25 3.25
1679 A392 £1.20 multi 3.25 3.25
Nos. 1672-1679 (8) 15.20 15.20

Souvenir Sheet

Celtic Kingdom Festival of Silk — A393

2014, Oct. 23 Litho. *Perf. 13x12¾*
1680 A393 £3 multi 7.75 7.75

Christmas — A394

Scenes from *The Snowman and the Snowdog,* by Raymond Briggs: Nos. 1681, 1687, Snowman, Snowdog and Billy flying. Nos. 1682, 1688, Snowman, Snowdog and Santa Claus. 75p, Snowman and Snowdog. 90p, Snowdog chasing ball. £1.21, Snowman skiing, Snowdog and Billy on toboggan. £2.21, Snowman, Snowdog and Billy.

2014, Oct. 23 Litho. *Perf. 13*
1681 A394 42p multi 1.15 1.15
1682 A394 42p multi 1.15 1.15
1683 A394 75p multi 1.90 1.90
1684 A394 90p multi 2.40 2.40
1685 A394 £1.21 multi 3.25 3.25
1686 A394 £2.21 multi 5.75 5.75
Nos. 1681-1686 (6) 15.60 15.60

Self-Adhesive

Serpentine Die Cut 11¼
1687 A394 42p multi 1.15 1.15
1688 A394 42p multi 1.15 1.15

Souvenir Sheet

New Year 2015 (Year of the Sheep) — A395

2015, Jan. 2 Litho. *Perf. 13¼*
1689 A395 Sheet of 2 7.75 7.75
a. 10p Ram .25 .25
b. £3 Ewe 7.25 7.25
c. Sheet of 16 #1689a + 4 labels 4.00 4.00

Sir Winston Churchill (1874-1965), Prime Minister — A396

Churchill: No. 1690, As young man wearing military uniform. No. 1691, Wearing top hat. No. 1692, With hand on hip. No. 1693, Reading while smoking cigar. No. 1694, Giving victory salute. No. 1695, Behind microphone. No. 1696, Painting picture. No. 1697, Building brick wall.

2015, Jan. 2 Litho. *Perf. 13¾x13½*
1690 A396 42p multi 1.10 1.10
1691 A396 42p multi 1.10 1.10
a. Vert. pair, #1690-1691 2.20 2.20
1692 A396 75p multi 2.00 2.00
1693 A396 75p multi 2.00 2.00
a. Vert. pair, #1692-1693 4.00 4.00
1694 A396 90p multi 2.25 2.25
1695 A396 90p multi 2.25 2.25
a. Vert. pair, #1694-1695 4.50 4.50
1696 A396 110p multi 2.75 2.75
1697 A396 110p multi 2.75 2.75
a. Vert. pair, #1696-1697 5.50 5.50
Nos. 1690-1697 (8) 16.20 16.20

World War I, Cent. Type of 2014

Photographs, memorial poppies and inscription: No. 1698, Home Front. No. 1699, Palestine. 75p, Western Front. £1.10, Eastern Front. £1.44, Gallipoli. £1.64, Italy.

2015, Feb. 17 Litho. *Perf. 14*
1698 A372 42p multi 1.10 1.10
1699 A372 42p multi 1.10 1.10
1700 A372 75p multi 1.90 1.90
1701 A372 £1.10 multi 2.75 2.75
1702 A372 £1.44 multi 3.75 3.75
1703 A372 £1.64 multi 4.00 4.00
Nos. 1698-1703 (6) 14.60 14.60

Nos. 1698-1703 each were printed in sheets of 8 + central label.

Penny Black, 175th Anniv. A397

Designs: 1p, Great Britain #1. 42p, Great Britain #2. 90p, Great Britain #3. £1.20, Stanley Gibbons (1840-1913), stamp dealer, and *Gibbons Stamp Monthly.* £1.60, William Mulready (1786-1863), designer of stamped envelopes, Great Britain #U1. £2.30, Sir Rowland Hill (1795-1879), inventor of postage stamp, cover bearing Great Britain #3.

2015, Feb. 17 Litho. *Perf. 13¾*
1704 A397 1p multi .25 .25
1705 A397 42p multi 1.00 1.00
1706 A397 90p multi 2.25 2.25
a. Sheet of 20, 16 #1704, 2 each #1705-1706 7.00 7.00
1707 A397 £1.20 multi 3.00 3.00
1708 A397 £1.60 multi 4.00 4.00
1709 A397 £2.30 multi 5.75 5.75
Nos. 1704-1709 (6) 16.25 16.25

Victory in World War II, 70th Anniv. — A398

No. 1710: a, Gurkha soldier. b, Soldier aiming rifle.
£1.50, Military medal, woman celebrating victory in Europe, newspaper.

2015, Feb. 26 Litho. *Perf. 13¾*
1710 A398 Sheet of 2 5.25 5.25
a.-b. £1 Either single 2.60 2.60
c. Sheet of 10 #1710a + 10 labels 26.00 26.00

Souvenir Sheet
1711 A398 £1.50 multi 4.00 4.00

Caesar Bacon (1791-1876) and Duke of Wellington (1769-1862) A399

2015, Mar. 9 Litho. *Perf. 13¼*
1712 A399 £1 multi 3.00 3.00

Napoleon's Hundred Days Campaign, 200th anniv.

Millennium of Tynwald Tapestry — A400

Inscriptions: Nos. 1713a, 1715, The Viking Arrival. Nos. 1713b, 1716, Manx Bill of Rights. Nos. 1713c, 1717, Tourist Industry. Nos. 1713d, 1718, Spuds 'n' Herring. Nos. 1713e, 1719, Fishing Industry. No. 1714a, TT. No. 1714b, Transport. No. 1714c, Old House of Keys in Castletown. No. 1714d, Woman's Suffrage. No. 1714e, Tynwald Hill.

2015, Apr. 10 Litho. *Perf. 14¼*
1713 Horiz. strip of 5 5.25 5.25
a.-e. A400 1st Any single 1.05 1.05
1714 Horiz. strip of 5 9.50 9.50
a.-e. A400 EU Any single 1.90 1.90
f. As "b," Queen's head 5mm tall 1.90 1.90

Booklet Stamps
Self-Adhesive

Die Cut Perf. 13¼
1715 A400 1st multi 1.25 1.25
1716 A400 1st multi 1.25 1.25
1717 A400 1st multi 1.25 1.25
1718 A400 1st multi 1.25 1.25
1719 A400 1st multi 1.25 1.25
a. Booklet pane of 12, 3 each #1715, 1717, 2 each #1716, 1718, 1719 15.00
Nos. 1715-1719 (5) 6.25 6.25

Europa (#1714b, 1714f). On day of issue, Nos. 1713a-1713e, 1715-1719 each sold for 42p, and Nos. 1714a-1714e each sold for 75p. Queen's head is 4½mm tall on No. 1714b. No. 1715f was printed in sheets of 10.

Women's Institute, Cent. — A401

Designs: No. 1720, Women with loudspeaker. No. 1721, Two women with signs supporting dairy farmers. No. 1722, Women protesting for equal pay. No. 1723, Women protesting for litter control. No. 1724, Group of women with signs supporting dairy farmers. No. 1725, Women with signs showing years and achievements.

2015, Apr. 25 Litho. *Perf. 13½*
1720 A401 1st multi 1.05 1.05
1721 A401 1st multi 1.05 1.05
1722 A401 £1 multi 2.75 2.75
1723 A401 £1 multi 2.75 2.75
1724 A401 £1.75 multi 4.75 4.75
1725 A401 £1.75 multi 4.75 4.75
Nos. 1720-1725 (6) 17.10 17.10

On day of issue, Nos. 1720-1721 each sold for 42p. Nos. 1720-1725 are impregnated with a rose scent.

Miniature Sheet

Paintings of Ships by John Halsall — A402

No. 1726: a, Master Frank. b, HMS Ramsey. c, HMS Ben my Chree. d, Lusitania and Wanderer.

2015, May 1 Litho. *Perf. 13½x13¾*
1726 A402 Sheet of 4 9.00 9.00
a.-b. 75p Either single 1.90 1.90
c.-d. £1 Either single 2.60 2.60

A403

A404

A405

Battle of Waterloo, 200th Anniv. — A406

No. 1727: a, Duke of Wellington on horseback. b, Battle of Quatre-Bras.
No. 1728: a, Fighting at La Haye-Sainte. b, Napoleon in the Battle of Waterloo.
No. 1729: a, Defense of Château de Hougoumont. b, Wellington defeats Ney at Quatre-Bras.
No. 1730: a, Wellington and Blücher. b, General Hill and the Last Stand of the French Imperial Guard.

2015, May 8 Litho. *Perf. 12¾*
1727 A403 Horiz. pair 4.00 4.00
a.-b. 75p Either single 2.00 2.00
1728 A404 Horiz. pair 4.00 4.00
a.-b. 75p Either single 2.00 2.00
1729 A405 Horiz. pair 4.50 4.50
a.-b. 90p Either single 2.25 2.25
1730 A406 Horiz. pair 4.50 4.50
a.-b. 90p Either single 2.25 2.25
Nos. 1727-1730 (4) 17.00 17.00

Queen Elizabeth II — A407

Various photographs of Queen Elizabeth II with inscriptions of: Nos. 1731, 1739a, The Coronation. Nos. 1732, 1739b, The Investiture. Nos. 1733, 1739c, The Silver Jubilee. Nos. 1734, 1739d, Order of the Garter. Nos. 1735, 1739e, Trooping the Color. Nos. 1736, 1739f, The Golden Jubilee. Nos. 1737, 1739g, The Diamond Jubilee. Nos. 1738, 1739h, Opening of Parliament.

Perf. 14¼x14¾
2015, June 18 Litho.
1731 A407 44p multi 1.10 1.10
1732 A407 44p multi 1.10 1.10
1733 A407 77p multi 1.90 1.90
1734 A407 77p multi 1.90 1.90
1735 A407 93p multi 2.40 2.40
1736 A407 93p multi 2.40 2.40
1737 A407 £1.24 multi 3.25 3.25
1738 A407 £1.24 multi 3.25 3.25
Nos. 1731-1738 (8) 17.30 17.30

Miniature Sheet
Self-Adhesive

Die Cut Perf. 11¾
1739 Sheet of 8 19.00
a.-b. A407 44p Either single 1.20 1.20
c.-d. A407 77p Either single 2.00 2.00
e.-f. A407 93p Either single 2.60 2.60
g.-h. A407 £1.24 Either single 3.50 3.50
i. Booklet pane of 2, #1739a-1739b 2.40
j. Booklet pane of 3, #1739c-1739e 6.60
k. Booklet pane of 3, #1739f-1739h 9.60
l. Booklet pane of 8, #1739a-1739h 18.60
Complete booklet, #1739i-1739l 37.50

No. 1739l has staple holes and other half of the folio. No. 1739 can be cut from No. 1739l.

Curraghs Wildlife Park, 50th Anniv. — A408

Designs: No. 1740, Humboldt penguin. No. 1741, Red panda. 93p, Ruffed lemur. £1.13, Waldrapp ibis. £1.24, Fishing cat. £2.38, Rodrigues fruit bat.

2015, July 3 Litho. *Perf. 13¾x13¼*
1740 A408 44p multi 1.10 1.10
1741 A408 44p multi 1.10 1.10
1742 A408 93p multi 2.60 2.60
1743 A408 £1.13 multi 3.00 3.00

1744 A408 £1.24 multi 3.50 3.50
1745 A408 £2.38 multi 6.50 6.50
Nos. 1740-1745 (6) 17.80 17.80

Buses
A409

Designs: 44p, Douglas Corporation Transport Leyland Cub KPZ1. 60p, Isle of Man Road Services Leyland/MCW Olympic HR40. 77p, Isle of Man Road Services Leyland Tiger PS1. 93p, Douglas Corporation Transport Daimler CWA6. 147p, Isle of Man Road Services Leyland Titan PD1. 186p, Douglas Corporation Transport AEC Regent 1.

2015, July 15 Litho. *Perf. 13¼*

1746 A409 44p multi 1.10 1.10
1747 A409 60p multi 1.60 1.60
1748 A409 77p multi 2.00 2.00
1749 A409 93p multi 2.60 2.60
1750 A409 147p multi 4.00 4.00
1751 A409 186p multi 5.00 5.00
Nos. 1746-1751 (6) 16.30 16.30

1865 Companies Act, 150th Anniv. — A410

Registration certificates and memorabilia of: 44p, Isle of Man Bank Limited. 77p, Isle of Man Steam Packet Company Limited. 93p, Finch Hill Pavilion and Bowling Club Limited. 113p, Heron and Brearley Limited. 154p, Farmers Combine Limited. 165p, Peel Golf Club Limited.

2015, Sept. 28 Litho. *Perf. 13¼*

1752 A410 44p multi 1.10 1.10
1753 A410 77p multi 2.00 2.00
1754 A410 93p multi 2.60 2.60
1755 A410 113p multi 3.00 3.00
1756 A410 154p multi 4.00 4.00
1757 A410 165p multi 4.25 4.25
Nos. 1752-1757 (6) 16.95 16.95

Art of Bryan Kneale — A411

No. 1758: a, Self-portrait, 1954. b, Pendulum, 1964. c, The Watcher, 1977. d, Three Legs of Man, 1979. e, Horse, 1985. f, The Deemster Fish, 1996. g, Captain Quilliam, 2005. h, Illiam Dhone, 2006. i, Triton III, 2009. j, Quince, 2015.

2015, Oct. 1 Litho. *Perf. 13¼x12½*

1758 Block of 10 12.00 12.00
a.-j. A411 44p Any single 1.20 1.20

Christmas — A412

Manx words from Manx Christmas Prayer Book: 44p, Niart (strength). 77p, Grayse (grace). 93p, Shee (peace). 124p, Graih (love). 320p, Credjue (faith).

Serpentine Die Cut 13½

2015, Oct. 23 Litho.

Self-Adhesive

1759 A412 44p multi 1.10 1.10
a. Booklet pane of 10 11.00
1760 A412 77p multi 2.00 2.00
1761 A412 93p multi 2.60 2.60
1762 A412 124p multi 3.50 3.50
1763 A412 320p multi 8.50 8.50
Nos. 1759-1763 (5) 17.70 17.70

Manx Christmas Prayer Book, 250th anniv.

Royal Aeronautical Society, 150th Anniv.
A413

No. 1764: a, 1784 balloon ascent of Vincenzo Lunardi. b, Sir George Cayley (1773-1857), and flying machine designs. c, Wright A Flyer at Reims, France, 1909. d, Yuri Gagarin (1934-68), first man in space.

No. 1765: a, Hawker P1127. b, British Airways Concorde. c, Rolls-Royce Trent 900 jet engine. d, International Space Station.

2016, Jan. 12 Litho. *Perf. 13¼*

1764 Horiz. strip of 4 7.00 7.00
a.-b. A413 1st Either single 1.25 1.25
c.-d. A413 77p Either single 2.25 2.25
1765 Horiz. strip of 4 13.00 13.00
a.-b. A413 93p Either single 2.75 2.75
c.-d. A413 124p Either single 3.75 3.75

Nos. 1764a-1764b each sold for 44p on day of issue.

New Year 2016 (Year of the Monkey) — A414

No. 1766: a, One monkey. b, Two monkeys.

2016, Jan. 20 Litho. *Perf. 13¼*

1766 A414 Sheet of 2 6.00 6.00
a. 10p multi .25 .25
b. £2 multi 5.75 5.75
c. Sheet of 20 #1766a 5.00 5.00

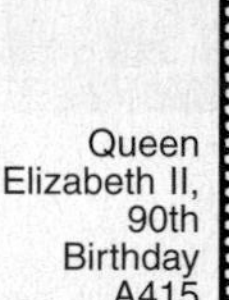

Queen Elizabeth II, 90th Birthday
A415

Queen Elizabeth II wearing: No. 1767, Purple coat and hat. No. 1768, Maroon coat, red and maroon hat. No. 1769, Bright green coat and hat. No. 1770, White dress and tiara. No. 1771, Royal blue and greenish blue coat and hat. No. 1772, Red dress. No. 1773, Pale blue coat and hat. No. 1774, Red coat and hat.

2016 Litho. *Perf. 13*

1767 A415 1st multi 1.25 1.25
1768 A415 1st multi 1.25 1.25
1769 A415 77p multi 2.25 2.25
1770 A415 77p multi 2.25 2.25
1771 A415 93p multi 2.60 2.60
1772 A415 93p multi 2.60 2.60
a. Souvenir sheet of 2, #1770, 1772 5.00 5.00
1773 A415 £1.24 multi 3.50 3.50
1774 A415 £1.24 multi 3.50 3.50
a. Souvenir sheet of 2, #1771, 1774 6.25 6.25
Nos. 1767-1774 (8) 19.20 19.20

Issued: Nos. 1767-1774, 2/6; Nos. 1772a, 1774a, 4/21. Nos. 1767-1768 each sold for 44p on day of issue.

Battle of the Somme, Cent.
A416

Poppies and: 1st, Soldiers near cannon. 77p, Aerial dogfight. 93p, Soldiers and cemetery. 124p, Tanks. 165p, Injured soldiers walking past dead soldiers. 186p, Memorial.

2016 Litho. *Perf. 14x14¼*

1775 A416 1st multi 1.25 1.25
1776 A416 77p multi 2.25 2.25
1777 A416 93p multi 2.60 2.60
1778 A416 124p multi 3.50 3.50
1779 A416 165p multi 4.75 4.75
1780 A416 186p multi 5.25 5.25
a. Souvenir sheet of 6, #1775-1780 18.50 18.50
Nos. 1775-1780 (6) 19.60 19.60

Issued: Nos. 1775-1780, 2/17; No. 1780a, 7/1. On day of issue, No. 1775 sold for 44p.

Souvenir Sheet

Battle of Jutland, Cent. — A417

No. 1781: a, British Admiral Sir John Jellicoe (1859-1935), German Admiral Reinhard Scheer (1863-1928), denomination at UL. b, British Vice Admiral Sir David Beatty (1871-1936), German Vice Admiral Franz Hipper (1863-1932), denomination at UR.

2016, Feb. 17 Litho. *Perf. 14x14¼*

1781 A417 Sheet of 2 10.00 10.00
a.-b. 175p Either single 5.00 5.00

Birds — A418

Designs: Nos. 1782a, 1784, Manx shearwater. Nos. 1782b, 1785, Robin. Nos. 1782c, 1786, Pheasant. Nos. 1782d, 1787, Goldfinch. Nos. 1782e, 1788, Tawny owl. No. 1783a, Starling. No. 1783b, Blue tit. No. 1783c, Puffin. No. 1783d, Hobby. No. 1783e, Cormorant.

2016, Mar. 24 Litho. *Perf. 12½*

1782 Horiz. strip of 5 6.25 6.25
a.-e. A418 1st Any single 1.25 1.25
1783 Horiz. strip of 5 11.50 11.50
a.-e. A418 EU Any single 2.25 2.25
f. Miniature sheet of 9, 3 each #1782a, 1783c, 1783e 17.50 17.50

Booklet Stamps
Self-Adhesive

Serpentine Die Cut 13

1784 A418 1st multi 1.25 1.25
1785 A418 1st multi 1.25 1.25
1786 A418 1st multi 1.25 1.25
1787 A418 1st multi 1.25 1.25
1788 A418 1st multi 1.25 1.25
a. Booklet pane of 10, 2 each #1784-1788 12.50
Nos. 1784-1788 (5) 6.25 6.25

On day of issue, Nos. 1782a-1782e, 1784-1788 each sold for 44p, and Nos. 1783a-1783e each sold for 77p.

Royal Artillery, 300th Anniv.
A419

Designs: 45p, Artilleryman, c. 1716. 50p, Royal Horse Artillery officer, c. 1800. 95p, Gunner of 4th Mountain Artillery Battery, 1890. £1.27, Major John Drinkwater of Royal Field Artillery in World War I uniform. £1.69, Officer from Royal Artillery Light Anti-Aircraft Regiment in World War II. £2.44, Major Kate Philp in Afghanistan, 2008.

2016, May 9 Litho. *Perf. 13½*

1789 A419 45p multi 1.40 1.40
1790 A419 50p multi 1.50 1.50
1791 A419 95p multi 2.75 2.75
1792 A419 £1.27 multi 3.75 3.75
1793 A419 £1.69 multi 5.00 5.00
1794 A419 £2.44 multi 7.00 7.00
Nos. 1789-1794 (6) 21.40 21.40

Booklet Stamps
Self-Adhesive

Die Cut Perf. 11¾

1795 A419 45p multi 1.40 1.40
1796 A419 50p multi 1.50 1.50
1797 A419 95p multi 2.75 2.75
a. Booklet pane of 3, #1795-1797 5.75
1798 A419 £1.27 multi 3.75 3.75
1799 A419 £1.69 multi 5.00 5.00
a. Booklet pane of 2, #1798-1799 8.75
1800 A419 £2.44 multi 7.00 7.00
a. Booklet pane of 1 7.00
b. Booklet pane of 6, #1795-1800 21.50
Complete booklet, #1797a, 1799a, 1800a, 1800b 43.00
Nos. 1795-1800 (6) 21.40 21.40

Souvenir Sheet

Antarctic Explorers — A420

No. 1801: a, Captain Frank Worsley of Endurance Expedition, 1914-17. b, Henry Worsley of Shackleton Solo Expedition, 2015-16.

2016, May 10 Litho. *Perf. 13½x13*

1801 A420 Sheet of 2 10.00 10.00
a.-b. £1.75 Either single 5.00 5.00

Imperial Trans-Antarctic Expedition, cent.

2016 Summer Olympics, Rio de Janeiro
A421

No. 1802: a, Cycling. b, Track and field. c, Gymnast putting chalk on hands. d, Swimming.

2016 Litho. *Perf. 13¼*

1802 Horiz. strip of 4 15.00 15.00
a.-d. A421 £1.27 Any single 3.75 3.75
e. Souvenir sheet of 4, #a-d, + 8 labels 15.00 15.00
f. Souvenir sheet of 4, #a-d, + 4 labels 12.50 12.50

Issued: Nos. 1802, 1802e, 5/23; No. 1802f, 10/21.

Churches on Manx Telecom Parish Walk Race Route — A422

No. 1803: a, St. Brendan's Church, Braddan. b, Marown Parish Church, Marown. c, St. Sanctain's Church, Santon. d, St. Lupus Church, Malew. e, Parish Church of St. Columba, Arbory. f, Holy Trinity Church, Rushen. g, Holy Trinity Church, Patrick. h, St. German's Cathedral, Peel. i, St. Michael's Church, Michael. j, St. Mary's Church, Ballaugh. k, St. Patrick's Church, Jurby. l, St. Bridget's Church, Bride. m, St. Andrew's Church, Andreas. n, Kirk Christ, Lezayre. o, Maughold Parish Church, Maughold. p, All Saints' Church, Lonan. q, St. Peter's Church, Onchan.

2016, June 15 Litho. *Perf. 13¼*

1803 Block of 17 + label 21.50 21.50
a.-q. A422 1st Any single 1.25 1.25

On day of issue, Nos. 1803a-1803q each sold for 45p. Nos. 1803a-1803q were also printed in a sheet of 108 stamps, lacking labels, which contains 12 No. 1803a and 6 each of Nos. 1803b-1803q, arranged in blocks of 6 of the same stamp.

Physics A423

Designs: 45p, Albert Einstein (1879-1955), mass-energy equivalence equation. 50p, Stephen Hawking, black hole entropy equation. 95p, Gravitational waves produced by two black holes. £1.27, Hawking radiation. £1.69, Two black holes colliding. £2.44, Black hole.

Litho. With Foil Application

2016 ***Perf. 13½***

1804 A423 45p multi 1.25 1.25
1805 A423 50p multi 1.40 1.40
1806 A423 95p multi 2.60 2.60
1807 A423 £1.27 multi 3.50 3.50
1808 A423 £1.69 multi 4.50 4.50
1809 A423 £2.44 multi 6.50 6.50
a. Souvenir sheet of 6, #1804-1809 20.00 20.00
Nos. 1804-1809 (6) 19.75 19.75

Booklet Stamps Self-Adhesive

Die Cut Perf. 15

1810 A423 45p multi 1.25 1.25
a. Booklet pane of 1 1.25 1.25
1811 A423 50p multi 1.40 1.40
a. Booklet pane of 1 1.40
1812 A423 95p multi 2.60 2.60
1813 A423 £1.27 multi 3.50 3.50
1814 A423 £1.69 multi 4.50 4.50
1815 A423 £2.44 multi 6.50 6.50
a. Booklet pane of 4, #1812-1815 17.50
b. Booklet pane of 6, #1810-1815 20.00
Complete booklet, #1810a, 1811a, 1815a, 1815b 41.00

Einstein's General Theory of Relativity, cent.
Issued: Nos. 1804-1809, 7/1; Nos. 1810-1815, 7/15.

Aardman Animation Characters A424

Inscriptions: No. 1816, Morph, Laxey tram. No. 1817, Wallace and Gromit, motorcycle and ladder. No. 1818, Shaun the Sheep, Bitzer the dog. No. 1819, Timmy Time. No. 1820, Shaun the Sheep jijack road line painting macine. No. 1821, Wallace and Gromit at the beach. No. 1822, Creature Comforts. No. 1823, Morph, Laxey wheel.

2016, Aug. 12 Litho. ***Perf. 15x14***

1816 A424 1st multi 1.25 1.25
1817 A424 1st multi 1.25 1.25
1818 A424 77p multi 2.10 2.10
1819 A424 77p multi 2.10 2.10
a. Souvenir sheet of 6 13.00 13.00
1820 A424 95p multi 2.60 2.60
a. Souvenir sheet of 6, 3 each #1818, 1820 14.50 14.50
1821 A424 95p multi 2.60 2.60
a. Souvenir sheet of 6, 3 each #1817, 1821 12.00 12.00
1822 A424 £1.24 multi 3.25 3.25
a. Souvenir sheet of 6 19.50 19.50
1823 A424 £1.24 multi 3.25 3.25
a. Souvenir sheet of 6, 3 each #1816, 1823 13.50 13.50
Nos. 1816-1823 (8) 18.40 18.40

On day of issue, Nos. 1816-1817 each sold for 45p.

Art of Roger Dean — A425

Designs: 45p, Meeting Place. 77p, Blind Owl Late Landing. 95p, Pathways. £1.24, Green Parrot Island. £1.69, Tales From Topographic Oceans. £2.08, Sea of Light.

2016, Aug. 19 Litho. ***Perf. 13***

1824 A425 45p multi 1.25 1.25
1825 A425 77p multi 2.10 2.10
1826 A425 95p multi 2.60 2.60
1827 A425 £1.24 multi 3.25 3.25
1828 A425 £1.69 multi 4.50 4.50
1829 A425 £2.08 multi 5.50 5.50
Nos. 1824-1829 (6) 19.20 19.20

Islands and Bridges Exhibition of Art by Dean, Manx Museum, Douglas.

Sand Castle A426

Europa A427

Recycling Emblem, Richmond Hill Waste-to-Energy Plant — A428

TT Zero Race Electric Motorcycle, Flora and Fauna — A429

Hydroelectic Power Emblem, Fish — A430

2016, Oct. 7 Litho. ***Perf. 13½***

1830 A426 45p multi 1.10 1.10
1831 A427 77p multi 1.90 1.90
a. Miniature sheet of 10 19.00 19.00
1832 A428 £1.13 multi 2.75 2.75
1833 A429 £1.47 multi 3.75 3.75
1834 A430 £2.33 multi 5.75 5.75
Nos. 1830-1834 (5) 15.25 15.25

Think Green Issue, Europa (No. 1831).

Souvenir Sheet

Circumnavigation of Solar Impulse 2 Solar-Powered Airplane — A431

2016, Oct. 14 Litho. ***Perf. 14¼x14***

1835 A431 £3 multi 7.50 7.50

Christmas Pantomime Shows — A432

Props from: 45p, The Wizard of Oz. 77p, Peter Pan. 95p, Aladdin. 113p, Snow White and the Seven Dwarfs. 124p, Dick Whittington. 186p, Robin Hood.

2016, Oct. 20 Litho. ***Perf. 13***

1836 A432 45p multi 1.10 1.10
1837 A432 77p multi 1.90 1.90
1838 A432 95p multi 2.40 2.40
1839 A432 113p multi 2.75 2.75
1840 A432 124p multi 3.00 3.00
1841 A432 186p multi 4.75 4.75
Nos. 1836-1841 (6) 15.90 15.90

Self-Adhesive

Serpentine Die Cut 13½

1842 A432 45p multi 1.10 1.10

Tourism — A433

Tourism art by Adam Berry for: 1st, Peel. EU, Castletown. 95p, Onchan. £1.24, Ramsey. £1.27, Port St. Mary. £2.33, Port Erin.

2017, Jan. 19 Litho. ***Perf. 13½x13¼***

1843 A433 1st multi 1.25 1.25
a. Miniature sheet of 10 12.50 12.50
1844 A433 EU multi 2.00 2.00
a. Miniature sheet of 10 20.00 20.00
1845 A433 95p multi 2.40 2.40
1846 A433 £1.24 multi 3.25 3.25
1847 A433 £1.27 multi 3.25 3.25
1848 A433 £2.33 multi 6.00 6.00
Nos. 1843-1848 (6) 18.15 18.15

On day of issue, No. 1843 sold for 45p; No. 1844, 77p.

Reign of Queen Elizabeth II, 65th Anniv. A434

Photograph of Queen Elizabeth II taken in: 45p, Australia, 1954. 77p, China, 1986. 95p, India, 1983. £1.13, Isle of Man, 1979. £1.24, Canada, 2010. £2.37, Tuvalu, 1982.
£3.75, Queen Elizabeth II receiving horse from Royal Canadian Mounted Police, 1969.

2017, Feb. 6 Litho. ***Perf. 13***

1849 A434 45p multi 1.10 1.10
1850 A434 77p multi 1.90 1.90
1851 A434 95p multi 2.40 2.40
1852 A434 £1.13 multi 2.75 2.75
1853 A434 £1.24 multi 3.00 3.00
1854 A434 £2.37 multi 6.00 6.00
Nos. 1849-1854 (6) 17.15 17.15

Souvenir Sheet

1855 A434 £3.75 multi 9.25 9.25
a. Overprinted in red in sheet margin with Canada 150th anniv. emblem 9.75 9.75

Issued: No. 1855a, 7/1.

First General Election of the House of Keys, 150th Anniv. — A435

Designs: 1st, Douglas Court House on Election Day, Register of Electors John Senhouse Goldie-Taubman, and poll book. £1, Castle Rushen, Proclamation for dissolving the House of Keys, and Lieutenant Governor Henry Loch. £1.50, Jail of Castle Rushen, *Isle of Man Times* newspaper and its owner, James Brown. £2, Journalist Robert Fargher, Castletown House of Keys, and Fargher's *Mona's Herald* newspaper.

2017, Feb. 13 Litho. ***Perf. 13¼***

1856 A435 1st multi 1.10 1.10
1857 A435 £1 multi 2.50 2.50
1858 A435 £1.50 multi 3.75 3.75
1859 A435 £2 multi 5.00 5.00
Nos. 1856-1859 (4) 12.35 12.35

On day of issue, No. 1856 sold for 45p.

Miniature Sheet

Festivals — A436

No. 1860: a, Conductor's hands (Mananan International Festival). b, Man reading book (Manx Litfest). c, Actress (Manx Music, Speech and Dance Festival). d, Dancer (Shennaghys Jiu). e, Accordion player (Celtfest).

2017, Apr. 6 Litho. ***Perf. 13¼x13***

1860 A436 Sheet of 5 10.00 10.00
a.-e. 75p Any single 2.00 2.00

Food Production — A437

Inscription: Nos. 1861, 1867, Farm to Yarn. Nos. 1862, 1868, Fish to Dish. EU, Welly to Belly. 98p, Cow to Cup. RoW, Tree to Table. £2.52, Field to Fork.

2017 Litho. ***Perf. 13¼x13***

1861 A437 1st multi 1.25 1.25
1862 A437 1st multi 1.25 1.25
1863 A437 EU multi 2.00 2.00
1864 A437 98p multi 2.50 2.50
1865 A437 RoW multi 3.25 3.25
1866 A437 £2.52 multi 6.50 6.50
Nos. 1861-1866 (6) 16.75 16.75

Booklet Stamps Self-Adhesive

Serpentine Die Cut 12½

1867 A437 1st multi 1.25 1.25
1868 A437 1st multi 1.25 1.25
a. Booklet pane of 10, 5 each #1867-1868 12.50

Issued: Nos. 1861-1866, 5/3; Nos. 1867-1868, 5/15. On day of issue, Nos. 1861-1862 each sold for 45p; No. 1863, 77p; No. 1865, £1.24, Nos. 1867-1868, 47p.

Symbols of Freemasonry — A438

Designs: 20p, Jewel of the Steward. 1st, Jewel of the Inner Guard. 50p, Jewel of the Junior and Senior Deacon. £1.30, Jewel of the Junior Warden. £1.74, Jewel of the Senior Warden. £3.40, Jewel of the Worshipful Master.

Litho. With Foil Application

2017, May 11 *Perf. 13½*

1869	A438	20p	gold & multi	.55	.55
1870	A438	1st	gold & multi	1.25	1.25
1871	A438	50p	gold & multi	1.40	1.40
1872	A438	£1.30	gold & multi	3.50	3.50
1873	A438	£1.74	gold & multi	4.50	4.50
1874	A438	£3.40	gold & multi	8.75	8.75
a.		Souvenir sheet of 6, #1869-1874		20.00	20.00
		Nos. 1869-1874 (6)		19.95	19.95

English Freemasonry, 300th anniv.

TT Motorcycle Race Winners — A439

Designs: 1st, Joey Dunlop, 1977. EU, Steve Hislop, 1987. RoW, Ian Simpson, 1997. £2.50, Ian Hutchinson, 2007.

2017, May 26 **Litho.** *Perf. 13*

1875	A439	1st	multi	1.25	1.25
1876	A439	EU	multi	2.10	2.10
1877	A439	RoW	multi	3.50	3.50
1878	A439	£2.50	multi	6.50	6.50
		Nos. 1875-1878 (4)		13.35	13.35

On day of issue, No. 1875 sold for 47p; No. 1876, 80p; No. 1877, £1.30.

Prince Philip — A440

Various photographs of Prince Philip.

2017, June 10 **Litho.** *Perf. 13*

1879	A440	Block of 6	18.50	18.50
a.		47p multi	1.25	1.25
b.		80p multi	2.10	2.10
c.		98p multi	2.60	2.60
d.		£1.18 multi	3.00	3.00
e.		£1.30 multi	3.50	3.50
f.		£2.33 multi	6.00	6.00

Birds A441

Designs: 47p, Oystercatchers. 80p, Eiders. 98p, Little tern. £1.18, Fulmars. £1.30, Black guillemots. £1.94, Razorbills.

2017, June 29 **Litho.** *Perf. 14*

1880	A441	47p	multi	1.25	1.25
1881	A441	80p	multi	2.10	2.10
1882	A441	98p	multi	2.60	2.60
1883	A441	£1.18	multi	3.00	3.00
1884	A441	£1.30	multi	3.50	3.50
1885	A441	£1.94	multi	5.00	5.00
		Nos. 1880-1885 (6)		17.45	17.45

70th Wedding Anniversary of Queen Elizabeth II and Prince Philip A442

Flowers and various photographs of Queen Elizabeth II and Prince Philip from: 1st, 1947. 80p, 1957. 98p, 1987. £1.30, 1997. £1.86, 2007. £2.33, 2017.

2017, July 9 **Litho.** *Perf. 14*

1886	A442	1st	multi	1.25	1.25
1887	A442	80p	multi	2.10	2.10
1888	A442	98p	multi	2.60	2.60
1889	A442	£1.30	multi	3.50	3.50
1890	A442	£1.86	multi	5.00	5.00
1891	A442	£2.33	multi	6.25	6.25
		Nos. 1886-1891 (6)		20.70	20.70

On day of issue, No. 1886 sold for 47p.

John C. Taylor, Inventor and Philanthropist — A443

Designs: 47p, Chronophage. 80p, Taylor's clock collection. £1.30, Bimetal kettle switch. £1.47, Otter G switch. £1.68, Arragon Mooar. £1.86, Taylor Library and statue.

Perf. 12x11¾ Syncopated

2017, Sept. 13 **Litho.**

1892	A443	47p	sil & multi	1.25	1.25
1893	A443	80p	sil & multi	2.25	2.25
1894	A443	£1.30	sil & multi	3.50	3.50
1895	A443	£1.47	sil & multi	4.00	4.00
1896	A443	£1.68	sil & multi	4.50	4.50
1897	A443	£1.86	sil & multi	5.00	5.00
		Nos. 1892-1897 (6)		20.50	20.50

Self-Adhesive

Die Cut Perf. 9½ Syncopated

1898	Sheet of 6	20.50	
a.	A443 47p sil & multi	1.25	1.25
b.	A443 80p sil & multi	2.25	2.25
c.	A443 £1.30 sil & multi	3.50	3.50
d.	A443 £1.47 sil & multi	4.00	4.00
e.	A443 £1.68 sil & multi	4.50	4.50
f.	A443 £1.86 sil & multi	5.00	5.00

Souvenir Sheet

Bloodhound SSC Supersonic Land Vehicle — A444

No. 1899: a, Blodhound SSC in motion (28x34mm). b, Silhouette of Bloodhound SSC (40x24mm)

Perf. 13½x13¼ (#1899a), 13x13¼ (#1899b)

Litho. & Silk-screened

2017, Sept. 22

1899	A444	Sheet of 2 + 2 labels	12.00	12.00
a.		£2 sil & multi	5.25	5.25
b.		£2.50 sil & multi	6.75	6.75

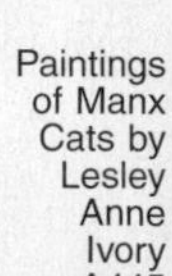

Paintings of Manx Cats by Lesley Anne Ivory A445

Various cats with frame color of: 47p, Red. £1.30, Lilac. £1.57, Green. £3.68, Gray blue.

2017, Oct. 10 **Litho.** *Perf. 12¾*

1900	A445	47p	multi	1.25	1.25
1901	A445	£1.30	multi	3.50	3.50
1902	A445	£1.57	multi	4.25	4.25
1903	A445	£3.68	multi	9.75	9.75
		Nos. 1900-1903 (4)		18.75	18.75

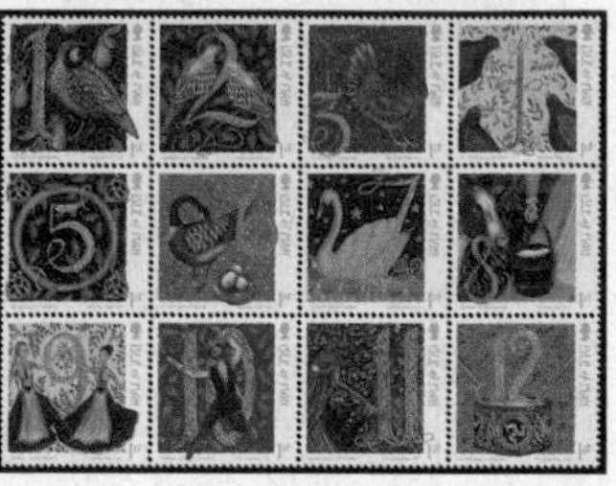

Christmas — A446

Nos. 1904 and 1905 — Items from Christmas song "The Twelve Days of Christmas": a, "1," partridge and pears. b, "2," turtle doves. c, "3," French hen. d, "4," calling birds. e, "5," golden rings. f, "6," goose and eggs. g, "7," swan. h, "8," cow and milkmaid with bucket. i, "9," ladies dancing. j, "10," leaping lord. k, "11," piper. l, "12," drum and sticks.

2017, Oct. 19 **Litho.** *Perf. 12½*

1904	A446	Block of 12	17.00	17.00
a.-l.		1st Any single	1.40	1.40

Self-Adhesive

Serpentine Die Cut 12¾

1905	A446	Sheet of 12	17.00	
a.-l.		1st Any single	1.40	1.40

On day of issue, Nos. 1904a-1904l and 1905a-1905l each sold for 52p.

Tholtans (Abandoned Structures) A447

Tholtan: 20p, Ballagale, Surby. 1st, Pairk Mooar, Maughold. EU, Cronk Dhoo, Kirk Michael. RoW, North Laxey Mines. £1.74, Carnagrie, Slieau Whallian. £2.08, Kirk Michael Mines.

2018, Jan. 5 **Litho.** *Perf. 13*

1906	A447	20p	multi	.60	.60
1907	A447	1st	multi	1.40	1.40
1908	A447	EU	multi	2.25	2.25
1909	A447	RoW	multi	3.75	3.75
1910	A447	£1.74	multi	5.00	5.00
1911	A447	£2.08	multi	6.00	6.00
		Nos. 1906-1911 (6)		19.00	19.00

On day of issue, No. 1907 sold for 47p; No. 1908, for 80p; and No. 1909, for £1.30.

Royal Air Force, Cent. A448

Designs: Nos. 1912, 1920a, Sopwith Camel. Nos. 1913, 1920b, Supermarine Spitfire. Nos. 1914, 1920c, Avro Lancaster. Nos. 1915, 1920d, Avro Vulcan. Nos. 1916, 1920e, Boeing Chinook helicopter. Nos. 1917, 1920f, Hawker Siddeley Harrier. Nos. 1918, 1920g, Eurofighter Typhoon. Nos. 1919, 1920h, Lockheed-Martin Lightning II.

2018, Jan. 15 **Litho.** *Perf. 14x13½*

1912	A448	1st	multi	1.40	1.40
1913	A448	1st	multi	1.40	1.40
1914	A448	EU	multi	2.25	2.25
1915	A448	EU	multi	2.25	2.25
1916	A448	£1	multi	3.00	3.00
1917	A448	£1	multi	3.00	3.00
1918	A448	RoW	multi	3.75	3.75
1919	A448	RoW	multi	3.75	3.75
		Nos. 1912-1919 (8)		20.80	20.80

Self-Adhesive

Die Cut Perf. 13½x13¼

1920	Sheet of 8	21.00	
a.-b.	A448 1st Either single	1.40	1.40
c.-d.	A448 EU Either single	2.25	2.25
e.-f.	A448 £1 Either single	3.00	3.00
g.-h.	A448 RoW Either single	3.75	3.75

On day of issue, Nos. 1912-1913, 1920a-1920b each sold for 47p; Nos. 1914-1915, 1920c-1920d, for 80p; and Nos. 1918-1919, 1920g-1920h, for £1.30.

Preen Line of Women's Clothing by Thornton and Bregazzi — A449

Designs: 1st, Red Finella. EU, Citrus power dress. £1, Quilted floral dress. RoW, Pink velvet hitch dress. £1.57, Striped Flintoff dress. £1.86, Pink silk wrap dress.

2018, Feb. 1 **Litho.** *Perf. 13*

1921	A449	1st	multi	1.40	1.40
1922	A449	EU	multi	2.25	2.25
1923	A449	£1	multi	3.00	3.00
1924	A449	RoW	multi	3.75	3.75
1925	A449	£1.57	multi	4.50	4.50
1926	A449	£1.86	multi	5.25	5.25
		Nos. 1921-1926 (6)		20.15	20.15

On day of issue, No. 1921 sold for 47p; No. 1922, for 80p; and No. 1924, for £1.30

New Year 2018 (Year of the Dog) — A450

Dog's head facing: £1.50, Right. £2, Left.

2018, Feb. 8 **Litho.** *Perf. 13*

1927	A450	£1.50	multi	4.25	4.25
1928	A450	£2	multi	5.50	5.50

Actors and Actresses Starring in Film Adaptations by Sir Thomas Hall Caine (1853-1931) A451

Designs: No. 1929, Pola Negri (1897-1987) in *Barbed Wire.* No. 1930, Anny Ondra (1902-87) in *The Manxman.* EU, Conrad Nagel (1897-1970) in *Name the Man.* 98p, Barbara La Marr (1896-1926) in *The Eternal City.* RoW, Richard Dix (1893-1949) in *The Christian.* £1.50, Norman Kerry (1894-1956) in *The Bondman.*

2018, Feb. 14 **Litho.** *Perf. 13*

1929	A451	1st	sil & multi	1.40	1.40
1930	A451	1st	sil & multi	1.40	1.40
1931	A451	EU	sil & multi	2.25	2.25
1932	A451	98p	sil & multi	2.75	2.75
1933	A451	RoW	sil & multi	3.75	3.75
1934	A451	£1.50	sil & multi	4.25	4.25
		Nos. 1929-1934 (6)		15.80	15.80

On day of issue, Nos. 1929-1930 each sold for 47p; No. 1931 sold for 80p; No. 1933, for £1.30.

Wedding of Prince Harry and Meghan Markle A452

Couple: £1.75, Legs visible. £2, Legs not visible.

2018, Mar. 28 Litho. ***Perf. 13x13¼***

No.	Description	Unused	Used
1935	A452 £1.75 multi	5.00	5.00
1936	A452 £2 multi	5.75	5.75
a.	Souvenir sheet of 4, 2 each #1935-1936, + 2 labels	21.50	21.50

Walkers Above Fleshwick A453

TT Fireworks and Light Show — A454

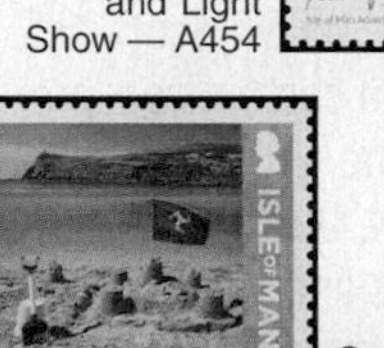

Sand Castle with Manx Flag, Port Erin — A455

Manx Telecom Parish Walk — A456

Michael Starkey Painting — A457

Niarbyl Coast — A458

Skeddan Jiarg Dance Group — A459

Sunset at Peel — A460

Lonan Cross — A461

Niarbyl Cottage and Kayaks — A462

2018, Apr. 10 Litho. ***Perf. 12½***

No.	Description	Unused	Used
1937	Horiz. strip of 5	7.00	7.00
a.	A453 1st multi	1.40	1.40
b.	A454 1st multi	1.40	1.40
c.	A455 1st multi	1.40	1.40
d.	A456 1st multi	1.40	1.40
e.	A457 1st multi	1.40	1.40
1938	Horiz. strip of 5	11.50	11.50
a.	A458 EU multi	2.25	2.25
b.	A459 EU multi	2.25	2.25
c.	A460 EU multi	2.25	2.25
d.	A461 EU multi	2.25	2.25
e.	A462 EU multi	2.25	2.25

Miniature Sheet
Self-Adhesive

Serpentine Die Cut 13

No.	Description	Unused	Used
1939	Sheet of 5	7.00	7.00
a.	A453 1st multi	1.40	1.40
b.	A454 1st multi	1.40	1.40
c.	A455 1st multi	1.40	1.40
d.	A456 1st multi	1.40	1.40
e.	A457 1st multi	1.40	1.40

On day of issue, Nos. 1937a-1937e, 1939a-1939e each sold for 52p, and Nos. 1938a-1938e each sold for 83p.

Isle of Man International Motor Scooter Rally, 60th Anniv. — A463

Designs: No. 1940, Sand races. No. 1941, Ramsey Sprint. No. 1942, Ride Out. No. 1943, Concours d'Elegance. £1, Team time trials. No. 1945, Display team. No. 1946, Sidecar hill climb. No. 1947, Scooter Girl.

2018, May 10 Litho. ***Perf. 14***

No.	Description	Unused	Used
1940	A463 1st multi	1.40	1.40
1941	A463 1st multi	1.40	1.40
1942	A463 EU multi	2.25	2.25
1943	A463 EU multi	2.25	2.25
1944	A463 £1 multi	2.75	2.75
1945	A463 RoW multi	3.75	3.75
1946	A463 RoW multi	3.75	3.75
1947	A463 RoW multi	3.75	3.75
	Nos. 1940-1947 (8)	21.30	21.30

On day of issue, Nos. 1940-1941 each sold for 52p; Nos. 1942-1943, for 83p; Nos. 1945-1947, for £1.40.

British Motorcycles — A464

No. 1948: a, 1920 Zenith JAP engine. b, Zenith racing. c, 1936 Excelsior Manxman engine. d, Excelsior Manxman in race. e, Douglas flat-twin in race. f, 1937 Douglas engine. g, AJS 500cc V-four in race. h, 1939 AJS engine. i, 1949 Vincent HRD chain drive. j, Vincent HRD 1000cc V-twin in race. k, 1961 Norton Manx engine. l, Norton Manx single in race.

2018, May 17 Litho. ***Perf. 12½***

No.	Description	Unused	Used
1948	A464 Block of 12	17.00	17.00
a.-l.	1st Any single	1.40	1.40

On day of issue, Nos. 1948a-1948l each sold for 52p.

Motion Picture *2001: A Space Odyssey,* 50th Anniv. of Premiere A465

Designs: 20p, Stanley Kubrick (1928-99), director, and actors. 30p, Arthur C. Clarke (1917-2008), screenplay writer, and props. 52p, Space Station V. 75p, Monolith. 83p, Zero gravity. £1.40, Starchild. £1.93, Dr. David Bowman. £2.01, HAL 9000.

2018, June 14 Litho. ***Perf. 14x13½***

No.	Description	Unused	Used
1949	A465 20p multi	.65	.65
1950	A465 30p multi	.80	.80
1951	A465 52p multi	1.40	1.40
1952	A465 75p multi	2.00	2.00
1953	A465 83p multi	2.25	2.25
1954	A465 £1.40 multi	3.75	3.75
1955	A465 £1.93 multi	5.00	5.00
1956	A465 £2.01 multi	5.25	5.25
	Nos. 1949-1956 (8)	21.10	21.10

Manx Electric Railway, 125th Anniv. A466

Designs: 1st, Cars 6, 22 and 16 at Derby Castle Terminus. EU, Car 9 on Ballure Viaduct. £1.25, Car 1 near Laxey. RoW, Car 16 with mail car, near Onchan Head. £1.87, Cars 1 and 2 at Derby Castle Terminus. £1.93, Car 7 at Bulgham Rocks.

2018, June 30 Litho. ***Perf. 13***

No.	Description	Unused	Used
1957	A466 1st multi	1.40	1.40
1958	A466 EU multi	2.25	2.25
1959	A466 £1.25 multi	3.25	3.25
1960	A466 RoW multi	3.75	3.75
1961	A466 £1.87 multi	5.00	5.00
1962	A466 £1.93 multi	5.00	5.00
	Nos. 1957-1962 (6)	20.65	20.65

Self-Adhesive

Serpentine Die Cut 13x14

No.	Description	Unused	Used
1963	Sheet of 6	21.00	
a.	A466 1st multi	1.40	1.40
b.	A466 EU multi	2.25	2.25
c.	A466 £1.25 multi	3.25	3.25
d.	A466 RoW multi	3.75	3.75
e.	A466 £1.87 multi	5.00	5.00
e.	A466 £1.87 multi	5.00	5.00
f.	A466 £1.93 multi	5.00	5.00
g.	Booklet pane of 2, #1963a-1963b	3.75	
h.	Booklet pane of 2, #1963c-1963d	7.00	
i.	Booklet pane of 2, #1963e-1963f	10.00	
j.	Booklet pane of 6, #1963a-1963f	21.00	
	Complete booklet, #1963g-1963j	42.00	

Europa (#1958, 1963b). On day of issue, Nos. 1957 and 1963a each sold for 52p; Nos. 1958 and 1963b, for 83p; and Nos. 1960 and 1963d, for £1.40. The complete booklet consists of pages folded and stapled in the center, with Nos. 1963g-1963h and 1963i-1963j, being connected on opposite sides of the fold when exploded from the booklet. No. 1963 is merely a cut down version of No. 1963j that was sold separately from the complete booklet.

ANZAC Memorials Sculpted by Rayner Hoff (1894-1937) — A467

Soldier and details from memorials in Sydney and Adelaide: 52p, Pioneer sculpture, waratah flower. 83p, Sacrifice sculpture, kangaroo paw flower and Hoff. £1.25, Aviator sculpture, rosemary sprig. £1.40, Soldiers and horse bas-relief, blue gum branch. £1.75, Female angel sculpture, poppy. £2.05, Male angel sculpture, golden wattle flower.

2018, Aug. 4 Litho. ***Perf. 13***

No.	Description	Unused	Used
1964	A467 52p multi	1.40	1.40
1965	A467 83p multi	2.25	2.25
1966	A467 £1.25 multi	3.25	3.25
1967	A467 £1.40 multi	3.75	3.75
1968	A467 £1.75 multi	4.50	4.50
1969	A467 £2.05 multi	5.25	5.25
	Nos. 1964-1969 (6)	20.40	20.40

Prince Charles, 70th Birthday A468

Paintings of Prince Charles by: 52p, Richard Stone. 83p, David Griffiths. £1.01, Stone, diff. £1.25, June Mendoza. £1.75, Mendoza, diff. £2.42, Michael Noakes.

2018, Sept. 26 Litho. ***Perf. 13***

No.	Description	Unused	Used
1970	A468 52p multi	1.40	1.40
1971	A468 83p multi	2.25	2.25
1972	A468 £1.01 multi	2.75	2.75
1973	A468 £1.25 multi	3.25	3.25
1974	A468 £1.75 multi	4.75	4.75
1975	A468 £2.42 multi	6.50	6.50
	Nos. 1970-1975 (6)	20.90	20.90

Manx Folk Traditions A469

Designs: 1st, Yn Melliah. EU, Hop-tu-naa. £1.01, Hunt the wren. £1.40, New Year's Eve. £1.75, Quaaltagh. £2.15, Eve of Old Christmas Day.

2018, Oct. 8 Litho. ***Perf. 13***

No.	Description	Unused	Used
1976	A469 1st brnz & multi	1.40	1.40
1977	A469 EU brnz & multi	2.25	2.25
1978	A469 £1.01 brnz & multi	2.60	2.60
1979	A469 £1.40 brnz & multi	3.75	3.75
1980	A469 £1.75 brnz & multi	4.50	4.50
1981	A469 £2.15 brnz & multi	5.50	5.50
	Nos. 1976-1981 (6)	20.00	20.00

On day of issue, No. 1976 sold for 52p and No. 1977 sold for 83p.

Lighthouses — A470

Designs: 52p, Point of Ayre Lighthouse and service buildings. £1.53, Winkie automatic light and Point of Ayre Lighthouse. £2.60, Upper and Lower Calf of Man Lighthouses. £3.10, Upper Calf of Man Lighthouse.

2018, Oct. 18 Litho. ***Perf. 13¼***

No.	Description	Unused	Used
1982	A470 52p multi	1.40	1.40
1983	A470 £1.53 multi	4.00	4.00
1984	A470 £2.60 multi	6.75	6.75
1985	A470 £3.10 multi	8.00	8.00
	Nos. 1982-1985 (4)	20.15	20.15

Point of Ayre Lighthouse and Calf of Man Lighthouse, bicent.

Christmas
A471

Characters from *The Beano* comic magazine by Nigel Parkinson: No. 1986, Dennis the Menace throwing pie at Santa Claus on steam locomotive. No. 1987, Dennis and Gnasher at Castle Rushen. No. 1988, Gnasher chsaing Manx cat at Douglas Sea Terminal. No. 1989, Dennis on Laxey Wheel pelting Santa Claus with snow. No. 1990, Dennis and Gnasher in cart with postman in mail sack. No. 1991, Santa Claus in car chasing Dennis and Gnasher at Marine Drive Toll Gate. No. 1992, Viking throwing snowball at Dennis and Gnasher building snow castle. No. 1993, Dennis and Gnasher with Minx fairies applying stamps to letters.

2018, Oct. 29 Litho. *Perf. 13¼*

1986	A471	1st multi	1.40	1.40
1987	A471	1st multi	1.40	1.40
a.		Vert. pair, #1986-1987	2.80	2.80
1988	A471	EU multi	2.25	2.25
1989	A471	EU multi	2.25	2.25
a.		Vert. pair, #1988-1989	4.50	4.50
1990	A471	£1.25 multi	3.25	3.25
1991	A471	£1.25 multi	3.25	3.25
a.		Vert. pair, #1990-1991	6.50	6.50
1992	A471	RoW multi	3.75	3.75
1993	A471	RoW multi	3.75	3.75
a.		Vert. pair, #1992-1993	7.50	7.50
		Nos. 1986-1993 (8)	21.30	21.30

On day of issue, Nos. 1986-1987 each sold for 52p; Nos. 1988-1989, for 83p; Nos. 1992-1993, for £1.40.

POSTAGE DUE STAMPS

Catalogue values for unused stamps in this section are for Never Hinged items.

D1

Imprint: "1973 Questa"

Perf. 13½

1973, July 5 Litho. Unwmk.

Inscriptions and Coat of Arms in Black and Red

J1	D1	½p yellow	.25	.25
J2	D1	1p buff	.25	.25
J3	D1	2p lt yellow grn	.90	.90
J4	D1	3p gray	1.60	1.60
J5	D1	4p dull rose	2.50	2.50
J6	D1	5p light blue	2.75	2.75
J7	D1	10p light violet	6.25	6.25
J8	D1	20p lt grnsh blue	15.00	15.00
		Nos. J1-J8 (8)	29.50	29.50

Inscribed: "1973 A Questa"

1973, Sept.

J1a	D1	½p	1.75	1.50
J2a	D1	1p	.90	.45
J3a	D1	2p	.25	.25
J4a	D1	3p	.25	.25
J5a	D1	4p	.25	.25
J6a	D1	5p	.25	.25
J7a	D1	10p	.45	.40
J8a	D1	20p	.90	.65
		Nos. J1a-J8a (8)	5.00	4.00

D2

1975, Jan. 8 Litho. *Perf. 14*

Inscriptions and Coat of Arms in Black and Red

J9	D2	½p yellow	.25	.25
J10	D2	1p buff	.25	.25
J11	D2	4p lilac rose	.25	.25
J12	D2	7p blue	.30	.30
J13	D2	9p sepia	.35	.35
J14	D2	10p lilac	.40	.40
J15	D2	50p orange	1.00	1.00
J16	D2	£1 bright green	2.00	2.00
		Nos. J9-J16 (8)	4.80	4.80

D3

D4

1982-92 Litho. *Perf. 15x14*

J17	D3	1p light green	.25	.25
J18	D3	2p bright pink	.25	.25
J19	D3	5p grnsh blue	.25	.25
J20	D3	10p bright lilac	.30	.30
J21	D3	20p gray	.55	.55
J22	D3	50p dull yellow	1.50	1.50
J23	D3	£1 brick red	2.25	2.25
J24	D3	£2 blue	4.50	4.50

Litho.

Perf. 13x13½

J25	D4	£5 multicolored	11.50	11.50
		Nos. J17-J25 (9)	21.35	21.35

Issued: £5, 9/16/92; others, 10/5/82.

GREECE

'grēs

(Hellas)

LOCATION — Southern part of the Balkan Peninsula in southeastern Europe, bordering on the Ionian, Aegean and Mediterranean Seas
GOVT. — Republic
AREA — 50,949 sq. mi.
POP. — 10,511,000 (1997 est.)
CAPITAL — Athens

In 1923 the reigning king was forced to abdicate and the following year Greece was declared a republic. In 1935, the king was recalled by a "plebiscite" of the people. Greece became a republic in June 1973. The country today includes the Aegean Islands of Chios, Mytilene (Lesbos), Samos, Icaria (Nicaria) and Lemnos, the Ionian Islands (Corfu, etc.) Crete, Macedonia, Western Thrace and part of Eastern Thrace, the Mount Athos District, Epirus and the Dodecanese Islands.

100 Lepta = 1 Drachma
100 Cents = 1 Euro (2002)

Catalogue values for unused stamps in this country are for Never Hinged items, beginning with Scott 472 in the regular postage section, Scott B1 in the semi-postal section, Scott C48 in the airpost section, Scott CB1 in the airpost semi-postal section, Scott RA69 in the postal tax section, and Scott N239 in the occupation and annexation section.

Values for unused stamps are for examples with original gum as defined in the catalogue introduction. Any exceptions will be noted.

Values for Large Hermes Head stamps with double control numbers on the back, Nos. 20e, 21c, 27a, et al, are for examples with two distinct and separate impressions, not for blurred or "slide doubles" caused by paper slippage on the press.

Watermarks

Wmk. 129 — Crown and ET

Wmk. 252 — Crowns

Paris Print

Hermes (Mercury) — A1

Paris Print, Fine Impression

The enlarged illustrations show the head in various states of the plates. The differences are best seen in the shading lines on the cheek and neck.

1861 Unwmk. Typo. *Imperf.*
Without Figures on Back

1 A1 1 l choc, *brnish* 600.00 550.00
a. 1 l red brown, *brnish* 725.00 600.00
b. 1 l brown 575.00 475.00
2 A1 2 l ol bis, *straw* 67.50 87.50
a. 2 l brown buff, *buff* 55.00 75.00
b. 2 l yellowish bister 55.00 75.00
3 A1 5 l yel grn, *grnsh* 700.00 150.00
a. 5 l emerald green 875.00 175.00
4 A1 20 l bl, *bluish* 1,150. 95.00
a. 20 l deep blue, *bluish* 1,100. 340.00
b. On pelure paper 1,350. *275.00*
5 A1 40 l vio, *bl* 325.00 130.00
6 A1 80 l rose, *pink* 250.00 120.00
a. 80 l carmine, *pink* 250.00 120.00

Large Figures, 8mm high, on Back

7 A1 10 l red org, *bl* 1,040. 500.00
a. "10" on back inverted — —
c. "0" of "10" invtd. on back — *1,850.*
d. "1" of "10" invtd. on back — *2,750.*

No. 7 without "10" on back is a proof.

Trial impressions of Paris prints exist in many shades, some being close to those of the issued stamps. The gum used was thin and smooth instead of thick, brownish and crackly as on the issued stamps.

See Nos. 8-58. For surcharges see Nos. 130, 132-133, 137-139, 141-143, 147-149, 153-154, 157-158.

Faint quadrille, horizontal or vertical lines are visible in the background of some Athens print large Hermes head stamps.

Nos. 16, 16a, 16b are the only 1 l stamps that have these lines.

Athens Prints

Athens Print, Typical Fine Impression

Athens Print, Typical Coarse Impression

Figures on Back
5 l:

#11

#18-45

Fine Printing (F)
Fine Printing (F, '62) see footnote
Coarse Printing (C)

1861-62 Without Figures on Back

8 A1 1 l choc, *brnish* (F, '62) 490.00 *490.00*
No gum 350.00
a. 1 l dk chocolate, *brnish* (F) 1,300. 1,325.
No gum 700.00
b. 1 l chocolate, *brnish* (F) 590.00 590.00
No gum 460.00
9 A1 2 l bis brn, *bister* (F) 75.00 *110.00*
No gum 40.00
a. 2 l dark brown, *straw*, (C) *6,750.* —
b. 2 l bister brown, *bister* (C) 90.00 *135.00*
c. 2 l bister brown, *bister* (F, '62) 90.00 *135.00*
10 A1 20 l dk bl, *bluish* (C) *15,000.*

With Figures on Back

11 A1 5 l grn, *grnsh* (F) 300.00 135.00
No gum 175.00
a. 5 l green, *greenish* (C) 375.00 190.00
b. As "a," double "5" on back (F, C) *2,850.*
c. 5 l green, *greenish*, bl grn figures on back (F, '62) 350.00 135.00
12 A1 10 l org, *grnsh* (F, '62) 600.00 90.00
No gum 325.00
a. 10 l orange, *greenish* (C) 1,950. 300.00
c. 10 l orange, *greenish* (F) 600.00 135.00
13 A1 20 l blue, *bluish* (F, '62) *475.00* 57.50
a. 20 l dull blue, *bluish* (C) *6,750.* 245.00
b. 20 l dark blue, *bluish*, (F) *3,500.* 110.00
14 A1 40 l red vio, *pale bl* (F, '62) *5,250.* 475.00
a. 40 l red violet, *blue* (C) *10,000.* 600.00
b. 40 l red violet, *blue*, (F) *5,250.* 475.00
15 A1 80 l car, *pink* (F, '62) 1,200. 165.00
a. 80 l carmine, *pink* (F) 1,200. 165.00
b. 80 l dl rose, *pink* (F) 1,200. 165.00

Nos. 8-15 are known as the "Athens Provisionals." The first printings were not very successful, producing the "coarse printings." Later printings used an altered printing method that gave better results (the "fine printings"). All these were issued in the normal manner by the Post Office.

Nos. 8, 9c, 11c, 12, 13, 14, 15 have uninterrupted and even shading lines that do not taper off at the ends. They were produced in May 1862 (F, '62). Other fine printing stamps were produced in Feb.-Apr. 1862 (F).

The numerals on the back are strongly shaded in the right lines with the corresponding left lines being quite thin. The colors of the numerals are generally strong and often show clumps of ink.

Nos. 15a and 15b have vermilion figures on the back, while those of all later printings are carmine.

Athens Print, Consecutive Print

With Figures on Back
Except 1 l, 2 l

1862-67

16 A1 1 l brn, *brnish* (poor print) 60.00 60.00
a. 1 l red brn, *brnish* (poor print) 150.00 150.00
b. 1 l choc, *brnish* 67.50 67.50
17 A1 2 l bister, *bister* 55.00 *60.00*
a. 2 l brnsh bis, *bister* 13.00 *24.00*
18 A1 5 l grn, *grnsh* 250.00 24.00
a. 5 l yellowish green, *grnsh* 250.00 12.00
19 A1 10 l org, *blue* ('64) 400.00 47.50
a. 10 l yel org, *bluish* 650.00 60.00
b. As "a," "10" inverted on front of stamp *23,500.*
c. 10 l red org, *bl* (Dec. '65) *650.00* 27.50
d. "01" on back *9,000.* *175.00*
20 A1 20 l bl, *bluish* 250.00 24.00
a. 20 l lt bl, *bluish* (fine print) 375.00 24.00
b. 20 l dark blue, *bluish* 2,000. 67.50
c. 20 l blue, *greenish* *1,700.* 37.50
d. "80" on back *2,450.*
e. Double "20" on back *1,500.*
f. Without "20" on back *5,500.*
21 A1 40 l lilac, *bl* 550.00 37.50
a. 40 l grayish lilac, *blue* 1,750. 37.50
b. 40 l lilac brown, *lil gray* *1,500.* 47.50
c. Double "40" on back 1,600.
22 A1 80 l car, *pale rose* 80.00 24.00
a. 80 l rose, *pale rose* 80.00 24.00
b. "8" on back inverted — 550.00
c. "80" on back inverted —
d. "8" only on back 700.00
e. "0" only on back 700.00

Nos. 16-22 represent a series of printings for each value, from 1862 through 1867, until a major cleaning of the plates was done in 1868. Impressions range from very fine and clear to coarse and blotchy.

Some printings of Nos. 16, 16a, 16b show faint vertical, horizontal or quadrilled lines in the background. Later 1 l stamps do not show these lines.

Many stamps of this and succeeding issues which are normally imperforate are known privately rouletted, pin-perforated, percé en scie, etc.

With Figures on Back, Except 1 l, 2 l

1868 From Cleaned Plates

23 A1 1 l gray brn, *brnish* 67.50 75.00
24 A1 2 l gray bis, *bister* 32.50 *47.50*
25 A1 5 l grn, *grnsh* *6,500.* 150.00
a. 5 l yellow green, *grnsh* 6,500. 50.00
26 A1 10 l pale org, *bluish* *1,650.* 40.00
a. "01" on back —
27 A1 20 l pale bl, *bluish* *1,500.* 24.00
a. Double "20" on back — *1,450.*
28 A1 40 l rose vio, *bl* 325.00 37.50
a. "20" on back, corrected to "40" — *2,750.*
29 A1 80 l rose car, *pale rose* 190.00 250.00

The "0" on the back of No. 29 is printed more heavily than the "8."

With Figures on Back, Except 1 l

1870

30 A1 1 l dp reddish brn, *brnish* 175.00 *200.00*
a. 1 l redsh brn, *brnish* 200.00 *240.00*
31 A1 20 l lt bl, *bluish* *1,900.* 24.00
a. 20 l blue, *bluish* *2,000.* 35.00
b. "02" on back 1,225.
c. "20" on back inverted 675.00

Nos. 30 and 30a have short lines of shading on cheek. The spandrels of No. 31 are very pale with the lines often broken or missing.

This was an Athens Printing made under supervision of German workmen.

Medium to Thin Paper
With Figures on Back, Except 1 l, 2 l

1870 Without Mesh

32 A1 1 l brn, *brnish* 325.00 325.00
a. 1 l purple brown, *brnish* 325.00 325.00
33 A1 2 l sal bis, *bister* 19.00 *45.00*
34 A1 5 l grn, *grnsh* *6,000.* 120.00
35 A1 10 l lt red org, *grnsh* — 240.00
a. "01" on back — —
b. "10" on back inverted — —
36 A1 20 l bl, *bluish* *1,400.* 24.00
a. "02" on back — 600.00
b. Double "20" on back — 1,375.
37 A1 40 l sal, *grnsh* 825.00 82.50
a. 40 l lilac, *greenish* *75,000.*

The stamps of this issue have rather coarse figures on back.

No. 37a is printed in the exact shade of the numerals on the back of No. 37.

Thin Transparent Paper With Figures on Back, Except 1 l

1872 **Showing Mesh**

38 A1 1 l grayish brn, *straw* 55.00 *75.00*
- *a.* 1 l red brn, *yelsh* 82.50 *115.00*

39 A1 5 l grn, *greenish* 675.00 30.00
- *a.* 5 l dark green, *grnsh* 725.00 40.00
- *b.* Double "5" on back 225.00

40 A1 10 l red org, *grnsh* *1,050.* 37.50
- *a.* 10 l red orange, *pale lilac* *7,750.* 150.00
- *b.* As #40, "10" on back inverted — 90.00
- *c.* Double "10" on back — 1,125.
- *d.* "0" on back — 525.00
- *e.* "01" on back — *2,100.*

41 A1 20 l dp bl, *bluish* 1,375. 30.00
- *a.* 20 l blue, *bluish* 1,375. 32.50
- *b.* 20 l dark blue, *bluish* 2,500. 55.00

42 A1 40 l brn, *bl* 45.00 *67.50*
- *a.* 40 l olive brown, *blue* 45.00 *70.00*
- *b.* 40 l red violet, *blue* 1,000. 95.00
- *c.* 40 l gray violet, *blue* 825.00 75.00
- *d.* Figures on back bister (#42b, 42c) 1,100. 95.00

The mesh is not apparent on Nos. 38, 38a.

On Cream Paper Unless Otherwise Stated With Figures on Back, Except 1 l, 2 l

1875

43 A1 1 l gray brn 15.00 12.00
- *a.* 1 l Deep red brown 35.00 20.00
- *b.* 1 l black brown, *yellowish* 175.00 *160.00*
- *c.* 1 l red brown 45.00 *60.00*
- *d.* 1 l dark red brown 75.00 *87.50*
- *e.* 1 l purple brown 75.00 *87.50*

44 A1 2 l bister 30.00 *32.50*

45 A1 5 l pale yel grn 200.00 30.00
- *a.* 5 l dk yel grn 275.00 40.00

46 A1 10 l orange 425.00 45.00
- *a.* 10 l orange, *yellow* 240.00 25.00
- *c.* "00" on back 925.00 200.00
- *d.* "1" on back — 260.00
- *e.* "0" on back — 225.00
- *f.* "01" on back — 535.00
- *g.* Double "10" on back — 800.00

47 A1 20 l ultra 160.00 24.00
- *a.* 20 l blue 290.00 24.00
- *b.* 20 l deep Prussian blue 1,600. 60.00
- *c.* "02" on back — 475.00
- *d.* "20" on back inverted — *11,000.*
- *e.* "2" instead of "20," inverted — *3,000.*
- *f.* Double "20" on back — 1,350.
- *g.* "20" inverted, on front of stamp 210,000.

48 A1 40 l salmon 30.00 *90.00*

The back figures are found in many varieties, including "1" and "0" inverted in "10."

Value for No. 47e is for example with "2" of "02" broken (deformed). Also known with unbroken "2"; value used about $600.

Paris Print, Clear Impression

1876 **Without Figures on Back**

49 A1 30 l ol brn, *yelsh* 290.00 60.00
- *a.* 30 l brown, *yellowish* 500.00 135.00

50 A1 60 l grn, *grnsh* 40.00 *115.00*

Athens Print, Coarse Impression, Yellowish Paper

51 A1 30 l dark brown 75.00 13.50
- *a.* 30 l black brown 75.00 13.50

52 A1 60 l green 625.00 67.50

Without Figures on Back

1880-82 **Cream Paper**

53 A1 5 l green 30.00 9.50

54 A1 10 l orange 27.50 9.50
- *a.* 10 l yellow 27.50 9.50
- *b.* 10 l red orange *8,250.* 75.00

55 A1 20 l ultra 450.00 190.00

56 A1 20 l pale rose (aniline ink) ('82) 8.25 8.25
- *a.* 20 l rose (aniline ink) ('82) 8.25 8.25
- *b.* 20 l deep carmine *275.00* 17.50

57 A1 30 l ultra ('82) 225.00 17.50
- *a.* 30 l slate blue 230.00 17.50

58 A1 40 l lilac 67.50 15.00
- *a.* 40 l violet 67.50 24.00

Stamps of type A1 were not regularly issued with perf. 11½ but were freely used on mail.

Hermes — A2

Lepta denominations have white numeral tablets.

Belgian Print, Clear Impression

1886-88 ***Imperf.***

64 A2 1 l brown ('88) 4.00 4.00

65 A2 2 l bister ('88) 9.50 *225.00*

66 A2 5 l yel grn ('88) 12.00 2.75

67 A2 10 l yellow ('88) 16.00 2.40

68 A2 20 l car rose ('88) 45.00 4.00

69 A2 25 l blue 160.00 2.75

70 A2 40 l violet ('88) 105.00 30.00

71 A2 50 l gray grn 8.25 2.75

72 A2 1d gray 120.00 4.00

Nos. 64-72 (9) 479.75 277.65

See Nos. 81-116. For surcharges see Nos. 129, 134, 140, 144, 150, 151-152, 155-156.

1891 ***Perf. 11½***

81 A2 1 l brown 8.25 3.50

82 A2 2 l bister 13.50 —

83 A2 5 l yel grn 27.50 13.00

84 A2 10 l yellow 40.00 13.00

85 A2 20 l car rose 55.00 18.00

86 A2 25 l blue 275.00 25.00

87 A2 40 l violet 190.00 190.00

88 A2 50 l gray grn 22.50 6.50

89 A2 1d gray 200.00 8.25

Nos. 81-89 (9) 831.75 277.25

The Belgian Printings perf. 13½ and most of the values perf. 11½ (Nos. 82-86) were perforated on request of philatelists at the main post office in Athens. While not regularly issued they were freely used for postage.

Athens Print, Poor Impression Wmk. Greek Words in Some Sheets

1889-95 ***Imperf.***

90 A2 1 l black brn 6.75 2.75
- *a.* 1 l brown 6.75 4.00

91 A2 2 l pale bister 1.75 1.60
- *a.* 2 l buff 2.75 *2.75*

92 A2 5 l green 11.00 1.60
- *a.* Double impression *200.00* —
- *b.* 5 l deep green 40.00 9.50

93 A2 10 l yellow 125.00 5.50
- *a.* 10 l orange 47.50 4.00
- *b.* 10 l dull yellow 125.00 5.50

94 A2 20 l carmine 11.00 8.25
- *a.* 20 l rose 75.00 40.00

95 A2 25 l dull blue 125.00 9.50
- *a.* 25 l indigo 150.00 6.75
- *b.* 25 l ultra 125.00 6.75
- *c.* 25 l brt blue 135.00 9.50

96 A2 25 l lilac 13.50 2.75
- *a.* 25 l red vio ('93) 20.00 4.00

97 A2 40 l red vio ('91) 125.00 27.50

98 A2 40 l blue ('93) 9.50 2.75

99 A2 1d gray ('95) 475.00 8.25

Perf. 13½

100 A2 1 l brown 80.00 —

101 A2 2 l buff 2.00 1.60

104 A2 20 l carmine 67.50 5.25
- *a.* 20 l rose 80.00 6.25

105 A2 40 l red violet 130.00 47.50

Other denominations of type A2 were not officially issued with perf. 13½.

Perf. 11½

107 A2 1 l brown 3.00 1.60
- *a.* 1 l black brown 7.25 5.75

108 A2 2 l pale bister 2.50 2.00
- *a.* 2 l buff 2.75 2.75

109 A2 5 l pale green 13.50 2.00
- *a.* 5 l deep green 55.00 3.00

110 A2 10 l yellow 95.00 1.25
- *a.* 10 l dull yellow 165.00 2.50
- *b.* 10 l orange 300.00 5.75

111 A2 20 l carmine 55.00 .75
- *a.* 20 l rose 160.00 1.60

112 A2 25 l dull blue 110.00 3.75
- *a.* 25 l indigo 300.00 21.00
- *b.* 25 l ultra 110.00 52.50
- *c.* 25 l bright blue 160.00 9.00

113 A2 25 l lilac 6.75 1.60
- *a.* 25 l red violet 20.00 2.75

114 A2 40 l red violet 160.00 37.50

115 A2 40 l blue 16.50 2.75

116 A2 1d gray 600.00 10.00

Partly-perforated varieties sell for about twice as much as normal stamps.

The watermark on Nos. 90-116 consists of three Greek words meaning Paper for Public Service. It is in double-lined capitals, measures 270x35mm, and extends across three panes.

Boxers — A3

Discobolus by Myron — A4

Vase Depicting Pallas Athene (Minerva) — A5

Chariot Driving A6

Stadium and Acropolis A7

Statue of Hermes by Praxiteles — A8

Statue of Victory by Paeonius — A9

Acropolis and Parthenon A10

Perf. 14x13½, 13½x14

1896 **Unwmk.**

117 A3 1 l ocher 4.00 3.00

118 A3 2 l rose 3.00 3.00
- *a.* Without engraver's name 30.00 21.00

119 A4 5 l lilac 12.50 5.25

120 A4 10 l slate gray 12.50 7.25

121 A5 20 l red brn 25.00 8.25

122 A6 25 l red 30.00 10.50

123 A5 40 l violet 14.50 9.50

124 A6 60 l black 42.50 21.00

125 A7 1d blue 115.00 26.00

126 A8 2d bister 325.00 105.00
- *a.* Horiz. pair, imperf. btwn. — —

127 A9 5d green 575.00 500.00

128 A10 10d brown 625.00 550.00

Nos. 117-128 (12) 1,784. 1,249.

1st intl. Olympic Games of the modern era, held at Athens. Counterfeits of Nos. 123-124 and 126-128 exist.

For surcharges see Nos. 159-164.

Preceding Issues Surcharged

1900 ***Imperf.***

129 A2 20 l on 25 l dl bl, #95c 3.00 1.60
- *a.* 20 l on 25 l indigo, #95a 67.50 47.50
- *b.* 20 l on 25 l ultra, #95b 70.00 55.00
- *c.* Double surcharge 57.50 57.50
- *d.* Triple surcharge 85.00 85.00
- *e.* Inverted surcharge 60.00 57.50
- *f.* "20" above word 110.00 105.00
- *g.* Pair, one without surcharge 250.00 250.00
- *h.* "20" without word 165.00 165.00

130 A1 30 l on 40 l vio, *cr*, #58a 6.50 6.25
- *a.* 30 l on 40 l lilac, #58 15.50 15.50
- *b.* Broad "0" in "30" 10.50 8.25
- *c.* First letter of word is "A" 135.00 135.00
- *d.* Double surcharge *625.00* *625.00*

132 A1 40 l on 2 l bis, *cr*, #44 8.50 8.25
- *a.* Broad "0" in "40" 12.50 12.50
- *b.* First letter of word is "A" 165.00 165.00

133 A1 50 l on 40 l sal, *cr*, #48 6.25 6.25
- *a.* Broad "0" in "50" 10.00 8.25
- *b.* First letter of word is "A" 135.00 135.00
- *c.* "50" without word 200.00 175.00
- *d.* "50" above word 200.00 175.00

134 A2 1d on 40 l red vio (No. 97) 15.50 6.25

137 A1 3d on 10 l org, *cr*, #54 52.50 52.50
- *a.* 3d on 10 l yellow, #54a 52.50 52.50

138 A1 5d on 40 l red vio, *bl*, #21 150.00 150.00
- *a.* 5d on 40 l red vio, *bl*, #28 190.00 *190.00*
- *b.* "20" on back corrected to "40" *1,400.*

139 A1 5d on 40 l red vio, *bl*, #42b 575.00

Perf. 11½

140 A2 20 l on 25 l dl bl, #112 3.25 3.25
- *a.* 20 l on 25 l indigo, #112a 100.00 90.00
- *b.* 20 l on 25 l ultra, #112b 80.00 77.50
- *c.* Double surcharge 67.50 70.00
- *d.* Triple surcharge 95.00 95.00
- *e.* Inverted surcharge 67.50 67.50
- *f.* "20" above word 150.00 150.00

141 A1 30 l on 40 l vio, *cr*, #58a 10.50 10.50
- *a.* 30 l on 40 l lilac, #58 17.50 17.50
- *b.* Broad "0" in "30" 12.50 12.50
- *c.* First letter of word is "A" 150.00 150.00
- *d.* Double surcharge

142 A1 40 l on 2 l bis, *cr*, #44 15.50 15.50
- *a.* Broad "0" in "40" 15.50 15.50
- *b.* First letter of word is "A" 165.00 165.00

143 A1 50 l on 40 l sal, *cr*, #48 10.50 10.50
- *a.* Broad "0" in "50" 12.50 12.50
- *b.* First letter of word is "A" 135.00 135.00
- *c.* "50" without word 200.00 175.00

144 A2 1d on 40 l red vio, #114 145.00 160.00

147 A1 3d on 10 l yel, *cream*, #54a 57.50 57.50
- *a.* 3d on 10 l org, *cr*, #54 60.00 *65.00*

148 A1 5d on 40 l red vio, *bl*, #21 150.00 175.00
- *a.* 5d on 40 l red vio, *bl*, #28 175.00 *225.00*

149 A1 5d on 40 l red vio, *bl*, #42b 625.00

Perf. 13½

150 A2 2d on 40 l red vio, #105 12.00 12.50

The 1d on 40 l perf. 13½ and the 2d on 40 l, both imperf. and perf. 13½, were not officially issued.

Surcharge Including "A M"

"A M" = "Axia Metalliki" or "Value in Metal (gold)."

1900 ***Imperf.***

151 A2 25 l on 40 l vio, #70 6.00 10.50

152 A2 50 l on 25 l bl, #69 26.50 24.00

153 A1 1d on 40 l brn, *bl*, #42b 125.00 *150.00*

154 A1 2d on 5 l grn, *cr*, #53 16.00 *21.00*

Perf. 11½

155 A2 25 l on 40 l vio, #87 12.00 15.50

156 A2 50 l on 25 l bl, #86 52.50 62.50

157 A1 1d on 40 l brn, *bl*, #42b 160.00 160.00

158 A1 2d on 5 l grn, *cr*, #53 20.00 26.00

Nos. 151-158 (8) 418.00 469.50

Partly-perforated varieties of Nos. 129-158 sell for about two to three times as much as normal stamps.

Surcharge in Red

1900-01 ***Perf. 14x13½***

159 A7 5 l on 1d blue 15.00 9.50
- *a.* Wrong font "M" with serifs 75.00 *80.00*
- *b.* Double surcharge 225.00 200.00

160 A5 25 l on 40 l vio 70.00 67.50
- *a.* Double surcharge 900.00

161 A8 50 l on 2d bister 80.00 62.50
- *a.* Broad "0" in "50" 80.00 62.50

162 A9 1d on 5d grn ('01) 250.00 200.00
- *a.* Greek "Δ" instead of "A" as 3rd letter 650.00 700.00

163 A10 2d on 10d brn ('01) 70.00 *100.00*
- *a.* Greek "Δ" instead of "A" as 3rd letter 275.00 250.00

Nos. 159-163 (5) 485.00 439.50

Black Surcharge on No. 160

164 A5 50 l on 25 l on 40 l vio (R + Bk) 500.00 475.00
- *a.* Broad "0" in "50" 475.00 *575.00*

Nos. 151-164 and 179-183, gold currency stamps, were generally used for parcel post and foreign money orders. They were also available for use on letters, but cost about 20 per cent more than the regular stamps of the same denomination.

Counterfeit surcharges exist of Nos. 159-164.

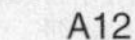

Giovanni da Bologna's Hermes

A11 A12

A13

Type I Type II

FIVE LEPTA.

Type I — Letters of "ΕΛΛΑΣ" not outlined at top and left. Only a few faint horizontal lines between the outer vertical lines at sides.

Type II — Letters of "ΕΛΛΑΣ" fully outlined. Heavy horizontal lines between the vertical frame lines.

Perf. 11½, 12½, 13½

1901 Engr. Wmk. 129

165	A11	1 l yellow brn	.40	.25
166	A11	2 l gray	.60	.25
167	A11	3 l orange	.65	.30
168	A12	5 l grn, type I	.80	.25
a.		5 l yellow green, type I	.60	.25
b.		5 l yellow green, type II	.60	.25
169	A12	10 l rose	3.25	.25
170	A11	20 l red lilac	6.50	.25
171	A12	25 l ultra	6.50	.25
172	A11	30 l dl vio	12.00	2.00
173	A11	40 l dk brn	25.00	3.00
174	A11	50 l brn lake	20.00	1.50

Perf. 12½, 14 and Compound

175	A13	1d black	47.50	3.00
a.		Horiz. pair, imperf. btwn.	325.00	
c.		Horiz. pair, imperf. vert.	300.00	
d.		Vert. pair, imperf. horiz.	300.00	

Litho.

Perf. 12½

176	A13	2d bronze	11.00	8.00
177	A13	3d silver	11.00	*12.00*
178	A13	5d gold	13.00	*15.00*
		Nos. 165-178 (14)	158.20	46.30
		Set, never hinged	325.00	

All values 1 l through 1d issued on both thick and thin paper. Nos. 173-174 are values for thin paper — values for thick paper are higher.

For overprints and surcharges see Nos. RA3-RA13, N16, N109.

Imperf., Pairs

165a	A11	1 l	12.00
166a	A11	2 l	15.00
167a	A11	3 l	15.00
168c	A12	5 l	12.00
169a	A12	10 l	19.00
170a	A11	20 l	15.00
171a	A12	25 l	15.00
172a	A11	30 l	250.00
173a	A11	40 l	300.00
174a	A11	50 l	70.00
175b	A13	1d	250.00

Nos. 165a-175a were issued on both thick and thin paper. Values are for the less expensive thin paper.

Hermes — A14

1902, Jan. 1 Engr. *Perf. 13½*

179	A14	5 l deep orange	2.00	1.10
a.		Imperf., pair	82.50	
180	A14	25 l emerald	30.00	3.00
181	A14	50 l ultra	30.00	3.75
a.		Imperf., pair	550.00	
182	A14	1d rose red	30.00	8.25
183	A14	2d orange brn	52.50	50.00
		Nos. 179-183 (5)	144.50	66.10
		Set, never hinged	375.00	

See note after No. 164. In 1913 remainders of Nos. 179-183 were used as postage dues.

Apollo Throwing Discus A15

Jumper, with Jumping Weights A16

Victory — A17

Atlas and Hercules A18

Struggle of Hercules and Antaeus A19

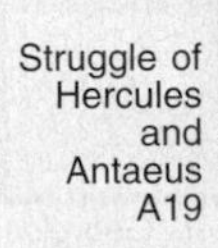

Wrestlers A20

Daemon of the Games A21

Foot Race A22

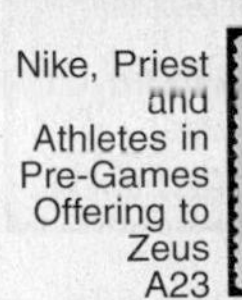

Nike, Priest and Athletes in Pre-Games Offering to Zeus A23

Wmk. Crown and ET (129)

1906, Mar. Engr. *Perf. 13½, 14*

184	A15	1 l brown	.55	.40
a.		Imperf., pair	*300.00*	
185	A15	2 l gray	.55	.40
a.		Imperf., pair	*300.00*	
186	A16	3 l orange	.55	.40
a.		Imperf., pair	300.00	
187	A16	5 l green	1.25	.40
a.		Imperf., pair	110.00	
188	A17	10 l rose red	3.00	.60
a.		Imperf., pair	*300.00*	
189	A18	20 l magenta	5.00	.60
a.		Imperf., pair	*575.00*	
190	A19	25 l ultra	6.00	.85
a.		Imperf., pair	*575.00*	
191	A20	30 l dl pur	5.00	2.75
a.		Double impression	*1,100.*	
192	A21	40 l dk brown	5.00	2.75
193	A18	50 l brn lake	10.00	3.25
194	A22	1d gray blk	65.00	13.00
a.		Imperf., pair	*1,100.*	
195	A22	2d rose	100.00	35.00
196	A22	3d olive yel	155.00	125.00
197	A23	5d dull blue	160.00	140.00
		Nos. 184-197 (14)	516.90	325.40
		Set, never hinged	1,500.	

Greek Special Olympic Games of 1906 at Athens, celebrating the 10th anniv. of the modern Olympic Games.

Surcharged stamps of this issue are revenues.

A24

Iris Holding Caduceus A25

Hermes Donning Sandals A26

Hermes Carrying Infant Arcas — A27

Hermes, from Old Cretan Coin — A28

Designs A24 to A28 are from Cretan and Arcadian coins of the 4th Century, B.C.

Serrate Roulette 13½

1911-21 Engr. Unwmk.

198	A24	1 l green	.65	.30
199	A25	2 l car rose	.65	.30
200	A24	3 l vermilion	.95	.30
201	A26	5 l green	2.00	.30
202	A24	10 l car rose	9.50	.30
203	A25	20 l gray lilac	3.00	.80
204	A25	25 l ultra	15.00	.80
a.		Rouletted in black	190.00	140.00
205	A26	30 l car rose	4.50	1.60
206	A25	40 l deep blue	10.00	4.00
207	A26	50 l dl vio	15.00	3.00
208	A27	1d ultra	20.00	.80
209	A27	2d vermilion	27.50	.95
210	A27	3d car rose	27.50	1.40
a.		Size 20¼x25½mm ('21)	100.00	50.00
211	A27	5d ultra	35.00	4.00
a.		Size 20¼x25½mm ('21)	200.00	25.00
212	A27	10d dp bl ('21)	140.00	70.00
a.		Size 20x26½mm ('11)	300.00	125.00
213	A28	25d deep blue	87.50	55.00
		Nos. 198-213 (16)	398.75	143.85
		Set, never hinged	750.00	

The 1921 reissues of the 3d, 5d and 10d measure 20¼x25½mm instead of 20x26½mm.

See Nos. 214-231. For overprints see Nos. 233-248B, N1, N10-N15, N17-N52A, N110-N148, Thrace 22-30, N26-N75.

Imperf., Pairs

198a	A24	1 l		[illegible]	[illegible]
200a	A24	3 l		240.00	240.00
201a	A26	5 l		30.00	30.00
202a	A24	10 l		52.50	52.50
203a	A25	20 l		225.00	225.00
204b	A25	25 l		300.00	300.00
206a	A25	40 l		350.00	
207a	A26	50 l		350.00	
208a	A27	1d		350.00	
209a	A27	2d		350.00	
210b	A27	3d		350.00	
211b	A27	5d		240.00	
212b	A27	10d	As "a"	*1,600.*	
213a	A28	25d		*2,250.*	

Serrate Roulette 10½x13½, 13½

1913-23 Litho.

214	A24	1 l green	.25	.25
a.		Without period after "ΕΛΛΑΣ"	77.50	—
215	A25	2 l rose	.25	.25
216	A24	3 l vermilion	.25	.25
217	A26	5 l green	.25	.25
218	A24	10 l carmine	.25	.25
219	A25	15 l dl bl ('18)	.35	.25
220	A25	20 l slate	.35	.25
221	A25	25 l ultra	4.00	.50
a.		25 l blue	.25	.25
c.		Double impression	—	
222	A26	30 l rose ('14)	.95	.40
223	A25	40 l indigo ('14)	2.10	.70
224	A26	50 l vio brn ('14)	4.25	.35
225	A26	80 l vio brn ('23)	5.25	1.40
226	A27	1d ultra ('19)	7.00	.70
227	A27	2d ver ('19)	6.50	.70
228	A27	3d car rose ('20)	8.50	.80
229	A27	5d ultra ('22)	12.00	1.00
230	A27	10d dp bl ('22)	12.00	1.25
231	A28	25d indigo ('22)	16.00	4.75
		Nos. 214-231 (18)	80.50	14.30
		Set, never hinged	225.00	

Nos. 221, 223 and 226 were re-issued in 1926, printed in Vienna from new plates. There are slight differences in minor details.

The 10 lepta brown, on thick paper, type A28, is not a postage stamp. It was issued in 1922 to replace coins of this denomination during a shortage of copper.

Imperf., Pairs

214b	A24	1 l	65.00	
215a	A25	2 l	110.00	
216a	A24	3 l	175.00	
217a	A26	5 l	65.00	
218a	A24	10 l	82.50	
220a	A25	20 l	82.50	
221b	A25	25 l	175.00	
222a	A26	30 l	175.00	
223a	A25	40 l	175.00	
224a	A26	50 l	[illegible]	
225b	A26	80 l	92.50	
226a	A27	1d		250.00
227a	A27	2d	100.00	
228b	A27	3d	300.00	
229a	A27	5d	360.00	

Raising Greek Flag at Suda Bay, Crete A29

1913, Dec. 1 Engr. *Perf. 14½*

232	A29	25 l blue & black	8.00	5.00
		Never hinged	16.00	
a.		Imperf., pair	*1,400.*	

Union of Crete with Greece. Used only in Crete.

Stamps of 1911-14 Overprinted in Red or Black

Serrate Roulette 13½

1916, Nov. 1 Litho.

233	A24	1 l green (R)	.25	.25
234	A25	2 l rose	.25	.25
235	A24	3 l vermilion	.25	.25
236	A26	5 l green (R)	.50	.40
237	A24	10 l carmine	.75	.40
238	A25	20 l slate (R)	1.50	.40
239	A25	25 l blue (R)	1.50	.40
a.		25 l ultra	140.00	26.00
240	A26	30 l rose	1.50	.90
a.		Pair, one without ovpt.		
241	A25	40 l indigo (R)	11.00	3.00
242	A26	50 l vio brn (R)	37.50	2.50

Engr.

243	A24	3 l vermilion	.50	.50
244	A26	30 l car rose	1.25	1.25
245	A27	1d ultra (R)	40.00	.80
a.		Rouletted in black	325.00	225.00
246	A27	2d vermilion	24.00	3.50
247	A27	3d car rose	14.00	3.50
248	A27	5d ultra (R)	95.00	15.00
248B	A27	10d dp bl (R)	24.00	22.50
		Nos. 233-248B (17)	253.75	55.80
		Set, never hinged	500.00	

Most of Nos. 233-248B exist with overprint double, inverted, etc. Minimum value of errors $18. Excellent counterfeits of the overprint varieties exist.

Issued by the Venizelist Provisional Government

Iris — A32

1917, Feb. 5 Litho. *Perf. 14*

249 A32 1 l dp green .40 .25
250 A32 5 l yel grn .40 .25
251 A32 10 l rose .80 .35
252 A32 25 l lt blue 1.10 .35
253 A32 50 l gray vio 9.00 2.50
254 A32 1d ultra 2.25 .75
255 A32 2d lt red 4.50 1.50
256 A32 3d claret 25.00 7.75
257 A32 5d gray bl 5.75 3.00
258 A32 10d dk blue 70.00 20.00
259 A32 25d slate 125.00 *160.00*
Nos. 249-259 (11) 244.20 196.70
Set, never hinged 400.00

The 4d was used only as a revenue stamp.

Imperf., Pairs

249a A32 1 l 9.50
250a A32 5 l 9.50
251a A32 10 l 9.50
252a A32 25 l 17.50
253a A32 50 l 25.00
254a A32 1d 22.50
255a A32 2d 30.00
256a A32 3d 65.00
257a A32 5d 65.00
258a A32 10d 110.00
259a A32 25d 125.00

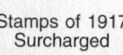

Stamps of 1917 Surcharged

1923

260 A32 5 l on 10 l rose .25 .25
a. Inverted surcharge 24.00 *35.00*
261 A32 50 l on 50 l gray vio .25 .25
262 A32 1d on 1d ultra .25 .25
a. 1d on 1d gray .25 .25
263 A32 2d on 2d lt red .55 .55
264 A32 3d on 3d claret 1.60 1.60
265 A32 5d on 5d dk bl 2.00 2.00
266 A32 25d on 25d slate 27.50 27.50
Nos. 260-266 (7) 32.40 32.40
Set, never hinged 125.00

Same Surcharge on Occupation of Turkey Stamps, 1913

Perf. 13½

267 O2 5 l on 3 l org .25 .25
a. Inverted surcharge 19.00
268 O1 10 l on 20 l vio 1.50 1.50
a. Inverted surcharge 82.50
269 O2 10 l on 25 l pale bl .25 .25
a. Inverted surcharge 60.00 35.00
270 O1 10 l on 30 l gray grn .25 .25
271 O2 10 l on 40 l ind 1.25 1.25
272 O1 50 l on 50 l dk bl .25 .25
a. Inverted surcharge 72.50 37.50
273 O1 2d on 2d gray brn 60.00 60.00
274 O2 3d on 3d dl bl 4.50 *6.00*
a. Imperf., pair 500.00
275 O1 5d on 5d gray 4.00 *7.00*
276 O2 10d on 10d vio brn 15.00 *22.50*
276A O2 10d on 10d car 800.00
Nos. 267-276 (10) 87.25 99.25
Set, never hinged 150.00

Dangerous counterfeits of No. 276A exist.

Same Surcharge on Stamps of Crete

Perf. 14

On Crete Nos. 50, 52, 59

276B A6 5 l on 1 l red brn 27.50 27.50
277 A8 10 l on 10 l red .25 .25
277B A8 10 l on 25 l bl 110.00 110.00

On Crete Nos. 66-69, 71

278 A8 10 l on 25 l blue .25 .25
279 A6 50 l on 50 l lilac .45 *.70*
279A A6 50 l on 50 l ultra 8.50 *14.00*
280 A9 50 l on 1d gray vio 3.00 *4.00*
280A A11 50 l on 5d grn & blk 27.50 27.50

On Crete Nos. 77-82

281 A15 10 l on 20 l bl grn 125.00 125.00
282 A16 10 l on 25 l ultra .45 .45
a. Double surcharge 50.00 50.00
283 A17 50 l on 50 l yel brn .25 .35
284 A18 50 l on 1d rose car & brn 2.00 1.75
a. Imperf., pair 425.00
285 A19 3d on 3d org & blk 14.00 14.00
286 A20 5d on 5d ol grn & blk 9.00 9.00

On Crete Nos. 83-84

287 A21 10 l on 25 l bl & blk 3.25 1.75
a. Imperf., pair
287B A22 50 l on 1d grn & blk 8.00 4.50

Surcharged on Crete No. 96

288 A23 10 l on 10 l brn red .25 .25
a. Inverted surcharge 45.00 40.00

On Crete No. 91

288B A17 50 l on 50 l yel brn *800.00*

Dangerous counterfeits of the overprint on No. 288B are plentiful.

On Crete No. 109

289 A19 3d on 3d org & blk 17.50 17.50

On Crete Nos. 111, 113-120

290 A6 5 l on 1 l vio brn .25 .25
a. Inverted surcharge 25.00
291 A13 5 l on 5 l grn .25 .25
a. Inverted surcharge 47.50
292 A23 10 l on 10 l brn red .25 .25
a. Inverted surcharge 47.50
293 A15 10 l on 20 l bl grn .30 .30
a. Inverted surcharge 47.50
294 A16 10 l on 25 l ultra .35 .35
a. Inverted surcharge 47.50
295 A17 50 l on 50 l yel brn .40 .40
296 A18 50 l on 1d rose car & brn 5.25 5.25
a. Inverted surcharge
b. Double surcharge 225.00
c. Double surch., one invtd.
d. Imperf., pair
297 A19 3d on 3d org & blk 16.00 16.00
298 A20 5d on 5d ol grn & blk 200.00 200.00

Dangerous counterfeits of No. 298 exist.

Crete Nos. J2-J9

299 D1 5 l on 5 l red .25 .25
a. Inverted surcharge 45.00 6.75
300 D1 5 l on 10 l red .30 .30
301 D1 10 l on 20 l red 12.00 12.00
a. Inverted surcharge
302 D1 10 l on 40 l red .30 .30
303 D1 50 l on 50 l red .30 *.55*
304 D1 50 l on 1d red .30 .50
a. Double surcharge
305 D1 50 l on 1d on 1d red 9.50 9.50
306 D1 2d on 2d red 1.25 1.25

On Crete Nos. J11-J13

307 D1 5 l on 5 l red 6.00 6.00
308 D1 5 l on 10 l red 1.50 1.50
a. "ΕΛΛΑΣ" inverted 6.50
309 D1 10 l on 20 l red 55.00 55.00

On Crete Nos. J20-J22, J24-J26

310 D1 5 l on 5 l red .25 .25
311 D1 5 l on 10 l red .25 .25
a. Inverted surcharge 12.00
312 D1 10 l on 20 l red .25 .25
313 D1 50 l on 50 l red .55 .55
314 D1 50 l on 1d red 4.00 4.00
315 D1 2d on 2d red 7.00 7.00

These surcharged Postage Due stamps were intended for the payment of ordinary postage.

Nos. 260 to 315 were surcharged in commemoration of the revolution of 1922.

Nos. 59, 91, 109, 111, 113-120, J11-J13, J20-J22, J24-J26 are on stamps previously overprinted by Crete.

Issues of the Republic

Lord Byron — A33

Byron at Missolonghi — A34

1924, Apr. 16 Engr. *Perf. 12*

316 A33 80 l dark blue .55 .25
317 A34 2d dk vio & blk 1.25 .65
Set, never hinged 3.25

Death of Lord Byron (1788-1824) at Missolonghi.

Tomb of Markos Botsaris — A35

Serrate Roulette 13½

1926, Apr. 24 Litho.

318 A35 25 l lilac .85 .50
Never hinged 1.75

Centenary of the defense of Missolonghi against the Turks.

Corinth Canal A36

Dodecanese Costume A37

Macedonian Costume A38

Monastery of Simon Peter on Mt. Athos A39

White Tower of Salonika A40

Temple of Hephaestus A41

The Acropolis — A42

Cruiser "Georgios Averoff" — A43

Academy of Sciences, Athens — A44

Temple of Hephaestus A45

Acropolis A46

Perf. 12½x13, 13, 13x12½, 13½, 13½x13

1927, Apr. 1 Engr.

321 A36 5 l dark green .25 .25
a. Vert. pair, imperf. horiz. 140.00 92.50
322 A37 10 l orange red .30 .25
a. Horiz. pair, imperf. between 140.00 92.50
c. Double impression 77.50
323 A38 20 l violet .30 .25
324 A39 25 l slate blue .50 .25
a. Imperf., pair 140.00 140.00
b. Vert. pair, imperf. between 150.00 110.00
325 A40 40 l slate blue .50 .25
326 A36 50 l violet 1.10 .25

327 A36 80 l dk bl & blk .95 .25
a. Imperf., pair 825.00
328 A41 1d dk bl & bis brn (I) 1.10 .25
a. Imperf., pair 150.00 125.00
b. Center inverted *6,500.*
c. Double impression of center 325.00 225.00
d. Double impression of frame 325.00 225.00
329 A42 2d dk grn & blk 6.50 .30
a. Imperf., pair 600.00 *800.00*
330 A43 3d dp vio & blk 6.00 .30
a. Double impression of center 225.00 *275.00*
b. Center inverted *8,000.*
331 A44 5d yel & blk 15.00 2.00
a. Imperf., pair 925.00 925.00
b. Center inverted 10,000. *4,500.*
c. 5d yellow & green 110.00 37.50
332 A45 10d brn car & blk 45.00 11.00
333 A44 15d brt yel grn & blk 57.50 16.00
334 A46 25d green & blk 110.00 18.00
a. Double impression of center —
Nos. 321-334 (14) 245.00 49.60
Set, never hinged 700.00

See Nos. 364-371 and notes preceding No. 364. For overprints see Nos. RA55, RA57, RA60, RA66, RA70-RA71.

This series as prepared, included a 1 lepton dark brown, type A37, but that value was never issued. Most stamps were burned. Value $300.

Gen. Charles N. Fabvier and Acropolis A47

1927, Aug. 1 *Perf. 12*

335 A47 1d red .30 .25
336 A47 3d dark blue 2.00 .60
337 A47 6d green 12.00 9.00
Nos. 335-337 (3) 14.30 9.85
Set, never hinged 42.50

Cent. of the liberation of Athens from the Turks in 1826.

For surcharges see Nos. 376-377.

Bay of Navarino and Pylos A48

Battle of Navarino A49

"Edward" omitted — A50

"Edward" added — A51

Admiral de Rigny — A52

Admiral van der Heyden — A53

Designs: Nos. 340-341, Sir Edward Codrington.

Perf. 13½x12½, 12½x13½, 13x12½, 12½x13

1927-28 **Litho.**

338 A48 1.50d gray green 1.60 .35
- *a.* Imperf., pair 275.00
- *b.* Horiz. pair, imperf. btwn. 875.00
- *c.* Horiz. pair, imperf. vert. 250.00

339 A49 4d dk gray bl ('30) 7.00 1.50
340 A50 5d dk brn & gray 5.50 *4.75*
- *a.* 5d blk brn & blk ('28) 13.00 6.50

341 A51 5d dk brn & blk ('28) 35.00 12.00
342 A52 5d vio bl & blk ('28) 35.00 12.00
343 A53 5d lake & blk ('28) 20.00 9.50
Nos. 338-343 (6) 104.10 40.10
Set, never hinged 275.00

Centenary of the naval battle of Navarino.
For surcharges see Nos. 372-375.

Admiral Lascarina Bouboulina A54

Athanasios Diakos A55

Map of Greece in 1830 and 1930 — A56

Sortie from Missolonghi A58

Patriots Declaring Independence — A57

Portraits: 10 l, Constantine Rhigas Ferreos. 20 l, Gregorios V. 40 l, Prince Alexandros Ypsilantis. No. 345, Bouboulina. No. 355, Diakos. No. 346, Theodoros Kolokotronis. No. 356, Konstantinos Kanaris. No.347, Georgios Karaiskakis. No. 357, Markos Botsaris. 2d, Andreas Miaoulis. 3d, Lazaros Koundouriotis. 5d, Count John Capo d'Istria (Capodistria), statesman and doctor. 10d, Petros Mavromichalis. 15d, Dionysios Solomos. 20d, Adamantios Korais.

Various Frames

1930, Apr. 1 **Engr.** ***Perf. 13½, 14***

Imprint of Perkins, Bacon & Co.

344 A55 10 l brown .25 .25
345 A54 50 l red .25 .25
346 A54 1d car rose .30 .30
347 A55 1.50d lt blue .40 .40
348 A55 2d orange .45 .45
349 A55 5d purple 1.50 1.50
350 A54 10d gray blk 6.50 6.50
351 A54 15d yellow grn 12.00 12.00
352 A55 20d blue blk 17.50 17.50

Imprint of Bradbury, Wilkinson & Co.

Perf. 12

353 A55 20 l black .25 .25
354 A55 40 l blue grn .25 .25
355 A55 50 l brt blue .25 .25
356 A55 1d brown org .30 .30
357 A55 1.50d dk red .40 .40
358 A55 3d dk brown .65 .65
359 A56 4d dk blue 3.00 3.00
360 A57 25d black 17.50 17.50
361 A58 50d red brn 45.00 45.00
Nos. 344-361 (18) 106.75 106.75
Set, never hinged 275.00

Greek independence, cent. Some exist imperf.

Arcadi Monastery and Abbot Gabriel (Mt. Ida in Background) A60

1930, Nov. 8 ***Perf. 12***

363 A60 8d deep violet 13.00 1.10
Never hinged 55.00

Issue of 1927 Re-engraved

Type I

Type II

1d. Type I — Greek letters "Λ," "Α," "Δ" have sharp pointed tops; numerals "1" are 1½mm wide at the foot, and have a straight slanting serif at top.

1d. Type II — Greek letters "Λ," "Α," "Δ" have flat tops; numerals "1" are 2mm wide at foot and the serif at top is slightly curved. Perf. 14.

There are many minor differences in the lines of the two designs.

1d. Type III — The "1" in lower left corner has no serif at left of foot. Lines of temple have been deepened, so details stand out more clearly.

2d. On 1927 stamp the Parthenon is indistinct and blurred. On 1933 stamp it is strongly outlined and clear. Between the two pillars at lower right are four blocks of marble. These blocks are clear and distinct on the 1933 stamp but run together on the 1927 issue.

3d. Design is clearer, especially vertical lines of shading in smoke stacks and reflections in the water. Two or more sides perf. 11½.

10d. Background and shading of entire stamp have been lightened. Detail of frame is clearer and more distinct.

15d. Many more lines of shading in sky and foreground. Engraving is sharp and clear, particularly in frame. Two or more sides perf. 11½.

25d. Background has been lightened and foreground reduced until base of larger upright column is removed and fallen column appears nearly submerged.

50 l, Design is clearer, especially "50" and the 10 letters.

Sizes in millimeters:
50 l, 1927, 18x24¾. 1933, 18½x24½.
1d, 1927, 24¾x17¾. 1931, 24¾x17¼. 1933, 24½x18¼.
2d, 1927, 24½x17¾. 1933, 24½x18½.

Perf. 11½, 11½x12½, 12½x10, 13, 13x12½, 14

1931-35

364 A36 50 l dk vio ('33) 4.00 1.00
365 A41 1d dk bl & org brn, type II 10.00 1.00
366 A41 1d dk bl & org brn, type III ('33) 5.75 .25
367 A42 2d dk grn & blk ('33) 2.75 .50
368 A43 3d red vio & blk ('34) 3.25 .25
- *a.* Imperf., pair

369 A45 10d brn car & blk ('35) 47.50 1.50
370 A44 15d pale yel grn & blk ('34) 82.50 17.50
- *a.* Imperf., pair *1,100.*

371 A46 25d dk grn & blk ('35) 25.00 17.00
Nos. 364-371 (8) 180.75 39.00
Set, never hinged 600.00

Nos. 336-337, 340-343 Surcharged in Red

1932 ***Perf. 12½x13½, 12½x13***

372 A52 1.50d on 5d 2.00 .25
373 A53 1.50d on 5d 2.00 .25
- *a.* Double surcharge 110.00

374 A50 2d on 5d 5.00 .25
375 A51 2d on 5d 9.00 .25

Perf. 12

376 A47 2d on 3d 2.25 .25
- *a.* Double surcharge 125.00

377 A47 4d on 6d 2.50 1.10
Nos. 372-377 (6) 22.75 2.35
Set, never hinged 50.00

Adm. Pavlos Koundouriotis and Cruiser "Averoff" — A61

Pallas Athene — A62

Youth of Marathon — A63

1933 ***Perf. 13½x13, 13x13½***

378 A61 50d black & ind 50.00 1.60
- *a.* Imperf., pair *2,250.*

379 A62 75d blk & vio brn 110.00 *175.00*
- *a.* Imperf., pair 825.00
- Never hinged 1,700.

380 A63 100d brn & dull grn 625.00 29.00
- *a.* Imperf., pair 2,750.

Nos. 378-380 (3) 785.00 *205.60*
Set, never hinged 1,800.

The imperf pairs are without gum.
For surcharges see Nos. 386-387.

Approach to Athens Stadium A64

Perf. 11½, 11½x10, 13x11½

1934, Dec. 10

381 A64 8d blue 65.00 2.25
Never hinged 200.00

Perforations on No. 381 range from 10½ to 13, including compounds.

Church of Pantanassa, Mistra — A65

1935, Nov. 1 ***Perf. 13x12½***

382 A65 4d brown 17.00 1.60
Never hinged 47.50
- *a.* Horiz. pair, imperf. between 725.00
- *b.* Imperf., pair 725.00

Issues of the Monarchy

J71, J76, J82, 380, 379 Surcharged in Red or Blue

Nos. 383-385

Nos. 386-387

Serrate Roulette 13½

1935, Nov. 24 **Litho.**

383 D3 50 l on 40 l indigo (R) .25 .25
- *a.* Double surcharge 27.50

384 D3 3d on 3d car (Bl) .55 .40

Perf. 13

385 D3 3d on 3d rose red (Bl) 2.75 2.00

Perf. 13x13½

386 A63 5d on 100d (R) 2.25 2.00
387 A62 15d on 75d (Bl) 6.50 6.00
Nos. 383-387 (5) 12.30 10.65
Set, never hinged 30.00

King Constantine — A66

Center Engr., Frame Litho.

Perf. 12x13½

1936, Nov. 18 **Wmk. 252**

389 A66 3d black & brown .55 .40
- *a.* Pair, printer's name in Greek 22.50
- *b.* Pair, printer's name in English 22.50

390 A66 8d black & blue 1.10 .90
- *a.* Pair, printer's name in Greek 22.50
- *b.* Pair, printer's name in English 22.50

Set, never hinged 3.25

Re-burial of the remains of King Constantine and Queen Sophia.

Two printings exist, the first containing varieties "a" and "b" with gray border; second with black border.

King George II — A67

1937, Jan. 24 **Engr.** ***Perf. 12½x12***

391 A67 1d green .25 .25
392 A67 3d red brown .25 .25
393 A67 8d dp blue .90 .40
394 A67 100d carmine lake 12.00 12.00
Nos. 391-394 (4) 13.40 12.90
Set, never hinged 30.00

For surcharges see Nos. 484-487, 498-500, RA86-RA87, N241-N242.

Pallas Athene — A68

1937, Apr. 17 **Unwmk.** ***Perf. 11½***

395 A68 3d yellow brown .55 .25
Never hinged 1.10

Centenary of the University of Athens.

Contest with Bull — A69

Lady of Tiryns — A70

Zeus of Dodona — A71

Coin of Amphictyonic League A72

Diagoras of Rhodes, Victor at Olympics A73

Venus of Melos — A74

Battle of Salamis A75

Chariot of Panathenaic Festival A76

Alexander the Great at Battle of Issos — A77

St. Paul Preaching to Athenians A78

St. Demetrius' Church at Salonika A79

Leo III Victory over Arabs — A80

Allegorical Figure of Glory — A81

Perf. 13½x12, 12x13½

1937, Nov. 1 Litho. Wmk. 252

396	A69	5 l brn red & bl	.25	.25
a.		Double impression of frame	60.00	
397	A70	10 l bl & brn red	.25	.25
a.		Double impression of frame	60.00	
398	A71	20 l black & grn	.25	.25
399	A72	40 l green & blk	.25	.25
a.		Green impression doubled	60.00	
400	A73	50 l brown & blk	.25	.25
401	A74	80 l ind & yel brn	.25	.25

Engr.

402	A75	2d ultra	.25	.25
403	A76	5d red	.25	.25
a.		Printer's name omitted	5.50	
404	A77	6d olive brn	.25	.25
405	A78	7d dk brown	.55	.50
406	A79	10d red brown	.25	.25
407	A80	15d green	.25	.25
408	A81	25d dk blue	.25	.25
		Nos. 396-408 (13)	3.55	3.50
		Set, never hinged	4.00	

See Nos. 413, 459-466. For overprints and surcharges see Nos. 455-458, 476-477, RA75-RA78, RA83-RA85, N202-N217, N246-N247.

Cerigo, Paxos, Lefkas

Greek stamps with Italian overprints for the islands of Cerigo (Kithyra), Paxos and Lefkas (Santa Maura) are fraudulent.

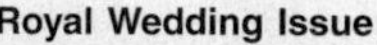

Royal Wedding Issue

Princess Frederika-Louise and Crown Prince Paul — A82

1938 Wmk. 252 *Perf. 13½x12*

409	A82	1d green	.25	.25
410	A82	3d orange brn	.30	.25
411	A82	8d dark blue	.55	.65
		Nos. 409-411 (3)	1.10	1.15
		Set, never hinged	2.75	

Arms of Greece, Romania, Yugoslavia and Turkey — A83

Perf. 12x12½

1938, Feb. 8 Litho. Unwmk.

412	A83	6d blue	5.50	1.75
		Never hinged	14.00	

Balkan Entente.

Tiryns Lady Type of 1937 Corrected Inscription

1938 Wmk. 252 *Perf. 12x13½*

413	A70	10 l blue & brn red	.50	*.70*
		Never hinged	.85	

The first four letters of the third word of the inscription read "TIPY" instead of "TYPI."

Statue of King Constantine — A84

Perf. 12x13½

1938, Oct. 8 Engr. Unwmk.

414	A84	1.50d green	.45	.25
415	A84	30d orange brn	2.25	*3.25*
		Set, never hinged	5.50	

For overprint see No. N218.

Coats of Arms of Ionian Islands — A85

Fort at Corfu — A86

King George I of Greece and Queen Victoria of England A87

Perf. 12½x12, 13½x12

1939, May 21 Engr. Unwmk.

416	A85	1d dk blue	.85	.25
417	A86	4d green	2.90	1.00
418	A87	20d yellow org	17.00	17.00
419	A87	20d dull blue	17.00	17.00
420	A87	20d car lake	17.00	17.00
		Nos. 416-420 (5)	54.75	52.25
		Set, never hinged	125.00	

75th anniv. of the union of the Ionian Islands with Greece.

Runner with Shield — A88

10th Pan-Balkan Games: 3d, Javelin thrower. 6d, Discus thrower. 8d, Jumper.

Perf. 12x13½

1939, Oct. 1 Litho. Unwmk.

421	A88	50 l slate grn & grn	.25	.25
422	A88	3d hen brn & dl rose	1.25	.55
423	A88	6d cop brn & dl org	3.00	2.25
424	A88	8d ultra & gray	3.00	2.50
		Nos. 421-424 (4)	7.50	5.55
		Set, never hinged	18.00	

Arms of Greece, Romania, Turkey and Yugoslavia — A92

Perf. 13x12½

1940, May 27 Wmk. 252

425	A92	6d blue	10.00	2.25
426	A92	8d blue gray	7.00	2.25
		Set, never hinged	45.00	

Balkan Entente.

Emblem of Youth Organization A93

Boy Member — A94

Designs: 3d, 100d, Emblem of Greek Youth Organization. 10d, Girl member. 15d, Javelin Thrower. 20d, Column of members. 25d, Flag bearers and buglers. 30d, Three youths. 50d, Line formation. 75d, Coat of arms.

Perf. 12½, 13½x12½

1940, Aug. 3 Litho. Wmk. 252

427	A93	3d sil, dp ultra & red	.85	*1.25*
428	A94	5d dk bl & blk	6.50	*7.50*
429	A94	10d red org & blk	7.50	*10.00*
430	A94	15d dk grn & blk	30.00	*32.50*
401	A94	20d lake & blk	25.00	25.00
432	A94	25d dk bl & blk	25.00	25.00
433	A94	30d rose vio & blk	25.00	25.00
434	A94	50d lake & blk	30.00	30.00
435	A94	75d dk bl, brn & gold	30.00	32.50
436	A93	100d sil, dp ultra & red	50.00	*37.50*
		Nos. 427-436,C38-C47 (20)	555.70	529.00
		Set, never hinged	1,000.	

4th anniv. of the founding of the Greek Youth Organization. The stamps were good for postal duty Aug. 3-5, 1940, only. They remained on sale until Feb. 3, 1941.

For overprints see Nos. N219-N238.

Windmills on Mykonos A103

Bourtzi Fort — A104

Aspropotamos River — A105

Candia Harbor, Crete — A106

Houses at Hydra — A107

Meteora Monasteries A108

Edessa A109

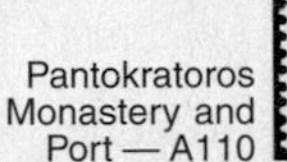

Pantokratoros Monastery and Port — A110

Bridge at Konitsa A111

Ekatontapiliani Church, Paros — A112

Ponticonissi, Corfu (Mouse Island) A113

Perf. 12½, 13½x12½

1942-44 Litho. Wmk. 252

437 A103 2d red brown .25 .25
438 A104 5d lt bl grn .25 .25
a. "ΝΑΥΟΔΙΟΝ" instead of "ΝΑΥΠΛΙΟΝ" 8.25 8.25
439 A105 10d lt blue .25 .25
440 A106 15d red vio .25 .25
441 A107 25d org red .25 .25
442 A108 50d sapphire .25 .25
443 A109 75d dp rose .25 .25
444 A110 100d black .25 .25
445 A110 200d ultra .25 .25
a. Imprint omitted 4.00 4.00
446 A111 500d dk olive .25 .25
447 A112 1000d org brn .25 .25
448 A113 2000d dp blue .25 .25
449 A111 5000d rose red .25 .25
450 A112 15,000d rose lil .25 .25
451 A113 25,000d green .25 .25
452 A105 500,000d blue .25 .25
453 A103 2,000,000d turq grn .25 .25
454 A104 5,000,000d rose brn .25 .30
Nos. 437-454 (18) 4.50 4.55
Set, never hinged 4.50

Double impressions exist of 10d, 25d, 50d, 100d, 200d, 1,000d and 2,000d. Value, each $30.

Issued: Nos. 439-442, 9/1; 200d, 12/1; Nos. 446-448, 3/15/44; Nos. 449-451, 7/1/44; Nos. 452-454, 9/15/44.

For surcharges and overprint see Nos. 472C, 473B-475, 478-481, 501-505, B1-B5, B11-B15, RA72-RA74, N239-N240, N243-N245, N248.

Imperf., Pairs

439a A105 10d 57.50
440a A106 15d 57.50
441a A107 25d 45.00
442a A108 50d 45.00
446a A111 500d 45.00
447a A112 1000d 45.00
448a A113 2000d 45.00
449a A111 5000d 45.00
450a A112 15,000d 45.00
451a A113 25,000d 45.00
452a A105 500,000d 45.00
454a A104 5,000,000d 45.00

Nos. 400, 402-404 Surcharged in Blue Black

1944-45 *Perf. 13½x12*

455 A73 50 l brn & blk .25 .25
a. Double surcharge 40.00 40.00
b. Pair, one without surcharge 65.00
456 A75 2d ultra .25 .25
a. Double surcharge 40.00
b. Pair, one without surcharge 65.00
457 A76 5d red .25 .25
a. Inverted surcharge 47.50
b. Double surcharge 47.50
c. Printer's name omitted (403a) 12.00 12.00
d. Pair, one without surcharge 20.00
458 A77 6d olive brn ('45) .25 .25
a. Double surcharge 55.00
Nos. 455-458 (4) 1.00
Set, never hinged .90

Glory Type of 1937

Perf. 12½x13½

1945 Litho. Wmk. 252

459 A81 1d dull rose vio .40 .25
460 A81 3d rose brown .40 .25
461 A81 5d ultra .40 .25
462 A81 10d dull brown .40 .25
463 A81 20d dull violet .40 .25
464 A81 50d olive black .40 .25
465 A81 100d pale blue 6.00 6.00
466 A81 200d slate 5.25 4.75
Nos. 459-466 (8) 13.65 12.25
Set, never hinged 27.50

Imperf., Pairs

459a A81 1d 145.00
460a A81 3d 145.00
461a A81 5d 145.00
462a A81 10d 145.00
463a A81 20d 145.00
464a A81 50d 145.00
465a A81 100d 160.00
466a A81 200d 175.00

Doric Column and Greek Flag — A114

1945, Oct. 28 Unwmk.

467 A114 20d orange brown .25 .25
a. Imperf., pair 50.00
468 A114 40d blue .25 .25
a. Double impression 00.00
b. Imperf., pair 50.00
Set, never hinged .75

Vote of Oct. 28, 1940, refusing Italy's ultimatum. "OXI" means "No."
Exist imperf.

Franklin D. Roosevelt — A115

1945, Dec. 21 Unwmk.

469 A115 30d blk & red brn .30 .25
a. Center double 27.00
c. Inverted frame 72.50
d. Imperf., pair 45.00
470 A115 60d blk & sl gray .30 .25
a. Center double 27.50
b. 60d black & blue gray 11.00 11.00
c. Imperf., pair 27.50
d. Inverted frame 65.00
471 A115 200d blk & vio brn .30 .25
a. Center double 27.50 77.50
b. Imperf., pair 45.00
Nos. 469-471 (3) .90 .75
Set, never hinged 1.50

Death of Pres. Franklin D. Roosevelt.

Catalogue values for unused stamps in this section, from this point to the end of the section, are for Never Hinged items.

Nos. C61, C63, 447-451, 453, 398, 401, 454 and 452 Surcharged in Black or Carmine

Perf. 12½, 12x13½, 13½x12½

1946 Wmk. 252

472 AP35 10d on 10d .40 .25
a. Inverted surcharge 100.00 —
b. Double surcharge 22.50
472C A113 10d on 2000d (C) .40 .25
473 AP35 20d on 50d (C) .40 .25
a. Inverted surcharge 125.00 —
c. Imperf., pair —
473B A112 20d on 1000d .40 .25
a. Double surcharge 125.00
474 A113 50d on 25,000d (C) .55 .25
a. Double surcharge 120.00
475 A103 100d on 2,000,000d (C) .95 .30
476 A71 130d on 20 l (C) 1.00 .25
b. Double surcharge 27.50
476A A71 250d on 20 l (C) 1.25 .25
c. Double surcharge 92.50
477 A74 300d on 80 l 1.00 .25
a. Purple brown surcharge 17.00 17.00
b. Double surcharge 90.00
c. Pair, #477 and #477a 45.00
478 A104 500d on 5,000,000d 4.00 .80
a. Inverted surcharge 85.00
b. Double surcharge 85.00
479 A105 1000d on 500,000d (C) 14.00 2.25
a. Double surcharge 45.00
480 A111 2000d on 5000d 52.50 4.50
a. Double surcharge 250.00
481 A112 5000d on 15,000d 160.00 35.00
a. Blue surcharge 160.00 140.00
Nos. 472-481 (13) 236.85 44.85

The surcharge exists in various shades on most denominations. A 150d on 20 l exists but was not officially issued. Value, unused $300. Examples are known used in Macedonia and Thrace; these are very scarce.

Eleutherios K. Venizelos — A116

Perf. 12x13½

1946, Mar. 25 Litho. Wmk. 252

482 A116 130d brn ol & buff .40 .25
a. Double impression of brn olive 7.25
b. Imperf., pair 45.00
483 A116 300d red brn & pale brn .40 .25
a. Double impression of red brown 14.00
b. Imperf., pair 45.00

Venizelos (1864-1936), statesman.

Nos. 391 to 394 Surcharged in Blue Black

1946, Sept. 28 *Perf. 12½x12*

484 A67 50d on 1d .70 .25
a. Double surcharge 100.00
485 A67 250d on 3d 1.60 .25
a. Date omitted 32.50
b. Inverted surcharge 32.50 —
c. Double surcharge 75.00
486 A67 600d on 8d 11.00 1.25
a. Additional surcharge on back, inverted 72.50
b. Carmine surcharge 150.00
487 A67 3000d on 100d 27.50 2.00
Nos. 484-487 (4) 40.80 3.75

Plebiscite of Sept. 1, 1946, which resulted in the return of King George II to Greece.

Panaghiotis Tsaldaris — A117

Perf. 12½x13½

1946, Nov. 15 Litho. Unwmk.

488 A117 250d red brn & buff 4.00 1.25
a. Imperf., pair 55.00
489 A117 600d dp bl & pale bl 4.00 1.25
a. Double impression 22.50
b. Imperf., pair 55.00

Naval Convoy A118

Torpedoing of Cruiser Helle — A119

Women Carrying Ammunition in Pindus Mountains A120

Troops in Albania A121

Campaign of Greek Troops in Italy — A122

Allegory of Flight — A123

Greek Torpedo Boat Towing Captive Submarine A124

Design: 5000d, Memorial Tomb, El Alamein.

1946-47 Unwmk. Engr. *Perf. 13*

490 A118 50d dk bl grn .25 .25
491 A119 100d dp ultra .65 .25
492 A120 250d yel grn ('46) .65 .25
493 A121 500d yel brn 1.05 .25
494 A122 600d dk brown 1.40 .85
495 A123 1000d dull lil 7.25 .40
496 A124 2000d dp ultra 30.00 2.50
497 A119 5000d dk car 40.00 2.50
a. Imperf., pair 1,500.
Nos. 490-497 (8) 81.25 7.25

1947 stamps issued May 1.

King George II Memorial Issue

Nos. 391-393 Surcharged in Black

Perf. 12½x12

1947, Apr. 15 Wmk. 252

498 A67 50d on 1d grn .60 .25
a. Double surcharge 72.50
499 A67 250d on 3d red brn 1.25 .25
a. Double surcharge 72.50
b. Pair, one without surcharge 72.50
500 A67 600d on 8d dp bl 10.00 .55
a. Double surcharge 72.50
Nos. 498-500 (3) 11.85 1.05

Nos. 446, 438, 442, 439 and 443 Surcharged in Carmine or Black

1947 *Perf. 12½*

501 A111 20d on 500d .30 .25
a. Double surcharge 27.50

No.	Type	Value	Description	Unused	Used
502	A104	30d	on 5d	.95	.40
a.			"ΝΑΥΟΛΙΟΝ" instead of "ΝΑΥΠΛΙΟΝ"	35.00	45.00
503	A108	50d	on 50d	.45	.25
504	A105	100d	on 10d	1.60	.25
a.			Double surcharge	150.00	
505	A109	450d	on 75d (Bk)	2.50	.25
			Nos. 501-505 (5)	5.80	1.40

Castellorizo Castle A126

Dodecanese Vase A127

Dodecanese Costume A128

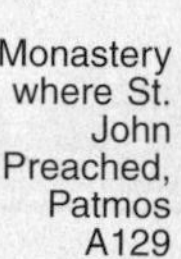

Monastery where St. John Preached, Patmos A129

Emanuel Xanthos — A130

Sailing Vessel of 1824 — A131

Revolutionary Stamp of 1912 — A132

Statue of Hippocrates A133

Colossus of Rhodes A134

Perf. 12½x13½, 13½x12½

1947-48 Litho. Wmk. 252

No.	Type	Value	Description	Unused	Used
506	A126	20d	ultra	.30	.25
507	A127	30d	blk brn & buff	.30	.25
508	A128	50d	chlky bl	.50	.25
509	A129	100d	blk grn & pale grn	.50	.25
510	A130	250d	gray grn & pale grn	1.00	.25
511	A132	450d	dp bl ('48)	2.25	.25
512	A131	450d	dp bl & pale bl ('48)	1.75	.25
513	A132	500d	red	1.40	.25
514	A133	600d	vio brn & pale pink	1.40	.25
515	A134	1000d	brn & cream	2.00	.25
			Nos. 506-515 (10)	11.40	2.50

Return of the Dodecanese to Greece. See Nos. 520-522, 525-534.

Imperf., Pairs

No.	Type	Value	Price
506a	A126	20d	250.00
507a	A127	30d	250.00
508a	A128	50d	250.00
509a	A129	100d	260.00
510a	A130	250d	260.00
512a	A131	450d	275.00
514a	A133	600d	300.00
515a	A134	1000d	250.00

Battle of Crete — A135

1948, Sept. 15 Engr. ***Perf. 13x13½***

No.	Type	Value	Description	Unused	Used
516	A135	1000d	dark green	6.50	.50

Battle of Crete, 7th anniversary.

Abduction of Children A136

Concentration Camp — A137

Protective Mother — A138

Perf. 13½x12½, 12½x13½

1949, Feb. 1 Litho. Wmk. 252

No.	Type	Value	Description	Unused	Used
517	A136	450d	dk & lt violet	3.75	.65
a.			Imperf., pair	360.00	
518	A137	1000d	dk & lt brown	13.50	4.00
519	A138	1800d	dk red & cream	17.50	.40
			Nos. 517-519 (3)	34.75	5.05

A variety of No. 519 exists in green and cream.

Types of 1947

1950, Apr. 5 ***Perf. 12½x13½***

No.	Type	Value	Description	Unused	Used
520	A127	2000d	org brn & sal	50.00	.55
a.			Imperf., pair	140.00	
521	A133	5000d	rose vio	55.00	.55
522	A134	10,000d	ultra	95.00	1.25
			Nos. 520-522 (3)	200.00	2.35

Map of Crete and Flags A139

Perf. 13½x13

1950, Apr. 28 Engr. Wmk. 252

No.	Type	Value	Description	Unused	Used
523	A139	1000d	deep blue	17.50	.40
a.			Imperf., pair	*1,500.*	

Battle of Crete, 9th anniversary.

Youth of Marathon — A140

Engraved and Lithographed

1950, May 21 ***Perf. 13x13½***

No.	Type	Value	Description	Unused	Used
524	A140	1000d	cream & dp grn	2.00	.60
a.			Without dates	450.00	
b.			"1949" only	450.00	
c.			Dates inverted	450.00	
d.			Dates doubled	450.00	

75th anniv. (in 1949) of the UPU.
No. 524 exists imperforate in used condition.

Types of 1947-48

Perf. 12½x13½, 13½x12½

1950 Litho. Wmk. 252

No.	Type	Value	Description	Unused	Used
525	A130	200d	orange	.70	.25
526	A128	300d	orange	.95	.25
a.			Imperf., pair	275.00	
527	A129	400d	blue	1.75	.25
528	A133	700d	lilac rose	2.25	.25
529	A133	700d	blue green	27.50	.25
a.			Imperf., pair	290.00	
530	A131	800d	pur & pale grn	2.75	.25
a.			Imperf., pair	275.00	
531	A132	1300d	carmine	12.00	.25
532	A126	1500d	brn org	82.50	1.10
533	A127	1600d	ultra & bl gray	8.50	.25
534	A134	2600d	emer & pale grn	11.50	.85
			Nos. 525-534 (10)	150.40	3.95

Altar and Sword A141

St. Paul — A142

St. Paul by El Greco — A143

Preaching to Athenians — A144

Perf. 13½x12, 12x13½

1951, June 15 Engr. Unwmk.

No.	Type	Value	Description	Unused	Used
535	A141	700d	red vio	3.50	1.00
536	A142	1600d	lt blue	14.50	8.75
537	A143	2600d	dk ol bis	25.00	9.00
538	A144	10,000d	red brn	175.00	80.00
			Nos. 535-538 (4)	218.00	98.75

1900th anniv. of St. Paul's visit to Athens.

Industrialization A145

Designs: 800d, Fishing. 1300d, Rebuilding. 1600d, Farming. 2600d, Home Industries. 5000d, Electrification and map of Greece.

Perf. 12½x13½

1951, Sept. 20 Wmk. 252

No.	Type	Value	Description	Unused	Used
539	A145	700d	red org	5.00	.30
540	A145	800d	aqua	7.25	.30
541	A145	1300d	grnsh bl	10.00	.30
542	A145	1600d	olive grn	30.00	.50
543	A145	2600d	vio gray	75.00	2.25
544	A145	5000d	dp plum	100.00	.50
			Nos. 539-544 (6)	227.25	4.15

Issued to publicize Greek recovery under the Marshall Plan.

King Paul I — A146

Allegorical Figure and Medal — A147

1952, Dec. 14 Engr. ***Perf. 12½x12***

No.	Type	Value	Description	Unused	Used
545	A146	200d	deep green	2.00	.25
546	A146	1000d	red	6.00	.35
547	A147	1400d	blue	20.00	2.25
548	A146	10,000d	dk red lil	60.00	14.00
			Nos. 545-548 (4)	88.00	16.85

50th birthday of King Paul I.

Oranges A148

Tobacco — A149

National Products: 1000d, Olive oil, Pallas Athene. 1300d, Wine. 2000d, Figs. 2600d, Grapes and bread. 5000d, Bacchus holding grapes.

1953, July 1 ***Perf. 13½x13, 13x13½***

No.	Type	Value	Description	Unused	Used
549	A148	500d	dp car & org	1.90	.25
550	A149	700d	dk brn & org yel	1.90	.25
a.			Imperf., pair	600.00	
551	A148	1000d	bl & lt ol grn	4.00	.25
a.			Imperf., pair	450.00	
552	A149	1300d	dp plum & org brn	5.50	.25
553	A149	2000d	dk brn & lt grn	13.50	.40
a.			Imperf., pair	600.00	
554	A149	2600d	vio & ol bis	37.50	1.75
555	A149	5000d	dk brn & yel grn	37.50	.90
			Nos. 549-555 (7)	101.80	4.05

Pericles A150

Homer A151

Hunting Wild Boar — A152

Shepherd Carrying Calf — A152a

Designs: 200d, Mycenaean oxhead vase. 500d, Zeus of Istiaea. 600d, Head of a youth. 1000d, Alexander the Great. 1200d, Charioteer of Delphi. 2000d, Vase of Dipylon. 4000d, Voyage of Dionysus. 20,000d, Pitcher bearers.

Perf. 13½x13, 12½x12, 13x13½

1954, Jan. 15 Litho.

No.	Type	Value	Description	Unused	Used
556	A150	100d	red brn	.50	.25
557	A150	200d	black	.50	.25
558	A151	300d	blue vio	1.25	.25
559	A151	500d	green	2.00	.25
560	A151	600d	rose pink	2.00	.25
561	A151	1000d	dl bl & blk	2.50	.25
562	A150	1200d	ol grn	2.50	.25

563	A150	2000d red brn	11.00	.25
564	A152	2400d grnsh bl	11.00	.40
a.		Double impression	150.00	
565	A152a	2500d dk bl grn	11.00	.25
566	A151	4000d dk car	27.50	.40
567	A150	20,000d rose lilac	225.00	1.25
		Nos. 556-567 (12)	296.75	4.30

See Nos. 574-581, 632-638, and 689.

British Parliamentary Debate and Ink Blot — A153

1954, Sept. *Perf. 12½*

Center in Black

568	A153	1.20d cream	4.00	.45
569	A153	2d orange	20.00	3.75
570	A153	2d lt bl	20.00	9.25
571	A153	2.40d lilac	20.00	2.50
572	A153	2.50d pink	20.00	2.50
573	A153	4d citron	60.00	3.75
		Nos. 568-573 (6)	144.00	22.20

Document in English on Nos. 569, 572, 573; in French on Nos. 570, 571 and in Greek on No. 568.

Issued to promote the proposed union between Cyprus and Greece.

Types of 1954

Designs: 20 l, Mycenaean oxhead vase. 30 l, Pericles. 50 l, Zeus of Istiaea. 1d, Head of a youth. 2d, Alexander the Great. 3d, Hunting wild boar. 3.50d, Homer. 4d, Voyage of Dionysus.

Perf. 13½x13, 12½x12, 13x13½

1955 **Litho.** **Wmk. 252**

574	A150	20 l dk green	.40	.25
575	A150	30 l yellow brn	.60	.25
576	A151	50 l car lake	.90	.25
577	A151	1d blue grn	2.25	.25
578	A151	2d brown & blk	7.25	.25
579	A152	3d red org	11.00	.25
580	A151	3.50d rose crim	11.00	.70
581	A151	4d violet bl	82.50	.45
		Nos. 574-581 (8)	115.90	2.65

Samos Coin Picturing Pythagoras A154

Pythagorean Theorem A155

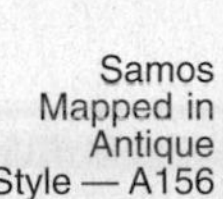

Samos Mapped in Antique Style — A156

1955, Aug. 20 *Perf. 12x13½*

582	A154	2d green	3.75	.40
583	A155	3.50d intense blk	13.50	3.00
584	A154	5d plum	45.00	2.00
585	A156	6d blue	57.50	32.50
		Nos. 582-585 (4)	119.75	37.90

2500th anniv. of the founding of the 1st School of Philosophy by Pythagoras on Samos.

Globe and Rotary Emblem — A157

Perf. 12x13½

1956, May 15 **Litho.** **Wmk. 252**

586	A157	2d ultra	17.50	.40

50th anniv. of Rotary Intl. (in 1955).

King Alexander A158

Crown Prince Constantine — A159

Portraits: 30 l, George I. 50 l, Queen Olga. 70 l, King Otto. 1d, Queen Amalia. 1.50d, King Constantine. 2d, 7.50d, King Paul. 3d, George II. 3.50d, Queen Sophia. 4d, Queen Frederica. 5d, King Paul and Queen Frederica. 10d, King, Queen and Crown Prince.

Perf. 13½x12, 12x13½

1956, May 21 **Engr.**

587	A158	10 l blue vio	.25	.25
588	A159	20 l dull pur	.25	.25
589	A159	30 l sepia	.25	.25
590	A159	50 l red brn	.30	.25
591	A159	70 l lt ultra	.50	.25
592	A159	1d grnsh bl	.50	.25
593	A159	1.50d gray bl	3.50	.25
594	A159	2d black	4.75	.25
595	A159	3d brown	3.50	.25
596	A159	3.50d copper brn	11.50	.25
597	A159	4d gray green	11.50	.25
598	A158	5d rose car	11.50	.25
599	A159	7.50d ultra	11.50	2.00
600	A158	10d dk blue	60.00	1.10
		Nos. 587-600 (14)	119.80	6.10

See Nos. 604-617.

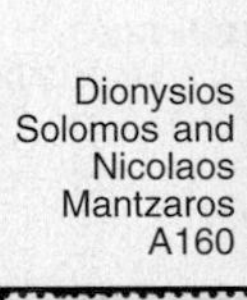

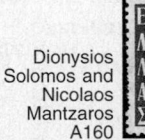

Dionysios Solomos and Nicolaos Mantzaros A160

Dionysios Solomos — A161

5d, View on Zante and bust of Solomos.

Perf. 13½x12, 12x13½

1957, Mar. 26 **Litho.** **Wmk. 252**

601	A160	2d red brn & ocher	4.25	.50
602	A161	3.50d bl & gray	6.75	3.25
603	A160	5d dk grn & ol bis	9.00	4.75
		Nos. 601-603 (3)	20.00	8.50

Centenary of the death of Dionysios Solomos (1798-1857), nationalist poet best known for the poem *Hymn to Liberty*, the first two stanzas of which were adopted as the lyrics of the Greek national anthem.

Types of 1956

Designs as before.

Perf. 13½x12

1957 **Wmk. 252** **Engr.**

604	A158	10 l rose lake	.50	.25
605	A159	20 l orange	.50	.25
606	A159	30 l gray blk	.50	.25
607	A159	50 l grnsh blk	.50	.25
608	A159	70 l rose lil	1.50	.65
609	A159	1d rose red	1.00	.25
610	A159	1.50d lt ol grn	1.75	.25
611	A159	2d carmine	3.25	.25
612	A159	3d dk blue	4.00	.25
613	A159	3.50d blk vio	10.00	.25
a.		Imperf., pair		
614	A159	4d red brn	10.00	.25
615	A158	5d gray blue	10.00	.25
616	A159	7.50d yel org	3.00	1.25
617	A158	10d green	75.00	.80
		Nos. 604-617 (14)	121.50	5.45

Oil Tanker A162

Ships: 1d, Ocean liner. 1.50d, Sailing ship, 1820. 2d, Byzantine vessel. 3.50d, Ship from 6th century B. C. 5d, "Argo."

1958, Jan. 30 **Litho.** *Perf. 13½x12*

618	A162	50 l multi	.50	.25
619	A162	1d ultra, blk & bis	.50	.25
620	A162	1.50d blk & car	1.50	.95
a.		Double impression of blk	160.00	
621	A162	2d vio bl, blk & red brn	.50	.30
622	A162	3.50d lt bl, blk & red	2.00	1.25
a.		Double impression of blk	160.00	125.00
623	A162	5d bl grn, blk & car	13.50	10.00
		Nos. 618-623 (6)	18.50	13.00

Issued to honor the Greek merchant marine.

Narcissus — A163

Designs: 30 l, Daphne (laurel) and Apollo. 50 l, Adonis (hibiscus) and Aphrodite. 70 l, Pitys (pine) and Pan. 1d, Crocus. 2d, Iris. 3.50d, Tulips. 5d, Cyclamen.

1958, Sept. 15 **Wmk. 252** *Perf. 13*

Size: 22½x38mm

624	A163	20 l multi	.25	.25
625	A163	30 l multi	.25	.25
626	A163	50 l multi	.25	.25
627	A163	70 l multi	.25	.25

Perf. 12½x12

Size: 21½x26mm

628	A163	1d multi	.45	.40

Perf. 12x13½

Size: 22x32mm

629	A163	2d multi	.25	.25
630	A163	3.50d multi	1.75	1.75
a.		Imperf., pair	325.00	
631	A163	5d multi	5.00	5.00
		Nos. 624-631 (8)	8.45	8.40

International Congress for the Protection of Nature, held in Athens.

Types of 1954

Designs: 10 l, Pericles. 20 l, Mycenaean oxhead vase. 50 l, Zeus of Istiaea. 70 l, Charioteer of Delphi. 1d, Head of a youth. 1.50d, Pitcher bearers. 2.50d, Alexander the Great.

Two types of 2.50d:

I — 9 dots in upper half of right border.

II — 10 dots.

Perf. 13½x13, 12½x12

1959 **Litho.** **Wmk. 252**

632	A150	10 l emerald	.50	.25
633	A150	20 l magenta	.80	.25
634	A151	50 l lt bl grn	1.75	.25
a.		Imperf., pair	1,500.	
635	A150	70 l red org	.50	.25
636	A151	1d reddish brn	4.60	.25
637	A150	1.50d brt bl	25.00	.25
638	A151	2.50d mag & blk (II)	17.50	.30
a.		Type I	60.00	.55
		Nos. 632-638 (7)	50.55	1.80

Zeus-Eagle Coin — A164

Helios-Rose Coin — A165

Ancient Greek Coins: 20 l, Athena & Owl. 50 l, Nymph Arethusa & Chariot. 70 l, Hercules & Zeus. 1.50d, Griffin & Square. 2.50d, Apollo & Lyre. 4.50d, Apollo & Labyrinth. 6d, Aphrodite & Apollo. 8.50d, Ram's Head & Incuse Squares.

1959, Mar. 24 **Wmk. 252** *Perf. 14*

Coins in Various Shades of Gray

639	A164	10 l red brn & blk	.45	.25
640	A164	20 l dp bl & blk	.45	.25
641	A164	50 l plum & blk	.60	.25
642	A164	70 l ultra & blk	1.10	.30
643	A165	1d dk car rose & blk	1.50	.25
644	A164	1.50d ocher & blk	1.75	.25
645	A164	2.50d dp mag & blk	2.50	.25
646	A165	4.50d Prus grn & blk	5.50	.40
647	A165	6d ol grn & blk	25.00	.25
648	A165	8.50d dp car & blk	10.00	1.75
		Nos. 639-648 (10)	48.85	4.20

See Nos. 750-758.

Audience, Vase 580 B. C. — A166

Theater, Delphi A167

Designs: 50 l, Clay tragedy mask, 3rd cent. B.C. 1d, Flute, drum and lyre. 2.50d, Clay statue of an actor, 3rd cent. B.C. 4.50d, Andromeda, vase, 4th cent. B.C. 6d, Actors, bowl 410 B.C.

Perf. 13x13½, 13½x13

1959, June 20 **Litho.** **Wmk. 252**

649	A166	20 l blk, fawn & gray	.30	.25
650	A166	50 l dk red brn & ol bis	.30	.25
651	A166	1d grn, brn & ocher	.30	.25
652	A166	2.50d brn & bl	.80	.65
653	A167	3.50d red brn, grn & sep	15.00	10.50
654	A167	4.50d blk & fawn	1.50	1.25
655	A166	6d blk, fawn & gray	1.75	1.50
		Nos. 649-655 (7)	19.95	14.65

Ancient Greek theater.

"Victory" and Soldiers — A168

Perf. 13x13½

1959, Aug. 29 **Wmk. 252**

656	A168	2.50d red brn, ultra & blk	5.00	.50

10th anniversary of civil war.

St. Basil — A169

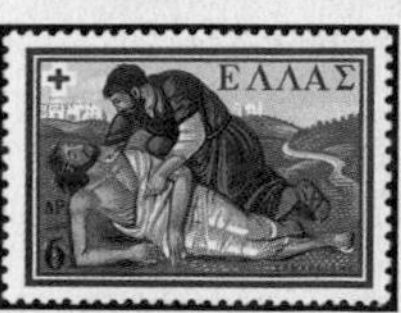

The Good Samaritan A170

Designs: 20 l, Plane tree of Hippocrates. 50 l, Aesculapius. 2.50d, Achilles and Patroclus. 3d, Globe and Red Cross over people receiving help. 4.50d, Henri Dunant.

Perf. 13½x12, 12x13½

1959, Sept. 21 **Litho.**

657 A170 20 l multi .25 .25
658 A169 50 l multi .25 .25
659 A169 70 l multi .25 .25
660 A169 2.50d multi .60 .50
661 A169 3d multi 10.00 10.00
662 A169 4.50d multi 1.60 1.60
663 A170 6d multi 1.50 1.50
Nos. 657-663 (7) 14.45 14.35

Cent. of the Red Cross idea. Sizes: Nos. 658-660, 662 24½x32mm, No. 661 32x47mm.

Imre Nagy — A171

Perf. 13x13½

1959, Dec. 8 **Wmk. 252**

664 A171 4.50d org brn & dk brn 1.75 1.75
665 A171 6d brt bl, bl & blk 1.75 1.75

3rd anniv. of the crushing of the 1956 Hungarian Revolution, and to honor Premier Imre Nagy, its leader.

Costis Palamas — A172

1960, Jan. 25 ***Perf. 12x13½***

666 A172 2.50d multi 7.00 .75

Centenary of the birth of Costis Palamas (1859-1943), poet.

Ship Battling Storm A173

4.50d, Ship in calm sea and rainbow.

Perf. 13½x13

1960, Apr. 7 **Wmk. 252**

667 A173 2.50d multi .50 .40
668 A173 4.50d multi 2.00 1.40

Issued to publicize World Refugee Year, July 1, 1959-June 30, 1960.

Boy Scout on Horseback, St. George and Dragon — A174

Scouts Planting Tree A175

30 l, Scout taking oath & boy of ancient Athens. 40 l, Scouts helping in disaster. 70 l, Scouts reading map & tent. 1d, Boy Scout, Sea Scout & Air Scout. 2.50d, Crown Prince Constantine. 6d, Scout flag of Greece & Military Merit medal.

Perf. 13x13½, 13½x13

1960, Apr. 23 **Litho.**

669 A174 20 l multi .25 .25
670 A174 30 l multi .25 .25
671 A174 40 l multi .25 .25
672 A175 50 l multi .25 .25
673 A175 70 l multi .25 .25
674 A175 1d multi .80 .40
675 A174 2.50d multi 2.00 1.25
676 A175 6d multi 2.50 1.50
Nos. 669-676 (8) 6.55 4.40

Greek Boy Scout Organization, 50th anniv.

Greek Holding Sacred Disk Proclaiming Armistice During Games — A176

Lighting Olympic Flame A177

Designs: 70 l, Youth taking oath. 80 l, Boy cutting olive branches for Olympic prizes. 1d, Judges entering stadium. 1.50d, Long jump. 2.50d, Discus thrower. 4.50d, Sprinters. 5d, Javelin thrower. 6d, Crowning the victors. 12.50d, Victor in chariot entering home town.

Perf. 13x13½, 13½x13

1960, Aug. 12 **Wmk. 252**

677 A176 20 l multi .25 .25
678 A177 50 l multi .25 .25
679 A176 70 l multi .25 .25
680 A177 80 l multi .25 .25
a. Imperf., pair 585.00
681 A177 1d multi .40 .30
682 A177 1.50d multi .40 .30
683 A176 2.50d multi .80 .50
684 A177 4.50d multi .95 .70
a. Dbl. impression of black 365.00 *450.00*
685 A176 5d multi 2.75 1.60
686 A177 6d multi 2.75 1.60
687 A177 12.50d multi 15.00 10.00
Nos. 677-687 (11) 24.05 16.00

17th Olympic Games, Rome, 8/25-9/11.

Common Design Types pictured following the introduction.

Europa Issue, 1960

Common Design Type

Perf. 13½x12

1960, Sept. 19 **Litho.** **Wmk. 252**

Size: 33x23mm

688 CD3 4.50d ultra *5.00* *2.00*
a. Double impression *325.00*

Shepherd Type of 1954

1960, Sept. 1 **Wmk. 252** ***Perf. 13***

689 A152a 3d ultra 2.25 .40
a. Imperf., pair 1,100.

Crown Prince Constantine and Yacht — A178

1961, Jan. 18 ***Perf. 13½x13***

690 A178 2.50d multi 1.00 .25

Victory of Crown Prince Constantine and his crew at the 17th Olympic Games, Rome (Gold medal, Yachting, Dragon class).

Castoria A179

Delphi — A180

Landscapes and Ancient Monuments: 20 l, Meteora. 50 l, Hydra harbor. 70 l, Acropolis, Athens. 80 l, Mykonos. 1d, St. Catherine's Church, Salonika. 1.50d, Olympia. 2.50d, Knossos. 3.50d, Rhodes. 4d, Epidauros amphitheater. 4.50d, Temple of Poseidon, Sounion. 5d, Temple of Zeus, Athens. 7.50d, Aslan's mosque, Ioannina. 8d, Mount Athos. 8.50d, Santorini. 12.50d, Marble lions, Delos.

Perf. 13½x12½, 12½x13½

1961, Feb. 15 **Engr.** **Wmk. 252**

691 A179 10 l dk gray bl .25 .25
692 A179 20 l dk purple .25 .25
693 A179 50 l blue .25 .25
694 A179 70 l dk purple .25 .25
695 A179 80 l brt ultra .40 .25
696 A179 1d red brn .70 .25
697 A179 1.50d brt grn 1.00 .25
698 A179 2.50d carmine 3.50 .25
699 A179 3.50d purple 1.40 .25
700 A179 4d sl grn 11.00 .25
701 A179 4.50d dk blue 1.25 .25
702 A179 5d claret 11.00 .25
703 A180 6d slate grn 2.50 .25
704 A179 7.50d black .70 .25
705 A180 8d dk vio bl 4.50 .25
706 A180 8.50d org ver 7.00 .65
707 A179 12.50d dk brn 2.75 1.50
Nos. 691-707 (17) 48.70 5.90

Issued for tourist publicity.

Lily Vase — A181

Partridge and Fig Pecker A182

Minoan Art: 1d, Fruit dish. 1.50d, Rhyton bearer. 2.50d, Ladies of Knossos Palace. 4.50d, Sarcophagus of Hagia Trias. 6d, Dancer. 10d, Two vessels with spouts.

Perf. 13x13½, 13½x13

1961, June 30 **Litho.**

708 A181 20 l multi .50 .25
709 A182 50 l multi .50 .25
710 A182 1d multi .50 .25
711 A181 1.50d multi 1.00 .25
712 A182 2.50d multi 7.00 .25
713 A181 4.50d multi 3.00 2.00
714 A182 6d multi 13.50 1.60
715 A182 10d multi 15.00 8.00
Nos. 708-715 (8) 41.00 12.85

Democritus Nuclear Research Center — A183

Democritus — A184

1961, July 31 ***Perf. 13½x13***

716 A183 2.50d dp lil rose & rose lil .50 .25
717 A184 4.50d vio bl & pale vio bl 1.00 .60

Inauguration of the Democritus Nuclear Research Center at Aghia Paraskevi.

Europa Issue, 1961

Common Design Type

1961, Sept. 18 ***Perf. 13½x12***

Size: 32½x22mm

718 CD4 2.50d ver & pink *.40* .25
a. Pink omitted (inscriptions white) *15.00* *18.00*
719 CD4 4.50d ultra & lt ultra *.40* .25

Nicephoros Phocas — A185

1961, Sept. 22 **Wmk. 252**

720 A185 2.50d multi 1.00 .60

1000th anniv. of the liberation of Crete from the Saracens by the Byzantine general (later emperor) Phocas.

Hermes Head of 1861 — A186

Each denomination shows a different stamp of 1861 issue.

1961, Dec. 20 **Litho.** ***Perf. 13x13½***

721 A186 20 l brn, red brn & cream .25 .25
722 A186 50 l brn, bis & straw .25 .25
723 A186 1.50d emer & gray .25 .25
724 A186 2.50d red org & ol bis .25 .25
725 A186 4.50d dk bl, bl & gray .45 .30
726 A186 6d rose lil, pale rose & bl .75 .50
727 A186 10d car, rose & cr 1.50 1.50
Nos. 721-727 (7) 3.70 3.30

Centenary of Greek postage stamps.

Tauropos Dam and Lake — A187

Ptolemais Power Station A188

Designs: 50 l, Ladhon river hydroelectric plant. 1.50d, Louros river dam. 2.50d, Aliverion power plant. 4.50d, Salonika hydroelectric sub-station. 6d, Agra river hydroelectric station, interior.

Perf. 13x13½, 13½x13

1962, Apr. 14 Wmk. 252

No.	Type	Value	Color	Unused	Used
728	A187	20 l	multi	.25	.25
729	A187	50 l	multi	.25	.25
730	A188	1d	multi	.25	.25
731	A188	1.50d	multi	.25	.25
732	A188	2.50d	multi	1.25	.25
733	A188	4.50d	multi	.95	.70
734	A188	6d	multi	4.00	4.00
			Nos. 728-734 (7)	7.20	5.95

National electrification project.

Youth with Shield and Helmet from Ancient Vase — A189

Designs: 2.50d, Zappion hall, horiz. 4.50d, Kneeling soldier from Temple of Aphaea, Aegina. 6d, Standing soldier from stele of Ariston.

Perf. 13¼x14, 12x13½

1962, May 3 Litho. Wmk. 252

Sizes: 22x33mm, 33x22mm

No.	Type	Value	Color	Unused	Used
735	A189	2.50d	grn, bl, red & brn	.25	.25
736	A189	3d	brn, buff & red brn	.25	.25
737	A189	4.50d	bl & gray	.40	.40

Size: 21x37mm

No.	Type	Value	Color	Unused	Used
738	A189	6d	brn red & blk	.40	.30
			Nos. 735-738 (4)	1.30	1.20

Ministerial congress of NATO countries, Athens, May 3-5.

Europa Issue, 1962

Common Design Type

1962, Sept. 17 ***Perf. 13½x12***

Size: 33x23mm

No.	Type	Value	Color	Unused	Used
739	CD5	2.50d	ver & blk	*.75*	*.40*
740	CD5	4.50d	ultra & blk	*1.50*	*.75*

Hands and Grain — A190

1962, Oct. 30 ***Perf. 13x13½***

No.	Type	Value	Color	Unused	Used
741	A190	1.50d	dp car, blk & brn	*.50*	.25
742	A190	2.50d	brt grn, blk & brn	*.75*	.25

Agricultural Insurance Program.

Demeter — A191

Design: 4.50d, Wheat and globe.

Perf. 12x13½

1963, Apr. 25 Wmk. 252

No.	Type	Value	Color	Unused	Used
743	A191	2.50d	brn car, gray & blk, gold	.40	.25
744	A191	4.50d	blue, gray, blk, tan	.85	.35

FAO "Freedom from Hunger" campaign.

George I, Constantine XII, Alexander I, George II and Paul I — A192

Perf. 13½x12½

1963, June 29 Engr.

No.	Type	Value	Color	Unused	Used
745	A192	50 l	rose car	.25	.25
746	A192	1.50d	green	.45	.25
747	A192	2.50d	redsh brn	1.00	.25
748	A192	4.50d	dk blue	1.60	1.25
749	A192	6d	violet	3.50	.60
			Nos. 745-749 (5)	6.80	2.60

Centenary of the Greek dynasty.

Coin Types of 1959

Ancient Greek Coins: 50 l, Nymph Arethusa & Chariot. 80 l, Hercules & Zeus. 1d, Helios & Rose. 1.50d, Griffin & Square. 3d, Zeus & Eagle. 3.50d, Athena & Owl. 4.50d, Apollo & Labyrinth. 6d, Aphrodite & Apollo. 8.50d, Ram's head & Incuse Squares.

Perf. 13½x13, 13x13½

1963, July 5 Litho. Wmk. 252

Coins in Various Shades of Gray

No.	Type	Value	Color	Unused	Used
750	A164	50 l	violet bl	.25	.25
751	A164	80 l	dp magenta	.25	.25
752	A165	1d	emerald	.25	.25
753	A164	1.50d	lilac rose	.85	.25
754	A164	3d	olive	.60	.25
755	A164	3.50d	vermilion	.70	.25
756	A165	4.50d	redsh brn	.85	.50
757	A165	6d	blue grn	1.10	.25
758	A165	8.50d	brt blue	2.00	.85
			Nos. 750-758 (9)	6.85	3.10

"Acropolis at Dawn" by Lord Baden-Powell — A193

Jamboree Badge (Boeotian Shield) — A194

Designs: 2.50d, Crown Prince Constantine, Chief Scout. 3d, Athanassios Lefkadites (founder of Greek Scouts) and Lord Baden-Powell. 4.50d, Scout bugling with conch shell.

1963, Aug. 1

No.	Type	Value	Color	Unused	Used
759	A193	1d	bl, sal & ol	.25	.25
760	A194	1.50d	dk bl, org brn & brn	.25	.25
761	A194	2.50d	multi	1.25	.25
762	A193	3d	multi	.50	.55
763	A194	4.50d	multi	1.25	.55
			Nos. 759-763 (5)	3.50	1.85

11th Boy Scout Jamboree, Marathon, July 29-Aug. 16, 1963.

Athenian Treasury, Delphi — A195

2d, Centenary emblem. 2.50d, Queen Olga, founder of Greek Red Cross. 4.50d, Henri Dunant.

1963, Sept. 16 ***Perf. 12x13½***

No.	Type	Value	Color	Unused	Used
764	A195	1d	multi	.50	.25
765	A195	2d	multi	.25	.25
766	A195	2.50d	multi	.30	.25
767	A195	4.50d	multi	.75	.50
			Nos. 764-767 (4)	1.80	1.25

International Red Cross Centenary.

Europa Issue, 1963

Common Design Type

1963, Sept. 16 ***Perf. 13½x12***

Size: 33x23mm

No.	Type	Value	Color	Unused	Used
768	CD6	2.50d	green	*2.25*	*.40*
769	CD6	4.50d	brt magenta	*3.00*	*1.50*

Vatopethion Monastery — A196

Designs: 80 l, St. Denys' Monastery. 1d, "Protaton" (Founder's) Church, horiz. 2d, Stavronikita Monastery. 2.50d, Jeweled cover of Nicephoros Phocas Gospel. 3.50d, Fresco of St. Athanassios, founder of community. 4.50d, Presentation of Christ, 11th century manuscript. 6d, Great Lavra Church, horiz.

Perf. 13x13½, 13½x13

1963, Dec. 5 Litho. Wmk. 252

No.	Type	Value	Color	Unused	Used
770	A196	30 l	multi	.25	.25
771	A196	80 l	multi	.25	.25
772	A196	1d	multi	.25	.25
773	A196	2d	multi	1.00	.25
774	A196	2.50d	multi	3.00	.25
775	A196	3.50d	multi	1.00	.85
776	A196	4.50d	multi	1.00	.55
777	A196	6d	multi	1.10	.55
			Nos. 770-777 (8)	7.85	3.20

Millennium of the founding of the monastic community on Mt. Athos.

King Paul I (1901-1964) — A197

1964, May 6 ***Perf. 12x13½***

No.	Type	Value	Color	Unused	Used
778	A107	30 l	brown	.25	.25
779	A197	50 l	purple	.25	.25
780	A197	1d	green	.75	.25
781	A197	1.50d	orange	.40	.25
782	A197	2d	blue	.75	.25
783	A197	2.50d	chocolate	.75	.25
784	A197	3.50d	red brn	.75	.25
785	A197	4d	ultra	2.00	.25
786	A197	4.50d	bluish blk	2.00	.80
787	A197	6d	rose pink	3.00	1.00
			Nos. 778-787 (10)	10.90	3.80

Archangel Michael — A198

Designs: 1d, Bulgaroctonus coin of Emperor Basil II. 1.50d, Two armed saints from ivory triptych by Harbaville, Louvre. 2.50d, Lady, fresco by Panselinos, Protaton Church, Mt. Athos. 4.50d, Angel, mosaic, Daphni Church, Athens.

1964, June 10 ***Perf. 12x13½***

No.	Type	Value	Color	Unused	Used
788	A198	1d	multi	.25	.25
789	A198	1.50d	multi	.25	.25
790	A198	2d	multi	.25	.25
791	A198	2.50d	multi	.25	.25
792	A198	4.50d	multi	.80	.50
			Nos. 788-792 (5)	1.80	1.50

Byzantine Art and for the Byzantine Art Exhibition, Athens, Apr.-June, 1964.

Exist imperf.

Birth of Aphrodite, Emblem of Kythera A199

Designs (emblems of islands): 20 l, Trident, Paxos. 1d, Head of Ulysses, Ithaca. 2d, St. George slaying dragon, Lefkas. 2.50d, Zakyntnos, Zante. 4.50d, Cephalus, dog and spear, Cephalonia. 6d, Trireme, Corfu.

Perf. 13½x12

1964, July 20 Litho. Wmk. 252

No.	Type	Value	Color	Unused	Used
793	A199	20 l	multi	.25	.25
794	A199	30 l	multi	.25	.25
795	A199	1d	multi	.25	.25
796	A199	2d	multi	.25	.25
797	A199	2.50d	sl grn & dl grn	.50	.25
798	A199	4.50d	multi	1.00	.75
799	A199	6d	multi	1.00	.40
			Nos. 793-799 (7)	3.50	2.40

Centenary of the union of the Ionian Islands with Greece.

Child and Sun — A200

1964, Sept. 10 Wmk. 252

No.	Type	Value	Color	Unused	Used
800	A200	2.50d	multi	.80	.25

50th anniv. of the Natl. Institute of Social Welfare for the Protection of Children and Mothers (P.I.K.P.A.).

Europa Issue, 1964

Common Design Type

1964, Sept. 14 Litho. ***Perf. 13x13½***

Size: 23x39mm

No.	Type	Value	Color	Unused	Used
801	CD7	2.50d	lt grn & dk red	*2.25*	*.40*
802	CD7	4.50d	gray & brn	*2.75*	*1.50*

King Constantine II and Queen Anne-Marie A201

1964, Sept. 18 Engr. ***Perf. 13½x14***

No.	Type	Value	Color	Unused	Used
803	A201	1.50d	green	.25	.25
804	A201	2.50d	rose car	.25	.25
805	A201	4.50d	brt ultra	.50	.25
			Nos. 803-805 (3)	1.00	

Wedding of King Constantine II anc cess Anne-Marie of Denmark, Sept. 18,

Peleus and Atalante Fighting, 6th Cent. B.C. Vase — A202

Designs: 1d, Runners on amphora, horiz. 2d, Athlete on vase, horiz. 2.50d, Discus thrower and judge, pitcher. 4.50d, Charioteer, sculpture, horiz. 6d, Boxers, vase, horiz. 10d, Apollo, frieze from Zeus Temple at Olympia.

Perf. 12x13½, 13½x12

1964, Oct. 24 Litho. Wmk. 252

806 A202 10 l multi .25 .25
807 A202 1d multi .25 .25
808 A202 2d multi .25 .25
809 A202 2.50d multi .25 .25
810 A202 4.50d multi .40 .30
811 A202 6d multi .25 .25
812 A202 10d multi .30 .25
Nos. 806-812 (7) 1.95 1.80

18th Olympic Games, Tokyo, Oct. 10-25.

Detail from "Christ Stripped of His Garments" by El Greco — A203

Paintings by El Greco: 1d, Concert of the Angels. 1.50d, El Greco's painted signature, horiz. 2.50d, Self-portrait. 4.50d, Storm-lashed Toledo.

Perf. 12x13½, 13½x12

1965, Mar. 6 Litho. Wmk. 252

813 A203 50 l sepia & multi .25 .25
814 A203 1d gray & multi .25 .25
a. Double impression of black *115.00*
815 A203 1.50d multi .25 .25
816 A203 2.50d sl & multi .25 .25
817 A203 4.50d multi .30 .25
Nos. 813-817 (5) 1.30 1.25

350th anniv. of the death of Domenico Theotocopoulos, El Greco (1541-1614).

Aesculapius Theatre, Epidauros — A204

Design: 4.50d, Herod Atticus Theatre, and Acropolis, Athens.

1965, Apr. 30 Litho. *Perf. 12x13½*

818 A204 1.50d multi .25 .25
819 A204 4.50d multi .30 .30

Epidauros and Athens theatrical festivals.

ITU Emblem, Old and New Telecommunication Equipment — A205

1965, Apr. 30 *Perf. 13½x12*

820 A205 2.50d multi .40 .25

Cent. of the ITU.

Swearing-in Ceremony A206

Flag of Philiki Hetaeria, the Friends' Society A207

Perf. 13½x12

1965, May 31 Litho. Wmk. 252

821 A206 1.50d multi .25 .25
822 A207 4.50d gray & multi .25 .25

150th anniv. of the Friends' Society, a secret organization for the liberation of Greece from Turkey.

Emblem of A.H.E.P.A. A208

1965, June 30

823 A208 6d lt bl, blk & ol .50 .25

Congress of the American Hellenic Educational Progressive Association, Athens.

Eleutherios Venizelos, Therissos, 1905 — A209

Designs: 2d, Venizelos signing Treaty of Sevres, 1920. 2.50d, Venizelos portrait.

1965, June 30 Engr. *Perf. 12½x13*

824 A209 1.50d green .25 .25
825 A209 2d dark blue .40 .30
826 A209 2.50d brown .25 .25
Nos. 824-826 (3) .90 .80

Cent. of the birth of Eleutherios Venizelos (1864-1936), statesman and prime minister.

Symbols of Planets — A210

Astronaut in Space — A211

Design: 6d, Two space ships over globe.

Perf. 12½x13½

1965, Sept. 11 Litho. Wmk. 252

827 A210 50 l multi .25 .25
828 A211 2.50d multi .25 .25
829 A211 6d multi .25 .25
Nos. 827-829 (3) .75 .75

16th Astronautical Cong., Athens, 9/12-18.

Victory Medal — A212

Stadium, Phaleron A213

Design: 1d, Games' emblem and "JBA."

Perf. 13½x13, 13x13½

1965, Sept. 11

830 A213 1d multicolored .25 .25
831 A212 2d multicolored .25 .25
832 A213 6d multicolored .25 .25
Nos. 830-832 (3) .75 .75

24th Balkan Games, Sept. 1-10.

Europa Issue, 1965

Common Design Type

1965, Oct. 21 *Perf. 13½x12*

Size: 33x23mm

833 CD8 2.50d bl gray, blk & dk bl .75 .40
834 CD8 4.50d olive, blk & grn 1.50 .75

Hipparchus and Astrolabe A214

1965, Oct. 21 Litho. Wmk. 252

835 A214 2.50d bl grn, blk & dk red .40 .25

Opening of the Evghenides Planetarium, Athens.

St. Andrew's Church, Patras — A215

St. Andrew — A216

1965, Nov. 30 *Perf. 12x13½*

836 A215 1d multicolored .25 .25
837 A216 5d multicolored .25 .25

Return of the head of St. Andrew from St. Peter's, Rome to St. Andrew's, Patras. The design of the 5d is from an 11th cent. mosaic at St. Luke's Monastery, Boeotia.

Ants and Anthill — A217

Savings Bank and Book — A218

1965, Nov. 30 Litho. Wmk. 252

838 A217 10 l grn, blk & bis .25 .25
839 A218 2.50d multi .30 .25

50th anniv. of the Post Office Savings Bank.

Theodore Brysakes — A219

Greek Painters: 1d, Nikeforus Lytras. 2.50d, Constantin Volonakis. 4d, Nicolas Gyses. 5d, George Jacobides.

Perf. 13x13½

1966, Feb. 28 Litho. Wmk. 252

840 A219 80 l multi .25 .25
841 A219 1d multi .25 .25
842 A219 2.50d multi .25 .25
843 A219 4d multi .25 .25
844 A219 5d multi .25 .25
Nos. 840-844 (5) 1.25 1.25

Jean Gabriel Eynard — A220

Banknote of 1867 — A221

2.50d, Georgios Stavros. 4d, Bank's 1st headquarters, etching by Yannis Kefallinos.

Perf. 12x13½

1966, Mar. 30 Engr. Wmk. 252

845 A220 1.50d gray grn .25 .25
846 A220 2.50d brown .25 .25
847 A221 4d ultra .25 .25
848 A221 6d black .25 .25
Nos. 845-848 (4) 1.00 1.00

National Bank of Greece, 125th anniv.

Symbolic Water Cycle — A222

UNESCO Emblem — A223

WHO Headquarters, Geneva — A224

Perf. 12x13½, 13½x12

1966, Apr. 18 Litho.

849 A222 1d multicolored .25 .25
850 A223 3d multicolored .25 .25
851 A224 5d multicolored .25 .25
Nos. 849-851 (3) .75 .75

Hydrological Decade (UNESCO), 1965-74, (1d); 20th anniv. of UNESCO (3d); inauguration of the WHO Headquarters, Geneva (5d).

Geannares Michael (Hatzes) — A225

Explosion at Arkadi Monastery A226

Map of Crete — A227

1966, Apr. 18

852	A225	2d multi	.25	.25
853	A226	2.50d multi	.25	.25
854	A227	4.50d multi	.25	.25
		Nos. 852-854 (3)	.75	.75

Cent. of the Cretan revolt against the Turks. Geannares Michael (Hatzes), the leader of the revolt, was a member of Cretan government and a writer.

Copper Mask, 4th Century, B.C. — A228

Dionysus on a Thespian Ship-Chariot A229

Designs: 2.50d, Old Theater of Dionysus, Athens, 6th Century B.C. 4.50d, Dancing Dionysus, from vase by Kleophrades, c. 500 B.C.

Perf. 12x13½, 13½x12

1966, May 26 Litho. Wmk. 252

855	A228	1d multi	.25	.25
856	A229	1.50d multi	.25	.25
857	A229	2.50d multi	.25	.25
858	A228	4.50d multi	.25	.25
		Nos. 855-858 (4)	1.00	1.00

2500th anniversary of Greek theater.

Boeing 707-320 over New York Buildings and Greek Column A230

1966, May 26 *Perf. 13x12½*

859	A230	6d blue & dark blue	.40	.25

Inauguration of transatlantic flights of Olympic Airways.

Tobacco Worker — A231

Design: 5d, Woman sorting tobacco leaves.

Perf. 12½x13½

1966, Sept. 19 Litho. Wmk. 252

860	A231	1d multicolored	.25	.25
861	A231	5d multicolored	.45	.25

Greek tobacco industry, and 4th Intl. Scientific Tobacco Congress, Athens, Sept. 19-26.

Europa Issue, 1966

Common Design Type

1966, Sept. 19 Litho. Wmk. 252

Size: 23x33mm

862	CD9	1.50d olive	*.75*	*.35*
863	CD9	4.50d lt red brown	*1.50*	*.70*

Carved Cases for Knitting Needles — A232

Bridegroom, Embroidery from Epirus A233

Designs (Popular Art): 50 l, Lyre, Crete. 1d, Massa (stringed instrument). 1.50d, Bas-relief (cross and angels). 2d, Icon (Sts. Constantine and Helena). 2.50d, Virgin (wood carving, Church of St. Nicholas, Galaxeidon). 3d, Embroidery (sailing ship from Skyros). 4d, Embroidery (wedding parade). 4.50d, Carved wooden distaff (Sts. George and Barbara). 5d, Silver and agate necklace and earrings. 20d, Handwoven cloth, Cyprus.

Perf. 12x13½, 13½x12

1966, Nov. 21 Litho. Wmk. 252

864	A232	10 l multi	.25	.25
865	A233	30 l multi	.25	.25
866	A232	50 l multi	.25	.25
867	A232	1d multi	.25	.25
868	A232	1.50d multi	.25	.25
869	A232	2d multi	1.60	.25
870	A232	2.50d multi	.25	.25
871	A233	3d multi	.25	.25
872	A233	4d multi	.65	.25
873	A232	4.50d multi	.30	.30
874	A232	5d multi	.70	.25
875	A233	20d multi	1.50	.50
		Nos. 864-875 (12)	6.50	3.30

King Constantine II, Queen Anne-Marie and Princess Alexia — A234

Designs: 2d, Princess Alexia. 3.50d, Queen Anne-Marie and Princess Alexia.

Perf. 13½x14

1966, Dec. 19 Engr. Wmk. 252

876	A234	2d green	.30	.25
877	A234	2.50d brown	.30	.25
878	A234	3.50d ultra	.40	.25
		Nos. 876-878 (3)	1.00	.75

Princess Alexia, successor to the throne of Greece.

"Night" by John Cossos (1830-73) — A235

Sculptures: 50 l, Penelope by Leonides Drosses (1836-1882). 80 l, Shepherd by George Fytales. 2d, Woman's torso by Constantine Demetriades (1881-1943). 2.50d, "Colocotrones" (equestrian statue) by Lazarus Sochos (1862-1911). 3d, Sleeping Young Lady by John Halepas (1851-1938), horiz. 10d, Woodcutter by George Filippotes (1839-1919), horiz.

Perf. 12x13½, 13½x12

1967, Feb. 28 Litho. Wmk. 252

879	A235	20 l Prus bl, gray & blk	.25	.25
880	A235	50 l brn, gray & blk	.25	.25
881	A235	80 l brn red, gray & blk	.25	.25
882	A235	2d vio bl, gray & blk	.25	.25
883	A235	2.50d ultra, blk & grn	.25	.25
884	A235	3d bl, lt bl, gray & blk	.40	.25
885	A235	10d bl & multi	.30	.25
		Nos. 879-885 (7)	1.95	1.75

Issued to honor modern Greek sculptors.

World Map and Olympic Rings A236

Discus Thrower by C. Demetriades A237

Designs: 1.50d, Runners on ancient clay vessel. 2.50d, Hurdler and map of Europe and Near East. 6d, Rising sun over Altis ruins at Olympia.

Perf. 13½x12, 12x13½

1967, Apr. 6 Litho. Wmk. 252

886	A236	1d multi	.25	.25
887	A236	1.50d multi	.25	.25
888	A236	2.50d multi	.25	.25
889	A237	5d multi	.40	.30
890	A236	6d multi	.45	.25
		Nos. 886-890 (5)	1.60	1.30

Olympic Games Day, Apr. 6 (1d); Classic Marathon Race, Apr. 6 (1.5d); athletic qualifying rounds for the Cup of Europe, June 24-25 (2.50d); 9th contest for the European Athletic Championships, 1969 (5d); founding of the Intl. Academy at Olympia and the 7th meeting of the Academy, July 29-Aug. 14, 1967 (6d).

Europa Issue, 1967

Common Design Type

Perf. 12x13½

1967, May 2 Litho. Wmk. 252

Size: 23x33½mm

891	CD10	2.50d buff, lt & dk brn	*1.00*	*.25*
892	CD10	4.50d grn, lt & dk grn	*2.75*	*.75*

Chapel, Skopelos Island A238

Plaka District, Athens — A239

Intl. Tourist Year: 4.50d, Doric Temple of Epicurean Apollo, by Itkinus, c. 430 B.C.

Perf. 13½x12, 12x13½

1967, June 26 Litho. Wmk. 252

893	A238	2.50d multi	.25	.25
894	A238	4.50d multi	.50	.30
a.		Double impression of black		
895	A239	6d multi	.50	.25
		Nos. 893-895 (3)	1.25	.80

Destroyer and Sailor A240

Training Ship, Merchant Marine Academy — A241

Maritime Week: 2.50d, Merchant Marine Academy, Aspropyrgos, Attica, and rowing crew. 3d, Cruiser Georgios Averoff and Naval School, Poros. 6d, Merchant ship and bearded figurehead.

1967, June 26

896	A240	20 l multi	.25	.25
897	A241	1d multi	.25	.25
898	A240	2.50d multi	.25	.25
899	A240	3d multi	.30	.25
900	A240	6d multi	.40	.25
		Nos. 896-900 (5)	1.45	1.25

Soldier and Rising Phoenix — A242

Perf. 12x13½

1967, Aug. 30 Litho. Wmk. 252

901	A242	2.50d blue & multi	.25	.25
902	A242	3d orange & multi	.25	.25
903	A242	4.50d multi	.25	.25
		Nos. 901-903 (3)	.75	.75

Revolution of Apr. 21, 1967.

Blast Furnaces — A243

1967, Nov. 29 *Perf. 13x14*

904	A243	4.50d brt bl & dk vio bl	.40	.40

1st meeting of the UN Industrial Development Organization, Athens, Nov. 29-Dec. 20.

Sailboats A244

Children's Drawings: 1.50d, Steamship and island. 3.50d, Farmhouse. 6d, Church on hill.

1967, Dec. 20 *Perf. 13½x12½*

905	A244	20 l multi	.25	.25
906	A244	1.50d grn, dk bl & blk	.25	.25
907	A244	3.50d multi	.40	.40
908	A244	6d multi	.40	.40
		Nos. 905-908 (4)	1.30	1.30

Javelin A245

Apollo, Olympic Academy Seal
A246

Discus Thrower by Demetriades
A247

Designs: 1d, Jumping. 2.50d, Attic vase showing lighting of Olympic torch. 4d, Olympic rings and world map, horiz. 6d, Long-distance runners, vert.

Wmk. 252

1968, Feb. 28 Litho. ***Perf. 12½***

909 A245 50 l ultra & bis .25 .25
910 A245 1d grn, yel, blk & gray .25 .25
911 A246 1.50d blk, bl & buff .25 .25
912 A246 2.50d ol grn, blk & org brn .25 .25
913 A246 4d gray & multi .35 .25
914 A247 4.50d bl, grn, yel & blk 1.25 .35
915 A245 6d brn, red & bl .30 .25
Nos. 909-915 (7) 2.90 1.85

50 l, 1d, 6d, 27th Balkan Games, Athens, Aug. 29-Sept. 1; 1.50d, Meeting of the Intl. Olympic Academy; 2.50d, Lighting of the Olympic torch for 19th Olympic Games, Mexico City; 4d, Olympic Day, Apr. 6; 4.50d, 9th European Athletic Championships, 1969.

Europa Issue, 1968

Common Design Type

Perf. 13½x12

1968, Mar. 29 Litho. Wmk. 252

Size: 33x23mm

916 CD11 2.50d cop red, bis & blk *1.25 .40*
917 CD11 4.50d vio, bister & blk *2.50 1.25*

Emblems of Greek and International Automobile Clubs — A248

1968, Mar. 29 ***Perf. 13x14***

918 A248 5d ultra & org brn 1.00 .40

General Assembly of the International Automobile Federation, Athens, Apr. 8-14.

Athena Defeating Alkyoneus, from Pergamos Altar, 180 B.C. — A249

Athena, 2nd Century, B.C. — A250

Winged Victory of Samothrace, c. 190 B.C. — A251

Designs: 50 l, Alexander the Great on horseback, from sarcophagus, c. 310 B.C. 1.50d, Emperors Constantine and Justinian bringing offerings to Virgin Mary, Byzantine mosaic. 2.50d, Emperor Constantine Paleologos, lithograph by D. Tsokos, 1859. 3d, Greece in Missolonghi, by Delacroix. 4.50d, Greek Soldier (evzone), by G. B. Scott.

Perf. 13½x13, 13x13½, 13½x14 (A249)

1968, Apr. 27

919 A249 10 l gray & multi .25 .25
920 A250 20 l grn & multi .25 .25
921 A250 50 l pur & multi .25 .25
922 A249 1.50d gray & multi .25 .25
923 A250 2.50d multi .25 .25
924 A251 3d multi .25 .25
925 A251 4.50d multi .25 .25
926 A251 6d multi .35 .30
Nos. 919-926 (8) 2.10 2.05

"The Hellenic Fight for Civilization" exhibition

Monument to the Unknown Priest and Teacher, Rhodes
A252

Map & Flag of Greece — A253

Perf. 14x13½, 13½x14

1968, July 11 Litho. Wmk. 252

927 A252 2d multicolored .40 .25
928 A253 5d multicolored .80 .80

20th anniv. of the union of the Dodecanese Islands with Greece.

Cross and Globe — A254

1968, July 11 ***Perf. 13½x14***

929 A254 6d multicolored .55 .40

19th Biennial Congress of the Greek Orthodox Archdiocese of North and South America.

Antique Lamp (GAPA Emblem)
A255

1968, July 11 ***Perf. 14x13½***

930 A255 6d multicolored .50 .30

Regional Congress of the Greek-American Progressive Association, G.A.P.A.

Fragment of Bas-relief, Temple of Aesculapius, Athens — A256

Perf. 13½x14

1968, Sept. 8 Litho. Wmk. 252

931 A256 4.50d multicolored 1.50 .90

Issued to publicize the 5th European Cardiology Congress, Athens, Sept. 8-14.

View of Olympia, Site of Ancient Games
A257

Pindar and Olympic Ode — A258

Design: 2.50d, Panathenaic Stadium, site of 1896 Olympic Games.

Perf. 14x13½, 13x13½

1968, Sept. 25 Litho. Wmk. 252

932 A257 2.50d multicolored .30 .25
933 A257 5d green & multi .60 .25
934 A258 10d bl, yel & brn 1.50 .80
Nos. 932-934 (3) 2.40 1.30

19th Olympic Games, Mexico City, 10/12-27.

On 10d, hyphen is omitted at end of 5th line of ode on 5 of 50 stamps in each sheet.

Hygeia and WHO Emblem — A259

1968, Nov. 8 ***Perf. 13½x14***

935 A259 5d gray & multi .70 .40

20th anniv. of WHO.

Mediterranean, Breguet 19 and Flight Route, 1928 — A260

Farman, 1912, Plane and F-104G Jet — A261

Design: 2.50d, Greek air force pilot ramming enemy plane over Langada.

1968, Nov. 8 ***Perf. 14x13½, 13½x14***

936 A260 2.50d ultra, blk & yel .25 .25
937 A260 3.50d multicolored .25 .25
938 A261 8d multicolored 1.25 .90
Nos. 936-938 (3) 1.75 1.40

Exploits of Royal Hellenic Air Force.

St. Zeno, The Letter Bearer — A262

Perf. 13½x14

1969, Feb. 10 Litho. Wmk. 252

939 A262 2.50d multicolored .50 .25

Establishment of the feast day of St. Zeno as the day of Greek p.o. personnel.

Hephaestus and Cyclops, Bas-relief
A263

Parade of Harvesters, Minoan Vase — A264

1969, Feb. 10 ***Perf. 13½x12½***

940 A263 1.50d multicolored .35 .25
941 A264 10d multicolored .90 .65

50th anniv. of the ILO.

Yachts in Vouliagmeni Harbor — A265

Athens Festival, Chorus of Elders — A266

View of Astypalaia — A267

Perf. 13½x12½, 12½x13½

1969, Mar. 3

942 A265 1d multicolored .25 .25
943 A266 5d multicolored .80 .70
944 A267 6d multicolored .40 .25
Nos. 942-944 (3) 1.45 1.20

Issued for tourist publicity.

Attic Shield and Helmet on Greek Coin, 461-450 B.C. — A268

Hoplites and Flutist, from Proto-Corinthian Pitcher, 640-630 B.C. — A269

Perf. 12½x13½, 13½x12½

1969, Apr. 4 Litho. Wmk. 252

945 A268 2.50d rose red, blk & sl .35 .25
946 A269 4.50d multi 1.00 .65

20th anniv. of NATO.

Europa Issue, 1969

Common Design Type

1969, May 5 ***Perf. 13½x12½***

Size: 33x23mm

947 CD12 2.50d multi *1.75* .25
948 CD12 4.50d multi *3.25* *1.25*

Victory Medal A270

Pole Vault and Pentathlon (from Panathenaic Amphora) A271

5d, Relay race and runners from amphora, 525 B.C., horiz. 8d, Modern and ancient (Panathenaic amphora, c. 480 B.C.) discus throwers.

Perf. 12½x13½, 13½x12½

1969, May 5

949 A270 20 l red & multi .25 .25
950 A271 3d gray & multi .25 .25
951 A271 5d multicolored .25 .25
952 A271 8d multicolored 1.40 .75
Nos. 949-952 (4) 2.15 1.50

Issued to publicize the 9th European Athletic Championships, Athens, Sept. 16-21.

Greece and the Sea Issue

Oil Tanker A272

Merchant Vessels and Warships, 1821 — A273

Designs: 80 l, Brig and steamship, painting by Ioannis Poulakas, vert. 4.50d, Warships on maneuvers. 6d, Battle of Salamis, 480 B.C., painting by Constantine Volonakis.

Perf. 12½x13½, 13½x12½, 13½x13

1969, June 28 Litho. Wmk. 252

953 A272 80 l multicolored .25 .25
954 A272 2d blk, bl & gray .25 .25
955 A273 2.50d dk bl & multi .25 .25
956 A272 4.50d brn, gray & bl 1.00 .35
957 A273 6d multicolored 1.50 .45
Nos. 953-957 (5) 3.25 1.55

Raising Greek Flag — A274

1969, Aug. 31 ***Perf. 13x13½***

958 A274 2.50d blue & multi .70 .25

20th anniv. of the Grammos-Vitsi victory.

Athena Promachos and Map of Greece A275

"National Resistance" A276

Greek Participation in World War II — A277

Perf. 13x13½, 13½x14

1969, Oct. 12 Litho. Wmk. 252

959 A275 4d multicolored .25 .25
960 A276 5d multicolored 1.50 .70
961 A277 6d multicolored .65 .25
Nos. 959-961 (3) 2.40 1.20

25th anniv. of the liberation of Greece in WW II.

No. 960 exists imperf.

Demetrius Tsames Karatasios, by G. Demetriades A278

Pavlos Melas, by P. Mathiopoulos A279

2.50d, Emmanuel Pappas, statue by Nicholas Perantinos. 4.50d, Capetan Kotas.

Perf. 12x13½

1969, Nov. 12 Litho. Wmk. 252

962 A278 1.50d multicolored .25 .25
963 A278 2.50d blue & multi .25 .25
964 A279 3.50d gray & multi .25 .25
965 A279 4.50d multicolored .95 .55
Nos. 962-965 (4) 1.70 1.30

Issued to honor Greek heroes in Macedonia's struggle for liberation.

Angel of the Annunciation, Daphni Church, 11th Century — A280

Dolphins, Delos, 110 B.C. A281

Christ's Descent into Hell, Nea Moni Church, 11th Cent. A282

Greek Mosaics: 1.50d, The Holy Ghost (dove), Hosios Loukas Monastery, 11th cent. 2d, The Hunter, Pella, 4th cent. B.C. 5d, Bird, St. George's Church, Salonica, 5th cent.

Perf. 12x13½, 13½x12 (1d), 13x13½ (6d)

1970, Jan. 16 Litho. Wmk. 252

966 A280 20 l multicolored .25 .25
967 A281 1d multicolored .25 .25
968 A280 1.50d blue & multi .25 .25
969 A280 2d gray & multi .45 .25
970 A280 5d bister & multi .55 .35
971 A282 6d multicolored .75 .75
Nos. 966-971 (6) 2.50 2.10

Hercules and the Cretan Bull — A283

Hercules and the Erymanthian Boar — A284

Labors of Hercules: 30 l, Capture of Cerberus. 1d, Capture of the golden apples of the Hesperides. 1.50d, Lernean Hydra. 2d, Slaying of Geryon. 3d, Centaur Nessus. 4.50d, Fight with the river god Achelos. 5d, Nemean lion. 6d, Stymphalian birds. 20d, Giant Antaeus. Designs of 20 l and 1d are from Temple of Zeus, Olympia; others from various vessels; all from 7th-5th cent. B.C.

Perf. 13½x12, 12x13½

1970, Mar. 16 Litho. Wmk. 252

972 A283 20 l gray, blk & yel .25 .25
973 A283 30 l ocher & multi .25 .25
974 A284 1d bl gray, blk & bl .25 .25
975 A283 1.50d dk brn, bls & sl grn .30 .25
976 A283 2d ocher & multi 2.25 .25
977 A284 2.50d ocher, dk brn & dl red .30 .25
978 A284 3d multicolored 2.25 .25
979 A283 4.50d dk bl & multi .50 .25
980 A283 5d multicolored .50 .25
981 A283 6d multicolored .50 .25
982 A283 20d black & multi 1.75 .85
Nos. 972-982 (11) 9.10 3.35

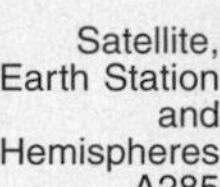

Satellite, Earth Station and Hemispheres A285

1970, Apr. 21 ***Perf. 13½x12***

983 A285 2.50d bl, gray & yel .50 .30
984 A285 4.50d brn, ol & bl 1.25 1.10

Opening of the Earth Satellite Telecommunications Station "Thermopylae," Apr. 21, 1970.

Europa Issue, 1970

Common Design Type and

Owl (Post Horns and CEPT) — A287

1970, Apr. 21 ***Perf. 13½x12, 12x13½***

985 CD13 2.50d rose red & org *2.00* .75
986 A287 3d brt bl, gray & vio bl *2.00* .75
987 CD13 4.50d ultra & org *5.75* *1.25*
Nos. 985-987 (3) 9.75 2.75
Nos. 985,987 (2) 7.75 2.00

St. Demetrius with Cyril and Methodius as Children A288

Emperor Michael III with Sts. Cyril and Methodius A290

A289

2d, St. Cyril. 10d, St. Methodius.

Perf. 13½x14 (50 l); 12x13½ (2d, 10d); 13x13½ (5d)

1970, Apr. 17 Litho. Wmk. 252

988 A288 50 l multi .25 .25
989 2d multi .60 .45
990 A290 5d multi .50 .25
991 10d multi .70 .50
a. A289 Pair, #989, 991 1.25 1.25
Nos. 988-991 (4) 2.05 1.45

Sts. Cyril and Methodius who translated the Bible into Slavonic.

Greek Fir A292

Jankaea Heldreichii A293

6d, Rock partridge, horiz. 8d, Wild goat.

Perf. 13x14, 14x13, 12x13½ (2.50d)

1970, June 16 Litho. Wmk. 252

992	A292	80 l multi	.35	.35
993	A293	2.50d multi	1.25	.25
994	A292	6d multi	2.40	.55
995	A292	8d multi	2.75	2.40
		Nos. 992-995 (4)	6.75	3.55

European Nature Conservation Year, 1970.

Map Showing Link Between AHEPA Members and Greece A294

1970, Aug. 1 *Perf. 13½x13*

996 A294 6d blue & multi 1.00 .40

48th annual AHEPA (American Hellenic Educational Progressive Assoc.) Cong., Athens, Aug. 1970.

UPU Headquarters, Bern — A295

Education Year Emblem — A296

Mahatma Gandhi — A297

United Nations Emblem — A298

Ludwig van Beethoven — A299

Perf. 13½x12, 13x14, 12x13½

1970, Oct. 7 Litho. Wmk. 252

997	A295	50 l bis & multi	.25	.25
998	A296	2.50d bl & multi	.40	.25
999	A297	3.50d multi	.25	.25
1000	A298	4d bl & multi	.75	.25
1001	A299	4.50d blk & multi	1.50	1.10
		Nos. 997-1001 (5)	3.15	2.10

Inauguration of the UPU Headquarters, Bern (50 l); Intl. Education Year (2.50d); cent. of the birth of Mohandas K. Gandhi (1869-1948), leader in India's struggle for independence (3.50d); 25th anniv. of the UN (4d); Ludwig van Beethoven (1770-1827), composer (4.50d).

The Shepherds (Mosaic) — A300

Christmas (from Mosaic in the Monastery of Hosios Loukas, Boetia, 11th cent.): 4.50d, The Three Kings and Angel. 6d, Nativity, horiz.

1970, Dec. 5 *Perf. 13x14, 14x13*

1002	A300	2d bister & multi	.25	.25
1003	A300	4.50d bister & multi	.40	.30
1004	A300	6d bister & multi	.80	.80
		Nos. 1002-1004 (3)	1.45	1.35

"Leonidas" A301

Priest Sworn in as Fighter, from Commemorative Medal — A302

Eugenius Voùlgaris (1716-1806) A303

Battle of Corinth A304

Kaltetsi Monastery, Seal of Peloponnesian Senate — A305

Death of Bishop Isaias, Battle of Alamana — A306

Designs: No. 1009, *Pericles.* No. 1010, Sacrifice of Kapsalis. 1.50d, *Terpsichore.* No. 1012, Patriarch Grigorius IV. No. 1013, Suliot women in battle, horiz. No. 1015, *Karteria.* No. 1016, Adamantios Korais, M.D. No. 1017, Memorial column, provincial administrative seal of Epidaurus. 3d, Naval battle, Samos, horiz. 5d, Battle of Athens. 6d, Naval battle, Yeronda. 6.50d, Battle of Maniaki. 9d, Battle of Karpenisi, death of Marcos Botsaris. 10d, Bishop Germanos blessing flag. 15d, *Secret School.* 20d, John Capodistrias' signature and seal.

1971 Litho. Wmk. 252

1005	A301	20 l multi	.25	.25
1006	A302	50 l multi	.25	.25
1007	A303	50 l multi	.25	.25
1008	A304	50 l multi	.25	.25
1009	A301	1d multi	.25	.25
1010	A304	1d multi	.25	.25
1011	A301	1.50d multi	.25	.25
1012	A302	2d multi	.25	.25
1013	A304	2d multi	.25	.25
1014	A305	2d multi	.25	.25
1015	A301	2.50d multi	.25	.25
1016	A303	2.50d multi	.25	.25
1017	A305	2.50d multi	.25	.25
1018	A304	3d multi	.65	.40
1019	A306	4d multi	.25	.25
1020	A304	5d multi	.40	.25
1021	A301	6d multi	1.25	.90
1022	A301	6.50d multi	.40	.25
1023	A301	9d multi	1.00	.90
1024	A306	10d multi	1.10	.90
1025	A306	15d multi	1.25	1.10
1026	A305	20d multi	2.25	1.40
		Nos. 1005-1026 (22)	11.80	9.60

Sesquicentennial of Greece's uprising against the Turks. Emphasize role of Navy (Nos. 1005, 1009, 1011, 1015, 1018, 1021), issued 3/15; Church (Nos. 1006, 1012, 1019, 1024), 2/8; Instructors (Nos. 1007, 1016, 1025), 6/21; Land Forces (Nos. 1008, 1010, 1013, 1020, 1022-1023), 9/21; Provincial Administrations (Nos. 1014, 1017, 1026), 10/19.

Sizes: 37x24mm: Nos. 1005, 1009, 1011, 1015; 40x27½mm, No. 1021; 48x33mm, Nos. 1022, 1023.

Perfs.: 14x13, Nos. 1005, 1009, 1011, 1013, 1015, 1018; 13½x14, Nos. 1006, 1012; 12x13½, Nos. 1007, 1016, 1019, 1022-1025; 13x14, Nos. 1008, 1010, 1020; 13½x13, Nos. 1014, 1017, 1021, 1026.

Spyridon Louis, Winner of 1896 Marathon Race, Arriving at Stadium A307

Pierre de Coubertin and Memorial Column — A308

Perf. 13½x13, 13x13½

1971, Apr. 10 Litho. Wmk. 252

1027	A307	3d multi	.50	.25
1028	A308	8d multi	1.25	.90

Olympic Games revival, 75th anniv.

Europa Issue, 1971

Common Design Type

1971, May 18 *Perf. 13½x12*

Size: 33x22½mm

1029	CD14	2.50d grn, yel & blk	*1.00*	*.30*
1030	CD14	5d org, yel & blk	*3.00*	*1.50*

Hosios Lukas Monastery A309

Monasteries and Churches: 1d, Daphni Church. 2d, St. John the Divine, Patmos. 2.50d, Koumbelidiki Church, Kastoria. 4.50d, Chalkeon Church, Thessalonica. 6.50d, Paregoritissa Church, Arta. 8.50d, St. Paul's Monastery, Mt. Athos.

1972, Jan. 17 *Perf. 14x13*

1031	A309	50 l multi	.25	.25
1032	A309	1d multi	.25	.25
1033	A309	2d multi	.25	.25
1034	A309	2.50d multi	.25	.25
1035	A309	4.50d multi	.25	.25
1036	A309	6.50d multi	.25	.25
1037	A309	8.50d multi	1.00	1.00
		Nos. 1031-1037 (7)	2.50	2.50

Cretan Costume — A310

Greek regional costumes: 1d, Woman, Pindus. 2d, Man, Missolonghi. 2.50d, Woman, Sarakatsan, Attica. 3d, Woman, Island of Nisyros. 4.50d, Woman, Megara. 6.50d, Woman, Trikeri. 10d, Woman, Pylaia, Macedonia.

1972, Mar. 1 *Perf. 12½x13½*

1038	A310	50 l shown	.25	.25
1039	A310	1d multi	.25	.25
1040	A310	2d multi	.25	.25
1041	A310	2.50d multi	.25	.25
a.		"1972" omitted	10.00	10.00
1042	A310	3d multi	.25	.25
1043	A310	4.50d multi	.25	.25
1044	A310	6.50d multi	.30	.25
1045	A310	10d multi	3.00	1.00
		Nos. 1038-1045 (8)	4.80	2.75

See Nos. 1073-1089, 1121-1135.

Memorial Medal, Science and Industry A311

Flag and Map of Greece — A312

Honeycomb, Transportation and Industry — A313

Perf. 13½x13, 13x13½

1972, Apr. 21 Wmk. 252

1046	A311	2.50d blue & multi	.25	.25
1047	A312	4.50d ocher & multi	.25	.25
1048	A313	5d multi	.40	.40
		Nos. 1046-1048 (3)	.90	.90

5th anniversary of the revolution.

Europa Issue 1972

Common Design Type

1972, May 2 *Perf. 12x13½*

Size: 23x33mm

1049	CD15	3d multi	*.50*	*.30*
1050	CD15	4.50d blue & multi	*1.50*	*1.25*

Acropolis and Car — A314

Route of Automobile Rally — A315

1972, May 26 *Perf. 13½x12*

1051	A314	4.50d multi	.60	.60
1052	A315	5d bl & multi	.60	.60

20th Acropolis Automobile Rally, May 26-29.

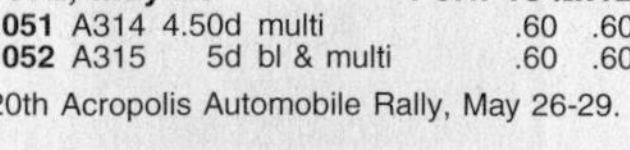

Gaia Handing Erecthonius to Athena, Cecrops A316

Designs: 2d, Uranus, from altar of Zeus at Pergamum. 2.50d, Gods defeating the Giants, Treasury of Siphnos. 5d, Zeus of Dodona.

1972, June 26 Litho. *Perf. 14x13½*

1053 A316 1.50d yel grn & blk .25 .25
1054 A316 2d dk bl & blk .25 .25
1055 A316 2.50d org brn & blk .25 .25
1056 A316 5d dk brn & blk .50 .40
a. Strip of 4, #1053-1056 2.00 2.00

Greek mythology. No. 1056 issued only se-tenant with Nos. 1053-1055 in sheets of 40 (4x10). Nos. 1053-1055 issued also in sheets of 50 each.

Olympic Rings, Wrestlers A317

50 l, Young athlete, crowning himself, c. 480 B.C., vert. 3.50d, Spartan woman running, Archaic period, vert. 4.50d, Episkyros ball game, 6th century B.C. 10d, Running youths, from Panathenaic amphora.

Perf. 13½x14, 14x13½

1972, July 28 Litho. Wmk. 252

1057 A317 50 l mar, blk & gray .25 .25
1058 A317 1.50d brn, gray & blk .25 .25
1059 A317 3.50d ocher & multi .50 .25
1060 A317 4.50d grn, buff & blk .25 .25
1061 A317 10d blk & fawn 1.00 .55
Nos. 1057-1061 (5) 2.25 1.55

20th Olympic Games, Munich, 8/26-9/11.

Young Stamp Collector — A318

1972, Nov. 15 *Perf. 13x14*

1062 A318 2.50d multi .25 .25

Stamp Day.

Three Kings and Angels — A319

1972, Nov. 15

1063 A319 2.50d shown .25 .25
1064 A319 4.50d Nativity .25 .25
a. Pair, #1063-1064 .40 .40

Christmas 1972.

Technical University, 1885, by Luigi Lanza — A320

1973, Mar. 30 *Perf. 13½x13*

1065 A320 2.50d multi .40 .25

Centenary of the Metsovion National Technical University.

"Spring," Fresco — A321

Breast-form Jug — A322

"Wooing and Twittering Swallows" Fresco — A323

Designs: 30 l, "Blue Apes" fresco. 1.50d, Jug decorated with birds. 5d, "Wild Goats" fresco. 6.50d, Wrestlers, fresco.

1973, Mar. 30 *Perf. 13x13½, 13½x13*

1066 A321 10 l multi .25 .25
1067 A322 20 l multi .25 .25
1068 A323 30 l multi .25 .25
1069 A322 1.50d grn & multi .25 .25
1070 A323 2.50d multi .25 .25
1071 A323 5d multi .25 .25
1072 A323 6.50d multi .80 .80
Nos. 1066-1072 (7) 2.30 2.30

Archaeological treasures from Santorini Island (Thera).

Costume Type of 1972

Women's costumes except 10 l, 20 l, 50 l, 5d, 15d.

1973, Apr. 18 *Perf. 12½x13½*

1073 A310 10 l Peloponnesus .25 .25
1074 A310 20 l Sterea Hellas .25 .25
1075 A310 30 l Locris .25 .25
1076 A310 50 l Skyros .25 .25
1077 A310 1d Spetsai .25 .25
1078 A310 1.50d Almyros .25 .25
1079 A310 2.50d Macedonia .25 .25
1080 A310 3.50d Salamis .25 .25
1081 A310 4.50d Epirus .25 .25
1082 A310 5d Lefkas .25 .25
1083 A310 6.50d Skyros .25 .25
1084 A310 8.50d Corinth .40 .25
1085 A310 10d Corfu .40 .25
1086 A310 15d Epirus .40 .25
1087 A310 20d Thessaly 1.25 .25
1088 A310 30d Macedonia 1.60 .35
1089 A310 50d Thrace 3.25 1.60
Nos. 1073-1089 (17) 10.05 5.70

Europa Issue 1973

Common Design Type

1973, May 2 *Perf. 13½x12½*

Size: 35x22mm

1090 CD16 2.50d dp bl & lt bl *.30* *.25*
1091 CD16 3d dp car & dp org *.30* *.30*
1092 CD16 4.50d ol grn & yel *1.50* *.85*
Nos. 1090-1092 (3) 2.10 1.40

Zeus Battling Typhoeus, from Amphora A324

1d, Mount Olympus, after photograph. 2.50d, Zeus battling Giants, from Pergamum Altar. 4.50d, Punishment of Atlas and Prometheus, from vase.

Perf. 14x13½

1973, June 25 Wmk. 252

1093 A324 1d gray & blk .25 .25
1094 A324 2d multi .25 .25
1095 A324 2.50d gray, blk & buff .25 .25
1096 A324 4.50d ocher & multi .45 .45
a. Strip of 4, #1093-1096 1.75 1.75

Greek mythology.

Dr. George Papanicolaou A325

Perf. 13x13½

1973, Aug. 10 Litho. Wmk. 252

1097 A325 2.50d multi .25 .25
1098 A325 6.50d multi .25 .25

Dr. George Papanicolaou (1883-1962), cytologist and cancer researcher.

Icon, The Annunciation A326

1973, Aug. 10

1099 A326 2.50d multi .40 .25

Miraculous icon of Our Lady of the Annunciation found on Tinos, 1823.

A327

Triptolemus holding wheat on chariot.

Perf. 13x14

1973, Oct. 22 Litho. Wmk. 252

1100 A327 4.50d buff, dk brn & red .30 .25

5th Symposium of the European Conf. of Transport Ministers, Athens, Oct. 22-25.

A328

National Benefactors: 1d, Georgios Averoff. 2d, Apostolos Arsakis. 2.50d, Constantine Zappas. 4d, Andrea Sygros. 6.50d, John Varvakis.

1973, Nov. 15 Engr.

1101 A328 1.50d dk red brn .25 .25
1102 A328 2d car rose .25 .25
1103 A328 2.50d slate green .25 .25
1104 A328 4d purple .25 .25
1105 A328 6.50d black .25 .25
Nos. 1101-1105 (5) 1.25 1.25

Child Examining Stamp — A329

1973, Nov. 15 Litho. *Perf. 14x13*

1106 A329 2.50d multi .25 .25

Stamp Day.

Lord Byron in Souliot Costume — A330

Byron Taking Oath at Grave of Botsaris — A331

Perf. 13x14

1974, Apr. 4 Wmk. 252 Litho.

1107 A330 2.50d multi .25 .25
1108 A331 4.50d multi .25 .25

George Gordon, Lord Byron (1788-1824), English poet involved in Greek struggle for independence.

Harpist of Keros, c. 2800-2200 B.C. — A332

Europa: 4.50d, Statue of Young Women, c. 510 B.C. 6.50d, Charioteer of Delphi, c. 480-450 B.C.

1974, May 10 *Perf. 13x14*

1109 A332 3d dp bl & multi *.45* *.25*
1110 A332 4.50d dl red & multi *.65* *.30*
1111 A332 6.50d yel & multi *1.75* *.80*
Nos. 1109-1111 (3) 2.85 1.35

Zeus and Hera Enthroned, and Iris — A333

Greek mythology (from Vases, 5th Cent. B.C.): 2d, Birth of Athena, horiz. 2.50d, Artemis, Apollo, Leto, horiz. 10d, Hermes, the messenger.

1974, June 24 *Perf. 13x14, 14x13*

1112 A333 1.50d ocher, blk & brn .25 .25
1113 A333 2d blk, ocher & brn .25 .25
1114 A333 2.50d blk, ocher & brn .25 .25

1115 A333 10d blk, ocher & brn .25 .25
Nos. 1112-1115 (4) 1.00 1.00

Design from Mycenean Vase and UPU Emblem — A334

UPU cent.: 4.50d, Hermes on the Move, horiz. 6.50d, Woman reading letter.

1974, Sept. 14 ***Perf. 12½x13½***

1116 A334 2d vio & blk .25 .25
1117 A334 4.50d vio & blk .25 .25
1118 A334 6.50d vio & blk .25 .30
Nos. 1116-1118 (3) .75 .80

Crete No. 80 A335

1974, Nov. 15 Litho. ***Perf. 13½x13***

1119 A335 2.50d multi .25 .25

Stamp Day.

Flight into Egypt — A336

1974, Nov. 15 ***Perf. 13½x14***

1120 A336 Strip of 3 .80 .80
a. 2d ocher & multi .25 .25
b. 4.50d ocher & multi .25 .25
c. 8.50d ocher & multi .25 .25

Christmas 1974. Design is from 11th cent. Codex of Dionysos Monastery on Mount Athos.

Costume Type of 1972

Designs: Women's costumes, except 1.50d.

1974, Dec. 5 ***Perf. 12½x13½***

1121 A310 20 l Megara .25 .25
1122 A310 30 l Salamis .25 .25
1123 A310 50 l Edipsos .25 .25
1124 A310 1d Kyme .25 .25
1125 A310 1.50d Sterea Hellas .25 .25
1126 A310 2d Desfina .25 .25
1127 A310 3d Epirus .25 .25
1128 A310 3.50d Naousa .25 .25
1129 A310 4d Hasia .25 .25
1130 A310 4.50d Thasos .25 .25
1131 A310 5d Skopelos .25 .25
1132 A310 6.50d Epirus .25 .25
1133 A310 10d Pelion .30 .25
1134 A310 25d Kerkyra .70 .25
1135 A310 30d Boeotia 2.25 .60
Nos. 1121-1135 (15) 6.25 4.10

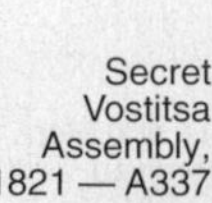

Secret Vostitsa Assembly, 1821 — A337

Grigorios Dikeos-Papaflessas A338

Aghioi Apostoli Church, Kalamata A339

Perf. 13½x12½, 12½x13½

1975, Mar. 24

1136 A337 4d multi .25 .25
1137 A338 7d multi .25 .25
1138 A339 11d multi .25 .25
Nos. 1136-1138 (3) .75 .75

Grigorios Dikeos-Papaflessas (1788-1825), priest and leader in Greece's uprising against the Turks, sesquicentennial of death.

Vase with Flowers — A340

Erotokritos and Aretussa — A341

Europa: 11d, Girl with Hat. All designs are after paintings by Theophilos Hatzimichael (d. 1934).

Perf. 12½x13½

1975, May 10 Litho. Wmk. 252

1139 A340 4d multi *.50* .45
1140 A341 7d multi *.70* .65
1141 A340 11d multi *2.00* 1.25
Nos. 1139-1141 (3) *3.20* 2.35

House, Kastoria A342

Greek Houses, 18th Cent.: 40 l, Arnea, Halkidiki. 4d, Veria. 6d, Siatista. 11d, Ambelakia, Thessaly.

1975, June 26 ***Perf. 13½x12½***

1142 A342 10 l brt bl & blk .25 .25
1143 A342 40 l red org & blk .25 .25
1144 A342 4d bister & blk .25 .25
1145 A342 6d ultra & multi .25 .25
1146 A342 11d org & blk .25 .25
Nos. 1142-1146 (5) 1.25 1.25

IWY Emblem, Neolithic Goddess — A343

"Looking to the Future" — A344

8.50d, Confrontation between Antigone & Creon.

Perf. 12½x13½

1975, Sept. 29 Litho. Wmk. 252

1147 A343 1.50d lilac & dk brn .25 .25
1148 A343 8.50d bis, blk & brn .25 .25
1149 A344 11d bl & blk .25 .25
Nos. 1147-1149 (3) .75 .75

International Women's Year 1975.

Papanastasiou and University Buildings — A345

First University Building A346

University City Plan A347

1975, Sept. 29 ***Perf. 14x13½***

1150 A345 1.50d tan & sepia .25 .25
1151 A346 4d multi .25 .25
1152 A347 11d multi .25 .25
Nos. 1150-1152 (3) .75 .75

Thessaloniki University, 50th anniversary. Alexandros Papanastasiou (1876-1936), founded University while Prime Minister.

Evangelos Zappas and Zappeion Building — A348

National Benefactors: 4d, Georgios Rizaris and Rizarios Ecclesiastical School. 6d, Michael Tositsas and Metsovion Technical University. 11d, Nicolaos Zosimas and Zosimea Academy.

Perf. 14x13

1975, Nov. 15 Litho. Wmk. 252

1153 A348 1d blk & grn .25 .25
1154 A348 4d blk & brn .25 .25
1155 A348 6d blk & org .25 .25
1156 A348 11d blk & brick red .25 .25
Nos. 1153-1156 (4) 1.00 1.00

Greece No. 380 — A349

1975, Nov. 15 ***Perf. 13x14***

1157 A349 11d dull grn & brn .40 .35

Stamp Day 1975.

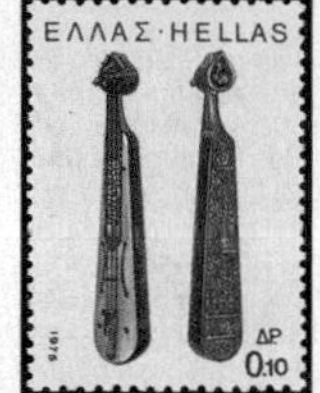

Pontos Lyre — A350

Musicians, Byzantine Mural — A351

Designs: 1d, Cretan lyre. 1.50d, Tambourine. 4d, Guitarist, from amphora, horiz. 6d, Bagpipes. 7d, Lute. 10d, Barrel organ. 11d, Pipes and zournadas. 20d, Musicians and singers praising God, Byzantine mural, horiz. 25d, Drums. 30d, Kanonaki, horiz.

Perf. 12½x13½, 13½x12½

1975, Dec. 15 Litho. Wmk. 252

1158 A350 10 l multi .25 .25
1159 A351 20 l multi .25 .25
1160 A350 1d ultra & multi .25 .25
1161 A350 1.50d multi .25 .25
1162 A351 4d multi .25 .25
1163 A350 6d multi .25 .25
1164 A350 7d multi .25 .25
1165 A350 10d multi .25 .25
1166 A350 11d red & multi .25 .25
1167 A351 20d multi .25 .25
1168 A350 25d multi .45 .25
1169 A350 30d multi 1.00 1.00
Nos. 1158-1169 (12) 3.95 3.75

Popular musical instruments.

Early Telephone, Globe, Waves A352

11d, Globe, waves, telephone 1976.

Perf. 13½x12½

1976, Mar. 23 Litho. Wmk. 252

1170 A352 7d blk & multi .25 .25
1171 A352 11d blk & multi .25 .25
a. Pair, Nos. 1170-1171 .50 .50

1st telephone call by Alexander Graham Bell, Mar. 10, 1876.

Sortie of Missolonghi — A353

1976, Mar. 23 ***Perf. 13½x13***

1172 A353 4d multi .25 .25

Sortie of the garrison of Missolonghi, sesquicentennial.

Florina Jugn — A354

Avramidis Plate — A355

Europa: 11d, Egina pitcher with Greek flags.

Perf. 13x14, 12½x12 (A355)

1976, May 10 Litho. Wmk. 252

1173 A354 7d buff & multi .40 .30
1174 A355 8.50d blk & multi .50 .30
1175 A354 11d gray & multi 1.50 .90
Nos. 1173-1175 (3) 2.40 1.50

Lion Attacking Bull — A356

Head of Silenus — A357

Designs: 4.50d, Flying aquatic birds. 7d, Wounded bull. 11d, Cow feeding calf, horiz. Designs from Creto-Mycenaean engraved seals, c. 1400 B.C.

Perf. 13x12½, 13½x14, 14x13½

1976, May 10

1176 A356 2d bis & multi .25 .25
1177 A356 4.50d multi .25 .25
1178 A356 7d multi .25 .25
1179 A357 8.50d pur & multi .25 .25
1180 A357 11d brn & multi .25 .25
Nos. 1176-1180 (5) 1.25 1.25

Long Jump A358

Montreal and Athens Stadiums — A359

Designs (Classical and Modern Events): 2d, Basketball. 3.50d, Wrestling. 4d, Swimming. 25d, Lighting Olympic flame and Montreal Olympic Games torch.

Perf. 14x13½, 12½x13½ (A359)

1976, June 25 Litho. Wmk. 252

1181 A358 50 l org & multi .25 .25
1182 A358 2d org & multi .25 .25
1183 A358 3.50d org & multi .25 .25
1184 A358 4d bl & multi .25 .25
1185 A359 11d multi .25 .25
1186 A358 25d org & multi .75 .75
Nos. 1181-1186 (6) 2.00 2.00

21st Olympic Games, Montreal, Canada, July 17-Aug. 1.

Lesbos, View and Map A360

Perf. 13½x14, 14x13½

1976, July 26 Litho. Wmk. 252

1187 A360 30d Lemnos, vert. .45 .25
1188 A360 50d shown .75 .25
1189 A360 75d Chios .90 .25
1190 A360 100d Samos 2.10 1.75
Nos. 1187-1190 (4) 4.20 2.50

Greek Aegean Islands.

Three Kings Speaking to the Jews — A361

Christmas: 7d, Nativity. Designs from manuscripts in Esfigmonou Monastery, Mount Athos.

1976, Dec. 8 ***Perf. 13½x14***

1191 A361 4d yellow & multi .25 .25
1192 A361 7d yellow & multi .25 .25

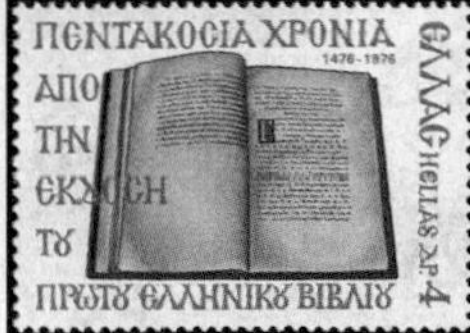

Greek Grammar of 1478 A362

1976, Dec. 8 ***Perf. 14x13***

1193 A362 4d multi .25 .25

500th anniversary of printing of first Greek book by Constantin Lascaris, Milan.

Heinrich Schliemann A363

Brooch with Figure of Goddess — A364

Designs: 4d, Gold bracelet, horiz. 7d, Gold diadem, horiz. 11d, Gold mask (Agamemnon). Treasures from Mycenaean tombs.

1976, Dec. 8 ***Perf. 13x14, 14x13***

1194 A363 2d multi .25 .25
1195 A364 4d multi .25 .25
1196 A364 5d grn & multi .25 .25
1197 A364 7d multi .25 .25
1198 A364 11d multi .50 .50
Nos. 1194-1198 (5) 1.50 1.50

Cent. of the discovery of the Mycenaean royal shaft graves by Heinrich Schliemann.

Aesculapius with Patients — A365

Patient in Clinic — A366

Designs: 1.50d, Aesculapius curing young man. 2d, Young Hercules with old nurse. 20d, Old man with votive offering of large leg.

Perf. 12½x13½ (A365); 13x12 (A366)

1977, Mar. 15 Litho. Wmk. 252

1199 A365 50 l multi .25 .25
1200 A366 1d multi .25 .25
1201 A366 1.50d multi .25 .25
1202 A366 2d multi .25 .25
1203 A365 20d multi .25 .25
Nos. 1199-1203 (5) 1.25 1.25

International Rheumatism Year.

Winged Wheel, Modern Transportation — A367

1977, May 16 Litho. ***Perf. 14x13½***

1204 A367 7d multi .25 .25

European Conference of Ministers of Transport (E.C.M.T.), Athens, June 1-3.

Mani Castle, Vathia A368

Europa: 7d, Santorini, vert. 15d, Windmills on Lasithi plateau.

Perf. 14x13½, 13½x14

1977, May 16 Litho. Wmk. 252

1205 A368 5d multicolored .45 .25
1206 A368 7d multicolored .45 .35
1207 A368 15d multicolored 1.50 .50
Nos. 1205-1207 (3) 2.40 1.10

Alexandria Lighthouse, from Roman Coin — A369

Designs: 1d, Alexander places Homer's works into Achilles' tomb, fresco by Raphael. 1.50d, Alexander descends to the bottom of the sea, Flemish miniature. 3d, Alexander searching for water of life, Hindu plate. 7d, Alexander on horseback, Coptic carpet. 11d, Alexander hearing oracle that his days are numbered, Byzantine manuscript. 30d, Death of Alexander, Persian miniature. All designs include gold coin of Lysimachus with Alexander's head.

1977, July 23 ***Perf. 14x13***

1208 A369 50 l silver & multi .25 .25
1209 A369 1d silver & multi .25 .25
1210 A369 1.50d silver & multi .25 .25
1211 A369 3d silver & multi .25 .25
1212 A369 7d silver & multi .25 .25
1213 A369 11d silver & multi .25 .25
1214 A369 30d silver & multi .35 .35
Nos. 1208-1214 (7) 1.85 1.85

Cultural influence of Alexander the Great (356-323 B.C.), King of Macedonia.

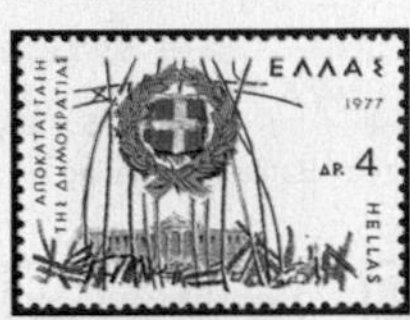

"Greece Rising Again" A370

People in Front of University A371

Greek Flags, Laurel, University A372

Perf. 13½x12½, 12x12½, 12½x12

1977, July 23 Unwmk.

1215 A370 4d multi .25 .25
1216 A371 7d multi .25 .25
1217 A372 20d multi .25 .25
Nos. 1215-1217 (3) .75 .75

Restoration of Democracy in Greece.

Archbishop Makarios, Map of Cyprus — A373

Design: 4d, Archbishop Makarios, vert.

Perf. 13x13½, 13½x13

1977, Sept. 10 Litho. Unwmk.

1218 A373 4d sepia & blk .25 .25
1219 A373 7d buff, brn & blk .25 .25

Archbishop Makarios (1913-1977), President of Cyprus.

Old Athens Post Office A374

Neo-Hellenic architecture: 1d, Institution for the Blind, Salonika. 1.50d, Townhall, Syros. 2d, National Bank of Greece, Piraeus. 5d, Byzantine Museum, Athens. 50d, Municipal Theater, Patras.

1977, Sept. 22 ***Perf. 13½x13***

1220 A374 50 l multi .25 .25
1221 A374 1d multi .25 .25
1222 A374 1.50d multi .25 .25
1223 A374 2d multi .25 .25
1224 A374 5d multi .25 .25
1225 A374 50d multi .35 .35
Nos. 1220-1225 (6) 1.60 1.60

Battle of Navarino, Lithograph — A375

Adm. Van Heyden, Sir Edward Codrington, Count de Rigny — A376

1977, Oct. 20 *Perf. 13½x13*

1226	A375 4d brn, buff & blk	.25	.25
1227	A376 7d multi	.25	.25

150th anniversary of Battle of Navarino.

Parthenon and Refinery — A377

Caryatid and Factories — A379

Fish and Birds Suffering from Pollution A378

Design: 7d, Birds and trees in polluted air.

1977, Oct. 20 *Perf. 13½x14, 14x13½*

1228	A377 3d org & blk	.25	.25
1229	A378 4d multi	.25	.25
1230	A378 7d multi	.25	.25
1231	A379 30d blk, gray & slate	.40	.40
	Nos. 1228-1231 (4)	1.15	1.15

Protection of the environment.

Map of Greece and Ships — A380

Globe and Swallows A381

Letter with Flags, Swallow A382

5d, Globe with Greek flag. 13d, World map showing dispersion of Greeks abroad.

1977, Dec. 15 *Perf. 13½x12½*

1232	A380 4d multi	.25	.25
1233	A380 5d multi	.25	.25
1234	A381 7d multi	.25	.25
1235	A382 11d multi	.25	.25
1236	A380 13d multi	.25	.25
	Nos. 1232-1236 (5)	1.25	1.25

Greeks living abroad.

Kalamata Harbor, by Constantine Parthenis — A383

Greek Paintings: 2.50d, Boats, Arsanas, by Spyros Papaloucas, vert. 4d, Santorini, by Constantine Maleas. 7d, The Engagement, by Nicolaus Gyzis. 11d, Woman with Straw Hat, by Nicolaus Lytras, vert. 15d, "Spring" (nude), by Georgio Iacovidis.

1977, Dec. 15 *Perf. 13½x13, 13x13½*

1237	A383 1.50d yel & multi	.25	.25
1238	A383 2.50d yel & multi	.25	.25
1239	A383 4d yel & multi	.25	.25
1240	A383 7d yel & multi	.25	.25
1241	A383 11d yel & multi	.25	.25
1242	A383 15d yel & multi	.25	.25
	Nos. 1237-1242 (6)	1.50	1.50

Ebenus Cretica — A384

Greek Flora: 2.50d, Dwarf lily. 3d, Campanula oreadum. 4d, Tiger lily. 7d, Viola delphinantha. 25d, Paeonia rhodia.

1978, Mar. 30 Litho. *Perf. 13x13½*

1243	A384 1.50d multi	.25	.25
1244	A384 2.50d multi	.25	.25
1245	A384 3d multi	.25	.25
1246	A384 4d multi	.25	.25
1247	A384 7d multi	.25	.25
1248	A384 25d multi	.30	.25
	Nos. 1243-1248 (6)	1.55	1.50

Postrider, Cancellation A385

5d, S.S. Maximilianos & Hermes Head. 7d, 19th cent. mail train & #122. 30d, Mailmen on motorcycles & #1062.

1978, May 15 *Perf. 13½x12½*

1249	A385 4d buff & multi	.25	.25
1250	A385 5d buff & multi	.25	.25
1251	A385 7d buff & multi	.25	.25
1252	A385 30d buff & multi	.25	.25
a.	Souvenir sheet of 4	1.00	1.00
	Nos. 1249-1252 (4)	1.00	1.00

150th anniv. of Greek postal service.

No. 1252a issued Sept. 25, contains Nos. 1249-1252 in slightly changed colors. Sold for 60d.

Lighting Olympic Flame, Olympia — A386

Start of 100-meter Race — A387

1978, May 15 *Perf. 13x14*

1253	A386 7d multi	.40	.25
1254	A387 13d multi	.85	.40

80th session of International Olympic Committee, Athens, May 10-21.

Europa Issue

St. Sophia, Salonica A388

Lysicrates Monument, Athens — A389

1978, May 15 *Perf. 13x14, 14x13*

1255	A388 4d multi	*.75*	.30
1256	A389 7d multi	*1.50*	.70

Aristotle, Roman Bust — A390

School of Athens, by Raphael — A391

Map of Chalcidice, Base of Statue from Attalus Arcade A392

Aristotle the Wise, Byzantine Fresco, St. George's Church, Ioannina A393

Perf. 13x13½, 13½x14 (20d)

1978, July 10 Litho.

1257	A390 2d multi	.25	.25
1258	A391 4d multi	.25	.25
1259	A392 7d multi	.25	.25
1260	A393 20d multi	.25	.25
	Nos. 1257-1260 (4)	1.00	1.00

Aristotle (384-322 B.C.), systematic philosopher.

Rotary Emblem A394

Surgeons Operating — A395

Ugo Foscolo, View of Zante — A396

Hellenistic Bronze Head — A397

Charioteer's Hand, Delphi — A398

Wright Brothers' Plane, Daedalus and Icarus — A399

1978, Sept. 21 Litho. *Perf. 12½*

1261	A394 1d multi	.25	.25
1262	A395 1.50d multi	.25	.25
1263	A396 2.50d multi	.25	.25
1264	A397 5d multi	.25	.25
1265	A398 7d multi	.40	.30
1266	A399 13d multi	.40	.40
	Nos. 1261-1266 (6)	1.80	1.70

Rotary in Greece, 50th anniv. (1d); 11th Greek Surgery Cong., Salonica (1.50d); Ugo Foscolo (1778-1827), Italian writer (2.50d); European Convention on Human Rights, 25th anniv. (5d); 2nd Conf. of Ministers of Culture of the Council of Europe member countries, Athens, Oct. 23-27 (7d); 75th anniv. of 1st powered flight (13d).

Poor Woman and her 5 Children A400

Scenes from Fairy Tale "The 12 Months": 3d, The poor woman and the 12 months. 4d, The poor woman and the gold coins. 20d, Punishment of the greedy woman.

1978, Nov. 6 Litho. *Perf. 13½x13*

1267	A400 2d multi	.25	.25
1268	A400 3d multi	.25	.25
1269	A400 4d multi	.25	.25
1270	A400 20d multi	.25	.25
	Nos. 1267-1270 (4)	1.00	1.00

"Transplants" A401

The Miracle of St. Anarghiri A402

1978, Nov. 6 *Perf. 12½x13½*

1271	A401 4d multi	.25	.25
1272	A402 10d multi	.25	.25

Advancements in organ transplants.

Cruiser A403

New and Old Greek Naval Ships: 1d, Torpedo boats. 2.50d, Submarine Papanicolis. 4d, Battleship Psara. 5d, Sailing ship "Madonna of Hydra." 7d, Byzantine corvette. 50d, Archaic trireme.

1978, Dec. 15 Litho. *Perf. 13½x12*

1273	A403 50 l multi	.25	.25
1274	A403 1d multi	.25	.25
1275	A403 2.50d multi	.25	.25
1276	A403 4d multi	.25	.25

1277	A403	5d multi	.25	.25
1278	A403	7d multi	.25	.25
1279	A403	50d multi	.45	.45
		Nos. 1273-1279 (7)	1.95	1.95

Cadet Officer, Military School, Nauplia A404

Cadet Officers' School Emblem — A405

Design: 10d, Cadet Officers Military School, Athens, Cadet's uniform, 1978.

1978, Dec. 15 ***Perf. 13½x12, 12x13½***

1280	A404	1.50d multi	.25	.25
1281	A405	2d multi	.25	.25
1282	A404	10d multi	.25	.25
		Nos. 1280-1282 (3)	.75	.75

Cadet Officers Military School, 150th anniv.

Virgin and Child — A406

Baptism of Christ — A407

Designs from 16th century icon stands in Stavronikita Monastery.

1978, Dec. 15 ***Perf. 13x13½***

1283	A406	4d multi	.25	.25
1284	A407	7d multi	.25	.25

Christmas 1978.

Map of Greece A408

1978, Dec. 28 ***Perf. 14x13***

1285	A408	7d multi	.25	.25
1286	A408	11d multi	.25	.25
1287	A408	13d multi	.25	.25
		Nos. 1285-1287 (3)	.75	.75

Kitsos Tzavellas — A409

Souli Castle A410

10d, Fighting Souliots. 20d, Fight of Zalongo.

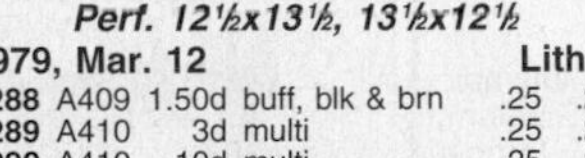

Perf. 12½x13½, 13½x12½

1979, Mar. 12 **Litho.**

1288	A409	1.50d buff, blk & brn	.25	.25
1289	A410	3d multi	.25	.25
1290	A410	10d multi	.25	.25
1291	A409	20d buff, blk & brn	.25	.25
		Nos. 1288-1291 (4)	1.00	1.00

Struggle of the Souliots, 18th century fighters for freedom from Turkey.

Cycladic Figure from Amorgos — A411

1979, Apr. 26 **Litho.** ***Perf. 12x13½***

1292	A411	20d multi	.35	.35

Aegean art.

Mailmen from Crete — A412

Europa: 7d, Rural mailman on horseback, Crete.

1979, May 11 ***Perf. 13½x14***

1293	A412	4d multi	*1.00*	.25
1294	A412	7d multi	*1.00*	.55
a.		Pair, #1293-1294	*2.25*	*2.25*

Nicolas Scoufas A413

Basketball A415

Locomotives — A414

Mene Psarianosi Symeonidis Fossil A416

Temple of Hephaestus and Byzantine Church A417

Victory of Paeonius Statue, Flags of Balkan Countries A418

1979, May 12 ***Perf. 13x14, 14x13***

1295	A413	1.50d multi	.25	.25
1296	A414	2d multi	.25	.25
1297	A415	3d multi	.25	.25
1298	A416	4d multi	.25	.25
1299	A417	10d multi	.25	.25
1300	A418	20d multi	.35	.35
		Nos. 1295-1300 (6)	1.60	1.60

Nicolas Scoufas (1779-1818), founder of (patriotic) Friendly Society; Piraeus-Athens-to-the-frontier railroad, 75th anniv.; European Basketball Championship; 7th Intl. Cong. for the Study of the Neocene Period in the Mediterranean; Balkan Tourist Year 1979; 50 years of track and field competitions in Balkan countries.

Wheat with Members' Flags, Greek Coins — A419

European Parliament, Strasbourg — A420

Perf. 13x14, 14x13

1979, May 28 **Litho.**

1301	A419	7d multi	.25	.25
1302	A420	30d multi	.35	.35

Greece's entry into European Economic Community and Parliament.

Statue of a Girl, IYC Emblem — A421

Intl. Year of the Child: 8d, Girl & pigeons. 20d, Mother & Children, painting by Iacovides.

1979, June 27 **Litho.** ***Perf. 13x14***

1303	A421	5d multi	.25	.25
1304	A421	8d multi	.25	.25
1305	A421	20d multi	.25	.25
		Nos. 1303-1305 (3)	.75	.75

Philip II, Bust — A422

Designs: 8d, Golden wreath. 10d, Copper vessel. 14d, Golden casket, horiz. 18d, Silver ewer. 20d, Golden quiver (detail). 30d, Gold and iron cuirass.

Perf. 13½x14, 14x13½

1979, Sept. 15 **Litho.**

1306	A422	6d multi	.25	.25
1307	A422	8d multi	.25	.25
1308	A422	10d multi	.25	.25
1309	A422	14d multi	.25	.25
1310	A422	18d multi	.25	.25
1311	A422	20d multi	.25	.25
1312	A422	30d multi	.40	.40
		Nos. 1306-1312 (7)	1.90	1.90

Archaeological finds from Vergina, Macedonia.

Purple Heron — A423

Protected Birds: 8d, Gull. 10d, Falcon, horiz. 14d, Kingfisher, horiz. 20d, Pelican. 25d, White-tailed sea eagle.

1979, Oct. 15

1313	A423	6d multi	.25	.25
1314	A423	8d multi	.25	.25
1315	A423	10d multi	.25	.25
1316	A423	14d multi	.25	.25
1317	A423	20d multi	.25	.25
1318	A423	25d multi	.75	.60
		Nos. 1313-1318 (6)	2.00	1.85

Council of Europe wildlife and natural habitat protection campaign.

Agricultural Bank A424

St. Cosmas — A425

Basil the Great — A426

Balkan Countries, Magnifier — A427

Aristotelis Valaoritis — A428

Golfer A429

Hippocrates A430

Parliament in Session A431

Perf. 14x13½, 13½x14

1979, Nov. 24 **Litho.**

1319	A424	3d multi	.25	.25
1320	A425	4d multi	.25	.25
1321	A426	6d multi	.25	.25
1322	A427	8d multi	.25	.25
1323	A427	10d multi, horiz.	.25	.25
1324	A428	12d multi	.25	.25
1325	A429	14d multi	.25	.25
1326	A430	18d multi	.30	.30
1327	A431	25d multi	.40	.40
		Nos. 1319-1327 (9)	2.45	2.45

Agricultural Bank of Greece, 50th anniv.; Cosmas the Aetolian (1714-79), Greek missionary and martyr; Basil the Great (330-379

Archbishop of Caesarea; Balkanfila, Balkan Stamp Exhibition, Athens, Nov. 24-Dec. 2; Aristotelis Valaoritis (1824-79), Greek poet; 27th World Golf Championship, Nov. 8-11; Intl. Hippocratic Foundation of Cos; Greek Parliament, 104th anniv.

Parnassus — A432

Tempe Valley A433

2d, Melos. 4d, Vikos Gorge. 5d, Missolonghi Salt Lake. 6d, Louros Aqueduct. 7d, Samothrace. 8d, Sithonia-Halkidiki. 10d, Samarias Gorge, vert. 12d, Siphnos. 14d, Kyme. 18d, Ios. 20d, Thasos. 30d, Paros. 50d, Cephalonia.

Perf. 12½x13½, 13½x12½

1979, Dec. 15 **Litho.**

1328 A432 50 l shown .25 .25
1329 A433 1d shown .25 .25
1330 A432 2d multicolored .25 .25
1331 A432 4d multicolored .25 .25
1332 A433 5d multicolored .25 .25
1333 A432 6d multicolored .25 .25
1334 A432 7d multicolored .25 .25
1335 A433 8d multicolored .25 .25
1336 A433 10d multicolored .25 .25
1337 A432 12d multicolored .25 .25
1338 A433 14d multicolored .25 .25
1339 A432 18d multicolored .25 .25
1340 A432 20d multicolored .25 .25
1341 A433 30d multicolored .30 .25
1342 A432 50d multicolored .50 .40
Nos. 1328-1342 (15) 4.05 3.90

Byzantine Castle of Thessalonica A434

4d, Aegosthena Castle, vert. 8d, Cave of Perama Ioannina, vert. 10d, Cave of Dyros, Mani, vert. 14d, Arta Bridge. 20d, Kalogiros Bridge, Epirus.

Perf. 12½x14, 14x12½

1980, Mar. 15 **Litho.**

1343 A434 4d multi .25 .25
1344 A434 6d multi .25 .25
1345 A434 8d multi .25 .25
1346 A434 10d multi .25 .25
1347 A434 14d multi .25 .25
1348 A434 20d multi .25 .25
Nos. 1343-1348 (6) 1.50 1.50

Gate of Galerius A435

1980, Mar. 15

1349 A435 8d multi .25 .25

1st Hellenic Congress of Nephrology, Thessalonica, Mar. 20-22.

Solar System A436

Design: 10d, Temple of Hera, Aristarchus' theory and diagram.

1980, May 5 **Litho.** *Perf. 13½x12½*

1350 A436 10d multi .25 .25
1351 A436 20d multi .40 .35

Aristarchus of Samos, first astronomer to discover heliocentric theory of universe, 2300th birth anniv.; Intl. Scientific Congress on Aristarchus, Samos, June 17-19.

Maria Callas (1923-1977), Opera Singer A437

Europa: 8d, Georges Seferis (1900-1971), writer and diplomat.

1980, May 5

1352 A437 8d multi *.40* .40
1353 A437 14d multi *1.60* 1.20

Energy Conservation Manual A438

20d, Candle in bulb, vert.

Perf. 13½x12½, 12½x13½

1980, May 5

1354 A438 8d shown .25 .25
1355 A438 20d multicolored .30 .30

Firemen A439

St. Demetrius, Angel, Fresco — A440

Ancient Vase, Olives — A442

Soldiers Marching through Crete — A441

Federation Emblem, Newspaper A443

Constantinos Ikonomos A444

1980, July 14 **Litho.** *Perf. 12½*

1356 A439 4d multi .25 .25
1357 A440 6d multi .25 .25
1358 A441 8d multi .25 .25
1359 A442 10d multi .25 .25
1360 A443 14d multi .25 .25
1361 A444 20d multi .40 .40
Nos. 1356-1361 (6) 1.65 1.65

Fire Brigade, 50th anniv.; St. Demetrius, 1700th birth anniv.; Therissos Revolution, 75th anniv.; 2nd Intl. Olive Oil Year; Intl. Federation of Journalists, 15th Cong., Athens, May 12-16; Constantinos Ikonomos (1780-1857), writer and revolutionary.

Olympic Stadium, Temple Coin, Olympia A445

Olympic Rings and: 14d, Stadium and coin of Delphi 18d, Epidaurus theater, coin of Olympia 20d, Rhodes Stadium, Cos coin. 50d, Panathenean Stadium; 1st Olympic Games medal.

1980, Aug. 11 **Litho.** *Perf. 13½x13*

1362 A445 8d multi .25 .25
1363 A445 14d multi .35 .30
1364 A445 18d multi .25 .25
1365 A445 20d multi .30 .25
1366 A445 50d multi .65 .55
Nos. 1362-1366 (5) 1.80 1.60

22nd Summer Olympic Games, Moscow, July 19-Aug. 3.

Asbestos A446

Perf. 13½x12½

1980, Sept. 22 **Litho.**

1367 A446 6d shown .25 .25
1368 A446 8d Gypsum, vert. .25 .25
1369 A446 10d Copper ore .25 .25
1370 A446 14d Barite, vert. .35 .35
1371 A446 18d Chromite .25 .25
1372 A446 20d Mixed sulphides, vert. .25 .25
1373 A446 30d Bauxite, vert. .35 .35
Nos. 1367-1373 (7) 1.95 1.95

Tow Truck — A447

Air Force Jet — A448

Airplane and Hangar A449

Ships in Port A450

Students' Association Headquarters A451

1980, Oct. 31 **Litho.** *Perf. 12½*

1374 A447 6d multi .25 .25
1375 A448 8d multi .25 .25
1376 A449 12d multi .25 .25
1377 A450 20d multi .35 .30
1378 A451 25d multi .40 .40
Nos. 1374-1378 (5) 1.50 1.45

Road Assistance Service of Automobile and Touring Club of Greece, 20th anniv.; Air Force, 50th anniv.; Flyers' Club of Thessaloniki, 50th anniv.; Piraeus Port Organization, 50th anniv.; Association for Macedon ian Studies, 40th anniv.

Madonna and Child, by Theodore Poulakis — A452

Christmas 1980: He is Happy Thanks to You, by Theodore Poulakis. No. 1381a has continuous design.

1980, Dec. 10 *Perf. 13½*

1379 6d multi .25 .25
1380 14d multi .25 .25
1381 20d multi .30 .30
a. A452 Strip of 3, #1379-1381 .75 .75

Vegetables for Export — A453

1981, Mar. 16 **Litho.** *Perf. 12½*

1382 A453 9d shown .25 .25
1383 A453 17d Fruits .25 .25
1384 A453 20d Cotton .25 .25
1385 A453 25d Marble .40 .40
Nos. 1382-1385 (4) 1.15 1.15

Europa Issue

Kira Maria Folk Dance, Alexandria — A454

17d, Cretan Sousta (dance).

1981, May 4 **Litho.** *Perf. 14x13*

1386 A454 12d shown *.50* .25
1387 A454 17d multicolored *1.00* .75

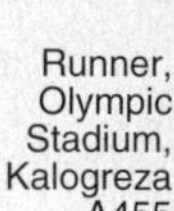

Runner, Olympic Stadium, Kalogreza A455

1981, May 4

1388 A455 12d shown .25 .25
1389 A455 17d Runners, Europe .40 .40

13th European Athletic Championship, Athens, 1982.

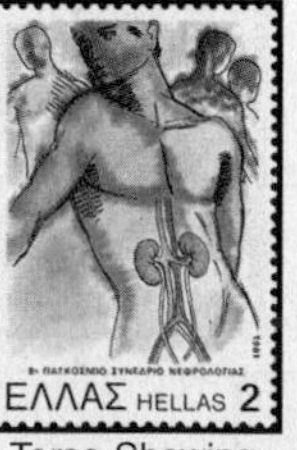

Torso Showing Kidneys A456

Sky Diver and Airplanes A457

Views of Thessaly and Epirus — A458

Oil Rig and Map of Thassos Island — A460

Vase with Painted Eyes A459

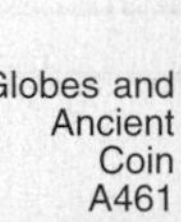

Globes and Ancient Coin A461

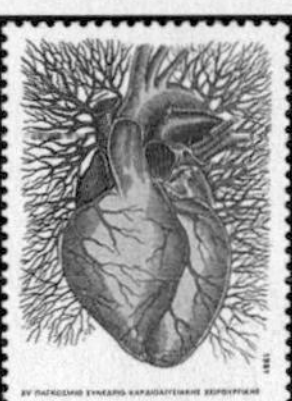

Heart and Vessels — A462

Perf. 13½x14, 14x13½

1981, May 22 **Litho.**

1390 A456 2d multi .25 .25
1391 A457 3d multi .25 .25
1392 A458 6d multi .25 .25
1393 A459 9d multi .25 .25
1394 A460 12d multi .25 .25
1395 A461 21d multi .50 .45
1396 A462 40d multi .75 .75
Nos. 1390-1396 (7) 2.50 2.45

8th Intl. Nephrology Conf., Athens, June 7-12; Greek National Air Club, 50th anniv.; Intl. Historical Symposium, Volos, Sept. 27-30; Greek Ophthalmological Society, 50th anniv.; inauguration of oil production at Thassos Island; World Assoc. for Intl. Relations, Athens, 2nd anniv.; 15th Intl. Cardiovascular Surgery Conference, Athens, Sept. 6-10.

Cockles A463

1981, June 30 **Litho.** ***Perf. 14x13½***

1397 A463 4d shown .25 .25
1398 A463 5d Parrot fish .25 .25
1399 A463 12d Painted comber .25 .25
1400 A463 15d Common dentex .25 .25
1401 A463 17d Parnassius apollo .50 .30
1402 A463 50d Colias hyale 1.10 .90
Nos. 1397-1402 (6) 2.60 2.20

Bell Tower, Epirus — A464

Altar Gate, St. Paraskevi's Church — A465

Bell Towers and Wood Altar Gates (Iconostases): 9d, Pelion, horiz. 12d, Church of Sts. Constantine and Helen, Epirus. 17d, St. Nicolas Church, Velvendos, horiz. 30d, St. Jacob icon, Church Museum, Alexandroupolis. 40d, St. Nicholas Church, Makrinitsa.

1981, Sept. 30 **Litho.**

1403 A464 4d multi .25 .25
1404 A465 6d multi .25 .25
1405 A465 9d multi .25 .25
1406 A464 12d multi .25 .25
1407 A465 17d multi .25 .25
1408 A465 30d multi .35 .35
1409 A465 40d multi .60 .60
Nos. 1403-1409 (7) 2.20 2.20

European Urban Renaissance Year — A466

St. Simeon, Archbishop of Thessalonica A467

Promotion of Breastfeeding A468

Gina Bachauer, Pianist, 5th Death Anniv. A469

Constantine Broumidis, Artist, Death Centenary A470

Sesquicentennial of Greek Banknotes — A471

Perf. 14x13½, 13½x14

1981, Nov. 20 **Litho.**

1410 A466 3d multi .25 .25
1411 A467 9d multi .25 .25
1412 A468 12d multi .25 .25
1413 A469 17d multi .40 .25
1414 A470 21d multi .45 .25
1415 A471 50d multi .75 .60
Nos. 1410-1415 (6) 2.35 1.85

Old Parliament Building, Athens A472

Angelos Sikelianos (1884-1951), Poet A473

Harilaos Tricoupis, Politician, Birth Sesquicentennial A474

Aegean Islands Exhib., Rhodes, Athens — A475

Petralona Cave and Skull — A477

Olympic Airlines, 25th Anniv. A476

Perf. 13½x12½, 12½x13½

1982, Mar. 15 **Litho.**

1416 A472 2d multi .25 .25
1417 A473 9d multi .25 .25
1418 A474 15d multi .25 .25
1419 A475 21d multi .40 .40
1420 A476 30d multi .65 .55
1421 A477 50d multi 1.10 1.00
Nos. 1416-1421 (6) 2.90 2.70

Historical and Ethnological Society centennial (2d); 3rd European Anthropology Congress, Halkidiki, Sept. (50d).

Europa 1982 — A478

21d, Battle of Marathon, 490 BC. 30d, 1826 Revolution.

1982, May 10 **Litho.** ***Perf. 13½x14***

1422 A478 21d multicolored *2.00* 1.00
1423 A478 30d multicolored *4.00* 2.00

13th European Athletic Championships, Athens — A479

21d, Pole vaulting, horiz. 25d, Running. 40d, Sports, horiz.

1982, May 10 ***Perf. 14x13½, 13½x14***

1424 A479 21d multicolored .30 .25
1425 A479 25d multicolored .40 .25
1426 A479 40d multicolored .80 .65
Nos. 1424-1426 (3) 1.50 1.15

Byzantine Book Illustrations A480

4d, Gospel book heading. 6d, Illuminated "E," vert. 12d, Illuminated "T," vert. 15d, Gospel reading canon table, vert. 80d, Zoology book heading.

Perf. 13½x12½, 12½x13½

1982, June 26 **Litho.**

1427 A480 4d multicolored .25 .25
1428 A480 6d multicolored .25 .25
1429 A480 12d multicolored .25 .25
1430 A480 15d multicolored .25 .25
1431 A480 80d multicolored 1.50 1.25
Nos. 1427-1431 (5) 2.50 2.25

Georgios Karaiskakis (1782-1827), Liberation Hero — A481

Designs: 12d, Camp in Piraeus, by von Krazeisen. 50d, Meditating.

1982, Sept. 20 **Litho.** ***Perf. 13x13½***

1432 A481 12d multicolored .40 .25
1433 A481 50d multicolored .80 .50

Amnesty Intl. — A482

1982, Sept. 20 ***Perf. 13x14***

1434 A482 15d Vigil .45 .25
1435 A482 75d Prisoners 1.25 1.00

Natl. Resistance Movement, 1941-44 A483

Designs: 1d, Demonstration of Mar. 24, 1942. 2d, Sacrifice of Inhabitants of Kalavrita, by S. Vasiliou. 5d, Resistance Fighters in Thrace, by A. Tassos. 9d, The Start of Resistance in Crete, by P. Gravalos. 12d, Partisan Men and Women, by P. Gravalos. 21d, Blowing up a Bridge, by A. Tassos. 30d, Fighters at a Barricade, by G. Sikeliotis. 50d, The Fight in Northern Greece, by B. Katraki, 5d, 9d, 12d, 21d vert.

1982, Nov. 8 **Litho.** ***Perf. 12½***

1436 A483 1d multi .25 .25
1437 A483 2d multi .25 .25
1438 A483 5d multi .25 .25
1439 A483 9d multi .25 .25
1440 A483 12d multi .25 .25
1441 A483 21d multi .25 .25
a. Souv. sheet, 5d, 9d, 12d, 21d 1.75 1.75
1442 A483 30d multi .50 .35
1443 A483 50d multi 1.25 .55
a. Souv. sheet, 1d, 2d, 30d, 50d 2.00 2.00
Nos. 1436-1443 (8) 3.25 2.40

Christmas 1982 — A484

Designs: Various Byzantine Nativity basreliefs, Byzantine Museum.

1982, Dec. 6 **Litho.** ***Perf. 13½x12½***

1444 A484 9d multi .25 .25
1445 A484 21d multi .30 .25
a. Pair, #1444-1445 .65 .65

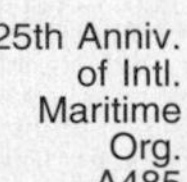

25th Anniv. of Intl. Maritime Org. A485

Ship Figureheads: 11d, Ares, Tsamados. 15d, Ares, Miaoulis, vert. 18d, Female figure, vert. 25d, Spetses, Bouboulina, vert. 40d, Epameinondas, K. Babas, vert. 50d, Carteria.

1983, Mar. 14 ***Perf. 14x13½, 13½x14***

1446 A485 11d multicolored .25 .30
1447 A485 15d multicolored .25 .2
1448 A485 18d multicolored .25 .2

1449 A485 25d multicolored .40 .25
1450 A485 40d multicolored .60 .35
1451 A485 50d multicolored 1.25 1.00
Nos. 1446-1451 (6) 3.00 2.40

Postal Code Inauguration A486

1983, Mar. 14 Litho. *Perf. 12½*
1452 A486 15d Cover, map .25 .25
1453 A486 25d Hermes, post horn, vert. .45 .40

Rowing A487

18d, Water skiing, vert. 27d, Wind surfing, vert. 50d, Skiers on chairlift, vert. 80d, Skiing.

1983, Apr. 28 *Perf. 14x13, 13x14*
1454 A487 15d shown .25 .25
1455 A487 18d multicolored .35 .25
1456 A487 27d multicolored .65 .60
1457 A487 50d multicolored .65 .60
1458 A487 80d multicolored 2.00 1.75
Nos. 1454-1458 (5) 3.90 3.45

Europa Issue

Acropolis — A488

Archimedes and His Hydrostatic Principle — A489

Perf. 12½x13½, 13x13½
1983, Apr. 28 Litho.
1459 A488 25d multi *2.00* 1.00
1460 A489 80d multi *4.00* 3.00

Marinos Antypas (1873-1907), Farmers' Movement Leader — A490

Designs: 9d, Nicholas Plastiras (1883-1953), prime minister. 15d, George Papandreou (1888-1968), statesman. 20d, Constantine Cavafy (1863-1933), poet. 27d, Nikos Kazantzakis (1883-1957), writer. 32d, Manolis Calomiris (1883-1962), composer. 40d, George Papanicolaou (1883-1962), medical researcher. 50d, Despina Achladioti (1890-1982), nationalist.

1983, July 11 Litho. *Perf. 13½x14*
1461 A490 6d multi .25 .25
1462 A490 9d multi .25 .25
1463 A490 15d multi .25 .25
1464 A490 20d multi .30 .25
1465 A490 27d multi .35 .25
1466 A490 32d multi .60 .30
1467 A490 40d multi .70 .30
1468 A490 50d multi .85 .60
Nos. 1461-1468 (8) 3.55 2.45

Portrait Bust — A491

1983, Sept. 26 Litho. *Perf. 13½x13*
1469 A491 50d multi 1.00 .50

1st Intl. Conf. on the Works of Democritus (Philosopher, 460-370 BC), Xanthe, Oct.

A492

1983, Nov. 17 Litho. *Perf. 13*
1470 A492 15d Poster .25 .25
1471 A492 30d Flight from school .45 .35

Polytechnic School Uprising, 1st anniv.

The Deification of Homer — A493

Homer Inspired Artworks: 3d, The Abduction of Helen by Paris, horiz. 4d, The Wooden Horse, horiz. 5d, Achilles Throwing Dice with Ajax, horiz. 6d, Achilles. 10d, Hector Receiving His Arms from His Parents. 14d, Single-handed Battle Between Ajax and Hector, horiz. 15d, Priam Requesting the Body of Hector, horiz. 20d, The Blinding of Polyphemus. 27d, Ulysses Escaping from Polyphemus' Cave, horiz. 30d, Ulysses Meeting with Nausica. 32d, Ulysses on the Island of the Sirens, horiz. 50d, Ulysses Slaying the Suitors, horiz. 75d, The Heroes of the Iliad, horiz. 100d, Homer.

1983, Dec. 19 Litho. *Perf. 13*
1472 A493 2d multi .25 .25
1473 A493 3d multi .25 .25
1474 A493 4d multi .25 .25
1475 A493 5d multi .25 .25
1476 A493 6d multi .25 .25
1477 A493 10d multi .25 .25
1478 A493 14d multi .25 .25
1479 A493 15d multi .25 .25
1480 A493 20d multi .25 .25
1481 A493 27d multi .30 .25
1482 A493 30d multi .40 .25
1483 A493 32d multi .50 .25
1484 A493 50d multi .60 .25
1485 A493 75d multi 1.25 .60
1486 A493 100d multi 1.90 .80
Nos. 1472-1486 (15) 7.20 4.65

Horse's Head from Chariot of Seline A494

Horsemen and Heroes A495

1984, Mar. 15 Litho. *Perf. 14½x14*
1487 A494 14d shown .25 .25
1488 A494 15d Dionysus .35 .25
1489 A494 20d Hestia, Dione, Aphrodite .65 .30
1490 A494 27d Ilissus .85 .30
1491 A494 32d Lapith, centaur 1.50 .75
Nos. 1487-1491 (5) 3.60 1.85

Souvenir Sheet

Perf. 13x13½
1492 Sheet of 4 4.50 4.50
a. A495 15d multi .75 .75
b. A495 21d multi .90 .90
c. A495 27d multi 1.00 1.00
d. A495 32d multi 1.25 1.25

Marble from the Parthenon. No. 1492 sold for 107d.

Nos. 1492a-1492b and 1492c-1492d have continuous designs.

Nos. 1492a-1492b, Equestrian scene. Nos. 1492c-1492d, Athenian Elders.

Europa (1959-84) A496

1984, Apr. 30 Litho. *Perf. 14x13½*
1493 A496 15d multi *.75* *.40*
1494 A496 27d multi *1.75* *1.00*
a. Pair, #1493-1494 *3.25* *3.25*

1984 Summer Olympics — A497

Designs: 14d, Ancient Olympic stadium crypt. 15d, Athletes training. 20d, Broad jump, discus thrower. 32d, Athletes, diff. 80d, Stadium, Demetrius Bikelos, poet, organizer of 1896 Athens games.

1984, Apr. 30 *Perf. 13½x14*
1495 A497 14d multi .30 .25
1496 A497 15d multi .40 .35
1497 A497 20d multi .50 .45
1498 A497 32d multi .75 .65
1499 A497 80d multi 1.75 1.40
a. Strip of 5, #1495-1499 4.50 4.50

Also issued in booklets.

Turkish Invasion of Cyprus, 10th Anniv. — A498

1984, July 10 Litho. *Perf. 13*
1500 A498 20d Tank, map, vert. .40 .25
1501 A498 32d Map, barbed wire .60 .50

Also issued in booklets.

Greek Railway Centenary A499

15d, Pelion. 20d, Papadia Bridge, vert. 30d, Piraeus-Peloponnese. 50d, Cogwheel Calavryta, vert.

Perf. 13x13½, 13½x13
1984, July 20 Litho.
1502 A499 15d multicolored .65 .35
1503 A499 20d multicolored 2.00 1.40
1504 A499 30d multicolored .65 .35
1505 A499 50d multicolored 2.00 1.40
Nos. 1502-1505 (4) 5.30 3.50

Sesquicentenary of Athens as Capital City — A500

15d, 4d silver coin, 5th cent. BC, city plan, vert. 100d, Views of ancient & modern Athens.

Perf. 13½x13, 13x13½
1984, Oct. 12 Litho.
1506 A500 15d multi .40 .25
1507 A500 100d multi 1.60 1.00

10th Anniv. of Democratic Govt. — A501

1984, Oct. 12 Litho. *Perf. 13x13½*
1508 A501 95d "10" on flag 1.75 .75

Christmas 1984 — A502

Scenes from 18th cent. icon by Athanasios Tountas: 14d, Annunciation. 20d, Nativity. 25d, Presentation in the Temple. 32d, Baptism of Christ.

1984, Dec. 6 Litho. *Perf. 13½x13*
1509 A502 14d multicolored .50 .30
1510 A502 20d multicolored .50 .30
1511 A502 25d multicolored .50 .40
1512 A502 32d multicolored .50 .50
a. Block of 4, #1509-1512 2.50 2.50

Also issued in booklets.

Runner A503

Palais des Sports A504

Perf. 13, 13x13½ (#1515)
1985, Mar. 1 Litho.
1513 A503 12d shown .25 .25
1514 A503 15d Shot put .35 .25
1515 A504 20d shown .35 .25
1516 A503 25d Hurdles .70 .25
1517 A503 80d Women's high jump 1.40 .80
Nos. 1513-1517 (5) 3.05 1.80

European Indoor Athletics Championships, Palais des Sports, New Phaleron.

Europa 1985 — A505

CEPT emblem and: 27d, Musical contest between Marsyas and Apollo. 80d, Dimitris

Mitropoulos (1896-1960) and Nikos Skalkottas (1904-1949), composers.

1985, Apr. 29 ***Perf. 14x14½***

1518	A505	27d multi	*.80*	.50
1519	A505	80d multi	*1.50*	1.00

Exist se-tenant as strip of 3, 27d+80d+27d in booklets.

Melos Catacombs, A.D. 2nd Cent., Trypete A506

15d, Niche. 20d, Altar, Central Gallery. 100d, Catacombs.

1985, Apr. 29 ***Perf. 14½x14***

1520	A506	15d multicolored	.25	.25
1521	A506	20d multicolored	.50	.25
1522	A506	100d multicolored	1.60	1.10
		Nos. 1520-1522 (3)	2.35	1.60

Republic of Cyprus, 25th Anniv. — A507

1985, June 24 ***Perf. 13x13½***

1523	A507	32d Map of Cyprus, urn	1.00	.50

Coin of King Cassander (315 B.C.), Personification of Salonika, Galerius Era Bas-relief — A508

Sts. Demetrius and Methodius, Mosaics — A509

Designs: 15d, Emperor sacrificing at Altar, Arch of Galerius, Roman era. 20d, Eastern walls of Salonika, Byzantine era. 32d, Houses in the Upper City. 50d, Liberation of Salonika by the Greek Army, 1912. 80d, German occupation, 1941-44, the Old Mosque. 95d, View of city, Trade Fair grounds, Aristotelian University tower.

Perf. 14½x14 (A508), 14x14½ (A509)

1985, June 24

1524	A508	1d multi	.25	.25
1525	A509	5d multi	.35	.25
1526	A508	15d multi	.40	.25
1527	A508	20d multi	.40	.25
1528	A508	32d multi	.45	.25
1529	A508	50d multi	.60	.25
1530	A508	80d multi	1.25	.50
1531	A509	95d multi	1.75	1.50
		Nos. 1524-1531 (8)	5.45	3.50

Salonika City, 2300th anniv. Aristotelian University, Trade Fair, 60th annivs.

Athenian Cultural Heritage A510

Ancient art and architecture: 15d, Democracy Crowning the City, bas-relief from a column, Ancient Agora of Athens, vert. 20d, Mosaic pavement of tritons, nereids, dolphins, etc., Roman baths at Hieratus, Isthmia, A.D. 2nd cent. 32d, Angel, fresco, Grotto of Pentheli, A.D. 13th cent., vert. 80d, Capodistrian University, Athens.

1985, Oct. 7 ***Perf. 13½x13, 13x13½***

1532	A510	15d multi	.25	.25
1533	A510	20d multi	.25	.25
1534	A510	32d multi	.65	.30
1535	A510	80d multi	1.40	1.10
		Nos. 1532-1535 (4)	2.55	1.90

Intl. Youth Year — A511

UN 40th Anniv. — A512

15d, Children, olive wreath. 25d, Children, doves. 27d, UN General Assembly, dove. No. 1539, 100d, UN building, emblem.

No. 1540, Girl crowned with flowers, Stadium of Peace and Friendship, Athens.

1985, Oct. 7 ***Perf. 14x14½***

1536	A511	15d multicolored	.25	.25
1537	A511	25d multicolored	.45	.25
1538	A512	27d multicolored	.55	.25
1539	A512	100d multicolored	1.60	1.50
		Nos. 1536-1539 (4)	2.85	2.25

Souvenir Sheet

1985, Nov. 22 ***Perf. 14x13***

1540	A511	100d multicolored	2.00	2.00

No. 1540 contains one 43x47mm stamp.

Pontic Hellenism Cultural Reformation A513

12d, Folk dance. 15d, Our Lady Soumela Monastery. 27d, Folk costumes, vert. 32d, Trapezus High School. 80d, Sinope Castle.

Perf. 14x12½, 12½x14

1985, Dec. 9 **Litho.**

1541	A513	12d multicolored	.25	.25
1542	A513	15d multicolored	.25	.25
1543	A513	27d multicolored	.45	.30
1544	A513	32d multicolored	.45	.30
1545	A513	80d multicolored	1.10	1.00
		Nos. 1541-1545 (5)	2.50	2.10

Greek Gods — A514

1986, Feb. 17 **Litho.** ***Perf. 13***

1546	A514	5d Hestia	.25	.25
1547	A514	18d Hermes	.25	.25
1548	A514	27d Aphrodite	.30	.25
1549	A514	32d Ares	.45	.35
1550	A514	35d Athena	.60	.35
1551	A514	40d Hephaestus	.70	.25
1552	A514	50d Artemis	.95	.35
1553	A514	110d Apollo	1.10	.35
1554	A514	150d Demeter	1.75	.35
1555	A514	200d Poseidon	2.50	.45
1556	A514	300d Hera	4.25	.95
1557	A514	500d Zeus	9.50	4.50
		Nos. 1546-1557 (12)	22.60	8.65

Booklet Stamps

Perf. 13 Horiz.

1546A	A514	5d Hestia	.25	.25
1547A	A514	18d Hermes	.25	.25
1548A	A514	27d Aphrodite	.40	.25
1549A	A514	32d Ares	.40	.25
1550A	A514	35d Athena	.40	.25
1551A	A514	40d Hephaestus	.40	.25
1552A	A514	50d Artemis	.55	.25
1553A	A514	110d Apollo	1.00	.25
1554A	A514	150d Demeter	3.25	.25
1555A	A514	200d Poseidon	3.25	.25
1556A	A514	300d Hera	4.75	.25
1557A	A514	500d Zeus	12.00	.25
		Nos. 1546A-1557A (12)	26.90	3.00

Nos. 1546A-1557A were each sold in booklets containing 20 panes of 5 stamps.

Youth of Antikythera A515

Soccer Players A517

Diadoumenos, by Polycleitus A516

Wrestlers, Hellenic Era Statue — A518

Cyclists — A520

Volleyball Players A519

Commemorative Design for 1st Modern Olympic Games — A521

1986, Mar. 3 ***Perf. 12***

1558	A515	18d multi	.40	.25
1559	A516	27d multi	1.40	.40
1560	A517	32d multi	2.75	.90
1561	A518	35d multi	1.40	1.25
1562	A519	40d multi	1.40	.45
1563	A520	50d multi	1.40	.45
1564	A521	110d multi	4.50	1.60
		Nos. 1558-1564 (7)	13.25	5.30

First World Junior Athletic Championships. Pan-European Junior Soccer Championships. Pan-European Free-style and Greco-Roman Wrestling Championships. Men's World Volleyball Championships. Sixth International Round-Europe Cycling Meet. Modern Olympic Games, 90th anniv.

European Traffic Safety Year — A522

1986, Mar. 3 ***Perf. 12½x14***

1565	A522	18d Seat belts	.25	.25
1566	A522	27d Motorcycle	.95	.95
1567	A522	110d Speed limits	1.50	.50
		Nos. 1565-1567 (3)	2.70	1.70

Prevention of Forest Fires A523

1986, Apr. 23 **Litho.** ***Perf. 14x13½***

1568	A523	35d shown	*3.00*	2.00
1569	A523	110d Prespa Lakes wetlands	*5.00*	4.00
a.		Pair, 35d, 110d	*9.00*	9.00

Booklet Stamps

Perf. 13½ Vert.

1568A	A523	35d shown	*5.50*	*5.50*
1569B	A523	110d Prespa Lakes wetlands	*5.50*	*5.50*
c.		Pair, #1568A, 1569B	12.50	12.50
d.		Bklt. pane, 2 each #1568A, 1569B	*25.00*	

Europa.

New Postal Services — A524

18d, Intelpost. 110d, Express mail, horiz.

1986, Apr. 23 ***Perf. 13½x14, 14x13½***

1570	A524	18d multicolored	.40	.25
1571	A524	110d multicolored	1.60	.80

May Day Strike, Chicago, Cent. — A525

40d, Strikers, monument.

1986, Apr. 23 ***Perf. 12½***

1572	A525	40d multicolored	.65	.50

Eleutherios K. Venizelos (1864-1936), Premier A526

18d, Venizelos, Ministers taking oath of office, 1917. 110d, Old Hania Harbor, Crete.

1986, June 30 **Litho.** ***Perf. 14x12½***

1573	A526	18d multi	.25	.25
1574	A526	110d multi	1.75	.70

6th Intl. Cretological Conference, Crete.

Intl. Peace Year — A527

18d, Dove, sun, vert. 35d, Flags, dove, vert. 110d, World cage, dove.

1986, Oct. 6 **Litho.** ***Perf. 12½***

1575	A527	18d multicolored	.25	.25
1576	A527	35d multicolored	.60	.40
1577	A527	110d multicolored	1.50	.70
		Nos. 1575-1577 (3)	2.35	1.35

Christmas — A528

Religious art in the Benaki Museum: 22d, Madonna and Child Enthroned, triptych center panel, 15th cent. 46d, Adoration of the M...

15th cent. 130d, Christ Enthroned with St. John the Evangelist, triptych panel.

1986, Dec. 1 Litho. *Perf. 13½x14*

1578	A528	22d multi	.30	.25
1579	A528	46d multi	.65	.50
1580	A528	130d multi	1.75	.40
		Nos. 1578-1580 (3)	2.70	1.15

Size of No. 1579: 27x35mm.

Aesop's Fables — A529

2d, Fox and the Grapes. 5d, North Wind and the Sun. 10d, Stag and the Lion. 22d, Zeus and the Snake. 32d, Crow and the Fox. 40d, Woodcutter and Hermes. 46d, Ass in a Lion's Skin. 130d, Tortoise and the Hare.

1987, Mar. 5 Litho. *Perf. 12½*

1581	A529	2d multicolored	.25	.25
1582	A529	5d multicolored	.25	.25
1583	A529	10d multicolored	.30	.30
1584	A529	22d multicolored	.60	.25
1585	A529	32d multicolored	1.10	.30
1586	A529	40d multicolored	1.25	.40
1587	A529	46d multicolored	2.10	.65
1588	A529	130d multicolored	4.50	1.60
		Nos. 1581-1588 (8)	10.35	4.00

Booklet Stamps
Perf. 13½ Horiz.

1581A	A529	2d multicolored	.25	.25
1582A	A529	5d multicolored	.25	.25
1583A	A529	10d multicolored	.40	.25
1584A	A529	22d multicolored	.80	.25
1585A	A529	32d multicolored	1.60	.25
1586A	A529	40d multicolored	2.00	.25
1587A	A529	46d multicolored	4.00	.25
1588A	A529	130d multicolored	20.00	.80
		Nos. 1581A-1588A (8)	29.30	2.55

Nos. 1581A-1588A were each sold in booklets containing 20 panes of 5 stamps.

Europa 1987 — A530

Modern art: 40d, Composition, by Achilleas Apergis. 130d, Delphic Light, by Gerassimos Sklavos.

1987, May 4 Litho. *Perf. 12½*

1589	A530	40d multi	3.00	2.00
1590	A530	130d multi	4.00	3.00
a.		Pair, #1589-1590	7.50	7.50

Booklet Stamps
Perf. 12½ Vert.

1589A	A530	40d multi	2.75	1.60
1590B	A530	130d multi	2.75	1.60
c.		Pair, #1589A, 1590B	10.00	10.00
d.		Bklt. pane, 2 each #1589A,1590B	21.00	

25th European Basketball Championships, Stadium of Peace and Friendship — A531

A532

22d, Jump shot, stadium, vert. 25d, Emblem, spectators. 130d, Two players, vert.

1987, May 4 *Perf. 13½x14, 12½*

1591	A531	22d multicolored	.60	.60
1592	A532	25d multicolored	.40	.25
1593	A531	130d multicolored	1.90	1.10
		Nos. 1591-1593 (3)	2.90	1.95

Higher Education Sesquicentenary — A533

3d, Students, tapestry. 23d, Owl, medallion. 40d, Institute, symbols of science. 60d, Institute, students.

Perf. 14x13½, 13½x14
1987, May 4 Litho.

1594	A533	3d multicolored	.25	.25
1595	A533	23d multicolored	.40	.25
1596	A533	40d multicolored	.70	.40
1597	A533	60d multicolored	1.00	.75
		Nos. 1594-1597 (4)	2.35	1.65

Capodistrias University of Athens (Nos. 1594-1595); The Natl. Metsovio Polytechnic Institute (Nos. 1596-1597). Nos. 1596-1597 vert.

Souvenir Sheet

25th European Men's Basketball Championships — A534

1987, June 3 Litho. *Perf. 13x14*

1598	A534	Sheet of 3	6.00	6.00
a.		40d Jump ball	.90	.90
b.		60d Layup	1.25	1.25
c.		100d Dunk shot	2.25	2.25

Architecture A535

Designs: 2d, Ionic and Corinthian capitals, Archaic Era. 26d, Doric capital, the Parthenon (detail). 40d, Ionic capital and the Erechteum. 60d, Corinthian capital and the Tholos in Epidaurus.

1987, July 1 Litho. *Perf. 13½x12½*

1599	A535	2d multi	.25	.25
1600	A535	26d multi	.35	.25
1601	A535	40d multi	.55	.35
1602	A535	60d multi	1.10	1.00
		Nos. 1599-1602 (4)	2.25	1.85

Engraving by Yiannis Kephalinos — A536

Panteios School A537

Perf. 12½x14, 14x12½
1987, Oct. 1 Litho.

1603	A536	26d multi	.35	.25
1604	A537	60d multi	.85	.75

School of Fine Arts, 150th anniv. (26d), and Panteios School of Political Science, 60th anniv. (60d).

Greek Natl. Team, Winner, 25th European Men's Basketball Championship A538

1987, Oct. 1 *Perf. 13x14*

1605	A538	40d multi	.90	.90

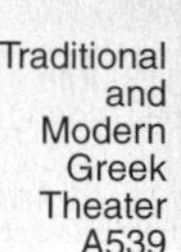

Traditional and Modern Greek Theater A539

Designs: 2d, Eleni Papadaki in Hecuba, by Euripides, and outdoor theater, Philippi. 4d, Christopher Nezer in The Wasps, by Aristophane, and outdoor theater, Dodona. 7d, Emilios Veakis in Oedipus Rex and theater, Delphi. 26d, Marika Cotopouli in The Shepherdess's Love, by Dimitris Koromilas. 40d, Katina Paxinou in Abraham's Sacrifice, by Vitzentzos Cornaros. 50d, Kyveli in Countess Valeraina's Secret, by Gregory Xenopoulos. 60d, Director Carolos Koun, stage setting. 100d, Dimitris Rontiris teaching ancient dance, Greek National Theater.

1987, Dec. 2 Litho. *Perf. 14x13½*

1606	A539	2d multi	.25	.25
1607	A539	4d multi	.25	.25
1608	A539	7d multi	.25	.25
1609	A539	26d multi	.35	.25
1610	A539	40d multi	.55	.25
1611	A539	50d multi	.65	.25
1612	A539	60d multi	.90	.30
1613	A539	100d multi	1.75	.35
		Nos. 1606-1613 (8)	4.95	2.75

Christmas — A540

1987, Dec. 2 *Perf. 13x12½*

1614	26d Angel facing right	.50	.25
1615	26d Angel facing left	.50	.25
a.	Bklt. pane, 5 each #1614-1615	5.00	—
b.	A540 Pair, #1614-1615	1.00	1.00

Marine Life — A541

30d, Codonellina. 40d, Diaperoecia major. 50d, Artemia. 60d, Posidonia oceanica. 100d, Padina pavonica.

1988, Mar. 2 *Perf. 14x12½*

1616	A541	30d multicolored	.80	.40
1617	A541	40d multicolored	1.25	.60
1618	A541	50d multicolored	1.75	.90
1619	A541	60d multicolored	4.00	2.00
1620	A541	100d multicolored	4.00	2.00
		Nos. 1616-1620 (5)	11.80	5.90

Booklet Stamps
Perf. 12½ Vert.

1616A	A541	30d multicolored	4.00	.40
1617A	A541	40d multicolored	2.40	.40
1618A	A541	50d multicolored	7.00	.40
1619A	A541	60d multicolored	8.00	.40
1620A	A541	100d multicolored	12.00	.40
		Nos. 1616A-1620A (5)	33.40	2.00

Nos. 1616A-1620A were each sold in booklets containing 20 panes of 5 stamps.

Europa 1988 — A542

Communication and transport: 60d, Telecommunications satellite, telephone and facsimile machine. 150d, Passenger trains.

1988, May 6 Litho. *Perf. 12½*

1621	60d multi	*5.00*	*3.00*
1622	150d multi	*5.50*	*4.00*
a.	A542 Pair, 60d, 150d	*11.50*	*11.50*

Booklet Stamps
Perf. 14 Vert.

1621A	60d multi	*4.00*	*2.75*
1622B	150d multi	*4.00*	*2.75*
c.	A542 Pair, #1621A, 1622B	*12.00*	*12.00*
d.	Bklt. pane of 4, 2 each #1621A, 1622B	*26.00*	—

1988 Olympics A543

Designs: 4d, Ancient Olympia and Temple of Zeus. 20d, Javelin thrower and and ancient Olympians in open-air gymnasium. 30d, Centenary emblem of the modern Games (cent. in 1996). 60d, Wrestlers, runners and other ancient athletes in training. 170d, Modern torch-bearer.

1988, May 6 *Perf. 14x12*

1623	A543	4d multi	.50	.35
1624	A543	20d multi	1.10	.60
1625	A543	30d multi	2.00	.90
1626	A543	60d multi	3.75	2.75
1627	A543	170d multi	5.25	3.25
a.		Strip of 5, #1623-1627	14.00	14.00

Booklet Stamps
Perf. 14 Vert.

1623A	A543	4d multi	.40	.25
1624A	A543	20d multi	.40	.40
1625A	A543	30d multi	2.40	1.60
1626A	A543	60d multi	4.00	3.25
1627B	A543	170d multi	7.25	4.50
c.		Bklt. pane of 5, #1623A-1626A, 1627B	19.00	19.00

Nos. 1623A-1626A, 1627B were sold in bklts. containing 20 panes of 5 stamps.

See Korea No. B53.

A544

Waterfalls: 10d, Catarractis village falls at the foot of the Tzoumerca Mountain Range. 60d, Edessa Waterfalls. 100d, Edessaios River cascades.

1988, July 4 Litho. *Perf. 12½x14*

1628	A544	10d multi	2.00	.40
1629	A544	60d multi	7.00	2.25
1630	A544	100d multi	10.00	2.25
		Nos. 1628-1630 (3)	19.00	4.90

Booklet Stamps
Perf. 14 Vert.

1628A	A544	10d multi	4.00	1.25
1629A	A544	60d multi	9.50	1.25
1630A	A544	100d multi	14.50	5.50
		Nos. (3)	28.00	8.00

Nos. 1628A-1630A were sold in booklets containing 20 panes of 5 stamps.

A545

1988, July 4 *Perf. 13x12½*

1631 A545 60d multi 8.00 2.50

Booklet Stamp
Perf. 14 Vert.

1631A A545 60d multi 12.00 1.25

20th Pan-European Postal Trade Unions Congress. No. 1631A was sold in booklets containing 20 panes of 5 stamps.

A546

Designs: 30d, Premier Eleutherios Venizelos (1864-1936), natl. flag and map. 70d, Lady liberty, flag and map.

1988, Oct. 7 Litho. *Perf. 12½x13*

1632 A546 30d shown .85 .30
1633 A546 70d multi 1.40 .75

Booklet Stamps
Perf. 14 Horiz.

1632A A546 30d shown 3.25 .40
1633A A546 70d multi 4.75 1.20

Union of Crete with Greece and liberation of Epirus and Macedonia from Turkish rule, 75th annivs.

Nos. 1632A-1633A were sold in booklets containing 20 panes of 5 stamps.

A547

Departmental Seats: 2d, Mytilene-Lesbos Harbor, painting by Theophilos. 3d, Alexandroupolis lighthouse. 4d, St. Nicholas bell tower, Kozane. 5d, Labor Center, Hermoupolis. 7d, Sparta Town Hall. 8d, Pegasus of Leukas. 10d, Castle of the Knights, Rhodes. 20d, The Acropolis, Athens. 25d, Kavalla aqueduct. 30d, Statue of Athanasios Diakos and castle, Lamia. 50d, Preveza cathedral bell tower and Venetian clock. 60d, Corfu promenade. 70d, Harbor view of Hagios Nicolaos. 100d, Poligiros public fountains. 200d, Church of the Apostle Paul, Corinth.

1988, Oct. 7 *Perf. 13*

1634 A547 2d multi .25 .25
1635 A547 3d multi .25 .25
1636 A547 4d multi .25 .25
1637 A547 5d multi .25 .25
1638 A547 7d multi .25 .25
1639 A547 8d multi .25 .25
1640 A547 10d multi .25 .25
1641 A547 20d multi .30 .25
1642 A547 25d multi .35 .25
1643 A547 30d multi .40 .25
1644 A547 50d multi .60 .25
1645 A547 60d multi 1.25 .60
1646 A547 70d multi 1.25 .60
1647 A547 100d multi 2.00 .40
1648 A547 200d multi 4.00 .70
Nos. 1634-1648 (15) 11.90 5.05

Booklet Stamps
Perf. 13 Horiz. or Vert.

1634A A547 2d multi .25 .25
1635A A547 3d multi .25 .25
1636A A547 4d multi .25 .25
1637A A547 5d multi .25 .25
1638A A547 7d multi .25 .25
1639A A547 8d multi .25 .25
1640A A547 10d multi .25 .25
1641A A547 20d multi .25 .25
b. Bklt. pane, 4 each 3d, 5d, 10d, 20d 4.25 —
1642A A547 25d multi .25 .25
1643A A547 30d multi .25 .25
1644A A547 50d multi .80 .25
1645A A547 60d multi 1.25 .60
1646A A547 70d multi 1.25 .60
1647A A547 100d multi 2.40 .40
1648A A547 200d multi 4.00 .80
Nos. 1634A-1648A (15) 12.20 5.15

Nos. 1634A-1648A, were each sold in booklets containing 20 panes of 5 stamps. Nos. 1634A, 1638A-1639A, 1642A, and 1645A-1648A are perforated horizontally. Nos. 1635A-1637A, 1640A-1641A, and 1643A-1644A are perforated vertically.

Council of Europe, Rhodes, Dec. 2-3 — A548

Designs: 60d, Map and Castle of the Knights, Rhodes. 100d, Head of Helios, Rhodian 2nd-3rd cent. B.C. coin, and flags.

1988, Dec. 2 Litho. *Perf. 12½*

1649 A548 60d multi 2.00 1.75
1650 A548 100d multi 3.00 1.25

Booklet Stamps
Perf. 14 Horiz.

1649A A548 60d multi 2.40 1.20
1650A A548 100d multi 4.00 .80

Nos. 1649A-1650A were sold in booklets containing 20 panes of 5.

Christmas — A549

Paintings: 30d, *Adoration of the Magi*, by El Greco. 70d, *The Annunciation*, by Costas Parthenis, horiz.

1988, Dec. 2 *Perf. 12½*

1651 A549 30d multi .80 .40
a. Bklt. pane of 10 24.00 —

Stamps in No. 1651a are perf 12½ on three sides.

1652 A549 70d multi 1.75 .85

Booklet Stamp
Perf. 14 Vert.

1652A A549 70d multi 3.25 1.60

No. 1652A was sold in booklets containing 20 panes of 5 stamps.

A550

Athens '96 emblem and: 30d, High jumper and ancient Olympia. 60d, Wrestlers and view of Delphi. 70d, Swimmers and The Acropolis, Athens. 170d, Sports complex.

1989, Mar. 17 Litho. *Perf. 13¼x14*

1653 A550 30d multi .50 .30
1654 A550 60d multi 1.00 .60
1655 A550 70d multi 1.50 1.40
1656 A550 170d multi 3.00 2.00
a. Strip of 4, Nos. 1653-1656 7.00 7.00

Booklet Stamps
Perf. 13¼ Vert.

1653A A550 30d multi .80 .40
1654A A550 60d multi 1.20 .95
1655A A550 70d multi 1.60 1.20
1656B A550 170d multi 2.75 1.05
c. Bklt. pane of 4, #1653A-1655A, 1656B 7.50 —

A551

Europa: Children's toys.

1989, May 22 Litho. *Perf. 12½x14*

1657 A551 60d Whistling bird *4.50 2.50*
1658 A551 170d Butterfly *5.00 2.50*
a. Pair, #1657-1658 *10.00 10.00*

Printed se-tenant in sheets of 16.

Booklet Stamps
Perf. 13¾ Vert.

1657A A551 60d Whistling bird *3.25 2.00*
1658B A551 170d Butterfly *3.25 2.00*
c. Pair, #1657A, 1658B *6.50 4.00*
d. Bklt. pane, 2 each #1657A,1658B 13.00 —

Perf. 13¼ Vert.

1657B A551 60d Whistling bird *2.00 1.20*
1658E A551 170d Butterfly *2.00 1.20*

Sold in booklets containing 20 panes of 5 stamps.

Anniversaries — A552

1989, May 22 *Perf. 14x13¼*

1659 A552 30d Flags .75 .40
1660 A552 50d Flag, La Liberte .75 .40
1661 A552 60d Flag, ballot box 1.75 1.10
1662 A552 70d Coin, emblem 1.75 1.10
1663 A552 200d Flag, "40" 4.00 1.50
Nos. 1659-1663 (5) 9.00 4.50

Booklet Stamps
Perf. 13 Horiz.

1659A A552 30d Flags .80 .40
1660A A552 50d Flag, La Liberte 8.00 3.25
1661A A552 60d Flag, ballot box 8.00 3.25
1662A A552 70d Coin, emblem 8.00 3.25
1663A A552 200d Flag, "40" 8.00 3.25
Nos. 1659A-1663A (5) 32.80 13.40

Six-nation Initiative for Peace and Disarmament, 5th anniv. (30d); French revolution, bicent. (50d); European Parliament Elections in Greece, 10th anniv. (60d); Interparliamentary Union, cent. (70d); and Council of Europe, 40th anniv. (200d).

Nos. 1659A-1663A were each issued in booklets containing 20 panes of 5 stamps.

A553

BALKANFILA XII, Sept. 30-Oct. 8, Salonica — A554

1989, Sept. 25 Litho. *Perf. 14x12½*

1664 A553 60d shown .85 .50
1665 A553 70d Eye, magnifying glass .85 .75

Souvenir Sheet
Perf. 14x13

1666 A554 200d shown 3.50 3.50

Wildflowers A555

1989, Dec. 8 Litho. *Perf. 14x12½*

1667 A555 8d Wild rose .25 .25
1668 A555 10d Common myrtle .25 .25
1669 A555 20d Field poppy .25 .25
1670 A555 30d Anemone .40 .25
1671 A555 60d Dandelion, chicory .80 .40
1672 A555 70d Mallow .90 .50
1673 A555 200d Thistle 2.50 1.90
Nos. 1667-1673 (7) 5.35 3.80

Ursus arctos A556

Rare and endangered species: 70d, Caretta caretta. 90d, Monachus monachus. 100d, Lynx lynx.

1990, Mar. 16 Litho. *Perf. 14x12½*

1674 A556 40d shown .55 .25
1675 A556 70d multicolored 1.90 .45
1676 A556 90d multicolored 2.40 .50
1677 A556 100d multicolored 2.50 1.10
Nos. 1674-1677 (4) 7.35 2.30

Europa 1990 — A557

Post offices: 70d, Old Central P.O. interior. 210d, Contemporary p.o. exterior.

1990, May 11 Litho. *Perf. 13¼x12¼*

1678 A557 70d multicolored *3.25 2.75*
1679 A557 210d multicolored *5.75 4.75*
a. Pair, #1678-1679 *9.50 9.50*

Nos. 1678-1679 were printed se-tenant in sheets of 16.

Booklet Stamps
Perf. 12¼ Vert.

1678A A557 70d multicolored *3.25 2.75*
1679B A557 210d multicolored *5.75 4.75*
c. Pair, #1678A, 1679B *10.00 10.00*
d. Bklt. pane, 2 each #1678A, 1679B *20.00*

Natl. Reconcilation A558

1990, May 11 *Perf. 12½x13½*

1680 A558 40d Flag, handshake .50 .25
1681 A558 70d Dove, ribbon .85 .35
1682 A558 100d Map, gift of flowers 1.25 1.25
Nos. 1680-1682 (3) 2.60 1.85

Political Reformers — A559

No. 1683, Gregoris Lambrakis (1912-63). No. 1684, Pavlos Bakoyiannis (1935-89).

1990, May 11

1683 A559 40d multicolored .65 .40
1684 A559 40d multicolored .65 .40

A560

Department Seats: 2d, Karditsa, the commercial-animal fair. 5d, Trikkala fort and clock tower. 8d, Veroia, street with traditional architecture. 10d, Mesolongion, Central Monument of Fallen Heroes in the Exodus. 15d, Chios, view. 20d, Tripolis, street with neoclassical architecture. 25d, Volos, view with town hall, woodcut by A. Tassou. 40d, Kalamata, neoclassical town hall. 50d, Pyrgos, central marketplace. 70d, Ioannina, view of lake and island. 80d, Rethymnon, sculpture at the port. 90d, Argostolion, view before earthquake. 100d, Nauplia, Bourtzi with Palamidi in the background. 200d, Patras, central lighthouse. 250d, Florina, street with neoclassical architecture. Nos. 1685, 1687, 1695, 1698 vert.

Perf. 12¾x12¼, 12¼x12¾

1990, June 20 **Litho.**

1685 A560 2d multicolored .25 .25
1686 A560 5d multicolored .25 .25
1687 A560 8d multicolored .25
1688 A560 10d multicolored .25 .25
1689 A560 15d multicolored .25 .25
1690 A560 20d multicolored .25 .25
1691 A560 25d multicolored .40 .25
1692 A560 40d multicolored .60 .25
1693 A560 50d multicolored .75 .25
1694 A560 70d multicolored 1.00 .40
1695 A560 80d multicolored 1.10 .45
1696 A560 90d multicolored 1.40 .50
1697 A560 100d multicolored 2.25 .60
1698 A560 200d multicolored 4.50 1.10
1699 A560 250d multicolored 6.00 1.50
Nos. 1685-1699 (15) 19.50 6.80

Booklet Stamps
Perf. 13½ Vert. or Horiz.

1685A A560 2d multicolored .25 .25
1686A A560 5d multicolored .25 .25
1687A A560 8d multicolored .25 .25
1688A A560 10d multicolored .25 .25
1689A A560 15d multicolored .25 .25
1690A A560 20d multicolored .25 .25
1691A A560 25d multicolored .40 .40
1692A A560 40d multicolored .40 .40
1693A A560 50d multicolored .40 .40
1694A A560 70d multicolored .40 .40
1695A A560 80d multicolored .80 .40
1696A A560 90d multicolored .80 .40
1697A A560 100d multicolored .80 .40
1698A A560 200d multicolored 2.40 .40
1699A A560 250d multicolored 3.25 .40
Nos. 1685A-1699A (15) 11.15 5.10

Nos. 1685A-1699A were each sold in booklets containing 20 panes of 5 stamps. Nos. 1685A, 1687A, 1695A, and 1698A are perforated vertically. Nos. 1686A, 1688A-1694A, 1696A-1697A, and 1699A are perforated horizontally.

See Nos. 1749-1760, 1792-1801.

1996 Summer Olympics — A561

1990, July 13 ***Perf. 12½x13½***

1700 A561 20d Sailing .25 .25
1701 A561 50d Wrestling .60 .25
1702 A561 80d Sprinting .90 .90
1703 A561 100d Basketball 1.25 .90
1704 A561 250d Soccer 3.00 1.50
a. Strip of 5, #1700-1704 7.00 7.00

Athens, proposed site for centennial Summer Olympic Games. Exists perf. 13½ vert.

Heinrich Schliemann (1822-1890), Archaeologist — A562

1990, Oct. 11 **Litho.** ***Perf. 14x13½***

1705 A562 80d multicolored 5.00 3.00

See Germany No. 1615.

Greco-Italian War, 50th Anniv. — A563

50d, Woman knitting. 80d, Virgin Mary, soldier. 100d, Women volunteers.

1990, Oct. 11 ***Perf. 12½***

1706 A563 50d multicolored .60 .25
1707 A563 80d multicolored 1.00 .80
1708 A563 100d multicolored 1.40 .80
Nos. 1706-1708 (3) 3.00 1.85

Souvenir Sheet

Stamp Day — A564

1990, Dec. 14 **Litho.** ***Perf. 14x13***

1709 A564 300d multicolored *10.00 10.00*

The Muses — A565

Designs: 50d, Calliope, Euterpe, Erato. 80d, Terpsichore, Polyhymnia, Melpomene. 250d, Thalia, Clio, Urania.

1991, Mar. 11 **Litho.** ***Perf. 12½***

1710 A565 50d multicolored .60 .25
1711 A565 80d multicolored .95 .40
1712 A565 250d multicolored 2.75 1.25
Nos. 1710-1712 (3) 4.30 1.90

Battle of Crete by Ioannis Anousakis — A566

300d, Map, flags of participating allied armies.

1991, May 20 **Litho.** ***Perf. 12½x13½***

1713 A566 60d multicolored 1.60 .40

Size: 32x24mm
Perf. 12½

1714 A566 300d multicolored 3.25 1.50

Battle of Crete, 50th anniv.

Europa A567

Designs: 80d, Icarus pushing modern satellite. 300d, Chariot of the Sun.

1991, May 20 ***Perf. 12½***

1715 A567 80d multicolored *4.00* 3.00
1716 A567 300d multicolored *5.50* 4.50
a. Pair, #1715-1716 *10.00* 10.00

No. 1716a printed in continuous design in sheets of 16.

Booklet Stamps
Perf. 12½ Vert.

1715A A567 80d multicolored *4.00* 3.25
1716B A567 300d multicolored *4.00* 3.25
c. Pair, #1715A, 1716B *11.00* 11.00
d. Bklt. pane, 2 ea. #1715A, 1716B *22.00* 22.00

A568

1991, June 25 **Litho.** ***Perf. 13½x14***

1717 A568 10d Swimming .25 .25
1718 A568 60d Basketball .50 .25
1719 A568 90d Gymnastics .90 .30
1720 A568 130d Weight lifting 1.25 .50
1721 A568 300d Hammer throw 3.50 2.00
Nos. 1717-1721 (5) 6.40 3.30

1991 Mediterranean Games, Athens.

A569

1991, Sept. 20 **Litho.** ***Perf. 13½x14***

1722 A569 100d multicolored 1.10 .60

Athenian Democracy, 2500th anniv.

Europa Souvenir Sheet

Greek Presidency of CEPT — A570

Europe with Zeus metmorphosed into a bull, from Attic vase, c. 500 B.C.

1991, Sept. 20 ***Perf. 14x13***

1723 A570 300d multicolored *20.00 20.00*

A571

Greek Membership in EEC, 10th anniv.: 50d, Pres. Konstantin Karamanlis signing Treaty of Greek entrance into EEC. 80d, Map showing EEC members, Pres. Karamanlis.

1991, Dec. 9 **Litho.** ***Perf. 13x14***

1724 A571 50d multicolored .55 .25
1725 A571 80d multicolored .90 .50

A572

1991, Dec. 9 ***Perf. 12½x13½***

1726 A572 80d Speed skaters .90 .80
1727 A572 300d Slalom skier 3.25 1.10
a. Pair, #1726-1727 4.25 4.25

16th Winter Olympics, Albertville.

A573

1992 Summer Olympics, Barcelona A574

Perf. 12½, 14x13½ (90d, 340d)

1992, Apr. 3 **Litho.**

1728 A573 10d Javelin .25 .25
1729 A573 60d Equestrian .90 .30
1730 A574 90d Runner 1.40 .75
1731 A573 120d Gymnastics 2.75 .80
1732 A574 340d Runners 4.50 2.25
Nos. 1728-1732 (5) 9.80 4.35

Health — A575

Designs: 60d, Protection against AIDS. 80d, Diseases of digestive system. 90d, Dying flower symbolizing cancer. 120d, Hephaestus at his forge, 6th century BC. 280d, Alexandros S. Onassis Cardiosurgical Center.

1992, May 22 **Litho.** ***Perf. 12½***

1733 A575 60d multicolored .60 .30
1734 A575 80d multicolored .85 .40
1735 A575 90d multicolored .90 .45
1736 A575 120d multicolored 1.50 .65
1737 A575 280d multicolored 3.25 1.75
Nos. 1733-1737 (5) 7.10 3.55

No. 1734, 1st United European Gastroenterology Week. No. 1736, European Year of Social Security, Hygiene and Health in the Workplace.

Discovery of America, 500th Anniv. A576

Europa: 340d, Map of 15th century Chios, Columbus.

1992, May 22 ***Perf. 13¾x12¼***

1738 A576 90d shown *2.75 2.00*
1739 A576 340d multicolored *6.50 4.75*
a. Pair, #1738-1739 *10.00 10.00*

No. 1739a was printed in continuous design in sheets of 16.

Booklet Stamps
Perf. 12½ Vert.

1738A A576 90d shown *3.00 2.25*
1739B A576 340d multicolored *6.75 5.50*
c. Bklt. pane, 2 each #1738A, 1739B *20.00 20.00*
d. Pair, #1738A, 1739B *10.00 10.00*

Souvenir Sheet

European Conference on Transportation — A577

1992, June 8 *Perf. 14x13*
1740 A577 300d multicolored *8.50 8.50*

Macedonian Treasures — A578

Designs: 10d, Head of Hercules wearing lion skin, Vergina treasures. 20d, Bust of Aristotle, map of Macedonia, horiz. 60d, Alexander the Great at Battle of Issus, horiz. 80d, Archaeologist Manolis Andronikos, tomb of King Philip II. 90d, Deer hunt mosaic, Pella. 120d, Macedonian tetradrachm. 340d, St. Paul, 4th century church near Philippi.

1992, July 17 **Litho.** *Perf. 12½*
1741 A578 10d multicolored .50 .25
1742 A578 20d multicolored .50 .25
1743 A578 60d multicolored .60 .25
1744 A578 80d multicolored 1.60 .25
1745 A578 90d multicolored 1.90 .25
1746 A578 120d multicolored 2.40 1.00
1747 A578 340d multicolored 8.50 2.50
Nos. 1741-1747 (7) 16.00 4.75

European Unification — A579

1992, Oct. 12 **Litho.** *Perf. 14x13*
1748 A579 90d multicolored *1.00 1.00*

Departmental Seat Type of 1990

Designs: 10d, Piraeus, the old clock. 20d, Amphissa, view of city with citadel. 30d, Samos (Vathy), the Heraion. 40d, Canea, city in 1800s. 50d, Zakinthos (Zante), view in 1800s. 60d, Karpenision, Velouchi and city. 70d, Kilkis, the cave, vert. 80d, Xanthe, door of Town Hall, vert. 90d, Salonika, Macedonian Struggle Museum. 120d, Komotine, Tsanakleous School. 340d, Drama, spring. 400d, Larissa, Pinios bridge.

1992, Oct. 12 *Perf. 12¾*
1749 A560 10d multicolored .25 .25
1750 A560 20d multicolored .25 .25
1751 A560 30d multicolored .25 .25
1752 A560 40d multicolored .35 .25
1753 A560 50d multicolored .40 .25
1754 A560 60d multicolored [illegible] [illegible]
1755 A560 70d multicolored .60 .35
1756 A560 80d multicolored .60 .35
1757 A560 90d multicolored 1.25 .40
1758 A560 120d multicolored 2.50 .65
1759 A560 340d multicolored 4.00 1.60
1760 A560 400d multicolored 5.50 2.25
Nos. 1749-1760 (12) 16.40 7.15

Booklet Stamps
Perf. 10½ Horiz. or Vert.

1749A A560 10d multicolored .25 .25
1750A A560 20d multicolored .25 .25
1751A A560 30d multicolored .25 .25
1752A A560 40d multicolored .25 .25
1753A A560 50d multicolored .25 .25
1754A A560 60d multicolored .40 .25
1755A A560 70d multicolored .40 .25
1756A A560 80d multicolored 1.60 .25
1757A A560 90d multicolored 1.60 .25
1758A A560 120d multicolored 2.40 .40
1759A A560 340d multicolored 4.00 .95
1760A A560 400d multicolored 5.25 1.60
Nos. 1749A-1760A (12) 16.90 5.20

Nos. 1749A-1760A were each sold in booklets containing 20 panes of 5 stamps. Nos. 1749A-1754A, and 1757A-1760A are perforated horizontally. Nos. 1755A-1756A are perforated vertically.

City of Rhodes, 2400th Anniv. — A580

Designs: 60d, Headstone, 4th cent. B.C. 90d, Bathing Aphrodite, 1st cent. B.C. 120d, St. Irene, Church of St. Catherine, 14th cent. 250d, St. Paul's Gate, 15th cent.

1993, Feb. 26 **Litho.** *Perf. 13x14*
1761 A580 60d multicolored .65 .35
1762 A580 90d multicolored 1.10 .80
1763 A580 120d multicolored 1.25 .70
1764 A580 250d multicolored 4.00 1.75
Nos. 1761-1764 (4) 7.00 3.60

Remembrances of Greek Wars — A581

Designs: 10d, Death of Georgakis Olympios, 1821. 30d, Theodore Kolokotronis in battle, 1821. 60d, Pavlos Melas. 90d, Glory lays wreath over graves of dead from Balkan Wars. 120d, Greek soldiers at Battle of El Alamein, 1942, horiz. 150d, Greek troops in Aegean Islands, 1943-45, horiz. 200d, Kalavryta Massacre Memorial.

Perf. 13x14, 14x13
1993, May 25 **Litho.**
1765 A581 10d multicolored .25 .25
1766 A581 30d multicolored .40 .25
1767 A581 60d multicolored .55 .30
1768 A581 90d multicolored 1.00 .40
1769 A581 120d multicolored 2.40 1.00
1770 A581 150d multicolored 2.40 1.60
1771 A581 200d multicolored 4.75 2.25
Nos. 1765-1771 (7) 11.75 6.05

The Benefits of Transportation, by K. Parthenis — A582

Europa: 90d, Tree, three people, ships. 350d, Woman and children, town.

1993, May 25 *Perf. 13x13¼*
1772 90d multicolored *1.50 1.25*
1773 350d multicolored *6.75 5.50*
a. A582 Pair, #1772-1773 *9.00 9.00*

No. 1773a was printed in continuous design in sheets of 16.

Booklet Stamps
Perf. 13¼ Vert.

1772A 90d multicolored *1.50 1.25*
1773B 350d multicolored *6.75 5.50*
c. Bklt. pane, 2 each #1772A, 1773B *18.00 18.00*
d. Pair, #1772A, 1773B *9.00 9.00*

Buildings in Athens A583

Designs: 30d, Concert Hall. 60d, Numismatic Museum (Iliou Melathron). 90d, Natl. Library of Greece. 200d, Opthalmology Hospital.

1993, Oct. 4 **Litho.** *Perf. 14*
1774 A583 30d multicolored .85 .25
1775 A583 60d multicolored .85 .30
1776 A583 90d multicolored 1.00 .80
1777 A583 200d multicolored 5.00 2.00
Nos. 1774-1777 (4) 7.70 3.35

Souvenir Sheet

Greek Presidency of the European Community Council of Ministers — A584

1993, Dec. 20 **Litho.** *Perf. 14*
1778 A584 400d multicolored *5.00 5.00*

Chariot of Selene Driven by Hermes A585

1994, Mar. 7 **Litho.** *Perf. 13x13½*
1779 A585 200d multicolored 2.25 1.50

2nd Pan-European Transportation Conference.

Passion of Christ A586

Designs: 30d, Last Supper, 16th cent. icon, St. Catherine's Church, Crete, vert. 60d, Crucifixion, detail from 1552 wall drawing, Great Meteoron, vert. 90d, Burial, 1620-45 icon, Church of the Presentation of the Lord, Patmos. 150d, Resurrection, illustrated manuscript of Mt. Athos, 11th cent.

1994, Apr. 8 **Litho.** *Perf. 14*
1780 A586 30d multicolored .40 .25
1781 A586 60d multicolored .50 .25
1782 A586 90d multicolored .75 .40
1783 A586 150d multicolored 1.60 .90
Nos. 1780-1783 (4) 3.25 1.80

European Inventors, Discoverers A587

Europa: 90d, Thales of Miletus (625?-547? B.C.), philosopher, mathematician. 350d, Konstantinos Karatheodoris (1873-1950).

1994, May 9 **Litho.** *Perf. 14x13½*
1784 A587 90d multicolored *1.75 1.50*
1785 A587 350d multicolored *3.75 3.25*
a. Pair, #1784-1785 *6.00 6.00*

Nos. 1784-1785 was issued in sheets of 16.

Booklet Stamps
Perf. 13¾ Vert.

1784A A587 90d multicolored *2.00 1.75*
1785B A587 350d multicolored *4.00 3.50*
c. Bklt. pane, 2 each #1784A-1785B *13.00 13.00*
d. Pair, #1784A, 1785B *6.50 6.50*

Athletic Events, Anniversaries A588

Designs: 60d, Demetrios Vikelas (1835-1908), first president Intl. Olympic Committee, vert. 90, Modern, ancient soccer players. 120d, Volleyball, net, vert. 400d, Statue of Liberty, modern, ancient soccer players.

1994, June 6 **Litho.** *Perf. 14*
1786 A588 60d multicolored .70 .30
1787 A588 90d multicolored .85 .60
1788 A588 120d multicolored 1.75 .90
Nos. 1786-1788 (3) 3.30 1.80

Souvenir Sheet
Perf. 14x13½

1789 A588 400d multicolored 4.50 4.50

Intl. Olympic Committee, cent. (No. 1786). 1994 World Cup Soccer Championships, US (Nos. 1787, 1789). World Volleyball Championships, Piraeus & Salonika (No. 1788).

No. 1789 contains one 42x52mm stamp.

Greek Presidency of European Community Council of Ministers A589

Designs: 90d, Winged chariot driven by Greece. 120d, Doric columns, European Community flag.

1994, June 21 *Perf. 13*
1790 A589 90d multicolored 1.00 .90
1791 A589 120d multicolored 1.25 .90

Departmental Seat Type of 1990

Designs: 10d, Katerine, Tsalopoulou mansion house, vert. 20d, Arta, Byzantine Church Parigoritissas. 30d, Lebadea, medieval bridge, tower of catalanian castle, Krias springs vert. 40d, Kastoria, Church of Panagia Koumbelidkis. 50d, Grevena, outdoor theatre. 60d, Edessa, waterfall. 80d, Chalcis, red house. 90d, Serrai, government house, Merarchias road, Acropolis of Koulas. 120d, Candia (Herakleion), town hall. 150d, Egoumenitsa, Church of Evangelistria, vert.

1994, Oct. 5 **Litho.** *Perf. 12¾*
1792 A560 10d multicolored .25 .25
1793 A560 20d multicolored .25 .25
1794 A560 30d multicolored .30 .25
1795 A560 40d multicolored .40 .25
1796 A560 50d multicolored .50 .25
1797 A560 60d multicolored .65 .25
1798 A560 80d multicolored .75 .30
1799 A560 90d multicolored .80 .30
1800 A560 120d multicolored 1.00 .40
1801 A560 150d multicolored 1.25 .50
Nos. 1792-1801 (10) 6.15 3.00

Booklet Stamps
Perf. 10½ Vert. or Horiz.

1792A A560 10d multicolored .25 .25
b. Perf. 13¼ vert. —
1793A A560 20d multicolored .25 .25
1794A A560 30d multicolored .25 .25
1795A A560 40d multicolored .40 .25
1796A A560 50d multicolored .50 .25
1797A A560 60d multicolored .65 .25
1798A A560 80d multicolored .75 .25
1799A A560 90d multicolored 2.00 .25
1800A A560 120d multicolored 2.00 .25
1801A A560 150d multicolored 2.40 .80
Nos. 1792A-1801A (10) 9.45 3.05

Nos. 1792A-1801A were each sold in booklets containing 20 panes of 5 stamps. Nos. 1792A, 1794A, and 1801A are perforated vertically. Nos. 1793A, and 1795A-1800A ar perforated horizontally.

Constitution, 150th Anniv. — A590

Designs: 60d, People, army demonstrating, by Carl Howpt, vert. 150d, Portraits of Ioannis Makriyannis, Andreas Metaxas, Demetrios Kallergis. 200d, Painting of night of Sept. 3, 1843. 340d, Article 107, seal of Greek Parliament, signature of President.

1994, Nov. 21 Litho. *Perf. 14x13*

1802 A590 60d multicolored .65 .40
1803 A590 150d multicolored 1.10 .65
1804 A590 200d multicolored 2.25 1.00
1805 A590 340d multicolored 4.25 2.00
Nos. 1802-1805 (4) 8.25 4.05

Melina Mercouri (1925-94), Actress, Politician — A591

90d, Portrait, Parthenon. 100d, Portraits as actress. 340d, Portrait, vert.

1995, Mar. 7 Litho. *Perf. 14x13*

1806 A591 60d shown .65 .25
1807 A591 90d multicolored .80 .40
1808 A591 100d multicolored 3.00 1.00
1809 A591 340d multicolored 6.75 2.25
Nos. 1806-1809 (4) 11.20 3.90

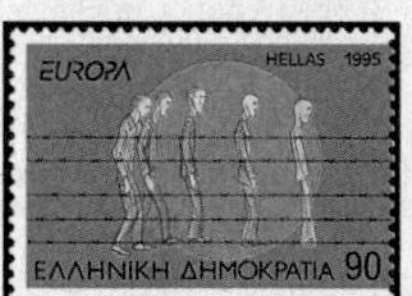
Liberation of Concentration Camps, 50th Anniv. A592

Europa: 90d, Prisoners. 340d, Peace doves, broken barbed wire fence.

1995, May 3 Litho. *Perf. 14*

1810 A592 90d multicolored 2.00
1811 A592 340d multicolored 4.00 4.00
a. Pair, #1810-1811 6.50 6.50

Booklet Stamps
Perf. 13½ Vert.

1810A A592 90d multicolored 2.00 2.00
1811B A592 340d multicolored 4.00 4.00
c. Bklt. pane, 2 each #1810A, 1811B 13.00 13.00
Complete booklet, #1811c 13.00
d. Pair, #1810A, 1811B 6.50 6.50

Anniversaries & Events — A593

Designs: 10d, Stylized emblem, basketball, vert. 70d, University building. 90d, Architectural ruins, vert. 100d, Flag, soldier, vert. 120d, Statue of Peace, by Kifissodotos, vert. 150d, Dolphins. 200d, Early telephone, push buttons, vert. 300d, Owl, basketball, vert.

Perf. 13½x13, 13x13½
1995, June 21 Litho.

1812 A593 10d multicolored .25 .25
1813 A593 70d multicolored 1.00 .30
1814 A593 90d multicolored 1.25 .40
1815 A593 100d multicolored 1.40 .45
1816 A593 120d multicolored 1.75 .55
1817 A593 150d multicolored 2.00 .65
1818 A593 200d multicolored 2.75 .90
1819 A593 300d multicolored 4.50 1.25
Nos. 1812-1819 (8) 14.90 4.75

5th World Junior Basketball Championships (No. 1812). Agricultural University of Athens, 75th anniv. (No. 1813). UN, 50th anniv. (Nos. 1814, 1816). End of World War II, 50th anniv. (No. 1815). European Nature Conservation Year (No. 1817). Telephone in Greece, cent. (No. 1818). 29th European Basketball Championships (No. 1819).

Book of Revelation, 1900th Anniv. — A594

Visions of the Apocalypse: 80d, First vision, Angels of the Seven Churches of Asia Minor, icon by Thomas Bathas, vert. 110d, Apostle John at Cave of the Apocalypse dictating to Prochoros, miniature from manuscript of Four Gospels, vert. 300d, First Angel with trumpet from silver gilded Gospel cover.

1995, Sept. 18 Litho. *Perf. 14*

1820 A594 80d multicolored 2.00 .35
1821 A594 110d multicolored 2.75 .90
1822 A594 300d multicolored 3.75 2.00
Nos. 1820-1822 (3) 8.50 3.25

Jason & the Argonauts A595

Designs: 80d, Argonauts, the Argus, goddess Athena setting out for Colchis. 120d, Phineas, Hermes, one of the Voreadae, Harpy. 150d, Jason taming the bull, Medea and Nike. 200d, Jason takes Golden Fleece, kills serpent with Medea's help. 300d, Medea watches, Jason, crowned by Nike, giving Golden Fleece to Pelias.

1995, Nov. 6 Litho. *Perf. 13x13½*

1823 A595 80d multicolored .90 .40
1824 A595 120d multicolored .90 .75
1825 A595 150d multicolored 1.10 .65
1826 A595 200d multicolored 1.60 .75
1827 A595 300d multicolored 4.50 1.60
Nos. 1823-1827 (5) 9.00 4.15

Lighthouses — A596

1995, Dec. 18 Litho. *Perf. 14*

1828 A596 80d Psyttaleia 1.00 .40
1829 A596 120d Sapienza 1.50 .60
1830 A596 150d Kastri (Othonoi) 2.00 1.10
1831 A596 500d Zourva (Hydra) 7.25 2.40
Nos. 1828-1831 (4) 11.75 4.50

Souvenir Sheets

Modern Olympic Games, Cent. — A597

Perf. 13½x13, 13x13½
1996, Mar. 25 Litho.

1832 A597 Sheet of 4 15.00 15.00
a. 80d like #117, vert. 3.00 3.00
b. 120d like #118, vert. 3.00 3.00
c. 150d like #119, vert. 3.00 3.00
d. 650d like #120, vert. 3.00 3.00
1833 A597 Sheet of 4 15.00 15.00
a. 80d like #122 3.00 3.00
b. 120d like #124 3.00 3.00
c. 150d like #125 3.00 3.00
d. 650d like #128 3.00 3.00
1834 A597 Sheet of 4 15.00 15.00
a. 80d like #121, vert. 3.00 3.00
b. 120d like #123, vert. 3.00 3.00
c. 150d like #126, vert. 3.00 3.00
d. 650d like #127, vert. 3.00 3.00

Famous Women — A598

Europa: 120d, Sappho (c.610-580BC), lyric poet. 430d, Amalia Fleming.

1996, Apr. 22 Litho. *Perf. 14x14½*

1835 A598 120d multicolored *1.50 1.50*
1836 A598 430d multicolored *4.50 4.50*
a. A598 Pair, #1835-1836 *6.25 6.25*

Booklet Stamps
Perf. 14½ Vert.

1835A A598 120d multicolored *1.50 1.50*
1836B A598 430d multicolored *4.50 4.50*
c. Booklet pane, 2 each #1835A, 1836B *12.50 12.50*
Complete booklet, #1836c *12.50*
d. Pair, #1835A, 1836B *6.25 6.25*

Modern Olympic Games, Cent. A599

Stylized designs: 10d, Greek runners, vert. 80d, Discus thrower, vert. 120d, Weight lifter, vert. 200d, Wrestlers.

Perf. 13½x14, 14x13½
1996, June 4 Litho.

1837 A599 10d multicolored .45 .25
1838 A599 80d multicolored 1.60 .45
1839 A599 120d multicolored 3.00 .75
1840 A599 200d multicolored 4.75 2.00
Nos. 1837-1840 (4) 9.80 3.45

First Intl. Medical Olympiad — A600

1996, July 8 Litho. *Perf. 13½*

1841 A600 80d Hippocrates 2.00 .80
1842 A600 120d Galen 2.50 1.25

Castles A601

1996, Oct. 7 Litho. *Perf. 13¼*

1843 A601 10d Mytilene .25 .25
1844 A601 20d Lindos .25 .25
1845 A601 30d Rethymnon .30 .25
1846 A601 70d Assos Cephalonia .65 .35
1847 A601 80d Serbs .80 .60
1848 A601 120d Monemvasia 1.00 .65
1849 A601 200d Didimotihon 1.75 1.00
1850 A601 430d Vonitsas 4.25 3.00
1851 A601 1000d Nikopolis 10.00 6.50
Nos. 1843-1851 (9) 19.25 12.85

Booklet Stamps
Perf. 13¼ Vert.

1843A A601 10d Mytilene .25 .25
1844A A601 20d Lindos .25 .25
1845A A601 30d Rethymnon .30 .25
1846A A601 70d Assos Cephalonia .65 .25
1847A A601 80d Serbs .80 .30
1848A A601 120d Monemvasia 1.10 .30
1849A A601 200d Didimotihon 1.75 .50
1850A A601 430d Vonitsas 4.25 1.50
1851A A601 1000d Nikopolis 10.00 3.25
Nos. 1843A-1851A (9) 19.35 6.85

Nos. 1843A-1851A were each sold in booklets containing 20 panes of 5 stamps.

Figures from Shadow Theatre — A602

100d, Four characters, diff. 120d, Three characters. 200d, Two characters, dragon.

1996, Nov. 15 Litho. *Perf. 14*

1852 A602 80d multicolored 1.00 .45
1853 A602 100d multicolored 1.00 .55
1854 A602 120d multicolored 2.00 .70
1855 A602 200d multicolored 3.00 1.10
Nos. 1852-1855 (4) 7.00 2.80

Hellenic Language A603

Designs: 80d, Oldest Hellenic inscription, wine pitcher, 720BC. 120d, Verse IX, 436-445 from Homer's Iliad, 1st-2nd cent. AD. 150d, Psalm of the Holy Apostles, 6th cent. AD. 350d, Reference to Hellenic language, Dionysios Solomos, 1824.

1996, Dec. 18 Litho. *Perf. 13x13½*

1856 A603 80d multicolored .85 .55
1857 A603 120d multicolored 1.10 .85
1858 A603 150d multicolored 1.75 1.40
1859 A603 350d multicolored 4.25 2.10
Nos. 1856-1859 (4) 7.95 4.90

Andreas G. Papandreou (1919-96), Prime Minister — A604

Papandreou at various ages and: 80d, Graduation cap, books, diploma. 120d, Leaving airplane. 150d, Building. 500d, Greek flag, dove.

1997, Feb. 12 Litho. *Perf. 13*

1860 A604 80d multicolored 1.10 .30
1861 A604 120d multicolored 1.10 .45
1862 A604 150d multicolored 1.75 .85
1863 A604 500d multicolored 4.00 .95
Nos. 1860-1863 (4) 7.95 2.55

Thessaloniki, European Cultural Capital A605

Designs: 80d, Frescoe of St. Dimitrios, patron saint of Thessaloniki, Church of Aghios Nikolaos Orphanos, vert. 100d, Hippocratic Hospital. 120d, Marble pedestal with inscription, medallion with woman's head, vert. 150d, Detail of mosaic from Rotunda cupola, vert. 300d, "laspis" chalice, 14th cent., Mt. Athos.

1997, Mar. 26 *Perf. 13½*

1864 A605 80d multicolored .90 .50
1865 A605 100d multicolored 1.40 .65
1866 A605 120d multicolored 1.50 .75
1867 A605 150d multicolored 1.75 1.00
1868 A605 300d multicolored 4.50 2.00
Nos. 1864-1868 (5) 10.05 4.90

Bridges of Macedonia
A606

80d, Village of Trikomo. 120d, Portitsa. 150d, Village of Ziakas. 350d, Village of Kastro.

1997, Apr. 24 Litho. *Perf. 14*

1869	A606	80d	multicolored	.70	.45
1870	A606	120d	multicolored	1.10	.65
1871	A606	150d	multicolored	2.00	.85
1872	A606	350d	multicolored	5.25	1.90
	Nos. 1869-1872 (4)			9.05	3.85

Stories and Legends
A607

Europa: 120d, Prometheus, the giver of fire. 430d, Digenis Akritas, Greek swordsmen on horseback.

1997, May 19 Litho. *Perf. 14*

1873	A607	120d	multicolored	*1.75*	*1.50*
1874	A607	430d	multicolored	*4.00*	*3.50*
a.	Pair, #1873-1874			*5.75*	*5.75*

Booklet Stamps
Perf. 13½ Vert.

1873A	A607	120d	multicolored	*1.75*	*1.50*
1874B	A607	430d	multicolored	*4.00*	*3.50*
c.	Booklet pane, 2 each #1873A, 1874B			*11.50*	*11.50*
	Complete booklet, #1874c			*11.50*	
d.	Pair, #1873A, 1874B			*5.75*	*5.75*

6th IAAF World Track & Field Championships, Athens — A608

Official IAAF emblem, Greek flag and: 20d, Runners. 100d, Nike. 140d, High jump. 170d, Hurdles. 500d, Olympic Stadium, Athens.

1997, July 11 Litho. *Perf. 13x13½*

1875	A608	20d	multicolored	.25	.25
1876	A608	100d	multicolored	.85	.40
1877	A608	140d	multicolored	1.25	.80
1878	A608	170d	multicolored	1.60	1.00
1879	A608	500d	multicolored	5.25	2.50
	Nos. 1875-1879 (5)			9.20	4.95

Famous People
A609

Designs: 20d, Alexandros Panagoulis (1939-76), resistance leader, vert. 30d, Grigorios Xenopoulos (1867-1951), novelist, vert. 40d, Odysseus Elytis (1911-96), poet. 50d, Panayiotis Kanellopoulos (1902-86), prime minister, vert. 100d, Harilaos Trikoupis (1832-96), politician. 170d, Maria Callas (1923-77), opera singer. 200d, Rigas Vélestinlis-Feraios (1757-98), revolutionary, vert.

Perf. 13½x13, 13x13½

1997, Oct. 01 Litho.

1880	A609	20d	multicolored	.25	.25
1881	A609	30d	multicolored	.50	.25
1882	A609	40d	multicolored	.60	.25
1883	A609	50d	multicolored	.90	.25
1884	A609	100d	multicolored	1.50	.75
1885	A609	170d	multicolored	3.00	1.40
1886	A609	200d	multicolored	3.50	1.60
	Nos. 1880-1886 (7)			10.25	4.75

Film Comedians
A610

Designs: 20d, Vassilis Avlonitis. 30d, Vassilis Argyropoulos. 50d, Georgia Vassileiadou. 70d, Lambros Constantaras. 100d, Vassilis Logothetidis. 140d, Dionysis Papagiannopoulos. 170d, Nikos Stavrides. 200d, Mimis Fotopoulos.

1997, Dec. 17 Litho. *Perf. 13x13½*

1887	A610	20d	multicolored	.25	.25
1888	A610	30d	multicolored	.40	.25
1889	A610	50d	multicolored	.60	.45
1890	A610	70d	multicolored	.85	.70
1891	A610	100d	multicolored	1.10	.85
1892	A610	140d	multicolored	1.60	1.60
1893	A610	170d	multicolored	2.40	1.60
1894	A610	200d	multicolored	5.00	1.60
	Nos. 1887-1894 (8)			12.20	7.30

Incorporation of the Dodecanese Islands into Greece, 50th Anniv. — A611

100d, German commander signing treaty turning islands over to English and Greek military, Symi (Simi), May 8, 1945. 140d, Greece and Colossus of Rhodes, Greek flag. 170d, English general turns islands over to Greek military command, Rhodes, 3/31/47. 500d, Greek flag raised over Dodecanese, Kasos (Caso), 3/7/47.

1998, Feb. 27 Litho. *Perf. 13½x13*

1895	A611	100d	multicolored	1.00	.65
1896	A611	140d	multicolored	1.40	1.40
1897	A611	170d	multicolored	2.00	1.75
1898	A611	500d	multicolored	5.50	1.25
	Nos. 1895-1898 (4)			9.90	5.05

Hagia Sophia General Children's Hospital, Cent. — A612

Holy Monastery of Xenon, 1000th Anniv.
A613

4th World Congress of Thracians, Nea Orestiada
A614

16th World Congress of Cardiology Research, Athens — A615

European Movement, 50th Anniv. — A616

Perf. 13x13½, 13½x13

1998, Apr. 30 Litho.

1899	A612	20d	multicolored	.25	.25
1900	A613	100d	multicolored	.90	.50
1901	A614	140d	multicolored	1.25	1.25
1902	A615	150d	Building, heart, horiz.	1.25	1.25
1903	A615	170d	multicolored	2.00	1.60
1904	A616	500d	multicolored	6.50	1.90
	Nos. 1899-1904 (6)			12.15	6.75

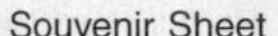

Souvenir Sheet

1998 FIBA World Basketball Championships, Greece — A617

1998, June 15 Litho. *Perf. 14*

1905	A617	300d	multicolored	3.50	3.50

Natl. Festivals
A618

Europa: 140d, Culture Festival, Grecian Theatre, Epidaurus. 500d, Culture Festival, Herod Atticus Theatre, Athens.

1998, May 29 Litho. *Perf. 14x13½*

1906	A618	140d	multicolored	*1.50*	*1.50*
1907	A618	500d	multicolored	*4.25*	*4.25*
a.	Pair, #1906-1907			*6.25*	*6.25*

Booklet Stamps
Perf. 13 Vert.

1906A	A618	140d	multicolored	*1.75*	*1.75*
1907B	A618	500d	multicolored	*5.00*	*5.00*
c.	Bklt. pane, 2 ea. #1906A, 1907B			*14.50*	*14.50*
	Complete booklet, #1907c			*14.50*	
d.	Pair, #1906A, 1907B			*7.25*	*7.25*

Castle Ruins in Greece
A619

30d, Hierapetra. 50d, Korfu. 70d, Limnos. 100d, Argolis. 150d, Iraklion. 170d, Navpaktos, vert. 200d, Ioannina, vert. 400d, Plataea. 550d, Karitainas, vert. 600d, Fragkokastello, Crete.

1998, July 15 Litho. *Perf. 13¼*

1908	A619	30d	multicolored	.25	.25
1909	A619	50d	multicolored	.40	.25
1910	A619	70d	multicolored	.55	.30
1911	A619	100d	multicolored	.75	.40
1912	A619	150d	multicolored	.75	.65
1913	A619	170d	multicolored	1.25	.90
1914	A619	200d	multicolored	2.00	1.00
1915	A619	400d	multicolored	4.50	1.50
1916	A619	550d	multicolored	6.25	2.25
1917	A619	600d	multicolored	6.50	2.75
	Nos. 1908-1917 (10)			23.20	10.25

Booklet Stamps
Perf. 13¼ Vert. or Horiz.

1908A	A619	30d	multicolored	.25	.25
1909A	A619	50d	multicolored	.40	.25
1910A	A619	70d	multicolored	.55	.30
1911A	A619	100d	multicolored	.75	.40
1912A	A619	150d	multicolored	.75	.65
1913A	A619	170d	multicolored	1.25	.90
1914A	A619	200d	multicolored	2.00	1.00
1915A	A619	400d	multicolored	4.50	1.50
1916A	A619	550d	multicolored	6.25	2.25
1917A	A619	600d	multicolored	6.50	2.75
	Nos. 1908A-1917A (10)			23.20	10.25

Nos. 1908A-1917A were each sold in booklets containing 20 panes of 5 stamps. Nos.1908A-1912A, 1915A, and 1917A are perforated horizontally. Nos. 1913A-1914A, and 1916A are perforated vertically.

Greek Orthodox Community of Venice, 500th Anniv. — A620

Designs: 30d, Cathedral. 40d, Icon, vert. 140d, Illuminated manuscript, vert. 230d, Icon of Madonna and Child surrounded by saints.

1998, Oct. 26 Litho. *Perf. 14*

1918	A620	30d	multicolored	.30	.25
1919	A620	40d	multicolored	.55	.35
1920	A620	140d	multicolored	1.50	.85
1921	A620	230d	multicolored	3.50	2.00
	Nos. 1918-1921 (4)			5.85	3.45

Greek Writers of Antiquity — A621

1998 Litho. *Perf. 13½x13*

1922	A621	20d	Homer	.25	.25
1923	A621	100d	Sophocles	1.60	1.60
1924	A621	140d	Thucydides	1.90	1.90
1925	A621	200d	Plato	2.40	2.40
1926	A621	250d	Demosthenes	3.75	3.75
	Nos. 1922-1926 (5)			9.90	9.90

Intl. Year of the Ocean
A622

Designs: 40d, Ancient ship, map of Mediterranean Sea. 100d, Sailing ship, Neptune. 200d, Modern ship . 500d, Silver tetradrachm of Antigonos Doson, 229-221 B.C.

1999, Feb. 19 Litho. *Perf. 13x13½*

1927	A622	40d	multicolored	.30	.25
1928	A622	100d	multicolored	.90	.40
1929	A622	200d	multicolored	1.60	1.00
1930	A622	500d	multicolored	3.25	1.50
	Nos. 1927-1930 (4)			6.05	3.15

Pres. Konstantin Karamanlis (1907-98) — A623

Various portraits of Karamanlis and: 100d, Representations of economic development, 1955-63. 170d, People celebrating. 200d, Emblem of European Union. 500d, National flag, vert.

1999, Apr. 19 Litho. *Perf. 14*

1931	A623	100d	multicolored	.70	.35
1932	A623	170d	multicolored	1.25	.75
1933	A623	200d	multicolored	1.50	.85
1934	A623	500d	multicolored	3.00	2.00
	Nos. 1931-1934 (4)			6.45	3.95

Europa
A624

Various views Mytikas peak (Mt. Olympus) and wildflowers.

1999, May 24 Litho. ***Perf. 14***

1935 A624 170d multicolored *1.75 1.75*
1936 A624 550d multicolored *4.50 4.00*
a. Pair, #1935-1936 *6.75 6.75*

Booklet Stamps
Perf. 13¼ Vert.

1935A A624 170d multicolored *2.00 1.75*
1936B A624 550d multicolored *4.75 4.00*
c. Booklet pane, 2 each #1935A, 1936B *14.00 14.00*
Complete booklet, #1936c *14.00*
d. Pair, #1935A, 1936B *7.00 7.00*

Greece-Japan Diplomatic Relations, Cent. — A625

1999, June 28 Litho. ***Perf. 13¾x14***

1937 A625 120d multicolored .90 .75

4000 Years of Hellenism — A626

Designs: a, Sanctuary of Apollo Hylates, Kourion. b, Mycenaean "Krater of the Warriors," Athens. c, Mycenaean amphoral krater, Cyprus Museum. d, Sanctuary of Apollo Epikourios, Delphi.

1999, June 28 Litho. ***Perf. 13½x13***

1938 A626 120d Block of 4, #a.-d. 3.50 3.50

See Cyprus No. 936.

Community Support Framework, 5th Anniv. A627

Designs: 20d, Modernization of Greek Railway Organization. 120d, Rio-Antirrio Bridge. 140d, Modernization of Greek Post Office. 250d, Athens Metro train. 500d, Eleftherios Venizelos Airport, Athens.

1999, Nov. 8 Litho. ***Perf. 13x13¼***

1939 A627 20d multi .25 .25
1940 A627 120d multi .75 .75
1941 A627 140d multi .85 .85
1942 A627 250d multi 1.50 1.50
1943 A627 500d multi 3.00 3.00
Nos. 1939-1943 (5) 6.35 6.35

Armed Forces A628

20d, Exercise with helicopters, rafts. 30d, Patrol boat. 40d, F-16s in flight. 50d, CL-215 dousing forest fire. 70d, Destroyers. 120d, Distribution of goods in Bosnia. 170d, Mirage 2000 in flight. 250d, Exercise with helicopters, tanks. 600d, Submarine Okeanos.

Perf. 13¾x13½

1999, Dec. 13 Litho.

1944 A628 20d multi .25 .25
1945 A628 30d multi .25 .25
1946 A628 40d multi .25 .25
1947 A628 50d multi .30 .30
1948 A628 70d multi .40 .40
1949 A628 120d multi .70 .50
1950 A628 170d multi 1.25 1.10
1951 A628 250d multi 1.75 1.50
1952 A628 600d multi 3.75 3.50
Nos. 1944-1952 (9) 8.90 8.05

Christianity, 2000th Anniv. A629

Designs: 20d, Birth of Christ, vert. 50d, Inter-religious dialogue, vert. 120d, Angels with instruments, vert. 170d, Dove. 200d, Communion. 500d, Providence, vert.

2000, Jan. 1 ***Perf. 14¼x14***

1953 A629 20d multi .25 .25
1954 A629 50d multi .30 .30
1955 A629 120d multi .70 .70

Perf. 14x14¼

1956 A629 170d multi 1.00 1.00

Size: 35x35mm
Perf. 13¾

1957 A629 200d multi 1.25 1.25

Size: 27x57mm
Perf. 13½x14

1958 A629 500d multi 3.00 3.00
Nos. 1953-1958 (6) 6.50 6.50

Europa, 2000
Common Design Type

2000, May 9 Litho. ***Perf. 13¼x13***

1959 CD17 170d multi *3.00 3.00*

Booklet Stamps
Perf. 13 Vert.

1959A CD17 170d multi *3.50 3.50*
b. Booklet pane, 4 #1959A *14.00 14.00*
Complete booklet, #1959b *14.00*

Ships — A630

Designs: 10d, Steamship Ilissos. 120d, Destroyer Adrias. 170d, Steamship Ia II. 400d, Destroyer Vas. Olga.

Perf. 14¼x13¾

2000, June 26 Litho.

1960 A630 10d multi .30 .25
1961 A630 120d multi 1.00 .65
1962 A630 170d multi 1.90 1.10
1963 A630 400d multi 4.75 3.00
Nos. 1960-1963 (4) 7.95 5.00

Stampin' the Future Children's Stamp Design Contest Winners A631

Art by: 130d, Spyros Dalakos (rainbow). 180d, Ornella Moshovaki-Chaiger (robots). 200d, Zisis Zariotis (building, tree, vehicles). 620d, Athina Limoudi (rocket).

2000, June 26

1964 A631 130d multi .70 .70
1965 A631 180d multi 1.10 1.10
1966 A631 200d multi 1.75 1.75
1967 A631 620d multi 4.25 4.25
Nos. 1964-1967 (4) 7.80 7.80

Sydney and Athens — A632

Olympic torch, flag and: 200d, Parthenon. 650d, Sydney Opera House.

Perf. 13¼x13¾

2000, Sept. 15 Litho.

1968-1969 A632 Set of 2 5.00 5.00

See Australia Nos. 1873-1874.

Emblem of 2004 Athens Olympic Games — A633

Various backgrounds. Denominations: 10d, 50d, 130d, 180d, 200d, 650d.

2000, Nov. 7 ***Perf. 14x14¼***

1970-1975 A633 Set of 6 8.00 8.00

Souvenir Sheet

Stamps of the Cretan Government, Cent. — A634

No. 1976: a, 200d, Crete #69. b, 650d, Crete #71.

2000, Dec. 18 Litho. ***Perf. 14x14¼***

1976 A634 Sheet of 2, #a-b 15.00 15.00

Christianity, 2000th Anniv. — A635

Designs: 20d, Sculpture of Christ as Orpheus, vert. 30d, Sculpture of The Good Shepherd, vert. 40d, Mosaic of Christ, vert. 100d, Mural of Christ. 130d, Icon of Christ (green frame), vert. 150d, Icon of Christ with open Bible, vert. 180d, Icon of Christ with closed Bible (dark blue frame), vert. 1000d, Byzantine coin depicting Christ.

2000, Dec. 18 ***Perf. 14x14¼, 14¼x14***

1977-1984 A635 Set of 8 10.00 10.00

Post Office Savings Bank, Cent. A636

Designs: 20d, Mother and child, vert. 130d, Emblem and 2-euro coin.

Perf. 13¼x13¾, 13¾x13¼

2001, May 15 Litho.

1985-1986 A636 Set of 2 1.10 1.10

UN High Commissioner for Refugees, 50th Anniv. — A637

2001, May 15 ***Perf. 13¾x13¼***

1987 A637 140d multi 1.25 1.25

Thessaloniki Intl. Trade Fair, 75th Anniv. — A638

2001, May 15 ***Perf. 13¼x13¾***

1988 A638 180d multi 1.25 1.25

Aristotle University, Thessaloniki, 75th Anniv. — A639

2001, May 15 ***Perf. 13¾x13¼***

1989 A639 200d multi 1.50 1.50

Academy of Athens, 75th Anniv. A640

2001, May 15

1990 A640 500d multi 3.75 3.75

Ioannis Zigdis (1913-97), Politician — A641

2001, May 15 ***Perf. 13¼x13¾***

1991 A641 700d multi 5.00 5.00

Europa — A642

Designs: Nos. 1992a, 1992c, Dry leaf, parched earth. Nos. 1992b, 1992d, Water, fresh leaves.

2001, May 15 ***Perf. 14¼x13¾***

1992 A642 Horiz. pair 8.50 8.50
a. 180d multi 2.00 2.00
b. 650d multi 6.50 6.50

Booklet Stamps
Perf. 13¼ Vert.

1992C A642 Horiz. pair 8.50 8.50
d. 180d multi 2.00 2.00
e. 650d multi 6.50 6.50
f. Booklet pane, 2 # 1992C 17.00
Booklet, #1992f 17.00

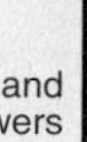

Birds and Flowers A643

Designs: 20d, Little egret. 50d, White stork. 100d, Bearded vulture. 140d, Orchid, vert. 150d, Dalmatian pelican, vert. 200d, Lily, Plastira Lake. 700d, Egyptian vulture. 850d, Black vulture.

Perf. 13¾x13¼, 13¼x13¾

2001, June 27

1993-2000	A643	Set of 8	17.00	17.00

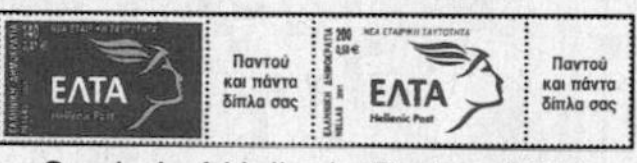

Symbol of Hellenic Post — A644

2001, Sept. 8 Litho. *Perf. 13x12¾*

2001	A644	Pair + 2 labels	2.50	2.50
a.		140d blue & yellow	1.00	1.00
b.		200d blue	1.50	1.50

Wording on label varies. No. 2001 could be personalized by adding photos to the labels.

Souvenir Sheet

Christianity in Armenia, 1700th Anniv. — A645

2001, Dec. 5 ***Perf. 13***

2002	A645 850d multi		9.50	9.50

Souvenir Sheet

2004 Summer Olympics, Athens — A646

2001, Dec. 5 ***Perf. 13¾***

2003	A646 1200d multi		9.50	9.50

100 Cents = 1 Euro (€)

Dances A647

Designs: 2c, Kamakaki. 3c, Bride's dowry. 5c, Zagorissios, vert. 10c, Balos. 15c, Synkathistos. 20c, Tsakonikos, vert. 30c, Pyrrichios. 35c, Fourles, vert. 40c, Apokriatikos. 45c, Kotsari. 50c, Pentozalis, vert. 55c, Karagouna. 60c, Hassapiko. 65c, Zalistos. 85c, Pogonissios. €1, Kalamatianos. €2, Maleviziotis. €2.15, Tsamikos. €2.60, Zeibekikos, vert. €3, Nyfiatikos. €4, Paschaliatikos.

Perf. 13x13¼, 13¼x13

2002, Jan. 2 Litho.

2004	A647	2c multi	.25	.25
2005	A647	3c multi	.25	.25
2006	A647	5c multi	.25	.25
2007	A647	10c multi	.30	.30
2008	A647	15c multi	.45	.45
2009	A647	20c multi	.60	.60
2010	A647	30c multi	.90	.90
2011	A647	35c multi	1.00	1.00
2012	A647	40c multi	1.25	1.25
2013	A647	45c multi	1.40	1.40
2014	A647	50c multi	1.50	1.50
2015	A647	55c multi	1.60	1.60
2016	A647	60c multi	1.75	1.75
2017	A647	65c multi	1.90	1.90
2018	A647	85c multi	2.50	2.50
2019	A647	€1 multi	3.00	3.00
2020	A647	€2 multi	6.00	6.00
2021	A647	€2.15 multi	6.50	6.50
2022	A647	€2.60 multi	7.75	7.75
2023	A647	€3 multi	9.00	9.00
2024	A647	€4 multi	12.00	12.00
	Nos. 2004-2024 (21)		60.15	60.15

Booklet Stamps

Perf. 13¼ Vert. or Horiz.

2004A	A647	2c multi	.25	.25
2005A	A647	3c multi	.25	.25
2006A	A647	5c multi	.25	.25
2007A	A647	10c multi	.30	.30
2008A	A647	15c multi	.45	.45
2009A	A647	20c multi	.60	.60
2010A	A647	30c multi	.90	.90
2011A	A647	35c multi	1.00	1.00
2012A	A647	40c multi	1.25	1.25
2013A	A647	45c multi	1.40	1.40
2014A	A647	50c multi	1.50	1.50
2015A	A647	55c multi	1.60	1.60
2016A	A647	60c multi	1.75	1.75
2017A	A647	65c multi	1.90	1.90
2018A	A647	85c multi	2.50	2.50
2019A	A647	€1 multi	3.00	3.00
2020A	A647	€2 multi	6.00	6.00
2021A	A647	€2.15 multi	6.50	6.50
2022A	A647	€2.60 multi	7.75	7.75
2023A	A647	€3 multi	9.00	9.00
2024A	A647	€4 multi	12.00	12.00
	Nos. 2004A-2024A (21)		60.15	60.15

Nos. 2004A-2024A were each sold in booklets containing 20 panes of 5 stamps.

2004 Summer Olympics, Athens A648

Ancient Olympics: 41c, Runners. 59c, Sculpture of charioteer, vert. 80c, Javelin thrower. €2.05, Doryphoros of Polycleitos, vert. €2.35, Weight lifter.
€5, Stadium archway.

Perf. 13¾x13¼, 13¼x13¾

2002, Mar. 15 Litho.

2025-2029	A648	Set of 5	19.00	19.00

Souvenir Sheet

Perf. 12¾

2030	A648	€5 multi	15.00	15.00

No. 2030 contains one 49x28mm stamp.

Europa — A649

2002, May 9 ***Perf. 13¼x13¾***

2031	A649	Horiz. pair, #a-b	*8.50*	*8.50*
a.		60c Elephant	*1.75*	*1.75*
b.		€2.60 Equestrian act	*6.75*	*6.75*

Booklet Stamp

Perf. 13¼ Vert.

2031C	A649	Horiz. pair, #d-e	*8.50*	*8.50*
d.		60c Elephant	*1.75*	*1.75*
e.		€2.60 Equestrian act	*6.75*	*6.75*
f.		Booklet pane, 2, #2031C	*17.00*	—
		Booklet, #2031f	*17.00*	

Scouting A650

Designs: 45c, Navy Scout, sailboats. 60c, Scout, emblem of World Conference. 70c, Scouts planting tree. €2.15, Scouts, map and mountain.

2002, June 26 Litho. *Perf. 13x13½*

2032-2035	A650	Set of 4	11.50	11.50
2035a		Miniature sheet, 2 each #2032-2035 + 4 labels	25.00	25.00

Greek Language A651

Designs: 45c, Hieros Nomos, Athens Acropolis, 5th cent. B.C. 60c, Linear B script, 13th cent. B.C., vert. 90c, The Memoirs of General Makriyiannis. €2.15, Byzantine script, 11th cent., vert.

Perf. 13¾x13¼, 13¼x13¾

2002, Sept. 23

2036-2039	A651	Set of 4	10.00	10.00

Ancient Olympic Winners With Laurel Wreaths — A652

Head color: 45c, Green. 60c, Dark blue. €2.15, Pink. €2.60, Light blue.

2002, Oct. 30 Litho. *Perf. 13¼x13¾*

2040-2043	A652	Set of 4	17.50	17.50
2043a		Miniature sheet, 2 each #2040-2043	35.00	35.00

Souvenir Sheet

Stadia of First Olympics — A653

2002, Oct. 30 ***Perf. 12¾***

2044	A653 €6 multi		18.00	18.00

Archbishops of Athens A654

Archbishop and years of reign: 10c, Chrysostomos I (1923-38). 45c, Chrysanthos (1938-41). €2.15, Damaskinos (1941-49). €2.60, Serapheim (1974-98).

2002, Dec. 10 ***Perf. 13x13½***

2045-2048	A654	Set of 4	16.00	16.00

Olympic Sports Equipment — A655

Designs: 2c, Discus. 5c, Hammer. 47c, Javelin. 65c, Pole vault pole and bar. €2.17, Hurdles. €2.85, Weights.

2003, Feb. 11 ***Perf. 13¾x14¼***

2049-2054	A655	Set of 6	13.00	7.00
2054a		Sheet, #2049-2054	20.00	20.00

2004 Summer Olympics, Athens.

Souvenir Sheet

Mascots for 2004 Summer Olympics, Athens — A656

No. 2055: a, €2.50, Mascot with red shirt. b, €2.85, Mascot with blue shirt.

2003, Feb. 11 ***Perf. 13¼***

2055	A656	Sheet of 2, #a-b	16.00	16.00

Greetings — A657

No. 2056: a, Globe. b, Athens 2004 Olympic Games emblem and Olympic rings. c, Ancient Greek athlete with laurel wreath. d, Roses and wedding headband. e, Spheres and grid. f, Child's drawing of train. g, Man and woman holding flowers. h, Stone carving of face. i, Acropolis.

2003, Mar. 18 Litho. *Perf. 14x13¾*

2056	A657	Sheet of 9	13.50	13.50
a.-g.		47c Any single	1.40	1.40
h.-i.		65c Either single	2.00	2.00
q.		No. 2056h + label	3.75	3.75
r.		#2056a + label	2.00	2.00
s.		#2056b + label	2.00	2.00
t.		#2056c + label	2.00	2.00
u.		#2056d + label	2.00	2.00
v.		#2056e + label	2.00	2.00
w.		#2056f + label	2.00	2.00
x.		#2056g + label	2.00	2.00
y.		#2056i + label	3.75	3.75

No. 2056q and 2056y were issued in sheets of 15 stamps and 15 labels that sold for €19.50. Labels could be personalized. No. 2056q exists dated "2004." Stamps dated "2004" were issued in sheets of 5 stamps + 5 preprinted labels that sold for €4 per sheet. Nos. 2056r-2056x were printed in sheets of 15 + 15 labels that sold for €14.10. Labels could be personalized.

Dove and Stars — A658

White Tower of Thessalon... Letters —

Fresco of Birds — A660

Jigsaw Puzzle Pieces — A661

2003, Apr. 16 ***Perf. 14x13¾***

2057 A658 47c multi 1.40 1.40
2058 A659 65c multi 2.00 2.00
2059 A660 €2.17 multi 6.50 6.50
2060 A661 €2.85 multi 8.50 8.50
2060a Sheet, 2 each #2057-2060 37.50 37.50
Nos. 2057-2060 (4) 10.40 10.40

Greek Presidency of European Union.

Europa — A662

Poster art: a, 65c, Abstract. b, €2.85, Tourist poster.

2003, May 9 Litho. ***Perf. 13¼x13¾***

2061 A662 Horiz. pair 10.50 10.50
a. 65c multi 2.00 2.00
b. €2.85 multi 8.50 8.50

Booklet Stamps
Perf. 13¼ Vert.

2061C A662 Horiz. pair 10.50 10.50
d. 65c multi 2.00 2.00
e. €2.85 multi 8.50 8.50
f. Booklet pane, 2 #2061C 21.00 —
Complete booklet, #2061f 21.00

A663

No. 2062: a, Water polo. b, Diving. c, Swimming.

No. 2063, vert.: a, Table tennis. b, Basketball. c, Soccer. d, Handball.

No. 2064: a, Kayak slalom. b, Windsurfing.

No. 2065, vert.: a, Rhythmic gymnastics. b, Judo. c, Archery. d, Trampoline.

No. 2066: a, Kayak (flatwater). b, Rowing (coxswain). c, Rowing (rower).

No. 2067, vert.: a, Badminton. b, Fencing. c, Tennis. d, Taekwondo.

No. 2068: a, Cycling. b, Triathlon.

No. 2069, vert.: a, Baseball. b, Beach volleyball. c, Field hockey. d, Boxing.

No. 2070, vert.: a, Weight lifting (figure in red) b, Weight lifting (figure in blue).

2003, May 9 Litho. ***Perf. 13¼***

2062 A663 Booklet pane of 3 + label 4.75 —
a.-c. 47c Any single 1.50 1.40
2063 A663 Booklet pane of 4 6.00 —
a.-d. 47c Any single 1.50 1.40
2064 A663 Booklet pane of 2 3.50 —
a.-b. 47c Either single 1.75 1.40
2065 A663 Booklet pane of 4 6.00 —
a. 30c multi 1.25 1.00
b.-d. 47c Any single 1.50 1.40
A663 Booklet pane of 3 + label 4.75 —
c. 47c Any single 1.50 1.40
A663 Booklet pane of 4 6.00 —
30c multi 1.25 1.00
47c Any single 1.50 1.40

2068 A663 Booklet pane of 2 3.50 —
a.-b. 47c Either single 1.75 1.40
2069 A663 Booklet pane of 4 6.00 —
a. 35c multi 1.25 1.10
b.-d. 47c Any single 1.50 1.40
2070 A663 Booklet pane of 2 3.50 —
a.-b. 47c Either single 1.75 1.40
Complete booklet, #2062-2070 50.00

Booklet containing Nos. 2062-2070 sold for €14.99.

Environmental Protection — A664

Designs: 15c, Apple falling from tree. 47c, Apple in water. 65c, Laurel wreath over seacoast. €2.85, Moon over tree.

2003, June 5 ***Perf. 13¼x13¾***

2071-2074 A664 Set of 4 12.50 12.50

Olympic Sports A665

Designs: 5c, High jump. 47c, Wrestling. 65c, Running. 80c, Cycling, vert. €4, Windsurfing, vert.

Perf. 13¾x13¼, 13¼x13¾

2003, Sept. 9

2075-2079 A665 Set of 5 18.00 18.00
2079a Miniature sheet, #2075-2079 18.00 18.00

Souvenir Sheet

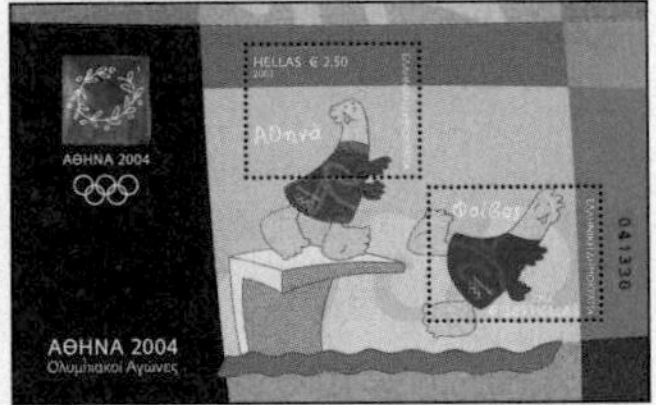

Mascots for 2004 Summer Olympics, Athens — A666

No. 2080: a, Figure in red. b, Figure in blue.

2003, Sept. 9 ***Perf. 13¼***

2080 A666 Sheet of 2 16.00 16.00
a. €2.50 multi 7.50 7.50
b. €2.85 multi 8.50 8.50

Trades of the Past — A667

Designs: 3c, Stair carving. 10c, Shoemaking. 50c, Blacksmithing. €1, Typesetting by hand. €1.40, Sponge fishing. €4, Weaving.

2003, Oct. 17 ***Perf. 13¾x13¼***

2081-2086 A667 Set of 6 21.00 21.00
2086a Miniature sheet, #2081-2086 21.00 21.00

Olympic Athletes — A668

Various athletes: 20c, 30c, 40c, 47c, €2, €2.85.

Perf. 13¼x13¾

2003, Nov. 28 Litho.

2087-2092 A668 Set of 6 19.00 19.00
2092a Miniature sheet, #2087-2092 19.00 19.00

Greek Olympians A669

Athletes: 3c, Spyridon Louis, marathon, 1896 gold medalist. 10c, Aristides Konstantinides, cycling road race, 1896 gold medalist. €2, Ioannis Fokianos, gymnastics coach. €2.17, Ioannis Mitropoulos, rings, 1896 gold medalist. €3.60, Konstantinos Tsiklitiras, standing long jump, 1912 gold medalist.

Litho. with Foil Application

2004, Jan. 15 ***Perf. 13x13½***

2093-2097 A669 Set of 5 24.00 24.00

Cities Hosting Events at 2004 Olympics A670

Designs: 1c, Volos. 2c, Patra. 5c, Iraklion. 47c, Athens. €1.40, Thessaloniki. €4, Athens, diff.

2004, Jan. 15 Litho.

2098-2103 A670 Set of 6 18.00 18.00
2103a Miniature sheet, #2098-2103 20.00 20.00

Olympic Sports A671

Designs: 5c, Swimmer. 10c, Gymnast chalking hands. 20c, Kayak. 47c, Relay race. €2, Rhythmic gymnastics, vert. €5, Men's rings, vert.

2004, Mar. 24 Litho. ***Perf. 13¼***

2104-2109 A671 Set of 6 24.00 24.00
2109a Miniature sheet, #2104-2109 24.00 24.00

Europa — A672

2004, May 4 ***Perf. 13¼x13¾***

2110 A672 Horiz. pair 10.50 10.50
a. 65c Sailboat 2.00 2.00
b. €2.85 Balloon 8.50 8.50

Booklet Stamps
Perf. 13¼ Vert.

2110C A672 Horiz. pair 10.50 10.50
d. 65c Sailboat 2.00 2.00
e. €2.85 Balloon 8.50 8.50
f. Booklet pane, 2 #2110C 21.00 —
Complete booklet, #2110f 21.00

Souvenir Sheets

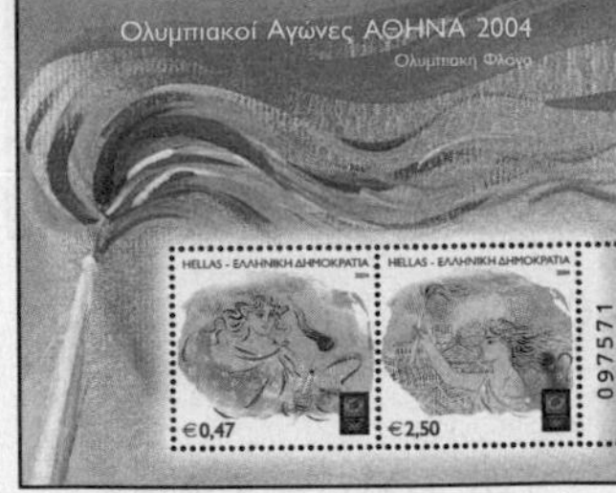

Olympic Flame — A673

Olympic Dove — A674

2004, May 4 ***Perf. 13¾x14***

2111 A673 Sheet of 2 9.00 9.00
a. 47c Torch bearer 1.40 1.40
b. €2.50 Torch bearer, city 7.50 7.50
c. #2111a + label, perf. 14x13¾ 2.40 2.40

Perf. 13¼

2112 A674 Sheet of 2 9.00 9.00
a. 47c Dove, Olympic rings 1.40 1.40
b. €2.50 Dove, people 7.50 7.50

No. 2111c was printed in sheets of 15 + 15 labels that sold for €15. Labels could be personalized.

Olympic Coins — A675

Obverse and reverse of: 47c, Silver three-drachma of Cos, 480-450 BC. 65c, Gold stater of Philip II of Macedonia. €2, Silver two-drachma of Elis, 460 BC. €2.17, Silver four-drachma of Philip II of Macedonia.

2004, June 15 ***Perf. 13¼***

2113-2116 A675 Set of 4 16.00 16.00
2116a Miniature sheet, #2113-2116 16.00 16.00

Souvenir Sheets

Modern Art and the Olympics — A676

2004, July 23 ***Perf. 13x13¼***

2117 A676 Sheet of 2 9.00 9.00
a. 50c Wavy lines 1.50 1.50
b. €2.50 Stripes of color 7.50 7.50

Perf. 13¼x13

2118 A676 Sheet of 2 9.00 9.00
a. €1 Paint brush, vert. 3.00 3.00
b. €2 Paint roller, vert. 6.00 6.00
c. Miniature sheet, #2117a-2117b, 2118a-2118b 18.00 18.00

Greece, 2004 European Soccer Champions A677

Designs: 47c, Greek flag, trophy. 65c, Greek players celebrating. €1, Greek players holding trophy. €2.88, Greek players, trophy.

2004, July 16 Litho. ***Perf. 13x13¼***

2119-2122	A677	Set of 4	15.00	15.00
a.	Souvenir sheet, #2119-2122		15.00	15.00

Greek Flag and Trophy — A678

2004, July Litho. ***Perf. 14x13¾***

2123	A678	47c multi + label	1.60	1.60
a.	Sheet of 5 + 5 labels		8.25	—
b.	Sheet of 10 + 10 labels		16.50	—

No. 2123 was printed in sheets of 15 + 15 labels that could be personalized. The sheet sold for €15. Nos. 2123a and 2123b have labels that depict soccer players or emblems, which cannot be personalized. Nos. 2123a and 2123b exist with two different sets of labels, and the set of 4 sheets sold for €20.

2004 Summer Olympics, Athens — A679

Designs: 50c, Hall of Good Harvest, Temple of Heaven, Beijing. 65c, Parthenon, Athens.

2004, Aug. 9 Litho. ***Perf. 14***

2124-2125	A679	Set of 2	4.00	4.00
2125a	Souvenir sheet, #2124-2125		4.00	4.00
2125b	#2125 + label		6.00	6.00

No. 2125b was issued in sheets of 15 + 15 labels thaty sold for €19.50. Labels could be personalized. See People's Republic of China Nos. 3376-3377.

Souvenir Sheet

Olymphilex 2004 Philatelic Exhibition — A680

2004, Aug. 13 ***Perf. 13½x13¼***

2126	A680	€6 multi	18.00	18.00

Nikos Syranidis and Thomas Bimis, Synchronized Diving Gold Medalists A681

Leonidas Sampanis, Disqualified Bronze Medalist in 62 Kilogram Weight Lifting — A682

Ilias Iliadis, Judo Gold Medalist A683

Sofia Bekatorou and Emilia Tsoulfa, Women's 470 Sailing Gold Medalists A684

Pyrros Dimas, 85 Kilogram Weight Lifting Bronze Medalist A685

Dimosthenis Tampakos, Rings Gold Medalist A686

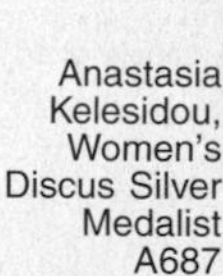

Anastasia Kelesidou, Women's Discus Silver Medalist A687

Vasilis Polymeros and Nikos Skiathitis, Lightweight Double Sculls Bronze Medalists A688

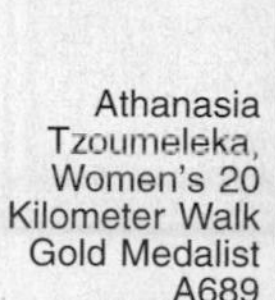

Athanasia Tzoumeleka, Women's 20 Kilometer Walk Gold Medalist A689

Chrysopigi Devezi, Women's Triple Jump Silver Medalist A690

Fani Chalkia, Women's 400-Meter Hurdles Gold Medalist A691

Nikos Kaklamanakis, Men's Mistral Sailing Silver Medalist A692

Artiom Kiouregian, 55 Kilogram Greco-Roman Wrestling Bronze Medalist A693

Women's Water Polo Team, Silver Medalist A694

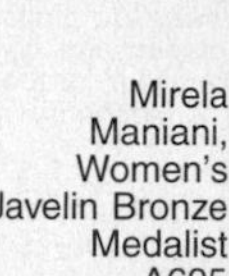

Mirela Maniani, Women's Javelin Bronze Medalist A695

Elisavet Mystakidou, Women's 67 Kilogram Taekwondo Silver Medalist A696

Alexandros Nikolaidis, Men's 80 Kilogram Taekwondo Silver Medalist A697

Digitally Printed

2004, Aug. ***Perf. 13¼***

2127	A681	65c multi	1.90	1.90
2128	A682	65c multi	19.00	19.00
2129	A683	65c multi	1.90	1.90
2130	A684	65c multi	1.90	1.90
2131	A685	65c multi	1.90	1.90
2132	A686	65c multi	1.90	1.90
2133	A687	65c multi	1.90	1.90
2134	A688	65c multi	1.90	1.90
2135	A689	65c multi	1.90	1.90
2136	A690	65c multi	1.90	1.90
2137	A691	65c multi	1.90	1.90
2138	A692	65c multi	1.90	1.90
2139	A693	65c multi	1.90	1.90
2140	A694	65c multi	1.90	1.90
2141	A695	65c multi	1.90	1.90
2142	A696	65c multi	1.90	1.90
2143	A697	65c multi	1.90	1.90
	Nos. 2127-2143 (17)		49.40	49.40

Litho.

2144	A681	65c multi	1.90	1.90
2145	A682	65c multi	15.00	15.00
2146	A683	65c multi	1.90	1.90
2147	A684	65c multi	1.90	1.90
2148	A685	65c multi	1.90	1.90
2149	A686	65c multi	1.90	1.90
2150	A687	65c multi	1.90	1.90
2151	A688	65c multi	1.90	1.90
2152	A689	65c multi	1.90	1.90
2153	A690	65c multi	1.90	1.90
2154	A691	65c multi	1.90	1.90
2155	A692	65c multi	1.90	1.90
2156	A693	65c multi	1.90	1.90
2157	A694	65c multi	1.90	1.90
2158	A695	65c multi	1.90	1.90
2159	A696	65c multi	1.90	1.90
2160	A697	65c multi	1.90	1.90
a.	Souvenir sheet, #2144, 2146-2160		30.00	30.00
	Nos. 2144-2160 (17)		45.40	45.40

Issued: Nos. 2127-2128, 8/17; No. 2129, 8/18; Nos. 2130-2131, 8/22; Nos. 2132-2134, 8/23, Nos. 2135-2136, 8/24, Nos. 2137-2139, 8/26, No. 2140, 8/27; No. 2141, 8/28; No. 2142, 8/29; No. 2143, 8/30. Nos. 2144-2160 were to have been issued within days of the digitally printed stamp with the same design. The digitally printed stamps have almost illegible lettering above the Olympic rings at upper right, and fuzzy, indistinct details in the emblem above this lettering. These details are clearer and more readable on the lithographed stamps.

Nos. 2128 and 2145 were withdrawn from circulation after the athlete shown was stripped of his medal after failing a drug test.

2004 Paralympics, Athens — A698

Designs: 20c, Horses and riders. 49c, Handicapped runner. €2, Wheelchair basketball. €2.24, Archer in wheelchair.

Perf. 13¼x13¾

2004, Sept. 22 Litho.

2161-2164	A698	Set of 4	12.50	12.50

Island Views — A699

2004, Dec. 27 ***Perf. 14x13¾***

2165	A699	2c	Santorini	.25	.25
2166	A699	3c	Karpathos	.25	.25
2167	A699	5c	Crete-Vai	.25	.25
2168	A699	10c	Mykonos	.30	.30
2169	A699	49c	Canea	1.50	1.50
2170	A699	50c	Castellorizo	1.50	1.50
2171	A699	€1	Astipalaia	3.00	3.00
2172	A699	€2	Serifos	6.00	6.00
2173	A699	€2.24	Melos	6.75	6.75
2174	A699	€4	Skiathos	12.00	12.00
	Nos. 2165-2174 (10)			31.80	31.80

Booklet Stamps

Perf. 13¼ Horiz.

2165A	A699	2c	Santorini	.25	.25
2166A	A699	3c	Karpathos	.25	.25
2167A	A699	5c	Crete-Vai	.25	.25
2168A	A699	10c	Mykonos	.30	.30
2169A	A699	49c	Canea	1.50	1.50
2170A	A699	50c	Castel-lorizo	1.50	1.50
2171A	A699	€1	Astipalaia	3.00	3.00
2172A	A699	€2	Serifos	6.00	6.00
2173A	A699	€2.24	Melos	6.75	6.75
2174A	A699	€4	Skiathos	12.00	12.00
	Nos. 2165A-2174A (10)			31.80	31.80

Jewelry A700

Designs: 1c, Necklace, 730 B.C. 15c, Snake-shaped bracelet, 2nd-3rd cent. B.C., vert. 30c, Necklace, 5th cent. 49c, Crown, 2nd cent. €4, Earring, 8th cent. B.C., vert.

Perf. 13¾x13¼, 13¼x13¾

2005, Feb. 25

2175-2179	A700	Set of 5	15.00	15.00

State Laboratory, 75th Anniv. — A701

European Diabetes Association, 41st Meeting — A702

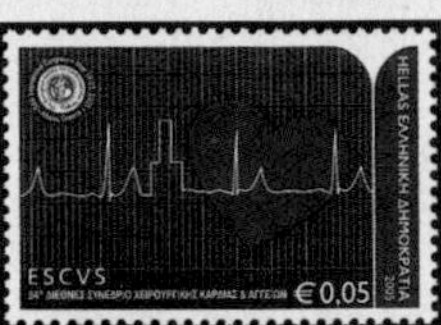

European Society for Cardiovascular Surgery, 54th Congress — A703

I. Kondilakis, First President of Athens Journalists Union — A704

Year of Economic Competitiveness — A705

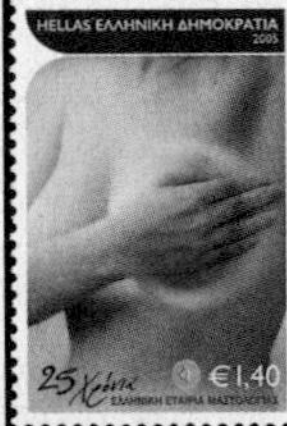

Greek Mastological Society, 25th Anniv. — A706

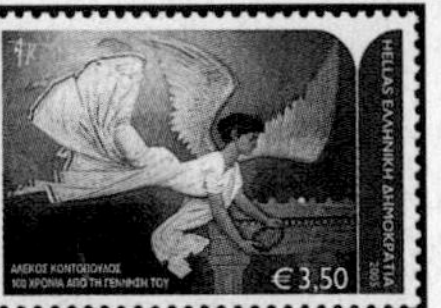

Angel, by Alekos Kontopoulos — A707

2005, Apr. 5 ***Perf. 13¼x13, 13x13¼***

2180 A701 1c multi .25 .25
2181 A702 4c multi .25 .25
2182 A703 5c multi .25 .25
2183 A704 40c multi 1.25 1.25
2184 A705 49c multi 1.50 1.50
2185 A706 €1.40 multi 4.25 4.25
2186 A707 €3.50 multi 10.50 10.50
Nos. 2180-2186 (7) 18.25 18.25

Flowers — A708

Designs: 20c, Gladiolus illyricus. 40c, Crocus sieberi. 49c, Narcissus tazetta. €1.40, Rhododendron luteum. €3, Tulipa boeotica.

2005, Apr. 5 ***Perf. 13¼x13¾***

2187-2191 A708 Set of 5 16.00 16.00

Europa — A709

2005, May 19 ***Perf. 14¼x13¾***

2192 A709 Horiz. pair 9.00 9.00
a. 65c Finished dish 2.00 2.00
b. €2.35 Ingredients 7.00 7.00

Booklet Stamps
Perf. 13¼ Vert.

2192C A709 Horiz. pair 9.00 9.00
d. 65c Finished dish 2.00 2.00
e. €2.35 Ingredients 7.00 7.00
f. Booklet pane, 2 #2192C 18.00 —
Complete booklet, #2192f 18.00

Wine Grapes A710

Designs: 20c, Agiorgitiko grapes and grape pickers, Peloponnisos. 49c, Assyrtiko grapes, Santorini. 65c, Xinomavro grapes and coin, Macedonia. €2.24, Robolla grapes, Cephalonia. €2.40, Moschofilero, Peloponnisos.

2005, May 19 ***Perf. 13¾x14***

2193-2197 A710 Set of 5 18.00 18.00

Blackboard A711

Girl Reading — A712

Envelope A713

Stylized People — A714

Grid — A715

Globe and Stylized Stamp — A716

Flowers — A717

Church — A718

2005, July 15 ***Perf. 14x13¾***

2198 A711 49c multi 1.50 1.50
a. #2198 + label 2.50 2.50
2199 A712 49c multi 1.50 1.50
a. #2199 + label 2.50 2.50
2200 A713 49c multi 1.50 1.50
a. #2200 + label 2.50 2.50
2201 A714 49c multi 1.50 1.50
a. #2201 + label 2.50 2.50
2202 A715 49c multi 1.50 1.50
a. #2202 + label 2.50 2.50
2203 A716 49c multi 1.50 1.50
a. #2203 + label 2.50 2.50
2204 A717 49c multi 1.50 1.50
a. #2204 + label 2.50 2.50
2205 A718 65c multi 1.90 1.90
a. #2205 + label 3.25 3.25
Nos. 2198-2205 (8) 12.40 12.40

Nos. 2198a, 2199a and 2200a were printed in sheets of 10 + 10 labels that sold for €10. Nos. 2201a, 2202a, 2203a and 2204a were printed in sheets of 15 + 15 labels that sold for €15. No. 2205a was printed in sheets of 10 + 10 labels that sold for €13. Labels could be personalized.

Drawing by Fokion Dimitriadis A719

Drawing by Archelaos A720

Drawing by Themos Anninos — A721

Drawing by Dimitris Galanis — A722

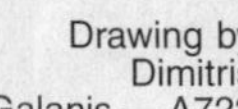

Drawing by Kostas Mitropoulos A723

Unattributed Odyssey Scene — A724

2005, Sept. 16 ***Perf. 13¼x13¾***

2206 A719 15c multi .45 .45
2207 A720 20c multi .60 .60
2208 A721 30c multi .90 .90
2209 A722 50c multi 1.50 1.50
2210 A723 65c multi 1.90 1.90
2211 A724 €4 multi 12.00 12.00
Nos. 2206-2211 (6) 17.35 17.35

Booklet Panes of 1
Self-Adhesive

2212 A719 15c multi .45 .45
2213 A720 20c multi .60 .60
2214 A721 30c multi .90 .90
2215 A722 50c multi 1.50 1.50
2216 A723 65c multi 1.90 1.90
2217 A724 €4 multi 12.00 12.00
Complete booklet, #2212-2217 17.50
Nos. 2212-2217 (6) 17.35 17.35

Greece, 2005 European Basketball Champions A725

Basketball, net and: 30c, Players in game. 50c, Championship bowl. 65c, Fans. €3.55, Players celebrating.

2005, Oct. 7 **Litho.** ***Perf. 13x13¼***

2218-2221 A725 Set of 4 15.00 15.00
2221a Souvenir sheet, #2218-2221 15.00 15.00

Greece, 2005 European Basketball Champions — A725a

2005, Oct. 7 **Litho.** ***Perf. 14x13¾***

2221B A725a 50c multi + label 5.00 5.00

No. 2221B was printed in sheets of 10 + 10 labels that sold for €10. Labels could be personalized.

Automobiles — A726

Designs: 1c, Mini Cooper. 30c, Fiat 500. 50c, Citroen 2CV. €2.25, Volkswagen Beetle. €2.85, Ford Model T.

2005, Nov. 4 ***Perf. 13x13¼***

2222-2226 A726 Set of 5 17.50 17.50
2226a As #2226, without inscription "Ford Model T" 15.00 15.00
2226b Booklet pane, #2222-2225, 2226a 20.00 —
Complete booklet, #2226b 20.00

Panathinaikos Soccer Team Emblem — A727

Panionios Soccer Team Emblem — A728

Iraklis Soccer Team Emblem — A729

PAOK Soccer Team Emblem — A730

Panellinios Sports Club Emblem — A731

Designs: 30c, Ethnikos Sports Club emblem. €4, Omilos Ereton emblem.

2005, Nov. 30 Litho. *Perf. 14x13¾*

2227	A727	30c multi	.90	.90
2228	A727	50c multi	1.50	1.50
a.		#2228 + label	2.40	2.40
2229	A728	50c multi	1.50	1.50
a.		#2229 + label	2.40	2.40
2230	A729	50c multi	1.50	1.50
a.		#2230 + label	2.40	2.40
2231	A730	65c multi	1.90	1.90
a.		#2231 + label	3.25	3.25
2232	A731	65c multi	1.90	1.90
a.		#2232 + label	3.25	3.25
2233	A727	€4 multi	12.00	12.00
		Nos. 2227-2233 (7)	21.20	21.20

Nos. 2228a, 2229a and 2230a were printed in sheets of 10 + 10 labels that sold for €10. Nos. 2231a and 2232a were printed in sheets of 10 + 10 labels that sold for €13. Labels could be personalized.

Christmas A732

Icons: 1c, Hodeghetria Virgin. 20c, Kardiotissa Virgin. 70c, Glykophiloussa Virgin. €3.20, Virgin with Symbols of the Passion.

Litho. With Foil Application

2005, Dec. 20 *Perf. 13¾*

2234-2237 A732 Set of 4 12.50 12.50

Souvenir Sheet

Europa Stamps, 50th Anniv. — A733

2006, Jan. 10 Litho. *Perf. 13x13¼*

2238	A733	Sheet of 2	12.00	12.00
a.		€1.50 Greece #1255	4.50	4.50
b.		€2.50 Greece #1459	7.50	7.50

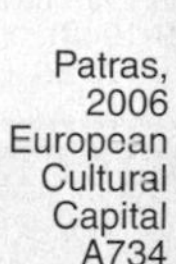

Patras, 2006 European Cultural Capital A734

Designs: 1c, Drama masks. 15c, Buildings, sailboat, lighthouse. 20c, Child. 50c, Carnival dragon and clown. 65c, Emblem, vert. €2.25, Jars, containers and boxes. €2.30, Icon, vert.

2006, Feb. 28 *Perf. 13x13¼, 13¼x13*

2239-2245 A734 Set of 7 18.00 18.00

Carnival Dragon and Clown — A734a

Emblem — A734b

2006, Feb. 28 Litho. *Perf. 14x13¾*

2245A	A734a	50c multi + label	2.40	2.40
2245B	A734b	65c multi + label	3.25	3.25

Patras, 2006 European Cultural Capital. Nos. 2245A and 2245B were issued in sheets of 10 stamps and 10 labels that could be personalized. Sheets of No. 2245A sold for €10; No. 2245B for €13.

Items in Greek Museums A735

Designs: 5c, Kouros of Anavissos, sculpture, 530 B.C., Natl. Archaeological Museum. 20c, Seated figure, 2800-2300 B.C., Museum of Cycladic Art. 50c, Spiral (28x28mm). 65c, Pediment from Parthenon, Acropolis Museum, horiz. €1.40, Greco-Roman portrait of an Egyptian, 4th cent. €2.25, Concert of the Angels, by El Greco, Natl. Art Gallery, horiz.

Litho with Foil Application, Litho. (50c)

2006, Apr. 7 *Perf. 14x13¾, 13¾x14*

2246-2251	A735	Set of 6	15.00	15.00
2248a		#2248 + label	2.50	2.50

No. 2248a was printed in sheets of 10 + 10 labels that sold for €10. Labels could be personalized.

Pediment From Parthenon — A735a

2006, Apr. 7 Litho. *Perf. 14x13¾*

2251A A735a 65c multi + label 3.25 3.25

No. 2251A was printed in sheets of 10 + 10 labels that sold for €13. Labels could be personalized.

Souvenir Sheets

Stamps Issued for 1906 Interim Olympic Games — A736

No. 2252: a, 20c, #187. b, 30c, #191. c, 50c, #188. d, €2, #192.

No. 2253: a, 50c, #189. b, 65c, #194. c, 85c, #197. d, €1, #190.

2006, Apr. 7 Litho. *Perf. 13x13¼*

Sheets of 4, #a-d

2252-2253 A736 Set of 2 18.00 18.00

Europa — A737

2006, May 15 *Perf. 13¾x14¼*

2254	A737	Horiz. pair	11.00	11.00
a.		65c Rope and moon	1.90	1.90
b.		€3 Rope and sun	9.00	9.00

Booklet Stamps

Perf. 13¼ Vert.

2254C	A737	Horiz. pair	11.00	11.00
d.		65c Rope and moon	1.90	1.90
e.		€3 Rope and sun	9.00	9.00
f.		Booklet pane, 2 #2254C	22.50	—
		Complete booklet, #2254f	22.50	

State General Archives — A738

Admission to European Union, 25th Anniv. — A739

2006 Eurovision Song Contest, Athens — A740

Olive and Olive Oil Year — A741

Tinia, Etruscan Sky God — A742

Greek Participation in 2005-06 UN Security Council — A743

2006, May 15 *Perf. 14x13¾*

2255	A738	15c multi	.45	.45
2256	A739	20c multi	.60	.60
2257	A740	50c multi	1.50	1.50
a.		#2257 + label	2.60	2.60
2258	A741	65c multi	1.90	1.90
a.		#2258 + label	3.50	3.50
2259	A742	€1.40 multi	4.25	4.25
2260	A743	€3 multi	9.00	9.00
		Nos. 2255-2260 (6)	17.70	17.70

No. 2257a was printed in sheets of 10 + 10 labels that sold for €10. No. 2258a was printed in sheets of 10 + 10 labels that sold for €13. Labels could be personalized.

Island Views A744

2006, June 16 Litho. *Perf. 14¼x14*

2261	A744	1c Lesbos	.25	.25
2262	A744	3c Hydra	.25	.25
2263	A744	10c Sifnos	.30	.30
2264	A744	20c Levkas	.60	.60
2265	A744	40c Samothrace	1.25	1.25
2266	A744	50c Syros	1.50	1.50
2267	A744	65c Rhodes	1.90	1.90
2268	A744	85c Cephalonia	2.50	2.50
2269	A744	€2.25 Corfu	6.75	6.75
2270	A744	€5 Naxos	15.00	15.00
		Nos. 2261-2270 (10)	30.30	30.30

Booklet Stamps

Perf. 13¼ Vert.

2261A	A744	1c Lesbos	.25	.25
2262A	A744	3c Hydra	.25	.25
2263A	A744	10c Sifnos	.30	.30
2264A	A744	20c Levkas	.60	.60
2265A	A744	40c Samothrace	1.25	1.25
2266A	A744	50c Syros	1.50	1.50
2267A	A744	65c Rhodes	1.90	1.90
2268A	A744	85c Cephalonia	2.50	2.50
2269A	A744	€2.25 Corfu	6.75	6.75
2270A	A744	€5 Naxos	15.00	15.00
		Nos. 2261A-2270A (10)	30.30	30.30

Syros — A744a

Rhodes — A744b

2006, June 16 Litho. ***Perf. 14x13¾***

2270B A744a 50c multi + label 2.60 2.60
2270C A744b 65c multi + label 5.00 5.00

No. 2270B was printed in sheets of 10 + 10 labels that sold for €10. No. 2270C was printed in sheets of 10 + 10 labels that sold for €13. Labels could be personalized.

Ancient Greek Technology A745

Designs: 3c, Trireme "Olympias." 5c, Odometer, by Hero of Alexandria. 50c, Piston water pump, vert. 65c, Antikythera Mechanism, vert. €3.80, Automatic temple gates, by Hero of Alexandria, vert.

Litho. With Foil Application
Perf. 13¾x13¼, 13¼x13¾

2006, Sept. 14

2271-2275 A745 Set of 5 15.00 15.00

Souvenir Sheet

Second Place Finish of Greek Team at 2006 World Basketball Championships — A746

Litho. With Foil Application

2006, Oct. 16 ***Perf. 13¼***

2276 A746 Sheet of 3 17.00 17.00
a. 50c Silver medal 1.50 1.50
b. €2 Team 6.00 6.00
c. €3 Team, medal ribbon 9.00 9.00

Silver Medal of 2006 Greek Team at World Basketball Championships — A746a

2006, Oct. 16 Litho. ***Perf. 14x13¾***

2276D A746a 50c multi + label 5.00 5.00

No. 2276D was printed in sheets of 5 + 5 labels that could not be personalized.

Soccer Team Emblems A747

Designs: 2c, Apollon Kalamaria. 3c, Atromitos Athinon. 52c, Aris Thessaloniki. €2.27, Ethnikos Piraeus. €3.20, Apollon Smyrnis.

2006, Nov. 29 Litho. ***Perf. 14x13¾***

2277-2281 A747 Set of 5 18.00 18.00
2279a #2279 + label 2.75 2.75

No. 2279a was printed in sheets of 10 + 10 labels that sold for €10. Labels could be personalized.

Items in Toys, Games and Childhood Section of Benaki Museum A748

Designs: 5c, Doll, chest and clothing from France, c. 1905. 15c, Wooden airplanes, c. 1940. 30c, Dolls made by Skonouchi Karopoulos, c. 1925. 40c, Horses on wheels made by Anesis Romeopoulos, c. 1920. 52c, Dominos, toy cat, duck on wheels. 72c, Parachutist, c. 1950, vert. €2.27, Airplane carousel, 1950s, vert. €4, Puppet theater of the Resistance, 1941-45, vert.

Perf. 13¾x13¼, 13¼x13¾

2006, Dec. 22

2282-2289 A748 Set of 8 25.00 25.00

Faces — A749

Globe — A750

Crescents A751

Artemis — A752

Ring Around Earth — A753

Parthenon A754

Phrasikleia Kore — A755

2007, Mar. 12 Litho. ***Perf. 14x13¾***

2290 A749 52c multi 1.40 1.40
a. #2290 + label 2.75 2.75
2291 A750 52c multi 1.40 1.40
a. #2291 + label 2.75 2.75
2292 A751 52c multi 1.40 1.40
a. #2292 + label 2.75 2.75
2293 A752 52c multi 1.40 1.40
a. #2293 + label 2.75 2.75
2294 A753 52c multi 1.40 1.40
a. #2294 + label 2.75 2.75
2295 A754 65c multi 1.75 1.75
a. #2295 + label 3.50 3.50
2296 A755 65c multi 1.75 1.75
a. Miniature sheet, #2290-2296 10.50 10.50
b. #2296 + label 3.50 3.50
Nos. 2290-2296 (7) 10.50 10.50

Nos. 2290a, 2292a amd 2293a were printed in sheets of 10 + 10 labels that sold for €10. Nos. 2291a and 2294a were printed in sheets of 15 + 15 labels that sold for €15. Nos. 2295a and 2296b were printed in sheets of 10 + 10 labels that sold for € 13. Labels could be personalized.

Kostis Palamas (1859-1943), Poet — A756

Greek Cultural Year in China A757

Symposium of Seven Cardiovascular Surgeons, Athens and Delphi — A758

2nd Union Network International World Postal Conference A759

Treaty of Rome, 50th Anniv. — A760

Georgios Kotzias (1918-77) A761

Rigas Velestinlis (1757-98), Poet — A762

Year of Innovation A763

State Legal Council, 125th Anniv. A764

Perf. 13¼x13¾, 13¾x13¼

2007, Apr. 25

2297 A756 2c multi .25 .25
2298 A757 10c multi .30 .30
2299 A758 20c multi .55 .55
2300 A759 52c multi 1.40 1.40
2301 A760 65c multi 1.75 1.75
2302 A761 85c multi 2.40 2.40
2303 A762 €1 multi 2.75 2.75
2304 A763 €2.27 multi 6.25 6.25
2305 A764 €3 multi 8.25 8.25
Nos. 2297-2305 (9) 23.90 23.90

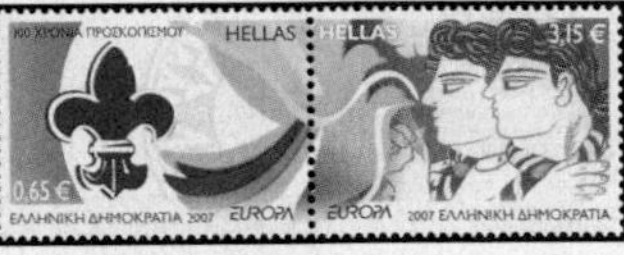

Europa — A765

No. 2306: a, Scouting fleur-de-lis, dove's tail. b, Scouts, dove's head.

2007, May 25 ***Perf. 14¼x14***

2306 A765 Horiz. pair 10.50 10.50
a. 65c multi 1.75 1.75
b. €3.15 multi 8.75 8.75

Booklet Stamps
Perf. 13¾ Vert.

2306C A765 Horiz. pair 10.50 10.50
d. 65c multi 1.75 1.75
e. €3.15 multi 8.75 8.75
f. Booklet pane, 2 #2306C 21.00 —
Complete booklet, #2306f 21.00

Scouting, cent.

Signs of the Zodiac A766

Litho. With Foil Application
Perf. 13¾x13¼, 13¼x13¾

2007, May 25

2307 A766 2c Scorpio .25 .25
2308 A766 3c Cancer .25 .25
2309 A766 5c Capricorn .25 .25
2310 A766 10c Taurus .30 .30
2311 A766 20c Sagittarius, vert. .55 .55
2312 A766 40c Leo, vert. 1.10 1.10
2313 A766 52c Virgo, vert. 1.40 1.40
2314 A766 65c Aries 1.75 1.75
2315 A766 85c Aquarius 2.40 2.40
2316 A766 €1 Libra 2.75 2.75
2317 A766 €2.27 Pisces 6.25 6.25
2318 A766 €2.80 Gemini 7.50 7.50
Nos. 2307-2318 (12) 24.75 24.75

Souvenir Sheet

Statues of Asclepius, Greek God of Medicine — A767

No. 2319: a, Statue from Museum of Ampurias, Spain. b, Statue from National Archaeological Museum, Athens.

2007, June 28 Litho. *Perf. 13¾*

2319 A767 Sheet of 2 13.50 13.50
a.-b. €2.50 Either single 6.75 6.75

See Spain No. 3521.

Discovery of the Tomb of St. Cyril, 150th Anniv. A768

University of Macedonia, 50th Anniv. A769

Konstantinos Tsatsos (1899-1987), Politician — A770

Litho. With Foil Application

2007, Sept. 28 *Perf. 13¾x14*

2320 A768 2c multi .25 .25

Litho.

2321 A769 3c multi .25 .25

Perf. 14x13¾

2322 A770 €4 multi 11.50 11.50
Nos. 2320-2322 (3) 12.00 12.00

Sports Team Emblems A771

Designs: 2c, Ergotelis Sports Club. 4c, OFI. 54c, Olympiacos C.F.P. €2.29, Doxa Dramas Sports Club. €5, Nautical Club of Mytilini.

2007, Nov. 2 Litho. *Perf. 14x13¾*

2323-2327 A771 Set of 5 23.00 23.00
2325a #2325 + label 3.00 3.00

No. 2325a was printed in sheets of 10 + 10 labels that sold for €10. Labels could be personalized.

Busts of Goddesses — A772

Designs: 54c, Bust of Aphrodite. €2.40, Bust of Goddess Anahit, Armenia.

2007, Dec. 14 *Perf. 14x14¼*

2328-2329 A772 Set of 2 8.75 8.75

See Armenia Nos. 774-775.

Islands A773

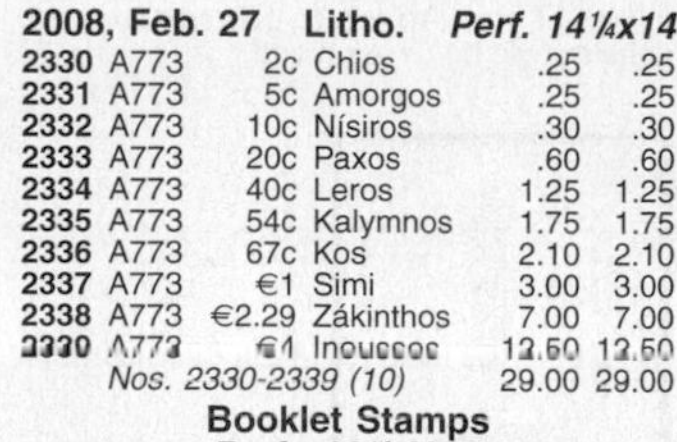

2008, Feb. 27 Litho. *Perf. 14¼x14*

2330 A773 2c Chios .25 .25
2331 A773 5c Amorgos .25 .25
2332 A773 10c Nísiros .30 .30
2333 A773 20c Paxos .60 .60
2334 A773 40c Leros 1.25 1.25
2335 A773 54c Kalymnos 1.75 1.75
2336 A773 67c Kos 2.10 2.10
2337 A773 €1 Simi 3.00 3.00
2338 A773 €2.29 Zákinthos 7.00 7.00
2339 A773 €4 Inousses 12.50 12.50
Nos. 2330-2339 (10) 29.00 29.00

Booklet Stamps
Perf. 13¼ Vert.

2330A A773 2c Chios .25 .25
2331A A773 5c Amorgos .25 .25
2332A A773 10c Nísiros .30 .30
2333A A773 20c Paxos .60 .60
2334A A773 40c Leros 1.25 1.25
2335A A773 54c Kalymnos 1.75 1.75
2336A A773 67c Kos 2.10 2.10
2337A A773 €1 Simi 3.00 3.00
2338A A773 €2.29 Zákinthos 7.00 7.00
2339A A773 €4 Inousses 12.50 12.50
Nos. 2330A-2339A (10) 29.00 29.00

2008 Summer Olympics, Beijing — A774

Designs: 3c, Discus thrower. 35c, Lighting of Olympic flame. No. 2342, 67c, Torch bearer. No. 2343, 67c, Three cyclists, horiz.

2008, Mar. 14 *Perf. 13½x13, 13x13½*

2340-2343 A774 Set of 4 5.50 5.50

Letter — A775

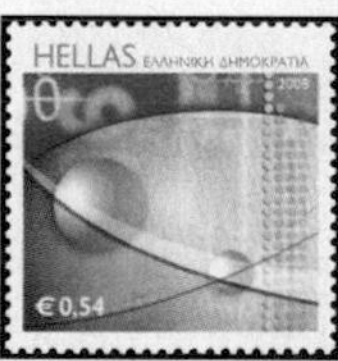

Numbers — A776

Heart — A777

Kites — A778

Pillar — A779

Greek Flag — A780

2008, Apr. 21 Litho. *Perf. 14x13¾*

2344 A775 54c multi 1.75 1.75
a. #2344 + label 4.75 4.75
2345 A776 54c multi 1.75 1.75
a. #2345 + label 4.75 4.75
2346 A777 54c multi 1.75 1.75
a. #2346 + label 4.75 4.75
2347 A778 54c multi 1.75 1.75
a. #2347 + label 4.75 4.75
2348 A779 67c multi 2.10 2.10
a. #2348 + label 5.75 5.75
2349 A780 67c multi 2.10 2.10
a. Miniature sheet, #2344-2349 11.50 11.50
b. #2349 + label 5.75 5.75
Nos. 2344-2349 (6) 11.20 11.20

Nos. 2344a, 2345a, 2346a and 2347a each were printed in sheets of 10 + 15 labels that sold for €10. Nos. 2348a and 2348b each were printed in sheets of 10 + 15 labels that sold for €13. Labels could be personalized.

Europa — A781

No. 2350: a, Inkwell, pen and papers. b, Fountain pen and papers.

2008, May 26 *Perf. 14¼x14*

2350 A781 Horiz. pair 12.50 12.50
a. 67c multi 2.25 2.25
b. €3.17 multi 10.00 10.00

Booklet Stamps
Perf. 13¾ Vert.

2350C A781 Horiz. pair 12.50 12.50
d. 67c multi 2.25 2.25
e. €3.17 multi 10.00 10.00
f. Booklet pane, 2 #2350C 25.00 —
Complete booklet, #2350f 25.00

Anniversaries A782

Curved lines and: 3c, Emblem of Hellenic Post. 5c, Posthorn, Greek men. 10c, Ioannis Kapodistrias (1776-1831), provisional president of Greece. 57c, M. Karagatsis (1908-60), writer. 70c, Fish. €1.85, Emblem of National Hellenic Research Foundation. €3, Emblem of National Council of Women.

2008, June 20 *Perf. 13¼x13¾*

2351-2357 A782 Set of 7 20.00 20.00

Hellenic Post, 180th anniv. (Nos. 2351-2352); Inauguration of Kapodistrias, 180th anniv. (No. 2353); Intl. Year of Planet Earth (No. 2355); National Hellenic Research Foundation, 50th anniv. (No. 2356), National Council of Women, cent. (No. 2357).

Greek Products — A783

Designs: 3c, Feta cheese and tomatoes. 5c, Mastic. 20c, Olive, bottle of olive oil, horiz. 57c, Bottle of ouzo, marine life and boat. €1, Pistachio nuts. €4, Bees, rose, jar of honey.

Perf. 13¼x13¾, 13¾x13¼

2008, Sept. 19

2358-2363 A783 Set of 6 16.50 16.50

Sports Team Emblems A784

Designs: 40c, Diagoras Rhodos Sports Club. 57c, A.E.K. soccer team. 70c, Asteras Tripolis soccer team. €2, Panserraoikos soccer team. €3, Kerkiraikos Sports Club.

2008, Oct. 20 *Perf. 14x13¾*

2364-2368 A784 Set of 5 17.00 17.00
2365a #2365 + label 4.00 4.00
2366a #2366 + label 4.00 4.00

Nos. 2365a and 2366a each were printed in sheets of 10 + 10 labels that sold for €13. Labels could be personalized.

Fairy Tales, Fables and Children's Literature A785

Designs: 10c, The Mermaid and Alexander the Great. 57c, Little Red Riding Hood. €1, The Fairies. €1.85, The Little Match Girl. €3, Arion and the Lyre.

2008, Dec. 16 *Perf. 13¾x14*

2369-2373 A785 Set of 5 18.00 18.00

Actors and Actresses A786

Designs: 1c, Manos Katrakis (1908-84). 20c, Dinos Iliopoulos (1915-2001). 35c, Elli Lambeti (1926-83). 40c, Alekos Alexandrakis (1928-2005). 50c, Aliki Vougiouklaki (1934-96). 57c, Jenny Karezi (1932-92). €1, Dimitris Horn (1921-98). €2.42, Nikos Kourkoulos (1934-2007). €3.50, Thanos Kotsopoulos (1911-94).

2009, Feb. 9 Litho. *Perf. 13¾x13¼*

2374-2382 A786 Set of 9 23.00 23.00
2382a Miniature sheet of 9, #2374-2382 23.00 23.00

Compare with type A828.

Souvenir Sheet

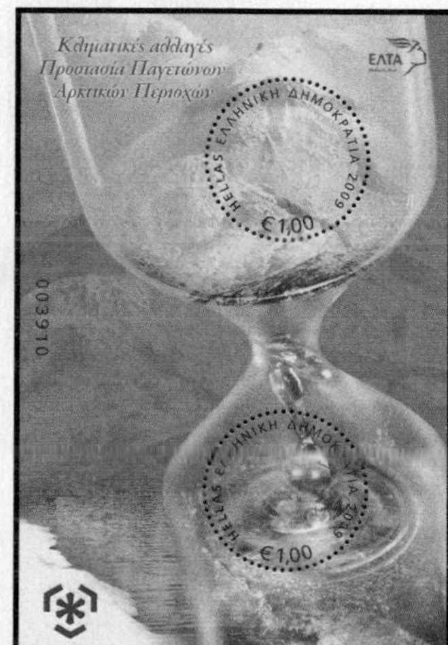

Preservation of Polar Regions and Glaciers — A787

No. 2383: a, Snow-covered mountain. b, Droplet of water.

2009, Mar. 3 *Perf.*

2383 A787 €1 Sheet of 2, #a-b 5.75 5.75

No. 2383 contains two 30mm diameter stamps.

Sivitanidios School, 80th Anniv. A788

University of Piraeus, 70th Anniv. — A789

Natl. Archaeological Museum, 180th Anniv. — A790

Greek Presidency of UPU Postal Operations Council A791

Eye, Braille Script, Hands Touching Braille Book A792

Introduction of Euro, 10th Anniv. A793

Lord Byron (1788-1824), Poet — A794

Natl. Real Estate Registry A795

Litho., Litho. With Foil Application (10c, 50c), Litho. & Embossed (57c)
Perf. 13¾x13¼, 13¼x13¾

2009, Mar. 30

2384	A788	5c multi	.25	.25
2385	A789	10c multi	.30	.30
2386	A790	20c multi	.60	.60
2387	A791	50c multi	1.50	1.50
2388	A792	57c multi	1.75	1.75
2389	A793	70c multi	2.10	2.10
2390	A794	€2.42 multi	7.25	7.25
2391	A795	€3 multi	9.00	9.00
		Nos. 2384-2391 (8)	22.75	22.75

Louis Braille (1809-52), educator of the blind (No. 2388), Hellenophile and Intl. Solidarity Day (No. 2390).

Europa — A796

No. 2392: a, Pulsar diagram. b, Aristarchos Telescope.

2009, May 11 Litho. ***Perf. 14¾x14***

2392	A796	Horiz. pair	11.00	11.00
a.		70c multi	2.00	2.00
b.		€3.20 multi	9.00	9.00

Booklet Stamps
Perf. 13¾ Vert.

2392C	A796	Horiz. pair	11.00	11.00
d.		70c multi	2.00	2.00
e.		€3.20 multi	9.00	9.00
f.		Booklet pane, 2 #2392C	22.00	—
		Complete booklet, #2392f	22.00	

Intl. Year of Astronomy.

UNESCO World Heritage Sites A797

Designs: No. 2393, 57c, Acropolis (denomination at LL). No. 2394, 57c, Meteora (denomination at UR). No. 2395, 70c, Delphi (denomination at UR). No. 2396, 70c, Mycenae (denomination at LL). €2, Mystras. €3, Delos.

Litho. With Foil Application

2009, June 20 ***Perf. 13¾x14***

2393-2398	A797	Set of 6	21.00	21.00
2398a		Miniature sheet of 6, #2393-2398	21.00	21.00

Acropolis — A797a

Meteora — A797b

Delphi — A797c

Mycenae — A797d

2009, June 20 Litho. ***Perf. 14x13¾***

2398B	A797a	57c multi + label	4.50	4.50
2398C	A797b	57c multi + label	4.50	4.50
2398D	A797c	70c multi + label	5.50	5.50
2398E	A797d	70c multi + label	5.50	5.50
		Nos. 2398B-2398E (4)	20.00	20.00

Nos. 2398B and 2398C each were printed in sheets of 10 + 10 labels that sold for €10. Nos, 2398D and 2398E each were printed in sheets of 10 + 10 labels that sold for €13. Labels could be personalized.

Lighthouses A798

Designs: 1c, Didimi Islet Lighthouse. 57c, Tourlitis Lighthouse. 70c, Chania Lighthouse. €1, Korakas Paros Lighthouse, horiz. €4.20, Strongyli Lighthouse, horiz.

Litho. With Foil Application
Perf. 13¼x13¾, 13¾x13¼

2009, Aug. 21

2399-2403	A798	Set of 5	19.00	19.00
2403a		Souvenir sheet, #2399-2403	19.00	19.00

Greek Mythology A799

Designs: 1c, Theseus against the Minotaur. 5c, Heracles and Triton. 57c, Odysseus and the Sirens, vert. 70c, Talos and the Dioskuroi. €5, Vellerofontis riding Pegasus, vert.

Perf. 13¾x14, 14x13¾

2009, Oct. 20 Litho.

2404-2408	A799	Set of 5	19.00	19.00

Convention on Rights of the Child, 20th Anniv. — A800

Designs: 20c, Hands of adult and child. 58c, Child standing against wall, horiz. 72c, Clasped hands of children, horiz. €1, Child looking through barred window. €4, Child in darkness.

Perf. 13¼x13, 13x13¼

2009, Dec. 7 Litho.

2409-2413	A800	Set of 5	19.00	19.00

Souvenir Sheets

Medals For Greek National Basketball Teams — A801

Designs: No. 2414, €2, Gold medal for men's under-20 team at 2009 European Basketball Championships. No. 2415, €2, Silver medal for men's under-19 team at 2009 World Basketball Championships. No. 2416, €2, Bronze medal for men's team at 2009 European Basketball Championships.

Litho. & Embossed With Foil Application

2009, Dec. 15 ***Perf. 13x13¼***

2414-2416	A801	Set of 3	17.50	17.50

20th Century Paintings by Greeks — A802

Designs: 1c, Stuffed Head, by Giannis Gaitis. 5c, Orpheus, Hermes and Eurydice, by Nikos Engonopoulos. 50c, Erotic, by Yannis Moralis. 58c, Sailor Sitting at the Table, Pink Background, by Yannis Tsarouchis. €2.43, Wattle Fences, by Nikos Hadjikyriakos-Ghika. €3, The Drawing, by Diamantis Diamantopoulos.

2010, Feb. 11 Litho. ***Perf. 14x13¾***

2417-2422	A802	Set of 6	18.00	18.00
2422a		Sheet of 6, #2417-2422	18.00	18.00

Renewable Energy Development A803

Designs: 1c, Solar energy. 40c, Water energy. 58c, Wind energy, horiz. 72c, Self-contained man. €2.43, Wave energy. €2.50, Bioenergy.

Perf. 13¼x13¾, 13¾x13¼

2010, Apr. 26

2423-2428	A803	Set of 6	18.00	18.00

Europa — A804

No. 2429: a, Boy in balloon, Puss in Boots. b, Girl on books.

2008, May 26 Litho. ***Perf. 14¼x14***

2429	A804	Horiz. pair	9.50	9.50
a.		72c multi	1.75	1.75
b.		€3.22 multi	7.75	7.75

Booklet Stamps
Perf. 13¾ Vert.

2429C	A804	Horiz. pair	9.50	9.50
d.		72c multi	1.75	1.75
e.		€3.22 multi	7.75	7.75
f.		Booklet pane, 2 #2429C	19.00	—
		Complete booklet, #2429f	19.00	

New Acropolis Museum — A805

Designs: 5c, Peplos kore. 58c, Parthenon gallery, horiz. 72c, Fragment of Parthenon frieze, horiz. €1, Entrance to new museum, horiz. €4, Marble sculpture of dog, horiz.

Perf. 13¼x13¾, 13¾x13¼

2010, June 21 Litho.

2430-2434	A805	Set of 5	16.00	16.00
2434a		Souvenir sheet, #2430-2434	16.00	16.00

Parthenon Gallery — A805a

Fragment of Parthenon Frieze — A805b

2010, June 21 Litho. *Perf. 14x13¾*

2435 A805a 58c multi + label 2.50 2.50
2436 A805b 72c multi + label 3.25 3.25

Nos. 2435-2436 each were printed in sheets of 10 stamps + 10 labels that could be personalized. The sheet containing No. 2435 sold for €10, and that of No. 2436 sold for €13.

Battle of Marathon, 2500th Anniv. A806

Designs: 50c, Athenian and Persian fighting. 58c, Phalanx marching into battle. 72c, Battle scene. €3, Bronze Corinthian helmet.

Litho. With Foil Application

2010, June 23 *Perf. 13¾x14*

2437-2440 A806 Set of 4 12.50 12.50

Popular Musicians A807

Designs: 10c, Vasilis Tsitsanis (1915-84). 20c, Giorgos Zampetas (1925-92). 58c, Stelios Kazantzidis (1931-2001). 72c, Grigoris Bithikotsis (1922-2005). €1, Vicky Moscholiou (1945-2005). €4.80, Sotiria Bellou (1921-97).

Perf. 13¾x13¼

2010, Sept. 16 Litho.

2441-2446 A807 Set of 6 21.00 21.00
2446a Souvenir sheet, #2441-2446 21.00 21.00

Paper Boat — A808

Spiral Staircase — A809

2010, Oct. 14 *Perf. 14x13¾*

2447 A808 (58c) multi 1.75 1.75
2448 A809 (72c) multi 2.10 2.10

Booklet Stamps

2447A A808 (58c) multi 1.75 1.75
2448A A809 (72c) multi 2.10 2.10

Islands A810

2010, Oct. 14 *Perf. 14¼x14*

2449 A810 2c Limnos .25 .25
2450 A810 5c Paros .25 .25
2451 A810 20c Ithaki .60 .60
2452 A810 40c Tinos 1.25 1.25
2453 A810 50c Skyros 1.40 1.40
2454 A810 €1 Evia-Chalkida 3.00 3.00
2455 A810 €2 Samos 5.75 5.75
2456 A810 €4 Kassos 11.50 11.50
Nos. 2449-2456 (8) 23.90 23.90

Booklet Stamps
Perf. 12¾ Vert.

2449A A810 2c Limnos .25 .25
2450A A810 5c Paros .25 .25
2451A A810 20c Ithaki .60 .60
2452A A810 40c Tinos 1.25 1.25
2453A A810 50c Skyros 1.40 1.40
2454A A810 €1 Evia-Chalkida 3.00 3.00
2455A A810 €2 Samos 5.75 5.75
2456A A810 €4 Kassos 11.50 11.50
Nos. 2449A-2456A (8) 24.00 24.00

Buildings A811

Designs: 20c, Municipal Theater of Piraeus. 58c, Benaki Museum. €2.43, National Theater. €2.50, National Gallery of Nafplio.

Litho. With Foil Application

2010, Nov. 16 *Perf. 13¾x14*

2457-2460 A811 Set of 4 15.50 15.50

Christmas — A812

Designs: 50c, Doves, holly leaves, stars. 58c, Angel with horn. €1, Ship with Christmas decorations. €3.50, Christmas tree, birds, holly leaves.

2010, Dec. 10 Litho. *Perf. 13¾x14*

2461-2464 A812 Set of 4 15.00 15.00

Self-Adhesive
Miniature Sheet
Die Cut Perf. 13¼

2465 Sheet of 4 15.00
a. A812 50c multi 1.40 1.40
b. A812 58c multi 1.60 1.60
c. A812 €1 multi 2.75 2.75
d. A812 €3.50 multi 9.25 9.25

20th Century Greek Engraving and Wood Cut Prints — A813

Designs: 3c, Aigaion V, by Kostas Grammatopoulos (1916-2003). 30c, To Pagoni, by Giannis Kefallinos (1894-1957), horiz. 60c, Maria, by A. Tassos (1914-85). €1, Plastikes Rimes, by Dimitris Galanis (1879-1966), horiz. €4, Mikros Kavalaris, by Vasso Katraki (1914-88).

Litho. with Foil Application

2011, Jan. 20 *Perf. 14x13¾, 13¾x14*

2466-2470 A813 Set of 5 16.50 16.50

European Year of Volunteers — A814

Academy of Athens, 85th Anniv. — A815

Alexandros Papadiamantis (1851-1911), Writer — A816

Battle of Crete, 70th Anniv. — A817

Organization for Economic Cooperation and Development, 50th Anniv. — A818

Spyros Samaras (1861-1917), Composer A819

Perf. 13¾x14, 14x13¾

2011, Feb. 23 Litho.

2471 A814 3c multi .25 .25
2472 A815 10c multi .30 .30
2473 A816 20c multi .55 .55
2474 A817 60c multi 1.75 1.75
2475 A818 €1.50 multi 4.25 4.25
2476 A819 €3 multi 8.50 8.50
Nos. 2471-2476 (6) 15.60 15.60

A820

2011 Special Olympics, Athens — A821

Special Olympics emblem and: 2c, Heart, stylized people, emblem of 2011 Athens Special Olympics. 4c, Stylized person, buildings, emblem of 2011 Athens Special Olympics. No. 2479, 60c, Emblem of 2011 Athens Special Olympics, vert. 75c, Sun, emblem of 2011 Athens Special Olympics, vert. €4.20, Emblem of 2011 Athens Special Olympics.

No. 2482, Emblems of Special Olympics and 2011 Athens Special Olympics.

2011, Mar. 18 *Perf. 13¾x14, 14x13¾*

2477-2481 A820 Set of 5 16.50 16.50

Booklet Stamp
Perf. 14x13¾

2482 A821 60c multi + label 2.00 2.00
a. Booklet pane of 1 + label 2.00 —
Complete booklet, 24 #2484a 52.50

Complete booklet sold for €18. Each booklet pane in booklet has a label with a different image.

Ancient Greek Ships — A822

Designs: 1c, Ship from a Thera wall painting, 1500 B.C. 20c, Polyreme, 4th-2nd cent. B.C., horiz. 60c, Triaconter, 15th-4th cent. B.C., horiz. 75c, Hellenic trireme, 7th-4th cent. B.C., horiz. €2.47, Macedonian hexareme, 4th-3rd cent. B.C., horiz. €2.50, Byzantine dromond, 5th-11th cent. A.D.

Litho. With Foil Application

2011, Apr. 18 *Perf. 13¾*

2483-2488 A822 Set of 6 19.00 19.00
2488a Souvenir sheet of 6, #2483-2488 19.00 19.00

Europa — A823

No. 2489 — Leaves and: a, Wildlife. b, Trees.

2011, May 17 *Perf. 13¼x13½*

2489 A823 Horiz. pair 12.00 12.00
a. 75c multi 2.25 2.25
b. €3.25 multi 9.50 9.50

Booklet Stamps
Perf. 12¾ Vert.

2489C A823 Horiz. pair 12.00 12.00
d. 75c multi 2.25 2.25
e. €3.25 multi 9.50 9.50
f. Booklet pane, 2 #2489C 24.00 —
Complete booklet, #2489f 24.00

Intl. Year of Forests.

Tourism A824

Text "www.visitgreece.gr" and: 1c, Stylized waves. 3c, Drama mask. 60c, Paper boat. 75c, Columns. €4, Town on cliff.

2011, June 22 Litho. *Perf. 13¾*

2490-2494 A824 Set of 5 15.50 15.50

Booklet Stamp
Self-Adhesive
Die Cut Perf. 12x11¼

2495 A824 75c multi 2.10 2.10
a. Booklet pane of 10 21.00

Primary School Book Cover Art — A825

Book cover art from: 2c, 1954 third grade reading book. 20c, *Little Children,* 1939 first grade reading book. 60c, *Alphavitario,* 1955 first grade reading book. 75c, 1955 second grade reading book. €1, *Krinoloulouda,* 1939 second grade reading book. €3.50, 1955 fifth grade reading book.

2011, Sept. 5 Litho. *Perf. 14x14¼*

2496-2501 A825 Set of 6 17.00 17.00
2501a Souvenir sheet of 6, #2496-2501 17.00 17.00

Booklet Stamp
Self-Adhesive
Die Cut Perf. 13¼

2502 A825 60c Like #2498 1.75 1.75
a. Booklet pane of 10 17.50

Alphavitario, 1955 First Grade Reading Book — A825a

2011, Sept. 5 Litho. *Perf. 14x13¾*

2503 A825a 60c multi + label 4.00 4.00

No. 2503 was printed in sheets of 10 + 10 labels that sold for €10. Labels could be personalized.

First Greek Postage Stamps, 150th Anniv. — A827

Type A1 stamp with original denominations removed in: 15c, Chocolate. 50c, Bister. 60c, Green. 75c, Orange. €1, Blue. €2, Violet. €5, Red.

Perf. 13¼x13¾
2011, Oct. 1 Litho. & Engr.

2504-2510 A827 Set of 7 27.50 27.50
2510a Souvenir sheet of 1, #2510 14.00 14.00

Actors and Actresses A828

Designs: 1c, Vassilis Diamantopoulos (1920-99). 5c, Rena Vlachopoulou (1923-2004). 50c, Orestis Makris (1898-1975). 60c, Thanasis Veggos (1927-2011). €2.47, Mary Aroni (1916-92). €2.50, Sapfo Notara (c. 1907-85).

Perf. 13¾x13½
2011, Nov. 22 Litho.

2511-2516 A828 Set of 6 16.50 16.50
2516a Souvenir sheet of 6, #2511-2516 16.50 16.50

Compare with type A786.

Souvenir Sheets

Gold Medalists at 2011 FINA World Championships — A829

Designs: No. 2517, €3, Greek flag and medal for Greek women's water polo team. No. 2518, €3, Spyros Gianniotis, swimmer, and gold medal.

2011, Dec. 15

2517-2518 A829 Set of 2 16.00 16.00

A830

A831

Marine Life A832

Designs: 2c, Palinurus elephas. 3c, Octopus vulgaris. 5c, Anemonia viridis. 20c, Caretta caretta. 35c, Epinephelus marginatus. 50c, Dentex dentex. (60c), Hippocampus guttulatus. €1, Aurelia aurita. (€2.47), Dasyatis pastinaca. €3, Charcharius taurus.

2012, Feb. 21 *Perf. 14¼x14*

2519 A830 2c multi .25 .25
2520 A830 3c multi .25 .25
2521 A830 5c multi .25 .25
2522 A830 20c multi .55 .55
2523 A830 35c multi .95 .95
2524 A830 50c multi 1.40 1.40
2525 A831 (60c) multi 1.60 1.60
2526 A830 €1 multi 2.60 2.60
2527 A832 (€2.47) multi 6.50 6.50
2528 A830 €3 multi 8.00 8.00
Nos. 2519-2528 (10) 22.35 22.35

Booklet Stamps
Perf. 12¾ Vert.

2519A A830 2c multi .25 .25
2520A A830 3c multi .25 .25
2521A A830 5c multi .25 .25
2522A A830 20c multi .55 .55
2523A A830 35c multi .95 .95
2524A A830 50c multi 1.40 1.40
2525A A831 (60c) multi 1.60 1.60
2526A A830 €1 multi 2.60 2.60
2527A A832 (€2.47) multi 6.50 6.50
2528A A830 €3 multi 8.00 8.00
Nos. 2519A-2528A (10) 22.35 22.35

A834

Children's Games — A835

Children and: 2c, Soccer ball. 10c, Scooter, vert. 35c, Jump rope. (60c), Marbles. €2, Tops. €3, Hopscotch.

Perf. 14¼x14, 14x14¼
2012, Apr. 18 Litho.

2530 A834 2c multi .25 .25
2531 A834 10c multi .30 .30
2532 A834 35c multi .95 .95
2533 A835 (60c) multi 1.60 1.60
2534 A834 €2 multi 5.25 5.25
2535 A834 €3 multi 8.00 8.00
Nos. 2530-2535 (6) 16.35 16.35

Booklet Stamp
Self-Adhesive
Die Cut Perf. 13¼

2536 A835 (60c) multi 1.60 1.60
a. Booklet pane of 10 16.00

Europa — A836

No. 2537 — Background color: a, Beige. b, White.

Litho. With Foil Application
2012, May 10 *Perf. 13½x13¼*

2537 A836 Horiz. pair 10.00 10.00
a. 75c multi 1.90 1.90
b. €3.25 multi 8.00 8.00

Booklet Stamps
Perf. 12¾ Vert.

2537C A836 Horiz. pair 10.00 10.00
d. 75c multi 1.90 1.90
e. €3.25 multi 8.00 8.00
f. Booklet pane, 2 #2537C 20.00 —
Complete booklet, #2537f 20.00

Nature Tourism A837

Designs: 1c, Tzoumerka Mountains, Epirus, rock climber. 10c, Rope bridge over Evinos River, backpacker. 62c, Samaria Gorge, Crete, hikers. 78c, Acheron River, Epirus, kayaker. €2, Rhodope Mountain stream, backpacker. €2.50, Field near Xanthi, backpacker.

2012, June 25 Litho. *Perf. 13¾*

2538-2543 A837 Set of 6 15.00 15.00

Booklet Stamps
Self-Adhesive
Die Cut Perf. 12x11½

2543A A837 62c multi 1.60 1.60
c. Booklet pane of 10 16.00
2543B A837 78c multi 1.90 1.90
d. Booklet pane of 10 19.00

2012 Summer Olympics, London A838

Emblem of 2012 Summer Olympics and: 78c, London landmarks and years London hosted previous Olympic Games. €1.70, Athletes and sporting equipment.

2012, July 2

2544-2545 A838 Set of 2 6.25 6.25

Souvenir Sheets

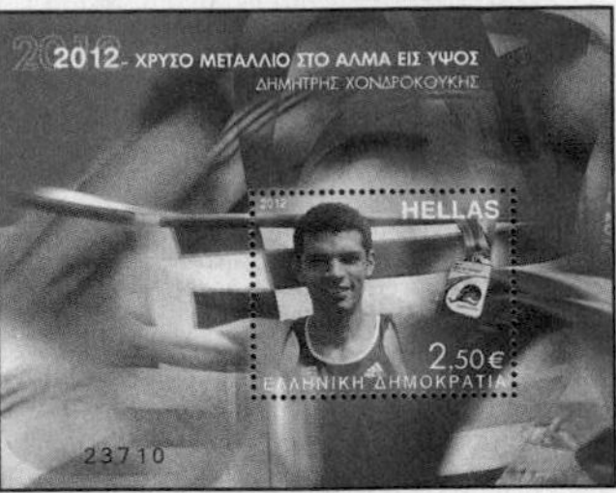

Dimitris Chondrokoukis, 2012 Intl. High Jump Champion — A839

Vlassis Maras, 2001-02 Intl. Horizontal Bar Champion — A840

2012, July 16 *Perf. 13¾x13¼*

2546 A839 €2.50 multi 6.25 6.25
2547 A840 €2.50 multi 6.25 6.25

Greek Ships — A841

Designs: 1c, Paron, 1821. 15c, Mistiko, 17th cent. 62c, Corvette, 18th cent. 78c, Ionian-Cretan galley, 16th cent. €2, Sakoleva, 19th cent. €2.40, latinadiko in shipyard, 18th cent.

Litho. With Foil Application
2012, Sept. 12

2548-2553 A841 Set of 6 15.50 15.50

Liberation of Thessalonica, Cent. — A842

Designs: 40c, Battle of Deskati. 62c, Greek Army entering Thessalonica (47x25mm). 85c, Cruiser G. Averof at sea. €2.50, Battle of Sarantaporo.

Perf. 13¾, 13½x13¼ (62c)
2012, Oct. 26

2554-2557 A842 Set of 4 11.50 11.50

See Nos. 2595-2597.

Christmas A843

Triangle, beater and Christmas ornament in shape of: 10c, Sphere. 62c, Christmas tree. 78c, Stocking. €3, Gift.

2012, Dec. 12 ***Perf. 14x14¼***
2558-2561 A843 Set of 4 12.00 12.00

Booklet Stamps
Self-Adhesive
Die Cut Perf. 13¼

2562 A843 62c multi 1.75 1.75
a. Booklet pane of 8 14.00
2563 A843 78c multi 2.10 2.10
a. Booklet pane of 8 17.00

No. 2562a sold for €4.90 and No. 2563a sold for €6.20.

Liberation of Ioannina, Cent. A844

Paintings by Kenan Messare: 3c, Women of Hepirus in Struggle. 55c, Campaign. 62c, Shell Blast.

Litho. With Foil Application
2013, Feb. 21 ***Perf. 13¾***
2564-2566 A844 Set of 3 3.25 3.25

Souvenir Sheet

Plato's Academy, 2400th Anniv. — A845

No. 2567: a, Circles and triangles. b, "N" and checkerboard pattern.

Perf. 13¼x13¾
2013, Mar. 28 **Litho.**
2567 A845 Sheet of 2 7.75 7.75
a. €1 multi 2.50 2.50
b. €2 multi 5.25 5.25

Greek Films — A846

Designs: 20c, Voyage to Cythera, 1984. 30c, Electra, 1962. 62c, The Travelling Players, 1975. €2.80, The Ogre of Athens, 1956.

Litho. With Foil Application
2013, Apr. 22 ***Perf. 13¾***
2568-2571 A846 Set of 4 10.50 10.50

Europa — A847

No. 2572: a, Postal van. b, Postal bicycle.

2013, May 9 **Litho.** ***Perf. 13¾***
2572 A847 Horiz. pair 11.00 11.00
a. 78c multi 2.10 2.10
b. €3.28 multi 8.75 8.75

Booklet Stamps
Perf. 13¾ Vert.

2572C A847 Horiz. pair 11.00 11.00
d. 78c multi 2.10 2.10
e. €3.28 multi 8.75 8.75
f. Booklet pane, 2 #2572C 22.00 —
Complete booklet, #2572f 22.00

Complete booklet sold for €8.10.

A848

A849

Sailboats A850

Various sailboats.

2013, June 4 ***Perf. 13½x13***
2573 A848 5c multi .25 .25
2574 A848 30c multi .80 .80
2575 A848 47c multi 1.25 1.25
a. Souvenir sheet of 3, #2573-2575 2.40 2.40
2576 A849 (62c) multi 1.75 1.75
2577 A850 (78c) multi 2.10 2.10
2578 A848 €3 multi 8.00 8.00
a. Souvenir sheet of 3, #2576-2578 12.00 12.00
Nos. 2573-2578 (6) 14.15 14.15

Booklet Stamps
Self-Adhesive
Die Cut Perf. 13

2579 A849 (62c) multi 1.75 1.75
a. Booklet pane of 10 17.50
2580 A850 (78c) multi 2.10 2.10
a. Booklet pane of 10 21.00

First Ascent of Mt. Olympus, Cent. A851

Centenary emblem and various photographs of Mt. Olympus: 5c, 10c, (78c), €3.50.

Litho. With Foil Application
2013, July 19 ***Perf. 13¼***
2581-2584 A851 Set of 4 12.00 12.00

Famous Men With Greek Heritage — A852

Designs: 5c, Andrew N. Liveris, President of Dow Chemical Company. 10c, Dr. Aristides A. N. Patrinos, head of U.S. National Human Genome Research Institute. 20c, James N. Gianopulos, chariman of Fox Entertainment Group. 72c, Stavros Niarchos (1909-96), shipping tycoon and philanthropist, horiz. 80c, Vangelis, composer. €3, Nikos A. Aliagas, French television host.

Perf. 14x14¼, 14¼x14
2013, Sept. 16 **Litho.**
2585-2590 A852 Set of 6 13.50 13.50

Classic Elements — A853

Designs: 5c, Earth. 47c, Water. €1, Air. €2.50, Fire.

2013, Oct. 3 **Litho.** ***Perf. 13¼***
2591-2594 A853 Set of 4 11.00 11.00
2594a Souvenir sheet of 4, #2591-2594 11.00 11.00

Liberation of Ioannia Type of 2013

Designs: 72c, Greek flag over Port of Chania in Crete. €1, Map of Crete from 1676, by Philippus Cluverius. €2.40, Surrender of Mount Athos to Greek Navy.

Litho. With Foil Application
2013 ***Perf. 13¾***
2595-2597 A844 Set of 3 11.50 11.50

Issued: 72c, €1, 12/2; €2.40, 10/3. International recognition of union of Greece and Crete, cent. (72c, €1); Surrender of Mount Athos, cent. (€2.40).

Evolution of Postal Services A854

Designs: 1c, Computer and cable, bar code. 10c, Computer cable, flash drive, fingerprint. 72c, Quick response code. €2.62, Key, wavy lines, stripes from airmail envelope.

2013, Dec. 2 **Litho.** ***Perf. 13¼x13¾***
2598-2601 A854 Set of 4 9.50 9.50

Booklet Stamp
Self-Adhesive
Serpentine Die Cut 12¼x13¼

2602 A854 72c multi 2.00 2.00
a. Booklet pane of 10 20.00

A855

A856

A857

Greek Presidency of the European Union A858

2014, Jan. 15 **Litho.** ***Perf. 14x13¼***
2603 A855 3c multi .25 .25
2604 A856 72c multi 2.00 2.00
2605 A857 €2 multi 5.50 5.50
a. Souvenir sheet of 2, #2604-2605 7.50 7.50
2606 A858 €2.15 multi 5.75 5.75
a. Souvenir sheet of 2, #2603, 2606 6.00 6.00
Nos. 2603-2606 (4) 13.50 13.50

Corinth Canal, 120th Anniv. A859

Filiki Eteria (Society of Friends) Independence Movement, 200th Anniv. — A860

Ionian Islands as Greek Territory, 150th Anniv. — A861

Thessaloniki, 2014 European Youth Capital — A862

University of Ioannina, 50th Anniv. A863

St. Cosmas of Aetolia (c. 1714-79) A864

Perf. 13¼x13¾, 13¾x13¼

2014, Feb. 17 **Litho.**

2607	A859	5c	multi	.25	.25
2608	A860	38c	blk & red	1.10	1.10
2609	A861	72c	multi	2.00	2.00
2610	A862	90c	multi	2.50	2.50
2611	A863	€1.50	multi	4.25	4.25
2612	A864	€1.95	multi	5.50	5.50
	Nos. 2607-2612 (6)			15.60	15.60

Booklet Stamp
Self-Adhesive

Die Cut Perf. 13¾x13¼

2613	A862	90c	multi	2.50	2.50
a.	Booklet pane of 10			25.00	

Songbirds A865

Designs: Nos. 2614, 2619, Luscinia megarhynchos. Nos. 2615, 2620, Carduelis chloris. €1, Carduelis cannabina. €1.62, Carduelis spinus. €2.62, Carduelis carduelis.

Perf. 13¾x13¼

2014, Mar. 20 **Litho.**

2614	A865	72c	multi	2.00	2.00
a.	Booklet pane of 1			3.50	—
2615	A865	72c	multi	2.00	2.00
a.	Booklet pane of 1			3.50	—
2616	A865	€1	multi	2.75	2.75
a.	Booklet pane of 1			5.00	—
2617	A865	€1.62	multi	4.50	4.50
a.	Booklet pane of 1			8.00	—
2618	A865	€2.62	multi	7.25	7.25
a.	Booklet pane of 1			13.00	—
	Complete booklet, #2614a, 2615a, 2616a, 2617a, 2618a			33.00	
	Nos. 2614-2618 (5)			18.50	18.50

Booklet Stamps
Self-Adhesive

Die Cut Perf. 13¾

2619	A865	72c	multi	2.00	2.00
a.	Booklet pane of 10			20.00	—
2620	A865	72c	multi	2.00	2.00
a.	Booklet pane of 10			20.00	—

Complete booklet sold for €12.

April A866

July — A867

December — A868

January A869

March A870

August A871

June — A872

November — A873

September — A874

May A875

February — A876

October A877

Perf. 13¼x13¾, 13¾x13¼

2014, Apr. 24 **Litho.**

2621	A866	2c	multi	.25	.25
2622	A867	20c	multi	.55	.55
2623	A868	40c	multi	1.10	1.10
2624	A869	50c	multi	1.40	1.40
2625	A870	72c	multi	2.00	2.00
2626	A871	80c	multi	2.25	2.25
2627	A872	85c	multi	2.40	2.40
2628	A873	90c	multi	2.50	2.50
2629	A874	€1	multi	2.75	2.75
2630	A875	€2.62	multi	7.25	7.25
2631	A876	€3	multi	8.25	8.25
2632	A877	€3.10	multi	8.75	8.75
	Nos. 2621-2632 (12)			39.45	39.45

Booklet Stamps

Perf. 13¾ Vert.

2621A	A866	2c	multi	.25	.25
2622A	A867	20c	multi	.55	.55
2623A	A868	40c	multi	1.10	1.10
2624A	A869	50c	multi	1.40	1.40
2625A	A870	72c	multi	2.00	2.00
2626A	A871	80c	multi	2.25	2.25
2627A	A872	85c	multi	2.40	
2628A	A873	90c	multi	2.50	2.50
2629A	A874	€1	multi	2.75	2.75
2630A	A875	€2.62	multi	7.25	7.25
2631A	A876	€3	multi	8.25	8.25
2632A	A877	€3.10	multi	8.75	8.75
	Nos. 2621A-2632A (12)			37.05	39.45

Booklet Stamps
Self-Adhesive

Die Cut Perf. 12x11½

2633	A870	72c	multi	2.00	2.00
a.	Booklet pane of 10			20.00	
2634	A871	80c	multi	2.25	2.25
a.	Booklet pane of 10			22.50	

Folk art depicting the months of the year.

Europa — A878

No. 2635: a, Musician bowing a stringed instrument. b, Lyrist.

2014, May 19 **Litho.** ***Perf. 13¼x13¾***

2635	A878	Horiz. pair	12.00	12.00
a.	90c multi		2.50	2.50
b.	€3.40 multi		9.25	9.25

Booklet Stamps

Perf. 13¾ Vert.

2635C	A878	Horiz. pair	12.00	12.00
d.	90c multi		2.50	2.50
e.	€3.40 multi		9.25	9.25
f.	Booklet pane, 2 #2635C		24.00	—
	Complete booklet, #2635f		24.00	

Bicycles A879

Designs: No. 2636, Bicycle with training wheels, children at play. Nos. 2637, 2640, Green and red adult men's bicycle. 80c, White women's bicycle. €2, Red and green child's bicycle.

Perf. 13¾x13¼

2014, June 12 **Litho.**

2636	A879	72c	multi	2.00	2.00
a.	Souvenir sheet of 1			2.00	2.00
2637	A879	72c	multi	2.00	2.00
a.	Souvenir sheet of 1			2.00	2.00
2638	A879	80c	multi	2.25	2.25
a.	Souvenir sheet of 1			2.25	2.25
2639	A879	€2	multi	5.50	5.50
a.	Souvenir sheet of 1			5.50	5.50
	Nos. 2636-2639 (4)			11.75	11.75

Booklet Stamps
Self-Adhesive

Die Cut Perf. 13¾

2640	A879	72c	multi	2.00	2.00
a.	Booklet pane of 10			20.00	
2641	A879	80c	multi	2.25	2.25
a.	Booklet pane of 10			22.50	

A booklet with panes containing one perf. 13¼x13¾ example each of Nos. 2636-2639 sold for €12.

2014 World Cup Soccer Championships, Brazil — A880

No. 2642: a, Mascot holding soccer ball. b, Silhouette of soccer player.

2014, June 12 **Litho.** ***Perf. 13¼x14***

2642	A880	Pair	6.00	6.00
a.	90c multi		2.50	2.50
b.	€1.30 multi		3.50	3.50
c.	Souvenir sheet of 1 #2642a		2.50	2.50
d.	Souvenir sheet of 1 #2642b		3.50	3.50

Euromed Postal Emblem and Mediterranean Sea — A881

2014, July 9 **Litho.** ***Perf. 13¼x13¾***

2643	A881	€3 multi	8.00	8.00
a.	Perf. 13¾ vert.		8.00	8.00
b.	Booklet pane of 2 #2643a		16.00	—
	Complete booklet, #2643b		16.00	

Fishing Boat A882

Rhodes A883

Santorini
A884

Die Cut Perf. 13

2014, Aug. 8 **Litho.**

Booklet Stamps Self-Adhesive

2647 A882 (80c) multi 2.25 2.25
a. Booklet pane of 10 22.50
2648 A883 (80c) multi 2.25 2.25
a. Booklet pane of 10 22.50
2649 A884 (80c) multi 2.25 2.25
a. Booklet pane of 10 22.50
Nos. 2647-2649 (3) 6.75 6.75

Souvenir Sheet

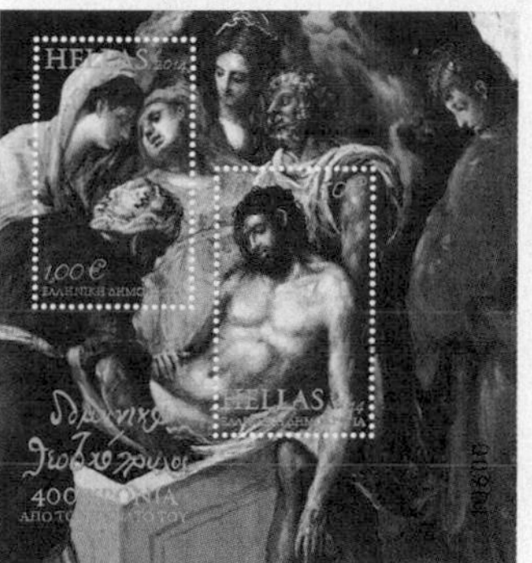

The Entombment of Christ, by El Greco (1541-1614) — A885

No. 2650 — Painting details: a, Grieving women, b, Jesus.

Litho. With Foil Application

2014, Sept. 10 ***Perf. 13½x13***

2650 A885 Sheet of 2 6.25 6.25
a. €1 multi 2.50 2.50
b. €1.50 multi 3.75 3.75

Writers
A886

Designs: 10c, Kostas Varnalis (1884-1974). 40c, Dido Sotiriou (1909-2004). €2, Antonis Samarakis (1919-2003). €2.10, Stratis Tsirkas (1911-80).

2014, Oct. 23 **Litho.** ***Perf. 13½x13¾***

2651-2654 A886 Set of 4 11.50 11.50

A887

Christmas
A888

Designs: No. 2655, Christmas tree and elves. No. 2656, Elf and toys. No. 2657, Reindeer and snowman. No. 2658, Toys in bag.

Die Cut Perf. 13 ½ (A887), 12½ (A888)

2014, Dec. 12 **Litho.**

Booklet Stamps Self-Adhesive Color of QR Code

2655 A887 72c red 1.75 1.75
2656 A888 72c purple 1.75 1.75
a. Booklet pane of 10, 5 each #2655-2656 17.50
2657 A887 90c blue 2.25 2.25
2658 A888 90c green 2.25 2.25
a. Booklet pane of 10, 5 each #2657-2658 22.50
Nos. 2655-2658 (4) 8.00 8.00

Advertisement for Misko Pasta — A889

Advertisement for Papadopoulos "Petit-Beurre" Biscuits
A890

2014, Dec. 18 **Litho.** ***Perf. 14x13¼***

2659 A889 72c multi 1.75 1.75
2660 A890 72c multi 1.75 1.75

Booklet Stamps Self-Adhesive

Die Cut Perf. 11½x12

2661 A889 72c multi 1.75 1.75
a. Booklet pane of 10 17.50
2662 A890 72c multi 1.75 1.75
a. Booklet pane of 10 17.50

Journalists' Union of Athens Daily Newspapers — A891

Designs: 1c, Paulos Palaiologos, Dimitris Psathas. 20c, Ioannis Iakovos Mager, Vlasis Gavriilidis. 50c, Maria Rezan, Nikos Karantinos. 72c, Aimilios Chourmouzios, Marios Ploritis. €2.62, Union emblem, quotation by Mager.

2015, Jan. 21 **Litho.** ***Perf. 13¼x13¾***

2663-2667 A891 Set of 5 9.25 9.25

Thermal Springs — A892

Designs: 5c, Methana. 10c, Loutraki Perachora. 23c, Lefkada Ikaria. 72c, Edipsos. 90c, Loutraki Aridaia (Pozar). €2, Vouliagmeni Lake.

2015, Feb. 26 **Litho.** ***Perf. 14x13¼***

2668-2673 A892 Set of 6 9.00 9.00

Locomotives of Greek Railways A893

Designs: 20c, German 40-45, 1951. 72c, Austrian La901-940, 1925-27. 80c, American G401-420, 1915. €2.50, French Z501-517, 1890-1901.

2015, Mar. 30 **Litho.** ***Perf. 14x13¼***

2674 A893 20c multi .45 .45
a. Souvenir sheet of 1 .45 .45
2675 A893 72c multi 1.60 1.60
a. Souvenir sheet of 1 1.60 1.60
2676 A893 80c multi 1.75 1.75
a. Souvenir sheet of 1 1.75 1.75
2677 A893 €2.50 multi 5.50 5.50
a. Souvenir sheet of 1 5.50 5.50
Nos. 2674-2677 (4) 9.30 9.30

Booklet Stamps Self-Adhesive

Die Cut Perf. 13¼x12¾

2678 A893 72c multi 1.60 1.60
a. Booklet pane of 10 16.00
2679 A893 80c multi 1.75 1.75
a. Booklet pane of 10 17.50

Sakis Karayorgas and Kostas Yorgakis — A894

Nikiforos Mandilaras and Panayotis Elis — A895

Dimitris Opropoulos and Spyros Moustaklis — A896

Design: 90c, Yorgos Tsarouhas and Yannis Halkidis.

Litho. With Foil Application

2015, Apr. 21 ***Perf, 13¼x13¾***

2680 A894 72c multi 1.60 1.60
2681 A895 72c multi 1.60 1.60
2682 A896 72c multi 1.60 1.60
2683 A896 90c multi 2.10 2.10
Nos. 2680-2683 (4) 6.90 6.90

Fighters against the 1967 junta.

Europa — A897

No. 2684 — Marbles and: a, Top, toy airplane. b, Toy car, slingshots.

2015, May 11 **Litho.** ***Perf. 13¾***

2684 A897 Horiz. pair 9.50 9.50
a. 90c multi 2.00 2.00
b. €3.40 multi 7.50 7.50

Booklet Stamps

Perf. 13¾ Vert.

2684C A897 Horiz. pair 9.50 9.50
d. 90c multi 2.00 2.00
e. €3.40 multi 7.50 7.50
f. Booklet pane, 2 #2684C 19.00 —
Complete booklet, #2684C 19.00

2015 European Sea Ports Organization Conference, Athens — A898

European Maritime Day
A899

Designs: 72c, Emblem and ships. No. 2686, Emblem, ship, rope and mooring bollard. No. 2687, Map of Piraeus harbor.

2015, May 20 **Litho.** ***Perf. 13¼x13¾***

2685 A898 72c multi 1.60 1.60
2686 A898 80c multi 1.75 1.75
2687 A899 80c multi 1.75 1.75
Nos. 2685-2687 (3) 5.10 5.10

Miniature Sheets

A901

A902

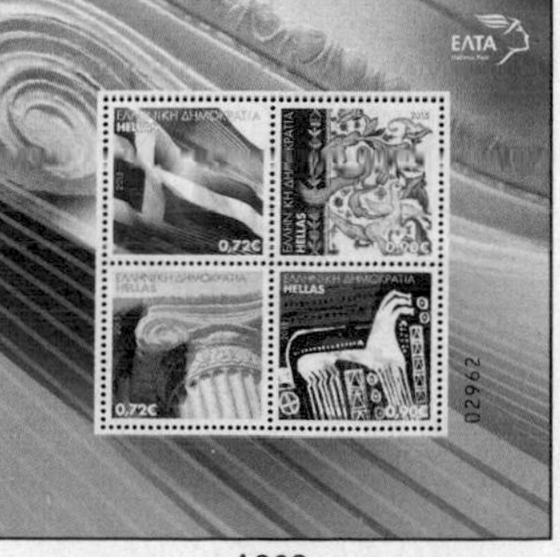

A903

No. 2689: a, Owls and books. b, Sun, flowers, birds with letters. c, Cogwheels, handshake. d, Letters, airplane, cogwheels, Sydney Opera House, Big Ben, Roman Colosseum, Eiffel Tower.

No. 2690: a, Birds on baby carriage. b, Birds and heart. c, Balloons and baby. d, Woman and man on penny-fathing bicycles, flowers.

No. 2691: a, Unofficial flag of Greece. b, Column and capital. c, Birds and flowers. d, Ancient art.

2015, June 11 Litho. *Perf. 14x13½*

2689	A901	Sheet of 4	7.00	7.00
a.-c.		72c Any single	1.60	1.60
d.		90c multi	2.00	2.00
2690	A902	Sheet of 4	7.00	7.00
a.-c.		72c Any single	1.60	1.60
d.		90c multi	2.00	2.00
2691	A903	Sheet of 4	7.25	7.25
a.-b.		72c Either single	1.60	1.60
c.-d.		90c Either single	2.00	2.00
		Nos. 2689-2691 (3)	21.25	21.25

Fishing Boat A904

2015, July 9 Litho. *Perf. 13¼x13¾*

2692	A904	€3 multi	6.75	6.75
a.		Perf. 13¾ vert.	6.75	6.75
b.		Booklet pane of 2 #2692a	13.50	—
		Complete booklet, #2692a	13.50	

Diving A905

Diver and: 10c, Shipwreck. 50c, Ancient jar. Nos. 2695, 2699, 80c, Fish and sponges. Nos. 2696, 2700, 80c, Byzantine shipwreck. €1.62, Shipwreck, diff. €2, Yellow gorgonians.

2015, July 20 Litho. *Perf. 13¼x13¾*

2693-2698 A905 Set of 6 13.00 13.00

Booklet Stamps
Self-Adhesive

Die Cut Perf. 13¾x14

2699	A905	80c multi	1.75	1.75
2700	A905	80c multi	1.75	1.75
a.		Booklet pane of 10, 5 each #2699-2700	17.50	

Volcanoes A906

Designs: 1c, Milos Volcano. 20c, Nisyros Volcano. €1, Santorini Volcano. €2, Nisyros Volcano, diff.

2015, Sept. 8 Litho. *Perf. 13¼x13¾*

2701-2704 A906 Set of 4 7.25 7.25

Flanghinis College, 350th Anniv. — A907

Designs: 3c, Tomasso Flangini (1578-1648), school founder. 72c, Our Lady of the Flanghinis College. €1.50, Flanghinis College building, Venice. €2, Emblem of Hellenic Institute of Byzantine and Post-Byzantine Studies of Venice.

Litho. With Foil Application

2015, Oct. 9 *Perf. 13¾x13¼*

2705-2708 A907 Set of 4 9.50 9.50

Souvenir Sheet

Greek Postal Savings Bank, 115th Anniv. — A908

Litho. With Foil Application

2015, Oct. 30 *Perf. 13¾*

2709 A908 €1 multi 2.25 2.25

Notos 2015 International Philatelic Exhibition, Athens — A909

Designs: 72c, Exhibition emblem. 90c, Exhibition emblem, map and origami bird.

2015, Nov. 4 Litho. *Perf. 13¾*

2710-2711	A909	Set of 2	3.50	3.50
2711a		Souvenir sheet of 2, #2710-2711	3.50	3.50

United Nations. 70th Anniv. — A910

2015, Nov. 4 Litho. *Perf. 13¾*

2712 A910 €1 multi 2.25 2.25

Souvenir Sheet

Maritime Cooperation Between Greece and People's Republic of China — A911

2015, Nov. 4 Litho. *Perf. 13¾*

2713 A911 €3 multi 6.50 6.50

Advertisement for Loumidis-Papagalos Coffee — A912

Advertisement for Sun Spices A913

Advertisement for Attiki Honey — A914

Advertisement for Pitsos Home Appliances A915

Advertisement for Hatzopoulos Flexible Packaging A916

Litho. With Foil Application

2015, Dec. 14 *Perf. 13¾*

2714 A912 72c multi 1.60 1.60

Litho.

2715	A913	72c multi	1.60	1.60
2716	A914	72c multi	1.60	1.60
2717	A915	72c multi	1.60	1.60
2718	A916	90c multi	2.00	2.00
		Nos. 2714-2718 (5)	8.40	8.40

Diplomatic Relations Between Greece and Israel, 25th Anniv. A917

2016, Feb. 9 Litho. *Perf. 14*

2719 A917 90c multi 2.00 2.00

See Israel No. 2091.

National Liberation Front, 75th Anniv. A918

Members of National Liberation Front (World War II resistance fighters): 20c, Kostas Maragkoudakis. 50c, Apostolos (Lakis) Santas (1920-2011). €1, Manolis Glezos. €2, Vardis Vardinogiannis. €2.10, Stelios Zamanos.

2016, Feb. 23 Litho. *Perf. 14¼x14*

2720-2724 A918 Set of 5 12.50 12.50

National Bank of Greece, 175th Anniv. A919

Designs: 5c, Drawing of Central Bank Office, by Eugène Troump, 1900. 10c, Ludwig Square, 1847, painting by Johannes Rabe. 50c, Design for 60th anniversary medal, by George Lakovidis, 1902. €2.62, Karatzas Building, 2002.

Litho. With Foil Application

2016, Mar. 30 *Perf. 13¾*

2725	A919	5c multi	.25	.25
a.		Souvenir sheet of 1	.25	.25
2726	A919	10c multi	.25	.25
a.		Souvenir sheet of 1	.25	.25
2727	A919	50c multi	1.25	1.25
a.		Souvenir sheet of 1	1.25	1.25
2728	A919	€2.62 multi	6.00	6.00
a.		Souvenir sheet of 1	6.00	6.00
		Nos. 2725-2728 (4)	7.75	7.75

A920

A921

A922

Year of Greece in Russia — A923

2016, Apr. 18 Litho. *Perf. 13¾*

2729	A920 80c multi	1.90	1.90
2730	A921 80c multi	1.90	1.90
2731	A922 80c multi	1.90	1.90
2732	A923 90c multi	2.10	2.10
a.	Souvenir sheet of 4, #2729-2732	8.00	8.00
	Nos. 2729-2732 (4)	7.80	7.80

Booklet Stamp Self-Adhesive

Die Cut Perf. 11½x12

2733	A922 80c multi	1.90	1.90
a.	Booklet pane of 10	19.00	

Labor Leaders A924

Designs: 5c, Napoleon Soukatzidis (1909-44), executed trade union leader. 50c, Tasos Toussis (1911-36), murdered striker. €1, Kostas Theos (1896-1958), exiled labor leader. €2, Sotiris Paraskevaidis, Communist activist killed at 1924 rally, denomination at LL.

2016, Apr. 21 Litho. *Perf. 13¾*

2734-2737	A924 Set of 4	8.25	8.25

A925

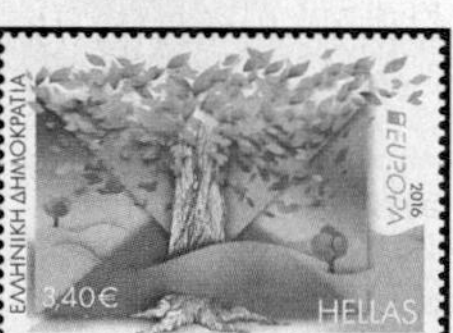

Europa A926

2016, May 11 Litho. *Perf. 14¼x14*

2738	A925 90c multi	2.00	2.00
2739	A926 €3.40 multi	7.75	7.75
b.	Horiz. pair, #2738-2739	9.75	9.75

Booklet Stamps

Perf. 14 Vert.

2738A	A925 90c multi	2.00	2.00
2739A	A926 €3.40 multi	7.75	7.75
c.	Horiz. pair, #2738A-2739A	9.75	9.75
d.	Booklet pane of 4, 2 each #2738A-2739A	19.50	—
	Complete booklet, #2739d	19.50	

Think Green Issue.

Aristotle (384-322 B.C.), Philosopher A927

Designs: 72c, Aristotle. 80c, Aristotle and his student, Alexander the Great. €1, Aristotle and his teacher, Plato.

2016, May 23 Litho. *Perf. 13¾*

2740	A927 72c multi	1.60	1.60
a.	Souvenir sheet of 1	1.60	1.60
2741	A927 80c multi	1.75	1.75
a.	Souvenir sheet of 1	1.75	1.75
2742	A927 €1 multi	2.25	2.25
a.	Souvenir sheet of 1	2.25	2.25
	Nos. 2740-2742 (3)	5.60	5.60

Booklet Stamps Self-Adhesive

Die Cut Perf. 11½x12

2743	A927 72c multi	1.60	1.60
a.	Booklet pane of 10	16.00	
2744	A927 80c multi	1.75	1.75
a.	Booklet pane of 10	17.50	

Personalized Stamps — A927a

Designs: 72c, Aristotle. 80c, Aristotle and his student, Alexander the Great.

2016, May 23 Litho. *Perf. 14*

2744B	A927a 72c multi + label	2.50	2.50
2744C	A927a 80c multi + label	2.75	2.75

Nos. 2744B and 2744C were each printed in sheets of 5 + 5 labels that could be personalized. The generic label is shown.

Souvenir Sheet

Patriarch Bartholomew of Constantinople, 25th Anniv. of Installation — A928

No. 2745: a, Patriarch Bartholomew. b, Emblem of Patriarchate.

Litho., Sheet Margin Litho. With Foil Application

2016, June 10 *Perf. 13¾*

2745	A928 Sheet of 2	4.25	4.25
a.	90c multi	2.00	2.00
b.	€1 multi	2.25	2.25

A929

Holy and Great Council of the Orthodox Church — A930

2016, June 16 Litho. *Perf. 14*

2746	A929 90c multi + label	3.75	3.75

Souvenir Sheet

Litho., Sheet Margin Litho. With Foil Application

Perf. 13¾

2747	A930 90c multi	2.00	2.00

No. 2746 was printed in sheets of 5 + 5 labels that sold for €8. Labels could be personalized. The generic label is shown.

A930a

Personalized Stamps — A930b

2016, June 15 Litho. *Perf. 14*

2747A	A930a 80c multi + label	2.75	2.75
2747B	A930b 80c multi + label	2.75	2.75

Nos. 2747A and 2747B were each printed in sheets of 5 + 5 labels that could be personalized. The generic labels are shown.

Fish of the Mediterranean Sea — A931

2016, July 8 Litho. *Perf. 13¾*

2748	A931 €3 multi	6.75	6.75

Booklet Stamps

Perf. 12¾ Vert.

2748A	A931 €3 multi	6.75	6.75
b.	Booklet pane of 2 #2748A	13.50	—
	Complete booklet, #2748b	13.50	

2016 Summer Olympics, Rio de Janeiro A932

Silhouette of Rio de Janeiro skyline, Christ the Redeemer statue, Greek Olympic Committe emblem, ancient Greek statues and: 80c, Gymnast on rings. 90c, Runner crossing finish line.

2016, July 8 Litho. *Perf. 13¾*

2749-2750	A932 Set of 2	3.75	3.75

Lambrakis Youth Movement — A933

Designs: 20c, Sotiris Petroulas (1942-65), student killed in protest. 72c, Andreas Lentakis (1935-97), politician. 80c, Mikis Theodorakis, composer and first president of Lambrakis Democratic Youth. €2, Christos Rekleitis (1937-2014), anti-junta protestor tortured by military, denomination at LR.

2016, July 8 Litho. *Perf. 13¾*

2751-2754	A933 Set of 4	8.50	8.50

2016 International Foundation for Greece Award Recipients A934

Emblem and: 72c, Rita Wilson, actress. 80c, Costa-Gavras, film director. 90c, John A. Catsimatidis, businessman. €1, George Stephanopoulos, television journalist. €1.20, Dr. Peter Diamandis, engineer and chairman of X PRIZE Foundation.

2016, Sept. 1 Litho. *Perf. 14x14¼*

2755-2759	A934 Set of 5	10.50	10.50

Siege of Corfu, 300th Anniv. A935

Litho. With Foil Application

2016, Oct. 20 *Perf. 13¼x13*

2760	A935 €2 multi	4.50	4.50

Souvenir Sheet

Marathon Race of Modern Olympics, 120th Anniv. — A936

No. 2761: a, Ancient naked marathon runner. b, Modern runner wearing cap.

Litho., Sheet Margin Litho. With Foil Application

2016, Nov. 10 *Perf. 13¾*

2761	A936 Sheet of 2	6.50	6.50
a.	90c multi	2.00	2.00
b.	€2.10 multi	4.50	4.50

Personalized Stamp — A936a

2016, Nov. 10 Litho. *Perf. 14*

2761C	A936a 90c multi + label	3.50	3.50

No. 2761C was printed in sheets of 5 + 5 labels that could be personalized. The sheet sold for €8. The generic label is shown.

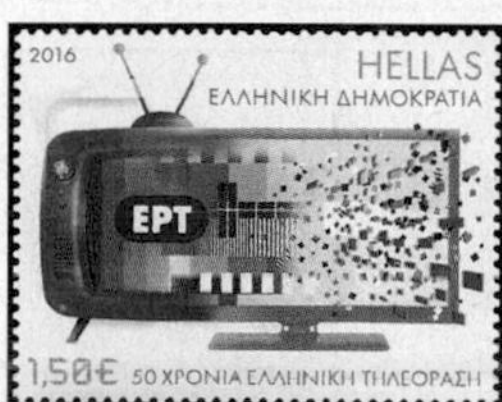

Television Broadcasting in Greece, 50th Anniv. — A937

2016, Nov. 24 Litho. *Perf. 13¾*

2762	A937 €1.50 multi	3.25	3.25

Herbs — A938

Designs: 20c, Cistus creticus. 40c, Origanum dictamus. 50c, Hypericum empetrifolium.

72c, Sideritis clandestina. €1, Origanum vulgare. €2.62, Salvia fruticosa.

2016, Dec. 15 Litho. ***Perf. 14x14¼***
2763-2768 A938 Set of 6 11.50 11.50

No. 2768 is impregnated with a Greek oregano scent.

National Archaeological Museum, 150th Anniv. (in 2016) — A939

Designs: 10c, The Kiss. 50c, Odysseus of Antikythera statue, vert. 72c, Diadoumenos sculpture, vert. 90c, Poseidon of Livadostra statue, vert. €1.50, Athenian Youth, vert. €2, Mycenaean Lady.

Litho. With Foil Application

2017, Mar. 15 ***Perf. 13¾***
2769-2774 A939 Set of 6 12.50 12.50
2769a Souvenir sheet of 1 .25 .25
2770a Souvenir sheet of 1 1.10 1.10
2771a Souvenir sheet of 1 1.60 1.60
2772a Souvenir sheet of 1 2.00 2.00
2773a Souvenir sheet of 1 3.25 3.25
2774a Souvenir sheet of 1 4.25 4.25

Booklet Stamp Self-Adhesive

Litho.

Die Cut Perf. 11½x12

2775 A939 72c multi 1.60 1.60
a. Booklet pane of 10 16.00

Sports A940

Arts — A941

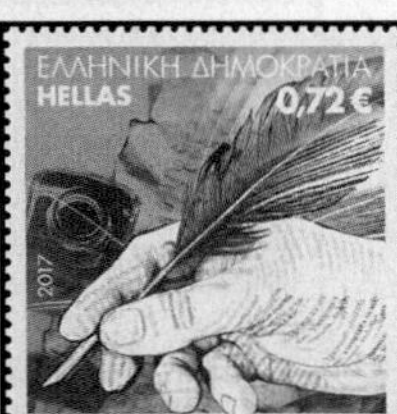

Literature A942

Music A943

Tourism A944

Wine A945

2017, Apr. 7 Litho. ***Perf. 13¾***
2776 A940 72c multi 1.60 1.60
2777 A941 72c multi 1.60 1.60
2778 A942 72c multi 1.60 1.60
2779 A943 72c multi 1.60 1.60
2780 A944 80c multi 1.75 1.75
2781 A945 90c multi 2.00 2.00
Nos. 2776-2781 (6) 10.15 10.15

Booklet Stamp Self-Adhesive

Die Cut Perf. 13¾

2782 A944 80c multi 1.75 1.75
a. Booklet pane of 10 17.50

Size: 30x30mm Water-Activated Gum

Perf. 13¼

2783 A940 72c multi + label 2.75 2.75
2784 A941 72c multi + label 2.75 2.75
2785 A942 72c multi + label 2.75 2.75
2786 A943 72c multi + label 2.75 2.75
2787 A944 80c multi + label 3.50 3.50
2788 A945 90c multi + label 3.50 3.50
Nos. 2783-2788 (6) 18.00 18.00

Nos. 2783-2788 were each printed in sheets of 5 + 5 labels that could be personalized. Sheets of Nos. 2783-2786 each sold for €6; Nos. 2787-2788, for €8.

Souvenir Sheet

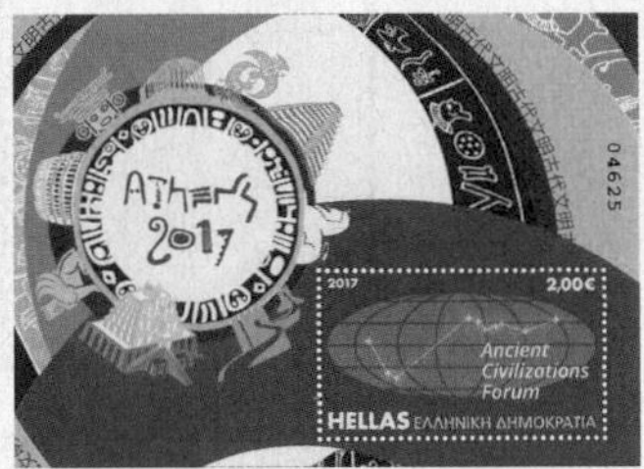
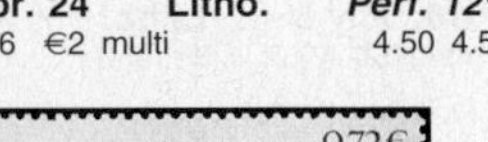

Ancient Civilizations Forum, Athens — A946

2017, Apr. 24 Litho. ***Perf. 12¾***
2789 A946 €2 multi 4.50 4.50

Cross and Initials of Apostoliki Diakonia — A947

St. Helen — A948

2017, May 11 Litho. ***Perf. 13¾***
2790 A947 72c multi 1.60 1.60

Souvenir Sheet

Litho. Margin Litho. With Foil Application

2791 A948 €2 multi 4.50 4.50

Apostoliki Diakonia of the Church of Greece, 80th anniv.

Europa — A949

No. 2792: a, Palamidi Castle, Nafplio. b, Methoni Castle.

2017, May 18 Litho. ***Perf. 14¼x14***
2792 A949 Horiz. pair 9.75 9.75
a. 90c multi 2.00 2.00
b. €3.40 multi 7.75 7.75
c. Horiz. pair, perf. 14 vert. 9.75 9.75
d. As "a," perf. 14 vert. 2.00 2.00
e. As "b," perf. 14 vert. 7.75 7.75
f. Booklet pane, 2 #2792c 19.50 —
Complete booklet, #2792f 19.50

Mastic Trees — A950

2017, June 27 Litho. ***Perf. 13¾***
2793 A950 €2.62 multi 6.00 6.00
a. Souvenir sheet of 1 6.00 6.00
b. Perf. 13¾ horiz. 6.00 6.00
c. Booklet pane of 2 #2793b 12.00 —
Complete booklet, #2793c 12.00

Seven Wise Men of Antiquity — A951

Designs: 5c, Chilon of Sparta. 10c, Cleobulus of Lindos. 20c, Periander of Corinth. 50c, Pittacus of Mytilene. 80c, Solon of Athens. €1, Thales of Miletus. €2, Bias of Priene.

2017, July 27 Litho. ***Perf. 14x14¼***
2794-2800 A951 Set of 7 11.00 11.00

Greek Theater Costume A952

Bamboo Shoot and Olive Branch A953

Chinese Theater Costume A954

2017, Sept. 8 Litho. ***Perf. 13¾***
2801 A952 50c multi 1.25 1.25
2802 A953 90c multi 2.10 2.10
c. Souvenir sheet of 1 2.10 2.10
2803 A954 €2 multi 4.75 4.75
a. Souvenir sheet of 2, #2801, 2803 6.00 6.00
Nos. 2801-2803 (3) 8.10 8.10

Year of Cultural Exchanges and Cooperation of Creative Industries of Greece and China.

Monument to Fighters in 1944 Battle of the Keratsini Power Station A955

Battle of the Keratsini Power Station A956

2017, Oct. 11 Litho. ***Perf. 13¾***
2804 A955 50c multi 1.25 1.25
a. Souvenir sheet of 1 1.25 1.25
2805 A956 €1 blk & car 2.40 2.40
a. Souvenir sheet of 1 2.40 2.40

Greek Philatelists A957

Designs: 5c, Alexander Argyropoulos (1883-1962). 20c, Charilis Binos (1909-78). 72c, Moses Konstantinis (1932-2018). 90c, Georgios Papastephanou (1890-1978). €1.50, Stephanos Makrymichalos (1902-83). €2, Nikolaus Atzaritis (1900-76).

Litho. With Gold Foil Application

2017, Nov. 16 ***Perf. 13¾***
2806-2811 A957 Set of 6 14.00 14.00

Discovery of Temple of Artemis Amarynthia A958

Litho. With Foil Application

2017, Nov. 24 ***Perf. 13¾***
2812 A958 €1 multi 2.40 2.40
a. Souvenir sheet of 1 2.40 2.40

Christmas A959

Children and: No. 2813, 72c, Penguin. No. 2814, 72c, Squirrel. Nos. 2815, 2817, 72c, Reindeer. Nos. 2816, 2818, 90c, Bear.

2017, Dec. 5 Litho. *Perf. 13¾*
2813-2816 A959 Set of 4 7.50 7.50

Booklet Stamps Self-Adhesive

Die Cut Perf. 11½x12

2817 A959 72c multi 1.75 1.75
a. Booklet pane of 10 17.50
2818 A959 90c multi 2.25 2.25
a. Booklet pane of 10 22.50

Civil Servants Joint Stock Fund Building, Athens A960

Dimitrios N. Levidis (1806-93), Founder of Civil Servants Joint Stock Fund — A961

Civil Servants Joint Stock Fund Building, Athens — A962

Litho. With Foil Application

2017, Dec. 8 *Perf. 13¾*
2819 A960 72c gold & multi 1.75 1.75
2820 A961 €2.50 gold & multi 6.00 6.00

Litho.

Perf. 14

2821 A962 72c gold & multi + label 2.40 2.40

Civil Servants Joint Stock Fund, 150th anniv. No. 2821 was printed in sheets of 10 + 10 labels that could be personalized. Sheets sold for €10.

Souvenir Sheet

Reconstructed Appearance of "Myrtis," Girl Who Died in 430 B.C. Typhoid Epidemic in Athens — A963

Litho., Sheet Margin Litho. With Foil Application

2018, Feb. 15 *Perf. 13¾*
2822 A963 €1.50 sil & multi 3.75 3.75

A964

International Women's Day — A965

2018, Mar. 8 Litho. *Perf. 14¼x14*
2823 A964 72c multi 1.75 1.75

Litho. With Foil Application

Perf. 14x14¼

2824 A965 90c multi 2.25 2.25

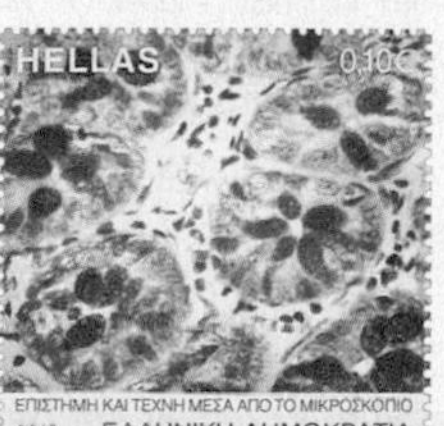

Art in Microscope Photography — A966

Artistic shapes found in microscope photography by Maria Lambropoulou: 10c, Flowers. 20c, Butterfly. 72c, Heart. €1, Wreath. €2, Deer.

2018, Mar. 19 Litho. *Perf. 13¼*
2825-2829 A966 Set of 5 10.00 10.00

A.E.K. Basketball Club Emblem, Basketball Player, Backboard, and European Basketball Winner's Cup — A967

Panathenaic Stadium — A968

2018, Mar. 30 Litho. *Perf. 13¾*
2830 A967 72c multi 1.75 1.75
a. Souvenir sheet of 1 1.75 1.75
2831 A968 90c multi 2.25 2.25
a. Souvenir sheet of 1 2.25 2.25

Victory of A.E.K. Basketball Club in European Championships, 50th anniv.

Souvenir Sheet

Juan de Fuca (1536-1602), Explorer — A969

Litho., Sheet Margin Litho. With Foil Application

2018, Apr. 24 *Perf. 13¾*
2832 A969 €2.50 multi 6.00 6.00

Juan de Fuca was born as Ioannis Phokas in Greece.

A.E.K. Basketball Club Emblem, Basketball Player, Backboard, and European Basketball Winner's Cup — A970

2018, Apr. 26 Litho. *Perf. 13¼*
2833 A970 72c multi + label 3.00 3.00

No. 2833 was printed in sheets of 5 + 5 labels that could be personalized. Sheets sold for €6.

Souvenir Sheets

Greek Holocaust Monument — A971

Monastir Synagogue — A972

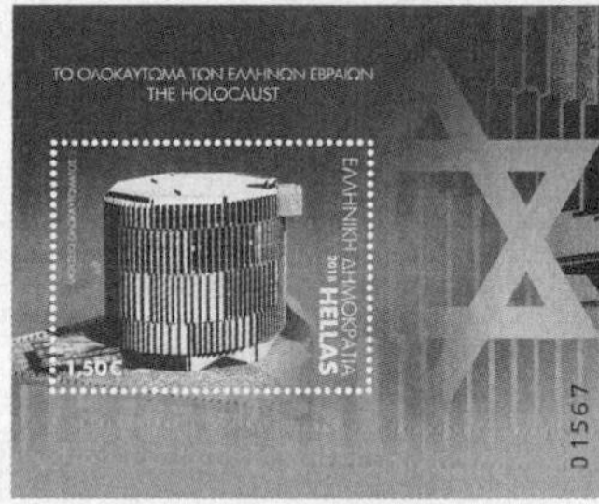

Holocaust Memorial Museum of Greece — A973

2018, May 16 Litho. *Perf. 13¾*
2834 A971 €1.50 multi 3.50 3.50
2835 A972 €1.50 multi 3.50 3.50
2836 A973 €1.50 multi 3.50 3.50
Nos. 2834-2836 (3) 10.50 10.50

World Bee Day — A974

Apis mellifera and: 50c, Lilac flower. 72c, Honeycomb. 80c, Plant. €2, Pink flower.

2018, May 20 Litho. *Perf. 13¾x13½*
2837 A974 50c multi 1.25 1.25
a. Souvenir sheet of 1 1.25 1.25
2838 A974 72c multi 1.75 1.75
a. Souvenir sheet of 1 1.75 1.75
2839 A974 80c multi 1.90 1.90
a. Souvenir sheet of 1 1.90 1.90
2840 A974 €2 multi 4.75 4.75
a. Souvenir sheet of 1 4.75 4.75
Nos. 2837-2840 (4) 9.65 9.65

Sheet margins on Nos. 2837a-3840a are litho. with foil application.

Souvenir Sheet

General Confederation of Greek Workers, Cent. — A975

No. 2841: a, Centenary emblem. b, Centenary emblem, workers and flag.

2018, May 21 Litho. *Perf. 13¾*
2841 A975 €1 Sheet of 2, #a-b 4.75 4.75

Europa — A976

No. 2842: a, Rio-Antirrio Bridge. b, Plaka Bridge.

2018, May 24 Litho. *Perf. 14¼x13¾*

2842	A976 Horiz. pair	10.00	10.00
a.	90c multi	2.00	2.00
b.	€3.40 multi	8.00	8.00
c.	Horiz. pair, perf. 13¾ vert.	10.00	10.00
d.	As "a," perf. 13¾ vert.	2.00	2.00
e.	As "b," perf. 13¾ vert.	7.75	7.75
f.	Booklet pane, 2 #2842c	20.00	—
	Complete booklet, #2842f	20.00	

Hellenic Army Academy, 190th Anniv. — A977

Designs: 72c, Academy emblem. 80c, Governor of Greece Ioannis Kapodistrias awarding decroation to cadet. €1, Soldiers at flag lowering ceremony at academy, horiz. €2.82, Cadet and new academy building.

Litho. With Gold Foil Application

2018, June 15 *Perf. 13¾*

2843-2846	A977 Set of 4	12.00	12.00

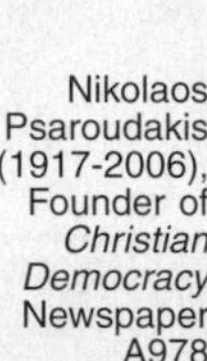

Nikolaos Psaroudakis (1917-2006), Founder of *Christian Democracy* Newspaper A978

2018, June 19 Litho. *Perf. 14*

2847	A978 72c multi	1.75	1.75

Hellenic Mathematical Society, Cent. — A979

2018, June 19 Litho. *Perf. 14*

2848	A979 80c multi	1.90	1.90

Inter-Parliamentary Assembly on Orthodoxy, 25th Anniv. — A980

Litho. With Foil Application

2018, June 19 *Perf. 13¾*

2849	A980 90c multi	2.10	2.10

Tower in Mani — A981

Mansion in Pelion — A982

Cycladic House — A983

Houses in Dodecanese A984

2018, July 20 Litho. *Perf. 13¼x13½*

2850	A981 72c multi	1.75	1.75
a.	Souvenir sheet of 1	1.75	1.75
b.	Perf. 13¾ vert.	1.75	1.75
2851	A982 72c multi	1.75	1.75
a.	Souvenir sheet of 1	1.75	1.75
b.	Perf. 13¾ vert.	1.75	1.75
2852	A983 80c multi	1.90	1.90
a.	Souvenir sheet of 1	1.90	1.90
b.	Perf. 13¾ vert.	1.90	1.90
2853	A984 90c multi	2.10	2.10
a.	Souvenir sheet of 1	2.10	2.10
b.	Perf. 13¾ vert.	2.10	2.10
c.	Booklet pane of 4, #2850b, 2851b, 2852b, 2853b	7.50	—
	Complete booklet, #2853c	7.50	
	Nos. 2850-2853 (4)	7.50	7.50

Souvenir Sheets

Alexander the Great, Painting by Theophilos Hatzimihail (1873-1934) — A985

Erotokritos and Aretousa, Painting by Hatzimihail — A986

Litho., Sheet Margin Litho. With Foil Application

2018, July 25 *Perf. 13¾*

2854	A985 €1 copper & multi	2.40	2.40
2855	A986 €1 copper & multi	2.40	2.40

Museum of Modern Greek Culture, Athens, cent.

Special Disaster Response Unit, 30th Anniv. — A988

2018, Sept. 5 Litho. *Perf. 13¾x14¼*

2857	A988 72c multi	1.75	1.75

Orthodox Academy of Crete, 50th Anniv. A989

2018, Sept. 5 Litho. *Perf. 14¼x13¾*

2858	A989 €1 multi	2.40	2.40

A990

83rd Thessaloniki International Trade Fair — A991

2018, Sept. 5 Litho. *Perf. 14¼x13¾*

2859	A990 80c multi	1.90	1.90

Perf. 13½

2860	A991 80c multi + label	3.75	3.75

No. 2860 was printed in sheets of 5 + 5 labels that could be personalized. The sheet sold for €8. The generic label is shown.

SEMI-POSTAL STAMPS

Catalogue values for unused stamps in this section are for Never Hinged items.

Nos. 440-444 Surcharged in Blue

1944 Wmk. 252 *Perf. 12½*

B1	A106 100,000d on 15d	1.25	*1.50*
B2	A107 100,000d on 25d	1.25	*1.50*
a.	Inverted surcharge	*50.00*	
b.	Double impression	*150.00*	
B3	A108 100,000d on 50d	1.25	*1.50*
a.	Double impression	*150.00*	
B4	A109 100,000d on 75d	1.25	*1.50*
B5	A110 100,000d on 100d	1.25	*1.50*
a.	Inverted surcharge	*50.00*	
b.	Double impression	*75.00*	
	Nos. B1-B5,CB1-CB5 (10)	12.50	*16.05*

The proceeds aided victims of the Piraeus bombing, Jan. 11, 1944. The exceptionally high face value discouraged the use of these stamps.

Nos. 437-441 Surcharged in Blue

1944, July 20 50,000d + 450,000d

B11	A103 on 2d	.75	*1.00*
B12	A104 on 5d	.75	*1.00*
a.	"NAYOLION" instead of "NAYPLION"	55.00	*60.00*
B13	A105 on 10d	.75	*1.00*
B14	A106 on 15d	.75	*1.00*
a.	Pair, one without surcharge	80.00	
b.	Inverted surcharge	*35.00*	
B15	A107 on 25d	.75	*1.00*
	Nos. B11-B15,CB6-CB10 (10)	10.00	*10.00*

The surtax aided children's camps.

AIR POST STAMPS

Italy-Greece-Turkey-Rhodes Service

Flying Boat off Phaleron Bay — AP1

Flying Boat over Acropolis — AP2

Flying Boat over Map of Southern Europe — AP3

Flying Boat Seen through Colonnade — AP4

Perf. 11½

1926, Oct. 20 Unwmk. Litho.

C1	AP1 2d multicolored	1.60	1.25
a.	Horiz. pair, imperf. vert.	725.00	
C2	AP2 3d multicolored	12.00	11.00
C3	AP3 5d multicolored	1.60	1.25
C4	AP4 10d multicolored	12.00	12.00
	Nos. C1-C4 (4)	27.20	25.50
	Set, never hinged	80.00	

Graf Zeppelin Issue

Zeppelin over Acropolis AP5

1933, May 2 *Perf. 13½x12½*

C5	AP5	30d rose red	13.00	13.00
C6	AP5	100d deep blue	52.50	52.50
C7	AP5	120d dark brown	52.50	52.50
		Nos. C5-C7 (3)	118.00	118.00
		Set, never hinged	325.00	

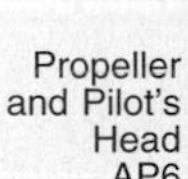

Propeller and Pilot's Head AP6

Temple of Apollo, Corinth AP7

Plane over Hermoupolis, Syros — AP8

Allegory of Flight
AP9 AP12

Map of Italy-Greece-Turkey-Rhodes Airmail Route — AP10

Head of Hermes and Airplane — AP11

1933, Oct. 10 **Engr.** *Perf. 12*

C8	AP6	50 l green & org	.25	.25
C9	AP7	1d bl & brn org	.30	.25
C10	AP8	3d dk vio & org brn	.50	.50
C11	AP9	5d brn org & dk bl	7.25	4.50
C12	AP10	10d dp red & blk	1.50	1.40
C13	AP11	20d black & grn	7.25	4.00
C14	AP12	50d dp brn & dp bl	50.00	*55.00*
		Nos. C8-C14 (7)	67.05	*65.90*
		Set, never hinged	200.00	

By error the 1d stamp is inscribed in the plural "ΔΡΑΧΜΑΙ" instead of the singular "ΔΡΑΧΜΗ." This stamp exists bisected, used as a 50 lepta denomination.

All values of this set exist imperforate but were not regularly issued.

For General Air Post Service

Airplane over Map of Greece — AP13 Airplane over Map of Icarian Sea — AP14

Airplane over Acropolis AP15

Perf. 13x13½, 13x12½, 13½x13, 12½x13

1933, Nov. 2

C15	AP13	50 l green	.25	.25
C16	AP13	1d red brown	.30	*.55*
C17	AP14	2d lt violet	.60	*.85*
C18	AP15	5d ultra	3.50	3.50
a.		Imperf., pair	650.00	550.00
b.		Horiz. pair, imperf. vert.	650.00	
C19	AP14	10d car rose	6.50	*7.75*
C20	AP13	25d dark blue	30.00	20.00
C21	AP15	50d dark brown	30.00	*42.50*
a.		Imperf., pair	775.00	650.00
		Nos. C15-C21 (7)	71.15	75.40
		Set, never hinged	225.00	

Helios Driving the Sun Chariot AP16

Iris — AP17

Daedalus Preparing Icarus for Flying — AP18 Pallas Athene Holding Pegasus — AP19

Hermes AP20 Zeus Carrying off Ganymede AP21

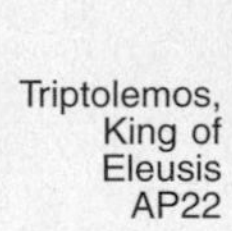

Triptolemos, King of Eleusis AP22

Bellerophon and Pegasus — AP23

Phrixos and Helle on the Ram Flying over the Hellespont AP24

Perf. 13x12½, 12½x13

1935, Nov. 10 **Engr.**

Grayish Paper

Size: 34x23½mm, 23½x34mm

C22	AP16	1d deep red	1.50	1.50
C23	AP17	2d dull blue	1.50	1.50
C24	AP18	5d dk violet	17.50	4.00
C25	AP19	7d blue violet	25.00	7.25
C26	AP20	10d bister brown	5.00	5.00
C27	AP21	25d rose	6.00	5.75
C28	AP22	30d dark green	2.00	2.00
C29	AP23	50d violet	8.00	6.00
C30	AP24	100d brown	2.50	2.25
		Nos. C22-C30 (9)	69.00	35.25
		Set, never hinged	150.00	

Re-engraved

Size: 34¼x24mm, 24x34¼mm

1937-39 **White Paper**

C31	AP16	1d red	.30	.25
C32	AP17	2d gray blue	.30	.25
C33	AP18	5d violet	.30	.25
C34	AP19	7d dp ultra	.30	.25
C35	AP20	10d brn org	2.40	*3.50*
		Nos. C31-C35 (5)	3.60	*4.50*
		Set, never hinged	7.00	

Issued: #C35, 3/1/39; others 8/3/37.

Postage Due Stamp, 1913, Overprinted in Red

Serrate Roulette 13½

1938, Aug. 8 **Litho.** **Unwmk.**

C36	D3	50 l violet brown	.25	.25
		Never hinged	.25	
a.		"O" for "P" in word at foot	30.00	30.00

Same Overprint on No. J79 in Red

1939, June 26 *Perf. 13½x12½*

C37	D3	50 l dark brown	.25	.25
		Never hinged	.25	

Meteora Monasteries, near Trikkala — AP25

Designs: 4d, Simon Peter Monastery. 6d, View of Santorin. 8d, Church of Pantanassa. 16d, Santorin view. 32d, Ponticonissi, Corfu. 40d, Acropolis, Athens. 55d, Erechtheum. 65d, Temple of Nike Apteros. 100d, Temple of the Olympian Zeus, Athens.

Wmk. Crowns (252)

1940, Aug. 3 **Litho.** *Perf. 12½*

C38	AP25	2d red org & blk	.85	*1.25*
C39	AP25	4d dk grn & blk	4.00	3.50
C40	AP25	6d lake & blk	7.25	6.50
C41	AP25	8d dk bl & blk	18.75	16.50
C42	AP25	16d rose vio & blk	30.00	25.00
C43	AP25	32d red org & blk	40.00	*47.50*
C44	AP25	45d dk grn & blk	52.50	47.50
C45	AP25	55d lake & blk	52.50	47.50
C46	AP25	65d dk bl & blk	52.50	47.50
C47	AP25	100d rose vio & blk	67.50	60.00
		Nos. C38-C47 (10)	325.85	302.75
		Set, never hinged	800.00	

4th anniv. of the founding of the Greek Youth Organization. The stamps were good for postal duty on Aug. 3-5, 1940, only. They remained on sale until Feb. 3, 1941.

For overprints see Nos. N229-N238.

Catalogue values for unused stamps in this section, from this point to the end of the section, are for Never Hinged items.

Postage Due Stamps Nos. J81 and J75 Surcharged in Red

1941-42 **Unwmk.** *Perf. 13x12½*

C48	D3	1d on 2d lt red	.25	.25
a.		Inverted surcharge	45.00	

Serrate Roulette 13½

C49	D3	1d on 2d ver ('42)	.25	.25
a.		Inverted surcharge	32.50	
b.		Double surcharge	22.50	

Nos. J83, J84, J86, J87 Overprinted in Red

1941-42 *Perf. 13, 12½x13*

C50	D3	5d gray bl ('42)	.25	.25
a.		Inverted overprint	45.00	
b.		Double overprint	32.50	
c.		Pair, one without ovpt.	22.50	
d.		Surcharge on back	22.50	
e.		On No. J78 ('42)	140.00	*160.00*
C51	D3	10d gray grn	.30	.30
a.		Inverted overprint	16.00	
b.		Vert. pair, imperf. btwn.	325.00	
C52	D3	25d lt red	.85	.85
a.		Inverted overprint	110.00	
C53	D3	50d orange	1.50	1.50
		Nos. C50-C53 (4)	2.90	2.90

Boreas, North Wind — AP35

Winds: 5d, Notus, South. 10d, Apeliotes, East. 20d, Lips, Southwest. 25d, Zephyrus, West. 50d, Kaikias, Northeast.

Wmk. 252

1942, Aug. 15 **Litho.** *Perf. 12½*

C55	AP35	2d emerald	.25	.25
C56	AP35	5d red org	.25	.25
a.		Imperf., pair	325.00	
b.		Double impression	55.00	—
C57	AP35	10d red brown	.45	.45
C58	AP35	20d brt blue	.50	.50
C59	AP35	25d dk red org	.50	.50
C60	AP35	50d gray blk	2.00	2.00
a.		Double impression	110.00	
		Nos. C55-C60 (6)	3.95	3.95

1943, Sept. 15

Winds: 10d, Apeliotes, East. 25d, Zephyrus, West. 50d, Kaikias, Northeast. 100d, Boreas, North. 200d, Eurus, Southeast. 400d, Skiron, Northwest.

C61	AP35	10d rose red	.25	.25
C62	AP35	25d Prus green	.25	.25
C63	AP35	50d violet blue	.25	.25
C64	AP35	100d slate black	.25	.25
C65	AP35	200d claret	.25	.25
C66	AP35	400d steel blue	.25	.25
		Nos. C61-C66 (6)	1.50	1.50

Double impressions exist of 10d and 400d. Value, each $30.

For surcharges see #472, 473, CB1-CB10.

Imperf., Pairs

C61a	AP35	10d	110.00
C62a	AP35	25d	110.0
C63a	AP35	50d	110.
C64a	AP35	100d	110
C65a	AP35	200d	11
C66a	AP35	400d	110.

Priest Blessing Troops on Summit of Mt. Grammos — AP36

Designs: 1700d, Victory above Mt. Vitsi. 2700d, Battle Scene. 7000d, Victory leading infantry.

1952, Aug. 29 Engr. *Perf. 12x13½*

C67	AP36	1000d deep blue	1.50	.30
C68	AP36	1700d dp blue grn	5.00	2.00
C69	AP36	2700d brown	15.00	6.00
C70	AP36	7000d olive green	45.00	15.00
		Nos. C67-C70 (4)	66.50	23.30

Greek army's struggle against communism.

Torchbearer — AP37

Designs: 2400dr, Coin of Amphictyonic League. 4000dr, Pallas Athene.

1954, May 15 *Perf. 13*

C71	AP37	1200d dp orange	7.50	.35
C72	AP37	2400d dk green	37.50	2.50
C73	AP37	4000d dp ultra	65.00	3.50
		Nos. C71-C73 (3)	110.00	6.35

5th anniv. of the signing of the North Atlantic Treaty.

Piraeus AP38

Harbors: 15d, Salonika. 20d, Patras. 25d, Hermoupolis (Syra). 30d, Volos. 50d, Cavalla. 100d, Herakleion (Candia).

Perf. 13½x13

1958, July 1 Wmk. 252 Litho.

C74	AP38	10d multicolored	12.50	.25
C75	AP38	15d multicolored	1.75	.40
C76	AP38	20d multicolored	12.50	.25
C77	AP38	25d multicolored	2.00	.80
C78	AP38	30d multicolored	2.25	.80
C79	AP38	50d multicolored	8.00	.80
C80	AP38	100d multicolored	40.00	4.00
		Nos. C74-C80 (7)	79.00	7.30

AIR POST SEMI-POSTAL STAMPS

Catalogue values for unused stamps in this section are for Never Hinged items.

Nos. C61-C65 Surcharged in Blue like Nos. B1-B5

1944, June Wmk. 252 *Perf. 12½*

CB1	AP35	100,000d on 10d	1.25	*1.75*
CB2	AP35	100,000d on 25d	1.25	*1.75*
CB3	AP35	100,000d on 50d	1.25	*1.75*
a.		Inverted overprint	55.00	
CB4	AP35	100,000d on 100d	1.25	*1.65*
a.		Double surcharge	*55.00*	
CB5	AP35	100,000d on 200d	1.25	*1.65*
		Nos. CB1-CB5 (5)	6.25	*8.55*

The exceptionally high face value discouraged the use of these stamps.

The proceeds aided victims of the Piraeus bombing, January 11, 1944.

No. CB2 exists with double impression of No. C62.

Nos. C61-C65 Surcharged in Blue like Nos. B11-B15

1944, July 50,000d + 450,000d

CB6	AP35	on 10d	1.25	*1.00*
a.		Inverted surcharge	*135.00*	
b.		Double surcharge	*55.00*	
CB7	AP35	on 25d	1.25	*1.00*
a.		Inverted surcharge	*70.00*	
b.		Double surcharge	*55.00*	
CB8	AP35	on 50d	1.25	*1.00*
a.		Inverted surcharge	*55.00*	
b.		Double surcharge	*55.00*	
CB9	AP35	on 100d	1.25	*1.00*
a.		Inverted surcharge	*55.00*	
b.		Double surcharge	*55.00*	
CB10	AP35	on 200d	1.25	*1.00*
a.		Inverted surcharge	*55.00*	
b.		Double surcharge	*55.00*	
		Nos. CB6-CB10 (5)	6.25	*5.00*

The surtax aided children's camps.

POSTAGE DUE STAMPS

D1

Perf. 9, 9½, and 10, 10½ and Compound

1875 Litho. Unwmk.

J1	D1	1 l green & black	1.50	1.50
J2	D1	2 l green & black	1.50	1.50
J3	D1	5 l green & black	1.75	1.25
J4	D1	10 l green & black	1.75	1.25
J5	D1	20 l green & black	42.50	30.00
J6	D1	40 l green & black	8.25	5.50
J7	D1	60 l green & black	42.50	30.00
J8	D1	70 l green & black	8.25	5.50
J9	D1	80 l green & black	17.50	14.50
J10	D1	90 l green & black	11.00	11.00
J11	D1	1d green & black	12.00	11.00
J12	D1	2d green & black	13.00	11.00
		Nos. J1-J12 (12)	161.50	124.00

Imperforate and part perforated, double and inverted center varieties of Nos. J1-J12 are believed to be printers' waste.

Perf. 12, 13 and 10½x13

J13	D1	1 l green & black	1.60	1.60
J14	D1	2 l green & black	22.50	22.50
J15	D1	5 l green & black	2.75	2.75
J16	D1	10 l green & black	3.25	3.25
J17	D1	20 l green & black	40.00	27.50
J18	D1	40 l green & black	10.00	7.75
J19	D1	60 l green & black	42.50	27.50
J20	D1	70 l green & black	7.75	7.75
J21	D1	80 l green & black	12.00	12.00
J22	D1	90 l green & black	17.50	12.00
J23	D1	1d green & black	27.50	17.50
J24	D1	2d green & black	22.50	17.50
		Nos. J13-J24 (12)	209.85	159.60

D2

Redrawn
"Lepton" or "Lepta" in Larger Greek Letters

1876 *Perf. 9, 9½, and 10, 10½*

J25	D2	1 l green & black	4.50	4.50
J26	D2	2 l dk grn & blk	6.00	5.75
J27	D2	5 l dk grn & blk	360.00	275.00
J28	D2	10 l green & black	3.00	2.10
J29	D2	20 l green & black	4.00	3.00
J30	D2	40 l green & black	32.50	25.00
J31	D2	60 l green & black	27.50	15.00
J32	D2	70 l green & black	22.50	25.00
J33	D2	80 l green & black	17.50	15.00
J34	D2	90 l green & black	17.50	16.00
J35	D2	100 l green & black	22.50	15.00
J36	D2	200 l green & black	22.50	15.00
		Nos. J25-J36 (12)	540.00	416.35

Perf. 11½ to 13

J37	D2	1 l yel grn & blk	1.75	.95
J38	D2	2 l yel grn & blk	1.75	.95
J39	D2	5 l yel grn & blk	4.75	1.25
J40	D2	10 l yel grn & blk	2.75	2.00
a.		Perf. 10-10½x11½-13	4.00	
J41	D2	20 l yel grn & blk	2.75	2.00
J42	D2	40 l yel grn & blk	15.00	11.00
J43	D2	60 l yel grn & blk	9.50	9.50
J47	D2	100 l yel grn & blk	12.00	12.00
J48	D2	200 l yel grn & blk	13.50	11.00
		Nos. J37-J48 (9)	63.75	50.65

Footnote below No. J12 applies also to Nos. J25-J48.

D3

1902 Engr. Wmk. 129 *Perf. 13½*

J49	D3	1 l chocolate	.30	.25
J50	D3	2 l gray	.30	.25
J51	D3	3 l orange	.30	.25
J52	D3	5 l yel grn	.30	.25
J53	D3	10 l scarlet	.30	.25
J54	D3	20 l lilac	.45	.25
J55	D3	25 l ultra	8.00	4.00
J56	D3	30 l dp vio	.50	.30
J57	D3	40 l dk brn	.60	.50
J58	D3	50 l red brn	.60	.40
J59	D3	1d black	1.50	.90

Litho.

J60	D3	2d bronze	2.00	1.25
J61	D3	3d silver	3.00	3.00
J62	D3	5d gold	6.50	*9.00*
		Nos. J49-J62 (14)	24.65	20.85

See Nos. J63-J88, J90-J93. For overprints and surcharges see Nos. 383-385, J89, RA56, RA58-RA59, NJ1-NJ31.

Imperf., Pairs

J50a	D3	2 l	90.00
J51a	D3	3 l	90.00
J52a	D3	5 l	90.00
J55a	D3	25 l	150.00
J56a	D3	30 l	150.00
J58a	D3	50 l	150.00
J59a	D3	1d	150.00

Serrate Roulette 13½

1913-26 Unwmk.

J63	D3	1 l green	.25	.25
J64	D3	2 l carmine	.25	.25
J65	D3	3 l vermilion	.25	.25
J66	D3	5 l green	.25	.25
a.		Imperf., pair	150.00	
b.		Double impression	60.00	
c.		"o" for "p" in lowest word	5.00	5.00
J67	D3	10 l carmine	.25	.25
J68	D3	20 l slate	.25	.25
J69	D3	25 l ultra	.25	.25
J70	D3	30 l carmine	.25	.25
J71	D3	40 l indigo	.25	.25
J72	D3	50 l vio brn	.30	.25
a.		"o" for "p" in lowest word	25.00	20.00
J73	D3	80 l lil brn ('24)	.40	.25
J74	D3	1d blue	8.00	1.25
a.		1d ultramarine	12.00	5.00
J75	D3	2d vermilion	8.00	1.50
J76	D3	3d carmine	8.00	1.50
J77	D3	5d ultra	30.00	12.00
J78	D3	5d gray bl ('26)	8.00	4.00
		Nos. J63-J78 (16)	64.95	23.00

In 1922-23 and 1941-42 some postage due stamps were used for ordinary postage.

In 1916 Nos. J52, and J63 to J75 were surcharged for the Mount Athos District (see note after No. N166) but were never issued there. By error some of them were put in use as ordinary postage due stamps in Dec., 1924. In 1932 the balance of them was burned.

Type of 1902 Issue

Perf. 13, 13½x12½, 13½x13

1930 Litho.

J79	D3	50 l dk brown	.30	.30
J80	D3	1d lt blue	.30	.30
J81	D3	2d lt red	.30	.30
J82	D3	3d rose red	27.50	25.00
J83	D3	5d gray blue	.30	.30
J84	D3	10d gray green	.30	.30
J85	D3	15d red brown	.30	.30
J86	D3	25d light red	.70	.65
		Nos. J79-J86 (8)	30.00	27.45

Type of 1902 Issue

1935 Engr. *Perf. 12½x13*

J87	D3	50d orange	.30	.30
J88	D3	100d slate green	.30	.30

No. J70 Surcharged with New Value in Black

1942

J89	D3	50 (l) on 30 l carmine	1.50	1.50

Type of 1902 Issue

1943 Wmk. 252 Litho. *Perf. 12½*

J90	D3	10d red orange	.25	.25
J91	D3	25d ultramarine	.25	.25
J92	D3	100d black brown	.25	.25
J93	D3	200d violet	.25	.25
		Nos. J90-J93 (4)	1.00	1.00

POSTAL TAX STAMPS

"The Tragedy of War" — PT1

Serrate Roulette 13½

1914 Litho. Unwmk.

RA1	PT1	2 l red ('18)	.30	.25
a.		2 l carmine	.45	.25
b.		Imperf., pair	265.00	
RA2	PT1	5 l blue	.50	*.50*
a.		Imperf., pair	375.00	

Red Cross, Nurses, Wounded and Bearers — PT1a

1915 *Serrate Roulette 13*

RA2B	PT1a	(5 l) dk bl & red	12.00	2.00

The tax was for the Red Cross.

Women's Patriotic League Badge — PT1b

1915, Nov. *Perf. 11½*

RA2C	PT1b	(5 l) dk bl & car	1.25	1.25
d.		Horiz. pair, imperf. btwn.	55.00	
e.		Imperf., pair	55.00	

The tax was for the Greek Women's Patriotic League.

Nos. 165, 167, 170, 172-175 Surcharged in Black or Brown

a

b

In type "b" the letters, especially those in the first line, are thinner than in type "a," making them appear taller.

Perf. 11½, 12½, 13½ and Compound

1917 Engr. Wmk. 129

RA3	A11(a)	1 l on 1 l	1.50	1.50
a.		Double surcharge	8.50	
b.		Inverted surcharge	10.00	
c.		Dbl. surch., one invtd.	10.00	
RA4	A11(a)	1 l on 1 l (Br)	24.00	*30.00*
RA5	A11(a)	1 l on 3 l	.30	.30
RA6	A11(b)	1 l on 3 l	.30	.30
a.		Triple surcharge	12.00	
b.		Dbl. surch., one invtd.	6.00	
c.		"K.M." for "K.Π."	20.00	
d.		Inverted surcharge	7.00	
e.		Double surcharge	7.00	
RA7	A11(a)	5 l on 1 l	2.00	2.00
a.		Double surcharge	12.00	
b.		Dbl. surch., one invtd.	12.00	
c.		Inverted surcharge	13.50	
RA8	A11(a)	5 l on 20 l	.65	.65
a.		Double surcharge	13.50	
b.		Dbl. surch., one invtd.	13.50	
c.		Inverted surcharge	15.00	
RA9	A11(b)	5 l on 40 l	.65	.65
a.		Imperf.	*200.00*	*250.00*
b.		Double surcharge	13.50	
c.		Dbl. surch., one invtd.	13.50	
d.		Triple surcharge	47.50	
RA10	A11(b)	5 l on 50 l	.65	.65
a.		Double surcharge	25.00	
b.		Dbl. surch., one invtd.	25.00	
c.		Inverted surcharge	15.00	
d.		Triple surcharge	24.00	
e.		Triple surch., two invtd.	30.00	
f.		Pair, imperf.	*225.00*	*185.00*

RA11 A13(b) 5 l on 1d 2.25 2.25
a. Imperf. *200.00*
b. Inverted surcharge 55.00
c. Double surcharge 35.00
d. Dbl. surch., one invtd. 55.00
e. Triple surcharge 55.00
f. Horiz. pair, imperf. vert. —
g. Vert. pair, imperf. horiz. —
RA12 A11(a) 10 l on 30 l .80 .80
a. Imperf.
b. Double surcharge 18.00
c. Dbl. surch., one invtd. 18.00
d. Inverted surcharge 35.00
RA13 A11(a) 30 l on 30 l .90 .90
a. Double surcharge 20.00
b. Dbl. surch., one invtd. 24.00
c. Triple surch., one invtd. 24.00
d. Inverted surcharge 17.00
Nos. RA3-RA13 (11) 34.00 40.00

Same Surcharge On Occupation Stamps of 1912

Serrate Roulette 13½

1917 Litho. Unwmk.

RA14 O2 (b) 5 l on 25 l pale bl .45 .45
a. Triple surch., one invtd. 15.00
b. Double surcharge 12.00
c. Dbl. surch., one invtd. 13.50
d. Dbl. surch., both invtd. 13.50
e. Inverted surcharge 15.50
RA15 O2 (b) 5 l on 40 l indigo .35 .35
a. Dbl. surch., one invtd. 10.00
b. Double surcharge 10.00
c. Dbl. surch., both invtd. 13.50
d. Inverted surcharge 13.50
e. Triple surcharge 13.50
f. Triple surch., one invtd. 20.00
RA16 O1 (b) 5 l on 50 l dk bl .25 .25
a. Double surcharge 12.00
b. Inverted surcharge 12.00
c. Dbl. surch., one invtd. 13.50
d. Triple surcharge 27.00
e. Triple surch., two invtd. 27.00
Nos. RA14-RA16 (3) 1.05 1.05

There are many wrong font, omitted and misplaced letters and punctuation marks and similar varieties in the surcharges on Nos. RA3 to RA16.

Revenue Stamps Surcharged in Brown

"Victory"

1917

RA17 R1 1 l on 10 l blue .70 *1.00*
RA18 R1 1 l on 80 l blue .70 *1.00*
RA19 R1 5 l on 10 l blue 18.00 *27.50*
RA20 R1 5 l on 60 l blue 6.00 *7.25*
a. Perf. vert. through middle 9.50 *15.00*
b. As "a," inverted surcharge
RA21 R1 5 l on 80 l blue 3.25 *4.50*
a. Perf. vert. through middle 9.50 *15.00*
b. Inverted surcharge
RA22 R1 10 l on 70 l blue 18.00 *25.00*
a. Perf. vert. through middle 7.25 *10.00*
RA23 R1 10 l on 90 l blue 13.50 37.50
a. Perf. vert. through middle 22.50 *45.00*
RA24 R1 20 l on 20 l blue *6,500. 3,600.*
RA25 R1 20 l on 30 l blue 12.00 9.50
RA26 R1 20 l on 40 l blue 14.50 *21.00*
RA27 R1 20 l on 50 l blue 12.00 12.00
RA28 R1 20 l on 60 l blue 500.00 375.00
RA29 R1 20 l on 80 l blue 60.00 *72.50*
RA30 R1 20 l on 90 l blue 5.00 *9.75*
a. Inverted surcharge *100.00*
b. Double surcharge
Nos. RA17-RA30 (14) 7,164. 4,204.

No. RA19 is known only with vertical perforation through the middle.

Counterfeits exist of Nos. RA17-RA43, used.

Surcharged in Brown or Black

RA31 R1 1 l on 50 l vio (Bk) .85 *1.40*
RA32 R1 5 l on 10 l bl (Br) .85 *1.40*
a. Inverted surcharge 85.00
b. Left "5" invert. 97.50
RA33 R1 5 l on 10 l vio (Br) .85 *1.40*
RA34 R1 10 l on 50 l vio (Br) 6.00 *12.00*
RA35 R1 10 l on 50 l vio (Bk) 25.00 *32.50*
a. Double surcharge *85.00*
RA36 R1 20 l on 2d bl (Bk) 9.75 9.75
a. Surcharged "20 lept. 30" 80.00 *120.00*
b. Horiz. pair, imperf. btwn.
Nos. RA31-RA36 (6) 43.30 58.45

The "T," fourth Greek letter of the denomination in the surcharge ("ΛΕΠΤ."), is normally omitted on Nos. RA31, RA34-RA36.

Corfu Issue

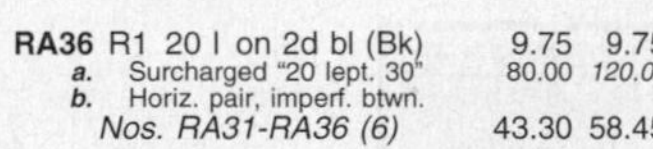

Surcharged in Black

1917

RA37 R1 1 l on 10 l blue 2.50 2.50
RA38 R1 5 l on 50 l blue 60.00 *80.00*
RA39 R1 10 l on 50 l blue 725.00 725.00
RA40 R1 20 l on 50 l blue 2,850. 1,075.

Surcharged in Black

RA41 R1 10 l on 50 l blue 13.50 *14.50*
RA42 R1 20 l on 50 l blue 30.00 30.00
RA43 R1 30 l on 50 l blue 18.00 18.00

Surcharged in Black

Without serifs

With serifs

RA44 R1 5 l on 10 l vio & red 9.75 *13.50*
a. "K" with serifs 13.50 *25.00*

Counterfeits exist of Nos. RA17-RA44.

Similar stamps with denominations higher than 30 lepta were for revenue use.

Wounded Soldier — PT2

1918 ***Serrate Roulette 13½, 11½***

RA45 PT2 5 l bl, yel & red 8.50 2.00

Overprinted

RA46 PT2 5 l blue, yel & red 11.00 2.00
e. Double overprint 290.00

The letters are the initials of Greek words equivalent to "Patriotic Relief Institution." The proceeds were given to the Patriotic League, for the aid of disabled soldiers.

Counterfeits exist of Nos. RA45-RA46.

PT3

Surcharge in Red

1922 Litho. ***Perf. 11½***

Dark Blue & Red

RA46A PT3 5 l on 10 l *325.00* 16.00
f. Double surcharge *410.00 410.00*
RA46B PT3 5 l on 20 l 97.50 57.50
RA46C PT3 5 l on 50 l 325.00 275.00
RA46D PT3 5 l on 1d 12.00 *60.00*

Counterfeit surcharges exist. Examples of Nos. RA46A-RA46C without surcharge, each 50 cents.

Value for No. RA46Af unused is for example without gum.

Red Cross Help to Soldier and Family — PT3a

1924 ***Perf. 13½ x 12½***

RA47 PT3a 10 l blue, buff & red .85 .25

Proceeds were given to the Red Cross.

1926 ***Perf. 11½***

RA47C PT3a 10 l blue, buff & red .30 .25
a. Imperf., pair 40.00
b. Horiz. pair, imperf. btwn. 40.00
d. Horiz. pair, imperf. vert. 45.00
e. Vert. pair, imperf. horiz. 50.00

St. Demetrius — PT4

1934 ***Perf. 11½***

RA48 PT4 20 l brown .35 .25
a. Horizontal pair, imperf. between 10.00
b. Vertical pair, imperf. between 16.00
c. Imperf., pair 18.00
d. Horiz. pair, imperf. vert. 16.00
e. Vert. pair, imperf. horiz. 16.00
f. Double impression *60.00*

No. RA48 was obligatory as a tax on all interior mail, including air post, mailed from Salonika.

For surcharge see No. RA69.

"Health" — PT5

1934, Dec. 28 ***Perf. 13, 13x13½***

RA49 PT5 10 l bl grn, org & buff .25 .25
a. Vert. pair, imperf. horiz.
RA50 PT5 20 l ultra, org & buff .25 .25
RA51 PT5 50 l grn, org & buff 2.00 .70
Nos. RA49-RA51 (3) 2.50 1.20

For surcharge see No. RA67.

"Health" — PT6

1935

RA52 PT6 10 l yel grn, org & buff .25 .25
RA53 PT6 20 l ultra, org & buff .30 .25
RA54 PT6 50 l grn, org & buff .70 .70
Nos. RA52-RA54 (3) 1.25 1.20

The use of #RA49-RA54 was obligatory on all mail during 4 weeks each year including Christmas, the New Year and Easter, and on parcel post packages at all times. For the benefit of the tubercular clerks and officials of the Post, Telephone and Telegraph Service.

See No. RA64. For surcharge see No. RA68.

No. 364 Overprinted in Red

1937, Jan. 20 Engr. ***Perf. 13x12½***

RA55 A36 50 l violet 1.40 .25
a. Inverted overprint .75 .25

No. RA55a first appeared as an error, then was issued deliberately in quantity to avoid speculation.

Same Overprint in Blue on No. J67

Litho.

Serrate Roulette 13½

RA56 D3 10 l carmine .80 .25
a. Inverted overprint 50.00
b. Without accent mark on "O" .90 .50

No. RA56 has accent mark on "O." No. RA56 with blue overprint double exists only with additional black overprint of Ionian Islands No. NRA1a.

Same Overprint in Green on No. 364

1937 Engr. ***Perf. 13x12½***

RA57 A36 50 l violet .30 .25

Nos. J66, J68 and 323 Surcharged in Blue or Black

Serrate Roulette 13½

1938 Litho. Unwmk.

RA58 D3 50 l on 5 l grn 1.50 .80
a. Accent mark on "O" 7.50 1.00
b. "O" for "P" in lowest word 30.00 25.00
c. As No. RA58, vert. pair, imperf. horiz. 65.00 120.00
RA59 D3 50 l on 20 l slate 1.50 .80
a. Accent mark on "O" 240.00 47.50

Nos. RA58 and RA59 have no accent mark on "O."

Engr. ***Perf. 13x12½***

RA60 A38 50 l on 20 l vio (Bk) .40 .25
Nos. RA58-RA60 (3) 3.40 1.85

Surcharge on No. RA60 is 14½x16½mm.

Queens Olga and Sophia PT7

1939, Feb. 1 Litho. ***Perf. 13½x12***

RA61 PT7 10 l brt rose, *pale rose* .25 .25
RA62 PT7 50 l gray grn, *pale grn* .25 .25
a. Double impression 120.00
b. Imperf., pair
RA63 PT7 1d dl bl, *lt bl* .25 .25
Nos. RA61-RA63 (3) .75 .75

For overprints and surcharges see Nos. RA65, RA79-RA81A, NRA1-NRA3.

"Health" Type of 1935

1939 ***Perf. 12½***

RA64 PT6 50 l brn & buff .40 .30

No. RA62 Overprinted in Red

1940 *Perf. 13½x12*

RA65 PT7 50 l gray grn, *pale grn* .25 .25
- *a.* Inverted overprint 27.50
- *b.* Pair, one without overprint 80.00
- *c.* Double impression 120.00

Proceeds of Nos. RA64-RA65 were used for the benefit of tubercular clerks and officials of the Post, Telephone and Telegraph Service. No. RA65 was used in Albania during the Greek occupation, 1940-41 without additional overprint.

No. 321 Surcharged in Carmine

1941 Unwmk. Engr. *Perf. 13½x13*

RA66 A36 50 l on 5 l dk grn .25 .25
- *a.* Inverted surcharge 18.00

No. RA49 and Type of 1935 Surcharged with New Value in Black

Perf. 12½x13, 13x13½

Litho.

RA67 PT5 50 l on 10 l .75 5.00
- *a.* Inverted surcharge 47.50

RA68 PT6 50 l on 10 l dp bl grn, dl org & buff .25 .25
- *a.* Inverted surcharge 40.00
- *b.* Double surcharge 40.00

Catalogue values for unused stamps in this section, from this point to the end of the section, are for Never Hinged items.

No. RA48 Surcharged in Green

1942 *Perf. 11½*

RA69 PT4 1d on 20 l brn .30 .25
- *a.* Pair, one without surcharge 37.50
- *b.* Imperf., pair
- *c.* Double surcharge 25.00 25.00
- *d.* Horiz. pair, imperf. vert. 37.50

Nos. 321, 324 Surcharged In Red or Carmine

1942-43 Engr. *Perf. 13½x13*

RA70 A36 10d on 5 l ('43) .25 .25
- *a.* Double surcharge 25.00
- *b.* Inverted surcharge *45.00*
- *c.* Imperf., pair *300.00*
- *d.* Horiz. pair, imperf. vert. *200.00*

RA71 A39 10d on 25 l (C) .25 .25
- *a.* Inverted surcharge 45.00
- *b.* Double surcharge *25.00*
- *c.* Imperf., pair *300.00*
- *d.* Horiz. pair, imperf. vert. 200.00

No. 444 Overprinted in Red

1944 Wmk. 252 Litho. *Perf. 12½*

RA72 A110 100d black .25 .25
- *a.* Double overprint 12.00
- *b.* Inverted overprint 10.00

No. 443 Surcharged in Blue

RA73 A109 5000d on 75d .25 .25
- *a.* Double surcharge 27.50
- *b.* Inverted surcharge 30.00

No. 437 Surcharged in Blue

RA74 A103 25000d on 2d .25 .25
- *a.* Double surcharge 30.00
- *b.* Additional surcharge on back 120.00
- *c.* Inverted surcharge
- *d.* Inv. surch. on back only *135.00*

No. 399 Surcharged in Blue or Carmine

1945 *Perf. 13½x12*

RA75 A72 1d on 40 l .25 .25
- *a.* Double surcharge 20.00
- *b.* Triple surcharge *50.00*

RA76 A72 2d on 40 l (C) .25 .25
- *a.* Vert. pair, one without surch. 30.00
- *b.* Surcharged on back
- *c.* Inverted surcharge 30.00
- *d.* Double surcharge 30.00

Tax on Nos. RA67, RA68-RA70 to RA76 aided the postal clerks' tuberculosis fund.

Nos. 396 and 399 Surcharged in Carmine

1946

RA77 A72 20d on 40 l .30 .25
- *a.* Pair, one without surcharge
- *b.* Inverted surcharge 40.00
- *c.* Double surcharge 40.00
- *d.* Violet surcharge 18.00

RA78 A69 20d on 5 l .75 .30

Same Surcharge in Carmine on Nos. RA62 and RA63

1946-47 Unwmk. *Perf. 13½x12*

RA79 PT7 50d on 50 l ('47) .50 .25
- *a.* Inverted surcharge 30.00
- *b.* Pair, one without surcharge *120.00*
- *c.* Double surcharge 20.00
- *d.* Imperf., pair *180.00*

RA80 PT7 50d on 1d .30 .25
- *a.* Red violet surcharge 8.00 3.00
- *b.* Brown violet surcharge 16.00 *20.00*
- *c.* Additional surcharge on back

The tax on Nos. RA77 to RA80 was for the Postal Clerks' Welfare Fund.

Nos. RA65 and RA62 Surcharged in Carmine

1947

RA81 50d on 50 l (RA65) 2.00 .25
- *b.* Double surcharge 130.00

RA81A 50d on 50 l (RA62) 40.00 *45.00*

Tax for the postal clerks' tuberculosis fund.

St. Demetrius — PT8

1948 Litho. *Perf. 12x13½*

RA82 PT8 50d yellow brown .25 .25
- *a.* Imperf., pair 40.00

Obligatory on all domestic mail. The tax was for restoration of historical monuments and churches destroyed during World War II.

Nos. 397 and 413 Surcharged In Blue

1950 **Wmk. 252**

RA83 A70 50d on 10 l (#397) 1.25 .30
- *a.* Stamp with double frame *165.00*
- *b.* Surcharge reading down 25.00 25.00
- *c.* Double surcharge 30.00

RA84 A70 50d on 10 l (#413) 1.00 .25
- *a.* Surcharge reading down 25.00 25.00
- *b.* Double surcharge 30.00
- *c.* Stamp with double frame *165.00*

Tax for the Postal Clerks' Welfare Fund.

No. 396 Surcharged in Carmine

1951 *Perf. 13½x12*

RA85 A69 50d on 5 l 2.00 .25
- *a.* Double surcharge

Tax for the Postal Employees' Welfare Fund.

No. 392 Surcharged in Black

1951 Wmk. 252 *Perf. 12½x12*

RA86 A67 50d on 3d red brn 1.25 .25
- *a.* Pair, one without surcharge *100.00*
- *b.* "50" omitted *75.00*
- *c.* Inverted surcharge *47.50*
- *d.* Cross of Lorraine omitted

Tax for the postal clerks' tuberculosis fund.

No. 393 Surcharged in Carmine

1952

RA87 A67 100d on 8d deep blue 1.00 .25
- *a.* Double surcharge *45.00*
- *b.* Add'l surch. on back (inverted) *120.00*

The tax was for the State Welfare Fund.

Ruins of Church of Phaneromeni, Zante — PT9

500d, Map & scene of destruction, Argostoli.

1953 Wmk. 252 Litho. *Perf. 12½*

RA88 PT9 300d indigo & pale grn 1.25 .25

RA89 PT9 500d dk brn & buff 3.75 .70

The tax was for the reconstruction of Cephalonia, Ithaca, and Zante, Ionian Islands destroyed by earthquake.

Zeus on Macedonian Coin of Philip II — PT10

Design: 1d, Aristotle.

1956 *Perf. 13½*

RA90 PT10 50 l dk car rose 1.25 .25
- *a.* Imperf., pair 275.00

RA91 PT10 1d brt blue 4.50 1.25

Tax for archaeological research in Macedonia. The coin on No. RA90 portrays Zeus despite inscription of Philip's name.

1958 *Perf. 12½x13½*

RA90B PT10 50 l dk car rose 20.00 .50

RA91A PT10 1d brt blue 55.00 4.50

POSTAL TAX SEMI-POSTAL STAMPS

Child — PTSP1

Mother and Child — PTSP2

Virgin and Christ Child — PTSP3

Perf. 12x13½

1943 Wmk. 252 Litho.

RAB1 PTSP1 25d + 25d bl grn .25 .50
- *a.* Imperf., pair *65.00*

RAB2 PTSP2 100d + 50d rose vio .25 .50
- *a.* Imperf., pair *65.00*

RAB3 PTSP3 200d + 100d red brn .25 .50
- *a.* Imperf., pair *65.00*

Nos. RAB1-RAB3 (3) .75 1.50

Surtax aided needy children. These stamps were compulsory on domestic mail in Oct. 1943.

OCCUPATION AND ANNEXATION STAMPS

During the Balkan wars, 1912-13, Greece occupied certain of the Aegean Islands and part of Western Turkey. She subsequently acquired these territories and they were known as the New Greece.

Most of the special issues for the Aegean Islands were made by order of the military commanders.

For Use in the Aegean Islands Occupied by Greece

CHIOS

Greece No. 221 Overprinted in Red

Serrate Roulette 13½

1913 Litho. Unwmk.

N1 A25 25 l ultramarine 60.00 *85.00*
a. Inverted overprint 200.00 *225.00*
b. "Λ" for "Δ" in overprint 225.00 *250.00*
c. As "b," overprint inverted 475.00 *525.00*

ICARIA (NICARIA)

Penelope — I1

1912 Unwmk. Litho. *Perf. 11½*

N2 I1 2 l orange 1.25 2.50
N3 I1 5 l blue green 1.25 2.50
N4 I1 10 l rose 1.25 2.50
N5 I1 25 l ultra 1.25 2.50
a. Pair, imperf. between 80.00 80.00
N6 I1 50 l gray lilac 1.50 3.50
a. Pair, imperf. between 80.00 80.00
N7 I1 1d dark brown 2.50 *9.00*
N8 I1 2d claret 3.50 *15.00*
N9 I1 5d slate 5.00 *22.50*
Nos. N2-N9 (8) 17.50 *60.00*

Counterfeits of Nos. N1-N15 are plentiful.

Stamps of Greece, 1911-23, Overprinted Reading Up

1913 On Issue of 1911-21 Engr.

N10 A25 2 l car rose 40.00 30.00
N11 A24 3 l vermilion 40.00 30.00

Litho.

On Issue of 1912-23

N12 A24 1 l green 40.00 30.00
N12A A25 2 l car rose 40.00 30.00
N13 A24 3 l vermilion 40.00 30.00
N14 A26 5 l green 40.00 30.00
N15 A24 10 l carmine 40.00 30.00
Nos. N10-N15 (6) 240.00 180.00

LEMNOS

Regular Issues of Greece Overprinted in Black

On Issue of 1901

1912 Wmk. 129 Engr. *Perf. 13½*

N16 A11 20 l red lilac 2.00 2.00
a. Inverted overprint 22.50
b. Double overprint 22.50

On Issue of 1911-21

Unwmk.

Serrate Roulette 13½

N17 A24 1 l green .60 .60
a. Inverted overprint 15.00
b. Double overprint 15.00
c. Double ovpt., one inverted 30.00
N18 A25 2 l carmine rose .70 .70
a. Inverted overprint 15.00
b. Double overprint 15.00
N19 A24 3 l vermilion .70 .70
a. Inverted overprint 15.00
b. Double overprint 15.00
c. Double ovpt., one inverted 20.00
d. Triple overprint 72.50
e. Triple ovpt., one inverted 72.50
f. Inverted ovpt. on face, upright ovpt. on reverse 120.00
N20 A26 5 l green .70 .70
a. Inverted overprint 15.00
b. Double overprint 15.00
N21 A24 10 l car rose 1.00 1.00
a. Inverted overprint 15.00
b. Double overprint 15.00
c. Double ovpt., one inverted 30.00
N22 A25 20 l gray lilac 1.50 1.75
a. Inverted overprint 15.00
b. Double overprint 27.00
N23 A25 25 l ultra 1.50 1.75
a. Inverted overprint 22.50
b. Double overprint 22.50
N24 A26 30 l car rose 3.00 3.00
a. Inverted overprint 50.00
b. Double overprint 50.00
N25 A25 40 l deep blue 4.75 *5.50*
a. Inverted overprint 55.00
N26 A26 50 l dl violet 5.00 *5.50*
N27 A27 1d ultra 6.00 6.00
b. Double overprint 60.00
N28 A27 2d vermilion 20.00 20.00
N29 A27 3d car rose 22.50 22.50
N30 A27 5d ultra 26.00 26.00
N31 A27 10d deep blue 80.00 *97.50*
N32 A28 25d deep blue 150.00 150.00
Nos. N17-N32 (16) 323.95 343.20

On Issue of 1912-23

Litho.

N33 A24 1 l green .60 .60
a. Inverted overprint 15.00
b. Double overprint 15.00
c. Double overprint, one inverted 22.50
d. Double overprint, both inverted 22.50
e. Inverted overprint on face, upright overprint on reverse 40.00
g. Triple ovpt, one inverted 40.00
N34 A26 5 l green .70 .70
a. Inverted overprint 12.00
b. Double overprint 12.00
N35 A24 10 l carmine .70 .70
a. Inverted overprint 120.00
b. Double overprint 13.50
N36 A25 25 l ultra 3.00 3.00
a. Inverted overprint 22.50
b. Double overprint 15.00
Nos. N33-N36 (4) 5.00 5.00

Red Overprint

On Issue of 1911-23

Engr.

N37 A25 40 l deep blue 2.00 2.00
N38 A26 50 l dull violet 2.00 2.00
N39 A27 1d ultramarine 3.00 3.00
N40 A27 3d car rose 15.00 15.00
N41 A27 5d gray blue 400.00 300.00
N42 A27 10d deep blue 120.00 120.00
N43 A28 25d deep blue 150.00 150.00

Litho.

N44 A24 5 l green .60 .60
a. Inverted overprint —
b. Double overprint —
N45 A25 25 l ultramarine 2.00 2.00
Nos. N37-N45 (9) 694.60 594.60

Carmine Overprint

Engr.

N46 A25 2 l carmine 3.00 3.00
a. Double overprint 30.00
b. Triple overprint 60.00
N47 A24 3 l vermilion 3.00 3.00
N48 A25 20 l gray blue 12.00 12.00
N49 A26 30 l carmine rose 6.00 6.00
a. Inverted overprint 30.00
b. Double overprint 30.00
N50 A27 2d vermilion 360.00 300.00
a. Inverted overprint —
b. Double overprint —
c. Double ovpt., both inverted —
N51 A27 3d car rose 120.00 90.00
N51A A27 5d ultramarine 60.00 60.00
b. Double overprint 120.00
N51B A28 25d deep blue 1,200. 475.00

Litho.

N51C A24 1 l green 2.00 2.00
a. Without period after "ΕΛ-ΛΑΣ" (on #214a) 175.00 185.00
b. As "a.," double overprint — —
e. As N51C, double ovpt. 15.00
N52 A24 10 l carmine 4.00 4.00
g. Double overprint 24.00
Nos. N46-N52 (10) 1,770. 955.00

No. N33 with Added "Greek Administration" Overprint, as on Nos. N109-N148, in Black

1913

N52A A24 1 l green 25.00 25.00
b. Period omitted after "ΕΛ-ΛΑΣ" (on #N33f) 360.00
c. Inverted "ΛΗΜΝΟΣ" overprint (on No. N33a) 90.00
d. Double "ΛΗΜΝΟΣ" overprint (on No. N33a) 90.00
e. As "b," double "ΛΗΜΝΟΣ" overprint (on No. N33f) —
f. As "b," inverted "ΛΗΜΝΟΣ" overprint (on No. N33f) —

Counterfeits of Nos. N16-N52A are plentiful.

MYTILENE (LESBOS)

Turkey Nos. 162, 158 Overprinted in Blue

Perf. 12, 13½ and Compound

1912 Typo. Unwmk.

N53 A21 20pa rose 22.50 22.50
N54 A21 10pi dull red 125.00 *135.00*

On Turkey Nos. P68, 151-155, 137, 157-158 in Black

N55 A21 2pa olive green 2.00 2.00
N56 A21 5pa ocher 2.00 2.00
N57 A21 10pa blue green 2.00 2.00
N58 A21 20pa rose 2.00 2.00
N59 A21 1pi ultra 4.00 4.00
N60 A21 2pi blue black 25.00 25.00
N61 A19 2½pi dk brown 12.00 12.00
N62 A21 5pi dk violet 26.00 26.00
N63 A21 10pi dull red 125.00 *135.00*
Nos. N55-N63 (9) 200.00 210.00

On Turkey Nos. 161-163, 145 in Black

N64 A21 10pa blue green 7.25 7.25
a. Double overprint 47.50 47.50
N65 A21 20pa rose 7.25 7.25
a. Blue overprint 40.00 40.00
N66 A21 1pi ultra 7.25 7.25
N67 A19 2pi blue black 65.00 65.00

Nos. N55, N58, N65, N59 Surcharged in Blue or Black

N68 A21 25 l on 2pa 12.00 12.00
a. New value inverted 45.00 *50.00*
N68C A21 25 l on 20pa 30.00 30.00
N68D A21 50 l on 2pa 30.00 30.00
N69 A21 50 l on 20pa 12.00 12.00
b. New value inverted 50.00 *55.00*
N70 A21 1d on 20pa (N65) (Bk) 40.00 40.00
a. New value inverted 72.50 72.50
c. Blue surcharge 37.50 40.00
d. As "c," new value inverted 120.00 120.00
N71 A21 2d on 1pi (Bk) 24.00 27.50
a. New value inverted

Same Overprint on Turkey No. J49

N72 A19 1pi blk, *dp rose* 60.00 72.50

The overprint is found on all values reading up or down with inverted "i" in the first word and inverted "e" in the third word.

No. N72 was only used for postage.

Counterfeits of Nos. N53-N72 are plentiful.

SAMOS

Issues of the Provisional Government

Map of Samos OS1

1912 Unwmk. Typo. *Imperf.*

N73 OS1 5 l gray green 24.00 10.00
N74 OS1 10 l red 20.00 10.00
a. 10 l pale green (error) 240.00 —
N75 OS1 25 l blue 55.00 20.00
a. 25 l pale green (error) *500.00* *600.00*
b. 25 l red (error) 500.00 —
Nos. N73-N75 (3) 99.00 40.00

Only one example of No. N75c is known.

Counterfeits exist of Nos. N73 to N75.

Hermes — OS2

1912 Litho. *Perf. 11½*

Without Overprint

N76 OS2 1 l gray 2.00 1.50
N77 OS2 5 l lt green 2.00 1.50
N78 OS2 10 l rose 3.50 1.80
b. Half used as 5 l on cover *240.00*
N79 OS2 25 l lt blue 8.50 2.25
N80 OS2 50 l violet brn 15.00 6.00

With Overprint

N81 OS2 1 l gray 1.00 1.20
b. Pair, imperf. between 120.00
N82 OS2 5 l blue grn 1.00 1.20
b. Pair, imperf. between 120.00
N83 OS2 10 l rose 1.00 1.20
b. Half used as 5 l on cover *240.00*
N84 OS2 25 l blue 2.00 1.50
N85 OS2 50 l violet brn 12.00 7.25
N86 OS2 1d orange 15.00 13.50
Nos. N76-N86 (11) 63.00 38.90

For overprints and surcharge see Nos. N92-N103.

Imperf., Pairs

Without Overprint

N76a OS2 1 l 37.50 30.00
N77a OS2 5 l 37.50 30.00
N78a OS2 10 l 37.50 30.00
N79a OS2 25 l 37.50 30.00
N80a OS2 50 l 37.50 30.00

With Overprint

N81a OS2 1 l 85.00 40.00
N82a OS2 5 l 85.00 40.00
N83a OS2 10 l 85.00 40.00
N85a OS2 50 l 85.00 40.00

Church in Savior's Name and Fort Ruins OS3

Manuscript Initials in Red or Black

1913

N87 OS3 1d brown (R) 18.00 15.00
a. Without initials 23.00 *42.50*
N88 OS3 2d deep blue (R) 18.00 15.00
a. Without initials 23.00 *42.50*
N89 OS3 5d gray grn (R) 37.50 30.00
a. Without initials 80.00 *120.00*
N90 OS3 10d yellow grn (R) 100.00 95.00
a. Without initials 180.00 *250.00*
c. Horiz. pair, imperf. vert. 800.00
N91 OS3 25d red (Bk) 100.00 85.00
a. Without initials 180.00 *225.00*
c. Horiz. pair, imperf. vert. 800.00
d. Initials in red
Nos. N87-N91 (5) 273.50 240.00

Victory of the Greek fleet in 1824 and the union with Greece of Samos in 1912. The manuscript initials are those of Pres. Themistokles Sofulis.

Exist imperf. Counterfeits of Nos. N87-N91 are plentiful.

For overprints see Nos. N104-N108.

Imperf., Pairs

Without Initials

N87b OS3 1 d 150.00
N88b OS3 2 d 150.00
N89b OS3 5 d 200.00
N90b OS3 10 d 800.00
N91b OS3 25 d 800.00

Nos. N76 to N80 Overprinted

1914

N92 OS2 1 l gray 7.25 6.00
a. Inverted overprint 200.00 160.00
b. Imperf., pair 90.00
N93 OS2 5 l lt green 7.25 6.00
a. Inverted overprint 200.00 160.00
b. Imperf., pair 90.00
N94 OS2 10 l rose 7.25 6.00
a. Double overprint 60.00
b. Inverted overprint 230.00 175.00
c. Imperf., pair 90.00

N95 OS2 25 l lt blue 12.00 12.00
b. Inverted overprint 230.00 175.00
c. Imperf., pair 90.00
N96 OS2 50 l violet brn 9.00 9.00
a. Double overprint 90.00 *100.00*
b. Inverted overprint 170.00 135.00
c. Imperf., pair 90.00
Nos. N92-N96 (5) 42.75 39.00

Charity Issues of Greek Administration

Nos. N81 to N86 Overprinted in Red or Black

1915
N97 OS2 1 l gray (R) 18.00 22.00
a. Black overprint 145.00 160.00
b. As N97, double overprint 180.00
N98 OS2 5 l blue grn (Bk) 1.50 *2.00*
a. Red overprint 105.00 *150.00*
b. As N98, double overprint 145.00 *220.00*
N99 OS2 10 l rose (Bk) 1.50 *2.00*
a. Red overprint 135.00 *160.00*
b. As N99, inverted overprint 125.00 *150.00*
N100 OS2 25 l blue (Bk) 1.50 *2.00*
a. Red overprint 135.00 *160.00*
N101 OS2 50 l violet brn (Bk) 1.50 *2.00*
a. Red overprint 135.00 *160.00*
N102 OS2 1d orange (R) 3.50 *4.00*
a. Inverted overprint 135.00 *220.00*
b. Black overprint 120.00 *190.00*
c. As "b," double overprint 160.00 *220.00*

No. N102 With Additional Surcharge in Black

N103 OS2 1 l on 1d orange 20.00 20.00
a. Black surcharge double 180.00 *325.00*
b. Black surcharge inverted 180.00
Nos. N97-N103 (7) 47.50 54.00

Issue of 1913 Overprinted in Red or Black

Without Sofoulis' Initials Above Overprint

1915
N104 OS3 1d brown (R) 28.00 17.00
a. With initials 40.00 25.00
N105 OS3 2d dp blue (R) 28.00 23.00
a. With initials 47.50 37.50
b. As "a," double overprint
N106 OS3 5d gray grn (R) 45.00 28.00
a. With initials 40.00 25.00
b. As "a," black overprint 1,500.
N107 OS3 10d yellow grn (Bk) 85.00 72.50
a. Inverted overprint 1,600.
N108 OS3 25d red (Bk) *600.00 650.00*
a. With initials 750.00 750.00
Nos. N104-N108 (5) 786.00 790.50

Nos. N97 to N108 inclusive have an embossed control mark, consisting of a cross encircled by a Greek inscription.

Counterfeits of Nos. N104-N108 are plentiful.

FOR USE IN PARTS OF TURKEY OCCUPIED BY GREECE (NEW GREECE)

Regular Issues of Greece Overprinted

Black Overprint Meaning "Greek Administration" On Issue of 1901

1912 Wmk. 129 Engr. *Perf. 13½*
N109 A11 20 l red lilac 3.25 2.75
a. Double overprint 45.00 45.00

On Issue of 1911-21

Unwmk.

Serrate Roulette 13½
N110 A24 1 l green 1.00 1.00
a. Double overprint 22.50 22.00
N111 A25 2 l car rose 1.00 1.00
a. Double overprint 6.75 *8.00*
b. Double ovpt., one inverted 70.00
N112 A24 3 l vermilion 1.00 1.00
a. Double overprint 6.75 *8.00*
N113 A26 5 l green 1.00 1.00
a. Double overprint 10.00 10.00
N114 A24 10 l car rose 1.50 2.00
a. Double overprint 10.00 10.00
N115 A25 20 l gray lilac 2.75 2.75
a. Double overprint 22.50 22.50
g. Imperf., pair 1,200.
N116 A25 25 l ultra 2.75 2.75
a. Double overprint 22.50 18.50
N117 A26 30 l car rose 2.75 *3.00*
a. Double overprint 25.00 25.00
N118 A25 40 l deep blue 3.75 *4.50*
a. Double overprint 27.50 24.00
N119 A26 50 l dl violet 4.50 *5.00*
a. Double overprint 30.00 *30.00*
N120 A27 1d ultra 11.00 3.50
b. Double overprint 90.00 90.00
N121 A27 2d vermilion 55.00 25.00
a. Double overprint 120.00 120.00
N122 A27 3d car rose 55.00 32.50
N123 A27 5d ultra 25.00 32.50
a. Double overprint 45.00 45.00
N124 A27 10d deep blue 265.00 265.00
N125 A28 25d dp bl, ovpt. horiz. 325.00 325.00

On Issue of 1913-23

Litho.
N126 A24 1 l green 1.00 1.00
a. Double overprint 5.50 *7.00*
b. Double ovpt., one inverted 55.00 55.00
c. Period omitted after "ΕΛ-ΛΑΣ" (on #214a) 145.00 75.00
f. As "c," double overprint
g. As "c," double ovpt., one inverted
N127 A26 5 l green 1.00 1.00
a. Double overprint 7.00 *8.00*
b. Imperf., pair
N128 A24 10 l carmine 4.00 3.00
a. Double overprint 7.00 *8.00*
b. Double overprint, one inverted 140.00 140.00
N129 A25 25 l blue 6.00 6.00
a. Double overprint 22.50 22.50
b. Triple overprint 225.00
Nos. N109-N129 (21) 773.25 721.25

Red Overprint, Reading Up On Issues of 1911-21

Engr.
N130 A24 1 l green 1.00 1.00
N131 A26 5 l green 1.00 1.00
a. Double overprint
N132 A25 20 l gray lilac 5.50 5.00
a. Inverted overprint (reading down) *3,000. 1,800.*
N133 A25 40 l deep blue 2.75 2.75
a. Double overprint 275.00 275.00
N134 A26 50 l dull violet 3.25 3.25
N135 A27 1d ultramarine 20.00 15.00
N136 A27 2d vermilion 90.00 *100.00*
N137 A27 3d carmine rose 32.50 *45.00*
N138 A27 5d ultramarine 550.00 400.00
N139 A27 10d deep blue 40.00 *55.00*
a. Double overprint 725.00
N140 A28 25d dp bl, ovpt. horiz. 75.00 100.00
a. Double overprint 1,800.
b. Inverted overprint (reading down) 550.00 550.00
c. Inverted overprint (reading up) 650.00 650.00

Litho.
N141 A26 5 l green 1.60 1.75
N142 A25 25 l ultra, ovpt. vert. (reading up) 2.75 1.75
Nos. N130-N142 (13) 825.35 731.50

Nos. N140b and N140c were the only horizontal or vertical overprints placed into normal circulation.

Engr.

Carmine Overprint, Reading Up

N143 A25 2 l carmine rose 12.00 *13.00*
a. Double overprint 40.00
N144 A24 3 l vermilion 11.00 *13.00*
N145 A25 20 l gray lilac 50.00 *80.00*
a. Double overprint 75.00
N146 A25 25 l ultramarine 90.00 90.00
N147 A26 30 l carmine rose 110.00 110.00
a. Double overprint 290.00
N148 A27 2d vermilion 200.00 165.00
N149 A27 5d ultramarine *550.00* 400.00
a. Double overprint 625.00

Litho.
N150 A24 1 l green 11.00 12.50
b. Period omitted after "ΕΛ-ΛΑΣ" (on #214a) *450.00*
e. Ovpt. reading down *1,575.*
f. As "e," period omitted after "ΕΛΛΑΣ" (on #214a)
N151 A24 10 l carmine rose 65.00 65.00
Nos. N143-N151 (9) 1,100. 948.50

There are numerous broken, missing and wrong font letters with a Greek "Λ" instead of "Δ" as the first letter of the second word.

Counterfeits exist of Nos. N109-N151.

Cross of Constantine
O1

Eagle of Zeus
O2

1912 Litho.
N150A O1 1 l brn, *grayish* .30 .30
c. 1 l brown, *yellowish* 5.50 5.50
N152 O2 2 l red, *yelwsh* .30 .30
N153 O2 3 l org, *grayish* .30 .30
a. 3 l orange, *yellowish* 5.50 5.50
N154 O1 5 l grn, *grayish* .30 .30
a. 5 l green, *yellowish* 6.50 6.50
N155 O1 10 l rose red, *grayish* .30 .30
a. 10 l rose red, *yellowish* 11.00 3.25
N156 O1 20 l vio, *grayish* 22.50 4.00
N157 O2 25 l pale bl, *yelwsh* 3.00 1.00
N158 O1 30 l gray grn, *yelwsh* 70.00 3.00
N159 O2 40 l indigo, *grayish* 11.00 5.00
a. 40 l indigo, *yellowish* 17.50 8.50
c. Double impression —
N160 O1 50 l dk bl, *yelwsh* 5.00 3.00
N161 O2 1d vio brn, *grayish* 15.00 4.50
a. 1d violet brn, *yellowish*
N162 O1 2d gray brn, *grayish* 55.00 9.00
a. 2d violet brn
N163 O2 3d dl bl, *yelwsh* 225.00 32.50
a. 3d dull blue, *grayish* 700.00 110.00
N164 O1 5d gray, *yelwsh* 200.00 32.50
N165 O2 10d car, *grayish* *225.00 325.00*
N166 O1 25d gray blk, *yelwsh* *225.00 350.00*
Nos. N150A-N166 (16) 1,058. 771.00

There are numerous broken, missing and wrong font letters with a Greek "Λ" instead of "Δ" as the first letter of the second word. Occupation of Macedonia, Epirus and some of the Aegean Islands.

Sold only in New Greece.

Dangerous forgeries of Nos. N165-N166 exist.

In 1916 some stamps of this issue were overprinted in Greek: "I (era) Koinotis Ag (iou) Orous" for the Mount Athos Monastery District. They were never placed in use and most of them were destroyed.

For surcharges and overprints see Nos. 267-276A, RA14-RA16, Thrace 31-33.

Imperf., Pairs Without Overprint

N150d	O1	1 l	(as #N150Ac)	500.00
N151b	O2	2 l		600.00
N152b	O2	2 l		500.00
N153b	O2	3 l	(as #153a)	450.00
N154b	O1	5 l	(as #154a)	200.00
N155b	O1	10 l	(as #155a)	200.00
N156b	O1	20 l		1,800.
N157b	O2	25 l		1,800.
N158b	O1	30 l		1,800.
N159b	O2	40 l		1,800.
N160b	O1	50 l		2,000.
N161b	O2	1d		2,000.
N163b	O2	3d		*2,800.*
N163c	O2	3d	(As #N163a)	
N164a	O1	5d		*2,800.*
N165a	O2	10d		*2,800.*

CAVALLA

Bulgaria Nos. 89-97 Surcharged in Red

1913 Unwmk. Engr. *Perf. 12*
N167 A20 5 l on 1s myr grn *30.00 30.00*
N168 A25 10 l on 10s red & blk *550.00 450.00*
Never hinged *850.00*
N169 A25 10 l on 15s brn bis *70.00 70.00*
N170 A26 10 l on 25s ultra & blk *35.00 35.00*
N171 A21 15 l on 2s car & blk *70.00 70.00*
N172 A22 20 l on 3s lake & blk *70.00 70.00*
N173 A23 25 l on 5s grn & blk *25.00 15.00*
N174 A24 50 l on 10s red & blk *45.00 35.00*
N175 A25 1d on 15s brn bis *300.00 250.00*
N176 A27 1d on 30s bl & blk *120.00 120.00*
N177 A28 1d on 50s ocher & blk *165.00 165.00*

Blue Surcharge

N178 A24 50 l on 10s red & blk *25.00 25.00*
Nos. N167-N178 (11) *955.00 885.00*

The counterfeits and reprints of Nos. N167-N178 are difficult to distinguish from originals. Many overprint varieties exist.

Some specialists question the status of Nos. N167-N178.

DEDEAGATCH

(Alexandroupolis)

D1-(10 lepta)

Control Mark in Red

1913 Unwmk. Typeset *Perf. 11½*
N179 D1 5 l black 40.00 30.00
N180 D1 10 l black 5.50 4.00
N181 D1 25 l black 6.50 5.00
a. Sheet of 8 135.00 110.00
Nos. N179-N181 (3) 52.00 39.00

Nos. N179-N181 issued without gum in sheets of 8, consisting of one 5 l, three 10 l normal, one 10 l inverted, three 25 l and one blank. The sheet yields se-tenant pairs of 5 l & 10 l, 10 l & 25 l; tete beche pairs of 5 l & 10 l, 10 l & 25 l and 10 l & 10 l.

Also issued imperf., value $200 unused, $160 canceled.

The 5 l reads "PENTE LEPTA" in Greek letters; the 10 l is illustrated; the 25 l carries the numeral "25."

Bulgaria Nos. 89-90, 92-93, 95 Surcharged

1913 Red Surcharge *Perf. 12*
N182 A20 5 l on 1s myr grn 65.00 45.00
a. "ΔΕΛΕΑΓΤΕ" instead of "ΔΕΔΕΑΓΤΕ" 150.00 110.00
N183 A26 1d on 25s ultra & blk 100.00 60.00
a. "ΔΕΛΕΑΓΤΕ" instead of "ΔΕΔΕΑΓΤΕ" 180.00 125.00

Blue Surcharge

N184 A24 10 l on 10s red & blk 32.50 25.00
N185 A23 25 l on 5s grn & blk 35.00 27.50
N187 A21 50 l on 2s car & blk 65.00 45.00
Nos. N182-N185,N187 (5) 297.50 202.50

The surcharges on Nos. N182 to N187 are printed from a setting of eight, which was used for all, with the necessary changes of value. No. 6 in the setting has a Greek "L" instead of "D" for the third letter of the third word of the surcharge.

The 25 l surcharge also exists on 8 examples of the 25s, Bulgaria No. 95.

D2

1913, Sept. 15 Typeset *Perf. 11½*

Control Mark in Blue

N188	D2	1 l blue	*200.00*	65.00
N189	D2	2 l blue	*200.00*	65.00
N190	D2	3 l blue	*200.00*	65.00
N191	D2	5 l blue	*200.00*	65.00
N192	D2	10 l blue	*200.00*	65.00
N193	D2	25 l blue	*200.00*	65.00
N194	D2	40 l blue	*200.00*	65.00
N195	D2	50 l blue	*200.00*	65.00
a.		Sheet of 8	*2,200.*	*1,000.*
		Nos. N188-N195 (8)	1,600.	520.00

Issued without gum in sheets of 8 containing all values.

Counterfeits of Nos. N188-N195 exist.

D3

1913, Sept. 25 Typeset

Control Mark in Blue

N196	D3	1 l blue, *gray blue*	175.00	55.00
N197	D3	5 l blue, *gray blue*	175.00	55.00
N198	D3	10 l blue, *gray blue*	175.00	55.00
N199	D3	25 l blue, *gray blue*	175.00	55.00
N200	D3	30 l blue, *gray blue*	175.00	55.00
N201	D3	50 l blue, *gray blue*	175.00	55.00
a.		Sheet of 6	*1,350.*	*500.00*
		Nos. N196-N201 (6)	1,050.	330.00

Nos. N196 to N201 were issued without gum in sheets of six containing all values.

Counterfeits of Nos. N182-N201 are plentiful.

FOR USE IN NORTH EPIRUS (ALBANIA)

Greek Stamps of 1937-38 Overprinted in Black

Perf. 13½x12, 12x13½

1940 Litho. Wmk. 252

N202	A69	5 l brn red & bl	.25	.30
a.		Inverted overprint	55.00	
b.		Double impression of frame		
N203	A70	10 l bl & brn red (No. 413)	.25	.30
a.		Double impression of frame	*150.00*	
b.		Double overprint		
N204	A71	20 l blk & grn	.25	.30
a.		Inverted overprint	55.00	
b.		Double impression of grn		
N205	A72	40 l grn & blk	.25	.30
a.		Inverted overprint	55.00	
b.		Double impression of grn		
N206	A73	50 l brn & blk	.25	.30
N207	A74	80 l ind & yel brn	.35	.35
a.		Double impression of frame	55.00	
N208	A67	1d green	.35	.35
a.		Inverted overprint	*90.00*	
b.		"ΛΙΟΙΚΗΕΙΕ" instead of "ΔΙΟΙΚΗΕΙΕ"	24.00	
c.		Double overprint	200.00	
N209	A75	2d ultra	.35	.40
N210	A67	3d red brn	.75	.80
a.		"ΛΙΟΙΚΗΕΙΕ" instead of "ΔΙΟΙΚΗΕΙΕ"	24.00	
N211	A76	5d red	.75	.80
N212	A77	6d ol brn	.85	.95
N213	A78	7d dk brn	.95	1.00
N214	A67	8d deep blue	.95	1.00
a.		"ΛΙΟΙΚΗΕΙΕ" instead of "ΔΙΟΙΚΗΕΙΕ"	24.00	
N215	A79	10d red brn	2.00	2.00
N216	A80	15d green	2.00	2.00
N217	A81	25d dark blue	5.00	*6.25*
a.		Inverted overprint	*100.00*	

Engr.

Unwmk.

N218	A84	30d org brn	8.00	*15.00*
a.		Double overprint		
		Nos. N202-N218 (17)	23.55	32.40

Same Overprinted in Carmine on National Youth Issue

1941 Litho. *Perf. 12½, 13½x12½*

N219	A93	3d sil, dp ultra & red	1.00	*1.00*
N220	A94	5d dk bl & blk	3.00	*4.50*
N221	A94	10d red org & blk	4.50	*6.75*
N222	A94	15d dk grn & blk	18.50	*20.00*
N223	A94	20d lake & blk	13.50	*15.00*
N224	A94	25d dk bl & blk	13.50	*15.00*
N225	A94	30d rose vio & blk	13.50	*15.00*
N226	A94	50d lake & blk	13.50	*15.00*
N227	A94	75d dk bl, brn & gold	15.00	15.00
N228	A93	100d sil, dp ultra & red	22.50	*20.00*
a.		Inverted overprint	*475.00*	
		Nos. N219-N228 (10)	118.50	127.25

Same Overprint in Carmine on National Youth Air Post Stamps

N229	AP25	2d red org & blk	1.00	*1.00*
a.		Inverted overprint	*165.00*	
N230	AP25	4d dk grn & blk	3.50	*4.50*
a.		Inverted overprint	*165.00*	
N231	AP25	6d lake & blk	6.50	*7.00*
a.		Inverted overprint	*165.00*	
N232	AP25	8d dk bl & blk	6.50	*7.00*
N233	AP25	16d rose vio & blk	11.00	9.00
N234	AP25	32d red org & blk	15.00	15.00
N235	AP25	45d dk grn & blk	16.00	14.00
N236	AP25	55d lake & blk	16.00	14.00
N237	AP25	65d dk bl & blk	16.00	14.00
N238	AP25	100d rose vio & blk	25.00	*30.00*
		Nos. N229-N238 (10)	116.50	115.50

Some specialists have questioned the status of Nos. N230a and N231a.

For other stamps issued by Greece for use in occupied parts of Epirus and Thrace, see the catalogue listings of those countries.

Catalogue values for unused stamps in this section, from this point to the end of the section, are for Never Hinged items.

FOR USE IN THE DODECANESE ISLANDS

Greece, No. 472C, with Additional Overprint in Carmine or Silver

1947 Wmk. 252 Litho. *Perf. 12½*

N239	A113	10d on 2,000d (C)	2.25	2.40
a.		Double overprint	70.00	
N240	A113	10d on 2,000d (S)	2.25	2.40
a.		Inverted overprint		
b.		Dbl. ovpt., one car. one sil.	145.00	

These stamps sold for 5 lire (100 drachmas) and paid postage for that amount.

King George II Memorial Issue

Greece, Nos. 484 and 485, With Additional Overprint in Black

1947 Engr. *Perf. 12½x12*

N241	A67	50d on 1d green	1.40	1.50
a.		Inverted overprint	110.00	
N242	A67	250d on 3d red brn	1.40	1.50
a.		Inverted overprint	145.00	

The letters are initials of the Greek words for "Military Administration of the Dodecanese."

Greece, Nos. 501 and 502 Overprinted in Carmine

1947 Wmk. 252 Litho. *Perf. 12½*

N243	A111	20d on 500d dk ol	2.00	2.25
N244	A104	30d on 5d lt bl grn	2.00	2.25
a.		"ΝΑΥΟΛΙΟΝ" instead of "ΝΑΥΠΛΙΟΝ"	32.50	*35.00*

Greece, Nos. 437, 406, 407 and 445, Surcharged in Black or Carmine

1947 *Perf. 12½, 13½x12*

N245	A103	50d on 2d	2.25	2.25

Engr.

N246	A79	250d on 10d	6.00	6.75
a.		Double overprint		
N247	A80	400d on 15d (C)	7.75	8.75
a.		Inverted surcharge	145.00	
b.		Double overprint	175.00	
c.		Surch. and ovpt. inverted	225.00	

Litho.

N248	A110	1000d on 200 (C)	4.50	5.50
a.		Imprint omitted	32.50	32.50
		Nos. N245-N248 (4)	23.90	23.90

POSTAGE DUE STAMPS

FOR USE IN PARTS OF TURKEY OCCUPIED BY GREECE (NEW GREECE)

1902 Postage Due Stamps of Greece Overprinted

1912 Wmk. 129 Engr. *Perf. 13½*

Black Overprint, Reading Up

NJ1	D3	1 l chocolate	.55	.65
a.		Double overprint	22.00	
NJ2	D3	2 l gray	.55	.65
a.		Double overprint	15.50	
NJ3	D3	3 l orange	.55	.65
a.		Double overprint	15.50	*20.00*
NJ4	D3	5 l yel grn	.95	1.10
a.		Double overprint	20.00	
NJ5	D3	10 l scarlet	1.45	1.60
a.		Double overprint	20.00	
NJ6	D3	20 l lilac	1.45	1.60
NJ7	D3	30 l dp vio	3.00	3.50
a.		Double overprint	75.00	
NJ8	D3	40 l dk brn	6.50	*7.00*
a.		Double overprint	122.50	
NJ9	D3	50 l red brn	9.50	10.00
NJ10	D3	1d black	45.00	*47.50*
NJ11	D3	2d bronze (overprint reading down)	72.50	82.50
NJ12	D3	3d silver (overprint reading down)	142.50	120.00
NJ13	D3	5d gold (overprint reading down)	225.00	250.00
		Nos. NJ1-NJ13 (13)	509.50	526.75

Red Overprint, Reading Up

NJ14	D3	1 l chocolate	1.00	1.00
NJ15	D3	2 l gray	1.00	1.00
a.		Double overprint	00.00	
NJ16	D3	5 l yellow green	1.00	1.00
NJ17	D3	20 l lilac	1.00	1.00
NJ18	D3	30 l deep violet	5.00	5.00
NJ19	D3	40 l dark brown	1.45	1.60
NJ20	D3	50 l red brown	1.45	1.60
NJ21	D3	1d black	10.00	10.50
NJ22	D3	2d bronze	20.00	*21.00*
NJ23	D3	3d silver	24.50	*27.00*
NJ24	D3	5d gold	60.00	*62.50*
		Nos. NJ14-NJ24 (11)	126.40	133.20

Carmine Overprint, Reading Up

NJ25	D3	2 l gray	10.00	11.00
NJ26	D3	3 l orange	147.50	*170.00*
NJ27	D3	1d black	82.50	*110.00*
a.		Double overprint, one inverted	245.00	
NJ28	D3	2d bronze	500.00	
NJ29	D3	3d silver		*2,000.*
		Nos. NJ25-NJ29 (5)	740.00	2,291.

Carmine Overprint, Reading Down

NJ30	D3	2 l gray	4.00	4.00
NJ31	D3	3 l orange	10.00	11.00
NJ32	D3	5 l yellow green	9.00	9.00
NJ33	D3	10 l scarlet	15.00	15.00
NJ34	D3	1d black	55.00	55.00
a.		Double overprint	275.00	
NJ35	D3	2d bronze	85.00	*90.00*
NJ36	D3	3d silver	385.00	*400.00*
NJ37	D3	5d gold	750.00	*775.00*
		Nos. NJ30-NJ37 (8)	1,313.	1,359.

Some of the varieties of lettering that occur on the postage stamps are also found on the postage due stamps.

FOR USE IN NORTH EPIRUS (ALBANIA)

Postage Due Stamps of Greece, 1930, Surcharged or Overprinted in Black:

a

b

Perf. 13, 13x12½

1940 Litho. Unwmk.

NJ38	D3(a)	50 l on 25d lt red	.45	.90
NJ39	D3(b)	2d light red	1.10	*1.75*
a.		Inverted overprint	67.50	
NJ40	D3(b)	5d blue gray	.55	*1.45*
NJ41	D3(b)	10d green	1.10	*1.90*
NJ42	D3(b)	15d red brown	1.10	*1.90*
		Nos. NJ38-NJ42 (5)	4.30	7.90

POSTAL TAX STAMPS

FOR USE IN NORTH EPIRUS (ALBANIA)

Postal Tax Stamps of Greece, Nos. RA61-RA63, Overprinted Type "b" in Black

1940 Unwmk. Litho. *Perf. 13½x12*

NRA1	PT7	10 l	.25	.35
NRA2	PT7	50 l	.35	.55
a.		Inverted overprint	65.00	
NRA3	PT7	1d	.95	*1.75*
		Nos. NRA1-NRA3 (3)	1.55	2.65

MOUNT ATHOS

Catalogue values for unused stamps in this section are for Never Hinged items.

All stamps also are available for postage in Greece.

Nikiforos Fokas A1

Ioannis Tsimiskis A2

Map of Mount Athos A3

Church of the Protaton A4

Staff of Protepistates — A5

Litho. With Foil Application

Perf. 13¼x13

2008, May 16			**Unwmk.**	
1	A1	40c multi + label	1.25	1.25
2	A2	60c multi + label	1.90	1.90
3	A3	70c multi + label	2.25	2.25
4	A4	€2 multi + label	6.50	6.50
5	A5	€4 multi + label	13.00	13.00
		Nos. 1-5 (5)	24.90	24.90

Megisti Lavra Monastery A6

Vatopedi Monastery A7

Koutloumousiou Monastery — A8

Iveron Monastery A9

Helandariou Monastery — A10

2008, June 13				
6	A6	57c multi + label	1.75	1.75
7	A7	70c multi + label	2.25	2.25
8	A8	€1 multi + label	3.25	3.25
9	A9	€1.85 multi + label	5.75	5.75
10	A10	€3 multi + label	9.25	9.25
		Nos. 6-10 (5)	22.25	22.25

Pantokratoros Monastery — A11

Xeropotamou Monastery — A12

Karakalou Monastery A13

Zografou Monastery A14

Docheiariou Monastery — A15

2008, July 4				
11	A11	57c multi + label	1.90	1.90
12	A12	70c multi + label	2.25	2.25
13	A13	80c multi + label	2.50	2.50
14	A14	€1.50 multi + label	4.75	4.75
15	A15	€3.50 multi + label	11.00	11.00
		Nos. 11-15 (5)	22.40	22.40

Agiou Pavlou Monastery A16

Dionysiou Monastery A17

Stavronikita Monastery — A18

Simonos Petras Monastery A19

Filotheou Monastery A20

2008, Aug. 22				
16	A16	57c multi + label	1.75	1.75
17	A17	70c multi + label	2.10	2.10
18	A18	€1.20 multi + label	3.50	3.50
19	A19	€1.80 multi + label	5.25	5.25
20	A20	€3 multi + label	9.00	9.00
		Nos. 16-20 (5)	21.60	21.60

Xenophontos Monastery — A21

Osiou Grigoriou Monastery A22

Esphigmenou Monastery — A23

Konstamonitou Monastery — A24

Agiou Panteleimon Monastery — A25

2008, Nov. 7				
21	A21	57c multi + label	1.50	1.50
22	A22	70c multi + label	1.90	1.90
23	A23	85c multi + label	2.25	2.25
24	A24	€2.42 multi + label	6.25	6.25
25	A25	€3 multi + label	7.75	7.75
		Nos. 21-25 (5)	19.65	19.65

Monk Ringing Talanton A26

Monk in Library A27

Protepistate Konstantinos Prigoumenos Vatopaidinos — A28

Monk Sculpting Wood A29

Monk Packing Mule A30

2009, May 11

No.	Type	Value		Unused	Used
26	A26	57c	multi + label	1.60	1.60
27	A27	70c	multi + label	2.00	2.00
28	A28	85c	multi + label	2.40	2.40
29	A29	€2.42	multi + label	6.75	6.75
30	A30	€3	multi + label	8.50	8.50
			Nos. 26-30 (5)	21.25	21.25

Monk Sewing Clothes A31

Monk Binding Book A32

Monk Cooking A33

Monk Watering Flowers A34

Monk Hiking A35

2009, June 12

No.	Type	Value		Unused	Used
31	A31	57c	multi + label	1.60	1.60
32	A32	70c	multi + label	2.00	2.00
33	A33	€1	multi + label	2.75	2.75
34	A34	€1.85	multi + label	5.25	5.25
35	A35	€3.30	multi + label	9.25	9.25
			Nos. 31-35 (5)	20.85	20.85

Olive Collecting, by Polykleitos Rengos A36

Old Apostolos with His Lines, by Fotis Kontoglou A37

Shipwright, by Kontoglou A38

Icon Painter on Mount Athos, by Theodoros Rallis A39

Monk at Study, by Dimitris Gioldasis A40

2009, Sept. 18

No.	Type	Value		Unused	Used
36	A36	57c	multi + label	1.75	1.75
37	A37	70c	multi + label	2.10	2.10
38	A38	80c	multi + label	2.40	2.40
39	A39	€1	multi + label	3.00	3.00
40	A40	€4.50	multi + label	13.50	13.50
			Nos. 36-40 (5)	22.75	22.75

Holy Epistiasia of the Holy Community of Mount Athos, 1938 — A41

Athonias School, 1936 — A42

Archimandrite Gabriel Celebrating Feast of the Holy Monastery of Xenophontos, 1967 — A43

Holy Community of Mount Athos, 1951 — A44

Archimandrite Vyssarion, 1998 — A45

2009, Nov. 17 ***Perf. 13½***

No.	Type	Value		Unused	Used
41	A41	58c	multi + label	1.75	1.75
42	A42	70c	multi + label	2.10	2.10
43	A43	€1.20	multi + label	3.75	3.75
44	A44	€1.85	multi + label	5.50	5.50
45	A45	€3	multi + label	9.00	9.00
			Nos. 41-45 (5)	22.10	22.10

Flora and Fauna A46

Designs: No. 46, 58c, Pansy. No. 47, 72c, Judas tree. No. 48, €1, Arbutus. No. 49, €2.43, European tree frog. No. 50, €3, Heath.

Litho. With Foil Application

2010, May 11 ***Perf. 13½x13***

Stamps + Label

46-50 A46 Set of 5 18.50 18.50

2010, June 21 **Stamps + Label**

Designs: No. 51, 50c, Silene orphanidis. No. 52, 58c, Nightingale. No. 53, 72c, European roe deer. No. 54, €2, Laurel. No. 55, €3.50, European green lizard.

51-55 A46 Set of 5 18.50 18.50

Flora and Fauna Type of 2010

Designs: No. 56, 58c, Two-tailed pasha butterfly. No. 57, 72c, Golden eagle. No. 58, €1, Mountain tea (white flowers and mountain). No. 59, €2.43, Amaranth (plant). No. 60, €3, Mediterranean monk seal.

Stamps + Label

Litho. With Foil Application

2010, Sept. 16 ***Perf. 13½x13***

56-60 A46 Set of 5 21.50 21.50

2010, Nov. 16 **Stamps + Label**

Designs: No. 61, 50c, Chestnut. No. 62, 58c, Fir tree. No. 63, 72c, Sage. No. 64, €2, Wild boar. No. 65, €3.50, Spiny puffball mushroom.

61-65 A46 Set of 5 19.50 19.50

A47

A48

A49

A50

A51

Illuminated Greek Letters — A52

Litho. With Foil Application

2011, Mar. 18 ***Perf. 13½x13***

No.	Type	Value		Unused	Used
66	A47	50c	multi + label	1.50	1.50
67	A48	60c	multi + label	1.75	1.75
68	A49	75c	multi + label	2.25	2.25
69	A50	€1	multi + label	3.00	3.00
70	A51	€1.50	multi + label	4.50	4.50
71	A52	€2.15	multi + label	6.25	6.25
			Nos. 66-71 (6)	19.25	19.25

A53

A54

A55

A56

A57

Illuminated Greek Letters — A58

2011, May 17

72	A53	50c multi + label	1.50	1.50
73	A54	60c multi + label	1.75	1.75
74	A55	75c multi + label	2.25	2.25
75	A56	€1 multi + label	3.00	3.00
76	A57	€1.47 multi + label	4.25	4.25
77	A58	€2 multi + label	5.75	5.75
		Nos. 72-77 (6)	18.50	18.50

A59

A60

A61

A62

A63

Illuminated Greek Letters — A64

2011, July 18

78	A59	50c multi + label	1.50	1.50
79	A60	60c multi + label	1.75	1.75
80	A61	75c multi + label	2.25	2.25
81	A62	85c multi + label	2.50	2.50
82	A63	€1.47 multi + label	4.25	4.25
83	A64	€2 multi + label	5.75	5.75
		Nos. 78-83 (6)	18.00	18.00

A65

A66

A67

A68

A69

Illuminated Greek Letters — A70

2011, Dec. 15

84	A65	50c multi + label	1.40	1.40
85	A66	60c multi + label	1.60	1.60
86	A67	85c multi + label	2.25	2.25
87	A68	€1 multi + label	2.60	2.60
88	A69	€1.47 multi + label	4.00	4.00
89	A70	€2 multi + label	5.25	5.25
		Nos. 84-89 (6)	17.10	17.10

Megisti Lavra Monastery Katholikon A71

Helandariou Monastery Katholikon — A72

Iveron Monastery Katholikon A73

Dionysiou Monastery Katholikon A74

Vatopedi Monastery Katholikon A75

Protaton Katholikon A76

2012, Jan. 26 *Perf. 13½x13*

90	A71	50c multi + label	1.40	1.40
91	A72	60c multi + label	1.60	1.60
92	A73	75c multi + label	2.00	2.00
93	A74	85c multi + label	2.25	2.25
94	A75	€1 multi + label	2.60	2.60
95	A76	€2.20 multi + label	5.75	5.75
		Nos. 90-95 (6)	15.60	15.60

Koutloumousiou Monastery Katholikon — A77

Pantokratoros Monastery Katholikon — A78

Xeropotamou Monastery Katholikon — A79

Zografou Monastery Katholikon
A80

Docheiariou Monastery Katholikon — A81

2012, Mar. 20

No.	Type	Denomination		Unused	Used
96	A77	50c	multi + label	1.40	1.40
97	A78	60c	multi + label	1.60	1.60
98	A79	€1	multi + label	2.60	2.60
99	A80	€1.50	multi + label	4.00	4.00
100	A81	€2	multi + label	5.25	5.25
		Nos. 96-100 (5)		14.85	14.85

Karakalou Monastery Katholikon
A82

Filotheou Monastery Katholikon
A83

Simonos Petras Monastery Katholikon
A84

Agiou Pavlou Monastery Katholikon
A85

Stavronikita Monastery Katholikon
A86

2012, Sept. 12

No.	Type	Denomination		Unused	Used
101	A82	62c	multi + label	1.60	1.60
102	A83	78c	multi + label	2.00	2.00
103	A84	85c	multi + label	2.25	2.25
104	A85	€1	multi + label	2.60	2.60
105	A86	€2.10	multi + label	5.50	5.50
		Nos. 101-105 (5)		13.95	13.95

Xenophontos Monastery Katholikon — A87

Osiou Grigoriou Monastery Katholikon
A88

Esphigmenou Monastery Katholikon — A89

Agiou Panteleimon Monastery Katholikon — A90

Konstamonitou Monastery Katholikon — A91

2012, Nov. 20

No.	Type	Denomination		Unused	Used
106	A87	50c	multi + label	1.40	1.40
107	A88	62c	multi + label	1.60	1.60
108	A89	€1	multi + label	2.60	2.60
109	A90	€1.50	multi + label	4.00	4.00
110	A91	€2.10	multi + label	5.50	5.50
		Nos. 106-110 (5)		15.10	15.10

17th Cent. Manuscript Illumination
A92

13th Cent. Manuscript Illumination
A93

17th Cent. Manuscript Illumination
A94

13th Cent. Manuscript Illumination
A95

14th Cent. Manuscript Illumination
A96

10th Cent. Manuscript Illumination
A97

2013, Apr. 22

No.	Type	Denomination		Unused	Used
111	A92	40c	multi + label	1.10	1.10
112	A93	50c	multi + label	1.40	1.40
113	A94	62c	multi + label	1.60	1.60
114	A95	78c	multi + label	2.10	2.10
115	A96	85c	multi + label	2.25	2.25
116	A97	€2	multi + label	5.25	5.25
		Nos. 111-116 (6)		13.70	13.70

13th Cent. Manuscript Illumination
A98

9th Cent. Manuscript Illumination
A99

17th Cent. Manuscript Illumination
A100

16th Cent. Manuscript Illumination
A101

17th Cent. Manuscript Illumination
A102

2013, May 9

No.	Type	Denomination		Unused	Used
117	A98	50c	multi + label	1.40	1.40
118	A99	62c	multi + label	1.75	1.75
119	A100	78c	multi + label	2.10	2.10
120	A101	€1	multi + label	2.75	2.75
121	A102	€2.20	multi + label	6.00	6.00
		Nos. 117-121 (5)		14.00	14.00

18th Cent. Manuscript Illumination
A103

12th Cent. Manuscript Illumination
A104

17th Cent. Manuscript Illumination
A105

14th Cent. Manuscript Illumination
A106

16th Cent. Manuscript Illumination
A107

Litho. With Foil Application

2013, Sept. 9 ***Perf. 13½x13***

122	A103	40c multi + label	1.10	1.10
123	A104	62c multi + label	1.75	1.75
124	A105	78c multi + label	2.10	2.10
125	A106	€1 multi + label	2.75	2.75
126	A107	€2.50 multi + label	6.75	6.75
	Nos. 122-126 (5)		14.45	14.45

17th Cent. Manuscript Illumination
A108

17th Cent. Manuscript Illumination
A109

11th Cent. Manuscript Illumination
A110

12th Cent. Manuscript Illumination
A111

17th Cent. Manuscript Illumination
A112

Litho. With Foil Application

2013, Nov. 5 ***Perf. 13½x13***

127	A108	62c multi + label	1.75	1.75
128	A109	72c multi + label	2.00	2.00
129	A110	80c multi + label	2.25	2.25
130	A111	90c multi + label	2.40	2.40
131	A112	€2.10 multi + label	5.75	5.75
	Nos. 127-131 (5)		14.15	14.15

Gold Embroidered Priest's Stole, 16th-17th Cent. — A113

Parament, 17th Cent.
A114

Liturgical Vestments, 20th Cent.
A115

Liturgical Vestments, 20th Cent.
A116

Priest's Stole, 17th Cent.
A117

Priest's Stole, 1813
A118

Litho. With Foil Application

2014, July 9 ***Perf. 13½x13¾***

132	A113	40c multi + label	1.10	1.10
133	A114	50c multi + label	1.40	1.40
134	A115	72c multi + label	2.00	2.00
135	A116	90c multi + label	2.40	2.40
136	A117	€1 multi + label	2.75	2.75
137	A118	€1.50 multi + label	4.00	4.00
	Nos. 132-137 (6)		13.65	13.65

Icon Case Parament, 16th Cent.
A119

Parament, 18th Cent.
A120

Embroidered Item, 20th Cent. — A121

Parament, 18th Cent.
A122

Icon Case Parament, 17th Cent.
A123

Litho. With Foil Application

2014, July 9 ***Perf. 13½x13¾***

138	A119	50c multi + label	1.40	1.40
139	A120	72c multi + label	2.00	2.00
140	A121	80c multi + label	2.10	2.10
141	A122	85c multi + label	2.25	2.25
142	A123	€1.62 multi + label	4.50	4.50
	Nos. 138-142 (5)		12.25	12.25

Priest's Vestment, 18th Cent.
A124

Liturgical Stole, 16th Cent.
A125

Parament, 1627
A126

Liturgical Cuffs, 18th Cent.
A127

Liturgical Fan, 17th Cent.
A128

Litho. With Foil Application

2014, Sept. 10 ***Perf. 13½x13¾***

143	A124	30c multi + label	.75	.75
144	A125	40c multi + label	1.00	1.00
145	A126	72c multi + label	1.90	1.90
146	A127	€1 multi + label	2.50	2.50
147	A128	€1.50 multi + label	3.75	3.75
	Nos. 143-147 (5)		9.90	9.90

Cloth Cover, 20th Cent.
A129

Liturgical Vestments
A130

Napoleon's Battle Tent
A131

Liturgical Fan, 19th Cent.
A132

Portable Icon, 19th Cent.
A133

Litho. With Foil Application

2014, Nov. 19 *Perf. 13½x13¾*

148 A129	50c multi + label	1.25	1.25
149 A130	72c multi + label	1.75	1.75
150 A131	85c multi + label	2.10	2.10
151 A132	90c multi + label	2.25	2.25
152 A133	€1.20 multi + label	3.00	3.00
Nos. 148-152 (5)		10.35	10.35

16th Cent. Wood Carving, Protaton Church A134

15th Cent. Wood Carving, Vatopedi Monastery A135

18th Cent. Wood Carving, Helandariou Monastery — A136

18th Cent. Wood Carving, Iveron Monastery A137

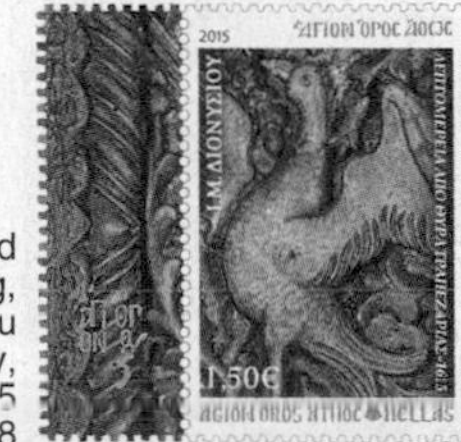

Wood Carving, Dionysiou Monastery, c. 1615 A138

Litho. With Foil Application

2015, May 20 *Perf. 13½x13¾*

153 A134	50c multi + label	1.10	1.10
154 A135	72c multi + label	1.60	1.60
155 A136	90c multi + label	2.00	2.00
156 A137	€1 multi + label	2.25	2.25
157 A138	€1.50 multi + label	3.50	3.50
Nos. 153-157 (5)		10.45	10.45

19th Cent. Wood Carving, Pantokratoros Monastery — A139

18th Cent. Wood Carving, Zografou Monastery A140

18th Cent. Wood Carving, Xeropotamou Monastery — A141

18th Cent. Wood Carving, Docheiariou Monastery — A142

18th Cent. Wood Carving, Koutloumousiou Monastery — A143

Litho. With Foil Application

2015, July 9 *Perf. 13½x13¾*

158 A139	40c multi + label	.90	.90
159 A140	72c multi + label	1.60	1.60
160 A141	80c multi + label	1.75	1.75
161 A142	85c multi + label	1.90	1.90
162 A143	€1.50 multi + label	3.25	3.25
Nos. 158-162 (5)		9.40	9.40

Wood Carving, Simonos Petras Monastery A144

14th Cent. Wood Carving, Filotheou Monastery A145

18th Cent. Wood Carving, Agiou Pavlou Monastery A146

16th Cent. Wood Carving, Stavronikita Monastery A147

18th Cent. Wood Carving, Karakalou Monastery A148

Litho. With Foil Application

2015, Sept. 8 *Perf. 13½x13¾*

163 A144	30c multi + label	.70	.70
164 A145	50c multi + label	1.10	1.10
165 A146	72c multi + label	1.60	1.60
166 A147	€1 multi + label	2.25	2.25
167 A148	€1.62 multi + label	3.75	3.75
Nos. 163-167 (5)		9.40	9.40

Wood Carving, Osiou Grigoriou Monastery A149

Wood Carving, Xenophontos Monastery — A150

18th Cent. Wood Carving, Agiou Panteleimon Monastery — A151

Wood Carving, Konstamonitou Monastery, c. 1870-1900 — A152

16th Cent. Wood Carving, Esphigmenou Monastery — A153

Litho. With Foil Application

2015, Nov. 5 *Perf. 13½x13¾*

168 A149	20c multi + label	.45	.45
169 A150	50c multi + label	1.10	1.10
170 A151	85c multi + label	1.90	1.90
171 A152	90c multi + label	1.90	1.90
172 A153	€1.20 multi + label	2.60	2.60
Nos. 168-172 (5)		7.95	7.95

Stone Relief, Protaton A154

Stone Relief, Megisti Lavra Monastery A155

Stone Relief, Vatopedi Monastery A156

Stone Relief, Iveron Monastery A157

Stone Relief, Helandariou Monastery — A158

Stone Relief, Dionysiou Monastery A159

Litho. With Foil Application

2016, Jan. 26 *Perf. 13½x13*

173 A154	20c multi + label	.45	.45
174 A155	72c multi + label	1.60	1.60
175 A156	80c multi + label	1.75	1.75
176 A157	90c multi + label	2.00	2.00
177 A158	€1 multi + label	2.25	2.25
178 A159	€1.20 multi + label	2.60	2.60
	Nos. 173-178 (6)	10.65	10.65

Stone Relief, Pantokratoros Monastery — A160

Stone Relief, Xeropotamou Monastery — A161

Stone Relief, Zografou Monastery A162

Stone Relief, Koutloumousiou Monastery — A163

Stone Relief, Docheiariou Monastery A164

Litho. With Foil Application

2016, Mar. 30 *Perf. 13½x13*

179 A160	50c multi + label	1.25	1.25
180 A161	72c multi + label	1.75	1.75
181 A162	80c multi + label	1.90	1.90
182 A163	85c multi + label	2.00	2.00
183 A164	€1.20 multi + label	2.75	2.75
	Nos. 179-183 (5)	9.65	9.65

Stone Relief, Stavronikita Monastery A165

Stone Relief, Karakalou Monastery A166

Stone Relief, Filotheou Monastery A167

Stone Relief, Agiou Pavlou Monastery A168

Stone Relief, Simonos Petras Monastery A169

Litho. With Foil Application

2016, Oct. 6 *Perf. 13½x13*

184 A165	30c multi + label	.70	.70
185 A166	50c multi + label	1.10	1.10
186 A167	72c multi + label	1.60	1.60
187 A168	€1 multi + label	2.25	2.25
188 A169	€1.62 multi + label	3.75	3.75
	Nos. 184-188 (5)	9.40	9.40

Stone Relief, Konstamonitou Monastery — A170

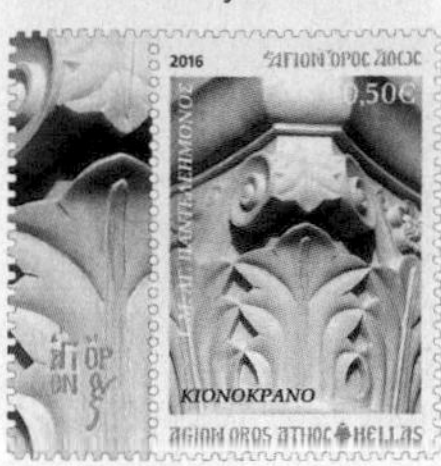
Stone Relief, Agiou Panteleimon Monastery — A171

Stone Relief, Xenophontos Monastery — A172

Stone Relief, Esphigmenou Monastery — A173

Stone Relief, Osiou Gregoriou Monastery A174

Litho. With Foil Application

2016, Nov. 10 *Perf. 13½x13*

189 A170	20c multi + label	.45	.45
190 A171	50c multi + label	1.10	1.10
191 A172	85c multi + label	1.90	1.90
192 A173	90c multi + label	2.00	2.00
193 A174	€1.20 multi + label	2.60	2.60
	Nos. 189-193 (5)	8.05	8.05

Xeropotamou Monastery — A175

Zografou Monastery A176

Filotheou Monastery A177

Xenophontos Monastery — A178

Konstamonitou Monastery — A179

Esphigmenou Monastery — A180

Osiou Grigoriou Monastery A181

Litho. With Foil Application

2017, July 27 *Perf. 13½x13*

194 A175	20c blk & gold + label	.50	.50
195 A176	50c blk & gold + label	1.25	1.25
196 A177	72c blk & gold + label	1.75	1.75
197 A178	80c blk & gold + label	1.90	1.90
198 A179	80c blk & gold + label	1.90	1.90
199 A180	€1 blk & gold + label	2.40	2.40
200 A181	€1.62 blk & gold + label	4.00	4.00
	Nos. 194-200 (7)	13.70	13.70

Engravings by Vassileios Grigorovic Barskij (c. 1701-47).

Megisti Lavra Monastery A182

Vatopedi Monastery A183

Iveron Monastery A184

Docheiariou Monastery A185

Agiou Pavlou Monastery A186

Agiou Panteleimon Monastery — A187

Litho. With Gold Foil Application

2017, Sept. 25 *Perf. 13½x13*

201	A182	72c multi + label	1.75	1.75
202	A183	80c multi + label	1.90	1.90
203	A184	90c multi + label	2.10	2.10
204	A185	€1 multi + label	2.40	2.40
205	A186	€1.50 multi + label	3.50	3.50
206	A187	€2.62 multi + label	6.25	6.25
		Nos. 201-206 (6)	17.90	17.90

Paintings by Vladimir Davydov (1871-1906).

Karyes A188

Chilandariou Monastery — A189

Dionysiou Monastery A190

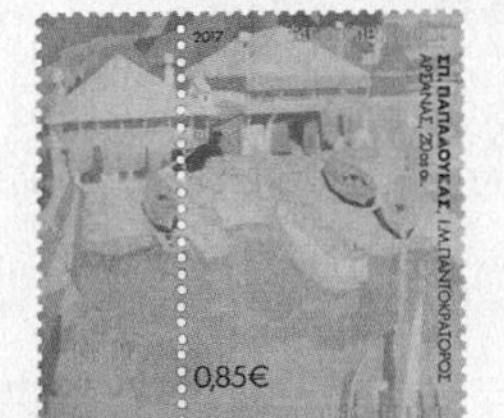

Pantokratoros Monastery — A191

Koutloumousiou Monastery — A192

Stavronikita Monastery A193

Karakalou Monastery A194

Simonos Petras Monastery A195

Litho. With Gold Foil Application

2017, Nov. 8 *Perf. 13½x13*

207	A188	20c multi + label	.50	.50
208	A189	72c multi + label	1.75	1.75
209	A190	80c multi + label	1.90	1.90
210	A191	85c multi + label	2.00	2.00
211	A192	90c multi + label	2.25	2.25
212	A193	€1 multi + label	2.40	2.40
213	A194	€1.50 multi + label	3.75	3.75
214	A195	€1.62 multi + label	4.00	4.00
		Nos. 207-214 (8)	18.55	18.55

Paintings by Spyros Papaloukas (1892-1957).

GREENLAND

ˈgrēn lənd

LOCATION — North Atlantic Ocean
GOVT. — Danish
AREA — 840,000 sq. mi.
POP. — 56,076 (1998)
CAPITAL — Nuuk (Godthaab)

In 1953 the colony of Greenland became an integral part of Denmark.

100 Ore = 1 Krone

Catalogue values for unused stamps in this country are for Never Hinged items, beginning with Scott 28 in the regular postage section, Scott B1 in the semi-postal section.

Christian X — A1

Polar Bear — A2

Perf. 13x12½

1938-46 **Unwmk.** **Engr.**

1	A1	1o olive black	2.00	*.30*
2	A1	5o rose lake	2.10	1.25
3	A1	7o yellow green	2.25	*3.75*
4	A1	10o dk violet	.85	.75
5	A1	15o red	.85	.75
6	A1	20o red ('46)	.95	*1.25*
7	A2	30o blue	4.00	*7.25*
8	A2	40o blue ('46)	18.00	8.50
9	A2	1k light brown	5.00	*8.50*
		Nos. 1-9 (9)	36.00	*32.30*
		Set, never hinged	90.00	

Issued: Nov. 1, 1938; Aug. 1, 1946.
For surcharges see Nos. 39-40.

Harp Seal — A3

Christian X — A4

Dog Team — A5

Designs: 1k, Polar bear. 2k, Eskimo in kayak. 5k, Eider duck.

1945, Feb. 1 *Perf. 12*

10	A3	1o ol blk & vio	18.50	*40.00*
11	A3	5o rose lake & ol bister	18.50	*40.00*
12	A3	7o green & blk	18.50	*40.00*
13	A4	10o purple & olive	18.50	*40.00*
14	A4	15o red & brt ultra	18.50	*40.00*
15	A5	30o dk blue & red brn	18.50	*40.00*
16	A5	1k brown & gray blk	18.50	*40.00*
17	A5	2k sepia & dp grn	18.50	*40.00*
18	A5	5k dk pur & dl brn	18.50	*40.00*
		Nos. 10-18 (9)	166.50	*360.00*
		Set, never hinged	325.00	

Nos. 10-18 Overprinted in Carmine or Blue

1945

19	A3	1o (C)	75.00	*75.00*
20	A3	5o (Bl)	75.00	*75.00*
21	A3	7o (C)	75.00	*75.00*
22	A4	10o (Bl)	95.00	*110.00*
	a.	Overprint in carmine	375.00	*700.00*
23	A4	15o (C)	95.00	*110.00*
	a.	Overprint in blue	200.00	*240.00*
24	A5	30o (Bl)	95.00	*110.00*
	a.	Overprint in carmine	200.00	*240.00*
25	A5	1k (C)	95.00	*110.00*
	a.	Overprint in blue	200.00	*240.00*
26	A5	2k (C)	95.00	*110.00*
	a.	Overprint in blue	200.00	*240.00*
27	A5	5k (Bl)	95.00	*110.00*
	a.	Overprint in carmine	200.00	*240.00*
		Nos. 19-27 (9)	795.00	*885.00*
		Set, never hinged	1,350.	
		Nos. 22a-27a (6)	1,375.	*1,900.*
		Set, never hinged	2,900.	

Liberation of Denmark from the Germans.

Overprint illustrated as on Nos. 19-21. Larger type and different settings used for Types A4 and A5. Overprint sizes: A3, 11.5 mm; A4, 13 mm; A5, 14.5 mm. A variety of No. 23 exists with overprint measuring 11.5 mm. Value: $3,300. Overprint often smudged.

Nos. 19-27 exist with overprint inverted. Values: 1k and 30o, each $1,200; others, each $1,000.

Catalogue values for unused stamps in this section, from this point to the end of the section, are for Never Hinged items.

Frederik IX — A6

Polar Ship "Gustav Holm" — A7

1950-60 Unwmk. Engr. *Perf. 13*

28 A6 1o dark olive green .35 .30
29 A6 5o deep carmine .30 .30
30 A6 10o green .35 .35
31 A6 15o purple .60 .40
a. 15o dull purple 4.25 1.50
32 A6 25o vermilion 2.60 1.00
33 A6 30o dark blue 40.00 2.25
34 A6 30o vermilion .70 .35
35 A7 50o deep blue 52.50 11.00
36 A7 1k brown 16.00 3.25
37 A7 2k dull red 8.75 3.25
38 A7 5k gray 2.75 2.00
Nos. 28-38 (11) 124.90 24.45

Issued: Nos. 28-30, 31a, 32, 35-37, 8/15/50; No. 33, 12/1/53; No. 38, 8/14/58; No. 34, 10/29/59; No. 31, 10/60.

For surcharges see Nos. B1-B2.

Nos. 8 and 9 Surcharged

1956, Mar. 8

39 A2 60o on 40o blue 8.50 1.60
40 A2 60o on 1k lt brown 67.50 9.00

Drum Dancer — A8

Designs: 50o, The Boy and the Fox. 60o, The Mother of the Sea. 80o, The Girl and the Eagle. 90o, The Great Northern Diver and the Raven.

1957-69 Engr. *Perf. 13*

41 A8 35o gray olive 1.10 1.00
42 A8 50o brown red 1.10 *1.25*
43 A8 60o blue 4.00 1.25
44 A8 80o light brown 1.25 *1.25*
45 A8 90o dark blue 3.50 3.50
Nos. 41-45 (5) 10.95 8.25

Issued: 35o, 3/16/61; 50o, 9/22/66; 60o, 5/2/57; 80o, 9/18/69; 90o, 11/23/67.

Hans Egede — A9

1958, Nov. 5

46 A9 30o henna brown 9.00 1.50

200th anniv. of death of Hans Egede, missionary to Eskimos in Greenland.

Knud Rasmussen — A10

1960, Nov. 24 *Perf. 13*

47 A10 30o dull red 1.60 1.00

50th anniv. of establishment by Rasmussen of the mission and trading station at Thule (Dundas).

Northern Lights and Crossed Anchors — A11

Frederick IX — A12

Polar Bear — A13

1963-68 Engr.

48 A11 1o gray .30 *.35*
49 A11 5o rose claret .30 *.35*
50 A11 10o green .40 *.50*
51 A11 12o yellow grn .40 *.40*
52 A11 15o rose vio .90 *1.25*
53 A12 20o ultra 4.25 3.50
54 A12 25o lt brown .75 *.75*
55 A12 30o green .30 *.50*
56 A12 35o dull red .30 *.30*
57 A12 40o gray .35 *.55*
58 A12 50o grnsh blue 9.00 *10.00*
59 A12 50o dark red .35 *.45*
60 A12 60o rose claret .40 *.45*
61 A12 80o orange .80 *.85*
62 A13 1k brown .65 .35
63 A13 2k dull red 3.25 1.10
64 A13 5k dark blue 2.75 2.25
65 A13 10k dull slate grn 5.00 1.10
Nos. 48-65 (18) 30.45 25.00

Issued: Nos. 48-52, 3/7/63; No. 53, 61, 7/25/63; Nos. 62-65, 9/17/63; Nos. 54, 56-58, 3/11/64; No. 59, 9/9/65; No. 60, 2/29/68; No. 55, 11/21/68.

Niels Bohr (1885-1962) and Atom Diagram — A14

1963, Nov. 21 Unwmk.

66 A14 35o red brown .40 .55
67 A14 60o dark blue 4.75 4.75

50th anniv. of atom theory of Prof. Bohr.

A15

1964, Nov. 26

68 A15 35o brown red .65 .65

Samuel Kleinschmidt (1814-1886), philologist.

A16

1967, June 10

69 A16 50o red 3.50 3.50

Wedding of Crown Princess Margrethe and Prince Henri de Monpezat.

Frederik IX and Map of Greenland A17

1969, Mar. 11 Engr. *Perf. 13*

70 A17 60o dull red 1.40 1.40

70th birthday of King Frederik IX.

Musk Ox — A18

Designs: 1k, Right whale diving off Disko Island. 2k, Narwhal. 5k, Polar bear. 10k, Walruses.

1969-76 Engr. *Perf. 13*

71 A18 1k dark blue .40 .40
72 A18 2k gray green .90 .60
73 A18 5k blue 2.00 .75
74 A18 10k sepia 4.00 1.90
75 A18 25k greenish gray 9.00 3.75
Nos. 71-75 (5) 16.30 7.40

Issued: 1k, 3/5/70; 2k, 2/20/75; 5k, 2/19/76; 10k, 2/15/73; 25k, 11/27/69.

Liberation Celebration at Jakobshaven A19

1970, May 4

76 A19 60o red brown 2.25 2.25

Hans Egede and Gertrude Rask on the Haabet — A20

1971, May 6 Engr. *Perf. 13*

77 A20 60o brown red 1.60 1.60

250th anniv. of arrival of Hans Egede in Greenland and the beginning of its colonization.

Mail-carrying Kayaks — A21

Designs: 70o, Umiak (women's rowboat). 80o, Catalina seaplane dropping mail by parachute. 90o, Dog sled. 1k, Coaster Kununguak and pilot boat. 1.30k, Schooner Sokongen. 1.50k, Longboat off Greenland coast. 2k, Helicopter over mountains.

1971-77 Engr. *Perf. 13*

78 A21 50o blue grn .30 .25
79 A21 70o dull red ('72) .35 .25
80 A21 80o black ('76) .40 .40
81 A21 90o blue ('72) .35 .25
82 A21 1k red ('76) .40 .40
83 A21 1.30k dl blue ('75) .85 .65
84 A21 1.50k gray grn ('74) .80 .55
85 A21 2k blue ('77) 1.00 .85
Nos. 78-85 (8) 4.45 3.60

Issued: No. 78, 11/4; No. 81, 2/29; No. 79, 9/21; No. 84, 2/21; No. 83, 4/17; No. 80, 10/11; No. 85, 2/24.

Queen Margrethe — A22

1973-79 Engr. *Perf. 13*

86 A22 5o car rose ('78) .30 .25
87 A22 10o gray green .30 .25
a. 10o emerald ('89) 5.00 5.00
88 A22 60o sepia .60 .45
89 A22 80o sepia ('79) .30 .30
90 A22 90o red brown ('74) .65 .55
91 A22 1k dark red ('77) .30 .30
a. Bklt. pane, 4 #87a, 6 #91b 32.50
b. 1k carmine ('89) 5.00 5.00
92 A22 1.20k dk blue ('74) .65 1.00
93 A22 1.20k maroon ('78) .75 .50
94 A22 1.30k dk blue ('77) .55 .60
95 A22 1.30k red ('79) .55 .50
96 A22 1.60k blue ('79) .65 .70
97 A22 1.80k dl green ('78) .85 .70
Nos. 86-97 (12) 6.45 6.10

Nos. 86, 89, 93, 95-97 inscribed "Kalaallit Nunaat."

The background lines on Nos. 87, 91 are sharp and complete. On No. 87a, 91b they are irregular and broken.

Issued: Nos. 87-88, 4/16. Nos. 90, 92, 10/24. Nos. 91, 94, 5/26. Nos. 86, 93, 97, 4/17. Nos. 89, 95-96, 3/29.

Trawler and Kayaks — A23

2k, Old Trade Buildings, Copenhagen, vert.

1974, May 16 Engr. *Perf. 13*

98 A23 1k lt red brown .55 *.90*
99 A23 2k sepia .65 .60

Royal Greenland Trade Dept. Bicentennial.

Falcon and Radar — A24

1975, Sept. 4 Engr. *Perf. 13*

100 A24 90o red .60 .60

50th anniversary of Greenland's telecommunications system.

Sirius Sled Patrol A25

1975, Oct. 16 Engr. *Perf. 13*

101 A25 1.20k sepia .40 .40

Sirius sled patrol in northeast Greenland, 25th anniversary.

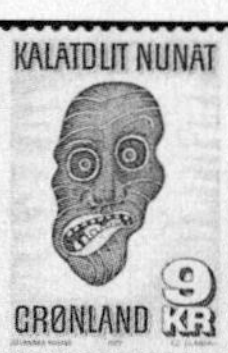

Inuit Cult Mask — A26

Designs: 6k, Tupilac, a magical creature, carved whalebone. 7k, Soapstone sculpture. 8k, Eskimo with Family, driftwood sculpture, by Johannes Kreutzmann (1862-1940).

1977-80

102 A26 6k deep rose lilac 2.25 1.90
103 A26 7k gray olive 2.50 2.25
104 A26 8k dark blue 3.00 2.50
105 A26 9k black 3.25 3.00
Nos. 102-105 (4) 11.00 9.65

Issue dates: 6k, Oct. 5, 1978. 7k, Sept. 6, 1979. 8k, Feb. 29, 1980. 9k, Sept. 6, 1977.

The 6k, 7k, 8k are inscribed "Kalaallit Nunaat."

Jorgen Bronlund, Jakobshavn, Disko Bay — A27

1977, Oct. 20

106 A27 1k red brown .40 .25

Jorgen Bronlund, arctic explorer, birth centenary.

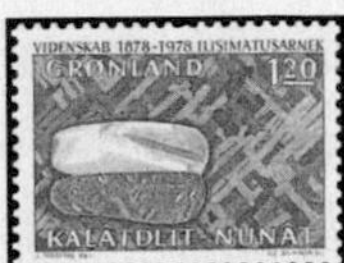
Meteorite — A28

1978, Jan. 20 **Engr.** ***Perf. 13***
107 A28 1.20k dull red .55 .45

Scientific Research Commission, centenary.

Sun Rising over Mountains — A29

1978, June 5 **Engr.** ***Perf. 13***
108 A29 1.50k dark blue .55 .55

25th anniversary of Constitution.

Hans Egede, Settlers, Troops and Drummer A30

1978, Aug. 29 **Engr.** ***Perf. 13***
109 A30 2.50k red brown .95 .65

Founding of Godthaab, 250th anniversary.

Navigator — A31

1979, May 1 **Engr.**
110 A31 1.10k brown .40 .40

Establishment of home rule, May 1, 1979.

A32

Eskimo Boy, aurora borealis, IYC emblem.

1979, Oct. 18 **Engr.** ***Perf. 13***
111 A32 2k olive green .80 .80

International Year of the Child.

The Legend of the Reindeer and the Larva, by Jens Kreutzmann, 1860 — A33

Designs: 2.70k, Harpooning a Walrus, Jakob Danielsen. No. 114, Life in Thule, c. 1900, by Aninaaq. No. 115, Landscape, Ammassalik Fjord, Eastern Greenland, Peter Rosing (1892-1965). 3k, Footrace, woodcut by Aron from Kagec (1822-1869). 3.70k, Polar Bear Killing Seal Hunter, K. Andreassen (1890-1934). 9k, Hares Hunting, Gerhard Kleist (1855-1931).

1980-87 **Engr.** ***Perf. 13***
112 A33 1.60k red .65 .65
113 A33 2.70k deep violet 1.10 1.00
114 A33 2.80k lake 1.10 .95
115 A33 2.80k lake 1.40 1.00
116 A33 3k black 1.25 1.10
117 A33 3.70k blue black 1.75 1.50
118 A33 9k dark green 4.00 2.75
Nos. 112-118 (7) 11.25 8.95

Issued: 1.60k, 3/26/81; 2.70k, 6/24/82; No. 114, 9/4/86; No. 115, 4/9/87; 3k, 9/4/80; 3.70k, 2/9/84; 9k, 9/5/85.

Queen Margrethe, Map of Greenland A34

1980-89 **Engr.** ***Perf. 13***
120 A34 50o purple ('81) .30 .30
a. 50o dull purple ('89) 5.75 5.75
121 A34 80o sepia .40 .40
122 A34 1.30k red .60 .60
123 A34 1.50k royal blue ('82) .70 .70
124 A34 1.60k ultra .90 .90
125 A34 1.80k dull red ('82) .90 .70
126 A34 2.30k dk grn ('81) .90 .75
127 A34 2.50k red ('83) 1.10 .75
128 A34 2.80k copper red ('85) 1.75 .80
129 A34 3k fawn ('88) 2.00 2.00
130 A34 3.20k rose ('89) 2.00 2.00
a. Bklt. pane of 10 (4 #120a, 6 #130) 32.50
131 A34 3.80k slate blue ('85) 1.75 1.75
132 A34 4.10k brt blue ('88) 2.25 2.25
133 A34 4.40k ultra ('89) 3.25 2.75
Nos. 120-133 (14) 18.80 16.65

Issued: Nos. 121-122, 124, 4/16; Nos. 120, 126, 1/29; Nos. 123, 125, 5/13; No. 127, 3/30; Nos. 128, 131, 2/7; Nos. 129, 132, 2/4; Nos. 130, 133, 1/30.

Rasmus Berthelsen (Teacher, Hymnist), in Training College Library, 1830 — A35

1980, May 29 **Engr.** ***Perf. 13***
134 A35 2k brown, *cream* .70 .70

Greenland Public Library Service, 150th anniv.

Ejnar Mikkelsen on board Gustav Holm, 1934 — A36

1980, Oct. 16 **Engr.** ***Perf. 13***
135 A36 4k slate green 1.40 1.40

Ejnar Mikkelsen, inspector of East Greenland, birth centenary.

Pandalus Borealis — A37

Designs: No. 137, Anarhicas minor. No. 138, Reinhardtius Hippoglossoides. No. 139, Mallotus villosus. 25k, Codfish. 50k, Salmo salar.

1981-86 **Engr.** ***Perf. 13***
136 A37 10k multicolored 3.50 2.00
137 A37 10k dk bl & blk 5.50 4.00
138 A37 10k multicolored 4.00 4.00
139 A37 10k grnsh blk & blk 4.25 4.75
140 A37 25k multicolored 8.75 4.25
141 A37 50k multicolored 18.00 10.00
Nos. 136-141 (6) 44.00 29.00

Issued: 25k, 5/21; No. 136, 4/1/82; 50k, 1/27/83; No. 137, 10/11/84; No. 138, 10/10/85; No. 139, 10/16/86.

Saqqaq Eskimo in Kayak, Reindeer — A38

5k, Tunit-Dorset hunters hauling seal.

1981, Oct. 15 **Engr.** ***Perf. 12½***
146 A38 3.50k dark blue 1.00 1.00
147 A38 5k brown 1.50 1.50

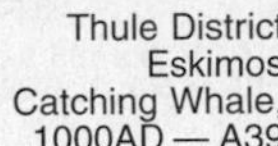

Thule District Eskimos Catching Whale, 1000AD — A39

Greenland history: No. 149, Bishop Joen Smyrill's house and staff, 12th cent. No. 150, Wooden dolls, 13th cent. No. 151, Eskimo mummy, sacrificial stones, 14th cent. No. 152, Hans Pothorst, explorer, 15th cent. No. 153, Glass pearls, 16th cent. No. 154, Apostle spoons, 17th cent. No. 155, Key, trading station, 18th cent. No. 156, Trade Ship Hvalfisken, masthead, 19th cent. No. 157, Communications satellite, Earth, 20th cent.

1982, Sept. 30
148 A39 2k brown red .75 .75
149 A39 2.70k dark blue 1.05 1.05

1983, Sept. 15
150 A39 2.50k red .85 .85
151 A39 3.50k brown 1.30 1.30
152 A39 4.50k blue 1.50 1.50

1984, Mar. 29
153 A39 2.70k red brown 1.50 1.50
154 A39 3.70k dark blue 1.50 1.50
155 A39 5.50k brown 1.90 1.90

1985, Mar. 21
156 A39 2.80k violet 1.50 1.50
157 A39 6k blue black 2.40 2.40
Nos. 148-157,B10 (11) 15.50 15.50

250th Anniv. of Settlement of New Herrnhut — A40

1983, Nov. 2 **Engr.**
158 A40 2.50k carmine lake .90 .90

Henrik Lund, Natl. Anthem Score, Lichtenau Fjord — A41

1984, Sept. 6 **Engr.**
159 A41 5k greenish blk 2.75 2.75

Henrik Lund (1875-1948), natl. anthem composer, artist, only Greenlander to win Ingenio et Arti medal.

A42

1984, June 6 **Engr.** ***Perf. 13***
160 A42 2.70k dull red 1.75 1.75

Prince Henrik, 50th birthday.

Danish Grenadier, 1734 — A43

1984, July 25 **Engr.** ***Perf. 13***
161 A43 3.70k vio brn 1.40 1.40

Town of Christianshab, 250th anniv.

Ingrid, Queen Mother of Denmark, Chrysanthemums — A44

1985, May 21 **Litho. & Engr.**
162 A44 2.80k multicolored 1.10 1.10

Arrival in Denmark of Princess Ingrid, 50th anniv. See Denmark No. 775.

Intl. Youth Year — A45

3.80k, Emblem, birds nesting, fiord.

1985, June 27 **Litho.**
163 A45 3.80k multicolored 1.25 1.25

Greenland Port Post Office, Flags — A46

1986, Mar. 6 Engr. *Perf. 13*

164	A46	2.80k dark red	1.05	1.05

Transfer of postal control under Greenland Home Rule, Jan. 1, 1986.

Artifacts — A47

2.80k, Sewing needles, case. 3k, Buckets, bowl, scoop. No. 166, 3.80k, Ulos. No. 167, 3.80k, Masks. 5k, Harpoon points. 6.50k, Lard lamps. 10k, Carved faces.

1986-88 Engr. *Perf. 13*

165	A47	2.80k multicolored	1.25	.95
165A	A47	3k multicolored	1.10	.90
166	A47	3.80k multicolored	1.25	1.25
167	A47	3.80k multicolored	1.60	1.60
168	A47	5k multicolored	1.75	1.50
169	A47	6.50k multicolored	2.50	2.50
172	A47	10k multicolored	4.00	3.25
		Nos. 165-172 (7)	13.45	11.95

Issued: No. 166, 6.50k, 5/22. 2.80k, 3.80k, 6/11, 1987. 3k, 5k, 10k, 10/27/88.

Souvenir Sheet

HAFNIA '87 — A48

1987, Jan. 23 Litho. *Perf. 13*

175	A48	Sheet of 3	8.00	8.00
	a.	2.80k Gull in flight	2.25	2.25
	b.	3.80k Mountain	2.75	2.75
	c.	6.50k Gulls in water	2.75	2.75

No. 175 sold for 19.50k. See No. 199.

Year of the Fishing, Sealing and Whaling Industries — A49

1987, Apr. 9 Litho. *Perf. 13*

176	A49	3.80k multi	1.50	1.50

Lagopus Mutus — A50

Birds of Prey — A51

3k, Falco rusticolus. 3.20k, Clangula hyemalis. 4k, Anser caerulescens. 4.10k, Corvus corax. 4.40k, Plectrophenax nivalis. No. 183, 5.50k, Haliaeetus albicilla. No. 184, 5.50k, Cepphus grylle. 6.50k, Uria lomvia. 7k, Gavia immer. 7.50k, Stercorarius longicaudus. 10k, Nyctea scandiaca.

1987-90 Litho. *Perf. 13*

177	A51	3k shown	1.50	1.50
178	A51	3.20k multicolored	2.10	1.25
179	A51	4k multicolored	1.50	1.25
180	A51	4.10k multicolored	1.90	1.90
181	A51	4.40k multicolored	2.10	2.10
182	A50	5k shown	2.60	2.40
183	A51	5.50k multicolored	3.25	3.00
184	A51	5.50k multicolored	2.60	2.25
185	A51	6.50k multicolored	3.50	2.60
186	A51	7k multicolored	3.25	3.50
187	A51	7.50k multicolored	3.00	3.00
188	A50	10k multicolored	3.75	3.75
		Nos. 177-188 (12)	31.05	28.50

Issued: 5k, 10k, 9/3; 3k, 4.10k, No. 183, 7k, 4/14/88; 3.20k, 4.40k, No. 184, 6.50k, 3/16/89; 4k, 7.50k, 1/15/90.

Plants — A52

No. 189, 4k, Campanula gieseckiana. No. 190, 4k, Pedicularis hirsuta. 5k, Eriophorum scheuchzeri. 5.50k, Ledum groenlandicum. 6.50k, Cassiope tetragona. 7.25k, Saxifraga oppositifolia. 10k, Papaver radicatum, vert.

1989-92 Litho. *Perf. 13*

189	A52	4k multicolored	1.60	1.50
190	A52	4k multicolored	1.90	1.50
191	A52	5k multicolored	.225	2.10
192	A52	5.50k multicolored	2.00	2.25
193	A52	6.50k multicolored	2.60	2.75
194	A52	7.25k multicolored	3.00	3.00
196	A52	10k multicolored	4.25	4.00
		Nos. 189-196 (7)	15.58	17.10

Issued: 5k, 10k, 10/12/89; No. 189, 5.50k, 6.50k, 6/7/90; No. 190, 7.25k, 3/26/92. Nos. 189-190 vert.

HAFNIA type of 1987

Souvenir Sheet

Uummannaq Mountain in winter, horiz.

1987, Oct. 16 Litho. *Perf. 13x12½*

199	A48	2.80k slate blue & lake	2.75	*3.75*

No. 199 sold for 4k.

Greenland Home Rule, 10th Anniv.
A53 A54

1989, May 1 Litho. *Perf. 13*

200	A53	3.20k Flag, landscape	1.25	1.25
201	A54	4.40k Coat of arms	2.25	1.75

Queen Margrethe — A55

and

Nos. 214, 217 Surcharged in Red or Blue

1990-96 Engr. *Perf. 13*

214	A55	25o green	.30	.30
217	A55	1k brown	.55	.45
	a.	Bklt. pane, 4 #214, 6 #217	35.00	
	b.	Bklt. pane, 4 each #214, 217	16.00	
224	A55	4k carmine rose	1.50	1.25
		Complete booklet, 217a, 10 #224	35.00	
225	A55	4.25k red	*2.60*	*2.60*
226	A55	4.25k on 25o #214 (R)	*5.00*	*5.00*
	a.	Inverted surcharge	*1,100.*	
227	A55	4.50k on 1k #217 (Bl)	5.00	5.00
228	A55	6.50k blue	2.75	2.75
229	A55	7k violet	3.50	3.50
		Nos. 214-229 (8)	21.20	20.85

Value for No. 225 is for stamp with yellow fluorescence. Value for stamp with white fluorescence, $5.50.

Issued: No. 217a, 5/3/90; No. 217b, 9/9/93; 7k, 2/10/94; No. 225, 1996; Nos. 226-227, 12/31/95; others, 4/5/90.

First-day covers of Nos. 226-227 are dated 1/2/96.

Frederik Lynge (1889-1957), Politician — A56

25k, Augo Lynge (1899-1959), politician

1990, Oct. 18 Engr. *Perf. 13x12½*

231	A56	10k rose brn & dk bl	5.00	3.00
232	A56	25k vio & dk bl	11.50	7.00

See Nos. 242-243, 249.

Phoca Hispida — A57

Walrus and Seals: No. 234, Pagophilus groenlandicus. No. 235, Cystophora cristata. No. 236, Odobenus rosmarus. No. 237, Erignatus barbatus. No. 238, Phoca vitulina.

Litho. & Engr.

1991, Mar. 14 *Perf. 13*

233	A57	4k shown	1.50	1.50
234	A57	4k multicolored	1.50	1.50
235	A57	7.25k multicolored	3.00	3.00
236	A57	7.25k multicolored	3.00	3.00
237	A57	8.50k multicolored	3.25	3.25
238	A57	8.50k multicolored	3.25	3.25
	a.	Miniature sheet of 6, #233-238	17.00	17.00
		Nos. 233-238 (6)	15.50	15.50

Village of Ilulissat, 250th Anniv. — A58

1991, May 15 Litho. *Perf. 13*

239	A58	4k multicolored	1.60	1.60

Tourism — A59

1991, May 15 *Perf. 12½x13*

240	A59	4k Iceberg	1.50	1.50
241	A59	8.50k Skiers, sled dogs	3.50	3.50

See Nos. 259-260, 289-290.

Famous Men Type of 1990

10k, Jonathan Petersen (1881-1961), musician. 50k, Hans Lynge (1906-88), artist & writer. 100k, Lars Moller (1842-1926), newspaper editor.

1991-92 Engr. *Perf. 13x12½*

242	A56	10k black & dk blue	4.75	3.00
243	A56	50k red brn & blue	20.00	15.00
249	A56	100k claret & slate	35.00	30.00
		Nos. 242-249 (3)	59.75	48.00

Issued: 10k, 50k, 9/5; 100k, 9/15/92.

Settlement of Paamiut, 250th Anniv. A60

1992, May 14 Engr. *Perf. 13*

252	A60	7.25k dk bl & ol brn	3.25	3.00

Denmark's Queen Margrethe and Prince Henrik, Silver Wedding Anniv. — A61

1992, June 10 Litho. *Perf. 12½x13*

253	A61	4k multicolored	2.40	2.40

See Denmark No. 946.

A62

1992, Nov. 12 Litho. *Perf. 13*

254	A62	4k Christmas	2.50	1.90

A63

1993, Feb. 4 Litho. *Perf. 13*

255	A63	4k multicolored	2.25	1.50

Intl. Year of Indigenous Peoples.

Crabs — A64

4k, Neolithodes grimaldii. 7.25k, Chionoecetes oiliqo. 8.50k, Hyas coarctatus, Hyas araneus.

Litho. & Engr.

1993, Mar. 25 *Perf. 13*

256	A64	4k multicolored	1.25	1.25
257	A64	7.25k multicolored	4.00	4.00
	a.	Chionoecetes opilio	10.00	10.00
	b.	Booklet pane, 4 each #256, 257a	45.00	
258	A64	8.50k multicolored	5.00	5.00
		Nos. 256-258 (3)	10.25	10.25

Issue date: No. 257b, Sept. 9.

Tourism Type of 1991

1993, May 6 Litho. *Perf. 12½x13*

259	A59	4k Village in winter	2.00	2.00
260	A59	8.50k Ruins, coastline	3.50	3.50

AIDS Research A66

1993, Sept. 9 Litho. *Perf. 13*
261 A66 4k multicolored 2.25 2.25

Native Animals — A67

5k, Canis lupus. 8.50k, Alopex lagopus. 10k, Rangifer tarandus.

Litho. & Engr.

1993, Oct. 14 *Perf. 13*
262 A67 5k multicolored 2.50 2.50
263 A67 8.50k multicolored 4.00 4.00
264 A67 10k multicolored 4.50 4.50
Nos. 262-264 (3) 11.00 11.00

See Nos. 270-272, 296-298.

Christmas A68

1993, Nov. 11 Litho. *Perf. 13*
265 A68 4k multicolored 2.00 2.00

Buksefjord Electrical Project — A69

Litho. & Engr.

1994, Mar. 24 *Perf. 13*
266 A69 4k multicolored 1.50 1.50

Ammassalik, Cent. — A70

1994, Mar. 24
267 A70 7.25k multicolored 3.00 3.00

Expedition to North East Greenland, 1906-08 A71

Europa: 4k, Icebound Danmark. 7.25k, Danmark, expedition car, dogs.

1994, May 5 Litho. *Perf. 13*
268 A71 4k multicolored *1.50 1.50*
269 A71 7.25k multicolored *3.25 3.25*

Native Animal Type of 1993

Designs: 5.50k, Mustela erminea. 7.25k, Dicrostonyx torquatus. 9k, Lepus arcticus.

Litho. & Engr.

1994, Sept. 8 *Perf. 13*
270 A67 5.50k multicolored 2.50 2.50
271 A67 7.25k multicolored 4.00 4.00
272 A67 9k multicolored 4.50 4.50
Nos. 270-272 (3) 11.00 11.00

Ship's Figureheads — A72

Litho. & Engr

1994, Oct. 13 *Perf. 13*
273 A72 4k Ceres 1.50 1.50
274 A72 8.50k Nordlyset 3.50 3.50

See Nos. 299-300, 309-310.

Christmas Paintings, by Julia Pars — A73

1994, Nov. 10 Litho. *Perf. 12½x13*
275 A73 4k shown 2.00 2.00
276 A73 5k Santa, dogs, igloo 3.00 3.00

Orchids — A74

4k, Listera cordata. 4.25k, Corallorhiza trifida. 4.50k, Amerorchis rotundifolia. 7.25k, Leucorchis albida. 7.50k, Plantanthera hyperborea.

Litho. & Engr.

1995-96 *Perf. 13x12½*
279 A74 4k multicolored 2.00 2.00
280 A74 4.25k multicolored 1.75 1.75
281 A74 4.50k multicolored 1.90 1.90
282 A74 7.25k multicolored 3.00 3.00
283 A74 7.50k multicolored 3.25 3.25
a. Booklet pane, #281, 283, 2 ea #225, 280 + 4 labels 12.50
Complete booklet, 2 #283a 25.00
Nos. 279-283 (5) 11.90 11.90

No. 283a exists with different labels and stamps in different order. Complete booklet contains one of each type of No. 283a.
Issued: 4k, 7.25k, 2/9/95.

Ilinniarfissuaq Seminarium, Nuuk (The Greenland Training College), 150th Anniv. — A75

Litho. & Engr.

1995, Mar. 23 *Perf. 13*
287 A75 4k multicolored 1.75 1.75

United Nations, 50th Anniv. — A76

1995, Mar. 23
288 A76 7.25k multicolored 3.75 3.75

Tourism Type of 1991

1995, Apr. 20 Litho. *Perf. 12½x13*
289 A59 4k Iceberg, inlet 2.10 2.10
290 A59 8.50k Mountains 4.25 4.25

Peace & Liberty A77

Europa: 4k, Envelope, simulated stamp. 8.50k, Doves flying over Greenland.

1995, May 5 *Perf. 12½x13*
291 A77 4k multicolored *1.75 1.75*
292 A77 8.50k multicolored *4.00 4.00*

Souvenir Sheets

Types A3-A5 Surcharged

America Series — A78

Designs: No. 295a, Dog team. b, Polar bear. c, Eskimo in kayak. d, Eider duck.

1995, May 5 Litho. *Perf. 13*
293 A78 Sheet of 2 + 4 labels *6.50 6.50*
a. 5k on 10o pur & ol (Type A4) *3.00 3.00*
b. 5k on 15o red & vio (Type A4) *3.00 3.00*
294 A78 Sheet of 3 *7.75 7.75*
a. 1k on 1o dk ol & vio bl (Type A3) *.60 .60*
b. 5k on 5o rose lake & brn (Type A3) *3.00 3.00*
c. 7k on 7o dk grn & blk (Type A3) *4.25 4.25*
295 A78 Sheet of 4 *10.00 10.00*
a. 4k on 30o dk bl & red brn (Type A5) *2.40 2.40*
b. 4k on 1k brn & gray blk (Type A5) *2.40 2.40*
c. 4k on 2k sep & dp grn (Type A5) *2.40 2.40*
d. 4k on 5k dp pur & dl brn (Type A5) *2.40 2.40*

Native Animal Type of 1993

Litho. & Engr.

1995, Sept. 7 *Perf. 13*
296 A67 4k Ursus maritimus 2.00 2.00
297 A67 7.25k Gulo gulo 3.25 3.25
298 A67 7.50k Ovibus moschatus 3.25 3.25
Nos. 296-298 (3) 8.50 8.50

Ship's Figureheads Type of 1994

Litho. & Engr.

1995, Oct. 12 *Perf. 13*
299 A72 4k Hvalfisken, vert. 1.60 1.60
300 A72 8.50k Tjalfe 3.75 3.75

Christmas A79

1995, Nov. 9 Litho. *Perf. 13*
301 A79 4k Boy running in snow 1.50 1.50
302 A79 5k Girl running in snow 2.00 2.00

Whales A80

Designs: 25o, Orcinus orca. 50o, Megaptera novaeangliae. 1k, Delphinapterus leucas. 4.50k, Physeter catodon. 6.50k, Balaena mysticetus. 9.50k, Balaenoptera acutorostrata.

1996, Apr. 25 Litho. *Perf. 13*
303 A80 25o blue, blk & red .25 .25
304 A80 50o blue, blk & red .25 .25
305 A80 1k blue, blk & red .65 .65
306 A80 4.50k blue, blk & red 2.00 2.00
a. Bklt. pane, #304, 2 ea #303, 306 5.00
Complete booklet, 2 #306a 10.00
307 A80 6.50k blue, blk & red 3.25 3.25
308 A80 9.50k blue, blk & red 4.50 4.50
a. Souvenir sheet, Nos. 303-308 11.50 11.50
Nos. 303-308 (6) 10.90 10.90

No. 306a exists with stamps in different order. Issued: No. 306a, 1/14/97.
See Nos. 319-322, 329-334.

Ship's Figureheads Type of 1994

Litho. & Engr.

1996, Sept. 5 *Perf. 13*
309 A72 15k Blaahejren, vert. 5.50 5.50
310 A72 20k Gertrud Rask 7.50 7.50

Arnarulunnguaq (1896-1933), Member of Thule Expedition — A81

1996, Sept. 5 Engr.
311 A81 4.50k dark blue *1.75 1.75*

Europa.

Christmas A82

Designs: 4.25k, Girl looking through frozen window pane, angels scratched in ice. 4.50k, Paper star, children singing.

1996, Nov. 7 Litho.
312 A82 4.25k multicolored 2.00 2.00
313 A82 4.50k multicolored 2.50 2.50
a. Booklet pane, 3 each #312-313 13.00
Complete booklet, 2 #313a 26.00

No. 313a was issued in two formats, one with No. 312 at the UL, the other with No. 313 at the UL. The complete booklet contains one of each format.

A83

Litho. & Engr.

1997, Jan. 14 *Perf. 13*
314 A83 4.50k multicolored 2.25 2.25

Coronation of Queen Margrethe II, 25th anniv.

A84

Butterflies: 2k, Clossiana chariclea. 3k, Colias hecla. 4.75k, Plebejus franklinii. 8k, Lycaena phlaeas.

1997, Jan. 14
315 A84 2k multicolored 1.10 1.10
316 A84 3k multicolored 1.75 1.75
317 A84 4.75k multicolored 1.75 1.75
318 A84 8k multicolored 3.50 3.50
a. Booklet pane of 6, 2 #314, 1 ea #315-318 + 2 labels 13.00
Complete booklet, 2 #318a 26.00
Nos. 315-318 (4) 8.10 8.10

Issued: No. 318a, 5/5.
No. 318a exists with stamps in two different orders and with two different backgrounds, one of green plants, the other of red flowers.

The complete booklet contains one of each type of pane.

Whale Type of 1996

Designs: 5k, Balaenoptera musculus. 5.75k, Balaenoptera physalus. 6k, Balaenoptera borealis. 8k, Monodon monoceros.

1997, May 5 Litho. ***Perf. 13***

319 A80 5k blue, blk & red 1.90 1.90
320 A80 5.75k blue, blk & red 2.25 2.25
321 A80 6k blue, blk & red 2.25 2.25
322 A80 8k blue, blk & red 3.25 3.25
a. Souvenir sheet of 4, #319-322 10.00 10.00
Nos. 319-322 (4) 9.65 9.65

Story of the "Bear of the Sea" — A85

1997, May 5 Litho. & Engr. ***Perf. 13***

323 A85 4.75k blk & blue blk *2.50 2.50*

Europa.

Town of Nanortalik, Bicent. A86

Litho. & Engr.

1997, Aug. 15 ***Perf. 13***

324 A86 4.50k multicolored 1.75 1.75

Paintings by Aage Gitz-Johansen (1897-1977) — A87

Designs: 10k, Native dancer, Thule. 16k, Nude woman, Ammassalik.

1997, Aug. 15 Litho. ***Perf. 13x12½***

325 A87 10k multicolored 3.75 3.75
326 A87 16k multicolored 5.75 5.75

Christmas A88

Designs: 4.50k, Child with dogs in snow. 4.75k, Family in sled with Christmas presents, tree, father preparing harness.

1997, Nov. 6 Litho. ***Perf. 13x12½***

327 A88 4.50k multicolored 2.00 2.00
328 A88 4.75k multicolored 2.00 2.00
a. Booklet pane, 3 each #327-328 14.00
Complete booklet, 2 #328a 28.00

No. 328a comes in two configurations. One has No. 327 at UL, the second has No. 328 at UL. Complete booklet has one of each pane.

Whale Type of 1996

Designs: 2k, Phocoena phocoena. 3k, Lagenorhynchus albirostris. No. 331, Globicephala melaena. No. 332, Hyperoodon ampullatus. No. 333, Lagenorhynchus acutus. No. 334, Eubalaena glacialis.

1998, Feb. 5 Litho. ***Perf. 13***

329 A80 2k multicolored .65 .65
330 A80 3k multicolored 1.25 1.25
331 A80 4.50k multicolored 2.00 2.00
332 A80 4.50k multicolored 2.00 2.00
333 A80 4.75k multicolored 2.00 2.00
334 A80 4.75k multicolored 2.00 2.00
a. Souvenir sheet of 6, #329-334 10.00 10.00
Nos. 329-334 (6) 9.90 9.90

Intl. Year of the Ocean.

New Order of 1950 — A89

Design: Augo Lynge, Frederik Lynge, first Greenland politicians in Danish Parliament.

1998, Feb. 5 Engr. ***Perf. 13***

335 A89 4.50k multicolored 1.75 1.75

Europa — A90

Children's drawings of "Children's Day in Greenland:" 4.75k, Happy faces beside lake. 10k, People celebrating across Greenland.

1998, May 29 Litho. ***Perf. 13***

336 A90 4.75k multicolored *1.50 1.50*
337 A90 10k multicolored *4.00 4.00*

Ships — A91

Litho. & Engr.

1998, Aug. 20 ***Perf. 13***

338 A91 4.50k Gertrud Rask 2.00 2.00
a. Booklet pane of 6 12.00
339 A91 4.75k Hans Egede 2.00 2.00
a. Booklet pane of 6 12.00
Complete booklet, #338a, 339a 24.00

Paintings by Hans Lynge (1906-88) — A92

Designs: 11k, "Brother Gets Breast-fed." 25k, "Refuelling" (men in boat).

1998, Aug. 20 Litho. ***Perf. 13***

340 A92 11k multicolored 3.75 3.75
341 A92 25k multicolored 8.75 8.75

Christmas A93

1998, Nov. 5 Litho. ***Perf. 13***

342 A93 4.50k Dickey, kamikker 2.00 2.00
a. Booklet pane of 6 15.00
343 A93 4.75k Kamikker, hat 2.50 2.50
a. Booklet pane of 6 15.00
Complete booklet, #342a, 343a 30.00

World Wildlife Fund — A94

Nyctea scandiaca (snowy owl): 1k, Nesting with young. 4.75k, In flight. 5.50k, Two adults. 5.75k, Perched on rock.

Litho. & Engr.

1999, Feb. 8 ***Perf. 13***

344 A94 1k multicolored .60 .60
345 A94 4.75k multicolored 2.00 2.00
a. Booklet pane, 3 each #344-345 8.50
346 A94 5.50k multicolored 2.25 2.25
347 A94 5.75k multicolored 2.50 2.50
a. Booklet pane, 3 each #346-347 14.50
Complete booklet, #345a, 347a 25.00
Nos. 344-347 (4) 7.35 7.35

Europa A95

1999, May 7 Litho. & Engr. ***Perf. 13***

348 A95 6k Polar bear *2.50 2.50*

Paintings, by Peter Rosing (1892-1965) — A96

Designs: 7k, The Man from Aluk, 1944. 20k, Homecoming, 1956.

1999, May 7 Litho. ***Perf. 12½x13***

349 A96 7k multicolored 2.00 2.00
350 A96 20k multicolored 7.00 7.00

Arctic Vikings A97

4.50k, Viking ship. 4.75k, Man on driftwood. 5.75k, Arrowhead, coins. 8k, Tjodhilde's church.

1999, Aug. 13 Engr. ***Perf. 13x13¼***

351 A97 4.50k multicolored 1.75 1.75
352 A97 4.75k multicolored 1.75 1.75
353 A97 5.75k multicolored 2.25 2.25
354 A97 8k multicolored 3.00 3.00
a. Souvenir sheet, #351-354 9.00 9.00
Nos. 351-354 (4) 8.75 8.75

See Nos. 358-361, 380-383.

Christmas A98

1999, Nov. 11 Litho. ***Perf. 13x13¼***

355 A98 4.50k Writing letter 1.50 1.50
a. Booklet pane of 6 9.00
356 A98 4.75k Handshake 1.75 1.75
a. Booklet pane of 6 10.50
Complete booklet, #355a, 356a 20.00

Millennium A99

1999, Nov. 11 Litho. ***Perf. 13x13¼***

357 A99 5.75k multicolored 2.00 2.00

Arctic Vikings Type of 1999

Designs: 25o, Hunter, four walruses. 3k, Storyteller. 5.50k, Dog chasing reindeer. 21k, Man, gyrfalcon, polar bear, narwhal tusk, items made from animals.

2000, Feb. 21 Engr. ***Perf. 13x13¼***

358 A97 25o bl gray & brn .25 .25
359 A97 3k bl gray & brn 1.40 1.40
360 A97 5.50k bl gray 2.25 2.25
361 A97 21k bl gray 9.00 9.00
a. Souvenir sheet, #358-361 13.00 13.00
Nos. 358-361 (4) 12.90 12.90

Navy Dog Sled Patrol A100

Litho. & Engr.

2000, Feb. 21 ***Perf. 12¾***

362 A100 10k multi 3.25 3.25

Europa, 2000

Common Design Type

2000, May 9 Litho. ***Perf. 13¼x13***

363 CD17 4.75k multi *1.90 1.90*

Queen Margrethe A101

2000-02 Engr. ***Perf. 13x13¼***

364 A101 25o blk & bl gray .30 .25
365 A101 50o red brn & bl gray .25 .25
367 A101 4.50k red & bl gray 1.60 1.60
368 A101 4.75k bl & bl gray 1.75 1.75
Complete booklet, 4 each #364, #368 8.00
372 A101 8k yel grn & bl gray 3.00 3.00
374 A101 10k grn & bl gray 3.50 3.50
375 A101 12k pur & bl gray 4.25 4.25
Nos. 364-375 (7) 14.65 14.60

Issued: 4.50k, 4.75k, 8k, 10k, 5/9/00. 25o, 12k, 5/9/01. 50o, 10/21/02.

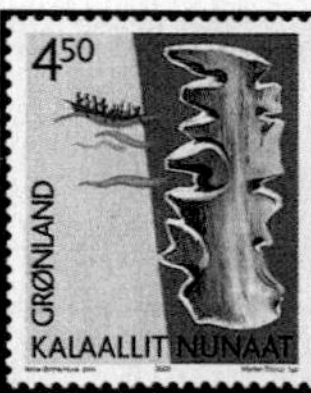

Cultural Heritage — A102

2000, Aug. 18 Litho. ***Perf. 13¼x13***

376 A102 4.50k Wooden map 1.50 1.50
a. Booklet pane of 6 + 2 labels 9.00
377 A102 4.75k Sealskin 1.75 1.75
a. Booklet pane of 6 + 2 labels 10.50
Booklet, #376a, 377a 20.00

See Nos. 384-385, 392-393, 414-415

Christmas A103

2000, Nov. 9 Litho. ***Perf. 13x13¼***

378 A103 4.50k Stars, candles 1.75 1.75
a. Booklet pane of 6 10.50

379 A103 4.75k Star 1.90 1.90
a. Booklet pane of 6 11.50
Booklet, #378a, 379a 22.50

Arctic Vikings Type of 1999

Designs: 1k, Hunter, dead seals. 4.50k, Mice eating food. 5k, Man and pack animals leaving. 10k, Birds on ruins.

2001, Feb. 5 Engr. ***Perf. 13x13¼***
380 A97 1k indigo & red 1.00 1.00
381 A97 4.50k indigo & blue 1.15 1.15
382 A97 5k indigo & blue 2.10 2.10
383 A97 10k indigo & red 4.25 4.25
a. Souvenir sheet, #380-383 8.00 8.00
Nos. 380-383 (4) 8.50 8.50

Cultural Heritage Type of 2000

Designs: 4.50k, Smoked fish. 4.75k, Fishing spear.

2001, May 9 Litho. ***Perf. 13¼x13***
384 A102 4.50k multi 1.50 1.50
a. Booklet pane of 6 + 2 labels 10.00
385 A102 4.75k multi 2.00 2.00
a. Booklet pane of 6 + 2 labels 10.00
Complete booklet, #384a, 385a 20.00

Europa A104

2001, May 9 Litho. & Engr. ***Perf. 13***
386 A104 15k Krill *4.75 4.75*

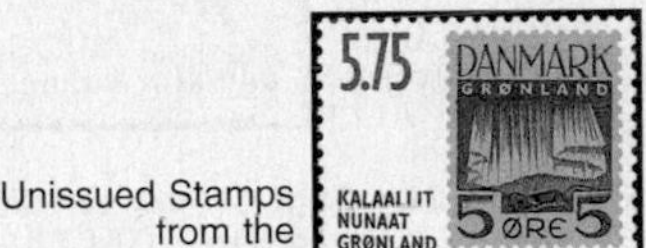

Unissued Stamps from the 1930s — A105

Designs: 5.75k, 5o Northern lights. 8k, 10o Seal. 21k, 15o Polar bear.

Litho. & Engr.
2001, Oct. 16 ***Perf. 12¾***
387 A105 5.75k blk & brn 2.25 2.25
388 A105 8k blk & brn 3.25 3.25
389 A105 21k blk & brn 8.25 8.25
a. Souvenir sheet, #387-389 + 3 labels 14.00 14.00

Christmas A106

Grouse and: 4.50k, Berries. 4.75k, Mountain.

2001, Oct. 16 Litho. ***Perf. 13x13¼***
390 A106 4.50k multi 1.50 1.50
a. Booklet pane of 6 9.00 —
391 A106 4.75k multi 1.75 1.75
a. Booklet pane of 6 10.50 —
Complete booklet, #390a, 391a 20.00

Cultural Heritage Type of 2000

Designs: 4.50k, Thule drum. 4.75k, Mask.

2002, Mar. 5 Litho. ***Perf. 13x13¼***
392 A102 4.50k multi 1.75 1.75
a. Miniature sheet of 8 + label 14.00 —
393 A102 4.75k multi 1.90 1.90
a. Miniature sheet of 8 + label 15.00 —

Sculptures A107

Designs: 1k, Stone and Man, by various sculptors. 31k, Nuuk Snow Festival snow sculpture.

2002, Mar. 5 ***Perf. 12¾***
394 A107 1k multi .40 .40
395 A107 31k multi 12.00 12.00

Europa — A108

2002, June 24 Litho. ***Perf. 12¾***
396 A108 11k multi *4.00 4.00*

Ships A109

2002, June 24 Engr. ***Perf. 13x13¼***
397 A109 2k Nordlyset .80 .80
398 A109 4k Hvidbjornen 1.60 1.60
399 A109 6k Staerkodder 2.40 2.40
a. Booklet pane of 4, 2 each #398-399 8.00 —
400 A109 16k Haabet 6.25 6.25
a. Booklet pane of 4, 2 each #397, 400 14.00 —
Complete booklet, #399a, 400a 22.50
Nos. 397-400 (4) 11.05 11.05

See Nos. 416-419, 434-437, 452-455.

Intl. Council for Exploration of the Seas, Cent. — A110

Designs: 7k, Somniosus microcephalus and iceberg. 19k, Sebastes mentella and exploration ship Paamiut.

Litho. & Engr.
2002, Oct. 21 ***Perf. 13¼x13***
401 A110 7k multi 2.25 2.25
402 A110 19k multi 6.25 6.25
a. Souvenir sheet, #401-402 8.50 8.50

See Denmark Nos. 1237-1238, Faroe Islands No. 426.

Christmas — A111

Designs: 4.50k, Man with gifts, children on sled with tree. 4.75k, Family with gifts near fire.

2002, Oct. 21 Litho. ***Perf. 12¾***
403 A111 4.50k multi 2.00 2.00
404 A111 4.75k multi 2.00 2.00

Booklet Stamps
Self-Adhesive
Serpentine Die Cut 14
405 A111 4.50k multi 2.00 2.00
406 A111 4.75k multi 2.25 2.25
a. Horiz. pair, #405-406 4.50
b. Booklet, 6 each #405-406 27.00

Danish Literary Greenland Expedition, Cent. — A112

Designs: 15k, Campsite. 21k, Knud Rasmussen.

2003, Mar. 12 Engr. ***Perf. 12¾***
407 A112 15k multi 6.00 6.00

Size: 28x21mm
408 A112 21k blue gray 8.00 8.00
a. Souvenir sheet, #407-408 + label 14.00 14.00

Sled Dogs A113

Designs: 4.50k, Puppies playing. 4.75k, Close-up of dog. 6k, Dog in harness.

2003, Mar. 12 ***Perf. 13x13¼***
409 A113 4.50k blue gray 1.90 1.90
a. Sheet of 8 + central label 15.00 15.00
410 A113 4.75k blue gray 2.00 2.00
a. Sheet of 8 + central label 16.00 16.00
411 A113 6k blue gray 2.60 2.60
a. Booklet pane, 2 each #409-411, with #411 at UL 15.00 —
b. Booklet pane, 2 each #409-411, with #409 at UL 15.00 —
Complete booklet, #411a, 411b 30.00
Nos. 409-411 (3) 6.50 6.50

Europa — A114

2003, June 16 Litho. ***Perf. 13¼x13***
412 A114 5.50k multi *2.60 2.60*

Town of Qaanaaq, 50th Anniv. — A115

2003, June 16 ***Perf. 12¾***
413 A115 15k multi 6.00 6.00

Cultural Heritage Type of 2000

Designs: 25o, Comb. 1k, Ice bucket.

2003, June 16 ***Perf. 13¼x13***
414 A102 25o multi .25 .25
415 A102 1k multi .55 .55

Ship Type of 2002

Litho. & Engr.
2003, Oct. 20 ***Perf. 13x13¼***
416 A109 6.75k Emma 2.75 2.75
417 A109 7.75k Gamle Fox 3.00 3.00
418 A109 8.75k Godthaab 3.50 3.50
419 A109 26k Sonja 10.00 10.00
Nos. 416-419 (4) 19.25 19.25

Christmas A116

Designs: Nos. 420, 422, Christmas tree. Nos. 421, 423, Church.

2003, Oct. 20 Litho. ***Perf. 12¾***
420 A116 5k multi 2.00 2.00
421 A116 5.50k multi 2.25 2.25

Booklet Stamps
Self-Adhesive
Serpentine Die Cut 12¼x12¾
422 A116 5k multi 2.50 2.50
423 A116 5.50k multi 2.50 2.50
b. Booklet pane of 12, 6 each #422-423 30.00
Nos. 420-423 (4) 9.25 9.25

Polar Air Route, 50th Anniv. — A117

2004, Mar. 26 Litho. ***Perf. 13¼x13***
424 A117 8.75k multi 3.25 3.25

Home Rule, 25th Anniv. — A118

2004, Mar. 26 ***Perf. 12¾x12½***
425 A118 11k multi 4.00 4.00

Landing Boat From Expedition of Arctic Explorer Otto Sverdrup (1854-1930) A119

Litho. & Engr.
2004, Mar. 26 ***Perf. 13¼x13***
426 A119 17.50k multi 7.50 7.50
a. Souvenir sheet of 1 + 2 labels 7.50 7.50

See Canada Nos. 2026-2027, Norway Nos. 1398-1399.

Norse Mythology A120

Designs: 5.50k, Moon Man. 6.50k, Northern Lights.

2004, Mar. 26 Litho. ***Perf. 12¾***
427 A120 5.50k multi 2.75 2.75
428 A120 6.50k multi 3.00 3.00
a. Souvenir sheet, #427-428 5.75 5.75

Wedding of Crown Prince Frederik and Mary Donaldson A121

Designs: 5k, Couple facing right. 5.50k, Couple facing left.

2004, May 14 ***Perf. 13¼***
429 A121 5k multi 2.00 2.00
430 A121 5.50k multi 2.25 2.25
a. Souvenir sheet, #429-430 + central label 4.25 4.25
b. Booklet pane, 3 each #429-430, with #429 at top 13.00 —
c. As "b," with #430 at top 13.00 —
Complete booklet, #430b-430c 26.00

Edible Plants A122

Designs: 5k, Angelica archangelica. 5.50' Thymus praecox. 17k, Empetr hermaphroditum.

2004, May 14 ***Perf. 1***
431 A122 5k multi 2.
a. Sheet of 8 + central label 1

432 A122 5.50k multi 2.25 2.25
a. Sheet of 8 + central label 18.00 18.00
433 A122 17k multi 6.75 6.75
Nos. 431-433 (3) 11.00 11.00

See Nos. 459-461

Ships Type of 2002

6.50k, Constance. 8.75k, Disko. 14k, Julius Thomsen. 21.75k, Misigssut.

Litho. & Engr.

2004, Oct. 18 ***Perf. 13x13¼***
434 A109 6.50k multicolored 2.25 2.25
435 A109 8.75k multicolored 3.25 3.25
436 A109 14k multicolored 5.00 5.00
437 A109 21.75k multi 8.00 8.00
Nos. 434-437 (4) 18.50 18.50

Europa — A123

2004, Oct. 18 **Litho.** ***Perf. 13¼x13***
438 A123 6.50k multi *2.75 2.75*

Christmas A124

Designs: 5k, Family, Christmas tree. 5.50k, Carolers with lanterns.

2004, Oct. 18 ***Perf. 12¾***
439 A124 5k multi 2.00 2.00
440 A124 5.50k multi 2.00 2.00

Booklet Stamps
Self-Adhesive

Serpentine Die Cut 12¼x12¾
441 A124 5k multi 2.00 2.00
442 A124 5.50k multi 2.00 2.00
a. Horiz. pair, #441-442 4.00 4.00
b. Complete booklet, 6 #442a 24.00
Nos. 439-442 (4) 8.00 8.00

Ilulissat Ice Fjord, UNESCO World Heritage Site — A125

2005, Jan. 17 **Litho.** ***Perf. 12¾***
443 A125 6k multi 2.40 2.40

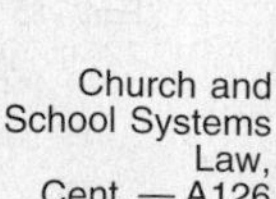

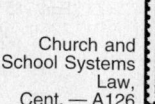

Church and School Systems Law, Cent. — A126

2005, Jan. 17 ***Perf. 12¾***
444 A126 9.25k multi 3.50 3.50

Europa — A127

2005, Jan. 17 ***Perf. 13¼x13***
445 A127 11.75k multi 4.50 4.50

Mushrooms — A128

Designs: 5.25k, Leccinum sp. 6k, Russula subrubens. 7k, Amanita groenlandica.

2005, Jan. 17 ***Perf. 13x13¼***
446 A128 5.25k multi 2.10 2.10
a. Sheet of 8 + central label 17.00 —
447 A128 6k multi 2.40 2.40
a. Sheet of 8 + central label 19.00 —
448 A128 7k multi 2.75 2.75
Nos. 446-448 (3) 7.25 7.25

Booklet Stamps
Self-Adhesive

Serpentine Die Cut 9¾x10¼
449 A128 5.25k multi 2.10 2.10
450 A128 6k multi 2.40 2.40
451 A128 7k multi 2.75 2.75
a. Booklet pane, 2 each #449-451 14.50
Complete booklet, 2 #451a 29.00
Nos. 449-451 (3) 7.25 7.25

No. 451a has two different marginal designs.
See Nos. 476-480.

Ships Type of 2002

Litho. & Engr.

2005, June 20 ***Perf. 13x13¼***
452 A109 5.25k Dannebrog 2.10 2.10
453 A109 6k Kista Arctica 2.40 2.40
454 A109 18.50k Sarpik Ittuk 7.25 7.25
455 A109 23k Triton 9.25 9.25
Nos. 452-455 (4) 21.00 21.00

Science In Greenland — A129

Designs: 7.25k, Geological map. 9.25k, Diver at limestone columns in Ikka Fjord, horiz. 10k, Limnognathia maerski, horiz.

Perf. 13¼x13, 13x13¼

2005, June 20
456 A129 7.25k multi 2.75 2.75
457 A129 9.25k multi 3.50 3.50
458 A129 10k multi 3.75 3.75
Nos. 456-458 (3) 10.00 10.00

Edible Plants Type of 2004

Designs: 75o, Ligusticum scoticum. 6.50k, Rhodiola rosea. 8.25k, Oxyria digyna.

2005, Oct. 31 **Litho.** ***Perf. 13x13¼***
459 A122 75o multi .30 .30
460 A122 6.50k multi 2.25 2.25
461 A122 8.25k multi 3.00 3.00
Nos. 459-461 (3) 5.55 5.55

Admiral Robert E. Peary (1856-1920), Explorer — A130

Litho. & Engr.

2005, Oct. 31 ***Perf. 13***
462 A130 27.50k multi 10.00 10.00
a. Souvenir sheet of 1 10.00 10.00

Parcel Post Stamps, Cent. — A131

2005-07 **Litho.** ***Perf. 14x13½***
463 A131 25k #Q3 10.00 10.00

Perf. 12¾x13
464 A131 50k #Q4 20.00 20.00
a. Perf. 14x13½, dated "2007" 18.00 18.00

Issued: 25k, 1/16/06; No. 464, 10/3; No. 464a, 2007.

No. 464a is found only in No. 497a, along with an example of No. 463 dated "2007." Issued: No. 464a, 5/21/07.
See No. 497.

Christmas A132

Designs: 5.25k, Boy at left. 6k, Girl at right.

2005, Oct. 31 ***Perf. 12¾***
465 A132 5.25k multi 2.00 2.00
466 A132 6k multi 2.00 2.00

Booklet Stamps
Self-Adhesive

Serpentine Die Cut 12¾x13
467 A132 5.25k multi 2.00 2.00
468 A132 6k multi 2.00 2.00
b. Booklet pane, 6 each #467-468 24.00

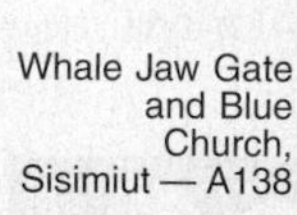

Whale Jaw Gate and Blue Church, Sisimiut — A138

2006, Jan. 16 ***Perf. 13¾x13¼***
469 A138 9.75k multi 3.50 3.50

Sisimiut, 250th anniv.

Nordic Union "Norden" Stamps, 50th Anniv. — A139

2006, Jan. 16
470 A139 19.50k multi 7.00 7.00

European Philatelic Cooperation, 50th Anniv. — A140

2006, Jan. 16 ***Perf. 14x13¼***
471 A140 26.50k #438 and stars 10.00 10.00

Europa stamps, 50th anniv.

Norse Mythology A141

Designs: 7.50k, The Mother of the Sea. 13.50k, Asiaq, Mistress of the Weather.

Perf. 13¾x13½

2006, Mar. 29 **Litho.**
472 A141 7.50k multi 2.75 2.75
473 A141 13.50k multi 4.75 4.75
a. Souvenir sheet, #472-473 7.50 7.50

Sheep Farming in Greenland, Cent. A142

2006, May 22
474 A142 7.50k multi 3.00 3.00

Alfred Wegener (1880-1930), Geophysicist A143

2006, May 22 **Engr.** ***Perf. 13x13¼***
475 A143 20.75k red & blue 8.00 8.00
a. Souvenir sheet of 1 8.00 8.00

Mushrooms Type of 2005

Designs: 5.50k, Rozites caperatus. 7k, Lactarius dryadophilus. 10k, Calvatia cretacea.

2006, May 22 **Litho.** ***Perf. 14x13¼***
476 A128 5.50k multi 2.25 2.25
a. Sheet of 8 + central label 18.00 18.00
477 A128 7k multi 2.75 2.75
a. Sheet of 8 + central label 22.00 22.00
478 A128 10k multi 4.00 4.00
Nos. 476-478 (3) 9.00 9.00

Self-Adhesive
Booklet Stamps

Serpentine Die Cut 12¼x12
479 A128 5.50k multi 2.25 2.25
480 A128 7k multi 2.75 2.75
a. Booklet pane, 3 each #479-480 15.00
Complete booklet, 2 #480a 30.00

No. 480a has two different marginal designs.

Galathea 3 Research Expedition — A144

2006, Sept. 9 **Litho.** ***Perf. 13½x14***
481 A144 9.75k multi 3.75 3.75

Science — A145

Designs: 50o, Larch tree preserved in Kap Kobenhavn Formation. 8k, Geologist obtaining rock sample from mountains at Isua. 15.50k, Qeqertarsuaq Arctic Station, cent.

Litho. & Engr.

2006, Nov. 6 *Perf. 13¼x13*

482	A145	50o multi	.25	.25
483	A145	8k multi	3.00	3.00
484	A145	15.50k multi	5.75	5.75
		Nos. 482-484 (3)	9.00	9.00

See Nos. 502-504, 524-526, 552-554.

Christmas A146

Music for hymn and: 5.50k, Angel. 7k, Candle.

2006, Nov. 6 Litho. *Perf. 13¾x13½*

485	A146	5.50k multi	2.10	2.10
486	A146	7k multi	2.50	2.50

Booklet Stamps
Self-Adhesive
Serpentine Die Cut 12¼x12

487	A146	5.50k multi	2.00	2.00
488	A146	7k multi	2.50	2.50
a.		Booklet pane, 3 each #487-488	13.50	—
		Complete booklet, 2 #488a	27.00	

Hydroelectric Power — A147

2007, Jan. 15 Litho. *Perf. 13¾x13½*

489	A147	5k multi	1.75	1.75

West Nordic Council, 10th anniv.

Crown Prince Frederik, Crown Princess Mary and Prince Christian — A148

2007, Jan. 15 *Perf. 13¼x14*

490	A148	14.25k multi	5.00	5.00

Intl. Polar Year A149

Designs: 7.50k, Scientists drilling ice cores. 8k, Urbanization.

Litho. & Engr.

2007, Jan. 15 *Perf. 13x13¼*

491	A149	7.50k multi	2.75	2.75
492	A149	8k multi	3.00	3.00
a.		Souvenir sheet, #491-492	5.75	5.75

Europa — A150

Scouts: 5.75k, And rock pile. 7.50k, At campsite.

2007, Jan. 15 Litho. *Perf. 13¾x13¼*

493	A150	5.75k multi	2.25	2.25
a.		Sheet of 8 + central label	18.00	18.00
494	A150	7.50k multi	2.75	2.75
a.		Sheet of 8 + central label	22.00	22.00

Booklet Stamps
Self-Adhesive
Serpentine Die Cut 12¼x12

495	A150	5.75k multi	2.25	2.25
496	A150	7.50k multi	2.75	2.75
a.		Booklet pane, 3 each #495-496	15.00	—
		Complete booklet, 2 #496a	30.00	

Parcel Post Stamp Centenary Type of 2005 06

2007, May 21 Litho. *Perf. 14x13½*

497	A131	100k #Q6	37.50	37.50
a.		Souvenir sheet, #463, 464a, 497	65.00	65.00

Examples of Nos. 463 and 464a in No. 497a are dated "2007."

A151

Contemporary Art — A152

Unnamed paintings by: 3k, Jens Rosing. 8.50k, Anne-Birthe Hove. 10.50k, Linda Riber Sorensen.

2007, May 21

498	A151	3k multi	1.25	1.25
499	A152	8.50k multi	3.50	3.50
500	A152	10.50k multi	4.00	4.00
		Nos. 498-500 (3)	8.75	8.75

Greenlandic Landscape — A153

2007, Oct. 1

501	A153	6.50k multi	2.75	2.75

Science Type of 2006

Designs: 75o, Planting of Greenlandic flag on Tubbiap Queqertaa. 2k, Soapstone bowl and quarry. 10.25k, Cyanobacteria.

Litho. & Engr.

2007, Oct. 1 *Perf. 13¼x13*

502	A145	75o multi	.35	.35
503	A145	2k multi	.85	.85
504	A145	10.25k multi	4.25	4.25
		Nos. 502-504 (3)	5.45	5.45

Ship Pourquoi-Pas? — A154

Paul-Emile Victor (1907-95), Arctic Explorer — A155

2007, Nov. 8 Engr. *Perf. 13½*

505	A154	5.75k multi	2.50	2.50
506	A155	7.50k multi	3.25	3.25
a.		Souvenir sheet, #505-506, + label	5.75	5.75

See France No. 3369.

Christmas — A156

Snowflakes and: 5.75k, Angel. 7.50k, Star.

2007, Nov. 8 Litho. *Perf. 13½x13¾*

507	A156	5.75k multi	2.25	2.25
508	A156	7.50k multi	3.00	3.00

Self-Adhesive
Booklet Stamps
Serpentine Die Cut 12x12¼

509	A156	5.75k multi	2.25	2.25
510	A156	7.50k multi	3.00	3.00
b.		Booklet pane of 12, 6 each #509-510	31.50	

Europa — A157

Envelope half and: 5.75k, Man. 7.50k, Woman.

2008, Jan. 31 Litho. *Perf. 13¾x13½*

511	A157	5.75k multi	2.40	2.40
a.		Sheet of 8 + central label	19.50	19.50
512	A157	7.50k multi	3.00	3.00
a.		Sheet of 8 + central label	24.00	24.00

Booklet Stamps
Self-Adhesive
Serpentine Die Cut 12¼x12

513	A157	5.75k multi	2.40	2.40
514	A157	7.50k multi	3.00	3.00
a.		Booklet pane, 6 each #513-514	32.50	

Contemporary Art — A158

Unnamed paintings by: 5.50k, Ina Rosing. 14.25k, Buuti Pedersen. 30.50k, Aka Hoegh.

2008, Jan. 31 *Perf. 14x13½*

515	A158	5.50k multi	2.25	2.25
516	A158	14.25k multi	5.75	5.75
517	A158	30.50k multi	12.50	12.50
		Nos. 515-517 (3)	20.50	20.50

Mythical Places — A159

Myths of: 7k, Kayaker and river rocks. 8k, Bear of the Lake.

Perf. 13¾x13½

2008, Mar. 27 Litho.

518	A159	7k multi	3.25	3.25
519	A159	8k multi	3.50	3.50
a.		Souvenir sheet, #518-519	6.75	6.75

Wedding of Prince Joachim and Marie Cavallier — A160

2008, May 24 Litho. *Perf. 13½x14*

520	A160	10.25k multi	4.75	4.75

Fossils A161

Designs: 1k, Halkieria evangelista. 20.50k, Ichthyostega stensioei. 25k, Eudimorphodon cromptonellus.

Litho. & Engr.

2008, May 24 *Perf. 13x13¼*

521	A161	1k multi	.45	.45
522	A161	20.50k multi	8.75	8.75
523	A161	25k multi	10.50	10.50
		Nos. 521-523 (3)	19.70	19.70

See Nos. 553-555.

Science Type of 2006

Designs: 6.50k, Scientist, equipment hauler, satellite above Greenland. 10.50k, French station at Scoresbysund. 28k, Danish Arctic station at Nuuk.

Litho. & Engr.

2008, Oct. 20 *Perf. 13¼x13*

524	A145	6.50k multi	2.50	2.50
525	A145	10.50k multi	4.00	4.00
526	A145	28k multi	10.50	10.50
a.		Souvenir sheet, #524-526	17.00	17.00
		Nos. 524-526 (3)	17.00	17.00

International Geophysical Year, 50th anniv. (No. 524); French station at Scoresbysund, 75th anniv. (No. 525); Danish Arctic station at Nuuk, 125th anniv. (No. 526).

Expedition Ship Sofia — A162

Adolf Erik Nordenskiöld (1832-1901), Arctic Explorer — A163

2008, Oct. 20 *Perf. 13¼x13*

527	A162	8.50k multi	3.00	3.00
528	A163	16.25k multi	5.75	5.75
a.		Souvenir sheet, #527-528, + label	8.75	8.75

See Finland No. 1321.

Christmas A164

Designs: 5.75k, Reindeer and house. 7.50k, Christmas tree and houses.

2008, Oct. 20 Litho. *Perf. 13¾x13¼*

529	A164	5.75k multi	2.25	2.25
530	A164	7.50k multi	2.75	2.75

Booklet Stamps
Self-Adhesive
Serpentine Die Cut 12¼x12

531 A164 5.75k multi 2.25 2.25
532 A164 7.50k multi 2.75 2.75
b. Booklet pane of 12, 6 each #531-532 30.00

Fossils Type of 2008

Designs: 2k, Schizoneura carcinoides. 11.50k, Scaphites rosenkrantzi. 22k, Mallotus villosus.

Litho. & Engr.
2009, Jan. 19 ***Perf. 13x13¼***

533 A161 2k multi .70 .70
534 A161 11.50k multi 4.00 4.00
535 A161 22k multi 7.75 7.75
Nos. 533-535 (3) 12.45 12.45

Preservation of Polar Regions and Glaciers — A165

2009, Jan. 19 Litho. ***Perf. 14x13¼***
536 A165 5k multi 2.00 2.00

Europa — A166

Designs: 6.25k, Ursa Major constellation. 8k, Ursa Major constellation and outline of bear.

2009, Jan. 19 ***Perf. 13¼x13¾***
537 A166 6.25k multi 2.25 2.25
a. Sheet of 8 + central label 18.00 18.00
538 A166 8k multi 2.75 2.75
a. Sheet of 8 + central label 22.00 22.00

Booklet Stamps
Self-Adhesive
Serpentine Die Cut 12x12¼

539 A166 6.25k multi 2.25 2.25
540 A166 8k multi 2.75 2.75
a. Booklet pane of 12, 6 each #539-540 30.00

Intl. Year of Astronomy.

Prince Henrik, 75th Birthday — A167

2009, June 11 Litho. ***Perf. 13¼x14***
541 A167 8k multi 3.25 3.25

Self-Governance — A168

2009, June 21 ***Perf. 14x13¼***
542 A168 6.25k multi 2.60 2.60

Matthew Henson (1866-1955), Polar Explorer — A169

2009, June 21 ***Perf. 13¼x13¾***
543 A169 9k multi 3.50 3.50

First Steps, Comic Strip by Nuka K. Godtfredsen — A170

2009, June 21 ***Perf. 14x13¼***
544 A170 15.50k multi 6.00 6.00
a. Souvenir sheet of 1 6.00 6.00

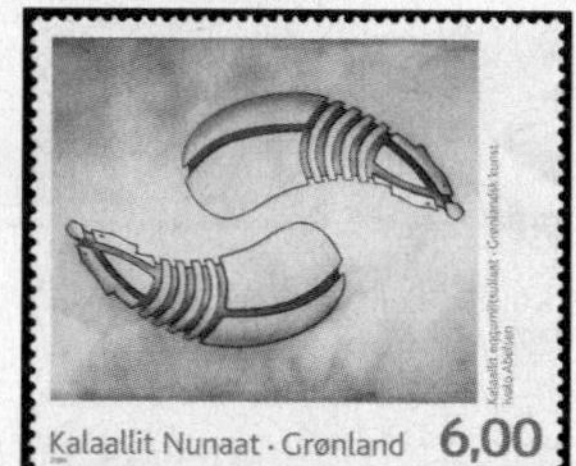

Contemporary Art — A171

Designs: 6k, Two Polar Bears From Above, by Ivalo Abelsen. 18k, Window to the World, by Camilla Nielsen. 33k, Gletscher, by Naja Abelsen.

2009, June 21
545 A171 6k multi 2.25 2.25
546 A171 18k multi 6.75 6.75
547 A171 33k multi 12.50 12.50
Nos. 545-547 (3) 21.50 21.50

Greenlandic Landscape — A172

2009, Sept. 16 Litho. ***Perf. 14x13¼***
548 A172 7k multi 2.75 2.75

North Star Mission Station, Thule, Cent. — A173

2009, Oct. 19 Engr. ***Perf. 13¼x13***
549 A173 15.25k blk & blue 6.25 6.25

Otto Nordenskjold (1869-1928), Arctic Explorer — A174

Litho. & Engr.
2009, Oct. 19 ***Perf. 13¼x13***
Sans-Serif Inscriptions
550 A174 30k multi 12.00 12.00

Souvenir Sheet
Serifed Inscriptions
551 A174 30k multi + label 12.00 12.00

Science Type of 2006

Designs: 1k, Cryolite mine, Ivittuut. 15.50k, Himantolophus groenlandicus. 23.50k, Gold mine, Nalunaq.

2009, Oct. 19 ***Perf. 13¼x14***
552 A145 1k multi .40 .40
553 A145 15.50k multi 6.25 6.25
554 A145 23.50k multi 9.50 9.50
a. Souvenir sheet, #552-554 16.50 16.50
Nos. 552-554 (3) 16.15 16.15

Christmas A175

Star and: 6.25k, Family. 8k, Baby.

2009, Oct. 19 Litho. ***Perf. 13¾x13¼***
555 A175 6.25k multi 2.50 2.50
556 A175 8k multi 3.25 3.25

Booklet Stamps
Self-Adhesive
Serpentine Die Cut 12¼x12

557 A175 6.25k multi 2.50 2.50
558 A175 8k multi 3.25 3.25
b. Booklet pane, 6 each #557-558 35.00

Air Greenland, 50th Anniv. — A176

2010, Jan. 18 Litho. ***Perf. 12½x12¾***
559 A176 16.50k multi 6.25 6.25

Contemporary Art — A177

Designs: 6.50k, Polar Bear, by Maria Panínguak' Kjaerulff. 7.50k, Sun, by Miki Jacobsen, vert. 50k, Greenland Razorbills, by Bolatta Silis-Hoegh.

2010, Jan. 18 ***Perf. 14x13¼, 13¼x14***
560 A177 6.50k multi 2.50 2.50
561 A177 7.50k multi 2.75 2.75
562 A177 50k multi 19.00 19.00
Nos. 560-562 (3) 24.25 24.25

Europa — A178

Designs: 8.50k, Boy reading book. 9.50k, Children reading book.

2010, Jan. 18 ***Perf. 13¾x13¼***
563 A178 8.50k multi 3.25 3.25
a. Sheet of 8 + central label 26.00 26.00
564 A178 9.50k multi 3.50 3.50
a. Sheet of 8 + central label 28.00 28.00

Booklet Stamps
Self-Adhesive
Serpentine Die Cut 12¼x12

565 A178 8.50k multi 3.25 3.25
566 A178 9.50k multi 3.50 3.50
a. Booklet pane of 12, 6 each #565-566 41.00

Intl. Women's Day, Cent. — A179

2010, Mar. 8 Litho. ***Perf. 13¼x14***
567 A179 12.50k multi 4.50 4.50

Life by the Sea — A180

Designs: 7k, Sea ice. 8.50k, Port and sea ice.

2010, Mar. 24 ***Perf. 13¾x13¼***
568 A180 7k multi 2.75 2.75
569 A180 8.50k multi 3.50 3.50
a. Souvenir sheet, #568-569 6.25 6.25

Queen Margrethe II, 70th Birthday — A181

2010, Apr. 16 ***Perf. 13¼x14***
570 A181 35k multi 12.00 12.00

Flag of Greenland, 25th Anniv. — A182

2010, May 1
571 A182 7k multi 2.50 2.50

Buuarsikkut, Comic Strip by Robert Holmene — A183

2010, May 1 ***Perf. 14x13¼***
572 A183 23.50k multi 8.25 8.25
a. Souvenir sheet of 1 8.25 8.25

Thule Trading Station, Cent. — A184

2010, Oct. 18 Engr. *Perf. 12¼x12½*

573 A184 25k blk & blue 9.50 9.50

Hans Sakaeus (c. 1797-1819), Interpreter for Explorer John Ross — A185

Ross Expedition Ships Isabella and Alexander — A186

2010, Oct. 18 *Perf. 12½x12*

574 A185 25o pur & bl blk .25 .25
575 A186 32k pur & bl blk 12.00 12.00
a. Souvenir sheet, #574-575, + label 12.50 12.50

Mining in Greenland A187

Designs: 50o, King Frederik VII's copper mine. 26.50k, Ivituut cryolite mine.

Die Cut Perf. 13x13¼

2010, Oct. 18 Litho.

Self-Adhesive

576 A187 50o multi .25 .25
577 A187 26.50k multi 10.00 10.00

See Nos. 601-602, 616-617, 634-635, 661-662, 688-689.

Christmas A188

Santa Claus and: 7k, Two children. 8.50k, One child.

2010, Oct. 18 *Perf. 13¾x13¼*

578 A188 7k multi 2.75 2.75
579 A188 8.50k multi 3.25 3.25

Booklet Stamps
Self-Adhesive

Serpentine Die Cut 12¼x12

580 A188 7k multi 2.75 2.75
581 A188 8.50k multi 3.25 3.25
b. Booklet pane of 12, 6 each #580-581 36.00

Herbs A189

Designs: 13.50k, Sorbus groenlandica. 25k, Vaccinium vitis-idaea.

2011, Jan. 17 *Perf. 13*

582 A189 13.50k multi 5.00 5.00
583 A189 25k multi 9.25 9.25

See Nos. 608-609.

Mail Delivery Man in Kamik A190

Atuagagdliutit Newspaper, 150th Anniv. — A191

Greenland Connect Submarine Cable, 2nd Anniv. A192

2011, Jan. 17 *Perf. 13*

584 A190 2k multi .75 .75
a. Perf. 12¾x12½ .75 .75
585 A191 7.50k multi 2.75 2.75
a. Perf. 12¾x12½ 2.75 2.75
586 A192 46.50k multi 17.00 17.00
a. Perf. 12¾x12½ 17.00 17.00
b. Souvenir sheet of 3, #584a, 585a, 586a 20.50 20.50
Nos. 584-586 (3) 20.50 20.50

Communications in Greenland.

Europa — A193

Trees in: 9k, Winter. 10k, Summer.

2011, Jan. 17 *Perf. 12¾x13*

587 A193 9k multi 3.25 3.25
a. Sheet of 8 + central label 26.00 26.00
588 A193 10k multi 3.75 3.75
a. Sheet of 8 + central label 30.00 30.00

Booklet Stamps
Self-Adhesive

Serpentine Die Cut 13x13¼

589 A193 9k multi 3.25 3.25
590 A193 10k multi 3.75 3.75
b. Booklet pane of 12, 6 each #589-590 42.00

Intl. Year of Forests.

Civil Aircraft — A194

Designs: 8k, Consolidated PBY-5A Catalina. 17.50k, De Havilland DHC-3 Otter.

2011, May 9 Engr. *Perf. 12½x12*

591 A194 8k multi 3.00 3.00
592 A194 17.50k multi 6.75 6.75

See Nos. 624-626, 653-654, 678, 695-697, 727-728.

Queen Margrethe II — A195

2011, May 9 Engr. *Perf. 13*

593 A195 50o claret 1.75 1.75
594 A195 1k blue green 3.75 3.75

Kaassassuk, Comic Strip by Christian Fleischer Rex — A196

2011, May 9 Litho. *Perf. 12¾x12½*

595 A196 20k multi 8.00 8.00
a. Souvenir sheet of 1 8.00 8.00

Commonwealth of the Realm Pause, by Julie Edel Hardenberg — A197

Painting by Naja Rosing-Asvid — A198

Painting by Anne-Lise Lovstrom — A199

2011, May 9

596 A197 3k multi 1.25 1.25
597 A198 7k multi 2.75 2.75
598 A199 34k multi 13.00 13.00
Nos. 596-598 (3) 17.00 17.00

Naomi Uemura (1941-84), Adventurer — A200

2011, July 28 Engr. *Perf. 12½x12*

599 A200 36.50k multi 15.00 15.00
a. Souvenir sheet of 1, perf. 12¾x12½ 15.00 15.00

Uemura was, in 1978, the first man to cross Greenland from north to south.

Dogsleds Near Iceberg — A201

2011, Sept. 28 Litho. *Perf. 12¾*

600 A201 8k multi 3.00 3.00

Mining Type of 2010

Designs: 75o, Shaft tower, Josva's copper mine. 28k, Miners and equipment, Qaarsuarsuk coal mine.

2011, Oct. 17 *Die Cut Perf. 13x13¼*

Self-Adhesive

601 A187 75o multi .30 .30
602 A187 28k multi 10.50 10.50

Christmas — A202

Girls: 7.50k, Looking at Christmas star through window. 9k, With dogsled carrying gifts, horiz.

2011, Oct. 17 *Perf. 12½x13*

603 A202 7.50k multi 2.75 2.75

Perf. 13x12½

604 A202 9k multi 3.50 3.50

Booklet Stamps
Self-Adhesive

Serpentine Die Cut 13x13¼

605 A202 7.50k multi 2.75 2.75

Serpentine Die Cut 13¼x13

606 A202 9k multi 3.50 3.50
a. Booklet pane of 12, 6 each #605-606 37.50

Reign of Queen Margrethe II, 40th Anniv. — A203

Litho. & Engr.

2012, Jan. 4 *Perf. 13¼*

607 A203 26.50k multi 9.50 9.50
a. Souvenir sheet of 1 9.50 9.50

Herbs Type of 2011

Designs: 14.50k, Vaccinium uliginosum. 18.50k, Ledum groenlandicum.

2012, Jan. 16 Litho. *Perf. 14x13¼*

608 A189 14.50k multi 5.25 5.25
609 A189 18.50k multi 6.50 6.50

Knud Rasmussen Folk High School, Sisimiut, 50th Anniv. — A204

2012, Jan. 16

610 A204 21k multi 7.50 7.50

Painting by Jessie Kleemann — A205

Iceberg by Frederik "Kunngi" Kristensen — A206

Map of Denmark With Ice Sheet, by Inuk Silis Hoegh — A207

2012, Jan. 16

611 A205 8.50k multi 3.00 3.00
612 A206 9.50k multi 3.50 3.50
613 A207 38.50k multi 14.00 14.00
a. Souvenir sheet of 1 14.00 14.00
Nos. 611-613 (3) 20.50 20.50

Marine Life — A208

Iceberg and: 8k, Seal. 9.50k, Whale.

2012, Mar. 21 ***Perf. 13¾x13¼***

614 A208 8k multi 3.00 3.00
615 A208 9.50k multi 3.50 3.50
a. Souvenir sheet of 2, #614-615 6.50 6.50

Mining Type of 2010

Designs: 25o, Eqalussuit graphite mine. 14.50k, Amitsoq graphite mine.

2012, May 7 ***Die Cut Perf. 13x13¼***

Self-Adhesive

616 A187 25o multi .25 .25
617 A187 14.50k multi 5.00 5.00

Agriculture A209

Designs: 75o, Field of vegetables. 49k, Cattle.

2012, May 7 ***Perf. 12¾x12½***

618 A209 75o multi .25 .25
619 A209 49k multi 17.50 17.50

Europa A210

Designs: 9.50k, Aurora Borealis. 10.50k, Ship and sea ice.

2012, May 7 ***Perf. 14x13½***

620 A210 9.50k multi 3.25 3.25
a. Sheet of 8 + central label 26.00 26.00
621 A210 10.50k multi 3.50 3.50
a. Sheet of 8 + central label 28.00 28.00

Booklet Stamps
Self-Adhesive

Serpentine Die Cut 13x12¾

622 A210 9.50k multi 3.25 3.25
623 A210 10.50k multi 3.50 3.50
a. Booklet pane of 12, 6 each #622-623 41.00

Civil Aircraft Type of 2011

Designs: 7.50k, Douglas DC-4. 28k, Sikorsky S61N helicopter. 36k, Bell 206 Jet Ranger helicopter.

Litho. & Engr.

2012, Oct. 22 ***Perf. 13***

624 A194 7.50k multi 2.60 2.60
625 A194 28k multi 9.75 9.75
626 A194 36k multi 12.50 12.50
Nos. 624-626 (3) 24.85 24.85

Queen Margrethe II — A211

Litho. & Engr.

2012, Oct. 22 ***Perf. 13¼x13***

627 A211 50o red & blue .25 .25
628 A211 1k green & blue .35 .35

See Nos. 655, 698-699, 729-730.

Hans Hendrik (Suersaq) (1834-89), Polar Explorer — A212

2012, Oct. 22 ***Perf. 13***

629 A212 29.50k mar & blk 10.00 10.00
a. Souvenir sheet of 1 10.00 10.00

Christmas — A213

Heads of Inuit girls: 8k, On Christmas trees. 9.50k, In circles, evergreen branches, flags of Greenland, horiz.

2012, Oct. 22 Litho. ***Perf. 13¼x13¾***

630 A213 8k multi 2.75 2.75

Perf. 13¾x13¼

631 A213 9.50k multi 3.25 3.25

Booklet Stamps
Self-Adhesive

Serpentine Die Cut 13x12½

632 A213 8k multi 2.75 2.75

Serpentine Die Cut 12½x13

633 A213 9.50k multi 3.25 3.25
a. Booklet pane of 12, 6 each #632-633 36.00

Mining Type of 2010

Designs: 38k, Coal mine, Qullissat. 49k, Marble quarry, Maarmorilik.

Die Cut Perf. 13¼x13½

2013, Jan. 14

Self-Adhesive

634 A187 38k multi 14.00 14.00
635 A187 49k multi 18.00 18.00

Contemporary Art — A214

Designs: 50o, Sculpture by Isle Hessner. 2k, Painting of iceberg by Niels "Mo" Motzfeldt. 40.50k, Painting by Kristian Olsen aaju.

2013, Jan. 14 ***Perf. 13¼***

636 A214 50o multi .25 .25
637 A214 2k multi .75 .75
638 A214 40.50k multi 15.00 15.00
Nos. 636-638 (3) 16.00 16.00

Europa A215

Postal conveyance: 10.50k, Dog sled. 11.50k, Truck, van and scooter.

2013, Jan. 14 ***Perf. 12½***

639 A215 10.50k multi 4.00 4.00
a. Miniature sheet of 9 36.00 36.00
640 A215 11.50k multi 4.25 4.25
a. Miniature sheet of 9 39.00 39.00

Booklet Stamps
Self-Adhesive

Serpentine Die Cut 13¼x13½

641 A215 10.50k multi 4.00 4.00
642 A215 11.50k multi 4.25 4.25
a. Booklet pane of 12, 6 each #641-642 50.00

Uummannaq, 250th Anniv. — A216

2013, June 11 ***Perf. 13¼x13***

643 A216 9k multi 3.25 3.25

Musk Ox A217

2013, June 11

644 A217 11.50k multi 4.25 4.25

Whale A218

2013, June 11 ***Perf. 12½***

645 A218 16k multi 5.75 5.75

Aasiaat, 250th anniv.

Polar Bear A219

2013, June 11 ***Perf. 13¼***

646 A219 19.50k multi 7.00 7.00
a. Souvenir sheet of 1 7.00 7.00

See Israel No. 1987.

Herbs — A220

Designs: 8.50k, Fucus vesiculosus. 28k, Juniperus communis var. saxatalis, horiz.

2013, June 11 ***Perf. 12½***

647 A220 8.50k multi 3.00 3.00
648 A220 28k multi 10.00 10.00

Agriculture A221

Designs: 20k, Sheep in meadow. 29.50k, Farm machinery in field.

2013, June 11 ***Perf. 13x12½***

649 A221 20k multi 7.25 7.25
650 A221 29.50k multi 11.00 11.00

Greenland Post Office, 75th Anniv. — A222

Litho. & Engr.

2013, Sept. 17 ***Perf. 14x13½***

651 A222 20k red & blk 7.25 7.25
a. Souvenir sheet of 1 7.25 7.25

Sheet margin of No. 651a contains and imperforate reproduction of Greenland No. 5 that is is invalid for postage.

Limited quantities of imperforate examples of No. 651a were sold at a stamp show and later given as gifts to standing order customers. Value, $32.50

Fishermen on Dock at Nordafar Fishery, Foroyinghavn, Greenland — A223

Perf. 13½x13¾

2013, Sept. 23 Litho. & Engr.

652 A223 22.50k multi 8.25 8.25

a. Souvenir sheet of 1 + 2 labels 8.25 8.25

See Faroe Islands No. 609.

Civil Aircraft Type of 2011

Designs: 1k, Sikorsky S58ET helicopter. 28k, De Havilland Canada DHC-6 Twin Otter.

Perf. 14¼x13¾

2013, Oct. 21 Litho. & Engr.

653 A194 1k multi .35 .35

654 A194 28k multi 10.00 10.00

Queen Margrethe II Type of 2012

Litho. & Engr.

2013, Oct. 21 ***Perf. 13¼x13***

Size: 26x36mm

655 A211 10k dk bl & blue 3.75 3.75

Carl Petersen (1813-80), Polar Explorer — A224

Perf. 14¼x13¾

2013, Oct. 21 Litho. & Engr.

656 A224 31.50k multi 11.50 11.50

a. Souvenir sheet of 1 11.50 11.50

Christmas A225

Christmas decorations with polar bear and: 9k, Candle. 10.50k, Lace, folded-paper stars.

2013, Oct. 21 Litho. ***Perf. 13x12½***

657 A225 9k multi 3.25 3.25

658 A225 10.50k multi 3.75 3.75

Booklet Stamps
Self-Adhesive

Serpentine Die Cut 13½x13¾

659 A225 9k multi 3.25 3.25

660 A225 10.50k multi 3.75 3.75

a. Booklet pane of 12, 6 each #659-660 42.00

Mining Type of 2010

Designs: 10k, Mine cars at lead mine, Mesters Vig. 56k, Cableway at Black Angel lead and zinc mine, Maarmorilik.

Die Cut Perf. 13¼x13½

2014, Jan. 20 Litho.

Self-Adhesive

661 A187 10k multi 3.75 3.75

662 A187 56k multi 20.50 20.50

Rhodiola Flowers A226

2014, Jan. 20 Litho. ***Perf. 12½***

663 A226 13k multi 4.75 4.75

A227

Illustrations of Song Lyrics by Camilla Nielsen — A228

2014, Jan. 20 Litho. ***Perf. 12½***

664 A227 5k multi 1.90 1.90

665 A228 12.50k multi 4.50 4.50

Europa — A229

Designs; 11.50k, Man with drum. 13k, Musicians with violin and accordion, horiz.

2014, Jan. 20 Litho. ***Perf. 12½***

666 A229 11.50k multi 4.25 4.25

a. Miniature sheet of 9 39.00 39.00

667 A229 13k multi 4.75 4.75

a. Miniature sheet of 9 43.00 43.00

Booklet Stamps
Self-Adhesive

Serpentine Die Cut 13¾

668 A229 11.50k multi 4.25 4.25

669 A229 13k multi 4.75 4.75

a. Booklet pane of 12, 6 each #668-669 54.00

Maritime Heritage — A230

Designs: 10k, People looking at boats at sea. 11.50k, Ship at night.

2014, Mar. 17 Litho. ***Perf. 12½***

670 A230 10k multi 3.75 3.75

671 A230 11.50k multi 4.25 4.25

a. Souvenir sheet of 2, #670-671 8.00 8.00

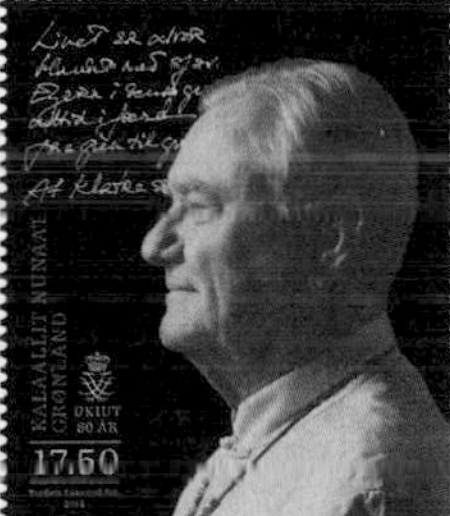

Prince Henrik, 80th Birthday A231

Perf. 13½x13¼

2014, June 11 Litho.

672 A231 17.50k multi 6.50 6.50

a. Souvenir sheet of 1 6.50 6.50

Sheep Farming — A232

Designs: 21.50k, Feeding of sheep in barn. 31.50k, Sheep mustering.

2014, June 11 Litho. ***Perf. 12½***

673 A232 21.50k multi 8.00 8.00

674 A232 31.50k multi 11.50 11.50

Contemporary Art — A233

Designs: 3k, Painting of face by Sissi Moller. 24k, Painting of snow hut by Lisa Kreutzmann, horiz. 30.50k, Painting by Isak Brandt, horiz.

2014, June 11 Litho. ***Perf. 13¼***

675 A233 3k multi 1.10 1.10

676 A233 24k multi 8.75 8.75

677 A233 30.50k multi 11.50 11.50

Nos. 675-677 (3) 21.35 21.35

Civil Aviation Type of 2011

Litho. & Engr.

2014, Oct. 20 ***Perf. 13¼***

678 A194 41k Bell 212 helicopter 14.00 14.00

Polar Bear and Map of Greenland A234

2014, Oct. 20 Litho. ***Perf. 14½***

679 A234 21.50k multi 7.25 7.25

a. Souvenir sheet of 1 + label 7.25 7.25

Value for No. 679 is for stamp with surrounding selvage. See New Zealand Ross Dependency No. L138a.

Hunter's Life A235

Hunters and prey from: 50ö, Northern Greenland. 45k, Southern Greenland.

2014, Oct. 20 Litho. ***Perf. 12½***

680 A235 50o multi .25 .25

681 A235 45k multi 15.00 15.00

Denmark Expedition of Greenland of 1906-08 — A236

Designs: 9k, Jorgen Bronlund (1877-1907), Niels Peter Hoeg Hagen (1877-1907), explorers, and dog team. 30.50k, Ludvig Mylius-Erichsen (1872-1907), expedition leader, and ship.

Litho. & Engr.

2014, Oct. 20 ***Perf. 13¼***

682 A236 9k multi 3.00 3.00

683 A236 30.50k multi 10.50 10.50

a. Souvenir sheet of 2, #682-683 13.50 13.50

Christmas A237

Christmas tree and: 10k, Musicians playing instruments. 11.50k, Choir.

2014, Oct. 20 Litho. ***Perf. 12½***

684 A237 10k multi 3.50 3.50

685 A237 11.50k multi 4.00 4.00

Booklet Stamps
Self-Adhesive

Serpentine Die Cut 13½x13¼

686 A237 10k multi 3.50 3.50

687 A237 11.50k multi 4.00 4.00

a. Booklet pane of 12, 6 each #686-687 45.00

Mining Type of 2010

Designs: 3k, Nalunaq Gold Mine, Nanortalik. 18.50k, Seqi Olivine Mine, Fiskefjord.

Die Cut Perf. 13¼x13½

2015, Jan. 19 Litho.

Self-Adhesive

688 A187 3k multi .95 .95

689 A187 18.50k multi 5.75 5.75

Hunter's Life — A238

Various hunters and prey.

2015, Jan. 19 Litho. ***Perf. 12½***

690 A238 11k multi 3.50 3.50

691 A238 19k multi 5.75 5.75

A239

Illustrations of Song Lyrics by Camilla Nielsen — A240

2015, Jan. 19 Litho. ***Perf. 12½***

692 A239 50o multi .25 .25

693 A240 49k multi 15.00 15.00

Queen Margrethe II, 75th Birthday — A241

2015, Apr. 16 Litho. ***Perf. 12½***

694 A241 23.50k multi 7.25 7.25

Civil Aircraft Type of 2011

Designs: 1k, DeHavilland Canada DHC7. 34.50k, Boeing B767-383ER. 45k, Boeing B727-100.

Litho. & Engr.

2015, May 13 *Perf. 13¼*

695 A194 1k multi .30 .30
696 A194 34.50k multi 10.50 10.50
697 A194 45k multi 13.50 13.50
Nos. 695-697 (3) 24.30 24.30

Queen Margrethe II Type of 2012

Litho. & Engr.

2015, May 13 *Perf. 13¼x13*

Size: 26x36mm

698 A211 5k purple & blue 1.50 1.50
699 A211 20k brown & blue 6.00 6.00

Nuuk Gay Pride — A242

2015, May 13 **Litho.** *Perf. 12½*

700 A242 11k multi 3.50 3.50

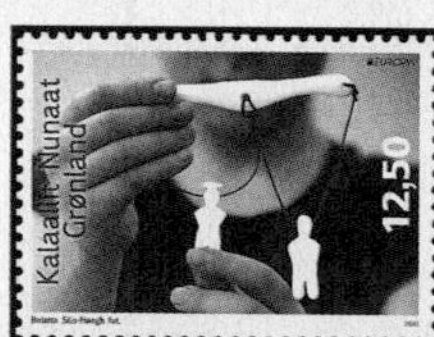

Europa A243

Toys: 12.50k, String puzzle. 14k, Wooden dolls.

2015, May 13 **Litho.** *Perf. 12½*

701 A243 12.50k multi 3.25 3.25
a. Miniature sheet of 9 29.50 29.50
702 A243 14k multi 3.75 3.75
a. Miniature sheet of 9 34.00 34.00

Booklet Stamps
Self-Adhesive

Serpentine Die Cut 13¼x13½

703 A243 12.50k multi 3.75 3.75
704 A243 14k multi 4.25 4.25
a. Booklet pane of 12, 6 each #703-704 48.00

Renewable Energy — A244

Designs: 13.50k, Sun and solar panel. 37.50k, Water turbine and high-tension wires.

2015, Oct. 19 **Litho.** *Perf. 12½*

705 A244 13.50k multi 4.00 4.00
706 A244 37.50k multi 11.00 11.00
a. Souvenir sheet of 2, #705-706 15.00 15.00

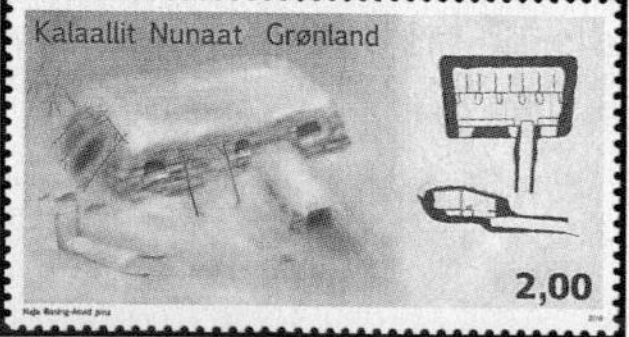

Architecture — A245

Designs: 2k, Winter house. 10k, Modern buildings in Nuuk and Sisimiut. 26k, High-rise apartment buildings, older apartment buildings, houses. 33.50k, Summer tent.

2015, Oct. 19 **Litho.** *Perf. 13¼*

707 A245 2k multi .60 .60
708 A245 10k multi 3.00 3.00
709 A245 26k multi 7.75 7.75
a. Souvenir sheet of 2, #708-709 11.00 11.00
710 A245 33.50k multi 10.00 10.00
a. Souvenir sheet of 2, #707, 710 11.00 11.00
Nos. 707-710 (4) 21.35 21.35

Christmas A246

Designs: 11k, Polar bear and cubs. 12.50k, Greenlandic family.

2015, Oct. 19 **Litho.** *Perf. 12½*

711 A246 11k multi 3.25 3.25
712 A246 12.50k multi 3.75 3.75

Booklet Stamps
Self-Adhesive

Serpentine Die Cut 13½x13¾

713 A246 11k multi 3.25 3.25
714 A246 12.50k multi 3.75 3.75
a. Booklet pane of 12, 6 each #713-714 42.00

Dog Sled in Winter A247

Hikers in Summer A248

2016, Jan. 18 **Litho.** *Perf. 12½*

715 A247 13k multi 3.00 3.00
716 A248 27k multi 6.50 6.50

Traditional Women's Clothing — A249

Woman from: 10.50k, Northern Greenland. 12k, Western Greenland. 13.50k, Eastern Greenland. 48.50k, Southern Greenland.

2016, Jan. 18 **Litho.** *Perf. 12½*

717 A249 10.50k multi 2.50 2.50
718 A249 12k multi 2.75 2.75
719 A249 13.50k multi 3.25 3.25
720 A249 48.50k multi 11.50 11.50
Nos. 717-720 (4) 20.00 20.00

Booklet Stamps
Self-Adhesive

Serpentine Die Cut 13¾x13¼

721 A249 10.50k multi 2.50 2.50
722 A249 12k multi 2.75 2.75
723 A249 13.50k multi 3.25 3.25
724 A249 48.50k multi 11.50 11.50
a. Booklet pane of 8, 2 each #721-724 40.00
Nos. 721-724 (4) 20.00 20.00

Greenlandic Foods — A250

Designs: 12k, Capelin. 13.50k, Whale skin.

2016, Mar. 21 **Litho.** *Perf. 12½*

725 A250 12k multi 3.00 3.00
a. Perf. 13x13¼ 3.00 3.00
726 A250 13.50k multi 3.50 3.50
a. Perf. 13x13¼ 3.50 3.50
b. Souvenir sheet of 2, #725a, 726a, + label 6.50 6.50

Civil Aircraft Type of 2011

Designs: 15k, Airbus 330-200. 24.50k, De Havilland DHC8-200 (Dash-8).

Litho. & Engr.

2016, May 12 *Perf. 13¼*

727 A194 15k multi 4.00 4.00
728 A194 24.50k multi 7.00 7.00

Queen Margrethe II Type of 2012

Litho. & Engr.

2016, May 12 *Perf. 13¼x13*

Size: 26x36mm

729 A211 2k blue .60 .60
730 A211 50k pur & bl 13.50 13.50

Sports A251

Designs: 75o, Arctic Circle Race. 25.50k, Alpine skier. 39k, Kayak race.

2016, May 12 **Litho.** *Perf. 12½*

731 A251 75o multi .25 .25
a. Perf. 13x13¼ .25 .25
732 A251 25.50k multi 6.25 6.25
a. Perf. 13x13¼ 6.25 6.25
733 A251 39k multi 9.50 9.50
a. Perf. 13x13¼ 9.50 9.50
b. Souvenir sheet of 3, #731a, 732a, 733a 16.00 16.00
Nos. 731-733 (3) 16.00 16.00

See Nos. 746-748, 772-774.

Crown Prince Frederik and His Family — A252

2016, Oct. 17 **Litho.** *Perf. 13*

734 A252 20.50k multi 6.25 6.25
a. Souvenir sheet of 1 6.25 6.25

Greenland in World War II — A253

Designs: 25o, National Assembly members. 36k, Family seated around table. 36.50k, Children holding fruit, ship, people carrying sacks.

Litho. & Engr.

2016, Oct. 17 *Perf. 13¼*

735 A253 25o multi .25 .25
736 A253 36k multi 11.00 11.00
737 A253 36.50k multi 11.00 11.00
Nos. 735-737 (3) 22.25 22.25

See Nos. 749, 792-793.

Zackenberg Research Station A254

Designs: 11.50k, Greenlandic wildlife. 14k, Scientists and research equipment.

2016, Oct. 17 **Litho.** *Perf. 12½*

738 A254 11.50k multi 3.50 3.50
a. Miniature sheet of 9 32.00 32.00
739 A254 14k multi 4.25 4.25
a. Miniature sheet of 9 39.00 39.00

Self-Adhesive

Die Cut Perf. 13½x13¼

740 A254 11.50k multi 3.50 3.50
741 A254 14k multi 4.25 4.25

Christmas — A255

Designs: 12k, Candles and iceberg. 13.50k, Christmas tree, star and sofa.

2016, Oct. 17 **Litho.** *Perf. 12½x13*

742 A255 12k multi 3.75 3.75
743 A255 13.50k multi 4.00 4.00

Booklet Stamps
Self-Adhesive

Serpentine Die Cut 13¾x13½

744 A255 12k multi 3.75 3.75
745 A255 13.50k multi 4.00 4.00
a. Booklet pane of 12, 6 each #744-745 46.50

Sports Type of 2016

Designs: 16k, National Dogsled Championships. 19.50k, Kang-Nu Race. 22k, Town relay race.

2017, Jan. 23 **Litho.** *Perf. 12½*

746 A251 16k multi 4.75 4.75
a. Perf. 13x13¼ 4.75 4.75
747 A251 19.50k multi 5.75 5.75
a. Perf. 13x13¼ 5.75 5.75
748 A251 22k multi 6.50 6.50
a. Perf. 13x13¼ 6.50 6.50
b. Souvenir sheet of 3, #746a-748a 17.00 17.00
Nos. 746-748 (3) 17.00 17.00

Greenland in World War II Type of 2016

Design: 36.50k, Cryolite in train cars awaiting shipping

Litho. & Engr.

2017, Jan. 23 *Perf. 13¼*

749 A253 36.50k multi 10.50 10.50

Music A256

Designs: 1k, Drum singing. 24.50k, Choral singing. 27k, Accordion player.

2017, Jan. 23 **Litho.** *Perf. 13x13¼*

750 A256 1k multi .30 .30
751 A256 24.50k multi 7.25 7.25
752 A256 27k multi 7.75 7.75
Nos. 750-752 (3) 15.30 15.30

Sealskin Coat — A257

2017, May 15 **Litho.** *Perf. 12½*

753 A257 15k multi 4.50 4.50

Queen Margrethe II and Prince Henrik, 50th Wedding Anniv. A258

2017, May 15 Litho. *Perf. 13½*

754 A258 50k multi 15.00 15.00
a. Souvenir sheet of 1 15.00 15.00

See Denmark No. 1777, Faroe Islands No. 686.

Flags at Abandoned Gronnedal Naval Base — A259

Barrels at Abandoned Ikateq Air Base A260

2017, May 15 Litho. *Perf. 12½*

755 A259 5k multi 1.50 1.50
756 A260 14k multi 4.25 4.25

Illustrations from Greenlandic Banknotes — A261

Designs: No. 757, Birds from 1911 25-ore banknote. No. 758, Seal from 1911 50-ore banknote (53x35mm).
No. 758A, As #757, but with partial letters from banknote above and below circle. No. 758B, As #758, but with partial letters from banknote above and below crest.

Litho. & Engr.

2017, May 17 *Perf. 13*

757 A261 20k multi 6.00 6.00
758 A261 39k multi 12.00 12.00

Souvenir Sheets

758A A261 20k multi 6.00 6.00
758B A261 39k multi 12.00 12.00

See Nos. 784-787.

Europa A262

Various paintings of icebergs by Buuti Pedersen.

2017, May 15 Litho. *Perf. 12½*

759 A262 15k multi 4.50 4.50
a. Miniature sheet of 9 41.00 41.00
760 A262 16k multi 5.00 5.00
a. Miniature sheet of 9 45.00 45.00

Booklet Stamps
Self-Adhesive

Serpentine Die Cut 13¼x13¾

761 A262 15k multi 4.50 4.50
762 A262 16k multi 5.00 5.00
a. Booklet pane of 12, 6 each #761-762 57.00

Birds of the Antarctic and Arctic A263

Designs: 10.50k, Sterna paradisaea. 27k, Haliaeetus albicilla.

Litho. & Engr.

2017, Oct. 27 *Perf. 13*

Stamps With White Frames

763 A263 10.50k multi 3.50 3.50
764 A263 27k multi 8.50 8.50

Souvenir Sheet
Stamps Without White Frames

765 Sheet of 2 + label 12.00 12.00
a. A263 10.50k multi 3.50 3.50
b. A263 27k multi 8.50 8.50

Dipolmatic relations bewteen Greenland and French Southern and Antarctic Territories.
See French Southern and Antarctic Territories Nos. 571-573.

Weather Balloon — A264

Laundry on Clothesline A265

Die Cut Perf. 13½

2017, Oct. 27 Litho.

Self-Adhesive

766 A264 2k multi .65 .65
767 A265 11.50k multi 3.75 3.75

A266

Christmas A267

2017, Oct. 27 Litho. *Perf. 13¼x12½*

768 A266 13k multi 4.25 4.25
769 A267 15k multi 4.75 4.75

Booklet Stamps
Self-Adhesive

Serpentine Die Cut 13½x13¾

770 A266 13k multi 4.25 4.25
771 A267 15k multi 4.75 4.75
a. Booklet pane of 12, 6 each #770-771 54.00

Sports Type of 2016

Inuit and Dene games: 50o, Arm pull. 14.50k, Two foot high kick. 28.50k, Pole push.

2018, Jan. 22 Litho. *Perf. 12½*

772 A251 50o multi .25 .25
a. Perf. 13x13¼ .25 .25
773 A251 14.50k multi 5.00 5.00
a. Perf. 13x13¼ 5.00 5.00
774 A251 28.50k multi 9.50 9.50
a. Perf. 13x13¼ 9.50 9.50
b. Souvenir sheet of 3, #772a, 773a, 774a 15.00 15.00
Nos. 772-774 (3) 14.75 14.75

Abandoned Camp Century A268

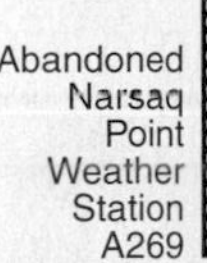

Abandoned Narsaq Point Weather Station A269

2018, Jan. 22 Litho. *Perf. 12½*

775 A268 11k multi 3.75 3.75
776 A269 40.50k multi 13.50 13.50

Polar Bear A270

Ice — A271

Die Cut Perf. 13½x13¼

2018, Jan. 22 Litho.

Self-Adhesive

777 A270 20k multi 6.75 6.75
778 A271 23.50k multi 8.00 8.00

Europa A272

Designs: 16k, Bridge in Qaqortok. 17k, Ice bridge.

2018, Jan. 22 Litho. *Perf. 12½*

779 A272 16k multi 5.50 5.50
a. Miniature sheet of 9 50.00 50.00
780 A272 17k multi 5.75 5.75
a. Miniature sheet of 9 52.00 52.00

Booklet Stamps
Self-Adhesive

Serpentine Die Cut 13¼x13½

781 A272 16k multi 5.50 5.50
782 A272 17k multi 5.75 5.75
a. Booklet pane of 12, 6 each #781-782 67.50

Mountains — A273

2018, May 25 Litho. *Perf. 12½*

783 A273 16k multi 5.00 5.00

SEPAC.

Illustrations From Greenlandic Banknotes Type of 2017

Designs: No. 784, Caribou from 1911 1-krone banknote (53x35mm). No. 785, Polar bear from 1911 5-krone banknote (45x35mm).
No. 786, As #784, but with partial letters from banknote at UL and UR. No. 787, As #785, but with partial lettering from banknote around circle.

Perf. 13¾ (38k), 13½x13¼ (40k)

2018, May 25 Litho. & Engr.

784 A261 38k multi 12.00 12.00
785 A261 40k multi 12.50 12.50

Souvenir Sheets

786 A261 38k multi 12.00 12.00
787 A261 40k multi 12.50 12.50

Fish A274

Designs: 12k, Two mackerel. 16k, Three herring.

2018, May 25 Litho. *Perf. 12¼x12½*

Stamps With Pale Buff Background

788 A274 12k multi 3.75 3.75
789 A274 16k multi 5.00 5.00

Souvenir Sheet
Stamps with Pale Blue Background

Perf. 12½x13

790 Sheet of 2 8.75 8.75
a. A274 12k multi 3.75 3.75
b. A274 16k multi 5.00 5.00

Crown Prince Frederik, 50th Birthday A275

2018, May 26 Litho. *Perf. 12½*

791 A275 50k multi 16.00 16.00
a. Souvenir sheet of 1, perf. 13x13¼ 16.00 16.00

Sheet margin on No. 791a is embossed.

Greenland In World War II Type of 2016

Designs: 5k, Military airplanes over airport. 20.50k, Men and women dancing, phonograph and record, advertisements from Sears Mail Order Catalog.

Perf. 14¼x13¾

2018, Oct. 22 Litho. & Engr.

792 A253 5k multi 1.60 1.60
793 A253 20.50k multi 6.25 6.25

Kujataa UNESCO World Heritage Site — A276

2018, Oct. 22 Litho. *Perf. 13x13¼*

794 A276 17k multi 5.25 5.25

Laarseeraw Svendsen (1926-75), Singer — A277

Jens Hendriksen (1928-2001), Musician — A278

First Record Album by Greenlanic Performers — A279

2018, Oct. 22 Litho. *Perf. 13¼*

795	A277	3k multi	.95	.95
796	A278	10k multi	3.00	3.00
797	A279	25.50k multi	7.75	7.75
		Nos. 795-797 (3)	11.70	11.70

A280

Christmas A281

2018, Oct. 22 Litho. *Perf. 12½*

798	A280	14k multi	4.25	4.25
799	A281	16k multi	5.00	5.00

Booklet Stamps
Self-Adhesive

Serpentine Die Cut 13¼x13½

800	A280	14k multi	4.25	4.25
801	A281	16k multi	5.00	5.00
a.		Booklet pane of 12, 6 each #800-801	56.00	

No. 798 is impregnated with a cinnamon scent. No. 799 is impregnated with a pine scent.

SEMI-POSTAL STAMPS

Catalogue values for unused stamps in this section are for Never Hinged items.

No. 35 Surcharged in Red

1958, May 22 Engr. *Perf. 13*

B1 A7 30o + 10o on 50o 4.50 1.90

The surtax was for the campaign against tuberculosis in Greenland.

No. 32 Surcharged

1959, Feb. 23 Unwmk.

B2 A6 30o + 10o on 25o 4.75 4.75

The surtax was for the benefit of the Greenland Fund.

Two Greenland Boys in Round Tower — SP1

1968, Sept. 12 Engr. *Perf. 13*

B3 SP1 60o + 10o dark red 1.00 *1.50*

Surtax for child welfare work in Greenland.

Hans Egede Explaining Bible to Natives — SP2

1971, July 3 Engr. *Perf. 13*

B4 SP2 60o + 10o red brown 2.75 2.75

See footnote after No. 77.

Frederik IX, "Dannebrog" off Umanak — SP3

1972, Apr. 20

B5 SP3 60o + 10o dull red 1.50 1.50

King Frederik IX (1899-1972). The surtax was for humanitarian and charitable purposes.

Heimaey Town and Volcano — SP4

1973, Oct. 18 Engr. *Perf. 13*

B6 SP4 70o + 20o blue & red 1.75 1.75

The surtax was for the victims of the eruption of Heimaey Volcano.

Arm Pulling, by Hans Egede — SP5

1976, Apr. 8 Engr. *Perf. 12½*

B7 SP5 100o + 20o multi .60 .60

Surtax for the Greenland Athletic Union.

Rasmussen and Eskimos — SP6

1979, June 7 Engr. *Perf. 13*

B8 SP6 1.30k + 20o brown red .75 .75

Knud Rasmussen (1879-1933), arctic explorer and ethnologist.

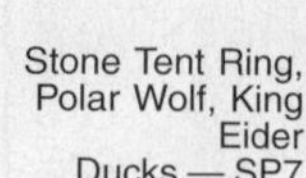

Stone Tent Ring, Polar Wolf, King Eider Ducks — SP7

1981, Sept. 3 Engr. *Perf. 13*

B9 SP7 1.60k + 20o lt red brn 1.10 1.10

Surtax was for Peary Land Expeditions.

History Type of 1982

Design: Eric the Red sailing for Greenland.

1982, Aug. 2 Engr. *Perf. 12½*

B10 A39 2k + 40o dk red brn 1.25 1.25

Surtax was for Cultural House, Julianehab.

Blind Man — SP8

1983, May 19 Engr.

B11 SP8 2.50k + 40o multi 1.50 1.50

Surtax was for the handicapped.

Greenland Sports Union — SP9

No. B12, Water game.

1986, Apr. 17 Litho.

B12 SP9 2.80k + 50o multi 2.00 2.00

Surtax for the Sports Union.

Greenland PO, 50th Anniv. — SP10

1988, Sept. 16 Litho. *Perf. 12½x13*

B13 SP10 300o +50o multi 2.75 2.75

Surtax for the purchase of postal artifacts.

Sled Dog, Common Eider — SP11

Litho. & Engr.

1990, Sept. 6 *Perf. 13*

B14 SP11 400o + 50o multi 3.75 3.75

Surtax for the Greenland Environmental Foundation.

SP12

1991, Sept. 5 Litho. *Perf. 13*

B15 SP12 4k +50o multi 15.00 15.00

Blue Cross of Greenland, 75th Anniv. Surtax benefits Blue Cross of Greenland.

Cancer Research in Greenland — SP13

1992, Oct. 8 Litho. *Perf. 13*

B16 SP13 4k +50o multi 3.75 *4.50*

Red Cross — SP14

Boy Scouts in Greenland, 50th Anniv. SP15

1993, June 17 Litho. *Perf. 13*

B17	SP14	4k +50o red & blue	2.50	2.50
B18	SP15	4k +50o multi	2.50	2.50
a.		Souv. sheet, 2 ea #B17-B18	22.50	22.50

1994 Winter Olympics, Lillehammer SP16

1994, Feb. 10 Litho. *Perf. 13*

B19	SP16	4k +50o Skiers	3.00	3.00
a.		Souvenir sheet of 4	12.00	12.00

Surtax to support Greenlandic athletes.

Natl. Flag, 10th Anniv. — SP17

1995, June 21 Litho. *Perf. 13*

B20	SP17	4k +50o multi	2.75	2.75
a.		Souvenir sheet of 4	11.00	11.00

Surtax for benefit of Greenland Flag Society.

Handicapped and Disabled in Greenland SP18

1996, Sept. 5 Litho. *Perf. 13*

B21	SP18	4.25k +50o multi	2.50	2.50
a.		Souvenir sheet of 4	10.00	10.00

Katuaq Cultural Center, Nuuk SP19

Litho. & Engr.

1997, Jan. 14 *Perf. 13*

B22	SP19	4.50k +50o multi	2.50	2.50
a.		Souvenir sheet of 4	10.00	10.00

SP20

Women's Society of Greenland: Kathrine Chemnitz (1894-1978), first Gen. Secretary.

1998, May 29 Litho. *Perf. 13*

B23 SP20 4.50k +50o multi	2.50	2.50
a. Souvenir sheet of 4	10.00	10.00

Pincushion, Natl. Museum — SP21

1999, May 7 Engr. *Perf. 13*

B24 SP21 4.50k +50o multi	1.60	1.60
a. Souvenir sheet of 4	7.00	7.00

Surtax for the benefit of Greenland National Museum & Archives.

Drum Dance — SP22

Litho. & Engr.

2000, Aug. 18 *Perf. 13¼x13*

B25 SP22 4.50k + 1k multi	1.75	1.75
a. Souvenir sheet of 4	7.00	7.00

Surtax to benefit the Hafnia 01 Philatelic Exhibition, Copenhagen.

2002 Arctic Winter Games — SP23

2001, Feb. 5 Litho. *Perf. 13¼x13*

B26 SP23 4.50k +50o multi	1.75	1.75
a. Souvenir sheet of 4	7.00	7.00

SP24

2002, Mar. 5 *Perf. 12¾*

B27 SP24 4.50k +50o multi	2.00	2.00
a. Souvenir sheet of 4	8.00	8.00

Surtax for "Children Are People, Too" Project of Paarisa.

Ornament With Santa Claus, Map of Greenland, House — SP25

2003, Oct. 20 *Perf. 13¼*

B28 SP25 5k +50o multi	2.25	2.25
a. Souvenir sheet of 4	9.00	9.00

Society of Greenlandic Children, 80th Anniv. — SP26

2004, May 14 *Perf. 13x13¼*

B29 SP26 5k +50o multi	2.25	2.25
a. Souvenir sheet of 4	9.00	9.00

Surtax for Society of Greenlandic Children.

Child — SP27

2005, Jan. 17 *Perf. 12¾*

B30 SP27 5.25k +50o multi	2.10	2.10
a. Souvenir sheet of 4	8.50	8.50

Surtax for Save the Children Fund.

Crown Prince Frederik and Crown Princess Mary — SP28

2006, Mar. 29 *Perf. 13¼x13¾*

B31 SP28 5.50k +50o multi	2.10	2.10
a. Souvenir sheet of 4	8.50	8.50

Surtax for children's charities.

Amnesty Greenland SP29

2007, Jan. 15 *Perf. 13¾x13¼*

B32 SP29 575o +50o multi	2.25	2.25
a. Souvenir sheet of 4	9.00	9.00

Fight Against Tuberculosis SP30

2008, May 24 *Perf. 13¾x13½*

B33 SP30 575o +50o multi	2.75	2.75
a. Souvenir sheet of 4	11.00	11.00

Fight Against Cancer — SP31

2009, Jan. 19 *Perf. 13¼x14*

B34 SP31 6.25k +50o blk & red	2.50	2.50
a. Souvenir sheet of 4	10.00	10.00

Surtax for Greenlandic Cancer Society.

Performer SP32

2010, Jan. 18 *Perf. 14x13¼*

B35 SP32 7k +50o multi	3.00	3.00
a. Souvenir sheet of 4	12.00	12.00

Surtax for Silamiut Theater Group.

SP33

2011, Jan. 17 Litho. *Perf. 13*

B36 SP33 7.50k+50o multi	3.00	3.00
a. Souvenir sheet of 4	12.00	12.00

Surtax for KIMIK (Association of Artists in Greenland).

Family — SP34

2012, Jan. 16 Litho. *Perf. 12½x12¾*

B37 SP34 800o+50o multi	3.00	3.00
a. Souvenir sheet of 4	12.00	12.00

Surtax for NAKUUSA, a collaborative children's rights project of Naalakersuisut and UNICEF.

Children and Boat — SP35

2013, Jan. 14 *Perf. 12½*

B38 SP35 9k+50o multi	3.50	3.50
a. Souvenir sheet of 4	14.00	14.00

Surtax for Better Childlife Organization.

Homeless Person — SP36

2014, Jan. 20 Litho. *Perf. 12½*

B39 SP36 10k+1k multi	4.00	4.00
a. Souvenir sheet of 4	16.00	16.00

Surtax for facilities for the homeless.

2016 Arctic Winter Games, Nuuk — SP37

2015, Jan. 19 Litho. *Perf. 12½x13¼*

B40 SP37 11k+1k multi	3.75	3.75
a. Perf. 12½	3.75	3.75

No. B40a was printed in sheets of 4.

Child's Face and Emblem of MIO — SP38

2016, Jan. 18 Litho. *Perf. 12½*

B41 SP38 12k+1k multi	3.75	3.75
a. Perf. 13¼x13	3.75	3.75

Surtax for MIO, Greenland's Children's Rights Institution. No. B41a was printed in sheets of 4.

Kofoed's School, Nuuk SP39

2017, Oct. 18 Litho. *Perf. 12½*

B42 SP39 13k+1k multi	4.50	4.50
a. Perf. 13x13¼	4.50	4.50

Surtax for Kofoed's School. No. B42a was printed in sheets of 4.

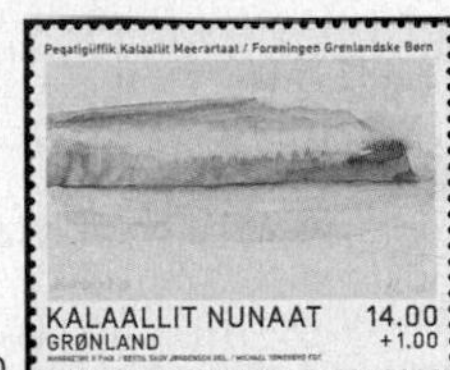

SP40

SP41

SP42

SP43

SP44

SP45

Watercolor Landscapes Painted by Queen Margrethe II — SP46

2018, Apr. 16 Litho. *Perf. 13x13¼*

B43 SP40 14k+1k multi 5.00 5.00
- *a.* Perf. 13xx13¼ (B44) 5.00 5.00

Miniature Sheet

Perf. 13¼

B44 Sheet of 7, #B43a, B44a-B44f, + 2 labels 17.00 17.00
- *a.* SP41 2k multi .70 .70
- *b.* SP42 2k multi .70 .70
- *c.* SP43 5k multi 1.75 1.75
- *d.* SP44 5k multi 1.75 1.75
- *e.* SP45 10k multi 3.50 3.50
- *f.* SP46 10k multi 3.50 3.50

No. B44 sold for 52k. Surtax for Association for Greenlandic Children. Labels on No. B44 are embossed.

PARCEL POST STAMPS

Arms of Greenland PP1

Perf. 10¾, 11½

1905-37 Unwmk. Typo.

Q1 PP1 1o ol grn ('15-'26) 45.00 *50.00*
- *a.* Perf. 12½ ('05) 600.00 650.00

Q2 PP1 2o yel ('15-'24) 300.00 110.00
Q3 PP1 5o brn ('18-'28) 120.00 120.00
- *a.* Perf. 12½ ('05) 600.00 650.00

Q4 PP1 10o blue ('37) 30.00 *60.00*
- *a.* Perf. 12½ ('05) 750.00 550.00
- *b.* Perf. 11½ ('18) 45.00 55.00

Q5 PP1 15o vio ('15-'28) 225.00 225.00
Q6 PP1 20o red ('15-'33) 10.00 12.00
- *a.* Perf. 11 ('37) 42.50 60.00

Q7 PP1 70o violet ('37) 25.00 *140.00*
- *a.* Perf. 11½ ('30) 225.00 200.00

Q8 PP1 1k yellow ('37) 32.50 *100.00*
- *a.* Perf. 11½ ('30) 40.00 55.00

Q9 PP1 3k brown ('30) 110.00 *160.00*
Nos. Q1-Q9 (9) 897.50 *977.00*
Nos. Q1-Q9, never hinged 3,000.

1937 Litho. *Perf. 11*

Q10 PP1 70o pale violet 27.50 *140.00*
Q11 PP1 1k yellow 30.00 *90.00*
Nos. Q10-Q11, never hinged 135.00

On lithographed stamps, PAKKE-PORTO is slightly larger, hyphen has rounded ends and lines in shield are fine, straight and evenly spaced.

On typographed stamps, hyphen has squared ends and shield lines are coarse, uneven and inclined to be slightly wavy.

Used values are for stamps postally used from Denmark. Numeral cancels indicate use as postal savings stamps and are usually worth as much or more than postally used examples. Greenland village cancels on Nos. Q6, Q6a and Q8a often reflect postal savings use. These are often worth as much or more than postally used examples. Parcel post stamps not regularly used for postal savings that have village cancellations are often worth much more.

Sheets of 25. Certain printings of Nos. Q1-Q2, Q3a, Q4a and Q5-Q6 were issued without sheet margins. Stamps from the outer rows are straight edged. Some of these sheets had the outer straight edges officially perforated in 1918. Stamps with falsified reperforations exist.

GRENADA

grə-ˈnā-də

LOCATION — Windward Islands, West Indies
GOVT. — Independent nation in the British Commonwealth
AREA — 133 sq. mi.
POP. — 98,600 (1998 est.)
CAPITAL — St. George's

Grenada consists of Grenada Island and the southern Grenadines, including Carriacou. This colony was granted associated statehood with Great Britain in 1967 and became an independent state Feb. 7, 1974.

12 Pence = 1 Shilling
100 Cents = 1 Dollar (1949)

Catalogue values for unused stamps in this country are for Never Hinged items, beginning with Scott 143 in the regular postage section, Scott B1 in the semi-postal section, Scott C1 in the air post section, Scott J15 in the postage due section, and Scott O1 in the official section.

Watermarks

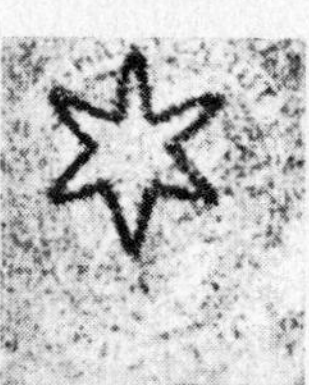
Wmk. 5 — Small Star

Wmk. 6 — Large Star

Wmk. 7 — Large Star with Broad Points

Values for unused stamps are for examples with original gum as defined in the catalogue introduction. Very fine examples of Nos. 1-19, 27-29, and 31-38 will have perforations touching the design on at least one side due to the narrow spacing of the stamps on the plates. Stamps with perfs clear of the design on all four sides are scarce and will command higher prices.

Queen Victoria — A1

Rough Perf. 14 to 16

1861 Engr. Unwmk.

1 A1 1p green 57.50 55.00
- *a.* 1p blue green 5,250. 350.00
- *b.* As No. 1, horiz. pair, imperf. btwn.

2 A1 6p rose 1,050. 110.00
- *b.* 6p lake red, perf. 11-12½ 1,000.

No. 2b was not issued. No. 2 imperf is a proof.

1863-71 Wmk. 5

3 A1 1p green ('64) 120.00 17.50
- *a.* 1p yellow green 145.00 30.00

4 A1 6p rose 775.00 20.00
5 A1 6p vermilion ('71) 875.00 20.00
- *a.* 6p dull red 4,000. 275.00
- *g.* Double impression 2,350.
- *i.* 6p orange red ('66) 750.00 14.00

No. 5a always has sideways watermark. Other colors sometimes have sideways watermark.

1873-78 *Clean-Cut Perf. about 15*

5B A1 1p deep green 140.00 55.00
- *j.* Pair, imperf between *14,000.*
- *c.* 1p blue green ('78) 275.00 45.00
- *h.* Half used as ½p on cover 11,000.

5D A1 6p vermilion ('75) 925.00 55.00
- *e.* 6p dull red 950.00 40.00
- *f.* Double impression 2,350.

1873 Wmk. 6

6 A1 1p blue green 110.00 28.00
- *a.* Diagonal half used as ½p on cover 11,000.

7 A1 6p vermilion 775.00 35.00

1875 *Perf. 14*

7A A1 1p yellow green 95.00 9.00
- *b.* Half used as ½p on cover 16,000.
- *c.* Perf. 15 10,000. *2,600.*

A2

A2a

Revenue Designs Surcharged in Black

Perf. 14, 14½

1875-81

8 A2 ½p purple ('81) 17.50 7.50
- *a.* "OSTAGE" 225.00 150.00
- *b.* Imperf., pair 350.00
- *c.* "ALF" *4,000.*
- *e.* No hyphen between "HALF" and "PENNY" 225.00 150.00
- *f.* Double surcharge 350.00 350.00

9 A2a 2½p lake ('81) 75.00 10.00
- *a.* Imperf., pair 650.00
- *b.* Imperf. vertically, pair 6,500.
- *c.* "PENCF" 525.00 225.00
- *d.* No period after "PENNY" 290.00 90.00

10 A2 4p blue ('81) 150.00 10.00

Revenue Designs Surcharged in Dark Blue

11 A2 1sh purple 775.00 20.00
- *a.* "SHLLIING" *6,500.* 800.00
- *b.* "NE SHILLING" *3,250.*
- *c.* "OSTAGE" 7,250. *3,000.*
- *d.* Invtd. "S" in "POSTAGE" *4,500.* *750.00*

See Nos. 27-35.

1881 Wmk. 7

12 A2 2½p lake 200.00 57.50
- *a.* 2½p claret 550.00 200.00
- *b.* As No. 12, "PENCF" 875.00 325.00
- *c.* As No. 12, No period after "PENNY" 650.00 230.00
- *d.* As "a," "PENCF" 1,850. 825.00
- *e.* As "a," no period after "PENNY" 1,275. 575.00

13 A2 4p blue 350.00 210.00

Revenue Stamp Overprinted "POSTAGE" in Black

A3

A4

A5

Revenue Stamp Handstamped "POSTAGE" in Manuscript

A6

1883 Wmk. 5

Denomination & Crown in 2nd Color

14 A3 ½p orange & grn 900.00 275.00
- *a.* Unsevered pair *5,000.* *1,500.*
- *b.* "POSTAGE" inverted 1,500.

15 A4 ½p orange & grn 325.00 150.00
- *a.* Unsevered pair *2,000.* *525.00*

16 A5 1p orange & grn *400.00* 65.00
- *a.* Inverted overprint 3,500. 2,600.
- *b.* Double overprint 1,625. 1,275.
- *c.* Inverted "S" in "Postage" 1,150. 700.00
- *d.* Diagonal half used as ½p on cover *3,500.*

"Postage" in Manuscript, Red or Black

18 A6 1p org & grn (R) *21,000.*
19 A6 1p org & grn — *15,000.*

On Nos. 14-19 the words "ONE PENNY" measure from 10-11¼mm in length.

On No. 15, the lower "POSTAGE" is always inverted.

It has been claimed that although Nos. 18 and 19 were used, they were not officially authorized by Grenada's postmaster.

A8

1883 Wmk. 2 *Perf. 14*

20 A8 ½p green 2.75 1.25
- *a.* Tete beche pair 5.50 *21.00*

21 A8 1p rose 90.00 4.00
- *a.* Tete beche pair 325.00 *375.00*

22 A8 2½p ultra 14.00 1.25
- *a.* Tete beche pair 35.00 *60.00*

23 A8 4p slate 15.00 2.25
- *a.* Tete beche pair 37.50 *65.00*

24 A8 6p red lilac 6.00 *6.50*
- *a.* Tete beche pair 21.00 *65.00*

25 A8 8p bister 10.50 *14.00*
- *a.* Tete beche pair 40.00 *90.00*

26 A8 1sh violet 160.00 65.00
- *a.* Tete beche pair 2,000. *2,250.*

Nos. 20-26 (7) 298.25 94.25

Stamps of types A8, A10 and D2 were printed with alternate horizontal rows inverted.

For surcharges see Nos. 36-38, J4-J7.

Revenue Stamps Surcharged

1886 Wmk. 6

27 A2 1p on 1½ org & grn 60.00 50.00
- *a.* Inverted surcharge 475.00 350.00
- *b.* Diagonal half used as ½ on cover 2,250.
- *c.* Double surcharge 775.00 350.00
- *d.* "HALH" instead of "HALF" 300.00 275.00
- *e.* "F" for first "E" in "THREE" 300.00 225.00
- *f.* "PFNCE" for "PENCE" 300.00 225.00

28 A2 1p on 1sh org & grn 50.00 45.00
- *a.* "SHILLNG" instead of "SHILLING" 525.00 450.00
- *b.* No period after "POSTAGE" *500.00*
- *c.* Half used as ½p on cover 2,350.

Wmk. 5

29 A2 1p on 4p org & grn 190.00 110.00

A10

1887 Wmk. 2

30 A10 1p rose 5.00 1.75
- *a.* Tete beche pair 11.00 *30.00*

Revenue Stamps Surcharged

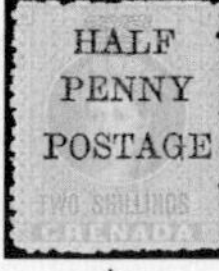

h

i

j

k

l

1888-91 Wmk. 5 *Perf. 14½*

31 A2 (h) ½p on 2sh org & grn ('89) 17.50 *32.50*
a. Double surcharge 350.00 *375.00*
b. First "S" in "SHILLINGS" inverted 325.00 *350.00*
32 A2 (i) 4p on 2sh org & grn 50.00 22.50
a. "4d" and "POSTAGE" 5mm apart 80.00 37.50
b. "S" inverted, as in #31b 550.00 400.00
c. As "a," inverted "S," as in #31b 750.00 650.00

"d" Vertical instead of Slanting

33 A2 (j) 4p on 2sh org & grn 875.00 475.00
34 A2 (k) 1p on 2sh org & grn ('90) 92.50 87.50
a. Inverted surcharge 875.00 —
b. "S" inverted 825.00 750.00
35 A2 (l) 1p on 2sh org & grn ('91) 75.00 70.00
b. No period after "d" 450.00 —
c. "S" inverted 575.00 575.00

No. 25 Surcharged in Black

Wmk. 2

36 A8 1p on 8p bister 12.00 *20.00*
a. Tete beche pair 50.00 *70.00*
b. Inverted surcharge 375.00 325.00
c. No period after "d" 300.00 300.00

"2" of "½" Upright

37 A8 2½p on 8p bister 11.00 *14.00*
a. Tete beche pair 50.00 *70.00*
c. Double surcharge 1,000. *925.00*
d. Triple surcharge 1,100.
e. Double surcharge, one inverted 650.00 575.00

"2" of "½" Italic

38 A8 2½p on 8p bister 22.00 *13.00*
a. Tete beche pair 50.00 *70.00*
b. Tete beche pair, #37, 38 125.00
c. Inverted surcharge
d. Double surcharge 875.00 *925.00*
e. Triple surcharge 1,050.
f. Triple surch., two inverted 1,000.
g. Double surcharge, one inverted 625.00 575.00

Queen Victoria — A17

1895-99 Wmk. 2 Typo. *Perf. 14*

39 A17 ½p lilac & green 4.75 2.00
40 A17 1p lilac & car rose 6.75 .90
41 A17 2p lilac & brown 47.50 37.50
42 A17 2½p lilac & ultra 12.50 1.75
43 A17 3p lilac & orange 8.00 *18.00*
44 A17 6p lilac & green 23.00 *65.00*
45 A17 8p lilac & black 15.00 *52.50*
46 A17 1sh green & org 22.50 65.00
Nos. 39-46 (8) 140.00 *242.65*

Numerals of ½p, 3p, 8p and 1sh of type A17 are in color on colorless tablet.

Issue dates: 1p, May, 1896; ½p, 2p, Sept. 1899; others, Sept. 5, 1895.

Columbus' Flagship, La Concepcion — A18

1898, Aug. 15 Engr. Wmk. 1

47 A18 2½p ultra 22.50 8.00
a. Bluish paper 40.00 *47.50*

Discovery of the island by Columbus, Aug. 15th, 1498.

King Edward VII — A19

1902 Wmk. 2 Typo.

48 A19 ½p violet & grn 4.50 1.50
49 A19 1p vio & car rose 10.00 .35
50 A19 2p vio & brown 6.50 *11.50*
51 A19 2½p vio & ultra 7.00 3.25
52 A19 3p vio & org 7.00 *10.50*
53 A19 6p vio & green 9.00 *20.00*
54 A19 1sh green & org 13.00 *40.00*
55 A19 2sh grn & ultra 40.00 *65.00*
56 A19 5sh grn & car rose 47.50 *85.00*
57 A19 10sh green & vio 160.00 *300.00*
Nos. 48-57 (10) 304.50 *537.10*

Numerals of ½p, 3p, 1sh, 2sh and 10sh of type A19 are in color on colorless tablet.

1904-06 Wmk. 3 *Perf. 14*

Ordinary Paper

58 A19 ½p vio & green 22.50 *47.50*
59 A19 1p vio & car rose 24.00 3.00
60 A19 2p vio & brown 65.00 *130.00*
61 A19 2½p vio & ultra 65.00 *75.00*
62 A19 3p vio & org 6.50 *15.00*
a. Chalky paper 7.50 *9.00*
63 A19 6p vio & green 17.00 *30.00*
a. Chalky paper 18.00 *40.00*
64 A19 1sh green & org 7.25 *40.00*
65 A19 2sh grn & ultra 60.00 *85.00*
a. Chalky paper 50.00 *80.00*
66 A19 5sh grn & car rose 80.00 *120.00*
67 A19 10sh green & vio 190.00 *300.00*
Nos. 58-67 (10) 537.25 *845.50*

Issued: Nos. 58, 60-62, 64, 1905; Nos. 63, 65-67, 1906.

Seal of Colony — A20

1906-11 Engr.

68 A20 ½p green 5.25 .35
69 A20 1p carmine 10.00 .25
70 A20 2p yellow 5.25 3.50
71 A20 2½p blue 7.00 2.00
a. 2½p ultramarine 11.00 3.75

Typo.

Chalky Paper

Numerals white on dark ground

72 A20 3p vio, *yel* ('08) 8.25 1.90
73 A20 6p violet ('08) 22.50 10.00
74 A20 1sh blk, *grn* ('11) 8.00 5.00
75 A20 2sh vio & blue, *blue* ('08) 40.00 14.00
76 A20 5sh red & grn, *yel* ('08) 80.00 *95.00*
Nos. 68-76 (9) 186.25 *132.00*

1908 Wmk. 2

77 A20 1sh black, *green* 50.00 *80.00*
78 A20 10sh red & grn, *grn* 160.00 *300.00*

King George V — A21

1913 Ordinary Paper Wmk. 3

79 A21 ½p green 1.25 1.60
80 A21 1p carmine 2.50 .35
a. 1p scarlet ('16) 14.00 2.00
81 A21 2p orange 1.90 .35
82 A21 2½p ultra 2.00 2.00

Chalky Paper

83 A21 3p violet, *yel* .75 *1.00*
84 A21 6p dl vio & red vio 1.75 *10.00*
85 A21 1sh black, *green* 1.10 *11.50*
a. 1sh black, *emerald* 1.75 *20.00*
b. 1sh blk, *bl grn*, olive back 52.50 *90.00*
c. As "a," olive back 1.75 *15.00*
86 A21 2sh vio & ultra, *bl* 7.25 *14.00*
87 A21 5sh grn & red, *yel* 20.00 *67.50*
88 A21 10sh grn & red, *grn* 70.00 *130.00*
a. 10sh grn & red, *emer* 70.00 *190.00*
Nos. 79-88 (10) 108.50 *238.30*

1914 Surface-colored Paper

89 A21 3p violet, *yel* .70 *1.60*
90 A21 1sh black, *green* 1.40 *8.50*

1921-29 Ordinary Paper Wmk. 4

91 A21 ½p green 1.40 .35
92 A21 1p rose red .90 .85
93 A21 1p brown ('23) 1.75 .35
94 A21 1½p rose red ('22) 1.75 1.75
95 A21 2p orange 1.40 .35
96 A21 2p gray ('26) 2.75 *3.00*
97 A21 2½p ultramarine 8.50 *10.00*
98 A21 2½p gray ('22) 1.10 *10.00*
99 A21 3p ultra ('22) 1.75 *12.50*

Chalky Paper

100 A21 3p vio, *yel* ('26) 3.50 *5.75*
101 A21 4p blk & red, *yel* ('26) 1.10 *4.25*
102 A21 5p gray vio & ol grn ('22) 1.75 *4.75*
103 A21 6p dl vio & red vio 1.50 *29.00*
104 A21 6p blk & red ('26) 2.50 *2.75*
105 A21 9p gray vio & blk ('22) 2.50 *11.00*
106 A21 1sh blk, *emer* ('23) 3.00 *60.00*
107 A21 1sh org brn ('26) 4.50 *11.00*
108 A21 2sh vio & ultra, *bl* ('22) 7.00 *19.00*
109 A21 2sh6p blk & red, *bl* ('29) 15.00 *24.00*
110 A21 3sh grn & vio ('22) 12.00 *30.00*
111 A21 5sh grn & red, *yel* ('23) 14.00 *40.00*
112 A21 10sh grn & red, *emer* ('23) 57.50 *150.00*
Nos. 91-112 (22) 147.15 *430.65*

Grand Anse Beach — A22

Seal of the Colony — A23

View of Grand Etang — A24

View of St. George's — A25

1934, Oct. 23 Engr. *Perf. 12½*

114 A22 ½p green .25 *1.25*
a. Perf. 12½x13 ('36) 11.00 *70.00*

Perf. 13½x12½

115 A23 1p blk brn & blk .65 .35
a. Perf 12½ 2.00 4.00

Perf. 12½x13½

116 A24 1½p car & black 1.25 .45
a. Perf 12½ ('36) 10.00 7.50

Perf. 12½

117 A23 2p org & black 1.10 .80
118 A25 2½p deep blue .55 .55
119 A23 3p ol grn & blk 1.10 *3.25*
120 A23 6p claret & blk 3.75 2.00
121 A23 1sh brown & blk 4.50 *4.50*
122 A23 2sh6p ultra & blk 9.00 *30.00*
123 A23 5sh vio & black 50.00 *55.00*
Nos. 114-123 (10) 72.15 *98.15*
Set, never hinged 130.00

Common Design Types pictured following the introduction.

Silver Jubilee Issue

Common Design Type

1935, May 6 *Perf. 11x12*

124 CD301 ½p green & blk 1.00 *1.35*
125 CD301 1p black & ultra 1.10 *2.00*
126 CD301 1½p car & blue 1.10 *3.25*
127 CD301 1sh brn vio & ind 13.50 *34.00*
Nos. 124-127 (4) 16.70 *40.60*
Set, never hinged 29.00

Coronation Issue

Common Design Type

1937, May 12 Wmk. 4 *Perf. 11x11½*

128 CD302 1p dark purple .25 .25
129 CD302 1½p dark carmine .25 .25
130 CD302 2½p deep ultra .50 .35
Nos. 128-130 (3) 1.00 .85
Set, never hinged 1.60

George VI — A26

Chalky Paper

1937, July 12 Photo. *Perf. 14½x14*

131 A26 ¼p chestnut 3.25 *.25*
a. Ordinary paper ('42) .65 3.00

Grand Anse Beach — A27

Seal of the Colony — A28

View of Grand Etang — A29

View of St. George's — A30

Seal of the Colony — A31

1938, Mar. 16 Engr. *Perf. 12½*
132 A27 ½p green .70 *1.40*
133 A28 1p blk brn & blk .50 .55
134 A29 1½p scarlet & blk .25 *.95*
135 A28 2p orange & blk .25 *.55*
136 A30 2½p ultramarine .25 *.35*
137 A28 3p ol grn & blk .25 *2.10*
138 A28 6p red vio & blk 2.10 .45
139 A28 1sh org brn & blk 3.00 .45
140 A28 2sh ultra & black 21.00 2.00
141 A28 5sh purple & blk 4.25 *2.75*

Perf. 14
142 A31 10sh rose car & gray blue 19.00 13.00
a. 10sh deep car & gray blue, perf. 12 ('43) 500.00 *1,900.*
b. Perf. 12x13 36.00 12.00
Nos. 131-142 (12) 54.80 24.80
Set, never hinged 72.50

1938-42 *Perf. 12½x13½, 13½x12½*
132a A27 ½p 3.00 .90
133a A28 1p .30 .25
134a A29 1½p car & blk 1.10 .40
135a A28 2p 1.25 .75
136a A30 2½p *7,500.* *200.00*
137a A28 3p 2.10 *1.00*
138a A28 6p ('42) 1.10 .35
139a A28 1sh ('42) 2.50 2.50
140a A28 2sh ('41) 21.00 2.00
141a A28 5sh ('47) 3.50 *4.50*

Catalogue values for unused stamps in this section, from this point to the end of the section, are for Never Hinged items.

Peace Issue
Common Design Type

1946, Sept. 25 *Perf. 13½x14*
143 CD303 1½p carmine .25 .25
144 CD303 3½p deep blue .25 *.70*

Silver Wedding Issue
Common Design Types

1948, Oct. 27 Photo. *Perf. 14x14½*
145 CD304 1½p scarlet .25 .25

Engr.; Name Typo.
Perf. 11½x11
146 CD305 10sh gray green 21.50 21.50

UPU Issue
Common Design Types
Engr.; Name Typo. on 6c, 12c
Perf. 13½, 11x11½

1949, Oct. 10 Wmk. 4
147 CD306 5c ultra .25 .25
148 CD307 6c deep olive 1.35 *2.25*
149 CD308 12c red lilac .30 *.50*
150 CD309 24c red brown .25 *.55*
Nos. 147-150 (4) 2.15 3.55

A32 A33

A34

1951, Jan. 8 Engr. *Perf. 11½*
Center in Black
151 A32 ½c chestnut .25 *1.30*
152 A32 1c blue green .25 *.55*
153 A32 2c dark brown .25 .25
154 A32 3c carmine .25 .25
155 A32 4c deep orange .40 .25
156 A32 5c purple .50 .30
157 A32 6c olive .50 .60
158 A32 7c blue 2.00 .30
159 A32 12c red violet 2.25 .70

Perf. 11½x12½
160 A33 25c dark brown 2.50 .85
161 A33 50c ultra 6.50 .55
162 A33 $1.50 orange 8.25 8.00

Perf. 11½x13
Center in Gray Blue
163 A34 $2.50 deep carmine 9.50 5.50
Nos. 151-163 (13) 33.40 19.40

See Nos. 180-183, 202. For overprints see Nos. 166-169.

University Issue
Common Design Types

1951, Feb. 16 *Perf. 14x14½*
164 CD310 3c dp car & gray blk .55 *1.00*
165 CD311 6c olive & black .65 .60

Nos. 154-156 and 159 Overprinted in Black or Carmine

1951, Sept. 21 *Perf. 11½*
166 A32 3c carmine & black .25 *.40*
167 A32 4c dp orange & black .25 *.40*
168 A32 5c purple & black (C) .30 *.65*
169 A32 12c red violet & black .30 *.90*
Nos. 166-169 (4) 1.10 *2.35*

Adoption of a new constitution for the Windward Islands.

Coronation Issue
Common Design Type

1953, June 3 *Perf. 13½x13*
170 CD312 3c carmine & black .30 .25

Types of 1951 Inscribed "E II R" and

Queen Elizabeth II — A35

1953-59 Engr. *Perf. 11½*
Center in Black
171 A35 ½c chestnut ('54) .25 .25
172 A35 1c blue green .25 .25
173 A35 2c dark brown .30 .25
174 A35 3c carmine ('54) .25 .25
175 A35 4c dp orange ('54) .25 .25
176 A35 5c purple ('54) .25 .25
177 A35 6c olive 2.00 *1.25*
178 A35 7c blue ('55) 2.50 .25
179 A35 12c red violet .30 .25

Perf. 11½x12½
180 A33 25c dk brn ('55) 1.40 .30
181 A33 50c ultra ('55) 6.00 .80
182 A33 $1.50 orange ('55) 12.50 *11.50*

Perf. 11½x13
Center in Gray Blue
183 A34 $2.50 deep car ('59) 25.00 9.00
Nos. 171-183 (13) 51.25 24.85

See Nos. 195-202.

No. 182 was locally surcharged "2" and two black horizontal lines and issued Dec. 23, 1965, for revenue use. It was used postally, though not authorized for postal use. The "2" is found in two type faces.

West Indies Federation
Common Design Type
Perf. 11½x11

1958, Apr. 22 Wmk. 314
184 CD313 3c green .35 .25
185 CD313 6c blue .55 *.70*
186 CD313 12c carmine rose .60 .25
Nos. 184-186 (3) 1.50 1.20

Victoria and Elizabeth II and Mail Truck A36

Queens and: 8c, "La Concepcion" and Dakota plane. 25c, Steam Packet "Solent" and B.O.A.C. plane.

1961, June 1 Photo. *Perf. 14½x14*
187 A36 3c gray & deep car .25 .25
188 A36 8c orange & ultra .50 .25
189 A36 25c blue & maroon .55 .25
Nos. 187-189 (3) 1.30 .75

Centenary of first Grenada postage stamps.

Freedom from Hunger Issue
Common Design Type

1963, June 4 *Perf. 14x14½*
190 CD314 8c green .30 .25

Red Cross Centenary Issue
Common Design Type

1963, Sept. 2 Litho. *Perf. 13*
191 CD315 3c black & red .25 .25
192 CD315 25c ultra & red .55 .25

Types of 1953-55
Wmk. 314

1963-64 Engr. *Perf. 11½*
Center in Black
195 A35 2c dark brown .25 .25
196 A35 3c carmine .25 .25
197 A35 4c dp orange .25 *.80*
198 A35 5c purple .25 .25
199 A35 6c olive 180.00 95.00
201 A35 12c red violet .30 .25

Perf. 11½x12½
202 A33 25c dark brown 2.50 1.00
Nos. 195-198,201-202 (6) 3.80 2.80

Issued: 8c, 1963; others, May 12, 1964.

ITU Issue
Common Design Type

1965, May 17 Litho. *Perf. 11x11½*
205 CD317 2c vermilion & olive .25 .25
206 CD317 50c yellow & ver .25 .25

Intl. Cooperation Year Issue
Common Design Type

1965, Oct. 25 Litho. *Perf. 14½*
207 CD318 1c blue grn & claret .25 .25
208 CD318 25c lt violet & green .25 .25

Churchill Memorial Issue
Common Design Type

1966, Jan. 24 Photo. *Perf. 14*
Design in Black, Gold and Carmine Rose
209 CD319 1c bright blue .25 .25
210 CD319 3c green .25 .25
211 CD319 25c brown .25 .25
212 CD319 35c violet .35 .35
Nos. 209-212 (4) 1.10 1.10

Royal Visit Issue
Common Design Type

1966, Feb. 4 Litho. *Perf. 11x12*
213 CD320 3c violet blue .25 .25
214 CD320 35c dark car rose .55 .25

Careenage, St. George's A37

Queen Elizabeth II — A38

Designs: 1c, Hillsborough, Carriacou. 2c, Bougainvillea. 3c, Flamboyant plant. 5c, Levera Beach. 8c, Annandale Falls. 10c, Cacao pods. 12c, Inner Harbor. 15c, Nutmeg. 25c, St. George's. 35c, Grand Anse Beach. 50c, Bananas. $1, Seal of Colony. $3, Map of Grenada.

Perf. 14½x13½, 14½ (A38)
1966, Apr. 1 Photo. Wmk. 314
215 A37 1c blue, grn & yel .25 .80
216 A37 2c dk grn & dp car rose .25 .25
217 A37 3c multicolored .90 .90
218 A37 5c multicolored 1.10 .25
219 A37 6c ultra, grn & car rose .95 .25
220 A37 8c dp grn, ind & yel .95 .25
221 A37 10c yel grn, brn & dk car .50 .25
222 A37 12c multicolored .30 *.90*
223 A37 15c multicolored .30 .90
224 A37 25c dk bl, grn & car rose .30 .25
225 A37 35c multicolored .40 .25
226 A37 50c violet & green 1.10 *2.00*
227 A38 $1 brn, ultra & dull grn 7.25 3.50
228 A38 $2 multicolored 4.50 *9.00*
229 A38 $3 brt grnsh bl, dk bl & dl yel 4.00 *15.00*
Nos. 215-229 (15) 23.05 *34.75*

For overprints and surcharges see Nos. 237-261, B1A-B1D.

World Cup Soccer Issue
Common Design Type

1966, July 1 Litho. *Perf. 14*
230 CD321 5c multicolored .25 .25
231 CD321 50c multicolored .40 *.70*

WHO Headquarters Issue
Common Design Type

1966, Sept. 20 Litho. *Perf. 14*
232 CD322 8c multicolored .25 .25
233 CD322 25c multicolored .55 .25

UNESCO Anniversary Issue
Common Design Type

1966, Dec. 1 Litho. *Perf. 14*
234 CD323 2c "Education" .25 .25
235 CD323 15c "Science" .25 .25
236 CD323 50c "Culture" .60 *.70*
Nos. 234-236 (3) 1.10 1.20

Nos. 216-217, 220 and 224 Overprinted "ASSOCIATED STATEHOOD 1967" in Silver
Perf. 14½x13½

1967, Mar. 3 Photo. Wmk. 314
237 A37 2c dk grn & dp car rose .25 .25
238 A37 3c multicolored .25 .25
239 A37 8c dp grn, ind & yel .25 .25
240 A37 25c dk bl, grn & car rose .25 .25
Nos. 237-240 (4) 1.00 1.00

Nos. 216, 221, 223 and 227-228 Surcharged

Perf. 14½x13½, 14½ (A38)
1967, July 1 Photo. Wmk. 314
241 A37 1c on 15c multi .25 .25
242 A37 2c dk grn & dp car rose .25 .25
243 A37 3c on 10c multi .25 .25
244 A38 $1 multicolored .25 .25
245 A38 $2 multicolored .35 .35
Nos. 241-245 (5) 1.35 1.35

EXPO '67 Intl. Exhib., Montreal, Apr. 28-Oct. 27.

Nos. 215-229 Ovptd. in Black

1967-68 Photo. Wmk. 314
246 A37 1c multicolored .25 .25
247 A37 2c multicolored .25 .25
248 A37 3c multicolored .25 .25
249 A37 5c multicolored .25 .25
250 A37 6c multicolored .25 .25
251 A37 8c multicolored .25 .25
252 A37 10c multicolored .25 .25
253 A37 12c multicolored .25 .25
254 A37 15c multicolored .25 .25
255 A37 25c multicolored .25 .25
256 A37 35c multicolored .50 .25
257 A37 50c multicolored .80 .30
258 A38 $1 multicolored 1.10 .60
259 A38 $2 multicolored 1.00 *2.40*
260 A38 $3 multicolored 2.00 *4.00*

Overprinted and Surcharged
261 A38 $5 on $2 multi 1.40 *3.75*
Nos. 246-261 (16) 9.30 *13.80*

Issued: $5, 5/18/68; others, 10/19/67.
For surcharges, see Nos. B1A-B1D.

Pres. John F. Kennedy — A39

Pres. Kennedy and: 25c, 50c, Bird-of-paradise flower. 35c, $1, Roses.

Perf. 14½x14

1968, Jan. 13 **Unwmk.**

262	A39	1c	lt blue & multi	.25	.25
263	A39	15c	orange & multi	.25	.25
264	A39	25c	violet & multi	.25	.25
265	A39	35c	multicolored	.25	.25
266	A39	50c	blue & multi	.30	.25
267	A39	$1	multicolored	.40	*.70*
			Nos. 262-267 (6)	1.70	1.95

50th anniv. of the birth of Pres. John F. Kennedy (1917-1963).

Bugler and Jamboree Emblem — A40

Jamboree Emblem and: 2c, 50c, Boy Scouts sitting in tent. 3c, $1, Lord Baden-Powell.

1968, Feb. 1 **Photo.** ***Perf. 13x14***

268	A40	1c	orange & multi	.25	.25
269	A40	2c	emer & multi	.25	.25
270	A40	3c	yellow & multi	.25	.25
271	A40	35c	multicolored	.30	.25
272	A40	50c	blue & multi	.40	.40
273	A40	$1	multicolored	.55	*.70*
			Nos. 268-273 (6)	2.00	2.10

12th Boy Scout Jamboree, Farragut State Park, Idaho, Aug. 1-9, 1967.

Seascape, by Winston Churchill — A41

Paintings: 12c, Pine at the shore. 15c, 35c, Houses at the shore. 50c, Churchill painting a seascape.

Perf. 14x14½

1968, Mar. 23 **Unwmk.**

274	A41	10c	multicolored	.25	.25
275	A41	12c	multicolored	.25	.25
276	A41	15c	multicolored	.25	.25
277	A41	25c	multicolored	.25	.25
278	A41	35c	multicolored	.25	.25
279	A41	50c	multicolored	.40	.25
			Nos. 274-279 (6)	1.65	1.50

Winston Churchill as a painter.

Edith McGuire, US, 200m. Dash, 1964 A42

Gold Medal Winners: 2c, 50c, Arthur Wint, Jamaica, 400m run, 1948. 3c, 60c, Adhemar Ferreira da Silva, Brazil, hop, step and jump, 1952 & 1956. 10c, Like 1c.

1968, Sept. 24 **Photo.** ***Perf. 12½***

280	A42	1c	ultra & multi	.25	*.30*
281	A42	2c	lilac & multi	.25	*.30*
282	A42	3c	green & multi	.25	*.30*
283	A42	10c	red org & multi	.25	*.30*
284	A42	50c	Prus blue & multi	.35	*.75*
285	A42	60c	orange & multi	.40	*.85*
			Nos. 280-285 (6)	1.75	*2.80*

19th Olympic Games, Mexico City, Oct. 12-27. Nos. 280-282 and 283-285 are printed in sheets of 9 (3 of each denomination).

For surcharges see Nos. 310-315.

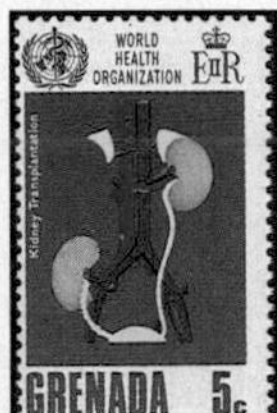

Transplant Operations — A43

Perf. 13x13½

1968, Nov. 25 **Photo.** **Unwmk.**

286	A43	5c	Kidney	.25	.25
287	A43	25c	Heart	.30	.25
288	A43	35c	Lung	.40	.25
289	A43	50c	Cornea	.45	*.60*
			Nos. 286-289 (4)	1.40	1.35

20th anniv. of WHO.

Adoration of the Magi, by Veronese A44

Paintings: 15c, Madonna and Child with St. John and St. Catherine, by Titian. 35c, Adoration of the Magi, by Botticelli. $1, "A Knight Adoring the Infant Christ" by Vincenzo di Biagio Catena.

1968, Dec. 3 ***Perf. 12½***

290	A44	5c	vio blue & multi	.25	.25
291	A44	15c	crimson & multi	.25	.25
292	A44	35c	dk green & multi	.25	.25
293	A44	$1	dk blue & multi	.25	.25
			Nos. 290-293 (4)	1.00	1.00

Christmas. For overprints see Nos. 341-344.

Hibiscus and "La Concepcion" A45

Yacht in St. George's Harbour — A45a

Designs: 2c, Bird-of-paradise flower. 3c, Bougainvillea. 5c, Rock hind (fish; horiz.). 6c, Sailfish. 8c, Red snapper, horiz. 10c, Giant toad, horiz. 12c, Yellowfoot tortoise. No. 302, Tree boa, horiz. No. 302A, Thunbergia. 25c, Mouse opossum. 35c Armadillo, horiz. 50c, Mona monkey. $1, Bananaquit (bird). $2, Brown pelican. $3, Magnificent frigate bird. $5, Bare-eyed thrush.

Perf. 14x14½, 14½x14; 14x13½ (#302A); 13½x14 (#305A)

Photo.; Litho. (#302A, 305A)

1968-71 **Unwmk.**

294	A45	1c	dl yel & multi	.25	.25
295	A45	2c	brt pink & multi	.25	.25
296	A45	3c	blue & multi	.25	.25
297	A45	5c	violet & multi	.25	.25
298	A45	6c	emer & multi	.25	.25
299	A45	8c	multicolored	.25	.25
300	A45	10c	multicolored	.25	.25
301	A45	12c	ver & multi	.25	.25
302	A45	15c	emer & multi	.90	.85
302A	A45	15c	gray & multi	5.00	3.25
303	A45	25c	multicolored	.30	.25
304	A45	35c	multicolored	.35	.25
305	A45	50c	ultra & multi	.45	.25
305A	A45a	75c	blue & multi	10.00	8.00
306	A45	$1	multicolored	3.00	2.40
307	A45	$2	multicolored	4.25	*10.00*
308	A45	$3	yel & multi	4.25	5.00
309	A45	$5	multicolored	6.00	*19.00*
			Nos. 294-309 (18)	36.50	*51.25*

Nos. 294-309 vary in size from 25x44mm to 29x46mm.

The overprint "VOTE/FEB. 28 1972" was applied to the 2c, 3c, 6c and 25c in Feb., 1972.

Issued: 5c, 10c, 25c, $2, 2/4/69; 3c, 8c, 35c, $5, 7/1/69; No. 302A, 1970; 75c, 10/9/71; others, 10/68.

For surcharges see Nos. 462-464. For overprints see Nos. 528-541, C3-C19.

Nos. 280-285 Surcharged in Carmine

1969, Feb. ***Perf. 12½***

310	A42	5c	on 1c multi	.25	.25
311	A42	8c	on 2c multi	.25	.25
312	A42	25c	on 3c multi	.25	.25
313	A42	35c	on 10c multi	.25	.25
314	A42	$1	on 50c multi	.25	.25
315	A42	$2	on 60c multi	.40	*.60*
			Nos. 310-315 (6)	1.65	1.85

Gov. Hilda Bynoe and View of St. George's A46

Designs: 15c, Premier Eric M. Gairy, fruits and St. George's. 60c, Emblems of Brussels, New York and Montreal World's Fairs.

1969, May 1 **Litho.** ***Perf. 13x13½***

316	A46	5c	multicolored	.25	.25
317	A46	15c	multicolored	.25	.25
318	A46	50c	multicolored	.25	.25
319	A46	60c	multicolored	.25	.30
			Nos. 316-319 (4)	1.00	1.05

Nos. 316-319 issued to publicize CARIFTA (Caribbean Free Trade Area) Exposition, St. George's, Apr. 5-30.

Gov. Hilda Bynoe — A47

Designs: 25c, Dr. Martin Luther King, Jr. $1, Belshazzar's Feast, by Rembrandt, horiz.

Perf. 13x12½, 12½x13

1969, June 8 **Photo.** **Unwmk.**

320	A47	5c	multicolored	.25	.25
321	A47	25c	multicolored	.25	.25
322	A47	35c	multicolored	.25	.25
323	A47	$1	multicolored	.30	.40
			Nos. 320-323 (4)	1.05	1.15

International Human Rights Year.

Batsman Playing Off-drive — A48

Cricket: 10c, Batsman playing defensive stroke. 25c, Batsman sweeping ball. 35c, Batsman playing on-drive.

1969, Aug. 1 ***Perf. 14x14½***

324	A48	3c	dk blue & multi	.25	*.95*
325	A48	10c	fawn & multi	.25	*.40*
326	A48	25c	dp green & multi	.45	*.80*
327	A48	35c	brt purple & multi	.60	*.85*
			Nos. 324-327 (4)	1.55	*3.00*

Astronaut Collecting Moon Rocks, Landing Module and Earth — A49

Designs: ½c, like $1. 1c, Apollo 11, moon and earth. 2c, Landing module "Eagle." 3c, Memorial tablet left on moon. 8c, Separation of rocket and spaceship. 25c, Take off from Cape Kennedy, vert. 35c, Apollo 11 circling the moon, vert. 50c, Splashdown, vert. ½c, 2c, 25c, 50c, $1 inscribed: "We came in peace for all mankind." 1c, 3c, 8c, 35c inscribed: "Like the moon it shall be established forever" Psalms 89:37.

Perf. 13x13½ (½c), 12½

1969, Sept. 24 **Litho.** **Unwmk.**

Size: 56x35mm

328	A49	½c	multicolored	.25	.25

Size: 44½x28mm, 28x44½mm

329	A49	1c	multicolored	.25	.25
330	A49	2c	multicolored	.25	.25
331	A49	3c	multicolored	.25	.25
332	A49	8c	multicolored	.25	.25
333	A49	25c	multicolored	.25	.25
334	A49	35c	multicolored	.25	.25
335	A49	50c	multicolored	.25	.25
336	A49	$1	multicolored	.40	.60
a.			Souvenir sheet of 2	2.00	2.00
			Nos. 328-336 (9)	2.40	2.60

Man's first moonlanding (Apollo 11), July 20, 1969.

No. 336a contains stamps similar to Nos. 331 and 336 with simulated perforations.

For surcharge and overprints see Nos. 349, 379-382.

Mahatma Gandhi — A50

Gandhi in various positions. 15c, 25c are vert.

1969, Oct. 8 ***Perf. 11½x12, 12x11½***

Queen's Head in Gold

337	A50	6c	multicolored	.25	.25
338	A50	15c	multicolored	.25	.25
339	A50	25c	multicolored	.55	.25
340	A50	$1	multicolored	.85	*1.10*
a.			Souvenir sheet of 4	5.00	5.00
			Nos. 337-340 (4)	1.90	1.85

Mohandas K. Gandhi (1869-1948), leader in India's fight for independence.

No. 340a contains stamps similar to Nos. 337-340 with simulated perforation.

Nos. 290-293 Overprinted in Black or Silver

1969, Dec. 23 Photo. *Perf. 12½*

341	A44	2c on 15c multi	.25	*.75*
342	A44	5c multi (S)	.25	.25
343	A44	35c multi (S)	.25	.25
344	A44	$1 multi (S)	.65	*1.75*
		Nos. 341-344 (4)	1.40	*3.00*

Christmas.

Edward Teach (Blackbeard) A51

Pirates: 25c, Anne Bonney and sailboats. 50c, Jean Lafitte and sailboats. $1, Mary Read, ships and fighting pirates.

1970, Feb. 1 Engr. *Perf. 13x13½*

345	A51	15c black	.60	.25
346	A51	25c emerald	1.00	.25
347	A51	50c purple	1.90	.25
348	A51	$1 carmine	3.00	.95
		Nos. 345-348 (4)	6.50	1.70

No. 328 Surcharged

Type I

Type II

1970, Mar. 18 Litho. *Perf. 13x13½*

349	A49	5c on ½c multi (I)	.40	.40
a.		Type II	1.25	*1.50*

Christ, from "The Last Supper," by Andrea del Sarto — A52

Paintings: No. 351 (5c), St. John, from Last Supper by Andrea del Sarto. Nos. 352-353 (15c), Christ Crowned with Thorns, by Anthony Van Dyck. Nos. 354-355 (25c), Passion of Christ, by Hans Memling. Nos. 356-357 (60c), Christ in the Tomb, by Peter Paul Rubens. Nos. 350, 352, 354 and 356 have denomination in lower right corner; others in lower left corner. The stamps of the same denomination are printed se-tenant without separating margin, reproducing continuous picture.

1970, Apr. 13 Litho. *Perf. 11½x11*

350		5c rose car & multi	.25	.25
351		5c rose car & multi	.25	.25
a.		A52 Pair, #350-351	.40	.40
352		15c ultra & multi	.25	*.25*
353		15c ultra & multi	.25	*.25*
a.		A52 Pair, #352-353	.40	*.50*
354		25c brt vio & multi	.25	*.25*
355		25c brt vio & multi	.25	*.25*
a.		A52 Pair, #354-355	.40	.50
356		60c dull org & multi	.25	*.55*
357		60c dull org & multi	.25	*.55*
a.		A52 Pair, #356-357	.40	1.10
b.		Souvenir sheet of 4, #354-357	1.25	1.25
		Nos. 350-357 (8)	2.00	*2.60*

Easter.

Girl Pushing Carriage with Kittens — A53

Designs: 15c, Girl playing with puppy and kitten. 30c, Boy fishing and cat. 60c, Children with pets.

1970, May 27 Litho. *Perf. 11*

358	A53	5c multicolored	.25	.25
359	A53	15c multicolored	.25	.25
360	A53	30c multicolored	.35	.35
a.		Souvenir sheet of 2	2.00	2.00
361	A53	60c multicolored	.75	*1.00*
a.		Souvenir sheet of 2	2.00	2.00
		Nos. 358-361 (4)	1.60	1.85

William Wordsworth (1770-1850). English poet. No. 360a contains stamps similar to Nos. 358 and 360; No. 361a contains stamps similar to Nos. 359 and 361. Sheets have simulated perforations.

Indian Parliament — A54

Commonwealth Parliamentary Association Emblem and: 25c, British Parliament. 50c, Canadian Parliament. 60c, Grenadian Parliament.

1970, June 15 *Perf. 14½x14*

362	A54	5c multicolored	.25	.25
363	A54	25c multicolored	.25	.25
364	A54	50c multicolored	.25	.25
365	A54	60c multicolored	.25	.25
a.		Souvenir sheet of 4, #362-365	1.00	1.00
		Nos. 362-365 (4)	1.00	1.00

7th Caribbean Regional Conf. of the Commonwealth Parliamentary Assoc., St. George's. June 13-20.

Sun Tower and EXPO Emblem A55

EXPO Emblem and: 2c, Livelihood Industry pavilion, horiz. 3c, Ikenobo, Japanese floral art, vert. 10c, Adam and Eve, by Tintoretto and Italian pavilion, horiz. 25c, UN pavilion and flags reflected in pool, 50c, Peace statue of St. Francis, San Francisco pavilion, cable car and Golden Gate Bridge, $1, Toshiba-Ihi pavilion, horiz.

1970, Aug. 8 Litho. *Perf. 13½*

366	A55	1c brt blue & multi	.25	.25
367	A55	2c multicolored	.25	.25
368	A55	3c buff & multi	.25	.25
369	A55	10c multicolored	.25	.25
370	A55	25c gray & multi	.25	.25
371	A55	50c gray & multi	.25	*1.00*
		Nos. 366-371 (6)	1.50	2.25

Souvenir Sheet

372	A55	$1 gold & multi	1.00	*1.75*

EXPO '70 Intl. Exhib., Osaka, Japan, Mar. 15-Sept. 13.

Pres. Roosevelt and Flag-Raising on Iwo Jima A56

Designs: 5c, Marshal Georgi K. Zhukov and fall of Berlin. 15c, Winston Churchill and evacuation of Dunkirk. 25c, Charles de Gaulle and liberation of Paris. 50c, General Dwight D. Eisenhower and D-Day landing. 60c, Field Marshal Bernard Montgomery and Battle of Alamein.

1970, Sept. 3 *Perf. 11*

373	A56	½c multicolored	.25	*.60*
374	A56	5c multicolored	1.00	.35
375	A56	15c multicolored	1.50	.55
376	A56	25c multicolored	1.75	.55
377	A56	50c multicolored	2.00	1.60
378	A56	60c multicolored	2.25	*3.00*
a.		Souv. sheet of 4 #373, 375, 377-378	5.75	5.75
		Nos. 373-378 (6)	8.75	6.65

End of World War II, 25th anniversary.

Nos. 333-336 Overprinted in Black or Silver: "PHILYMPIA / LONDON 1970"

1970, Sept. 18 *Perf. 12½*

379	A49	25c multicolored	.25	.25
380	A49	35c multicolored	.25	.25
381	A49	50c multicolored	.25	.25
382	A49	$1 multi (S)	.40	.40
		Nos. 379-382 (4)	1.15	1.15

Philympia 1970, London philatelic exhibition, Sept. 18-26. The overprint on No. 382 is vertical, reading up.

This overprint was applied in silver to No. 336a. Value $45.

UPU Headquarters, Emblem and Old Transportation — A57

UPU Headquarters, emblem and: 25c, Jet plane, ship and diesel train. 50c, Rowland Hill, vert. $1, Abraham Lincoln, vert.

1970, Oct. 17 Litho. *Perf. 14½*

383	A57	15c orange & multi	.65	.25
384	A57	25c blue & multi	.65	.25
385	A57	50c multicolored	.40	.40
386	A57	$1 rose & multi	.60	*2.00*
a.		Souvenir sheet of 2	1.90	*3.00*
		Nos. 383-386 (4)	2.30	2.90

Opening of the new UPU Headquarters in Bern. No. 386a contains stamps similar to Nos. 385-386.

Madonna of the Goldfinch, by Tiepolo — A58

Christmas (Paintings): No. 388, 35c, Virgin and Child with Sts. Peter and Paul, by Dirk Bouts. No. 389, $1, Virgin and Child, by Bellini. 3c, Like No. 387. 2c, 50c, Madonna of the Basket, by Correggio.

1970, Dec. 5 *Perf. 14x13½*

387	A58	½c yel grn & multi	.25	.25
388	A58	½c pink & multi	.25	.25
389	A58	½c yellow & multi	.25	.25
390	A58	2c lt blue & multi	.25	.25
391	A58	3c dp rose & multi	.25	.25
392	A58	35c dk green & multi	.25	.40
393	A58	50c brown & multi	.35	.50
394	A58	$1 purple & multi	.50	1.10
a.		Souvenir sheet of 2, #393-394	2.25	*3.00*
		Nos. 387-394 (8)	2.35	3.25

Nursing in 19th Century A59

Designs: 15c, Horse-drawn ambulance, Northern France, 1918. 25c, First aid station, 1941. 60c, Red Cross truck loaded on plane, 1970 emergency aid.

1970, Dec. 12 Litho. *Perf. 14½x14*

395	A59	5c red & multi	.25	.25
396	A59	15c red & multi	.30	.25
397	A59	25c red & multi	.50	.35
398	A59	60c red & multi	1.00	*1.25*
a.		Souvenir sheet of 4, #395-398	2.50	2.25
		Nos. 395-398 (4)	2.05	2.10

Centenary of the British Red Cross Society.

John Dewey, Children Learning to Paint — A60

Designs: 10c, Jean-Jacques Rousseau and students. 50c, Moses Maimonides and biology student. $1, Bertrand Russell and boys.

1971, May 8 Litho. *Perf. 13½*

399	A60	5c multicolored	.25	.25
400	A60	10c multicolored	.25	.25
401	A60	50c multicolored	.50	.50
402	A60	$1 multicolored	1.10	.75
a.		Souvenir sheet of 2, #401-402	2.00	2.25
		Nos. 399-402 (4)	2.10	1.75

International Education Year.

Jennifer Hosten and Map of Grenada A61

1971, June 1 Litho. *Perf. 13½*

403	A61	5c vio blue & multi	.25	.25
404	A61	10c red lilac & multi	.25	.25
405	A61	15c brt rose & multi	.25	.25
406	A61	25c violet & multi	.25	.25
407	A61	35c blue & multi	.30	.45
408	A61	50c red & multi	.65	.65
a.		Souvenir sheet of 1	1.90	2.00
		Nos. 403-408 (6)	1.95	2.10

Honoring Miss Jennifer Hosten of Grenada, Miss World, 1971. No. 408a, printed on silk, contains imperf. stamp similar to No. 408.

Nos. 403-408 and 408a were overprinted "INTERPEX/1972" in Mar. 1972. Value $9.50.

For surcharge and overprints Nos. 465, C23-C26.

Canadian and French Boy Scouts — A62

Boy Scouts from: 35c, West Germany and US. 50c, Australia and Japan. 75c, Grenada and Great Britain.

1971, Aug. Litho. *Perf. 11*

409	A62	5c multicolored	.25	.25
410	A62	35c multicolored	.40	.40
411	A62	50c multicolored	.50	.60
412	A62	75c multicolored	.65	.90
a.		Souvenir sheet of 2, #411-412	2.00	*2.75*
		Nos. 409-412 (4)	1.80	2.15

13th Boy Scout World Jamboree, Asagiri Plain, Japan, Aug. 2-10.

Napoleon, by Edouard Détaille A63

Paintings of Napoleon: 15c, Outside Madrid, by Carle Vernet. 35c, Crossing the Alps, by Jacques Louis David. $2, Portrait, by David.

1971, Sept. *Perf. 13x13½*

413	A63	5c multicolored	.25	.25
414	A63	15c multicolored	.25	.25
415	A63	35c multicolored	.40	.40
a.		Souvenir sheet of 1	2.50	*3.25*
416	A63	$2 multicolored	1.25	1.60
		Nos. 413-416 (4)	2.15	2.50

Sesquicentennial of the death of Napoleon Bonaparte (1769-1821).

No. 415a contains stamp similar to No. 415 with simulated perforations.

Grenada No. 1 — A64

15c, Grenada #2 & Queen Elizabeth II. 35c, Grenada #1, 2. 50c, Grenada #1 & scroll.

1971, Nov. 6 Litho. *Perf. 11*

417	A64	5c dk red & multi	.25	.25
418	A64	15c multicolored	.35	.25
419	A64	35c dull org & multi	.55	.25
420	A64	50c dk green & multi	.75	*1.75*
a.		Souvenir sheet of 2, #419-420	1.75	1.75
		Nos. 417-420 (4)	1.90	*2.50*

110th anniversary of postal service.

Splashdown, Apollo 13 — A65

Designs: 2c, Capsule and rafts in ocean, Apollo 13. 3c, Separation of landing module from rocket, Apollo 14. 10c, Astronauts collecting moon rocks, Apollo 14. 25c, Astronauts in moon rover, Apollo 15. 50c, $1, Rocket blast-off, Apollo 15, vert.

1971, Nov.

421	A65	1c multicolored	.25	.30
422	A65	2c multicolored	.25	.30
423	A65	3c black & multi	.25	.30
424	A65	10c black & multi	.35	.25
425	A65	25c multicolored	1.10	.35
426	A65	$1 multicolored	2.25	*3.50*
		Nos. 421-426 (6)	4.45	*5.00*

Souvenir Sheet

427	A65	50c multicolored	2.50	2.50

US moon missions of Apollo 10, 14 and 15.

67th Regiment of Foot, 1787 — A66

Designs: 1c, 45th Regiment of Foot, 1792. 2c, 29th Regiment of Foot, 1794. 10c, 9th Regiment of Foot, 1801. 25c, 2nd Regiment of Foot, 1815. $1, 70th Regiment of Foot, 1764.

1971, Dec. *Perf. 13½x14*

428	A66	½c red & multi	.25	.25
429	A66	1c red & multi	.25	.25
430	A66	2c red & multi	.25	.25
431	A66	10c red & multi	.50	.25
432	A66	25c red & multi	.90	.30
433	A66	$1 red & multi	2.75	2.75
a.		Souv. sheet of 2, #432-433, perf. 15	4.00	4.00
		Nos. 428-433 (6)	4.90	4.05

Uniforms of British units stationed in Grenada.

For surcharges see Nos. 439, C1-C2.

Adoration of the Kings, by Memling — A67

Christmas: 25c, Madonna and Child, sculpture by Michelangelo. 35c, Madonna and Child, by Murillo. 50c, Madonna with the Apple, by Memling. $1, Adoration of the Kings, by Jan Mostaert.

1971, Dec. *Perf. 14x13½*

434	A67	15c gold & multi	.25	.25
435	A67	25c gold & multi	.25	.25
436	A67	35c gold & multi	.30	.25
437	A67	50c gold & multi	.40	.75
		Nos. 434-437 (4)	1.20	1.50

Souvenir Sheet

438	A67	$1 gold & multi	1.00	1.00

No. 430 Surcharged

1972, Feb. 3 *Perf. 13½x14*

439	A66	$2 on 2c red & multi	1.25	1.25
a.		Souvenir sheet of 2	2.00	2.00

11th Winter Olympic Games, Sapporo, Japan, Feb. 3-13. See Nos. C1-C2.

No. 439a is overprinted in red on No. 433a (no surcharge); margin inscribed in red: "SAPPORO 1972."

King Arthur, UNICEF Emblem A68

UNICEF Emblem and: 1c, 50c, Robin Hood. 2c, 75c, Robinson Crusoe, vert. 25c, like ½c. $1, Mary and her Little Lamb, vert.

1972, Mar. 4 *Perf. 14½x14, 14x14½*

450	A68	½c dp blue & multi	.25	.25
451	A68	1c yellow & multi	.25	.25
452	A68	2c dp yel & multi	.25	.25
453	A68	25c salmon & multi	.25	.25
454	A68	50c multicolored	.25	.35
455	A68	75c blue & multi	.30	.60
456	A68	$1 multicolored	.40	.85
a.		Souvenir sheet of 1	1.00	1.00
		Nos. 450-456 (7)	1.95	2.80

25th anniv. (in 1971) of UNICEF.

Yachting A69

1c, 50c, Equestrian. 2c, 35c, Running, vert.

1972, Sept. 8 Litho. *Perf. 14*

457	A69	½c multicolored	.25	.25
458	A69	1c lt blue & multi	.25	.25
459	A69	2c orange & multi	.25	.25
460	A69	35c yellow & multi	.40	.80
461	A69	50c yel grn & multi	.60	1.10
		Nos. 457-461,C20-C21 (7)	3.15	3.70

20th Olympic Games, Munich, Aug. 26-Sept. 11. See No. C22.

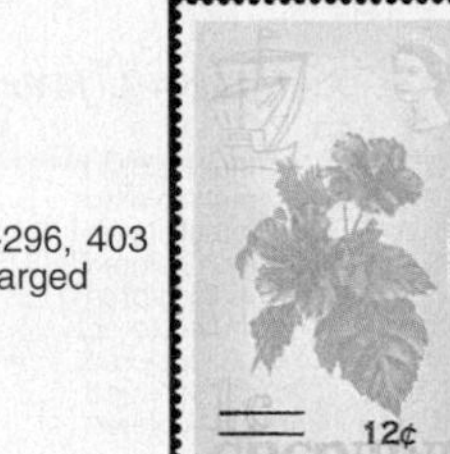

Nos. 294-296, 403 Surcharged

Perf. 14x14½, 13½

1972, Oct. Photo.

462	A45	12c on 1c multi	.50	.55
463	A45	12c on 2c multi	.50	.55
464	A45	12c on 3c multi	.50	.55
465	A61	12c on 5c multi	.50	.55
		Nos. 462-465 (4)	2.00	2.20

Silver Wedding Issue, 1972

Common Design Type

Design: Queen Elizabeth II, Prince Philip, seal of Grenada and myristica fragrans.

Perf. 14x14½

1972, Nov. 20 Wmk. 314

466	CD324	8c olive & multi	.25	.25
467	CD324	$1 multicolored	.45	.45

Boy Scout Saluting A70

Designs: 1c, Two Scouts knotting ropes. 2c, 70c, 75c, Scouts from different nations. 3c, 60c, $1, Lord Baden-Powell.

Unwmk.

1972, Dec. 2 Litho. *Perf. 14*

468	A70	½c yellow & multi	.25	.25
469	A70	1c red & multi	.25	.25
470	A70	2c yellow & multi	.25	.25
471	A70	3c brt lilac & multi	.25	.25
472	A70	75c lt blue & multi	.80	.80
473	A70	$1 multicolored	1.25	1.25
		Nos. 468-473,C27-C28 (8)	4.05	3.95

Souvenir Sheet

474		Sheet of 2	2.75	2.75
a.		A70 60c ocher & multi	1.25	1.25
b.		A70 70c pale lilac & multi	1.50	1.50

Boy Scouts, 65th anniversary.

Virgin and Child, Crosier — A71

Christmas: 3c, 35c, 70c, The Three Kings. 5c, $1, Holy Family. 25c, 60c, Like 1c.

1972, Dec. 9 Litho. *Perf. 14x13½*

475	A71	1c blue & multi	.25	.25
476	A71	3c gray & multi	.25	.25
477	A71	5c multicolored	.25	.25
478	A71	25c multicolored	.25	.25
479	A71	35c lt blue & multi	.25	.25
480	A71	$1 ocher & multi	.60	.60
		Nos. 475-480 (6)	1.85	1.85

Souvenir Sheet

Perf. 15

481		Sheet of 2	1.10	1.10
a.		A71 60c blue & multi	.45	.45
b.		A71 70c bright pink & multi	.60	.60

Flamingos — A72

1973, Jan. 5 Litho. *Perf. 14*

482	A72	25c shown	1.00	.25
483	A72	35c Tapir	.80	.25
484	A72	60c Macaws	1.75	1.75
485	A72	70c Ocelot	1.60	*2.25*
		Nos. 482-485 (4)	5.15	4.50

National Zoo of Grenada.

Class II Ocean Racing Yacht — A73

35c, Boats in St. George's Harbour. 60c, Yacht "Bloodhound". 70c, St. George's Harbour.

1973, Jan. 26 Litho. *Perf. 13½x14*

486	A73	25c shown	.40	.35
487	A73	35c multicolored	.55	.50
488	A73	60c multicolored	.90	.85
489	A73	70c multicolored	.95	*1.10*
		Nos. 486-489 (4)	2.80	2.80

Yachting off Grenada.

Sun God Helios, Equinoxes and Solstices — A74

WMO Emblem and: 1c, Poseidon and Nomad automatic storm detector. 2c, Zeus and radarscope. 3c, Goddess Iris, rainbow, weather balloon. 35c, Hermes, ATS 3 satellite. 50c, Zephyr and circulation of atmosphere. 75c, Demeter, space photograph of storm. $1, Selene, globe showing world rainfall. $2, Computer weather map (42x31mm).

1973, July 6 Litho. *Perf. 13½*

No.	Type	Value / Color	Unused	Used
490	A74	½c multicolored	.25	.25
491	A74	1c multicolored	.25	.25
492	A74	2c multicolored	.25	.25
493	A74	3c multicolored	.25	.25
494	A74	35c multicolored	.30	.25
495	A74	50c multicolored	.45	.25
496	A74	75c multicolored	.55	.45
497	A74	$1 multicolored	.55	.55
		Nos. 490-497 (8)	2.85	2.50

Souvenir Sheet

498	A74	$2 multicolored	1.75	1.75

Intl. meteorological cooperation, cent.

Racing Class Yachts — A75

1c, Cruising class. 2c, Open-decked sloops. 35c, Sloop Mermaid. 50c, St. George's Harbour. 75c, Map of Carriacou. $1, Boat building. $2, End of race.

1973, Aug. 3 Litho. *Perf. 13½*

No.	Type	Value / Color	Unused	Used
499	A75	½c shown	.25	.25
500	A75	1c multicolored	.25	.25
501	A75	2c multicolored	.25	.25
502	A75	35c multicolored	.35	.25
503	A75	50c multicolored	.45	.25
504	A75	75c multicolored	.65	.65
505	A75	$1 multicolored	.80	.80
		Nos. 499-505 (7)	3.00	2.70

Souvenir Sheet

506	A75	$2 multicolored	1.50	1.75

Carriacou Regatta, August 1973.

Ignaz Philipp Semmelweiss A76

Designs: Physicians and scientists.

1973, Sept. 17 Litho. *Perf. 14½*

No.	Type	Value / Design	Unused	Used
507	A76	½c shown	.25	.25
508	A76	1c Louis Pasteur	.25	.25
509	A76	2c Edward Jenner	.25	.25
510	A76	3c Sigmund Freud	.25	.25
511	A76	25c Emil von Behring	.45	.45
512	A76	35c Carl Jung	.60	.60
513	A76	50c Charles Calmette	.90	.90
514	A76	$1 William Harvey	1.75	1.75
		Nos. 507-514 (8)	4.70	4.70

Souvenir Sheet

515	A76	$2 Marie Curie	3.50	3.50

WHO, 25th anniv.

Princess Anne and Mark Phillips — A77

1973, Nov. 14 Wmk. 314 *Perf. 13½*

No.	Type	Value / Color	Unused	Used
516	A77	25c dp orange & multi	.30	.80
517	A77	$2 green & multi	.30	.80
a.		Souv. sheet of 2 (75c, $1)	.60	.60

Wedding of Princess Anne and Capt. Mark Phillips.

Nos. 516-517 were issued only in sheets of 5 plus label. Colors of 75c and $1 are as those of 25c and $2.

Virgin and Child, by Carlo Maratti — A78

Christmas (Paintings): 1c, Virgin and Child, by Carlo Crivelli. 2c, Virgin and Child, by Verrocchio. 3c, Adoration of the Shepherds, by Roberti. 25c, Holy Family, by Federigo Baroccio. 35c, Holy Family, by Bronzino. 75c, Mystic Nativity, by Botticelli. $1, Adoration of the Kings, by Geertgen tot Sint Jans. $2, Adoration of the Kings, by Jan Mostaert (30x45mm).

1973, Nov. Unwmk. *Perf. 14½*

No.	Type	Value / Color	Unused	Used
519	A78	½c lt brown & multi	.25	.25
520	A78	1c citron & multi	.25	.25
521	A78	2c blue & multi	.25	.25
522	A78	3c green & multi	.25	.25
523	A78	25c multicolored	.25	.25
524	A78	35c multicolored	.25	.25
525	A78	75c vio blue & multi	.25	.80
526	A78	$1 multicolored	.30	1.00
		Nos. 519-526 (8)	2.05	3.30

Souvenir Sheet

Perf. 13½x14

527	A78	$2 red & multi	2.00	2.00

Nos. 294-297, 299-301, 303-304, 305A-309 Overprinted

Perf. 14x14½, 14½x14

1974, Feb. 7 Photo.

No.	Type	Value / Color	Unused	Used
528	A45	1c multicolored	.25	.25
529	A45	2c multicolored	.25	.25
530	A45	3c multicolored	.25	.25
531	A45	5c multicolored	.25	.25
532	A45	8c multicolored	.25	.25
533	A45	10c multicolored	.25	.25
534	A45	12c multicolored	.25	.25
535	A45	25c multicolored	.40	.40
536	A45	35c multicolored	.60	.60

Litho.

Perf. 13½x14

537	A45a	75c multicolored	*2.10*	*1.50*

Photo.

Perf. 14x14½

No.	Type	Value / Color	Unused	Used
538	A45	$1 multicolored	*3.75*	*1.75*
539	A45	$2 multicolored	*5.75*	*6.50*
540	A45	$3 multicolored	*7.25*	*8.25*
541	A45	$5 multicolored	*11.50*	*18.50*
		Nos. 528-541 (14)	*33.10*	*39.25*

Grenada's independence, Feb. 7, 1974. Size of overprint on vertical stamps 16x5mm; on horizontal stamps 20x6mm.

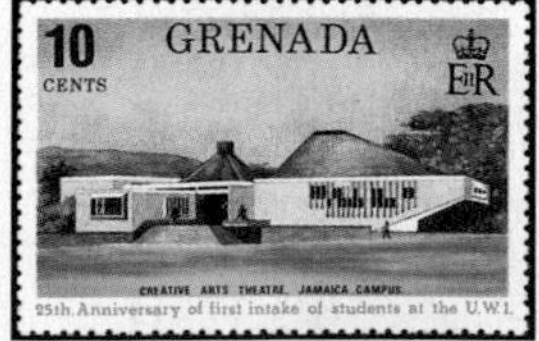

Creative Arts Theater, Jamaica Campus — A79

Designs: 25c, Marryshow House, University Center. 50c, Chapel, vert. $1, $2, University coat of arms, vert.

1974, Apr. 10 Litho. *Perf. 13½*

No.	Type	Value / Color	Unused	Used
542	A79	10c multicolored	.25	.25
543	A79	25c multicolored	.25	.25
544	A79	50c multicolored	.25	.25
545	A79	$1 multicolored	.30	.30
		Nos. 542-545 (4)	1.05	1.05

Souvenir Sheet

546	A79	$2 multicolored	.90	.90

25th anniv. of the University of the West Indies.

Prime Minister Eric M. Gairy — A80

3c, Nutmeg and mace. 8c, Map of Grenada. 35c, Anse Beach and Flag. $1, Coat of arms. $2, Coat of arms.

1974, Aug. 19 Litho. *Perf. 13½*

No.	Type	Value / Color	Unused	Used
547	A80	3c multicolored	.25	.25
548	A80	8c multicolored	.25	.25
549	A80	25c shown	.30	.30
550	A80	35c multicolored	.35	.35
551	A80	$1 multicolored	.85	.85
		Nos. 547-551 (5)	2.00	2.00

Souvenir Sheet

552	A80	$2 multicolored	1.10	1.10

Grenada's independence.

Soccer, Flags of West Germany and Chile — A81

Soccer Games and Flags: 1c, East Germany and Australia. 2c, Yugoslavia and Brazil. 10c, Scotland and Zaire. 25c, Netherlands and Uruguay. 50c, Sweden and Bulgaria. 75c, Italy and Haiti. $1, Poland and Argentina. $2, Flags of participating nations, horiz.

1974, Sept. 3 Litho. *Perf. 14½*

No.	Type	Value / Color	Unused	Used
553	A81	½c multicolored	.25	.25
554	A81	1c multicolored	.25	.25
555	A81	2c multicolored	.25	.25
556	A81	10c multicolored	.25	.25
557	A81	25c multicolored	.25	.25
558	A81	50c multicolored	.25	.25
559	A81	75c multicolored	.30	.30
560	A81	$1 multicolored	.45	.45
		Nos. 553-560 (8)	2.25	2.25

Souvenir Sheet

Perf. 13

561	A81	$2 multicolored	1.60	1.60

World Cup Soccer Championship, Munich, June 13-July 7.

19th Century US Mail Train, Concorde and UPU Emblem — A82

UPU Emblem and: 1c, Sailing ship "Caesar," 1839, and helicopter. 2c, Zeppelin, jet and early planes. 8c, Pigeon post, 1480, telephone dial. 15c, Bellman, 18th cent. and radar. 25c, German Imperial messenger, 1450, satellite. 35c, French pillar box and ocean liner. $1, German mailman, 18th cent., and futuristic mail train. $2, St. Gotthard mail coach, 1735, vert.

1974, Oct. 8 Litho. *Perf. 14½*

No.	Type	Value / Color	Unused	Used
562	A82	½c rose & multi	.25	.25
563	A82	1c gray & multi	.25	.25
564	A82	2c dull pink & multi	.25	.25
565	A82	8c yellow & multi	.25	.25
566	A82	15c yel grn & multi	.40	.25
567	A82	25c dull yel & multi	.45	.25
568	A82	35c lilac & multi	.70	.25
569	A82	$1 lt blue & multi	1.75	1.60
		Nos. 562-569 (8)	4.30	3.35

Souvenir Sheet

Perf. 13

570	A82	$2 multicolored	1.75	*2.25*

UPU, cent.

Sir Winston Churchill — A83

Design: $2, Churchill, different portrait.

1974, Oct. 28 Litho. *Perf. 13½*

No.	Type	Value / Color	Unused	Used
571	A83	35c multicolored	.25	.25
572	A83	$2 multicolored	.65	.65

Souvenir Sheet

No.		Description	Unused	Used
573		Sheet of 2	1.10	1.10
a.		A83 75c like 35c	.45	.45
b.		A83 $1 like $2	.65	.65

Winston Churchill (1874-1965).

Virgin and Child, by Botticelli — A84

Christmas: Paintings of the Virgin and Child.

1974, Nov. 18 *Perf. 14½*

No.	Type	Value / Design	Unused	Used
574	A84	½ shown	.25	.25
575	A84	1c Niccolo di Pietro	.25	.25
576	A84	2c Van der Weyden	.25	.25
577	A84	3c Bastiani	.25	.25
578	A84	10c Giovanni	.25	.25
579	A84	25c Van der Weyden	.25	.25
580	A84	50c Botticelli	.25	.25
581	A84	$1 Mantegna	.40	.40
		Nos. 574-581 (8)	2.15	2.15

Souvenir Sheet

Perf. 13½

582	A84	$2 Niccolo di Pietro	1.40	1.40

Yachts and Point Saline A85

1c, Grenada Yacht Club race, St. George's. 2c, Carenage taxi (boat). 3c, Large working boats. 5c, Deep Water Dock, St. George's. 6c, Cacao beans in drying trays. 8c, Nutmeg branch. 10c, River Antoine Estate rum distillery, c. 1785. 12c, Cacao branch. 15c, Fishermen landing catch at Fontenoy. 20c, Parliament Building, St. George's. 25c, Fort George cannons. 35c, Pearls Airport. 50c, General Post Office. 75c, Carib Leap, Sauteurs Bay. $1, Careenage, St. George's. $2, St. George's harbor at night. $3, Grand Anse Beach. $5, Canoe Bay and Black Bay from Point Saline Lighthouse. $10, Sugar-loaf Island from Levera Beach.

1975 Litho. *Perf. 14½*

Size: 38x25mm

No.	Type	Value / Color	Unused	Used
583	A85	½c multicolored	.25	*.55*
584	A85	1c multicolored	.25	.25
585	A85	2c multicolored	.25	.25
586	A85	3c multicolored	.25	.25
587	A85	5c multicolored	.25	.25
588	A85	6c multicolored	.25	.25
589	A85	8c multicolored	1.00	.25
590	A85	10c multicolored	.25	.25
591	A85	12c multicolored	.35	.25
592	A85	15c multicolored	.25	.25
593	A85	20c multicolored	.25	.25
594	A85	25c multicolored	.25	.25
595	A85	35c multicolored	.25	.25
596	A85	50c multicolored	.25	.25

Perf. 13½x14

Size: 45x28mm

No.	Type	Value / Color	Unused	Used
597	A85	75c multicolored	.50	.40
598	A85	$1 multicolored	.55	.60
599	A85	$2 multicolored	.55	*1.25*
600	A85	$3 multicolored	.60	*1.75*
601	A85	$5 multicolored	.70	*2.50*
602	A85	$10 multicolored	2.00	*5.50*
		Nos. 583-602 (20)	9.25	15.80

Issue dates: Nos. 583-596, Jan. 13; Nos. 597-601, Jan. 22; No. 602, Mar. 26.

For overprints, see Nos. 965-979.

1978 *Perf. 13*

No.	Type	Denom.	Unused	Used
584a	A85	1c	.25	.25
585a	A85	2c	.25	.25
586a	A85	3c	.25	.25
587a	A85	5c	.25	.25
588a	A85	6c	.25	.25
590a	A85	10c	.25	.25
592a	A85	15c	.25	.30
593a	A85	20c	.25	.40
594a	A85	25c	.25	.50
596a	A85	50c	.40	.55
		Nos. 584a-596a (10)	2.65	3.25

Sailfish A86

Designs: Big game fish.

1975, Feb. 3 *Perf. 14½*

603	A86	½c shown	.25	.25
604	A86	1c Blue marlin	.25	.25
605	A86	2c White marlin	.25	.25
606	A86	10c Yellowfin tuna	.25	.25
607	A86	25c Wahoo	.35	.30
608	A86	50c Dolphin	.55	.40
609	A86	70c Grouper	.75	.40
610	A86	$1 Great barracuda	.90	.50
		Nos. 603-610 (8)	3.55	2.60

Souvenir Sheet

Perf. 13

611	A86	$2 Mako shark	2.40	2.40

Passiflora Quadrangularis — A87

Flowers of Grenada: 1c, Bleeding heart. 2c, Poinsettia. 3c, Obroma cacao. 10c, Gladioli. 25c, Red head-yellow head. 50c, Plumbago. $1, Orange blossoms.
$2, Barbados gooseberry.

1975, Feb. 26 **Litho.** *Perf. 14½*

612	A87	½c shown	.25	.25
613	A87	1c multicolored	.25	.25
614	A87	2c multicolored	.25	.25
615	A87	3c multicolored	.25	.25
616	A87	10c multicolored	.25	.25
617	A87	25c multicolored	.45	.25
618	A87	50c multicolored	.65	.25
619	A87	$1 multicolored	.95	.45
		Nos. 612-619 (8)	3.30	2.20

Souvenir Sheet

Perf. 13½

620	A87	$2 multicolored	1.75	1.75

Grenada Flag and UN Emblem — A88

Designs: 1c, UN and Grenada flags. 2c, $1, UN emblem and Grenada coat of arms. 35c, UN emblem over map of Grenada. 50c, Grenada flag in front of UN Headquarters. 75c, like ½c. $2, UN emblem and scroll.

1975, Mar. 10 *Perf. 14½*

621	A88	½c multicolored	.25	.25
622	A88	1c multicolored	.25	.25
623	A88	2c multicolored	.25	.25
624	A88	35c multicolored	.25	.25
625	A88	50c multicolored	.25	.25
626	A88	$2 multicolored	.50	.50
		Nos. 621-626 (6)	1.75	1.75

Souvenir Sheet

Perf. 13½

627	Sheet of 2	1.40	1.40
a.	A88 75c multicolored	.55	.55
b.	A88 $1 multicolored	.90	.90

Grenada's admission to the United Nations, Sept. 17, 1974.

> Remainders of Grenada stamps between Scott Nos. 630 and 872, except Nos. 747-748 and 802-804, were later canceled to order and sold at a fraction of their face value. Our used values for these stamps are for c-t-o examples. Postally used stamps are worth the same as unused, never hinged examples.

Midnight Ride of Paul Revere — A89

1c, Crispus Attucks at Boston Massacre. 2c, Patrick Henry. 3c, Franklin visiting Washington at the front. 5c, Lexington-Concord. 10c, John Paul Jones. No. 634, Arms of Grenada & US. No. 635, Flags of Grenada & US.

1975, May 6 **Litho.** *Perf. 14½, 13*

628	A89	½c Prus blue & multi	.25	*.25*
629	A89	1c buff & multi	.25	*.25*
630	A89	2c dp org & multi	.25	*.25*
631	A89	3c orange & multi	.25	*.25*
632	A89	5c Prus blue & multi	.25	*.25*
633	A89	10c ultra & multi	.25	*.25*
		Nos. 628-633,C29-C32 (10)	3.40	*2.50*

Souvenir Sheets

Perf. 13½

634	A89	$2 tan & multi	1.00	*.45*
635	A89	$2 gray & multi	1.00	*.45*

American Revolution Bicentennial. Size of stamps on Nos. 634-635: 47x34mm.

Nos. 628-633 issued in sheets of 40. Each denomination was also printed in sheets of 5 plus label, perf. 13.

Angel Collecting Jesus' Blood in Grail, by Bellini — A90

Easter (Paintings): 1c, Pieta, by Bellini. 2c, The Deposition, by Rogier van der Weyden. 3c, Pieta, by Bellini. 35c, Descent from the Cross, by Bellini. 75c, Jesus Rising from the Tomb, by Bellini. $1, Descent from the Cross, by Procaccini. $2, Pieta, by Botticelli.

1975, May 21

636	A90	½c multicolored	.25	*.25*
637	A90	1c multicolored	.25	*.25*
638	A90	2c multicolored	.25	*.25*
639	A90	3c multicolored	.25	*.25*
640	A90	35c multicolored	.30	*.25*
641	A90	75c multicolored	.35	*.25*
642	A90	$1 multicolored	.45	*.25*
		Nos. 636-642 (7)	2.10	*1.75*

Souvenir Sheet

Perf. 13½

643	A90	$2 multicolored	1.40	*.65*

Scouts Studying Wildlife, Nordjamb 75 Emblem A91

Nordjamb 75 Emblem and: 1c, Seamanship; Scouts in sailboat. 2c, Survival; Scouts reading map. 35c, First aid. 40c, Physical fitness; gymnastics. 75c, Mountaineering. $1, Emergency boat building. $2, Scouts singing.

1975, July 2 **Litho.** *Perf. 14*

644	A91	½c blue & multi	.25	*.25*
645	A91	1c blue & multi	.25	*.25*
646	A91	2c blue & multi	.25	*.25*
647	A91	35c blue & multi	.45	*.25*
648	A91	40c blue & multi	.50	*.25*
649	A91	75c blue & multi	.60	*.25*
650	A91	$2 blue & multi	1.25	*.35*
		Nos. 644-650 (7)	3.55	*1.85*

Souvenir Sheet

651	A91	$1 blue & multi	1.00	*.35*

Nordjamb 75, 14th Boy Scout World Jamboree, Lillehammer, Norway, July 29-Aug. 7.

Leafy Jewel Box — A92

Sea shells — 1c, Emerald nerite. 2c, Yellow cockle. 25c, Purple sea snail. 50c, Turkey wing. 75c, West Indian fighting conch. $1, Noble wentletrap.
$2, Music volute.

1975, Aug. 1 **Litho.** *Perf. 14*

652	A92	½c shown	.25	*.25*
653	A92	1c multicolored	.25	*.25*
654	A92	2c multicolored	.25	*.25*
655	A92	25c multicolored	1.00	*.25*
656	A92	50c multicolored	2.00	*.40*
657	A92	75c multicolored	2.75	*.50*
658	A92	$1 multicolored	2.75	*.50*
		Nos. 652-658 (7)	9.25	*2.40*

Souvenir Sheet

659	A92	$2 multicolored	4.50	*.90*

Butterflies — A93

½c, Large tiger. 1c, Five continents. 2c, Large striped blue. 35c, Gonatryx. 45c, Spear-winged cattle heart. 75c, Risty nymula. $2, Blue night.
$1, Lycrophon.

1975, Sept. 22 **Litho.** *Perf. 14*

660	A93	½c multicolored	.25	*.25*
661	A93	1c multicolored	.25	*.25*
662	A93	2c multicolored	.25	*.25*
663	A93	35c multicolored	.85	*.25*
664	A93	45c multicolored	1.00	*.30*
665	A93	75c multicolored	1.50	*.40*
666	A93	$2 multicolored	3.75	*.75*
		Nos. 660-666 (7)	7.85	*2.45*

Souvenir Sheet

667	A93	$1 multicolored	3.00	*1.00*

Crew Race — A94

1c, Women's swimming. 2c, Steeplechase. 35c, Gymnastics. 45c, Soccer. 75c, Boxing. $2, Bicycling.
$1, Sailing.

1975, Oct. 13 **Litho.** *Perf. 14*

668	A94	½c shown	.25	*.25*
669	A94	1c multicolored	.25	*.25*
670	A94	2c multicolored	.25	*.25*
671	A94	35c multicolored	.25	*.25*
672	A94	45c multicolored	.25	*.25*
673	A94	75c multicolored	.30	*.25*
674	A94	$2 multicolored	1.10	*.40*
		Nos. 668-674 (7)	2.65	*1.90*

Souvenir Sheet

675	A94	$1 multicolored	2.00	*.45*

7th Pan-American Games, Mexico City, Oct. 13-26.

Young Man, by Michelangelo A95

Works by Michelangelo (except 50c): ½c, David. 2c, Moses. 40c, Zachariah. 50c, St. John the Baptist (sculpture). 75c, Judith and Holofernes (detail). $1, Madonna (head from Pietà). $2, Doni Madonna (detail from Holy Family).

1975, Nov. 3

676	A95	½c black & multi	.25	*.25*
677	A95	1c black & multi	.25	*.25*
678	A95	2c black & multi	.25	*.25*
679	A95	40c black & multi	.40	*.25*
680	A95	50c black & multi	.50	*.25*
681	A95	75c black & multi	.75	*.25*
682	A95	$2 black & multi	1.25	*.45*
		Nos. 676-682 (7)	3.65	*1.95*

Souvenir Sheet

683	A95	$1 black & multi	2.25	*.40*

Michelangelo Buonarroti (1475-1564), Italian painter, sculptor and architect.

Virgin and Child Paintings — A96

½c, Filippino Lippi. 1c, Mantegna. 2c, Luis de Morales. 35c, G. M. Morandi. 50c, Antonello da Messina. 75c, Durer. $1, Velazquez.
$2, Bellini.

1975, Dec. 8

684	A96	½c multicolored	.25	*.25*
685	A96	1c multicolored	.25	*.25*
686	A96	2c multicolored	.25	*.25*
687	A96	35c multicolored	.25	*.25*
688	A96	50c multicolored	.25	*.25*
689	A96	75c multicolored	.30	*.25*
690	A96	$1 multicolored	.35	*.25*
		Nos. 684-690 (7)	1.90	*1.75*

Souvenir Sheet

691	A96	$2 multicolored	1.60	*.45*

Christmas.

Bananaquit — A97

Designs: 1c, Orange-rumped agouti. 2c, Hawksbill turtle, horiz. 5c, Dwarf poinciana. 35c, Albacores, horiz. 40c, Cardinal's guard flower. $1, Belted kingfisher. $2, Antillean armadillo, horiz.

1976, Jan. 20 **Litho.** *Perf. 14*

692	A97	½c multicolored	.25	*.25*
693	A97	1c multicolored	.25	*.25*
694	A97	2c multicolored	.25	*.25*
695	A97	5c multicolored	.25	*.25*
696	A97	35c multicolored	1.10	*.25*

697	A97	40c multicolored	1.25	*.25*
698	A97	$2 multicolored	3.00	*.75*
		Nos. 692-698 (7)	6.35	*2.25*

Souvenir Sheet

699	A97	$1 multicolored	7.25	*1.00*

Carnival Dancers A98

Designs: 1c, Scuba diving. 2c, Cruise ship in St. George's Harbor. 35c, Game fishing. 50c, St. George's Golf Course. 75c, Tennis. $1, Mount Rich rock carvings. $2, Sailboats.

1976, Feb. 25 Litho. *Perf. 14*

700	A98	½c multicolored	.25	*.25*
701	A98	1c multicolored	.25	*.25*
702	A98	2c multicolored	.25	*.25*
703	A98	35c multicolored	.90	*.25*
704	A98	50c multicolored	0.00	*.25*
705	A98	75c multicolored	3.25	*.35*
706	A98	$1 multicolored	3.50	*.35*
		Nos. 700-706 (7)	11.40	*1.95*

Souvenir Sheet

707	A98	$2 multicolored	2.75	*.75*

Tourist publicity.

Descent from the Cross, by Master of Okolicsno — A99

Easter (Paintings): 1c, Pieta, by Correggio. 2c, Crucifixion, by van der Weyden. 3c, Burial of Christ, by Dürer. 35c, God the Father Holding Crucified Christ, by unknown master (Florence). 75c, Ascension, by Raphael. $1, Burial of Christ, by Raphael. $2, Pieta, by Crespi.

1976, Mar. 29

708	A99	½c multicolored	.25	*.25*
709	A99	1c multicolored	.25	*.25*
710	A99	2c multicolored	.25	*.25*
711	A99	3c multicolored	.25	*.25*
712	A99	35c multicolored	.25	*.25*
713	A99	75c multicolored	.30	*.25*
714	A99	$1 multicolored	.40	*.25*
		Nos. 708-714 (7)	1.95	*1.75*

Souvenir Sheet

715	A99	$2 multicolored	1.25	*1.25*

Sharpshooters, 1780 — A100

First Stars and Stripes and: 1c, Defense of Liberty Pole. 2c, Men loading muskets. 35c, 75c, Fight for Liberty. 50c, $2, Peace Treaty, 1783. $1, Drumming march on Breed's Hill. $3, Gunboat, c. 1776.

1976, Apr. 15 Litho. *Perf. 14*

716	A100	½c multicolored	.25	*.25*
717	A100	1c multicolored	.25	*.25*
718	A100	2c multicolored	.25	*.25*
719	A100	35c multicolored	.45	*.25*
720	A100	50c multicolored	.55	*.25*
721	A100	$1 multicolored	.90	*.25*
722	A100	$3 multicolored	2.25	*.25*
		Nos. 716-722 (7)	4.90	*1.75*

Souvenir Sheet

723		Sheet of 2	2.00	*1.40*
a.		A100 75c multicolored	.65	*.55*
b.		A100 $2 multicolored	1.40	*.75*

American Bicentennial.

Girl Guide Emblems, Nature Study — A101

Various Girl Guide Emblems and: 1c, Cooking. 2c, $2, First aid, diff. 50c, Tenting. 75c, Home economics. $1, Drawing.

1976, June 1 Litho. *Perf. 14*

724	A101	½c multicolored	.25	*.25*
725	A101	1c multicolored	.25	*.25*
726	A101	2c multicolored	.25	*.25*
727	A101	50c multicolored	.50	*.25*
728	A101	75c multicolored	.75	*.25*
729	A101	$2 multicolored	1.75	*.45*
		Nos. 724-729 (6)	3.75	*1.70*

Souvenir Sheet

730	A101	$1 multicolored	1.75	*.80*

Girl Guides of Grenada, 50th anniv.

Volleyball — A102

Olympic Rings and: 1c, Bicycling. 2c, Rowing. 35c, Judo. 45c, Hockey. 75c, Women's gymnastics. $1, High jump. $3, Equestrian.

1976, June 21 Litho. *Perf. 14*

731	A102	½c multicolored	.25	*.25*
732	A102	1c multicolored	.25	*.25*
733	A102	2c multicolored	.25	*.25*
734	A102	35c multicolored	.30	*.25*
735	A102	45c multicolored	.55	*.25*
736	A102	75c multicolored	.60	*.40*
737	A102	$1 multicolored	.70	*.40*
		Nos. 731-737 (7)	2.90	*2.05*

Souvenir Sheet

738	A102	$3 multicolored	1.75	*1.25*

21st Olympic Games, Montreal, Canada, July 17-Aug. 1.

Moulin Rouge, by Toulouse-Lautrec A103

Paintings by Toulouse-Lautrec: 1c, Start of the Quadrille. 2c, Woman's Head. 3c, Hall at the Moulin Rouge. 40c, Man Delivering Laundry. 50c, Dancing the Bolero. $1, Lady with Boa. $2, Signor Boileau at the Cafe.

1976, July 20 Litho. *Perf. 14*

739	A103	½c multicolored	.25	*.25*
740	A103	1c multicolored	.25	*.25*
741	A103	2c multicolored	.25	*.25*
742	A103	3c multicolored	.25	*.25*
743	A103	40c multicolored	.75	*.25*
744	A103	50c multicolored	.95	*.25*
745	A103	$2 multicolored	2.50	*.50*
		Nos. 739-745 (7)	5.20	*2.00*

Souvenir Sheet

746	A103	$1 multicolored	4.50	*1.25*

Henri de Toulouse-Lautrec (1864-1901), painter, 75th death anniv.

Map of West Indies, Bats, Wicket and Ball A103a

Prudential Cup — A103b

1976, July 26

747	A103a	35c lt blue & multi	.60	.60
748	A103b	$1 lilac rose & blk	1.50	1.50

World Cricket Cup, won by West Indies Team, 1975.

Piper Apache A104

Airplanes: 1c, Beech Twin Bonanza. 2c, D.H. Twin Otter. 40c, Britten Norman Islander. 50c, D.H. Heron. $2, Hawker Siddeley Avro 748. $3, B.A.C. One-Eleven.

1976, Aug. 18

749	A104	½c multicolored	.25	*.25*
750	A104	1c multicolored	.25	*.25*
751	A104	2c multicolored	.25	*.25*
752	A104	40c multicolored	.75	*.25*
753	A104	50c multicolored	.80	*.25*
754	A104	$2 multicolored	2.50	*.75*
		Nos. 749-754 (6)	4.80	*2.00*

Souvenir Sheet

755	A104	$3 multicolored	3.00	*1.10*

Helios Mission, Assembly — A105

Designs: 1c, Helios spacecraft in space. 2c, Helios assembled. 15c, Helios, system test and checkout. 45c, Viking nearing Mars, horiz. 75c, Viking on Mars. $2, Viking spacecraft assembled. $3, Helios orbiter and Viking lander.

1976, Sept. 1 Litho. *Perf. 14*

756	A105	½c multicolored	.25	*.25*
757	A105	1c multicolored	.25	*.25*
758	A105	2c multicolored	.25	*.25*
759	A105	15c multicolored	.25	*.25*
760	A105	45c multicolored	.25	*.25*
761	A105	75c multicolored	.35	*.25*
762	A105	$2 multicolored	.65	*.35*
		Nos. 756-762 (7)	2.25	*1.85*

Souvenir Sheet

763	A105	$3 multicolored	1.75	*1.00*

Helios (solar probe) mission and Viking Mars missions.

S.S. Geestland, Geest Line Flag — A106

Ships: 1c, M.V. Federal Palm, West Indies Shipping Service. 2c, H.M.S. Blake and ship's crest. 25c, M.V. Vistafjord and Norwegian-American Line flag. 75c, S.S. Canberra and P. & O. Line flag. $1, S.S. Regina and Chandris Line flag. $2, Santa Maria and Spanish flag, 1492. $5, S.S. Arandora and Blue Star Line flag.

1976, Nov. 3 Litho. *Perf. 14½*

764	A106	½c blue & multi	.25	*.25*
765	A106	1c blue & multi	.25	*.25*
766	A106	2c blue & multi	.25	*.25*
767	A106	25c blue & multi	.55	*.25*
768	A106	75c blue & multi	1.00	*.25*
769	A106	$1 blue & multi	1.25	*.30*
770	A106	$5 blue & multi	2.50	*.65*
		Nos. 764-770 (7)	6.05	*2.20*

Souvenir Sheet

771	A106	$2 multicolored	2.50	*2.50*

Ships connected with Grenada's development.

Altarpiece of San Barnaba, by Botticelli A107

Christmas (Paintings): 1c, Annunciation, by Botticelli. 2c, Madonna with Chancellor Rolin, by Jan van Eyck. 35c, Annunciation, by Fra Filippo Lippi. 50c, Madonna of the Magnificat, by Botticelli. 75c, Madonna of the Pomegranate, by Botticelli. $2, Gipsy Madonna, by Titian. $3, Madonna with St. Cosmas and Saints, by Botticelli.

1976, Dec. 8 Litho. *Perf. 14*

772	A107	½c multicolored	.25	*.25*
773	A107	1c multicolored	.25	*.25*
774	A107	2c multicolored	.25	*.25*
775	A107	35c multicolored	.25	*.25*
776	A107	50c multicolored	.25	*.25*
777	A107	75c multicolored	.35	*.25*
778	A107	$3 multicolored	.75	*.40*
		Nos. 772-778 (7)	2.35	*1.90*

Souvenir Sheet

779	A107	$2 multicolored	1.60	*.75*

Globe and Telephone Users A108

Designs: ½c, A. G. Bell, 1876 and modern telephones. 2c, Satellites around globe, world map. 18c, Videophone. 40c, Satellite and ground stations. $1, Satellite and telephone communication with ships. $2, British "Trimphone" and radar station. $5, Flags of the world surrounding globe, and telephone.

1976, Dec. 17 Litho. *Perf. 14*

780	A108	½c multicolored	.25	*.25*
781	A108	1c multicolored	.25	*.25*
782	A108	2c multicolored	.25	*.25*
783	A108	18c multicolored	.25	*.25*
784	A108	40c multicolored	.30	*.25*
785	A108	$1 multicolored	.40	*.25*
786	A108	$2 multicolored	.65	*.45*
		Nos. 780-786 (7)	2.35	*1.95*

Souvenir Sheet

787	A108	$5 multicolored	2.25	*.90*

Centenary of first telephone conversation by Alexander Graham Bell, Mar. 10, 1876.

Coronation of Elizabeth II — A109

Designs: ½c, Coronation. 1c, $1, Orb and scepter. 35c, $3, Trooping of the Guards. 50c, $2, Spoon and ampulla. 35c, (bklt.), $2.50, Elizabeth II and Prince Philip. $5, Royal visit to Grenada.

1977, Feb. 8 **Litho.** *Perf. 14, 12*

788	A109	½c	multicolored	.25	*.25*
789	A109	1c	multicolored	.25	*.25*
790	A109	35c	multicolored	.25	*.25*
791	A109	$2	multicolored	.30	*.30*
792	A109	$2.50	multicolored	.35	*.30*
a.			Booklet pane of 6 (35c)	.95	
b.			Booklet pane of 3 (50c, $1, $3)	3.25	
			Nos. 788-792 (5)	1.40	*1.35*

Souvenir Sheet

793	A109	$5	multicolored	1.10	*1.10*

Reign of Queen Elizabeth II, 25th anniv.

Nos. 792a-792b are self-adhesive, roulette x imperf. Marginal inscriptions.

Nos. 788-792 were printed in sheets of 40 (10x4), perf. 14, and sheets of 5 plus label, perf. 12, in changed colors.

For overprints see Nos. 821-826.

Water Skiing, One-ski Slalom A110

Designs: 1c, Speedboat racing around Grand Anse. 2c, Crew racing, St. George's. 22c, Swimming, Grand Anse. 35c, Local work boat races. 75c, Water polo, careenage, St. George's. $2, Game fishing. $3, South Coast yacht race.

1977, Apr. 13 **Litho.** *Perf. 14*

794	A110	½c	multicolored	.25	*.25*
795	A110	1c	multicolored	.25	*.25*
796	A110	2c	multicolored	.25	*.25*
797	A110	22c	multicolored	.25	*.25*
798	A110	35c	multicolored	.35	*.25*
799	A110	75c	multicolored	.55	*.25*
800	A110	$2	multicolored	1.10	*.35*
			Nos. 794-800 (7)	3.00	*1.85*

Souvenir Sheet

801	A110	$3	multicolored	1.75	*1.25*

1977 Easter Water Parade.

Tent, OAS Emblem A111

1977, June 14 **Litho.** *Perf. 14*

802	A111	35c	multicolored	.25	.25
803	A111	$1	multicolored	.35	.35
804	A111	$2	multicolored	.60	.60
			Nos. 802-804 (3)	1.20	1.20

7th Regular Session, General Assembly of Organization of American States.

Scouts on Raft A112

Designs: 1c, Tug-of-war. 2c, Boy Scout regatta. 18c, Scouts around camp fire. 40c, Field kitchen. $1, Boy Scouts and Sea Scouts. $2, Hiking and map reading. $3, Semaphore.

1977, Sept. 6 **Litho.** *Perf. 14*

805	A112	½c	multicolored	.25	*.25*
806	A112	1c	multicolored	.25	*.25*
807	A112	2c	multicolored	.25	*.25*
808	A112	18c	multicolored	.30	*.25*
809	A112	40c	multicolored	.45	*.25*
810	A112	$1	multicolored	1.10	*.35*
811	A112	$2	multicolored	2.00	*.55*
			Nos. 805-811 (7)	4.60	*2.15*

Souvenir Sheet

812	A112	$3	multicolored	2.75	*1.25*

6th Caribbean Jamboree, Kingston, Jamaica, Aug. 5-14.

Annunciation to the Shepherds — A113

Ceiling Paintings, St. Martin's Church, Zillis, Switzerland, 12th Century: 1c, Joseph on his way. 2c, Virgin and Child, Flight into Egypt. 22c, Angel leading the way. 35c, King on way to Herod. 75c, Three horses. $2, Virgin and Child. $3, Adoration of the Kings.

1977, Nov. 3 **Litho.** *Perf. 14*

813	A113	½c	multicolored	.25	*.25*
814	A113	1c	multicolored	.25	*.25*
815	A113	2c	multicolored	.25	*.25*
816	A113	22c	multicolored	.25	*.25*
817	A113	35c	multicolored	.25	*.25*
818	A113	75c	multicolored	.25	*.25*
819	A113	$2	multicolored	.35	*.25*
			Nos. 813-819 (7)	1.85	*1.75*

Souvenir Sheet

820	A113	$3	multicolored	1.50	*1.00*

Christmas.

Nos. 788-793 Overprinted

1977, Nov. 10 *Perf. 12, 14*

821	A109	½c	multicolored	.25	.25
822	A109	1c	multicolored	.25	.25
823	A109	35c	multicolored	.25	.25
824	A109	$2	multicolored	.25	*.35*
825	A109	$2.50	multicolored	.25	*.45*
			Nos. 821-825 (5)	1.25	*1.55*

Souvenir Sheet

Perf. 14

826	A109	$5	multicolored	.75	1.40

Caribbean visit of Queen Elizabeth II. Nos. 821-822 are perf. 12, others perf. 12 and 14.

Christjaan Eijkman — A114

Portraits: 1c, Winston Churchill, Literature, 1953. 2c, Woodrow Wilson, Peace, 1919. 35c, Frederic Passy, Peace 1901. $1, Albert Einstein, Physics, 1921. $2, Alfred Nobel, founder. $3, Carl Bosch, Chemistry, 1931.

1978, Jan. 25 **Litho.** *Perf. 14*

827	A114	½c	multicolored	.25	*.25*
828	A114	1c	multicolored	.25	*.25*
829	A114	2c	multicolored	.25	*.25*
830	A114	35c	multicolored	.30	*.25*
831	A114	$1	multicolored	.85	*.30*
832	A114	$3	multicolored	2.25	*.55*
			Nos. 827-832 (6)	4.15	*1.85*

Souvenir Sheet

833	A114	$2	multicolored	2.00	*1.00*

Nobel Prize winners.

Early Zeppelin and Count Zeppelin A115

Designs: 1c, Lindbergh and Spirit of St. Louis. 2c, "Deutschland" airship. 22c, Lindbergh landing in Paris. 35c, Lindbergh in cockpit. 75c, Lindbergh and Spirit of St. Louis in flight. $1, Zeppelin over Alps. $2, Count Zeppelin and early airship. $3, Zeppelin over Capitol.

1978, Feb. 13 **Litho.** *Perf. 14*

834	A115	½c	multicolored	.25	*.25*
835	A115	1c	multicolored	.25	*.25*
836	A115	2c	multicolored	.25	*.25*
837	A115	22c	multicolored	.40	*.25*
838	A115	75c	multicolored	.75	*.25*
839	A115	$1	multicolored	.90	*.25*
840	A115	$3	multicolored	2.00	*.50*
			Nos. 834-840 (7)	4.80	*2.00*

Souvenir Sheet

841			Sheet of 2	3.25	*1.00*
a.			A115 35c multicolored	.75	
b.			A115 $2 multicolored	2.50	

Aviation history.

Launching of Space Shuttle — A116

Space Shuttle: 1c, Booster separation. 2c, External tank separation. 18c, In orbit. 75c, Satellite placement. $2, Landing approach. $3, On landing pad.

1978, Feb. 28

842	A116	½c	multicolored	.25	*.25*
843	A116	1c	multicolored	.25	*.25*
844	A116	2c	multicolored	.25	*.25*
845	A116	18c	multicolored	.40	*.25*
846	A116	75c	multicolored	.90	*.25*
847	A116	$2	multicolored	1.75	*.40*
			Nos. 842-847 (6)	3.80	*1.65*

Souvenir Sheet

848	A116	$3	multicolored	2.10	*1.00*

US space shuttle.

Black-headed Gulls — A117

Wild Birds of Grenada and Wildlife Fund Emblem: 1c, Wilson's petrels. 2c, Killdeers. 50c, White-necked jacobin and hibiscus. 75c, Blue-faced booby. $1, Broad-winged hawk. $2, Scaley-necked pigeon. $3, Scarlet ibis.

1978, Mar. 8 **Litho.** *Perf. 14*

849	A117	½c	multicolored	.30	*.25*
850	A117	1c	multicolored	.30	*.25*
851	A117	2c	multicolored	.30	*.25*
852	A117	50c	multicolored	2.50	*.40*
853	A117	75c	multicolored	3.00	*.60*
854	A117	$1	multicolored	4.00	*.80*
855	A117	$2	multicolored	6.50	*1.50*
			Nos. 849-855 (7)	16.90	*4.05*

Souvenir Sheet

856	A117	$3	multicolored	11.00	*2.00*

Marquise de Spinola, by Rubens — A118

Paintings by Peter Paul Rubens (1577-1640): 5c, Reception of Marie de Medicis. 15c, Rubens and Helena Fourment. 25c, Ludovicus Nonnius. 45c, Helena Fourment with her Children. 75c, Child's head. $3, Suzanne Fourment in Velvet Hat.

1978, Mar. 30 **Litho.** *Perf. 13½x14*

857	A118	5c	lt blue & multi	.30	*.25*
858	A118	15c	lt blue & multi	.30	*.25*
859	A118	18c	lt blue & multi	.30	*.25*
860	A118	25c	lt blue & multi	.30	*.25*
861	A118	45c	lt blue & multi	.55	*.25*
862	A118	75c	lt blue & multi	.80	*.25*
863	A118	$3	lt blue & multi	1.75	*.55*
			Nos. 857-863 (7)	4.30	*2.05*

Souvenir Sheet

864	A118	$5	lt blue & multi	3.75	*1.00*

Ludwig van Beethoven — A119

Designs: 15c, Woman violinist playing concerto. 18c, Various musical instruments. 22c, Piano. 50c, Two violins. 75c, Beethoven's piano and score. $2, Beethoven and score. $3, Beethoven and his house. 15c, 18c, 22c, 75c, $2, $3, horiz.

1978, Apr. 24 *Perf. 14*

865	A119	5c	multicolored	.25	*.25*
866	A119	15c	multicolored	.25	*.25*
867	A119	18c	multicolored	.50	*.25*
868	A119	22c	multicolored	.50	*.25*
869	A119	50c	multicolored	.85	*.35*
870	A119	75c	multicolored	1.60	*.50*
871	A119	$3	multicolored	2.75	*.65*
			Nos. 865-871 (7)	6.70	*2.50*

Souvenir Sheet

872	A119	$2	multicolored	3.25	*1.25*

Ludwig van Beethoven (1770-1827), composer, death sesquicentennial.

Elizabeth II with Crown, Scepter and Orb — A120

Trooping of the Colors — A121

Designs: 35c, Coronation. $2.50, St. Edward's crown. $5, Elizabeth II and Prince Philip.

1978, June 2 **Litho.** *Perf. 14*

873	A120	35c	multicolored	.25	.25
874	A120	$2	multicolored	.45	.45
875	A120	$2.50	multicolored	.45	.45
			Nos. 873-875 (3)	1.15	1.15

Souvenir Sheet

876	A120	$5	multicolored	.85	.85

Imperf

Self-adhesive

35c, Elizabeth II at Maundy Money distribution ceremony. $5, Elizabeth II and Prince Philip.

877		Souvenir booklet	3.25
a.	A121	Bklt. pane, 3 each 25c, 35c	1.00
b.	A121	Booklet pane of 1, $5	2.50

Coronation of Queen Elizabeth II, 25th anniv.

Nos. 873-875 were printed in sheets of 40 (10x4), perf. 14, and sheets of 3 plus label, perf. 12, in changed colors. Labels show royal insignia.

No. 877 contains 2 booklet panes printed on peelable paper backing showing coins.

Goalkeeper Reaching for Ball — A122

Designs: Goalkeeper reaching for ball, various stages of motion.

1978, Aug. 1 Litho. *Perf. 15*

878	A122	40c multicolored	.25	.25
879	A122	60c multicolored	.25	.25
880	A122	90c multicolored	.35	.35
881	A122	$2 multicolored	.85	.85
		Nos. 878-881 (4)	1.70	1.70

Souvenir Sheet

882	A122	$2.50 multicolored	1.75	1.75

11th World Cup Soccer Championship, Argentina, June 1-25.

Flying Objects, 16th Century Drawing and Flying Saucer, 1962
A123

Designs: 35c, Radar probing skies, and Mars surface. $2, Prime Minister Eric Gairy and UN General Assembly Building. $3, Flying saucer with downwards beam, and UFO photograph.

1978, Aug. 17

883	A123	5c multicolored	.30	.30
884	A123	35c multicolored	.55	.40
885	A123	$3 multicolored	3.50	3.25
		Nos. 883-885 (3)	4.35	3.95

Souvenir Sheet

886	A123	$2 multicolored	3.50	3.50

Proposal by Prime Minister Eric Gairy of Grenada to the UN General Assembly to study unidentified flying objects, Oct. 7, 1977.

Wright Glider and Allegory of Flight
A124

15c, Flyer I, 1903, & eagle. 18c, Flyer III & allegory of flight. 22c, Flyer III & eagle. 50c, Orville Wright, Flyer & allegory of flight. 75c, Flyer, 1908, & eagle. $2, Flyer & allegory of flight. $3, Wilbur Wright, Flyer & allegory of flight.

1978, Aug. 24 *Perf. 14*

887	A124	5c multicolored	.25	.25
888	A124	15c multicolored	.25	.25
889	A124	18c multicolored	.25	.25
890	A124	22c multicolored	.25	.25
891	A124	50c multicolored	.45	.35
892	A124	75c multicolored	.55	.45
893	A124	$3 multicolored	1.35	1.35
		Nos. 887-893 (7)	3.35	3.15

Souvenir Sheet

894	A124	$2 multicolored	3.75	3.75

75th anniversary of first powered flight by Wright brothers, Dec. 17, 1903.

Hawaiian Feast in Capt. Cook's Honor
A125

Capt. Cook and: 35c, Hawaiian warriors' dance. 75c, Honolulu harbor. $3, "Resolution." $4, Death scene.

1978, Dec. 5 Litho. *Perf. 14*

895	A125	18c multicolored	.90	.50
896	A125	35c multicolored	1.10	.60
897	A125	75c multicolored	2.00	1.90
898	A125	$3 multicolored	2.75	*4.50*
		Nos. 895-898 (4)	6.75	7.50

Souvenir Sheet

899	A125	$4 multicolored	5.00	5.00

Bicentenary of Capt. Cook's arrival in Hawaii and 250th anniversary of his birth.

Detail from Paumgartner Altar, by Dürer — A126

Dürer Paintings: 60c, The Three Kings. 90c, Virgin and Child. $2, Head of the Virgin. $4, Virgin and Child.

1978, Dec. 20 Litho. *Perf. 14*

900	A126	40c multicolored	.25	.25
901	A126	60c multicolored	.35	.35
902	A126	90c multicolored	.40	.40
903	A126	$2 multicolored	.75	.75
		Nos. 900-903 (4)	1.75	1.75

Souvenir Sheet

904	A126	$4 multicolored	2.00	2.00

Christmas and 450th death anniv. of Albrecht Dürer (1471-1528), German painter.

Convention and Cultural Center — A127

18c, Geodesic Dome. 22c, Rowboat race, Easter parade, St. George's. 35c, Prime Minister Eric M. Gairy. $3, Cross at Fort Frederick at night.

1979, Feb. 8 Litho. *Perf. 14*

905	A127	5c multicolored	.25	.25
906	A127	18c multicolored	.25	.25
907	A127	22c multicolored	.25	.25
908	A127	35c multicolored	.25	.25
909	A127	$3 multicolored	.40	.40
		Nos. 905-909 (5)	1.40	1.40

5th anniversary of independence.

Chenille Plant — A128

Native Flowers: 50c, Red hibiscus. $1, Skyflower. $2, Pink pride of India. $3, Rosebay.

1979, Feb. 26

910	A128	18c multicolored	.25	.25
911	A128	50c multicolored	.30	.25
912	A128	$1 multicolored	.50	.45
913	A128	$3 multicolored	1.25	1.10
		Nos. 910-913 (4)	2.30	2.05

Souvenir Sheet

914	A128	$2 multicolored	1.60	1.60

Birds in Flight — A129

$2, Bird in flight & Human Rights emblem.

1979, Mar. 15

915	A129	15c multicolored	.25	.25
916	A129	$2 multicolored	.75	.75

Universal Declaration of Human Rights, 30th anniversary.

Children Playing Cricket — A130

IYC Emblem and: 22c, Boys playing baseball. $4, Children with model spaceship. $5, Three children.

1979, Apr. 23 Litho. *Perf. 14*

917	A130	18c multicolored	1.00	.50
918	A130	22c multicolored	.50	.30
919	A130	$5 multicolored	4.50	*6.00*
		Nos. 917-919 (3)	6.00	6.80

Souvenir Sheet

920	A130	$4 multicolored	2.25	2.25

Intl. Year of the Child.

Balloon and Space Shuttle
A131

Designs: 35c, Octopus holding sailors, nuclear submarine. 75c, Rocket and moon. $3, Imaginary plane and space ship. $4, Multi-propellered ship and US space shuttle.

1979, May 4

921	A131	18c multicolored	.40	.25
922	A131	35c multicolored	.70	.25
923	A131	75c multicolored	.90	.65
924	A131	$3 multicolored	2.40	*3.00*
		Nos. 921-924 (4)	4.40	4.15

Souvenir Sheet

925	A131	$4 multicolored	2.25	2.25

Jules Verne (1828-1905), science fiction writer.

African Mail Runner
A132

Sir Rowland Hill (1795-1879), originator of penny postage, and: 40c, American Pony Express. $1, Oriental pigeon post. $3, European mail coach. $5, Tete-beche stamps with revenue surcharge, 1883.

1979, July 23 Litho. *Perf. 14*

926	A132	20c multicolored	.25	.25
927	A132	40c multicolored	.25	.25
928	A132	$1 multicolored	.25	.25
929	A132	$3 multicolored	.40	.40
		Nos. 926-929 (4)	1.15	1.15

Souvenir Sheet

930	A132	$5 multicolored	1.00	1.00

Nos. 926-929 were printed in sheets of 40, perf. 14, and in sheets of 5 plus label, perf. 12, in changed colors.

For overprints see Nos. 989A-989D.

Boys, Map of Grenada, Vaccination Gun — A133

1979, Aug. 2 Litho. *Perf. 14*

931	A133	5c multicolored	.25	.25
932	A133	$1 multicolored	.90	.90

Intl. Year of the Child, immunization of children.

Reef Shark
A134

Designs: 45c, Spotted eagle ray. 50c, Many-tooth conger. 60c, Golden olive shells. 70c, West Indian murex. 75c, Giant tuns. 90c, Brown boobies. $1, Magnificent frigate bird. $2.50, Sooty tern.

1979, Aug. 22 Litho. *Perf. 14*

933	A134	40c multicolored	.40	.35
934	A134	45c multicolored	.40	.35
935	A134	50c multicolored	.45	.40
936	A134	60c multicolored	.75	.60
937	A134	70c multicolored	.90	.70
938	A134	75c multicolored	1.10	*1.10*
939	A134	90c multicolored	1.75	*2.25*
940	A134	$1 multicolored	1.75	*2.25*
		Nos. 933-940 (8)	7.50	8.00

Souvenir Sheet

941	A134	$2.50 multicolored	3.25	3.25

Flight into Egypt, Tapestry
A135

Tapestries: 25c, Virgin and Child. 30c, Angel, vert. 40c, Infant Jesus, by Doge Marino Grimani, vert. 90c, Shepherds, vert. $1, Flight into Egypt, vert. $2, Virgin in Glory, vert. $4, Virgin and Child, by Grimani, vert.

1979, Oct. 16 Litho. *Perf. 14*

942	A135	6c multicolored	.25	.25
943	A135	25c multicolored	.25	.25
944	A135	30c multicolored	.25	.25
945	A135	40c multicolored	.25	.25
946	A135	90c multicolored	.25	.25
947	A135	$1 multicolored	.25	.25
948	A135	$2 multicolored	.30	.30
		Nos. 942-948 (7)	1.80	1.80

Souvenir Sheet

949	A135	$4 multicolored	1.25	1.25

Christmas.

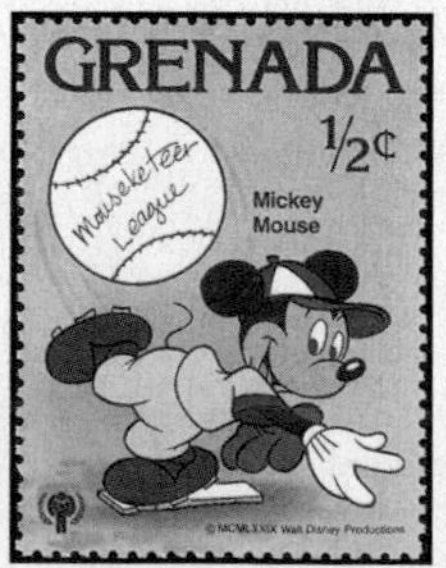

Disney Characters and IYC Emblem
A135a

Sport scenes: ½c, Mickey Mouse, baseball. 1c, Donald, high jump. 2c, Goofy, basketball. 3c, Goofy, hurdles. 4c, Donald Duck, golf. 5c, Mickey, cricket. 10c, Mickey, soccer. $2, Mickey, tennis. $2.50, Minnie, equestrian.
$3, Goofy in riding habit.

1979, Nov. 2 Litho. *Perf. 11*

950	A135a	½c multi	.25	.25
951	A135a	1c multi	.25	.25
952	A135a	2c multi	.25	.25

953 A135a 3c multi .25 .25
954 A135a 4c multi .25 .25
955 A135a 5c multi .25 .25
956 A135a 10c multi .25 .25
957 A135a $2 multi 3.00 *3.50*
958 A135a $2.50 multi 3.00 *3.50*
Nos. 950-958 (9) 7.75 8.75

Souvenir Sheet

Perf. 13½

959 CD329 $3 multi 2.50 2.50

See Nos. 1031-1032.

Hands, Paul P. Harris, Rotary Emblem — A136

Rotary Emblem and Hands Holding: 30c, Caduceus. 90c, Wheat. $2, Family. $4, Emblem.

1980, Feb. 25 Litho. *Perf. 14*
960 A136 6c multicolored .25 .25
961 A136 30c multicolored .25 .25
962 A136 90c multicolored .25 .25
963 A136 $2 multicolored .60 .60
Nos. 960-963 (4) 1.35 1.35

Souvenir Sheet

964 A136 $4 multicolored 1.60 1.60

Rotary International, 75th anniversary.

Nos. 585-586, 588-591, 593-594, 596-602 Overprinted in Black

1980 *Perf. 15, 13½*
965 A85 2c multicolored .25 .25
966 A85 3c multicolored .25 .25
967 A85 6c multicolored .25 .25
968 A85 8c multicolored .25 .25
969 A85 10c multicolored .25 .25
970 A85 12c multicolored .25 .25
971 A85 20c multicolored .25 .25
972 A85 25c multicolored .40 .60
973 A85 50c multicolored .40 .60
974 A85 75c multicolored .65 .95
975 A85 $1 multicolored 1.00 1.25
976 A85 $2 multicolored 1.75 2.40
977 A85 $3 multicolored 2.25 3.25
978 A85 $5 multicolored 3.00 5.50
979 A85 $10 multicolored 4.25 8.00
Nos. 965-979 (15) 15.45 24.30

Issue dates: 25c, Apr. 7; others, Feb. 28.

Boxing, Kremlin, Olympic Rings A137

1980, Mar. 24 *Perf. 14*
980 A137 25c shown .25 .25
981 A137 40c Bicycling .25 .25
982 A137 90c Equestrian .25 .25
983 A137 $2 Running .60 .60
Nos. 980-983 (4) 1.35 1.35

Souvenir Sheet

984 A137 $4 Yachting 1.25 1.25

22nd Summer Olympic Games, Moscow, July 19-Aug. 3.

Tropical Kingbirds — A138

40c, Rufous-breasted hermits. $1, Troupials. $2, Ruddy quail doves. $3, Prairie warblers.

1980, Apr. 8
985 A138 20c shown 1.00 .80
986 A138 40c multicolored 1.40 1.10
987 A138 $1 multicolored 1.90 1.60
988 A138 $2 multicolored 2.25 *4.00*
Nos. 985-988 (4) 6.55 7.50

Souvenir Sheet

989 A138 $3 multicolored 5.00 5.00

Nos. 926-929 Overprinted: "LONDON 1980"

1980, May 6 Litho. *Perf. 12*
989A A132 20c multicolored .25 .25
989B A132 40c multicolored .30 .30
989C A132 $1 multicolored .50 .50
989D A132 $3 multicolored 1.40 1.40
Nos. 989A-989D (4) 2.45 2.45

London '80 Intl. Stamp Exhib., May 6-14.

Free School Hot Lunches A139

1980, May 19 Litho. *Perf. 14*
990 A139 10c shown .25 .25
991 A139 40c Food canning .25 .25
992 A139 $1 Health care .40 .40
993 A139 $2 Housing projects .65 .65
Nos. 990-993 (4) 1.55 1.55

Souvenir Sheet

994 A139 $5 Prime Minister Bishop, vert. 1.50 1.50

People's Revolution, 1st anniv.

Jamb Statues, West Portal, Chartres Cathedral — A140

Masterpieces: 10c, Les Desmoiselles d'Avignon, by Picasso. 40c, Winged Victory of Samothrace. 50c, The Night Watch, by Rembrandt. $1, Edward VI as a Child, by Holbein, the Younger. $3, Queen Nefertiti. $4, Weier Haws, by Dürer, vert.

1980, June Litho. *Perf. 14*
995 A140 8c multicolored .25 .25
996 A140 10c multicolored .25 .25
997 A140 40c multicolored .25 .25
998 A140 50c multicolored .25 .25
999 A140 $1 multicolored .35 .35
1000 A140 $2 multicolored .90 .90
Nos. 995-1000 (6) 2.25 2.25

Souvenir Sheet

1001 A140 $4 multicolored 1.50 1.50

Carib Canoes A141

Designs: 1c, Boat building. 2c, Small workboat. 4c, "Santa Maria." 5c, West India man barque, 1840. 6c, "Orinoco," 1851. 10c, Schooner. 12c, Trimaran. 15c, "Petite Amie," Spice Island cruising yacht. 20c, Fishing pirogue. 25c, Harbor police launch. 30c, Grand Anse speedboat. 40c, "Seimstrand." 50c, "Ariadne," 3-masted schooner. 90c, "Geestide," banana boat. $1, "Cunard Countess," cruise ship. $3, Rumrunner. $5, "Statendam." $10, Coast Guard patrol boat.

1980, Sept. 9 Litho. *Perf. 14*
1002 A141 ½c multicolored .25 .25
1003 A141 1c multicolored .25 .25
1004 A141 2c multicolored .25 .25
1005 A141 4c multicolored .40 .55
1006 A141 5c multicolored .40 .55
1007 A141 6c multicolored .40 .55
1008 A141 10c multicolored .45 .25
1009 A141 12c multicolored .90 .70
1010 A141 15c multicolored .50 .25
1011 A141 20c multicolored .90 .25
1012 A141 25c multicolored 1.75 .45
1013 A141 30c multicolored 1.25 .45
1014 A141 40c multicolored 2.00 .55
1015 A141 50c multicolored .60 .70
1016 A141 90c multicolored 1.75 .70
1017 A141 $1 multicolored 3.00 1.25
1018 A141 $3 multicolored 2.50 *4.50*
1019 A141 $5 multicolored 3.50 *7.25*
1020 A141 $10 multicolored 4.25 *9.50*
Nos. 1002-1020 (19) 25.30 29.20

No. 1017 reprinted inscribed 1982, No. 1015, 1984.

For overprints see Nos. O1-O10, O12-O13, O15, O17.

1982-84 *Perf. 12½x12*
1002a A141 ½c .45 .45
1006a A141 5c 1.05 1.05
1008a A141 10c 1.15 1.15
1011a A141 20c 1.75 1.75
1012a A141 25c 3.50 3.50
1013a A141 30c 2.75 2.75
1014a A141 40c 3.50 3.50
1015a A141 50c ('84) 1.45 1.45
1018a A141 $3 5.25 5.25
1019a A141 $5 7.50 7.50
1020a A141 $10 ('84) 17.00 17.00
Nos. 1002a-1020a (11) 45.35 45.35

Snow White at Well — A142

Christmas: Various scenes from Walt Disney's Snow White and the Seven Dwarfs.

1980, Sept. 25 Litho. *Perf. 11*
1021 A142 ½c multicolored .25 .25
1022 A142 1c multicolored .25 .25
1023 A142 2c multicolored .25 .25
1024 A142 3c multicolored .25 .25
1025 A142 4c multicolored .25 .25
1026 A142 5c multicolored .25 .25
1027 A142 10c multicolored .25 .25
1028 A142 $2.50 multicolored 2.75 2.75
1029 A142 $3 multicolored 3.25 3.25
Nos. 1021-1029 (9) 7.75 7.75

Souvenir Sheet

1030 A142 $4 multicolored 5.25 5.25

No. 1030 contains a vertical stamp.

Disney Type of 1980

50th anniversary of Pluto character: $2, Pluto and birthday cake. $4, Pluto.

1981, Jan. 19 Litho. *Perf. 14*
1031 A135a $2 multicolored 2.50 2.50

Souvenir Sheet

1032 A135a $4 multicolored 3.50 3.50

No. 1031 issued in sheets of 8.

Adult Education — A143

5c, Flags of the Revolution and Grenada. 15c, Food processing plant. 25c, Agriculture. 40c, Fishing boat, crawfish. 90c, Ships. $1, Palm trees. $3, Map.

1981, Mar. 13 Litho. *Perf. 12½*
1033 A143 5c multicolored .25 .25
1034 A143 10c shown .25 .25
1035 A143 15c multicolored .25 .25
1036 A143 25c multicolored .25 .25
1037 A143 40c multicolored .25 .25
1038 A143 90c multicolored .65 .65
1039 A143 $1 multicolored .70 .70
1040 A143 $3 multicolored 2.10 2.10
Nos. 1033-1040 (8) 4.70 4.70

2nd Festival of the Revolution.

Mickey Mouse and Goofy with Easter Basket A144

Easter: Various Disney characters with Easter baskets.

1981, Apr. 7 *Perf. 11*
1041 A144 35c multi .30 .30
1042 A144 40c multi .30 .30
1043 A144 $2 multi 1.60 1.60
1044 A144 $2.50 multi 2.10 2.10
Nos. 1041-1044 (4) 4.30 4.30

Souvenir Sheet

1045 A144 $4 multi 3.25 3.25

Large Heads, by Picasso — A145

Paintings by Pablo Picasso (1881-1973): 25c, Woman-Flower. 30c, Portrait of Madame. 90c, Cavalier with Pipe. $5, Woman on the Bank of the Seine.

1981, Apr. 28 *Perf. 14*
1046 A145 25c multicolored .25 .25
1047 A145 30c multicolored .25 .25
1048 A145 90c multicolored .45 .45
1049 A145 $4 multicolored 2.25 2.25
Nos. 1046-1049 (4) 3.20 3.20

Souvenir Sheet

1050 A145 $5 multicolored 4.75 4.75

Royal Wedding Issue

Common Design Type

1981, June 16 Litho. *Perf. 15*
1051 CD331a 50c Couple .25 .25
1052 CD331a $2 Holyrood House .30 .30
1053 CD331a $4 Charles .40 .40
Nos. 1051-1053 (3) .95 .95

Souvenir Sheet

1054 CD331 $5 Glass coach .90 .90

Souvenir Booklet

1055 CD331 multi 8.00
a. Pane of 6 (3x$1, Lady Diana, 3x$2, Charles) 5.50
b. Pane of 1, $5, Couple 2.50

No. 1055 contains imperf., self-adhesive stamps.

Sheets of 5 plus label contain 30c, 40c or $4 in changed colors, perf. 14x14½.

For overprints see Nos. O11, O14, O16,

The Bath, by Mary Cassatt (1845-1926) A146

Decade for Women (Paintings by Women): 40c, Mademoiselle Charlotte du Val d'Ognes, by Constance Marie Charpentier. 60c, Self-portrait, by Mary Beale. $3, Woman in White Stockings, by Suzanne Valadon. $5, The Artist Hesitating between the Arts of Music and Painting, horiz.

1981, Oct. 13 Litho. *Perf. 14*

No.	Type	Description	Unused	Used
1058	A146	15c multicolored	.25	.25
1059	A146	40c multicolored	.30	.30
1060	A146	60c multicolored	.45	.45
1061	A146	$3 multicolored	2.00	2.00
		Nos. 1058-1061 (4)	3.00	3.00

Souvenir Sheet

No.	Type	Description	Unused	Used
1062	A146	$5 multicolored	3.00	3.00

Cinderella and Prince Charming Dancing at the Ball — A147

Christmas: Scenes from Walt Disney's Cinderella.

1981, Nov. 2 Litho. *Perf. 14x13½*

No.	Type	Description	Unused	Used
1063	A147	½c multi	.25	.25
1064	A147	1c multi	.25	.25
1065	A147	2c multi	.25	.25
1066	A147	3c multi	.25	.25
1067	A147	4c multi	.25	.25
1068	A147	5c multi	.25	.25
1069	A147	10c multi	.25	.25
1070	A147	$2.50 multi	3.00	3.00
1071	A147	$3 multi	3.50	3.50
		Nos. 1063-1071 (9)	8.25	8.25

Souvenir Sheet

No.	Type	Description	Unused	Used
1072	A147	$5 multi	6.75	6.75

Columbia Space Shuttle — A148

Views of the Columbia space shuttle.

1981, Nov. 12

No.	Type	Description	Unused	Used
1073	A148	30c multicolored	.25	.25
1074	A148	60c multicolored	.40	.40
1075	A148	70c multicolored	.50	.50
1076	A148	$3 multicolored	2.00	2.00
		Nos. 1073-1076 (4)	3.15	3.15

Souvenir Sheet

No.	Type	Description	Unused	Used
1077	A148	$5 multicolored	3.25	3.25

UPU Membership Centenary — A149

1981, Dec. 10 Litho. *Perf. 15*

No.	Type	Description	Unused	Used
1078	A149	25c St. George's P.O.	.25	.25
1079	A149	30c No. 1	.25	.25
1080	A149	90c No. 384	.50	.50
1081	A149	$4 No. 189	2.25	2.25
		Nos. 1078-1081 (4)	3.25	3.25

Souvenir Sheet

No.	Type	Description	Unused	Used
1082	A149	$5 No. 562	4.00	4.00

Intl. Year of the Disabled (1981) — A150

30c, Artist. 40c, Computer operator. 70c, Teaching Braille. $3, Drummer.
$4, Auto mechanic.

1982, Feb. 4 *Perf. 14*

No.	Type	Description	Unused	Used
1083	A150	30c multicolored	.25	.25
1084	A150	40c multicolored	.30	.30
1085	A150	70c multicolored	.50	.50
1086	A150	$3 multicolored	2.00	2.00
		Nos. 1083-1086 (4)	3.05	3.05

Souvenir Sheet

No.	Type	Description	Unused	Used
1087	A150	$4 multicolored	3.50	3.50

Scouting Year A151

1982, Feb. 19 *Perf. 15*

No.	Type	Description	Unused	Used
1088	A151	70c Gardening	.60	.60
1089	A151	90c Map reading	.75	.75
1090	A151	$1 Bee keeping	.85	.80
1091	A151	$4 Hospital reading	2.75	2.75
		Nos. 1088-1091 (4)	4.95	4.90

Souvenir Sheet

No.	Type	Description	Unused	Used
1092	A151	$5 Trophy presentation	3.50	3.50

Flambeaux A152

60c, Large orange sulphurs. $1, Red anartias. $3, Polydamas swallowtails.
$5, Caribbean buckeyes.

1982, Mar. 24 Litho. *Perf. 14*

No.	Type	Description	Unused	Used
1093	A152	10c shown	.70	.25
1094	A152	60c multicolored	2.50	1.25
1095	A152	$1 multicolored	3.00	2.10
1096	A152	$3 multicolored	8.00	7.25
		Nos. 1093-1096 (4)	14.20	10.85

Souvenir Sheet

No.	Type	Description	Unused	Used
1097	A152	$5 multicolored	8.75	8.75

Norman Rockwell A153

1982, Apr. 12 Litho. *Perf. 14x13½*

No.	Type	Description	Unused	Used
1098	A153	15c shown	.40	.25
1099	A153	30c Card Tricks	.65	.25
1100	A153	60c Pharmacist	1.10	1.00
1101	A153	70c Pals	1.40	1.25
		Nos. 1098-1101 (4)	3.55	2.75

Princess Diana Issue

Common Design Type

50c, Kensington Palace. $1, Couple in field. $3, Diana in green dress.
$5, Diana, diff.

1982, July 1 Litho. *Perf. 14½x14*

No.	Type	Description	Unused	Used
1101A	CD332	50c multicolored	.55	*.75*
1102	CD332	60c like 50c	.60	.50
1102A	CD332	$1 multi	.90	.80
1103	CD332	$2 like $1	2.25	1.75
1103A	CD332	$3 multi	2.50	2.50
1104	CD332	$4 like $3	3.25	3.25
		Nos. 1101A-1104 (6)	10.05	9.55

Souvenir Sheet

No.	Type	Description	Unused	Used
1105	CD332	$5 multi	6.00	6.00

For overprints see Nos. 1115A-1119.

Franklin Roosevelt Birth Centenary A154

Designs: 10c, Mary McLeod Bethune, director of Negro Affairs, 1942. 60c, Leadbelly (Huddie Ledbetter, Works Progress Administration). $1.10, Signing Fair Employment Act, 1941. $3, Farm Security Administration.

1982, July 27 Litho. *Perf. 14*

No.	Type	Description	Unused	Used
1106	A154	10c multi	.25	.25
1107	A154	60c multi	.30	.30
1108	A154	$1.10 multi	.50	.50
1109	A154	$3 multi	1.40	1.40
		Nos. 1106-1109 (4)	2.45	2.45

Souvenir Sheet

No.	Type	Description	Unused	Used
1110	A154	$5 multi	2.50	2.50

Easter A155

Details from Raphael's "On the Way to Calvary." 70c, $1.10, $4, $5, vert.

1982, Sept. 2 *Perf. 14½*

No.	Type	Description	Unused	Used
1111	A155	40c multi	.25	.25
1112	A155	70c multi	.30	.30
1113	A155	$1.10 multi	.55	.55
1114	A155	$4 multi	1.75	1.75
		Nos. 1111-1114 (4)	2.85	2.85

Souvenir Sheet

No.	Type	Description	Unused	Used
1115	A155	$5 multi	3.00	3.00

Nos. 1101A-1105 Overprinted in Black

1982, Sept. 27 Litho. *Perf. 14½x14*

No.	Type	Description	Unused	Used
1115A	CD332	50c multi	.35	.35
1116	CD332	60c multi	.40	.40
1116A	CD332	$1 multi	.65	.65
1117	CD332	$2 multi	1.25	1.25
1117A	CD332	$3 multi	2.00	2.00
1118	CD332	$4 multi	2.50	2.50
		Nos. 1115A-1118 (6)	7.15	7.15

Souvenir Sheet

No.	Type	Description	Unused	Used
1119	CD332	$5 multi	4.50	4.50

Birth of Prince William of Wales, June 21.

Orient Express A156

60c, Trans-Siberian Express. 70c, Fleche D'or. 90c, Flying Scotsman. $1, German Federal Railways. $3, German Natl. Railways.
$5, 20th Century Limited, US.

1982, Oct. 4

No.	Type	Description	Unused	Used
1120	A156	30c shown	.35	*.40*
1121	A156	60c multicolored	.65	.65
1122	A156	70c multicolored	.75	.75
1123	A156	90c multicolored	.95	.95
1124	A156	$1 multicolored	1.25	1.25
1125	A156	$3 multicolored	3.00	*4.00*
		Nos. 1120-1125 (6)	6.95	*8.00*

Souvenir Sheet

No.	Type	Description	Unused	Used
1126	A156	$5 multicolored	3.75	3.75

Christmas — A157

Scenes from Walt Disney's Robin Hood.

1982, Dec. 7 Litho. *Perf. 14*

No.	Type	Description	Unused	Used
1127	A157	½c multi	.25	.25
1128	A157	1c multi	.25	.25
1129	A157	2c multi	.25	.25
1130	A157	3c multi	.25	.25
1131	A157	4c multi	.25	.25
1132	A157	5c multi	.25	.25
1133	A157	10c multi	.25	.25
1134	A157	$2.50 multi	2.75	2.75
1135	A157	$3 multi	3.00	3.00
		Nos. 1127-1135 (9)	7.50	7.50

Souvenir Sheet

No.	Type	Description	Unused	Used
1136	A157	$5 multi	7.25	7.25

Italy's Victory in 1982 World Cup A158

60c, Stolen ball. $4, Captain holding trophy.
$5, Flags.

1982, Dec. 2 *Perf. 14x13½*

No.	Type	Description	Unused	Used
1137	A158	60c multicolored	.50	.50
1138	A158	$4 multicolored	3.25	3.25

Souvenir Sheet

No.	Type	Description	Unused	Used
1139	A158	$5 multicolored	3.75	3.75

Killer Whale — A159

40c, Sperm whale. 70c, Blue whale. $3, Common dolphins.
$5, Humpback whale.

1982, Dec. 15 *Perf. 14*

No.	Type	Description	Unused	Used
1140	A159	15c shown	1.50	.50
1141	A159	40c multicolored	2.50	.75
1142	A159	70c multicolored	3.50	2.75
1143	A159	$3 multicolored	6.00	6.00
		Nos. 1140-1143 (4)	13.50	10.00

Souvenir Sheet

No.	Type	Description	Unused	Used
1144	A159	$5 multicolored	11.00	11.00

GRENADA 25c

500th Birth Anniv. of Raphael — A160

25c, Construction of the Ark. 30c, Jacob's Vision. 90c, Joseph Interprets the Dreams. $4, Joseph Interprets Pharaoh's Dream.
$5, Creation of the Animals.

1983, Feb. 15 Litho. *Perf. 14*

No.	Type	Value	Description	Unused	Used
1145	A160	25c	multicolored	.25	.25
1146	A160	30c	multicolored	.25	.25
1147	A160	90c	multicolored	.55	.55
1148	A160	$4	multicolored	1.75	1.75
			Nos. 1145-1148 (4)	2.80	2.80

Souvenir Sheet

No.	Type	Value	Description	Unused	Used
1149	A160	$5	multicolored	2.75	2.75

A161

10c, Dental care. 70c, Airport runway construction. $1.10, Beach. $3, Boat building.

1983, Mar. 14

No.	Type	Value	Description	Unused	Used
1150	A161	10c	multicolored	.25	.25
1151	A161	70c	multicolored	.40	.40
1152	A161	$1.10	multicolored	.65	.65
1153	A161	$3	multicolored	1.25	1.75
			Nos. 1150-1153 (4)	2.55	3.05

Commonwealth Day.

World Communication Year — A162

30c, Ship-satellite communication. 40c, Rural telephone installation. $2.50, Weather map. $3, Airport control tower.
$5, Satellite.

1983, Apr. 18

No.	Type	Value	Description	Unused	Used
1154	A162	30c	multicolored	.25	.25
1155	A162	40c	multicolored	.25	.25
1156	A162	$2.50	multicolored	1.25	1.25
1157	A162	$3	multicolored	1.50	1.50
			Nos. 1154-1157 (4)	3.25	3.25

Souvenir Sheet

No.	Type	Value	Description	Unused	Used
1158	A162	$5	multicolored	2.75	2.75

For overprints see Nos. 1248-1250.

Franklin Sport Sedan, 1928 A163

10c, Delage D8, 1933. 40c, Alvis, 1938. 60c, Invicta S-type Tourer, 1931. 70c, Alfa-Romeo 1750 Gran Sport, 1930. 90c, Isotta Fraschini, 1930. $1, Bugatti Royal Type 41, 1941. $2, BMV 328, 1938. $3, Marmon V-16, 1931. $4, Lincoln KB Saloon, 1932.
$5, Cougar XR-7, 1972.

1983, May 4 Litho. *Perf. 15*

No.	Type	Value	Description	Unused	Used
1159	A163	6c	shown	.25	.25
1160	A163	10c	multicolored	.25	.25
1161	A163	40c	multicolored	.25	.25
1162	A163	60c	multicolored	.40	.40
1163	A163	70c	multicolored	.45	.45
1164	A163	90c	multicolored	.65	.60
1165	A163	$1	multicolored	.70	.70
1166	A163	$2	multicolored	1.25	1.25
1167	A163	$3	multicolored	1.75	1.75
1168	A163	$4	multicolored	2.50	2.50
			Nos. 1159-1168 (10)	8.45	8.40

Souvenir Sheet

No.	Type	Value	Description	Unused	Used
1169	A163	$5	multicolored	3.25	3.25

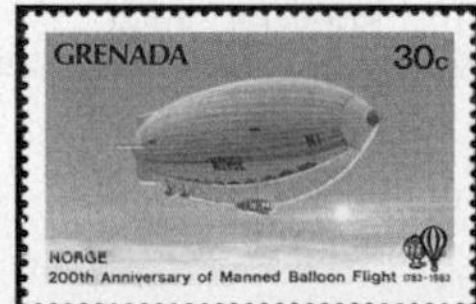

Manned Flight Bicentenary — A164

30c, Norge blimp. 60c, Gloster-VI sea plane. $1.10, Curtiss NC-4. $4, Dornier Do-18.
$5, Hot air ballooning, vert.

1983, July 18 Litho. *Perf. 14*

No.	Type	Value	Description	Unused	Used
1170	A164	30c	multicolored	.60	.60
1171	A164	60c	multicolored	1.00	1.00
1172	A164	$1.10	multicolored	1.75	1.75
1173	A164	$4	multicolored	4.25	4.25
			Nos. 1170-1173 (4)	7.60	7.60

Souvenir Sheet

No.	Type	Value	Description	Unused	Used
1174	A164	$5	multicolored	4.25	4.25

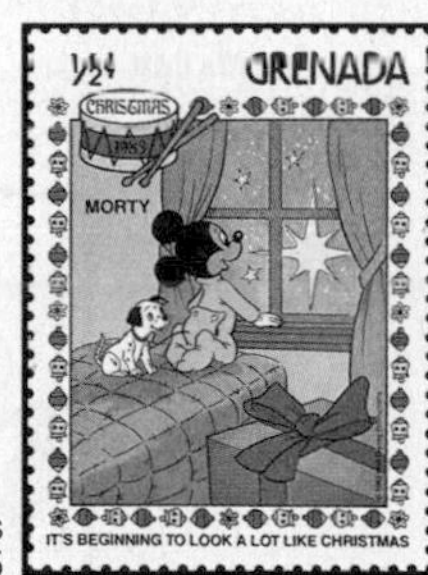

Christmas A165

Walt Disney's It's Beginning to look a lot like Christmas: ½c, Morty and Patches. 1c, Ludwig von Drake. 2c, Gyro Gearloose. 3c, Pluto and Figaro. 4c, Morty and Ferdy. 5c, Mickey Mouse and Gooty. 10c, Chip'n'Dale. $2.50, Mickey and Minnie. $3, Donald and Grandma Duck.
$5, Goofy.

1983, Nov. *Perf. 11*

No.	Type	Value	Description	Unused	Used
1175	A165	½c	multicolored	.25	.25
1176	A165	1c	multicolored	.25	.25
1177	A165	2c	multicolored	.25	.25
1178	A165	3c	multicolored	.25	.25
1179	A165	4c	multicolored	.25	.25
1180	A165	5c	multicolored	.30	.25
1181	A165	10c	multicolored	.30	.25
1182	A165	$2.50	multicolored	2.75	2.75
1183	A165	$3	multicolored	2.75	2.75
			Nos. 1175-1183 (9)	7.35	7.25

Souvenir Sheet

No.	Type	Value	Description	Unused	Used
1184	A165	$5	multicolored	7.50	7.50

1984 Olympics — A166

Designs: Various Disney characters.

1983, Dec. 19 Litho. *Perf. 13½*

No.	Type	Value	Description	Unused	Used
1185	A166	½c	Pommel Horse	.25	.25
1186	A166	1c	Boxing	.25	.25
1187	A166	2c	Archery	.25	.25
1188	A166	3c	Uneven bars	.25	.25
1189	A166	4c	Hurdles	.25	.25
1190	A166	5c	Weightlifting	.25	.25
1191	A166	$1	Kayak	1.75	1.75
1192	A166	$2	Marathon	2.50	2.50
1193	A166	$3	Pole Vault	3.00	*3.50*
			Nos. 1185-1193 (9)	8.75	9.25

Souvenir Sheet

No.	Type	Value	Description	Unused	Used
1194	A166	$5	Medley Relay, vert.	8.00	8.00

Inscribed with Olympic Rings Emblem

1984 *Perf. 12½x12*

No.	Type	Value	Description	Unused	Used
1185a	A166	½c		.25	.25
1186a	A166	1c		.25	.25
1187a	A166	2c		.25	.25
1188a	A166	3c		.25	.25
1189a	A166	4c		.25	.25
1190a	A166	5c		.25	.25
1191a	A166	$1		1.75	1.75
1192a	A166	$2		2.50	2.50
1193a	A166	$3		3.00	*3.50*
			Nos. 1185a-1193a (9)	8.75	9.25

Souvenir Sheet

No.	Type	Value	Description	Unused	Used
1194a	A166	$5	Olympic rings emblem inscribed	8.00	8.00

Nos. 1185a-1193a printed in sheets of 5.

Banana Boat A167

70c, Queen Elizabeth 2. 90c, Working sailboats. $4, Amerikanis.
$5, Spanish galleon, flotilla.

1984, July 16 Litho. *Perf. 15*

No.	Type	Value	Description	Unused	Used
1195	A167	40c	shown	1.00	.60
1196	A167	70c	multicolored	1.50	1.00
1197	A167	90c	multicolored	1.60	2.00
1198	A167	$4	multicolored	6.00	*8.00*
			Nos. 1195-1198 (4)	10.10	11.60

Souvenir Sheet

No.	Type	Value	Description	Unused	Used
1199	A167	$5	multicolored	6.75	6.75

King William I, 1066-87 — A168

British Kings or Queens and Years of their reigns: No. 1200b, William II, 1087-1100. c, Henry I, 1100-35. d, Stephen, 1135-54. e, Henry II, 1154-89. f, Richard I, 1189-99. g, John, 1199-1216.

No. 1201a, Henry III, 1216-72. b, Edward I, 1272-1307. c, Edward II, 1307-27. d, Edward III, 1327-77. e, Richard II, 1377-99. f, Henry IV, 1399-1413. g, Henry V, 1413-22.

No. 1202a, Henry VI, 1422-61. b, Edward IV, 1461-83. c, Edward V, 1483. d, Richard III, 1483-85. e, Henry VII, 1485-1509. f, Henry VIII, 1509-47. g, Edward VI, 1547-53.

No. 1203a, Jane Grey, 1553. b, Mary I, 1553-58. c, Elizabeth I, 1558-1603. d, James I, 1603-25. e, Charles I, 1625-49. f, Charles II, 1660-85. g, James II, 1685-88.

No. 1204a, William III, 1688-1702. b, Mary II, 1688-94. c, Anne, 1702-14. d, George I, 1714-27. e, George II, 1727-60. f, George III, 1760-1820. g, George IV, 1820-30.

No. 1205a, William IV, 1830-37. b, Victoria, 1837-1901. c, Edward VII, 1901-10. d, George V, 1910-36. e, Edward VIII, 1936. f, George VI, 1936-52. g, Elizabeth II, since 1952. Size: 141x128mm.

1984, Jan. 25 Litho. *Perf. 14*

No.	Type	Value	Description	Unused	Used
1200			Sheet of 7 + label	19.00	19.00
a.-g.	A168	$4	any single	2.75	2.75
1201			Sheet of 7 + label	19.00	19.00
a.-g.	A168	$4	any single	2.75	2.75
1202			Sheet of 7 + label	19.00	19.00
a.-g.	A168	$4	any single	2.75	2.75
1203			Sheet of 7 + label	19.00	19.00
a.-g.	A168	$4	any single	2.75	2.75
1204			Sheet of 7 + label	19.00	19.00
a.-g.	A168	$4	any single	2.75	2.75
1205			Sheet of 7 + label	19.00	19.00
a.-g.	A168	$4	any single	2.75	2.75

Local Flowers A169

1984, May *Perf. 15*

No.	Type	Value	Description	Unused	Used
1206	A169	25c	Lantana	.25	.25
1207	A169	30c	Plumbago	.30	.25
1208	A169	90c	Spider lily	.70	.60
1209	A169	$4	Giant alocasia	2.75	2.75
			Nos. 1206-1209 (4)	4.00	3.85

Souvenir Sheet

No.	Type	Value	Description	Unused	Used
1210	A169	$5	Orange trumpet vine	3.25	3.25

For overprints see Nos. 1216-1218.

Coral Reef Fish, World Wildlife Fund Emblem A170

10c, Blue parrot fish. 30c, Flame-back cherub fish. 70c, Painted wrasse. 90c, Straight-tailed razorfish.
$5, Spanish hogfish.

1984, May Litho. *Perf. 14*

No.	Type	Value	Description	Unused	Used
1211	A170	10c	multicolored	3.25	.95
1212	A170	30c	multicolored	5.25	1.60
1213	A170	70c	multicolored	9.00	4.00
1214	A170	90c	multicolored	12.00	5.25
			Nos. 1211-1214 (4)	29.50	11.80

Souvenir Sheet

No.	Type	Value	Description	Unused	Used
1215	A170	$5	multicolored	10.00	10.00

Nos. 1208-1210 Overprinted in Black

1984 Litho. *Perf. 15*

No.	Type	Value	Description	Unused	Used
1216	A169	90c	multi	.70	.70
1217	A169	$4	multi	3.00	3.00

Souvenir Sheet

No.	Type	Value	Description	Unused	Used
1218	A169	$5	multi	3.50	3.50

AUSIPEX '84 — A171

1984, Sept. 21 *Perf. 14*

No.	Type	Value	Description	Unused	Used
1219	A171	$1.10	Puffing Billy	1.10	1.10
1220	A171	$4	Australia II	5.25	5.25

Souvenir Sheet

No.	Type	Value	Description	Unused	Used
1221	A171	$5	Melbourne tram	6.75	6.75

Correggio & Degas — A171a

Paintings by Correggio: 10c, The Night (detail). 30c, Virgin Adoring the Child. 90c, Mystical Marriage of St. Catherine with St. Sebastian. $4, Madonna and the Fruit Basket. No. 1230, Madonna at the Spring.

Paintings by Degas: 25c, L'Absinthe. 70c, Pouting, horiz. $1.10, The Millinery Shop. $3, The Bellelli Family, horiz. No. 1231, The Cotton Market.

1984, Aug. Litho. *Perf. 14*

No.	Type	Value	Description	Unused	Used
1222	A171a	10c	multi	.45	.25
1223	A171a	25c	multi	.60	.30
1224	A171a	30c	multi	.80	.40
1225	A171a	70c	multi	1.25	1.00
1226	A171a	90c	multi	1.50	1.00
1227	A171a	$1.10	multi	1.75	1.75
1228	A171a	$3	multi	3.00	*4.00*
1229	A171a	$4	multi	4.00	*5.00*
			Nos. 1222-1229 (8)	13.35	13.70

Souvenir Sheets

No.	Type	Value	Description	Unused	Used
1230	A171a	$5	multi	6.25	6.25
1231	A171a	$5	multi	6.25	6.25

450th Anniversary of the Death of Correggio (Painter), 1494-1534 and 150th Anniversary of the Birth of Edgar Degas (Painter), 1834-1917.

19th Cent. Locomotives — A172

30c, Locomotion, 1825. 40c, Novelty, 1829. 60c, Washington Farmer, 1836. 70c, French Crampton, 1859. 90c, Dutch State, 1873.

$1.10, Champion, 1882. $2, Webb Compound, 1893. $4, Berlin 74, 1900.

No. 1240, Crampton Phoenix, 1863. No. 1241, 2-8-2 Mikado, 1897.

1984, Oct. ***Perf. 14½***

No.	Type	Description	Unused	Used
1232	A172	30c multicolored	.80	.35
1233	A172	40c multicolored	.90	.45
1234	A172	60c multicolored	1.00	.70
1235	A172	70c multicolored	1.00	1.00
1236	A172	90c multicolored	1.25	1.00
1237	A172	$1.10 multicolored	1.50	*2.00*
1238	A172	$2 multicolored	2.40	*3.00*
1239	A172	$4 multicolored	4.75	*5.00*
		Nos. 1232-1239 (8)	13.60	*13.50*

Souvenir Sheets

No.	Type	Description	Unused	Used
1240	A172	$5 multicolored	4.25	4.25
1241	A172	$5 multicolored	4.25	4.25

Christmas and 50th Anniv. of Donald Duck A173

Scenes from various Donald Duck movies.

Perf. 13½x14, 12 ($2)

1984, Nov. **Litho.**

No.	Type	Description	Unused	Used
1242	A173	45c multicolored	1.00	.65
1243	A173	60c multicolored	1.25	.95
1244	A173	90c multicolored	2.00	1.50
1245	A173	$2 multicolored	3.25	3.25
1246	A173	$4 multicolored	6.50	6.50
		Nos. 1242-1246 (5)	14.00	12.85

Souvenir Sheet

No.	Type	Description	Unused	Used
1247	A173	$5 multicolored	8.50	8.50

Nos. 1155. 1157, and 1158 Overprinted

1984, Oct. 28 **Litho.** ***Perf. 14½x14***

No.	Type	Description	Unused	Used
1248	A162	40c on #1155	.50	.50
1249	A162	$3 on #1157	3.00	3.00

Souvenir Sheet

Same Overprint in Margin in 2 Lines

No.	Type	Description	Unused	Used
1250	A162	$5 on #1158	4.50	4.50

Audubon Birth Bicentenary A174

50c, Clapper Rail. 70c, Hooded Warbler. 90c, Flicker. $4, Bohemian Waxwing.

$5, Pigeon Hawk, horiz.

1985, Feb. **Litho.** ***Perf. 14***

No.	Type	Description	Unused	Used
1251	A174	50c multi	2.00	.75
1252	A174	70c multi	2.50	1.50
1253	A174	90c multi	3.00	1.75
1254	A174	$4 multi	6.50	*7.50*
		Nos. 1251-1254 (4)	14.00	11.50

Souvenir Sheet

No.	Type	Description	Unused	Used
1255	A174	$5 multi	11.00	11.00

See Nos. 1352-1356.

Motorcycle Centenary — A175

25c, Honda XL500R. 50c, Suzuki GS1100ES. 90c, Kawasaki KZ700. $4, BMW K100.

$5, Yamaha 500CC.

1985, Mar. 11 **Litho.** ***Perf. 14***

No.	Type	Description	Unused	Used
1256	A175	25c multicolored	1.50	.75
1257	A175	50c multicolored	1.75	1.50
1258	A175	90c multicolored	2.50	1.60
1259	A175	$4 multicolored	5.75	*7.50*
		Nos. 1256-1259 (4)	11.50	11.35

Souvenir Sheet

No.	Type	Description	Unused	Used
1260	A175	$5 multicolored	9.00	9.00

Girl Guides, 75th Anniv. A176

25c, Nature hike. 60c, Cookout. 90c, Singing around campfire. $3, Public service. $5, Flags.

1985, Apr. 15

No.	Type	Description	Unused	Used
1261	A176	25c multicolored	.65	.40
1262	A176	60c multicolored	1.00	.90
1263	A176	90c multicolored	1.50	1.25
1264	A176	$3 multicolored	4.50	4.50
		Nos. 1261-1264 (4)	7.65	7.05

Souvenir Sheet

No.	Type	Description	Unused	Used
1265	A176	$5 multicolored	4.75	4.75

Opening of Point Saline Intl. Airport, Oct. 28, 1984 — A177

Inaugural flights.

1985, Apr. 30

No.	Type	Description	Unused	Used
1266	A177	70c From Barbados	2.50	1.40
1267	A177	$1 From New York	3.50	2.00
1268	A177	$4 To Miami	7.50	*8.50*
		Nos. 1266-1268 (3)	13.50	11.90

Souvenir Sheet

No.	Type	Description	Unused	Used
1269	A177	$5 Point Saline Intl. Airport	7.75	7.75

Intl. Civil Aviation Org., 40th Anniv. A178

10c, McDonnell Douglas DC-8. 50c, Super Constellation. 60c, Vickers Vanguard. $4, DeHavilland Twin Otter.

$5, Avro 748 Turboprop.

1985, May 15

No.	Type	Description	Unused	Used
1270	A178	10c multicolored	.40	.25
1271	A178	50c multicolored	1.00	.65
1272	A178	60c multicolored	1.50	.80
1273	A178	$4 multicolored	5.00	*6.50*
		Nos. 1270-1273 (4)	7.90	8.20

Souvenir Sheet

No.	Type	Description	Unused	Used
1274	A178	$5 multicolored	5.00	5.00

Water Sports A179

10c, Model boat racing. 50c, Snorkeling, Sandy Island carriacou. $1.10, Sailing, Grand Anse Beach. $4, Windsurfing. $5, Snorkelers, surfers, sailboats.

1985, June 15 ***Perf. 15***

No.	Type	Description	Unused	Used
1275	A179	10c multicolored	.25	.25
1276	A179	50c multicolored	.40	.40
1277	A179	$1.10 multicolored	.90	.90
1278	A179	$4 multicolored	2.75	2.75
		Nos. 1275-1278 (4)	4.30	4.30

Miniature Sheet

No.	Type	Description	Unused	Used
1279	A179	$5 multicolored	4.75	4.75

Island Flowers — A180

½c, Strelitzia reginae. 1c, Passiflora coccinea. 2c, Nerium oleander. 4c, Ananas comosus. 5c, Anthurium andraeanum. 6c, Bougainvillea glabra. 10c, Hibiscus rosa-sinensis. 15c, Alpinia purpurata. 25c, Euphorbia pulcherrima. 30c, Antigonon leptopus. 40c, Datura candida. 50c, Hippeastrum puniceum. 60c, Opuntia megacantha. 70c, Acalypha hispida. 75c, Cordia sebestina. $1, Catharan-thus roseus. $1.10, Ixora macrothyrsa. $3, Justicia brandegeeana. $5, Plumbago capensis. $10, Lantana camara. $20, Jatropha integerrima.

1985-88 ***Perf. 14***

No.	Type	Description	Unused	Used
1280	A180	½c multi	.25	.25
1281	A180	1c multi	.25	.25
1282	A180	2c multi	.25	.25
1283	A180	4c multi	.25	.25
1284	A180	5c multi	.25	.25
1285	A180	6c multi	.25	.25
1286	A180	10c multi	.25	.25
1287	A180	15c multi	.25	.25
1288	A180	25c multi	.25	.25
1289	A180	30c multi	.25	.25
1290	A180	40c multi	.50	.50
1291	A180	50c multi	.60	.60
1292	A180	60c multi	.70	.70
1293	A180	70c multi	.75	.75
1293B	A180	75c multi	1.00	1.00
1294	A180	$1 multi	1.20	1.20
1295	A180	$1.10 multi	1.30	1.30
1296	A180	$3 multi	3.25	3.25
1297	A180	$5 multi	5.25	5.25
1297A	A180	$10 multi	11.00	11.00
1297B	A180	$20 multi	21.50	21.50
		Nos. 1280-1297B (21)	49.55	49.55

Issued: Nos. 1280-1293, 1294-1297, 7/1; $10, 11/11; $20, 8/1/86; 75c, 1/12/88.

For overprints see Nos. 1357-1358, 1558-1560.

1986 ***Perf. 12x12½***

No date inscription

No.	Type	Description	Unused	Used
1280a	A180	½c	.25	.25
1281a	A180	1c	.25	.25
1282a	A180	2c	.25	.25
1283a	A180	4c	.25	.25
1284a	A180	5c	.25	.25
1285a	A180	6c	.25	.25
1286a	A180	10c	.25	.25
b.		Inscribed "1988"	2.75	2.75
1287a	A180	15c	.25	.25
1288a	A180	25c	.25	.25
1289a	A180	30c	.25	.25
1290a	A180	40c	.25	.25
1291a	A180	50c	.30	.30
1292a	A180	60c	.35	.35
1293a	A180	70c	.40	.40
1294a	A180	$1	.60	.60
1295a	A180	$1.10	.65	.65
1296a	A180	$3	2.75	2.75
1297c	A180	$5	3.75	3.75
1297d	A180	$10	6.75	6.75
		Nos. 1280a-1297d (19)	18.30	18.30

Issued: Nos. 1280a-1285a, 1287a-1292a, 1294a-1296a, Mar.; 10c, 70c, $5, July; $10, Dec.

1987 **Inscribed "1987"**

No.	Type	Description	Unused	Used
1289b	A180	30c	.95	.65
1291b	A180	50c	1.25	.80
1292b	A180	60c	1.60	1.25
1294b	A180	$1	2.25	1.25
		Nos. 1289b-1294b (4)	6.05	3.95

Queen Mother, 85th Birthday A181

Photographs: $1, At the Royal Opera, vert. $1.50, Playing pool, London Press Club. $2.50, At Epsom for the Oaks Day races, vert. $5, In open carriage with Prince Charles, Thanksgiving Day, 1980, vert.

1985, July 5

No.	Type	Description	Unused	Used
1298	A181	$1 multicolored	.60	.60
1299	A181	$1.50 multicolored	.90	.90
1300	A181	$2.50 multicolored	1.40	1.40
		Nos. 1298-1300 (3)	2.90	2.90

Souvenir Sheet

No.	Type	Description	Unused	Used
1301	A181	$5 multicolored	3.50	3.50

1986, Jan. 20 **Litho.** ***Perf. 12x12½***

No.	Type	Description	Unused	Used
1301A	A181	90c like #1298	.55	.55
1301B	A181	$1 like #1299	.65	.65
1301C	A181	$3 like #1300	1.90	1.90
		Nos. 1301A-1301C (3)	3.10	3.10

Nos. 1301A-1301C issued in sheets of 5 + label.

Intl. Youth Year — A182

1985, Aug. 21 ***Perf. 15***

No.	Type	Description	Unused	Used
1302	A182	25c Gardening	.40	.25
1303	A182	50c At the beach	.50	.40
1304	A182	$1.10 Education	1.00	1.00
1305	A182	$3 Health care	2.10	2.10
		Nos. 1302-1305 (4)	4.00	3.75

Souvenir Sheet

No.	Type	Description	Unused	Used
1306	A182	$5 Harmonizing	4.00	4.00

4th Caribbean Cuboree, Aug. 17-23 A183

1985, Sept. 5 ***Perf. 14***

No.	Type	Description	Unused	Used
1307	A183	10c Pitching tents	.40	.25
1308	A183	50c Swimming	.80	.65
1309	A183	$1 Stamp collecting	1.90	1.40
1310	A183	$4 Bird watching	5.25	5.25
		Nos. 1307-1310 (4)	8.35	7.55

Souvenir Sheet

No.	Type	Description	Unused	Used
1311	A183	$5 Grand Circle ritual	5.75	5.75

GRENADA 300th Birth Anniversary of Johann Sebastian Bach — Crumhorn — 25c

Johann Sebastian Bach — A184

Portrait, signature, music from Ciaccona and: 25c, Crumhorn. 70c, Oboe d'amore. $1, Violin. $3, Harpsichord. $5, Portrait.

1985, Sept. 19

No.	Type	Description	Unused	Used
1312	A184	25c multicolored	.75	.25
1313	A184	70c multicolored	1.40	.85
1314	A184	$1 multicolored	1.75	1.25
1315	A184	$3 multicolored	3.50	3.50
		Nos. 1312-1315 (4)	7.40	5.85

Souvenir Sheet

No.	Type	Description	Unused	Used
1316	A184	$5 multicolored	5.75	5.75

The Prince & the Pauper — A185

Walt Disney characters: 25c, Prince & Pauper meet. 50c, Exchange clothes. $1.10, Prince as the Pauper. $1.50, Prince rescued. $2, Pauper as the Prince.
$5, Prince & Pauper celebrate.

1985, Oct. 30

1317	A185	25c	multicolored	1.25	.40
1318	A185	50c	multicolored	1.50	.80
1319	A185	$1.10	multicolored	2.00	1.75
1320	A185	$1.50	multicolored	2.75	2.50
1321	A185	$2	multicolored	4.00	4.00
	Nos. 1317-1321 (5)			11.50	9.45

Souvenir Sheet

1322	A185	$5	multicolored	9.50	9.50

IYY, Mark Twain (1835-1910), author.

Elizabeth II, Royal Visit to Spice Island — A186

50c, Flags of Grenada, U.K. $1, Elizabeth II, vert. $4, HMS Britannia.
$5, Map.

1985, Oct. 31 *Perf. 14½*

1323	A186	50c	multicolored	1.00	.50
1324	A186	$1	multicolored	1.00	1.25
1325	A186	$4	multicolored	3.50	3.50
	Nos. 1323-1325 (3)			5.50	5.25

Souvenir Sheet

1326	A186	$5	multicolored	3.75	3.75

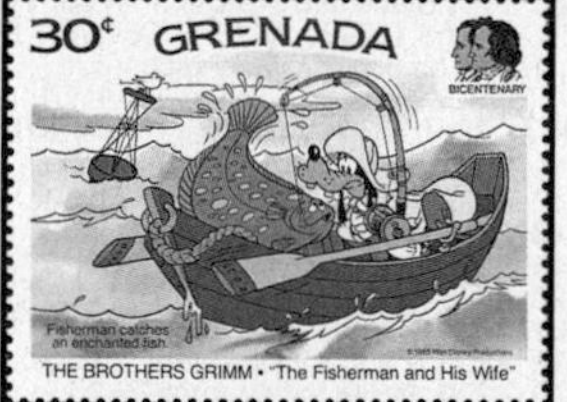
The Brothers Grimm — A187

Disney characters in The Fisherman and His Wife.

1985, Nov. 4 **Litho.** *Perf. 14*

1327	A187	30c	multicolored	1.00	.50
1328	A187	60c	multicolored	1.50	1.00
1329	A187	70c	multicolored	2.00	1.10
1330	A187	$1	multicolored	3.00	1.60
1331	A187	$3	multicolored	5.00	5.00
	Nos. 1327-1331 (5)			12.50	9.20

Souvenir Sheet

1332	A187	$5	multicolored	9.50	9.50

Indigenous Fish and Coral — A188

25c, Red-spotted hawkfish. 50c, Spotfin butterflyfish. $1.10, Fire coral, orange sponge. $3, Pillar coral.
$5, Bigeye.

1985, Nov. 15

1333	A188	25c	multicolored	1.75	.80
1334	A188	50c	multicolored	2.75	1.25
1335	A188	$1.10	multicolored	5.00	3.25
1336	A188	$3	multicolored	8.75	8.75
	Nos. 1333-1336 (4)			18.25	14.05

Souvenir Sheet

1337	A188	$5	multicolored	7.00	7.00

UN, 40th Anniv. A189

UN stamps and famous people: 50c, No. 258, Mary McLeod Bethune (1875-1955), American educator. $2, No. 156, Maimonides (1135-1204), Judaic scholar. $2.50, No. 41, Alexander Graham Bell (1847-1922), inventor of the telephone. $5, Dag Hammarskjold (1905-1961), 2nd UN secretary general.

1985, Nov. 22 *Perf. 14½*

1338	A189	50c	multicolored	.75	.65
1339	A189	$2	multicolored	3.25	3.25
1340	A189	$2.50	multicolored	3.25	3.75
	Nos. 1338-1340 (3)			7.25	7.65

Souvenir Sheet

1341	A189	$5	multicolored	4.25	4.25

Christmas A190

Religious paintings: 25c, Adoration of the Shepherds, by Andre Mantegna (1431-1506). 60c, Journey of the Magi, by Sassetta (d. 1450). 90c, Madonna and Child Enthroned with Saints, by Raphael (1483-1520). $4, Nativity, by Monaco. $5, Madonna and Child Enthroned with Saints, by Agnolo Gaddi (c. 1350-1396).

1985, Dec. 23 *Perf. 15*

1342	A190	25c	multicolored	.25	.25
1343	A190	60c	multicolored	.35	.35
1344	A190	90c	multicolored	.55	.55
1345	A190	$4	multicolored	2.50	2.50
	Nos. 1342-1345 (4)			3.65	3.65

Souvenir Sheet

1346	A190	$5	multicolored	3.25	3.25

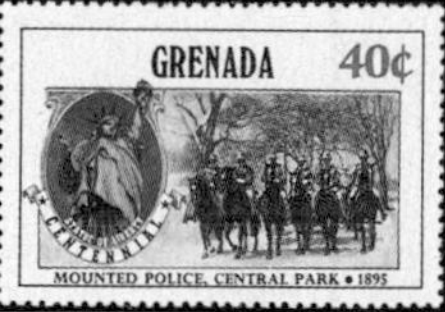
Statue of Liberty, Cent. A191

Views of New York City: 5c, Columbus Circle, 1893. 25c, Circle, 1986. 40c, Central Park Mounted Police, 1895. $4, Mounted Police, 1986.
$5, Statue of Liberty.

1986, Jan. 6

1347	A191	5c	multicolored	.50	.25
1348	A191	25c	multicolored	1.00	.45
1349	A191	40c	multicolored	1.75	1.25
1350	A191	$4	multicolored	6.50	*8.00*
	Nos. 1347-1350 (4)			9.75	9.95

Souvenir Sheet

1351	A191	$5	multicolored	5.50	5.50

Nos. 1347-1348, 1351 vert.

Audubon Type of 1985

50c, Snowy egret. 90c, Red flamingo. $1.10, Barnacle goose. $3, Smew.
$5, Brant Goose, horiz.

1986, Jan. 20 *Perf. 12x12½*

1352	A174	50c	multi	2.00	1.00
1353	A174	90c	multi	2.75	1.60
1354	A174	$1.10	multi	3.00	2.50
1355	A174	$3	multi	5.50	5.50
	Nos. 1352-1355 (4)			13.25	10.60

Souvenir Sheet

Perf. 14

1356	A174	$5	multi	16.00	16.00

Nos. 1291 and 1297 Overprinted in Black

1986, Feb. 20 *Perf. 14*

1357	A180	50c	multicolored	.45	.45
1358	A180	$5	multicolored	4.50	4.50

St. George Methodist Church, Bicent. A192

1986, Feb. 24 *Perf. 15*

1359	A192	60c	multicolored	.80	.80

Souvenir Sheet

1360	A192	$5	multicolored	3.50	3.50

Heritage Year.

1986 World Cup Soccer Championships, Mexico — A193

Various soccer plays.

1986, Mar. 6 *Perf. 14*

1361	A193	50c	multicolored	.80	.70
1362	A193	70c	multicolored	1.00	1.00
1363	A193	90c	multicolored	1.50	1.50
1364	A193	$4	multicolored	5.25	5.25
	Nos. 1361-1364 (4)			8.55	8.45

Souvenir Sheet

1365	A193	$5	multicolored	6.00	6.00

For overprints see Nos. 1399-1403.

Halley's Comet A194

5c, Clyde Tombaugh, discovered Pluto, 1930, & Dudley Observatory. 20c, US X-24B space shuttle prototype, 1973. 40c, Medallic art, Catholic Church, 1618. $4, Lot & his daughters fleeing Sodom & Gomorrah, 1949 B.C. $5, Comet over Grand Anse Beach.

1986, Mar. 20

1366	A194	5c	multicolored	.50	.50
1367	A194	20c	multicolored	.75	.25
1368	A194	40c	multicolored	1.00	.40
1369	A194	$4	multicolored	4.25	4.25
	Nos. 1366-1369 (4)			6.50	5.40

Souvenir Sheet

1370	A194	$5	multicolored	7.75	7.75

For overprints see Nos. 1416-1420.

Queen Elizabeth II, 60th Birthday
Common Design Type

2c, Signing the log, 1951. $1.50, Presenting polo trophy, Windsor, 1965. $4, Derby Day, 1977. $5, Royal family portrait, 1939.

1986, Apr. 21 *Perf. 14*

1371	CD339	2c	yel & blk	.25	.25
1372	CD339	$1.50	pale grn & multi	.90	.90
1373	CD339	$4	dl lil & multi	2.40	2.40
	Nos. 1371-1373 (3)			3.55	3.55

Souvenir Sheet

1374	CD339	$5	tan & blk	3.25	3.25

AMERIPEX '86 — A195

Walt Disney characters playing baseball.

1986, May 22 **Litho.** *Perf. 11*

1375	A195	1c	Pitcher	.25	.25
1376	A195	2c	Catcher	.25	.25
1377	A195	3c	Strike	.25	.25
1378	A195	4c	Force out	.25	.25
1379	A195	5c	Fly ball	.25	.25
1380	A195	6c	Third base	.25	.25
1381	A195	$2	Manager	2.10	1.90
1382	A195	$3	Error	3.00	3.00
	Nos. 1375-1382 (8)			6.60	6.40

Souvenir Sheets

Perf. 14

1383	A195	$5	Batter	6.50	6.50
1384	A195	$5	Grand slam	6.50	6.50

Royal Wedding Issue, 1986
Common Design Type

Designs: 2c, Prince Andrew and Sarah Ferguson. $1.10, Andrew. $4, Andrew in flight suit, helicopter. $5, Couple, diff.

1986, July 23 *Perf. 14*

1385	CD340	2c	multicolored	.25	.25
1386	CD340	$1.10	multicolored	.80	.80
1387	CD340	$4	multicolored	3.00	3.00
	Nos. 1385-1387 (3)			4.05	4.05

Souvenir Sheet

1388	CD340	$5	multicolored	4.25	4.25

Seashells A196

Designs: 25c, Gmelin brown-lined latirus. 60c, Lamarck lamellose wentletrap. 70c, Swainson turkey wing. $4, Linne rooster-tail conch. $5, Linne angular triton.

1986, July 15 **Litho.** *Perf. 15*

1389	A196	25c	multicolored	.50	.25
1390	A196	60c	multicolored	.75	.55
1391	A196	70c	multicolored	.90	.90
1392	A196	$4	multicolored	3.50	3.50
	Nos. 1389-1392 (4)			5.65	5.20

Souvenir Sheet

1393	A196	$5	multicolored	3.50	3.50

Mushrooms A197

10c, Lepiota roselamellata. 60c, Lentinus bertieri. $1, Lentinus retinervis. $4, Eccilia cystiophorus.
$5, Cystolepiota eriophora.

1986, Aug. 1 *Perf. 15*

1394	A197	10c	multicolored	.65	.40
1395	A197	60c	multicolored	1.25	1.00
1396	A197	$1	multicolored	2.75	2.00
1397	A197	$4	multicolored	6.50	6.50
	Nos. 1394-1397 (4)			11.15	9.90

Souvenir Sheet

1398	A197	$5	multicolored	13.50	13.50

Nos. 1361-1365 Ovptd. in Gold

1986, Sept. 15 Litho. *Perf. 14*

1399 A193 50c multicolored .95 .95
1400 A193 70c multicolored 1.25 1.25
1401 A193 90c multicolored 1.50 1.50
1402 A193 $4 multicolored 5.50 5.50
Nos. 1399-1402 (4) 9.20 9.20

Souvenir Sheet

1403 A193 $5 multicolored 5.75 5.75

Disarmament Week and Intl. Peace Year — A198

60c, Mahatma Gandhi, rifles, dove. $4, Martin Luther King, Jr., hands, olive branch.

1986, Sept. 15 *Perf. 15*

1404 A198 60c multi, vert. .40 .40
1405 A198 $4 multi 2.75 2.75

Christmas — A199

Disney characters: 30c, Mickey, hearth. 45c, Mickey, Santa. 60c, Donald, Mickey Mouse phone. 70c, Goofy, toy band. $1.10, Daisy, dolls. $2, Goofy as Santa. $2.50, Goofy playing piano. $3, Train ride.

No. 1414, Donald, Goofy, Mickey. No. 1415, Dewey.

Nos. 1406-1407, 1411-1412 vert.

1986, Nov. 3 *Perf. 11*

1406 A199 30c multi .50 .30
1407 A199 45c multi .75 .45
1408 A199 60c multi .90 .60
1409 A199 70c multi 1.10 .70
1410 A199 $1.10 multi 1.25 1.10
1411 A199 $2 multi 1.90 1.90
1412 A199 $2.50 multi 2.10 2.10
1413 A199 $3 multi 2.50 2.50
Nos. 1406-1413 (8) 11.00 9.65

Souvenir Sheets

1414 A199 $5 multi 6.75 6.75
1415 A199 $5 multi 6.75 6.75

Nos. 1366-1370 Ovptd. with Halley's Comet Emblem

1986, Oct. 15 Litho. *Perf. 14*

1416 A194 5c multicolored .60 .60
1417 A194 20c multicolored .80 .60
1418 A194 40c multicolored 1.10 .70
1419 A194 $4 multicolored 7.00 7.00
Nos. 1416-1419 (4) 9.50 8.90

Souvenir Sheet

1420 A194 $5 multicolored 5.00 5.00

Fauna and Flora A200

10c, Chicken, rooster. 30c, Fish-eating bat. 60c, Goat. 70c, Cow. $1, Anthurium. $1.10, Royal poinciana. $2, Frangipani. $4, Orchid.

No. 1429, Horse. No. 1430, Trees.

1986, Nov. 17 *Perf. 14*

1421 A200 10c multicolored .25 .25
1422 A200 30c multicolored .40 .25
1423 A200 60c multicolored .85 .75
1424 A200 70c multicolored 1.00 .90
1425 A200 $1 multicolored 1.50 1.10
1426 A200 $1.10 multicolored 1.50 1.25
1427 A200 $2 multicolored 2.50 2.50
1428 A200 $4 multicolored 5.00 *6.50*
Nos. 1421-1428 (8) 13.00 13.50

Souvenir Sheets

1429 A200 $5 multicolored 4.75 4.75
1430 A200 $5 multicolored 4.75 4.75

Automobile, Cent. — A202

1886 Daimler and modern automobiles: 10c, 1984 Maserati Biturbo. 30c, 1960 AC Cobra. 60c, 1963 Corvette. 70c, 1932 Duesenberg SJ7. 90c, 1957 Porsche. $1.10, 1930 Stoewer. $2, 1957 VW Beetle. $3, 1963 Mercedes 600 Limo.

No. 1439, 1914 Stutz. No. 1440, 1941 Packard.

1986, Nov. 20 *Perf. 15*

1431 A202 10c multicolored .25 .25
1432 A202 30c multicolored .35 .35
1433 A202 60c multicolored .55 .55
1434 A202 70c multicolored .65 .65
1435 A202 90c multicolored .75 .75
1436 A202 $1.10 multicolored 1.00 1.00
1437 A202 $2 multicolored 1.60 1.60
1438 A202 $3 multicolored 2.40 *2.75*
Nos. 1431-1438 (8) 7.55 7.90

Souvenir Sheets

1439 A202 $5 multicolored 3.75 3.75
1440 A202 $5 multicolored 3.75 3.75

Song of Songs, by Marc Chagall (1887-1984) — A203

Paintings: No. 1441, The Rooster. No. 1442, Lovers in the Moonlight. No. 1443, Woman and Haystack. No. 1444, Snow-Covered Church. No. 1445, Peasant Life. No. 1446, Moses Receiving the Tablets. No. 1447, Vitebsk: From Mt. Zadunuv. No. 1449, Song of Songs, diff. No. 1450, The Creation of Man. No. 1451, Spring. No. 1452, Jacob's Struggle with the Angel. No. 1453, Song of Songs (wedding detail). No. 1454, The Painter to the Moon, 1917. No. 1455, Moses Striking the Rock. No. 1456, To My Betrothed, 1911. No. 1457, Sacrifice of Isaac. No. 1458, Monkey Acting as Judge Over Dispute Between Wolf and Fox, 1925. No. 1459, Song of Songs (bride riding Pegasus). No. 1460, Lovers in the Lilac, 1930. No. 1461, Song of Songs (sun, spirits). No. 1462, Jacob's Dream (figures with ladder). No. 1463, Purim, 1916. No. 1464, Fantastic Horsecart. No. 1465, Listening to the Cock, 1944. No. 1466, Self-portrait, 1914. No. 1467, The Juggler, 1943. No. 1468, Noah and the Rainbow. No. 1469, Moses Before the Burning Bush. No. 1470, Around Her, 1945. No. 1471, The Trough, 1925. No. 1472, The Poet of Half-Past-Three. No. 1473, The Tree of Life, 1948. No. 1474, Bride with the Blue Face, 1932. No. 1475, Chrysanthemums, 1926. No. 1476, Spoonful of Milk, 1912. No. 1477, The Soldier Drinks, 1911. No. 1478, Noah's Ark. No. 1479, Flowers and Fruit. No. 1480, Adam and Eve Expelled fron Paradise. No. 1481, Return from Synagogue. No. 1482, Aleko: A Fantasy of St. Petersburg. No. 1483, The Orchard. No. 1484, Solitude. No. 1485, Paris Through the Window, 1913. No. 1486, The Wedding (bridal couple, musicians), 1910. No. 1487, Paradise. No. 1488, The Dream, 1939. No. 1489, Abraham and the Three Angels. No. 1490, Water Carrier Under the Moon, 1914.

1986-87

1441-1480 A203 $1 Set of 40 40.00 40.00

Size: 110x95mm

Imperf

1481-1490 A203 $5 Set of 10 40.00 40.00

Nos. 1441-1446, 1450-1452 1455-1458, 1464-1467 and 1470-1479 vert.

Issued: Nos. 1441-1452, 1481-1483, 1986; Nos. 1453-1480, 1484-1490, 1987.

A204

America's Cup — A205

1987, Feb. 5 Litho. *Perf. 15*

1491 A204 10c Columbia, 1958 .25 .25
1492 A204 60c Resolute, 1920 .45 .45
1493 A204 $1.10 Endeavor, 1934 .80 .80
1494 A204 $4 Rainbow, 1934 3.00 3.00
Nos. 1491-1494 (4) 4.50 4.50

Souvenir Sheet

1495 A205 $5 Weatherly, 1962 3.75 3.75

Virgin Mary — A206

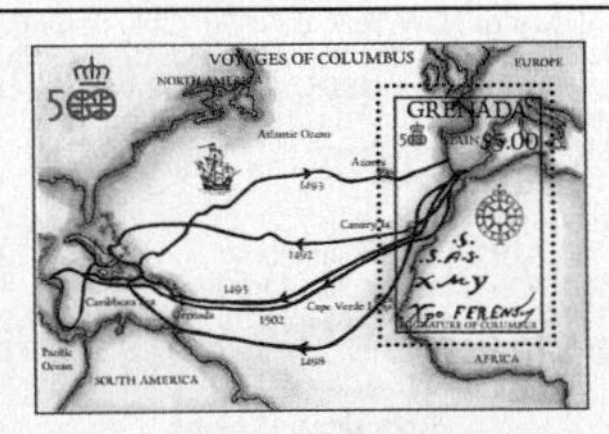

Map of Voyage, Columbus' Signature — A207

30c, Nina, Pinta, Santa Maria. 50c, Columbus, map. 60c, Columbus. 90c, Isabella, Ferdinand. $1.10, Discovering the Antilles. $2, Carib Indians. $3, American Indians, 1493.

No. 1505, Columbus, Christ child.

1987, Apr. 27 *Perf. 15*

1496 A206 10c shown .30 .25
1497 A206 30c multicolored .55 .25
1498 A206 50c multicolored .65 .40
1499 A206 60c multicolored .75 .45
1500 A206 90c multicolored .85 .70
1501 A206 $1.10 multicolored .90 .80
1502 A206 $2 multicolored 1.50 1.50
a. Souv. sheet of 3, 30c, 90c, $2 2.40 2.40
1503 A206 $3 multicolored 2.25 2.25
a. Souv. sheet of 5 + label, 10c, 50c, 60c, $1.10, $3 4.00 4.00
Nos. 1496-1503 (8) 7.75 6.60

Souvenir Sheets

1504 A207 $5 shown 3.75 3.75
1505 A207 $5 multicolored 3.75 3.75

Discovery of America 500th anniv. (in 1992). Nos. 1497, 1500 and 1502 horiz.

CAPEX '87 A208

Fish: 10c, Black grouper, vert. 30c, Blue marlin. 60c, White marlin, vert. 70c, Big-eye thresher shark. $1, Bonefish. $1.10, Wahoo. $2, Sailfish. $4, Albacore.

No. 1514, Barracuda. No. 1515, Yellowfin tuna, vert.

1987, June 15

1506 A208 10c multicolored .40 .25
1507 A208 30c multicolored .60 .25
1508 A208 60c multicolored .75 .50
1509 A208 70c multicolored .85 .60
1510 A208 $1 multicolored 1.25 1.00
1511 A208 $1.10 multicolored 1.50 1.25
1512 A208 $2 multicolored 2.25 2.00
1513 A208 $4 multicolored 3.50 3.50
Nos. 1506-1513 (8) 11.10 9.35

Souvenir Sheets

1514 A208 $5 multicolored 4.50 4.50
1515 A208 $5 multicolored 4.50 4.50

Transportation Innovations — A209

10c, Cornu's Helicopter, 1907. 15c, The Monitor and Merrimack, 1862. 30c, LZ1 Zeppelin, c. 1900. 50c, S.S. Sirius, 1838. 60c, Trans-Siberian Railway. 70c, USS Enterprise, 1960. 90c, Blanchard's Balloon, 1785. $1.50, USS Holland 1, 1900. $2, S.S. Oceanic, 1871. $3, 1984 Lamborghini Countach.

1987, May 18 *Perf. 14*

1516 A209 10c multicolored .80 .60
1517 A209 15c multicolored .80 .60
1518 A209 30c multicolored 1.00 .80
1519 A209 50c multicolored 1.10 .85
1520 A209 60c multicolored 1.25 1.00
1521 A209 70c multicolored 1.40 1.10
1522 A209 90c multicolored 1.50 1.40
1523 A209 $1.50 multicolored 2.25 2.25
1524 A209 $2 multicolored 3.00 3.00
1525 A209 $3 multicolored 4.50 4.50
Nos. 1516-1525 (10) 17.60 16.10

For overprints see Nos. 1599-1602.

Statue of Liberty, Cent. A210

10c, Computer structural diagrams. 25c, Fireworks around statue. 50c, Fireworks in front of statue. 60c, Statue, boats. 70c, Structural diagram, close-up. $1, Rear of statue, close-up. $1.10, Liberty and Manhattan Islands. $2, Statue, boats, diff. $4, Ocean liner, New York Harbor.

1987, Aug. 5

1526 A210 10c multicolored .25 .25
1527 A210 25c multicolored .25 .25
1528 A210 50c multicolored .50 .50
1529 A210 60c multicolored .65 .60
1530 A210 70c multicolored .90 .65
1531 A210 $1 multicolored 1.00 .95
1532 A210 $1.10 multicolored 1.10 1.25
1533 A210 $2 multicolored 2.00 2.25
1534 A210 $4 multicolored 3.25 *4.50*
Nos. 1526-1534 (9) 9.90 11.20

Nos. 1529, 1531-1534 vert.

Inventors and Innovators A211

Designs: 50c, Sir Isaac Newton (1642-1727), law of gravity. $1.10, Jons Jakob Berzelius (1779-1848), symbols of chemical elements. $2, Robert Boyle (1627-1691), and Boyle's Law of pressure and volume. $3, James Watt (1736-1819), and diagram of steam engine. $5, Wright Flyer, Voyager.

1987, Sept. 9

1535 A211 50c multicolored .90 .90
1536 A211 $1.10 multicolored 2.00 2.00
1537 A211 $2 multicolored 2.75 2.75
1538 A211 $3 multicolored 5.00 5.00
Nos. 1535-1538 (4) 10.65 10.65

Souvenir Sheet

1539 A211 $5 multicolored 5.25 5.25

No. 1536 inscribed with incorrect spelling of inventors name, "John Jacob Berzelius." No. 1538 inscribed with incorrect caption; James Watt and Watt engine are pictured, not Rudolf Diesel and the Diesel engine.

Miniature Sheets

Fairy Tales — A212

Snow White (50th Anniv.): No. 1540a, Snow White scrubs stairs. b, Wicked Queen, looking glass. c, Snow White fleeing. d, Dwarfs, mine. e, Snow White at cottage. f, Snow White, dwarfs. g, Snow White dancing with dwarfs. h, Eating poison apple. i, Prince kissing Snow White.

Sleeping Beauty: No. 1541a, Royal family. b, Maleficent cursing infant (Aurora). c, Merryweather altering curse. d, Three good fairies. e, Briar Rose (Aurora), forest animals. f, Aurora, spinning wheel. g, Sleeping Beauty (Aurora). h, Prince Phillip battling dragon (Maleficent). i, Sleeping Beauty awakes.

Cinderella: No. 1542a, Ella (Cinderella) and father. b, Cinderella sweeping. c, Cinderella, animals in barn. d, Cinderella, stepmother, stepsisters. e, Mice. f, Fairy Godmother. g, Cinderella transformed, coach. h, i, Duke puts glass slipper on Cinderella's foot.

Pinocchio: No. 1543a, Geppetto and puppet. b, Jiminy Cricket. c, Pinocchio, J. Worthington Foulfellow and Gideon. d, Pinocchio, Master Stromboli. e, Blue Fairy rescues Pinocchio. f, Pinocchio, donkeys. g, Pinocchio riding fish. h, Pinocchio and Geppetto at sea. i, Pinocchio transformed into a boy.

Alice in Wonderland: No. 1544a, Alice, rabbit hole. b, Alice in bottle. c, Walrus and Carpenter. d, White Rabbit in pink house. e, Alice, pink butterfly. f, March Hare, Mad Hatter. g, Alice in garden. h, Queen of Hearts. i, Alice on trial.

Peter Pan: No. 1545a, Nana. b, Peter Pan. c, Peter Pan, Tinker Bell, Wendy, John and Michael Darling flying. d, In NeverNever Land. e, Peter Pan and Tiger Lily. f, Captain Hook and First Mate Smee. g, Pater Pan dueling with Captain Hook. h, Tinker Bell, pirate ship. i, Captain Hook, crocodile.

No. 1546, Snow White and Prince riding off into sunset. No. 1547, Aurora and Prince Phillip dancing. No. 1548, Cinderella and Prince Charming marry. No. 1549, Pinocchio, Jiminy Cricket and Gepetto. No. 1550, Alice, cat, mother. No. 1551, Darling children waving goodbye to Peter Pan.

1987, Sept. 9 *Perf. 14x13½*

1540 A212 Sheet of 9 4.25 4.25
a.-i. 30c any single .45 .45
1541 A212 Sheet of 9 4.25 4.25
a.-i. 30c any single .45 .45
1542 A212 Sheet of 9 4.25 4.25
a.-i. 30c any single .45 .45
1543 A212 Sheet of 9 4.25 4.25
a.-i. 30c any single .45 .45
1544 A212 Sheet of 9 4.25 4.25
a.-i. 30c any single .45 .45
1545 A212 Sheet of 9 4.25 4.25
a.-i. 30c any single .45 .45
Nos. 1540-1545 (6) 25.50 25.50

Souvenir Sheets

1546-1551 A212 $5 each 6.75 6.75

Souvenir Sheet

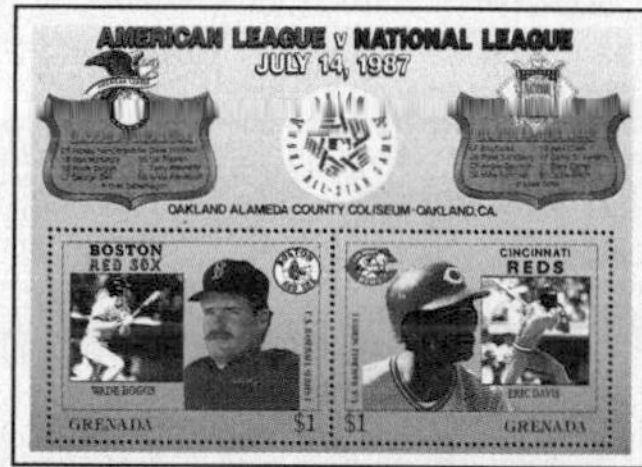

Baseball All-Star Game, Oakland, July 14 — A213

Athletes, team emblems: a, Wade Boggs, Boston Red Sox. b, Eric Davis, Cincinnati Reds.

1987, Nov. 2 **Litho.** *Perf. 14*

1552 A213 Sheet of 2 2.00 2.00
a.-b. $1 any single .95 .95

Massachusetts State Crest — A214

Designs: 15c, Independence Hall, Philadelphia. 50c, Benjamin Franklin. $4, Robert Morris (1734-1806), financier of American Revolution. $5, Pres. James Madison.

1987, Nov. 2

1553 A214 15c multi, vert. .25 .25
1554 A214 50c multi, vert. .30 .30
1555 A214 60c shown .40 .40
1556 A214 $4 multi, vert. 2.50 2.50
Nos. 1553-1556 (4) 3.45 3.45

Souvenir Sheet

1557 A214 $5 multi, vert. 3.25 3.25

US Constitution bicent.

Nos. 1286, 1291 and 1296 Overprinted

1987, Nov. 2

1558 A180 10c multicolored .25 .25
1559 A180 50c multicolored .35 .35
1560 A180 $3 multicolored 2.00 2.00
Nos. 1558-1560 (3) 2.60 2.60

HAFNIA '87 — A215

Disney animated characters in adaptation of fairy tales by Hans Christian Andersen: 25c, The Shadow. 30c, The Storks. 50c, The Emperor's New Clothes. 60c, The Tinderbox. 70c, The Shepherdess and the Chimney Sweep. $1.50, The Little Mermaid. $3, The Princess and the Pea. $4, The Marsh King's Daughter.

No. 1569, The Flying Trunk, horiz. No. 1570, The Sandman, horiz.

1987, Nov. 16 **Litho.** *Perf. 14*

1561 A215 25c multicolored .50 .30
1562 A215 30c multicolored .50 .35
1563 A215 50c multicolored .75 .60
1564 A215 60c multicolored 1.00 .65
1565 A215 70c multicolored 1.25 .80
1566 A215 $1.50 multicolored 2.25 1.75
1567 A215 $3 multicolored 3.25 3.25
1568 A215 $4 multicolored 4.25 4.25
Nos. 1561-1568 (8) 13.75 11.95

Souvenir Sheets

1569 A215 $5 multicolored 7.50 7.50
1570 A215 $5 multicolored 7.50 7.50

Christmas — A216

Religious paintings: 15c, The Annunciation, by Fra Angelico. 30c, The Annunciation, attributed to Hubert van Eyck (c. 1370-1426). 60c, Adoration of the Magi, by Januarius Zick (1730-1797). $4, The Flight Into Egypt, by David. $5, The Circumcision, produced by artists of the Giovanni Bellini Studio, 14th cent.

1987, Dec. 15

1571 A216 15c multicolored .55 .45
1572 A216 30c multicolored 1.00 .50
1573 A216 60c multicolored 1.75 1.40
1574 A216 $4 multicolored 6.75 6.75
Nos. 1571-1574 (4) 10.05 9.10

Souvenir Sheet

1575 A216 $5 multicolored 8.00 8.00

T. Albert Marryshow (b. 1887) — A217

1988, Jan. 22 **Litho.** *Perf. 14*

1576 A217 25c scarlet, red brn & brn blk .30 .30

40th Wedding Anniv. of Queen Elizabeth II and Prince Philip — A218

15c, Wedding portrait, 1947. 50c, Elizabeth, Charles, Anne. $1, Elizabeth, Anne. $4, Elizabeth, c. 1980.

$5, Elizabeth, 1947.

1988, Feb. 15

1577 A218 15c multicolored .30 .25
1578 A218 50c multicolored .60 .45
1579 A218 $1 multicolored 1.00 1.00
1580 A218 $4 multicolored 3.00 3.00
Nos. 1577-1580 (4) 4.90 4.70

Souvenir Sheet

1581 A218 $5 multicolored 3.75 3.75

Disney Animated Characters and 1988 Summer Olympics, Seoul A219

1c, Lighting torch, Olympia. 2c, Torch bearers. 3c, Flag bearers. 4c, Releasing doves. 5c, Opening ceremony. 10c, Olympic motto. $6, Tiger character trademark. $7, Oldest Korean p.o.

No. 1590, Sportsmanship oath. No. 1591, Closing ceremony.

1988, Apr. 13 **Litho.** *Perf. 13½x14*

1582 A219 1c multicolored .25 .25
1583 A219 2c multicolored .25 .25
1584 A219 3c multicolored .25 .25
1585 A219 4c multicolored .25 .25
1586 A219 5c multicolored .25 .25
1587 A219 10c multicolored .25 .25
1588 A219 $6 multicolored 5.50 5.50
1589 A219 $7 multicolored 6.00 5.50
Nos. 1582-1589 (8) 13.00 12.50

Souvenir Sheets

1590 A219 $5 multicolored 5.50 5.50
1591 A219 $5 multicolored 5.50 5.50

Boy Scouts A220

1988, May 3 **Litho.** *Perf. 14*

1592 A220 20c Fishing, vert. .40 .25
1593 A220 70c Hiking 1.25 1.00
1594 A220 90c First-aid 1.75 1.40
1595 A220 $3 Canoeing, vert. 4.00 4.00
Nos. 1592-1595 (4) 7.40 6.65

Souvenir Sheet

1596 A220 $5 Scout holding koala, vert. 3.75 3.75

Rotary Conference, District 405, St. George, May 5-7 — A221

Rotary Intl. emblem and: $2, Map of District 405 island nations (Grenada, Guyana, Surinam and French Guiana), 15th cent. Spanish galleon Santa Maria, vert. $10, Motto "Service Above Self."

1988, May 5 *Perf. 13½x14*

1597 A221 $2 multicolored 1.50 1.50

Souvenir Sheet

Perf. 14x13½

1598 A221 $10 shown 7.25 7.25

Nos. 1522-1525 Overprinted for Philatelic Exhibitions

a

b

c

d

1988, Apr. 19 Litho. *Perf. 14*

1599	A209 (a)	90c multi	1.25	.85
1600	A209 (b)	$1.50 multi	1.75	1.50
1601	A209 (c)	$2 multi	2.25	2.25
1602	A209 (d)	$3 multi	2.75	2.75
		Nos. 1599-1602 (4)	8.00	7.35

Birds — A222

10c, Roseate tern. 25c, Laughing gull. 50c, Osprey. 60c, Rose-breasted grosbeak. 90c, Purple gallinule. $1.10, White-tailed tropicbird. $3, Blue-faced booby. $4, Northern shoveler.

No. 1611, Belted kingfisher. No. 1612, Rusty-tailed flycatcher.

1988, May 31

1603	A222	10c multicolored	.80	.30
1604	A222	25c multicolored	1.00	.30
1605	A222	50c multicolored	1.25	.60
1606	A222	60c multicolored	1.25	.60
1607	A222	90c multicolored	1.25	.95
1608	A222	$1.10 multicolored	1.25	1.10
1609	A222	$3 multicolored	3.00	3.00
1610	A222	$4 multicolored	4.25	4.25
		Nos. 1603-1610 (8)	14.05	11.10

Souvenir Sheet

1611	A222	$5 multicolored	5.00	5.00
1612	A222	$5 multicolored	5.00	5.00

Miniature Sheets

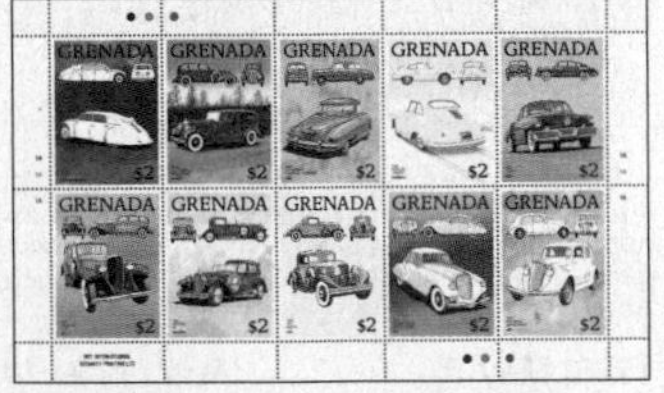

Classic Automobiles — A223

Cars (U.S. unless otherwise stated): No. 1613a, 1934 Tatra Type 77, Czechoslovakia. b, 1938 Rolls-Royce Phantom III, Britain. c, 1947 Studebaker Champion Starlight. d, 1948 Porsche Gmund, Germany. e, 1948 Tucker. f, 1931 Peerless V-16. g, 1931 Minerva AL, Belgium. h, 1933 REO Royale. i, 1933 Pierce-Arrow Silver Arrow. j, 1934 Hupmobile Aerodynamic.

No. 1614a, 1925 Vauxhall Type OE30/98, Britain. b, 1926 Wills Sainte Claire. c, 1928 Bucciali, France. d, 1929 Irving Napier Golden Arrow, Britain. e, 1930 Studebaker President. f, 1907 Thomas Flyer. g, 1908 Isotta-Fraschini Tipo J, Italy. h, 1910 Fiat 10/14HP, Italy. i, 1911 Mercer Type 35 Raceabout. j, 1917 Marmon Model 34 Cloverleaf.

No. 1615a, 1965 Peugeot 404, France. b, 1969 Ford Capri, Britain. c, 1975 Ferrari 312T, Italy. d, 1978 Lotus T-79, Britain. e, 1979 Williams-Cosworth FW07, Britain. f, 1948 H.R.G. 1500 Sports, Britain. g, 1949 Crosley Hotshot. h, 1955 Volvo PV444, Sweden. i, 1960 Maserati Tipo 61, Italy. j, 1963 Saab 96, Sweden.

1988, June 1 *Perf. 13x13½*

1613	A223	Sheet of 10	13.00	13.00
a.-j.		$2 any single	1.25	1.25
1614	A223	Sheet of 10	13.00	13.00
a.-j.		$2 any single	1.25	1.25
1615	A223	Sheet of 10	13.00	13.00
a.-j.		$2 any single	1.25	1.25

Paintings by Titian (c. 1488-1576) A224

Paintings by Titian: 10c, Lavinia Vecellio, c. 1546. 20c, Portrait of a Man, c. 1510. 25c, Andrea De Franceschi, 1532. 90c, Head of a Soldier, 1511. $1, Man With a Flute. $2, Lucrezia and Tarquinius, c. 1515. $3, Duke of Mantua with Dog, 1525. $4, La Bella Di Tiziano, 1536. No. 1624, Allegory of Alfonso D'Avalos. No. 1625, Fall of Man, 1570, horiz.

1988, June 15 *Perf. 13½x14*

1616	A224	10c multicolored	.25	.25
1617	A224	20c multicolored	.25	.25
1618	A224	25c multicolored	.25	.25
1619	A224	90c multicolored	.60	.60
1620	A224	$1 multicolored	.65	.65
1621	A224	$2 multicolored	1.40	1.40
1622	A224	$3 multicolored	2.10	2.10
1623	A224	$4 multicolored	2.50	2.50
		Nos. 1616-1623 (8)	8.00	8.00

Souvenir Sheets

1624	A224	$5 multicolored	3.75	3.75

Perf. 14x13½

1625	A224	$5 multicolored	3.75	3.75

Zeppelins A225

Designs: 10c, Graf Zeppelin over the Federal Building, Chicago, 1933 World's Fair, vert. 15c, LZ-1 over Lake Constance, 1900. 25c, Washington aerial balloon lifting off the aircraft carrier USS George Washington Parke Custis off Port Royal, South Carolina, 1862, vert. 45c, Hindenburg over a Maybach Zeppelin automobile, Friedrichshaven, 1936. 50c, Goodyear Blimp over the Statue of Liberty, 1986, vert. 60c, Hindenburg passing over the Statue of Liberty during its final flight, 1937. 90c, Experimental docking of aircraft (piloted by Ernst Udet) with the Hindenburg, 1936. $2, Hindenburg over the Olympic stadium, Berlin, 1936, vert. $3, Hindenburg over Christ the Redeemer statue, Rio de Janeiro, 1937, vert. $4, Hindenburg over mail plane catapult ship Bremen, 1936. No. 1636, Zepplin over DLH base, Bathurst, Gambia, 1935. No. 1637, Graf Zeppelin over St. Basil's Cathedral, Moscow, 1930.

1988, July 1 *Perf. 14*

1626	A225	10c multicolored	.50	.25
1627	A225	15c multicolored	.60	.25
1628	A225	25c multicolored	.70	.35
1629	A225	45c multicolored	.75	.40
1630	A225	50c multicolored	.80	.45
1631	A225	60c multicolored	.85	.50
1632	A225	90c multicolored	1.00	.80
1633	A225	$2 multicolored	1.75	1.75
1634	A225	$3 multicolored	2.50	2.50
1635	A225	$4 multicolored	3.50	3.50
		Nos. 1626-1635 (10)	12.95	10.75

Souvenir Sheets

1636	A225	$5 multicolored	3.75	3.75
1637	A225	$5 multicolored	3.75	3.75

The ship name on No. 1628 is incorrect.

SYDPEX '88, Sydney, Australia — A226

Walt Disney characters in Australian settings: 1c, Camping in the Outback, a howling Tasmanian wolf. 2c, Offering peanuts to wallabies. 3c, With a kangaroo and joey against Ayers Rock. 4c, Riding emus, emu-wrens. 5c, Camp and wombat. 10c, Duck-billed platypuses. No. 1644, Photographing a kookaburra. $6, Koala and Mickey waving flags of Grenada, Australia and the United States, map. No. 1646, Flags and candles atop Cake in the shape of Australia. No. 1647, Mickey, Minnie Pluto and Goofy taking a break during a walkabout.

1988, Aug. 1 Litho. *Perf. 14x13½*

1638	A226	1c multicolored	.25	.25
1639	A226	2c multicolored	.25	.25
1640	A226	3c multicolored	.25	.25
1641	A226	4c multicolored	.25	.25
1642	A226	5c multicolored	.25	.25
1643	A226	10c multicolored	.25	.25
1644	A226	$5 multicolored	5.50	5.50
1645	A226	$6 multicolored	6.50	6.50
		Nos. 1638-1645 (8)	13.50	13.50

Souvenir Sheet

1646	A226	$5 multicolored	6.50	6.50
1647	A226	$5 multicolored	6.50	6.50

Mickey Mouse, 60th anniversary.

Intl. Fund for Agricultural Development, 10th Anniv. — A227

1988, Aug. 11 Litho. *Perf. 14*

1648	A227	25c Pineapple, vert.	.40	.40
1649	A227	75c Banana, vert.	.80	.80
1650	A227	$3 Mace, nutmeg	2.50	2.25
		Nos. 1648-1650 (3)	3.70	3.45

Flowering Trees and Shrubs of the Caribbean A228

15c, Lignum vitae. 25c, Saman. 35c, Red frangipani. 45c, Flowering maple. 60c Yellow poui. $1, Wild chestnut. $3, Mountain immortelle. $4, Queen of flowers.

No. 1659, Flamboyant. No. 1660, Orchid tree.

1988, Sept. 30 Litho.

1651	A228	15c multicolored	.25	.25
1652	A228	25c multicolored	.25	.25
1653	A228	35c multicolored	.25	.25
1654	A228	45c multicolored	.35	.35
1655	A228	60c multicolored	.45	.45
1656	A228	$1 multicolored	.75	.75
1657	A228	$3 multicolored	2.25	2.25
1658	A228	$4 multicolored	3.00	3.00
		Nos. 1651-1658 (8)	7.55	7.55

Souvenir Sheets

1659	A228	$5 multicolored	3.75	3.75
1660	A228	$5 multicolored	3.75	3.75

Miniature Sheet

Christmas, Mickey Mouse 60th Anniv. — A229

Designs: a, Huey draping garland. b, Goofy stringing popcorn. c, Chip'n'Dale decorating tree. d, Santa Claus in his sleigh. e, Dewey hanging stockings. f, Louie unpacking decorations. g, Donald Duck. h, Mickey Mouse. No. 1662, Morty and Ferdie leaving milk and cookies for Santa, horiz. No. 1663, Morty and Ferdie dreaming of presents, horiz.

Perf. 13½x14, 14x13½

1988, Dec. 1 Litho.

1661	A229	Sheet of 8	7.50	7.50
a.-h.		$1 any single	.90	.90

Souvenir Sheets

1662	A229	$5 multicolored	5.00	5.00
1663	A229	$5 multicolored	5.00	5.00

Miniature Sheets

Major League Baseball Players — A230

No. 1664: a, Mickey Mantle. b, Roger Clemens. c, Rod Carew. d, Ryne Sandberg. e, Mike Scott. f, Tim Raines. g, Willie Mays. h, Bret Saberhagen. i, Honus Wagner.

No. 1665: a, Roberto Clemente. b, Cal Ripken, Jr. c, Bob Feller. d, George Bell. e, Mark McGwire. f, Alvin Davis. g, Pete Rose. h, Dan Quisenberry. i, Babe Ruth.

No. 1666: a, Jackie Robinson. b, Dwight Gooden. c, Brooks Robinson, Jr. d, Nolan Ryan. e, Mike Schmidt. f, Gary Gaetti. g, Nellie Fox. h, Tony Gwynn. i, Dizzy Dean.

No. 1667: a, Ernie Banks. b, National League emblem. c, Julio Franco. d, Jack Morris. e, Fernando Valenzuela. f, Lefty Grove. g, Ted Williams. h, Darryl Strawberry. i, Dale Murphy.

No. 1668: a, Johnny Bench. b, Dave Stieb. c, Reggie Jackson. d, Harold Baines. e, Wade Boggs. f, Pete O'Brien. g, Stan Musial. h, Wally Joyner. i, Grover Cleveland Alexander.

No. 1669: a, Jose Cruz. b, American League emblem. c, Al Kaline. d, Chuck Klein. e, Don Mattingly. f, Mike Witt. g, Mark Langston. h, Hubie Brooks. i, Harmon Killebrew.

No. 1670: a, George Brett. b, Joe Carter. c, Frank Robinson. d, Mel Ott. e, Benito Santiago. f, Teddy Higuera. g, Lloyd Moseby. h, Bobby Bonilla. i, Warren Spahn.

No. 1671: a, Gary Carter. b, Hank Aaron. c, Gaylord Perry. d, Ty Cobb. e, Andre Dawson. f, Charlie Hough. g, Kirby Puckett. h, Robin Yount. i, Don Drysdale.

No. 1672: a, Luis Aparicio. b, Paul Molitor. c, Lou Gehrig. d, Jeffrey Leonard. e, Eric Davis. f, Pete Incaviglia. g, Steve Rogers. h, Ozzie Smith. i, Randy Jones.

1988, Nov. 28 Litho. *Perf. 14*

1664	A230	Sheet of 9	1.75	1.75
a.-i.		30c any single	.25	.25
1665	A230	Sheet of 9	1.75	1.75
a.-i.		30c any single	.25	.25
1666	A230	Sheet of 9	1.75	1.75
a.-i.		30c any single	.25	.25
1667	A230	Sheet of 9	1.75	1.75
a.-i.		30c any single	.25	.25
1668	A230	Sheet of 9	1.75	1.75
a.-i.		30c any single	.25	.25
1669	A230	Sheet of 9	1.75	1.75
a.-i.		30c any single	.25	.25
1670	A230	Sheet of 9	1.75	1.75
a.-i.		30c any single	.25	.25
1671	A230	Sheet of 9	1.75	1.75
a.-i.		30c any single	.25	.25
1672	A230	Sheet of 9	1.75	1.75
a.-i.		30c any single	.25	.25
		Nos. 1664-1672 (9)	15.75	15.75

No. 1665 was reprinted with No. 1665g replaced by a label inscribed "U.S. Baseball Series."

Singers — A231

10c, Tina Turner. 25c, Lionel Ritchie. 45c, Whitney Houston. 60c, Joan Armatrading. 75c, Madonna. $1, Elton John. $3, Bruce Springsteen. $4, Bob Marley.

No. 1681: a, Yoko Minamino. b, Yoko Minamino, diff.

1988, Dec. 5 Litho. *Perf. 14*

1673	A231	10c	multicolored	.30	.25
1674	A231	25c	multicolored	.30	.25
1675	A231	45c	multicolored	.45	.40
1676	A231	60c	multicolored	.60	.50
1677	A231	75c	multicolored	1.00	.65
1678	A231	$1	multicolored	1.25	.85
1679	A231	$3	multicolored	2.25	2.25
1680	A231	$4	multicolored	3.00	3.00
	Nos. 1673-1680 (8)			9.15	8.15

Souvenir Sheet

1681	Sheet of 4 (2 55c, 2 $1)	3.50	3.50
a.	A231 55c multicolored	.75	.75
b.	A231 $1 multicolored	2.50	2.50

Armatrading is misspelled "Ammertrading."

Car Type of 1988

Miniature Sheets

Locomotives.

No. 1682: a, 1889 Canada Atlantic Railway No. 2 0-6-0, Canada. b, 1875 Virginia & Truckee Railroad J.W. Bowker 2-4-0, US. c, 1872 Philadelphia & Reading Railway Ariel 2-2-2, US. d, 1867 Chicago & Rock Is. Railroad America 4-4-0, US. e, 1866 Lehigh Valley Railroad Consolidation No. 63 2-8-0, US. f, 1860 Great Western Railway Scotia 0-6-0, Canada. g, 1854 Grand Trunk Railway Birkenhead Class 4-4-0, Canada. h, 1837 Camden & Amboy Railroad Monster 0-8-0, US. i, 1834 B&O Railroad Grasshopper Class 0-4-0, US. j, 1829 B&O Railroad Tom Thumb 0-2-2, US.

No. 1683: a, 1925 United Railways of Yucatan Yucatan 4-4-0, Mexico. b, 1924 Canadian Natl. Railways Class T2 2-10-2, Canada. c, 1919 St. Louis-San Francisco Railroad USRA Light Mikado 2-8-2, US. d, 1919 Atlantic Coast Line Railroad USRA Light Pacific 4-6-2, US. e, 1913 Edaville Railroad (Bridgton & Saco River Railroad) No. 7 2-4-4-T, US. f, 1903 Denver & Rio Grande Western Railroad Mudhens Class K27 2-8-2, US. g, 1902 PRR Class E-2 No. 7002 4-4-2, US. h, 1899 PRR Class H6 2-8-0, US. i, 1893 Mohawk & Hudson Railroad De Witt Clinton 0-4-0, US. j, 1891 St. Clair Tunnel Company No. 598 0-10-0, Canada.

No. 1684: a, 1947 Chesapeake & Ohio Railroad M-1 Class No. 500 steam turbine electric, US. b, 1946 Rutland Railroad No. 93 4-8-2, US. c, 1942 PRR Class T1 4-4-4-4, US. d, 1942 Chesapeake & Ohio Railroad Class H-8 2-6-6-6, US. e, 1941 Atchison, Topeka & Santa Fe Railway EMD Model FT Bo-Bo, US. f, 1940 Gulf, Mobile & Ohio Railroad ALCO Models S-1 & S-2 Bo-Bo, US. g, 1937 New York, New Haven & Hartford Railroad Class 15 4-6-4, US. h, 1936 Seaboard Air Line Railroad Class R 2-6-6-4, US. i, 1930 Newfoundland Railway Class R-2 2-8-2, Canada. j, 1928 Canadian Natl. Railway No. 9000 2-Do-1 + 1-Do-2, Canada.

1989, Jan. 23 Litho. *Perf. 13x13½*

1682	A223	Sheet of 10	14.00	14.00
a.-j.		$2 any single	1.40	1.40
1683	A223	Sheet of 10	14.00	14.00
a.-j.		$2 any single	1.40	1.40
1684	A223	Sheet of 10	14.00	14.00
a.-j.		$2 any single	1.40	1.40

Medalists of the 1988 Summer Olympics, Seoul — A232

Designs: 10c, Jackie Joyner-Kersee, US, long jump. 25c, Steffi Graf, Federal Republic of Germany, women's singles tennis. 45c, Peter Rono, Kenya, 1500m run. 75c, Greg Barton, US, kayak singles. $1, Italy, women's team foil. $2, Kristin Otto, German Democratic Republic, women's 100m freestyle swimming. $3, Holger Behrendt, German Democratic Republic, still rings. $4, Japan, duet synchronized swimming. No. 1693, Yukio Iketani, Japan, men's floor exercise. No. 1694, West Germany, 400m relay, and (Olympic) flame over track.

1989, Apr. 6 Litho. *Perf. 14*

1685	A232	10c	multicolored	.30	.30
1686	A232	25c	multicolored	.70	.35
1687	A232	45c	multicolored	.80	.40
1688	A232	75c	multicolored	.90	.60
1689	A232	$1	multicolored	1.00	.75
1690	A232	$2	multicolored	1.50	1.50
1691	A232	$3	multicolored	2.25	2.25
1692	A232	$4	multicolored	2.75	2.75
	Nos. 1685-1692 (8)			10.20	8.90

Souvenir Sheets

1693	A232	$6	multicolored	4.75	4.75
1694	A232	$6	multicolored	4.75	4.75

"The Fifty-three Stations on the Tokaido" — A233

Prints by Hiroshige (1797-1858): 10c, Shinagawa on Edo Bay. 25c, Pine Trees on the Road to Totsuka. 60c, Kanagawa on Edo Bay. 75c, Crossing Banyu River to Hiratsuka. $1, Windy Shore at Odawara. $2, Snow-covered Post Station of Mishima. $3, Full Moon at Fuchu. $4, Crossing the Stream at Okitsu. No. 1703, Mt. Uzu at Okabe. No. 1704, Mountain Pass at Nissaka.

1989, May 15 Litho. *Perf. 14x13½*

1695	A233	10c	multicolored	.25	.25
1696	A233	25c	multicolored	.25	.25
1697	A233	60c	multicolored	.45	.45
1698	A233	75c	multicolored	.65	.65
1699	A233	$1	multicolored	1.00	.75
1700	A233	$2	multicolored	1.50	1.50
1701	A233	$3	multicolored	2.25	2.25
1702	A233	$4	multicolored	3.00	3.00
	Nos. 1695-1702 (8)			9.35	9.10

Souvenir Sheets

1703	A233	$5	multicolored	3.75	3.75
1704	A233	$5	multicolored	3.75	3.75

Hirohito (1901-1989) and enthronement of Akihito as emperor of Japan.

Indigenous Birds — A234

5c, Great blue heron. 10c, Green heron. 15c, Ruddy turnstone. 25c, Blue-winged teal. 35c, Ring-necked plover. 45c, Emerald-throated hummingbird. 50c, Hairy hermit. 60c, Lesser Antillean bullfinch. 75c, Brown pelican. $1, Black-crowned night heron. $3, Sparrow hawk. $5, Barn swallow. $10, Red-billed tropicbird. $20, Barn owl.

1989, June 6 Litho. *Perf. 14*

1705	A234	5c	multicolored	.75	*1.00*
1706	A234	10c	multicolored	.75	.60
1707	A234	15c	multicolored	.80	.60
1708	A234	25c	multicolored	.90	.30
1709	A234	35c	multicolored	1.10	.30
1710	A234	45c	multicolored	1.10	.40
1711	A234	50c	multicolored	1.25	.45
1712	A234	60c	multicolored	1.40	.55
1713	A234	75c	multicolored	1.50	.65
1714	A234	$1	multicolored	1.60	1.00
1715	A234	$3	multicolored	2.40	2.40
1716	A234	$5	multicolored	4.00	4.00
1717	A234	$10	multicolored	8.00	8.00
1718	A234	$20	multicolored	21.50	21.50
	Nos. 1705-1718 (14)			47.05	41.75

Nos. 1709-1718 vert.

1990-93 Litho. *Perf. 11½x13*

1705a	A234	5c	.70	.70
1706a	A234	10c	.70	.60
1707a	A234	15c	.75	.60
1708a	A234	25c	.85	.30

Perf. 13x11½

1709a	A234	35c	1.00	.30
1710a	A234	45c	1.00	.35
1711a	A234	50c	1.10	.45
1712a	A234	60c	1.25	.50
1713a	A234	75c	1.40	.55
1714a	A234	$1	1.50	.90
1715a	A234	$3	2.40	2.40
1716a	A234	$5	4.00	4.00
1717a	A234	$10	8.00	8.00
1718a	A234	$20	21.50	21.50
	Nos. 1705a-1718a (14)		46.15	41.15

Issued: No. 1718a, 1/22/90.

1990 World Cup Soccer Championships, Italy — A235

10c, Scotland. 25c, England vs. Brazil. 60c, Paolo Rossi, Italy. 75c, Jairzinho of Brazil. $1, Swedish Striker. $2, Pele, Brazil. $3, Mario Kempes, Argentina. $4, Pat Jennings.

No. 1727, Argentina vs. Holland. No. 1728, Goalie.

1989, June 12 *Perf. 14*

1719	A235	10c	multicolored	.50	.30
1720	A235	25c	multicolored	.60	.50
1721	A235	60c	multicolored	.80	.70
1722	A235	75c	multicolored	1.00	.80
1723	A235	$1	multicolored	1.25	1.00
1724	A235	$2	multicolored	2.50	2.00
1725	A235	$3	multicolored	2.75	2.75
1726	A235	$4	multicolored	3.75	3.75
	Nos. 1719-1726 (8)			13.15	11.80

Souvenir Sheets

1727	A235	$6	multicolored	5.50	5.50
a.		$6 1990 score ovptd. in margin		7.50	7.50
1728	A235	$6	multicolored	5.50	5.50

Issue date: No. 1727a, Nov. 30, 1990.

PHILEXFRANCE '89 — A236

19th Cent. ships and cargo: 25c, Chebeck, sugarcane. 75c, Lugger, cotton. $1, Merchantman, cocoa. $4, Ketch, coffee. $6, Vue du Fort et Ville de St. George dans l'Isle de la Grenade et du Morne, 1779.

1989, July 7 *Perf. 14*

1729	A236	25c	multicolored	.90	.30
1730	A236	75c	multicolored	1.10	.85
1731	A236	$1	multicolored	1.40	1.10
1732	A236	$4	multicolored	5.50	5.50

Size: 114x71mm

Imperf

1733	A236	$6	multicolored	6.00	6.00
	Nos. 1729-1733 (5)			14.90	13.75

First Moon Landing, 20th Anniv. A237

Space achievements: 15c, Alan Shepard, 1st American in space, 1961. 35c, Friendship 7, piloted by John Glenn, 1st manned orbit of the Earth, 1962. 45c, Apollo 8 mission, 1st manned orbit of the Moon, 1968. 70c, Lunar rover on Moon, 1972. $1, Apollo 11 mission emblem and Eagle lunar module on the Moon, 1969. $2, Gemini 8-Agena, 1st space docking, 1969. $3, Edward White, 1st American to walk in space, 1965. $4, Apollo 7 mission emblem. No. 1742, Simple flight plan for the Apollo 11 mission. No. 1743, Raising of the American flag on the Moon.

1989, July 20 *Perf. 14*

1734	A237	15c	multicolored	.50	.40
1735	A237	35c	multicolored	.60	.45
1736	A237	45c	multicolored	.80	.60
1737	A237	70c	multicolored	1.00	.70
1738	A237	$1	multicolored	1.50	1.10
1739	A237	$2	multicolored	2.50	2.10
1740	A237	$3	multicolored	3.00	3.00
1741	A237	$4	multicolored	4.00	4.00
	Nos. 1734-1741 (8)			13.90	12.35

Souvenir Sheets

1742	A237	$5	multicolored	5.50	5.50
1743	A237	$5	multicolored	5.50	5.50

Mushrooms A238

15c, Hygrocybe occidentalis scarletina. 40c, Marasmius haematocephalus. 50c, Hygrocybe hypohaemacta. 70c, Lepiota pseudoignicolor. 90c, Cookeina tricholoma. $1.10, Leucopaxillus gracillimus. $2.25, Hygrocybe nigrescens. $4, Clathrus crispus.

No. 1752, Mycena holoporphyra. No. 1753, Xeromphalina tenuipes.

1989, Aug. 17 Litho. *Perf. 14*

1744-1751	A238	Set of 8	15.00	15.00

Souvenir Sheets

1752-1753	A238	$6 Set of 2	15.00	15.00

YWCA, Cent. — A239

1989, Sept. 11 *Perf. 14*

1754	A239	50c shown	.70	.70
1755	A239	75c Emblem, horiz.	.90	.90

Butterflies A240

6c, Orion. 30c, Southern daggertail. 40c, Soldier. 60c, Silver spot. $1.10, Gulf fritillary. $1.25, Monarch. $4, Polydamas swallowtail. $5, Flambeau.

No. 1764, St. Christopher hairstreak. No. 1765, White peacock.

1989, Oct. 2 *Perf. 14*

1756	A240	6c	multicolored	.35	.35
1757	A240	30c	multicolored	.50	.50
1758	A240	40c	multicolored	.65	.65
1759	A240	60c	multicolored	1.00	1.00
1760	A240	$1.10	multicolored	1.60	1.60
1761	A240	$1.25	multicolored	1.90	1.90
1762	A240	$4	multicolored	4.00	4.00
1763	A240	$5	multicolored	4.75	4.75
	Nos. 1756-1763 (8)			14.75	14.75

Souvenir Sheets

1764	A240	$6	multicolored	6.00	6.00
1765	A240	$6	multicolored	6.00	6.00

Discovery of America, 500th Anniv. (in 1992) — A241

Anniv. and UPAE emblems and various pre-Columbian petroglyphs.

1989, Oct. 16 Litho. *Perf. 14*

1766	A241	45c	multicolored	.90	.90
1767	A241	60c	multi, diff.	1.10	1.10
1768	A241	$1	multi, diff.	1.25	1.25
1769	A241	$4	multi, diff.	4.75	4.75
	Nos. 1766-1769 (4)			8.00	8.00

Souvenir Sheet

1770	A241	$6	multi, diff.	5.50	5.50

World Stamp Expo '89, Scenes from *Ben and Me* — A242

Walt Disney characters, story of the American Revolution: 1c, Amos leaves home. 2c, Amos meets young Benjamin Franklin. 3c, Invention of the Franklin stove. 4c, Invention of bifocals. 5c, *Pennsylvania Gazette*. 6c, Franklin at printing press. 10c, Experimenting with electricity. $5, As an American diplomat in England. No. 1779, Amos's "Document of Agreement." No. 1780, Franklin presiding over meeting of the Ben Franklin Stamp Club. No. 1781, 2nd Continental Congress, Philadelphia, 1775.

Perf. 14x13½, 13½x14

1989, Nov. 17 **Litho.**

1771	A242	1c multi	.25	.25
1772	A242	2c multi	.25	.25
1773	A242	3c multi	.25	.25
1774	A242	4c multi	.25	.25
1775	A242	5c multi	.25	.25
1776	A242	6c multi	.25	.25
1777	A242	10c multi	.25	.25
1778	A242	$5 multi	5.50	5.50
1779	A242	$6 multi	5.75	6.00
		Nos. 1771-1779 (9)	13.00	13.25

Souvenir Sheets

1780	A242	$6 multi, vert.	5.50	5.50
1781	A242	$6 multi	5.50	5.50

Christmas — A243

Paintings by Rubens: 20c, *Christ in the House of Mary and Martha*. 35c, *The Circumcision*. 60c, *Trinity Adored by Duke of Mantua and Family*. $2, *Holy Family with St. Francis*. $3, *The Ildefonso Altarpiece*. $4, *Madonna and Child with Garland and Putti*, by Rubens and Jan Brueghel. No. 1788, *Adoration of the Magi*. No. 1789, *Virgin and Child Adored by Angels*.

1990, Jan. 4 **Litho.** ***Perf. 14***

1782	A243	20c multicolored	.50	.25
1783	A243	35c multicolored	.65	.45
1784	A243	60c multicolored	1.00	.65
1785	A243	$2 multicolored	2.00	2.00
1786	A243	$3 multicolored	2.50	2.50
1787	A243	$4 multicolored	3.50	3.50
		Nos. 1782-1787 (6)	10.15	9.35

Souvenir Sheets

1788	A243	$5 multicolored	4.50	4.50
1789	A243	$5 multicolored	4.50	4.50

Anniversaries and Events (in 1989) — A244

Designs: 10c, Alexander Graham Bell, early telephone, telephone lines. 25c, George Washington, the Capitol Building. 35c, William Shakespeare, birthplace, Stratford-on-Avon. 75c, Jawaharlal Nehru, Mahatma Gandhi. $1, Hugo Eckener, Ferdinand von Zeppelin, zeppelin *Delag*. $2, Charlie Chaplin. $3, Ship in port. $4, Pres. Friedrich Ebert, Heidelberg Gate. No. 1798, Concorde jet. No. 1799, Ship, 13th century, vert.

1990, Feb. 12 **Litho.** ***Perf. 14***

1790	A244	10c multicolored	.35	.25
1791	A244	25c multicolored	.35	.25
1792	A244	35c multicolored	1.10	.55
1793	A244	75c multicolored	2.00	1.60
1794	A244	$1 multicolored	1.40	1.40
1795	A244	$2 multicolored	2.75	2.75
1796	A244	$3 multicolored	3.00	3.00
1797	A244	$4 multicolored	4.25	4.25
		Nos. 1790-1797 (8)	15.20	14.05

Souvenir Sheets

1798	A244	$6 multicolored	6.00	6.00
1799	A244	$6 multicolored	6.00	6.00

Invention of the telephone, 1876 (10c); American presidency, 200th anniv. (25c); 425th birth anniv. of Shakespeare (35c); birth cent. of Nehru (75c); 1st passenger zeppelin, 80th anniv. ($1); birth cent. of Charlie Chaplin ($2); Hamburg, 800th anniv. ($3, No. 1799); Federal Republic of Germany, 40th anniv. ($4); and test flight of the Concorde supersonic jet, 20th anniv. (No. 1798).

Orchids — A245

1c, Odontoglossum triumphans. 25c, Oncidium splendidum. 60c, Laelia anceps. 75c, Cattleya trianaei. $1, Odontoglossum rossii. $2, Brassia gireoudiana. $3, Cattleya dowiana. $4, Sobralia macrantha.

No. 1808, Laelia rubescens. No. 1809, Oncidium lanceanum.

1990, Mar. 6 **Litho.** ***Perf. 14***

1800	A245	1c multicolored	.25	.25
1801	A245	25c multicolored	.30	.30
1802	A245	60c multicolored	.65	.65
1803	A245	75c multicolored	.80	.80
1804	A245	$1 multicolored	1.25	1.25
1805	A245	$2 multicolored	1.75	1.75
1806	A245	$3 multicolored	2.50	2.50
1807	A245	$4 multicolored	3.25	3.25
		Nos. 1800-1807 (8)	10.75	10.75

Souvenir Sheets

1808	A245	$6 multicolored	5.50	5.50
1809	A245	$6 multicolored	5.50	5.50

EXPO '90 Intl. Garden and Greenery Exposition, Japan.

America Issue — A246

Butterflies, UPAE and discovery of America 500th anniv. emblems: 15c, Southern dagger tail. 25c, Caribbean buckeye. 75c, Malachite. 90c, Orion. $1, St. Lucia mestra. $2, Red rim. $3, Flambeau. $4, Red anartia. No. 1818, Giant hairstreak. No. 1819, Orange-barred sulphur.

1990, Mar. 16 **Litho.** ***Perf. 14***

1810	A246	15c multicolored	.65	.25
1811	A246	25c multicolored	.80	.25
1812	A246	75c multicolored	1.25	.80
1813	A246	90c multicolored	1.40	.95
1814	A246	$1 multicolored	1.50	1.00
1815	A246	$2 multicolored	2.00	2.00
1816	A246	$3 multicolored	3.00	3.00
1817	A246	$4 multicolored	4.00	4.00
		Nos. 1810-1817 (8)	14.60	12.25

Souvenir Sheets

1818	A246	$6 multicolored	7.00	7.00
1819	A246	$6 multicolored	7.00	7.00

Wildlife A247

10c, Caribbean monk seal. 15c, Little brown bat. 45c, Norway rat. 60c, Old-world rabbit. $1, Water opossum. $2, White-nosed ichneumon. $3, Little big-eared bat. $4, Mouse opossums.

No. 1828, Old-world rabbit. diff. No. 1829, Water opossum.

1990, Apr. 3 **Litho.** ***Perf. 14***

1820	A247	10c multicolored	.50	.30
1821	A247	15c multicolored	.55	.30
1822	A247	45c multicolored	.65	.50
1823	A247	60c multicolored	.75	.60
1824	A247	$1 multicolored	1.00	.90
1825	A247	$2 multicolored	1.60	1.60
1826	A247	$3 multicolored	2.40	2.40
1827	A247	$4 multicolored	3.25	3.25
		Nos. 1820-1827 (8)	10.70	9.85

Souvenir Sheets

1828	A247	$6 multicolored	5.50	5.50
1829	A247	$6 multicolored	5.50	5.50

No. 1826 is vert. Nos. 1828-1829 have multicolored decorative margins contininuing the designs and picturing little brown bat, prehensile-tailed porcupine and mouse opossum (No. 1828) or four-eyed opossum, West Indies manatee and Norway rat (No. 1829).

World War II A248

Designs: 25c, Operation Battleaxe, June 15, 1941. 35c, Allied landing in southern France, Aug. 15, 1944. 45c, US invasion of Guadalcanal, Aug. 7, 1942. 50c, Allied defeat of Japanese army in New Guinea, Jan. 22, 1943. 60c, US forces secure Leyte, Dec. 11, 1944. 75c, US forces enter Cologne, Mar. 5, 1945. $1, Allied offensive to break out of Anzio, May 23, 1944. $2, Battle of the Bismarck Sea, Mar. 3, 1943. $3, US fleet under Adm. Nimitz, Dec. 17, 1941. $4, Allied landing at Salerno, Sept. 9, 1943. $6, German U-boat.

1990, Apr. 30 **Litho.** ***Perf. 14x13½***

1830	A248	25c multicolored	.40	.40
1831	A248	35c multicolored	.50	.50
1832	A248	45c multicolored	.60	.60
1833	A248	50c multicolored	.70	.70
1834	A248	60c multicolored	.80	.80
1835	A248	75c multicolored	1.00	1.00
1836	A248	$1 multicolored	1.50	1.50
1837	A248	$2 multicolored	1.75	1.75
1838	A248	$3 multicolored	2.50	2.50
1839	A248	$4 multicolored	3.50	3.50
		Nos. 1830-1839 (10)	13.25	13.25

Souvenir Sheet

1840	A248	$6 multicolored	7.00	7.00

Souvenir Sheet

Penny Black, 150th Anniv. — A249

1990, May 3 **Litho.** ***Perf. 14***

1841	A249	$6 violet	5.50	5.50

Stamp World London '90.

Stamp World London '90 — A250

Walt Disney characters and British trains: 5c, 1925 King Arthur Class. 10c, 1813 Puffing Billy. 20c, 1765 Colliery Tram-wagon. 45c, 1935 No. 2509 Silver Link. $1, 1948 No. 60149 Amadis. $2, 1830 Liverpool. $4, 1870 Flying Scotsman. $5, 1972 Advanced Passenger Train.

No. 1852, Stockton & Darlington Railway Opening, 1825, vert. No. 1853, 1809 *Catch-Me-Who-Can.*

1990, June 21 ***Perf. 14***

1844	A250	5c multicolored	.45	.25
1845	A250	10c multicolored	.45	.25
1846	A250	20c multicolored	.60	.25
1847	A250	45c multicolored	1.00	.55
1848	A250	$1 multicolored	1.50	1.10
1849	A250	$2 multicolored	2.25	2.10
1850	A250	$4 multicolored	4.00	4.00
1851	A250	$5 multicolored	4.75	4.50
		Nos. 1844-1851 (8)	15.00	13.00

Souvenir Sheets

1852	A250	$6 multicolored	6.50	6.50
1853	A250	$6 multicolored	6.50	6.50

Queen Mother, 90th Birthday A251

1990, July 5 **Litho.** ***Perf. 14***

1854	A251	$2 Wearing black hat	2.10	2.10
1855	A251	$2 shown	2.10	2.10
1856	A251	$2 Wearing crown	2.10	2.10
		Nos. 1854-1856 (3)	6.30	6.30

Souvenir Sheet

1857	A251	$6 Like No. 1855	5.00	5.00

1992 Summer Olympics, Barcelona — A252

Character trademark and: 10c, Men's steeplechase. 15c, Equestrian. 45c, Men's 200 meter butterfly. 50c, Field hockey. 65c, Balance beam. 75c, Flying Dutchman Class yachting. $2, Freestyle wrestling. $3, Men's diving. $4, Women's cycling. $5, Men's basketball. No. 1863, Three-day equestrian event. No. 1863A, Men's 10,000 M race.

1990, July 9

1858	A252	10c multicolored	.35	.30
1858A	A252	15c multicolored	.45	.35
1859	A252	45c multicolored	.55	.40
1859A	A252	50c multicolored	.80	.60
1860	A252	65c multicolored	.80	.60
1860A	A252	75c multicolored	1.00	.80
1861	A252	$2 multicolored	1.75	1.75
1861A	A252	$3 multicolored	2.50	2.50
1862	A252	$4 multicolored	3.75	3.75
1862A	A252	$5 multicolored	4.00	4.00
		Nos. 1858-1862A (10)	15.95	15.05

Souvenir Sheet

1863	A252	$8 multicolored	6.00	6.00
1863A	A252	$8 multicolored	6.00	6.00

Nos. 1858A, 1859A, 1860A, 1861A, 1862A, 1863A were not available until 1991.

US Airborne, 50th Anniv. A253

75c, Mass jump.

$2.50, Paratrooper landing. $6, Paratroopers 1940, 1990.

1990, July 3

1864	A253	75c multicolored	2.50	2.50

Souvenir Sheets

1865	A253	$2.50 multicolored	2.50	2.50
1866	A253	$6 multicolored	5.50	5.50

Yellow Goatfish A254

25c, Black margate. 65c, Bluehead wrasse. 75c, Puddingwife. $1, Foureye butterflyfish. $2, Honey damselfish. $3, Queen angelfish. $5, Cherubfish.

No. 1875, Smooth trunkfish. No. 1876, Sergeant major.

1990, Aug. 8

No.	Type	Description	Unused	Used
1867	A254	10c shown	.40	.40
1868	A254	25c multicolored	.60	.60
1869	A254	65c multicolored	1.00	1.00
1870	A254	75c multicolored	1.25	1.25
1871	A254	$1 multicolored	1.50	1.50
1872	A254	$2 multicolored	1.90	1.90
1873	A254	$3 multicolored	2.50	2.50
1874	A254	$5 multicolored	4.50	4.50
		Nos. 1867-1874 (8)	13.65	13.65

Souvenir Sheets

No.	Type	Description	Unused	Used
1875	A254	$6 multicolored	6.50	6.50
1876	A254	$6 multicolored	6.50	6.50

Birds A255

15c, Tropical mockingbird. 25c, Gray kingbird. 65c, Bare-eyed thrush. 75c, Antillean crested hummingbird. $1, House wren. $2, Purple martin. $4, Hooded tanager. $5, Common ground dove.

No. 1885, Fork-tailed flycatcher. No. 1886, Smooth-billed ani.

1990, Sept. 10 Litho. *Perf. 14*

No.	Type	Description	Unused	Used
1877	A255	15c multicolored	.45	.45
1878	A255	25c multicolored	.50	.50
1879	A255	65c multicolored	.80	.80
1880	A255	75c multicolored	1.00	1.00
1881	A255	$1 multicolored	1.50	1.50
1882	A255	$2 multicolored	1.90	1.90
1883	A255	$4 multicolored	3.50	3.50
1884	A255	$5 multicolored	4.25	4.25
		Nos. 1877-1884 (8)	13.90	13.90

Souvenir Sheets

No.	Type	Description	Unused	Used
1885	A255	$6 multicolored	7.50	7.50
1886	A255	$6 multicolored	7.50	7.50

Crustaceans — A256

5c, Coral crab. 10c, Smoothtail spiny lobster. 15c, Flamestreaked box crab. 25c, Spotted swimming crab. 75c, Sally lightfoot rock crab. $1, Spotted spiny lobster. $3, Longarm spiny lobster. $20, Caribbean spiny lobster.

No. 1895, Spanish lobster. No. 1896, Caribbean furry lobster.

1990, Sept. 17

No.	Type	Description	Unused	Used
1887	A256	5c multicolored	.25	.25
1888	A256	10c multicolored	.25	.25
1889	A256	15c multicolored	.25	.25
1890	A256	25c multicolored	.25	.25
1891	A256	75c multicolored	.70	.70
1892	A256	$1 multicolored	.90	.90
1893	A256	$3 multicolored	2.60	2.60
1894	A256	$20 multicolored	16.50	16.50
		Nos. 1887-1894 (8)	21.70	21.70

Souvenir Sheets

No.	Type	Description	Unused	Used
1895	A256	$6 multicolored	6.75	6.75
1896	A256	$6 multicolored	6.75	6.75

World Cup Soccer Championships, Italy — A257

Players from participating countries.

1990, Sept. 24

No.	Type	Description	Unused	Used
1897	A257	10c Cameroun	.25	.25
1898	A257	25c Spain	.25	.25
1899	A257	$1 West Germany	.80	.80
1900	A257	$5 Scotland	3.75	3.75
		Nos. 1897-1900 (4)	5.05	5.05

Souvenir Sheets

No.	Type	Description	Unused	Used
1901	A257	$6 Uruguay	6.00	6.00
1902	A257	$6 Italy	6.00	6.00

Christmas A258

Paintings by Raphael: 10c, The Ansidei Madonna. 15c, The Sistine Madonna. $1, Madonna of the Baldacchino. $2, The Large Holy Family. $5, Madonna in the Meadow. No. 1908, Madonna of the Veil. No. 1909, Madonna of the Diadem.

1990, Dec. 31 Litho. *Perf. 14*

No.	Type	Description	Unused	Used
1903	A258	10c multicolored	.30	.25
1904	A258	15c multicolored	.30	.25
1905	A258	$1 multicolored	1.50	1.00
1906	A258	$2 multicolored	2.40	2.40
1907	A258	$5 multicolored	5.00	5.00
		Nos. 1903-1907 (5)	9.50	8.90

Souvenir Sheets

No.	Type	Description	Unused	Used
1908	A258	$6 multicolored	6.75	6.75
1909	A258	$6 multicolored	6.75	6.75

Peter Paul Rubens (1577-1640), Painter — A259

Entire paintings or different details from: 5c, $1, $4, The Brazen Serpent. 10c, Garden of Love. 25c, Head of Cyrus. 75c, Tournament in Front of a Castle. $2, Judgement of Paris. $5, The Kermesse. No. 1918, The Prodigal Son. No. 1919, Anger of Neptune.

1991, Jan. 31 Litho. *Perf. 14*

No.	Type	Description	Unused	Used
1910	A259	5c multicolored	.35	.25
1911	A259	10c multicolored	.35	.25
1912	A259	25c multicolored	.60	.25
1913	A259	75c multicolored	.80	.60
1914	A259	$1 multicolored	1.00	.90
1915	A259	$2 multicolored	1.60	1.60
1916	A259	$4 multicolored	3.00	3.00
1917	A259	$5 multicolored	4.00	4.00
		Nos. 1910-1917 (8)	11.70	10.75

Souvenir Sheets

No.	Type	Description	Unused	Used
1918	A259	$6 multicolored	6.50	6.50
1919	A259	$6 multicolored	6.50	6.50

Disney Film *Fantasia*, 50th Anniv. — A260

5c, Mickey as Sorcerer's apprentice, walking broom. 10c, Mushroom Dance Ensemble from The Nutcracker Suite. 20c, Pterodactyls from The Rite of Spring. 45c, Centaurs from The Pastoral Symphony. $1, Bacchus & Jacchus from The Pastoral Symphony. $2, Ostrich ballerina in Dance of the Hours. $4, Elephant dance from Dance of the Hours. $5, Diana, Goddess of the Moon from Dance of the Hours. No. 1928, Mickey as Sorcerer's apprentice. No. 1929, Mickey, Leopold Stokowski. $12, Mickey as Sorcerer's Apprentice, vert.

1991, Feb. 4 Litho. *Perf. 14*

No.	Type	Description	Unused	Used
1920	A260	5c multicolored	.75	.25
1921	A260	10c multicolored	.75	.25
1922	A260	20c multicolored	1.10	.25
1923	A260	45c multicolored	1.25	.55
1924	A260	$1 multicolored	1.75	1.75
1925	A260	$2 multicolored	2.75	2.75
1926	A260	$4 multicolored	5.00	5.00
1927	A260	$5 multicolored	6.50	6.50
		Nos. 1920-1927 (8)	19.85	17.30

Souvenir Sheets

No.	Type	Description	Unused	Used
1928	A260	$6 multicolored	8.50	8.50
1929	A260	$6 multicolored	8.50	8.50
1930	A260	$12 multicolored	16.50	16.50

Butterflies A261

5c, Adelphia iphicla. 10c, Nymphalidae claudina. 15c, Brassolidae polyxena. 20c, Zebra longwing. 25c, Marpesia corinna. 30c, Morpho hecuba. 45c, Morpho rhetenor. 50c, Dismorphia spio. 60c, Prepona omphale. 70c, Morpho anaxibia. 75c, Marpesia iole. $1, Metalmark. $2, Morpho cisseis. $3, Danaidae plexippus. $4, Morpho achilleana. $5, Calliona argenissa. No. 1947, Anteos clorinde. No. 1948, Haetera piera. No. 1949, Papilio cresphontes. No. 1950, Prepona pheridames.

1991, Apr. 8 Litho. *Perf. 14*

No.	Type	Description	Unused	Used
1931	A261	5c multicolored	.55	.45
1932	A261	10c multicolored	.60	.45
1933	A261	15c multicolored	.65	.45
1934	A261	20c multicolored	.70	.35
1935	A261	25c multicolored	.75	.35
1936	A261	30c multicolored	.85	.35
1937	A261	45c multicolored	.95	.60
1938	A261	50c multicolored	1.00	.65
1939	A261	60c multicolored	1.20	.75
1940	A261	70c multicolored	1.30	.95
1941	A261	75c multicolored	1.75	1.75
1942	A261	$1 multicolored	1.90	1.90
1943	A261	$2 multicolored	2.60	2.60
1944	A261	$3 multicolored	4.00	4.00
1945	A261	$4 multicolored	5.50	5.50
1946	A261	$5 multicolored	7.00	7.00
		Nos. 1931-1946 (16)	31.30	28.10

Souvenir Sheets

No.	Type	Description	Unused	Used
1947	A261	$6 multicolored	8.50	8.50
1948	A261	$6 multicolored	8.50	8.50
1949	A261	$6 multicolored	8.50	8.50
1950	A261	$6 multicolored	8.50	8.50

Voyages of Discovery A262

Explorer's ships: 5c, Vitus Bering, 1728-1729. 10c, Louis de Bougainville, 1766-1769. 25c, Polynesians. 50c, Alvaro de Mendana, 1567-1569. $1, Charles Darwin, 1831-1835. $2, Capt. James Cook, 1768-1771. $4, Capt. Willem Schouten, 1615-1617. $5, Abel Tasman, 1642-1644. No. 1959, Columbus' ship Santa Maria. No. 1960, Loss of Santa Maria.

1991, Apr. 29

No.	Type	Description	Unused	Used
1951	A262	5c multicolored	.50	.40
1952	A262	10c multicolored	.50	.40
1953	A262	25c multicolored	.50	.30
1954	A262	50c multicolored	.90	.50
1955	A262	$1 multicolored	1.50	1.25
1956	A262	$2 multicolored	2.75	2.50
1957	A262	$4 multicolored	3.75	3.75
1958	A262	$5 multicolored	4.75	4.75
		Nos. 1951-1958 (8)	15.15	13.85

Souvenir Sheets

No.	Type	Description	Unused	Used
1959	A262	$6 multicolored	6.50	6.50
1960	A262	$6 multicolored	6.50	6.50

Discovery of America, 500th anniv. (in 1992).

PHILANIPPON '91 — A263

Walt Disney characters celebrating festivals of Japan: 5c, Daisy Duck and Minnie Mouse, Peach Fete, Festival of the Dolls. 10c, Morty and Ferdie, Tango Festival, Boys' Day Festival. 20c, Mickey, Minnie Mouse, Hoshi-Matsuri, Star Festival. 45c, Minnie, Daisy folk dancing at Bon-Odori Summer Festival. $1, Huey, Dewey and Louie wearing Eboshi headdresses at Yari-Matsuri, Spear Festival of Ohji. $2, Mickey, Goofy pulling Daisy, Minnie in Yamaboko, Gion Festival of Kyoto. $4, Minnie, Daisy preparing rice broth for Nanakusa, Festival of the Seven Plants. $5, Huey, Dewey floating straw boat at O-Bon, Festival of Lanterns. No. 1969, Goofy, Tori-No-Hichi or Rake Festival, vert. No. 1970, Minnie Mouse, Japanese New Year, vert. No. 1971, Mickey, Snow Festival, vert.

1991, May 6 Litho. *Perf. 13½x14*

No.	Type	Description	Unused	Used
1961	A263	5c multicolored	.45	.25
1962	A263	10c multicolored	.45	.25
1963	A263	20c multicolored	.95	.25
1964	A263	45c multicolored	1.25	.80
1965	A263	$1 multicolored	2.25	1.25
1966	A263	$2 multicolored	3.00	3.00
1967	A263	$4 multicolored	4.25	4.25
1968	A263	$5 multicolored	5.00	5.00
		Nos. 1961-1968 (8)	17.60	15.05

Souvenir Sheets

No.	Type	Description	Unused	Used
1969	A263	$6 multicolored	5.75	5.75
1970	A263	$6 multicolored	5.75	5.75
1971	A263	$6 multicolored	5.75	5.75

Paintings by Vincent Van Gogh — A264

Designs: 20c, Blossoming Almond Branch in a Glass, vert. 25c, La Mousme, Sitting, vert. 30c, Still Life with Red Cabbages and Onions. 40c, Japonaiserie: Flowering Plum Tree, vert. 45c, Japonaiserie: Bridge in Rain, vert. 60c, Still Life with Basket of Apples. 75c, Italian Woman (Agostina Segatori), vert. $1, The Painter on His Way to Work, vert. $2, Portrait of Pere Tanguy, vert. $3, Still Life with Plaster Statuette, a Rose and Two Novels, vert. $4, Still Life: Bottle, Lemons and Oranges. $5, Orchard with Blossoming Apricot Trees. No. 1984, Farmhouse in a Wheatfield. No. 1985, The "Roubine du Roi" Canal with Washerwoman, vert. No. 1986, Japonaiserie: Oiran, vert. No. 1987, The Gleize Bridge over the Viguerat Canal. No. 1988, Rocks with Oak Tree.

1991, May 13 Litho. *Perf. 13½*

No.	Type	Description	Unused	Used
1972	A264	20c multicolored	.50	.25
1973	A264	25c multicolored	.50	.25
1974	A264	30c multicolored	.55	.30
1975	A264	40c multicolored	.75	.40
1976	A264	45c multicolored	.75	.50
1977	A264	60c multicolored	1.00	.70
1978	A264	75c multicolored	1.10	1.00
1979	A264	$1 multicolored	1.25	1.25
1980	A264	$2 multicolored	1.60	1.60
1981	A264	$3 multicolored	2.40	2.40
1982	A264	$4 multicolored	3.25	3.25
1983	A264	$5 multicolored	4.00	4.00
		Nos. 1972-1983 (12)	17.65	15.90

Size: 100x75mm, 75x100mm

Imperf

1984-1988	A264	$6 each	5.00	5.00

Mushrooms A265

Designs: 15c, Psilocybe cubensis. 25c, Leptonia caeruleocapitata. 65c, Cystolepiota eriophora. 75c, Chlorophyllum molybdites. $1, Xerocomus hypoxanthus. $2, Volvariella cubensis. $4, Xerocomus coccolobae. $5, Pluteus chrysophlebius. No. 1997, Hygrocybe miniata. No. 1998, Psathyrella tuberculata.

1991, June 1 ***Perf. 14***

1989	A265	15c multicolored	.70	.30
1990	A265	25c multicolored	.85	.30
1991	A265	65c multicolored	1.25	.75
1992	A265	75c multicolored	1.50	1.00
1993	A265	$1 multicolored	1.75	1.00
1994	A265	$2 multicolored	2.00	2.00
1995	A265	$4 multicolored	4.25	4.25
1996	A265	$5 multicolored	4.75	4.75
		Nos. 1989-1996 (8)	17.05	14.35

Souvenir Sheet

1997	A265	$6 multicolored	8.25	8.25
1998	A265	$6 multicolored	8.25	8.25

Miniature Sheets

Exploration of Mars — A266

Designs (all different): No. 1999: a, Johannes Kepler, 1571-1630. b, Galileo Galilei, 1564-1642. c, Martian canals drawn by Giovanni Schiaparelli, 1886. d, Sir William Herschel, 1738-1882. e, Mars, planets. f, Percival Lowell at telescope. g, Mariner 4. h, Mars 2. i, Mars 3.

No. 2000: a, e, Profiles of Mars. b, Olympus Mons. c, Dusty face of Mars. d, Martian moon Phobos. f, Martian moon Deimos. g, Nix Olympica. h, Terrain feature resembling human face. i, South Polar Cap.

No. 2001: a, Mars from Phobus. b, Martian dusk. c, "Voyager descent." d, Viking 2 lander on Mars. e, f, Martian landscape. g, h, i, Panorama view from Viking 2 lander.

No. 2002: a, b, Mariner 9. c, Mars. d, Polar cycle. e, Plain of Sinai. f, South pole. g, Nix Olympica. h, Martian surface. i, Outflow channel.

No. 2003, Phobos spacecraft over Mars. No. 2004, Future spacecraft. No. 2005, Future spacecraft, Mars.

1991, June 21 ***Perf. 14x13½***

Sheets of 9

1999	A266	75c #a.-i.	4.25	4.25
2000	A266	$1.25 #a.-i.	6.75	6.75
2001	A266	$2 #a.-i.	11.00	11.00
2002	A266	$7 #a.-i.	37.50	37.50

Souvenir Sheets

2003	A266	$6 multicolored	5.00	5.00
2004	A266	$6 multicolored	5.00	5.00
2005	A266	$6 multicolored	5.00	5.00

Royal Family Birthday, Anniversary

Common Design Type

1991, July 5 Litho. ***Perf. 14***

2006	CD347	10c multicolored	.50	.25
2007	CD347	15c multicolored	.50	.25
2008	CD347	40c multicolored	.95	.35
2009	CD347	50c multicolored	1.50	.50
2010	CD347	$1 multicolored	1.75	1.50
2011	CD347	$2 multicolored	2.75	1.75
2012	CD347	$4 multicolored	3.25	3.25
2013	CD347	$5 multicolored	3.75	3.75
		Nos. 2006-2013 (8)	14.95	11.60

Souvenir Sheet

2014	CD347	$5 Philip, Elizabeth	5.25	5.25
2015	CD347	$5 Diana, sons, Charles	5.25	5.25

10c, 50c, $1, Nos. 2013, 2015, Charles and Diana, 10th Wedding anniversary. Others, Queen Elizabeth II, 65th birthday.

University of West Indies, 40th Anniv. — A266a

Designs: 45c, Marryshow House, Grenada. 50c, Administrative Building, Barbados.

1991, July 19

2016	A266a	45c multicolored	.85	.50
2017	A266a	50c multicolored	.90	.90

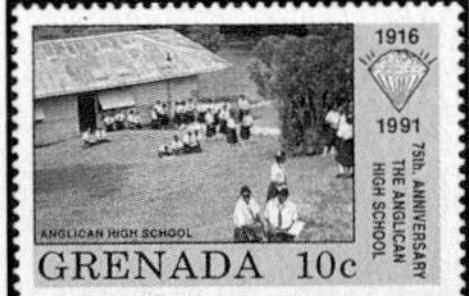

Anglican High School, 75th Anniv. A267

1991, July 29

2018	A267	10c Existing school	.35	.25
2019	A267	25c New school design	.60	.25

Railways of the World — A269

Railways of Great Britain: No. 2020a, Stephenson's first engine, 1814. b, George Stephenson (1781-1848). c, Stephenson's Killingworth engine, 1816. d, Locomotion No. 1, 1825. e, Locomotion in Darlington, 1825. f, Opening of Stockton & Darlington Railway, 1825. g, Royal George No. 5, 1827. h, Northumbrian Rocket, 1829. i, Planet Class engine, 1830.

No. 2021a, Old Ironsides, US, 1832. b, Wilberforce, Stockton & Darlington Railway, Great Britain, 1832. c, Stephenson's Der Adler, Germany, 1835. d, Stephenson's North Star, Great Britain, 1837. e, London & Birmingham No. 1, Great Britain, 1838. f, Stephenson's 1st Austrian locomotive, 1838. g, Mud Digger, US, 1840. h, Standard Norris, US, 1840. i, Fire Fly Class, Great Britain, 1840.

No. 2022a, Lion, Liverpool and Manchester, Great Britain, 1841. b, Beuth 2-2-2, Berlin-Anhalt Railway, Germany, 1843. c, Derwent No. 25, Stockton & Darlington Railway, Great Britain, 1845. d, MKpV, WCB, Vienna, 1846. e, First railway in Hungary, Budapest to Vac, 1846. f, Stockton & Darlington, 1846. g, Stephenson's long boiler type, Paris, 1847. h, Baldwin 4-4-0, US, 1850. i, 2-4-0, Germany, 1850. No. 2023, Boiler of Locomotion No. 1. No. 2024, Liverpool & Manchester Railway, Great Britain, 1833.

1991-92 Litho. ***Perf. 14***

Sheets of 9

2020	A269	75c #a.-i.	6.50	6.50
2021	A269	$1 #a.-i.	9.00	9.00
2022	A269	$2 #a.-i.	17.00	17.00

Souvenir Sheet

2023	A269	$6 multicolored	7.50	7.50
2024	A269	$6 multicolored	7.50	7.50

Issued: 75c, No. 2023, 12/2; others, 5/7/92.

Miniature Sheet

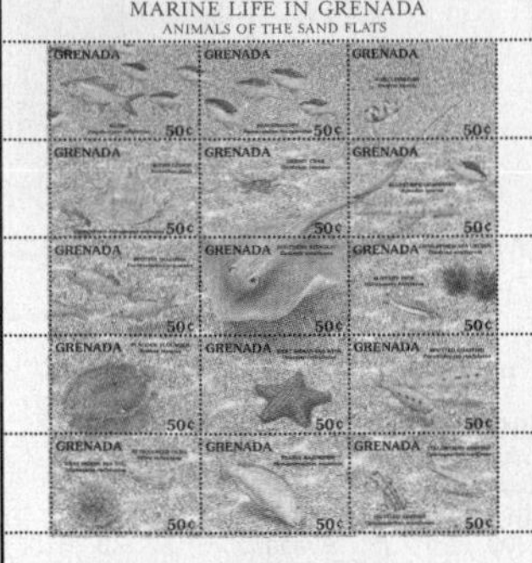

Marine Life in the Sand Flats — A270

Designs: No. 2025a, Barbu. b, Beaugregory. c, Porcupinefish. d, Conchfish, queen conch. e, Hermit crab. f, Bluestripe lizardfish. g, Spotfin mojarra. h, Southern stingray. i, Slippery dick, long-spined sea urchin. j, Peacock flounder. k, West Indian sea star. l, Spotted goatfish. m, West Indian sea egg, reticulated olive. n, Pearly razorfish. o, Mottled and yellowhead jawfish. $6, Shortnose batfish.

1991, Dec. 5 Litho. ***Perf. 14***

2025	A270	50c Sheet of 15, #a.-o.	12.00	12.00

Souvenir Sheet

2026	A270	$6 multicolored	11.00	11.00

Christmas A271

Details from paintings by Albrecht Durer: 10c, Adoration of the Magi. 35c, The Madonna with the Siskin. 50c, The Feast of the Rose Garlands. 75c, Madonna and Child (Virgin with the Pear). $1, The Virgin in Half-Length. $2, Madonna and Child. $4, Virgin and Child with St. Anne. $5, Virgin and Child, diff. No. 2035, Virgin with a Multitude of Animals. No. 2036, The Nativity.

1991, Dec. 9 ***Perf. 12***

2027	A271	10c multicolored	.40	.25
2028	A271	35c multicolored	.60	.35
2029	A271	50c multicolored	.65	.45
2030	A271	75c multicolored	1.00	.70
2031	A271	$1 multicolored	1.10	.90
2032	A271	$2 multicolored	1.75	1.75
2033	A271	$4 multicolored	4.00	4.00
2034	A271	$5 multicolored	4.50	4.50
		Nos. 2027-2034 (8)	14.00	12.90

Souvenir Sheets

Perf. 14½

2035	A271	$6 multicolored	7.00	7.00
2036	A271	$6 multicolored	7.00	7.00

Thrill Sports — A272

Walt Disney characters enjoying thrill sports: 5c, Windsurfing. 10c, Skateboarding. 20c, Gliding. 45c, Stunt kite flying. $1, Mountain biking. $2, Parachuting. $4, Go-carting. $5, Water skiing.

No. 2045, Roller blade hockey. No. 2046, Bungee jumping. No. 2046A, Hang gliding. No. 2046B, River rafting.

1992, Feb. 11 Litho. ***Perf. 14x13½***

2037	A272	5c multicolored	.45	.35
2038	A272	10c multicolored	.55	.35
2039	A272	20c multicolored	.80	.35
2040	A272	45c multicolored	1.25	.35
2041	A272	$1 multicolored	1.50	1.00
2042	A272	$2 multicolored	2.25	2.25
2043	A272	$4 multicolored	4.50	4.50
2044	A272	$5 multicolored	5.00	5.00
		Nos. 2037-2044 (8)	16.30	14.15

Souvenir Sheets

2045	A272	$6 multicolored	6.00	6.00
2046	A272	$6 multicolored	6.00	6.00
2046A	A272	$6 multicolored	6.00	6.00
2046B	A272	$6 multicolored	6.00	6.00

Queen Elizabeth II's Accession to the Throne, 40th Anniv.

Common Design Type

1992, Feb. 6 ***Perf. 14***

2047	CD348	10c multicolored	.25	.25
2048	CD348	50c multicolored	.40	.40
2049	CD348	$1 multicolored	.80	.80
2050	CD348	$5 multicolored	3.50	3.50
		Nos. 2047-2050 (4)	4.95	4.95

Souvenir Sheets

2051	CD348	$6 Queen at left	5.50	5.50
2052	CD348	$6 Queen at right	5.50	5.50

Spanish Art — A273

Paintings: 10c, The Corpus Christi Procession in Seville, by Manuel Cabral y Aguado, horiz. 35c, The Mancorbo Channel, by Carlos de Haes. 50c, Countess of Vilches, by Federico de Madrazo y Kuntz. 75c, Countess of Santovenia, by Eduardo Rosales Gallina. $1, Queen Maria Isabel de Braganza, by Bernardo Lopez Piquer. $2, $4, The Presentation of Don John of Austria to Charles V (different details), by Gallina. $5, The Testament of Isabella the Catholic, by Eduardo Rosales Gallina, horiz. No. 2061, Meeting of Poets in Antonio Maria Esquivel's Studio, by Antonio Maria Esquivel y Suarez de Urbina. No. 2062, The Horse Corral in the Old Madrid Bullring, by Manuel Castellano, horiz.

1992, Apr. 30 Litho. ***Perf. 13***

2053	A273	10c multicolored	.35	.25
2054	A273	35c multicolored	.45	.35
2055	A273	50c multicolored	.55	.45
2056	A273	75c multicolored	.80	.65
2057	A273	$1 multicolored	1.25	.85
2058	A273	$2 multicolored	1.75	1.75
2059	A273	$4 multicolored	3.25	3.25
2060	A273	$5 multicolored	4.00	4.00

Size: 120x95mm

Imperf

2061	A273	$6 multicolored	5.50	5.50
2062	A273	$6 multicolored	5.50	5.50
		Nos. 2053-2062 (10)	23.40	22.55

Granada '92.

A274

10c, Green-winged parrot. 25c, Santa Maria. 35c, Columbus. 50c, Hourglass. 75c, Queen Isabella. $4, Cantino map, 1502.

No. 2069, Map, ship, fish. No. 2070, Map, arms, Genoa.

1992, May 7 Litho. ***Perf. 14***

2063	A274	10c multicolored	.50	.25
2064	A274	25c multicolored	.50	.25
2065	A274	35c multicolored	.50	.45
2066	A274	50c multicolored	.70	.60
2067	A274	75c multicolored	1.25	1.00
2068	A274	$4 multicolored	4.50	4.50
		Nos. 2063-2068 (6)	7.95	7.05

Souvenir Sheets

2069 A274 $6 multicolored 6.75 6.75
2070 A274 $6 multicolored 6.75 6.75

World Columbian Stamp Expo '92, Chicago.

Discovery of America, 500th Anniv. — A275

1992 *Perf. 14½*

2071 A275 $1 Coming ashore 1.40 1.40
2072 A275 $2 Native, ships 2.50 2.50

Organization of East Caribbean States.

Hummingbirds A276

10c, Ruby-throated. 25c, Vervain. 35c, Blue-headed. 50c, Cuban Emerald. 75c, Antillean Mango. $2, Purple-throated carib. $4, Puerto Rican emerald. $5, Green-throated carib.

No. 2081, Rufous-breasted hermit. No. 2082, Antillean crested.

1992, May 28

2073 A276 10c multicolored .75 .30
2074 A276 25c multicolored .90 .30
2075 A276 35c multicolored .95 .35
2076 A276 50c multicolored 1.25 .50
2077 A276 75c multicolored 1.50 .75
2078 A276 $2 multicolored 1.60 1.60
2079 A276 $4 multicolored 3.25 3.25
2080 A276 $5 multicolored 4.00 4.00
Nos. 2073-2080 (8) 14.20 11.05

Souvenir Sheets

2081 A276 $6 multicolored 8.00 8.00
2082 A276 $6 multicolored 8.00 8.00

Genoa '92.

USO, 50th Anniv. — A277

15c, Gracie Fields. 25c, Jack Benny. 35c, Jinx Falkenburg. 50c, Frances Langford. 75c, Joe E. Brown. $1, Phil Silvers. $2, Danny Kaye. $5, Frank Sinatra.

No. 2091, Anna May Wong. No. 2092, Bob Hope.

1992, June 1 *Perf. 14*

2083 A277 15c multicolored .35 .25
2084 A277 25c multicolored .45 .25
2085 A277 35c multicolored .50 .40
2086 A277 50c multicolored .65 .50
2087 A277 75c multicolored 1.00 1.00
2088 A277 $1 multicolored 1.25 1.25
2089 A277 $2 multicolored 2.50 2.50
2090 A277 $5 multicolored 5.75 5.75
Nos. 2083-2090 (8) 12.45 11.90

Souvenir Sheets

2091 A277 $6 multicolored 6.50 6.50
2092 A277 $6 multicolored 6.50 6.50

1992 Summer Olympics, Barcelona — A278

10c, Badminton. 25c, Women's long jump. 35c, Women's 100-meter dash. 50c, Cycling. 75c, Decathlon (pole vault), horiz. $2, Judo, horiz. $4, Women's gymnastics. $5, Javelin.

No. 2101, Men's floor exercise. No. 2102, Men's vault.

1992

2093 A278 10c multicolored .50 .30
2094 A278 25c multicolored .50 .25
2095 A278 35c multicolored .50 .30
2096 A278 50c multicolored 1.00 .50
2097 A278 75c multicolored 1.00 .70
2098 A278 $2 multicolored 1.60 1.60
2099 A278 $4 multicolored 3.25 3.25
2100 A278 $5 multicolored 4.00 4.00
Nos. 2093-2100 (8) 12.35 10.90

Souvenir Sheets

2101 A278 $6 multicolored 5.50 5.50
2102 A278 $6 multicolored 5.50 5.50

Model Trains A279

Designs: 10c, The Blue Comet, standard gauge, US, 1933. 35c, Switching locomotive, 2-inch gauge, 1906. 40c, B & O Tunnel locomotive, 2-inch gauge, 1905. 75c, Grand Canyon, standard gauge, US, 1931. $1, Lithographed tin streamliner, O gauge, 1930's. $2, Switching locomotive #237, No. 1 gauge, US, 1911. $4, Parlor car, standard gauge, US, 1928. $5, Locomotive #4687 of Improved President's Special, standard gauge, 1927. No. 2111, Engine #3239, No. 1 gauge, US, 1912. No. 2112, Ives engine #1132, 1921.

1992, Oct. 22 **Litho.** *Perf. 14*

2103 A279 10c multicolored .45 .25
2104 A279 35c multicolored .50 .30
2105 A279 40c multicolored .50 .35
2106 A279 75c multicolored .90 .50
2107 A279 $1 multicolored 1.25 1.00
2108 A279 $2 multicolored 1.50 1.50
2109 A279 $4 multicolored 3.00 3.00
2110 A279 $5 multicolored 3.75 3.75
Nos. 2103-2110 (8) 11.85 10.65

Souvenir Sheet
Perf. 13

2111 A279 $6 multicolored 6.00 6.00
2112 A279 $6 multicolored 6.00 6.00

Nos. 2111-2112 contains one 51x40mm stamp.

Souvenir Sheet

Guggenheim Museum, NYC — A280

1992, Oct. 28 *Perf. 14*

2113 A280 $6 multicolored 5.00 5.00

Postage Stamp Mega Event '92, NYC.

Christmas A281

Details or entire paintings: 10c, The Adoration of the Magi, by Fra Filippo Lippi. 15c, Madonna Adoring Child in a Wood, by Fra Filippo Lippi. 25c, Adoration of the Magi, by Botticelli. 35c, The Epiphany-Adoration of the Magi, by Hieronymus Bosch. 50c, Adoration of the Magi, by Giovanni de Paolo. 75c, The Adoration of the Magi, by Gentile da Fabriano. 90c, Adoration of the Magi, by Juan Batista Maino. $1, The Adoration of the Child, by Master of Liesborn. $2, The Adoration of the Kings, by Master of Liesborn. $3, The Adoration of the Three Wise Men, by Pedro Berruguete. $4, The Adoration of the Child, by Filippo Lippi. $5, Adoration of the Child, by Correggio. No. 2126, Adoration of the Magi, by Hans Memling. No. 2127, Adoration of the Magi, by Andrea Mantegna. No. 2128, Adoration of the Shepherds, by De La Tour.

1992, Nov. 16 **Litho.** *Perf. 13½x14*

2114 A281 10c multicolored .45 .25
2115 A281 15c multicolored .50 .25
2116 A281 25c multicolored .55 .25
2117 A281 35c multicolored .75 .40
2118 A281 50c multicolored .90 .50
2119 A281 75c multicolored 1.10 .80
2120 A281 90c multicolored 1.25 .90
2121 A281 $1 multicolored 1.50 1.00
2122 A281 $2 multicolored 1.75 1.75
2123 A281 $3 multicolored 2.75 2.75
2124 A281 $4 multicolored 3.75 3.75
2125 A281 $5 multicolored 4.75 4.75
Nos. 2114-2125 (12) 20.00 17.35

Souvenir Sheet

2126 A281 $6 multicolored 6.00 6.00
2127 A281 $6 multicolored 6.00 6.00
2128 A281 $6 multicolored 6.00 6.00

Regattas of the World — A282

Yachts, races: 15c, Matador, Newport News Regatta. 25c, Awesome, Antigua Regatta. 35c, Mistress Quickly, Bermuda Regatta. 50c, Emeraude, St. Tropez Regatta. $1, Diva G, German Admirals Cup. $2, Lady Be, French Admirals Cup. $4, Midnight Sun, Admirals Cup Regatta. $5, Carat, Sardinia Cup Regatta. No. 2137, 1979 Fastnet Race, horiz. No. 2138, Grenada Regatta, horiz.

1992, Oct. **Litho.** *Perf. 14*

2129 A282 15c multicolored .25 .25
2130 A282 25c multicolored .25 .25
2131 A282 35c multicolored .30 .30
2132 A282 50c multicolored .75 .40
2133 A282 $1 multicolored 1.00 .75
2134 A282 $2 multicolored 1.40 1.40
2135 A282 $4 multicolored 3.00 3.00
2136 A282 $5 multicolored 3.75 3.75
Nos. 2129-2136 (8) 10.70 10.10

Souvenir Sheets

2137 A282 $6 multicolored 7.00 7.00
2138 A282 $6 multicolored 7.00 7.00

A283

Anniversaries and Events — A284

Designs: 25c, LZ1 on maiden flight, 1900. 50c, Endosat, proposed robot plane. 75c, Konrad Adenauer, factory. $1.50, Golden lion tamarin. No. 2143 Mountain gorilla. No. 2144, WHO emblem and "Heartbeat-the Rhythm of Health." $3, Wolfgang Amadeus Mozart. No. 2146, German flag, map, Adenauer. No. 2147, Voyager 2, Neptune. $5, Count Zeppelin, Graf Zeppelin. $6, Lion's Club emblem, Admiral Richard E. Byrd. No. 2150, Scene from "The Magic Flute." No. 2151, Konrad Adenauer. No. 2152, Earth Summit emblem, northern spotted owl. No. 2153, Count Zeppelin. No. 2154, Satellite rescue, vert.

1992 **Litho.** *Perf. 14*

2139 A283 25c multicolored 1.50 1.50
2140 A283 50c multicolored 1.50 1.50
2141 A283 75c multicolored 1.50 1.50
2142 A283 $1.50 multicolored 3.50 3.50
2143 A283 $2 multicolored 4.00 4.00
2144 A283 $2 multicolored 4.75 4.75
2145 A284 $3 multicolored 5.75 5.75
2146 A283 $4 multicolored 4.00 4.00
2147 A283 $4 multicolored 5.50 5.50
2148 A283 $5 multicolored 8.00 8.00
2149 A283 $6 multicolored 5.50 5.50
Nos. 2139-2149 (11) 45.50 45.50

Souvenir Sheets

2150 A284 $6 multicolored 6.25 6.25
2151 A283 $6 multicolored 5.75 5.75
2152 A283 $6 multicolored 5.50 5.50
2153 A283 $6 multicolored 5.75 5.75
2154 A283 $6 multicolored 5.50 5.50

Count Ferdinand von Zeppelin, 75th anniv. of death (Nos. 2139, 2148, 2153). Intl. Space Year (Nos. 2140, 2147, 2154). Konrad Adenauer, 25th anniv. of death (Nos. 2141, 2146, 2151). Earth Summit, Rio de Janeiro (Nos. 2142-2143, 2152). Mozart, bicent. of death (in 1991) (Nos. 2145, 2150). Lions Intl., 75th anniv. (No. 2149).

Issue dates: Nos. 2145, 2150, Oct. Nos. 2140-2141, 2144, 2146-2147, 2149, 2151, 2154, Nov. Nos. 2139, 2142-2143, 2148, 2152-2153, Dec.

Grenada Dove — A285

1992

2155 A285 10c multicolored 2.00 2.00

Entertainers — A286

Gold record award winners: No. 2156a, Cher. b, Michael Jackson. c, Elvis Presley. d, Dolly Parton. e, Johnny Mathis. f, Madonna. g, Nat King Cole. h, Janis Joplin.

No. 2157a, Frank Sinatra. b, Perry Como.

No. 2158a, Chuck Berry. b, James Brown.

1992, Nov. 19 **Litho.** *Perf. 14*

Miniature Sheet

2156 A286 90c Sheet of 8, #a.-h. 11.50 11.50

Souvenir Sheets

2157 A286 $3 Sheet of 2, #a.-b. 7.50 7.50
2158 A286 $3 Sheet of 2, #a.-b. 7.50 7.50

Care Bears Promote Conservation — A287

75c, Bear on uncontaminated beachfront. $2, Bear with parasol, butterfly on flower, vert.

1992, Dec. 15 Litho. *Perf. 14*

2159 A287 75c multicolored 1.00 1.00

Souvenir Sheet

2160 A287 $2 multicolored 4.00 4.00

Dogs A288

Designs: 10c, Samoyed, St. Basil's Cathedral, Moscow. 15c, Chow chow, Ling Yin Monastery, China. 25c, Boxer, Traitor's Gate, United Kingdom. 90c, Basenji, Yamma Mosque, Niger. $1, Golden Labrador Retriever, Parliament, Ottawa, Canada. $3, Saint Bernard, Parsenn, Switzerland. $4, Rhodesian ridgeback, Melrose House, South Africa. $5, Afghan, Mazar-i-Sharif, Afghanistan. No. 2169, Alaskan malamute, Alaska. No. 2170, Australian cattle dog, Australia.

1993, Jan. 20 Litho. *Perf. 14*

2161 A288 10c multicolored .70 .40
2162 A288 15c multicolored .85 .40
2163 A288 25c multicolored .90 .40
2164 A288 90c multicolored 1.25 .75
2165 A288 $1 multicolored 1.50 1.00
2166 A288 $3 multicolored 2.25 2.25
2167 A288 $4 multicolored 3.00 3.00
2168 A288 $5 multicolored 3.75 3.75
Nos. 2161-2168 (8) 14.20 11.95

Souvenir Sheet

2169 A288 $6 multicolored 5.75 5.75
2170 A288 $6 multicolored 5.75 5.75

Miniature Sheet

Louvre Museum, Bicent. — A289

Paintings by Jean-Antoine Watteau (1684-1721): a, The Faux-Pas. b, A Gentleman. c, Young Lady with Archlute. d, Young Man Dancing. e, Autumn. f, The Judgement of Paris. g-h, Pierrot (diff. details).

No. 2172, The Embarkation for Cythera, horiz.

1993, Mar. 8 Litho. *Perf. 12*

2171 A289 $1 Sheet of 8, #a.-h. + label 9.50 9.50

Souvenir Sheet

Perf. 14½

2172 A289 $6 multicolored 7.25 7.25

No. 2172 contains one 88x55mm stamp.

Moths A290

10c, Magnificant. 35c, Metzl's io. 45c, Owl. 75c, Pink-spotted hawk. $1, Faithful beauty. $2, Green geometrid. $4, Gaudy sphinx. $5, Black witch.

No. 2181, Titan hawk, vert. No. 2182, Avocado, vert.

1993, Apr. 13 Litho. *Perf. 14*

2173 A290 10c multicolored .35 .25
2174 A290 35c multicolored .50 .35
2175 A290 45c multicolored .60 .40
2176 A290 75c multicolored 1.00 .60
2177 A290 $1 multicolored 1.25 .75
2178 A290 $2 multicolored 2.50 1.50
2179 A290 $4 multicolored 2.75 2.75
2180 A290 $5 multicolored 3.50 3.50
Nos. 2173-2180 (8) 12.45 10.10

Souvenir Sheets

2181 A290 $6 multicolored 5.25 5.25
2182 A290 $6 multicolored 5.25 5.25

Flowers — A291

10c, Heliconia. 35c, Pansy. 45c, Water lily. 75c, Bougainvillea. $1, Calla lily. $2, California poppy. $4, Red ginger. $5, Anthurium.

No. 2191, Christmas rose, horiz. No. 2192, Moth orchids, horiz.

1993, May 17 Litho. *Perf. 14*

2183 A291 10c multicolored .35 .25
2184 A291 35c multicolored .50 .35
2185 A291 45c multicolored .60 .40
2186 A291 75c multicolored .85 .60
2187 A291 $1 multicolored 1.00 .75
2188 A291 $2 multicolored 1.50 1.50
2189 A291 $4 multicolored 3.00 3.00
2190 A291 $5 multicolored 3.75 3.75
Nos. 2183-2190 (8) 11.55 10.60

Souvenir Sheet

2191 A291 $6 multicolored 5.75 5.75
2192 A291 $6 multicolored 5.75 5.75

Baha'i Shrine, Haifa, Israel — A292

1993, May Litho. *Perf. 13½x14*

2193 A292 75c multicolored 1.90 1.90

Baha'i faith in Grenada, cent.

Miniature Sheet

Coronation of Queen Elizabeth II, 40th Anniv. — A293

Designs: a, 35c, Official coronation photograph. b, 70c, Queen Consort's Ivory Rod, Queen Consort's Scepter. c, $1, Elizabeth accepting scepter during ceremony. $5, Queen, family, 1960s.

$6, Portrait, by Peter George Greenham, 1965.

1993, June 2 *Perf. 13½x14*

2194 A293 Sheet, 2 each #a.-d. 12.00 12.00

Souvenir Sheet

Perf. 14

2195 A293 $6 multicolored 6.25 6.25

No. 2195 contains one 28x42mm stamp.

A294

Anniversaries and Events — A295

Designs: 35c, Telescope. 50c, Willy Brandt, Sen. Edward Kennedy, Mrs. Robert Kennedy, 1973. $4, Astronaut standing on moon. No. 2199, Willy Brandt, Kurt Waldheim. No. 2200, Copernicus. $6, Newspaper headline announcing Brandt's resignation.

1993, July 1 Litho. *Perf. 14*

2196 A294 35c multicolored .50 .50
2197 A295 50c black & brown .75 .75
2198 A294 $4 multicolored 4.50 4.50
2199 A295 $5 black & brown 4.25 4.25
Nos. 2196-2199 (4) 10.00 10.00

Souvenir Sheets

2200 A294 $5 multicolored 5.50 5.50
2201 A295 $6 brown & black 5.75 5.75

Nicolaus Copernicus, 450th anniv. of death (Nos. 2196, 2198, 2200). Willy Brandt, 1st anniv. of death (Nos. 2197, 2199, 2201).

Grenada Carnival, 1992 A296

35c, Public Library, vert. 75c, Dancers.

1993, July 1

2202 A296 35c multicolored .50 .50
2203 A296 75c multicolored .95 .95

Public Library, cent. (in 1992) (No. 2202).

Miniature Sheet

Songbirds — A297

Designs: No. 2204a, 15c, Red-eyed vireo. b, 25c, Scissor-tailed flycatcher (g). c, 35c, Palmchat. d, 35c, Chaffinch. e, 45c, Yellow wagtail. f, 45c Painted bunting. g, 50c, Short-tailed pygmy flycatcher. h, 65c, Rainbow bunting. i, 75c, Red crossbill. j, 75c, Kauai akialoa. k, $1, Yellow-throated wagtail. l, $4, Barn swallow.

No. 2205, Song thrush. No. 2206, White-crested laughing thrush.

1993, July 13

2204 A297 Sheet of 12, #a.-l. 13.00 13.00

Souvenir Sheets

2205 A297 $6 multicolored 5.25 5.25
2206 A297 $6 multicolored 5.25 5.25

Miniature Sheet

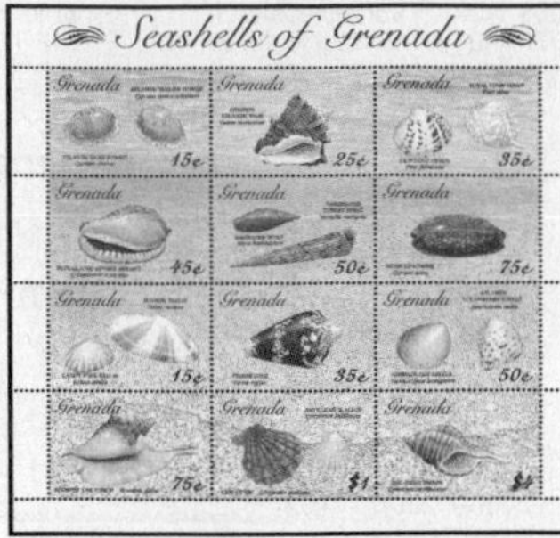

Seashells — A298

Designs: No. 2207a, 15c, Atlantic gray cowrie, Atlantic yellow cowrie. b, 15c, Candy stick tellin, sunrise tellin. c, 25c, Common Atlantic vase. d, 35c, Lightning venus, royal comb venus. e, 35c, Crown cone. f, 45c, Reticulated cowrie-helmet. g, 50c, Barbados miter, variegated turret shell. h, 50c, Common egg cockle, Atlantic strawberry cockle. i, 75c, Measled cowrie. j, 75c, Rooster tail conch. k, $1, Lion's paw, Antillean scallop. l, $4, Dog-head triton.

No. 2208, Dyson's keyhole limpet. No. 2209, Virgin nerite, emerald nerite.

1993, July 19 Litho. *Perf. 14*

2207 A298 Sheet of 12, #a.-l. 14.00 14.00

Souvenir Sheets

2208 A298 $6 multicolored 7.00 7.00
2209 A298 $6 multicolored 7.00 7.00

A299

Picasso (1881-1973): 25c, Woman with Loaves, 1906. 90c, Weeping Woman, 1937. $4, Woman Seated in Armchair, 1947. $6, Three Women at the Spring, 1921.

1993, July 1 Litho. *Perf. 14*

2210 A299 25c multicolored .35 .35
2211 A299 90c multicolored 1.25 1.00
2212 A299 $4 multicolored 4.00 4.00
Nos. 2210-2212 (3) 5.60 5.35

Souvenir Sheet

2213 A299 $6 multicolored 4.75 4.75

A300

1994 Winter Olympics, Lillehammer, Norway: 35c, Gaeten Boucher, speedskating gold medalist, 1984. $5, Norbert Schramm, figure skater. $6, Michela Figini, Sigrid Wolf, Karen Percy, Super G medalists, 1988, horiz.

1993, July 1

2214 A300 35c multicolored .50 .30
2215 A300 $5 multicolored 4.50 4.50

Souvenir Sheet

2216 A300 $6 multicolored 5.75 5.75

Polska '93 — A301

Paintings: $1, Portrait of Marii Prohaska, by Tytus Czyzewski, 1923. $3, Marysia et Burek a Geylan, by S.I. Wirkiewicz, 1920-21. $6, Parting, by Witold Wojtkiewicz, 1908.

1993, July 1 Litho. *Perf. 14*

2217 A301 $1 multicolored 1.25 1.25
2218 A301 $3 multicolored 3.75 3.75

Souvenir Sheet

2219 A301 $6 multicolored 6.25 6.25

Taipei '93 — A302

Designs: 35c, Fire-breathing dragon, New Year's Fair, Chongqing. 45c, Stone elephant, Spirit Way to Ming Tomb, Nanjing. $2, Marble peifang, Ming Tombs, Beijing. $4, Stone pillar, Nanjing.
Paintings by Han Meilin: No. 2224a, Ornamental cock. b, Tiger cub. c, Owl. d, Cat. e, Gorillas. f, Leopard.
No. 2225, Orangutan.

1993, Aug. 13 Litho. *Perf. 14*

2220 A302 35c multicolored .25 .25
2221 A302 45c multicolored .75 .75
2222 A302 $2 multicolored 3.25 3.25
2223 A302 $4 multicolored 6.25 6.25
Nos. 2220-2223 (4) 10.50 10.50

Miniature Sheet

2224 A302 $1.50 Sheet of 6, #a.-f. 6.75 6.75

Souvenir Sheet

2225 A302 $6 multicolored 5.50 5.50

With Bangkok '93 Emblem

Designs: 35c, Nora Nair, Prasad Phra Thepidon, Wat Phra Kaew. 45c, Stucco deities, Library, Wat Phra Singh. $2, Naga snake, Chiang Mai's Temple. $4, Stucco elephants, Wat Chang Lom.
Thai sculpture: No. 2230a, Horses. b, Wheel of the Law, 7th-8th cent. c, Lanna bronze elephant, 1575. d, Kendi in form of elephant. e, Bronze duck, 14th-15th cent. f, Horseman, 14th-15th cent.
No. 2231, Elephants, horiz.

1993, Aug. 13

2226 A302 35c multicolored .25 .25
2227 A302 45c multicolored .35 .35
2228 A302 $2 multicolored 1.50 1.50
2229 A302 $4 multicolored 3.00 3.00
Nos. 2226-2229 (4) 5.10 5.10

Miniature Sheet

2230 A302 $1.50 Sheet of 6, #a.-f. 6.75 6.75

Souvenir Sheet

2231 A302 $6 multicolored 4.50 4.50

With Indopex '93 Emblem

35c, Megalithic carving, Sumba Island, Indonesia. 45c, Entrance to Gao Gaja (Elephant Cave), Bali. $2, Loving Mother Bridge, Taroko Gorge Natl. Park. $4, Kala head gateway to Balinese Temple, Northern Bali.
Indonesian sculpture - No. 2236: a, Kris holder and Kris, 19th cent. b, Hanuman protecting Sita, I. Dojotan of Mas. c, Sendi of Visnu mounted on Garuda, 19th cent. d, Wahana (mini vehicle for votive fig.), 20th cent. e, Mercurial monkey warrior Hanuman, Rodja of Mas. f, Singa (polychrome lion).
No. 2237, Loris.

1993, Aug. 13 *Perf. 13½x14*

2232 A302 35c multicolored .25 .25
2233 A302 45c multicolored .35 .35
2234 A302 $2 multicolored 1.50 1.50
2235 A302 $4 multicolored 3.00 3.00
Nos. 2232-2235 (4) 5.10 5.10

Miniature Sheet

2236 A302 $1.50 Sheet of 6, #a.-f. 11.00 11.00

Souvenir Sheet

2237 A302 $6 multicolored 5.50 5.50

Miniature Sheet

Italian Soccer Assoc. and Genoa Soccer Club, Cent. — A303

Players for Genoa Soccer Club, each $3: No. 2238a, Vittorio Sardelli. b, Juan Carlos Verdeal. c, Fosco Becattini. d, Julio Cesar Abadie. e, Luigi Meroni. f, Roberto Pruzzo.
No. 2239a, each $3: James K. Spensley. b, Renzo de Vecchi. c, Giovanni de Pra. d, Luigi Burlando. e, Felice Levratto. f, Guglielmo Stabile.
Each $15: No. 2240, 1991 Genoa team photo, horiz. No. 2241, Genoa team emblem.

1993, Sept. 7 Litho. *Perf. 14*

Sheets of 6, #a-f

2238-2239 A303 Set of 2 40.00 40.00

Souvenir Sheets

2240-2241 A303 Set of 2 37.00 37.00

No. 2240 contains one 48x35mm stamp. No. 2241 contains one 29x45mm stamp.

1994 World Cup Soccer Championships, US — A304

Designs: 10c, Nikolai Larionov, Russia. 25c, Andrea Carnevale, Italy. 35c, Enzo Scifo, Belgium, Soon-Ho Choi, South Korea. 45c, Gary Lineker, England. $1, Diego Maradona, Argentina. $2, Lothar Matthaeus, Germany. $4, Jan Karas, Poland, Julio Cesar Silva, Brazil. $5, Claudio Caniggia, Argentina.
Each $6: No. 2250, Wlodzimierz, Poland. No. 2251, Jose Basualdo, Argentina.

1993, Sept. 7 Litho. *Perf. 14*

2242-2249 A304 Set of 8 12.00 12.00

Souvenir Sheets

2250-2251 A304 Set of 2 11.00 11.00

Mickey Mouse, 65th Birthday — A305

Movie clips: 25c, The Band Concert, 1935. 35c, Mickey's Circus, 1936. 50c, Magician Mickey, 1937. 75c, Moose Hunters, 1937. $1, Mickey's Amateurs, 1937. $2, Tugboat Mickey, 1940. $4, Orphan's Benefit, 1941. $5, Mickey's Christmas, 1983.
Each $6: No. 2260, Mickey's Birthday Party, 1942. No. 2261, Mickey's Trailer, 1938.

1993, Nov. 11 Litho. *Perf. 14x13½*

2252-2259 A305 Set of 8 12.50 12.50

Souvenir Sheets

2260-2261 A305 Set of 2 13.00 13.00

Christmas A306

Woodcuts by Durer: 10c, The Nativity. 25c, "The Annunciation." $1, "Adoration of the Magi." $5, "The Virgin Mary in the Sun."
Paintings by Leonardo Da Vinci: 35c, The Litta Madonna. 60c, Madonna and Child with St. Anne and the Infant St. John. 90c, Madonna with the Carnation. $4, The Benois Madonna.
Each $6: No. 2270, The Holy Family with Three Hares, by Durer. No. 2271, Adoration of the Magi, by Da Vinci.
The 25c actually shows the Adoration of the Magi. The $1 actually shows The Virgin Mary in the Sun. The $5 actually shows The Annunciation.

1993, Nov. 22 Litho. *Perf. 13½x14*

2262-2269 A306 Set of 8 10.50 10.50

Souvenir Sheets

2270-2271 A306 Set of 2 10.50 10.50

Hugo Eckener (1868-1954) — A307

Graf Zeppelin over: 35c, Vienna. 75c, Pyramids at Giza. $5, Rio de Janeiro. No. 2275, Flensburg.

1993, Dec. 21 *Perf. 14*

2272-2274 A307 Set of 3 5.50 5.50

Souvenir Sheet

2275 A307 $6 multicolored 5.50 5.50

Royal Air Force, 75th Anniv. A308

1993, Dec. 21

2276 A308 50c Lysander 1.00 1.00
2277 A308 $3 Hawker Typhoon 4.25 4.25

Souvenir Sheet

2278 A308 $6 Hawker Hurricane 5.50 5.50

Automotive Anniversaries — A309

35c, 1932 Mercedes Benz 370 S Cabriolet. 45c, 1966 Ford Mustang. $3, 1930 Model A Ford Phaeton. $4, Mercedes Benz 300 SL Gullwing.
Each $6: No. 2283, 1903 Ford Model A. No. 2284, 1934 Mercedes Benz 290.

1993, Dec. 21 Litho. *Perf. 14*

2279-2282 A309 Set of 4 10.00 10.00

Souvenir Sheets

2283-2284 A309 Set of 2 10.50 10.50

1st Benz 4-wheel car, cent. 1st Ford engine, cent.

First Gas Balloon Flight in America, Bicent. A310

Designs: 45c, Lift-off from Philadelphia. $2, Balloon in flight, vert. $6, Blanchard's balloon in flight, diff., vert.

1993, Dec. 21 Litho. *Perf. 14*

2285-2286 A310 Set of 2 3.00 3.00

Souvenir Sheet

2287 A310 $6 multicolored 6.50 6.50

Fine Art — A311

Self-portraits, by Matisse: 15c, 1900. 45c, 1918. $2, 1906. $4, 1900, diff.
Self-portraits, by Rembrandt: 35c, 1629. 50c, 1640. 75c, 1652. $5, 1625-31.
No. 2296, The Painter in His Studio, by Matisse. No. 2297, The Sampling Officials of the Draper's Guild, by Rembrandt, horiz.

1993, Dec. 31 Litho. *Perf. 13½x14*

2288 A311 15c multicolored .40 .25
2289 A311 35c multicolored .50 .25
2290 A311 45c multicolored .55 .40
2291 A311 50c multicolored .65 .45
2292 A311 75c multicolored 1.00 .60
2293 A311 $2 multicolored 1.75 1.60
2294 A311 $4 multicolored 3.25 3.25
2295 A311 $5 multicolored 4.00 4.00
Nos. 2288-2295 (8) 12.10 10.80

Souvenir Sheets

2296 A311 $6 multicolored 5.25 5.25

Perf. 14x13½

2297 A311 $6 multicolored 5.25 5.25

Spice Islands Billfish Tournament, 25th Anniv. — A312

15c, Blue marlin. 25c, Sailfish with angler. 35c, Yellowfin tuna with angler. 50c, White marlin with angler. 75c, Catching a sailfish.

1993, Dec. Litho. *Perf. 14*

2302-2306 A312 Set of 5 1.00 1.00

A313

Hong Kong '94 — A314

Stamps, painting, Hong Kong Post Office-1846, by M. Bruce: No. 2307, Hong Kong #263, left detail. No. 2308, Right detail, #1597.
Porcelain ware, Qing Dynasty: No. 2309a, Vase with dragon decor. b, Hat stand. c, Gourd-shaped vase. d, Rotating vase with openwork. e, Candlestick with dogs. f, Hat stand, diff.

1994, Feb. 18 Litho. *Perf. 14*

2307	40c multicolored	.65	.65
2308	40c multicolored	.65	.65
a.	A313 Pair, #2307-2308	1.40	1.40

Miniature Sheet

2309	A314 45c Sheet of 6, #a.-f.	3.75	3.75

Nos. 2307-2308 issued in sheets of 5 pairs. No. 2308a is a continuous design.
New Year 1994 (Year of the Dog) (No. 2309e).

Independence, 20th Anniv. — A315

1994, Feb. 8 Litho. *Perf. 14*

2310	A315 35c Natl. flag, boat	.80	.80

Souvenir Sheet

2311	A315 $6 Map of Grenada	6.25	6.25

Miniature Sheets

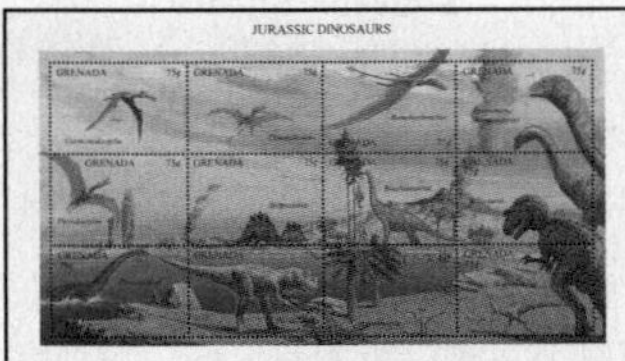

Dinosaurs — A316

Jurassic: No. 2312a, Germanodactylus. b, Dimorphodon. c, Ramphorhynchus. d, Apatosaurus (h). e, Pterodactylus. f, Stegosaurus. g, Brachiosaurus. h, Allosaurus (l). i, Plesiosaurus. j, Ceratosaurus. k, Compsognathus. l, Elaphosaurus.
Cretaceous: No. 2313a, Quetzalcoatlus. b, Pteranodon ingens (c). c, Tropeognathus. d, Phobetor. e, Alamosaurus (i). f, Triceratops (e). g, Tyrannosaurus rex (h). h, Tyrannosaurus rex (up close) (l). i, Lambeosaurus. j, Spinosaurus. k, Parasaurolophus (l). l, Hadrosaurus.
No. 2314, Plateosaurus, vert. No. 2315, Pteranodon ingens.

1994, Apr. 13 Sheets of 12

2312	A316 75c #a.-l.	8.00	8.00
2313	A316 75c #a.-l.	8.00	8.00

Souvenir Sheets

2314	A316 $6 multicolored	5.25	5.25
2315	A316 $6 multicolored	5.25	5.25

Mushrooms A317

Designs: 35c, Hygrocybe acutoconica. 45c, Leucopaxillus gracillimus. 50c, Leptonia caeruleocapitata. 75c, Leucoprinus birnbaumii. $1, Marasmius atrorubens. $2, Boletellus cubensis. $4, Chlorophyllum molybdites. $5, Psilocybe cubensis.
No. 2324, Mycena pura. No. 2325, Pyrrhoglossum lilaceipes.

1994, Apr. 6

2316	A317 35c multicolored	.50	.25
2317	A317 45c multicolored	.60	.35
2318	A317 50c multicolored	.70	.40
2319	A317 75c multicolored	.90	.50
2320	A317 $1 multicolored	1.25	.75
2321	A317 $2 multicolored	1.60	1.25
2322	A317 $4 multicolored	3.25	3.25
2323	A317 $5 multicolored	3.75	3.75
	Nos. 2316-2323 (8)	12.55	10.50

Souvenir Sheets

2324	A317 $6 multicolored	6.00	6.00
2325	A317 $6 multicolored	6.00	6.00

D-Day, 50th Anniv. A318

Designs: 40c, Sherman Dual-Drive swimming tanks. $2, Churchill "Ark" in operation. $3, Churchill "Bobbin" lays path over soft ground.
$6, Churchill "Avre."

1994, Aug. 4 Litho. *Perf. 14*

2326-2328	A318 Set of 3	6.50	6.50

Souvenir Sheet

2329	A318 $6 multicolored	6.25	6.25

Miniature Sheet

First Manned Moon Landing, 25th Anniv. — A319

Tribute to crew of space shuttle Challenger: No. 2330a, Flame erupting before explosion. b, Judith A. Resnick. c, Aircraft flyover in "Missing Man" formation. d, Dick Scobee. e, Challenger 51-L patch. f, Michael J. Smith.
$6, Crew of mission 51-L.

1994, Aug. 4

2330	A319 $2 Sheet of 6, #a.-f.	8.50	8.50

Souvenir Sheet

2331	A319 $6 multicolored	5.25	5.25

A320

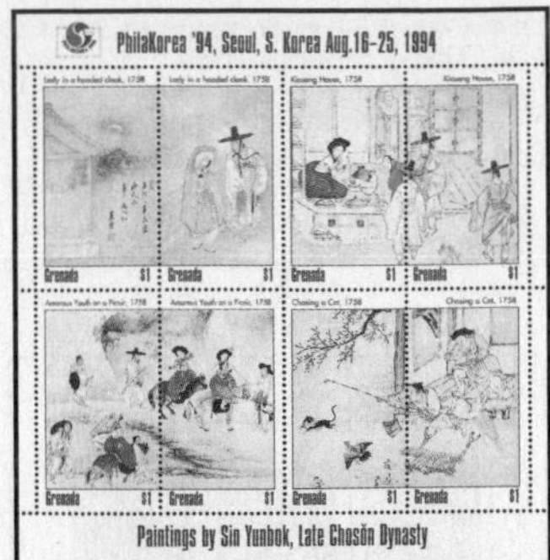

PHILAKOREA '94 — A321

Designs: 40c, Wonson Park & Garden. $1, Port of Pusan. $4, National Theatre, Seoul.
Paintings by Sin Yunbok, Late Choson Dynasty: No. 2335a-2335b, Lady in a Hooded Cloak. c-d, Kiaseng House. e-f, Amorous Youth on a Picnic. g-h, Chasing a Cat.
$6, Roof Tiling, by Kim Hongdo, vert.

1994, Aug. 4 *Perf. 14, 13½ (#2335)*

2332-2334	A320 Set of 3	4.00	4.00

Miniature Sheet

2335	A321 $1 Sheet of 8, #a.-h.	6.00	6.00

Souvenir Sheet

2336	A320 $6 multicolored	4.50	4.50

A322

Orchids: 15c, Brassavola cuculatta. 25c, Comparettia falcata. 45c, Epidendrum ciliare. 75c, Epidendrum cochleatum. $1, Ionopsis utricularioides. $2, Oncidium cebolleta. $4, Oncidium luridium. $5, Rodriquezia secunda.
Each $6: No. 2345, Ionopsis utricularioides, diff. No. 2346, Onicium luridum, diff.

1994, Aug. 7 *Perf. 14*

2337-2344	A322 Set of 8	11.50	11.50

Souvenir Sheets

2345-2346	A322 Set of 2	12.00	12.00

A323

1994 World Cup Soccer Championships, US: No. 2347a, Tony Meola, US. b, Steve Mark, Grenada. c, Gianluigi Lentini, Italy. d, Belloumi, Algeria. e, Nunoz, Spain. f, Lothar Matthaus, Germany.
Each $6: No. 2348, Steve Mark, diff. No. 2349, Poster from 1st World Cup Championships, Uruguay, 1930.

1994, Aug. 11 *Perf. 14*

Miniature Sheet

2347	A323 75c Sheet of 6, #a.-f.	5.50	5.50

Souvenir Sheet

2348-2349	A323 Set of 2	10.00	10.00

Fish A324

Designs: 15c, Yellowtail snapper. 20c, Blue tang. 25c, Porkfish, vert. 75c, Foureye butterflyfish. $1, Longsnout seahorse, vert. $2, Spotted moray eel, vert. $4, Fairy basslet. $5, Queen triggerfish, vert.
Each $6: No. 2358, Queen angelfish. No. 2359, Squirrelfish.

1994, Sept. 1

2350-2357	A324 Set of 8	9.25	9.25

Souvenir Sheets

2358-2359	A324 Set of 2	11.00	11.00

A325

Intl. Olympic Committee, Cent. — A326

Designs: 50c, Heike Drechsler, Germany, long jump, 1992. $1.50, Nadia Comaneci, Romania, Gymnastics, 1976, 1980.
$6, Dan Jansen, US, 1000-meters long track speed skating, 1994.

1994, Aug. 4

2360	A325 50c multicolored	1.00	1.00
2361	A325 $1.50 multicolored	2.25	2.25

Souvenir Sheet

2362	A326 $6 multicolored	5.00	5.00

1994, Year of the Dog — A327

Scenes from Disney's Society Dog Show: 2c, Mickey bathing Pluto. 3c, Using atomizer. 4c, Having tail "set." 5c, Putting on mascara. 10c, Having nails done. 15c, Mickey using flea powder on Pluto. 20c, On judge's stand. $4, Judge looking at Pluto. $5, Pluto in chair with first prize.
No. 2372, Pluto wearing "13," first prize ribbon. No. 2373, Little dog beside judge. No. 2374, Pluto with first prize ribbon.

1994, Sept. 22 Litho. *Perf. 14x13½*

2363-2371	A327 Set of 9	10.00	10.00

Souvenir Sheets

2372-2374	A327 $6 each	4.75	4.75

Butterflies — A328

10c, Red anartia. 15c, Ruddy daggerwing. 25c, Fiery skipper. 35c, Caribbean buckeye. 45c, Giant hairstreak. 50c, Zebra longwing. 75c, Diadem. $1, Blue night. $2, Orion. $3, Orange-barred sulphur. $4, Long-tail skipper. $5, Polydamas swallowtail. $10, Bamboo page. $20, Queen cracker.

1994, Sept. 28 *Perf. 14*

2375	A328	10c	multicolored	.35	.25
2376	A328	15c	multicolored	.35	.25
2377	A328	25c	multicolored	.40	.25
a.	Inscribed "1996"			.40	.25
2378	A328	35c	multicolored	.45	.40
a.	Inscribed "1996"			.45	.25
2379	A328	45c	multicolored	.50	.40
2380	A328	50c	multicolored	.60	.50
2381	A328	75c	multicolored	.70	.70
2382	A328	$1	multicolored	1.25	1.25
2383	A328	$2	multicolored	2.25	2.25
2384	A328	$3	multicolored	3.50	3.50
2385	A328	$4	multicolored	4.50	4.50
2386	A328	$5	multicolored	5.25	5.25
2386A	A328	$10	multicolored	10.00	10.00
2386B	A328	$20	multicolored	16.50	16.50
	Nos. 2375-2386B (14)			46.60	46.00

See Nos. 2585-2586.

Intl. Year of the Family A329

1994, Aug. 4

2387 A329 $1 multicolored .90 .90

Order of the Caribbean Community — A330

First award recipients: 15c, Sir Shridath Ramphal, statesman, Guyana. 65c, William Demas, economist, Trinidad & Tobago. $2, Derek Walcott, writer, St. Lucia.

1994, Sept. 1

2388-2390 A330 Set of 3 3.00 3.00

Christmas A331

Paintings, by Zurbaran: 10c, The Virgin and Child with St. John. 15c, The Circumcision. 25c, Adoration of St. Joseph. 35c, Adoration of the Magi. 75c, The Portiuncula. $1, The Virgin and Child with St. John, 1662. $2, The Virgin and Child with St. John, 1658-64. $4, The Flight into Egypt.

Each $6: No. 2399, Adoration of the Shepherds, horiz. No. 2400, Our Lady of Ransom and Two Mercedarians.

1994, Dec. 5 **Litho.** *Perf. 13½x14*

2391-2398 A331 Set of 8 7.25 7.25

Souvenir Sheets

2399-2400 A331 Set of 2 10.00 10.00

A332

Birds: 25c, Grenada dove, horiz. 35c, Grenada doves, horiz. 45c, Cuban tody. No. 2404, 75c, Grenada dove, diff. No. 2405, 75c, Painted bunting, horiz. No. 2406, $1, Grenada dove, in flight. No. 2407, $1, Red-legged honeycreeper, horiz. $5, Green jay, horiz.

Each $6: No. 2409, Chestnut-sided shrike-vireo, horiz. No. 2410, Chaffinch, horiz.

1995, Jan. 10 **Litho.** *Perf. 14*

2401-2408 A332 Set of 8 15.00 15.00

Souvenir Sheet

2409-2410 A332 Set of 2 11.50 11.50

World Wildlife Fund (Nos. 2401-2402, 2404, 2406).

A333

Designs: 25c, Junior Murray, Grenada/W. Indies. 35c, R.B. Richardson, Leeward Isl./W. Indies. $2, A.J. Steward, England, horiz.

No. 2414, West Indies team, horiz.

1995, Jan. 12

2411-2413 A333 Set of 3 3.00 3.00

Souvenir Sheet

2414 A333 $3 multicolored 4.00 4.00

English Touring Cricket, cent.

Water Birds A334

25c, Hooded merganser. 35c, Teal. $1, Harlequin duck. $3, European wigeon.

No. 2419a, King eider. b, Shoveler. c, Long-tailed duck. d, Chiloe wigeon. e, Red-breasted merganser. f, Falcated teal. g, Vericolor teal. h, Smew. i, Red-crested pochard. j, Northern pintail. k, Barrow's goldeneye. l, Stellar's eider.

No. 2420, European wigeon, diff. No. 2421, Egyptian goose.

1995, Mar. 27 **Litho.** *Perf. 14*

2415-2418 A334 Set of 4 5.00 5.00

Miniature Sheet

2419 A334 75c Sheet of 12, #a.-l. 9.00 9.00

Souvenir Sheets

2420 A334 $5 multicolored 4.00 4.00
2421 A334 $6 multicolored 4.50 4.50

New Year 1995 (Year of the Boar) — A335

a, 50c, Pig priest, China. b, 75c, Porcelain pig, Scotland. c, $1, Porcelain pig, Italy.

$2, Jade pig, China.

1995, Apr. 21 **Litho.** *Perf. 14*

2422 A335 Strip of 3, #a.-c. 3.00 3.00

Souvenir Sheet

2423 A335 $2 multicolored 3.25 3.25

No. 2422 was issued in miniature sheets containing 3 No. 2422.

Miniature Sheets of 6 and 8

End of World War II, 50th Anniv. — A336

No. 2423A: b, Great Marianas Turkey Shoot. c, Battle of Midway. d, Battle of the Bismarck Sea. e, Musashi sinks at Leyte Gulf. f, Henderson Field. g, Battle of Guadalcanal.

Fighter planes: No. 2424a, Lavochkin LA7, Soviet Air Force. b, Hawker Hurricane, Royal Air Force (RAF). c, North American P-51D, US Army Air Force (USAAF). d, Messerschmitt ME 109F, Luftwaffe. e, Bristol Beaufighter, RAF. f, Messerschmitt ME 262, Luftwaffe. g, Republic P-47D, USAAF. h, Hawker Tempest V, RAF.

No. 2425, Nose of P-47D. No. 2425A, B-29 bomber.

1995, May 8

2423A A336 $2 #b.-g. + label 12.00 12.00
2424 A336 $2 #a.-h. + label 15.00 15.00

Souvenir Sheets

2425 A336 $6 multicolored 7.00 7.00
2425A A336 $6 multicolored 6.50 6.50

18th World Scout Jamboree, Holland — A337

Designs: a, 75c, Palm trees, scout. b, $1, Mountain climbing. c, $2, Scout salute, flag.

$6, Canoeing.

1995, May 8

2426 A337 Strip of 3, #a.-c. 3.25 3.25

Souvenir Sheet

2427 A337 $6 multicolored 5.25 5.25

No. 2426 issued in sheets of 9 stamps.

UN, 50th Anniv. A338

Designs: a, 75c, Man bending sword into plowshare. b, $1, Earth, dove. c, $2, UN Headquarters.

$6, Emblem.

1995, May 8

2428 A338 Strip of 3, #a.-c. 3.25 3.25

Souvenir Sheet

2429 A338 $6 multicolored 5.00 5.00

No. 2428 is a continuous design and was issued in sheets of 9 stamps.

Grenada-Republic of China Friendship — A339

Designs: 75c, Flags of Grenada, Republic of China. $1, Prime Minister Nicholas Brathwaite, Grenada, Pres. Lee Teng-hui, Republic of China.

1995, Apr. 27 **Litho.** *Perf. 14*

2430 A339 75c multicolored 1.25 1.25
2431 A339 $1 multicolored 1.50 1.50
a. Souvenir sheet, #2430-2431 2.75 2.75

Domesticated Animals — A340

Designs: 10c, Cocker spaniel. 15c, Pinto. 25c, Rottweiler. 35c, German shepherd. 45c, Persian. 50c, Snowshoe. 75c, Percheron. $1, Scottish fold. $2, Arabian. $3, Andalusian. $4, C.P. shorthair. $5, Chihuahua.

No. 2444, $5, Manx. No. 2445, $5, Donkey. No. 2446, $6, Shar pei.

1995, May 3

2432-2443 A340 Set of 12 16.00 16.00

Souvenir Sheets

2444-2445 A340 Set of 2 8.00 8.00
2446 A340 multi 5.25 5.25

Miniature Sheet

Sierra Club, Cent. — A341

No. 2447, vert, each $1: a, Margay, mouth open. b, Margay seated. c, Margay up close. d, Condor facing left. e, Condor facing right. f, Condor looking back. g, White-faced saki on tree limb. h, White-faced saki, face in light. i, Patagonia Region, South America.

No. 2448, each $1: a, Darwin's rhea, two facing right. b, Darwin's rhea, two facing left. c, One Darwin's rhea. d, Snow covered mountains, Patagonia Region. e, Mountain peaks, Patagonia Region. f, White-faced saki. g, Crested caracara facing right. h, Two crested caracara. i, Crested caracara facing left.

1995, May 5 **Sheets of 9, #a.-i.**

2447-2448 A341 Set of 2 22.00 22.00

FAO, 50th Anniv. — A342

No. 2449: a, 75c, Woman with baskets. b, $1, Boy with basket. c, $2, Men working in field.

$6, FAO emblem.

1995, May 8

2449 A342 Strip of 3, #a.-c. 3.25 3.25

Souvenir Sheet

2450 A342 $6 multicolored 5.00 5.00

No. 2449 was issued in sheets of 9 stamps.

Rotary Intl., 90th Anniv. — A343

$6, Paul Harris, emblem.

1995, May 8

2451 A343 $5 shown 4.25 4.25

Souvenir Sheet

2452 A343 $6 multicolored 5.00 5.00

Queen Mother, 95th Birthday — A344

No. 2453: a, Drawing. b, Holding flower. c, Formal portrait. d, Blue hat, white coat.
$6, As younger woman.

1995, May 8 ***Perf. 13½x14***

2453 A344 $1.50 Strip or block of 4, #a.-d. 6.75 6.75

Souvenir Sheet

2454 A344 $6 multicolored 6.25 6.25

No. 2453 was issued in sheets of 8 stamps.
Sheets of Nos. 2453 and 2454 exist with black border and text "In Memoriam 1900-2002" overprinted in sheet margins.

1996 Summer Olympics, Atlanta — A345

No. 2455: a, Tian Bingyi, China, badminton. b, Waldemar Leigien, Poland, Frank Wieneke, Germany, judo. c, Nelli Kim, USSR, women's gymnastics. d, Allessandro Andri, Italy, shot put.

No. 2456: a, Jackie Joyner, US, heptathlon. b, Mitsuo Tsukahara, Japan, gymnastics. c, Flo Hyman, US, Zhang Rung Fang, China, volleyball. d, Steffi Graf, Germany, tennis.

Each $6: No. 2457, Sailing. No. 2458, Wilma Rudolph, US, track.

1995, June 23

2455 A345 75c Strip of 4, #a.-d. 3.00 3.00

2456 A345 $2 Strip of 4, #a.-d. 7.75 7.75

Souvenir Sheets

2457-2458 A345 Set of 2 10.00 10.00

Anniversaries & Events — A346

25c, Junior Murray, cricket player. 75c, Spices. No. 2461, $1, Sendall Tunnel, cent. No. 2462, $1, Caribbean Development Bank, 25th anniv.

1995, Aug. 18 **Litho.** ***Perf. 14***

2459-2462 A346 Set of 4 3.50 3.50

Miniature Sheet

Trains of the World — A347

No. 2463: a, ETR 450, Italy. b, Isparta to Bozanonu, Turkey. c, TGV, France. d, ICE Inter-City Express, Germany. e, Nishi Nippon Rail, Japan. f, Bullet Train, Japan. g, Standard 4-4-0, Central Pacific RR, US. h, Amatrak 900 Bo-Bo Electric, US. i, Sir Nigel Gresley LNER, Great Britain.

No. 2464: a, Bi Level Vista Dome, Kinki Nippon Rail, Japan. b, Rolios Rail, South Africa. c, Class 160 Bo Bo, Switzerland. d, The Central, Peru. e, X2000 Tilt Body Train, Sweden. f, Toronto-Vancouver, Canada. g, Talisman 125 Class 31, Great Britain. h, Flying Scotsman, Great Britain. i, Indian Pacific, Australia.

$5, Diesel Hydraulic, Korea. $6, Trans-Mongolian Beijing to Ulan Bator.

1995, Sept. 5 **Sheet of 9, #a.-i.**

2463-2464 A347 $1 Set of 2 17.50 17.50

Souvenir Sheets

2465 A347 $5 multicolored 4.25 4.25

2466 A347 $6 multicolored 5.00 5.00

Singapore '95 (No. 2463).

Miniature Sheet

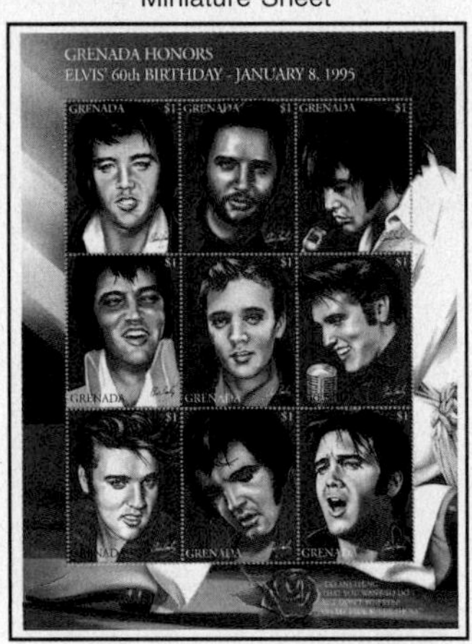

Elvis Presley (1935-77) — A348

Various portraits.

1995, Sept. 5 ***Perf. 13½x14***

2467 A348 $1 Sheet of 9, #a.-i. 7.50 7.50

A349

Motion Picture, Cent. — A350

No. 2470: a, Film reel, Oscar statuette. b, "HOLLYWOOD" sign. c, Charlie Chaplin. d, Shirley Temple. e, Spencer Tracy, Katherine Hepburn. f, Marilyn Monroe. g, John Wayne. h, Marlon Brando. i, Tom Cruise.
$5, Orson Welles as Citizen Kane, horiz.

1995, Sept. 5 ***Perf. 14***

2468 A349 75c Marilyn Monroe 1.00 1.00

2469 A349 75c Elvis Presley 1.00 1.00

Miniature Sheet

Perf. 13½x14

2470 A350 $1 Sheet of 9, #a.-i. 8.00 8.00

Souvenir Sheet

Perf. 14x13½

2471 A350 $5 multicolored 8.75 8.75

Nos. 2468-2469 were each issued in miniature sheets of 16. No. 2470 is a continuous design.

Local Entertainers A351

Designs: No. 2472, 35c, Ajamu, white outfit. No. 2473, 35c, Mighty Sparrow, blue suit. 50c, Mighty Sparrow, black tuxedo. 75c, Ajamu, checkered shirt, sailor hat.

1995, Sept. 5 **Litho.** ***Perf. 14***

2472-2475 A351 Set of 4 2.75 2.75

Miniature Sheets

Marine Life — A352

No. 2476: a, Yellowtail damselfish. b, Bluehead wrasse. c, Balloonfish. d, Shy hamlet. e, Orange tube coral. f, Rock beauty.

No. 2477: a, Creole wrasse. b, Queen angelfish. c, Trumpetfish (e, f). d, Barred hamlet. e, Tube sponge (b, f, h, i). f, Porcupine fish. g, Fire coral (d, e, h). h, Fairy basslet. i, Anemone.

Each $6: No. 2478, Elkhorn coral. No. 2479, Common seahorse, gulfweed.

1995, Apr. 24

2476 A352 $1 Sheet of 6, #a.-f. 5.25 5.25

2477 A352 $1 Sheet of 9, #a.-i. 7.25 7.25

Souvenir Sheets

2478-2479 A352 Set of 2 9.00 9.00

Issued: No. 2477, 2478, 4/24/95; Nos. 2476, 2479, 9/19/95.

Mickey's High Sea Adventure A353

Designs: 15c, Mickey sword fighting with pirate. 25c, Mickey with treasure chest. 35c, Minnie trying on jewelry from chest. 75c, Pluto with telescope, Mickey over barrel. $3, Pirate. $5, Mickey holding scarf with Minnie's name.

Each $6: No. 2486, Pirate fox fighting on ratlines. No. 2487, Minnie lowered from pirate ship to Mickey.

1995, Oct. 2 ***Perf. 13½x14***

2480-2485 A353 Set of 6 8.50 8.50

Souvenir Sheets

2486-2487 A353 Set of 2 10.00 10.00

Miniature Sheets

Nobel Prize Fund Established, Cent. — A354

Recipients: No. 2488a, Albert A. Michelson, physics, 1907. b, Ralph Bunche, peace, 1950. c, Edwin Neher, physiology or medicine, 1991. d, Klaus von Klitzing, physics, 1985. e, Johann Deisenhofer, chemistry, 1988. f, Max Delbrück, physiology or medicine, 1969. g, J. Georg Bednorz, physics, 1987. h, Feodor Lynen, physiology or medicine, 1964. i, Walther Bothe, physics, 1954.

No. 2489: a, Hans G. Dehmelt, physics, 1989. b, Heinrich Böll, literature, 1972. c, Georges Köhler, physiology or medicine, 1984. d, Wolfgang Pauli, physics, 1945. e, Sir Bernard Katz, physiology or medicine, 1970. f, Ernest Ruska, physics, 1986. g, William Golding, literature, 1983. h, Hartmut Michel, chemistry, 1988. i, Hans A. Bethe, physics, 1967.

No. 2490: a, James Franck, physics, 1925. b, Gustav Hertz, physics, 1925. c, Friedrich Bergius, chemistry, 1931. d, Otto Loewi, physiology or medicine, 1936. e, Fritz Lipmann, physiology or medicine, 1953. f, Otto Meyerhof, physiology or medicine, 1922. g, Paul Heyse, literature, 1910. h, Jane Addams, peace, 1931. i, Carl F. Braun, physics, 1909.

Each $6: No. 2491, Winston Churchill, literature, 1953. No. 2492, Woodrow Wilson, peace, 1919. No. 2493, Theodore Roosevelt, peace, 1906.

1995, Oct. 18 **Litho.** ***Perf. 14***

Sheets of 9, #a.-i.

2488-2490 A354 $1 Set of 3 25.00 25.00

Souvenir Sheets

2491-2493 A354 Set of 3 14.50 14.50

Teresa Teng, Chinese Entertainer A355

Nos. 2495-2496: Various portraits.

1995, Sept. 29
2494 A355 75c shown 1.00 1.00

Miniature Sheets

2495 A355 35c Sheet of 16, #a.-p. 5.50 5.50
2496 A355 75c Sheet of 9, #a.-i. 7.00 7.00

Nos. 2495a-2495p are 24x38mm.

Christmas A356

Details or entire paintings: 15c, The Madonna, by Montagna. 25c, Sacred Conversation Piece, by dei Pitati. 35c, Nativity, by Van Loo. 75c, The Virgin of the Fountain, Van Eyck. $2, Apparition of the Virgin, by Tiepolo. $5, The Holy Family, by Ribera.

Each $6: No. 1503, Madonna with the Christ Child, by Van Dyck. No. 1504, Vision of St. Anthony, by Van Dyck.

1995, Nov. 28 Litho. ***Perf. 13½x14***
2497-2502 A356 Set of 6 6.50 6.50

Souvenir Sheets

2503-2504 A356 Set of 2 10.50 10.50

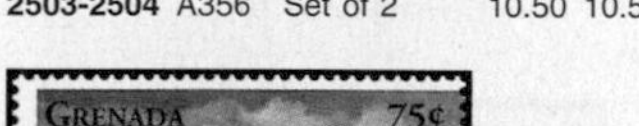

Liberation of Grenada, 12th Anniv. A357

US Pres. Ronald Reagan and: No. 2505: a, Fort George. b, US, Grenada flags. c, St. George. No. 2506, Island scene, map. No. 2507, Waterfall.

1995, Dec. 8 ***Perf. 14***
2505 A357 75c Strip of 3, #a.-c. 2.50 2.50

Souvenir Sheets

2506 A357 $5 multicolored 5.00 5.00
2507 A357 $6 multicolored 6.00 6.00

No. 2505 was issued in sheets of 9 stamps.

Pope John Paul II, 1995 Visit to New York City — A358

A358a

Pope John Paul II and: No. 2508, Statue of Liberty. No. 2509, St. Patrick's Cathedral. No. 2510, New York skyline.

1995, Dec. 13
2508 A358 $1 multicolored 1.00 1.00
2509 A358 $1 multicolored 1.00 1.00

Souvenir Sheet

2510 A358 $6 multicolored 5.25 5.25

Litho. & Embossed

Perf. 9

2510A A358a $30 gold & multi 32.50

Nos. 2508-2509 were each issued in sheets of 9.

New Year 1996 (Year of the Rat) — A359

Stylized rats: a, green & multi. b, red & multi. c, orange brown & multi.

$1, Two rats, horiz.

1996, Jan. 2 Litho. ***Perf. 14***
2511 A359 75c Strip of 3, #a.-c. 2.50 2.50

Miniature Sheet

2512 A359 75c Sheet of 1 #2511 2.50 2.50

Souvenir Sheet

2513 A359 $1 multicolored 1.75 1.75

No. 2511 was issued in sheets of 9 stamps.

Woodcuts by Dürer and Paintings by Rubens A360

Details or entire works: 15c, Young Woman, by Dürer. 25c, Four Horsemen from Apocalypse, by Dürer. 35c, Assumption and Coronation of Virgin, by Dürer. 75c, Mulay Ahmed, by Rubens. $1, Anthony Van Dyck Aged 15, by Rubens. $2, Head of a Young Monk, by Rubens. $3, A Scholar Inspired by Nature, by Rubens. $5, Hanns Dürer, by Dürer.

$5, Martrydom of St. Ursula, by Rubens. $6, The Death and Life of a Virgin, by Dürer.

1996. Jan. 29 Litho. ***Perf. 13½x14***
2514-2521 A360 Set of 8 10.50 10.50

Souvenir Sheets

2522 A360 $5 multicolored 5.00 5.00
2523 A360 $6 multicolored 5.50 5.50

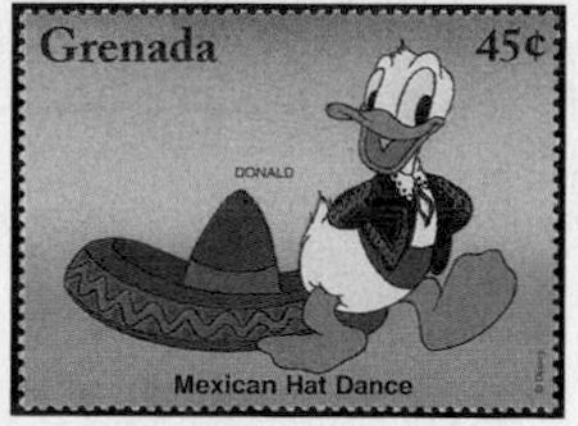

Disney Dancers — A361

Character, dance: 35c, Goofy, tap dance, vert. 45c, Donald, Mexican hat dance. 75c, Daisy, hula, vert. 90c, Mickey, Minnie, tango. $1, Daisy, Donald, jitterbug, vert. $2, Mickey, Minnie, Ukrainian folk dance. $3, Goofy, Pluto, ballet. $4, Minnie, Mickey, line dancing.

$5, Minnie, the can-can. $6, Scrooge McDuck, Scottish sword dance.

Perf. 13½x14, 14x 13½

1996, Feb. 26 Litho.
2524-2531 A361 Set of 8 11.50 11.50

Souvenir Sheets

2532 A361 $5 multicolored 5.00 5.00
2533 A361 $6 multicolored 6.00 6.00

Queen Elizabeth II, 70th Birthday — A362

Designs: No. 2534a, 35c, In blue dress. b, 75c, In white hat. c, $4, In black hat.

$6, Younger picture with Prince Phillip.

1996, May 8 Litho. ***Perf. 13½x14***
2534 A362 Strip of 3, #a.-c. 4.50 4.50

Souvenir Sheet

2535 A362 $6 multicolored 5.25 5.25

No. 2534 was issued in sheets of 9 stamps.

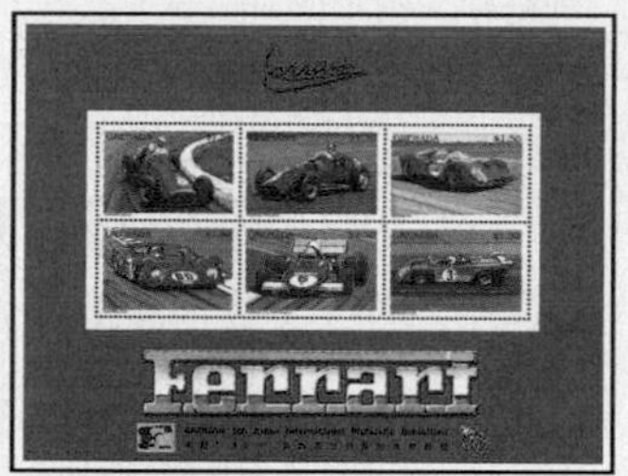

Ferrari Race Cars — A363

Designs: a, 125-F1. b, Tipo 625. c, P4. d, 312P. e, 312, Formula 1. f, 312B.

$6, F333 SP.

1996, May 8 ***Perf. 14***
2536 A363 $1.50 Sheet of 6, #a.-f. 10.00 10.00

Souvenir Sheet

2537 A363 $6 multicolored 5.75 5.75

China '96, 9th Asian Intl. Philatelic Exhibition (No. 2536). No. 2537 contains one 85x28mm stamp.

Modern Olympic Games, Cent. A364

Designs: 35c, 1896 Olympic Gold Medal, vert. 75c, Olympic Stadium, Athens, 1896. $2, Ancient Greek Olympic runners. $3, Spiridon Louis, 1896 marathon winner.

1996, May 8 Litho. ***Perf. 14***
2538-2541 A364 Set of 4 5.00 5.00

See Nos. 2599-2602.

Jerusalem, 3000th Anniv. — A365

Various city gates: 75c, $2, $3.

$5, Buildings inside city, horiz.

1996, June 26
2542-2544 A365 Set of 3 4.75 4.75

Souvenir Sheet

2545 A365 $5 multicolored 4.75 4.75

UNICEF, 50th Anniv. A366

Designs: 35c, Child writing in book. $2, Child planting seedling. $3, Faces of boy, girl.

$5, Boy, vert.

1996, June 26
2546-2548 A366 Set of 3 4.25 4.25

Souvenir Sheet

2549 A366 $5 multicolored 4.00 4.00

Radio, Cent. A367

Entertainers: 35c, Jack Benny. 75c, Gertrude Berg. $1, Eddie Cantor. $2, Groucho Marx.

$6, George Burns, Gracie Allen, horiz.

Perf. 13½x14, 14x13½

1996, June 26
2550-2553 A367 Set of 4 4.25 4.25

Souvenir Sheet

2554 A367 $6 multicolored 5.25 5.25

Classic Cars A368

No. 2555: a, 1939 Type 57C Atalante. b, 1900 Cannstatt-Daimler. c, 1925 Delage. d, 1899 Coventry Daimler. e, 1900 Vauxhall. f, 1912 T-15 Hispano-Suza.

No. 2556: a, 35c, 1929 Mercedes-Benz. b, 1935 J. Duesenberg. c, 1914 Mercer. d, 1927 Bugatti Type 35. e, 1929 Alfa Romeo. f, 1910 Rolls Royce.

Each $6: No. 2557, 1915 L-Head Mercer. No. 2558, 1937 Mercedes.

1996, July 25 Litho. ***Perf. 14***
2555 A368 $1 Sheet of 6, #a.-f. 5.00 5.00
2556 A368 Sheet of 6, #a.-f. 6.25 6.25

Souvenir Sheets

2557-2558 A368 Set of 2 10.50 10.50

Nos. 2557-2558 each contain one 57x43mm stamp.

Ships A369

War ships, No. 2559, each $1: a, Bounty, Britain, 1788. b, Bismark, Germany, 1941. c, Chuii Apoo, China, 1849. d, F224 Lubeck, Germany, 1970. e, Barbary Corsair, France, 1655. f, Augsburg, Germany, 1970. g, Henri Grace A Dieu, 1514, France. h, Prince of Wales, Britain, 1941. i, Santa Anna, Spain, 1512.

Sailing ships, each $1: No. 2560a, Gorch Fock, Germany, 1916. b, Henry B. Hyde, US, 1886. c, Resolution, Britain, 1652. d, USS Constitution, 1797. e, Nippon Maru, Japan,

1930. f, Preussen, Germany, 1902. g, Taeping, Britain, 1852. h, Chariot of Fame, US, 1853. i, Star of India, US, 1861.
$5, Victory, Britain, 1805. $6, Cutty Sark, Britain, 1869.

1996, Aug. 14 Sheets of 9, #a-i

2559-2560 A369 Set of 2 16.00 16.00

Souvenir Sheets

2561 A369 $5 multicolored 4.50 4.50
2562 A369 $6 multicolored 5.25 5.25

Trains A370

Designs: 35c, C51 Imperial Train, Japan. 75c, Reingold, Germany. $2, Pioneer, US. $3, LA France, France.
Trains of the Orient, each $1: No. 2567: a, C62 4-6-4, Japanese Natl. Railways. b, 4-6-0, Shantung Railways, China. c, C57 Light 4-6-2, Japanese Natl. Railways. d, Diesel Express, Japanese Natl. Railways. e, 4-6-2, Shanghai-Nanking Railway, China. f, 051 2-8-2, Japanese Natl. Railways.
Trains of the world, each $1: No. 2568a, Atlantic Coast Line, US. b, #1619, Pioneer Smith Compound, England. c, 4-8-4 Trans-Siberian Railway. d, "Atlantic type," Palatinate Railway, Germany. e, 4-6-0 Paris, Lyons and Mediterranean Railway, France. f, 0341 Diesel Electric, Italian State Railways.
$5, Baden State Railways, Germany. $6, C11 2-6-4, Japanese National Railways.

1996, Aug. 28

2563-2566 A370 Set of 4 4.50 4.50

Sheets of 6, #a-f

2567-2568 A370 Set of 2 9.00 9.00

Souvenir Sheets

2569 A370 $5 multicolored 4.25 4.25
2570 A370 $6 multicolored 5.00 5.00

Flowers A371

No. 2571, each $1: a, Winter jasmine. b, Chrysanthemum. c, Lilac. d, Japanese iris. e, Hibiscus. f, Sacred lotus. g, Apple blossom. h, Gladiolus. i, Japanese quince.
No. 2572, vert, each $1: a, Canterbury bell. b, Rose. c, Nasturtium. d, Daffodil. e, Tulip. f, Snapdragon. g, Zinnia. h, Sweetpea. i, Pansy.
$5, Aster. $6, Peony, vert.

1996, Sept. 9 Litho. *Perf. 14*

Sheets of 9, #a-i

2571-2572 A371 Set of 2 15.00 15.00

Souvenir Sheets

2573 A371 $5 multicolored 5.00 5.00
2574 A371 $6 multicolored 5.50 5.50

Zeppelins A372

No. 2575: a, 30c, L31, Germany. b, 30c, L35, Germany. c, 50c, L30, Germany. d, 75c, LZ10, Germany. e, $3, L3, Germany. f, $3, Beardmore No. 24, British.
No. 2576: a, Zeppelin L21, Germany. b, Zodiac Type 13 Spiess, France. c, NI "Norge." d, D-LZ 127 "Graf Zeppelin," Germany. e, D-LZ 129 "Hindenburg," Germany. f, Zeppelin NT, Germany, 1996.
Each $6: No. 2577, L13, Germany. No. 2578, Zeppelin ZT, Germany.

1996, Sept. 9 Sheets of 6

2575 A372 #a.-f. 7.50 7.50
2576 A372 $1.50 #a.-f. 8.00 8.00

Souvenir Sheets

2577-2578 A372 Set of 2 10.00 10.00

Birds A373

No. 2579: a, Horned guan. b, St. Lucia parrot. c, Black penelopina. d, Grenada dove. e, St. Vincent parrot. f, White-breasted thrasher.
$5, Barbados yellow warbler. $6, Semper's warbler.

1996

2579 A373 $1.50 Sheet of 6, #a.-f. 8.75 8.75

Souvenir Sheets

2580 A373 $5 multicolored 4.50 4.50
2581 A373 $6 multicolored 5.25 5.25

Endangered Species — A374

Designs: a, Blue whale. b, Humpback whale. c, Right whale. d, Hawksbill turtle. e, Leatherback turtle. f, Green turtle.

1996, Sept. 18 Litho. *Perf. 14*

2582 A374 $1.50 Sheet of 6, #a.-f. 11.50 11.50

Jacqueline Kennedy Onassis (1929-94) — A375

Various portraits.

1996, Aug. 26

2583 A375 $1 Sheet of 9, #a.-i. 8.75 8.75

Souvenir Sheet

2584 A375 $6 multicolored 5.25 5.25

Butterfly Type of 1994

90c, Tropical chequered skipper. $1.50, Godman's hairstreak.

1996, Nov. 7 Litho. *Perf. 12*

2585 A328 90c multicolored .80 .80
2586 A328 $1.50 multicolored 1.25 1.25

A376

Sea Creatures: No. 2587, each $1: a, Killer whale. b, Dolphin. c, Dolphins. d, Sea lion, royal angelfish. e, Dolphins, hawksbill turtle. f, Hawksbill turtles (e). g, Royal angelfish. h, Pennant butterflyfish. i, Sea lion, squirrel fish.
No. 2588, each $1: a, Brown pelican. b, Killer whale. c, Whale (c). d, Dolphins, sea lion. e, Shortfin pilot whale, blue ringed octopus, sea lion (d, f, h). f, Hammerhead sharks, sea lion. g, Blue striped grunts. h, Stingray, Van Gogh fusiliers (i). i, Van Gogh fusiliers, golden coney, ribbon moray eel (h).
Each $6: No. 2589, Sea lions, horiz. No. 2590, Dolphins, horiz.

1996, Nov. 7 *Perf. 14*

Sheets of 9, #a-i

2587-2588 A376 Set of 2 16.00 16.00

Souvenir Sheets

2589-2590 A376 Set of 2 10.00 10.00

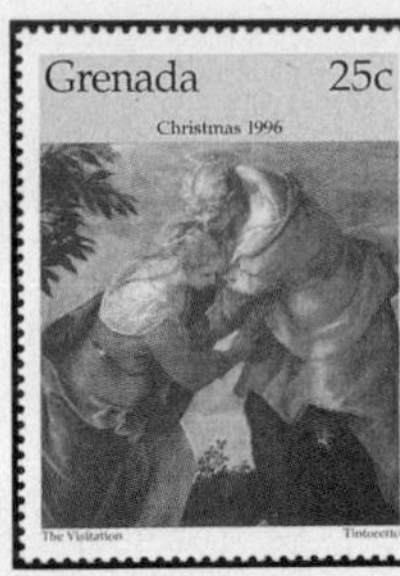

Christmas A377

Details or entire paintings: 25c, The Visitation, by Tintoretto. 35c, Virgin with the Child, by Palma Vecchio. 50c, The Adoration of the Magi, by Botticeli. 75c, The Annunciation, by Titian. $1, The Flight into Egypt, by Tintoretto. $3, The Holy Family with the Infant Saint John, by Andrea Del Sarto.
Each $6: No. 2597, Adoration of the Magi, by Paolo Schiavo. No. 2598, Madonna and Child with Saints, by Vincenzo Foppa.

1996, Nov. 18 *Perf. 13½x14*

2591-2596 A377 Set of 6 5.50 5.50

Souvenir Sheets

2597-2598 A377 Set of 2 10.50 10.50

Modern Olympic Games Type of 1996

Marathon medalists: No. 2599: a, Boughera El Quafi, 1928. b, Gustav Jansson, 1952. c, Spiridon Louis, 1896. d, Basil Heatley, 1964. e, Emil Zatopek, 1952. f, Frank Shorter, 1972. g, Alain Mimoun, 1956. h, Kokichi Tsuburaya, 1964. i, Delfo Cabrera, 1948.
Weight lifting medalists: No. 2600: a, Harald Sakata, 1948. b, Tom Kono, 1952. c, Naim Suleymanoglu, 1988. d, Lee Hyung Kun, 1988. e, Vassily Alexeyev, 1972. f, Chen Weiqiang, 1984. g, Ye Huanming, 1988. h, Manfred Nerlinger, 1984. i, Joseph Depietro, 1948.
$5, Manfred Nerlinger, vert. $6, Thomas Hicks, 1904, vert.

1996, July 8 Litho. *Perf. 14*

Sheets of 9

2599-2600 A364 $1 #a.-i., each 7.75 7.75

Souvenir Sheets

2601 A364 $5 multicolored 4.25 4.25
2602 A364 $6 multicolored 5.00 5.00

US Pres. Ronald Reagan A378

Various portraits.

1996, Aug. 26 *Perf. 13½*

2603 A378 $1 Sheet of 9, #a.-i. 7.25 7.25

Sylvester Stallone in Movie, "Rocky" — A379

1996, Nov. 21 Litho. *Perf. 14*

2604 A379 $2 Sheet of 3 5.25 5.25

New Year 1997 (Year of the Ox) — A380

Oxen: Nos. 2605a, 2606a, Horns pointed down. Nos. 2605b, 2606b, Horns pointed up. Nos. 2605c, 2606c, Shown.

Self-Adhesive

Serpentine Die Cut 11

1997, Jan. 2 Litho. Sheets of 3

2605 A380 $2 #a.-c., gold & multi 4.50 4.50
2606 A380 $2 #a.-c., sil & multi 4.50 4.50

Mickey Visits Hong Kong — A381

No. 2607: a, Pet birds. b, Kung-fu tea. c, Chinese Wet Market. d, Handmade grasshopper. e, Mid-Autumn Festival. f, Tai-chi.
No. 2608: a, 35c, Tram. b, 50c, Victoria Harbor. c, 75c, Buddha. d, 90c, Bank of China. e, $2, Bottle gas. f, $3, Seafood restaurant.
No. 2609, Mickey at The Peak, vert. $4, Minnie, Mickey, Hong Kong mail, vert. $5, Mickey pulling rickshaw, vert. $6, Mickey at Peking Noodle Show, vert.

1997, Feb. 12 Litho. *Perf. 14x13½*

2607 A381 $1 Sheet of 6, #a.-f. 7.00 7.00
2608 A381 Sheet of 6, #a.-f. 8.75 8.75

Souvenir Sheets

Perf. 13½x14

2609 A381 $3 multicolored 3.50 3.50
2610 A381 $4 multicolored 4.25 4.25
2611 A381 $5 multicolored 5.25 5.25
2612 A381 $6 multicolored 6.00 6.00

Hong Kong '97.

UNESCO, 50th Anniv. — A382

Designs: 35c, Kyoto, Japan. 75c, Quedlinburg, Germany. 90c, Dubrovnik, Croatia. $1, Ruins, Delphi, Greece. $2, Tomar, Portugal. $3, Palace of Chaillot, Paris, France.
No. 2619, Chinese sites, vert, each $1: a, Entrance to caves, Desert of Taklamakan. b, House, Taklamakan. c, Monument, Taklamakan. d, Palace of Cielos Purpuras, Wudang. e, House, Wudang. f, Stone Guard, Great Wall. g, Ming Dynasty, Wudang. h, Section, Great Wall.
No. 2620, vert, each $1: a, Bryggen Wharf, Bergen, Norway. b, Old City of Bern, Switzerland. c, Warsaw, Poland. d, Fortress Walls, Luxembourg. e, Palace of Drottningholm, Sweden. f, Petäj ävesi Old Church, Finland. g, Vilnius, Lithuania. h, Church of Jelling, Denmark.
No. 2621: a, Cathedral, Segovia, Spain. b, Würzburg, Germany. c, Lakes of Plitvice, Croatia. d, Monastery of Batalha, Portugal. e, River Seine, Paris, France.
Each $6: No. 2622, Monastery of Popocatepetl, Mexico. No. 2623, Shirakami-Sanchi, Japan. No. 2624, Monastery of the Hieronymites and Tower of Belem, Portugal.

1997, Apr. 3 Litho. *Perf. 14*

2613-2618 A382 Set of 6 7.50 7.50

Sheets of 8 or 5 + Label

2619-2620 A382 Set of 2 15.00 15.00
2621 A382 $1.50 #a.-e. 7.00 7.00

Souvenir Sheets

2622-2624 A382 Set of 3 11.00 11.00

Cats — A383

Cats: 35c, Devon rex. 90c, Japanese bobtail. $2, Cornish rex.
No. 2628: a, Turkish van. b, Ragdoll. c, Siberian. d, Egyptian mau. e, American shorthair. f, Bengal. g, Asian longhair. h, Somali. i, Turkish angora.

1997, Apr. 10
2625-2627 A383 Set of 3 3.50 3.50
Sheet of 9
2628 A383 $1 #a.-i. 8.50 8.50
Souvenir Sheet
2629 A383 $6 Singapura 5.75 5.75

Dogs — A384

Dogs: 75c, Cavalier King Charles spaniel. $1, Afghan hound. $3, Pekingese.
No. 2633: a, Lhasa apso. b, Rough collie. c, Norwich terrier. d, America cocker spaniel. e, Chinese crested dog. f, Old English sheepdog. g, Standard poodle. h, German shepherd. i, German shorthaired pointer.
No. 2634, Bernese mountain dog.

1997, Apr. 10
2630-2632 A384 Set of 3 4.00 4.00
Sheet of 9
2633 A384 $1 #a.-i. 8.50 8.50
Souvenir Sheet
2634 A384 $6 multicolored 5.75 5.75

Prehistoric Animals — A385

Designs: 35c, Dunkleosteus. 75c, Tyrannosaurus rex. $2, Askeptosaurus, vert. $3, Triceratops, vert.
No. 2639: a, Sordes. b, Dimorphodon. c, Diplodocus. d, Allosaurus. e, Pentaceratops. f, Protoceratops.
Each $6: No. 2640, Maiasaura, vert. No. 2641, Tristychius, Cladoselache, vert.

1997, Apr. 15
2635-2638 A385 Set of 4 6.50 6.50
2639 A385 $1.50 Sheet of 6, #a.-f. 8.25 8.25
Souvenir Sheets
2640-2641 A385 Set of 2 12.50 12.50

Marine Life A386

Designs: 45c, Porcelain crab. 75c, Humpback whale. 90c, Hermit crab. $1, Great white shark. $3, Green sea turtle. $4, Whale shark.
No. 2648, vert: a, Octopus. b, Lei triggerfish. c, Lionfish. d, Harlequin wrasse. e, Clown fish. f, Moray eel.
Each $6: No. 2649, Pacific barracudas. No. 2650, Scalloped hammerhead shark.

1997, May 2
2642-2647 A386 Set of 6 9.00 9.00
2648 A386 $1.50 Sheet of 6, #a.-f. 8.50 8.50
Souvenir Sheets
2649-2650 A386 Set of 2 11.50 11.50

Queen Elizabeth II, Prince Philip, 50th Wedding Anniv. A386a

No. 2651: a, Queen, Prince waving. b, Royal Arms. c, Formal portrait in royal attire. d, Formal portrait in street clothes. e, Windsor Castle. f, Prince Philip.
$6, Formal portrait in royal attire, diff.

1997, May 28 Litho. *Perf. 14*
2651 A386a $1 Sheet of 6, #a.-f. 6.00 6.00
Souvenir Sheet
2652 A386a $6 multicolored 6.00 6.00

Paintings by Hiroshige (1797-1858) A387

No. 2653: a, Nihon Embankment, Yoshiwara. b, Asakusa Ricefields and Torinomachi Festival. c, Senju Great Bridge. d, Dawn Inside the Yoshiwara. e, Tile Kilns and Hasiba Ferry, Sumida River. f, View from Massaki of Suijin Shrine, Uchigawa Inlet and Sekiya.
Each $6: No. 2654, Kinryuzan Temple, Asakusa. No. 2655, Night View of Saruwakamachi.

1997, May 28 *Perf. 13½x14*
2653 A387 $1.50 Sheet of 6, #a.-f. 9.50 9.50
Souvenir Sheets
2654-2655 A387 Set of 2 11.50 11.50

Heinrich von Stephan (1831-97), Founder of UPU A388

No. 2656: a, Postal delivery on motorcycle. b, UPU emblem. c, Postal delivery on skis and snowshoes, Rockies, 1900. $6, Chinese long distance carrier.

1997, May 28 Litho. *Perf. 14*
2656 A388 $2 Sheet of 3, #a.-c. 6.00 6.00
Souvenir Sheet
2657 A388 $6 multicolored 6.00 6.00
PACIFIC 97.

Paul P. Harris (1868-1947), Founder of Rotary, Intl. — A389

Designs: $3, Rotary emblem, vocational training service program, The Philippines, portrait of Harris.
$6, Doves, hands holding globe inscribed "Act with Integrity, Serve with love, Work for Peace".

1997, May 28
2658 A389 $3 multicolored 2.75 2.75
Souvenir Sheet
2659 A389 $6 multicolored 5.25 5.25

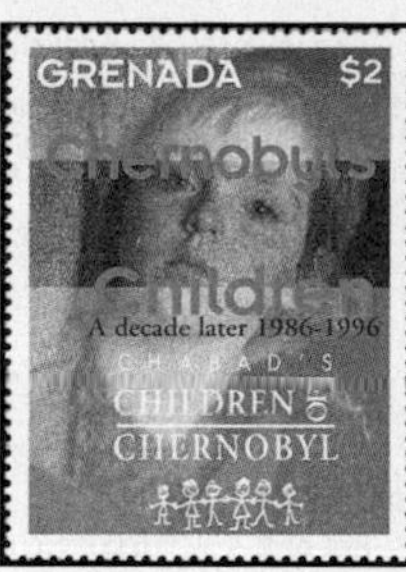

Chernobyl Disaster, 10th Anniv. A390

Designs: No. 2660, Chabad's Children of Chernobyl. No. 2661, UNESCO.

1997, May 28 *Perf. 13½x14*
2660 A390 $2 multicolored 2.00 2.00
2661 A390 $2 multicolored 2.00 2.00

Grimm's Fairy Tales A391

Mother Goose — A392

Scenes from "Snow White and the Seven Dwarfs:" No. 2662: a, Witch as woman looking into mirror. b, Dwarfs looking at Snow White as she sleeps. c, Snow White awakening, Prince. $6, Witch holding out apple for Snow White.
$5, "Little Johnny" walking in rain with umbrella.

1997, May 28 *Perf. 13½x14*
2662 A391 $2 Sheet of 3, #a.-c. 6.25 6.25
Souvenir Sheets
Perf. 14, 13½x14
2663 A392 $5 multicolored 4.00 4.00
2664 A391 $6 multicolored 5.00 5.00

1998 Winter Olympics Games, Nagano A393

Designs: 45c, Luge. 75c, Speed skater in red. $2, Male figure skater. $3, Slalom skier.
No. 2669: a, Luge, diff. b, Ski jumper. c, Downhill skier. d, Speed skater in blue. e, Two-man bobsled. f, Female figure skater. g, Biathlon. h, Hockey. i, Freestyle skier upside down.
Each $6: No. 2670, Downhill skier in air, vert. No. 2671, 4-Man bobsled.

1997, June 26 *Perf. 14*
2665-2668 A393 Set of 4 6.50 6.50
2669 A393 $1 Sheet of 9, #a.-i. 9.00 9.00
Souvenir Sheets
2670-2671 A393 Set of 2 11.50 11.50

Return of Hong Kong to China — A394

Views of city, Chinese flag as Chinese inscription: 90c, Bank of China, night scene. $1, Skyscrapers. $1.75, "Hong Kong," city in lights, horiz. $2, Deng Xiaoping (1904-97), Hong Kong, horiz.

1997, July 1
2672-2675 A394 Set of 4 7.00 7.00
Nos. 2672-2673 were issued in sheets of 4. Nos. 2674-2675 are 59x28mm and were issued in sheets of 3.

Disney's Hercules A395

No. 2676: a, Hercules. b, Pegasus. c, Megara. d, Philoctetes. e, Nessus. f, Hydra. g, Pain and Panic. h, Hades.
Each $6: No. 2677, Young Hercules. No. 2678, Calliope surrounded by Terpsichore, Melpomene, Clio, Thalia.

1997, Aug. 7 Litho. *Perf. 13½x14*
2676 A395 $1 Sheet of 8, #a.-h. 7.75 7.75
Souvenir Sheets
2677-2678 A396 Set of 2 13.00 13.00

Butterflies A396

Designs: 45c, Peacock. 75c, Orange flambeau. 90c, Eastern tailed blue. $2, Black and red. $3, Large white. $4, Oriental swallowtail.
No. 2685: a, Brimstone. b, Mocker swallowtail. c, American painted lady. d, Tiger swallowtail. e, Long wing. f, Sunset moth. g, Australian blue mountain swallowtail. h, Bird wing.
Each $5: No. 2686, Monarch. No. 2687, Blue morpho.

1997, Aug. 12 *Perf. 14*
2679-2684 A396 Set of 6 10.00 10.00
2685 A396 $1 Sheet of 8, #a.-h. 7.50 7.50
Souvenir Sheets
2686-2687 A396 Set of 2 10.50 10.50

1998 World Cup Soccer Championships, France — A397

Various actions scenes from Italy v. West Germany, 1982. 15c, 75c, 90c, $2, $3, $4, vert.

Winning teams: No. 2694, each $1: a, Uruguay. b, Brazil, 1958. c, Germany. d, Argentina. e, Italy. f, West Germany. g, Italy. h, Brazil, 1970.

Soccer players: No. 2695, each $1: a, Seaman, England. b, Klinsmann, Germany. c, Berger, Czech Rep. d, McCoist, Scotland. e, Gascoigne, England. f, Djorkaeff, France. g, Sammer, Germany. h, Futre, Portugal.

Each $6: No. 2696, Beckenbauer, Germany, vert. No. 2697, Moore, England.

1997 ***Perf. 13½x14***

2688-2693 A397 Set of 6 10.00 10.00

Sheets of 8, #a-h

Perf. 14x13½

2694-2695 A397 Set of 2 14.50 14.50

Souvenir Sheets

2696-2697 A397 Set of 2 12.00 12.00

Minnie Mouse in Hawaiian Holiday — A398

Stamps in flip book sequence showing Minnie doing Hula dance: No. 2698: a, 1. b, 2. c, 3. d, 4. e, 5. f, 6. g, 7. h, 8.

No. 2699: a, 9. b, 10. c, 11. d, 12. e, 13. f, 14. g, 15. h, 16. i, 17.

$6, 18.

1997, Aug. 7 Litho. ***Perf. 14x13½***

Sheets of 8 or 9

2698 A398 50c #a.-h. + label 5.50 5.50

2699 A398 50c #a.-i. 6.00 6.00

Souvenir Sheet

2700 A398 $6 multicolored 8.50 8.50

PACIFIC 97.

Mushrooms — A399

Designs: 35c, Boletus erythropus. 75c, Armillariella mellea. 90c, Amanita flavorubens. $1, Indigo milky. $2, Tylopilus balloui. $4, Boletus parasiticus.

No. 2707, each $1.50: a, Boletus parasiticus, diff. b, Frostis bolete. c, Amanita myscara flavilolvata. d, Volvariella volvacea. e, Stuntz's blue legs. f, Orange-latex milky.

No. 2708, each $1.50: a, Agaricus solidipes. b, Salmon waxy cap. c, Fused marasmius. d, Shellfish-scented russula. e, Red-capped scaber stalk. f, Calocybe tricholoma gambosum.

Each $6: No. 2709, Omphalotus illudens. No. 2710, Agaricus agrenteus.

1997, Sept. 4 ***Perf. 14***

2701-2706 A399 Set of 6 8.75 8.75

Sheets of 6, #a-f

2707-2708 A399 Set of 2 16.50 16.50

Souvenir Sheets

2709-2710 A399 Set of 2 11.50 11.50

Orchids A400

Designs: 20c, Paphiopedilum urbanianum. 35c, Trichoceros parviflorus. 45c, Euanthe sanderiana, vert. 75c, Oncidium macranthum, vert. 90c, Psychopsis kramerianum, vert. $1, Oncidium hastatum, vert. $3, Masdevallia saltatrix, vert. $4, Cattleya luteola.

No. 2719, vert, each $2: a, Odontoglossum crispum. b, Cattleya brabantiae. c, Cattleya bicolor. d, Trichopilia suavia. e, Encyclia mariae. f, Angraecum leonis.

No. 2720, vert, each $2: a, Broughtonia sanguinea. b, Anguloa virginalis. c, Dendrobium Bigibbum. d, T. forcia, L. lucasiana. e, Cymbidium. f, Cymbidium, diff.

Each $6: No. 2721, Oncidium onustum. No. 2722, Laelia milleri.

1997, Sept. 4

2711-2718 A400 Set of 8 13.00 13.00

Sheets of 6, #a-f

2719-2720 A400 Set of 2 26.00 26.00

Souvenir Sheets

2721-2722 A400 Set of 2 15.00 15.00

Diana, Princess of Wales (1961-97) — A401

Various portraits.

1997, Oct. 15 Litho. ***Perf. 14½***

2723 A401 $1.50 Sheet of 6, #a.-f. 7.75 7.75

Souvenir Sheet

2724 A401 $5 multicolored 4.75 4.75

Christmas — A402

Works of art, entire paintings, or details: 35c, Angel, by Matthias Grunewald. 50c, Saint Demetrius (icon). 75c, Reliquary in the Form of a Triptych. $1, Angel of the Annunciation, by Jan van Eyck. $3, The Annunciation, by Simone Martini. $4, Saint Michael (mosaic).

Each $6: No. 2731, The Annunciation, by Titian, horiz. No. 2732, The Coronation of the Virgin, by Fra Angelico.

1997, Dec. 5 Litho. ***Perf. 14***

2725-2730 A402 Set of 6 8.75 8.75

Souvenir Sheets

2731-2732 A402 Set of 2 12.50 12.50

New Year 1998 (Year of the Tiger) — A403

Designs: a, shown, b, With mouth open. c, With ears rolled back.

1998, Jan. 5 Litho. ***Die Cut Perf. 9***

Self-Adhesive

Sheets of 3, #a.-c.

2733 A403 $1.50 gold & multi *30.00*

2734 A403 $1.50 sil & multi *30.00*

Nos. 2733b, 2734b have point of triangle down.

Fish A404

65c, Black-tailed humbug. 90c, Yellow sweetlips. $1, Common squrrelfish. $2, Powder blue surgeon.

No. 2739, each $1.50: a, Blue tang. b, Porkfish. c, Banded butterflyfish. d, Threadfin butterflyfish. e, Red-headed. f, Emperor angelfish.

No. 2740, each $1.50: a, Scribbled angelfish. b, Lemonpeel angelfish. c, Bandit angelfish. d, Bicolor cherub. e, Regal tang. f, Yellow tang.

Each $6: No. 2741, Two-banded anemonefish. No. 2742, Long-nosed butterflyfish.

1998, Feb. 10 Litho. ***Perf. 14***

2735-2738 A404 Set of 4 6.00 6.00

Sheets of 6, #a.-f.

2739-2740 A404 Set of 2 18.50 18.50

Souvenir Sheets

2741-2742 A404 Set of 2 15.00 15.00

Orchids A405

No. 2743, each $1.50: a, Arachnis clarkei. b, Cymbidium eburneum. c, Dendrobium chrysotoxum. d, Paphiopedilum insigne. e, Paphiopedilum venustum. f, Renanthera imschootiana.

No. 2744, each $1.50: a, Sophronitis grandiflora. b, Phalaenopsis amboinensis. c, Zygopetalum intermedium. d, Paphiopedilum purpuratum. e, Miltonia regnellii. f, Dendrobium parishii.

Each $6: No. 2745, Lycaste aromatica. No. 2746, Pleione maculata.

1998, Apr. 21 Litho. ***Perf. 14***

Sheets of 6, #a.-f.

2743-2744 A405 Set of 2 21.00 21.00

Souvenir Sheets

2745-2746 A405 Set of 2 14.00 14.00

Ships A406

No. 2747, each $1: a, Brig. b, Clipper. c, Caique. d, Mississippi Riverboat. e, Luxury liner. f, The Mayflower. g, Frigate. h, Janggolan. i, Junk.

No. 2748, each $1: a, Dhow. b, Galleon. c, Felucca. d, Schooner. e, Aircraft carrier. f, Knau. g, Destroyer. h, Longship. i, Queen Elizabeth 2.

Each $6: No. 2749, The Lusitania. No. 2750, Submarine.

1998, Apr. 26 Litho. ***Perf. 14***

Sheets of 9, #a-i

2747-2748 A406 Set of 2 19.00 19.00

Souvenir Sheets

2749-2750 A406 Set of 2 12.50 12.50

No. 2749 contains one 85x28mm stamp; No. 2750 one 56x42mm stamp.

Disney's Hercules A407

Hercules grows up — No. 2751: a, Hercules, Zeus. b, Hercules and Pegasus walking past creature. c, Phil, Hercules. d, Hercules swinging through air. e, Centaur carrying captured Meg. f, Hercules attacking centaur. g, Hercules fighting lion. h, Hercules, Pegasus looking at prints.

Birth and childhood of Hercules — No. 2752, each $1: a, Zeus and Hera with newborn Hercules. b, Hades finds baby. c, Hades in the night. d, Baby sleeping. e, Baby swept away by Pain and Panic. f, Old couple with Baby Hercules. g, Hercules pulling cart. h, Hercules looking into mirror.

Hercules triumphant — No. 2753, each $1: a, Hercules carrying Meg. b, Meg, Hades. c, Hercules being trained by Phil. d, Hercules meeting Hades. e, Monster coming through city. f, Zeus. g, Hercules lifting column off Meg. h, Hercules diving into water.

Each $6: No. 2754, Hercules with sword, fighting Hydra. No. 2755, Hades on fire. No. 2756, Hercules, Meg on Pegasus, horiz. No. 2757, Zeus, Hercules, horiz. No. 2758, Hades. No. 2759, Zeus with baby Pegasus.

1998, June 16 Litho. ***Perf. 13½x14***

Sheets of 8

2751 A407 10c #a.-h. 3.75 3.75

2752-2753 A407 Set of 2 19.00 19.00

Souvenir Sheets

2754-2759 A407 Set of 6 40.00 40.00

Sea Birds — A408

Designs: 90c, Arctic skua. $1.10, Humboldt penguin. $2, Herring gull. $3, Red knot.

No. 2764, horiz.: a, Northern fulmar. b, Black-legged kittiwake. c, Cape petrel. d, Mediterranean gull. e, Brandt's cormorant (h). f, Greater shearwater. g, Black-footed albatross. h, Red-necked phalarope. i, Black skimmer (f).

Each $5: No. 2765, Black-browed albatross. No. 2766, King penguin.

1998, June 30 Litho. ***Perf. 14***

2760-2763 A408 Set of 4 6.00 6.00

2764 A408 $1 Sheet of 9, #a.-i. 10.00 10.00

Souvenir Sheets

2765-2766 A408 Set of 2 11.50 11.50

Diana, Princess of Wales (1961-97) — A409

Portrait of Diana with rose: No. 2767, Wearing hat. No. 2768, Without hat.

Litho. & Embossed

1998, July 14 ***Die Cut 7½***

2767 A409 $20 gold & multi

2768 A409 $20 gold & multi

Supermarine Spitfires — A410

No. 2769, each $1.50: a, MK IX. b, MK XIV. c, MK XII. d, MK XI. e, H.F. MK VIII. f, MK VB.

No. 2770, each $1.50: a, MK I. b, MK VIII. c, MK III. d, MK XVI. e, MK V. f, MK XIX.

Each $6: No. 2771, MK IX. No. 2772, MK IA.

1998, July 20 Litho. ***Perf. 14***

Sheets of 6, #a.-f.

2769-2770 A410 Set of 2 15.00 15.00

Souvenir Sheets

2771-2772 A410 Set of 2 12.00 12.00

Nos. 2771-2772 each contain one 57x43mm stamp.

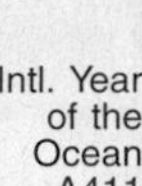

Intl. Year of the Ocean A411

No. 2773: a, Walrus. b, African black footed penguins. c, African black-footed penguin. d, California sea lion. e, Green turtle. f, Redfin anthias. g, Sperm whale. h, French angelfish, Australian sea lion. i, Jellyfish. j, Sawfish. k, Male and female cuckoo wrasse. l, Garibaldi. m, Spinecheek anemonefish. n, Leafy seadragon. o, Blue-spotted goatfish. p, Two-spot gobies.
No. 2774, Atlantic spotted dolphins. No. 2775, Octopus.

1998, Aug. 19
2773 A411 75c Sheet of 16, #a.-p. 13.50 13.50

Souvenir Sheets
2774 A411 $5 multicolored 5.00 5.00
2775 A411 $6 multicolored 6.25 6.25

CARICOM, 25th Anniv. — A412

1998, Sept. 15 Litho. *Perf. 13½*
2776 A412 $1 multicolored 1.10 1.10

Mahatma Gandhi (1869-1948) A413

Design: $6, Portrait, head down.

1998, Sept. 13 *Perf. 14*
2777 A413 $1 multicolored 1.50 1.50

Souvenir Sheet
2778 A413 $6 multicolored 6.50 6.50

No. 2777 was issued in sheets of 4.

Paintings by Pablo Picasso (1881-1973) — A414

45c, The Bathers, 1918, vert. $2, Luncheon on the Grass, 1960. $3, The Swimmer, 1929. $5, Woman Reading, 1944, vert.

Perf. 14½x14, 14x14½
1998, Sept. 15
2779-2781 A414 Set of 3 [illegible]

Souvenir Sheet
2782 A414 $5 multicolored 5.25 5.25

Paintings by Eugéne Delacroix (1798-1863) — A415

No. 2783: a, Horsemen Fighting in the Plain. b, The Assassination of the Bishop of Liege. c, Still-life with Lobsters. d, The Battle of Nancy. e, The Shipwreck of Don Juan. f, The Death of Ophelia. g, Attila and the Barbarians. h, Entertaining the Arabians.
$5, Entry of the Crusaders into Constantinople.

1998, Sept. 15 *Perf. 14*
Sheet of 8
2783 A415 $1 #a.-h. 7.75 7.75

Souvenir Sheet
2784 A415 $5 multicolored 5.25 5.25

Organization of American States, 50th Anniv. A416

1998, Sept. 15 Litho. *Perf. 14*
2785 A416 $1 multicolored 1.10 1.10

Diana, Princess of Wales (1961-97) A417

1998 *Perf. 14½*
2786 A417 $1 multicolored 1.25 1.25

Self-Adhesive
Serpentine Die Cut Perf. 11½
Sheet of 1
Size: 52x65mm
2786A A417 $6 Diana, buildings *6.00*

No. 2786 was issued in sheets of 6.
Soaking in water may affect the multi-layer image of No. 2786A.
Issued: $1, 9/15; $6, 11/5/98.

Enzo Ferrari (1898-1988), Automobile Manufacturer — A418

No. 2787: a, 250 GT Berlinetta Lusso. b, 250 GTO. c, 250 GT Boano/Ellena cabriolet.
$5, Dino 246 GTS.

1998, Sept. 15 *Perf. 14*
2787 A418 $2 Sheet of 3, #a.-c. 6.00 6.00

Souvenir Sheet
2788 A418 $5 multicolored 6.00 6.00

No. 2786 was issued in sheets of 6. No. 2788 contains one 91x35mm stamp.

1998 World Scouting Jamboree, Chile — A419

Designs: $2, Scout salute. $3, World Scout flag. $4, Scout first aid. $6, World Scout flag.

1998, Sept. 15
2789-2791 A419 Set of 3 8.75 8.75

Souvenir Sheet
2792 A419 $6 multi, horiz. 7.00 7.00

Royal Air Force, 80th Anniv. A420

No. 2793, each $2: a, Vickers Supermarine Spitfire Mk2a. b, Vickers Supermarine Spitfire HF Mk1XB flying right. c, Vickers Supermarine Spitfire HF Mk1Xb flying left. d, Hawker Hurricane 11C.
No. 2794, each $2: a, EF-2000 Eurofighter prototype. b, Nimrod MR2P. c, Eurofighter 2000, diff. d, C-47 Dakota.
Each $6: No. 2795, Eurofighter 2000, VC10. No. 2796, Biplane, hawk's head. No. 2797, Biplane, hawk. No. 2798, Eurofighter 2000, Jet Provost.

1998, Sept. 15 Sheets of 4, #a-d
2793-2794 A420 Set of 2 16.00 16.00

Souvenir Sheets
2795-2798 A420 Set of 4 25.00 25.00

Tennis Stars A421

45c, Arthur Ashe. 75c, Martina Hingis. 90c, Chris Evert. $1, Steffi Graf. $1.50, Arantxa Sanchez Vicario. $3, Martina Navratilova. $2, Monica Seles. $6, Martina Hingis, diff.

1998, Oct. 28
2799-2805 A421 Set of 7 8.75 8.75

Souvenir Sheet
2806 A421 $6 multicolored 7.00 7.00

Peacekeepers, Beirut, Lebanon, 1982-84 — A422

1998, Nov. 30 Litho. *Perf. 14*
2807 A422 $1 multicolored 1.25 1.25

Christmas A423

Birds: 45c, Blue-hooded Euphonia. 75c, Black-bellied whistling duck. 90c, Purple martin. $1, Imperial parrot. $2, Adelaide's warbler. $3, Roseate flamingo.
$5, Green-throated carib. $6, Purple-throated carib, Canada #85.

1998, Dec. 1
2808-2813 A423 Set of 6 7.75 7.75

Souvenir Sheet
2814 A423 $5 multicolored 5.25 5.25
2815 A423 $6 multicolored 8.00 8.00

No. 2815 contains one 38x61mm stamp.

Christmas — A424

Works of art: 35c, Painting, The Angel's Parting from Tobias, by Jean Bilevelt. 45c, Painting, Allegory of Faith, by Moretto da Brescia. 90c, Painting, Cross, with Depiction of the Crucifixion, by Ugolino di Tedice. $1, The Triumphal Entry into Jerusalem, Master of the Thuison Altarpiece.

1998, Dec. 1
2816-2819 A424 Set of 4 2.75 2.75

New Year 1999 (Year of the Rabbit) — A425

Various rabbits, color of country name: a, green. b, orange. c, red.

1999, Jan. 4 Litho. *Die Cut Perf. 9*
Self-Adhesive
Sheet of 3
2820 A425 $1 sil & multi, #a.-c. 4.00 4.00

No. 2820b has point of triangle down.

A426

Famous People: No. 2821: a, Martin Luther King, Jr. (1929-68). b, Socrates (470-399BC). c, Thomas Moore (1478-1535). d, Chaim Weizmann (1874-1952). e, Alexander Solzhenitsyn (1918-2008). f, Galileo Galilei (1564-1642). g, Michael Servetus (1511-53). h, Salman Rushdie (b. 1947).
$6, Mother Teresa (1910-97).

1999, Mar. 1 Litho. *Perf. 14*
2821 A426 $1 Sheet of 8, #a.-h. 10.00 10.00

Souvenir Sheet
2822 A426 $6 multicolored 7.00 7.00

Nos. 2821b-2821c, 2821e-2821f are 53x38mm.

A427

Space Exploration — No. 2823, each $1.50: a, Robert H. Goddard. b, Werner von Braun. c, Yuri Gagarin. d, Freedom 7 rocket. e, Aleksei Leonov. f, Apollo 11 astronauts on moon.
No. 2824, each $1.50: a, Mariner 9. b, Voyager 1. c, Bruce McCandless. d, Giotto probe. e, Space Shuttle. f, Magellan probe.
Each $6: No. 2825, John H. Glenn, Jr. No. 2826, Neil A. Armstrong.

1999, Mar. 5 Sheets of 6, #a-f
2823-2824 A427 Set of 2 16.00 16.00

Souvenir Sheets
2825-2826 A427 Set of 2 12.00 12.00

Mickey's Dream Wedding A428

No. 2827: a, Goofy. b, Mickey. c, Minnie. d, Daisy Duck. e, Donald Duck. f, Pluto. g, Huey, Dewey & Louie. h, Dog.

Each $6: No. 2828, Mickey eating cake. No. 2829, Mickey, Minnie in back of carriage, horiz.

1999, Mar. 12 ***Perf. 13½x14, 14x13½***

2827 A428 $1 Sheet of 8, #a.-h. 8.00 8.00

Souvenir Sheets

2828-2829 A428 Set of 2 14.50 14.50

Mickey Mouse, 70th anniv.

Trains A429

Designs: 25c, Grand Trunk Western. 35c, Louisville & Nashville. 45c, Gulf, Mobile & Ohio. 75c, Missouri Pacific. 90c, RTG, French Natl. Railway. $1, Florida East Coast. $3, Kansas City Southern. $4, New Haven.

No. 2838, each $1.50: a, Western Pacific. b, Union Pacific. c, Chesapeake & Ohio. d, Southern Pacific. e, Baltimore & Ohio. f, Wabash.

No. 2839, each $1.50: a, Burlington Route. b, Texas Special, Missouri, Kansas & Texas. c, City of Los Angeles. d, Northwestern. e, Canadian National. f, Rock Island.

No. 2840, each $1.50: a, Rio Grande. b, Erie Lackawanna. c, New York Central. d, Pennsylvania. e, Milwaukee Road. f, Illinois Central.

No. 2841, each $1.50: a, TGV, French National Railways. b, HST, British Railways. c, TEE, Trans Europe Express. d, Ancona Express Itay. e, XPT, Australia. f, APT-P, British Railways.

Each $6: No. 2842, Bullet Train, Japan. No. 2843, Inter City Express, Germany. No. 2844, Santa Fe. No. 2845, ELD 4, Netherlands.

1999, Mar. 15 ***Perf. 14***

2830-2837 A429 Set of 8 9.00 9.00

Sheets of 6, #a-f

2838-2841 A429 Set of 4 34.00 34.00

Souvenir Sheets

2842-2845 A429 Set of 4 24.00 24.00

Australia '99, World Stamp Expo A430

Flora and fauna: $1, Orangutan. $2, Dourocouli. $3. Black caiman. $4, Black leopard, vert.

No. 2850, vert, each 75c: a, African binturong. b, Two elephants. c, One elephant. d, Garkulax mitratus. e, Vanda hookeriana (a, f). f, Heron. g, Fur seal (f). h, Pied shag (g). i, Round batfish (e). j, Loggerhead turtle (f, k). k, Three harlequin sweet lips (l). l, Two harlequin sweet lips (k).

No. 2851, each 75c: a, Papilio blumei (d). b, Egret (e). c, Kumarahou (b, f). d, Javan rhinoceros (g). e, Silver eye. f, Kiore (i). g, Cyclorana novaehollandiae. h, Caterpillar. i, Grey duck (h). j, Honey blue-eye. k, Krefft's tortoise. l, Archer fish.

Each $6: No. 2852, Impalas. No. 2853, Ring-tailed lemurs.

1999, Apr. 12 **Litho.** ***Perf. 14***

2846-2849 A430 Set of 4 9.50 9.50

Sheets of 12, #a-l

2850-2851 A430 Set of 2 17.50 17.50

Souvenir Sheets

2852-2853 A430 Set of 2 12.50 12.50

Paintings by Hokusai (1760-1849) A431

Entire paintings or details — No. 2854, each $1.50: a, The Actor Ichikawa Danjuro as Tomoe Gozen. b, E-Tehon drawings (washing clothes). c, The Prostitute of Eguchi. d, Sudden Shower from a Fine Sky. e, E-tehon drawings (hanging clothes up to dry). f, Shimada.

No. 2855, each $1.50: a, Head of Old Man. b, Horse Drawings (with head down). c, Girl Making Cord for Binding Hats. d, Li Po Admiring the Waterfall of Lo-Shan. e, Horse drawings (with head up). f, Potted Dwarf Pine with Basin.

Each $6: No. 2856, Women on the Beach at Enoshima. No. 2857, The Guardian God Fudo Myoo and His Two Young Attendants.

1999, May 24 **Litho.** ***Perf. 13½x14***

Sheets of 6, #a-f

2854-2855 A431 Set of 2 17.00 17.00

Souvenir Sheets

2856-2857 A431 Set of 2 12.50 12.50

Johann Wolfgang von Goethe (1749-1832), Poet — A432

No. 2858: a, Faust contempates the moon in his story. b, Portrait of Goethe and Freidrich von Schiller (1759-1805). c, Faust converses with Wagner outside the town gate.

No. 2860, Margaret Muses in "Faust."

1999, May 24 ***Perf. 14***

2858 A432 $3 Sheet of 3, #a.-c. 8.75 8.75

Souvenir Sheet

2860 A432 $6 multi 6.75 6.75

IBRA '99, World Philatelic Exhibition, Nuremberg — A433

IBRA'99 emblem, 1893 4-4-0 locomotive and: No. 2862, 75c, Prussia #2. No. 2864, $1, Saxony #1.

Emblem, Humboldt sailing ship and: No. 2863, 90c, Mecklenburg-Schwerin #1. No. 2865, $2, Mecklenburg-Strelitz #1.

$6, Saxony #1.

1999, May 24 **Litho.** ***Perf. 14***

2862-2865 A433 Set of 4 5.25 5.25

Souvenir Sheet

2866 A433 $6 multicolored 7.75 7.75

Apollo 11 Moon Landing, 30th Anniv. — A434

No. 2867, each $1.50: a, Footprint on moon. b, V2 Rocket. c, Command module, Columbia. d, Lunar rover. e, Lunar lander, Eagle. f, Command module during re-entry.

No. 2868, each $1.50: a, Moon. b, Edward H. White during first spacewalk. c, Edwin "Buzz" Aldrin. d, Earth. e, Michael Collins. f, Neal A. Armstrong, first man to walk on moon.

Each $6: No. 2869, Launch of Apollo 11, vert. No. 2870, US flag, Armstrong on Moon.

1999, May 24 **Sheets of 6, #a-f**

2867-2868 A434 Set of 2 19.00 19.00

Souvenir Sheets

2869-2870 A434 Set of 2 12.50 12.50

Souvenir Sheets

PhilexFrance '99, World Philatelic Exhibition — A435

Designs, each $6: No. 2871, 2-8-0 Heavy freight locomotive, French State Railways. No. 2872, 4 Cylinder Compound Pacific, Paris-Lyons and Mediterranean Railway.

1999, May 24 ***Perf. 13¾***

2871-2872 A435 Set of 2 12.50 12.50

A436

Wedding of Prince Edward and Sophie Rhys-Jones — No. 2873: a, Edward. b, Sophie and Edward. c, Sophie.

$6, Couple, horiz.

1999, June 18 **Litho.** ***Perf. 13½***

2873 A436 $3 Sheet of 3, #a.-c. 8.75 8.75

Souvenir Sheet

2874 A436 $6 multicolored 7.00 7.00

A437

Children: a, Two with fur hats. b, One with pink hat. c, Boy without shirt, girl with shawl.

$6, Wearing white shirt.

1999, May 24 **Litho.** ***Perf. 14***

2875 A437 $3 Sheet of 3, #a.-c. 8.75 8.75

Souvenir Sheet

2876 A437 $6 multicolored 7.00 7.00

UN Rights of the Child, 10th anniv.

British Comedy "Carry On" — A438

a, Dick. b, Doctor. c, England. d, Matron. e, Round the Bend. f, Up the Jungle. g, Loving. h, Up the Khyber.

$6, Various characters.

1999, May 24 ***Perf. 13½x14***

2877 A438 $1 Sheet of 8, #a.-h. 8.75 8.75

Perf. 13¾

2877I A438 $6 multicolored 6.75 6.75

Variety Club of Great Britain, 50th anniv.

UPU, 125th Anniv. A439

Mail from space: a, Cosmonaut with letter from home. b, Supply and mail ship, "Progress." c, Postmark of space station Mir. d, Buran shuttle, Mir in space.

$6, Space station Mir.

1999, May 24 ***Perf. 14***

2878 A439 $2 Sheet of 4, #a.-d. 8.75 8.75

Souvenir Sheet

2879 A439 $6 multicolored 7.00 7.00

Queen Mother, 100th Birthday (in 2000) — A440

A440a

No. 2880: a, Queen Mother, Prince Charles, 1948. b, Queen Mother, 1970. c, Queen Mother in Australia, 1958. d, Queen Mother.

$6, Queen Mother, 1953.

1999, Aug. 16 **Gold Frames**

Sheet of 4

2880 A440 $2 #a.-d. + label 8.75 8.75

Souvenir Sheet

2881 A440 $6 multicolored 7.00 7.00

Litho. & Embossed
Die Cut Perf. 8¾
Without Gum

2881A A440a $20 gold & multi *20.00*

No. 2881 contains one 38x50mm stamp. Margins of sheet are embossed.
See Nos. 3212-3213.

Birth of the Silver Screen A441

Musicians — No. 2882, each $1: a, George Gershwin, 1929. b, Florence Mills, 1928. c, Sam Beckett, 1925. d, Bessie Smith, 1923. e, Billie Holiday, 1933. f, Bert Williams, 1914. g, Cole Porter, 1934. h, Sophie Tucker, 1915.

Actors — No. 2883, each $1: a, Lon Chaney, 1930. b, Buster Keaton, 1930. c, Norma Shearer, 1934. d, James Cagney, 1930. e, Hedda Hopper, 1933. f, Jean Harlow, 1931. g, Marlene Dietrich, 1930. h, Ramon Novarro, 1928.

Each $6: No. 2884, Louis Armstrong. No. 2885, Clark Gable, 1932,

1999, Aug. 18 **Sheets of 8, #a-h**

2882-2883 A441 Set of 2 16.00 16.00

Souvenir Sheets

2884-2885 A441 Set of 2 14.00 14.00

Star Trek A442

Various starships.

1999, July 20 **Litho.** ***Perf. 13¼***

2886 A442 $1.50 Sheet of 9, #a.-i. 14.50 14.50

Dinosaurs A443

35c, Ouranosaurus. 45c, Struthiomimus, vert. 75c, Parasaurolophus, vert. $2, Triceratops. $3, Stegoceras. $4, Stegosaurus.

No. 2893, each $1: a, Agathaumus. b, Camarosaurus. c, Quetzalcoatlus. d, Alioramus. e, Camptosaurus. f, Albertosaurus. g, Anatosaurus. h, Spinosaurus. i, Centrosaurus.

No. 2894, each $1: a, Archaeopteryx. b, Brachiosaurus. c, Dilophosaurus. d, Dimetrodon. e, Psittacosaurus. f, Acrocanthosaurus. g, Stenonychosaurus. h, Dryosaurus. i, Compsognathus.

Each $6: No. 2895, Velociraptor, vert. No. 2896, Tyrannosaurus, vert.

1999, Sept. 1 **Litho.** ***Perf. 14***

2887-2892 A443 Set of 6 10.00 10.00

Sheets of 9, #a-i

2893-2894 A443 Set of 2 18.00 18.00

Souvenir Sheets

2895-2896 A443 Set of 2 12.50 12.50

Christmas — A444

Candle and: 20c, Rose. 75c, Tulip. 90c, Pear. $1, Hibiscus. $4, Lily.
$6, The Nativity, by Sandro Botticelli.

1999, Dec. 7 **Litho.** ***Perf. 14***

2897-2901 A444 Set of 5 6.75 6.75

Souvenir Sheet

2902 A444 $6 multi 7.00 7.00

Flowers A445

Various flowers making up a photomosaic of Princess Diana.

1999, Dec. 31 **Litho.** ***Perf. 13¾***

2903 A445 $1 Sheet of 8, #a.-h. 9.50 9.50

See No. 3055.

New Year 2000 (Year of the Dragon) — A446

Inscription color: a, Blue green. b, Red. c, Violet.

2000, Feb. 5 ***Perf. 12½x12¾***

2904 A446 $2 Sheet of 3, #a.-c. 8.00 8.00

No. 2904b has point of triangle down.

Birds A447

Designs: 75c, Roseate spoonbill. 90c, Scarlet ibis. $1.50, Sparkling violet-ear. $2, Northern jacana.

No. 2909, each $1: a, Blue-headed euphonia. b, Troupial. c, Caribbean parakeet. d, Forest thrush. e, Hooded tanager. f, Stripe-headed tanager. g, Ringed kingfisher. h, Zenaida dove.

No. 2910, each $1: a, Adelaide's warbler. b, Hispaniolan trogon. c, Sun parakeet. d, Black-necked stilt. e, Sora rail. f, Fulvous tree duck. g, Blue-headed parrot. h, Tropical mockingbird.

Each $6: No. 2911, Antillean siskin. No. 2912, Cedar waxwing, vert.

2000, Mar. 1 **Litho.** ***Perf. 14***

2905-2908 A447 Set of 4 5.00 5.00

Sheets of 8, #a-h

2909-2910 A447 Set of 2 14.00 14.00

Souvenir Sheets

2911-2912 A447 Set of 2 11.00 11.00

No. 2911 contains one 50x37mm stamp. No. 2912 contains one 37x50mm stamp.

Mushrooms A448

Designs: 35c, Clitocybe geotropa. 45c, Psalliota augusta. $1, Amanita rubescens. $4, Boletus satanas.

No. 2917, each $1.50: a, Ungulina marginata. b, Pleurotus ostreatus. c, Flammula penetrans. d, Morchella crassipes. e, Lepiota procera. f, Tricholoma aurantium.

No. 2918, each $1.50: a, Pholiota spectabilis. b, Mycena polygramma. c, Collybia iocephala. d, Corinus cornatus. e, Amanita muscaria. f, Boletus aereus.

Each $6: No. 2919, Lepiota acutesquamosa. No. 2920, Daedala quercina.

2000, May 1 ***Perf. 14***

2913-2916 A448 Set of 4 6.25 6.25

Sheets of 6, #a-f

2917-2918 A448 Set of 2 17.00 17.00

Souvenir Sheets

2919-2920 A448 Set of 2 12.00 12.00

Paintings of Anthony Van Dyck — A449

No. 2921, each $1: a, Young Woman Resting Her Head on Her Hand. b, Self-portrait. c, Woman Looking Upwards. d, Head of an Old Man, c. 1621. e, Head of a Boy. f, Head of an Old Man, 1616-18.

No. 2922, each $1: a, Charles I on Horseback with Seigneur de St. Antoine. b, St. Martin Dividing His Cloak. c, Giovanni Paolo Balbi on Horseback. d, Marchese Anton Giulio Brignole-Sale on Horseback. e, Study of a Horse. f, An Oriental on Horseback.

No. 2923, each $1.50: a, Portrait of a Man. b, Portrait of a Man Aged Seventy. c, Portrait of a Woman. d, An Elderly Man. e, Portrait of a Young Man. f, Man with a Glove.

No. 2924, each $1.50: a, St. John the Baptist. b, St. Anthony of Padua and the Ass of Rimini. c, The Stoning of St. Stephen. d, The Martyrdom of St. Sebastian. e, St. Sebastian Bound for Martyrdom. f, St. Jerome.

No. 2925, each $1.50: a, Inscribed "Portrait of Anthony Van Dyck," actually a self-portrait of Rubens. b, Inscribed "Self-portrait (after Peter Paul Rubens)." c, Isabella Brant, Wife of Peter Paul Rubens. d, The Penitent Apostle Peter. e, Head of a Robber. f, The Heads of the Apostles, by Rubens.

Each $5: No. 2926, Prince Thomas-Francis of Savoy-Carignan on Horseback. No. 2927, Charles I on Horseback. No. 2928, The Emperor Theodosius Refused Entry in Milan Cathedral, horiz.

Each $6: No. 2929, St. Jerome (in the Wilderness). No. 2930, St. Martin Dividing His Cloak, horiz. No. 2931, Portrait of a Man and His Wife.

2000, May 1 ***Perf. 13¾***

Sheets of 6, #a.-f.

2921-2922 A449 Set of 2 10.50 10.50
2923-2925 A449 Set of 3 22.50 22.50

Souvenir Sheets

2926-2928 A449 Set of 3 13.00 13.00
2929-2931 A449 Set of 3 14.50 14.50

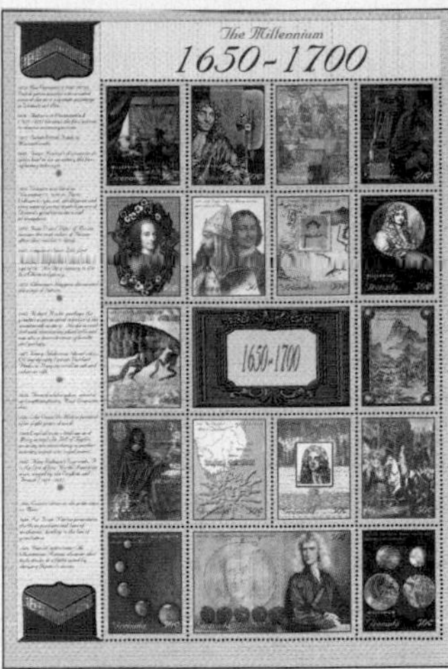

Millennium — A450

Highlights of 1650-1700: a, Painter Jan Vermeer dies. b, Birth of microbiology. c, Salem Witch Trials. d, Sir Isaac Newton builds first reflecting telescope. e, Voltaire born. f, Ivan V and Peter become joint rulers of Russia. g, First Qing Dynasty Emperor, Shun Zhi, dies. h, Christiaan Huygens discovers rings of Saturn. i, Robert Hooke identifies cells. j, Wang Shih-min paints "Verdant Peaks." k, René Descartes dies. l, Canal du Midi completed. m, Glorious Revolution. n, King William's War ends. o, Gian Domenico Cassini observes polar caps on Mars. p, Newton formulates law of gravitation (60x40mm). q, Ole Roemer discovers that light moves at a finite speed.

2000, May 1 ***Perf. 12½***

2932 A450 50c Sheet of 17, #a.-q., + label 8.75 8.75

Orchids — A451

Designs: 75c, Brassolaeliocattleya. 90c, Maxilbera. $1, Isochilius. $2, Oncidium.

No. 2937, each $1.50: a, Laeliocattleya. b, Sophrocattleya (red). c, Epidendrum. d, Cattleya. e, Ionopsis. f, Brassoepidendrum.

No. 2938, each $1.50: a, Lycaste. b, Cochleanthes. c, Brassocattleya. d, Brassolaeliacattleya, diff. e, Iwanagaara. f, Sophrocattleya (orange).

Each $6: No. 2939, Vanilla. No. 2940, Brassocattleya, diff.

2000, May 15 **Litho.** ***Perf. 14***

2933-2936 A451 Set of 4 5.00 5.00

Sheets of 6, #a.-f.

2937-2938 A451 Set of 2 19.00 19.00

Souvenir Sheets

2939-2940 A451 Set of 2 12.50 12.50

100th Test Match at Lord's Ground — A452

90c, Junior Murray. $5, Rawl Lewis.
$6, Lord's Ground, horiz.

2000, May 15 **Litho.** ***Perf. 14***

2941-2942 A452 Set of 2 4.75 4.75

Souvenir Sheet

2943 A452 $6 multi 5.25 5.25

Prince William, 18th Birthday — A453

No. 2944: a, In suit. b, In suit, with person in tan suit. c, In suit, waving. d, In ski jacket.
$6, In suit, diff.

2000, May 15 *Perf. 14*

2944 A453 $1.50 Sheet of 4, #a-d 4.50 4.50

Souvenir Sheet

Perf. 13¾

2945 A453 $6 multi 4.50 4.50

No. 2944 contains four 28x42mm stamps.

First Zeppelin Flight, Cent. — A454

No. 2946 — Ferdinand von Zeppelin and: a, LZ-130. b, LZ-2. c, LZ-127.
$6, LZ-129.

2000, May 15 *Perf. 14*

2946 A454 $3 Sheet of 3, #a-c 8.00 8.00

Souvenir Sheet

2947 A454 $6 multi 5.25 5.25

No. 2946 contains three 42x28mm stamps.

Berlin Film Festival, 50th Anniv. — A455

No. 2948: a, Alphaville. b, Rod Steiger. c, Os Fuzis. d, Jean-Pierre Leaud. e, Cul-de-sac. f, Ikiru.
$6, Hsi Yen.

2000, May 15

2948 A455 $1.50 Sheet of 6, #a-f 6.75 6.75

Souvenir Sheet

2949 A455 $6 multi 4.50 4.50

Apollo-Soyuz Mission, 25th Anniv. — A456

No. 2950, vert.: a, Soyuz launch vehicle. b, Soyuz 19. c, Apollo 18 and Soyuz 19 docked.
$6, Valeri Kubasov and Thomas Stafford.

2000, May 15

2950 A456 $3 Sheet of 3, #a-c 7.75 7.75

Souvenir Sheet

2951 A456 $6 multi 5.75 5.75

Souvenir Sheets

2000 Summer Olympics, Sydney — A457

No. 2952: a, Archibald Hahn. b, Show jumping. c, Sports Palace, Rome, and Italian flag. d, Ancient Greek chariot racing.

2000, May 15

2952 A457 $2 Sheet of 4, #a-d 7.00 7.00

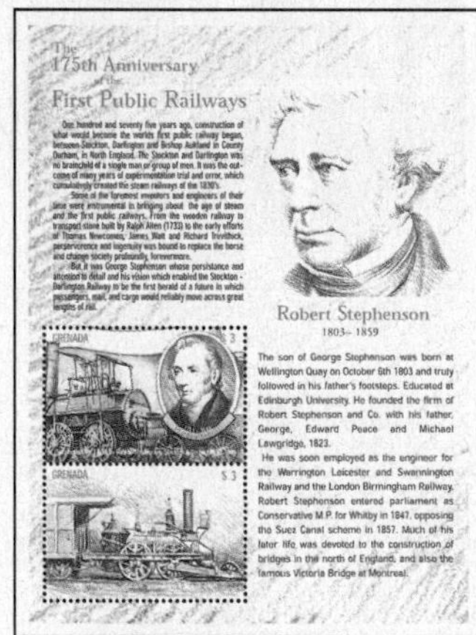

Public Railways, 175th Anniv. — A458

No. 2953: a, Locomotion No. 1, George Stephenson. b, John Bull.

2000, May 15

2953 A458 $3 Sheet of 2, #a-b 5.75 5.75

Johann Sebastian Bach (1685-1750) — A459

2000, May 15

2954 A459 $6 multi 4.50 4.50

Souvenir Sheet

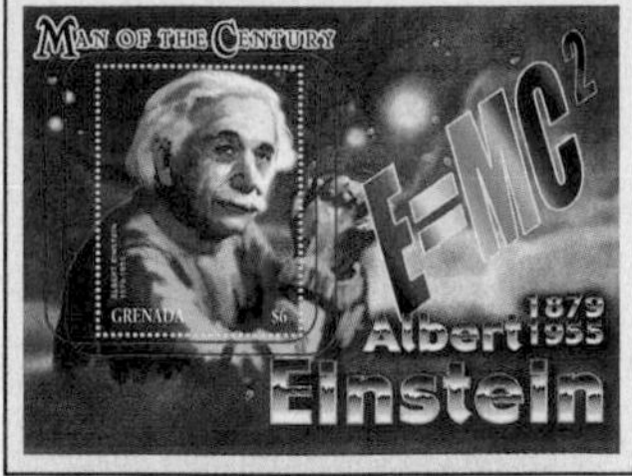

Albert Einstein (1879-1955) — A460

2000, May 15 Litho. *Perf. 14¼*

2955 A460 $6 multi 4.50 4.50

Space — A461

No. 2956: a, Luna 4. b, Clementine. c, Luna 12. d, Luna 16. e, Apollo 11 Lunar module. f, Ranger 7.
$6, Apollo command and service modules.

2000, May 15 Litho. *Perf. 14*

2956 A461 $1.50 Sheet of 6, #a-f 7.75 7.75

Souvenir Sheet

2957 A461 $6 multi 5.25 5.25

World Stamp Expo 2000, Anaheim

Marine Life A462

Designs: 45c, Porkfish. 75c, Short bigeye. 90c, Red snapper. $1, Creole wrasse. $2, Indigo hamlet. $3, Blue tang.
No. 2964: a, Juvenile French angelfish. b, Beaugregory. c, Queen angelfish. d, Sergeant major. e, Bank butterflyfish. f, Spanish hogfish. g, Porkfish. h, Banded butterflyfish. i, Longsnout seahorse.
No. 2965: a, Hawksbill turtle. b, Foureye butterflyfish. c, Porcupinefish. d, Yellowtail damselfish. e, Adult French angelfish. f, Yellow goatfish. g, Blue-striped grunt. h, Spanish grunt. i, Queen triggerfish.
No. 2966, Queen angelfish. No. 2967, Blue tang.

2000, Aug. 8

2958-2963 A462 Set of 5 7.00 7.00

Sheets of 9, #a-i

2964-2965 A462 $1 Set of 2 14.50 14.50

Souvenir Sheets

2966-2967 A462 $6 Set of 2 9.00 9.00

Grenada National Stadium A463

Designs: $2, Aerial view.
No. 2969: a, Cricket team photo. b, Cricketers playing.

2000, Aug. 8

2968 A463 $2 multi 1.50 1.50

Souvenir Sheet

2969 A463 $1 Sheet of 2, #a-b 1.50 1.50

European Soccer Championships — A464

No. 2970, horiz. — Belgium: a, Vanderhaege. b, Belgian team. c, Ronny Gaspercic. d, Lorenzo Staelens. e, Stadium Koning Boudewijn. f, Strupar and Mpenza.
No. 2971, horiz. — Spain: a, Sergi Barjuan. b, Spanish team. c, Luis Enrique. d, Hierro. e, De Kuip Stadium. f, Raul Gonzales.
No. 2972, horiz. — Yugoslavia: a, Dejan Savicevic. b, Yugoslavian team. c, Predrag Migatovic. d, Savo Milosevic. e, Jan Breydel Stadium. f, Darko Kovacevic.
No. 2973, Belgian coach Robert Waseige. No. 2974, Spanish coach José Antonio Camacho. No. 2975, Yugoslavian coach Vujadin Boskov.
Illustration reduced.

2000, Aug. 8 *Perf. 13¾*

Sheets of 6, #a-f

2970-2972 A464 $1.50 Set of 3 20.00 20.00

Souvenir Sheets

2973-2975 A464 $6 Set of 3 13.50 13.50

Ferrari Automobiles — A465

20c, 1953 500 Mondial. 45c, 1948 166 Inter. 75c, 1953 340 MM. 90c, 1964 500 Superfast. $1, 1948 166 MM. $1.50, 1952 250 S. $2, 1957 250 California. $3, 1966 365 California.

2000, Sept. 5 *Perf. 14*

2976-2983 A465 Set of 8 8.00 8.00

Antique Automobiles — A466

45c, 1921 Marmon Model 34. 75c, 1917 Buick D44. 90c, 1918 Hudson Runabout Landau. $1, 1915 Chevrolet Royal Mail. $2, 1925 Kissel Speedster. $3, 1915 Ford Model T.
No. 2990: a, 1925 Cadillac V63. b, 1939 Plymouth. c, 1934 Franklin Club Sedan. d, 1933 Fiat Ardita. e, 1929 Essex Speedabout. f, 1932 Stutz Bearcat.
No. 2991: a, 1929 Rolls Royce. b, 1932 Graham Convertible. c, 1937 Mercedes-Benz 540K. d, 1948 Jaguar MkV. e, 1939 Lagonda Drophead Coupe. f, 1930 Alfa Romeo Gran Sport.
No. 2992, 1915 Dodge Tourer. No. 2993, 1924 Chrysler.

2000, Sept. 5

2984-2989 A466 Set of 6 6.00 6.00

Sheets of 6, #a-f

2990-2991 A466 $1.50 Set of 2 13.50 13.50

Souvenir Sheets

2992-2993 A466 $6 Set of 2 9.00 9.00

Popes — A467

No. 2994: a, Stephen VIII, 939-42. b, Theodore I, 642-49. c, Theodore II, 897. d, Valentine, 827. e, Vitalian, 657-72. f, Zacharias, 741-52.
$6, Sylvester II, 999-1003.

2000, Sept. 5 *Perf. 13¾*
2994 A467 $1.50 Sheet of 6, #a-f 6.75 6.75

Souvenir Sheet

2995 A467 $6 multi 4.50 4.50

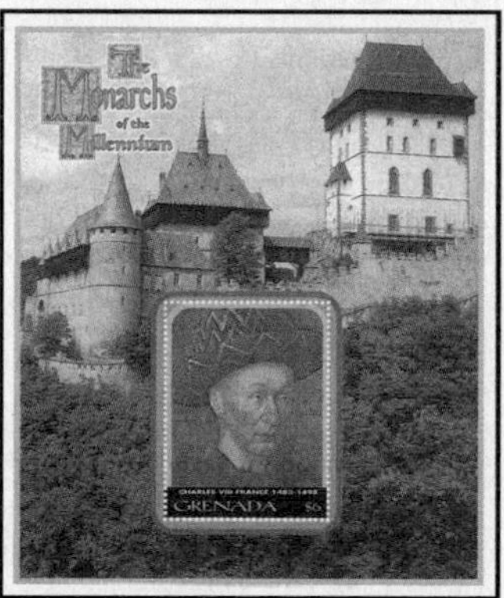

Monarchs — A468

No. 2996: a, George III of Great Britain, 1760-1820. b, George IV of Great Britain, 1820-30. c, Duchess Charlotte of Luxembourg, 1964-present. d, Grand Duke Jean of Luxembourg, 1964-present.
$6, Charles VIII of France, 1483-98.

2000, Sept. 5 *Perf. 13¾*
2996 A468 $1.50 Sheet of 4, #a-d 4.50 4.50

Souvenir Sheet

2997 A468 $6 multi 4.50 4.50

Shirley Temple in "Heidi" — A469

No. 2998, horiz.: a, With woman holding candle. b, With girl in green dress c, On stairs. d, With Christmas gift.
No. 2999, horiz.: a, Walking with woman. b, Touching bearded man. c, Holding goat. d, With doves. e, With bearded man. f, Seated with woman.

2000, Oct. 6 **Litho.** *Perf. 13¾*
2998 A469 $1.50 Sheet of 4, #a-d 4.50 4.50
2999 A469 $1.50 Sheet of 6, #a-f 6.75 6.75

Souvenir Sheet

3000 A469 $6 Seated near tree 4.50 4.50

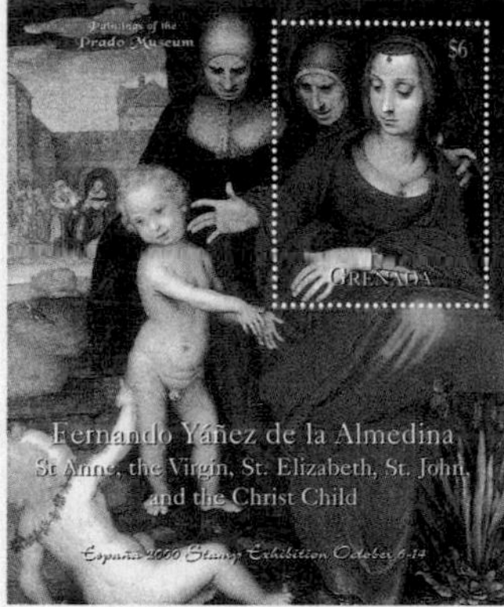

Paintings from the Prado — A470

No. 3001: a, Monk and king from The Virgin of the Catholic Monarchs, by an Anonymous Castilian. b, Madonna and child from The Virgin of the Catholic Monarchs. c, Monk and queen from The Virgin of the Catholic Monarchs. d, The Flagellation, by Alexo Fernandez. e, The Virgin and Souls in Purgatory, by Pedro Machuca. f, The Holy Trinity, by El Greco.
No. 3002: a, Playing at Giants, by El Greco. b, The Holy Family Under the Oak Tree, by Raphael. c, Don Gaspar Melchior de Jovellanos, by Francisco de Goya. d, Man with arm on hip from Joseph in the Pharaoh's Palace, by Jacopo Amiconi. e, Man and woman from Joseph in the Pharaoh's Palace. f, Man on bended knee from Joseph in the Pharaoh's Palace.
No. 3003: a, The Savior Blessing, by Francisco de Zurbarán. b, St. John the Baptist, by Francisco Solimena. c, Noli Me Tangere, by Corregio. d, St. Casilda, by Zurbarán. e, Nicolás Omazur by Bartolomé Esteban Murillo. f, Juan Martínez Montañés, by Diego Velázquez.
No. 3004, St. Anne, the Virgin, St. Elizabeth, St. John and the Christ child, by Fernando Yáñez de la Almedina. No. 3005, The Virgin of the Catholic Monarchs. No. 3006, Joseph in the Pharaoh's Palace, horiz.
Illustration reduced.

2000, Oct. 19 *Perf. 12x12¼, 12¼x12*

Sheets of 6, #a-f

3001-3003 A470 $1.50 Set of 3 20.00 20.00

Souvenir Sheets

3004-3006 A470 $6 Set of 3 13.50 13.50

Espana 2000 Intl. Philatelic Exhibition.

Battle of Britain, 60th Anniv. — A471

No. 3007: a, Messerschmitt BF 109E and bomb blast. b, Supermarine Spitfire MK XI. c, V1 flying bomb. d, U-boat. e, Ack-ack gun unit. f, Bedford field ambulance.
No. 3008: a, Messerschmitt BF 109E. b, German paratrooper. c, Hawker Hurricane HK 1. d, RAF airfield. e, Heinkel HE 111 H. f, Nose of Supermarine Spitfire MK XI.
No. 3009, Line of Hawker Hurricanes. No. 3010, Supermarine Spitfire MK XI.

2000, Oct. 30 *Perf. 14*

Sheets of 6, #a-f

3007-3008 A471 $1.50 Set of 2 16.00 16.00

Souvenir Sheets

3009-3010 A471 $6 Set of 2 12.00 12.00

A472

Birds: 25c, Purple gallinule. 40c, Limpkin. 50c, Black-necked stilt. 60c, Painted bunting. 75c, Yellow-breasted warbler. $1, Blackburnian warbler. $1.25, Blue grosbeak. $1.50, Black-and-white warbler. $1.60, Blue whistling thrush. $3, Common yellowthroat. $4, Indigo bunting. $5, Gray catbird. $10, Bananaquit. $20, Blue-gray gnatcatcher.

2000, Oct. 30 *Perf. 14¾x14*
3011-3024 A472 Set of 14 37.50 37.50

See No. 3540.

A473

Dogs: $2, Shetland sheepdog. $3, Central Asian sheepdog.
No. 3027, horiz.: a, Labrador retriever. b, Standard poodle. c, Boxer. d, Rough-coated Jack Russell terrier. e, Tibetan terrier. f, Welsh corgi.
$6, Irish red and white setter, horiz.

2000, June 23 **Litho.** *Perf. 14*
3025-3026 A473 Set of 2 3.75 3.75
3027 A473 $1.50 Sheet of 6, #a-f 6.75 6.75

Souvenir Sheet

3028 A473 $6 multi 4.50 4.50

Butterflies A474

45c, Marpesia eleuchea bahamaensis. 75c, Pterourus palamedes. 90c, Dryas julia framptoni. $1, Hypna clytemnestra iphegenia.
No. 3033, $1.50: a, Danaus plexippus. b, Anartia amathea. c, Colobura dirce. d, Parides gundiachianus. e, Spiroeta stelenes. f, Hamadryas feronia.
No. 3034, $1.50: a, Merchantis isthmia. b, Colias eurytheme. c, Papilio troilus d, Junonia coenia. e, Doxocopa laure. f, Pierella hyalinus.
No. 3035, $6, Agraulis vanilae insularis. No. 3036, $6, Danaus gilippus.

2000, June 26
3029-3032 A474 Set of 4 3.00 3.00

Sheets of 6, #a-f

3033-3034 A474 Set of 2 17.00 17.00

Souvenir Sheets

3035-3036 A474 Set of 2 10.00 10.00

A475

Trains — A476

No. 3037, $1.50: a, Diesel-electric locomotive, Royal State Railway of Thailand. b, Diesel-electric locomotive, Danish Railways. c, French-built Turbo train. d, Diesel, Spanish Railways. e, Virgen del Rosario, Spanish Railways. f, 22 Class Co-Co Diesel-electric locomotive, Malayan Railways.
No. 3038, $1.50: a, Class 87 electric locomotive, British Railways. b, Electric-Diesel locomotive, Iraqi Railway. c, Electric locomotive, Austrian Railways. d, 1.4 meter gauge locomotive, South Australia Railways. e, Automated electric locomotive, Black Mesa & Lake Powell Railroad. f, Diesel-electric, Yugoslav Railways.
No. 3039, $1.50: a, Class 10 4-6-2, German Federal Railway. b, Class E.10 Bo-Bo Electric locomotive, German Federal Railways. c, Class 23 2-6-2, German Federal Railway. d, 2-8-4 locomotive, German Federal Railway. e, Rebuilt 01 Class Pacific, East German State Railway. f, High speed Diesel railcar, Deutschen Reichsbahn.
No. 3040, $1.50: a, Borsig Standard 2-2-2. b, Austerity 2-10-0 Series 52, German Federal Railway. c, Adler, facing right, Nuremburg-Furth Railway. d, Bardenia, Baden State Railways. e, Drache. f, Adler, facing left.
No. 3041, $6, Diesel T.E.E. Parsifal. No. 3042, $6, High speed electric, Netherlands Railway. No. 3043, $6, Electric train, Swiss Railways. No. 3044, $6, Silver Fern, New Zealand Railways. No. 3045, $6, Borsig locomotive, Berlin and Anhalt Railway. No. 3046, $6, Krauss-Maffei V.200 Diesel hydraulic locomotive, German Federal Railway.
Illustrations reduced.

2000, Sept. 5 **Sheets of 6, #a-f**
3037-3038 A475 Set of 2 15.00 15.00
3039-3040 A476 Set of 2 15.00 15.00

Souvenir Sheets

3041-3044 A475 Set of 4 21.00 21.00
3045-3046 A476 Set of 2 11.00 11.00

Descriptions of trains are in margins on Nos. 3039-3040, 3045-3046.

Nursery Rhymes — A477

No. 3047, Little Bo Peep, $1.50, vert.: a, Crook, tree, dove. b, Little Bo Peep. c, Sheep. d, Geese. e, Goose, Little Bo Peep's leg. f, Dog.
No. 3048, The Old Woman Who Lived in a Shoe, $1.50, vert.: a, Child, roof. b, Child with hat, rainbow. c, Cow, sun, rainbow. d, Child at door. e, Old woman, child. f, Child on shoe.
No. 3049, Little Boy Blue, $1.50, vert.: a, Sheep, house. b, Sun. c, Cow. d, Geese, path. e, Dog, Little Boy Blue's leg. f, Little Boy Blue.
No. 3050, The Cat and the Fiddle, $1.50, vert. a, Bird, house. b, Cow jumping over moon. c, Spoon. d, Dog, house. e, Cat and fiddle. f, Dish.
No. 3051, $6, Little Bo Peep. No. 3052, $6, The Old Woman Who Lived in a Shoe. No. 3053, $6, Little Boy Blue. No. 3054, Cow jumping over the moon.
Illustration reduced.

2000, Sept. 8 *Perf. 13¾x13¼*

Sheets of 6, #a-f

3047-3050 A477 Set of 4 27.50 27.50

Souvenir Sheets

Perf. 13¼x13¾

3051-3054 A477 Set of 4 18.00 18.00

Flower Photomosaic Type of 1999

Queen Mother

Various flowers making up photomosaic.

2000, Nov. 20 *Perf. 13¾*
3055 A445 $1 Sheet of 8, #a-h 6.00 6.00

Cats — A478

75c, Maine Coon cat. 90c, Selkirk Rex.
No. 3058, horiz.: a, Spotted tabby British shorthair. b, Burmilla. c, British blue shorthair. d, Siamese. e, Japanese bobtail. f, Oriental shorthair.

2000, June 23 Litho. *Perf. 14*
3056-3057 A478 Set of 2 1.75 1.75
3058 A478 $1.50 Sheet of 6, #a-f 8.00 8.00

Souvenir Sheet

3059 A478 $6 Scottish Fold 5.75 5.75

Queen Mother, 100th Birthday — A479

2000, Nov. 20
3060 A479 $1.50 multi 1.10 1.10

Printed in sheets of 6.

Christmas — A480

Designs: 15c, 50c, No. 3065b, Angel looking left. 25c, $5, No. 3065a, Angel looking right.

2000, Dec. 4
3061-3064 A480 Set of 4 4.50 4.50
3065 A480 $2 Sheet, 2 ea #a-b 6.00 6.00

Souvenir Sheet

3066 A480 $6 Baby Jesus 4.50 4.50

Souvenir Sheets

Betty Boop — A481

Designs: No. 3067, $6, Wearing lei. No. 3068, $6, Holding fishing pole and fish. No. 3069, $6, Wearing polka dot hat. No. 3070, $6, Holding castanets. No. 3071, $6, At Japanese tea ceremony. No. 3072, $6, Wearing pink hat. No. 3073, $6, In mountains, wearing flowered hat. No. 3074, $6, Wearing beret. No. 3075, $6, As Statue of Liberty. No. 3076, $6, In Hollywood. No. 3077, $6, On horse. No. 3078, $6, On camel's back.

2000, Oct. 11 Litho. *Perf. 13¾*
3067-3078 A481 Set of 12 60.00 60.00

Souvenir Sheet

New Year 2001 (Year of the Snake) — A482

No. 3079: a, Blue green denomination. b, Red denomination. c, Purple denomination.

2001, Jan. 2 *Perf. 12½x13*
3079 A482 $2 Sheet of 3, #a-c 4.50 4.50

Rijksmuseum, Amsterdam, Bicent. — A483

No. 3080, $1.50: a, William I, Prince of Orange, by Adriaen Thomasz Key. b, Rutger Jan Schimmelpennick and Family, by Pierre Paul Prud'hon. c, Johan Rudolf Thorbecke, by Johan Heinrich Neuman. d, St. Sebastian, by Joachim Wtewael. e, St. Sebastian, by Hendrick ter Brugghen. f, Portrait of a Man With a Ring, by Werner Van Den Valckert.
No. 3081, $1.50: a, The Syndics of the Amsterdam Goldsmith's Guild, by Thomas de Keyser. b, Portrait of a Gentleman, by de Keyser. c, Portrait of Eva Wtewael, by Wtewael. d, The Cattle Ferry, by Esaias van de Velde. e, Landscape With the Parable of the Tares Among the Wheat, by Abraham Bloemaert. f, Princess Henrietta Marie Stuart, by Bartholomeus van der Helst.
No. 3082, $1.50: a, The Merry Fiddler, by Gerard van Honthorst. b, The Merry Drinker, by Frans Hals. c, Granida and Daifilo, by van Honthorst. d, Vertumnus and Pomona, by Paulus Moreelse. e, Flutist from The Concert, by ter Brugghen. f, A Young Student at His Desk: Melancholy, by Pieter Codde.
No. 3083, $1.50: a, The Haarlem Painter Abraham Casteleyn and His Wife Margarieta van Bancken, by Jan de Bray. b, Two figures from The Concert. c, The Procuress, by Dirck van Baburen. d, Woman Seated at a Virginal, by Johannes Vermeer. e, Dignified Couples Courting, by Willem Buytewech. f, The Young Flute Player, by Judith Leyster.
No. 3084, $6, Interior of the Portuguese Synagogue in Amsterdam, by Emanuel de Witte. No. 3085, $6, The Denial of St. Peter, by Rembrandt, horiz. No. 3086, $6, Winter Landscape With Skaters, by Hendrick Avercamp, horiz. No. 3087, $6, The Raampoortje, by Wouter Johannes van Troostwijk, horiz.

2001, Jan. 15 *Perf. 13¾*

Sheets of 6, #a-f

3080-3083 A483 Set of 4 27.50 27.50

Souvenir Sheets

3084-3087 A483 Set of 4 18.00 18.00

Pokémon — A484

No. 3088: a, Rattata. b, Sandshrew. c, Wartortle. d, Primeape. e, Golduck. f, Persian.

2001, Feb. 1
3088 A484 $1.50 Sheet of 6, #a-f 6.75 6.75

Souvenir Sheet

3089 A484 $6 Jolteon 4.50 4.50

Waterfowl — A485

No. 3090, $1.25: a, African pygmy goose. b, Silver teal. c, Marbled teal. d, Garganey. e, Wandering whistling duck. f, Northern shoveler.
No. 3091, $1.25: a, Female flightless steamer duck. b, Radjah. c, Cape teal. d, Hartlaub's duck. e, Ruddy shelduck. f, White-cheeked pintail.
No. 3092, $1.25, vert.: a, Fulvous whistling duck. b, African black duck. c, Madagascar white-eye. d, Female pygmy goose. e, Female wood duck. f, Male wood duck.
No. 3093, $6, Flightless steamer duck. No. 3094, $6, Flying steamer duck. No. 3095, $6, Australian shelduck, vert.

Perf. 13¼x13¾, 13¾x13¼
2001, Mar. 5 Litho.

Sheets of 6, #a-f

3090-3092 A485 Set of 3 17.00 17.00

Souvenir Sheets

3093-3095 A485 Set of 3 13.50 13.50

Hong Kong 2001 Stamp Exhibition.

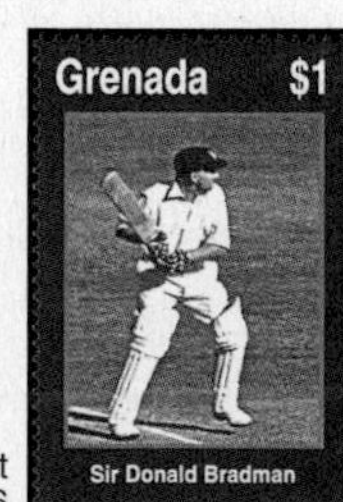

Cricket Players — A486

No. 3096: Various photos of Sir Donald Bradman swinging bat.
No. 3097, Various photos of Shane Warne bowling.
No. 3098, Various photos of Sir Jack Hobbs.
No. 3099, Various photos of Sir Vivian Richards.
No. 3100, Various photos of Sir Garfield Sobers.
No. 3101, oval vignettes: a, Bradman. b, Sobers. c, Hobbs. d, Warne. e, Richards.

2001, May 15 *Perf. 14*

3096	Sheet of 8, #a-h	6.00	6.00
a.-h.	A486 $1 Any single	.75	.75
3097	Sheet of 8, #a-h	6.00	6.00
a.-h.	A486 $1 Any single	.75	.75
3098	Sheet of 4, #a-d	6.00	6.00
a.-d.	A486 $2 Any single	1.50	1.50
3099	Sheet of 4, #a-d	6.00	6.00
a.-d.	A486 $2 Any single	1.50	1.50
3100	Sheet of 4, #a-d	6.00	6.00
a.-d.	A486 $2 Any single	1.50	1.50
3101	Sheet of 5, #a-e	7.50	7.50
a.-e.	A486 $2 Any single	1.50	1.50
	Nos. 3096-3101 (6)	37.50	37.50

A487

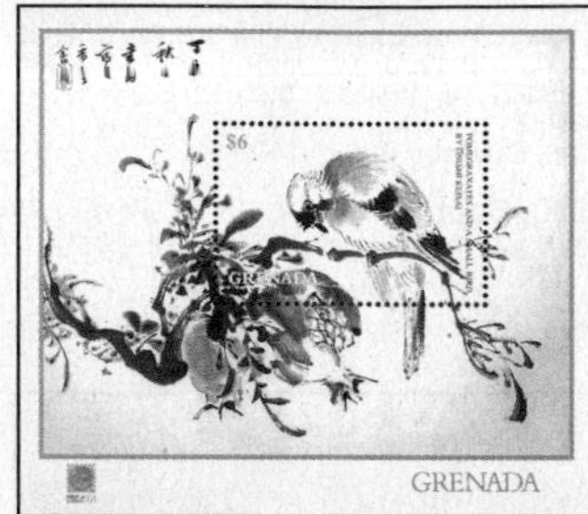

Phila Nippon '01, Japan — A488

Art: 75c, Scenes of Daily Life in Edo, by Miyagawa Choshun. 90c, Twelve Famous Places in Japan, by Kano Isenin Naganobu. $1, After the Rain, by Kawai Gyokudo. $1.25, Ryogoku Bridge Crowded With People, by Kano Kyuei. No. 3106, $2, A Courtesan of Fukagawa, by Katsukawa Shunei. $3, Rite of Bear Killing, by unknown artist.
No. 3108 — Details from the Lotus Sutra, $2, vert.: a, Figure in white at left. b, Figure with flag at lower right. c, Water in center. d, White pagoda at top right.
No. 3109 — Details from the Tale of Genji, $2 (size: 84x28mm): a, Yugao Chapter. b, Suetsumuhana Chapter. c, Wakamurasaki Chapter. d, Momiji-no-ga Chapter.
No. 3110, $6, Pomegranates and a Small Bird, by Onishi Keisai. No. 3111, $6, Bodhisattva from the Lotus Sutra, vert.

2001, May 1 Litho. *Perf. 14*
3102-3107 A487 Set of 6 6.75 6.75

Sheets of 4, #a-d

3108-3109 A488 Set of 2 12.00 12.00

Souvenir Sheets

3110-3111 A488 Set of 2 9.00 9.00

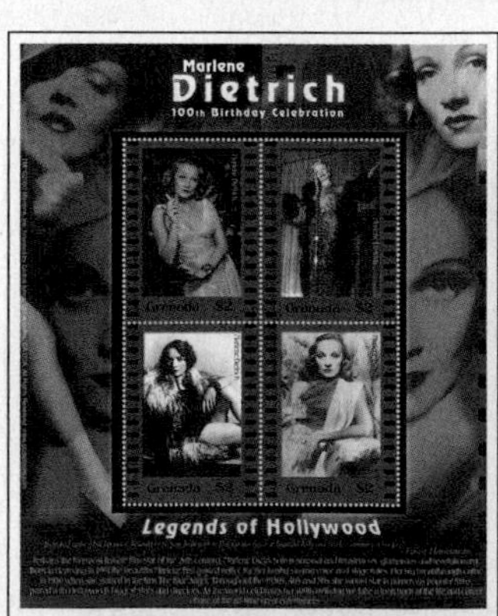

Marlene Dietrich — A489

No. 3112: a, With cigarette. b, Behind microphone. c, Seated, showing legs. d, Seated.

2001, May 15 *Perf. 13¾*
3112 A489 $2 Sheet of 4, #a-d 6.00 6.00

Queen Victoria (1819-1901) — A490

No. 3113: a, In white, as young girl. b, Wearing crown as young woman. c, Wearing crown as old woman.
$6, On throne.

2001, May 15 ***Perf. 14***

3113 A490 $3 Sheet of 3, #a-c 6.75 6.75

Souvenir Sheet

3114 A490 $6 multi 4.50 4.50

Queen Elizabeth II, 75th Birthday — A491

No. 3115: a, Straw hat. b, Red hat. c, Flowered hat. d, Blue hat.
$6, Blue hat with brim.

2001, May 15 ***Perf. 14***

3115 A491 $2 Sheet of 4, #a-d 6.00 6.00

Souvenir Sheet

Perf. 13¾

3116 A491 $6 multi 4.50 4.50

No. 3116 contains one 38x51mm stamp.

UN Women's Human Rights Campaign — A492

Designs: 90c, Woman, bird, torch. $1, Woman.

2001, May 15 **Litho.** ***Perf. 14***

3117-3118 A492 Set of 2 1.40 1.40

Mao Zedong (1893-1976) — A493

No. 3119 — background colors: a, Deep purple. b, Pinkish gray. c, Mottled red violet.
$6, Mao with cap.

2001, May 15 ***Perf. 13¾***

3119 A493 $2 Sheet of 3, #a-c 4.50 4.50

Souvenir Sheet

3120 A493 $3 multi 2.25 2.25

Giuseppe Verdi (1813-1910), Opera Composer — A494

No. 3121: a, Actor with crown. b, Score from Ernani. c, Verdi. d, La Scala Theater, Milan.
$6, Verdi with hat.

2001, May 15 ***Perf. 14***

3121 A494 $2 Sheet of 4, #a-d 6.00 6.00

Souvenir Sheet

3122 A494 $6 multi 4.50 4.50

Toulouse-Lautrec Paintings — A495

No. 3123: a, Alone. b, Two Half-naked Women. c, The Toilette. d, Justine Dieuhl.
$6, Mademoiselle Dihau at the Piano.

2001, May 15 ***Perf. 13¾***

3123 A495 $2 Sheet of 4, #a-d 6.00 6.00

Souvenir Sheet

3124 A495 $6 multi 4.50 4.50

A496

Ships — A497

Designs: 45c, Phoenician trading ship. 75c, Portuguese caravel. 90c, Marblehead schooner. No. 3128, $1, Mala pansi. $1.50, US corvette. $2, Racing schooner.

No. 3131, $1: a, English carrack. b, Mediterranean carrack. c, Spanish galleon. d, Elizabeth Grumster. e, British East Indiaman. f, Clipper ship. g, British gunship. h, British flagship. i, English hoy.

No. 3132, $1: a, English cog. b, Roman merchantman. c, Greek war galley. d, Greek merchantman. e, Norse Oseberg ship. f, Egyptian sailboat. g, Egyptian oared ship. h, 16th cent. galleass. i, Norman sailing ship.

No. 3133, $1: a, Gloucester fishing schooner. b, Racing sloop. c, Chinese junk. d, Sambuk. e, Baltimore clipper schooner. f, Schooner yacht. g, US Clipper ship. h, US frigate. i Steam naval packet.

No. 3134, $6, Gulf Streamer. No. 3135, $6, Suhaili.

2001, June 18 ***Perf. 14***

3125-3130 A496 Set of 6 5.00 5.00

Sheets of 9, #a-i

3131-3133 A496 Set of 3 21.00 21.00

Miniature Sheets

3134-3135 A497 Set of 2 9.00 9.00

Belgica 2001 Intl. Stamp Exhibition, Brussels (Nos. 3131-3133).

A498

Flowers A499

Designs: 25c, Brassavola nodosa. No. 3137, $1, Allamanda cathartica. No. 3138, $2, Aspasia epidendroides. $3, Oncidium splendidum.

35c, Flor de San Miguel. 75c, Red frangipani. No. 3142, $1, Paper flower. No. 3143, $2, Flor de muerto.

No. 3144, $1.50: a, Candlebush. b, Flamingo flower. c, Bush morning glory. d, Laelia anceps. e, Galeandra baueri. f, Chinese hibiscus.

No. 3145, $1.50: a, Red ginger. b, Bird of paradise. c, Psychlis atropurpurea. d, Cattleya velutina. e, Caularthron bicornutum. f, Cattleya warneri.

No. 3146, $1.50, vert.: a, Mandeville. b, Tithonia rotundifolia. c, June rose. d, Columnea argentea. e, Chameleon plant. f, Protlandia albiflora.

No. 3147, $1.50, vert.: a, Wild chestnut. b, Jatropha integerrima. c, Fern tree. d, Geiger tree. e, Golden trumpet. f, Saman.

No. 3148, $6, Ipomoea learii, horiz. No. 3149, $6, Anthurium scherzerianum, horiz.

No. 3150, $6, Ladies eardrops. No. 3151, $6, Heliconia psittacorum, vert.

2001

3136-3139 A498 Set of 4 6.25 6.25

3140-3143 A499 Set of 4 4.75 4.75

Sheets of 6, #a-f

3144-3145 A498 Set of 2 15.00 15.00

3146-3147 A499 Set of 2 15.00 15.00

Souvenir Sheets

3148-3149 A498 Set of 2 11.00 11.00

3150-3151 A499 Set of 2 11.00 11.00

Kane — A500

No. 3152 — Kane: a, In air, above ring ropes. b, On one knee. c, In air. d, With red background. e, With gradiated gray and yellow background. f, Holding up opponent with both hands. g, With spotlight background. h, Holding up shirtless opponent. i, Holding up opponent with one hand.

No. 3153, $5, With red background, diff. No. 3154, $5, With opponent.

2001 ***Perf. 13¾***

3152 A500 $1 Sheet of 9, #a-i 6.75 6.75

Souvenir Sheets

3153-3154 A500 Set of 2 7.50 7.50

The Three Stooges — A501

No. 3155, $1: a, Larry, Moe, two cowboys. b, Moe and Shemp with hats, Larry. c, Shemp and Larry in drag, Moe with mustache. d, Moe with gun, Larry, Shemp, woman. e, Larry, Moe, Shemp with certificate. f, Shemp, Moe. g, Larry, picture. h, Moe, picture. i, Shemp.

No. 3156, $1: a, Larry, Curly, Moe with tool. b, Joe DeRita eating hay, horse, Larry, Moe. c, Shemp, Larry with flowers, Moe. d, Moe, Shemp, Larry, reading paper. e, Larry, Moe, Shemp with pots. f, Moe, Shemp, Larry with money. g, Shemp with knight. h, Joe DeRita, horse, Moe, Larry. i, Larry with knight.

No. 3157, $5, Larry, Moe, Shemp, woman from movie poster. No. 3158, $5, Shemp pulling Moe's arm. No. 3159, $5, Joe DeRita and Larry. No. 3160, $5, Larry and Joe DeRita, jet engine. No. 3161, $5, Moe, Larry holding woman's hand. No. 3162, $5, Larry, Moe listening to jet engine, horiz. No. 3163, $5, Larry, Moe, Shemp and cowboy, horiz. No. 3164, $5, Shemp behind bar, cowboys fighting Larry and Moe, horiz. No. 3165, $5, Curly, Moe, Larry and propeller, horiz. No. 3166, $5, Moe, Larry, woman with drink, horiz. No. 3167, $6, Moe, Larry with knight, horiz. No. 3168, $6, Curly in wringer, Moe, horiz.

2001 Sheets of 9, #a-i

3155-3156 A501 Set of 2 13.50 13.50

Souvenir Sheets

3157-3168 A501 Set of 12 47.50 47.50

Lighthouses
A502

Designs: 25c, Montauk Point, NY. 50c, Alcatraz, CA. $1, Barnegat, NJ. $2, St. Augustine, FL.

No. 3173, $1.50: a, Admiralty Head, WA. b, Hooper's Strait, MD. c, Hunting Island, SC. d, Key West Lighthouse Museum, FL. e, Old Point Loma, CA. f, Old Mackinac Point, MI.

No. 3174, $1.50: a, Point Amour, Canada. b, Inubo-Saki, Japan. c, Belle-Ile. France. d, Faerder, Norway. e, Cape Agulhas, South Africa. f, Minicoy, India.

No. 3175, $1.50: a, Keri, Estonia. b, Anholt, Denmark. c, Porer, Croatia. d, Laotieshan, China. e, Sapientza Methoni, Greece. f, Arkona, Germany.

No. 3176, $6, Boston, MA. No. 3177, $6, Pellworm, Germany. No. 3178, $6, Kvitsoy, Norway. No. 3179, Mahota Pagoda, China.

2001, Aug. 27 Litho. *Perf. 14*

3169-3172 A502 Set of 4 2.75 2.75

Sheets of 6, #a-f

3173-3175 A502 Set of 3 20.00 20.00

Souvenir Sheets

3176-3179 A502 Set of 4 18.00 18.00

Marine Mammals
A503

Designs: 25c, Commerson's dolphin. 50c, Pacific white-sided dolphin. $2, Northern bottlenosed whale. $3, Baird's beaked whale.

No. 3184, $1.50: a, Risso's dolphin. b, Fraser's dolphin. c, Dall's porpoise. d, Right whale. e, Gray whale. f, Minke whale.

No. 3185, $1.50: a, Common dolphin. b, Antillean beaked whale. c, Killer whale. d, Bryde's whale. e, Cuvier's beaked whale. f, Sei whale.

No. 3186, $1.50: a, Harbor porpoise. b, Beluga. c, White-beaked dolphin. d, Narwhal. e, Bowhead whale. f, Fin whale.

No. 3187, $6, Sperm whale. No. 3188, $6, Blue whale. No. 3189, $6, Southern right whale. No. 3190, $6, Humpback whale.

2001, Sept. 10

3180-3183 A503 Set of 4 4.25 4.25

Sheets of 6, #a-f

3184-3186 A503 Set of 3 20.00 20.00

Souvenir Sheets

3187-3190 A503 Set of 4 18.00 18.00

Monet Paintings — A504

No. 3191, horiz.: a, Boats in Winter Quarters, Etretat. b, Regatta at Sainte Adresse. c, The Bridge at Bougival. d, The Beach at Sainte Adresse.

$6, Monet's Garden at Vétheuil.

2001, May 15 Litho. *Perf. 13¾*

3191 A504 $2 Sheet of 4, #a-d 6.00 6.00

Souvenir Sheet

3192 A504 $6 multi 4.50 4.50

2002 World Cup Soccer Championships, Japan and Korea — A505

No. 3193, $1.50: a, Poster, 1950. b, West German championship team, 1954. c, Just Fontaine, 1958. d, Garrincha, Brazil, 1962. e, Bobby Moore, England, 1966. f, Pelé, Brazil, 1970.

No. 3194, $1.50: a, Osvaldo Ardiles, Argentina, 1978. b, Lakhdar Belloumi, Algeria, 1982. c, Diego Maradona, Argentina, 1986. d, Matthaüs and Völler, West Germany, 1990. e, Seo Jung Won, South Korea, 1994. f, Ronaldo, Brazil, 1998.

No. 3195, $6, Face from Jules Rimet trophy. No. 3196, $6, Face and globe from World Cup trophy.

2001, Nov. 29 *Perf. 13¾x14¼*

Sheets of 6, #a-f

3193-3194 A505 Set of 2 13.50 13.50

Souvenir Sheet

3195-3196 A505 Set of 2 9.00 9.00

Christmas
A506

Santa Claus and: 15c, House, Christmas tree. 50c, Trees, snowman. $1, Tree, ice skates. $4, Children.

$6, Santa eating cookie.

2001, Dec. 3 *Perf. 14*

3197-3200 A506 Set of 4 4.25 4.25

Souvneir Sheet

3201 A506 $6 multi 4.50 4.50

A507

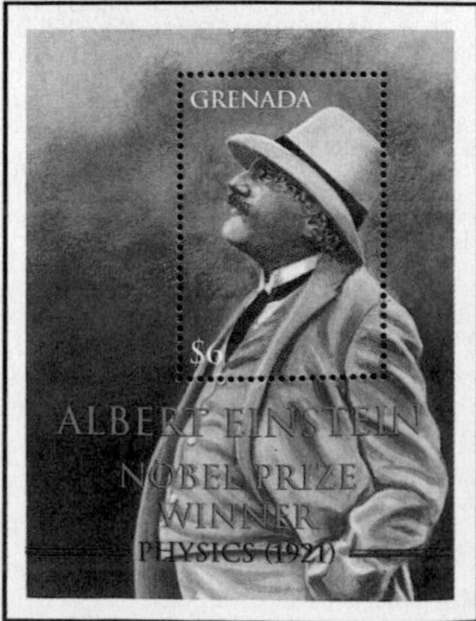

Nobel Prizes, Cent. — A508

1901 Laureates: 75c, Emil A. von Behring, Medicine. 90c, Wilhelm C. Röntgen, Physics. $1, Jacobus H. van't Hoff, Chemistry. No. 3205, $1.50, Frederic Passy, Peace. $2, Jean-Henri Dunant, Peace. $3, René Sully-Prudhomme, Literature.

No. 3208, horiz. — Albert Einstein, 1921 Physics laureate, with: a, Dark hair, black suit. b, Pipe. c, Gray suit. d, Pink sweater. e, Gray hair, black suit. f, Blue sweater.

$6, Einstein wearing hat.

2001, Dec. 13

3202-3207 A507 Set of 6 7.00 7.00

3208 A508 $1.50 Sheet of 6, #a-f 6.75 6.75

Souvenir Sheet

3209 A508 $6 multi 4.50 4.50

Princess Diana (1961-97) — A509

No. 3210: a, Blue gown. b. White gown. c, Red gown.

$6, With pink curtain.

2001, Dec. 13

3210 A509 $1.50 Sheet, 2 each #a-c 6.75 6.75

Souvenir Sheet

3211 A509 $6 multi 4.50 4.50

Queen Mother Type of 1999

No. 3212: a, Queen Mother, Prince Charles, 1948. b, Queen Mother, 1970. c, Queen Mother in Australia, 1958. d, Queen Mother.

$6, Queen Mother, 1953.

2001, Dec. 13 *Perf. 14*

Yellow Orange Frames

3212 A440 $2 Sheet of 4, #a-d, + label 6.00 6.00

Souvenir Sheet

Perf. 13¾

3213 A440 $6 multi 4.50 4.50

Queen Mother's 101st birthday. No. 3213 contains one 38x50mm stamp with a redder backdrop than that found on No. 2881. Sheet margins of Nos. 3212-3213 lack embossing and gold arms found on Nos. 2880-2881.

New Year 2002 (Year of the Horse) — A510

Ceramic horses of T'ang dynasty — No. 3214: a, Brown horse with long, tan mane. b, Blue horse with pink hooves. c, Black horse with gray mane. d, Tan horse with round ornaments.

$4, Brown horse with gray and green saddle.

2001, Dec. 17 *Perf. 13¾*

3214 A510 $1.50 Sheet of 4, #a-d 4.50 4.50

Souvenir Sheet

3215 A510 $4 multi 4.00 4.00

A511

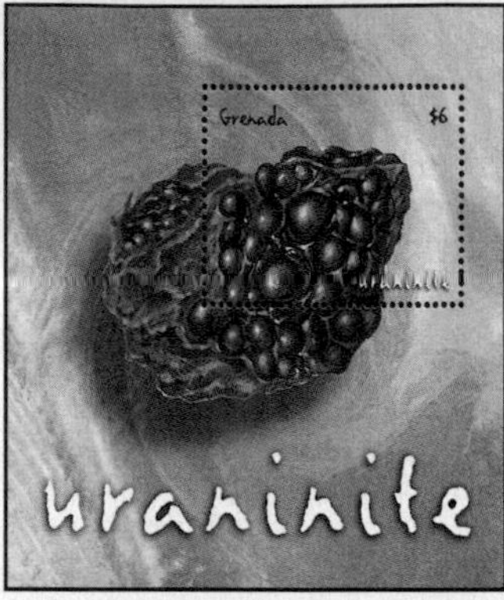

Gemstones and Minerals — A512

Monthly gemstones — No. 3216, $1.50: a, Garnet (January). b, Amethyst (February). c, Aquamarine (March). d, Diamond (April). e, Emerald (May). f, Pearl (June).

No. 3217, $1.50: a, Ruby (July). b, Sardonyx (August). c, Sapphire (September). d, Opal (October). e, Topaz (November). f, Turquoise (December).

Gemstones in mineral form — No. 3218: a, Ruby. b, Diamond. c, Sapphire. d, Opal. e, Turquoise. f, Jade.

No. 3219, $6, Uraninite. No. 3220, $6, Calcite. No. 3221, $6, Quartz, vert.

2001, Dec. 31 *Perf. 14*

Sheets of 6, #a-f

3216-3217 A511 Set of 2 14.50 14.50

3218 A512 $1.50 Sheet of 6, #a-f 7.50 7.50

Souvenir Sheets

3219-3221 A512 Set of 3 14.50 14.50

US Presidents — A513

No. 3222, $1.50 — John F. Kennedy and: a, Field. b, Flag, building, microphone. c, Airplane.

No. 3223, $1.50 — Ronald Reagan: a, In uniform with binoculars. b, With red tie. c, With flag.

No. 3224, $6, Kennedy. No. 3225, $6, Reagan.

2001, Dec. 31

Sheets, 2 each #a-c

3222-3223 A513 Set of 2 13.50 13.50

Souvenir Sheets

3224-3225 A513 Set of 2 9.00 9.00

Souvenir Sheets

I Love Lucy — A514

Designs: No. 3226, $6, Ethel watching Lucy and Ricky dance. No. 3227, $6, Desi, Lucy, Fred and Ethel near door. No. 3228, $6, Desi holding Lucy. No. 3229, $6, Lucy in plaid shirt.

2001 ***Perf. 13¾***
3226-3229 A514 Set of 4 18.00 18.00

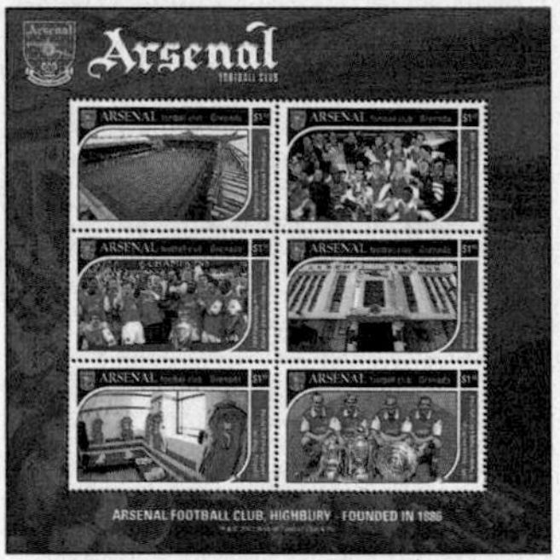

English Soccer Teams — A515

No. 3230, $1.50 — Arsenal: a, Inside of Highbury Stadium. b, Players celebrate 1994 European Cup and Winner's Cup. c, Players celebrate 1998 premiership. d, East stands, Highbury Stadium. e, Locker rooms. f, Four players with trophies, 1998.

No. 3231, $1.50 — Aston Villa: a, Sign on Villa Park. b, Fans watching night game. c, Empty stadium, field at right. d, Empty stadium, field at left. e, Holte End of stadium. f, Fans in stands.

No. 3232, $1.50 — Bolton Wanderers: a, Empty Reebok Stadium. b, Players celebrating 2001 Division 1 playoff win. c, Promotion to Premier League. d, Fans celebrate. e, Players, coaches with trophy. f, Game played in Reebok Stadium.

No. 3233, $1.50 — Everton: a, 2001-02 team. b, Re-signing of Duncan Ferguson. c, Statue of Wiliam Ralph "Dixie" Dean. d, Fans. e, Goodison Park. f, 1969-70 league championship team.

No. 3234, $1.50 — Ipswich Town: a, Players holding banner and trophy after 2000 Division 1 playoff final. b, 2001-02 team. c, Manager George Burley and Chairman David Sheepshanks. d, Pablo Counago fights for ball. e, Captain Matt Holland. f, George Burley receives Manager of the Year award.

No. 3235, $1.50 — Liverpool: a, Anfield. b, 2000-01 Worthington Cup winners. c, 2000-01 FA Cup winners. d, Fans. e, 2000-01 UEFA Cup winners. f, Treble Cup parade.

No. 3236, $1.50 — Manchester United: a, Legends Meredith, Law and Charlton. b, Three 1998-99 trophies. c, Views of Old Trafford, 1948, 1956. d, Recent views of Old Trafford. e, Third premiership in three years, 2000-01. f, Heroes, Best, Robson and Beckham.

No. 3237, $1.50 — Rangers: a, View of Ibrox Stadium from street. b, 1972 European Cup and Winner's Cup team. c, Scottish FA Cup, Scottish Premier League Trophy. d, Aerial view of Ibrox Stadium. e, Fans in stadium. f, Nine consecutive Scottish League wins.

2001, Sept. 12 **Litho.** ***Perf. 13¼***
Sheets of 6, #a-f
3230-3237 A515 Set of 8 55.00 55.00

See Nos. 3286-3294.

Reign of Queen Elizabeth II, 50th Anniv. — A516

No. 3238: a, With Prince Philip. b, Wearing flowered hat. c, Wearing tiara. d, Wearing gray coat with white collar.
$6, Wearing uniform.

2002, Feb. 6 ***Perf. 14½***
3238 A516 $2 Sheet of 4, #a-d 6.00 6.00

Souvenir Sheet
3239 A516 $6 multi 4.50 4.50

United We Stand — A517

2002, Feb. ***Perf. 13¾x13½***
3240 A517 $2 multi 1.50 1.50

Issued in sheets of 4.

Dale Earnhardt, Race Car Driver — A518

Years of Winston Cup Championships: No. 3241, $2, 1980. No. 3242, $2, 1986. No. 3243, $2, 1987. No. 3244, $2, 1990. No. 3245, $2, 1991. No. 3246, $2, 1993. No. 3247, $2, 1994.

2002, Mar. 4 **Litho.** ***Perf. 14x13¾***
3241-3247 A518 Set of 7 12.00 12.00

Mickey Mouse A519

No. 3249 — Scenes from: a, The Nifty Nineties, 1941. b, Magician Mickey, 1937. c, Steamboat Willie, 1928. d, Fantasia, 1940. e, Mickey Mouse Club, 1955. f, Cactus Kid, 1930. g, The Prince and the Pauper, 1990. h, Brave Little Tailor, 1938. i, Canine Caddy, 1941.

2002, Apr. 24 ***Perf. 13¾***
3248 A519 $1 shown .90 .90
3249 A519 $1 Sheet of 9, #a-i 8.75 8.75

No. 3248 was printed in sheets of nine.

American Civil War Naval History — A520

No. 3250, $1: a, CSS Teaser. b, US gunboats on the James River. c, USS Tyler. d, USS Maratanza. e, USS Metacomet. f, USS Rattler.

No. 3251, $1.25: a, CSS Tennessee. b, USS Hartford. c, USS Chickasaw. d, USS Ossipee. e, Battle of Mobile Bay. f, USS Chickasaw at Mobile Bay.

No. 3252, $1.50: a, CSS H.L. Hunley. b, USS Cumberland. c, CSS Old Dominion. d, USS Housatonic. e, USS Hartford. f, USS Essex.

No. 3253, $1.50: a, CSS Alabama. b, USS Kearsarge and CSS Alabama. c, USS Hatteras. d, CSS Alabama and decoy. e, CSS Sumter. f, USS Kearsarge.

No. 3254, $6, USS Monitor. No. 3255, $6, CSS Florida. No. 3256, $6, CSS Tennessee. No. 3257, $6, Capt. Raphael Semmes aboard CSS Alabama.

2002, Apr. 8 **Litho.** ***Perf. 13¼x13½***
Sheets of 6, #a-f
3250-3253 A520 Set of 4 28.00 28.00

Souvenir Sheets
3254-3257 A520 Set of 4 22.00 22.00

Chiune Sugihara, Japanese Diplomat Who Saved Jews in World War II — A521

2002, July 1 ***Perf. 13½x13¾***
3258 A521 $2 multi 1.50 1.50

Printed in sheets of 4.

2002 Winter Olympics, Salt Lake City A522

Skier with: No. 3259, $2, Red skis. No. 3260, $2, Yellow skis.

2002, July 1 ***Perf. 13¼x13½***
3259-3260 A522 Set of 2 3.00 3.00
a. Souvenir sheet, #3259-3260 3.00 3.00

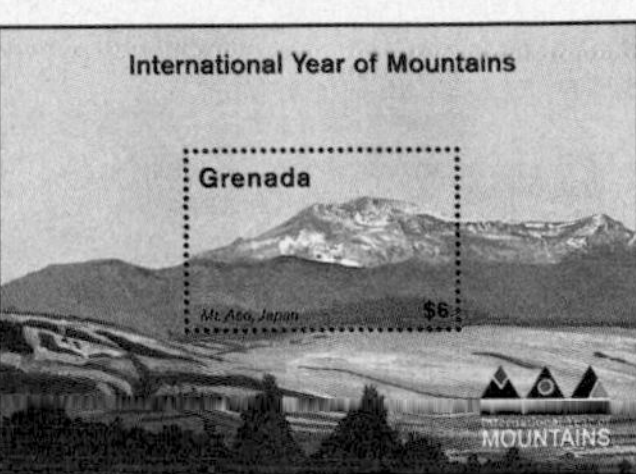

Intl. Year of Mountains — A523

No. 3261: a, Mt. Mawensi, Kenya. b, Mt. Stanley, Uganda. c, Mt. Taweche, Nepal. d, Mt. San Exupery, Argentina.
$6, Mt. Aso, Japan.

2002, July 1
3261 A523 $2 Sheet of 4, #a-d 6.00 6.00

Souvenir Sheet
3262 A523 $6 multi 4.50 4.50

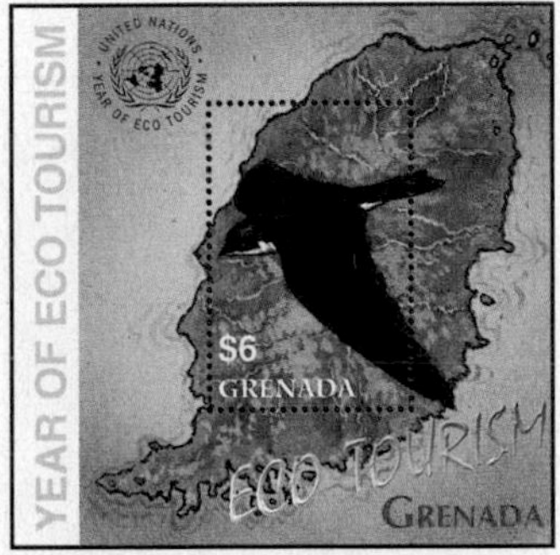

Intl. Year of Ecotourism — A524

No. 3263, horiz.: a, Tower and pennants. b, Bird. c, Flower, vacationer on chair. d, Diver, fish. e, Fish. f, Sailboats.
$6, Map of Grenada, bird.

2002, July 1 ***Perf. 13¼x13½***
3263 A524 $1 Sheet of 6, #a-f 4.50 4.50

Souvenir Sheet
Perf. 13½x13¼
3264 A524 $6 multi 4.50 4.50

No. 3263 was overprinted in sheet margin "Hurricane Relief 2004" in 2005.

20th World Scout Jamboree, Thailand — A525

No. 3265, horiz.: a, Scout in canoe with oar out of water. b, Scout in canoe with oar in water. c, Bugler. d, Scout making Scout sign.
$6, Scout saluting.

2002, July 1 ***Perf. 13¼x13½***
3265 A525 $2 Sheet of 4, #a-d 7.50 7.50

Souvenir Sheet
Perf. 13½x13¼
3266 A525 $6 multi 5.00 5.00

Model Heidi Klum — A526

No. 3267: a, Arms up. b, Arms down. c, No arms shown.

2002, Aug. 16 *Perf. 14*

3267 A526 $1.50 Horiz. strip of 3, #a-c 3.50 3.50

Printed in sheets containing two strips.

Elvis Presley (1935-77) A527

2002, Aug. 26 *Perf. 13½x13¾*

3268 A527 $1 multi .75 .75

Printed in sheets of 9.

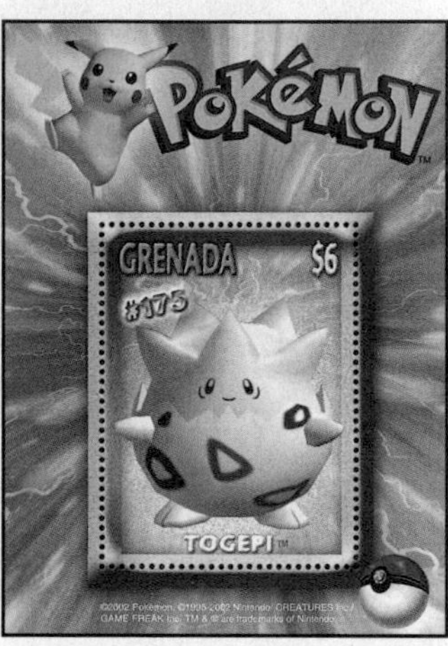

Pokémon — A528

No. 3269: a, Mareep. b, Sunkern. c, Teddiursa. d, Swinub. e, Murkrow. f, Snubbull. $6, Togepi.

2002, Aug. 26 *Perf. 13¾*

3269 A528 $1.50 Sheet of 6, #a-f 6.75 6.75

Souvenir Sheet

3270 A528 $6 multi 4.50 4.50

A529

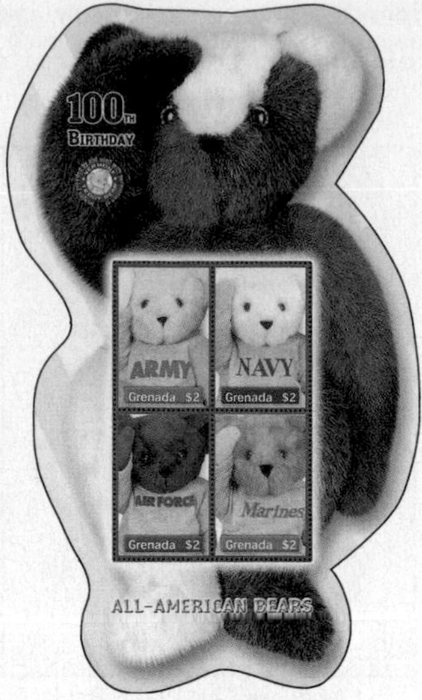

A530

Teddy Bears, Cent. — A531

No. 3271: a, 25c, Bear with red hat, lace collar, cheese wheels. b, $1.25, Bear with black cap. c, $3, Bear with wooden shoes. d, $5, Bear with red hat and ribbon.

No. 3272: a, Army bear. b, Navy bear. c, Air Force bear. d, Marines bear.

No. 3273: a, Basketball bear. b, Martial arts bear. c, Golf bear. d, Baseball bear.

2002, Aug. 26 *Perf. 14*

3271 A529 Sheet of 4, #a-d 7.25 7.25

Perf. 14¼

3272 A530 $2 Sheet of 4, #a-d 6.00 6.00
3273 A531 $2 Sheet of 4, #a-d 6.00 6.00

Dutch Nobel Prize Winners — A532

Dutch Lighthouses — A533

Traditional Dutch Women's Costumes — A534

No. 3274: a, Jacobus H. van't Hoff, Chemistry, 1901. b, Nobel Peace medal. c, Pieter Zeeman, Physics, 1902. d, Johannes D. van der Waals, Physics, 1910. e, Tobias M. C. Asser, Peace, 1911. f, Heike Kammerlingh-Onnes, Physics, 1913.

No. 3275: a, Schiermonnikoog. b, Texel. c, Egmond. d, Scheveningen. e, Schouwen. f, Hellevoetsluis.

No. 3276: a, Zeeland (woman with red necklace, patterned dress). b, Noord-Brabant (woman with black shawl). c, Noord-Holland (woman with flowered neckpiece).

2002, Aug. 29 *Perf. 13½x13¼*

3274 A532 $1.50 Sheet of 6, #a-f 6.75 6.75
3275 A533 $1.50 Sheet of 6, #a-f 6.75 6.75

Perf. 13¼

3276 A534 $3 Sheet of 3, #a-c 6.75 6.75

Amphilex 2002 Intl. Stamp Exhibition, Amsterdam.

Shirley Temple — A535

Scenes from "Our Little Girl" — No. 3277, horiz.: a, With man. b, With man and woman. c, With dog and man. d, With woman and two men. e, On seesaw with dog. f, With dog.

No. 3278: a, With woman. b, with man and clown. c, Kneeling beside chair. d, With man and woman.

$6, In pink dress.

2002, Sept. 3 *Perf. 14¼*

3277 A535 $1.50 Sheet of 6, #a-f 6.75 6.75
3278 A535 $2 Sheet of 4, #a-d 6.00 6.00

Souvenir Sheet

3279 A535 $6 multi 4.50 4.50

Souvenir Sheet

Terrorist Attack on World Trade Center, 1st Anniv. — A536

2002, Sept. 11 *Perf. 13¾*

3280 A536 $6 multi 4.50 4.50

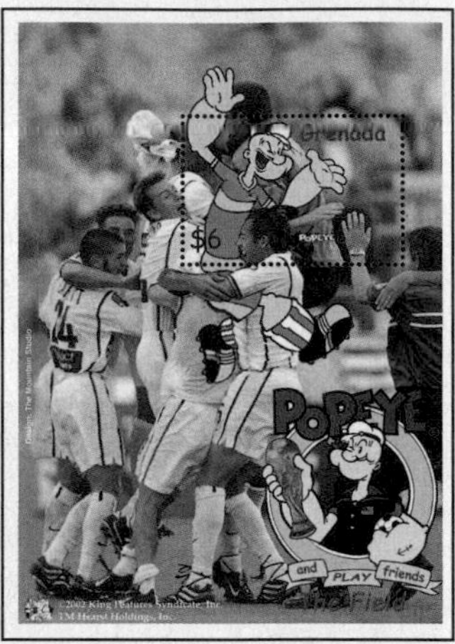

Popeye — A537

No. 3281, vert.: a, Popeye in Florence, Italy. b, Popeye and Brutus in Paris, France. c, Popeye in Athens, Greece. d, Popeye and Olive Oyl in Venice, Italy. e, Popeye in London, England. f, Popeye in Norway.

No. 3282, vert. — At soccer match: a, Swee'Pea. b, Jeep. c, Popeye. d, Brutus.

No. 3283, $6, Popeye playing soccer. No. 3284, $6, Brutus playing soccer. No. 3285, $6, Popeye at Leaning Tower of Pisa, vert.

Perf. 14¼ (#3281, 3285), 14

2002, Sept. 23

3281 A537 $1.50 Sheet of 6, #a-f 6.75 6.75
3282 A537 $2 Sheet of 4, #a-d 6.00 6.00

Souvenir Sheets

3283-3285 A537 Set of 3 13.50 13.50

No. 3218 contains six 38x50mm stamps; No. 3285 contains one 50x75mm stamp.

English Soccer Teams Type of 2001

No. 3286, $1.50 — Tottenham Hotspur: a, Fans watching match in White Hart Lane Stadium. b, Sheringham and Anderton in action against Fulham. c, Poyet scoring against Liverpool. d, Tottenham Hotspur wins UEFA Cup, 1972. e, Celebrations after win against Chelsea. f, Fans in stadium, team insignia.

No. 3287, $1.50 — Manchester City: a, Maine Road Stadium from stands. b, Fans celebrate becoming Division One champions. c, Manager Kevin Keegan and trophy. d, Team with trophy. e, Players wearing medals, with trophy. f, Field level view of Maine Road Stadium.

No. 3288, $1.50 — Norwich City: a, Match at the Nest. b, Promotion to the Top Flight, 1971-72. c, Milk Cup win, 1985. d, Carrow Road Stadium. e, Win against Bayern Munich, 1993. f, Action from 1958-59 Cup run.

No. 3289, $1.50 — Arsenal, Double Winners: a, Tony Adams and Patrick Vieira hold FA Cup. b, Team wearing tan shirts, holding championship bannners. c, Team without banners, at Premiership trophy presentation. d, Photo of 2001-02 Premiership team, standing and wearing red shirts. e, Four players celebrate winning goal against Chelsea. f, Manager Arsene Wenger and Tony Adams at Double Winners Parade.

No. 3290, $1.50 — Arsenal, Premiership Winners: a, Inside of Highbury Stadium, team emblem and name in red panels. b, Celebrations after Gilberto scores winning goal. c, Team with FA Community Shield sign. d, Team photo, empty stands. e, Gilberto with FA Community Shield. f, Highbury Stadium with fans, team emblem.

No. 3291, $1.50 — Manchester United: a, David Beckham after free kick. b, Team photo, empty stands. c, Aerial view of Old Trafford Stadium. d, Celebration after Ole Gunnar Solskjaer's 100th goal for Manchester United. e, Fans at Old Trafford Stadium. f, North stand of Old Trafford Stadium.

No. 3292, $1.50 — Liverpool: a, Anfield's Centenary stand, as seen from Main stand. b, 2002-03 team photo. c, Gerard Houllier and Phil Thompson. d, Milan Baros celebrates goal. e, Vladimir Smicer congratulating Danny Murphy. f, The Kop, as seen from Anfield Road end.

No. 3293, $1.50 — Celtic: a, Interior of Celtic Park. b, Martin O'Neill with SPL Trophy. c, Henrik Larsson celebrating goal. d, 2002-03 team photo. e, Players celebrating a goal. f, Exterior of Celtic Park.

No. 3294, $1.50 — Chelsea: a, Night match at Stamford Bridge Stadium. b, Team with 1998 Cup Winners' Cup Final trophy. c, Fans in stadium. d, Sign for the Shed End. e, Field level view of Stamford Bridge Stadium. f, Players celebrating 2000 FA Cup victory.

2002 *Perf. 14x13¾*

Sheets of 6, #a-f

3286-3294 A515 Set of 9 60.00 60.00

Issued: Nos. 3286-3289, 9/23; Nos. 3290-3294, 11/14.

Butterflies, Insects, Mushrooms and Whales — A538

No. 3295, $1.50 — Butterflies: a, Common morpho. b, Blue night. c, Small flambeau. d, Grecian shoemaker. e, Orange-barred sulphur. f, Cramer's mesene.

No. 3296, $1.50 — Insects: a, Honeybees. b, Dragonfly. c, Milkweed bug. d, Bumblebee. e, Migratory grasshopper. f, Monarch caterpillar.

No. 3297, $1.50 — Mushrooms: a, Boletus crocipodius. b, King bolete. c, Velvet shank. d, Death cap. e, Golden cavalier. f, Fly agaric.

No. 3298, $1.50 — Whales: a, Blue. b, Pygmy sperm. c, Humpback. d, Killer. e, Bowhead. f, Gray.

No. 3299, $6, Figure-of-eight butterfly. No. 3300, $6, Hercules beetle. No. 3301, $6, Sharp-scaled parasol mushroom. No. 3302, $6, Blue whale, horiz.

2002, Oct. 21 *Perf. 14*

Sheets of 6, #a-f

3295-3298 A538 Set of 4 27.50 27.50

Souvenir Sheets

3299-3302 A538 Set of 4 18.00 18.00

Sir Norman Wisdom, British Comedian A539

2002, Nov. 3 *Perf. 13¾*

3303 A539 $1.50 multi 1.10 1.10

Printed in sheets of 6.

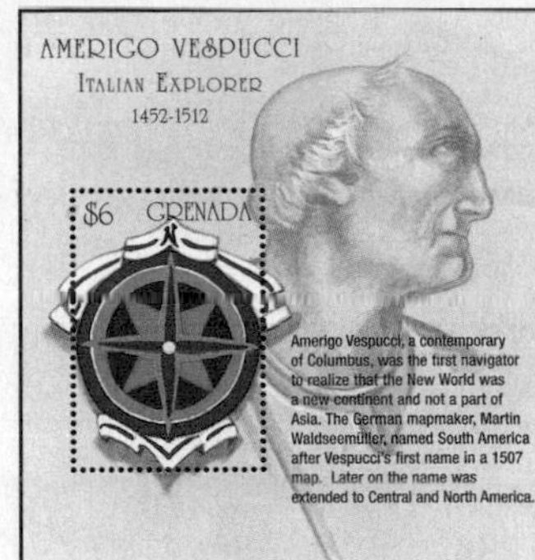

Amerigo Vespucci (1454-1512), Explorer — A540

No. 3304, $3: a, Map of South America, ship. b, Compass rose, ship. c, Map of Europe and Africa.

No. 3305, $3, horiz.: a, Sextant, map of northern South America. b, Vespucci, map of central South America. c, Ship, map of southern South America.

No. 3306, $6, Compass rose. No. 3307, $6, Globe.

2002, Nov. 4 *Perf. 13¾*

Sheets of 3, #a-c

3304-3305 A540 Set of 2 13.50 13.50

Souvenir Sheets

Perf. 14

3306-3307 A540 Set of 2 9.00 9.00

No. 3304 contains three 38x50mm stamps; No. 3305 contains three 50x38mm stamps.

Christmas A541

Cimabue paintings: 15c, Madonna and Child, Four Angels and St. Francis, entire. 25c, Madonna and Child and Two Angels, vert. 50c, Madonna Enthroned, detail, vert. $1, Madonna Enthroned, entire, vert. $4, Madonna and Child, Four Angels and St. Francis, detail, vert.

$6, Nativity by Perugino, vert.

2002, Nov. 4 *Perf. 14*

3308-3312 A541 Set of 5 4.50 4.50

Souvenir Sheet

3313 A541 $6 multi 4.50 4.50

Second Round Matches of 2002 World Cup Soccer Championships, Japan and Korea — A542

No. 3314, $1.50 — Sweden vs. Senegal: a, Johan Mjalby. b, Magnus Hedman. c, Fredrik Ljungberg. d, Khalilou Fadiga. e, El Hadji Diouf. f, Papa Bouba Diop.

No. 3315, $1.50 — Brazil vs. Belgium: a, Roberto Carlos. b, Juninho Paulista. c, Ronaldinho. d, Johan Walem. e, Marc Wilmots. f, Bart Goor.

No. 3316, $3 — Swedish players: a, Henrik Larsson. b, Niclas Alexandersson.

No. 3317, $3 — Senegal players: a, Fadiga. b, Coach Bruno Metsu.

No. 3318, $3 — Brazil players: a, Coach Luiz Felipe Scolari. b, Ronaldo.

No. 3319, $3 — Belgium players: a, Wesley Sonck. b, Coach Robert Waseige.

2002, Nov. 18 *Perf. 13¼*

Sheets of 6, #a-f

3314-3315 A542 Set of 2 13.50 13.50

Souvenir Sheets of 2, #a-b

3316-3319 A542 Set of 4 18.00 18.00

Souvenir Sheet

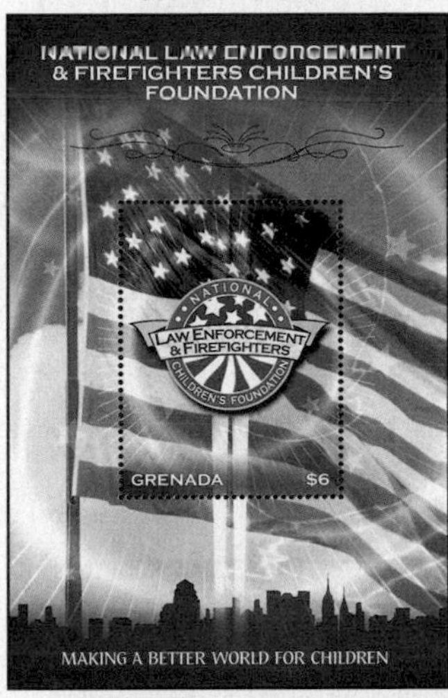

United States Natl. Law Enforcement and Firefighters Children's Foundation — A543

2002, Nov. 28 *Perf. 14¼*

3320 A543 $6 multi 4.50 4.50

Pres. John F. Kennedy (1917-63) — A544

No. 3321, horiz.: a, Meeting with Cabinet. b, Signing bill into law. c, Meeting civil rights leaders. d, With Astronaut John Glenn. e, On campaign trail. f, Arrival in Dallas, Nov. 22, 1963.

$6, At microphone.

2002, Dec. 4 *Perf. 14*

3321 A544 $1.50 Sheet of 6, #a-f 6.75 6.75

Souvenir Sheet

3322 A544 $6 multi 4.50 4.50

Intl. Federation of Stamp Dealers Associations, 50th Anniv. — A545

2002, Dec. 16 **Litho.**

3323 A545 $2 multi 1.50 1.50

Princess Diana (1961-97) — A546

No. 3324: a, Wearing bow tie. b, Wearing blue dress. c, Wearing red and white hat. d, Holding flowers.

$6, Wearing earphones and microphone.

2002 *Perf. 14*

3324 A546 $2 Sheet of 4, #a-d 6.00 6.00

Souvenir Sheet

3325 A546 $6 multi 4.50 4.50

I Love Lucy Type of 2001

Souvenir Sheets

No. 3326, $6, Lucy standing near fireplace. No. 3327, $6, Lucy and Ethel at desk. No. 3328, $6, Fred and Desi standing. No. 3329, $6, Fred and Desi at desk, horiz.

2002 *Perf. 13¾*

3326-3329 A514 Set of 4 18.00 18.00

New Year 2003 (Year of the Ram) A547

2003, Jan. 27 *Perf. 13¾*

3330 A547 $1.25 multi .95 .95

Printed in sheets of 4.

M-Gears — A548

No. 3331: a, Airplane. b, Vehicle. c, Monster. d, Race car.

2003, Feb. 16 **Litho.** *Perf. 14¼*

3331 A548 $2 Sheet of 4, #a-d 6.00 6.00

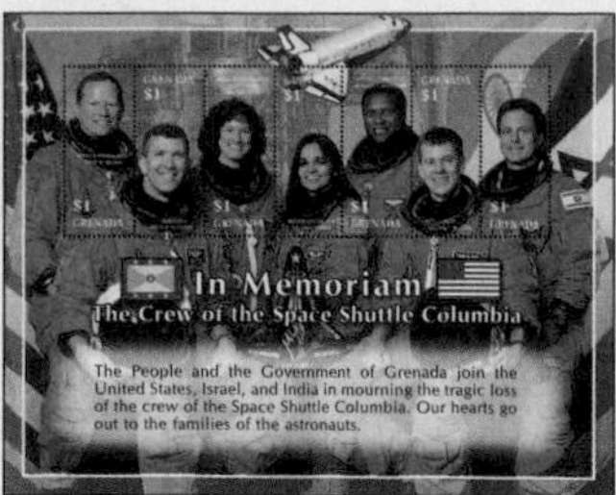

Astronauts Killed in Space Shuttle Columbia Accident — A549

No. 3332: a, Mission Specialist 1 David M. Brown. b, Commander Rick D. Husband. c, Mission Specialist 4 Laurel Blair Salton Clark. d, Mission Specialist 4 Kalpana Chawla. e, Payload Commander Michael P. Anderson. f, Pilot William C. McCool. g, Payload Specialist 4 Ilan Ramon.

2003, Apr. 7 ***Perf. 13¼***
3332 A549 $1 Sheet of 7, #a-g 0.00 0.00

Paintings of Gustav Klimt (1862-1918) A550

Designs: 15c, Jardin aux Tournesols. 25c, L'allée aux Poulets. 75c, Allée dans le Parc du Schloss Kammer. $1, Portrait of Johanna Staude. $1.25, Portrait of Friederike Maria Beer. $3, Portrait of Mäda Primavesi.
No. 3339: a, La Jeune Fille. b, Les Amies. c, Le Berceau. d, La Vie et la Mort.
$6, Portrait of Margaret Stonborough-Wittgenstein.

2003, Apr. 28 ***Perf. 14¼***
3333-3338 A550 Set of 6 5.00 5.00
3339 A550 $2 Sheet of 4, #a-d 6.00 6.00

Size: 82x103mm

Imperf

3340 A550 $6 multi 4.50 4.50

Art of Yoshitoshi Taiso (1839-92) A551

Designs: 75c, A Harlot in Repose. $1, A "Shakuni," or Geisha, Who Serves Wine or Sake. $1.25, A "Joro," or Low Ranking Prostitute, Having a Snack. $3, A Geisha Known as a "Geiko," or Entertainer Relaxing.
No. 3345: a, Enjoying a Cool Evening Breeze in a Pleasure Boat. b, A Fukagawa Waitress Carrying a Wooden Table Laden With Food. c, A Spoiled Unmarried Woman Pretending to Be Displeased With an Admirer. d, A Coy Young Girl, Biting Her Sleeve Pretending to Be Embarrassed.
$6, A Geisha About to Board a Party Boat.

2003, Apr. 28 ***Perf. 14¼***
3341-3344 A551 Set of 4 4.50 4.50
3345 A551 $2 Sheet of 4, #a-d 6.00 6.00

Souvenir Sheet

3346 A551 $6 multi 4.50 4.50

Paintings by Lucas Cranach the Elder (1472-1553) — A552

Details from St. Catherine Altarpiece: 50c, Sts. Dorothy, Agnes and Cunigonde. 75c, St. Margaret, vert. $1.25, St. Barbara, vert. $3, Detail from left wing, vert.
No. 3351 — Painting details: a, Lot and His Daughters. b, David and Bathsheba. c, The Agony in the Garden. d, The Adoration of the Magi.
$6, Detail of Samson and Delilah, vert.

2003, Apr. 28
3347-3350 A552 Set of 4 4.25 4.25
3351 A552 $2 Sheet of 4, #a-d 0.00 0.00

Souvenir Sheet

3352 A552 $6 multi 4.50 4.50

Teddy Bear A553

2003, Apr. 29 Embroidered ***Imperf.***
Self-Adhesive
3353 A553 $15 multi 11.50 11.50

Issued in sheets of 4.

Reading Rods — A554

No. 3354 — Children and: a, Bulletin board. b, Blackboard. c, Globe. d, Teacher.

2003, May 5 Litho. ***Perf. 13¾***
3354 A554 $2 Sheet of 4, #a-d 6.00 6.00

Tour de France Bicycle Race, Cent. — A555

No. 3355, $2: a, Sylvére Maes, 1939. b, Jean Lazaridés, 1946. c, Jean Robic, 1947. d, Gino Bartali, 1948.
No. 3356, $2: a, Fausto Coppi, 1949. b, Ferdinand Kubler, 1950. c, Hugo Koblet, 1951. d, Coppi, 1952.
No. 3357, $2: a, Roger Walkowiak, 1956. b, Jacques Anquetil, 1957. c, Charly Gaul, 1958. d, Federico Bahamontes, 1959.
No. 3358, $6, Coppi, 1949, diff. No. 3359, $6, Kubler, 1950, diff. No. 3360, $6, Anquetil, 1964.

2003, June 17 ***Perf. 13¼***
Sheets of 4, #a-d
3355-3357 A555 Set of 3 18.00 18.00

Souvenir Sheets

3358-3360 A555 Set of 3 13.50 13.50

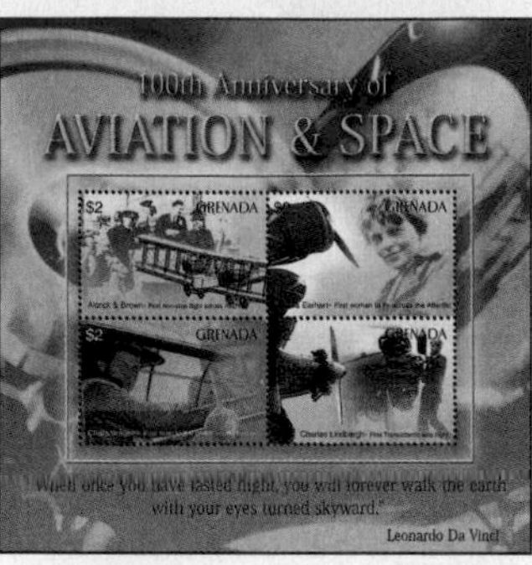

Powered Flight, Cent. — A556

No. 3361, $2: a: First non-stop transatlantic flight by Alcock & Brown. b, Amelia Earhart, first woman to fly across Atlantic. c, Chuck Yeager, first man to break sound barrier. d, Charles Lindbergh, first solo transatlantic flight.
No. 3362, $2: a, Louis Bleriot, first flight across English Channel. b, Johnnie Johnson, ace pilot in World War II. c, Wright Brothers, first powered flight. d, Jacqueline Cochran, first woman to break sound barrier.

2003, June 24 ***Perf. 13¼x13½***
Sheets of 4, #a-d
3361-3362 A556 Set of 2 12.00 12.00

Coronation of Queen Elizabeth II, 50th Anniv. — A557

Designs: No. 3363, $2, Enthroning of the Queen. No. 3364, $2, Duke pays homage to the Queen. No. 3365, $2, Celebration of Holy Communion. No. 3366, $2, Floodlit mall. No. 3367, $2, Queen on balcony. No. 3368, $2, St. Edward's Chair. No. 3369, $2, Official coronation portrait. No. 3370, $2, Queen leaves Abbey.
$6, Queen in coach.

2003, June 30 ***Perf. 13½x14***
3363-3370 A557 Set of 8 12.00 12.00

Souvenir Sheet

3371 A557 $6 multi 4.50 4.50

No. 3371 contains one 38x51mm stamp.

CARICOM, 30th Anniv. — A558

2003, July 4 ***Perf. 14***
3372 A558 $1 multi .75 .75

Intl. Year of Fresh Water — A559

No. 3373: a, Levera Pond. b, Concord Falls. c, Lake Antoine.
$6, Lake Grand Etang.

2003, July 4 ***Perf. 13½x13¼***
3373 A559 $2 Sheet of 3, #a-c 4.50 4.50

Souvenir Sheet

3374 A559 $6 multi 4.50 4.50

Circus Performers — A560

No. 3375, $2: a, Clive Andrews. b, Bell Bozo. c, Bumpsy. d, Annie Frattellini.
No. 3376, $2: a, Stag. b, Olga and Regina Kolpensky. c, Brad Byers. d, Tiger.

2003, July 14 ***Perf. 14***
Sheets of 4, #a-d
3375-3376 A560 Set of 2 12.00 12.00

St. George's University School of Medicine A561

Designs: 75c, Aerial view of campus. $1, Campus buildings.

2003, July 23
3377-3378 A561 Set of 2 1.40 1.40

Prince William, 21st Birthday — A562

No. 3379, vert.: a, With bouquet of flowers. b, Wearing blue shirt. c, Wearing blue shirt, close-up.
$6, Wearing plaid shirt.

2003, Aug. 25
3379 A562 $3 Sheet of 3, #a-c 6.75 6.75

Souvenir Sheet

3380 A562 $6 multi 4.50 4.50

Operation Iraqi Freedom — A563

No. 3381, $1: a, Gazelle helicopter. b, Hovercraft. c, Jaguar. d, HMS Liverpool. e, Harrier GR7. f, Challenger 2 tank. g, Chinook helicopters. h, Tornado F3.

No. 3382, $1: a, Gen. Sir Mike Jackson. b, Air Vice-marshal Glenn Torpy. c, Air Marshal Brian Burridge. d, Maj. Gen. Tony Milton. e, Maj. Gen. Peter Wall. f, Maj. Gen. Barney White-Spunner. g, Adm. Sir Alan West. h, Air Chief Marshal Sir Peter Squire.

2003, Aug. 29 **Sheets of 8, #a-h**

3381-3382 A563 Set of 2 12.00 12.00

Pres. Ronald Reagan — A564

No. 3383: a, On Korean demilitarized zone, 1983. b, With British Prime Minister Margaret Thatcher. c, Speaking at the Berlin Wall, 1987. d, Signing IMF treaty with Soviet Secretary General Mikhail Gorbachev. e, With Egyptian President Anwar Sadat, 1981. f, At home with his horse.

$6, Addressing the nation.

2003

3383 A564 $1.50 Sheet of 6, #a-f 6.75 6.75

Souvenir Sheet

3384 A564 $6 multi 4.50 4.50

Souvenir Sheet

Anatoly Karpov, Chess Champion — A565

2003 ***Perf. 13¼***

3385 A565 $20 multi 15.00 15.00

Prehistoric Animals — A566

No. 3386, $2, horiz.: a, Spinosaurus. b, Herrerasaurus. c, Protarchaeopteryx. d, Sinosauropteryx.

No. 3387, $2, horiz.: a, Allosaurus. b, Crylophosaurus. c, Eoraptor. d, Caudipteryx.

No. 3388, $6, Archaeopteryx. No. 3389, $6, Triceratops.

2003, Oct. 23 Litho. ***Perf. 13¼x13½***

Sheets of 4, #a-d

3386-3387 A566 Set of 2 14.00 14.00

Souvenir Sheets

Perf. 13½x13¼

3388-3389 A566 Set of 2 10.00 10.00

Flowers A567

Designs: 25c, Yellow allamanda. 50c, Queen of the night. 75c, Anthurium. $3, Oleander.

No. 3394: a, Blue passion flower. b, Chinese hibiscus. c, Poinsettia. d, Bird of paradise.

$6, Shrimp flower.

2003, Oct. 23 ***Perf. 14***

3390-3393 A567 Set of 4 3.50 3.50
3394 A567 $2 Sheet of 4, #a-d 6.00 6.00

Souvenir Sheet

3395 A567 $6 multi 4.50 4.50

Fish A568

Designs: No. 3396, $1, Gold coney. No. 3397, $1, Spotfin butterflyfish. No. 3398, $1, Smallmouth grunt. $3, Night sergeant.

No. 3400: a, Cuban hogfish. b, Bluehead wrasse. c, Black cap gramma. d, Cherubfish.

$6, Banded butterflyfish.

2003, Oct. 23

3396-3399 A568 Set of 4 4.50 4.50
3400 A568 $2 Sheet of 4, #a-d 6.00 6.00

Souvenir Sheet

3401 A568 $6 multi 4.50 4.50

Birds A569

Designs: No. 3402, $1.25, Osprey. No. 3403, $1.25, Northern oriole. No. 3404, $1.25, Red-eyed vireo. $3, Bahama pintail.

No. 3406: a, Slaty-capped shrike vireor. b, Northern flicker. c, Blackburnian warbler. d, Common tody-flycatcher.

$6, Blue grosbeak, vert.

2003, Oct. 23

3402-3405 A569 Set of 4 5.00 5.00
3406 A569 $2 Sheet of 4, #a-d 6.00 6.00

Souvenir Sheet

3407 A569 $6 multi 4.50 4.50

Christmas A570

Paintings by Giotto: 35c, Madonna and Child, from the Church of the Ognissanti. 75c, Ognissanti Madonna. $1, Madonna of the Angels. $4, Madonna and Child, from the Florentine Church of San Giorgio alla Costa.

$6, Holy Family with John the Baptist and St. Elizabeth, horiz.

2003, Nov. 17 ***Perf. 14¼***

3408-3411 A570 Set of 4 4.75 4.75

Souvenir Sheet

3412 A570 $6 multi 4.50 4.50

St. Petersburg, Russia, 300th anniv. (No. 3412).

Paintings by Norman Rockwell (1894-1978) — A571

No. 3413, vert.: a, The Spring Tonic. b, The Facts of Life. c, The Proper Gratuity. d, The Runaway.

$6, Boy with Carriage.

2003, Dec. 8 ***Perf. 13¼***

3413 A571 $2 Sheet of 4, #a-d 6.00 6.00

Souvenir Sheet

3414 A571 $6 multi 4.50 4.50

Paintings in the Hermitage, St. Petersburg, Russia — A572

Designs: 45c, At the Palmist's, by Jean-Baptiste Le Prince, vert. $1, A Visit to Grandmother, by Louis Le Nain. $1.50, Musicale, by Dirck Hals. $3, A Young Woman in the Morning, by Frans van Mieris the Elder, vert.

No. 3419, vert.: a, Louis, Grand Dauphin de France, by Louis Tocqué. b, Count P. A. Stroganov as a Child, by Jean-Baptiste Greuze. c, A Boy with a Book, by Jean-Baptiste Perronneau. d, A Girl with a Doll, by Greuze.

No. 3420, The Lute Player, by Caravaggio. No. 3421, The Spoiled Child, by Greuze, vert.

2003, Dec. 8 ***Perf. 13¼***

3415-3418 A572 Set of 4 4.50 4.50
3419 A572 $2 Sheet of 4, #a-d 6.00 6.00

Imperf

Size: 78x65mm

3420 A572 $6 multi 4.50 4.50

Size: 67x78mm

3421 A572 $6 multi 4.50 4.50

Paintings by Pablo Picasso (1881-1973) — A573

No. 3422: a, Claude Drawing. b, Claude and Paloma at Play. c, Paloma at Three Years Old. d, Paloma with an Orange.

$6, Paloma in Blue.

2003, Dec. 8 Litho. ***Perf. 13¼***

3422 A573 $2 Sheet of 4, #a-d 6.00 6.00

Imperf

3423 A573 $6 multi 4.50 4.50

No. 3422 contains four 37x50mm stamps.

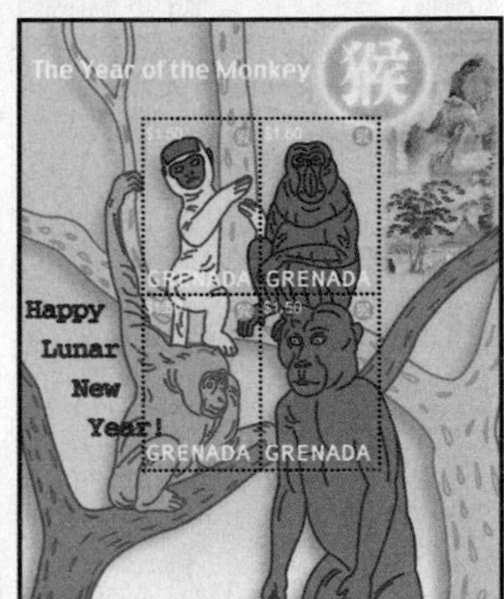

New Year 2004 (Year of the Monkey) — A574

No. 3424: a, Buff monkey with brown features. b, Brown monkey. c, Tan monkey. d, Gray monkey.

2004, Jan. 4 ***Perf. 14***

3424 A574 $1.50 Sheet of 4, #a-d 4.50 4.50

Souvenir Sheet

Training Ship "Lissy" — A575

2004, Jan. 16 Litho. ***Perf. 14¼***

3425 A575 $6 multi 4.50 4.50

Opening of Weser Tunnel, Dedesdorf, Germany.

Paintings by Pu Hsin-yu (1896-1963) — A576

No. 3426: a, Woman. b, Monkeys in tree. c, Landscape. d, Bird in tree. e, Man seated. f, Man standing.
No. 3427: a, Branch. b, Man.

2004, Jan. 29 ***Perf. 13½x13¼***

3426 A576 $1.50 Sheet of 6, #a-f 6.75 6.75
3427 A576 $3 Sheet of 2, #a-b 4.50 4.50

2004 Hong Kong Stamp Expo.

Arthur and Friends — A577

No. 3428, $1.50: a, Arthur. b, D. W. with Valentine's Day card. c, Binky. d, Muffy. e, D. W. as Cupid. f, Francine.
No. 3429, $1.50: a, Muffy giving speech about butterflies. b, Francine giving presentation about butterflies. c, Brain with plants. d, D. W. in space. e, Sue Ellen with insects. f, Arthur with model of solar system.
No. 3430, $2: a, Robinson Crusoe. b, Treasure Island. c, Tom Sawyer. d, Jungle Book.
No. 3431, $2: a, Robin Hood. b, Rumplestiltskin. c, How Arthur Drew Forth His Sword. d, King Arthur.

2004, Jan. 29 ***Perf. 13¼***

Sheets of 6, #a-f

3428-3429 A577 Set of 2 13.50 13.50

Sheets of 4, #a-d

3430-3431 A577 Set of 2 12.00 12.00

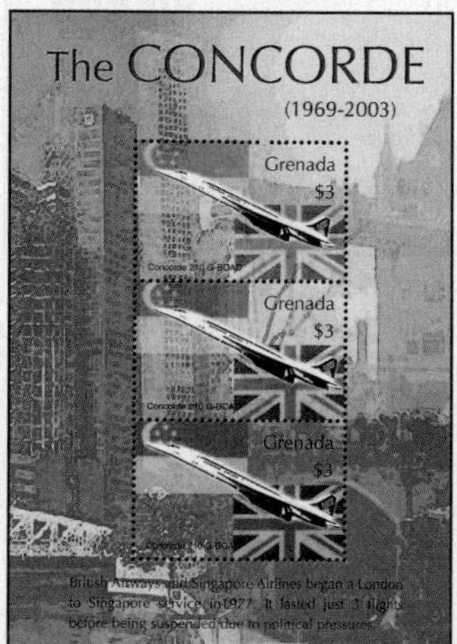

Cessation of Conorde Flights (in 2003) — A578

No. 3432, $3 — Concorde 210 G-BOAD, British and Singapore flags and: a, Roof line of buildings at UR. b, Curved and jagged lines at UR. c, Dark gray background at UR.
No. 3433, $3 — Concorde 001 F-WTSS, French flag and: a, Concorde above runway. b, Spectators near airport fence. c, Cockpit control panel.
No. 3434, $3 — Concorde 203 F-BVFA and: a, Top of US Capitol. b, Middle part of Capitol dome, head of statue. c, Base of Capitol and statue.

2004, Feb. 16 ***Perf. 13¼x13½***

Sheets of 3, #a-c

3432-3434 A578 Set of 3 21.00 21.00

2004 Summer Olympics, Athens A579

Designs: 75c, Lord Killanin, Intl. Olympic Committee President, 1972-80. $1, 10,000 meter run, 1928 Olympics, horiz. $1.25, Commemorative plaque from 1900 Paris Olympics. $3, Presentation of olive wreath.

2004, Apr. 8 ***Perf. 13¼***

3435-3438 A579 Set of 4 4.50 4.50

American Indian Chiefs — A580

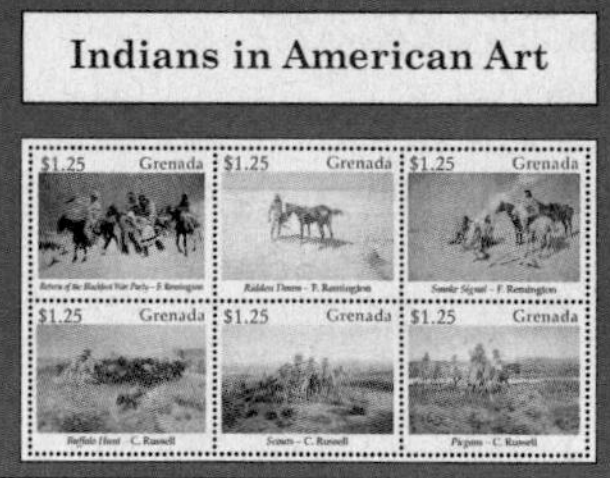

Paintings of American Indians — A581

No. 3439: a, American Horse. b, Blue Bird. c, Crow King. d, Crow Man. e, Gall. f, Good Horse. g, Goose. h, John Grass. i, Rain-in-the-Face. j, Red Cloud. k, Sitting Bull. l, Wild Horse.
No. 3440: a, Return of the Blackfoot War Party, by Frederic Remington. b, Ridden Down, by Remington. c, Smoke Signal, by Remington. d, Buffalo Hunt, by Charles Russell. e, Scouts, by Russell. f, Piegans, by Russell.

2004, Apr. 19 ***Perf. 13¾***

3439 A580 75c Sheet of 12, #a-l 6.75 6.75
3440 A581 $1.25 Sheet of 6, #a-f 5.75 5.75

Souvenir Sheet

Deng Xiaoping (1904-97), Chinese Communist Party Leader — A582

2004, May 3 ***Perf. 13½x13¼***

3441 A582 $6 multi 4.50 4.50

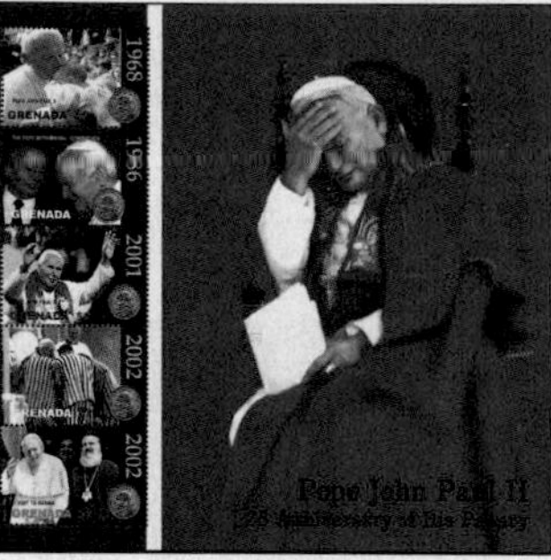

Election of Pope John Paul II, 25th Anniv. — A583

No. 3442: a, Kissing baby. b, With Mikhail Gorbachev. c, Waving to crowd. d, Meeting with Polish deportees. e, Visit to Russia.

2004, May 3 ***Perf. 13¼x13½***

3442 A583 $2 Sheet of 5, #a-e 7.50 7.50

Marilyn Monroe (1926-62) — A584

No. 3444: a, Wearing red dress with strap over shoulder, mouth wide open. b, Wearing orange red dress, mouth closed. c, Wearing white dress. d, Wearing red dress, mouth partially open.

2004, May 3 ***Perf. 14***

3443 A584 50c shown .60 .60

Perf. 13½x13¼

3444 A584 $2 Sheet of 4, #a-d 7.50 7.50

No. 3443 printed in sheets of 16.

European Soccer Championships, Portugal — A585

No. 3445, vert.: a, Jan Svehlik. b, Franz Beckenbauer. c, Karol Dobias. d, Crvena Zvezda Stadium, Belgrade.
$6, 1976 Czechoslovakian team.

2004, May 3 ***Perf. 13½x13¼***

3445 A585 $2 Sheet of 4, #a-d 6.00 6.00

Souvenir Sheet

Perf. 13¼

3446 A585 $6 multi 4.50 4.50

No. 3445 contains four 28x42mm stamps.

D-Day, 60th Anniv. A586

Designs: 45c, Don Sheppard, Royal Engineers. $1, Air Chief Marshall Sir Arthur Tedder. $1.50, Douglas Kay, 13th/18th Royal Hussars. $3, Gen. Bernard Montgomery.
No. 3451, $2: a, Germans detect Allied invasion. b, Germans prepare to engage Allied invasion fleet. c, Soldier, Merville Battery. d, Paratroopers capture Merville Battery.
No. 3452, $2: a, HMS Belfast fires on German shore batteries. b, Allies pound German coastal defenses. c, Air strikes over Utah Beach. d, Allied troops head towards Omaha Beach.
No. 3453, $6, Fake landing craft. No. 3454, $6, Pipeline under the ocean.

2004, May 3 ***Perf. 14***

Stamps + Labels (#3447-3450)

3447-3450 A586 Set of 4 4.50 4.50

Sheets of 4, #a-d

3451-3452 A586 Set of 2 12.00 12.00

Souvenir Sheets

3453-3454 A586 Set of 2 9.00 9.00

Locomotives and Famous Men — A587

No. 3455, $1: a, Sir Lord Nelson 4-6-0. b, South African 16CR Class Pacific. c, Florisdorf 0-6-0 Fireless, Austria. d, GWR 57XX Class 0-6-0. e, GWR Castle Class 4-6-0. f, GWR Saint Class 4-6-0. g, GWR Star Class 4-6-0. h, GWR 28XX Class 2-8-0. i, GWR 51XX Class 2-6-2T.
No. 3456, $1, vert.: a, GN Stirling Single 4-2-2. b, Beyer Peacock Mogul 2-6-0. c, Prussian G8 0-8-0. d, George Stephenson. e, James Nasmyth. f, Nasmyth's steam hammer. g, Raven Z Class 4-4-2. h, Sir Vincent Raven. i, Thomas Cook.
No. 3457, $1, vert.: a, SR Schools Class 4-4-0. b, Indian Railways SGS Class 0-6-0. c, Borsig 0-4-0 Tram, Paraguay. d, Richard Trevithick. e, Herbert Garratt. f, Isambard Kingdom Brunel. g, Replica of Trevithick's Coalbrookdale Engine. h, Rhodesian 20th Class Garratt. i, Train on Brunel's Royal Saltash Bridge.
No. 3458, $6, California Zephyr. No. 3459, $6, Indian Pacific. No. 3460, $6, Cumbres and Toltec.

2004, July 19 **Litho.**

Sheets of 9, #a-i

3455-3457 A587 Set of 3 21.00 21.00

Souvenir Sheets

3458-3460 A587 Set of 3 13.50 13.50

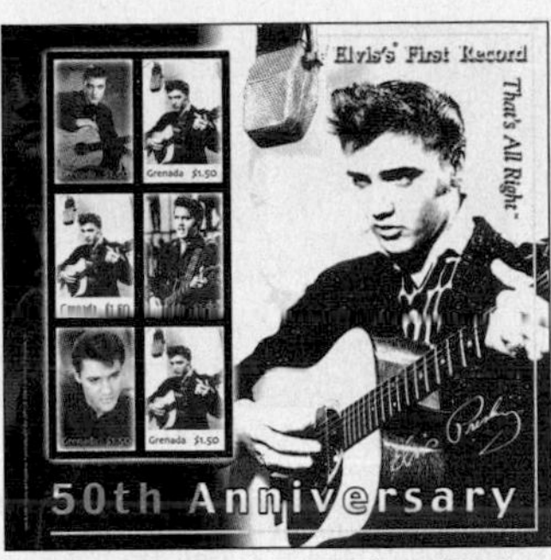

Elvis Presley (1935-77) — A588

No. 3461: a, Holding guitar (brown). b, Playing guitar (green). c, Playing guitar, diff. (red violet). d, Portrait (brown). e, Like #3461b, (blue).

2004, Aug. 3 ***Perf. 14***
3461 A588 $1.50 Sheet, #a-d, 2 #e 7.25 7.25

Operation Iraqi Freedom — A589

No. 3462: a, Pres. George W. Bush. b. Paul Bremer. c, Col. James Hickey, US Special Forces. d, A friendly welcome.

2004, Aug. 25 ***Perf. 13¼x13½***
3462 A589 $2 Sheet of 4, #a-d 6.00 6.00

Queen Juliana of the Netherlands (1909-2004) — A590

2004, Aug. 25 Litho. ***Perf. 13¼***
3463 A590 $2 multi 1.50 1.50

Printed in sheets of 6.

Miniature Sheet

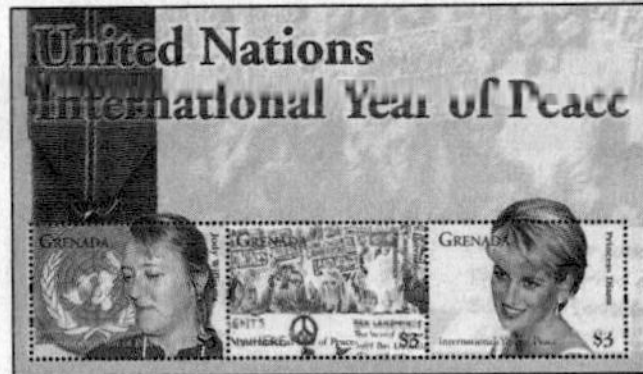

Intl. Year of Peace — A591

No. 3464: a, Jody Williams, 1997 Nobel Peace laureate. b, Protesters against landmines. c, Princess Diana.

2004, Sept. 7 ***Perf. 14***
3464 A591 $3 Sheet of 3, #a-c 6.75 6.75

Miniature Sheet

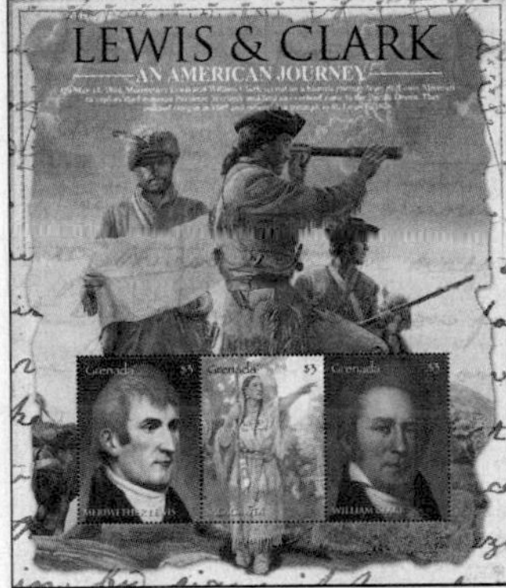

Lewis and Clark Expedition, Bicent. — A592

No. 3465: a, Meriwether Lewis. b, Sacajawea. c, William Clark.

2004, Sept. 7 ***Perf. 14¼***
3465 A592 $3 Sheet of 3, #a-c 6.75 6.75

Miniature Sheet

Mars Rover Mission — A593

No. 3466: a, Delta II rocket blasts off. b, Entering Mars atmosphere. c, Parachute descent. d, Landing on the surface. e, Rover leaving lander. f, Rover on Mars surface.

2004, Sept. 7
3466 A593 $1.50 Sheet of 6, #a-f 6.75 6.75

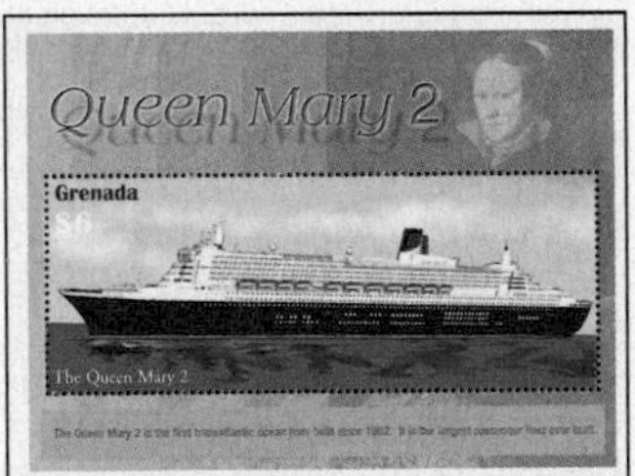

Ocean Liners — A594

No. 3467, $2: a, RMS Titanic. b, TSS Normandie. c, Mauritania. d, Lusitania.
No. 3468, $2: a, Queen Mary 2. b, Queen Elizabeth II. c, Queen Mary. d, Queen Elizabeth.
$6, Queen Mary 2, diff.

2004, Sept. 7 ***Perf. 13¼x13***
Sheets of 4, #a-d
3467-3468 A594 Set of 2 12.00 12.00

Souvenir Sheet
3469 A594 $6 multi 4.50 4.50

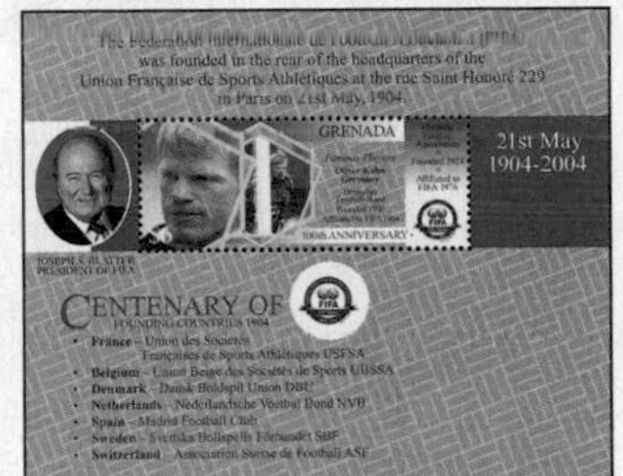

FIFA (Fédération Internationale de Football Association), Cent. — A595

No. 3470: a, Gabriel Batistuta. b, Cafu. c, Michel Platini. d, Gianluca Vialli.
$6, Oliver Kahn.

2004, Nov. 1 ***Perf. 12¾x12½***
3470 A595 $2 Sheet of 4, #a-d 6.00 6.00

Souvenir Sheet
3471 A595 $6 multi 4.50 4.50

National Basketball Association Players — A596

Designs: No. 3472, 75c, Pau Gasol, Memphis Grizzlies. No. 3473, 75c, Allen Iverson, Philadelphia 76ers. No. 3474, 75c, Stephon Marbury, New York Knicks.

2004 ***Perf. 14***
3472-3474 A596 Set of 3 1.75 1.75

Issued: No. 3472, 11/3; No. 3473, 11/5; No. 3474, 11/6. Each printed in sheets of 12.
See Nos. 3485-3487.

Miniature Sheet

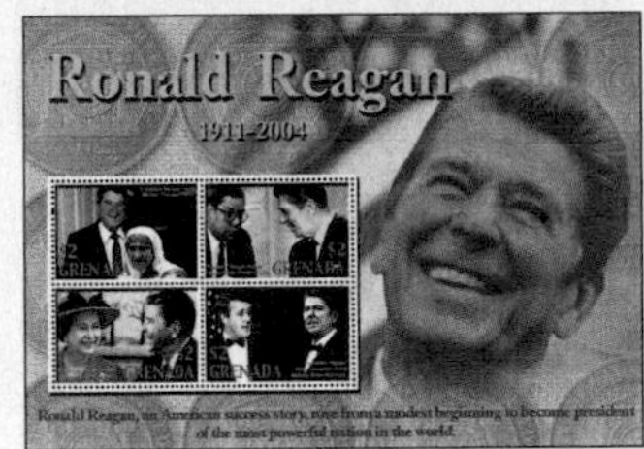

Pres. Ronald Reagan (1911-2004) — A597

No. 3475: a, With Mother Teresa. b, With Colin Powell. c, With Queen Elizabeth II. d, With Brian Mulroney.

2004 ***Perf. 13½***
3475 A597 $2 Sheet of 4, #a-d 6.00 6.00

A598

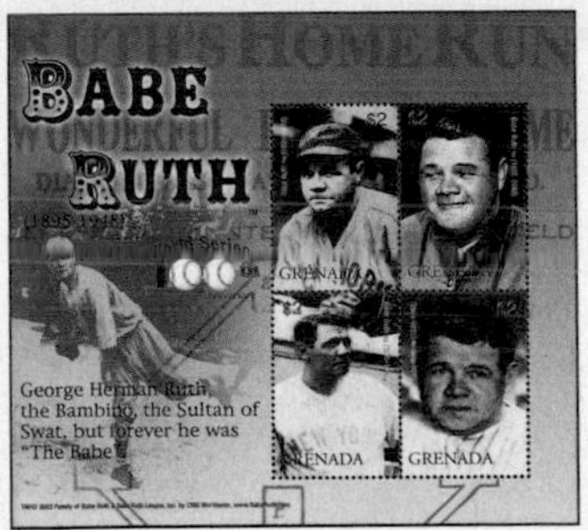

George Herman "Babe" Ruth (1895-1948), Baseball Player — A599

Various portraits.

2004 ***Perf. 14***
3476 A598 $2 Sheet of 4, #a-d 6.00 6.00

Perf. 13¾x13¼
3477 A599 $2 Sheet of 4, #a-d 6.00 6.00

Christmas A600

Paintings by Norman Rockwell: 35c, Merry Christmas. 75c, Yuletide Merriment. $1, Dressing Up. $4, Christmas.
$6, The London Coach.

2004, Dec. 9 ***Perf. 12***
3478-3481 A600 Set of 4 4.75 4.75

Souvenir Sheet
3482 A600 $6 multi 4.50 4.50

New Year 2005 (Year of the Rooster) — A601

Paintings by Qi Baishi: $1, Chrysanthemums, Cocks and Hens. $4, Taro Leaves and Double Hens.

2005, Jan. 17 Litho. ***Perf. 11¾x12¼***
3483 A601 $1 multi 1.25 1.25

Souvenir Sheet
Perf. 12¾x13
3484 A601 $4 multi 5.00 5.00

No. 3483 printed in sheets of 4. No. 3484 contains one 22x76mm stamp.

Basketball Players Type of 2004

Designs: No. 3485, 75c, Zydrunas Ilgauskas, Cleveland Cavaliers. No. 3486, 75c, Dwyane Wade, Miami Heat. $3, Tracy McGrady, Orlando Magic.

2005, Feb. 10 ***Perf. 14***
3485-3487 A596 Set of 3 3.50 3.50

Souvenir Sheet

Intl. Year of Rice — A602

No. 3488: a, Detail from Deities Overseeing the Transplanting of Rice, by unknown artist. b, Detail from the Taoist God Overseeing the Rice Planting, by unknown artist. c, Women Transplanting Rice in Late Spring Rain, by Hiroshige.

2005, Feb. 10
3488 A602 $3 Sheet of 3, #a-c 6.75 6.75

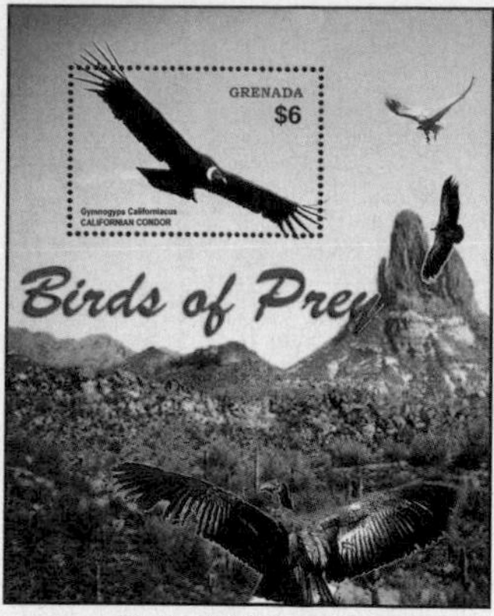

Birds, Wild Cats and Butterflies — A603

No. 3489, $1.50, vert. — Birds: a, Turkey vulture. b, Bald eagle. c, Peregrine falcon. d, Prairie falcon. e, Northern goshawk. f, Cooper's hawk.

No. 3490, $1.50, vert. — Wild cats: a, Cheetah. b, Lion. c, White tiger. d, Leopard. e, Bobcat. f, Bengal tiger.

No. 3491, $1.50 — Butterflies: a, Machaonides's swallowtail. b, Viceroy. c, Glasswing satyr. d, Birdwing. e, Ornithoptera goliath procus. f, Ornithoptera priamus alberio.

No. 3492, $6, California condor. No. 3493, $6, Jaguar, vert. No. 3494, $6, Lime butterfly.

2005, Feb. 10 **Litho.**

Sheets of 6, #a-f

3489-3491 A603 Set of 3 21.00 21.00

Souvenir Sheets

3492-3494 A603 Set of 3 13.50 13.50

A604

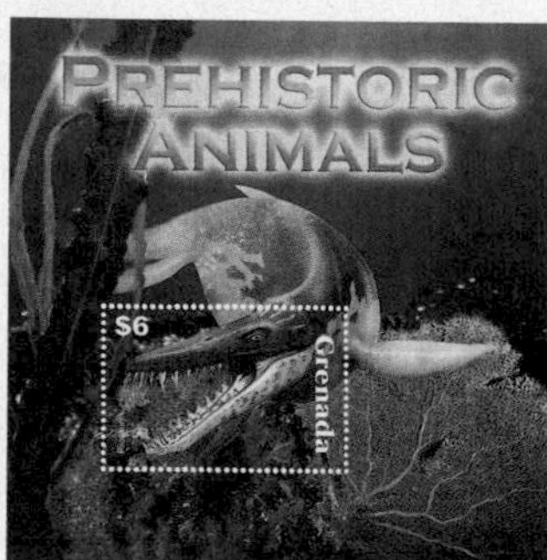

Prehistoric Animals — A605

No. 3495: a, Majungatholus. b, Diplodocus. c, Willo. d, Velociraptor.

No. 3496, $2: a, Archelon. b, Ammonite. c, Plesiosaur. d, Xiphactinus.

No. 3497, $2: a, Pteranodon. b, Dimorphodon. c, Pterodactylus. d, Rhamphorhynchus.

No. 3498, Spinosaurus.

No. 3499, $6, Pliosaur. No. 3500, $6, Tapejara imperator.

2005, Feb. 10

3495 A604 $2 Sheet of 4, #a-d 6.00 6.00

Sheets of 4, #a-d

3496-3497 A605 Set of 2 12.00 12.00

Souvenir Sheets

3498 A604 $6 multi 4.50 4.50

3499-3500 A605 Set of 2 9.00 9.00

Souvenir Sheet

Buildings Damaged in Hurricane Ivan — A606

No. 3501: a, Cathedral of Immaculate Conception. b, Anglican Church. c, York House. d, Springs Sub-office.

2005, Mar. 8 ***Perf. 12¾***

3501 A606 $2 Sheet of 4, #a-d 6.00 6.00

Elvis Presley (1935-77) — A607

No. 3502, $1.50: a, Singing, 1955. b, Holding microphone, 1957. c, Playing guitar, 1959. d, Singing, 1961. e, Singing, 1968. f, With guitar, 1970.

No. 3503, $1.50: a, Dancing, 1957. b, Playing guitar, 1964. c, On saddle, 1965. d, Playing guitar, 1968. e, Playing piano, 1969. f, Singing, 1970.

2005, Apr. 4 ***Perf. 13¾***

Sheets of 6, #a-f

3502-3503 A607 Set of 2 13.50 13.50

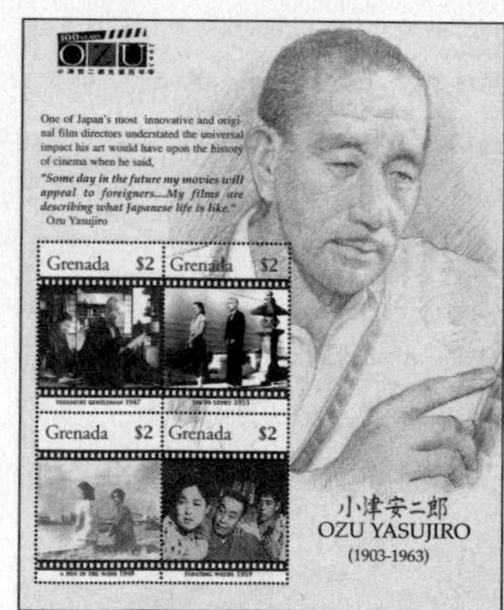

Yasujiro Ozu (1903-63), Film Director — A608

No. 3504: a, Tenement Gentleman, 1947. b, Tokyo Story, 1953. c, A Hen in the Wind, 1948. d, Floating Weeds, 1959.

2005, Apr. 8 ***Perf. 14¼***

3504 A608 $2 Sheet of 4, #a-d 6.00 6.00

Dutch Royalty — A609

No. 3505: a, King William I. b, King William II. c, King William III. d, Queen Wilhelmina. e, Queen Juliana. f, Queen Beatrix. g, Prince Willem-Alexander. h, Princess Catharina-Amalia.

2005, Apr. 14 **Litho.** ***Perf. 12***

3505 A609 $2 Sheet of 8, #a-h 12.00 12.00

End of World War II, 60th Anniv. — A610

No. 3506, $2 — Burma Campaign: a, "21 Curves" Road. b, British advance through the jungle of Burma. c, Troops at Magwe airstrip. d, Allied troops escorting prisoners.

No. 3507, $2 — Operation Market Garden: a, Allied troops landing behind enemy lines. b, Allied troops fire on German defenders. c, German troops move up to counterattack. d, Bridges still remain in German hands.

No. 3508, $6, Troops discuss next move.

No. 3509, $6, Allied troops meet stiff resistance.

2005, May 10 ***Perf. 13¼***

Sheets of 4, #a-d

3506-3507 A610 Set of 2 12.00 12.00

Souvenir Sheets

3508-3509 A610 Set of 2 9.00 9.00

V-E Day, 60th Anniv. — A611

No. 3510: a, D-Day. b, Allied troops break through enemy lines. c, German troops begin to surrender. d, The war in Europe is over.

$6, Berlin falls to the armies of the Soviet Union.

2005, May 10 ***Perf. 14***

3510 A611 $2 Sheet of 4, #a-d 6.00 6.00

Souvenir Sheet

3511 A611 $6 multi 4.50 4.50

V-J Day, 60th Anniv. — A612

No. 3512: a, Airplanes over islands of the Pacific. b, Allied forces storm the beaches of Japanese-held islands. c, Gen. Douglas MacArthur returns to the Philippines. d, The Japanese armies surrender.

$6, Allies enjoy victory celebration.

2005, May 10

3512 A612 $2 Sheet of 4, #a-d 6.00 6.00

Souvenir Sheet

3513 A612 $6 multi 4.50 4.50

Rotary International, Cent. — A613

No. 3514: a, Child receiving polio vaccination. b, District 7030 Governor David Edwards and wife, Donna. c, Paul P. Harris, Rotary International founder.

$6, 2001-02 Rotary President Richard D. King, children.

2005, May 10 ***Perf. 14***

3514 A613 $3 Sheet of 3, #a-c 6.75 6.75

Souvenir Sheet

3515 A613 $6 multi 4.50 4.50

Miniature Sheet

Expo 2005, Aichi, Japan — A614

No. 3516: a, Victoria Falls. b, Bald eagle. c, Caribbean coral reef. d, Childbirth. e, First man on the moon. f, Pollination.

2005, June 27 ***Perf. 12***

3516 A614 $1.50 Sheet of 6, #a-f 6.75 6.75

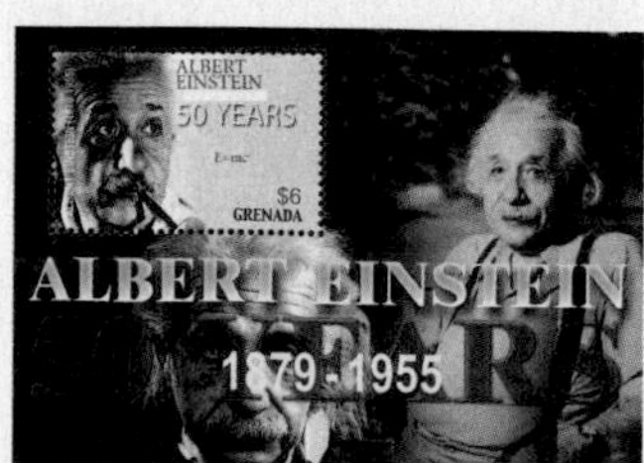

Albert Einstein (1879-1955), Physicist — A615

No. 3517 — Einstein and country name in: a, Blue. b, Black. c, White. d, Red

$6, Einstein with pipe.

2005, June 27 ***Perf. 12¾***

3517 A615 $2 Sheet of 4, #a-d 6.00 6.00

Souvenir Sheet

3518 A615 $6 multi 4.50 4.50

Souvenir Sheet

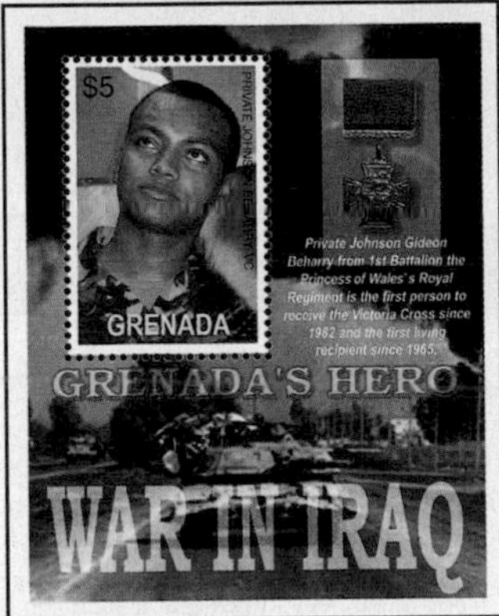

Private Johnson Beharry, Victoria Cross Recipient in Iraq War — A616

2005, July 11 **Litho.**
3519 A616 $5 multi 3.75 3.75

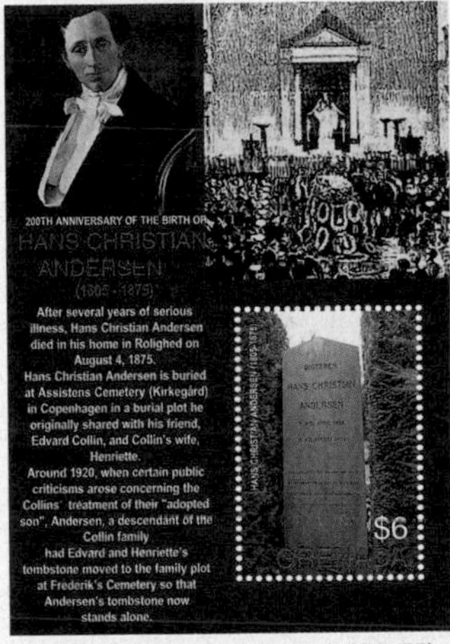

Hans Christian Andersen (1805-75), Author — A617

No. 3520: a, Andersen, with hands shown. b, Photograph of Andersen. c, Andersen, with white tie.
$6, Andersen's tombstone, Copenhagen.

2005, July 11
3520 A617 $3 Sheet of 3, #a-c 6.75 6.75

Souvenir Sheet

3521 A617 $6 multi 4.50 4.50

Friedrich von Schiller (1759-1805), Writer — A618

No. 3522, vert.: a, William Tell Memorial, Altdorf, Switzerland. b, Animated movie of William Tell. c, Stage production of William Tell.
$6, Scene from William Tell story.

2005, July 11 ***Perf. 14***
3522 A618 $3 Sheet of 3, #a-c 6.75 6.75

Souvenir Sheet

3523 A618 $6 multi 4.50 4.50

Jules Verne (1828-1905), Writer — A619

No. 3524: a, Photograph of Verne. b, Photograph of Verne in oval. c, Drawing of Verne.
$6, From the Earth to the Moon.

2005, July 11 ***Perf. 12¾***
3524 A619 $3 Sheet of 3, #a-c 6.75 6.75

Souvenir Sheet

3525 A619 $6 multi 4.50 4.50

Battle of Trafalgar, Bicent. — A620

No. 3526, vert.: a, Admiral Horatio Nelson. b, Napoleon Bonaparte. c, HMS Victory. d, The Nelson Touch.
$6, Sailors on ship.

2005, July 11 ***Perf. 12¾***
3526 A620 $2 Sheet of 4, #a-d 6.00 6.00

Souvenir Sheet

3527 A620 $6 multi 4.50 4.50

Miniature Sheets

Dennis The Menace, Comic Strip by Hank Ketcham — A621

No. 3528, $2: a, "Grandpa got a now knee. . ." b, "Joey an' me don't have any money. . ." c, "Good news, Mrs. Wilson! . ." d, "I think the boy's . ."
No. 3529, $2: a, "How 'bout a trade. . ." b, "It's not a good idea. . ." c, "I'll bet you were the top . ." d, "Boy, I'm glad I don't have to. . ."

2005, July 11 ***Perf. 14¼***

Sheets of 4, #a-d

3528-3529 A621 Set of 2 12.00 12.00

Souvenir Sheet

Taipei 2005 Intl. Stamp Exhibition — A622

No. 3530: a, Shalom Meir Tower, Tel Aviv. b, Empire State Building, New York. c, Taipei 101 Building, Taipei. d, Eiffel Tower, Paris.

2005, Aug. 19 ***Perf. 14***
3530 A622 $2 Sheet of 4, #a-d 6.00 6.00

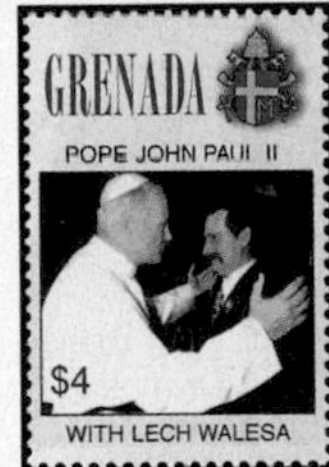

Pope John Paul II (1920-2005) and Lech Walesa — A623

2005, Aug. 22 ***Perf. 12¾***
3531 A623 $4 multi 3.00 3.00

Printed in sheets of 4.

Wedding of Prince Charles and Camilla Parker Bowles — A624

Various pictures of couple with oval in: No. 3532, $2, Lemon. No. 3533, $2, Light blue. No. 3534, $2, Pink, horiz.

2005, Sept. 7 ***Perf. 13½***
3532-3534 A624 Set of 3 4.50 4.50

Each stamp printed in sheets of 4.

Christmas — A625

Designs: 25c, The Nativity, by Correggio. 75c, Virgin and Child, by Lorenzo Lotto. $1, The Holy Family, by Lotto. $5, Madonna and Child with the Saints, by Lotto.
$6, Allegory of Music, by Fra Filippo Lippi.

2005, Nov. 15 ***Perf. 12¾***
3535-3538 A625 Set of 4 5.25 5.25

Souvenir Sheet

3539 A625 $6 multi 4.50 4.50

Bird Type of 2000

2005 **Litho.** ***Perf. 12x11¾***

Size:22x26mm

3540 A472 10c Purple-throated Carib .25 .25

Miniature Sheets

Chelsea Soccer Team, Cent. — A626

Liverpool Soccer Team — A627

No. 3541: a, Stadium and field. b, Stadium, field, team emblem and years. c, Players holding English League Championship award. d, Players in bus with cup and flag. e, Fans with flag. f, Aerial view of bus carrying players. g, Players. h, Coach. i, Stadium, field, team emblem. j, Team with award.
No. 3542: a, Crowd watching bus carrying players near stadium. b, Player and coach holding UEFA Cup. c, Gate. d, Aerial view of stadium. e, Banner. f, Players waving. g, Fans. h, Soccer match. i, Players celebrating. j, Crowd cheering players in bus.

2005, Dec. 28 **Litho.** ***Perf. 13¼***
3541 A626 $1.50 Sheet of 10, #a-j 11.50 11.50
3542 A627 $1.50 Sheet of 10, #a-j 11.50 11.50

The Two Hounds, by Hui-Tsung A628

2006, Jan. 3
3543 A628 $1 shown .75 .75

Souvenir Sheet

3544 A628 $4 Entire painting 3.00 3.00

No. 3544 contains one 50x37mm stamp.

Pope Benedict XVI — A629

2006, Jan. 10
3545 A629 $2 multi 1.50 1.50

Printed in sheets of 4.

A630

Elvis Presley (1935-77) — A631

No. 3546 — Movie posters: a, Girls! Girls! Girls! b, Jailhouse Rock. c, Paradise - Hawaiian Style. d, It Happened at the World's Fair.

2006 Litho. *Perf. 13¼*
3546 A630 $3 Sheet of 4, #a-d 9.00 9.00

Litho. & Embossed
Die Cut Perf. 7¾
Without Gum

3547 A631 $20 shown 15.00 15.00

Issued: No. 3546, 7/11, No. 3547, 2/21.

Queen Elizabeth II, 80th Birthday — A632

No. 3548: a, Wearing necklace, no earrings. b, Wearing blue jacket. c, Portrait. d, Wearing jacket and earrings.
$6, Wearing hat.

2006, Feb. 21 Litho. *Perf. 13¼*
3548 A632 $3 Sheet of 4, #a-d 9.00 9.00

Souvenir Sheet
Perf. 12¼x12

3549 A632 $6 multi 4.50 4.50

Teams Competing in 2006 World Cup Soccer Championships, Germany — A633

Designs: No. 3550, $1.50, Angola. No. 3551, $1.50, Argentina. No. 3552, $1.50, Australia. No. 3553, $1.50, Brazil. No. 3554, $1.50, Costa Rica. No. 3555, $1.50, Croatia. No. 3556, $1.50, Czech Republic. No. 3557, $1.50, Ecuador. No. 3558, $1.50, England. No. 3559, $1.50, France. No. 3560, $1.50, Germany. No. 3561, $1.50, Ghana. No. 3562, $1.50, Iran. No. 3563, $1.50, Italy. No. 3564, $1.50, Ivory Coast. No. 3565, $1.50, Japan. No. 3566, $1.50, Mexico. No. 3567, $1.50, Netherlands. No. 3568, $1.50, Paraguay. No. 3569, $1.50, Poland. No. 3570, $1.50, Portugal. No. 3571, $1.50, Saudi Arabia. No. 3572, $1.50, Serbia and Montenegro. No. 3573, $1.50, South Korea. No. 3574, $1.50, Spain. No. 3575, $1.50, Sweden. No. 3576, $1.50, Switzerland. No. 3577, $1.50, Togo. No. 3578, $1.50, Trinidad and Tobago. No. 3579, $1.50, Tunisia. No. 3580, $1.50, Ukraine. No. 3581, $1.50, United States.

2006, Mar. 29 *Perf. 12¼x12*
3550-3581 A633 Set of 32 36.00 36.00

Nos. 3550-3581 each printed in sheets of 6. Stamps other than Nos. 3550, 3553, 3554, 3560, 3561, 3566, 3575, 3579 and 3581, which have solid color backgrounds, have multicolored backgrounds that vary within the sheet.

Marilyn Monroe (1926-62), Actress — A634

2006, Mar. 30 *Perf. 13¼*
3582 A634 $3 multi 2.25 2.25

Printed in sheets of 4.

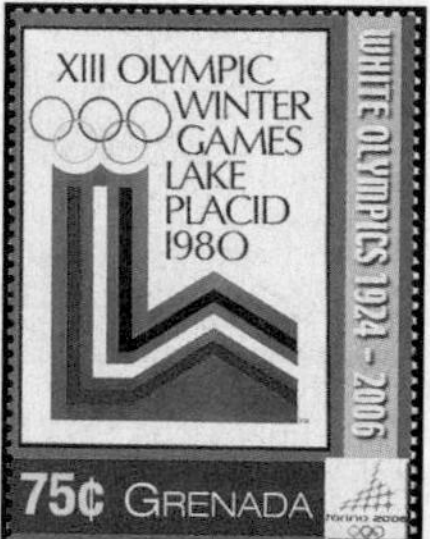

2006 Winter Olympics, Turin A635

Designs: No. 3583, Poster for 1980 Lake Placid Winter Olympics. No. 3583A, Poster for 2006 Turin Winter Olympics. No. 3584, Switzerland #B173. No. 3584A, Italy #2722. $2, Poster for 1948 St. Moritz Winter Olympics. $3, Switzerland #B172.

2006, May 10 *Perf. 14¼*
3583 A635 75c multicolored .55 .55
3583A A635 75c multicolored .55 .55
3584 A635 90c multicolored .70 .70
3584A A635 90c multicolored .70 .70
3585 A635 $2 multicolored 1.50 1.50
3586 A635 $3 multicolored 2.25 2.25
Nos. 3583-3586 (6) 6.25 6.25

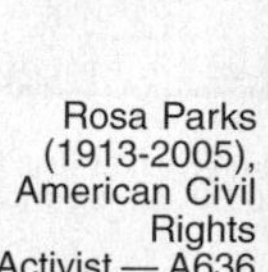

Rosa Parks (1913-2005), American Civil Rights Activist — A636

2006, May 27 *Perf. 11½x12*
3587 A636 $3 multi 2.25 2.25

Printed in sheets of 3.

Flags and Uniforms of World Cup Soccer Champions A637

Designs: 75c, Brazil, 2002. 90c, Germany, 1990. $3, France, 1998.

2006, June 9 *Perf. 13¼*
3588-3590 A637 Set of 3 3.50 3.50

World Cup Trophy — A638

2006, June 9 *Die Cut*
Self-Adhesive

3591 A638 $6 multi 4.50 4.50

Rembrandt (1606-69), Painter A639

Designs: 50c, The Little Jewish Bride. $1, Young Man in Velvet Cap. $1.50, Old Woman Sleeping. No. 3595, $3, Woman Reading. No. 3596, $6, Portrait of a Seated Man (70x100mm). No. 3597, $6, Portrait of a Scholar (70x100mm).

No. 3598, $3: a, Young Woman with Flowers in Her Hair. b, Portrait of a Seated Woman. c, Alijdt Adriaensor. d, Amalia van Solms.

Perf. 12, 12½x12¼ (#3596, 3597)
2006, June 16
3592-3597 A639 Set of 6 13.50 13.50
3597a Imperf. 4.50 4.50

Miniature Sheet
Perf. 13x13¼

3598 A639 $3 Sheet of 4, #a-d 9.00 9.00

Souvenir Sheet

Wolfgang Amadeus Mozart (1756-91), Composer — A640

2006, June 22 *Perf. 12¾*
3599 A640 $6 multi 4.50 4.50

Souvenir Sheet

Ludwig Durr (1878-1956), Engineer, and Zeppelins — A641

No. 3600 — Durr and: a, Graf Zeppelin D-LZ-127. b, Graf Zeppelin LT. c, Graf Zeppelin L-26.

2006, June 22
3600 A641 $4 Sheet of 3, #a-c 9.00 9.00

Space — A642

No. 3601, $2 — Sputnik 1: a, Sergei Korolev. b, Sputnik 1 in space. c, Inside Sputnik 1. d, Sputnik 1 capsule.

No. 3602, $2, vert. — Apollo-Soyuz: a, Apollo rocket. b, Apollo command module and adapter. c, Soyuz rocket on launchpad. d, Soyuz.

No. 3603 — Giotto Comet Probe: a, Halley's Comet, round head in yellow at right. b, Tip of Giotto Probe launcher Ariane V14. c, Halley's Comet, head at left, thin tail. d, Halley's Comet, head in white at right. e, Bottom of Giotto Probe launcher Ariane V14. f, Halley's Comet, head at left, wide tail.

No. 3604, $6, Stardust Comet Probe. No. 3605, $6, Comet Tempel 1 Deep Impact Mission. No. 3606, $6, Space Shuttle Discovery's return to space.

2006, Sept. 14 Litho. *Perf. 12¾*
Sheets of 4, #a-d

3601-3602 A642 Set of 2 12.00 12.00
3603 A642 $2 Sheet of 6, #a-f 9.00 9.00

Souvenir Sheets

3604-3606 A642 Set of 3 13.50 13.50

Christopher Columbus (1451-1506), Explorer — A643

Designs: $1.50, Sinking of the Santa Maria. $2, Santa Maria, vert. $3, Columbus, sailor and ship, vert. $4, Columbus and ships, vert.
$6, Fleet of ships, 1493.

2006, Oct. 26 *Perf. 12¾*
3607-3610 A643 Set of 4 8.00 8.00

Souvenir Sheet

3611 A643 $6 multi 4.50 4.50

Butterflies A644

Designs: 10c, Mourning cloak butterfly. 25c, Snout butterfly. $1, Tithorea pinthias. $2, Diadem butterfly. $4, Red satyr butterfly. $5, Taygetis chrysogone. $10, Pierella hortona. $20, Morpho aega.

2006, Dec. 1 Litho. *Perf. 12½*
3612 A644 10c multi .25 .25
3613 A644 25c multi .25 .25
3614 A644 $1 multi .75 .75
3615 A644 $2 multi 1.50 1.50
3616 A644 $4 multi 3.00 3.00
3617 A644 $5 multi 3.75 3.75
3618 A644 $10 multi 7.50 7.50
3619 A644 $20 multi 15.00 15.00
Nos. 3612-3619 (8) 32.00 32.00

Princess Maxima of the Netherlands — A645

No. 3620: a, Head of Princess Maxima. b, Princess Maxima holding purse.

2006, Dec. 7 *Perf. 13½*
3620 A645 $1.50 Pair, #a-b 2.25 2.25

Printed in sheets containing 3 of each stamp.

Christmas — A646

Details of The Adoration of the Shepherds, by Peter Paul Rubens: 25c, Man with hat. 50c, Mary. 75c, Shepherd. $1, Baby Jesus.

No. 3625: a, Like 25c. b, Like 50c. c, Like 75c. d, Like $1.

2006, Dec. 21 *Perf. 14*
3621-3624 A646 Set of 4 1.90 1.90

Souvenir Sheet

3625 A646 $2 Sheet of 4, #a-d 6.00 6.00

Betty Boop — A647

No. 3626 — Betty Boop: a, Sitting on "E." b, With hands on thighs, between "Y" and "B." c, With one leg elevated. d, With hands clasped, Standing behind "E." e, With arms at side, standing in front of "Y." f, With arms raised upwards.

No. 3627: a, With hands clasped, blue circles. b, With arms at side, red and blue circles. c, With arms raised upwards, pink and blue circles. d, At microphone, blue circles.

No. 3628, $3: a, Holding mirror. b, Wearing fruited hat.

No. 3629, $3, horiz.: a, Head and upper torso. b, Lower torso.

2006, Dec. 22 *Perf. 14*
3626 A647 $1.50 Sheet of 6, #a-f 6.75 6.75
3627 A647 $2 Sheet of 4, #a-d 6.00 6.00

Souvenir Sheets of 2, #a-b

3628-3629 A647 Set of 2 9.00 9.00

Arsenal Soccer Team — A648

No. 3630: a, $1, Players and crowd. b, $1, Soccer field at night. c, $1, Fans in seats at end of stadium. d, $1, Emirates Stadium exterior. e, $1, Players. f, $2, Players. g, $2, Aerial view of stadium exterior. h, $2, Fans. i, $2, Soccer field and fans. j, $2, Stadium exterior at night.

2007, Jan. 16
3630 A648 Sheet of 10, #a-j 11.50 11.50

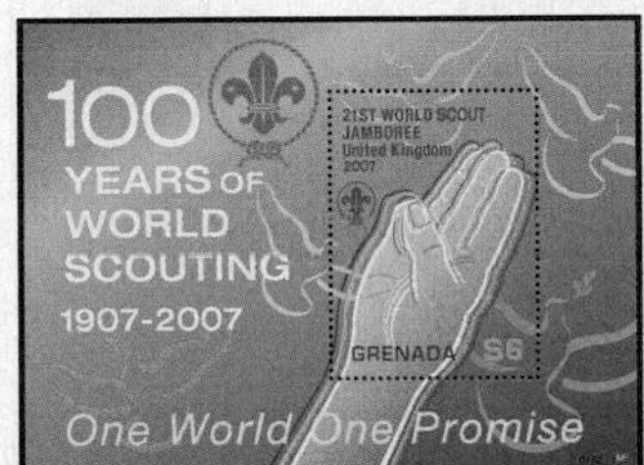

Concorde Test Pilots and Flags — A649

No. 3631: a, Amore Turcat, French flag. b, Brian Trubshaw, British flag.

2007, Feb. 15
3631 A649 $2 Pair, #a-b 3.00 3.00

Printed in sheets containing three of each stamp.

Scouting, Cent. — A650

No. 3632 — Scout sign and denomination in: a, Blue. b, Orange. c, Red violet. d, Green

$6, Orange.

2007, Feb. 15
3632 A650 $3 Sheet of 4, #a-d 9.00 9.00

Souvenir Sheet

3633 A650 $6 multi 4.50 4.50

Pres. John F. Kennedy (1917-63) — A651

No. 3634, $2 — First meeting with Soviet Premier Nikita Khrushchev: a, Khrushchev at the Simferopol Space Control Center. b, Kennedy greeting Khrushchev. c, Kennedy and Khrushchev on sofa. d, Kennedy and Khrushchev at residence of US Ambassador in Vienna.

No. 3635, $2 — Cuban Missile Crisis: a, Khrushchev and Fidel Castro. b, Kennedy addressing nation. c, Completed SA-2 missile site. d, Kennedy and Khrushchev shaking hands in Vienna.

2007, Feb. 15 **Sheets of 4, #a-d**
3634-3635 A651 Set of 2 12.00 12.00

Souvenir Sheet

New Year 2007 (Year of the Pig) — A652

No. 3636 — Text "Traditional Chinese New Year Paper Cutting" in: a, $1, Black. b, $1, White. c, $2, Beige. d, $2, Yellow.

2007, Feb. 18 *Perf. 14*
3636 A652 Sheet of 4, #a-d 4.50 4.50

Pope Benedict XVI — A653

2007, June 4 **Litho.** *Perf. 13¼*
3637 A653 $1 multi .75 .75

Printed in sheets of 8.

2007 Cricket World Cup, West Indies — A654

Designs: $1, Cricket World Cup emblem, flag and map of Grenada. $2, Rawl Lewis. $3, Queen's Park, horiz.

$6, Cricket World Cup emblem.

2007, June 18
3638-3640 A654 Set of 3 4.50 4.50

Souvenir Sheet

3641 A654 $6 multi 4.50 4.50

Wedding of Queen Elizabeth II and Prince Philip, 60th Anniv. — A655

No. 3642: a, Queen and Prince, orange panel. b, Queen, orange panel. c, Queen, light blue panel. d, Queen and Prince, light blue panel. e, Queen and Prince, lilac panel. f, Queen, lilac panel.

$6, Queen and Prince, diff.

2007, June 25
3642 A655 $2 Sheet of 6, #a-f 9.00 9.00

Souvenir Sheet

3643 A655 $6 multi 4.50 4.50

Princess Diana (1961-97) — A656

No. 3644 — Diana with: a, Red dress. b, Light blue and white dress. c, White gown. d, Green and white dress.

No. 3645, $6, Scarf on head. No. 3646, $6, Red dress, horiz.

2007, June 25
3644 A656 $2 Sheet of 4, #a-d 6.00 6.00

Souvenir Sheets

3645-3646 A656 Set of 2 9.00 9.00

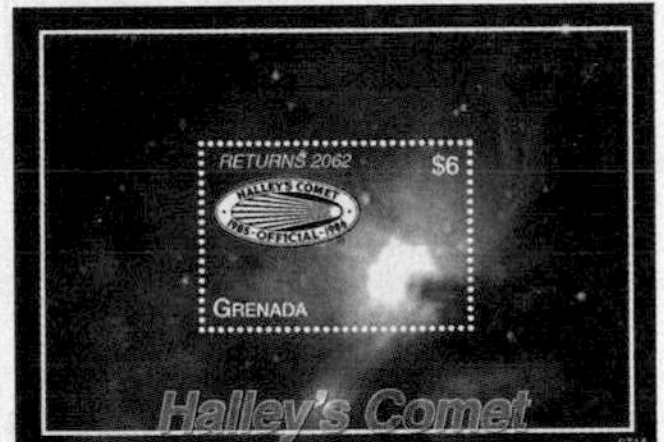

Intl. Polar Year — A657

No. 3647, vert.: a, Adult penguin with head raised. b, Three penguins in distance. c, Adult penguin with head lowered. d, Juvenile penguin, ball. e, Juvenile penguin with wings extended. f, Juvenile penguin with head raised.

$6, Penguin on skis.

2007, June 25
3647 A657 $2 Sheet of 6, #a-f 9.00 9.00

Souvenir Sheet

3648 A657 $6 multi 4.50 4.50

1986 Halley's Comet Merchandising Emblem — A658

No. 3649: a, Orange brown frame. b, Dark blue frame. c, Purple frame. d, Red frame.

$6, Emblem, night sky.

2007, July 11
3649 A658 $2 Sheet of 4, #a-d 6.00 6.00

Souvenir Sheet

3650 A658 $6 multi 4.50 4.50

U.S. Presidents — A659

No. 3651: a, 1c, George Washington. b, 2c, John Adams. c, 3c, Thomas Jefferson. d, 4c, James Madison. e, 5c, James Monroe. f, 6c, John Quincy Adams. g, 7c, Andrew Jackson. h, 8c, Martin Van Buren. i, 9c, William Henry Harrison. j, 10c, John Tyler. k, 11c, James Knox Polk. l, 12c, Zachary Taylor. m, 13c, Millard Fillmore. n, 14c, Franklin Pierce. o, $4, Presidential seal.

No. 3652: a, 15c, James Buchanan. b, 16c, Abraham Lincoln. c, 17c, Andrew Johnson. d, 18c, Ulysses S. Grant. e, 19c, Rutherford B. Hayes. f, 20c, James A. Garfield. g, 21c, Chester A. Arthur. h, 22c, Grover Cleveland. i,

23c, Benjamin Harrison. j, 24c, Grover Cleveland. k, 25c, William McKinley. l, 26c, Theodore Roosevelt. m, 27c, William Howard Taft. n, 28c, Woodrow Wilson. o, $2, Capitol Dome.

No. 3653: a, 29c, Warren G. Harding. b, 30c, Calvin Coolidge. c, 31c, Herbert Hoover. d, 32c, Franklin D. Roosevelt. e, 33c, Harry S Truman. f, 34c, Dwight D. Eisenhower. g, 35c, John F. Kennedy. h, 36c, Lyndon B. Johnson. i, 37c, Richard M. Nixon. j, 38c, Gerald R. Ford. k, 39c, Jimmy Carter. l, 40c, Ronald Reagan. m, 41c, George H. W. Bush. n, 42c, William J. Clinton. o, 43c, George W. Bush.

2007, July 16 ***Perf. 12***

3651 A659 Sheet of 15, #a-o 3.75 3.75
3652 A659 Sheet of 15, #a-o 3.75 3.75
3653 A659 Sheet of 15, #a-o 4.00 4.00
Nos. 3651-3653 (3) 11.50 11.50

Worldwide Fund for Nature (WWF) — A660

No. 3654 — Clymene dolphins with denomination in: a, Orange. b, Bluish green. c, Yellow. d, Aquamarine.

2007, July 23 ***Perf. 13¼***

3654 Strip of 4 3.75 3.75
a.-d. A660 $1.20 Any single .90 .90
e. Miniature sheet, 2 each #3654a-3654d 7.50 7.50

Souvenir Sheet

St. George's University, 30th Anniv. — A661

2007, Oct. 26 ***Perf. 12¾***

3655 A661 $6 multi 4.50 4.50

Souvenir Sheet

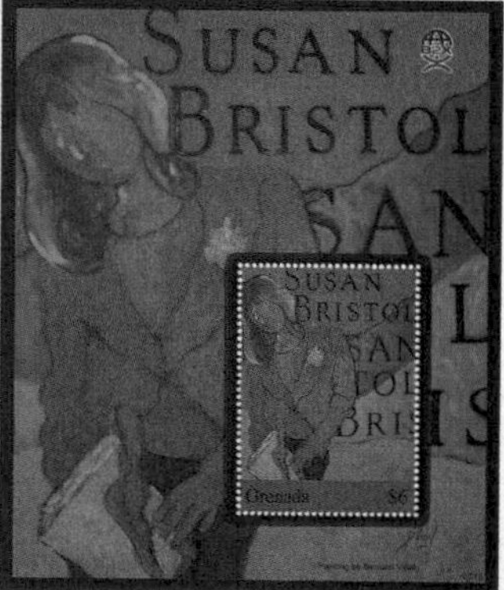

Susan Bristol, Painting by Bernard Vidal — A662

2007, Oct. 26 ***Perf. 13¼***

3656 A662 $6 multi 4.50 4.50

Victoria Cross, 150th Anniv. — A663

No. 3657, vert.: a, Corporal Bryan Budd. b, Brigadier General James Forbes-Robertson. c, Private Johnson Beharry. d, Sergeant William J. Gordon. e, Private Henry Tandey. f, Private Jorgen Christian Jensen.

$6, Seaman Jack Mantel.

2007, Oct. 26 **Litho.**

3657 A663 $1.50 Sheet of 6, #a-f 6.75 6.75

Souvenir Sheet

3658 A663 $6 multi 4.50 4.50

First Helicopter Flight, Cent. — A664

No. 3659, horiz.: a, S-65/RH-53D. b, Autogyro and bird. c, BK 117. d, AS-64.

$6, AH-64 Apache.

2007, Oct. 26

3659 A664 $2 Sheet of 4, #a-d 6.00 6.00

Souvenir Sheet

3660 A664 $6 multi 4.50 4.50

Miniature Sheets

Intl. Holocaust Remembrance Day — A665

No. 3661 $1.40 — United Nations diplomats and delegates: a, Srgian Kerim, President of 62nd General Assembly. b, Andrei Dapkiunas, Belarus. c, Jean-Marie Ehouzou, Benin. d, Milos Prica, Bosnia & Herzegovina. e, Samuel O. Outlule, Botswana. f, Francis K. Butagira, Uganda. g, Valeriy P. Kuchinsky, Ukraine. h, Jean Ping, President of 59th General Assembly.

No. 3662, $1.40: a, Erasmo Lara-Peña, Dominican Republic. b, Diego Cordovez, Ecuador. c, Carmen M. Gallardo-Hernandez, El Salvador. d, Lino Sima Ekua Avomo, Equatorial Guinea. e, Tina Intelmann, Estonia. f, Dawit Yohannes, Ethiopia. g, Isikia Rabiei Savua, Fiji. h, Lars Wide, Chef de Cabinet of 60th General Assembly.

No. 3663, $1.40: a, Angus Friday, Grenada. b, Alfredo Lopes Cabral, Guinea-Bissau. c, Samuel Rudolph Insanally, Guyana. d, Lèo Mérorès, Haiti. e, Ivan Romero-Martinez, Honduras. f, Gabor Brodi, Hungary. g, Hjalmar W. Hannesson, Iceland. h, Dan Gillerman, Israel.

No. 3664, $1.40: a, Colin Beck, Solomon Islands. b, Dumisani S. Kumalo, South Africa. c, Juan Antonio Yáñez-Barnueva, Spain. d, Anders Liden, Sweden. e, Peter Maurer, Switzerland. f, K. Laxanachantorn Laohaphan, Thailand. g, José Luis Guterres, East Timor. h, Fekitamoeloa 'Utoikamanu, Tonga.

2007, Oct. 26 **Litho.**

Sheets of 8, #a-h

3661-3664 A665 Set of 4 35.00 35.00

Christmas A666

Various details from Nativity with the Annunciation to the Shepherds, by Follower of Jan Joest: 25c, 50c, 75c, $1.

2007, Nov. 1 ***Perf. 14¾x14***

3665-3668 A666 Set of 4 1.90 1.90

New Year 2008 (Year of the Rat) A667

2007, Dec. 3 **Litho.** ***Perf. 13x13¼***

3669 A667 $2 multi 1.50 1.50

Printed in sheets of 4.

Souvenir Sheet

Breast Cancer Prevention — A668

2007, Dec. 11 ***Perf. 14***

3670 A668 $6 multi 4.50 4.50

Princess Diana (1961-97) — A669

Serpentine Die Cut 7¾

2007, Dec. 11 **Litho. & Embossed**

Without Gum

3671 A669 $20 gold & multi 15.00 15.00

Miniature Sheets

A670

Elvis Presley (1935-77) — A671

No. 3672 — Presley: a, Holding guitar at neck. b, Singing, not touching microphone. c, Wearing green shirt. d, Facing right, playing guitar. e, Singing, holding microphone. f, Facing right, playing guitar.

No. 3673 — Presley: a, Holding microphone. b, Wearing necktie. c, Holding guitar over shoulder. d, And guitar head.

2008 **Litho.** ***Perf. 13¼***

3672 A670 $1.50 Sheet of 6, #a-f 6.75 6.75
3673 A671 $2 Sheet of 4, #a-d 6.00 6.00

Issued: No. 3672, 1/14; No. 3673, 6/13.

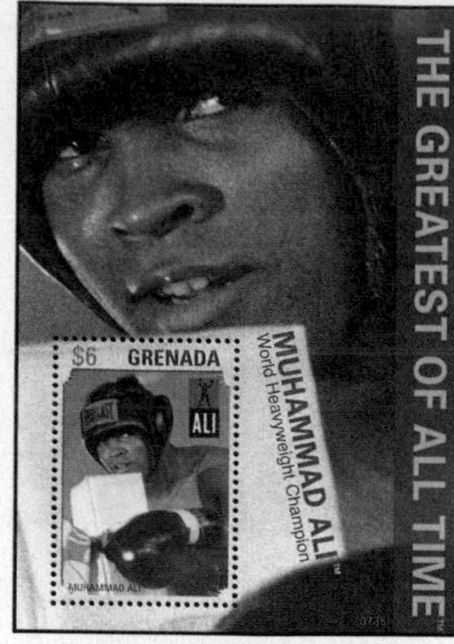

Muhammad Ali, Boxer — A672

No. 3674, $2 — Ali: a, With towel on head, bank of microphones at left. b, With towel on head, bank of microphone at right. c, With fist raised. d, With towel off head, bank of microphones at right.

No. 3675, $2, horiz. — Ali: a, With arms raised. b, Wearing robe. c, At punching bag. d, Boxing.

No. 3676, $6, Ali wearing protective headgear. No. 3677, $2, Ali with fan's hand on shoulder.

Perf. 12x11½, 11½ (#3675)

2008, Jan. 14

Sheets of 4, #a-d

3674-3675 A672 Set of 2 12.00 12.00

Souvenir Sheets

Perf. 13¼

3676-3677 A672 Set of 2 9.00 9.00

Paintings by Qi Baishi (1864-1957) — A673

No. 3678: a, Magnolias and Bees. b, Mother Hen, Chicks and Banana Leaves. c, Fish, Crabs and Watergrass. d, Crows Returning to Wintry Trees.

$4, Morning Glories.

2008. Feb. 6 ***Perf. 12½***

3678 A673 $1 Sheet of 4, #a-d 3.00 3.00

Souvenir Sheet

Perf. 11¼x11½

3679 A673 $4 multi 3.00 3.00

Miniature Sheet

2008 Summer Olympics, Beijing — A674

No. 3680: a, Greece #123. b, Poster for 1896 Olympic Games, Athens. c, Germany #B88. d, Poster for 1936 Olympic Games, Berlin.

2008, Feb. 6 ***Perf. 14¼***

3680 A674 $3 Sheet of 4, #a-d 9.00 9.00

Flora of Taiwan — A675

No. 3681, horiz.: a, Oolong tea. b, Pink lotus. c, Japanese maple. d, Bitter melon. e, Rice field. f, Lychees.
$5, Shitou Forest.

2008, May 8 ***Perf. 11½***

3681 A675 $1 Sheet of 6, #a-f 4.50 4.50

Souvenir Sheet

Perf. 13½

3682 A675 $5 multi 3.75 3.75

No. 3681 contains six 40x30mm stamps. 2008 Taipei Intl. Stamp Exhibition.

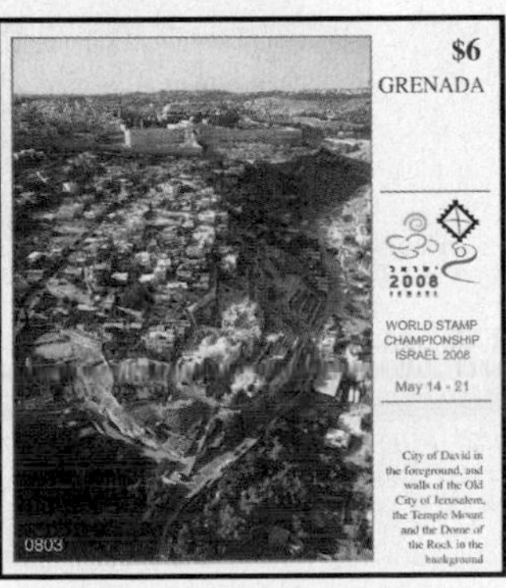

2008 World Stamp Championship, Israel — A676

2008, May 14 ***Imperf.***

3683 A676 $6 multi 4.50 4.50

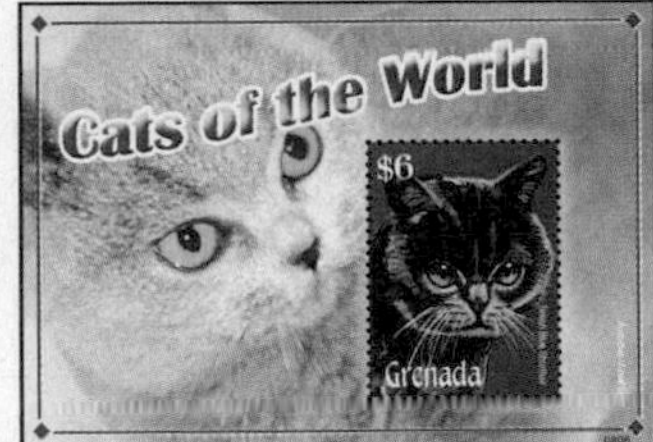

Cats — A677

No. 3684: a, Tortoiseshell. b, Korat. c, Turkish Van. d, Manx.
$6, British blue shorthair.

2008, June 18 ***Perf. 11½***

3684 A677 $1.40 Sheet of 4, #a-d 4.25 4.25

Souvenir Sheet

3685 A677 $6 multi 4.50 4.50

Miniature Sheet

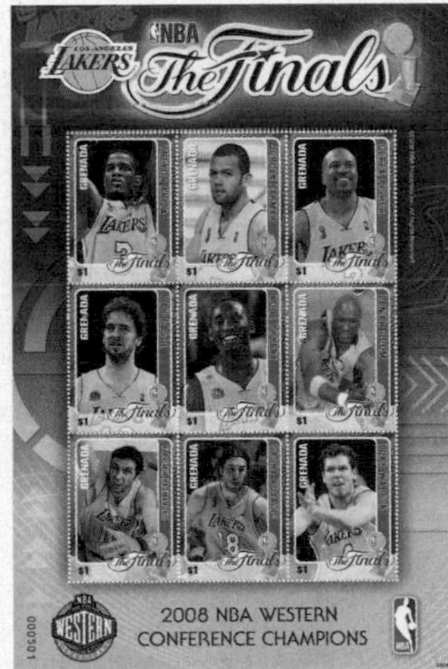

Players on 2008 Los Angeles Lakers Basketball Team — A678

No. 3686: a, Trevor Ariza. b, Jordan Farmar. c, Derek Fisher. d, Pau Gasol. e, Kobe Bryant. f, Lamar Odom. g, Vladimir Radmanovic. h, Sasha Vujacic. i, Luke Walton.

2008, June 17 **Litho.** ***Perf. 13½***

3686 A678 $1 Sheet of 9, #a-i 6.75 6.75

Miniature Sheet

Visit of Pope Benedict XVI to United States — A679

No. 3687 — Pope Benedict XVI and faded background showing: a, Bishop's red zucchetto under LL flourish. b, White ceiling tiles at top. c, Bishop's ear at UL. d, Bishop's hands at R.

2008, June 18 ***Perf. 13½***

3687 A679 $2 Sheet of 4, #a-d 6.00 6.00

Miniature Sheet

Pres. John F. Kennedy (1917-63) — A680

No. 3688 — Kennedy and background designs of: a, Flag's white stripe and blue field. b, Flag's white and red stripes. c, Necktie. d, Flag's red and white stripes, with blue in UL corner.

2008, Oct. 10 ***Perf. 11½x11¼***

3688 A680 $1.50 Sheet of 4, #a-d 4.50 4.50

Miniature Sheets

A681

A682

A683

A684

A685

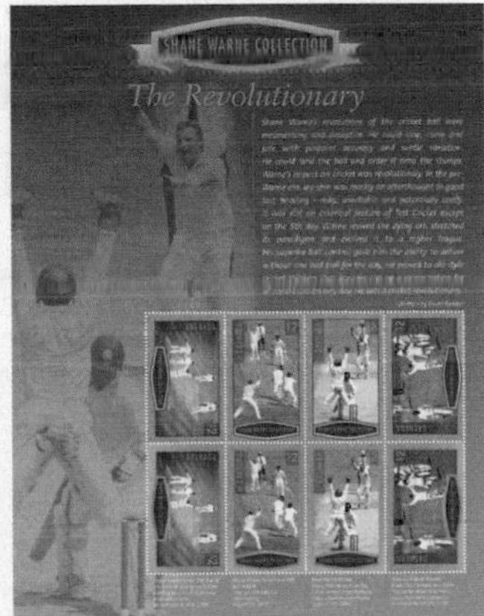

Shane Warne, Cricket Player — A686

No. 3689 — Warne: a, Holding ball, tan frame. b, Waving to crowd, tan frame. c, Close-up, tan frame. d, Wearing white shirt, green frame. e, As "b," green frame. f, As "c," green frame.

No. 3690 — Warne: a, Bowling in Australia uniform, tan frame. b, Holding trophy, tan frame. c, Celebrating, tan frame. d, As "a," green frame. e, As "b," green frame. f, As "c," green frame.

No. 3691 — Drawings of Warne by Phillip Howe: a, The Mastery (tan frame). b, The Revolutionary (tan frame). c, The Appeal (tan frame). d, The Natural (tan frame). e, As "a," green frame. f, As "b," green frame. g, As "c," green frame. h, As "d," green frame. Titles are in sheet margin.

No. 3692 — Warne bowling: a, Left arm horizontal, tan frame. b, Leg lifted, hands even, tan frame. c, Leg lifted, right hand higher than left hand, tan frame. d, Arm above head, tan frame. e, As "a," green frame. f, As "b," green frame. g, As "c," green frame. h, As "d," green frame.

No. 3693 — Warne: a, Celebrating and making fist, tan frame. b, With ball near ear, tan frame. c, After releasing ball, tan frame. d, With arm above head, umpire in background, tan frame. e, As "a," green frame. f, As "b," green frame. g, As "c," green frame. h, As "d," green frame.

No. 3694 — Match scenes: a, Warne bowling against Mike Gatting, tan frame, horiz. b, Warne taking 600th test wicket, tan frame. c, Warne capturing 533rd wicket. d, Warne taking 356th test wicket. e, As "a," green frame. f, As "b," green frame. g, As "c," green frame. h, As "d," green frame. Match descriptions are in sheet margin.

2008, Dec. 3 ***Perf. 14x14½, 14½x14***

3689 A681 $2 Sheet of 6, #a-f 9.25 9.25
3690 A682 $2 Sheet of 6, #a-f 9.25 9.25
3691 A683 $2 Sheet of 8, #a-h 12.50 12.50
3692 A684 $2 Sheet of 8, #a-h 12.50 12.50
3693 A685 $2 Sheet of 8, #a-h 12.50 12.50
3694 A686 $2 Sheet of 8, #a-h 12.50 12.50
Nos. 3689-3694 (6) 68.50 68.50

Miniature Sheet

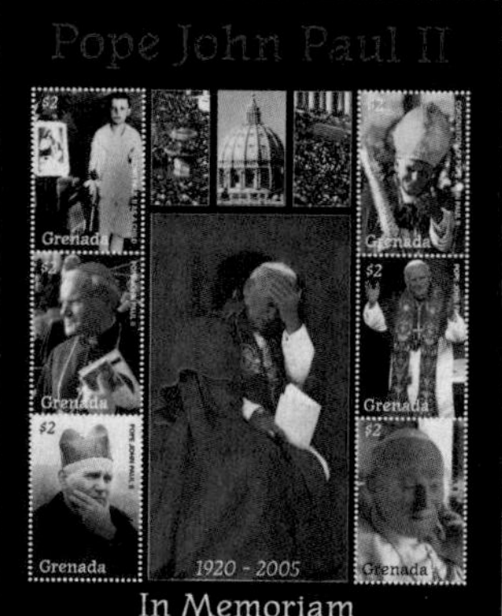

Pope John Paul II (1920-2005) — A687

No. 3695 — Pope John Paul II: a, As child. b, At coronation. c, Holding books. d, With hands raised. e, Wearing biretta, hand on chin. f, Wearing zucchetto, hand touching face.

2008, Dec. 8 ***Perf. 13½***

3695 A687 $2 Sheet of 6, #a-f 9.25 9.25

Coat of Arms — A688

2008, June 18 Litho. ***Perf. 14x15***

3696 A688 250c multi + label 1.90 1.90

Printed in sheets of 8 + 8 labels.

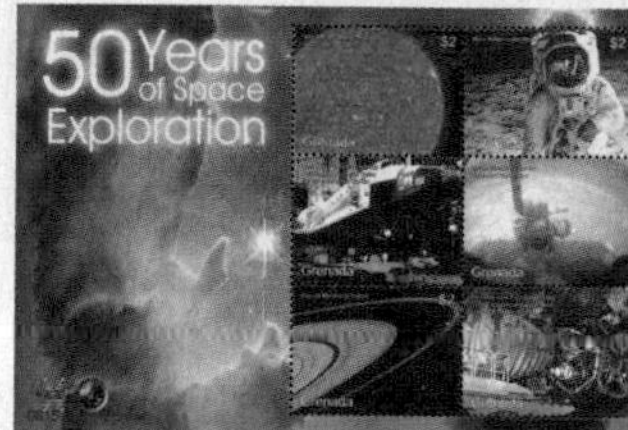

Inauguration of US Pres. Barack Obama — A689

2009, Jan. 20 ***Perf. 12¼x11¾***

3697 A689 $2.75 multi 2.10 2.10

Printed in sheets of 4.

Miniature Sheets

Space Exploration, 50th Anniv. (in 2007) — A690

No. 3698, $2: a, Ultraviolet photograph of Sun. b, Buzz Aldrin on Moon. c, Crane lifting Space Shuttle Atlantis at Kennedy Vehicle Assembly Building. d, Mars Orbiter looking at Victoria Crater. e, Cassini Mission to Saturn. f, Engines being installed on Space Shuttle Atlantis.

No. 3699, $2: a, International Space Station. b, Concept for new lunar truck. c, Milky Way over Ontario. d, M16 and the Eagle Nebula. e, Astronaut in space on Expedition 16. f, Dextre robot working on the Space Station.

No. 3700, $2.50, vert.: a, Canadarm 2 (robotic arm on Space Station). b, Space Shuttle Atlantis on launch pad in daylight. c, Cat's Eye Nebula. d, Orion crew capsule.

No. 3701, $2.50, vert.: a, Space Shuttle Atlantis at Kennedy Space Center at night. b, International Space Station as seen from Space Shuttle Discovery. c, Aurora over Saturn. d, Kibo pressurized and logistic modules.

2009, Jan. 22 ***Perf. 12***

Sheets of 6, #a-f

3698-3699 A690 Set of 2 18.50 18.50

Sheets of 4, #a-d

Perf. 12½

3700-3701 A690 Set of 2 15.50 15.50

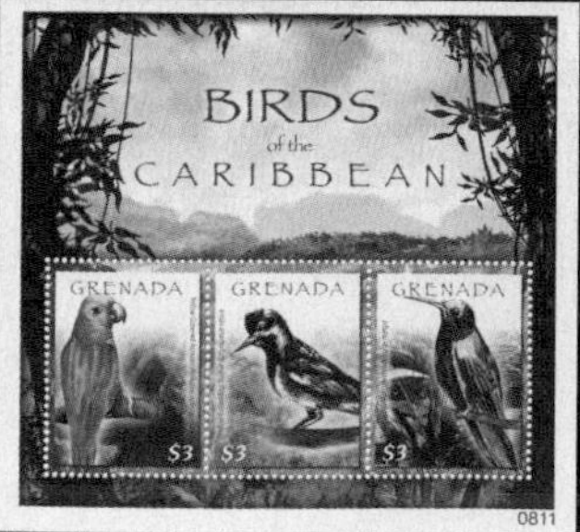

A691

A692

Birds — A693

Designs: $1, White-crowned pigeon. $2, Blue-winged warbler. $4, Bananaquit. $5, Monk parakeet.

No. 3706: a, Yellow-crowned amazon. b, Yellow-bellied sapsucker. c, Jamaican mango.

No. 3707: a, Tree swallow. b, Ringed kingfisher. c, Black-and-white warbler.

2009, Jan. 22 ***Perf. 12½***

3702-3705 A691 Set of 4 9.25 9.25
3706 A692 $3 Sheet of 3, #a-c 7.00 7.00

Perf. 12¾x13

3707 A693 $3 Sheet of 3, #a-c 7.00 7.00

New Year 2009 (Year of the Ox) — A694

2009, Jan. 26 ***Perf. 12***

3708 A694 $2.50 multi 2.25 2.25

Printed in sheets of 4.

A695

Mushrooms — A696

Designs: 25c, Panaeolus papilionaceus. 50c, Panaeolus cyanescens. 75c, Panaeolus sphintrinus. 90c, Panaeolus fimicola. $1, Copelandia cyanescens. $4, Psilocybe cubensis.

No. 3715: a, Panaleus subbalteatus. b, Alboleptonia earlei. c, Porphyrellus portoricensis. d, Psilocybe caerulescens.

2009, Feb. 9 ***Perf. 11½***

3709-3714 A695 Set of 6 5.75 5.75
3715 A696 $2.50 Sheet of 4, #a-d 7.75 7.75

Miniature Sheet

Marilyn Monroe (1926-62), Actress — A697

No. 3716 — Monroe: a, With arm extended. b, Touching wall. c, With chair in background. d, Resting on arms.

2009, Feb. 9

3716 A697 $2.50 Sheet of 4, #a-d 7.75 7.75

Flag of Grenada, and Designer Anthony C. George — A698

Frame color: 10c, Blue green. 25c, Blue. 50c, Red. 75c, Yellow.
$6, Flag and George, vert.

2009, Feb. 25 ***Perf. 13¼***

3717-3720 A698 Set of 4 1.25 1.25

Souvenir Sheet

Perf. 12

3721 A698 $6 multi 4.75 4.75

No. 3721 contains one 30x40mm stamp.

Peony on Vase — A699

2009, Apr. 10 ***Perf. 13¼***

3722 A699 75c multi .55 .55

Souvenir Sheet

3723 A699 $5 Peony, diff. 3.75 3.75

No. 3723 contains one 44x44mm stamp. No. 3722 was printed in sheets of 12.

Miniature Sheet

Olympic Track and Field Events — A700

No. 3724: a, Pole vault. b, Hurdles. c, Relay race. d, High jump.

2009, Apr. 29 ***Perf. 12***
3724 A700 $1.40 Sheet of 4, #a-d 4.25 4.25

China 2009 World Stamp Exhibition, Luoyang.

Miniature Sheet

First Man on the Moon, 40th Anniv. — A701

No. 3725: a, Proposed upper stages of Orion spacecraft, Wernher von Braun. b, Crew of Apollo 11. c, Lunar Orbiter. d, Ranger 7. e, Lunar Module, Pres. John F. Kennedy. f, Proposed Orion lunar module.

2009, Apr. 29 ***Perf. 11½***
3725 A701 $2 Sheet of 6, #a-f 9.00 9.00

Miniature Sheet

Joseph Haydn (1732-1809), Composer — A702

No. 3726: a, Haydn's birthplace, Rohrau, Austria. b, Johann Peter Salomon, impresario. c, Austro-Hungarian Haydn Orchestra. d, Wolfgang Amadeus Mozart, composer. e, Haydn's house, Vienna. f, Ludwig van Beethoven, composer and student of Haydn.

2009, Apr. 29
3726 A702 $2.25 Sheet of 6, #a-f 10.00 10.00

Miniature Sheet

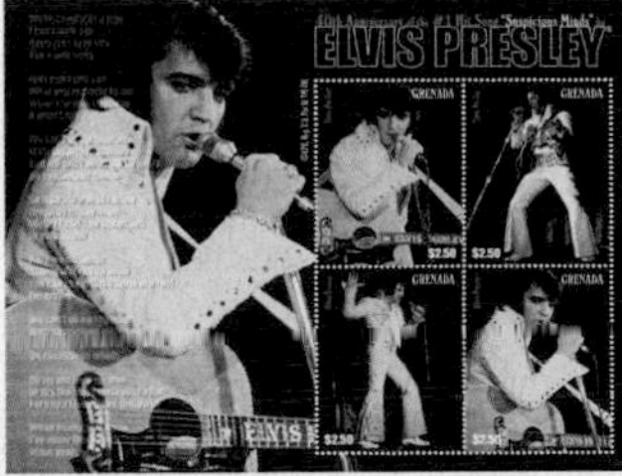

Elvis Presley (1935-77) — A703

No. 3727 — Presley: a, With guitar strap on both sides. b, Facing left. c, With hand raised. d, With guitar strap at right.

2009, Apr. 29 ***Perf. 13¼***
3727 A703 $2.50 Sheet of 4, #a-d 7.50 7.50

Miniature Sheets

Dogs — A704

No. 3728, $2.30 — Golden retriever: a, On outdoor chair. b, On lawn, with pumpkin and gourds. c, On sofa. d, Two dogs in basket.

No. 3729, $2.50 — Beagle: a, On desktop. b, Face. c, On lawn. d, Near stone wall.

2009, Apr. 29 ***Perf. 11½***
Sheets of 4, #a-d
3728-3729 A704 Set of 2 14.50 14.50

American Kennel Club, 125th anniv.

Miniature Sheet

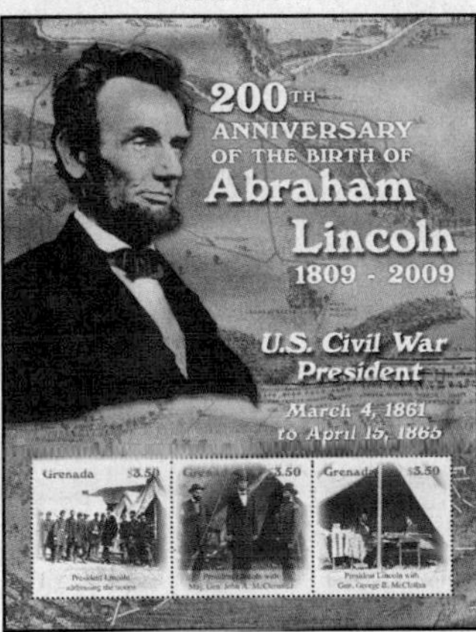

Pres. Abraham Lincoln (1809-65) — A705

No. 3730 — Lincoln: a, Addressing Union troops. b, With Major General John A. McClernand. c, With General George B. McClellan.

2009, July 21 **Litho.** ***Perf. 13½***
3730 A705 $3.50 Sheet of 3, #a-c 8.00 8.00

Miniature Sheet

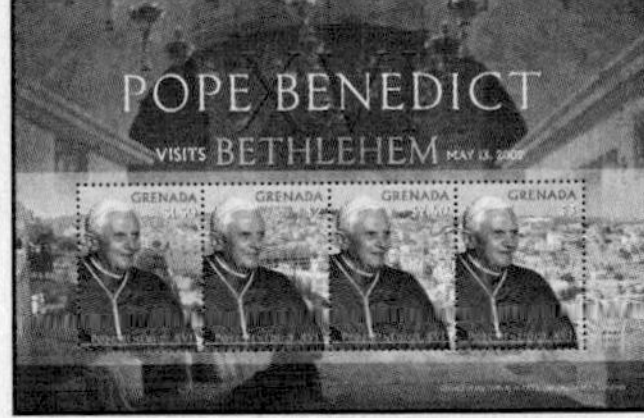

Visit of Pope Benedict XVI to Bethlehem — A706

No. 3731 — Pope Benedict and buildings in Bethlehem: a, $1.50. b, $2. c, $2.50. d, $3.

2009, July 21 ***Perf. 11½***
3731 A706 Sheet of 4, #a-d 6.75 6.75

Miniature Sheet

Charles Darwin (1809-82), Naturalist — A707

No. 3732 — Darwin and: a, Bird. b, Wolf. c, Fossil. d, Tortoise.

2009, July 21
3732 A707 $2.50 Sheet of 4, #a-d 7.50 7.50

Chinese Aviation, Cent. — A708

No. 3733: a, J-5. b, J-6. c, J-7G. d, J-7. $6, JF-17.

2009, Nov. 13 **Litho.** ***Perf. 14***
3733 A708 $2 Sheet of 4, #a-d 6.50 6.50

Souvenir Sheet
Perf. 14¼
3734 A708 $6 multi 4.75 4.75

2009 Aeropex, Beijing. No. 3733 contains four 42x28mm stamps.

Miniature Sheet

Chinese Zodiac Animals — A709

No. 3735: a, Rat. b, Ox. c, Tiger. d, Rabbit. e, Dragon. f, Snake. g, Horse. h, Ram. i, Monkey. j, Cock. k, Dog. l, Pig.

2010, Jan. 4 ***Perf. 12***
3735 A709 60c Sheet of 12, #a-l 5.50 5.50

Miniature Sheet

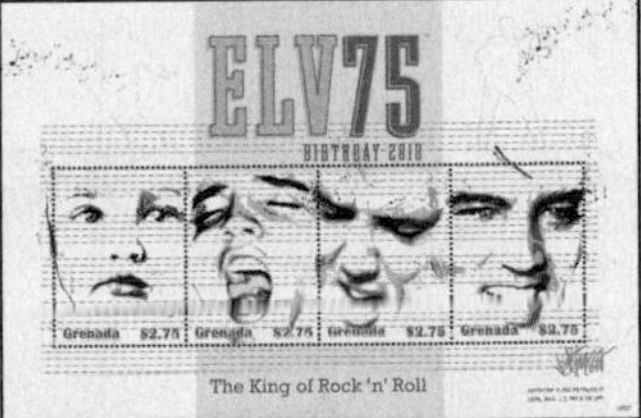

Elvis Presley (1935-77) — A710

Various views of Presley's face.

2010, Jan. 7 ***Perf. 13¼***
3736 A710 $2.75 Sheet of 4, #a-d 8.50 8.50

Christmas 2009 A711

Designs: $1, Fish wearing stocking caps. $2, Christmas tree, lights, fruit. $4, Bells. $5, Map of Grenada, stars, Christmas ornaments.

2010, Jan. 13 ***Perf. 12½***
3737-3740 A711 Set of 4 9.25 9.25

Orchids — A712

Designs: $1.20, Brassia caudata. $1.80, Epidendrum imatophyllum. No. 3743, $3, Ionopsis utriculoides. $5, Habenaria bractescens.

No. 3745, horiz.: a, Vanilla pompona. b, Caularthron bicornutum. c, Epidendrum nocturnum. d, Aspasia variegata.

No. 3746, $3, horiz.: a, Epidendrum hartii. b, Brassavola cucullata.

2010, Jan. 13 ***Perf. 13¼x13***
3741-3744 A712 Set of 4 8.50 8.50

Perf. 13x13¼
3745 A712 $2.75 Sheet of 4, #a-d 8.50 8.50

Souvenir Sheet
3746 A712 $3 Sheet of 2, #a-b 4.75 4.75

Ferrari Automobiles and Their Parts — A713

No. 3747, $1.25: a, Engine of 1989 F1-89. b, 1989 F1-89.

No. 3748, $1.25: a, Engine of 1994 F355 Berlinetta. b, 1994 F355 Berlinetta.

No. 3749, $1.25: a, Wires and parts to 1997 355 F1 Berlinetta. b, 1997 355 F1 Berlinetta.

No. 3750, $1.25: a, Steering wheel of 1997 F310 B. b, 1997 F310 B.

2010, Mar. 1 ***Perf. 12***

Vert. Pairs, #a-b

3747-3750 A713 Set of 4 7.75 7.75

Miniature Sheet

Pres. John F. Kennedy (1917-63), 50th Anniv. of Election — A714

No. 3751: a, Facing left, black and white photograph. b, Standing, black and white photograph. c, Color photograph. d, With flag in background, black and white photograph.

2010, Apr. 9 ***Perf. 12x11½***

3751 A714 $2.75 Sheet of 4, #a-d 8.25 8.25

Miniature Sheets

A715

Princess Diana (1961-97) — A716

No. 3752: a, Wearing black hat, gray and white along left margin of stamp. b, Wearing blue hat, with black frame at LL over gray area. c, As "b," with black frame at LL over white area. d, As "a," with hand of Princess Diana (from central illustration) touching black frame at left.

No. 3753: a, Wearing white hat, gray and white along left margin. b, Wearing no hat, with black frame at LL over red area (Diana's jacket from central illustration). c, As "b," with LL corner over gray area. d, As "a," with entire left margin over red area (Diana's jacket from central illustration).

2010, Apr. 9

3752 A715 $2.75 Sheet of 4, #a-d 8.25 8.25

3753 A716 $2.75 Sheet of 4, #a-d 8.25 8.25

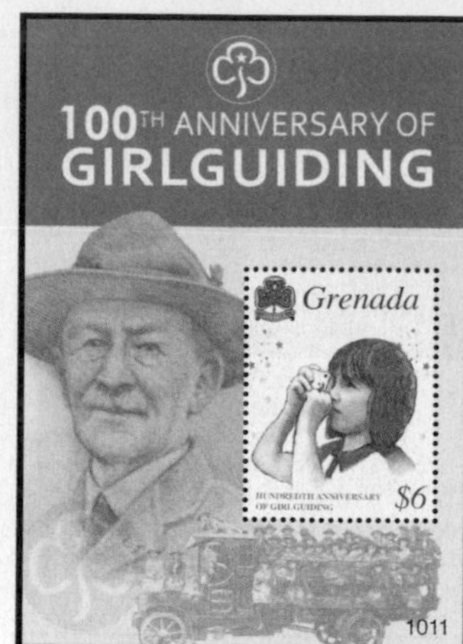

Girl Guides, Cent. — A717

No. 3754, horiz. — Girl Guides: a, Looking at image taken by camera. b, With cameras. c, With movie clapboard. d, Looking at image take by camera with telephoto lens.

$6, Girl Guide with camera.

2010, June 11 ***Perf. 13x13¼***

3754 A717 $2.75 Sheet of 4, #a-d 8.25 8.25

Souvenir Sheet

Perf. 13¼x13

3755 A717 $6 multi 4.50 4.50

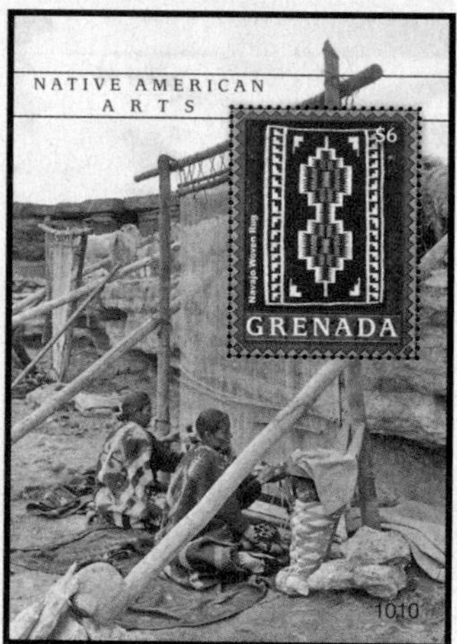

Native American Arts — A718

No. 3756: a, Apache woven basket. b, Sioux beaded moccasins. c, Iroquois cornhusk mask. d, Tlingit totem pole. e, Inuit hunter doll. f, Hopi pottery.

$6, Navajo woven rug.

2010, June 11 ***Perf. 13¼x13***

3756 A718 $2 Sheet of 6, #a-f 9.00 9.00

Souvenir Sheet

3757 A718 $6 multi 4.50 4.50

Souvenir Sheet

New Year 2010 (Year of the Tiger) — A719

No. 3758 — Half of tiger's head with denomination at: a, UL. b, UR.

2010, Jan. 4 **Litho.** ***Perf. 12***

3758 A719 $5 Sheet of 2, #a-b 7.75 7.75

2010 World Cup Soccer Championships, South Africa — A720

No. 3759, $1.50 — Group A first-round matches: a, South Africa vs. Mexico. b, Uruguay vs. France. c, Uruguay vs. South Africa. d, France vs. Mexico. e, Mexico vs. Uruguay. f, France vs. South Africa.

No. 3760, $1.50 — Group B first-round matches: a, South Korea vs. Greece. b, Argentina vs. Nigeria. c, South Korea vs. Argentina. d, Nigeria vs. Greece. e, Nigeria vs. South Korea. f, Greece vs. Argentina.

No. 3761, $1.50 — Group C first-round matches: a, England vs. United States. b, Algeria vs. Slovenia. c, United States vs. Slovenia. d, England vs. Algeria. e, Slovenia vs. England. f, Algeria vs. United States.

No. 3762, $1.50 — Group D first-round matches: a, Serbia vs. Ghana. b, Germany vs. Australia. c, Germany vs. Serbia. d, Ghana vs. Australia. e, Ghana vs. Germany. f, Australia vs. Serbia.

No. 3763, $3.50: a, Nelson Mandela Bay Stadium, Port Elizabeth. b, Cape Town Stadium, Cape Town.

No. 3764, $3.50: a, Soccer City Stadium, Johannesburg. b, Moses Mabhida Stadium, Durban.

2010, June 11 ***Perf. 13¼***

Sheets of 6, #a-f

3759-3762 A720 Set of 4 27.00 27.00

Sheets of 2, #a-b

3763-3764 A720 Set of 2 10.50 10.50

Miniature Sheet

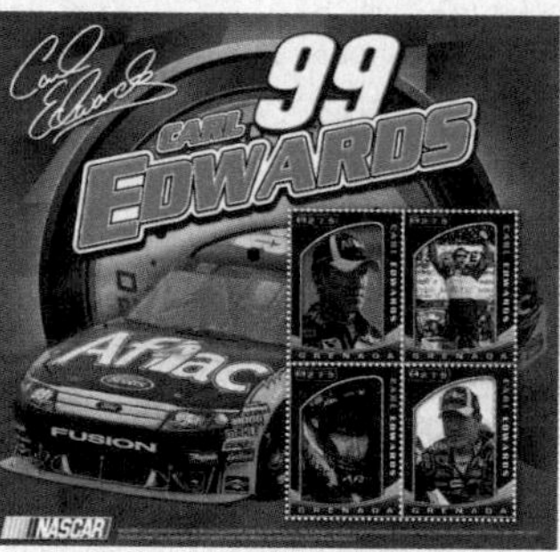

Carl Edwards, NASCAR Driver — A721

No. 3765 — Edwards: a, Wearing baseball cap, arms not visible. b, Without hat, arms raised. c, Wearing racing helmet. d, Wearing baseball cap, arms visible.

2010, July 26 ***Perf. 12***

3765 A721 $2.75 Sheet of 4, #a-d 8.25 8.25

Frédéric Chopin (1810-49), Composer — A722

No. 3766: a, Sketch of Chopin facing left. b, George Sand, writer. c, Chopin, with arms folded. d, Chopin's birthplace.

$6, Chopin and musical notes.

2010, Sept. 1

3766 A722 $2.50 Sheet of 4, #a-d 7.50 7.50

Souvenir Sheet

3767 A722 $6 multi 4.50 4.50

Henri Dunant (1828-1910), Founder of the Red Cross — A723

No. 3768 — Dunant and members of Red Cross "Committee of Five" founding members: a, Louis Appia. b, Gustave Moynier. c, Théodore Maunoir. d, Henri Dufour.

$6, Dunant and the First Geneva Convention, 1894.

2010, Sept. 1

3768 A723 $2.50 Sheet of 4, #a-b 7.50 7.50

Souvenir Sheet

3769 A723 $6 multi 4.50 4.50

Miniature Sheet

Pope John Paul II (1920-2005) — A724

No. 3770 — Pope John Paul II: a, With crucifix. b, Without crucifix.

2010, Nov. 4

3770 A724 $2.75 Sheet of 4, #3770a, 3 #3770b 8.25 8.25

Boy Scouts of America, Cent. — A725

No. 3771, $2.75: a, Scout saluting. b, Scout rescuing child.

No. 3772, $2.75: a, Scout assisting woman with groceries. b, Scout reading from book.

2010, Nov. 4 ***Perf. 12½***

Pairs, #a-b

3771-3772 A725 Set of 2 8.25 8.25

Nos. 3771-3772 each were printed in sheets containing two pairs.

A726

Pres. Abraham Lincoln (1809-65) — A727

No. 3773 — Lincoln: a, With mouth to right of "resting." b, With mouth to right of "endure." c, Seated.

No. 3774 — Lincoln: a, Standing. b, With son, Tad. c, Seated.

2010, Nov. 4

3773 A726 $2 Horiz. strip of 3, #a-c 4.50 4.50
3774 A727 $2 Horiz. strip of 3, #a-c 4.50 4.50

Nos. 3773-3774 each were printed in sheets containing two strips.

Miniature Sheets

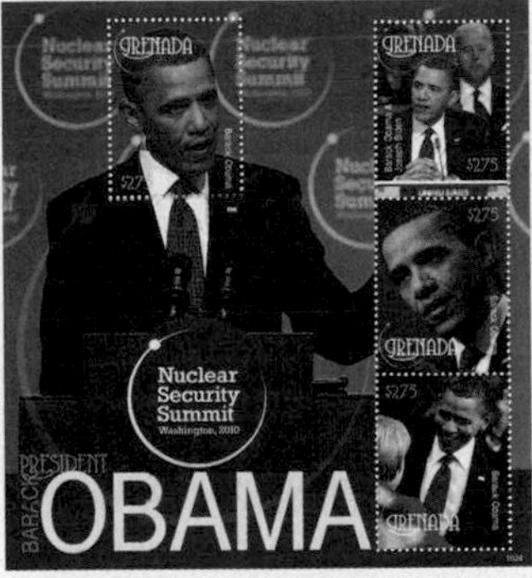

Pres. Barack Obama at Nuclear Security Summit — A728

Pres. Obama and Mexican President Felipe Calderón — A729

No. 3775 — Pres. Obama: a, Facing right. b, With Vice-President Joseph Biden. c, Facing left. d, Greeting person.

No. 3776: a, Obama and Calderón shaking hands. b, Calderón. c, Obama. d, Calderón and Obama standing together.

2010, Nov. 4 ***Perf. 12***

3775 A728 $2.75 Sheet of 4, #a-d 8.25 8.25
3776 A729 $2.75 Sheet of 4, #a-d 8.25 8.25

St. George's, 300th Anniv. A730

Photographs from the mid-1900s: 25c, St. George's Lagoon. 50c, Church Street, St. George's, Grenada #91, vert. $1, Market Day, St. George's.

2010, Dec. 9 **Litho.** ***Perf. 12***

3777-3779 A730 Set of 3 1.40 1.40

Nos. 3777-3779 each were printed in sheets of 4.

Sickle Cell Association of Grenada — A731

No. 3780 — Flowers, text, orange ribbon: a, 25c. b, 50c. c, $1. d, $2. $6, Flowers, text, blue ribbon.

2010, Dec. 9

3780 A731 Sheet of 4, #a-d 3.00 3.00

Souvenir Sheet

3781 A731 $6 multi 4.50 4.50

Souvenir Sheets

A732

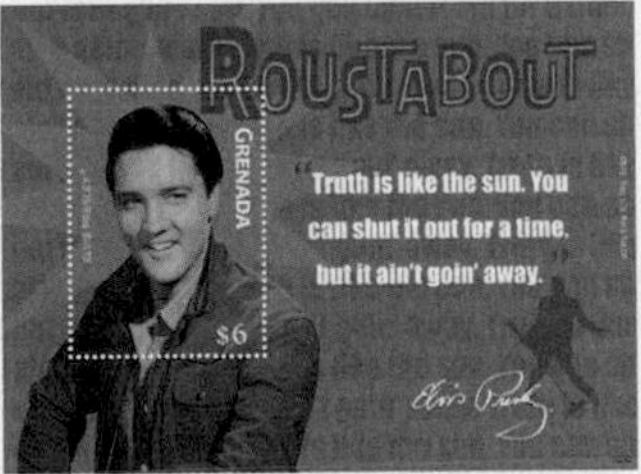

A733

A734

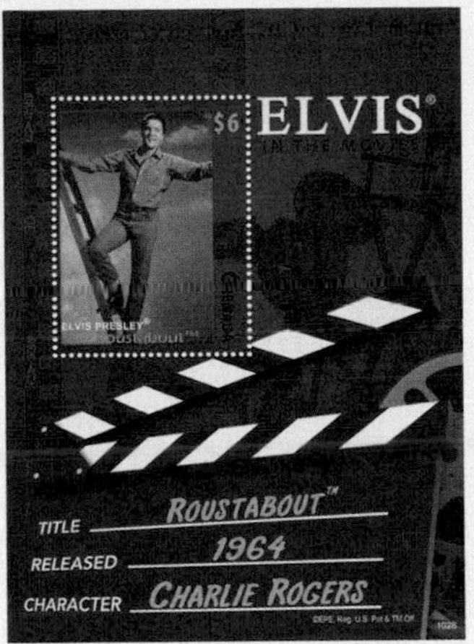

Elvis Presley (1935-77) — A735

2010, Dec. 9 ***Perf. 12½***

3782 A732 $6 multi 4.50 4.50
3783 A733 $6 multi 4.50 4.50
3784 A734 $6 multi 4.50 4.50
3785 A735 $6 multi 4.50 4.50
Nos. 3782-3785 (4) 18.00 18.00

Christmas A736

Designs: 25c, Three Wise Men. 50c, Adoration of the Shepherds, by Guido Reni. $1, Anbetung der Hirten, by Jusepe de Ribera. $2, Star of Bethlehem.

$6, Geburt Christi, by Max Bentele, horiz.

2010, Dec. 9 ***Perf. 12***

3786-3789 A736 Set of 4 3.00 3.00

Souvenir Sheet

Perf. 12½

3790 A736 $6 multi 4.50 4.50

Nos. 3786-3789 each were printed in sheets of 4. No. 3790 contains one 50x38mm stamp.

Souvenir Sheet

New Year 2011 (Year of the Rabbit) — A737

No. 3791 — Background above rabbit's ears in: a, Tan. b, Green.

2011, Feb. 1 ***Perf. 12***

3791 A737 $2.50 Sheet of 2, #a-b 3.75 3.75

Fish — A738

Designs: 25c, Rock beauty. $1.25, Graysby. $1.50, Beaugregory damselfish. $2, Juvenile Pomacanthus paru.

$100, Longsnout butterflyfish.

2011, Feb. 1 **Litho.** ***Perf. 13¼***

3792-3795 A738 Set of 4 3.75 3.75

Souvenir Sheet

Perf. 14¾x14

3796 A738 $100 multi 75.00 75.00

No. 3796 contains one 40x30mm stamp.

Forbidden City, Beijing — A739

No. 3797: a, Aerial view. b, Ancient sundial. c, Temple roof. d, Canal.

$5, Golden lion, vert.

2011, Feb. 1 ***Perf. 12***

3797 A739 $2 Sheet of 4, #a-d 6.00 6.00

Souvenir Sheet

Perf. 12½

3798 A739 $5 multi 3.75 3.75

2010 Beijing Intl. Stamp and Coin Exhibition. No. 3798 contains one 38x51mm stamp.

Engagement of Prince William and Catherine Middleton A740

Designs: No. 3799, Couple.

No. 3800: a, Prince William. b, Catherine Middleton.

2011, Feb. 18 ***Perf. 13 Syncopated***

3799 A740 $2.50 multi 1.90 1.90
3800 A740 $2.50 Horiz. pair, #a-b 3.75 3.75

No. 3799 was printed in sheets of 4; No. 3800, in sheets containing 2 pairs.

Miniature Sheet

Chinese Zodiac Animals — A741

No. 3801: a, Rat. b, Ox. c, Tiger. d, Snake. e, Dragon. f, Rabbit. g, Horse. h, Ram. i, Monkey. j, Pig. k, Dog. l, Rooster.

2011, Apr. 1 ***Perf. 12***

3801 A741 $1 Sheet of 12, #a-l 9.00 9.00

Miniature Sheets

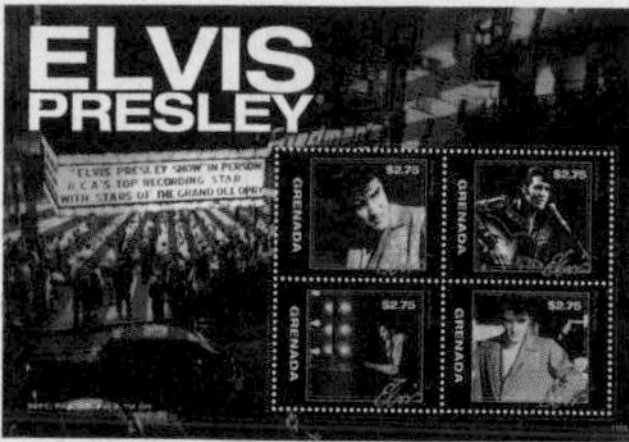

A742

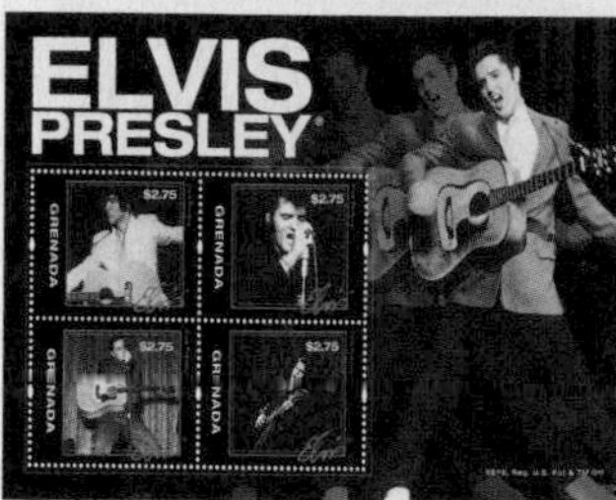

Elvis Presley (1935-77) — A743

No. 3802 — Signature in lilac with Presley: a, Wearing checked jacket, head tilted. b, Playing guitar. c, At dressing room table. d, Wearing checked jacket, head straight.

No. 3803 — Signature in blue with Presley: a, Wearing white jacket. b, Holding microphone, no guitar visible. c, Holding microphone, guitar visible. d, Playing guitar.

2011, Apr. 6

3802 A742 $2.75 Sheet of 4, #a-d 8.25 8.25

Perf. 13 Syncopated

3803 A743 $2.75 Sheet of 4, #a-d 8.25 8.25

Miniature Sheets

A744

Princess Diana (1961-97) — A745

No. 3804 — Princess Diana wearing: a, Black hat and black jacket. b, White and pink hat with veil. c, Gray striped jacket. d, Black hat and white scarf.

No. 3805 — Princess Diana: a, Sniffing flowers. b, Wearing white veil around head. c, Wearing plaid jacket. d, Wearing black hat and black dress with white ruffled collar.

Perf. 13 Syncopated

2011, Apr. 15 **Litho.**

3804 A744 $2.75 Sheet of 4, #a-d 8.25 8.25

Perf. 12

3805 A745 $2.75 Sheet of 4, #a-d 8.25 8.25

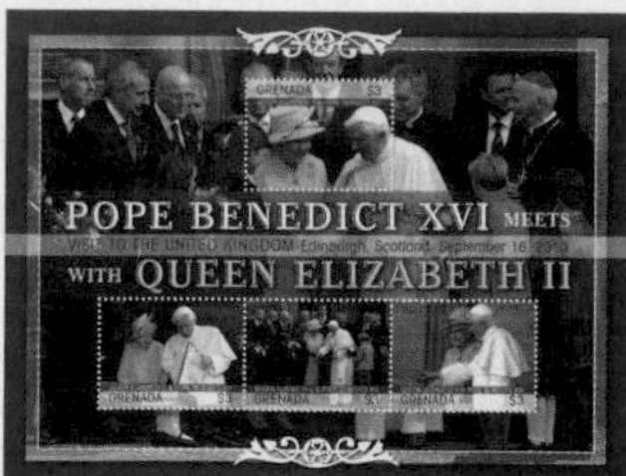

Meeting of Pope Benedict XVI and Queen Elizabeth II — A746

No. 3806: a, Pope Benedict XVI, Queen Elizabeth II and girl. b, Pope and Queen looking at book. c, Pope and Queen with children and dignitaries. d, Pope and Queen, Pope pointing.

No. 3807, vert.: a, Queen. b, Pope.

2011, Apr. 15 ***Perf. 11½x12***

3806 A746 $3 Sheet of 4, #a-d 9.00 9.00

Souvenir Sheet

Perf. 11½

3807 A746 $3.50 Sheet of 2, #a-b 5.25 5.25

First Man in Space, 50th Anniv. — A747

No. 3808, $2.75: a, Bust of Yuri Gagarin. b, Aluminum medal depicting Gagarin. c, Vostok rocket. d, U.S. astronaut L. Gordon Cooper.

No. 3809, $2.75: a, Monument to the Conquerors of Space, Moscow. b, U.S. astronaut Walter Schirra. c, Gagarin wearing decorations. d, Vostok spaceship.

No. 3810, $6, Gagarin wearing military uniform and decorations, diff. No. 3811, $6, Vostok spaceship, horiz.

2011, Apr. 15 ***Perf. 12x12½***

Sheets of 4, #a-d

3808-3809 A747 Set of 2 16.50 16.50

Souvenir Sheets

Perf. 11¼x11½, 11½x11¼

3810-3811 A747 Set of 2 9.00 9.00

Large Hadron Collider, France and Switzerland — A748

No. 3812: a, Galileo Galilei. b, Sir Isaac Newton. c, Large Hadron Collider. d, Albert Einstein. $6, Collider, diff.

2011, July 22 ***Perf. 12***

3812 A748 $2.75 Sheet of 4, #a-d 8.25 8.25

Souvenir Sheet

Perf. 12½

3813 A748 $6 multi 4.50 4.50

No. 3813 contains one 51x38mm stamp.

Souvenir Sheets

Chinese Civil Engineering Projects — A749

No. 3814, $6, Qingdao Cross-Sea Bridge. No. 3815, $6, Diagram of Qingdao Haozhouwan Tunnel.

2011, July 22 ***Perf. 12***

3814-3815 A749 Set of 2 9.00 9.00

Parrots — A750

No. 3816 — Map of Caribbean islands and: a, Scarlet macaw. b, Hyacinth macaw. c, Slender-billed parakeet. d, Blue-and-yellow macaw. e, Olive-throated parakeet. f, Burrowing parrot.

$6, Red-and-green macaw.

2011, Sept. 15 **Litho.** ***Perf. 12***

3816 A750 $2 Sheet of 6, #a-f 9.00 9.00

Souvenir Sheet

3817 A750 $6 multi 4.50 4.50

Miniature Sheets

Mother Teresa (1910-97), Humanitarian — A751

No. 3818, $2.50: a, Mother Teresa, curved frame at LR. b, Mother Teresa and Pope John Paul II. c, Mother Teresa and Princess Diana. d, Mother Teresa, curved frame at UL.

No. 3819, $2.50: a, Mother Teresa and Prince Charles. b, Mother Teresa, curved frame at LL. c, Motehr Teresa, curved frame at UR. d, Mother Teresa and Senator Edward M. Kennedy.

Sheets of 4, #a-d

2011, Sept. 15 ***Perf. 12***

3818-3819 A751 Set of 2 15.00 15.00

Miniature Sheets

Pres. Abraham Lincoln (1809-65) — A752

No. 3820, $2.75 — Photograph of Lincoln with background color of: a, Green. b, Blue black. c, Gray black. d, Red brown.

No. 3820, $2.75, horiz. — Photograph of Lincoln with background color of: a, Black. b, Dark red. c, Brown. d, Purple.

2011, Sept. 15 ***Perf. 13 Syncopated***

Sheets of 4, #a-d

3820-3821 A752 Set of 2 14.50 14.50

Chocolate Candy A753

Chocolate Frosting — A754

No. 3822 — Candy with: a, Country name in gray, denomination in pink. b, Country name and denomination in pink. c, "GRE" in pink, "NADA" and denomination in gray.

No. 3823 — Teardrop-shaped swirl in frosting at: a, Left of "NA" in panel at right, above "ho" in "Chocolate," curved frame at UL. b, Left of "A $" in panel at right, above "Ch" in "Chocolate." c, Left of "EN" in panel at right, above "oc" in "Chocolate." d, Left of "RE" in panel at right, above "ho" in "Chocolate." e, Left of "GR" in panel at right, above "e" in "Chocolate." f, Left of "GR" in panel at right, above "oc" in "Chocolate." g, Left of "G" in panel at right (touching edge of stamp), above "ho" in "Chocolate," curved frame at LL. h, Left of "G" in panel at right (touching edge of stamp), above "e" in "Chocolate." i, Left of "G" in panel at right (touching edge of stamp), above "oc" in "Chocolate."

2011, Oct. 26 **Litho.**

3822 Horiz. strip of 3 5.25 5.25

a.-c. A753 $2.25 Any single 1.75 1.75

3823 A754 $2.25 Sheet of 9, #a-i 15.00 15.00

No. 3822 is printed in sheets containing 3 strips. Nos. 3822-3823 are impregnated with a chocolate aroma.

British Monarchs A755

Designs: No. 3824, $2, King William II (c. 1056-1100). No. 3825, $2, King Richard I (1157-99). No. 3826, $2, King Edward III (1312-77). No. 3827, $2, King Edward IV (1442-83). No. 3828, $2, King Henry VIII (1491-1547). No. 3829, $2, King Charles I (1600-49). No. 3830, $2, King George I (1660-

1727). No. 3831, $2, King George V (1865-1936).

2011, Oct. 26 ***Perf. 14***
3824-3831 A755 Set of 8 12.00 12.00

Nos. 3824-3831 each were printed in sheets of 8 + central label.

Sept. 11, 2011 Terrorist Attacks, 10th Anniv. — A756

No. 3832: a, Tribute in light at World Trade Center site. b, Pentagon Memorial. c, September 11 Memorial, New York. d, September 11 Memorial, New Jersey.
$6, World Trade Center towers, vert.

2011, Oct. 26 ***Perf. 12***
3832 A756 $2.75 Sheet of 4, #a-d 8.25 8.25

Souvenir Sheet

3833 A756 $6 multi 4.50 4.50

Mao Zedong (1893-1976), Chinese Leader — A757

2011, Nov. 8 **Litho.**
3834 A757 $3 shown 2.25 2.25

Souvenir Sheet

3835 A757 $6 Portrait, diff. 4.50 4.50

China 2011 Intl. Philatelic Exhibition, Wuxi (No. 3835). No. 3834 was printed in sheets of 3.

Miniature Sheets

Visit of Pope Benedict XVI to Germany — A758

No. 3836: a, Pope Benedict XVI wearing miter, facing left, building. b, Red City Hall, Berlin. c, Madonna in the Rose Bower, by Stefan Lochner. d, Pope Benedict XVI with arms extended, building.
No. 3837 — Various buildings and Pope Benedict XVI: a, Praying. b, Holding crucifix in his left hand, waving. c, Holding crucifix in his right hand.

2011, Nov. 8 ***Perf. 13¼x13***
3836 A758 $2.75 Sheet of 4, #a-d 8.25 8.25
3837 A758 $3 Sheet of 3, #a-c 6.75 6.75

Chinese Zodiac Animals — A759

New Year 2012 (Year fo the Dragon) — A760

No. 3838: a, Rat. b, Ox. c, Tiger. d, Rabbit. e, Dragon. f, Snake. g, Horse. h, Sheep. i, Monkey. j, Rooster. k, Dog. l, Boar.
$8, Dragon.

Litho. With Foil Application

2011 ***Perf. 13 Syncopated***
3838 A759 65c Sheet of 12, #a-l 5.75 5.75

Souvenir Sheet

Litho.

Perf. 12

3839 A760 $8 multi 6.00 6.00

Issued: No. 3838, 11/8; No. 3839, 10/26.

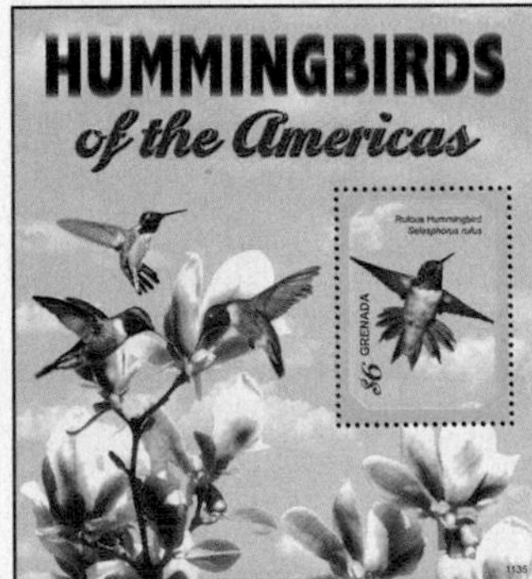

Hummingbirds — A761

No. 3840, horiz.: a, Calliope hummingbird. b, Anna's hummingbird. c, Black-chinned hummingbird. d, Ruby-throated hummingbird. e, Costa's hummingbird. f, Broad-billed hummingbird.
$6, Rufous hummingbird.

2011, Dec. 16 **Litho.** ***Perf. 12***
3840 A761 $2 Sheet of 6, #a-f 9.00 9.00

Souvenir Sheet

3841 A761 $6 multi 4.50 4.50

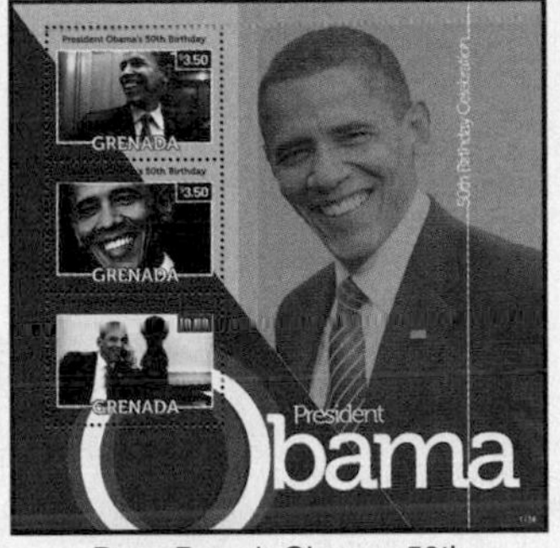

Pres. Barack Obama, 50th Birthday — A762

No. 3842 — Pres. Obama: a, Looking left. b, Close-up. c, Holding hand to face.
$6, Pres. Obama, diff.

2011, Dec. 16 ***Perf. 12***
3842 A762 $3.50 Sheet of 3, #a-c 7.75 7.75

Souvenir Sheet

Perf. 12¾

3843 A762 $6 multi 4.50 4.50

No. 3843 contains one 51x38mm stamp.

Souvenir Sheets

Pres. John F. Kennedy (1917-63) — A763

No. 3844, $3 — Pres. Kennedy: a, Sitting in rocking chair. b, Standing behind microphone. c, Signing document.
No. 3855, $3 — Pres. Kennedy: a, Close-up photograph of head. b, On campaign posters at convention. c, Standing.

2011, Dec. 16 ***Perf. 13 Syncopated***

Sheets of 3, #a-c

3844-3845 A763 Set of 2 13.50 13.50

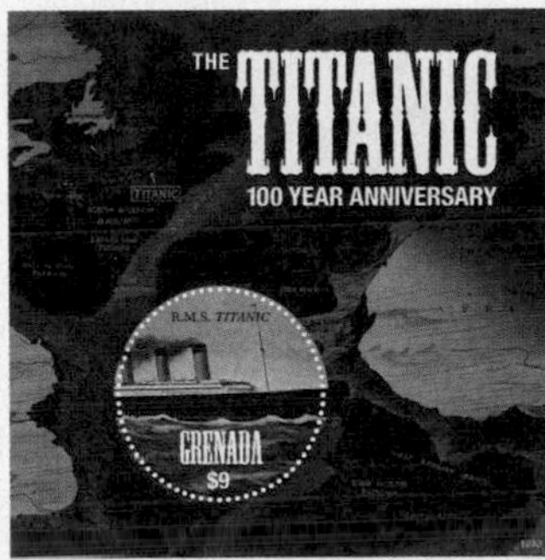

Sinking of the Titanic, Cent. — A764

No. 3846: a, Family waits for survivors. b, Survivors arrive at the docks. c, Captain Edward J. Smith. d, Titanic sinks into the sea.
$9, Titanic at sea.

2012, Feb. 8 ***Perf.***
3846 A764 $3.50 Sheet of 4, #a-d 10.50 10.50

Souvenir Sheet

3847 A764 $9 multi 6.75 6.75

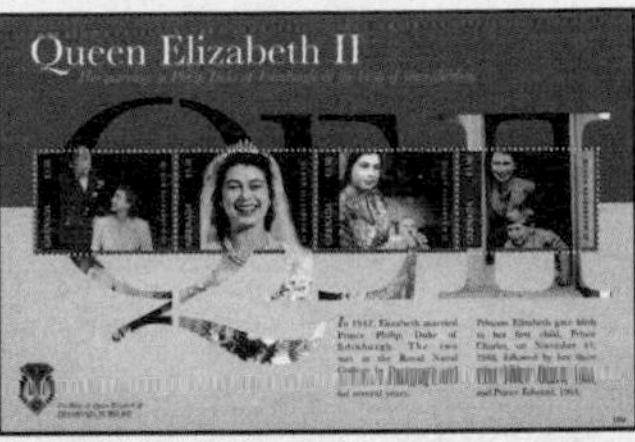

Reign of Queen Elizabeth II, 60th Anniv. — A765

No. 3848 — Queen Elizabeth II: a, With Prince Philip. b, In wedding dress. c, Holding infant Prince Charles. d, With young Prince Andrew.
$9, With two children, vert.

2012, Feb. 8 ***Perf. 12***
3848 A765 $3.50 Sheet of 4, #a-d 10.50 10.50

Souvenir Sheet

3849 A765 $9 multi 6.75 6.75

Mother Teresa (1910-97), Humanitarian — A766

No. 3850, $4 — Various photos of Mother Teresa with: a, Black denomination, white at UL corner of frame. b, Brown denomination. c, Black denomination, purple at UL corner of frame.
No. 3851, $4, Mother Teresa in truck.

2012, Apr. 5 ***Perf. 13 Syncopated***
3850 A766 $4 Sheet of 3, #a-c 9.00 9/00

Souvenir Sheet

3851 A766 $4 multi 3.00 3.00

Souvenir Sheets

A767

A768

A769

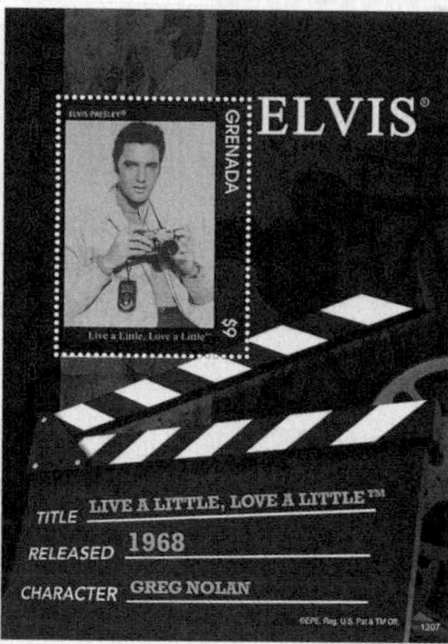

Elvis Presley (1935-77) — A770

2012, Apr. 5 *Perf. 12¾*

3852 A767 $9 multi 6.75 6.75
3853 A768 $9 multi 6.75 6.75
3854 A769 $9 multi 6.75 6.75
3855 A770 $9 multi 6.75 6.75
Nos. 3852-3855 (4) 27.00 27.00

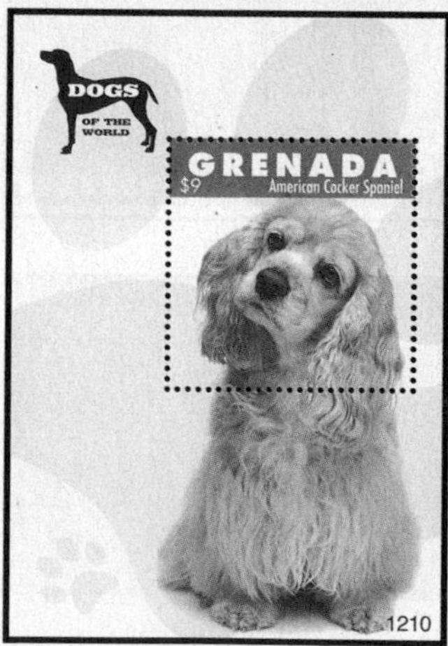

Dogs — A771

No. 3856, vert.: a, Labrador retriever. b, Bernese mountain dog. c, Bordeaux mastiff. No. 3857: a, Great Dane. b, Chocolate Labrador retriever. c, Chihuahua. d, Miniature pinscher. No. 3858, $9, American cocker spaniel. No. 3859, $9, Shih tzu.

2012, Apr. 24 *Perf. 13½x13¼*

3856 A771 $3.50 Sheet of 3, #a-c 7.75 7.75

Perf. 12¾

3857 A771 $3.50 Sheet of 4, #a-d 10.50 10.50

Souvenir Sheets

Perf. 12

3858-3859 A771 Set of 2 13.50 13.50

No. 3856 contains three 30x50mm stamps. No. 3857 contains four 25x25mm stamps.

Emblem of the 2012 Summer Olympics, London A772

No. 3860 — Emblem color: a, Pink. b, Orange. c, Blue. d, Green.

2012, July 27 *Perf. 13¼*

3860 Horiz. strip of 4 4.50 4.50
a.-d. A772 $1.50 Any single 1.10 1.10

No. 3860 was printed in sheets containing three strips.

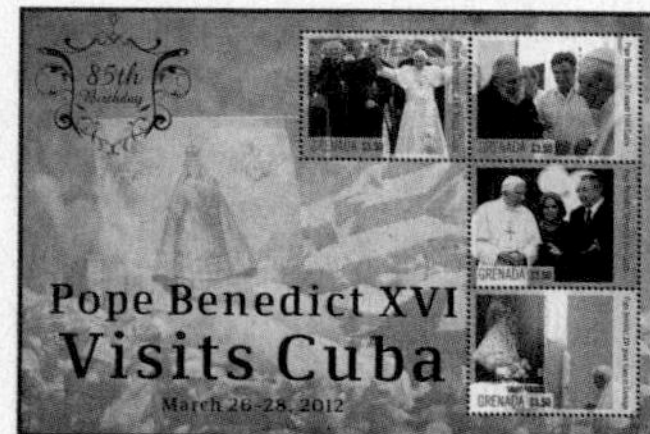

Visit of Pope Benedict XVI to Cuba — A773

No. 3861: a, Pope with arms extended, with other clerics. b, Pope meeting with Fidel Castro. c, Pope meeting with Cuban Pres. Raul Castro and woman. d, Pope kneeling at altar. $9, Pope carrying crucifix before crowd.

2012, Nov. 28 *Perf. 14*

3861 A773 $3.50 Sheet of 4, #a-d 10.50 10.50

Souvenir Sheet

Perf. 12

3862 A773 $9 multi 6.75 6.75

Chinese Zodiac Animals — A774

Designs: No. 3863, 55c, Ram. No. 3864, 55c, Horse.

2012, Nov. 28 **Litho.** *Perf. 13¼x13*

3863-3864 A774 Set of 2 .85 .85

Christmas 2012 A775

Paintings by Fra Angelico: No. 3865, $1, Annunciation. No. 3866, $1, Archangel Gabriel Annunciate. No. 3867, $2, Virgin Mary Annunciate. No. 3868, $2, The Virgin of the Annunciation. No. 3869, $5, Virgin and Child. No. 3870, $5, Adoration of the Magi.

2013, Jan. 3 *Perf. 12¾*

3865-3870 A775 Set of 6 12.00 12.00

A776

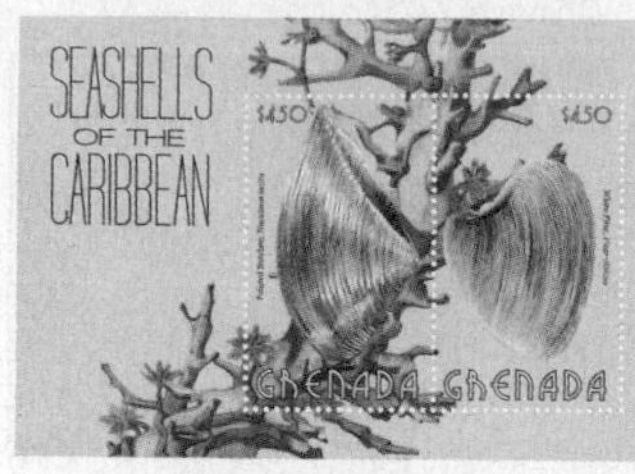

Seashells A777

No. 3871: a, Short abbreviate coral shell (30x40mm). b, Winged surfclam (30x40mm). c, Brown-line niso (60x40mm).

No. 3872: a, Spotted Brazilian top shell. b, Accuminate phos. c, Florida fighting conch. d, Jasper cone.

No. 3873: a, Pointed nut clam. b, White pitar.

$9, Boring turret snail, horiz.

2013, Jan. 3 *Perf. 12*

3871 A776 $3.50 Sheet of 3, #a-c 7.75 7.75
3872 A776 $3.50 Sheet of 4, #a-d 10.50 10.50

Souvenir Sheets

3873 A777 $4.50 Sheet of 2, #a-b 6.75 6.75
3874 A777 $9 multi 6.75 6.75

No. 3874 contains one 80x30mm stamp.

Michelangelo's Completion of the Painting of the Sistine Chapel Ceiling, 500th Anniv. — A778

No. 3875: a, The Creation of Adam (detail of Adam). b, The Creation of Adam (detail of God). c, Deluge. d, The Downfall of Adam and Eve and Their Expulsion from the Garden of Eden.

$8, The Sacrifice of Noah, vert.

2013, Jan. 3 *Perf. 12¾*

3875 A778 $3.25 Sheet of 4, #a-d 9.75 9.75

Souvenir Sheet

3876 A778 $8 multi 6.00 6.00

Amelia Earhart (1897-1937), Aviator — A779

No. 3877 — Earhart in: a, 1921. b, 1928. c, 1930. d, 1932. e, 1935. f, 1937.

$9, Earhart and airplane.

2013, Jan. 3

3877 A779 $2.25 Sheet of 6, #a-f 10.00 10.00

Souvenir Sheet

3878 A779 $9 multi 6.75 6.75

Miniature Sheets

Princess Diana (1961-97) — A780

No. 3879, $3.50 — Black-and-white photographs of Princess Diana: a, Looking left. b, Wearing hat with veil. c, Looking up. d, Wearing pearl necklace.

No. 3880, $3.50 — Color photographs of Princess Diana wearing: a, Dark blue hat and jacket. b, Red and white hat and dress. c, Black hooded raincoat. d, Red dress, no hat.

2013, Jan. 3 *Perf. 13 Syncopated*

Sheets of 4, #a-d

3879-3880 A780 Set of 2 21.00 21.00

Butterflies — A781

No. 3881: a, Heliconius mimicry. b, Junonia evarete. c, Heliconius erato petiveranus. d, Agraulis vanillae.

$9, Anartia jatrophae, vert.

2013, Jan. 3 *Perf. 13¾*

3881 A781 $3.50 Sheet of 4, #a-d 10.50 10.50

Souvenir Sheet

Perf. 12½

3882 A781 $9 multi 6.75 6.75

No. 3882 contains one 38x51mm stamp.

Souvenir Sheets

Elvis Presley (1935-77) — A782

Frame color: No. 3883, $9, Red. No. 3884, $9, Gray. No. 3885, $9, Red (Presley holding microphone). No. 3886, $9, Purple. No. 3887, $9, Black.

2013, Mar. 11 *Perf. 12½*

3883-3887 A782 Set of 5 34.00 34.00

Souvenir Sheet

Elvis Presley (1935-77) — A783

Litho., Margin Embossed

2013 ***Imperf.***

Without Gum

3888 A783 $25 multi 18.50 18.50

Souvenir Sheets

History of Art — A784

No. 3889, $3.75 — The Birth of Venus, by Sandro Botticelli (details): a, Man and woman. b, Venus. c, Woman facing left.

No. 3890, $3.75, vert. — Paintings by Fra Angelico: a, Noli Me Tangere. b, Lamentation Over the Dead Christ. c, Presentation in the Temple.

No. 3891, $3.75, vert. — Details of paintings of the Early Renaissance period: a, The Annunciation with St. Emidius, by Carlo Crivelli. b, The Crucified Christ, by Fra Angelico. c, The Baptism of Chirst, by Andrea del Verrocchio.

2013, Apr. 4 **Litho.** ***Perf. 12¾***

Sheets of 3, #a-c

3889-3891 A784 Set of 3 25.00 25.00

Ancient Roman Structures — A785

No. 3892: a, Colosseum. b, Roman Forum. c, Ostia Antica. d, Trajan's Market. e, Baths of Caracalla. f, Pantheon.

$9, View of Roman Forum from Palatine Hill, horiz.

2013, Apr. 29 **Litho.** ***Perf. 13¾***

3892 A785 $2.50 Sheet of 6, #a-f 11.50 11.50

Souvenir Sheet

Perf. 12¾

3893 A785 $9 multi 6.75 6.75

No. 3893 contains one 51x38mm stamp.

Pope Benedict XVI — A786

No. 3894, $3.25 — 2008 World Youth Day celebration photographs of Pope Benedict XVI with: a, Australian Prime Minister Kevin Rudd and his wife, Thérèse Rein. b, Youths, waving. c, Cross. d, Two priests celebrating Mass.

No. 3895, $3.25 — Photographs of Pope Benedict XVI at Lourdes, France: a, With French President Nicolas Sarkozy. b, Waving, wearing white vestments. c, With priests celebrating Mass. d, Waving, wearing red vestments.

No. 3896, $3.25, Pope Benedict XVI walking in front of cardinal at World Youth Day celebration. No. 3897, $9, Pope Benedict XVI praying at Lourdes.

Perf. 13 Syncopated

2013, Apr. 29 **Litho.**

Sheets of 4, #a-d

3894-3895 A786 Set of 2 19.50 19.50

Souvenir Sheets

3896-3897 A786 Set of 2 9.25 9.25

A787

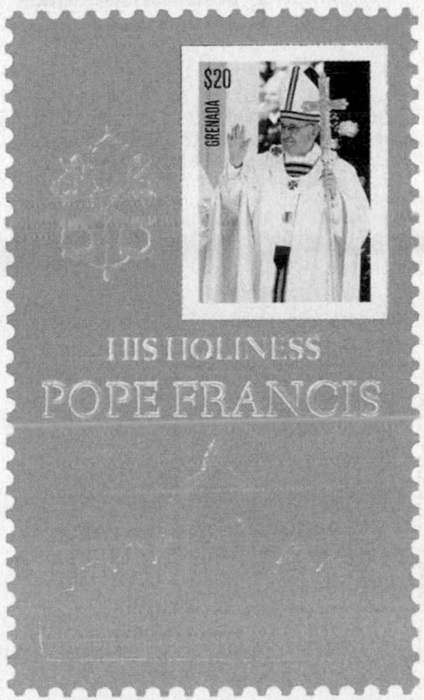

Election of Pope Francis — A788

No. 3898 — Pope Francis: a, Waving to crowd. b, Delivering first Urbi et Orbi blessing at Easter Mass. c, Preparing to celebrate Mass. d, Delivering weekly address.

2013, June 3 **Litho.** ***Perf. 12***

3898 A787 $3.25 Sheet of 4, #a-d 9.75 9.75

Litho., Margin Embossed

Souvenir Sheet

Without Gum

Imperf

3899 A788 $20 multi 15.00 15.00

Birth of Prince George of Cambridge — A789

No. 3900 — Crown and: a, Prince George, Duke and Duchess of Cambridge. b, Prince George and Duchess of Cambridge. c, Baby carriage. d, Prince George and Duke of Cambridge.

$9, Prince George, Duke and Duchess of Cambridge, diff.

2013, Sept. 27 **Litho.** ***Perf. 12***

3900 A789 $3.25 Sheet of 4, #a-d 9.75 9.75

Souvenir Sheet

3901 A789 $9 multi 6.75 6.75

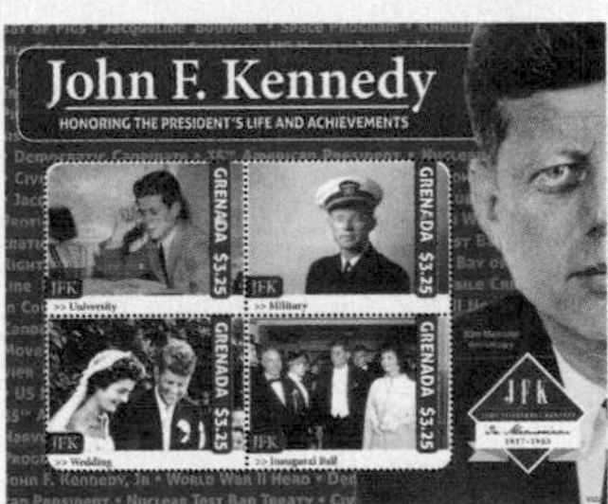

Pres. John F. Kennedy (1917-63) — A790

No. 3902 — John F. Kennedy: a, At desk as university student. b, In Navy uniform. c, With wife, Jacqueline, at wedding. d, With wife at inaugural ball.

No. 3903, vert.: a, Pres. Kennedy. b, Jacqueline Kennedy.

2013, Oct. 10 **Litho.** ***Perf. 12¾***

3902 A790 $3.25 Sheet of 4, #a-d 9.75 9.75

Souvenir Sheet

Perf. 14

3903 A790 $4.75 Sheet of 2, #a-b 7.00 7.00

No. 3903 contains two 30x40mm stamps.

Constellations — A791

No. 3904, $3.75: a, Aries. b, Taurus. c, Gemini.

No. 3905, $3.75: a, Cancer. b, Virgo. c, Leo.

No. 3906, $3.75: a, Sagittarius. b, Scorpio. c, Libra.

No. 3907, $3.75: a, Aquarius. b, Pisces. c, Capricorn.

$9, Ophiuchus.

2013, Oct. 10 **Litho.** ***Perf. 13¾***

Sheets of 3, #a-c

3904-3907 A791 Set of 4 33.50 33.50

Souvenir Sheet

3908 A791 $9 multi 6.75 6.75

A792

Coronation of Queen Elizabeth II, 60th Anniv. — A793

No. 3909 — Blue panels at bottom with photographs of Queen Elizabeth II: a, Wearing blue hat. b, At coronation. c, Wearing tiara, black-and-white photograph. d, Wearing tiara, color photograph.

No. 3910 — Maroon panels at bottom with photographs of Queen Elizabeth II: a, Wearing pink and white hat and white jacket. b, At coronation, holding scepter. c, At coronation, seated on throne. d, Wearing pinkish orange and white hat and pinkish orange jacket.

No. 3911, $9, Queen Elizabeth II wearing white hat. No. 3912, $9, Queen Elizabeth II wearing tiara, horiz.

2013, Oct. 10 **Litho.** ***Perf. 14***

3909 A792 $3.50 Sheet of 4, #a-d 10.50 10.50

3910 A793 $3.50 Sheet of 4, #a-d 10.50 10.50

Souvenir Sheets
Perf. 12

3911-3912 A793 Set of 2 13.50 13.50

Lady Margaret Thatcher (1925-2013), British Prime Minister — A794

No. 3913 — Thatcher: a, On telephone. b, Wearing blue jacket and pearl necklace. c, Laughing. d, Wearing scarf around neck.
$9, Like No. 3913a.

2013, Oct. 10 Litho. *Perf. 13¾*
3913 A794 $3.25 Sheet of 4, #a-d 9.75 9.75

Souvenir Sheet
3914 A794 $9 multi 6.75 6.75

Shells — A795

No. 3915: a, Brassica phyllonotus. b, Lyropecten subnodosus. c, Lobatus gigas. d, Cymatium lotorium.
$9, Charonia variegata.

2013, Oct. 16 Litho. *Perf. 14*
3915 A795 $3.25 Sheet of 4, #a-d 9.75 9.75

Souvenir Sheet
Perf. 12
3916 A795 $9 multi 6.75 6.75

Cats — A796

No. 3917, $3.25 — Wild cats: a, Puma. b, Snow leopard. c, Jaguar. d, Fishing cat.
No. 3918, $3.25 — Domestic cat breeds: a, Bengal. b, Maine Coon. c, Russian Blue. d, Egyptian Mau.
No. 3919, $9, Lioness. No. 3920, $9, Persian cat.

2013, Oct. 16 Litho. *Perf. 13¾*
Sheets of 4, #a-d
3917-3918 A796 Set of 2 19.50 19.50

Souvenir Sheets
3919-3920 A796 Set of 2 13.50 13.50

Minerals — A797

No. 3921: a, Azurite. b, Rhodonite. c, Baryte. d, Ruby in matrix. e, Chalcedony. f, Sodalite.
No. 3922, $4.50: a, Jade. b, Jasper.
No. 3923, $4.50: a, Hornblende. b, Turquenite.

2013, Oct. 16 Litho. *Perf. 13¾*
3921 A797 $2.50 Sheet of 6, #a-f 11.50 11.50

Sheets of 2, #a-b
3922-3923 A797 Set of 2 13.50 13.50

A798

Mao Zedong (1893-1976), Chinese Communist Leader — A799

No. 3924 — Mao Zedong: a, Walking with Liu Shaoqi. b, Looking at document with Zhou Enlai. c, Standing with Zhu De in winter military uniforms.
No. 3925: a, Mao Zedong. b, Chinese text, people and flags. c, Chinese text, people seated and standing. d, Chinese text, three Chinese people. e, Chinese text, flag, group of people with horn player. f, Great Wall of China.

2013, Oct. 18 Litho. *Perf. 14*
3924 A798 55c Horiz. strip of 3, #a-c 1.25 1.25
3925 A799 55c Sheet of 6, #a-f 2.50 2.50

No. 3924 was printed in sheets containing 2 of each stamp.

Parrots A800

Designs: 25c, Blue-and-yellow macaw. 35c, Blue-cheeked amazon. 40c, Scarlet macaw. 75c, Blue-fronted amazon. $1, Blue-winged macaw. $1.25, Festive amazon. $1.50, Gold-capped conure. $2, Hyacinth macaw. $4, Military macaw. $5, White-eared conure. $10, Yellow-headed amazon. $50, Hispaniolan parakeet. $100, Mealy amazon.

2013, Oct. 21 Litho. *Perf. 13¾*

3926	A800	25c	multi	.25	.25
3927	A800	35c	multi	.25	.25
3928	A800	40c	multi	.30	.30
3929	A800	75c	multi	.55	.55
3930	A800	$1	multi	.75	.75
3931	A800	$1.25	multi	.95	.95
3932	A800	$1.50	multi	1.10	1.10
3933	A800	$2	multi	1.50	1.50
3934	A800	$4	multi	3.00	3.00
3935	A800	$5	multi	3.75	3.75
3936	A800	$10	multi	7.50	7.50
3937	A800	$50	multi	37.00	37.00
3937A	A800	$100	multi	75.00	75.00
	Nos. 3926-3937A (13)			131.90	131.90

World Radio Day — A801

No. 3938 — Scientists and flags: a, Heinrich Hertz (1857-94), flag of Germany. b, Jagadish Bose (1858-1937), flag of India. c, Alexander Popov (1859-1906), flag of Russia. d, Reginald Fessenden (1866-1932), flag of Canada.
$9, Guglielmo Marconi (1874-1937), flag of Italy.

2013, Oct. 10 Litho. *Perf. 12½*
3938 A801 $3.50 Sheet of 4, #a-d 10.50 10.50

Souvenir Sheet
Perf.
3939 A801 $9 multi 6.75 6.75

No. 3939 contains one 38mm diameter stamp.

Coronation of Queen Elizabeth II, 60th Anniv. — A802

2013, Oct. 10 Embroidered *Imperf.*
Self-Adhesive
3940 A802 $20 multi 15.00 15.00

Christmas A803

Paintings: $1.10, The Annunciation, by Bernardo Daddi. $2.25, The Annunciation, by Jan de Beer. $2.50, Coronation of the Virgin, by Giovanni da Milano. $2.75, Madonna and Child, by Masolino da Panicale.
$9, The Baptism of Christ, by Joachim Patinir.

2013, Dec. 25 Litho. *Perf. 12½*
3941-3944 A803 Set of 4 6.50 6.50

Souvenir Sheet
3945 A803 $9 multi 6.75 6.75

New Year 2014 (Year of the Horse) A804

2014 Litho. *Perf. 13¾*
3946 A804 $1.50 multi 1.10 1.10

Embroidered
Size: 50x50mm
Self-Adhesive
3947 A804 $22 pink & red 16.50 16.50

Issued: $1.50, 1/14; $22, 1/20. No. 3946 was printed in sheets of 9.

Animals of China — A805

No. 3948: a, Red panda. b, Crested ibis. c, Golden pheasant. d, South China tiger.
$9, Giant panda.

2014, Jan. 20 Litho. *Perf. 14*
3948 A805 $3.25 Sheet of 4, #a-d 9.75 9.75

Souvenir Sheet
Perf. 12
3949 A805 $9 multi 6.75 6.75

Turtles — A806

No. 3950: a, Chelus fimbriata. b, Trachemys terrapen. c, Dermochelys coriacea. d, Lepidochelys kempii.
$9, Eretmochelys imbricata.

2014, Jan. 20 Litho. *Perf. 14*
3950 A806 $3.25 Sheet of 4, #a-d 9.75 9.75

Souvenir Sheet
Perf. 12
3951 A806 $9 multi 6.75 6.75

Last Flight of the Concorde — A807

No. 3952: a, Concorde returns to Filton Airfield. b, Concorde at Manchester Airport. c, G-BOAC Concorde on display. d, Front end of the Concorde.
$9, Alpha-Foxtrot final flight over Bristol.

2014, Jan. 20 Litho. *Perf. 12*
3952 A807 $3.25 Sheet of 4, #a-d 9.75 9.75

Souvenir Sheet
3953 A807 $9 multi 6.75 6.75

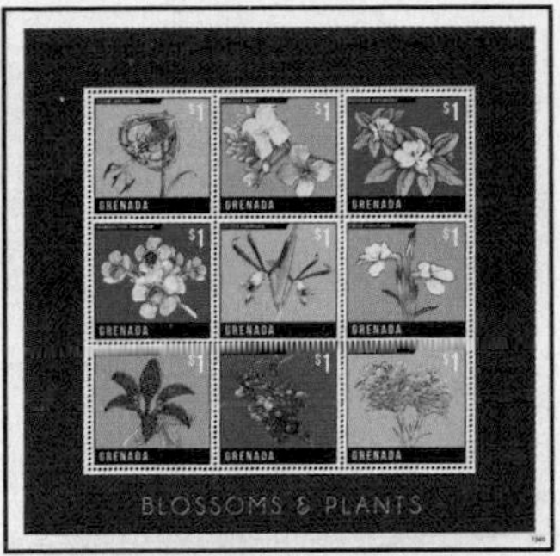

Flowers — A808

No. 3954: a, Lilium lancifolium. b, Brassica napus. c, Magnolia virginiana. d, Chamelaucium uncinatum. e, Cleistes divaricata. f, Striga densiflora. g, Lilium philadelphicum. h, Nerium oleander. i, Platanthera cristata.
$9, Calopogon pulchellus.

2014, Jan. 20 Litho. *Perf. 13¾*

3954 A808 $1 Sheet of 9, #a-i 6.75 6.75

Souvenir Sheet

3955 A808 $9 multi 6.75 6.75

Sir Eric Gairy (1922-97), First Prime Minister of Grenada — A809

Frame color: 40c, Green. 75c, Yellow. $1, Red. $1.25, Blue.
$10, Gairy, no frame.

2014, Feb. 7 Litho. *Perf. 14*

3956-3959 A809 Set of 4 2.50 2.50

Souvenir Sheet

Perf. 12

3960 A809 $10 multi 7.50 7.50

Characters From *Downton Abbey* Television Series — A810

No. 3961: a, Earl of Grantham. b, Dowager Countess of Grantham. c, Lady Rosamund Painswick. d, Isobel Crawley.
$9, Earl and Countess of Grantham, horiz.

2014, Apr. 7 Litho. *Perf. 14*

3961 A810 $3.25 Sheet of 4, #a-d 9.75 9.75

Souvenir Sheet

3962 A810 $9 multi 6.75 6.75

A811

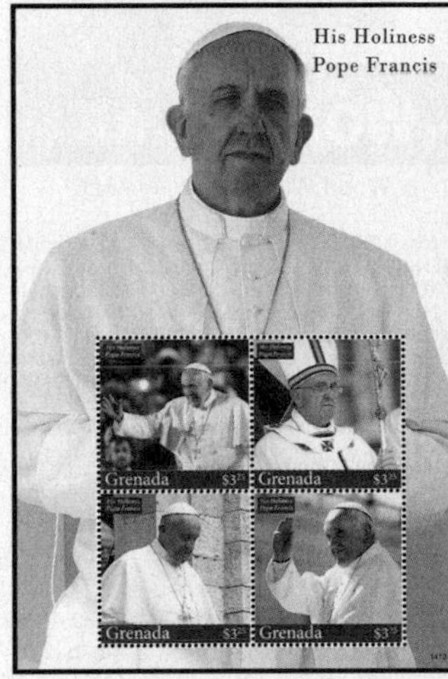

Pope Francis — A812

No. 3963 — Pope Francis: a, Wearing zucchetto and glasses. b, Wearing zucchetto, waving, archway in background. c, Wearing miter with gold trim. d, Wearing zucchetto, man in background.
No. 3964 — Pope Francis: a, Wearing zucchetto, waving, crowd in background. b, Wearing miter with black and gold trim, holding crucifix. c, Wearing zucchetto, leaving building. d, Wearing zucchetto, waving, building in background.
No. 3965, $5, horiz.: a, Pope Francis and King Letsie III of Lesotho. b, Pope Francis and party balloons.
No. 3966, $5, horiz.: a, Pope Francis with Congo President Denis Sassou Nguesso. b, Pope Francis wearing flower necklace.

2014, Apr. 7 Litho. *Perf. 13¾*

3963 A811 $3.25 Sheet of 4, #a-d 9.75 9.75

3964 A812 $3.25 Sheet of 4, #a-d 9.75 9.75

Souvenir Sheets of 2, #a-b

Perf. 14

3965-3966 A812 Set of 2 15.00 15.00

Nos. 3965-3966 both contain two 40x30mm stamps.

A813

Nelson Mandela (1918-2013), President of South Africa — A814

No. 3967: a, Mandela wearing blue shirt with fist raised. b, Mandela wearing gray shirt, smiling.
No. 3968: a, Mandela with Queen Elizabeth II. b, Mandela wearing black and tan checked shirt. c, Mandela wearing sweater, with fist raised. d, Mandela wearing blue and white shirt, standing in front of wall. e, Mandela wearing black and gray patterned shirt. f, Mandela wearing suit and tie.
No. 3969, $9, Mandela wearing red shirt, with arm raised, vert. No. 3970, $9, Black-and-white photograph of Mandela as young man in suit and tie, vert.

2014, Apr. 17 Litho. *Perf. 13¾*

3967 A813 $2.50 Pair, #a-b 3.75 3.75

3968 A814 $2.50 Sheet of 6, #a-f 11.50 11.50

Souvenir Sheets

Perf. 12½

3969-3970 A814 Set of 2 13.50 13.50

Nos. 3969-3970 both contain one 38x51mm stamp. No. 3967 was printed in sheets of 6 containing three each of Nos. 3967a and 3967b.

Pres. Barack Obama and Wife, Michelle — A815

Designs: No. 3972, $9, Pres. Obama and Vice-President Joe Biden. No. 3973, $9, Pres. Obama holding football, horiz.

2014, Apr. 23 Litho. *Perf. 14*

3971 A815 $3.25 multi 2.40 2.40

Souvenir Sheets

Perf. 12½

3972-3973 A815 Set of 2 13.50 13.50

No. 3971 was printed in sheets of 4. No. 3972 contains one 38x51mm stamp. No. 3973 contains one 51x38mm stamp.

A816

Flowers — A817

No. 3974, $4.75: a, Magnolias. b, Lilies. c, Calla lilies. d, Geraniums.
No. 3975, $4.75: a, Roses. b, Hydrangeas. c, Peonies. d, Oriental poppies.
No. 3976, $9.50: a, Magnolias, pink petal at UR corner. b, Magnolias, green leaf at UR corner.
No. 3977, $9.50: a, Hydrangeas, diff. b, Violets.

2014, Apr. 23 Litho. *Perf. 13¾*

Sheets of 4, #a-d

3974-3975 A816 Set of 2 28.50 28.50

Souvenir Sheets of 2, #a-b

Perf. 12½

3976-3977 A817 Set of 2 28.50 28.50

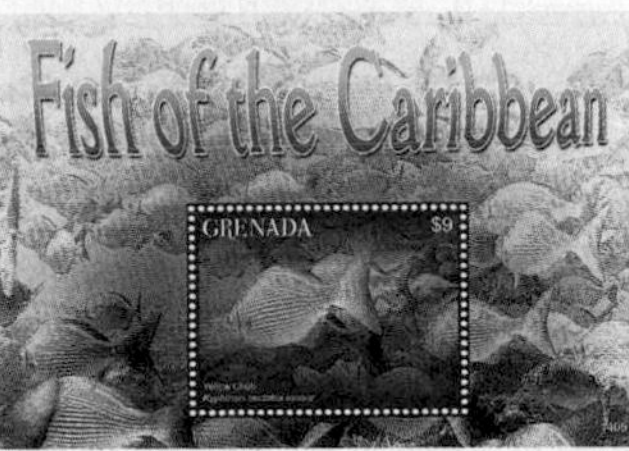

Fish — A818

No. 3978, $3.25: a, Yellowhead wrasses. b, Pintanos. c, Queen angelfish. d, Stoplight parrotfish.
No. 3979, $3.25: a, Four-eyed butterflyfish. b, French angelfish. c, Juvenile French angelfish. d, Great barracudas.
No. 3980, $9, Yellow chubs. No. 3981, $9, Banded butterflyfish.

Perf. 14, 12 (#3981)

2014, Apr. 23 Litho.

Sheets of 4, #a-d

3978-3979 A818 Set of 2 19.50 19.50

Souvenir Sheets

3980-3981 A818 Set of 2 13.50 13.50

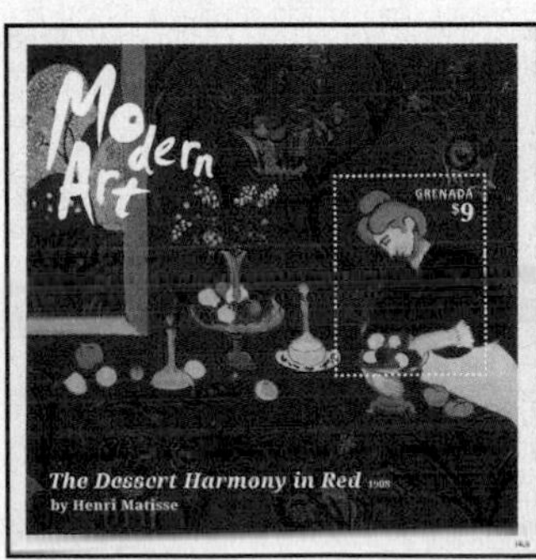

Modern Art — A819

No. 3982, $3.50 — Paintings by Henri Matisse (1869-1954): a, A Glimpse of Notre-Dame in the Late Afternoon. b, Dishes and Fruit. c, Fruit and Coffeepot.
No. 3983, $3.50 — Paintings by Adolf Dehn (1895-1968): a, Central Park. b, Landscape. c, Into the Rigging.
No. 3984, $9, The Dessert: Harmony in Red, by Matisse. No. 3985, $9, Cosmic Synchromy, by Morgan Russell (1886-1953).

2014, Apr. 23 Litho. *Perf. 12½*

Sheets of 3, #a-c

3982-3983 A819 Set of 2 15.50 15.50

Souvenir Sheets

3984-3985 A819 Set of 2 13.50 13.50

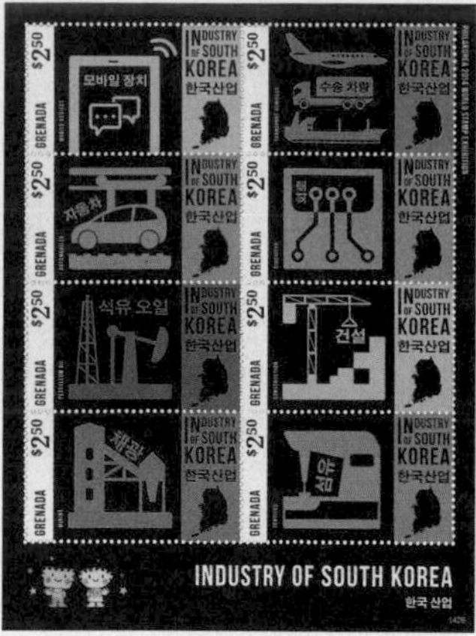

Industry of South Korea — A820

No. 3986: a, Mobile devices. b, Transport vehicles. c, Automobiles. d, Circuitry. e, Petroleum. f, Construction. g, Mining. h, Textiles. $10, Tourism.

2014, May 29 Litho. *Perf. 12*

3986 A820 $2.50 Sheet of 8, #a-h 15.00 15.00

Imperf

Size: 70x70mm

3987 A820 $10 multi 7.50 7.50

A821

Canonization of Pope John Paul II — A822

No. 3988 — Pope John Paul II: a, Waving. b, Wearing miter, holding crucifix. c, Standing in Popemobile, holding post. d, Touching hands of people in crowd.

No. 3989 — Pope John Paul II: a, Standing in Popemobile, wearing miter. b, With arm raised. c, Touching wall. d, Standing in Popemobile, with arm extended, without miter.

No. 3990, $10, Pope John Paul II with arm raised, horiz. No. 3991, $10, Face of Pope John Paul II, horiz.

2014, May 29 Litho. *Perf. 12*

3988 A821 $3.25 Sheet of 4, #a-d 9.75 9.75

3989 A822 $3.25 Sheet of 4, #a-d 9.75 9.75

Souvenir Sheets

Perf. 12¾

3990-3991 A822 Set of 2 15.00 15.00

Nos. 3990-3991 each contain one 51x38mm stamp.

Paintings by Henri de Toulouse-Lautrec (1864-1901) — A823

No. 3992, $3.25: a, Self-portrait Before a Mirror. b, Ball at the Moulin de la Galette. c, Queen of Joy. d, Portrait of Vincent van Gogh.

No. 3993, $3.25: a, Self-portrait caricature. b, Au Moulin Rouge. c, La Revue Blanche. d, Hangover.

No. 3994, $5 — Details from At the Moulin Rouge: a, Dancing woman. b, Woman wearing hat.

No. 3995, $5 — Women from Salon at the Rue des Moulins with panel color of: a, Yellow brown. b, Gray.

2014, May 29 Litho. *Perf. 12*

Sheets of 4, #a-d

3992-3993 A823 Set of 2 19.50 19.50

Souvenir Sheets of 2, #a-b

3994-3995 A823 Set of 2 15.00 15.00

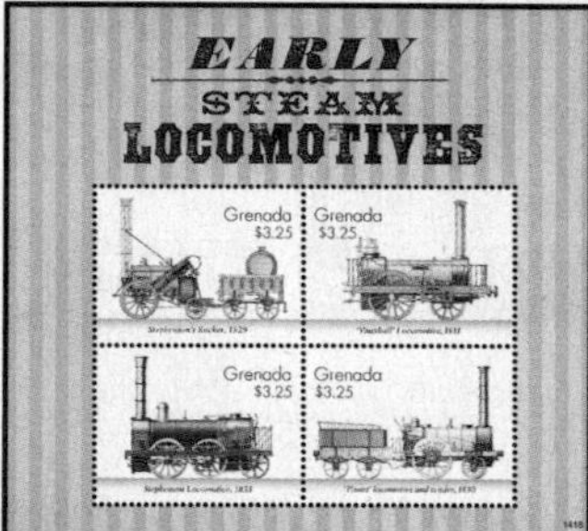

Early Steam Locomotives — A824

No. 3996: a, Stephenson's Rocket, 1829. b, Vauxhall locomotive, 1831. c, Stephenson locomotive, 1833. d, Planet locomotive and tender, 1830.

No. 3997: a, Blenkinsop's rack locomotive, 1812. b, North Star locomotive, 1837.

2014, June 23 Litho. *Perf. 14*

3996 A824 $3.25 Sheet of 4, #a-d 9.75 9.75

Souvenir Sheet

3997 A824 $5 Sheet of 2, #a-b 7.50 7.50

Moths — A825

No. 3998: a, Common silver line moth. b, Cream-spotted tiger moth. c, Great tiger moth. d, Hebe moth. e, Magpie moth. f, Margate beauty moth. g, Pink under-wing moth. h, Small tiger moth. i, Argent and sable moth.

No. 3999, $5, horiz.: a, Clear-winged humming sphinx. b, Drury's sphinx.

No. 4000, $5, horiz.: a, Elephant sphinx. b, Spurge sphinx.

2014, June 23 Litho. *Perf. 13¾*

3998 A825 $2 Sheet of 9, #a-i 13.50 13.50

Souvenir Sheets of 2, #a-b

Perf. 12¾

3999-4000 A825 Set of 2 15.00 15.00

Nos. 3999-4000 each contain two 51x38mm stamps.

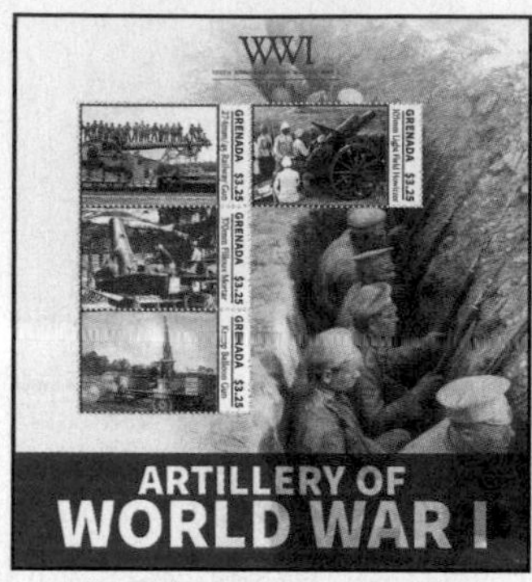

World War I, Cent. — A826

No. 4001, $3.25 — Artillery: a, 274mm/45 railway gun. b, 105mm light field howitzer. c, 370mm Filloux mortar. d, Krupp balloon gun.

No. 4002, $3.25, vert. — World leaders: a, Woodrow Wilson, flag of United States. b, King Albert I, flag of Belgium. c, Emperor Taisho, flag of Japan. d, King Victor Emmanuel III, flag of Italy.

No. 4003, $5 — Artillery: a, 2-inch mortar bombs. b, 6-inch mortar bombs.

No. 4004, $5 — World leaders: a, Tsar Nicholas II, flag of Russia. b, King George V, flag of Great Britain.

2014, June 23 Litho. *Perf. 12*

Sheets of 4, #a-d

4001-4002 A826 Set of 2 19.50 19.50

Souvenir Sheets of 2, #a-b

4003-4004 A826 Set of 2 15.00 15.00

Paintings — A827

No. 4005, $3.50: a, Meekness, by Eustache Le Sueur. b, Midsummer Eve, by Edward Robert Hughes. c, The Lion Polyptych, by Lorenzo Veneziano.

No. 4006, $3.50: a, Lady with a Unicorn, by Raphael. b, Portrait of a Woman, by Paolo Uccello. c, Flowers in a Brown Vase, by Odilon Redon.

No. 4007, $10, Portrait of a Man in Front of a Rose Hedge, by Hans Baldung. No. 4008, $10, Les Muses, by Maurice Denis.

2014, June 23 Litho. *Perf. 12¾*

Sheets of 3, #a-c

4005-4006 A827 Set of 2 15.50 15.50

Size: 100x100mm

Imperf

4007-4008 A827 Set of 2 15.00 15.00

Souvenir Sheets

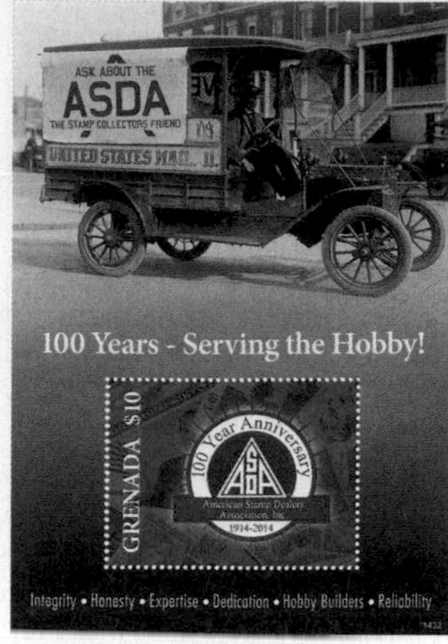

American Stamp Dealers' Association, Cent. — A828

Centennial emblem and background of: No. 4009, $10, Postage stamps. No. 4010, $10, Post office boxes, vert.

2014, Oct. 24 Litho. *Perf. 12¾*

4009-4010 A828 Set of 2 15.00 15.00

Gulls — A829

No. 4011, $3.25: a, Gray-headed gull. b, Hartlaub's gull. c, Red-billed gull. d, Silver gull.

No. 4012, $3.25: a, Black-billed gull. b, Andean gull. c, Brown-headed gull. d, Bonaparte's gull.

No. 4013, $5, horiz.: a, Black-headed gull, diff. b, Slender-billed gull.

No. 4014, $5, horiz.: a, Brown-hooded gull. b, Andean gull, diff.

2014, Nov. 3 Litho. *Perf. 14*

Sheets of 4, #a-d

4011-4012 A829 Set of 2 19.50 19.50

Souvenir Sheets of 2, #a-b

4013-4014 A829 Set of 2 15.00 15.00

A830

A831

A832

Monarch Butterflies — A833

Various butterflies, as depicted.

2014, Nov. 3 Litho. *Perf. 13¾*
4015 A830 $3.50 Sheet of 3, #a-c 7.75 7.75
4016 A831 $3.50 Sheet of 3, #a-c 7.75 7.75

Souvenir Sheets
4017 A832 $5 Sheet of 2, #a-b 7.50 7.50
4018 A833 $5 Sheet of 2, #a-b 7.50 7.50

Deng Xiaoping (1904-97), Chinese Leader — A834

No. 4019 — Flags, buildings and symbols of People's Republic of China and Macao with various images of Deng Xiaoping, numbered: a, (110-1). b, (110-2). c, (110-3). d, (110-4). e, (110-5). f, (110-6). g, (110-7). h, (110-8). i, (110-9). j, (110-10). k, (110-11). l, (110-12). m, (110-13). n, (110-14). o, (110-15). p, (110-16). q, (110-17). r, (110-18). s, (110-19). t, (110-20). u, (110-21). v, (110-22). w, (110-23). x, (110-24). y, (110-25). z, (110-26). aa, (110-27). ab, (110-28). ac, (110-29). ad, (110-30). ae, (110-31). af, (110-32). ag, (110-33). ah, (110-34). ai, (110-35). aj, (110-36). ak, (110-37). al, (110-38). am, (110-39). an, (110-40). ao, (110-41). ap, (110-42). aq, (110-43). ar, (110-44). as, (110-45). at, (110-46). au, (110-47). av, (110-48). aw, (110-49). ax, (110-50). ay, (110-51). az, (110-52). ba, (110-53). bb, (110-54). bc, (110-55). bd, (110-56). be, (110-57). bf, (110-58). bg, (110-59). bh, (110-60). bi, (110-61). bj, (110-62). bk, (110-63). bl, (110-64). bm, (110-65). bn, (110-66). bo, (110-67). bp, (110-68). bq, (110-69). br, (110-70). bs, (110-71). bt, (110-72). bu, (110-73). bv, (110-74). bw, (110-75). bx, (110-76). by, (110-77). bz, (110-78). ca, (110-79). cb, (110-80). cc, (110-81). cd, (110-82). ce, (110-83). cf, (110-84). cg, (110-85). ch, (110-86). ci, (110-87). cj, (110-88). ck, (110-89). cl, (110-90). cm, (110-91). cn, (110-92). co, (110-93). cp, (110-94). cq, (110-95). cr, (110-96). cs, (110-97). ct, (110-98). cu, (110-99). cv, (110-100). cw, (110-101). cx, (110-102). cy, (110-103). cz, (110-104). da, (110-105). db, (110-106). dc, (110-107). dd, (110-108). de, (110-109). df, (110-110).

2014, Dec. 8 Litho. *Perf. 14¼x14¾*
4019 Sheet of 110 97.50 97.50
a.-df. A834 $1.20 Any single .85 .85

Worldwide Fund for Nature (WWF) — A835

Nos. 4020 and 4021: a, Oceanic whitetip shark and fish. b, Oceanic whitetip shark and ocean ripples. c, Two Oceanic whitetip sharks. d, Head of Oceanic whitetip shark.

2014, Dec. 8 Litho. *Perf. 14¾x14*
4020 A835 $1.25 Block or vert. strip of 4, #a-d 3.75 3.75
4021 A835 $2.75 Block or vert. strip of 4, #a-d 8.25 8.25

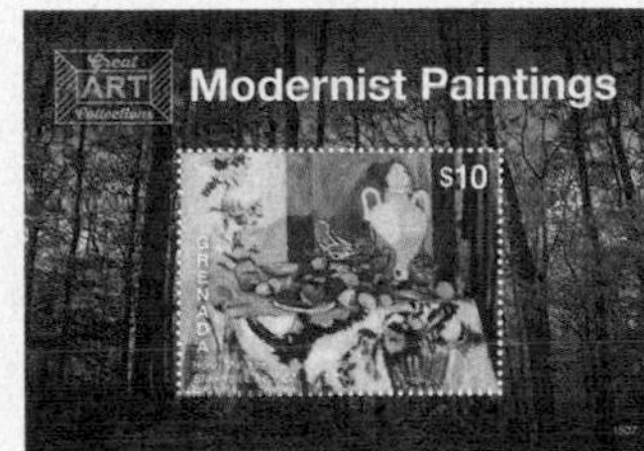

Modernist Paintings — A836

No. 4022, vert.: a, Red Madras Headdress, by Henri Matisse. b, The Studio Boat, by Claude Monet. c, Mr. Loulou (Louis Le Ray), by Paul Gauguin. d, The Smoker, by Vincent van Gogh. e, Woman with Pigeons, by Gustave Courbet. f, Mussel Fishers at Berneval, by Pierre-Auguste Renoir. g, Woman Walking in an Exotic Forest, by Henri Rousseau. h, Peasant Standing with Arms Crossed, by Paul Cézanne.
$10, Blue Still Life, by Matisse.

2015, May 18 Litho. *Perf. 12½*
4022 A836 $3.15 Sheet of 8, #a-h 14.00 14.00

Souvenir Sheet
4023 A836 $10 multi 7.50 7.50

St. John Paul II (1920-2005) — A837

No. 4024 — Pope John Paul II: a, Waving to crowd, wearing miter. b, Waving, black-and-white photograph. c, At Western Wall, Jerusalem. d, In Popemobile.
$10, Pope John Paul II, horiz.

2015, May 18 Litho. *Perf. 14*
4024 A837 $3.25 Sheet of 4, #a-d 9.75 9.75

Souvenir Sheet
Perf. 12½
4025 A837 $10 multi 7.50 7.50
No. 4025 contains one 51x38mm stamp.

Large Cruise Ships — A838

No. 4026: a, Oasis of the Seas. b, Allure of the Seas. c, Independence of the Seas.
$10, Allure of the Seas, diff.

2015, May 18 Litho. *Perf. 12*
4026 A838 $3.50 Sheet of 3, #a-c 7.75 7.75

Souvenir Sheet
Perf. 14
4027 A838 $10 multi 7.50 7.50
No. 4026 contains three 50x30mm stamps.

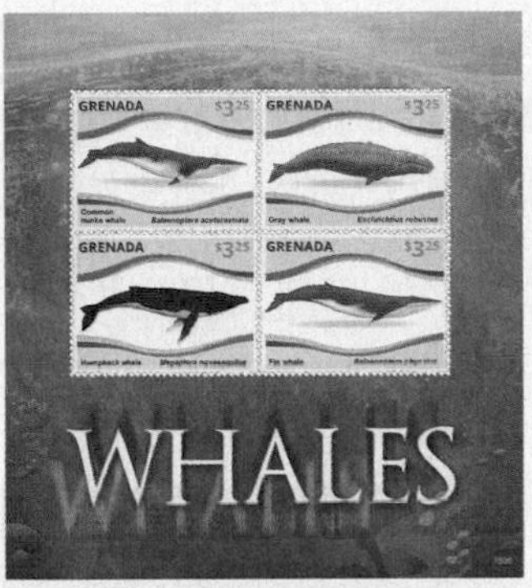

Whales — A839

No. 4028, $3.25: a, Common minke whale. b, Gray whale. c, Humpback whale. d, Fin whale.
No. 4029, $3.25: a, Bowhead whale. b, Narwhal. c, Beluga whale. d, Pilot whale.
No. 4030, $10, Sperm whales. No. 4031, $10, Killer whale.

2015, May 18 Litho. *Perf. 14*
Sheets of 4, #a-d
4028-4029 A839 Set of 2 19.50 19.50

Souvenir Sheets
Perf. 13¾
4030-4031 A839 Set of 2 15.00 15.00
Nos. 4030-4031 each contain one 35x35mm stamp.

Horses in Art — A840

No. 4032, $3.25 — Details from *The Horse Fair,* by Rosa Bonheur: a, Man holding bit of horse. b, Black horse rearing. c, Man standing, two riders on horses. d, Heads of two white horses.
No. 4033, $3.25, horiz.: a, *Before the Race,* by Eugène Delacroix. b, *Horses,* by Francis Picabia. c, *Horse Frightened by Lightning,* by Delacroix. d, *The Red Horses,* by Franz Marc.
No. 4034, $10, *Whistlejacket,* by George Stubbs. No. 4035, $10, *The Three Horses,* by Xu Beihong, horiz.

2015, May 18 Litho. *Perf. 14*
Sheets of 4, #a-d
4032-4033 A840 Set of 2 19.50 19.50

Souvenir Sheets
Perf. 12½
4034-4035 A840 Set of 2 15.00 15.00
No. 4034 contains one [illegible] stamp. No. 4035 contains one 51x38mm stamp.

Flag of People's Republic of China and Battle Scene A841

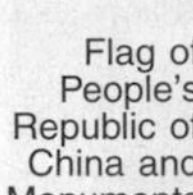

Flag of People's Republic of China and Monuments A842

Flag of People's Republic of China and Japanese World War II Surrender A843

Flag of People's Republic of China and Islands A844

2015, May 28 Litho. *Perf. 14¾x14*
4036 A841 $1.20 multi .90 .90
4037 A842 $1.20 multi .90 .90
4038 A843 $1.20 multi .90 .90
4039 A844 $1.20 multi .90 .90
Nos. 4036-4039 (4) 3.60 3.60

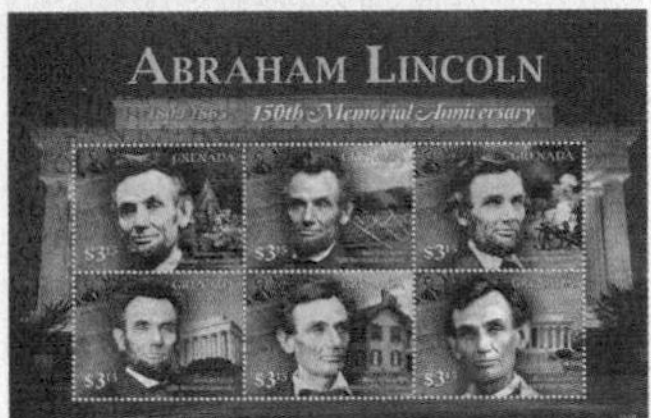

Pres. Abraham Lincoln (1809-65) — A845

No. 4040 — Lincoln and: a, Sculpture of soldiers riding horses into battle. b, Fence. c, Soldiers and cannon. d, Corner of Lincoln Memorial. e, Lincoln's home, Springfield, Illinois. f, Lincoln Memorial and steps.
$10, Lincoln and cannon.

2015, May 28 Litho. *Perf. 14*
4040 A845 $3.15 Sheet of 6, #a-f 14.00 14.00

Souvenir Sheet
Perf. 12½
4041 A845 $10 multi 7.50 7.50
No. 4041 contains one 51x38mm stamp.

Paintings by Vincent van Gogh — A846

No. 4042: a, The Church in Auvers-sur-Oise, View from the Chevet, 1890. b, Self-portrait, 1887. c, Café Terrace at Night, 1888. d, Three Sunflowers in a Vase, 1888. e, Portrait of Dr. Gachet, 1890. f, Still Life with Decanter and Lemons on a Plate, 1887.
$10, The Starry Night, 1889, horiz.

2015, May 28 Litho. *Perf. 14*
4042 A846 $3.15 Sheet of 6, #a-f 14.00 14.00

Souvenir Sheet
Perf. 12
4043 A846 $10 multi 7.50 7.50
No. 4043 contains one 60x40mm stamp.

The 1960's British "Invasion" — A847

No. 4044: a, Acoustic guitar. b, Moptop hair-cut. c, Mod fashion. d, Drum kit.
$10, Electric guitar.

2015, May 28 Litho. *Perf. 14*

4044 A847 $3.15 Sheet of 4, #a-d 9.50 9.50

Souvenir Sheet

Perf. 12

4045 A847 $10 multi 7.50 7.50

Europhilex 2015 Stamp Exhibition, London.

Sailboats in Art — A848

No. 4046: a, Fishing Boats at Sea, by Claude Monet. b, Thunder Storm on Narragansett Bay, by Martin Johnson Heade. c, Yellow Boat, by Odilon Redon. d, Fishing Boats, by Joaquín Sorolla. e, Sailboats at Argenteuil, by Pierre-Auguste Renoir. f, Sailboats Racing on the Delaware, by Thomas Eakins.
$10, Fishing Boats on the Beach at Saintes-Maries-de-la-Mer, by Vincent van Gogh.

2015, May 28 Litho. *Perf. 12¾*

4046 A848 $3.15 Sheet of 6, #a-f 14.00 14.00

Souvenir Sheet

4047 A848 $10 multi 7.50 7.50

World Leaders — A849

Designs: No. 4048, $4.50, Chinese leader Mao Zedong (1893-1976) and flag of People's Republic of China (5-1). No. 4049, $4.50, Soviet leader Joseph Stalin (1879-1953) and Russian flag (5-2). No. 4050, $4.50, Pres. Franklin D. Roosevelt (1882-1945) and flag of United States (5-3). No. 4051, $4.50, British Prime Minister Sir Winston Churchill (1874-1965) and British flag (5-4). No. 4052, $4.50, French Pres. Charles de Gaulle (1890-1970) and French flag (5-5).

2015, Aug. 3 Litho. *Perf. 14*

4048-4052 A849 Set of 5 17.00 17.00

People's Republic of China, 66th Anniv. — A850

Flag of People's Republic of China, various scenes from Chinese military parade, and stamp number at bottom: No. 4053, $4.50, (15-1). No. 4054, $4.50, (15-2). No. 4055, $4.50, (15-3). No. 4056, $4.50, (15-4). No. 4057, $4.50, (15-5). No. 4058, $4.50, (15-6). No. 4059, $4.50, (15-7). No. 4060, $4.50, (15-8). No. 4061, $4.50 (15-9). No. 4062, $4.50, (15-10). No. 4063, $4.50, (15-11). No. 4064, $4.50, (15-12). No. 4065, $4.50, (15-13). No. 4066, $4.50, (15-14). No. 4067, $4.50, (15-15).

2015, Aug. 3 Litho. *Perf. 14*

4053-4067 A850 Set of 15 50.00 50.00

Miniature Sheets

A851

A852

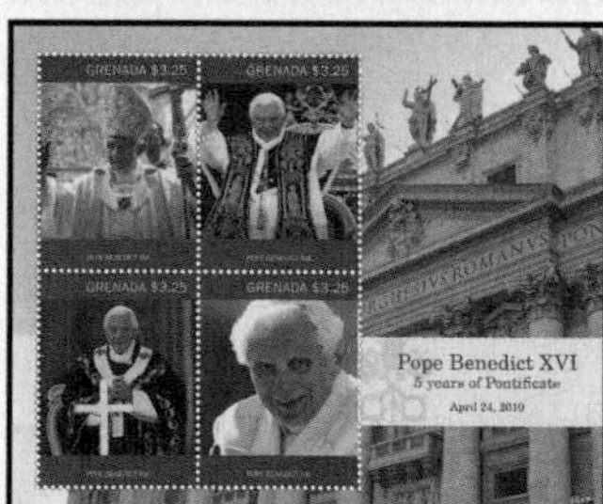

Popes — A853

No. 4068: a, Pope John Paul II wearing miter, waving. b, Pope Benedict XVI wearing miter. c, Pope Benedict XVI wearing zucchetto, praying. d, Pope John Paul II wearing zucchetto, in crowd.

No. 4069 — Pope Benedict XVI wearing: a, Black cassock. b, Miter and red vestments. c, Zucchetto and green vestments. d, Red cassock.

No. 4070 — Pope Benedict XVI wearing: a, Miter and white vestments. b, Stole, waving with both hands. c, Purple vestments. d, White cassock.

2015, Aug. 26 Litho. *Perf. 14*

4068 A851 $3.25 Sheet of 4, #a-d 9.75 9.75
4069 A852 $3.25 Sheet of 4, #a-d 9.75 9.75
4070 A853 $3.25 Sheet of 4, #a-d 9.75 9.75
Nos. 4068-4070 (3) 29.25 29.25

Birth of Princess Charlotte of Cambridge — A854

No. 4071: a, King George V. b, Queen Elizabeth II. c, Princess Diana and Prince Charles. d, Duke and Duchess of Cambridge with Princess Charlotte. e, Prince George of Cambridge. f, Duchess of Cambridge holding Princess Charlotte.
$10, King George V, Queen Elizabeth II, Princess Diana, Prince Charles, Duke and Duchess of Cambridge with Princess Charlotte, horiz.

2015, Aug. 26 Litho. *Perf. 14*

4071 A854 $3.15 Sheet of 6, #a-f 14.00 14.00

Souvenir Sheet

Perf. 13¾

4072 A854 $10 multi 7.50 7.50

No. 4072 contains one 70x35mm stamp.

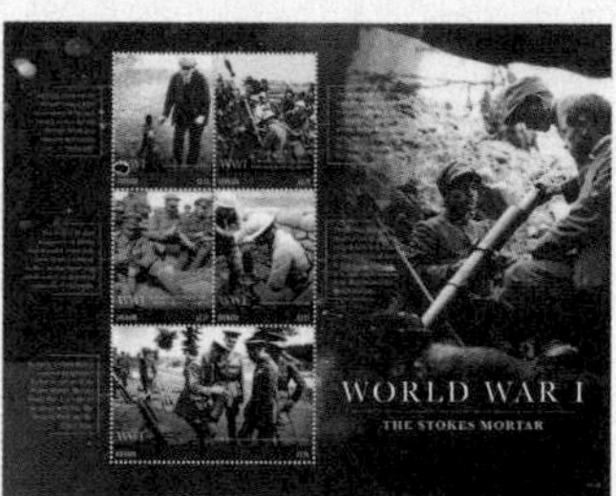

World War I, Cent. — A855

No. 4073: a, Sir Wilfred Stokes and mortar (30x40mm). b, British troops firing a Stokes mortar (30x40mm). c, Members of King's Own Yorkshire Light Infantry fusing Stokes shells (30x40mm). d, Soldier loading a Stokes mortar (30x40mm). e, King George V inspecting Stokes mortar (60x40mm).
$10, Soldier loading Stokes mortar, diff., vert.

2015, Aug. 26 Litho. *Perf. 14*

4073 A855 $3.25 Sheet of 5, #a-e 12.00 12.00

Souvenir Sheet

Perf. 12½

4074 A855 $10 multi 7.50 7.50

No. 4074 contains one 38x51mm stamp.

Queen Elizabeth II, Longest-Reigning British Monarch — A856

No. 4075: Various depictions of Queen Elizabeth II.
No. 4076, $10, Queen Elizabeth II, in coach. No. 4077, $10, Queen Elizabeth II and Prince Philip, horiz.

Perf. 14, 12 (#4077)

2015, Nov. 1 Litho.

4075 A856 $3.15 Horiz. strip of 3, #a-c 7.00 7.00

Souvenir Sheets

4076-4077 A856 Set of 2 15.00 15.00

No. 4075 was printed in sheets containing two each Nos. 4075a-4075c.

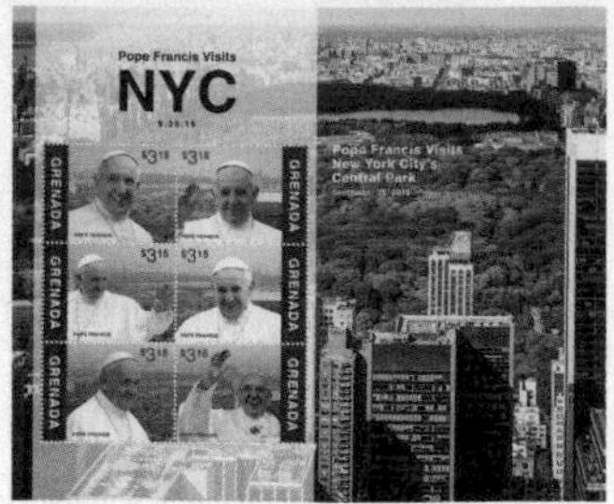

Visit of Pope Francis to New York City — A857

No. 4078: Various photographs of Pope Francis and Central Park, as shown.
$10, Pope Francis, diff.

2015, Nov. 1 Litho. *Perf. 14*

4078 A857 $3.15 Sheet of 6, #a-f 14.00 14.00

Souvenir Sheet

Perf. 12

4079 A857 $10 multi 7.50 7.50

A858

A859

New Year 2016 (Year of the Monkey) A860

Various depictions of monkeys.

2015, Nov. 2 Litho. *Perf. 14*

4080 A858 $1.40 multi 1.00 1.00
4081 A859 $1.50 multi 1.10 1.10
4082 A860 $1.50 multi 1.10 1.10
4083 A859 $2 multi 1.50 1.50
4084 A860 $2 multi 1.50 1.50
4085 A858 $2.40 multi 1.75 1.75
4086 A860 $2.50 multi 1.90 1.90
4087 A858 $3 multi 2.25 2.25
4088 A858 $3.50 multi 2.60 2.60
4089 A859 $3.50 green & multi 2.60 2.60
4090 A859 $3.50 multi (white background) 2.60 2.60
4091 A860 $3.50 multi 2.60 2.60
Nos. 4080-4091 (12) 22.50 22.50

Miniature Sheet

New Year 2016 (Year of the Monkey) — A861

No. 4092 — Monkey on: a, Horse, turquoise green background. b, Horse, rose background. c, Elephant, yellow background. d, Elephant, dull green background.

2015, Nov. 2 Litho. *Perf. 13¾*
4092 A861 $3.25 Sheet of 4, #a-d 9.75 9.75

Christmas A862

Paintings by Sandro Botticelli: 90c, Madonna of the Sea. $2.25, The Virgin Adoring the Child. $3.50, The Virgin and Child with Two Angels and the Young St. John the Baptist. $5, Mystic Nativity.

2015, Nov. 2 Litho. *Perf. 12½*
4093-4096 A862 Set of 4 8.75 8.75

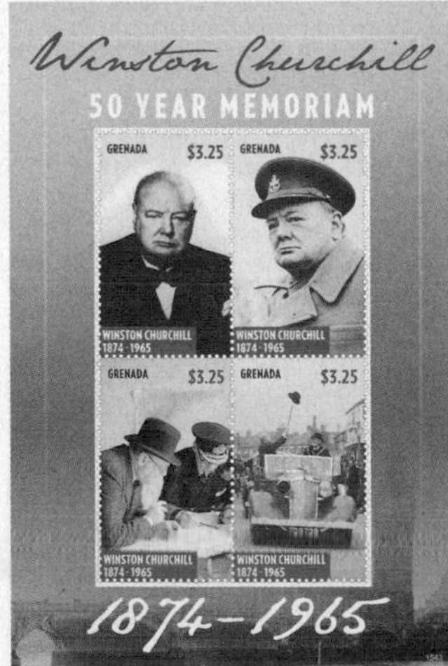

Sir Winston Churchill (1874-1965), British Prime Minister — A863

No. 4097 — Churchill: a, Wearing bowtie. b, Wearing military cap. c, Wearing hat, with military officer. d, In automobile.
$10, Churchill wearing hat.

2015, Dec. 21 Litho. *Perf. 12*
4097 A863 $3.25 Sheet of 4, #a-d 9.75 9.75

Souvenir Sheet
4098 A863 $10 multi 7.50 7.50

Star Trek Television Series, 50th Anniv. — A864

No. 4099 — Scene from episode: a, Dagger of the Mind. b, Spectre of the Gun. c, The City on the Edge of Forever. d, Mirror, Mirror. e, Spock's Brain. f, The Trouble with Tribbles.
$10, Amok Time.

2015, Dec. 21 Litho. *Perf. 12*
4099 A864 $3.15 Sheet of 6, #a-f 14.00 14.00

Souvenir Sheet
Perf. 12½
4100 A864 $10 multi 7.50 7.50

No. 4100 contains one 38x51mm stamp.

Manatees — A865

No. 4101: a, Florida manatee swimming forward, entire manatee shown. b, Florida manatee swimming upside down, denomination on manatee. c, Two Caribbean manatees. d, Florida manatee swimming forward, tips of tail and flippers not on stamp. e, Head of Florida manatee, denomination near nose. f, Profile view of caribbean manatee.
$10, Caribbean manatee, diff.

2015, Dec. 21 Litho. *Perf. 12*
4101 A865 $3.15 Sheet of 6, #a-f 14.00 14.00

Souvenir Sheet
4102 A865 $10 multi 7.50 7.50

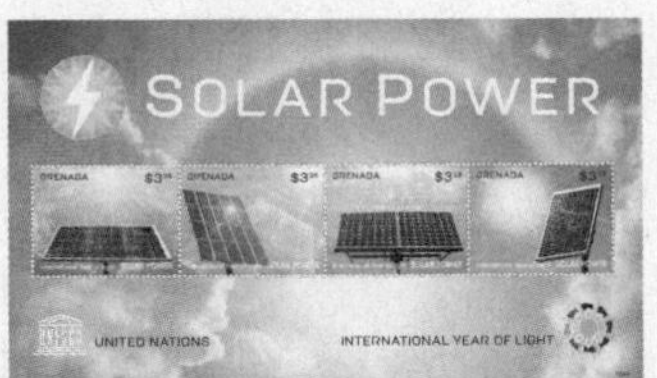

International Year of Light — A866

No. 4103 — a, Solar panel with single post, Sun at top center. b, Solar panel with single post at left, Sun at UR. c, Double array of solar panels with support and single post. d, Solar panel with single post at right, Sun at left.
$10, Solar panels, diff.

2015, Dec. 21 Litho. *Perf. 14*
4103 A866 $3.25 Sheet of 4, #a-d 9.75 9.75

Souvenir Sheet
Perf. 12
4104 A866 $10 multi 7.50 7.50

No. 4104 contains one 50x30mm stamp.

Airplanes of World War I — A867

No. 4105 — Bombers: a, One Caproni Ca 33 450hp biplane. b, Two Ansaldo SVA5 biplanes. c, Two Caproni Ca 33 450hp biplanes. d, One Ansaldo SVA5 biplane.
$10, Two Caproni Ca 33 450 hp biplanes, diff.

2015, Dec. 21 Litho. *Perf. 13¾*
4105 A867 $3.25 Sheet of 4, #a-d 9.75 9.75

Souvenir Sheet
Perf. 12½
4106 A867 $10 multi 7.50 7.50

No. 4106 contains one 51x38mm stamp.

Birds — A868

No. 4107: a, Egyptian goose. b, Woodpecker. c, Cedar waxwing. d, American avocet.
$10, Western tanager.

2015, Dec. 21 Litho. *Perf. 14*
4107 A868 $3.25 Sheet of 4, #a-d 9.75 9.75

Souvenir Sheet
4108 A868 $10 multi 7.50 7.50

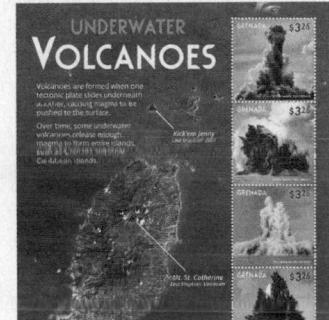

Underwater Volcanoes — A869

Volcanoes as shown.

2015, Dec. 21 Litho. *Perf. 13¾*
4109 A869 $3.25 Sheet of 4, #a-d 9.75 9.75

Souvenir Sheet
Perf. 12
4110 A869 $10 multi 7.50 7.50

No. 4110 contains one 40x30mm stamp.

Fish — A870

No. 4111, $3.25: a, Queen angelfish. b, Foureye butterflyfish. c, Gray angelfish. d, Yellowtail snapper.
No. 4112, $3.25: a, Bar jack. b, Spotted trunkfish. c, Sergeant major. d, Rock beauty.
No. 4113, $10, Great barracuda. No. 4114, $10, Yellowtail damsel.

2015, Dec. 21 Litho. *Perf. 14*
Sheets of 4, #a-d
4111-4112 A870 Set of 2 19.50 19.50

Souvenir Sheets
4113-4114 A870 Set of 2 15.00 15.00

A871

A872

Nos. 4115-4116: Various starfish, as shown.
No. 4117, $10, White starfish, vert. No. 4118, $10, Orange starfish, vert.

2015, Dec. 21 Litho. *Perf. 14*
4115 A871 $3.25 Sheet of 4, #a-d 9.75 9.75
4116 A872 $3.25 Sheet of 4, #a-d 9.75 9.75

Souvenir Sheets
4117-4118 A872 Set of 2 15.00 15.00

Owls — A873

No. 4119, $3.25: a, Long-eared owl. b, Barn owl. c, Great gray owl. d, Burrowing owl.
No. 4120, $3.25: a, Eurasian eagle owl. b, Spotted owl. c, Short-eared owl. d, Spectacled owl.

No. 4121, $10, Northern hawk owl. No. 4122, $10, Barred owl, horiz.

Perf. 12, 14 (#4120)

2015, Dec. 21 Litho.

Sheets of 4, #a-d

4119-4120 A873 Set of 2 19.50 19.50

Souvenir Sheets

Perf. 12½

4121-4122 A873 Set of 2 15.00 15.00

No. 4121 contains one 38x51mm stamp. No. 4122 contains one 51x38mm stamp.

A874

A875

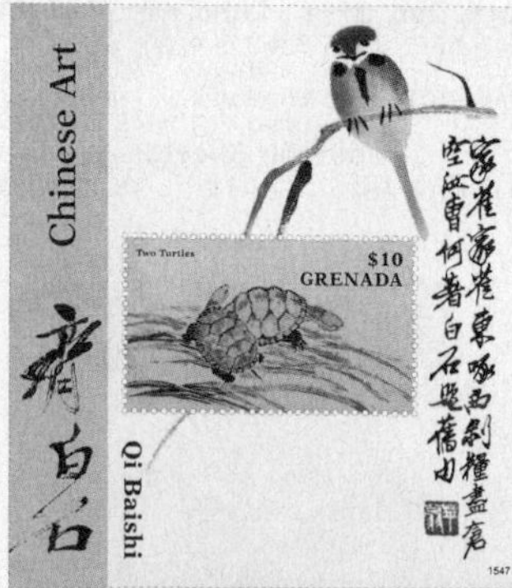

Chinese Art — A876

Nos. 4123-4124: Various paintings by Chang Dai Chien, as shown.

No. 4125, $10, Two Turtles, by Qi Baishi, horiz. No. 4126, $10, Wisteria and Goldfish, by Qi Baishi, horiz.

2015, Dec. 21 Litho. *Perf. 12½*

4123 A874 $3.25 Sheet of 4, #a-d 9.75 9.75

4124 A875 $3.25 Sheet of 4, #a-d 9.75 9.75

Souvenir Sheets

Perf. 12

4125-4126 A876 Set of 2 15.00 15.00

Miniature Sheets

Stamps of United Nations Countries — A877

No. 4127, $3.15: a, Afghanistan #1. b, Albania #1. c, Algeria #1. d, Andorra (Spanish Administration) #1, Andorra (French Administration) #1. e, Angola #1. f, Antigua #1.

No. 4128, $3.15: a, Argentina #1. b, Armenia #1. c, Australia #1. d, Austria #1. e, Azerbaijan #1. f, Bahamas #5.

No. 4129, $3.15: a, Bahrain #1. b, Bangladesh #1. c, Barbados #1. d, Belarus #1. e, Belgium #1. f, Belize #312.

No. 4130, $3.15: a, Benin #1. b, Bhutan #1. c, Bolivia #1. d, Bosnia and Herzegovina #1. e, Botswana #1. f, Brazil #1.

No. 4131, $3.15: a, Honduras #1. b, Hungary #1. c, Iceland #1. d, India #1. e, Indonesia #1. f, Iran #1.

No. 4132, $3.15: a, Iraq #9. b, Ireland #1. c, Israel #1. d, Italy #17. e, Ivory Coast #1. f, Jamaica #1.

No. 4133, $3.15: a, Japan #1. b, Jordan #1. c, Kazakhstan #1. d, Kenya #1. e, Kiribati #325. f, Korean Republic #1.

No. 4134, $3.15: a, Democratic People's Republic of Korea #1. b, Kuwait #1. c, Kyrgyzstan #1. d, Laos #1. e, Latvia #1. f, Lebanon #1.

2015, Dec. 21 Litho. *Perf. 12½*

Sheets of 6, #a-f

4127-4134 A877 Set of 8 115.00 115.00

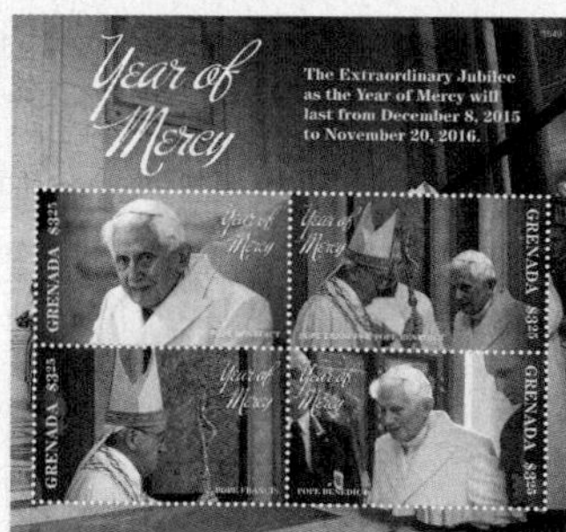

Extraordinary Jubilee of Mercy — A878

No. 4135: a, Pope Benedict XVI. b, Popes Francis and Benedict XVI. c, Pope Francis. d, Pope Benedict XVI and attendants.

$10, Popes Francis and Benedict XVI.

2016, Jan. 31 Litho. *Perf. 12*

4135 A878 $3.25 Sheet of 4, #a-d 9.75 9.75

Souvenir Sheet

4136 A878 $10 multi 7.50 7.50

Chinese Battle Scene A879

2016, Feb. 2 Litho. *Perf. 14*

4137 A879 $2.50 multi 1.90 1.90

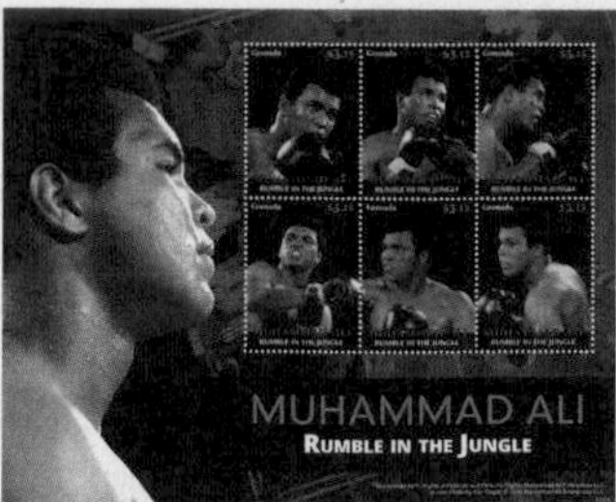

Muhammad Ali (1942-2016), Boxer — A880

No. 4138 — Various photographs of Ali, as shown.

$10, Ali jumping rope.

Perf. 13¼x12½

2016, Feb. 20 Litho.

4138 A880 $3.15 Sheet of 6, #a-f 14.00 14.00

Souvenir Sheet

Perf. 11¼x11¾

4139 A880 $10 multi 7.50 7.50

No. 4139 contains one 30x50mm stamp.

Jimi Hendrix (1942-70), Rock Guitarist — A881

No. 4140 — Paintings depicting Hendrix with panel color of: a, Purple. b, Blue. c, Pink. d, Orange brown.

$10, Hendrix, vert.

2016, Mar. 8 Litho. *Perf. 13¾*

4140 A881 $3.25 Sheet of 4, #a-d 9.75 9.75

Souvenir Sheet

Perf. 12½

4141 A881 $10 multi 7.50 7.50

No. 4141 contains one 38x51mm stamp.

Souvenir Sheets

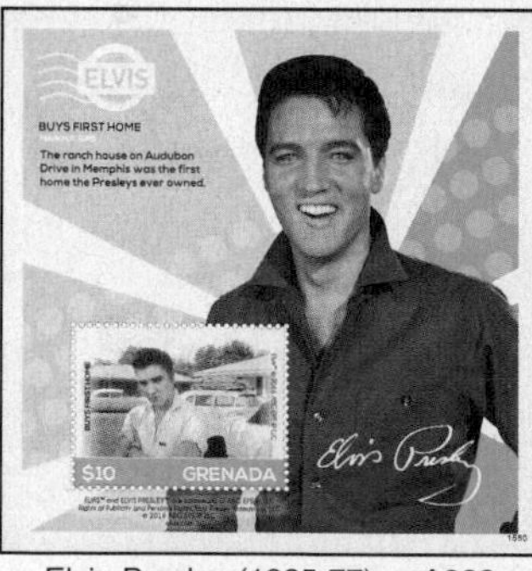

Elvis Presley (1935-77) — A882

Designs: No. 4142, $10, Presley buying first home. No. 4143, $10, Grammy Lifetime Achievement Award. No. 4144, $10, Presley's first public performance. No. 4145, $10, Presley wearing lei in Hawaii.

2016, Mar. 8 Litho. *Perf. 12½x13¼*

4142-4145 A882 Set of 4 30.00 30.00

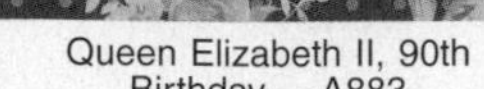

Queen Elizabeth II, 90th Birthday — A883

No. 4146 — Queen Elizabeth wearing: a, Purple hat and coat. b, Purple dress, denomination at UR. c, Purple dress, denomination at UL. d, Purple kerchief and coat.

$13, Queen Elizabeth II holding flowers, vert.

2016, May 16 Litho. *Perf. 13¾*

4146 A883 $3.25 Sheet of 4, #a-d 9.75 9.75

Souvenir Sheet

Perf. 12½

4147 A883 $13 multi 9.75 9.75

No. 4147 contains one 38x51mm stamp.

World Stamp Show 2016, New York — A884

No. 4148 — World Stamp Show 2016 and New York landmarks: a, Bethesda Fountain, Central Park. b, Statue of Liberty. c, Grand Central Terminal. d, Williamsburg Bridge.

$8, New Yourk City skyline, horiz.

2016, May 16 Litho. *Perf. 12*

4148 A884 $4 Sheet of 4, #a-d 12.00 12.00

Souvenir Sheet

Perf. 14

4149 A884 $8 multi 6.00 6.00

No. 4149 contains one 90x80mm stamp.

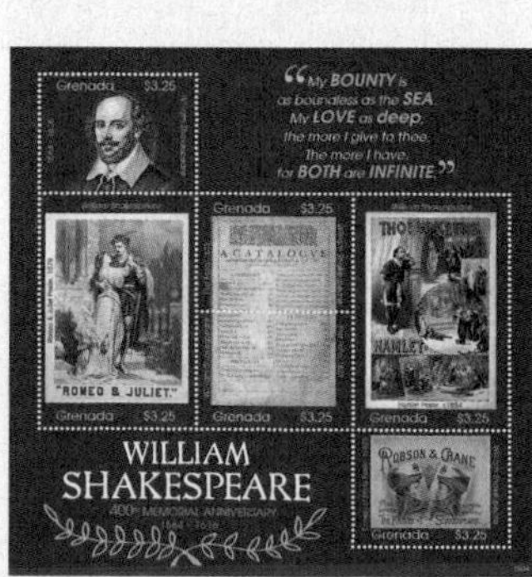

William Shakespeare (1564-1616), Writer — A885

No. 4150: a, Shakespeare (40x30mm). b, 1879 poster for *Romeo and Juliet* (40x60mm). c, Top of front page of Shakespeare's *First Folio* (40x30mm). d, Bottom of front page of Shakespeare's *First Folio* (40x30mm). e, Poster for *Hamlet*, c. 1884 (40x60mm). f, Poster for *The Comedy of Errors*, c. 1879 (40x30mm).

No. 4151 — Shakespeare and line from: a, *Othello*. b, *King Lear*. c, *Measure for Measure*. d, *Twelfth Night*.

$14, Shakespeare and line from *Richard III*.

2016, May 30 Litho. *Perf. 14*

4150 A885 $3.25 Sheet of 6, #a-f 14.50 14.50

Perf. 12

4151 A885 $3.50 Sheet of 4, #a-d 10.50 10.50

Souvenir Sheet

4152 A885 $14 multi 10.50 10.50

No. 4151 contains four 30x50mm stamps. No. 4152 contains one 30x50mm stamp.

A886

A887

A888

A889

A890

A891

A892

A893

A894

A895

A896

A897

A898

Chinese Paintings — A899

2016, June 20 Litho. *Perf. 14*

4153 A886 $1.20 multi .90 .90
4154 A887 $1.20 multi .90 .90
4155 A888 $1.20 multi .90 .90
4156 A889 $1.20 multi .90 .90
4157 A890 $1.20 multi .90 .90
4158 A891 $1.20 multi .90 .90
4159 A892 $1.20 multi .90 .90
4160 A893 $1.20 multi .90 .90
4161 A894 $1.20 multi .90 .90
4162 A895 $1.20 multi .90 .90
4163 A896 $1.20 multi .90 .90
4164 A897 $1.20 multi .90 .90
4165 A898 $1.20 multi .90 .90
4166 A899 $1.20 multi .90 .90
Nos. 4153-4166 (14) 12.60 12.60

Nos. 4155-4160 were printed in sheets of 24 containing six of each stamp. Nos. 4161-4166 were printed in sheets of 24 containing six of each stamp.

15TH MEMORIAL ANNIVERSARY 9/11
We will never forget

Sept. 11, 2001 Terrorist Attacks in New York, 15th Anniv. — A900

No. 4167: a, World Trade Center in daylight. b, World Trade Center in daylight as seen from base. c, World Trade Center with lights on at dusk. d, World Trade Center with lights on at night. e, Tribute in Light. f, World Trade Center with lights on as seen from base.

No. 4168, vert. — World Trade Center: a, Orange sky. b, At night.

$14, Tribute in Light, vert.

2016, June 30 Litho. *Perf. 14*

4167 A900 $3.25 Sheet of 6, #a-f 14.50 14.50

Souvenir Sheets

Perf. 12

4168 A900 $7 Sheet of 2, #a-b 10.50 10.50

Perf. 12½

4169 A900 $14 multi 10.50 10.50

No. 4169 contains one 38x51mm stamp.

Chinese Aerospace Day — A901

No. 4170 — Various satellites over Earth with denomination at: a, LL. b, LR.

2016, July 29 Litho. *Perf. 14*

4170 A901 $5 Horiz. pair, #a-b 7.50 7.50

A902

A903

A904

A905

A906

A907

A908

Gates of the Great Wall of China A909

2016, Aug. 15 Litho. *Perf. 12*

4171 A902 $1.20 multi .90 .90
4172 A903 $1.20 multi .90 .90
4173 A904 $1.20 multi .90 .90
4174 A905 $1.20 multi .90 .90
a. Block of 4, #4171-4174 3.60 3.60
4175 A906 $1.20 multi .90 .90
4176 A907 $1.20 multi .90 .90
4177 A908 $1.20 multi .90 .90
4178 A909 $1.20 multi .90 .90
a. Block of 4, #4175-4178 3.60 3.60
Nos. 4171-4178 (8) 7.20 7.20

Nos. 4174-4174 and Nos. 4175-4178 were printed together in sheets of 16, with one block of four containing all four stamps at the center of the sheet.

A910

A911

A912

A913

A914

A915

A916

Chinese Long March A917

2016, Sept. 6 Litho. *Perf. 14¾x14¼*

4179 A910 $1.20 multi (8-1) .90 .90
4180 A911 $1.20 multi (8-2) .90 .90
4181 A912 $1.20 multi (8-3) .90 .90
4182 A913 $1.20 multi (8-4) .90 .90
4183 A914 $1.20 multi (8-5) .90 .90
4184 A915 $1.20 multi (8-6) .90 .90
4185 A916 $1.20 multi (8-7) .90 .90
4186 A917 $1.20 multi (8-8) .90 .90
Nos. 4179-4186 (8) 7.20 7.20

Launch of New Horizons Space Probe, 10th Anniv. — A918

No. 4187 — New Horizons probe and: a, APL asteroid. b, Charon. c, Neptune. d, Pluto. $10, Launch, vert.

2016, Sept. 9 Litho. *Perf. 14*

4187 A918 $3.25 Sheet of 4, #a-d 9.75 9.75

Souvenir Sheet

Perf. 12

4188 A918 $10 multi 7.50 7.50

Sea Birds — A919

No. 4189: a, Royal tern. b, Red-billed tropicbird. c, Magnificent frigatebird. d, Brown noddy.
No. 4190, vert.: a, Masked booby. b, Red-footed booby.

2016, Sept. 16 Litho. *Perf. 14*

4189 A919 $4 Sheet of 4, #a-d 12.00 12.00

Souvenir Sheet

Perf. 12

4190 A919 $7 Sheet of 2, #a-b 10.50 10.50

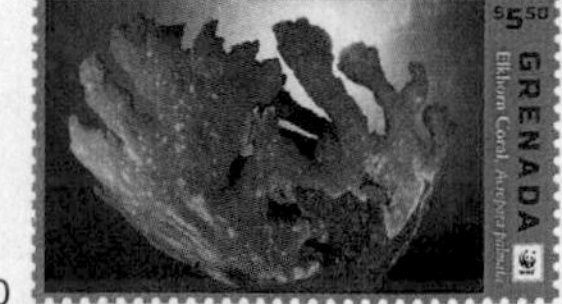

A920

A921

A922

Worldwide Fund for Nature (WWF) — A923

2016, Nov. 3 Litho. *Perf. 12*

4191 Strip of 4 17.00 17.00
a. A920 $5.50 multi 4.25 4.25
b. A921 $5.50 multi 4.25 4.25
c. A922 $5.50 multi 4.25 4.25
d. A923 $5.50 multi 4.25 4.25
e. Miniature sheet of 8, 2 each #4191a-4191d 34.00 34.00

Paintings by Hieronymus Bosch (c. 1450-1516) — A924

No. 4192: a, Ecce Homo. b, St. John the Baptist in the Wilderness. c, Christ Carrying the Cross. d, St. John, the Evangelist, on Patmos.
No. 4193: a, Crucifixion with a Donor. b, Christ Crowned with Thorns.

2016, Nov. 14 Litho. *Perf. 14*

4192 A924 $5.50 Sheet of 4, #a-d 16.50 16.50

Souvenir Sheet

Perf. 12½

4193 A924 $7.50 Sheet of 2, #a-b 11.50 11.50

No. 4193 contains two 38x51mm stamps.

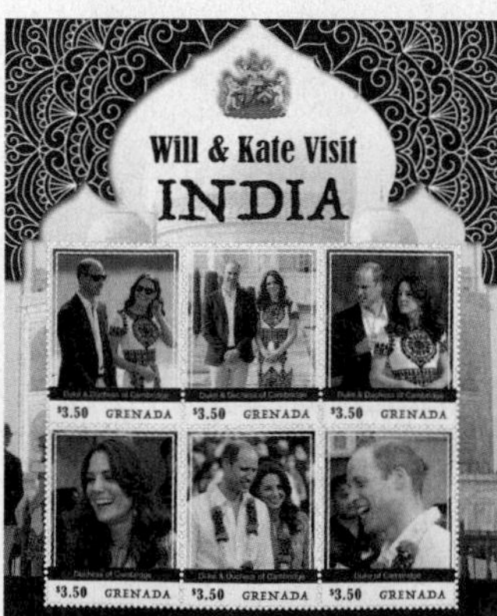

Duke and Duchess of Cambridge in India — A925

No. 4194: a, Duke and Duchess, Duchess touching ear. b, Duke and Duchess in front of building. c, Duke and Duchess, Duke's hand behind shoulder of Duchess. d, Duchess. e, Duke and Duchess standing in front of crowd. f, Duke.

No 4195: a, Princess Diana seated on bench. b, Duke and Duchess seated on bench.

2016, Nov. 25 Litho. *Perf. 14*

4194 A925 $3.50 Sheet of 6, #a-f 15.50 15.50

Souvenir Sheet

Perf. 12

4195 A925 $7.50 Sheet of 2, #a-b 11.50 11.50

Christmas A926

Christmas tree-shaped items: No. 4196, $5.50, Ornament. No. 4197, $5.50, Decorated cookie. No. 4198, $10, Ornament, diff. No. 4199, $10, Cookie, diff.

2016, Dec. 1 Litho. *Perf. 12½*

4196-4199 A926 Set of 4 23.00 23.00

Monkey King — A927

No. 4200: a, Monkey King looking towards LR. b, Cloud, orange stairway in background. c, Monkey King looking towards LL. d, Cloud, orange background. e, Monkey King with grass in mouth. f, Cloud, over temple. g, Monkey King over temple, rod pointing to LR. h, Cloud over temple, Monkey King in background. i, Monkey King over temple, looking left.
No. 4201 — Monkey King wearing: a, Carrying rod, b, Juggling fruit.

2016, Dec. 1 Litho. *Perf. 13¾*

4200 A927 $1.50 Sheet of 9, #a-i 10.00 10.00

Souvenir Sheet

Perf. 12

4201 A927 $7.50 Sheet of 2, #a-b 11.50 11.50

No. 4201 contains two 30x40mm stamps.

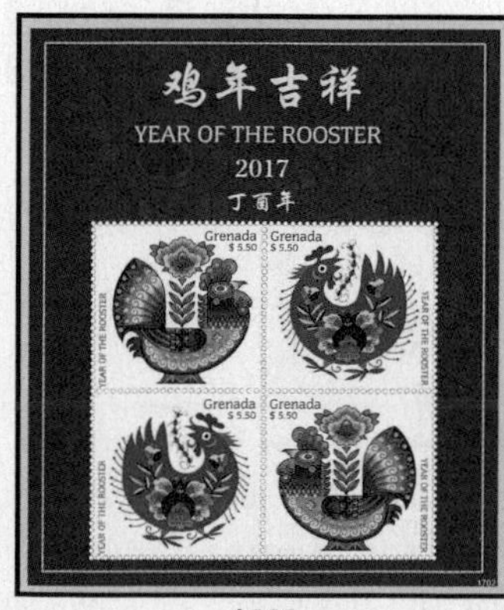

A928

New Year 2017 (Year of the Rooster) — A929

No. 4202: a, Flower over rooster, denomination at UR. b, Centipede over rooster, denomination at UL. c, Centipede over rooster, denomination at UR. d, Flower over rooster, denomination at UL.
No. 4203 — Rooster with: a, Blue neck facing right. b, Green neck facing right. c, Green neck facing left. d, Blue neck facing left.

2016, Dec. 5 Litho. *Perf. 13¾*

4202 A928 $5.50 Sheet of 4, #a-d 16.50 16.50

Perf.

4203 A929 $5.50 Sheet of 4, #a-d 16.50 16.50

Attack on Pearl Harbor, 75th Anniv. — A930

No. 4204: a, USS Arizona. b, USS Utah. c, USS Oklahoma. d, USS Nevada.
No. 4205, vert.: a, Pres. Franklin D. Roosevelt. b, Pres. Harry S. Truman.

2016, Dec. 13 Litho. *Perf. 14*

4204 A930 $3.50 Sheet of 4, #a-d 10.50 10.50

Souvenir Sheet

Perf. 12½

4205 A930 $4 Sheet of 2, #a-b 6.00 6.00

No. 4205 contains two 38x51mm stamps.

A931

A932

A933

A934

A935

New Year 2017 (Year of the Rooster) A936

2016, Dec. 21 Litho. *Perf. 13¾*

4206	A931 $1.20 multi		.90	.90
4207	A932 $1.20 multi		.90	.90
4208	A933 $1.50 multi		1.10	1.10
4209	A934 $1.50 multi		1.10	1.10
4210	A935 $1.60 multi		1.25	1.25
4211	A936 $1.60 multi		1.25	1.25
	Nos. 4206-4211 (6)		6.50	6.50

Swarovski Crystal Rooster A937

2016, Dec. 1 Litho. *Perf. 14*

4212 A937 $3.50 multi 2.60 2.60

Miniature Sheets

A938

Pres. John F. Kennedy (1917-63) — A939

No. 4213 — Pres. Kennedy: a, At inauguration, mouth open. b, On telephone. c, At inauguration, mouth closed. d, With wife, Jacqueline (wearing lt blue dress and hat). e, With wife, Jacqueline (black-and-white photograph). f, With wife, Jacqueline (with crowd in background).

No. 4214 — Presidential seal and: a, Pres. Kennedy with wife, Jacqueline. b, Pres. Kennedy, red frame. c, Pres. Kennedy, flag at right. d, Pres. Kennedy, flag at left.

2017, Feb. 7 Litho. *Perf. 14*

4213	A938 $4 Sheet of 6, #a-f		18.00	18.00
4214	A939 $5 Sheet of 4, #a-d		15.00	15.00

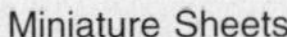

Miniature Sheets

A940

Ranger 7, 50th Anniv. (in 2014) — A941

No. 4215: a, Launch, text in black at right. b, Ranger 3 above Moon, text in white at right. c, Measurement gauge and Ranger 7 photograph of Moon before impact, text on one line at left. d. Ranger 7 above Moon, text in white at right.

No. 4216: a, Launch, text in white at left. b, Ranger 7 photograph of Moon before impact, text on two lines at left. c, Ranger 3 above Moon. text in white at left. d, Ranger 7 above Moon, text in white at left.

2017, Feb. 28 Litho. *Perf. 14*

4215	A940 $3.25 Sheet of 4, #a-d		9.75	9.75
4216	A941 $3.25 Sheet of 4, #a-d		9.75	9.75

Bats — A942

No. 4217: a, Great fruit-eating bat. b, Pallas's mastiff bat. c, Seba's short-tailed bat. d, Little yellow-shouldered bat. e, Mexican fruit bat. f, Greater bulldog bat.

No. 4218: a, Tree bat. b, Long-tailed skipper butterfly.

2017, Feb. 28 Litho. *Perf. 13¾*

4217 A942 $3.50 Sheet of 6, #a-f 15.50 15.50

Souvenir Sheet

Perf.

4218 A942 $7.50 Sheet of 2, #a-b 11.00 11.00

No. 4218 contains two 38mm diameter stamps.

A943

A944

A945

A946

A947

A948

A949

A950

A951

Return of Hong Kong to People's Republic of China, 20th Anniv. A952

2017 Litho. *Perf. 13½x13¼*

4219	A943 $1.20 multi		.90	.90
4220	A944 $1.20 multi		.90	.90

Perf. 14

4221	A945 $1.20 multi		.90	.90
4222	A946 $1.20 multi		.90	.90
4223	A947 $1.20 multi		.90	.90
4224	A948 $1.20 multi		.90	.90
4225	A949 $1.50 multi		1.10	1.10
4226	A950 $1.50 multi		1.10	1.10
4227	A951 $1.50 multi		1.10	1.10
4228	A952 $1.50 multi		1.10	1.10
	Nos. 4219-4228 (10)		9.80	9.80

Issued: Nos. 4219-4220, 3/21; Nos. 4221-4228, 5/9.

Beaches — A953

No. 4229: a, Whitehaven Beach, Australia. b, Grand Anse Beach, Grenada. c, Railay West Beach, Thailand. d, Hanalei Bay, Hawaii. e, Boulders Beach, South Africa. f, Cinque Terre, Italy.

$10, Navagio Beach, Greece.

2017, Mar. 30 Litho. *Perf. 13½*

4229 A953 $3.50 Sheet of 6, #a-f 15.50 15.50

Souvenir Sheet

Perf. 12½x13¼

4230 A953 $10 multi 7.50 7.50

No. 4230 contains one 80x30mm stamp.

Miniature Sheets

Royal Air Force, Cent. — A954

No. 4231, $4: a, Red Arrow Hawk T1 in flight. b, Nine Red Arrow planes in diamond formation. c, Five Red Arrow planes flying to right. d, Nine Red Arrow planes flying forward. e, Ten Red Arrow planes in arc. f, Five Red Arrow planes flying to left.

No. 4232: a, $3, Westland Sea King helicopter. b, $3, Duke of Cambridge in helicopter. c, $3, Prince George of Cambridge wearing ear protection. d, $5, Emblem of Search and Rescue Force. e, $5, Princes William and Harry. f, $5, Queen Elizabeth II.

2017, Apr. 1 Litho. *Perf. 14*

Sheets of 6, #a-f

4231-4232 A954 Set of 2 36.00 36.00

Animals — A955

No. 4233: a, Caspian pond turtle. b, Pallid bat. c, Purple-banded sunbird. d, Bactrian camel.

$9, Dwarf rabbit, vert.

2017, Apr. 3 Litho. *Perf. 12½*

4233 A955 $6 Sheet of 4, #a-d 18.00 18.00

Souvenir Sheet

4234 A955 $9 multi 6.75 6.75

A956

Princess Diana (1961-97) — A957

No. 4235 — Princess Diana wearing: a, Lilac suit, hands not visible (30x40mm). b, Strapless gown (30x40mm). c, White shirt with ruffles, hands visible (30x40mm). d, Lilac dress (30x40mm). e, Green dress with white stripes and dots, white hat (30x40mm). f, Dark purple dress and lilac hat, (30x80mm).

No. 4236 — Princess Diana: a, Wearing dull rose blouse (30x40mm). b, Holding purse, wearing white dress (30x80mm). c, Wearing gown and jacket (30x80mm).

2017, Apr. 14 Litho. *Perf. 14*

4235 A956 $3.50 Sheet of 6, #a-f 15.50 15.50

Souvenir Sheet

4236 A957 $5 Sheet of 3, #a-c 11.00 11.00

Miniature Sheets

A958

A959

Inauguration of Pres. Donald Trump — A960

No. 4237 — Inaugural Ball photographs of: a, Pres. Trump and wife, Melania, black background. b, Ivanka Trump and Jared Kushner. c, Vice-President Mike Pence and wife, Karen. d, Pres. Trump and wife, colored background.

No. 4238 — Barron Trump with: a, Father, 2007. b, Father, 2014. c, Father, 2017. d, Mother, 2007. e, Mother, 2010. f, Mother, 2017.

No. 4239: a, Melania Trump in black dress. b, Melania Trump in white dress. c, Ivanka Trump in pink dress. d, Ivanka Trump in black dress. e, Pres. Trump, flag in background, f, Pres. Trump, door in background.

2017, June 26 Litho. *Perf. 14*

4237 A958 $4.50 Sheet of 4, #a-d 13.50 13.50
4238 A959 $4.50 Sheet of 6, #a-f 20.00 20.00
4239 A960 $4.50 Sheet of 6, #a-f 20.00 20.00

New Year 2018 (Year of the Dog) A961

Chinese Zodiac Animals — A962

No. 4240 — Dog facing: a, Left. b, Right.

No. 4241: a, Rat. b, Ox. c, Tiger. d, Rabbit. e, Dragon. f, Snake. g, Horse. h, Goat. i, Monkey. j, Rooster. k, Dog. l, Pig.

2017, Aug. 8 Litho. *Perf. 14*

4240 A961 $5.50 Vert. pair, #a-b 8.25 8.25

Miniature Sheet

4241 A962 $1.80 Sheet of 12, #a-l 16.00 16.00

No. 4240 was printed in sheets containing two pairs.

Dogs and Cats — A963

No. 4242, $7: a, Dog and squirrel in tree. b, Dog, sitting. c, Dog and ball.

No. 4243, $7: a, Cat and bird in cage. b, Cat, sitting. c, Cat and fish in tank.

No. 4244, $12, Dog with tongue out. No. 4245, $12, Cat and ball of yarn.

2017, Aug. 9 Litho. *Perf. 14*

Sheets of 3, #a-c

4242-4243 A963 Set of 2 31.00 31.00

Souvenir Sheets

Perf. 12½

4244-4245 A963 Set of 2 18.00 18.00

Nos. 4244-4245 each contain one 38x51mm stamp.

Starfish — A964

No. 4246: a, Common starfish. b, Common sunstar. c, Brittle star. d, West Indian seastar. $12, Starfish and coral, horiz.

2017, Aug. 9 Litho. *Perf. 13¾*

4246 A964 $7 Sheet of 4, #a-d 21.00 21.00

Souvenir Sheet

Perf. 14

4247 A964 $12 multi 9.00 9.00

No. 4247 contains one 80x30mm stamp.

Souvenir Sheets

A965

Coral Reefs — A966

No. 4248: a, Corals (40x360mm). b, Coral, fish and sea horse (80x30mm).

No. 4249: a, Shell. b, Octopus.

2017, Aug. 9 Litho. *Perf. 12½x13¼*

4248 A965 $7.50 Sheet of 2, #a-b 11.00 11.00

Perf. 13¾

4249 A966 $7.50 Sheet of 2, #a-b 11.00 11.00

70th Wedding Anniversary of Queen Elizabeth II and Prince Philip — A967

No. 4250 — Photographs of couple on wedding day: a, Princess Elizabeth waving. b, In wedding procession. c, Passing soldiers. d, Standing in front of curtain.

$18, Couple and attendants, vert.

2017, Aug. 11 Litho. *Perf. 14*

4250 A967 $6 Sheet of 4, #a-d 18.00 18.00

Souvenir Sheet

Perf. 12½

4251 A967 $18 multi 13.50 13.50

No. 4251 contains one 38x51mm stamp.

Tropical Fish — A968

No. 4252: a, Kole tang. b, Spotbase burrfish. c, Coral trout. d, Yellow tang.

No. 4253: a, Discus. b, Palette surgeonfish. c, Copperband butterflyfish.

Perf. 12½x13¼

2017, Aug. 16 Litho.

4252 A968 $7 Sheet of 4, #a-d 21.00 21.00

Souvenir Sheet

4253 A968 $7 Sheet of 3, #a-c 15.50 15.50

Miniature Sheets

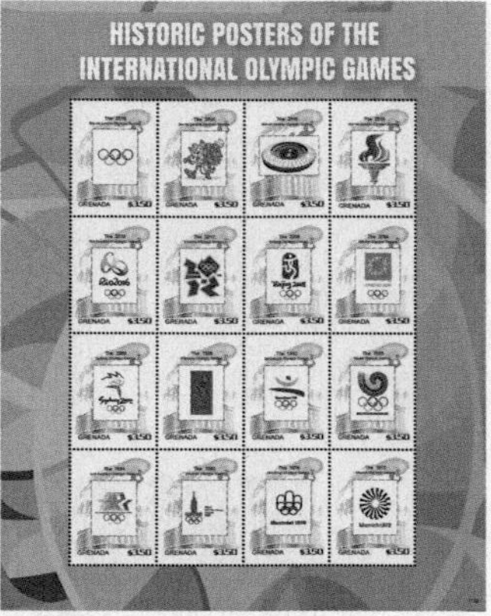

Emblems and Posters of the Summer Olympics — A969

No. 4254, $3.50: a, Olympic rings, 2016. b, Mascots, 2016. c, Stadium, 2016. d, Olympic torch, 2016. e, 2016 emblem. f, 2012 emblem. g, 2008 emblem. h, 2004 emblem, i, 2000 emblem. j, 1996 emblem. k, 1992 emblem. l, 1988 emblem. m, 1984 emblem. n, 1980 emblem. o, 1976 emblem. p, 1972 emblem.

No. 4255, $3.50: a, 1968 emblem. b, 1964 emblem. c, 1960 emblem. d, 1956 emblem. e, 1952 emblem. f, 1948 emblem. g, 1936 emblem. h, 1932 emblem. i, 1928 poster. j, 1924 poster. k, 1920 poster. l, 1912 poster. m, 1908 poster. n, 1904 poster. o, 1900 poster. p, 1896 poster (erroneously inscribed "1986").

2017, Sept. 14 Litho. *Perf. 14*

Sheets of 16, #a-p

4254-4255 A969 Set of 2 85.00 85.00

Study of Two Characters from *Los Borrachos*, by Diego Velázquez — A970

2017, Oct. 6 Litho. *Perf. 12½*

4256 A970 $50 multi 37.50 37.50

Souvenir Sheets

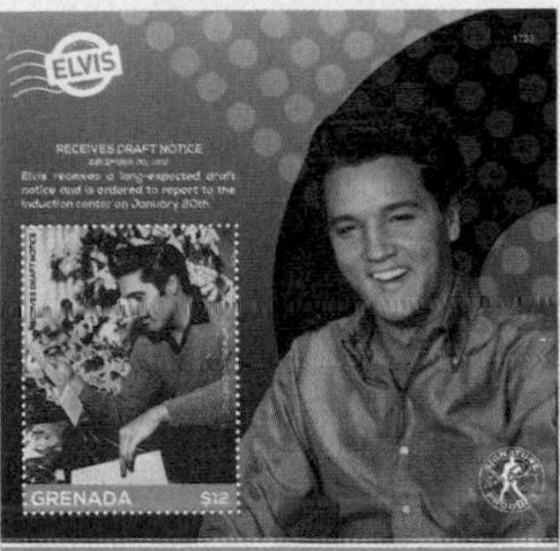

Elvis Presley (1935-77) — A971

Inscriptions: No. 4257, $12, Receives draft notice. No. 4258, $12, Elvis dances despite the "wiggle ban." No. 4259, $12, Shower of Stars Benefit.

2017, Oct. 26 Litho. *Perf. 12½*
4257-4259 A971 Set of 3 27.00 27.00

Muhammad Ali (1942-2016), Boxer — A972

No. 4260 — Various photographs of Ali, as shown.
$12, Ali looking right, fists ungloved.

2017, Oct. 26 Litho. *Perf. 12*
4260 A972 $7 Sheet of 3, #a-c 15.50 15.50

Souvenir Sheet
Perf. 12½

4261 A972 $12 multi 9.00 9.00

No. 4261 contains one 38x51mm stamp.

Miniature Sheet

World War II, 75th Anniv. — A973

No. 4262: a, Buy War Bonds poster. b, U.S. Marines recruitment poster. c, Woman Ordnance Worker poster. d, We Can Do It! poster. e, Save Your Cans poster. f, Keep Buying War Bonds poster.

2017, Dec. 4 Litho. *Perf. 14*
4262 A973 $4 Sheet of 6, #a-f 18.00 18.00

Christmas — A974

Religious paintings: $1, The Adoration of the Shepherds, by Philippe de Champaigne. $2, The Adoration of the Kings, by Peter Paul Rubens. $5, The Adoration of the Kings, by Giuseppe Chiara. $10, Adoration of the Kings, by Abraham Bloemaert.

2017, Dec. 17 Litho. *Perf. 12½*
4263-4266 A974 Set of 4 13.50 13.50

Red Fox — A975

No. 4267 — Various depictions of red fox with denominations of: a, $5.50. b, $6.50. c, $7.50. d, 8.50.
No. 4268, $12, One red fox. No. 4269, $12, Two red foxes.

Perf. 12½, 13¾ (#4269)
2017, Dec. 18 Litho.
4267 A975 Sheet of 4, #a-d 21.00 21.00

Souvenir Sheets

4268-4269 A975 Set of 2 18.00 18.00

No. 4269 contains one 35x35mm stamp.

Miniature Sheet

Chinese Paintings — A976

Various Chinese paintings depicting dogs (Nos. 4270a-4270j) or flowers (Nos. 4270k-4270t) numbered: a, 2018-1. b, 2018-2. c, 2018-3. d, 2018-4. e, 2018-5. f, 2018-6. g, 2018-7. h, 2018-8. i, 2018-9. j, 2018-10. k, 2018-11. l, 2018-12. m, 2018-13. n, 2018-14. o, 2018-15. p, 2018-16. q, 2018-17. r, 2018-18. s, 2018-19. t, 2018-20.

2018, Jan. 1 Litho. *Perf. 14*
4270 A976 $1.20 Sheet of 20, #a-t 18.00 18.00

Visit to People's Republic of China of Pres. Donald Trump — A977

No. 4271: a, Melania Trump. b, Pres. Donald Trump. c, Chinese Pres. Xi Jinping. d, Peng Liyuan.
$12, Pres. Xi Jinping and the Trumps, horiz.

2018, Jan. 24 Litho. *Perf. 12*
4271 A977 $8 Sheet of 4, #a-d 24.00 24.00

Souvenir Sheet
Perf. 12½

4272 A977 $12 multi 9.00 9.00

No. 4272 contains one 51x38mm stamp.

Miniature Sheet

Engagement of Prince Harry and Meghan Markle — A978

No. 4273: a, Prince William. b, Catherine, Duchess of Cambridge. c, Prince Harry. d, Markle.

2018, Mar. 5 Litho. *Perf. 14*
4273 A978 $7 Sheet of 4, #a-d 21.00 21.00

Miniature Sheet

Solar System — A979

No. 4274: a, $4, Neptune, Pluto. b, $5, Saturn, Uranus. c, $6, Earth, Mars, Jupiter. d, $7, Sun, Mercury, Venus.

2018, May 22 Litho. *Perf. 13¾*
4274 A979 Sheet of 4, #a-d 16.50 16.50

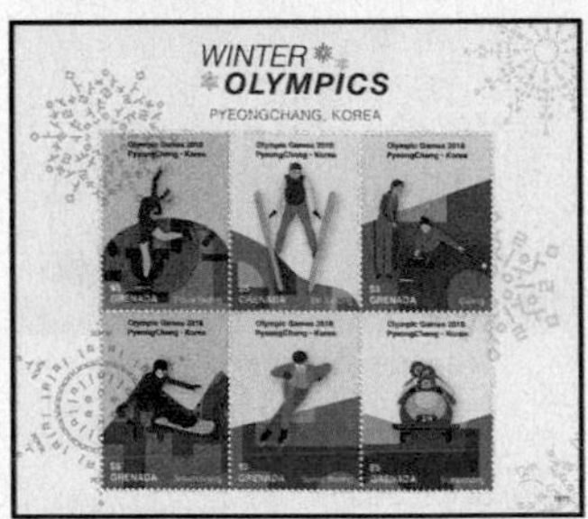

2018 Winter Olympics, Pyeongchang, South Korea — A980

No. 4275: a, Figure skating. b, Ski jumping. c, Curling. d, Snowboarding. e, Speed skating. f, Bobsledding.
No. 4276: a, Ice hockey. b, Freestyle skiing.

2018, May 22 Litho. *Perf. 14*
4275 A980 $5 Sheet of 6, #a-f 22.50 22.50

Souvenir Sheet
Perf. 12½

4276 A980 $8 Sheet of 2, #a-b 12.00 12.00

No. 4276 contains two 38x51mm stamps.

Souvenir Sheets

Coronation of Queen Elizabeth Ii, 65th Anniv. — A981

No. 4277 — Queen Elizabeth II: a, Standing. b, Seated in coach.
$10, Queen Elizabeth II waving.

2018, May 22 Litho. *Perf. 14*
4277 A981 $8 Sheet of 2, #a-b 12.00 12.00

Perf. 12

4278 A981 $10 multi 7.50 7.50

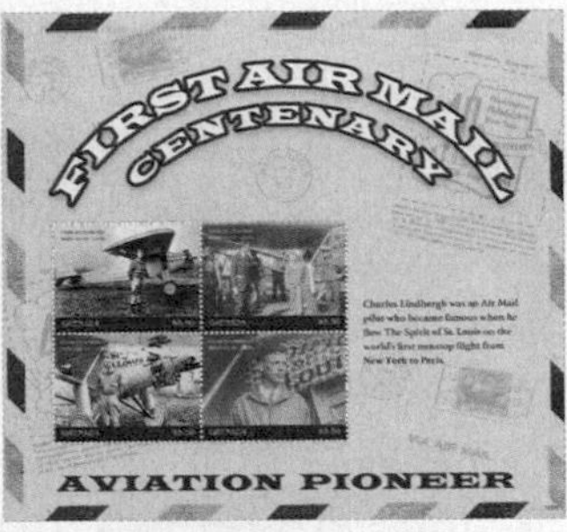

Airmail, Cent. — A982

No. 4279 — Charles Lindbergh and the Spirit of St. Louis: a, Lindbergh standing under wing. b, Lindbergh with other people near airplane. c, Lindbergh standing behind wheel. d, Close-up of Lindbergh and name of airplane.
$10, U.S. #C10.

2018, May 22 Litho. *Perf. 14*
4279 A982 $5.50 Sheet of 4, #a-d 16.50 16.50

Souvenir Sheet
Perf. 12½

4280 A982 $10 multi 7.50 7.50

No. 4280 contains one 51x38mm stamp.

Theobroma Cacao — A983

No. 4281: a, $3, Branch with brown pods. b, $4, Branch with yellow pod.
$10, Branch with pod, diff.

2018, June 18 Litho. *Perf. 14*
4281 A983 Pair, #a-b 5.25 5.25

Souvenir Sheet
Perf. 12½

4282 A983 $10 multi 7.50 7.50

No. 4281 was printed in sheets containing three pairs. No. 4282 contains one 38x51mm stamp.

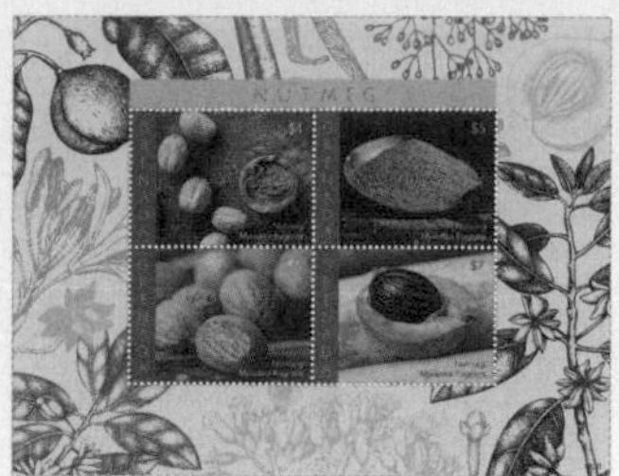

Nutmeg — A984

No. 4283: a, $4, Ground nutmeg and nutmeg seeds. b, $5. Ground nutmeg. c, $6, Nutmeg seeds. d, $7, Mace aril surrounding nutmeg kernel.
$10, Nutmeg tree branch and seeds.

2018, June 18 Litho. *Perf. 14*
4283 A984 Sheet of 4, #a-d 16.50 16.50

Souvenir Sheet
Perf. 12½
4284 A984 $10 multi 7.50 7.50

No. 4284 contains one 51x38mm stamp.

Wedding of Prince Harry and Meghan Markle — A985

No. 4285: a, Prince Charles escorting bride. b, Bride and groom in church. c, Bride and groom holding hands. d, Bride and groom waving in car.
$10, Bride holding flower bouquet.

2018, July 27 Litho. *Perf. 12*
4285 A985 $5 Sheet of 4, #a-d 15.00 15.00

Souvenir Sheet
Perf. 12½
4286 A985 $10 multi 7.50 7.50

No. 4286 contains one 51x38mm stamp.

Flora and Fauna — A986

Designs: $5, Cacao tree. $10, West Indian manatee. $20, Nine-banded armadillo. $40, Bougainvillea. $60, Nutmeg. $80, Grenada dove.

2018, Aug. 3 Litho. *Perf. 14*
4287 A986 $5 multi 3.75 3.75
4288 A986 $10 multi 7.50 7.50
4289 A986 $20 multi 15.00 15.00
4290 A986 $40 multi 30.00 30.00
4291 A986 $60 multi 45.00 45.00
4292 A986 $80 multi 60.00 60.00
Nos. 4287-4292 (6) 161.25 161.25

Souvenir Sheets

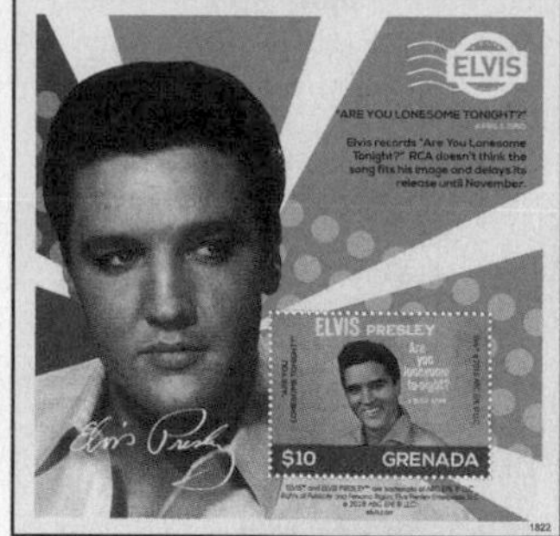

Elvis Presley (1935-77) — A987

Inscriptions: No. 4293, $10, "Are You Lonesome Tonight?" No. 4294, $10, Elvis's first army leave. No. 4295, $10, Elvis trading cards, vert. No. 4296, $10, Memphis Music Hall of Fame.

2018, Aug. 3 Litho. *Perf. 14*
4293-4296 A987 Set of 4 30.00 30.00

Miniature Sheet

Equids — A988

No. 4297: a, $5, Donkeys. b, $6, Mules. c, $7, Horses.

2018, Oct. 10 Litho. *Perf. 12*
4297 A988 Sheet of 3, #a-c 13.50 13.50

Grenada Waterfalls — A989

No. 4298: a, Annandale Falls. b, Concord Falls. c, Royal Mt. Carmel Falls.
$10, Seven Sisters Falls.

2018, Oct. 10 Litho. *Perf. 12*
4298 A989 $5 Sheet of 3, #a-c 11.00 11.00

Souvenir Sheet
4299 A989 $10 multi 7.50 7.50

No. 4299 contains one 30x50mm stamp.

Fish — A990

No. 4300: a, $4, Queen triggerfish. b, $5, French angelfish. c, $6, Cherubfish. d, $7, Queen parrotfish.
$10, Queen angelfish.

2018, Oct. 10 Litho. *Perf. 14*
4300 A990 Sheet of 4, #a-d 16.50 16.50

Souvenir Sheet
Perf. 12½
4301 A990 $10 multi 7.50 7.50

No. 4301 contains one 51x38mm stamp.

Tropical Fruit — A991

No. 4302: a, $5, Tamarinds. b, $5, Passion fruits. c, $6, Mangos. d, $6, Starfruits.
No. 4303: a, Guavas. b, Soursops.

2018, Oct. 10 Litho. *Perf. 14*
4302 A991 Sheet of 4, #a-d 16.50 16.50

Souvenir Sheet
Perf. 12
4303 A991 $8 Sheet of 2, #a-b 12.00 12.00

Miniature Sheet

Christening of Prince Louis of Cambridge — A992

No. 4304: a, $5, Prince Louis. b, $6, Prince Louis in arms of Duchess of Cambridge, clergyman. c, $7, Princes William, Charles, and Harry with wives and children. d, $8, Princes William, Charles and Harry with wives, children and other family members.

2018, Oct. 17 Litho. *Perf. 14*
4304 A992 Sheet of 4, #a-d 19.50 19.50

Flight of Apollo 11, 50th Anniv. (in 2019) — A993

No. 4305: a, Launch. b, Lunar Module and astronaut on Moon. c, Astronaut on moon. d, Earth. e, Earth and Moon. f, Moon.
$11, Lunar Module above Moon, mission patch, horiz.

2018, Oct. 17 Litho. *Perf. 12*
4305 A993 $5 Sheet of 6, #a-f 22.50 22.50

Souvenir Sheet
Perf. 12½
4306 A993 $11 multi 8.25 8.25

No. 4306 contains one 51x38mm stamp.

New Year 2019 (Year of the Pig) — A994

No. 4307 — Pig facing: a, $5, Right, dark red flower on hindquarters. b, $5, Right, orange red flower on hindquarters. c, $6, Left, orange red flower on hindquarters. d, $6, Left, dark red flower on hindquarters.
$8, Pig, diff.

2018, Oct. 17 Litho. *Perf. 14*
4307 A994 Sheet of 4, #a-d 16.50 16.50

Souvenir Sheet
Perf. 12
4308 A994 $8 multi 6.00 6.00

No. 4308 contains one 50x30mm stamp.

Cats — A995

No. 4309: a, Abyssinian. b, Kurilian Bobtail. c, British Shorthair. d, Cornish Rex. e, Russian Blue. f, American Curl.
$10, Balinese, horiz.

2018, Nov. 9 Litho. *Perf. 14*
4309 A995 $4 Sheet of 6, #a-f 18.00 18.00

Souvenir Sheet
Perf. 12
4310 A995 $10 multi 7.50 7.50

SEMI-POSTAL STAMPS

Catalogue values for unused stamps in this section are for Never Hinged items.

Nos. 227-229 Overprinted

Type I

Type II

1968 Type I
B1A A38 2c + 3c on $2 #228 .25 .25
B1B A38 3c + 3c on $3 #229 .25 .25

Type II

B1C A38 1c + 3c on $1 #227 .25 .25
B1D A38 2c + 3c on $2 #228 26.00 *55.00*
Nos. B1A-B1D (4) 26.75 *55.75*

Issued: B1A-B1B, 7/22; B1C-B1D, 8/19.

ESPANA '82 World Cup Soccer SP1

Players and Flags of Winning Countries — No. B1, West Germany, 1974. No. B2, Argentina, 1978. No. B3, Brazil, 1970. No. B4, Grt. Britain, 1966.

No. B5, World Cup, ESPANA '82.

Unwmk.

1981, Nov. 30 Litho. *Perf. 14*

B1 SP1 25c + 10c multi .50 .50
B2 SP1 40c + 20c multi .70 .70
B3 SP1 50c + 25c multi 1.00 1.00
B4 SP1 $1 + 50c multi 1.75 1.75
Nos. B1-B4 (4) 3.95 3.95

Souvenir Sheet

B5 SP1 $5 + 50c multi 4.00 4.00

Nos. B1-B4 each issued in sheets of 12 with sheet background showing soccer ball.

1988 Seoul Olympics — SP2

No. B6, Pole vault. No. B7, Balance beam. No. B8, Shot put. No. B9, High jump.

No. B10, Swimming.

1986, Dec. 1 Litho. *Perf. 15*

B6 SP2 10c + 5c multi .25 .30
B7 SP2 50c + 20c multi .55 *.65*
B8 SP2 70c + 30c multi .85 .85
B9 SP2 $2 + $1 multi 1.75 *2.50*
Nos. B6-B9 (4) 3.40 *4.30*

Souvenir Sheet

B10 SP2 $3 + $1 multi 3.50 3.50

Surtax for natl. Olympic team.

World Philatelic Programs SP3

Halley's Comet or Stamp Collecting emblem and: No. B11, Halley's initial work on nebulae, 1676. No. B12, Experiments at sea (tall ship, manned capsule). No. B13, Halley observes complete lunar cycle, 1720-1738. No. B14, Halley publishes Newton's Principia, 1687. No. B15, Halley charts the southern skies, 1676.

1989, Apr. 25 Litho. *Perf. 14*

B11 SP3 25c +5c multi .85 .85
B12 SP3 75c +5c multi 1.45 1.45
B13 SP3 90c +5c multi 1.75 1.75
B14 SP3 $2 +5c multi 2.25 2.25

Size: 111x78mm

Imperf

B15 SP3 $5 +5c multi 5.00 5.00
Nos. B11-B15 (5) 11.30 11.30

AIR POST STAMPS

Catalogue values for unused stamps in this section are for Never Hinged items.

Nos. 428-429 Surcharged with New Value, Olympic Rings, "Air Mail" and "WINTER OLYMPICS / FEB. 3 13, 1972 / SAPPORO, JAPAN"

Perf. 13½x14

1972, Feb. 3 Litho. Unwmk.

C1 A66 35c on ½c multi .40 .40
C2 A66 50c on 1c multi .60 .60

11th Winter Olympic Games, Sapporo, Japan, Feb. 3-13.

Nos. 294-300, 302A, 303-309 Surcharged Type "a" or Overprinted Type "b"

a

b

Perfs. as Before

1972, May 2 Photo.; Litho.

C3 A45 5c violet & multi .25 .25
C4 A45 8c multicolored .25 .25
C5 A45 10c orange & multi .25 .25
C6 A45 15c gray & multi .25 .25
C7 A45 25c multicolored .40 .30
C8 A45 30c on 1c multi .50 .35
C9 A45 35c multicolored .55 .40
C10 A45 40c on 2c multi .60 .45
C11 A45 45c on 3c multi .65 .50
C12 A45 50c multicolored .70 .55
C13 A45 60c on 5c multi .80 .70
C14 A45 70c on 6c multi .95 .90
C15 A45 $1 multicolored 6.50 1.25
C16 A45 $1.35 on 8c multi 3.25 3.00
C17 A45 $2 multicolored 8.00 7.00
C18 A45 $3 multicolored 10.00 9.00
C19 A45 $5 multicolored 13.00 *16.00*
Nos. C3-C19 (17) 46.90 41.40

"AIR MAIL" reading down on 5c, 15c, 25c, 35c, 60c and $5.

Olympic Type of Regular Issue

Olympic Rings and: 25c, 60c, $1, Boxing. 70c, Equestrian (not inscribed air mail).

1972, Sept. 8 Litho. *Perf. 14*

C20 A69 25c blue & multi .50 .30
C21 A69 $1 green & multi .90 .75

Souvenir Sheet

C22 Sheet of 2 1.50 1.50
a. A69 60c blue & multi .50 .50
b. A69 70c deep yellow & multi 1.00 1.00

Nos. 409-412 Overprinted Vertically, Reading Up "AIR MAIL"

1972, Oct. Litho. *Perf. 11*

C23 A62 5c multicolored .60 .25
C24 A62 35c multicolored 1.50 .60
C25 A62 50c multicolored 1.75 1.00
C26 A62 75c multicolored 2.50 2.00
Nos. C23-C26 (4) 6.35 3.85

Boy Scout Type of Regular Issue

Designs: 25c, Scout saluting. 35c, Two Scouts knotting ropes.

1972, Nov. *Perf. 14*

C27 A70 25c dp blue & multi .40 .35
C28 A70 35c brn org & multi .60 .55

John Hancock — AP1

Designs: 50c, Benjamin Franklin. 75c, John Adams. $1, Marquis de Lafayette.

1975, May 6 Litho. *Perf. 14½, 13*

C29 AP1 40c multicolored .25 *.25*
C30 AP1 50c multicolored .45 *.25*
C31 AP1 75c multicolored .55 *.25*
C32 AP1 $1 multicolored .65 *.25*
Nos. C29-C32 (4) 1.90 *1.00*

American Revolution Bicentennial.

Nos. C29-C32 issued in sheets of 40. Each denomination was also printed in sheets of 5 plus label, perf. 13.

POSTAGE DUE STAMPS

D1

1892 Typo. Wmk. 2 *Perf. 14*

J1 D1 1p black 30.00 2.75
J2 D1 2p black 225.00 3.25
J3 D1 3p black 200.00 4.00
Nos. J1-J3 (3) 455.00 10.00

Nos. 24 & 25 Surcharged in Black

J4 A8 1p on 6p red lilac 110.00 2.25
a. Tete beche pair 2,750. *1,800.*
b. Double surcharge 225.00
c. Same as "b," tete beche pair
J5 A8 1p on 8p bister 1,600. 6.00
a. Tete beche pair *8,500.* *2,500.*
J6 A8 2p on 6p red lilac 190.00 4.50
a. Tete beche pair *3,500.* 1,800.
J7 A8 2p on 8p bister 3,200. 12.00
a. Tete beche pair *7,500.* 5,000.
Nos. J4-J7 (4) 5,100. 24.75

Nos. J4-J7 were printed with alternate horizontal rows inverted.

1906-11 Wmk. 3

J8 D1 1p black ('11) 3.75 *7.50*
J9 D1 2p black 12.50 3.75
J10 D1 3p black 15.00 6.50
Nos. J8-J10 (3) 31.25 17.75

D3

1921-22 Wmk. 4

J11 D3 1p black 2.00 *1.40*
J12 D3 1½p black 10.00 *25.00*
J13 D3 2p black 3.00 *4.50*
J14 D3 3p black 3.00 *4.75*
Nos. J11-J14 (4) 18.00 *35.65*

Issued: 1½p, Dec. 15, 1922, others, Dec. 1921.

Catalogue values for unused stamps in this section, from this point to the end of the section, are for Never Hinged items.

1952, Mar. 1

J15 D3 2c black .50 *9.00*
a. Wmk. 4a (error) 55.00
J16 D3 4c black .50 *17.00*
a. Wmk. 4a (error) 60.00
J17 D3 6c black .65 *13.00*
a. Wmk. 4a (error) 100.00
J18 D3 8c black .75 *14.00*
a. Wmk. 4a (error) 200.00
Nos. J15-J18 (4) 2.40 *53.00*

WAR TAX STAMPS

Nos. 80a, 80 Overprinted

1916 Wmk. 3 *Perf. 14*

MR1 A21 1p carmine 2.50 2.00
a. 1p scarlet 3.00 3.00
b. Double overprint 325.00
c. Inverted overprint 325.00

No. 80 Overprinted

MR2 A21 1p scarlet .30 .25

OFFICIAL STAMPS

Catalogue values for unused stamps in this section are for Never Hinged items.

Nos. 1006-1018, 1020, 1051-1053 Overprinted: "P.R.G."

1982, July 15 Litho. *Perf. 14, 15*

O1 A141 5c multicolored .25 .25
O2 A141 6c multicolored .25 .25
O3 A141 10c multicolored .25 .25
O4 A141 12c multicolored .25 .25
O5 A141 15c multicolored .25 .25
O6 A141 20c multicolored .25 .25
O7 A141 25c multicolored .25 .25
O8 A141 30c multicolored .25 .25
O9 A141 40c multicolored .30 .30
O10 A141 50c multicolored .40 .40
O11 CD331 50c multicolored .40 .40
O12 A141 90c multicolored .75 .75
O13 A141 $1 multicolored .80 .80
O14 CD331 $2 multicolored 1.75 1.75
O15 A141 $3 multicolored 2.25 2.25
O16 CD331 $4 multicolored 4.00 4.00
O17 A141 $10 multicolored 7.00 7.00
Nos. O1-O17 (17) 19.65 19.65

PRG stands for People's Revolutionary Government.

GRENADA GRENADINES

grə-ˈnā-də ˌgre-nə-ˈdēnz

LOCATION — North of Grenada
GOVT. — Part of Grenada
CAPITAL — None

Main islands are Carriacou and Ronde.

Catalogue values for all unused stamps in this country are for Never Hinged items.

All stamps are a type of Grenada unless otherwise noted or illustrated. Nos. 15-58 have the additional inscription Grenadines.

Grenada Nos. 516-517a Overprinted

Perf. 13½x14

1973, Dec. 23 Litho. Wmk. 314

No.	Type	Description	Unused	Used
1	A77	25c dp orange & multi	.25	.25
2	A77	$2 green & multi	.50	.50
a.		Souvenir sheet of 2 (75c, $1)	.75	.50

Grenada Nos. 294-297, 299-301, 303, 306-309 Overprinted

Perf. 14x14½, 14½x14

1974, May 29 Photo. Unwmk.

Size: 25x44mm

No.	Type	Description	Unused	Used
3	A45	1c multicolored	.25	.25
4	A45	2c multicolored	.25	.25
5	A45	3c multicolored	.25	.25
6	A45	5c multicolored	.25	.25
7	A45	8c multicolored	.25	.25
8	A45	10c multicolored	.25	.25
9	A45	12c multicolored	.25	.25
10	A45	25c multicolored	.30	.30

Size: 25x47mm

No.	Type	Description	Unused	Used
11	A45	$1 multicolored	2.50	1.40
12	A45	$2 multicolored	3.75	2.00
13	A45	$3 multicolored	3.75	2.90
14	A45	$5 multicolored	4.50	3.50
		Nos. 3-14 (12)	16.55	11.85

World Cup Soccer Type

Designs: Soccer matches and flags. ½c, West Germany-Chile. 1c, East Germany-Australia. 2c, Yugoslavia-Brazil. 10c, Scotland-Zaire. 25c, Netherlands-Uruguay. 50c, Sweden-Bulgaria. 75c, Italy-Haiti. $1, Poland-Argentina. $2, Flags of participating nations.

1974, Sept. 17 Litho. *Perf. 14½*

No.	Type	Description	Unused	Used
15	A81	½c multicolored	.25	.25
16	A81	1c multicolored	.25	.25
17	A81	2c multicolored	.25	.25
18	A81	10c multicolored	.25	.25
19	A81	25c multicolored	.25	.25
20	A81	50c multicolored	.35	.25
21	A81	75c multicolored	.35	.25
22	A81	$1 multicolored	.40	.30
		Nos. 15-22 (8)	2.35	2.05

Souvenir Sheet

No.	Type	Description	Unused	Used
23	A81	$2 multicolored	2.00	2.00

UPU Centenary Type

UPU Emblem and: 8c, Mailboat *Caesar*, 1839, helicopter. 25c, German messenger, 1540, satellite. 35c, Biplanes, zeppelin, jet. No. 27, US Mail train, 19th cent., Concorde. No. 28a, Bellman, 18th cent., radar. $2, German postman, 18th cent., mail train, 1980's.

1974, Oct. 8 *Perf. 14½*

No.	Type	Description	Unused	Used
24	A82	8c multicolored	.25	.25
25	A82	25c multicolored	.25	.25
26	A82	35c multicolored	.25	.25
27	A82	$1 multicolored	.95	.50
		Nos. 24-27 (4)	1.70	1.25

Souvenir Sheet

Perf. 13

No.	Type	Description	Unused	Used
28		Sheet of 2	1.75	1.75
a.		A82 $1 multicolored	.50	.50
b.		A82 $2 multicolored	1.25	1.25

Churchill Type

Design: $2, Churchill, different portrait.

1974, Nov. 11 *Perf. 13½*

No.	Type	Description	Unused	Used
29	A83	35c multicolored	.25	.25
30	A83	$2 multicolored	.35	.35

Souvenir Sheet

No.	Type	Description	Unused	Used
31		Sheet of 2	.80	.80
a.		A82 75c like 35c	.30	.30
b.		A82 $1 like $2	.35	.35

Christmas Type

Paintings of the Virgin and Child: ½c, Botticelli. 1c, Niccolo di Pietro. 2c, Van der Weyden. 3c, Bastiani. 10c, Giovanni. 25c, Van der Weyden, diff. 50c, Botticelli. $1, Mantegna. $2, Niccolo di Pietro.

1974, Nov. 27 *Perf. 14½*

No.	Type	Description	Unused	Used
32	A84	½c multicolored	.25	.25
33	A84	1c multicolored	.25	.25
34	A84	2c multicolored	.25	.25
35	A84	3c multicolored	.25	.25
36	A84	10c multicolored	.25	.25
37	A84	25c multicolored	.25	.25
38	A84	50c multicolored	.25	.25
39	A84	$1 multicolored	.30	.25
		Nos. 32-39 (8)	2.05	2.00

Souvenir Sheet

Perf. 13½

No.	Type	Description	Unused	Used
40	A84	$2 multicolored	1.00	1.00

Big Game Fish Type

½c, Sailfish. 1c, Blue marlin. 2c, White marlin. 10c, Yellowfin tuna. 25c, Wahoo. 50c, Dolphin. 70c, Grouper. $1, Great barracuda. $2, Mako shark.

1975, Feb. 17 *Perf. 14½*

No.	Type	Description	Unused	Used
41	A86	½c multicolored	.25	.25
42	A86	1c multicolored	.25	.25
43	A86	2c multicolored	.25	.25
44	A86	10c multicolored	.25	.25
45	A86	25c multicolored	.25	.25
46	A86	50c multicolored	.25	.25
47	A86	70c multicolored	.40	.30
48	A86	$1 multicolored	.60	.50
		Nos. 41-48 (8)	2.50	2.30

Souvenir Sheet

Perf. 13

No.	Type	Description	Unused	Used
49	A86	$2 multicolored	2.50	2.50

Flowers of Grenada Type

½c, Grandilla barbadine. 1c, Bleeding heart. 2c, Poinsettia. 3c, Cocoa. 10c, Gladioli. 25c, Red head-yellow head. 50c, Plumbago. $1, Orange blossoms. $2, Barbados gooseberry.

1975, Mar. 11 *Perf. 14½*

No.	Type	Description	Unused	Used
50	A87	½c multicolored	.25	.25
51	A87	1c multicolored	.25	.25
52	A87	2c multicolored	.25	.25
53	A87	3c multicolored	.25	.25
54	A87	10c multicolored	.25	.25
55	A87	25c multicolored	.25	.25
56	A87	50c multicolored	.35	.35
57	A87	$1 multicolored	.60	.55
		Nos. 50-57 (8)	2.45	2.40

Souvenir Sheet

Perf. 13½

No.	Type	Description	Unused	Used
58	A87	$2 multicolored	1.50	1.50

Remainders of Grenada Grenadines stamps between Scott Nos. 59 and 269, except Nos. 109-128, 217-220, 237-240 and some souvenir sheets, were later canceled to order and sold at a fraction of their face value. Our used values for these stamps are for c-t-o examples. Postally used stamps are worth the same as unused, never hinged examples.

Christ Crowned with Thorns, by Titian — G1

Easter paintings of the Crucifixion by various artists: 1c, Giotto. 2c, Tintoretto. 3c, Cranach. 35c, Caravaggio. 75c, Tiepolo. $2, Velasquez.
$1, Titian, diff.

1975, June 24 *Perf. 14½*

No.	Type	Description	Unused	Used
59	G1	½c shown	.25	.25
60	G1	1c multicolored	.25	.25
61	G1	2c multicolored	.25	.25
62	G1	3c multicolored	.25	.25
63	G1	35c multicolored	.25	.25
64	G1	75c multicolored	.25	.25
65	G1	$2 multicolored	.30	.25
		Nos. 59-65 (7)	1.80	1.75

Souvenir Sheet

Perf. 13½

No.	Type	Description	Unused	Used
66	G1	$1 multicolored	1.10	1.10

Works by Michelangelo (1475-1564) — G2

Designs: ½c, Dawn (sculpture, detail from Medici tomb). 1c, Delphic Sibyl. 2c, Giuliano de Medici (sculpture). 40c, The Creation. 50c, Lorenzo de Medici (sculpture). 75c, Persian Sibyl. $1, The Prophet Jeremiah. $2, Head of Christ (sculpture).

1975, July 16 *Perf. 14½*

No.	Type	Description	Unused	Used
67	G2	½c violet & multi	.25	.25
68	G2	1c multicolored	.25	.25
69	G2	2c green & multi	.25	.25
70	G2	40c multicolored	.25	.25
71	G2	50c brt red & multi	.30	.25
72	G2	75c multicolored	.45	.25
73	G2	$2 brt blue & multi	.75	.25
		Nos. 67-73 (7)	2.50	1.75

Souvenir Sheet

Perf. 13½

No.	Type	Description	Unused	Used
74	G2	$1 multicolored	1.25	.75

Butterflies — G3

½c, Emperor. 1c, Queen. 2c, Tiger pierid. 35c, Cracker. 45c, Scarlet bamboo page. 75c, Apricot. $2, Purple king shoemaker.
$1, Bamboo page.

1975, Aug. 12 *Perf. 15*

No.	Type	Description	Unused	Used
75	G3	½c multicolored	.25	.25
76	G3	1c multicolored	.25	.25
77	G3	2c multicolored	.25	.25
78	G3	35c multicolored	.55	.25
79	G3	45c multicolored	.70	.25
80	G3	75c multicolored	1.25	.25
81	G3	$2 multicolored	3.25	.25
		Nos. 75-81 (7)	6.50	1.75

Souvenir Sheet

Perf. 13½

No.	Type	Description	Unused	Used
82	G3	$1 multicolored	6.00	6.00

Jamboree Scenes and Badges G4

Nordjamb 75 Emblem and: ½c, Progress badge. 1c, Boating badge. 2c, Coxswain badge. 35c, Interpreter badge. 45c, Ambulance badge. 75c, Chief scout's award. $1, Venture award. $2, Queen's scout award.

1975, Aug. 22 *Perf. 15*

No.	Type	Description	Unused	Used
83	G4	½c lemon yel & multi	.25	.25
84	G4	1c vio blue & multi	.25	.25
85	G4	2c green & multi	.25	.25
86	G4	35c dull vio & multi	.25	.25
87	G4	45c org brown & multi	.25	.25
88	G4	75c brown & multi	.25	.25
89	G4	$2 green & multi	.60	.25
		Nos. 83-89 (7)	2.10	1.75

Souvenir Sheet

Perf. 13½

No.	Type	Description	Unused	Used
90	G4	$1 dull vio & multi	1.00	.40

Nordjamb 75, 14th Boy Scout World Jamboree, Lillehammer, Norway, July 29-Aug. 7.

Surrender of Lord Cornwallis G5

Designs: 1c, Minuteman. 2c, Paul Revere's Ride. 3c, Battle of Bunker Hill. 5c, *Spirit of '76.* 45c, Backwoodsman. 75c, Boston Tea Party. No. 98, Naval engagement. No. 99, George Washington. No. 100, White House, flags.

1975, Sept. 30 *Perf. 14*

Size: 39x25mm

No.	Type	Description	Unused	Used
91	G5	½c multicolored	.25	.25
92	G5	1c multicolored	.25	.25
93	G5	2c multicolored	.25	.25
94	G5	3c multicolored	.25	.25
95	G5	5c multicolored	.25	.25
96	G5	45c multicolored	.25	.25
97	G5	75c multicolored	.25	.25
98	G5	$2 multicolored	.45	.45

Size: 59x39mm

Perf. 11

No.	Type	Description	Unused	Used
99	G5	$2 multicolored, vert.	.45	.45
a.		Souvenir sheet of 1, imperf.	1.00	1.00
100	G4	$2 multicolored	.45	.45
a.		Souvenir sheet of 1, imperf.	1.00	1.00
		Nos. 91-100 (10)	3.10	3.10

American Revolution Bicentennial.
Nos. 99a, 100a have simulated perfs.

Fencing G6

1975, Oct. 27 *Perf. 15*

No.	Type	Description	Unused	Used
101	G6	½c shown	.25	.25
102	G6	1c Hurdling	.25	.25
103	G6	2c Pole vault	.25	.25
104	G6	35c Weightlifting	.25	.25
105	G6	45c Javelin	.25	.25
106	G6	75c Discus	.25	.25
107	G6	$2 Diving	.35	.25
		Nos. 101-107 (7)	1.85	1.75

Souvenir Sheet

No.	Type	Description	Unused	Used
108	G6	$1 Sprinter	.80	.80

Pan American Games, Mexico City, Oct. 12-26, 1975.

Type of 1975

Designs: ½c, Cruising Yachts, Point Saline. 1c, Yacht Club race, St. George's. 2c, Careenage Taxi. 3c, Working boats. 5c, Deep water dock, St. George's. 6c, Cocoa beans drying. 8c, Nutmegs. 10c, Rum distillery, River Antoine Estate. 12c, Cocoa tree. 15c, Landing catch at Fontenoy. 20c, Parliament building, St. George's. 25c, Fort George cannons. 35c, Pearls airport. 50c, General Post Office. 75c, Caribs Leap, Sauteurs Bay. $1, Careenage, St. George's. $2, St. George's harbor at night. $3, Grand Anse beach. $5, Canoe and Black

Bays from Point Saline lighthouse. $10, Sugar Loaf Island from Levera beach.

1975-76 Size: 38x25mm ***Perf. 14½***

109 A85 ½c multicolored .25 *.35*
110 A85 1c multicolored .25 .25
111 A85 2c multicolored .25 .25
112 A85 3c multicolored .25 .25
113 A85 5c multicolored .25 .25
114 A85 6c multicolored .25 .25
115 A85 8c multicolored .25 .25
116 A85 10c multicolored .25 .25
117 A85 12c multicolored .25 .25
118 A85 15c multicolored .25 .25
119 A85 20c multicolored .25 *.65*
120 A85 25c multicolored .25 .25
121 A85 35c multicolored 1.00 .25
122 A85 50c multicolored .25 *1.00*

Perf. 13½x14

Size: 45x28mm

123 A85 75c multicolored .55 *.65*
124 A85 $1 multicolored .85 *.95*
125 A85 $2 multicolored 1.25 *2.25*
126 A85 $3 multicolored 1.50 *2.75*
127 A85 $5 multicolored 1.75 *5.50*
128 A85 $10 multicolored 3.00 *6.00*
Nos. 109-128 (20) 13.15 22.85

Issued: Nos. 109-127, 11/5/75; No. 128, 1/1/76.

For overprints see Nos. 360-372.

Madonna and Child by Durer — G8

Christmas: Paintings showing Madonna and Child by various artists — 1c, Durer, diff. 2c, Correggio. 40c, Botticelli. 50c, Niccolo da Cremona. 75c, Correggio, diff. $2, Correggio, diff. $1, Bellini.

1975, Dec. 17 ***Perf. 14***

129 G8 ½c shown .25 .25
130 G8 1c multicolored .25 .25
131 G8 2c multicolored .25 .25
132 G8 40c multicolored .25 .25
133 G8 50c multicolored .25 .25
134 G8 75c multicolored .25 .25
135 G8 $2 multicolored .35 .25
Nos. 129-135 (7) 1.85 1.75

Souvenir Sheet

136 G8 $1 multicolored .80 .60

Sea Shells G9

1976, Jan. 13

137 G9 ½c Bleeding Tooth .25 .25
138 G9 1c Wedge clam .25 .25
139 G9 2c Hawk wing conch .25 .25
140 G9 3c Distorsio clathrata .25 .25
141 G9 25c Scotch bonnet .45 .25
142 G9 50c King helmet .90 .25
143 G9 75c Queen conch 1.50 .25
Nos. 137-143 (7) 3.85 1.75

Souvenir Sheet

144 G9 $2 Atlantic triton 2.75 1.00

Lignum Vitae G10

Designs: 1c, Cocoa thrush. 2c, Tarantula. 35c, Hooded tanager. 50c, Nyctaginaceae. 75c, Grenada dove. $1, Marine toad. $2, Blue-hooded euphonia.

1976, Feb. 4

145 G10 ½c multicolored .25 .25
146 G10 1c multicolored .25 .25
147 G10 2c multicolored .25 .25
148 G10 35c multicolored 1.25 .25
149 G10 50c multicolored 1.25 .25
150 G10 75c multicolored 2.50 .30
151 G10 $1 multicolored 2.50 .30
Nos. 145-151 (7) 8.25 1.85

Souvenir Sheet

152 G10 $2 multicolored 5.75 1.25

Hooked Sailfish G11

Designs: 1c, Careened schooner, Carriacou. 2c, Annual regatta. 18c, Boat building. 22c, Workboat race. 75c, Cruising off Petit Martinique. $1, Water skiing. $2, Yacht racing.

1976, Feb. 17

153 G11 ½c multicolored .25 .25
154 G11 1c multicolored .25 .25
155 G11 2c multicolored .25 .25
156 G11 18c multicolored .25 .25
157 G11 22c multicolored .25 .25
158 G11 75c multicolored .40 .25
159 G11 $1 multicolored .55 .25
Nos. 153-159 (7) 2.20 1.75

Souvenir Sheet

160 G11 $2 multicolored .90 .90

Making a Camp Fire G12

50th anniv. of Girl Guides of Grenada: 1c, First aid. 2c, Nature study. 50c, Cooking. $1, Drawing. $2, Playing guitar.

1976, Mar. 17

161 G12 ½c multicolored .25 .25
162 G12 1c multicolored .25 .25
163 G12 2c multicolored .25 .25
164 G12 50c multicolored .45 .25
165 G12 $1 multicolored 1.00 .30
Nos. 161-165 (5) 2.20 1.30

Souvenir Sheet

166 G12 $2 multicolored 1.40 1.00

Christ Mocked, by Bosch — G13

Easter Paintings: 1c, Christ Crucified by Messina. 2c, Adoration by Durer. 3c, Lamentation of Christ by Durer. 35c, The Entombment by Van Der Weyden. $2, Blood of the Redeemer by Bellini. $3, The Deposition by Raphael.

1976, Apr. 28

167 G13 ½c multicolored .25 .25
168 G13 1c multicolored .25 .25
169 G13 2c multicolored .25 .25
170 G13 3c multicolored .25 .25
171 G13 35c multicolored .25 .25
172 G13 $3 multicolored .30 .30
Nos. 167-172 (6) 1.55 1.55

Souvenir Sheet

173 G13 $2 multicolored .80 .80

Frigate South Carolina G14

1c, Schooner Lee. 2c, HMS Roebuck. 35c, Andrew Doria. 50c, Sloop Providence. $1, Flagship Alfred. $2, Frigate Confederacy. $3, Cutter Revenge.

1976, May 18

174 G14 ½c multicolored .25 .25
175 G14 1c multicolored .25 .25
176 G14 2c multicolored .25 .25
177 G14 35c multicolored .55 .25
178 G14 50c multicolored .70 .25
179 G14 $1 multicolored 1.25 .25
180 G14 $2 multicolored 1.75 .40
Nos. 174-180 (7) 5.00 1.90

Souvenir Sheet

181 G14 $3 multicolored 2.25 1.25

American Revolution Bicentennial.

Piper Apache G15

Designs: 1c, Beech Twin Bonanza. 2c, de Havilland Twin Otter. 40c, Britten Norman Islander. 50c, de Havilland Heron. $2, Hawker Siddeley Avro 748. $3, BAC 1-11.

1976, June 10

182 G15 ½c multicolored .25 .25
183 G15 1c multicolored .25 .25
184 G15 2c multicolored .25 .25
185 G15 40c multicolored .40 .25
186 G15 50c multicolored .55 .25
187 G15 $2 multicolored 1.25 .30
Nos. 182-187 (6) 2.95 1.55

Souvenir Sheet

188 G15 $3 multicolored 2.25 1.50

Olympic Games, Montreal G16

1976, July 1

189 G16 ½c Cycling .25 .25
190 G16 1c Gymnastics .25 .25
191 G16 2c Hurdling .25 .25
192 G16 35c Shot put .25 .25
193 G16 45c Diving .25 .25
194 G16 75c Sprinting .25 .25
195 G16 $2 Rowing .65 .30
Nos. 189-195 (7) 2.15 1.80

Souvenir Sheet

196 G16 $3 Sailing 1.25 1.00

Virgin and Child by Cima — G17

Christmas: 1c, 2c, The Nativity by Romanino. 35c, Adoration of the Kings by Brueghel. 50c, Madonna and Child by Girolamo. 75c, Adoration of the Magi by Giorgione, horiz. $2, The Adoration of the Kings by Angelico, horiz. $3, The Holy Family by Garofalo.

1976, Oct. 19

197 G17 ½c multicolored .25 .25
198 G17 1c multicolored .25 .25
199 G17 2c multicolored .25 .25
200 G17 35c multicolored .25 .25
201 G17 50c multicolored .25 .25
202 G17 75c multicolored .25 .25
203 G17 $2 multicolored .75 .35
Nos. 197-203 (7) 2.25 1.85

Souvenir Sheet

204 G17 $3 multicolored 1.60 1.60

Alexander Graham Bell, First Telephone G18

Portraits of Bell and Telephone from: 1c, 1895. 2c, 1900. 35c, 1915. 75c, 1920. $1, 1929. $2, 1963. $3, 1976.

1977, Jan. 28

205 G18 ½c multicolored .25 .25
206 G18 1c multicolored .25 .25
207 G18 2c multicolored .25 .25
208 G18 35c multicolored .25 .25
209 G18 75c multicolored .25 .25
210 G18 $1 multicolored .30 .25
211 G18 $2 multicolored .55 .25
Nos. 205-211 (7) 2.10 1.75

Souvenir Sheet

212 G18 $3 multicolored 1.75 1.00

Centenary of 1st telephone conversation, Mar. 10, 1876.

Coronation Coach — G19

Royal Visit — G20

Designs: 50c, Crown of St. Edward. No. 214, Queen entering Abbey. No. 219, Queen and Prince Charles. $4, Queen is crowned. No. 216, Mall on Coronation Night. No. 220, Queen's Flag.

Litho. and Embossed

1977, Feb. 7 ***Perf. 13½***

213 G19 35c multicolored .25 .25
214 G19 $2 multicolored .25 .25
215 G19 $4 multicolored .35 .25
Nos. 213-215 (3) .85 .75

Souvenir Sheet

Perf. 14

216 G19 $5 multicolored .90 .90

Booklet Stamps

Roulette x imperf.

Self-adhesive

217 G20 35c multicolored .25 .25
a. Booklet pane of 6 .75
218 G20 50c multicolored .35 .35
219 G20 $2 multicolored .55 .55
220 G20 $5 multicolored .65 .65
a. Bklt. pane of 3, #218, #219, #220 1.25

Reign of Queen Elizabeth II, 25th anniv.

Nos. 213-215, perf. 11, have different background colors and come from sheetlets of 3 stamps plus label.

For overprints see Nos. 237-240.

Easter — G21

Paintings of the Crucifixion by various artists: ½c, Fra Angelico. 1c, Fra Angelico, diff. 2c, El Greco. 18c, El Greco, diff. 35c, Fra Angelico, diff. 50c, Giottino. $2, da Messina. $3, Fra Angelico, diff.

1977, July 5 Litho. ***Perf. 14***

221 G21 ½c multicolored .25 .25
222 G21 1c multicolored .25 .25
223 G21 2c multicolored .25 .25
224 G21 18c multicolored .25 .25
225 G21 35c multicolored .25 .25

226 G21 50c multicolored .25 .25
227 G21 $2 multicolored .25 .25
Nos. 221-227 (7) 1.75 1.75

Souvenir Sheet

228 G21 $3 multicolored 1.10 .80

Adoration of Jesus by Correggio — G22

Christmas: Paintings of the Madonna and Child by various artists.

1977, Nov. 17 *Perf. 14*

229 G22 ½c shown .25 .25
230 G22 1c Giorgione .25 .25
231 G22 2c Morales .25 .25
232 G22 18c Raphael .25 .25
233 G22 35c Van Dyck .25 .25
234 G22 50c Filippo Lippi .25 .25
235 G22 $2 Filippo Lippi, diff. .25 .25
Nos. 229-235 (7) 1.75 1.75

Souvenir Sheet

236 G22 $3 Ghirlandaio 1.10 .80

Nos. 213-216 Overprinted

1977, Nov. 23 *Perf. 13½*

237 G19 35c multicolored .25 .25
238 G19 $2 multicolored .25 .25
239 G19 $4 multicolored .55 .55
Nos. 237-239 (3) 1.05 1.05

Souvenir Sheet

240 G19 $5 multicolored .80 .80

Caribbean visit of Queen Elizabeth II. Nos. 237-239 exist perf. 11.

Swimming and Life Saving G23

6th Caribbean Jamboree, Kingston, Jamaica, Aug. 5-14: 1c, Hiking. 2c, Ropes and Knots. 22c, Erecting Tent. 35c, Limbo dance. 75c, Cooking. $2, Pioneer bridge building. $3, Sea Scouts' race.

1977, Dec. 7 *Perf. 14*

241 G23 ½c multicolored .25 .25
242 G23 1c multicolored .25 .25
243 G23 2c multicolored .25 .25
244 G23 22c multicolored .25 .25
245 G23 35c multicolored .25 .25
246 G23 75c multicolored .60 .25
247 G23 $3 multicolored 1.10 .40
Nos. 241-247 (7) 2.95 1.90

Souvenir Sheet

248 G23 $2 multicolored 1.75 1.25

Space Shuttle Blast-off G24

Designs: 1c, Booster separation. 2c, External tank separation. 22c, Working in orbit. 50c, Re-entry. $2, Towing in. $3, Landing.

1978, Feb. 3

249 G24 ½c multicolored .25 .25
250 G24 1c multicolored .25 .25
251 G24 2c multicolored .25 .25
252 G24 22c multicolored .25 .25
253 G24 50c multicolored .25 .25
254 G24 $3 multicolored 1.25 .50
Nos. 249-254 (6) 2.50 1.75

Souvenir Sheet

255 G24 $2 multicolored 1.00 1.00

US Space Shuttle.

Alfred Nobel, Medicine Medal G25

Alfred Nobel and: 1c, Physics, Chemistry Medal. 2c, Peace Medal. 22c, Nobel Institute, Oslo. 75c, Peace Prize committee. $2, Peace Medal, Nobel's will. $3, Literature Medal.

1978, Feb. 22

256 G25 ½c multicolored .25 .25
257 G25 1c multicolored .25 .25
258 G25 2c multicolored .25 .25
259 G25 22c multicolored .30 .25
260 G25 75c multicolored .70 .25
261 G25 $3 multicolored 2.25 .40
Nos. 256-261 (6) 4.00 1.65

Souvenir Sheet

262 G25 $2 multicolored 2.50 .90

Nobel Prize awards.

Germany No. C37 — G26

15c, France #C43. 25c, Liechtenstein #C8 specimen. 35c, Panama #257. 50c, Russia #C15. 75c, US #C10. $2, Germany #C57. $3, Spain #C56.

1978, Mar. 15

263 G26 5c multicolored .25 .25
264 G26 15c multicolored .65 .25
265 G26 25c multicolored .25 .25
266 G26 35c multicolored .40 .25
267 G26 50c multicolored .75 .25
268 G26 $3 multicolored 1.90 .40
Nos. 263-268 (6) 4.20 1.65

Souvenir Sheet

269 Sheet of 2 2.50 1.25
a. G26 75c multicolored .50 .30
b. G26 $2 multicolored 1.50 .80

50th anniv. of Lindbergh's solo trans-Atlantic flight. 75th anniv. of 1st Zeppelin flight.

Coronation Ring — G27

Designs: $2, Queen's Orb. $2.50, Imperial State Crown. $5, Queen Elizabeth II.

1978, Apr. 12 *Perf. 14*

270 G27 50c multicolored .25 .25
271 G27 $2 multicolored .25 .25
272 G27 $2.50 multicolored .35 .35
Nos. 270-272 (3) .85 .85

Souvenir Sheet

273 G27 $5 multicolored .80 .80

Nos. 270-272, perf 12, printed in sheets of 3 + label, have different background colors. Issue date; June 2, 1978.

G28

Designs: 18c, Drummer, Royal Regiment of Fusiliers. 50c, Drummer, Royal Anglian Regiment. $5, Drum Major, Queen's Regiment.

1978, Apr. 12 ***Roulette x imperf.***

Booklet Stamps
Self-Adhesive

274 Souvenir booklet 2.50 *3.00*
a. G28 Pane of 6 (3 ea 18c, 50c) .75 .75
b. G28 Pane of 1 ($5) 1.50 1.50

G29

Paintings by Rubens: 5c, Le Chapeau de Paille. 15c, Hector Killed by Achilles. 18c, Helene Fourment and Her Children. 22c, Rubens and Isabella Brandt. 35c, Ildefonso Altarpiece. $2, Self-portrait. $3, Four Negro Heads.

1978, May 18 *Perf. 14*

275 G29 5c multicolored .25 .25
276 G29 15c multicolored .25 .25
277 G29 18c multicolored .25 .25
278 G29 22c multicolored .30 .25
279 G29 35c multicolored .30 .25
280 G29 $3 multicolored 2.40 1.50
Nos. 275-280 (6) 3.75 2.75

Souvenir Sheet

281 G29 $2 multicolored 1.40 1.40

400th birth anniv. of Rubens.

Wright Flyer G30

Designs: 15c, Orville Wright, vert. 18c, Wilbur Wright, vert. 25c, 35c, 75c, $2, $3, various Wright airplanes.

1978, Aug. 10

282 G30 5c multicolored .25 .25
283 G30 15c multicolored .25 .25
284 G30 18c multicolored .25 .25
285 G30 25c multicolored .25 .25
286 G30 35c multicolored .25 .25
287 G30 75c multicolored .25 .25
288 G30 $3 multicolored 1.00 1.00
Nos. 282-288 (7) 2.50 2.50

Souvenir Sheet

289 G30 $2 multicolored 1.75 1.75

75th anniv. of first powered flight by the Wright brothers, Dec. 17, 1903.

Audubon's Shearwater — G31

10c, Northern ring-necked plover. 18c, Garnet-throated hummingbird. 22c, Black-bellied tree duck. 40c, Purple martin. $1, Yellow-billied tropic bird. $2, Long-billed curlew. $5, Snowy egret.

1978, Sept. 28

290 G31 5c multi *1.00* *.25*
291 G31 10c multi *1.25* *.25*
292 G31 18c multi, horiz. *1.50* *.30*
293 G31 22c multi, horiz. *2.00* *.30*
294 G31 40c multi, horiz. *3.00* *.50*
295 G31 $1 multi *4.25* *.60*
296 G31 $2 multi *5.75* *1.10*
Nos. 290-296 (7) *18.75* *3.30*

Souvenir Sheet

297 G31 $5 multicolored *17.00* *17.00*

Players, Soccer Ball — G32

Soccer players in action.

1978, Nov. 2

298 G32 15c multicolored .25 .25
299 G32 35c multicolored .25 .25
300 G32 50c multicolored .25 .25
301 G32 $3 multicolored .65 .65
Nos. 298-301 (4) 1.40 1.40

Souvenir Sheet

302 G32 $2 multicolored 1.50 1.50

World Cup Soccer Championships, Argentina, June 1-25.

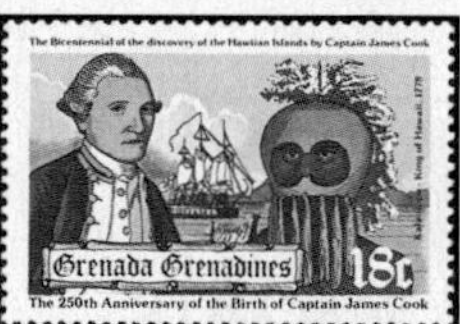

Captain Cook, Kalaniopu (King of Hawaii), 1778 G33

22c, Cook, Hawaiian native. 50c, Cook, death scene, 2/14/79. $3, Cook and offering ceremony. $4, Cook, HMS Resolution.

1978, Dec. 13

303 G33 18c multicolored .50 .25
304 G33 22c multicolored .65 .25
305 G33 50c multicolored 1.10 .50
306 G33 $3 multicolored 2.75 2.00
Nos. 303-306 (4) 5.00 3.00

Souvenir Sheet

307 G33 $4 multicolored 3.00 3.00

250th birth anniv. of Captain James Cook and Bicentennial of his discovery of the Hawaiian Islands.

Durer Paintings — G34

Christmas: 40c, The Virgin at Prayer. 60c, Dresden Alterpiece. 90c, Madonna and Child. $2, Madonna and Child. $4, Salvator Mundi.

1978, Dec 20

308 G34 40c multicolored .25 .25
309 G34 60c multicolored .25 .25
310 G34 90c multicolored .25 .25
311 G34 $2 multicolored .70 .70
Nos. 308-311 (4) 1.45 1.45

Souvenir Sheet

312 G34 $4 multicolored 1.40 1.40

Strelitzia Reginae — G35

40c, Euphorbia pulcherrima. $1, Heliconia humilis. $3, Thunbergia alata. $2, Bougainvillea glabra.

1979, Feb. 15

313 G35 22c shown .25 .25
314 G35 40c multicolored .40 .40
315 G35 $1 multicolored .80 .45
316 G35 $3 multicolored 1.40 .80
Nos. 313-316 (4) 2.85 1.90

Souvenir Sheet

317 G35 $2 multicolored 2.10 2.10

Children with Pig G36

International Year of the Child: 50c, Children with donkey. $1, Children with goats. $3, Children fishing. $4, Child with coconuts.

1979, Mar. 22

318 G36 18c multicolored .25 .25
319 G36 50c multicolored .25 .25
320 G36 $1 multicolored .40 .40
321 G36 $3 multicolored .60 .60
Nos. 318-321 (4) 1.50 1.50

Souvenir Sheet

322 G36 $4 multicolored 1.00 1.00

150th Birth Anniv. of Jules Verne G37

Designs: 18c, 20,000 Leagues Under the Sea. 38c, From the Earth to the Moon. 75c, From the Earth to the Moon, diff. $3, Five Weeks in a Balloon. $4, Around the World in 80 Days.

1979, Apr. 20

323 G37 18c multicolored .65 .25
324 G37 38c multicolored .75 .25
325 G37 75c multicolored .90 .40
326 G37 $3 multicolored 1.75 1.75
Nos. 323-326 (4) 4.05 2.65

Souvenir Sheet

327 G37 $4 multicolored 3.00 3.00

Sir Rowland Hill, Mail Truck G38

Designs: $1, Ocean liner. $2, Mail train. $3, Concorde. $4, Sir Rowland Hill.

1979, July 30 *Perf. 14*

328 G38 15c multicolored .25 .25
329 G38 $1 multicolored .25 .25
330 G38 $2 multicolored .55 .55
331 G38 $3 multicolored .70 .70
Nos. 328-331 (4) 1.75 1.75

Souvenir Sheet

332 G38 $4 multicolored 1.25 1.25

Death centenary of Sir Rowland Hill.
Nos. 328-331, perf. 12, printed in sheets of 5 + label, have different colored backgrounds.

Virgin and Child Enthroned (Byzantine Era, 11th Cent.) — G39

Christmas sculptures: 25c, Presentation in the Temple by Beauneveu c. 1390. 30c, Flight to Egypt (Utrecht, c. 1510). 40c, Madonna and Child by della Quercia, 1047-48. 90c, Madonna della Mela by della Robbia, c. 1455. $1, Madonna and Child by Rossellino, 1461-66. $2, Madonna (Antwerp, 1700). $4, Virgin (Krumau, c. 1390).

1979, Oct. 23 *Perf. 14*

333 G39 6c multicolored .25 .25
334 G39 25c multicolored .25 .25
335 G39 30c multicolored .25 .25
336 G39 40c multicolored .25 .25
337 G39 90c multicolored .25 .25
338 G39 $1 multicolored .25 .25
339 G39 $2 multicolored .25 .25
Nos. 333-339 (7) 1.75 1.75

Souvenir Sheet

340 G39 $4 multicolored 1.00 1.00

Great Hammerhead Shark — G40

Designs: 45c, Banded butterflyfish. 50c, Permit. 60c, Threaded turban. 70c, Milk conch. 75c, Great blue heron. 90c, Colored Atlantic natica. $1, Red footed booby. $2.50, Collared plover.

1979, Nov. 9

341 G40 40c multicolored .50 .50
342 G40 45c multicolored .55 .55
343 G40 50c multicolored .65 .65
344 G40 60c multicolored .75 .75
345 G40 70c multicolored .90 .90
346 G40 75c multicolored 1.50 1.00
347 G40 90c multicolored 1.30 1.30
348 G40 $1 multicolored 1.90 1.90
Nos. 341-348 (8) 8.05 7.55

Souvenir Sheet

349 G40 $2.50 multicolored 2.50 2.50

Doctor Goofy G41

International Year of the Child: 1c, Admiral Mickey Mouse. 2c, Fireman Goofy. 3c, Nurse Minnie Mouse. 4c, Drum Major Mickey Mouse. 5c, Policeman Donald Duck. 10c, Pilot Donald Duck. $2, Mailman Goofy, horiz. $2.50 Engineer Donald Duck, horiz. $3, Fireman Mickey Mouse.

1979, Dec. 12 *Perf. 11*

350 G41 ½c multicolored .25 .25
351 G41 1c multicolored .25 .25
352 G41 2c multicolored .25 .25
353 G41 3c multicolored .25 .25
354 G41 4c multicolored .25 .25
355 G41 5c multicolored .25 .25
356 G41 10c multicolored .25 .25
357 G41 $2 multicolored 2.50 2.50
358 G41 $2.50 multicolored 2.75 2.75
Nos. 350-358 (9) 7.00 7.00

Souvenir Sheet

Perf. 13½

359 G41 $3 multicolored 3.50 3.50

Nos. 114, 117-128 Overprinted

1980, Mar. 10 *Perf. 15*

360 A85 6c multicolored .25 .25
361 A85 12c multicolored .25 .25
362 A85 15c multicolored .25 .25
363 A85 20c multicolored .25 .25
364 A85 25c multicolored .25 .25
365 A85 35c multicolored .25 .25
366 A85 50c multicolored .30 .35

Perf. 13½x14

367 A85 75c multicolored .35 .40
368 A85 $1 multicolored .45 .60
369 A85 $2 multicolored .70 .90
370 A85 $3 multicolored 1.25 1.60
371 A85 $5 multicolored 1.75 2.40
372 A85 $10 multicolored 3.00 3.75
Nos. 360-372 (13) 9.30 11.50

Classroom G42

Rotary Intl., 75th anniv.: 30c, Rotary emblem, people. 60c, Rotary executive making contribution to physician. $3, Young patients, nurses. $4, Paul P. Harris, founder of Rotary.

1980, Mar. 12 *Perf. 14*

373 G42 6c multicolored .25 .25
374 G42 30c multicolored .25 .25
375 G42 60c multicolored .45 .45
376 G42 $3 multicolored 1.90 1.60
Nos. 373-376 (4) 2.85 2.55

Souvenir Sheet

377 G42 $4 multicolored 1.25 1.25

Yellow-bellied Seedeater — G43

40c, Blue-hooded euphonia. 90c, Yellow warbler. $2, Tropical mockingbird. $3, Barn owl.

1980, Apr. 14

378 G43 25c multicolored .65 .25
379 G43 40c multicolored .70 .25
380 G43 90c multicolored 1.50 .85
381 G43 $2 multicolored 2.00 1.60
Nos. 378-381 (4) 4.85 2.95

Souvenir Sheet

382 G43 $3 multicolored 5.50 5.50

Running G44

Designs: 40c, Soccer. 90c, Boxing. $2, Wrestling. $4, Runners in silhouette.

1980, Apr. 21

383 G44 30c multicolored .25 .25
384 G44 40c multicolored .25 .25
385 G44 90c multicolored .40 .40
386 G44 $2 multicolored .85 .85
Nos. 383-386 (4) 1.75 1.75

Souvenir Sheet

387 G44 $4 multicolored .90 .90

22nd Summer Olympic Games, Moscow, July 19-Aug. 3.

Nos. 328-331 Overprinted

1980, May 6 *Perf. 12*

388 G38 15c multicolored .25 .25
389 G38 $1 multicolored 1.10 .50
390 G38 $2 multicolored 2.25 1.75
391 G38 $3 multicolored 3.75 3.00
Nos. 388-391 (4) 7.35 5.50

Issued in sheets of 5 + label.

Longspine Squirrelfish — G45

Designs: 1c, Blue chromis. 2c, Foureye butterflyfish. 4c, Sergeant major. 5c, Yellowtail snapper. 6c, Mutton snapper. 10c, Cocoa damselfish. 12c, Royal gramma. 15c, Cherubfish. 20c, Blackbar soldierfish. 25c, Comb grouper. 30c, Longsnout butterflyfish. 40c, Pudding wife. 50c, Midnight parrotfish. 90c, Redspotted hawkfish. $1, Hogfish. $3, Beau gregory. $5, Rock beauty. $10, Barred hamlet.

1980, Aug. 6 *Perf. 14*

No imprint date below design

392 G45 ½c multicolored .25 .25
a. Perf. 12, inscribed 1982 10.00 10.00
393 G45 1c multicolored .25 .25
394 G45 2c multicolored .25 .25
395 G45 4c multicolored .25 .25
396 G45 5c multicolored .25 .25
397 G45 6c multicolored .25 .25
398 G45 10c multicolored .25 .25
a. Inscribed "1984" .50 .50
399 G45 12c multicolored .25 .25
400 G45 15c multicolored .25 .25
401 G45 20c multicolored .25 .25
a. Inscribed "1987" 3.25 3.25
402 G45 25c multicolored .25 .25
403 G45 30c multicolored .25 .25
404 G45 40c multicolored .25 .25
405 G45 50c multicolored .30 .35
406 G45 90c multicolored .45 .50
407 G45 $1 multicolored .55 .60
408 G45 $3 multicolored 1.40 1.75
409 G45 $5 multicolored 1.75 2.25
410 G45 $10 multicolored 3.00 3.75
Nos. 392-410 (19) 10.70 12.45

Bambi with Mother — G46

Various scenes from Walt Disney's Bambi.

1980, Oct. 7 *Perf. 11*

411 G46 ½c multicolored .25 .25
412 G46 1c multicolored .25 .25
413 G46 2c multicolored .25 .25
414 G46 3c multicolored .25 .25
415 G46 4c multicolored .25 .25
416 G46 5c multicolored .25 .25
417 G46 10c multicolored .25 .25

418 G46 $2.50 multicolored 1.50 1.50
419 G46 $3 multicolored 1.50 1.50
Nos. 411-419 (9) 4.75 4.75

Souvenir Sheet

420 G46 $4 multicolored 3.00 3.00

Christmas.

The Unicorn in Captivity by Unknown 15th Cent. Artist — G47

Designs: 10c, The Fighting Temeraire by J.M.W. Turner. 25c, Sunday Afternoon on the Ile De La Grande-Jatte by Seurat. 90c, Max Schmitt in a Single Scull by Eakins. $2, The Burial of the Count of Orgaz by El Greco. $3, George Washington by Stuart. $5, Kaiser Karl the Great by Durer. Nos. 425-427 are vert.

1981, Jan. 25 *Perf. 14*

421 G47 6c multicolored .25 .25
422 G47 10c multicolored .25 .25
423 G47 25c multicolored .25 .25
424 G47 90c multicolored .50 .50
425 G47 $2 multicolored .90 .90
426 G47 $3 multicolored 1.25 1.25
Nos. 421-426 (6) 3.40 3.40

Souvenir Sheet

427 G47 $5 multicolored 2.75 2.75

Disney Type of 1979

50th anniv. of Pluto character: $2, Mickey Mouse, Pluto and birthday cake. $4, Pluto.

1981, Jan. 26

428 A135a $2 multicolored 1.10 1.10

Souvenir Sheet

429 A135a $4 multicolored 2.50 2.50

No. 428 issued in sheets of 8.

Chip Coloring Easter Eggs — G48

Easter: Various Disney characters coloring Easter eggs.

1981, Apr. 14 *Perf. 11*

430 G48 35c multicolored .25 .25
431 G48 40c multicolored .25 .25
432 G48 $2 multicolored .90 .90
433 G48 $2.50 multicolored 1.40 1.40
Nos. 430-433 (4) 2.80 2.80

Souvenir Sheet

Perf. 14

434 G48 $4 multicolored 2.75 2.75

Bust of a Woman — G49

Paintings by Pablo Picasso (1881-1973): 40c, Woman (Study for Les Demoiselles d'Avignon). 90c, Nude with Raised Arms (The Dancer of Avignon). $4, The Dryad. $5, Les Demoiselles d'Avignon.

1981, May 5 *Perf. 14*

435 G49 6c multicolored .30 .30
436 G49 40c multicolored .30 .30
437 G49 90c multicolored .45 .45
438 G49 $4 multicolored 2.25 2.25

Size: 103x128mm

Imperf

439 G49 $5 multicolored 3.00 3.00
Nos. 435-439 (5) 6.30 6.30

Common Design Types pictured following the introduction.

Royal Wedding Issue

Common Design Type

1981, June 16 *Perf. 15*

440 CD331a 40c Couple .25 .25
441 CD331a $2 Balmoral Castle .25 .25
442 CD331a $4 Charles .45 .45
Nos. 440-442 (3) .95 .95

Souvenir Sheet

443 CD331a $5 Royal Coach 1.40 1.40

Sheets of 5 plus label contain 30c (like No. 440), 40c (like No. 441), or $4 in changed colors, perf 15x14½.

Diana — G50

$1, Diana. $2, Charles. $5, Diana and Charles.

Booklet Stamps

Roulette x imperf. (#444a), Imperf. (#444b)

1981, June 16 **Self-Adhesive**

444 G50 Souvenir Booklet 4.00
a. Pane of 6 (3 each $1, $2) 2.25
b. Pane of 1, $5 1.75

Royal wedding.

Amy Johnson, Pilot of 1st Britain-Australia Solo Flight by a Woman, May 1930 — G51

Decade for Women: 70c, Mme. la Baronne de Laroche, 1st qualified aviatrix, May 1910. $1.10, Ruth Nichols. $3, Amelia Earhart, 1st Atlantic solo flight by woman, May 1932. $5, Valentina Tereshkova, 1st woman in space, June 1963.

1981, Oct. 13 *Perf. 14*

445 G51 30c multicolored .45 .45
446 G51 70c multicolored .70 .70
447 G51 $1.10 multicolored .85 .85
448 G51 $3 multicolored 1.75 1.75
Nos. 445-448 (4) 3.75 3.75

Souvenir Sheet

449 G51 $5 multicolored 2.00 2.00

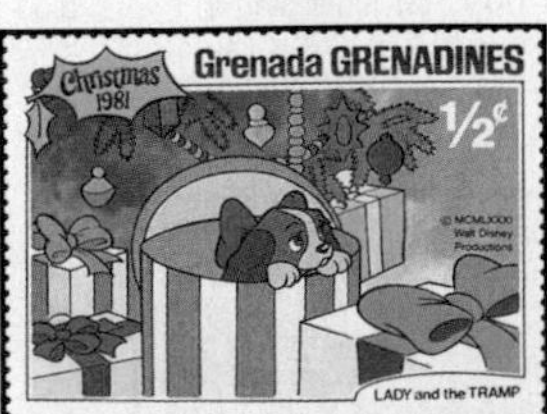

Lady and the Tramp — G52

Christmas. Various scenes from Walt Disney's film Lady and the Tramp.

1981, Nov. 2

450 G52 ½c multicolored .25 .25
451 G52 1c multicolored .25 .25
452 G52 2c multicolored .25 .25
453 G52 3c multicolored .25 .25
454 G52 4c multicolored .25 .25
455 G52 5c multicolored .25 .25
456 G52 10c multicolored .25 .25
457 G52 $2.50 multicolored 3.50 1.75
458 G52 $3 multicolored 3.50 2.25
Nos. 450-458 (9) 8.75 5.75

Souvenir Sheet

459 G52 $5 multicolored 7.00 6.00

747 Carrying Space Shuttle — G53

Designs: 40c, Re-entry. $1.10, External tank separation. $3, Touchdown. $5, Lift-off.

1981, Nov. 2 *Perf. 14½*

460 G53 10c multicolored .40 .25
461 G53 40c multicolored .75 .30
462 G53 $1.10 multicolored 1.40 .80
463 G53 $3 multicolored 2.25 1.50
Nos. 460-463 (4) 4.80 2.85

Souvenir Sheet

464 G53 $5 multicolored 5.00 4.00

Soccer Player — G54

World Cup Soccer Championships, Spain, 1982: Soccer players in various positions.

1981, Nov. 30 *Perf. 14*

465 G54 20c multicolored .25 .25
466 G54 40c multicolored .25 .25
467 G54 $1 multicolored .45 .30
468 G54 $2 multicolored .90 .60
Nos. 465-468 (4) 1.85 1.40

Souvenir Sheet

469 G54 $4 multicolored 1.75 1.50

Stagecoach, Mail Truck — G55

UPU Membership Cent.: 40c, UPU Emblem. $2.50, Sailing ship, ocean liner. $4, Biplane, Concorde. $5, Steam train, high-speed trains.

1982, Jan. 13 *Perf. 15*

470 G55 30c multicolored .40 .25
471 G55 40c multicolored .40 .25
472 G55 $2.50 multicolored 1.75 1.00
473 G55 $4 multicolored 3.00 2.00
Nos. 470-473 (4) 5.55 3.50

Souvenir Sheet

474 G55 $5 multicolored 4.75 4.25

Sprinting G56

90c, Sea scouts sailing. $1.10, Hand crafts. $3, Animal husbandry. $5, Music around campfire.

1982, Feb. 19

475 G56 6c multicolored .25 .25
476 G56 90c multicolored .70 .60
477 G56 $1.10 multicolored .90 .70
478 G56 $3 multicolored 1.90 1.90
Nos. 475-478 (4) 3.75 3.45

Souvenir Sheet

479 G56 $5 multicolored 3.00 3.00

Boy Scouts, 75th anniv. Lord Baden-Powell, 125th birth anniv.

White Peacock G57

Designs: 40c, St. Vincent long-tail skipper. $1.10, Painted lady. $3, Orion. $5, Silver spot.

1982, Mar. 24 *Perf. 14*

480 G57 30c multicolored 1.25 .60
481 G57 40c multicolored 1.25 .85
482 G57 $1.10 multicolored 3.00 2.25
483 G57 $3 multicolored 5.25 5.25
Nos. 480-483 (4) 10.75 8.95

Souvenir Sheet

484 G57 $5 multicolored 6.50 6.50

Princess Diana Issue

Common Design Type

1982, July 1 *Perf. 14½x14*

485 CD332 50c Blenheim Palace 1.25 1.25
486 CD332 60c Like 50c .75 .75
487 CD332 $1 Couple in field 1.75 1.75
488 CD332 $2 Like $1 1.90 1.90
489 CD332 $3 Diana 2.50 2.50
490 CD332 $4 Like $3 2.50 2.50
Nos. 485-490 (6) 10.65 10.65

Souvenir Sheet

491 CD332 $5 Diana, diff. 7.00 7.00

50c, $1, $3 issued in sheets of 5 plus label.

Overprinted

1982, Aug. 30

492 CD332 50c multicolored .75 .75
493 CD332 60c multicolored .80 .80
494 CD332 $1 multicolored 1.00 1.00
495 CD332 $2 multicolored 1.50 1.50
496 CD332 $3 multicolored 1.90 1.90
497 CD332 $4 multicolored 2.25 2.25
Nos. 492-497 (6) 8.20 8.20

Souvenir Sheet

498 CD332 $5 multicolored 5.25 5.25

Birth of Prince William of Wales, June 21.

Roosevelt Type of 1982

Designs: 30c, New Deal soil conservation. 40c, Roosevelt, George Washington Carver. 70c, Civilian Conservation Corps. $3, Roosevelt, Liberian Pres. Edwin Barclay. $5, Roosevelt addressing Howard University.

1982, July 27 *Perf. 14*

499 A154 30c multicolored .50 .25
500 A154 40c multicolored .50 .25
501 A154 70c multicolored .60 .30
502 A154 $3 multicolored 1.40 1.40
Nos. 499-502 (4) 3.00 2.20

Souvenir Sheet

503 A154 $5 multicolored 3.25 3.25

Presentation of Christ in the Temple — G58

Easter Paintings by Rembrandt: 60c, Descent from the Cross. $2, Raising of the Cross. $4, Resurrection of Christ. $5, The Risen Christ.

1982, Sept. 2 *Perf. 14½*
504 G58 30c multicolored .50 .25
505 G58 60c multicolored .60 .25
506 G58 $2 multicolored .80 .80
507 G58 $4 multicolored 1.50 1.50
Nos. 504-507 (4) 3.40 2.80

Souvenir Sheet

508 G58 $5 multicolored 3.50 3.50

G59

1982, Oct. 4 *Perf. 15*
509 G59 10c Santa Fe .65 .25
510 G59 40c Mistral .90 .30
511 G59 70c Rheingold 1.00 .65
512 G59 $1 ET 403 1.25 .70
513 G59 $1.10 Mallard 1.50 .75
514 G59 $2 Tokaido 1.75 1.25
Nos. 509-514 (6) 7.05 3.90

Souvenir Sheet

515 G59 $5 Settebello 3.25 3.25

Soccer Players G60

Italy, World Cup Soccer Champions: $4, Soccer players, diff. $5, Map of Italy.

1982, Dec. 2 *Perf. 14*
516 G60 60c multicolored 1.00 .45
517 G60 $4 multicolored 2.75 2.75

Souvenir Sheet

518 G60 $5 multicolored 2.50 2.50

Christmas Type of 1982

Scenes from Walt Disney's film The Rescuers.

1982, Dec. 14 *Perf. 13½*
519 A157 ½c multicolored .25 .25
520 A157 1c multicolored .25 .25
521 A157 2c multicolored .25 .25
522 A157 3c multicolored .25 .25
523 A157 4c multicolored .25 .25
524 A157 5c multicolored .25 .25
525 A157 10c multicolored .25 .25
526 A157 $2.50 multicolored 3.00 3.25
527 A157 $3 multicolored 3.00 3.25
Nos. 519-527 (9) 7.75 8.25

Souvenir Sheet

528 A157 $5 multicolored 6.75 6.75

Whales Type of 1982

Designs: 10c, Pilot whale. 60c, Dall porpoise. $1.10, Humpback whale. $3, Bowfin whale. $5, Spotted dolphin.

1983, Jan. 10 *Perf. 14*
529 A159 10c multicolored 1.25 1.10
530 A159 60c multicolored 3.00 2.75
531 A159 $1.10 multicolored 5.25 4.50
532 A159 $3 multicolored 8.50 7.00
Nos. 529-532 (4) 18.00 15.35

Souvenir Sheet

533 A159 $5 multicolored 9.00 7.50

Raphael Paintings Type

Designs: 25c, David and Goliath. 30c, David Sees Bathsheba. 90c, Triumph of David. $4, Anointing of Solomon. $5, Anointing of David.

1983, Feb. 15 *Perf. 14*
534 A160 25c multicolored .25 .25
535 A160 30c multicolored .25 .25
536 A160 90c multicolored .35 .35
537 A160 $4 multicolored .80 .80
Nos. 534-537 (4) 1.65 1.65

Souvenir Sheet

538 A160 $5 multicolored 1.25 1.25

Audio and Video Communication — G61

World Communications Year: 60c, Ambulance. $1.10, Helicopters. $3, Satellite. $5, Diver, bottle-nose porpoise.

1983, Apr. 7 *Perf. 14*
539 G61 30c multicolored .25 .25
540 G61 60c multicolored .45 .45
541 G61 $1.10 multicolored .80 .80
542 G61 $3 blk, red & blue 1.50 1.50
Nos. 539-542 (4) 3.00 3.00

Souvenir Sheet

543 G61 $5 multicolored 3.50 3.00

For overprints see Nos. 629-630A.

Car Type of 1983

Designs: 10c, 1931 Chrysler Imperial Roadster. 30c, 1925 Doble Steam Car. 40c, 1965 Ford Mustang. 60c, 1930 Packard Tourer. 70c, 1913 Mercer Raceabout. 90c, 1963 Corvette Stingray. $1.10, 1935 Auburn 851 Supercharger Speedster. $2.50, 1933 Pierce Arrow Silver Arrow. $3, 1929 Duesenberg Dual Cowl Phaeton. $4, 1928 Mercedes-Benz SSK. $5, 1923 McFarlan Knickerbocker Cabriolet.

1983, May 4 *Perf. 14½*
544 A163 10c multicolored .25 .25
545 A163 30c multicolored .35 .35
546 A163 40c multicolored .35 .35
547 A163 60c multicolored .50 .50
548 A163 70c multicolored .50 .50
549 A163 90c multicolored .50 .50
550 A163 $1.10 multicolored .50 .50
551 A163 $2.50 multicolored .80 .80
552 A163 $3 multicolored .90 .90
553 A163 $4 multicolored .90 .90
Nos. 544-553 (10) 5.55 5.55

Souvenir Sheet

554 A163 $5 multicolored 3.25 3.25

Anniversary of Manned Flight Type

Designs: 40c, Short Solent flying boat. 70c, Curtiss R3C-2 seaplane. 90c, Hawker Nimrod biplane. $4, Montgolfier balloon. $5, Victoria Luise airship.

1983, July 18 *Perf. 14*
555 A164 40c multicolored 1.00 .25
556 A164 70c multicolored 1.25 .50
557 A164 90c multicolored 1.50 1.50
558 A164 $4 multicolored 3.75 3.25
Nos. 555-558 (4) 7.50 5.50

Souvenir Sheet

559 A164 $5 multicolored 3.50 3.50

Christmas G62

Walt Disney characters in scenes from "Jingle Bells."

1983, Nov. 7 *Perf. 11*
560 G62 ½c multicolored .25 .25
561 G62 1c multicolored .25 .25
562 G62 2c multicolored .25 .25
563 G62 3c multicolored .25 .25
564 G62 4c multicolored .25 .25
565 G62 5c multicolored .25 .25
566 G62 10c multicolored .25 .25
567 G62 $2.50 multicolored 5.25 5.25
568 G62 $3 multicolored 5.75 5.75
Nos. 560-568 (9) 12.75 12.75

Souvenir Sheet

Perf. 13½

569 G62 $5 multicolored 11.00 11.00

G63

1984, Jan. 9 *Perf. 14*
570 G63 30c Weightlifting .25 .25
571 G63 60c Gymnastics .55 .50
572 G63 70c Archery .75 .60
573 G63 $4 Sailing 2.25 2.25
Nos. 570-573 (4) 3.80 3.60

Souvenir Sheet

574 G63 $5 Basketball 3.50 3.50

Olympic Games, Los Angeles.

G64

Designs: 15c, Frangipani. 40c, Dwarf poinciana. 70c, Walking iris. $4, Lady's slipper. $5, Brazilian glory vine.

1984, Apr. 9 *Perf. 15*
575 G64 15c multicolored .25 .25
576 G64 40c multicolored .30 .30
577 G64 70c multicolored .75 .55
578 G64 $4 multicolored 2.75 2.75
Nos. 575-578 (4) 4.05 3.85

Souvenir Sheet

579 G64 $5 multicolored 3.75 3.75

For overprints see Nos. 598-600.

Easter G65

Walt Disney characters with Easter hats.

1984, May 1 *Perf. 11*
580 G65 ½c multicolored .25 .25
581 G65 1c multicolored .25 .25
582 G65 2c multicolored .25 .25
583 G65 3c multicolored .25 .25
584 G65 4c multicolored .25 .25
585 G65 5c multicolored .25 .25
586 G65 10c multicolored .25 .25
587 G65 $2 multicolored 1.90 1.90
588 G65 $4 multicolored 2.75 2.75
Nos. 580-588 (9) 6.40 6.40

Souvenir Sheet

589 G65 $5 multicolored 5.25 5.25

Bobolink G66

Birds: 50c, Eastern kingbird. 60c, Barn swallow. 70c, Yellow warbler. $1, Rose-breasted grosbeak. $1.10, Yellowthroat. $2, Catbird. $5, Fork-tailed flycatcher.

1984, May 21 *Perf. 14*
590 G66 40c multicolored 2.50 2.00
591 G66 50c multicolored 2.90 2.25
592 G66 60c multicolored 3.25 2.90
593 G66 70c multicolored 3.25 2.90
594 G66 $1 multicolored 3.50 3.50
595 G66 $1.10 multicolored 4.00 4.00
596 G66 $2 multicolored 5.00 5.00
Nos. 590-596 (7) 24.40 22.55

Souvenir Sheet

597 G66 $5 multicolored 11.00 11.00

Nos. 577-579 Overprinted

1984, June 19 *Perf. 15*
598 G64 70c multicolored 1.10 1.10
599 G64 $4 multicolored 5.00 5.00

Souvenir Sheet

600 G64 $5 multicolored 4.50 4.50

Geeststar G67

60c, Daphne. $1.10, Schooner Southwind. $4, Oceanic.
$5, Privateer.

1984, July 16 *Perf. 15*
601 G67 30c shown .85 .85
602 G67 60c multicolored 1.10 1.10
603 G67 $1.10 multicolored 1.40 1.40
604 G67 $4 multicolored 2.40 2.40
Nos. 601-604 (4) 5.75 5.75

Souvenir Sheet

605 G67 $5 multicolored 5.25 5.25

Correggio Paintings Type

Designs: 10c, The Hunt — Blowing the Horn. 30c, St. John the Evangelist, horiz. 90c, The Hunt — The Deer's Head. $4, The Virgin Crowned by Christ, horiz. $5, Martyrdom of the Four Saints.

1984, Aug. 22 *Perf. 14*
606 A171a 10c multicolored .25 .25
607 A171a 30c multicolored .25 .25
608 A171a 90c multicolored .70 .70
609 A171a $4 multicolored 2.50 2.50
Nos. 606-609 (4) 3.70 3.70

Souvenir Sheet

610 A171a $5 multicolored 3.50 3.50

The Song of the Dog — G68

Paintings by Edgar Degas: 70c, Cafe-Concert. $1.10, The Orchestra of the Opera. $3, The Dance Lesson. $5, Madame Camus at the Piano.

1984, Aug. 22
611 G68 25c multicolored .45 .25
612 G68 70c multicolored .75 .60
613 G68 $1.10 multicolored 1.60 1.60
614 G68 $3 multicolored 3.00 3.00
Nos. 611-614 (4) 5.80 5.45

Souvenir Sheet

615 G68 $5 multicolored 4.00 4.00

150th birth anniv. of Degas.

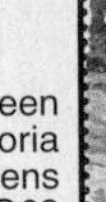

Queen Victoria Gardens G69

$4, Ayers Rock. $5, Yarra River, Melbourne.

1984, Sept. 21

616 G69 $1.10 multicolored .85 .85
617 G69 $4 multicolored 3.25 3.25

Souvenir Sheet

618 G69 $5 multicolored 4.00 4.00

AUSIPEX International Stamp Exhibition, Melbourne, Australia.

Colonel Steven's Model, "1825" G70

Locomotives: 50c, Royal George, 1827. 60c, Stourbridge Lion, 1829. 70c, Liverpool, 1830. 90c, South Carolina, 1832. $1.10, Monster, 1836. $2, Lafayette, 1837. $4, Lion, 1838.

No. 627, Sequin's Engine, 1829. No. 628, Der Adler, 1835.

1984, Oct. 3 ***Perf. 15***

619 G70 20c multicolored .80 .30
620 G70 50c multicolored 1.00 .60
621 G70 60c multicolored 1.10 .75
622 G70 70c multicolored 1.25 1.25
623 G70 90c multicolored 1.40 1.40
624 G70 $1.10 multicolored 1.40 1.40
625 G70 $2 multicolored 1.75 1.75
626 G70 $4 multicolored 2.25 2.25
Nos. 619-626 (8) 10.95 9.70

Souvenir Sheets

627 G70 $5 multicolored 4.00 4.00
628 G70 $5 multicolored 4.00 4.00

Nos. 539, 541, 543 Overprinted

1984, Oct. 28 ***Perf. 14***

629 G61 30c multicolored .35 .25
630 G61 $1.10 multicolored 1.25 .95

Souvenir Sheet

630A G61 $5 multicolored 6.25 5.25

Opening of the Point Saline International Airport. No. 630A is overprinted in the margin.

Christmas Type of 1984

Scenes from various Donald Duck movies.

1984, Nov. 26 ***Perf. 13½x14***

631 A173 45c multicolored .95 .55
632 A173 60c multicolored 1.10 .75
633 A173 90c multicolored 1.50 1.25
634 A173 $2 multi, perf. 12 2.25 2.25
635 A173 $4 multicolored 4.50 4.50
Nos. 631-635 (5) 10.30 9.30

Souvenir Sheet

636 A173 $5 multicolored 6.50 6.00

No. 634 issued in sheets of 8.

Audubon Type of 1985

Designs: 50c, Blue-winged teal. 90c, White ibis. $1.10, Swallow-tailed kite. $3, Common Gallinule. $5, Mangrove cuckoo.

1985, Feb. 11 ***Perf. 14***

637 A174 50c multicolored 2.25 .90
638 A174 90c multicolored 2.75 1.60
639 A174 $1.10 multicolored 3.50 2.10
640 A174 $3 multicolored 4.50 4.50
Nos. 637-640 (4) 13.00 9.10

Souvenir Sheet

641 A174 $5 multicolored 6.00 6.00

See Nos. 732-736.

Motorcycle Centenary — G71

Anniv. emblem and: 30c, Kawasaki 750, 1972. 60c, Honda Goldwing GL1000, 1974, horiz. 70c, Kawasaki Z650, 1976, horiz. $4, Honda CBX, 1977. $5, BMW R100RS, 1978.

1985, Mar. 11

642 G71 30c multicolored .75 .50
643 G71 60c multicolored 1.00 1.00
644 G71 70c multicolored 1.25 1.25
645 G71 $4 multicolored 4.50 4.50
Nos. 642-645 (4) 7.50 7.25

Souvenir Sheet

646 G71 $5 multicolored 5.75 5.75

Intl. Youth Year G72

Designs: 50c, Folding bandages (health). 70c, Diver, turtle (environment). $1.10, Sailing (leisure). $3, Boys playing chess (education). $5, Hands touching globe.

1985, Apr. 15

647 G72 50c multicolored .65 .45
648 G72 70c multicolored 1.00 .85
649 G72 $1.10 multicolored 1.50 1.40
650 G72 $3 multicolored 7.50 7.50
Nos. 647-650 (4) 10.65 10.20

Souvenir Sheet

651 G72 $5 multicolored 4.75 4.75

Intl. Civil Aviation Org., 40th Anniv. G73

Designs: 5c, Lockheed Lodestar. 70c, Avro 748 Turboprop. $1.10, Boeing 727. $4, Boeing 707. $5, Pilatus Britten-Norman Islander.

1985, Apr. 30

652 G73 5c multicolored .50 .25
653 G73 70c multicolored 2.10 .70
654 G73 $1.10 multicolored 2.50 1.10
655 G73 $4 multicolored 4.25 3.25
Nos. 652-655 (4) 9.35 5.30

Souvenir Sheet

656 G73 $5 multicolored 5.50 5.00

Girl Guides Type

Designs: 30c, Lady Baden-Powell, Guide leaders. 50c, Botany field trip. 70c, Making camp, vert. $4, Sailing, vert. $5, Lord and Lady Baden-Powell, vert.

1985, May 30

657 A176 30c multicolored .50 .25
658 A176 50c multicolored 1.25 .35
659 A176 70c multicolored 1.25 .55
660 A176 $4 multicolored 5.00 2.75
Nos. 657-660 (4) 8.00 3.90

Souvenir Sheet

661 A176 $5 multicolored 5.50 5.50

Grenadine Grizzled Skipper G74

Butterflies: 1c, Red anartia. 2c, Lesser Antillean giant hairstreak. 4c, Santa Domingo longtail skipper. 5c, Spotted Manuel's skipper. 6c, Grenada's polydamus swallowtail. 10c, Palmira sulphur. 12c, Pupillated orange sulphur. 15c, Migrant sulphur. 20c, St. Christopher's hairstreak. 25c, St. Lucia mestra. 30c, Insular gulf fritillary. 40c, Michael's Caribbean buckeye. 60c, Frampton's flambeau. 70c, Bamboo page. $1.10, Antillean cracker. $2.50, Red crescent hairstreak. $5, Single colored Antillean white. $10, Lesser whirlabout. $20, Blue night.

1985-86 ***Perf. 14***

662 G74 ½c multicolored .25 .25
663 G74 1c multicolored .25 .25
664 G74 2c multicolored .25 .25
665 G74 4c multicolored .25 .25
666 G74 5c multicolored .25 .25
667 G74 6c multicolored .25 .25
668 G74 10c multicolored .40 .25
669 G74 12c multicolored .60 .25
670 G74 15c multicolored .60 .25
671 G74 20c multicolored .80 .25
672 G74 25c multicolored .80 .25
673 G74 30c multicolored .80 .30
674 G74 40c multicolored 1.00 .60
675 G74 60c multicolored 1.40 .95
676 G74 70c multicolored 1.60 1.00
677 G74 $1.10 multicolored 2.50 1.90
678 G74 $2.50 multicolored 4.50 3.75
679 G74 $5 multicolored 6.75 6.25
680 G74 $10 multicolored 11.00 11.00
681 G74 $20 multicolored 15.50 15.50
Nos. 662-681 (20) 49.75 44.00

Issued: Nos. 662-679, 6/17; No. 680, 11/11; No. 681, 1/8/86.

For overprints see Nos. 737-738.

1986 ***Perf. 12½x12***

662a G74 ½c multicolored .40 .40
663a G74 1c multicolored .40 .40
664a G74 2c multicolored .40 .40
665a G74 4c multicolored .40 .40
666a G74 5c multicolored .40 .40
667a G74 6c multicolored .40 .40
668a G74 10c multicolored .40 .40
669a G74 12c multicolored .40 .40
670a G74 15c multicolored .40 .40
671a G74 20c multicolored .40 .40
672a G74 25c multicolored .40 .40
673a G74 30c multicolored .60 .60
674a G74 40c multicolored .70 .70
675a G74 60c multicolored 1.25 1.25
676a G74 70c multicolored 1.25 1.25
677a G74 $1.10 multicolored 2.00 2.00
678a G74 $2.50 multicolored 7.00 7.00
679a G74 $5 multicolored 12.00 12.00
680a G74 $10 multicolored 20.00 20.00
681a G74 $20 multicolored 26.00 26.00
Nos. 662a-681a (20) 75.20 75.20

Issued: Nos. 662a-677a, 679a, 1986; Nos. 678a, 680a, 9/1986; No. 681a, 5/1989.

Queen Mother Birthday Type

$1, Portrait. $1.50, At Ascot, horiz. $2.50, Queen Mother, Prince Charles. $5, Portrait, diff.

1985, July 3 ***Perf. 14***

682 A181 $1 multicolored .65 .65
683 A181 $1.50 multicolored 1.10 1.10
684 A181 $2.50 multicolored 1.75 1.75
Nos. 682-684 (3) 3.50 3.50

Souvenir Sheet

685 A181 $5 multicolored 3.75 3.75

1986, Jan. 28 ***Perf. 12x12½***

686 A181 70c like #682 .60 .60
687 A181 $1.10 like #683 .75 .75
688 A181 $3 like #684 2.50 2.50
Nos. 686-688 (3) 3.85 3.85

Issued in sheets of 5 plus label.

Water Sports Type

Designs: 15c, Scuba diving. 70c, Playing in waterfall. 90c, Water skiing. $4, Swimming. $5, Skin diver, sailboat.

1985, July 15 ***Perf. 15***

689 A179 15c multicolored .25 .25
690 A179 70c multicolored .55 .55
691 A179 90c multicolored 1.00 1.00
692 A179 $4 multicolored 3.50 3.50
Nos. 689-692 (4) 5.30 5.30

Souvenir Sheet

693 A179 $5 multicolored 4.50 4.50

Queen Conch G75

Marine Life: 90c, Porcupine fish, fire coral. $1.10, Ghost crab. $4, West Indies spiny lobster. $5, Long-spined urchin.

1985, Aug. 1 ***Perf. 14***

694 G75 60c multicolored .85 .70
695 G75 90c multicolored 1.50 1.00
696 G75 $1.10 multicolored 1.75 1.25
697 G75 $4 multicolored 4.25 4.25
Nos. 694-697 (4) 8.35 7.20

Souvenir Sheet

698 G75 $5 multicolored 8.50 8.50

Bach Anniversary Type

Portrait, signature, music from Invention No. 9 and: 15c, Natural trumpet. 60c, Bass viol. $1.10, Flute. $3, Double flageolet. $5, Portrait.

1985, Sept. 3 ***Perf. 14***

699 A184 15c multicolored .65 .25
700 A184 60c multicolored 1.10 .60
701 A184 $1.10 multicolored 2.00 1.00
702 A184 $3 multicolored 3.00 2.50
Nos. 699-702 (4) 6.75 4.35

Souvenir Sheet

703 A184 $5 multicolored 4.50 4.50

Royal Visit Type

10c, Arms of Great Britain, Grenada. $1, Queen Elizabeth II. $4, HMY Britannia. $5, Map.

1985, Nov. 4 ***Perf. 14½***

704 A186 10c multicolored .25 .25
705 A186 $1 multi, vert. 1.50 1.50
706 A186 $4 multicolored 4.50 4.50
Nos. 704-706 (3) 6.25 6.25

Souvenir Sheet

707 A186 $5 multicolored 5.25 5.25

UN Anniversary Type

UN stamps and famous people: $1, #373, Neil Armstrong. $2, #221, Mahatma Gandhi. $2.50, #43, Maimonides. $5, Ralph Bunche.

1985, Nov. 22

708 A189 $1 multicolored 1.50 1.25
709 A189 $2 multicolored 4.00 4.00
710 A189 $2.50 multicolored 4.75 4.75
Nos. 708-710 (3) 10.25 10.00

Souvenir Sheet

711 A189 $5 multicolored 5.00 5.00

Twain & Disney Type

Walt Disney characters in scenes from "Letters From Hawaii": 25c, Mickey, Minnie on beach. 50c, Donald Duck surfing. $1.50, Donald roasting marshmallow. $3, Mickey canoeing. $5, Mickey, cat.

1985, Nov. 27 ***Perf. 14x13½***

712 A185 25c multicolored .85 .40
713 A185 50c multicolored 1.25 .90
714 A185 $1.50 multicolored 3.25 3.25
715 A185 $3 multicolored 5.00 5.00
Nos. 712-715 (4) 10.35 9.55

Souvenir Sheet

716 A185 $5 multicolored 7.00 7.00

Brothers Grimm & Disney Type

Walt Disney characters in scenes from "The Elves and the Shoemaker": 30c, Mickey as shoemaker. 60c, Elves helping. 70c, Mickey, new shoes. $4, Minnie at sewing machine. $5, Minnie & Mickey.

1985, Nov. 27 ***Perf. 13½x14***

717 A187 30c multicolored .85 .45
718 A187 60c multicolored 1.25 1.00
719 A187 70c multicolored 1.60 1.25
720 A187 $4 multicolored 4.75 4.75
Nos. 717-720 (4) 8.45 7.45

Souvenir Sheet

721 A187 $5 multicolored 7.00 7.00

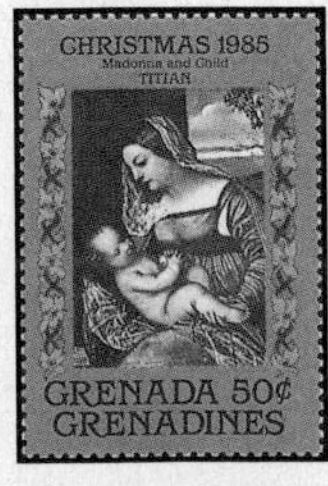

Madonna and Child by Titian — G76

Christmas paintings: 70c, Madonna and Child with St. Mary and John the Baptist by Bugiardini. $1.10, Adoration of the Magi by Di Fredi. $3, Madonna and Child with Young St. John the Baptist by Bartolomeo. $5, The Annunciation by Botticelli.

1985, Dec. 23 *Perf. 15*

722	G76	50c	multicolored	.60	.45
723	G76	70c	multicolored	.70	.55
724	G76	$1.10	multicolored	1.10	.90
725	G76	$3	multicolored	2.10	2.10
			Nos. 722-725 (4)	4.50	4.00

Souvenir Sheet

726	G76	$5	multicolored	3.50	3.50

Statue of Liberty Type of 1985

Designs: 5c, Croton Reservoir, 1875. 10c, NY Public Library, 1986. 70c, Old Boathouse, Central Park, 1894. $4, Boating, Central Park, 1986. $5, Statue of Liberty, vert.

1986, Jan. 6 *Perf. 15*

727	A191	5c	multicolored	.25	.25
728	A191	10c	multicolored	.25	.25
729	A191	70c	multicolored	.40	.40
730	A191	$4	multicolored	2.40	2.40
			Nos. 727-730 (4)	3.30	3.30

Souvenir Sheet

731	A191	$5	multicolored	5.00	5.00

Audubon Type of 1985

Designs: 50c, Louisiana heron. 70c, Black-crowned night heron. 90c, Bittern. $4, Glossy ibis. $5, King eider.

1986, Jan. 28 *Perf. 12½x12*

732	A174	50c	multicolored	2.25	1.10
733	A174	70c	multicolored	2.75	1.60
734	A174	90c	multicolored	3.00	2.40
735	A174	$4	multicolored	5.50	5.50
			Nos. 732-735 (4)	13.50	10.60

Souvenir Sheet

Perf. 14

736	A174	$5	multicolored	8.00	8.00

Nos. 732-735 issued in sheets of 5 plus label.

Nos. 676, 679 Overprinted

1986, Feb. 20 *Perf. 14*

737	G74	70c	multicolored	1.50	1.50
738	G75	$5	multicolored	6.50	6.50

World Cup Soccer Championships, Mexico — G77

Various soccer plays.

1986, Mar. 18

739	G77	10c	multicolored	.65	.40
740	G77	70c	multicolored	1.75	1.40
741	G77	$1	multicolored	2.10	1.90
742	G77	$4	multicolored	5.00	5.00
			Nos. 739-742 (4)	9.50	8.70

Souvenir Sheet

743	G77	$5	multicolored	6.00	6.00

For overprints see Nos. 772-776.

Halley's Comet Type

Designs: 5c, Nicolaus Copernicus, Earl of Rossi's six foot reflector. 20c, Sputnik. 40c, Tycho Brahe's notes, sketch of comet of 1577. $4, Edmond Halley, comet of 1682. $5, Halley's comet. Captions on 40c and $4 are reversed.

1986, Mar. 26

744	A194	5c	multicolored	.55	.50
745	A194	20c	multicolored	.90	.50
746	A194	40c	multicolored	1.10	.75
747	A194	$4	multicolored	5.25	5.25
			Nos. 744-747 (4)	7.80	7.00

Souvenir Sheet

748	A194	$5	multicolored	4.50	4.50

"Tycho," on 40c, and "Nicolaus" on 5c misspelled.

For overprints see Nos. 787-791. Compare No. 748 with No. 913.

Queen Elizabeth II, 60th Birthday

Common Design Type

Designs: 2c, At Windsor Park, 1933. $1.50, Queen Elizabeth II. $4, In Sydney, Australia, 1970. $5, Family portrait, Coronation Day, 1937.

1986, Apr. 21

749	CD339	2c	yel & blk	.25	.25
750	CD339	$1.50	pale grn & multi	.85	.85
751	CD339	$4	dl lil & multi	2.40	2.40
			Nos. 749-751 (3)	3.50	3.50

Souvenir Sheet

752	CD339	$5	tan & blk	3.25	3.25

AMERIPEX '86 Type

Walt Disney characters visiting: 30c, Grand Canyon. 60c, Golden Gate Bridge. $1, Chicago Watertower. $3, The White House. $5, NY Harbor, Statue of Liberty.

1986, May 22 *Perf. 11*

753	A195	30c	multicolored	.80	.50
754	A195	60c	multicolored	1.20	1.20
755	A195	$1	multicolored	2.00	2.00
756	A195	$3	multicolored	4.00	4.00
			Nos. 753-756 (4)	8.00	7.70

Souvenir Sheet

Perf. 14

757	A195	$5	multicolored	6.00	6.00

Royal Wedding Issue, 1986

Common Design Type

Designs: 60c, Prince Andrew and Sarah Ferguson. 70c, Andrew. $4, Andrew in dress uniform, helicopter. $5, Couple, diff.

1986, July 1 *Perf. 14*

758	CD340	60c	multicolored	.45	.45
759	CD340	70c	multicolored	.55	.55
760	CD340	$4	multicolored	3.00	3.00
			Nos. 758-760 (3)	4.00	4.00

Souvenir Sheet

761	CD340	$5	multicolored	5.00	5.00

Mushrooms — G78

Designs: 15c, Hygrocybe firma. 50c, Xerocomus coccolobae. $2, Volvariella cubensis. $3, Lactarius putidus. $5, Leponia caeruleocapitata.

1986, July 15 *Perf. 15*

762	G78	15c	multicolored	1.25	.80
763	G78	50c	multicolored	2.60	2.40
764	G78	$2	multicolored	5.00	5.00
765	G78	$3	multicolored	6.25	6.25
			Nos. 762-765 (4)	15.10	14.45

Souvenir Sheet

766	G78	$5	multicolored	13.00	13.00

Seashells — G79

Designs: 15c, Giant Atlantic pyram. 50c, Beau's murex. $1.10, West Indian fighting conch. $4, Alphabet coral. $5, Brown-lined paper bubble.

1986, Aug. 1

767	G79	15c	multicolored	1.25	.60
768	G79	50c	multicolored	3.00	1.75
769	G79	$1.10	multicolored	3.25	3.25
770	G79	$4	multicolored	5.75	5.75
			Nos. 767-770 (4)	13.25	11.35

Souvenir Sheet

771	G79	$5	multicolored	11.50	11.50

Nos. 739-743 Overprinted in Gold

1986, Sept. 15 *Perf. 14*

772	G77	10c	multicolored	.75	.45
773	G77	70c	multicolored	1.25	1.25
774	G77	$1	multicolored	1.75	1.50
775	G77	$4	multicolored	4.25	4.25
			Nos. 772-775 (4)	8.00	7.45

Souvenir Sheet

776	G77	$5	multicolored	7.50	7.50

Manicou G80

Wildlife: 30c, Giant toad. 60c, Land tortoise. 70c, Murine opossum. 90c, Burmese mongoose. $1.10, Antillean armadillo. $2, Agouti. $3, Humpback whale.

No. 785, Mona monkey. No. 786, Iguana.

1986, Sept. 15 *Perf. 15*

777	G80	10c	shown	.25	.25
778	G80	30c	multicolored	.50	.50
779	G80	60c	multicolored	1.00	1.00
780	G80	70c	multicolored	1.10	1.10
781	G80	90c	multicolored	1.25	1.25
782	G80	$1.10	multicolored	1.60	1.60
783	G80	$2	multicolored	2.50	2.50
784	G80	$3	multicolored	5.75	5.75
			Nos. 777-784 (8)	13.95	13.95

Souvenir Sheets

785	G80	$5	multicolored	6.50	6.50
786	G80	$5	multicolored	6.50	6.50

Nos. 744-748 Overprinted in Silver or Black

1986, Oct. 15 *Perf. 14*

787	A194	5c	multi (Bk)	.90	.75
788	A194	20c	multicolored	1.10	.65
789	A194	40c	multi (Bk)	1.25	.75
790	A194	$4	multicolored	6.50	6.50
			Nos. 787-790 (4)	9.75	8.65

Souvenir Sheet

791	A194	$5	multicolored	8.50	8.50

Christmas Type of 1986

25c, Chip 'n' Dale. 30c, Mickey Mouse. 50c, Piglet, Pooh, Jose Carioca. 60c, Daisy. 70c, A kiss under the mistletoe. $1.50, Huey, Dewey, and Louie. $3, Mickey Mouse, Morty. $4, Kittens on the keys.

No. 800, Mickey Mouse. No. 801, Bambi.

1986 Nov. 3 *Perf. 11*

792	A199	25c	multicolored	.55	.25
793	A199	30c	multicolored	.55	.30
794	A199	50c	multicolored	.70	.40
795	A199	60c	multicolored	.80	.50
796	A199	70c	multicolored	.95	.60
797	A199	$1.50	multicolored	1.75	1.75
798	A199	$3	multicolored	2.00	2.00
799	A199	$4	multicolored	3.50	3.50
			Nos. 792-799 (8)	10.80	9.30

Souvenir Sheets

800	A199	$5	multicolored	5.00	5.00
801	A199	$5	multicolored	5.00	5.00

Nos. 793, 795-796, 799 vert.

Automobile Centenary Type

Designs: 10c, 1984 Aston-Martin Volante. 30c, 1948 Jaguar Mk V. 60c, 1956 Nash Ambassador. 70c, 1984 Toyota Supra. 90c, 1985 Ferrari Testarossa. $1, 1955 BMW 501B. $2, 1968 Mercedes-Benz 280SL. $3, 1932 Austro-Daimler ADR8.

No. 810, 1977 Morgan +8. No. 811, Checker Taxi.

1986, Nov. 20 *Perf. 15*

802	A202	10c	multicolored	.30	.30
803	A202	30c	multicolored	.55	.55
804	A202	60c	multicolored	.75	.75
805	A202	70c	multicolored	.75	.75
806	A202	90c	multicolored	.90	.90
807	A202	$1	multicolored	.90	.90
808	A202	$2	multicolored	1.25	1.25
809	A202	$3	multicolored	1.60	1.60
			Nos. 802-809 (8)	7.00	7.00

Souvenir Sheets

810	A202	$5	multicolored	4.25	4.25
811	A202	$5	multicolored	4.25	4.25

Chagall Type

Paintings.: $1.10 — No. 812, The Mirror. No. 813, Dancer with a Fan. No. 814, The Acrobat. No. 815, Abraham's Sacrifice. No. 816, The Fruit Seller. No. 817, The Rooster, 1947. No. 818, The Wedding. No. 819, Horsewoman. No. 820, The Aged Lion from Fables of La Fontaine. No. 821, The Fruit Basket. No. 822, The Satyr and the Wayfarer. No. 823, Self-portrait with Seven Fingers. No. 824, Fruit and Flowers. No. 825, Lovers and Flowers. No. 826, The Wedded with an Angel. No. 827, In the Cafe, 1936. No. 828, The Equestrian. No. 829, Blue Violinist, 1947. No. 830, Zemphira costume design from Aleko scene I (dancer with red dress). No. 831, Portrait of Vava, 1955. No. 832, I and the Village, 1911. No. 833, The Accordion Player. No. 834, The Violinist, 1913. No. 835, Mother and Child, 1968. No. 836. Sunday, 1953. No. 837, Red and Black World, 1951. No. 838, Double Portrait with Wineglass, 1917. No. 839, Unknown (blonde woman in a blue dress). No. 840, Time is a River without Banks, 1930. No. 841, Homage to Apollinaire. No. 842, Unknown (rooster behind Eiffel tower). No. 843, The Blue Home, 1926, horiz. No. 844, Still-life, 1912, horiz. No. 845, Autumn Village. No. 846, Bonjour Paris. No. 847, The Jew in Pink, 1914. No. 848, Unknown (clown with violin). No. 849, War, 1943. No. 850, The Artist Angel. No. 851, Unknown (vase of flowers, woman at window).

$5 — No. 852, Birthday, 1915. No. 853, Wheatfield on a Summer Afternoon, 1942. No. 854, The Nude Above Vitebsk. No. 855, Aleko and Zemphira by Moonlight. No. 856, The Family Dinner. No. 857, Life (couple with baby, sun, celebrants). No. 858, The Flying Carriage, 1913. No. 859, The Studio. No. 860, Birth. No. 861, Rain.

1986-87 *Perf. 14x13½*

812-851	A203	Set of 40	55.00	55.00

Size: 110x95mm

Imperf

852-861	A203	Set of 10	42.50	42.50

Issued: Nos. 824-851, 855-861, 1987.

America's Cup Type

25c, Defender, 1895. 45c, Caleta, 1886. 70c, Azzurra, 1981. $4, Australia II, 1983.

$5, Columbia, Shamrock, 1899.

1987, Feb. 5 *Perf. 15*

862	A204	25c	multicolored	.85	.55
863	A204	45c	multicolored	1.10	.85
864	A204	70c	multicolored	1.40	1.40
865	A204	$4	multicolored	2.75	2.75
			Nos. 862-865 (4)	6.10	5.55

Souvenir Sheet

866	A204	$5	multicolored	6.50	6.50

Discovery of America Type

15c, Columbus. 30c, Queen Isabella. 50c, Santa Maria. 60c, Landing in New World. 90c, Lesser Antilles. $1, King Ferdinand. $2, Fort of La Navidad. $3, Galley off Hispaniola.

No. 875, Native Canoe. No. 876, Santa Maria at anchor.

1987, Apr. 27

867	A206	15c	multicolored	.25	.25
868	A206	30c	multicolored	.25	.25
869	A206	50c	multicolored	.40	.40
870	A206	60c	multicolored	.45	.45
871	A206	90c	multicolored	.75	.75
872	A206	$1	multicolored	.80	.80
873	A206	$2	multicolored	1.75	1.75
874	A206	$3	multicolored	2.50	2.50
a.			Sheet of 8	12.00	12.00
			Nos. 867-874 (8)	7.15	7.15

Souvenir Sheets

875	A207	$5	multicolored	6.00	6.00
876	A207	$5	multicolored	6.00	6.00

Transportation Innovations Type

Designs: 10c, Saunders Roe SR-N1 Hovercraft, 1959. 15c, Bugatti Royale, 1931. 30c, Aleksei Leonov, 1st space walk, 1965. 50c, CSS Hunley, submarine, 1864. 60c, Rolls Royce Flying Bedstead, VTOL aircraft, 1954. 70c, Jenny Lind, locomotive, 1854. 90c, Duryea, 1893. $1.50, Steam locomotive, London subway, 1863. $2, SS Great Britain, screw-driven steamship, 1843. $3, Budweiser rocket, 1979.

1987, May 18 *Perf. 14*

877 A209 10c multicolored .55 .30
878 A209 15c multicolored .60 .40
879 A209 30c multicolored .80 .50
880 A209 50c multicolored 1.10 .75
881 A209 60c multicolored 1.25 .90
882 A209 70c multicolored 1.40 1.25
883 A209 90c multicolored 1.50 1.25
884 A209 $1.50 multicolored 2.25 2.25
885 A209 $2 multicolored 2.75 2.75
886 A209 $3 multicolored 3.00 3.00
Nos. 877-886 (10) 15.20 13.35

Capex '87 Type

Fish.

1987, June 15

887 A208 6c Yellow chub .25 .25
888 A208 30c Kingfish .55 .40
889 A208 50c Mako shark .75 .65
890 A208 60c Dolphinfish .85 .85
891 A208 90c Bonito 1.10 1.10
892 A208 $1.10 Cobia 1.40 1.40
893 A208 $3 Great tarpon 3.25 3.25
894 A208 $4 Swordfish 3.50 3.50
Nos. 887-894 (8) 11.65 11.40

Souvenir Sheets

895 A208 $5 Jewfish 5.00 5.00
896 A208 $5 Amberjack 5.00 5.00

Statue of Liberty Type

10c, Washing statue's face. 15c, Commemorative medals. 25c, Band facing right. 30c, Band facing forward. 45c, Liberty's face. 50c, Washing statue's hair, horiz. 60c, Commemorative statuettes, horiz. 70c, Boats in NY Harbor, horiz. $1, Re-opening. $1.10, Blimps, Liberty & Manhattan Islands. $2, Warship. $3, Commemorative flags.

1987, Aug. 5

897 A210 10c multicolored .25 .25
898 A210 15c multicolored .30 .30
899 A210 25c multicolored .45 .45
900 A210 30c multicolored .50 .50
901 A210 45c multicolored .55 .55
902 A210 50c multicolored .60 .60
903 A210 60c multicolored .70 .70
904 A210 70c multicolored .80 .80
905 A210 $1 multicolored .95 .95
906 A210 $1.10 multicolored 1.00 1.00
907 A210 $2 multicolored 1.90 1.90
908 A210 $3 multicolored 2.10 2.10
Nos. 897-908 (12) 10.10 10.10

Inventors Type

Designs: 60c, Isaac Newton, Newton Medal. $1, Louis Daguerre, inventor of Daguerreotype. $2, Antoine Lavoisier, French chemist, apparatus. $3, Rudolf Diesel, German engineer, Diesel engine. $5, Halley's comet.

1987, Sept. 9

909 A211 60c multicolored 1.00 .80
910 A211 $1 multicolored 1.25 1.25
911 A211 $2 multicolored 2.60 2.60
912 A211 $3 multicolored 6.00 6.00
Nos. 909-912 (4) 10.85 10.65

Souvenir Sheet

913 A211 $5 multicolored 8.00 8.00

No. 913 inscribed "Great Scientific Discoveries" in margin.

No. 912 incorrectly inscribed "James Watt, Steam Engine." See Grenada No. 1538.

US Constitution Bicentennial Type

10c, Constitutional Convention, Philadelphia. 50c, Georgia state flag. 60c, Capitol, vert. $4, Thomas Jefferson, vert. $5, Alexander Hamilton, vert.

1987, Nov. 1

914 A214 10c multicolored .25 .25
915 A214 50c multicolored .85 .75
916 A214 60c multicolored .85 .80
917 A214 $4 multicolored 4.50 4.50
Nos. 914-917 (4) 6.45 6.30

Souvenir Sheet

918 A214 $5 multicolored 4.00 4.00

Hafnia '87 Type

Walt Disney characters in adaptations of Hans Christian Andersen Fairy Tales: 25c, The Swineherd. 30c, What the Good Man Does is Always Right. 50c, Little Tuk. 60c, The World's Fairest Rose. 70c, The Garden of Paradise. $1.50, The Naughty Boy. $3, What the Moon Saw. $4, Thumbelina. No. 927, Hans Clodhopper. No. 928, Elder Tree Mother.

1987, Nov. 16

919 A215 25c multicolored .55 .30
920 A215 30c multicolored .60 .40
921 A215 50c multicolored .80 .80
922 A215 60c multicolored .80 .80
923 A215 70c multicolored .85 .85
924 A215 $1.50 multicolored 2.25 2.25
925 A215 $3 multicolored 3.00 3.00
926 A215 $4 multicolored 3.50 3.50
Nos. 919-926 (8) 12.35 11.90

Souvenir Sheets

927 A215 $5 multicolored 6.25 6.25
928 A215 $5 multicolored 6.25 6.25

Christmas — G81

Paintings by El Greco: 10c, Virgin and Child with Saints Martin and Agnes. 50c, Detail from Virgin and Child with Saints Martin and Agnes. 60c, The Annunciation. $4, Holy Family with St. Anne. $5, Adoration of the Shepherds.

1987, Dec. 15

929 G81 10c multicolored .45 .25
930 G81 50c multicolored 1.40 .95
931 G81 60c multicolored 1.40 1.10
932 G81 $4 multicolored 5.50 5.50
Nos. 929-932 (4) 8.75 7.80

Souvenir Sheet

933 G81 $5 multicolored 9.25 9.25

Wedding Anniv. Type

20c, Elizabeth, Anne. 30c, Wedding portrait. $2, Elizabeth, Charles, Anne. $3, Elizabeth wearing tiara.

$5, Elizabeth in wedding gown.

1988, Feb. 15

934 A218 20c multicolored .25 .25
935 A218 30c multicolored .25 .25
936 A218 $2 multicolored 1.40 1.40
937 A218 $3 multicolored 2.00 2.00
Nos. 934-937 (4) 3.90 3.90

Souvenir Sheet

938 A218 $5 multicolored 4.00 4.00

1988 Summer Olympics Type

Walt Disney characters in modern and ancient events: 1c, Rhythmic gymnastics. 2c, Pankration. 3c, Synchronized swimming. 4c, Hoplite race. 5c, Baseball. 10c, Horse race. $6, Windsurfing. $7, Chariot race.

No. 947, Tennis. No. 948, Pentathlon.

1988, Apr. 13 *Perf. 13½x14, 14x13½*

939 A219 1c multicolored .25 .25
940 A219 2c multicolored .25 .25
941 A219 3c multicolored .25 .25
942 A219 4c multicolored .25 .25
943 A219 5c multicolored .25 .25
944 A219 10c multicolored .25 .25
945 A219 $6 multicolored 5.00 5.00
946 A219 $7 multicolored 5.75 5.75
Nos. 939-946 (8) 12.25 12.25

Souvenir Sheet

947 A219 $5 multicolored 5.00 5.00
948 A219 $5 multicolored 5.00 5.00

Boy Scout Type

50c, Semaphore, vert. 70c, Canoeing, vert. $1, Cook-out. $3, Campfire.

$5, Pitching tent.

1988, May 3 *Perf. 14*

949 A220 50c multicolored .50 .50
950 A220 70c multicolored .60 .60
951 A220 $1 multicolored .90 .90
952 A220 $3 multicolored 2.50 2.50
Nos. 949-952 (4) 4.50 4.50

Souvenir Sheet

953 A220 $5 multicolored 4.50 4.50

Bird Type

20c, Yellow-crowned night heron. 25c, Brown pelican. 45c, Audubon's shearwater. 60c, Red-footed booby. 70c, Bridled tern. 90c, Red-billed tropicbird. $3, Blue-winged teal. $4, Sora.

No. 962, Little blue heron. No. 963, Purple-throated carib.

1988, May 31

954 A222 20c multicolored .30 .30
955 A222 25c multicolored .30 .30
956 A222 45c multicolored .45 .40
957 A222 60c multicolored .65 .45
958 A222 70c multicolored .65 .60
959 A222 90c multicolored .90 .90
960 A222 $3 multicolored 2.50 2.50
961 A222 $4 multicolored 3.50 3.50
Nos. 954-961 (8) 9.25 8.95

Souvenir Sheets

962 A222 $5 multicolored 5.00 5.00
963 A222 $5 multicolored 5.00 5.00

Titian Type

Paintings by Titian: 15c, Man with Blue Eyes, 1545. 30c, The Three Ages of Man, 1512. 60c, Don Diego Mendoza, 1545. 75c, Emperor Charles V Seated, 1548. $1, A Young Man in a Fur, 1515. $2, Tobias and the Angel, 1543. $3, Pietro Bembo, 1540. $4, Pier Luigi Farnese, 1546. No. 972, Sacred and Profane Love. No. 973, Venus and Adonis.

1988, June 15 *Perf. 13½x14*

964 A224 15c multicolored .25 .25
965 A224 30c multicolored .25 .25
966 A224 60c multicolored .40 .40
967 A224 75c multicolored .55 .55
968 A224 $1 multicolored .75 .75
969 A224 $2 multicolored 1.40 1.40
970 A224 $3 multicolored 2.00 2.00
971 A224 $4 multicolored 2.75 2.75
Nos. 964-971 (8) 8.35 8.35

Souvenir Sheet

972 A224 $5 multicolored 5.00 5.00
973 A224 $5 multicolored 5.00 5.00

Airship Type

Historic flights: 10c, Hindenburg over Rio de Janeiro, 1937. 20c, Hindenburg over NYC, 1937. 30c, US Navy airships, WWII convoy to Europe, 1944. 40c, Hindenburg docking at Lakehurst, NJ, 1937, vert. 60c, Joint flight, Hindenburg and Graf Zeppelin, 1936, vert. 70c, DC-3, Hindenburg, Los Angeles at Lakehurst, 1936. $1, Graf Zeppelin II over England, 1939, vert. $2, Deutschland, 1st passenger flight, 1912. $3, Graf Zeppelin over Dome of the Rock, Jerusalem, 1931. $4, Hindenburg Olympic flight, 1936. No. 984, Graf Zeppelin over Vatican City, 1933, vert. No. 985, Graf Zeppelin Polar flight, 1931.

1988, July 1 *Perf. 14*

974 A225 10c multicolored .25 .25
975 A225 20c multicolored .25 .25
976 A225 30c multicolored .25 .25
977 A225 40c multicolored .35 .35
978 A225 60c multicolored .80 .60
979 A225 70c multicolored 1.10 .80
980 A225 $1 multicolored 1.10 .90
981 A225 $2 multicolored 1.75 1.75
982 A225 $3 multicolored 2.50 2.50
983 A225 $4 multicolored 3.25 3.25
Nos. 974-983 (10) 11.60 10.90

Souvenir Sheets

984 A225 $5 multicolored 6.00 6.00
985 A225 $5 multicolored 6.00 6.00

Fairy Tales Type

Miniature Sheets

Bambi: No. 986a, Newborn Bambi, mother and forest animals. b, Bambi, Flower and Thumper. c, Bambi and opossum family hanging from tree. d, Bambi, his mother, and Faline, a female fawn. e, Foraging in a snow storm. f, Meeting his father, the Great Stag. g, Competing for Faline's attention. h, The Great Stag leading animals to safety during forest fire. i, Bambi, grown, becomes the Great Stag.

The Fox and the Hound: No. 987a, Big Mama, consoling the orphaned baby fox, Tod. b, Widow Tweed feeding Tod. c, Tod playing with Copper, the hound. d, Copper leashed. e, Copper and Chief. f, Chief barking at Tod, Copper shocked. g, Porcupine. h, Vixey, a female fox. i, Bear attacking Copper.

101 Dalmatians: No. 988a, Pongo, Perdita and their masters. b, Pongo and Perdita, courting. c, Three puppies. d, Cruella de Ville and henchmen. e, Captain the Horse, Colonel the Sheepdog and Tibbs the Cat. f, Dalmatians following Tibbs to freedom. g, Cruella racing car in pursuit. h, Dalmatians disguised in soot. i, Nanny dusting off the soot.

Dumbo: No. 989a, Stork delivering Dumbo. b, Elephant making fun of Dumbo's large ears. c, Dumbo, Mrs. Jumbo performing. d, Timothy the Mouse. e, Timothy and Dumbo. f, Crows pushing Dumbo off a cliff. g, Dumbo flying away from burning building. h, Dumbo flying with the crows. i, Dumbo and Mrs. Jumbo on train.

Lady and the Tramp: No. 990a, Darling holding Lady. b, Lady meets the Tramp. c, Lady looking in bassinet. d, Siamese cats, Lady. e, Lady, Tramp, crocodiles. f, Tramp kisses Lady. g, Lady in dog catcher's carriage. h, Lady and Tramp attacking rat. i, Trusty and Jock overturning dog catcher's carriage where Tramp is imprisoned.

The Aristocats: No. 991a, Edgar driving Madame Mornfamille's carriage. b, Dutchess and kittens. c, Edgar feeding the cats cream spiked with sleeping pills. d, Edgar transporting cats on motorcycle. e, Walter O'Malley discovers the abandoned cats. f, Three geese. g, Scat Cat and friends holding a jam session. h, Edgar attacks O'Malley with a pitch fork. i, Frau-Frau kicking Edgar.

No. 992, Faline and newborn twin fawns. No. 993, Tod and Vixey. No. 994, Pongo, Perdita and puppies. No. 995, Dumbo flying with Timothy the Mouse. No. 996, Lady and Tramp's puppies. No. 997, Walter O'Malley, Dutchess and kittens.

1988, July 25 *Perf. 14x13½*

986 Sheet of 9 4.00 4.00
a.-i. A212 30c any single .40 .40
987 Sheet of 9 4.00 4.00
a.-i. A212 30c any single .40 .40
988 Sheet of 9 4.00 4.00
a.-i. A212 30c any single .40 .40
989 Sheet of 9 4.00 4.00
a.-i. A212 30c any single .40 .40
990 Sheet of 9 4.00 4.00
a.-i. A212 30c any single .40 .40
991 Sheet of 9 4.00 4.00
a.-i. A212 30c any single .40 .40
Nos. 986-991 (6) 24.00 24.00

Souvenir Sheets

992-997 A212 $5 each 6.25 6.25

SYDPEX '88 Type

Walt Disney characters: 1c, Conducting at Sydney Opera House. 2c, Climbing Ayers Rock. 3c, Working at a sheep station. 4c, Visiting Lone Pine Koala Sanctuary. 5c, Playing Australian football. 10c, Racing camels. No. 1004, Lawn bowling. $6, America's Cup trophy and Australia II. No. 1006, The Great Barrier Reef. No. 1007, Beach party.

1988, Aug. 1 *Perf. 14x13½*

998 A226 1c multicolored .25 .25
999 A226 2c multicolored .25 .25
1000 A226 3c multicolored .25 .25
1001 A226 4c multicolored .25 .25
1002 A226 5c multicolored .25 .25
1003 A226 10c multicolored .25 .25
1004 A226 $5 multicolored 5.50 5.50
1005 A226 $6 multicolored 6.50 6.50
Nos. 998-1005 (8) 13.50 13.50

Souvenir Sheets

1006 A226 $5 multicolored 5.00 5.00
1007 A226 $5 multicolored 5.00 5.00

Flowering Trees Type

10c, Potato tree, vert. 20c, Wild cotton. 30c, Shower of gold, vert. 60c, Napoleon's button, vert. 90c, Geiger tree. $1, Fern tree. $2, French cashew. $4, Amherstia, vert.

No. 1016, African tulip tree, vert. No. 1017, Swamp immortelle.

1988, Sept. 30 *Perf. 14*

1008 A228 10c multicolored .25 .25
1009 A228 20c multicolored .25 .25
1010 A228 30c multicolored .25 .25
1011 A228 60c multicolored .50 .45
1012 A228 90c multicolored .75 .65
1013 A228 $1 multicolored .85 .85
1014 A228 $2 multicolored 1.75 1.75
1015 A228 $4 multicolored 3.00 3.00
Nos. 1008-1015 (8) 7.60 7.45

Souvenir Sheets

1016 A228 $5 multicolored 3.75 3.75
1017 A228 $5 multicolored 3.75 3.75

Car Type

Miniature Sheets

Designs: No. 1018a, 1925 Doble Series E, US. b, 1926 Alvis 12/50, United Kingdom. c, 1927 Sunbeam 3-liter, UK. d, 1928 Franklin Airman, US. e, 1929 Delage D8S, France. f, 1897 Mors, France. g, 1904 Peerless Green Dragon, US. h, 1909 Pope-Hartford, US. i, 1920 Daniels Submarine Speedster, US. j, 1922 McFarlan 9.3 liter, US.

No. 1019a, 1949 Frazer Nash Lemans Replica, UK. b, 1953 Pegaso Z102, Spain. No. 1019c, 1953 Siata Spyder V-8, Italy. d, 1953 Kurtis-Offenhauser, US. No. 1019e, 1954 Kaiser-Darrin, US. f, 1930 Tracta, France. g, 1932 Maybach Zeppelin, Germany. h, 1934 Railton Light Sports, UK. i, 1936 Hotchkiss, France. j, 1939 Mercedes-Benz W163, Germany.

No. 1020a, 1982 Aston Martin Vantage V8, UK. b, 1982 Porsche 956, Germany. No. 1020c, 1983 Lotus Esprit Turbo, UK. d, 1984 McLaren MP4/2, UK. e, 1985 Mercedes-Benz 190E 2-3-16, Germany. f, 1963 Ferrari 250 GT Lusso, Italy. g, 1964 Porsche 904, Germany. h, 1967 Volvo P1800, Sweden. i, 1970 McLaren-Chevrolet M8D, US. j, 1981 Jaguar XJ6, UK.

1988, Oct. 7 *Perf. 13x13½*

1018 Sheet of 10 15.00 15.00
a.-j. A223 $2 any single 1.50 1.50
1019 Sheet of 10 15.00 15.00
a.-j. A223 $2 any single 1.50 1.50
1020 Sheet of 10 15.00 15.00
a.-j. A223 $2 any single 1.50 1.50

Christmas and Mickey Mouse 60th Anniv. Type

Miniature Sheet

"Mickey's Christmas Parade": No. 1021a, Dumbo. b, Goofy. c, Minnie Mouse. d, Morty, Ferdy and Clarabelle Cow. e, Huey, Dewey and Louie. f, Donald Duck. g, Wooden soldiers marching. h, Mickey Mouse leading parade.

No. 1022, Capt. Hook on float. No. 1023, Mickey and Donald on float.

1988, Dec. 1 *Perf. 13½x14*

1021 Sheet of 8 6.00 6.00
a.-h. A229 $1 any single .75 .75

Souvenir Sheets

Perf. 14x13

1022 A229 $7 multicolored 6.50 6.50
1023 A229 $7 multicolored 6.50 6.50

Japanese Painting Type

"The Fifty-three Stations on the Tokaido" by Hiroshige (1979-1858): 15c, Crossing the Oi at Shimada by Ferry. 20c, Daimyo and Entourage at Arai. 45c, Cargo Portage through Goyu. 75c, Snowfall at Fujigawa. $1, Horses for the Emperor at Chiryu. $2, Rainfall at Tsuchiyama. $3, At Inn of Ishibe. $4, On the Shore of Lake Biwa at Otsu. No. 1032, Pilgrimage to Atsuta Shrine at Miya. No. 1033, Fishing Village of Yokkaichi on the Mie.

1989, May 15 *Perf. 14x13½*

1024 A233 15c multicolored .30 .30
1025 A233 20c multicolored .35 .35
1026 A233 45c multicolored .60 .60
1027 A233 75c multicolored 1.00 1.00
1028 A233 $1 multicolored 1.00 1.00
1029 A233 $2 multicolored 1.75 1.75
1030 A233 $3 multicolored 2.75 2.75
1031 A233 $4 multicolored 3.75 3.75
Nos. 1024-1031 (8) 11.50 11.50

Souvenir Sheets

1032 A233 $5 multicolored 4.50 4.50
1033 A233 $5 multicolored 4.50 4.50

1988 Olympic Medalists Type

Designs: 15c, Henry Maske, East Germany, boxing (165 lbs.). 50c, Andreas Schroeder, East Germany, freestyle wrestling (286 lbs.). 60c, East German team, women's gymnastics. 75c, Greg Louganis, US, men's springboard and platform diving. $1, Mitsuru Sato, Japan, freestyle wrestling (115 lbs.). $2, West German team, 4x200m freestyle relay. $3, Dieter Baumann, West Germany, 5000m race. $4, Jackie Joyner-Kersee, US, heptathlon. No. 1042, Joachim Kunz, East Germany, weight lifting (149 lbs.). No. 1043, West German equestrian team, 3-day event.

1989, Apr. 13 *Perf. 14*

1034 A232 15c multicolored .30 .25
1035 A232 50c multicolored .40 .35
1036 A232 60c multicolored .50 .40
1037 A232 75c multicolored .70 .55
1038 A232 $1 multicolored .85 .75
1039 A232 $2 multicolored 1.50 1.50
1040 A232 $3 multicolored 2.25 2.25
1041 A232 $4 multicolored 3.00 3.00
Nos. 1034-1041 (8) 9.50 9.05

Souvenir Sheets

1042 A232 $6 multicolored 4.75 4.75
1043 A232 $6 multicolored 4.75 4.75

World Cup Soccer Championships, Italy — G82

Designs: 15c, World Cup, vert. 45c, Kaiser Franz, West Germany, vert. 75c, Like 20c, flag of Italy, 1982 champions. $1, Pele, Brazil, vert. $2, Like 20c, flag of West Germany, 1974 champions. $3, Like 20c, flag of Brazil, 1970 champions. $4, Jules Rimet Cup, vert. No. 1052, Pele, Jules Rimet Cup, vert. No. 1053, Goalie.

1989, June 12

1044 G82 15c multicolored .25 .25
1045 G82 20c multicolored .25 .25
1046 G82 45c multicolored .30 .30
1047 G82 75c multicolored .55 .55
1048 G82 $1 multicolored 1.40 1.40
1049 G82 $2 multicolored 2.60 2.60
1050 G82 $3 multicolored 2.10 2.10
1051 G82 $4 multicolored 2.60 2.60
Nos. 1044-1051 (8) 10.05 10.05

Souvenir Sheets

1052 G82 $6 multicolored 4.50 4.50
1053 G82 $6 multicolored 4.50 4.50

Car Type of 1988

Miniature Sheets

North American locomotives: No. 1054a, Morris & Essex, Dover, 1841. No. 1054b, B&O, Memmon No. 57, 1848. No. 1054c, Camden & Amboy, John Stevens, 1849. No. 1054d, Lawrence Machine Shop, Lawrence, 1853. No. 1054e, South Carolina, James S. Corry, 1859. No. 1054f, Mine Hill & Schuylkill Haven, Flexible Beam No. 3, 1860. No. 1054g, DL&W, Montrose, 1861. No. 1054h, Central Pacific, Pequop No. 68, 1868. No. 1054i, Boston & Providence, Daniel Nason, 1863. No. 1054j, Morris & Essex, Joe Scranton, 1870.

No. 1055a, Central Railroad of New Jersey, No. 124, 1871. No. 1055b, Baldwin Steam Motor for Street Railways, 1876. No. 1055c, Lackawanna & Bloomsburg, Luzerne, 1878. No. 1055d, Central Mexicano, No. 150, 1892. No. 1055e, Denver, South Park & Pacific, Breckenridge No. 15, 1879. No. 1055f, Miles Planting & Manufacturing Co., "Daisy" Plantation locomotive, 1894. No. 1055g, Central of Georgia, Baldwin 854 No. 1136, 1895. No. 1055h, Savannah, Florida & Western, No. 111, 1900. No. 1055i, Douglas, Gilmore, & Co. No. 3, 1902. No. 1055j, Lehigh Valley Coal Co., Compressed Air locomotive No. 900, 1903.

No. 1056a, Morgan's Louisiana & Texas, McKeen Motorcar, 1908. No. 1056b, Clear Lake Lumber Co., Type B Climax, 1910. No. 1056c, Blue Jay Lumber Co., Heisler No. 10, 1912. No. 1056d, Stewartstown, Gasoline Engine No. 6, 1920's. No. 1056e, Bangor & Aroostook, Class G No. 186, 1921. No. 1056f, Hammond Lumber Co., No. 6, 1923. No. 1056g, Central Railroad of New Jersey, No. 1000, 1925. No. 1056h, Atchison, Topeka & Santa Fe, Super Chief No. 1-1A, 1935. No. 1056i, Norfolk & Western, Class Y-6, 1948. No. 1056i, Boston & Maine, Budd Railcar, 1949.

1989, June 28 *Perf. 13x13½*

1054 Sheet of 10 19.00 19.00
a.-j. A223 $2 any single 1.60 1.60
1055 Sheet of 10 19.00 19.00
a.-j. A223 $2 any single 1.60 1.60
1056 Sheet of 10 19.00 19.00
a.-j. A223 $2 any single 1.60 1.60

PHILEXFRANCE '89 — G83

Walt Disney characters in Paris: 1c, Military school. 2c, Conciergerie. 3c, Hotel de Ville, vert. 4c, Genie of the Bastille, vert. 5c, The Opera. 10c, Gardens of Luxembourg. $5, Arche de la Defense, vert. No. 1064, $6, Place Vendome, vert.

No. 1065, $6, Riding moped. No. 1066, $6, Hot air ballooning.

1989, July 7 *Perf. 14x13½, 13½x14*

1057 G83 1c multicolored .25 .25
1058 G83 2c multicolored .25 .25
1059 G83 3c multicolored .25 .25
1060 G83 4c multicolored .25 .25
1061 G83 5c multicolored .25 .25
1062 G83 10c multicolored .25 .25
1063 G83 $5 multicolored 7.00 7.00
1064 G83 $6 multicolored 7.00 7.00
Nos. 1057-1064 (8) 15.50 15.50

Souvenir Sheets

1065 G83 $6 multicolored 7.00 7.00
1066 G83 $6 multicolored 7.00 7.00

Moon Landing Anniv. Type

Apollo 11 mission, 1969: 25c, Liftoff, vert. 50c, Splashdown. 60c, Spacecraft approaching moon, vert. 75c, Buzz Aldrin conducting experiment on lunar surface. $1, Leaving Earth orbit. $2, Transport of launch vehicle to pad, vert. $3, Lunar module liftoff. $4, Eagle lands on moon, vert. No. 1075, Footprint on moon. No. 1076, Armstrong stepping onto the moon, vert.

1989, July 20 *Perf. 14*

1067 A237 25c multicolored .30 .30
1068 A237 50c multicolored .50 .50
1069 A237 60c multicolored .60 .60
1070 A237 75c multicolored .75 .75
1071 A237 $1 multicolored .90 .90
1072 A237 $2 multicolored 2.00 2.00
1073 A237 $3 multicolored 2.50 2.50
1074 A237 $4 multicolored 3.50 3.50
Nos. 1067-1074 (8) 11.05 11.05

Souvenir Sheets

1075 A237 $5 multicolored 4.50 4.50
1076 A237 $5 multicolored 4.50 4.50

Mushroom Type

6c, Collybia aurea. 10c, Podaxis pistillaris. 20c, Hygrocybe firma. 30c, Agaricus rufoaurantiacus. 75c, Leptonia howellii. $2, Marasmiellus purpureus. $3, Marasmius trinitatis. $4, Hygrocybe martinicensis.

No. 1086, Lentinus crinitus. No. 1087, Agaricus purpurellus.

1989, Aug. 17

1078 A238 6c multicolored .40 .25
1079 A238 10c multicolored .40 .25
1080 A238 20c multicolored .65 .50
1081 A238 30c multicolored .75 .65
1082 A238 75c multicolored 1.60 1.60
1083 A238 $2 multicolored 3.00 3.00
1084 A238 $3 multicolored 3.50 3.50
1085 A238 $4 multicolored 4.00 4.00
Nos. 1078-1085 (8) 14.30 13.75

Souvenir Sheets

1086 A238 $6 multicolored 8.00 8.00
1087 A238 $6 multicolored 8.00 8.00

Butterflies Type

25c, Androgeus swallowtail. 35c, Cloudless sulpher. 45c, Cracker. 50c, Painted lady. 75c, Great southern white. 90c, Little sulpher. $2, Migrant sulpher. $3, Mimic.

No. 1096, Giant hairstreak. No. 1097, Red anartia.

1989, Oct. 2 *Perf. 14*

1088 A239 25c multicolored .85 .85
1089 A239 35c multicolored 1.00 1.00
1090 A239 45c multicolored 1.10 1.10
1091 A239 50c multicolored 1.10 1.10
1092 A239 75c multicolored 1.75 1.75
1093 A239 90c multicolored 1.90 1.90
1094 A239 $2 multicolored 4.25 4.25
1095 A239 $3 multicolored 5.00 5.00
Nos. 1088-1095 (8) 16.95 16.95

Souvenir Sheets

1096 A239 $6 multicolored 8.50 8.50
1097 A239 $6 multicolored 8.50 8.50

World Stamp Expo Type

Scenes from Walt Disney animated films and quotes from Poor Richard's Almanack by Benjamin Franklin: 1c, "Beware of little expenses, a small leak will sink a great ship." 2c, "Trust thyself and another shall not betray thee." 3c, "A spoonful of honey will catch more flies than a gallon of vinegar." 4c, "No gain without pain." 5c, "A true friend is the best possession." 6c, "Haste makes waste." 8c, "A quiet conscience sleeps in thunder, but rest and guilt live far asunder." 10c, "The muses love the morning." $5, "An egg today is better than a hen tomorrow." No. 1107, "He that riseth late, must trot all day." No. 1108, "If you'd be belov'd, make yourself amiable." No. 1109, "In Christmas feasting pray take care; let not your table be a snare; but with the poor God's bounty share. Adieu my friends! Till the next year," vert.

1989, Nov. **Litho.** *Perf. 14x13½*

1098 A242 1c multicolored .25 .25
1099 A242 2c multicolored .25 .25
1100 A242 3c multicolored .25 .25
1101 A242 4c multicolored .25 .25
1102 A242 5c multicolored .25 .25
1103 A242 6c multicolored .25 .25
1104 A242 8c multicolored .25 .25
1105 A242 10c multicolored .25 .25
1106 A242 $5 multicolored 4.50 4.50
1107 A242 $6 multicolored 5.50 5.50
Nos. 1098-1107 (10) 12.00 12.00

Souvenir Sheet

1108 A242 $6 multicolored 7.50 7.50
1109 A242 $6 multicolored 7.50 7.50

World Stamp Expo '89, Washington, D.C.

Shakespearean Actors and Theater Masks — G84

15c, Ethel Barrymore (1879-1959). $1.10, Richard Burton (1925-1984). $2, John Barrymore (1882-1942). $3, Paul Robeson (1898-1976). $6, Bando Tamasaburo & Nakamura Kanzaburo.

1989, Oct. 9 **Litho.** *Perf. 14*

1110 G84 15c multicolored .40 .30
1111 G84 $1.10 multicolored 1.75 1.50
1112 G84 $2 multicolored 2.50 2.50
1113 G84 $3 multicolored 2.75 2.75
Nos. 1110-1113 (4) 7.40 7.05

Souvenir Sheet

1114 G84 $6 multicolored 6.50 6.50

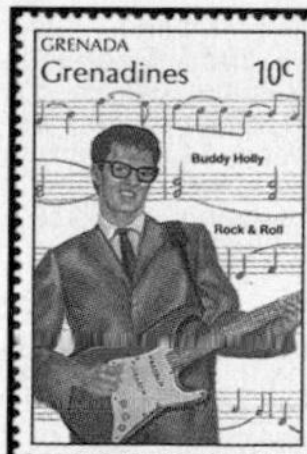

20th Century Musicians — G85

1989, Oct. 9

1115 G85 10c Buddy Holly .40 .30
1116 G85 25c Jimi Hendrix .65 .50
1117 G85 75c Mighty Sparrow .95 .95
1118 G85 $4 Katsutoji Kineya 4.25 4.25
Nos. 1115-1118 (4) 6.25 6.00

Souvenir Sheet

1119 G85 $6 Lotte Lenya, Kurt Weill 6.25 6.25

Jimi is spelled incorrectly as "Jimmy."

Discovery of America Type

1989, Oct. 16

1120 A241 15c Canoeing .40 .30
1121 A241 75c Cooking 1.25 1.25
1122 A241 90c Using stone tools 1.75 1.75
1123 A241 $3 Eating 4.50 4.50
Nos. 1120-1123 (4) 7.90 7.80

Souvenir Sheet

1124 A241 $6 Building fire 6.25 6.25

Christmas Type

Religious paintings by Rubens: 10c, The Annunciation. 15c, The Flight of the Holy Family into Egypt. 25c, The Presentation in the Temple. 45c, The Holy Family Under the Apple Tree. $2, Madonna and Child with Saints. $4, The Virgin and Child Enthroned with Saints. No. 1132, The Holy Family. No. 1132, Adoration of the Magi. No. 1133, Adoration of the Magi, diff.

1990, Jan. 4 *Perf. 14*

1125 A243 10c multicolored .40 .25
1126 A243 15c multicolored .45 .25
1127 A243 25c multicolored .65 .25
1128 A243 45c multicolored .85 .40
1129 A243 $2 multicolored 2.40 2.40
1130 A243 $4 multicolored 3.50 3.50
1131 A243 $5 multicolored 3.50 3.50
Nos. 1125-1131 (7) 11.75 10.55

Souvenir Sheets

1132 A243 $5 multicolored 7.00 7.00
1133 A243 $5 multicolored 7.00 7.00

America Issue (Insects) G86

35c, Hercules beetle. 40c, Click beetle. 50c, Harlequin beetle. 60c, Gold rim butterfly. $1, Red skimmer dragonfly. $2, Buprestid beetle. $3, Mimic butterfly. $4, Scarab beetle.

No. 1142, Canna skipper butterfly. No. 1143, Monarch butterfly.

1990, Mar. 16 *Perf. 14*

1134 G86 35c multicolored .45 .45
1135 G86 40c multicolored .45 .45
1136 G86 50c multicolored .60 .60
1137 G86 60c multicolored 1.10 1.10
1138 G86 $1 multicolored 1.25 1.25
1139 G86 $2 multicolored 2.40 2.40
1140 G86 $3 multicolored 3.50 3.50
1141 G86 $4 multicolored 3.50 3.50
Nos. 1134-1141 (8) 13.25 13.25

Souvenir Sheets

1142 G86 $6 multicolored 6.50 6.50
1143 G86 $6 multicolored 6.50 6.50

Orchids — G87

15c, Brassocattleya thalie. 20c, Odontocidium tigersun. 50c, Odontioda hambuhren. 75c, Paphiopedium delrosi. $1, Vuylstekeara yokara. $2, Paphiopedilum geelong. $3, Wilsonara tigerwood. $4, Cymbidium ormoulu.

No. 1152, Odontonia sappho. No. 1153, Cymbidium vieux rose.

1990, Mar. 6 Litho. *Perf. 14*

1144 G87 15c multicolored .35 .35
1145 G87 20c multicolored .35 .35
1146 G87 50c multicolored .55 .55
1147 G87 75c multicolored .65 .65
1148 G87 $1 multicolored 1.10 1.10
1149 G87 $2 multicolored 2.10 2.10
1150 G87 $3 multicolored 2.75 2.75
1151 G87 $4 multicolored 3.50 3.50
Nos. 1144-1151 (8) 11.35 11.35

Souvenir Sheets

1152 G87 $6 multicolored 7.00 7.00
1153 G87 $6 multicolored 7.00 7.00

EXPO '90 Intl. Garden and Greenery Exposition, Osaka, Japan.

Wildlife Type

5c, West Indies giant rice rat. 25c, Agouti. 30c, Humpback whale. 40c, Pilot whale. $1, Spotted dolphin. $2, Mongoose. $3, Prehensile-tailed porcupine. $4, West Indies manatee.

No. 1162, Caribbean monk seal. No. 1163, Egyptian mongoose.

1990, Apr. 3

1154 A247 5c multicolored .30 .30
1155 A247 25c multicolored .45 .45
1156 A247 30c multicolored 1.00 1.00
1157 A247 40c multicolored 1.00 1.00
1158 A247 $1 multicolored 1.25 1.25
1159 A247 $2 multicolored 2.40 2.40
1160 A247 $3 multicolored 3.25 3.25
1161 A247 $4 multicolored 3.75 3.75
Nos. 1154-1161 (8) 13.40 13.40

Souvenir Sheets

1162 A247 $6 multicolored 7.00 7.00
1163 A247 $6 multicolored 7.00 7.00

World War II Type

Designs: 6c, First British troops arrive in France, Sept. 6, 1939. 10c, British launch "Operation Crusader", Nov. 18, 1941. 20c, Rommel begins retreat from El Alamein, Nov. 4, 1942. 45c, US forces land on Aleutian Islands, May 11, 1943. 50c, US Marines land on Tarawa, Nov. 20, 1943. 60c, US 5th Army enters Rome, June 4, 1944. 75c, US troops reach River Seine, Aug. 19, 1944. $1, Battle of the Bulge, Dec. 16, 1944. $5, Allies launch final phase of Italian Campaign, Apr. 9, 1945. No. 1173, Atom bomb dropped on Hiroshima, Aug. 6, 1945. No. 1174, St. Paul's Catherdral during London blitz, Battle of Britain, 1940.

1990, Apr. 30

1164 A248 6c multicolored .40 .40
1165 A248 10c multicolored .40 .40
1166 A248 20c multicolored .65 .65
1167 A248 45c multicolored .70 .70
1168 A248 50c multicolored .80 .80
1169 A248 60c multicolored .85 .85
1170 A248 75c multicolored .95 .95
1171 A248 $1 multicolored 1.25 1.25
1172 A248 $5 multicolored 4.00 4.00
1173 A248 $6 multicolored 5.00 5.00
Nos. 1164-1173 (10) 15.00 15.00

Souvenir Sheet

1174 A248 $6 multicolored 7.50 7.50

Disney Type

Disney characters portraying Shakespearian characters: 15c, Daisy Duck at Ann Hathaway's Cottage, Shottery. 30c, Minnie Mouse and a young Shakespeare walking in Stratford birthplace, vert. 50c, Minnie as Mary Arden, Shakespeare's mother in Wilmcote, vert. 60c, Mickey in front of New Place, Stratford. $1, Mickey walking in Great Garden of New Place. $2, Mickey at Guild Chapel, Scholars Lane, vert. $4, Mickey at the Royal Shakespeare Theater, Stratford, vert. $5, Ludwig von Drake instructing Shakespeare. No. 1183, Mickey at Edge Hill, Stratford, vert. No. 1184, Mickey and Minnie rowing past Holy Trinity Church, Stratford-Upon-Avon.

1990, May *Perf. 14x13½*

1175 A250 15c multicolored .50 .25
1176 A250 30c multicolored .65 .45
1177 A250 50c multicolored .95 .85
1178 A250 60c multicolored 1.10 1.10
1179 A250 $1 multicolored 1.50 1.50
1180 A250 $2 multicolored 2.75 2.75
1181 A250 $4 multicolored 4.00 4.00
1182 A250 $5 multicolored 4.00 4.00
Nos. 1175-1182 (8) 15.45 14.90

Souvenir Sheets

Perf. 14

1183 A250 $6 multicolored 7.50 7.50
1184 A250 $6 multicolored 7.50 7.50

Penny Black Type

Souvenir Sheet

1990, May 3 Litho. *Perf. 14*

1185 A249 $6 Globe with South America 8.00 8.00

Stamp World London '90.

Queen Mother, 90th Birthday Type

1990, July 5

1186 A251 $2 Pink hat 1.40 1.40
1187 A251 $2 With Charles 1.40 1.40
1188 A251 $2 Blue outfit 1.40 1.40
Nos. 1186-1188 (3) 4.20 4.20

Souvenir Sheet

1189 A251 $6 like #1187 4.25 4.25

Bird Type

25c, Yellow-bellied seedeater. 45c, Carib grackle. 50c, Black-whiskered vireo. 75c, Bananaquit. $1, Collared swift. $2, Yellow-bellied elaenia. $3, Blue-hooded euphonia. $5, Eared dove.

No. 1198, Mangrove cuckoo. No. 1199, Scaly breasted thrasher.

1990, Sept. 10 Litho. *Perf. 14*

1190 A255 25c multicolored .45 .45
1191 A255 45c multicolored .65 .65
1192 A255 50c multicolored .75 .75
1193 A255 75c multicolored .85 .85
1194 A255 $1 multicolored 1.25 1.25
1195 A255 $2 multicolored 1.90 1.90
1196 A255 $3 multicolored 2.50 2.50
1197 A255 $5 multicolored 4.50 4.50
Nos. 1190-1197 (8) 12.85 12.85

Souvenir Sheets

1198 A255 $6 multicolored 5.75 5.75
1199 A255 $6 multicolored 5.75 5.75

Crustaceans Type of 1990

10c, Slipper lobster. 25c, Green reef crab. 65c, Caribbean lobsterette. 75c, Blind deep sea lobster. $1, Flattened crab. $2, Ridged slipper lobster. $3, Land crab. $4, Mountain crab.

No. 1208, Caribbean king crab. No. 1209, Purse crab.

1990, Sept. 17

1200 A256 10c multicolored .25 .25
1201 A256 25c multicolored .35 .35
1202 A256 65c multicolored .70 .70
1203 A256 75c multicolored .80 .80
1204 A256 $1 multicolored 1.10 1.10
1205 A256 $2 multicolored 2.00 2.00
1206 A256 $3 multicolored 2.25 2.25
1207 A256 $4 multicolored 2.75 2.75
Nos. 1200-1207 (8) 10.20 10.20

Souvenir Sheets

1208 A256 $6 multicolored 5.00 5.00
1209 A256 $6 multicolored 5.00 5.00

G88

Players from participating countries.

1990, Sept. 24

1210 G88 15c England .25 .25
1211 G88 45c Argentina .50 .50
1212 G88 $2 Sweden 1.75 1.75
1213 G88 $4 South Korea 3.00 3.00
Nos. 1210-1213 (4) 5.50 5.50

Souvenir Sheets

1214 G88 $6 Yugoslavia 4.50 4.50
1215 G88 $6 United States 4.50 4.50

World Cup Soccer Championships, Italy.

G89

10c, Boxing. 25c, Olympic flame. 50c, Soccer. 75c, Discus. $1, Pole vault. $2, Equestrian 3-day event. $4, Women's basketball. $5, Men's gymnastics.

No. 1224, Sailboarding. No. 1225, Decathlon.

1990, Nov. 11 Litho. *Perf. 14*

1216 G89 10c multicolored .25 .25
1217 G89 25c multicolored .25 .25
1218 G89 50c multicolored .50 .50
1219 G89 75c multicolored .65 .65
1220 G89 $1 multicolored .90 .90
1221 G89 $2 multicolored 2.00 2.00
1222 G89 $4 multicolored 4.00 4.00
1223 G89 $5 multicolored 3.50 3.50
Nos. 1216-1223 (8) 12.05 12.05

Souvenir Sheets

1224 G89 $6 multicolored 6.00 6.00
1225 G89 $6 multicolored 6.00 6.00

1992 Summer Olympics, Barcelona.

Rubens Type

Entire paintings or different details from: 5c, 25c, Adam and Eve, vert. 15c, Esther before Ahasuerus. 50c, Expulsion from Eden. $1, Cain Slaying Abel, vert. $2, Lot's Flight. $4, Samson and Delilah. $5, Abraham and Melchizedek. No. 1234, The Meeting of David and Abigail. No. 1235, Daniel in the Lions Den.

1991, Jan. 31 Litho. *Perf. 14*

1226 A259 5c multicolored .25 .25
1227 A259 15c multicolored .40 .25
1228 A259 25c multicolored .50 .25
1229 A259 50c multicolored .85 .65
1230 A259 $1 multicolored 1.50 1.25
1231 A259 $2 multicolored 2.00 2.00
1232 A259 $4 multicolored 3.00 3.00
1233 A259 $5 multicolored 3.50 3.50
Nos. 1226-1233 (8) 12.00 11.15

Souvenir Sheets

1234 A259 $6 multicolored 6.00 6.00
1235 A259 $6 multicolored 6.00 6.00

Fish Type of 1990

15c, Barred hamlet. 35c, Squirrelfish. 45c, Red-spotted hawkfish. 75c, Bigeye. $1, Spiny puffer. $2, Smallmouth grunt. $3, Harlequin bass. $4, Creole fish.

No. 1244, Fairy basslet. No. 1245, Copper sweeper.

1991, Feb. 5

1236 A254 15c multicolored .55 .30
1237 A254 35c multicolored .90 .60
1238 A254 45c multicolored 1.00 .70
1239 A254 75c multicolored 1.60 1.25
1240 A254 $1 multicolored 1.90 1.50
1241 A254 $2 multicolored 2.75 2.75
1242 A254 $3 multicolored 3.50 3.50
1243 A254 $4 multicolored 3.75 3.75
Nos. 1236-1243 (8) 15.95 14.35

Souvenir Sheets

1244 A254 $6 multicolored 6.50 6.50
1245 A254 $6 multicolored 6.50 6.50

Hummel Figurines — G90

10c, Angel, star. 15c, Angel, guitar, Christ Child. 25c, Shepherd. 50c, Angel, lantern, horn. $1, Angel, children, Christ Child. $2, Angel, candle, Christ Child. $4, Angel with baskets. $5, Angels singing.

1991, Mar. 1 Litho. *Perf. 14*

1246 G90 10c multicolored .25 .25
1247 G90 15c multicolored .35 .25
1248 G90 25c multicolored .50 .25
1249 G90 50c multicolored 1.00 .55
1250 G90 $1 multicolored 1.25 1.00
1251 G90 $2 multicolored 2.25 2.25
1252 G90 $4 multicolored 3.25 3.25
1253 G90 $5 multicolored 3.50 3.50
Nos. 1246-1253 (8) 12.35 11.30

Souvenir Sheets

1254 Sheet of 4 5.00 5.00
a. G90 5c like No. 1247 .25 .25
b. G90 40c like No. 1249 .30 .30
c. G90 60c like No. 1250 .50 .50
d. G90 $3 like No. 1253 2.75 2.75
1255 Sheet of 4 7.00 7.00
a. G90 20c like No. 1246 .25 .25
b. G90 30c like No. 1248 .25 .25
c. G90 75c like No. 1251 .70 .70
d. G90 $6 like No. 1252 4.50 4.50

Christmas 1990.

Orchids — G91

Designs: 5c, Brassia maculata. 10c, Oncidium lanceanum. 15c, Broughtonia sanguinea. 25c, Diacrium bicornutum. 35c, Cattleya labiata. 45c, Epidendrum fragrans. 50c, Oncidium papilio. 75c, Neocogniauxia monophylla. $1, Epidendrum polybulbon. $2, Spiranthes speciosa. $4, Epidendrum ciliare. $5, Phais tankervilliae. $10, Brassia caudata. $20, Brassavola cordata.

1991-92 Litho. *Perf. 14*

1256 G91 5c multicolored .70 .70
1257 G91 10c multicolored .70 .70
1258 G91 15c multicolored .75 .30
1259 G91 25c multicolored .90 .30
1260 G91 35c multicolored .90 .30
1261 G91 45c multicolored 1.25 .45
1262 G91 50c multicolored 1.25 .50
1263 G91 75c multicolored 1.50 .80
1264 G91 $1 multicolored 2.00 1.25
1265 G91 $2 multicolored 3.25 3.25
1266 G91 $4 multicolored 5.25 5.25
1267 G91 $5 multicolored 5.50 5.50
1268 G91 $10 multicolored 10.50 10.50
1269 G91 $20 multicolored 21.00 21.00
Nos. 1256-1269 (14) 55.45 50.80

Issued: $20, 6/92; others, 4/1/91.

Butterfly Type

Designs: 5c, Crimson-patched longwing. 10c, Morpho helena. 15c, Morpho sulkowskyi. 20c, Dynastor napoleon. 25c, Pieridae callinira. 30c, Anartia amathea. 35c, Heliconiidae dido. 45c, Papilionidae columbus. 50c, Nymphalidae praeneste. 60c, Panacea prola. 75c, Julia. $1, Papilionidae orthosilaus. $2, Pyrrhopyge cometes. $3, Papilionidae paeon. $4, Morpho cypris. $5, Choringa. No. 1286, Caligo idomenides. No. 1287, Monarch. No. 1287A, Nymphalidae amydon. No. 1287B, Papilio childrenae.

1991, Apr. 8 Litho. *Perf. 14*

1270 A261 5c multicolored .60 .45
1271 A261 10c multicolored .60 .45
1272 A261 15c multicolored .85 .50
1273 A261 20c multicolored .95 .55
1274 A261 25c multicolored .95 .60
1275 A261 30c multicolored 1.10 .70
1276 A261 35c multicolored 1.10 .70
1277 A261 45c multicolored 1.25 .95
1278 A261 50c multicolored 1.40 1.00
1279 A261 60c multicolored 1.60 1.10
1280 A261 75c multicolored 1.60 1.25
1281 A261 $1 multicolored 2.00 1.60
1282 A261 $2 multicolored 2.75 2.75
1283 A261 $3 multicolored 3.50 3.50
1284 A261 $4 multicolored 4.00 4.00
1285 A261 $5 multicolored 5.00 5.00
Nos. 1270-1285 (16) 29.25 25.10

Souvenir Sheets

1286 A261 $6 multicolored 6.50 6.50
1287 A261 $6 multicolored 6.50 6.50
1287A A261 $6 multicolored 6.50 6.50
1287B A261 $6 multicolored 6.50 6.50

Save Our Planet — G100

Walt Disney characters and ecology themes: 10c, Daisy and Donald, alternate forms of transportation. 15c, Goofy saving water. 25c, Donald, Daisy camping simply. 45c, Donald protecting birds. $1, Donald holding ascending balloons. $2, Minnie, Daisy using natural coolers. $4, Mickey, nephews cleaning beaches. $5, Scrooge McDuck using pedal power. No. 1296, Little Hiawatha and Iron Eyes Cody viewing destroyed forest. No. 1297, Donald, recycling. No. 1298, Minnie, Mickey planting trees.

1991, Apr. 22 Litho. *Perf. 14*

1288 G100 10c multicolored .65 .25
1289 G100 15c multicolored .75 .25
1290 G100 25c multicolored 1.00 .40

1291 G100 45c multicolored 1.40 .60
1292 G100 $1 multicolored 2.25 1.40
1293 G100 $2 multicolored 3.25 3.00
1294 G100 $4 multicolored 4.00 4.00
1295 G100 $5 multicolored 4.00 4.00
Nos. 1288-1295 (8) 17.30 13.90

Souvenir Sheets

1296 G100 $6 multicolored 6.50 6.50
1297 G100 $6 multicolored 6.50 6.50
1298 G100 $6 multicolored 6.50 6.50

Voyages of Discovery Type

Discovery of America, 500th anniv. (in 1992).: 15c, Ferdinand Magellan, 1519-1521. 20c, Sir Francis Drake, 1577-1580. 50c, Capt. James Cook, 1768-1771. 60c, Douglas World Cruiser, 1924. $1, Sputnik, 1957. $2, Yuri Gagarin, 1961. $4, John Glenn, 1962. $5, Space Shuttle, 1981. No. 1307, Columbus' fleet. No. 1308, The Pinta, vert.

1991, Apr. 29 Litho. *Perf. 14*
1299 A262 15c multicolored .40 .30
1300 A262 20c multicolored .30 .30
1301 A262 50c multicolored .60 .60
1302 A262 60c multicolored .70 .70
1303 A262 $1 multicolored 1.10 1.10
1304 A262 $2 multicolored 2.25 2.25
1305 A262 $4 multicolored 4.25 4.25
1306 A262 $5 multicolored 5.25 5.25
Nos. 1299-1306 (8) 14.85 14.75

Souvenir Sheets

1307 A262 $6 multicolored 6.00 6.00
1308 A262 $6 multicolored 6.00 6.00

Disney Phila Nippon '91 Type

Walt Disney characters demonstrating arts, crafts and industries of Japan: 15c, Minnie, silkworms. 30c, Mickey, Minnie, Morty and Ferdie photographing the Torii. 50c, Donald, Mickey, origami. 60c, Mickey, Minnie diving for pearls. $1, Minnie modeling kimono. $2, Mickey making masks. $4, Donald, Mickey making paper. $5, Minnie, Pluto, pottery. No. 317, Mickey making prints, vert. No. 1318, Mickey arranging flowers, vert. No. 1319, Mickey, tea ceremony, vert. No. 1320, Mickey carving ivory and wood into netsukes, vert.

1991, May 6
1309 A263 15c multi .50 .25
1310 A263 30c multi .85 .35
1311 A263 50c multi 1.00 .55
1312 A263 60c multi 1.10 .60
1313 A263 $1 multi 2.00 1.00
1314 A263 $2 multi 2.75 2.50
1315 A263 $4 multi 3.75 3.75
1316 A263 $5 multi 4.50 4.50
Nos. 1309-1316 (8) 16.45 13.50

Souvenir Sheets

1317 A263 $6 multi 5.00 5.00
1318 A263 $6 multi 5.00 5.00
1319 A263 $6 multi 5.00 5.00
1320 A263 $6 multi 5.00 5.00

Mushrooms Type

5c, Pyrrhoglossum pyrrhum. 45c, Agaricus purpurellus. 50c, Amanita craseoderma. 90c, Hygrocybe acutoconica. $1, Limacella guttata. $2, Lactarius hygrophoroides. $4, Boletellus cubensis. $5, Psilocybe caerulescens.
No. 1329, Marasmius haemato- cephalus. No. 1330, Lepiota spiculata.

1991, June 1 Litho. *Perf. 14*
1321 A265 5c multicolored .40 .25
1322 A265 45c multicolored 1.00 .55
1323 A265 50c multicolored 1.00 .60
1324 A265 90c multicolored 1.75 1.25
1325 A265 $1 multicolored 1.75 1.25
1326 A265 $2 multicolored 2.50 2.50
1327 A265 $4 multicolored 4.00 4.00
1328 A265 $5 multicolored 4.00 4.00
Nos. 1321-1328 (8) 16.40 14.40

Souvenir Sheets

1329 A265 $6 multicolored 7.50 7.50
1330 A265 $6 multicolored 7.50 7.50

Royal Family Birthday, Anniversary
Common Design Type

No. 1339, Elizabeth, Philip. No. 1340, Diana, Charles, with sons.

1991, July 5 Litho. *Perf. 14*
1331 CD347 5c multi .50 .30
1332 CD347 20c multi .30 .30
1333 CD347 25c multi .30 .25
1334 CD347 60c multi 1.00 .75
1335 CD347 $1 multi 1.00 1.00
1336 CD347 $2 multi 1.75 1.75
1337 CD347 $4 multi 3.00 3.00
1338 CD347 $5 multi 4.50 4.50
Nos. 1331-1338 (8) 12.35 11.85

Souvenir Sheet

1339 CD347 $5 multi 5.75 5.75
1340 CD347 $5 multi 5.75 5.75

5c, 60c, $1, Nos. 1338, 1340, Charles and Diana, 10th wedding anniversary. Others, Queen Elizabeth II, 65th birthday.

Van Gogh Painting Type

Designs: 5c, Two Thistles, vert. 10c, The Baby Marcelle Roulin, vert. 15c, Still Life: Basket with Six Oranges. 25c, Orchard in Blossom, vert. 45c, Portrait of Armand Roulin, vert. 50c, Wood Gatherers in the Snow (detail). 60c, Almond Tree in Blossom, vert. $1, Portrait of an Old Man, vert. $2, The Seine Bridge at Asnieres. $3, Vase with Lilacs, Daisies & Anemones, vert. $4, Self-portrait, vert. $5, Portrait of Patience Escalier, vert. No. 1353, Les Alyscamps, vert. No. 1354, Quay with Men Unloading Sand Barges. No. 1355, Sunset: Wheat Fields Near Arles.

Perf. 13½x14, 14x13½
1991, Nov. 18 Litho.
1341 A264 5c multicolored .40 .25
1342 A264 10c multicolored .40 .25
1343 A264 15c multicolored .40 .25
1344 A264 25c multicolored .40 .25
1345 A264 45c multicolored .50 .40
1346 A264 50c multicolored .65 .50
1347 A264 60c multicolored .70 .60
1348 A264 $1 multicolored 1.25 1.00
1349 A264 $2 multicolored 2.25 2.25
1350 A264 $3 multicolored 3.00 3.00
1351 A264 $4 multicolored 4.25 4.25
1352 A264 $5 multicolored 4.75 4.75
Nos. 1341-1352 (12) 18.95 17.75

Size: 102x127mm, 127x102mm
Imperf

1353 A264 $6 multicolored 5.00 5.00
1354 A264 $6 multicolored 5.00 5.00
1355 A264 $6 multicolored 5.00 5.00

Marine Life Type
Miniature Sheet

Marine life of the deeper reef: No. 1356a, Sargassum triggerfish. b, Tobaccofish. c, Longsnout butterflyfish. d, Cherubfish. e, Black jack head. f, Black jack tail, masked goby. g, Spotfin hogfish. h, Fairy basslet. i, Orangeback bass. j, Candy basslet. k, Blackcap basslet. l, Longspine squirrelfish. m, Jackknife fish. n, Bigeye. o, Short Bigeye. $6, Caribbean flashlight fish.

1991, Dec. 5 Litho. *Perf. 14*
1356 A270 50c Sheet of 15, #a.-o. 20.00 20.00

Souvenir Sheet

1357 A270 $6 multicolored 14.00 14.00

Christmas Art Type

Details, entire paintings or engravings by Martin Schongauer: 10c, Angel of the Annunciation. 35c, Madonna of the Rose Hedge. 50c, Madonna of the Rose Hedge, diff. 75c, Nativity. $1, Adoration of the Shepherds. $2, Nativity, diff. $4, Nativity, diff. $5, Symbol of St. Matthew. No. 1366, Nativity, diff. No. 1367, Adoration of the Shepherds.

1991, Dec. 9 *Perf. 12*
1358 A271 10c multicolored .45 .25
1359 A271 35c multicolored .80 .25
1360 A271 50c multicolored 1.10 .45
1361 A271 75c multicolored 1.40 .75
1362 A271 $1 multicolored 1.50 1.25
1363 A271 $2 multicolored 2.25 2.25
1364 A271 $4 multicolored 2.75 2.75
1365 A271 $5 multicolored 2.75 2.75
Nos. 1358-1365 (8) 13.00 10.70

Souvenir Sheets
Perf. 14½

1366 A271 $6 multicolored 6.25 6.25
1367 A271 $6 multicolored 6.25 6.25

Queen Elizabeth II's Accession to the Throne, 40th Anniv.
Common Design Type

1992, Feb. 6 Litho. *Perf. 14*
1368 CD348 60c multicolored .90 .35
1369 CD348 75c multicolored 1.00 .40
1370 CD348 $2 multicolored 2.10 1.60
1371 CD348 $4 multicolored 3.00 3.00
Nos. 1368-1371 (4) 7.00 5.35

Souvenir Sheets

1372 CD348 $6 Queen, rural scene 5.00 5.00
1373 CD348 $6 Queen, harbor 5.00 5.00

Railways of the World Type

Steam locomotives: No. 1379a, Medoc Class, Switzerland, 1857. b, Sterling, Great Britain, 1870. c, No. 90, France, 1877. d, Standard, US, 1880. e, Vittorio Emanuel II, Italy, 1884. f, Johnson Single, Great Britain, 1887. g, No. 999, US, 1893. h, Q1 Class, Great Britain, 1896. i, Claud Hamilton, Great Britain, 1900.

No. 1380a, Class P8, Germany, 1906. b, Class P, Denmark, 1935. c, Class Ps, US, 1926. d, Class 4-4-0, Ireland, 1932. e, Class GS, US, 1937. f, Class 12, Belgium, 1938. g, Class J, US, 1941. h, PA series, US, 1946. i, Class 4E1, South Africa, 1954.

No. 1381a, Tee 4-car train, Europe, 1957. b, FL9B, US, 1960. c, Shin-Kansen 16-car train, Japan, 1964. d, Class 103.1, Germany 1970. e, RTG 4-car train set, France, 1972. f, ETR 401 Pendolino 4-car train, Italy, 1976. g, Class 370, Great Britain, 1981. h, LRC, Canada, 1982. i, Mav BZMOT 601 1B1, Hungary, 1983.

No. 1382, ETR 401 four-car train, Italy, 1976. No. 1382A, Werner von Siemens' first electric locomotive, Germany, 1879.

1992, Feb. 13 Litho. *Perf. 14*
Sheets of 9
1379 A269 75c #a.-i. 6.00 6.00
1380 A269 $1 #a.-i. 8.00 8.00
1381 A269 $2 #a.-i. 16.00 16.00
Nos. 1379-1381 (3) 30.00 30.00

Souvenir Sheets

1382 A269 $6 multicolored 5.50 5.50
1382A A269 $6 multicolored 5.50 5.50

1992 Summer Olympics, Barcelona — G101

Designs: 10c, Women's 100-meter backstroke. 15c, Women's handball. 25c, 4x100-meter relay. 35c, Hammer throw. 50c, 110-meter hurdles. 75c, Pole vault. $1, Volleyball. $2, Weight lifting. $5, Stationary rings. $6, Soccer. No. 1393, Baseball. No. 1394, Finn class single-handed dinghy.

1992, Mar. 23 Litho. *Perf. 14*
1383 G101 10c multicolored .65 .30
1384 G101 15c multicolored .70 .30
1385 G101 25c multicolored .80 .30
1386 G101 35c multicolored .85 .35
1387 G101 50c multicolored 1.00 .65
1388 G101 75c multicolored 1.40 .85
1389 G101 $1 multicolored 1.50 1.10
1390 G101 $2 multicolored 2.50 2.50
1391 G101 $5 multicolored 3.50 3.50
1392 G101 $6 multicolored 3.75 3.75
Nos. 1383-1392 (10) 16.65 13.60

Souvenir Sheets

1393 G101 $15 multicolored 10.50 10.50
1394 G101 $15 multicolored 10.50 10.50

Spanish Art Type

Paintings: 10c, The Surrender of Seville, by Francisco de Zurbaran. 35c, The Liberation of Saint Peter by an Angel, by Antonio de Pereda. 50c, Joseph Explains the Dreams of the Pharaoh, by Antonio del Castillo Saavedra, horiz. 75c, The Flower Vase, by Juan de Arellano. $1, The Duke of Pastrana, by Juan Carreno de Miranda. $2, $4, The Annunciation (diff. details), by Francisco Rizi. $5, Old Woman Seated, attributed to Antonio Puga. No. 1403, The Triumph of Saint Hermenegildo, by Francisco de Herrera, the Younger, vert. No. 1404, Relief of Genoa by the Second Marquis of Santa Cruz, by de Pereda, horiz.

1992, Apr. 30 *Perf. 13*
1395 A273 10c multicolored .30 .25
1396 A273 35c multicolored .50 .35
1397 A273 50c multicolored .75 .60
1398 A273 75c multicolored 1.00 .75
1399 A273 $1 multicolored 1.10 .90
1400 A273 $2 multicolored 1.75 1.75
1401 A273 $4 multicolored 2.75 2.75
1402 A273 $5 multicolored 2.75 2.75
Nos. 1395-1402 (8) 10.90 10.10

Size: 95x110mm
Imperf

1403 A273 $6 multicolored 10.00 10.00
1404 A273 $6 multicolored 10.00 10.00

Granada '92.

Discovery of America, 500th Anniv. G102

Designs: 10c, Don Isaac Abarbanel (1437-1508), Spanish Minister of Finance. 25c, Columbus. 35c, Crewman sighting land. 50c, King Ferdinand and Queen Isabella. 60c, Columbus and Queen Isabella. $5, Santa Maria and map. No. 1411, Portrait of Columbus. No. 1412, Columbus at first landfall.

1992, May 7 Litho. *Perf. 14*
1405 G102 10c multicolored .25 .25
1406 G102 25c multicolored .35 .30
1407 G102 35c multicolored .55 .45
1408 G102 50c multicolored .85 .85
1409 G102 60c multicolored 1.00 1.00
1410 G102 $5 multicolored 7.00 7.00
Nos. 1405-1410 (6) 10.00 9.85

Souvenir Sheets

1411 G102 $6 multicolored 5.25 5.25
1412 G102 $6 multicolored 5.25 5.25

World Columbian Expo '92, Chicago.

USO Anniv. Type of 1992

10c, James Cagney. 15c, Ann Sheridan. 35c, Jerry Colonna. 50c, Spike Jones. 75c, Edgar Bergen, Charlie McCarthy. $1, Andrews Sisters. $2, Dinah Shore. $5, Bing Crosby.
No. 1421, Marlene Dietrich. No. 1422, Fred Astaire.

1992, May 7
1413 A277 10c multicolored .55 .25
1414 A277 15c multicolored .55 .25
1415 A277 35c multicolored .55 .25
1416 A277 50c multicolored .65 .35
1417 A277 75c multicolored .80 .50
1418 A277 $1 multicolored 1.25 .75
1419 A277 $2 multicolored 1.90 1.90
1420 A277 $5 multicolored 4.25 4.25
Nos. 1413-1420 (8) 10.50 8.50

Souvenir Sheets

1421 A277 $6 multicolored 5.25 5.25
1422 A277 $6 multicolored 5.25 5.25

Hummingbird Type of 1992

Designs: 5c, Blue-headed male. 10c, Rufous-breasted hermit female. 20c, Blue-headed female. 45c, Green-throated carib male. 90c, Antillean crested male. $2, Purple-throated carib male. $4, Purple-throated carib female. $5, Antillean crested female. No. 1431, Rufous-breasted hermit female. No. 1432, Green-throated carib female.

1992, May 7
1423 A276 5c multicolored .25 .25
1424 A276 10c multicolored .25 .25
1425 A276 20c multicolored .25 .25
1426 A276 45c multicolored .40 .40
1427 A276 90c multicolored .85 .85
1428 A276 $2 multicolored 2.00 2.00
1429 A276 $4 multicolored 4.00 4.00
1430 A276 $5 multicolored 5.00 5.00
Nos. 1423-1430 (8) 13.00 13.00

Souvenir Sheets

1431 A276 $6 multicolored 6.00 6.00
1432 A276 $6 multicolored 6.00 6.00

Genoa '92.

Discovery of America Type

1992 *Perf. 14½*
1433 A275 $1 Coming ashore 1.25 1.25
1434 A275 $2 Natives, ships 2.75 2.75

Walt Disney's Goofy, 60th Anniv. — G103

Scenes from Disney cartoon films: 5c, Father's Day Off, 1953. 10c, Cold War, 1951. 15c, Home Made Home, 1951. 25c, Get Rich Quick, 1951. 50c, Man's Best Friend, 1952. 75c, Aquamania, 1961. 90c, Tomorrow We Diet, 1951. $1, Teachers Are People, 1952. $2, The Goofy Success Story, 1955. $3, Double Dribble, 1946. $4, Hello Aloha, 1952. $5, Father's Lion, 1952. No. 1447, Father's Weekend, 1953, vert. No. 1448, Motor Mania, 1950. No. 1449, Hold That Pose, 1950, vert.

1992, Nov. 24 Litho. *Perf. 14x13½*
1435 G103 5c multicolored .25 .25
1436 G103 10c multicolored .25 .25
1437 G103 15c multicolored .25 .25
1438 G103 25c multicolored .25 .25
1439 G103 50c multicolored .40 .40
1440 G103 75c multicolored .60 .60
1441 G103 90c multicolored .70 .70
1442 G103 $1 multicolored .75 .75
1443 G103 $2 multicolored 1.50 1.50
1444 G103 $3 multicolored 2.25 2.25
1445 G103 $4 multicolored 2.75 2.75
1446 G103 $5 multicolored 3.50 3.50
Nos. 1435-1446 (12) 13.45 13.45

Souvenir Sheets

Perf. 13½x14

1447 G103 $6 multicolored 4.25 4.25
1448 G103 $6 multicolored 4.25 4.25
1449 G103 $6 multicolored 4.25 4.25

Model Trains Type of 1992

Designs: 15c, #2220 Switcher locomotive, 2-inch gauge, US, 1910. 25c, 0-4-0 Engine, Bridge Port Line, O gauge, US, 1907. 50c, First Ives Co. electric toy locomotive, O gauge, US, 1910. 75c, J. C. Penney Special, standard gauge, US, 1920. $1, Cast metal locomotive, O gauge, US, 1916. $2, Copper-plated cast iron locomotive & tender pull toy, US, 1900. $4, Chromium plated locomotive #4689, standard gauge, US, 1928. $5, Ives long cab locomotive of the Olympian set, standard gauge, US, 1929.

No. 1458, Clockwork model, O gauge, US, 1910. No. 1459, American Flyer Statesman passenger train.

1992, Oct. 22 Litho. *Perf. 14*

1450 A279 15c multicolored .25 .25
1451 A279 25c multicolored .40 .25
1452 A279 50c multicolored .70 .45
1453 A279 75c multicolored .90 .65
1454 A279 $1 multicolored 1.00 .90
1455 A279 $2 multicolored 1.75 1.75
1456 A279 $4 multicolored 3.25 3.25
1457 A279 $5 multicolored 3.25 3.25
Nos. 1450-1457 (8) 11.50 10.75

Souvenir Sheet

Perf. 13

1458 A279 $6 multicolored 5.00 5.00
1459 A279 $6 multicolored 5.00 5.00

Nos. 1458-1459 contain one 51x40mm stamp.

New York City Type

Souvenir Sheet

1992, Oct. 28 *Perf. 14*

1460 A280 $6 Brooklyn Bridge 5.50 5.50

Postage Stamp Mega Event '92, New York City.

Christmas Type of 1992

Details or entire paintings of The Annunciation by: 5c, Robert Campin. 15c, Melchior Broederlam. 25c, The Annunciation (2 panels), by Fra Filippo Lippi. 35c, Simone Martini. 50c, Fra Filippo Lippi, detail of angel. 75c, The Annunciation (Mary), by Fra Filippo Lippi. 90c, Albert Bouts. $1, D. Di Michelino. $2, Van der Weyden. $3, Sandro Botticelli, detail of angel. $4, Botticelli, detail of Mary. $5, Bernardo Daddi, horiz. No. 1472, Rogier Van der Weyden, vert. No. 1473, Hubert Van Eyck. No. 1474, Botticelli.

Perf. 13½x14, 14x13½

1992, Nov. 16

1461 A281 5c multicolored .25 .25
1462 A281 15c multicolored .30 .25
1463 A281 25c multicolored .35 .25
1464 A281 35c multicolored .45 .30
1464A A281 50c multicolored .65 .50
1465 A281 75c multicolored .85 .70
1466 A281 90c multicolored .90 .90
1467 A281 $1 multicolored .90 .90
1468 A281 $2 multicolored 1.90 1.90
1469 A281 $3 multicolored 2.50 2.50
1470 A281 $4 multicolored 3.00 3.00
1471 A281 $5 multicolored 3.25 3.25
Nos. 1461-1471 (12) 15.30 14.70

Souvenir Sheets

1472 A281 $6 multicolored 4.75 4.75
1473 A281 $6 multicolored 4.75 4.75
1474 A281 $6 multicolored 4.75 4.75

America's Cup Yacht Race — G104

Designs: 15c, Atalanta, Mischief, 1881. 25c, Valkyrie III, Defender. 35c, Shamrock IV, Resolute. 75c, Endeavour II, Ranger, 1937. $1, Sceptre, Columbia, 1958. $2, Australia II, Liberty. $4, Stars and Stripes, Kookaburra III. $5, New Zealand, Stars and Stripes, 1988. No. 1483, America, Aurora, 1851. No. 1484, Emblems of 1992 participants.

1992, Oct. *Perf. 14*

1475 G104 15c multicolored .55 .25
1476 G104 25c multicolored .70 .25
1477 G104 35c multicolored .85 .40
1478 G104 75c multicolored 1.10 .70
1479 G104 $1 multicolored 1.25 .90
1480 G104 $2 multicolored 1.75 1.75
1481 G104 $4 multicolored 2.75 2.75
1482 G104 $5 multicolored 3.00 3.00
Nos. 1475-1482 (8) 11.95 10.00

Souvenir Sheets

1483 G104 $6 multicolored 5.50 5.50
1484 G104 $6 multicolored 5.50 5.50

Nos. 1483-1484 contains one 58x43mm stamp.

G105

Anniversaries and Events — G106

Designs: 25c, Zeppelin Viktoria Luise over Kiel Harbor. 50c, Space Shuttle Columbia. 75c, Flag, arms of Germany, Konrad Adenauer. $1.50, Giant anteater. No. 1489, Scarlet macaw, vert. No. 1490, Emblem of Intl. Conf. on Nutrition. $3, Wolfgang Amadeus Mozart. No. 1492, Berlin airlift. No. 1493, Space Shuttle Endeavour crew repairing Intelsat VI. $5, Hindenburg disaster. No. 1495, Adm. Richard E. Byrd's Ford Trimotor flying over North Pole, 1926. No. 1496, Map of Federal Republic of Germany, vert. No. 1497, Zeppelin Z.4 above clouds. No. 1498, First flight of space shuttle Endeavour. No. 1499, Scene from "The Marriage of Figaro." No. 1500, Jaguar.

1992 Litho. *Perf. 14*

1485 G105 25c multicolored .65 .25
1486 G105 50c multicolored .75 .35
1487 G105 75c multicolored .75 .60
1488 G105 $1.50 multicolored 1.10 1.10
1489 G105 $2 multicolored 2.50 2.00
1490 G105 $2 multicolored 1.50 1.50
1491 G106 $3 multicolored 2.25 2.25
1492 G105 $4 multicolored 3.00 3.00
1493 G105 $4 multicolored 3.00 3.00
1494 G105 $5 multicolored 3.75 3.75
1495 G105 $5 multicolored 3.75 3.75
Nos. 1485-1495 (11) 23.00 21.55

Souvenir Sheets

Perf. 13½

1496 G105 $6 multicolored 4.75 4.75
1497 G105 $6 multicolored 4.75 4.75
1498 G105 $6 multicolored 4.75 4.75

Perf. 14

1499 G106 $6 multicolored 4.75 4.75
1500 G105 $6 multicolored 4.75 4.75

Count Zeppelin, 75th anniv. of death (Nos. 1485, 1494, 1497). Intl. Space Year (Nos. 1486, 1493). Konrad Adenauer, 25th anniv. of death (Nos. 1487, 1492, 1496).Earth Summit, Rio de Janeiro (Nos. 1488-1489, 1500). Intl. Conf. on Nutrition, Rome (No. 1490). Wolfgang Amadeus Mozart, bicent. of death (in 1991) (Nos. 1491, 1499). Intl. Lions Intl., 75th anniv. (No. 1495). Space Year (No. 1498).

Issue dates: Nos. 1491, 1499, Oct. Nos. 1485-1486, 1490, 1493-1495, 1497, Nov. Nos. 1487-1489, 1492, 1496, 1500, Dec.

No. 1496 contains one 39x50mm stamp, Nos. 1497-1498 one 50x39mm stamp, No. 1500 one 52x40mm stamp.

Entertainers Type of 1992

Miniature Sheet

Grammy award winners: No. 1501a, Leonard Bernstein. b, Ray Charles. c, Bob Dylan. d, Barbra Streisand. e, Frank Sinatra. f, Harry Belafonte. g, Aretha Franklin. h, Garth Brooks.

No. 1502a, Johnny Cash. b, Willie Nelson. No. 1503a, Charlie Parker. b, Miles Davis.

1992, Nov. 19 *Perf. 14*

1501 A286 90c Sheet of 8, #a.-h. 17.50 17.50

Souvenir Sheets

1502 A286 $3 Sheet of 2, #a.-b. 6.50 6.50
1503 A286 $3 Sheet of 2, #a.-b. 6.50 6.50

Dogs — G107

Designs: 35c, Irish Setter, Glendalough, Ireland. 50c, Boston terrier, State House, Boston, US. 75c, Beagle, Temple to Athena, Greece. $1, Weimaraner, Nesselwang, Germany. $3, Norwegian elkhound, Urnes Stave Church, Norway. $4, Mastiff, Great Sphinx, Egypt. No. 1510, Akita, Kyoto torii, Japan. No. 1511, Saluki, Rub'al Khali, Saudi Arabia. No. 1512, Shar pei, China. No. 1513, Bulldog, United Kingdom.

1993, Jan. 20 Litho. *Perf. 14*

1504 G107 35c multicolored .65 .35
1505 G107 50c multicolored .90 .65
1506 G107 75c multicolored 1.25 .75
1507 G107 $1 multicolored 1.60 1.10
1508 G107 $3 multicolored 3.25 3.25
1509 G107 $4 multicolored 3.50 3.50
1510 G107 $5 multicolored 3.50 3.50
1511 G107 $5 multicolored 3.50 3.50
Nos. 1504-1511 (8) 18.15 16.60

Souvenir Sheets

1512 G107 $6 multicolored 4.75 4.75
1513 G107 $6 multicolored 4.75 4.75

Louvre Painting Type

Miniature Sheet

Details or entire paintings: No. 1514a, The Virgin and Child with Young St. John the Baptist, by Botticelli. b, The Buffet, by Chardin. c, The Provider, by Chardin. d, Erasmus, by Durer. e, Self-Portrait, by Durer. f, Jeanne of Aragon, by Raphael. g-h, La Belle Jardiniere (diff. details), by Raphael.

$6, Charles I, King of England, Hunting, by Van Dyck.

1993, Mar. 8 Litho. *Perf. 12*

1514 A289 $1 Sheet of 8, #a.-h. + label 12.00 12.00

Souvenir Sheet

Perf. 14½

1515 A289 $6 multicolored 7.75 7.75

No. 1515 contains one 55x88mm stamp.

Butterflies — G108

15c, Polydamas swallowtail. 35c, Guaraguao skipper. 45c, Giant hairstreak. 75c, Malachite. $1, Cloudless sulphur. $2, Silver spot. $4, St. Christopher's hairstreak. $5, Common long-tail skipper.

No. 1524, Orion. No. 1525, Zebra.

1993, Apr. 13 Litho. *Perf. 14*

1516 G108 15c multicolored .35 .35
1517 G108 35c multicolored .50 .50
1518 G108 45c multicolored .55 .55
1519 G108 75c multicolored 1.00 1.00
1520 G108 $1 multicolored 1.25 1.25
1521 G108 $2 multicolored 2.50 2.50
1522 G108 $4 multicolored 5.00 5.00
1523 G108 $5 multicolored 6.50 6.50
Nos. 1516-1523 (8) 17.65 17.65

Souvenir Sheets

1524 G108 $6 multicolored 8.00 8.00
1525 G108 $6 multicolored 8.00 8.00

Flowers Type of 1993

No. 1526, Hibiscus. No. 1527, Columbine. No. 1528, Red ginger. No. 1529, Bougainvillea. No. 1530, Crown imperial. No. 1531, Fairy orchid. No. 1532, Heliconia. No. 1533, Tulip. No. 1534, Balloonflower, horiz. No. 1535, Blackberry lily, horiz.

1993, May

1526 A291 35c multicolored .65 .30
1527 A291 35c multicolored .65 .30
1528 A291 45c multicolored .65 .35
1529 A291 75c multicolored .90 .60
1530 A291 $1 multicolored 1.00 .75
1531 A291 $2 multicolored 1.60 1.60
1532 A291 $4 multicolored 2.75 2.75
1533 A291 $5 multicolored 3.00 3.00
Nos. 1526-1533 (8) 11.20 9.65

Souvenir Sheets

1534 A291 $6 multicolored 4.50 4.50
1535 A291 $6 multicolored 4.50 4.50

No. 1536 will not be assigned.

Coronation of Queen Elizabeth II Type of 1993

Miniature Sheet

Designs: a, 35c, Official coronation photograph. b, 50c, Ampulla, spoon. c, $2, Queen, following coronation. d, $4, Queen, Prince Charles and his family, c. 1984.

$6, Portrait, by Pietro Annigoni, 1954.

1993, June 2 Litho. *Perf. 13½x14*

1537 A293 Sheet, 2 each #a.-d. 10.50 10.50

Souvenir Sheet

Perf. 14

1538 A293 $6 multicolored 5.50 5.50

No. 1538 contains one 28x42mm stamp.

Anniversaries and Events Types of 1993

Designs: 50c, Telescope. 75c, Willy Brandt, Lyndon Johnson, 1961. $4, Radio telescope. $5, Willy Brandt, Eleanor Hulles, 1957. No. 1543, Copernicus. No. 1544, Willy, Rut Brandt.

1993, July 1 Litho. *Perf. 14*

1539 A294 50c multicolored 1.40 .50
1540 A295 75c multicolored 1.60 1.60
1541 A294 $4 multicolored 4.00 4.00
1542 A295 $5 multicolored 4.00 4.00
Nos. 1539-1542 (4) 11.00 10.10

Souvenir Sheets

1543 A294 $6 multicolored 5.50 5.50
1544 A295 $6 multicolored 5.50 5.50

Copernicus, 450th death anniv. (Nos. 1539, 1541, 1543). Willy Brandt, 1st death anniv. (Nos. 1540, 1542, 1544).

Songbird Type of 1993

Miniature Sheet

Designs: No. 1545a, 15c, Painted bunting. b, 15c, White-throated sparrow. c, 25c, Common grackle. d, 25c, Royal flycatcher. e, 35c, Swallow tanager. f, 35c, Vermilion flycatcher. g, 45c, Black headed bunting. h, 50c, Rosebreasted grosbeak. i, 75c, Corn bunting. j, 75c, Rosebreasted thrush tanager. k, $1, Buff-throated saltator. l, $4, Plush-capped finch.

No. 1546, Bohemian waxwing. No. 1547, Pine grosbeak.

1993, July 13

1545 A297 Sheet of 12, #a.-l. 14.00 14.00

Souvenir Sheets

1546 A297 $6 multicolored 7.25 7.25
1547 A297 $6 multicolored 7.25 7.25

Seashell Type of 1993

Miniature Sheet

Designs: No. 1548a, 15c, Hawk wing conch. b, 15c, Music volute. c, 25c, Globe vase, deltoid rock shell. d, 35c, Spiny vase. e, 35c, Common sundial, common purple snail. f, 45c, Caribbean donax, gaudy asaphis. g, 45c, Mouse cone. h, 50c, Gold-mouthed triton. i, 75c, Tulip mussel, trigonal tivela. j, 75c, Common dove shell, chestnut latirus. k, $1, Wide-mouthed purpura. l, $4, Atlantic thorny oyster, Atlantic wing oyster.

No. 1549, Turkey wing. No. 1550, Zebra periwinkle.

1993, July 19 Litho. *Perf. 14*

1548 A298 Sheet of 12, #a.-l. 13.00 13.00

Souvenir Sheet

1549 A298 $6 multicolored 6.50 6.50
1550 A298 $6 multicolored 6.50 6.50

Picasso Type of 1993

Paintings: 15c, Painter and Model, 1928. $1, The Artist and His Model, 1963. $4, The Drawing Lession, 1925. $6, Picasso seated in front of canvas, 1956.

1993, July 1 Litho. *Perf. 14*

1551	A299	15c multi, horiz.	.60	.35
1552	A299	$1 multi, horiz.	1.50	1.50
1553	A299	$4 multi, horiz.	3.75	3.75
		Nos. 1551-1553 (3)	5.85	5.60

Souvenir Sheet

1554	A299	$6 multi, horiz.	5.00	5.00

Olympics Type of 1993

Design: $6, Emil Zografski, ski jump.

1993, July 1

1554A	A300	35c multi	.30	.30
1554B	A300	$5 multi	3.75	3.75
1555	A300	$6 multicolored	5.00	5.00
		Nos. 1554A-1555 (3)	9.05	9.05

Polska '93 Type of 1993

Paintings: 75c, Gra w Gudziki, by Ludomir Slendzinski, 1928. $2, Pocalunek Mongoskiego Ksiecia, by S.I. Witkiewicz, 1915. $6, Allegory, by Jan Wydra, 1929.

1993, July 1

1556	A301	75c multi, horiz.	1.25	1.25
1557	A301	$2 multi, horiz.	3.50	3.50

Souvenir Sheet

1558	A301	$6 multicolored	5.25	5.25

Taipei '93 Type

Designs: 35c, Macao Palace, Hong Kong. 45c, Stone pixie, Ming Tomb, Nanjing. $1, Stone camels, Ming Tomb, Nanjing. $5, Stone lion and elephant, Ming Tomb, Nanjing.

Sculpture: No. 1563a, Nesting quail incense burner. b, Standing quail incense burner. c, Seated qilin incense burner. d, Pottery horse, Han Dynasty. e, Seated caparisoned elephant. f, Cow (imitation delft).

No. 1564, Sumatran tiger.

1993 Litho. *Perf. 14x13½*

1559	A302	35c multi, horiz.	.25	.25
1560	A302	45c multi, horiz.	.35	.35
1561	A302	$1 multi, horiz.	.75	.75
1562	A302	$5 multi, horiz.	3.75	3.75
		Nos. 1559-1562 (4)	5.10	5.10

Miniature Sheet

1563	A302	$1.50 Sheet of 6, #a.-f.	11.00	11.00

Souvenir Sheet

Perf. 13½x14

1564	A302	$6 multicolored	7.50	7.50

Nos. 1563a-1563f are horiz.

With Bangkok '93 Emblem

Designs: 35c, Naga snakes, Chiang Mai's Temple, Thailand. 45c, Sri Mariamman Temple, Singapore. $1, Topiary, Hua Hin Resort, Thailand. $5, Pak Tai Temple, Cheung Chau Island.

Thai paintings: No. 1569a, Buddha's victory over Mara. b, Mythological elephant. c, Battle with Mara. d, Untitled work, by Panya Wijinthanasarn, 1984. e, Temple mural. f, Elephants in Pahcekha Buddha's Heaven.

No. 1570, Monkey.

1993 *Perf. 14x13½*

1565	A302	35c multi, horiz.	.25	.25
1566	A302	45c multi, horiz.	.35	.35
1567	A302	$1 multi, horiz.	.75	.75
1568	A302	$5 multi, horiz.	3.75	3.75
		Nos. 1565-1568 (4)	5.10	5.10

Miniature Sheet

1569	A302	$1.50 Sheet of 6, #a.-f.	11.00	11.00

Souvenir Sheet

Perf. 13½x14

1570	A302	$6 multicolored	6.50	6.50

Nos. 1569a-1569f are horiz.

Indopex '93 Type

Designs: 35c, Natl. Museum, Central Jakarta, Indonesia. 45c, Sacred Wheel & Deer, Monastery. $1, Ramayana relief, Panataran Temple. $5, Candi Tikus, Trawulan, East Java.

Paintings: No. 1575a, Bullock Carts, bu Batara Lubis, 1951. b, Surat Irsa II, by A.D. Pirous, 1983. c, Self-portrait with Goat, by Kartika, 1987. d, The Cow-est Cow, by Ivan Sagito, 1987. e, Rain Storm, by Sudjana Kerton, 1984. f, Story of Pucuk Flower, by Effendi, 1972.

No. 1576, Banteng cattle.

1993, Aug. 13 Litho. *Perf. 14x13½*

1571	A302	35c multicolored	.25	.25
1572	A302	45c multicolored	.35	.35
1573	A302	$1 multicolored	.75	.75
1574	A302	$5 multicolored	3.75	3.75
		Nos. 1571-1574 (4)	5.10	5.10

Miniature Sheet

1575	A302	$1.50 Sheet of 6, #a.-f.	11.00	11.00

Souvenir Sheet

1576	A302	$6 multicolored	5.25	5.25

Nos. 1571-1576 are horiz.

1994 World Cup Soccer Championships, US — G109

Designs: 15c, Stuart McCall, Carlos Verri. 25c, Carlos Verri, Diego Maradona. 35c, S. Schillaci, J.P. Saldana. 45c, Ruud Gullit, Mark Wright. $1, Carlos Verri, Diego Maradona. $2, Zubizarreta, Fernandez, Albert. $4, Gheorghe Hagi, Paul McGrath. $5, Alberto Gorriz, Enzo Scifo. No. 1585, Schaefer Stadium, Foxboro, MA. No. 1586, Rudi Voeller, vert.

1993, Sept. 7 Litho. *Perf. 14*

1577	G109	15c multicolored	.45	.25
1578	G109	25c multicolored	.45	.25
1579	G109	35c multicolored	.45	.25
1580	G109	45c multicolored	.45	.40
1581	G109	$1 multicolored	.75	.75
1582	G109	$2 multicolored	1.50	1.50
1583	G109	$4 multicolored	3.00	3.00
1584	G109	$5 multicolored	3.75	3.75
		Nos. 1577-1584 (8)	10.80	10.15

Souvenir Sheets

1585	G109	$6 multicolored	5.00	5.00
1586	G109	$6 multicolored	5.00	5.00

Mickey Mouse, 65th Anniv. Type

Movie clips: 15c, The Worm Turns, 1937. 35c, Mickey's Rival, 1936. 50c, The Pointer, 1939. 75c, Society Dog Show, 1939. $1, A Gentleman's Gentleman, 1941. $2, The Little Whirlwind, 1941. $4, Mickey Down Under, 1948. $5, R'coon Dawg, 1951.

No. 1595, Mickey's Garden, 1935, vert. No. 1596, Lonesome Ghosts, 1937.

Perf. 13½x14, 14x13½

1993, Nov. 11 Litho.

1587	A305	15c multicolored	.60	.25
1588	A305	35c multicolored	.80	.35
1589	A305	50c multicolored	1.00	.60
1590	A305	75c multicolored	1.40	1.00
1591	A305	$1 multicolored	1.60	1.10
1592	A305	$2 multicolored	2.25	2.25
1593	A305	$4 multicolored	3.25	3.25
1594	A305	$5 multicolored	3.25	3.25
		Nos. 1587-1594 (8)	14.15	12.05

Souvenir Sheets

1595	A305	$6 multicolored	5.50	5.50
1596	A305	$6 multicolored	5.50	5.50

Christmas Type of 1993

Various details from Adoration of the Shepherds by Durer: 10c, 75c, $1, $4. No. 1605, $6, horiz.

Various details from Oddi Altarpiece by Raphael: 25c, 35c, 50c, $5. No. 1606, $6.

Perf. 13½x14, 14x13½ (#1605)

1993, Nov. 22 Litho.

1597-1604	A306	Set of 8	11.00	11.00

Souvenir Sheets

1605-1606	A306	Set of 2	11.00	11.00

Eckener Type of 1993

Designs: 50c, Graf Zeppelin over Rio De Janeiro. 75c, Dr. Hugo Eckener. $5, Eckener commanding Graf Zeppelin. $6, Eckener, Pres. Herbert Hoover.

1993, Dec. 21 Litho. *Perf. 14*

1607-1609	A307	Set of 3	5.25	5.25

Souvenir Sheet

1610	A307	$6 multicolored	5.00	5.00

Royal Air Force Anniv. Type of 1993

Designs: 15c, Avro Lancaster. $5, Short Sunderland. $6, Supermarine Spitfire.

1993, Dec. 21

1611	A308	15c multicolored	.35	.25
1612	A308	$5 multicolored	6.50	6.50

Souvenir Sheet

1613	A308	$6 multicolored	7.00	7.00

Automobile Anniv. Type

Designs: 25c, 1955 Mercedes Benz 300SLR. 45c, 1957 Ford Thunderbird. $4, 1929 Ford 150A Station Wagon. $5, Mercedes Benz 540K.

Each $6: No. 1618, 1929 Mercedes Benz SSK. No. 1619, 1924 Ford Model T.

1993, Dec. 21 Litho. *Perf. 14*

1614-1617	A309	Set of 4	10.00	10.00

Souvenir Sheets

1618-1619	A309	Set of 2	11.00	11.00

1st Benz 4-wheel car, 1st Ford engine, cent.

First Gas Balloon Flight in America Type

Designs: 35c, Blanchard's balloon crossing Delaware River. $3, Blanchard delivering Washington's passport of introduction. $6, Balloon in flight, vert.

1993, Dec. 21 Litho. *Perf. 14*

1620-1621	A310	Set of 2	3.50	3.50

Souvenir Sheet

1622	A310	$6 multicolored	5.00	5.00

Fine Art Type

Details or entire paintings by Rembrandt: 15c, Hendrickje Stoffels as Flora. 35c, Lady & Gentlemen in Black. 50c, Aristotle with Bust of Homer. $5, Christ & the Woman of Samaria.

Details or entire paintings by Matisse: 75c, Interior: Flowers and Parakeets. $1, Goldfish. $2, The Girl with Green Eyes. $3, Still Life with a Plaster Figure.

Each $6: No. 1631, Anna Accused of Stealing the Kid, by Rembrandt. No. 1632, Tea in the Garden by Matisse, horiz.

Perf. 13½x14, 14x13½

1993, Dec. 31 Litho.

1623-1630	A311	Set of 8	11.00	11.00

Souvenir Sheets

1631-1632	A311	Set of 2	11.00	11.00

Hong Kong '94 Type

Designs: No. 1633, Hong Kong #426, jet at Kai Tak Airport. No. 1634, Junk, Kwaloon Bay, #975.

Chinese jade: No. 1635a, White jade brush washer. b, Archaic jade brush washer. c, Dark green jade brush washer. d, Green jade alms bowl. e, Archaic jade dog. f, Yellow jade brush washer.

1994, Feb. 18 Litho. *Perf. 14*

1633	A313	40c multicolored	.90	.90
1634	A313	40c multicolored	.90	.90
a.		Pair, #1633-1634	2.40	2.40

Miniature Sheet

1635	A314	45c Sheet of 6, #a.-f.	7.50	7.50

Nos. 1633-1634 issued in sheets of of 5 pairs. No. 1634a is a continuous design. Nos. 1635a-1635f are horiz.

New Year 1994 (Year of the Dog) (No. 1635e).

Dinosaurs G110

15c, Spinosaurus. 35c, Apatosaurus. 45c, Tyrannosaurus rex. 55c, Triceratops. $1, Pachycephalosaurus. $2, Pteranodon. $4, Parasaurolophus. $5, Brachiosaurus.

Each $6: No. 1644, Brachiosaurus, vert. No. 1645, Tyrannosaurus, spinosaurus, vert.

1994 Litho. *Perf. 14*

1636-1643	G110	Set of 8	12.50	12.50

Souvenir Sheets

1644-1645	G110	Set of 2	11.00	11.00

Mushrooms G111

Designs: 35c, Hygrocybe hypohaemacta. 45c, Cantherellus cinnabarinus. 50c, Marasmius haematocephalus. 75c, Mycena pura. $1, Gymnopilus russipes. $2, Galocybe cyanocephala. $4, Pleuteus chrysophlebius. $5, Chlorophyllum molybdites.

Each $6: No. 1654, Collybia fibrosipes. No. 1655, Xeromphalina tenuipes.

1994

1646-1653	G111	Set of 8	10.00	10.00

Souvenir Sheets

1654-1655	G111	Set of 2	9.50	9.50

D-Day Type of 1994

40c, Churchill bridgelayer in action. $2, Sherman "Firefly" attacks beach. $3, Churchill Crocodile flame thrower. $6, Sherman "Crab" flail tank.

1994, Aug. 4 Litho. *Perf. 14*

1656-1658	A318	Set of 3	5.00	5.00

Souvenir Sheet

1659	A318	$6 multicolored	5.25	5.25

First Manned Moon Landing, 25th Anniv. Type of 1994

Miniature Sheet of 6

Tribute to Challenger crew: No. 1660a, Slidewire escape training. b, Christa A. McAuliffe. c, Challenger 51-L on pad LC39B. d, Gregory B. Jarvis. e, Ellison S. Onizuka. f, Ronald E. McNair.

$6, Judith A. Resnick, vert.

1994, Aug. 4

1660	A319	$1.10 #a.-f.	7.50	7.50

Souvenir Sheet

1661	A319	$6 multicolored	6.50	6.50

PHILAKOREA '94 Type

Designs: 40c, Onung Tomb, Korea. $1, Stone pagoda, Mt. Nansan, Kyongju. $4, Pusan Port.

Paintings, by Sin Yunbok, late Choson Dynasty, 1758: No. 1665a-1665b, Admiring spring in the Country. c-d, Women on Dano Day. e-f, Enjoying Lotuses While Listening to Music. g-h, Women by a Crystal Stream.

$6, Blacksmith's Shop, by Kim Duksin (1754-1822).

1994, Aug. 4 *Perf. 14, 13½ (#1665)*

1662-1664	A320	Set of 3	4.25	4.25

Miniature Sheet of 8

1665	A321	$1 #a.-h.	9.50	9.50

Souvenir Sheet

1666	A320	$6 multicolored	5.00	5.00

Orchid Type of 1994

15c, Cattleya aurantiaca. 25c, Blettia patula. 45c, Sobralia macrantha. 75c, Encyclia belizensis. $1, Sophrolaeliocattleya. $2, Encyclia frangrans. $4, Schombocattleya. $5, Brassolaeliocattleya.

Each $6: No. 1675, Brassavola nodosa. No. 1676, Ornithidium coccineum.

1994, Aug. 7 *Perf. 14*

1667-1674	A322	Set of 8	11.00	11.00

Souvenir Sheets

1675-1676	A322	Set of 2	10.00	10.00

1994 World Cup Soccer Type

Miniature Sheet of 6

Designs: No. 1677a, Steve Mark, Grenada. b, Jurgen Kohler, Germany. c, Almir, Brazil. d, Michael Windischmann, US. e, Guiseppe Giannini, Italy. f, Rashidi Yekini, Nigeria.

Each $6: No. 1678, Kemari. No. 1679, The World Cup.

1994, Aug. 11 *Perf. 14*

1677	A323	75c #a.-f.	5.25	5.25

Souvenir Sheets

1678-1679	A323	Set of 2	9.50	9.50

Disney's PHILAKOREA '94 — G112

15c, Mickey, Unjin Miruk, Kwanch Ok Temple. 35c, Goofy, statue of Admiral Yi, Chonju. 50c, Cousin Gus, Donald. 75c, Mickey playing flute. $1, Goofy, Tolharubang Grandfather statue. $2, Mickey, Minnie, Hyang-Wonjong. $4, Mickey, Unsan Pyolshin Festival. $5, Minnie, ceremonial fan.

Each $6: No. 1688, Minnie, Buk drum, vert. No. 1689, Mickey, Pugok Hawaii, vert.

1994, Aug. 16 Litho. *Perf. 14x13½*
1680-1687 G112 Set of 8 15.00 15.00

Souvenir Sheets
Perf. 13½x14

1688-1689 G112 Set of 2 12.00 12.00

This set exists with very low face values.

Fish Type of 1994

Designs, each 75c: No. 1690a, Yellowtail snapper (b, e). b, Caribbean reef shark (a). c, Great barracuda. d, Redtail parrotfish. e, Blue tang. f, Queen angelfish. g, Red hind (h). h, Rock beauty. i, Queen parrotfish. j, Spanish hogfish. k, Spotted moray. l, Queen triggerfish (i).

Each 75c: No. 1691a, Pork fish (b). b, Blue chromis (a). c, Caribbean reef shark. d, Long-spine squirrelfish. e, Foureye butterflyfish. f, Blue head. g, Royal gramma. h, Sharpnose puffer. i, Longsnout seahorse. j, Blackbar soldierfish (g, k). k, Redlip blenny. l, Rainbow wrasse.

Each $6: No. 1692, Rainbow wrasse, diff. No. 1693, Queen angelfish, diff.

1994, Sept. 1 *Perf. 14*
Miniature Sheets of 12

1690-1691 A324 Set of 2 24.00 24.00

Souvenir Sheets

1692-1693 A324 Set of 2 12.00 12.00

Intl. Olympic Committee Type of 1994

Designs: 50c, Silke Renk, Germany, javelin, 1992. $1.50, Mark Spitz, US, swimming, 1972. $6, Team Japan, Nordic combined, 1994.

1994 *Perf. 14*
1694 A325 50c multi, horiz. .40 .40
1695 A325 $1.50 multi, horiz. 1.10 1.10

Souvenir Sheet

1696 A326 $6 multicolored 5.00 5.00

Intl. Year of the Family Type of 1994

1994
1697 A329 $1 Family of 5 .80 .80

Order of the Caribbean Community Type

Designs: 25c, Sir Shridath Ramphal, statesman, Guyana. 50c, William Demas, economist, Trinidad & Tobago. $2, Derek Walcott, writer, St. Lucia.

1994, Sept. 1
1698-1700 A330 Set of 3 3.00 3.00

Christmas Type of 1994

Paintings, by Bartolome Murillo: 15c, The Annunciation. 35c, The Adoration of the Shepherds. No. 1703, 50c, Flight into Egypt. No. 1704, 50c, Virgin and Child with St. Rose. 75c, Virgin and Child. $1, Virgin of the Rosary. $4, The Holy Family.

Each $6: No. 1708, Adoration of the Shepherds. No. 1709, The Holy Family with a Little Bird.

1994, Dec. 5 Litho. *Perf. 13½x14*
1701-1707 A331 Set of 7 7.50 7.50

Souvenir Sheets

1708-1709 A331 Set of 2 10.00 10.00

Bird Type of 1995

25c, Ground dove. 50c, White-winged dove, horiz. $2, Inca dove. $4, Mourning dove, horiz.

1995, Jan. 10 *Perf. 14*
1710-1713 A332 Set of 4 9.50 9.50

English Touring Cricket, Cent. Type

Designs: 50c, M.A. Atherton, England, horiz. 75c, C.E.L. Ambrose, Leeward Isl./W. Indies. $1, B.C. Lara, Trinidad/W. Indies. $3, West Indies Team, horiz.

1995, Jan. 12
1715-1717 A333 Set of 3 4.00 4.00

Souvenir Sheet

1718 A333 $3 multicolored 4.00 4.00

Miniature Sheet

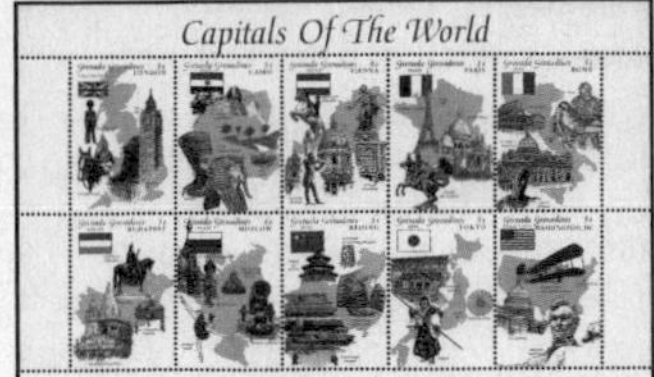

Capitals of the World — G113

Designs: a, London. b, Cairo. c, Vienna. d, Paris. e, Rome. f, Budapest. g, Moscow. h, Beijing. i, Tokyo. j, Wasington.

1995, Mar. 10 Litho. *Perf. 14*
1719 G113 $1 #a.-j. 10.00 10.00

New Year 1995 (Year of the Boar) — G114

Various stylized boars with different Chinese inscriptions: a, Smiling, purple legs. b, Smiling, red legs. c, Brown legs. d, Red legs.

$2, Two boars, horiz.

1995, Apr. 21 Litho. *Perf. 14½*
1720 G114 75c Block or horiz. strip of 4, #a.-d. 2.25 2.25
e. Souvenir sheet of 4, #1720a-1720d 3.00 3.00

Souvenir Sheet

1721 G114 $2 multicolored 2.25 2.25

No. 1720 was issued in miniature sheets of 16 stamps.

VE Day Type of 1995

No. 1721A: b, Mitsubishi G4M1 "Betty." c, Aircraft carrying submarine I-14. d, Mitsubishi G3M1. e, Destroyer Akizuki. f, Battleship Kirishima. g, Cruiser Asigari.

Bombers: No. 1722: a, Avro Lancaster, Tallboy bomb. b, Junkers JU-88. c, B-25 Mitchell. d, B-17 Flying Fortress. e, Petlyakov Pe-2. f, Martin B-26 Marauder. g, Henkel He-111. h, Consolidated B-24 Liberator.

No. 1723, Pres. Truman displaying newspaper headline. No. 1723A, Aichi D3A1 "Val" dive bomber.

1995, May 8 *Perf. 14*
Miniature Sheets of 6 and 8

1721A A336 $2 #b.-g. + label 9.50 9.50
1722 A336 $2 #a.-h. + label 13.00 13.00

Souvenir Sheets

1723 A336 $6 multicolored 5.25 5.25
1723A A336 $6 multicolored 6.00 6.00

Inscription in central label of No. 1721A misidentifies a Yokosuka MXY-7 Okha kamikaze plane.

No. 1723 contains one 57x42mm stamp.

Scout Jamboree Type of 1995

a, 75c, Beach scene, scout. b, $1, Mountains, sea, scout with pole. c, $2, Flag, scout salute.

$6, Snorkeling, fish.

1995, May 8
1724 A337 Strip of 3, #a.-c. 3.00 3.00

Souvenir Sheet

1725 A337 $6 multicolored 5.50 5.50

No. 1724 was issued in sheets of 9 stamps.

UN, 50th Anniv. Type of 1995

Designs: a, 75c, Building, UN flag. b, $1, Trygve Lie (1896-1968), Norway, 1st Secretary General. c, $2, Flag, member of UN peacekeeping force.

$6, Dove, emblem.

1995, May 8
1726 A338 Strip of 3, #a.-c. 3.00 3.00

Souvenir Sheet

1727 A338 $6 multicolored 4.75 4.75

No. 1726 is a continuous design and was issued in sheets of 9 stamps.

Marine Life of the Caribbean G115

No. 1728, each $1: a, Dolphins. b, Scorpion fish. c, Sea turtle, rock beauty. d, Butterflyfish, nurse shark. e, Angel fish. f, Grouper coney. g, Rainbow eel, moray eel. h, Sun flower-star, coral crab. i, Octopus.

No. 1729, each $1: a, Bull shark. b, Big white shark. c, Octopus. d, Barracuda (e). e, Moray eel (f, h, i). f, Spotted eagle ray. g, Gold-spotted snake. h, Stingray. i, Grouper.

$5, French angelfish. $6, Hammerhead shark.

1995, May 3 Litho. *Perf. 14*
Miniature Sheets of 9, #a-i

1728-1729 G115 Set of 2 18.00 18.00

Souvenir Sheets

1730 G115 $5 multicolored 4.25 4.25
1731 G115 $6 multicolored 5.00 5.00

Domesticated Animals — G116

Horses: 15c, Suffolk punch. 25c, Shetland pony. $1, Arab. $3, Shire horse.

Dogs, each 75c: No. 1736a, Shetland sheepdog. b, Bull terrier. c, Afghan. d, Scottish terrier. e, Labrador retriever. f, English springer spaniel. g, Samoyed. h, Irish setter. i, Border collie. j, Pekingese. k, Dachshund. l, Weimaraner.

Cats, each 75c: No. 1737a, Blue persian. b, Sorrel abyssinian. c, White angora. d, Brown burmese. e, Red tabby exotic shorthair. f, Seal-point birman. g, Korat. h, Norwegian forest cat. i, Lilac-point Balinese. j, British shorthair. k, Red self longhair. l, Calico manx.

Each $6: No. 1738, English setter. No. 1739, Seal-point colorpoint.

1995, May 3
1732-1735 G116 Set of 4 3.50 3.50

Miniature Sheets of 12, #a-l

1736-1737 G116 Set of 2 14.00 14.00

Souvenir Sheets

1738-1739 G116 Set of 2 11.00 11.00

Sierra Club, Cent. — G117

No. 1740, each $1: a, Brown pelican. b, Northern spotted owl. c, Northern spotted owl in winter. d, Jaguarundi. e, Central American spider monkeys facing forward. f, Two Central American spider monkeys. g, Central American spider monkey. h, Wood stork. i, Maned wolves.

No. 1741, each $1, vert: a, Northern spotted owl. b, Brown pelican. c, Brown pelican up close. d, Jaguarundi up close. e, Jaguarundi. f, Maned wolf. g, Wood stork facing right. h, Wood stork facing left. i, Maned wolf up close.

Miniature Sheets of 9, #a-i

1995, May 5
1740-1741 G117 Set of 2 25.00 25.00

FAO, 50th Anniv. — G118

No. 1742: a, 75c, Man working in field. b, $1, Woman working in field. c, $2, Two workers in field.

$6, Child with chopsticks.

1995, May 8
1742 G118 Strip of 3, #a.-c. 3.00 3.00

Souvenir Sheet

1743 G118 $6 multicolored 4.50 4.50

No. 1742 was issued in sheets of 9 stamps.

Rotary Intl., 90th Anniv. G119

1995, May 8
1744 G119 $5 Paul Harris, emblem 3.75 3.75

Souvenir Sheet

1745 G119 $6 Old, new emblems 4.50 4.50

Queen Mother, 95th Anniv. Type of 1995

No. 1746: a, Drawing. b, In black outfit. c, Formal portrait. d, In green outfit.

No. 1747, Speaking at Blitz Memorial.

1995, May 8
1746 A344 $1.50 Strip or block of 4, #a.-d. 5.50 5.50

Souvenir Sheet

1747 A344 $6 multicolored 5.50 5.50

No. 1746 was issued in sheets of 8 stamps.

Sheets of Nos. 1746-1747 exist with black border and text "In Memoriam - 1900-2002" in sheet margins.

1996 Summer Olympics Type

No. 1748, horiz: a, Rosemary Ackerman, East Germany, high jump. b, Li Ning, China, gymnastics. c, Denise Parker, US, archery.

No. 1749, horiz: a, Terry Carlisle, US, skeet shooting. b, Kathleen Nord, East Germany, 200-meter butterfly. c, Brigit Schmidt, East Germany, kayaking.

Each $6: No. 1750, George Foreman, US, boxing. No. 1751, Dan Gable US, Kikuo Wada, Japan, wrestling.

1995, June 23
1748 A345 15c Strip of 3, #a.-c. .60 .60
1749 A345 $3 Strip of 3, #a.-c. 9.50 9.50

Souvenir Sheets

1750-1751 A345 Set of 2 11.00 11.00

G120

Designs: 10c, Brown pelican. 15c, Common stilt. 25c, Cuban trogan. 35c, Flamingo. 75c, Parrot. $1, Pintail duck. $2, Ringed kingfisher. $3, Strip-headed tanager.

No. 1760: a, Great blue heron. b, Jamaican tody. c, Laughing gull. d, Purple-throated carib. e, Red-legged thrush. f, Ruddy duck. g, Shoveler duck. h, West Indian red-bellied woodpecker.

Each $5: No. 1761, Blue-hooded Euphonia. No. 1762, Village weaver.

1995, Sept. 5 Litho. *Perf. 14*
1752-1759 G120 Set of 8 8.00 8.00

Miniature Sheet of 8

1760 G120 $1 #a.-h. 8.00 8.00

Souvenir Sheets

1761-1762 G120 Set of 2 10.50 10.50

Singapore '95 (Nos. 1760-1762). No. 1760d is misspelled.

Mickey's High Sea Adventure — G121

10c, Goofy carrying treasure chests, Donald. 35c, Mickey, Minnie at helm. 75c, Mickey, Donald, Goofy opening treasure chest. $1, Pirates confronting Mickey. $2, Mickey, Goofy, Donald in life boat. $5, Goofy using mop to fight enemy.

Each $6: No. 1769, Cannonballs being shot at Goofy, vert. No. 1770, Mickey on island, monkey pinching his nose, vert.

1995, Oct. 2 Litho. ***Perf. 14x13½***

1763-1768 G121 Set of 6 7.00 7.00

Souvenir Sheets

Perf. 13½x14

1769-1770 G121 Set of 2 10.00 10.00

Nobel Prize Recipients Type of 1995

No. 1770A, Derek Walcott, literature, 1992. No. 1770B, W. Arthur Lewis, economics, 1979.

No. 1771, each $1: a, Heike Kamerlingh Onnes, physics, 1913. b, Fridtjof Nansen, 1922. c, Sir Ronald Ross, physiology or medicine, 1902. d, Paul Müller, physiology or medicine, 1948. e, Allvar Gullstrand, physiology or medicine, 1911. f, Gerhart Hauptmann, literature, 1912. g, Hans Spemann, physiology or medicine, 1935. h, Cecil F. Powell, physics, 1950. i, Walther Bothe, physics, 1954.

No. 1772, each $1: a, Jules Bordet, physiology or medicine, 1919. b, René Cassin, peace, 1968. c, Verner von Heidenstam, literature, 1916. d, Jose Echegaray, literature, 1904. e, Otto Wallach, chemistry, 1910. f, Corneille Heymans, physiology or medicine, 1938. g, Ivar Giaever, physics, 1973. h, Sir William Cremer, peace, 1903. i, John W. Strutt, physics, 1904.

No. 1773, each $1: a, James Franck, physics, 1925. b, Tobias M.C. Asser, peace, 1911. c, Carl F.G. Spitteler, literature, 1919. d, Christiaan Eijkman, physiology or medicine, 1929. e, Ragnar Granit, physiology or medicine, 1967. f, Frederic Passy, peace, 1901. g, Louis Neel, physics, 1970. h, Sir William Ramsay, chemistry, 1904. i, Philip Noel-Baker, peace, 1959.

Each $6: No. 1774, Albert Schweitzer, peace, 1952. No. 1775, Willy Brandt, peace, 1971. No. 1776, Winston Churchill, literature, 1953.

1995, Oct. 18 Litho. ***Perf. 14***

1770A A354 75c multicolored .55 .55
1770B A354 75c multicolored .55 .55

Miniature Sheets of 9, #a-i

1771-1773 A354 Set of 3 20.00 20.00

Souvenir Sheets

1774-1776 A354 Set of 3 18.00 18.00

Miniature Sheets

Motion Pictures, Cent. — G122

Actresses, each $1: No. 1777a, Marion Davies. b, Marlene Dietrich. c, Lillian Gish. d, Bette Davis. e, Elizabeth Taylor. f, Veronica Lake. g, Ava Gardner. h, Grace Kelly. i, Kim Novak.

Romantic couples, each $1: No. 1778a, Nita Naldi, Rudolph Valentino. b, Ramon Novarro, Alice Terry. c, Frederic March, Joan Crawford. d, Clark Gable, Vivien Leigh. e, Barbara Stanwyck, Burt Lancaster. f, Warren Beatty, Natalie Wood. g, Spencer Tracy, Katharine Hepburn. h, Humphrey Bogart, Lauren Bacall. i, Omar Sharif, Julie Christie.

Each $6: No. 1779, Sophia Loren. No. 1780, Greta Garbo, John Gilbert, horiz.

1995, Nov. 3 ***Perf. 13½x14***

Sheets of 9, #a-i

1777-1778 G122 Set of 2 15.00 15.00

Souvenir Sheets

Perf. 13½x14, 14x13½

1779-1780 G122 Set of 2 10.00 10.00

Classic Racing Cars G123

Designs: 10c, 1990's Williams-Renault Formula 1. 25c, 1980's Le Mans Porsche 956. 35c, 1970's Lotus "John Player Special." 75c, 1960's Ford GT 40. $2, 1950's Mercedes Benz W196. $3, 1920's Mercedes SSK.

$6, 1971 Tyrrell-Ford Fourmula 1.

1995, Nov. 7 ***Perf. 14***

1781-1786 G123 Set of 6 6.75 6.75

Souvenir Sheet

1787 G123 $6 multicolored 6.00 6.00

Local Transportation — G124

1995, Nov. 7

1788 G124 35c Donkey .60 .30
1789 G124 75c Bus 1.50 1.00

Miniature Sheet

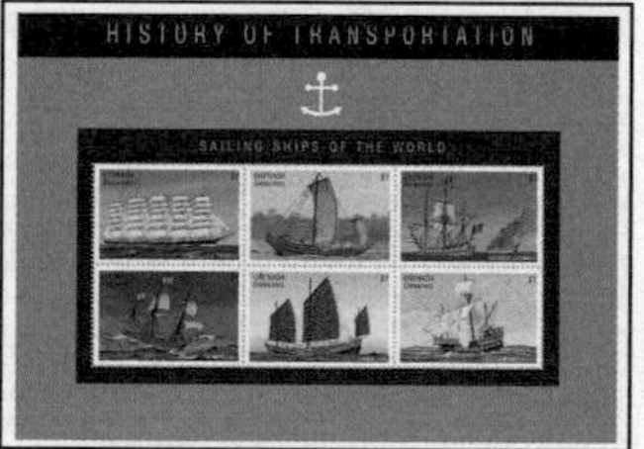

Sailing Ships — G125

Designs: No. 1790a, Preussen. b, Japanese junk. c, Pirate ship. d, Mayflower. e, Chinese junk. f, Santa Maria.

$5, Spanish galleon.

1995, Nov. 7

1790 G125 $1 Sheet of 6, #a.-f. 6.00 6.00

Souvenir Sheet

1791 G125 $5 multicolored 5.00 5.00

No. 1791 contains one 57x42mm stamp.

Christmas Type of 1995

Details or entire paintings. 10c, Immaculate Conception, by De Cosimo. 15c, St. Michel Dedicating Arms to the Madonna, by Le Nain. 35c, Annunciation, by de Credi. 60c, The Holy Family, by Jordaens. $3, Madonna and Child, by Lippi. $5, Madonna and Child with Ten Saints, by Fiorentino.

Each $6: No. 1798, Adoration of the Shepherds, by Van Oost. No. 1799, Holy Family, by Del Sart.

1995, Nov. 28 ***Perf. 13½x14***

1792-1797 A356 Set of 6 8.00 8.00

Souvenir Sheets

1798-1799 A356 Set of 2 11.00 11.00

New Year 1996 (Year of the Rat) — G126

Stylized rats: No. 1800: a, blue & multi. b, violet & multi. c, red & multi. d, green & multi.

$2, Two rats, horiz.

1996, Jan. 2 Litho. ***Perf. 14½***

1800 G126 75c Block of 4, #a.-d. 2.25 2.25

Miniature Sheet

1801 G126 75c Sheet of 1 #1800 2.25 2.25

Souvenir Sheet

1802 G126 $2 multicolored 1.75 1.75

No. 1800 was issued in sheets of 16 stamps.

Works by Dürer and Rubens Type of 1996

Details or entire work: 15c, The Centaur Family, by Dürer. 35c, Oriental Ruler Seated, by Dürer. 50c, The Entombment, by Dürer. 75c, Man in Armor, by Rubens. $1, Peace Embracing Plenty, by Rubens. $2, Departure of Lot, by Rubens. $3, The Four Evangelists, by Rubens. No. 1810, $5, Knight, Death and Devil, by Dürer.

No. 1811, The Father of the Church, by Rubens. $6, St. Jerome, 1514 engraving, by Dürer.

1996, Jan. 29 Litho. ***Perf. 14***

1803-1810 A360 Set of 8 10.00 10.00

Souvenir Sheets

1811 A360 $5 multicolored 4.50 4.50
1812 A360 $6 multicolored 4.50 4.50

Disney Holidays — G127

Disney characters celebrating: 25c, New Year's Day, "Hopping John" Feast. 50c, May Day. 75c, Independence Day. 90c, Halloween. $3, Thanksgiving. $4, Hanukkah.

Each $6: No. 1819, Caribbean Carnival. No. 1820, St. Patrick's Day Parade, vert.

1996, Apr. 17 Litho. ***Perf. 14x13½***

1813-1818 G127 Set of 6 10.00 10.00

Souvenir Sheets

Perf. 14x13½, 13½x14

1819-1820 G127 Set of 2 13.00 13.00

Sites in China — G128

No. 1821, each $1: a, Entryway to hall, Imperial Palace. b, Great Wall's eastern end, Shanhaiguan. c, Fortress in Great Wall, Shanhaiguan. d, Gate of Heavenly Peace, Tiananmen, main entrance to Imperial City.

No. 1822, each $1: a, Mausoleum of Dr. Sun Yat-Sen, Nanjing. b, Summer Palace, Beijing. c, Temple of Heaven, Beijing. d, Hall of Supreme Harmony, Forbidden City, Beijing.

Each $6: No. 1823, Great Wall of China. No. 1824, Marble boat, Summer Palace, Beijing.

Illustration reduced.

1996, May 8 ***Perf. 13***

Sheets of 4, #a-d

1821-1822 G128 Set of 2 13.00 13.00

Souvenir Sheets

1823-1824 G128 Set of 2 10.50 10.50

China '96, 9th Asian Intl. Philatelic Exhibition (Nos. 1821-1822).

No. 1823 contains one 40x51mm stamp, No. 1824 one 51x40mm stamp.

See No. 1881.

Queen Elizabeth II, 70th Birthday Type of 1996

Designs: a, 35c, Portrait in blue dress. b, $2, Wearing crown. c, $4, Windsor Castle.

$6, Standing in front of palace.

1996, May 8 Litho. ***Perf. 13½x14***

1825 A362 Strip of 3, #a.-c. 4.75 4.75

Souvenir Sheet

1826 A362 $6 multicolored 4.50 4.50

No. 1825 was issued in sheets of 9 stamps with each strip in a different order.

Flowers — G129

35c, Camellia "Apple Blossom." 90c, Camellia japonica "Extravaganza." $1, Chrysanthemum "Primrose Dorothy Else." $2, Dahlia "Brandaris."

No. 1831: a, Odontoglossum. b, Cattleya. c, Paphiopedilum "Venus's Slipper." d, Laellocattleya "Marysville."

No. 1832: a, Fushcia "Citation." b, Fuchsia "Amy Lye." c, Clysonimus butterfly. d, Digitalis purpurea "Foxglove" (h). e, Lilium martagon "Martagon Lily." f, Tulip "Couleur Cardinal." g, Galanthus nivalis "Snowdrop." h, Rose "Superstar." i, Crocus "Dutch Yellow Mammouth." j, Lilium speciosum Japanese lily. k, Lilium "Joan Evans." l, Rose "Rosemary Harkness."

$5, Narcissus "Rembrandt." $6, Gladiollus "Flowersong."

1996, June 12 Litho. ***Perf. 14***

1827-1830 G129 Set of 4 4.50 4.50
1831 G129 75c Strip of 4, #a.-d. 3.50 3.50
1832 G129 75c Sheet of 12, #a.-l. 9.00 9.00

Souvenir Sheets

1833 G129 $5 multicolored 4.50 4.50
1834 G129 $6 multicolored 5.00 5.00

No. 1831 issued in sheets of 12 stamps.

UNICEF, 50th Anniv. G130

Letters spelling UNICEF and: 75c, Child smiling. $2, Child eating. $3, Child reading.

$6, Child on mother's back.

1996, June 26

1836-1838 G130 Set of 3 4.50 4.50

Souvenir Sheet

1839 G130 $6 multicolored 4.50 4.50

Jerusalem, 3000th Anniv. — G131

Flowers and: a, $1, Pool of Bethesda. b, $2, Damascus Gate. c, $3, Church of All Nations, Gethsemane.

$6, Church of the Holy Sepulchre.

1996, June 26
1840 G131 Sheet of 3, #a.-c. 4.50 4.50

Souvenir Sheet

1841 G131 $6 multicolored 4.50 4.50

Radio, Cent. Type of 1996

Entertainers: 35c, Ed Wynn. 75c, Red Skelton. $1, Joe Penner. $3, Jerry Colonna.
$6, Bob Elliott, Ray Goulding, horiz.

1996, June 26 ***Perf. 13½x14***
1842-1845 A367 Set of 4 3.75 3.75

Souvenir Sheet
Perf. 14x13½

1846 A367 $6 multicolored 4.50 4.50

Olympics Type of 1996

35c, Memorial Coliseum, Los Angeles, 1994. 75c, Connie Carpenter-Phinney, US. $2, Mohamed Bouchighe, Algeria, vert. $3, Jackie Joyner-Kersee, US.

No. 1851, Gymnasts, vert, each $1: a, Julianne McNamara, US. b, Takuti Hayata, Japan. c, Nikolai Andrianov, Russia. d, Mitch Gaylord, US. e, Ludmilla Tourischeva, Russia. f, Karin Janz, Germany. g, Peter Kormann, US. h, Sawao Kato, Japan. i, Nadia Comaneci, Romania.

No. 1852, Equestrian participants, vert, each $1: a, Josef Neckermann, Germany. b, Harry Boldt, Germany. c, Elena Petouchkova, Russia. d, Alwin Schockemoehle, Germany. e, Hans Winkler, Germany. f, Joe Fargis, US. g, David Broome, Great Britain. h, Reiner Klimke, Germany. i, Richard Meade, Great Britain.

No. 1853, Young Japanese girl, vert. No. 1854, William Steinkraus, US.

1996, July 15 ***Perf. 14***
1847-1850 A364 Set of 4 4.50 4.50

Sheets of 9, #a-i

1851-1852 A364 Set of 2 13.50 13.50

Souvenir Sheets

1853 A364 $5 multicolored 3.75 3.75
1854 A364 $6 multicolored 4.50 4.50

Classic Cars — G132

No. 1855: a, Delaunay-Belleville HB6, France. b, Bugatti Type-15, Italy. c, Mazda Type 800, Japan. d, Mercedes 24/100/140 Sport, Germany. e, MG K3 Rover, England. f, Plymouth Fury, US.

No. 1856: a, 35c, Chevrolet Belair Convertible, US. b, 75c, Rolls Royce Torpedo, England. c, $1, Nissan Type "Cepric," Japan. d, 50c, VIP car. e, $2, Mercedes Benz 500k, Germany. f, $3, Bugatti Type-13, Italy.

$5, Bugatti "Roadster" Type-55. $6, Lincoln Type-L, US.

1996, July 25 **Litho.** ***Perf. 14***
1855 G132 $1 Sheet of 6, #a.-f. 4.50 4.50
1856 G132 Sheet of 6, #a.-f. 5.75 5.75

Souvenir Sheets

1857 G132 $5 multicolored 3.75 3.75
1858 G132 $6 multicolored 4.50 4.50

Nos. 1857-1858 each contain one 51x39mm stamp.

Ships G133

Traditional Grenada schooners: 35c, Red and white. 75c, Blue and white.

No. 1861, Ancient ships, each $1: a, Athenian war triremes, 1000BC. b, Egyptian Nile trader, 30BC. c, Bangladesh dinghi, 3100BC. d, Queen Hatshepsut warship, 1476BC. e, Chinese junk, 200BC. f, Polynesian voyager, 600BC.

No. 1862, Ocean liners, each $1: a, Europa, Germany, 1957. b, Lusitania, England, 1906. c, Queen Mary, England, 1936. d, Bianca C, Italy. e, SS France, 1932. f, Orion, England, 1915.

$5, Queen Elizabeth 2, England, 1969. $6, Viking ship, 610BC.

1996, Aug. 14
1859 G133 35c multicolored .25 .25
1860 G133 75c multicolored .55 .55

Sheets of 6, #a-f

1861-1862 G133 Set of 2 9.00 9.00

Souvenir Sheets

1863 G133 $5 multicolored 3.75 3.75
1864 G133 $6 multicolored 4.50 4.50

No. 1863 contains one 51x42mm stamp, No. 1864 one 42x51mm stamp.

Famous Composers G134

Composer, work illustrated: No. 1865, each $1: a, Bèla Bartòk, "Mikrokosmos," 1926. b, Giacomo Puccini, "Madame Butterfly," 1904. c, George Gershwin, "Rhapsody in Blue," 1923. d, Leonard Bernstein, "West Side Story", 1957. e, Kurt Weill, "Three Penny Opera," 1928. f, John Cage, "Music of Changes," 1951. g, Aaron Copland, "El Salón Mexico," 1936. h, Sergei Prokofiev, "Peter and the Wolf," 1936. i, Igor Stravinsky, "Rite of Spring," 1913.

No. 1866, each $1: a, Felix Mendelssohn, overture to "Midsummer Night's Dream," 1826. b, Franz Schubert, "Die Forelle" (The Trout) D.550, 1817. c, Franz Joseph Haydn, "String Quartet in D Major," Op. 64 No. 5 (Lark), 1790. d, Robert Schumann, "Spring," Symphony No. 1, Op. 38, 1841. e, Ludwig Van Beethoven, "Moonlight" sonata Op. 27, No. 2. f, Gioacchino Rossini, "William Tell," 1829. g, George Frederick Handel, "Royal Fireworks Music," 1749. h, Peter Ilyich Tchaikovsky, "Swan Lake," Op.20, 1876. i, Frederic Chopin, "Fantasia," in F minor, Op. 49, 1840-41.

$5, Richard Strauss. $6, Mozart, "Jupiter" symphony in C major.

1996, Aug. 26 **Sheets of 9, #a-i**
1865-1866 G134 Set of 2 14.00 14.00

Souvenir Sheets

1867 G134 $5 multicolored 3.75 3.75
1868 G134 $6 multicolored 4.50 4.50

Trains G135

No. 1869, each $1.50: a, Pacific Blue Peter, British Eastern. b, Class P36 4-8-4, Russia. c, Class OJ 2-10-2, China. d, Class 12 4-4-2, Belgium. e, Challenger Class 4-6-6-4, US. f, Class 25 4-8-4 Condenser, South Africa.

No. 1870, each $1.50: a, Federal Railways Class 38 4-6-0, Germany. b, Duchess of Hamilton Class 4-6-2, London & Glasgow. c, Class WP 4-6-2, Indian State Railways. d, Class 141R "L'Americane" 282, France (American-built). e, Class A4 4-6-2 Mallard, England. f, Deutche Reichsbahn Class 18 4-6-2, Germany.

$5, Cornish Rivera Express, King Class 4-6-2, Britain. $6, Caledonian "Royal Scot Class," 4-6-0, Britain.

1996, Aug. 28 **Sheets of 6, #a-f**
1869-1870 G135 Set of 2 13.50 13.50

Souvenir Sheets

1871 G135 $5 multicolored 3.75 3.75
1872 G135 $6 multicolored 4.50 4.50

Christmas Type of 1996

Details of painting, Suffer Little Children to Come Unto Me, by Van Dyck: 15c, Child with beads over shoulder. 25c, Christ anointing head of child. $1, Mother holding infant, father, children. $1.50, Christ, disciples. $2, Father, infant. $4, Christ, children, family.

Each $6: No. 1879, Entire painting, horiz. No. 1880, Adoration of the Shepherds, by Bernaldo Strozzi, horiz.

1996, Nov. 18 **Litho.** ***Perf. 13½x14***
1873-1878 A377 Set of 6 7.00 7.00

Souvenir Sheets

1879-1880 A377 Set of 2 9.00 9.00

Souvenir Sheet

China '96 — G136

Painting depicting scene from "Hong Lou Meng."

1996, May 8 **Litho.** ***Perf. 13x13½***
1881 G136 $2 multicolored 4.00 4.00

No. 1881 was not available until March 1997.

Hong Kong Past and Present G137

No. 1882, Man Ho Temple, each $3: a, 1841. b, 1983.

No. 1883, City of Victoria with view of St. John's Cathedral, each $3: a, 1886. b, 1983.

No. 1884, Victoria Harbor, Hong Kong, each $3: a, 1858. b, 1983.

No. 1885, each $3: a, Treaty of Nanking, 1842. b, Margaret Thatcher signing Joint Declaration, 1984.

No. 1886, Victoria Harbor, each $3: a, Older black & white photograph. b, Modern photograph.

1997, Feb. 12 **Litho.** ***Perf. 14***

Sheets of 2, #a-b

1882-1886 G137 Set of 5 25.00 25.00

Hong Kong '97.

UNESCO Type of 1997

Designs: 15c, Kyoto, Japan. 25c, Roman ruins at Trier, Germany. $1, Mount Taishan, China. $1.50, Scandola Nature Reserve, France. $2, Fortress Wall, Dubrovnik, Croatia. $4, Angra Do Heroismo, Portugal.

No. 1893, vert, each $1: a, Sanctuary of Congonhas, Brazil. b, Cartagena, Colombia. c, City of Puebla, Mexico. d, Mayan Ruins, Copan, Honduras. e, Monastery of Popocatepetl, Mexico. f, Galapagos Islands, Ecuador. g, Waterfall, La Amisted Natl. Park, Costa Rica. h, Glaciares Natl. Park, Argentina.

No. 1894, vert, each $1: a, b, c, Kyoto, Japan. d, Ayutthaya, Thailand. e, Temple of Borobudur, Indonesia. f, Monuments, Pattadakal, India. g, Polonnaruwa, Sri Lanka. h, Sagarmatha Natl. Park, Nepal.

No. 1895, each $1.50: a, Cathedral of Notre Dame, France. b, Timbered house, Maulbronn, Germany. c, Himeji-Jo, Japan. d, Ruins, Delphi, Greece. e, Palace of Fontainebleau, France.

Each $6: No. 1896, Temple, Chengde, China. No. 1897, Pre-hispanic city of Teotihuacan, Mexico. No. 1898, Mont St. Michel, France.

1997, Apr. 3 **Litho.** ***Perf. 14***
1887-1892 A382 Set of 6 6.75 6.75

Sheets of 8

1893-1894 A382 Set of 2 12.00 12.00

Sheet of 5 + Label

1895 A382 #a.-e. 5.75 5.75

Souvenir Sheets

1896-1898 A382 Set of 3 15.00 15.00

Dogs and Cats G138

Dogs: 35c, Springer spaniel. 75c, Doberman pinscher. $1, Italian spinone, vert. $2, Cocker spaniel, vert.

No. 1903: a, Leonberger. b, Newfoundland. c, Boxer. d, St. Bernard. e, Silky terrier. f, Miniature schnauzer.

No. 1904, Golden retriever puppy.

1997, Apr. 10
1899-1902 G138 Set of 4 3.00 3.00

Sheet of 6

1903 G138 $1.50 #a.-f. 6.75 6.75

Souvenir Sheet

1904 G138 $6 multicolored 6.75 6.75

1997, Apr. 10

Cats: 45c, Abyssinian blue. 50c, Bermese cream, vert. 90c, Persian tortoiseshell and white. $3, Oriental shorthair red Agouti tabby, vert.

No. 1909: a, Siamese chocolate point. b, Oriental shorthair white. c, Burmese sable. d, Abysinian tabby. e, Persian shaded silver. f, Tonkinese natural mink.

1905-1908 G138 Set of 4 3.75 3.75

Sheet of 6

1909 G138 $1.50 #a.-f. 6.75 6.75

Souvenir Sheet

1910 G138 $6 Sphinx, vert. 6.75 6.75

Prehistoric Animal Type of 1997

Designs: 45c, Stegosaurus. 90c, Diplodocus. $1, Pteranodon, vert. $2, Deinonychus, ankylasaurus, vert.

No. 1915: a, Rhamphorhynchus, brachiosaurus (c, d, e,). b, Archaeopteryx. c, Anurognathus. d, Albertosaurus (f). e, Herrerasaurus. f, Platyhystrix.

Each $6: No. 1916, Hypacrosaurus. No. 1917, Apatosaurus, allosaurus, vert.

1997, Apr. 15 **Litho.** ***Perf. 14***
1911-1914 A385 Set of 4 3.00 3.00
1915 A385 $1.50 Sheet of 6, #a.-f. 6.75 6.75

Souvenir Sheets

1916-1917 A385 Set of 2 9.00 9.00

Queen Elizabeth II, Prince Philip, 50th Wedding Anniv. Type of 1997

No. 1918: a, Colored portrait. b, Royal Arms. c, Black and white portrait. d, Black and white portrait in royal attire. e, Sandringham House. f, Queen in blue dress, Prince in uniform.

$6, Wedding portrait.

1997, May 28 **Litho.** ***Perf. 14***
1918 A386a $1 Sheet of 6, #a.-f. 4.75 4.75

Souvenir Sheet

1919 A386a $6 multicolored 4.75 4.75

Paintings by Hiroshige Type of 1997

No. 1920: a, Koume Embankment. b, Azuma Shrine and the Entwined Camphor. c, Yanagishima. d, Inside Akiba Shrine, Ukeji. e, Distant View of Kinryuzan Temple and Azuma Bridge. f, Night View of Matsuchiyama and the San'ya Canal.

Each $6: No. 1921, Five Pines, Onagi Canal. No. 1922, Spiral Hall, Five Hundred Rakan Temple.

1997, May 28 ***Perf. 13½x14***
1920 A387 $1.50 Sheet of 6, #a.-f. 8.50 8.50

Souvenir Sheets

1921-1922 A387 Set of 2 11.00 11.00

Heinrich von Stephan Type of 1997

1997, May 28 **Litho.** ***Perf. 14***

Portrait of Von Stephan and: No. 1923: a, The Pony Express, 1860-61. b, UPU emblem. c, Steam locomotive postal delivery, 1800's.

$6, Camel courier, Baghdad.

1923 A388 $1.50 Sheet of 3, #a.-c. 2.75 2.75

Souvenir Sheet

1924 A388 $6 multicolored 4.50 4.50

PACIFIC 97.

Paul P. Harris Type of 1997

Designs: $3, Women in Burkina Faso pumping well water, portrait of Harris.

$6, Early Rotary parade float.

1997, May 28
1925 A389 $3 multicolored 2.25 2.25

Souvenir Sheet

1926 A389 $6 multicolored 4.50 4.50

Grimm's Fairy Tale and Mother Goose Types of 1997

Scenes from "The Fox and the Geese:" No. 1927: a, Fox, geese. b, Geese singing as fox waves knife, fork. c, Fox asleep, geese celebrating. No. 1928, Fox lurking in forest, horiz. No. 1929, Girl with black sheep.

1997, May 28 ***Perf. 13½x14***
1927 A391 $2 Sheet of 3, #a.-c. 4.50 4.50

Souvenir Sheets
Perf. 14x13½, 14

1928 A391 $6 multicolored 4.50 4.50
1929 A392 $6 multicolored 4.50 4.50

1998 Winter Olympic Games, Nagano G139

Designs: 90c, Downhill skier. $2, Luge. $3, Male figure skater. $5, Speed skater in blue hat.
No. 1934: a, Downhill skier in air. b, Freestyle skier. c, Curling. d, Ski jumper. e, Bobsled. f, Biathlon. g, Speed skater in yellow and red hat. h, Hockey. i, Cross-country skier.
Each $6: No. 1935, Luge, diff., vert. No. 1936, Female figure skater.

1997, June 26 ***Perf. 14***
1930-1933 G139 Set of 4 8.25 8.25
1934 G139 $1 Sheet of 9, #a.-i. 6.75 6.75

Souvenir Sheets

1935-1936 G139 Set of 2 9.50 9.50

Return of Hong Kong to China Type

Chinese flag in foreground, "Hong Kong" in English and Chinese with city scene showing through words: $1, Night scene. $1.25, Daytime view of skyscrapers. $1.50, Skyline at night, horiz. $2, View of harbor, horiz.

1997, July 1
1937-1940 A394 Set of 4 4.50 4.50

Nos. 1937-1938 were issued in sheets of 4. Nos. 1939-1940 are 59x28mm and were issued in sheets of 3.

Fish G140

Designs: 10c, Wimplefish. 15c, Clown triggerfish. 25c, Ringed emperor angelfish. 35c, Hooded butterfly fish. 45c, Semicircle angelfish. 75c, Scribbled angelfish. 90c, Threadfin butterfly fish. $1, Clown surgeonfish.

1997, July 22 **Litho.** ***Perf. 14***
1941 G140 10c multicolored .30 .30
1942 G140 15c multicolored .30 .30
1943 G140 25c multicolored .30 .30
1944 G140 35c multicolored .30 .30
1945 G140 45c multicolored .45 .45
1946 G140 75c multicolored .70 .70
1947 G140 90c multicolored .90 .90
1948 G140 $1 multicolored .95 .95
Nos. 1941-1948 (8) 4.20 4.20

Winnie the Pooh G141

No. 1949: a, Winnie the Pooh. b, Kanga & Roo. c, Eeyore. d, Tigger. e, Piglet & Gopher. f, Rabbit.
$6, Christopher Robin.

1997, Aug. 7 **Litho.** ***Perf. 13½x14***
1949 G141 $1 Sheet of 6, #a.-f. 6.00 6.00

Souvenir Sheet

1950 G141 $6 multicolored 6.00 6.00

1998 World Cup Soccer Type of 1997

Team pictures: 10c, Italy, 1934. 20c, Angola. 45c, Brazil, 1958. $1, Uruguay, 1950. $1.50, West Germany, 1974. $5, Italy, 1938.
World Cup winners: No. 1951, $1: a, England. b, W. Germany, 1954. c, Uruguay. d, West Germany, 1990. e, Argentina, 1986. f, Brazil. g, Argentina, 1978. h, W. Germany 1974.
Tournament stars, vert.: No. 1952, $1: a, Ademir, Brazil. b, Kocsis, Hungary. c, Leonidas, Brazil. d, Nejedly, Czechoslovakia. e, Schiavio, Italy. f, Stabile, Uruguay. g, Pele, Brazil. h, Walter, W. Germany.
Each $6: No. 1953, Shearer, England, vert. No. 1954, Paulao, Angola.

1997, Aug. 11
1950A-1950F A397 Set of 6 6.25 6.25

Sheets of 8, #a-h

1951-1952 A397 Set of 2 12.50 12.50

Souvenir Sheets

1953-1954 A397 Set of 2 9.50 9.50

Fish Type of 1997

$2, Tursiops truncatus. $5, Balistes vetula. $10, Pterois volitans. $20, Equetus lanceolatus.

1997, July 22 **Litho.** ***Perf. 14***
1955 G140 $2 multicolored 1.50 1.50
1956 G140 $5 multicolored 3.75 3.75
1957 G140 $10 multicolored 7.50 7.50
1958 G140 $20 multicolored 15.00 15.00
Nos. 1955-1958 (4) 27.75 27.75

Sealed with a Kiss — G142

Characters from Disney's classic animated films: No. 1959: a, Snow White, 1937. b, Pinocchio, 1940. c, Peter Pan, 1953. d, Cinderella, 1950. e, The Little Mermaid, 1989. f, Beauty and the Beast, 1991. g, Aladdin, 1992. h, Pocahontas, 1995. i, Hunchback of Notre Dame, 1996.
$5, The Artistocats, 1970, vert.

1997, Aug. 7 **Litho.** ***Perf. 14x13½***
1959 G142 $1 Sheet of 9, #a.-i. 7.00 7.00

Souvenir Sheet
Perf. 13½x14

1960 G142 $5 multicolored 4.00 4.00

Butterflies of the World G143

75c, Polyura dehaani. 90c, Polyura dolon. $1, Charaxes candiope. $1.50, Pantaporia punctata. $2, Charaxes etesippe. $3, Charaxes castor.
No. 1967, Euphaedra, each $1.50: a, Francina. b, Eleus. c, Harpalyce. d, Cyparissa. e, Gausape. f, Imperialis.
No. 1968, each $1.50: a, Euthalia confucius. b, Euthalia kardama. c, Limenitis albomaculata. d, Hestina assimilis. e, Kalima inachus. f, Euthalia teutoides.
Each $6: No. 1969, Charaxes numenes, vert. No. 1970, Charaxes nobilis, vert.

1997, Aug. 12 ***Perf. 14***
1961-1966 G143 Set of 6 7.25 7.25

Sheets of 6, #a-f

1967-1968 G143 Set of 2 16.00 16.00

Souvenir Sheets

1969-1970 G143 Set of 2 10.00 10.00

James Dean (1931-55), Actor — G144

Various portraits.

1997, Aug. 22 ***Perf. 14x13½***
1971 G144 $1 Sheet of 9, #a.-i. 7.25 7.25

Mushrooms — G145

Designs: 75c, Clitocybe metachroa. 90c, Clavulinopsis helvola. $1, Lycoperdon pyriforme. $1.50, Auricularia auricula-judae. $2, Clathrus archeri. $3, Lactarius trivialis.
No. 1978: a, Entoloma incanum. b, Coprinus atramentarius. c, Mycena polygramma. d, Lepista nuda. e, Pleurotis cornucopiae. f, Laccaria amethystina.
Each $6: No. 1979, Amanita muscaria. No. 1980, Morchella esculenta.

1997, Sept. 4 ***Perf. 14***
1972-1977 G145 Set of 6 7.00 7.00
1978 G145 $1.50 Sheet of 6, #a.-f. 7.00 7.00

Souvenir Sheets

1979-1980 G145 Set of 2 10.00 10.00

G146

Orchids — G147

Designs: 35c, Symphyglossum sanguineum. 45c, Doritaenopsis "Mythic Beauty." 75c, Odontoglossum cervantesii. 90c, Cattleya "Pumpernickel." $1, Vanda "Patricia Law." $1.50, Odontonia "Debutante." $2, Laeliocattleya "Mini Purple." $3, Phragmipedium "Dominiarium."
No. 1989, each $1: a, Cymbidium "Showgirl." b, Disa "Blackii." c, Phalaenopsis aphrodite. d, Iwanagaara "Apple Blossom." e, Masdevallia "Copper Angel." f, Paphiopedilum micranthum. g, Paphiopedilum "Claire de Lune." h, Cattleya forbesii. i, Dendrobium "Dawn Maree."
No. 1990, each $1: a, Lycaste "Aquila." b, Brassolaeliocattleya "Dorothy Bertsch." c, Phalaenopsis "Zuma Urchin." d, Promenaea xanthina. e, Amesiella philippinensis. f, Brassocattleya "Angel Lace." g, Brassoepidsendrum "Peggy Ann." h, Miltonia seine. i, Sophralaeliocattleya "Precious Stones."
No. 1991, each $1.50: a, Miltonlosis "Jean Sabourin." b, Cymbididium "Red Beauty." c, Brassocattleya "Green Dragon." d, Phalaenopsis hybrid. e, Laelio cattleya "Mary Ellen Carter." f, Disa hybrid.
No. 1992, each $1.50: a, Lycaste macrobulbon. b, Cochleanthes discolor. c, Cymbidium "Nang Carpenter." d, Paphiopedilum "Clair de Lune." e, Masdevallia caudata. f, Cymbidum "Showgirl."
$5, Phalenopsis "Medford Star." $6, Brassolaeliocattleya "Mem. Dorothy Bertsch."

1997, Sept. 4
1981-1988 G146 Set of 8 7.50 7.50

Sheets of 9, #a-i

1989-1990 G147 Set of 2 13.50 13.50

Sheets of 6, #a-f

1991-1992 G146 Set of 2 13.50 13.50

Souvenir Sheets

1993 G146 $5 multicolored 3.75 3.75
1994 G146 $6 multicolored 4.50 4.50

Famous Composers, Musicians G148

No. 1995, each $1: a, Beethoven. b, Tchaikovsky. c, J.S. Bach. d, Chopin. e, Stravinsky. f, Haydn. g, Mahler. h, Rossini.
Each $6: No. 1996, Mozart. No. 1997, Schubert.

1997, Oct. 10 **Litho.** ***Perf. 14½x14***

Sheet of 8

1995 G148 #a.-h. + label 6.50 6.50

Souvenir Sheets

1996-1997 G148 Set of 2 10.00 10.00

Diana, Princess of Wales (1961-97) G149

Various portraits of Diana wearing various hats, scenes following her death: No. 1998: a, Buckingham Palace. b, Island, Spencer Estate, Althorp. c, Westminster Abbey. d, Gate, Spencer Estate. e, Gate, Kensington Palace. g, Spencer Estate, Althorp.
$6, Diana smelling flowers in front of Kensington Palace.

1997, Nov. 10 ***Perf. 14***
1998 G149 $1.50 Sheet of 6, #a.-f. 6.75 6.75

Souvenir Sheet

1999 G149 $6 multicolored 4.75 4.75

No. 1999 contains one 60x40mm stamp.

Christmas Art Type of 1997

Entire paintings, details, or sculptures: 20c, Choir of Angels, by Simon Marmion. 75c, The Annunciation, by Giotto. 90c, Festival of the Rose Garlands, by Albrecht Durer. $1.50, Madonna with Two Angels, by Hans Memling. $2, The Ognissanti Madonna, by Giotto. $3, Angel with Candlestick, by Michelangelo.
Each $6: No. 2006, Cupid Commemorating a Marriage by Incising on a Table, by Jean-Baptiste Huet, horiz. No. 2007, The Rising of the Sun, by Francois Boucher, horiz.

1997, Dec. 5 **Litho.** ***Perf. 14***
2000-2005 A402 Set of 6 12.50 12.50

Souvenir Sheets

2006-2007 A402 Set of 2 9.00 9.00

Marine Life Type of 1997

No. 2008, each $1: a, Holocanthus ciliaris. b, Balistoides conspicillum. c, Chaetodon quadrimaculatus. d, Microspathodon chrysurus. e, Halichoeres garnoti. f, Gramma loreto. g, Liopropoma carmabi. h, Lactophrys triqueter. i, Cephalopolis miniatus.
Each $6: No. 2009, Carcharhinus melanopterus. No. 2010, Obistognathus aurifrons, vert.

1997, Dec. 12 **Litho.** ***Perf. 14***
2008 A386 Sheet of 9, #a.-i. 7.00 7.00

Souvenir Sheets

2009-2010 A386 Set of 2 9.00 9.00

New Year 1998 (Year of the Tiger) — G150

Die Cut Perf. 11

1998, Feb. 10 **Litho.**

Self-Adhesive

2011 G150 $1.50 Hologram 3.25

Souvenir Sheet

2012 G150 $3 like #2011 5.50

No. 2011 was issued in sheets of 4. No. 2012 contains one 52x65mm stamp.

Great Ships, Shipwrecks — G151

Ships — No. 2013: a, CSS Alabama. b, Persia. c, Ariel. d, CSS Florida. e, Great Eastern. f, Jacob Bell. g, Star of India. h, Robert E. Lee. i, US Monitor Passaic. j, Madagascar. k, HMS Devastation. l, General Grant.

"Gone with the Wind," vert. — No. 2014: a, Clark Gable. b, Blockade runner wrecked on Sullivan's Island, North Carolina, 1863. c, Margaret Mitchell. d, George Alfred Trenholm, model for character Rhett Butler. e, Dock Street Theater, confiscated from Trenholm after Civil War. f, Howlet sinks off Charleston, South Carolina, 1865. g, USS Tecumseh sunk by Confederate gunboats, 1864. h, City jail, where Trenholm was imprisioned, 1865.

Each $6: No. 2015, Nashville sinks the Union clipper, Harvey Birch, vert. No. 2016, Dr. Lee Spence, expert on shipwrecks and sunken treasures, Alabama sinking Hatteras off Texas coast.

1998, May 7 **Litho.** ***Perf. 14***

2013 G151 75c Sheet of 12, #a.-l. 7.25 7.25
2014 G151 $1 Sheet of 8, #a.-h. 6.50 6.50

Souvenir Sheets

2015-2016 G151 Set of 2 9.50 9.50

Nos. 2015-2016 each contain one 57x43mm stamp.

Modern, Future Aircraft G152

70c, Concept strike fighter. 90c, Concept space shuttle. $2, Concept air & space jet. $3, V Jet II.

No. 2021: a, Velocity 173 RG Elite. b, Davis DA 9. c, Concorde. d, Voyager. e, Factimobile. f, RAF 2000. g, Boomerang. h, N1M Flying Wing.

Each $6: No. 2022, Gee-Bee replica. No. 2023, Concept Aeropod.

1998, May 13

2017-2020 G152 Set of 4 5.50 5.50
2021 G152 $1 Sheet of 8, #a.-h. 6.50 6.50

Souvenir Sheets

2022-2023 G152 Set of 2 9.00 9.00

No. 2022 is inscribed "Delmar."

Orchids — G153

Designs: $1, Laclia tenebrosa. $1.50, Phragmipedium besseae. $2, Pschopsis papilio. $3, Masdevallia coccinea.

No. 2028, each $1: a, Lycaste deppei. b, Dendrobium victoriae. c, Dendrobium nobile. d, Cymbidium danyanum. e, Cymbidium starbright. f, Cymbidium giganteum. g, Chysis aurea. h, Broughtonia sanguinea. i, Cattleya guttata.

No. 2029, each $1: a, Calanthe vestita. b, Cattleya bicolor. c, Laelia anceps. d, Epidendrum prismatocarpum. e, Coelogyne ochcracea. f, Doritaenopsis eclantant. g, Laelia gouldiana. h, Encyclia vitellina. i, Maxillaria praestans.

Each $6: No. 2030, Masdevallia ignea. No. 2031, Encyclia brassavolae.

1998, May 19

2024-2027 G153 Set of 4 6.25 6.25

Sheets of 9, #a-i

2028-2029 G153 Set of 2 14.00 14.00

Souvenir Sheets

2030-2031 G153 Set of 2 9.50 9.50

Sea Birds Type of 1998

75c, Bonaparte's gull. 90c, Western sandpiper. $2, Great black-backed gull. $3, Dotterell.

No. 2036, each $1.50: a, Terns. b, Brown pelican. c, Black-legged kittiwake. d, Herring gull. e, Lesser noddy. f, Kittiwake.

No. 2037, each $1.50: a, Whimbrels. b, Golden white-tailed tropic bird. c, Arctic tern. d, Ruddy turnstones. e, Imperial shag. f, Magellan gull.

Each $5: No. 2038, Yellow-nosed albatross, vert. No. 2039, Broad-billed prion.

1998, June 30 **Litho.** ***Perf. 14***

2032-2035 A408 Set of 4 6.00 6.00

Sheets of 6, #a-f

2036-2037 A408 Set of 2 15.00 15.00

Souvenir Sheets

2038-2039 A408 Set of 2 9.00 9.00

Diana, Princess of Wales (1961-97) — G155

Diana in front of Kensington Palace: No. 2040, Wearing tiara, ruffled dress. No. 2041, Wearing white dress, pearls.

Litho. & Embossed

1998, July 14 ***Die Cut 7½***

2040 G155 $20 gold
2041 G155 $20 gold & multi

Intl. Year of the Ocean Type

No. 2042: a, Great black-backed gull. b, Common dolphin. c, Seal. d, Amazonian catfish. e, Shark. f, Goldfish. g, Cyathopharynx. h, Whale. i, Telmatochromis. j, Crab. k, Octopus. l, Turtle.

No. 2043: a, Dolphins. b, Seal. c, Turtle. d, Leopard shark. e, Flame angelfish. f, Syndontis. g, Lamprologus. h, Kryptopterus bicirrhus. i, Pterophyllum scalare. j, Swimming pancake. k, Cowfish. l, Sea horse.

Each $6: No. 2044, Tetraodon mbu. No. 2045, Goldfish.

1998, Aug. 19 **Litho.** ***Perf. 14***

Sheets of 12

2042 A411 75c #a.-l. 7.25 7.25
2043 A411 90c #a.-l. 8.50 8.50

Souvenir Sheets

2044-2045 A411 Set of 2 9.50 9.50

Gandhi Type of 1998

Portraits of Gandhi.

1998, Sept. 15 **Litho.** ***Perf. 14***

2046 A413 $1 multicolored .75 .75

Souvenir Sheet

2047 A413 $6 multicolored 4.75 4.75

No. 2046 was issued in sheets of 4.

Picasso Type of 1998

Paintings: 45c, Bust of a Woman, 1943, vert. $2, Three Musicians, 1921. $3, Studio at La Californie, 1956.

$5, Woman with a Blue Hat, 1901.

Perf. 14½x14, 14x14½

1998, Sept. 15

2048-2050 A414 Set of 3 4.25 4.25

Souvenir Sheet

2051 A414 $5 multicolored 3.75 3.75

Delacroix Type of 1998

Paintings — No. 2052: a, The Natchez. b, Christ and His Disciples Crossing the Sea of Galilee. c, Sunset. d, Moroccans Outside the Walls of Tangier. e, The Fireplace. f, Forest View with a Oak Tree. g, View of the Harbor at Dieppe. h, Arabs Skirmishing in the Mountains.

$5, Orphan Girl in a Cemetary, vert.

1998, Sept. 15 **Litho.** ***Perf. 14***

2052 A415 $1 Sheet of 8, #a.-h. 6.50 6.50

Souvenir Sheet

2053 A415 $5 multicolored 4.75 4.75

Organization of American States Type

1998, Sept. 15

2054 A416 $1 multicolored .90 .90

Diana Type of 1998

1998 ***Perf. 14½***

2055 A417 $1.50 multicolored 1.25 1.25

Self-Adhesive

Serpentine Die Cut Perf. 11½

Sheet of 1

Size: 53x65mm

2055A A417 $8 Diana, buildings

No. 2055 was issued in sheets of 6.

Soaking in water may affect the multi-layer image of No. 2055A.

Issued: $1.50, 9/15; $8, 11/5/98.

Ferrari Type of 1998

No. 2056: a, 275 GTB. b, 340 MM. c, 250 GT SWB Berlinetta SEFAC "Hot Rod."

$5, First Ferrari Cabriolet (011-S).

1998, Sept. 15 ***Perf. 14***

2056 A418 $2 Sheet of 3, #a.-c. 4.75 4.75

Souvenir Sheet

2057 A418 $5 multicolored 4.75 4.75

No. 2057 contains one 91x35mm stamp.

Scout Jamboree Type of 1998

Designs: 90c, Scout sign. $1.50, Lord Baden-Powell. $5, Scout salute.

$6, Lord Baden-Powell, diff., vert.

1998, Sept. 15

2058-2060 A419 Set of 3 5.75 5.75

Souvenir Sheet

2061 A419 $6 multicolored 4.75 4.75

Royal Air Force Type of 1998

No. 2062, each $2: a, Chinook. b, BAe Harrier GR5. c, Panavia Tornado F3 ADV. d, Chinook HC2 carrying 105mm light gun.

No. 2063, each $2: a, Tornado GR1. b, BAe Hawk TIA. c, Sepecat Jaguar GRI. d, Harrier GR7.

Each $6: No. 2064, Eurofighter 2000, Hunter. No. 2065, Biplane, hawk in flight. No. 2066, Head of hawk, biplane. No. 2067, Eurofighter 2000, Tornado.

1998, Sept. 15 **Sheets of 4, #a-d**

2062-2063 A420 Set of 2 12.00 12.00

Souvenir Sheets

2064-2067 A420 Set of 2 17.00 17.00

Disney Christmas Trains — G156

Silly Symphony Railroad — No. 2068, each $1: a, Santa in locomotive, rabbit. b, Giraffe, elephant, tiger. c, Wolf, Three Little Pigs. d, Robin Hood blowing horn, Jiminy Cricket, penguins, children. e, Geese, Indian boy, turtle in caboose.

Mickey's Toontown Christmas Train — No. 2069, each $1: a, Mickey in locomotive. b, Pluto, chipmunks in coal car. c, Donald, Daisy Duck in passenger car. d, Goofy leading Huey, Dewey, & Louie in caroling. e, Minnie in caboose.

Pooh's Railroad — No. 2070, each $1: a, Piglet as engineer. b, Winnie the Pooh shoveling honey. c, Rabbit, Owl. d, Kanga, Roo, Christopher Robin. e, Eeyore, Tigger.

Each $6: No. 2071, Santa setting up toy train under Christmas tree. No. 2072, Mickey as engineer. No. 2073, Winnie the Pooh reading paper, Rabbit, Piglet.

1998, Oct. 15 ***Perf. 14x13½***

Sheets of 5, #a-e

2068-2070 G156 Set of 3 11.00 11.00

Souvenir Sheets

2071-2073 G156 Set of 3 13.00 13.00

New Year 1999 (Year of the Rabbit) Type

Various rabbits, color of country name: a, green. b, orange. c, red.

Sheet of 3

Self-Adhesive

1999, Jan. 4 **Litho.** ***Die Cut Perf. 9***

2074 A425 $1.50 gold & multi, #a.-c. 3.50 3.50

No. 2074b has point of triangle down.

Queen Elizabeth II and Prince Philip, 50th Wedding Anniv. — G157

Litho. & Embossed

1999, Jan. 8 ***Die Cut Perf. 7***

Without Gum

2075 G157 $20 gold & multi

Australia '99, World Stamp Expo G158

Dinosaurs — No. 2076: a, Troodon. b, Camptosaurus. c, Parasaurolophus. d, Dryosaurus. e, Gallimimus. f, Camarasaurus (all vert.).

No. 2077: a, Duckbill. b, Lambeosaurus. c, Iguanodon. d, Euoplocephalus. e, Triceratops. f, Brachiosaurus. g, Ponoptosaurus. h, Stegosaurus.

Each $6: No. 2078, Edmontosaurus. No. 2079, Tyrannosaurus, vert. No. 2080, Halticosaurus, vert.

1999, Mar. 1 **Litho.** ***Perf. 14***

2076 G158 $1 Sheet of 6, #a.-f. 4.50 4.50
2077 G158 $1.50 Sheet of 8, #a.-h. 9.25 9.25

Souvenir Sheets

2078-2080 G158 Set of 3 13.50 13.50

Trains G159

Designs: 15c, India, 4-4-0 express passenger and mail engine. 75c, Ireland, 4-4-0. 90c, Canada, 4-6-0. $1.50, India, 4-4-0 express. $2, Australia, 4-6-2. $3, Great Britain, Stirling 0-4-2.

No. 2087, each $2: a, Belgium, type 4-4-0. b, Sweden, class "Cc" type 4-4-0. c, Chile, 0-6-4. d, Bolivia, Fairlie-type double engine.

No. 2088, each $2: a, Belgium, 4-cylinder 4-6-0. b, England, 4-cylinder 4-6-0. c, Northern Ireland, 2-cylinder compound 4-4-0. d, Holland, 4-4-0.

No. 2089, each $2: a, Switzerland, 0-8-0. b, Ireland, 0-6-0. c, US 4-6-0. d, Great Britain, Prince of Wales class 4-2-2.

No. 2090, each $2: a, Ireland, narrow gauge 2-4-2. b, Russia, 0-8-0. c, England, Ivatt large-boilered Atlantic. d, Germany, Atlantic type express.

No. 2091, each $2: a, France, 4-6-0. b, New Zealand, 2-6-4. c, Burma, 4-4-4. d, Malaya, 4-6-0.

Each $6: No. 2092, France, 4-4-0. No. 2093, Italy, 0-6-4.

1999, Apr. 12 Litho. *Perf. 14*

2081-2086 G159 Set of 6 6.25 6.25

Sheets of 4, #a-d

2087-2091 G159 Set of 5 30.00 30.00

Souvenir Sheets

2092-2093 G159 Set of 2 9.00 9.00

Flora and Fauna Type of 1999

Designs: 75c, Porkfish. 90c, Leatherback turtle. $1.50, Ruby-throated hummingbird. $2, Theope eudocia.

No. 2098, vert, each $1: a, White-tailed tropicbird. b, Laughing gull. c, Palm tree. d, Humpback whale. e, Painted bunting. f, Common grackle. g, Green anole. h, Morpho peleides. i, Prepoua meandor.

No. 2099, vert, each $1: a, Common dolphin. b, Catonephele numiti. c, Sooty tern. d, Vermilion flycatcher. e, Blue grosbeak. f, Great egret. g, Actinote pellenea. h, Anteos clorinade. i, Common iguana.

Each $6: No. 2100, Bannaquit. No. 2101, Beay gregory.

1999, Apr. 26

2094-2097 A430 Set of 4 4.00 4.00

Sheets of 9, #a-i

2098-2099 A430 Set of 2 14.00 14.00

Souvenir Sheets

2100-2101 A430 Set of 2 9.25 9.25

Hokusai Type of 1999

Entire paintings or details, horiz. — No. 2102, each $1.50: a, A Breeze on a Fine Day. b, Ejiri. c, Horse drawings (kicking up hind legs). d, Horse drawings (with head down). e, View Along the Bank of the Sumida River. f, Thunderstorm Below the Mountain.

No. 2103, each $1.50: a, Fuchû. b, Doll Fair at Fikkendana. c, Sumo Wrestlers (with arms locked). d, Sumo Wrestlers (one head butting). e, Sôjô Henjô. f, Twin Gardens Gateway of the Asakusa Kannon Temple.

Each $6: No. 2104 Kôbô Daishi Exorcising Demon that Causes Sickness. No. 2105, Stretching Cloth.

1999, May 24 Litho. *Perf. 14x13½*

Sheets of 6, #a-f

2102-2103 A431 Set of 2 13.50 13.50

Souvenir Sheet

2104-2105 A431 Set of 2 9.00 9.00

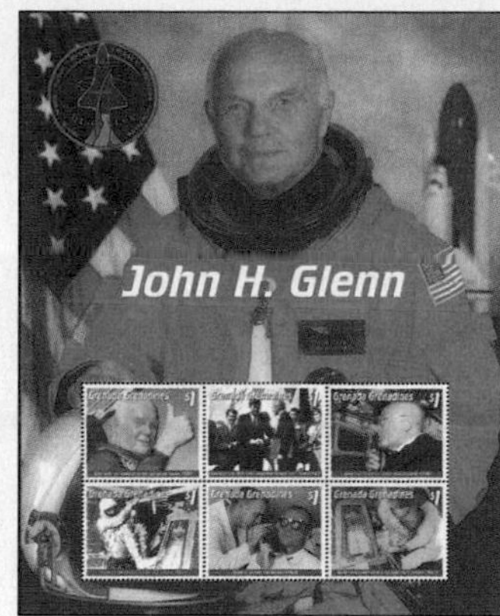

John H. Glenn's Return to Space — G160

Portraits — No. 2106: a, Thumbs up, 1998 flight. b, Receiving NASA Service Award from Pres. Kennedy, 1962. c, Talking to Ground Control from Discovery, 1998. d, Climbing out of Friendship 7, 1962. e, Being checked for balance, 1998. f, Climbing into Friendship 7, 1962.

No. 2107, vert.: a, Portrait as Ohio Senator, 1974. b, Official portrait, 1962. c, Suit-up test, 1998. d, Suiting up for Discovery, 1998. e, Meeting press after Discovery flight, 1998. f, Smiling aboard Discovery, 1998. g, Medical research, 1998. h, Official portrait, 1998.

1999, May 24 *Perf. 14x14½*

Sheets of 6 and 8

2106 G160 $1 #a.-f. 5.00 5.00
2107 G160 $1 #a.-h. 6.50 6.50

Goethe Type of 1999

No. 2108: a, Peasants dancing under the linden tree. b, Faust dreams of soaring above the mortal.

No. 2109, Portrait of Goethe.

1999, May 24 *Perf. 14*

2108 A432 $3 Sheet of 3, #a.-b., Grenada #2858b 6.75 6.75

Souvenir Sheet

2109 A432 $6 multi 4.50 4.50

IBRA '99 World Stamp Expo Type of 1999

IBRA '99 emblem, Luckenbach sailing ship and: No. 2110, 35c, Thurn and Taxis #1. No. 2113, $3, North German Confederation #1.

Emblem, Leipzig-Dresden Railway and: No. 2111, 45c, Schleswig-Holstein #1. No. 2112, $1.50, Oldenburg #4.

$6, Cover showing pair of Thurn & Taxis #1.

1999, May 24 Litho. *Perf. 14*

2110-2113 A433 Set of 4 4.00 4.00

Souvenir Sheet

2114 A433 $6 multicolored 4.75 4.75

Philexfrance '99 Type

Souvenir Sheets

Designs, each $6: No. 2115, Co-co 7000 class high speed electric locomotive. No. 2116, Cha Pelon 4 8 0.

1999, May 24 Litho. *Perf. 14*

2115-2116 A435 Set of 2 7.00 7.00

Beginning with Nos. 2117-2118, stamps from Grenada Grenadines will be inscribed GRENADA / Carriacou & Petite Martinique.

Wedding of Prince Edward and Sophie Rhys-Jones Type

No. 2117: a, Edward. b, Sophie, Edward. c, Sophie.

$6, Couple.

1999, June 18 Litho. *Perf. 13½*

2117 A436 $3 Sheet of 3, #a.-c. 6.75 6.75

Souvenir Sheet

2118 A436 $6 multicolored 4.50 4.50

UN Rights of the Child Type of 1999

No. 2119: a, Boy. b, Liv Ullman, UNICEF's first woman ambassador. c, Woman.

$6, Maurice Pate, founding director of UNICEF.

1999, May 24 Litho. *Perf. 14*

2119 A437 $3 Sheet of 3, #a.-c. 6.75 6.75

Souvenir Sheet

2120 A437 $6 multicolored 4.50 4.50

Queen Mother Type of 1999

No. 2121: a, Lady Elizabeth Bowles-Lyon. b, Queen Elizabeth in Rhodesia, 1957. c, Queen Elizabeth, Princess Elizabeth, and Princess Anne, 1950. d, Queen Mother, 1988.

$6, Queen Mother, Berlin.

Gold frames

1999, Aug. 16 Sheet of 4

2121 A440 $2 #a.-d. + label 6.00 6.00

Souvenir Sheet

2122 A440 $6 multicolored 4.50 4.50

No. 2122 contains one 38x50mm stamp. Margins of sheets are embossed.

See Nos. 2369-2370.

Litho. & Embossed

Die Cut Perf. 8¾

Without Gum

2122A A440a $20 gold & multi

Famous People Type of 1999

Actors — No. 2123: a, George Raft (1895-1980). b, Raft in movie scene. c, Fatty Arbuckle (1887-1933) in movie scene. d, Portrait of Arbuckle. e, Buster Keaton (1895-1966). f, Keaton in movie scene. g, Harold Lloyd (1893-1971) in movie scene. h, Portrait of Lloyd.

No. 2124: a, James Cagney (1899-1986). b, Cagney in movie scene. c, Edward G. Robinson (1893-1973). d, Robinson in movie scene.

$6, Charlie Chaplin (1889-1977).

1999, Aug. 20 Litho. *Perf. 14*

2123 A426 $1 Sheet of 8, #a.-h. 6.00 6.00
2124 A426 $2 Sheet of 4, #a.-d. 6.00 6.00

Souvenir Sheet

2125 A426 $6 multicolored 4.50 4.50

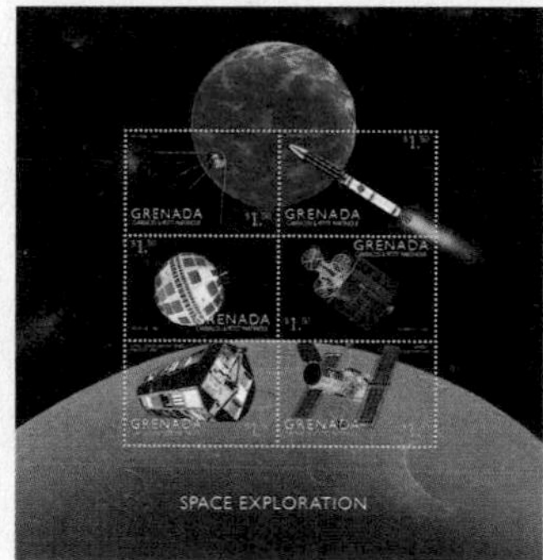

Space Exploration — G161

No. 2126, each $1.50: a, Sputnik I. b, Explorer I. c, Telstar I. d, Marisat I. e, Long Duration Exposure Facility. f, Hubble Space Telescope.

No. 2127, vert, each $1.50: a, X-15. b, Mercury Redstone 3 rocket, Freedom 7. c, Mercury Atlas 6 rocket, Friendship 7. d, Gemini 4, Edward H. White II. e, Saturn V rocket, Edwin Aldrin. f, Lunar rover.

Each $6: No. 2128, Space Shuttle Columbia. No. 2129, Mars Pathfinder.

1999, Oct. 8 Litho. *Perf. 14*

Sheets of 6, #a.-f.

2126-2127 G161 Set of 2 13.50 13.50

Souvenir Sheets

2128-2129 G161 Set of 2 9.00 9.00

Christmas Type of 1999

Christmas plants: 15c, Poinsettia. 35c, Holly. 75c, Fir tree. $1.50, Ivy. $3, Geranium.

$6, The Adoration of the Magi.

1999, Nov. 23 Litho. *Perf. 13¾*

2130-2134 A444 Set of 5 4.25 4.25

Souvenir Sheet

2135 A444 $6 multicolored 4.50 4.50

Kirk Douglas (b. 1916), Actor G162

Douglas in various poses.

1999 Litho. *Perf. 13¾*

2136 G162 $1.50 Sheet of 6, #a.-f. 6.75 6.75

Souvenir Sheet

2137 G162 $6 multi 4.50 4.50

Elvis Presley G163

Presley in various poses.

1999 Sheet of 6

2138 G163 $1.50 #a.-f. 6.75 6.75

Millennium Type of 2000

Highlights of 1970s — No. 2139: a, Salvador Allende elected Pres. of Chile. b, Earth Day. c, CAT scan introduced. d, Pres. Nixon goes to China. e, Massacre at Olympics. f, Gas shortages. g, Sydney Opera House opens. h, Pres. Nixon resigns. i, New theory of black holes. j, US bicentennial. k, 1st "Test tube" baby. l, Pope John Paul II visits Poland. m, Iran's Islamic Revolution. n, Concorde makes 1st flight. o, Charles de Gaulle dies. p, Camp David agreements (60x40mm). q, Mother Teresa wins Nobel Peace Prize.

Highlights of 1300-1350 — No. 2140: a, Robert the Bruce crowned King of Scotland. b, Giotto paints frescoes. c, Mansa Musa rules Mali. d, Dante completes "The Divine Comedy." e, Noh theater developed in Japan. f, Tenochtitlan founded by Aztecs. g, Ibn Battutah journeys to Africa and Asia. h, Munich fire. i, Ivan I of Russia increases Moscow's importance. j, Hundred Years' War begins. k, First use of cannons in Europe. l, Black Death devastates Europe. m, Boccaccio begins writing "Decameron." n, Eyeglasses developed in Italy. o, Plate armor replaces chain mail. p, Grand Canal of China completed. (60x40mm). q, Migration of Maoris to New Zealand.

Sea Exploration — No. 2141: a, Ferdinand Magellan. b, Restless seas. c, Queen Elizabeth I. d, Albatrosses. e, Penguins. f, Tahiti. g, Breadfruit. h, Easter Island. i, Maori carving. j, Lobster. k, Orchid. l, Walrus. m, Kangaroo. n, The Beagle. o, Frigatebird. p, Strait of Magellan (60x40mm). q, Capt. James Cook.

2000 Litho. *Perf. 12¾x12½*

Sheets of 17

2139 A450 20c #a.-q., + label 2.50 2.50
2140 A450 50c #a.-q. + label 6.25 6.25
2141 A450 50c #a.-q., + label 6.25 6.25

Issued: Nos. 2139, 3/28; Nos. 2140-2141, 2/1.

Souvenir Sheet

New Year 2000 (Year of the Dragon) — G164

2000, Feb. 5 *Perf. 13¾*
2142 G164 $4 multi 3.00 3.00

G165

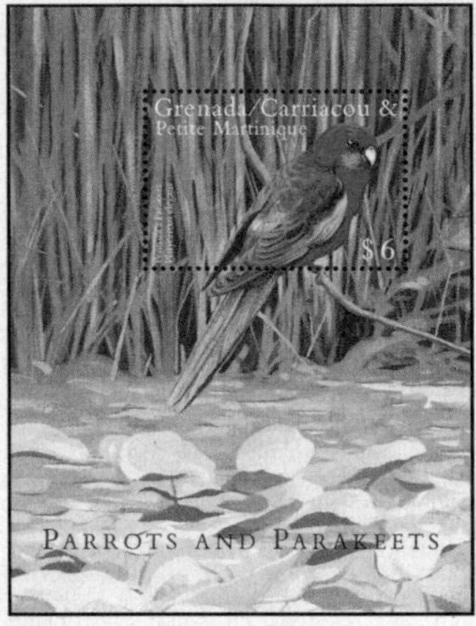

Birds — G166

Designs: 75c, Barn swallow. 90c, Caribbean coot. $2, Common moorhen. $3, Orange-winged parrot.

No. 2147, each $1: a, Red-collared lorikeet. b, Citron-crested cockatoo. c, Stella's lorikeet. d, Leadbeator's cockatoo. e, Golden conure. f, Red-spotted parakeet. g, Nobel macaw. h, Goffins cockatoo. i, Sun conure.

No. 2148, each $1: a, Turquoise parakeet. b, Scarlet-chested parakeet. c, Red-capped parakeet. d, Eastern rosella. e, Budgerigar. f, Orange-flanked parakeet. g, Mallee ringneck. h, Red-rumped parakeet. i, Yellow-fronted parakeet.

No. 2149, each $1.50: a, Puerto Rican emerald. b, Green mango. c, Red-legged thrush. d, Red-crowned parrot. e, Hispaniolan parrot. f, Yellow-crowned parrot.

No. 2150, each $1.50: a, Yellow-shouldered blackbird. b, Troupial. c, Green-throated Carib. d, Black-hooded parakeet. e, Scarlet tanager. f, Yellow-crowned bishop.

Each $6: No. 2151, Puerto Rican lizard-cuckoo. No. 2152, Pin-tailed whydah, vert. No. 2153, Pennant's parakeet. No. 2154, Scarlet macaw, vert.

2000, Mar. 1 **Litho.** *Perf. 14*
2143-2146 G165 Set of 4 6.00 6.00

Sheets of 9, #a.-i.

2147-2148 G166 Set of 2 16.00 16.00

Sheets of 6, #a.-f.

2149-2150 G165 Set of 2 16.00 16.00

Souvenir Sheets

Perf. 13¾

2151-2152 G165 Set of 2 11.00 11.00

Perf. 14

2153-2154 G166 Set of 2 11.00 11.00

No. 2151 contains one 48x32mm stamp; No. 2152 contains one 32x48mm stamp.

Tropical Fish G167

35c, Slender mbuna. 45c, Pygoplite diacanthus. No. 2157, 75c, Siamese fighting fish. No. 2158, 75c, Pomacanthus semicirclatus. 90c, Zanclus canescens. #No. 160, $1, Dwarf pencilfish. No. 2161, $1, Xiphophorus maculatus. No. 2162, $2, Wimplefish. No. 2163, $2, Gramma loreto. $3, Zebrasoma xanthurum.

No. 2165, each $1: a, Emperor angelfish. b, Strawberryfish. c, Jackknife fish. d, Flame angelfish. e, Clarke's anemonefish. f, Flashback dottyback. g, Coral trout. h, Foxface.

No. 2166, each $1: a, Bumbelbee goby. b, Black-headed blenny. c, Boarfish. d, Achilles tang. e, Swordtail. f, Moorish idol. g, Banded pipefish. h, Striped sea catfish.

No. 2167, each $1.65: a, Bodianus rufus. b, Coris aygula. c, Centropyge bicolor. d, Balistoides conspicillum. e, Poecilia reticulata. f, Heniochus acuminatus.

No. 2168, each $1.65: a, Plectorhynchus chaetodonoids. b, Bodianus puchellus. c, Acanthurus leucosternon. d, Chromileptis altivelis. e, Pterophyllum scalare f, Premnas biaculeatus.

Each $6: No. 2169, Equetus punctatus. No. 2170, Harlequin tuskfish. No. 2171, Purplequeen. No. 2172, Pomacanthius imperator, vert.

2000, Mar. 28 *Perf. 14*
2155-2164 G167 Set of 10 10.00 10.00

Sheets of 8, #a.-h.

2165-2166 G167 Set of 2 13.00 13.00

Sheets of 6, #a.-f.

2167-2168 G167 Set of 2 16.00 16.00

Souvenir Sheets

2169-2172 G167 Set of 4 19.00 19.00

Van Dyck Painting Type of 2000

No. 2173, $1.50: a, Cardinal Bentivoglio. b, Cardinal Infante Ferdinand. c, Cesare Alessandro Scaglia. d, A Roman Clergyman. e, Jean-Charles della Faille. f, Cardinal Domenico Rivarola.

No. 2174, $1.50: a, Portrait of an Elderly Woman. b, Head of a Young Woman. c, Portrait of a Man. d, Jan van den Wouwer. e, Portrait of a Young Man. f, Portrait of Everhard Jabach.

No. 2175, $1.50: a, A Man in Armor. b, Portrait of a Young General. c, Emanuele Filiberto, Prince of Savoy. d, Donna Polixena Spinola Guzman de Leganes. e, Luigia Cattaneo Gentile. f, Portrait of Giovanni Battista Cattaneo.

No. 2176, $1.50: a, Marchesa Paolina Adorno Brignole-Sale, 1623-25. b, Marchesa Geronima Spinola. c, Marchesa Paolina Adorno Broignole-Sale, 1627. d, Marcello Durazzo. e, Marchesa Grimaldi Cattaneo with a Black Page. f, Young Man of the House of Spinola.

No. 2177, $5, Portrait of Jacques le Roy. No. 2178, $5, Hendrik van der Bergh.

No. 2179, $6, Frederik Hendrik, Prince of Orange. No. 2180, $6, Justus van Meerstraeten. No. 2181, $6, The Abbot Scaglia Adoring the Virgin and Child, horiz. No. 2182, $6, Maria Louisa de Tassis, horiz.

2000, May 1 *Perf. 13¾*

Sheets of 6, #a.-f.

2173-2176 A449 Set of 4 27.00 27.00

Souvenir Sheets

2177-2178 A449 Set of 2 7.50 7.50
2179-2182 A449 Set of 4 18.00 18.00

Prince William Type of 2000

No. 2183: a, Wearing scarf. b, Wearing suit with vest. c, Wearing casual shirt. d, Wearing gray suit.

$6, Wearing sweater.

2000, May 15 **Litho.** *Perf. 14*
2183 A453 $1.50 Sheet of 4, #a-d 4.50 4.50

Souvenir Sheet

Perf. 13¾

2184 A453 $6 multi 4.50 4.50

No. 2183 contains four 28x42mm stamps.

Zeppelin Type of 2000

No. 2185 — Ferdinand von Zeppelin and: a, LZ-3. b, LZ-56. c, LZ-88.

$6, LZ-1.

2000, May 15 *Perf. 14*
2185 A454 $3 Sheet of 3, #a-c 6.75 6.75

Souvenir Sheet

2186 A454 $6 multi 4.50 4.50

No. 2185 contains three 42x28mm stamps.

Berlin Film Festival Type of 2000

No. 2187: a, James Stewart. b, Sachiko Hidari. c, Juliette Mayniel. d, Le Bonheur. e, La Notte. f, Lee Marvin.

$6, The Thin Red Line.

2000, May 15
2187 A455 $1.50 Sheet of 6, #a-f 6.75 6.75

Souvenir Sheet

2188 A455 $6 multi 4.50 4.50

Olympics Type of 2000

Souvenir Sheets

No. 2189: a, Frantz Reichel. b, Discus throw. c, Seoul Sports Complex and Korean flag. d, Ancient Greek wrestlers.

2000, May 15
2189 A457 $2 Sheet of 4, #a-d 6.00 6.00

Public Railways Type of 2000

No. 2190: a, Locomotion No. 1 and George Stephenson. b, Rocket.

2000, May 15
2190 A458 $3 Sheet of 2, #a-b 4.50 4.50

Bach Type of 2000

2000, May 15
2191 A459 $6 Statue of Bach 4.50 4.50

G168

Butterflies and Moths — G169

No. 2192, each $1.50: a, Clara satin moth. b, Spanish festoon. c, Giant silkmoth. d, Oak eggar. e, Common wall. f, Large oak blue.

No. 2193, each $1.50: a, Jersey tiger. b, Boisduval's autumnal moth. c, Orange swallow-tailed moth. d, Regent skipper. e, Hoop pine moth. f, Coppery oysphania.

No. 2194, each $1.50: a, Grecian shoemaker. b, 88. c, Cramer's mesene. d, Salt marsh moth. e, Ruddy dagger wing. f, Blue night.

No. 2195, each $1.50: a, Heliconius charitonius. b, Tiger pierid. c, Hewiton's blue hairstreak. d, Esmeralda. e, California dogface. f, Orange theope.

No. 2196, each $2: a, Hummingbird gleariwing. b, Gold-drop helicopis. c, Great tiger moth. d, Staudinger's longtail.

No. 2197, each $2: a, Common map. b, Papilio machaon. c, Purple emperor. d, Redlined geometrid.

Each $6: No. 2198, Peacock royal. No. 2199, Queen Alexandra's birdwing. No. 2200, Giant leopard moth. No. 2201, Robin moth, vert.

2000, May 29 *Perf. 14*

Sheets of 6, #a-f

2192-2193 G168 Set of 2 13.50 13.50
2194-2195 G169 Set of 2 13.50 13.50

Sheets of 4, #a-d

2196-2197 G168 Set of 2 12.00 12.00

Souvenir Sheets

2198-2199 G168 Set of 2 9.00 9.00
2200-2201 G169 Set of 2 9.00 9.00

Apollo-Soyuz Type

No. 2202, vert.: a, Thomas P. Stafford. b, Mission badge. c, Donald K. Slayton.

$6, Alexei Leonov, vert.

2000, May 15 **Litho.** *Perf. 14*
2202 A456 $3 Sheet of 3, #a-c 6.75 6.75

Souvenir Sheet

2203 A456 $6 Alexei Leonov 4.50 4.50

Einstein Type

Souvenir Sheet

2000, May 15 *Perf. 14¼*
2204 A460 $6 multi 4.50 4.50

Space Type

Nos. 2205, each $1.50: a, Foton (green and orange background). b, Sub-satellite and comet tail. c, NEAR Eros (green background). d, Explorer 16 and sun. e, Astro Challenger (green and orange background). f, Giotto (green background).

No. 2206, each $1.50: a, Foton and asteroid. b, Sub-satellite and asteroid. c, NEAR Eros and asteroid. d, Explorer 16 and planet surface. e, Space Shuttle. f, Giotto (blue background).

Each $6: No. 2207, Lunar Prospector. No. 2208, Pegasus Saturn.

2000, May 15 *Perf. 14*

Sheets of 6, #a-f

2205-2206 A461 Set of 2 13.50 13.50

Souvenir Sheets

2207-2208 A461 Set of 2 9.00 9.00

Nos. 2205-2206 depict different satellites, but have the same inscriptions. World Stamp Expo 2000, Anaheim.

Trains G170

Designs: 90c, Golsdorf 2-6-2, Vienna Metropolitan Railways. $1, Forrester 2-2-0, Dublin & Kingstown Railway. $2, Metro-Cammell Co-Co, Nigerian Railways. $3, TGV 001, French Natl. Railways.

No. 2213, each $1.50: a, Braithwait 0-4-0, Eastern Counties Railway. b, The Philadelphia, Austria. c, Stephenson 2-2-2, Russia. d, L'aigle, Western Railway of France. e, Borsig Standard 2-2-2, Germany. f, The Ajax, Great Western Railway.

No. 2214, each $1.50: a, Co-Co locomotive, Norwegian State Railways. b, Diesel-electric locomotive, Jamaica Railway. c, Diesel-electric locomotive, Railway of the People's Republic of China. d, Electric locomotive, Portuguese Railways. e, Re 6/6, Swiss Federal Railways. f, Dual-purpose Electric locomotive, Turkish State Railways.

No. 2215, each $1.50: a, 4-4-0 engine, Perak Government Railway. b, 2-4-2 tank engine, Rhondda & Swansea Railway. c, 2-4-2 tank engine, Lancashire & Yorkshire Railway. d, 2-8-2 tank engine, Northwestern Railway of India. e, 4-2-2 Imperial Yellow Mail engine, Shanghai-Nanking Railway. f, 2-4-2 tank engine, Danish State Railway.

No. 2216, each $1.50: a, Electric railcar, South Jersey Transit. b, Metroliner, US. c, HSST Mag-lev train. d, E60C, Amtrak. e, TEE Express "Parsifal." f, 2-Co-Co-2 electric, Amtrak.

No. 2217, $6, The Experiment, US. No. 2218, 2-8-2 locomotive, Central South African Railway. No. 2219, $6, The Prospector, Western Australian Government Railways. No. 2220, Diesel-electric locomotive, South African Railways.

2000, June 13
2209-2212 G170 Set of 4 5.25 5.25

Sheets of 6, #a-f

2213-2216 G170 Set of 4 26.00 26.00

Souvenir Sheets

2217-2220 G170 Set of 4 18.00 18.00

European Soccer Championships Type

No. 2221, horiz, each $1.50 — Denmark: a, Tofting. b, Team photo. c, Michael Laudrup. d, Jorgensen. e, Philips Stadium, Eindhoven. f, Moller.

No. 2222, horiz, each $1.50 — France: a, Thuram. b, Team photo. c, Barthez. d, Zidane. e, Jan Breydel Stadium, Brugge. f, Michel Platini.

No. 2223, horiz, each $1.50 — Netherlands: a, Giovanni Van Bronckhorst. b, Team photo. c, Patrick Kluivert. d, Johan Cruyff. e, Amsterdam Arena Stadium. f, Zenden.

Each $6: No. 2224, Denmark coach Bo Johansson. No. 2225, France coach Roger Lemerre. No. 2226, Netherlands coach Frank Rijkaard.

2000, Aug. 8 ***Perf. 13¾***

Sheets of 6, #a-f

2221-2223 A464 Set of 3 20.00 20.00

Souvenir Sheets

2224-2226 A464 Set of 3 13.50 13.50

Popes Type

No. 2227, each $1.50: a, Adrian VI, 1522-23. b, Paul II, 1464-71. c, Calixtus III, 1455-58. d, Eugenius IV, 1431-47.

2000, Aug. 22

2227 A467 Sheet of 4, #a-d 4.50 4.50

Souvenir Sheet

2228 A467 $6 Gregory IX, 1370-78 4.50 4.50

Monarchs Type

No. 2229, each $1.50: a, Louis XVI of France, 1774-92. b, Louis XVIII of France, 1814-24. c, Queen of Kublai Khan, China. d, Mary Tudor of England, 1553-58. e, Mohammed Ali of Iran, 1907-09. f, Ch'ien-lung (Qianlong, Hung-li) of China, 1735-96.

$6, Vladimir I, Grand Prince of Kiev, 980-1015.

2000, Aug. 22

2229 A468 Sheet of 6, #a-f 6.75 6.75

Souvenir Sheet

2230 A468 $6 Vladimir I 4.50 4.50

Fauna G171

Designs: 75c, St. Lucia Amazon. 90c, Three-toed sloth. $1, Hispaniolan solenodon. $2,Thick-billed parrot.

No. 2235, each $1.50: a, Jaguarundi. b, Andean condor. c, Darwin's rhea. d, Central American tapir. e, Jaguar. f, Jamaican hutia.

No. 2236, each $1.50: a, Red vakari. b, San Andreas vireo. c, Golden lion tamarin. d, American crocodile. e, Spectacled caiman. f, Rhinoceros iguana.

Each $6: No. 2237, Pronghorn. No. 2238, Kemp Ridley sea turtle.

2000, Sept. 5 ***Perf. 14***

2231-2234 G171 Set of 4 4.25 4.25

Sheets of 6, #a-f

2235-2236 G171 Set of 2 17.00 17.00

Souvenir Sheets

2237-2238 G171 Set of 2 12.00 12.00

The Stamp Show 2000, London (Nos. 2235-2238).

Souvenir Sheet

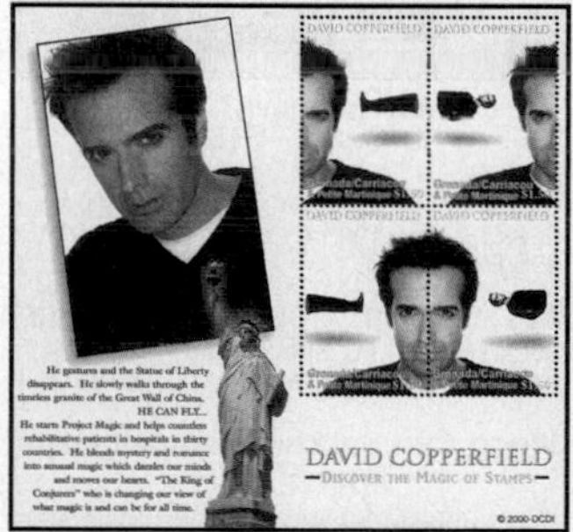

David Copperfield, Magician — G172

No. 2239, each $1.50: a, Copperfield's face at L, legs at R. b, Upper torso at L, face at R. c, Legs at L, face at R. d, Face at L, upper torso at R.

2000, Sept. 14

2239 G172 Sheet of 4, #a-d 4.50 4.50

Prado Paintings Type

No. 2240, each $1.50: a, St. John the Baptist and the Franciscan Maestro Henricus Werl, by Robert Campin. b, Justice and Peace, by Corrado Giaquinto. c, St. Barbara, by Campin. d, John Fane, 10th Count of Westmoreland, by Thomas Lawrence. e, The Marchioness of Manzanedo, by Jean-Louis-Ernest Meissonier. f, Mr. Storer, by Martin Archer Shee.

No. 2241, each $1.50: a, Isabella Carla Eugenia, by Alonso Sánchez Coello. b, Portrait of a Nobleman with His Hand on His Chest, by El Greco. c, Philip III, by Juan Pantoja de la Cruz. d, Madonna & child from The Holy Family with Saints Ildefons & John the Evangelist, & the Master Alonso de Villegas, by Blas del Prado. e, The Last Supper, by Bartolomé Carducci. f, Man with goblet from The Holy Family with Saints Ildefons & John the Evangelist, & the Master Alonso de Villegas.

No. 2242, each $1.50: a, Dominic of Silos, by Bartolomé Bermejo. b, Head of a Prophet, by Jaime Huguet. c, Christ Giving His Blessing, by Fernando Gallego. d, The Mystic Marriage of St. Catherine, by Alonso Sánchez Coello. e, St. Catherine of Alexandria, by Fernando Yáñez de la Almedina. f, Virgin and Child, by Luis de Morales.

Each $6: No. 2243, The Holy Family with Saints Ildefons & John the Evangelist, & the Master Alonso de Villegas. No. 2244, The Last Supper, horiz. No. 2245, The Coronation of the Virgin, by El Greco, horiz.

2000, Oct. 19 ***Perf. 12x12¼, 12¼x12***

Sheets of 6, #a-f

2240-2242 A470 Set of 3 20.00 20.00

Souvenir Sheets

2243-2245 A470 Set of 3 13.50 13.50

Espana 2000, Intl. Philatelic Exhibition.

Mushroom Type of 2000

No. 2246, $2: a, Cinnabar chanterelle. b, Blackening wax cap. c, Edible cort. d, Orange scaber-stalk bolete.

No. 2247, $2: a, Crab russula. b, Steel blue entoloma. c, Tiger lentinus. d, Yellow-white mycena.

No. 2248, $2, horiz.: a, Le Gal's bolete. b, Emetic russula. c, Silvery violet cort. d, Tree volvarlella.

No. 2249, $6, Scaly vase chanterelle, horiz. No. 2250, $6, Common collybia, horiz.

2000, Mar. 3 **Litho.** ***Perf. 14***

Sheets of 4, #a-d

2246-2248 A448 Set of 3 18.00 18.00

Souvenir Sheets

2249-2250 A448 Set of 2 9.00 9.00

Dog Type of 2000

Designs: 45c, Irish setter. 90c, Dalmatian. $2, German shepherd.

No. 2254, $1.50: a, Alaskan malamute. b, Golden retriever. c, Afghan hound. d, Long-haired dachshund. e, Irish terrier. f, Miniature poodle.

No. 2255, $1.50: a, Great Dane. b, Newfoundland. c, Rottweiler. d, Bulldog. e, Japanese spitz. f, Bull terrier.

No. 2256, $6, Labrador retriever. No. 2257, $6, Basset hound, horiz.

2000, June 23

2251-2253 A473 Set of 3 2.50 2.50

Sheets of 6, #a-f

2254-2255 A473 Set of 2 13.50 13.50

Souvenir Sheets

2256-2257 A473 Set of 2 9.00 9.00

Cat Type of 2000

Designs: 75c, Blue point snowshoe. $3, Black and white Maine coon cat. $4, Brown tabby British shorthair.

No. 2261, $1.50: a, California spangled cat. b, Russian blue. c, Seal point Siamese. d, Black Devon rex. e, Silver tabby British shorthair. f, Tricolor Japanese bobtail.

No. 2262, $1.50: a, British white shorthair. b, Blue cream American shorthair. c, Bombay. d, Red Burmese. e, Sorrel Abyssinian. f, Ocicat.

$5, Silver classic tabby Persian, horiz.

No. 2263A, $5, Red-white bicolored British shorthair.

2000, June 23

2258-2260 A478 Set of 3 5.75 5.75

Sheets of 6, #a-f

2261-2262 A478 Set of 2 13.50 13.50

Souvenir Sheet

2263 A478 $5 multi 3.75 3.75

2263A A478 $5 multi 3.75 3.75

Battle of Britain Type of 2000

No. 2264, each $1: a, Women fire fighters, London. b, Family leaving after the Blitz. c, Searchlights, London. d, Winston Churchill in Coventry after German raid. e, Rescue after German bombing. f, Rescue after London bombing. g, Terror hits Buckingham Gate. h, After a German raid on Coventry.

No. 2265, each $1: a, Pilots scramble to their planes. b, Balloons to catch low-flying planes. c, Spitfire B. d, Speech by Princess Elizabeth. e, Fire Watchers, auxiliary fire service. f, Painting stripes to see at night. g, Bombed buildings in Britain. h, Air raid wardens, auxiliary police force.

Each $6: No. 2266, Hawker Hurricane. No. 2267, British family survives German bombing, vert.

2000, Oct. 30 **Sheets of 8, #a-h**

2264-2265 A471 Set of 2 12.00 12.00

Souvenir Sheets

2266-2267 A471 Set of 2 9.00 9.00

Queen Mother Type of 2000

2000, Oct. 30

2268 A479 $1.50 multi 1.10 1.10

Printed in sheets of 6.

Photomosaic Type of 1999

No. 2269, $1: Various flowers making up a photomosaic of the Queen Mother.

No. 2270, $1: Various photographs with religious theme making up a photomosaic of Pope John Paul II.

2000, Oct. 30 ***Perf. 13¾***

2269-2270 A445 Set of 2 12.00 12.00

Harry Houdini, Magician — G173

2000 **Litho.** ***Perf. 14***

2271 G173 $1.50 multi 1.10 1.10

Issued in sheets of 4.

Souvenir Sheet

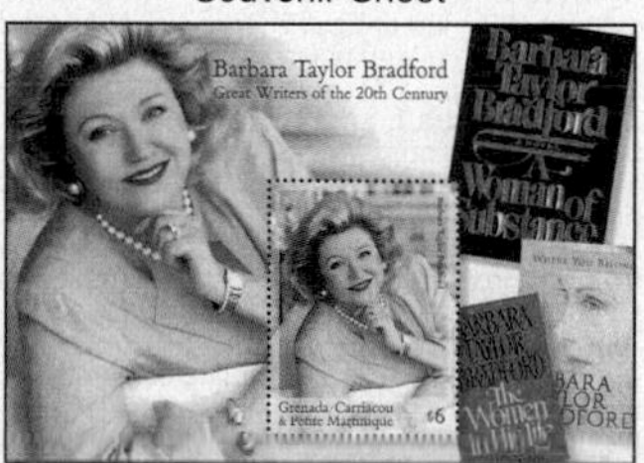

Barbara Taylor Bradford, Author — G174

2000 **Litho.** ***Perf. 12¼***

2272 G174 $6 multi 4.50 4.50

Souvenir Sheet

Hong Kong Comic Strip "The Storm Riders" — G175

No. 2273: a, Character with arms folded. b, Character with sword. c, Character in brown cape. d, Character in green.

2000 ***Perf. 13½***

2273 G175 $4 Sheet of 4, #a-d 9.00 9.00

New Year 2001 (Year of the Snake) — G176

No. 2274: a, Rat snake. b, Mangrove snake. c, Boomslang. d, Emerald tree boa. e, African egg-eating snake. f, Chinese green tree viper.

2001, Jan. 2 ***Perf. 14***

2274 G176 90c Sheet of 6, #a-f 4.00 4.00

Souvenir Sheet

2275 G176 $4 King cobra 3.00 3.00

Rijksmuseum Type of 2001

No. 2276, $1.50: a, Person with red shirt from Dune Landcape, by Jan van Goyen. b, The Raampoortje, by Wouter Johannes van Troostwijk. c, House and horse from The Cattle Ferry, by Esaias van de Velde. d, The Departure of a Senior Functionary from Middleburg, by Adriaen van de Venne. e, Steeple and ferry from The Cattle Ferry. f, Four people near rock from Dune Landscape.

No. 2277, $1.50: a, Building, statue and dog from Garden Party, by Dirck Hals. b, Still Life with Gilt Cup, by Willem Claesz Heda. c, Cloud of smoke from Orestes and Pylades Disputing at the Altar, by Pieter Lastman. d, Buildings from Orestes and Pylades Disputing at the Altar. e, Self-portrait in a Yellow Robe, by Jan Lievens. f, Birds in sky from Garden Party.

No. 2278, $1.50: a, Beatrix from Marriage Portrait of Isaac Massa and Beatrix van der Laen, by Frans Hals. b, Winter Landscape With Ice Skaters, by Hendrick Avercamp. c, Man and woman from The Spendthrift, by Cornelis Troost. d, Men in brown from The Spendthrift. e, Men and woman from The Art Gallery of Jan Gildermeester Jansz, by Adriaan de Lelie. f, Three men from The Art Gallery of Jan Gildermeester Jansz.

No. 2279, $1.50: a, Man from A Music Party, by Rembrandt. b, Woman from A Music Party. c, Girl and boy from Rutger Jan Schimmelpennick With His Wife and Children, by Pierre-Paul Prud'hon. d, Girl from Rutger Jan Schimmelpennick With His Wife and Children. e, Two men from The Syndics, by Thomas de Keyser. f, Isaac and Beatrix from Marriage Portrait of Isaac Massa and Beatrix van der Laen.

No. 2280, $6, A Music Party. No. 2281, $6, Anna Accused by Tobit of Stealing a Kid, by Rembrandt. No. 2282, $6, Cleopatra's Banquet, by Gerard Lairesse, horiz. No. 2283, $6, View of Tivoli, by Isaac de Moucheron.

2001, Jan. 15 ***Perf. 13¾***

Sheets of 6, #a-f

2276-2279 A483 Set of 4 27.50 27.50

Souvenir Sheets

2280-2283 A483 Set of 4 18.00 18.00

Pokémon Type of 2001

No. 2284, each $1.50: a, Bellsprout. b, Vulpix. c, Dewgong. d, Oddish. e, Dratini. f, Jigglypuff.

2001, Feb. 1

2284 A484 Sheet of 6, #a-f 6.75 6.75

Souvenir Sheet

2285 A484 $6 Pikachu 4.50 4.50

Animals of the Tropics G177

Designs: 75c, Greater flamingo, vert. 90c, Cuban crocodile. $1, Jaguarundi, vert. $2, Wedge-capped capuchin monkey.

No. 2290, $1.50, vert.: a, Cuban pygmy owl. b, Woody spider monkey. c, Bee hummingbirds. d, Dragonfly, poison dart frog. e, Red brocket deer. f, Cuban stream anole.

No. 2291, $1.50, vert.: a, Red-breasted toucan. b, Mexican black howler monkey. c, Fleck's pygmy boa. d, Red-eyed tree frog. e, Caiman. f, Jaguar.

No. 2292, $6, Ocelot, vert. No. 2293, $6, Western knight anole, vert.

2001, Feb. 1 *Perf. 14*

2286-2289 G177 Set of 4 4.25 4.25

Sheets of 6, #a-f

2290-2291 G177 Set of 2 17.00 17.00

Souvenir Sheets

2292-2293 G177 Set of 2 13.00 13.00

Hong Kong 2001 Stamp Exhibition.

Fish Type of 2000 with Added WWF Emblem

No. 2294: a, Sparisoma rubripinne. b, Scarus vetula. c, Scarus taeniopterus. d, Sparisoma viride.

2001, Mar. 28 **Litho.** *Perf. 14*

2294 G167 75c Strip of 4, #a-d 4.25 4.25

Waterfowl — G178

No. 2295, horiz, each $1.50: a, Falklands streamer duck. b, Black-crowned night heron. c, Muscovy duck. d, Ruddy duck. e, Black-necked screamer. f, White-faced whistling duck.

2001, Mar. 28

2295 G178 Sheet of 6, #a-f 7.00 7.00

Souvenir Sheet

2296 G178 $6 Great egret 5.00 5.00

Scenes From "The Littlest Rebel," Starring Shirley Temple — G179

Temple with — No. 2297, horiz.: a, Pointing soldier. b, Black woman. c, Soldier in carriage. d, Pres. Lincoln.

No. 2298: a, Spoon. b, Woman near tree. c, Soldier with hat. d, Woman. e, Black man and soldier. f, Man.

$6, Black man.

2001, Apr. 25 *Perf. 13¾*

2297 G179 $2 Sheet of 4, #a-d 6.00 6.00

2298 G179 $2 Sheet of 6, #a-f 9.00 9.00

Souvenir Sheet

2299 G179 $6 multi 4.50 4.50

Clark Gable (1901-60) — G180

No. 2300, $1.50 — Color of photo: a, Purple. b, Sepia (wearing suit and tie). c, Yellow. d, Sepia (wearing sweater). e, Blue. f, Sepia (wearing bow tie).

No. 2301, $1.50 — Signature of Gable and Gable with: a, Cigar. b, Vest. c, Chair. d, Pen. e, Suit and tie. f, Pinstriped suit.

No. 2302, $6, Blue background. No. 2303, $6, Gable in uniform.

2001, Apr. 25 *Perf. 14*

Sheets of 6, #a-f

2300-2301 G180 Set of 2 13.50 13.50

Souvenir Sheets

2302-2303 G180 Set of 2 9.00 9.00

Betty Boop Type of 2000

No. 2304 — Boop: a, With comb. b, With veil. c, With lei. d, At carnival. e, With flower in hair. f, With cowboy hat. g, With beret. h, In automobile. i, As Statue of Liberty.

No. 2305, $6, In sari. No. 2306, $6, In gondola.

2001, Apr. 25 *Perf. 13¾*

2304 A481 $1 Sheet of 9, #a-i 6.75 6.75

Souvenir Sheets

2305-2306 A481 Set of 2 9.00 9.00

Phila Nippon Type of 2001

Designs: 75c, Scenes of Daily Life in Edo, by Choshun Miyagawa. 90c, Twelve Famous Places in Japan, by Eisenin Naganobu Kano. $1, Scenery Along the Length of the Sumida River, by Kyuei Kano. $1.25, Cranes, by Eisenin Michinobu Kano. No. 2311, $2, A Courtesan of Yoshiwara, by Shunei Katsukawa. $3, Rite of Bear Killing: Praying to the Bear's Spirit, by unknown artist.

No. 2313, $2, vert. — Bodhisattva Samantabhadra from the Lotus Sutra with: a, Surrounding rings, yellow elephant. b, White elephant. c, Temple at left. d, Surrounding rings with rays.

No. 2314, $2 (85x28mm) — Chapter illustrations from Genji Monogatari Emaki, by Ryusetsu Hidenobu Kano: a, Kiritsubo. b, Akashi. c, Hatsune. d, E-Awase.

No. 2315, $6, A Sage Pointing at the Moon, by Ranseki Katagiri. No. 2316, $6, Frontispiece for Devadatta, Lotus Sutra, vert.

2001, May 1 *Perf. 14*

2307-2312 A487 Set of 6 6.75 6.75

Sheets of 4, #a-d

2313-2314 A488 Set of 2 12.00 12.00

Souvenir Sheets

2315-2316 A488 Set of 2 9.00 9.00

Marlene Dietrich Type of 2001

Dietrich with: a, Microphone. b, Robe. c, Flowered dress. d, Hat.

2001, May 15 *Perf. 13¾*

2317 A489 $2 Sheet of 4, #a-d 6.00 6.00

Queen Victoria Type of 2001

No. 2318 — Queen Victoria with: a, Scepter. b, Flower. c, Sash.

$6, Sash, diff.

2001, May 15 *Perf. 14*

2318 A490 $3 Sheet of 3, #a-c 6.75 6.75

Souvenir Sheet

2319 A490 $6 multi 4.50 4.50

Queen Elizabeth II Type of 2001

No. 2320, each $1.25 — Predominant background colors: a, Brown and yellow. b, Green. c, Blue. d, Black. e, Red and violet. f, Red and light blue.

No. 2320G, each $2: h, Green background. i, Purple background. j, Brown background.

$6, Tan.

2001, May 15 *Perf. 14*

2320 A491 Sheet of 6, #a-f 5.75 5.75

2320G A491 Sheet of 3, #h-j 4.50 4.50

Souvenir Sheet

Perf. 13¾

2321 A491 $6 multi 3.75 3.75

No. 2321 contains one 38x51mm stamp.

Ship Type of 2001

Designs: 90c, Creole. $1, Britannia. $2, Ariel. $3, Sindia.

No. 2326, $1.25: a, William Fawcett. b, Sirius. c, S.S. Great Britain. d, Oriental. e, Lightning. f, Great Eastern.

No. 2327, $1.25: a, Santa Maria and Christopher Columbus. b, Sao Gabriel and Vasco da Gama. c, Victoria and Ferdinand Magellan. d, Golden Hind and Sir Francis Drake. e, Endeavour and Capt. James Cook. f, HMS Erebus and John Franklin.

No. 2328, $1.25, vert.: a, Mayflower. b, Gabriel. c, Beagle. d, Challenger. e, Vega. f, Fram.

No. 2329, $6, Challenge. No. 2330, $6, Cutty Sark.

2001, June 18 *Perf. 14*

2322-2325 A497 Set of 4 5.25 5.25

Sheets of 6, #a-f

2326-2328 A497 Set of 3 17.00 17.00

Miniature Sheets

2329-2330 A497 Set of 2 9.00 9.00

Magician Type of Grenada Grenadines of 2000

Designs: No. 2331, $1.50, Howard Thurston. No. 2332, $1.50, Harry Kellar.

2001

2331-2332 G173 Set of 2 2.25 2.25

Issued in sheets of 4.

Mao Zedong Type of 2001

No. 2333, horiz.: a, Mao on stairs. b, Mao at right, with soldiers. c, Mao at left, with peasants. d, Mao seated, with officers.

$3, Portrait.

2001, May 15 **Litho.** *Perf. 14*

2333 A493 $1.50 Sheet of 4, #a-d 4.50 4.50

Souvenir Sheet

2334 A493 $3 multi 2.25 2.25

Verdi Type of 2001

No. 2335 — Verdi and score: a, 25c. b, 75c. c, $2. d, $3.

$6, Portrait.

2001, May 15 *Perf. 14*

2335 A494 Sheet of 4, #a-d 4.50 4.50

Souvenir Sheet

2336 A494 $6 multi 4.50 4.50

Toulouse-Lautrec Type of 2001

No. 2337, horiz.: a, Helene V. b, The Clownesse. c, Madame Berthe Bady. d, The Woman With The Black Boa.

$6, Loie Fuller at the Folies Bergére.

2001, May 15 *Perf. 13¾*

2337 A495 $1 Sheet of 4, #a-d 3.00 3.00

Souvenir Sheet

2338 A495 $6 multi 4.50 4.50

Monet Type of 2001

No. 2339, horiz.: a, The Magpie. b, La Pointe de la Hève at Low Tide. c, Boats: Regatta at Argenteuil. d, La Grenouillère.

$6, Portrait of J. F. Jaquemart with Parasol.

2001, May 15

2339 A504 $1 Sheet of 4, #a-d 3.00 3.00

Souvenir Sheet

2340 A504 $6 multi 4.50 4.50

Orchids G181

Designs: 25c, Vanda Singapore. 50c, Vanda Joan Warne. 75c, Vanda lamellata. $2, Vanda merrillii.

No. 2345, $1.50: a, Papilionanthe teres. b, Vanda flabellata. c, Vanda tessellata (name at LL). d, Vanda pumila. e, Rhynchostylis gigantea. f, Vandopsis gigantea.

No. 2346, $1.50: a, Vanda tessellata (name at center left). b, Vanda helvola. c, Vanda brunnea. d, Vanda stangeana. e, Vanda limbata. f, Vandopsis tricolor.

No. 2347, $6, Vanda insignis. No. 2348, $6, Vandopsis lissochiloides.

2001, Oct. 15 *Perf. 14*

2341-2344 G181 Set of 4 2.60 2.60

Sheets of 6, #a-f

2345-2346 G181 Set of 2 13.50 13.50

Souvenir Sheets

2347-2348 G181 Set of 2 9.00 9.00

Souvenir Sheets

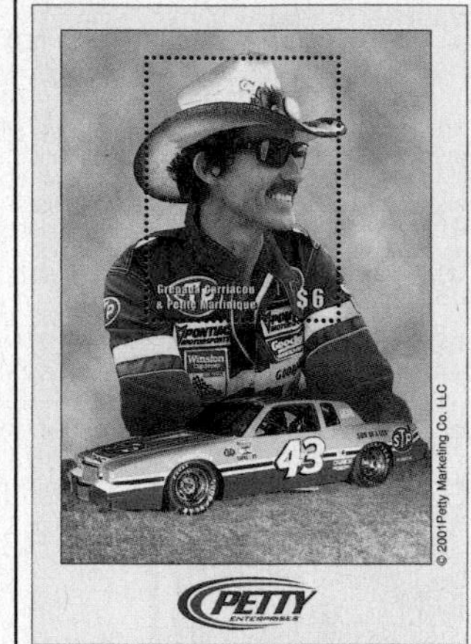

Richard Petty, Stock Car Racer — G182

Designs: No. 2349, $6, shown. No. 2350, $6, Petty speaking into microphone.

2001, Oct. 15 *Perf. 13¾*

2349-2350 G182 Set of 2 9.00 9.00

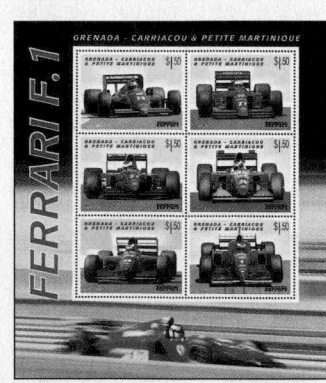

Ferrari Formula 1 Racing Cars — G183

No. 2351: a, 1986 F1 86. b, 1989 F1 89. c, 1992 F92A. d, 1993 F1 93. e, 1994 412T1. f, 1996 F310.

2001, Nov. 19 *Perf. 13¾*

2351 G183 $1.50 Sheet of 6, #a-f 6.75 6.75

World Cup Soccer Championships Type of 2001

No. 2352, $1.50 — World Cup posters and badges from: a, 1950. b, 1954. c, 1958. d, 1962. e, 1966. f, 1970.

No. 2353, $1.50 — World Cup posters and badges from: a, 1978. b, 1982. c, 1986. d, 1990. e, 1994. f, 1998.

No. 2354, $6, World Cup poster and badge, 1930. No. 2355, $6, Head and globe from World Cup trophy.

2001, Nov. 29 ***Perf. 13¾x14¼***

Sheets of 6, #a-f

2352-2353 A505 Set of 2 13.50 13.50

Souvenir Sheets

2354-2355 A505 Set of 2 9.00 9.00

Christmas — G184

Designs: 25c, Coronation of the Virgin, by Filippo Lippi. 75c, Virgin and Child, by Mantegna. $1.50, Madonna and Child, by Masaccio. $3, Madonna and Child, by Raphael.

$6, Virgin and child Enthroned with Angels, by Mantegna.

2001, Dec. 3 ***Perf. 14***

2356-2359 G184 Set of 4 4.25 4.25

Souvenir Sheet

2360 G184 $6 multi 4.50 4.50

Royal Navy Ships — G185

Designs: 75c, HMS Renown in Portsmouth Harbor, 1922. 90c, Battle of the Saintes, 1782. $2, Battle of Trafalgar, 1805. $3, Embarkation at Dover, 1520.

No. 2365, $1.50, horiz.: a, Battle of Solebay, 1672. b, HMS Royal Prince, 1679. c, Battle of Texel, 1673. d, Battle of Scheveningen, 1653. e, Barbary Pirates, 1600s. f, Royal Charles, 1667.

No. 2366, $1.50, horiz.: a, Skirmishing preceding the Battle of the First of June. b, Moonlight Battle, 1780. c, Great ships of the Jacobean Navy, 1623. d, Battle of the Gulf of Genoa, 1795. e, Battle of the Nile, 1798. f, St. Lucia, 1778.

No. 2367, $6, Battle of Navarino, 1827, horiz. No. 2368, $6, HMS Repulse, 1924, horiz.

2001, Dec. 10 **Litho.**

2361-2364 G185 Set of 4 5.00 5.00

Sheets of 6, #a-f

2365-2366 G185 Set of 2 13.50 13.50

Souvenir Sheets

2367-2368 G185 Set of 2 9.00 9.00

Queen Mother Type of 1999 Redrawn

No. 2369: a, Lady Elizabeth Bowles-Lyon. b, In Rhodesia, 1957. c, With Princesses Elizabeth and Anne, 1950. d, In 1988.

$6, In Berlin.

2001, Dec. 13 ***Perf. 14***

Yellow Orange Frames

2369 A440 $2 Sheet of 4, #a-d, + label 6.00 6.00

Souvenir Sheet

Perf. 13¾

2370 A440 $6 multi 4.50 4.50

Queen Mother's 101st birthday. No. 2370 contains one 38x50mm stamp with a slightly darker appearance than that found on No. 2122. Sheet margins of Nos. 2369-2370 lack embossing and gold arms and frames found on Nos. 2121-2122.

Princess Diana Type of 2001

Souvenir Sheet

Diana in: a, Yellow dress. b, Red jacket. c, White pinstriped suit.

2001, Feb. 15 ***Perf. 14***

2371 A509 $1.50 Sheet of 2 each #a-c 6.75 6.75

Pres. John F. Kennedy — G187

No. 2372, vert. — Pres. Kennedy: a, In boat. b, In chair. c, Profile. d, Close-up, smiling. e, Close-up. f, Looking down.

$6, With Nikita Khrushchev.

2001, Dec. 15 ***Perf. 13¾***

2372 G187 $1.50 Sheet of 6, #a-f 6.75 6.75

Souvenir Sheet

2373 G187 $6 multi 4.50 4.50

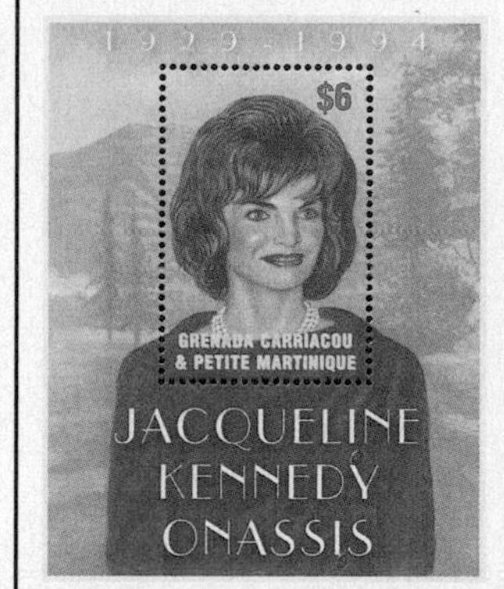

Jacqueline Kennedy Onassis (1929-94) — G188

No. 2374: a, Blue jacket, blue blouse. b, Red jacket, blue blouse. c, Green dress. d, Blue cape. e Pink and blue jacket. f, Blue jacket, yellow blouse.

No. 2375, $6, Mountain in background. No. 2376, $6, Beige background.

2001, Dec. 15 ***Perf. 14***

2374 G188 $1.50 Sheet of 6, #a-f 6.75 6.75

Souvenir Sheets

2375-2376 G188 Set of 2 9.00 9.00

G189

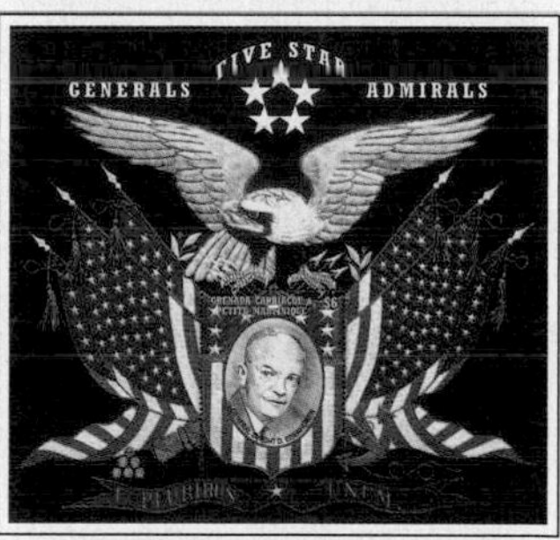

US Generals and Admirals — G190

No. 2377: a, Gen. Omar N. Bradley. b, Gen. George C. Marshall. c, Gen. Douglas MacArthur. d, Adm. William F. Halsey. e, Gen. Dwight D. Eisenhower. f, Adm. Chester Nimitz. g, Adm. William D. Leahy. h, Gen. Henry H. Arnold. i, Adm. Ernest J. King. j, Gen. George Washington. k, Gen. John J. Pershing.

No. 2378: a, Gen. George S. Patton, Jr. b, Gen. Joseph W. Stilwell. c, Adm. Thomas C. Kinkaid. d, Gen. Jonathan Wainwright. e, Lt. Gen. James H. Doolittle. f, Gen. Matthew B. Ridgway. g, Gen. Maxwell D. Taylor. h, Adm. Richmond Kelly Turner. i, Gen. Curtis E. LeMay. j, Gen. Hoyt S. Vandenberg. k, Gen. Carl Spaatz. l, Adm. Raymond Spruance.

No. 2379, $6, Eisenhower. No. 2380, $6, Douglas MacArthur.

2001, Dec. 15 ***Perf. 14***

2377 G189 75c Sheet of 11, #a-k, + label 6.25 6.25

2378 G189 75c Sheet of 12, #a-l 6.75 6.75

Souvenir Sheets

Perf. 13¾

2379-2380 G190 Set of 2 9.00 9.00

Moths G191

Designs: 75c, Pine emperor. 90c, Inquisitive monkey. $2, Oak eggar. $3, Madagascan sunset moth.

No. 2385, $1.50: a, Spanish moon moth. b, Coppery dysphania. c, Io moth. d, Large agarista. e, Millar's tiger. f, Tropical fruit-piercer.

No. 2386, $1.50: a, Indian moon moth. b, Beautiful tiger. c, Regal moth. d, Great tiger moth. e, Venus moth. f, Zodiac moth.

No. 2387, $6, Diva moth, vert. No. 2388, $6, African moon moth, vert.

2001, Dec. 17 ***Perf. 14***

2381-2384 G191 Set of 4 5.00 5.00

Sheets of 6, #a-f

2385-2386 G191 Set of 2 13.50 13.50

Souvenir Sheets

2387-2388 G191 Set of 2 9.00 9.00

Vegaspex (No. 2386).

Reign of Queen Elizabeth II, 50th Anniv. Type of 2002

No. 2389: a, White hat. b, Red hat. c, Tiara. d, Hatless.

$6, With Princes Philip, Charles, Princess Anne.

2002, Feb. 6 ***Perf. 14¼***

2389 A516 $2 Sheet of 4, #a-d 6.00 6.00

Souvenir Sheet

2390 A516 $6 multi 4.50 4.50

New Year 2002 (Year of the Horse) — G192

Various horses with background colors of — No. 2391: a, 75c, Light brown and light orange. b, $1.25, Light blue and olive green. c, $2, Tan and bister.

$6, Light orange and orange.

2002, Mar. 4 **Litho.** ***Perf. 13¾***

2391 G192 Sheet of 3, #a-c 3.00 3.00

Souvenir Sheet

2392 G192 $6 multi 4.50 4.50

United We Stand — G193

2002, May 21 ***Perf. 14***

2393 G193 80c multi .60 .60

Printed in sheets of 4.

Chiune Sugihara Type of 2002

Souvenir Sheets

Sugihara and: No. 2394, $6, Map of Asia. No. 2395, $6, Pink background.

2002, July 1 ***Perf. 13½x13¼***

2394-2395 A521 Set of 2 9.00 9.00

Winter Olympics Type of 2002

Montages of: No. 2396, $3, Skier in air, course flag, vert. No. 2397, $3, Skier, no flag, vert.

2002, July 1 ***Perf. 13½x13¼***

2396-2397 A522 Set of 2 4.50 4.50

2397a Souvenir sheet, #2396-2397 4.50 4.50

Intl. Year of Mountains Type of 2002

No. 2398: a, Mt. Kilimanjaro, Tanzania. b, Mt. Kenya, Kenya. c, Mauna Kea, Hawaii. d, Mt. Fuji, Japan.

$6, Koolau Mountains, Hawaii.

2002, July 1 ***Perf. 13¼x13½***

2398 A523 $2 Sheet of 4, #a-d 6.00 6.00

Souvenir Sheet

2399 A523 $6 multi 4.50 4.50

Intl. Year of Ecotourism Type of 2002

No. 2400, horiz.: a, Tourists at waterfall. b, Bird. c, Butterfly. d, Fish. e, Cactus. f, Orchid.

$6, Birds, horiz.

2002, July 1 ***Perf. 13¼x13½***

2400 A524 $1.50 Sheet of 6, #a-f 6.75 6.75

Souvenir Sheet

2401 A524 $6 multi 4.50 4.50

Nos. 2400-2401 were each overprinted in sheet margins "Hurricane Relief 2004" in 2005.

Scout Jamboree Type of 2002

No. 2402, horiz.: a, Campfire, Scout emblem. b, Scout with walking stick and backpack. c, Scout feeding calf. d, Girl giving Scout sign.

No. 2403, $6, Scout with hat.

2002, July 1 ***Perf. 13¼x13½***

2402 A525 $2 Sheet of 4, #a-d 6.00 6.00

Souvenir Sheet

Perf. 13½x13¼

2403 A525 $2 multi 1.50 1.50

Amerigo Vespucci (1454-1512), Explorer — G194

Various portraits with background colors of: $1, Purple. $2, Orange brown. $3, Green.

$6, Vespucci and map.

2002, July 1 ***Perf. 13½x13¼***

2404-2406 G194 Set of 3 4.50 4.50

Souvenir Sheet

2407 G194 $6 multi 4.50 4.50

Butterflies, Insects, Mushrooms and Whales Type of 2002

No. 2408, $1 — Whales: a, Sperm. b, Bottlenose. c, Sei. d, Killer. e, Humpback. f, Pygmy sperm.

No. 2409, $1 — Insects: a, Bumblebee. b, Dragonfly. c, Hercules beetle. d, Ladybug. e, Figure-of-eight butterfly. f, Praying mantis.

No. 2410, $2 — Butterflies: a, White peacock. b, Orange-barred sulphur. c, Blue night. d, Banded king shoemaker. e, Cramer's mesene. f, Common morpho.

No. 2411, $2 — Mushrooms: a, Shaggy mane. b, Shaggy parasol. c, Purple coincap. d, Sharp-scaled parasol. e, Thick-footed morel. f, Rosy-gill fairy helmet.

No. 2412, $6, Blue whale, horiz. No. 2413, $6, Dragonfly, horiz. No. 2414, $6, Blue night butterfly, horiz. No. 2415, $6, Death cap mushroom.

2002, Aug. 12 *Perf. 14*

Sheets of 6, #a-f

2408-2411 A538 Set of 4 27.50 27.50

Souvenir Sheets

2412-2415 A538 Set of 4 18.00 18.00

Elvis Presley Type of 2002 and

Elvis Presley — G195

No. 2416, Color portrait.

No. 2417: a, Wearing light plaid shirt. b, Holding microphone. c, Wearing dark shirt. d, Holding guitar with neck up. e, Wearing suit, holding guitar. f, Wearing short-sleeve shirt, holding guitar. g, Wearing shirt with flowers on shoulders. h, Wearing wrist watch and short-sleeve shirt. i, Wearing dark plaid shirt, holding guitar.

2002, Aug. 26 *Perf. 13¾*

2416 A527 $1 multi .75 .75
2417 G195 $1 Sheet of 9, #a-i 6.75 6.75

No. 2416 printed in sheets of 9.

Dutch Nobel Prize Winners, Lighthouses and Women's Costumes Types of 2002

No. 2418 — Nobel Prize winners: a, Paul Crutzen, Chemistry, 1995. b, Nobel Medal for Physics, Chemistry, Physiology or Medicine, and Literature. c, Martinus J. G. Veltman, Physics, 1999. d, Hendrik A. Lorentz, Physics, 1902. e, Christiaan Eijkman, Physiology or Medicine, 1929. f, Gerardus 't Hooft, Physics, 1999.

No. 2419 — Lighthouses: a, Ameland. b, Vlieland. c, Julianadorp. d, Noordwijk. e, Hoek van Holland. f, Goeree.

No. 2420 — Women's costumes: a, Noord-Holland (woman with child). b, Overijssel (woman with blue dress and plaid neckerchief). c, Zeeland (woman with necklace).

2002, Aug. 29 *Perf. 13½x13¼*

2418 A532 $1.50 Sheet of 6, #a-f 6.75 6.75
2419 A533 $1.50 Sheet of 6, #a-f 6.75 6.75

Perf. 13¼

2420 A534 $3 Sheet of 3, #a-c 6.75 6.75

Amphilex 2002 Intl. Stamp Exhibition, Amsterdam.

Teddy Bear Centenary Types of 2002

No. 2421 — Bear with: a, 15c, Tasseled helmet. b, $2, Black hat with red bullseye. c, $3, Hat and neck ruffle. d, $4, Gray hat.

No. 2422 — Bear with: a, 50c, Happy birthday heart. b, $1, Flower, vest, hat, and violin case. c, $2, Hat and trench coat. d, $5, Shorts.

2002, Sept. 23 *Perf. 14*

2421 A529 Sheet of 4, #a-d 7.00 7.00
2422 A530 Sheet of 4, #a-d 6.50 6.50

Christmas Type of 2002

Carpaccio paintings: 15c, The Redeemer and the Four Apostles. 25c, The Miracle of the Relic of the Cross, vert. 50c, The Presentation in the Temple. $2, The Visitation. $3, The Birth of the Virgin.

$6, Madonna and Child and Two Angels, by Cimabue, vert.

2002, Nov. 4 *Perf. 14*

2423-2427 A541 Set of 5 4.50 4.50

Souvenir Sheet

2428 A541 $6 multi 4.50 4.50

World Cup Soccer Matches Type of 2002

No. 2429, $1.50: a, Oliver Neuville, Eddie Pope. b, Claudio Reyna, Miroslav Klose. c, Christian Ziege, Frankie Hejduk. d, Nadal, Jung Hwan Ahn. e, Luis Enrique, Chong Gug Song. f, Park Ji Sung, Mendieta Gaizka.

No. 2430, $1.50: a, Danny Mills, Ronaldo. b, Roque Junior, Emile Heskey. c, Sol Campbell, Rivaldo. d, Lamine Diatta, Hakan Sukur. e, Umit Davala, Khalilou Fadiga. f, El Hadji Diouf, Tugay Kerimoglu.

No. 2431, $3: a, Oliver Kahn. b, Brad Friedel.

No. 2432, $3: a, Chun Soo Lee. b, Juan Carlos Valeron.

No. 2433, $3: a, David Beckham, Roberto Carlos. b, Ronaldinho, Nicky Butt.

No. 2434, $3: a, Alpay Ozalan. b, Fadiga.

2002, Nov. 18 *Perf. 13¼*

Sheets of 6, #a-f

2429-2430 A542 Set of 2 13.50 13.50

Souvenir Sheets of 2, #a-b

2431-2434 A542 Set of 4 18.00 18.00

Dale Earnhardt Type of 2002

No. 2435: a, $2, 1980 photo. b, $2, 1986 photo. c, $2, 1987 photo. d, $2, 1990 photo. e, $2, 1991 photo. f, $2, 1993 photo. g, $2, 1994 photo. h, $4, Two cars (75x50mm).

2002 *Perf. 13½x13¾*

2435 A518 Sheet of 8, #a-h 13.50 13.50

New Year 2003 (Year of the Ram) — G196

2003, Jan. 27 *Perf. 14*

2436 G196 $1.25 multi 1.25 1.25

Printed in sheets of 4.

G197

Coronation of Queen Elizabeth II, 50th Anniv. — G198

No. 2437: a, As child. b, In blue dress. c, On horse.

$6, Wearing sash and tiara.

$20, Wearing tiara.

2003 **Litho.** *Perf. 14*

2437 G197 $3 Sheet of 3, #a-c 6.75 6.75

Souvenir Sheet

2438 G197 $6 multi 4.50 4.50

Miniature Sheet

Litho. & Embossed

Perf. 13¼x13

2439 G198 $20 gold & multi 15.00 15.00

Issued: Nos. 2437-2438, 8/25; No. 2439, 2/24.

Space Shuttle Columbia Type of 2003

No. 2440: a, Mission Specialist 1 David M. Brown. b, Commander Rick D. Husband. c, Mission Specialist 4 Laurel Blair Salton Clark. d, Mission Specialist 4 Kalpana Chawla. e, Payload Commander Michael P. Anderson. f, Pilot William C. McCool. g, Payload Specialist 4 Ilan Ramon.

2003, Apr. 7 **Litho.** *Perf. 13¼*

2440 A549 $1 Sheet of 7, #a-g 5.25 5.25

Klimt Paintings Type of 2003

Designs: 15c, Le Chapeau de Plumes Noires. 25c, Le Schloss Kammer am Attersee. 50c, Malcesine sue le Lac de Garde. 75c, Ferme en Haute Autriche. $1.25, Portrait d'une Dame. $4, La Frise Beethoven.

No. 2447: a, Portrait de la Baronne Elisabeth Bachofen-Echt. b, Portrait d'une Dame, diff. c, Portrait d'Emilie Floge. d, Portrait d'Adele Bloch-Bauer.

$6, Le Baiser.

2003, Apr. 28 *Perf. 14¼*

2441-2446 A550 Set of 6 5.25 5.25

Perf. 13¼

2447 A550 $2 Sheet of 4, #a-d 6.00 6.00

Size: 83x103mm

Imperf

2448 A550 $6 multi 4.50 4.50

Japanese Art Type of 2003

Paintings by Kunichika Toyohara: 50c, The Actor Danjuro Ichikawa IX as the Beggar Kagekiyo Akushichibyoe. 75c, The Actor Danjuro Ichikawa IX as the Female Demon Uwanari. $1.25, The Actor Tossho Sawamura II as Sutewakamaru. $3, The Actor Hikosaburo Bando V as Danjo Nikki.

No. 2453: a, The Actor Shikan Nakamura IV as Rokusuke Keyamura. b, The Actor Hikosaburo Bando V as Ichimisair No Musume Osono. c, The Actor Sadanji Ichikawa I as Wada No Shimobe Busuke. d, The Actor Sandanji Ichikawa I as Kiyomizu no Yoshitaka.

$6, The Actor Kikugoro Onoe V as Tsuneemon Torii Retruning to Mikawa, horiz.

2003, Apr. 28 *Perf. 14¼*

2449-2452 A551 Set of 4 4.25 4.25
2453 A551 $2 Sheet of 4, #a-d 6.00 6.00

Souvenir Sheet

2454 A551 $6 multi 4.50 4.50

Cranach Paintings Type of 2003

Details from paintings by Lucas Cranach the Elder: 25c, The St. Mary Altarpiece, vert. $1, The St. Mary Altarpiece, diff., vert. $1.25, Duke John with St. James the Greater, from Altarpiece of the Princes, vert. $3, Frederick the Wise with St. Bartholomew, vert.

No. 2459: a, Judith at the Table of Holofernes. b, Central panel of St. Catherine Altarpiece. c, Judith Killing Holofernes. d, The Martyrdom of St. Catherine.

$6, Cardinal Albrecht of Brandenbourg as St. Jerome in the Wilderness, vert.

2003, Apr. 28

2455-2458 A552 Set of 4 4.25 4.25
2459 A552 $2 Sheet of 4, #a-d 6.00 6.00

Souvenir Sheet

2460 A552 $6 multi 4.50 4.50

Teddy Bear Type of 2003

2003, Apr. 29 Embroidered *Imperf.*

Self-Adhesive

2461 A553 $15 multi 11.50 11.50

Issued in sheets of 4.

Tour de France Type of 2003

No. 2462, $2: a, Ferdinand Kubler, 1950. b, Hugo Koblet, 1951. c, Fausto Coppi, 1952. d, Louison Bobet, 1953.

No. 2463, $2: a, Bobet, 1954. b, Bobet, 1955. c, Roger Walkowiak, 1956. d, Jacques Anquetil, 1957.

No. 2464, $2: a, Gastone Nencini, 1960. b, Anquetil, 1961. c, Anquetil, 1962. d, Anquetil, 1963.

No. 2465, $6, Bobet, 1953-55. No. 2466, $6, Anquetil, 1957, diff. No. 2467, $6, Eddy Merckx, 1969.

2003, June 17 *Perf. 13¼*

Sheets of 4, #a-d

2462-2464 A555 Set of 3 18.00 18.00

Souvenir Sheets

2465-2467 A555 Set of 3 13.50 13.50

John F. Kennedy Type of 2002

No. 2468, $2: a, As Choate graduate, 1935. b, As congressman, 1946. c, With wife, Jacqueline, on tennis court. d, With son, John, Jr.

No. 2469, $2: a, With wife, Jacqueline. b, Announcing Cuban blockade, 1962. c, Seated in White House, 1962. d, Wife and children at funeral, 1963.

2003, July 1 *Perf. 14*

Sheets of 4, #a-d

2468-2469 A544 Set of 2 12.00 12.00

Intl. Year of Fresh Water Type of 2003

No. 2470 — Flag and: a, La Sagesse. b, Annadale Falls. c, Grand Etang.

$6, Flag and St. George, horiz.

2003, July 4 *Perf. 13½x13¼*

2470 A559 $2 Sheet of 3, #a-c 4.50 4.50

Souvenir Sheet

Perf. 13¼x13½

2471 A559 $6 multi 4.50 4.50

Circus Performers Type of 2003

No. 2472, $2 — Clowns: a, Anton Pilossian. b, Victor Vashnikov. c, Dan Rice. d, Tom Comet.

No. 2473, $2: a, Dog. b, Macaw. c, Monique. d, Vassily Trofimov.

2003, July 14 *Perf. 14*

Sheets of 4, #a-d

2472-2473 A560 Set of 2 12.00 12.00

Powered Flight Type of 2003

No. 2474, $2: a, Wright Brothers Flyer. b, NC-4. c, Douglas World Cruiser. d, Fokker Eindecker.

No. 2475, $2: a, Hawker Hart. b, Martin B-10. c, Armstrong Whitworth Siskin IIIA. d, Loening OL-8.

No. 2476, $2: a, Hansa-Brandenberg D.1. b, B.E. 2e. c, Handley Page 0/400. d, Avro 504.

No. 2477, $6, Wright Brothers No. 3 glider. No. 2478, $6, Wright Brothers Flyer No. 2. No. 2479, $6, Gloster Gamecock.

2003, July 14 *Sheets of 4, #a-d*

2474-2476 A556 Set of 3 18.00 18.00

Souvenir Sheets

2477-2479 A556 Set of 3 13.50 13.50

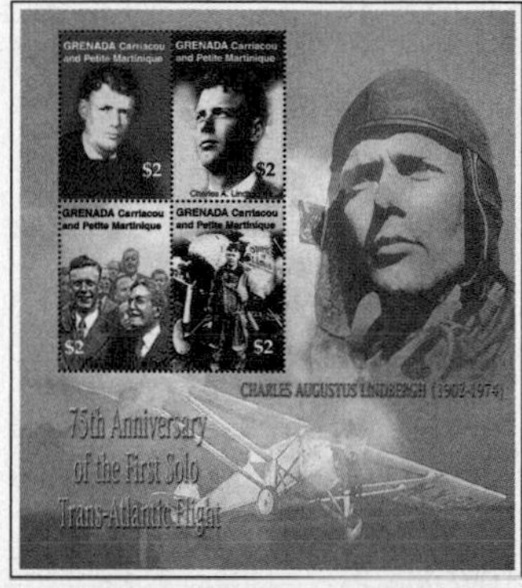

First Nonstop Solo Transatlantic Flight, 75th Anniv. — G199

No. 2480, $2: a, Charles Lindbergh (white denomination, blue background). b, Lindbergh (blue denomination, brown background. c, Lindbergh's arrival in Paris, 1927. d, Lindbergh and Spirit of St. Louis (white denomination, country name in blue)

No. 2481, $2: a, Lindbergh (blue denomination and background). b, Lindbergh and Spirit of St. Louis, blue denomination, red violet background). c, Lindbergh and Spirit of St. Louis (white denomination and country name). d, Lindbergh (white denomination, blue country name).

2003, July 14 *Sheets of 4, #a-d*

2480-2481 G199 Set of 2 12.00 12.00

Prince William Type of 2003

No. 2482, vert.: a, Looking right. b, Looking forward. c, Looking left.

$6, In ski jacket, vert.

2003, Sept. 22

2482 A562 $3 Sheet of 3, #a-c 6.75 6.75

Souvenir Sheet

2483 A562 $6 multi 4.50 4.50

Flowers Type of 2003

Designs: 75c, Wild rhododendron, vert. $1, Peony, vert. $1.25, Camellia, vert. No. 2487, $2, Laurel, vert.

No. 2488, $2, vert.: a, Apple blossom. b, Mock orange. c, Wild rose. d, Hibiscus.

$6, Violets, vert.

2003, Oct. 23 *Perf. 13½*

2484-2487 A567 Set of 4 3.75 3.75

2488 A567 $2 Sheet of 4, #a-d 6.00 6.00

Souvenir Sheet

2489 A567 $6 multi 4.50 4.50

ASDA Postage Stamp Mega-event (No. 2489).

Fish Type of 2003

Designs: 25c, Domino damsel. 75c, Porcupine fish. $1.25, Damselfish. No. 2493, $2, Clownfish.

No. 2494, $2: a, Triggerfish. b, Half-and-half wrasse. c, Long-fin bannerfish. d, Butterflyfish.

$6, Blue-girdled angelfish.

2003, Oct. 23

2490-2493 A568 Set of 4 3.25 3.25

2494 A568 $2 Sheet of 4, #a-d 6.00 6.00

Souvenir Sheet

2495 A568 $6 multi 4.50 4.50

Birds Type of 2003

Designs: 25c, Rose-breasted grosbeak. No. 2497, 50c, Gray catbird. No. 2498, 50c, Bullock's oriole. $1, Blue grosbeak.

No. 2500, $2, vert.: a, Lazuli bunting. b, Indigo bunting. c, Broad-tailed hummingbird. d, Scarlet tanager.

$6, Barn swallow.

2003, Oct. 23

2496-2499 A569 Set of 4 2.25 2.25

2500 A569 $2 Sheet of 4, #a-d 6.00 6.00

Souvenir Sheet

2501 A569 $6 multi 4.50 4.50

Christmas Type of 2003

Designs: 35c, Madonna and Child, from Carnesecchi Tabernacle, by Domenico Veneziano. 75c, Madonna and Child, from Magnoli altarpiece, by Veneziano. 90c, Crevole Madonna, by Duccio di Buoninsegna. $3, Madonna and Child, by Veneziano.

$6, Madonna and Child by the Fireplace, by Robert Campin.

2003, Nov. 17 *Perf. 14¼*

2502-2505 A570 Set of 4 3.75 3.75

Souvenir Sheet

2506 A570 $6 multi 4.50 4.50

Hermitage Paintings Type of 2003

Designs: 75c, Abraham and Isaac, by Rembrandt, vert. $1, David and Jonathan, by Rembrandt, vert. $1.25, St. Onuphrius, by Jusepe de Ribera, vert. No. 2510, $2, Pope Paul III, by Titian, vert.

No. 2511, $2: a, Rest on the Flight into Egypt, by Bartolomé Estéban Murillo. b, Esther Before Ahasuerus, by Nicolas Poussin. c, Abraham's Servant and Rebecca, by Jacob Hogers. d, The Prophet Elisha and Naaman, by Lambert Jacobsz.

No. 2512, Hagar Flees Abram's House, by Peter Paul Rubens. No. 2513, The Building of Noah's Ark, by Guido Reni, vert.

2003, Dec. 8 *Perf. 13½*

2507-2510 A572 Set of 4 3.75 3.75

2511 A572 $2 Sheet of 4, #a-d 6.00 6.00

Imperf

Size: 78x65mm

2512 A572 $6 multi 4.50 4.50

Size: 67x78mm

2513 A572 $6 multi 4.50 4.50

Norman Rockwell Type of 2003

No. 2514, vert.: a, The Trumpeter. b, Waiting for the Vet. c, The Diving Board. d, The Discovery.

$6, Day in a Boy's Life.

2003, Dec. 8 Litho. *Perf. 13¼*

2514 A571 $2 Sheet of 4, #a-d 6.00 6.00

Souvenir Sheet

2515 A571 $6 multi 4.50 4.50

Pablo Picasso Type of 2003

No. 2516: a, Jacqueline Sitting. b, Jacqueline with Flower. c, Seated Nude. d, Woman in Armchair.

$6, Head of a Woman.

2003, Dec. 8 *Perf. 13¼*

2516 A573 $2 Sheet of 4, #a-d 6.00 6.00

Imperf

2517 A573 $6 multi 4.50 4.50

No. 2516 contains four 37x50mm stamps.

New Year (Year of the Monkey) Type of 2004

No. 2518: a, White, blue and orange monkey. b, Blue monkey. c, Brown monkey. d, Monkey with orange face.

2004, Jan. 4 *Perf. 14*

2518 A574 $1.50 Sheet of 4, #a-d 4.50 4.50

Zhoa Mengfu (1254-1322), Artist — G200

No. 2519: a, The Mind Landscape of Xie Youyu. b, Scroll with green backround and large mountains at left and right. c, Twin Pines. d, Scroll with brown background and large mountain at left.

$6, Autumn.

2004, Jan. 29 Litho. *Perf. 13½x13¼*

2519 G200 $2 Sheet of 4, #a-d 6.00 4.50

Souvenir Sheet

2520 G200 $6 multi 4.50 4.50

Arthur and Friends Type of 2004

No. 2521: a, Brain. b, Binky. c, Francine. d, Prunella. e, Arthur. f, Muffy.

No. 2522, $2: a, Francine, diff. b, Buster. c, Muffy, diff. d, Sue Ellen.

No. 2523, $2: a, Francine and butterfly. b, Binky and map. c, Brain and blackboard. d, Arthur and model of solar system.

2004, Jan. 29 *Perf. 13¼*

2521 A577 $1.50 Sheet of 6, #a-f 6.75 6.75

Sheets of 4, #a-d

2522-2523 A577 Set of 2 12.00 12.00

Olympics Type of 2004

Designs: 25c, Long jumper, 1924 Paris Olympics. 50c, Avery Brundage, Intl. Olympic Committee President, 1952-72. $1, Commemorative medal for 1972 Munich Olympics. $4, Paidotribai.

2004, Apr. 8 **Litho.**

2524-2527 A579 Set of 4 4.50 4.50

Deng Xiaoping Type of 2004

Souvenir Sheet

2004, May 3 *Perf. 13½x13¼*

2528 A582 $6 Wearing cap 4.50 4.50

Pope John Paul II Type of 2004

No. 2529: a, With Lech Walesa. b, With Meir Lau, Chief Rabbi of Israel. c, Blessing children. d, At computer. e, Wearing miter.

2004, May 3 *Perf. 13½*

2529 A583 $2 Sheet of 5, #a-e 7.50 7.50

Marilyn Monroe Type of 2004

Designs: 50c, Portrait, diff.

No. 2531 — Various portraits with color and location of denomination of: a, Black, UL. b, Black, UR. c, White, UR. d, White, UL.

2004, May 3 *Perf. 13½x13¼*

2530 A584 50c multi .40 .40

2531 A584 $2 Sheet of 4, #a-d 6.00 6.00

No. 2530 was printed in sheets of 16.

D-Day Type of 2004

Designs: 25c, Admiral Sir Bertram Ramsay. 50c, Lt. Gen. Miles Dempsey. 75c, Bob Shrimpton, Submarine Detector on HMS Belfast. $4, Denis Edwards, 6th Airborne Division.

No. 2536, $2: a, Sir Winston Churchill without hat. b, Churchill with hat. c, British link up with Airborne troops. d, Link up at Orne River.

No. 2537, $2: a, US troops move inland. b, Troops move inland from Omaha Beach. c, Heavy fighting on Sword Beach. d, German generals meet.

No. 2538, $6, Assault landing craft head for invasion beaches. No. 2539, $6, Gunner in a British bomber.

2004, July 19 *Perf. 14*

Stamps + Labels (#2532-2535)

2532-2535 A586 Set of 4 4.25 4.25

Sheets of 4, #a-d

2536-2537 A586 Set of 2 12.00 12.00

Souvenir Sheets

2538-2539 A586 Set of 2 9.00 9.00

Locomotives Type of 2004

No. 2540, $1: a, Liner V2 Class 2-6-2. b, Sudan Railways 2-8-2. c, China Railways DF4 Co-Co. d, LMS 2F 0-6-0 with Black 5 4-6-0. e, LMS Lickey Banker 0-10-0. f, LMS Princess Royal Pacific. g, LMS Rebuilered Claughton Class 4-6-0. h, LMS Stanier 8F 2-8-0. i, Midland Railway Compound 4-4-0.

No. 2541, $1: a, Britannia Class 4-6-2. b, Indian Railways XD Class 2-8-2. c, China Railways KD6 2-8-0 (USATC S160). d, SE+CR 01 Class 0-6-0. e, Battle of Britain Light Pacific. f, SR King Arthur Class 4-6-0. g, SR Marsh 13 Class 4-4-2T. h, SR N Class 2-6-0. i, SR School Class 4-4-0.

No. 2542, $1: a, SR Morchant Navy Pacific 4-6-2. b, Gazira Cotton Railway, Sudan. c, Spanish Railways 4-8-4. d, LNER 04-1 Class 2-8-0. e, LNER A1 4-6-2 Pacific. f, LNER A3 Class 4-6-2. g, LNER A4 Class 4-6-2 Pacific. h, LNER B1 Class 4-6-0. i, LNER Ivatt Large Atlantic 4-4-2 A4 Pacific 4-6-2.

No. 2543, $6, Aberdeen to Penzance train. No. 2544, $6, London to Holyhead train. No. 2545, $6, Dublin to Tralee train.

2004, July 19 *Perf. 14*

Sheets of 9, #a-i

2540-2542 A587 Set of 3 21.00 21.00

Souvenir Sheets

2543-2545 A587 Set of 3 13.50 13.50

Queen Juliana Type of 2004

2004, Aug. 25 Litho. *Perf. 13¼*

2546 A590 $2 1937 portrait 1.50 1.50

Printed in sheets of 6

Carriacou Regatta Festival, 40th Anniv. G201

Designs: 75c, Parade. 90c, People, boats in water. $1, Sailboats, vert.

2004, Oct. 11 *Perf. 14*

2547-2549 G201 Set of 3 2.00 2.00

FIFA Type of 2004

No. 2550: a, David Beckham. b, Marcel Desailly. c, Guido Buchwald. d, Alfonso.

$6, Bobby Charlton.

2004, Nov. 1 *Perf. 12¾x12½*

2550 A595 $2 Sheet of 4, #a-d 6.00 6.00

Souvenir Sheet

2551 A595 $6 multi 4.50 4.50

Ocean Liners — G202

Designs: 25c, Titanic. 75c, Michelangelo. $1, America. $1.25, Vaterland. $2, Deutschland. $3, Mauritania.

$6, Ile de France.

2004, Nov. 29 *Perf. 14¼*

2552-2557 G202 Set of 6 6.25 6.25

Souvenir Sheet

2558 G202 $6 multi 4.50 4.50

Elvis Presley Type of 2004

No. 2559, $2: a, Wearing purple shirt. b, Playing guitar, wearing polka dot shirt, "Elvis Presley" at right. c, With guitar hanging from neck, "Elvis Presley" at right. d, Wearing patterned shirt.

No. 2560, $2: a, Wearing brown shirt. b, Playing guitar, wearing polka dot shirt, "Elvis Presley" at left. c, With guitar hanging from neck, "Elvis Presley" at left. d, Wearing gray suit and black shirt, playing guitar.

2004, Nov. 29 *Perf. 13¼*

Sheets of 4, #a-d

2559-2560 A588 Set of 2 12.00 12.00

Christmas Type of 2004

Paintings by Norman Rockwell: 35c, Follow Me in Merry Measure. 75c, The Merrie Old Coach Driver. 90c, Joy to the World. $3, Santa Reading His Mail.

$6, Wartime Santa.

2004, Dec. 9 *Perf. 12*

2561-2564 A600 Set of 4 3.75 3.75

Size: 63x81mm

Imperf

2565 A600 $6 multi 4.50 4.50

Babe Ruth Type of 2004

No. 2566: a, Blue background. b, White background.

No. 2567: a, Swinging bat. b, Looking forward. c, Looking to right. d, With glove.

2004, Jan. 29 Litho. *Perf. 14*

2566 A598 50c Pair, #a-b .75 .75

2567 A598 $2 Sheet of 4, #a-d 6.00 6.00

Moths — G202a

Designs: 75c, Scarlet-bodied wasp moth. 90c, Bella moth. $1, Sphinx moth. $3, Faithful beauty moth.
$6, Empyreuma affinis.

2004, Nov. 17 *Perf. 12¾*
2568-2571 G202a Set of 4 4.25 4.25

Souvenir Sheet

2572 G202a $6 multi 4.50 4.50

Ronald Reagan Type of 2004

No. 2573: a, With Press Secretary James Brady. b, With German Chancellor Helmut Kohl. c, With family. d, With Princess Diana.

2004, Nov. 29 *Perf. 13¼x13½*
2573 A597 $2 Sheet of 4, #a-d 6.00 6.00

Year of the Rooster Type of 2005

Paintings by Ren Yi: 75c, Double Chickens and Peony. $3, A Rooster, horiz.

2005, Jan. 17 *Perf. 12¾x13*
2574 A601 75c multi .60 .60

Souvenir Sheet

2575 A601 $3 multi 2.25 2.25

No. 2574 printed in sheets of 4. No. 2575 contains one 56x35mm stamp.

Intl. Year of Rice Type of 2005 and

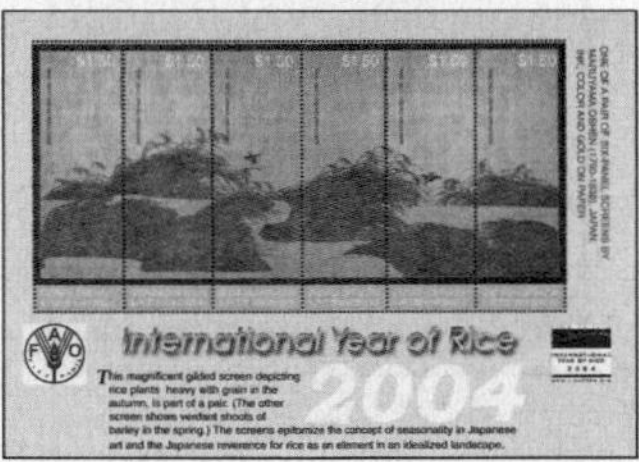

Screen Panels by Oshen Maruyama — G203

No. 2576 — Various panels depicting rice plants and birds.
$6, Rice Farming in Bali, by unknown artist, horiz.

2005, Feb. 10 *Perf. 14*
2576 G203 $1.50 Sheet of 6, #a-f 6.75 6.75

Souvenir Sheet

2577 A602 $6 multi 4.50 4.50

Prehistoric Animals Type of 2005

No. 2578: a, Psittacosaurus. b, Deinonychus. c, Suchomimus. d,Smilodon.
$6, Tenotosaurus.

2005, Feb. 10 *Perf. 13¼x13½*
2578 A604 $2 Sheet of 4, #a-d 6.00 6.00

Souvenir Sheet

2579 A604 $6 multi 4.50 4.50

See Nos. 2598-2601.

Reptiles and Amphibians — G204

No. 2580: a, Poison dart frog. b, Western Antillean anole. c, Black iguana. d, American crocodile.
$6, Anolis lizard.

2005, Feb. 10 *Perf. 12¾*
2580 G204 $2 Sheet of 4, #a-d 8.75 8.75

Souvenir Sheet

2581 G204 $6 multi 6.50 6.50

Carnivorous Plants — G205

No. 2582: a, Heliamphora tatei. b, Sarracenia flava, Genlisea pygmaea. c, Nepenthes bicalcarata. d, Utricularia intermedia.
$6, Dionaea muscipula.

2005, Feb. 10
2582 G205 $2 Sheet of 4, #a-d 6.00 6.00

Souvenir Sheet

2583 G205 $6 multi 4.50 4.50

Elvis Presley Type of 2005

No. 2584, $1.50: a, With guitar, 1955. b, Singing, 1956. c, With hand on chin, 1958. d, In suit, 1962. e, With guitar, 1968. f, Singing, 1972.
No. 2585, $1.50: a, In Army uniform, 1958. b, Wearing Hawaiian shirt, 1961. c, Wearing cap, 1963. d, Wearing turban, 1965. e, Sitting on sports car, 1966. f, With stethoscope, 1969.

2005, Apr. 4 *Perf. 13½*

Sheets of 6, #a-f

2584-2585 A607 Set of 2 13.50 13.50

Battle of Trafalgar, Bicent. — G206

Designs: 75c, Swiftsure. $1, British sail near Cape Trafalgar, horiz. $2, Capt. Alexander Ball. $3, Vice-Admiral Francedillaois Brueys d'Aigalliers.
$6, Admiral Aristide du Petit-Thouars.

2005, Apr. 4 *Perf. 14*
2586-2589 G206 Set of 4 5.25 5.25

Souvenir Sheet

2590 G206 $6 multi 4.50 4.50

Yasujiro Ozu Type of 2005

No. 2591: a, A Mother Should Be Loved, 1934. b, An Inn in Tokyo, 1935. c, Dragnet Girl, 1933. d, There Was a Father, 1942.

2005, Apr. 8 *Perf. 14¼*
2591 A608 $2 Sheet of 4, #a-d 6.00 6.00

Basketball Players Type of 2004

Designs: No. 2592, 75c, Steve Francis, Orlando Magic. No. 2593, 75c, Allan Houston, New York Knicks. No. 2594, 75c, Tracy McGrady, Houston Rockets. No. 2595, 75c, Steve Nash, Phoenix Suns. No. 2596, 75c, Shaquille O'Neal, Miami Heat. No. 2597, 75c, Chris Webber, Sacramento Kings.

2005, Mar. 8 **Litho.** *Perf. 14*
2592-2597 A596 Set of 6 3.50 3.50

Each stamp printed in sheets of 12.

Prehistoric Animals Type of 2005

No. 2598, $2: a, Eurypholis. b, Ichthyosaurus. c, Plesiosaur. d, Varnerxiphactinus.
No. 2599, $2: a, Pterosaurus. b, Archaeopteryx. c, Pterosaurian. d, Microraptor.
No. 2600, $6, Uintatherium. No. 2601, $6, Mammoth, vert.

Perf. 13¼x13¾, 13¾x13¼

2005, Apr. 15 **Sheets of 4, #a-d**
2598-2599 A604 Set of 2 12.00 12.00

Souvenir Sheets

2600-2601 A604 Set of 2 9.00 9.00

End of World War II Type of 2005

No. 2602, $2 — Battle of El Alamein: a, Field Marshal Bernard Montgomery directs troops forward. b, Field Marshal Erwin Rommel ready for battle. c, Troops move forward into battle. d, Line of German prisoners after battle.
No. 2603, $2 — Fall of Berlin: a, Russians at the gates of Berlin. b, German soldiers surrender. c, Berlin in ruins. d, Picking up the pieces.
No. 2604, $6, Troops attacking. No. 2605, $6, Sign with quote by Adolf Hitler, vert.

2005, May 10 *Perf. 13¼*

Sheets of 4, #a-d

2602-2603 A610 Set of 2 12.00 12.00

Souvenir Sheets

2604-2605 A610 Set of 2 9.00 9.00

Albert Einstein Type of 2005

No. 2606, vert.: a, Einstein, planet, diagram of Earth and Moon. b, Einstein. c, Israeli Prime Minister David Ben Gurion.

2005, June 27 *Perf. 13¼*
2606 A615 $3 Sheet of 3, #a-c 6.75 6.75

No. 2606 contains three 38x50mm stamps.

V-J Day Type of 2005

No. 2607, $2: a, P-38J Lightning. b, P-51D Mustang. c, F-4 fighter plane. d, Douglas C-47 Skytrain.
No. 2608, $2: a, Officer reads V-J Day message to his troops. b, Chaplain's prayer. c, Rejoicing the victory. d, USS Missouri in Tokyo Bay.

2005, July 11 *Perf. 12¾*

Sheets of 4, #a-d

2607-2608 A612 Set of 2 12.00 12.00

Rotary International Type of 2005

No. 2609, horiz.: a, People in front of National Polio Laboratory. b, People in National Polio Laboratory. c, Rotary International emblem.

2005, July 11 *Perf. 14*
2609 A613 $3 Sheet of 3, #a-c 6.75 6.75

Pope John Paul II (1920-2005) — G207

2005, Sept. 22 *Perf. 13¼x13½*
2610 G207 $3 multi 2.25 2.25

Printed in sheets of 6.

Maimonides (1135-1204), Philosopher — G208

2005 *Perf. 12*
2611 G208 $2 multi 1.50 1.50

Christmas Type of 2005

Designs: 35c, Madonna and Child, by Andrea del Sarto. 75c, Madonna Pesaro, by Titian. 90c, Madonna and Child, by Titian. $3, Madonna and Child, by Peter Paul Rubens.
$6, Madonna and Child, by Domenico Veneziano.

2005 *Perf. 12¾*
2612-2615 A625 Set of 4 3.75 3.75

Souvenir Sheet

2616 A625 $6 multi 4.50 4.50

Dog, by Chang Dai-Chien — G209

2006, Jan. 3 **Litho.** *Perf. 11½x11¼*
2617 G209 $1 multi .75 .75

New Year 2006 (Year of the Dog). Printed in sheets of 4.

Pope Benedict XVI Type of 2006

2006, Jan. 10 *Perf. 13¼*
2618 A629 $2 Pope, diff. 1.50 1.50

Printed in sheets of 4.

Elvis Presley Type of 2006

Variable Die Cut Perf.

2006, Feb. 21 **Litho. & Embossed**

Without Gum

2619 A631 $20 multi 15.00 15.00

Queen Elizabeth II, 80th Birthday Type of 2006

No. 2620: a, Queen wearing hat, sepia photograph. b, Queen wearing tiara. c, Queen with Princess Anne. d, Queen wearing hat, color photograph.
$6, Portrait of Queen in robe.

2006, Feb. 21 **Litho.** *Perf. 13¼*
2620 A632 $3 Sheet of 4, #a-d 9.00 9.00

Souvenir Sheet

Perf. 12

2621 A632 $6 multi 4.50 4.50

Marilyn Monroe Type of 2006

2006, Mar. 30 *Perf. 13½*
2622 A634 $3 Monroe, diff. 2.25 2.25

Printed in sheets of 4.

Rembrandt Type of 2006

Designs: 75c, The Strolling Musicians. 90c, The Great Jewish Bride. $1, Old Haaringh. $4, Beggars Receiving Alms at the Door of a House. No. 2627, $6, Young Woman in a Pearl-trimmed Beret (70x100mm). No. 2628, $6, Portrait of a Boy (70x100mm).
No. 2629: a, Man from Lady and Gentleman in Black. b, Woman from Lady and Gentleman in Black. c, Man from The Shipbuilder and His Wife. d, Woman from The Shipbuilder and His Wife.

Perf. 12, 12½x12¼ (#2627-2628)

2006, June 16
2623-2628 A639 Set of 6 14.00 14.00

Miniature Sheet

2629 A639 $3 Sheet of 4, #a-d 9.00 9.00

Mozart Type of 2006

2006, June 22 **Litho.** *Perf. 12¾*
2630 A640 $6 Don Giovanni 4.50 4.50

Space Type of 2006

No. 2631 — First Flight of Space Shuttle Columbia: a, Columbia on launchpad. b, Astronauts John W. Young and Robert L. Crippen. c, Liftoff of Columbia. d, Columbia in space. e, Crew in cabin. f, Columbia landing.
No. 2632, $3 — Apollo-Soyuz: a, Liftoff of Soyuz 19. b, Apollo-Soyuz crew. c, Crew in cabin. d, Soyuz 19.
No. 2633, $3 — Space Shuttle Discovery's return to space: a, Discovery on launchpad. b, Crew of Mission STS-114. c, Discovery and International Space Station. d, STS-114 space walk.
No. 2634, $6, Luna 9. No. 2635, $6, Venus Express. No. 2636, $6, Mars Reconnaissance Orbiter.

2006, Sept. 14
2631 A642 $2 Sheet of 6, #a-f 9.00 9.00

Sheets of 4, #a-d

2632-2633 A642 Set of 2 18.00 18.00

Souvenir Sheets

2634-2636 A642 Set of 3 13.50 13.50

Columbus Type of 2006

Designs: 75c, Pinta, vert. $1.50, Nina, Pinta and Santa Maria set sail. $2, Ship and map. $3, Columbus discovers San Salvador.
$6, Columbus.

2006, Oct. 26
2637-2640 A643 Set of 4 5.50 5.50

Souvenir Sheet

2641 A643 $6 multi 4.50 4.50

Christmas Type of 2006

Details of St. Willibrod in Adoration Before Mary, Mother of God, by Peter Paul Rubens: 25c, Man. 50c, Angels. 75c, Mary and Jesus. $1, St. Willibrod.

No. 2646: a, Like 25c. b, Like 50c. c, Like 75c. d, Like $1.

2006, Dec. 21 ***Perf. 14***
2642-2645 A646 Set of 4 1.90 1.90

Souvenir Sheet

2646 A646 $2 Sheet of 4, #a-d 6.00 6.00

Souvenir Sheet

Airships — G210

No. 2647: a, LZ-127. b, Dining room of the Hindenburg. c, Marine airship L53.

2007, Jan. 16 ***Perf. 13¼***
2647 G210 $3 Sheet of 3, #a-c 6.75 6.75

Souvenir Sheet

Elvis Presley (1935-77) — G211

No. 2648 — Various portraits with: a, Black denomination. b, Red denomination, playing guitar. c, White denomination. d, Red denomination, hands off guitar.

2007, Jan. 16 ***Perf. 14¼***
2648 G211 $3 Sheet of 4, #a-d 9.00 9.00

Pres. John F. Kennedy (1917-63) — G212

No. 2649, $2: a, On crutches, running for Congress. b, Campaigning for Congress. c, Campaigning in New Hampshire. d, As president.

No. 2650, $2.50: a, Naru Island. b, As Navy lieutenant on Solomon Islands, wearing cap. c, As lieutenant on Solomon Islands, without cap. d, SOS coconut carved by Kennedy.

2007, Jan. 16 ***Perf. 13½***

Sheets of 4, #a-d

2649-2650 G212 Set of 2 13.50 13.50

Scouting Type of 2007

Scout fleur-de-lis, "100," years "1907 / 2007," and background colors of: $2, Blue and green, horiz. $6, Orange and green, horiz.

2007, Jan. 16
2651 A650 $2 multi 1.50 1.50

Souvenir Sheet

2652 A650 $6 multi 4.50 4.50

No. 2651 printed in sheets of 4.

Year of the Pig Type of 2007

Miniature Sheet

No. 2653 — Wild Boar, by Liu Jiyou and painting name in: a, $1, Black. b, $1, Brown. c, $2, Black. d, $2, Red.

2007, Feb. 15 **Litho.** ***Perf. 14***
2653 A652 Sheet of 4, #a-d 4.50 4.50

G213

G214

Mushrooms — G215

Designs: 75c, Morchella semilibera. No. 2655, $1, Ganoderma resinaceum. No. 2656, $1, Helvella crispa. $4, Ganoderma sp.

No. 2658, $2: a, Russula sardonia. b, Amanita cruzii. c, Macrocybe titans. d, Amanita microspora.

No. 2659, $2: a, Aleuria aurantia. b, Boletus sp. c, Boletellus russellii. d, Otidea onotica.

No. 2660, $5, Amanita polypyramis. No. 2661, $5, Boletellus ananas. No. 2662, $5, Cantharellus cibarius.

2007, May 16 **Litho.** ***Perf. 14***
2654-2657 G213 Set of 4 5.25 5.25

Sheets of 4, #a-d

2658-2659 G214 Set of 2 12.00 12.00

Souvenir Sheets

2660 G214 $5 multi 3.75 3.75
2661-2662 G215 Set of 2 7.50 7.50

Birds — G216

Designs: 75c, Pied-billed grebe. No. 2664, $1, Black-crowned night heron. No. 2665, $1, Turkey vulture. $4, Green honeycreeper.

No. 2667, $2, horiz.: a, Caspian tern. b, Scarlet tanager. c, Common nighthawk. d, Osprey.

No. 2668, $2, horiz.: a, Hooded warbler. b, Northern flicker. c, Mockingbird. d, Blue tit.

No. 2669, $5, White-winged parakeet. No. 2670, $5, Blackpoll warbler, horiz. No. 2671, $5, Yellow-green vireo, horiz.

2007, May 16
2663-2666 G216 Set of 4 5.75 5.75

Sheets of 4, #a-d

2667-2668 G216 Set of 2 12.00 12.00

Souvenir Sheets

2669-2671 G216 Set of 3 13.00 13.00

Orchids — G217

Designs: 75c, Goodyera tesselata. $1.50, Oncidium floridanum. No. 2674, $2, Hexalectris spicata. $3, Pogonia ophioglossoides.

No. 2676, $2: a, Platanthera blephariglottis. b, Epipactis helleborine. c, Cypripedium alaskanum. d, Zeuxine strateumatica.

No. 2677, $2: a, Platanthera grandiflora. b, Platanthera peramoena. c, Cyrtopodium punctatum. d, Spiranthes odorata.

No. 2678, $6, Platanthera chapmanii. No. 2679, $6, Bletilla striata, horiz. No. 2680, $6, Macradenia lutescens, horiz.

2007, May 16 ***Perf. 12¾***
2672-2675 G217 Set of 4 5.50 5.50

Sheets of 4, #a-d

2676-2677 G217 Set of 2 12.00 12.00

Souvenir Sheets

2678-2680 G217 Set of 3 13.50 13.50

Betty Boop in "Snow White" — G218

No. 2681, horiz.: a, Queen looking at ring in snow. b, Green witch looking at mirror, dog and clown. c, Dancing ghost. d, Betty Boop asleep, frozen skull.

No. 2682, horiz.: a, $1, Queen looking in mirror. b, $1, Angry queen. c, $1, Knights and tree stump. d, $2, Betty Boop with alarm clock. e, $2, Betty Boop with mirror, dog, clown. f, $2, Betty Boop in snow.

$6, Betty Boop running.

2007, June 4 ***Perf. 13½***
2681 G218 $2 Sheet of 4, #a-d 6.00 6.00
2682 G218 Sheet of 6, #a-f 6.75 6.75

Souvenir Sheet

2683 G218 $6 multi 4.50 4.50

Intl. Polar Year Type of 2007

No. 2684, vert. — Royal penguins with: a, Country name at UR, denomination at LR. b, Country name at top, denomination at LR. c, Country name at LR, denomination at UL. d, Country name at bottom, denomination at UL. e, Country name at bottom, denomination at UR. f, Country name at UL, denomination at LR.

$6, African penguin, vert.

2007, June 25 ***Perf. 13½***
2684 A657 $2 Sheet of 6, #a-f 9.00 9.00

Souvenir Sheet

2685 A657 $6 multi 4.50 4.50

First Helicopter Flight, Cent. Type of 2007

No. 2686, horiz.: a, BK 117. b, UH-1 Iroquois. c, S-65/RH-53D. d, UH-1B/C Iroquois. e, Autogyro. f, BO 105.

$6, AH-64 Apache, horiz.

2007, June 25
2686 A664 $1.50 Sheet of 6, #a-f 6.75 6.75

Souvenir Sheet

2687 A664 $6 multi 4.50 4.50

Pope Benedict XVI Type of 2007

2007, July 11
2688 A653 $1 Pope, diff. .75 .75

Printed in sheets of 8.

Christmas G219

Paintings: 25c, Virgin and Child with Saints Jerome and Bartholomew, by Alessandro Bonvicino. 50c, Virgin and Child Between Saints Thomas and Jerome, by Guido Reni. 75c, Virgin and Child, by Giovanni Batista Salvi. $1, Madonna of Decemviri, by Pietro Perugino.

2007, Oct. 26 ***Perf. 14¼x14¾***
2689-2692 G219 Set of 4 1.90 1.90

Wedding of Queen Elizabeth II and Prince Philip, 60th Anniv. Type of 2007

Miniature Sheet

No. 2693: a, Couple, denomination at left, dull maroon panel. b, Queen, denomination at right, dull maroon panel. c, Queen, denomination at left, maroon panel. d, Couple, denomination at right, maroon panel. e, Couple, denomination at left, maroon panel. f, Queen, denomination at right, maroon panel.

2007, June 25 **Litho.** ***Perf. 13¼***
2693 A655 $1.50 Sheet of 6, #a-f 6.75 6.75

Year of the Rat Type of 2007

2007, Dec. 3 ***Perf. 13x13¼***
2694 A667 $1 multi .75 .75

Printed in sheets of 4.

Princess Diana Type of 2007

No. 2695 — Diana wearing: a, Plaid jacket. b, Purple feathered hat. c, Green dress. d, Plaid jacket, close-up in frame. e, Purple feathered hat, close-up in frame. f, Green dress, close-up in frame.

$6, Princess Diana, Prince Charles and infant, horiz.

2008, Jan. 14 ***Perf. 13¼***
2695 A656 $1.50 Sheet of 6, #a-f 6.75 6.75

Souvenir Sheet

2696 A656 $6 multi 4.50 4.50

Elvis Presley Type of 2008

No. 2697 — Presley: a, Silhouette, holding microphone, gray background. b, Wearing green shirt. c, Silhouette, holding microphone, olive green background. d, Playing guitar. e, Silhouette, playing guitar. f, Wearing orange shirt.

2008, Jan. 14 ***Perf. 13¼***
2697 A671 $1.50 Sheet of 6, #a-f 6.75 6.75

World Stamp Championship Type of 2008

Design: Aerial view of Jerusalem, horiz. (149x125mm).

2008, May 14 ***Imperf.***
2698 A676 $6 multi 4.50 4.50

Basketball Type of 2008

Miniature Sheet

No. 2699 — Members of 2008 Boston Celtics basketball team: a, Ray Allen. b, Rajon Rondo. c, Paul Pierce. d, Kendrick Perkins. e, Kevin Garnett. f, Leon Powe. g, James Posey. h, Sam Cassell. i, P. J. Brown.

2008, June 17 **Litho.** ***Perf. 13½***
2699 A678 $1 Sheet of 9, #a-i 6.75 6.75

Cats Type of 2008

No. 2700: a, Havana. b, Scottish Fold. c, American Curl. d, American Bobtail. e, Balinese. f, Singapura.

$6, Burmese, horiz.

2008, June 18 ***Perf. 11½***
2700 A677 $1 Sheet of 6, #a-f 4.50 4.50

Souvenir Sheet

2701 A677 $6 multi 4.50 4.50

Elvis Presley Type of 2008
Miniature Sheet

No. 2702 — Presley: a, Wearing lei, holding microphone in right hand. b, Playing guitar, red striped background. c, Wearing lei, holding microphone in left hand, right arm extended with hand in fist. d, Playing guitar, olive green and black background. e, Wearing lei, holding microphone in left hand, right hand at side. f, Wearing red shirt.

2008, Oct. 10 ***Perf. 13¼***
2702 A670 $1.50 Sheet of 6, #a-f 6.75 6.75

Christmas G220

Designs: 25c, Christmas ornament washing up on beach. 50c, Gift boxes hanging ornaments and electric Christmas lights. 75c, "Merry Christmas" written on beach. $1, Starfish and shells hanging ornaments, vert.

Perf. 14¾x14¼, 14¼x14¾
2008, Dec. 3 **Litho.**
2703-2706 G220 Set of 4 1.90 1.90

Space Exploration Type of 2009
Miniature Sheets

No. 2707, $2: a, Venus and Mercury. b, Jupiter. c, Earth and Mars. d, Saturn. e, Neptune. f, Uranus.
No. 2708, $2, vert. — Mariner 9: a, And the Valles Marineris on Mars. b, And technicians. c, And the Olympus Mons on Mars. d, Photograph of Valles Marineris. e, Lifting off on Atlas-Centaur rocket. f, And Phobos.
No. 2709, $2.50, vert. — Mariner 10: a, And Mars at UR. b, Lifting off on Atlas-Centaur rocket. c, And technicians. d, And Moon at UL.
No. 2710, $2.50, vert.: a, Pillars of Creation in Eagle Nebula. b, Orion Nebula. c, Crab Nebula. d, Horsehead Nebula.

2008, Dec. 24 ***Perf. 14***
Sheets of 6, #a-f
2707-2708 A690 Set of 2 18.00 18.00
Sheets of 4, #a-d
2709-2710 A690 Set of 2 15.00 15.00

Fish G221

Designs: $1, Blue chromis. No. 2712, $2, Clown wrasse. No. 2713, $4, Orange-spotted filefish. $5, Palometa.
No. 2715, $2: a, Tiger grouper. b, Bluehead wrasse. c, Squirrel fish. d, Queen parrotfish. e, Yellowtail snapper. f, Barred hamlet.

2009, Jan. 9 ***Perf. 12½***
2711-2714 G221 Set of 4 9.00 9.00
Perf. 12
2715 G221 $2 Sheet of 6, #a-f 9.00 9.00

G222

Shells — G223

Designs: 25c, True tulip. 50c Twisted plait olive. 75c, Junonia. $1, Royal comb venus.
No. 2720: a, Lion's paw. b, Banded tulip. c, Flame auger. d, Miniature melo, e, West Indian worm shell. f, Mouse cowry.

2009, Jan. 9 ***Perf. 12½***
2716-2719 G222 Set of 4 2.25 2.25
Perf. 12
2720 G223 $2 Sheet of 6, #a-f 9.00 9.00

Obama Type of 2009

No. 2721 — Pres. Barack Obama: a, Pointing. b, Wearing blue tie, hands not shown. c, Touching thumb to index finger. d, Wearing red tie, hands not shown.
$10, Pres. Obama and US Capitol.

2009, Jan. 20 ***Perf. 11½***
2721 A689 $2.75 Sheet of 4, #a-d 8.50 8.50

Souvenir Sheet
Perf. 13¼
2722 A689 $10 multi 7.75 7.75

No. 2722 contains one 38x51mm stamp.

New Year 2009 (Year of the Ox) — G224

2009, Jan. 26 ***Perf. 11½***
2723 G224 $2.50 multi 1.90 1.90

Olympic Sports Type of 2009
Miniature Sheet

No. 2724, vert.: a, Archery. b, Track cycling. c, Wrestling. d, Boxing.

2009, Apr. 26 ***Perf. 12***
2724 A700 $1.40 Sheet of 4, #a-d 4.25 4.25

China 2009 World Stamp Exhibition, Luoyang.

Miniature Sheet

Qianglong (1711-99), Chinese Emperor — G225

No. 2725: a, Qianglong as young man, with chop at UR. b, Qianglong, women, table and tree. c, Qianglong at desk. d, Qianglong as older man.

2009, Apr. 29 ***Perf. 12***
2725 G225 $1.40 Sheet of 4, #a-d 4.25 4.25

China 2009 World Stamp Exhibition, Luoyang.

Elvis Presley Type of 2009
Miniature Sheet

No. 2726, horiz. — Presley: a, Singing, with hand raised near mouth, denimination in yellow brown. b, Holding microphone, denomination in purple. c, Holding microphone, diff., denomination in red violet. d, Singing and holding microphone, denomination in Prussian blue.

2009, Apr. 29 ***Perf. 13½***
2726 A703 $2.50 Sheet of 4, #a-d 7.50 7.50

Worldwide Fund for Nature (WWF) — G226

No. 2727 — Various depictions of Caribbean spiny lobster with denomination in: a, Orange. b, Green. c, Pink. d, Yellow.

2009, June 23 ***Perf. 13½***
2727 Strip of 4 9.00 9.00
a.-d. G226 $3 Any single 2.25 2.25
e. Sheet of 8 2 each #2727a-2727d 18.00 18.00

G227

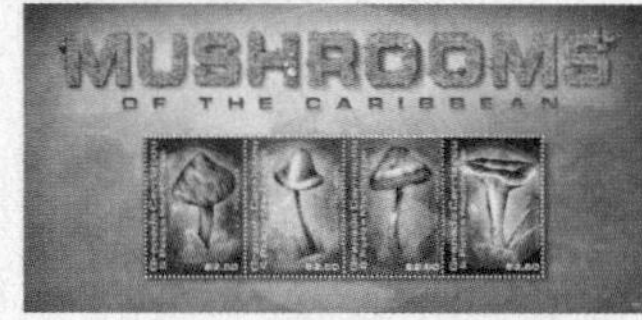

G228

Mushrooms — G229

Designs: 25c, Psilocybe mexicana. $1, Crinipellis piceae. $2, Psilocybe subcubensis. $5, Psilocybe cubensis.
No. 2732: a, Panacolus fimicola. b, Psilocybe yungensis. c, Panacolus subbalteatus. d, Russula cremeolilacina.
No. 2733: a, Psilocybe guilartensis. b, Psilocybe aztecorum.

2009, July 2 ***Perf. 14x14¾***
2728-2731 G227 Set of 4 6.25 6.25
Perf. 14¼x14¾
2732 G228 $2.50 Sheet of 4, #a-d 7.50 7.50

Souvenir Sheet
Perf. 14x14¾
2733 G229 $3 Sheet of 2, #a-b 4.50 4.50

Miniature Sheet

Pres. Abraham Lincoln (1809-65) — G230

No. 2734 — Photograph of Lincoln: a, Without beard, ear showing at right. b, Without beard, ear showing at left. c, With beard, wearing vest. d, With beard, without vest.

2009, July 21 **Litho.** ***Perf. 13¼***
2734 G230 $2.50 Sheet of 4, #a-d 7.50 7.50

Miniature Sheet

Visit of Pope Benedict XVI to Israel — G231

No. 2735: a, Pope Benedict XVI. b, Pope and Israeli President Shimon Peres. c, Pope at Temple Mount, Jerusalem. d, Pope and Heichal Shlomo.

2009, Sept. 15 ***Perf. 11½x12***
2735 G231 $2.50 Sheet of 4, #a-d 7.50 7.50

Miniature Sheet

Teenage Mutant Ninja Turtles, 25th Anniv. — G232

No. 2736: a, Donatello. b, Leonardo. c, Raphael. d, Michelangelo.

2009, Sept. 15 ***Perf. 12x11½***
2736 G232 $2.50 Sheet of 4, #a-d 7.50 7.50

Miniature Sheet

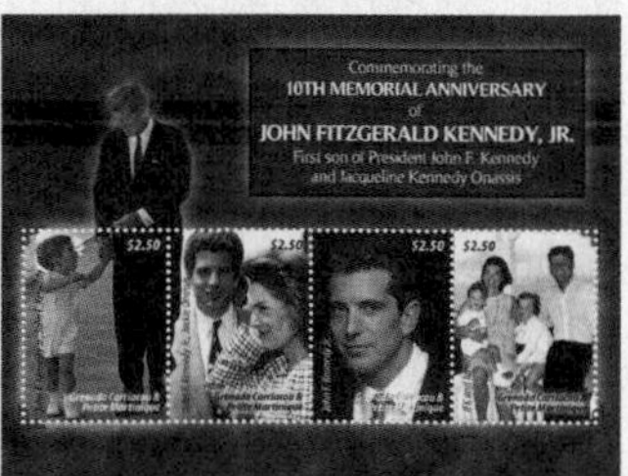

John F. Kennedy, Jr. (1960-99), Magazine Publisher — G233

No. 2737: a, As child, with father Pres. John F. Kennedy. b, With mother, Jacqueline. c, Alone. d, As child with mother, father and sister Caroline.

2009, Dec. 7 **Litho.** ***Perf. 11¼x11½***
2737 G233 $2.50 Sheet of 4, #a-d 7.75 7.75

First Man on the Moon, 40th Anniv. Type of 2009

No. 2738, vert.: a, Saturn, Titan and Voyager I. b, Apollo 11 Lunar Module. c, Voyager I, Europa, Jupiter, Io, Callisto and Ganymede. $6, Apollo 11 Lunar Module, diff., vert.

2009, Dec. 7 *Perf. 13¼*

2738 A701 $2 Horiz. strip of 3, #a-c 4.75 4.75

Souvenir Sheet

2739 A701 $6 multi 4.75 4.75

No. 2738 was printed in sheets containing 2 strips of three stamps.

G234

G235

G236

G237

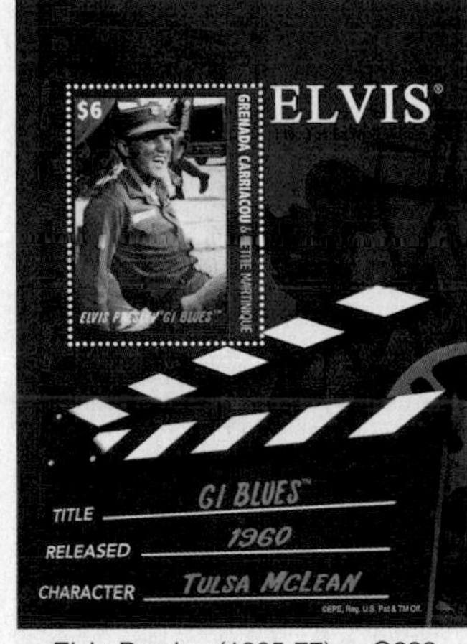

Elvis Presley (1935-77) — G238

No. 2740 — Presley: a, Facing crowd, with guitar at right. b, Facing crowd, with guitar in front of him. c, Close-up with crowd in background. d, Holding microphone, no crowd.

2010, Jan. 7

2740 G234 $2.75 Sheet of 4, #a-d 8.50 8.50

Souvenir Sheets

2741 G235 $6 multi 4.75 4.75
2742 G236 $6 multi 4.75 4.75
2743 G237 $6 multi 4.75 4.75
2744 G238 $6 multi 4.75 4.75
Nos. 2741-2744 (4) 19.00 19.00

Miniature Sheet

Awarding of 2009 Nobel Peace Prize to Pres. Barack Obama — G239

No. 2745 — Various photographs of Pres. Obama and gray map in background showing: a, Alaska, Western and Central United States. b, Greenland, Northeastern United States, Great Lakes. c, Southwestern United States, Mexico. d, Southeastern United States, Northern South America.

2010, Mar. 4 *Perf. 12x11½*

2745 G239 $2.50 Sheet of 4, #a-d 7.75 7.75

Orchids G240

Designs: $1.20, Dendrophylax lindenii. $1.80, Scaphyglottis imbricata. No. 2748, $3, Encyclia ceratistes. $5, Scaphyglottis stellata.

No. 2750: a, Oncidium excavatum. b, Brassavola nodosa. c, Cattleya gaskelliana. d, Phalaenopsis cultivars.

No. 2751, $3: a, Lepanthopsis floripecten. b, Equitant oncidium.

Perf. 11½x11¼, 11½x12 (#2750)

2010, Mar. 4

2746-2749 G240 Set of 4 8.50 8.50

2750 G240 $2.50 Sheet of 4, #a-d 7.75 7.75

Souvenir Sheet

2751 G240 $3 Sheet of 2, #a-b 4.75 4.75

Miniature Sheets

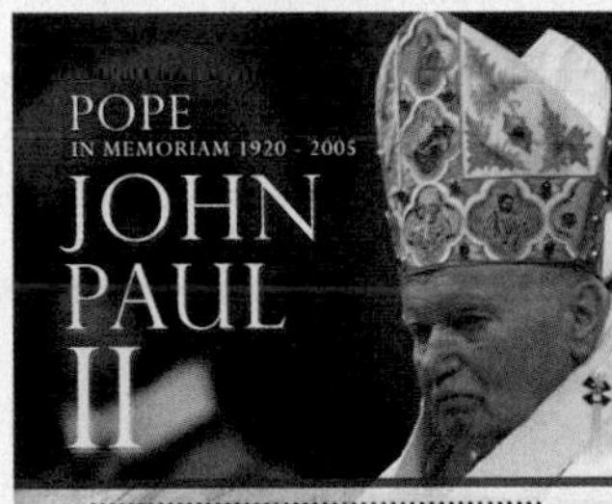

G241

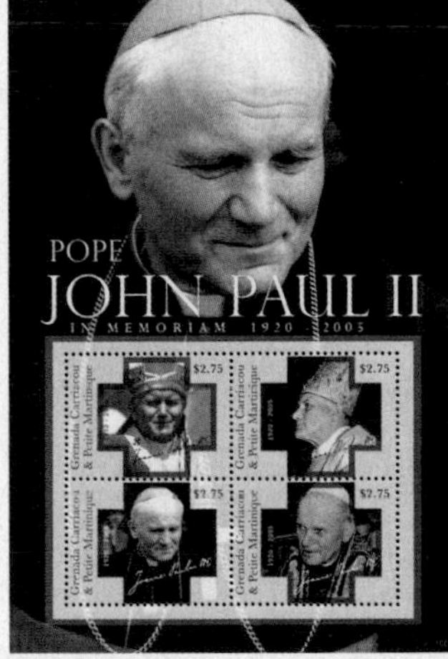

Pope John Paul II (1920-2005) — G242

No. 2752: a, Pope wearing zucchetto, country name over colored area. b, Pope wearing miter, white area under and below denomination. c, As "b," with colored area under and below denomination. d, As "a," country name over white area.

No. 2753: a, Pope wearing miter, looking forward. b, Pope wearing miter, looking left. c, Pope wearing zucchetto, looking right. d, Pope wearing zucchetto, looking left.

2010, Apr. 9 *Perf. 11½x12*

2752 G241 $2.75 Sheet of 4, #a-d 8.25 8.25

2753 G242 $2.75 Sheet of 4, #a-d 8.25 8.25

Girl Guides Type of 2010

No. 2754, horiz. — Girl Guides: a, And adult leader. b, In tent. c, Sitting in field of flowers. d, looking at young Girl Guide pointing.

$6, Girl Guides wearing hooded sweatshirts.

2010, June 11 *Perf. 13x13¼*

2754 A717 $2.75 Sheet of 4, #a-d 8.25 8.25

Souvenir Sheet

Perf. 13¼x13

2755 A717 $6 multi 4.50 4.50

World Cup Type of 2010

No. 2756, $1.50 — Group E first-round matches: a, Netherlands vs. Denmark. b, Japan vs. Cameroun. c, Netherlands vs. Japan. d, Denmark vs. Cameroun. e, Japan vs. Denmark. f, Cameroun vs. Netherlands.

No. 2757, $1.50 — Group F first-round matches: a, Italy vs. Paraguay. b, New Zealand vs. Slovakia. c, Slovakia vs. Paraguay. d, New Zealand vs. Italy. e, Slovakia vs. Italy. f, Paraguay vs. New Zealand.

No. 2758, $1.50 — Group G first-round matches: a, Ivory Coast vs. Portugal. b, Brazil vs. North Korea. c, Brazil vs. Ivory Coast. d, Portugal vs. North Korea. e, North Korea vs. Ivory Coast. f, Portugal vs. Brazil.

No. 2759, $1.50 — Group H first-round matches: a, Honduras vs. Chile. b, Spain vs. Switzerland. c, Chile vs. Switzerland. d, Honduras vs. Spain. e, Spain vs. Chile. f, Switzerland vs. Honduras.

No. 2760, $3.50: a, Ellis Park Stadium, Johannesburg. b, Mbombela Stadium, Nelspruit.

No. 2761, $3.50: a, Loftus Versfeld Stadium, Pretoria. b, Free State Stadium, Bloemfontein.

No. 2762, $3.50: a, Peter Mokaba Stadium, Polokwane. b, Royal Bafokeng Stadium, Rustenburg.

2010, June 11 **Litho.** *Perf. 13¼*

Sheets of 6, #a-f

2756-2759 A720 Set of 4 27.00 27.00

Sheets of 2, #a-b

2760-2762 A720 Set of 3 16.00 16.00

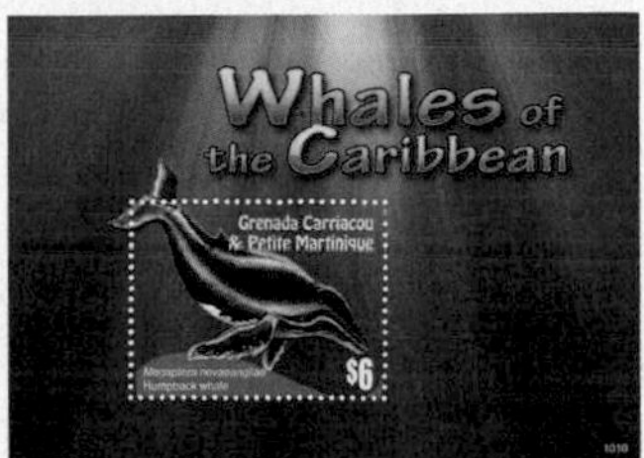

Whales — G243

No. 2763: a, Gervais's beaked whale. b, Cuvier's beaked whale. c, Pygmy sperm whale. d, Melon-headed whale. e, Bryde's whale. f, Sperm whale.

$6, Humpback whale.

2010, Sept. 1 *Perf. 12*

2763 G243 $2 Sheet of 6, #a-f 9.00 9.00

Souvenir Sheet

2764 G243 $6 multi 4.50 4.50

Leonardo da Vinci (1452-1519), Artist — G244

No. 2765, vert.: a, Reputed self-portrait. b, Statue of da Vinci outside of Uffizi Gallery, Florence. c, Vitruvian Man. d, La Scapigliata. e, Mona Lisa. f, Study of Horses.

$6, The Last Supper.

2010, Nov. 4

2765 G244 $2 Sheet of 6, #a-f 9.00 9.00

Souvenir Sheet

2766 G244 $6 multi 4.50 4.50

Miniature Sheets

G245

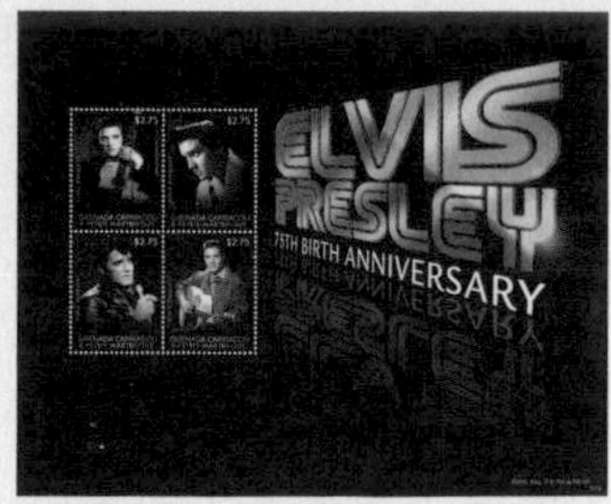

Elvis Presley (1935-77) — G246

No. 2767 — Presley: a, Standing behind microphone. b, With guitar, no microphone visible. c, Holding microphone, no guitar visible. d, With guitar, holding microphone.

No. 2768 — Presley: a, With guitar neck by face. b, Without microphone. c, Holding microphone. d, Playing guitar.

2010, Nov. 4

2767 G245 $2.75 Sheet of 4, #a-d 8.25 8.25
2768 G246 $2.75 Sheet of 4, #a-d 8.25 8.25

Engagement of Prince William and Catherine Middleton G247

Engagement ring emblem and: No. 2769, Couple.

No. 2770: a, Middleton wearing fur hat. b, Prince William wearing military uniform and beret. c, Middleton without hat. d, Prince William in suit.

No. 2771: a, Middleton wearing beret. b, Prince William.

No. 2772, horiz.: a, Middleton wearing hat. b, Prince William, diff.

2011, Feb. 18 Litho. ***Perf. 12***

2769 G247 $2.50 multi 1.90 1.90
2770 G247 $2.50 Sheet of 4, #a-d 7.50 7.50

Souvenir Sheets

Perf. 12¾x13 Syncopated

2771 G247 $3 Sheet of 2, #a-b 4.50 4.50

Perf. 13x12¾ Syncopated

2772 G247 $3 Sheet of 2, #a-b 4.50 4.50

No. 2769 was printed in sheets of 4.

Miniature Sheet

Pres. Barack Obama in India — G248

No. 2773: a, Obama holding microphone. b, Indian Prime Minister Manmohan Singh, Obama, woman. c, Obama and Singh. d, Obama at lectern.

Perf. 12¾x13 Syncopated

2011, Mar. 30

2773 G248 $2.75 Sheet of 4, #a-d 8.25 8.25

Indipex 2011, New Delhi.

Miniature Sheet

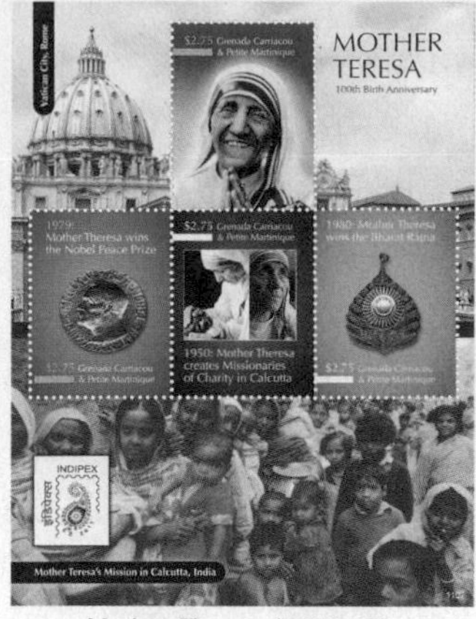

Mother Teresa (1910-97), Humanitarian — G249

No. 2774: a, Mother Teresa with hands together in prayer. b, Nobel Prize medal. c, Photographs of Mother Teresa. d, Bharat Ratna award.

2011, Mar. 30 ***Perf. 12***

2774 G249 $2.75 Sheet of 4, #a-d 8.25 8.25

Indipex 2011, New Delhi.

Miniature Sheets

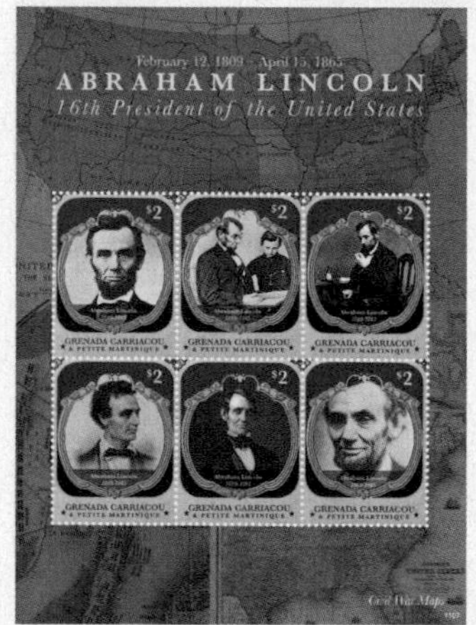

G250

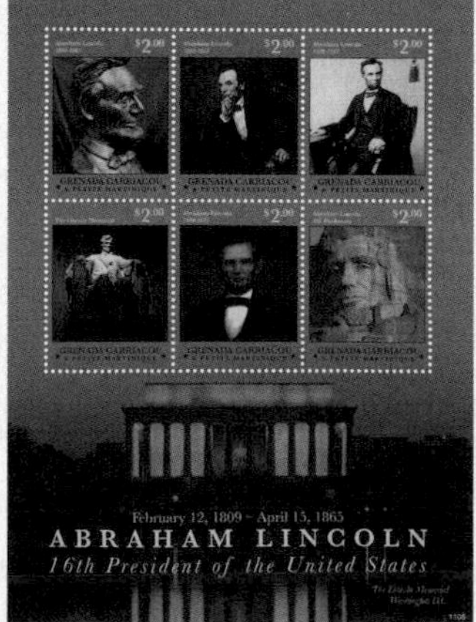

Pres. Abraham Lincoln (1809-65) — G251

No. 2775 — Photographs of Lincoln: a, With beard, both ears visible. b, Reading to son, Tad. c, Sitting in chair. d, Without beard, facing right. e, Without beard, facing forward. f, With beard, one ear visible.

No. 2776: a, Bust of Lincoln. b, Painting of Lincoln with hand at chin. c, Photograph of Lincoln sitting in chair. d, Statue in Lincoln Memorial. e, Painting of Lincoln, hands not visible. f, Mt. Rushmore sculpture of Lincoln.

2011, Apr. 1 ***Perf. 12***

2775 G250 $2 Sheet of 6, #a-f 9.00 9.00
2776 G251 $2 Sheet of 6, #a-f 9.00 9.00

G252

Pres. John F. Kennedy (1917-63) — G253

Designs: No. 2777, Kennedy at desk in Oval Office.

No. 2778: a, Kennedy and family in hallway. b, Kennedy and wife, Jacqueline, in formal wear. c, Kennedy and wife at stadium. d, Kennedy and family on porch.

No. 2779, Kennedy, window at side. No. 2780, Kennedy walking and reviewing papers with aides.

2011, Apr. 1 ***Perf. 12***

2777 G252 $2.75 multi 2.10 2.10
2778 G253 $2.75 Sheet of 4, #a-d 8.25 8.25

Souvenir Sheets

Perf. 12¾x13 Syncopated

2779 G252 $6 multi 4.50 4.50
2780 G253 $6 multi 4.50 4.50

No. 2777 was printed in sheets of 4.

Miniature Sheets

Dogs — G254

No. 2781, $2.50: a, King Charles spaniel. b, Labador retriever. c, German shepherd. d, Weimaraner.

No. 2782, $2.50: a, Border collie. b, Briard. c, Great Dane. d, Afghan hound.

2011, Apr. 15 Litho. ***Perf. 12x12½***

Sheets of 4, #a-d

2781-2782 G254 Set of 2 15.00 15.00

Miniature Sheets

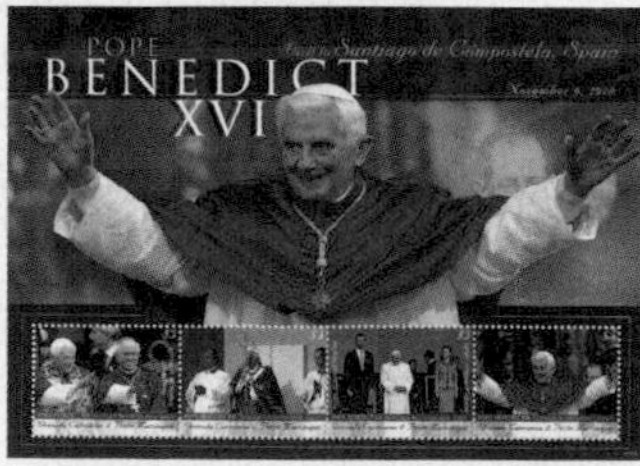

Visit to Spain of Pope Benedict XVI — G255

No. 2783, $3 — Visit to Santiago de Compostela: a, Pope Benedict XVI and Archbishop Julian Barrio. b, Pope holding crucifix, c, Pope with Prince and Princess of Asturias. d, Pope extending arms.

No. 2784, $3 — Visit to Barcelona: a, Pope holding Bible. b, Pope and priest in procession. c, Pope with King Juan Carlos and Queen Sofia. d, Pope at pulpit reading.

Perf. 11½x12, 11½x11¼ (#2784)

2011, Apr. 15

Sheets of 4, #a-d

2783-2784 G255 Set of 2 18.00 18.00

Beatification of Pope John Paul II — G256

No. 2785 — Pope John Paul II. a, Wearing miter. b, Kneeling in prayer. c, With arm extended.

$6, Pope with arms clasped.

2011, Apr. 15 ***Perf. 13 Syncopated***

2785 G256 $3.30 Sheet of 3, #a-c 7.50 7.50

Souvenir Sheet

Perf. 12

2786 G256 $6 multi 4.50 4.50

Princess Diana Type of 2011

No. 2787 — Princess Diana: a, Wearing hat. b, With children. c, As young girl. d, Walking with Prince Charles. $6, Princess Diana wearing red hat.

2011, Apr. 15 ***Perf. 12***

2787 A744 $2.75 Sheet of 4, #a-d 8.25 8.25

Souvenir Sheet

Perf. 13 Syncopated

2788 A744 $6 multi 4.50 4.50

Wedding of Prince William and Catherine Middleton — G257

No. 2789, $2.75: a, Couple in coach waving. b, Bride facing left. c, Groom wearing hat. d, Couple holding hands.

No. 2790, $2.75: a, Groom without hat. b, Bride, diff. c, Soldiers on horseback. d, Couple waving.

No. 2791, vert.: a, Bride, diff. b, Groom, diff.

2011, Sept. 15 ***Perf. 13 Syncopated***

Sheets of 4, #a-d

2789-2790 G257 Set of 2 16.50 16.50

Souvenir Sheet

2791 G257 $3 Sheet of 2, #a-b 4.50 4.50

Birds — G258

No. 2792, $2.50: a, Troupial. b, Green-throated carib. c, Osprey. d, Green heron.

No. 2793, $2.50: a, Village weaver. b, Belted kingfisher. c, Scarlet tanager. d, Semipalmated plover.

No. 2794, $6, Rose-breasted grosbeak. No. 2795, $6, Merlin.

2011, Oct. 26 ***Perf. 13 Syncopated***

Sheets of 4, #a-d

2792-2793 G258 Set of 2 15.00 15.00

Souvenir Sheets

Perf. 12

2794-2795 G258 Set of 2 9.00 9.00

Chinese Musical Instruments — G259

No. 2796: a, Pipa. b, Guqin. c, Dizi. d, Yangqin. e, Dagu.
$6, Erhu, vert.

2011, Nov. 8 ***Perf. 13¼***

2796 G259 $2 Sheet of 5, #a-e 7.50 7.50

Souvenir Sheet

Perf. 13¼x13

2797 G259 $6 multi 4.50 4.50

China 2011 Intl. Philatelic Exhibition, Wuxi. No. 2797 contains one 30x80mm stamp.

Christmas G260

Paintings: 25c, Annunciation, by Niccolò di Pietro Gerini. 50c, The Annunciation, by Melchior Broederlam. $1, Coronation of the Virgin, by Giovanni da Milano. $2, Madonna, by André Beauneveu.

2011, Nov. 1 ***Perf. 12***

2798-2801 G260 Set of 4 2.75 2.75

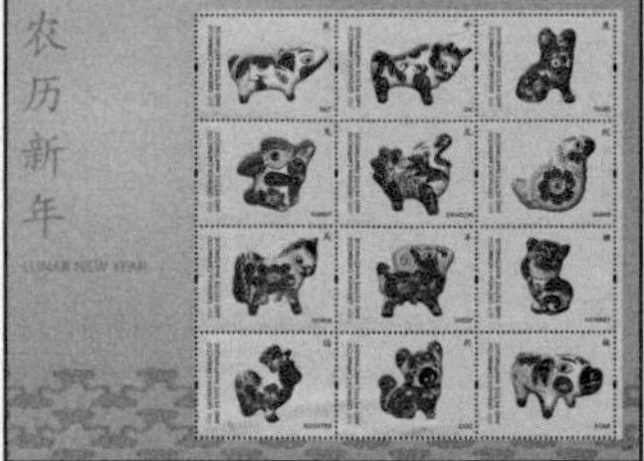

Chinese Zodiac Animals — G261

New Year 2012 (Year of the Dragon) — G262

No. 2802: a, Rat. b, Ox. c, Tiger. d, Rabbit. e, Dragon. f, Snake. g, Horse. h, Sheep. i, Monkey. j, Rooster. k, Dog. l, Boar.
$8, Dragon.

Litho. With Foil Application

2011 ***Perf. 13 Syncopated***

2802 G261 65c Sheet of 12, #a-l 5.75 5.75

Souvenir Sheet

Litho.

Perf. 13¼

2803 G262 $8 multi 6.00 6.00

Issued: No. 2802, 11/8; No. 2803, 10/26.

G263

Mushrooms — G264

No. 2804: a, Coltriciella navispora. b, Tylopilus rufonigricans. c, Chroogomphus rutilus. d, Entoloma rugostriatum. e, Xerocomus amazonicus. f, Coltricia oblectabilis.
No. 2805: a, Tylopilus exiguus. b, Mycena acicula. c, Panaeolus papilionaceus. d, Chroomogomphus ochraceus.
No. 2806, Amanita calochroa. No. 2807, Psilocybe cubensis.

2011, Dec. 16 ***Perf. 13 Syncopated***

2804 G263 $2 Sheet of 6, #a-f 9.00 9.00
2805 G264 $2.50 Sheet of 4, #a-d 7.50 7.50

Souvenir Sheets

2806 G263 $6 multi 4.50 4.50
2807 G264 $6 multi 4.50 4.50

Reptiles — G265

No. 2808, $3.50: a, Puerto Rican crested anole. b, Tropical house gecko. c, Dominican ground lizard. d, Eyed anole.
No. 2809, $3.50: a, Giant ditch frog. b, Coqui antillano. c, Gounouj. d, Tink frog.
No. 2810, $9, Lesser Antillean Iguana. No. 2811, $9, Red-footed tortoise.

2012, Feb. 8 ***Perf. 13 Syncopated***

Sheets of 4, #a-d

2808-2809 G265 Set of 2 21.00 21.00

Souvenir Sheets

2810-2811 G265 Set of 2 13.50 13.50

Miniature Sheet

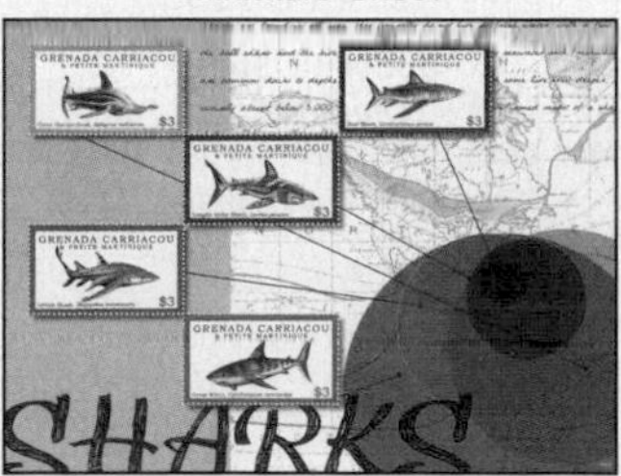

Sharks — G266

No. 2812: a, Great hammerhead shark. b, Reef shark. c, Longfin mako shark. d, Lemon shark. e, Great white shark.

2012, Apr. 5 ***Perf. 12***

2812 G266 $3 Sheet of 5, #a-e 11.00 11.00

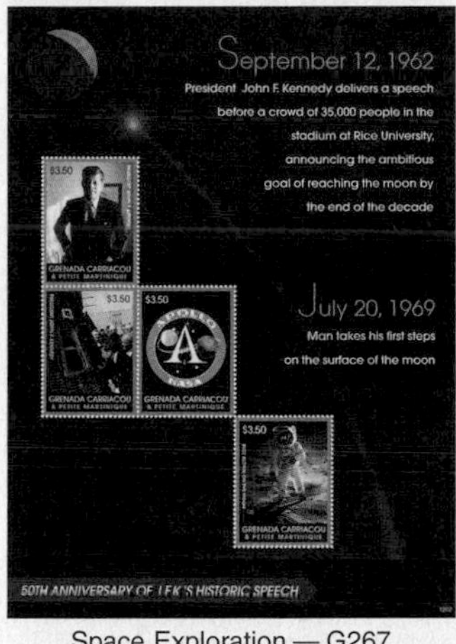

Space Exploration — G267

No. 2813: a, Pres. John F. Kennedy. b, Pres. Kennedy looking into space capsule. c, Emblem for NASA's Apollo program. d, Buzz Aldrin on the Moon.
$9, Pres. Kennedy greeting men under rocket.

2012, Apr. 5 ***Perf. 14***

2813 G267 $3.50 Sheet of 4, #a-d 10.50 10.50

Souvenir Sheet

Perf. 12

2814 G267 $9 multi 6.75 6.75

No. 2814 contains one 30x50mm stamp.

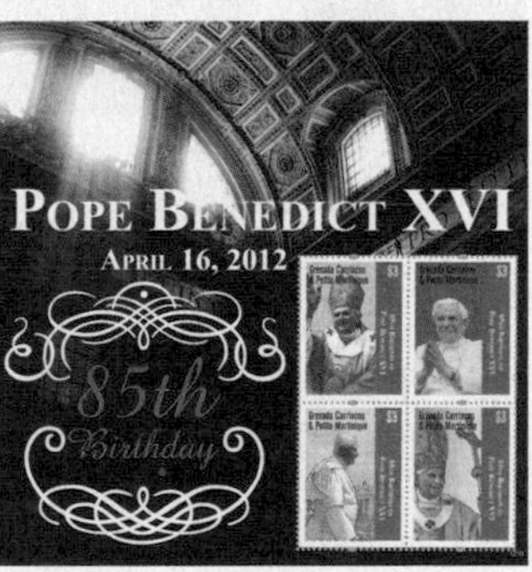

G268

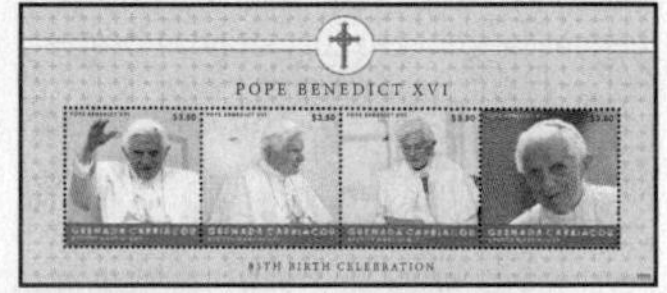

Pope Benedict XVI, 85th Birthday — G269

No. 2815 — Pope Benedict XVI: a, Waving. b, With hands together. c, At Vatican City. d, With crucifix.
No. 2816 — Pope Benedict XVI: a, Waving. b, Facing right. c, In front of microphone. d, Facing forward.
$9, Pope facing right wearing red vestments.

Perf. 13 Syncopated (G268), 13¾

2012, Nov. 28

2815 G268 $3 Sheet of 4, #a-d 9.00 9.00
2816 G269 $3.50 Sheet of 4, #a-d 10.50 10.50

Souvenir Sheet

2817 G268 $9 multi 6.75 6.75

Sinking of the Titanic, Cent. (in 2012) — G270

No. 2818 — Inscriptions: a, The investigation on the R.M.S. Titanic begins. b, R.M.S. Titanic (at sea, viewed from side). c, R.M.S. Titanic (viewed from above). d, R.M.S. Titanic (with lowered lifeboat).
$9, Newsboy with newspapers with headline about sinking.

2013, Jan. 3 ***Perf. 13¾***

2818 G270 $3.50 Sheet of 4, #a-d 10.50 10.50

Souvenir Sheet

Perf. 12

2819 G270 $9 multi 6.75 6.75

No. 2819 contains one 30x50mm stamp.

Whales — G271

No. 2820: a, Pygmy right whale. b, Gray whale. c, Pygmy killer whale. d, Bowhead whale.
$9, Humpback whale.

2013, Jan. 3 ***Perf. 13¾***

2820 G271 $3.50 Sheet of 4, #a-d 10.50 10.50

Souvenir Sheet

2821 G271 $9 multi 6.75 6.75

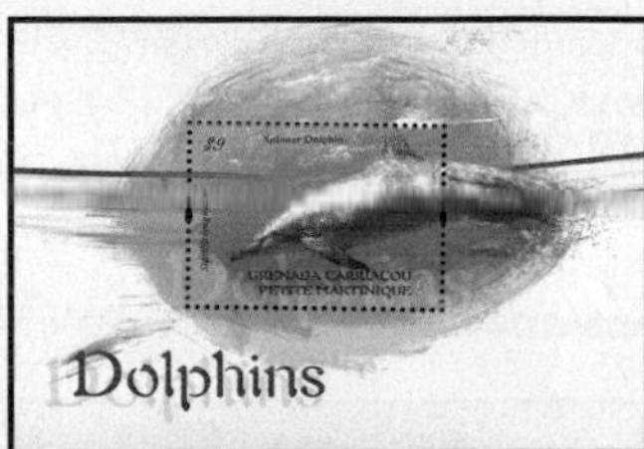

Dolphins — G272

No. 2822: a, Dusky dolphin. b, Indo-Pacific humpback dolphin. c, Commerson's dolphin. d, Hector's dolphin. e, Atlantic spotted dolphin. f, Striped dolphin.
$9, Spinner dolphin.

2013, Jan. 3 *Perf. 13 Syncopated*
2822 G272 $2.75 Sheet of 6, #a-f 12.50 12.50

Souvenir Sheet

2823 G272 $9 multi 6.75 6.75

Princess Diana (1961-97) — G273

No. 2824 — Princess Diana wearing: a, Pink hat. b, Tiara. c, Checked dress. d, Lilac jacket.
$9, Princess Diana wearing pink hat, diff.

2013, Jan. 3 *Perf. 14*
2824 G273 $3.50 Sheet of 4, #a-d 10.50 10.50

Souvenir Sheet
Perf. 12

2825 G273 $9 multi 6.75 6.75

Elvis Presley Type of 2013
Souvenir Sheets

Frame color: No. 2826, $9, Gray. No. 2827, $9, Black. No. 2828, $9, Purple. No. 2829, $9, Red (Presley without guitar). No. 2830, $9, Red (Presley with guitar).

2013, Jan. 3 *Perf. 12¾*
2826-2830 A782 Set of 5 34.00 34.00

History of Art — G274

No. 2831 — Holy Allegory, by Giovanni Bellini (details): a, Buildings in distance. b, Virgin Mary, two women and man. c, Old man, child shaking tree. d, Job and St. Sebastian.
No. 2832, vert.: a, The Annunciation, by Matthias Grünewald. b, St. Jerome in the Desert, by Bellini. c, Lady with an Ermine, by Leonardo da Vinci.
$9, Mona Lisa, by Leonardo, vert.

2013, Apr. 4 **Litho.**
2831 G274 $3.25 Sheet of 4, #a-d 9.75 9.75
2832 G274 $3.75 Sheet of 3, #a-c 8.50 8.50

Souvenir Sheet

2833 G274 $9 multi 6.75 6.75

G275

Reign of Queen Elizabeth II, 60th Anniv. (in 2012) — G276

No. 2834 — Various images of Queen Elizabeth II with name at: a, Left in blue. b, Left in white. c, Right in blue (black-and-white photograph). d, Right in blue (color photograph).

2013, Apr. 25 *Perf. 14*
2834 G275 $3.25 Sheet of 4, #a-d 9.75 9.75

Souvenir Sheet
Perf. 12

2835 G276 $9 black 6.75 6.75

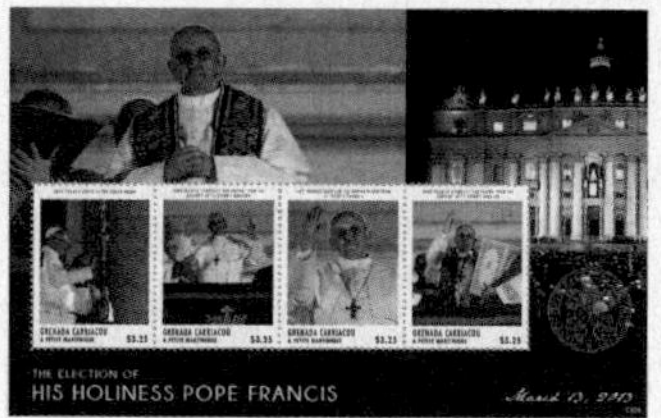

Election of Pope Francis — G277

No. 2836 — Pope Francis: a, Facing right, assistant holding crucifix. b, With arms raised. c, Waving. d, Blessing crowd, assistant holding book.
$9, Pope Francis on balcony with cardinals.

2013, June 3 *Perf. 12*
2836 G277 $3.25 Sheet of 4, #a-d 9.75 9.75

Souvenir Sheet
Perf. 12½

2837 G277 $9 multi 6.75 6.75

No. 2837 contains one 38x51mm stamp.

Pres. John F. Kennedy (1917-63) — G278

No. 2838 — Photographs of Pres. Kennedy: a, Touching lapel pocket of his jacket. b, Standing between two women. c, Sitting and pointing. d, Standing behind microphones, men and women in background. e, Sitting with legs crossed. f, Standing behind lectern with Presidential seal.
$9, Drawing of Pres. Kennedy, vert.

Perf. 13 Syncopated

2013, Jan. 1 **Litho.**
2838 G278 $2.50 Sheet of 6, #a-f 11.50 11.50

Souvenir Sheet

2839 G278 $9 multi 6.75 6.75

Birth of Prince George of Cambridge — G279

No. 2840: a, Duchess of Cambridge holding Prince George. b, Duke of Cambridge holding Prince George. c, Prince Charles and Princess Diana holding infant Prince William. d, Prince Gerorge, Duke and Duchess of Cambridge.
$9, Prince George, Duke and Duchess of Cambridge, diff.

2013, Sept. 27 **Litho.** *Perf. 14*
2840 G279 $3.25 Sheet of 4, #a-d 9.75 9.75

Souvenir Sheet

2841 G279 $9 multi 6.75 6.75

War Ships — G280

No. 2842: a, USS Arizona. b, Japanese battleship Yamato. c, USS Enterprise. d, German battleship Bismarck.
$9, HMS Victory, vert.

2013, Oct. 10 **Litho.** *Perf. 12*
2842 G280 $3.25 Sheet of 4, #a-d 9.75 9.75

Souvenir Sheet
Perf. 12½

2843 G280 $9 multi 6.75 6.75

No. 2843 contains one 38x51mm stamp.

Marine Life — G281

No. 2844: a, Blacktip sharks. b, Flying fish. c, Spotted eagle ray. d, Hammerhead sharks.
$9, Humpback whale, vert.

2013, Oct. 16 **Litho.** *Perf. 13¾*
2844 G281 $3.50 Sheet of 4, #a-d 10.50 10.50

Souvenir Sheet
Perf. 12½

2845 G281 $9 multi 6.75 6.75

No. 2845 contains one 38x51mm stamp.

Birds — G282

No. 2846, $3.75: a, American white ibis. b, Swallow-tailed kite. c, Sora.
No. 2847, $3.75: a, Red-billed tropicbird. b, Scarlet ibis. c, Stilt sandpiper.
No. 2848, $9, Tree swallow, horiz. No. 2849, $9, Purple gallinule, horiz.

2013, Oct. 16 **Litho.** *Perf. 12½*

Sheets of 3, #a-c

2846-2847 G282 Set of 2 17.00 17.00

Souvenir Sheets

2848-2849 G282 Set of 2 13.50 13.50

World Environment Day — G283

No. 2850: a, Rocks, denomination at LL. b, Mountains and clouds, denomination at UR. c, Plant, denomination at LL. d, Rocks, plants and clouds, denomination at UR.
$9, Fruits and vegetables, horiz.

2013, Oct. 10 **Litho.** *Perf. 14*
2850 G283 $3.25 Sheet of 4, #a-d 9.75 9.75

Souvenir Sheet
Perf. 12

2851 G283 $9 multi 6.75 6.75

Bats — G284

No. 2852: a, Chilonycteris gymnonotus (30x40mm). b, Vespertilio murinus (30x40mm). c, Rhinolophus clivosus (60x40mm). d, Vespertilio sinensis (30x40mm).
$9, Leptonycteris yerbabuenae.

2013, Oct. 16 **Litho.** *Perf. 14*
2852 G284 $3.50 Sheet of 4, #a-d 10.50 10.50

Souvenir Sheet
Perf. 12

2853 G284 $9 multi 6.75 6.75

No. 2853 contains one 30x50mm stamp.

Christmas Type of 2013

Paintings: $2, The Annunciation, by Paolo Uccello. $2.25, Center panel of Triptych with the Birth of Christ, by Rogier van der Weyden. $2.50, The Flight into Egypt, by Annibale Carracci. $2.75, Madonna and Child with Angels, by Giottino.

2013, Dec. 25 Litho. *Perf. 12¾*
2854-2857 A800 Set of 4 7.00 7.00

Coronation of Queen Elizabeth II, 60th Anniv. (in 2013) — G285

No. 2858 — Color of coat worn by Queen Elizabeth II: a, Dark Blue. b, Lilac. c, Pink. d, Light blue.
$9, Queen Elizabeth II wearing tiara.

2014, Jan. 14 Litho. *Perf. 14*
2858 G285 $3.25 Sheet of 4, #a-d 9.75 9.75

Souvenir Sheet

2859 G285 $9 multi 6.75 6.75

100th Tour de France Bicycle Race (in 2013) — G286

No. 2860: a, Map of 2013 race. b, Cyclist facing left. c, Cyclists in peloton in Paris, van and building in background. d, Cyclists in peloton in Paris, buildings in background.
$9, Cyclist facing right, map, Eiffel Tower, airplane.

2014, Jan. 14 Litho. *Perf. 13¾*
2860 G286 $3.25 Sheet of 4, #a-d 9.75 9.75

Souvenir Sheet

2861 G286 $9 multi 6.75 6.75

Final New York to London Flight of the Concorde — G287

No. 2862: a, Concorde, stairs and crowd. b, Concorde taking off. c, Concorde, member of ground crew. d, Concorde in flight.
$9, Nose of Concorde.

2014, Jan. 20 Litho. *Perf. 14*
2862 G287 $3.25 Sheet of 4, #a-d 9.75 9.75

Souvenir Sheet
Perf. 12

2863 G287 $9 multi 6.75 6.75

Chinese Folk Art — G288

No. 2864: a, The Seven Fairy Maidens. b, Fairy Maiden. c, Lady of Heaven. d, Chang'e.
$9, Magu.

2014, Jan. 20 Litho. *Perf. 12½*
2864 G288 $2.50 Sheet of 4, #a-d 7.50 7.50

Souvenir Sheet

2865 G288 $9 multi 6.75 6.75

Nos. 2864-2685 exist with overprint "CHINA INTERNATIONAL COLLECTION EXPO" under the expo logo.

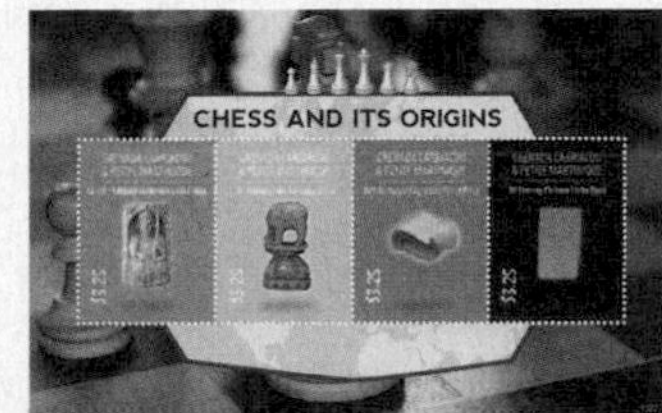

Chess and its Origins — G289

No. 2866: a, European chess piece, 12th-16th cent. b, Russian chess piece, 18th cent. c, Egyptian senet piece, 30th cent. B.C. d, Chinese liubo piece, 2nd cent.
$9, Modern queen chess piece.

2014, Jan. 20 Litho. *Perf. 14*
2866 G289 $3.25 Sheet of 4, #a-d 9.75 9.75

Souvenir Sheet
Perf. 12

2867 G289 $9 multi 6.75 6.75

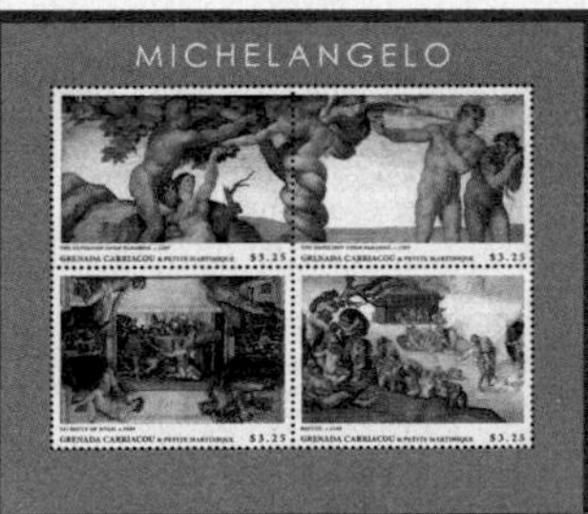

Details From Ceiling of Sistine Chapel Painted by Michelangelo — G290

No. 2868: a, The Expulsion from Paradise (tree at right). b, The Expulsion from Paradise (tree at left). c, Sacrifice of Noah. d, Deluge.
$9, The Entombment, vert.

2014, Jan. 20 Litho. *Perf. 12½*
2868 G290 $3.25 Sheet of 4, #a-d 9.75 9.75

Souvenir Sheet

2869 G290 $9 multi 6.75 6.75

Sea Turtles — G291

No. 2870: a, Hawksbill turtle. b, Loggerhead turtle. c, Green turtle.
$9, Olive ridley turtle.

2014, Jan. 20 Litho. *Perf. 14*
2870 G291 $3.75 Sheet of 3, #a-c 8.50 8.50

Souvenir Sheet
Perf. 12

2871 G291 $9 multi 6.75 6.75

Purebred Cat Breeds — G292

No. 2872, $3.25: a, Bengal. b, Egyptian Mau. c, Somali. d, Burmese.
No. 2873, $3.25: a, Savannah. b, Scottish Fold. c, British Shorthair. d, Bombay.
No. 2874, $9, Sphynx. No. 2875, $9, Siamese.

2014, Jan. 20 Litho. *Perf. 14*
Sheets of 4, #a-d
2872-2873 G292 Set of 2 19.50 19.50

Souvenir Sheets

2874-2875 G292 Set of 2 13.50 13.50

Butterflies — G293

No. 2876, $3.25: a, Astraptes anaphus. b, Danaus plexippus. c, Agraulis vanillae. d, Hypolimnas misippus.
No. 2877, $3.25: a, Urbanus proteus. b, Pyrgus oileus. c, Leptotes cassius. d, Hylephila phyleus.
No. 2878, $9, Dryas julia. No. 2879, $9, Heliconius charithonia.

2014, Jan. 20 Litho. *Perf. 14*
Sheets of 4, #a-d
2876-2877 G293 Set of 2 19.50 19.50

Souvenir Sheets
Perf. 12

2878-2879 G293 Set of 2 13.50 13.50

Chocolate Labrador Retrievers — G294

No. 2880: Various photograps of chocolate Labrador retrievers.
$9, Dog running.

2014, Apr. 7 Litho. *Perf. 14*
2880 G294 $3.25 Sheet of 4, #a-d 9.75 9.75

Souvenir Sheet
Perf. 12½

2881 G294 $9 multi 6.75 6.75

No. 2881 contains one 51x38mm stamp.

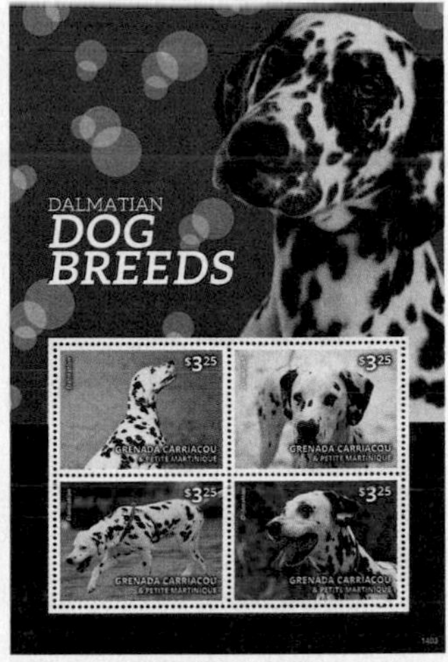

Dalmatians — G295

No. 2882: Various photograps of Dalmatians.
$9, Dalmatian, diff.

2014, Apr. 7 Litho. *Perf. 14*
2882 G295 $3.25 Sheet of 4, #a-d 9.75 9.75

Souvenir Sheet
Perf. 12½

2883 G295 $9 multi 6.75 6.75

No. 2883 contains one 51x38mm stamp.

Rocks and Minerals — G296

No. 2884, $3.25: a, Wulfenite, mimetite. b, Calcite, Mercenaria permagna fossil. c, Hubnerite, cookeite, quartz. d, Heulandite, rose mordenite.
No. 2885, $3.25: a, Fluorapophyllite, stilbite. b, Garnet, epidote. c, Tourmaline. d, Uncut ruby crystal.
No. 2886, $9, Malachite, goethite. No. 2887, $9, Pyromorphite, baryte.

2014, Apr. 7 Litho. *Perf. 14*
Sheets of 4, #a-d
2884-2885 G296 Set of 2 19.50 19.50

Souvenir Sheets
Perf. 12

2886-2887 G296 Set of 2 13.50 13.50

Downton Abbey Characters Type of 2014

No. 2888, $4.75: a, Lady Mary Crawley. b, Sarah O'Brien. c, Alfred Nugent. d, Lady Rosamund Painswick.
No. 2889, $4.75. a, Lady Edith Crawley. b, Daisy. c, Isobel Crawley. d, Earl of Grantham.

2014, May 26 Litho. *Perf. 14*
Sheets of 4, #a-d
2888-2889 A810 Set of 2 28.50 28.50

Early Locomotives — G297

No. 2890: a, Four-wheel locomotive, c. 1878. b, 1880 Forney locomotive. c, 1885 passenger locomotive. d, 1890 Uncle Dick locomotive.

No. 2891: a, 1878 Forney locomotive. b, 1881 Fontaine locomotive.

2014, June 23 Litho. *Perf. 14*

2890 G297 $3.25 Sheet of 4, #a-d 9.75 9.75

Souvenir Sheet

2891 G297 $5 Sheet of 2, #a-b 7.50 7.50

World War I, Cent. — G298

No. 2892, $3.25 — Ships and submarines: a, U-14, Germany. b, U-9, Germany. c, RMS Lusitania, United Kingdom. d, HMS Aboukir, United Kingdom.

No. 2893, $3.25 — Airplanes: a, Albatros D.III, Germany. b, SPAD S.XIII, France. c, LFG Roland C.II, Germany. d, Nieuport 27, France.

No. 2894, $5 — Ships: a, USS New York, U.S. b, HMS Monarch, United Kingdom.

No. 2895, $5 — Airplanes: a, Siemens-Schuckert D.III, Germany. b, Sopwith 1½ Strutter, United Kingdom.

2014, June 23 Litho. *Perf. 14*

Sheets of 4, #a-d

2892-2893 G298 Set of 2 19.50 19.50

Souvenir Sheets of 2, #a-b

2894-2895 G298 Set of 2 15.00 15.00

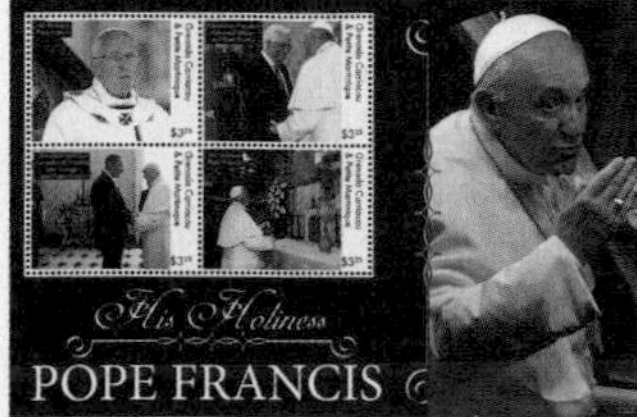

G299

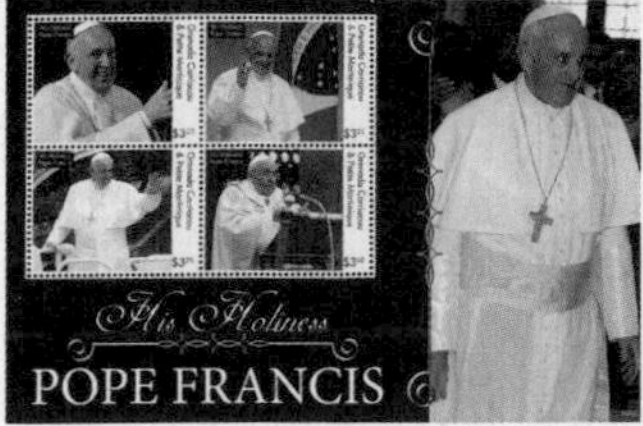

G300

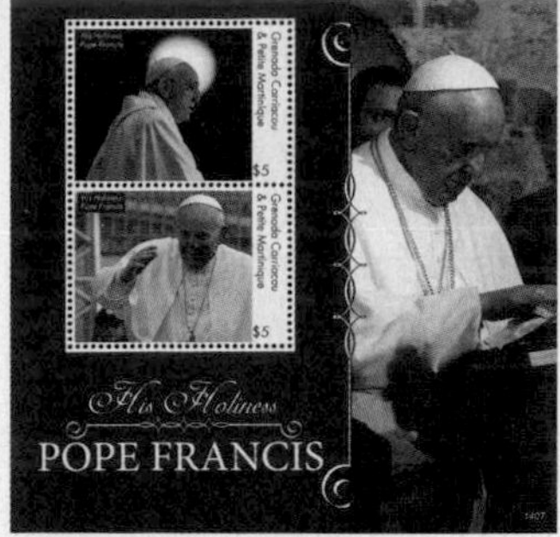

G301

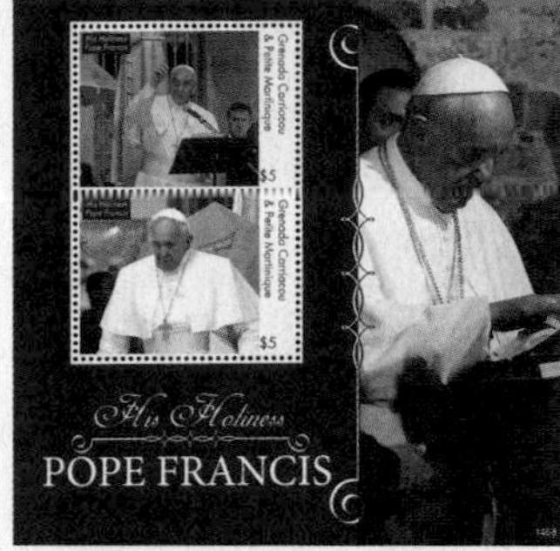

Pope Francis — G302

No. 2896 — Pope Francis: a, Wearing zucchetto and glasses. b, Meeting with Palestinian Authority President Mahmoud Abbas. c, Meeing Trinidad and Tobago President Anthony Carmona. d, Kneeling at altar.

No. 2897 — Pope Francis: a, Wearing zucchetto, with arm raised. b, With arm raised, flag of Brazil in background. c, Holding railing in Popemobile. d, At microphone.

No. 2898 — Pope Francis: a, With spotlight behind head. b, With arm raised.

No. 2899 — Pope Francis: a, At microphone, with hand raised. b, With arms at side.

2014, June 23 Litho. *Perf. 14*

2896 G299 $3.25 Sheet of 4, #a-d 9.75 9.75

2897 G300 $3.25 Sheet of 4, #a-d 9.75 9.75

Souvenir Sheets

2898 G301 $5 Sheet of 2, #a-b 7.50 7.50

2899 G302 $5 Sheet of 2, #a-b 7.50 7.50

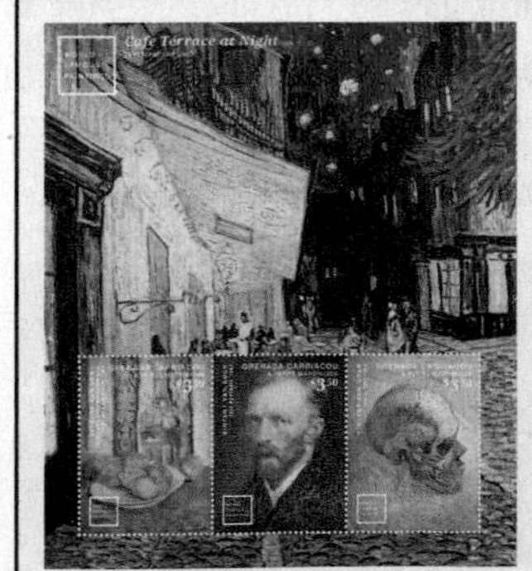

Paintings — G303

No. 2900, $3.50 — Paintings by Vincent van Gogh: a, Still Life with Decanter and Lemons on a Plate. b, Self-portrait, 1887. c, Skull.

No. 2901, $3.50: a, Ballerina and Lady with a Fan, by Edgar Degas. b, Strawberries in a Wan-li Bowl, by Adriaen Coorte. c, The Inspiration of Saint Matthew, by Caravaggio.

No. 2902, $10, Portrait of Dr. Gachet, by van Gogh. No. 2903, $10, Cardsharps, by Caravaggio.

2014, June 23 Litho. *Perf. 12½*

Sheets of 3, #a-c

2900-2901 G303 Set of 2 15.50 15.50

Size: 100x100mm

Imperf

2902-2903 G303 Set of 2 15.00 15.00

Nuremberg, Germany — G304

No. 2904: a, Skyline of Nuremberg. b, Albrecht Dürer House. c, Buildings in Old Town.

$10, Skyline of Nuremberg, horiz.

2014, Oct. 24 Litho *Perf. 13¾*

2904 G304 $3.50 Sheet of 3, #a-c 7.75 7.75

Souvenir Sheet

Perf. 14

2905 G304 $10 multi 7.50 7.50

Fall of the Berlin Wall, 25th anniv. No. 2905 contains one 80x30mm stamp.

Cattleya Mossiae — G305

No. 2906, $3.25: a, Purple flower, green leaves at LL. b, Pink flower, green leaves at center and LL. c, Pink flower, green leaf under denomination. d, White flower, stem at LL.

No. 2907, $3.25, vert.: a, White flower, green leaf at center, gray background. b, White flower, no leaf, gray background. c, Lilac flower, leaf behind denomination. d, Lilac flower, green leaves at LR.

No. 2908, $5, vert.: a, Pink flower, green leaf at top. b, Pink flower, green leaf at bottom.

No. 2909, $5: a, White flower with yellow accents, green leaf at top center and LR. b, White flower with pink accents, green leaf at center.

Perf. 14, 12 (#2909)

2014, Oct. 24 Litho.

Sheets of 4, #a-d

2906-2907 G305 Set of 2 19.50 19.50

Souvenir Sheets of 2, #a-b

2908-2909 G305 Set of 2 15.00 15.00

Miniature Sheets

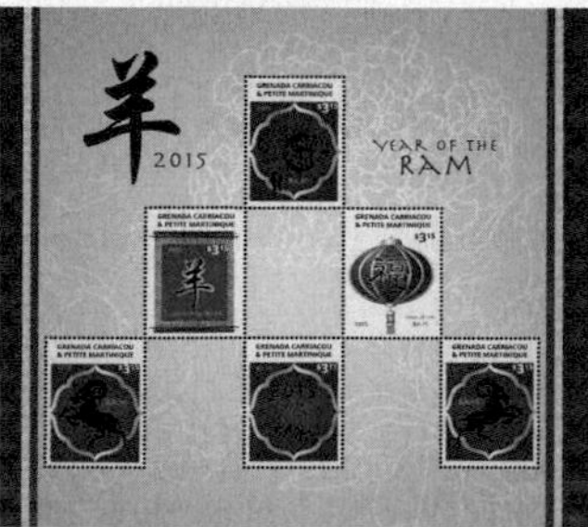

G306

New Year 2015 (Year of the Ram) — G307

No. 2910: a, Ram's head. b, Chinese character for "ram." c, Chinese lantern with Chinese characters. d, Ram facing left. e, "2015 Year of the Ram" f, Ram facing right.

No. 2911 — Ram's head in; a, Green. b, Dark red. c, Purple and blue. d, Orange red and pale yellow.

2014, Oct. 24 Litho. *Perf. 14*

2910 G306 $3.15 Sheet of 6, #a-f, + label 14.00 14.00

2911 G307 $3.25 Sheet of 4, #a-d 9.75 9.75

Nos. 2910-2911 are dated 2015.

Fruits and Vegetables — G308

No. 2912, $3.25: a, European pears. b, Peaches. c, Bananas. d, Apricot. e, Apples.

No. 2913, $3.25: a, Eggplant. b, Garlic. c, Bell pepper. d, Avocado. e, Tomato.

No. 2914, $10, Strawberries. No. 2915, $10, Mango and slice.

2014, Nov. 3 Litho. *Perf. 12½*

Sheets of 5, #a-e

2912-2913 G308 Set of 2 24.00 24.00

Souvenir Sheets

2914-2915 G308 Set of 2 15.00 15.00

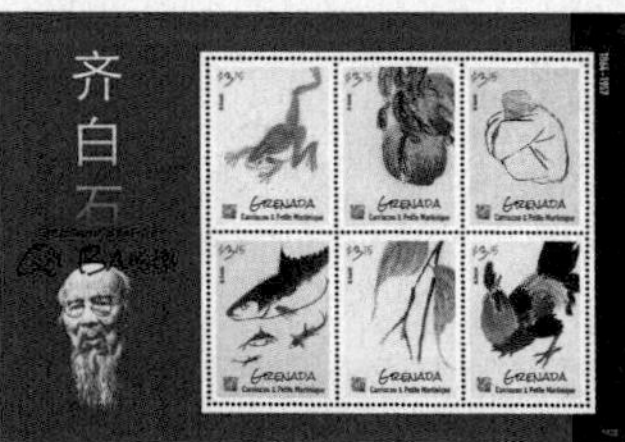

G309

Art of Qi Baishi (1864-1957) — G310

No. 2916: a, Frog. b, Peaches. c, Seated man. d, Fish. e, Leaves and twigs. f, Rooster.

No. 2917: a, Crabs. b, Frogs. c, Shrimp. d, Insect on leaf.

No. 2918, $10, Frog and tadpoles. No. 2929, $10, Chicks.

Perf. 14, 12 (#2917)

2015, May 18 **Litho.**

2916 G309 $3.15 Sheet of 6, #a-f 14.00 14.00

2917 G310 $3.25 Sheet of 4, #a-d 9.75 9.75

Souvenir Sheets

2918-2919 G310 Set of 2 15.00 15.00

International Year of Light — G311

Various depictions of the Aurora Borealis.

2015, May 28 **Litho.** ***Perf. 14***

2920 G311 $3.25 Sheet of 5, #a-e 12.00 12.00

Souvenir Sheet

Perf. 12

2921 G311 $10 multi 7.50 7.50

Paintings of Vincent van Gogh (1853-90) — G312

No. 2922: a, Two Women in the Moor. b, The Cottage. c, Weaver Near an Open Window. d, Still Life with Three Birds Nests. e, Cart with Red and White Ox.
$10, The Potato Eaters.

2015, Aug. 26 **Litho.** ***Perf. 14***

2922 G312 $3.15 Sheet of 5, #a-e 12.00 12.00

Souvenir Sheet

Perf. 12

2923 G312 $10 multi 7.50 7.50

Orchids — G313

No. 2924: a, Bletilla striata. b, Serapias lingua. c, Brasiliorchis picta. d, Phaius flavus.
$10, Aerangis luteoalba var. rhodosticta.

2015, Aug. 26 **Litho.** ***Perf. 14***

2924 G313 $3.25 Sheet of 4, #a-d 9.75 9.75

Souvenir Sheet

Perf. 12

2925 G313 $10 multi 7.50 7.50

Miniature Sheets

G314

G315

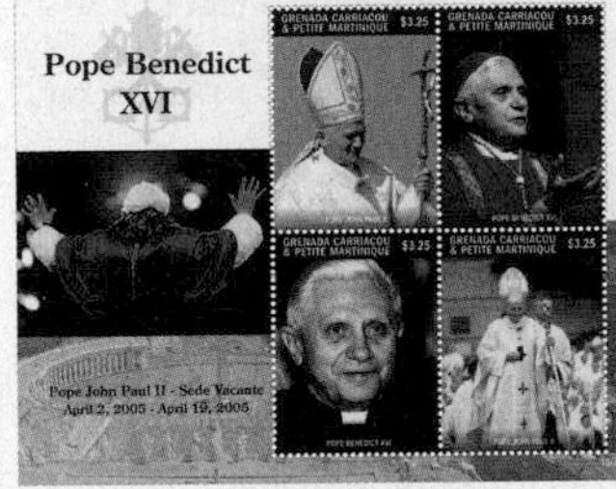

Pope Benedict XVI — G316

No. 2926 — Pope Benedict XVI: a, Wearing green vestments and miter. b, Without head covering, wearing white alb, waving. c, With mountain in background. d, With candle.

No. 2927 — Pope Benedict XVI at inauguration: a, Wearing miter, waving. b, Wearing miter, holding crucifix, waving. c, Flowers in background, without head covering, waving, d, Holding crucifix, attendant in background.

No. 2928: a, Pope John Paul II holding crucifix. b, Pope Benedict XVI wearing red vestments and zucchetto. c, Pope Benedict XVI wearing black vestments. d, Pope John Paul II and attendants.

2015, Aug. 26 **Litho.** ***Perf. 14***

2926 G314 $3.25 Sheet of 4, #a-d 9.75 9.75

2927 G315 $3.25 Sheet of 4, #a-d 9.75 9.75

2928 G316 $3.25 Sheet of 4, #a-d 9.75 9.75

Nos. 2926-2928 (3) 29.25 29.25

Queen Elizabeth II, Longest-Reigning British Monarch — G317

No. 2929 — Various photographs of Queen Elizabeth II, as shown.
$10, Queen Elizabeth II and Prince Philip, horiz.

2015, Nov. 1 **Litho.** ***Perf. 14***

2929 G317 $3.15 Sheet of 6, #a-f 14.00 14.00

Souvenir Sheet

Perf. 12

2930 G317 $10 multi 7.50 7.50

Paintings by El Greco (1541-1614) — G318

No. 2931, $3.50: a, Portrait of Fray Hortensio Felix Paravicino. b, Madonna of Charity. c, St. Martin and the Beggar.

No. 2932, $3.50: a, Portrait of Diego de Covarrubias. b, Christ in the Olive Garden. c, St. Ildefonso.

No. 2933, $10, Mount Sinai. No. 2934, $10, Deposition in the Tomb.

Perf. 12, 14 (#2932)

2015, Dec. 1 **Litho.**

Sheets of 3, #a-c

2931-2932 G318 Set of 2 15.50 15.50

Size: 81x120mm

Imperf

2933-2934 G318 Set of 2 15.00 15.00

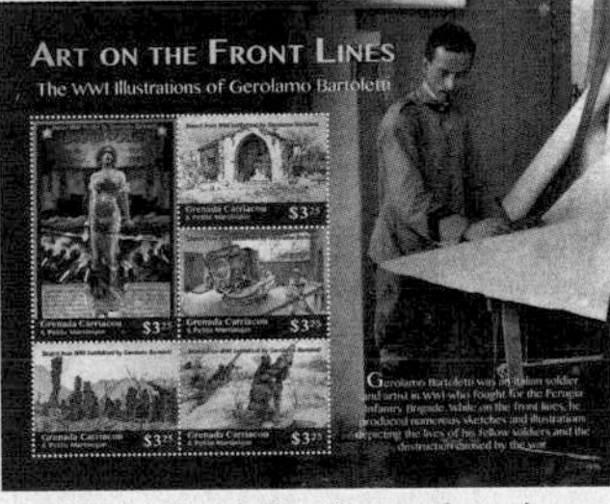

World War I Era Illustrations by Gerolamo Bartoletti — G319

No. 2935: a, Italian poster (40x60mm). b, House and graves (40x30mm). c, Gun battery (40x30mm). d, Damaged building (40x30mm) e, Soldiers in battle (40x30mm).
$10, Cover of collection of illustrations, horiz.

2015, Dec. 21 **Litho.** ***Perf. 14***

2935 G319 $3.25 Sheet of 5, #a-e 12.00 12.00

Souvenir Sheet

Perf. 12

2936 G319 $10 multi 7.50 7.50

No. 2936 contains one 60x40mm stamp.

Birds — G320

No. 2937: a, Purple-throated Carib. b, Lesser Antillean tanager. c, Grenada flycatcher. d, Bananaquit.
$10, Grenada dove, vert.

2015, Dec. 21 **Litho.** ***Perf. 14***

2937 G320 $3.25 Sheet of 4, #a-d 9.75 9.75

Souvenir Sheet

Perf. 12

2938 G320 $10 multi 7.50 7.50

No. 2938 contains one 30x50mm stamp.

Characters from *Star Trek: The Next Generation* Television Series — G321

No. 2939: a, Deanna Troi. b, Jean-Luc Picard. c, William Riker. d, Geordi La Forge. e, Worf. f, Beverly Crusher. g, Data.
$10, Picard, horiz.

2015, Dec. 21 **Litho.** ***Perf. 12***

2939 G321 $3.15 Sheet of 7, #a-g 16.50 16.50

Souvenir Sheet

2940 G321 $10 multi 7.50 7.50

No. 2940 contains one 40x30mm.

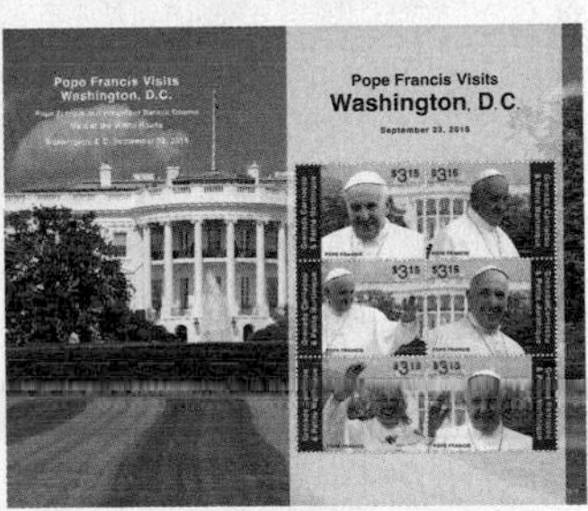

Visit of Pope Francis to Washington, D.C. — G322

No. 2941 — Various photographs of Pope Francis and White House, as shown.
$10, Pope Francis, Pres. Barack Obama and wife, Michelle.

2016, Jan. 31 **Litho.** ***Perf. 14***

2941 G322 $3.15 Sheet of 6, #a-f 14.00 14.00

Souvenir Sheet

2942 G322 $10 multi 7.50 7.50

No. 2942 contains one 80x30mm stamp.

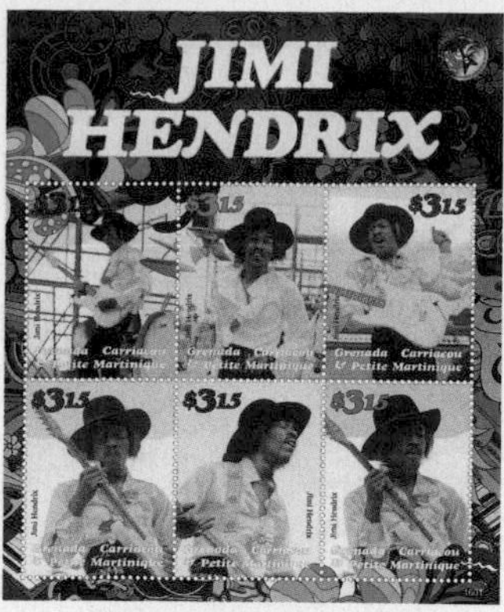

Jimi Hendrix (1942-70), Rock Guitarist — G323

No. 2943 — Hendrix: a, Picking guitar strings. b, Without guitar. c, With hand raised. d, With hand on guitar neck, "Jimi Hendrix" at left, orange red denomination. e, With hand on guitar neck, "Jimi Hendrix" at right, scarlet denomination. f, With hand on guitar neck, "Jimi Hendrix " at left, blue denomination.
$10, Hendrix and microphone.

2016, Mar. 8 Litho. *Perf. 14*
2943 G323 $3.15 Sheet of 6, #a-f 14.00 14.00

Souvenir Sheet
Perf. 12½

2944 G323 $10 multi 7.50 7.50

No. 2944 contains one 38x51mm stamp.

Elvis Presley Type of 2016 Souvenir Sheets

Designs: No. 2945, $10, Presley buys motorcycle. No. 2946, $10, Presley kissing woman. No. 2947, $10, Presley appearing on *The Steve Allen Show.* No. 2948, $14, Presley rents out Memphis amusement park. No. 2949, $14, Presley begins tour with Andy Griffith, vert. No. 2950, $14, Presley meets future wife at party, vert. No. 2951, $14, Presley's first press interview, vert.

Perf. 14, 13x13¼ (#2948), 13¼x13 (#2949-2951)

2016 Litho.
2945-2951 A882 Set of 7 65.00 65.00

Issued: Nos. 2945-2947, 3/8; Nos. 2948-2951, 6/30.

Queen Elizabeth II, 90th Birthday — G324

No. 2952 — Photograph of Queen Elizabeth II from: a, 1972. b, 1946. c, 1943. d, 1965.
No. 2953, vert. — Photograph of Queen Elizabeth II from: a, 1971. b, 2015.

2016, Apr. 1 Litho. *Perf. 12*
2952 G324 $3.25 Sheet of 4, #a-d 9.75 9.75

Souvenir Sheet

2953 G324 $7 Sheet of 2, #a-b 10.50 10.50

Space Flight of Valentina Tereshkova, 50th Anniv. (in 2013) — G325

No. 2954: a, Launch. b, Tereshkova wearing space helmet. c, Wedding of Tereshkova, 1963. d, Space capsule after re-entry.
$12, Tereshkova, vert.

2016, May 2 Litho. *Perf. 12*
2954 G325 $3.25 Sheet of 4, #a-d 9.75 9.75

Souvenir Sheet

2955 G325 $12 multi 9.00 9.00

World Stamp Show 2016, New York — G326

No. 2956 — World Stamp Show emblem and New York City landmarks: a, New York Stock Exchange. b, New York Public Library. c, St. Patrick's Cathedral. d, Bethesda Terrace.
$14, Empire State Building and other buildings, vert.

2016, May 2 Litho. *Perf. 12½*
2956 G326 $4 Sheet of 4, #a-d 12.00 12.00

Souvenir Sheet
Perf. 12

2957 G326 $14 multi 10.50 10.50

No. 2957 contains one 60x80mm stamp.

Souvenir Sheet

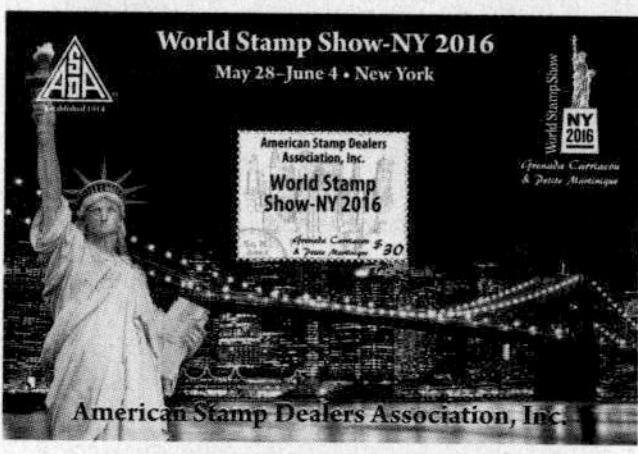

World Stamp Show 2016, New York — G327

2016, May 30 Litho. *Perf. 12½x12*
2958 G327 $30 multi 22.50 22.50

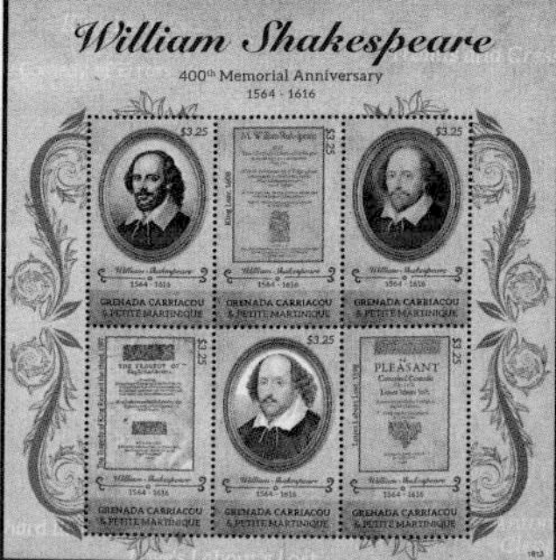

William Shakespeare (1564-1616), Writer — G328

No. 2959: a, Shakespeare, 6mm collar strings. b, Front page of *King Lear.* c, Shakespeare, 3mm collar strings. d, Front page of *King Richard III.* e, Shakespeare, 5mm collar strings. f, Front page of *Love's Labour's Lost.*
No. 2960: a, Shakespeare, collar with strings. b, Front page of *Hamlet.* c, Shakespeare, collar without strings. d, Front page of *Othello.*
$14, Shakespeare, diff.

2016, May 30 Litho. *Perf. 12*
2959 G328 $3.25 Sheet of 6, #a-f 14.50 14.50
2960 G328 $3.50 Sheet of 4, #a-d 10.50 10.50

Souvenir Sheet
Perf. 12½

2961 G328 $14 multi 10.50 10.50

No. 2961 contains one 38x51mm stamp.

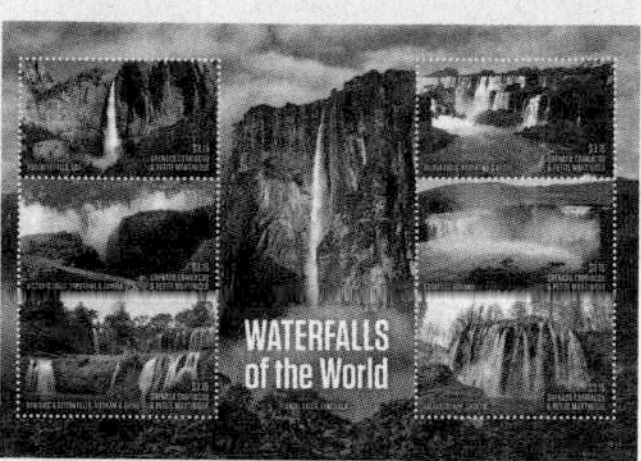

Waterfalls — G329

No. 2962: a, Yosemite Falls, U.S. b, Iguazu Falls, Argentina and Brazil. c, Victoria Falls, Zimbabwe and Zambia. d, Godhafoss, Iceland. e, Ban Gioc-Detian Falls, Viet Nam and People's Republic of China. f, Galovac Falls, Croatia.
$13, Niagara Falls, U.S. and Canada.

2016, June 21 Litho. *Perf. 12*
2962 G329 $3.15 Sheet of 6, #a-f 14.00 14.00

Souvenir Sheet

2963 G329 $13 multi 9.75 9.75

No. 2963 contains one 80x30mm stamp.

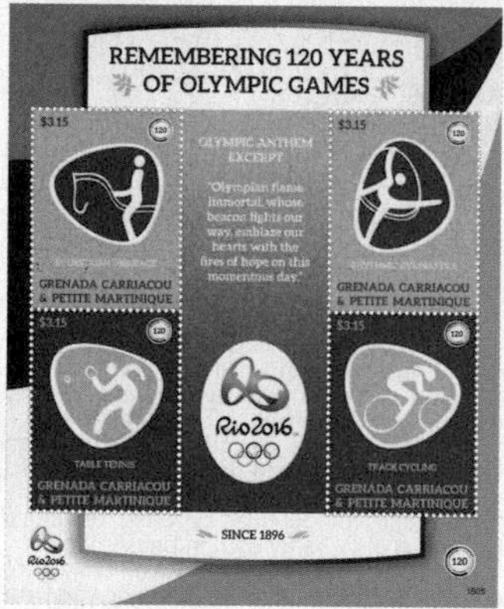

2016 Summer Olympics, Rio de Janeiro — G330

No. 2964: a, Equestrian dressage. b, Rhythmic gymnastics. c, Table tennis. d, Track cycling.
No. 2965: a, Fencing. b, Helene Mayer, Olympic fencer.

2016, July 7 Litho. *Perf. 14*
2964 G330 $3.15 Sheet of 4, #a-d 9.50 9.50

Souvenir Sheet
Perf. 12½

2965 G330 $12 Sheet of 2, #a-b 18.00 18.00

No. 2965 contains two 38x51mm stamps.

Crabs and Birds — G331

No. 2966: a, Glossy ibis. b, Zombie crab. c, Yellow-crowned night heron. d, Blue land crab. e, Great blue heron. f, Red land crab.
No. 2967: a, Coral crab. b, Batwing coral crab.

2016, Sept. 9 Litho. *Perf. 14*
2966 G331 $3.25 Sheet of 6, #a-f 14.50 14.50

Souvenir Sheet
Perf. 12

2967 G331 $7 Sheet of 2, #a-b 10.50 10.50

G332

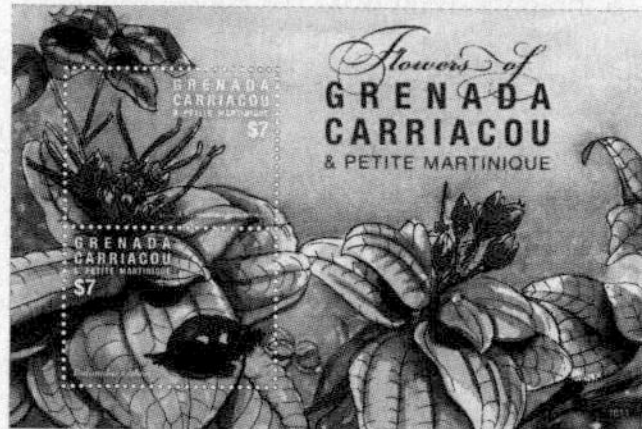

Flowers — G333

No. 2968: a, Royal poinciana. b, Golden trumpet. c, Painted brasiliorchis. d, Flamingo flower. e, Barbados lily. f, Great bougainvillea.
No. 2969: a, Charianthus grenadensis. b, Bulimulus wiebesi snail.

2016, Sept. 9 Litho. *Perf. 14*
2968 G332 $3.25 Sheet of 6, #a-f 14.50 14.50

Souvenir Sheet
Perf. 12

2969 G333 $7 Sheet of 2, #a-b 10.50 10.50

Christmas G334

Designs: No. 2970, $5.50, Conifer branch and cones, Christmas ornaments. No. 2971, $5.50, Snowflake ornament. No. 2972, $10, Christmas tree, gift box. No. 2973, $10, Christmas ornaments.

2016, Dec. 1 Litho. *Perf. 12½*
2970-2973 G334 Set of 4 23.00 23.00

G335

G336

New Year 2017 (Year of the Rooster) — G337

No. 2974: a, Bird wing at top center. b, Butterflies at top center.

2016, Dec. 5 Litho. *Perf. 12*

2974 G335 $5.50 Pair, #a-b 8.25 8.25

Souvenir Sheets

Perf.

2975 G336 $10 multi 7.50 7.50
2976 G337 $10 multi 7.50 7.50

No. 2974 was printed in sheets containing two each Nos. 2974a-2974b.

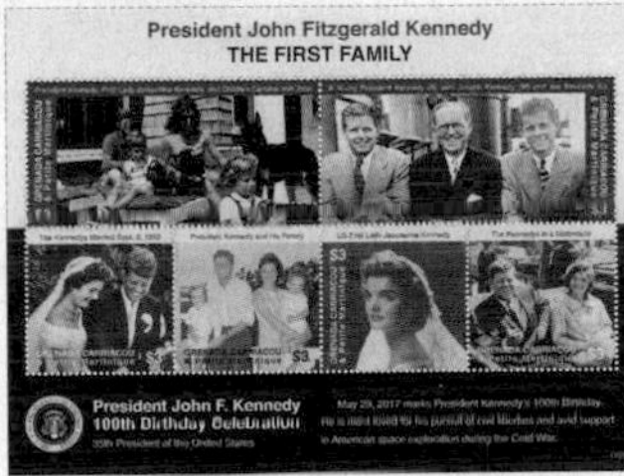

G338

G339

Pres. John F. Kennedy (1917-63) and His Family — G340

No. 2977: a, Pres. Kennedy with wife, Jacqueline, and children, Caroline and John, Jr. (70x35mm). b, Pres. Kennedy with father, Joseph, and brother, Joe (70x35mm). c, Pres. Kennedy and wife at their wedding (35x35mm). d, Pres. Kennedy with wife and children (35x35mm). e, Jacqueline Kennedy (35x35mm). f, Pres. Kennedy and wife in limousine (35x35mm).

No. 2978: a, Pres. Kennedy and son. b, Jacqueline Kennedy and daughter. c, Pres. Kennedy with his children and horse. d, Caroline Kennedy and doll.

No. 2979: a, Pres. Kennedy and son under desk. b, Pres. Kennedy and daughter. c, Pres. Kennedy with wife and daughter.

2017, Feb. 28 Litho. *Perf. 13¾*

2977 G338 $3 Sheet of 6, #a-f 13.50 13.50
2978 G339 $5.50 Sheet of 4, #a-d 16.50 16.50

Souvenir Sheet

Perf. 12½

2979 G340 $5 Sheet of 3, #a-c 11.00 11.00

Miniature Sheets

G341

G342

Princess Diana (1961-97) — G343

Various photographs of Princess Diana, as shown.

2017, May 15 Litho. *Perf. 14*

2980 G341 $5.50 Sheet of 4, #a-d 16.50 16.50
2981 G342 $5.50 Sheet of 4, #a-d 16.50 16.50
2982 G343 $5.50 Sheet of 4, #a-d 16.50 16.50
Nos. 2980-2982 (3) 49.50 49.50

Bats — G344

No. 2983: a, Mexican long-tongued bat. b, Hairy big-eyed bat. c, Little yellow-shouldered bat. d, Greater bulldog bat.

$12, Velvety free-tailed bat, horiz.

2017, July 24 Litho. *Perf. 14*

2983 G344 $7 Sheet of 4, #a-d 21.00 21.00

Souvenir Sheet

Perf. 12½

2984 G344 $12 multi 9.00 9.00

No. 2984 contains one 51x38mm stamp.

New Year 2018 (Year of the Dog) — G345

Chinese Zodiac Animals — G346

No. 2986: a, Rat. b, Ox. c, Tiger, d, Rabbit. e, Dragon. f, Snake. g, Horse. h, Ram. i, Monkey. j, Rooster. k, Dog. l, Pig.

2017, Aug. 8 Litho. *Perf. 12*

2985 G345 $8 multi 6.00 6.00

Miniature Sheet

Perf. 14

2986 G346 $1.80 Sheet of 12, #a-l 16.00 16.00

No. 2985 was printed in sheets of 4.

Paintings by Gustav Klimt (1862-1918) — G347

No. 2987: a, Adele Bloch-Bauer I. b, Portrait of Fritza Riedler. c, Eugenia Primavesi. d, Māda Gertrude Primavesi.

$15, The Kiss.

2017, Aug. 11 Litho. *Perf. 14*

2987 G347 $7 Sheet of 4, #a-d 21.00 21.00

Souvenir Sheet

2988 G347 $15 multi 11.00 11.00

No. 2988 contains one 30x80mm stamp.

Elvis Presley Type of 2017

Souvenir Sheets

Inscriptions: No. 2989, $12, Last pre-Army concert. No. 2990, $12, Transatlantic interview. No. 2991, $12, Getting Army haircut. No. 2992, $12, First rock'n'roll gold record.

2017, Oct. 26 Litho. *Perf. 12½*

2989-2992 A971 Set of 4 36.00 36.00

Muhammad Ali (1942-2016), Boxer — G348

No. 2993 — Ali: a, With arm raised. b, Fighting, lights in background. c, Leaning over boxing ring rope, no robe.

$12, Ali leaning on boxing ring rope, with robe.

2017, Oct. 26 Litho. *Perf. 12*

2993 G348 $7 Sheet of 3, #a-c 15.50 15.50

Souvenir Sheet

Perf. 12½

2994 G348 $12 multi 9.00 9.00

No. 2994 contains one 38x51mm stamp.

Miniature Sheet

World War I, Cent. — G349

No. 2995 — Poster: a, U.S. Official War Pictures. b, Men Wanted for the Army. c, For Liberty's Sake. d, Hello! This is Liberty Speaking. e, Adventure and Action. f, First in France U.S. Marines.

2017, Nov. 14 Litho. *Perf. 12x11½*
2995 G349 $4 Sheet of 6, #a-f 18.00 18.00

Miniature Sheets

Ospreys — G350

Broad-winged Hawks — G351

Barn Owls — G352

No. 2996 — Various photographs of ospreys: a, $3. b, $5. c, $7. d, 9.
No. 2997 — Various photographs of broad-winged hawks: a, $5.50. b, $6.50. c, $7.50. d, $8.50.
No. 2998, $7, Various photographs of barn owls, as shown.

2017, Dec. 31 Litho. *Perf. 14*
2996 G350 Sheet of 4, #a-d 18.00 18.00
2997 G351 Sheet of 4, #a-d 21.00 21.00
2998 G352 Sheet of 4, #a-d 21.00 21.00
Nos. 2996-2998 (3) 60.00 60.00

Miniature Sheets

Jellyfish — G353

No. 2999: a, $5, Cannonball jellyfish. b, $6, Comb jellyfish. c, $7, Moon jellyfish. d, $8, Mangrove upside-down jellyfish.
No. 3000: a, $6, Mauve jellyfish. b, $7, Box jellyfish. c, $8, Atlantic sea nettle. d, $9, Portuguese man-of-war.

2018, Mar. 7 Litho. *Perf. 12*
2999 G353 Sheet of 4, #a-d 19.50 19.50
3000 G353 Sheet of 4, #a-d 22.50 22.50

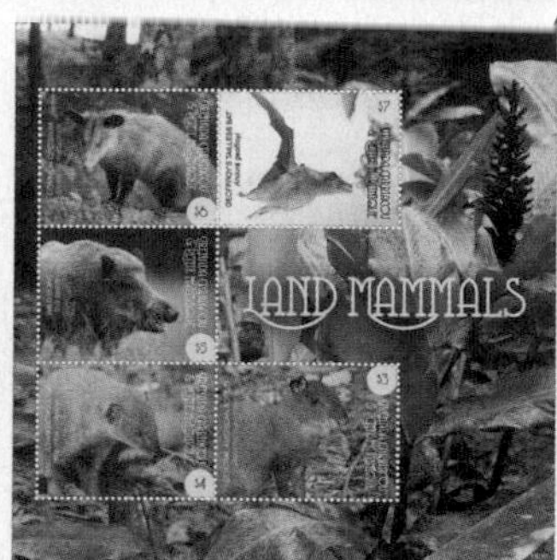

Mammals — G354

No. 3001: a, $3, Central American agouti. b, $4, Small Asian mongoose. c, $5. Wild boar. d, $6, Common opossum. e, $7, Geoffroy's tailless bat.
$14, Mona monkey, vert.

2018, Mar. 7 Litho. *Perf. 14*
3001 G354 Sheet of 5, #a-e 18.50 18.50

Souvenir Sheet

Perf. 12½

3002 G354 $14 multi 10.50 10.50

No. 3002 contains one 38x51mm stamp.

Mao Zedong (1893-1976), Chairman of Communist Party of China — G355

No. 3003 — Various depictions of Mao: a, $6. b, $7. c, $8.
$11, Mao, diff.

2018, Mar. 7 Litho. *Perf. 12*
3003 G355 Sheet of 3, #a-c 15.50 15.50

Souvenir Sheet

3004 G355 $11 multi 8.25 8.25

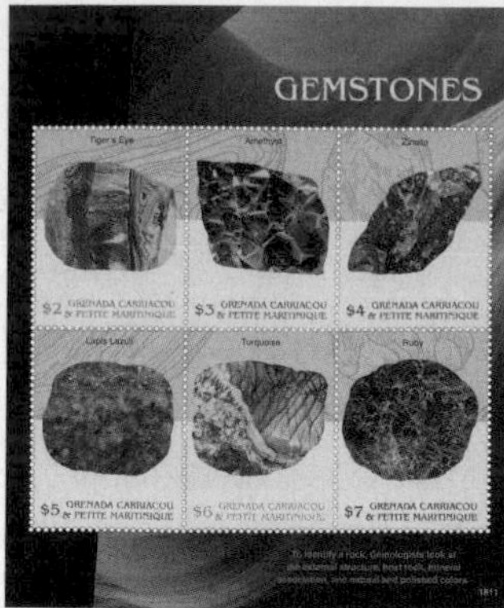

Gemstones — G356

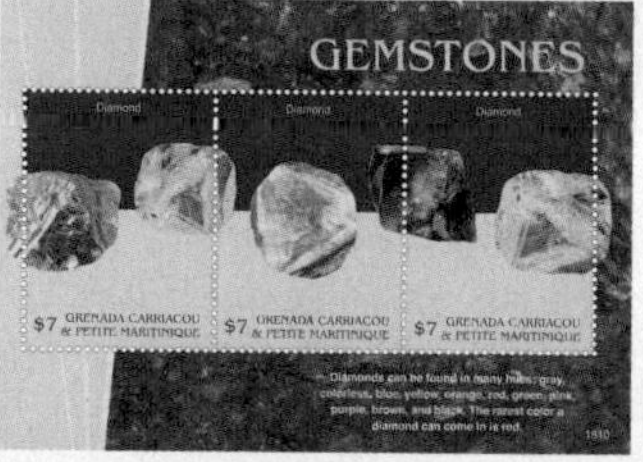

Diamonds — G357

No. 3005: a, $2, Tiger's eye. b, $3, Amethyst. c, $4, Zincite. d, $5, Lapis lazuli. e, $6, Turquoise. f, $7, Ruby.
No. 3006: a, Colored diamond at left, below colorless diamond. b, Colored diamond at right. c, Colored diamond at left, above colorless diamond.

2018, Mar. 21 Litho. *Perf. 14*
3005 G356 Sheet of 6, #a-f 20.00 20.00

Souvenir Sheet

3006 G357 $7 Sheet of 3, #a-c 15.50 15.50

Miniature Sheet

Engagement of Prince Harry and Meghan Markle — G358

No. 3007 — Couple: a, $5, Tree in background. b, $5, Prince Harry pointing. c, $6, Markle with hand raised near head. d, $6, Sign in background.

2018, July 27 Litho. *Perf. 14*
3007 G358 Sheet of 4, #a-d 16.50 16.50

Prince George of Cambridge, 5th Birthday — G359

No. 3008 — Prince George: a, $5, Wearing shirt with buttons. b, $5, Wearing shirt without buttons. c, $5, With great-grandmother, Queen Elizabeth II. d, $6, As infant, with parents, Duke and Duchess of Cambridge.
$11, Prince George, with father, Prince William.

2018, July 27 Litho. *Perf. 14*
3008 G359 Sheet of 4, #a-d 15.50 15.50

Souvenir Sheet

Perf. 12½

3009 G359 $11 multi 8.25 8.25

No. 3009 contains one 38x51mm stamp.

Elvis Presley (1935-77) — G360

2018, Aug. 3 Litho. *Perf. 12*
3010 G360 $5.50 multi 4.25 4.25

No. 3010 was printed in sheets of 3.

G361

New Year 2019 (Year of the Pig) — G362

2018, Oct. 17 Litho. *Perf. 12*
3011 G361 $8 multi 6.00 6.00

Souvenir Sheet

Perf. 13¾

3012 G362 $6 multi 4.50 4.50

G363

Wedding of Prince Harry and Meghan Markle — G364

No. 3013: a, $3, Prince Harry removing veil from face of wife. b, $3, Couple in car. c, $4, Couple holding hands. d, $5, Prince Harry. e, $5, Markle.
$10, Couple, vert.

2018, Nov. 9 Litho. *Perf. 13¾*

3013	G363	Sheet of 5, #a-e	15.00	15.00

Souvenir Sheet
Perf. 12

3014	G364	$10 multi	7.50	7.50

SEMI-POSTAL STAMPS

1988 Seoul Olympics Type

No. B1, Cycling. No. B2, Sailing. No. B3, Uneven Parallel Bars. No. B4, Dressage.
No. B5, Marathon.

1986, Dec. 1 *Perf. 15*

B1	SP2	10c +5c multi	.90	.45
B2	SP2	50c +20c multi	.90	.90
B3	SP2	70c +30c multi	.90	.90
B4	SP2	$2 +$1 multi	2.40	2.40
		Nos. B1-B4 (4)	5.10	4.65

Souvenir Sheet

B5	SP2	$3 +$1 multi	4.00	4.00

OFFICIAL STAMPS

Grenada Grenadines Nos. 396-408, 410, 440-442, 465-468 Overprinted "P.R.G."

1982, June *Perf. 14, 15*

O1	G45	5c multicolored	.25	.25
O2	G45	6c multicolored	.25	.25
O3	G45	10c multicolored	.25	.25
O4	G45	12c multicolored	.25	.25
O5	G45	15c multicolored	.25	.25
O6	G45	20c multicolored	.25	.25
O7	G54	20c multicolored	.25	.25
O8	G45	25c multicolored	.25	.25
O9	G45	30c multicolored	.25	.25
O10	G45	40c multicolored	.25	.25
O11	CD331	40c multicolored	.25	.25
O12	G54	40c multicolored	.25	.25
O13	G45	50c multicolored	.30	.30
O14	G45	90c multicolored	.55	.55
O15	G45	$1 multicolored	.60	.60
O16	G54	$1 multicolored	.60	.60
O17	CD331	$2 multicolored	1.10	1.10
O18	G54	$2 multicolored	1.10	1.10
O19	G45	$3 multicolored	1.60	1.60
O20	CD331	$4 multicolored	2.10	2.10
O21	G45	$10 multicolored	5.75	5.75
		Nos. O1-O21 (21)	16.70	16.70

Royal Wedding stamps in changed colors, perf 15x14½ were also overprinted.

GRIQUALAND WEST

'gri-kwə-ˌland 'west

LOCATION — In South Africa west of the Orange Free State and north of the Orange River
GOVT. — British Crown Colony
AREA — 15,197 sq. mi.
POP. — 83,375 (1891)
CAPITAL — Kimberley

Originally a territorial division of the Cape of Good Hope Colony, Griqualand West was declared a British Crown Colony in 1873 and together with Griqualand East was annexed to the Cape Colony in 1880.

12 Pence = 1 Shilling

Beware of forgeries.

Stamps of Cape of Good Hope 1864-65 (Type I, 4p, 6p, 1sh) and 1871-76 (Type II, ½p, 1p, 4p, 5sh) Surcharged or Overprinted

Type I — With frame line around stamp.
Type II — Without frame line.

Manuscript Surcharge in Dark Red

1874 Wmk. 1 *Perf. 14*

1	A3 1p on 4p blue (type I)		1,900.	*2,600.*

Overprinted

1877 Black Overprint

2	1p rose	800.00	115.00
a.	Double overprint		*3,250.*

Red Overprint

3	4p blue (type II)	425.00	85.00

Overprinted In Black on the One Penny, in Red on the Other Values

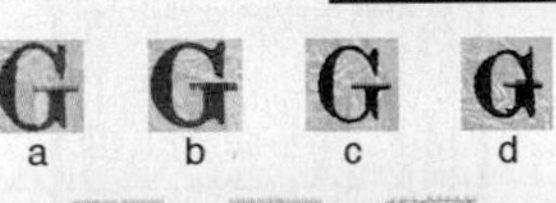

a b c d

e f g

Cape of Good Hope No. 17 Surcharged

4	(a)	½p gray black	45.00	*47.50*
5	(a)	1p rose	45.00	30.00
6	(a)	4p blue (type I)	475.00	75.00
7	(a)	4p blue (type II)	425.00	50.00
8	(a)	6p dull violet	325.00	57.50
9	(a)	1sh green	375.00	47.50
a.		Inverted overprint		1,000.
10	(a)	5sh orange	1,150.	57.50
11	(b)	½p gray black	105.00	125.00
12	(b)	1p rose	115.00	67.50
13	(b)	4p blue (type I)	1,150.	190.00
14	(b)	4p blue (type II)	900.00	145.00
15	(b)	6p dull violet	625.00	155.00
16	(b)	1sh green	800.00	115.00
17	(b)	5sh orange	1,900.	135.00
18	(c)	½p gray black	800.00	*850.00*
19	(c)	1p rose	115.00	52.50
20	(c)	4p blue (type I)	*3,750.*	1,000.
21	(c)	4p blue (type II)	*3,400.*	800.00
22	(c)	6p dull violet	*3,250.*	950.00
23	(c)	1sh green	*4,250.*	950.00
24	(c)	5sh orange	*4,750.*	1,050.
25	(d)	½p gray black	62.50	*75.00*
26	(d)	1p rose	62.50	42.50
27	(d)	4p blue (type I)	800.00	105.00
28	(d)	4p blue (type II)	575.00	75.00
29	(d)	6p dull violet	425.00	80.00
30	(d)	1sh green	575.00	62.50
31	(d)	5sh orange	1,575.	80.00
32	(e)	½p gray black	105.00	*125.00*
33	(e)	1p rose	115.00	67.50
34	(e)	4p blue (type I)	1,150.	190.00
35	(e)	4p blue (type II)	900.00	145.00
36	(e)	6p dull violet	[illegible]	[illegible]
37	(e)	1sh green	800.00	115.00
a.		Inverted overprint		1,600.
38	(e)	5sh orange	1,900.	135.00
39	(f)	½p gray black	115.00	*135.00*
40	(f)	1p rose	125.00	85.00
41	(f)	4p blue (type I)	1,250.	235.00
42	(f)	4p blue (type II)	950.00	165.00
43	(f)	6p dull violet	750.00	175.00
44	(f)	1sh green	900.00	145.00
45	(f)	5sh orange	2,900.	165.00
46	(g)	½p gray black	57.50	67.50
47	(g)	1p rose	45.00	30.00
48	(g)	4p blue (type I)	575.00	95.00
49	(g)	4p blue (type II)	525.00	62.50
50	(g)	6p dull violet	400.00	77.50
51	(g)	1sh green	525.00	57.50
a.		Inverted overprint	—	1,150.
52	(g)	5sh orange	1,475.	67.50

There are minor varieties of types e and f.

Overprinted in Black

i k l m n

o p q r

1878

54	(g)	4p blue (type II)	625.00	100.00
55	(g)	6p dull violet	900.00	145.00
56	(i)	1p rose	57.50	35.00
57	(i)	4p blue (type II)	325.00	47.50
58	(i)	6p dull violet	525.00	95.00
a.		Double overprint		*1,600.*
59	(k)	1p rose	115.00	52.50
60	(k)	4p blue (type II)	575.00	90.00
61	(k)	6p dull violet	850.00	135.00
62	(l)	1p rose	50.00	32.50
63	(l)	4p blue (type II)	290.00	47.50
64	(l)	6p dull violet	475.00	85.00
a.		Double overprint		*1,100.*
65	(m)	1p rose	80.00	70.00
66	(m)	4p blue (type II)	400.00	82.50
67	(m)	6p dull violet	550.00	150.00
68	(n)	1p rose	145.00	95.00
69	(n)	4p blue (type II)	750.00	125.00
70	(n)	6p dull violet	1,000.	190.00
a.		Double overprint		*1,750.*
71	(o)	1p rose	125.00	75.00
72	(o)	4p blue (type II)	625.00	105.00
73	(o)	6p dull violet	900.00	175.00
74	(p)	1p rose	200.00	135.00
75	(p)	4p blue (type II)	1,000.	190.00
76	(p)	6p dull violet	1,375.	300.00
77	(q)	1p rose	125.00	85.00
78	(q)	4p blue (type II)	625.00	105.00
79	(q)	6p dull violet	900.00	175.00
80	(r)	1p rose	625.00	425.00
81	(r)	4p blue (type II)	*3,000.*	625.00
82	(r)	6p dull violet	*3,750.*	950.00

There are two minor varieties of type l and one of type p.

s

t

1878 Overprinted in Red

83	(s)	½p gray black	28.00	30.00
a.		Double overprint	85.00	*100.00*
b.		Inverted overprint	30.00	30.00
c.		Double overprint, inverted	165.00	*190.00*
84	(s)	4p blue (type II)	625.00	165.00
a.		Inverted overprint	700.00	135.00
85	(t)	½p gray black	30.00	30.00
a.		Double overprint	135.00	135.00
b.		Inverted overprint	30.00	*30.00*
86	(t)	4p blue (type II)	—	150.00
a.		Inverted overprint	625.00	150.00

Black Overprint

87	(s)	½p gray black	375.00	190.00
a.		Inverted overprint	400.00	*400.00*
b.		With 2nd ovpt. *(s)* in red, invtd.	625.00	
c.		With 2nd ovpt. *(t)* in red, invtd.	350.00	
88	(s)	1p rose	30.00	20.00
a.		Double overprint	375.00	90.00
b.		Inverted overprint	30.00	30.00
c.		Double overprint, both inverted	375.00	115.00
d.		With second overprint *(s)* in red, both inverted	70.00	75.00
89	(s)	4p blue (type I)		300.00
90	(s)	4p blue (type II)	265.00	50.00
a.		Double overprint	—	400.00
b.		Inverted overprint	425.00	150.00
c.		Double overprint, both inverted	—	475.00
91	(s)	6p dull violet	290.00	50.00
92	(t)	½p gray black	85.00	85.00
a.		Inverted overprint	180.00	125.00
b.		With 2nd ovpt. inverted	350.00	
93	(t)	1p rose	30.00	22.50
a.		Double overprint	—	160.00
b.		Inverted overprint	145.00	50.00
c.		Double overprint, both inverted	—	190.00
d.		With 2nd ovpt. *(t)* in red, both invtd.	150.00	150.00
94	(t)	4p blue (type I)		300.00
95	(t)	4p blue (type II)	300.00	27.50
a.		Double overprint	—	375.00
b.		Inverted overprint	450.00	50.00
c.		Double overprint, both inverted	—	200.00
96	(t)	6p dull violet		50.00

Overprinted in Black

97	½p gray black	35.00	12.00
a.	Double overprint	550.00	350.00
98	1p rose	37.50	9.00
a.	Double overprint	—	175.00
b.	Triple overprint	—	325.00
c.	Inverted overprint	—	115.00
99	4p blue (type II)	70.00	9.00
a.	Double overprint	—	150.00
100	6p brt violet	300.00	15.00
a.	Double overprint	1,150.	210.00
b.	Inverted overprint	—	150.00
101	1sh green	275.00	10.00
a.	Double overprint	650.00	140.00
102	5sh orange	850.00	27.50
a.	Double overprint	1,050.	140.00
b.	Triple overprint	—	425.00

These stamps were declared obsolete in 1880 and the remainders were used in Cape of Good Hope offices as ordinary stamps. Prices for used stamps are for examples with such cancels.

GUADELOUPE

ˈgwä-dəl-ˌüp

LOCATION — In the West Indies lying between Montserrat and Dominica
GOVT. — French colony
AREA — 688 sq. mi.
POP. — 271,262 (1946)
CAPITAL — Basse-Terre

Guadeloupe consists of two large islands, Guadeloupe proper and Grande-Terre, together with five smaller dependencies. Guadeloupe became an integral part of the Republic, acquiring the same status as the departments in metropolitan France, under a law effective Jan. 1, 1947.

100 Centimes = 1 Franc

Catalogue values for unused stamps in this country are for Never Hinged items, beginning with Scott 168 in the regular postage section, Scott B12 in the semi-postal section, Scott C1 in the airpost section, and Scott J38 in the postage due section.

See France Nos. 850, 909, 1280, 1913 for French stamps inscribed "Guadeloupe."

Stamps of French Colonies Surcharged

1884 Unwmk. *Imperf.*
1 A8 20c on 30c brn, *bis* 70.00 55.00
a. Large "2" 325.00 260.00
2 A8 25c on 35c blk, *org* 57.50 55.00
a. Large "2" 325.00 260.00
b. Large "5" 160.00 125.00

The 5c on 4c (French Colonies No. 40) was not regularly issued. Three examples exist. Value $42,500.

The 5c on 4c also exists as an essay, surcharge similar to the issued values. Value $1,000.

c

d

1889 *Perf. 14x13½*

Surcharged Type c
3 A9 3c on 20c red, *grn* 5.25 5.25
4 A9 15c on 20c red, *grn* 32.50 27.50
5 A9 25c on 20c red, *grn* 32.50 27.50
Nos. 3-5 (3) 70.25 60.25

Surcharged Type d
6 A9 5c on 1c blk, *lil bl* 14.50 13.50
a. Inverted surcharge — *1,400.*
b. Double surcharge *450.00* *450.00*
7 A9 10c on 40c red, *straw* 40.00 35.00
a. Double surcharge 475.00 475.00
8 A9 15c on 20c red, *grn* 32.50 30.00
a. Double surcharge 475.00 475.00
9 A9 25c on 30c brn, *bis* 52.50 40.00
a. Double surcharge 475.00 475.00
Nos. 6-9 (4) 139.50 118.50

The word "centimes" in surcharges "b" and "c" varies from 10 to 12½mm.

Issue dates: No. 6, June 25; others, Mar. 22.

Stamps of French Colonies Surcharged

1891
10 A9 5c on 10c blk, *lav* 15.00 12.00
11 A9 5c on 1fr brnz grn, *straw* 16.00 11.00

Stamps of French Colonies Overprinted in Black

1891 *Imperf.*
12 A7 30c brn, *yelsh* 350.00 *375.00*
a. Double overprint 725.00 725.00
13 A7 80c car, *pnksh* 1,100. *1,300.*

Perf. 14x13½
14 A9 1c blk, *lil bl* 1.75 1.60
a. Double overprint 40.00 40.00
b. Inverted overprint 150.00 150.00
15 A9 2c brn, *buff* 2.60 2.00
a. Double overprint 45.00 40.00
16 A9 4c claret, *lav* 6.00 5.25
17 A9 5c grn, *grnsh* 8.75 7.25
a. Double overprint 45.00 40.00
b. Inverted overprint 160.00 160.00
18 A9 10c blk, *lavender* 17.00 13.50
19 A9 15c blue 52.50 6.00
a. Double overprint — 110.00
20 A9 20c red, *grn* 45.00 30.00
a. Double overprint 240.00 240.00
21 A9 25c blk, *rose* 47.50 5.25
a. Double overprint 240.00 240.00
b. Inverted overprint 225.00 225.00
22 A9 30c brn, *bister* 45.00 30.00
a. Double overprint 240.00 240.00
23 A9 35c dp vio, *org* 87.50 72.50
a. Double overprint 675.00 675.00
24 A9 40c red, *straw* 65.00 52.50
a. Double overprint 675.00 675.00
25 A9 75c car, *rose* 130.00 125.00
26 A9 1fr brnz grn, *straw* 92.50 72.50
Nos. 14-26 (13) 601.10 423.35

Navigation and Commerce — A7

Perf. 14x13½
1892-1901 Typo. Unwmk.
Colony Name in Blue or Carmine
27 A7 1c blk, *lil bl* 1.40 1.40
28 A7 2c brn, *buff* 1.50 1.40
29 A7 4c claret, *lav* 1.75 1.50
30 A7 5c grn, *grnsh* 3.50 1.50
31 A7 5c yel grn ('01) 6.00 1.60
32 A7 10c blk, *lavender* 10.00 3.25
33 A7 10c red ('00) 8.75 2.40
a. Imperf. 120.00
b. As "a," country name omitted 150.00
34 A7 15c blue, quadrille paper 18.00 1.75
35 A7 15c gray, *lt gray* ('00) 13.00 1.60
36 A7 20c red, *grn* 11.00 6.50
37 A7 25c blk, *rose* 11.00 3.00
38 A7 25c blue ('00) 100.00 100.00
39 A7 30c brn, *bister* 24.00 15.00
40 A7 40c red, *straw* 24.00 15.00
41 A7 50c car, *rose* 30.00 16.00
42 A7 50c brn, *az* ('00) 45.00 42.50
43 A7 75c dp vio, *org* 32.50 22.50
44 A7 1fr brnz grn, *straw* 32.50 30.00
Nos. 27-44 (18) 373.90 266.90

Perf. 13½x14 stamps are counterfeits.
For surcharges see Nos. 45-53, 83-85.

Nos. 39-41, 43-44 Surcharged in Black

f

g

h

1903
45 A7 (f) 5c on 30c 4.00 4.00
a. "C" instead of "G" 32.50 32.50
b. Inverted surcharge 45.00 45.00
c. Double surcharge 140.00 140.00
d. Double surch., inverted 160.00
46 A7 (g) 10c on 40c 9.50 9.50
a. "C" instead of "G" 40.00 40.00
b. "1" inverted 60.00 60.00
c. Inverted surcharge 55.00 55.00
d. Double surcharge 200.00 200.00
47 A7 (f) 15c on 50c 13.00 13.00
a. "C" instead of "G" 40.00 40.00
b. Inverted surcharge 110.00 110.00
c. "15" inverted 375.00 375.00
e. Double surcharge 200.00 200.00
48 A7 (g) 40c on 1fr 13.00 13.00
a. "C" instead of "G" 52.50 52.50
b. "4" inverted 120.00 120.00
c. Inverted surcharge 110.00 110.00
d. Double surcharge 240.00 240.00
e. Triple surcharge 450.00 *500.00*
49 A7 (h) 1fr on 75c 42.50 42.50
a. "C" instead of "G" 160.00 160.00
b. "1" inverted 160.00 160.00
c. Value above "G & D" 300.00 300.00
d. Inverted surcharge 125.00 125.00
Nos. 45-49 (5) 82.00 82.00

Letters and figures from several fonts were used for these surcharges, resulting in numerous minor varieties.

Nos. 48-49 With Additional Overprint "1903" in a Frame

1904, Mar. Red Overprint
50 A7 (g) 40c on 1fr 75.00 85.00
b. Inverted surcharge 600.00 650.00
c. Double surcharge 1,250. 1,250.
51 A7 (h) 1fr on 75c 92.50 100.00
a. Double surcharge 950.00 950.00

Overprinted in Blue

52 A7 (g) 40c on 1fr 60.00 65.00
53 A7 (h) 1fr on 75c 87.50 95.00
Nos. 50-53 (4) 315.00 345.00

The date "1903" may be found in 19 different positions and type faces within the frame. These stamps may also be found with the minor varieties of Nos. 48-49.

The 40c exists with black overprint. Value, $500 unused or used.

Harbor at Basse-Terre — A8

View of La Soufrière A9

Pointe-à-Pitre, Grand-Terre — A10

1905-27 Typo. *Perf. 14x13½*
54 A8 1c blk, *bluish* .30 .30
55 A8 2c vio brn, *straw* .30 .30
56 A8 4c bis brn, *az* .30 .30
57 A8 5c green 2.40 .65
58 A8 5c dp blue ('22) .25 .25
59 A8 10c rose 2.25 .65
60 A8 10c green ('22) 1.40 1.25
61 A8 10c red, *bluish* ('25) .25 .25
62 A8 15c violet .55 .50
63 A9 20c red, *grn* .55 .40
64 A9 20c bl grn ('25) .65 .65
65 A9 25c blue .95 .55
66 A9 25c ol grn ('22) .65 .65
67 A9 30c black 5.00 3.25
68 A9 30c rose ('22) .70 .70
69 A9 30c brn ol, *lav* ('25) .55 .55
70 A9 35c blk, *yel* ('06) .80 .80
71 A9 40c red, *straw* .80 .80
72 A9 45c ol gray, *lil* ('07) 1.40 .80
73 A9 45c rose ('25) .80 .80
74 A9 50c gray grn, *straw* 5.50 4.00
75 A9 50c dp bl ('22) 1.25 1.10
76 A9 50c violet ('25) .70 .70
77 A9 65c blue ('27) .70 .70
78 A9 75c car, *bl* .90 .80
79 A10 1fr blk, *green* 1.75 1.50
80 A10 1fr lt bl ('25) 1.00 .95
81 A10 2fr car, *org* 2.25 2.00
82 A10 5fr dp bl, *org* 7.50 7.50
Nos. 54-82 (29) 42.40 33.65

Nos. 57, 59 and 82 exist imperf. Value, Nos. 57 and 59 each $60, No. 82 $140.

For surcharges see #86-95, 167, B1-B2.

Nos. 29, 39 and 40 Surcharged in Carmine or Black

1912, Nov.
83 A7 5c on 4c claret, *lav* (C) 1.50 1.50
84 A7 5c on 30c brn, *bis* (C) 2.00 2.00
85 A7 10c on 40c red, *straw* 2.25 2.25
Nos. 83-85 (3) 5.75 5.75

Two spacings between the surcharaged numerals are found on Nos. 83 to 85. For detailed listings, see the *Scott Classic Specialized Catalogue of Stamps and Covers.*

Stamps & Types of 1905-27 Surcharged

No. 89

No. 94

1924-27
86 A10 25c on 5fr dp bl, *org* .75 .70
87 A10 65c on 1fr gray grn 1.40 1.25
88 A10 85c on 1fr gray grn 1.50 1.40
89 A9 90c on 75c dl red 1.40 1.25
90 A10 1.05fr on 2fr ver (Bl) 1.00 .85
91 A10 1.25fr on 1fr lt bl (R) .65 .65
92 A10 1.50fr on 1fr dk bl 1.25 1.25
93 A10 3fr on 5fr org brn 1.50 1.50
94 A10 10fr on 5fr vio rose, *org* 11.00 11.00
95 A10 20fr on 5fr rose lil, *pnksh* 14.00 13.00
Nos. 86-95 (10) 34.45 32.85

Years issued: Nos. 87-88, 1925. Nos. 90-91, 1926. Nos. 89, 92-95, 1927.

Sugar Mill — A11

Saints Roadstead A12

Harbor Scene A13

Perf. 14x13½
1928-40 Unwmk. Typo.
96 A11 1c yel & vio .25 .25
97 A11 2c blk & lt red .25 .25
98 A11 3c yel & red vio ('40) .30 .30
99 A11 4c yel grn & org brn .25 .25
100 A11 5c ver & grn .25 .25

101	A11	10c bis brn & dp bl	.25	.25
102	A11	15c brn red & blk	.30	.30
103	A11	20c lil & ol brn	.50	.50
104	A12	25c grnsh bl & olvn	.55	.55
105	A12	30c gray grn & yel grn	.40	.40
106	A12	35c bl grn ('38)	.40	.40
107	A12	40c yel & vio	.40	.40
108	A12	45c vio brn & slate	.95	.80
109	A12	45c bl grn & dl grn ('40)	1.10	1.00
110	A12	50c dl grn & org	.30	.30
111	A12	55c ultra & car ('38)	1.40	1.25
112	A12	60c ultra & car ('40)	.65	.65
113	A12	65c gray blk & ver	.55	.55
114	A12	70c gray blk & ver ('40)	.70	.70
115	A12	75c dl red & bl grn	.70	.70
116	A12	80c car & brn ('38)	.85	.65
117	A12	90c dl red & dl rose	2.00	1.75
118	A12	90c rose red & bl ('39)	1.25	1.10
119	A13	1fr lt rose & lt bl	5.25	3.75
120	A13	1fr rose red & org ('38)	1.75	1.50
121	A13	1fr bl gray & blk brn ('40)	.70	.70
122	A13	1.05fr lt bl & rose	1.25	1.10
123	A13	1.10fr lt red & grn	4.00	2.75
124	A13	1.25fr bl gray & blk brn ('33)	.65	.65
125	A13	1.25fr brt rose & red org ('39)	.95	.95
126	A13	1.40fr lt bl & lil rose ('40)	.70	.70
127	A13	1.50fr dl bl & bl	.40	.40
128	A13	1.60fr lil rose & yel brn ('40)	.70	.70
129	A13	1.75fr lil rose & yel brn ('33)	5.75	3.25
130	A13	1.75fr vio bl ('38)	6.00	4.00
131	A13	2fr bl grn & dk brn	.40	.40
132	A13	2.25fr vio bl ('39)	1.25	1.25
133	A13	2.50fr pale org & grn ('40)	1.25	1.25
134	A13	3fr org brn & sl	.65	.65
135	A13	5fr dl bl & org	1.25	1.00
136	A13	10fr vio & ol brn	1.25	1.00
137	A13	20fr green & mag	1.50	1.40
		Nos. 96-137 (42)	50.20	40.95

Nos. 96-103, 110, 119, 123, 134, 137 exist imperf. Values each $30-$60.

For surcharges see Nos. 161-166.

For 10c, type A11, without "RF," see No. 163A.

Common Design Types pictured following the introduction.

Colonial Exposition Issue

Common Design Types

1931, Apr. 13 Engr. ***Perf. 12½***

Name of Country in Black

138	CD70	40c deep green	4.75	4.75
139	CD71	50c violet	4.75	4.75
140	CD72	90c red orange	4.75	4.75
141	CD73	1.50fr dull blue	4.75	4.75
		Nos. 138-141 (4)	19.00	19.00

Cardinal Richelieu Establishing French Antilles Co., 1635 — A14

Victor Hugues and his Corsairs — A15

1935 ***Perf. 13***

142	A14	40c gray brown	10.00	10.00
143	A14	50c dull red	10.00	10.00
144	A14	1.50fr dull blue	10.00	10.00
145	A15	1.75fr lilac rose	10.00	10.00
146	A15	5fr dark brown	10.00	10.00
147	A15	10fr blue green	10.00	10.00
		Nos. 142-147 (6)	60.00	60.00

Tercentenary of the establishment of the French colonies in the West Indies.

Paris International Exposition Issue

Common Design Types

1937 ***Perf. 13***

148	CD74	20c deep violet	1.90	1.90
149	CD75	30c dark green	1.75	1.75
150	CD76	40c car rose	1.50	1.50
151	CD77	50c dk brn & blk	1.50	1.50
152	CD78	90c red	1.50	1.50
153	CD79	1.50fr ultra	1.90	1.90
		Nos. 148-153 (6)	10.05	10.05

Colonial Arts Exhibition Issue

Souvenir Sheet

Common Design Type

1937 ***Imperf.***

154	CD75	3fr dark blue	9.50	*11.00*

New York World's Fair Issue

Common Design Type

1939 Engr. ***Perf. 12½x12***

155	CD82	1.25fr car lake	1.25	1.25
156	CD82	2.25fr ultra	1.25	1.25

For surcharges see Nos. 159-160.

La Soufrière View and Marshal Pétain A16

1941 Engr. ***Perf. 12½x12***

157	A16	1fr lilac	.80	
158	A16	2.50fr blue	.80	

Nos. 157-158 were issued by the Vichy government in France, but were not placed on sale in Guadeloupe.

For surcharges, see Nos. B11A-B11B.

Nos. 155, 156, 113, 117 and 118 Surcharged in Black

1943 ***Perf. 14x13½, 12½x12***

159	CD82	40c on 1.25fr	.80	.80
160	CD82	40c on 2.25fr	1.60	1.60
161	A12	50c on 65c	1.00	1.00
162	A12	1fr on 90c (#117)	1.40	1.40
163	A12	1fr on 90c (#118)	1.25	1.25
		Nos. 159-163 (5)	6.05	6.05

Type of 1928 Without "RF"

1943 ***Perf. 14x13½***

163A	A11	10c bis brn & dp blue	.65	

No. 163A was issued by the Vichy government in France, and was not placed on sale in Guadeloupe.

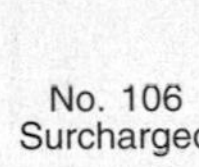

No. 106 Surcharged

No. 104 Surcharged

No. 113 Surcharged

No. 90 Surcharged

1944 ***Perf. 14x13½***

164	A12	40c on 35c	1.10	1.10
165	A12	50c on 25c	.30	.30
166	A12	1fr on 65c	1.25	1.25
a.		Double surcharge	200.00	150.00
167	A10	4fr on 1.05fr on 2fr	1.75	1.75
		Nos. 164-167 (4)	4.40	4.40

Catalogue values for unused stamps in this section, from this point to the end of the section, are for Never Hinged items.

Dolphins A17

1945 Unwmk. Photo. ***Perf. 11½***

168	A17	10c chlky bl & red org	.30	.25
169	A17	30c lt yel grn & red	.30	.25
170	A17	40c lt bl & car	.85	.65
171	A17	50c red org & yel grn	.40	.30
172	A17	60c ol bis & lt bl	.40	.30
173	A17	70c lt gray & yel grn	.85	.65
174	A17	80c lt bl grn & yel	.85	.65
175	A17	1fr brn vio & grn	.40	.30
176	A17	1.20fr brt red vio & yel grn	.40	.30
177	A17	1.50fr dl brn & car	.90	.55
178	A17	2fr cer & bl	.90	.55
179	A17	2.40fr sal & yel grn	1.50	.95
180	A17	3fr gray brn & bl vio	.85	.55
181	A17	4fr ultra & buff	.70	.30
182	A17	4.50fr brn org & grn	.90	.55
183	A17	5fr dk vio & grn	1.10	.65
184	A17	10fr gray grn & red vio	1.10	.65
185	A17	15fr sl gray & org	1.50	.85
186	A17	20fr pale gray & dl org	2.50	1.00
		Nos. 168-186 (19)	16.70	10.25

Eboue Issue

Common Design Type

1945 Engr. ***Perf. 13***

187	CD91	2fr black	.65	.50
188	CD91	25fr Prussian green	1.40	1.10

Basse-Terre Harbor and Woman A18

Cutting Sugar Cane — A19

Pineapple Bearer — A20

Guadeloupe Woman — A21

Gathering Coffee — A22

Guadeloupe Woman — A23

1947 Unwmk. Engr. ***Perf. 13***

189	A18	10c red brown	.30	.25
190	A18	30c sepia	.30	.25
191	A18	50c blue grn	.40	.30
192	A19	60c black brn	.75	.50
193	A19	1fr dp carmine	1.00	.65
194	A19	1.50fr dk gray bl	1.50	.85
195	A20	2fr blue grn	1.50	.85
196	A20	2.50fr dp car	1.40	.95
197	A20	3fr deep blue	1.50	.95
198	A21	4fr violet	1.40	.95
199	A21	5fr blue grn	1.40	.95
200	A21	6fr red	1.40	.95
201	A22	10fr deep blue	1.50	1.00
202	A22	15fr dk vio brn	2.50	1.25
203	A22	20fr rose red	2.75	1.50
204	A23	25fr blue green	7.00	3.00
205	A23	40fr red	8.00	4.00
		Nos. 189-205 (17)	34.60	19.15

SEMI-POSTAL STAMPS

Nos. 59 and 62 Surcharged in Red

1915-17 Unwmk. ***Perf. 14 x 13½***

B1	A8	10c + 5c rose	5.25	3.50
B2	A8	15c + 5c violet	5.25	3.50
a.		Double surcharge	225.00	225.00
b.		Triple surcharge	240.00	240.00
c.		Inverted surcharge	240.00	240.00
d.		In pair with unovptd. stamp	275.00	

Curie Issue

Common Design Type

1938, Oct. 24 ***Perf. 13***

B3	CD80	1.75fr + 50c brt ultra	11.00	10.50

French Revolution Issue

Common Design Type

Name and Value Typo. in Black

1939, July 5 Photo. ***Perf. 13***

B4	CD83	45c + 25c green	10.00	10.00
B5	CD83	70c + 30c brown	10.00	10.00
B6	CD83	90c + 35c red org	10.00	10.00
B7	CD83	1.25fr + 1fr rose pink	10.00	10.00
B8	CD83	2.25fr + 2fr blue	10.00	10.00
		Nos. B4-B8 (5)	50.00	50.00

Common Design Type and

Colonial Artillery SP1

Colonial Infantry — SP2

1941 Photo. ***Perf. 13½***

B9	SP1	1fr + 1fr red	1.00	
B10	CD86	1.50fr + 3fr maroon	1.00	
B11	SP2	2.50fr + 1fr blue	1.50	
		Nos. B9-B11 (3)	3.50	

Nos. B9-B11 were issued by the Vichy government in France, but were not placed on sale in Guadeloupe.

Nos. 157-158 Surcharged in Black or Red

1944 Engr. *Perf. 12½x12*
B11A 50c + 1.50fr on 2.50fr blue (R) .80
B11B + 2.50fr on 1fr lilac .80

Colonial Development Fund.

Nos. B11A-B11B were issued by the Vichy government in France, but were not placed on sale in Guadeloupe.

Catalogue values for unused stamps in this section, from this point to the end of the section, are for Never Hinged items.

Red Cross Issue
Common Design Type

1944 *Perf. 14½x14*
B12 CD90 5fr + 20fr ultra 1.40 1.00

The surtax was for the French Red Cross and national relief.

AIR POST STAMPS

Catalogue values for unused stamps in this section are for Never Hinged items.

Common Design Type

1945 Unwmk. Photo. *Perf. 14½x14*
C1 CD87 50fr green 1.50 1.00
C2 CD87 100fr deep plum 2.25 1.50

Victory Issue
Common Design Type

1946, May 8 Engr. *Perf. 12½*
C3 CD92 8fr redsh brn 1.25 1.00

Chad to Rhine Issue
Common Design Types

1946, June 6
C4 CD93 5fr dk slate grn 2.00 1.60
C5 CD94 10fr deep blue 2.00 1.60
C6 CD95 15fr brt violet 2.00 1.60
C7 CD96 20fr brown car 2.00 1.60
C8 CD97 25fr black 2.00 1.60
C9 CD98 50fr red brown 2.00 1.60
Nos. C4-C9 (6) 12.00 9.60

Gathering Bananas — AP1

Seaplane at Roadstead — AP2

Pointe-a-Pitre Harbor and Guadeloupe Woman — AP3

1947 Unwmk. *Perf. 13*
C10 AP1 50fr dk brown violet 6.00 2.75
C11 AP2 100fr deep blue 8.75 5.25
C12 AP3 200fr red 11.50 5.50
Nos. C10-C12 (3) 26.25 13.50

AIR POST SEMI-POSTAL STAMPS

Mother & Nurse with Children — SPAP1

1942, June 22 Engr. *Perf. 13*
CB1 SPAP1 1.50fr + 3.50fr green 1.00
CB2 SPAP1 2fr + 6fr brn & red 1.00

Native children's welfare fund.

Nos. CB1-CB2 were issued by the Vichy government in France, but were not placed on sale in Guadeloupe.

Colonial Education Fund
Common Design Type

1942, June 22
CB3 CD86a 1.20fr + 1.80fr blue & red 1.10

No. CB3 was issued by the Vichy government in France, but was not placed on sale in Guadeloupe.

POSTAGE DUE STAMPS

D1 D2 D3

1876 Unwmk. Typeset *Imperf.*
J1 D1 25c black 1,350. 925.
J2 D2 40c black, *blue* *37,500.*
J3 D3 40c black 1,500. 1,200.

Twenty varieties of each.

Nos. J1 and J3 have been reprinted on thinner and whiter paper than the originals.

D4

1879
J4 D4 15c black, *blue* 55.00 52.50
a. Period after "c" omitted 175.00 175.00
J5 D4 30c black 110.00 87.50
a. Period after "c" omitted 240.00 225.00

Twenty varieties of each.

D5

1884
J6 D5 5c black 35.00 35.00
a. Double impression 100.00 100.00
J7 D5 10c black, *blue* 75.00 65.00
a. Double impression 150.00 150.00
J8 D5 15c black, *violet* 110.00 87.50
a. Double impression 225.00 225.00
J9 D5 20c black, *rose* 160.00 100.00
a. Italic "2" in "20" 1,000. 950.00
J10 D5 30c black, *yellow* 160.00 160.00
a. Double impression 450.00 450.00
J11 D5 35c black, *gray* 60.00 52.50
a. Double impression 225.00 225.00
J12 D5 50c black, *green* 32.50 27.50
a. Double impression 200.00 200.00
Nos. J6-J12 (7) 632.50 527.50

There are ten varieties of the 35c, and fifteen of each of the other values, also numerous wrong font and missing letters.

Postage Due Stamps of French Colonies Surcharged in Black

Two surcharge types: I, wide font, "3" with rounded top; II, narrow font, "3" with flat top.

1903 Type I
J13 D1 30c on 60c brn, *cr* 325.00 325.00
a. Inverted surcharge 1,100. 1,100.
b. Bee corner ornament turned 1,150. 1,150.
c. As "b," inverted surcharge 1,700.
d. "G" omitted 800.00 800.00
e. As "d," inverted surcharge 1,250.
f. Corrected surcharge, "30" over "33" 10,500. 10,500.
J14 D1 30c on 1fr rose, *cr* 400.00 400.00
a. Inverted surcharge 1,150. 1,150.
b. "30" sideways 10,000. 10,000.
c. As "b," inverted surcharge 10,000. 10,000.

Type II
J13A D1 30c on 60c brn, *cr* 1,000. 1,000.
a. Inverted surcharge 1,900. 1,900.
b. Bee corner ornament turned 1,600. 1,600.
c. As "b," inverted surcharge 2,200.
d. "G" omitted 1,000 1,000.
e. As "d," inverted surcharge 1,500.
f. Corrected surcharge, "30" over "33" 10,500. 10,500.
J14A D1 30c on 1fr rose, *cr* 400.00 400.00
a. Inverted surcharge 1,200. 1,200.
b. "30" sideways 10,500. 10,500.
c. As "b," inverted surcharge 10,500. 10,500.

Gustavia Bay — D6

1905-06 Typo. *Perf. 14x13½*
J15 D6 5c blue .55 .55
J16 D6 10c brown .55 .55
J17 D6 15c green 1.00 1.00
J18 D6 20c black, *yel* ('06) 1.00 1.00
J19 D6 30c rose 1.25 1.25
J20 D6 50c black 3.25 3.25
J21 D6 60c brown orange 1.75 1.75
J22 D6 1fr violet 3.25 3.25
Nos. J15-J22 (8) 12.60 12.60

Type of 1905-06 Issue Surcharged

1926-27
J23 D6 2fr on 1fr gray 2.00 2.00
J24 D6 3fr on 1fr ultra ('27) 2.75 2.75

Avenue of Royal Palms — D7

1928, June 18
J25 D7 2c olive brn & lil .25 .25
J26 D7 4c bl & org brn .25 .25
J27 D7 5c gray grn & dk brn .25 .25
J28 D7 10c dl vio & yel .30 .30
J29 D7 15c rose & olive grn .30 .30
J30 D7 20c brn org & ol grn .50 .50
J31 D7 25c brn red & bl grn .50 .50
J32 D7 30c slate & olivine .80 .80
J33 D7 50c ol brn & lt red .80 .80
J34 D7 60c dp bl & blk .80 .80
J35 D7 1fr green & orange 3.00 2.60
J36 D7 2fr bis brn & lt red 2.25 1.90
J37 D7 3fr vio & bl blk 1.25 1.10
Nos. J25-J37 (13) 11.25 10.35

Type of 1928 Without "RF"

1944
J37A D7 60c dp bl & blk .30
J37B D7 1fr green & orange .65
J37C D7 2fr bis brn & lt red .65
Nos. J37A-J37C (3) 1.60

Nos. J37A-J37C were issued by the Vichy government in France, but were not placed on sale in Guadeloupe.

Catalogue values for unused stamps in this section, from this point to the end of the section, are for Never Hinged items.

D8

Perf. 14x13
1947, June 2 Unwmk. Engr.
J38 D8 10c black .30 .25
J39 D8 30c dull blue green .40 .30
J40 D8 50c bright ultra .40 .30
J41 D8 1fr dark green .65 .50
J42 D8 2fr dark blue .85 .70
J43 D8 3fr black brown 1.25 1.00
J44 D8 4fr lilac rose 1.40 1.25
J45 D8 5fr purple 1.90 1.60
J46 D8 10fr red 2.60 2.10
J47 D8 20fr dark violet 3.00 2.25
Nos. J38-J47 (10) 12.75 10.25

GUATEMALA

ˌgwä-lə-ˈmä-lə

LOCATION — Central America, bordering on Atlantic and Pacific Oceans
GOVT. — Republic
AREA — 42,042 sq. mi.
POP. — 12,335,580 (1999 est.)
CAPITAL — Guatemala City

100 Centavos = 8 Reales = 1 Peso
100 Centavos de Quetzal = 1 Quetzal (1927)

Catalogue values for unused stamps in this country are for Never Hinged items, beginning with Scott 316 in the regular postage section, Scott B5 in the semi-postal section, Scott C137 in the air post section, Scott CB5 in the air post semi-postal section and Scott E2 in the special delivery section.

Coat of Arms — A1

Two types of 10c:
Type I — Both zeros in "10" are wide.
Type II — Left zero narrow.

Perf. 14x13½

1871, Mar. 1 — Typo. — Unwmk.

No.	Type	Description	Unused	Used
1	A1	1c ocher	2.00	*50.00*
a.		Imperf., pair	10.00	
b.		Printed on both sides, imperf.	135.00	
2	A1	5c lt bister brn	9.00	*22.50*
a.		Imperf. pair	50.00	
b.		Tête bêche pair	350.00	
c.		Tête bêche pair, imperf.	*3,500.*	
3	A1	10c blue (I)	11.00	*25.00*
a.		Imperf., pair (I)	75.00	
b.		Type II	25.00	*50.00*
c.		Imperf. pair (II)	110.00	
4	A1	20c rose	9.00	*24.00*
a.		Imperf., pair	75.00	
b.		20c blue (error)	350.00	*125.00*
c.		As "b," imperf.	*1,750.*	
		Nos. 1-4 (4)	31.00	*121.50*

Forgeries exist. Forged cancellations abound. See No. C458.

Coat of Arms — A2

1873 — Litho. — *Perf. 12*

No.	Type	Description	Unused	Used
5	A2	4r dull red vio	675.00	175.00
6	A2	1p dull yellow	350.00	215.00

Forgeries exist. Only one pair of No. 5 is known on cover.

Liberty
A3 A4

A5

A6

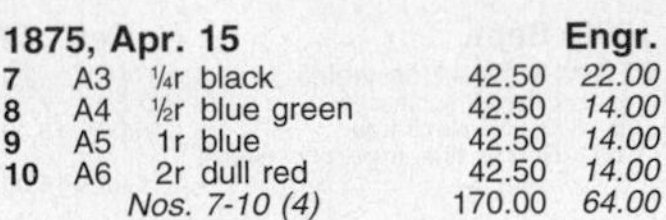

1875, Apr. 15 — Engr.

No.	Type	Description	Unused	Used
7	A3	¼r black	42.50	*22.00*
8	A4	½r blue green	42.50	*14.00*
9	A5	1r blue	42.50	*14.00*
10	A6	2r dull red	42.50	*14.00*
		Nos. 7-10 (4)	170.00	*64.00*

Nos. 7-10 normally lack gum. Unused values are for examples without gum.

Forgeries and forged cancellations exist.

Indian Woman — A7

Typographed on Tinted Paper

1878, Jan. 10 — *Perf. 13*

No.	Type	Description	Unused	Used
11	A7	½r yellow grn	2.75	*6.75*
12	A7	2r carmine rose	4.25	*13.00*
13	A7	4r violet	4.25	*14.50*
14	A7	1p yellow	5.00	*35.00*
		Nos. 11-14 (4)	16.25	*69.25*

Some sheets of Nos. 11-14 have papermaker's watermark, "LACROIX FRERES," in double-lined capitals appearing on six stamps.

Part perforate pairs of Nos. 11, 12 and 14 exist. Value for each, about $100.

Forgeries of Nos. 11-14 are plentiful. Forged cancellations exist.

For surcharges see Nos. 18, 20.

One pair of No. 14 is known to exist on cover.

Imperf., Pairs

No.	Type	Description	Unused
11a	A7	½r yellow green	215.00
12a	A7	2r carmine rose	215.00
13a	A7	4r violet	215.00
14a	A7	1p yellow	215.00

Quetzal — A8

1879 — Engr. — *Perf. 12*

No.	Type	Description	Unused	Used
15	A8	¼r brown & green	16.00	*20.00*
16	A8	1r black & green	24.00	*30.00*

For similar types see A11, A72, A103, A121, A146. For surcharges see Nos. 17, 19.

Nos. 11, 12, 15, 16 Surcharged in Black

1881 — *Perf. 12 and 13*

No.	Type	Description	Unused	Used
17	A8	1c on ¼r brn & grn	25.00	*35.00*
a.		"ecntavo,"	87.50	*100.00*
b.		Pair, one without surcharge	125.00	
c.		Period omitted	87.50	*100.00*
18	A7	5c on ½r yel grn	19.00	*30.00*
a.		"ecntavos,"	80.00	*110.00*
b.		"5" omitted	215.00	
c.		Double surcharge	200.00	*260.00*
19	A8	10c on 1r blk & grn	40.00	*50.00*
a.		"s" of "centavos" missing	115.00	135.00
b.		"ecntavos"	145.00	*190.00*
20	A7	20c on 2r car rose	100.00	*145.00*
a.		Horiz. pair, imperf. between	750.00	
b.		Period omitted	125.00	*175.00*
c.		Comma for period	200.00	*260.00*
		Nos. 17-20 (4)	184.00	*260.00*

The 5c had three settings.

Surcharge varieties found on Nos. 17-20 include: Period omitted; comma instead of period; "ecntavo." or "ecntavos."; "s" omitted; spaced "centavos."; wider "0" in "20."

Counterfeits of Nos. 17-20 are plentiful.

Quetzal — A11

1881, Nov. 7 — Engr. — *Perf. 12*

No.	Type	Description	Unused	Used
21	A11	1c black & grn	6.00	4.25
22	A11	2c brown & grn	6.00	4.50
a.		Center inverted	*725.00*	*550.00*
23	A11	5c red & grn	13.00	5.50
a.		Center inverted	*7,000.*	*2,500.*
24	A11	10c gray vio & grn	6.00	4.50
25	A11	20c yellow & grn	6.00	5.25
a.		Center inverted	*825.00*	*575.00*
		Nos. 21-25 (5)	37.00	24.00

Surcharged in Black

Gen. Justo Rufino Barrios — A12

A12a

A12b

1886, Mar. 6

No.	Type	Description	Unused	Used
26	A12	25c on 1p ver	1.00	1.00
a.		"centovos"	20.00	20.00
b.		"centanos"	20.00	20.00
c.		"255" instead of "25"	150.00	225.00
d.		Inverted "S" in "Nacionales"	20.00	22.50
f.		"cen avos"	40.00	
h.		"Corre cionales"	25.00	
i.		Inverted surcharge	*100.00*	
27	A12	50c on 1p ver	1.00	1.00
a.		"centovos"	10.00	10.00
b.		"centanos"	10.00	10.00
c.		"Carreos"	10.00	10.00
d.		Inverted surcharge	100.00	100.00
e.		Double surcharge	110.00	
f.		Inverted "S" in "Nacionales"	110.00	
g.		"centavo"	22.50	
h.		"cen avos"	40.00	
28	A12	75c on 1p ver	1.00	1.00
a.		"centovos"	10.00	10.00
b.		"centanos"	10.00	10.00
c.		"Carreos"	10.00	10.00
d.		"50" for "75" at upper right	10.00	10.00
e.		Inverted "S" in "Nacionales"	10.00	10.00
f.		Double surcharge	100.00	
g.		"ales" inverted	100.00	
29	A12a	100c on 1p ver	2.00	3.00
a.		"110" at upper left and "á" at lower left, instead of "100"	17.50	25.00
b.		Inverted surcharge	100.00	*100.00*
c.		"Guatemala" bolder; 23mm instead of 18½mm wide	9.00	*10.00*
d.		Double surcharge, one diagonal	100.00	
30	A12b	150c on 1p ver	2.00	3.50
a.		Inverted "G"	7.50	7.50
b.		"Guetemala" and italic "5" in upper 4 numerals	10.00	10.00
d.		Inverted surcharge	125.00	
e.		Pair, one without surcharge	150.00	
f.		Double surcharge	130.00	
		Nos. 26-30 (5)	7.00	9.50

There are many other minor varieties, such as wrong font letters, etc.

Used values of Nos. 26-30 are for canceled to order stamps. Postally used sell for much more.

National Emblem — A13

1886, July 1 — Litho. — *Perf. 12*

No.	Type	Description	Unused	Used
31	A13	1c dull blue	7.50	3.00
32	A13	2c brown	8.50	4.50
33	A13	5c purple	55.00	1.50
34	A13	10c red	25.00	1.50
35	A13	20c emerald	25.00	2.00
36	A13	25c orange	27.50	2.00
37	A13	50c olive green	15.00	4.50
38	A13	75c carmine rose	17.50	4.50
39	A13	100c red brown	17.50	10.00
40	A13	150c dark blue	20.00	12.50
41	A13	200c orange yellow	25.00	12.50
		Nos. 31-41 (11)	243.50	58.50

Used values of Nos. 38-41 are for canceled to order stamps. Postally used sell for more.

See Nos. 43-50, 99-107. For surcharges see Nos. 42, 51-59, 75-85, 97-98, 108-110, 124-130.

No. 32 Surcharged in Black

Two settings:
I — "1886" (no period).
II — "1886." (period).

1886, Nov. 12

No.	Type	Description	Unused	Used
42	A13	1c on 2c brown, I	5.50	*10.00*
a.		Date inverted, I	125.00	
b.		Date double, I	125.00	
c.		Date omitted, I	125.00	
d.		Date double, one invtd., I	135.00	
e.		Date triple, one inverted, I	*135.00*	
f.		Setting II	3.50	2.00
g.		Inverted surcharge, II	10.00	
h.		Double surcharge, II	125.00	

Forgeries exist.

Type I

Type II

Two types of 5c:
I — Thin "5"
II — Larger, thick "5"

1886-95 — Engr. — *Perf. 12*

No.	Type	Description	Unused	Used
43	A13	1c blue	1.50	.50
44	A13	2c yellow brn	3.50	.50
a.		Half used as 1c on cover		125.00
45	A13	5c purple (I)	200.00	5.00
46	A13	5c vio (II) ('88)	4.50	.75
47	A13	6c lilac ('95)	4.50	.50
48	A13	10c red ('90)	4.50	.50
49	A13	20c green ('93)	7.50	1.00
50	A13	25c red org ('93)	12.50	2.00
		Nos. 43-44,46-50 (7)	38.50	5.75

The impression of the engraved stamps is sharper than that of the lithographed. On the engraved stamps the top four lines at left are heavier than those below them. (This is also true of the 1c litho., which is distinguished from the engraved only by a slight color difference and the impression.)

The "2" and "5" (I) are more open than the litho. numerals. The "10" of the engraved is wider. The 20c and 25c of the engraved have a vertical line at right end of the "centavos" ribbon.

No. 38 Surcharged in Blue Black

"1894" 14½mm wide

1894, Apr. 25

No.	Type	Description	Unused	Used
51	A13	10c on 75c car rose	9.00	7.50
a.		Double surcharge	175.00	
b.		Inverted surcharge	90.00	

Same on Nos. 38-41 in Blue or Red "1894" 14mm wide

1894, June 13

No.	Type	Description	Unused	Used
52	A13	2c on 100c	7.50	6.00
53	A13	6c on 150c (R)	8.00	6.50
54	A13	10c on 75c	1,000.	900.00
a.		Thick "1" in "10"	1,100.	1,100.
55	A13	10c on 200c	10.00	5.00
c.		Inverted surcharge	125.00	
d.		"207" (position 29)	50.00	
e.		Thick "1" in "10"	12.50	7.50

Nos. 54-55 exist with thick or thin "1" in new value.

Same on Nos. 39-41 in Black or Red "1894" 12mm wide

1894, July 14

No.	Type	Description	Unused	Used
52a	A13	2c on 100c red brn (Bk)	12.50	6.50
b.		Vert. pair, one without surcharge	*250.00*	
53a	A13	6c on 150c dk bl (R)	12.50	6.50
55a	A13	10c on 200c org yel (Bk)	12.50	6.50
d.		Inverted surcharge	110.00	
e.		Vert. pair, one without surcharge	160.00	
f.		"207" (position 29)	*250.00*	

Nos. 44 and 46 Surcharged in Black, Blue Black, or Red

b

c

d

e

1894-96

56 A13 (b) 1c on 2c (Bk) .75 .30
a. "Centav" 5.00 5.00
b. Double surcharge 75.00
c. As "a," dbl. surcharge 150.00
d. Blue black surcharge 20.00 20.00
e. Dbl. surch., one inverted 150.00
57 A13 (c) 1c on 5c (R) ('95) .50 .25
a. Inverted surcharge 3.00 3.00
b. "1894" instead of "1895" 3.50 3.00
c. Double surcharge 50.00
58 A13 (d) 1c on 5c (R) ('95) .75 .25
a. Inverted surcharge 50.00 50.00
b. Double surcharge 50.00
59 A13 (e) 1c on 5c (R) ('96) 1.25 .40
a. Inverted surcharge 50.00 50.00
b. Double surcharge 50.00
Nos. 56-59 (4) 3.25 1.20

Nos. 56-58 may be found with thick or thin "1" in the new value.

National Arms and President J. M. Reyna Barrios
A21

1897, Jan. 1 **Engr.** **Unwmk.**

60 A21 1c blk, *gray* .55 .55
61 A21 2c blk, *grnsh gray* .55 .55
62 A21 6c blk, *brn org* .55 .55
63 A21 10c blk, *dl bl* .55 .55
64 A21 12c blk, *rose red* .55 .55
65 A21 18c blk, *grysh white* 9.50 9.50
66 A21 20c blk, *scarlet* 1.00 1.00
67 A21 25c blk, *bis brn* 1.60 1.00
68 A21 50c blk, *redsh brn* 1.00 1.00
69 A21 75c blk, *gray* 52.50 52.50
70 A21 100c blk, *bl grn* 1.00 1.00
71 A21 150c blk, *dl rose* 105.00 *135.00*
72 A21 200c blk, *magenta* 1.00 1.00
73 A21 500c blk, *yel grn* 1.00 1.00
Nos. 60-73 (14) 176.35 *205.75*

Issued for Central American Exposition.

Stamps often sold as Nos. 65, 69 and 71 are examples with telegraph overprint removed.

Used values for Nos. 60-73 are for canceled-to-order stamps. Postally used examples are worth more.

The paper of Nos. 64 and 66 was originally colored on one side only, but has "bled through" on some examples.

No. 64 Surcharged in Violet

1897, Nov.

74 A21 1c on 12c *rose red* 1.00 1.00
a. Inverted surcharge 30.00 30.00
b. Pair, one without surcharge 75.00
c. Dbl. surch., one invtd. 100.00

Stamps of 1886-93 Surcharged in Red

f

g

1898

75 (f) 1c on 5c violet 1.00 1.00
a. Inverted surcharge 75.00
76 (f) 1c on 50c ol grn 1.50 1.25
a. Inverted surcharge 100.00 100.00
77 (f) 6c on 5c violet 4.50 1.50
78 (f) 6c on 150c dk bl 4.50 3.25
79 (g) 10c on 20c emerald 5.00 4.00
a. Double surch., one inverted 125.00 125.00
Nos. 75-79 (5) 16.50 11.00

Black Surcharge

80 (f) 1c on 25c red org 2.00 2.00
81 (f) 1c on 75c car rose 1.50 1.50
a. Double surcharge 100.00
82 (f) 6c on 10c red 10.00 9.00
83 (f) 6c on 20c emer 5.00 4.00
84 (f) 6c on 100c red brn 5.00 4.00
85 (f) 6c on 200c org yel 5.00 4.00
a. Inverted surcharge 50.00 50.00
Nos. 80-85 (6) 28.50 24.50

Information indicates that No. 77 inverted and double surcharges are counterfeits.

National Emblem — A24

Revenue Stamp Overprinted or Surcharged in Carmine

Perf. 12, 12x14, 14x12

1898, Oct. 8 **Litho.**

86 A24 1c dark blue 1.40 1.40
a. Inverted overprint 12.50 12.50
87 A24 2c on 1c dk bl 2.25 2.25
a. Inverted surcharge 12.50 12.50

Counterfeits exist.

See type A26.

National Emblem — A25

Revenue Stamps Surcharged in Carmine

1898 **Engr.** ***Perf. 12½ to 16***

88 A25 1c on 10c bl gray .75 .75
a. "ENTAVO" 5.00 5.00
89 A25 2c on 5c pur 1.25 1.00
90 A25 2c on 10c bl gray 6.50 *7.00*
a. Double surch., car & blk 100.00 75.00
91 A25 2c on 50c dp bl 9.25 *9.25*
a. Double surch., car & blk 100.00 100.00
Nos. 88-91 (4) 17.75 *18.00*

Black Surcharge

92 A25 2c on 1c lil rose 3.50 2.00
93 A25 2c on 25c red 7.50 8.00
94 A25 6c on 1p purple 4.00 4.50
95 A25 6c on 5p gray vio 7.50 7.50
96 A25 6c on 10p emer 7.50 7.50
Nos. 92-96 (5) 30.00 29.50

Nos. 88 and 90 are found in shades ranging from Prussian blue to slate blue.

Varieties other than those listed are bogus. Counterfeits exist of No. 92.

Soaking in water causes marked fading.

See type A27.

No. 46 Surcharged in Red

1899, Sept. ***Perf. 12***

97 A13 1c on 5c violet .40 .25
a. Inverted surcharge 7.50 7.50
b. Double surcharge 15.00 15.00
c. Double surcharge, one inverted 15.00 15.00

No. 48 Surcharged in Black

1900, Jan.

98 A13 1c on 10c red .65 .50
a. Inverted surcharge 10.00 10.00
b. Double surcharge 75.00 75.00

Quetzal Type of 1886

1900-02 **Engr.**

99 A13 1c dark green .60 .25
100 A13 2c carmine .60 .25
101 A13 5c blue (II) 2.25 1.25
102 A13 6c lt green .75 .25
103 A13 10c bister brown 7.50 1.00
104 A13 20c purple 7.50 7.50
105 A13 20c bister brn ('02) 7.50 7.50
106 A13 25c yellow 7.50 7.50
107 A13 25c blue green ('02) 7.50 7.50
Nos. 99-107 (9) 41.70 33.00

No. 49 Surcharged in Black

1901, May

108 A13 1c on 20c green .50 .50
a. Inverted surcharge 22.50 22.50
b. Double surch., one diagonal 50.00
109 A13 2c on 20c green 1.50 1.50

No. 50 Surcharged in Black

1901, Apr.

110 A13 1c on 25c red org .60 .60
a. Inverted surcharge 25.00 25.00
b. Double surcharge 50.00 50.00

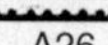
A26

A27

Revenue Stamps Surcharged in Carmine or Black

1902, July ***Perf. 12, 14x12, 12x14***

111 A26 1c on 1c dk blue 1.10 1.10
a. Double surcharge 20.00
b. Inverted surcharge 20.00
112 A26 2c on 1c dk blue 1.10 1.10
a. Double surcharge 90.00
b. Inverted surcharge 25.00

Perf. 14, 15

113 A27 6c on 25c red (Bk) 2.50 2.50
a. Double surch., one invtd. 75.00 75.00
Nos. 111-113 (3) 4.70 4.70

National Emblem — A28

Statue of Justo Rufino Barrios — A29

"La Reforma" Palace — A30

Temple of Minerva — A31

Lake Amatitlán — A32

Cathedral in Guatemala — A33

Columbus Theater — A34

Artillery Barracks — A35

Monument to Columbus — A36

School for Indians — A37

1902 **Engr.** ***Perf. 12 to 16***

114 A28 1c grn & claret .25 .25
a. Horiz. pair, imperf. vert. 100.00
115 A29 2c lake & blk .25 .25
a. Horiz. or vert. pair, imperf. btwn. 150.00
116 A30 5c blue & blk .30 .25
a. 5c ultra & blk .75 .40
b. Imperf., pair 100.00 100.00
c. Horiz. pair, imperf. vert. 100.00
117 A31 6c bister & grn .30 .25
a. Horiz. pair, imperf. btwn. 150.00
118 A32 10c orange & bl .40 .40
a. Horiz. pair, imperf. vert. 100.00
119 A33 20c rose lil & blk .60 .40
a. Horiz. pair, imperf. vert. 100.00
120 A34 50c red brn & bl .45 .40
a. Vert. pair, imperf. btwn. 350.00
121 A35 75c gray lil & blk .55 .40
a. Horiz. pair, imperf. btwn. 150.00
b. Horiz. pair, imperf. vert. 100.00
122 A36 1p brown & blk .85 .40
a. Horiz. pair, imperf. btwn. 150.00
123 A37 2p ver & blk 1.00 .85
Nos. 114-123 (10) 4.95 3.85

See Nos. 210, 212-214, 219, 223, 239-241, 243. For overprints and surcharges see Nos. 133, 135-139, 144-157, 168, 170-171, 178, 192-194, 298-299, 301, C19, C27, C123.

Issues of 1886-1900 Surcharged in Black or Carmine

1903, Apr. 18 *Perf. 12*

124 A13 25c on 1c dk grn 1.25 .55
a. Inverted surcharge 50.00 50.00
125 A13 25c on 2c carmine 1.50 .55
126 A13 25c on 6c lt grn 2.50 1.75
a. Inverted surcharge 40.00 40.00
127 A13 25c on 10c bis brn 7.50 7.00
128 A13 25c on 75c rose 10.00 10.00
129 A13 25c on 150c dk bl (C) 9.00 9.00
130 A13 25c on 200c yellow 10.00 10.00
Nos. 124-130 (7) 41.75 38.85

Forgeries and bogus varieties exist.

Declaration of Independence A38

1907, Jan. 1 *Perf. 13½ to 15*

132 A38 12½c ultra & blk .45 .45
a. Horiz. pair, imperf. btwn. 150.00

For surcharge see No. 134.

Nos. 118, 119 and 132 Surcharged in Black or Red

1908, May

133 A32 1c on 10c org & bl .30 .30
a. Double surcharge 25.00
b. Inverted surcharge 15.00 15.00
c. Pair, one without surcharge 50.00
134 A38 2c on 12½c ultra & blk (R) .25 .25
a. Horiz. or vert. pair, imperf. btwn. 100.00
b. Inverted surcharge 15.00 10.00
c. Double surcharge 30.00
135 A33 6c on 20c rose lil & blk .45 .25
a. Inverted surcharge 20.00 20.00
Nos. 133-135 (3) 1.00 .80

Similar Surcharge, Dated 1909, in Red or Black on Nos. 121 and 120

1909, Apr.

136 A35 2c on 75c (R) .55 .55
137 A34 6c on 50c (R) 62.50 62.50
a. Double surcharge 125.00 125.00
138 A34 6c on 50c (Bk) .30 .30
Nos. 136-138 (3) 63.35 63.35

Counterfeits exist of Nos. 137, 137a.

No. 123 Surcharged in Black

139 A37 12½c on 2p ver & blk .30 .30
a. Inverted surcharge 25.00 25.00
b. Period omitted after "1909" 12.50 12.50

Counterfeits exist.

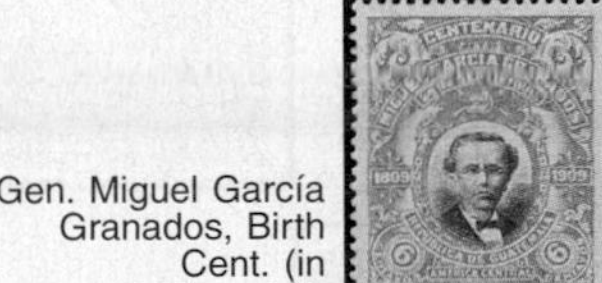

Gen. Miguel García Granados, Birth Cent. (in 1909) — A39

1910, Feb. 11 *Perf. 14*

140 A39 6c bis & indigo .55 .40
a. Imperf., pair 55.00

Some sheets used for this issue contained a two-line watermark, "SPECIAL POSTAGE PAPER / LONDON." For surcharge see No. 143.

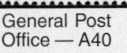

General Post Office — A40

Pres. Manuel Estrada Cabrera — A41

1911, June *Perf. 12*

141 A40 25c bl & blk .55 .25
a. Center inverted 1,750. 900.00
142 A41 5p red & blk .65 .65
a. Center inverted 30.00 27.50

Nos. 116, 118 and 140 Surcharged in Black or Red

h

i

j

1911 *Perf. 14*

143 A39 (h) 1c on 6c 25.00 9.75
a. Double surcharge 75.00 75.00
144 A30 (i) 2c on 5c (R) 1.60 .85
145 A32 (j) 6c on 10c 1.25 1.25
a. Double surcharge 50.00
Nos. 143-145 (3) 27.85 11.85

See watermark note after No. 140. Forgeries exist.

Nos. 119-121 Surcharged in Black

k

l

m

1912, Sept.

147 A33 (k) 1c on 20c .40 .40
a. Inverted surcharge 12.50 12.50
b. Double surcharge 15.00 15.00
148 A34 (l) 2c on 50c .40 .40
a. Inverted surcharge 12.50 12.50
b. Double surcharge 12.50
c. Double inverted surcharge 25.00
149 A35 (m) 5c on 75c .80 .80
a. "191" for "1912" 7.50 7.50
b. Double surcharge 15.00 15.00
c. Inverted surcharge 10.00
Nos. 147-149 (3) 1.60 1.60

Forgeries exist.

Nos. 120, 122 and 123 Surcharged in Blue, Green or Black

n

o

p

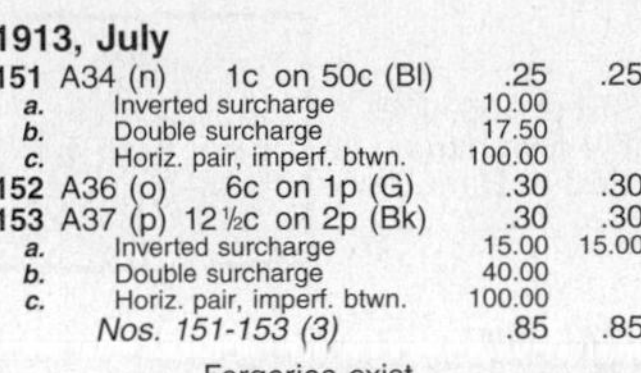

1913, July

151 A34 (n) 1c on 50c (Bl) .25 .25
a. Inverted surcharge 10.00
b. Double surcharge 17.50
c. Horiz. pair, imperf. btwn. 100.00
152 A36 (o) 6c on 1p (G) .30 .30
153 A37 (p) 12½c on 2p (Bk) .30 .30
a. Inverted surcharge 15.00 15.00
b. Double surcharge 40.00
c. Horiz. pair, imperf. btwn. 100.00
Nos. 151-153 (3) .85 .85

Forgeries exist.

Nos. 114 and 115 Surcharged in Black

q

r

s

t

1916-17

154 A28 (q) 2c on 1c ('17) .25 .25
155 A28 (r) 6c on 1c .25 .25
156 A28 (s) 12½c on 1c .25 .25
157 A29 (t) 25c on 2c .25 .25
Nos. 154-157 (4) 1.00 1.00

Numerous errors of value and color, inverted and double surcharges and similar varieties are in the market. They were not regularly issued, but were surreptitiously made and sold.

Counterfeit surcharges abound.

"Liberty" and President Estrada Cabrera — A51

1917, Mar. 15 *Perf. 14, 15*

158 A51 25c dp blue & brown .25 .25

Re-election of President Estrada Cabrera.

Estrada Cabrera and Quetzal — A52

1918 *Perf. 12*

161 A52 1.50p dark blue .30 .25

Radio Station — A54

"Joaquina" Maternity Hospital — A55

"Estrada Cabrera" Vocational School — A56

National Emblem — A57

1919, May 3 *Perf. 14, 15*

162 A54 30c red & blk 2.75 .75
163 A55 60c ol grn & blk .80 .50
164 A56 90c red brn & blk .80 .75
165 A57 3p dp grn & blk 1.75 .50
Nos. 162-165 (4) 6.10 2.50

See Nos. 215, 227. For surcharges see Nos. 166-167, 179-185, 188, 195-198, 245-246, C8-C11, C21-C22.

No. 162 Ovptd. in Blue & Srchd. in Black

1920, Jan. **Unwmk.**

166 A54 2c on 30c red & blk .30 .25
a. Inverted surcharge 12.50 12.50
b. "1920" double 10.00 10.00
c. "1920" omitted 15.00 15.00
d. "2 centavos" omitted 20.00
e. Imperf, pair 100.00
f. Pair, imperf. btwn. 100.00

Nos. 123 and 163 Surcharged

u

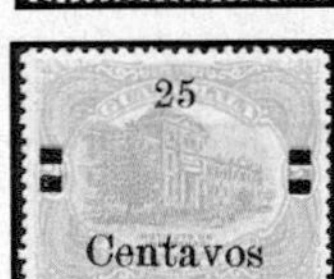

v

1920

167 A55 2c on 60c (Bk & R) .25 .25
a. Inverted surcharge 10.00 10.00
b. "1920" inverted 7.50 7.50
c. "1920" omitted 10.00 10.00
d. "1920" only 10.00
e. Double surcharge 25.00
168 A37 25c on 2p (Bk) .30 .25
a. "35" for "25" 10.00 10.00
b. Large "5" in "25" 10.00 10.00
c. Inverted surcharge 15.00 15.00
d. Double surcharge 25.00

A61

1920

169 A61 25c green .25 .25
a. Double overprint 50.00
b. Double overprint, inverted 75.00

See types A65-A66.

No. 119 Surcharged

1921, Apr.

170 A33 12½c on 20c .25 .25
a. Double surcharge 15.00
b. Inverted surcharge 15.00

No. 121 Surcharged

1921, Apr.
171 A35 50c on 75c lil & blk .50 .30
a. Double surcharge 22.50
b. Inverted surcharge 25.00 25.00

Mayan Stele at Quiriguá — A62

Monument to President Granados — A63

"La Penitenciaria" Bridge — A64

1921, Sept. 1 *Perf. 13½, 14, 15*
172 A62 1.50p blue & org .85 .25
173 A63 5p brown & grn 2.75 1.25
174 A64 15p black & red org 22.50 12.50
Nos. 172-174 (3) 26.10 14.00

See Nos. 216, 228, 229. For surcharges see Nos. 186-187, 189-191, 199-201, 207, 231, 247-251, C1-C5, C12, C23-C24.

Telegraph Stamps Overprinted or Surcharged in Black or Red

A65

A66

1921 *Perf. 14*
175 A65 25c green .25 .25
176 A66 12½c on 25c grn (R) .25 .25
177 A66 12½c on 25c grn 15.00 15.00
Nos. 175-177 (3) 15.50 15.50

Nos. 119, 163 and 164 Surcharged in Black or Red

w

x

1922, Mar.
178 A33(w) 12½c on 20c .25 .25
a. Inverted surcharge 10.00
179 A55(w) 12½c on 60c (R) .50 .50
a. Inverted surcharge 25.00
180 A56(w) 12½c on 90c .50 .50
a. Inverted surcharge 25.00
181 A55(x) 25c on 60c 1.00 1.00
a. Inverted surcharge 20.00
182 A55(x) 25c on 60c (R) 125.00 125.00
183 A56(x) 25c on 90c 1.00 1.00
a. Inverted surcharge 25.00
184 A56(x) 25c on 90c (R) 4.00 4.00
Nos. 178-181,183-184 (6) 7.25 7.25

Counterfeits exist.

Nos. 165, 173-174 Surcharged in Red or Dark Blue

1922, May
185 A57 12½c on 3p grn & blk (R) .25 .25
186 A63 12½c on 5p brn & grn .50 .45
187 A64 12½c on 15p blk & ver .50 .45
Nos. 185-187 (3) 1.25 1.15

Nos. 165, 173-174 Surcharged in Red or Black

Type I

Type II

Type III

Type IV

1922
188 A57 25c on 3p (I) (R) .25 .25
a. Type II .60 .60
b. Type III .60 .60
c. Type IV .30 .30
d. Inverted surcharge 40.00
e. Horiz. or vert. pair, imperf. btwn. (I) 125.00
189 A63 25c on 5p (I) 1.00 2.00
a. Type II 2.00 3.00
b. Type III 2.00 3.00
c. Type IV 1.00 2.00
190 A64 25c on 15p (I) 1.00 1.50
a. Type II 2.00 3.00
b. Type III 2.00 3.00
c. Type IV 1.00 1.50
191 A64 25c on 15p (I) (R) 22.50 30.00
a. Type II 40.00 45.00
b. Type III 45.00 45.00
c. Type IV 30.00 35.00
Nos. 188-191 (4) 24.75 33.75

Stamps of 1902-21 Surcharged in Dark Blue or Red

Type V

Type VI

Type VII

Type VIII

Type IX

1922, Aug. **On Nos. 121-123**
192 A35 25c on 75c (V) .40 .40
a. Type VI .40 .40
b. Type VII 1.75 1.75
c. Type VIII 5.50 4.75
d. Type IX 6.50 6.00
193 A36 25c on 1p (V) .30 .30
a. Type VI .30 .30
b. Type VII 1.25 1.25
c. Type VIII 2.50 2.50
d. Type IX 4.00 3.50
e. Inverted surcharge 40.00
194 A37 25c on 2p (V) .45 .45
a. Type VI .45 .45
b. Type VII 1.25 1.25
c. Type VIII 4.00 4.00
d. Type IX 6.50 6.50

On Nos. 162-165
195 A54 25c on 30c (V) .45 .45
a. Type VI .45 .45
b. Type VII 1.25 1.25
c. Type VIII 5.50 5.50
d. Type IX 6.50 6.50
196 A55 25c on 60c (V) 1.00 1.50
a. Type VI 1.25 1.50
b. Type VII 6.25 7.75
c. Type VIII 8.50 9.50
d. Type IX 10.00 11.00
197 A56 25c on 90c (V) 1.00 1.50
a. Type VI 1.50 2.00
b. Type VII 6.00 6.75
c. Type VIII 8.50 9.50
d. Type IX 10.00 11.00
198 A57 25c on 3p (R) (V) .40 .40
a. Type VI .40 .40
b. Type VII 1.25 1.00
c. Type VIII 6.00 4.50
d. Type IX 6.50 6.00
e. Inverted surcharge 50.00

On Nos. 172-174
199 A62 25c on 1.50p (V) .30 .30
a. Type VI .30 .30
b. Type VII 1.25 1.00
c. Type VIII 3.00 3.00
d. Type IX 4.50 4.50
e. Inverted surcharge 40.00
200 A63 25c on 5p (V) .75 .90
a. Type VI .80 1.00
b. Type VII 3.00 3.50
c. Type VIII 5.50 6.00
d. Type IX 8.00 8.50
201 A64 25c on 15p (V) .85 .90
a. Type VI 1.50 1.50
b. Type VII 5.00 5.50
c. Type VIII 6.50 6.50
d. Type IX 12.00 12.00
Nos. 192-201 (10) 5.90 7.10

Centenary Palace — A69

National Palace at Antigua — A70

Printed by Waterlow & Sons

1922 *Perf. 14, 14½*
202 A69 12½c green .30 .25
a. Horiz. or vert. pair, imperf. btwn. 100.00
203 A70 25c brown .30 .25

See Nos. 211, 221, 234.

Columbus Theater A71

Quetzal A72

Granados Monument — A73

Litho. by Castillo Bros.

1924, Feb. *Perf. 12*
204 A71 50c rose .50 .25
a. Imperf., pair 7.50
b. Horiz. or vert. pair, imperf. btwn. 25.00
205 A72 1p dark green 2.25 .25
a. Imperf. vertically 15.00
b. Vert. pair, imperf. btwn. 20.00
c. Imperf., pair 7.50
206 A73 5p orange 1.25 .50
a. Imperf., pair 8.50
b. Horiz. pair, imperf. btwn. 20.00
Nos. 204-206 (3) 4.00 1.00

For surcharges see Nos. 208-209.

Nos. 172 and 206 Surcharged

1924, July
207 A62 1p on 1.50p bl & org .30 .25
208 A73 1.25p on 5p orange .50 .50
a. "UN PESO 25 Cents." omitted 40.00
b. Horiz. pair, imperf. btwn. 25.00

No. 208 Overprinted

1924
209 A73 1p on 5p orange .50 .50

Types of 1902-22 Issues Engr. by Perkins Bacon & Co.

1924, Aug. **Re-engraved** *Perf. 14*
210 A31 6c bister .25 .25
211 A70 25c brown .25 .25
212 A34 50c red .25 .25
213 A36 1p orange brn .25 .25
214 A37 2p orange .35 .25
215 A57 3p deep green 2.00 .50
216 A64 15p black 5.00 2.75
Nos. 210-216 (7) 8.35 4.50

The designs of the stamps of 1924 differ from those of the 1902-22 issues in many details which are too minute to illustrate. The re-engraved issue may be readily distinguished by the imprint "Perkins Bacon & Co. Ld. Londres."

Pres. Justo Rufino Barrios A74

Lorenzo Montúfar A75

1924, Aug.
217 A74 1.25p ultra .25 .25
218 A75 2.50p dk violet 1.00 .25

See Nos. 224, 226. For surcharges see Nos. 232, C6, C20.

Aurora Park — A76

National Post Office — A77

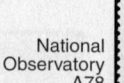

National Observatory A78

Types of 1921-24 Re-engraved and New Designs Dated 1926

Engraved by Waterlow & Sons, Ltd.

1926, July-Aug. *Perf. 12½*
219 A31 6c ocher .25 .25
220 A76 12½c green .25 .25
221 A70 25c brown .25 .25

222	A77	50c red	.25	.25
223	A36	1p orange brn	.25	.25
224	A74	1.50p dk blue	.25	.25
225	A78	2p orange	1.25	1.00
226	A75	2.50p dk violet	1.50	1.25
227	A57	3p dark green	.45	.25
228	A63	5p brown vio	1.00	.40
229	A64	15p black	6.00	2.75
		Nos. 219-229 (11)	11.70	7.15

These stamps may be distinguished from those of the same designs in preceding issues by the imprint "Waterlow & Sons, Limited, Londres," the date, "1926," and the perforation.

See Nos. 233, 242. For surcharge see No. 230.

Nos. 225-226, 228 Surcharged in Various Colors

1928

230	A78	½c on 2p (Bl)	.65	.50
a.		Inverted surcharge	12.50	
231	A63	½c on 5p (Bk)	.35	.25
a.		Inverted surcharge	10.00	10.00
b.		Double surcharge	50.00	
c.		Blue surcharge	45.00	45.00
d.		Blue and black surcharge	50.00	50.00
232	A75	1c on 2.50p (R)	.35	.25
b.		Double surcharge		50.00
		Nos. 230-232 (3)	1.35	1.00

Barrios — A79

Montúfar — A80

Granados A81

General Orellana A82

Coat of Arms of Guatemala City — A83

Engraved by T. De la Rue & Co.

1929, Jan. *Perf. 14*

233	A78	½c yellow grn	.75	.25
234	A70	1c dark brown	.25	.25
235	A79	2c deep blue	.25	.25
236	A80	3c dark violet	.25	.25
237	A81	4c orange	.25	.25
238	A82	5c dk carmine	.50	.25
239	A31	10c brown	.40	.25
240	A36	15c ultra	.50	.25
241	A29	25c brown org	1.00	.25
242	A76	30c green	.90	.30
243	A32	50c pale rose	2.00	.60
244	A83	1q black	3.00	.40
		Nos. 233-244 (12)	10.05	3.55

Nos. 233, 234 and 239 to 243 differ from the illustrations in many minor details, particularly in the borders.

See No. 300 for bisect of No. 235. For overprints and surcharges see Nos. 297, C13, C17-C18, C25-C26, C28, E1, RA17-RA18.

No. 227 Surcharged in Black or Red

1929, Dec. 28 *Perf. 12½, 13*

245	A57	3c on 3p dk grn (Blk)	1.25	*1.90*
a.		Inverted surcharge	15.00	15.00
246	A57	5c on 3p dk grn (R)	1.25	*1.90*
a.		Inverted surcharge	15.00	15.00

Inauguration of the Eastern Railroad connecting Guatemala and El Salvador.

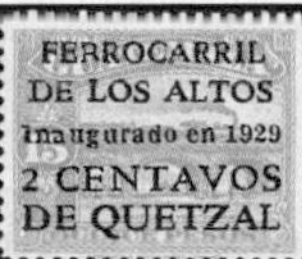

No. 229 Surcharged in Red

1930, Mar. 30 **Unwmk.**

247	A64	1c on 15p black	1.25	*1.40*
248	A64	2c on 15p black	1.25	*1.40*
249	A64	3c on 15p black	1.25	*1.40*
250	A64	5c on 15p black	1.25	*1.40*
251	A64	15c on 15p black	1.25	1.40
		Nos. 247-251 (5)	6.25	*7.00*

Opening of Los Altos electric railway.

Hydroelectric Dam — A85

Los Altos Railway A86

Railroad Station A87

1930, Mar. 30 **Typo.** *Perf. 12*

252	A85	2c brn vio & blk	1.40	*1.90*
a.		Horiz. pair, imperf. btwn.	125.00	
253	A86	3c dp red & blk	2.75	*2.75*
a.		Vert. pair, imperf. btwn.	125.00	
254	A87	5c buff & dk bl	2.75	*2.75*
		Nos. 252-254 (3)	6.90	*7.40*

Opening of Los Altos electric railway. Exist imperf.

Mayan Stele at Quiriguá — A91

1932, Apr. 8 **Engr.**

258	A91	3c carmine rose	1.90	.40

See Nos. 302-303.

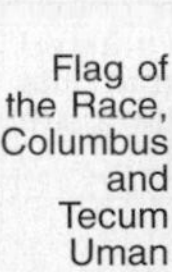

Flag of the Race, Columbus and Tecum Uman A92

1933, Aug. 3 **Litho.** *Perf. 12½*

259	A92	½c dark green	.75	*.75*
260	A92	1c dull brown	1.25	1.10
261	A92	2c deep blue	1.25	1.10
262	A92	3c dull violet	1.25	.75
263	A92	5c rose	1.25	1.10
		Nos. 259-263 (5)	5.75	*4.80*

Day of the Race and 441st anniv. of the sailing of Columbus from Palos, Spain, Aug. 3, 1492, on his 1st voyage to the New World. The 3c and 5c exist imperf.

Birthplace of Barrios A93

View of San Lorenzo A94

Justo Rufino Barrios A95

National Emblem and Locomotive A96

General Post Office — A97

Telegraph Building and Barrios A98

Military Academy A99

National Police Headquarters — A100

Jorge Ubico and J. R. Barrios A101

1935, July 19 **Photo.**

264	A93	½c yel grn & mag	.40	*.45*
265	A94	1c org red & pck bl	.40	*.45*
266	A95	2c orange & blk	.40	*.55*
267	A96	3c car rose & pck bl	4.50	2.25
268	A97	4c pck bl & org red	4.50	*10.00*
269	A98	5c bl grn & brn	3.25	*4.25*
270	A99	10c slate grn & rose lake	4.50	*5.50*
271	A100	15c ol grn & org brn	4.50	*4.75*
272	A101	25c scarlet & bl	4.50	*4.75*
		Nos. 264-272 (9)	26.95	*32.95*

General Barrios. See Nos. C29-C31.

Lake Atitlán A102

Quetzal A103

Legislative Building — A104

1935, Oct. 10

273	A102	1c brown & crim	.25	.25
274	A103	3c rose car & pck grn	.70	.25
275	A103	3c red org & pck grn	.70	.25
276	A104	4c brt bl & dp rose	.35	.25
		Nos. 273-276 (4)	2.00	1.00

See No. 277. For surcharges see Nos. B1-B3.

No. 273 perforated diagonally through the center

1936, June *Perf. 12½x12*

277	A102	(½c) brown & crimson	.25	.25
a.		Unsevered pair	.50	.60

Bureau of Printing — A105

Map of Guatemala A106

1936, Sept. 24 *Perf. 12½*

278	A105	½c green & pur	.25	.25
279	A106	5c blue & dk brn	.90	.25

For surcharge see No. B4.

Quetzal A107

Union Park, Quezaltenango A108

Gen. Jorge Ubico on Horseback A109

1c, Tower of the Reformer. 3c, National Post Office. 4c, Government Building, Retalhuleu. 5c, Legislative Palace entrance. 10c, Custom House. 15c, Aurora Airport Custom House. 25c, National Fair. 50c, Residence of Presidential Guard. 1.50q, General Ubico, portrait standing, no cap.

1937, May 20

280 A107 ½c pck bl & car rose .70 *.45*
281 A107 1c ol gray & red brn .70 .35
282 A108 2c vio & car rose .60 .35
283 A108 3c brn vio & brt bl .50 .25
284 A108 4c yel & dl ol grn 3.00 *3.00*
285 A107 5c crim & brt vio 3.00 3.00
286 A107 10c mag & brn blk 4.00 *4.00*
287 A108 15c ultra & cop red 3.00 *3.00*
288 A108 25c red org & vio 4.00 *4.00*
289 A108 50c dk grn & org red 6.00 *6.00*
290 A109 1q mag & blk *50.00 50.00*
291 A109 1.50q red brn & blk *50.00 50.00*
Nos. 280-291 (12) 125.50 124.40

Second term of President Ubico.

Mayan Calendar A119

Natl. Flower (White Nun Orchid) A120

Quetzal — A121

Map of Guatemala A122

1939, Sept. 7 ***Perf. 13x12, 12½***

292 A119 ½c grn & red brn *.85* .25
293 A120 2c bl & gray blk *5.00* 1.00
294 A121 3c red org & turq grn *6.50* 1.75
295 A121 3c ol bis & turq grn *6.50* 1.75
296 A122 5c blue & red *5.75* 5.75
Nos. 292-296 (5) 24.60 10.50

For overprints see Nos. 324, C157.

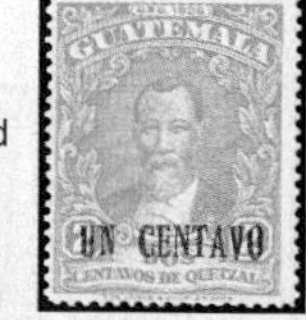

No. 235 Surcharged in Red

1939, Sept. ***Perf. 14***

297 A79 1c on 2c deep blue .25 .25

Stamps of 1929 Surcharged in Blue

y

z

1940, June

298 A29 (y) 1c on 25c brn org .25 .25
299 A32 (z) 5c on 50c pale rose (bar 10x¾mm) .25 .25
a. Bar 12½x2mm .30 .25
b. Bar 12½x1mm 50.00 5.00

No. 235 perforated diagonally through the center

1941, Aug. 16 ***Perf. 14x11½***

300 A79 (1c) deep blue .30 .25
a. Unsevered pair .80 .80

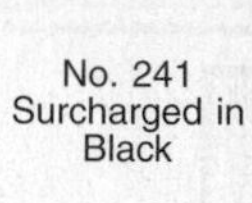

No. 241 Surcharged in Black

1941, Dec. 24 ***Perf. 14***

301 A29 ½c on 25c brn org .30 .30

Type of 1932 Inscribed "1942"

1942 Engr. *Perf. 12*

302 A91 3c green .95 .25
303 A91 3c deep blue .95 .25

Issued to publicize the coffee of Guatemala.

Vase of Guastatoya A123

Home for the Aged A124

1942, July 13 **Unwmk.**

304 A123 ½c red brown .35 .25
305 A124 1c carmine rose .35 .25

National Printing Works — A125

1943, Jan. 25 Engr. *Perf. 11, 12*

307 A125 2c scarlet .25 .25
a. Vert. pair, imperf. horiz. 35.00

Rafael Maria Landivar — A126

1943, Aug. ***Perf. 11***

308 A126 5c brt ultra .25 .25

Death of Rafael Landivar, poet, 150th anniv.

National Palace A127

1944, June 30 ***Perf. 11***

309 A127 3c dk blue green .30 .30

Inauguration of the Natl. Palace, Nov. 10, 1943.

See Nos. C137A-C139. For overprints see Nos. 311-311A, C133.

Ruins of Zakuleu A128

1945, Jan. 6

310 A128 ½c black brown .25 .25

Type of 1944 Overprinted in Blue

1945, Jan. 15

311 A127 3c deep blue .30 .25

Overprint Bar 1mm Thick

311A A127 3c deep blue 1.00 .70

Allegory of the Revolution — A129

1945, Feb. 20

312 A129 3c grayish blue .30 .25
Nos. 312,C128-C131 (5) 2.50 1.25

Revolution of 10/20/44.

Torch — A130

1945, Oct. 20

313 A130 3c deep blue .25 .25

1st anniv. of the Revolution of Oct. 20, 1944. See No. C135-C136.

José Milla y Vidaurre A131

Payo Enriquez de Rivera A132

1945 ***Perf. 11, 12½***

314 A131 1c deep green .25 .25
315 A132 2c dull lilac .25 .25
Nos. 314-315,C134-C134A (4) 2.20 1.80

See Nos. 343-346, 379, C137, C269, C311-C315.

Catalogue values for unused stamps in this section, from this point to the end of the section, are for Never Hinged items.

José Batres y Montufar — A133

1946 **Unwmk.**

316 A133 ½c sepia .30 .25
317 A133 3c deep blue .30 .25

See Nos. 319, C142.

UPU Monument Bern, Switzerland A134

1946, Aug. 5 Photo. *Perf. 14x13*

318 A134 1c vio & gray brn .35 .25
Nos. 318,C140-C141 (3) 1.50 .80

Centenary of the first postage stamp.

Batres Type of 1946

1947, Nov. 11 Engr. *Perf. 11, 12½*

319 A133 3c dull green .30 .25

Symbolical of Labor — A135

1948, May 14 Unwmk. *Perf. 11*

320 A135 1c deep green .50 .25
a. Perf. 12½ 5.00
321 A135 2c sepia .50 .25
a. Perf. 12½ 5.00
322 A135 3c deep ultra .50 .25
a. Perf. 12½ 5.00
323 A135 5c rose carmine .50 .25
a. Perf. 12½ 5.00
Nos. 320-323 (4) 2.00 1.00

Labor Day, May 1, 1948. Other perfs. and compound perfs. exist.

No. 296 Overprinted in Carmine at Lower Right

1948, May 14 ***Perf. 12½***

324 A122 5c blue & red .50 .30

Bartolomé de las Casas and Indian — A136

1949, Oct. 8 Engr. *Perf. 12½, 13½*

325 A136 ½c red .25 .25
326 A136 1c black brown .25 .25
327 A136 2c dk blue grn .25 .25
a. 2c green, perf. 11, 11½ ('60) .25 .25
328 A136 3c rose pink .25 .25
a. 3c car, perf. 11, 12½, 13½ ('64) .30 .25
329 A136 4c ultra .25 .25
Nos. 325-329 (5) 1.25 1.25

See Nos. 384-386.

Gathering Coffee — A137

1c, Poptun Agricultural Colony. 2c, Banana trees. 3c, Sugar cane field. 6c, Intl. Bridge.

1950, Feb. **Photo.** ***Perf. 14***

330 A137 ½c vio bl, pink & ol gray .35 .25
331 A137 1c red brn, yel & grnsh gray .35 .25
332 A137 2c ol grn, pink & bl gray .35 .25
333 A137 3c pur, bl & org brn .35 .25
334 A137 6c dp org, aqua & vio .60 .25
Nos. 330-334 (5) 2.00 1.25

See Nos. 347-349.

Badge of Public and Social Assistance Ministry — A138

Nurse — A139

Map Showing Hospitals — A140

1950-51 **Litho.** ***Perf. 12, 12½x12***

335 A138 1c car rose & bl .25 .25
336 A139 3c dl grn & rose red .35 .25

Perf. 12

337 A140 5c dk bl & choc ('51) .50 .25
a. Souvenir sheet, #335-337 8.00 8.00
Nos. 335-337 (3) 1.10 .75

Issued to publicize the National Hospitals Fund.

No. 337a exists perf. and imperf., same values.

A perforated souvenir sheet is known which is similar to No. 337a, but with the 5c stamp like the basic stamp of No. C232 (with "BRITISH HONDURAS" inscription).

See Nos. C177-C180a. For overprint see No. C232.

Motorcycle Messenger A141

1951, May 22 ***Perf. 14x12½***

337B A141 4c bl grn & gray blk .65 .25

Issued for regular postage, although inscribed "Expreso." See No. E2.

Souvenir Sheet

A142

Typographed and Engraved

1951, Oct. 22 ***Imperf.***

338 A142 Sheet of 2 5.00 5.00
a. 1c rose carmine 2.00 1.50
b. 10c deep ultramarine 2.00 1.50

75th anniv. (in 1949) of the UPU.
For overprint see No. 419.

A143

Modern Model Schools A144

1951, Oct. 22 **Photo.** ***Perf. 13½x14***

339 A143 ½c purple & sepia .35 .25
340 A144 1c brn car & dl grn .35 .25
341 A143 2c grnsh bl & red brn .35 .25
342 A144 4c blk brn & rose vio .35 .25
Nos. 339-342 (4) 1.40 1.00

Enriquez de Rivera Type of 1945 Re-engraved

1952, June 4 ***Perf. 12½***

343 A132 ½c violet .25 .25
344 A132 1c rose carmine .25 .25
345 A132 2c green .25 .25
346 A132 4c orange .45 .25
Nos. 343-346 (4) 1.20 1.00

A panel containing the dates "1660-1951" has been added below the portrait.

Produce Type of 1950

Designs: ½c, Sugar cane field. 1c, Banana trees. 2c, Poptun Agricultural Colony.

1953, Feb. 11 **Photo.** ***Perf. 13½***

347 A137 ½c dk brn & dp bl .70 .25
348 A137 1c red org & ol grn .70 .25
349 A137 2c dk car & gray blk .70 .25
Nos. 347-349 (3) 2.10 .75

Issued to publicize farming.

Rafael Alvarez Ovalle and José Joaquin Palma A145

1953, May 13

350 A145 ½c purple & blk .55 .40
351 A145 1c dk grn & org brn .55 .40
352 A145 2c org brn & ol grn .55 .40
353 A145 3c dk bl & ol brn .55 .40
Nos. 350-353 (4) 2.20 1.60

Authors of Guatemala's national anthem.
For overprints see Nos. 374-378.

Quetzal — A146

1954, Sept. 27 **Engr.** ***Perf. 12½, 11***

354 A146 1c dp violet blue 1.75 .25

See Nos. 367-373, 380-382A, 434-444. For overprint see No. 395.

Mario Camposeco — A147

10c, Carlos Aguirre Matheu. 15c, Goalkeeper.

1955-56 **Unwmk.** ***Perf. 12½***

355 A147 4c violet 1.00 .25
356 A147 4c carmine ('56) 1.00 .25
357 A147 4c blue grn ('56) 1.00 .25
358 A147 10c bluish grn 3.25 .75
359 A147 15c dark blue 3.25 2.00
Nos. 355-359 (5) 9.50 3.50

50 years of Soccer in Guatemala.

Globe and Red Cross — A148

Designs: 3c, Red Cross, Telephone and "5110." 4c, Nurse, patient and Red Cross flag.

1956, May 23 ***Perf. 13x12½***

360 A148 1c brown & car .30 .25
361 A148 3c dk green & red .30 .25
362 A148 4c dk sl grn & red .35 .25
Nos. 360-362 (3) .95 .75

Red Cross. See Nos. B5-B7, CB5-CB7. For surcharges see Nos. CB8-CB10.

Dagger-Cross of the Liberation — A149

1c, Map showing 2,000 km. (1,243 miles) of new roads. 3c, Oil production.

1956 **Engr.** ***Perf. 12½***

363 A149 ½c violet .30 .25
364 A149 1c dk blue grn .30 .25

Perf. 11

365 A149 3c sepia .30 .25
Nos. 363-365 (3) .90 .75

Liberation of 1954-55. Issue dates: ½c, 1c, July 27; 3c, Oct. 31. See Nos. C210-C218.

Quetzal Type of 1954

1957-58 ***Perf. 11, 12½***

367 A146 2c violet .85 .25
368 A146 3c carmine rose 1.00 .25
369 A146 3c ultra 1.00 .25
a. 3c dark blue, perf. 11½ ('72) — —
370 A146 4c orange 1.25 .25
371 A146 5c brown 1.75 .25
372 A146 5c org ver ('58) 1.75 .25
373 A146 6c yellow grn 2.25 .25
Nos. 367-373 (7) 9.85 1.75

No. 368 is only perf. 12½. The 2c, 4c and No. 369 are found in perf. 11 and 12½. Other values are only perf. 11.

No. 350 Ovptd. in Blue, Black, Carmine, Red Orange or Green

1958, Nov.-Dec. **Photo.** ***Perf. 13½***

374 A145 ½c purple & blk (Bl) .65 *.65*
375 A145 ½c purple & blk (Bk) .65 *.65*
376 A145 ½c purple & blk (C) .65 *.65*
377 A145 ½c purple & blk (RO) .65 *.65*
378 A145 ½c purple & blk (G) .65 *.65*
Nos. 374-378 (5) 3.25 *3.25*

Cent. of the birth of Rafael Alvarez Ovalle, composer of Guatemala's national anthem.

Re-engraved Rivera Type of 1945

1959, Sept. 12 **Engr.** ***Perf. 11, 12½***

379 A132 4c gray blue .30 .25

See note after No. 346.

Quetzal Type of 1954

1960-63 **Unwmk.** ***Perf. 11***

380 A146 2c brown ('61) .90 .35
381 A146 4c lt violet 1.50 .35
382 A146 5c blue green 1.75 .35

Perf. 12½

382A A146 5c slate gray ('63) 2.75 .55
Nos. 380-382A (4) 6.90 1.60

Romulus and Remus Statue, Rome — A150

1961 **Photo.** ***Perf. 14***

383 A150 3c blue .65 .25

Inauguration of the Plaza Italia.

Las Casas Type of 1949

Perf. 11, 11½, 12½, 13½

1962-64 **Engr.**

384 A136 ½c blue .25 .25
385 A136 1c brt violet ('64) .25 .25
386 A136 4c brown ('64) .25 .25
Nos. 384-386 (3) .75 .75

1871 Stamp — A151

1963-66 **Unwmk.** ***Perf. 11***

387 A151 10c carmine .40 .25
388 A151 10c slate ('64) .40 .25

Perf. 11½

389 A151 10c olive brn ('66) .40 .25
390 A151 20c dp purple ('64) .65 .30
391 A151 20c dk blue ('65) .65 .30
Nos. 387-391 (5) 2.50 1.35

For souvenir sheet, see No. C310.

Pedro Bethancourt Comforting Sick Man — A152

1964, Jan. 6 **Engr.** ***Perf. 11***

394 A152 2½c olive bister .50 .25

Beatification (1962-63) of Pedro Bethancourt (1626-67). See Nos. C319-C322. For overprints see Nos. C381-C382.

Quetzal Type of 1957-58 Overprinted in Blue

1964, Dec. 29 **Engr.** ***Perf. 12½***

395 A146 4c orange .50 .25

15th anniv. (in 1963) of the Intl. Soc. of Guatemala Collectors.

Map of Guatemala and British Honduras A153

1967, Apr. 28 **Litho.** ***Perf. 14x13½***

396 A153 4c ol, vio bl & dp rose .55 .30
397 A153 5c ocher, vio bl & dp org .45 .30
398 A153 6c dp org, vio bl & gray .45 .30
Nos. 396-398 (3) 1.45 .90

Issued to state Guatemala's claim to British Honduras.

For overprints see Nos. C411-C413.

Quetzal, Mayan Ball Game Goal — A154

Lithographed and Engraved

1968, Oct. 15 ***Perf. 11½***

399 A154 1c blk, lt grn & red .40 .25
400 A154 5c yel, lt grn & red .55 .25
401 A154 8c org, lt grn & red .65 .25
402 A154 15c bl, lt grn & red 1.10 .25
403 A154 30c lt vio, lt grn & red 2.00 1.10
Nos. 399-403 (5) 4.70 2.10

19th Olympic Games, Mexico City, 10/12-27.
The 1c, 5c, 8c, 15c also exist perf 12½, 1c, 8c, perf 13½.
See Nos. 412-415. For overprints see Nos. 408-411, C431-C435.

Child and Poinsettia — A155

1968-70 **Typo.** ***Perf. 13½***

404 A155 2½c grn, dp bis & car .30 .25
405 A155 2½c grn, org & car ('70) .45 *.55*
406 A155 5c green, gray & car .45 .25
407 A155 21c green, lil & car 1.00 .85
Nos. 404-407 (4) 2.20 1.90

Issued to help abandoned children.

Type of 1968 Overprinted in Black or Red

1970, Mar. 19 **Litho.** ***Perf. 13½***

408 A154 8c org, lt grn & red .50 *1.25*
409 A154 8c org, lt grn & red (R) .50 *1.25*

Perf. 12½

410 A154 15c bl, lt grn & red .75 *1.25*
411 A154 15c bl, lt grn & red (R) .75 *1.25*
Nos. 408-411 (4) 2.50 *5.00*

50th anniv. of ILO. Gold overprint believed to be a trial color.

Type of 1968

1971 **Typo. & Engr.** ***Perf. 11½***

412 A154 1c gray, yel grn & red .30 .25

Typo.

413 A154 5c brt pink, yel grn & red .55 .25
414 A154 5c brown, grn & red .55 .25
415 A154 5c dk bl, grn & red .55 .55
Nos. 412-415 (4) 1.95 1.30

Mayas and CARE Package — A156

1971-72 **Typo.** ***Perf. 13½***

416 A156 1c black & multi .30 .25

Perf. 11½

417 A156 1c violet & multi ('72) .30 .25
418 A156 1c brown & multi ('72) .30 .25
Nos. 416-418 (3) .90 .75

10th anniv. of CARE in Guatemala, a US-Canadian Cooperative for American Relief Everywhere. Exist imperf. See No. C459.

No. 338 (trimmed) Overprinted in Orange

Souvenir Sheet

Typo. & Engr.

1972, Oct. 23 ***Imperf.***

419 A142 Sheet of 2 1.50 *1.50*
a. 1c rose carmine ("Munich") .40 *.40*
b. 10c deep ultra ("1972") .50 *.50*

20th Olympic Games, Munich, Aug. 26-Sept. 11. Commemorative inscriptions on No. 338 at left, top and right have been trimmed off. Size: 61x45mm (approximately). Many varieties exist. Gold overprints probably are proofs.

Pres. Carlos Arana Osorio A157

Designs: 3c, 5c, President Osorio seated, vert. 8c, Pres. Osorio standing, vert.

1973-74 **Typo.** ***Perf. 12½***

420 A157 2c blue & blk .80 .25
421 A157 3c orange & brn 1.00 .25
422 A157 5c rose car & blk 1.25 .25
423 A157 8c black & brt grn 1.50 .25
a. Lithographed ('74) 1.00 .25
Nos. 420-423 (4) 4.55 1.00

8th population and 3rd dwellings census, Mar. 26-Apr. 7, 1973.

Francisco Ximenez — A158

Typographed, Lithographed (#426)

1973-77 ***Perf. 11½, 13½ (#426)***

424 A158 2c black & emer .25 .25
425 A158 3c dk brn & org .25 .25
426 A158 3c black & yellow .45 .25
427 A158 6c black & brt bl .45 .25
Nos. 424-427 (4) 1.40 1.00

Brother Francisco Ximenez, discoverer and translator of National Book of Guatemala. No. 427 issued for Intl. Book Year 1972.
Issued: 6c, 8/2; 2c, 1/14/75; No. 425, 3/5/75; No. 426, 9/26/77.

Sculpture of Christ, by Pedro de Mendoza, 1643 — A159

8c, Sculpture by Lanuza Brothers, 18th century.

1977, Apr. 4 **Litho.** ***Perf. 11***

428 A159 6c purple & multi .45 .25
429 A159 8c purple & multi .45 .25
Nos. 428-429,C614-C619 (8) 4.75 2.80

Holy Week 1977.

INTERFER 77 Emblem — A160

1977, Oct. 31 **Litho.** ***Perf. 11½***

430 A160 7c black & multi .45 .25

INTERFER 77, 4th International Fair, Guatemala, Oct. 31-Nov. 13.

Rotary Intl., 75th Anniv. A161

6c, Diamond and Quetzal. 10c, Paul P. Harris.

1980, July 31 **Litho.** ***Perf. 11½***

431 A161 4c shown .85 .25
432 A161 6c multicolored .85 .25
433 A161 10c multicolored 1.20 .60
Nos. 431-433 (3) 2.90 1.10

Quetzal Type of 1954

1984-86 **Engr.** ***Perf. 12½***

434 A146 1c deep green *2.75* .90
435 A146 2c deep blue *2.75* .90
436 A146 3c olive green *2.75* *2.75*
437 A146 3c sepia *2.75* .90
438 A146 3c blue *2.75* .90
439 A146 3c red *2.75* *2.75*
440 A146 3c orange *2.75* *2.75*
441 A146 3c vermilion *2.75* *2.75*
442 A146 4c lt red brn *2.75* .90
443 A146 5c magenta *2.75* .90
444 A146 6c deep blue *2.75* *2.75*
Nos. 434-444 (11) *30.25* *19.15*

Issued: Nos. 436-439, 2/20; No. 441, 6c, 4/25/86; 1c, 4c, 5c, 2/16/87; 2c, 3/25/87.

Miguel Angel Asturias Cultural Center — A162

Perf. 12½, 11½ (5c, 9c), 12½x11½ (4c), 13x12½ (6c)

1987-96 **Litho.**

445 A162 1c light blue .30 .25
446 A162 2c bister brown .30 .25
447 A162 3c ultra .30 .25
448 A162 4c bright pink .30 .25
449 A162 5c orange .30 .25
450 A162 6c pale green .30 .25
451 A162 7c vermilion .30 .25
452 A162 8c brt pink .30 .25
453 A162 9c black .30 .25
454 A162 10c pale green .40 .25
Nos. 445-454 (10) 3.10 2.50

Miguel Angel Asturias (1899-1974), 1967 Nobel laureate in literature.
Issued: 3c, 11/24; 7c, 11/17; 8c, 11/27; 10c, 12/8; 2c, 3/2/88; 5c, 3/23/90; 9c, 10/1/91; 4c, 6c, 3/16/93; 1c, 7/9/96.
For surcharge see No. 573.

Central American and Caribbean University Games A163

Toucan as a participant in various events.

1990 **Litho.** ***Perf. 12½***

455 A163 15c shown .30 .25
456 A163 20c Torch bearer, vert. .45 .25
457 A163 25c Volleyball .65 .25
458 A163 30c Soccer .70 .25
459 A163 45c Karate 1.10 .30
460 A163 1q Baseball 2.50 .70
461 A163 2q Basketball 4.50 1.50
462 A163 3q Hurdles 7.50 2.50
Nos. 455-462 (8) 17.70 6.00

Issued: 20c, 8/22; 30c, 3q, 7/10; others, 4/25.

A164

Oct. 20 Revolution, 50th Anniv. A165

A166

Designs: 1q, Student holding book, rifle. 2q, Constitution, city buildings, San Carlos University, social security building.

1994, Nov. 8 **Litho.** ***Perf. 11½***

463 A164 40c multicolored .30 .25
464 A165 60c multicolored .50 .35
465 A164 1q multicolored .95 .65
466 A166 2q multicolored 1.75 1.25
467 A166 3q multicolored 3.00 1.75
Nos. 463-467 (5) 6.50 4.25

UNICEF, 50th Anniv. — A167

Designs: 10c, Soldier hugging child, vert. 20c, Children flying on doves.

1997, May 21 **Litho.** ***Perf. 12½***

468 A167 10c multicolored .25 .25

Perf. 11½x12½

469 A167 20c multicolored .25 .25

Landmark Buildings A168

Designs: 50c, Paraninfo University. 1q, Central American Brewery Building, vert.

1997, Mar. 6 *Perf. 12½*
470 A168 50c multicolored .60 .30
471 A168 1q multicolored 1.00 .65

Famous Guatemalans With 1999 Birth Anniversaries A169

Designs: 3q, Francisco Marroquin (b. 1499), first Guatemalan bishop. 4q, Jacinto Rodriguez Diaz (b. 1899), aviator. 8.75q, Miguel Angel Asturias (1899-1974), 1967 Nobel Laureate for Literature. 10q, Cesar Brañas (b. 1899), writer.

2001, Oct. 9 **Litho.** *Perf. 12½x11½*
472-475 A169 Set of 4 27.50 10.00

Visit of Pope John Paul II and Canonization of St. Peter of San José Betancur (1626-67) — A170

Designs: Nos. 476, 483a, 20c, Saint and churches, vert. Nos. 477, 483b, 25c, Saint and bell, vert. Nos. 478, 483c, 50c, Pope, Saint and church. Nos. 479, 483d, 1q, Saint, painting of nativity, and bell, vert. Nos. 480, 483e, 2q, Pope and Guatemala Archbishop Quezada Toruño. Nos. 481, 483f, 5q, Pope, fountain and church decoration. Nos. 482, 483g, 8.75q, Pope and churches.

2002, July 16 **Litho.** *Perf. 12½*
476-482 A170 Set of 7 18.50 8.00

Souvenir Sheet

Rouletted 8½

483 A170 Sheet of 7, #a-g 20.00 20.00

Universal Postal Union, 125th Anniv. (in 1999) — A171

Designs: 20c, Quetzal, air mail envelopes, globe, flags. 2q, UPU emblem, quetzal, envelopes. 5q, Globe, quetzal, UPU emblem. 6q, Map of Guatemala, globe, envelopes and flags.

2002, Oct. 31 **Litho.** *Perf. 12½*
484-487 A171 Set of 4 8.50 4.25

2001 Ascent of Mt. Everest by Jaime Viñals — A172

2002, Nov. 22
488 A172 3q multi 2.50 1.25

Pan-American Health Organization, Cent. — A173

2002, Dec. 18
489 A173 4q multi 3.25 1.60

St. Josemaría Escrivá de Balaguer (1902-75) A174

Balaguer and: 20c, Farmer. 50c, Fisherman with boatful of fish. 3q, Fisherman, mountain. 10q, Church.

2003 **Litho.** *Perf. 12¼*
490-493 A174 Set of 4 11.50 5.75

Masks for Dances — A175

Mask for: 20c, Dance of the Conquest. 2q, Dance of the Moors and Christians. 3q, Dance of the Deer. 4q, Dance of the Jaguar.
5q, Dance of Paabanc.

2003, July 9 **Litho.** *Perf. 12½*
494-497 A175 Set of 4 11.00 8.00

Souvenir Sheet

Rouletted 8½

498 A175 5q multi 5.50 5.50

No. 498 was issued in sheets of 18 and has perf. 12½ margins.

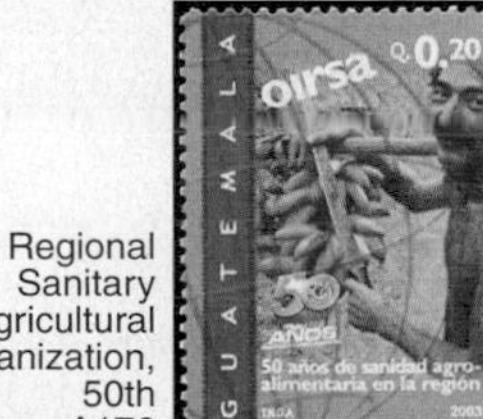
Regional Sanitary Agricultural Organization, 50th Anniv. — A176

Designs: 20c, Banana picker. 1q, Hands in corn. 2q, Cow. 4q, Cultivated field. 5q, Sliced meat. 10q, Eye, map, ear of corn.
3q, Basket of vegetables.

2003, Dec. 8 **Litho.** *Perf. 12½*
499-504 A176 Set of 6 16.00 8.00

Souvenir Sheet

Rouletted 8¼

505 A176 3q multi 3.00 3.00

Tourist Attractions of Izabal Department A177

Designs: 20c, Punta de Manabique. 50c, Siete Altares. 1q, Las Escobas. 1.50q, View between Barrios and Pichilingo. 2q, Acropolis, Quiriguá. 3q, Livingston on the Río Dulce. No. 512, 4q, Castle of San Felipe. 5q, El Estor. 8.75q, Agua Caliente. 10q, Río Polochic.
No. 516, Quiriguá.

2004, Jan. 30 *Perf. 12½*
506-515 A177 Set of 10 26.50 13.50

Souvenir Sheet

Rouletted 6½

516 A177 4q multi 4.25 4.25

Elevation to Cardinal of Archbishop Rodolfo Quezada Toruño A178

Designs: 20c, Cardinal, cathedral. 25c, Cardinal holding crucifix, cathedral. 50c, Cardinal wearing biretta kneeling before Pope John Paul II. 1q, Cardinal wearing zucchetto kneeling before Pope. 2q, Cardinal holding biretta, wearing zucchetto. No. 522, 3q, Cardinal wearing zucchetto. 4q, Cardinal wearing miter. 5q, Cardinal kissing hand of Pope. 8.75q, Cardinal and bishops. 10q, Coat of arms
No. 527, 3q, Statue of Virgin Mary.

2004, Nov. 5 **Litho.** *Perf. 12½*
517-526 A178 Set of 10 25.00 12.50

Souvenir Sheet

Rouletted 6½

527 A178 3q multi 4.25 4.25

America Issue, Flora and Fauna — A179

Designs: 50c, Sarcoramphus papa. 3q, Heliconia collinsiana, vert. 5q, Felis concolor. 10q, Heliconius potiveranus.
12q, Tapirus vairdii.

2005, Apr. 29 **Litho.** *Perf. 12½*
528 A179 50c multi .80 .80
529 A179 3q multi 6.00 6.00
530 A179 5q multi 10.00 10.00
531 A179 10q multi 20.00 20.00
Nos. 528-531 (4) 36.80 36.80

Souvenir Sheet

Rouletted 6½

532 A179 12q multi 21.00 21.00

Diplomatic Relations Between Guatemala and Japan A180

Flags of Guatemala and Japan and: 1q, Child, flowing well pipe, San Pedro La Laguna. 8q, Child, hospital, Puerto Barrios.
14q, Mt. Fuji.

2005, July 29 **Litho.** *Perf. 12½*
533-534 A180 Set of 2 5.75 5.75

Souvenir Sheet

Rouletted 8½

535 A180 14q multi 8.50 8.50

Majolica A181

Designs: 1q, Incense burner. 2q, Jars. 6.50q, Bowls. 8q, Lantern.
12q, Covered jar and sugar bowls.

2005, Oct. 4 *Perf. 12½*
536-539 A181 Set of 4 11.00 11.00

Souvenir Sheet

Rouletted 8½

540 A181 12q multi 7.75 7.75

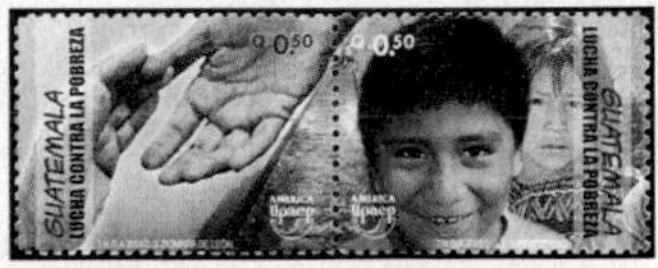
Rotary International, Cent. — A182

Designs: 2q, Emblem, handshake, Western Hemisphere. 6.50q, Emblem, Polio Plus emblem.
8q, Emblem.

2005, Nov. 15 *Perf. 12½*
541-542 A182 Set of 2 5.25 5.25

Souvenir Sheet

Rouletted 8½

543 A182 8q multi 5.00 5.00

America Issue, Fight Against Poverty — A183

No. 544, 50c: a, Open hands. b, Two children
No. 545, 5q: a, Clasped hands. b, Two children, diff.

2006, Feb. 22 *Perf. 12½*

Horiz. Pairs, #a-b

544-545 A183 Set of 2 7.25 7.25

Prof. José Joaquín Pardo, Historian, Cent. of Birth — A184

2006, Feb. 28
546 A184 3q multi 2.00 2.00

Churches A185

Designs: 50c, Santa Cruz Hermitage, Antigua Guatemala. 1q, San Jacinto Church, Salcajá. 2q, San Andres Xecul Church, Totonicapan, vert. 3q, El Calvario Church, Chichicastenango, vert. 4q, San Cristobal Acasaguastlán, El Progreso, vert. 5q, Antigua Cathedral, Antigua Guatemala. 8q, San Pedro Church and Hospital, Antigua Guatemala. 10q, San Pedro Las Huertas Church, Antigua Guatemala.

14q, Metropolitan Cathedral, Guatemala City.

2006, Mar. 15 *Perf. 12½*
547-554 A185 Set of 8 21.00 21.00

Souvenir Sheet
Rouletted 8½

555 A185 14q multi 11.00 11.00

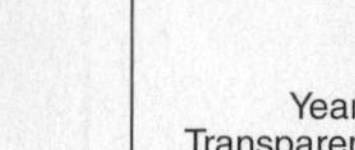

Christmas A186

Various ceramic creche figurines: 20c, 6.50q.

2006, Nov. 27 **Litho.** *Perf. 12½*
556-557 A186 Set of 2 4.50 4.50

Coffee Growing Regions A187

Designs: 50c, Acatenango. 1q, Antigua. 2q, Atitlán. 6.50q, Cobán. 8q, Fraijanes. 10q, Huehue.
No. 564: a, 5q, Oriente. b, 20q, San Marcos.

2006, Nov. 29 *Perf. 12½*
558-563 A187 Set of 6 18.00 18.00

Souvenir Sheet
Rouletted 6½

564 A187 Sheet of 2, #a-b 15.00 15.00

America Issue, Energy Conservation A188

Designs: 3q, Oil wells, gasoline pump nozzle. 10q, Light switch, solar panels.

2006, Dec. 7 *Perf. 12½*
565-566 A188 Set of 2 8.25 8.25

Diplomatic Relations Between Guatemala and Brazil, Cent. — A189

No. 567: a, Baile de la Conquista dancers. b, Maracatu dancers.

2006, Dec. 12
567 A189 4q Horiz. pair, #a-b 15.00 15.00

Nos. 453, C850-C852, C863, C865, C870-C871 Surcharged

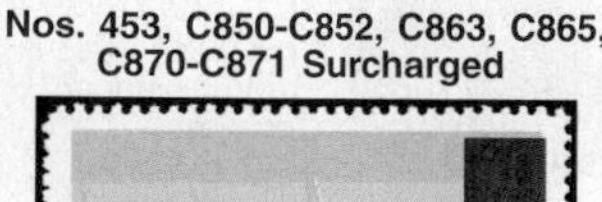

Methods and Perfs As Before

2007, Jan. 23
568 AP186 50c on 40c #C850 .35 .35
569 AP188 50c on 40c #C863 .35 .35
570 AP186 1q on 60c #C851 .60 .60
571 AP191 2q on 80c #C871 1.35 1.35
572 AP188 3q on 60c #C865 2.10 2.10
573 A162 5q on 9c #453 4.25 4.25
574 AP186 8q on 80c #C852 5.75 5.75
575 AP191 10q on 60c #C870 6.75 6.75
Nos. 568-575 (8) 21.50 21.50

"Aereo" on Nos. 568-572, 574-575 is not obliterated.

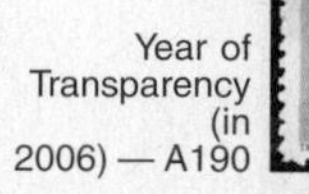

Year of Transparency (in 2006) — A190

Designs: 20c, Hand holding ball with map of Guatemala. 6.50q, Magnifying glass, fingerprint (45x25mm)

2007, Jan. 23 **Litho.** *Perf. 12½*
576-577 A190 Set of 2 5.50 5.50

Dated 2006.

Guatemala Philatelic Association, 75th Anniv. — A191

Designs: 1q, Guatemala #21. 3q, Guatemala #22. 6.50q, Guatemala #23. 8q, Guatemala #24.
25q, Guatemala #25.

2007, July 19 **Litho.** *Perf. 12½*
578-581 A191 Set of 4 9.50 9.50

Souvenir Sheet

582 A191 25q multi 18.00 18.00

Diplomatic Relations Between Guatemala and Uruguay, Cent. — A192

No. 583: a, Santa Catarina Arch, Antigua, Guatemala. b, City gate, Colonia del Sacramento, Uruguay.

2007, Sept. 7
583 A192 4q Horiz. pair, #a-b 6.25 6.25

See Uruguay No. 2205.

America Issue, Education For All — A193

No. 584 — Stick figure children and: a, Blue panel. b, Red panel. c, Yellow orange panel. d, Green panel.

2007, Oct. 25
584 A193 4q Block of 4, #a-d 8.75 8.75

Christmas — A194

Creche figures: 20c, Holy Family. 6.50q, Magi, horiz. (36x31mm).

2007, Dec. 4
585-586 A194 Set of 2 3.75 3.75

Scouting, Cent. — A195

2007, Dec. 5
587 A195 20c multi .60 .40

Institute For Municipal Development, 50th Anniv. (in 2007) — A196

2008, Jan. 30
588 A196 3q multi 1.60 1.60

Dated 2007.

Monsignor Juan Gerardi Conedera (1922-98) A197

2008, Apr. 25 **Litho.** *Perf. 12½*
589 A197 8q multi 3.50 3.50

19th Cent. Defensive Bulwarks of Guatemala City — A198

No. 590: a, San Rafael de Matamoros. b, San José de Buena Vista.

2008, June 27
590 A198 1q Horiz. pair, #a-b 1.25 .90

2008 Summer Olympics, Beijing — A199

2008, Oct. 17 **Litho.** *Perf. 12½*
591 A199 6.50q multi 2.40 2.40

Birds — A200

Designs: 50c, Trogon violaceus braccatus. 1q, Amarilia beryllina viola. 2q, Turdus rufitorques. 4q, Glaucidium brasilianum ridgwayi. 20q, Brotogeris jugularis.

2008, Nov. 14
592-595 A200 Set of 4 4.00 4.00

Souvenir Sheet

596 A200 20q multi 9.25 9.25

Christmas — A201

Needlepoint: 20c, Flower. 8q, Christmas tree.

2008, Dec. 2 **Litho.**
597-598 A201 Set of 2 3.75 3.75

Franciscan Order, 800th Anniv. (in 2009) — A202

2008, Dec. 16
599 A202 3q multi 1.50 1.40

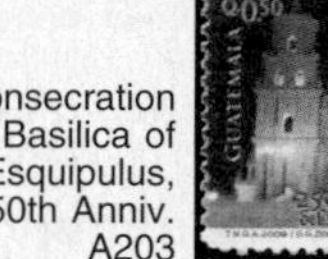

Consecration of Basilica of Esquipulus, 250th Anniv. A203

2009, Jan. 3
600 A203 50c multi .60 .50

Natl. Marine Defense, 50th Anniv. A204

2009, Jan. 12
601 A204 1q multi *2.25 2.00*

America Issue, National Festivals — A205

Designs: 50c, Dancers, Comalapa. 2q, All Saints Day Festival, Santiago Sacatepequez. 3q, Dancers and marimba players. 5q, Dancers.
8q, Cofrades y Capitanas.

2009, Feb. 6
602-605 A205 Set of 4 5.00 5.00

Souvenir Sheet

606 A205 8q multi 3.50 3.50

Native Costumes A206

Designs: 50c, San Juan Atitán man. 1q, San Juan Sacatepéquez woman. 2q, Tamahú woman. 3q, San Rafael Petzal woman. 4q, Totonicapán man. 5q, Patzicia woman. 8q, San Pedro San Marcos woman.
10q, San Juan Cotzal man and woman.

2009, Apr. 14 Litho. *Perf. 12½*
607-613 A206 Set of 7 *21.00 21.00*

Souvenir Sheet

614 A206 10q multi *30.00 30.00*

See Nos. 645-648.

Marimbas
A207

Designs: 3q, Gourd marimba. 4q, 18th cent. marimba. 5q, Double marimba. 8q, Concert marimba. 10q, Man playing marimba.

2009, Oct. 30
615-619 A207 Set of 5 12.00 12.00

Louis Braille (1809-52), Educator of the Blind — A208

2009, Nov. 13 Litho. & Embossed
620 A208 1q multi 1.00 .75

Christmas
A209

Beaded ornaments: 20c, Spheres. 50c, Reindeer. 1q, Angels. 6.50q, Star.

2009, Dec. 4 Litho.
621-624 A209 Set of 4 4.00 4.00

Battle of La Arada, 150th Anniv. (in 2011) — A210

No. 625: a, Sword and arms. b, Pres. Rafael Carrera.
10q, Carrera, vert.

2010, Feb. 12 *Perf. 12½*
625 A210 5q Horiz. pair, #a-b 3.75 3.75

Souvenir Sheet

626 A210 10q multi 3.50 3.50

America
Issue
A211

Traditional toys and games: 50c, Capitucho. 1q, Barillete (kite). 6.50q, Yo-yo. 8q, Trompo (top).

2010, Mar. 17
627-630 A211 Set of 4 6.25 6.25

Dated 2009.

José Ernesto Monzón (1917-2003), Musician — A212

2010, Aug. 6 Litho. *Perf. 12½*
631 A212 2q multi 1.00 .75

Tourist Sites in Chiquimula Department — A213

No. 632: a, Ipala Volcano. b, Ipala Lake.

2010, Sept. 11
632 A213 8q Vert. pair, #a-b 5.75 5.75

Christmas — A214

No. 633: a, Joseph. b, Infant Jesus and Star of Bethlehem. c, Mary.

2010, Dec. 2
633 A214 3q Horiz. strip of 3, #a-c 3.75 3.75

Textile Art
by Priscilla
Bianchi
A215

Various designs.

2010, Dec. 15 *Perf. 12½*

634	A215	20c multi	.25	.25
a.		Dated "2016"	.25	.25
635	A215	50c multi	.25	.25
a.		Dated "2016"	.25	.25
636	A215	1q multi	.25	.25
a.		Dated "2016"	.25	.25
637	A215	2q multi	.70	.70
a.		Dated "2016"	.55	.55
638	A215	3q multi	1.00	1.00
639	A215	4q multi	1.30	1.30
640	A215	5q multi	1.60	1.60
a.		Dated "2016"	1.40	1.40
641	A215	6.50q multi	2.25	2.25
642	A215	8q multi	2.60	2.60
a.		Dated "2016"	2.10	2.10
643	A215	10q multi	3.25	3.25
a.		Dated "2016"	2.75	2.75
		Nos. 634-643 (10)	13.45	13.45

See Nos. 709-711.

Postal Union of the Americas, Spain and Portugal (UPAEP), Cent. — A216

2011, Mar. 23 Litho. *Perf. 12½*
644 A216 2q multi 1.00 .75

Native Costumes Type of 2009

Designs: 50c, San Mateo Ixtatán woman. 5q, Almolonga man. 6.50q, Tecpán woman. 10q, Palín man and women.

2011, May 17
645-647 A206 Set of 3 5.00 5.00

Souvenir Sheet

648 A206 10q multi 3.75 3.75

National
Journalism
Library, 50th
Anniv. — A217

2011, May 17 Litho. *Perf. 12½*
649 A217 5q multi 2.00 2.00

Phragmipedium Humboltii — A218

2011, June 29
650 A218 5q multi 2.00 2.00

Alexander von Humboldt (1769-1859), naturalist.

America
Issue,
National
Symbols
A219

Designs: 20c, Ceiba tree. 10q, White nun orchids.

2011, Sept. 14 Litho. *Perf. 12½*
651-652 A219 Set of 2 4.00 4.00

Republic of China, Cent. — A220

2011, Oct. 3
653 A220 2q multi 1.00 .75

Civil Aviation in Guatemala, Cent. — A221

2011, Dec. 8
654 A221 8q multi 3.25 3.25

Christmas
A222

Creche scenes from: 4q, Señora de las Misericordias Church. 10q, Merced Parish Church.

2011, Dec. 9
655-656 A222 Set of 2 5.25 5.25

José Joaquín Palma (1844-1911), Poet — A223

2011, Dec. 23
657 A223 1q multi .60 .35

Mailbox — A224

2012, Oct. 22
658 A224 5q multi 1.90 1.90

America issue.

Museums in a Changing World — A225

No. 659: a, Pre-Columbian figurines (goat at right). b, Modern figurines (goat at left).

2012, Dec. 11
659 A225 4q Horiz. pair, #a-b 3.00 3.00

Max Tott Half Marathon, Guatemala City, 75th Anniv. — A226

2012, Dec. 12
660 A226 8q multi 2.75 2.75

Daughters of Charity of St. Vincent de Paul, 150th Anniv. in Guatemala A227

2012, Dec. 13
661 A227 6.50q multi 2.25 2.25

Beginning of 13th Cycle of Mesoamerican Long Count Calendar A228

Designs: 1q, Calendar wheel. 2q, Leiden Plate. 3q, Zoomorph P, Quiriguá. 4q, Pelota player holding calendar wheel. No. 666, Stela D, Quiriguá. No. 667, Pelota player holding ball. 8q, Stela C, Quiriguá. No. 669, Mayan Ab' calendar. No. 670, Mixco Viejo Archaeological Site.

2012, Dec. 17 Litho. *Perf. 12½*

662	A228	1q multi	.40	.40
663	A228	2q multi	.85	.85
664	A228	3q multi	1.20	1.20
665	A228	4q multi	1.60	1.60
a.		Booklet pane of 3, #662, 663, 665	4.50	—
666	A228	5q multi	2.10	2.10
667	A228	5q multi	2.10	2.10
668	A228	8q multi	3.00	3.00
669	A228	10q multi	4.00	4.00
a.		Booklet pane of 3, #666, 668, 669	11.00	—
670	A228	10q multi	4.00	4.00
a.		Booklet pane of 3, #664, 667, 670	9.50	—
		Complete booklet, #665a, 669a, 670a	27.50	
		Nos. 662-670 (9)	19.25	19.25

Caravana del Zorro Motorcycle Ride from Guatemala City to Esquipulas, 50th Anniv. A229

Emblem and motorcyclists with: No. 671, Pale orange color at lower corners. No. 672, Gray color at lower corners.

2013, Feb. 2 Litho. *Perf. 12½*
671 A229 10q multi 2.75 2.60

Souvenir Sheet

672 A229 10q multi 2.75 2.60

Rodolfo Galeotti Torres (1912-88), and His Sculpture "La Puerta del Saber" — A230

2013, Sept. 27 Litho. *Perf. 12½*
673 A230 50c multi 1.00 .25

America Issue — A231

Myths and legends: 1q, El Sombrerón. 5q, La Tatuana. 8q, La Llorona. 10q, Xocomil.

2013, Oct. 11 Litho. *Perf. 12½*
674-677 A231 Set of 4 6.50 6.00

Christmas — A232

Designs: 2q, Angels. 3q, Nativity scene.

2013, Nov. 14 Litho. *Perf. 12½*
678-679 A232 Set of 2 1.50 1.25

Villa Nueva, 250th Anniv. — A233

2013, Dec. 13 Litho. *Perf. 12½*
680 A233 6.50q multi 3.00 1.75

Abies Guatemalensis — A234

No. 681: a, Grove of trees (48x30mm). b, Cones on tree (28x30mm).

2014, Jan. 13 Litho. *Perf. 12½*
681 A234 5q Horiz. pair, #a-b 2.60 2.60

Jesus Nazareno de Candelaria Statue, 450th Anniv. — A235

2014, Feb. 5 Litho. *Perf. 12½*
682 A235 20c multi .75 .25

Native Cuisine A236

Designs: 2q, Plátanos en mole (plantains in mole sauce). 5q, Kaq Ik (turkey in tomato sauce). 6q, Pepián (chicken in vegetable sauce). 10q, Jocón (chicken in tomatillo and cilantro sauce).

2014, Mar. 4 Litho. *Perf. 12½*
683-686 A236 Set of 4 6.00 6.00

Numismatic Museum of Guatemala — A237

2014, Mar. 28 Litho. *Perf. 12½*
687 A237 50c multi .65 .25

Items Made of Jade — A238

No. 688: a, Bracelet with jaguar heads, sculpture of God of Corn, three carved jaguars. b, Carved jaguar, Tikal funerary mask, nahuales. c, Ring, nahuales, sculpture of King of Corn.

2014, Apr. 3 Litho. *Perf. 12½*
688 A238 50c Horiz. strip of 3, #a-c 1.25 .40

Lizards A239

Designs: 1q, Abronia vasconcelosi. 5q, Abronia fimbriata. 6.50q, Abronia meledona. 10q, Abronia frosti.

2014, July 4 Litho. *Perf. 12½*
689-692 A239 Set of 4 6.00 5.75

Campaign Against Discrimination — A240

2014, Aug. 6 Litho. *Perf. 12½*
693 A240 1q multi 2.00 .25

America issue.

Landscapes — A241

Designs: 1q, Volcán de Fuego and Acatenango. 3q, El Pino Lake. 6.50q, Magdalena Lake. 8q, Lake Chicabal.

2014, Aug. 12 Litho. *Perf. 12½*
694-697 A241 Set of 4 4.75 4.75

Souvenir Sheet

Virgen del Carmen Chapel, Guatemala City, 400th Anniv. — A242

2014, Nov. 21 Litho. *Perf. 12½*
698 A242 10q multi 2.60 2.60

Christmas A243

Religious paintings from Our Lady of Peace Church and text: 6.50q, Feliz Navidad. 8q, Bendicianes.

2014, Nov. 25 Litho. *Perf. 12½*
699-700 A243 Set of 2 4.00 4.00

America Issue A244

Designs: 20c, Juan José Arévalo (1904-90), first democratically elected president of Guatemala. 10q, Juan Matalbatz, K'iche' chief converted to Christianity, Spanish provincial governor.

2014, Dec. 10 Litho. *Perf. 12½*
701-702 A244 Set of 2 2.75 2.75

Guatemala, 2015 Iberoamerican Capital of Culture — A245

Designs: 2q, Parrot holding torch. 8q, Stylized birds in flight (46x31mm).

2015, Feb. 26 Litho. *Perf. 12½*

703-704	A245	Set of 2	2.75	2.75
704a		Booklet pane of 8, 4 each #703-704	13.00	—
		Complete booklet, #704a	15.00	

Complete booklet sold for 50q.

Metropolitan Cathedral, Guatemala City, Bicent. — A246

Designs: 50c, Dome. 5q, Interior. 6.50q, Clock tower.

2015, Apr. 24 Litho. *Perf. 12½*
705-707 A246 Set of 3 3.25 3.25

A booklet containing panes of one of each stamp sold for 40q. Value, $15.

Postal Headquarters — A247

No. 708 — Postal Headquarters in: a, Guatemala (denomination at left). b, Paraguay (denomination at right).

2015, Aug. 13 Litho. *Perf. 12½*
708 A247 4q Horiz. pair, #a-b 2.10 2.10

See Paraguay No. 3030.

Textile Art Type of 2010

Various designs.

2015, Feb. 15 Litho. *Perf. 12½*
709 A215 25q multi 8.75 8.75
a. Dated "2016" 8.75 8.75
710 A215 50q multi 17.50 17.50
a. Dated "2016" 17.50 17.50
711 A215 100q multi 34.00 34.00
a. Dated "2016" 34.00 34.00

Coral Reef Marine Life — A248

Designs: 50c, Panulirus argus. 5q, Pomacanthus paru. 6.50q, Sparisoma viride. 10q, Chelonia mydas.

2015, Sept. 25 Litho. *Perf. 12½*
712-715 A248 Set of 4 5.75 5.75
715a Souvenir sheet of 4, #712-715 *19.50 19.50*

Guatemala No. C260 — A249

2015, Nov. 6 Litho. *Perf. 12½*
716 A249 6.50q multi 1.75 .80

Discovery of onchocerciasis in Central America by Dr. Rodolfo Robles, cent.

Campaign to End Violence Against Women — A250

2015, Nov. 25 Litho. *Perf. 12½*
717 A250 8q multi 2.10 1.10

See Dominican Republic No. 1583, Ecuador No. 2173, El Salvador No. 1747, Venezuela No. 1731.

Christmas A251

Designs: 50c, Wreath and toy horse. 5q, Christmas tree decorated with ornaments (30x56mm).

2015, Dec. 1 Litho. *Perf. 12½*
718-719 A251 Set of 2 1.50 .75

Guatemala Military Engineers, 125th Anniv. — A252

No. 720: a, Military engineers and building (45x30mm). b, Surveyors and vehicles (25x30mm). c, Vehicles and bridge (45x30mm).

2015, Dec. 3 Litho. *Perf. 12½*
720 A252 1q Horiz. strip of 3, #a-c .80 .40

Campaign Against Human Trafficking — A253

No. 721: a, Black hand, broken chain. b, Orange hand, Sun.

2015, Dec. 11 Litho. *Perf. 12½*
721 A253 4q Horiz. pair, #a-b 2.10 1.10

America Issue.

SEMI-POSTAL STAMPS

Regular Issues of 1935-36 Surcharged in Blue or Red

1937, Mar. 15 Unwmk. *Perf. 12½*
B1 A102 1c + 1c brn & crim .75 *1.00*
B2 A103 3c + 1c rose car & pck grn .75 *1.00*
B3 A103 3c + 1c red org & pck grn .75 *1.00*
B4 A106 5c + 1c bl & dk brn (R) .75 *1.00*
Nos. B1-B4 (4) 3.00 *4.00*

1st Phil. Exhib. held in Guatemala, Mar. 15-20.

Catalogue values for unused stamps in this section, from this point to the end of the section, are for Never Hinged items.

Type of Regular Issue, 1956

Designs: 5c+15c, Nurse, Patient and Red Cross Flag. 15c+50c, Red Cross, telephone and "5110." 25c+50c, Globe and Red Cross.

1956, June 19 Engr. *Perf. 13x12½*
B5 A148 5c + 15c ultra & red 1.00 *1.40*
a. Imperf., pair 75.00
B6 A148 15c + 50c dk vio & red 2.25 *2.75*
B7 A148 25c + 50c bluish blk & car 2.25 *2.75*
Nos. B5-B7 (3) 5.50 *0.90*

The surtax was for the Red Cross.

Jesus and Esquipulas Cathedral — SP1

1957, Oct. 29 *Perf. 13*
B8 SP1 1½c + ½c blk & brn .60 .25

The surtax was for the Esquipulas highway. See Nos. CB12-CB14.

Type of Air Post Semi-Postal Stamps and

Arms — SP2

3c+3c, Wounded man, Battle of Solferino.

1960, Apr. 9 Photo. *Perf. 13½x14*
Cross in Rose Red
B9 SP2 1c + 1c red brn & bl .35 .25
B10 SPAP2 3c + 3c lil, bl & pink .35 .25
B11 SP2 4c + 4c blk & bl .35 .25
Nos. B9-B11 (3) 1.05 .75

Cent. (in 1959) of the Red Cross idea. The surtax went to the Red Cross. Exist imperf. See Nos. CB15-CB21.

AIR POST STAMPS

No. 229 Surcharged in Red

1929, May 20 Unwmk. *Perf. 12½*
C1 A64 3c on 15p blk 1.10 *1.40*
C2 A64 5c on 15p blk .55 .45
C3 A64 15c on 15p blk 1.50 .45
a. Double surcharge (G & R) 100.00
C4 A64 20c on 15p blk 2.25 2.25
a. Inverted surcharge 100.00
b. Double surcharge 100.00

No. 216 Surcharged in Red

1929, May 20 *Perf. 14*
C5 A64 5c on 15p black 3.25 2.25
Nos. C1-C5 (5) 8.65 6.80

No. 218 Surcharged in Black

1929, Oct. 9
C6 A75 3c on 2.50p dk vio 1.00 1.00

Airplane and Mt. Agua AP3

1930, June 4 Litho. *Perf. 12½*
C7 AP3 6c rose red 5.00 *5.00*
a. Double impression 25.00 25.00
b. Imperf., pair 350.00

For overprint see No. C14.

Nos. 227, 229 Surcharged in Black or Red

1930, Dec. 9 *Perf. 12½*
C8 A57 1c on 3p grn (Bk) .40 .40
a. Double surcharge 100.00
C9 A57 2c on 3p grn (Bk) 1.10 *1.50*
C10 A57 3c on 3p grn (R) 1.10 *1.50*
C11 A57 4c on 3p grn (R) 1.10 *1.50*
C12 A64 10c on 15p blk (R) 5.00 *5.00*
a. Double surcharge 125.00
Nos. C8-C12 (5) 8.70 *9.90*

No. 237 Overprinted

1931, May 19 *Perf. 14*
C13 A81 4c orange .40 .30
a. Double overprint 40.00 *50.00*

No. C7 Overprinted

Perf. 12½
C14 AP3 6c rose red *2.00 2.00*
a. On No. C7a 30.00 30.00
b. Inverted overprint 7.00 *7.00*

Nos. 240, 242 Overprinted in Red

1931, Oct. 21 *Perf. 14*
C15 A36 15c ultra 2.00 .25
a. Double overprint 125.00 125.00
C16 A76 30c green 3.00 .95
a. Double overprint 75.00 75.00

Nos. 235-236 Overprinted in Red or Green

1931, Dec. 5
C17 A79 2c dp bl (R) 2.50 *3.00*
C18 A80 3c dk vio (G) 2.50 *3.00*

No. 240 Overprinted in Red

C19 A36 15c ultra 2.75 *3.00*

Nos. C17-C19 were issued in connection with the 1st postal flight from Barrios to Miami.

No. 224 Surcharged in Red

1932-33 *Perf. 12½*
C20 A74 2c on 1.50p dk bl .80 .55

Nos. 227, 229 Surcharged in Violet, Red or Blue

C21 A57 3c on 3p grn (V) .80 .25
a. Inverted surcharge 45.00 45.00
b. Vert. pair, imperf. horiz. 900.00
C22 A57 3c on 3p grn (R) .80 .25
C23 A64 10c on 15p blk (R) 7.75 6.25
b. First "I" of "Interior" missing 10.00 10.00

C24 A64 15c on 15p blk (Bl) 9.00 8.50
a. First "I" of "Interior" missing 15.00 15.00
Nos. C20-C24 (5) 19.15 15.80

Issued: No. C22, 1/1/33; others, 2/11/32.

No. 237 Overprinted in Green

1933, Jan. 1 *Perf. 14*
C25 A81 4c orange .40 .35
a. Double overprint 40.00 40.00

Nos. 235, 238 and 240 Overprinted in Red or Black

1934, Aug. 7
C26 A82 5c dk car (Bk) 1.50 .25
C27 A36 15c ultra (R) 1.50 .25

Overprinted in Red

C28 A79 2c deep blue .55 .25

View of Port Barrios — AP7

Designs: 15c, Tomb of Barrios. 30c, Equestrian Statue of Barrios.

1935, July 19 Photo. *Perf. 12½*
C29 AP7 10c yel brn & pck grn 6.00 4.50
C30 AP7 15c gray & brn 1.50 *1.75*
C31 AP7 30c car rose & bl vio 1.50 1.25
Nos. C29-C31 (3) 9.00 7.50

Birth cent. of Gen. Justo Rufino Barrios.

Lake Amatitlán AP10

Designs: Nos. C36, C37, C45, C46. Different views of Lake Amatitlan. 3c, Port Barrios. No. C34, C35, Ruins of Fort San Felipe. 10c, Port Livingston. No. C39, C40, Port San Jose. No. C41, C42, View of Atitlan. No. C43, C44, Aurora Airport.

Overprinted with Quetzal in Green

1935-37 **Size: 37x17mm**
C32 AP10 2c org brn .25 .25
C33 AP10 3c blue .25 .25
C34 AP10 4c black .25 .25
C35 AP10 4c ultra ('37) .25 .25
C36 AP10 6c yel grn .25 .25
C37 AP10 6c blk vio ('37) 4.00 .25
C38 AP10 10c claret .50 .25
C39 AP10 15c red org .65 .40
C40 AP10 15c yel grn ('37) .65 .65
C41 AP10 30c olive grn 6.00 6.50
C42 AP10 30c ol bis ('37) .75 .50
C43 AP10 50c rose vio 17.50 15.00
C44 AP10 50c Prus bl ('36) 4.00 3.00
C45 AP10 1q scarlet 17.50 20.00
C46 AP10 1q car ('36) 4.50 3.00
Nos. C32-C46 (15) 57.30 50.80

Issue dates follow No. C69.

For overprints and surcharges see Nos. C70-C79, CB1-CB2.

Central Park, Antigua AP11

Designs: 1c, Guatemala City. 2c, Central Park, Guatemala City. 3c, Monastery. Nos. C50-C51, Mouth of Dulce River. Nos. C52-C53, Plaza Barrios. Nos. C54-C55, Los Proceres Monument. No. C56, Central Park, Antigua. No. C57, Dulce River. Nos. C58-C59, Quezaltenango. Nos. C60-C61, Ruins at Antigua. Nos. C62-C63, Dock at Port Barrios. Nos. C64-C65, Port San Jose. Nos. C66-C67, Aurora Airport. 2.50q, Island off Atlantic Coast. 5q, Atlantic Coast view.

Overprinted with Quetzal in Green

Size: 34x15mm
C47 AP11 1c yel brn .25 .25
C48 AP11 2c vermilion .25 .25
C49 AP11 3c magenta .50 .25
C50 AP11 4c org yel ('36) 1.75 1.40
C51 AP11 4c car lake ('37) 1.00 .75
C52 AP11 5c dl bl .25 .25
C53 AP11 5c org ('37) .25 .25
C54 AP11 10c red brn .50 .35
C55 AP11 10c ol grn ('37) .50 .30
C56 AP11 15c rose red .25 .25
C57 AP11 15c ver ('37) .25 .25
C58 AP11 20c ultra 2.50 *3.00*
C59 AP11 20c dp cl ('37) .50 .25
C60 AP11 25c gray blk 3.00 *3.50*
C61 AP11 25c bl grn ('37) .45 .25
a. Quetzal omitted *1,100.*
C62 AP11 30c yel grn 1.50 1.50
C63 AP11 30c rose red ('37) 1.00 .25
C64 AP11 50c car rose 7.00 *8.00*
C65 AP11 50c pur ('36) 6.50 *7.50*
C66 AP11 1q dk bl 22.50 *25.00*
C67 AP11 1q dk grn ('36) 7.50 7.50

Size: 46x20mm
C68 AP11 2.50q rose red & ol grn ('36) 5.00 3.00
C69 AP11 5q org & ind ('36) 7.00 4.00
a. Quetzal omitted 1,500. 1,250.
Nos. C47-C69 (23) 70.20 *68.30*

Issued: Nos. C32-C34, C36, C38-C39, C41, C43, C45, C47-C49, C52, C54, C56, C58, C60, C62, 11/1/35; Nos. C44, C50, C67-C69, 10/1/36; Nos. C35, C37, C40, C42, C51, C53, C55, C57, C59, C61, C63, 1/1/37.

Value for No. C61a is for a sound stamp.

For overprints and surcharges see Nos. C80-C91, CB3-CB4.

Progressive Colony, Lake Amatitlan — AP11a

2c, Quezaltenango. 3c, Lake Atitian. 6c, Carmen Hill. 10c, Relief map. 15c, National University. 30c, Espana Plaza. 50c, Police Station, Aurora Airport. 75c, Amphitheater, Aurora Airport. 1q, Aurora Airport.

Center in Brown Black

1937, May 18

Overprinted with Airplane in Blue

Size: 34x15mm
C70 AP11a 2c carmine .25 .25
C71 AP11a 3c blue 1.00 *1.25*
C72 AP11a 4c citron .25 .25
C73 AP11a 6c yel grn .35 .25
C74 AP11a 10c red vio 2.00 *2.25*
C75 AP11a 15c orange 1.50 1.00
C76 AP11a 30c ol grn 3.75 3.00
C77 AP11a 50c pck bl 5.00 4.25
C78 AP11a 75c dk vio 10.00 *11.00*
C79 AP11a 1q dp rose 11.00 *12.00*
Nos. C70-C79 (10) 35.10 *35.50*

7th Ave., Guatemala City — AP11b

2c, Los Proceres Monument. 3c, Natl. Printing Office. 5c, Natl. Museum. 10c, Central Park. 15c, Escuintla. 20c, Motorcycle Police. 25c, Slaughterhouse, Escuintla. 30c, Exhibition Hall. 50c, Barrios Plaza. 1q, Polytechnic School. 1.50q, Aurora Airport.

Overprinted with Airplane in Black

Size: 33x15mm
C80 AP11b 1c yel brn & brt bl .25 .25
C81 AP11b 2c crim & dp vio .25 .25
C82 AP11b 3c red vio & red brn .50 .50
C83 AP11b 5c pck grn & cop red 4.00 3.00
C84 AP11b 10c car & grn 1.25 1.00
C85 AP11b 15c rose & dl ol grn .50 .25
C86 AP11b 20c ultra & blk 3.00 1.75
C87 AP11b 25c dk gray & scar 2.50 2.50
C88 AP11b 30c grn & dp vio 1.25 1.25
C89 AP11b 50c mag & ultra 10.00 *12.00*

Size: 42x19mm
C90 AP11b 1q ol grn & red vio 10.00 *12.00*
C91 AP11b 1.50q scar & ol brn 10.00 *12.00*
Nos. C80-C91 (12) 43.50 *46.75*

Second term of President Ubico.

Souvenir Sheet

AP12

1938, Jan. 10 *Perf. 12½*
C92 AP12 Sheet of 4 8.00 8.00
a. 15c George Washington 1.50 1.50
b. 4c Franklin D. Roosevelt 1.50 1.50
c. 4c Map of the Americas 1.50 1.50
d. 15c Pan American Union Building, Washington, DC .75 .75

150th anniv. of US Constitution.

President Arosemena, Panama AP13

Flags of Central American Countries — AP19

Designs: 2c, Pres. Cortés Castro, Costa Rica. 3c, Pres. Somoza, Nicaragua. 4c, Pres. Carias Andino, Honduras. 5c, Pres. Martinez, El Salvador. 10c, Pres. Ubico, Guatemala.

1938, Nov. 20 **Unwmk.**
C93 AP13 1c org & ol brn .25 .25
C94 AP13 2c scar, pale pink & sl grn .30 .25
C95 AP13 3c grn, buff & ol brn .40 .30
C96 AP13 4c dk cl, pale lil & brn .55 .35
C97 AP13 5c bis, pale grn & ol brn .50 *.60*
C98 AP13 10c ultra, pale bl & brn 1.00 *1.25*
Nos. C93-C98 (6) 3.00 *3.00*

Souvenir Sheet

C99 AP19 Sheet of 6 8.00 8.00
a. 1c Guatemala .80 .80
b. 2c El Salvador .80 .80
c. 3c Honduras 1.10 1.10
d. 4c Nicaragua 1.40 1.40
e. 5c Costa Rica 1.40 1.40
f. 10c Panama 2.40 2.40

1st Central American Phil. Exhib., Guatemala City, Nov. 20-27.

For overprints see Nos. CO1-CO7.

La Merced Church, Antigua AP20

Designs: 2c, Ruins of Christ School, Antigua. 3c, Aurora Airport. 4c, Drill ground, Guatemala City. 5c, Cavalry barracks. 6c, Palace of Justice. 10c, Customhouse, San José. 15c, Communications Building, Retalhuleu. 30c, Municipal Theater, Quezaltenango. 50c, Customhouse, Retalhuleu. 1q, Departmental Building.

Inscribed "Aéreo Interior"

Overprinted with Quetzal in Green

1939, Feb. 14
C100 AP20 1c ol bis & chnt .25 .25
C101 AP20 2c rose red & sl grn .25 .25
C102 AP20 3c dl bl & bis .25 .25
C103 AP20 4c rose pink & yel grn .25 .25
C104 AP20 5c brn lake & brt ultra .30 .25
C105 AP20 6c org & gray brn .35 .25
C106 AP20 10c bis brn & gray blk .50 .25
C107 AP20 15c dl vio & blk .75 .25
C108 AP20 30c dp bl & dk car 1.10 .25
C109 AP20 50c org & brt vio 1.50 .40
a. Quetzal omitted *1,750.*
C110 AP20 1q yel grn & brt ultra 2.50 1.25
Nos. C100-C110 (11) 8.00 3.90

See Nos. C111-C122. For overprint and surcharge see No. C124, C132.

View of Antigua — AP20a

Inscribed "Aéreo Internacional" or "Aérea Exterior"

Designs: 1c, Mayan Altar, Aurora Park. 2c, Sanitation Building. 3c, Lake Amatitlan. 4c, Lake Atitlan. 5c, Tamazulapa River bridge. 10c, Los proceres Monument. 15c, Palace of Captains General. 20c, Church on Carmen Hill. 25c, Barrios Park. 30c, Mayan Altar. 50c, Charles III fountain.

Overprinted with Quetzal in Green

1939, Feb. 14
C111 AP20a 1c ol grn & gldn brn .25 .25
C112 AP20a 2c lt grn & blk .30 .25
C113 AP20a 3c ultra & cob bl .25 .25
C114 AP20a 4c org brn & yel grn .25 .25
C115 AP20a 5c sage grn & red org .35 .25
C116 AP20a 10c lake & sl blk 1.75 .25
C117 AP20a 15c ultra & brt rose 1.75 .25
C118 AP20a 20c yel grn & ap grn .60 .25
C119 AP20a 25c dl vio & lt ol grn .60 .25
C120 AP20a 30c dl rose & blk .80 .25
C121 AP20a 50c scar & brt yel 1.50 .25
C122 AP20a 1q org & yel grn 2.50 .35
Nos. C111-C122 (12) 10.90 3.10

No. 240 Overprinted in Carmine

1940, Apr. 14 *Perf. 14*
C123 A36 15c ultra .60 .25

Pan American Union, 50th anniversary.

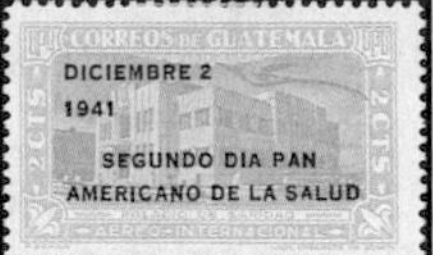

No. C112 Overprinted in Carmine

1941, Dec. 2 ***Perf. 12½***

C124 AP20 2c lt grn & blk .40 .25

Second Pan American Health Day.

San Carlos University, Antigua AP21

1943, June 25 **Engr.** ***Perf. 11***

C125 AP21 15c dk red brn .55 .25
a. Imperf., pair 100.00

Don Pedro de Alvarado AP22

Type I — Diagonal shading lines running from lower left to upper right at inner edges of commemorative tablet.

Type II — Additional diagonal shading lines running from upper left to lower right added throughout tablet, resulting in crosshatched lines at inner edges.

1943, Mar. 10 **Unwmk.** ***Perf. 11½***

C126 AP22 15c dp ultra (II) .60 .25
a. Type I 25.00 17.50

400th anniv. of the founding of Antigua.

National Police Building AP23

1943, Aug. 3 ***Perf. 11***

C127 AP23 10c dp rose vio .35 .25

Allegory of Revolution Type

1945, Apr. 27 **Engr.**

C128 A129 5c dp rose .55 .25
C129 A129 6c dk bl grn .55 .25
a. Imperf., pair 110.00
C130 A129 10c violet .55 .25
C131 A129 15c aqua .55 .25
Nos. C128-C131 (4) 2.20 1.00

No. C113 Surcharged in Red

1945, July 25 ***Perf. 12½***

C132 AP20 2½c on 3c *5.00 5.00*

The 1945 Book Fair.

Type of 1947 Overprinted in Carmine

1945, Aug. **Engr.** ***Perf. 11***

C133 A127 5c rose car .35 .25
a. Triple ovpt., one inverted 50.00 25.00
b. Double ovpt., one inverted 65.00

See Nos. C137A-C139.

José Milla y Vidaurre Type

1945

C134 A131 7½c sepia 1.10 1.00
C134A A131 7½c dark blue .60 .30

Issued: No. C134, 9/28; No. C134A, 12/6.
For overprint see No. C230.

Torch Type

1945, Oct. 19

C135 A130 5c brt red vio .40 .25

Souvenir Sheet

Imperf

C136 A130 Sheet of 2 5.00 4.00
a. 5c bright red violet .40 .40

1st anniv. of the Revolution of Oct. 20, 1944.
See Nos. C147-C150.

Catalogue values for unused stamps in this section, from this point to the end of the section, are for Never Hinged items.

Payo Enriquez de Rivera Type

1946, Jan. 22 **Unwmk.** ***Perf. 11***

C137 A132 5c rose pink .55 .25

See Nos. C269, C311-C315.

Palace Type of 1944

1946-47

C137A A127 5c rose car ('47) .60 .25
C138 A127 10c deep lilac .35 .25
a. Imperf., pair 100.00
C139 A127 15c blue .60 .25
a. Imperf., pair 100.00
Nos. C137A-C139 (3) 1.55 .75

For overprint see No. C133.

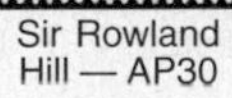
Sir Rowland Hill — AP30

Globes, Quetzal — AP31

1946, Aug. 5 **Photo.** ***Perf. 14x13***

C140 AP30 5c slate & brn (blk ovpt.) .50 .25
a. Without "AEREO" ovpt. *400.00 400.00*
C141 AP31 15c car lake, ultra & emer .65 .30

Centenary of the first postage stamp.

José Batres y Montufar — AP32

1946, Sept. 16 **Engr.** ***Perf. 11***

C142 AP32 10c Prus grn .55 .25
a. Perf. 12½ 10.00 .25

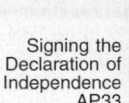

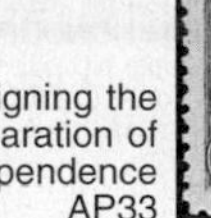

Signing the Declaration of Independence AP33

1946, Dec. 19 ***Perf. 11***

C143 AP33 5c rose car .25 .25
C144 AP33 6c ol brn .25 .25
C145 AP33 10c violet .35 .25
C146 AP33 20c blue .45 .25
Nos. C143-C146 (4) 1.30 1.00

125th anniv. of the signing of the Declaration of Independence.

Torch Type of 1945
Dated 1944-1946

1947, Feb. 3 **Engr.**

C147 A130 1c green .50 .25
C148 A130 2c carmine .50 .25
C149 A130 3c violet .50 .25
C150 A130 5c dp bl .50 .25
Nos. C147-C150 (4) 2.00 1.00

Inscribed "II Aniversario de la Revolucion." "Aereo" in color on a white background.
2nd anniv. of the Revolution of 10/20/44.

Franklin D. Roosevelt — AP34

1947, June 6

C151 AP34 5c rose car .25 .25
C152 AP34 6c blue .25 .25
C153 AP34 10c dp ultra .35 .25
C154 AP34 30c gray blk 1.60 .90
C155 AP34 50c lt violet 2.50 2.25
a. Imperf., pair 125.00
C156 AP34 1q gray grn 4.25 3.75
a. Imperf., pair 125.00
Nos. C151-C156 (6) 9.20 7.65

No. 296 Overprinted in Carmine

1948, May 14 ***Perf. 12½***

C157 A122 5c blue & red .40 .25

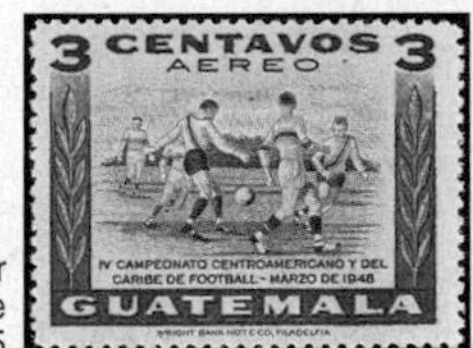
Soccer Game AP35

1948, Aug. 31 **Engr.**

Center in Black

C158 AP35 3c brt carmine .75 .30
C159 AP35 5c blue green .90 .40
C160 AP35 10c dk violet 1.00 .95
C161 AP35 30c dp blue 2.25 *3.50*
C162 AP35 50c bister 4.50 4.50
Nos. C158-C162 (5) 9.40 9.65

4th Central American and Caribbean Soccer Championship, Mar. 1948.

Seal, University of Guatemala — AP36

1949, Nov. 29 ***Perf. 12½***

Center in Blue

C163 AP36 3c carmine .70 .40
C164 AP36 10c green 1.00 .75
C165 AP36 50c yellow 3.75 3.25
Nos. C163-C165 (3) 5.45 *4.40*

1st Latin American Cong. of Universities.

Lake Atitlan — AP37

Tecum Uman Monument — AP38

Designs: 8c, San Cristobal Church. 13c, Weaver. 35c, Momostenango Cliffs.

1950, Feb. 17 **Photo.** ***Perf. 14***

Multicolored Centers

C166 AP37 3c car rose .35 .25
C167 AP38 5c red brn .35 .25
C168 AP37 8c dk sl grn .40 .25
C169 AP38 13c brown .70 .25
C170 AP37 35c purple 2.50 *3.00*
Nos. C166-C170 (5) 4.30 4.00

See No. C181.

Soccer — AP39

Pole Vault — AP40

Designs: 3c, Foot race. 8c, Tennis. 35c, Diving. 65c, Stadium.

1950, Feb. 25 **Engr.** ***Perf. 12½***

Center in Black

C171 AP39 1c purple .65 .25
C172 AP39 3c carmine .70 .25
C173 AP40 4c orange brn .95 .30
C174 AP39 8c red violet 1.10 .40
C175 AP40 35c lt blue 2.50 *3.25*

Center in Green

C176 AP40 65c dk slate grn 5.00 *5.50*
Nos. C171-C176 (6) 10.90 9.95

6th Central American and Caribbean Games.

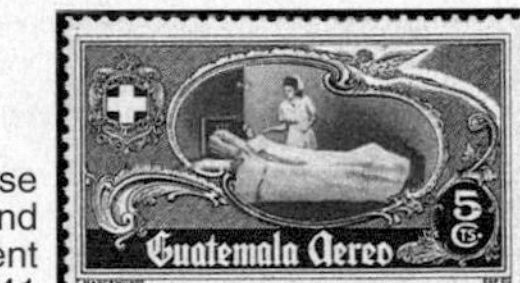
Nurse and Patient AP41

Designs: 10c, School of Nurses. 50c, Zacapa Hospital. 1q, Roosevelt Hospital.

1950, Sept. 6 **Litho.** ***Perf. 12***

Quetzal in Blue Green

C177 AP41 5c rose vio & car .25 .25
a. Double impression (frame) 25.00
C178 AP41 10c ol brn & emer .70 .35
C179 AP41 50c ver & red vio 3.50 *3.50*
C180 AP41 1q org yel & sage grn 5.00 *5.00*
a. Souv. sheet, #C177-C180 12.00 *12.00*
Nos. C177-C180 (4) 9.45 *9.10*

National Hospital Fund.
Nos. C177-C180 exist with colors reversed, perf. and imperf. These are proofs.

No. C168 Perf. 12½ or 12 diagonally through center

1951, Apr. ***Perf. 14***

C181 AP37 (4c) multi 15.00 9.00
a. Unsevered pair 37.50 22.50

Counterfeits of diagonal perforation exist.

Ceremonial Stone Ax — AP42

1953, Feb. 11 Photo. *Perf. 14x13½*

C182	AP42	3c dk bl & ol gray	.50	.45
C183	AP42	5c dk gray & hn brn	.60	.45
C184	AP42	10c dk pur & slate	.90	.45
		Nos. C182-C184 (3)	2.00	1.35

National Flag and Emblem — AP43

1953, Mar. 14 *Perf. 13½*

Multicolored Center

C185	AP43	1c maroon	.30	.25
C186	AP43	2c slate green	.30	.25
C187	AP43	4c dark brown	.35	.25
		Nos. C185-C187 (3)	.95	.75

Issued to mark the passing of the presidency from J. J. Arevalo to Col. Jacobo Arbenz Guzman.

Regional Dance — AP44

Horse Racing AP45

Designs: 4c, White nun — national flower. 5c, Allegory of the fair. 20c, Zakuleu ruins. 30c, Symbols of Agriculture. 50c, Champion bull. 65c, Bicycle racing. 1q, Quetzal.

1953, Dec. 18 Engr. *Perf. 12½*

C188	AP44	1c dp ultra & car	.25	.25
C189	AP44	4c org & grn	1.25	.30
C190	AP44	5c emer & choc	.80	.40
C191	AP45	15c choc & dk pur	1.10	1.00
C192	AP45	20c car & ultra	1.00	1.00
C193	AP44	30c dp ultra & choc	1.25	*1.25*
C194	AP45	50c pur & blk	1.25	1.25
C195	AP45	65c lt bl & dk grn	2.50	*2.50*
C196	AP44	1q dk bl grn & dk red	25.00	*15.00*
		Nos. C188-C196 (9)	34.40	*22.95*

National Fair, Oct. 20, 1953.

Indian — AP46

1954, Apr. 21 Unwmk. *Perf. 12½*

C197	AP46	1c carmine	.30	.25
C198	AP46	2c dp blue	.30	.25
C199	AP46	4c yellow grn	.30	.25
C200	AP46	5c aqua	.55	.25
C201	AP46	6c orange	.55	.25
C202	AP46	10c violet	1.10	.30
C203	AP46	20c black brn	3.25	3.25
		Nos. C197-C203 (7)	6.35	4.80

Guatemala and ODECA Flags — AP47

1954, Oct. 13 Photo. *Perf. 14x13½*

C204	AP47	1c multicolored	.55	.50
C205	AP47	2c multicolored	.55	.50
C206	AP47	4c multicolored	.55	.50
		Nos. C204-C206 (3)	1.65	1.50

3rd anniv. of the formation of the Organization of Central American States.

Rotary Emblem, Map of Guatemala AP48

1956, Sept. 8 Engr.

C207	AP48	4c bl & dl yel	.30	.25
C208	AP48	6c lt bl grn & dl yel	.30	.25
C209	AP48	35c pur & dl yel	1.50	*1.75*
		Nos. C207-C209 (3)	2.10	*2.25*

50th anniv. of Rotary Intl. (in 1955).

Mayan Warrior Holding Dagger Cross of the Liberation AP49

4c, Family looking into the sun. 5c, The dagger of the Liberation destroying communist symbols. 6c, Hands holding cogwheel & map of Guatemala. 20c, Monument to the victims of communism & flag. 30c, Champerico harbor. 65c, Radio tower, Mercury & map of Guatemala. 1q, Flags of the American nations. 5q, Pres. Carlos Castillo Armas.

1956, Oct. 10 Photo. *Perf. 14x13½*

C210	AP49	2c dp grn, red, bl & brn	.25	.25
C211	AP49	4c dp car & gray blk	.25	.25
C212	AP49	5c bl & red brn	.25	.25
C213	AP49	6c dk brn & dp ultra	.30	.25
C214	AP49	20c vio, brn & bl	1.40	*1.75*
C215	AP49	30c dp bl & ol	1.75	*2.00*
C216	AP49	65c chnt brn & grn	2.50	*3.00*
C217	AP49	1q dk brn & multi	3.50	*4.00*
C218	AP49	5q multi	14.00	*15.00*
		Nos. C210-C218 (9)	24.20	*26.75*

Liberation of 1954-55.

For overprints see Nos. C233, C243, C265-C266, C417.

Red Cross, Map and Quetzal AP50

Designs: 2c, José Ruiz Angulo and woman with child, vert. 3c, Pedro de Bethancourt with sick man. 4c, Rafael Ayau.

Perf. 13½x14, 14x13½

1958, May 13 Unwmk.

C219	AP50	1c multicolored	.75	.40
C220	AP50	2c multicolored	.45	.25
C221	AP50	3c multicolored	.45	.25
C222	AP50	4c multicolored	.45	.25
		Nos. C219-C222 (4)	2.10	1.15

Issued in honor of the Red Cross.

For overprints and surcharges see Nos. C235-C242, C251-C254, C283-C298, C390-C395.

Col. Carlos Castillo Armas — AP51

1959, Feb. 27 *Perf. 14x13½*

Center in Dark Blue and Yellow

C223	AP51	1c black	.30	.25
C224	AP51	2c rose red	.30	.25
C225	AP51	4c brown	.30	.25
C226	AP51	6c dk bl grn	.30	.25
C227	AP51	10c dk purple	.45	.30
C228	AP51	20c blue grn	1.25	.75
C229	AP51	35c gray	1.75	1.40
		Nos. C223-C229 (7)	4.65	3.45

Pres. Carlos Castillo Armas (1914-1957).

No. C134A Overprinted in Carmine

1959, Mar. 4 Engr. *Perf. 11*

C230	A131	7½c dk blue	1.25	*1.25*

Issued to honor the United Nations.

Galleon of 1532 and Freighter "Quezaltenango" AP52

1959, May 15 Litho. *Perf. 11*

C231	AP52	6c ultra & rose red	1.00	.30

Issued to honor the formation of the Guatemala-Honduras merchant fleet.

For overprint see No. C467.

Type of 1950 Overprinted in Dark Blue

1959, Oct. 9 *Perf. 12*

C232	A140	5c dk bl & lt brn	.75	.25
a.		Inverted overprint	200.00	35.00

Issued to state Guatemala's claim to British Honduras. Overprint reads: "Belize is ours." Map includes "BRITISH HONDURAS" and its borderline, and excludes bit extending above "A" of "GUATEMALA" on No. 337.

No. C232 is known without overprint in multiples.

No. C213 Overprinted in Red

1959, Oct. 26 Photo. *Perf. 14x13½*

C233	AP49	6c dk brn & dp ultra	.65	.30

Centenary of coffee export.

Pres. and Mrs. Villeda of Honduras AP53

1959, Nov. 3 Litho. *Perf. 11*

C234	AP53	6c pale brown	.70	.30

Visit of President Ramon Villeda Morales of Honduras, Oct. 12, 1958.

For overprint see No. C415.

Nos. C219-C222 Overprinted in Green, Violet, Blue or Brown

No. C235

No. C236

Perf. 13½x14, 14x13½

1960, Apr. 23 Photo. Unwmk.

C235	AP50	1c multi (G)	2.00	1.75
C236	AP50	2c multi (V)	.95	.95
C237	AP50	3c multi (Bl)	.95	.95
C238	AP50	4c multi (Br)	.95	.95

Nos. C219-C222 Overprinted

C239	AP50	6c on 1c multi	5.00	2.50
C240	AP50	7c on 2c multi	2.50	2.25
C241	AP50	10c on 3c multi	4.00	4.25
C242	AP50	20c on 4c multi	4.50	4.50
		Nos. C235-C242 (8)	20.85	18.10

Nos. C235-C242 issued to publicize World Refugee Year, July 1, 1959-June 30, 1960.

No. C213 Overprinted in Red

1960, Apr. 30 *Perf. 14x13½*

C243	AP49	6c dk brn & dp ultra	1.40	1.25

Founding of the city of Melchor de Mencos.

UNESCO and Eiffel Tower, Paris AP54

1960, Nov. 4 Photo. *Perf. 12½*

C244	AP54	5c dp mag & vio	.25	.25
C245	AP54	6c ultra & vio brn	.25	.25
C246	AP54	8c emer & magenta	.40	.25
C247	AP54	20c red brn & dl bl	1.40	1.40
		Nos. C244-C247 (4)	2.30	2.15

Issued to honor UNESCO.

For overprints see Nos. C258, C267-C268.

Abraham Lincoln — AP55

1960, Oct. 29 Engr. *Perf. 11*

C248 AP55 5c violet blue .25 .25
C249 AP55 30c violet 1.10 *1.40*
C250 AP55 50c gray 5.50 *6.50*
Nos. C248-C250 (3) 6.85 *8.15*

Sesquicentenary of the birth of Abraham Lincoln.
An 8c was also printed, but was not issued and all copies were destroyed.

Nos. C219-C222 Overprinted in Green, Blue or Brown

Perf. 13½x14, 14x13½
1961, Apr. 20 Photo. Unwmk.

C251 AP50 1c multi (G) .60 .45
C252 AP50 2c multi (Bl) .60 .45
C253 AP50 3c multi (Bl) .60 .45
C254 AP50 4c multi (Br) .60 .45
Nos. C251-C254 (4) 2.40 1.80

Issued to honor the Red Cross.

Proclamation of Independence — AP56

1962 Engr. *Perf. 11*

C255 AP56 4c sepia .25 .25
C256 AP56 5c violet blue .40 .25
C257 AP56 15c brt violet 1.40 .65
Nos. C255-C257 (3) 2.05 1.15

140th anniv. of Independence (in 1961).
Issue dates: 4c, 5c, May 23; 15c, Aug. 10.

No. C245 Overprinted in Red

1962, Oct. 4 Photo. *Perf. 12½*

C258 AP54 6c ultra & vio brn 1.00 *1.40*

WHO drive to eradicate malaria.

Dr. José Luna — AP57

Guatemalan physicians: 4c, Rodolfo Robles. 5c, Narciso Esparragoza y Gallardo. 6c, Juan J. Ortega. 10c, Dario Gonzalez. 20c, José Felipe Flores.

1962, Dec. 12 Photo. *Perf. 14x13½*

C259 AP57 1c ol bis & dl pur .80 .25
C260 AP57 4c org yel & gray ol .80 .25
C261 AP57 5c pale bl & red brn .80 .25
C262 AP57 6c salmon & blk .80 .25
C263 AP57 10c pale grn & red brn 1.10 .25
C264 AP57 20c pale pink & bl 1.25 .80
Nos. C259-C264 (6) 5.55 2.05

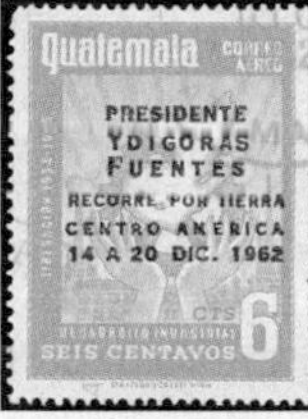

No. C213 Overprinted in Red

1962, Dec. Photo. *Perf. 14x13½*

C265 AP49 6c dk brn & dp ultra 1.25 .80

Pres. Ydigoras' tour of Central America, Dec. 14-20, 1962.

No. C213 Overprinted in Vermilion

Perf. 14x13½
1963, Mar. 18 Unwmk.

C266 AP49 6c dk brn & dp ultra 6.00 3.00

Meeting of Pres. John F. Kennedy with the Presidents of the Central American Republics, San Jose, Costa Rica, Mar. 18-21.

Nos. C245-C246 Overprinted in Magenta or Black

1963, Mar. 14 *Perf. 12½*

C267 AP54 6c ultra & vio brn (M) .55 .25
C268 AP54 8c emerald & mag .60 .25

Signing of the new charter of the Organization of Central American States (ODECA).

Enriquez de Rivera Type of 1946
Perf. 11, 11½, 12½
1963, Mar. 26 Engr.

C269 A132 5c olive bister .35 .25

Woman Carrying Fruit Basket — AP58

1963, Mar. 14 Litho. *Perf. 11, 12½*

C270 AP58 1c multicolored .35 .25

Spring Fair, 1960.

Reaper — AP59

1963, July 25 Photo. *Perf. 14*

C271 AP59 5c Prus green .35 .25
C272 AP59 10c dark blue .65 .30

FAO "Freedom from Hunger" campaign.

Ceiba Tree — AP60

1963 Unwmk. *Perf. 12*

C273 AP60 4c brown & green 1.40 .25

Patzun Palace AP61

Buildings: 3c, Coban. 4c, Retalhuleu. 5c, San Marcos. 6c, Captains General of Antigua.

1964, Jan. 15 *Perf. 13½x14*

C274 AP61 1c rose red & brn .50 .25
C275 AP61 3c rose cl & Prus grn .50 .25
C276 AP61 4c vio bl & rose lake .50 .25
C277 AP61 5c brown & blue .65 .25
C278 AP61 6c green & slate .65 .25
Nos. C274-C278 (5) 2.80 1.25

City Hall, Guatemala City AP62

Design: 4c, Social Security Institute.

1964, Jan. 15 Photo. *Perf. 12x11½*

C279 AP62 3c brt bl & brn .45 .25
C280 AP62 4c brn & brt bl .55 .25

See Nos. C281-C282A. For overprints see Nos. C360-C361, C421.

1964-65 Engr. *Perf. 11½*

Designs: 3c, Social Security Institute. 4c, University administration building. No. C282, City Hall, Guatemala City. No. C282A, Engineering School.

Different Frames

C281 AP62 3c dull green .55 .25
C281A AP62 4c gray ('65) .55 .25
C282 AP62 7c blue .60 .25
C282A AP62 7c olive bis ('65) .60 .25
Nos. C281-C282A (4) 2.30 1.00

Nos. C219-C222 Ovptd. in Green, Blue or Black

1964 Photo. *Perf. 13½x14, 14x13½*

C283 AP50 1c multi (G) 1.25 *1.40*
C284 AP50 2c multi (Bl) 1.25 *1.40*
C285 AP50 3c multi (G) 1.25 *1.40*
C286 AP50 4c multi (Bk) 1.25 *1.40*
Nos. C283-C286 (4) 5.00 *5.60*

18th Olympic Games, Tokyo, 10/10-25/64.

Nos. C219-C222 Surcharged in Green, Blue or Black

1964

C287 AP50 7c on 1c multi (G) .30 .25
C288 AP50 9c on 2c multi (Bl) .40 *.40*
C289 AP50 13c on 3c multi (Bl) .55 .45
C290 AP50 21c on 4c multi (Bk) 1.00 *.85*
Nos. C287-C290 (4) 2.25 *1.95*

Nos. C219-C222 Ovptd. in Green, Blue or Black

1964, June 25

C291 AP50 1c multi (G) .80 *.85*
C292 AP50 2c multi (Bl) .80 *.85*
C293 AP50 3c multi (G) .80 *.85*
C294 AP50 4c multi (Bk) .80 *.85*
Nos. C291-C294 (4) 3.20 *3.40*

New York World's Fair.

Nos. C219-C222 Ovptd. in Green, Blue or Black

1964

C295 AP50 1c multi (G) 1.60 *1.40*
C296 AP50 2c multi (Bl) 1.60 *1.40*
C297 AP50 3c multi (G) 1.60 *1.40*
C298 AP50 4c multi (Bk) 2.50 *2.25*
Nos. C295-C298 (4) 7.30 *6.45*

Eighth Bicycle Race.

Pres. John F. Kennedy — AP63

1964 Engr. *Perf. 11½*

C299 AP63 1c violet 1.10 .70
C300 AP63 2c yellow grn 1.10 .70
C301 AP63 3c brown 1.10 .70
C302 AP63 7c deep blue 1.10 .70
C303 AP63 50c dk gray 8.50 *7.50*
Nos. C299-C303 (5) 12.90 *10.30*

Minute letters "TEOK" are in lower right corner of 1c, 2c, 3c and 50c.
Issue dates: 7c, July 10; others, Aug. 21.

Centenary Emblem — AP64

Perf. 11x12
1964, Sept. 9 Unwmk. Photo.

C304 AP64 7c ultra, sil & red .90 .25
C305 AP64 9c org, sil & red .90 .40
C306 AP64 13c pur, sil & red 1.40 .55
C307 AP64 21c brt grn, sil & red 1.10 *1.00*
C308 AP64 35c brn, sil & red 2.10 *1.40*
C309 AP64 1q lem, sil & red 3.75 3.00
Nos. C304-C309 (6) 10.15 *6.60*

Centenary (in 1963) of the Intl. Red Cross.
For overprints see Nos. C323-C327, C395-C400.

Type of Regular Issue 1963
Souvenir Sheet

1964 Engr. *Imperf.*

C310 Sheet of 2 9.50 *10.00*
a. A151 10c violet blue 4.00 4.00
b. A151 20c carmine 4.00 4.00

15th UPU Congress, Vienna, May-June, 1964.

Enriquez de Rivera Type of 1946

1964, Dec. 18 Engr. *Perf. 11½*

C311	A132 5c gray	.30	.25
C312	A132 5c orange	.30	.25
C313	A132 5c lt green	.30	.25
C314	A132 5c lt ultra	.30	.25
C315	A132 5c dull violet	.30	.25
	Nos. C311-C315 (5)	1.50	1.25

Bishop Francisco Marroquin AP65

1965, Jan. 21 Photo. Unwmk.

C316	AP65 4c lilac & brn	.25	.25
C317	AP65 7c gray & sepia	.60	.25
C318	AP65 9c vio bl & blk	.70	.25
	Nos. C316-C318 (3)	1.55	.75

Issued to honor Bishop Francisco Marroquin.

Bethancourt Type of Regular Issue, 1964

1965, Apr. 20 Engr. *Perf. 11½*

C319	A152 2½c violet blue	.30	.25
C320	A152 3c orange	.30	.25
C321	A152 4c purple	.30	.25
C322	A152 5c yellow grn	.35	.25
	Nos. C319-C322 (4)	1.25	1.00

For overprints see Nos. C381-C382.

Nos. C304-C308 Overprinted in Red

1965, June 18 Photo. *Perf. 11x12*

C323	AP64 7c ultra, sil & red	.45	.45
C324	AP64 9c org, sil & red	.55	.55
C325	AP64 13c pur, sil & red	.60	.55
C326	AP64 21c brt grn, sil & red	.85	.80
C327	AP64 35c brn, sil & red	1.00	*1.25*
	Nos. C323-C327 (5)	3.45	3.60

Guatemalan Boy Scout Emblem — AP66

Designs: 9c, Campfire and Scouts. 10c, Scout emblem and Scout carrying torch and flag. 15c, Scout emblem, flags and Scout giving Scout sign. 20c, Lord Baden-Powell.

1966, Mar. 3 Photo. *Perf. 14x13½*

C328	AP66 5c multicolored	.60	.55
C329	AP66 9c multicolored	.75	.70
C330	AP66 10c multicolored	.95	.85
C331	AP66 15c multicolored	1.25	1.10
C332	AP66 20c multicolored	1.75	1.50
	Nos. C328-C332 (5)	5.30	4.70

5th Interamerican Regional Training Conf., Guatemala City, Mar. 1-3.
For overprints see Nos. C376-C380.

Central American Independence Issue

Flags of Central American States — AP67

1966, Mar. 9 *Perf. 12½x13½*

C333	AP67 6c multicolored	.45	.25

Queen Nefertari Temple, Abu Simbel AP68

1966, Oct. 3 Photo. *Perf. 12*

C334	AP68 21c violet & ocher	.95	.45

UNESCO world campaign to save historic monuments in Nubia.

Coat of Arms — AP69

1966-70 Engr. *Perf. 13½*

C335	AP69 5c orange	.90	.30
C336	AP69 5c green	.90	.30
a.	5c yel grn, perf. 11½ ('69)	1.00	.30

Perf. 11½

C337	AP69 5c blue ('67)	.90	.30
a.	5c dk bl, perf. 12½ ('69)	.35	.30

Perf. 12½

C338	AP69 5c gray ('67)	.90	.30
C339	AP69 5c purple ('67)	.90	.30
a.	5c bright violet ('69)	.35	.30

Perf. 11½

C339B	AP69 5c dp mag ('70)	1.50	.30
C339C	AP69 5c grn, *yel* ('70)	1.75	.30
	Nos. C335-C339C (7)	7.75	2.10

Issued: No. C335, 10/31; No. C336, 12/15/66; No. C337, 2/9/67; Nos. C338-C339, 4/28/67; No. C336a, 12/3/69; No. C339a, 12/11/69; No. C339B, 7/8/70; No. C339C, 10/16/70.

Msgr. Mariano Rossell y Arellano AP70

1966, Nov. 3 Engr. *Perf. 13½*

C340	AP70 1c dp violet	.25	.25
C341	AP70 2c green	.30	.25
C342	AP70 3c brown	.30	.25
C343	AP70 7c blue	.45	.40
C344	AP70 50c gray	2.00	2.00
	Nos. C340-C344 (5)	3.30	3.15

Issued to honor Msgr. Mariano Rossell y Arellano, apostolic delegate.

Mario Mendez Montenegro AP71

1966-67 *Perf. 13½*

C345	AP71 2c rose red ('67)	.25	.25
C346	AP71 3c orange ('67)	.30	.25
C347	AP71 4c rose claret ('67)	.40	.25
C348	AP71 5c gray	.55	.25
C349	AP71 5c lt ultra ('67)	.55	.25
C350	AP71 5c green ('67)	.55	.25
C351	AP71 5c bluish blk ('67)	.55	.25
	Nos. C345-C351 (7)	3.15	1.75

Mario Mendez Montenegro (1910-65), founder of the Revolutionary Party.

Morning Glory and Map of Guatemala AP72

Flowers: 8c, Bird of paradise, horiz. 10c, White nun orchid, national flower, horiz. 20c, Nymphs of Amatitlan.

1967, Jan. 12 Photo. *Perf. 12*

Flowers in Natural Colors

C352	AP72 4c orange	1.40	.60
C353	AP72 8c green	1.40	.60
C354	AP72 10c dk blue	1.60	1.10
C355	AP72 20c dk red	3.50	2.40
	Nos. C352-C355 (4)	7.90	4.70

Pan-American Institute Emblem — AP73

1967, Apr. 13 Photo. *Perf. 13½*

C356	AP73 4c lt brn, lil & blk	.40	.25
C357	AP73 5c ol, bl & blk	.75	.25
C358	AP73 7c org yel, bl & blk	1.10	.40
	Nos. C356-C358 (3)	2.25	.90

8th Gen. Assembly of the Pan-American Geographical and Historical Institute in 1965.

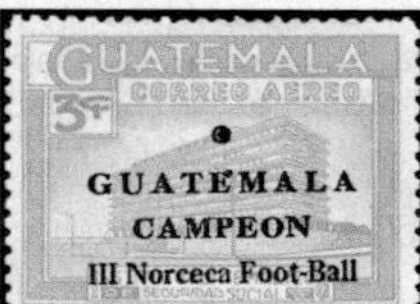

No. C281 Overprinted

1967, Apr. 28 Engr. *Perf. 11½*

C360	AP62 3c dull green	1.60	1.10

Guatemala's victory in the 3rd Norceca Soccer Games (Caribbean, Central and North American).

No. C281A Overprinted in Red

1967, June 28 Engr. *Perf. 11½*

C361	AP62 4c gray	1.10	1.10

Meeting of American Presidents, Punta del Este, Apr. 10-12.

Handshake AP74

1967, June 28 Photo. *Perf. 12*

C362	AP74 7c pink, brn & grn	.55	.25
C363	AP74 21c lt bl, grn & brn	.85	.55

"Peace and Progress through Cooperation."
For overprint see No. C416.

Church of Santo Domingo AP75

1c, Yurrita Church, vert. 3c, Church of St. Francis. 4c, Antonio José de Irisarri, vert. 5c, Church of the Convent, vert. 7c, Mercy Church, Antigua. 10c, Metropolitan Cathedral.

1967, Aug. *Perf. 11½x12, 12x11½*

C364	AP75 1c grn, lt bl & dk brn	.40	.25
C365	AP75 2c plum, sal pink & brn	.45	.25
C366	AP75 3c brt rose, gray & blk	.45	.25
C367	AP75 4c mar, sl grn & org	.45	.25
C368	AP75 5c lil, pale grn & dk brn	.45	.25
C369	AP75 7c ultra, lil rose & blk	.55	.25
C370	AP75 10c pur, yel & blk	.95	.30
	Nos. C364-C370 (7)	3.70	1.80

Abraham Lincoln (1809-1865) AP76

1967 Engr. *Perf. 13½, 11½ (9c)*

C371	AP76 7c gray & dp org	.45	.25
C372	AP76 9c dk grn & grysh	.55	.25
C373	AP76 11c brn org & slate	.45	.30
C374	AP76 15c ultra & vio brn	.65	.40
C375	AP76 30c magenta & grn	1.50	1.50
	Nos. C371-C375 (5)	3.60	2.70

Issued: 7c, 9c, Oct. 9; others, Dec. 12.
For surcharge see No. C554.

Nos. C328-C332 Overprinted

1967, Dec. 1 Photo. *Perf. 14x13½*

C376	AP66 5c multicolored	.50	.40
C377	AP66 9c multicolored	.85	.65
C378	AP66 10c multicolored	1.10	.85
C379	AP66 15c multicolored	1.10	.85
C380	AP66 20c multicolored	1.40	1.00
	Nos. C376-C380 (5)	4.95	3.75

Issued to commemorate the 8th Central American Boy Scout Camporee, Dec. 1-8.

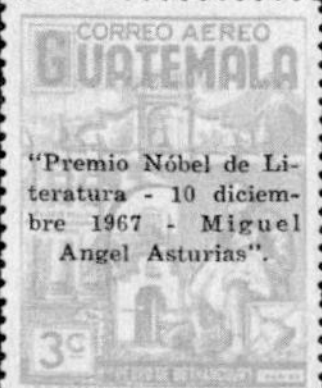

Nos. C320-C321 Overprinted

1967, Dec. 11 Engr. *Perf. 11½*

C381	A152 3c orange	.55	.55
C382	A152 4c purple	.55	.55

Awarding of the Nobel Prize for Literature to Miguel Angel Asturias, Guatemalan writer.

Institute Emblem — AP77

1967, Dec. 12 **Engr.** ***Perf. 11½***

C383	AP77	9c black & grn	3.75	3.75
C384	AP77	25c car & brn	5.00	5.00
C385	AP77	1q ultra & bl	17.50	*19.00*
		Nos. C383-C385 (3)	26.25	27.75

Inter-American Agriculture Institute, 25th anniv.

UNESCO Emblem and Children AP78

1967, Dec. 12

C386	AP78	4c blue green	.30	.25
C387	AP78	5c blue	.35	.25
C388	AP78	7c gray	.50	.35
C389	AP78	21c brt rose lil	1.10	1.10
		Nos. C386-C389 (4)	2.25	1.95

20th anniv. (in 1966) of UNESCO.

Nos. C219-C221 and C304-C308 Ovptd. in Black or Yellow Green

Perf. 13½x14, 14x13½, 11x12

1968, Jan. 23 **Photo.**

C390	AP50	1c multi	.80	.55
C391	AP50	1c multi (G)	.80	.80
C392	AP50	2c multi	.80	.80
C393	AP50	2c multi (G)	.80	.80
C394	AP50	3c multi	.80	.80
C395	AP50	3c multi (G)	.80	.80
C396	AP64	7c multi	.80	.80
C397	AP64	9c multi	1.10	1.10
C398	AP64	13c multi	1.60	1.10
C399	AP64	21c multi	2.25	1.10
C400	AP64	35c multi	1.90	1.90
		Nos. C390-C400 (11)	12.45	10.55

3rd meeting of Central American Presidents, Nov. 15-18, 1967.

Our Lady of the Coro — AP79

1968-74 **Engr.** ***Perf. 13½, 11½***

C403	AP79	4c ultra	.55	.25
C404	AP79	7c slate	.50	.25
C405	AP79	9c green	.50	.25
C406	AP79	9c lilac ('74)	.55	.25
C407	AP79	10c brick red	.95	.25
C408	AP79	10c gray	.60	.25
C408A	AP79	10c vio bl ('74)	.40	.25
C409	AP79	1q vio brn	4.00	3.50
C410	AP79	1q org yel	4.00	3.50
		Nos. C403-C410 (9)	12.05	8.75

Perf. 13½ applies to 4c and Nos. C407, C409-C410; perf. 11½ to 4c, 7c, 9c and Nos. C408, C408A.

Nos. 396-398 Overprinted

1968, Mar. 25 **Litho.** ***Perf. 14x13½***

C411	A153	4c multicolored	.85	.85
C412	A153	5c multicolored	.85	.85
C413	A153	6c multicolored	.70	.70
		Nos. C411-C413 (3)	2.40	2.40

The 11th Bicycle Race.

Miguel Angel Asturias, Flags of Guatemala and Sweden — AP80

1968, June 18 **Engr.** ***Perf. 11½***

C414	AP80	20c ultra	*5.50*	*5.50*

Awarding of the Nobel Prize for Literature to Miguel Angel Asturias.

No. C234 Overprinted in Carmine

1968, July 18 **Litho.** ***Perf. 11***

C415	AP53	6c pale brown	.80	.40

International Human Rights Year.

No. C362 Overprinted

1968, July 18 **Photo.** ***Perf. 12***

C416	AP74	7c pink, brn & grn	.70	.40

Issued to publicize forest conservation.

No. C213 Overprinted in Brown

1968, Aug. 23 **Photo.** ***Perf. 14x13½***

C417	AP49	6c dk brn & dp ultra	.70	.65

Nahakin scientific expedition along the route of the Mayas undertaken jointly with Peru.

Views, Quetzal and White Nun Orchid — AP81

1968, Aug. 23 **Engr.** ***Perf. 13½***

C418	AP81	10c dp cl & grn	3.00	2.00
C419	AP81	20c dp org & blk	4.00	3.00
C420	AP81	50c ultra & car	5.00	5.00
		Nos. C418-C420 (3)	12.00	10.00

Issued for tourist publicity.

No. C281A Overprinted in Carmine

1968, Nov. 4 ***Perf. 11½***

C421	AP62	4c gray	.65	.55

20th anniv. of the Federation of Central American Universities.

Presidents Gustavo Diaz Ordaz and Julio Cesar Mendez Montenegro AP82

1968, Dec. 3 **Litho.** ***Perf. 14x13½***

C422	AP82	5c multicolored	.25	.25
C423	AP82	10c multicolored	.40	.25
C424	AP82	25c multicolored	.95	.85
		Nos. C422-C424 (3)	1.60	1.35

Mutual visits of the Presidents of Mexico and Guatemala.

ITU Emblem, Old and New Communication Equipment — AP83

Engraved and Photogravure

1968-74 ***Perf. 11½, 12½ (21c)***

C425	AP83	7c violet blue	.25	.25
C426	AP83	15c gray & emer	.45	.25
C426A	AP83	15c vio brn & org ('74)	.60	.25
C427	AP83	21c magenta	.70	.45
C428	AP83	35c rose red & emer	.95	.45
C429	AP83	75c green & red	2.40	2.40
C430	AP83	3q brown & red	9.25	7.75
		Nos. C425-C430 (7)	14.60	11.80

Cent. (in 1965) of the ITU.

Nos. C425, C427 are engr. only; on others denominations are photo. No. C426A is on thin, toned paper.

Issued: No. C426A, 2/18/74; others 12/13/68.

For surcharges see Nos. C454, C516.

Nos. 399-403 Overprinted in Red, Black or Gold

Lithographed and Engraved

1969 ***Perf. 11½, 13½ (1c)***

C431	A154	1c blk, lt grn & red (R)	.80	*2.00*
C432	A154	5c yel, lt grn & red	1.10	*2.00*
C433	A154	8c org, lt grn & red	1.25	*4.00*
C434	A154	15c bl, lt grn & red	1.40	*4.00*
C435	A154	30c lt vio, lt grn & red (G)	1.75	*4.00*
		Nos. C431-C435 (5)	6.30	*16.00*

Dante Alighieri — AP84

1969, July 17 **Engr.** ***Perf. 12½***

C436	AP84	7c rose vio & ultra	.40	.25
C437	AP84	10c dk blue	.45	.25
C438	AP84	20c green	.70	.25
C439	AP84	21c gray & brn	1.10	.80
C440	AP84	35c pur & brt grn	2.75	1.75
		Nos. C436-C440 (5)	5.40	3.30

Dante Alighieri (1265-1321), Italian poet.

Map of Latin America — AP85

Design: 9c, Seal of University.

1969, Oct. 29 **Typo.** ***Perf. 13***

Size: 44x27mm

C441	AP85	2c brt pink & blk	.25	.25

Size: 35x27mm

C442	AP85	9c gray & blk	.55	.25

Souvenir Sheet

Imperf

C443	AP85	Sheet of 2	1.40	1.40
a.		2c light blue & black	.60	.60
b.		9c orange & black	.60	.60

20th anniv. of the Union of Latin American Universities.

Moon Landing Issue

Moon Landing — AP86

1969-70 **Engr.** ***Perf. 11½***

C444	AP86	50c maroon & blk	2.75	2.75
C445	AP86	1q ultra & blk	4.75	4.75

Souvenir Sheet

Imperf

C446	AP86	1q yel grn & ultra	6.75	6.75

See note after US No. C76. No. C446 contains one stamp with simulated perforations.

Issued: Nos. C445-C446, 12/19/69; No. C444, 1/6/70.

Giant Grebe Family on Lake Atitlan AP87

Designs: 4c, Lake Atitlan. 20c, Grebe chick, eggs atop floating nest, vert.

1970, Mar. 31 Litho. *Perf. 13½*

C447 AP87 4c red & multi 1.00 .25
C448 AP87 9c red & multi 1.60 .30
a. Souv. sheet of 2, #C447-C448 17.50 17.50
C449 AP87 20c red & multi 2.75 .85
Nos. C447-C449 (3) 5.35 1.40

Protection of zambullidor ducks.

Dr. Victor Manuel Calderon — AP88

1970 Litho. & Engr. *Perf. 13, 12½*

C450 AP88 1c lt bl & blk .30 .25
C451 AP88 2c pale grn & blk .30 .25

Perf. 13

C452 AP88 9c yellow & blk .65 .25
Nos. C450-C452 (3) 1.25 .75

Dr. Victor Manuel Calderon (1889-1969), who described microfilaria, a blood parasite.

Hand Holding Bible — AP89

1970 Litho. & Typo. *Perf. 13x13½*

C453 AP89 5c red & multi .35 .25

Fourth centenary of the Bible in Spanish.

No. C430 Surcharged

1971, Mar. 11 Engr. *Perf. 11½*

C454 AP83 50c on 3q brn & red 2.00 2.00

Arms of Guatemala, Newspapers — AP90

Official Decree of First Issue — AP91

1971 Litho. *Perf. 11½, 12½*

C455 AP90 2c dk bl & red .30 .25
C456 AP90 5c brn & red .30 .25
C457 AP90 25c brt bl & red .70 .40
Nos. C455-C457 (3) 1.30 .90

Souvenir Sheet

Lithographed and Engraved

Imperf

C458 AP91 Sheet of 5 2.00 2.00

Cent. of Guatemala's postage stamps. Nos. C456-C457 have white value tablet.

No. C458 contains a litho. 4c black and engr. reproductions of Nos. 1-4 in colors similar to 1871 issue. Simulated perforations.

In 1974 No. C458 was overprinted "Conmemorativa / al Campeonato Mundial de Foot Ball / Munich 1974" and Munich Games emblem in black. Value $12. Overprint in gold or other colors was not authorized.

See Nos. C569-C570.

Mayas with CARE Package — AP92

1971 Typo. *Perf. 11½*

C459 AP92 5c multi .45 .40
a. Souv. sheet of 2 2.50 2.50

25th aniversary of CARE, a US-Canadian Cooperative for American Relief Everywhere.

No. C459a contains imperf. stamps similar to Nos. 416 and C459.

J. Rufino Barrios, M. Garcia Granados, Map of Guatemala, Quetzal — AP93

1971, June 30 *Perf. 11½*

C460 AP93 2c multi, perf 13½ .80 .25
a. Value in pink ('72) .70 .25
C461 AP93 10c multi 1.50 .30
a. Value in pink, perf. 12½ ('72) 1.50 .30
C462 AP93 50c multi 8.00 3.25
C463 AP93 1q multi 12.00 6.50
Nos. C460-C463 (4) 22.30 10.30

Centenary of the liberal revolution of 1871.

Chavarry Arrué and León Bilak — AP94

Perf. 11½, 11x12½, 12½

1971-72 Engr.

C464 AP94 1c grn & blk ('72) .25 .25
C465 AP94 2c lt brn & blk ('72) .30 .25
C466 AP94 5c org & blk .45 .30
Nos. C464-C466 (3) 1.00 .80

Honoring J. Arnoldo Chavarry Arrué, stamp engraver; León Bilak, philatelist.

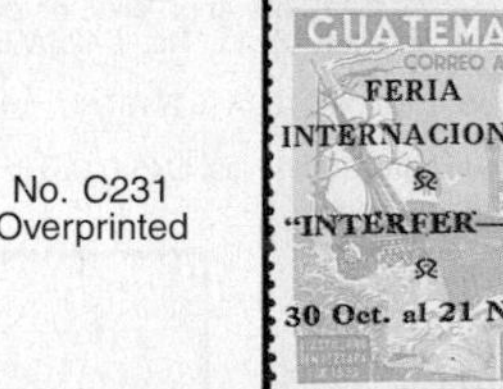

No. C231 Overprinted

1971, Oct. 25 Litho. *Perf. 11½*

C467 AP52 6c ultra & rose red *5.00 3.00*

INTERFER 71, Intl. Fair, Guatemala, Oct. 30-Nov. 21.

Flag and Map of Guatemala AP95

Perf. 13½ (1c), 12½ (3c, 9c), 11 (5c)

1971-75 Typo.

C468 AP95 1c blk, bl & lil .30 .25
a. Lithographed ('75) .30 .25
C469 AP95 3c brn, brt pink & bl .30 .25
C470 AP95 5c brn, org & bl .30 .25
a. Lithographed, perf. 12½ ('74) .30 .25
C471 AP95 9c blk, emer & bl .30 .25
Nos. C468-C471 (4) 1.20 1.00

Central American independence, sesqui. Issued: Nos. C469-C471, 7/10/72.

UNICEF Emblem and Mayan Figure — AP96

1971-75 Engr. *Perf. 11½*

C472 AP96 1c yel grn .25 .25
C472A AP96 2c purple .25 .25
C473 AP96 50c vio brn 1.90 1.90
C474 AP96 1q ultra 3.00 3.00
Nos. C472-C474 (4) 5.40 5.40

25th anniv. UNICEF.
Issued: 2c, 2/24/75; others, 11/71.

Early Boeing Planes — AP97

Design: 10c, Bleriot's plane.

1972 Typo. *Perf. 11½*

C475 AP97 5c lt brn & brt bl .75 .30
C476 AP97 10c dark blue 1.25 .30

Military aviation in Guatemala, 50th anniv.

Arches, Antigua — AP98

Nos. C481, C487, C493, C501, Cathedral. Nos. C482, C490, C496, C498 Fountain, Central Park. Nos. C483, C491, C497, C499, Capuchin Monastery. Nos. C484, C488, C494, C502, Fountain and Santa Clara. Nos. C485, C489, C495, C503, Portal of San Francisco.

1972-73 Typo. *Perf. 11½*

Dark Blue and Light Blue

C480 AP98 1c multicolored .25 .25
C481 AP98 1c multicolored .25 .25
C482 AP98 1c multicolored .25 .25
C483 AP98 1c multicolored .25 .25
C484 AP98 1c multicolored .25 .25
C485 AP98 1c multicolored .25 .25
a. Block of 6, #C480-C485 1.75 1.60

Black, Lilac Rose, and Silver

C486 AP98 2½c multicolored .45 .25
C487 AP98 2½c multicolored .45 .25
C488 AP98 2½c multicolored .45 .25
C489 AP98 2½c multicolored .45 .25
C490 AP98 2½c multicolored .45 .25
C491 AP98 2½c multicolored .45 .25
a. Block of 6, #C3486-C491 3.00 1.60

Blue, Orange and Black

C492 AP98 5c shown .95 .25
C493 AP98 5c multicolored .95 .25
C494 AP98 5c multicolored .95 .25
C495 AP98 5c multicolored .95 .25
C496 AP98 5c multicolored .95 .25
C497 AP98 5c multicolored .95 .25
a. Block of 6, #C492-C497 6.00 3.00

Nos. C492-C497 exist perf. 12½, same value.

Perf. 12½

Red, Blue and Black

C498 AP98 1q multicolored 4.75 2.50
C499 AP98 1q multicolored 4.75 2.50
C500 AP98 1q multicolored 4.75 2.50
C501 AP98 1q multicolored 4.75 2.50
C502 AP98 1q multicolored 4.75 2.50
C503 AP98 1q multicolored 4.75 2.50
a. Block of 6, #C498-C503 27.50 15.00
Nos. C480-C503 (24) 38.40 19.50

Earthquake ruins of Antigua. 1c printed se-tenant in sheets of 90 (10x9); 2½c, 5c se-tenant in sheets of 30 (5x6); 1q se-tenant in sheets of 6 (3x2).

On Nos. C498-C503 the inks were applied by a thermographic process giving a shiny raised effect.

Issued: Nos. C480-C485, 12/14; Nos. C486-C491, 1/22/73; Nos. C492-C497, 3/12/73; Nos. C498-C503, 8/22/73.

Nos. C480-C485 were overprinted "II Feria Internacional / INTERFER/73 / 31 Octubre — Noviembre 18 / 1973 / GUATEMALA" in black or lilac rose and issued 11/3/73. Value, each set $3.

See Nos. C528-C545, C770-C775F. For overprints see Nos. C517-C523.

Simon Bolivar and Map of Americas AP99

1973-74 *Perf. 11½*

C504 AP99 3c brt lil rose & blk .25 .25
C505 AP99 3c org & dk bl ('74) *5.00 2.00*
C506 AP99 5c yel & multi .25 .25
C507 AP99 5c brt grn & blk .25 .25
Nos. C504-C507 (4) 5.75 2.75

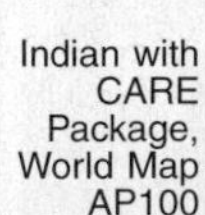

Indian with CARE Package, World Map AP100

CARE Package AP101

1973, June 14 Typo. *Perf. 12½*

C508 AP100 2c blk & multi .25 .25
C509 AP101 10c blk & multi .55 .40
a. Souvenir sheet of 2 1.50 1.50

25th anniversary of CARE (in 1971), a US-sponsored relief organization and 10th anniversary of its work in Guatemala.

No. C509a contains 2 stamps similar to Nos. C508-C509 with simulated perforations.

Guatemala No. 1, Laurel AP102

1973-74 Engr. ***Perf. 12½, 11½ (1q)***
C510 AP102 1c yel brn ('74) .25 .25
C511 AP102 1q rose claret 3.00 2.50

Centenary (in 1971) of Guatemala postage stamps. See Nos. C574-C576A.

Oak Wreath and Star AP103

1973, Aug. 22 Typo. ***Perf. 12½***
C512 AP103 5c brn, yel & bl .55 .25

Centenary of Escuela Politecnica, Guatemala's military academy.
See Nos. C552-C553.

Eleanor Roosevelt AP104

Perf. 11½, 12½
1973, Sept. 11 Engr.
C513 AP104 7c blue .45 .25

Eleanor Roosevelt (1884-1962), lecturer, writer, UN delegate.

Boys' School, Chiquimula AP105

1973-74 Typo. ***Perf. 12½***
C514 AP105 3c blk & bl .50 .25
C515 AP105 5c blk & dp lil rose .50 .25

Centenary of the Instituto Varones in Chiquimula.
Issued: 5c, 12/5/73; 3c, 6/13/74.

No. C430 Surcharged in Red

1974 Engr. & Photo. ***Perf. 11½***
C516 AP83 50c on 3q brn & red 2.00 2.00

Nos. C480-C485 and C509a Overprinted

1974, June 13 Typo. ***Perf. 11½***
C517 AP98 1c dk bl & lt bl .40 .30
C518 AP98 1c dk bl & lt bl .40 .30
C519 AP98 1c dk bl & lt bl .40 .30
C520 AP98 1c dk bl & lt bl .40 .30
C521 AP98 1c dk bl & lt bl .40 .30
C522 AP98 1c dk bl & lt bl .40 .30
Nos. C517-C522 (6) 2.40 1.80

Souvenir Sheet
C523 Sheet of 2 13.50 13.50

Centenary of Universal Postal Union.
No. C523 consists of an overprint on No. C509a, including "UNIVERSAL POSTAL UNION" instead of "UPU."
The overprint on No. C523 in red was not authorized by the Post Office. Value $28.

Antigua Type of 1972-73

No. C528, Capuchin Monastery. No. C529, Arches. No. C530, Cathedral. No. C531, Fountain and Santa Clara. No. C532, Portal of San Francisco. No. C533, Fountain.

1974, Oct. 8 Typo. ***Perf. 11½***
Black and Light Brown
C528 AP98 2c multicolored .25 .25
C529 AP98 2c multicolored .25 .25
C530 AP98 2c multicolored .25 .25
C531 AP98 2c multicolored .25 .25
C532 AP98 2c multicolored .25 .25
C533 AP98 2c multicolored .25 .25
Nos. C528-C533 (6) 1.50 1.50

Antigua Type of 1972-73

No. C540, Capuchin Monastery. No. C541, Arches. No. C542, Cathedral. No. C543, Fountain and Santa Clara. No. C544, Portal of San Francisco. No. C545, Fountain.

1974, Sept. 24 Black and Yellow
C540 AP98 20c multicolored .55 .55
C541 AP98 20c multicolored .55 .55
C542 AP98 20c multicolored .55 .55
C543 AP98 20c multicolored .55 .55
C544 AP98 20c multicolored .55 .55
C545 AP98 20c multicolored .55 .55
Nos. C540-C545 (6) 3.30 3.30

Earthquake ruins of Antigua. Each group of six printed se-tenant in sheets of 30 (5x6). Value $2.
Nos. C528-C533 were printed in 1975 in black and bister se-tenant in sheets of 24 (4x6) on whiter paper. Value $5.

Generals Justo Rufino Barrios and M. Garcia Granados — AP106

Polytechnic School AP107

1974-75 Typo. ***Perf. 12½, 11½ (25c)***
C552 AP106 6c red, gray & bl .35 .25
C553 AP107 25c multi .50 .30

Centenary (in 1973) of Escuela Politecnica, Guatemala's military academy.
Issued: 6c, 9/17; 25c, 1/1/75.

No. C373 Surcharged in Black and Green

1974, Dec. 3 Engr. ***Perf. 13½***
C554 AP76 10c on 11c multi 1.10 .50

Nature protection. The quetzal, Guatemala's national bird.

Costume San Martin Sacatepequez AP108

Costumes of Women: 2c, Solola. 9c, Coban. 20c, Chichicastenango.

1974-75 Typo. ***Perf. 12½***
C556 AP108 2c car & multi .25 .25
C557 AP108 2½c bl, car & brn .25 .25
C559 AP108 9c bl & multi .35 .25
a. Perf. 12½x13½ .35 .25
C561 AP108 20c red & multi .65 .25
Nos. C556-C561 (4) 1.50 1.00

Issue dates: 2½c, Dec. 16, 1974; 20c, Jan. 14, 1975; 2c, 9c, May 19, 1975.

Quetzals and Maya Quekchi Woman Wearing Huipil — AP109

1975, June 25 Litho. ***Perf. 13½***
C565 AP109 8c bl & multi .70 .25
C566 AP109 20c red & multi 1.25 .40

International Women's Year 1975.

Rotary Emblem AP110

1975-76 Typo. ***Perf. 13½***
C567 AP110 10c bl & multi .45 .25
Perf. 11½
C568 AP110 15c bl & multi .50 .25

Guatemala City Rotary Club, 50th anniv.
Issued: 10c, 10/1; 15c, 12/21/76.

Gaceta Type of 1971 Redrawn

1975-76 Typo. ***Perf. 12½***
C569 AP90 5c brn & red .25 .25
C570 AP90 50c brt rose & brn 1.40 .55

The white background around numeral and on right of arms has been filled in.
Issued: 5c, 12/12; 50c, 12/1/76.

IWY Emblem and White Nun Orchid — AP111

1975-76 ***Perf. 12½x13½, 11½ (8c)***
C571 AP111 1c multi .30 .25
C572 AP111 8c yel & multi .40 .25
C573 AP111 26c rose & multi .95 .30
Nos. C571-C573 (3) 1.65 .80

International Women's Year 1975.
Issued: 1c, 12/19; 8c, 12/12; 26c, 5/10/76.

Stamp Centenary Type of 1973

1975-77 Engr. ***Perf. 11½***
C574 AP102 6c orange .30 .25
C575 AP102 6c green ('76) .30 .25
C576 AP102 6c gray ('77) .30 .25
C576A AP102 6c vio bl ('77) .30 .25
Nos. C574-C576A (4) 1.20 1.00

Issued: No. C574, 12/31; No. C575, 5/10; others, 8/10.

Destroyed Joyabaj Village — AP112

Designs (Guatemala Flag and): 3c, Emergency food distribution. 5c, Jaguar Temple, Tikal. 10c, Destroyed bridge. 15c, Outdoors emergency hospital. 20c, Sugar cane harvest. 25c, Destroyed house. 30c, New building, Tecpan. 50c, Destroyed Cerro del Carmen church. 75c, Cleaning up debris. 1q, Military help. 2q, Lake Atitlan.

1976, June 4 Litho. ***Perf. 12½***
C577 AP112 1c red & multi .25 .25
C578 AP112 3c multi .25 .25
C579 AP112 5c pink & multi .25 .25
C580 AP112 10c red & multi .30 .25
C581 AP112 15c multi .45 .25
C582 AP112 20c pink & multi .45 .30
C583 AP112 25c red & multi .80 .35
C584 AP112 30c multi .95 .50
C585 AP112 50c red & multi 1.25 1.00
C586 AP112 75c multi 2.00 1.75
C587 AP112 1q multi 3.00 2.50
C588 AP112 2q multi 5.75 5.75
Nos. C577-C588 (12) 15.70 13.40

Earthquake of Feb. 4, 1976, and gratitude for foreign help. Inscriptions in colored panels vary. 3 imperf. souvenir sheets exist (50c, 1q, 2q). Size: 112x83mm. Value, each $15.

Allegory of Independence — AP113

Designs: 2c, Boston Tea Party. 3c, Thomas Jefferson, vert. 4c, 20c, 35c, Allegory of Independence (each different; 4c, 35c, vert.). 5c, Warren's Death at Bunker Hill. 10c, Washington at Valley Forge. 15c, Washington at Monmouth. 25c, The Generals at Yorktown. 30c, Washington Crossing the Delaware. 40c, Declaration of Independence. 45c, Patrick Henry, vert. 50c, Congress Voting Independence. 1q, Washington, vert. 2q, Lincoln, vert. 3q, Franklin, vert. 5q, John F. Kennedy, vert. The historical designs and portraits are after paintings.

1976, July 30 Litho. ***Perf. 12½***
Size: 46x27mm, 27x46mm
C592 AP113 1c multicolored .30 .25
C593 AP113 2c multicolored .30 .25
C594 AP113 3c multicolored .30 .25
C595 AP113 4c multicolored .30 .25
C596 AP113 5c multicolored .30 .25
C597 AP113 10c multicolored .30 .25
C598 AP113 15c multicolored .30 .25
C599 AP113 20c multicolored .45 .25
C600 AP113 25c multicolored .45 .25
C601 AP113 30c multicolored .80 .25
C602 AP113 35c multicolored .85 .45
C603 AP113 40c multicolored .85 .55
C604 AP113 45c multicolored 1.00 .65
C605 AP113 50c multicolored 1.40 .45
C606 AP113 1q multicolored 2.40 2.00
a. Souvenir sheet 2.75 2.75
C607 AP113 2q multicolored 4.00 4.00
a. Souvenir sheet 5.00 5.00

C608 AP113 3q multicolored 5.50 5.50
a. Souvenir sheet 6.25 6.25

Size: 35x55mm

C609 AP113 5q multicolored 9.50 3.50
a. Souvenir sheet 12.00 12.00
Nos. C592-C609 (18) 29.30 19.60

American Bicentennial. Souvenir sheets contain one imperf. stamp each.

1974 Quetzal Coin AP114

Lithographed and Engraved

1976, Dec. 1 *Perf. 11½*
C610 AP114 8c org, blk & bl .30 .25

Perf. 13½
C611 AP114 20c brt rose, bl & blk .75 .25

50th anniv. of introduction of Quetzal currency.

Engineers at Work AP115

1976, Dec. 21 **Engr.** *Perf. 11½*
C612 AP115 9c ultra .35 .25
C613 AP115 10c green .35 .25

School of Engineering, Guatemala City, centenary.

Holy Week Type of 1977

Designs: Sculptures of Christ from various Guatemalan churches. 4c, 7c, 9c, 20c, vert.

1977, Apr. 4 **Litho.** *Perf. 11*
C614 A159 3c pur & multi .40 .25
C615 A159 4c pur & multi .40 .25
C616 A159 7c pur & multi .40 .25
C617 A159 9c pur & multi .45 .25
C618 A159 20c pur & multi .95 .60
C619 A159 26c pur & multi 1.25 .70
Nos. C614-C619 (6) 3.85 2.30

Souvenir Sheet

Roulette 7½

C620 A159 30c pur & multi 4.00 4.00

Holy Week 1977.

City Hall and Bank of Guatemala — AP116

Designs: 6c, Deed to original site, vert. 8c, Church and farm house, site of first legislative session. 9c, Coat of arms of Pedro Cortes, first archbishop. 22c, Arms of Guatemala City, vert.

Perf. 13½ (6c); 11½ (others)

1977, Aug. 10 **Litho.**
C621 AP116 6c multicolored .40 .25
C622 AP116 7c multicolored .40 .25
C623 AP116 8c multicolored .40 .25
C624 AP116 9c multicolored .55 .25
a. Souvenir sheet 1.00 .80
C625 AP116 22c multicolored .85 .25
a. Souvenir sheet 1.10 1.10
Nos. C621-C625 (5) 2.60 1.25

Bicentenary of the founding of Nueva Guatemala de la Asuncion (Guatemala City). Nos. C624a-C625a contain one stamp each with simulated perforations.

Arms of Quetzaltenango AP117

City Hall and Torch AP118

1977, Sept. 11 **Litho.** *Perf. 11½*
C626 AP117 7c blk & sil .30 .25
C627 AP118 30c bl & yel .85 .30

Founding of Quetzaltenango, 150th anniv.

Mayan Bas-relief — AP119

1977, Nov. 7
C628 AP119 10c brt car & blk .80 .25

14th Intl. Cong. of Latin Notaries.

Children Bringing Gifts to Christ Child — AP120

Christmas: 1c, Mother and children, horiz. 4c, Guatemalan children's Nativity scene.

1977, Dec. 16 **Litho.** *Perf. 11½*
C629 AP120 1c multicolored .60 .25
C630 AP120 2c multicolored .60 .25
C631 AP120 4c multicolored .60 .25
Nos. C629-C631 (3) 1.80 .75

Almolonga Costume, Cancer League Emblem — AP121

Regional Costumes after Paintings by Carlos Mérida and Cancer League Emblem: 2c, Nebaj woman. 5c, San Juan Cotzal couple. 6c, Todos Santos couple. 20c, Regidores men. 30c, San Cristobal woman.

Perf. 14 (1c, 5c, No. C636); Perf. 12 (2c, 6c, No. C636a, 30c)

1978, Apr. 3 **Litho.**
C632 AP121 1c gold & multi .30 .25
C633 AP121 2c gold & multi .30 .25
C634 AP121 5c gold & multi .30 .25
C635 AP121 6c gold & multi .35 .25
C636 AP121 20c gold & multi 1.20 .25
a. Souv. sheet of 1 4.00 4.00
C637 AP121 30c gold & multi 1.20 .30
Nos. C632-C637 (6) 3.65 1.55

Part of proceeds from sale of stamps went to National League to Fight Cancer.

Virgin of Sorrows, Antigua — AP122

Statues from Various Churches: 4c, Virgin of Mercy, Antigua. 5c, Virgin of Anguish, Yurrita. 6c, Virgin of the Rosary, Santo Domingo. 8c, Virgin of Sorrows, Santo Domingo. 9c, Virgin of the Rosary, Quetzaltenango. 10c, Virgin of the Immaculate Conception, Church of St. Francis. 20c, Virgin of the Immaculate Conception, Cathedral Church.

1978 **Litho.** *Perf. 11½*
C638 AP122 2c multicolored .45 .30
C639 AP122 4c multicolored .45 .30
C640 AP122 5c multicolored .45 .30
C641 AP122 6c multicolored .45 .30
C642 AP122 8c multicolored .45 .30
C643 AP122 9c multicolored .45 .30
C644 AP122 10c multicolored .45 .30
C645 AP122 20c multicolored 1.25 .30
Nos. C638-C645 (8) 4.40 2.40

Holy Week 1978. A 30c imperf. souvenir sheet shows the Pietà from Calvary Church, Antigua. Size: 71x101mm. Value $4.50.

Issued: 6c, 10c, 20c, 9/28; others, 5/22.

Soccer Player, Argentina '78 Emblem AP123

1978, July 3 **Litho.** *Perf. 12*
C646 AP123 10c multicolored .50 .25

11th World Cup Soccer Championship, Argentina, June 1-25.

Gymnastics AP124

1978, Sept. 4 *Perf. 12*
C647 AP124 6c shown .25 .25
C648 AP124 6c Volleyball .25 .25
C649 AP124 6c Target shooting .25 .25
C650 AP124 6c Weight lifting .25 .25
a. Block of 4, #C647-C650 4.00 4.00
C651 AP124 8c Track & field .25 .25
Nos. C647-C651 (5) 1.25 1.25

13th Central American and Caribbean Games, Medellin, Colombia.

Cattleya Pachecoi AP125

Orchids: No. C653, Sobralia. No. C654, Cypripedium. No. C655, Oncidium. No. C656, Cattleya bowrigiana. No. C657, Encyclia. No. C658, Epidendrum. No. C659, Barkeria. No. C660, Spiranthes. No. C661, Lycaste.

1978, Dec. 7 **Litho.** *Perf. 12*
C652 AP125 1c shown 1.40 1.40
C653 AP125 1c multi 1.40 1.40
C654 AP125 1c multi 1.40 1.40
C655 AP125 1c multi 1.40 1.40
a. Block of 4, #C652-C655 20.00 20.00
C656 AP125 3c multi 1.60 1.60
C657 AP125 3c multi 1.60 1.60
C658 AP125 3c multi 1.60 1.60
C659 AP125 3c multi 1.60 1.60
a. Block of 4, #C656-C659 20.00 20.00
C660 AP125 8c multi 8.00 3.00
C661 AP125 20c multi 12.50 10.50
Nos. C652-C661 (10) 32.50 25.50

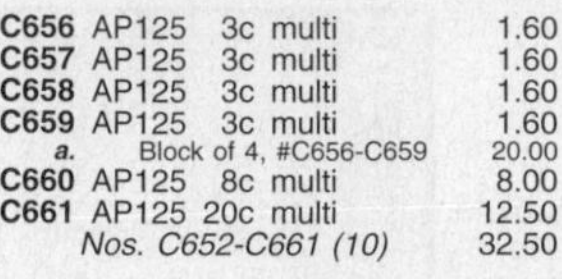

Seal of University AP126

Students of Different Departments AP127

Designs: 12c, Student in 17th cent. clothes. 14c, Students, 1978, and molecular model.

1978, Dec. 7
C662 AP126 6c multicolored .30 .25
C663 AP127 7c multicolored .30 .25
C664 AP126 12c multicolored .35 .25
C665 AP126 14c multicolored .50 .25
Nos. C662-C665 (4) 1.45 1.00

San Carlos University of Guatemala, tercentenary.

Brown and White Children AP128

A Helping Hand — AP129

Designs: 7c, Child at play. 14c, Hands sheltering Indian girl.

1978, Dec. 7
C666 AP128 6c multicolored .30 .25
C667 AP128 7c multicolored .30 .25
C668 AP129 12c multicolored .35 .25
C669 AP129 14c multicolored .50 .25
Nos. C666-C669 (4) 1.45 1.00

Year of the Children of Guatemala.

Tree Planting and FAO Emblem — AP130

Forest protection: 8c, Burnt forest. 9c, Watershed, river and trees. 10c, Sawmill. 26c, Forests, river and cultivated terraces.

1979, Apr. 16 Litho. *Perf. 13½*

C670	AP130	6c multicolored	.45	.25
C671	AP130	8c multicolored	.45	.25
C672	AP130	9c multicolored	.45	.25
C673	AP130	10c multicolored	.45	.25
C674	AP130	26c multicolored	.85	.25
a.		Souv. sheet of 5, #C670-C674	9.50	*9.50*
		Nos. C670-C674 (5)	2.65	1.25

Peten Wild Turkey — AP131

Wildlife conservation: 3c, White-tailed deer, horiz. 5c, King buzzard. 7c, Horned owl. 9c, Young wildcat. 30c, Quetzal.

1979, June 14 Litho. *Perf. 13½*

C675	AP131	1c multicolored	1.90	.70
C676	AP131	3c multicolored	1.10	.70
C677	AP131	5c multicolored	5.75	.70
C678	AP131	7c multicolored	12.50	2.75
C679	AP131	9c multicolored	2.75	.70
		Nos. C675-C679 (5)	24.00	5.55

Souvenir Sheet

C680	AP131	30c multicolored	16.00	16.00

Clay Jar, 50-100 A.D. — AP132

Archaeological Treasures from Tikal: 3c, Mayan woman, ceramic head, 900 A.D. 4c, Earring, 450 A.D. 5c, vase, 700 A.D. 6c, Boy, 200-50 B.C. 7c, Bone carving, 700 A.D. 8c, Striped vase, 700 A.D. 10c, Covered vase on tripod, 450 A.D.

1979, Sept. 19 Litho. *Perf. 13*

C681	AP132	2c multi	.50	.25
C682	AP132	3c multi	.75	.40
C683	AP132	4c multi	.95	.55
C684	AP132	5c multi	1.25	.55
C685	AP132	6c multi	1.60	.80
C686	AP132	7c multi	1.90	.95
C687	AP132	8c multi	2.00	1.00
C688	AP132	10c multi	2.25	1.25
		Nos. C681-C688 (8)	11.20	5.75

Presidential Guard Patches AP133

Presidential Guard, 30th anniv.: 10c, Guard Headquarters.

1979, Dec. 6 Litho. *Perf. 11½*

C689	AP133	8c multi	.30	.25
C690	AP133	10c multi	.30	.25

National Coat of Arms — AP134

Arms of Guatemalan Municipalities: No. C692, Alta Verapaz. No. C693, Baja Verapaz. No. C694, Chimal Tenango. No. C695, Chiquimula. No. C696, Escuintla. No. C697, Flores. No. C698, Guatemala. No. C699, Huehuetenango. No. C700, Izabal. No. C701, Jalapa. No. C702, Jutiapa. No. C703, Mazatenango. No. C704, Progreso. No. C705, Quezaltenango. No. C706, Quiche. No. C707, Retalhuleu. No. C708, Sacatepequez. No. C709, San Marcos. No. C710, Santa Rosa. No. C711, Solola. No. C712, Totonicapan. No. C713, Zacapa.

No. C714, 1st & current national arms.

1979, Dec. 27 Litho. *Perf. 13½*

C691	AP134	8c shown	.60	.25
C692	AP134	8c multi	.60	.25
C693	AP134	8c multi	.60	.25
C694	AP134	8c multi	.60	.25
C695	AP134	8c multi	.60	.25
C696	AP134	8c multi	.60	.25
C697	AP134	8c multi	.60	.25
C698	AP134	8c multi	.60	.25
C699	AP134	8c multi	.60	.25
C700	AP134	8c multi	.60	.25
C701	AP134	8c multi	.60	.25
C702	AP134	8c multi	.60	.25
C703	AP134	8c multi	.60	.25
C704	AP134	8c multi	.60	.25
C705	AP134	8c multi	.60	.25
C706	AP134	8c multi	.60	.25
C707	AP134	8c multi	.60	.25
C708	AP134	8c multi	.60	.25
C709	AP134	8c multi	.60	.25
C710	AP134	8c multi	.60	.25
C711	AP134	8c multi	.60	.25
C712	AP134	8c multi	.60	.25
C713	AP134	8c multi	.60	.25
		Nos. C691-C713 (23)	13.80	5.75

Miniature Sheet

Imperf

C714	AP134	50c multi	5.25	3.50

No. C714 is horizontal.

Scenes from Popul Vuh (Sacred Book of the Ancient Quiches of Guatemala) AP135

Designs: No. C715, Creation of the World. No. C716, Origin of the Twin Semi-gods. No. C717, Populating the earth. No. C718, Balam Quitze. No. C719, Quiche monarch Cotuha. No. C720, Birth of the Stick Men. No. C721, Princess Xquic's punishment. No. C722, Caha Paluma. No. C723, Cotuha and Iztayul invincible. No. C724, Odyssey of Hun Ahpu and Xbalanque. No. C725, Balam Acab. No. C726, Chief of all Nations. No. C727, Destruction of the Stick Men. No. C728, The Test in Xibalba. No. C729, Chomiha. No. C730, Warrior with captive. No. C731, Creation of the Corn Men. No. C732, Multiplication of the Prodigies. No. C733, Mahucutah. No. C734, Undefeatable king. No. C735, Thanksgiving. No. C736, Deification of Hun Ahpu and Xbalanque. No. C737, Tzununiha. No. C738, Greatness of the Quiches (battle scene).

1981 Litho. *Perf. 12*

Background Color

C715	AP135	1c lilac	.40	.75
C716	AP135	1c pink	.40	.75
C717	AP135	2c green	.40	.75
C718	AP135	2c brt lilac	.40	.75
C719	AP135	3c blue	.50	.75
C720	AP135	4c dk blue	.95	.75
C721	AP135	4c blue vio	.95	.75
C722	AP135	4c blue	.95	.75
C723	AP135	4c lilac	.95	.75
C724	AP135	6c brown	.95	.75
C725	AP135	6c pink	.80	.75
C726	AP135	6c org brn	.50	.50
C727	AP135	8c citron	1.25	1.00
C728	AP135	8c green	1.25	1.00
C729	AP135	8c yel grn	1.25	1.00
C730	AP135	8c gray	1.25	1.00
C731	AP135	10c orange	1.25	1.00
C732	AP135	10c brt yellow	1.25	1.00
C733	AP135	10c blue green	1.25	1.00
C734	AP135	10c dull green	1.25	1.00
C735	AP135	22c brown	1.25	1.25
C736	AP135	26c dull bl grn	1.40	1.25
C737	AP135	30c gray grn	2.25	1.50
C738	AP135	50c red violet	3.50	2.00
		Nos. C715-C738 (24)	26.55	22.75

Issued: Nos. C715, C717, 3c, C727, C731, 22c, 1/29; Nos. C716, C718, C721-C722, C724-C725, C728-C729, C732-C733, 26c, 30c, 3/16; others, 1981.

Thomas Edison (Phonograph Centenary) AP136

Talking Movies, 50th Anniv. — AP137

Telephone Centenary (1976) — AP138

Lindbergh's Atlantic Flight, 50th Anniv. (1977) AP139

12c, Jose Cecilio del Valle, patriot. 25c, Jesus Castillo (1877-1949), composer.

Perf. 11½, 12½ (25c)

1981, June 1 Litho.

C739	AP136	3c multi	.25	.25
C740	AP137	5c multi	.30	.25
C741	AP138	6c multi	.40	.25
C742	AP139	7c multi	.45	.30
C743	AP139	12c multi	.80	.45
C744	AP139	25c multi	1.50	1.00
		Nos. C739-C744 (6)	3.70	2.50

First Police Chief Roderico Toledo and Present Chief German Chupina AP140

1981, Sept. 12 Litho. *Perf. 11½*

C745	AP140	2c shown	.45	.25
C746	AP140	4c Headquarters	.45	.25

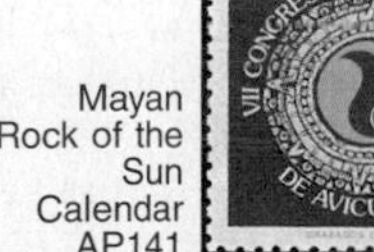

Mayan Rock of the Sun Calendar AP141

1981, Oct. 9

C747	AP141	1c multi	.30	.25

Gen. Jose Gervasio Artigas of Uruguay AP142

Liberators of the Americas: 2c, Bernardo O'Higgins (Chile). 4c, Jose de San Martin (Argentina). 10c, Miguel Garcia Granados. 2c, 4c, 10c, 31x47mm.

1982, Apr. 2 Litho. *Perf. 11½*

C748	AP142	2c multi	*1.00*	*1.00*
C749	AP142	3c multi	.25	.25

Perf. 12½

C750	AP142	4c multi	*1.00*	*1.00*
C751	AP142	10c tan & blk	.25	.25
		Nos. C748-C751 (4)	2.50	2.50

Occidents Bank Centenary (1981) AP143

1c, Justo Rufino Barrios (1st pres.), Main Office, Quezaltenango. 2c, Main Office, 3c, Emblem, vert. 4c, Commemorative medals, vert.

1982, July 28 Litho. *Perf. 11½*

C752	AP143	1c multi	.40	.25
C753	AP143	2c multi	.40	.25
C754	AP143	3c multi	.40	.25
C755	AP143	4c multi	.40	.25
		Nos. C752-C755 (4)	1.60	1.00

50th Anniv. of Natl. Mortgage Bank (1980) AP144

Various emblems. 5c vert.

1982, Oct. 18 Litho. *Perf. 11½*

C756	AP144	1c multi	.40	.25
C757	AP144	2c multi	.40	.25
C758	AP144	5c multi	.40	.25
C759	AP144	10c multi	.40	.25
		Nos. C756-C759 (4)	1.60	1.00

AP145

1983, May 16 Litho. *Perf. 11½*

C760	AP145	1c Portrait	.30	.25
C761	AP145	20c Aparition, horiz.	.65	.40

20th Anniv. of Beatification of Pedro Bethancourt (1626-1667).

AP146

1983, July 25 Litho. *Perf. 11½*

C762	AP146	10c multi	.50	.25

World Telecommunications and Health Day, May 17, 1981

Evangelical Church Centenary (1982) — AP147

3c, Hands holding bible. 5c, Church.

1983, Aug. 9

C763 AP147 3c multi .45 .25
C764 AP147 5c multi .55 .25

Natl. Railroad Centenary — AP148

10c, 1st locomotive crossing Puenta de Las Vacas. 25c, General Justo Rufino Barrios, Railroad Yard. 30c, Spanish Diesel, Amatitlan crossing.

1983, Sept. 28 Litho. *Perf. 11½*

C765 AP148 10c multi 1.20 .80
C766 AP148 25c multi 2.75 1.75
C767 AP148 30c multi 3.50 2.00
Nos. C765-C767 (3) 7.45 4.55

World Food Day AP149

8c, Globe, wheat, vert.

1983, Oct. 16 Photo. *Perf. 11½*

C768 AP149 8c multi 1.25 .75
C769 AP149 1q shown 8.00 4.00

Architecture Type of 1972

1984, Feb. 20 Typo. *Perf. 12½*

Black and Green

C770 AP98 1c like #C480 .30 .25
C771 AP98 1c like #C481 .30 .25
C772 AP98 1c like #C482 .30 .25
C773 AP98 1c like #C483 .30 .25
C774 AP98 1c like #C484 .30 .25
C775 AP98 1c like #C485 .30 .25
g. Strip of 6, #C770-C775 1.50 1.50

Black, Brown and Orange Brown

C775A AP98 5c like #C484 .30 .25
C775B AP98 5c like #C485 .30 .25
C775C AP98 5c like #C482 .30 .25
C775D AP98 5c like #C483 .30 .25
C775E AP98 5c like #C480 .30 .25
C775F AP98 5c like #C481 .30 .25
h. Strip of 6, #C775A-C775F 2.25 2.25

Visit of Pope John Paul II, Mar. 8-9, 1983 AP150

4c, Pope, arms. 8c, Receiving Mayan indian, vert.

1984, Mar. 26 Litho. *Perf. 11½*

C776 AP150 4c multi .45 .35
C777 AP150 8c multi .55 .35

Rafael Landivar (1731-93), Poet — AP151

2c, Portrait. 4c, Tomb, horiz.

1984, Aug. 6 Litho. *Perf. 11½*

C778 AP151 2c multi .30 .25
C779 AP151 4c multi .35 .25

Cardinal Mario Casariego y Acevedo AP152

10c, 16th archbishop of Guat. (1909-83).

1984, Aug. 6

C780 AP152 10c multicolored .50 .25

Central American Bank for Economic Integration, 20th Anniv. — AP153

30c, Bank emblem, map.

1984, Sept. 10 Litho. *Perf. 11½*

C781 AP153 30c multicolored 1.10 .60

Coffee Production, 1870 AP154

Natl. Scouting Assoc. — AP156

Scouting emblems and: 5c, Beaver scout, Pyramid of Tikal. 6c, Wolf scout, Palace of the Captains-General and Ahua Volcano. 8c, Scout, San Pedro Volcano and Marimba player. 10c, Rover scout and conquest mask dance. 20c, Lord Baden-Powell and Col. Carlos Cipriani, natl. founder.

1985, July 1

C792 AP156 5c multi .60 .25
C793 AP156 6c multi .70 .25
C794 AP156 8c multi .80 .30
C795 AP156 10c multi 1.00 .40
C796 AP156 20c multi 2.00 .85
Nos. C792-C796 (5) 5.10 2.05

Inter-American Family Unity Year — AP157

1985, Oct. 16

C797 AP157 10c multi .50 .30

Central American Aeronautics Admin., 25th Anniv. — AP158

1985, Nov. 11

C798 AP158 10c multi 1.00 .25

Natl. Telegraph, Cent. — AP159

Portraits: Samuel Morse, telegraph inventor, and Justo Rufino Barrios, communications pioneer.

1985, Nov. 20 *Perf. 12*

C799 AP159 4c brn & blk .50 .25

Intl. Olympic Committee, 90th Anniv. — AP160

Designs: 8c, Mayan bust of ancient sportsman. 10c, Baron Pierre de Coubertin (1863-1937), father of modern Games, 1st committee president.

1986, Jan. 28 Litho. *Perf. 11½*

C800 AP160 8c multi .55 .45
C801 AP160 10c multi .75 .45

Volunteer Fire Department AP161

1986, Feb. 6 Litho. *Perf. 11½*

C802 AP161 6c multi 1.75 .25

Temple of Minerva — AP162

Quetzaltenango Coat of Arms, City Hall — AP163

1986, July 16 Litho. *Perf. 12½, 11½*

C803 AP162 8c multi .30 .25
C804 AP163 10c multi .50 .25

Quetzaltenango Independence Fair, cent.

Volunteer Fire Department AP164

1986, Oct. 10 Litho. *Perf. 11½*

C805 AP164 8c Rescue 1.25 .30
C806 AP164 10c Ruins 1.75 .30

Assoc. of Telegraphers and Radio-Telegraph Operators, 25th Anniv. — AP165

1986, Oct. 10 *Perf. 12*

C807 AP165 6c multi .50 .25

San Carlos University School of Architecture, 25th Anniv. — AP166

1987, Feb. 16 Litho. *Perf. 11½*

C808 AP166 10c multi .80 .25

ICAO, 40th Anniv. (in 1984) AP167

Modern Coffee Production AP155

Designs: 1c, Planting coffee. 2c, Harvesting. 3c, Drying beans. 4c, Loading beans on steamer. 5c, Reyna plant grafting method. 10c, Picking beans, coffee cup. 12c, Drying unripened beans, Gardiola Freeze-drying machine. 25c, Cargo transports.

1984, Dec. 19 *Perf. 11½*

C782 AP154 1c sep & pale brn .25 .25
C783 AP154 2c sep & pale org brn .25 .25
C784 AP154 3c sep & beige .25 .25
C785 AP154 4c sep & pale yel brn .25 .25
C786 AP155 5c multi .30 .25
C787 AP155 10c multi .60 .40
C788 AP155 12c multi .80 .45
C789 AP155 25c multi 1.50 1.00
Nos. C782-C789 (8) 4.20 3.10

Natl. coffee production and export. An 86x112mm 25c stamp of Type AP154 and a 105x85mm 30c stamp of Type AP155 exist, value $100 and $125 respectively.

8c, Aviateca Airlines jet. 10c, Jet, vert.

1987, Apr. 2 Litho. *Perf. 11½*
C809 AP167 8c multicolored .40 .25
C810 AP167 10c multicolored .50 .25

Chixoy Hydroelectric Power Plant — AP168

1987, May 18 Litho. *Perf. 11½*
C811 AP168 2c multi .80 .40

Nat'l. Electrification Institute inauguration (in 1985).

San Jose de los Infantes College, 200th Anniv. (in 1981) AP169

8c, Portrait of Archbishop Cayetano Francos y Monroy, founder. 10c, College crest.

1987, June 10
C812 AP169 8c multi, vert. .25 .25
C813 AP169 10c multi .30 .25

Promotion of Literacy in Latin America and Caribbean AP170

1987, Aug. 20 Litho. *Perf. 11½*
C814 AP170 12c apple grn, blk & brt org .40 .25

19th Natl. Folklore Carnival of Coban, Alta Verapaz, July 25 — AP171

1q, Three girls from Tamahu.

1987, Oct. 12
C815 AP171 1q multicolored 5.50 2.00

1987, Dec. 8
C816 AP171 50c Girl weaving 2.75 .95

See No. C831.

9th Pan American Games, Caracas AP172

1987, Nov. 5 *Perf. 12½*
C817 AP172 10c blk & sky blue *10.00 5.00*

Writers and Historians AP173

Designs: 1c, Flavio Herrera, poet, novelist. 2c, Rosendo Santa Cruz, novelist. 3c, Werner Ovalle Lopez, poet. 4c, Enrique A. Hidalgo, poet, humorist. 5c, Enrique Gomez Carrillo (1873-1927), novelist. 6c, Cesar Branas (1899-1976), journalist. 7c, Clemente Marroquin Rojas, historian. 8c, Rafael Arevalo Martinez (1884-1975), poet. 9c, Jose Milla y Vidaurre (1822-1882), historian. 10c, Miguel Angel Asturias, Nobel laureate for literature.

1987-90 *Perf. 11½*
C818 AP173 1c blk & lil .30 .25
C819 AP173 2c blk & dl org .30 .25
C820 AP173 3c blk & brt bl .30 .25
C821 AP173 4c blk & ver .30 .25
C822 AP173 5c blk & org brn .30 .25
C823 AP173 6c blk & org .30 .25
C824 AP173 7c blk & grn .30 .25
C825 AP173 8c blk & brt red .30 .25
C826 AP173 9c blk & brt rose lil .30 .25
C827 AP173 10c blk & yel .30 .25
Nos. C818-C827 (10) 3.00 2.50

Issued: 6c, 8c, 9c, 11/5/87; 4c, 5c, 1/13/88; 7c, 3/23/90; 1c, 2c, 3c, 10c, 4/9/90.

Esquipulas II — AP174

1988, Jan. 15 *Perf. 12½*
C828 AP174 10c dark olive grn .40 .25
C829 AP174 40c plum 1.50 1.00
C830 AP174 60c deep blue vio 2.40 1.50
Nos. C828-C830 (3) 4.30 2.75

2nd Meeting of the Central American Peace Plan. Nos. C828-C829 horiz.

Folklore Festival Type of 1987 Souvenir Sheet

1988, Dec. 6 Litho. *Imperf.*
C831 AP171 2q Music ensemble, horiz. 10.00 10.00

St. John Bosco (1815-1888), Educator AP175

1989, Feb. 1 Litho. *Perf. 11½*
C832 AP175 40c gold & blk 1.00 .55

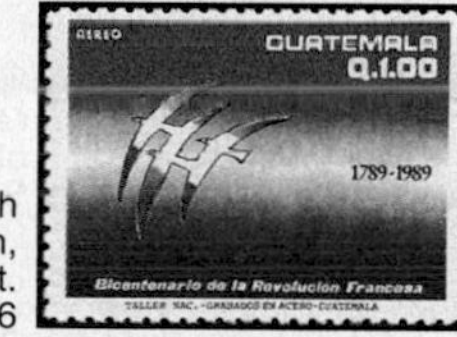

French Revolution, Bicent. AP176

1989, Oct. 18 Litho. *Perf. 11½*
C833 AP176 1q dk red, blk & dp blue 5.00 2.00

America Issue — AP177

UPAE emblem and: 10c, Detail of the *Madrid Codex*. 20c, Temple of the Gran Jaguar of Tikal, Tikal Natl. Park.

1990, Jan. 25 Litho. *Perf. 11½*
C834 AP177 10c shown 1.75 1.10
C835 AP177 20c brown & multi 3.50 2.40

Institute of Nutrition of Central America and Panama, 40th Anniv. AP178

1990, May 18
C837 AP178 20c multicolored .80 .25

Red Cross, Red Crescent Societies, 125th Anniv. — AP179

1990, June 8
C838 AP179 50c multicolored 1.60 .40

Defense Ministry General Staff, Cent. AP180

1991, May 8 Litho. *Perf. 11½*
C839 AP180 20c multicolored .80 .25

America AP181

UPAE: 10c, Pacaya Volcano Erupting at Night. 60c, Lake Atitlan.

1991, July 30 Litho. *Perf. 11½*
C840 AP181 10c multicolored .25 .25
C841 AP181 60c multicolored 2.25 .50

America Issue AP182

Designs: 40c, Pinzon brothers, Nina. 60c, Columbus, Santa Maria, vert.

1992, July 27 Litho. *Perf. 11½*
C842 AP182 40c green & black .95 .45
C843 AP182 60c green & black 1.40 .70

AP183

1992, Oct. 6 Litho. *Perf. 12½*
C844 AP183 10c multicolored *5.00 5.00*

Interamerican Institute for Agricultural Cooperation, 50th anniv.

AP184

1992, Dec. 1 Photo. *Perf. 11½*
C845 AP184 1q multicolored 4.00 .80

World campaign against AIDS.

Orchids AP185

AP185a

AP185b

AP185c

AP185d

20c, Phragmipedium caudatum. 50c, Encyclia cochleata. 1q, Encyclia vitellina. 1.50q, Odontoglossum laeve 2q, Odontoglossum uroskinneri.

1994, Aug. 9 Litho. *Perf. 11½*

C845A	AP185	20c multi	.60	.60
C846	AP185a	50c multi	1.10	.80
C847	AP185b	1q multi	2.40	.80
C847A	AP185c	1.50q multi	4.75	4.75
C848	AP185d	2q multi	4.25	1.50
		Nos. C845A-C848 (5)	13.10	8.45

Nos. C845A, C847A put on sale 8/16/96.
Font sizes differ slightly on Nos. C845A-C848.

Tourism — AP186

Designs: 20c, Rafting. 40c, Water sports. 60c, Boats on Lake Atitlan, volcanic mountain. 80c, Tourist boat on Lake Atitlan. 1q, Mt. Pacaya erupting. 2q, Guatemala City. 3q, Macaws, vert. 4q, Temple of the Gran Jaguar, vert. 5q, Holy Week procession from Antigua, carpet of colored saw dust, vert.

1995-96 Litho. *Perf. 12½*

C849	AP186	20c multicolored	.50	.25
C850	AP186	40c multicolored	.80	.25
C851	AP186	60c multicolored	.70	.30
C852	AP186	80c multicolored	1.60	.40
C853	AP186	1q multicolored	.80	.30
C854	AP186	2q multicolored	1.60	.60
C855	AP186	3q multicolored	2.00	.85
C856	AP186	4q multicolored	2.75	1.25
C857	AP186	5q multicolored	3.50	1.75
		Nos. C849-C857 (9)	14.25	5.95

Issued: No. C850, 7/5/96; No. C852, 7/9/96.
For surcharges see Nos. 568-570, 574.

Visit of Pope John Paul II — AP187

Papal arms, quotation, Pope John Paul II: 10c, With arms outstreached, dove, "That all the people join hands for peace." 1q, Kissing infant, "Let the children come unto me." 1.75q, Holding crucifix, "The house of the Lord is my house." 1.90q, Looking forward, "Blessed is he who comes in the name of the Lord." 2.90q, Waving hand, "Remember that all men are our brothers."

1996, Jan. 5 Litho. *Perf. 12½*

C858	AP187	10c multicolored	.40	.25
C859	AP187	1q multicolored	.95	.45
C860	AP187	1.75q multicolored	1.60	.85
C861	AP187	1.90q multicolored	1.75	.95
C862	AP187	2.90q multicolored	2.75	1.50
		Nos. C858-C862 (5)	7.45	4.00

Distinguished Guatemalans AP188

Designs: 40c, Carlos Merida (Self-portrait). 50c, José Eulalio Samayoa. 60c, Manuel Montufar y Coronado.

1996, Oct. 21 Litho. *Perf. 12½*

C863	AP188	40c blue, black	.40	.25
C864	AP188	50c red brn, blk, blue	.50	.25
C865	AP188	60c brn, blue, blk	.55	.30
		Nos. C863-C865 (3)	1.45	.80

For surcharge see No. 572.

Mother Breastfeeding — AP190

1997, Mar. 6 *Perf. 11½*

C868	AP190	1q multicolored	1.00	.60

Public Finance Projects — AP191

Designs: 20c, Education. 60c, Health care. 80c, Road construction. 1q, Family security.

1997, Oct. 6 Litho. *Perf. 11½x12½*

C869	AP191	20c multicolored	.50	.25
C870	AP191	60c multicolored	.55	.25
C871	AP191	80c multicolored	.80	.40
C872	AP191	1q multicolored	.95	.45
		Nos. C869-C872 (4)	2.80	1.35

For surcharges see Nos. 571, 575.

Jorge Rybar and Machine — AP192

1998 Litho. *Perf. 12½*

C873	AP192	10c multi	.80	.25

Plastics industry in Guatemala, 50th anniv.

Intl. Society of Guatemala Collectors, 50th Anniv. — AP193

1999, May 14 Litho. *Perf. 11½x12½*

C874	AP193	1q Quetzel note	1.40	.60

1993 Census AP194

2001, Dec. 6 Litho. *Perf. 11½*

C875	AP194	10c multi	100.00	90.00

No. C875 was withdrawn from sale 12/11/01.

AIR POST SEMI-POSTAL STAMPS

Air Post Stamps of 1937 Surcharged in Red or Blue

1937, Mar. 15 Unwmk. *Perf. 12½*

CB1	AP10	4c + 1c ultra (R)	.90	*1.25*
CB2	AP10	6c + 1c blk vio (R)	.90	*1.25*
CB3	AP11	10c + 1c ol grn (Bl)	.90	*1.25*
CB4	AP11	15c + 1c ver (Bl)	.90	*1.25*
		Nos. CB1-CB4 (4)	3.60	*5.00*

1st Phil. Exhib. held in Guatemala, Mar. 15-20.

Catalogue values for unused stamps in this section, from this point to the end of the section, are for Never Hinged items.

Type of Regular Issue, 1956

Designs: 35c+1q, Red Cross, Ambulance and Volcano. 50c+1q, Red Cross, Hospital and Nurse. 1q+1q, Nurse and Red Cross.

Perf. 13x12½

1956, June 19 Engr. Unwmk.

CB5	A148	35c + 1q red & ol grn	5.50	*5.75*
CB6	A148	50c + 1q ultra & red	5.50	*5.75*
CB7	A148	1q + 1q dk grn & dk red	5.50	*5.75*
		Nos. CB5-CB7 (3)	16.50	*17.25*

The surtax was for the Red Cross.

Nos. B5-B7 Overprinted

1957, May 11

CB8	A148	5c + 15c	7.00	*8.00*
a.		Imperf., pair	225.00	
CB9	A148	15c + 50c	7.00	*8.00*
a.		Overprint inverted	275.00	
CB10	A148	25c + 50c	7.00	*8.00*
		Nos. CB8-CB10 (3)	21.00	*24.00*

The surtax was for the Red Cross.

Type of Semi-Postal Stamps, 1957 and

Esquipulas Cathedral SPAP1

15c+1q, Cathedral & crucifix. 20c+1q, Christ with crown of thorns and part of globe. 25c+1q, Archbishop Mariano Rossell y Arellano.

Perf. 13½x14½, 13

1957, Oct. 29 Engr. Unwmk.

CB11	SPAP1	10c + 1q choc & emer	7.00	*7.50*
CB12	SP1	15c + 1q dl grn & sep	7.00	*7.50*
CB13	SP1	20c + 1q bl gray & brn	7.00	*7.50*
CB14	SP1	25c + 1q lt vio & car	7.00	*7.50*
		Nos. CB11-CB14 (4)	28.00	*30.00*

The tax was for the Esquipulas highway.

Wounded Man, Battle of Solferino SPAP2

Designs: 6c+6c, 20c+20c, Flood disaster. 10c+10c, 25c+25c, Earth, moon and stars. 15c+15c, 30c+30c, Red Cross headquarters.

1960, Apr. 9 Photo. *Perf. 13½x14*

CB15	SPAP2	5c + 5c multi	2.50	*2.75*
CB16	SPAP2	6c + 6c multi	2.50	*2.75*
CB17	SPAP2	10c + 10c multi	2.50	*2.75*
CB18	SPAP2	15c + 15c multi	2.50	*2.75*
CB19	SPAP2	20c + 20c multi	2.50	*2.75*
CB20	SPAP2	25c + 25c multi	2.50	*2.75*
CB21	SPAP2	30c + 30c multi	2.50	*2.75*
		Nos. CB15-CB21 (7)	17.50	*19.25*

Cent. (in 1959) of the Red Cross idea. The surtax went to the Red Cross. Exist imperf.

AIR POST OFFICIAL STAMPS

Nos. C93-C98 Overprinted in Black

1939, Apr. 29 Unwmk. *Perf. 12½*

CO1	AP13	1c org & ol brn	1.60	1.60
CO2	AP13	2c multi	1.60	1.60
CO3	AP13	3c multi	1.60	1.60
CO4	AP13	4c multi	1.60	1.60
CO5	AP13	5c multi	1.60	1.60
CO6	AP13	10c multi	1.60	1.60
		Nos. CO1-CO6 (6)	9.60	9.60

No. C99 Overprinted in Black

1939

CO7	AP19	Sheet of 6	5.00	5.00
a.		1c yel org, blue & blk	.75	.75
b.		2c lake, org, blue & blk	.75	.75
c.		3c olive, blue & orange	.75	.75
d.		4c dk claret, bl, org & blk	.75	.75
e.		5c grnsh bl, bl, red, org & blk	.75	.75
f.		10c olive bister, red & org	.75	.75

SPECIAL DELIVERY STAMPS

No. 237 Overprinted in Red

1940, June Unwmk. *Perf. 14*

E1	A81	4c orange	1.50	.35

No. E1 paid for express service by motorcycle messenger between Guatemala City and Coban.

Catalogue values for unused stamps in this section, from this point to the end of the section, are for Never Hinged items.

Motorcycle Messenger SD1

Black Surcharge

1948, Sept. 3 Photo. *Perf. 14x12½*

E2	SD1	10c on 4c bl grn & gray blk	3.25	.85

No. E2 without surcharge was issued for regular postage, not special delivery. See No. 337B.

OFFICIAL STAMPS

O1

1902, Dec. 18 Typeset *Perf. 12*

O1	O1	1c green	9.00	5.50
O2	O1	2c carmine	9.00	5.50
O3	O1	5c ultra	9.00	4.50
O4	O1	10c brown violet	12.00	4.50
O5	O1	25c orange	12.00	4.50
a.		Horiz. pair, imperf. between	125.00	
		Nos. O1-O5 (5)	51.00	24.50

Nos. O1-O5 printed on thin paper with sheet watermark "AMERICAN LINEN BOND." Nos. O1-O3 also printed on thick paper with sheet watermark "ROYAL BANK BOND." Values are for copies that do not show the watermark. Counterfeits of Nos. O1-O5 exist.

During the years 1912 to 1926 the Post Office Department perforated the word "OFICIAL" on limited quantities of the following stamps: Nos. 114-123, 132, 141-149, 151-153, 158, 202, 210-229 and RA2. The perforating was done in blocks of four stamps at a time and was of two types.

A rubber handstamp "OFICIAL" was also used during the same period and was applied in violet, red, blue or black to stamps No. 117-118, 121-123, 163-165, 172 and 202-218.

Both perforating and handstamping were done in the post office at Guatemala City and use of the stamps was limited to that city.

National Emblem — O2

1929, Jan. Engr. *Perf. 14*

O6	O2	1c pale grnsh bl	.30	.30
O7	O2	2c dark brown	.30	.30
O8	O2	3c green	.30	.30
O9	O2	4c deep violet	.40	.35
O10	O2	5c brown car	.40	.35
O11	O2	10c brown orange	.70	.70
O12	O2	25c dark blue	1.40	1.10
		Nos. O6-O12 (7)	3.80	3.40

POSTAL TAX STAMPS

National Emblem — PT1

Perf. 13½, 14, 15

1919, May 3 Engr. Unwmk.

RA1 PT1 12½c carmine .30 .25

Tax for rebuilding post offices.

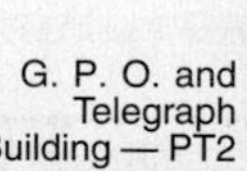

G. P. O. and Telegraph Building — PT2

1927, Nov. 10 Typo. *Perf. 14*

RA2 PT2 1c olive green .55 .25

Tax to provide a fund for building a post office in Guatemala City.

No. RA2 Overprinted in Green

1936, June 30

RA3 PT2 1c olive green *5.75 4.00*

Liberal revolution, 65th anniversary.

No. RA2 Overprinted in Blue

1936, Sept. 15

RA4 PT2 1c olive green .55 .55

115th anniv. of the Independence of Guatemala.

No. RA2 Overprinted in Red Brown

1936, Nov. 15

RA5 PT2 1c olive green .55 .45

National Fair.

No. RA2 Overprinted in Red

1937, Mar. 15

RA6 PT2 1c olive green .55 .55

No. RA2 Overprinted in Blue

1938, Jan. 10 *Perf. 14x14½*

RA7 PT2 1c olive green .30 .25

a. "1937-1939" omitted 110.00

150th anniv. of the US Constitution.

No. RA2 Overprinted in Blue or Red

1938 *Perf. 14*

RA8 PT2 1c olive green (Bl) .40 .30

RA9 PT2 1c olive green (R) .40 .30

No. RA2 Overprinted in Violet

1938, Nov. 20

RA10 PT2 1c olive green .40 .25

1st Central American Philatelic Exposition.

No. RA2 Overprinted in Green or Black

1939

RA11 PT2 1c olive green (G) .40 .25

RA12 PT2 1c olive green (Bk) .40 .25

No. RA2 Overprinted in Violet or Brown

1940

RA13 PT2 1c olive green (V) .40 .25

RA14 PT2 1c olive green (Br) .40 .25

No. RA2 Overprinted in Red

1940, Apr. 14

RA15 PT2 1c olive green .40 .25

Pan American Union, 50th anniversary.

No. RA2 Overprinted in Red

1941

RA16 PT2 1c olive green .55 .25

No. 235 Surcharged in Red

RA17 A79 1c on 2c deep blue .30 .25

No. 235 Surcharged in Carmine

1942, Jan.

RA18 A79 1c on 2c deep blue .55 .25

PT3

With Imprint Below Design

1942, June 3 Engr. *Perf. 11, 12x11*

RA19 PT3 1c black brown 14.50 8.00

No imprint; Thin Paper

Perf. 11, 12x11, 11x12, 11x12x11x11

1942, July 18

RA20 PT3 1c black brown .40 .25

Arch of Communications Building — PT4

1943 *Perf. 11, 12x11, 12*

RA21 PT4 1c orange .40 .25

PT5

Perf. 11, 12½ and Compound

1945, Feb. Unwmk.

RA22 PT5 1c orange .30 .25

1949 *Perf. 12½*

RA23 PT5 1c deep ultra .30 .25

GUINEA

'gi-nē

LOCATION — Coast of West Africa, between Guinea-Bissau and Sierra Leone
GOVT. — Republic
AREA — 94,926 sq. mi.
POP. — 7,538,953 (1999 est.)
CAPITAL — Conakry

This former French Overseas Territory of French West Africa proclaimed itself an independent republic on October 2, 1958.

100 Centimes = 1 Franc
100 Caury = 1 Syli (1973)
100 Centimes = 1 Guinean Franc (1986)

Catalogue values for all unused stamps in this country are for Never Hinged items.

Common Design Types pictured following the introduction.

French West Africa No. 79 Overprinted

1959 Unwmk. Photo. *Perf. 12x12½*

168	CD104	10fr multi	3.00	2.50

French West Africa No. 78 Surcharged in Red

Engr.
Perf. 13

169	A33	45fr on 20fr multi	3.50	2.25

Map, Dove and Pres. Sékou Touré — A12

1959 Unwmk. Engr. *Perf. 13*

170	A12	5fr rose car	.30	.25
171	A12	10fr ultramarine	.40	.25
172	A12	20fr orange	.70	.30
173	A12	65fr slate green	2.10	.95
174	A12	100fr violet	3.50	2.10
		Nos. 170-174 (5)	7.00	3.85

Proclamation of independence, Oct. 2, 1958.

Bananas — A13

1959 Litho. *Perf. 11½*

175	A13	10fr shown	.25	.25
176	A13	15fr Grapefruit	.40	.25
177	A13	20fr Lemons	.70	.25
178	A13	25fr Avocados	.80	.25
179	A13	50fr Pineapple	1.75	.25
		Nos. 175-179 (5)	3.90	1.25

For overprints see Nos. 209-213.

Fishing Boats and Tamara Lighthouse A14

5fr, Coco palms & sailboat, vert. 10fr, Launching fishing pirogue. 15fr, Elephant's head. 20fr, Pres. Sékou Touré & torch, vert. 25fr, Elephant.

1959 Engr. *Perf. 13½*

180	A14	1fr rose	.25	.25
181	A14	2fr green	.25	.25
182	A14	3fr brown	.25	.25
183	A14	5fr blue	.40	.25
184	A14	10fr claret	.40	.25
185	A14	15fr light brn	1.20	.30
186	A14	20fr claret	1.20	.35
187	A14	25fr red brown	2.25	.60
		Nos. 180-187 (8)	6.20	2.50

Flag Raising, Labé — A15

1959 Litho. *Perf. 12*

188	A15	50fr multicolored	1.10	.25
189	A15	100fr multicolored	2.00	.50

For overprints see Nos. 201-202.

UN Headquarters, New York, and People of Guinea — A16

1959 *Perf. 12*

190	A16	1fr vio blue & org	.25	.25
191	A16	2fr red lil & emer	.25	.25
192	A16	3fr brn & crimson	.25	.25
193	A16	5fr brn & grnsh bl	.25	.25
		Nos. 190-193,C22-C23 (6)	3.40	2.65

Guinea's admission to the UN, first anniv.
For overprints see Nos. 205-208, C27-C28.

Uprooted Oak Emblem — A17

1960 Photo. *Perf. 11½*
Granite Paper

194	A17	25fr multicolored	.80	.25
195	A17	50fr multicolored	1.10	.25

World Refugee Year, 7/1/59-6/30/60.
For surcharges see Nos. B17-B18.

UPU Monument, Bern — A18

1960 Granite Paper Unwmk.

196	A18	10fr gray brn & blk	.25	.25
197	A18	15fr lil & purple	.45	.25
198	A18	20fr ultra & dk blue	.65	.25
199	A18	25fr yel grn & sl grn	.85	.25
200	A18	50fr red org & brown	.90	.25
		Nos. 196-200 (5)	3.10	1.25

Nos. 199-200 are vertical.
Admission to the UPU, first anniv.

Nos. 188-189 Overprinted in Black, Orange or Carmine: "Jeux Olympiques Rome 1960" and Olympic Rings

1960 Litho. *Perf. 12*

201	A15	50fr multi (Blk)	8.00	6.00
202	A15	100fr multi (O or C)	12.50	9.00
		Nos. 201-202,C24-C26 (5)	92.25	67.25

17th Olympic Games, Rome, 8/25-9/11. See note after No. C26.

Map and Flag of Guinea — A19

1960 Photo. *Perf. 11½*

203	A19	25fr multicolored	.60	.30
204	A19	30fr multicolored	.80	.30

Second anniversary of independence.

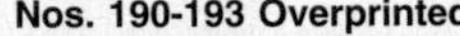

Nos. 190-193 Overprinted

1961 Litho. *Perf. 12*

205	A16	1fr vio blue & org	.25	.25
206	A16	2fr red lil & emer	.25	.25
207	A16	3fr brn & crimson	.25	.25
208	A16	5fr brn & grnsh bl	.25	.25

Nos. 175-179 Overprinted in Black or Orange

Perf. 11½
Fruits in Natural Colors

209	A13	10fr red	.25	.25
210	A13	15fr grn & pink	.40	.25
211	A13	20fr red brn & bl	.50	.25
212	A13	25fr bl & yel (O)	.50	.25
213	A13	50fr dk vio blue	1.00	.40
		Nos. 205-213,C27-C28 (11)	6.15	3.35

15th anniversary of United Nations.

Defassa Waterbuck A20

1961, Sept. 1 Photo. *Perf. 11½*
Multicolored Design; Granite Paper

214	A20	5fr bright grn	.25	.25
215	A20	10fr emerald	.35	.25
216	A20	25fr lilac	.40	.25
217	A20	40fr orange	.60	.25
218	A20	50fr red orange	1.20	.30
219	A20	75fr ultramarine	2.25	.75
		Nos. 214-219 (6)	5.05	2.05

For surcharges see Nos. B19-B24.

Exhibition Hall — A21

1961, Oct. 2 *Perf. 11½*
Flag in Red, Yellow & Green
Granite Paper

220	A21	5fr ultra & red	.25	.25
221	A21	10fr brown & red	.25	.25
222	A21	25fr gray grn & red	.30	.25
		Nos. 220-222 (3)	.80	.75

First Three-Year Plan.

Gray-breasted Helmet Guinea Fowl — A22

1961 Unwmk. *Perf. 13x14*

223	A22	5fr rose lil, sepia & bl	.25	.25
224	A22	10fr dp org, sepia & bl	.30	.25
225	A22	25fr cerise, sepia & bl	.35	.25
226	A22	40fr ocher, sepia & bl	.70	.25
227	A22	50fr lemon, sepia & bl	1.00	.25
228	A22	75fr apple grn, sep & bl	1.40	.30
		Nos. 223-228 (6)	4.00	1.55

For surcharges see Nos. B30-B35.

Patrice Lumumba and Map of Africa — A23

1962, Feb. 13 Photo. *Perf. 11½*

229	A23	10fr multicolored	.25	.25
230	A23	25fr multicolored	.55	.25
231	A23	50fr multicolored	.75	.25
		Nos. 229-231 (3)	1.55	.75

Death anniv. (on Feb. 12, 1961) of Patrice Lumumba, Premier of the Congo Republic.

King Mohammed V of Morocco and Map of Africa — A24

1962, Mar. 15 Litho. *Perf. 13*

232	A24	25fr multicolored	.75	.25
233	A24	75fr multicolored	2.25	.60

First anniv. of the conference of African heads of state at Casablanca.
For surcharges see Nos. B36-B37.

African Postal Union Issue

Map of Africa and Post Horn — A25

1962, Apr. 23 Photo. *Perf. 13½x13*

234	A25	25fr org, blk & grn	.60	.25
235	A25	100fr deep brn & org	1.90	.55

Establishment of African Postal Union.

Bolon Player A26

Musical Instruments: 30c, 25fr, 50fr, Bote, vert. 1fr, 10fr, Flute, vert. 1.50fr, 3fr, Koni. 2fr, 20fr, Kora. 40fr, 75fr, Bolon.

Perf. 13½x13, 13x13½

1962, June 15

236 A26 30c bl, dk grn & red .25 .25
237 A26 50c sal, brn & brt grn .25 .25
238 A26 1fr yel grn, grn & lil .25 .25
239 A26 1.50fr yel, red & bl .25 .25
240 A26 2fr rose lil, red lil & grn .25 .25
241 A26 3fr brn grn, grn & lil .25 .25
242 A26 10fr org, brn & bl .25 .25
243 A26 20fr ol, dk ol & car .45 .25
244 A26 25fr ol, dk ol & lil .55 .25
245 A26 40fr bl, grn & red lil .80 .25
246 A26 50fr rose, dp rose & Prus bl 1.10 .25
247 A26 75fr dl yel, brn & Prus bl 1.50 .60
Nos. 236-247,C32-C34 (15) 16.10 9.10

Hippopotamus — A27

25fr, 75fr, Lion. 30fr, 100fr, Leopard.

1962, Aug. 25 Litho. *Perf. 13x13½*

248 A27 10fr org, grn & brn .35 .25
249 A27 25fr emer, blk & brn .55 .25
250 A27 30fr yel grn, dk brn & yel .90 .25
251 A27 50fr vio bl, dk brn & grn 1.10 .30
252 A27 75fr lil, lt lil & red brn 1.75 .50
253 A27 100fr grnsh bl, dk brn & yel 2.40 .60
Nos. 248-253 (6) 7.05 2.15

See Nos. 340-345

Child at Blackboard — A28

Designs: 10fr, 20fr, Adult class.

1962, Sept. 19 Photo. *Perf. 13½x13*

254 A28 5fr yel, dk brn & org .25 .25
255 A28 10fr org & dk brn .25 .25
256 A28 15fr yel grn, dk brn & red .30 .25
257 A28 20fr bl & dk brn .40 .25
Nos. 254-257 (4) 1.20 1.00

Campaign against illiteracy.

Imperforates
From late 1962 onward, most Guinea stamps exist imperforate.

Alfa Yaya — A29

30fr, King Behanzin. 50fr, King Ba Bemba. 75fr, Almamy Samory. 100fr, Tierno Aliou.

1962, Oct. 2 *Perf. 13½*

Gold Frame

258 A29 25fr brt bl & sepia .25 .25
259 A29 30fr yel & sepia .40 .25
260 A29 50fr brt pink & sepia .65 .30
261 A29 75fr yel grn & sepia 1.25 .45
262 A29 100fr org, red & sepia 1.90 .70
Nos. 258-262 (5) 4.45 1.95

Heroes and martyrs of Africa.

Gray Parrot A30

Birds: 00c, 0fr, 50fr, Crowned crane (vert). 1fr, 20fr, Abyssinian ground hornbill. 1.50fr, 25fr, White spoonbill. 2fr, 40fr, Bateleur eagle.

1962, Dec. *Perf. 13½x13, 13x13½*

263 A30 30c multicolored .25 .25
264 A30 50c multicolored .25 .25
265 A30 1fr multicolored .25 .25
266 A30 1.50fr multicolored .25 .25
267 A30 2fr multicolored .25 .25
268 A30 3fr multicolored .65 .25
269 A30 10fr multicolored .80 .25
270 A30 20fr multicolored .90 .25
271 A30 25fr multicolored .95 .25
272 A30 40fr multicolored 1.10 .25
273 A30 50fr multicolored 1.60 .35
274 A30 75fr multicolored 2.10 .50
Nos. 263-274,C41-C43 (15) 27.10 11.60

Wheat Emblem and Globe A31

1963, Mar. 21 Photo. *Perf. 13x14*

275 A31 5fr red & yellow .25 .25
276 A31 10fr emerald & yel .25 .25
277 A31 15fr brown & yel .25 .25
278 A31 25fr dark ol & yel .25 .25
Nos. 275-278 (4) 1.00 1.00

FAO "Freedom from Hunger" campaign.

Basketball — A32

50c, 4fr, 30fr, Boxing. 1fr, 5fr, Running. 1.50fr, 10fr, Bicycling. 2fr, 20fr, Single sculls.

1963, Mar. 16 Unwmk. *Perf. 14*

279 A32 30c ver, dp claret & grn .25 .25
280 A32 50c lilac & blue .25 .25
281 A32 1fr dl org, sep & grn .25 .25
282 A32 1.50fr org, ultra & mag .25 .25
283 A32 2fr aqua, dk bl & mag .25 .25
284 A32 3fr ol, dp cl & grn .25 .25
285 A32 4fr car rose, pur & bl .25 .25
286 A32 5fr brt grn, ol & mag .25 .25
287 A32 10fr lil rose, ultra & mag .25 .25
288 A32 20fr red org, dk bl & crim .25 .25
289 A32 25fr emer, dp cl & dk grn .35 .25
290 A32 30fr gray, pur & bl .35 .25
Nos. 279-290,C44-C46 (15) 15.20 7.60

For overprints and surcharges see Nos. 312-314, C58-C60.

A33

Various Butterflies.

1963, May 10 Photo. *Perf. 12*

291 A33 10c dp rose, blk & gray .25 .25
292 A33 30c rose, blk & yel .25 .25
293 A33 40c yel grn, brn & yel .25 .25
294 A33 50c pale vio, blk & grn .25 .25
295 A33 1fr yel, blk & emer .40 .25
296 A33 1.50fr bluish grn, blk & sep .40 .25
297 A33 2fr multi .40 .25
298 A33 3fr multi 1.10 .25
299 A33 10fr rose lil, blk & grn 1.25 .25
300 A33 20fr gray, blk & grn 1.40 .25
301 A33 25fr yel grn, blk & gray 1.60 .25
302 A33 40fr multi 2.00 .45
303 A33 50fr ultra, blk & yel 2.50 .55
304 A33 75fr yel, blk & grn 3.25 .80
Nos. 291-304,C47-C49 (17) 30.40 11.80

Handshake, Map and Dove — A34

1963, May 22 *Perf. 13½x14*

305 A34 5fr bluish grn & dk brn .25 .25
306 A34 10fr org yel & dk brn .25 .25
307 A34 15fr ol & dk brn .25 .25
308 A34 25fr bis brn & dk brn .30 .25
Nos. 305-308 (4) 1.05 1.00

Conference of African heads of state for African Unity, Addis Ababa.

Globe Encircled by Satellite — A35

1963, July 25 Engr. *Perf. 10½*

309 A35 5fr green & car .25 .25
310 A35 10fr vio bl & car .40 .25
311 A35 15fr yellow & car .50 .25
Nos. 309-311,C50 (4) 1.90 1.00

Centenary of the International Red Cross.

Nos. 279-281 Surcharged in Carmine, Yellow or Orange

1963, Nov. 20 Photo. *Perf. 14*

312 A32 40fr on 30c (C or Y) 1.40 1.10
313 A32 50fr on 50c (C or O) 2.10 1.75
314 A32 75fr on 1fr (C or O) 3.50 2.50
Nos. 312-314,C58-C60 (6) 18.00 13.75

Meeting of the Olympic Games Preparatory Commission at Conakry. The overprint is in a circular line on #312, in 3 lines on each side on #313-314.

Jewelfish A36

Fish: 40c, 30fr, Golden pheasant. 50c, 40fr, Blue gularis. 1fr, 75fr, Banded Jewelfish. 1.50fr, African lyretail. 2fr, Six-barred epiplatys. 5fr, Jewelfish.

1964, Feb. 15 Litho. *Perf. 14x13½*

315 A36 30c car rose & multi .25 .25
316 A36 40c pur & multi .25 .25
317 A36 50c car rose & multi .25 .25
318 A36 1fr blue & multi .25 .25
319 A36 1.50fr blue & multi .25 .25
320 A36 2fr pur & multi .60 .25
321 A36 5fr blue & multi .65 .25
322 A36 30fr grn & multi .85 .25
323 A36 40fr pur & multi 1.75 .40
324 A36 75fr multi 2.50 .55
Nos. 315-324,C54-C55 (12) 17.60 4.90

John F. Kennedy A37

1964, Mar. 5 Engr. *Perf. 10½*

Flag in Red and Blue

325 A37 5fr blk & pur .25 .25
326 A37 25fr grn & pur .40 .25
327 A37 50fr brn & pur .70 .30
Nos. 325-327,C56 (4) 2.85 1.60

Issued in sheets of 20 with marginal quotations in English and French. Two sheets for each denomination. See No. C56.

Workers Welding Pipe — A38

5fr, Pipe line over mountains, vert. 10fr, Waterworks. 30fr, Transporting pipe. 50fr, Laying pipe.

1964, May 1 Photo. *Perf. 11½*

328 A38 5fr deep mag .25 .25
329 A38 10fr bright pur .25 .25
330 A38 20fr org red .30 .25
331 A38 30fr ultra .50 .25
332 A38 50fr yel grn .70 .25
Nos. 328-332 (5) 2.00 1.25

Completion of the water-supply pipeline to Conakry, Mar. 1964.

Ice Hockey — A39

1964, May 15 ***Perf. 13x12½***

333 A39 10fr shown .40 .25
334 A39 25fr Ski jump .60 .25
335 A39 50fr Slalom 1.10 .40
Nos. 333-335,C57 (4) 4.35 1.30

9th Winter Olympic Games, Innsbruck, Jan. 29-Feb. 9, 1964.

Eleanor Roosevelt Reading to Children — A40

1964, June 1 **Engr.** ***Perf. 10½***

336 A40 5fr green .25 .25
337 A40 10fr red org .25 .25
338 A40 15fr bright bl .25 .25
339 A40 25fr car rose .25 .25
Nos. 336-339,C61 (5) 1.75 1.25

Eleanor Roosevelt, 15th anniv. of the Universal Declaration of Human Rights (in 1963).

Animal Type of 1962

Designs: 5fr, 30fr, Striped hyenas. 40fr, 300fr, Black buffaloes. 75fr, 100fr, Elephants.

1964, Oct. 8 **Litho.** ***Perf. 13x13½***

340 A27 5fr yellow & blk .25 .25
341 A27 30fr light bl & blk .45 .25
342 A27 40fr lil rose & blk 1.00 .25
343 A27 75fr yel grn & blk 2.25 .40
344 A27 100fr bister & blk 2.50 .75
345 A27 300fr orange & blk 6.50 2.75
Nos. 340-345 (6) 12.95 4.65

Guinea Exhibit, World's Fair — A41

1964, Oct. 26 **Engr.** ***Perf. 10½***

346 A41 30fr vio & emerald .35 .25
347 A41 40fr red lil & emer .50 .25
348 A41 50fr sepia & emer .65 .25
349 A41 75fr rose red & dk bl .95 .25
Nos. 346-349 (4) 2.45 1.00

New York World's Fair, 1964-65.
See Nos. 372-375, C62-C63, C69-C70.

Queen Nefertari Crowned by Isis and Hathor — A42

Designs: 25fr, Ramses II in battle. 50fr, Submerged sphinxes, sailboat, Wadies-Sebua. 100fr, Ramses II holding crook and flail, Abu Simbel. 200fr, Feet and legs of Ramses statues, Abu Simbel.

1964, Nov. 19 **Photo.** ***Perf. 12***

350 A42 10fr dk bl, red brn & cit .25 .25
351 A42 25fr blk, dl red & brn .30 .25
352 A42 50fr dk brn, bl & vio .55 .25
353 A42 100fr dk brn, yel & pur 1.10 .40
354 A42 200fr pur, dl grn & buff 2.00 .75
Nos. 350-354,C64 (6) 7.70 3.30

UNESCO campaign to preserve Nubian monuments.
For overprint see No. 415.

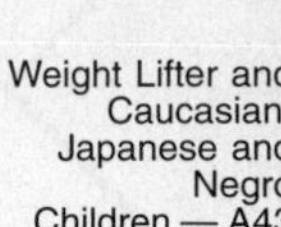
Weight Lifter and Caucasian, Japanese and Negro Children — A43

10fr, Runner carrying torch. 25fr, Pole vaulting and flags. 40fr, Runners. 50fr, Judo. 75fr, Japanese woman, flags and stadium.

1965, Jan. 18 **Photo.** ***Perf. 13x12½***

355 A43 5fr gold, claret & blk .25 .25
356 A43 10fr gold, blk, ver & bl .40 .25
357 A43 25fr gold, blk, yel grn & red .45 .25
358 A43 40fr gold, blk, brn & yel .50 .25
359 A43 50fr gold, blk & grn .70 .30
360 A43 75fr gold & multi 1.50 .40
Nos. 355-360,C65 (7) 5.55 2.05

18th Olympic Games, Tokyo, 10/10-25/64.
For overprints see Nos. 410-414.

Doudou Mask, Boké — A44

Designs: 40c, 1fr, 15fr, Various Niamou masks, N'Zérékoré region. 60c, "Yoki," wood-carved statuette of a girl, Boke. 80c, Masked woman dancer from Guekedou. 2fr, Masked dancer from Macenta. 20fr, Beater from Tam-tam. 60fr, Bird dancer from Macenta. 80fr, Bassari dancer from Koundara. 100fr, Sword dancer from Karana.

1965, Feb. 15 **Unwmk.** ***Perf. 14***

361 A44 20c multicolored .25 .25
362 A44 40c multicolored .25 .25
363 A44 60c multicolored .25 .25
364 A44 80c multicolored .25 .25
365 A44 1fr multicolored .25 .25
366 A44 2fr multicolored .25 .25
367 A44 15fr multicolored .30 .25
368 A44 20fr multicolored .35 .25
369 A44 60fr multicolored 1.10 .40
370 A44 80fr multicolored 1.50 .50
371 A44 100fr multicolored 1.75 .50
Nos. 361-371,C68 (12) 11.75 6.15

World's Fair Type of 1964 Inscribed "1965"

1965, Mar. 24 **Engr.** ***Perf. 10½***

372 A41 30fr grn & orange .30 .25
373 A41 40fr car & brt grn .45 .25
374 A41 50fr brt grn & vio .60 .25
375 A41 75fr brown & vio .90 .35
Nos. 372-375 (4) 2.25 1.10

See Nos. C69-C70.

Blacksmith A45

Handicrafts: 20fr, Potter. 60fr, Cloth dyers. 80fr, Basketmaker.

1965, May 1 **Photo.** ***Perf. 14***

376 A45 15fr multicolored .25 .25
377 A45 20fr multicolored .50 .25
378 A45 60fr multicolored .80 .30
379 A45 80fr multicolored .95 .40
Nos. 376-379,C71-C72 (6) 9.25 2.80

ITU Emblem, Old and New Communication Equipment — A46

1965, May 17 **Unwmk.**

380 A46 25fr yel, gray, gold & blk .45 .25
381 A46 50fr yel, grn, gold & blk .70 .25
Nos. 380-381,C73-C74 (4) 4.75 1.55

ITU centenary. Exist in tete-beche pairs.

Maj. Virgil I. Grissom — A47

Moon from 258mi. — A48

Sputnik Over Earth A49

American Achievements in Space: 10fr, Lt. Com. John W. Young. 25fr, Moon from 115mi. 30fr, Moon from 58mi. 100fr, Grissom and Young in Gemini 3 spaceship.

1965, July 19 **Photo.** ***Perf. 13***

Size: 21x29mm

382 A47 5fr dk red & multi .25 .25
383 A47 10fr dk red & multi .25 .25
384 A48 15fr gold, bl & dk bl .25 .25

Size: 39x28mm

385 A48 25fr gold, bl & dk bl .25 .25

Size: 21x29mm

386 A48 30fr gold, bl & dk bl .25 .25

Size: 39x28mm

387 A47 100fr multi & dk red .50 .40
a. Sheet of 15, #382-387 9.00

Russian Achievements in Space: 5fr, Col. Pavel Belyayev. 10fr, Lt. Col. Alexei Leonov. 15fr, Vostoks 3 & 4 in space. 30fr, Vostoks 5 & 6 over Earth. 100fr, Leonov floating in space.

Size: 21x29mm

388 A47 5fr bl & multi .25 .25
389 A47 10fr bl & multi .25 .25
390 A49 15fr bl & multi .25 .25

Size: 39x28mm

391 A49 25fr bl & multi .25 .25

Size: 21x29mm

392 A49 30fr bl & multi .25 .25

Size: 39x28mm

393 A47 100fr blk, dk red & gold .50 .40
a. Sheet of 15, #388-393 9.00
Nos. 382-393 (12) 3.50 3.30

American and Russian achievements in space. Nos. 387a and 393a contain five triptychs each: four rows with 5fr, 100fr and 10fr, and a center row with 15fr, 25fr and 30fr stamps each.

ICY Emblem, UN Headquarters and Skyline, New York — A50

1965, Sept. 8 ***Perf. 10½***

394 A50 25fr yel grn & ver .35 .25
395 A50 45fr vio & orange .40 .25
396 A50 75fr red brn & org .65 .25
Nos. 394-396,C75 (4) 2.65 1.10

Intl. Cooperation Year, 1965.

Polytechnic Institute, Conakry — A51

New Projects, Conakry: 30fr, Hotel Camayenne. 40fr, Gbessia Airport. 75fr, Stadium "28 September."

1965, Oct. 2 **Photo.** ***Perf. 13½***

397 A51 25fr multicolored .30 .25
398 A51 30fr multicolored .35 .25
399 A51 40fr multicolored .60 .30
400 A51 75fr multicolored .75 .40
Nos. 397-400,C76-C77 (6) 8.75 5.20

Seventh anniversary of independence.

Photographing Far Side of Moon — A52

10fr, Trajectories of Ranger VII on flight to moon. 25fr, Relay satellite. 45fr, Vostoks I & II & globe.

1965, Nov. 15 **Litho.** ***Perf. 14x13½***

401 A52 5fr blk, pur & ocher .25 .25
402 A52 10fr red brn, lt grn & yel .25 .25
403 A52 25fr blk, bl & bis .50 .25
404 A52 45fr blk, lt ultra & bis 1.00 .25
Nos. 401-404,C78-C79 (6) 5.50 2.50

For overprints and surcharges see Nos. 529-530, C112-C112B.

Sword Dance, Karana — A53

Designs: 30c, Dancing girls, Lower Guinea. 50c, Behore musicians of Tiekere playing "Eyoro," horiz. 5fr, Doundouba dance of Kouroussa. 40fr, Bird man's dance of Macenta.

1966, Jan. 5 **Photo.** ***Perf. 13½***

Size: 26x36mm

405 A53 10c multicolored .25 .25
406 A53 30c multicolored .25 .25

Size: 36x28½mm

407 A53 50c multicolored .45 .25

Size: 26x36mm

408 A53 5fr multicolored .45 .25
409 A53 40fr multicolored .75 .25
Nos. 405-409,C80 (6) 3.40 1.75

Festival of African Art and Culture. See Nos. 436-441.

Engraved Overprint in Red or Orange on Nos. 355-356 and Nos. 358-360

1966, Mar. 14 ***Perf. 13x12½***

410 A43 5fr multi (R) .40 .25
411 A43 10fr multi (R) .50 .25
412 A43 40fr multi (O) .85 .25
413 A43 50fr multi (R) 1.10 .40
414 A43 75fr multi (R) 2.00 .65
Nos. 410-414,C81 (6) 6.10 2.25

4th Pan Arab Games, Cairo, Sept. 2-11, 1965. The same overprint was also applied to imperf. sheets of No. 357.

Engraved Red Orange Overprint on No. 352

1966, Mar. 14 ***Perf. 12***

415	A42	50fr dk brn, bl & vio	1.00	.50

1st Egyptian postage stamps, cent. See #C82.

Vonkou Rock, Telimélé — A54

Views: 25fr, Artificial lake, Coyah. 40fr, Kalé waterfalls. 50fr, Forécariah bridge. 75fr, Liana bridge.

1966, Apr. 4 **Photo.** ***Perf. 13½***

416	A54	20fr multicolored	.25	.25
417	A54	25fr multicolored	.45	.25
418	A54	40fr multicolored	.50	.25
419	A54	50fr multicolored	.70	.25
420	A54	75fr multicolored	.90	.30
		Nos. 416-420,C83 (6)	4.20	1.90

See Nos. 475-478, C83, C90-C91. For overprints see Nos. 482-488, C93-C95.

UNESCO Emblem A55

1966, May 2 **Photo.** **Unwmk.**

421	A55	25fr multicolored	.70	.25

20th anniv. of UNESCO. See Nos. C84-C85.

Woman of Guinea and Morning Glory — A56

Designs: Women and Flowers of Guinea.

1966, May 30 **Photo.** ***Perf. 13½***

Size: 23x34mm

422	A56	10c multicolored	.25	.25
423	A56	20c multicolored	.25	.25
424	A56	30c multicolored	.25	.25
425	A56	40c multicolored	.25	.25
426	A56	3fr multicolored	.25	.25
427	A56	4fr multicolored	.25	.25
428	A56	10fr multicolored	.25	.25
429	A56	25fr multicolored	.65	.25

Size: 28x43mm

430	A56	30fr multicolored	.80	.25
431	A56	50fr multicolored	1.00	.35
432	A56	80fr multicolored	1.50	.45
		Nos. 422-432,C86-C87 (13)	14.20	5.85

Symbolic Water Cycle and UNESCO Emblem — A57

1966, Sept. 26 **Engr.** ***Perf. 10½***

433	A57	5fr bl & dp org	.25	.25
434	A57	25fr grn & dp org	.30	.25
435	A57	100fr brt rose lil & dp org	.85	.35
		Nos. 433-435 (3)	1.40	.85

Hydrological Decade (UNESCO), 1965-74.

Dance Type of 1966

Various folk dances. 25fr, 75fr, horizontal.

1966, Oct. 24 **Photo.** ***Perf. 13½***

Sizes: 26x36mm, 36x28½mm

436	A53	60c multicolored	.25	.25
437	A53	1fr multicolored	.25	.25
438	A53	1.50fr multicolored	.25	.25
439	A53	25fr multicolored	.75	.25
440	A53	50fr multicolored	.95	.25
441	A53	75fr multicolored	1.40	.50
		Nos. 436-441 (6)	3.85	1.75

Guinean National Dancers.

Child's Drawing and UNICEF Emblem — A58

Children's Drawings: 2fr, Elephant. 3fr, Girl. 20fr, Village, horiz. 25fr, Boy playing soccer. 40fr, Still life. 50fr, Bird in a tree.

1966, Dec. 12 **Photo.** ***Perf. 13½***

442	A58	2fr multicolored	.25	.25
443	A58	3fr multicolored	.25	.25
444	A58	10fr multicolored	.25	.25
445	A58	20fr multicolored	.25	.25
446	A58	25fr multicolored	.40	.25
447	A58	40fr multicolored	.45	.25
448	A58	50fr multicolored	.65	.25
		Nos. 442-448 (7)	2.50	1.75

20th anniv. of UNICEF. Printed in sheets of 10 stamps and 2 labels with ornamental borders and inscriptions.

Laboratory Technician — A59

WHO Emblem and: 50fr, Physician examining infant. 75fr, Pre-natal care & instruction. 80fr, WHO Headquarters, Geneva.

1967, Jan. 20 **Photo.** ***Perf. 13½***

449	A59	30fr multicolored	.30	.25
450	A59	50fr multicolored	.40	.25
451	A59	75fr multicolored	.60	.25
452	A59	80fr multicolored	.70	.35
		Nos. 449-452 (4)	2.00	1.10

Inauguration (in 1966) of WHO Headquarters, Geneva.

Niamou Mask, N'Zerekore — A60

Designs: 10c, 1fr, 30fr, Small Banda mask, Kanfarade, Boké region. 1.50fr, 50fr, Like 30c. 50c, 5fr, 75fr, Bearded Niamou mask. 60c, 25fr, 100fr, Horned Yinadjinkele mask, Kankan region.

1967, Mar. 25 **Photo.** ***Perf. 14x13***

453	A60	10c org & multi	.25	.25
454	A60	30c cit & brn blk	.25	.25
455	A60	50c dp lil rose, blk & red	.25	.25
456	A60	60c dp org, blk & bis	.25	.25
457	A60	1fr yel grn & multi	.25	.25
458	A60	1.50fr sal pink & brn blk	.25	.25
459	A60	5fr ap grn, blk & red	.25	.25
460	A60	25fr red lil, blk & bis	.45	.25
461	A60	30fr bis & multi	.50	.25
462	A60	50fr grnsh bl & brn blk	.70	.25
463	A60	75fr yel, blk & red	1.00	.35
464	A60	100fr lt ultra, blk & bis	1.60	.55
		Nos. 453-464 (12)	6.00	3.40

Ball Python — A61

20c, Pastoria Research Institute. 50c, 75fr, Extraction of snake venom. 1fr, 50fr, Rock python. 2fr, Men holding rock python. 5fr, 30fr, Gaboon viper. 20fr, West African mamba.

1967, May 15 **Litho.** ***Perf. 13½***

Size: 43½x20mm

465	A61	20c multicolored	.25	.25
466	A61	30c multicolored	.25	.25
467	A61	50c multicolored	.25	.25
468	A61	1fr multicolored	.25	.25
469	A61	2fr multicolored	.25	.25
470	A61	5fr multicolored	.25	.25

Size: 56x26mm

471	A61	20fr multicolored	.65	.25
472	A61	30fr multicolored	.90	.25
473	A61	50fr multicolored	1.00	.25
474	A61	75fr multicolored	1.60	.25
		Nos. 465-474,C88-C89 (12)	12.65	6.00

Research Institute for Applied Biology of Guinea (Pastoria). For souvenir sheet see No. C88a.

Scenic Type of 1966

Views: 5fr, Loos Island. 30fr, Tinkisso Waterfalls. 70fr, "The Elephant's Trunk" Hotel, Mt. Kakoulima. 80fr, Evening at the shore, Ratoma.

1967, June 20 **Photo.** ***Perf. 13½***

475	A54	5fr multicolored	.25	.25
476	A54	30fr multicolored	.25	.25
477	A54	70fr multicolored	.60	.25
478	A54	80fr multicolored	.85	.25
		Nos. 475-478,C90-C91 (6)	4.30	2.55

People's Palace, Conakry — A62

Elephant A63

1967, Sept. 28 **Photo.** ***Perf. 13½***

479	A62	5fr silver & multi	.25	.25
480	A63	30fr silver & multi	.30	.25
481	A62	55fr gold & multi	.50	.25
		Nos. 479-481 (3)	1.05	.75

20th anniv. of the Democratic Party of Guinea and the opening of the People's Palace, Conakry. See No. C92.

Nos. 418-420 and 475-478 Overprinted

1967, Nov. 6

482	A54	5fr multicolored	.45	.25
483	A54	30fr multicolored	.90	.25
484	A54	40fr multicolored	.75	.25
485	A54	50fr multicolored	.80	.25
486	A54	70fr multicolored	1.00	.30
487	A54	75fr multicolored	1.45	.50
488	A54	80fr multicolored	1.90	.50
		Nos. 482-488,C93-C95 (10)	12.90	5.60

50th anniversary of Lions International.

WHO Office for Africa — A64

1967, Dec. 4 **Photo.** ***Perf. 13½***

489	A64	30fr lt ol grn, bis & dk grn	.45	.25
490	A64	75fr red org, bis & dk bl	.80	.30

Inauguration of the WHO Regional Office for Africa in Brazzaville, Congo.

Human Rights Flame — A65

1968, Jan. 15 **Photo.** ***Perf. 13½***

491	A65	30fr ocher, grn & dk car	.50	.25
492	A65	40fr vio, grn & car	.60	.25

International Human Rights Year, 1968.

Coyah, Dubréka Region A66

Homes and People: 30c, 30fr, Kankan Region. 40c, Kankan, East Guinea. 50c, 15fr, Woodlands Region. 60c, Fulahmori, Gaoual Region. 5fr, Cognagui, Kundara Region. 40fr, Fouta Djallon, West Guinea. 100fr, Labé, West Guinea.

1968, Apr. 1 Photo. *Perf. 13½x14*
Size: 36x27mm

493 A66 20c gold & multi .25 .25
494 A66 30c gold & multi .25 .25
495 A66 40c gold & multi .25 .25
496 A66 50c gold & multi .25 .25

Perf. 14x13½
Size: 57x36mm

497 A66 60c gold & multi .25 .25
498 A66 5fr gold & multi .25 .25
499 A66 15fr gold & multi .25 .25
500 A66 20fr gold & multi .35 .25
501 A66 30fr gold & multi .40 .25
502 A66 40fr gold & multi .55 .25
503 A66 100fr gold & multi 1.50 .30
Nos. 493-503,C100 (12) 9.05 4.05

The Storyteller — A67

African Legends: 15fr, The Little Genie of Mt. Nimba. No. 506, The Legend of the Moons and the Stars. No. 507, Lan, the Child Buffalo, vert. 40fr, Nianablas and the Crocodiles. 50fr, Leuk the Hare Playing the Drum, vert. 75fr, Leuk the Hare Selling his Sister, vert. 80fr, The Hunter and the Antelope-woman. The designs are from paintings by students of the Academy of Fine Arts in Bellevue.

1968 Photo. *Perf. 13½*

504 A67 15fr multicolored .25 .25
505 A67 25fr multicolored .25 .25
506 A67 30fr multicolored .25 .25
507 A67 30fr multicolored .25 .25
508 A67 40fr multicolored .40 .25
509 A67 50fr multicolored .65 .25
a. Souv. sheet of 4 5.50 5.50
510 A67 75fr multicolored .65 .25
511 A67 80fr multicolored 1.10 .25
Nos. 504-511,C101-C104 (12) 12.85 4.80

Issued in sheets of 10 plus 2 labels. No. 509a contains 4 imperf. stamps similar to Nos. 508-509, C101 and C104. "Poste Aerienne" omitted on the 70fr and 300fr of the souvenir sheet.

Issued: #505-506, 510-511, 5/16; #504, 507-509, 9/16.

Anubius Baboon — A68

African Animals: 10fr, Leopards. 15fr, Hippopotami. 20fr, Nile crocodile. 30fr, Ethiopian wart hog. 50fr, Defassa waterbuck. 75fr, Cape buffaloes.

1968, Nov. 25 Photo. *Perf. 13½*
Size: 44x31mm

512 A68 5fr gold & multi .25 .25
513 A68 10fr gold & multi .60 .25
514 A68 15fr gold & multi .65 .25
a. Souv. sheet of 3, #512-514 1.50 1.50
515 A68 20fr gold & multi .75 .25
516 A68 30fr gold & multi .75 .25
517 A68 50fr gold & multi .90 .25
a. Souv. sheet of 3, #515-517 3.75 3.75
518 A68 75fr gold & multi 1.45 .30
a. Souv. sheet of 3 10.50 10.50
Nos. 512-518,C105-C106 (9) 10.60 4.45

No. 518a contains one No. 518 and one each similar to Nos. C105-C106 without "POSTE AERIENNE" inscription. The three souvenir sheets contain 3 stamps and one green and gold label inscribed "FAUNE AFRICAINE."

Senator Robert F. Kennedy A69

Portraits: 75fr, Rev. Martin Luther King, Jr. 100fr, Pres. John F. Kennedy.

1968, Dec. 16

519 A69 30fr yel & multi .55 .25
520 A69 75fr multicolored 1.00 .25
521 A69 100fr multicolored 1.40 .30
Nos. 519-521,C107-C109 (6) 9.75 2.55

Robert F. Kennedy, John F. Kennedy and Martin Luther King, Jr., martyrs for freedom.

The stamps are printed in sheets of 15 (3x5) containing 10 stamps and five yellow-green and gold center labels. Sheets come either with English or French inscriptions on label.

Sculpture and Runner A70

Sculpture and Soccer — A71

Designs (Sculpture and): 10fr, Boxing. 15fr, Javelin. 30fr, Steeplechase. 50fr, Hammer throw. 75fr, Bicycling.

1969, Feb. 18 Photo. *Perf. 13½*

522 A70 5fr multicolored .25 .25
523 A70 10fr multicolored .25 .25
524 A70 15fr multicolored .40 .25
525 A71 25fr multicolored .40 .25
526 A70 30fr multicolored .40 .25
527 A70 50fr multicolored .50 .25
528 A70 75fr multicolored .75 .25
Nos. 522-528,C110-C111A (10) 11.45 4.05

19th Olympic Games, Mexico City, 10/12-27.

No. 404 Srchd. and Ovptd. in Red

1969, Mar. 17 Litho. *Perf. 14x13½*

529 A52 30fr on 45fr multi .60 .35
530 A52 45fr multicolored .60 .35
Nos. 529-530,C112-C112B (5) 4.60 2.60

US Apollo 8 mission, the first men in orbit around the moon, Dec. 21-27, 1968.

Nos. 529-530 also exist with surcharge and overprint in black. These sell for about 10% more.

Tarzan — A72

Designs: 30fr, Tarzan sitting in front of Pastoria Research Institute gate. 75fr, Tarzan and his family. 100fr, Tarzan sitting in a tree.

1969, June 6 Photo. *Perf. 13½*

531 A72 25fr orange & multi .45 .25
532 A72 30fr bl grn & multi .60 .25
533 A72 75fr yel grn & multi 1.25 .25
534 A72 100fr yellow & multi 1.90 .35
Nos. 531-534 (4) 4.20 1.10

Tarzan was a Guinean chimpanzee with superior intelligence and ability.

Campfire A73

25fr, Boy Scout & tents. 30fr, Marching Boy Scouts. 40fr, Basketball. 45fr, Senior Scouts, thatched huts & mountain. 50fr, Guinean Boy Scout badge.

1969, July 1

535 A73 5fr gold & multi .25 .25
536 A73 25fr gold & multi .30 .25
537 A73 30fr gold & multi .30 .25
538 A73 40fr gold & multi .45 .25
539 A73 45fr gold & multi .60 .25
540 A73 50fr gold & multi .65 .25
a. Min. sheet of 6, #535-540 3.50 3.50
Nos. 535-540 (6) 2.55 1.50

Issued to honor the Boy Scouts of Guinea.

Launching Apollo 11 — A74

Designs: 30fr, Earth showing Africa as seen from moon. 50fr, Separation of lunar landing module and spaceship. 60fr, Astronauts and module on moon. 75fr, Module on moon and earth. 100fr, Module leaving moon. 200fr, Splashdown.

"a" stamps are inscribed in French. "b" stamps are inscribed in English.

1969, Aug. 20 Photo. *Perf. 13½*
Size: 34x55mm

541 A74 25fr Pair, #541a, 541b .40 .25
542 A74 30fr Pair, #542a, 542b .50 .25
543 A74 50fr Pair, #543a, 543b .75 .25
544 A74 60fr Pair, #544a, 544b 1.25 .35
545 A74 75fr Pair, #545a, 545b 1.50 .40

Size: 34x71mm

546 A74 100fr Pair, #546a, 546b 2.50 .60

Size: 34x55mm

547 A74 200fr Pair, #547a, 547b 5.00 1.50
Nos. 541-547 (7) 11.90 3.60

Man's 1st landing on the moon, 7/20/69.

Harvest and ILO Emblem A75

ILO, 50th Anniv.: 25fr, Power lines and blast furnaces. 30fr, Women in broadcasting studio. 200fr, Potters.

1969, Oct. 28 Photo. *Perf. 13½*

548 A75 25fr gold & multi .25 .25
549 A75 30fr gold & multi .30 .25
550 A75 75fr gold & multi .65 .25
551 A75 200fr gold & multi 1.90 .60
Nos. 548-551 (4) 3.10 1.35

Mother and Sick Child — A76

25fr, Sick child. 40fr, Girl receiving vaccination. 50fr, Boy receiving vaccination. 60fr, Mother receiving vaccination. 200fr, Edward Jenner, M.D.

1970, Jan. 15 Photo. *Perf. 13½*

552 A76 25fr multicolored .25 .25
553 A76 30fr multicolored .35 .25
554 A76 40fr multicolored .40 .25
555 A76 50fr multicolored .50 .25
556 A76 60fr multicolored .60 .25
557 A76 200fr multicolored 2.00 1.00
Nos. 552-557 (6) 4.10 2.25

Campaign against smallpox and measles.

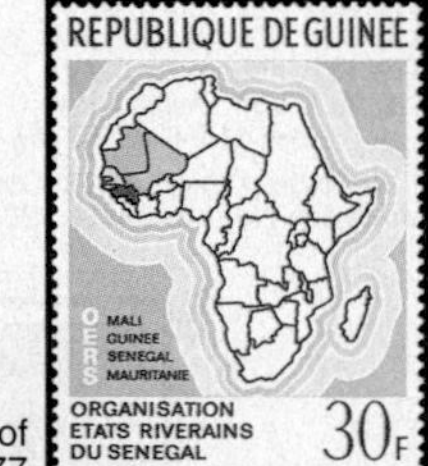

Map of Africa — A77

1970, Feb. 3 Litho. *Perf. 14½x14*

558 A77 30fr lt bl & multi .25 .25
559 A77 200fr lt vio & multi 1.75 .75

Meeting of statesmen of countries bordering on Senegal River: Mali, Guinea, Senegal and Mauritania.

Open Book and Radar A78

1970, July 6 Litho. *Perf. 14*

560 A78 5fr lt bl & blk .25 .25
561 A78 10fr rose & blk .25 .25
562 A78 50fr yellow & blk .60 .25
563 A78 200fr lilac & blk 2.10 .90
Nos. 560-563 (4) 3.20 1.65

International Telecommunications Day.

Lenin — A79

Designs: 20fr, Meeting with Lenin, by V. Serov. 30fr, Lenin Addressing Workers, by V. Serov. 40fr, Lenin with Red Guard Soldier and Sailor, by P. V. Vasiliev. 100fr, Lenin Speaking from Balcony, by P. V. Vasiliev. 200fr, Like 5fr.

1970, Nov. 16 Photo. *Perf. 13*

564 A79 5fr gold & multi .25 .25
565 A79 20fr gold & multi .40 .25
566 A79 30fr gold & multi .50 .25
567 A79 40fr gold & multi .70 .25

No.	Type	Denomination / Color	Unused	Used
568	A79	100fr gold & multi	1.60	.30
569	A79	200fr gold & multi	3.00	.75
		Nos. 564-569 (6)	6.45	2.05

Lenin (1870-1924), Russian communist leader.

Phenecogrammus Interruptus — A80

Designs: Various fish from Guinea.

1971, Apr. 1 Photo. *Perf. 13*

No.	Type	Denomination / Color	Unused	Used
570	A80	5fr gold & multi	.25	.25
571	A80	10fr gold & multi	.25	.25
572	A80	15fr gold & multi	.30	.25
573	A80	20fr gold & multi	.30	.25
574	A80	25fr gold & multi	.30	.25
575	A80	30fr gold & multi	.45	.25
576	A80	40fr gold & multi	.60	.25
577	A80	45fr gold & multi	.70	.25
578	A80	50fr gold & multi	1.00	.25
579	A80	75fr gold & multi	1.75	.55
580	A80	100fr gold & multi	2.25	.65
581	A80	200fr gold & multi	5.00	1.10
		Nos. 570-581 (12)	13.15	4.55

Violet-crested Touraco — A81

Birds: 20fr, European golden oriole. 30fr, Blue-headed coucal. 40fr, Northern shrike. 75fr, Vulturine guinea fowl. 100fr, Southern ground hornbill.

1971, June 18 Photo. *Perf. 13*
Size: 34x34mm

No.	Type	Denomination / Color	Unused	Used
582	A81	5fr gold & multi	.25	.25
583	A81	20fr gold & multi	.35	.25
584	A81	30fr gold & multi	.55	.25
585	A81	40fr gold & multi	.65	.25
586	A81	75fr gold & multi	2.00	.55
587	A81	100fr gold & multi	2.50	.80
		Nos. 582-587,C113-C113B (9)	14.15	4.80

UNICEF Emblem, Map of Africa — A82

1971, Dec. 24 *Perf. 12x12½*
Map in Olive

No.	Type	Denomination / Color	Unused	Used
588	A82	25fr orange & blk	.25	.25
589	A82	30fr pink & black	.35	.25
590	A82	50fr gray grn & blk	[illegible]	[illegible]
591	A82	60fr gray bl & blk	.70	.25
592	A82	100fr lil rose & blk	1.10	.25
		Nos. 588-592 (5)	3.00	1.25

UNICEF, 25th anniv.
For overprints see Nos. 625-629.

Imaginary Prehistoric Space Creature — A83

Various imaginary prehistoric space creatures.

1972, Apr. 1 *Perf. 13½x13*

No.	Type	Denomination / Color	Unused	Used
593	A83	5fr multicolored	.25	.25
594	A83	20fr multicolored	.25	.25
595	A83	30fr multicolored	.25	.25
596	A83	40fr multicolored	.50	.25
597	A83	100fr multicolored	1.00	.35
598	A83	200fr multicolored	2.10	.75
		Nos. 593-598 (6)	4.35	2.10

Black Boy, Men of 4 Races, Emblem — A84

Designs: 20fr, Oriental boy. 30fr, Indian youth. 50fr, Caucasian girl. 100fr, Men of 4 races and Racial Equality emblem.

1972, May 14 *Perf. 13x13½*

No.	Type	Denomination / Color	Unused	Used
599	A84	15fr gold & multi	.25	.25
600	A84	20fr gold & multi	.25	.25
601	A84	30fr gold & multi	.25	.25
602	A84	50fr gold & multi	.40	.25
603	A84	100fr gold & multi	.75	.30
		Nos. 599-603,C119 (6)	3.00	2.30

Intl. Year Against Racial Discrimination, 1971.

Map of Africa, Syncom Satellite — A85

Designs (Map of Africa and Satellites): 30fr, Relay. 75fr, Early Bird. 80fr, Telstar.

1972, May 17 Litho. *Perf. 13*

No.	Type	Denomination / Color	Unused	Used
604	A85	15fr multicolored	.25	.25
605	A85	30fr red org & multi	.30	.25
606	A85	75fr grn & multi	.80	.25
607	A85	80fr multicolored	.90	.45
		Nos. 604-607,C120-C121 (6)	5.85	2.80

4th World Telecommunications Day.

Carrier Pigeon, UPAF Emblem — A86

1972, July 10

No.	Type	Denomination / Color	Unused	Used
608	A86	15fr brt bl & multi	.25	.25
609	A86	30fr multicolored	.25	.25
610	A86	75fr lil & multi	.65	.25
611	A86	80fr multicolored	.80	.45
		Nos. 608-611,C122-C123 (6)	4.60	3.00

Book Year Emblem, Reading Child — A87

Designs (Book Year Emblem and): 15fr, Book as sailing ship. 40fr, Young woman with flower and book. 50fr, Book as key. 75fr, Man reading and globe. 200fr, Book and laurel.

1972, Aug. 2 Photo. *Perf. 14x13½*

No.	Type	Denomination / Color	Unused	Used
612	A87	5fr red & multi	.25	.25
613	A87	15fr multicolored	.25	.25
614	A87	40fr yel & multi	.45	.25
615	A87	50fr blue & multi	.65	.25
616	A87	75fr dk red & multi	.75	.45
617	A87	200fr org & multi	1.50	.90
		Nos. 612-617 (6)	3.85	2.35

International Book Year 1972.

Javelin, Olympic Emblems, Arms of Guinea A88

1972, Aug. 26 Photo. *Perf. 13*

No.	Type	Denomination / Color	Unused	Used
618	A88	5fr shown	.25	.25
619	A88	10fr Pole vault	.25	.25
620	A88	25fr Hurdles	.35	.25
621	A88	30fr Hammer throw	.50	.25
622	A88	40fr Boxing	.65	.25
623	A88	50fr Vaulting	.80	.35
624	A88	75fr Running	1.20	.45
		Nos. 618-624,C124-C125 (9)	9.00	3.75

20th Olympic Games, Munich, 8/26-9/11.

Nos. 588-592 Overprinted

1972, Sept. 28 Photo. *Perf. 12x12½*
Map in Olive

No.	Type	Denomination / Color	Unused	Used
625	A82	25fr org & blk	.40	.25
626	A82	30fr pink & blk	.60	.25
627	A82	50fr gray grn & blk	.90	.25
628	A82	60fr gray bl & blk	1.50	.25
629	A82	100fr lil rose & blk	2.10	.80
		Nos. 625-629 (5)	5.50	1.80

UN Conference on Human Environment, Stockholm, June 5-16.

Dimitrov at Leipzig Trial — A89

25fr, In Moabit Prison, 1933. 40fr, Writing his memoirs. 100fr, Portrait.

1972, Sept. 28 *Perf. 13*
Gold, Dark Green & Black

No.	Type	Denomination / Color	Unused	Used
630	A89	5fr shown	.25	.25
631	A89	25fr multicolored	.25	.25
632	A89	40fr multicolored	.50	.25
633	A89	100fr multicolored	1.20	.30
		Nos. 630-633 (4)	2.20	1.05

George Dimitrov (1882-1949), Bulgarian Communist party leader and Premier.

Emperor Haile Selassie — A90

Design: 200fr, Emperor facing right.

1972, Oct. 2

No.	Type	Denomination / Color	Unused	Used
634	A90	40fr blk & multi	.50	.25
635	A90	200fr multicolored	2.50	.95

Syntomeida Epilais — A91

Designs: Various insects.

1973, Mar. 5 Photo. *Perf. 14x13½*

No.	Type	Denomination / Color	Unused	Used
636	A91	5fr shown	.25	.25
637	A91	15fr Ladybugs	.35	.25
638	A91	30fr Green locust	1.00	.30
639	A91	40fr Honey bee	1.40	.40
640	A91	50fr Photinus pyralis	1.75	.60
641	A91	200fr Ancyluris formosissima	5.50	1.75
		Nos. 636-641 (6)	10.25	3.55

Kwame Nkrumah A92

Various portraits of Kwame Nkrumah.

1973, May 25 Photo. *Perf. 13½*

No.	Type	Denomination / Color	Unused	Used
642	A92	1.50s lt grn, gold & brn	.25	.25
643	A92	2.50s lt grn, gold & brn	.35	.25
644	A92	5s lt grn, gold & brn	.60	.25
645	A92	10s gold & dark vio	1.75	.45
		Nos. 642-645 (4)	2.95	1.20

OAU, 10th anniversary.

Institute for Applied Biology, Kindia A93

WHO Emblem and: 2.50s, Technicians inoculating egg. 3s, Filling vaccine into ampules. 4s, Sterilization of vaccine. 5s, Assembling of vaccine and vaccination gun. 10s, Inoculation of steer. 20s, Vaccination of woman.

1973, Nov. 16 Photo. *Perf. 13½*
Size: 40x36mm

No.	Type	Denomination / Color	Unused	Used
646	A93	1s gold & multi	.25	.25
647	A93	2.50s gold & multi	.35	.25
648	A93	3s gold & multi	.35	.25
649	A93	4s gold & multi	.50	.25

Size: 47½x31mm

650 A93 5s gold & multi .80 .25
651 A93 10s gold & multi 1.20 .40
652 A93 20s gold & multi 2.75 1.00
Nos. 646-652 (7) 6.20 2.65

WHO, 25th anniversary.

Copernicus, Heliocentric System, Primeval Landscape — A94

Nicolaus Copernicus — A95

Designs (Copernicus and): 2s, Sun rising over volcanic desert, and spacecraft. 4s, Earth, moon and spacecraft. 5s, Moon scape and spacecraft. 10s, Jupiter and spacecraft. 20s, Saturn and heliocentric system.

1973, Dec. 17 Photo. *Perf. 13½*

653 A94 50c gold & multi .25 .25
654 A94 2s gold & multi .25 .25
655 A94 4s gold & multi .40 .25
656 A94 5s gold & multi .50 .25
657 A94 10s gold & multi 1.10 .40
658 A94 20s gold & multi 2.40 .90
Nos. 653-658 (6) 4.90 2.30

Souvenir Sheet

659 Sheet of 4 16.00 16.00
a. A95 20s Single stamp 3.00 3.00

Nicolaus Copernicus (1473-1543), Polish astronomer. No. 659 contains center label showing rocket and heliocentric system in gold margin.

Loading Bauxite on Freighter — A96

1974, Mar. 1 Litho. *Perf. 13½*

660 A96 4s shown .60 .25
661 A96 6s Freight train 1.20 .25
662 A96 10s Mining 2.00 .65
Nos. 660-662 (3) 3.80 1.15

Bauxite mining, Boke.

Clappertonia Ficifolia — A97

1s, Rothmannia longiflora. 2s, Oncoba spinosa. 3s, Venidium fastuosum. 4s, Bombax costatum. 5s, Clerodendrum splendens. 7.50s, Combretuni grandiflorum. 10s, Mussaendra erythrophylla. 12s, Argemone mexicana.

1974, May 20 Photo. *Perf. 13*

Size: 25x36mm

663 A97 50c shown .25 .25
664 A97 1s multicolored .25 .25
665 A97 2s multicolored .25 .25
666 A97 3s multicolored .30 .25

Size: 31x42mm

667 A97 4s multicolored .40 .25
668 A97 5s multicolored .75 .25
669 A97 7.50s multicolored .85 .30
670 A97 10s multicolored 1.00 .35

Size: 38x38mm (Diamond)

671 A97 12s multicolored 1.25 .45
Nos. 663-671,C127-C129 (12) 18.80 7.40

Drummers, Pigeon, UPAF and UPU Emblems — A98

Designs (Carrier Pigeon, African Postal Union and UPU Emblems): 6s, Runner with letter stick. 7.50s, Monorail and mail truck. No. 675, Jet and ocean liner.

No. 676, Balloon and dugout canoe. 20s, Satellites over earth.

1974, Oct. 16 Photo. *Perf. 13½x14*

672 A98 5s mag & multi .60 .25
673 A98 6s grn & multi .80 .25
674 A98 7.50s ver & multi 1.25 .35
675 A98 10s Prus bl & multi 1.75 .60
Nos. 672-675 (4) 4.40 1.45

Souvenir Sheets

Perf. 13½

676 A98 10s ocher & multi *6.00* 6.00
677 Sheet of 4, multi 12.00 12.00
a. A98 20s Single stamp 1.60 1.60

Centenary of Universal Postal Union. No. 676 contains one 70x60mm stamp.

Rope Bridge — A99

Designs (Pioneers): 2s, Field observation. 4s, Communication. 5s, Cooking in camp. 7.50s, Salute. 10s, Basketball.

1974, Nov. 22 Photo. *Perf. 14x13½*

678 A99 50c multicolored .25 .25
679 A99 2s multicolored .35 .25
680 A99 4s multicolored .45 .25
681 A99 5s multicolored .75 .25
682 A99 7.50s multicolored 1.10 .25
683 A99 10s multicolored 1.90 .45
a. Souv. sheet of 2, #682-683 4.00 4.00
Nos. 678-683 (6) 4.80 1.70

National Pioneer Movement.

Souvenir Sheet

Fruit — A100

1974, Nov. 22 Photo. *Perf. 13x14*

684 A100 Sheet of 5 *12.00* 12.00
a. 4s Limes 1.00 .75
b. 4s Oranges 1.00 .85
c. 5s Bananas 1.50 1.25
d. 5s Mangos 1.50 1.25
e. 12s Pineapple 2.75 2.50

Chimpanzee — A101

2s, Impala. 3s, Wart hog. 4s, Kobus defassa. 5s, Leopard. 6s, Greater kudu. 6.50s, Zebra. 7.50s, Cape buffalo. 8s, Hippopotamus. 10s, Lion. 12s, Black rhinoceros. 15s, Elephant.

1975, May 14 Photo. *Perf. 13½*

685 A101 1s shown .25 .25
686 A101 2s multi .35 .25
687 A101 3s multi .50 .25
688 A101 4s multi .65 .25
a. Souv. sheet of 4, #685-688 7.00 7.00
689 A101 5s multi .80 .25
690 A101 6s multi 1.00 .25
691 A101 6.50s multi 1.10 .25
692 A101 7.50s multi 1.75 .25
a. Souv. sheet of 4, #689-692 7.00 7.00
693 A101 8s multi 2.40 .85
694 A101 10s multi 2.75 .85
695 A101 12s multi 3.75 1.00
696 A101 15s multi 4.75 1.50
a. Souv. sheet of 4, #693-696 17.50 17.50
Nos. 685-696 (12) 20.05 6.20

Sheets exist perf. and imperf.

Stamps in Nos. 692a, 696a are inscribed "Poste Aerienne."

Lions, Pipe Line and ADB Emblem A102

Designs (African Development Bank Emblem, Pipe Line and): 7s, Elephants. 10s, Male lions. 20s, Elephant and calf.

1975, June 16 Photo. *Perf. 13½*

697 A102 5s gold & multi .70 .25
698 A102 7s gold & multi .95 .25
699 A102 10s gold & multi 1.40 .35
700 A102 20s gold & multi 2.50 .70
Nos. 697-700 (4) 5.55 1.55

African Development Bank, 10th anniv.

Women Musicians, IWY Emblem A103

IWY Emblem and: 7s, Women banjo & guitar players. 9s, Woman railroad shunter & train. 15s, Woman physician examining infant. 20s, Male & female symbols.

1976, Apr. 12 Photo. *Perf. 13½*

701 A103 5s multicolored .55 .25
702 A103 7s multicolored .90 .25
703 A103 9s blue & multi 1.25 .45
704 A103 15s multicolored 2.00 .75
a. Souvenir sheet 3.00 3.00
705 A103 20s vio bl & multi 2.50 1.00
a. Souvenir sheet of 4 13.00 13.00
Nos. 701-705 (5) 7.20 2.70

International Women's Year 1975. No. 704a contains one stamp similar to No. 704 with gold frame. No. 705a contains 4 stamps similar to No. 705 with gold frame.

Woman Gymnast A104

Montreal Olympic Games Emblem and: 4s, Long jump. 5s, Hammer throw. 6s, Discus. 6.50s, Hurdles. 7s, Javelin. 8s, Running. 8.50s, Bicycling. 10s, High jump. 15s, Shot put. 20s, Pole vault. No. 717, Soccer.

No. 718, Swimming.

1976, May 17 Photo. *Perf. 13½*

Size: 38x38mm

706 A104 3s multicolored .35 .25
707 A104 4s grn & multi .45 .25
708 A104 5s yel & multi .55 .25
709 A104 6s multicolored .70 .25
710 A104 6.50s plum & multi .80 .25
711 A104 7s blue & multi .90 .30
712 A104 8s ultra & multi 1.10 .30
713 A104 8.50s org & multi 1.10 .35
714 A104 10s multicolored 1.25 .40
715 A104 15s multicolored 2.25 .75
716 A104 20s multicolored 2.75 .95
717 A104 25s grn & multi 3.50 1.00
Nos. 706-717 (12) 15.70 5.30

Souvenir Sheet

718 A104 25s multicolored 4.50 4.50

21st Olympic Games, Montreal, Canada, July 17-Aug. 1. No. 718 contains one 32x32mm stamp. See No. C130.

A. G. Bell, Telephone, 1900 — A105

7s, Wall telephone, 1910. 12s, Syncom telecommunications satellite. No. 722, Telstar satellite.

No. 723, Telephone switchboard operator, 1914.

1976, Nov. 15 Photo. *Perf. 13*

719 A105 5s multicolored .75 .25
720 A105 7s multicolored 1.00 .25
721 A105 12s multicolored 1.40 .45
722 A105 15s multicolored 1.75 .60
a. Souvenir sheet of 4, #719-722 7.00 7.00
Nos. 719-722 (4) 4.90 1.55

Souvenir Sheet

723 A105 15s multicolored 6.25 6.25

Centenary of first telephone call by Alexander Graham Bell, Mar. 10, 1876.

Collybia Fusipes — A106

Mushrooms: 7s, Lycoperdon perlatum. 9s, Boletus edulis. 9.50s, Lactarius deliciosus. 11.50s, Agaricus campestris.

1977, Feb. 6 Photo. *Perf. 13*

Size: 48x26mm

724 A106 5s multicolored 1.75 .25
725 A106 7s multicolored 2.25 .25
726 A106 9s multicolored 3.25 .55
a. Souvenir sheet of 2, #724, 726 7.00 7.00
727 A106 9.50s multicolored 3.50 .65

Size: 48x31mm

728 A106 11.50s multicolored 4.50 1.10
Nos. 724-728,C131-C133 (8) 30.50 6.50

Hexaplex Hoplites — A107

Sea Shells: 2s, Perrona lineata. 4s, Marginella pseudofaba. 5s, Tympanotonos radula. 7s, Marginella strigata. 8s, Harpa doris. 10s, Demoulia pinguis. 20s, Bursa scrobiculator. 25s, Marginella adansoni.

1977, Apr. 25 Photo. *Perf. 13*

Size: 50x25mm

729	A107	1s gold & multi	.25	.25
730	A107	2s gold & multi	.30	.25
731	A107	4s gold & multi	.75	.30
732	A107	5s gold & multi	1.15	.35
733	A107	7s gold & multi	1.60	.40
734	A107	8s gold & multi	1.90	.60

Size: 50x30mm

735	A107	10s gold & multi	2.50	.90
736	A107	20s gold & multi	5.00	1.25
737	A107	25s gold & multi	6.50	1.75
		Nos. 729-737 (9)	19.95	6.05

Farmers and Ox Plow A108

Designs: 5s, Pres. Touré addressing rally. 20s, Soldier driving farm tractor. 25s, Pres. Touré addressing UN General Assembly. 30s, 40s, Pres. Sékou Touré, vert.

1977, May 14 *Perf. 13½x13, 13x13½*

738	A108	5s gold & multi	.55	.25
739	A108	10s gold & multi	1.00	.40
740	A108	20s gold & multi	2.00	.90
741	A108	25s gold & multi	2.40	1.25
a.		Souvenir sheet of 4, #738-741	7.00	7.00
742	A108	30s gold & dk brn	3.25	1.25
743	A108	40s gold & sl grn	5.25	1.50
a.		Souvenir sheet of 2, #742-743	10.00	10.00
		Nos. 738-743 (6)	14.45	5.55

Democratic Party of Guinea, 30th anniv.

Nile Monitor — A109

Reptiles and Snakes: 4s, Frogs. 5s, Lizard (uromastix). 6s, Sand skink. 6.50s, Agama. 7s, Black-lipped spitting cobra. 8.50s, Ball python. 20s, Toads.

1977, Oct. 10 Photo. *Perf. 13½*

Size: 46x20mm

744	A109	3s multi	.50	.25
745	A109	4s multi	.70	.25
746	A109	5s multi	.70	.25

Size: 46x30mm

747	A109	6s multi	1.15	.25
748	A109	6.50s multi	1.45	.25
749	A109	7s multi	1.90	.55
750	A109	8.50s multi	2.10	.65
751	A109	20s multi	5.00	1.40
		Nos. 744-751,C134-C136 (11)	28.50	7.35

Eland — A110

Endangered Animals: 2s, Chimpanzee. 2.50s, Pygmy elephant. 3s, Lion. 4s, Palm squirrel. 5s, Hippopotamus. Each animal shown male, female and young.

1977, Dec. 12 Photo. *Perf. 14x13½*

752	A110	Strip of 3	.95	.25
a.-c.		1s any single	.25	
753	A110	Strip of 3	1.50	.25
a.-c.		2s any single	.35	
754	A110	Strip of 3	1.90	.30
a.-c.		2.50s any single	.50	
755	A110	Strip of 3	2.50	.40
a.-c.		3s any single	.60	
756	A110	Strip of 3	3.00	.55
a.-c.		4s any single	.95	
757	A110	Strip of 3	4.00	.65
a.-c.		5s any single	1.25	
		Nos. 752-757,C137-C142 (12)	50.60	22.40

Russian October Revolution, 60th Anniv. — A111

Designs: 2.50s, First Lenin debate, Moscow. 5s, Lenin speaking, 1917. 7.50s, Lenin and people. 8s, Lenin in first parade on Red Square.

1978, Feb. 27 Photo. *Perf. 14*

758	A111	2.50s gold & multi	.60	.25
759	A111	5s gold & multi	1.00	.25
760	A111	7.50s gold & multi	1.50	.30
761	A111	8s gold & multi	1.60	.35
		Nos. 758-761,C143-C144 (6)	14.10	4.05

Pres. Giscard d'Estaing at Microphones — A112

Pres. Valery Giscard d'Estaing of France and Pres. Sekou Toure of Guinea: 5s, 10s, In conference. 6.50s, Signing agreement. 7s, Attending official meeting. 8.50s, With their wives. 20s, Drinking a toast.

1979, Sept. 14 Photo. *Perf. 13*

762	A112	3s lt brn & brn	.80	.25
763	A112	5s green & brn	1.40	.25
764	A112	6.50s red lil & brn	1.75	.25
765	A112	7s ultra & brn	1.90	.30
766	A112	8.50s dk red & brn	2.25	.55
767	A112	10s vio & brown	2.40	.80
768	A112	20s yel grn & brn	4.00	1.10
		Nos. 762-768,C145 (8)	18.50	5.50

Visit of Pres. Valery Giscard d'Estaing to Guinea.

Twenty Thousand Leagues Under the Sea — A113

Jules Verne Stories: 3s, Children of Capt. Grant. 5s, Mysterious Island. 7s, A Captain at Fifteen. 10s, The Borsac Mission.

1979, Nov. 8 Litho. *Perf. 12x12½*

769	A113	1s multicolored	.25	.25
770	A113	3s multicolored	.35	.25
771	A113	5s multicolored	.65	.25
772	A113	7s multicolored	1.10	.30
773	A113	10s multicolored	1.60	.40
		Nos. 769-773,C146-C147 (7)	10.05	2.65

Jules Verne (1828-1905), French science fiction writer.

"Aerial Steam Carriage," 1842 A114

Aviation Retrospect: 5s, Wright's Flyer 1 1903. 6.50s, Caudron, 1934. 7s, Spirit of St. Louis, 1927. 8.50s, Bristol Beaufighter, 1940. 10s, Bleriot XI, 1909. No. 780, Concorde. No. 781, Boeing 727, 1963.

1979, Nov. 22 Photo. *Perf. 14*

774	A114	3s multicolored	.45	.25
775	A114	5s multicolored	.70	.25
776	A114	6.50s multicolored	.85	.25
777	A114	7s multicolored	1.00	.25
778	A114	8.50s multicolored	1.10	.30
779	A114	10s multicolored	1.75	.30
780	A114	20s multicolored	3.00	.65
781	A114	20s multicolored	3.00	.65
		Nos. 774-781 (8)	11.85	2.90

Hafia Soccer Team — A115

Designs: 2s, Players and Sekou Touré cup, vert. 5s, Pres. Touré presenting cup. 7s, Pres. Touré and player holding cup, vert. 8s, Sekou Touré cup, vert. 10s, Team captains and referees, vert. 20s, The winning goal.

Perf. 12½x12, 12x12½

1979, Dec. 18 Litho.

782	A115	1s multicolored	.25	.25
783	A115	2s multicolored	.25	.25
784	A115	5s multicolored	.65	.25
785	A115	7s multicolored	1.00	.35
786	A115	8s multicolored	1.25	.40
787	A115	10s multicolored	1.50	.45
788	A115	20s multicolored	3.00	.75
		Nos. 782-788 (7)	7.90	2.70

Hafia Soccer Team, African triple champions, 1977.

Train, IYC Emblem A116

IYC Emblem and: 2s, Children dancing around tree, vert. 4s, "1979" and leaves, vert. 7s, Village. 10s, Boy climbing tree. 25s, Boys of different races, flowers, sun.

1980, Jan. 14 *Perf. 13x13½, 13½x13*

789	A116	2s multicolored	.25	.25
790	A116	4s multicolored	.50	.25
791	A116	5s multicolored	.70	.25
792	A116	7s multicolored	1.00	.30
793	A116	10s multicolored	1.40	.40
794	A116	25s multicolored	4.00	1.10
		Nos. 789-794 (6)	7.85	2.55

International Year of the Child (1979).

Butterflyfish — A117

2s, Porgy. 3s, Zeus conchifer, vert. 4s, Grouper. 5s, Sea horse, vert. 6s, Hatchet fish. 7s, Pisodonophis semicinctus. 8s, Flying gurnard, vert. 9s, Squirrelfish. 10s, Psettus sebae, vert. 12s, Abudefuf hoeffleri. 15s, Triggerfish.

1980, Apr. 1 *Perf. 12½x12, 12x12½*

795	A117	1s shown	.25	.25
796	A117	2s multicolored	.25	.25
797	A117	3s multicolored	.45	.25
798	A117	4s multicolored	.60	.25
799	A117	5s multicolored	.75	.25
800	A117	6s multicolored	1.00	.35
801	A117	7s multicolored	1.25	.40
802	A117	8s multicolored	1.60	.50
803	A117	9s multicolored	1.75	.65
804	A117	10s multicolored	2.10	.65
805	A117	12s multicolored	3.00	.75
806	A117	15s multicolored	5.00	1.00
		Nos. 795-806 (12)	18.00	5.55

Apollo 11 Take-Off — A118

2s, Earth from moon. 4s, Armstrong leaving module. 5s, Armstrong on moon. 7s, Collecting samples. 8s, Re-entry. 12s, Recovery. 20s, Crew.

1980, July 20 Photo. *Perf. 14*

807	A118	1s shown	.25	.25
808	A118	2s multicolored	.25	.25
809	A118	4s multicolored	.45	.25
810	A118	5s multicolored	.70	.25
811	A118	7s multicolored	.85	.35
812	A118	8s multicolored	1.25	.45
813	A118	12s multicolored	2.10	.45
814	A118	20s multicolored	3.75	.75
		Nos. 807-814 (8)	9.60	3.00

Apollo 11 moon landing, 10th anniv. (1979).

Intl. Palestinian Solidarity Day — A119

1981, Nov. 21 Photo. *Perf. 13½*

815	A119	8s multicolored	1.20	.45
816	A119	11s multicolored	2.00	.60

Soccer — A120

1982 Litho. *Perf. 12½x12*

817	A120	1s shown	.25	.25
818	A120	2s Basketball	.45	.25
819	A120	3s Diving	.60	.25
820	A120	4s Gymnast	.75	.25
821	A120	5s Boxing	.90	.25
822	A120	6s Pole vault	1.10	.30
823	A120	7s Running	1.25	.35
824	A120	8s Long jump	1.40	.40
		Nos. 817-824,C148-C152 (13)	17.55	5.00

22nd Summer Olympic Games, Moscow, July 19-Aug. 3, 1980.

5th Anniv. of West African Economic Community — A121

1982, May 14 *Perf. 13½*

825 A121 6s multicolored 1.00 .25
826 A121 7s multicolored 1.20 .35
827 A121 9s multicolored 1.75 .55
Nos. 825-827 (3) 3.95 1.15

Kemal Ataturk Birth Centenary A122

Designs: 10s, Ataturk in formal attire. 25s, Equestrian statue, horiz.

1982, July 19 **Photo.** *Perf. 13½*

828 A122 7s multi 1.00 .35
829 A122 10s multi 1.50 .45
830 A122 25s multi 4.25 .85
Nos. 828-830,C153 (4) 11.00 2.45

1982 World Cup A123

Designs: Various soccer players.

1982, Aug. 23

831 A123 6s multicolored .85 .25
832 A123 8s multicolored 1.25 .25
833 A123 9s multicolored 1.75 .45
834 A123 10s multicolored 2.10 .60
Nos. 831-834,C154-C156 (7) 18.80 4.90

Nos. 831-834 Overprinted in Red and Green

1982, Aug. 23 **Photo.** *Perf. 13½*

835 A123 6s multicolored .85 .25
836 A123 8s multicolored 1.25 .25
837 A123 9s multicolored 1.75 .45
838 A123 10s multicolored 2.10 .60
Nos. 835-838,C157-C159 (7) 18.80 4.90

Italy's victory in 1982 World Cup.

23rd Olympic Games, Los Angeles, July 28-Aug. 12, 1984 A124

1983, July 1 **Litho.** *Perf. 13½*

839 A124 5s Wrestling 1.10 .25
840 A124 7s Weightlifting 1.40 .30
841 A124 10s Gymnastics 2.00 .55
842 A124 15s Discus 3.25 .95
843 A124 20s Kayak 4.50 1.40
844 A124 25s Equestrian 5.00 1.60
Nos. 839-844 (6) 17.25 5.05

Litho. & Embossed

Size: 39x58mm

844A A124 100s Running 45.00 37.50

Souvenir Sheets

Litho.

845 A124 30s Running 5.00 1.60

Litho. & Embossed

845A A124 100s Show jumping 15.00 12.50

Nos. 844A, 845A are airmail. No. 845A contains one 58x39mm stamp.

First Manned Balloon Flight, 200th Anniv. — A125

Designs: 5s, Marquis D'Arlandes, Pilatre de Rozier. 7s, Marie Antoinette Balloon, Rozier. 10s, Dirigible, Dupuy De Lome, horiz. 15s, Dirigible, Major A. Perseval, horiz.

1983, Aug. 1 **Litho.** *Perf. 13½*

846 A125 5s multicolored .65 .25
847 A125 7s multicolored .95 .25
848 A125 10s multicolored 1.40 .45
849 A125 15s multicolored 2.10 .75
Nos. 846-849,C160-C161 (6) 10.95 3.85

Intl. Year of the Handicapped — A126

1983, Aug. 24 **Litho.**

850 A126 10s multicolored 2.75 1.00
851 A126 20s multicolored 5.50 1.50

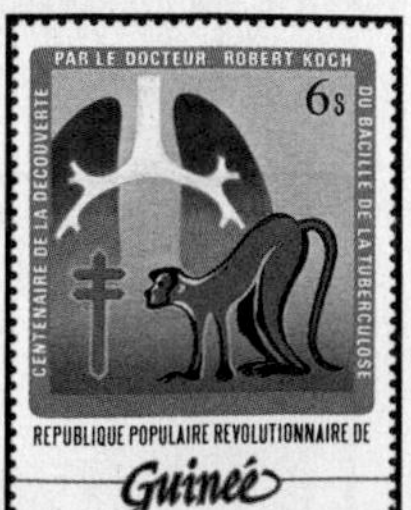

Dr. Robert Koch (1843-1910), TB Bacillus A127

Various phases of research.

1983, Aug. 24 **Litho.**

852 A127 6s multicolored 1.25 .30
853 A127 10s multicolored 1.75 .40
854 A127 11s multicolored 2.10 .50
855 A127 12s multicolored 2.50 .80
856 A127 15s multicolored 3.50 .95
857 A127 20s multicolored 4.25 1.10
858 A127 25s multicolored 5.00 1.40
Nos. 852-858 (7) 20.35 5.45

Mosque, Conakry A128

1983, Oct. 2 **Litho.** *Perf. 13½*

859 A128 1s grn & multi .25 .25
860 A128 2s yel & multi .35 .25
861 A128 5s org & multi .75 .25
862 A128 10s pink & multi 1.40 .55
Nos. 859-862 (4) 2.75 1.30

Souvenir Sheet

863 A128 25s white & multi 4.00 1.90

Natl. independence, 25th anniv. No. 863 airmail.

Mano River Union, 10th Anniv. A129

2s, Development program graduates. 7s, Emblem. 8s, Pres. Toure of Guinea, Stevens of Sierra Leone, Doe of Liberia. 10s, 20s, Signing treaty.

1983, Oct. 3

864 A129 2s blue & multi .30 .25
865 A129 7s org & multi .70 .30
866 A129 8s yel & multi .85 .40
867 A129 10s lt. org & multi 1.00 .40
Nos. 864-867 (4) 2.85 1.35

Souvenir Sheet

868 A129 20s lt. org & multi 2.50 1.50

No. 868 airmail.

14th Winter Olympics, Sarajevo, Feb. 8-19, 1984 — A130

5s, Biathlon. 7s, Bobsledding. 10s, No. 874A, 100s, Downhill skiing. 15s, Speed skating. 20s, Ski jumping. 25s, Figure skating.
30s, Hockey. No. 875A, 4-man bobsled.

1983, Dec. 5 **Litho.** *Perf. 13½*

869 A130 5s multicolored .75 .25
870 A130 7s multicolored .95 .30
871 A130 10s multicolored 1.40 .40
872 A130 15s multicolored 2.25 .65
873 A130 20s multicolored 3.00 .85
874 A130 25s multicolored 3.50 1.10
Nos. 869-874 (6) 11.85 3.55

Litho. & Embossed

Size: 58x39mm

874A A130 100s multicolored 15.00 5.00

Souvenir Sheets

Litho.

875 A130 30s multicolored 5.00 1.60

Litho. & Embossed

875A A130 100s multicolored 15.00 12.50
875B A130 100s as No. 874A 40.00 32.50

Nos. 873-875A airmail. No. 875A contains one 58x39mm stamp.

Self-portrait and Virgin with Blue Diadem, by Raphael A131

Designs: 7s, Self-portrait and Holy Family, by Rubens. 10s, Self-portrait and Portrait of Saskia, by Rembrandt. 15s, Portrait of Goethe and scene from Young Werther. 20s, Scouting Year. 25s, Paul Harris, Rotary emblem.
30s, J.F. Kennedy, Apollo XI. 100s, Paul Harris, 3 other men in Rotary meeting.

1984, Jan 2 **Litho.** *Perf. 13*

876 A131 5s multicolored .50 .30
877 A131 7s multicolored .80 .35
878 A131 10s multicolored 1.25 .45
879 A131 15s multicolored 1.75 .60
880 A131 20s multicolored 2.40 .75
881 A131 25s multicolored 3.25 .90
Nos. 876-881 (6) 9.95 3.35

Souvenir Sheets

882 A131 30s multicolored 4.50 1.50

Litho. & Embossed

Perf. 13½

882A A131 100s gold & multi 9.00 9.00

Nos. 880-882A airmail. No. 882A contains one 51x42mm stamp.
For overprints see Nos. C164-C165.

Transportation — A132

5s, Congo River steamer. 7s, Graf Zeppelin LZ 127. 10s, Daimler automobile, 1886. 15s, E. African RR Beyer-Garratt. 20s, Latecoere 28, 1929. 25s, Sial Marchetti S.M. 73, 1934.
30s, Series B locomotive.

1984, May 7 **Litho.** *Perf. 13½*

883 A132 5s multicolored .65 .25
884 A132 7s multicolored 1.00 .25
885 A132 10s multicolored 1.50 .30
886 A132 15s multicolored 2.10 .65
887 A132 20s multicolored 2.50 .65
888 A132 25s multicolored 2.75 .85
Nos. 883-888 (6) 10.50 2.95

Souvenir Sheet

889 A132 30s multicolored 4.50 2.00

Nos. 887-889 airmail.

Anniversaries and Events — A133

Famous men: 5s, Abraham Lincoln, log cabin, the White House. 7s, Jean-Henri Dunant, Red Cross at Battle of Solferino. 10s, Gottlieb Daimler, 1892 Motor Carriage. 15s, Louis Bleriot, monoplane. 20s, Paul Harris, Rotary Intl. 25s, Auguste Piccard, bathyscaphe Trieste. 100s, Paul Harris, Rotary Intl. emblem.
30s, Anatoly Karpov, world chess champion, chessboard and knight.

1984, Aug. 20 **Litho.** *Perf. 13½*

890 A133 5s multicolored .50 .25
891 A133 7s multicolored .95 .25
892 A133 10s multicolored 1.40 .35
893 A133 15s multicolored 2.10 .50
894 A133 20s multicolored 2.75 .65
895 A133 25s multicolored 3.50 .80
Nos. 890-895 (6) 11.20 2.80

Litho. & Embossed

Size: 60x30mm

895A A133 100s gold & multi 16.00 —
b. Min. sheet of 1, 91x70mm 60.00 —
c. Min. sheet of 1, 121x70mm 16.00 12.50

Souvenir Sheet

896 A133 30s multicolored 5.00 1.50

Nos. 894-896 are airmail.
For overprints see Nos. C163, C166.

The Holy Family, by Durer — A134

Painting details: 5s, The Mystic Marriage of St. Catherine and St. Sebastian, by Correggio. 10s, The Veiled Woman, by Raphael. 15s, Portrait of a Young Man, by Durer. 20s, Portrait of Soutine, by Modigliani. 25s, Esterhazy Madonna, by Raphael.
30s, Impannata Madonna, by Raphael.

1984, Aug. 23

897 A134 5s multicolored .55 .25
898 A134 7s multicolored .90 .30
899 A134 10s multicolored 1.60 .35
900 A134 15s multicolored 2.25 .75
901 A134 20s multicolored 2.75 .85
902 A134 25s multicolored 3.25 1.00
Nos. 897-902 (6) 11.30 3.50

Souvenir Sheet

903 A134 30s multicolored 4.75 1.50

Nos. 901-903 airmail.

1984 Winter Olympics, Sarajevo A135

Gold medalists: 5s, East German two-man bobsled. 7s, Thomas Wassberg, Sweden, 50-kilometer cross-country. 10s, Gaetan Boucher, Canada, 1000 and 1500-meter speed skating. 15s, Katarina Witt, DDR, singles figure skating. 20s, Bill Johnson, US, men's downhill. 25s, Soviet Union, ice hockey. No. 909A, 100s, Phil Mahre, US, slalom skiing.
No. 910, 30s, Jens Weissflog, DDR, 70-meter ski jump. No. 910A, 100s, Jayne Torvill & Christopher Dean, Great Britain, ice dancing.

1985, Sept. 23 Litho. *Perf. 13½*

904 A135 5s multicolored .60 .25
905 A135 7s multicolored .75 .25
906 A135 10s multicolored 1.20 .30
907 A135 15s multicolored 1.75 .45
908 A135 20s multicolored 2.25 .60
909 A135 25s multicolored 3.00 .75
Nos. 904-909 (6) 9.55 2.60

Litho. & Embossed

Size: 51x36mm

909A A135 100s gold & multi 60.00 30.00

Souvenir Sheets

Litho.

910 A135 30s multicolored 6.00 2.10

Litho. & Embossed

910A A135 100s gold & multi 18.00 15.00

Nos. 908A-910A are airmail. No. 910A contains one 51x36mm stamp.

1984 Los Angeles Summer Olympics — A136

Medalists: 5s, T. Ruiz and C. Costie, US, synchronized swimming. 7s, West Germany, team dressage. 10s, US, yachting, flying Dutchman class. 15s, Mark Todd, New Zealand, individual 3-day equestrian event. 20s, Daley Thompson, G.B., decathlon. 25s, US, team jumping.
30s, Carl Lewis, US, long jump, 100 and 200-meter run, 4x100 relay.

1985, Mar. 18 Litho. *Perf. 13½*

911 A136 5s multicolored .45 .25
912 A136 7s multicolored .70 .25
913 A136 10s multicolored .90 .25
914 A136 15s multicolored 1.40 .40
915 A136 20s multicolored 1.60 .45
916 A136 25s multicolored 2.40 .60
Nos. 911-916 (6) 7.45 2.20

Souvenir Sheet

917 A136 30s multicolored 6.00 2.10

Nos. 915-917 airmail.

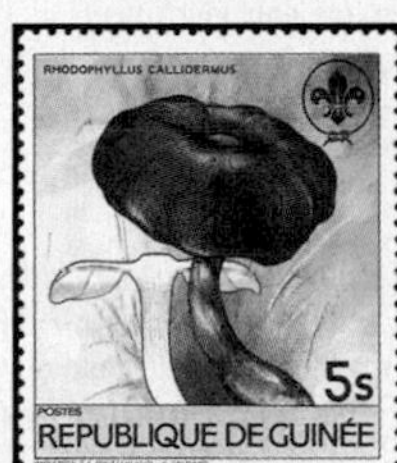

Fungi — A137

5s, Rhodophyllus callidermus. 7s, Agaricus niger. 10s, Thermitomyces globulus. 15s, Amanita robusta. 20s, Lepiota subradicans. 25s, Cantharellus rhodophyllus.
30s, Phlebopus sylvaticus.

1985, Mar. 21 Litho. *Perf. 13½*

918 A137 5s multicolored 1.25 .30
919 A137 7s multicolored 1.60 .45
920 A137 10s multicolored 2.00 .75
921 A137 15s multicolored 2.75 1.00
922 A137 20s multicolored 3.75 1.25
923 A137 25s multicolored 4.75 1.50
Nos. 918-923 (6) 16.10 5.25

Souvenir Sheet

924 A137 30s multicolored 5.50 4.00

Nos. 922-924 airmail.
For surcharges see Nos. 962-968.

Scientist Herman J. Oberth, and Two-Stage Rocket A138

Space achievements: 10s, Lunik 1, USSR, 1959. 15s, Lunik 2 on the Moon, 1959. 20s, Lunik 3 photographing the Moon, 1959. 30s, US astronauts Armstrong, Aldrin, Collins and Apollo 11, 1969. 35s, Sally Ride, 1st American woman in space, 1983. No. 930A, 200s, Guion S. Bluford, 1st black American astronaut.
50s, Recovering a Palapa B satellite, 1984. No. 931A, 200s, Viking probe on Mars.

1985, May 26 Litho. *Perf. 13½*

925 A138 7s multicolored .65 .25
926 A138 10s multicolored 1.10 .25
927 A138 15s multicolored 1.75 .40
928 A138 20s multicolored 2.40 .60
929 A138 30s multicolored 4.00 1.00
930 A138 35s multicolored 4.75 1.25
Nos. 925-930 (6) 14.65 3.75

Litho. & Embossed

Size: 51x36mm

930A A138 200s gold & multi 37.50 —

Souvenir Sheet

Litho.

931 A138 50s multicolored 6.50 3.25

Litho. & Embossed

931A A138 200s gold & multi 27.50 —

Nos. 929-931A are airmail. No. 931A contains one 51x36mm stamp.

Maimonides (1135-1204), Jewish Scholar, Cordoba Jewish Quarter — A139

Anniversaries and events: 10s, Christopher Columbus departing from Palos for New World, 1492. 15s, Frederic Auguste Bartholdi (1834-1904), sculptor, architect, and Statue of Liberty, cent. 20s, Queen Mother, 85th birthday. 30s, Ulf Merbold, German physicist, US space shuttle Columbia. 35s, Wedding of Prince Charles and Lady Diana, 1981. 100s, Queen Mother Elizabeth's 85th birthday.
50s, Charles, Diana, Princes Henry and William.

1985, Sept. 23

932 A139 7s multicolored .80 .25
933 A139 10s multicolored 1.10 .25
934 A139 15s multicolored 1.75 .40
935 A139 20s multicolored 2.25 .55
936 A139 30s multicolored 3.25 .80
937 A139 35s multicolored 4.00 .90
Nos. 932-937 (6) 13.15 3.15

Litho. & Embossed

Size: 42x51mm

937A A139 100s gold & multi 13.00 12.50

Souvenir Sheet

Litho.

938 A139 50s multicolored 6.50 3.25

Nos. 936-938 airmail. No. 938 contains one 51x36mm stamp. Nos. 934 and 937A exist in souvenir sheets of one.

Audubon Birth Bicent. — A140

Illustrations of bird species from Birds of America: 7s, Coccyzus erythrophtalmus. 10s, Conuropsis carolinensis. 15s, Anhinga anhinga. 20s, Buteo lineatus. 30s, Otus asio. 35s, Toxostoma rufum.
50s, Zenaidura macroura.

1985, Sept. 23 Litho. *Perf. 13½*

939 A140 7s multicolored .75 .25
940 A140 10s multicolored 1.20 .30
941 A140 15s multicolored 2.00 .50
942 A140 20s multicolored 2.50 .70
943 A140 30s multicolored 4.25 1.25
944 A140 35s multicolored 4.50 1.50
Nos. 939-944 (6) 15.20 4.50

Souvenir Sheet

945 A140 50s multicolored 6.50 3.00

Nos. 941, 944 vert. Nos. 943-945 are airmail. No. 945 contains one 51x36mm stamp. Nos. 939-944 exist in souvenir sheets of one. Value, set $90.

1986 World Cup Soccer Championships, Mexico — A141

Famous soccer players: 7s, Bebeto, Brazil. 10s, Rinal Dassaev, USSR. 15s, Phil Neal, Great Britain. 20s, Jean Tigana, France. 30s, Fernando Chalana, Portugal. 35s, Michel Platini, France.
50s, Karl Heinz Rummenigge, West Germany.

1985, Oct. 26

946 A141 7s multicolored .95 .25
947 A141 10s multicolored 1.25 .25
948 A141 15s multicolored 1.90 .40
949 A141 20s multicolored 2.50 .60
950 A141 30s multicolored 3.50 .85
951 A141 35s multicolored 4.50 .95
Nos. 946-951 (6) 14.60 3.30

Souvenir Sheet

952 A141 50s multicolored 7.50 3.00

Nos. 950-952 airmail.

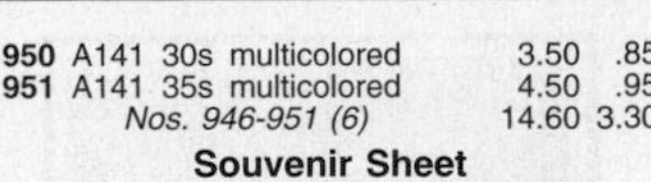

Cats and Dogs A142

7s, Blue-point Siamese. 10s, Cocker spaniel. 15s, Poodles. 20s, Blue Persian. 25s, European red-and-white tabby. 30s, German shepherd. 35s, Abyssinians. 40s, Boxer.
50s, Pyrenean mountain dog, chartreux cat.

1985, Oct. 26

953 A142 7s multicolored .80 .25
954 A142 10s multicolored 1.25 .25
955 A142 15s multicolored 2.00 .40
956 A142 20s multicolored 2.75 .60
957 A142 25s multicolored 3.75 .70
958 A142 30s multicolored 4.00 .85
959 A142 35s multicolored 4.50 .95
960 A142 40s multicolored 4.75 1.25
Nos. 953-960 (8) 23.80 5.25

Souvenir Sheet

961 A142 50s multicolored 6.50 2.50

Nos. 958-961 airmail. No. 961 contains one 51x30mm stamp.

Nos. 918-924 Surcharged

1985, Nov. 15

962 A137 1s on 5s multi .80 .25
963 A137 2s on 7s multi .85 .25
964 A137 8s on 10s multi 1.75 .40
965 A137 30s on 15s multi 6.50 1.60
966 A137 35s on 20s multi 7.50 2.25
967 A137 40s on 25s multi 9.00 2.75
Nos. 962-967 (6) 26.40 7.50

Souvenir Sheet

968 A137 50s on 30s multi 9.50 4.00

Nos. 966-968 airmail.

Locomotives — A143

Designs: 7s, 8F Class steam, Great Britain. 15s, Bobo 5500 Series III electric, German Fed. Railways. 25s, Pacific A Mazout No. 270, African Railways. 35s, Serie 420 electric train set, Suburban S Bahn, Germany.
50s, ICE high-speed train, German Fed. Railways.

1985, Dec. 18 Litho. *Perf. 13½*

969 A143 7s multicolored .95 .25
970 A143 15s multicolored 2.10 .70
971 A143 25s multicolored 3.50 .90
972 A143 35s multicolored 5.00 1.25
Nos. 969-972 (4) 11.55 3.10

Souvenir Sheet

973 A143 50s multicolored 6.50 2.75

Nos. 972-973 airmail.
For surcharges see Nos. 991-995.

Columbus Discovering America, 1492 — A144

10s, Pinta. 20s, Santa Maria. 30s, Nina. 40s, Santa Maria, sighting land.
50s, Columbus and Nina.

1985, Dec. 18

974	A144	10s multicolored	1.25	.25
975	A144	20s multicolored	2.50	.65
976	A144	30s multicolored	4.00	.95
977	A144	40s multicolored	5.75	1.25
		Nos. 974-977 (4)	13.50	3.10

Souvenir Sheet

978	A144	50s multicolored	6.50	3.00

Nos. 976-978 airmail.

Intl. Youth Year — A145

1986, Jan. 21

979	A145	10s Chopin	1.20	.40
980	A145	20s Botticelli	2.40	.85
981	A145	25s Picasso	4.00	1.10
982	A145	35s Rossini	2.75	1.50
		Nos. 979-982 (4)	10.35	3.85

Souvenir Sheet

983	A145	50s Michelangelo	6.50	2.75

Nos. 981, 983 airmail.
For surcharges see Nos. 996-1000.

Halley's Comet — A146

Sightings: 5fr, Bayeux Tapestry (detail), c. 1092, France. 30fr, Arab, astrolabe, 1400. 40fr, Montezuma II, Aztec deity. 50fr, Edmond Halley, trajectory diagram. 300fr, Halley, Sir Isaac Newton. 500fr, Giotto, Soviet and NASA space probes, comet. 600fr, Hally commemorative medal, Giotto probe.

1986, July 1 Litho. *Perf. 13½*

5fr-500fr Surcharged with New Currency in Silver or Black

984	A146	5fr multi	.25	.25
985	A146	30fr multi	.25	.25
986	A146	40fr multi	.30	.25
987	A146	50fr multi	.40	.25
988	A146	300fr multi	2.10	.75
989	A146	500fr multi	4.00	1.25
		Nos. 984-989 (6)	7.30	3.00

Souvenir Sheet

990	A146	600fr multi	5.50	2.50

Nos. 988-990 are airmail. Nos. 984-989 not issued without surcharge.

No. 969 Surcharged

Nos. 970-973 Surcharged

1986, Aug. 25 Litho. *Perf. 13½*

991	A143	2fr on 7s multi (B on S)	.30	.25
992	A143	25fr on 15s multi	.50	.25
993	A143	50fr on 25s multi	1.00	.25
994	A143	90fr on 35s multi	1.60	.55
		Nos. 991-994 (4)	3.40	1.30

Souvenir Sheet

995	A143	500fr on 50s multi	5.00	2.10

Nos. 979-983 Surcharged

1986, Aug. 25

996	A145	5fr on 10s multi	.40	.25
997	A145	35fr on 20s multi	.50	.25
998	A145	50fr on 25s multi	1.10	.30
999	A145	90fr on 35s multi	1.25	.40
		Nos. 996-999 (4)	3.25	1.20

Souvenir Sheet

1000	A145	500fr on 50s multi	6.00	2.10

Locomotives — A147

Designs: 20fr, Dietrich 640 CV. 100fr, T.13 7906. 300fr, Vapeur 01220. 400fr, ABH Type 3 5020. 600fr, Renault ABH 3 (300 CV).

1986, Nov. 1

1001	A147	20fr multi	.35	.25
1002	A147	100fr multi	1.00	.35
1003	A147	300fr multi	3.00	.95
1004	A147	400fr multi	4.25	1.25
		Nos. 1001-1004 (4)	8.60	2.80

Souvenir Sheet

1005	A147	600fr multi	7.00	2.50

Nos. 1004-1005 are airmail.

Discovery of America, 500th Anniv. (in 1992) — A148

Designs: 40fr, Columbus at Ft. Navidad construction, Santa Maria, 1492. 70fr, Landing at Hispaniola, 2nd voyage, 1494. 200fr, Aboard ship, 3rd voyage, 1498. 500fr, Trading with Indians. 600fr, At court of Ferdinand and Isabella, 1493.

1986, Nov. 1

1006	A148	40fr multi	.50	.25
1007	A148	70fr multi	.80	.25
1008	A148	200fr multi	2.25	.70
1009	A148	500fr multi	5.50	1.75
		Nos. 1006-1009 (4)	9.05	2.95

Souvenir Sheet

1010	A148	600fr multi	7.00	2.50

Nos. 1009-1010 are airmail.

Anniversaries & Events A149

30fr, Prince Charles and Diana, 5th wedding anniv. 40fr, Alain Prost, San Marino, 1985 Formula 1 Grand Prix world champion. 100fr, Wedding of Prince Andrew and Sarah Ferguson. 300fr, Elvis Presley. 500fr, Michael Jackson. 600fr, M. Dassault (1892-1986), aerospace engineer.

1986, Nov. 12

1011	A149	30fr multi	.35	.25
1012	A149	40fr multi	.45	.25
1013	A149	100fr multi	1.10	.40
1014	A149	300fr multi	3.00	1.25
1015	A149	500fr multi	5.00	2.40
		Nos. 1011-1015 (5)	9.90	4.55

Souvenir Sheet

1016	A149	600fr multi	6.50	2.75

Nos. 1015-1016 are airmail.

1986 World Cup Soccer Championships — A150

Various players and final scores.

1986, Nov. 12

1017	A150	100fr Pfaff	1.00	.35
1018	A150	300fr Platini	3.00	.95
1019	A150	400fr Matthaus	4.00	1.50
1020	A150	500fr D. Maradona	5.00	2.10
		Nos. 1017-1020 (4)	13.00	4.90

Souvenir Sheet

1021	A150	600fr Maradona, trophy	7.00	2.50

Nos. 1020-1021 are airmail. No. 1021 contains one 51x42mm stamp.
For surcharge see No. 1182A.

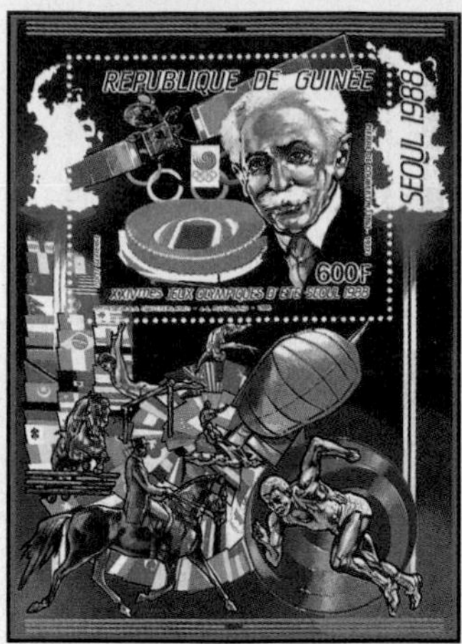

1988 Summer Olympics, Seoul — A151

Pierre de Coubertin (1863-1937), Seoul Stadium, Telecommunications Satellite — A151a

20fr, Judo. 30fr, High jump. 40fr, Team handball. 100fr, Women's gymnastics. 300fr, Javelin. 500fr, Equestrian.

1987, Jan. 17 Litho. *Perf. 13½*

1022	A151	20fr multicolored	.25	.25
1023	A151	30fr multicolored	.35	.25
1024	A151	40fr multicolored	.45	.25
1025	A151	100fr multicolored	1.00	.25
1026	A151	300fr multicolored	3.00	.90
1027	A151	500fr multicolored	5.00	2.10
		Nos. 1022-1027 (6)	10.05	4.00

Souvenir Sheet

1028	A151a	600fr multi	6.50	2.50

Dated 1986. Nos. 1026-1028 are airmail.

1988 Winter Olympics, Calgary — A152

50fr on 40fr, Biathlon. 100fr, Cross-country skiing. 400fr, Ski jumping. 500fr, Two-man bobsled.
600fr, Woman skater, satellite.

1987, Mar. 23 Litho. *Perf. 13½*

1029	A152	50fr on 40fr multi	.50	.25
1030	A152	100fr multicolored	1.00	.35
1031	A152	400fr multicolored	4.00	2.50
1032	A152	500fr multicolored	5.00	2.10
		Nos. 1029-1032 (4)	10.50	5.20

Souvenir Sheet

1033	A152	600fr multicolored	6.50	2.50

No. 1029 not issued without overprint. Nos. 1031-1033 are airmail.

1988 Winter Olympics, Calgary A153

Telecommunications satellite, athletes and emblem: 25fr, Women's slalom. 50fr, Hockey. 100fr, Men's figure skating. 150fr, Men's downhill skiing. 300fr, Speed skating. 500fr, Four-man bobsled.
600fr, Ski jumping.

1987, May 1

1034	A153	25fr multicolored	.25	.25
1035	A153	50fr multicolored	.40	.25
1036	A153	100fr multicolored	.80	.30
1037	A153	150fr multicolored	1.20	.45

1038	A153	300fr multicolored	2.25	1.25
1039	A153	500fr multicolored	4.00	2.10
		Nos. 1034-1039 (6)	8.90	4.60

Souvenir Sheet

1040	A153	600fr multicolored	5.50	2.00

Nos. 1038-1040 are airmail.

Famous Men — A154

Intl. Cardiology Congresses in Chicago, Washington and New York — A155

Designs: 50fr, Lafayette, military leader during American and French revolutions. 100fr, Ettore Bugatti (1881-1947), Italian automobile manufacturer, 200fr, Garri Kasparov, Russian chess champion. 300fr, George Washington. 400fr, Boris Becker, 1987 Wimbledon tennis champion. 500fr, Sir Winston Churchill.

1987, Nov. 1 Litho. *Perf. 13½*

1041	A154	50fr multi	.45	.25
1042	A154	100fr multi	1.00	.40
1043	A154	200fr multi	1.90	.80
1044	A154	300fr multi	2.75	1.25
1045	A154	400fr multi	3.75	1.60
1046	A154	500fr multi	4.75	2.00
		Nos. 1041-1046 (6)	14.60	6.30

Souvenir Sheet

1047	A155	1500fr multi	16.00	12.50

Nos. 1045-1047 are airmail. Stamp in No. 1047 divided into three sections by simulated perforations.

For surcharge see No. 1182B.

Cave Bear — A156

Prehistoric Animals — A157

50fr, Dimetrodon. 100fr, Iguanodon. 200fr, Tylosaurus. 400fr, Saber-tooth tiger. 500fr, Stegosaurus.

600fr, Triceratops.

1987, Nov. 1

1048	A156	50fr multicolored	.90	.25
1049	A156	100fr multicolored	1.75	.50
1050	A156	200fr multicolored	3.50	1.00
1051	A156	300fr shown	5.25	1.50
1052	A156	400fr multicolored	3.75	2.10
1053	A156	500fr multicolored	4.75	2.50
		Nos. 1048-1053 (6)	19.90	7.85

Souvenir Sheet

1054	A157	600fr multicolored	7.00	2.00

Nos. 1052-1054 are airmail.

For surcharge see No. 1182C.

1988 Summer Olympics, Seoul — A158

Male and female tennis players in action.

1987, Nov. 28

1055	A158	50fr multi	.40	.25
1056	A158	100fr multi, diff.	.80	.35
1057	A158	150fr multi, diff.	1.20	.60
1058	A158	200fr multi, diff.	1.60	.75
1059	A158	300fr multi, diff.	2.40	1.25
1060	A158	500fr multi, diff.	4.00	1.90
		Nos. 1055-1060 (6)	10.40	5.10

Souvenir Sheet

1061	A158	600fr multi	5.50	2.00

Reintroduction of tennis as an Olympic event. Nos. 1059-1061 are airmail.

1992 Summer Olympics, Barcelona A159

Athletes participating in events, Barcelona highlights: 50fr, Discus, courtyard of St. Croix and St. Paul Hospital. 100fr, High jump, Pablo Casals playing cello. 150fr, Long jump, Labyrinth of Horta. 170fr, Javelin, lizard from Guell Park. 400fr, Gymnastics, Mercy Church. 500fr, Tennis, Picasso Museum.

600fr, Running, tapestry by Miro.

1987, Dec. 28 Litho. *Perf. 13½*

1062	A159	50fr multi	.45	.25
1063	A159	100fr multi	.90	.35
1064	A159	150fr multi	1.25	.55
1065	A159	170fr multi	1.40	.60
1066	A159	400fr multi	3.50	1.40
1067	A159	500fr multi	4.50	1.75
		Nos. 1062-1067 (6)	12.00	4.90

Souvenir Sheet

1068	A159	600fr multi	6.50	2.00

Nos. 1066-1068 are airmail.

For surcharges see Nos. 1182D-1182E.

Wildlife A160

50fr, African wild dog pups. 70fr, Adult. 100fr, Adults circling gazelle. 170fr, Chasing gazelle. 400fr, Crown cranes. 500fr, Derby elands.

600fr, Vervet monkeys.

1987, Dec. 28

1069	A160	50fr multicolored	1.75	.75
1070	A160	70fr multicolored	2.25	1.00
1071	A160	100fr multicolored	2.75	1.25
1072	A160	170fr multicolored	3.25	1.50
1073	A160	400fr multicolored	4.00	1.40
1074	A160	500fr multicolored	5.00	2.50
		Nos. 1069-1074 (6)	19.00	8.40

Souvenir Sheet

1075	A160	600fr multicolored	7.00	5.50

Nos. 1069-1072 picture World Wildlife Fund emblem; Nos. 1073, 1075, picture Scouting trefoil and No. 1074 pictures Rotary Intl. emblem. Nos. 1073-1075 are airmail.

Nos. 1069-1072 exist in a souvenir sheet of 4. Value, $30.

For surcharges see Nos. 1182F-1182G.

Reconciliation Summit Conference, July 11-12, 1986 — A161

Heads of state and natl. flags: Dr. Samuel Kanyon Doe of Liberia, Colonel Lansana Conte of Guinea and Maj.-Gen. Joseph Saidu Momoh of Sierra Leone.

1987 Litho. *Perf. 13½*

1076	A161	40fr multi	.65	.25
1077	A161	50fr multi	.80	.45
1078	A161	75fr multi	1.10	.60
1079	A161	100fr multi	1.60	.75
1080	A161	150fr multi	2.40	.85
		Nos. 1076-1080 (5)	6.55	2.90

Space Exploration — A162

50fr, Galaxie-Grasp. 150fr, Energia-Mir. 200fr, NASA Space Station. 300fr, Ariane 5-E.S.A. 400fr, Mars-Rover. 450fr, Venus-Vega. 500fr, Mars-Phobos.

1988, Apr. 16

1081	A162	50fr multicolored	.45	.25
1082	A162	150fr multicolored	1.25	.50
1083	A162	200fr multicolored	1.75	.35
1084	A162	300fr multicolored	2.50	.60
1085	A162	400fr multicolored	3.50	.75
1086	A162	450fr multicolored	4.00	1.00
		Nos. 1081-1086 (6)	13.45	3.45

Souvenir Sheet

1087	A162	500fr multicolored	5.00	2.00

Nos. 1085-1087 are airmail.

A163

Boy Scouts watching birds and butterflies: 50fr, Spermophaga ruficapilla. 100fr, Medon nymphalidae. 150fr, Euplecte orix. 300fr, Nectarinia pulchella. 400fr, Sophia nymphalidae. 450fr, Rumia nymphalidae.

750fr, Opis nymphalidae, Psittacula krameri.

1988, July 5 Litho. *Perf. 13½*

1088	A163	50fr multicolored	.50	.25
1089	A163	100fr multicolored	1.05	.35
1090	A163	150fr multicolored	1.45	.60
1091	A163	300fr multicolored	3.00	1.25
1092	A163	400fr multicolored	3.75	1.50
1093	A163	450fr multicolored	4.50	1.75
		Nos. 1088-1093 (6)	14.25	5.70

Souvenir Sheet

1094	A163	750fr multicolored	7.50	6.50

Druya antimachus — A163a

1990, Aug. 3 Litho. & Embossed

1094A	A163a	1500fr multi	20.00	12.50

Nos. 1092-1094A are airmail. No. 1094 contains one 35x50mm stamp.

#1094A exists in souvenir sheet of 1. Value $45.

For surcharge and overprints see Nos. 1182H, 1240-1246.

A164

Famous People: 200fr, Queen Elizabeth II, Prince Philip and crown jewels. 250fr, Fritz von Opel (1899-1971), German automotive industrialist, and 1928 RAK 2 Opel. 300fr, Wolfgang Amadeus Mozart, composer, and Masonic emblem. 400fr, Steffi Graf, tennis champion. 450fr, Buzz Aldrin and Masonic emblem. 500fr, Paul Harris, Rotary Intl. founder, and organization emblem.

750fr, Thomas Jefferson, horiz.

1988, July 5

1095	A164	200fr multi	1.75	.45
1096	A164	250fr multi	2.25	.45
1097	A164	300fr multi	2.25	.60
1098	A164	400fr multi	3.50	.75
1099	A164	450fr multi	4.00	.90
1100	A164	500fr multi	4.75	1.00
		Nos. 1095-1100 (6)	18.50	4.15

Souvenir Sheet

1101	A164	750fr multi	7.00	2.00

40th wedding anniv. of Queen Elizabeth II and Prince Philip (200fr).

Nos. 1099-1101 are airmail. No. 1101 contains one 42x36mm stamp.

For surcharges see Nos. 1182I, 1182Q.

1988 Winter Olympics Gold Medalists A165

Designs: 50fr, Vreni Schneider, Switzerland, women's giant slalom and slalom. 100fr, Frank-Peter Roetsch, East Germany, 10 and 20-kilometer biathlon. 150fr, Matti Nykaenen, Finland, 70 and 90-meter ski jumping. 250fr, Marina Kiehl, West Germany, women's downhill. 400fr, Frank Piccard, France, super giant slalom. 450fr, Katarina Witt, East Germany, women's figure skating.

750fr, Pirmin Zurbriggen, Switzerland, men's downhill.

1988, Oct. 2 Litho. *Perf. 13½*

1102	A165	50fr multi, vert.	.45	.25
1103	A165	100fr multi, vert.	1.25	.25
1104	A165	150fr multi, vert.	2.10	.45
1105	A165	250fr multi, vert.	3.50	.75
1106	A165	400fr multi, vert.	.85	.45
1107	A165	450fr multi, vert.	3.75	1.00
		Nos. 1102-1107 (6)	11.90	3.15

Souvenir Sheet

1108	A165	750fr multi	6.75	2.00

Nos. 1103, 1107-1108 are airmail.

For surcharge see No. 1182J.

African Postal Union, 25th Anniv. A165a

1988 Litho. *Perf. 13½*

1108A A165a 50fr multicolored .45 .25
1108B A165a 75fr multicolored .75 .25
1108C A165a 100fr multicolored .85 .25
1108D A165a 150fr multicolored 1.25 .40
Nos. 1108A-1108D (4) 3.30 1.15

World Health Day — A165b

50fr, Medical research. 150fr, Immunization. 500fr, Dentistry.

1988, Oct. 2 Litho. *Perf. 13½*

1108E A165b 50fr multi .45 .25
1108F A165b 150fr multi 1.25 .35
1108G A165b 500fr multi 4.25 1.00
Nos. 1108E-1108G (3) 5.95 1.60

For surcharge see No. 1182K.

Opening of MT 20 Intl. Communications Center — A165c

1988, Dec. 8 Litho. *Perf. 13½*

1108H A165c 50fr multicolored .45 .25
1108I A165c 100fr multicolored .85 .25
1108J A165c 150fr multicolored 1.25 .45

Pierre de Coubertin, Founder of Intl. Olympic Committee A165d

1988 Litho. *Perf. 13½y*

1108K A165d 50fr multi .45 .25
1108L A165d 100fr multi .85 .25
1108M A165d 150fr multi 1.25 .35
1108N A165d 500fr multi 4.25 1.10
Nos. 1108K-1108N (4) 6.80 1.95

For surcharge see No. 1182L.

1992 Summer Olympics, Barcelona — A166

50fr, Diving. 100fr, Running, vert. 150fr, Shooting. 250fr, Tennis, vert. 400fr, Soccer. 500fr, Equestrian, vert.
750fr, Yachting, vert.

1989, May 3 Litho. *Perf. 13½*

1109 A166 50fr multi .45 .25
1110 A166 100fr multi 1.00 .55
1111 A166 150fr multi 1.75 .95
1112 A166 250fr multi 2.75 1.50
1113 A166 400fr multi 4.25 2.40
1114 A166 500fr multi 5.25 3.00
Nos. 1109-1114 (6) 15.45 8.65

Souvenir Sheet

1115 A166 750fr multi 7.50 2.50

Nos. 1113-1115 are airmail.
For surcharge see No. 1182M.

French Revolution, Bicent. — A167

Personalities of and scenes from the revolution: 250fr, Jean-Sylvain Bailly (1736-1793) leading proceedings in Tennis Court, June 20, 1789. 300fr, Count Mirabeau (1749-1791) at royal session, June 23, 1789. 400fr, Lafayette (1757-1834), federation anniversary celebration, July 18, 1790. 450fr, Jerome Petion de Villeneuve (1756-1794), king's arrest at Varennes-en-Argonne, June 21, 1791.
750fr, Camille Desmoulins (1760-1794), destruction of the Bastille, July 1789.

1989, July 7 Litho. *Perf. 13½*

1116 A167 250fr multi 2.40 .60
1117 A167 300fr multi 2.90 .75
1118 A167 400fr multi 4.00 1.10
1119 A167 450fr multi 4.75 1.20
Nos. 1116-1119 (4) 14.05 3.65

Souvenir Sheet

1120 A167 750fr multi 8.00 2.50

Nos. 1119-1120 airmail.
Nos. 1116-1119 exist in souvenir sheets of 1. Sold for 100fr extra.
For surcharge and overprints see Nos. 1182N, 1216-1220.

Planting A168

50fr, Irrigation. 75fr, Milking. 100fr, Fishing. 150fr, Farmers in corn field. 300fr, Public well.

1989 Litho. *Perf. 13½*

1121 A168 25fr shown .25 .25
1122 A168 50fr multi .40 .25
1123 A168 75fr multi .65 .25
1124 A168 100fr multi .80 .30
1125 A168 150fr multi 1.20 .40
1126 A168 300fr multi 2.40 .80
Nos. 1121-1126 (6) 5.70 2.25

Natl. Campaign for Self-sufficiency in Food Production and 10th anniv. of the Intl. Fund for Agricultural Development (in 1988). Dated 1988.

African Development Bank, 25th Anniv. — A169

1989, Nov. 4 Litho. *Perf. 13½*

1127 A169 300fr multicolored 3.00 1.10

Mano River Union, 15th Anniv. A170

Design: 300fr, Map of Guinea, Sierra Leone and Liberia, leaders' portraits.

1989, Nov. 4

1128 A170 150fr multicolored 1.50 .65
1129 A170 300fr multicolored 3.00 1.25

World Cup Soccer, Italy — A171

Various soccer plays and: 200fr, Spire of San Domenico, Naples. 250fr, Piazza San Carlo, Turin. 300fr, Church of San Cataldo. 450fr, Church of San Francesco, Utine.
750fr, Statue of Dante, Florence and World Cup Soccer Trophy.

1990, Aug. 3 Litho. *Perf. 13½*

1130 A171 200fr multicolored 1.50 .80
1131 A171 250fr multicolored 2.00 1.00
1132 A171 300fr multicolored 2.50 1.25
1133 A171 450fr multicolored 4.00 1.90
Nos. 1130-1133 (4) 10.00 4.95

Souvenir Sheet

1134 A171 750fr multicolored 7.25 2.75

No. 1133-1134 airmail.
For overprints see Nos. 1221-1225.

Concorde, TGV Atlantic — A172

1990, Aug. 3

1135 A172 400fr multicolored 4.00 1.50

No. 1135 exists in a souvenir sheet of 1.
For surcharge see No. 1182O.

Pope John Paul II, Pres. Gorbachev — A173

1990, Aug. 3

1136 A173 300fr multicolored 3.00 .60

Summit Meeting, Dec. 2, 1989. No. 1136 exists in a souvenir sheet of 1. Value $10.

1992 Winter Olympics, Albertville — A174

150fr, Downhill skiing. 250fr, Cross country skiing. 400fr, Two-man bobsled. 500fr, Speedskating.
750fr, Slalom skiing.

1990, Aug. 3

1137 A174 150fr multicolored .80 .25
1138 A174 250fr multicolored 2.10 .45
1139 A174 400fr multicolored 3.50 .75
1140 A174 500fr multicolored 4.50 1.00
Nos. 1137-1140 (4) 10.90 2.45

Souvenir Sheet

1141 A174 750fr multicolored 6.50 2.00

Nos. 1140-1141 airmail. Nos. 1137-1140 exist in souvenir sheets of 1. Value, set $16.
For overprints and surcharge see Nos. 1182P, 1225-1230.

Pres. Bush, Pres. Gorbachev — A175

1990, Aug. 3 Litho. *Perf. 13½*

1142 A175 200fr multicolored .40 .75

Summit Meeting Dec. 3, 1989. No. 1142 exists in a souvenir sheet of 1.

De Gaulle's Call for French Resistance, 50th Anniv. — A176

1990

1143 A176 250fr multi .45 1.00

No. 1143 exists in a souvenir sheet of 1.

A177

World Cup Soccer Championships, Italy 1990 — A178

200fr, Rudi Voller. 250fr, Uwe Bein. 300fr, Pierre Littbarski. 400fr, Jurgen Klinsmann. 450fr, Lothar Matthaus. 500fr, Andreas Brehme.
750fr, Brehme, diff. No. 1152, Player, Chateau Saint-Ange.

1991, Apr. 1 Litho. *Perf. 13½*

1144 A177 200fr multi 1.60 .80
1145 A177 250fr multi 2.00 1.00
1146 A177 300fr multi 2.40 1.25
1147 A177 400fr multi 3.25 1.90
1148 A177 450fr multi 3.25 1.90
1149 A177 500fr multi 4.75 2.00
Nos. 1144-1149 (6) 17.25 8.85

Litho. & Embossed

1150 A178 1500fr gold & multi 24.00 18.00

Souvenir Sheets

Litho.

1151 A177 750fr multi 6.50 2.00

Litho. & Embossed

1152 A178 1500fr gold & multi 16.00 12.50

Nos. 1148-1152 are airmail. Nos. 1144-1150 exist in souvenir sheets of 1.

Christmas A179

Paintings by Raphael: 50fr, Della Tenda Madonna. 100fr, Cowper Madonna. 150fr, Tempi Madonna. 250fr, Niccolini Madonna. 300fr, Orleans Madonna. 500fr, Solly Madonna.

750fr, Madonna of the Fish.

1991, Apr. 1 Litho.

1153 A179 50fr multi .40 .25
1154 A179 100fr multi .80 .45
1155 A179 150fr multi 1.20 .65
1156 A179 250fr multi 2.00 1.00
1157 A179 300fr multi 2.40 1.25
1158 A179 500fr multi 4.00 2.00
Nos. 1153-1158 (6) 10.80 5.60

Souvenir Sheet

1159 A179 750fr multi 6.50 2.00

Nos. 1157-1159 are airmail. Nos. 1153-1158 exist in souvenir sheets of 1.

A180

World War II Battles — A181

Designs: 100fr, Sinking of the Bismarck, May 27, 1941, Adm. Raeder and Adm. Tovey. 150fr, Battle of Midway, June 3, 1942, Adm. Yamamoto and Adm. Nimitz. 200fr, Guadalcanal, Oct. 7, 1942, Adm. Kondo and Adm. Halsey. 250fr, Battle of El Alamein, Oct. 23, 1942, Field Marshal Erwin Rommel, Field Marshal Montgomery. 300fr, Battle of the Bulge, Dec. 16, 1944, Gen. Guderian and Gen. Patton. 450fr, Sinking of the Yamato, Apr., 7, 1945, Adm. Kogo and Gen. MacArthur. No. 1166, 1500fr, Review of Free French Forces, July 14, 1940, Gen. Charles De Gaulle.

750fr, Boeing B-17G, Gen. Dwight Eisenhower. No. 1168, 1500fr, De Gaulle's Call for French Resistance, June 18, 1940.

1991, Apr. 8 Litho. *Perf. 13½*

1160 A180 100fr multicolored .90 .45
1161 A180 150fr multicolored 1.25 .70
1162 A180 200fr multicolored 1.75 .90
1163 A180 250fr multicolored 2.25 1.10
1164 A180 300fr multicolored 2.75 1.25
1165 A180 450fr multicolored 6.00 3.00
a. Sheet of 6, #1160-1165 16.00 8.00

Litho. & Embossed

1166 A181 1500fr gold & multi 17.00 11.00

Souvenir Sheets

Litho.

1167 A180 750fr multicolored 8.00 3.00

Litho. & Embossed

1168 A181 1500fr gold & multi 15.00 10.00

Nos. 1164-1168 are airmail. No. 1160-1166 exist in souvenir sheets of 1. Value, set $32.

For overprint see No. C177.

Doctors Without Borders A182

1991, Feb. 22 Litho. *Perf. 13½*

1169 A182 300fr multicolored 3.25 1.50

Telecom '91 A183

1991, Jan. 15

1170 A183 150fr multi, vert. 1.50 1.25
1171 A183 300fr shown 2.75 2.40

6th World Forum and Exposition on Telecommunications, Geneva, Switzerland.

American Entertainers and Films — A184

Designs: 100fr, Nat King Cole Trio. 150fr, Yul Brynner, The Magnificent Seven. 250fr, Judy Garland, The Wizard of Oz. 300fr, Steve McQueen, Papillon. 500fr, Gary Cooper, Sergeant York. 600fr, Bing Crosby, High Society.

750fr, John Wayne, How the West Was Won.

1991, Oct. 2 Litho. *Perf. 13½*

1172 A184 100fr multicolored .75 .45
1173 A184 150fr multicolored 1.10 .60
1174 A184 250fr multicolored 2.00 1.00
1175 A184 300fr multicolored 2.40 1.25
1176 A184 500fr multicolored 4.00 2.00
1177 A184 600fr multicolored 8.75 4.25
Nos. 1172-1177 (6) 19.00 9.55

Souvenir Sheet

1178 A184 750fr multicolored 8.00 3.00

Nos. 1176-1178 are airmail. No. 1172-1177 exist in souvenir sheets of 1.

Care Bears Promoting Environmental Protection — A184a

Designs: 50fr, Care Bears circling earth, vert. 100fr, Save water, vert. 200fr, Recycle, vert. 300fr, Control noise, vert. 400fr, Elephant.

500fr, Care Bear emblem, end of rainbow. 600fr, Scout, tent, Lord Baden Powell.

1991 Litho. *Perf. 13½*

1178A A184a 50fr multi .40 .25
1178B A184a 100fr multi .85 .40
1178C A184a 200fr multi 1.75 .85
1178D A184a 300fr multi 2.50 1.25
1178E A184a 400fr multi 3.50 1.75
Nos. 1178A-1178E (5) 9.00 4.50

Souvenir Sheets

1178F A184a 500fr multi 4.25 2.25
1178G A184a 600fr multi 5.00 2.50

Nos. 1178F-1178G each contain one 39x27mm stamp. No. 1178G is airmail.

African Tourism Year A185

100fr, Dancer, vert. 150fr, Baskets. 250fr, Drum. 300fr, Flute player, vert.

1991, Aug. 16 Litho. *Perf. 13½*

1179 A185 100fr multi 1.25 .60
1180 A185 150fr multi 2.00 .90
1181 A185 250fr multi 3.25 1.25
1182 A185 300fr multi 3.50 1.60
Nos. 1179-1182 (4) 10.00 4.35

Stamps of 1986-92 Surcharged in Black or Silver

Nos. 1182A, 1182M, 1182P, 1182R Surcharged

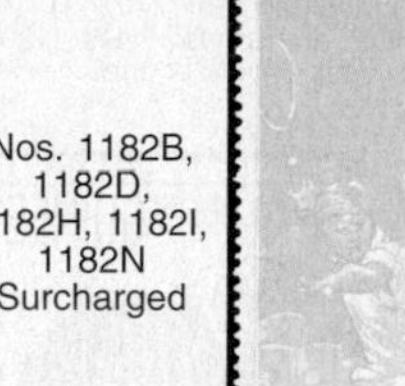
Nos. 1182B, 1182D, 1182H, 1182I, 1182N Surcharged

Nos. 1182C, 1182E, 1182G, 1182O Surcharged

Nos. 1182F, 1182J, 1182K, 1182L, 1182Q Surcharged

1991 Litho. *Perfs. as Before*

1182A A150 100fr on 400fr #1019 .85 .40
1182B A154 100fr on 400fr #1045 .85 .40
1182C A156 100fr on 400fr #1052 .85 .40
1182D A159 100fr on 170fr #1065 .85 .40
1182E A159 100fr on 400fr #1066 .85 .40
1182F A160 100fr on 170fr #1072 125.00 —
1182G A160 100fr on 400fr #1073 4.00 1.00
1182H A163 100fr on 400fr #1092 .85 .40
1182I A164 100fr on 400fr #1098 .85 .40
1182J A165 100fr on 400fr #1106 .85 .40
1182K A165b 100fr on 500fr #1108G .85 .40
1182L A165d 100fr on 500fr #1108N .85 .40
1182M A166 100fr on 400fr #1113 .85 .40
1182N A167 100fr on 250fr #1116 .85 .40
1182O A172 100fr on 400fr #1135 .85 .40
1182P A174 100fr on 400fr #1139 .85 .40
1182Q A164 300fr on 450fr #1099 2.50 1.25
1182R AP14 300fr on 450fr #C170 2.50 1.25
Nos. 1182A-1182R (18) 145.90 9.10

Nos. 1182B-1182C, 1182E, 1182G, 1182M, 1182Q-1182R are airmail.

Visit by Pope John Paul II — A185a

1992, Feb. 24 Litho. *Perf. 13½*

1182S A185a 150fr multicolored 3.00 1.75

1994 World Cup Soccer, US — A186

A186a

Player, World Cup Trophy and scenes of Atlanta: 100fr, Little Five Points. 300fr, Fulton County Stadium. 400fr, Inman Park. 500fr, High Museum of Art.

1000fr, Intelsat VI, Capitol. No. 1187A, Player in white shirt. No. 1187B, Player in red.

1992, Apr. 27 Litho. *Perf. 13½*

1183 A186 100fr multi 1.10 .40
1184 A186 300fr multi 3.25 1.25
1185 A186 400fr multi 4.50 1.75
1186 A186 500fr multi 5.50 2.25
Nos. 1183-1186 (4) 14.35 5.65

Souvenir Sheets

1187 A186 1000fr multi 8.00 4.00

Litho. & Embossed

1187A A186a 1500fr gold & multi 12.00 12.00

Souvenir Sheet

1187B A186a 1500fr gold & multi 20.00 20.00

Nos. 1186-1187B are airmail. Nos. 1183-1187A exist in souvenir sheets of 1.

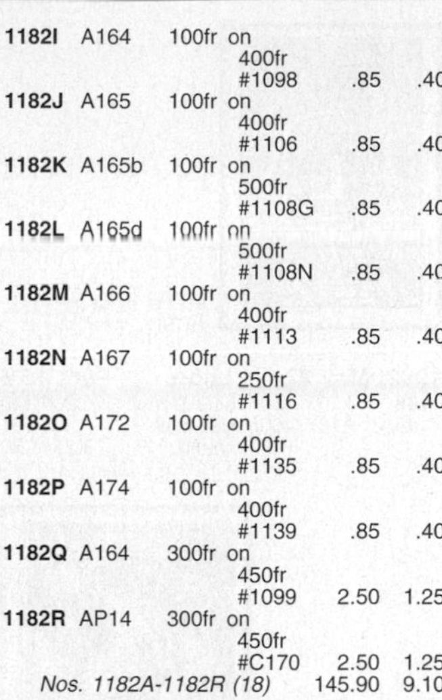

Lions Intl., 75th Anniv. — A187

1992, May 22 Litho. *Perf. 13½*

1188	A187	150fr blue & multi	1.20	.45
1188A	A187	400fr lilac rose & multi	3.25	1.50

Anniversaries and Events — A188

Designs: 100fr, Satellite ERS-1 in orbit. 150fr, Vase with Fourteen Sunflowers, by Vincent van Gogh. 200fr, Napoleon Bonaparte. 250fr, Henri Dunant, Red Cross workers. 300fr, Brandenburg Gate. 400fr, Pope John Paul II. 450fr, Garry Kasparov, Anatoly Karpov, chess pieces. 500fr, African child, dove, emblems of Rotary and Lions Clubs.

1992, Nov. 10 Litho. *Perf. 13½*

1189	A188	100fr multicolored	1.00	.45
1190	A188	150fr multicolored	1.50	.75
1191	A188	200fr multicolored	2.25	1.00
1192	A188	250fr multicolored	2.50	1.25
1193	A188	300fr multicolored	3.25	1.50
1194	A188	400fr multicolored	4.25	2.10
1195	A188	450fr multicolored	4.75	2.25
1196	A188	500fr multicolored	5.50	2.50
		Nos. 1189-1196 (8)	25.00	11.80

Intl. Space Year (#1189). Vincent van Gogh, cent. of death (in 1990) (#1190). Napolean Bonaparte, 170th anniv. of death (in 1991) (#1191). Founding of Red Cross (in 1864) (#1192). Brandenburg Gate, bicent. (#1193). Pope John Paul II's visit to Africa in 1989 (#1194). World Chess Championships (#1195). Lions Intl., 75th anniv. (#1196).

Nos. 1195-1196 are airmail. Nos. 1189-1196 exist in souvenir sheets of one.

For overprint see No. C178.

Anniversaries and Events — A189

Designs: 200fr, The Devil and Kate, Antonin Dvorak. 300fr, Antonio Vivaldi. 350fr, Graf Zeppelin, flying boat, Count Ferdinand von Zeppelin. 400fr, English Channel Euro-Tunnel Train. 450fr, Konrad Adenauer, Brandenburg Gate. 500fr, Japanese naval ensign, Emperor Hirohito.

750fr, Tunnel Train, diff.

1992, Nov. 10

1197	A189	200fr multicolored	2.00	.40
1198	A189	300fr multicolored	2.75	.40
1199	A189	350fr multicolored	3.25	.45
1200	A189	400fr multicolored	3.50	.65
1201	A189	450fr multicolored	4.00	.75
a.		Souvenir sheet of 2, #1199, 1201	6.50	1.50
1202	A189	500fr multicolored	4.50	1.10
		Nos. 1197-1202 (6)	20.00	3.75

Souvenir Sheet

1203	A189	750fr multicolored	6.50	1.50

Antonin Dvorak, 90th anniv. of death (in 1994) (#1197). Antonio Vivaldi, 250th anniv. of death (in 1991) (#1198). Count Ferdinand von Zeppelin, 75th anniv. of death (#1199). Opening of English Channel Tunnel (in 1994) (#1200, 1203). Konrad Adenauer, 25th anniv. of death, Brandenburg Gate, bicent. (#1201). Death of Emperor Hirohito (in 1989) (#1202).

Nos. 1201-1203 are airmail. Nos. 1197-1202 exist imperf. and in souvenir sheets of one. No. 1203 exists imperf. and contains one 60x42mm stamp.

Anniversaries and Events A190

Designs: 50fr, Modern Times, film by Charlie Chaplin. 100fr, Expo '92 Seville, Columbus. 150fr, St. Peter's Square, Rome. 200fr, Marlene Dietrich, roses. 250fr, Michael Schumacher, Benetton Ford B192. 300fr, Mercury rocket, John Glenn. 400fr, Bill Koch, America 3. 450fr, Mark Rypien, quarterback of Washington Redskins. 500fr, Rescue of Intelsat VI by shuttle Endeavour.

1992, Dec. 3

1204	A190	50fr multicolored	.45	.25
1205	A190	100fr multicolored	.90	.40
1206	A190	150fr multicolored	1.40	.65
1207	A190	200fr multicolored	1.90	.85
1208	A190	250fr multicolored	2.25	1.10
1209	A190	300fr multicolored	2.75	1.25
1210	A190	400fr multicolored	3.50	1.75
1211	A190	450fr multicolored	4.00	1.90
1212	A190	500fr multicolored	4.50	2.10
		Nos. 1204-1212 (9)	21.65	10.25

Discovery of America, 500th anniv. (#1205). First US orbital space flight, 30th anniv. (#1209). Americas Cup yacht race (#1210). Super Bowl XXVI football game (#1211).

Nos. 1210-1212 are airmail. Nos. 1204-1212 exist in souvenir sheets of one.

Intl. Conference on Nutrition, Rome — A191

1992, Nov. 10 Litho. *Perf. 13½*

1213	A191	150fr multi	1.20	.70
1214	A191	400fr multi	3.25	1.90
1215	A191	500fr multi	4.00	2.25
		Nos. 1213-1215 (3)	8.45	4.85

Nos. 1116-1120 Ovptd. in Silver

1992, Feb. 24 Litho. *Perf. 13½*

1216	A167	250fr multicolored	2.50	1.10
1217	A167	300fr multicolored	3.00	1.40
1218	A167	400fr multicolored	4.00	1.75
1219	A167	450fr multicolored	4.75	2.00
		Nos. 1216-1219 (4)	14.25	6.25

Souvenir Sheet

1220	A167	750fr multicolored	9.00	4.50

Nos. 1219-1220 are airmail. Nos. 1216-1219 exist in souvenir sheets of 1. Sold for 100fr extra.

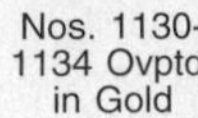

Nos. 1130-1134 Ovptd. in Gold

1992, Feb. 24 Litho. *Perf. 13½*

1221	A171	200fr multicolored	2.00	.80
1222	A171	250fr multicolored	2.50	1.00
1223	A171	300fr multicolored	3.00	1.25
1224	A171	450fr multicolored	5.00	2.00
		Nos. 1221-1224 (4)	12.50	5.05

Souvenir Sheet

1225	A171	750fr multicolored	8.00	3.00

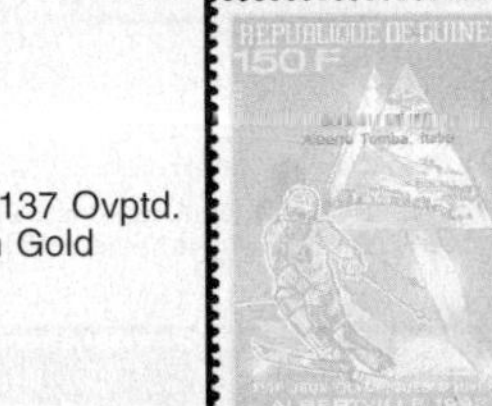

Nos. 1137 Ovptd. in Gold

Nos. 1138 Ovptd. in Gold

Nos. 1139 Ovptd. in Gold

Nos. 1141 Ovptd. in Gold

1992 Litho. *Perf. 13½*

1226	A174	150fr multicolored	1.45	.70
1227	A174	250fr multicolored	2.00	1.10
1228	A174	400fr multicolored	3.25	1.75
1229	A174	500fr multicolored	4.25	2.10
		Nos. 1226-1229 (4)	10.95	5.65

Souvenir Sheet

1230	A174	750fr multicolored	6.25	3.00

Overprints read: 150fr, 750fr, "SLALOM GEANT / Alberto Tomba, Italie." 250fr, "SKI NORDIQUE / Vegard Ulvang, Norvege." 400fr, "BOB A DEUX / G. Weder / D Acklin, Suisse." 500fr, "PATINAGE DE VITESSE / Olaf Zinke 1000m., Allemagne."

A192

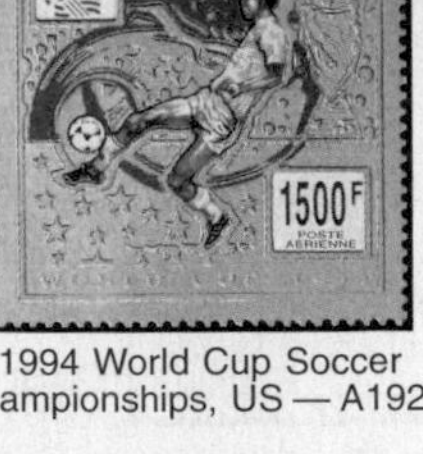

1994 World Cup Soccer Championships, US — A192a

Soccer player, city skyline: 100fr, San Francisco. 300fr, Washington, DC. 400fr, Detroit. 500fr, Dallas.

1000fr, New York.

1993, Sept. 24 Litho. *Perf. 13½*

1233	A192	100fr multicolored	1.20	.45
1234	A192	300fr multicolored	2.00	1.50
1235	A192	400fr multicolored	3.25	1.90
1236	A192	500fr multicolored	4.00	2.40
		Nos. 1233-1236 (4)	10.45	6.25

Souvenir Sheet

1237	A192	1000fr multicolored	8.00	5.50

Litho. & Embossed

1237A	A192a	1500fr gold & multi	16.00	12.50

Nos. 1236-1237A are airmail. No. 1237A exists in a souvenir sheet of 1.

Miniature Sheet

Dinosaurs — A193

No. 1238: a, 50fr, Euparkeria. b, 50fr, Plateosaurus. c, 50fr, Anchisaurus. d, 50fr, Ornithosuchus. e, 100fr, Megalosaurus. f, 100fr, Scelidosaurus. g, 100fr, Camptosaurus. h, 100fr, Ceratosaurus. i, 250fr, Ouranosaurus. j, 250fr, Dicraeosaurus. k, 250fr, Tarbosaurus. l, 250fr, Gorgosaurus. m, 250fr, Polacanthus. n, 250fr, Deinonychus. o, 250fr, Corythosaurus. p, 250fr, Spinosaurus.

1000fr, Tyrannosaurus rex.

1993, Oct. 27

1238	A193	Sheet of 16, #a.-p.	25.00	15.00

Souvenir Sheet

1239	A193	1000fr multicolored	10.00	4.50

No. 1239 is airmail and contains one 50x60mm stamp.

Nos. 1088-1094 Ovptd. in Silver

1993, Feb. 24 Litho. *Perf. 13½*

1240	A163	50fr multicolored	.45	.25
1241	A163	100fr multicolored	1.10	.50
1242	A163	150fr multicolored	1.75	.65
1243	A163	300fr multicolored	3.25	1.40

1244	A163	400fr multicolored	3.75	1.90
1245	A163	450fr multicolored	4.75	2.00
		Nos. 1240-1245 (6)	15.05	6.70

Souvenir Sheet

1246	A163	750fr multicolored	8.00	3.25

Nos. 1244-1246 are airmail.

A194

1994 Winter Olympic Games, Lillehammer A195

Views of Lillehammer: 150fr, Ice hockey. 250fr, Bobsled. 400fr, Biathlon. 450fr, Ski jump.
1000fr, Slalom skiing. 1500fr, Ice skating.

1993, July 16 Litho. *Perf. 13½*

1247	A194	150fr multicolored	1.25	.65
1248	A194	250fr multicolored	2.75	1.25
1249	A194	400fr multicolored	4.25	2.10
1250	A194	450fr multicolored	4.75	2.25
		Nos. 1247-1250 (4)	13.00	6.25

Souvenir Sheet

1251	A194	1000fr multicolored	10.00	5.00

Litho. & Embossed

1252	A195	1500fr gold & multi	16.00	12.50

Nos. 1249-1252 are airmail.
For overprints see #1267A-1267E.

A196

1996 Summer Olympic Games, Atlanta — A197

Event, scenes of Atlanta: 150fr, Soccer, "Little White House." 250fr, Cycling, Georgia World Congress Center. 400fr, Basketball, underground Atlanta. 500fr, Baseball, new Georgia Railroad.
1000fr, Table tennis, Atlanta at night. 1500fr, Running, Georgia State Capitol, Olympic torch.

1993, July 16 Litho. *Perf. 13½*

1253	A196	150fr multi	1.50	.65
1254	A196	250fr multi	2.75	1.25
1255	A196	400fr multi	4.75	2.10
1256	A196	500fr multi	6.00	2.50
		Nos. 1253-1256 (4)	15.00	6.50

Souvenir Sheet

1257	A196	1000fr multi	10.00	5.00

Litho. & Embossed

1257A	A197	1500fr gold & multi	16.00	12.50

Nos. 1256-1257A are airmail.
#1253-1256 exist in souvenir sheets of 1.

First Manned Moon Landing, 25th Anniv. — A197a

d, Luna 3, 1959. e, Ranger 7, 1964. f, Luna 9, 1966. g, Surveyor 1, 1966. h, Lunar Orbiter 1, 1966. i, Launch of Apollo 11, Neil Armstrong, 1969. j, Michael Collins, Apollo 11 command module. k, Apollo 11 landing on Moon, "Buzz" Aldrin. l, Apollo 12, 1969. m, Apollo 13, 1969. n, Luna 16, 1970. o, Luna 17, 1970. p, Apollo 14, 1971. q, Apollo 15, 1971. r, Apollo 16, 1972. s, Apollo 17, 1972.

1993, July 27 Litho. *Perf. 13½*
Sheet of 16

1257B	A197a	150fr #d.-s.	25.00	12.25

D-Day Landings, Normandy, 50th Anniv. — A198

Battle scenes and: No. 1258a, 150fr, Field Marshal Irwin Rommel (1891-1944), Germany. b, 600fr, Gen. Dwight D. Eisenhower (1890-1969), Allies. c, 150fr, Gen. George S. Patton, Jr. (1885-1945), Allies.
Battle of the Bulge, 1944: No. 1259a, 150fr, Lt. Gen. William H. Simpson. b, 600fr, Battle scene. c, 150fr, Gen. Heinz Guderian (1888-1954).
Austerlitz, Dec. 2, 1805: No. 1260a, 150fr, John I, Prince of Liechtenstein (1760-1836). b, 600fr, Napoleon I. c, 150fr, Marshal Joachim Murat (1767-1815)
Battle of Borodino, Sept. 7, 1812: No. 1261a, 150fr, Marshal Michael Ney (1769-1815). b, 600fr, Battle scene. c, 150fr, Prince Pyotr Ivanovich Bagration (1765-1812).

1994, Jan. 26 Litho. *Perf. 13½*

1258	A198	Strip of 3, #a.-c.	11.00	4.75
1259	A198	Strip of 3, #a.-c.	11.00	4.75
1260	A198	Strip of 3, #a.-c.	11.00	4.75
1261	A198	Strip of 3, #a.-c.	11.00	4.75
		Nos. 1258-1261 (4)	44.00	19.00

No. 1258b, 1259b, 1260b, 1261b are 60x46mm. Nos. 1258-1261 are each a continuous design.

Astronomers and Spacecraft — A199

Designs: a, 300fr, Johannes Kepler, Pluto probe. b, 500fr, Copernicus, Galileo probe. b, 300fr, Sir Isaac Newton, Voyager.

1994, Jan. 26

1262	A199	Strip of 3, #a.-c.	15.00	6.75

No. 1262b is 60x46mm. No. 1262 has a continuous design.

Nos. 1233-1237 Ovptd. in Silver

1994, Sept. 14 Litho. *Perf. 13½*

1263	A192	100fr multicolored	1.00	.50
1264	A192	300fr multicolored	3.00	1.75
1265	A192	400fr multicolored	4.00	2.25
1266	A192	500fr multicolored	4.75	2.50
		Nos. 1263-1266 (4)	12.75	7.00

Souvenir Sheet

1267	A192	1000fr multicolored	10.00	5.00

Nos. 1266-1267 are airmail.

No. 1247 Overprinted in Gold

No. 1248 Overprinted in Gold

No. 1249 Overprinted in Gold

No. 1250 Overprinted in Gold

1994, Sept. 14 Litho. *Perf. 13½*

1267A	A194	150fr multi	1.25	.65
1267B	A194	250fr multi	2.40	1.25
1267C	A194	400fr multi	3.75	1.90
1267D	A194	450fr multi	4.50	2.10
		Nos. 1267A-1267D (4)	11.90	5.90

Souvenir Sheet

1267E	A194	1000fr multi	10.00	5.00

Overprints read: 1000fr, T. MOE / U.S.A.
Nos. 1267C-1267E are airmail.

Birds — A200

150fr, Carduelis carduelis. 250fr, Luscinia megarhynchos. No. 1270, Serinus canaria. No. 1271, Fringilla coelebs. No. 1272, Carduelis chloris.
No. 1273, Erithacus rubecula.

1995, Aug. 31 Litho. *Perf. 13*

1268	A200	150fr multicolored	.50	.25
1269	A200	250fr multicolored	.80	.35
1270	A200	500fr multicolored	1.60	.80
1271	A200	500fr multicolored	1.60	.80
1272	A200	500fr multicolored	1.60	.80
		Nos. 1268-1272 (5)	6.10	3.00

Souvenir Sheet

1273	A200	1000fr multicolored	*6.00*	*3.00*

No. 1273 contains one 32x40mm stamp.

1996 Summer Olympics, Atlanta — A201

1995, Aug. 5

1274	A201	150fr Javelin	.50	.25
1275	A201	250fr Boxing	.80	.40
1276	A201	500fr Basketball	1.60	.80
1277	A201	500fr Weight lifting	1.60	.80
1278	A201	500fr Soccer	1.60	.80
		Nos. 1274-1278 (5)	6.10	3.05

Souvenir Sheet

1279	A201	1000fr Archery	*4.75*	*2.50*

No. 1279 contains one 32x40mm stamp.

African Animals A202

Designs: 150fr, Cercopithecus mona, vert. 250fr, Cercopithecus aethiops, vert. No. 1282, Galagoides demidovi, vert. No. 1283, Manis gigantea. No. 1284, Lepus crawshayi.
1000fr, Aonyx capensis, vert.

1995, Sept. 25

1280	A202	150fr multicolored	.50	.25
1281	A202	250fr multicolored	.80	.35
1282	A202	500fr multicolored	1.60	.80
1283	A202	500fr multicolored	1.60	.80
1284	A202	500fr multicolored	1.60	.80
		Nos. 1280-1284 (5)	6.10	3.00

Souvenir Sheet

1285	A202	1000fr multicolored	*6.00*	*3.00*

1998 World Cup Soccer Championships, France — A203

Opposing two players wearing: No. 1288, Yellow shirt & blue shorts, red shirt & white shorts. No. 1289, Red & white uniform, red shirt & white shorts. No. 1290, Striped shirt & blue shorts, red & yellow shirt & green shorts.

1000fr, Three players.

1995, Oct. 30 Litho. *Perf. 13*

1286	A203	150fr multicolored	.50	.25
1287	A203	250fr multicolored	.80	.35
1288	A203	500fr multicolored	1.60	.80
1289	A203	500fr multicolored	1.60	.80
1290	A203	500fr multicolored	1.60	.80
		Nos. 1286-1290 (5)	6.10	3.00

Souvenir Sheet

1291	A203	1000fr multicolored	*6.00*	*3.00*

No. 1291 contains one 32x40mm stamp.

Domestic Cats A204

150fr, Tortoiseshell. 250fr, Tabby and white. No. 1294, Tortoiseshell and white longhair. No. 1295, Red tabby. No. 1296, Smoke long-haired.
1000fr, Chinchilla.

1995, July 25

1292	A204	150fr multicolored	.65	.40
1293	A204	250fr multicolored	1.10	.55
1294	A204	500fr multicolored	2.10	1.25
1295	A204	500fr multicolored	2.10	1.25
1296	A204	500fr multicolored	2.10	1.25
		Nos. 1292-1296 (5)	8.05	4.70

Souvenir Sheet

Perf. 12½

1297	A204	1000fr multicolored	*4.50*	*2.50*

No. 1297 contains one 40x32mm stamp.

Production of Electrical Power — A205

Designs: 100fr, Banéa Dam. 150fr, Water Chamber, Donkea. 200fr, Tinkisso Spillway, vert. 250fr, Cascades of Grand Falls. 500fr, Building, Kinkon.

1995, July 18 *Perf. 12½*

1298	A205	100fr multicolored	.40	.25
1299	A205	150fr multicolored	.65	.35
1300	A205	200fr multicolored	.80	.50
1301	A205	250fr multicolored	1.00	.65
1302	A205	500fr multicolored	2.25	1.25
		Nos. 1298-1302 (5)	5.10	3.00

FAO, 50th Anniv. A206

Designs: 200fr, Man, oxen, boy. 750fr, Instructing women, children on nutrition.

1995, Oct. 16 *Perf. 13*

1303	A206	200fr multicolored	.80	.40
1304	A206	750fr multicolored	3.25	1.10

Light Aircraft — A207

100fr, Pup-150, UK. 150fr, Gardan GY-80 Horizon, France. 250fr, Piper Cub J-3, US. No. 1308, Valmet L-90TP Redigo, Finland. No. 1309, Pilatus PC-6 Porter, Switzerland. No. 1310, Piper PA-28 Cherokee Arrow, US.
1000fr, Stol DO-27, Germany.

1995, Oct. 1 *Perf. 12½*

1305	A207	100fr multicolored	.40	.25
1306	A207	150fr multicolored	.65	.25
1307	A207	250fr multicolored	1.10	.40
1308	A207	500fr multicolored	2.10	.75
1309	A207	500fr multicolored	2.10	.75
1310	A207	500fr multicolored	2.10	.75
		Nos. 1305-1310 (6)	8.45	3.15

Souvenir Sheet

1311	A207	1000fr multicolored	*4.50*	*2.50*

No. 1311 contains one 40x32mm stamp.

Flowers — A208

100fr, Sprekelia formosissima. 150fr, Rudbeckia purpurea. 250fr, Meconopsis betonicifolia. No. 1315, Gail Borden rose. No. 1316, Lathyrus odoratus. No. 1317, Iris starshine.
1000fr, Cypripedium alma gaevert.

1995, Oct. 12

1312	A208	100fr multicolored	.40	.25
1313	A208	150fr multicolored	.65	.25
1314	A208	250fr multicolored	1.10	.40
1315	A208	500fr multicolored	2.10	.75
1316	A208	500fr multicolored	2.10	.75
1317	A208	500fr multicolored	2.10	.75
		Nos. 1312-1317 (6)	8.45	3.15

Souvenir Sheet

1318	A208	1000fr multicolored	*4.50*	*2.50*

No. 1318 contains one 32x40mm stamp.

Historic Buses — A209

250fr, 1832 Omnibus. 300fr, 1898 Daimler. 400fr, 1904 V.H. Bussing. 450fr, 1906 Autobus M.A.N. 500fr, 1904 Autocar M.A.N.

1995, Dec. 3 Litho. *Perf. 12½*

1319	A209	250fr multicolored	.65	.35
1320	A209	300fr multicolored	.75	.45
1321	A209	400fr multicolored	.80	.60
1322	A209	450fr multicolored	.90	.60
1323	A209	500fr multicolored	.95	.75
		Nos. 1319-1323 (5)	4.05	2.75

Arabian Horses A210

Various horses.

1995 Background Colors

1324	A210	100fr dk bl, vert.	.40	.25
1325	A210	150fr tan, vert.	.65	.25
1326	A210	250fr lt bl, vert.	.90	.40
1327	A210	500fr pink, vert.	1.20	.75
1328	A210	500fr lilac, vert.	1.20	.75
1329	A210	500fr sage	1.20	.75
		Nos. 1324-1329 (6)	5.55	3.15

Souvenir Sheet

1330	A210	1000fr white & gray	*4.75*	*3.00*

No. 1330 contains one 32x40mm stamp.

Mushrooms A211

150fr, Leccinum nigrescens. 250fr, Boletus rhodoxanthus. No. 1333, Paxillus involutus. No. 1334, Cantharellus lutescens. No. 1335, Xerocomus rubellus.
1000fr, Gymnopilus junonius.

1995 Litho. *Perf. 12½*

1331	A211	150fr multicolored	.40	.25
1332	A211	250fr multicolored	.75	.40
1333	A211	500fr multicolored	.95	.75
1334	A211	500fr multicolored	.95	.75
1335	A211	500fr multicolored	.95	.75
		Nos. 1331-1335 (5)	4.00	2.00

Souvenir Sheet

1336	A211	1000fr multicolored	*5.00*	*3.00*

No. 1336 contains one 32x40mm stamp.

Tourism — A212

200fr, Mountain cliff. 750fr, Young child. 1000fr, Women carrying wood.

1996, Sept. 5 Litho. *Perf. 12½*

1337	A212	200fr multicolored	.80	.40
1338	A212	750fr multicolored	3.50	1.20
1339	A212	1000fr multicolored	4.50	1.75
		Nos. 1337-1339 (3)	8.80	3.35

Dogs — A213

200fr, Bull terrier. 250fr, Elkhound. 300fr, Akita. 400fr, Collie. 450fr, Rottweiler. 500fr, Boxer.
1000fr, German pointer.

1996, Oct. 20

1340	A213	200fr multi	.80	.30
1341	A213	250fr multi	.95	.35
1342	A213	300fr multi	1.20	.45
1343	A213	400fr multi	1.40	.60
1344	A213	450fr multi	1.60	.65
1345	A213	500fr multi	2.10	.75
		Nos. 1340-1345 (6)	8.05	3.10

Souvenir Sheet

Perf. 13

1346	A213	1000fr multi	4.00	2.50

No. 1346 contains one 32x40mm stamp.

Mushrooms A214

200fr, Chestnut. 250fr, Granular. 300fr, Destroying angel. 400fr, Milky blue. 450fr, Violet cortinarius. 500fr, Rough-stemmed.
1000fr, Hygrophorus.

1996, Dec. 20 Litho. *Perf. 12½*

1347	A214	200fr multicolored	.80	.30
1348	A214	250fr multicolored	.95	.35
1349	A214	300fr multicolored	1.20	.45
1350	A214	400fr multicolored	1.40	.60
1351	A214	450fr multicolored	1.50	.65
1352	A214	500fr multicolored	2.00	.75
		Nos. 1347-1352 (6)	7.85	3.10

Souvenir Sheet

Perf. 13

1353	A214	1000fr multicolored	*4.00*	*2.50*

No. 1353 contains one 32x40mm stamp.

Locomotives — A215

Designs: 200fr, Tom Thumb, 1829. 250fr, Genf, 1858. 300fr, Dübs and Company, 1873. 400fr, W.G. Bagnall of Castle Engine Works, 1932. 450fr, Werner von Siemens, 1879. 500fr, North London Tramways Co., 1885-89.
1000fr, General, 1862.

1996, Aug. 30 *Perf. 12½*

1354	A215	200fr multicolored	.80	.30
1355	A215	250fr multicolored	1.00	.40
1356	A215	300fr multicolored	1.25	.45
1357	A215	400fr multicolored	1.40	.60
1358	A215	450fr multicolored	1.75	.65
1359	A215	500fr multicolored	2.25	.75
		Nos. 1354-1359 (6)	8.45	3.15

Souvenir Sheet

1360	A215	1000fr multicolored	*4.50*	*2.50*

Nos. 1355, 1358 are each 68x27mm. No. 1360 contains one 40x32mm stamp.

Cats A216

200fr, Tortoiseshell short-hair. 250fr, Black and white short-hair. 300fr, Japanese. 400fr, Himalayan. 450fr, Brown long-hair. 500fr, Blue Persian.
1000fr, Tortoiseshell long-hair.

1996, Nov. 15 *Perf. 12½*

1361	A216	200fr multicolored	.80	.30
1362	A216	250fr multicolored	.95	.40
1363	A216	300fr multicolored	1.20	.45
1364	A216	400fr multicolored	1.40	.60
1365	A216	450fr multicolored	1.60	.65
1366	A216	500fr multicolored	2.10	.75
		Nos. 1361-1366 (6)	8.05	3.15

Souvenir Sheet

1367	A216	1000fr multicolored	*4.00*	*2.50*

No. 1367 contains one 32x40mm stamp.

Birds — A217

Designs: 200fr, Carduelis cucullata. 250fr, Uraeginthus bengalus. 300fr, Lonchura castaneothorax. 400fr, Amadina erythrocephala. 450fr, Chloebia gouldiae. 500fr, Euplectes orix.
1000fr, Poephila guttata.

1996, Sept. 28 *Perf. 12½*

1368	A217	200fr multicolored	.80	.30
1369	A217	250fr multicolored	.95	.40
1370	A217	300fr multicolored	1.20	.45

1371	A217	400fr	multicolored	1.40	.60
1372	A217	450fr	multicolored	1.60	.65
1373	A217	500fr	multicolored	2.10	.75
			Nos. 1368-1373 (6)	8.05	3.15

Souvenir Sheet

1374	A217	1000fr	multicolored	*4.00*	*2.50*

No. 1374 contains one 32x40mm stamp.

Orchids A218

Designs: 200fr, Paphiopedilum millmoore. 250fr, Paphiopedilum ernest read. 300fr, Paphiopedilum harrisianum. 400fr, Paphiopedilum gaudianum. 450fr, Paphiopedilum papa röhl. 500fr, Paphiopedilum sea cliffl.
1000fr, Paphiopedilum gowenanum.

1997, Mar. 3 Litho. *Perf. 12½*

1375	A218	200fr	multicolored	.80	.30
1376	A218	250fr	multicolored	.95	.40
1377	A218	300fr	multicolored	1.20	.45
1378	A218	400fr	multicolored	1.40	.60
1379	A218	450fr	multicolored	1.60	.65
1380	A218	500fr	multicolored	2.10	.75
			Nos. 1375-1380 (6)	8.05	3.15

Souvenir Sheet

1381	A218	1000fr	multicolored	4.00	2.50

No. 1381 contains one 32x40mm stamp.

1998 World Cup Soccer Championships, France — A219

Various soccer plays.

1997, Jan. 15

1382	A219	200fr	multi, vert.	.80	.25
1383	A219	250fr	multi, vert.	.95	.25
1384	A219	300fr	multi, vert.	1.20	.30
1385	A219	400fr	multicolored	1.40	.40
1386	A219	450fr	multicolored	1.60	.45
1387	A219	500fr	multicolored	2.10	.75
			Nos. 1382-1387 (6)	8.05	2.40

Souvenir Sheet

1388	A219	1000fr	Goalie at net	4.00	2.50

No. 1388 contains one 32x40mm stamp.

Wild Animals A220

Designs: 200fr, Giraffa camelopardalis. 250fr, Cerothoterium simun, vert. 300fr, Phacochoerus aethiopicus. 400fr, Acinonyx jubatus. 450fr, Loxodonta africana, vert. 500fr, Choeropsis liberiensis.
1000fr, Okapia johnstoni.

1997, Apr. 15 Litho. *Perf. 12½*

1389	A220	200fr	multicolored	.80	.25
1390	A220	250fr	multicolored	.95	.30
1391	A220	300fr	multicolored	1.20	.35
1392	A220	400fr	multicolored	1.40	.60
1393	A220	450fr	multicolored	1.60	.50
1394	A220	500fr	multicolored	2.10	.75
			Nos. 1389-1394 (6)	8.05	2.75

Souvenir Sheet

1395	A220	1000fr	multicolored	*4.00*	*2.00*

19th Century Warships — A221

Designs: 200fr, Captain, England, 1870. 250fr, Konig Wilhelm, Germany, 1869. 300fr, Téméraire, England, 1877. 400fr, Mouillage, Italy, 1866. 450fr, Inflexible, England, 1881. 500fr, Magenta, France, 1862.
1000fr, Redoutable, France, 1878.

1997, May 20 Litho. *Perf. 12½*

1396	A221	200fr	multicolored	.80	.25
1397	A221	250fr	multicolored	.95	.35
1398	A221	300fr	multicolored	1.20	.35
1399	A221	400fr	multicolored	1.40	.50
1400	A221	450fr	multicolored	1.60	.50
1401	A221	500fr	multicolored	2.10	.75
			Nos. 1396-1401 (6)	8.05	2.70

Souvenir Sheet

1402	A221	1000fr	multicolored	4.00	2.50

No. 1402 contains one 32x40mm stamp.

Fish A222

Designs: 200fr, Siganus trispilos. 250fr, Scarus niger. 300fr, Choerodon fasciata. 400fr, Naso lituratus. 450fr, Hypoplectrus gemma. 500fr, Acanthurus achilles.
1000fr, Zebrasoma flavescens.

1997, June 15 Litho. *Perf. 13*

1403	A222	200fr	multicolored	.35	.25
1404	A222	250fr	multicolored	.80	.50
1405	A222	300fr	multicolored	1.00	.60
1406	A222	400fr	multicolored	1.50	.80
1407	A222	450fr	multicolored	1.75	.90
1408	A222	500fr	multicolored	1.75	.95
			Nos. 1403-1408 (6)	7.15	4.00

Souvenir Sheet

Perf. 12½

1409	A222	1000fr	multicolored	3.50	2.50

No. 1409 contains one 40x32mm stamp.

Chess Pieces A222a

200fr, Thailand, 14th cent. 250fr, China, 1930. 300fr, Portugal, 1920. 400fr, Germany. 450fr, Russia. 500fr, Pieces by Max Ernst.
1000fr, France, 18th cent.

1997, Oct. 20 Litho. *Perf. 13*

1409A	A222a	200fr	multi	.65	.45
1409B	A222a	250fr	multi	.75	.55
1409C	A222a	300fr	multi	1.00	.70
1409D	A222a	400fr	multi	1.25	.90
1409E	A222a	450fr	multi	1.50	1.00
1409F	A222a	500fr	multi	1.75	1.10
			Nos. 1409A-1409F (6)	6.90	4.70

Souvenir Sheet

Perf. 12½

1409G	A222a	1000fr	multi	3.50	2.75

No. 1409G contains one 32x40mm stamp.

Dogs A223

200fr, Siberian husky. 250fr, Dachshund. 300fr, Boston terrier. 400fr, Basset hound. 450fr, Dalmatian. 500fr, Rottweiler.
1000fr, Golden retriever.

1997, Nov. 10 Litho. *Perf. 12½*

Stamp + Label

1410	A223	200fr	multi	.50	.35
1411	A223	250fr	multi	.65	.45
1412	A223	300fr	multi	.80	.50
1413	A223	400fr	multi	.95	.70
1414	A223	450fr	multi	1.10	.75
1415	A223	500fr	multi	1.25	.85
			Nos. 1410-1415 (6)	5.25	3.60

Souvenir Sheet

1416	A223	1000fr	multi	4.50	2.75

Nos. 1410-1415 are each printed with se-tenant label.

Prehistoric Animals — A224

200fr, Dilophosaurus. 250fr, Psittacosaurus. 300fr, Dromiceiomimus. 400fr, Stenonychosaurus. 450fr, Opisthocoelicaudia. 500fr, Ornitholestes.
1000fr, Anchiceratops.

1997 Litho. *Perf. 12½*

1417	A224	200fr	multi	.50	.40
1418	A224	250fr	multi, vert.	.65	.50
1419	A224	300fr	multi	.85	.55
1420	A224	400fr	multi, vert.	1.00	.75
1421	A224	450fr	multi	1.20	.80
1422	A224	500fr	multi	1.40	.90
			Nos. 1417-1422 (6)	5.60	3.90

Souvenir Sheet

1423	A224	1000fr	multicolored	3.00	2.00

No. 1423 contains one 40x32mm stamp.

UNICEF — A224a

Design: 200fr, Children at school, horiz. 300fr, Baby receiving inoculation, horiz. 750fr, Mother nursing child. 1500fr, Women reading, horiz.

1997 Litho. *Perf. 13¼*

1423A	A224a	200fr	multi	—	—
1423B	A224a	300fr	multi	—	—
1423C	A224a	750fr	multi	—	—
1423D	A224a	1500fr	multi	—	—

Butterflies — A225

200fr, Eueides cleobaea. 250fr, Danaus cleophile. 300fr, Dryas julia. 400fr, Dismorphia cubana. 450fr, Pyrrhocalles antiga. 500fr, Phoebis orbis.
1000fr, Morpho adonis.

1998

1424	A225	200fr	multicolored	.50	.40
1425	A225	250fr	multicolored	.70	.50
1426	A225	300fr	multicolored	.85	.55
1427	A225	400fr	multicolored	1.00	.75
1428	A225	450fr	multicolored	1.20	.80
1429	A225	500fr	multicolored	1.40	.90
			Nos. 1424-1429 (6)	5.65	3.90

Souvenir Sheet

1430	A225	1000fr	multicolored	3.00	2.00

No. 1430 contains one 40x32mm stamp.

Environmental Protection Week A225a

Mount Nimba and frame in: 200fr, Brown. 300fr, Blue. 750fr, Green.

1998 Litho. *Perf. 13¼x13½*

1430A-1430C	A225a	Set of 3	—	—

Domestic Cats — A226

200fr, English shorthair bicolor. 250fr, Scottish fold. 300fr, Birman. 400fr, American coarse hair. 450fr, Snowshoe. 500fr, Maine coon.
1000fr, Malaysian.

1998 Litho. *Perf. 12½*

1431	A226	200fr	multicolored	.65	.30
1432	A226	250fr	multicolored	.70	.45
1433	A226	300fr	multicolored	.85	.60
1434	A226	400fr	multicolored	1.20	.75
1435	A226	450fr	multicolored	1.40	.90
1436	A226	500fr	multicolored	1.50	1.00
			Nos. 1431-1436 (6)	6.30	4.00

Souvenir Sheet

Perf. 13

1437	A226	1000fr	multicolored	3.00	2.00

No. 1437 contains one 32x40mm stamp.

Diana, Princess of Wales (1961-97) — A227

Various portraits.

1998 Litho. *Perf. 13½*

Sheets of 9

1438	A227	200fr	#a.-i.	8.00	4.00
1439	A227	300fr	#a.-i	12.00	6.00
1440	A227	750fr	#a.-i.	30.00	15.00

Souvenir Sheets

1441 A227 1500fr multicolored 10.00 5.00
1442 A227 2000fr multicolored 10.00 5.00

Dated 1997.

1998 World Cup Soccer Championships, France — A228

Various soccer plays.

1998	**Litho.**	***Perf. 12½***	
1443 A228	200fr multi, vert.	.55	.40
1444 A228	250fr multi, vert.	.70	.50
1445 A228	300fr multi, vert.	.95	.55
1446 A228	400fr multi, vert.	1.20	.75
1447 A228	450fr multi	1.40	.80
1448 A228	500fr multi	1.50	.90
	Nos. 1443-1448 (6)	6.30	3.90

Souvenir Sheet

Perf. 13

1449 A228 1000fr multi 4.50 2.75

No. 1449 contains one 32x40mm stamp.

Old Germanic Military Uniforms A228a

Designs: 200fr, Officer, Von Witerfeldt's Regiment. 250fr, Non-commissioned officer, Von Kanitz's Regiment. 300fr, Private, Prince Franz von Anhalt-Dessau's Regiment. 400fr, Private, Von Kalnein's Regiment. 450fr, Grenadier, Duke Ferdinand of Brunswick's Regiment. 500fr, Musician, Rekow's Guards Battalion.

1000fr, Pioneer.

1997, Aug. 17 **Litho.** ***Perf. 12½***
1449A-1449F A228a Set of 6 8.00 5.00

Souvenir Sheet

1449G A228a 1000fr multi 4.00 2.25

No. 1449G contains one 32x40mm stamp.

Steam Locomotives — A229

200fr, Baldwin Locomotive Works, 0-4-2. 250fr, American Locomotive Co., 0-6-0. 300fr, Vulcan Iron Works, 0-6-0. 400fr, Baldwin Locomotive Works, 0-6-0. 450fr, H.K. Porter Co., 0-6-0. 500fr, Vulcan Iron Works, 0-6-0, diff.

1000fr, Baldwin Locomotive Works, 0-6-0, diff.

1997, Sept. 10 **Litho.** ***Perf. 12½***
1450-1455 A229 Set of 6 6.00 3.50

Souvenir Sheet

1456 A229 1000fr multicolored 5.00 3.00

No. 1456 contains one 40x32mm stamp.

Nectophrynoides Occidentalis — A230

Color of border: 200fr, green. 300fr, blue. 750fr, pale rose.

1998 ***Perf. 13½***
1457-1459 A230 Set of 3 5.50 2.75

Intl. Year of the Ocean A231

Marine life — No. 1460: a, Physeter macrocephalus, neophova cinerea. b, Melanogrammus aeglefinus. c, Delphinapterus leucas. d, Megaptera novaengliae. e, Notorhynchus cependianus. f, Manta birostris. g, Delphinaterusleucas, macrozoarces americanus. h, Physalia physalis, pollachius virens. i, Manta birostris. j, Odontapis taurus. k, Thalassoma ruppelli, octopus vulgaris. l, Sebestes marinus.

1500fr, Megaptera novaengliae, diff.

1998
1460 A231 200fr Sheet of 12, #a.-l. 11.00 11.00

Souvenir Sheet

1461 A231 1500fr multicolored 9.00 4.25

Antique Cars A232

200fr, 1932 Chrysler, 8 cylinders, US. 300fr, 1907 Napier, 60HP, England. 450fr, 1903 Mercedes, 60HP, Germany. 750fr, 1925 Fiat 509, Italy.

No. 1466: a, 1929 Alfa Romeo 6C 1750 Zagato, Italy. b, 1932 Hispano-Suiza Type 68, Spain. c, 1931 Horsch V12, Germany. d, 1909 Rolland Pilain, 16hp, France. e, 1920 McLaughlin, Canada. f, 1930 Walter 6B, Czechoslovakia.

No. 1467: a, 1914 Fischer SS, Switzerland. b, 1922 Excelsior Adex C, Belgium. c, 1912 Pilain Torpedo, France. d, 1932 Franklin, 6 cylinders, US. e, 1912 Abadal 18/24hp, Spain. f, 1923 Alvis 12/50, England.

No. 1468, 1500fr, 1925 Rolls Royce Phantom 1, England. No. 1468A, 1500fr, 1932 Ford V8, US.

1998, Aug. 21
1462-1465 A232 Set of 4 8.50 4.25

Sheets of 6

1466 A232 450fr #a.-f. 13.00 6.50
1467 A232 750fr #a.-f. 24.00 11.50

Souvenir Sheets

1468-1468A A232 Set of 2 18.00 8.50

Nos. 1468-1468A each contain one 56x42mm stamp.

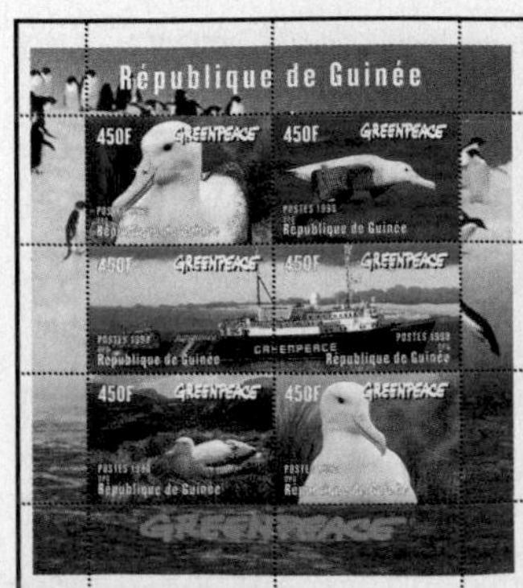

Greenpeace — A233

Designs: a, Albatross looking left. b, Albatross in flight. c, Stern of Greenpeace ship, helicopter. d, Bow of Greenpeace ship. e, Albatross nesting. f, Albatross looking right.

2000fr, Albatross with chick.

1998 **Litho.** ***Perf. 13½***
1469 A233 450fr Sheet of 6, #a.-f. 10.00 8.00

Souvenir Sheet

1470 A233 2000fr multicolored 9.50 4.75

No. 1470 contains one 40x46mm stamp.

Endangered Species — A234

Designs, vert: 200fr, Lynx pardellus. 300fr, Lepilemur mustelinus. 450fr, Canis rufus. 750fr, Bison bonasus.

No. 1475: a, Leopard. b, Civet (f). c, Bird (d). d, Hawk. e, Rhinoceros, impala. f, Okapi (e, h, i). g, Lion. h, Chimpanzee. i, Gorilla. j, Bird (long, curved beak). k, Hippopotamus (l). l, Antelope (h).

No. 1476: a, Falco pereginus. b, Acinonyx jubatus. c, Antilocapre americana. d, Mustela nigripes. e, Ursus maritimus. f, Rhinoceros unicornis.

No. 1477: a, Gymnobelideus leadbeater. b, Felis concolor. c, Felis pardalis. d, Panthera pardus. e, Bufo hemiophyrs. f, Mustela rutorius.

No. 1478, 1500fr, Muscardinus avellanarius. No. 1479, 1500fr, Aepyceros melampus, vert. No. 1480, 1500fr, Panthera uncia.

1998, Sept. 8
1471-1474 A234 Set of 4 9.00 4.50

Sheets of 12 & 6

1475 A234 200fr #a.-l. 10.00 5.00
1476 A234 450fr #a.-f. 12.00 5.75
1477 A234 750fr #a.-f. 18.00 9.00

Souvenir Sheets

1478-1480 A234 Set of 3 24.00 12.00

Locomotives of the World — A235

No. 1481: a, Sir Nigel Gresley, England. b, Switzerland. c, Canada. d, EMU 102-6 Tobu Railway Spacia, Japan. e, Krauss Maffei V200, Germany. f, IC 580 Portugal. g, Amtrak No. 5, US. h, TGV, France.

No. 1482: a, Nippon Pacific No. 82, Middle East. b, Russia. c, Freight train, Albania. d, Dart No. 8319, Ireland. e, No. 141-F-177, France. f, EMU No. 69625, Norway. g, Bo-Bo, New Zealand. h, Azusa, Japan.

No. 1483: a, Syrian Railways 2-8-0, Iraq. b, The Irish Mail, England. c, Four car EMU, Italy. d, Sprinter, England. e, Van Golu Express, Turkey. f, No. 11.2110, Norway. g, Two-car EMU, New Zealand. h, Grey Mouse, France.

No. 1484: a, The Flying Scotman, United Kingdom. b, National Railways, Japan. c, North Africa. d, F-40M Winnebago, US. e, Federal Railways Class 10, three cylinder 4-6-2, Germany. f, DX5500, New Zealand. g, CIE, Ireland. h, Intercity class 43, England.

No. 1485, 1500fr, D2157, New Zealand. No. 1486, 1500fr, 140.7410, German Railways. No. 1487, 1500fr, JR Shinkansen 221-204, Japan. No. 1488, Egyptian Railways, Bo-Bo.

Sheets of 8

1998, Oct. 30
1481 A235 200fr #a.-h. 8.00 3.75
1482 A235 300fr #a.-h. 12.00 5.75
1483 A235 450fr #a.-h. 16.00 7.75
1484 A235 750fr #a.-h. 24.00 12.00

Souvenir Sheets

1485-1488 A235 Set of 4 30.00 15.00

Aircraft — A236

Amphibians & flying boats — No. 1489: a, Boeing Model 1, 1916. b, Grumman G-21 Goose, 1937. c, Latecoere 631, 1942. d, Cessna Model 205. e, Sikorsky S-42, 1934. f, Boeing Model 314 Clipper. g, De Havilland Canada DHC-2 Beaver, 1947. h, Lake Buccaneer, 1979.

Balloons and Dirigibles — No. 1490: a, Henri Giffard, 1852. b, Santos-Dumont "Baladeuse," 1903. c, Zeppelin L37. d, R101, 1930. e, Santos-Dumont, 1898. f, Baldwin, 1908. g, Norge, 1926. h, Hindenburg, 1936.

Helicopters — No. 1491: a, Sikorsky VS-300, 1940. b, Sikorsky S-61, 1957. c, Bell Long Ranger, 1966. d, Dauphin SA 365, 1972. e, Bell 47, 1946. f, Boeing Vertol 243LR, 1958. g, Aerospatial SA 315 Blama. h, Bell Model 222, 1981.

Spacecraft — No. 1492: a, Mercury Capsule, 1961. b, Gemini 8, 1966. c, Apollo Lunar Module, 1968. d, Soviet Vostok, 1961. e, Apollo Command Module, 1968. f, Soviet Soyuz, 1975.

No. 1493, 1500fr, Cessna 208 Caravan, 1980. No. 1494, 1500fr, Goodyear Blimp. No. 1495, 1500fr, Miles Mi-26, 1983. No. 1496, 1500fr, Space Shuttle Columbia, 1981.

Sheets of 8 & 6

1998, Oct. 30
1489 A236 200fr #a.-h. 9.00 4.25
1490 A236 300fr #a.-h. 13.00 6.25
1491 A236 450fr #a.-h. 18.00 9.00
1492 A236 750fr #a.-f. 22.50 11.00

Souvenir Sheets

1493-1496 A236 Set of 4 20.00 10.00

No. 1489a incorrectly inscribed "1961."

Dinosaurs — A237

No. 1497: a, Dicraeosaurus. b, Parasaurolophus. c, Sauronithoides. d, Dilophosaurus. e, Titanosaurus, bagaceratops. f, Iguanodon. g, Tenontosaurus. h, Dryosaurus. i, Ceratosaurus.

1500fr, Yangchuanosaurus, brachiosaurus.

1998 **Litho.** ***Perf. 13½***
1497 A237 750fr Sheet of 9, #a.-i. 27.50 13.50

Souvenir Sheet

1498 A237 1500fr multicolored 6.00 3.00

Minerals — A238

a, Calcite. b, Wolframite. c, Spodumene.

No. 1500D: e, Psilomelane. f, Heterosite. g, Columbo-tantalite.

1998 Litho. *Perf. 13½*

Strip of 3

1499 A238 750fr Green background, #a.-c. 10.50 5.25

Souvenir Sheets of 3

1500 A238 750fr Gray blue background, #a.-c. 10.50 5.25
1500D A238 1500fr #e-g 21.00 21.00

Sailing Ships — A239

No. 1501, each 450fr: a, "Theseus." b, "Euphrates." c, Phoenician War Galley. d, Chinese Junk.

No. 1502, each 450fr: a, "Juan Sebastian." b, "Santa Maria." c, Frigate. d, Madurese Jukung rig.

No. 1503, vert, each 750fr: a, Windjammer, "Wavertree." b, British frigate, "Rose." c, Tromp's flagship, "Golden Leeuw." d, Danish Timber Barque.

No. 1504, vert, each 750fr: a, Kraeck. b, Clipper ship, "Golden State." c, English ship, "Resolution." d, "Eagle."

No. 1505, 1500fr, British barque, "Garthpool." No. 1506, 1500fr, HMS Victory.

1998, Nov. 10 *Perf. 14*

Sheets of 4, #a.-d.

1501-1502 A239 Set of 2 16.00 7.75
1503-1504 A239 Set of 2 30.00 15.00

Souvenir Sheets

1505-1506 A239 Set of 2 15.00 15.00

Novotel Hotel, Conakry — A239a

1998 Litho. *Perf. 13x13½*

1506A A239a 200fr multi — —
1506B A239a 750fr multi — —

The editors suspect that additional stamps may have been issued in this set and would like to examine any examples. Numbers may change.

Modern Guinean Arts

A239b

A239c

A239d

A239e

A239f

A239g

A239h

A239i

1998, Dec. 8 Litho. *Perf. 13¼x13*

1506D A239b 750fr Dance — —
1506E A239c 750fr Painting — —
1506F A239d 750fr Ceramics — —
1506G A239e 750fr Sculpture — —
1506H A239f 750fr Sculpture — —
1506I A239g 750fr Dance — —
1506J A239h 750fr Painting — —
1506K A239i 750fr Painting — —

Horses A240

Designs: 150fr, Trotteur Russe. 200fr, Brabant. 300fr, Camargue. No. 1510, 450fr, Unidentified breed. No. 1511, 450fr, Dales pony. No. 1512, 750fr, Fjord.

No. 1513, vert.: a, Kabardin. b, Shire. c, Arabian. d, Mustang. e, Quarter horse. f, Appaloosa.

No. 1514, vert.: a, Thoroughbred. b, Lipizzaner. c, Belgian. d, Palomino. e, Haflinger. f, Fjord, diff.

No. 1515, 1500fr, Mustang, diff. No. 1516, 1500fr, Thoroughbred colt.

1999, May 1 Litho. *Perf. 14*

1507-1512 A240 Set of 6 11.00 11.00

Sheets of 6

1513 A240 450fr #a.-f. 12.00 12.00
1514 A240 750fr #a.-f. 21.00 21.00

Souvenir Sheets

1515-1516 A240 Set of 2 17.00 17.00

Guinea — People's Republic of China Diplomatic Relations, 40th Anniv. — A240a

Designs: 200fr, Shown. 300fr, Building with flat roof, horiz. 750fr, Building with slanted roof, horiz.

1999 Litho. *Perf. 13¼x13*

1516A A240a 200fr multi — —
1516B A240a 300fr multi — —
1516C A240a 750fr multi — —

Dogs A241

Designs: 200fr, Newfoundland. No. 1518, 750fr, St. Bernard.

No. 1519, vert.: a, Bulldog. b, Miniature schnauzer. c, Dachshund. d, Beagle. e, Bloodhound. f, Miniature pinscher.

1500fr, Irish setter.

1999, May 1

1517-1518 A241 Set of 2 5.00 5.00

Sheet of 6

1519 A241 750fr #a.-f. 18.00 18.00

Souvenir Sheet

1520 A241 1500fr multi 8.00 8.00

Modern Guinean Sculptures — A241a

Various sculptures.

1999, Aug. 9 Litho. *Perf. 13¼x13*

1520A A241a 200fr multi 2.40 2.40
1520B A241a 250fr multi 2.40 2.40
1520C A241a 300fr multi 2.40 2.40
1520D A241a 500fr shown 2.40 2.40
1520E A241a 750fr multi 2.40 2.40

PhilexFrance '00.

A242

Dinosaurs & Prehistoric Animals — A243

Designs: 300fr, Ouranosaurus. No. 1522, 450fr, Centrosaurus. No. 1523, 450fr, Dilophosaurus, vert.

No. 1524: a, Cymbospondylus. b, Kronosaurus. c, Ichthyosaurus. d, Eurhinosaurus. e, Stenopterygius. f, Ophthalmosaurus. g, Shonisaurus. h, Temnodontosaurus. i, Mixosaurus.

No. 1525, vert.: a, Eudimorphodon. b, Sordes. c, Dimorphodon. d, Albertosaurus. e, Triceratops. f, Alioramus. g, Mesosaurus. h, Labidosaurus. i, Struthiomimus.

No. 1526: a, Saltosaurus. b, Corythosaurus. c, Protoceratops. d, Baryonyx. e, Pachycephalosaurus. f, Maiasaurus. g, Spinosaurus. h, Lambeosaurus.

2500fr, Elasmosaurus, vert. No. 1528, Tyrannosaurus Rex. No. 1529, Utahraptor. No. 1530, Parasaurolophus, vert.

1999, Aug. 12

1521-1523 A242 Set of 3 5.00 5.00

Sheets of 9

1524 A243 350fr #a.-i. 15.00 15.00
1525 A243 450fr #a.-i. 18.00 18.00

Sheet of 8

1526 A242 450fr #a.-h 18.00 18.00

Souvenir Sheets

1527 A243 2500fr multi 13.00 13.00
1528 A243 3000fr multi 13.00 13.00
1529-1530 A242 3000fr Set of 2 28.00 28.00

No. 1527 contains one 42x56mm stamp. No. 1528 contains one 56x42mm stamp.

Return of Macao to People's Republic of China, Dec. 20, 1999 A244

No. 1531, each 650fr: a, Current view of Nam Van (tall buildings). b, Nam Van in 1850s (hilltop and bay). c, Current view of Largo de Senado. d, Largo de Senado in 1900s.

No. 1532, each 650fr: a, Current view of Nam Van (highway). b, Nam Van in 1850s (buildings at water's edge). c, Current view of Nam Van (boat). d, Nam Van in 1850s (ships).

1999, Aug. 20 *Perf. 14¼x14½*

Sheets of 4, #a.-d.

1531-1532 A244 Set of 2 24.00 24.00

China 1999 World Philatelic Exhibition.

Paintings of Zhang Daqian (1899-1983) — A245

No. 1500. a, Ink Lotus. b, Ink Peony. c, Red Cliff Excursion at Night. d, Poetic Landscape. e, Landscape in the Evening. f, Spring Landscape. g, Chatting at Leisure in Mountains. h, Pine Nesting. i, Pine in Thunder. j, Blue and Green Landscape.

No. 1534: a, Landscape. b, Versing in the Landscape.

1999, Aug. 20 Litho. *Perf. 13¼*

1533 A245 330fr Sheet of 10, #a.-j. 15.00 15.00

Souvenir Sheet of 2

Perf. 13

1534 A245 1150fr #a.-b. 4.50 4.50

No. 1534 contains two 51x39mm stamps. China 1999 World Philatelic Exhibition

First French Postage Stamp, 150th Anniv. — A245a

Litho. with Hologram Applied

1999, Sept. 10 *Perf. 13*

1534C A245a 750fr multi *4.75 4.75*

Trains A246

100fr, Diesel TGV, East Germany. No. 1536, 200fr, 1900 horsepower Diesel-electric, Finland. No. 1537, 200fr, Type MLW 3000 horsepower Diesel-electric. No. 1538, 250fr, A-4, Britain. No. 1539, 250fr, Class R 4-6-4. No. 1540, 250fr, Class M, 4-6-2, Tasmania. No. 1541, 450fr, Class 68000 Diesel-electric, France. No. 1542, 450fr, 4-8-4 Daylight Express. No. 1543, 450fr, Electric TGV, Italy. No. 1544, 450fr, Western Class Hydraulic-Diesel.

No. 1545: a, Class 10 3-cylinder 4-6-2. b, SD18 Diesel-electric. c, Hikari Super Express Train, Japan. d, Diesel-electric No. 10000. e, PA-1 Diesel-electric. f, 2500 horsepower experimental gas turbine locomotive.

No. 1546: a, YP Class, India. b, Class 47, Standard Type 4 Diesel-electric. c, DSI Class 2-8-2, Japan. d, Class D-341 Diesel-electric. e, S1 Class 2-6-4. f, 3600 horsepower electric, India.

No. 1547: a, 2000 horsepower GP-20 Diesel-electric. b, Class C-53 3-cylinder, Japan. c, Multiple-unit Diesel, Japan. d, Royal Scot Class 4-6-0. e, Deltic electric prototype. f, W.P. Standard 4-6-2.

No. 1548: 2500fr, Class 40 electric, England.

Each 3000fr: No. 1549, GP-40 Diesel-electric. No. 1550, 9780 horsepower DM-3, Sweden. No. 1551, 1750 horsepower Diesel-electric, Denmark.

1999, Oct. 25 *Perf. 14*

1535-1544 A246 Set of 10 13.00 13.00

Sheets of 6

1545 A246 300fr #a.-f. 8.50 8.50
1546 A246 450fr #a.-f. 12.00 12.00
1547 A246 750fr #a.-f. 21.00 21.00

Souvenir Sheets

1548 A246 2500fr multi 11.00 11.00
1549-1551 A246 Set of 3 40.00 40.00

Mushrooms and Insects — A247

Mushrooms and unidentified insects: No. 1552, 100fr, Lentinellus cochleatus. No. 1553, 100fr, Lactarius blennius. No. 1554, 150fr, Lactarius sanguifluus. No. 1555, 150fr, Leucocortinarius bulbiger. No. 1556, 300fr, Clitocybe phyllophila. No. 1557, 300fr, Calocybe ionides. No. 1558, 300fr, Lactarius porninsis. No. 1559, 300fr, Cystoderma amianthinum. No. 1560, 300fr, Limacella guttata. No. 1561, 450fr, Suillus placidus. No. 1562, 450fr, Suillus grevillei. No. 1563, 450fr, Suillus luteus. No. 1564, 450fr, Suillus granulatus. No. 1565, 450fr, Pleurotus cornuscopiae. No. 1566, 450fr, Calocybe carnea. No. 1567, 450fr, Panus tigrinus.

Mushrooms and insects — No. 1568: a, Hygrocybe nigreseens, Argynnis paphia. b, Hygrocybe subglobispora, Pterophoridae. c, Oudemansiella mucida, Tettigonia viridissima. d, Amanita rubescens, unidentified insect. e, Amanita muscaria, Oedipoda caerulescens. f, Suillus luteus, Happarchia fagi. g, Coprinus picaceus, Aphantopus hyperantus. h, Gymnopilus junonius, Ourapteryx sambucaria. i, Amanita muscaria, Catocala nupta.

No. 1569: a, Macrolepiota procera, Pieris brassicae. b, Lactarius britannicus, Pyrochroa cocci. c, Cortinarius sanguineus, Tabicina haematodes. d, Amanita muscaria, Sympetrum. e, Aerocomus badius, Issoria lathonia. f, Laccaria amethystea, Sympetrum. g, Paxillus atrotomentosus, Inachis io. h, Armillaria mellea, Chrystoxum cautum. i, Amanita echinocephala, Vanessa atalanta.

Each 2500fr: No. 1570, Lactarius brittanicus, Coccinella punctala. No. 1571, Amanita phalloides, Ochlodes venatus. No. 1572, Coprinus atramentarius, unidentified insect.

Each 3000fr: No. 1573, Amanita citrina, unidentified insect. No. 1574, Amanita pantherina, Aperia syringaria.

1999, Nov. 11

1552-1567 A247 Set of 16 24.00 24.00

Sheets of 9

1568 A247 300fr #a.-i. 12.00 12.00
1569 A247 450fr #a.-i. 18.00 18.00

Souvenir Sheets

1570-1572 A247 Set of 3 35.00 35.00
1573-1574 A247 Set of 2 24.00 24.00

A248

Birds — A249

Designs: No. 1575, 200fr, Catamblyrhychus diadema. No. 1576, 200fr, Tichodrome. No. 1577, 300fr, Turtle dove. No. 1578, 300fr, Flamingo. No. 1579, 300fr, Duck. No. 1580, 300fr, Woodpecker. No. 1581, 450fr, Warbler. No. 1582, 450fr, Bullfinch.

No. 1583: a, Wild turkey. b, Ring-necked pheasant. c, Gray partridge. d, Woodcock. e, Capercaillie. f, Rock partridge.

No. 1584: a, Cuban hummingbird. b, Rufous-breated hermit. c, Green-throated hummingbird. d, Bee-eater. e, Puerto Rican hummingbird. f, Antillean hummingbird.

No. 1585: a, Gould's finch. b, Oriole. c, Psarisomus dalhousiae. d, Woodchat shrike. e, Pitta guajana. f, Neodreponis coruscans.

No. 1586, horiz.: a, Purple-throated Carib. b, Bahamas hummingbird. c, Blue-bearded hummingbird. d, Green hummingbird. e, Jamaican hummingbird. f, Vervaine.

Each 2500fr: No. 1587, Spotted waxwing. No. 1588, Red-banded bee-eater.

Each 2500fr: No. 1589, Bahamas hummingbird, horiz. No. 1590, Antillean crested hummingbird.

No. 1591, 3000fr, Emerald hummingbird.

1999, Nov. 22

1575-1582 A248 Set of 8 10.00 10.00

Sheets of 6

1583 A248 450fr #a.-f. 12.00 12.00
1584 A249 500fr #a.-f. 15.00 15.00
1585 A248 600fr #a.-f. 16.00 16.00
1586 A249 750fr #a.-f. 20.00 20.00

Souvenir Sheets

1587-1588 A248 Set of 2 24.00 24.00
1589-1590 A249 Set of 2 24.00 24.00
1591 A249 3000fr multi 14.00 14.00

Butterflies A250

Designs: No. 1592, 300fr, Acraea acerata. No. 1593, 300fr, Charaxes protoclea. No. 1594, 300fr, Charaxes hadrianus. No. 1595, 300fr, Colotis halimede. No. 1596, 300fr, Colotis eucharis. No. 1597, 300fr, Papilio dardanus.

No. 1598, vert.: a, Papilio charopus. b, Papilio dardanus. c, Acraea zetes. d, Hypolimnas salmacis. e, Cymothoe beckeri. f, Papilio nobilis.

No. 1599, vert.: a, Iolaus lalos. b, Graphium gudenusi. c, Hewitsonia boisduvali. d, Graphium ucalegon. e, Danaus chrysippus. f, Acraea satis.

Each 2500fr: No. 1600, Euxanthe tiberius. No. 1601, Colotis danae.

1999, Nov. 22

1592-1597 A250 Set of 6 7.50 7.50

Sheets of 6

1598 A250 450fr #a.-f. 12.00 12.00
1599 A250 750fr #a.-f. 20.00 20.00

Souvenir Sheets

1600-1601 A250 Set of 2 24.00 24.00

Wedding of Prince Edward and Sophie Rhys-Jones A251

No. 1602: a, Edward in blue striped shirt. b, Sophie with scarf. c, Edward looking left. d, Sophie looking right. e, Edward with blue checked shirt. f, Sophie with black blouse.

3000fr, Couple.

1999, Dec. 6

1602 A251 750fr Sheet of 6, #a.-f. 21.00 21.00

Souvenir Sheet

1603 A251 3000fr multi 14.00 14.00

Hokusai Paintings A252

No. 1604, each 750fr: a, Actor Ichikawa Ebizo. b, Drawings (man with fan). c, Actor Sakata Hangoro. d, Geisha and Madam. e, Drawings (man with sword). f, Kabuki Actor Hanshiro IV.

No. 1605, each 750fr: a, Kintaro and Wild Animals. b, Drawings (man with clasped hands). c, Lady Walking in the Snow. d, Lady and Maiden on an Outing. e, Drawings (man with incense burner). f, Girls at Their Toilette.

Each 3000fr: No. 1606, Sumo Wrestlers. No. 1607, Geisha House and Madam at Leisure with Child.

1999, Dec. 6 *Perf. 12¼*

Sheets of 6, #a.-f.

1604-1605 A252 Set of 2 35.00 35.00

Souvenir Sheets

1606-1607 A252 Set of 2 27.50 27.50

Johann Wolfgang von Goethe (1749-1832), German Poet — A253

No. 1608, each 1000fr: a, Mephistopheles tempts Faust with Margaret. b, Goethe and Friedrich von Schiller. c, The witches' kitchen, a potion brewed.

3000fr, Euphorion.

1999, Dec. 6 *Perf. 14*

1608 A253 Sheet of 3, #a.-c. 14.00 14.00

Souvenir Sheet

1609 A253 3000fr multi 14.00 14.00

A254

A255

Space Exploration — A256

Designs: No. 1610, 300fr, Pioneer 10. No. 1611, 300fr, Viking 1.

No. 1612: a, Takao Doi. b, Frank Borman. c, Alan B. Shepard, Jr. d, M. Scott Carpenter. e, Ulf Merbold. f, David R. Scott. g, Mamoru Mohri. h, Gherman Titov. i, Sally K. Ride. j, Walter M. Schirra. k, John L. Swigert, Jr. l, Yuri A. Gagarin.

No. 1613, each 500fr: a, Venus. b, Neptune. c, Jupiter. d, Uranus. e, Saturn. f, Mercury.

No. 1614, each 500fr: a, Mariner 4. b, HL-20. c, Mariner 2. d, Voyager 1. e, Venture Star. f, Phobos.

No. 1615, each 750fr: a, 1961 drawing of lunar ferry. b, 1960 drawing of lunar lander. c, 1959 drawing of lunar lander. d, 1962 drawing of lunar lander. e, 1962 drawing of lunar lander trainer. f, 1961 drawing of lunar lander.

No. 1616, vert, each 750fr: a, Apollo 5. b, Apollo 6, c, Apollo 7. d, Apollo escape test. e, Apollo "Little Joe." f, Apollo 4.

No. 1617, 1500fr, John Glenn.

No. 1618, 1500fr, Apollo 11 command module, vert. No. 1619, 1500fr, Collecting moon rocks.

No. 1620, 2000fr, Viking, diff. No. 1621, 2000fr, Mars Global Surveyor. No. 1622, 2000fr, Sojourner.

1999, Dec. 9

1610-1611 A254 Set of 2 3.00 3.00

Sheet of 12, #a.-l.

1612 A255 450fr multi 27.50 27.50

Sheets of 6, #a.-f.

1613-1614 A254 Set of 2 24.00 24.00
1615-1616 A256 Set of 2 40.00 40.00

Souvenir Sheets

1617 A255 1500fr multi 8.00 8.00
1618-1619 A256 Set of 2 15.00 15.00
1620-1622 A254 Set of 3 26.50 26.50

Nos. 1620-1622 each contain one 50x37mm stamp.

Queen Mother (b. 1900) — A257

No. 1623: a, In 1934. b, With tiara. c, Lady of the Garter. d, In 1997.

3000fr, With tiara, diff.

1999, Dec. 6 *Perf. 14*

1623 A257 1000fr Sheet of 4, #a.-d., + label 19.00 19.00

Souvenir Sheet
Perf. 13¾

1624 A257 3000fr multi 14.00 14.00

No. 1624 contains one 38x50mm stamp.

Cats A257a

Designs: 300fr, Ragdoll. No. 1626, 400fr, Egyptian Mau.

No. 1627, vert.: a, Tonkinese. b, Korat. c, Siamese. d, British Shorthair. e, Bengal. f, Persian.

1500fr, Calico Shorthair, vert.

1999 *Perf. 14*

1625-1626 A257a Set of 2 3.25 3.25

Sheet of 6

1627 A257a 450fr #a.-f. 12.00 12.00

Souvenir Sheet

1628 A257a 1500fr multi 8.00 8.00

Romance of the Three Kingdoms — A258

No. 1629, each 460fr: a, Archer and four men. b, Two men and tea pot. c, Spear carrier, man, woman. d, Horsemen jousting. e, Four men.

No. 1630, each 460fr: a, Swordsman on white horse. b, Spear carrier on black horse. c, Bed chamber. d, Man being speared. e, At sea.

2000fr, Three men with tea cups.

1999 Sheets of 5, #a.-e. *Perf. 13¼*

1629-1630 A258 Set of 2 20.00 20.00

Souvenir Sheet

1631 A258 2000fr multi 9.00 9.00

No. 1631 contains one 48x58mm stamp.

Millennium — A354

No. 1823 — Marco Polo's Voyage: a, Young Marco Polo. b, Piazza San Marco. c, Polo's ship. d, Priest buying incense. e, Houses in Syria. f, Ruins of Saveh. g, Persian ventilator. h, Moncia costume. i, Ulan Bator Abbey. j, Buddha, 5th cent. k, Great Wall of China. l, Warrior of Kublai Khan's Army. m, Ship on the Yangtze. n, Japanese archer. o, Golden plate. p, Medallion of Marco Polo, horiz. (60x40mm). q, Kublai Khan.

No. 1824 — Expansion of Knowledge: a, Election of King Sigismund I of Hungary as Holy Roman Emperor, 1411. b, Filippo Brunelleschi wins architectural contest to build the dome of the Santa Maria de Fiore, 1420. c, Lorenzo Ghiberti sculpts human forms on doors of the Florence Baptistry, 1425. d, Death of Juliana of Norwich, c. 1443. e, Chinese Ming capital moves from Nanjing to Beijing, 1420. f, Europeans begin to use Chinese method of black printing, 1423. g, King Henry V of England defeats French at Battle of Agincourt, 1415. h, Tamerlane defeats Ottomans at Battle of Ankyra, 1402. i, Joan of Arc leads French forces at Siege of Orleans, 1429. j, Korea prospers under rule of King Sejong, 1419. k, Thomas à Kempis writes *The Imitation of Christ*, 1427. l, King Casimir IV of Poland unites Polish Kingdom with Grand Duchy of Lithuania, 1447. m, End of the Great Schism, 1417. n, John Hus burnt at the stake, 1415. o, Medici family dominates the government of Florence, 1434. p, Chaucer completes *Canterbury Tales,* 1400, horiz. (60x40mm). q, Shogun Yoshima Ashikaga begins rule in Japan, 1449.

No. 1825 — Across the Continents: a, Engraving, c. 1598. b, Caribbean warriors. c, Viking ship, 12th cent. d, Ship of Vasco da Gama. e, Detail from Italian engraving. f, Columbus's letter of 1493. g, Kokyrboom tree, h, Megalzina virens. i, Details from a map, Moon between Earth and Sun. j, Details from a map, Earth between Sun and Moon. k, Maori wood carving. l, Astrolabes. m, Frilled lizard (inscribed "Gila monster"). n, White ibises. o, Tahitian utensils. p, Ocean monsters, horiz. (60x40mm). q, Samoan boat.

Perf. 12¾x12½

2000, Feb. 18 **Litho.**

Sheets of 17, #a-q, + Label

1823	A354 200fr multi		16.00	16.00
1824	A354 250fr multi		21.00	21.00
1825	A354 300fr multi		24.00	24.00
	Nos. 1823-1825 (3)		61.00	61.00

New Year 2000 (Year of the Dragon) — A355

No. 1826 — Dragon with background in: a, Red, claws near "Office." b, Green. c, Blue. d, Red, tail near "Office."

2000fr, Light blue.

2000, Feb. 18 *Perf. 13¾*

1826 A355 400fr Sheet of 4, #a-d 7.50 7.50

Souvenir Sheet

1827 A355 2000fr multi 9.50 9.50

No. 1826 contains four 48x32mm stamps.

Miniature Sheet

Vacation Photographs — A356

No. 1828: Various photographs making up a photomosaic of the Titanic.

2000, Feb. 18

1828 A356 750fr Sheet of 8, #a-h 24.00 24.00

2000 Summer Olympics, Sydney — A357

No. 1829: a, Women's discus. b, Javelin. c, Men's discus. d, Shot put. e, Hammer throw.

No. 1830: a, Women's volleyball. b, Water polo. c, Women's beach volleyball. d, Handball. e, Women's soccer.

No. 1831: a, Women's judo. b, Wrestling. c, Men's judo. d, Boxing, pink background. e, Boxing, green background.

No. 1832: a, Women's diving. b, Synchronized swimming. c, Women's swimming. d, Women's sailing. e, Kayaking.

No. 1833: a, Badminton. b, Field hockey. c, Baseball. d, Fencing. e, Weight lifting.

No. 1834: a, Dressage. b, Archery. c, Show jumping. d, Rifle shooting. e, Pistol shooting.

No. 1835: a, Table tennis, two men. b, Table tennis, one man, blue and purple background. c, Table tennis, one man, green and yellow background. d, Women's table tennis. e, Table tennis, four players.

No. 1836: a, Women's tennis, blue background. b, Men's tennis, green background. c, Women's tennis, bister background. d, Men's tennis, gray background. e, Men's tennis, blue background.

No. 1837: a, Women's basketball. b, Men's basketball (Michael Jordan dunking basketball). c, Men's basketball, two players. d, Men's basketball (Jordan dribbling). e, Men's basketball, blue background.

No. 1838: a, Cycling Road Race (Route). b, Cycling Sprint Race (Vitesse). c, Cycling Team Pursuit. d, Cycling Points Race (Kilometre). e, Cycling Time Trial (Contre la montre).

2000, Nov. 14 *Perf. 13¼*

Sheets of 5, #a-e, + Label

1829	A357 150fr multi	3.50	3.50
1830	A357 150fr multi	3.50	3.50
1831	A357 200fr multi	4.50	4.50
1832	A357 200fr multi	4.50	4.50
1833	A357 300fr multi	7.00	7.00
1834	A357 300fr multi	7.00	7.00
1835	A357 600fr multi	13.50	13.50
1836	A357 600fr multi	13.50	13.50
1837	A357 750fr multi	17.00	17.00
1838	A357 750fr multi	17.00	17.00
	Nos. 1829-1838 (10)	91.00	91.00

Sports and Chess — A358

No. 1839 — Golf: a, Golfer with purple cap. b, Golfer with white pants. c, Golfer with white cap. d, Golfer with green shirt.

No. 1840 — Soccer: a, Marcel Dessally. b, Zinedine Zidane. c, Youri Djorkaeff. d, Thierry Henry.

No. 1841 — Auto racing: a, Ayrton Senna. b, Mika Hakkinen. c, Alain Prost. d, Michael Schumacher.

No. 1842 — Chess: a, Player with hands on forehead. b, Player with blue jacket. c, Player with gray jacket. d, Female player.

2000, Nov. 14 **Sheets of 4, #a-d**

1839	A358 450fr multi	8.00	8.00
1840	A358 450fr multi	8.00	8.00
1841	A358 750fr multi	14.00	14.00
1842	A358 750fr multi	14.00	14.00
	Nos. 1839-1842 (4)	44.00	44.00

Locomotives — A359

No. 1843, horiz.: a, De Witt Clinton. b, American 220. c, Triplet Mallet. d, Philadelphia & Reading 422 Baldwin. e, Mason Bogie. f, Promontory Point 220 No. 119. g, Mogul. h, Best Friend of Charleston. i, John Bull.

No. 1844, horiz.: a, Union Pacific Bo-Bo-Bo-Bo. b, Bipolar No. 2. c, Burlington Northern-Series SD 40-2 No. 7044. d, Amtrak Metroliner No. 880. e, Rio Grande Western Series F. f, Union Pacific Series DD 40AX. g, Lake Superior & Ishpeming Co-Co 025C No. 2500. h, Chicago, Milwaukee, St. Paul & Pacific Bipolar 3000V No. 4. i, Southern Pacific Krauss-Maffei C-C No. 9006.

No. 1845, horiz.: a, Southern Pacific GM-EMD Series F No. 98. b, Union Pacific M-10001. c, Union Pacific Switcher No. 4466. d, Chesapeake & Ohio Series M No. 500. e, Amtrak Series P32 No. 513. f, Southern Pacific EMD SD 40-2 No. 9368. g, Great Northern Series W-1 No. 5018. h, Grand Canyon 140. i, Pennsylvania Railroad 6100.

No. 1846, horiz.: a, Burlington Northern Santa Fe No. 4326. b, Conrail Series GP EMD No. 8194. c, Kansas City Southern No. 6639. d, Southern Pacific No. 9800. e, Pennsylvania Railroad 661 No. 4835. f, Union Pacific No. 8182. g, Burlington Northern No. 2917. h, Gulf, Mobile & Ohio Railroad Series F. i, Santa Fe No. 627.

No. 1847, horiz.: a, Norfolk Southern No. 6627. b, Grand Trunk No. 6219. c, Soo Line No. 6401. d, Santa Fe BNSF No. 2512. e, Chessie System No. 6035. f, Utah Railway No. 9010. g, Chicago & Northwestern No. 6866. h, Norfolk Southern No. 3328. i, Canadian National No. 4634.

No. 1848, horiz.: a, Canadian Pacific Budd Autorail Diesel No. 9112. b, New York Central 2-Do-2 No. 113. c, British Columbia Railway Series C630 No. 703. d, Chesapeake & Ohio Series GP9 No. 6137. e, Amtrak 661 No. 902. f, Santa Fe GP9 No. 2293. g, Trainmaster Type Co-Co. h, Chicago, Burlington & Quincy Pioneer Zephyr. i, Denver & Rio Grande Western No. 5350.

No. 1849, 2000fr, Tom Thumb, 2-2-0. No. 1850, 2000fr, Norfolk & Western Class J. No. 1851, 2000fr, Royal Gorge CC No. 403. No. 1852, 2000fr, Hudson 4-6-4 No. 490.

2000, Dec. 7 **Sheets of 9, #a-i**

1843	A359 200fr multi	5.25	5.25
1844	A359 300fr multi	8.00	8.00
1845	A359 350fr multi	10.00	10.00
1846	A359 400fr multi	11.00	11.00
1847	A359 450fr multi	12.00	12.00
1848	A359 500fr multi	14.00	14.00
	Nos. 1843-1848 (6)	60.25	60.25

Souvenir Sheets

1849-1852 A359 Set of 4 22.50 22.50

Nos. 1843-1848 each contain nine 51x36mm stamps.

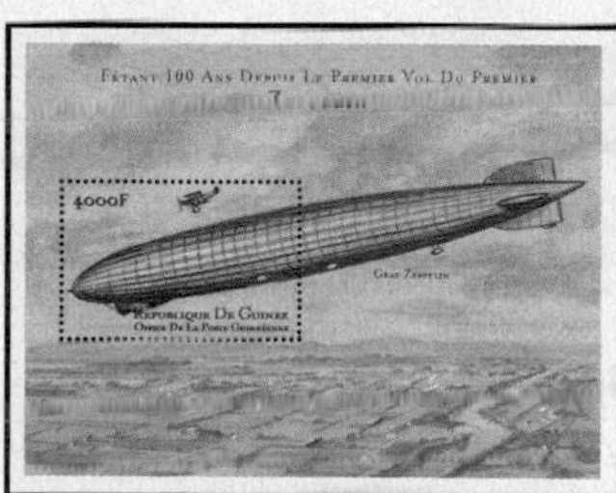
A360

First Zeppelin flight, Cent. — A361

No. 1853: a, Zeppelin LZ-11 Viktoria Luise. b, E. T. Willows. c, Hindenburg. d, Astra-Torres 1. e, Beta. f, Schutte-Lanz SL3.

No. 1854: a, Gross-Basenach M1. b, Schutte-Lanz SL1. c, Parseval PL25. d, Siemens-Schuckert. e, Delta. f, Parseval PL VIII.

No. 1855: a, LZ-9. b, LZ-10 Schwaben. c, LZ-11 Viktoria Luise, diff. d, LZ-127 Graf Zeppelin. e, LZ-129 Hindenburg. f, LZ-130.

No. 1856: a, LZ-1. b, LZ-2. c, LZ-3. d, LZ-4. e, LZ-5. f, LZ-6.

No. 1857, Graf Zeppelin and airplane. No. 1858, LZ-1, diff.

2000, Dec. 11 *Perf. 14*

Sheets of 6, #a-f

1853	A360	300fr multi		8.50	8.50
1854	A360	450fr multi		12.00	12.00
1855	A361	1000fr multi		27.50	27.50
1856	A361	1000fr multi		27.50	27.50
	Nos. 1853-1856 (4)			75.50	75.50

Souvenir Sheets

1857	A360	4000fr multi	20.00	20.00
1858	A361	4000fr multi	20.00	20.00

Miniature Sheet

Flowers — A362

No. 1859: Various photographs making up a photomosaic of Queen Mother Elizabeth.

2000, Dec. 11

1859	A362	750fr	Sheet of 8, #a-h	20.00	20.00

Prince William of Wales, 18th Birthday — A363

No. 1860: a, Wearing red tie. b, Wearing black and white checked tie. c, With Prince Harry. d, Wearing blue sweater.

4000fr, Wearing scarf.

2000, Dec. 11 *Perf. 14*

1860	A363	1000fr	Sheet of 4, #a-d	18.00	18.00

Souvenir Sheet

Perf. 13¾

1861	A363	4000fr multi	19.00	19.00

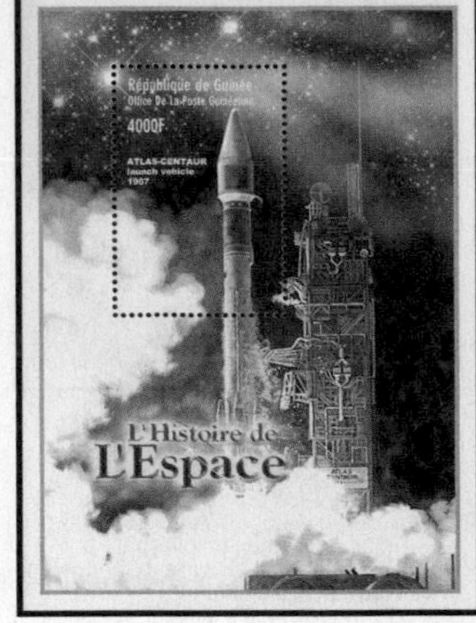

History of Space Exploration — A364

No. 1862, 200fr: a, Discovery of gunpowder. b, Fire arrows. c, Wan Hu's rocket glider. d, Konstantin Tsiolkovsky. e, Telescope of William Herschel. f, Galileo Galilei. g, Nicolaus Copernicus. h, Robert H. Goddard. i, Paper hot air balloons. j, Wernher von Braun. k, Launch of first rocket by Goddard. l, V-1 missile buzz-bomb.

No. 1863, 200fr: a, First American spacewalk by Ed White, Gemini 4. b, First man on the Moon, Apollo 11. c, Space Shuttle Atlantis. d, Voskhod 2. e, Sputnik 1. f, Apollo-Soyuz. g, John Glenn, first American to orbit Earth. h, Valentina Tereshkova, first woman in space. i, Yuri Gagarin, first man in space. j, Apollo 17. k, Robotic lunar explorer. l, Hubble Space Telescope.

No. 1864, 4000fr, Atlas-Centaur launch vehicle. No. 1865, 4000fr, International Space Station.

2000, Dec. 11 *Perf. 14*

Sheets of 12, #a-l

1862-1863	A364	Set of 2	17.00	17.00

Souvenir Sheets

1864-1865	A364	Set of 2	12.00	12.00

Apollo-Soyuz Mission, 25th Anniv. — A365

No. 1866, 1000fr: a, Saturn IB rocket. b, Apollo 18 command and service modules with docking adapter. c, Apollo 18 Commander Thomas P. Stafford. d, A-2 Soyuz rocket. e, Soyuz 19 spacecraft. f, Soyuz 19 Commander Alexei Leonov.

No. 1867, 1000fr, vert.: a, Lunar Module Eagle, upside-down. b, Lunar Module Eagle, with thrusters firing. c, Apollo 11 command module Columbia. d, Edwin E. Aldrin, Jr. on lunar module ladder. e, Apollo 11 Saturn V rocket. f, Re-entry of Apollo 11 capsule.

4000fr, Aldrin and lunar module on Moon.

2000, Dec. 11 **Sheets of 6, #a-f**

1866-1867	A365	Set of 2	42.50	42.50

Souvenir Sheet

1868	A365	4000fr multi	6.00	6.00

Marine Life — A367

Designs: No. 1873, 400fr, Coral grouper. No. 1874, 400fr, Candy cane sea star. 450fr, Hippocampus kuda.

No. 1876, 750fr: a, Chromis caerulea. b, Brittle star. c, Calloplesiops altivelis. d, Ewa blenny. e, Coral polyp. f, Butterflyfish.

No. 1877, 750fr: a, Chelonia mydas. b, Ptereleotris evides. c, Halichoeres iridis. d, Sea fan. e, Florometra serratissima. f, Gramma loreto.

No. 1878, 5000fr, Clownfish. No. 1879, 5000fr, Bigeye scad, horiz.

Perf. 13½x13¼, 13¼x13½

2001, Feb. 28

1873-1875	A367	Set of 3	5.50	5.50

Sheets of 6, #a-f

1876-1877	A367	Set of 2	40.00	40.00

Souvenir Sheets

1878-1879	A367	Set of 2	42.50	42.50

Marine Life A368

Designs: No. 1880, 400fr, Chaetodon semilarvatus. No. 1881, 400fr, Amphiprion ocellarus. No. 1882, 450fr, Gramma malecara. No. 1883, 450fr, Amphiprion bicinctuc.

No. 1884, 200fr: a, Diodon hystrix. b, Synchiropus splendidos. c, Lactoria cornuta. d, Canthigaster solandri. e, Gymnothorax tesselatus. f, Gramma loreto.

No. 1885, 200fr: a, Synchiropus picturatus. b, Pygoplytes diacanthus. c, Pomocanthus imperator. d, Holocanthus ciliaris. e, Phinecanthus aculeatus. f, Lienardella fasciatus.

No. 1886, 5000fr, Pterois antennata, vert. No. 1887, 5000fr, Hippocampus kuda, vert.

Perf. 13¼x13½, 13½x13¼

2001, Feb. 28

1880-1883	A368	Set of 4	6.00	6.00

Sheets of 6, #a-f

1884-1885	A368	Set of 2	9.00	9.00

Souvenir Sheets

1886-1887	A368	Set of 2	35.00	35.00

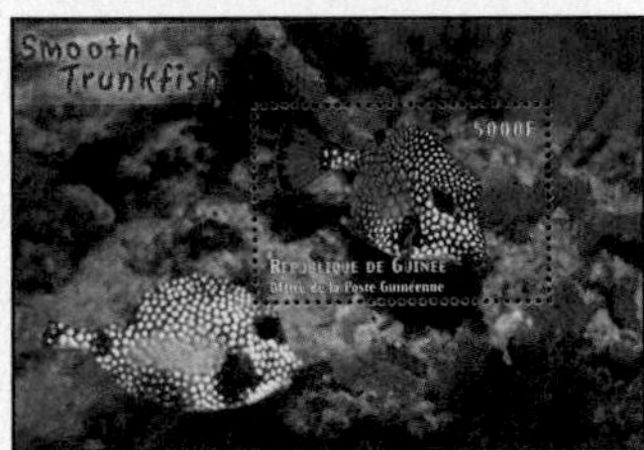

Marine Life — A369

No. 1888, 1000fr: a, Jackknife fish. b, Requiem shark. c, Great white shark (Grand blanc). d, Holocanthus ciliaris. e, Brain coral. f, Bluehead wrasse.

No. 1889, 1000fr: a, Sergeant major. b, Bottlenose dolphin. c, Swordfish. d, Sea horse. e, Slate pencil urchin. f, Gold-spotted snake eel.

No. 1890, 1000fr: a, Great white shark (Grand requin blanc). b, Baird's beaked whale. c, Butterflyfish. d, Turtle. e, Solenostomus paradoxus. f, Australian pineapple fish.

No. 1891, 1000fr: a, Hawksbill turtle. b, Killer whale. c, Manta ray. d, Filefish. e, Graysby. f, Striped-eel catfish.

No. 1892, 5000fr, Smooth trunkfish. No. 1879, 5000fr, Dolphin.

2001, Feb. 28 *Perf. 13¼x13½*

Sheets of 6, #a-f

1888-1891	A369	Set of 4	80.00	80.00

Souvenir Sheets

1892-1893	A369	Set of 2	35.00	35.00

Flora and Fauna — A370

No. 1894, 300fr — Bears: a, Spectacled bear. b, Giant panda. c, Silver bear. d, Cannelle (Pyreneean bear). e, Syrian bear. f, Grizzly bear.

No. 1895, 300fr — Primates: a, Howler monkey. b, Macaque. c, Drill. d, Yellow baboon. e, Anubis baboon. f, Gelada.

No. 1896, 300fr, vert. — Lemurs: a, Crowned lemur (couronné). b, Black lemur (macao). c, Albifrons lemur. d, Mongoz lemur. e, Sanfordi lemur. f, Fulvus lemur.

No. 1897, 300fr, vert. — Fish: a, Sebastes nigrocinctus. b, Lampris guttatus. c, Cyclopterus lumpus. d, Carnegiella strigata. e, Parosphromenus dreissneri. f, Syncniropus splendidus.

No. 1898, 300fr, vert. — Flowers: a, Peony (Pivoine des rocheuses). b, Hypericum richeri. c, Flamboyant. d, Bird of paradise (oiseau du paradis). e, Hesperantha petitiana. f, Moraea neopavonia.

No. 1899, 750fr — Lemurs: a, Lepilemur leucopus. b, Wooly avahi (avahi laineux). c, Black lemur (macao). d, Verreaux's sifaka (Propithecus verreauxi deckeni). e, Phaner. f, Verreaux's sifaka (Propithecus verrauxi majori).

No. 1900, 750fr — Flowers: a, Thunia alba. b, Eulophia guineensis. c, Polystacha bella. d, Oeceoclades maculata. e, Serapias cordigera. f, Angraecum distichum.

No. 1901, 750fr — Birds: a, Black cockatoo. b, Rosalbin cockatoo. c, Leadbetter's cockatoo. d, Goffin's cockatoo. e, Gray parrot. f, Senegal parrot.

No. 1902, 750fr, vert. — Owls: a, Hibou des marais. b, Hibou petit duc. c, Grand duc Americain. d, Chouette chevechette perlée. e, Hibou grand duc. f, Harphang des neiges.

No. 1903, 750fr, vert. — Insects: a, Giant Himalayan bee. b, Phyllium. c, Magicicada septemdecim. d, Petasida ephippigera. e, Graphosoma semipunctatum. f, Honeybee.

2001, Mar. 28 **Litho.** *Perf. 13¼*

Sheets of 6, #a-f

1894-1903	A370	Set of 10	125.00	125.00

Guinean Railways Locomotive A371

Design: 200fr, Front view. 300fr, Side view, horiz. 750fr, Rear view.

2001, May 16

1904-1906	A371	Set of 3	5.50	5.50

Nos. 1904-1906 each exist in souvenir sheets of 1, containing stamps lacking printer's inscription.

Locomotives — A372

Designs: 300fr, Union Pacific Jupiter. 400fr, No. 7200 Philadelphia. 600fr, C-28 Type 2-8-0. 800fr, Wainwright P Type 0-6-0. 1300fr, Union Pacific Rogers 119. 1600fr, Northwestern 4-6-0 steam engine.

No. 1913, 950fr: a, Oliver Cromwell. b, Big Boy 4-8-8-4 No. 4019. c, 1858 Rogers. d, Gray Lady. e, Old No. 1. f, Jones Goods 4-6-0.

No. 1914, 950fr: a, Jubilee Type No. SS96. b, Iron Horse. c, 4-6-0. d, Type OS2 2-10-0. e, Single Driver 1887 Johnson. f, King George V 4-6-0.

No. 1915, 950fr: a, Hardwicke Western 2-4-0, No. 790. b, High-wheeled Pacific, Texas State Railroad. c, Longhorne. d, City of Truro 4-4-0 No. 3440. e, Leander Type Jubilee. f, The American.

No. 1916, 4000fr, Stanier Black 5-4-6-0. No. 1917, 4000fr, LMS 5305. No. 1918, 4000fr, Duchess of Hamilton.

2001, June 8 *Perf. 13¼x13½*

1907-1912 A372 Set of 6 21.00 21.00

Sheets of 6, #a-f

1913-1915 A372 Set of 3 70.00 70.00

Souvenir Sheets

1916-1918 A372 Set of 3 55.00 55.00

Locomotives — A373

Designs: 500fr, Ae 6/6 Co-Co electric. 750fr, Hikari Super Express. 1000fr, Krauss-Maffei V200 Diesel-electric. 1250fr, 46 Type electric.

No. 1923, 950fr: a, EW Type Bo-Bo-Bo electric. b, 68000 Type Diesel-electric. c, Type Ge 6/6 electric. d, 19,000 horsepower Diesel-electric. e, Express Co-Co electric. f, AL6 Bo-Bo electric.

No. 1924, 950fr: a, 1,750 horsepower Diesel-electric. b, 7000 Co-Co electric. c, Type E10 Bo-Bo electric. d, D341 Type Diesel-electric. e, Diesel-hydraulic express. f, 5E1 electric.

No. 1925, 4000fr, Santa Fe F9 Diesel-electric. No. 1926, 4000fr, Type SSI Co-Co electric. No. 1918, 4000fr, Union Pacific electric.

2001, June 8

1919-1922 A373 Set of 4 15.00 15.00

Sheets of 6, #a-f

1923-1924 A373 Set of 2 45.00 45.00

Souvenir Sheets

1925-1927 A373 Set of 3 55.00 55.00

Belgica 2001 Intl. Stamp Exhibition, Brussels.

Locomotives — A374

Designs: 750fr, Type 18 4-6-2. 1000fr, ICE. 1250fr, Type G.

No. 1931, 950fr: a, Type WP 4-6-2. b, ETR 450. c, EU-07 Bo-Bo. d, Type 25 4-8-4. e, TGV. f, Type 345 Bo-Bo.

No. 1932, 950fr: a, Type SY 2-6-2. b, GM F7 War Bonnet. c, Type 4-4-0. d, Type A2/1 4-6-2. e, Type BB 22200. f, Type OL-49 4-6-2.

No. 1933, 4000fr, VT601. No. 1934, 4000fr, Type QJ 2-10-2.

2001, June 8

1928-1930 A374 Set of 3 13.00 13.00

Sheets of 6, #a-f

1931-1932 A374 Set of 2 45.00 45.00

Souvenir Sheets

1933-1934 A374 Set of 2 37.50 37.50

Belgica 2001 Intl. Stamp Exhibition, Brussels.

Famous People — A375

No. 1935 — Explorers: a, Vasco da Gama. b, Sir Francis Drake. c, Ferdinand Magellan. d, Capt. James Cook. e, Jacques Cartier. f, Christopher Columbus.

No. 1936: a, Albert Einstein. b, Albert Schweitzer. c, Henri Dunant. d, Sir Alexander Fleming. e, Marie Curie. f, Louis Pasteur.

No. 1937 — Space pioneers: a, Yuri Gagarin. b, John Glenn. c, Edward White. d, Neil Armstrong. e, John Young. f, Thomas Stafford and Alexei Leonov.

No. 1938 — Pope John Paul II: a, As baby, with mother and dove. b, Wearing miter and holding crucifix. c, In garden. d, Kneeling. e, Holding crucifix, with dove. f, With arms raised.

No. 1939 — Lord Robert Baden-Powell, Scouts and: a, Psittacus enthacus. b, Charaxes eupale. c, Pluvianus aegyptius. d, Catacroptera cloanthe. e, Merops albicollis. f, Euphaedra eupalus.

2001, June 14 *Perf. 13¼*

Sheets of 6, #a-f

1935 A375 350fr multi 10.00 10.00
1936 A375 450fr multi 12.00 12.00
1937 A375 475fr multi 13.00 13.00
1938 A375 600fr multi 16.00 16.00
1939 A375 750fr multi 21.00 21.00
Nos. 1935-1939 (5) 72.00 72.00

Nos. 1936a-1936f and 1939a-1939f each exist in souvenir sheets of one.

Birds — A377

Designs: 200fr, Guinea fowl (pintade vulturine). 250fr, African fish eagle (pygarve vocifer). 300fr, Striped hoopoe (huppe fasciée). 350fr, Jacana. 400fr, Secretary bird (serpentaire). 450fr, Wild Guinea fowl (pintade sauvage).

No. 1948, 950fr: a, Verreaux's eagle (aigle de verreaux). b, White pelican. c, Swallow (hirondelle de rivage). d, Egyptian geese (ouette d'Egypte). e, Crane (grue cendrée). f, Heron.

No. 1949, 950fr: a, Swallow (hirondelle de fenetre). b, Dwarf bee-eater (guepier nain). c, Blue rock thrush (merle solitaire rouge). d, Senegal jabiru. e, Ibis. f, Purple swamphen (talève sultane).

No. 1950, 950fr: a, Vulture (vautour chaugoun). b, Red and yellow barbet (barbican à tete rouge). c, Buzzard (buse rounoir). d, Tufted lark (cochevis). e, Gray wagtail (bergeronnette des ruisseaux). f, Red-heades shrike (pie grieche à tete rouge).

No. 1951, 4000fr, Flamingo (petit flamant). No. 1952, 4000fr, Anhinga. No. 1953, 4000fr, Marabout. No. 1954, 4000fr, Ostrich (autriche).

2001, Aug. 27 *Perf. 13½x13¼*

1942-1947 A377 Set of 6 8.50 8.50

Sheets of 6, #a-f

1948-1950 A377 Set of 3 52.50 52.50

Souvenir Sheets

1951-1954 A377 Set of 4 16.50 16.50

Phila Nippon '01, Japan (#1948-1954).

Birds — A378

Designs: 200fr, Heron. 300fr, Ibis. 500fr, Stonechat (tarier patre). 550fr, Sparrow (hirondelle striée). 600fr, Egyptian courser (pluvian fluviatile). 650fr, Jacana.

No. 1961, 750fr: a, Variable sunbird (soui-manga à ventre jaune). b, Long-tailed sunbird (soui-manga à longue queue). c, Scarlet-chested sunbird (soui-manga à poitrine rouge). d, Abyssinian roller (rollier d'Abyssinie). e, Blue-breasted roller (rollier à ventre bleu). f, Broad-billed roller (rolle violet).

No. 1962, 750fr: a, Black bee-eater (guepier noir). b, Blue-headed bee-eater (guepier à tete bleue). c, White-throated bee-eater (guepier à gorge blanche). d, Red-throated bee-eater (guepier à gorge rouge). e, Rosy bee-eater (guepier gris-rose). f, Carmine bee-eater (guepier supreme).

No. 1963, 750fr: a, Blue-breasted kingfisher (martin-chasseur à poitrine bleue). b, Gray-headed kingfisher (martin-chasseur à tete grise). c, Chocolate-backed kingfisher (martin-chasseur marron). d, Dwarf kingfisher (martin-pécheur à tete rousse). e, Malachite kingfisher (martin-pécheur huppé). f, Giant kingfisher (alcyon géant).

No. 1964, 4000fr, Touraco. No. 1965, 4000fr, White-faced whistling duck (dendrocygne veuf). No. 1966, 4000fr, Denham's bustard (outarde du Denham).

2001, Aug. 27

1955-1960 A378 Set of 6 11.00 11.00

Sheets of 6, #a-f

1961-1963 A378 Set of 3 55.00 55.00

Souvenir Sheets

1964-1966 A378 Set of 3 52.50 52.50

Phila Nippon '01, Japan (#1961-1966).

A379

Butterflies — A380

Designs: 700fr, Icolotis zoe. 750fr, Catopsilia florella. 800fr, Kallimoides rumia. 850fr, Charaxes eupale. No. 1971, 950fr, Physcaeneura leda. 1000fr, Mylothris chloris.

No. 1973, 900fr: a, Papilio demodocus. b, Anaphaeis auroto. c, Charaxes superbus. d, Amauris echeria. e, Euxanthe wakefieldi. f, Papilio dardanus.

No. 1974, 900fr: a, Hypolimnas salmacis. b, Myrena silenus. c, Charaxes smagardus. d, Papilio zalmoxis. e, Salamis parnassus. f, Charaxes bohemani.

No. 1975, 900fr: a, Charaxes fournierae. b, Eurema floricola. c, Mimacraea marshalli. d, Charaxes candiope. e, Catacroptera cloanthe. f, Danaus chrysippus.

No. 1976, 950fr: a, Castalius isis. b, Axioceres amanga. c, Eurema brenda. d, Epamera stenogrammica. e, Pseudaletis agrippina. f, Alaena margaritalea.

No. 1977, 950fr: a, Papilio dardanus, diff. b, Charaxes eupale, diff. c, Acraea cerasa. d, Precis clelia. e, Colotis celimene. f, Pseudacraea poggei.

No. 1978, 4000fr, Papilio antimachus. No. 1979, 4000fr, Acraea zetes. No. 1980, 4000fr, Colotis danae.

No. 1981, 4000fr, Hypolimnas deceptor. No. 1982, 4000fr, Euphaedra perseis.

2001, Aug. 27 *Perf. 13¼x13½*

1967-1972 A379 Set of 6 20.00 20.00

Sheets of 6, #a-f

1973-1975 A379 Set of 3 21.00 21.00
1976-1977 A380 Set of 2 35.00 35.00

Souvenir Sheets

1978-1980 A379 Set of 3 52.50 52.50
1981-1982 A380 Set of 2 35.00 35.00

Phila Nippon '01, Japan (#1973-1982). Rectangles replace the accented "e's" on all stamps of type A380.

Hummingbirds — A387

Designs: No. 2038, 900fr, Anthracothorax manga. No. 2039, 900fr, Eulampis holosericeus. No. 2040, 1000fr, Archilochus colubris. No. 2041, 1000fr, Chlorostilbon ricordii.

No. 2042, 1000fr: a, Selasphorus rufus. b, Mellisuga helenae. c, Eutoxeres aquila. d, Anthracothorax viridis. e, Allamanda cathartica. f, Orthorhynchus cristatus.

No. 2043, 1000fr: a, Archilochus alexandri. b, Calliphlox evelynae. c, Chlorostilbon maugaeus. d, Musta ornata. e, Phaethornis superciliosus. f, Eulampis jugularis.

No. 2044, 1000fr: a, Cyanophaia bicolor. b, Glaucis hirsuta. c, Chlorostilbon swainsonn. d, Heliconia. e, Heliconia bihal. f, Anthracothorax dominicus.

No. 2045, 4000fr, Amazilia violiceps. No. 2046, 4000fr, Trochilus scitulus. No. 2047, 4000fr, Trochilus polytmus, vert.

Perf. 13¼x13½, 13½x13¼

2001 **Litho.**

2038-2041 A387 Set of 4 14.00 14.00

Sheets of 6, #a-f

2042-2044 A387 Set of 3 65.00 65.00

Souvenir Sheets

2045-2047 A387 Set of 3 47.50 47.50

Trains of Africa
A390

Designs: No. 2050, 750fr, 0-6-4, Z.A.S.M, Transvaal, 1858. No. 2051, 750fr, 4-6-2, Central South Africa, 1858. No. 2052, 750fr, 4-4-0, Cape Province, 1903. No. 2053, 750fr, 4-8-2 Class 12, South Africa, 1920. No. 2054, 750fr, 4-6-2 Class 10 RB, South Africa, 1950. No. 2055, 750fr, 4-8-2, Benguela, 1951. No. 2056, 750fr, 4-6-4+4-6-4 Class 15A, South Africa, 1952. No. 2057, 750fr, 4-8-4 Class 25 NC, South Africa, 1953.

No. 2058, 200fr: a, Cape Province locomotive, 1895. b, 2-8-2, Central South Africa, 1920. c, 4-4-2, Cape Province, 1898. d, 4-8-2 Class 23, South Africa, 1930. e, Natal Province locomotive, 1901. f, 2-8-4 Class 24, South Africa, 1940.

No. 2059, 300fr: a, 4-6-2 Class 16E, South Africa, 1935. b, 4-8-4 Class 25, South Africa, 1953. c, 2-D-1+1-D-2 Class 20, South Africa, 1954. d, 4-8-2+2-8-4 Class 59, East Africa, 1955. e, 1-Co-Co-1 Class 92, East Africa, 1971. f, 2-D-2 Class 26, South Africa, 1982.

No. 2060, 750fr: a, 4-8-2 Class 15F, South Africa, 1948. b, 4-8-2+2-8-4 GEA Beyer-Garret, South Africa, 1950. c, 4-8-2 Class 11, South Africa, 1951. d, 4-8-2+2-8-4 GEA Beyer-Garrot, South Africa, 1954. e, 1-Co-Co-1 Class 4E, South Africa, 1954. f, Co-Co Class 9E, South Africa, 1978.

No. 2061, 4000fr, Umtali-Salisbury Class 4-4-0, 1897. No. 2062, 4000fr, Bo-Bo Class 5E, Blue Train, South Africa, 1969.

2002, Feb. 8 **Litho.** *Perf. 13¼x13½*

2050-2057 A390 Set of 8 21.00 21.00

Sheets of 6, #a-f

2058-2060 A390 Set of 3 26.50 26.50

Souvenir Sheets

2061-2062 A390 Set of 2 12.00 12.00

Watercraft — A391

Designs: No. 2063, 750fr, Three-masted schooner, 1866. No. 2064, 750fr, Two-masted schooner, 1932. No. 2065, 750fr, Bark, 1968. No. 2066, 750fr, Sailboard. No. 2067, 750fr, Galleass, 16th cent., horiz. No. 2068, 750fr, Sailboat, horiz.

No. 2069, 750fr: a, Galleon, 16th cent. b, 17th cent. ship. c, Corvette, 18th cent. d, Gaffrig yacht. e, Dinghy. f, Catamaran.

No. 2070, 4000fr, Full-rigged ship, 20th cent., horiz. No. 2071, 4000fr, Pinnace, 17th cent., horiz.

Perf. 13½x13¼, 13¼x13½

2002, Feb. 8

2063-2068 A391 Set of 6 16.00 16.00
2069 A391 750fr Sheet of 6, #a-f 17.00 17.00

Souvenir Sheets

2070-2071 A391 Set of 2 12.00 12.00

Nos. 2070-2071 each contain one 56x42mm stamp.

Airplanes and Ships — A392

No. 2072, 750fr: a, Wright Brothers Flyer. b, Super Sabre F-100. c, Junkers J1. d, De Havilland Comet. e, Douglas DC-3. f, Boeing 747.

No. 2073, 750fr: a, Egyptian wooden boat. b, 18th cent. sailboat. c, Viking longboat. d, Great Eastern. e, Spanish galleon, 16th cent. f, Savannah.

No. 2074, 4000fr, Concorde. No. 2075, 4000fr, Ocean Princess.

2002, Feb. 8 ***Perf. 13¼x13½***

Sheets of 6, #a-f

2072-2073 A392 Set of 2 9.25 9.25

Souvenir Sheets

2074-2075 A392 Set of 2 8.25 8.25

First Zeppelin Flight, Cent. — A393

No. 2076: a, LZ-3. b, LZ-5. c, USS Macon. d, Zeppelin NT.

No. 2077, 4000fr, LZ-4. No. 2078, 4000fr, LZ-129.

2002, Feb. 8

2076 A393 750fr Sheet of 4, #a-d 12.00 12.00

Souvenir Sheets

2077-2078 A393 Set of 2 12.00 12.00

Airplanes — A394

No. 2079: a, Lockheed Streamliner. b, Dornier Do-X. c, Lockheed Vega. d, Boeing 707. e, Douglas DC-3. f, De Havilland Comet.

4000fr, Concorde.

2002, Feb. 8

2079 A394 750fr Sheet of 6, #a-f 17.00 17.00

Souvenir Sheet

2080 A394 4000fr multi 6.00 6.00

Airplanes A395

Designs: No. 2081, 750fr, Tupelov TU-144. No. 2082, 750fr, Tri-star L-1011. No. 2083, 750fr, Airbus A-300-B. No. 2084, 750fr, Boeing 777-200.

No. 2085, 750fr: a, Junkers G-24. b, Armstrong Whitworth XV Atalanta. c, Aerospatiale SE 210 Caravelle III. d, De Havilland D. H. 106 Comet 4B. e, Armstrong Whitworth 650 Argosy 100. f, Douglas DC-9.

No. 2086, 750fr: a, Wright Brothers Flyer. b, Vickers Vimy. c, Spirit of St. Louis. d, Junkers G-38. e, Douglas DC-3. f, Vickers-Armstrong Viscount 700.

No. 2087, 4000fr, Boeing 747. No. 2088, 4000fr, Airbus A-3XX.

2002, Feb. 8

2081-2084 A395 Set of 4 11.00 11.00

Sheets of 6, #a-f

2085-2086 A395 Set of 2 32.50 32.50

Souvenir Sheets

2087-2088 A395 Set of 2 12.00 12.00

Military Aircraft A396

Designs: No. 2089, 750fr, Sopwith Camel. No. 2090, 750fr, Fokker Dr-1. No. 2091, 750fr, Messerschmitt Bf-109 E. No. 2092, 750fr, Mitsubishi Zero. No. 2093, 750fr, Northrop F-20 Tigershark. No. 2094, 750fr, Dassault-Breguet Mirage 2000.

No. 2095, 750fr: a, S.E. 5A. b, Fokker D-VII. c, Thomas Morse S4C. d, De Havilland D.H. 2. e, Boeing PW-9D. f, Spad XIII.

No. 2096, 750fr: a, Mustang P-51. b, Junkers Ju-87R. c, Curtiss Hawk 75A. d, Hawker Hurricane. e, Nakajima Ki-43 Hayabusa. f, Macchi M.C. 200 Saetta.

No. 2097, 750fr: a, Panavia Tornado Gr. Mk1. b, Mikoyan-Gurevich MiG-15. c, Vought A-7D Corsair 11. d, BAe Sea Harrier FRS Mk1. e, General Dynamics F-111. f, Dassault/Breguet Dornier Alpha Jet.

No. 2098, 4000fr, Saab Draken J35. No. 2099, 4000fr, Supermarine Spitfire.

2002, Feb. 8

2089-2094 A396 Set of 6 16.00 16.00

Sheets of 6, #a-f

2095-2097 A396 Set of 3 52.50 52.50

Souvenir Sheets

2098-2099 A396 Set of 2 12.00 12.00

Antique Automobiles — A397

No. 2100, 1000fr: a, 1920 Rolls-Royce. b, 1896 Ford. c, 1930 Hispano-Suiza. d, 1924 Stoewer Allemagne D10 D12. e, 1924 Chrysler. f, 1912 Hudson.

No. 2101, 1000fr: a, 1930 Bugatti SIA. b, 1901 Mercedes. c, 1926 Jordan Playboy. d, 1936 Cadillac V-16. e, 1914 Stutz Bearcat. f, 1904 Daimler.

No. 2102, 4000fr, 1886 Daimler-Benz. No. 2103, 4000fr, 1903 Ford Model A.

2002, Feb. 8 ***Perf. 13¼x13½***

Sheets of 6, #a-f

2100-2101 A397 Set of 2 42.50 42.50

Souvenir Sheets

2102-2103 A397 Set of 2 12.00 12.00

Race Cars A398

Designs: No. 2104, 750fr, Marmon Wasp, 1911 Indianapolis 500. No. 2105, 750fr, Ferrari Dino 246, 1958 French Grand Prix. No. 2106, 750fr, Lotus 49, 1967 German Grand Prix. No. 2107, Tyrell 003, 1971 American Grand Prix.

No. 2108, 750fr: a, Mercedes, 1914 French Grand Prix. b, Duesenberg, 1921 French Grand Prix. c, Bugatti, 1924 French Grand Prix. d, Alfa Romeo P3, 1934 French Grand Prix. e, Auto Union, 1937 Nürburgring Rally. f, Maserati 8C, 1939 German Grand Prix.

No. 2109, 750fr: a, Vanwall, 1957 British Grand Prix. b, Cooper T43, 1958 Argentine Grand Prix. c, Lotus 25, 1965 British Grand Prix. d, Brabham-Repro BT-19, 1966 French Grand Prix. e, Renault RS 01, 1977 British Grand Prix. f, Ferrari 640, 1989 Brazilian Grand Prix.

No. 2110, 4000fr, Coventry Daimler, 1899 Paris-Ostende Race. No. 2111, 4000fr, Penske PC-23, 1994 Portland Race.

2002, Feb. 8

2104-2107 A398 Set of 4 11.00 11.00

Sheets of 6, #a-f

2108-2109 A398 Set of 2 17.00 17.00

Souvenir Sheets

2110-2111 A398 Set of 2 12.00 12.00

Pres. John F. Kennedy (1917-63) — A400

No. 2113: a, With ship's wheel. b, With doves. c, With arch.

4000fr, At podium with flag and map.

Perf. 13½x13¼

2002, Feb. 20 **Litho.**

2113 A400 750fr Horiz. strip of 3, #a-c 8.00 8.00

Souvenir Sheet

2114 A400 4000fr multi 7.00 7.00

No. 2113 printed in sheets of 2 strips.

Pres. Ronald Reagan (1911-2004) — A401

No. 2115: a, With stars. b, With curtain. c, With US Capitol.

4000fr, With Statue of Liberty and Presidential seal.

2002, Feb. 20

2115 A401 750fr Horiz. strip of 3, #a-c 8.00 8.00

Souvenir Sheet

2116 A401 4000fr multi 7.00 7.00

No. 2115 printed in sheets of 2 strips.

Princess Diana (1961-97) — A402

No. 2117: a, Wearing tiara. b, Holding flowers. c, Wearing hat.

4000fr, Wearing black dress.

2002, Feb. 20

2117 A402 750fr Horiz. strip of 3, #a-c 8.00 8.00

Souvenir Sheet

2118 A402 4000fr multi 7.00 7.00

No. 2117 printed in sheets of 2 strips.

Prince William of Wales — A403

No. 2119, 750fr: a, Wearing brown checked shirt. b, Wearing jacket and bow tie. c, Wearing green sweater. d, Wearing lilac sweater. e, Wearing brown suit, white shirt and blue tie. f, Wearing brown suit, striped shirt and blue gray tie.

No. 2120, 750fr: a, Wearing blue shirt. b, Wearing blue suit, blue background. c, Wearing riding helmet. d, Wearing blue suit, white background. e, Wearing blue sweater. f, Wearing ski gear.

No. 2121, 4000fr, With Prince Harry. No. 2122, 4000fr, With Prince Charles, horiz.

Perf. 13½x13¼, 13¼x13½

2002, Feb. 20 **Sheets of 6, #a-f**

2119-2120 A403 Set of 2 32.50 32.50

Souvenir Sheets

2121-2122 A403 Set of 2 14.00 14.00

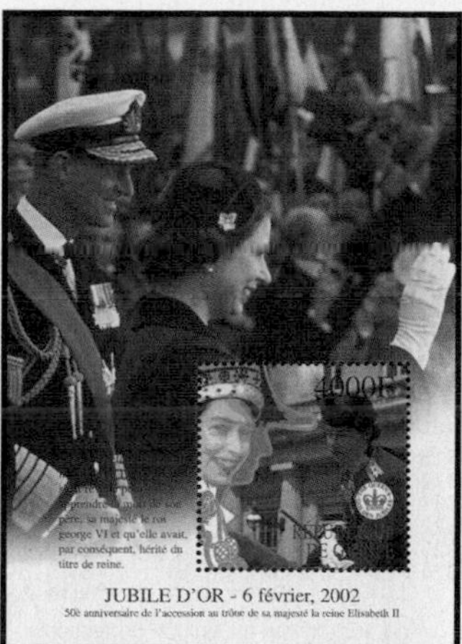

Queen Elizabeth II, 50th Anniv. of Reign — A404

No. 2123: a, Wearing blue coat and gloves. b, With Prince Philip. c, Wearing gray coat and hat. d, Wearing yellow suit and hat.
4000fr, Wearing red uniform.

2002, Feb. 20 ***Perf. 14¼***

2123 A404 1400fr Sheet of 4, #a-d 12.00 12.00

Souvenir Sheet

2124 A404 4000fr multi 7.00 7.00

A405

A406

Elvis Presley (1935-77) — A407

No. 2125 — Background color: a, Blue. b, Yellow. c, Red. d, Pink. e, Lilac. f, Yellow green.
No. 2126: a, Red and white shirt. b, Blue shirt. c, Black and brown shirt. d, Purple shirt. e, Red jacket with neckerchief. f, Red shirt.
No. 2127: a, Wearing red and white shirt with scarf. b, Wearing black jacket and gray shirt. c, Holding guitar on shoulder. d, With hands resting on guitar. e, Singing. f, Wearing army uniform.

2002, Feb. 20 ***Perf. 13½x13¼***

2125 A405 750fr Sheet of 6, #a-f 18.00 18.00
2126 A406 750fr Sheet of 6, #a-f 18.00 18.00
2127 A407 750fr Sheet of 6, #a-f 18.00 18.00

Nobel Prize Physics Laureates — A408

No. 2128, each 750fr: a, Hendrik Lorentz, 1902. b, Pieter Zeeman, 1902. c, Sir Joseph Thomson, 1906. d, Gabriel Lippman, 1908. e, Max von Laue, 1914. f, Jean B. Perrin, 1926.
No. 2129, each 750fr: a, Owen Richardson, 1928. b, Sir Chandrasekhara Venkata Raman, 1930. c, Victor F. Hess, 1936. d, Carl D. Anderson, 1936. e, Sir George Thompson, 1937. f, Clinton Davisson, 1937.
No. 2130, each 750fr: a, Enrico Fermi, 1938. b, Ernest Lawrence, 1939. c, Isidor I. Rabi, 1944. d, Patrick Blackett, 1948. e, Fritz Zernike, 1953. f, Donald A. Glaser, 1960.
No. 2131, each 750fr: a, Alfred Kastler, 1966. b, Luis W. Alvarez, 1968. c, Murray Gell-Mann, 1969. d, John Bardeen, 1972. e, Leon N. Cooper, 1972. f, John R, Schrieffer, 1972.
No. 2132: 4000fr, Wilhelm Röntgen, 1901. No. 2133, 4000fr, Marie Curie, 1903. No. 2134, 4000fr, Pierre Curie, 1903. No. 2135, 4000fr, Antoine Henri Becquerel, 1903.

2002, Feb. 20 **Litho.**

Sheets of 6, #a-f

2128-2131 A408 Set of 4 72.50 72.50

Souvenir Sheets

2132-2135 A408 Set of 4 27.50 27.50

Nobel Prizes, cent. (in 2001).

Albert Einstein (1879-1955), Physicist — A409

No. 2136: a, Smoking pipe. b, Wearing black jacket and tie, facing left. c, Wearing blue sweater. d, Wearing black jacket and tie, facing right. e, Wearing black sweater. f, Wearing brown jacket.
4000fr, With wife, Elsa.

2002, Feb. 20

2136 A409 750fr Sheet of 6, #a-f 17.00 17.00

Souvenir Sheet

2137 A409 4000fr multi 7.00 7.00

Pres. Theodore Roosevelt (1858-1919) — A410

No. 2138: a, As Assistant Navy Secretary. b, In Cuba, 1898. c, In Yellowstone Park, 1903. d, As President, 1901-09. e, Campaigning for war preparedness, 1916. f, In 1917.
4000fr, As colonel in Rough Riders.

2002, Feb. 20 ***Perf. 13¼***

2138 A410 950fr Sheet of 6, #a-f 21.00 21.00

Souvenir Sheet

2139 A410 4000fr multi 7.00 7.00

Jacqueline Kennedy Onassis (1929-94), First Lady — A411

Designs: No. 2140, 1000fr, Wearing white blouse, yellow background. 2000fr, With Pres. John F. Kennedy, horiz. No. 2142, 4000fr, Wearing Inaugural Ball gown.
No. 2143: a, Wearing necklace, shoulders showing, green background. b, Wearing hat. c, Facing left, green background. d, Wearing necklace, orange background. e, Wearing necklace, shoulders covered, green background. f, Wearing sunglasses.
No. 2144, 4000fr, As child.

Perf. 13½x13¼, 13¼x13½

2002, Feb. 20

2140-2142 A411 Set of 3 26.00 26.00
2143 A411 1000fr Sheet of 6, #a-f 24.00 24.00

Souvenir Sheet

2144 A411 4000fr multi 7.00 7.00

Famous People — A412

Designs: No. 2145, 750fr, Pres. John F. Kennedy (1917-63). No. 2146, 750fr, Pres. Ronald Reagan (1911-2004). No. 2147, 750fr, Chiune Sugihara, Japanese diplomat who saved Jews in World War II. No. 2148, 750fr, Queen Elizabeth II as younger woman, denomination at right. No. 2149, 750fr, Queen Elizabeth II wearing tiara, denomination at left. No. 2150, 750fr, Princess Diana (1961-97). No. 2151, 750fr, Queen Mother Elizabeth (1900-2002). No. 2152, 750fr, Prince William of Wales, denomination in red. No. 2153, 750fr, Prince William of Wales, denomination in yellow. No. 2154, 750fr, Prince William of Wales, denomination in violet. No. 2155, 750fr, Hereditary Prince Haakon and Princess Mette-Marie of Norway, horiz. No. 2156, 750fr, Prince Philippe and Princess Mathilde of Belgium, horiz.

2002, Feb. 20 ***Perf. 14***

2145-2156 A412 Set of 12 32.50 32.50

2002 Winter Olympic Games, Salt Lake City A413

Designs: No. 2157, 750fr, Biathlon. No. 2158, 750fr, Luge. No. 2159, 750fr, Skiing. No. 2160, 750fr, Snowboarding, vert.

Perf. 13¼x13½, 13½x13¼

2002, Feb. 20

2157-2160 A413 Set of 4 11.00 11.00

Japanese Entertainment — A414

No. 2161, 750fr — Film stars: a, Miyoshi Umeki. b, Kimiko Ikegami. c, Masahiro Takashima. d, Sessue Hayakawa. e, Toshiro Mifune. f, Kaho Minami.
No. 2162, 750fr — Kabuki actors: a, Shinnosuke as Sukeroku. b, Kikugoro as Genkuro Kitsune. c, Ganjiro as Izaemon. d, Kikunosuke as Shiratama. e, Kikunosuke as Keisei. f, Shinnosuke as Matsuomaru.
No. 2163, 4000fr, Akira Kurosawa, film director. No. 2164, 4000fr, Danjuro as Kampei and Tamasaburo as Okaru, horiz.

Perf. 13½x13¼, 13¼x13½

2002, Feb. 20 **Sheets of 6, #a-f**

2161-2162 A414 Set of 2 32.50 32.50

Souvenir Sheets

2163-2164 A414 Set of 2 14.00 14.00

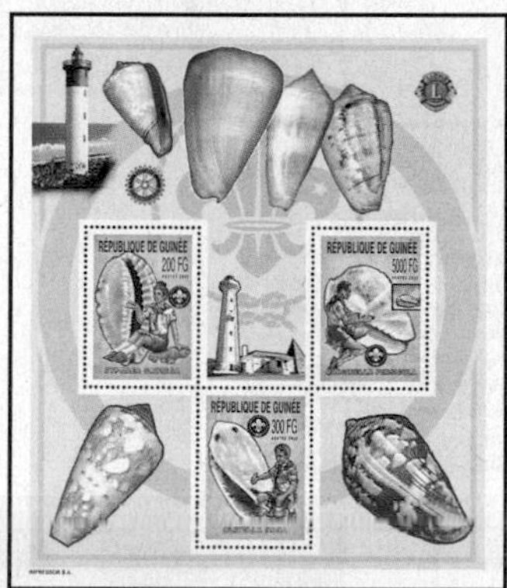

Scouts — A422

No. 2208 — Scouts and shells: a, 200fr, Cypraea caurica. b, 300fr, Olivella nana. c, 5000fr, Marginella persicula.
No. 2209 — Scouts and sea mammals: a, 200fr, Balaena mysticetus. b, 300fr, Tursiops truncatus. c, 5000fr, Delphinus delphis.
No. 2210 — Scouts and dinosaurs: a, 200fr, Spinosaurus. b, 300fr, Ouranosaurus. c, 5000fr, Kentrosaurus.
No. 2211 — Scouts and dogs: a, 200fr, Bouvier Bernois. b, 750fr, Chihuahua. c, 5000fr, Irish wolfhound.
No. 2212 — Scouts and meteorites from: a, 200fr, Tatahouine. b, 750fr, Gao-Guenie. c, 5000fr, Great Sand Sea.
No. 2213 — Scouts and cats: a, 300fr, Japanese bobtail. b, 750fr, Egyptian Mau. c, 5000fr, Bombay.
No. 2214 — Scouts and minerals: a, 300fr, Anglesite. b, 750fr, Brucite. c, 5000fr, Beudantite.
No. 2215 — Scouts and mushrooms: a, 300fr, Aseroe rubra. b, 750fr, Boletus edulis. c, 5000fr, Hygrocybe punicea.
No. 2216 — Scouts and butterflies: a, 300fr, Anaphe panda. b, 750fr, Eurema brigitta. c, 5000fr, Acraea zetes.

2002, Dec. 27 Litho. *Perf. 13¼*
Sheets of 3, #a-c

2208-2216 A422 Set of 9 62.50 62.50

Each stamp exists in souvenir sheet of 1.

Nicolaus August Otto (1832-91), Engineer A423

Wright Brothers and Wright Flyer A424

Astronaut Spacewalking — A425

Pierre de Coubertin (1863-1937), Intl. Olympic Committee President A426

Winston Churchill, Franklin D. Roosevelt and Joseph Stalin A427

Newspaper Mastheads A428

Ferris Wheels on Film A429

2002 *Perf. 13½x13¼, 13¼x13½*

2217	A423	200fr multi	1.60	1.60
2218	A424	300fr multi	1.60	1.60
2219	A425	750fr multi	1.60	1.60
2220	A426	1000fr multi	1.60	1.60
2221	A427	1250fr multi	1.60	1.60
2222	A428	1500fr multi	1.60	1.60
2223	A429	2000fr multi	1.60	1.60

Space — A430

Designs: No. 2224, 3000fr, Multi-scout Mars Lander. No. 2225, 3000fr, Stardust Probe. No. 2226, 3000fr, Mars Rover. No. 2227, 3000fr, Ceres-Vesta Probe. No. 2228, 3000fr, Deep Space Probe. No. 2229, 3000fr, NGST Space Telescope. No. 2230, 3000fr, Rosetta Probe. No. 2231, 3000fr, NEAR Probe.

No. 2232, 1500fr, horiz.: a, Newton Space Telescope. b, Darwin Space Telescope. c, Kepler Space Telescope. d, Herschel Space Telescope. e, Plank Space Telescope. f, Xeus Space Telescope. g, Mars Orbiter. h, Net Lander.

No. 2233, 1500fr, horiz.: a, Mission Specialist 4 Kalpana Chawla. b, Payload Commander Michael P. Anderson. c, Mission Specialist 1 David M. Brown. d, Pilot William C. McCool. e, Mission Specialist 4 Laurel B. Clark. f, Payload Specialist 4 Ilan Ramon. g, Commander Rick D. Husband. h, Columbia Space Shuttle.

No. 2234, 3000fr, Chawla, diff. No. 2235, 3000fr, Anderson, diff. No. 2236, 3000fr, Brown, diff. No. 2237, 3000fr, McCool, diff. No. 2238, 3000fr, Clark, diff. No. 2239, 3000fr, Ramon, diff. No. 2240, 3000fr, Husband, diff. No. 2241, 3000fr, Columbia Space Shuttle, diff. No. 2242, 6000fr, Corot Space Telescope, horiz. No. 2243, 6000fr, Crew of ill-fated Columbia Space Shuttle mission STS-107, horiz.

2003, Mar. 3 *Perf. 13¼*

2224-2231 A430 Set of 8 25.00 25.00

Sheets of 8, #a-h

2232-2233 A430 Set of 2 30.00 30.00

Souvenir Sheets

2234-2243 A430 Set of 10 37.50 37.50

Nos. 2242 and 2243 each contain one 50x41mm stamp. Nos. 2224-2231 each exist in souvenir sheets of 1.

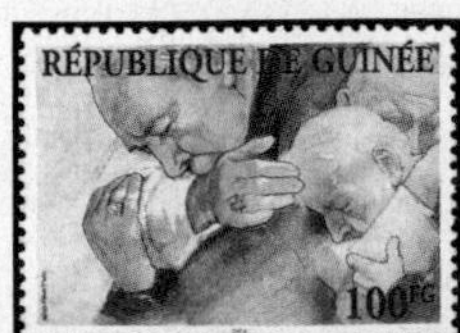

2004 Summer Olympics, Athens — A431

Designs: No. 2244, 750fr, No. 2252, 3000fr, Triathlon and Pentathlon. No. 2245, 750fr, No. 2253, 3000fr, Archery. No. 2246, 1500fr, No. 2254, 3000fr, Table tennis. No. 2247, 1500fr, No. 2255, 3000fr, Taekwondo and Judo. No. 2248, 1500fr, No. 2256, 3000fr, Equestrian. No. 2249, 1500fr, No. 2257, 3000fr, Women's tennis. No. 2250, 1500fr, No. 2258, 3000fr, Swimming. No. 2251, 1500fr, No. 2259, 3000fr, Track and field.

No. 2260, 6000fr, Soccer.

2003, Nov. 12 *Perf. 13¼*

2244-2251 A431 Set of 8 15.00 15.00

Souvenir Sheets

2252-2260 A431 Set of 9 30.00 30.00
2259a Souvenir sheet, #2252, 2257-2259 12.00 12.00

No. 2260 contains one 36x51mm stamp.

Pope John Paul II (1920-2005) — A433

Pope: 100fr, Hugging man. 150fr, In vestments, with open arms. 200fr, Face. 300fr, Praying at microphone. 350fr, Praying. 400fr, Holding crucifix. 450fr, Blessing bishop. 500fr, Kissing ground and with arms raised. 550fr, With Black Madonna of Czestochowa. 600fr, Wounded in assassination attempt. 650fr, With man. 1000fr, With children and Virgin Mary. 1500fr, Handshake. 2000fr, With Lech Walesa. 2500fr, With people tearing down Berlin Wall. 3000fr, Washing feet. 3500fr, Shaking hands of Fidel Castro. 4000fr, Meeting other religious leaders. 4500fr, Praying near town. 5000fr, With Mother Teresa. 5500fr, Holding crucifix, near church and statue. 6000fr, With crosses. 6500fr, With his coat of arms. 7000fr, With United Nations emblem. 7500fr, With crowd. 8000fr, Holding staff, in prayer. 8500fr, Holding crucifix and offering blessing.

2004 Litho. *Perf. 13x13¼*

2263	A433	100fr multi	—	—
2264	A433	150fr multi	—	—
2265	A433	200fr multi	—	—
2266	A433	300fr multi	—	—
2267	A433	350fr multi	—	—
2268	A433	400fr multi	—	—
2269	A433	450fr multi	—	—
2270	A433	500fr multi	—	—
2271	A433	550fr multi	—	—
2272	A433	600fr multi	—	—
2273	A433	650fr multi	—	—
2274	A433	1000fr multi	—	—
2275	A433	1500fr multi	—	—
2276	A433	2000fr multi	—	—
2277	A433	2500fr multi	—	—
2278	A433	3000fr multi	—	—
2279	A433	3500fr multi	—	—
2280	A433	4000fr multi	—	—
2281	A433	4500fr multi	—	—
2282	A433	5000fr multi	—	—
2283	A433	5500fr multi	—	—
2284	A433	6000fr multi	—	—
2285	A433	6500fr multi	—	—
2286	A433	7000fr multi	—	—
2287	A433	7500fr multi	—	—
2288	A433	8000fr multi	—	—
2289	A433	8500fr multi	—	—

SEMI-POSTAL STAMPS

Eye Examination — SP1

Microscopic Examination SP2

#B13, Medical laboratory. #B14, Insect control. #B16, Surgical operation.

Engraved and Lithographed

1960 Unwmk. *Perf. 11½*

B12	SP1	20fr + 10fr ultra & car	.95	.60
B13	SP1	30fr + 20fr brn org & violet	.95	.60
B14	SP1	40fr + 20fr rose lil & blue	1.25	.80
B15	SP2	50fr + 50fr grn & brn	1.90	1.25
B16	SP2	100fr + 100fr lil & grn	2.25	1.50
		Nos. B12-B16 (5)	7.30	4.75

Issued for national health propaganda. For overprints see Nos. B25-B29.

Nos. 194-195 Surcharged in Red or Orange

1961, June 6 Photo.

B17	A17	25fr + 10fr (R or O)	5.50	3.50
B18	A17	50fr + 20fr (R or O)	5.50	3.50

Nos. B17-B18 exist with orange surcharges transposed: "1961 + 10FRS." on 50fr and "1961 + 20FRS." on 25fr.

Nos. 214-219 Surcharged in Green, Lilac, Orange or Blue

Photo., Surcharge Engr.

1961, Dec. 8

Multicolored Design; Granite Paper

B19	A20	5fr + 5fr brt grn (G)	.70	.25
B20	A20	10fr + 5fr emer (G)	.75	.25
B21	A20	25fr + 5fr lilac (L)	1.90	.35
B22	A20	40fr + 5fr org (O)	2.50	.45
B23	A20	50fr + 5fr red org (O)	3.50	.65
B24	A20	75fr + 5fr ultra (B)	4.75	.90
		Nos. B19-B24 (6)	14.10	2.85

The surtax was for animal protection.

Nos. B12-B16 Overprinted in Red or Orange

Engr. & Litho.

1962, Feb. *Perf. 11½*

B25	SP1	20fr + 10fr (R or O)	.35	.25
B26	SP1	30fr + 20fr (R or O)	.50	.35
B27	SP1	40fr + 20fr (R or O)	.60	.40
B28	SP2	50fr + 50fr (R or O)	1.25	.80
B29	SP2	100fr + 100fr (R or O)	2.40	1.60
		Nos. B25-B29 (5)	5.10	3.40

WHO drive to eradicate malaria.
No. B25 also exists with black overprint.

Nos. 223-228 Srchd. in Red

Photo., Surcharge Engr.

1962, May 14 *Perf. 13x14*

B30	A22	5fr + 5fr multi	.40	.25
B31	A22	10fr + 5fr multi	.50	.25
B32	A22	25fr + 5fr multi	.65	.25
B33	A22	40fr + 5fr multi	.90	.45
B34	A22	50fr + 5fr multi	1.50	.75
B35	A22	75fr + 5fr multi	3.50	1.75
		Nos. B30-B35 (6)	7.45	3.70

The surtax was for bird protection.

Nos. 232-233 Surcharged & Overprinted in Orange or Red

1962, Nov. 1 Litho. *Perf. 13*

B36	A24	25fr + 15fr multi	.60	.45
B37	A24	75fr + 25fr multi	1.40	.90

Issued to help Algerian refugees.

Astronomers and Space Phenomena — SP3

No. B38, Helical nebula. No. B39, Orion nebula. No. B40, Eagle nebula. No. B41, Trifide nebula. No. B42, Eta-carinae nebula. No. B43, NGC-2264 nebula.
No. B44, Horse's Head nebula.

1989, Mar. 7 Litho. *Perf. 13½*

B38 SP3 100fr +25fr multi 1.00 .40
B39 SP3 150fr +25fr multi 1.50 .80
B40 SP3 200fr +25fr multi 2.25 1.00
B41 SP3 250fr +25fr multi 2.75 1.10
B42 SP3 300fr +25fr multi 3.25 1.50
B43 SP3 500fr +25fr multi 5.25 2.40
Nos. B38-B43 (6) 16.00 7.20

Souvenir Sheet

B44 SP3 750fr +50fr multi 7.25 3.00

Nos. B42-B44 are airmail.

AIR POST STAMPS

Lockheed Constellation — AP1

Design: 500fr, Plane on ground.

Lithographed and Engraved

1959, July 13 Unwmk. *Perf. 11½*

Size: 52½x24mm

C14 AP1 100fr dp car, ultra & emer 2.10 1.00
C15 AP1 200fr emer, brn & lil 2.75 2.00

Size: 56½x26mm

C16 AP1 500fr multicolored 7.25 3.50
Nos. C14-C16 (3) 12.10 6.50

For overprints see Nos. C24-C26, C52-C53.

Doves with Letter and Olive Twig — AP2

1959, Oct. 16 Engr. *Perf. 13½*

C17 AP2 40fr blue .30 .25
C18 AP2 50fr emerald .60 .40
C19 AP2 100fr dk car rose 1.00 1.00
C20 AP2 200fr rose red 1.90 1.75
C21 AP2 500fr red orange 5.25 3.00
Nos. C17-C21 (5) 9.05 6.40

For overprints see Nos. C35-C38.

Admission to UN Type of 1959

Engr. & Litho.

1959, Dec. 12 *Perf. 12*

Size: 44x26mm

C22 A16 50fr multicolored 1.00 .75
C23 A16 100fr multicolored 1.40 .90

For overprints see Nos. C27-C28.

Nos. C14-C16 Overprinted in Carmine, Orange or Blue

1960 Litho. & Engr. *Perf. 11½*

Size: 52½x24mm

C24 AP1 100fr multi (C or O) 9.75 4.25
C25 AP1 200fr multi (Bl) 17.00 8.00

Size: 56½x26mm

C26 AP1 500fr multi (C or O) 45.00 40.00
Nos. C24-C26 (3) 71.75 52.25

17th Olympic Games, Rome, 8/25-9/11.
No. 201 overprinted in green and Nos. C24 and C26 overprinted in black were included in a souvenir gift booklet celebrating Guinea's 3rd anniversary of independence. The booklet was sold at the NY World's Fair, but the stamps were not valid for postage.

Nos. C22-C23 Overprinted

Engr. & Litho.

1961, Oct. 24 *Perf. 12*

C27 A16 50fr multicolored 1.00 .40
C28 A16 100fr multicolored 1.50 .55

United Nations, 15th anniversary.

Mosquito and Malaria Eradication Emblem AP3

1962, Apr. 7 Engr. *Perf. 10½*

C29 AP3 25fr orange & blk .50 .25
C30 AP3 50fr car rose & blk .80 .35
C31 AP3 100fr green & blk 1.40 .60
Nos. C29-C31 (3) 2.70 1.20

WHO drive to eradicate malaria.
A souvenir sheet exists containing a 100fr green & sepia stamp, imperf. Sepia coat of arms in margin. Size: 102x76mm. Value $10.

Musician Type of Regular Issue

Musical Instruments: 100fr, 200fr, Kora. 500fr, Balafon.

1962, June 15 Photo. *Perf. 13x13½*

C32 A26 100fr brt pink, dk car & Prus bl 1.10 .50
C33 A26 200fr lt & dk ultra & car rose 2.10 1.25
C34 A26 500fr dl org, pur & Prus bl 6.75 4.00
Nos. C32-C34 (3) 9.95 5.75

Nos. C17-C20 Ovptd. in Carmine, Orange or Black

Perf. 13½

1962, Nov. 15 Unwmk. Engr.

C35 AP2 40fr blue (C or O) .60 .25
C36 AP2 50fr emer (C or O) .60 .35
C37 AP2 100fr dk car rose (B) 1.35 .70
C38 AP2 200fr rose red (B) 2.40 1.25
Nos. C35-C38 (4) 4.95 2.55

The conquest of space. Two types of overprint: Straight lines on 40fr and 50fr in carmine, 100fr (black). Curved lines on 40fr and 50fr in orange, 200fr (black).

Bird Type of Regular Issue

Birds: 100fr, Hornbill. 200fr, White spoonbill. 500fr, Bateleur eagle.

1962, Dec. Photo. *Perf. 13x13½*

C41 A30 100fr multicolored 2.50 1.10
C42 A30 200fr multicolored 4.25 2.40
C43 A30 500fr multicolored 11.00 4.75
Nos. C41-C43 (3) 17.75 8.25

Sports Type of Regular Issue, 1963

Designs: 100fr, Running. 200fr, Bicycling. 500fr, Single sculls.

1963, Mar. 16 *Perf. 14*

C44 A32 100fr dp rose, sep & grn 1.50 .60
C45 A32 200fr ol bis, ultra & mag 3.00 1.00
C46 A32 500fr ocher, dk bl & red 7.50 3.00
Nos. C44-C46 (3) 12.00 4.60

Butterfly Type of Regular Issue

Various Butterflies.

1963, May 10 Unwmk. *Perf. 12*

C47 A33 100fr cit, dk brn & gray 1.60 .35
C48 A33 200fr sal pink, blk & green 5.00 2.40
C49 A33 500fr multicolored 8.50 4.50
Nos. C47-C49 (3) 15.10 7.25

Red Cross Type of Regular Issue

1963, July 25 Engr. *Perf. 10½*

C50 A35 25fr black & car .75 .25

Souvenir Sheet

Imperf

C51 A35 100fr green & car 4.00 3.00

Nos. C14-C15 Overprinted

Lithographed and Engraved

1963, Oct. 28 *Perf. 11½*

C52 AP1 100fr dp car, ultra & emer 1.60 .70
C53 AP1 200fr emer, brn & lil 3.75 1.25

1st Pan American air service from Conakry to New York, July 30, 1963.

Fish Type of Regular Issue, 1964

100fr, African lyretail. 300fr, Six-barred epiplatys.

1964, Feb. 15 Litho. *Perf. 14x13½*

C54 A36 100fr grn & multi 2.25 .55
C55 A36 300fr brn & multi 7.75 1.40

Kennedy Type of Regular Issue, 1964

1964, Mar. 5 Engr. *Perf. 10½*

C56 A37 100fr multicolored 1.50 .80

See note after No. 327.

Olympic Type of Regular Issue

Design: 100fr, Women's ice skating.

1964, May 15 Photo. *Perf. 13x12½*

C57 A39 100fr gold, brn org & ind 2.25 .40

Nos. C44-C46 Overprinted in Carmine or Orange

1964, May 15 Unwmk. *Perf. 14*

C58 A32 100fr (C or O) 1.75 1.40
C59 A32 200fr (C or O) 2.75 2.00
C60 A32 500fr (C or O) 6.50 5.00
Nos. C58-C60 (3) 11.00 8.40

18th Olympic Games, Tokyo, Oct. 10-25.

Mrs. Roosevelt Type of Regular Issue

1964, June 1 Engr. *Perf. 10½*

C61 A40 50fr violet .75 .25

Souvenir Sheets

Unisphere, "Rocket Thrower" and Guinea Pavilion — AP4

1964, Oct. 26 Engr. *Imperf.*

C62 AP4 100fr dk bl & org 1.60 .80
C63 AP4 200fr rose red & emer 3.75 1.90

NY World's Fair, 1964-65. See Nos. C69-C70.

Nubian Monuments Type of Regular Issue

300fr, Queen Nefertari, Abu Simbel.

1964, Nov. 19 Photo. *Perf. 12*

C64 A42 300fr gold, dl red brn & sal 3.50 1.40

For overprint see No. C82.

Japanese Hostess, Plane and Map of Africa AP5

1965, Jan. 18 *Perf. 12½x13*

C65 AP5 100fr gold, blk & red lil 1.75 .35

18th Olympic Games, Tokyo, Oct. 10-25, 1964. Two multicolored souvenir sheets (200fr vert. and 300fr horiz.) exist, showing different views of Mt. Fuji. Sizes: 86x119mm, 119x86mm. Value, both: $12.50 perf; $40 imperf.
For overprint see No. C81.

Mask Type of Regular Issue

300fr, Niamou mask from N'Zérékoré.

1965, Feb. 15 Photo. *Perf. 14*

C68 A44 300fr multicolored 5.25 2.75

World's Fair Type of 1964

Souvenir Sheets

1965, Mar. 24 Engr. *Imperf.*

C69 AP4 100fr green & brn 2.40 1.00
C70 AP4 200fr grn & car rose 4.75 2.50

Handicraft Type of Regular Issue

100fr, Cabinetmaker. 300fr, Ivory carver.

1965, May 1 Photo. *Perf. 14*

C71 A45 100fr multicolored 1.50 .35
C72 A45 300fr multicolored 5.25 1.25

ITU Type of Regular Issue, 1965

1965, May 17 Unwmk.

C73 A46 100fr multicolored 1.10 .30
C74 A46 200fr multicolored 2.50 .75

Exist imperf.

ICY Type of Regular Issue, 1965

1965, Sept. 8 Engr. *Perf. 10½*

C75 A50 100fr bl & yel org 1.25 .35

West Facade, Polytechnic Institute — AP6

Design: 200fr, North facade.

1965, Oct. 2 Photo. *Perf. 13½*

C76 AP6 200fr gold & multi 1.75 1.00
C77 AP6 500fr gold & multi 5.00 3.00

Seventh anniversary of independence.
For overprints see Nos. C84-C85.

Moon Type of 1965

100fr, Ranger VII approaching moon, vert. 200fr, Launching of Ranger VII, Cape Kennedy, vert.

1965, Nov. 15 Litho. *Perf. 13½x14*
C78 A52 100fr rose red, yel & dk brown 1.00 .50
C79 A52 200fr multicolored 2.50 1.00

For overprints & surcharge see Nos. C112-C112B.

Dancer Type of Regular Issue, 1966

100fr, Kandia Kouyate, national singer.

1966, Jan. 5 Photo. *Perf. 13½*
Size: 36x28½mm
C80 A53 100fr multi, horiz. 1.25 .50

Engraved Overprint on No. C65

1966, Mar. 14 Photo. *Perf. 12½x13*
C81 AP5 100fr gold, blk & red lil 1.25 .45

Fourth Pan Arab Games, Cairo, Sept. 2-11, 1965. The same overprint was applied to two souvenir sheets noted after No. C65 (red ovpt. on 200fr, black ovpt. on 300fr).

Engraved Dark Blue Overprint on No. C64

1966, Mar. 14 *Perf. 12*
C82 A42 300fr gold, dl red brn & sal 2.75 1.50

Centenary of first Egyptian postage stamp.

Scenic Type of Regular Issue

View: Boulbinet Lighthouse.

1966, Apr. 4 *Perf. 13½*
C83 A54 100fr multicolored 1.40 .60

See Nos. C90-C91. For overprints see Nos. C93-C95.

Nos. C76-C77 Ovptd. in Blue or Yellow

1966, May 2 Photo. *Perf. 13½*
C84 AP6 200fr multi (Bl) 2.25 1.10
C85 AP6 500fr multi (Y) 5.00 2.75

UNESCO, 20th anniv.

Woman-Flower Type of Regular Issue

Designs: Women and flowers of Guinea.

1966, May 30 Photo. *Perf. 13½*
Size: 28x34mm
C86 A56 200fr multicolored 3.50 .70
C87 A56 300fr multicolored 5.00 2.10

Snake Type of Regular Issue

Designs: 200fr, Pastoria Research Institute. 300fr, Men holding rock python.

1967, May 15 Litho. *Perf. 13½*
Size: 56x20mm
C88 A61 200fr multicolored 2.50 1.25
a. Souv. sheet of 3, #471, 474, C88 9.00 6.50
C89 A61 300fr multicolored 4.50 2.25

Scenic Type of Regular Issue

Views: 100fr, House of explorer Olivier de Sanderval. 200fr, Conakry.

1967, June 20 Photo. *Perf. 13½*
C90 A54 100fr multicolored .75 .45
C91 A54 200fr multicolored 1.60 1.10

For overprints see Nos. C94-C95.

Elephant Type of Regular Issue, 1967

1967, Sept. 28 Photo. *Perf. 13½*
C92 A63 200fr gold & multi 1.60 .75

Nos. C83 and C90-C91 Overprinted

1967, Nov. 6
C93 A54 100fr multi (#C83) 1.45 .90
C94 A54 100fr multi (#C90) 1.45 .90
C95 A54 200fr multi (#C91) 2.75 1.50
Nos. C93-C95 (3) 5.65 3.30

50th anniversary of Lions International.

Detail from Mural by José Vela Zanetti — AP7

Family, Mural by Per Krohg — AP8

The designs of the 30fr, 50fr and 200fr show mankind's struggle for a lasting peace after the mural in the lobby of the UN Conference Building, NY. The designs of the 100fr and of Nos. C98a-C98b show mankind's hope for the future after a mural in the UN Security Council Chamber.

1967, Nov. 11
C96 AP7 30fr multicolored .30 .25
C97 AP7 50fr multicolored .40 .25
C98 AP8 100fr multicolored .85 .35
a. Souv. sheet of 3, English inscription 2.25 2.25
b. As "a," French inscription 2.25 2.25
C99 AP7 200fr multi 1.90 .50
Nos. C96-C99 (4) 3.45 1.35

Nos. C98a and C98b each contain a 100fr stamp similar to No. C98 and two 50fr stamps showing festival scenes. The 50fr stamps have not been issued individually.

People and Dwellings Type of Regular Issue

Design: 300fr, People and village of Les Bassari, Kundara Region.

1968, Apr. 1 Photo. *Perf. 14x13½*
Size: 57x36mm
C100 A66 300fr gold & multi 4.50 1.25

Legends Type of Regular Issue

70fr, The Girl and the Hippopotamus. 100fr, Old Faya's Inheritance, vert. 200fr, Soumangourou Kante Killed by Djegue (woman on horseback). 300fr, Little Gouné, Son of the Lion, vert.

1968 Photo. *Perf. 13½*
C101 A67 70fr multicolored .90 .25
C102 A67 100fr multicolored 1.40 .30
C103 A67 200fr multicolored 2.75 1.00
a. Souv. sheet of 4 7.00 7.00
C104 A67 300fr multicolored 4.00 1.25
Nos. C101-C104 (4) 9.05 2.80

Issued in sheets of 10 plus 2 labels. No. C103a contains 4 imperf. stamps similar to Nos. 510-511 and C102-C103.;
For souvenir sheet see No. 509a.
Issued: Nos. C102-C103, 5/16; Nos. C101, C104, 9/16.

African Animal Type of Regular Issue

1968, Nov. 25 Photo. *Perf. 13½*
Size: 49x35mm
C105 A68 100fr Lions 1.75 .55
C106 A68 200fr Elephant 3.50 2.10

For souvenir sheet see No. 518a.

Robert F. Kennedy Type of Regular Issue, 1968

Portraits: 50fr, Senator Robert F. Kennedy. 100fr, Rev. Martin Luther King, Jr. 200fr, Pres. John F. Kennedy.

1968, Dec. 16
C107 A69 50fr yel & multi .90 .25
C108 A69 100fr multicolored 1.90 .25
C109 A69 200fr multicolored 4.00 1.25
Nos. C107-C109 (3) 6.80 1.75

The stamps are printed in sheets of 15 (3x5) containing 10 stamps and five green and gold center labels. Sheets come either with English or French inscriptions on label.

Olympic Type of Regular Issue

Sculpture &: 100fr, Gymnast on pommel horse. 200fr, Gymnast on rings. 300fr, Pole vault.

1969, Feb. 1 Photo. *Perf. 13½*
C110 A71 100fr multicolored 1.25 .30
C111 A71 200fr multicolored 2.75 .90
C111A A71 300fr multicolored 4.50 1.10
Nos. C110-C111A (3) 8.50 2.30

Nos. C78-C79 Surcharged and Overprinted in Red

1969, Mar. 17 Litho. *Perf. 13½x14*
C112 A52 25fr on 200fr multi .40 .25
C112A A52 100fr multicolored 1.00 .65
C112B A52 200fr multicolored 2.00 1.00
Nos. C112-C112B (3) 3.40 1.90

See note after No. 530.
Nos. C112-C112B also exist with surcharge and overprint in orange (25fr, 200fr) or black (100fr). These sell for a small premium.

Bird Type of Regular Issue

Birds: 50fr, Violet-crested touraco. 100fr, European golden oriole. 200fr, Vulturine guinea fowl.

1971, June 18 Photo. *Perf. 13*
Size: 41x41mm
C113 A81 50fr gold & multi 1.10 .40
C113A A81 100fr gold & multi 2.25 .80
C113B A81 200fr gold & multi 4.50 1.25
Nos. C113-C113B (3) 7.85 2.45

John and Robert Kennedy, Martin Luther King, Jr. — AP9

Embossed on Metallic Foil

1972 *Die Cut Perf. 10½*
C114 AP9 300fr silver 35.00 35.00

Embossed & Typo.

C114A AP9 1500fr gold, cream & green 55.00 55.00

Jules Verne, Moon Rocket — AP10

Embossed on Metallic Foil

1972 *Die Cut Perf. 10½*
C115 AP10 300fr silver 35.00 35.00
C115A AP10 1200fr gold 85.00 85.00

Richard Nixon — AP11

Nixon and Mao — AP12

Nixon's Trip to People's Republic of China: a, Nixon. b, Chinese table tennis player. c, American table tennis player, Capitol dome. d, Mao Tse-tung.

Embossed on Metallic Foil

1972 *Die Cut Perf. 10½*
C116 AP11 90fr Block of 4, #a.-d., silver 27.50 27.50
C117 AP11 290fr Block of 4, #a.-d., gold 45.00 45.00

Embossed & Typo.

C118 AP12 1200fr gold & red 70.00 70.00

Perforations within blocks of 4 are perf. 11.

Racial Equality Year Type of Regular Issue

Design: 100fr, Men of 4 races and racial equality emblem (like No. 603).

1972, May 14 Photo. *Perf. 13x13½*
C119 A84 100fr gold & multi 1.10 1.00

Satellite Type of Regular Issue

Designs: 100fr, Map of Africa and Relay. 200fr, Map of Africa and Early Bird.

1972, May 17 Litho. *Perf. 13*
C120 A85 100fr yel & multi 1.20 .70
C121 A85 200fr multicolored 2.40 .90

African Postal Union Type of Regular Issue

Air mail envelope and UPAF emblem.

1972, July 10
C122 A86 100fr multicolored .90 .55
C123 A86 200fr multicolored 1.75 1.25

Olympic Type of Regular Issue

100fr, Gymnast on rings. 200fr, Bicycling. 300fr, Soccer.

1972, Aug. 26 Photo. *Perf. 13*
C124 A88 100fr multi 1.75 .60

C125 A88 200fr multi 3.25 1.10

Souvenir Sheet

C126 A88 300fr multi 7.00 7.00

Flower Type of 1974

20s, Thunbergia alata. 25s, Diascia barberae. 50s, Kigelia africana.

1974, May 20 Photo. *Perf. 13*
Size: 38x38mm (Diamond)

C127 A97 20s multi 2.75 .95
C128 A97 25s multi 3.50 1.10
C129 A97 50s multi 7.25 2.75
Nos. C127-C129 (3) 13.50 4.80

Olympic Games Type of 1976
Souvenir Sheet

1976, May 17 Photo. *Perf. 13½*

C130 Sheet of 4 16.00 12.50
a. A104 25s Soccer 2.50 2.50

No. C130 contains 32x32mm stamps.

Mushroom Type of 1977

Mushrooms: 10s, Morchella esculenta. 12s, Lepiota procera. 15s, Cantharellus cibarius.

1977, Feb. 6 Photo. *Perf. 13*
Size: 48x31mm

C131 A106 10s multicolored 3.50 .70
C132 A106 12s multicolored 5.00 .90
C133 A106 15s multicolored 6.75 2.10
Nos. C131-C133 (3) 15.25 3.70

Reptile Type of 1977

Reptiles: 10s, Flap-necked chameleon. 15s, Nile crocodiles. 25s, Painted tortoise.

1977, Oct. 10 Photo. *Perf. 13½*
Size: 46x30mm

C134 A109 10s multicolored 3.50 .80
C135 A109 15s multicolored 4.50 1.10
C136 A109 25s multicolored 7.00 1.60
Nos. C134-C136 (3) 15.00 3.50

Animal Type of 1977

Endangered Animals: 5s, Eland. 8s, Pygmy elephant. 9s, Hippopotamus. 10s, Chimpanzee. 12s, Palm squirrel. 13s, Lion. Male, female and young of each animal shown.

1977, Dec. 12 Photo. *Perf. 14x13½*

C137 A110 Strip of 3 3.50 1.75
a.-c. 5s any single .95
C138 A110 Strip of 3 5.50 2.75
a.-c. 8s any single 1.60
C139 A110 Strip of 3 5.75 3.00
a.-c. 9s any single 1.75
C140 A110 Strip of 3 6.00 3.50
a.-c. 10s any single 1.75
C141 A110 Strip of 3 7.50 4.00
a.-c. 12s any single 2.25
C142 A110 Strip of 3 8.50 5.00
a.-c. 13s any single 2.50
Nos. C137-C142 (6) 36.75 20.00

Russian Revolution Type, 1978

10s, Russian ballet. 30s, Pushkin Monument.

1978, Feb. 27 Photo. *Perf. 14*

C143 A111 10s gold & multi 2.40 .80
C144 A111 30s gold & multi 7.00 2.10

Giscard d'Estaing Type of 1979

Pres. Valery Giscard d'Estaing of France, vert.

1979, Sept. 14 Photo. *Perf. 13*

C145 A112 25s multicolored 4.00 2.00

Jules Verne Type of 1979

Designs: 20s, Five Weeks in a Balloon. 25s, Robur the Conqueror.

1979, Nov. 8 Litho. *Perf. 12x12½*

C146 A113 20s multicolored 2.60 .45
C147 A113 25s multicolored 3.50 .75

Olympic Type of 1982

1982 Litho. *Perf. 12½x12, 12x12½*

C148 A120 9s Fencing 1.40 .45
C149 A120 10s Soccer, vert. 1.60 .45
C150 A120 11s Basketball, vert. 1.75 .45
C151 A120 20s Diving, vert. 2.60 .60
C152 A120 25s Boxing, vert. 3.50 .75
Nos. C148-C152 (5) 10.85 2.70

Ataturk Type of 1982

1982, July 19 Photo. *Perf. 13½*

C153 A122 25s like #830 4.25 .80

World Cup Type of 1982

Designs: Various soccer players.

1982, Aug. 23

C154 A123 10s multicolored 2.60 .75
C155 A123 20s multicolored 4.25 1.10
C156 A123 25s multicolored 6.00 1.50
Nos. C154-C156 (3) 12.85 3.35

Nos. C154-C156 Overprinted

1982, Aug. 23 Photo. *Perf. 13½*

C157 A123 10s multicolored 2.60 .75
C158 A123 20s multicolored 4.25 1.10
C159 A123 25s multicolored 6.00 1.50
Nos. C157-C159 (3) 12.85 3.35

Location of flag in overprint varies.

Balloon Type

Designs: 20s, Graf Zeppelin, Airship, horiz. 25s, Double Eagle II, L. Newman, B. Abruzzo, M. Anderson. 30s, Le Geant Hot Air Balloon, Nadar; Dirigible, Dumont.

1983, Aug. 1 Litho. *Perf. 13½*

C160 A125 20s multicolored 2.60 .90
C161 A125 25s multicolored 3.25 1.25

Souvenir Sheet

C162 A125 30s multicolored 4.50 1.75

Nos. 894, 880-881 & 896 Overprinted

No. C163

No. C164

30s, "Kasparov / champion / du Monde".

1985, Nov. 5 Litho. *Perf. 13½*

C163 A133 20s multi 2.75 1.25
C164 A131 20s multi 2.75 1.25
C165 A131 25s Ovpt. like #C163 3.50 1.50
Nos. C163-C165 (3) 9.00 4.00

Souvenir Sheet

C166 A133 30s multi 15.00 10.00

US Space Shuttle Challenger Explosion, Jan. 28, 1986 — AP13

Designs: 100fr, Lift-off, crew names. 170fr, Shuttle design, Christa McAuliffe holding shuttle model. 600fr, Lift-off, vert.

100fr, 170fr Surcharged in Silver and Black

1986, July 1

C167 AP13 100fr multicolored 1.10 .30
C168 AP13 170fr multicolored 1.60 .50

Souvenir Sheet

C169 AP13 600fr multicolored 7.00 2.75

Nos. C167-C168 not issued without surcharge.

Souvenir sheets of one exist containing Nos. C167 and C168.

Robin Yount, Milwaukee Brewers Baseball Player — AP14

1990, Aug. 3 Litho. *Perf. 13½*

C170 AP14 450fr multicolored 5.00 2.10

No. C170 exists in a souvenir sheet of 1. For surcharge see No. 1182R.

Souvenir Sheet

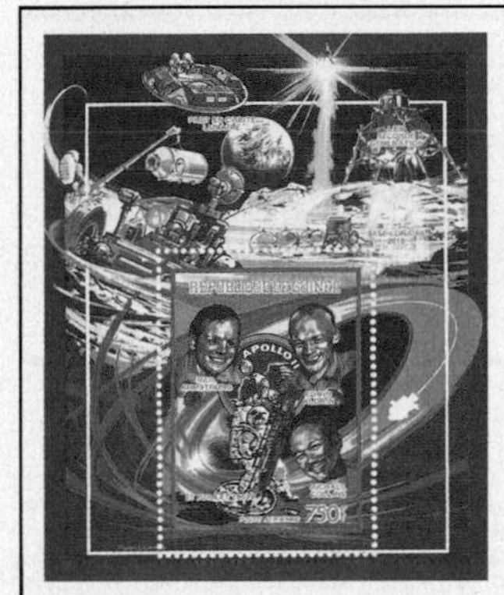

Armstrong, Aldrin, Collins and Apollo 11 Emblem — AP15

1990, Aug. 3 Litho. *Perf. 13½*

C171 AP15 750fr multicolored 8.00 3.25

Galileo Spacecraft — AP16

1990, Aug. 3

C172 AP16 500fr multicolored 5.25 2.25

No. C172 exists as a souvenir sheet of 1.

Pope John Paul II, Visit to Africa AP18

Portrait and: No. C174, Raising hand in benediction. No. C175, Child.

Litho. & Embossed

1992, Oct. 26 *Perf. 13½*

C174 AP18 1500fr gold & multi 24.00 19.00

Souvenir Sheet

C175 AP18 1500fr gold & multi 18.00 15.00

No. C175 exists imperf.

Elvis Presley, 15th Anniv. of Death — AP19

1992, Nov. 10

C176 AP19 1500fr gold & multi 24.00 20.00

No. C176 exists in miniature sheet of one.

De Gaulle Type of 1991 Overprinted "6 JUNE 1944 / DEBARQUEMENT"

1994 Litho. & Embossed *Perf. 13½*

C177 A181 1500fr like #1168 15.00 12.50

No. 1195 Overprinted in Silver

1993, Feb. 24 Litho. *Perf. 13½*

C178 A188 450fr multicolored 4.50 2.25

No. C178 exists in souvenir sheet of 1.

POSTAGE DUE STAMPS

D5

1959 Unwmk. Litho. *Perf. 11½*

J36 D5 1fr emerald .30 .25
J37 D5 2fr lilac rose .30 .25
J38 D5 3fr brown .55 .25
J39 D5 5fr blue 1.40 .25
J40 D5 10fr orange 2.10 .55
J41 D5 20fr rose lilac 4.25 .95
Nos. J36-J41 (6) 8.90 2.50

D6

1960 Engr. *Perf. 13½*

J42 D6 1fr dark carmine .25 .25
J43 D6 2fr brown orange .25 .25
J44 D6 3fr dark car rose .30 .25
J45 D6 5fr bright green .70 .35
J46 D6 10fr dark brown 1.50 .55
J47 D6 20fr dull blue 3.00 1.25
Nos. J42-J47 (6) 6.00 2.90

GUINEA-BISSAU

ˈgi-nē-bi-ˈsau̇ⁿ

LOCATION — West coast of Africa between Senegal and Guinea
GOVT. — Republic
AREA — 13,948 sq. mi.
POP. — 1,234,555 (1999 est.)
CAPITAL — Bissau

Guinea-Bissau, the former Portuguese Guinea, attained independence September 10, 1974. The state includes the Bissagos Islands.

100 Centavos = 1 Escudo
100 Centavos = 1 Peso
100 Centimes = 1 Franc (1997)

Catalogue values for all unused stamps in this country are for Never Hinged Items.

Amilcar Cabral, Map of Africa and Flag — A27

Design: Flag of the PAIGC (African Party of Independence of Guinea-Bissau and Cape Verde) shows location of Guinea-Bissau on map of Africa.

Perf. 11x10½

1974, Sept. 10 Litho. Unwmk.

345	A27	1p brown & multi	1.00	.55
346	A27	2.50p brown & multi	1.40	.80
347	A27	5p brown & multi	*22.50*	*8.00*
348	A27	10p brown & multi	3.75	*6.00*
		Nos. 345-348 (4)	28.65	15.35

First anniv. of Proclamation of Independence, Sept. 24, 1973.

Portuguese Guinea No. 344 Overprinted in Black

1975 Litho. *Perf. 13*

349	CD61 2c brown & multi	2.00	1.25

No. 349 exists with overprint in brown. Value, $5.

Amilcar Cabral, Map of Africa, Flag — A29

1975, Sept. Litho. *Perf. 11*

350	A29	1p brown & multi	.75	.75
351	A29	2.50p brown & multi	1.25	1.25
352	A29	5p brown & multi	8.00	7.00
353	A29	10p brown & multi	8.00	7.00
		Nos. 350-353 (4)	18.00	16.00

Nos. 350-353 are dated Sept. 24, 1973, in the design. Also exist dated Sept. 21, 1973. Value of latter set, $20.

Flag and Arms of Guinea-Bissau and Amilcar Cabral — A30

Flag, Arms and: 2e, No. 358, Family. 3e, 5e, Pres. Luiz Cabral. No. 359, like 1e.

1975, Sept. *Perf. 14*

354	A30	1e yel & multi	1.75	1.15
355	A30	2e multicolored	1.75	1.50
356	A30	3e red & multi	2.60	1.75
357	A30	5e yel & multi	7.25	4.50
358	A30	10e red & multi	11.00	5.75
359	A30	10e brt grn & multi	11.00	5.75
		Nos. 354-359 (6)	35.35	20.40

Amilcar Cabral's 51st birth anniv. (1e, No. 359); African Party of Independence of Guinea-Bissau and Cape Verde, 19th anniv. (2e, No. 358); Proclamation of Independence, 2nd anniv. (3e, 5e).

For surcharges see Nos. 367-367E.

Henry Knox, Cannons of Ticonderoga — A30a

Designs: 10e, Israel Putnam, Battle of Bunker Hill. 15e, Washington crossing the Delaware. 20e, Tadeusz Kosciuszko, Battle of Saratoga. 30e, Von Steuben, winter at Valley Forge. 40e, Lafayette, Washington rallying troops at Monmouth. 50e, Signing the Declaration of Independence.

1976, May 5 Litho. *Perf. 13½*

360	A30a	5e multicolored	.45	.25
360A	A30a	10e multicolored	.45	.25
360B	A30a	15e multicolored	.90	.40
360C	A30a	20e multicolored	2.00	.85
360D	A30a	30e multicolored	2.50	1.00
360E	A30a	40e multicolored	2.75	1.10
		Nos. 360-360E (6)	9.05	3.85

Souvenir Sheet

360F	A30a	50e multicolored	13.50	

American Revolution, bicentennial. Nos. 360D-360F are airmail.

Nos. 360-360E exist in miniature sheets of 1, perf. and imperf. Value, set of six perf or imperf sheets, $37.50. No. 360F contains one 75x45mm stamp and exists imperf. Value, $22.50.

See Nos. 371-371A.

Masked Dancer A30b

3p, Dancer, drummer. 5p, Dancers on stilts. 10p, Dancer with spear, bow. 15p, Masked dancer, diff. 20p, Dancer with striped cloak.

1976, May 10 *Perf. 11*

Denomination in Black on Silver Block

361	A30b	2p shown	.35	.25
361A	A30b	3p multicolored	.40	.25
361B	A30b	5p multicolored	.60	.25
361C	A30b	10p multicolored	.65	.25
361D	A30b	15p multicolored	2.00	.75
361E	A30b	20p multicolored	4.00	1.25
		Nos. 361-361E (6)	8.00	3.00

Souvenir Sheet

361F	A30b	50p Like No. 361E	7.00	7.00

Nos. 361C-361F are airmail. Silver block obliterates original denomination. Not issued without surcharge.

Nos. 361-361F Ovptd. in Black

1976, June 8 *Perf. 11*

362	A30b	2p on No. 361	.50	.25
362A	A30b	3p on No. 361A	.60	.25
362B	A30b	5p on No. 361B	.90	.25
362C	A30b	10p on No. 361C	1.25	.45
362D	A30b	15p on No. 361D	1.75	.65
362E	A30b	20p on No. 361E	2.50	.95
		Nos. 362-362E (6)	7.50	2.80

Souvenir Sheet

362F	A30b	50p on No. 361F	4.25	4.25

UPU cent. (in 1974). Nos. 362C-362F are airmail.

Nos. 362-362F exist imperf, and Nos. 362-362E in imperf miniature sheets of 1, all with black or red overprints.

Cabral, Guinean Mother and Children — A31

1976, Sept. 3 Litho. *Perf. 13½*

363	A31	3p multicolored	.25	.25
364	A31	5p multicolored	.25	.25
365	A31	6p multicolored	.45	.25
366	A31	10p multicolored	.55	.25
		Nos. 363-366 (4)	1.50	1.00

Third anniv. of assassination of Amilcar Cabral (1924-1973), revolutionary leader.

Nos. 363-366 exist in souvenir sheets of one. Value, set of four sheets $25.

Nos. 354-359 Surcharged in Black on Silver

1976, Sept. 12 Litho. *Perf. 14*

367	A30	1p on 1e No. 354	.40	.25
367A	A30	2p on 2e No. 355	.40	.25
367B	A30	3p on 3e No. 356	.40	.25
367C	A30	5p on 5e No. 357	1.40	.25
367D	A30	10p on 10e No. 358	1.45	.25
367E	A30	10p on 10e No. 359	1.45	.25
		Nos. 367-367E (6)	5.50	1.50

1876 Bell Telephone and Laying First Trans-Atlantic Cable — A31a

Telephones of: 3p, France, 1890, and first telephone booth, 1893. 5p, Germany, 1903, and automatic telephone, 1898. 10p, England, 1910, and relay station, 1963. 15p, France, 1924, and communications satellite. 20p, Modern telephone, 1970, and Molniya satellite. 50p, Picture phone.

1976, Oct. 18 *Perf. 13½*

368	A31a	2p multicolored	.25	.25
368A	A31a	3p multicolored	.25	.25
368B	A31a	5p multicolored	.25	.25
368C	A31a	10p multicolored	.75	.45
368D	A31a	15p multicolored	1.25	.70
368E	A31a	20p multicolored	1.75	.85
		Nos. 368-368E (6)	4.50	2.75

Souvenir Sheet

368F	A31a	50p multicolored	4.50	4.50

Nos. 368C-368F are airmail. No. 368F contains one 68x42mm stamp. No. 368F exists imperf. Nos. 368-368E exist in souvenir sheets of one, perf. and imperf.

1976 Winter Olympics, Innsbruck — A31b

1p, Women's figure skating. 3p, Ice hockey. 5p, Two-man bobsled. 10p, Pairs figure skating. 20p, Cross country skiing. 30p, Speed skating.

50p, Downhill skiing.

1976, Nov. 3 *Perf. 14x13½*

369	A31b	1p multicolored	.25	.25
369A	A31b	3p multicolored	.25	.25
369B	A31b	5p multicolored	.40	.25
369C	A31b	10p multicolored	.90	.25
369D	A31b	20p multicolored	1.45	.65
369E	A31b	30p multicolored	1.75	.85
		Nos. 369-369E (6)	5.00	2.50

Souvenir Sheet

369F	A31b	50p multicolored	4.50	4.50

Nos. 369C-369F are airmail. No. 369F exists imperf. Nos. 369-369E exist in souvenir sheets of one, perf. and imperf.

1976 Summer Olympics, Montreal A31c

1976, Nov. 24 *Perf. 13½*

370	A31c	1p Soccer	.25	.25
370A	A31c	3p Pole vault	.25	.25
370B	A31c	5p Women's hurdles	.40	.25
370C	A31c	10p Discus	.75	.40
370D	A31c	20p Sprinting	1.40	.60
370E	A31c	30p Wrestling	2.00	.75
		Nos. 370-370E (6)	5.05	2.50

Souvenir Sheet

370F	A31c	50p Cycling, horiz.	5.25	5.25

Nos. 370E-370F are airmail. No. 370F contains one 47x38mm stamp. No. 370F exists imperf. Nos. 370-370E exist in souvenir sheets of one, perf. and imperf.

American Revolution Type of 1976

Designs: 3.50p, Crispus Attucks, Boston Massacre. 5p, Martin Luther King, US Capitol.

1977, Jan. 27 *Perf. 13½*

Denomination in Black on Gold Block

371	A30a	3.50p multicolored	.35	.25
371A	A30a	5p multicolored	.45	.25
		Nos. 371-371A (2)	.80	.50

Gold block obliterates original denomination. Not issued without surcharge. Exist in souvenir sheets of one, perf. and imperf.

Cabral Addressing UN General Assembly — A32

Design: 50c, Cabral and guerrilla fighters.

1977, July **Litho.** ***Perf. 13½***

372	A32	50c	multicolored	.25	.25
373	A32	3.50p	multicolored	.45	.25

For surcharges see Nos. C12-C13.

Henri Dunant, Nobel Peace Prize, 1901 A32a

Nobel Prize Winners: 5p, Einstein, Physics, 1921. 6p, Irene and Frederic Joliot-Curie, Chemistry, 1935. 30p, Fleming, Medicine, 1945. 35p, Hemingway, Literature, 1954. 40p, J. Tinbergen, Economics, 1969. 50p, Nobel Prize Medal.

1977, July 27

374	A32a	3.50p	multicolored	.35	.25
374A	A32a	5p	multicolored	.40	.25
374B	A32a	6p	multicolored	.65	.25
374C	A32a	30p	multicolored	1.75	1.20
374D	A32a	35p	multicolored	3.25	1.40
374E	A32a	40p	multicolored	5.00	1.90
			Nos. 374-374E (6)	11.40	5.25

Souvenir Sheet

374F	A32a	50p	multicolored	4.50	4.50

Nos. 374D-374F are airmail. No. 374F contains one 57x39mm stamp. No. 374F exists imperf. Nos. 374-374E exist in souvenir sheets of one, perf. and imperf.

Postal Runner, Telstar Satellite — A32b

UPU Centenary (in 1974): 5p, Biplane, satellites encircle globe. 6p, Mail truck, satelite control room. 30p, Stagecoach, astronaut canceling letters on Moon. 35p, Steam locomotive, communications satellite. 40p, Space shuttle, Apollo-Soyuz link-up. 50p, Semaphore signalling system, satellite dish.

1977, Sept. 30

375	A32b	3.50p	multicolored	.25	.25
375A	A32b	5p	multicolored	.25	.25
375B	A32b	6p	multicolored	.35	.25
375C	A32b	30p	multicolored	2.25	.75
375D	A32b	35p	multicolored	2.40	1.25
375E	A32b	40p	multicolored	3.00	1.50
			Nos. 375-375E (6)	8.50	4.25

Souvenir Sheet

375F	A32b	50p	multicolored	4.00	4.00

Nos. 375D-375F are airmail. No. 375F exists imperf. Nos. 375-375E exist in souvenir sheets of one, perf. and imperf.

Torch and Party Emblem — A33

1977, Sept. **Litho.** ***Perf. 14***

376	A33	3p	yel & multi	.25	.25
377	A33	15p	sal & multi	.95	.60
378	A33	50p	lt grn & multi	2.25	1.50
			Nos. 376-378 (3)	3.45	2.35

African Party of Independence of Guinea-Bissau and Cape Verde, 20th anniversary.

Queen Elizabeth II, Silver Jubilee — A33a

Designs: 5p, Coronation ceremony. 10p, Yeoman of the Guard, Crown Jewels. 20p, Trumpeter. 25p, Royal Horse Guard. 30p, Royal Family. 50p, Queen Elizabeth II.

1977, Oct. 15

379	A33a	3.50p	multicolored	.35	.25
379A	A33a	5p	multicolored	.40	.25
379B	A33a	10p	multicolored	.85	.25
379C	A33a	20p	multicolored	1.90	.40
379D	A33a	25p	multicolored	2.75	.60
379E	A33a	30p	multicolored	3.25	1.00
			Nos. 379-379E (6)	9.50	2.75

Souvenir Sheet

379F	A33a	50p	multicolored	4.00	4.00

Nos. 379D-379F are airmail. No. 379F contains one 42x39mm stamp. No. 379F exists imperf. Nos. 379-379E exist in souvenir sheets of one, perf. and imperf.

Massacre of the Innocents by Rubens A33b

Paintings by Peter Paul Rubens: 5p, Rape of the Daughters of Leukippos. 6p, Lamentation of Christ, horiz. 30p, Francisco IV Gonzaga, Prince of Mantua. 35p, The Four Continents. 40p, Marquise Brigida Spinola Doria. 50p, The Wounding of Christ.

1977, Nov. 15

380	A33b	3.50p	multicolored	.40	.25
380A	A33b	5p	multicolored	.55	.25
380B	A33b	6p	multicolored	.65	.30
380C	A33b	30p	multicolored	2.25	1.20
380D	A33b	35p	multicolored	2.75	1.40
380E	A33b	40p	multicolored	3.75	1.60
			Nos. 380-380E (6)	10.35	5.00

Souvenir Sheet

380F	A33b	50p	multicolored	4.50	4.50

Nos. 380D-380F are airmail. Nos. 380-380F exist imperf. Nos. 380-380E exist in souvenir sheets of one, perf. and imperf.

Congress Emblem — A34

1977, Nov. 15 **Litho.** ***Perf. 14***

381	A34	3.50p	multicolored	.30	.25

3rd PAIGC Congress, Bissau, Nov. 15-20.

Santos-Dumont's Airship, 1901 — A34a

Airships: 5p, R-34 crossing the Atlantic, 1919. 10p, Norge over North Pole, 1926. 20p, Graf Zeppelin over Abu Simbel, 1931. 25p, Hindenburg over New York, 1937. 30p, Graf Zeppelin, Concorde, space shuttle. 50p, Ferdinand von Zeppelin, horiz.

1978, Feb. 27

382	A34a	3.50p	multicolored	.25	.25
382A	A34a	5p	multicolored	.35	.25
382B	A34a	10p	multicolored	.65	.25
382C	A34a	20p	multicolored	1.40	.50
382D	A34a	25p	multicolored	1.75	1.00
382E	A34a	30p	multicolored	2.10	1.40
			Nos. 382-382E (6)	6.50	3.65

Souvenir Sheet

382F	A34a	50p	multicolored	4.00	4.00

Nos. 382D-382F are airmail. No. 382F exists imperf. Nos. 382-382E exist in souvenir sheets of one, perf. and imperf.

World Cup Soccer Championships, Argentina — A34b

Soccer players and posters from previous World Cup Championships: 3.50p, 1930. 5p, 1938. 10p, 1950. 20p, 1962. 25p, 1970. 30p, 1974. 50p, Argentina '78 emblem.

1978, Mar. 15

383	A34b	3.50p	multicolored	.25	.25
383A	A34b	5p	multicolored	.25	.25
383B	A34b	10p	multicolored	.65	.35
383C	A34b	20p	multicolored	1.35	.75
383D	A34b	25p	multicolored	1.75	1.25
383E	A34b	30p	multicolored	2.10	1.50
			Nos. 383-383E (6)	6.35	4.35

Souvenir Sheet

383F	A34b	50p	multicolored	4.00	4.00

Nos. 383D-383F are airmail. Nos. 383-383F exist imperf. Nos. 383-383E exist in miniature sheets of one, perf. and imperf.

For surcharges see Nos. 393-393F.

Endangered Species — A34c

3.50p, Black antelope. 5p, Fennec. 6p, Secretary bird. 30p, Hippopotami. 35p, Cheetahs. 40p, Gorillas.

50p, Cercopithecus erythotis.

1978, Apr. 17

384	A34c	3.50p	multicolored	.25	.25
384A	A34c	5p	multicolored	.40	.25
384B	A34c	6p	multicolored	.60	.30
384C	A34c	30p	multicolored	3.00	1.45
384D	A34c	35p	multicolored	3.25	1.75
384E	A34c	40p	multicolored	3.50	2.00
			Nos. 384-384E (6)	11.00	6.00

Souvenir Sheet

384F	A34c	50p	multicolored	6.00	6.00

Nos. 384D-384F are airmail. No. 384F contains one 39x42mm stamp. No. 384F exists imperf. Nos. 384-384E exist in souvenir sheets of one, perf. and imperf.

Antenna, ITU Emblem A35

1978, May 17 **Litho.** ***Perf. 13½***

385	A35	3.50p	silver & multi	.25	.25
386	A35	10p	gold & multi	.65	.45

10th World Telecommunications Day.

Boy — A36

3p, Infant and grandfather. 5p, Boys. 30p, Girls.

1978 ***Perf. 14***

387	A36	50c	yel grn & dk bl	.25	.25
388	A36	3p	claret & car rose	.25	.25
389	A36	5p	ocher & brown	.30	.25
390	A36	30p	car & ocher	1.60	1.10
			Nos. 387-390 (4)	2.40	1.85

Children's Day.

Queen Elizabeth II, Silver Jubilee A36a

Elizabeth, Imperial State Crown — A36b

Designs: 5p, Queen, Prince Philip in Coronation Coach. 10p, Queen, Prince Philip. 20p, Mounted drummer. 25p, Imperial State Crown, St. Edward's Crown. 30p, Queen holding orb and scepter. 50p, Queen on Throne flanked by Archbishops. No. 391H, Coronation Coach.

1978, June 15

391	A36a	3.50p	multicolored	.25	.25
391A	A36a	5p	multicolored	.25	.25
391B	A36a	10p	multicolored	.55	.40
391C	A36a	20p	multicolored	1.30	.80
391D	A36a	25p	multicolored	1.60	1.00
391E	A36a	30p	multicolored	1.75	1.10
			Nos. 391-391E (6)	5.70	3.80

Litho. & Embossed

391F	A36b	100p	gold & multi	16.00	—

Souvenir Sheets

391G	A36a	50p	multicolored	4.00	4.00

Litho. & Embossed

391H	A36b	100p	gold & multi	11.00	—

Nos. 391D-391H are airmail. Nos. 391-391E exist in souvenir sheets of one, perf. and imperf. Nos. 391F-391H exist imperf.

History of Aviation — A36c

3.50p, Wright Brothers. 10p, Santos-Dumont. 15p, Bleriot. 20p, Lindbergh, Spirit of St. Louis. 25p, Lunar module. 30p, Space shuttle.
50p, Concorde.

1978, June 15 Litho. *Perf. 13½*

No.	Type	Value	Description	Unused	Used
392	A36c	3.50p	multicolored	.25	.25
392A	A36c	10p	multicolored	.70	.25
392B	A36c	15p	multicolored	.95	.45
392C	A36c	20p	multicolored	1.35	.60
392D	A36c	25p	multicolored	1.60	.70
392E	A36c	30p	multicolored	2.00	.95
			Nos. 392-392E (6)	6.85	3.20

Souvenir Sheet

No.	Type	Value	Description	Unused	Used
392F	A36c	50p	multicolored	4.50	4.50

Nos. 392D-392F are airmail. Nos. 392-392E exist in souvenir sheets of one, perf. and imperf. No. 392F exists imperf.

Nos. 383-383F Ovptd. in Gold

1978, Oct. 2

No.	Type	Value	Description	Unused	Used
393	A34b	3.50p	on No. 383	.25	.25
393A	A34b	5p	on No. 383A	.25	.25
393B	A34b	10p	on No. 383B	.65	.45
393C	A34b	20p	on No. 383C	1.45	.60
393D	A34b	25p	on No. 383D	1.90	.70
393E	A34b	30p	on No. 383E	2.50	.95
			Nos. 393-393E (6)	7.00	3.20

Souvenir Sheet

No.	Type	Value	Description	Unused	Used
393F	A34b	50p	on No. 383F	4.00	4.00

Nos. 393D-393F are airmail. Nos. 393-393F exist imperf. Nos. 393-393E exist in miniature sheets of 1 perf. and imperf. No. 393F exists overprinted in silver.

Virgin and Child by Albrecht Durer — A36d

Different Paintings of the Virgin and Child (Virgin only on 30p) by Durer.

1978, Nov. 14

No.	Type	Value	Description	Unused	Used
394	A36d	3.50p	multicolored	.25	.25
394A	A36d	5p	multicolored	.35	.25
394B	A36d	6p	multicolored	.40	.25
394C	A36d	30p	multicolored	2.10	.75
394D	A36d	35p	multicolored	2.40	1.10
394E	A36d	40p	multicolored	2.75	1.40
			Nos. 394-394E (6)	8.25	4.00

Souvenir Sheet

No.	Type	Value	Description	Unused	Used
394F	A36d	50p	multicolored	4.50	4.50

Nos. 394D-394F are airmail. No. 394F contains one 51x56mm stamp. Nos. 394-394E exist in souvenir sheets of one, perf. and imperf. No. 394F exists imperf.

Sir Rowland Hill (1795-1879), Wurttemberg No. 53 — A36e

Hill and: 5p, Belgium #1. 6p, Monaco #10. 30p, Spain 2r stamp of 1851 in blue. 35p, Switzerland #5. 40p, Two Sicilies #8. 50p, Portuguese Guinea #13 in brown.

1978, Dec. 15

No.	Type	Value	Description	Unused	Used
395	A36e	3.50p	multicolored	.25	.25
395A	A36e	5p	multicolored	.50	.25
395B	A36e	6p	multicolored	.75	.25
395C	A36e	30p	multicolored	2.50	.25
395D	A36e	35p	multicolored	4.00	.30
395E	A36e	40p	multicolored	4.50	.70
			Nos. 395-395E (6)	12.50	2.00

Souvenir Sheet

No.	Type	Value	Description	Unused	Used
395F	A36e	50p	multicolored	5.00	5.00

Nos. 395D-395F are airmail. No. 395F contains one 51x42mm stamp. Nos. 395-395E exist in souvenir sheets of one, perf. and imperf. No. 395F exists imperf.

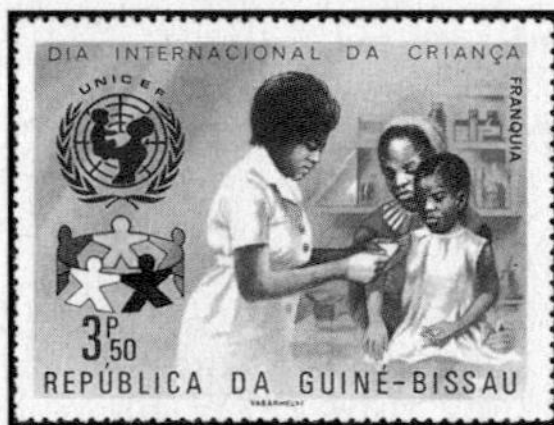

Intl. Day of the Child — A36f

10p, Children drinking. 15p, Child with book. 20p, Space plane. 25p, Skylab. 30p, Children playing chess.
50p, Children watching spaceship.

1979, Jan. 15 *Perf. 14*

No.	Type	Value	Description	Unused	Used
396	A36f	3.50p	shown	.25	.25
396A	A36f	10p	multicolored	.75	.25
396B	A36f	15p	multicolored	1.10	.55
396C	A36f	20p	multicolored	1.30	.65
396D	A36f	25p	multicolored	1.60	.85
396E	A36f	30p	multicolored	1.75	.95
			Nos. 396-396E (6)	6.75	3.50

Souvenir Sheet

No.	Type	Value	Description	Unused	Used
396F	A36f	50p	multicolored	5.00	5.00

Nos. 396C-396F are airmail. Nos. 396-396E exist in souvenir sheets of one, perf. and imperf. No. 396F exists imperf.

A36g

1979, Aug. 3 Litho. *Perf. 13*

No.	Type	Value	Description	Unused	Used
397	A36g	4.50p	multicolored	.45	.25

Massacre of Pindjiguiti, 20th anniv.

A36h

1979, May 17 Litho. *Perf. 14*

No.	Type	Value	Description	Unused	Used
397A	A36h	50c	shown	.25	.25
397B	A36h	4p	People, rainbow, diff.	.30	.25

World Telecommunications Day.

Family A37

1979, April 16 Litho. *Perf. 12x11½*

No.	Type	Value	Description	Unused	Used
398	A37	50c	multicolored	.25	.25
399	A37	2p	multicolored	.45	.25
400	A37	4p	multicolored	.90	.25
			Nos. 398-400 (3)	1.60	.75

General population census, Apr. 16-30.

Cassaca Conference, 16th Anniv. — A37a

1980, Feb. 13 Litho. *Perf. 14x14¼*

No.	Type	Value	Description	Unused	Used
400A	A37a	3.50p	multi	.25	.25
400B	A37a	6.50p	multi	.30	.25
400C	A37a	10p	multi	.65	.30

Ernst Udet and Fokker D.VII — A38

5p, Charles Nungesser, Nieuport 17. 6p, von Richthofen, Fokker DR.1. 30p, Francesco Baracca, Spad XIII.

1979, Sept. 3 Litho. *Perf. 13½*

No.	Type	Value	Description	Unused	Used
401	A38	3.50p	shown	.30	.25
401A	A38	5p	multicolored	.40	.25
401B	A38	6p	multicolored	.50	.30
401C	A38	30p	multicolored	2.00	1.00
			Nos. 401-401C,C14-C14A (6)	8.60	4.40

Lake Placid Emblem, Speed Skating — A39

1980, Dec. 10

No.	Type	Value	Description	Unused	Used
402	A39	3.50p	shown	.35	.25
402A	A39	5p	Downhill skiing	.55	.25
402B	A39	6p	Luge	.65	.25
402C	A39	30p	Cross-country skiing	2.10	.70
			Nos. 402-402C,C15-C16 (6)	9.05	4.05

13th Winter Olympic Games, Lake Placid, NY, Feb. 12-24.

Shot-put A40

5p, Athlete on rings. 6p, Running. 30p, Fencing.

1980, Jan. 21 Litho. *Perf. 13½*

No.	Type	Value	Description	Unused	Used
403	A40	3.50p	shown	.30	.25
403A	A40	5p	multi	.60	.25
403B	A40	6p	multi	.80	.25
403C	A40	30p	multi	3.00	.70
			Nos. 403-403C,C18-C19 (6)	12.45	4.05

22nd Summer Olympic Games, Moscow, July 19-Aug. 3.

Pres. Luis Cabral, Children and Workers A41

5p, Pres. Cabral holding books.

1980, Feb. 4 Litho. *Perf. 13½*

No.	Type	Value	Description	Unused	Used
404	A41	3.50p	multicolored	.35	.25
405	A41	5p	multicolored	.50	.25

Literacy campaign. See Nos. C21-C22.

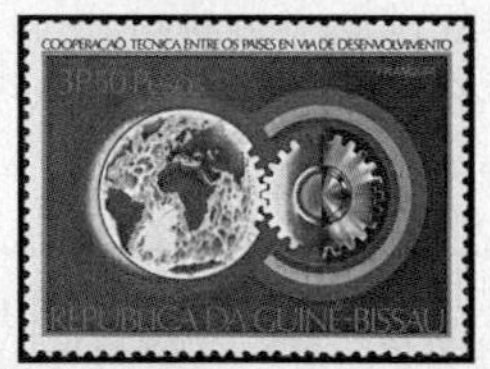

Cooperation Among Developing Countries — A42

1980, Feb. 14

No.	Type	Value	Description	Unused	Used
406	A42	3.50p	multicolored	.50	.25
407	A42	6p	multicolored	.55	.25
408	A42	10p	multicolored	1.50	.25
			Nos. 406-408 (3)	2.55	.75

Baskets — A43

3p, Bird, family wood statues, vert. 20p, Head, doll carvings.

1980, Feb. 26 Litho. *Perf. 13½*

No.	Type	Value	Description	Unused	Used
409	A43	3p	multi	.25	.25
410	A43	6p	shown	.30	.25
411	A43	20p	multi	1.10	.45
			Nos. 409-411 (3)	1.65	.95

Infant and Toy Train, Locomotive, IYC Emblem A44

6p, Classroom, horiz. 10p, Boy reading Jules Verne story. 35p, Archer, boy with bow. 50p, Students in lab.

1979, April 12

412	A44	6p	multi	.40	.30
412A	A44	10p	multi	.65	.55
412B	A44	25p	shown	1.50	.80
412C	A44	35p	multi	2.40	1.25
			Nos. 412-412C (4)	4.95	2.90

Souvenir Sheet

412D	A44	50p	multi	4.25	4.25

International Year of the Child (1979).

Columbia Space Shuttle and Crew — A45

Space Exploration: 3.50p, Galileo, satellites. 5p, Wernher von Braun. 6p, Jules Verne, rocket.

1981, Feb. 5 **Litho.** ***Perf. 13½***

413	A45	3.50p	multicolored	.35	.25
413A	A45	5p	multicolored	.40	.25
413B	A45	6p	multicolored	.45	.30
413C	A45	30p	multicolored	2.10	1.10
			Nos. 413-413C,C23-C24 (6)	9.05	5.15

Soccer Players, World Cup, Argentina '78 and Espana '82 Emblems — A46

Soccer scenes and famous players: 3.50p, Platini, France. 5p, Bettega, Italy. 6p, Rensenbrink, Netherlands. 30p, Rivelino, Brazil.

1981, March 11

414	A46	3.50p	multicolored	.35	.25
414A	A46	5p	multicolored	.40	.25
414B	A46	6p	multicolored	.45	.30
414C	A46	30p	multicolored	2.10	1.10
			Nos. 414-414C,C26-C27 (6)	9.05	5.15

Prince Charles and Lady Diana, St. Paul's Cathedral A47

Royal Wedding (Couple and): 3.50p, Diana leading horse. 5p, Charles crowned Prince of Wales. 6p, Diana with kindergarten children.

1981, Aug. 5 **Litho.** ***Perf. 13½***

415	A47	3.50p	multicolored	.40	.25
415A	A47	5p	multicolored	.40	.25
415B	A47	6p	multicolored	.50	.30
415C	A47	30p	multicolored	2.10	1.25
			Nos. 415-415C,C29-C30 (6)	10.65	5.30

Woman Before a Mirror, by Picasso (1881-1973) A48

Picasso Birth Cent.: Various paintings.

1981, Sept. 22 **Litho.** ***Perf. 13½***

416	A48	3.50p	multi	.30	.25
417	A48	5p	multi	.45	.25
418	A48	6p	multi	.65	.30
419	A48	30p	multi	3.00	1.25
			Nos. 416-419,C32-C33 (6)	14.65	5.45

Henrique Vermelho and his Ship, Drakkar A49

Navigators and their ships: 5p, Vasco de Gama, St. Gabriel. 6p, Ferdinand Magellan, Victoria. 30p, Jacques Cartier, Emerillon.

1981, Aug. 28 **Litho.** ***Perf. 13½***

420	A49	3.50p	multicolored	.30	.25
421	A49	5p	multicolored	.45	.25
422	A49	6p	multicolored	.55	.30
423	A49	30p	multicolored	2.50	1.25
			Nos. 420-423,C35-C36 (6)	11.30	5.65

Christmas — A50

Designs: Virgin and Child paintings.

1981, Nov. 19

424	A50	3.50p	Mantegna	.30	.25
425	A50	5p	Bellini	.45	.25
426	A50	6p	Mantegna, diff.	.55	.30
427	A50	25p	Correggio	2.50	1.25
			Nos. 424-427,C38-C39 (6)	11.05	5.65

Scouting Year — A51

1982, June 9 **Litho.** ***Perf. 13½***

428	A51	3.50p	Archery	.30	.25
429	A51	5p	First aid training	.35	.25
430	A51	6p	Bugler	.45	.30
431	A51	30p	Cub scouts	2.25	.85
			Nos. 428-431,C41-C42 (6)	9.35	4.90

1982 World Cup — A52

Various soccer players and cup.

1982, June 13 **Litho.** ***Perf. 13½***

432	A52	3.50p	Keegan	.30	.25
433	A52	5p	Rossi	.35	.25
434	A52	6p	Zico	.45	.30
435	A52	30p	Arconada	2.25	.85
			Nos. 432-435,C44-C45 (6)	9.35	4.90

21st Birthday of Princess Diana — A53

Portraits and scenes of Diana.

1982, Oct. 21

436	A53	3.50p	multicolored	.35	.25
437	A53	5p	multicolored	.35	.25
438	A53	6p	multicolored	.45	.25
439	A53	30p	multicolored	2.50	.65
			Nos. 436-439,C47-C48 (6)	10.15	4.25

For overprints see Nos. 450-456.

Visit by Portuguese President Eanes — A54

4.50p, Portugal and Guinea-Bissau flags.

1982, Dec. 2 **Litho.** ***Perf. 13½***

440	A54	4.50p	multicolored	.40	.25
441	A54	20p	multicolored	1.60	1.10

Manned Flight Bicentenary — A55

Various hot air balloons.

1983, Jan. 15 **Litho.** ***Perf. 11***

442	A55	50c	multicolored	.25	.25
443	A55	2.50p	multicolored	.25	.25
444	A55	3.50p	multicolored	.30	.25
445	A55	5p	multicolored	.50	.25
446	A55	10p	multicolored	.55	.25
447	A55	20p	multicolored	1.25	.35
448	A55	30p	multicolored	1.60	.45
			Nos. 442-448 (7)	4.70	2.05

Souvenir Sheet

Perf. 12½

449	A55	50p	multicolored	4.00	2.00

No. 449 contains one 47x47mm stamp.

Nos. 436-439, C47-C49B Overprinted

1982, Dec. 28 **Litho.** ***Perf. 13½***

450	A53	3.50p	multicolored	.45	.25
451	A53	5p	multicolored	.55	.25
452	A53	6p	multicolored	.65	.25
453	A53	30p	multicolored	2.75	.70
454	A53	35p	multicolored	3.25	.90
455	A53	40p	multicolored	3.75	1.25
			Nos. 450-455 (6)	11.40	3.60

Souvenir Sheet

456	A53	50p	multicolored	6.75	1.25

Litho. & Embossed

456A	A53a	200p	gold & multi	14.50	

Souvenir Sheet

456B	A53a	200p	gold & multi, vert.	32.50	

Nos. 454-456A are airmail.

African Apes and Monkeys A56

1p, Comopithecus hamadryas. 1.50p, Gorilla gorilla. 3.50p, Theropithecus gelada. 5p, Mandrillus sphinx. 8p, Pan trogladytes. 20p, Colobus abyssinicus. 30p, Cercopithecus diana.

1983, Mar. 15 **Litho.** ***Perf. 13½***

457	A56	1p	multicolored	.25	.25
458	A56	1.50p	multicolored	.25	.25
459	A56	3.50p	multicolored	.30	.25
460	A56	5p	multicolored	.40	.25
461	A56	8p	multicolored	.90	.25
462	A56	20p	multicolored	1.45	.30
463	A56	30p	multicolored	2.00	.45
			Nos. 457-463 (7)	5.55	2.00

Souvenir Sheet

TEMBAL '83, Stamp Exhibition, Basel — A57

1983, May 21

464	A57	50p	Space shuttle	5.00	1.50

A58

Designs: Various telecommunications satellites and space shuttles.

1983, May 25 **Litho.** ***Perf. 13½***

465	A58	1p	multicolored	.25	.25
466	A58	1.50p	multicolored	.25	.25
467	A58	3.50p	multicolored	.25	.25
468	A58	5p	multicolored	.35	.25
469	A58	8p	multicolored	.45	.25
470	A58	20p	multicolored	1.10	.40
471	A58	30p	multicolored	1.60	.65
			Nos. 465-471 (7)	4.25	2.30

Souvenir Sheet

472	A58	50p	multicolored	3.50	1.10

History of Chess — A59

Early Chess Game — A60

Various chess pieces.

1983, June 13 **Litho.** ***Perf. 12***

473	A59	1p	multicolored	.25	.25
474	A59	1.50p	multicolored	.25	.25
475	A59	3.50p	multicolored	.25	.25
476	A59	5p	multicolored	.35	.25
477	A59	10p	multicolored	.70	.25
478	A59	20p	multicolored	1.25	.25
479	A59	40p	multicolored	3.00	.60
			Nos. 473-479 (7)	6.05	2.10

Souvenir Sheet

480	A60	50p	brown & blk	4.00	1.25

Raphael, 500th Birth Anniv. A61

Various paintings.

1983, June 30 **Litho.** ***Perf. 12½***

481	A61	1p	gold & multi	.25	.25
482	A61	1.50p	gold & multi	.25	.25
483	A61	3.50p	gold & multi	.25	.25
484	A61	5p	gold & multi	.30	.25
485	A61	8p	gold & multi	.45	.25
486	A61	15p	gold & multi	.75	.25
487	A61	30p	gold & multi	1.75	.45
			Nos. 481-487 (7)	4.00	1.95

Souvenir Sheet

488	A61	50p	gold & multi	3.25	1.25

1984 Summer Olympics, Los Angeles — A62

1983, July 20 **Litho.** ***Perf. 12½***

489	A62	1p	Swimming	.25	.25
490	A62	1.50p	Jumping	.25	.25
491	A62	3.50p	Fencing	.35	.25
492	A62	5p	Weightlifting	.35	.25
493	A62	10p	Running	.45	.25
494	A62	20p	Equestrian	1.05	.25
495	A62	40p	Bicycling	2.10	.70
			Nos. 489-495 (7)	4.80	2.20

Souvenir Sheet

496	A62	50p	Stadium	4.00	1.25

Souvenir Sheet

BRASILIANA '83, Philatelic Exhibition — A63

1983, July 29 **Litho.** ***Perf. 13***

497	A63	50p	multicolored	*7.50*	*7.50*

Local Fish — A64

1p, Monodactylus sebae, vert. 1.50p, Botia macracanthus. 3.50p, Ctenopoma acutirostre. 5p, Roloffia bertholdi. 8p, Aphyosemion bualanum. 10p, Aphyosemion bivittatum. 30p, Aphyosemion australe.

Perf. 12x11½, 11½x12

1983, Dec. 8 **Litho.**

498	A64	1p	multicolored	.25	.25
499	A64	1.50p	multicolored	.25	.25
500	A64	3.50p	multicolored	.30	.25
501	A64	5p	multicolored	.35	.25
502	A64	8p	multicolored	.50	.25
503	A64	10p	multicolored	.75	.25
504	A64	30p	multicolored	2.25	.95
			Nos. 498-504 (7)	4.65	2.45

1984 Winter Olympics, Sarajevo — A65

1983, Oct. 10 **Litho.** ***Perf. 13***

505	A65	1p	Speed skating	.25	.25
506	A65	1.50p	Ski jumping	.25	.25
507	A65	3p	Biathlon	.35	.25
508	A65	5p	Bobsledding	.45	.25
509	A65	10p	Hockey	.55	.25
510	A65	15p	Figure skating	1.00	.25
511	A65	20p	Luge	1.40	.30
			Nos. 505-511 (7)	4.25	1.80

Souvenir Sheet

512	A65	50p	Downhill skiing	4.50	4.50

No. 512 contains one 31x40mm stamp.

A66

1983, Nov. 7 ***Perf. 12½***

513	A66	4.50p	Emblem	.50	.25
514	A66	7.50p	Woman, flag	.70	.25
515	A66	9p	Sewing	.95	.25
516	A66	12p	Farm workers	1.25	.25
			Nos. 513-516 (4)	3.40	1.00

First anniv. of Women's Federation.

A67

Designs: Local flowers: 1p, Canna coccinea. 1.50p, Bouganville litoralis. 3.50p, Euphorbia milii. 5p, Delonix regia. 8p, Bauhinia variegata. 10p, Spathodea campanulata. 30p, Hibiscus rosa-sinensis.

1983, Nov. 12 **Litho.** ***Perf. 13***

517	A67	1p	multicolored	.25	.25
518	A67	1.50p	multicolored	.25	.25
519	A67	3.50p	multicolored	.25	.25
520	A67	5p	multicolored	.30	.25
521	A67	8p	multicolored	.45	.25
522	A67	10p	multicolored	.60	.25
523	A67	30p	multicolored	1.75	.80
			Nos. 517-523 (7)	3.85	2.30

JAAC Congress, Sept. 8-12 — A68

1983, Sept. 1 **Litho.** ***Perf. 13***

524	A68	4p	shown	1.00	.25
524A	A68	5p	Emblem	1.00	.25

World Food Day A69

10p, Hoeing, vert.

1983, Oct. 16 **Litho.** ***Perf. 12½x12***

Frame Color

525	A69	1.50p	green	.25	.25
526	A69	2p	blue	.30	.25
527	A69	4p	red	.40	.25

Imperf

Size: 61x62mm

528	A69	10p	lt. blue	2.50	1.10
			Nos. 525-528 (4)	3.45	1.85

1984 Winter Olympics, Sarajevo A70

1984, Jan. 8 ***Perf. 12***

529	A70	50c	Ski jumping	.25	.25
530	A70	2.50p	Speed skating	.30	.25
531	A70	3.50p	Hockey	.40	.25
532	A70	5p	Biathlon	.45	.25
533	A70	6p	Downhill skiing	.50	.25
534	A70	20p	Figure skating	1.20	.40
535	A70	30p	Bobsledding	2.00	.45
			Nos. 529-535 (7)	5.10	2.10

Souvenir Sheet

Perf. 11½

536	A70	50p	Skiing	4.00	4.00

No. 536 contains one 32x43mm stamp.

World Communications Year — A71

50c, Rowland Hill. 2.50p, Samuel Morse. 3.50p, H.R. Hertz. 5p, Lord Kelvin. 10p, Alex. Graham Bell. 20p, G. Marconi. 30p, V. Zworykin.
50p, Satellites.

1983, Aug. 30 **Litho.** ***Perf. 12½***

537	A71	50c	multicolored	.30	.25
538	A71	2.50p	multicolored	.35	.25
539	A71	3.50p	multicolored	.40	.25
540	A71	5p	multicolored	.55	.25
541	A71	10p	multicolored	1.00	.25
542	A71	20p	multicolored	2.00	.60
543	A71	30p	multicolored	3.00	.75
			Nos. 537-543 (7)	7.60	2.60

Souvenir Sheet

544	A71	50p	multicolored	4.00	3.25

No. 544 contains one stamp 31x39mm.

Vintage Cars A72

5p, Duesenberg, 1928. 8p, MG Midget, 1932. 15p, Mercedes, 1928. 20p, Bentley, 1928. 24p, Alfa Romeo, 1929. 30p, Datsun, 1932. 35p, Lincoln, 1932.
100p, Gottlieb Daimler.

1984, Mar. 20 ***Perf. 12***

545	A72	5p	multicolored	.25	.25
546	A72	8p	multicolored	.40	.25
547	A72	15p	multicolored	.55	.25
548	A72	20p	multicolored	.65	.30
549	A72	24p	multicolored	.75	.35
550	A72	30p	multicolored	1.10	.50
551	A72	35p	multicolored	1.25	.55
			Nos. 545-551 (7)	4.95	2.45

Souvenir Sheet

552	A72	100p	multicolored	6.00	4.25

No. 552 contains one stamp 50x42mm.

Madonna and Child, by Morales — A73

Paintings by Spanish Artists (Espana '84): 6p, Dona Tadea Arias de Enriquez, by Goya. 10p, Santa Cassilda, by Zurbaran. 12p, Saints Andrew and Francis, by El Greco. 15p, Infanta Isabel Clara Eugenia, by Coello. 35p, Queen Maria of Austria, by Velazquez. 40p, Holy Trinity, by El Greco. 100p, Clothed Maja, by Goya.

1984, Apr. 20

553	A73	3p	multicolored	.25	.25
554	A73	6p	multicolored	.25	.25
555	A73	10p	multicolored	.25	.25
556	A73	12p	multicolored	.45	.25

557	A73	15p multicolored	.60	.25
558	A73	35p multicolored	1.45	.60
559	A73	40p multicolored	1.75	.65
		Nos. 553-559 (7)	5.00	2.50

Souvenir Sheet

560	A73	100p multicolored	5.00	4.75

No. 560 contains one stamp 29x50mm.

Carnivorous Animals — A74

1984, June 28

561	A74	3p Panthera tigris	.25	.25
562	A74	6p Panthera leo	.40	.25
563	A74	10p Neofelis nebulosa	.45	.25
564	A74	12p Acinonyx jubatus	.60	.30
565	A74	15p Lynx lynx	.65	.30
566	A74	35p Panthera pardus	1.75	.60
567	A74	40p Uncia uncia	1.90	.70
		Nos. 561-567 (7)	6.00	2.65

Intl. Civil Aviation Org., 40th Anniv. — A75

1984, Apr. 4 Litho. *Perf. 12½*

568	A75	8p Caravelle	.40	.25
569	A75	22p DC-6B	.85	.35
570	A75	80p IL-76	3.00	1.25
		Nos. 568-570 (3)	4.25	1.85

1984 Summer Olympics, Los Angeles — A76

6p, Soccer. 8p, Dressage. 15p, Yachting. 20p, Field hockey. 22p, Women's team handball. 30p, Canoeing. 40p, Boxing. 100p, Windsurfing.

1984, May 24 *Perf. 12*

571	A76	6p multicolored	.25	.25
572	A76	8p multicolored	.25	.25
573	A76	15p multicolored	.55	.25
574	A76	20p multicolored	.70	.25
575	A76	22p multicolored	.75	.25
576	A76	30p multicolored	1.10	.40
577	A76	40p multicolored	1.40	.80
		Nos. 571-577 (7)	5.00	2.45

Souvenir Sheet

Perf. 11½

578	A76	100p multicolored	5.50	3.75

World Heritage — A77

Wood sculptures: 3p, Pearl throne, Cameroun and Central Africa. 6p, Antelope, South Sudan. 10p, Kneeling woman, East Africa. 12p, Mask, West African coast. 15p, Leopard, Guinea coast. 35p, Standing woman, Zaire. 40p, Funerary statues, Southeast Africa and Madagascar.

1984, Aug. 15 *Perf. 12½*

579	A77	3p multicolored	.35	.25
580	A77	6p multicolored	.40	.25
581	A77	10p multicolored	.45	.25
582	A77	12p multicolored	.75	.25
583	A77	15p multicolored	.95	.30
584	A77	35p multicolored	1.90	.65
585	A77	40p multicolored	2.10	.70
		Nos. 579-585 (7)	6.90	2.65

Amilcar Cabral, 60th Birth Anniv. — A78

5p, Public speaking. 12p, In combat fatigues. 20p, Memorial building, Bafata. 50p, Mausoleum, Bissau.

1984, Sept. 12 *Perf. 13*

586	A78	5p multicolored	.50	.25
587	A78	12p multicolored	.55	.25
588	A78	20p multicolored	1.00	.35
589	A78	50p multicolored	2.25	.80
		Nos. 586-589 (4)	4.30	1.65

Independence, 11th Anniv. — A79

3p, Mechanic. 6p, Student. 10p, Mason. 12p, Health care, vert. 15p, Seamstress, vert. 35p, Telecommunications. 40p, PAIGC building.

1984, Sept. 24

590	A79	3p multi	.30	.25
591	A79	6p multi	.35	.25
592	A79	10p multi	.45	.25
593	A79	12p multi	.60	.30
594	A79	15p multi	.75	.30
595	A79	35p multi	1.50	.70
596	A79	40p multi	1.75	.75
		Nos. 590-596 (7)	5.70	2.80

Whales A80

5p, Eschrichtius gibbosus. 8p, Balaenoptera musculus. 15p, Tursiops truncatus. 20p, Physeter macrocephalus. 24p, Orcinus orca. 30p, Balaena mysticetus. 35p, Balaenoptera borealis.

1984, Sept. 30 *Perf. 12*

597	A80	5p multicolored	.45	.25
598	A80	8p multicolored	.60	.25
599	A80	15p multicolored	.90	.35
600	A80	20p multicolored	1.75	.35
601	A80	24p multicolored	2.75	.45
602	A80	30p multicolored	2.75	.55
603	A80	35p multicolored	2.75	.60
		Nos. 597-603 (7)	11.95	2.80

Butterflies A81

3p, Hypolimnas dexithea. 6p, Papilio arcturus. 10p, Morpho menelaus terrestris. 12p, Apaturina erminea papuana. 15p, Prepona praeneste. 35p, Ornithoptera paradisea. 40p, Morpho hecuba obidona.

1984, Oct. 6 *Perf. 12½x13*

604	A81	3p multicolored	.35	.25
605	A81	6p multicolored	.45	.25
606	A81	10p multicolored	.50	.25
607	A81	12p multicolored	.65	.25
608	A81	15p multicolored	.85	.35
609	A81	35p multicolored	1.20	.65
610	A81	40p multicolored	1.75	.75
		Nos. 604-610 (7)	5.75	2.75

1984 Los Angeles Summer Olympic Winners — A82

National flag, medal and: 6p, Carl Lewis, 4x100 relay, US. 8p, Koji Gushiken, gymnastics, Japan. 15p, Reiner Klimke, equestrian, Federal Republic of Germany. 20p, Tracie Ruiz, synchronized swimming, US. 22p, Mary Lou Retton, gymnastics, US. 30p, Michael Gross, swimming, Federal Republic of Germany. 40p, Edwin Moses, hurdler, US. 100p, Daley Thompson, decathlon, Great Britain.

1984, Nov. 27 *Perf. 13*

611	A82	6p multicolored	.25	.25
612	A82	8p multicolored	.30	.25
613	A82	15p multicolored	.50	.25
614	A82	20p multicolored	.75	.25
615	A82	22p multicolored	.80	.30
616	A82	30p multicolored	1.25	.45
617	A82	40p multicolored	1.60	.65
		Nos. 611-617 (7)	5.45	2.40

Souvenir Sheet

Perf. 12½

618	A82	100p multicolored	5.25	3.75

No. 618 contains one stamp 32x40mm.

Locomotives — A83

5p, White Mountain Central No. 4. 8p, Kessler 2-6-OT, 1886. 15p, Langen tram, 1901. 20p, Gurjao No. 6. 24p, Achenseebahn. 30p, Vitznau-Rigi steam locomotive. 35p, Riggenbach rackrail, 1873.

1984, Dec. 15 *Perf. 13*

619	A83	5p multicolored	.30	.25
620	A83	8p multicolored	.40	.25
621	A83	15p multicolored	.50	.30
622	A83	20p multicolored	.65	.35
623	A83	24p multicolored	.85	.40
624	A83	30p multicolored	1.05	.55
625	A83	35p multicolored	1.25	.85
		Nos. 619-625 (7)	5.00	2.95

Souvenir Sheet

Perf. 12½

625A	A83	100p like #621	5.75	3.50

No. 625A contains one stamp 40x32mm.

Native Crafts — A83a

LUBRAPEX '84: a, Numbe mask. b, Sono statue. c, Erande statue. d, Kokumba arms. e, Oma mask. f, Koni mask.

1984, May 9 Litho. *Perf. 13½*

626	A83a	7.50p Strip of 6, #a.-f.	5.00	3.50

Motorcycle Cent. — A84

1985, Feb. 20 *Perf. 13x12½*

627	A84	5p Harley-Davidson	.30	.25
628	A84	8p Kawasaki	.45	.25
629	A84	15p Honda	.70	.25
630	A84	20p Yamaha	1.10	.35
631	A84	25p Suzuki	1.60	.40
632	A84	30p BMW	1.90	.55
633	A84	35p Moto Guzzi	2.75	.60
		Nos. 627-633 (7)	8.80	2.65

Souvenir Sheet

Perf. 12½

634	A84	100p Daimler Motorized Bicycle, 1885, vert.	9.00	6.00

No. 634 contains one 32x40mm stamp.

Miniature Sheet

Mushrooms — A85

1985, May 15 *Perf. 13*

635	A85	Sheet of 6	6.50	2.10
a.		7p Clitocybe gibba	.35	.25
b.		9p Morchella elata	.40	.25
c.		12p Lepista nuda	.55	.30
d.		20p Lactarius deliciosus	.95	.35
e.		30p Russula virescens	1.35	.45
f.		35p Chroogomphus rutilus	1.50	.55

Henri Dunant (1828-1910), Red Cross Founder, Plane — A87

1985, June 12 *Perf. 12½*

643	A87	20p shown	.60	.25
644	A87	25p Ambulance	.70	.25
645	A87	40p Helicopter	1.50	.45
646	A87	80p Speed boat	3.00	.80
		Nos. 643-646 (4)	5.80	1.75

Cats — A88

1985, July 5 *Perf. 13*

647	A88	7p multicolored	.25	.25
648	A88	10p multicolored	.25	.25
649	A88	12p multicolored	.35	.25
650	A88	15p multicolored	.55	.25
651	A88	20p multicolored	.80	.25

652 A88 40p multicolored 1.15 .25
653 A88 45p multicolored 1.75 .40
Nos. 647-653 (7) 5.10 1.90

Souvenir Sheet

654 A88 100p multicolored 5.50 4.00

ARGENTINA '85. No. 654 contains one 40x32mm stamp.

Composers and Musical Instruments
A89

Designs: 4p, Vincenzo Bellini (1801-1835), harp, 1820, and descant viol, 16th cent. 5p, Schumann (1810-1856) and Viennese pyramid piano, 1829. 7p, Chopin (1810-1849) and piano-forte, 1817. 12p, Luigi Cherubini (1760-1842) and 18th cent. Baryton violin and Quinton viol. 20p, G. B. Pergolesi (1710-1736) and double-manual harpsichord, 1734. 30p, Handel (1685-1759), valve trumpet, 1825, and timpani drum, 18th cent. 50p, Heinrich Schutz (1585-1672), bass viol and two-stop oboe, 17th cent. 100s, Bach (1685-1750) and St. Thomas Church organ, Leipzig.

1985, Aug. 5 *Perf. 12*

655 A89 4p multicolored .25 .25
656 A89 5p multicolored .30 .25
657 A89 7p multicolored .45 .25
658 A89 12p multicolored .70 .25
659 A89 20p multicolored 1.00 .25
660 A89 30p multicolored 1.60 .30
661 A89 50p multicolored 2.50 .60
Nos. 655-661 (7) 6.80 2.15

Souvenir Sheet

Perf. 11½

662 A89 100p multicolored 6.50 4.25

No. 662 contains one 30x50mm stamp.

Santa Maria, 15th Cent., Spain — A90

Ships: 15p, Carack, 16th cent., Netherlands. 20p, Mayflower, 17th cent., Great Britain. 30p, St. Louis, 17th cent., France. 35p, Royal Sovereign, 1635, Great Britain. 45p, Soleil Royal, 17th cent., France. 80p, English brig, 18th-19th cent.

1985, Sept. 12 *Perf. 13*

663 A90 8p multicolored .30 .25
664 A90 15p multicolored .45 .25
665 A90 20p multicolored .60 .25
666 A90 30p multicolored 1.00 .30
667 A90 35p multicolored 1.15 .30
668 A90 45p multicolored 1.50 .45
669 A90 80p multicolored 3.00 .75
Nos. 663-669 (7) 8.00 2.55

UN, 40th Anniv.
A91

10p, Emblem, doves, vert. 20p, Emblem, 40.

1985, Oct. 17

670 A91 10p multicolored .60 .25
671 A91 20p multicolored 1.40 .50

Venus and Mars, by Sandro Botticelli (1445-1510)
A92

Botticelli paintings (details): 7p, Virgin with Child and St. John. 12p, St. Augustine in the Work Hall. 15p, Awakening of Spring. 20p, Virgin and Child. 40p, Virgin with Child and St. John, diff. 45p, Birth of Venus. 100p, Virgin and Child with Two Angels.

1985, Oct. 25 *Perf. 12½x13*

672 A92 7p multicolored .35 .25
673 A92 10p multicolored .40 .25
674 A92 12p multicolored .50 .25
675 A92 15p multicolored .55 .25
676 A92 20p multicolored .75 .25
677 A92 40p multicolored 1.50 .40
678 A92 45p multicolored 1.90 .45

Size: 73x106mm

Imperf

679 A92 100p multicolored 7.00 5.50
Nos. 672-679 (8) 12.95 7.60

ITALIA '85.

Intl. Youth Year
A93

1985, Nov. 29 **Litho.** *Perf. 12½*

680 A93 7p Dance .25 .25
681 A93 13p Wind surfing .30 .25
682 A93 15p Rollerskating .35 .25
683 A93 25p Hang gliding .65 .25
684 A93 40p Surfing 1.00 .30
685 A93 50p Skateboarding 1.25 .50
686 A93 80p Parachuting 2.25 .70
Nos. 680-686 (7) 6.05 2.50

Souvenir Sheet

Perf. 13

687 A93 100p Self-defense 6.00 4.50

No. 687 contains one 40x32mm stamp.

Halley's Comet — A94

1986 World Cup Soccer Championships, Mexico — A95

24th Summer Olympics, Seoul, 1988
A96

Italian Automobile Industry, Cent.
A97

German Railways, 150th Anniv.
A98

Discovery of America, 500th Anniv. (in 1992)
A99

First American Manned Space Flight, 25th Anniv. — A100

1986 Wimbledon Tennis Championships — A101

1986 Masters Tennis Championships — A102

Giotto Space Probe — A103

Designs: a, Comet tail. b, Comet. c, Trophy. d, Trophy base. e, Five-ring Olympic emblem. f, Alfa Tourer, Italy, c. 1905. g, Railway station, Frankfurt-on Main, c. 1914. h, Barcelona, site of Discovery of America exhibition and 1992 Olympics. i, Space station solar panels and tanks. j, Space station. k, Removing cargo from space shuttle. l, Docking facility, station panels. m, Boris Becker swinging tennis racket. n, Becker, diff. o, Ivan Lendl holding racket. p, Lendl, diff.

Miniature Sheet

1986, Dec. 30 **Litho.** *Perf. 13½*

688 Sheet of 16 *100.00*
a.-p. A94-A102 15p any single 6.00 3.25

Souvenir Sheet

689 A103 100p multicolored 14.00 10.00

Nos. 688a-688b, 688c-688d, 688i-688l, 688m-688n, 688o-688p are se-tenant in continuous designs. Inscription on Nos. 688i-688l incorrect; should read "TRIPULADO MERCURY / 5-5-1961."

Discovery of America, 500th Anniv. (in 1992) — A104

Designs: No. 690, Christopher Columbus aboard caravelle. No. 691, Guadalquivir Port, Seville, c. 1490. No. 692, Pedro Alvars Cabral landing at Bahia, Brazil. No. 693, Bridge over the Guadalquivir River, Seville. No. 694, Port, Lisbon, 15th cent.

1987, Feb. 27

690 A104 50p multicolored 3.50 1.20
691 A104 50p multicolored 3.50 1.20
692 A104 50p multicolored 3.50 1.20
693 A104 50p multicolored 3.50 1.20
Nos. 690-693 (4) 14.00 4.80

Souvenir Sheet

694 A104 150p multicolored 14.00 9.00

No. 694 exists with pink or yellow anniv. emblem pictured in vignette. Values are the same.

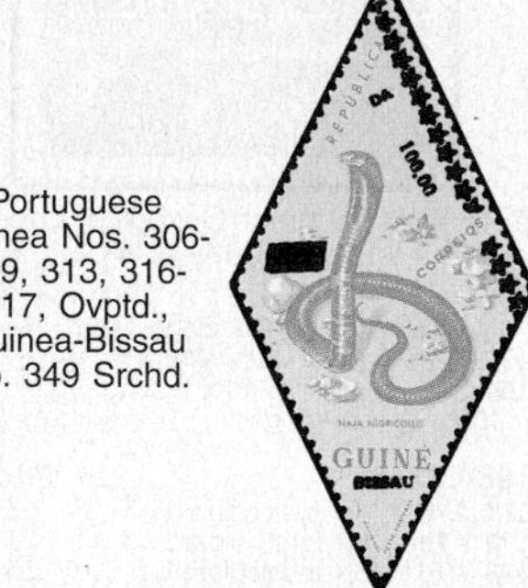

Portuguese Guinea Nos. 306-309, 313, 316-317, Ovptd., Guinea-Bissau No. 349 Srchd.

1987, July **Litho.** *Perf. 13½*

696 A21 100p on 20c #306 1.75 .60
697 A21 200p on 35c #307 3.25 1.25
698 A21 300p on 70c #308 5.00 1.60
699 A21 400p on 80c #309 5.50 2.00
700 A21 500p on 3.50e #313 7.75 2.75
701 A21 1000p on 15e #316 20.00 5.50
702 A21 2000p on 20e #317 40.00 13.50

Perf. 13

703 CD61 2500p on 2e #349 50.00 14.50
Nos. 696-703 (8) 133.25 41.70

Placement of "Bissau," new denomination and obliterating bar varies. No. 698 is known to have been sold in April 1986.

1988 Winter Olympics, Calgary — A106

5p, Pairs figure skating. 10p, Luge. 50p, Skiing. 200p, Slalom skiing. 300p, Skibobbing. 500p, Ski jumping, vert. 800p, Speed skating, vert.
900p, Two-man luge.

1988, Jan. 15 Litho. *Perf. 13*

704	A106	5p	multicolored	.30	.25
705	A106	10p	multicolored	.50	.25
706	A106	50p	multicolored	.60	.25
707	A106	200p	multicolored	.75	.35
708	A106	300p	multicolored	1.35	.50
709	A106	500p	multicolored	2.00	.65
710	A106	800p	multicolored	3.50	2.25
			Nos. 704-710 (7)	9.00	4.50

Souvenir Sheet

710A	A106	900p	multicolored	7.00	3.50

No. 710A contains one 40x32mm stamp.

Soccer — A107

Various soccer plays.

1988, Apr. 14 Litho. *Perf. 13*

711	A107	5p	multi	.25	.25
712	A107	10p	multi, diff.	.25	.25
713	A107	50p	multi, diff.	.55	.25
714	A107	200p	multi, diff.	1.10	.40
715	A107	300p	multi, diff.	1.75	.50
716	A107	500p	multi, diff.	2.00	.65
717	A107	800p	multi, diff.	4.00	1.75
			Nos. 711-717 (7)	9.90	4.05

Souvenir Sheet

718	A107	900p	multi, diff.	7.00	4.75

ESSEN '88 stamp exhibition. No. 718 contains one 32x40mm stamp.

1988 Summer Olympics, Seoul — A108

5p, Yachting, vert. 10p, Equestrian. 50p, High jump. 200p, Shooting. 300p, Long jump, vert. 500p, Tennis, vert. 800p, Women's archery, vert.
900p, Soccer.

Perf. 12½x12, 12x12½

1988, Feb. 26 Litho.

719	A108	5p	multi	.25	.25
720	A108	10p	multi	.25	.25
721	A108	50p	multi	.35	.25
722	A108	200p	multi	1.15	.50
723	A108	300p	multi	1.75	.60
724	A108	500p	multi	2.75	.75
725	A108	800p	multi	4.50	1.50
			Nos. 719-725 (7)	11.00	4.10

Souvenir Sheet

Perf. 12½

726	A108	900p	multi	5.00	2.25

No. 726 contains one 40x32mm stamp.

Ancient Ships — A109

Designs: 5p, Egyptian, c. 3300 B.C. 10p, Pharaoh Sahure's ship, c. 2700 B.C. 50p, Queen Hatsepsowe's ship, c. 1500 B.C. 200p, Ramses III's ship, c. 1200 B.C. 300p, Greek trireme, 480 B.C. 500p, Etruscan bireme, 600 B.C. 800p, Venetian galley, 12th cent.

1988 Litho. *Perf. 13x12½*

727	A109	5p	multi	.25	.25
728	A109	10p	multi	.25	.25
729	A109	50p	multi	.45	.25
730	A109	200p	multi	1.10	.35
731	A109	300p	multi	1.50	.40
732	A109	500p	multi	2.50	.60
733	A109	800p	multi	4.00	1.00
			Nos. 727-733 (7)	10.05	3.10

FINLANDIA '88 — A110

Chess champions, board and chessmen: 5p, Philidor. 10p, Staunton. 50p, Anderssen. 200p, Morphy. 300p, Steinitz. 500p, Lasker. 800p, Capablanca.
900p, Ruy Lopez.

1988 Litho. *Perf. 12x12½*

734	A110	5p	multi	.25	.25
735	A110	10p	multi	.25	.25
736	A110	50p	multi	.50	.25
737	A110	200p	multi	1.25	.25
738	A110	300p	multi	1.60	.30
739	A110	500p	multi	3.00	.40
740	A110	800p	multi	4.50	.65
			Nos. 734-740 (7)	11.35	2.35

Souvenir Sheet

Perf. 13

741	A110	900p	multi	7.00	4.75

No. 741 contains one 40x32mm stamp.

Dogs A111

5p, Basset hound. 10p, Great blue of Gascony. 50p, Sabujo of Italy. 200p, Yorkshire terrier. 300p, Small musterlander. 500p, Pointer. 800p, German setter.
900p, German shepherd.

1988, Sept. 29 *Perf. 13x12½*

742	A111	5p	multicolored	.25	.25
743	A111	10p	multicolored	.35	.25
744	A111	50p	multicolored	.35	.25
745	A111	200p	multicolored	.85	.40
746	A111	300p	multicolored	1.40	.70
747	A111	500p	multicolored	2.25	1.25
748	A111	800p	multicolored	3.50	1.75
			Nos. 742-748 (7)	8.95	4.85

Souvenir Sheet

Perf. 12½

749	A111	900p	multicolored	5.50	2.50

No. 749 contains one 40x32mm stamp.

Intl. Red Cross and Red Crescent Organizations, 125th Annivs. — A112

10p, Jean-Henri Dunant. 50p, Dr. T. Maunoir. 200p, Dr. Louis Appia. 800p, Gustave Moynier.

1988 *Perf. 13*

750	A112	10p	multicolored	.25	.25
751	A112	50p	multicolored	.50	.25
752	A112	200p	multicolored	.85	.50
753	A112	800p	multicolored	4.00	.90
			Nos. 750-753 (4)	5.60	1.90

Maps and Fauna — A113

5p, Panthera leo. 10p, Glaucidium brasilianum. 50p, Upupa epops. 200p, Equus burchelli antiquorum. 300p, Loxodonta africana. 500p, Acryllium vulturinum. 800p, Diceros bicornis.

1988 *Perf. 12½x13, 13x12½*

754	A113	5p	multicolored	.25	.25
755	A113	10p	multicolored	.25	.25
756	A113	50p	multicolored	.50	.25
757	A113	200p	multicolored	1.10	.25
758	A113	300p	multicolored	1.60	.30
759	A113	500p	multicolored	2.50	.75
760	A113	800p	multicolored	4.25	1.75
			Nos. 754-760 (7)	10.45	3.80

Nos. 754-755, 758-760 vert. The genus "Upupa" is misspelled on the 50p and "Loxodonta" is misspelled on the 300p.

Samora Machel (1933-1986), Pres. of Mozambique A114

50p, Raising fist. 200p, With sentry. 300p, Wearing earphones at UN.

1988 *Perf. 13*

761	A114	10p	shown	.25	.25
762	A114	50p	multicolored	.40	.25
763	A114	200p	multicolored	1.25	.50
764	A114	300p	multicolored	2.10	.80
			Nos. 761-764 (4)	4.00	1.80

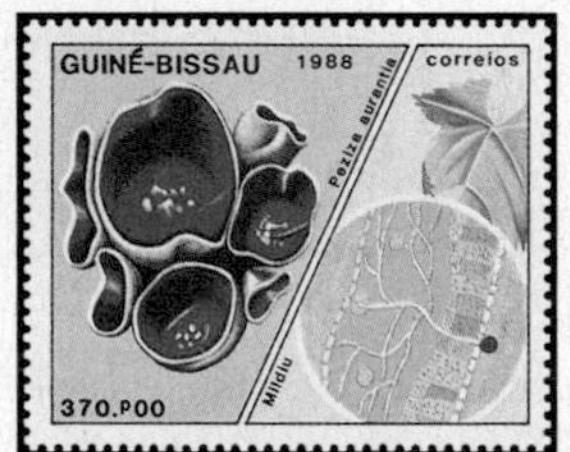

Mushrooms — A115

370p, Peziza aurantia. 470p, Morchella. 600p, Amanita caesarea. 780p, Amanita muscaria. 800p, Amanita phalloides. 900p, Agaricus bisporus. 945p, Cantharellus cibarius.

1988 Litho. *Perf. 13x12½*

765	A115	370p	multicolored	1.40	.35
766	A115	470p	multicolored	1.75	.40
767	A115	600p	multicolored	2.75	.60
768	A115	780p	multicolored	4.00	.70
769	A115	800p	multicolored	4.00	.70
770	A115	900p	multicolored	4.75	.90
771	A115	945p	multicolored	4.25	.95
			Nos. 765-771 (7)	22.90	4.60

1992 Winter Olympics, Albertville — A116

50p, Speed skating. 100p, Women's figure skating. 200p, Ski jumping. 350p, Skiing. 500p, Skiing, diff. 800p, Bobsled. 1000p, Ice hockey.
1500p, Ice hockey, diff.

1989, Oct. 12 Litho. *Perf. 12½x12*

772	A116	50p	multicolored	.40	.25
773	A116	100p	multicolored	.55	.25
774	A116	200p	multicolored	1.10	.25
775	A116	350p	multicolored	1.25	.40
776	A116	500p	multicolored	2.10	.55
777	A116	800p	multicolored	3.25	.95
778	A116	1000p	multicolored	4.25	1.10
			Nos. 772-778 (7)	12.90	3.75

Souvenir Sheet

Perf. 12½

779	A116	1500p	multicolored	6.00	5.00

No. 779 contains one 32x40mm stamp.

World Cup Soccer Championships, Italy — A117

Various soccer players.

1989, Aug. 14 Litho. *Perf. 12½*

780	A117	50p	multicolored	.25	.25
781	A117	100p	multicolored	.45	.25
782	A117	200p	multicolored	.60	.25
783	A117	350p	multicolored	1.00	.35
784	A117	500p	multicolored	1.20	.45
785	A117	800p	multicolored	2.50	.80
786	A117	1000p	multicolored	3.00	.90
			Nos. 780-786 (7)	9.00	3.25

Souvenir Sheet

Perf. 13

786A	A117	1500p	multicolored	4.50	3.00

No. 786A contains one 40x32mm stamp.

Lilies (Lilium) — A118

50p, Limelight. 100p, Candidum. 200p, Pardalinum. 350p, Auratum. 500p, Canadense. 800p, Enchantment. 1000p, Black Dragon.
1500p, Lilium pyrenaicum.

1989, June 15 *Perf. 12½*

787	A118	50p	multi	.25	.25
788	A118	100p	multi	.40	.25
789	A118	200p	multi	.70	.35
790	A118	350p	multi	1.15	.65
791	A118	500p	multi	1.35	.70
792	A118	800p	multi	2.75	1.50
793	A118	1000p	multi	3.50	1.90
			Nos. 787-793 (7)	10.10	5.60

Souvenir Sheet

794	A118	1500p	multi	5.25	3.00

No. 794 contains one 32x40mm stamp.

Trains A119

Various railroad engines.

1989, May 24 Litho. *Perf. 13*

795	A119	50p	multicolored	.25	.25
796	A119	100p	multicolored	.35	.25
797	A119	200p	multicolored	.60	.35
798	A119	350p	multicolored	1.25	.70
799	A119	500p	multicolored	1.75	.95
800	A119	800p	multicolored	2.50	1.60

Perf. 12½

Size: 68x27mm

801	A119	1000p	multicolored	3.25	.85
			Nos. 795-801 (7)	9.95	4.95

Souvenir Sheet

Perf. 12½

802 A119 1500p multicolored 5.00 3.00

No. 802 contains one 32x40mm stamp.

La Marseillaise by Francois Rude — A120

Paintings: 100p, Armed mob. 200p, Storming the Bastille. 350p, Lafayette, Liberty, vert. 500p, Dancing around the Liberty tree. 800p, Rouget de Lisle singing La Marseillaise by Pils. 1000p, Storming the Bastille, diff. 1500p, Arms of the Republic of France.

Perf. 12½, 12x12½ (350p)

1989, July 5

803 A120 50p shown .25 .25
804 A120 100p multicolored .25 .25
805 A120 200p multicolored .55 .40
806 A120 350p multicolored, 27x44mm 1.10 .50
807 A120 500p multicolored 1.60 .90
808 A120 800p multicolored 2.50 1.40
809 A120 1000p multicolored 3.00 1.75
Nos. 803-809 (7) 9.25 5.45

Souvenir Sheet

Perf. 13

810 A120 1500p multicolored 5.00 2.75

Birds A121

Designs: 50p, Alectroenas pulcherrima. 100p, Streptopelia senegalensis. 200p, Oena capensis. 350p, Claravis mondetoura. 500p, Streptopelia roseogrisea. 800p, Otidiphaps nobilis. 1000p, Chalcophaps indica. 1500p, Reinwardtoena Reinwardtsi.

1989, Apr. 28 **Litho.** *Perf. 12½*

811 A121 50p multicolored .25 .25
812 A121 100p multicolored .30 .25
813 A121 200p multicolored .60 .40
814 A121 350p multicolored 1.10 .50
815 A121 500p multicolored 1.60 .90
816 A121 800p multicolored 2.50 1.50
817 A121 1000p multicolored 3.00 1.75
Nos. 811-817 (7) 9.35 5.55

Souvenir Sheet

818 A121 1500p multicolored 6.50 3.00

Pioneers Organization — A122

10p, Children presenting flag, vert. 50p, Children saluting, vert. 300p, Children playing ball.

1989, Sept. 24 *Perf. 13*

819 A122 10p multicolored .25 .25
820 A122 50p multicolored .55 .25
821 A122 200p shown 2.25 .75
822 A122 300p multicolored 3.00 1.10
Nos. 819-822 (4) 6.05 2.35

Town of Cacheu, 400th Anniv. A123

1989, Nov. 30

823 A123 10p Monument, vert. .25 .25
824 A123 50p shown .25 .25
825 A123 200p Old building .40 .40
826 A123 300p Church 1.75 .60
Nos. 823-826 (4) 2.65 1.50

Dated 1988.

A124

Prehistoric creatures: 50p, Trachodon. 100p, Edaphosaurus. 200p, Mesosaurus. 350p, Elephas primigenius. 500p, Tyrannosaurus. 800p, Stegosaurus. 1000p, Cervus megaceros.

Perf. 13, 12½x12 (100p)

1989, Sept. 15

827 A124 50p multicolored .25 .25
828 A124 100p multi, 68x27mm .35 .25
829 A124 200p multicolored .60 .35
830 A124 350p multicolored 1.05 .50
831 A124 500p multicolored 1.75 .80
832 A124 800p multicolored 2.75 1.20
833 A124 1000p multicolored 3.25 1.50
Nos. 827-833 (7) 10.00 4.85

Nos. 828, 831-833 horiz.

A125

Designs: Musical instruments.

1989, Apr. 10 **Litho.** *Perf. 13*

834 A125 50p Bombalon .30 .25
835 A125 100p Flauta .45 .25
836 A125 200p Tambor .90 .30
837 A125 350p Dondon 1.45 .40
838 A125 500p Balafon 1.75 .75
839 A125 800p Kora 2.25 1.10
840 A125 1000p Nhanhero 2.40 1.25
Nos. 834-840 (7) 9.50 4.30

A126

Indian artifacts — 50p, Teotihuacan. 100p, Mochica. 200p, Jaina. 350p, Nayarit. 500p, Inca. 800p, Hopewell. 1000p, Taina.

1500p, Indian statuette.

1989, July 13 *Perf. 12x12½*

841 A126 50p multicolored .25 .25
842 A126 100p multicolored .30 .25
843 A126 200p multicolored .55 .35
844 A126 350p multicolored 1.25 .40
845 A126 500p multicolored 1.75 .80
846 A126 800p multicolored 2.75 1.20
847 A126 1000p multicolored 3.25 1.40
Nos. 841-847 (7) 10.10 4.65

Souvenir Sheet

Perf. 12½

848 A126 1500p multicolored 4.50 2.50

Brasiliana '89 Philatelic Exhibition. Nos. 841-847 printed se-tenant with multicolored label showing scenes of colonization. No. 848 contains one 32x40mm stamp.

1992 Summer Olympics, Barcelona A127

50p, Hurdles. 100p, Boxing. 200p, High jump. 350p, Sprinters in the blocks. 500p, Woman sprinter. 800p, Gymnastics. 1000p, Pole vault.

1500p, Soccer.

1989, June 3 *Perf. 12½x13*

849 A127 50p multicolored .30 .25
850 A127 100p multicolored .40 .25
851 A127 200p multicolored .60 .25
852 A127 350p multicolored .95 .40
853 A127 500p multicolored 1.60 .80
854 A127 800p multicolored 2.50 1.20
855 A127 1000p multicolored 3.25 1.40
Nos. 849-855 (7) 9.60 4.55

Souvenir Sheet

856 A127 1500p multicolored 4.50 2.40

No. 856 contains one 32x40mm stamp.

Wild Animals — A128

50p, Syncerus caffer. 100p, Equus quagga. 200p, Diceros bicornis. 350p, Okapia johnstoni. 500p, Macaca mulatta. 800p, Hippopotamus amphibius. 1000p, Acinonyx jubatus. 1500p, Panthera leo.

1989, Nov. 24 *Perf. 12½*

857 A128 50p multicolored .30 .25
858 A128 100p multicolored .45 .25
859 A128 200p multicolored .60 .25
860 A128 350p multicolored 1.00 .40
861 A128 500p multicolored 1.25 .60
862 A128 800p multicolored 2.10 1.00
863 A128 1000p multicolored 2.40 1.25
864 A128 1500p multicolored 3.75 1.75
Nos. 857-864 (8) 11.85 5.75

Christmas A129

Paintings of the Madonna and Child (50p) and the Adoration of the Magi: 50p, Fra Filippo Lippi. 100p, Pieter Brueghel. 200p, Mostaert. 350p, Durer. 500p, Rubens. 800p, Van der Weyden. 1000p, Francia, horiz.

1989, Dec. 10 *Perf. 13*

865 A129 50p multicolored .35 .25
866 A129 100p multicolored .45 .25
867 A129 200p multicolored .60 .25
868 A129 350p multicolored .95 .35
869 A129 500p multicolored 1.60 .60
870 A129 800p multicolored 2.75 .90
871 A129 1000p multicolored 3.25 1.25
Nos. 865-871 (7) 9.95 3.85

Womens' Hairstyles A130

Various hairstyles.

1989, Mar. 8 *Perf. 12½x13*

872 A130 50p multicolored .25 .25
873 A130 100p multicolored .40 .25
874 A130 200p multicolored .65 .35
875 A130 350p multicolored 1.15 .40
875A A130 500p multicolored 1.50 .80
876 A130 800p multicolored 2.75 1.20
877 A130 1000p multicolored 3.25 1.40
Nos. 872-877 (7) 9.95 4.65

Vegetables — A131

50p, Capisium annum. 100p, Solanium. 200p, Curcumis peco. 350p, Solanium licopersicum. 500p, Solanium itiopium. 800p, Hibiscus esculentus. 1000p, Oseille de guine.

1989, May 20 *Perf. 12½*

878 A131 50p blue .25 .25
879 A131 100p purple .25 .25
880 A131 200p blue grn .70 .25
881 A131 350p org red 1.30 .40
882 A131 500p brown 1.75 .60
883 A131 800p org brn 2.75 .95
884 A131 1000p olive grn 3.50 1.25
Nos. 878-884 (7) 10.50 3.95

Visit of Pope John Paul II — A132

1990, Jan. 27 **Litho.** *Perf. 13½*

885 A132 500p shown 1.75 1.60
886 A132 1000p multi, diff. 3.25 3.25

Souvenir Sheet

887 A132 1500p multi, diff., vert. 4.50 3.25

Souvenir Sheet

Belgica '90 — A133

1990, June 1 *Perf. 14½*

888 A133 3000p multicolored 5.50 3.50

World Meteorology Day — A134

1000p, Radar weather map. 3000p, Heliograph.

1990, Oct. 1 Litho. *Perf. 13*

889 A134 1000p multicolored	1.75	.70
890 A134 3000p multicolored	6.25	2.25

LUBRAPEX '90 — A135

1990, Sept. 21 *Perf. 14*

891 A135 500p Rooster, hen	.85	.40
892 A135 800p Turkey	1.60	.60
893 A135 1000p Duck, ducklings	2.00	.80
Nos. 891-893 (3)	4.45	1.80

Souvenir Sheet

Perf. 13½

894 A135 1500p Rooster, turkey, ducks	5.00	2.75

UN Development Program, 40th Anniv. — A136

1990 Litho. *Perf. 14*

895 A136 1000p multicolored	2.25	.65

Fight against AIDS.

Textile Manufacturing A137

No. 896: a, Gossypium hirsutum. b, Processing cotton. c, Spinning thread. d, Picking cotton. e, Moth, silkworms. f, Dyeing thread. g, Weaving. h, Animal design. i, Multicolored stripes design. j, Stripes, dots design.

1990

896 Sheet of 10	2.00	
a.-j. A137 150p any single	.25	.25
897 A137 400p like #896a	.30	.25
898 A137 500p like #896g	.40	.25
899 A137 600p like #896h	.50	.35
Nos. 896-899 (4)	3.20	.85

Carnival Masks A138

1990 Litho. *Perf. 14*

900 A138 200p Mickey Mouse	.45	.25
901 A138 300p Hippopotamus	.55	.25
902 A138 600p Bull	1.15	.35
903 A138 1200p Bull, diff.	2.25	.60
Nos. 900-903 (4)	4.40	1.45

Fish A139

Designs: 300p, Pentanemus quinquarius. 400p, Psettias sabae. 500p, Chaetodipterus goreensis. 600p, Trachinotus goreensis.

1991, Mar. 10 Litho. *Perf. 14*

904 A139 300p multicolored	.65	.35
905 A139 400p multicolored	1.00	.45
906 A139 500p multicolored	1.10	.55
907 A139 600p multicolored	1.25	.70
Nos. 904-907 (4)	4.00	2.05

Fire Trucks A140

1991, Aug. 19 Litho. *Perf. 14*

908 A140 200p shown	.40	.25
909 A140 500p Ladder truck	.85	.45
910 A140 800p Rescue vehicle	1.25	.70
911 A140 1500p Ambulance	2.50	1.25
Nos. 908-911 (4)	5.00	2.65

Birds — A141

Designs: 100p, Kaupifalco monogrammicus. 250p, Balearica pavonina. 350p, Bucorvus abyssinicus. 500p, Ephippiorhynchus senegalensis. 1500p, Kaupifalco monogrammicus, diff.

1991, Sept. 10

912 A141 100p multicolored	.75	.25
913 A141 250p multicolored	1.10	.25
914 A141 350p multicolored	1.75	.55
915 A141 500p multicolored	2.40	.75
Nos. 912-915 (4)	6.00	1.80

Souvenir Sheet

Perf. 14½

916 A141 1500p multicolored	5.00	5.00

No. 916 contains one 40x50mm stamp.

Messages A142

1991, Oct. 28 Litho. *Perf. 14*

917 A142 250p Congratulations	.35	.25
918 A142 400p With love	.65	.40
919 A142 800p Happiness	1.15	.80
920 A142 1000p Seasons Greetings	1.40	.95
Nos. 917-920 (4)	3.55	2.40

Fruits — A143

Designs: 500p, Landolfia owariensis. 1500p, Dialium guineensis. 2000p, Adansonia digitata. 3000p, Parkia biglobosa.

1992, Mar. 25 Litho. *Perf. 14*

921 A143 500p multicolored	.30	.30
922 A143 1500p multicolored	.75	.75
923 A143 2000p multicolored	1.10	1.10
924 A143 3000p multicolored	1.75	1.75
Nos. 921-924 (4)	3.90	3.90

For surcharges, see Nos. 1022, 1027.

Healthy Hearts — A144

Designs: 1500p, Cigarette butts, healthy heart. 4000p, Heart running over junk food.

1992, Apr. 7

925 A144 1500p multicolored	1.75	.80
926 A144 4000p multicolored	3.75	2.10

Traditional Costumes — A145

Designs: a, 400p, Fula. b, 600p, Balanta. c, 1000p, Fula, diff. d, 1500p, Manjaco.

1992, Feb. 28 Litho. *Perf. 14*

927 A145 Strip of 4, #a.-d.	3.00	2.10

Canoes A146

Designs: Nos. 928-931, Various types of canoes. No. 932, Alcedo cristata galerita.

1992, May 10

928 A146 750p multicolored	.40	.40
929 A146 800p multicolored	.55	.55
930 A146 1000p multicolored	.65	.65
931 A146 1300p multicolored	.80	.80
Nos. 928-931 (4)	2.40	2.40

Souvenir Sheet

Perf. 13½

932 A146 1500p multicolored	5.75	5.75

For surcharges, see No. 1018, 1021.

Trees — A147

a, 100p, Cassia alata. b, 400p, Perlebia purpurea. c, 1000p, Caesalpina pulcherrima. d, 1500p, Adenanthera pavonina. 3000p, Caesalpina pulcherrima, diff.

1992, May 8 *Perf. 14*

933 A147 Block of 4, #a.-d.	5.50	5.50

Souvenir Sheet

Perf. 13½

934 A147 3000p multicolored	5.00	5.00

1992 Summer Olympics, Barcelona A148

1992, July 28 Litho. *Perf. 14*

935 A148 600p Basketball	.25	.25
936 A148 1000p Volleyball	.55	.30
937 A148 1500p Team handball	.80	.35
938 A148 2000p Soccer	1.10	.65
Nos. 935-938 (4)	2.70	1.55

Trees A149

Designs: 1000p, Afzelia africana Smith. 1500p, Kaya senegalenses. 2000p, Militia regia. 3000p, Pterocarpus erinaceus.

1992, Sept. 11 *Perf. 12*

939 A149 1000p multicolored	.45	.45
940 A149 1500p multicolored	.60	.60
941 A149 2000p multicolored	.85	.80
942 A149 3000p multicolored	1.25	1.10
Nos. 939-942 (4)	3.15	2.95

For surcharge, see No. 1023.

Souvenir Sheet

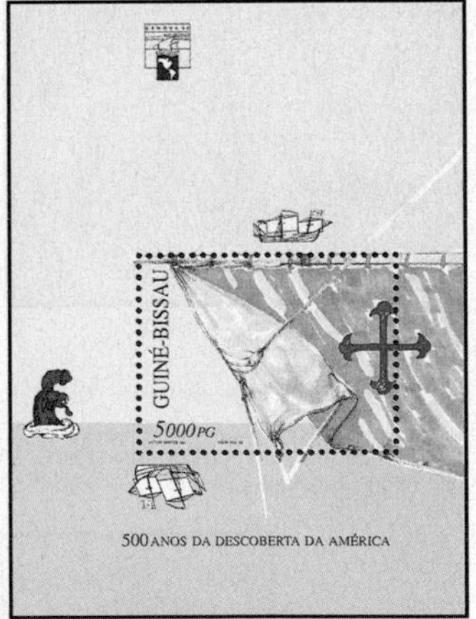

Discovery of America, 500th Anniv. — A150

1992, Sept. 18

943 A150 5000p multicolored	3.75	3.75

Genoa '92.

Procolobus Badius Temminckii — A151

Designs: a, Pair in tree. b, Adult seated in vegetation c, Adult seated in tree fork. d, Female with young.

1992 Litho. *Perf. 12x11½*

944 A151 2000p Strip of 4, #a.-d.	5.25	5.25

World Wildlife Fund.

Reptiles A152

1500p, Bitis sp. 3000p, Osteolaemus tetraspis. 4000p, Varanus nitolicus. 5000p, Agama agama.

1993, May 18 Litho. *Perf. 14*

945	A152	1500p multicolored	.50	.25
946	A152	3000p multicolored	1.10	.55
947	A152	4000p multicolored	1.50	.70
948	A152	5000p multicolored	1.90	.85
a.		Souvenir sheet of 4, #945-948	5.50	5.50
		Nos. 945-948 (4)	5.00	2.35

Souvenir Sheet

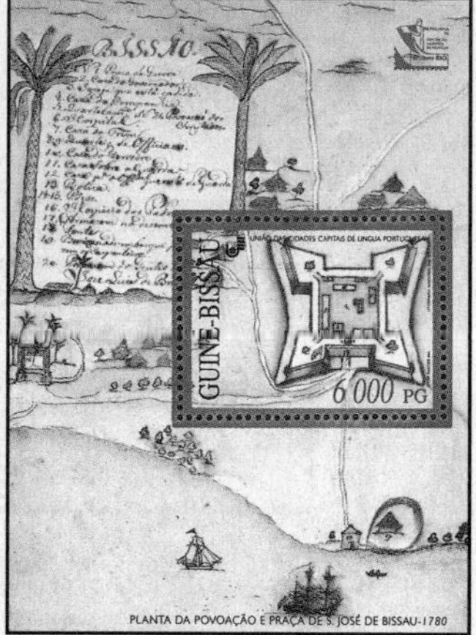

Union of Portuguese Speaking Capitals — A153

1993, July 30 Litho. *Perf. 13½*

949 A153 6000p Fort 1.75 1.75

Brasiliana '93.

Tourism — A154

Designs: a, 1000p. b, 2000p. c, 4000p. d, 5000p.

1993, Nov. 15 Litho. *Perf. 14*

950 A154 Block of 4, #a.-d. 4.50 4.50

Traditional Jewelry A155

1993, Nov. 30 *Perf. 14½*

951	A155	1500p Bracelet	.45	.25
952	A155	3000p Mask pendant	1.10	.50
953	A155	4000p Circle pendant	1.50	.65
954	A155	5000p Filigree pendant	1.75	.80
		Nos. 951-954 (4)	4.80	2.20

1994, Nov. 30 Souvenir Sheet

955 A155 18,000p like #952 8.00 8.00

Hong Kong '94 (No. 955). No. 955 has continuous design.

1994 World Cup Soccer Championships, US — A156

Various stylized designs of player, ball, net.

1994, June 17 Litho. *Perf. 14*

956	A156	4000p multicolored	1.00	.85
957	A156	5000p multicolored	1.25	1.10
958	A156	5500p multicolored	1.60	1.25
959	A156	6500p multicolored	2.00	1.60
		Nos. 956-959 (4)	5.85	4.80

Flowering Plants — A157

Designs: 2000p, Erythrina senegalensis. 3000p, Cassia occidentalis. 4000p, Gardenia ternifolia. 6000p, Cochlospermum tinctorium.

1994, May 30 Litho. *Perf. 14*

960	A157	2000p multicolored	.90	.45
961	A157	3000p multicolored	1.25	.70
962	A157	4000p multicolored	1.60	.90
963	A157	6000p multicolored	2.75	1.50
		Nos. 960-963 (4)	6.50	3.55

Snakes — A158

No. 964: a, Dasypeltis scabra. b, Philothamnus. c, Naja melanoleuca. d, Python sebae.

15,000p, Thelotornis kirtlandii.

1994, Aug. 16 Litho. *Perf. 14*

964 A158 5000p Block of 4, #a.-d. 8.00 8.00

Souvenir Sheet

Perf. 13½

965 A158 15,000p multicolored 6.50 6.50

PHILAKOREA '94, SINGPEX '94. No. 965 contains one 60x50mm stamp.

Palmeira Dendem — A159

3000p, Climbing tree to pick fruit. 6500p, Hand processing palm fruit into baskets. 7500p, Mechanical processing. 8000p, Palm oil, uses.

1995, Feb. 27 Litho. *Perf. 14*

966	A159	3000p multicolored	.75	.35
967	A159	6500p multicolored	1.50	.70
968	A159	7500p multicolored	1.75	.80
969	A159	8000p multicolored	2.00	.85
		Nos. 966-969 (4)	6.00	2.70

FAO, 50th Anniv. A160

3000p, Net fishing. 6500p, Disking field. 7500p, Hands holding fruit. 8000p, Vendors along road.

1995 Litho. *Perf. 13½*

970	A160	3000p multicolored	.70	.45
971	A160	6500p multicolored	1.25	.85
972	A160	7500p multicolored	1.50	1.00
973	A160	8000p multicolored	1.75	1.10
a.		Souvenir sheet of 2, #972-973	4.00	4.00
		Nos. 970-973 (4)	5.20	3.40

UN, 50th Anniv. — A161

1995, Oct. 24 Litho. *Perf. 13½*

974	A161	4000p shown	1.00	.55
975	A161	5500p UN flag	1.25	.75
976	A161	7500p Natl. flag	1.75	1.00
977	A161	8000p Hand on dove	2.00	1.10
		Nos. 974-977 (4)	6.00	3.40

Souvenir Sheet

978 A161 15,000p UN emblem 1.50 1.50

100 Centimes = 1 Franc (1997)

Endangered Animals — A166

No. 995: a, 5000p, Hippopotamus. b, 7500p, Crocodile. c, 10,000p, Chelonia mydas. d, 12,000p, Trichechus senegalensis.

1997 Litho. *Perf. 12x11¾*

995 A166 Block of 4, #a-d *75.00* —

Despite change to franc currency on May 2, 1997, Nos. 995-997 have denominations in pesos.

Venomous Animals — A167

No. 996: a, 7500p, Pandinus imperator. b, 8000p, Naja nigricollis. c, 10,000p, Scolopendra morsitans. d, 11,000p, Lycosa tarentula.

1997

996 A167 Block of 4, #a-d *75.00* —

Economic Community of West African States, 20th Anniv. (in 1995) — A168

1997, Dec. 26

997 A168 25,000p multi *5.00 5.00*

Native Foods A169

Designs: 100fr, Caldo branco. 120fr, Siga. 160fr, Caldo de amendoin. 190fr, Caldo de chabeu.

1998, June 1

998-1001 A169 Set of 4 *5.00 5.00*

No. 1001 Overprinted in Brown

1998, Sept. 4 Litho. *Perf. 12x11¾*

1002 A169 190fr on No. 1001 *2.00 2.00*

Maritime Discoveries — A170

1998, Oct. 9 *Perf. 12x11¾*

1003 A170 200fr multi *2.00 2.00*

a. Souvenir sheet of 1, perf. 12½ *5.00 5.00*

Marine Life A171

Designs: 150fr, Cultellus tenuis. 170fr, Penaeus keraethurus. 200fr, Periophthalmus papilio. 250fr, Istiophorus albicans.

1998, Dec. 28 *Perf. 12x11¾*

1004-1007 A171 Set of 4 *6.00 6.00*

1007a Souvenir sheet, #1004-1007, perf. 12½ *6.00 6.00*

SOS Children's Villages, 50th Anniv. (in 1999) A172

Designs: 130fr, Children, map of Guinea-Bissau. 160fr, Children in school, child in wheelchair, children at table. 170fr, Children playing in playground. 300fr, 50th anniv. emblem.

Perf. 12¼x11¾

2000, June 15 Litho.

1008	A172	130fr multi	—	*4.00*
1009	A172	160fr multi	—	*4.00*
1010	A172	170fr multi	—	*4.00*
1011	A172	300fr multi	—	*4.00*

Millennium A173

Designs: 100fr, Dove, trees, dancers. 190fr, Circle of people around tree. 200fr, Drummer, dancers, and traditional house. 350fr, Head of dove, map of Guinea-Bissau.

Perf. 11¾x12¼

2000, Sept. 24 **Litho.**

1012 A173 100fr multi *2.50*
1013 A173 190fr multi *2.50*
1014 A173 200fr multi *3.00*
1015 A173 350fr multi —

Souvenir Sheet

España 2000 World Philatelic Exhibition — A174

2000 **Litho.** *Perf. 13x12¾*

1016 A174 1000fr multi — —

Nos. 922, 924, 931, 940 & 963 Srchd.

Methods and Perfs As Before

2000 ?

1017 A143 100fr on 500p #921 —
1018 A146 150fr on 1000p #930 —
1019 A146 200fr on 800p #929 —
1020 A149 1000fr on 1000p #939 —
1021 A146 250fr on 1300p #931 — —
1022 A143 450fr on 1500p #922 —
1023 A149 450fr on 1500p #940 —
1024 A155 450fr on 1500p #951 —
1025 A143 500fr on 2000p #923 — —
1026 A157 500fr on 2000p #960 — —
1027 A143 1000fr on 3000p #924 — —
1028 A155 1000fr on 3000p #952 — —
1029 A157 1000fr on 3000p #961 —
1029A A157 1500fr on 4000p #962 —
1030 A157 2000fr on 6000p #963 — —

AIR POST STAMPS

Liftoff of Soyuz Spacecraft AP1

Apollo-Soyuz mission: 10p, Launch of Apollo spacecraft. 15p, Leonov, Stafford and meeting in space. 20p, Eclipse of the sun. 30p, Infra-red photo of Earth. 40p, Return to Earth. 50p, Apollo and Soyuz docked, horiz.

1976, Oct. 4 *Perf. 13½*

C10 AP1 5p multicolored .50 .30
C10A AP1 10p multicolored .65 .40
C10B AP1 15p multicolored 1.30 .55
C10C AP1 20p multicolored 1.75 .80
C10D AP1 30p multicolored 2.25 1.20
C10E AP1 40p multicolored 3.25 1.50
Nos. C10-C10E (6) 9.70 4.75

Souvenir Sheet

C10F AP1 50p multicolored 4.75 4.75

No. C10F contains one 60x42mm stamp. Nos. C10-C10E exist in souvenir sheets of one, perf. and imperf.

Viking Spacecraft Orbiting Mars AP2

35p, Viking gathering Martian soil samples.

1977, Jan. 27

C11 AP2 25p multicolored 3.00 1.10
C11A AP2 35p multicolored 3.00 1.25

Nos. 372-373 Surcharged in Black on Silver Panels

1978 **Litho.** *Perf. 13½*

C12 A32 15p on 3.50p multi .95 .40
C13 A32 30p on 50c multi 1.45 .60

History of Aviation Type of 1980

35p, Willy de Houthulst, Hanriot HD.1. 40p, Charles Guynemer, Spad S. VII. 50p, Comdr. de Rose, Nieuport.

1980 **Litho.** *Perf. 13½*

C14 A38 35p multicolored 2.40 1.20
C14A A38 40p multicolored 3.00 1.40

Souvenir Sheet

C14B A38 50p multicolored 5.25 4.00

No. C14B contains one stamp 37x55mm.

Winter Olympics Type of 1980

1980

C15 A39 35p Slalom 2.40 1.20
C16 A39 40p Figure skating 3.00 1.40

Souvenir Sheet

C17 A39 50p Ice hockey, horiz. 5.50 4.00

Summer Olympics Type of 1980

1980, Aug. **Litho.** *Perf. 13½*

C18 A40 35p Somersault 3.50 1.20
C19 A40 40p Running 4.25 1.40

Souvenir Sheet

C20 A40 50p Emblem 5.50 4.25

Literacy Type of 1980

1980, Aug. **Litho.** *Perf. 13½*

C21 A41 15p like #404 1.60 .60
C22 A41 25p like #405 2.75 .80

Space Type of 1981

35p, Viking 1 & 2. 40p, Apollo-Soyuz craft & crew. 50p, Apollo 11 crew, craft & emblem.

1981, May **Litho.** *Perf. 13½*

C23 A45 35p multicolored 2.75 1.50
C24 A45 40p multicolored 3.00 1.75

Souvenir Sheet

C25 A45 50p multicolored 7.00 4.75

No. C25 contains one stamp 60x42mm.

Soccer Type of 1981

Designs: 35p, Rummenigge, Germany. 40p, Kempes, Argentina. 50p, Juanito, Spain.

1981, May

C26 A46 35p multicolored 2.75 1.50
C27 A46 40p multicolored 3.00 1.75

Souvenir Sheet

C28 A46 50p multicolored 8.75 6.00

No. C28 contains one stamp 56x40mm.

Royal Wedding Type of 1981

1981 **Litho.** *Perf. 13½*

C29 A47 35p Palace 3.25 1.50
C30 A47 40p Prince of Wales arms 4.00 1.75

Souvenir Sheet

C31 A47 50p Couple 7.25 4.75

Picasso Type of 1981

1981, Dec. **Litho.** *Perf. 13½*

C32 A48 35p multicolored 4.50 1.50
C33 A48 40p multicolored 5.75 1.90

Souvenir Sheet

C34 A48 50p multicolored 7.25 4.75

No. C34 contains one stamp 41x50mm.

Navigator Type of 1981

35p, Francis Drake, Golden Hinde. 40p, James Cook, Endeavor. 50p, Columbus, Santa Maria.

1981 **Litho.** *Perf. 13½*

C35 A49 35p multicolored 3.50 1.60
C36 A49 40p multicolored 4.00 2.00

Souvenir Sheet

C37 A49 50p multicolored 10.00 7.25

Christmas Type of 1981

1981

C38 A50 30p Memling 3.25 1.60
C39 A50 35p Bellini, diff. 4.00 2.00

Souvenir Sheet

C40 A50 50p Fra Angelico 7.25 4.75

No. C40 contains one 35x59mm stamp.

Scout Type of 1982

1982, June 9 **Litho.** *Perf. 13½*

C41 A51 35p Canoeing 2.75 1.50
C42 A51 40p Flying model planes 3.25 1.75

Souvenir Sheet

C43 A51 50p Playing chess 14.00 5.00

No. C43 contains one 48x38mm stamp.

Soccer Type of 1982

1982, June 13 **Litho.** *Perf. 13½*

C44 A52 35p Kempes 2.75 1.50
C45 A52 40p Kaltz 3.25 1.75

Souvenir Sheet

C46 A52 50p Stadium 7.25 4.75

Diana Type of 1982 and

Princess Diana, 21st Birthday — AP3

1982

C47 A53 35p multicolored 3.00 1.25
C48 A53 40p multicolored 3.50 1.60

Souvenir Sheet

C49 A53 50p multi, vert. 8.00 4.25

1982, Oct. 1 **Litho. & Embossed**

C49A AP3 200p gold & multi 14.50

Souvenir Sheet

C49B AP3 200p gold & multi, vert. 32.50

For overprints see Nos. 456A-456B.

Audubon Birth Bicent. — AP4

5p, Brown pelican. 10p, American white pelican. 20p, Great blue heron. 40p, American flamingo.

1985, Apr. 16 **Litho.** *Perf. 12*

C50 AP4 5p multicolored .60 .25
C51 AP4 10p multicolored 1.00 .30
C52 AP4 20p multicolored 1.25 .80
C53 AP4 40p multicolored 2.50 1.00
Nos. C50-C53 (4) 5.35 2.35

GUYANA

gī-'a-nə

LOCATION — Northeast coast of South America
GOVT. — Republic
AREA — 83,000 sq. mi.
POP. — 705,156 (1999 est.)
CAPITAL — Georgetown

The former Crown Colony of British Guiana became an independent member of the British Commonwealth May 26, 1966, taking the name Guyana. On February 23, 1970, Guyana became a republic, remaining a Commonwealth nation.

100 Cents = 1 Dollar

Catalogue values for all unused stamps in this country are for Never Hinged items.

Watermark

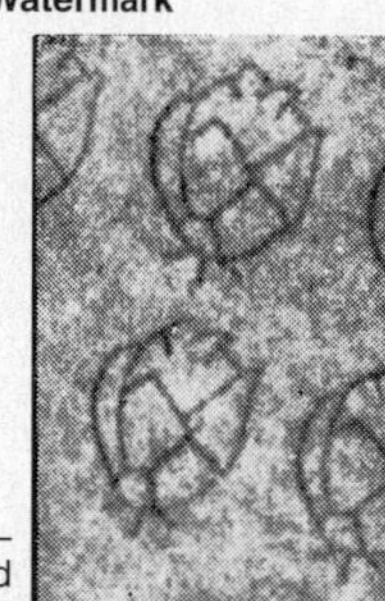

Wmk. 364 — Lotus Bud Multiple

British Guiana #254-256, 258-260, 267 Overprinted

Perf. 12½x13, 13

1966, May 26 — Wmk. 4 — Engr.

No.	Type	Value	Description	Unused	Used
1	A60	2c	dark green	.55	*.45*
1A	A60	3c	red brn & ol	2.50	*6.00*
2	A61	4c	violet	3.00	.90
3	A60	6c	yellow green	.55	.25
4	A60	8c	ultra	3.00	1.75
5	A61	12c	brn & blk	4.00	1.25
6	A61	$5	blk & ultra	27.50	*57.50*
			Nos. 1-6 (7)	41.10	*68.10*

Same Overprint on British Guiana Stamps and Types of 1954

Engr.; Center Litho. on $1

1966-67 — Wmk. 314 Upright

No.	Type	Value	Description	Unused	Used
7	A60	1c	black ('67)	.25	*.40*
8	A60	3c	red brn & ol (#279)	1.40	.25
9	A61	4c	violet ('67)	.35	*1.25*
10	A60	5c	blk & red (#280)	.50	.25
10A	A60	6c	yel green ('67)	.35	.30
11	A60	8c	ultra ('67)	3.00	*1.90*
12	A61	12c	brn & blk (#281)	.25	.25
13	A60	24c	org & blk (#282)	6.50	1.00
14	A60	36c	blk & rose (#283)	.40	.40
15	A61	48c	red brn & ultra (#284)	4.75	*12.50*
16	A61	72c	emer & rose (#285)	.90	.90
17	A60	$1	blk & multi (#286)	7.50	.50
18	A60	$2	mag (#287)	2.00	1.25
19	A61	$5	black & ultra	1.75	*5.00*
			Nos. 7-19 (14)	29.90	26.15

For surcharges see Nos. 543, 544A, 625-626, 1446.

1966-67 — Wmk. 314 Sideways

No.	Type	Value	Description	Unused	Used
7a	A60	1c	black	.25	.25
9a	A61	4c	violet	.25	.25
11a	A60	8c	ultramarine	.25	.25
12a	A61	12c	brown & black ('67)	.25	.25
13a	A60	24c	orange & black	2.50	.60
14a	A60	36c	black & rose ('67)	.35	*2.00*
15a	A61	48c	red brown & ultra	.35	.35
16a	A61	72c	emerald & rose ('67)	3.25	*7.00*
17a	A60	$1	black & multi ('67)	9.00	*6.00*
18a	A60	$2	magenta ('67)	3.00	*3.75*
19a	A61	$5	black & ultra ('67)	1.50	*3.75*
			Nos. 7a-19a (11)	20.95	24.45

See Nos. 32-32T and note. For surcharges see Nos. 544, 627-628, 1447.

Flag and Map of Guyana — A1

Designs: 25c, $1, Arms of Guyana.

Unwmk.

1966, May 26 — Photo. — *Perf. 14*

No.	Type	Value	Description	Unused	Used
20	A1	5c	violet & multi	.25	.25
21	A1	15c	dk red brown & multi	.30	.25
22	A1	25c	brt blue & multi	.30	.25
23	A1	$1	sepia & multi	.85	.85
			Nos. 20-23 (4)	1.70	1.60

Guyana's independence, May 26, 1966.

Bank of Guyana A2

1966, Oct. 11 — *Perf. 13½x14*

No.	Type	Value	Description	Unused	Used
24	A2	5c	yel grn, blue, blk & gold	.25	.25
25	A2	25c	blue, black & gold	.25	.25

Establishment of the Bank of Guyana.

British Guiana No. 13 — A3

1967, Feb. 23 — Litho. — *Perf. 12½*

No.	Type	Value	Description	Unused	Used
26	A3	5c	multicolored	.25	.25
a.			Imperf., pair		
27	A3	25c	multicolored	.25	.25

Issued to honor the unique British Guiana 1c black on magenta stamp of 1856.

Canceled to Order

Remainders of Nos. 26-30, 33-38 and 54-67 were canceled and sold by the Post Office in 1969. Values are for these canceled to order stamps. Postally used examples do not command a significant premium.

Chateau Margot — A4

Designs: 15c, Independence Arch. 25c, Guyana Fort, Fort Island, horiz. $1, Parliament, National Assembly Hall, horiz.

Perf. 14, 14½x14, 14x14½

1967, May 26 — Photo. — Unwmk.

No.	Type	Value	Description	Unused	Used
28	A4	6c	multicolored	.25	.25
29	A4	15c	multicolored	.25	.25
30	A4	25c	multicolored	.25	.25
31	A4	$1	multicolored	.25	.25
			Nos. 28-31 (4)	1.00	1.00

First anniversary of independence.

British Guiana Stamps and Types of 1954 Locally Overprinted

1967 — Wmk. 4

No.	Type	Value	Description	Unused	Used
32	A60	1c	black	.25	.25
32A	A60	2c	dark green	.25	.25
32B	A60	3c	red brown & ol	.40	.25
32C	A61	4c	violet	.30	.25
32D	A60	6c	yellow green	.30	.25
32E	A60	8c	ultramarine	.30	.25
32F	A61	12c	brown & black	.30	.25
32G	A60	$2	magenta	1.75	3.00
32H	A61	$5	black & ultra	2.25	2.75
			Nos. 32-32H (9)	6.10	7.50

The 24c with Wmk. 4 also exists with this overprint. Value: unused $450; used $110.

1967-68 — Wmk. 314 Upright

No.	Type	Value	Description	Unused	Used
32I	A60	1c	black ('68)	.25	*1.00*
32J	A60	2c	dk green ('68)	.80	*2.00*
32K	A60	3c	red brown & ol	.35	.25
32L	A61	4c	violet ('68)	.25	*1.25*
32M	A60	5c	black & red	1.50	*2.50*
32N	A60	6c	yel green ('68)	.40	*.90*
32O	A60	24c	orange & blk	6.00	.25
32P	A60	36c	black & rose	2.50	.25
32Q	A61	48c	red brn & ultra	1.25	*1.50*
32R	A61	72c	emer & rose	2.50	1.10
32S	A60	$1	black & multi	4.00	.60
32T	A60	$2	magenta	4.25	4.00
			Nos. 32I-32T (12)	24.05	15.60

The 1c, 4c, 6c, 8c and $5 with Wmk. 314 were not issued without overprint.
For surcharges see Nos. 540, 542, 543A.

Christmas Issues

"Millie," the Bilingual Macaw — A5

1967, Nov. 6 — *Perf. 14½x14*

No.	Type	Value	Description	Unused	Used
33	A5	5c	olive green & multi	.25	.25
33A	A5	25c	purple & multi	.25	.25

1968, Jan. 22

No.	Type	Value	Description	Unused	Used
34	A5	5c	red & multi	.25	.25
35	A5	25c	yel green & multi	.25	.25

Wicketkeeper, Emblem of West Indies Cricket Team — A6

Designs: 6c, Batsman and emblem of Marylebone Cricket Club. 25c, Bowler and emblem of West Indies Cricket Team.

1968, Jan. 8 — Photo. — *Perf. 14*

No.	Type	Value	Description	Unused	Used
36	A6	5c	multicolored	.25	.25
37	A6	6c	multicolored	.25	.25
38	A6	25c	multicolored	.35	.25
a.			Strip of 3, #36-38	1.00	1.00

Visit of the Marylebone Cricket Club to the West Indies, Jan.-Feb. 1968. Printed in sheets of 9.

Pike Cichlid — A7

Marail Guan — A8

Designs: 2c, Piranha. 3c, Cichla ocellaris (fish). 5c, Armored catfish. 6c, Two-spotted cichlid. 15c, Harpy eagle. 20c, Hoatzin. 25c, Andean cock-of-the-rock. 40c, Great kiskadee. 50c, Agouti. 60c, Peccary. $1, Paca. $2, Armadillo. $5, Ocelot.

Perf. 14x14½, 14½x14

1968, Mar. 4 — Photo. — Unwmk.

No.	Type	Value	Description	Unused	Used
39	A7	1c	chalky blue & multi	.25	.25
40	A7	2c	gray & multi	.25	.25
41	A7	3c	grnsh bl & multi	.25	.25
42	A7	5c	ultra & multi	.25	.25
43	A7	6c	brt olive & multi	.60	.25
44	A8	10c	yel green & multi	.75	.25
45	A8	15c	green & multi	1.60	.25
46	A8	20c	ap grn & multi	1.00	.25
47	A8	25c	brt green & multi	.75	.25
48	A8	40c	pale brn & multi	3.00	.80
49	A7	50c	rose brn & multi	1.50	.75
50	A7	60c	lilac rose & multi	1.50	.25
51	A7	$1	dp orange & multi	1.50	.25
52	A7	$2	ocher & multi	1.75	*3.50*
53	A7	$5	red & multi	2.50	*4.25*
			Nos. 39-53 (15)	17.45	12.05

See Nos. 68-82.

For overprints & surcharges see Nos. 357, 410-413, 603, 752, 756, 761a, 1463, 1501, 1839, 2045.

Christ of St. John of the Cross, by Salvador Dali — A9

1968, Mar. 25 — *Perf. 14x14½*

No.	Type	Value	Description	Unused	Used
54	A9	5c	car rose & multi	.25	.25
55	A9	25c	brt violet & multi	.25	.25

Easter.

"Efficiency Year" — A10

Designs: 30c, 40c, "Savings bonds."

1968, July 22 — Litho. — *Perf. 14*

No.	Type	Value	Description	Unused	Used
56	A10	6c	green & multi	.25	.25
57	A10	25c	fawn & multi	.25	.25
58	A10	30c	multicolored	.25	.25
59	A10	40c	multicolored	.25	.25
			Nos. 56-59 (4)	1.00	1.00

Issued to promote the sale of savings bonds and to publicize Efficiency Year.

Open Koran A11

Perf. 14x13½

1968, Oct. 9 — Photo. — Unwmk.

No.	Type	Value	Description	Unused	Used
60	A11	6c	sal pink, gold & blk	.25	.25
61	A11	25c	pale vio, gold & blk	.25	.25
62	A11	30c	pale yel grn, gold & blk	.25	.25
63	A11	40c	pale blue, gold & blk	.25	.25
			Nos. 60-63 (4)	1.00	1.00

Koran's 1400th anniversary.

For overprints & surcharges see Nos. 354, 355, 441, 445, 487-488, 575, 630, 1464-1465.

Dish Aerials, Thomas Lands, Guyana — A12

Designs: 30c, 40c, Map showing connection between Guyana and Trinidad. All stamps are inscribed: "Guyana Sends Christmas Greetings to the World."

Wmk. 364

1968, Nov. 11 Litho. *Perf. 14*

No.	Type		Description		
64	A12	6c	blue, gray, ocher & emer	.25	.25
65	A12	25c	brt rose lil, brn & emer	.25	.25
66	A12	30c	blue grn & dk blue grn	.25	.25
67	A12	40c	blue grn & red	.25	.25
			Nos. 64-67 (4)	1.00	1.00

Christmas; communications link with Trinidad by the tropospheric scatter system.

Types of 1968

Designs as before.

Perf. 14x14½, 14½x14

1968 Photo. Wmk. 364

No.	Type		Description		
68	A7	1c	chalky bl & multi	.25	.25
69	A7	2c	gray & multi	.25	*.25*
70	A7	3c	grnsh bl & multi	.25	*.25*
71	A7	5c	ultra & multi	.25	.25
72	A7	6c	brt olive & multi	.25	*.25*
73	A8	10c	yel grn & multi	.35	.25
74	A8	15c	green & multi	.50	.25
75	A8	20c	apple grn & multi	.50	.40
76	A8	25c	brt green & multi	.50	.25
77	A8	40c	pale brn & multi	1.00	.65
78	A7	50c	rose brn & multi	.55	.25
79	A7	60c	lilac rose & multi	.55	*.90*
80	A7	$1	dp org & multi	1.10	1.10
81	A7	$2	ocher & multi	1.75	*3.00*
82	A7	$5	red & multi	2.10	*4.50*
			Nos. 68-82 (15)	10.15	12.80

For overprints & surcharges see Nos. 373, 376-377, 413D, 565-566, 633, 635, 704-705, 744, 749, 752a, 757-758, 761-762, 1862-1863, 1981, 4107, 4164, 4187, O2.

Celebrants Spraying Perfumed Powder — A13

Phagwah (Holi) Hindu Festival: 25c, 40c, Two celebrants spraying colored water.

1969, Feb. 26 Litho. *Perf. 13½*

No.	Type		Description		
83	A13	6c	multicolored	.25	.25
84	A13	25c	multicolored	.25	.25
85	A13	30c	multicolored	.25	.25
86	A13	40c	multicolored	.25	.25
			Nos. 83-86 (4)	1.00	1.00

The Last Supper, by Salvador Dali A14

1969, Mar. 10 Photo. *Perf. 13*

No.	Type		Description		
87	A14	6c	dp carmine & multi	.25	.25
88	A14	25c	green & multi	.25	.25
89	A14	30c	org brown & multi	.25	.25
90	A14	40c	dp violet & multi	.25	.25
			Nos. 87-90 (4)	1.00	1.00

Easter. For overprints and surcharges see Nos. 393-394, 482-485, 572, 576, 634, 765, 772, 1407-1410, 1813, 1815-1817, 2050, 4108.

Map of Caribbean — A15

Design: 25c, "Strength in Unity," horiz.

Wmk. 364

1969, Apr. 30 Litho. *Perf. 13½*

No.	Type		Description		
91	A15	6c	violet blue & multi	.25	.25
92	A15	25c	brt rose, yel & brown	.25	.25

1st anniv. of CARIFTA (Caribbean Free Trade Area).

Prow of Aluminum Ship — A16

50th Anniv. of the ILO: 40c, Bauxite processing plant, horiz.

1969, Apr. 30 *Perf. 12x11, 11x12*

No.	Type		Description		
93	A16	30c	black, blue & silver	.40	.25
94	A16	40c	multicolored	.60	.25

Flag Raising A17

Designs: 8c, 30c, Campfire.

1969, Aug. 13 Litho. *Perf. 13½x13*

No.	Type		Description		
95	A17	6c	pale green & multi	.25	.25
96	A17	8c	orange & multi	.25	.25
97	A17	25c	pale brown & multi	.25	.25
98	A17	30c	multicolored	.25	.25
99	A17	50c	rose & multi	.25	.25
			Nos. 95-99 (5)	1.25	1.25

60th anniv. of Scouting in Guyana; 3rd Caribbean Scout Jamboree, Georgetown, Aug. 13-22. For overprints and surcharges see Nos. 392, 395, 397, 402, 404-405, 453.

Gandhi and Spinning Wheel A18

1969, Oct. 1 *Perf. 14½x14*

No.	Type		Description		
100	A18	6c	olive, blk & lt brn	.30	*.65*
101	A18	15c	rose lilac, blk & lt brn	1.00	.65

Mohandas K. Gandhi (1868-1948), leader in India's fight for independence.

Mother Sally Troupe — A19

City Hall, Georgetown — A20

1969, Nov. 17 *Perf. 14x13½*

No.	Type		Description		
102	A19	5c	multicolored	.25	.25
103	A20	6c	blue & multi	.25	.25
104	A19	25c	multicolored	.25	.25
105	A20	60c	orange & multi	.25	.25
			Nos. 102-105 (4)	1.00	1.00

Christmas. The 5c, 6c, and 25c exist without the "Christmas 1969" overprint.

Prime Minister Forbes Burnham and Map — A21

6c, "Rural Self Help Project" (man & woman building house). 15c, University of Guyana, horiz. 25c, President's Residence, horiz.

1970, Feb. 23 Litho. *Perf. 14*

No.	Type		Description		
106	A21	5c	blue, brn & ocher	.25	.25
107	A21	6c	blue, blk ocher & brn	.25	.25
108	A21	15c	apple grn & multi	.25	.25
109	A21	25c	multicolored	.25	.25
			Nos. 106-109 (4)	1.00	1.00

Issued for Republic Day, Feb. 23, 1970.

Descent from the Cross, by Rubens — A22

Easter: 6c, 25c, Christ on the Cross, by Rubens.

1970, Mar. 24 *Perf. 14x14½*

No.	Type		Description		
110	A22	5c	blue & multi	.25	.25
111	A22	6c	rose lilac & multi	.25	.25
112	A22	15c	dark red & multi	.25	.25
113	A22	25c	yellow & multi	.25	.25
			Nos. 110-113 (4)	1.00	1.00

"Peace" and UN Emblem A23

UN 25th Anniv.: 6c, 25c, UN emblem, panning for gold and drilling for minerals.

1970, Oct. 26 *Perf. 14½x14*

No.	Type		Description		
114	A23	5c	red & multi	.25	.25
115	A23	6c	blue & multi	.25	.25
116	A23	15c	multicolored	.25	.25
117	A23	25c	brown & multi	.25	.25
			Nos. 114-117 (4)	1.00	1.00

Mother and Child, by Philip Moore — A24

1970, Dec. 8 Litho. *Perf. 13½*

No.	Type		Description		
118	A24	5c	violet & multi	.25	.25
119	A24	6c	brown & multi	.25	.25
120	A24	15c	dk green & multi	.25	.25
121	A24	25c	maroon & multi	.25	.25
			Nos. 118-121 (4)	1.00	1.00

Christmas.

National Cooperative Bank — A25

1971, Feb. 23 Wmk. 364 *Perf. 14*

No.	Type		Description		
122	A25	6c	red & multi	.25	.25
123	A25	15c	yellow & multi	.25	.25
124	A25	25c	ultra & multi	.25	.25
			Nos. 122-124 (3)	.75	.75

Republic Day.

"Togetherness, Vision, Understanding" A26

1971, Mar. 22 *Perf. 14½x14*

No.	Type		Description		
125	A26	5c	yel grn & multi	.25	.25
126	A26	6c	lil rose & multi	.25	.25
127	A26	15c	multicolored	.25	.25
128	A26	25c	yellow & multi	.25	.25
			Nos. 125-128 (4)	1.00	1.00

Intl. year against racial discrimination.

Volunteer Felling Tree, by John Criswick — A27

1971, July 19 *Perf. 14*

No.	Type		Description		
129	A27	5c	blue & multi	.25	.25
130	A27	20c	green & multi	.25	.25
131	A27	25c	yellow & multi	.25	.25
132	A27	50c	brown & multi	.40	*1.25*
			Nos. 129-132 (4)	1.15	2.00

1st anniv. of the Natl. Self-help Road Project.

Yellow Allamanda — A28

Flora: 1c, Pitcher plant of Mt. Roraima. 3c, Heliconia collinsiana. 5c, Annatto tree. 6c, Cannonball tree. 10c, Cattleya violacea. 15c, Christmas orchid. 20c, Paphinia cristata. 25c, Gongora quinquinervis. 40c, Tiger beard. 50c, Guzmania lingulata. 60c, Soldier's cap. $1, Chelonanthus uliginoides. $2, Norantea guianensis. $5, Odontadenia grandiflora.

1971-76 Litho. *Perf. 13x13½*

No.	Type		Description		
133	A28	1c	multi ('72)	.25	.25
134	A28	2c	lilac & multi	.25	.25
135	A28	3c	multicolored	.25	.25
136	A28	5c	lt blue & multi	.25	.25
137	A28	6c	dull rose & multi	.25	.25

Perf. 13½

No.	Type		Description		
138	A28	10c	multi ('72)	3.50	.25
a.			Perf. 13	5.25	.25
139	A28	15c	multi ('72)	1.10	.25
a.			Perf. 13 ('76)	1.00	.25
140	A28	20c	multi ('72)	3.25	.40
a.			Perf. 13	5.00	.40
141	A28	25c	multi, 25c at center ('72)	5.00	*9.00*
141A	A28	25c	multi, 25c right of center ('73)	.45	.55
b.			Perf. 13 ('76)	.45	.30
142	A28	40c	multi ('72)	3.50	.25
143	A28	50c	multi ('73)	.50	*.80*
144	A28	60c	multi ('73)	.40	*.65*

145 A28 $1 multi ('73) .40 .40
146 A28 $2 multi ('73) .60 .60
147 A28 $5 multi ('73) .75 .75
Nos. 133-147 (16) 20.70 15.15

No. 141 has 2 blossoms at left, 3 at right; this is reversed on No. 141A.

The overprint "REVENUE / ONLY" between rules was applied to Nos. 134-136, 141A, 142-147 in 1975. Postal use was permitted in Nov.-Dec., 1975. Value, set $20.

See Nos. 433-434, 731-732, 4125-4126.

For overprints and surcharges see Nos. 192, 209, 234, 331-335, 351, 358-359, 367, 370, 372, 374-375A, 379-383, 385-390A, 401, 407, 422-425, 433-434, 438-440, 447, 450, 451, 457-458, 460-461, 464-466, 497-500, 545-546, 549b, 550, 563-564, 597, 602, 618, 631-632, 641-642, 666-667, 727, 747-748, 750-751, 753-754, 759-760, 803, 805, 807-808, 810-812, 847-848, 910-911, 995, 1361, 1382-1383, 1385-1386, 1391-1392, 1452, 1454, 1456-1460, 1466, 1499, 1778-1779, 1781-1784, 1837-1838, 1870-1872, 1898-1900, 2046-2049, 2225-2227, 4133, 4165, 4185, 4195, 4196, C2-C4, O1, O3-O5, O7, O13-O14, Q1-Q4, QO1.

The Lord's Prayer, by School Girl Veronica Bassoo — A29

Guyana Masker, by School Boy Michael Austin — A30

Perf. 13½x14, 14x13½

1971, Nov. 15 Litho. Wmk. 364

148 A29 5c brt green & multi .25 .25
149 A29 20c brt green & multi .25 .25
150 A30 25c multicolored .25 .25
151 A30 50c multicolored .30 .30
Nos. 148-151 (4) 1.05 1.05

Christmas.

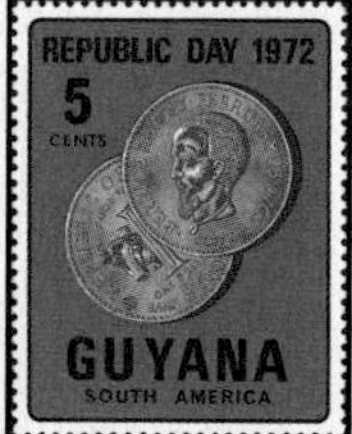

Guyana Dollar — A31

1972, Feb. 23 Litho. *Perf. 14½x14*

152 A31 5c blk, dp org & silver .25 .25
153 A31 20c blk, dp lil rose & sil .25 .25
154 A31 25c black, ultra & silver .25 .25
155 A31 50c black, emer & sil .25 .25
Nos. 152-155 (4) 1.00 1.00

Republic Day.

Handclasp and Mosque — A32

1972, Apr. 3 *Perf. 14*

156 A32 5c brown & multi .25 .25
157 A32 25c blue & multi .25 .25
158 A32 30c green & multi .25 .25
159 A32 60c yellow brn & multi .25 .25
Nos. 156-159 (4) 1.00 1.00

Youman Nabi (Peaceful Prophet), Mohammedan festival.

Map of South America, Emblem of Non-aligned Countries — A33

1972, July 20

160 A33 8c violet & multi .25 .25
161 A33 25c yellow grn & multi .25 .25
162 A33 40c orange & multi .25 .25
163 A33 50c red brown & multi .25 .25
Nos. 160-163 (4) 1.00 1.00

Conf. of Foreign Ministers of Nonaligned Countries, Georgetown, Aug. 7-12.

For overprints & surcharges see Nos. 573, 611, O17.

CARIFESTA '72 Emblem — A34

1972, Aug. 25

164 A34 8c orange & multi .25 .25
165 A34 25c orange & multi .25 .25
166 A34 40c orange & multi .25 .25
167 A34 50c orange & multi .25 .35
Nos. 164-167 (4) 1.00 1.10

Caribbean Festival of Arts (CARIFESTA), Georgetown, Aug. 25-Sept. 15.

Holy Family — A35

1972, Oct. 18 Litho. *Perf. 13x13½*

168 A35 8c blue & multi .25 .25
169 A35 25c blue & multi .25 .25
170 A35 40c blue & multi .25 *.25*
171 A35 50c blue & multi .25 *.30*
Nos. 168-171 (4) 1.00 1.05

Christmas.

Umana Yana (Meeting Place of Wai Wai Chiefs) — A36

Designs: 25c, 40c, Bethel Chapel.

1973, Feb. 23 Litho. *Perf. 14x14½*

172 A36 8c brt blue & multi .25 .25
173 A36 25c rose red & multi .25 .25
174 A36 40c emerald & multi .25 .25
175 A36 50c black & multi .35 .25
Nos. 172-175 (4) 1.10 1.00

Republic Day.

Pomegranate, Fertility and Church Symbol — A37

Map of Guyana and People Looking to the Cross — A38

1973, Apr. 19 *Perf. 14x14½, 13½*

176 A37 8c pink & multi .25 .25
177 A38 25c yellow & multi .25 .25
178 A38 40c ultra & multi .25 .25
179 A37 50c yellow & multi .25 .25
Nos. 176-179 (4) 1.00 1.00

Easter.

Symbolic of Blood Donation — A39

Perf. 14x14½

1973, Oct. 1 Wmk. 364

180 A39 8c red & black .25 .25
181 A39 25c red & lilac .25 .25
182 A39 40c red & vio blue .40 *.50*
183 A39 50c red & brown .65 *.90*
Nos. 180-183 (4) 1.55 1.90

Guyana Red Cross, 25th anniversary.

Steel Band, Star, Pegasus Hotel — A40

Madonna and Child, St. Philip's Anglican Church, Georgetown A41

1973, Nov. 20 Litho. *Perf. 14x14½*

184 A40 8c lilac & multi .25 .25
185 A40 25c lilac & multi .25 .25

Perf. 13½x14

186 A41 40c violet blue & multi .40 *.70*
187 A41 50c violet blue & multi .40 *.70*
Nos. 184-187 (4) 1.30 1.90

Christmas.

"One People, One Nation, One Destiny" A42

Designs: 25c, 50c, Wai Wai Indian.

1974, Feb. 23 Litho. *Perf. 13½*

188 A42 8c multicolored .25 .25
189 A42 25c multicolored .25 .25
190 A42 40c multicolored .25 *.30*
191 A42 50c multicolored .25 *.40*
Nos. 188-191 (4) 1.00 1.20

Republic Day.

No. 137 Surcharged with New Value and 2 Bars

Perf. 13x13½

1974, Mar. 18 Wmk. 364

192 A28 8c on 6c multi .30 .30

For overprints and surcharges see Nos. 424, 459, 474-478, 1453, 1500, 1780.

Crucifix Super-imposed on Eddy Bow Kite — A43

Crucifix in Pre-Columbian Timehri Style — A44

1974, Apr. 8 *Perf. 13½x14*

193 A43 8c green & multi .25 .25
194 A44 25c black, green & gray .25 .25
195 A44 40c black, gray & car .25 .25
196 A43 50c gold & multi .25 .25
Nos. 193-196 (4) 1.00 1.00

Easter.

UPU Emblem and British Guiana Type of 1863 — A45

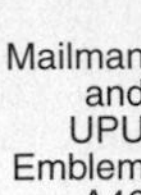

Mailman and UPU Emblem A46

1974, June 18 Litho. *Perf. 14, 14½*

197 A45 8c rose & multi	.30	.25
198 A46 25c yellow green & multi	.45	.25
199 A45 40c blue & multi	.45	.30
200 A46 50c yellow green & multi	.55	.55
Nos. 197-200 (4)	1.75	1.35

Centenary of Universal Postal Union.

Girl Guides Holding Banner A47

Designs: 25c, 40c, Guides in camp cooking and carrying water. 50c, Like 8c.

1974, Aug. 1 *Perf. 14½*

201 A47 8c multicolored	.25	.25
202 A47 25c multicolored	.35	.25
203 A47 40c multicolored	.50	.40
204 A47 50c multicolored	.50	.50
a. Souvenir sheet of 4, #201-204	2.00	2.00
Nos. 201-204 (4)	1.60	1.40

Girl Guides of Guyana, 50th anniv. For overprints see Nos. 574, 1352.

Buck Toyeau — A48

Christmas (Fruit): 35c, Carambola (starfruit) and awaras. 50c, Pawpaw and tangerine. $1, Pineapple and sapodillas.

1974, Nov. 18 Litho. *Perf. 14x13½*

205 A48 8c multicolored	.25	.25
206 A48 35c multicolored	.25	.25
207 A48 50c multicolored	.25	.25
208 A48 $1 multicolored	.40	.75
a. Souvenir sheet of 4, #205-208	1.00	*3.00*
Nos. 205-208 (4)	1.15	1.50

For overprints & surcharges see Nos. 551, 612, 716, 4173.

No. 135 Surcharged with New Value and Two Bars

1975, Jan. 20 Litho. *Perf. 13x13½*

209 A28 8c on 3c multi	.25	.25

For surcharge see No. 423.

Golden Arrow of Courage — A49

Republic Day: 35c, Cacique's Crown of Honour. 50c, Cacique's Crown of Valour. $1, Order of Excellence.

1975, Feb. 23 *Perf. 13x13½*

210 A49 10c brown & multi	.25	.25
211 A49 35c brown red & multi	.25	.25
212 A49 50c green & multi	.25	.35
213 A49 $1 violet bl & multi	.50	.65
Nos. 210-213 (4)	1.25	1.50

For overprints and surcharges see Nos. 360, 368, 398, 637, 1359.

Old Sluice Gate — A50

Modern Sluice Gate A51

1975, May 2 *Perf. 14*

214 A50 10c bister & multi	.25	.25
215 A51 35c brown & multi	.25	.25
216 A50 50c bister & multi	.25	.40
217 A51 $1 green & multi	.50	.75
a. Souvenir sheet of 4, #214-217	1.25	*3.50*
Nos. 214-217 (4)	1.25	1.65

Intl. Commission on Irrigation and Drainage, 25th anniv.

For overprints see Nos. 361, 592, 794-795, 1374-1375.

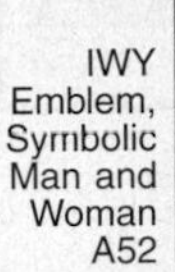

IWY Emblem, Symbolic Man and Woman A52

Designs: IWY emblem and petroglyph designs of men and women.

1975, July 1 Litho. Wmk. 364

218 A52 10c yellow & dull grn	.25	.25
219 A52 35c Prus blue & pur	.25	.25
220 A52 50c orange & dk blue	.25	.25
221 A52 $1 ultra & brown	.40	*.50*
a. Souvenir sheet of 4, #218-221, perf. 14½	1.50	*3.50*
Nos. 218-221 (4)	1.15	1.25

Intl. Women's Year. For overprints and surcharges see Nos. 362, 399, 555.

Freedom Monument, Georgetown — A53

Designs: Various views of Freedom Monument, Georgetown.

1975, Aug. 26 Litho. *Perf. 14*

222 A53 10c gray & multi	.25	.25
223 A53 35c yellow & multi	.25	.25
224 A53 50c lilac & multi	.30	.30
225 A53 $1 olive & multi	.40	.40
Nos. 222-225 (4)	1.20	1.20

Namibia Day (independence for South-West Africa).

For overprints and surcharges see Nos 330, 582, 593, 619, 1360.

"GNS," Flower and Clasped Hands — A54

"GNS" and Clasped hands: 35c, Wheel. 50c, Soccer ball. $1, Uniform cap.

1975, Oct. 2 Wmk. 364 *Perf. 14*

226 A54 10c violet, yel & grn	.25	.25
227 A54 35c brt bl, org & grn	.25	.25
228 A54 50c lt brn, brt bl & grn	.25	.25
229 A54 $1 grn, vio & brt grn	.40	.40
a. Souvenir sheet of 4, #226-229	1.25	*3.00*
Nos. 226-229 (4)	1.15	1.15

Guyana National Service, 1st anniv. For overprint & surcharges see Nos. 448, 636, 638.

Foresters' Building and Badge A55

35c, Rock painting of hunter. 50c, Crossed axes and hunting horn. $1, Bow and arrow.

1975, Nov. 14 Litho. Wmk. 364

230 A55 10c red, black & gold	.25	.25
231 A55 35c red, black & gold	.25	.25
232 A55 50c gold & multi	.25	.25
233 A55 $1 gold & multi	.45	.45
a. Souvenir sheet of 4, #230-233	1.00	*3.00*
Nos. 230-233 (4)	1.20	1.20

Ancient Order of Foresters, centenary.

For overprints and surcharges see Nos. 356, 363, 400, 422, 583, 4170.

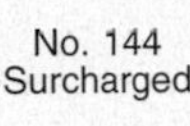

No. 144 Surcharged

1976, Feb. 10 *Perf. 13½*

234 A28 35c on 60c multi	.40	.40

For overprints see Nos. 703-703a, 852.

St. John Ambulance Emblem — A56

1976, Mar. 29 Litho. *Perf. 14*

235 A56 8c black, lil rose & sil	.25	.25
236 A56 15c black, orange & sil	.25	.25
237 A56 35c black, emer & silver	.25	.25
238 A56 40c black, blue & sil	.30	.30
Nos. 235-238 (4)	1.05	1.05

Guyana St. John Ambulance, 50th anniv. For surcharges see Nos. 715, 717, 1411.

Independence Arch, 1966 — A57

Stylized Designs: 15c, Victoria regia. 35c, Letter "S" for socialism. 40c, Worker with pitchfork.

1976, May 25 *Perf. 13½*

239 A57 8c silver & multi	.25	.25
240 A57 15c silver & multi	.25	.25
241 A57 35c silver & multi	.25	.25
242 A57 40c silver & multi	.25	.25
a. Souvenir sheet of 4, #239-242, perf. 14	1.00	*1.50*
Nos. 239-242 (4)	1.00	1.00

10th anniv. of independence. For surcharges see Nos. 567, 639, 1444.

Map of West Indies, Bats, Wicket and Ball A57a

Prudential Cup — A57b

Unwmk.

1976, Aug. 3 Litho. *Perf. 14*

243 A57a 15c light blue & multi	1.25	*1.75*
244 A57b 15c lilac rose & black	1.25	*1.75*

World Cricket Cup, won by West Indies Team, 1975.

For overprints & surcharges see Nos. 352-353, 653-654.

Lamp — A58

Designs: 15c, Hand and flame. 35c, Flame. 40c, Lakshmi, Hindu goddess of wealth.

1976, Oct. 21 *Perf. 14*

245 A58 8c multicolored	.25	.25
246 A58 15c orange & multi	.25	.25
247 A58 35c purple & multi	.25	.25
248 A58 40c ultra & multi	.30	.30
a. Souvenir sheet of 4, #245-248	1.25	*1.75*
Nos. 245-248 (4)	1.05	1.05

Deepavali, Hindu Festival of Lights.

For surcharges see Nos. 719-721.

Guitar-Sitar, Benin Head — A59

1977, Feb. 1 Litho. *Perf. 14½*

249 A59 10c gold & multi	.25	.25
250 A59 35c gold & multi	.25	.25
251 A59 50c gold & multi	.35	.35
252 A59 $1 gold & multi	.50	.50
a. Souvenir sheet of 4, #249-252	1.60	*3.50*
Nos. 249-252 (4)	1.35	1.35

2nd World Black and African Festival, Lagos, Nigeria, Jan. 15-Feb. 12. Nos. 249-252a were not issued without black bar.

For overprints see Nos. 364, 369, 584.

1c and 5c Coins A60

Coins (Obverse): 15c, 10c and 25c. 35c, 50c and $1. 40c, $5 and $10. $1, $50 and $100. $2, Reverse, Coat of arms.

1977, May 26 *Perf. 14*

253 A60 8c multicolored	.35	.35
254 A60 15c multicolored	.40	.40
255 A60 35c multicolored	.70	.70
256 A60 40c multicolored	.85	.85

257 A60 $1 multicolored 1.25 1.25
258 A60 $2 multicolored 2.00 2.00
Nos. 253-258 (6) 5.55 5.55

New coinage. For overprints and surcharges see Nos. 539, 541A, 568, 594, O18, O20, Q5.

Hand Pump, c. 1850
A61

National Fire Prevention Week: 15c, Steam engine, c. 1860. 35c, Fire engine, c. 1930. 40c, Fire engine, 1977.

Perf. 14x14½

1977, Nov. 15 Litho. Wmk. 364

259 A61 8c multicolored 1.25 .25
260 A61 15c multicolored 2.00 .25
261 A61 35c multicolored 2.25 1.10
262 A61 40c multicolored 2.50 1.25
Nos. 259-262 (4) 8.00 2.85

For surcharges see Nos. 1370-1371.

Cuffy Monument — A62

8c, 35c, Cuffy statue from monument.

1977, Dec. 7 Litho. *Perf. 14*

263 A62 8c multicolored .25 .25
264 A62 15c multicolored .25 .25
265 A62 35c multicolored .25 .25
266 A62 40c multicolored .25 .25
Nos. 263-266 (4) 1.00 1.00

Cuffy, Guyana's national hero, led a slave revolution in 1763. The monument was unveiled in 1976. For overprints see Nos. 446, 569, 613.

Wildlife Protection — A63

1978, Feb. 15 *Perf. 14*

267 A63 8c Manatee 1.00 .25
268 A63 15c Giant sea turtle 1.25 .40
269 A63 35c Harpy eagle 6.00 2.75
270 A63 40c Iguana 4.75 2.75
Nos. 267-270 (4) 13.00 6.15

8c, 15c are horiz. For overprints and surcharges see Nos. 443, 722-723, 1416.

Parliament and Prime Minister Burnham — A64

Prime Minister and: 15c, Student and school children. 35c, Bauxite mine. 40c, Cooperative village.

1978, Apr. 27 Litho. *Perf. 13½x14*

271 A64 8c violet & black .25 .25
272 A64 15c gray, blk & bl .25 .25
273 A64 35c multicolored .25 .25
274 A64 40c gray, blk & org .25 .25
a. Souvenir sheet of 4, #271-274 .90 *1.75*
Nos. 271-274 (4) 1.00 1.00

Prime Minister Linden Forbes Burnham, 25th anniv. of his entry into parliament. For surcharges see Nos. 648-649.

Dr. George Giglioli, Anopheles Mosquito — A65

30c, Institute of Applied Science & Technology, proposed for University of Guyana. 50c, Map of Guyana & National Science Research Council emblem. 60c, Commonwealth Science Council emblem.

Perf. 13½x14, 14x13½

1978, Sept. 4 Litho. Wmk. 364

275 A65 10c multi .25 .25
276 A65 30c multi, horiz. .25 .25
277 A65 50c multi .30 .30
278 A65 60c multi, horiz. .30 .30
Nos. 275-278 (4) 1.10 1.10

For overprints see Nos. 577, 585, 590.

Agrias Claudina — A66

5c, Prepona pheridamas. 10c, Archonias bellona. 15c, Eryphanis polyxena. 20c, Helicopis cupido. 25c, Nessaea batesli. 30c, Nymphidium mantus. 35c, Siderone galanthis. 40c, Morpho rhetenor, male. 50c, Hamadryas amphinone. 60c, Papilio androgeus. $1, Agrias claudina, vert. $2, Morpho rhetenor, female. $5, Morpho deidamia. $10, Elbella patrobas.

1978-80 *Perf. 14x13½*

Size: 22x16mm

279 A66 5c multicolored 1.50 .25
280 A66 10c multicolored 1.50 .25
281 A66 15c multicolored 1.50 .25
282 A66 20c multicolored 1.75 .25
283 A66 25c multicolored 1.75 .25
283A A66 30c multi ('80) 1.25 *3.25*
284 A66 35c multicolored 1.75 .25
285 A66 40c multicolored 1.75 .25
286 A66 50c multicolored 1.75 .30
286A A66 60c multi ('80) 1.25 1.75

Perf. 13½x13

287 A66 $1 multicolored 3.75 .35
288 A66 $2 multicolored 5.50 .70
289 A66 $5 multicolored 6.50 1.50
289A A66 $10 multi, perf. 14 ('80) 4.50 6.25
Nos. 279-289A (14) 36.00 15.85

Issued: Nos. 279-283, 284-286, 287-289, 10/1/78. For overprints and surcharges see Nos. 391, 406, 436-436A, 481, 486, 554, 668-670, 733-743, 871, 936-939, 944, 969, 1373, 1418, 1455, 1786, 1812, 1814, 1832-1833, 1873, 1901, 1912-1913, 1984-1988, 2051, 2053, 2054C, 2055, 2057, 2057B-2057C, 2058-2059, 2081-2111, 4188, 4189, C5-C6, O15-O16, O23-O29.

Indian Making Stone Chip Grater — A67

UNESCO Emblem and: 30c, Arawak Cassiri jar and decorated Amerindian jar. 50c, Gate to old Dutch fort, Kykover-al. 60c, Fort Island, Dutch ruins.

1978, Dec. 27 Wmk. 364 *Perf. 14*

290 A67 10c green & multi .25 .25
291 A67 30c green & multi .25 .25
292 A67 50c green & multi .25 .25
293 A67 60c green & multi .25 .25
Nos. 290-293 (4) 1.00 1.00

National and International Heritage Year. For surcharges see Nos. 604-606.

Earth Station at Dawn, Georgetown
A68

Designs: 30c, Earth Station in daylight, Georgetown. 50c, Intelsat V. $3, Intelsat IVa.

1979, Feb. 7 Litho. *Perf. 14x14½*

294 A68 10c multicolored .25 .25
295 A68 30c multicolored .25 .25
296 A68 50c multicolored .40 .25
297 A68 $3 multicolored 1.00 .90
Nos. 294-297 (4) 1.90 1.65

For surcharges see Nos. 384, 655, 714, 1376-1377, 1380, O9.

British Guyana No. 5 — A69

Designs: 30c, British Guiana No. 13, vert. 50c, British Guiana No. 152. $3, Printing press used for 1c Magenta, vert.

1979, June 11 Wmk. 364 *Perf. 14*

298 A69 10c multicolored .25 .25
299 A69 30c multicolored .30 .25
300 A69 50c multicolored .40 .25
301 A69 $3 multicolored .50 .50
Nos. 298-301 (4) 1.45 1.25

Sir Rowland Hill (1795-1879), originator of penny postage.
For overprints & surcharges see Nos. 409, 426, 428, 449, 479, 480, 578, 586, 598, 614, O6.

"Fun with the Fowls" and IYC Emblem — A70

Children's Drawings and IYC Emblem: 10c, "Me and my sister," vert. 50c, "Two boys catching ducks." $3, "Mango season."

1979, Aug. 20 Litho. *Perf. 13½*

302 A70 10c multicolored .25 .25
303 A70 30c multicolored .25 .25
304 A70 50c multicolored .25 .25
305 A70 $3 multicolored .50 *1.25*
Nos. 302-305 (4) 1.25 2.00

Intl. Year of the Child. For overprints and surcharges see Nos. 435, 579, 587, 599, 615, 943.

H. N. Critchlow, Worker Hauling Sack — A71

Critchlow and: 30c, Baker, horiz. 50c, Flag and crowd. $3, Portrait only.

1979, Sept. 27 Litho. *Perf. 14*

306 A71 10c multicolored .25 .25
307 A71 30c multicolored .25 .25
308 A71 50c multicolored .25 .25
309 A71 $3 multicolored .60 *.90*
Nos. 306-309 (4) 1.35 1.65

Guyana Labor Union, 60th anniversary. For surcharges see Nos. 403, 429, 718.

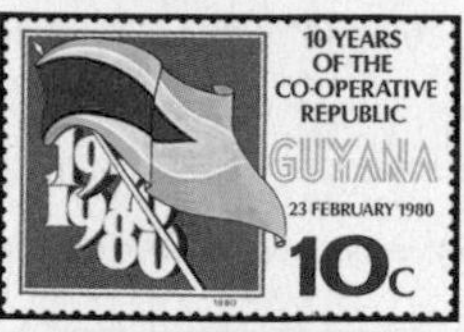

Cooperative Republic, 10th Anniv. — A72

35c, Demerara River Bridge. 60c, Kaieteur Falls. $3, Makanaima, American Indian.

Wmk. 364

1980, Feb. 23 Litho. *Perf. 14*

313 A72 10c shown .25 .25
314 A72 35c multicolored .30 .25
315 A72 60c multicolored .50 .25
316 A72 $3 multicolored .75 .75
Nos. 313-316 (4) 1.80 1.50

For overprints and surcharges see Nos. 365, 371, 450A, 442, 591, 656.

Miniature Sheet

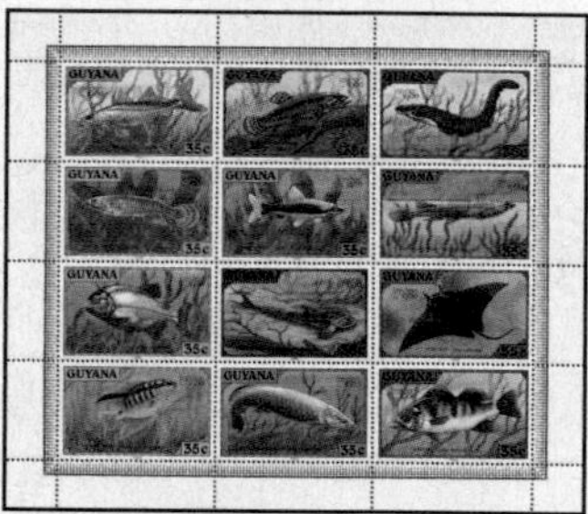
Snoek, London 1980 Emblem — A73

London 80 Emblem and Fish; a, Snoek. b, Haimara. c, Electric eel. d, Golden rivulus. e, Pencil fish. f, Four-eyed fish. g, Pirai. h, Smoking hassar. i, Devil ray. j, Flying patwa. k, Arapaima. l, Lukanani.

1980, May 6 Wmk. 373 *Perf. 14*

317 A73 Sheet of 12 4.75 4.75
a.-l. 35c any single .35 .35

London 1980 Intl. Stamp Exhib., May 6-14. For overprints & surcharges see Nos. 444, 725-726, 1414.

Children's Convalescent Home, Rotary Emblem — A74

Rotary International, 75th anniversary (Emblem and): 30c, Georgetown club emblem. 50c, District 404 emblem (hibiscus), vert. $3, Anniversary emblem, vert.

Perf. 14x14½, 14½x14

1980, June 23 Litho. Wmk. 364

318 A74 10c multicolored .25 .25
319 A74 30c multicolored .25 .25
320 A74 50c multicolored .35 .35
321 A74 $3 multicolored .75 .75
Nos. 318-321 (4) 1.60 1.60

For overprints and surcharges see Nos. 552, 580, 601, C1.

Emblem and Caduceus
A75

60c, Scientist, beach scene. $3, Emblems over island.

Wmk. 364

1980, Sept. 23 Litho. ***Perf. 13½***

322	A75	10c shown	.25	.25
323	A75	60c multicolored	.40	.25
324	A75	$3 multicolored	1.25	1.00
		Nos. 322-324 (3)	1.90	1.50

Commonwealth Caribbean Medical Research Council, 25th anniversary. For overprints and surcharges see Nos. 366, 427, 430, 494, 553.

Virola Surinamensis (Christmas 1980) — A76

1980, Nov. 1 Wmk. 373 ***Perf. 14***

325	A76	10c shown	.25	.25
326	A76	30c Hymenaea courbaril	.30	.25
327	A76	50c Mora excelsa	.40	.25
328	A76	$3 Peltogyne venosa	1.00	*1.60*
		Nos. 325-328 (4)	1.95	2.35

For overprints and surcharges see Nos. 431, 773, 790, 792-793, 4169, 4175.

Miniature Sheet

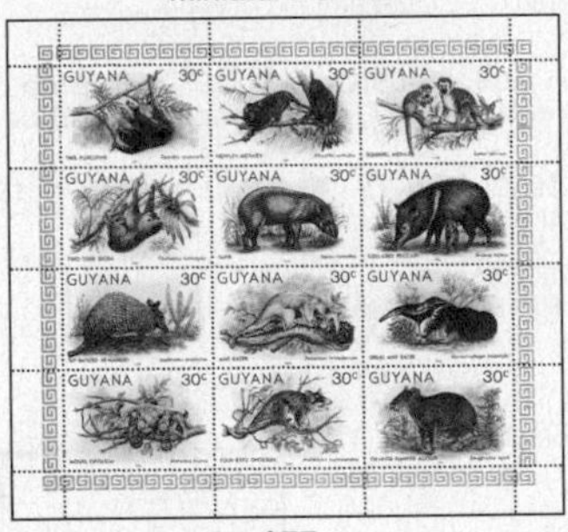

A77

Designs: a, Tree porcupine. b, Howler monkeys. c, Squirrel monkeys. d, Two-toed sloth. e, Tapir. f, Collared peccary. g, Six-banded armadillo. h, Anteater. i, Great anteaters. j, Mouse opossums. k, Four-eyed opossum. l, Orange-rumped agouti.

1981, Mar. 2 Wmk. 364 ***Perf. 14***

329	A77	Sheet of 12	8.00	8.00
a.-l.		30c any single	.40	.40
m.		As #329g, perf. 12	3.00	.40

For overprints see Nos. 581, 819, 1399, 1503, 1844.

During 1981-91, there were numerous sources creating stamps for Guyana, with as many as 5-7 parties being active at any given time.

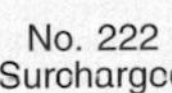

No. 222 Surcharged

1981, May 4

330	A53	$1.05 on 10c multi	.60

For surcharges see Nos. 396, 620.

Nos. 135, 145-147 Surcharged

No. 331

No. 332

No. 333

No. 334

No. 335

1981 Litho. Wmk. 364 ***Perf. 13½***

331	A28	60c on 3c #135	3.00
332	A28	75c on $5 #147	3.00
333	A28	$1.10 on $2 #146	3.00
334	A28	$3.60 on $5 #147 (Blk)	4.00
a.		Blue overprint	4.00
335	A28	$7.20 on $1 #145 (Bl)	4.00
a.		Black overprint	6.00

No. 333 is airmail. Issue dates: $3.60, $7.20, 5/6. Others 7/22. Diagonal overprint on No. 332. Vertical overprint on No. 333. Location of surcharge varies.

See Nos. 621, 666-667, Q4, QO5. For overprints and surcharges see Nos. 378, 489-496, 547, 549, 646, 818, 867-868, O11, Q3, QO3.

Map of Guyana — A78

1981, May 11 Photo. ***Perf. 13½***

Color of Map

336	A78	10c on 3c dl brn	1.20
337	A78	30c on 2c gray	1.20
338	A78	50c on 2c gray	1.20
339	A78	60c on 2c gray	1.20
340	A78	75c on 3c dl brn	1.20
		Nos. 336-340 (5)	6.00

Revenue stamps surcharged for postal use. For surcharge, see No. 503. For similar revenue stamps surcharged, see Nos. 501-502, 504-538, 934a. For surcharge see No. 503.

Nos. J5-J8 Surcharged in Red, Black, or Brown

a

b

Type "a"

1981, June 8 Typo. ***Perf. 13½x14***

341	D1	10c on 2c #J6	
342	D1	15c on 12c #J8 (Blk)	
343	D1	20c on 1c #J5	
344	D1	45c on 2c #J6	
345	D1	55c on 4c #J7	
346	D1	60c on 4c #J7 (Brn)	
347	D1	65c on 2c #J6	
348	D1	70c on 4c #J7	
349	D1	80c on 4c #J7	
		Nos. 341-349 (9)	11.00

Type "b"

341a	D1	10c on 2c #J6	
342a	D1	15c on 12c #J8 (Blk)	
343a	D1	20c on 1c #J5	
344a	D1	45c on 2c #J6	
345a	D1	55c on 4c #J7	
347a	D1	65c on 2c #J6	
348a	D1	70c on 4c #J7	
349a	D1	80c on 4c #J7	
		Nos. 341a-349a (8)	11.00

Pairs with types a and b exist for all values except the 60c.

Nos. 48, 61-62, 74, 139, 142-143, 145-147, 212-213, 216, 220, 231-232, 243-244, 251-252, 315-316, and 323 Overprinted in Black or Red

1981 ***Perfs. as Before***

Watermarks & Printing Methods as Before

350	A8	15c on #74 (R)	17.50
351	A28	15c on #139	
a.		Red overprint	7.00
b.		On #139a, red overprint	8.00
352	A57a	15c on #243	8.50
353	A57b	15c on #244	5.00
354	A11	25c on #61 (R)	.75
355	A11	30c on #62 (R)	.75
356	A55	35c on #231 (R)	3.00
357	A8	40c on #48	12.00
358	A28	40c on #142	
359	A28	50c on #143	4.00
360	A49	50c on #212	3.25
361	A50	50c on #216	1.50
362	A52	50c on #220	26.00
363	A55	50c on #232	3.25
364	A59	50c on #251	15.00
365	A72	60c on #315	.90
366	A75	60c on #323	.90
367	A28	$1 on #145	3.50
a.		Red overprint	2.00
368	A49	$1 on #213	7.50
369	A59	$1 on #252	6.50
370	A28	$2 on #146	8.00
a.		Red overprint	2.00
b.		Black ovpt. with serifs	25.00
371	A72	$3 on #316	3.00
372	A28	$5 on #147	4.25
		Nos. 350-372 (23)	50.00

Issued: Nos. 354-356, 367, 6/8; Nos. 350, 357, 370, 7/1; Nos. 351-353, 359-366, 368-369, 371-372, 7/7.

Location and size of overprint varies. Refer to second paragraph in footnote following No. 147 for Nos. 358-359.

For surcharges and overprints see Nos. 556, 607, 659, 745, 849-850, 1362, 4132.

Nos. 68, 135-136, 139, 145-147, 297, 333 Surcharged or Overprinted

1981 Litho. ***Perfs. as Before***

Watermarks & Printing Methods as Before

373	A7	15c on 1c #68	1.10	
374	A28	50c on 5c #136	3.00	
375	A28	75c on 5c #136	35.00	
375A	A28	80c on 15c #139		
376	A7	100c on 1c #68	1.00	
377	A7	110c on 1c #68	1.00	
a.		Strip of 3, #373, 376-377	5.50	4.00
378	A28	$1.10 on #333	15.00	
379	A28	120c on $1 #145	2.50	
380	A28	140c on $1 #145	2.50	
381	A28	150c on $2 #146	2.50	
382	A28	210c on $5 #147	35.00	
383	A28	220c on 5c #136	30.00	
384	A68	220c on $3 #297	5.00	
385	A28	250c on $5 #147	2.75	
386	A28	280c on $5 #147	2.75	
387	A28	360c on $2 #146	3.50	
388	A28	375c on $5 #147	3.00	
389	A28	$7.20 on 3c #135	100.00	
390	A28	720c on 60c #144	3.75	
390A	A28	$20 on 5c #136		

Location and size of surcharge and obliterator varies. Obliterator is an "X" on Nos. 381-388, 390, two solid boxes on Nos. 379-380, and five bars on No. 389. Numeral "7" is placed before 5 to make surcharge on No. 375. "Royal Wedding 1981" obliterated by three bars on No. 378. New denomination on No. 375A does not have cent sign. Obliterator on No. 390A is three horizontal bars.

Refer to second paragraph in footnote following No. 147 for Nos. 381, 387 and 390. Nos. 376-378 are airmail.

Issued: #375, 382, 6/8; #373-374, 376-388, 390, 7/1.

For overprint and surcharges see Nos. 408, 788, 859-860, 863-864, 1379, 1417.

No. 281 Overprinted "ESSEQUIBO / IS OURS"

1981, July Litho. ***Perf. 14x13½***

391	A66	15c on #281	8.50
a.		Ovpt. without serifs	

Nos. 87, 95-96, 142, 146, 210, 218, 230, 309, 330, O15 Surcharged

1981 ***Perfs. as Before***

Watermarks & Printing Methods as Before

392 A17 55c on 6c #95 4.50
393 A14 70c on 6c #87 1.25
394 A14 100c on 6c #87 1.50
395 A17 100c on 8c #96 4.50
396 A53 100c on #330 (surcharge reading down) 40.00
a. Surcharge reading up 50.00
397 A17 110c on 6c #95 3.00
398 A49 110c on 10c #210 3.00
399 A52 110c on 10c #218 7.00
400 A55 110c on 10c #230 7.00
401 A28 125c on $2 #146 15.00
402 A17 180c on 6c #95 4.50
403 A71 240c on $3 #309 12.00
404 A17 400c on 6c #95 4.50
405 A17 $4.40 on 6c #95 2.25
a. Fours same size 11.00
406 A66 550c on $10 #O15 10.00
407 A28 625c on 40c #142 17.50

Issued: Nos. 392, 394-395, 397-399, 405, 405a, 407, 7/7; Nos. 393, 402-404, 406, 9/15. Refer to 2nd paragraph in footnote following No. 147 for No. 407. For overprints and surcharges see Nos. 651-652, 996, 1858-1859, 1861, O8, O10, O12.

No. 383 Ovptd. "Espana 82" No. 301 Surcharged "1831-1981 / Von Stephan"

Perfs. as Before

1981, July 22 Litho. Wmk. 364

408 A28 220c on #383 7.00
409 A69 330c on $3 #301 10.00

For surcharges see Nos. 616, 622.

Nos. 43, 72 Surcharged

1981 Photo. Unwmk. ***Perf. 14x14½***

410 A7 12c on 12c on 6c #43
411 A7 Pair, #a.-b.
a. 15c on 10c on 6c #43
b. 15c on 30c on 6c #43
412 A7 Pair, #a.-b.
a. 15c on 50c on 6c #43
b. 15c on 60c on 6c #43
413 A7 Strip of 3, #a.-c.
a. 12c On 6c #43
b. 50c On 6c #43
c. $1 On 6c #43

Wmk. 364

413D A7 Strip of 3, #e.-g.
e. 12c On 6c #72
f. 50c On 6c #72
g. $1 On 6c #72

Issue dates: Nos. 410-412, Aug. 24. No. 413-413D, Nov. 10.

Nos. 410-412 were not issued without large numeral surcharges. Obliterator is black box on Nos. 410-412, "X" on Nos. 413a & 413De. Nos. 413b-413c, 413Df-g are airmail.

For overprints and surcharges see Nos. 728-728a, 914, 994, 994a, 1400-1401, 4174.

16th Anniv. of the Guyana Defense Force — A79

15c on 10c, Armed Ranger, 1772. 50c, Private, Foot Regiment, 1825. $1 on 30c, Marine Private, 1775. $1.10 on $3, Defense Force officers, 1966.

1981, Oct. 1 Wmk. 364 ***Perf. 13½***

414 A79 15c on 10c multi .35 .25
415 A79 50c multicolored .90 .45
416 A79 $1 on 30c multi 1.75 1.75
417 A79 $1.10 on $3 multi 2.00 2.00
Nos. 414-417 (4) 5.00 4.45

Nos. 414, 416-417 not issued without surcharge. For overprints see Nos. 570, 588, 595, 1368-1369.

Louis Braille and Boy Reading Braille — A80

Intl. Year of the Disabled: 50c, Helen Keller and Rajkumari Singh. $1, Beethoven and Sonny Thomas. $1.10, Renoir and painting.

1981, Nov. 2 ***Perf. 13½x14***

418 A80 15c on 10c multi .25 .25
419 A80 50c multi .75 .75
420 A80 $1 on 60c multi 1.25 1.25
421 A80 $1.10 on $3 multi 2.00 2.00
Nos. 418-421 (4) 4.25 4.25

Nos. 418, 420-421 not issued without surcharge. For overprints and surcharge see Nos. 571, 589, 596, 1913A.

Nos. 192, 209, 230, 298, 301, 309, 322, 324, 328, O1 Surcharged in Blue or Red

Watermarks & Printing Methods as Before

1981, Nov. 14 ***Perfs. as Before***

422 A55 110c on 10c #230 6.00
423 A28 110c on #209 5.00
424 A28 110c on #192 5.00
425 A28 110c on #O1 5.00
426 A69 110c on 10c #298 (R) 3.00
427 A75 110c on 10c #322 15.00
428 A69 110c on $3 #301 (R) 3.50
429 A71 110c on $3 #309 8.50
430 A75 110c on $3 #324 6.00
a. Red surcharge 9.00
431 A76 110c on $3 #328 9.00
a. Red surcharge 60.00
Nos. 422-431 (10) 66.00

Nos. 423-424 were issued with two 110c surcharges of different sizes. Refer to second paragraph in footnote below No. 147 for No. 425. For overprints and surcharges see Nos. 791, 820, 855, 1000, 1364-1366.

Flower Type of 1971-76 Surcharged

1981, Nov. 24 Photo. ***Perf. 15x14***

Size: 20x23mm

Coil Stamps

433 A28 15c on 2c like #134 .35
434 A28 15c on 8c Mazaruni Pride .35
a. Pair, #433-434 1.10

Nos. 433-434 were not issued without surcharge. See Nos. 731-732.

No. 305 Surcharged "U.N.I.C.E.F. / 1946-1981"

Wmk. 364

1981, Nov. 14 Litho. ***Perf. 13½***

435 A70 125c on $3 #305 4.00

For surcharge see No. 942.

No. 279 Surcharged "Nov. 81" (#436) or "Cancun 81" (#436A)

1981, Nov. 14 ***Perf. 14x13½***

436 A66 50c on 5c #279
436A A66 50c on 5c #279 6.50

Conversion to Metric System, Jan. 2 — A81

a, Tape measure. b, Juggler. c, Man, envelope. d, Baby on scale. e, Canje Bridge. f, Liter bucket.

Perf. 14½x14

1982, Jan. 18 Wmk. 364

437 A81 15c Sheet of 6, #a.-f. 3.25 3.25

For surcharge see No. 557.

Nos. 61, 63, 139, 140, 141A, 143-144, 146-147, 228, 266, 269, 300, 314 and 316-317 Ovptd. "1982" Vertically or Horizontally in Blue or Violet

Watermarks & Printing Methods as Before

1982-83 ***Perfs. as Before***

438 A28 15c on #139 8.00
a. On #139a 65.00
439 A28 20c on #140 4.00
440 A28 25c on #141A 7.50
441 A11 25c on #61 (V) 2.00
442 A72 35c on #314 1.00
443 A63 35c on #269 6.00
444 A73 35c on block of 6, #317a-317f 20.00
445 A11 40c on #63 (V) 1.00
446 A62 40c on #266 1.00
447 A28 50c on #143 3.00
448 A54 50c on #228 2.00
449 A69 50c on #300 1.00
449A A28 60c on #144 7.00
450 A28 $2 on #146 1.50
450A A72 $3 on #316 2.25
451 A28 $5 on #147 1.50
Nos. 438-451 (16) 68.75

Issued: Nos. 439-441, 2/8; Nos. 450-451, 4/23; Nos. 445-446, 4/27; No. 438, 6/17; Nos. 443-444, 8/16; No. 442, 9/15; Nos. 447-449, 10/11; No. 449A, 7/1/83; No. 450A, 11/3/83.

For other stamps overprinted "1982" only, see Nos 482-483, 555.

For overprints and surcharges see Nos. 806, 809, 813-814, 851, 999, 1354, 1415, 4134, 4171.

Nos. 97, O3, O4, O9-O10 Ovptd. "POSTAGE" in Blue

Watermarks and Printing Methods as Before

1982 ***Perfs. as Before***

452 A28 15c on #O3 10.00
453 A17 25c on #97 *6.00*
454 A28 50c on #O4 1.50
455 A68 100c on #O9 2.50
456 A17 110c on #O10 *3.00*

For surcharge see No. 853. For similar overprints see Nos. 729-730. Refer to second paragraph in footnote following No. 147 for No. 454.

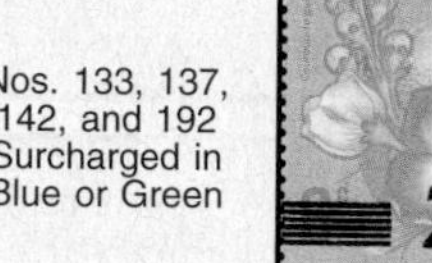

Nos. 133, 137, 142, and 192 Surcharged in Blue or Green

Perfs. as Before

1982 Litho. Wmk. 364

457 A28 20c on 6c #137 1.00
458 A28 20c on 6c #137 (G) 1.00
459 A28 125c on #192 1.00
460 A28 180c on #142 ovpt. "1982" 6.00
461 A28 220c on 1c #133 2.00
Nos. 457-461 (5) 11.00

No. 458 has no obliterator, "20c" is 23mm long.

Issued: Nos. 457-459, 2/8; No. 460, 4/8; No. 461, 4/23.

Refer to 2nd paragraph in footnote following No. 147 for No. 460.

For overprints see Nos. 755, 856, 862.

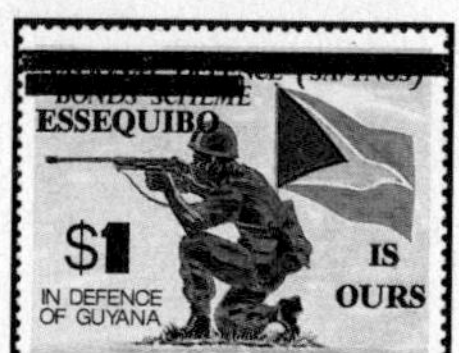

Savings Campaign A81a

No. 462, Soldier & flag. No. 463, Two soldiers, flag.

1982 Litho. ***Perf. 14½***

462 A81a $1 multi 1.00
463 A81a $1.10 on $5 multi 7.50
a. Inverted comma before "OURS"

Size of obliterator differs on Nos. 463 and 463a. Nos. 462-463a are revenue stamps ovptd. for postal use.

Issued: No 462, 2/8; No. 463, 3/3; No. 463a, 7/13.

Nos. 134, 136, & 192 Surcharged in Black or Green

Surcharges read: Nos. 464a, 465a, 466a: "BADEN-POWELL / 1857-1982".
Nos. 464b, 465b, 466b: "Scout Movement / 1907-1982"
Nos. 464c, 465c, 466c: "1907-1982"
Nos. 464d, 465d, 466d: "1857-1982"
Nos. 464e, 465e, 466e: "1982"

Perf. 13x13½

1982, Feb. 22 Litho. Wmk. 364

Sheets of 25

464 8 #a.-b., 4 #c.-d., 1 #e. 20.00
a.-e. A28 15c on 2c #134, any single .70
465 8 #a.-b., 4 #c.-d., 1 #e. 35.00
a.-e. A28 110c on 5c #136, any single 1.00
466 8 #a.-b., 4 #c.-d., 1 #e. 35.00
a.-e. A28 125c on #192, any single (G) 1.00

Lord Robert Baden-Powell, 125th anniv. of birth. Boy Scout Movement, 75th anniv.

For overprints and surcharges see Nos. 558, 778-784, 836-837, 1347.

Nos. 289, 299, 301 Surcharged or Overprinted in Black or Blue

Perfs. as Before

1982, Feb. 15 Litho. Wmk. 364

479 A69 100c on $3 #301 2.00 1.00
480 A69 400c on 30c #299 3.00 2.00
481 A66 $5 #289 (Bl) 15.00 10.00
Nos. 479-481 (3) 20.00 13.00

For surcharges see Nos. 617, 904-906, 937-939, O22-O29.

Nos. 88-89 Ovptd. "1982" in Blue and Nos. 87, 90 Surcharged in Blue or Red

1982, Mar. 15 Photo. ***Perf. 13***

482 A14 25c on #88
483 A14 30c on #89
484 A14 45c on 6c #87
485 A14 75c on 40c #90 (R)
Nos. 482-485 (4) 3.00

For overprints see Nos. 766-767.

Nos. 60, 284, 324, and 331-333 Surcharged in Black or Blue

Watermarks & Printing Methods as Before

1982 ***Perfs. as Before***

486 A66 20c on 35c #284 7.50
487 A11 80c on 6c #60 (Bl) 3.00
488 A11 85c on 6c #60 (Bl) 3.00
489 A28 85c on #331 6.00
490 A28 130c on #331 4.00
491 A28 160c on #333 (Bl) 3.00
a. Black surcharge 5.00
492 A28 170c on #333 15.00
493 A28 210c on #332 (Bl) 3.00
494 A75 210c on $3 #324 (Bl) 4.00
495 A28 235c on #332 5.00
a. Blue surcharge 9.00
496 A28 330c on #333 4.00
Nos. 486-496 (11) 57.50

Nos. 491-491a, 492, & 496 are airmail. Obliterators differ.

Issue dates: No. 486, 3/15. Others, 4/27.

For surcharges see Nos. 647, 1367.

Nos. 135, 137, 144 & 145 Overprinted or Surcharged in Blue or Black

Overprints read: Nos. 497-498, 500: "ESPANA / 1982". No. 499: "ESPANA / 1982" and "ITALY".

1982 Litho. Wmk. 364 ***Perf. 13½***

497 A28 $1 on #145 (Blk) 1.50
498 A28 110c on 3c #135 1.50
499 A28 $2.35 on 180c on 60c #144 *14.00*
500 A28 250c on 6c #137 2.00

Refer to second paragraph in footnote below No. 147 for No. 499.

No. 499 not issued without $2.35 surcharge.

See No. 597 for stamp with one-line Espana 1982 overprint. For surcharges see Nos. 774-777.

Issued: Nos. 497-498, 500, 5/15; No. 499, 7/15.

Map Revenue Surcharged in Black, Blue, or Red

1982-83 Photo. Wmk. 364 ***Perf. 13***
Color of Map
501 A78 15c on 2c gray (Bl)
502 A78 20c on 2c gray (Bl)
503 A78 20c on 10c #336 dl brn (Bl)
504 A78 25c on 2c gray
a. Blue surcharge
b. Red surcharge 1.00
505 A78 30c on 2c gray (Bl)
506 A78 40c on 2c gray
a. Blue surcharge
507 A78 45c on 2c gray (Bl)
508 A78 50c on 2c gray (Bl)
509 A78 60c on 2c gray (Bl)
510 A78 75c on 2c gray (Bl)
511 A78 80c on 2c gray (Bl)
512 A78 85c on 2c gray (Bl)
513 A78 $1.00 on 3c dl brn
514 A78 $1.10 on 3c dl brn
515 A78 $1.20 on 3c dl brn
516 A78 $1.25 on 3c dl brn
517 A78 $1.30 on 3c dl brn
518 A78 $1.50 on 3c dl brn
519 A78 $1.60 on 3c dl brn
520 A78 $1.70 on 3c dl brn
521 A78 $1.75 on 3c dl brn
522 A78 $1.80 on 3c dl brn
523 A78 $2.00 on 3c dl brn
524 A78 $2.10 on 3c dl brn
525 A78 $2.20 on 3c dl brn
526 A78 $2.35 on 3c dl brn
527 A78 $2.40 on 3c dl brn
528 A78 $2.50 on 3c dl brn
529 A78 $3.00 on 3c dl brn
530 A78 $3.30 on 3c dl brn
531 A78 $3.75 on 3c dl brn
532 A78 $4.00 on 3c dl brn
533 A78 $4.40 on 3c dl brn
534 A78 $5.00 on 3c dl brn
535 A78 $5.50 on 3c dl brn
536 A78 $6.25 on 3c dl brn
537 A78 $15 on 2c gray (R)
538 A78 $20 on 2c gray (R)
Nos. 501-538 (38) 210.00

Revenue stamps surcharged for postal use. Issue dates: Nos. 501-502, 504-538, May 17, 1982; No. 503, Mar. 14, 1983.
For surcharges see Nos. 935, 4135, 4186, 4191, 4192, 4197.

British Guiana Nos. 254, 255, 279, Guyana 10A, 13, 13a, 32J, 32K, 32N Surcharged "H.R.H. / Prince William / 21st June 1982" in Blue

British Guiana stamps also have "GUYANA."

1982, July 12 ***Perfs. as Before***
Watermarks & Printing Methods as Before
539 A60 50c on 2c #254 1.00 .45
540 A60 50c on 2c #32J 10.00 4.50
541 A66 $1.10 on 5c #279 3.00 .65
541A A60 $1.10 on 3c #255 2.00 .55
542 A60 $1.10 on 3c #32K 32.50 4.50
543 A60 $1.25 on 6c #10A
543A A60 $1.25 on 6c #32N .85 .85
544 A60 $2.20 on 24c #13a 4.00
544A A60 $2.20 on 24c #13 2.00 2.00

For surcharges see Nos. 797-800.

Nos. 133-134 Surcharged "C.A. & CARIB / Games / 1982"
Perf. 13x13½
1982, Aug. 16 Litho. Wmk. 364
545 A28 50c on 2c #134 2.25 .40
546 A28 60c on 1c #133 2.75 .25
Nos. 545-546 (2) 5.00

Central American and Caribbean Games, Havana. For overprint see No. 816.

Nos. 135, 331, C2 Surcharged
1982, Sept. 15
547 A28 130c on #331 3.00
548 A28 170c on #C2 4.00
549 A28 440c on 60c on 3c #331 ovptd. "1982" 3.50
a. Without "1982" 80.00
b. As No. 549, but with Royal Wedding overprint like No. 332 — —
Nos. 547-549 (3) 10.50

For surcharge see No. 802.

No. 137 Surcharged "Commonwealth / GAMES / AUSTRALIA / 1982" in Blue
1982, Sept. 27
550 A28 $1.25 on 6c #137 2.25 .50

For surcharge see No. 789.

Nos. 207, 221, 287, 320, 323, 332 Ovptd. in Blue, Dark Blue, Green or Blue Green

Overprints or Surcharges read: No. 551, "INT. / FOOD DAY / 1982"; No. 552, "INT. YEAR / OF THE / ELDERLY"; No. 553, "Dr. R. KOCH / CENTENARY / TBC BACILLUS / DISCOVERY"; No. 554, "F.D. ROOSEVELT / 1882-1982 "; No. 555, "1982"; No. 556, "GAC Inaug. Flight / Georgetown- / Boa Vista, Brasil" in Blue and "1982" in Blue Green.

Watermarks & Printing Methods as Before
1982, Oct. 15 ***Perfs. as Before***
551 A48 50c on #207 (DB) 21.00 1.00
552 A74 50c on #320 (DB) 9.00 1.00
553 A75 60c on #323 (DB) 6.00 .55
554 A66 $1 on #287 (G) 6.00 1.00
555 A52 $1 on #221 (Bl) 6.00 1.25
556 A28 200c on #332 (Bl, Bl G) 24.00 2.75
Nos. 551-556 (6) 72.00 7.55

For surcharges see Nos. 895, 902, 936, 1363.

No. 437 Surcharged "CARICOM / Heads of Gov't / Conference / July 1982"
Perf. 14½x14
1982, Jan. 18 Litho. Wmk. 364
557 Sheet of 6 15.00 12.50
a.-f. A81 50c on 15c, any single 2.25 .50

Nos. 464 Ovptd. "CHRISTMAS / 1982" in Red
1982, Dec. 1 ***Perf. 13x13½***
558 Sheet of 25, 8 #a.-b., 4 #c.-d., 1 #e. 32.50 32.50
a.-b. A28 15c on #464a-464b, either single .90 .45
c.-d. A28 15c on #464c-464d, either single 2.10 .45
e. A28 15c on #464e 24.00 24.00

Nos. 134, 137 Surcharged

Perf. 13x13½
1982-83 Litho. Wmk. 364
563 A28 15c on 2c #134 (Bl) .75
a. Red surcharge 2.00
b. Black surcharge .75
564 A28 20c on 6c #137 (Bk) .75
a. Green surcharge .75

Issued: No. 563, 12/15; No. 564, 1/5/83.
Compare No. 564 with Nos. 631-632. For surcharges see Nos. 846, 846a, 846b.

No. 72 Surcharged
1982, Dec. 15 Photo. ***Perf. 14x14½***
565 A7 50c on 6c #72 .75 .25
566 A7 $1.00 on 6c #72 1.25 .45
Nos. 565-566 (2) 2.00 .70

Nos. 62, 88-89, 144, 161, 202, 217, 224-225, 232, 240, 251, 254, 257, 264, 276-278, 299-301, 303-305, 315, 319, 321, 329m, 414-416, and 418-420 Ovptd. "1983" Vertically or Horizontally
1983 ***Perfs. as Before***
Watermarks & Printing Methods as Before
567 A57 15c on #240 6.00
568 A60 15c on #254 1.50
569 A62 15c on #264 1.00
570 A79 15c on 10c #414 1.00
571 A80 15c on 10c #418 .25
572 A14 25c on #88 .50
573 A33 25c on #161 14.00
574 A47 25c on #202
575 A11 30c on #62 1.50
576 A14 30c on #89 .50
577 A65 30c on #276 12.50
578 A69 30c on #299 5.00
579 A70 30c on #303 10.00
580 A74 30c on #319 6.00
581 A77 30c on #329m 3.00
582 A53 50c on #224 2.00
583 A55 50c on #232 5.00
584 A59 50c on #251 7.00
585 A65 50c on #277 5.00
586 A69 50c on #300 2.00
587 A70 50c on #304 30.00
588 A79 50c on #415 1.00
589 A80 50c on #419 2.00
590 A65 60c on #278 5.50
591 A72 60c on #315 7.00
592 A51 $1 on #217 10.00
593 A53 $1 on #225 10.00
594 A60 $1 on #257 6.00
595 A79 $1 on 30c #416 2.75
596 A80 $1 on 60c #420 7.50
597 A28 180c on 60c #144 2.00
598 A69 $3 on #301 12.00
599 A70 $3 on #305 15.00
601 A74 $3 on #321 75.00
602 A28 360c on $2 #146 2.25

Issued: Nos. 567-571, 583, 585-586, 2/1; No. 596, 3/7; No. 573, 3/11; Nos. 572, 576, 3/17; Nos. 582, 584, 587, 588, 589, 592-595, 598-599, 601, 4/1; No. 574, 5/23; Nos. 575, 577-580, 590-591, 7/1; No. 602, 11/3; No. 581, 11/15; No. 597, 12/14.
Refer to the second paragraph in footnote under No. 147 for Nos. 597 & 602. No. 597 contains unissued overprint, "ESPANA 1982."
For overprints and surcharges see Nos. 724, 901, 940, 943A.

No. O2 Ovptd. "POSTAGE" in Red
Perf. 14½x14
1983, Feb. 1 Photo. Wmk. 364
603 A8 15c on #O2 16.00 .50

For surcharge see Nos. 746-746a.

Nos. 291-293, 356 Surcharged in Blue or Black
Wmk. 364
1983, Feb. 8 Litho. ***Perf. 14***
604 A67 90c on 30c #291 (Blk) 2.00 1.00
605 A67 90c on 50c #292 1.25 .30
606 A67 90c on 60c #293 2.00 1.00
607 A55 90c on #356 4.75 .50
Nos. 604-607 (4) 10.00 2.80

For overprints and surcharges see Nos. 763-764, 768-769, 770-771.

Flag A82

Cooperative Youth Palace — A83

1983, Feb. 19 ***Perf. 14½x14***
608 A82 Pair 1.00 1.00
a. 25c Flag flying right .40 .40
b. 25c Flag flying left .40 .40
Perf. 13½
609 A83 $1.30 shown 1.00 1.00
Size: 43x25mm
Perf. 14½
610 A83 $6 Map 3.75 3.75

60th birthday of Pres. Linden Forbes Burnham. No. 608a inscribed for birthday; No. 608b for Burnham's 30th anniv. of election to parliament.
See Nos. 660, 913. For overprints & surcharges see Nos. 826-835, 924-926, 1404-1406.

Nos. 160, 205, 222, 263, 298, 302, 330, 333, 408-409, 480, C4, O1 and Q3 Ovptd. in Blue or Red

Watermarks & Printing Methods as Before
1983 Litho. ***Perfs. as Before***
611 A33 50c on 8c #160 (R) 25.00
612 A48 50c on 8c #205 2.25
613 A62 50c on 8c #263 8.00
614 A69 50c on 10c #298 (R) 1.50
615 A70 50c on 10c #302 4.00
616 A69 50c on #409 4.50
617 A69 50c on #480 2.00
618 A28 50c on #O1 5.00
619 A53 $1 on #222 8.50
620 A53 $1 on #330 5.00
621 A28 $1 on #333 5.00
622 A28 $1 on #408 10.00
623 A28 $1 on #C4 1.50
624 A28 $1 on #Q3 25.00

No. 621 has Royal Wedding ovpt. similar to No. 331. No. 624 also ovptd. "1982." See Nos. 648-649 for similar surcharges. For overprint see Nos. 815, 941. Issued: Nos. 614, 617, 619-624, 3/7; No. 611, 3/11; others, 4/1.

Nos. 10A, 13a Surcharged "Commonwealth / Day / 14 March 1983" and Emblem in Blue or Black
Wmk. 314 Upright
1983, Mar. 14 Engr. ***Perf. 12½x13***
625 A60 25c on 6c #10A
626 A60 $1.20 on 6c #10A (Bl)
Wmk. 314 Sideways
627 A60 $1.30 on 24c #13a
628 A60 $2.40 on 24c #13a (Bl)
Nos. 625-628 (4) 5.00

For overprints see Nos. 1823-1825.

Intl. Maritime Organization, 25th Anniv. — A84

Red Overprint on British Guiana Revenue Stamp
Perf. 14
1983, Mar. 17 Typo. Wmk. 3
629 A84 $4.80 grn & blue 7.50

Nos. 60, 72, 87 & 137 Surcharged in Black or Blue
1983 ***Perfs. as Before***
Watermarks & Printing Methods as Before
630 A11 15c on 6c #60 .75
a. Blue surcharge 1.00
631 A28 20c on 6c #137, two obliterators 1.00
632 A28 20c on 6c #137 1.00
633 A7 50c on 6c #72 .75
634 A14 50c on 6c #87 1.00
Nos. 630-634 (5) 4.50

Issued: Nos. 630, 632-633, 5/23; No. 630a, 631, 634, 5/2.
Surcharge on No. 632 has "c" after value. No. 564 does not.
For surcharge see No. 916.

No. 72 Surcharged in Black or Red
Perf. 14x14½
1983 Photo. Wmk. 364
635 A7 $1 on 6c #72 1.60
a. Red overprint, 4mm high 1.60

Issued: No. 635, 5/2. No. 635a, 5/23.
For surcharge see No. 916A.

Nos. 142, 147, 211, 226-227, 239 & 249 Surcharged in Blue
1983 ***Perfs. as Before***
Watermarks & Printing Methods as Before
636 A54 110c on 10c #226 3.00
637 A49 120c on 35c #211 4.50
638 A54 120c on 35c #227 4.50
639 A57 120c on 8c #239 4.50
640 A59 120c on 10c #249 4.50
641 A28 250c on 40c #142 12.00
642 A28 400c on $5 #147 9.00
Nos. 636-642 (7) 42.00

Issued: Nos. 636, 641-642, 5/2. Others, 7/1.
For surcharge see No. 865.

Nos. 332, 495a, C3 Surcharged in Red or Blue

Surcharges read: No. 643, "ITU / 1983"; No. 644, "WHO / 1983"; No. 645, "17 MAY '83 / ITU/WHO"; Nos. 646-647, "ITU/WHO / 17 MAY / 1983".

1983, May 17 ***Perfs. as Before***
Watermarks & Printing Methods as Before

643 A28 25c on #C3 4.00 .90
644 A28 25c on #C3 4.00 .90
645 A28 25c on #C3 4.00 .90
a. Strip of 3, #643-645 22.50 10.00
646 A28 $4.50 on #332 (Bl) 16.00 2.00
647 A28 $4.50 on #495a (Bl) 16.00

Nos. 643-645 issued in sheets of 25 with 8 each Nos. 643-644 and 9 No. 645.

Nos. 272, 274 Surcharged in Dark Blue

Perf. 13½x14

1983, May 18 Litho. Wmk. 364

648 A64 $1 on 15c #272 5.50 1.00
649 A64 $1 on 40c #274 9.00 1.00
Nos. 648-649 (2) 14.50 2.00

Surcharge on No. 648 also contains overprint "1983."

Nos. 402, 404, O8 Surcharged or Overprinted "CANADA 1983"

1983, June 15 ***Perf. 13½x13***

650 A17 $1.30 on #O8 4.50 3.00
651 A17 180c on #402 4.50 4.50
652 A17 $3.90 on #404 10.00 10.00
Nos. 650-652 (3) 19.00 17.50

For surcharge see No. 1860.

Nos. 243-244 Surcharged

1983, June 22 Unwmk. ***Perf. 14***

653 A57a 60c on 15c #243 15.00 1.00
654 A57b $1.50 on 15c #244 22.50 2.50
Nos. 653-654 (2) 37.50 3.50

Nos. 297, 313 Surcharged

Perfs. as Before

1983, July 1 Wmk. 364

655 A68 120c on #297 7.50 1.25
656 A72 120c on 10c #313 (R) 7.50 1.25

No. 655 has unissued surcharge, "INTERNATIONAL / SCIENCE YEAR / 375."

British Guiana No. J1 and Guyana No. J5 Surcharged "120 / GUYANA" in Dark Blue

1983, July 1 Wmk. 4 ***Perf. 13½x14***

657 D1 120c on 1c #J1 6.00 1.25

Wmk. 364

658 D1 120c on 1c #J5 6.00 1.25

No. 371 Surcharged in Red "CARICOM DAY 1983"

1983, July 1 Wmk. 364 ***Perf. 14***

659 A72 60c on $3 #371 3.00

Type A82 Without Inscription

1983, July 1 Litho. ***Perf. 14½x14***

660 A82 Pair 1.00 1.00
a. 25c, Flag flying right .40 .40
b. 25c, Flag flying left .40 .40

River Steamers A85

1983, July 11 Litho. ***Perf. 14***

661 A85 30c Kurupukari .25 .25
a. Tete-beche pair — —
662 A85 60c Makouria .50 .50
a. Tete-beche pair — —
663 A85 120c Powis 1.00 1.00
a. Tete-beche pair — —
664 A85 130c Pomeroon 1.25 1.25
665 A85 150c Lukanani 1.50 1.50
a. Tete-beche pair — —
Nos. 661-665 (5) 4.50 4.50

For surcharge, see No. 4020J.

No. 146 Surcharged in Dark Blue

1983, July 22 ***Perf. 13½***

666 A28 $2.30 on $1.10 on $2
667 A28 $3.20 on $1.10 on $2
Nos. 666-667 (2) 8.00

Nos. 666-667 have unissued surcharge of "$1.10 / Royal Wedding / 1981" similar to No. 331.

Nos. 282-283 & 283A Overprinted as Shown or with Various Initials in Red or Blue

Overprints: No. 668a, BW. b, LM. c, GY 1963 / 1983. d, JW. e, CU. f. Mont Golfier / 1783-1983.

No. 669a, BGI. b, GEO. c, MIA. d, BVB. e, PBM. f, Mont Golfier / 1783-1983. g, POS. h, JFK.

No. 670a, AHL. b, BCG. c, BMJ. d, EKE. e, GEO. f, GFO. g, IBM. h, Mont Golfier / 1783-1983. i, KAI. j, KAR. k, KPG. l, KRG. m, KTO. n, LTM. o, MHA. p, MWI. q, MYM. r, NAI. s, ORJ. t, USI. u, VEG.

1983, Sept. 5 ***Perf. 14x13½***

Sheets of 25

668 A66 20c 4 each #a.-e., 5 #f *30.00*
669 A66 25c 2 each #a., c.-e., g.-h., 8 #b., 5 #f. *45.00*
670 A66 30c #a.-e., g.-u., 5 #f., (Bl) *40.00*

Manned flight, bicentennial and Guyana Airways, 20th anniv. For ovpts. see Nos. 871, 969.

No. 234 Surcharged in Dark Blue

1983, Sept. 14 ***Perf. 13½***

703 A28 240c on #234 3.00 1.25
a. "4" with serif 3.50 1.50

Nos. 703, 703a appear in same sheet.

Nos. 68, 70 Surcharged "FAO 1983" in Red

Perf. 14x14½

1983, Sept. 15 Photo. Wmk. 364

704 A7 30c on 1c #68 .50 .25
705 A7 $2.60 on 3c #70 2.50 2.50
Nos. 704-705 (2) 3.00 2.75

For overprints see Nos. 1497-1498.

Great Britain, Postal Use In British Guiana, 150th Anniv. — A86

Stamps: a, #20. b, #26. c, #27. d, #28.

1983, Oct. 1 Litho. ***Perf. 14***

Inscribed in Black

706 A86 25c #20 .25 .25
707 A86 30c #26 .25 .25
708 A86 60c #27 .30 .30
709 A86 120c #28 1.00 1.00

Inscribed in Blue

710 Block of 4 .80 .80
a.-d. A86 25c any single .25 .25
711 Block of 4 1.00 1.00
a.-d. A86 30c any single .25 .25
712 Block of 4 1.00 1.00
a.-d. A86 45c any single .25 .25
713 Block of 4 3.50 3.50
a. A86 120c #20 .65 .65
b. A86 130c #26, Demerara .75 .75
c. A86 150c #27, Berbice .90 .90
d. A86 200c #28, Essequibo 1.20 1.20
Nos. 706-713 (8) 8.10 8.10

Nos. 706-709 printed in sheets with bottom two rows inverted. Nos. 710-712 printed in sheets of 60. No. 713 printed in sheets with blue marginal text.

For overprints and surcharges see Nos. 796, 903, 912, 1448, 1982.

Nos. 206, 235, 238, 297 & 309 Surcharged

Surcharges read: No. 714, "INT. / COMMUNICATIONS / YEAR"; No. 716, "Int. Food Day / 1983"; No. 718, "1918-1983 / I.L.O.".

1983, Oct. 15 ***Perfs. as Before***
Watermarks & Printing Methods as Before

714 A68 50c on 375c on $3 #297 6.00
715 A56 75c on 8c #235 7.50
716 A48 $1.20 on 35c #206 1.75
717 A56 $1.20 on 40c #238 7.50
718 A71 240c on $3 #309 2.25
Nos. 714-718 (5) 25.00

No. 714 was not issued without 375c surcharge. For overprint see No. 821.

Nos. 245, 247-248 Surcharged

Unwmk.

1983, Nov. 1 Litho. ***Perf. 14***

719 A58 25c on 8c #245 .35 .25
720 A58 $1.50 on 35c #247 2.40 1.00
721 A58 $1.50 on 40c #248 1.25 1.00
Nos. 719-721 (3) 4.00 2.25

Nos. 268 & 270 Surcharged

1983, Nov. 15 Wmk. 364

722 A63 60c on 15c #268 2.50 .50
723 A63 $1.20 on 40c #270 2.50 .90

No. 601 Ovptd. "Human Rights / Day"

1983, Dec. 1 ***Perf. 14½x14***

724 A74 $3 on #601 3.50 1.75

For surcharge see footnote following No. 998.

Nos. 317 and 726 Surcharged "LOS ANGELES / 1984"

1983, Dec. 6 Wmk. 373

725 Sheet of 12 80.00
a.-l. A73 55c on 125c on 35c #726a-726l, any single —
726 Sheet of 12 120.00
a.-l. A73 125c on 35c #317a-317l, any single —

For surcharge see No. 1897.

No. 133 Surcharged "COMMONWEALTH / HEADS OF GOV'T / MEETING--INDIA / 1983"

Perf. 13x13½

1983, Dec. 14 Litho. Wmk. 364

727 A28 150c on 1c #133 4.00 1.00

Nos. 413a, 413e Surcharged "CHRISTMAS / 1983"

1983, Dec. 14 Photo. ***Perf. 14x14½***
Watermarks as before

728 A7 20c on #413a 1.50 .25
a. 20c on #413De .50 .25

Nos. 146, O15 Ovptd. "POSTAGE" in Blue

1984, Jan. 8 ***Perfs. as before***

729 A28 $2 on #146 4.25 1.00
730 A66 550c on $10 #O15 22.00 10.00

Refer to second paragraph in footnote following No. 147 for No. 729.

Flower Type of 1971-76 Surcharged in Blue

Perf. 15x14

1984, Jan. Photo. Unwmk.
Size: 20x23mm
Coil Stamps

731 A28 17c on 2c, like #134 2.00 1.50
732 A28 17c on 8c, Mazaruni Pride 2.00 1.50
a. Pair, #731-732 4.00 4.00

Nos. 731-732 were intended for use on 8c envelopes to increase postage rate to 25c and were not issued without surcharge.

Nos. 284, 286A Surcharged in Black or Overprinted in Dark Blue

Surcharges or Overprints Read: Nos. 733, 741, "ALL / OUR HERITAGE"; Nos. 734, 743, "1984" 7mm long; Nos. 735, 742, "REPUBLIC / DAY"; No. 737, "BERBICE"; No. 738, "DEMERARA"; No. 739, "ESSEQUIBO"; No. 740, "1984" 18mm long.

Perf. 14x13½

1984, Feb. 24 Litho. Wmk. 364

733 A66 25c on 35c .75 .25
734 A66 25c on 35c 1.25 .50
735 A66 25c on 35c 1.25 .50
736 A66 25c on 35c #284 1.25 .50
737 A66 25c on 35c 6.00 4.50
738 A66 25c on 35c 6.00 4.50
739 A66 25c on 35c 6.00 4.50
740 A66 25c on 35c 14.00 14.00
741 A66 60c on #286A (DBl) 3.50 1.00
742 A66 60c on #286A (DBl) 3.50 1.00
743 A66 60c on #286A (DBl) 3.50 1.00

Nos. 733-740 were issued in sheets of 25, 6 No. 733, 4 each Nos. 734-736, 2 each Nos. 737-739, 1 No.740. Nos. 741-743 were issued in sheets of 25, 8 each Nos. 741-742, 9 No. 743.

Nos. 49-50, 52, 73-74, 77-80, 82, 139, 141A-143, 350, 603 Surcharged or Overprinted in Black and/or Blue "Protecting Our Heritage"

1984, Mar. 5 ***Perfs. as Before***
Watermarks & Printing Methods as Before

744 A8 20c on 15c #74 8.00 .50
a. Blue surcharge (value and words) 20.00
745 A8 20c on 15c #350 8.50 .50
746 A8 20c on 15c #603 (Bl) 15.00 2.00
a. "Protecting our Heritage" in black 40.00
747 A28 25c on #141A 12.50 .50
a. 25c on #141b 65.00 .60
748 A28 30c on 15c #139 24.00 .60
749 A8 40c on #77 10.00 .60
750 A28 50c on #143 1.75 .60
751 A28 50c on #143 (Revenue Ovpt.) 1.75 .60
752 A7 60c on #50 12.00 .60
a. 60c on #79 90.00
753 A28 90c on 40c #142 17.50 .90
754 A28 90c on 40c #142 (Revenue ovpt.) 125.00
755 A28 180c on #460 17.50 1.50
756 A7 $2 on #52 65.00 2.25
757 A8 225c on 10c on #73 21.00 1.75
758 A7 260c on $1 #80 15.00 1.50
759 A28 320c on 40c #142 15.00 3.25
760 A28 350c on 40c #142 25.00 4.25
761 A7 390c on 50c #78 8.00 4.00
a. 390c on #49 125.00
762 A7 450c on $5 #82 10.00 4.00
Nos. 744-762 (19) 412.50

Nos. 748, 753-754, 759-760 use row of "X", 6mm high, as obliterator. Nos. 744-746, 757 have new value printed vertically over old value. Nos. 758, 761-762 have new value printed horizontally over old value. Refer to second paragraph in footnote under No. 147 for Nos. 751, 754-755.

No. 87 Surcharged
Nos. 89, 484-485, 606 Overprinted or Surcharged in Dark Blue

Overprint or Surcharges read: Nos. 765-767, 773, "1984"; Nos. 764a, 769a, 771a, "INT. / CHESS / FED. / 1924-1984".

1984 ***Perfs. as Before***
Watermarks & Printing Methods as Before

763 A67 25c on #606 2.00
764 A67 25c on #606 4.00
a. Pair, #763-764 10.00
765 A14 30c on #89 .75
766 A14 45c on 6c #484 .75
767 A14 75c on 40c #485 .75
768 A67 75c on #606 1.00
769 A67 75c on #606 3.00
a. Pair, #768-769 8.00
770 A67 90c on #606 1.00
771 A67 90c on #606 3.00
a. Pair, #770-771 9.00
772 A14 130c on 6c #87 .50
773 A76 $3 on #328 3.00
Nos. 763-773 (11) 19.75

Issued: Nos. 765-767, 772, 3/17; No. 773, 6/15; Nos. 763-764, 768-769, 770-771, 7/20.

No. 767 exists with surcharge either above old value or in center of stamp.

Nos. 497-500 Surcharged

1984, Apr. 2 Litho. ***Perf. 13½***

774 A28 75c on #497 11.00 .55
775 A28 75c on #498 13.00 .55
776 A28 225c on #500 3.50 1.75
777 A28 230c on #499 4.00 1.25
Nos. 774-777 (4) 31.50 4.10

Nos. 464e, 465a, 465b, 465e, 466a, 466b, 466e Surcharged Like No. 748

1984, May 2

778 A28 20c on #464e 1.75 .50
779 A28 75c on #465e 8.75 1.00
780 A28 90c on #465a 5.25 1.25
781 A28 90c on #465b 7.25 1.25
782 A28 120c on #466a 8.25 1.50
783 A28 120c on #466e 8.25 1.50
784 A28 120c on #466b 2.75 1.50

Nos. C3, 386 Surcharged

Surcharges read: No. 785, "ITU DAY / 1984"; No. 786, "WHO DAY / 1984"; Nos. 787-788, "ITU/WHO / DAY / 1984".

1984, May 17

785 A28 25c on #C3 1.60 1.60
786 A28 25c on #C3 1.60 1.60
787 A28 25c on #C3 1.60 1.60
788 A28 $4.50 on #386 2.50 2.50
Nos. 785-788 (4) 7.30 7.30

The surcharge is vertical on Nos. 785-787, horizontal on No. 788.

No. 550 Surcharged

1984, June 11
789 A28 120c on #550 8.75 1.00

Nos. 325-327, 431 Surcharged in Blue or Black

Wmk. 373

1984, June 15 Litho. *Perf. 14*
790 A76 55c on 30c #326 (Blk) 5.00 .50
791 A76 75c on #431 1.10 .75
792 A76 160c on 50c #327 1.50 1.25
793 A76 260c on 10c #325 2.50 1.75
Nos. 790-793 (4) 10.10 4.25

No. 214 Surcharged

1984, June 18 Litho. Wmk. 364
794 A50 55c on 110c on 10c 1.25 .50
795 A50 90c on 110c on 10c 1.50 .75

No. 214 surcharged 110c only was never issued.

No. 713 Ovptd. "UPU / Congress 1984 / Hamburg"

1984, June 19
796 Block of 4 5.00 5.00
a. A86 120c on #713a .75 .75
b. A86 130c on #713b .90 .90
c. A86 150c on #713c 1.00 1.00
d. A86 200c on #713d 1.25 1.25

Nos. 539, 541, 543-544 Surcharged in Black, Blue or Dark Green

1984, June 21 *Perfs. as Before*
Watermarks & Printing Methods as Before
797 A60 45c on #539 .50 .50
798 A66 60c on #541 (DkG) 2.50 .60
a. 60c on British Guiana #255 (DkG)
799 A60 120c on #543 .75 .55
800 A60 200c on #544 (Bl) 6.75 1.50
Nos. 797-800 (4) 10.50 3.15

Nos. 135, 548, C2-C3 Surcharged in Blue or Black
No. C4 Overprinted "1984"

Perf. 13x13½
1984, June 30 Litho. Wmk. 364
801 A28 75c on #C2 (Blk) 1.50 .50
802 A28 120c on #548 (Blk) 1.90 .75
803 A28 150c on #135 1.60 .80
804 A28 200c on #C3 17.50 2.50
804A A28 330c on #C4 3.00 3.00
Nos. 801-804A (5) 25.50 7.55

Surcharge on Nos. 801-802, 804 is like No. 748. Surcharge on No. 803 is like No. 457.

Nos. 135, 450A Surcharged

Surcharges read: No. 805, "CARICOM / HEADS OF GOV'T / CONFERENCE / JULY 1984"; No. 806, "CARICOM DAY 1984".

1984, June 30 *Perfs. as Before*
Watermarks & Printing Methods as Before
805 A28 60c on 3c #135 .75 .60
806 A72 60c on #450A .75 .60

Nos. 140-141, 141A, 329, 334, 427, 439a-440, 546, 611, 718, O13 Ovptd. "1984" in Black or Blue

1984 *Perfs. as Before*
Watermarks & Printing Methods as Before
807 A28 20c on #140 12.50
a. On #140a 150.00
808 A28 20c on #140 55.00
a. On #140a 150.00
809 A28 20c on #439, 1984 omitted 60.00
810 A28 25c on #141 100.00
a. 1984 omitted 100.00
811 A28 25c on #141 (Revenue Only) 6.00
812 A28 25c on #141A
813 A28 25c on #141, 1982 ovpt., 1984 omitted 40.00
814 A28 25c on #440, 1984 omitted 40.00
815 A33 50c on #611 (Bl) 10.00
816 A28 60c on #546 (Bl) 1.00
817 A28 $2 on #O13 (Bl) 2.50
818 A28 $3.60 on #334 10.00
c. As #818, fleur-de-lis omitted 5.00
d. On #334a (Bl) 5.00
e. As "d," fleur-de-lis omitted 5.00
819 Sheet of 12 6.00
a.-l. A77 30c on #329a-329l, any single
820 A71 240c on #429 4.75
821 A71 240c on #718 4.75

Overprint on Nos. 808-814, 818 contains fleur-de-lis. Refer to second paragraph in footnote below No. 147 for Nos. 811-812, 817.

Issued: No. 819, 9/15; Nos. 820-821, 10/15.

Teachers' Assoc. Centenary — A87

1984, July 16 Wmk. 364 *Perf. 14*
822 A87 25c Children dancing .25 .25
823 A87 25c Torch, graduate .25 .25
824 A87 25c Torch concentric circles .25 .25
825 A87 25c Teachers, school .25 .25
a. Block of 4 1.00 1.00

No. 609 Surcharged in Blue:

Surcharges read: Nos. 826, 831, "CYCLING"; Nos. 827, 832, "TRACK / AND / FIELD";Nos. 828, 833, "OLYMPIC / GAMES / 1984"; Nos. 829, 834, "BOXING"; Nos. 830, 835, "OLYMPIC / GAMES / 1984 / LOS ANGELES".

Perf. 14½x14
1984, July 28 Litho. Wmk. 364
826 A83 25c on $1.30 1.00 .80
827 A83 25c on $1.30 1.00 .80
828 A83 25c on $1.30 1.00 .80
829 A83 25c on $1.30 3.75 2.00
830 A83 25c on $1.30 3.75 2.25
831 A83 $1.20 on $1.30 3.00 2.50
832 A83 $1.20 on $1.30 3.00 2.50
833 A83 $1.20 on $1.30 3.00 2.50
834 A83 $1.20 on $1.30 5.50 3.00
835 A83 $1.20 on $1.30 5.50 4.00

Nos. 826-828 and 831-833 exist in strips of 3. Nos. 827, 829-830 and 832, 834-835 exists in booklets.

Nos. 465-466 Surcharged "GIRL / GUIDES / 1924-1984" in Blue

1984, Aug. 15 *Perf. 13x13½*
Sheets of 25
836 8 #a.-b., 4 #c.-d., 1 #e.
a.-e. A28 25c on #465a-465e, any single
837 8 #a.-b., 4 #c.-d., 1 #e.
a.-e. A28 25c on #466a-466e, any single
Nos. 836-837 (2) 28.00

Nos. 138-139, 234, 335, 351, 378, 380, 388, 401, 423, 438, 452, 459, 461, 563, 642, O3, O11-O12, O14 Surcharged

1984 *Perfs. as Before*
Watermarks & Printing Methods as Before
846 A28 20c on #563 1.00
a. 20c on #563a (Blk over R) 1.00
b. 20c on #563b (Blk over Bl) 1.00
847 A28 25c on #138 27.50
a. 25c on #138a 55.00
848 A28 25c on #139 150.00
849 A28 25c on #351a 20.00
a. 25c on #351 70.00
850 A28 25c on #351b 8.50
851 A28 25c on #438 8.00
a. 25c on #438a 150.00
852 A28 25c on #234 100.00
853 A28 25c on #452 8.00
854 A28 25c on #O3 8.00
855 A28 60c on #423, two obliterators, small 110 only 45.00
a. Single obliterator, small 110 only
856 A28 120c on #459 5.00
857 A28 120c on #401 35.00
858 A28 120c on #O12 2.00
859 A28 120c on #380 6.00
860 A28 120c on #370 100.00
861 A28 130c on #O11 12.50
862 A28 200c on #461 5.00
863 A28 320c on #378 5.50
864 A28 350c on #388 5.00
865 A28 390c on #642 6.00
866 A28 450c on #O14 5.75
867 A28 600c on #335 15.00
a. 600c on #335a 10.00
868 A28 600c on #335a 17.50
a. 600c on #335 1.00
Nos. 846-868 (23) 596.25

Nos. 860-861 are airmail. Obliterator on Nos. 846, 856-859, 862-866 is row of "X", on Nos. 847, 850, 852 is single line, on Nos. 848-849, 851, 853-854 is fleur-de-lis, on No. 855 is a block of 6 lines, on No. 867 is 3 lines, on No. 868 is 3 lines and fleur-de-lis.

Nos. 556, 670, C4 Overprinted in Blue or Surcharged in Blue and Black

Overprints — No. 871:a-f, ICAO on #670a-f. g, IMB/ICAO on #670g. h, KCV/ICAO on #670h. i, KAI/ICAO on #670i. j-k, ICAO on #670j-670k. l, 1984 on #670h. m, KPM/ICAO on #670h. n-p, ICAO on #670 l-670n. q, PMT/ICAO on #670h. r-x, ICAO on #670o-670u.

Perf. 14x13½
1984, Sept. 6 Litho. Wmk. 364
871 A66 30c Sheet of 25, #a.-k., m.-x., 2 #l 65.00 65.00
895 A28 200c ICAO on #556 5.50 2.25
896 A28 200c ICAO on #C4 (Bl & Blk) 3.00 2.00

No. 896 is airmail with unissued "GAC" overprint. For surcharge see No. 1470.

Nos. J3-J4, J7-J8 Surcharged "120 / GUYANA" in Blue

Perf. 13½x14
1984, Oct. 1 Typo. Wmk. 314
897 D1 120c on 4c #J3 5.25 .80
898 D1 120c on 12c #J4 5.25 .80

Wmk. 364
899 D1 120c on 4c #J7 20.00 .80
900 D1 120c on 12c #J8 5.25 1.25
Nos. 897-900 (4) 35.75 3.65

Nos. 551, 571 Surcharged in Black or Blue

Perfs. as Before
1984, Oct. 15 Wmk. 364
901 A80 $1.50 on #571 (Bl) 14.00 1.50
902 A48 150c on 50c #551 3.00 1.00

Obliterator is "X" on No. 901. Surcharge on No. 902 places "1" before existing 50c value, obliterates "1982" and adds "1984."

Nos. 712, 479-481 Surcharged

1984, Oct. 22 *Perf. 14*
903 Block of 4 1.25 1.25
a.-d. A86 25c on 45c on #712a-712d, any single .25 .25
904 A69 120c on #479 9.50 .75
905 A69 120c on #480 1.25 .75
906 A66 320c on #481 20.00 2.75
Nos. 903-906 (4) 32.00 5.50

Nos. 135-136 Surcharged "MAHA SABHA / 1934-1984" in Blue

1984, Nov. 1 *Perf. 13x13½*
910 A28 25c on 5c #136 .75 .25
911 A28 $1.50 on 3c #135 4.25 1.50
Nos. 910-911 (2) 5.00 1.75

No. 713 Ovptd. "Philatelic Exhibition / New York 1984" in Red

1984, Nov. 15 *Perf. 14*
912 Block of 4 5.00 5.00
a. A86 120c on No. 713a 1.00 .80
b. A86 130c on No. 713b 1.10 .90
c. A86 150c on No. 713c 1.25 1.00
d. A86 200c on No. 713d 1.50 1.25

Type A83 Inscribed with Olympic Rings and "OLYMPIC GAMES 1984 / LOS ANGELES"

1984, Nov. 16 *Perf. 13½*
913 A83 $1.20 multicolored 3.00 3.00

Copies with numbers stamped on back are coils.

For similar stamp overprinted see No. 923.

For surcharges see Nos. 1953-1957.

Nos. 410, 413e, 633, 635a Surcharged

1984, Nov. 24 Photo. *Perf. 14x14½*
Watermarks as Before
914 A7 20c on #410 1.00 .25
915 A7 20c on #413De 92.50 7.50
916 A7 25c on #633 .50 .25
916A A7 60c on #635a .70 .45

No. 914 has an "X" obliterating a "1" and no obliterating lines. No. 1400 has obliterating lines and small "20" in UR.

Elanoides Forficatus A88

Designs: a, Pair in tree. b, Landing on branch. c, In flight, wings up. d, In flight, wings down. e, In flight, wings outstretched.

1984, Dec. 3 Wmk. 364 *Perf. 14½*
917 A88 60c Strip of 5, #a.-e. 18.00 18.00

Inscribed "Christmas 1982."

For surcharges see Nos. 1502, 1840.

High Street Architecture — A89

Designs: 25c, St. George's Cathedral, 1892, Colonial Life Insurance Co. 60c, No. 920a, Demerara Mutual Life Assurance Soc., Ltd. No. 920b, 200c, Town Hall, 1888, City Engineers Office. No. 920c, 300c, Victoria Law Courts, 1887.

1985, Feb. 8 *Perf. 14*
918 A89 25c multi .25 .25
919 A89 60c multi .25 .25
920 Triptych 1.40 1.40
a.-c. A89 120c, any single .45 .45
d. Triptych, unwmkd. 1.75 1.75
e.-g. As "d," any single .60 .60
921 A89 200c multi .90 .90
922 A89 300c multi 1.40 1.40
Nos. 918-922 (5) 4.20 4.20

For surcharge see No. 1850.

Type A83 Ovptd. "INTERNATIONAL / YOUTH YEAR 1985"

Wmk. 364
1985, Feb. 15 Litho. *Perf. 14½*
923 A83 $1.20 multi 3.00 .75

Bars obliterate Olympic Games inscription with second line spelled "LOS ANGELLES." No. 913 spells "Los Angeles" correctly.

Nos. 608, 610 Ovptd. in Red

Overprint reads "Republic / Day / 1970-1985" or "1970 / 1985 / Republic / Day"

1985, Feb. 22 *Perfs. as Before*
924 A82 25c on #608
925 A83 120c on $6 #610
926 A83 130c on $6 #610
Nos. 924-926 (3) 3.00 2.25

Ocelot Cub Xica — A90

Macaw Nena — A90a

Perf. 12½x13
1985, Mar. 11 Wmk. 364
927 A90 25c multi 1.10 .30
928 A90 60c multi .30 .30
929 Triptych 2.75 2.75
a.-c. A90 120c, like #927-928, 930 1.10 1.10
930 A90 130c multi .70 .70

Perf. 14½
931 A90a 320c shown 4.25 2.00
932 A90a 330c Cub on hind legs 2.00 2.00
Nos. 927-932 (6) 11.10 8.05

No. 929, perf. 14, inscribed "1986," were from the liquidation of stock held by the printer, value 75c.

For overprints see Nos. 1903-1905, 1983, 2032.

Map Revenue Type A78 and Nos. 481, 501, 554, O6 Surcharged in Black or Blue

1985 *Perfs as Before*
Watermarks & Printing Methods as Before
933 A69 30c on 50c on #O6 (Bl) 1.00 .25
934 A78 55c on 2c gray 1.00 .25
a. "ESSEQUIBO IS OURS" omitted 15.00

935 A78 55c on #501 1.00 .40
936 A66 90c on #554 (Bl) 7.00 .65
937 A66 225c on #481 10.00 2.00
938 A66 230c on #481 (Bl) 10.00 2.25
939 A66 260c on #481 (Bl) 10.00 2.50
Nos. 933-939 (7) 40.00 8.30

Issued: Nos. 933-936, 938-939, 3/11; No. 937, 4/11.

Obliterator on Nos. 934-935 is fleur-de-lis.

Nos. 305, 435, 587, 599, & 615 Ovptd. "INTERNATIONAL / YOUTH YEAR / 1985" in Blue

Wmk. 364

1985, Apr. 15 Litho. *Perf. 13½*

940 A70 50c on #587 2.00 .30
941 A70 50c on #615 7.00 .30
942 A70 120c on #435 2.25 .55
943 A70 $3 on #305 35.00 —
943A A70 $3 on #599 2.25 1.25
Nos. 940-943A (5) 48.50 2.40

No. 280 Surcharged with Names of 1860 Post Offices or Postal Agencies in Blue

Overprints: a, Airy Hall. b, Belfield / Arab. Coast. c, Belfield / E.C. Dem. d, Belladrum. e, Beterver- / wagting. f, Blairmont / Ferry. g, Boeraserie. h, Brahn. i, Bushlot. j, De / Kinderen. k, Fort / Wellington. l, Georgetown. m, Hague. n, Leguan. o, Mahaica. p, Mahaicony. q, New / Amsterdam. r, Plaisance. s, No. 6 Police / Station. t, Queenstown. u, Vertenoegen. v, Vigilance. w, Vreed-en- / Hoop. x, Wakenaam. y, Windsor / Castle.

Perf. 14x13½

1985, May 2 Litho. Wmk. 364

Sheet of 25

944 A66 25c on 10c, #a.-y. 27.50 27.50

Colonial Post Office, 125th anniv.

Nos. 670 Ovptd. "1985" or with Letters in Red

Overprints: a-f, 1985 on #670a-670f. g, I on #670g. h, T on #670h. i, U on #670i. j-k, 1985 on #670j-670k. l, W on #670h. m, H on #670h. n, O on #670h. o-p, 1985 on #670 l-670m. q, D on #670n. r, A on #670h. s, Y on #670o. t-y, 1985 on #670p-#670u.

1985, May 17 Sheet of 25

969 A66 30c #a.-y. 20.00 20.00

Nos. 413a & 413e Surcharged

1985, May 21 Photo. *Perf. 14x14½*

Watermarks as Before

994 A7 20c on #413a 10.00 .30
a. 20c on #413De 14.00 2.00

No. 994a has "20" at left and 11 obliterating lines. No. 1401 has "20" at right and 12 lines.

No. 135 Surcharged "CARDI / 1975-1985"

Perf. 13x13½

1985, May 29 Litho. Wmk. 364

995 A28 60c on 3c #135 1.75 .40

Caribbean Agricultural Research Development Institute, 10th anniv.

No. 407 Surcharged

1985, June 3

996 A28 600c on #407 40.00 5.00

Nos. 288, 724, C1 Surcharged "ROTARY / INTERNATIONAL / 1905-1985" in Red

1985, June 21 *Perfs. as Before*

Watermarks & Printing Methods as Before

997 A74 120c on #C1 14.50 1.00
998 A66 300c on #288 10.00 3.50

No. 724 with a similar surcharge is usually found on first day covers.

Nos. 426 and 450A Surcharged in Red

Surcharges read: No. 999, "CARICOM DAY / 1985"; No. 1000, "135th Anniversary / Cotton Reel / 1850-1985".

1985, June 28 *Perfs. as Before*

Watermarks & Printing Methods as Before

999 A72 60c on #450A 1.00 .50
1000 A69 120c on #426 1.00 .50

Orchids from Reichenbachia, by Sanders — A91

Wmk. 364 (#1027, 1031, 1036, 1046, 1049, 1052, 1054, 1071, 1074, 1076, 1079, 1084, 1091, 1108), Unwmkd.

1985-87 Series 1 *Perf. 14*

1021 A91 120c Plate No. 1 1.75 .80
1022 A91 60c Plate No. 2 1.10 .80
1023 A91 130c Plate No. 3 1.75 1.00
1024 A91 200c Plate No. 4 2.10 1.60
1025 A91 60c Plate No. 5 1.25 .90
1026 A91 75c like #1025 .80 .60
a. Wmk. 364 ('87) 12.50 12.50
1027 A91 100c Plate No. 6 1.25 1.00
a. Wmk. 364 — —
1028 A91 130c like #1027 2.40 1.00
a. Wmk. 364 ('86) 1.25 1.25
1029 A91 60c Plate No. 7 1.10 .60
1030 A91 25c Plate No. 8 1.25 .60
1031 A91 50c Plate No. 9 .60 .60
a. Wmk. 364 — —
1032 A91 55c like #1031 1.00 .75
a. Wmk. 364 ('86) .60 .60
1033 A91 60c Plate No. 10 1.10 .60
1034 A91 120c Plate No. 11 1.75 .80
1035 A91 25c Plate No. 12 .80 .80
1036 A91 100c Plate No. 13 1.25 1.00
a. Wmk. 364 — —
1037 A91 130c like #1036 1.75 1.00
a. Wmk. 364 ('86) 5.00 3.00
1038 A91 200c Plate No. 14 1.75 1.00
1039 A91 55c Plate No. 15 .60 .60
1040 A91 180c like #1039 1.60 1.60
a. Wmk. 364 ('87) 11.00 9.00
Nos. 1021-1040 (20) 26.95 17.65

Issued: Nos. 1022-1024, 1028-1029, 1033, 1035, 1037, 7/9; No. 1032, 8/12; Nos. 1021, 1030, 1034, 1038, 9/16; No. 1026, 2/26/86; No. 1040, 7/24/86; Nos. 1025, 1027, 1031, 1036, 1039, 8/21/86.

Nos. 1021, 1034 horiz.

1041 A91 130c Plate No. 16 1.50 1.10
1042 A91 55c Plate No. 17 .60 .60
a. Wmk. 364 ('87) 7.50 7.50
1043 A91 80c like #1042 2.25 .70
1044 A91 130c Plate No. 18 3.50 1.00
1045 A91 60c Plate No. 19 1.10 .60
1046 A91 100c Plate No. 20 2.25 1.00
a. Wmk. 364 — —
1047 A91 130c like #1046 1.25 1.00
a. Wmk. 364 ('86) 4.00 2.50
1048 A91 200c Plate No. 21 1.75 1.00
1049 A91 50c Plate No. 22 .60 .60
a. Wmk. 364 — —
1050 A91 55c like #1049 1.00 .75
a. Wmk. 364 ('86) .60 .60
1051 A91 25c Plate No. 23 1.25 .60
1052 A91 50c Plate No. 24 4.00 1.50
a. Wmk. 364 — —
1053 A91 225c like #1052 2.00 1.60
a. Wmk. 364 ('86) 6.50 4.00
1054 A91 100c Plate No. 25 .90 .90
a. Wmk. 364 — —
1055 A91 130c like #1054 1.75 1.00
a. Wmk. 364 ('86) 6.50 4.00
1056 A91 150c Plate No. 26 2.75 .75
1057 A91 120c Plate No. 27 1.75 1.00
1058 A91 120c Plate No. 28 1.75 .80
1059 A91 130c Plate No. 29 2.60 1.00
1060 A91 130c Plate No. 30 2.60 1.00
Nos. 1041-1060 (20) 37.15 18.50

Issued: Nos. 1044-1045, 1047, 1055, 1057, 1059-1060, 7/9; Nos. 1041, 1050, 8/12; Nos. 1048, 1051, 1058, 9/16; Nos. 1042, 1053, 1056, 7/10/86; Nos. 1046, 1049, 1052, 1054, 8/21/86; No. 1043, 11/25/86.

Nos. 1048, 1058 horiz.

1061 A91 60c Plate No. 31 1.10 .60
1062 A91 150c Plate No. 32 1.50 1.10
1063 A91 200c Plate No. 33 3.50 1.40
1064 A91 150c Plate No. 34 1.50 1.10
1065 A91 150c Plate No. 35 1.50 1.10
1066 A91 120c Plate No. 36 1.50 1.10
1067 A91 120c Plate No. 37 2.60 .60
1068 A91 130c Plate No. 38 1.50 1.10
1069 A91 80c Plate No. 39 .60 .60
1070 A91 260c like #1069 2.50 2.00
a. Wmk. 364 ('87) 6.50 5.50
1071 A91 100c Plate No. 40 .80 .80
1072 A91 150c like #1071 1.25 1.00
a. Wmk. 364 ('86) 6.50 3.50
1073 A91 150c Plate No. 41 1.50 1.10
1074 A91 100c Plate No. 42 .90 .90
1075 A91 150c like #1074 1.25 1.00
a. Wmk. 364 ('86) 6.50 3.50
1076 A91 100c Plate No. 43 .80 .80
1077 A91 200c like #1076 1.75 1.25
a. Wmk. 364 ('86) 6.50 3.25
1078 A91 60c Plate No. 44 1.00 1.00
1079 A91 100c Plate No. 45 .90 .90
1080 A91 150c like #1079 1.25 1.00
a. Wmk. 364 ('86) 6.50 3.50
Nos. 1061-1080 (20) 29.20 20.45

Issued: No. 1061, 7/9; Nos. 1062, 1064-1066, 1068, 1073, 1078, 8/12; Nos. 1072, 1075, 1077, 1080, 9/16; Nos. 1063, 1067, 1070, 7/10/86; Nos. 1069, 1071, 1074, 1076, 1079, 8/21/86.

Nos. 1063, 1071-1072, 1074-1077, 1079-1080 horiz.

1081 A91 120c Plate No. 46 2.60 .60
1082 A91 60c Plate No. 47 1.00 .75
1083 A91 150c Plate No. 48 1.50 1.10
1084 A91 50c Plate No. 49 1.50 .75
a. Wmk. 364 — —
1085 A91 55c like #1084 1.00 .75
a. Wmk. 364 ('86) 4.00 4.00
1086 A91 60c Plate No. 50 3.00 2.60
1087 A91 320c like #1086 4.00 2.10
a. Wmk. 364 ('87) 10.00 9.50
1088 A91 25c Plate No. 51 1.25 .60
1089 A91 25c Plate No. 52 1.00 1.00
1090 A91 30c Plate No. 53 1.40 .60
a. Wmk. 364 ('86) 3.25 3.25
1091 A91 50c like #1090 .60 .60
a. Wmk. 364 — —
1092 A91 45c Plate No. 54 .75 .60
a. Wmk. 364 ('87) 10.00 10.00
1093 A91 60c like #1092 .60 .60
1094 A91 50c Plate No. 55 2.60 1.10
a. Wmk. 364 — —
1095 A91 60c like #1094 1.40 1.40
1096 A91 75c like #1094 .60 .60
a. Wmk. 364 3.25 3.25
1097 A91 120c Plate No. 56 2.60 .70
1098 A91 60c Plate No. 57 1.60 .60
1099 A91 120c Plate No. 58 2.60 .70
1100 A91 25c Plate No. 59 1.25 .50
a. Dark red flowers ('86) 4.00 4.00
Nos. 1081-1100 (20) 32.85 18.25

Issued: Nos. 1082-1083, 1085, 1089, 8/12; No. 1088, 9/16; No.1095, 10/7; Nos. 1087, 1092, 2/26/86; Nos. 1081, 1090, 1096-1100, 7/10/86; Nos. 1086, 1091, 1093, 8/21/86; No. 1084, 12/22/86; No. 1094, 1/16/87.

No. 1098 horiz.

1101 A91 75c Plate No. 60 .70 .70
1102 A91 225c like #1101 3.00 1.75
a. Wmk. 364 ('87) 13.00 13.00
1103 A91 25c Plate No. 61 1.25 .60
1104 A91 150c Plate No. 62 1.50 1.10
1105 A91 25c Plate No. 63 1.25 .60
1106 A91 50c Plate No. 64 1.50 1.25
a. Wmk. 364 — —
1107 A91 55c like #1106 1.00 .75
a. Wmk. 364 ('86) 4.25 4.25
1108 A91 50c Plate No. 65 2.60 .60
a. Wmk. 364 — —
1109 A91 100c like #1108 .60 .60
a. Wmk. 364 4.00 4.00
1110 A91 130c Plate No. 66 2.75 .65
1111 A91 120c Plate No. 67 2.60 .60
1112 A91 40c Plate No. 68 1.40 1.00
1113 A91 100c like #1112 .60 .60
a. Wmk. 364 ('87) 6.50 6.50
1114 A91 60c Plate No. 69 .60 .60
1115 A91 120c like #1114 2.00 1.10
a. Wmk. 364 ('87) 14.00 14.00
1116 A91 25c Plate No. 70 1.25 .60
1117 A91 25c Plate No. 71 .80 .60
a. Wmk. 364 ('87) 15.00 15.00
1118 A91 60c like #1117 .70 .70
1119 A91 25c Plate No. 72 1.25 .60
1120 A91 60c Plate No. 73 1.60 .60
Nos. 1101-1120 (20) 28.95 15.60

Issued: Nos. 1104, 1107, 8/12; Nos. 1103, 1105, 1116, 1119, 9/16; Nos. 1102, 1115, 1117, 4/4/86; Nos. 1109-1111, 1113, 1120, 7/10/86; Nos. 1101, 1108, 1114, 1118, 8/21/86; No. 1112, 11/25/86.

No. 1114-1115, 1117-1118, 1120 horiz.

1121 A91 80c Plate No. 74 .70 .70
1122 A91 250c like #1121 2.25 2.00
a. Wmk. 364 ('87) 6.50 6.50
1123 A91 60c Plate No. 75 1.60 .60
1124 A91 65c Plate No. 76 .60 .60
1125 A91 150c like #1124 1.25 1.25
a. Wmk. 364 ('87) 14.00 14.00
1126 A91 40c Plate No. 77 .75 .60
a. Wmk. 364 ('87) 12.00 12.00
1127 A91 45c like #1126 1.00 1.00
1128 A91 45c Plate No. 78 1.40 1.25
1129 A91 150c like #1128 1.25 .75
a. Wmk. 364 ('87) 14.00 14.00
1130 A91 60c Plate No. 79 .60 .60
1131 A91 200c like #1130 1.75 1.60
a. Wmk. 364 ('87) 14.00 14.00
1132 A91 65c Plate No. 80 .60 .60
1133 A91 330c like #1132 3.00 2.75
a. Wmk. 364 ('87) 15.00 15.00
1134 A91 45c Plate No. 81 .50 .50
a. Wmk. 364 ('87) 15.00 15.00
1135 A91 55c like #1134 1.00 1.00
1136 A91 55c Plate No. 82 .60 .60
1137 A91 320c like #1136 3.00 2.50
a. Wmk. 364 ('87) 15.00 15.00
1138 A91 75c Plate No. 83 .70 .70
1139 A91 300c like #1138 3.00 2.50
a. Wmk. 364 ('87) 15.00 15.00
1140 A91 45c Plate No. 84 1.10 .75
1141 A91 90c like #1140 .60 .60
a. Wmk. 364 ('87) 14.00 14.00
Nos. 1121-1141 (21) 27.25 23.45

Issued: Nos. 1126, 1129, 1131, 1139, 1141, 2/26/86; Nos. 1122-1123, 7/10/86; Nos. 1125, 1133-1134, 1137, 7/24/86; Nos. 1121, 1124, 1127-1128, 1130, 1132, 1135-1136, 1138, 1140, 8/21/86.

No. 1123 horiz.

1142 A91 45c Plate No. 85 1.00 1.00
1143 A91 360c like #1142 3.50 3.00
a. Wmk. 364 ('87) 15.00 15.00
1144 A91 30c Plate No. 86 .60 .60
a. Wmk. 364 ('87) 7.50 7.50
1145 A91 40c like #1144 1.10 1.10
1146 A91 60c Plate No. 87 .60 .60
1147 A91 150c like #1146 2.50 1.25
a. Wmk. 364 ('87) 17.50 17.50
1148 A91 65c Plate No. 88 .60 .60
1149 A91 100c like #1148 .65 .65
a. Wmk. 364 ('87) 15.00 15.00
1150 A91 55c Plate No. 89 .75 .75
1151 A91 90c like #1150 .60 .60
a. Wmk. 364 ('87) 15.00 15.00
1152 A91 40c Plate No. 90 .60 .60
1153 A91 375c like #1152 3.00 3.00
a. Wmk. 364 ('87) 8.00 8.00
1154 A91 40c Plate No. 91 3.50 2.50
1155 A91 130c like #1154 1.25 1.00
a. Wmk. 364 ('87) 7.50 7.50
1156 A91 50c Plate No. 92 .75 .60
a. Wmk. 364 ('87) 15.00 15.00
1157 A91 75c like #1156 .70 .70
1158 A91 60c Plate No. 93 .60 .60
a. Wmk. 364 ('87) 7.50 7.50
1159 A91 80c like #1158 .70 .70
1160 A91 60c Plate No. 94 .60 .60
1161 A91 350c like #1160 4.00 3.00
a. Wmk. 364 ('87) 15.00 15.00
1162 A91 60c Plate No. 95 .80 .70
a. Wmk. 364 ('87) 15.00 15.00
1163 A91 75c like #1162 .70 .70
1164 A91 40c Plate No. 96 .60 .60
a. Wmk. 364 ('87) 14.00 14.00
1165 A91 65c like #1164 .70 .70
Nos. 1142-1165 (24) 30.40 26.15

See note below No. 1341. Issued: Nos. 1143, 1156, 1162, 2/26/86; Nos. 1147, 1161, 4/4/86; Nos. 1144, 1153, 1155, 1158, 7/10/86; Nos. 1149, 1151, 1164, 7/24/86; Nos. 1142, 1146, 1148, 1150, 1152, 1157, 1159-1160, 1163, 1165, 8/21/86; No. 1154, 9/26/86; No. 1145, 10/23/86.

Some stamps printed in sheets of 25, blocks of 4 each of different stamps separated by gutter containing 2 No. 1337 and strip of 5 No. 1339. Margin contains separation marks for Nos. 1337, 1339.

Nos. 1146-1147, 1160-1161 horiz.

Nos. 1025, 1027, 1031, 1036, 1039, 1046, 1049, 1052, 1054, 1069, 1071, 1074, 1076, 1079, 1086, 1091, 1093, 1101, 1108, 1114, 1118, 1121, 1124, 1127-1128, 1130, 1132, 1135-1136, 1138, 1140, 1142, 1146, 1148, 1150, 1152, 1157, 1159-1160, 1163, 1165 sold as singles in booklets only. Two booklets of 48 stamps each contain these numbers and previous values issued in the series. Value, each booklet, $80.

See No. 1372. For overprints and surcharges see Nos. 1342-1346, 1393, 1402-1403, 1412-1413, 1494, 1511-1670F, 1731-1740, 1742-1750, 1755-1759, 1761, 1764-1773, 1785, 1845-1849, 1906-1909, 1914-1933, 1939-1941, 1943-1947, 1958-1959, 1960-1979, 2000, 2619A-2619E, 4205-4210, C7, C9-C12, E2, E4.

1986-89 Litho. Unwmk. *Perf. 14*

Series 2

1166 A91 175c Plate No. 1 1.50 .65
1167 A91 560c like #1166 4.50 1.60
1168 A91 90c Plate No. 2 1.25 1.25
1169 A91 200c like #1168 2.75 1.25
1170 A91 50c Plate No. 3 .50 .50
1171 A91 90c like #1170 .75 .75
1172 A91 90c Plate No. 4 1.25 .60
1173 A91 140c like #1172 1.25 .50
1174 A91 130c Plate No. 5 1.10 .50
1175 A91 160c like #1174 1.60 .80
1176 A91 50c Plate No. 6 .50 .50
1177 A91 390c like #1176 3.75 2.00
1178 A91 30c Plate No. 7 .50 .50
1179 A91 40c like #1178 .50 .50
1180 A91 70c Plate No. 8 .50 .50
1181 A91 75c like #1180 1.00 .60
1182 A91 70c Plate No. 9 .50 .50
1183 A91 200c like #1182 2.00 1.00
1184 A91 90c Plate No. 10 3.25 1.40
1185 A91 320c like #1184 3.00 1.75
Nos. 1166-1185 (20) 31.95 17.65

Issued: Nos. 1172, 1175, 1181, 1183, 9/23; No. 1184, 10/23; Nos. 1177, 1185, 10/31; No. 1169, 11/25; Nos. 1171, 1179, 12/27; No. 1168, 1/5/87; No. 1167, 4/24/87; Nos. 1166, 1170, 1173-1174, 1176, 1178, 1180, 1182, 8/23/88.

Nos. 1174-1175 horiz.

1186 A91 200c Plate No. 11 1.75 .75
1187 A91 70c Plate No. 12 .50 .50
1188 A91 320c like #1187 3.50 1.60
1189 A91 50c Plate No. 13 1.50 1.50
1190 A91 90c like #1189 .60 .60
1191 A91 30c Plate No. 14 .60 .60
1192 A91 120c like #1191 1.00 1.00
1193 A91 50c Plate No. 15 4.25 4.25
1194 A91 85c like #1193 .60 .60
1195 A91 260c Plate No. 16 2.25 .75
1196 A91 320c like #1195 3.25 1.40
1197 A91 45c Plate No. 17 .50 .50
1198 A91 70c like #1197 .50 .50
1199 A91 85c Plate No. 18 .60 .60
1200 A91 320c like #1199 3.00 3.00
1201 A91 175c Plate No. 19 1.50 .65
1202 A91 450c like #1201 3.75 1.25

1203 A91 25c Plate No. 20 .50 .50
1204 A91 50c like #1203 .50 .50
1205 A91 45c Plate No. 21 2.00 2.00
Nos. 1186-1205 (20) 32.65 23.05

Issued: Nos. 1188, 1205, 9/23; Nos. 1190, 1197, 10/31; No. 1189, 12/3; Nos. 1192, 1194, 1200, 1203, 12/27; Nos. 1193, 1199, 1/5/87; No. 1202, 4/24/87; No. 1196, 6/1/88. Nos. 1186-1187, 1191, 1198, 1201, 1204, 8/23/88; No. 1195, 7/7/89.

Nos. 1201-1202, 1205, horiz.

1206 A91 30c Plate No. 22 .50 .50
1207 A91 150c like #1206 1.25 1.25
1208 A91 200c Plate No. 23 1.75 .75
1209 A91 85c Plate No. 24 2.25 1.60
1210 A91 225c like #1209 4.75 4.75
1211 A91 140c Plate No. 25 1.25 .55
1212 A91 230c like #1211 2.25 1.10
1213 A91 200c Plate No. 26 1.75 .75
1214 A91 60c Plate No. 27 .80 .50
1215 A91 90c like #1214 2.25 1.10
1216 A91 30c Plate No. 28 .50 .50
1217 A91 330c like #1216 3.00 3.00
1218 A91 130c Plate No. 29 1.00 .50
1219 A91 350c like #1218 3.75 1.75
1220 A91 30c Plate No. 30 3.25 3.25
1221 A91 875c Plate No. 31 6.00 3.50
1222 A91 50c Plate No. 32 .50 .50
1223 A91 130c like #1222 1.00 1.00
1224 A91 50c Plate No. 33 .50 .50
1225 A91 100c like #1224 .90 .90
Nos. 1206-1225 (20) 39.20 28.25

Issued: Nos. 1219, 1220, 9/23; Nos. 1214, 1224, 10/31; No. 1210, 11/25; Nos. 1209, 1215, 12/15; Nos. 1207, 1217, 1223, 12/27; No. 1212, 2/14/87; No. 1221, 6/15/88; Nos. 1206, 1208, 1211, 1213, 1216, 1218, 1222, 1225, 8/23/88.

Nos. 1218-1219 horiz.

1226 A91 140c Plate No. 34 1.10 .50
1227 A91 360c like #1226 3.75 1.75
1228 A91 380c Plate No. 35 3.25 1.40
1229 A91 525c Plate No. 36 4.00 2.25
1230 A91 175c Plate No. 37 1.25 .65
1231 A91 390c like #1230 3.00 1.25
1232 A91 130c Plate No. 38 1.00 .65
1233 A91 140c like #1232 1.25 .50
1234 A91 175c Plate No. 39 1.50 .65
1235 A91 260c like #1234 2.00 .75
1236 A91 250c Plate No. 40 4.50 1.90
1237 A91 $10 like #1236 7.50 5.75
1238 A91 140c Plate No. 41 1.10 .50
1239 A91 180c like #1238 1.75 1.00
1240 A91 80c Plate No. 42 1.00 .50
1241 A91 130c like #1240 1.10 .50
1242 A91 200c Plate No. 43 3.50 1.00
1243 A91 100c Plate No. 44 .80 .80
1244 A91 200c like #1243 2.00 1.00
1245 A91 35c Plate No. 45 .75 .50
1246 A91 85c like #1245 1.00 .60
Nos. 1226-1246 (21) 47.10 24.40

Issued: Nos. 1227, 1232, 1240, 9/23; Nos. 1244, 1246, 10/31; No. 1245, 1/5/87; No. 1239, 2/14/87; Nos. 1231, 1235, 4/24/87; No. 1242, 9/29/87; No. 1237, 3/24/88; No. 1229, 6/1/88; Nos. 1226, 1228, 1230, 1233-1234, 1236, 1238, 1241, 1243, 8/23/88.

Nos. 1230-1231, 1240-1241 horiz.

1247 A91 225c Plate No. 46 1.50 .80
1248 A91 175c Plate No. 47 1.25 .65
1249 A91 240c like #1248 1.75 .70
1250 A91 200c Plate No. 48 3.50 1.00
1251 A91 200c Plate No. 49 1.40 .55
1252 A91 720c like #1251 6.50 6.00
1253 A91 160c Plate No. 50 2.10 1.00
1254 A91 300c like #1253 3.00 1.50
1255 A91 175c Plate No. 51 2.25 1.25
1256 A91 500c like #1255 3.00 1.50
1257 A91 140c Plate No. 52 1.00 .40
1258 A91 590c like #1257 4.00 2.60
1259 A91 200c Plate No. 53 1.25 .55
1260 A91 290c like #1259 3.25 2.00
1261 A91 175c Plate No. 54 1.25 .60
1261A A91 400c like #1261 2.75 1.40
1262 A91 120c Plate No. 55 .90 .35
1263 A91 75c Plate No. 56 1.00 .50
1264 A91 100c like #1263 .50 .50
1265 A91 225c Plate No. 57 1.25 .60
Nos. 1247-1265 (20) 43.40 24.45

Issued: Nos. 1254, 1263, 10/31; No. 1258, 2/14/87; Nos. 1249, 1256, 1261A, 4/24/87; No. 1250, 9/29/87; Nos. 1252, 1260, 11/23/87; Nos. 1247-1248, 8/23/88; Nos. 1253, 1255, 11/3/88; Nos. 1251, 1257, 1259, 1261-1262, 1264-1265, 1/3/89.

Nos 1261, 1261A horiz.

1266 A91 175c Plate No. 58 1.25 .50
1267 A91 275c like #1266 2.00 .85
1268 A91 775c Plate No. 59 4.00 3.25
1269 A91 200c Plate No. 60 1.50 .55
1270 A91 575c like #1269 5.00 3.50
1271 A91 255c Plate No. 61 3.25 1.75
1272 A91 280c Plate No. 62 2.60 1.75
1273 A91 700c like #1272 4.75 4.25
1274 A91 285c Plate No. 63 3.25 1.75
1275 A91 200c Plate No. 64 1.00 .55
1276 A91 680c like #1275 6.00 3.50
1277 A91 140c Plate No. 65 .70 .40
1278 A91 650c like #1277 5.00 3.50
1279 A91 280c Plate No. 66 1.25 .75
1280 A91 750c like #1279 6.50 6.00
1281 A91 280c Plate No. 67 1.25 .75
1282 A91 $15 like #1281 8.50 7.50
1283 A91 325c Plate No. 68 4.00 1.40
1284 A91 530c Plate No. 69 3.00 2.75
1285 A91 550c Plate No. 70 3.75 3.75
Nos. 1266-1285 (20) 68.55 49.00

Issued: No. 1278, 2/14/87; No. 1267, 4/24/87; Nos. 1270, 1283, 10/26/87; Nos. 1271, 1276, 1280, 11/23/87; Nos. 1282, 1284, 6/1/88; Nos. 1268, 1273, 6/15/88; No. 1285, 8/15/88; Nos. 1272, 1274, 11/3/88; Nos. 1266, 1269, 1275, 1277, 1279, 1281, 1/3/89.
No. 1266 1267, 1280, 1285 horiz.

1286 A91 670c Plate No. 71 4.50 4.25
1287 A91 300c Plate No. 72 1.50 .80
1288 A91 $25 like #1287 12.00 12.00
1289 A91 130c Plate No. 73 .80 .25
1290 A91 475c like #1289 2.75 2.50
1291 A91 350c Plate No. 74 2.25 2.00
1291A A91 900c like #1291 6.50 6.00
1291B A91 600c on 900c #1291A
1292 A91 200c Plate No. 75 2.25 1.25
1293 A91 250c Plate No. 76 1.25 .65
1294 A91 850c like #1293 8.00 6.50
1295 A91 300c Plate No. 77 1.50 .80
1296 A91 480c like #1295 2.75 1.75
1297 A91 280c Plate No. 78 1.40 .75
1298 A91 950c like #1298 6.50 6.00
1299 A91 250c Plate No. 79 2.60 1.60
1300 A91 800c like #1299 7.50 6.50
1301 A91 300c Plate No. 80 1.50 .80
1302 A91 400c like #1301 2.25 1.40
1303 A91 305c Plate No. 81 1.50 .80
1304 A91 250c Plate No. 82 1.25 .65
1305 A91 330c like #1304 3.25 1.25
Nos. 1286-1291A,1292-1305 (21) 73.80 58.50

Issued: No. 1305, 2/14/87; Nos. 1288, 1296, 1302, 7/22/87; Nos. 1291A-1291B, 10/9/87; Nos. 1294, 1300, 11/23/87; No. 1290, 6/1/88; No. 1298, 6/15/88; No. 1291, 6/22/88; No. 1286, 8/15/88; Nos. 1292, 1299, 11/3/88; Nos. 1287, 1293, 1295, 1297, 1301, 1303-1304, 1/3/89; No. 1289, 7/7/89.
No. 1286 horiz.

1306 A91 350c Plate No. 83 1.75 .95
1307 A91 $20 like #1306 10.00 10.00
1308 A91 360c Plate No. 84 2.25 2.00
1309 A91 250c Plate No. 85 1.25 .65
1310 A91 300c like #1309 3.00 1.10
1311 A91 350c Plate No. 86 1.75 .95
1312 A91 500c like #1311 3.00 2.00
1313 A91 250c Plate No. 87 1.25 .65
1314 A91 425c like #1313 3.75 1.50
1315 A91 250c Plate No. 88 1.25 .65
1316 A91 440c like #1315 3.75 1.50
1317 A91 350c Plate No. 89 1.75 .95
1318 A91 520c like #1317 3.00 2.00
1319 A91 270c Plate No. 90 1.25 1.25
1320 A91 250c Plate No. 91 1.10 .65
1321 A91 $12 like #1320 7.50 7.00
1322 A91 200c Plate No. 92 3.50 1.00
1323 A91 200c Plate No. 93 2.25 1.25
1324 A91 300c Plate No. 94 1.50 .80
1325 A91 600c like #1324 3.50 2.75
1326 A91 420c Plate No. 95 4.25 2.00
1327 A91 200c Plate No. 96 1.60 .50
1328 A91 375c like #1327 4.25 2.25
Nos. 1306-1328 (23) 68.45 44.35

Issued: Nos. 1310, 1314, 1316, 2/14/87; Nos. 1307, 1312, 1318, 6/2/87; No. 1325, 7/22/87/ No. 1322, 9/29/87; No. 1326, 10/26/87; No. 1328, 11/23/87; No. 1321, 3/24/88; Nos. 1308, 1319, 8/15/88, No. 1323, 11/3/88; Nos. 1306, 1309, 1311, 1313, 1315, 1317, 1320, 1324, 1/3/89; No. 1327, 7/7/89.
No. 1326, horiz.
Nos. 1166, 1170, 1174, 1176, 1178, 1180, 1182, 1187, 1191, 1193, 1198, 1201, 1204, 1206, 1211, 1216, 1218, 1222, 1225-1226, 1230, 1233-1234, 1236, 1238, 1248, 1257, 1261, 1264, 1266, 1277, 1279, 1281, 1287, 1293, 1295, 1297, 1301, 1304, 1306, 1308-1309, 1311, 1313, 1315, 1317, 1320, 1324 sold as singles in booklets only. Two booklets of 48 stamps each contain these numbers and previous values issued in the series. Value, each booklet, $80.

Miniature Sheets of 4

Designs: Nos. 1329a, 1330b, 1331b, like #1303. Nos. 1329b, 1330a, 1332a, like #1265. Nos. 1329c, 1330c, 1332b, like #1247. Nos. 1330d, 1331a, 1332c, like #1262.

1329 #1262, 1329a-1329c 4.50 4.50
a.-c. A91 120c any single 1.00 1.00
1330 #a.-d. 4.50 4.50
a.-d. A91 150c any single 1.00 1.00
1331 #1247, 1265, 1331a-1331b 5.00 5.00
a.-b. A91 225c any single .95 .95
1332 #1303, 1332a-1332c 5.00 5.00
a.-c. A91 305c any single .95 .95
1333 7.00 7.00
a. A91 320c like #1262 1.25 1.25
b. A91 330c like #1247 1.25 1.25
c. A91 350c like #1303 1.50 1.50
d. A91 500c like #1265 2.40 2.40
1334 7.00 7.00
a. A91 320c like #1247 1.25 1.25
b. A91 330c like #1262 1.25 1.25
c. A91 350c like #1265 1.50 1.50
d. A91 500c like #1303 2.40 2.40
1335 7.00 7.00
a. A91 320c like #1303 1.25 1.25
b. A91 330c like #1265 1.25 1.25
c. A91 350c like #1262 1.50 1.50
d. A91 500c like #1247 2.40 2.40
1336 7.00 7.00
a. A91 320c like #1265 1.25 1.25
b. A91 330c like #1303 1.25 1.25
c. A91 350c like #1247 1.50 1.50
d. A91 500c like #1262 2.40 2.40

Issued: Nos. 1329-1332, 7/7/89; others, 2/26/88.
For surcharges & overprints see Nos. 1671-1727, 1776-1777, 1834-1835, 1942, 1948-1952, 1998-1999, 2031, 2033-2044, 2064, 2619A-2619D, 2578A-2578C, 2907A-2907G, 2928A-2928D, E3, E5, O40-O56.

Natl. Arms — A92

1985-87 *Perf. 14 Vert.*
1337 A92 25c multi .50 .50
1338 A92 25c multi ('87) 1.25 .75

Perf. 14 Horiz.
1339 A92 25c multi .25 .25
1340 A92 25c multi ('87) 1.25 .75
Nos. 1337-1340 (4) 3.25 2.25

Perf. 14
1341 A92 25c multi

Nos. 1337-1340 were cut from orchid sheet gutters. Stamps vary considerably in size.
Nos. 1338, 1340 are Nos. 1337 and 1339 redrawn to include black border.
Issue dates: Nos. 1337, 1339, 1341, July 1985. No. 1338, 1340 June 2, 1987.
See Nos. 1467-1468. For surcharges see Nos. 1777A-1777C, 4166-4168, 4190, 4193, 4194, 4199, 4203.

Nos. 1024, 1044, 1047, 1059, 1060 Surcharged or Overprinted in Blue or Black "QUEEN MOTHER 1900-1985" on 1 or 2 Lines

Nos. 1345a, 1346a overprinted "LADY BOWES-LYON 1900-1923". Nos. 1345b, 1346b overprinted "DUCHESS OF YORK 1923-1937". Nos. 1345c, 1346c overprinted "QUEEN ELIZABETH 1937-1952". Surcharge on No. 1346 sans serif.

1985 *Perfs. as Before*
1342 A91 130c on #1044
1343 A91 130c on #1059
1344 A91 130c on #1060
Nos. 1342-1344 (3) 6.25

Miniature sheets
1345 Sheet of 4 7.50
a.-d. A91 200c on #1024, any single
1346 Sheet of 4 12.00
a.-d. A91 200c on 130c #1047, any single (Blk)

Issued: Nos. 1342-1345, 7/9; No. 1346, 9/12.
For overprints see Nos. 1741, 1751-1754, 1774-1775.

Nos. 465 Surcharged in Red "INTERNATIONAL / YOUTH YEAR / 1985"

Perf. 13x13½
1985, July 18 **Litho.** **Wmk. 364**
1347 Sheet of 25, 8 #a.-b., 4 #c.-d., 1 #e. 175.00
a.-e. A28 25c on #465a-465e, any single

Nos. 203 and 443 Surcharged

1985, July 26 *Perfs. as Before*
Watermarks & Printing Methods as Before
1352 A47 225c on #203 55.00 6.50
1354 A63 240c on #443 55.00 8.00

Girl Guides, 75th anniv. (No. 1352), John J. Audubon, bicentennial of birth. No. 203 surcharged only with 350c, $2.25 or surcharged with both was not issued.

Abolition of Slavery, Sesquicent. — A93

Designs: 25c, Revolution leaders, 1763. 60c, Damon's execution, 1834. 130c, Demerara Uprising, 1823. 150c Den Arendt slave ship.

Unwmk.
1985, July 29 **Litho.** *Perf. 14*
1355 A93 25c gray & black .40 .25
1356 A93 60c pink & black .25 .25
1357 A93 130c blue grn & blk .45 .45
1358 A93 150c lilac & blk .85 .60
Nos. 1355-1358 (4) 1.95 1.55

See Nos. 1994-1997 for changed colors.

Nos. 135, 210 Surcharged; No. 223 Surcharged in Brown

Surcharges read: No. 1359, "Guyana/Libya / Friendship 1985"; No. 1361, "Mexico / 1986".

1985, Aug. 16 *Perfs. as Before*
Watermarks and Printing Methods as Before
1359 A49 150c on #210 10.00 3.00
1360 A53 150c on #223 3.50 .85
1361 A28 275c on 3c #135 9.00 1.75
Nos. 1359-1361 (3) 22.50 5.60

Refer to 2nd paragraph under No. 147 for No. 1361. See No. 1452 for 225c Mexico 1986 surcharge.

Nos. 366, 427, 430, 430a, 494, & 553 Ovptd. or Surcharged "1955-1985" Vertically or Horizontally

Wmk. 364
1985, Sept. 23 **Litho.** *Perf. 13½*
1362 A75 60c on #366 .35 .35
1363 A75 60c on #553 .35 .35
1364 A75 120c on #427 .70 .70
1365 A75 120c on #430 .70 .70
1366 A75 120c on #430a .70 .70
1367 A75 120c on #494 .70 .70
Nos. 1362-1367 (6) 3.50 3.50

No. 417 Surcharged "1965-1985" Vertically

1985, Sept. 30
1368 A79 25c on #417 .80 .30
1369 A79 225c on #417 2.75 1.50

Nos. 260 & 262 Surcharged "1985"

1985, Oct. 5 **Litho.** *Perf. 14x14½*
1370 A61 25c on 40c #262 20.00 1.00
1371 A61 320c on 15c #260 30.00 9.50

Orchid Type of 1985 Surcharged in Red "CRISTOBAL COLON / 1492-1992"

1985, Oct. 12 *Perf. 14*
1372 A91 350c on 120c like #1108 13.00 6.00

No. 1372 not issued without surcharge. For overprint see No. E1. For surcharge see No. 1591A.

No. 288 Overprinted "SIR WINSTON CHURCHILL / 1965-1985"

1985, Oct. 15 *Perf. 13½x13*
1373 A66 $2 on #288 26.00 8.00

No. 214 Surcharged "1950-1985"

1985, Oct. 15 *Perf. 14*
1374 A50 25c on 110c on 10c .25 .25
1375 A50 200c on 110c on 10c 1.00 1.00

No. 214 with 110c surcharge only was not issued.

Nos. 295-297, 384, and O9 Overprinted or Surcharged "United / Nations / 1945-1985"

1985, Oct. 28 *Perf. 14x14½*
1376 A68 30c on #295 1.75 .25
1377 A68 50c on #296 1.75 .30
1378 A68 100c on #O9 1.75 .50
1379 A68 225c on #384 30.00 4.00
1380 A68 $3 on #297 4.00 4.00
Nos. 1376-1380 (5) 39.25 9.05

Nos. 142-144, 289A, O4-O5, O7, O15, and QO1-QO2 Ovptd. "POSTAGE"

1985, Oct. 29 *Perfs. as Before*
Watermarks and Printing Methods as Before
1381 A28 30c on #O4 1.00 .30
1382 A28 40c on #142 60.00 1.50
1383 A28 50c on #143 1.00 .50
1384 A28 50c on #O5 1.00 .40
1385 A28 60c on #144 4.25 .50
1386 A28 60c on #144 (Revenue Only) 1.00 .35
1387 A28 60c on #O7 3.00 .40
1388 A66 $10 on #O15 35.00 9.00
1389 A28 $15 on #QO1 17.50 12.00
1390 A28 $20 on #QO2 17.50 13.00
Nos. 1381-1390 (10) 141.25 37.95

Refer to 2nd paragraph in footnote following No. 147 for Nos. 1381, 1384, 1386-1387.

Nos. 133-134 Surcharged "Deepavali / 1985"

1985, Nov. 1
1391 A28 25c on 2c #134 2.00 .35
1392 A28 150c on 1c #133 4.50 1.75

No. 1050 Ovptd. in Red

Overprinted: a, "Christmas 1985." b, "Happy New Year." c, "Merry Christmas." d, "Happy Holidays."

1985, Nov. 3 **Unwmk.** *Perf. 14*
1393 A91 55c Sheet of 4, #a.-d. 12.00 7.00

For surcharge see No. 1670F.

Clive Lloyd, Cricketer — A94

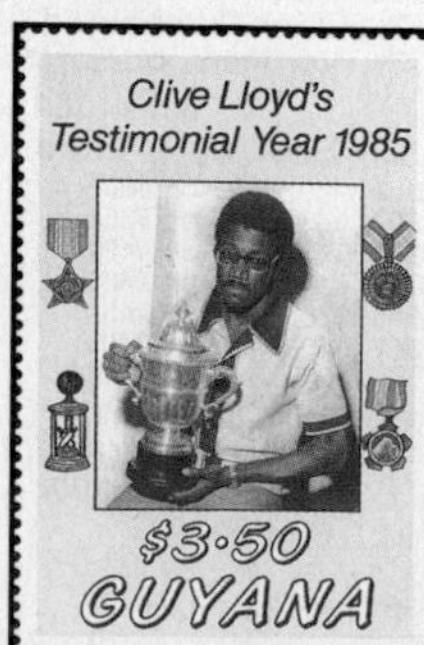

Lloyd Holding Intl. Cup — A95

No. 1394s: a, $2.25, Lloyd playing cricket. b, $1.30, Lloyd, bat and wicket. c, 60c, Gloves, wicket, bat, natl. flag.

1985, Nov. 7 *Perf. 14½x14*
1394 A94 Triptych 1.50 1.50
a.-c. 25c any single .45 .45

Size: 30x38mm

Perf. 14x14½
1395 A94 60c multi .55 .55
1396 A94 $1.30 multi .90 .90
1397 A94 $2.25 multi 1.60 1.60
1398 A95 $3.50 multi 2.60 2.60
Nos. 1394-1398 (5) 7.15 7.15

For surcharge see No. 1504.

No. 329 Ovptd. "1985" in Red

Wmk. 364

1985, Nov. 15 **Litho.** *Perf. 14*
1399 A77 30c Sheet of 12, #a.-l. 17.50 17.50

Nos. 410 and 413e Surcharged

1985, Dec. 23 **Photo.** *Perf. 14x14½*
Watermarks as Before
1400 A7 20c on #410 8.00 .50
1401 A7 20c on #413De 8.00 .50

Compare No. 1400 with No. 914 and 1401 with No. 994a.

Nos. 1075, 1077 Ovptd. "REICHENBACHIA 1886-1986" in Purple

1986, Jan. 13 **Litho.** *Perf. 14*
1402 A91 150c on #1075 9.00 1.00
1403 A91 200c on #1077 9.00 1.10

For surcharge and overprints see Nos. 1553, 1760, 1762-1763.

Nos. 608, 610 Surcharged "Republic Day / 1986"

Perfs. as Before

1986, Feb. 22 **Wmk. 364**
1404 A82 25c on #608
1405 A83 120c on $6 #610
1406 A83 225c on $6 #610
Nos. 1404-1406 (3) 2.00

No. 87 Surcharged "1986"

1986, Mar. 24 **Photo.** *Perf. 13*
1407 A14 25c on 6c #87 .30 .25
1408 A14 50c on 6c #87 .50 .45
1409 A14 100c on 6c #87 .90 .85
1410 A14 200c on 6c #87 1.75 1.50
Nos. 1407-1410 (4) 3.45 3.05

No. 237 Surcharged "1926 / 1986"

1986, Mar. 27 **Litho.** *Perf. 14*
1411 A56 150c on 35c #237 5.50 1.00

St. John Ambulance, 60th anniv.

Nos. 1028, 1037 Surcharged "Queen Elizabeth / 1926 1986"

1986, Apr. 21 **Unwmk.**
1412 A91 Sheet of 4 8.50 8.50
a. 130c on 130c #1028 1.75 1.50
b. 200c on 130c #1028 1.75 1.50
c. 260c on 130c #1028 1.75 1.50
d. 330c on 130c #1028 1.75 1.50
1413 A91 130c on #1037 7.50 2.75

Location of overprint on No. 1413 differs from No. 1412.
For overprints & surcharges see Nos. 1670A, 1738B.

Nos. 267, 317g-317 l, 444a-444f Surcharged "Protect the"

Wmk. 373

1986, May 3 **Litho.** *Perf. 14*
1414 A73 60c on 35c #317g-317l, block of 6, #a.-f. 3.00 3.00
1415 A73 60c on 35c #444, block of 6, #a.-f. 65.00 25.00

Wmk. 364
1416 A63 $6 on 8c #267 5.00 4.00

No. 390 Surcharged

1986, May 5 **Litho.** *Perf. 13*
1417 A28 600c on #390 24.00 2.75

No. 283A Surcharged

Overprints: a, Abary. b, Anna Regina. c, Aurora. d, Bartica Grove. e, Bel Air. f, Belle Plaine. g, Clonbrook. h, T.P.O. Dem. / Railway. i, Enmore. j, Fredericks / burg. k, Good Success. l, 1986. m, Mariabba. n, Massaruni. o, Nigg. p, No. 50. q, No. 63 / Benab. r, Philadelphia. s, Sisters. t, Skeldon. u, Suddie. v, Taymouth / Manor. w, Wales. x, Whim.

Perf. 14x13½

1986, May 15 **Litho.** **Wmk. 364**
1418 Sheet of 25, #a.-k., m.-x., 2 #l. 32.50 32.50
a.-x. A66 25c on 30c, any single 1.00 .75

Nos. 10A, 13a, 241, 713a-713d, British Guiana No. 254 Surcharged

Surcharges read: Nos. 1443, 1445, "GUYANA / INDEPENDENCE 1966-1986"; Nos. 1446-1447, "1986"; Nos. 1448a-1448d, "INDEPENDENCE / 1966-1986".

1986, May 26 *Perfs. as Before*
Watermarks and Printing Methods as Before
1443 A60 25c on 2c British Guiana #254 .25 .25
1444 A57 25c on 35c #241 .25 .25
1445 A60 60c on 2c British Guiana #254 .45 .30
1446 A60 120c on 6c #10A .50 .35
1447 A60 130c on 24c #13a 9.00 .75
1448 Block of 4 1.75 1.75
a. A86 25c on 120c #713a .35 .25
b. A86 25c on 130c #713b .35 .25
c. A86 25c on 150c #713c .35 .25
d. A86 225c on 200c #713d .70 .70
Nos. 1443-1448 (6) 12.20

No. 135 Surcharged "MEXICO / 1986" in Blue

Perf. 13x13½

1986, May 31 **Litho.** **Wmk. 364**
1452 A28 225c on 3c #135 20.00 3.75

World Cup Soccer Championships, Mexico City.

Nos. 136, 192 and 266A Surcharged or Ovptd. in Blue

Surcharge and Overprint Read: Nos. 1453-1454, "CARICOM HEADS OF GOV'T / CONFERENCE / JULY 1986"; No. 1455, "CARICOM / DAY 1986".

1986 *Perfs. as Before*
Watermarks and Printing Methods as Before
1453 A28 25c on #192 2.75 .75
1454 A28 60c on 3c #135 3.50 .30
1455 A66 60c on #286A 11.00 .75
Nos. 1453-1455 (3) 17.25

Issued: No. 1455, 6/28; Nos. 1453-1454, 7/1.

Nos. 133 and 137 Surcharged "INT. YEAR / OF PEACE" in Black or Blue

1986, July 14 **Litho.** *Perf. 13x13½*
1456 A28 25c on 1c #133 (Bl) .75 .45
1457 A28 60c on 6c #137 1.75 1.75
1458 A28 120c on 6c #137 1.75 1.75
1459 A28 130c on 6c #137 1.75 1.75
1460 A28 150c on 6c #137 1.75 1.75
Nos. 1456-1460 (5) 7.75

Halley's Comet — A96

Designs: a, Br. Guiana #172. b, Guyana #931.

1986, July 19 *Perf. 14*
1461 A96 320c Pair, #a.-b. 3.00 3.00
c. Imperf. 7.50

No. 1461 has continuous design. No. 1461 exists imperf. between. Most were overprinted.
For overprints and surcharges see Nos. 1822, 1836, 2029, E5-E6, E11, E14.

No. 43 Surcharged

1986, July 28 **Photo.** *Perf. 14x14½*
1463 A7 20c on 6c #43 11.00 .40

Nos. 60-61 Surcharged "GUSIA / 1936-1986"

Perf. 14x13½

1986, Aug. 15 **Photo.** **Unwmk.**
1464 A11 25c on #61 6.00 .50
1465 A11 $1.50 on 6c #60 11.00 4.50

No. 136 Surcharged "REGIONAL / PHARMACY / CONFERENCE / 1986" in Blue

Perf. 13x13½

1986, Aug. 15 **Litho.** **Wmk. 364**
1466 A28 130c on 5c #136 12.00 1.75

Nos. 1337, 1339, 1341 Inscribed "1966-1986"

Perfs. as Before

1986, Sept. 23 **Unwmk.**
1467 A92 25c on #1337 2.50 .30
1468 A92 25c on #1339 2.50 .30
1469 A92 25c on #1341 2.50 .30
Nos. 1467-1469 (3) 7.50 .90

For surcharges, see Nos. 4200-4201.

No. 871 Surcharged

Perf. 14x13½

1986, Oct. 1 **Litho.** **Wmk. 364**

Sheet of 25
1470 #a.-k., m.-x., 2 #l 55.00 40.00
a.-x. A66 120c any single 2.00 1.25

No. 1145 Surcharged "12th World Orchid Conference" / "TOKYO JAPAN MARCH 1987"

Unwmk.

1986, Oct. 6 **Litho.** *Perf. 14*
1494 A91 650c on 40c #1145 19.00 6.50

For overprint see No. 1851.

Orchid Type like No. 1052 Surchd. in Black and Red or Red

Surcharge reads: "1492-1992" and "CHRISTOPHER COLUMBUS".

1986, Oct.
1495 A91 320c on 150c 7.50 3.00
1496 A91 320c on 150c (R) 7.50 3.00

Issued: No. 1495, 10/10; No. 1496, 10/30. Nos. 1495-1496 not issued without surcharge.

Nos. 704 and 705 Surcharged "1986"

Perf. 14x14½

1986, Oct. 15 **Photo.** **Wmk. 364**
1497 A7 50c on #704 6.50 .60
1498 A7 225c on #705 18.00 5.50

Nos. 134, 192 Surcharged "Deepavali /1986"

1986, Nov. 3 **Litho.** *Perf. 13x13½*
1499 A28 25c on 2c #134 3.00 .50
1500 A28 200c on #192 11.00 4.00

No. 43 Surcharged "CHRISTMAS / 1986" in Red

1986, Nov. 26 *Perfs. as Before*
Watermarks and Printing Methods as Before
1501 A7 20c on 6c #43 5.00 .30

Miniature Sheet

No. 917 Surcharged in Red
1502 A88 120c on 60c on #a.-e. 8.50 8.50

No. 1502 is surcharged on an unissued miniature sheet containing No. 917. No. 1501 exists on a 2013 cover with "cents" obliterated with a felt-tip marker.

No. 329 Ovptd. "1986" in Blue

Wmk. 364

1986, Nov. 26 **Litho.** *Perf. 14*
1503 A77 30c Sheet of 12, #a.-l. 27.50 27.50

No. 1398 Surcharged in Red

1986, Dec. 1 **Litho.** *Perf. 14x14½*
1504 A95 $15 on $3.50 #1398 47.50 22.50

L.F.S. Burnham, President 1980-85 A97

25c, Tomb. 120c, Flags, map.130c, Government building. $6, Portrait, necklace, vert.

1986, Dec. 13 Litho. *Perf. 12½x13*

1505 A97 25c multi .25 .25
1506 A97 120c multi .35 .35
1507 A97 130c multi .45 .45
1508 A97 $6 multi 2.00 2.00
Nos. 1505-1508 (4) 3.05 3.05

Orchid Type of 1985-87 Surcharged "GPOC / 1977 - 1987"

1987, Jan. 19 *Perf. 14*

1509 A91 225c on 25c like #1090 4.50 1.00
1510 A91 $10 on 50c like #1052 11.00 11.00

Nos. 1509-1510 not issued without surcharge. No. 1509 adds "2" to 25c value, No. 1510 uses flower as obliterator.

Stamps of Type A91 Surcharged in Black or Red

a

b

c

d

e

f

g

h

i

j

k

l

1987-89 *Perfs. as Before*

Design A91
Series 1
(Plate Number in Parentheses)
On Nos. 1022-1039

1511 (a) 120c on 60c (2) 2.75
1512 (b) 120c on 60c (2) 1.10
1513 (a) 120c on 60c (5) 2.10
1514 (c) 200c on 60c (5) 1.10
1515 (c) 200c on 75c (5) 1.10

Obliterator invtd. in surch. on Nos. 1514-1515.

1516 (d) 200c on 60c (7) 1.10
1517 (d) 200c on 25c (8) 1.60
1518 (e) 200c on 25c (8) 1.10
1519 (a) 120c on 50c (9) 1.10
1520 (b) 120c on 50c (9)
1521 (f) 120c on 50c (9) 1.10
1522 (g) 120c on 50c (9)
1523 (a) 120c on 55c (9) 2.25
1524 (f) 120c on 55c (9) 1.60
a. 120c on 55c #1032a 2.00
1525 (g) 120c on 55c (9) 1.10
1526 (a) 120c on 60c (10) 2.25
1527 (d) 200c on 60c (10) 1.10
1528 (h) $2 on 25c (12) 1.10

Surcharge on No. 1528 lacks obliterator.

1529 (f) 120c on 55c (15) 1.40
1530 (a) 200c on 55c (15) 5.50

Issued: Nos. 1518, 1528, 3/6; Nos. 1514-1515, 3/17; Nos. 1516-1517, 1522, 1525, 1527, 3/87; Nos. 1521, 1524, 1529, 7/87; Nos. 1511, 1513, 1519, 1523, 1526, 1530, 9/87; Nos. 1512, 1520, 7/88.

On Nos. 1042-1061

1531 (b) 120c on 55c (17)
1532 (d) 200c on 55c (17) 1.60
1533 (a) 600c on 80c (17) 3.25
1534 (a) 120c on 60c (19) 2.25
1535 (d) 200c on 60c (19) 1.10
1536 (a) 120c on 50c (22)
1537 (b) 120c on 50c (22)
1538 (f) 120c on 50c (22) 1.10
1539 (c) 200c on 50c (22) 1.10
1540 (i) 225c on 50c (22) 1.60
1541 (a) 120c on 55c #1050a (22) 2.25
1542 (f) 120c on 55c #1050a (22) 1.75
1543 (c) 200c on 55c #1050a (22) 1.10
1544 (h) $2 on 25c (23) 1.40
1545 (a) 120c on 50c (24) 2.25
1546 (a) 200c on 50c (24)
1547 (d) 200c on 50c (24) 1.10
1548 (a) 120c on 60c (31) 2.25
1549 (d) 200c on 60c (31) 1.10

Issued: No. 1544, 3/6; Nos. 1539, 1543, 3/17; Nos. 1532, 1535, 1547, 1549, 3/87; No. 1540, 6/87; Nos. 1538, 1542, 7/87; Nos. 1533-1534, 1536, 1541, 1545-1546, 1548, 9/87; Nos. 1531, 1537, 7/88.

On Nos. 1069-1091

1550 (b) 120c on 80c (39)
1551 (a) 600c on 80c (39) 3.25
1552 (g) $15 on 80c (39) 4.50
1553 (i) 225c on #1402 (42) 1.60
1554 (d) 200c on 60c (44) 1.10
1555 (d) 200c on 60c (47) 1.10
1556 (a) 120c on 50c (49)
1557 (f) 120c on 50c (49) 1.60
1558 (a) 120c on 55c #1085a (49) 2.25
1559 (f) 120c on 55c (49) 1.40
a. 120c on 55c on #1085a 2.50
1560 (d) 200c on 55c (49) 1.25
a. 200c on 55c on #1085a 4.50
1561 (a) 120c on 60c (50) 2.25
1562 (b) 120c on 60c (50)
1563 (e) 200c on 25c (51) 1.40
1564 (d) 200c on 25c (52) 1.10
1565 (b) 120c on 30c (53)
a. 120c on 30c on #1090a
1566 (a) 120c on 50c (53) 2.25
1567 (d) 200c on 30c #1090a (53) 1.10
1568 (a) 200c on 50c (53)
1569 (d) 200c on 50c (53) 1.10
1570 (g) $10 on 25c (53) 3.25
1571 (g) $25 on 25c (53) 6.50

Surcharge on No. 1571 lacks obliterator and places a "$" in front of original denomination. Nos. 1570-1571 not issued without surcharge.

Issued: No. 1563, 3/6; Nos. 1552, 1554-1555, 1560, 1564, 1567, 1569-1571, 3/87; No. 1553, 6/87; Nos. 1557, 1559, 7/87; Nos. 1551, 1556, 1558, 1561, 1566, 1568, 9/87; Nos. 1550, 1562, 1565, 7/88.

On Nos. 1092-1108, 1372

1572 (b) 120c on 45c (54)
1573 (a) 120c on 60c (54) 2.25
1574 (b) 120c on 60c (54) 1.10
1575 (a) 200c on 50c (55)
1576 (i) 225c on 60c (55) 1.60
1577 (b) 120c on 60c (57) 1.10
a. New value at bottom
1578 (d) 200c on 60c (57) 1.10
1579 (b) 120c on 25c (59) 1.10
1580 (a) 120c on 75c (60) 2.25
1581 (c) 200c on 75c (60) 2.75
1582 (b) 120c on 25c (61)
1583 (b) 120c on 25c (63) 1.10
1584 (a) 120c on 50c (64)
1585 (f) 120c on 50c (64) 1.60
1586 (a) 120c on 55c, wmkd. (64) 2.25
1587 (f) 120c on 55c (64) 1.10
a. 120c on 55c on #1107a 1.40
1588 (g) 120c on 55c (64) 1.10
a. 120c on 55c on #1107a 1.25

Surcharge on Nos. 1522, 1525, 1588-1588a does not contain date.

1589 (a) 120c on 50c (65) 2.25
1590 (a) 200c on 50c (65)
1591 (d) 200c on 50c (65) 1.10
1591A (i) 225c on #1372 (65)

Issued: No. 1581, 3/17; Nos. 1578, 1588, 1591, 3/87; No. 1576, 6/87; Nos. 1585, 1587, 7/87; Nos. 1573, 1575, 1580, 1584, 1586, 1589-1590, 9/87; No. 1591A, 10/9/87; Nos. 1572, 1574, 1577, 1579, 1582-1583, 7/88.

On Nos. 1112-1124

1592 (b) 120c on 40c (68) 1.10
a. New value at LL
1593 (c) 200c on 40c (68) 1.10
a. Obliterator inverted 1.25
1594 (a) 225c on 40c (68) 2.75
1595 (a) 120c on 60c (69)
1596 (b) 120c on 60c (69) 1.10
1597 (b) 120c on 25c (70)
1598 (b) 120c on 25c (71)
1599 (a) 120c on 60c (71) 2.25
1600 (d) 200c on 25c (71) 1.10
1601 (d) 200c on 60c (71) 1.10
1602 (j) 120c on 25c (72)
1603 (d) 200c on 25c (72) 1.10
1604 (b) 120c on 60c (73)
1605 (d) 200c on 60c (73) .80
1606 (b) 120c on 80c (74)
1607 (a) 600c on 80c (74) 3.25
1608 (g) $12 on 80c (74) 3.75
1609 (b) 120c on 60c (75)
a. New value at bottom
1610 (d) 200c on 60c (75) 1.10
1611 (a) 225c on 65c (76) 2.75

Issued: No. 1593, 3/17; Nos. 1600-1601, 1603, 1605, 1608, 1610, 3/87; Nos. 1594-1595, 1599, 1611, 9/87; Nos. 1592, 1596-1598, 1604, 1606-1607, 1609, 7/88; No. 1602, 9/88.

On Nos. 1126-1142

1612 (b) 120c on 40c (77)
a. New value at UL
1613 (d) 200c on 40c (77) 1.10
1614 (a) 200c on 45c (77) 3.25
1615 (d) 200c on 45c (77) 1.10
1616 (a) 200c on 45c (78) 3.25
1617 (d) 200c on 45c (78) 1.10
1618 (a) 120c on 60c (79) 3.25
1619 (b) 120c on 60c (79)
1620 (a) 225c on 65c (80) 3.25
1621 (b) 120c on 45c (81)
1622 (f) 120c on 55c (81) 1.40
1623 (d) 200c on 45c (81) 1.10
1624 (a) 200c on 55c (81) 4.50
1625 (f) 120c on 55c (82) 1.75
1626 (a) 200c on 55c (82) 11.50
1627 (a) 120c on 75c (83) 3.25
1628 (b) 120c on 90c (84)
1629 (a) 200c on 45c (84) 3.25
1630 (a) 200c on 45c (85) 3.25
1631 (d) 200c on 45c (85) 1.10

Issued: Nos. 1613, 1615, 1617, 1623, 1631, 3/87; Nos. 1622, 1625, 7/87; Nos. 1614, 1616, 1618, 1620, 1624, 1626-1627, 1629-1630, 9/87; Nos. 1612, 1619, 1621, 1628, 7/88.

On Nos. 1144-1153

1632 (b) 120c on 30c (86)
1633 (b) 120c on 40c (86) 1.10
1634 (d) 200c on 30c (86) 1.10
1635 (d) 200c on 40c (86)
1636 (a) 225c on 40c (86) 3.25
a. Inscribed "ONTOGLOSSUM" 2.75
1637 (a) 120c on 60c (87) 2.25
a. Surcharge reading up
1638 (d) 200c on 60c (87) 1.10
1639 (a) 225c on 65c (88) 2.75
1640 (f) 120c on 55c (89) 1.40
1641 (b) 120c on 90c (89)
1642 (a) 200c on 55c (89) 5.25
1643 (d) 225c on 90c (89) 1.10
1644 (a) 120c on 40c (90) 2.25
1645 (b) 120c on 40c (90) 1.10
1646 (c) 200c on 40c (90) 1.10
1647 (d) 200c on 40c (R) (90) 1.40

1648 (c) 200c on 375c (90) 1.10
a. 200c on 375c #1153a 4.50
1649 (a) 225c on 40c (90) 2.75
1650 (i) 225c on 40c (90) 1.75
1651 (k) 260c on 375c (90) 1.10

Issued: No. 1647, 2/9/87; Nos. 1646, 1648, 3/17/87; Nos. 1634-1635, 1638, 1643, 3/87; No. 1650, 6/87; No. 1640, 7/87; Nos. 1636-1637, 1639, 1642, 1644, 1649, 9/87; Nos. 1632-1633, 1641, 1645, 7/88; No. 1651, 10/88.

Surcharge on No. 1651 is placed over original value and has no obliterator.

On Nos. 1154-1165

1652 (a) 120c on 40c (91) 2.25
1653 (b) 120c on 40c (91) 1.10
a. New value at LR
1654 (a) 225c on 40c (91) 3.25
1655 (i) 225c on 40c (91) 1.60
1656 (b) 120c on 50c (92)
1657 (a) 120c on 75c (92) 2.75
1658 (c) 200c on 50c (92)
1659 (c) 200c on 75c (92) 1.10
1660 (b) 120c on 60c (93)
1661 (b) 120c on 80c (93)
1662 (i) 225c on 60c (93) 1.75
1663 (i) 225c on [illegible] ([illegible]) 1.75
1664 (a) 600c on 80c (93)
1665 (a) 120c on 60c (94)
1666 (b) 120c on 60c (94)
1667 (b) 120c on 60c (95) 1.10
1668 (a) 120c on 75c (95) 3.50
1669 (b) 120c on 40c (96)
1670 (a) 225c on 65c (96) 2.75

Miniature Sheets

1670A Sheet of 4 27.50
b. (a) 600c on 130c #1412a (6)
c. (a) 600c on 200c #1412b (6)
d. (a) 600c on 260c #1412c (6)
e. (a) 600c on 330c #1412d (6)
1670F Sheet of 4 15.00
g. (i) 225c on #1393a (22)
h. (i) 225c on #1393b (22)
i. (i) 225c on #1393c (22)
j. (i) 225c on #1393d (22)

Issued: Nos. 1658-1659, 3/17/87; Nos. 1655, 1662-1663, 6/87; Nos. 1652, 1654, 1657, 1664-1665, 1668, 1670, 9/87; No. 1670F, 11/9/87; No. 1670A, 11/20/87; Nos. 1653, 1656, 1660-1661, 1666-1667, 1669, 7/88.

For overprints see Nos. 1975, 1979.

Series 2

On Nos. 1168-1204

1671 (b) 120c on 90c (2) 1.10
1672 (b) 120c on 50c (3) 1.10
1673 (f) 120c on 50c (3) 1.10
1674 (b) 200c on 90c (4)
1675 (b) 120c on 50c (6) 1.10
1676 (f) 120c on 50c (6) 1.10
1677 (b) 120c on 30c (7) 1.10
1678 (b) 120c on 70c (8) 1.10
1679 (b) 120c on 70c (9) 1.10
a. New value at LR
1680 (b) 120c on 90c (10) 1.10
1681 (b) 120c on 70c (12) 1.10
a. New value at LL
1682 (b) 120c on 50c (13) 1.10
1683 (b) 120c on 90c (13)
1684 (b) 120c on 30c (14) 1.10
a. New value at UR
1685 (b) 120c on 50c (15) 1.10
1686 (b) 120c on 85c (15)
1687 (b) 120c on 70c (17) 13.50
1688 (b) 120c on 85c (18) 1.10
1689 (c) 200c on 85c (18)
1690 (b) 120c on 50c (20) 1.10
1691 (f) 120c on 50c (20) 1.75

Issued: No. 1689, 3/17/87; Nos. 1673, 1676, 1691, 7/87; Nos. 1671-1672, 1674-1675, 1677-1688, 1690, 7/88.

On Nos. 1205-1240

1692 (b) 120c on 45c (21) 1.10
1693 (b) 120c on 30c (22) 1.10
1694 (l) 350c on 330c #O52 (23) 1.10
1695 (b) 120c on 85c (24) 1.10
1696 (j) 120c on 140c (R) (25) 1.10
1697 (l) 250c on 225c #O46 (26) 1.10
a. New value at UL
1698 (b) 120c on 60c (27) 2.25
1699 (b) 120c on 90c (27)
1700 (b) 120c on 30c (28) 1.10
a. New value at UL 2.25
1701 (b) 120c on 30c (30) 1.10
1702 (k) 240c on 140c (30) 1.10

No. 1702 not issued without surcharge.

1703 (l) 150c on 175c #O44 (31) 1.10
1704 (b) 120c on 50c (32) 1.10
1705 (f) 120c on 50c (32) 1.10
1706 (k) 240c on 140c (34) 1.10
1707 (l) 125c on 140c #O42 (36) 1.10
1708 (k) 120c on 140c (38) 1.10
1709 (k) 120c on 140c (41) 1.10
1710 (b) 200c on 80c (42)
1711 (l) 150c on #O43 (43) 1.10

Issued: No. 1705, 7/87; Nos. 1692-1693, 1695, 1698-1701, 1704, 1710, 7/88; Nos. 1702, 1706, 10/88; Nos. 1696, 1708-1709, 2/22/89; Nos. 1694, 1697, 1703, 1707, 1711, 3/89.

On Nos. 1245-1314

1712 (b) 120c on 35c (45) 1.10
1713 (b) 120c on 85c (45)
1714 (j) 120c on 140c (R) (52) 1.10
1715 (k) 300c on 290c (53) 1.10
1716 (j) 120c on 175c (R) (54) 1.10
1717 (k) 170c on 175c (58) 1.10
1718 (l) 250c on #O48 (59) 1.10
1719 (j) 120c on 140c (R) (65) 1.10
1720 (k) 250c on 280c (66) 1.10
1721 (k) 250c on 280c (67) 1.10
1722 (l) 250c on 230c #O47 (68) 1.10
1723 (l) 250c on 260c #O49 (69) 1.10
a. New value at UR 1.10
1724 (l) 600c on #O54 (70) 1.10
1725 (l) $12 on #O55 (71) 1.10
1726 (l) $15 on #O56 (84) 1.10
1727 (k) 240c on 425c (87) 1.10
1728 (l) 300c on 275c #O50 (90) 1.10
1729 (l) 125c on 130c #O41 (92) 1.10
1730 (l) 350c on #O53 (95) 1.10

On No. 1730 "Postage" reads up or down.

Issued: Nos. 1712-1713, 7/88; No. 1727, 10/88; Nos. 1714, 1716, 1719, 2/22/89; Nos. 1715, 1717-1718, 1720-1726, 1728-1730, 3/89.

Obliterator on Nos. 1708-1709, 1715, 1717, 1720-1721 has two thick bars.

Stamps of Type A91 Overprinted

m

n

o

p

1987 *Perfs. as Before*

Series 1

1731 (m) 120c on #1021 (1) 5.25
1732 (n) 130c on #1023 (3) 2.50
1733 (m) 130c on #1028a (6) 5.00
1734 (n) 130c on #1028 (6) 2.50
a. 130c on #1028a 2.50
1735 (m) 120c on #1034 (11) 3.25
1736 (m) [illegible] on #10[illegible]7a (1[illegible]) [illegible]
1737 (n) 130c on #1413 (13) 5.00
1738 (o) 130c on #1037 (13) 1.10
a. 130c on #1037a 1.10
1738B (p) 130c on #1413 (13)
1739 (n) 200c on #1038 (14) 2.50
1740 (n) 130c on #1041 (16) 1.10
1741 (n) 130c on #1342 (18) 1.10
1742 (p) 130c on #1342 (18) 1.10
1743 (m) 130c on #1047a (20) 2.25
1744 (n) 130c on #1047a (20) 2.50
a. 130c on #1047 4.00
1745 (m) 200c on #1048 (21) 2.25
1746 (n) 200c on #1048 (21)
1747 (m) 130c on #1055a (25) 4.50
1748 (o) 130c on #1055 (25) 1.10
a. 130c on #1055a 1.10
1749 (p) 150c on #1056 (26) 1.10
1750 (m) 120c on #1058 (28) 5.00
1751 (n) 130c on #1343 (29) 1.10
1752 (p) 130c on #1343 (29) 1.10

Issued: Nos. 1732, 1734, 1737-1741, 1744, 1746, 1748, 1751, Mar; Nos. 1731, 1733, 1735-1736, 1743, 1745, 1747, 1750, July; No. 1738B, 11/20; Nos. 1742, 1749, 1752, Dec.

1753 (n) 130c on #1344 (30) 1.10
1754 (p) 130c on #1344 (30) 1.10
1755 (n) 200c on #1063 (33) 1.10
1756 (m) 120c on #1067 (37) 1.60
1757 (n) 260c on #1070 (39) 2.25
1758 (m) 150c on #1072a, ovpt. reading up (40) 2.00
a. 150c on #1072 3.25
1759 (m) 150c on #1075a (42) 3.50
1760 (m) 150c on #1402 (42) 5.50
1761 (m) 200c on #1077a (43) 5.50
1762 (m) 200c on #1403 (43) 5.50
1763 (n) 200c on #1403 (43) 3.50
1764 (m) 150c on #1080 reading down (45) 2.25
a. 150c on #1080a reading up 3.25
1765 (m) 120c on #1081 (46) 8.50
1766 (m) 120c on #1097 (56) 3.25
1767 (m) 120c on #1099 (58) 3.25
1768 (n) 130c on #1110 (66) 3.25
1769 (p) 130c on #1110 (66) 1.10
1770 (p) 120c on #1111 (67) 1.10
1771 (n) 250c on #1122 (74) 1.40
1772 (n) 200c on #1131 (79) 1.10
1773 (o) 130c on #1155 (91) 1.60

Miniature Sheets of 4

1774 (n) 200c on #1345 (4) 4.00
1775 (n) 200c on 130c #1346 (20) 5.50

Series 2

1776 (n) 200c on #1169 (2) 7.00
1777 (n) 200c on #1183 (9) 1.75

Issued: Nos. 1753, 1755, 1757, 1763, 1768, 1771-1777, Mar.; Nos. 1756, 1758, 1759-1762, 1764-1767, July. Nos. 1754, 1769-1770, Dec.

Overprint reads up on Nos. 1759, 1761. Overprint reads down on Nos. 1731, 1735, 1745, 1750, 1755, 1758a, 1760, 1762, 1763.

See Nos. 1813-1814, 1844 for other stamps overprinted "1987" only.

Nos. 1337, 1339, 1341 Surcharged

1987, Mar. 6 *Perfs. as Before*

1777A A92 200c on #1337 6.00 2.00
1777B A92 200c on #1339 6.00 2.00
1777C A92 200c on #1341 6.00 2.00
Nos. 1777A-1777C (3) 18.00 6.00

See note following No. 1341.

Nos. 134, 136, 139a, and 192 Surcharged "Post Office / Corp. / 1977-1987" in Blue

Perfs. as Before

1987, Feb. 17 Litho. Wmk. 364

1778 A28 25c on 2c #134 .25 .25
1779 A28 25c on 5c #136 .25 .25
1780 A28 25c on #192 .25 .25
1781 A28 25c on 15c #139a 5.50 .50
1782 A28 60c on 15c #139a 12.00 .40
1783 A28 $1.20 on 2c #134 .85 .85
1784 A28 $1.30 on 15c #139a 13.00 3.75
Nos. 1778-1784 (7) 32.10 6.25

Nos. 1032, 1032a Surcharged "12th World Orchid Conference" and "TOKYO JAPAN"

1987, Mar. 12 Unwmk. *Perf. 14*

1785 A91 650c on 55c #1032 11.00 6.50
a. 650c on 55c #1032a 12.00 7.00

No. 280 Surcharged with Names of Post Offices Operating in 1885

Overprints: a, AGRICOLA. b, BAGOTVILLE. c, BOURDA. d, BUXTON. e, CABACABURI. f, CAR- / MICHAEL STREET. g, COTTON / TREE. h, DUNOON. i, FELLOW- / SHIP. j, GROVE. k, HACKNEY. l, LEONORA. m, 1987. n, MALLALI. o, PROVI- / DENCE. p, RELIANCE. q, SPARTA. r, STEWART- / VILLE. s, TARLOGY. t, T.P.O. / BERBICE RIV. u, T.P.O. / DEM. RIV. v, T.P.O. / ESSEQ. RIV. w, T.P.O. / MASSARUNI / RIV. x, TUSCHEN / (De / VRIENDEN). y, ZORG.

Perf. 14x13½

1987, Mar. 17 Wmk. 364

1786 Sheet of 25, #a.-y. 42.50 35.00
a.-y. A66 25c on 10c, any single 1.50 1.25

British Guiana Post Office, 125th Anniv.

Columbus' Discovery of America, 500th Anniv. (in 1992) — A98

Paintings: 120c, Discovery of America, by Dali. 225c, Preparations Before the Journey, by unknown artist. 360c, Catholic Kings from Prado Museum.

$6, Columbus' Fleet, by R. Monleon.

1987, Mar. 30 Litho. *Perf. 13½*

1787 A98 120c multicolored 1.75 1.00
1788 A98 225c multicolored 4.00 3.00
1789 A98 360c multicolored 6.25 3.00
a. Strip of 3, #1787-1789 13.50 13.50

Souvenir Sheet

1790 A98 $6 gold & multi 15.00 15.00

No. 1790 exists with silver border.

No. 289A Ovptd. "28 MARCH 1927 / PAA / GEO-POS"

1987, Mar. 28 *Perf. 13½x13*

1811 A66 $10 on #289A 24.00 13.00

First Georgetown to Port-of-Spain Flight, 50th Anniv.

No. 285 Surcharged

1987, Apr. 6 *Perf. 14x13½*

1812 A66 25c on 40c #285 16.00 .50

Nos. 87-88, 90, 287 Surcharged or Overprinted "1987"

1987, Apr. *Perfs. as Before*

Watermarks and Printing Methods as Before

1813 A14 25c on #88 .75 .10
1814 A66 $1 on #287 17.00 1.00
1815 A14 120c on 6c #87 .90 .25
1816 A14 320c on 6c #87 1.50 .75
1817 A14 500c on 40c #90 2.00 2.00
Nos. 1813-1817 (5) 22.15 4.10

Issued: Nos. 1813, 1815-1817, 4/21; No. 1814, Apr.

No. 1461 Ovptd. "CAPEX '87"

1987, June 10 Litho. *Perf. 14*

1822 A96 320c Pair, #a.-b. 5.50 5.50
c. on #1461, imperf. between 11.00

For surcharges see Nos. 2030, E15.

Nos. 626-628 Ovptd. "1987"

Wmk. 314 Upright

1987, July 15 Engr. *Perf. 12½x13*

1823 A60 $1.20 on #626 1.00 .25

Wmk. 314 Sideways

1824 A60 $1.30 on #627 12.00 1.00
1825 A60 $2.40 on #628 15.00 5.00
Nos. 1823-1825 (3) 28.00 6.25

A99

A100

Locomotives — A101

Nos. 1826a, 1827a, Alexandra 4. Nos. 1826b, 1827b, Diesel locomotive facing right. Nos. 1826c, 1827c, Steam locomotive facing right. Nos. 1826d, 1827d, Diesel locomotive No. 21 facing left.

Nos. 1829a, 1830b, Alexandra 4. Nos. 1829b, 1830a, Diesel locomotive. Nos. 1829c, 1830d, Steam locomotive facing right. Nos. 1829d, 1830c, Diesel locomotive No. 21. No. 1830e, Photograph of trains in Georgetown Station. No. 1831, Steam locomotive pulling cattle cars, map of routes from Parika to Vreedenhoop and from Georgetown to Rosignol.

1987, Aug. 3 *Perf. 15*

1826 Block of 4 2.00 2.00
a.-d. A99 $1.20 green, any single .40 .40
1827 Block of 5 5.00 5.00
a.-d. A99 $3.20 blue, any single .85 .85
e. A100 $3.20 blue .85 .85
1828 A101 $12 shown 4.00 4.00
Nos. 1826-1828 (3) 11.00 11.00

1987, Dec. 4

1829 Block of 4 2.40 2.40
a.-d. A99 $1.20 rose lake, any single .50 .50
1830 Block of 5 6.25 6.25
a.-d. A99 $3.30 blk, any single 1.10 1.10
e. A100 $3.30 black 1.10 1.10
1831 A101 $10 multi 4.50 4.50
Nos. 1829-1831 (3) 13.15 13.15

Sizes: Nos. 1827e, 1830e, 84x57mm. Nos. 1828, 1831, 90x40mm.

For surcharges see Nos. E12-E13. For overprints see Nos. 1910-1911, 1935-1938, 2024-2028F, 2054, 2056.

No. 287 Overprinted

Overprints read: No. 1832, "FAIREY NICHOLL / 15 AUG 1927 / GEO-MAB"; No. 1833, "FAIREY NICHOLL / 8 AUG 1927 / GEO-MAZ".

1987, Aug. 7 Litho. *Perf. 13½x13*

1832 A66 $1 "MAB" on #287 16.00 11.00
1833 A66 $1 "MAZ" on #287 16.00 11.00
a. Pair, #1832-1833 32.50 27.50

Nos. 1291A and 1461c Surcharged

Surcharges Read: No. 1834, "CRISTOVAO COLOMBO / 1492 — 1992"; No. 1835, "CHRISTOPHE COLOMB / 1492 — 1992"; No. 1836, "THE PASSING OF HALLEY'S COMET: / PROPHESY OF THE ARRIVAL OF / HERNAN CORTES 1519. / V CENTENARY OF THE LANDING OF / CHRISTOPHER COLUMBUS / IN THE AMERICAS".

Unwmk.

1987, Oct. 9 Litho. *Perf. 14*

1834 A91 950c on 900c #1291A 3.00 3.50
1835 A91 950c on 900c #1291A 3.00 3.50
a. Pair, #1834-1835 7.50 7.50

Imperf

1836 A96 $20 on 320c #1461c 8.50 8.50

Nos. 135-136 Surcharged "DEEPAVALI / 1987"

1987, Nov. 2 Litho. *Perf. 13x13½*

1837 A28 25c on 3c #135 3.00 .40
1838 A28 $3 on 5c #136 9.00 5.00

No. 43 Surcharged "CHRISTMAS / 1987" in Red

1987, Nov. 9 *Perfs. as Before*

Watermarks and Printing Methods as Before

1839 A7 20c on 6c #43 5.00 .50

No. 1502 Surcharged "1987" in Blue Miniature Sheet

1840 A88 120c on 60c #1502 1.75 1.75

No. 920 surcharged in Red Nos. 329, 1037, 1040, 1056, 1110-1111, 1494 Overprinted or Surcharged

Overprint or Surcharges read: No. 1844, "1987"; Nos. 1845-1849, 1851, "PROTECT OUR HERITAGE '87"; No. 1850, "Protect Our Heritage '87".

1987, Dec. 9 *Perfs. as Before*

Watermarks and Printing Methods as Before

1844 A77 30c Sheet of 12, #a.-l, on #329 7.00 7.00
1845 A91 120c on #1111 1.50 1.50
1846 A91 130c on #1110 1.75 1.75
1847 A91 150c on #1056 2.25 2.25
1848 A91 180c on #1040 2.50 2.50
1849 A91 320c on #1137 3.00 3.00
1850 A89 320c Triptych, #a.-c, on 120c #920 9.00 9.00
1851 A91 650c on #1494 5.00 5.00
Nos. 1844-1851 (8) 32.00 32.00

1988 Summer Olympics, Seoul — A102

1987, Dec. 30 Litho. *Perf. 13½x14*

1852 A102 $2 Jumping 2.50 2.25
1853 A102 $3 Discus 3.75 3.25
1854 A102 $5 Vase 6.50 5.50
a. Strip of 3, #1852-1854 13.50 13.50

Souvenir Sheet

Perf. 14

1855 A102 $3.50 Olympic Rings, horiz. 10.00 10.00

Christmas 1987 — A103

Paintings — No. 1856: a, The Virgin of the Rocks, by Da Vinci. b, Virgin with Grapes, by Mignard. c, Sacred Family, by Raphael. d, Virgin Mary, by Lucas Cranach. No. 1857, Adoration of Three Kings, by Rubens.

1988, Jan. 7 Litho. *Perf. 14*

1856 A103 $2 Strip of 4, #a.-d. 7.50 7.50

Souvenir Sheet

1857 A103 $10 Sheet of 1 13.50 13.50

Dated 1987.

Nos. 397, 405 and 651 Ovptd. or Surcharged "*AUSTRALIA* / 1987 JAMBOREE 1988" in Red

1988, Jan. 7 Litho. *Perf. 13½x13*

1858 A17 $4.40 on #405
1859 A17 $10 on #397
1860 A17 $10 on #651
1861 A17 $10 on #405
a. $10 on #405a
Nos. 1858-1861 (4) 10.00

Obliterator on Nos. 1859-1861 is red fleur-de-lis. Size and location of overprint varies.

Nos. 68 and 70 Surcharged "IFAD / For a World / Without Hunger"

Perf. 14x14½

1988, Jan. 26 Photo. Wmk. 364

1862 A7 25c on 1c #68 2.00 .30
1863 A7 $5 on 3c #70 7.00 3.00
Nos. 1862-1863 (2) 9.00 3.30

No. 1862 uses new denomination as obliterator and No. 1863 uses "X."

Flora and Fauna — A104

Mushrooms — No. 1864: a, Corprinus comatus. b, Amanita muscaria. c, Pholiota aurivella. d, Laccaria amethstina.

Birds — No. 1865: a, Starling. b, Reed warbler. c, Kingfisher. d, Goldcrest.

Cats — No. 1866: a, Himalayan. b, American shorthaired. c, Maine coon. d, Abyssinian.

Cactus flowers — No. 1866: e, Sulcorebutia densiseta. f, Subutia hyalacantha. g, Echinopsic. h, Lobivia polycephala.

Nos. 1866a-1866h horiz.

1988, Jan. 28 *Perf. 14*

1864 A104 $2 Strip of 4, #a.-d. 10.50 10.50
1865 A104 $2 Strip of 4, #a.-d. 9.50 9.50

Miniature Sheet

Perf. 14x13½

1866 A104 $2 Sheet of 8, #a.-h. 13.00 13.00

Dated 1987.

Santa Maria — A105

Ships: a, Santa Maria. b, Grande Francoise. No. 1869, San Martin, horiz.

1988, Feb. 10 Litho. *Perf. 13½x14*

1867 A105 $7 Pair, #a.-b., pale yel & multi 6.00 6.00
1868 A105 $7 Pair, #a.-b., bl & multi 6.00 6.00

Souvenir Sheet

Perf. 14

1869 A105 $7 silver & multi 12.00 12.00

Discovery of America, 500th anniv. (in 1992). Nos. 1867-1868 printed checkerwise with se-tenant labels describing ship dimensions. No. 1869 exists with gold border.

Nos. 136, 139a, and 146 Surcharged "Republic / Day / 1988" in Blue

Perfs. as Before

1988, Feb. 23 Litho. Wmk. 364

1870 A28 25c on 5c #136 .25 .25
1871 A28 120c on 15c #139a 4.50 .75
1872 A28 $10 on $2 #146 2.00 2.00
Nos. 1870-1872 (3) 6.75 3.00

No. 283A Surcharged with Names of Post Offices Operating in 1900

Overprints: a, Albouystown. b, Anns Grove c, Amacura. d, Arakaka. e, Baramanni. f, Cuyuni. g, Hope Placer. h, HMPS. i, Kitty. j, M'M'Zorg. k, Maccaseema. l, 1988. m, Morawhanna. n, Naamryck. o, Purini. p, Potaro / Landing. q, Rockstone. r, Rosignol. s, Stanleytown. t, Santa Rosa. u, Tumatumari. v, Weldaad. w, Wismar. x, TPO Berbice / Railway.

1988, Apr. 5 *Perf. 14x13½*

1873 A66 25c Sheet of 25, #a.-k., m.-x., 2 #l. 40.00 32.50

British Guiana Post Office, 125th Anniv.

No. 725 Surcharged "Olympic / Games / 1988"

Perf. 14½x14

1988, May 3 Litho. Wmk. 373

1897 A73 120c Sheet of 12, #a.-l. *18.00 18.00*

Nos. 136-137 and 146 Surcharged "Caricom Day / 1988"

Perf. 13x13½

1988, June 15 Litho. Wmk. 364

1898 A28 25c on 5c #136 .90 .25
1899 A28 $1.20 on 6c #137 .90 .25
1900 A28 $10 on $2 #146 4.50 6.00
Nos. 1898-1900 (3) 6.30 6.50

No. 286A Overprinted

Overprints: a, 1988. b, WHO / 1948-1988.

1988, June 17 Litho. *Perf. 14x13½*

1901 Sheet of 25, 24 #a., 1 #b. 27.50 25.00
a. A28 60c any single .40 .25
b. A28 60c 17.50 17.50

World Health Day, 40th anniv.

Nos. 929, 1053a, 1063, 1131 and 1161 Overprinted

Overprints: No. 1903, "CONSERVE TREES" on ocher stamp, "CONSERVE ELECTRICITY on green stamp, "CONSERVE WATER on brown stamp. No. 1904, "CONSERVE ELECTRICITY" on ocher stamp, "CONSERVE WATER on green stamp, "CONSERVE TREES on brown stamp. No. 1905, "CONSERVE WATER" on ocher stamp, "CONSERVE TREES on green stamp, "CONSERVE ELECTRICITY on brown stamp. Nos. 1906-1909, "CONSERVE / WATER".

Perfs. as Before

1988, July 15 Litho.

Watermarks as Before

1903 Triptych 3.50 3.50
a.-c. A90 120c any single .90 .60
1904 Triptych 3.50 3.50
a.-c. A90 120c any single .90 .60
1905 Triptych 3.50 3.50
a.-c. A90 120c any single .90 .90
1906 A91 200c on #1063 1.10 1.10
1907 A91 200c on #1131 1.10 1.10
1908 A91 225c on #1053a 1.10 1.10
1909 A91 350c on #1161 1.10 1.10
Nos. 1903-1909 (7) 14.90 14.90

Location and size of overprint varies.

Nos. 1826 and 1829 Overprinted

Overprints read: Nos. 1910a, 1911a, "BEWARE / OF ANIMALS"; Nos. 1910b, 1911b, "BEWARE / OF CHILDREN"; Nos. 1910c, 1911c, "DRIVE SAFELY"; Nos. 1910d, 1911d, "DO NOT / DRINK AND DRIVE".

Unwmk.

1988, July 15 Litho. *Perf. 15*

Block of 4, #a.-d.

1910 A99 $1.20 on #1826 7.50 7.50
1911 A99 $1.20 on #1829 7.50 7.50
Nos. 1910-1911 (2) 15.00 15.00

No. 287 Ovptd. or Surcharged

Perf. 13½x13

1988, July Litho. Wmk. 364

1912 A66 $1 "1988" on #287 13.00 1.50
1913 A66 120c on $1 #287 13.00 1.50

No. 421 Surcharged with New Value and "1988"

1988? Litho. *Perf. 13½x14*

1913A A80 $1.20 on $1.10 on $3 #421

Nos. 1037a, 1047a, 1056-1057, 1066-1068, 1097, 1099, 1109-1109a, 1110-1111, 1113, 1115, 1122, 1125, 1129, 1147, 1149, and 1155 Ovptd. "CONSERVE / OUR RESOURCES"

1988, July *Perf. 14*

Watermarks as Before

Series 1

Plate Numbers in Parentheses

1914 130c on #1037a (13) 1.25 .75
a. Overprint inverted *2.00*

No. 1914a probably is as common as No. 1914.

1915 A91 130c on #1047a (20) 1.25 .75
1916 A91 150c on #1056 (26) 1.25 .75
1917 A91 120c on #1057 (27) 1.25 .75
1918 A91 120c on #1066 (36) 1.25 .75
1919 A91 120c on #1067 (37) 1.25 .75
1920 A91 130c on #1068 (38) 1.25 .75
1921 A91 120c on #1097 (56) 1.25 .75
1922 A91 120c on #1099 (58) 1.25 .75

1923 A91 100c on #1109 (65) 1.25 .75
a. 100c on #1109a
1924 A91 130c on #1110 (66) 1.25 .75
1925 A91 120c on #1111 (67) 1.25 .75
1926 A91 100c on #1113 (68) 1.25 .75
1927 A91 120c on #1115 (69) 1.25 .75
1928 A91 250c on #1122 (74) 1.25 .75
1929 A91 150c on #1125 (76) 1.25 .75
1930 A91 150c on #1129 (78) 1.25 .75
1931 A91 150c on #1147 (87) 1.25 .75
1932 A91 100c on #1149 (88) 1.25 .75
1933 A91 130c on #1155 (91) 1.25 .75

Nos. 1827a-1827d and 1830a-1830d Ovptd. with Red Cross

1988, Aug. 3 Litho. *Perf. 15*

1935 A99 $3.20 Pair, #a.-b., on #1827a, 1827c 3.50 3.50
1936 A99 $3.20 Pair, #a.-b., on #1827b, 1827d 3.50 3.50
1937 A99 $3.30 Pair, #a.-b., on #1830a, 1830c 3.50 3.50
1938 A99 $3.30 Pair, #a.-b., on #1830b, 1830d 3.50 3.50
Nos. 1935-1938 (4) 14.00 14.00

Nos. 1038, 1131 Ovptd. and Nos. 1147, 1175 Surcharged "1928-1988 / CRICKET / JUBILEE"

1988, Sept. 5 Litho. *Perf. 14*
Watermarks as Before
Plate Numbers in Parentheses

1939 A91 200c on #1038 (14) 25.00 30.00
1940 A91 200c on #1131 (79) 1.25 .50
1941 A91 800c on 150c #1147 (87) 10.00 14.00
1942 A91 800c on 160c #1175 (5) 3.75 3.75
Nos. 1939-1942 (4) 40.00 48.25

Series 1
Plate Numbers in Parentheses

Nos. 1063, 1081, 1139, 1147, 1161, 1185, 1219, 1232, and 1305 Ovptd. and No. 1227 Surcharged "OLYMPIC GAMES / 1988"

1988, Sept. 16 Unwmk.

1943 A91 200c on #1063 (33) .70 .70
1944 A91 120c on #1081 (46) .70 .70
1945 A91 300c on #1139 (83) .70 .70
1946 A91 150c on #1147 (87) .70 .70
1947 A91 350c on #1161 (94) .90 .90

Series 2

1948 A91 320c on #1185 (10) .90 .90
1949 A91 350c on #1219 (29) .90 .90
1950 A91 300c on 360c #1227 (34) .90 .90
1951 A91 130c on #1232 (38) .90 .90
1952 A91 330c on #1305 (82) .90 .90

Overprint reads up on No. 1947.

Type A83 Ovptd. or Surcharged "OLYMPICS 1988" (a.) or "KOREA 1988" (b.)

1988 Litho. Wmk. 364 *Perf. 13½*

1953 A83 $1.20 Pair, #a.-b. 1.25 1.25
1954 A83 130c on $1.20, pair, #a.-b. 1.25 1.25
1955 A83 150c on $1.20, pair, #a.-b. 1.25 1.25
1956 A83 200c on $1.20, pair, #a.-b. 1.50 1.50
1957 A83 350c on $1.20, pair, #a.-b. 1.75 1.75
c. Strip of 5, #1953a-1957a 7.00 7.00
d. Strip of 5, #1953b-1957b 7.00 7.00

Overprint obliterates inscription spelled "LOS ANGELLES."

No. 1087 Overprinted, No. 1143 Surcharged

Overprint or Surcharge reads: "V CENTENARY OF / THE LANDING OF / CHRISTOPHER COLUMBUS / IN THE AMERICAS".

Unwmk.

1988, Oct. 12 Litho. *Perf. 14*

1958 A91 320c on #1087 2.50 .75
1959 A91 $15 on 360c #1143 5.00 5.00
Nos. 1958-1959 (2) 7.50 5.75

Nos. 1027, 1036, 1040, 1046, 1054, 1062, 1070, 1071, 1074, 1076, 1079, 1102, 1104, 1133, 1137 and 1143 Surcharged in Blue or Black; Nos. 1053, 1053a, 1102, 1591A and 1670F Ovptd. or Surcharged in Blue

Overprints read: Nos. 1960-1963, 1965-1974, 1976-1978, "SEASON's / GREETINGS"; Others, "SEASON'S / GREETINGS / 1988".

1988, Nov. 10 *Perfs. as Before*
Watermarks and Printing Methods as Before
Plate Numbers in Parentheses

1960 A91 120c on 100c #1027 (6) 2.00
1961 A91 120c on 100c #1036 (13) 2.00
1962 A91 240c on 180c #1040 (15) (Bk) 1.00
1963 A91 120c on 100c #1046 (20) 2.00
1964 A91 225c on #1053 (24) 1.00
a. 225c on #1053a 2.50
1965 A91 120c on 100c #1054 (25) 2.00
1966 A91 150c on #1062 (32) (Bk) 1.00
1967 A91 260c on #1070 (39) (Bk) 1.00
1968 A91 120c on 100c #1071 (40) 2.00
1969 A91 120c on 100c #1074 (42) 2.00
1970 A91 120c on 100c #1076 (43) 2.00
1971 A91 120c on 100c #1079 (45) 2.00
1972 A91 225c on #1102 (60) (Bk) 1.00
1973 A91 225c on #1102 (60) 1.00
1974 A91 150c on #1104 (62) (Bk) 1.00
1975 A91 225c on #1591A (65) 1.50
1976 A91 330c on #1133 (80) (Bk) 1.00
1977 A91 320c on #1137 (82) (Bk) 1.00
1978 A91 360c on #1143 (85) (Bk) 1.00
Nos. 1960-1978 (19) 27.50

Miniature Sheet

1979 A91 225c on #1670F (22) 4.75 4.75

Size and location of overprint varies.

Nos. 72, 713 and 932 Surcharged or Ovptd. "CHRISTMAS / 1988" in Red or Black

1988, Nov. 16 *Perfs. as Before*
Watermarks and Printing Methods as Before

1981 A7 20c on 6c #72 .35 .25
1982 A86 Block of 4 (Bk) 4.00 6.00
a. 120c on #713a 1.00 1.50
b. 120c on 130c #713b 1.00 1.50
c. 120c on 150c #713c 1.00 1.50
d. 120c on 200c #713d 1.00 1.50
1983 A90a 500c on 330c #932 2.50 3.00
Nos. 1981-1983 (3) 6.85 9.25

Overprint reads up on No. 1983.

Nos. 288, 289, and 289A Surcharged or Ovptd. for Prevention of AIDS

Beginnning of overprint reads: Nos. 1984a, 1985e, "Get information..." Nos. 1984b, 1985a, "Get the facts..." Nos. 1984c, 1985b, "Say no to drugs..." Nos. 1984d, 1985c, $2, $5, $10, "Protect yourself..." Nos. 1984e, 1985d, "Be compassionate..."

Perf. 13½x13

1988, Dec. 1 Litho. Wmk. 364

1984 A66 120c Strip of 5, #a.-e., on #289 18.50 18.50
1985 A66 120c Strip of 5, #a.-e., on #289A 18.50 18.50
1986 A66 $2 on #288 12.00 3.00
1987 A66 $5 on #289 14.00 7.50
1988 A66 $10 on #289A 16.00 12.00
Nos. 1984-1988 (5) 79.00 59.50

For surcharge, see No. 4176.

1988 Winter Olympics, Calgary
A106

Design: $3.50, Olympic rings.

1988, Dec. 1 *Perf. 14*

1989 A106 $7 Downhill skiing 11.00 11.00

Souvenir Sheet

1990 A106 $3.50 Sheet of 1 6.00 6.00

No. 1989 exists in souvenir sheet of 1. Value $40.

Christmas — A107

Paintings: No. 1991a, Virgin and Child Between St. George and St. Catherine, by Titian. b, Adoration of the Magi, by Titian.
No. 1992a, Holy Family, by Rubens. b, Adoration of the Shepherds, by Rubens.
$8, The Madonna, by Titian.

Perf. 14x13½, 13½x14

1988, Dec. 15 Litho.

1991 A107 $2 Pair, #a.-b. 7.00 7.00
1992 A107 $2 Pair, #a.-b. 7.00 7.00

Souvenir Sheet
Perf. 13½x14

1993 A107 $8 multicolored 17.00 17.00

Nos. 1991a-1991b, 1992a-1992b exist in souvenir sheets of 1.

Abolition of Slavery Type of 1985

1988, Dec. 16 Litho. *Perf. 14*
Designs as Before

1994 A93 25c brown & black .25 .25
1995 A93 60c magenta & black .50 .50
1996 A93 130c green & black 1.00 1.00
1997 A93 150c blue & black 1.25 1.25
Nos. 1994-1997 (4) 3.00 3.00

Nos. 1087, 1167, and 1200 Surcharged "SALUTING WINNERS / OLYMPIC GAMES / 1988"

Unwmk.

1989, Jan. 3 Litho. *Perf. 14*

1998 A91 $5.50 on 560c #1167 1.75 1.25
1999 A91 $9 on 320c #1200 2.25 2.25
2000 A91 $10.50 on 320c #1087 3.00 3.00
Nos. 1998-2000 (3) 7.00 6.50

Miniature Sheets

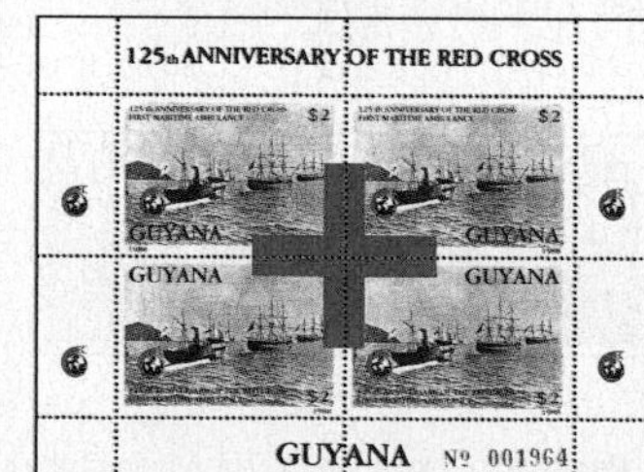

Red Cross, 125th Anniv. — A108

Designs: No. 2001, Henri Dunant, vert. No. 2002, First maritime ambulance. No. 2003, Red Cross hospital ship in African War. No. 2004, Red Cross air ambulance. No. 2005, Red Cross train.
Nos. 2001-2004 printed with red cross in center of sheet. Each stamp contains part of the red cross at the: a, LR. b, LL. c, UR. d, UL.

Perf. 13½x14, 14x13½

1989, Jan. 5 Litho.

2001 A108 $2 Sheet of 4, #a.-d. 10.00 10.00
2002 A108 $2 Sheet of 4, #a.-d. 10.00 10.00
2003 A108 $2 Sheet of 4, #a.-d. 10.00 10.00
2004 A108 $2 Sheet of 4, #a.-d. 10.00 10.00
Nos. 2001-2004 (4) 40.00 40.00

Souvenir Sheet
Perf. 14x13½

2005 A108 $7 Sheet of 1 11.00 11.00

Dated 1988.

Trains — A109

Designs: a, Hernalser sleeping carriage. b, 5 Forney locomotive. c, Austrian sleeping carriage. d, Pacific 231 locomotive.
$10, First Japanese imperial train.

1989, Jan. 5 Litho. *Perf. 14*

2006 A109 $2 Sheet of 4, #a.-d. 18.00 18.00

Souvenir Sheet

2007 A109 $10 multicolored 12.00 12.00

Nos. 2006a-2006d exist in souvenir sheets of 1. Value, each $3.75.
Dated 1988.

Naval Airship LZ 92, 1916 — A110

No. 2008: a, Astronaut on moon. b, Graf Zeppelin over San Francisco Bay, 1929. c, Testu-Brissy on horseback ascending in balloon, 1798.
No. 2009, Graf Zeppelin LZ 127.

1989, Jan. 26 *Perf. 14*

2007A A110 $2 black 3.00 3.00
2008 A110 $2 Strip of 3, #a.-c. 8.00 8.00

Souvenir Sheet

2009 A110 $2 Sheet of 1 10.00 6.00

Nos. 2007A, 2008b, 2009, Ferdinand von Zeppelin, 150th birth anniv. in 1988. No. 2008a, 1st moon landing, 20th anniv. in 1989. The inscriptions on Nos. 2007A and 2009 are in error. Dated 1988.

Mushrooms — A111

No. 2010: a, Cortinarius bolaris. b, Cortinarius laniger. c, Tricholoma sulphureum. d, Lepiota cristata.
No. 2011, Sarcoscypha coccinea, vert.

1989, Feb. 1 *Perf. 14x13½*

2010 A111 $2 Block of 4, #a.-d. 15.00 15.00

Souvenir Sheet
Perf. 13½x14

2011 A111 $5 Sheet of 1 11.00 11.00

Dated 1988.

Boy Scout Jamboree, Australia — A112

Design: $8, Scouts of different races.

1989, Feb. 10
2012 A112 $10 grn, black & yel 15.00 15.00

Souvenir Sheet
2013 A112 $8 Sheet of 1 15.00 15.00

Dated 1988. No. 2012 exists in souvenir sheet of 1.

1988 Summer Olympics, Seoul — A113

Emblem of South American Soccer Federation — A113a

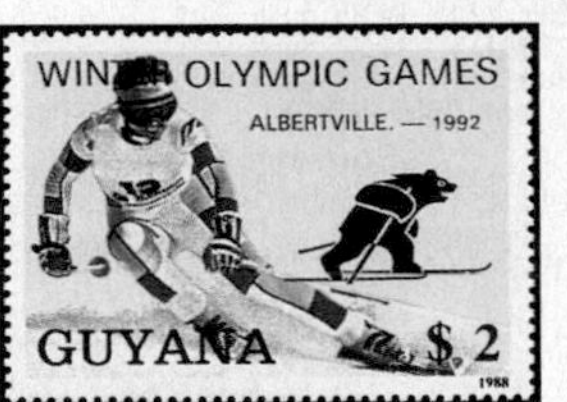

1992 Winter Olympics, Albertville — A113b

Designs: No. 2014, Florence Griffith-Joyner. No. 2015, Carl Lewis. No. 2016, Equestrian. No. 2017, Runners, horiz. No. 2018, City skyline, Olympic Rings, horiz. No. 2019, 1988 & 1992 Olympic mascots, horiz. No. 2022, Griffith-Joyner, Lewis, horiz. No. 2023, Cosmic Athlete by Dali, horiz.

1989, Feb. 15 Litho. *Perf. 14*
2014 A113 $2 multicolored 3.50 3.50
2015 A113 $2 multicolored 3.50 3.50
2016 A113 $2 multicolored 3.50 3.50
2017 A113 $2 multicolored 3.50 3.50
2018 A113 $2 multicolored 3.50 3.50
2019 A113 $2 multicolored 3.50 3.50
2020 A113a $2 multicolored 3.50 3.50
2021 A113b $2 multicolored —

Souvenir Sheets
2022 A113 $3.50 multicolored 15.00 15.00
2023 A113 $3.50 multicolored 15.00 15.00

No. 2023 exists with gold border and inscriptions. Nos. 2014-2020 inscribed 1988.

Nos. 1826, 1829 and 1831 Ovptd. "REPUBLIC DAY 1989" in Red

1989, Feb. 22 Litho. *Perf. 15*
2024 A99 $1.20 Block of 4, #a.-d. on #1826 4.50 4.50
2025 A99 $1.20 Block of 4, #a.-d., on #1829 4.50 4.50
2026 A101 $10 on #1831 7.50 7.50
Nos. 2024-2026 (3) 16.50 16.50

Nos. 1827a-1827d and 1830a-1830d Surcharged in Red

1989, Feb. 22
2027 A99 $5 Pair, #a.-b., on $3.20 #a., c. 7.50 7.50
2028 A99 $5 Pair, #a.-b., on $3.20 #b., d. 7.50 7.50
2028C A99 $5 Pair, #d.-e., on $3.30 #a., c. 7.50 7.50
2028F A99 $5 Pair, #g-h., on $3.30 #b., d. 7.50 7.50

Nos. 1461, 1822 Surcharged in Red

1989, Feb. 22 Litho. *Perf. 14*
2029 A96 $10 #a.-b. on #1461 10.00 10.00
2030 A96 $10 #a.-b. on #1822 10.00 10.00

No. 1188 Surcharged "EASTER"

1989, Mar. 22 *Perf. 14*
2031 A91 Sheet of 4 on #1100 5.00 5.00
a. 125c on 320c #1188 .50 .50
b. 250c on 320c #1188 1.00 1.00
c. 300c on 320c #1188 1.25 1.25
d. 350c on 320c #1188 1.50 1.50

No. 927 Surcharged

1989, Mar. Wmk. 364 *Perf. 14*
2032 A90 250c on 25c #927 6.00 1.25

Inscribed "1986."

No. 1197 Surcharged "RED CROSS / 1948 / 1988"

1989, Apr. Unwmk. *Perf. 14*
2033 A91 375c on 45c #1197 5.50 5.50
2034 A91 425c on 45c #1197 5.50 5.50

Guyana Red Cross, 40th anniv.

Nos. 1263 & 1252 Surcharged in Pairs

Surcharges read: a, "ALL FOR / HEALTH"; b, "HEALTH / FOR ALL".

1989, Apr. 3
2035 A91 250c on 75c #1263 (56), pair 8.00 8.00
2036 A91 675c on 720c #1252 (49), pair 10.00 10.00

For surcharge see No. 2052.

Nos. 1224-1225, 1254, 1272-1273 Overprinted or Surcharged

Overprint or Surcharges read: Nos. 2037a-2039a, "BOY SCOUTS / 1909 1989"; Nos. 2037b-2039b, "GIRL GUIDES / 1924 1989"; Nos. 2040-2041, "LADY BADEN POWELL / 1889-1989".

1989, Apr. 11
2037 A91 250c on 100c, pair, #a.-b. 5.00 5.00
2038 A91 $2.50 on 50c, pair, #a.-b. 5.00 5.00
2039 A91 300c Pair, #a.-b. 5.00 5.00
c. Pair, #d.-e., Prussian bl ovpt.
2040 A91 $25 on 280c #1272 7.00 7.00
a. Prussian blue overprint
2041 A91 $25 on 700c #1273 7.00 7.00
a. Prussian blue overprint
Nos. 2037-2041 (5) 29.00 29.00

Nos. 2037-2039, Boy Scouts in Guyana, 80th anniversary and Girl Guides, 65th anniversary. Nos. 2040-2041, Lady Baden Powell, birth centenary.

No. 1177 Surcharged "PHOTOGRAPHY / 1839-1989"

1989, Apr. 15
2042 A91 550c on 390c 7.00 7.00
2043 A91 650c on 390c, 2 bar obliterator 7.00 7.00
a. 6 bar obliterator 7.00 7.00
Nos. 2042-2043, 2043a (3) 21.00 21.00

Nos. 2042-2043 printed in sheets of 4 with alternating overprints.

No. 1263 Surcharged "I.L.O. / 1919-1989"

1989, May 2
2044 A91 300c on 75c #1263 12.00 3.00

Intl. Labor Organization, 70th anniversary.

Nos. 43, 87, 134-137, 279-280, 284-285, and 286A 288, 1827, 1830, and 2035-2036 Surcharged in Black or Blue

q

s

r

t

u

1989-92 *Perfs. as Before*
Watermarks and Printing Methods as Before

2045 A7(q) 80c on 6c #43 .60 .35
a. A7(u) 80c on 6c #43 .60 .35
2045B A28(r) 80c on 2c #134 —
2045C A28(r) 80c on 3c #135 —
2046 A28(q) $1 on 2c #134 .60 .35
a. A28(r) $1 on 2c #134 .60 .35
2047 A28(q) $2.05 on 3c #135 .60 .35
2048 A28(q) $2.55 on 5c #136 .60 .35
a. A28(r) $2.55 on 5c #136 .60 .35
2049 A28(q) $3.25 on 6c #137 .60 .40
a. A28(r) $3.25 on 6c #137 .60 .40
2050 A14(q) $5 on 6c #87 .60 .35
a. A14(s) $5 on 6c #87 .60 .35
b. A14(r) $5 on 6c #87 —
2051 A66(q) $6 on 5c #279
2052 A91 640c Pair, #2036 5.00 5.00
2053 A66(q) $6.40 on 10c #280 9.00 1.00
a. A66(u) $6.40 on 10c #280 6.00 .90
b. A66(r) $6.40 on 10c #280 6.00 .90
2054 Block of 5, #a.-e. on #1830 42.50 42.50
a.-d. A99(t) $6.40 on $3.30 #a.-d. 5.00 2.00
e. A100(t) $190 on $3.30 #e. 22.50 20.00
2054F A66(r) $7.65 on 35c #284 9.00 1.50
g. on 35c #284 —
2055 A66(u) $7.65 on 40c #285 8.25 1.50
2056 Block of 5, #a.-e. on #1827 42.50 42.50
a.-d. A99(t) $7.65 on $3.20 #a.-d. 5.00 2.00
e. A100(t) $225 on $3.20 #e. 22.50 20.00
2057 A66(q) $8.90 on 60c #286A 11.00 1.50
a. A66 $8.90 on 60c #286A 1.00 .60
2057B A66(q) $30 on 10c #280 1.00 .60
2057C A66(q) $35 on 35c #284 1.00 .60
2058 A66(r) $50 on $2 #288 (Bl) 22.00 11.00
2059 A66(r) $100 on $2 #288 32.00 24.00

Issued: Nos. 2045a, 2053-2053a, 2054F, 2055, 5/18; No. 2057, 5/26; Nos. 2058-2059, 6/5; Nos. 2045, 2049, 2046a, 2048a, 2049a, 6/15; Nos. 2050-2050a, 2051, 2052, 2054, 2056, 8/16; No. 2050b, 1992.

Nos. 2045a, 2053a, 2055, 2057a have no obliterator. New denominations are larger on Nos. 2045a, 2053a and 2057a. No. 2045a has no cent sign. Denomination on No. 2050b is above "X" obliterator.

Nos. 2054e, 2056b additionally overprinted "SPECIAL DELIVERY."

No. 1244 Surcharged "CARICOM / DAY"

Unwmk.

1989, June 26 Litho. *Perf. 14*
2064 A91 125c on 200c #1244, 2 bar obliterator 8.00 1.50
a. 6 bar obliterator 10.00 1.75

No. 280 Overprinted in Silver for 40th Birthday of Prince Charles

No. 2081 — Overprints read: a, "1948- / 1988." b, "H.R.H. / Prince / of Wales." c, "H.R.H / Prince / Charles." d, "40th / Birthday." e, "1948."

Perf. 14x13½

1989, Apr. Litho. Wmk. 364
2081 Sheet of 25, 4 #2081a, 8 #2081b, 6 #2081c, 5 #2081d, 2 #2081e — —
a.-e. A66 10c on #280, any single — —

No. 280 Ovptd. in Gold or Silver for Gold Medalists at 1988 Summer Olympics

Overprints read: Nos. 2082a, 2083a, "SEOUL / OLYMPICS." Nos. 2082b, 2083b, "Men's 800M / Ereng / Kenya." Nos. 2082c, 2083c, "KOREA." Nos. 2082d, 2083d, "Men's / Gymnastics / Artemov / USSR." Nos. 2082e, 2083e, "Men's / Swimming / Louganis / USA." Nos. 2082f, 2083f, "Woman's / Swimming / Otto / DDR." Nos. 2082g, 2083g, "Men's Fencing / Lamour / France." Nos. 2082h, 2083h, "Men's / Gymnastics / Lou / China." Nos. 2082i, 2083i, "Women's / Cycling / Knol / Holland." Nos. 2082j, 2083j, "Men's / Swimming / Szabo / Hungary." Nos. 2082k, 2083k, "1988." Nos. 2082l, 2083l, "Men's / Swimming / Nesty / Suriname." Nos. 2082m, 2083m, "Men's Boxing / Lewis / Canada." Nos. 2082n, 2083n, "Men's Javelin / Korjus / Finland." Nos. 2082o, 2083o, "Basketball / USA." Nos. 2082p, 2083p, "Men's / Equestrian / Klimke / W. Germany." Nos. 2082q, 2083q, "Men's Boxing / Park / Korea." Nos. 2082r, 2083r, "Women's / Marathon / Mota / Portugal." Nos. 2082s, 2083s, "Men's / Swimming / Suzuki / Japan." Nos. 2084a, 2085a, "Men's 100M / Lewis / USA." Nos. 2084b, 2085b, "Men's / Pole Vault / Bubka / USSR." Nos. 2084c, 2085c, "Women's / 100-200m / Joyner / USA." Nos. 2084d, 2085d, "Men's Pentathlon / Martinek / Hungary." Nos. 2084e, 2085e, "Men's Wrestling / Sako / Japan." Nos. 2084f, 2085f, "Men's Judo / Saito / Japan." Nos. 2084g, 2085g, "Women's 800M / Wodars / DDR." Nos. 2084h, 2085h, "Men's Boxing / Gross / W. Germany." Nos. 2084i, 2085i, "Men's Boxing / Maske / DDR." Nos. 2084j, 2085j, "Men's Boxing / Kim / Korea." Nos. 2084k, 2085k, "Woman's / Swimming / Evans / USA." Nos. 2084l, 2085l, "Soccer / USSR." Nos. 2084m, 2085m, "Woman's / Gymnastics / Silivas / Romania." Nos. 2084n, 2085n, "Men's Boxing / Mercer / USA." Nos. 2084o, 2085o, "Men's Marathon / Bordin / Italy." Nos. 2084p, 2085p, "Women's Tennis / Graf / W. Germany."

Perf. 14x13½

1989, Apr. Litho. Wmk. 364

Sheets of 25
2082 5 #a., 3 #c., #b., d.-s. 12.50 12.50
a.-s. A66 10c on #280, any single .45 .45
2083 5 #a., 3 #c., #b., d.-s. (S) 12.50 12.50
a.-s. A66 10c on #280, any single .45 .45
2084 #a.-p., 5 #2082a, 3 #2082c, #2082k 12.50 12.50
a.-p. A66 10c on #280, any single .45 .45
2085 #a.-p., 5 #2083a, 3 #2083c, #2083k (S) 12.50 12.50
a.-p. A66 10c on #280, any single .45 .45

Nos. 280 Ovptd. in Gold or Silver for Gold Medalists at 1988 Winter Olympics

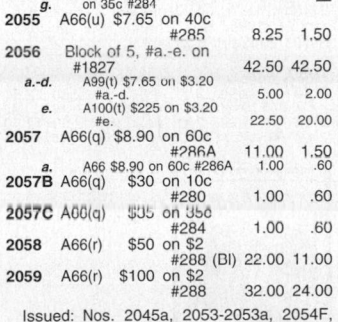

Overprints read: Nos. 2086a, 2087a, "Gold Medal / Winners." Nos. 2086b, 2087b, "Ice Hockey / USSR." Nos. 2086c, 2087c, "CALGARY / OLYMPICS." Nos. 2086d, 2087d, "Bobsled / Kipours-Kozlov / USSR." Nos. 2086e, 2087e, "Womens Skating / 1500-3000-5000M / Gennip / Netherlands." Nos. 2086f, 2087f, "Men's / Speed / Skating / 5000-10000M / Gustafson / Sweden." Nos. 2086g, 2087g, "Men's Figure / Skating / Boitano / USA." Nos. 2086h, 2087h, "Women's / 500M Skating / Blair / USA." Nos. 2086i, 2087i, "Women's / Figure Skating / Witt / DDR." Nos. 2086j, 2087j, "Men's Giant / Slalom / Tomba / Italy." Nos. 2086k, 2087k, "CANADA." Nos. 2086l, 2087l, "Men's Super / Giant Slalom / Picard / France." Nos. 2086m, 2087m, "Women's / Downhill Skiing / Kiehl / W. Germany." Nos. 2086n, 2087n, "Men's 50km Skiing Svan / Sweden." Nos. 2086o, 2087o, "Men's Nordic / Combined Skiing / Mueller-Pohl / Schwarz / W. Germany." Nos. 2086p, 2087p, "Women's / Giant Slalom / Schneider / Switzerland." Nos. 2086q, 2087q, "Women's / 5-km Skiing / Matikainen / Finland." Nos. 2086r, 2087r, "Men's Downhill / Alpine Skiing /

Zurbriggen / Switzerland." Nos. 2086s, 2087s, "Men's Ski / Jumping / Nykanen / Finland."

1989, Apr.

2086 4 #a., 3 #c., #b., d.-s., #2082k 12.50 12.50
a.-s. A66 10c on #280, any single .45 .45
2087 4 #a., 3 #c., #b., d.-s., #2083k (S) 12.50 12.50
a.-s. A66 10c on #280, any single .45 .45

No. 281 Ovptd. in Gold or Silver in Memory of Hirohito, Emperor of Japan

Overprints read: Nos. 2088a, 2089a, "Emperor / Hirohito." Nos. 2088b, 2089b, "Showa / Era." Nos. 2088c, 2089c, "Chrysanthemum / Dynasty." Nos. 2088d, 2089d, "Emperor / of Japan." Nos. 2088e, 2089e, "1901." Nos. 2088f, 2089f, "1989." Nos. 2088g, 2089g, "Emperor / Hirohito / 1901-1989."

1989, Apr.

2088 5 #a., 4 #c.-d., 9 #b., #e.-g. 12.50 12.50
a.-g. A66 15c on #281, any single .45 .45
2089 5 #a., 4 #c.-d., 9 #b., #e.-g. (S) 12.50 12.50
a.-g. A66 15c on #281, any single .45 .45

No. 280 Ovptd. in Gold or Silver for Enthronment of Akihito, Emperor of Japan

Overprints reads: Nos. 2090a, 2091a, "Honoring / His / Majesty." Nos. 2090b, 2091b, "Emperor / of / Japan." Nos. 2090c, 2091c, "1989." Nos. 2090d, 2091d, "HEISI / ERA."

1989, Apr.

2090 12 #a, 8 #b., 4 #c., #d. 12.50 12.50
a.-d. A66 10c on #280, any single .45 .45
2091 12 #a., 8 #b., 4 #c., #d. (S) 12.50 12.50
a.-d. A66 10c on #280, any single .45 .45

Overprint is 10mm long on Nos. 2090c, 2091c.

Nos. 280-281 and 283 Ovptd. with Emblems of Scouts, Rotary Intl., and Lions Intl. in Gold, Silver, Metallic Red, Metallic Green and Black

Overprints: Nos. 2092a, 2093a, 2094a, 2095a, 2096b, 2097b, 2098b, 2099b, 2100c, 2101c, 2102c, 2103c, Scouting emblem. Nos. 2092b, 2093b, 2094b, 2095b, 2096a, 2097a, 2098a, 2099a, 2100b, 2101b, 2102b, 2103b, Rotary emblem. Nos. 2092c, 2093c, 2094c, 2095c, 2096c, 2097c, 2098c, 2099c, 2100a, 2101a, 2102a, 2103a, Lions emblem. Nos. 2092d, 2093d, 2094d, 2095d, 2096d, 2097d, 2098d, 2099d, 2100d, 2101d, 2102d, 2103d, "1989." Nos. 2092e, 2093e, 2094e, 2095e, Large scouting emblem. Nos. 2096e, 2097e, 2098e, 2099e, Large Rotary emblem. Nos. 2100e, 2101e, 2102e, 2103e, Large Lions emblem.

1989, Apr.

2092 8 #a.-b., 6 #c., 2 #d., #e. 12.50 12.50
a.-e. A66 10c on #280, any single .45 .45
2093 8 #a.-b., 6 #c., 2 #d., #e. (S) 12.50 12.50
a.-e. A66 10c on #280, any single .45 .45
2094 8 #a.-b., 6 #c., 2 #d., #e. (R) 12.50 12.50
a.-e. A66 10c on #280, any single .45 .45
2095 8 #a.-b., 6 #c., 2 #d., #e. (Bk) 12.50 12.50
a.-e. A66 10c on #280, any single .45 .45
2096 8 #a.-b., 6 #c., 2 #d., #e. 12.50 12.50
a.-e. A66 15c on #281, any single .45 .45
2097 8 #a.-b., 6 #c., 2 #d., #e. (S) 12.50 12.50
a.-e. A66 15c on #281, any single .45 .45
2098 8 #a.-b., 6 #c., 2 #d., #e. (R) 12.50 12.50
a.-e. A66 15c on #281, any single .45 .45
2099 8 #a.-b., 6 #c., 2 #d., #e. (Gr) 12.50 12.50
a.-e. A66 15c on #281, any single .45 .45
2100 8 #a.-b., 6 #c., 2 #d., #e. 12.50 12.50
a.-e. A66 25c on #283, any single .45 .45
2101 8 #a.-b., 6 #c., 2 #d., #e. (S) 12.50 12.50
a.-e. A66 25c on #283, any single .45 .45
2102 8 #a.-b., 6 #c., 2 #d., #e. (R) 12.50 12.50
a.-e. A66 25c on #283, any single .45 .45
2103 8 #a.-b., 6 #c., 2 #d., #e. (Gr) 12.50 12.50
a.-e. A66 25c on #283, any single .45 .45

"1989" overprints are 7½mm long.

No. 280 Ovptd. in Gold or Silver for Halley's Comet

Overprints read: Nos. 2104a, 2105a, "Halley's / Comet." Nos. 2104b, 2105b, "Famous / Space Event." Nos. 2104c, 2105c, "Edmund / Halley / 1656-1742." Nos. 2104d, 2105d, "1910." Nos. 2104e, 2105e, "1986."

1989, Apr.

2104 11 #a., 6 #b., 4 #c., 2 #d.-e. 12.50 12.50
a.-e. A66 10c on #280, any single .45 .45
2105 11 #a., 6 #b., 4 #c., 2 #d.-e. (S) 12.50 12.50
a.-e. A66 10c on #280, any single .45 .45

No. 280 Ovptd. in Gold or Silver for Space Achievements

Overprints read: Nos. 2106a, 2107a, "Sputnik I / Oct. 4, 1957." Nos. 2106b, 2107b, "Explorer I / Jan. 31, 1958." Nos. 2106c, 2107c, "Sputnik II / Laika / Spacedog / Nov. 3, 1957." Nos. 2106d, 2107d, "Alan Shepard, Jr. / Mercury III / May 5, 1961." Nos. 2106e, 2107e, "Yuri Gagarin / Vostok I / April 12, 1961." Nos. 2106f, 2107f, "John Glenn / Mercury VI / Feb. 20, 1962." Nos. 2106g, 2107g, "Vostok III / Vostok IV / Aug. 12, 1962." Nos. 2106h, 2107h, "Grissom-Young / Gemini III / March 23, 1965." Nos. 2106i, 2107i, "Luna III / Oct. 4, 1959." Nos. 2106j, 2107j, "Edward H. White II / Gemini IV / June 3, 1965." Nos. 2106k, 2107k, "V. Tereshkova / First Woman / in Space / June 16-19, 1963." Nos. 2106 l, 2107 l, "Surveyor I / June 2, 1966." Nos. 2106m, 2107m, "Space / Achievements." Nos. 2106n, 2107n, "Voskod I / First 3 Man Crew / Oct. 12-13, 1964." Nos. 2106o, 2107o, "Apollo I / Jan. 27, 1967." Nos. 2106p, 2107p, "Alexei A. Leonov / First Walk in Space / March 18-19, 1965." Nos. 2106q, 2107q, "Apollo VIII / Dec. 21-27, 1968." Nos. 2106r, 2107r, "V. Komarov / Soyuz I / April 24, 1967." Nos. 2106s, 2107s, "Apollo XI / First Man on Moon / July 20, 1969." Nos. 2106t, 2107t, "Lunokhod I / Dec. 10, 1970." Nos. 2106u, 2107u, "Apollo XIII / April 11-17, / 1970." Nos. 2106v, 2107v, "Soyuz XI / June 30, 1971." Nos. 2106w, 2107w, "Viking I / July 20, 1976." Nos. 2106x, 2107x, "Vega I / March 6, 1986." Nos. 2106y, 2107y, "Columbia Sts-1 / April 12-14, / 1981."

1989, Apr.

2106 #a.-y. 12.50 12.50
a.-y. A66 10c on #280, any single .45 .45
2107 #a.-y. (S) 12.50 12.50
a.-y. A66 10c on #280, any single .45 .45

No. 280 Ovptd. in Gold or Silver

Overprints read: Nos. 2108a, 2109a, "1969- / 1989." Nos. 2108b, 2109b, "Apollo XI." Nos. 2108c, 2109c, "First Man / on Moon." Nos. 2108d, 2109d, "USA." Nos. 2108e, 2109e, "Neil A. / Armstrong." Nos. 2108f, 2109f, "Col. Edwin E. / Aldrin, Jr." Nos. 2108g, 2109g, "Lt. Col. / Michael / Collins."

1989, Apr.

2108 5 #a, 7 b, 4 c, 6 d, e-g 12.50 12.50
a.-g. A66 10c on #280, any single .45 .45
2109 5 #a, 7 b, 4 c, 6 d, e-g (S) 12.50 12.50
a.-g. A66 10c on #280, any single .45 .45

Moon Landing, 20th anniv.

No. 281 Ovptd. in Gold or Silver for Space Shuttle Program

Overprints read: Nos. 2110a, 2111a, "Enterprise / Aug. 12, 1977." Nos. 2110b, 2111b, "Columbia / April 12, 1981." Nos. 2110c, 2111c, "Space / Shuttles." Nos. 2110d, 2111d, "Discovery / Aug. 30, 1984." Nos. 2110e, 2111e, "Atlantis / Oct. 3, 1985." Nos. 2110f, 2111f, "Challenger / Heroes." Nos. 2110g, 2111g, "Resnik / McAuliffe / Jarvis." Nos. 2110h, 2111h, "In Memoriam / Challenger / Jan. 28, 1986." Nos. 2110i, 2111i, "Onizuka / Smith / McNair / Scobee."

1989, Apr.

2110 4 #a.-e., 2 #f., #g.-i. 12.50 12.50
a.-i. A66 15c on #281, any single .45 .45
2111 4 #a.-e., 2 #f., #g.-i. (S) 12.50 12.50
a.-i. A66 15c on #281, any single .45 .45

Butterflies — A115

80c, Stalachtis calliope. $2.25, Morpho rhetenor. $5, Agrias claudia. $6.40, Marpesia marcella. $7.65, Papilio zagreus. $8.90, Chorinea faunus. $25, Cepheuptychia cephus. $100, Nessaea regina.

1989, Sept. 7 Litho. *Perf. 14*

2208 A115 80c multicolored .50 .25
2209 A115 $2.25 multicolored .60 .25
2210 A115 $5 multicolored .75 .40
2211 A115 $6.40 multicolored .85 .70
2212 A115 $7.65 multicolored 1.00 .90
2213 A115 $8.90 multicolored 1.25 1.10
2214 A115 $25 multicolored 4.00 3.00
2215 A115 $100 multicolored 13.50 12.50
Nos. 2208-2215 (8) 22.45 19.10

See Nos. E16-E17. For overprints see Nos. 2251-2254, 2256-2257, 2260-2261, 2283-2290, E19-E22, E24, E26-E27, E31.

A116

Women in Space, 25th Anniv. (in 1988): $6.40, Kathryn Sullivan, 1st US woman to walk in space. $12.80, Svetlana Savitskaya, 1st Soviet woman to walk in space. $15.30, Judy Resnik & Christa McAuliffe, astronauts killed in Challenger explosion. $100, Sally Ride, 1st US woman astronaut.

1989, Nov. 8

2216 A116 $6.40 multicolored 1.00 .25
2217 A116 $12.80 multicolored 1.75 1.25
2218 A116 $15.30 multicolored 2.00 1.50
2219 A116 $100 multicolored 11.50 11.50
Nos. 2216-2219 (4) 16.25 14.50

See No. E18. For overprints see Nos. 2255, 2258-2259, 2262, E23, E25, E28, E32.

1990 World Cup Soccer Championships, Italy — A117

Various soccer players: No. 2221, Yellow shirt, vert. No. 2222, Goalie. No. 2223, Green shirt, vert.

No. 2224, Championships emblem, vert.

Perf. 14x13½, 13½x14

1989, Nov. 20

2220 A117 $2.55 shown 5.00 5.00
2221 A117 $2.55 multi 5.00 5.00
2222 A117 $2.55 multi 5.00 5.00
2223 A117 $2.55 multi 5.00 5.00
Nos. 2220-2223 (4) 20.00 20.00

Souvenir Sheet

2224 A117 $20 multi 17.50 17.50

Nos. 2220-2223 exist in souvenir sheets of 1.

For surcharges see Nos. 2263-2267.

No. 134-136 Surcharged "AHMADIYYA / CENTENARY / 1889-1989"

Perf. 13x13½

1989, Nov. 22 Litho. Wmk. 364

2225 A28 80c on 2c #134 4.50 .60
2226 A28 $6.40 on 3c #135 13.50 5.50
2227 A28 $8.90 on 5c #136 15.00 8.00
Nos. 2225-2227 (3) 33.00 14.10

1992 Summer Olympics, Barcelona
A118

No. 2229, Boxing, horiz. No. 2230, Chariot racing, horiz. No. 2231, Javelin, horiz. No. 2232, Running, horiz. No. 2233, Wrestling.

No. 2234, Running, horiz., diff. No. 2235, Columbus Walk by Picasso.

1989, Dec. 5 *Perf. 13½x14, 14x13½*

2228 A118 $2.55 shown 4.50 4.50
2229 A118 $2.55 multicolored 4.50 4.50
2230 A118 $2.55 multicolored 4.50 4.50
2231 A118 $2.55 multicolored 4.50 4.50
2232 A118 $2.55 multicolored 4.50 4.50
2233 A118 $2.55 multicolored 4.50 4.50
Nos. 2228-2233 (6) 24.00 24.00

Souvenir Sheets

2234 A118 $10 multicolored 15.00 15.00
2235 A118 $10 multicolored 15.00 15.00
Nos. 2234-2235 (2) 30.00 30.00

Nos. 2228-2233 exist in souvenir sheets of 1.

Christmas — A119

Paintings: No. 2236, Child Declaring in Favor of His Mother, by Titian. No. 2237, The Sacred Family, by Rubens. No. 2238, Saint Anne, the Virgin and Child, by Durer. No. 2239, Madonna Enthroned, Surrounded by Saints, by Rubens. $20, Saint Ildefonso, by Rubens.

1989, Dec. 26 *Perf. 14x13½, 13½x14*

2236 A119 $2.55 multi 4.50 4.50
2237 A119 $2.55 multi, vert. 4.50 4.50
2238 A119 $2.55 multi, vert. 4.50 4.50
2239 A119 $2.55 multi, vert. 4.50 4.50
Nos. 2236-2239 (4) 16.00 16.00

Souvenir Sheet

2240 A119 $20 multi, vert. 20.00 20.00

Nos. 2236-2239 exist in souvenir sheets of 1.

Harpy Eagle — A120

Channel-billed Toucan — A121

$2.25, Eagle's head. $5, Eagle with prey. $8.90, Eagle facing right. $25, Blue & yellow macaw. $30, Eagle facing left. $50, Wattled jacana, horiz. $60, Hoatzin, horiz.

No. 2249, Great kiskadee, horiz. No. 2250, Amazon kingfisher, horiz.

1990, Jan. 23 Litho. *Perf. 14*

2241 A120 $2.25 multicolored 1.00 .50
2242 A120 $5 multicolored 1.25 .75
2243 A120 $8.90 multicolored 1.50 1.00
2244 A121 $15 shown 1.00 .90
2245 A121 $25 multicolored 1.50 1.00
2246 A120 $30 multicolored 3.75 3.50
2247 A121 $50 multicolored 2.50 2.25
2248 A121 $60 multicolored 3.00 2.75
Nos. 2241-2248 (8) 15.50 12.65

Souvenir Sheets

2249 A121 $100 multicolored 5.25 5.25
2250 A121 $100 multicolored 5.25 5.25

Nos. 2241-2243, 2246, World Wildlife Fund.

Nos. 2208-2184 Ovptd. in Silver

Overprint includes Rotary Emblem and "ROTARY INTERNATIONAL 1905-1990" on 2 or 3 Lines.

1990, Mar. 15

2251	A115	80c on #2208	
2252	A115	$2.25 on #2209	
2253	A115	$5 on #2210	
2254	A115	$6.40 on #2211	
2255	A116	$6.40 on #2216	
2256	A115	$7.65 on #2212	
2257	A115	$8.90 on #2213	
2258	A116	$12.80 on #2217	
2259	A116	$15.30 on #2218	
2260	A115	$25 on #2214	
2261	A115	$100 on #2215	
2262	A116	$100 on #2219	
	Nos. 2251-2262 (12)		37.50

Nos. 2220-2224 Surcharged

Surcharges read: Nos. 2263-2265, 2267, "GERMANY / CHAMPION"; No. 2266, "GERMANY / CHAMPION / ARGENTINA / SUB-CHAMPION"

1990 ***Perfs. as Before***

2263	A117	$75 on #2220	
2264	A117	$75 on #2221	
2265	A117	$75 on #2222	
2266	A117	$75 on #2223	
	Nos. 2263-2266 (4)		10.00

Souvenir Sheet

2267	A117	$225 on #2224	8.00

Nos. 2263-2266 exist in souvenir sheets of 1.

Miniature Sheets

Penny Black, 150th Anniv., 500th Anniv. of Thurn & Taxis Postal Service — A122

No. 2268: a, Banghy Post runner, 1832. b, Penny Black, Sir Rowland Hill. c, Dutch mail ship. d, Paddle steamer Monarch, 1830. e, Paddle steamer Hindostan, 1842. f, Mail steamer Chusan. g, Sailing ship Madagascar, 1853. h, Paddle steamer Orinoco, 1855. i, Packet Orpheus, 1835.

No. 2269: a, Imperial postal messenger. b, Swiss messenger, 1499. c, River messenger, 15th century. d, Russian courier, Middle Ages. e, Oldenburg postilions, 1820. f, Indian mail coach, 1829. g, Baden mail coach postilions, 1820. h, Pony Express, 1860. i, Camel rider.

No. 2270: a, Mail coach, 1840. b, Danish Ball Post, 1815. c, Australian Bush mailman, 1838. d, Japanese postmen, 1870. e, Mail cart, 1857. f, Russian mail troika. g, Wells, Fargo Overland Express. h, Phantoms of the Night, 1853. i, Cobb & Co. coach, Australia.

No. 2271: a, Postilions, 1850. b, Mounted postilion, Holland. c, Paddle steamer Arctic, 1850. d, Peruvian swimming couriers. e, First London post box, 1855. f, Indian mail cart, 1870. g, Balloon post, 1870. h, Bath Mail Coach. i, Postrider, 1837.

No. 2272: a, Northeastern Railway post office. b, Traveling post office, 1838. c, American Express. d, Graf Zeppelin. e, Columbia Post airplane, 1925. f, Calcutta flying boat. g, Junkers JU-52/3M mail plane. h, Douglas M2 mail plane. i, US air mail service, DH-4.

No. 2273: a, First Atlantic Airways. b, Morris post office van, 1931. c, Swiss post-passenger bus. d, Westland-Sikorsky S51 helicopter mail flight. e, Union Pacific Railway. f, Boeing Model 314 flying boat, Yankee Clipper. g, Boeing 747. h, Concorde. i, Apollo 11, US #C76.

No. 2274, Mounted postilion. No. 2275, Thurn & Taxis #7. No. 2276, Thurn & Taxis #45.

1990, May 3

2268	A122	$15.30 Sheet of 9, #a.-i.	9.00	9.00
2269	A122	$15.30 Sheet of 9, #a.-i.	9.00	9.00
2270	A122	$15.30 Sheet of 9, #a.-i.	9.00	9.00
2271	A122	$17.80 Sheet of 9, #a.-i.	10.00	10.00
2272	A122	$20 Sheet of 9, #a.-i.	11.00	11.00
2273	A122	$20 Sheet of 9, #a.-i.	11.00	11.00
	Nos. 2268-2273 (6)		59.00	59.00

Souvenir Sheets

2274	A122	$150 multi	7.00	7.00
2275	A122	$150 multi	7.00	7.00
2276	A122	$150 multi	7.00	7.00

For overprint see No. 2551.

Nos. 1028, 1032, 1055, 1085, 1107 Surcharged

Surcharge reads "ROTARY / DISTRICT 405 / 9th CONFERENCE / MAY 1990 / GEORGETOWN".

Unwmk.

1990, May 8 **Litho.** ***Perf. 14***

Design A91

Plate Numbers in Parentheses

2277	80c on 55c #1032 (9)	
2278	80c on 55c #1085 (49)	
2279	80c on 55c #1107 (64)	
2280	$6.40 on 130c #1028 (6)	
2281	$6.40 on 130c #1055 (25)	
2282	$7.65 on 130c #1055 (25)	
	Nos. 2277-2282 (6)	10.00

Nos. 2208-2215 Overprinted

1990, June 8 **Litho.** ***Perf. 14***

2283	A115	80c on #2208	2.00	.50
2284	A115	$2.25 on #2209	2.25	.60
2285	A115	$5 on #2210	2.75	.70
2286	A115	$6.40 on #2211	3.00	.75
2287	A115	$7.65 on #2212	3.25	.90
2288	A115	$8.90 on #2213	3.25	1.00
2289	A115	$25 on #2214	9.00	6.50
2290	A115	$100 on #2215	20.00	20.00
	Nos. 2283-2290 (8)		45.50	30.95

See Nos. E26-E27.

Locomotives — A123

No. 2291, Class 3F. No. 2292, Class A4. No. 2293, Liner Class A34. No. 2294, Pacific Class. No. 2295, Grange Class.

No. 2296, Castle Class, vert. No. 2297, Southern Railway.

1990, July 15 ***Perf. 14x13½***

2291	A123	$2.55 multi	3.00	3.00
2292	A123	$2.55 multi	3.00	3.00
2293	A123	$2.55 multi	3.00	3.00
2294	A123	$2.55 multi	3.00	3.00
2295	A123	$2.55 multi	3.00	3.00
	Nos. 2291-2295 (5)		13.50	

Souvenir Sheets

Perf. 13½x14, 14x13½

2296	A123	$20 multi	12.50	12.50
2297	A123	$20 multi	12.50	12.50
	Nos. 2296-2297 (2)		22.50	

Still Life with Guitar, by Picasso — A124

Paintings: No. 2299, Horseman, by Velazquez. No. 2300, Sunflowers, by Van Gogh, vert. No. 2301, Man Wearing Striped Shirt, by Miro, vert. No. 2302, Franz von Taxis, by Durer, vert. No. 2303, Virgin and Child, by Titian, vert. No. 2304, Presentation of Marie de Medici, by Rubens, vert.

Perf. 14x13½, 13½x14

1990, Aug. 1 **Litho.**

2298	A124	$2.55 multicolored	3.00	3.00
2299	A124	$2.55 multicolored	3.00	3.00
2300	A124	$2.55 multicolored	3.00	3.00
2301	A124	$2.55 multicolored	3.00	3.00
2302	A124	$2.55 multicolored	3.00	3.00
	Nos. 2298-2302 (5)		11.50	

Souvenir Sheets

2303	A124	$20 multicolored	12.50	12.50
2304	A124	$20 multicolored	12.50	12.50
	Nos. 2303-2304 (2)		18.00	

Postal System of Thurn and Taxis, 500th anniv. (No. 2302). Titian, 500th birth anniv. (No. 2303). Rubens, 350th death anniv. (No. 2304).

Birds — A125

Designs: 80c, Guiana partridge, horiz. $2.55, Collared trogon. $3.25, Derby aracari. $5, Black-necked aracari. $5.10, Green aracari. $5.80, Ivory-billed aracari. $6.40, Guiana toucanet. $6.50, Sulphur-breasted toucan. $7.55, Red-billed toucan. $7.65, Toco toucan. $8.25, Natterers toucanet. $8.90, Welcome trogon. $9.75, Doubtful trogon. $11.40, Banded aracari. $12.65, Golden-headed train bearer. $12.80, Rufus-breasted hermit. $13.90, Band-tail barbthroat. $15.30, White-tipped sickle bill. $17.80, Black jacobin. $19.20, Fiery topaz. $22.95, Tufted coquette. $26.70, Ecuadorian pied-tail. $30, Quetzal. $50, Green-crowned brilliant. $100, Emerald-chinned hummingbird. $190, Lazuline sabre-wing. $225, Berylline hummingbird.

1990, Sept. 12 **Litho.** ***Perf. 14***

2305	A125	80c multi	.25	.25
2306	A125	$2.55 multi	.25	.25
2307	A125	$3.25 multi	.25	.25
2308	A125	$5 multi	.25	.25
2309	A125	$5.10 multi	.25	.25
2310	A125	$5.80 multi	.25	.25
2311	A125	$6.40 multi	.25	.25
2312	A125	$6.50 multi	.25	.25
2313	A125	$7.55 multi	.35	.35
2314	A125	$7.65 multi	.45	.45
2315	A125	$8.25 multi	.55	.55
2316	A125	$8.90 multi	.65	.65
2317	A125	$9.75 multi	.65	.65
2318	A125	$11.40 multi	.70	.70
2319	A125	$12.65 multi	.75	.75
2320	A125	$12.80 multi	.80	.80
2321	A125	$13.90 multi	.90	.90
2322	A125	$15.30 multi	1.10	1.10
2323	A125	$17.80 multi	1.25	1.25
2324	A125	$19.20 multi	1.40	1.40
2325	A125	$22.95 multi	1.60	1.60
2326	A125	$26.70 multi	1.90	1.90
2327	A125	$30 multi	2.00	2.00
2328	A125	$50 multi	3.25	3.25
2329	A125	$100 multi	6.00	6.00
2330	A125	$190 multi	11.50	11.50
2331	A125	$225 multi	14.00	14.00
	Nos. 2305-2331 (27)		51.80	51.80

For surcharge, see No. 4020M.

Butterflies — A126

Designs: 80c, Melinaea idae. $2.55, Rhetus dysonii. $5, Actinote anteas. $6.40, Heliconius tales. $7.65, Thecla telemus. $8.90, Theope eudocia. $50, Heliconius vicini. $100, Amarynthis meneria.

No. 2340, vert.: a, Thecla falerina. b, Pheles heliconides. c, Echenais leucocyana. d, Heliconius xanthocles. e, Mesopthalma idotea. f, Parides aeneas. g, Heliconius numata. h, Thecla critola. i, Themone pais. j, Nymula agle. k, Adelpha cocala. l, Anaea eribotes. m, Prepona demophon. n, Selenophanes cassiope. o, Consul hippona. p, Antirrhaea avernus.

No. 2341, vert.: a, Thecla telemus. b, Thyridia confusa. c, Heliconius burneyi. d, Parides lysander. e, Eunica orphise. f, Adelpha melona. g, Morpho menelaus. h, Nymula phylleus. i, Stalachtis phlegia. j, Theope barea. k, Morpho perseus. l, Lycorea ceres. m, Archonias bellona. n, Caerois chorinaeus. o, Vila azeca. p, Nessaea batesii.

No. 2342: a, Heliconius silvana. b, Eunica alcmena. c, Mechanitis polymnia. d, Mesosemia ephyne. e, Thecla erema. f, Callizona acesta. g, Stalachtis phaedusa. h, Battus belus. i, Nymula phliasus. j, Parides childrenae. k, Stalachtis euterpe. l, Dysmathia portia. m, Tithorea hermias. n, Prepona pheridamas. o, Dismorphia fortunata. p, Hamadryas amphinome.

No. 2343. a, Heliconius vetustus. b, Mesosemia eumene. c, Parides phosphorus. d, Polystichtis emylius. e, Xanthocleis aedesia. f, Doxocopa agathina. g, Adelpha plesaure. h, Heliconius wallacei. i, Notheme eumeus. j, Melinaea mediatrix. k, Theritas coronata. l, Dismorphia orise. m, Phyciodes ianthe. n, Morpho aega. o, Zaretis isidora. p, Pierella lena.

No. 2344, Heliconius aoede. No. 2345, Phyciodes clio, horiz. No. 2346, Nymphidium caricae. No. 2347, Thecla hemon.

1990, Sept. 26 **Litho.** ***Perf. 14***

2332	A126	80c multicolored	.85	.85
2333	A126	$2.55 multicolored	.85	.85
2334	A126	$5 multicolored	.85	.85
2335	A126	$6.40 multicolored	.85	.85
2336	A126	$7.65 multicolored	.85	.85
2337	A126	$8.90 multicolored	1.10	1.10
2338	A126	$50 multicolored	4.50	4.50
2339	A126	$100 multicolored	9.50	9.50
	Nos. 2332-2339 (8)		19.35	19.35

Miniature Sheets

2340	A126	$10 Sheet of 16, #a.-p.	16.00	16.00
2341	A126	$10 Sheet of 16, #a.-p.	16.00	16.00
2342	A126	$10 Sheet of 16, #a.-p.	16.00	16.00
2343	A126	$10 Sheet of 16, #a.-p.	16.00	16.00

Souvenir Sheets

2344	A126	$150 multicolored	10.00	10.00
2345	A126	$150 multicolored	10.00	10.00
2346	A126	$190 multicolored	15.00	15.00
2347	A126	$190 multicolored	15.00	15.00

For surcharges see Nos. 2415-2425, 2596-2606.

Mushrooms A127

Designs: No. 2348, Oudemanseilla mucida. No. 2349, Pholiota squarosa. No. 2350, Coprinus comatus. No. 2351, Anellaria semi-ovaja. $20, Phallus impudicus.

1990, Oct. 12

2348	A127	$2.55 multicolored	
2349	A127	$2.55 multicolored	
2350	A127	$2.55 multicolored	
2351	A127	$2.55 multicolored	
	Nos. 2348-2351 (4)		14.00

Souvenir Sheet

2352	A127	$20 multicolored	14.00

Sailing Ships — A128

No. 2353, Brig century. No. 2354, Dutch marine ship. No. 2355, Galleon, 1588. No. 2356, Warship, 16th cent. No. 2357, Hulk, 17th cent.

No. 2358, Dutch ships, 16th-17th cent.

1990, Oct. 12

2353	A128	$2.55 multicolored
2354	A128	$2.55 multicolored
2355	A128	$2.55 multicolored
2356	A128	$2.55 multicolored
2357	A128	$2.55 multicolored

Nos. 2353-2357 (5) 13.00

Souvenir Sheet

2358 A128 $20 multicolored 13.00

No. 2358 printed in continuous design. Discovery of America, 500th anniv. (in 1992).

Flora — A129

Orchids: $7.65, Vanilla inodora. $8.90, Epidendrum ibaguense. No. 858, Maxillaria parkeri. $15.30, Epidendrum nocturnum. $17.80, Catasetum discolor. $20, Scuticaria hadwenii. $25, Epidendrum fragrans. $100, Epistephium parviflorum.

No. 2367: a, Dichea muricata. b, Octomeria erosilabia. c, Spiranthes orchiodes. d, Brassavola nodosa. e, Epidendrum rigidum. f, Brassia caudata. g, Pleurothallis diffusa. h, Aspasia variegata. i, Stenia pallida. j, Cyrtopodium punctatum. k, Cattleya deckeri. l, Cryptarrhena lunata. m, Cattleya violacea. n, Caularthron bicornutum. o, Oncidium carthagenense. p, Galeandra devoniana.

No. 2368: a, Bifrenaria aurantiaca. b, Epidendrum ciliare. c, Dichaea picta. d, Scaphyglottis violacea. e, Cattleya percivaliana. f, Map of Guyana (no flower). g, Epidendrum difforme. h, Eulophia maculata. i, Spiranthes tenuis. j, Peristeria guttata. k, Pleurothallis pruinosa. l, Cleistes rosea. m, Maxillaria variabilis. n, Brassavola cucullata. o, Epidendrum moyobambae. p, Oncidium orthostates.

No. 2369: a, Brassavola martiana. b, Paphinia cristata. c, Aganisia pulchella. d, Oncidium lanceanum. e, Lockhartia imbricata. f, Caularthron bilamellatum. g, Oncidium nanum. h, Pleurothallis ovalifolia. i, Galeandra dives. j, Cycnoches loddigesii. k, Ada aurantiaca. l, Catasetum barbatum. m, Palmorchis pubescens. n, Epidendrum anceps. o, Hunteya meleagris. p, Sobralia sessilis.

No. 2370: a, Maxillaria camaridii. b, Vanilla pompona. c, Stanhopea grandiflora. d, Oncidium pusillum. e, Polycycnis vittata. f, Cattleya lawrenceana. g, Menadenium labiosum. h, Rodriguezia secunda. i, Mormodes buccinator. j, Otostylis brachystalix. k, Maxillaria discolor. l, Liparis elata. m, Gongora maculata. n, Koellensteinia graminea. o, Rudolfiella aurantiaca. p, Scuticaria steelei.

Flowering Trees: No. 2371: a, Cochlospermum vitifolium. b, Eugenia malaccensis. c, Plumiera rubra. d, Erythrina glauca. e, Spathodea campanulata. f, Jacaranda filicifolia. g, Samanea saman. h, Cassia fistula. i, Abutilon integerrimum. j, Lagerstroemia speciosa. k, Tabebuia serratifolia. l, Guaiacum officinale. m, Solanum macranthum. n, Peltophorum roxburghii. o, Bauhinia variegata. p, Plumiera alba.

Flowering Vines: No. 2372: a, Gloriosa rothschildiana. b, Pseudocalymma alliaceum. c, Callichlamys latifolia. d, Distictis riversii. e, Maurandya barclaiana. f, Beaumontia fragrans. g, Phaseolus caracalla. h, Mandevilla splendens. i, Solandra longiflora. j, Passiflora coccinea. k, Allamanda cathartica. l, Bauhinia galpini. m, Verbena maritima. n, Mandevilla suaveolens. o, Phryganocydia corymbosa. p, Jasminum sambac.

No. 2373, Galeandra devoniana. No. 2374, Delonix regia. No. 2375, Hexisea bidentata. No. 2376, Lecythis ollaria. No. 2377, Ionopsis utricularioides.

1990, Oct. 16 Litho. *Perf. 14*

2359 A129 $7.65 multicolored .40 .40
2360 A129 $8.90 multicolored .55 .55
2361 A129 $12.80 multicolored .85 .85
2362 A129 $15.30 multicolored .90 .90
2363 A129 $17.80 multicolored 1.00 1.00
2364 A129 $20 multicolored 1.25 1.25
2365 A129 $25 multicolored 1.50 1.50
2366 A129 $100 multicolored 6.50 6.50
Nos. 2359-2366 (8) 12.95 12.95

Miniature Sheets

2367 A129 $10 Sheet of 16, #a.-p. 8.00 8.00
2368 A129 $10 Sheet of 16, #a.-p. 8.00 8.00
2369 A129 $12.80 Sheet of 16, #a.-p. 12.00 12.00
2370 A129 $12.80 Sheet of 16, #a.-p. 12.00 12.00
2371 A129 $12.80 Sheet of 16, #a.-p. 12.00 12.00
2372 A129 $12.80 Sheet of 16, #a.-p. 12.00 12.00
Nos. 2367-2372 (6) 64.00 64.00

Souvenir Sheets

2373 A129 $150 multicolored 9.00 9.00
2374 A129 $150 multicolored 9.00 9.00
2375 A129 $150 multicolored 9.00 9.00
2376 A129 $150 multicolored 9.00 9.00
2377 A129 $190 multicolored 11.00 11.00
Nos. 2373-2377 (5) 47.00 47.00

Nos. 2370-2375 are horiz. For surcharges see Nos. 2487A-2487B, 2593-2595, 4020N, 4119, 4120, 4121, 4178, 4179, 4181, 4181Q, 4202.

Souvenir Sheet

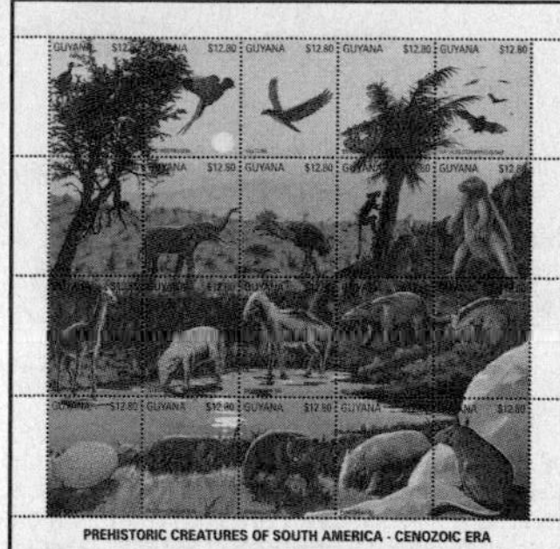

Cenozoic Era Wildlife — A130

Designs: a, Palaelodus. b, Archaeotrogon. c, Vulture. d, Bradyrus tridactylus. e, Natalus stramineus bat. f, Cebidae. g, Cuvieronius. h, Phororhacos. i, Smilodectes. j, Megatherium. k, Titanotylopus. l, Teleoceras. m, Macrauchenia. n, Mylodon. o, Smilodon. p, Glyptodon. q, Protohydrocherus. r, Archaeohyrax. s, Pyrotherium. t, Platypittamys.

1990, Nov. 6

2378 A130 $12.80 Sheet of 20, #a.-t. 15.00 15.00

Miniature Sheets

Endangered Wildlife — A131

No. 2379: a, Ivory-billed woodpecker. b, Cauca guan. c, Sun conure. d, Quetzal. e, Long-wattled umbrellabird. f, Banded cotinga. g, Blue-chested parakeet. h, Rufous-bellied chachalaca. i, Yellow-faced amazon. j, Toucan barbet. k, Red siskin. l, Cock-of-the-rock. m, Hyacinth macaw. n, Yellow cardinal. o, Bare-necked umbrellabird. p, Saffron toucanette. q, Red-billed curassow. r, Spectacled parrotlet. s, Lovely cotinga. t, Black-breasted gnateater.

No. 2380: a, Swallow-tailed kite. b, Hoatzin. c, Ruby topaz hummingbird. d, Black vulture. e, Rufous-tailed jacamar. f, Scarlet macaw. g, Rose-breasted thrush tanager. h, Toco toucan. i, Bearded bellbird. j, Blue-crowned motmot. k, Green oropendola. l, Pompadour cotinga. m, Vermilion flycatcher. n, Blue and yellow macaw. o, White-barred piculet. p, Great razor-billed curassow. q, Ruddy quail-dove. r, Paradise tanager. s, Anhinga. t, Greater flamingo.

No. 2381: a, Harpy eagle. b, Andean condor. c, Amazonian umbrellabird. d, Spider monkeys. e, Hyacinth macaw, diff. f, Red siskin, diff. g, Toucan barbet, diff. h, Three-toed sloth. i, Guanaco. j, Spectacled bear. k, White-lipped peccary. l, Maned wolf. m, Jaguar. n, Spectacled caiman. o, Giant armadillo. p, Giant anteater. q, South American river otter. r, Yapok. s, Central American river turtle. t, Cauca guan, diff.

Perf. 14x13½, 13½x14

1990, Nov. 6 Litho.

2379 A131 $12.80 Sheet of 20, #a.-t. 17.00 17.00
2380 A131 $12.80 Sheet of 20, #a.-t. 17.00 17.00
2381 A131 $12.80 Sheet of 20, #a.-t. 17.00 17.00

Nos. 2381a-2381t are horiz. No. 2380s incorrectly inscribed Anhigna. See Nos. E29-E30.

Numbers have been reserved for additional values in this set.

Independence, 25th Anniv. — A132

1991, June 25 Litho. *Imperf.*

2389 A132 $225 multicolored 9.00 9.00

Miniature Sheets

Olympic Gold Medal Winners — A133

No. 2390: a, Ramon Fonst. b, Lucien Gaudin. c, Ole A. Lilloe-Olsen. d, Morris Fisher. e, Ray C. Ewry. f, Hubert Van Innes. g, Alvin Kraenzlein. h, Johnny Weissmuller. i, Hans Winkler.

No. 2391: a, Viktor Chukarin. b, Agnes Keleti. c, Barbel Wochel. d, Eric Heiden. e, Alvodar Gerevich. f, Guiseppe Delfino. g, Alexander Tikhonov. h, C.F. Pahud de Mortanges. i, Patricia McCormick.

No. 2392: a, Nelli Kim. b, Viktor Krovopuskov. c, Viktor Sidiak. d, Nikolai Andrianov. e, Nadia Comaneci. f, Mitsuo Tsukahara. g, Yelena Novikova-Belova. h, John Naber. i, Kornelia Ender.

No. 2393: a, Olga Korbut. b, Lyudmila Turischeva. c, Lasse Viren. d, George Miez. e, Roland Matthes. f, Pal Kovaks. g, Jesse Owens. h, Mark Spitz. i, Eduardo Mangiarotti.

No. 2394: a, Sawao Kato. b, Rudolf Karpati. c, Jeno Fuchs. d, Emil Zatopek. e, Fanny Blankers-Koen. f, Melvin Sheppard. g, Gert Fredriksson. h, Paul Elvstrom. i, Harrison W. Dillard.

No. 2395: a, Lydia Skoblikova. b, Ivar Ballangrud. c, Clas Thunberg. d, Anton Heida. e, Akinori Nakayama. f, Sixten Jernberg. g, Yevgeniy Grischin. h, Paul Radmilovic. i, Charles Daniels.

No. 2396: a, Betty Cuthbert. b, Vera Caslavska. c, Galina Kulakova. d, Yukio Endo. e, Vladimir Morozov. f, Boris Shaklin. g, Don Schollander. h, Gyozo Kulscar. i, Christian D'Oriola.

No. 2397: a, Al Oerter. b, Polina Astakhova. c, Takashi Ono. d, Valentin Muratov. e, Henri St. Cyr. f, Iain Murray Rose. g, Larissa Latynina. h, Carlo Pavesi. i, Dawn Fraser.

No. 2398, Paavo Nurmi, vert. No. 2399, Johannes Kolehmainen, vert. $190. Nedo Nadi, vert.

1991, Aug. 12 Litho. *Perf. 14x13½*

2390 A133 $15.30 Sheet of 9, #a.-i. 5.00 5.00
2391 A133 $17.80 Sheet of 9, #a.-i. 5.50 5.50
2392 A133 $20 Sheet of 9, #a.-i. 6.00 6.00
2393 A133 $20 Sheet of 9, #a.-i. 6.00 6.00
2394 A133 $25 Sheet of 9, #a.-i. 6.50 6.50
2395 A133 $25 Sheet of 9, #a.-i. 6.50 6.50
2396 A133 $30 Sheet of 9, #a.-i. 7.50 7.50
2397 A133 $30 Sheet of 9, #a.-i. 7.50 7.50
Nos. 2390-2397 (8) 50.50 50.50

Souvenir Sheets

Perf. 13x13½

2398 A133 $150 multicolored 4.50 4.50
2399 A133 $150 multicolored 4.50 4.50
2400 A133 $190 multicolored 7.00 7.00

For overprints see Nos. 2552-2557.

Discovery of America, 500th Anniv. (in 1992) — A134

Birds: $6.40, Phoenicopterus ruber. $7.65, Ostinops decumanus. $50, Falco peregrinus. $100, Nymphicus hollandicus. $190, Vultur ferphus. $260, Merganetta armata, horiz.

1991, Sept. 15 Litho. *Perf. 13½x14*

2401 A134 $6.40 multicolored
2402 A134 $7.65 multicolored
2403 A134 $50 multicolored
2404 A134 $100 multicolored
2405 A134 $190 multicolored
Nos. 2401-2405 (5) 16.50

Souvenir Sheet

Perf. 14x13½

2406 A134 $360 multicolored 15.00

A135

Various orchids: No. 2411, Odontoglossum. No. 2413, Cycnoches ventricosum. No. 2414, Miltonia hibrida, horiz.

Perf. 13½x14, 14x13½

1991, Sept. 30

2407 A135 $6.40 multicolored
2408 A135 $7.65 multi, horiz.
2409 A135 $50 multicolored
2410 A135 $100 multicolored
2411 A135 $190 multicolored
Nos. 2407-2411 (5) 8.00

Souvenir Sheets

2412 A135 $360 multicolored
2413 A135 $360 multicolored
2414 A135 $360 multicolored
Nos. 2412-2414 (3) 22.50

Nos. 2332-2339, 2343-2345 Ovptd. or Surcharged

Overprints: 80c, $2.55, Nos. 2421-2422, 2423a, 2423p, Rotary emblem and "1905-1990." $5.00, $6.40, $7.65, Nos. 2420, 2423d, 2423m, Rotary emblem and "Paul Percy Harris Founder 1868-1947" on 2 or 3 lines. Nos. 2423b, 2423l, 2423n, Boy Scout emblem and "1907-1992." Nos. 2423c, 2423i, 2423o, Lions Intl. emblem and "1917-1992." Nos. 2423e, 2423h, Red Cross emblem and "125 Years / Red Cross." Nos. 2423f-2423g, 2423j-2423k have parts of larger Rotary emblem. Nos. 2424-2425 ovptd. with service emblems in sheet margins.

1991, Oct. 29 *Perfs. as Before*

2415 A126 80c on #2332 .25 .25
2416 A126 $2.55 on #2333 .25 .25
2417 A126 $5 on #2334 .25 .25
2418 A126 $6.40 on #2335 .25 .25
2419 A126 $7.65 on #2336 .25 .25
2420 A126 $100 on $8.90 #2337 1.75 1.75
2421 A126 $190 on $50 #2338 2.75 2.75
2422 A126 $225 on $100 #2339 3.00 3.00
Nos. 2415-2422 (8) 8.75 8.75

Miniature Sheet

2423 A126 Sheet of 16 8.00 8.00
a.-l. $10 any single .25 .25
m. $50 on $10 #2343m .90 .90

n. $75 on $10 #2343n 1.00 1.00
o. $100 on $10 #2343o 1.50 1.50
p. $190 on $10 #2343p 3.25 3.25

Souvenir Sheets

2424 A126 $400 on $150 #2344 12.00 12.00
2425 A126 $500 on $150 #2345 13.00 13.00

Swiss Confederation, 700th Anniv. — A136

Designs: $6.40, Painting by Diego Giacometti. $7.65, Swiss puppets. $50, Man in top hat by Goya. $100, Stained glass window of Mary & Joseph. $190, Stained glass window of Jesus healing the sick.

No. 2431, Ship's cross-section, by Le Corbusier. No. 2432, Portrait of Giovanna Tornabuoni.

1991, Oct. 30 ***Perf. 13½x14***

2426 A136 $6.40 multicolored
2427 A136 $7.65 multicolored
2428 A136 $50 multicolored
2429 A136 $100 multicolored
2430 A136 $190 multicolored
a. Sheet of 5 + label, #2426-2430 9.00

Souvenir Sheets

2431 A136 $360 multicolored
2432 A136 $360 multicolored
Nos. 2431-2432 (2) 16.00

Phila Nippon '91 — A137

Trains: $6.40, Class 581 12-car. $7.65, Class EF-81. $50, Class 381 9-car. $100, Kodama 8-car. $190, Shin-Kansen 16-car. No. 2438, Shin-Kansen 16-car, diff. No. 2439, Japanese locomotives in Calcutta.

1991, Nov. 16 ***Perf. 14x13½***

2433 A137 $6.40 multicolored
2434 A137 $7.65 multicolored
2435 A137 $50 multicolored
2436 A137 $100 multicolored
2437 A137 $190 multicolored
Nos. 2433-2437 (5) 15.00

Souvenir Sheets

2438 A137 $360 multicolored
2439 A137 $360 multicolored
Nos. 2438-2439 (2) 30.00

Swiss Confederation, 700th anniv., No. 2439.

Common Design Types pictured following the introduction.

Royal Family Birthday, Anniversary
Common Design Type

1991, Nov. **Litho.** ***Perf. 14***

2440 CD347 $8.90 multi .30 .25
2441 CD347 $12.80 multi .30 .30
2442 CD347 $15.30 multi .30 .30
2443 CD347 $50 multi 1.00 .80
2444 CD347 $75 multi 1.25 1.25
2445 CD347 $100 multi 1.25 1.25
2446 CD347 $130 multi 1.50 1.50
2447 CD347 $150 multi 2.50 2.50
2448 CD347 $190 multi 3.00 3.00
2449 CD347 $200 multi 2.50 2.50
Nos. 2440-2449 (10) 13.90 13.65

Souvenir Sheets

2450 CD347 $225 Elizabeth 3.50 3.50
2451 CD347 $225 Charles, Diana, sons 4.00 4.00

$8.90, $50, $75, $190, No. 2451, Charles and Diana, 10th wedding anniversary. $130, $150, Prince Philip, 70th birthday. Others, Queen Elizabeth II, 65th birthday.

Miniature Sheet

Japanese Attack on Pearl Harbor, 50th Anniv. — A138

No. 2452: a, Akagi launches attack planes. b, Sakamaki's midget submarine beached. c, Mistubishi ASM Zero fighter. d, USS Arizona under attack. e, Aichi D3A1 Val dive bomber. f, USS California. g, P40 defends Pearl Harbor. h, USS Cassin and Downes hit at dry dock. i, B17 crash lands at Bellows Field. j, USS Nevada burns at Hospital Point.

1991, Dec. 7 ***Perf. 14½x15***

2452 A138 $50 Sheet of 10, #a.-j. 10.00 10.00

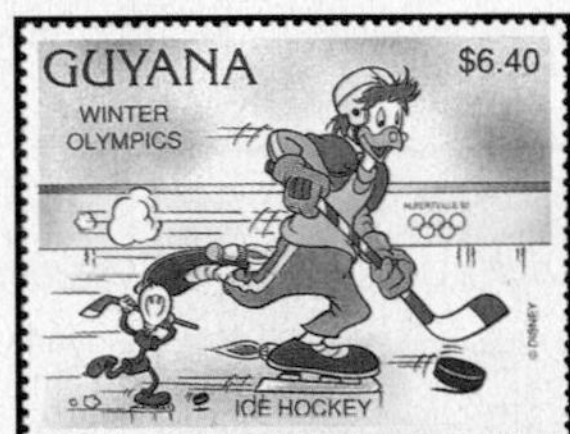

1992 Winter Olympics, Albertville — A139

Walt Disney characters at the Olympics: $6.40, Gus Gander playing ice hockey. $7.65, Mickey, Minnie in bobsled. $8.90, Huey, Dewey, Louie pretending to luge. $12.80, Goofy freestyle skiing. $50, Goofy ski jumping. $100, Donald, Daisy Duck speed skating. $130, Pluto cross-country skiing. $190, Mickey, Minnie ice dancing. No. 2461, Scrooge McDuck slalom skiing. No. 2462, Huey curling.

1991, Dec. 12 ***Perf. 13½x13***

2453 A139 $6.40 multi .35 .35
2454 A143 $7.65 multi .40 .40
2455 A139 $8.90 multi .45 .45
2456 A143 $12.80 multi .65 .65
2457 A143 $50 multi 1.40 1.40
2458 A139 $100 multi 2.25 2.25
2459 A139 $130 multi 2.75 2.75
2460 A143 $190 multi 4.00 4.00
Nos. 2453-2460 (8) 12.25 12.25

Souvenir Sheets

2461 A139 $225 multi 6.50 6.50
2462 A143 $225 multi 6.50 6.50

Mushrooms — A140

Designs: $6.40, Boletus satanoides. $7.65, Russula nigricans. $50, Cortinarius glaucopus. $100, Lactarius camphoratus. $190, Cortinarius callisteus. No. 2468, Russula integra. No. 2469, Coprinus micaceus, vert.

1991, Dec. 16 **Litho.** ***Perf. 14x13½***

2463 A140 $6.40 multicolored
2464 A140 $7.65 multicolored
2465 A140 $50 multicolored
2466 A140 $100 multicolored
2467 A140 $190 multicolored
Nos. 2463-2467 (5) 15.00

Souvenir Sheets
Perf. 14x13½, 13½x14

2468 A140 $360 multicolored
2469 A140 $360 multicolored
Nos. 2468-2469 (2) 28.00 28.00

Walt Disney Christmas Cards — A141

Designs and year of issue: 80c, Mickey, friends singing carols, 1989. $2.55, Mickey, friends riding trolley car, 1962. $5, Donald, Pluto wrapping package, 1971. $6.40, Mickey holding candle, 1948. $7.65, Mickey with Santa mask, 1947. $8.90, Pinocchio's shadow, 1939. $50, Three Little Pigs, dancing on wolf's back, 1933. $200, Mickey, mice singing carols, 1949.

No. 2478: a, Conductor, Donald. b, Elephant with book. c, Goofy, centaurs. d, Snow White, dwarfs. e, Pluto, dinosaur.

No. 2479: a, Mickey in sleigh. b, Three little pigs, Winnie-the-Pooh, Bambi. c, Dalmatian, bear, monkey, Lady and the Tramp. d, Alice, Goofy, Mad Hatter. e, Pinocchio, Tinker Bell, Peter Pan, Seven Dwarfs, Donald Duck. f, Pluto, 1974.

No. 2480, Mickey and friends riding in coach, 1932. No. 2481, Mickey, Pluto greeting friends, 1935. No. 2482, Donald, Jose Carioca, 1944. No. 2483, Couple dancing, baseball batter, 1945. No. 2484, Mickey, Donald, Goofy, 1946. No. 2485, Santa in chimney, 1969. No. 2486, Portrait of Winnie-the-Pooh hanging on wall, 1969. No. 2487, Mickey, 1978.

1991, Dec. 17 ***Perf. 14x13½***

2470 A141 80c multi .25 .25
2471 A141 $2.55 multi .25 .25
2472 A141 $5 multi .25 .25
2473 A141 $6.40 multi .35 .25
2474 A141 $7.65 multi .35 .25
2475 A141 $8.90 multi .35 .25
2476 A141 $50 multi 1.40 1.40
2477 A141 $200 multi 5.25 5.25
2478 A141 $50 Strip of 5, #a.-e. 7.00 7.00
2479 A141 $50 Strip of 6, #a.-f. 8.50 8.50
Nos. 2470-2479 (10) 23.95 23.65

Souvenir Sheets

2480 A141 $260 multi 6.00 6.00
2481 A141 $260 multi 6.00 6.00
2482 A141 $260 multi 6.00 6.00
2483 A141 $260 multi 6.00 6.00
2484 A141 $260 multi 6.00 6.00
2485 A141 $260 multi 6.00 6.00
2486 A141 $260 multi 6.00 6.00
2487 A141 $260 multi 6.00 6.00
Nos. 2480-2487 (8) 48.00 48.00

Nos. 2478a-2478e, 2479a-2479f, 2480-2481, 2485 and 2487 are vert.

No. 2373 Surcharged

1991, Dec. 19 **Litho.** ***Perf. 14***

2487A A129 $600 on $150 #2373 — —

No. 2377 Surcharged

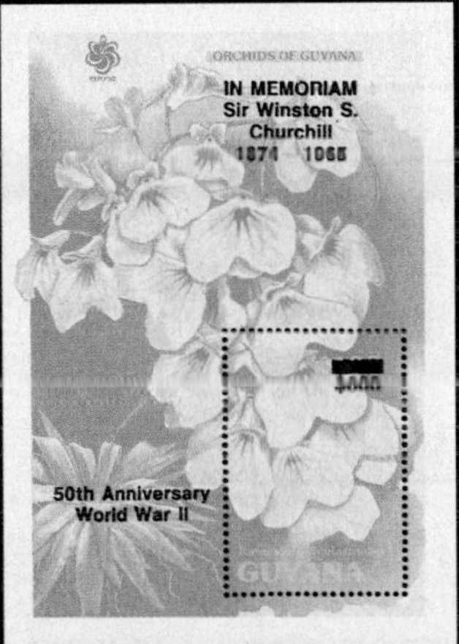

1991, Dec. 19 **Litho.** ***Perf. 14***

2487B A129 $600 on $190 #2377 — —

Christmas A142

Paintings: $6.40, Madonna and Child with Angels, by Titian, horiz. $7.65, Madonna and Child with Angels, by Rubens. $50, Madonna and Child, by Raphael. $100, Madonna and Child, by Durer. $190, Madonna, by Durer. No. 2493, Madonna and Child, by Rubens, horiz. No. 2494, Madonna, by Durer, diff.

1991, Dec. 30 ***Perf. 14x13½, 13½x14***

2488 A142 $6.40 multicolored
2489 A142 $7.65 multicolored
2490 A142 $50 multicolored
2491 A142 $100 multicolored
2492 A142 $190 multicolored
Nos. 2488-2 92(5) 15.00

Souvenir Sheets

2493 A142 $360 multicolored
2494 A142 $360 multicolored
Nos. 2493-2494 (2) 35.00

Brandenburg Gate, Bicent. — A143

Designs: $10, Map of Berlin. $25, US Pres. George Bush, Polish Pres. Lech Walesa. $100, German Chancellor Helmut Kohl, Foreign Minister Hans-Dietrich Genscher. $190, Armored helmet.

1991, Dec. ***Perf. 14***

2495 A143 $10 multicolored .30 .30
2496 A143 $25 multicolored .75 .75
2497 A143 $100 multicolored 2.50 2.50
Nos. 2495-2497 (3) 3.55 3.55

Souvenir Sheet

2498 A143 $190 multicolored 4.00 4.00

Wolfgang Amadeus Mozart, Death Bicent. A144

Portrait of Mozart and: $75, Laxenburg. $80, Death of Leopold II. $100, Mozart's birthplace, Salzburg.

1991, Dec.

2499 A144 $75 multicolored 2.00 2.00
2500 A144 $80 multicolored 2.25 2.25
2501 A144 $100 multicolored 2.50 2.50
Nos. 2499-2501 (3) 6.75 6.75

Souvenir Sheet

2502 A144 $190 Bust of Mozart, vert. 4.00 4.00

17th World Scout Jamboree, Korea — A145

Designs: $30, Scouts hiking. $40, Emblems, flag. $100, Lord Baden-Powell, vert. $190, Rocket cover with US No. 1145.

1991, Dec.

2503 A145 $25 multicolored .80 .80
2504 A145 $30 multicolored 1.00 1.00
2505 A145 $40 multicolored 1.10 1.10
2506 A145 $100 multicolored 2.50 2.50
Nos. 2503-2506 (4) 5.40 5.40

Souvenir Sheet

2507 A145 $190 multicolored 4.00 4.00

Charles de Gaulle A146

De Gaulle: $60, In Venice, 1944. $75, With Khrushchev, 1960. $80, In Algiers, 1958. $100, With Pope John VI, 1967.

1991, Dec.

2508 A146 $60 multicolored 2.00 2.00
2509 A146 $75 multicolored 2.50 2.50
2510 A146 $80 multicolored 2.75 2.75
2511 A146 $100 multicolored 3.25 3.25
Nos. 2508-2511 (4) 10.50 10.50

Souvenir Sheets

2512 A146 $150 Portrait, vert. 7.50 7.50
2513 A146 $190 Portrait, diff, vert. 9.75 9.75

Anniversaries and Events — A147

Designs: No. 2515, Caroline Herschel, astronomer, Old Town Hall, Hanover. No. 2516, Map of Switzerland, woman in traditional dress. $80, Otto Lilienthal's glider No. 3. $100, Locomotive. $190, Arms of Bern and Solothurn.

1991, Dec.

2515 A147 $75 multicolored 2.00 2.00
2516 A147 $75 multicolored 2.00 2.00
2517 A147 $80 multicolored 2.25 2.25
2518 A147 $100 multicolored 2.50 2.50
Nos. 2515-2518 (4) 8.75 8.75

Souvenir Sheet

2519 A147 $190 multicolored 4.00 4.00

Hanover, 750th anniv. (No. 2515), Swiss Confederation, 700th anniv. (Nos. 2516, 2519), first glider flight, cent. (No. 2517), Trans-Siberian Railway, cent. (No. 2518).

Discovery of America, 500th Anniv. A148

Designs: $6.40, Columbus lands on Trinidad. $7.65, Columbus, globe. $8.90, Ships blown off course by hurricane. $12.80, Map, hands in chains. $15.30, Land sighted. $50, Nina, Pinta. $75, Santa Maria. $100, Columbus trading with natives. $125, Superstitions & sea monsters. $130, Map, Columbus ashore. $140, Priest & natives. $150, Columbus kneeling before King Ferdinand and Queen Isabella. No. 2532, Map of New World. No. 2533, One of Columbus' ships, vert. No. 2534, Columbus.

1992, Jan. 2 *Perf. 14*

2520 A148 $6.40 multi .40 .35
2521 A148 $7.65 multi .45 .40
2522 A148 $8.90 multi .50 .45
2523 A148 $12.80 multi .55 .50
2524 A148 $15.30 multi .60 .55
2525 A148 $50 multi 1.75 1.75
2526 A148 $75 multi 2.25 2.25
2527 A148 $100 multi 3.00 3.00
2528 A148 $125 multi 3.75 3.75
2529 A148 $130 multi 4.00 4.00
2530 A148 $140 multi 4.25 4.25
2531 A148 $150 multi 4.50 4.50
Nos. 2520-2531 (12) 26.00 25.75

Souvenir Sheets

2532 A148 $280 multi 8.50 8.50
2533 A148 $280 multi 8.50 8.50
2534 A148 $280 multi 8.50 8.50

Movie Posters — A149

Designs: $8.90, The Great K & A Train Robbery. $12.80, Cimarron. $15.30, Buzzin' Around. $25, Adventures of Captain Marvel. $30, The Mummy. $50, A Sainted Devil. $75, A Tale of Two Cities. $100, A Tugboat Romeo. $130, Thief of Bagdad. $150, Bacon Grabbers. $190, A Night at the Opera. $200, Citizen Kane. No. 2547, She Done Him Wrong. No. 2548, The Circus. No. 2549, Babe Comes Home. No. 2550, Zeppelin, horiz.

1992, Mar. 11 **Litho.** *Perf. 14*

2535 A149 $8.90 multi .60 .50
2536 A149 $12.80 multi .65 .55
2537 A149 $15.30 multi .70 .65
2538 A149 $25 multi .80 .75
2539 A149 $30 multi .90 .85
2540 A149 $50 multi 1.50 1.40
2541 A149 $75 multi 2.25 2.00
2542 A149 $100 multi 3.00 2.75
2543 A149 $130 multi 3.75 3.50
2544 A149 $150 multi 4.50 4.25
2545 A149 $190 multi 5.75 5.50
2546 A149 $200 multi 6.00 5.75
Nos. 2535-2546 (12) 30.40 28.45

Size: 70x100mm, 100x70mm

Imperf

2547 A149 $225 multi 6.75 6.75
2548 A149 $225 multi 6.75 6.75
2549 A149 $225 multi 6.75 6.75
2550 A149 $225 multi 6.75 6.75

No. 2273 Overprinted or Surcharged with Olympic Rings and "ALBERTVILLE '92" or "XVIth Olympic Winter / Games in Albertville" (No. 2551e)

1992 *Perfs. as Before*

2551 A122 Sheet of 9
a.-f. $20 on #2273a-2273f
g. $70 on $20 #2273g
h. $100 on $20 #2273h
i. $190 on $20 #2273i

Nos. 2391g, 2395c, 2396c, 2398, 2400 Ovptd. "ALBERTVILLE '92" No. 2399 Ovptd. "Barcelona '92" and emblems in Sheet Margin

1992 *Perfs. as Before*

2552 A133 $17.80 on #2391g 12.00 12.00
2553 A133 $25 on #2395c 12.00 12.00
2554 A133 $30 on #2396c 12.00 12.00

Souvenir Sheets

2555 A133 $150 on #2398 7.00 7.00
2556 A133 $150 on #2399 7.00 7.00
2557 A133 $190 on #2400 7.00 7.00

Nos. 2552-2554 printed in sheets of 9, overprint applied to only one stamp per sheet. Overprint on Nos. 2555, 2557 applied to sheet margin.

Easter A150

Various details from paintings by Durer: $6.40, $12.80, $50, $130, No. 2567, The Martyrdom of Ten Thousand. $7.65, $15.30, $100, $190, No. 2566, Adoration of the Trinity.

1992 **Litho.** *Perf. 13½x14*

2558 A150 $6.40 multi .30 .25
2559 A150 $7.65 multi .30 .25
2560 A150 $12.80 multi .45 .25
2561 A150 $15.30 multi .55 .45
2562 A150 $50 multi 1.50 1.25
2563 A150 $100 multi 2.75 2.75
2564 A150 $130 multi 3.75 3.75
2565 A150 $190 multi 5.75 5.75
Nos. 2558-2565 (8) 15.35 14.70

Souvenir Sheets

2566 A150 $225 multi 6.50 6.50
2567 A150 $225 multi 6.50 6.50

A151

Queen Elizabeth II: $8.90, With Prince Philip. $12.80, In uniform. $100, At coronation. $130, Wearing black cape and hat. No. 2572, Coronation portrait. No. 2573, Fortieth anniv. portrait.

1992 **Litho.** *Perf. 14*

2568 A151 $8.90 multicolored 1.00 .50
2569 A151 $12.80 multicolored 1.25 .60
2570 A151 $100 multicolored 5.00 4.00
2571 A151 $130 multicolored 6.00 5.00
Nos. 2568-2571 (4) 13.25 10.10

Souvenir Sheets

2572 A151 $225 multicolored 6.50 6.50
2573 A151 $225 multicolored 6.50 6.50

Queen Elizabeth II's Accession to the Throne, 40th Anniv.

Diocese of Guyana, 150th Anniv. A152

Designs: $6.40, Holy Cross Church, Annai Bupununi. $50, St. Peter's Church. $100, St. George's Cathedral, interior, vert. $190, Map, vert. $225, Religious symbols.

1992 **Litho.** *Perf. 14*

2574 A152 $6.40 multicolored .35 .30
2575 A152 $50 multicolored 1.00 1.00
2576 A152 $100 multicolored 2.40 2.40
2577 A152 $190 multicolored 3.75 3.75
Nos. 2574-2577 (4) 7.50 7.45

Souvenir Sheet

2578 A152 $225 multicolored 6.50 6.50

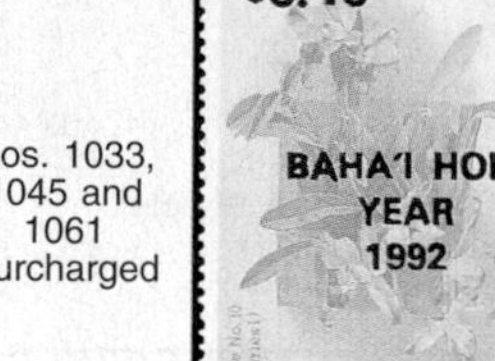

Nos. 1033, 1045 and 1061 Surcharged

Method, Perfs, and Watermarks As Before

1992, May 29

2578A A91 $6.40 on 60c #1033 — —
2578B A91 $7.65 on 60c #1061 — —
2578C A91 $8.90 on 60c #1045 — —

An additional stamp was issued in this set. The editors would like to examine any example of it.

Miniature Sheet

Horses — A153

No. 2579: a, Palomino. b, Appaloosa. c, Clydesdale. d, Arab. e, Morgan. f, Friesian. g, Pinto. h, Thoroughbred. No. 2580, Lipizzaner.

1992, Aug. 10

2579 A153 $190 Sheet of 8, #a.-h. 30.00 30.00

Souvenir Sheet

2580 A153 $190 multicolored 7.50 7.50

No. 2580 contains one 58x29mm stamp.

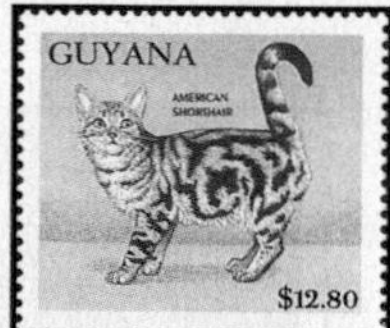

Cats — A154

$5, Burmese. $6.40, Turkish van. $12.80, American shorthair. $15.30, Egyptian. $50, Egyptian mau. $100, Japanese bobtail. $130, Abyssinian. $225, Oriental shorthair.

No. 2588A: b, Russian blue. c, Havana brown. d, Himalayan. e, Manx. f, Cornish rex. g, Black Persian. h, Scottish fold. i, Siamese.

No. 2589, Chartreuse, vert. No. 2590, Turkish angora. No. 2591, Maine coon. No. 2592, Chinchilla.

1992, Aug. 10 *Perf. 14½x14*

2581 A154 $5 multi .30 .25
2582 A154 $6.40 multi .30 .25
2583 A154 $12.80 multi .40 .35
2584 A154 $15.30 multi .55 .50
2585 A154 $50 multi 1.75 1.50
2586 A154 $100 multi 3.25 3.25
2587 A154 $130 multi 4.00 4.00
2588 A154 $225 multi 7.50 7.50
Nos. 2581-2588 (8) 18.05 17.60

Miniature Sheet

Perf. 14x13½

2588A A154 $50 Sheet of 8, #b.-i. 12.00 12.00

Souvenir Sheets

Perf. 14x14½

2589 A152 $250 multi 7.25 7.25
2590 A154 $250 multi 7.25 7.25
2591 A154 $250 multi 7.25 7.25
2592 A154 $250 multi 7.25 7.25

No. 2589 has continuous design. Nos. 2590-2592 are vert. and have continous design.

Nos. 2368-2369 Surcharged on 4 stamps and Overprinted in Red

Surcharge and overprint reads: "PHILA NIPPON '91 / WORLD STAMP EXHIBITION NIPPON '91" and Show Emblem in Sheet Margin

1992 *Perfs. as Before*

2593 A129 Sheet of 12, #a.-d., #2368a-2368l 19.00
a. $25 on $10 #2368m
b. $50 on $10 #2368n
c. $75 on $10 #2368o
d. $130 on $10 #2368p

2594 A129 Sheet of 16, #a.-d., 2369a-2369l 19.00
a. $25 on $12.80 #2369m
b. $50 on $12.80 #2369n
c. $75 on $12.80 #2369o
d. $100 on $12.80 #2369p

No. 2376 Surcharged in Red Souvenir Sheet

2595 A129 $250 on $150 #2376

Nos. 2332-2340, 2346-2347 Overprinted or Surcharged

Overprints: 80c, $2.55, Nos. 2602-2603, Lions emblem and Lions International / 1917-1992." $5, $6.40, $7.65, Nos. 2601, 2604d, 2604m, Lions emblem and "Melvin Jones Founder 1880-1961" on 2 or 3 lines. Nos. 2604a, 2604p, Lions emblem and "1917-1992." Nos. 2604b, 2604i, 2604o, Rotary emblem and "1905-1990." Nos. 2604c, 2604l, 2604n, Boy Scout emblem and "1907-1992." Nos. 2604e, 2604h, Red Cross emblem and "125 Years Red Cross." Nos. 2604f-2604g, 2604j-2604k have parts of larger Lions emblem. Nos. 2605-2606 have service organization emblems in sheet margins.

1992 *Perfs. as Before*

2596 A126 80c on #2332
2597 A126 $2.55 on #2333
2598 A126 $5 on #2334
2599 A126 $6.40 on #2335
2600 A126 $7.65 on #2336
2601 A126 $100 on $8.90 #2337
2602 A126 $190 on $50 #2338
2603 A126 $225 on $100 #2339

Miniature Sheet

2604 Sheet of 16 45.00
a.-l. A126 $10 any single
m. A126 $50 on $10 #2340m
n. A126 $75 on $10 #2340n
o. A126 $100 on $10 #2340o
p. A126 $190 on $10 #2340p

Souvenir Sheets

2605 A126 $400 on $190 #2346
2606 A126 $500 on $190 #2347

Elephants — A155

No. 2607: a, Mammoth, Oligocene Epoch. b, Stegodon, mid- Miocene Epoch. c, Mammoth, Pliocene Epoch. d, Hannibal's army crossing Alps. e, Royal elephant of the Maharaja of Mysore, India. f, Elephant pulling tree trunks, Burma. g, Tiger hunt, India. h, Elephant towing raft on River Kwai, Thailand.
$225, African elephants, Kenya.

1992, Aug. 10 **Litho.** *Perf. 14*

2607 A155 $50 Sheet of 8, #a.-h. 16.00 16.00

Souvenir Sheet

2608 A155 $225 multicolored 11.00 11.00

No. 2607 has continuous design.

Animals of Guyana A156

$8.90, Red howler monkey. $12.80, Ring-tailed coati. $15.30, Jaguar. $25, Two-toed sloth. $50, Giant armadillo. $75, Giant ant-eater. $100, Capybara. $130, Ocelot.
No. 2617, Wooly opossum, vert. No. 2618, Three-striped night monkey.

1992, Aug. 10

2609 A156 $8.90 multicolored .25 .25
2610 A156 $12.80 multicolored .30 .25
2611 A156 $15.30 multicolored .40 .35
2612 A156 $25 multicolored .65 .60
2613 A156 $50 multicolored 1.40 1.25
2614 A156 $75 multicolored 2.00 2.00
2615 A156 $100 multicolored 2.75 2.75
2616 A156 $130 multicolored 3.50 3.50
Nos. 2609-2616 (8) 11.25 10.95

Souvenir Sheets

2617 A156 $225 multicolored 7.00 7.00
2618 A156 $225 multicolored 7.00 7.00

Souvenir Sheet

Statue of Liberty, New York — A157

1992, Oct. 28

2619 A157 $325 multicolored 11.00 11.00

Postage Stamp Mega Event '92, New York City.

Nos. 1072a, 1075a, 1077a and 1080a Surcharged

Methods, Perfs, and Watermarks As Before

1992, Nov. 2

2619A A91 $6.40 on 150c #1080a — —
2619B A91 $7.65 on 150c #1075a — —
2619C A91 $8.90 on 150c #1072a — —
2619D A91 $10 on 200c #1077a — —
2619E A91 $50 on 60c #1022 — —

Miniature Sheets

Model Trains — A158

Marklin toy locomotives: No. 2620a, 2-4-4-2 Crocodile locomotive, 1 gauge, 1933. b, French prototype streetcar, 1 gauge, 1933. c, British prototype Flatiron 2-4-4 tank engine, O gauge, 1913. d, German National Railways 0-6-0 switching engine, Z gauge, 1970. e, Smoking/non-smoking third class car, 1 gauge, 1909. f, American style 0-4-0 locomotive, O gauge, 1904. g, Zurich, Switzerland prototype streetcar, O gauge, 1928. h, Central London Railway Bo-Bo, 1 gauge, 1904. i, "The Great Bear" Pacific, 1 gauge, 1909.

No. 2621: a, 0-4-4 American style locomotive, 2 gauge, 1907. b, German first and second class passenger car, 1 gauge, 1908. c, British Great Eastern Railway 4-4-0, 1 gauge, 1908. d, English prototype steeplecab, O gauge, 1904. e, Santa Fe Railroad diesel, 1962. f, British Great Northern 4-4-0, 3 gauge, live steam model, 1903. g, Caledonian Railway "Cardean" of Scotland, 1 gauge, 1904. h, British LNWR passenger car, 1 gauge, 1903. i, Swiss Gotthard Rwy. 0-4-0 locomotive, O gauge, 1920.

No. 2622: a, British LB & SCR tank engine, O gauge, 1920. b, Central London Railway, tunnel locomotive, 1 gauge, 1904. c, "Borsig" 4-6-4 streamliner, O gauge, 1935. d, French PLM first class car, 1 gauge, 1929. e, American style 0-4-0 locomotive #1021, 1 gauge, 1904. f, "Paris-Orsay" long-nose steeplecab, 1 gauge, 1920. g, British "Cock O' The North," 1 gauge, 1936. h, Prussian State Railways P8 4-6-0 live steam model, 1 gauge, 1975. i, 1937 German "Schnell Treibwagen," O gauge, 1937.

No. 2623: a, Marklin North British Railway "Atlantic," 1 gauge, 1913. b, Bing British London & Western Railway 4-4-2 "Precursor," O gauge, clockwork model, 1916. c, Marklin British Great Western "King George V," O gauge, 1937. d, Marklin passenger car, "Kaiser Train," 1 gauge, 1901. e, Bing 4-4-0 side tank engine, 1 gauge, live steam model, 1904. f, Marklin short-nose steeplecab, 1 gauge, 1912. g, Marklin "Der Adler", 1 gauge, 1935. h, Bing British Great Western Railway "County of Northampton," 1 gauge, live steam model, 1909. i, Bing British Midland Railway "Black Prince," 3 gauge, live steam model, 1908.

Bing toy locomotives: No. 2624: a, Midland Railway "Deeley Type" 4-4-0, 1 gauge clockwork model, 1909. b, No. 2631, British Midland Railway 0-4-0, 3 gauge clockwork model, 1903. c, German 4-6-2 Pacific, O gauge clockwork model, 1927. d, British Great Western Railway, third class coach, O gauge, 1926. e, British London & Southwestern "M7" 0-4-4, 1 gauge clockwork model, 1909. f, "Pilot" 4-4-0 side tank engine, 3 gauge live steam model, 1901. g, British London & Northwestern Railway Webb "Cauliflower," O gauge clockwork model, 1912. h, No. 112, 4-4-0 side tank locomotive, 1 gauge live steam model, 1910. i, British Great Northern Railway, "Stirling Single," 2 gauge live steam model, 1904.

Carette toy locomotives: No. 2625: a, Lithographed tin "Penny Bazaar" train, 1904. b, Winteringham 0-4-0 locomotive, O gauge, 1917. c, British Northeastern Railway, Smith Compound, 3 gauge, 1905. d, SE & CR 2-2-4 steam railcar, 1 gauge, live steam model, 1908. e, No. 776 British Great Northern Railway Stirling "Single," 3 gauge, live steam model, 1903. f, British Midland Railway 4-4-0, O gauge, clockwork model, 1911. g, London Metropolitan Railway "Westinghouse," 1 gauge, 1908. h, Clestory coach, 1 gauge, 1907. i, Steam railcar No. 1, O gauge, live steam model, 1906.

Marklin toy locomotives: No. 2626: a, LMS "Precursor" 4-4-2 tank engine, O gauge clockwork model, 1923. b, American "Congressional Limited" passenger car, 1 gauge, 1908. c, Swiss prototype "Ae 3/6" locomotive, O gauge, 1934. d, German National Railways class 80, 0-6-0, 1 gauge, 1975. e, British Southern Railway third class coach, O gauge, 1926. f, "Bowen-Cooke" 4-6-2 tank engine, O gauge, 1913. g, First electric prototype model, "Two Penny Tube," London, 1 gauge clockwork model, 1901. h, "Paris-Orsay" steeplecab, 1 gauge, 1920. i, 0-2-2 Passenger engine, O gauge clockwork model, 1895.

Bing toy locomotives: No. 2627: a, 2-2-0 engine and tender, 2 gauge live steam model, 1895. b, British Midland Railway "single," O gauge clockwork model, 1913. c, #524/510 reversible express passenger locomotive, 1 gauge, 1916. d, "Kaiser Train" passenger car with Gothic windows, 1 gauge, 1902. e, Tinplate model, British rural station, 1 gauge, 1915. f, British LSMR "M7" side tank locomotive, O gauge clockwork model, 1909. g, 4-4-4 "Windcutter," 1 gauge live steam model, 1912. h, British Great Central Railway "Sir Sam Fay," 1 gauge clockwork model, 1914. i, "Dunalastair" locomotive Caledonian Railway, 1 gauge clockwork model, 1910.

No. 2628, German National Railroad class 0-1 Pacific, O gauge, 1937. No. 2629, Bing 0-4-0 Contractor's locomotive, 4 gauge, 1904. No. 2630, Rack Railway "Steeplecab" locomotive, 2 gauge, 1908. No. 2631, Bing Pabst Blue Ribbon Beer refrigerator car, O gauge, 1925. No. 2632, Marklin "Commodore Vanderbilt," O gauge, 1937. No. 2633, Bing British Great Western Railway "County of Northampton," 1 gauge, live steam model, 1909. No. 2634, Marklin French Prototype PLM Pacific, 1 gauge, live steam model, 1912. No. 2635, Marklin "Mountain Etat" second series, O gauge, 1933.

1992, Nov. 19 *Perf. 14*

2620 A158 $45 Sheet of 9, #a.-i. 8.00 8.00
2621 A158 $45 Sheet of 9, #a.-i. 8.00 8.00
2622 A158 $45 Sheet of 9, #a.-i. 8.00 8.00
2623 A158 $45 Sheet of 9, #a.-i. 8.00 8.00
2624 A158 $45 Sheet of 9, #a.-i. 8.00 8.00
2625 A158 $45 Sheet of 9, #a.-i. 8.00 8.00
2626 A158 $45 Sheet of 9, #a.-i. 8.00 8.00
2627 A158 $45 Sheet of 9, #a.-i. 8.00 8.00

Souvenir Sheets

2628 A158 $350 multicolored 7.00 7.00
2629 A158 $350 multicolored 7.00 7.00

Perf. 14x13½

2630 A158 $350 multicolored 7.00 7.00

Perf. 13x13½, 13½x13

2631 A158 $350 multicolored 7.00 7.00
2632 A158 $350 multicolored 7.00 7.00
2633 A158 $350 multicolored 7.00 7.00
2634 A158 $350 multicolored 7.00 7.00
2635 A158 $350 multicolored 7.00 7.00

Genoa '92. Nos. 2628-2635 each contain one 50x39mm stamp.
While Nos. 2622-2623 & 2631 have the issue date as Nos. 2620-2621 & 2628-2630, the face value of of Nos. 2622-2623 & 2631 was lower when they were released.

Anniversaries and Events — A159

Designs: $12.80, Zeppelin over Lake Constance, 1909. No. 2638, Voyager 1, Jupiter. No. 2639, Konrad Adenauer, John F. Kennedy. No. 2640, Aeromedical airlift. No. 2641, Amazon dolphins. No. 2642, Lift-off of Voyager 1, 1977. No. 2643, Baby gorilla. No. 2644, America's Cup yacht Stars and Stripes. No. 2644A, Eye screening van, doctor with patient. $190, Adenauer, Charles de Gaulle. $225, Zeppelin preparing for takeoff. No. 2647, Count Zeppelin, vert. No. 2648 View of Earth from space, vert. No. 2649, Konrad Adenauer, vert. No. 2650, Tree frog, vert.

1993, Jan. **Litho.** *Perf. 14*

2637 A159 $12.80 multi .75 .75
2638 A159 $50 multi 1.75 1.75
2639 A159 $50 multi 2.00 2.00
2640 A159 $100 multi 4.50 4.50
2641 A159 $100 multi 3.00 3.00
2642 A159 $130 multi 4.25 4.25
2643 A159 $130 multi 3.75 3.75
2644 A159 $130 multi 4.75 4.75
2644A A159 $130 multi 4.75 4.75
2645 A159 $190 multi 6.00 6.00
2646 A159 $225 multi 6.50 6.50
Nos. 2637-2646 (11) 42.00 42.00

Souvenir Sheets

2647 A159 $225 multi 7.50 7.50
2648 A159 $225 multi 7.00 7.00
2649 A159 $225 multi 7.00 7.00
2650 A159 $225 multi 7.00 7.00

Count Zeppelin, 75th anniv. of death (Nos. 2637, 2646-2647). Intl. Space Year (Nos. 2638, 2642, 2648). Konrad Adenauer, 25th anniv. of death (Nos. 2639, 2645, 2649). World Health Organization (No. 2640). Earth Summit, Rio (Nos. 2641, 2643, 2650). America's Cup Yacht Race (No. 2644). Lions Intl., 75th anniv. (No. 2644A).

Miniature Sheet

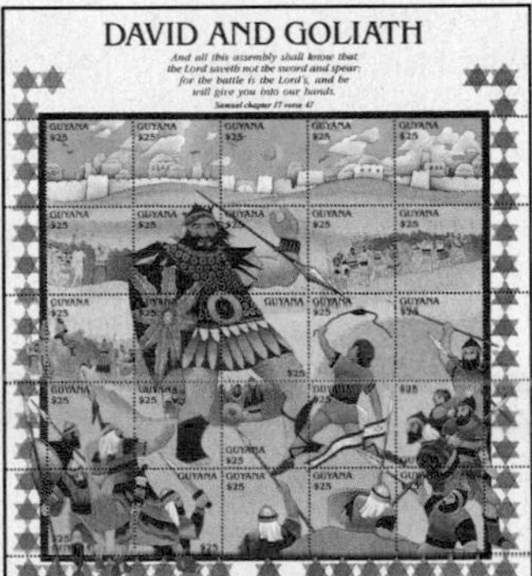

Biblical Story of David and Goliath — A160

No. 2651: a, City of Jerusalem, two birds in flight. b, City, bird in flight at right. c, City, sun above. d, City, bird in flight at left. e, City with clouds above. f, Philistine army (i-k, q-r). g, Goliath. h, Goliath's arm, spear shaft (b, i, n). l, Goliath's leg (m, q-s), shield. n, David (r-t, w) with slingshot. o, Jewish soldiers with spears or swords (p-y).

1992, Dec. 29 **Litho.** *Perf. 14*

2651 A160 $25 Sheet of 25, #a.-y. 18.00 18.00

No. 2651 has a continuous design.

Parrots
A161

80c, Hyacinth macaw. $6.40, Scarlet macaw. $7.65, Green macaw, vert. $15.30, Tovi parakeet. $50, Blue & yellow macaw. $100, Military macaw, vert. $130, Red & green macaw, vert. $190, Severa macaw.

No. 2660, Scarlet macaw, diff. No. 2661, Green parakeet, vert.

1993, Mar. 10

2652 A161 80c multicolored .35 .25
2653 A161 $6.40 multicolored .60 .30
2654 A161 $7.65 multicolored .60 .30
2655 A161 $15.30 multicolored .80 .60
2656 A161 $50 multicolored 1.25 .95
2657 A161 $100 multicolored 2.50 2.40
2658 A161 $130 multicolored 3.25 3.25
2659 A161 $190 multicolored 3.75 3.75
Nos. 2652-2659 (8) 13.10 11.80

Souvenir Sheet

2660 A161 $225 multicolored 6.00 6.00
2661 A161 $225 multicolored 6.00 6.00

While Nos. 2654-2656, 2659, 2661 have the same issue date as Nos. 2652-2653, 2657-2658, 2660, the value of Nos. 2654-2656, 2659, 2661 was lower when released.

For surcharge, see No. 4172.

Miniature Sheets

Dinosaurs — A162

No. 2662: a, Archaeopteryx. b, Pteranodon. c, Quetzalcoatlus. d, Protoavis. e, Dicraeosaurus. f, Moschops. g, Lystrosaurus. h, Dimetrondon. i, Staurikosaurus. j, Cacops. k, Diarthrognathus. l, Estemmenosuchus.

No. 2663: a, Pteranodon. b, Cearadactylus. c, Eudimorphodon. d, Pterodactylus. e, Stauirkosaurus. f, Euoplocephalus. g, Tuojiangosaurus. h, Oviraptor. i, Protoceratops. j, Panaoplosaurus. k, Psittacosaurus. l, Corythosaurus.

No. 2664: a, Sordes. b, Quetzalcoatlus. c, Archaeopteryx. d, Rhamphorynchus. e, Spinosaurus. f, Anchisaurus. g, Stegosaurus. h, Leaellynosaurus. i, Minmi. j, Heterdontosaurus. k, Lesothosaurus. l, Deninonychus.

1993, Mar. 10 Litho. *Perf. 14*

2662 A162 $30 Sheet of 12, #a.-l. 7.00 7.00
2663 A162 $30 Sheet of 12, #a.-l. 7.00 7.00
2664 A162 $30 Sheet of 12, #a.-l. 7.00 7.00

For surcharge, see No. 4117.

Miniature Sheet

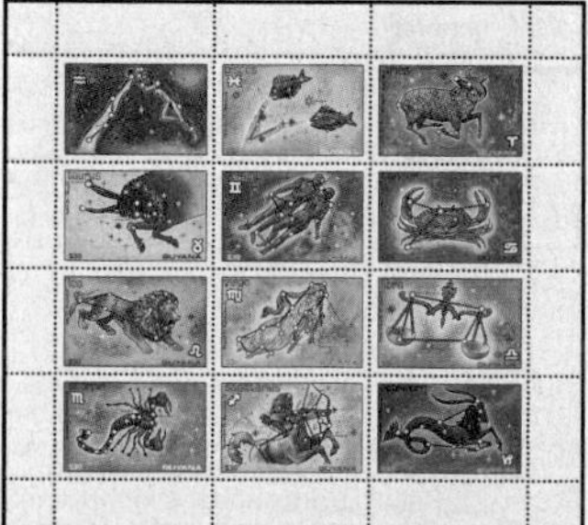

Signs of the Zodiac — A163

No. 2665: a, Aquarius. b, Pisces. c, Aries. d, Taurus. e, Gemini. f, Cancer. g, Leo. h, Virgo. i, Libra. j, Scorpio. k, Sagittarius. l, Capricorn.

1992, Dec. 29 Litho. *Perf. 14x13½*

Sheet of 12

2665 A163 $30 Sheet of 12, #a.-l. 17.00 17.00

Caribbean Manatee
A164

Designs: $6.40, Adult sticking head out of water. $7.65, Adult, eating, with young. $8.90, Adult swimming underwater. $50, Adult swimming with young.

1993, Mar. 10 Litho. *Perf. 15x14½*

2666 A164 $6.40 multicolored 1.10 1.00
2667 A164 $7.65 multicolored 1.10 1.00
2668 A164 $8.90 multicolored 1.10 1.00
2669 A164 $50 multicolored 4.25 4.25
Nos. 2666-2669 (4) 7.55 7.25

World Wildlife Federation. Exists imperf. Value, set $36.

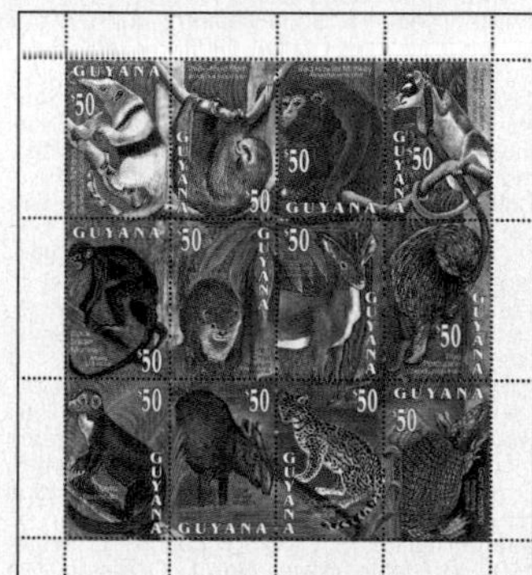

Fauna — A165

No. 2670: a, Southern tamandua. b, Three-toed sloth. c, Red howler monkey. d, Four-eyed opossum. e, Black spider monkey. f, Giant otter. g, Red brocket. h, Tree porcupine. i, Tayra. j, Tapir. k, Ocelot. l, Giant armadillo.

No. 2671: a, Crimson topaz hummingbird. b, Bearded bellbird (f). c, Amazonian umbrellabird. d, Paradise jacamar (h). e, Paradise tanager. f, White-tailed trogon (i-j). g, Scarlet macaw (k). h, Red fan parrot. i, Red-billed toucan. j, White plumed antbird. k, Crimson-hooded manakin. l, Guyanan cock-of-the-rock.

No. 2672, Paca. No. 2673, Tufted coquettes, horiz.

1993, Mar. 10 *Perf. 14*

2670 A165 $50 Sheet of 12, #a.-l. 10.00 10.00
2671 A165 $50 Sheet of 12, #a.-l. 10.00 10.00

Souvenir Sheets

2672 A165 $325 multicolored 6.00 6.00
2673 A165 $325 multicolored 6.00 6.00

Coronation of Queen Elizabeth II, 40th Anniv. — A166

No. 2674: a, $25, Official coronation photograph. b, $50, Gems from royal collection. c, $75, Queen, Duke of Edinburgh. d, $130, Queen opening Parliament.

$325, State Portrait, by Sir James Gunn, 1954-56.

1993, June 2 Litho. *Perf. 13½x14*

2674 A166 Sheet, 2 each #a.-d. 14.00 14.00

Souvenir Sheet

Perf. 14

2675 A166 $325 multicolored 9.00 9.00

No. 2675 contains one 28x42mm stamp.

For overprints see Nos. 2793-2795.

Jurassic Period Animals — A166a

No. 2675A — Animals from Jurassic period similar in appearance to animals from recent periods: b, Bird in flight. c, Ostriches. d, Mammoth. e, Reptile on shore, foliage and tree in background. f, Koala. g, Ape. h, Aquatic reptile, head at right. i, Reptile standing in water, head at left. j, Crocodile.

No. 2675K, Allosaurus, horiz. No. 2675L, Diplodocus, horiz. No. 2675M, Plateosaurus, horiz. No. 2675N, Stegosaurus, horiz. No. 2675O, Styracosaurus, horiz. No. 2675P, Tyrannosaurus rex, horiz.

1993, July 21 Litho. *Perf. 14*

2675A A166a $25 Block of 9, #b-j 7.50 7.50

Souvenir Sheets

2675K A166a $250 multi —
2675L A166a $250 multi —
2675M A166a $250 multi —
2675N A166a $250 multi —
2675O A166a $250 multi —
2675P A166a $250 multi —

A167

Famous People — A168

Athletes: No. 2676: a, O. J. Simpson, football. b, Rohan B. Kanhai, cricket. c, Gabriela Sabatini, tennis. d, Severiano Ballesteros, golf. e, Peace dove, blue background. f, Franz Beckenbauer, soccer. g, Pele, soccer. h, Wilt Chamberlain, basketball, i, Nadia Comaneci, gymnastics.

Scientists: No. 2677: a, Louis Leakey, archaeology. b, Jonas Salk, polio vaccine. c, Hideyo Noguchi, yellow fever. d, Karl Landsteiner, blood transfusions. e, Peace dove, blue green background. f, Sigmund Freud, psychoanalysis. g, Louis Pasteur. h, Madame Curie, radium tubes. i, Jean Baptiste Perrin, physics.

Artists, entertainers: No. 2678: a, Gabriel Marquez, writer. b, Pablo Picasso, artist. c, Cecil DeMille, film director. d, Martha Graham, dance. e, Peace dove, purple background. f, Charles Chaplin, actor. g, Paul Robeson, singer. h, Rudolph Dunbar, musician. i, Louis Armstrong, musician.

Politicians: No. 2679: a, Jawaharlal Nehru. b, Dr. Eric Williams, first prime minister of Trinidad and Tobago. c, John F. Kennedy. d, Hugh Desmond Hoyte, president of Guyana. e, Peace dove over map. f, Friedrich Ebert. g, Franklin D. Roosevelt. h, Mikhail Gorbachev. i, Winston Churchill.

Humanitarians: No. 2680: a, Gandhi. b, Dalai Lama. c, Michael Manley, prime minister of Jamaica. d, Javier Perez de Cuellar, former UN Secretary General. e, Peace dove, globe. f, Mother Teresa. g, Martin Luther King, Jr. h, Nelson Mandela. i, Raoul Wallenberg.

Transportation, communication: No. 2681: a, DC-3 cargo plane. b, Space shuttle. c, Concorde. d, Ferdinand von Zeppelin. e, Peace dove. f, Guglielmo Marconi. g, Adrian Thompson, mountaineer. h, Bullet train, Japan. i, John von Neumann, mathematician.

No. 2682, UN Flag, natl. flags. No. 2683, Jackie Robinson. No. 2684, Einstein's formula. No. 2685, Elvis Presley. No. 2686, Nobel Peace Prize certificate. No. 2687, Apollo Moon Landing.

1993, July 26 Litho. *Perf. 14*

2676 A167 $50 Sheet of 9, #a.-i. 12.00 12.00
2677 A167 $50 Sheet of 9, #a.-i. 12.00 12.00
2678 A167 $50 Sheet of 9, #a.-i. 12.00 12.00
2679 A168 $100 Sheet of 9, #a.-i. 12.00 12.00
2680 A168 $100 Sheet of 9, #a.-i. 12.00 12.00
2681 A168 $100 Sheet of 9, #a.-i. 12.00 12.00

Souvenir Sheets

2682 A168 $250 multi, vert. 7.00 7.00
2683 A167 $250 multi, vert. 7.00 7.00
2684 A167 $250 multi, vert. 7.00 7.00
2685 A167 $250 multi, vert. 7.00 7.00
2686 A168 $250 multi, vert. 7.00 7.00
2687 A168 $250 multi 7.00 7.00

Mushrooms — A168a

Designs: $7.65, Amanita phalloides. $8.90, Boletus satanas. $50, Suillus granulatus. $100, Gymnopilus spectabilis. $250, Pluteus leoninus.

No. 2687F, Coprinus plicatilis. No. 2687G, Hypholoma fasciculare. No. 2687H, Hygrocybe chlorophana. No. 2687I, Omphalotus illudens. No. 2687J, Kuehnevomyces mutabilis, vert.

1993, July 28 Litho. *Perf. 14x13½*

2687A A168a $7.65 multi .25 .25
2687B A168a $8.90 multi .25 .25
2687C A168a $50 multi 1.00 1.00
2687D A168a $100 multi 2.00 2.00
2687E A168a $250 multi 5.00 5.00
Nos. 2687A-2687E (5) 8.50 8.50

Souvenir Sheet

Perf. 14

2687F A168a $500 multi 2.50 2.50
2687G A168a $500 multi 2.50 2.50
2687H A168a $500 multi 2.50 2.50
2687I A168a $500 multi 2.50 2.50
2687J A168a $500 multi 2.50 2.50
Nos. 2687F-2687J (5) 12.50 12.50

Nos. 2687A-2687E exist perf. 10.

Willy Brandt (1913-1992), German Chancellor — A169

Designs: $25, Brandt, Golda Meir, 1969. $190, Brandt at steel mill, 1969. $325, Brandt.

1993, Aug. 16 Litho. *Perf. 14*

2688 A169 $25 multicolored 1.00 1.00
2689 A169 $190 multicolored 5.00 5.00

Souvenir Sheet

2690 A169 $325 multicolored 7.50 7.50

Armillary Sphere — A170

Copernicus (1473-1543): $190, Satellite antenna. $300, Copernicus.

1993, Aug. 16

2691	A170	$50	multicolored	1.50	1.50
2692	A170	$190	multicolored	5.50	5.50

Souvenir Sheet

2693	A170	$300	multicolored	7.00	7.00

Georg Hackl, Luge Gold Medalist, 1992 — A171

1994 Winter Olympics, Lillehammer, Norway: $130, Karen Magnussen, figure skater, 1972. $325, German bobsled team, 1992.

1993, Aug. 16

2694	A171	$50	multicolored	1.00	1.00
2695	A171	$130	multicolored	3.00	3.00

Souvenir Sheet

2696	A171	$325	multicolored	7.50	7.50

A172

World War II — A173

Designs: $6.40, Audie Murphy. $7.65, British, US forces link up in France, June 8, 1944. $8.90, Monte Cassino falls to Allies, May 18, 1944. $12.80, Battleship Yamato attacked by US in Battle of East China Sea, Apr. 7, 1945. $15.30, St. Basil's Cathedral, Moscow, Foreign Ministers Conf., Oct. 19, 1943. $50, US forces cross Rhine River, Mar. 7, 1945. $100, B-29s begin bombing raids on Japan from China, June 15, 1944. $130, Gen. George S. Patton, Jr., Battle of Sicily ends, Aug. 17, 1943. $190, Battleship Tirpitz sunk, Nov. 12, 1944. $200, US Sherman tank, US forces enter Brittany after taking Normandy, Aug. 1, 1944. $225, End of fighting in Italy, May 2, 1945.

No. 2708 — War at Sea, 1943: a, Adm. Yamamoto launches air offensive, Apr. 7. b, PT-109 in Blackett Strait, Aug. 1. c, USS Enterprise. d, Allied ships attack Rabaul, Oct. 12. e, US troops land at Cape Gloucester, Dec. 26. f, USS Bogue enters service, Feb. g, Wildcat fighters sink U-118. h, Battle of Atlantic reaches peak, U-boats sink 108 ships. i, Italian fleet surrenders at Malta, Sept. 10. j, Battleship Duke of York sinks Scharnhorst, Dec. 26.

No. 2709 — War in the Air, 1943: a, Royal Australian Air Force Beaufighter, Battle of Bismark Sea, Mar. 2-4. b, P-38 Lightening shoots down Adm. Yamamoto's plane over Bougainville, Apr. 7. c, B-24 Liberators bomb Tarawa prior to landings, Sept. 17-19. d, B-25 Mitchell of Fifth Air Force bombs Rabaul, Oct. 12. e, US Navy aircraft attack Makin, Nov. 19. f, US Army Air Force's first daylight raid over Germany, Jan. 27. g, Royal Air Force Mosquito bombers make first daylight raid on Berlin, Jan. 30. h, Allies devastate Hamburg with first firestorm, July 24-30. i, B-24 bombers raid Ploesti oil refineries in Romania, Aug. 1. j, Battle of Berlin begins, Nov. 18.

No. 2710, $325, US, Russian infantry meeting at Elbe River, Apr. 25, 1945.

1993, Oct. 18 Litho. *Perf. 14*

2697	A172	$6.40	multicolored	.30	.30
2698	A172	$7.65	multicolored	.30	.30
2699	A172	$8.90	multicolored	.30	.30
2700	A172	$12.80	multicolored	.30	.30
2701	A172	$15.30	multicolored	.30	.30
2702	A172	$50	multicolored	1.25	1.25
2703	A172	$100	multicolored	2.50	2.50
2704	A172	$130	multicolored	3.00	3.00
2705	A172	$190	multicolored	4.00	4.00
2706	A172	$200	multicolored	4.50	4.50
2707	A172	$225	multicolored	5.25	5.25
	Nos. 2697-2707 (11)			22.00	22.00

Miniature Sheets

Perf. 15

2708	A173	$50	Sheet of 10, #a.-j.	12.00	12.00
2709	A172	$50	Sheet of 10, #a.-j.	12.00	12.00

Nos. 2709a-2709j are 35½x22mm.

Souvenir Sheet

Perf. 14

2710	A172	$325	multicolored	8.00	8.00

1994 World Cup Soccer Championships, U.S. — A174

Player, country: $5, Stuart Pearce, England. $6.40, Ronald Koeman, Holland. $7.65, Gianluca Vialli, Italy. $12.80, McStay, Scotland, Alemao, Brazil. $15.30, Ceulemans, Belgium, Butcher, England. $50, Dragan Stojkovic, Yugoslovia. $100, Ruud Gullit, Holland. $130, Miloslav Kadlec, Czechoslovakia. $150, Ramos, Uruguay, Berthold, Germany. $190, Baggio, Italy; Wright, England. $200, Yarentchuck, Russia, Renquin, Belgium. $225, Timofte, Romania; Aleinikov, Russia. No. 2724, Rene Higuita, Colombia. No. 2723, Salvatore Schillaci, Italy, horiz.

1993, Oct. 18 Litho. *Perf. 14*

2711	A174	$5	multicolored	.25	.25
2712	A174	$6.40	multicolored	.25	.25
2713	A174	$7.65	multicolored	.25	.25
2714	A174	$12.80	multicolored	.25	.25
2715	A174	$15.30	multicolored	.25	.25
2716	A174	$50	multicolored	.90	.90
2717	A174	$100	multicolored	2.00	2.00
2718	A174	$130	multicolored	2.50	2.50
2719	A174	$150	multicolored	2.75	2.75
2720	A174	$190	multicolored	3.50	3.50
2721	A174	$200	multicolored	3.75	3.75
2722	A174	$225	multicolored	4.25	4.25
	Nos. 2711-2722 (12)			20.90	20.90

Souvenir Sheets

2723	A174	$325	multicolored	7.00	7.00
2724	A174	$325	multicolored	7.00	7.00

Order of the Caribbean Community A175

No. 2725, William Demas. No. 2726, Derek Walcott. No. 2727, Sir Shridath Ramphal.

1993, Sept. 27 Litho. *Perf. 14*

2725	A175	$7.65	multi	1.00	.75
2726	A175	$7.65	multi	1.00	.75
2727	A175	$7.65	multi	2.00	1.00
	Nos. 2725-2727 (3)			4.00	2.50

Christmas A176

Details from Holy Family Under the Apple Tree, by Rubens: No. 2728, $6.40, No. 2730, $12.80, No. 2733, $130, No. 2734, $190.

Details from The Virgin in Glory, by Durer: No. 2729, $7.65, No. 2731, $15.30, No. 2732, $50, No. 2735, $250.

No. 2736, Holy Family Under the Apple Tree (entire). No. 2737, The Virgin in Glory (entire).

1993, Dec. 1 *Perf. 13½x14*

2728-2735	A176	Set of 8	10.00	10.00

Souvenir Sheets

2736	A176	$325	multicolored	6.00	6.00
2737	A176	$325	multicolored	6.00	6.00

For surcharge, see No. 4177.

Louvre Museum, Bicent. A177

Details or entire paintings: No. 2738, Mona Lisa, by Da Vinci.

No. 2739, $50: a, La Femme à la Puce, by Crespi. b, La Femme Hydropique, by Dou. c, Portrait d'un Couple, by Ittenbach. d, Cléopâtre Assise, Demi Face, sur un Trône Élevé , by Moreau. e, La Richesse, by Vouet. f, Vieillard et Jeune Garçon, by Ghirlandaio. g, Louis XIV, by Rigaud. h, La Buveuse, by Pieter De Hooch.

No. 2740, $50: a, Autoportrait aux Besicles, by Chardin. b, L'Infante Marie-Thérèse, by Velasquez. c, Le Printemps, by Arcimboldo. d, La Vierge de Douleur, by Bouts. e, L'Etude, by Fragonard. f. François 1er, by Clouet. g, Le Condottière, by Antonello Da Messina. h, La Bohémienne, by Hals.

No. 2741, $50: a, La Femme à la Puce, entire, by Crespi. b, Autoportrait au Chevalet, by Rembrandt. c, Femmes d'Alger dans Leur Appartement, by Delacroix. d, Tête de Jeune Homme, by Raphael. e, Vénus et les Grâces, by Botticelli. f, Nature Morte à l'Échiquier, by Lubin Baugin. g, Lady MacBeth Somnambule, by Fussli. h, La Tabagie, by Chardin.

Nos. 2742, $50: a-c, L'Accordée de Village (left, center, right), by Greuze. d, Autoportrait, by Melendez. e, Le Chevalier, La Jeune Fille et La Mont, by Baldung-Grien. f, Le Jeune Mendiant, by Murillo. g-h, Les Pèlerins d'Emmaus (left, right), by Mathieu Le Nain.

No. 2743, $50: a-b, Le Vierge au Lapin (diff. details), by Titian. c, La Belle Jardinière, by Raphael. d, La Dentellière, by Vermeer. e, Jeanne d'Aragon, by Raphael. f, L'Astronome, by Vermeer. g, Le Pont du Rialto, by Canaletto. h, Sigismond Malatesta, by Piero Della Francesca.

No. 2744, $325, Cour de Ferme, by Jan Brueghel, the Younger. No. 2745, $325, Le Pont du Rialto, by Canaletto. No. 2746, $325, Le Sacre de Napoléon 1er, by David. No. 2747, $325, Details and painting of Mona Lisa. No. 2748, $325, Le Diseuse de Bonne Aventure, by Caravaggio. No. 2749, $325, Les Noces de Cana, by Veronese.

1993, Dec. 6 Litho. *Perf. 13½x14*

2738	A177	$50	multicolored	.75	.75
a.	Sheet of 8 + label			6.00	6.00

Sheets of 8, #a-h, + Label

2739-2743	A177	Set of 5	35.00	35.00

Souvenir Sheets

Perf. 12

2744-2749	A177	Set of 6	30.00	30.00

Nos. 2744-2746 each contain one 80x47mm stamp. Nos. 2747-2749 one 80x53mm stamp.

Christmas A177a

Entire paintings or details: $7.65, St. Anne with Mary and the Child Jesus, by Dürer. $8.90, Mary Being Crowned by Two Angels, by Dürer. $50, Pentecost, by Titian. $100, Samson and Delilah, by Rubens. $250, Origin of the Milky Way, by Rubens.

No. 2749F, $500, The Descent from the Cross, by Rubens, horiz. No. 2749G, $500, The Descent from the Cross, by Dürer, horiz.

1993 Litho. *Perf. 13½x14, 14x13½*

2749A-2749E	A177a	Set of 5	12.00	12.00

Souvenir Sheets

2749F-2749G	A177a	Set of 2	13.00	13.00

Polska '93 (Paintings) — A178

Designs: $50, $130, Pantaloons, by Tadeusz Brzozowski, 1966. $75, Photo of fortress in Miedzyrecz. $325, Children in the Garden, by Wladyslaw Podkowinski, 1892, horiz.

1993 *Perf. 14*

2750		$50	multicolored	1.25	1.25
2751	A178	$75	multicolored	1.75	1.75
2752		$130	multicolored	4.00	4.00
a.	A178 Pair, #2750, #2752			6.00	6.00
	Nos. 2750-2752 (3)			7.00	7.00

Souvenir Sheet

2753	A178	$325	multicolored	7.00	7.00

Picasso (Paintings) — A179

Designs: $15.30, Bather, Paris, 1909. $100, Two Nudes, 1906. $190, Nude Seated on a Rock, 1921. $325, The Rescue, 1922.

1993, Nov. Litho. *Perf. 14*

2754	A179	$15.30	multi	.40	.40
2755	A179	$100	multi	2.40	2.40
2756	A179	$190	multi	4.50	4.50
	Nos. 2754-2756 (3)			7.30	7.30

Souvenir Sheet

2756A	A179	$325	multi	7.00	7.00

Rebirth of Democracy, 1st Anniv. — A180

Designs: $6.40, Dr. Cheddie B. Jagan, Guyana Pres. $325, Sunburst, "REBIRTH OF DEMOCRACY," horiz.

1993, Dec. 17 Litho. *Perf. 13½x14*

2757	A180	$6.40 multicolored	.70	.70

Souvenir Sheet

Perf. 13

2757A	A180	$325 multicolored	6.50	6.50

Aladdin — A181

Nos. 2758: a-h, Various characters from Disney animated film, vert.

Nos. 2759: a-i, Various film scenes.

Nos. 2760: a-i, Various scenes from Disney animated film.

No. 2761, Genie, Jasmine, and Aladdin. No. 2762, Aladdin, the Genie, Abu, Magic Carpet. No. 2763, Aladdin as Prince Ali Ababwa. No. 2764, Aladdin, Abu, Jasmine.

1993, Dec. 20 Litho. *Perf. 14x13½*

2758	A181	$7.65 Sheet of 8, #a.-h.	2.00	2.00
2759	A181	$50 Sheet of 9, #a.-i.	8.00	7.00
2760	A181	$65 Sheet of 9, #a.-i.	11.00	8.00
		Nos. 2758-2760 (3)	21.00	17.00

Souvenir Sheets

2761	A181	$325 multicolored	6.50	6.50
2762	A181	$325 multicolored	6.50	6.50
2763	A181	$325 multicolored	6.50	6.50
2764	A181	$325 multicolored	6.50	6.50

A182

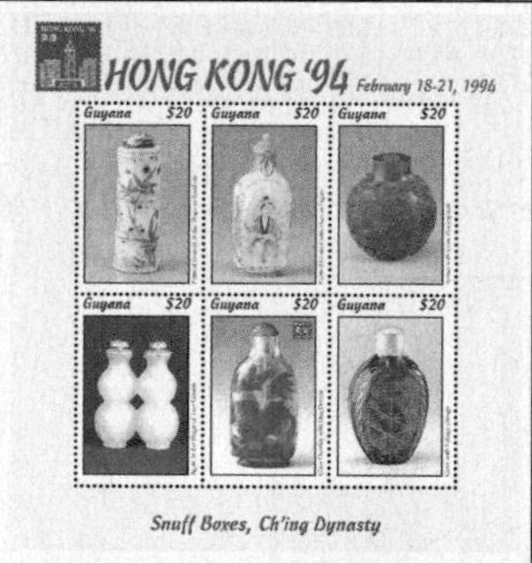

Hong Kong '94 — A183

Stamps, photograph of Happy Valley Horse Race Course: No. 2765, Hong Kong #437, scoreboard. No. 2766, Track, horses, #2545.

No. 2767 — Snuff boxes, Qing Dynasty: a, Painted enamel in shape of bamboo. b, Painted enamel with human figure. c, Amber with lions playing ball. d, Agate in shape of two gourds. e, Glass overlay with dog. f, Glass, foliage design.

No. 2768 — Porcelain, Ch'ing Dynasty: a, Covered jar with dragon. b, Rotating brush holder. c, Covered jar with horses. d, Amphora vase with bats & peaches. e, Tea caddy with Fo dogs. f, Vase with wild camellia & peaches.

1994, Feb. 18 *Perf. 14*

2765	A182	$50 multicolored	.80	.80
2766	A182	$50 multicolored	.80	.80
a.		Pair, #2765-2766	1.75	1.75

Miniature Sheets

2767	A183	$20 Sheet of 6, #a.-f.	5.00	5.00
2768	A183	$20 Sheet of 6, #a.-f.	5.00	5.00

Nos. 2765-2766 issued in sheets of 5 pairs. No. 2766a is continuous design.

New Year 1994 (Year of the Dog) (Nos. 2767e, #2768e).

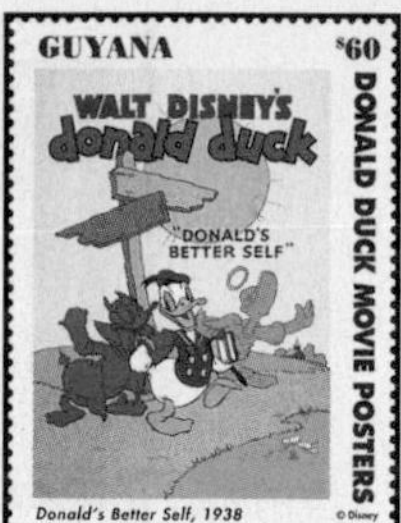

Vintage Donald Duck — A184

No. 2769, $60 — Movie posters: a, Donald's Better Self, 1938. b, Donald's Golf Game, 1938. c, Sea Scouts, 1939. d, Donald's Penguin, 1939. e, A Good Time for a Dime, 1941. f, Truant Officer Donald. g, Orphan's Benefit, 1941. h, Chef Donald, 1941.

No. 2770, $60: a, The Village Smithy, 1942. b, Donald's Snow Fight, 1942. c, Donald's Garden, 1942. d, Donald's Gold Mine, 1942. e, The Vanishing Private, 1942. f, Sky Trooper, 1942. g, Bellboy Donald, 1942. h, The New Spirit, 1942.

No. 2771, $60: a, Saludos Amigos, 1943. b, The Eyes Have It, 1945. c, Donald's Crime, 1945. d, Straight Shooters, 1947. e, Donald's Dilemma, 1947. f, Bootle Beetle, 1947. g, Daddy Duck, 1948. h, Soup's On, 1948.

No. 2772 — Story boards from Pirate Gold, horiz.: a, Pirate ship. b, Carrying treasure chest. c, Donald Duck with map. d, Donald, souvenir shop. e, Donald following Aracuan bird. f, Angry Donald.

No. 2773, $80 — Movie posters: a, Donald's Happy Birthday, 1949. b, Sea Salts, 1949. c, Honey Harvester, 1949. d, All in a Nutshell, 1949. e, The Greener Yard, 1949. f, Slide, Donald, Slide, 1949. g, Lion Around, 1950. h, Trailer Horn, 1950.

No. 2774, $80: a, Bee at the Beach, 1950. b, Out on a Limb, 1950. c, Corn Chips, 1951. d, Test Pilot Donald, 1951. e, Lucky Number, 1951. f, Out of Scale, 1951. g, Bee on Guard, 1951. h, Let's Stick Together, 1952.

No. 2775, $80: a, Trick or Treat, 1952. b, Don's Fountain of Youth, 1953. c, Rugged Bear, 1953. d, Canvas Back Duck, 1953. e, Dragon Around, 1954. f, Grin and Bear It, 1954. g, The Flying Squirrel, 1954. h, Up a Tree, 1955.

No. 2776, Studio Fan Card, Melody Time, 1948.

No. 2777, $500, Scene from picture book of first movie, The Wise Little Hen, 1944, horiz. No. 2778, $500, Sketch for closing scene of Timber, 1941. No. 2779, $500, Donald Duck, horiz. No. 2780, $500, Studio fan card, The Three Caballeros, 1945, horiz.

Movie posters contained in No. 2780A are listed as designs for Nos. 2769-2771, 2774-2775, 2777, 2780.

Perf. 14x13½, 13½x14

1993, Dec. 6 Litho.

Sheets of 8, #a-h

2769-2771	A184	Set of 3	25.00	25.00
2772	A184	$80 Sheet of 6, #a.-f.	8.00	8.00

Sheets of 8, #a-h

2773-2775	A184	Set of 3	27.50	27.50

Size: 130x104mm

Imperf

2776	A184	$500 multi	10.00	10.00

Souvenir Sheets

Perf. 14x13½, 13½x14

2777-2780	A184	Set of 4	40.00	40.00

Imperf

Self-Adhesive

Size: 64x89mm

2780A	A184	$60 Set of 50	70.00

No. 2780A exists with backing labels printed in English or French. Value is for either set. No. 2780A was printed on thin card and sold in sealed cellophane packages containing 10 stamps. To affix stamps, backing containing film information must be removed.

Nos. 2769-2771, 2773-2775 exist in sheets of 7 $5 stamps + label. The label replaces Nos. 2769f, 2770b, 2771h, 2773a, 2774d, 2775e. These sheets became available Nov. 20, 1996.

Tropical Flowers A185

Designs: $6.40, Cestrum parqui. $7.65, Brunfelsia calycina. $12.80, Datura rosei. $15.30, Ruellia macrantha. No. 2785, $50, Portlandia albiflora. $130, Pachystachys coccinea. $190, Beloperone guttata. $250, Ferdinandusa speciosa.

No. 2789, $50: a, Clusia grandiflora. b, Begonia haageana. c, Fuchsia simplicicaulis. d, Guaiacum officinale (a). e, Pithecoctenium cynanchoides. f, Sphaeralcea umbellata. g, Erythrina poeppigiana. h, Steriphoma paradoxa. i, Allemanda violacea (f). j, Centropogon cornutus (g). k, Passiflora quadrangularis. l, Victoria amazonica.

No. 2790, $50: a, Cobaea scandens. b, Pyrostegia venusta (c). c, Petrea kohautiana (b). d, Hippobroma longiflora (a). e, Cleome hassleriana (b, d, f, h, i). f, Verbena peruviana (c). g, Tropaeolum peregrinum. h, Plumeria rubra (g, i). i, Selenicereus grandiflorus. j, Mandevilla splendens (g). k, Pereskia aculeata. l, Ipomoea learii.

No. 2791, $325, Columnea fendleri. No. 2792, $325, Lophospermum erubescens.

1994, Feb. 10 Litho. *Perf. 13½*

2781-2788	A185	Set of 8	10.00	10.00

Sheets of 12, #a-l

Perf. 14

2789-2790	A185	Set of 2	20.00	20.00

Souvenir Sheets

Perf. 13

2791-2792	A185	Set of 2	10.00	10.00

For surcharges, see Nos. 4110, 4111, 4113, 4114.

Nos. 2674-2675 Ovptd. "ROYAL VISIT FEB 19-22, 1994" in One or Two Lines

1994 Litho. *Perf. 13½x14*

2793	A166	Sheet, 2 each #a.-d.	14.00	14.00

Souvenir Sheet

Perf. 14

2794	A166	$325 multicolored	7.50	7.50

Hummel Figurines — A186

Designs: No. 2795, $20, No. 2803a, $30, Girl holding basket and heart. No. 2796, $25, Boy holding heart. No. 2797, $35, No. 2804a, $20, Chef holding dessert. No. 2798, $50, No. 2804b, $130, Girl holding planter of mushrooms. No. 2799, $60, Girl holding plant, horn. No. 2800, $130, No. 2803b, $6, Four girls. No. 2801, $190, Two girls, boy and puppy. No. 2802, $250, No. 2804c, $35, Boy holding covered dish, puppy.

1994, May 5 Litho. *Perf. 14*

2795-2802	A186	Set of 8	12.00	12.00

Souvenir Sheets

2803	A186	Sheet of 4, #a.-b, #2796, 2801	4.00	4.00
2804	A186	Sheet of 4, #a.-c, #2799	4.00	4.00

Sierra Club, Cent. A187

No. 2805 — Various animals or scenic places: a-b, American alligator. c-d, Italian Alps. e-f, Mono Lake.

No. 2806: a, Red kangaroo. b-d, Whooping crane. e-f, Alaskan brown bear. g, Bald eagle. h, Giant panda.

No. 2807, vert.: a-b, Red kangaroo. c, American alligator. d, Alaskan brown bear. e-f, Bald eagle. g-h, Giant panda.

No. 2808, vert.: a-c, Sea lion. d, Mono Lake. e, Sierra Club centennial emblem. f, Italian Alps. g-i, Matterhorn.

1994, May 20 Litho. *Perf. 14*

2805	A187	$70 Sheet of 6, #a.-f.	7.50	7.50
2806	A187	$70 Sheet of 8, #a.-h.	10.00	10.00
2807	A187	$70 Sheet of 8, #a.-h.	10.00	10.00
2808	A187	$70 Sheet of 9, #a.-i.	11.00	11.00
		Nos. 2805-2808 (4)	38.50	38.50

First Manned Moon Landing, 25th Anniv. A188

No. 2809, $60: a, Robert R. Gilruth, Apollo 16. b, Ernst Stuhlinger, Apollo 17. c, Christopher C. Kraft, X-30 National Aero-Space Plane. d, Rudolf Opitz, Me-163, July 24, 1943. e, Clyde W. Tombaugh, "Face on Mars." f, Hermann Oberth, Scene from "The Girl in the Moon."

No. 2810, $60: a, Wernher von Braun, Apollo 11. b, Rocco A. Petrone, Apollo 11. c, Eberhard Rees, Apollo 12. d, Charles A. Berry, Apollo 13. e, Thomas O. Paine, Apollo 14. f, A.F. Staats, Apollo 15.

No. 2811, $60: a, Walter Dornberger, 1st A-4 launch. b, Rudolph Nebel, Surveyor 1. c, Robert H. Goddard, Apollo 7. d, Kurt Debus, Apollo 8. e, James T. Webb, Apollo 9. f, George E. Mueller, Apollo 10.

No. 2812, Frank J. Everest, Jr.

1994, July 20 Litho. *Perf. 14*

Sheets of 6, #a-f

2809-2811	A188	Set of 3	20.00	20.00

Souvenir Sheet

2812	A188	$325 multicolored	7.00	7.00

A189

World War II — A190

Designs: $6, Photo reconnaissance Spitfire. $35, 226 Squadron B-25. $190, 76 Squadron P-47 Thunderbolts.

No. 2816 — Europe and North Africa, 1944: a, Allied landings, Anzio, Jan. 22. b, RAF bombs Amiens prison, Feb. 18. c, Sevastopol falls to Red Army, May 9. d, Allies breach Gustav Line, May 19. e, D-Day, June 6. f, V-1 attacks on London begin, June 13. g, Cease fire declared for Paris, Aug. 19. h, Germany launches V-2 rockets, Sept. 8. i, German battleship Tirpitz sunk, Nov. 12. j, Siege of Bastogne lifted, Dec. 29.

No. 2817 — D-Day: a, Paratroops drop behind enemy lines. b, Glider-born commandos land behind enemy lines. c, USS Arkansas shells Omaha beach defenses. d, Allied aircraft attack enemy movements. e, Allied landing craft hit the beach. f, Allied troops pinned down by enemy fire. g, Commandos exit landing craft. h, Specialized Allied tanks destroy enemy mines. i, Allies break through beach defenses. j, Consolidation of position.

No. 2818, RAF Lancaster bomber.

1994, June 20 *Perf. 14*

2813	A189	$6 multicolored	.30	.25
2814	A189	$35 multicolored	.85	.50
2815	A189	$190 multicolored	3.75	3.25
		Nos. 2813-2815 (3)	4.90	4.00

Perf. 13

2816	A190	$60 Sheet of 10, #a.-j.	12.00	10.00
2817	A190	$60 Sheet of 10, #a.-j.	12.00	10.00

Souvenir Sheet

Perf. 14

2818	A189	$325 multicolored	7.00	7.00

A191

Butterflies A192

Designs: $6, Heliconius melpomene. $20, Helicopius cupido. $25, Agrias claudina. $30, Parides coelus. $50, Heliconius hecale. $60, Morpho diana. $190, Dismorphia orise. $250, Morpho deidamia.

No. 2827: a, Anaea marthesia. b, Brassolis astyra. c, Heliconius melpomene. d, Haetera piera. e, Morpho diana dixey. f, Parides coelus. g, Catagramma pitheas. h, Nessaea obrinus. i, Automeris janus. j, Papilio torquatus. k, Eunica sophonisba. l, Ceratinia nise. m, Panacea procilla. n, Pyrrhogyra neaerea. o, Morpho deidamia. p, Dismorphia orise.

No. 2829, $325, Eunica sophonisba. No. 2830, $325, Anaea eribotes.

No. 2831, $325, Hamadryas velutina. No. 2832, $325, Agrias claudina.

1994, July 5 Litho. *Perf. 14*

2819-2826 A191 Set of 8 13.00 13.00
2827 A192 $50 Sheet of 16, #a.-p. 12.00 12.00

Souvenir Sheets

2829-2830 A191 Set of 2 10.00 10.00
2831-2832 A192 Set of 2 10.00 10.00

Nos. 2829-2830 each contain one 43x28mm stamp.

Bible Stories — A193

No. 2833 — Story of Ruth and Naomi: a-f: Ruth & Naomi preparing to leave Moab & return to Israel. g-l: Ruth harvesting grain in fields of Boaz. m-r: Boaz receives a man's sandal, finalizing sale of Naomi's field. s-x: Naomi, Boaz, Ruth and Obed, who was David's grandfather.

No. 2834 — Story of Joseph: a-d, Jacob made Joseph a coat of many colors. e-h, Joseph's brothers take his coat and cast him into pit. i-l, Joseph is sold to the Ishmaelites. m-p, Joseph is accused by Potiphar's wife and thrown into prison. q-t, Joseph interprets Pharoah's dreams. u-x, Joseph is reunited with his brothers.

No. 2835 — Parting of the Red Sea: a-x, Moses leading Israelites through sea, Pharoah's army drowning.

No. 2836 — Daniel and the Lions: a-x, Daniel in lion's den surrounded by various animals, angel.

1994, Aug. 4 Litho. *Perf. 14*

Sheets of 24, #a-x

2833-2836 A193 $20 Set of 4 40.00 40.00

Nos. 2835-2836 have continuous design.

A194 A195

Philakorea '94: $6, Statues of socialist ideals, Pyongyang. $25, Statue of Adm. Yi Sunsin. $120, Sokkat'ap Pagoda, Pulguksa. $130, Village guardian, Chejudo Island.

No. 2841, $60 — Ten-fold screens: a, Shown. b-e, Cranes. h-i, Deer. j, Deer, mushrooms, waterfall.

No. 2842, $60: b-d, Cranes. f-h, Deer. c, h, Waterfalls. i-j, Mushrooms.

No. 2843, $325, Falled Rock, horiz. No. 2844, $325, Westerners at Korean Court, horiz.

1994, June 20 Litho. *Perf. 14*

2837-2840 A194 Set of 4 5.00 5.00

Sheets of 10, #a-j

Perf. 13

2841-2842 A195 Set of 2 20.00 20.00

Souvenir Sheets

Perf. 14

2843-2844 A194 Set of 2 10.00 10.00

Nos. 2841-2842 have continuous design.

Entertainers of Takarazuka Revue, Japan A196

No. 2845: a, $60, Mira Anju. b, $60, Yuki Amami. c, $60, Maki Ichiro. d, $60, Yu Shion. e, $20, Miki Maya. f, $20, Fubuki Takane. g, $20, Seika Juze. h, $20, Saki Asaji.

1994 *Perf. 14½*

2845 A196 Sheet of 8, #a.-h. + 4 labels 8.00 8.00

Nos. 2845a-2845d are 34x47mm.

A197

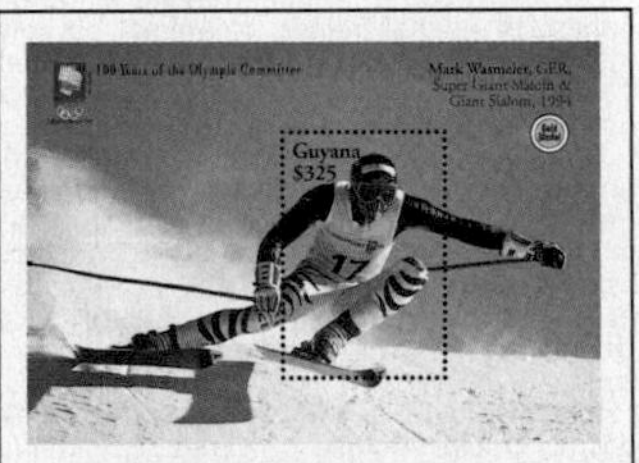

Intl. Olympic Committee, Cent. — A198

Designs: $20, Nancy Kerrigan, US, figure skating, 1994. $35, Sawao Kato, Japan, gymnastics, 1976. $130, Florence Griffith-Joyner, US, 100-, 200-meters, 1988.

$325, Mark Wasmeier, Germany, super giant & giant slalom, 1994.

1994, June 20

2846-2848 A197 Set of 3 4.00 4.00

Souvenir Sheet

2849 A198 $325 multicolored 7.00 7.00

1994 World Cup Soccer Championships, U.S. — A199

Player, country: $6, Paulo Futre, Portugal. $35, Lyndon Hooper, Canada. $60, Enzo Francescoli, Uruguay. $190, Freddy Rincon, Colombia.

No. 2854, $60: a, Paolo Maldini, Italy. b, Guyana player. c, Bwalya Kalusha, Zambia. d, Diego Maradona, Argentina. e, Andreas Brehme, Germany. f, Eric Wynalda, US.

No. 2855, $60: a, John Doyle, US. b, Eric Wynalda, US, diff. c, Thomas Dooley, US. d, Ernie Stewart, US. f, Marcelo Balboa, US. g, Coach Bora Milutinovic, US.

No. 2856, $325, 1994 World Cup program cover. No. 2857, $325,Oiler Watson.

1994, Aug. 8

2850-2853 A199 Set of 4 5.00 5.00

Sheets of 6, #a-f

2854-2855 A199 Set of 2 15.00 15.00

Souvenir Sheets

2856-2857 A199 Set of 2 14.00 14.00

Birds — A200

No. 2858, $35: a, Goshawk. b, Lapwing. c, Ornate umbrellabird. d, Slatey-headed parakeet. e, Regent bowerbird. f, Egytian goose. g, White-winged crossbill. h, Waxwing. i, Ruff. j, Hoopoe. k, Superb starling. l, Great jacamar.

No. 2859, $35: a, Peregrine falcon. b, Great spotted woodpecker. c, White-throated kingfisher. d, Peruvian cock-of-the-rock. e, Yellow-headed Amazon. f, Victoria crowned pigeon. g, Little owl. h, Pheasant. i, Goldfinch. j, Jay. k, Sulphur-brasted toucan. l, Japanese blue flycatcher.

No. 2860, $325, Gould's violet-ear. No. 2861, $325, Bald eagle.

1994, Sept. 15 Sheets of 12, #a.-l.

2858-2859 A200 Set of 2 17.00 17.00

Souvenir Sheets

2860-2861 A200 Set of 2 16.00 16.00

PHILAKOREA '94. For surcharges, see Nos. 4118, 4184.

1996 Summer Olympics, Atlanta — A201

German athletes: $6, Anja Fichtel, fencing, 1988, horiz. $25, Annegret Richter, 100-meter dash, 1976. $30, Heike Henkel, high jump, 1982. $35, Armin Hary, 100-meter dash, 1960. $50, Heide Rosendahl, long jump, 1972. $60, Josef Neckermann, equestrian grand prix, 1968. $130, Heike Drechsler, long jump, 1988. $190, Ulrike Mayfarth, high jump, 1984. $250, Michael Gross, swimming, 1984, horiz.

No. 2870A: b, $135, Markus Wasmeier, skiing, 1994. c, $190, Katja Seizinger, skiing, 1994.

No. 2871, $325, Franziska van Almsick, swimming, 1992. No. 2872, $325, Steffi Graf, tennis, 1992.

1994, Sept. 28

2862-2870 A201 Set of 9 13.00 13.00

Souvenir Sheets

2870A A201 Sheet of 2, #b.-c. 5.50 5.50
2871-2872 A201 Set of 2 11.00 11.00

Space Missions, First Manned Moon Landing, 25th Anniv. A202

No. 2873, $60: a, Laika, first dog in space. b, Yuri Gagarin, first man in space. c, John Glenn, first American to orbit earth. d, Edward White, first American to walk in space. e, Neil Armstrong, first to step foot onto moon. f, Luna 16. g, Luna 17. h, Skylab 1. i, 1975 Apollo-Soyuz.

No. 2874, $60 — Unmanned probes: a, Mars 3, Mars. b, Mariner 10, Mercury. c, Voyager, planetary grand tour. d, Pioneer, Venus. e, Giotto, Halley's Comet. f, Megellan, Venus. g, Galileo, Jupiter. h, Ulysses, Sun. i, Cassini, Titan.

No. 2875, $325, "Buzz" Aldrin, Neil Armstrong, Michael Collins. No. 2876, $325, Pioneer 1, 2.

1994, Nov. 10 Litho. *Perf. 13½*

Sheets of 9, #a-i

2873-2874 A202 Set of 2 18.00 18.00

Souvenir Sheets

2875-2876 A202 Set of 2 11.00 11.00

Steam Locomotives — A203

Designs: No. 2877, $25, South Eastern Railway #285, 1882. No. 2878, $25, West Point Foundry, 1830. No. 2879, $300, Mt. Washington Cog Railway, 1886. No. 2880, $300, Stroudley-Brighton, 1872.

No. 2881, $30: a, "John Bull," 1831. b, Stephenson, 1837. c, "Atlantic," 1832. d, Stourbridge Lion, 1829. e, Polonceau, 1854. f, Rogers, 1856. g, "Vulcan," 1858. h, "Namur," 1846.

No. 2882, $30: a, West Point Foundry, 1832. b, Sequin, 1830. c, Stephenson's Planet, 1830. d, Norris 4-2-0, 1840. e, Union Iron Works os San Francisco, 1867. f, Andrew Jackson, 1832. g, Herald, 1831. h, Cumberland, 1845.

No. 2883, $30: a, Pennsylvania's Class K, 1880. b, Cooke, 1885. c, John B. Turner, 1867. d, Baldwin, 1871. e, Richard Trevithick, 1804. f, John Stephens, 1825. g, John Blenkinsop, 1814. h, Pennsylvania, 1803.

$250, Est Railway, 1878. $300, "Claud Hamilton," 1840.

1994, Nov. 15 *Perf. 14*

2877-2880 A203 Set of 4 10.00 10.00

Sheets of 8, #a-h, + Label

2881-2883 A203 Set of 3 14.00 14.00

Souvenir Sheets

2884 A203 $250 multicolored 5.00 5.00
2885 A203 $300 multicolored 6.00 6.00

For surcharge, see No. 4116.

English Touring Cricket, Cent. A204

Designs: $20, C.H. Lloyd, Guyana/West Indies, vert. $35, C.W. Hooper, Guyana/West Indies, Wisden Trophy. $60, G.A. Hick, England, Wisden Trophy.

$200, First English Team, 1895.

1994, June 20 Litho. *Perf. 14*

2886-2888 A204 Set of 3 2.00 2.00

Souvenir Sheet

2889 A204 $200 multicolored 3.25 3.25

Christmas A205

Paintings: $6, Joseph with the Christ Child, by Guido Reni. $20, Adoration of the Christ Child, by Girolamo Romanino. $25, Adoration of the Christ Child with St. Barbara and St. Martin, by Raffaello Botticini. $30, Holy Family, by Pompeo Girolam Batoni. $35, Flight into Egypt, by Bartolommeo Carducci. $60, Holy Family and the Baptist, by Andrea del Sarto. $120, Sacred Conversation, by Cesare de Sesto. $190, Madonna and Child with Sts. Joseph & John the Baptist, by Pontormo.

No. 2898, $325, Holy Family and St. Elizabeth and St. John the Baptist, by Francisco Primaticcio. No. 2899, $325, Presentation of Christ in the Temple, by Fra Bartolommeo.

1994, Dec. 5 ***Perf. 13½x14***
2890-2897 A205 Set of 8 12.00 6.00

Souvenir Sheets

2898-2899 A205 Set of 2 10.00 10.00

Order of the Caribbean Community — A206

First award recipients: No. 2900, $60, Sir Shridath Ramphal, statesman, Guyana. No. 2901, $60, William Demas, economist, Trinidad & Tobago. No. 2902, $60, Derek Walcott, writer, St. Lucia.

1994 ***Perf. 14***

2900-2902 A206 Set of 3 4.00 4.00

Motion Picture, Star Trek Generations A207

A207a

No. 2903, "Boldly Go," Starship Enterprise.
No. 2904, $100: a, Capt. Picard. b, Cmdr. Riker. c, Capt. Kirk. d, Villain with phaser. e, Kirk, Picard on horseback. f, Klingons L'rsa and B'tor. g, Kirk, Picard, diff. h, Counselor Troi. i, Picard, Lt. Cmdr. Data.
No. 2905, $100: a, Troi, Riker. b, Worf. c, Picard. d, Worf, Lt. Cmdr. LaForge. e, Sailing ship, Enterprise. f, Picard, Riker. g, Data. h, Worf. i, Dr. Crusher.
No. 2906, Like No. 2903, horiz.
$1000, Kirk and Picard.
No. 2906D: e, Capt. Picard. f, Capt. Kirk.

1994 **Litho.** ***Perf. 13½x14***
2903 A207 $100 multicolored 1.50 1.50

Sheets of 9, #a-i

2904-2905 A207 Set of 2 40.00 40.00

Souvenir Sheet

Perf. 14x13½

2906 A207 $500 multicolored 8.00 8.00

Litho. & Embossed

Die Cut Perf. 9

2906C A207a $1000 gold & multi *25.00 25.00*

Souvenir Sheet

Die Cut Perf. 9 on Outside

2906D A207a $500 Sheet of 2, #e.-f. *25.00 25.00*

Issued: No. 2906C, 11/18, others 12/7. No. 2903 was issued in sheets of 9. Nos. 2906e-2906f are imperf.

Sisters of Mercy of Guyana, Cent. — A208

1994, Dec. 12 ***Perf. 14***
2907 A208 $60 multicolored 1.90 1.90

Nos. 1037a, 1097, 1099 Surcharged

Surcharge reads: "ILO / 75th Anniversary / 1919-1994".

Perfs & Printing Methods as Before

1994
2907A A91 $6 on 130c #1037a
2907B A91 $30 on 120c #1099
2907C A91 $35 on 120c #1097

Nos. 1063, 1098, 1120, 1123 Surcharged in Blue

Surcharge reads: "CENTENARY / Sign For The / MAHDI / 1894-1994".

Perfs. & Printing Methods as Before

1994
2907D A91 $6 on 60c #1120
2907E A91 $20 on 200c #1063
2907F A91 $30 on 60c #1098
2907G A91 $35 on 60c #1123

Cricket A209

Designs: $20, Sobers congratulates Lara. $30, Brian Lara setting world record, vert. $375, Lara, Chanderpaul.
$300, Brian Lara walking under "avenue of bats," vert.

1995, Feb. 3 **Litho.** ***Perf. 14***
2908-2910 A209 Set of 3 7.00 7.00

Souvenir Sheet

2911 A209 $300 multicolored 5.50 5.50

A210

A211

Babe Ruth (1895-1948) — A212

Type A211 various portraits like #2914.
$2000, Portrait, Ruth holding bat, vert.

1995, Feb. 6 **Litho.** ***Perf. 14***
2912 A210 $65 multi 1.40 1.40

Self-Adhesive (#2913)

Size: 64x89mm (#2913)

2913 A211 $350 Set of 12 50.00 50.00

Litho. & Embossed

Perf. 12

2914 A212 $1000 gold & sep *25.00*

Embossed

2914A A212 $2000 gold *29.00*

Litho.

Perf. 14

2915 A211 $65 Sheet of 12, #a.-l. 12.00 12.00

Souvenir Sheet

2916 A211 $500 like #2912a, horiz. 10.00 10.00

No. 2912 issued in sheets of 9. Portraits of Babe Ruth in No. 2913 are same as in No. 2915, but surrounded by gold frame, gold autograph, baseballs, and simulated perfs. No. 2913 was sold in sealed celophane package. To affix stamps, backing containing biographical information must be removed.

Disney Characters at Work — A213

No. 2917, $30 — Animal workers: a, Veterinarian. b, Animal trainer. c, Animal psychiatrist. d, Ornithologist. e, Dog groomer. f, Herpetologist. g, Pet shop keeper. h, Park ranger. i, Aquarist.
No. 2918, $30 — Arts & crafts: a, Mickey the animator, Pluto. b, Goofy the tailor, Mickey. c, Pete the glass blower, Morty. d, Clarabelle modeling for Minnie the artist. e, Daisy sculpts Donald. f, Donald, nephews working with clay. g, Watchmakers, Chip & Dale. h, Locksmith Donald, nephews. i, Grandma Duck makes a quilt.
No. 2919, $30 — Medical group: a, Family doctor. b, Optometrist. c, Nurse. d, Psychiatrist. e, Physical therapist. f, Dentist. g, Radiologist. h, Pharmacist. i, Chiropractor.
No. 2920, $35 — Hard hat & company, vert.: a, Mickey, Pluto in truck. b, Mickey at work. c, Goofy jackhammer. d, Minnie at work. e, Forklifters. f, Construction contractor. g, Carpenter. h, Bulldozer.
No. 2921, $35 — Home services, vert.: a, Mickey, plumber. b, Mickey, paperboy. c, Huey, Dewey, Louie, moving service. d, Pete, handyman. e, Donald, newphews' house painting service. f, Goofy, washer repairman. g, Minnie, babysitter. h, Daisy cares for Grandma Duck.
No. 2922, $35 — Public service workers, vert.: a, Policeman. b, Fireman. c, Ambulance driver. d, Crossing guard. e, Museum docent. f, Census taker. g, Street maintenance workers. h, Sanitation worker.
No. 2923, $200, Goofy, zoo keeper. No. 2924, $200, Camera, Pluto, vert. No. 2925, $200, Goofy, surgeon. No. 2926, $200, Minnie, pups, tool chest. No. 2927, $200, Minnie, maid. No. 2928, $200, Horace, politician.

1995, Feb. 23 **Litho.** ***Perf. 13½x14***

Sheets of 9, #a-i

2917-2919 A213 Set of 3 15.00 15.00

Sheets of 8, #a-h

Perf. 14x13½

2920-2922 A213 Set of 3 15.00 15.00

Souvenir Sheets

2923-2928 A213 Set of 6 32.50 32.50

Nos. 2917-2922 exist in sheets of 7 or 8 $5 stamps + label. The label replaces Nos. 2917e, 2918e, 2919g, 2920h, 2921h, 2922e. These sheets became available Nov. 20, 1996.

For sucharges, see Nos. 4122, 4123, 4124.

Nos. 1022, 1033, 1045, 1061 Surcharged in Red

Surcharge reads: "SALVATION / ARMY / 1895-1995".

1995, Apr. 24 **Litho.** ***Perf. 14***
2928A A91 $6 on 60c #1033
2928B A91 $20 on 60c #1045
2928C A91 $30 on 60c #1022
2928D A91 $35 on 60c #1061

New Year 1995 (Year of the Boar) — A214

No. 2929 — Stylized boars: a, $20. b, $30. c, $50, Facing forward. denomination LR. d, $100. f, $50, "Abundant Year of the Pig." g, $50, "Fortunate Year of the Pig." h, $50, Facing forward, denomination LL.
$150, Face, Chinese inscriptions.

1995, May 4 **Litho.** ***Perf. 14½***
2929 Block of 4, #a.-d. 5.00 5.00
e. A214 Souvenir sheet of 4, #c, f.-h. 6.00 6.00

Souvenir Sheet

2930 A214 $150 multicolored 5.00 5.00

No. 2929 was issued in miniature sheets of 4.

A215

Birds: $5, Goshawk. $6, Lapwing. $8, Ornate umbrellabird. $15, Slatey-headed parakeet. $19, Regent bowerbird. $20, Egyptian goose. $25, White-winged crossbill. $30, Waxwing. $35, Ruff. $60, Hoopoe. $100, Superb starling. $500, Great jacamar.

1995, May 8 **Litho.** ***Perf. 14½x13½***

2931	A215	$5	multicolored	.25	.25
2932	A215	$6	multicolored	.25	.25
2933	A215	$8	multicolored	.25	.25
2934	A215	$15	multicolored	.25	.25
2935	A215	$19	multicolored	.30	.30
2936	A215	$20	multicolored	.30	.30
2937	A215	$25	multicolored	.30	.30
2938	A215	$30	multicolored	.40	.40
2939	A215	$35	multicolored	.50	.50
2940	A215	$60	multicolored	.80	.80
2941	A215	$100	multicolored	1.60	1.60
2942	A215	$500	multicolored	7.00	7.00
	Nos. 2931-2942 (12)			12.20	12.20

For surcharges, see Nos. 4020K, 4020O, 4112, 4136, 4204.

Lapwing — A215a

1995 ? **Litho.** ***Perf. 13¼***
2942A A215a $6 multi —

For surcharges see Nos. 4020L, 4020P.

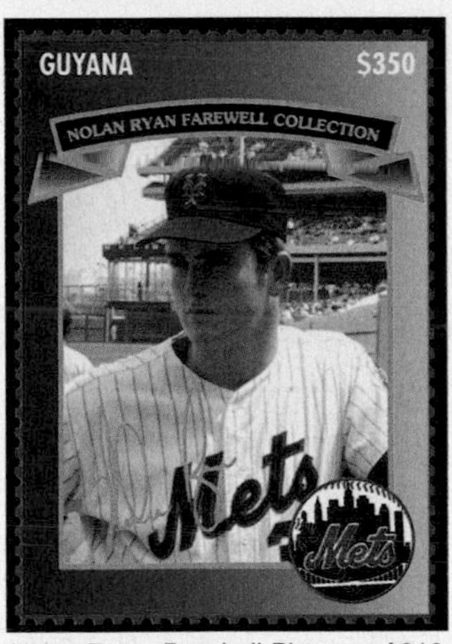

Nolan Ryan, Baseball Player — A216

No. 2943: a, Looking left, Mets. b, With bat, Mets. c, Pitching, Mets. d, Looking toward home plate, Angels. e, Pitching, Angels. f, Without hat, Angels. g, In red cap, Astros. h, Pitching, Astros. i, In black cap, Astros. j, Pitching, Rangers. k, Getting ready to pitch, Rangers. l, Up close, Rangers.

1995 Litho. *Imperf.*
Self-Adhesive
Size: 64x89mm

2943 A216 $350 Set of 12, #a.-l. 60.00 60.00

Nos. 2943a-2943l are printed on thin cards, distributed in boxed sets containing certificate of authenticity and sealed in cellophane packages. To affix stamps, backing containing biographical information must be removed.

Miniature Sheets

Singapore '95 — A217

No. 2944, $35 — Dogs: a, Gordon setter. b, Long-haired chihuahua. c, Dalmation. d, Afghan. e, English bulldog. f, Miniature schnauzer. g, Clumber spaniel. h, Pekingese. i, St. Bernard. j, English cocker spaniel. k, Alaskan malamute. l, Rottweiler.

No. 2945, $35 — Cats: a, Norwegian forest cat. b, Scottish fold. c, Red burmese. d, British blue-hair. e, Abyssinian. f, Siamese. g, Exotic shorthair. h, Turkish van cat. i, Black Persian. j, Black-tipped burmilla. k, Singapura. l, Calico shorthair.

No. 2946, $35 — Horses: a, Chestnut thoroughbred colt. b, Liver chestnut quarter horse. c, Black Freisian. d, Chestnut Belgian. e, Appaloosa. f, Lipizzanas. g, Chestnut hunter. h, British shire. i, Palomino. j, Seal brown point. k, Arab. l, Afghanistan Kabardin.

No. 2947, $300, Golden retriever. No. 2948, $300, Maine coon. No. 2949, $300, American Anglo-Arab.

1995, June 1 *Perf. 14*
Sheets of 12, #a-l

2944-2946 A217 Set of 3 20.00 20.00

Souvenir Sheets

2947-2949 A217 Set of 3 12.00 12.00

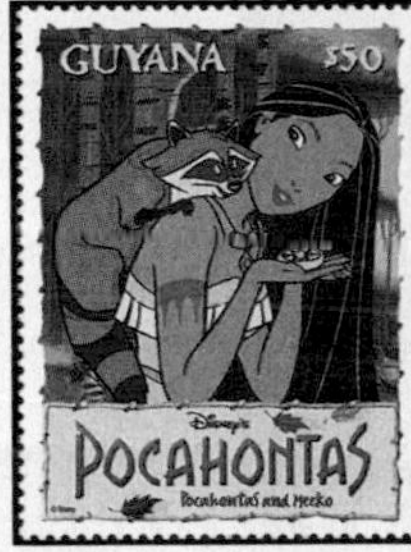

Pocahontas A218

No. 2950 — Characters from Disney animated film: a, Pocahontas, Meeko. b, John Smith. c, Chief Powhatan. d, Kocoum. e, Ratcliffe. f, Wiggins. g, Nakoma. h, Thomas.
No. 2951, Meeko, horiz.

1995, June 23 Litho. *Perf. 13½x14*

2950 A218 $50 Sheet of 8, #a.-h. 7.00 7.00

Souvenir Sheet
Perf. 14x13½

2951 A218 $300 multicolored 5.00 5.00

See Nos. 2985-2990.

UN, 50th Anniv. — A219

No. 2952 — Map of: a, $35, North, South America. b, $60, Europe, Africa. c, $200, Asia, Australia.
$300, Secretary General Boutros Boutros-Ghali.

1995, July 6 *Perf. 14*

2952 A219 Strip of 3, #a.-c. 4.50 4.50

Souvenir Sheet

2953 A219 $300 multicolored 4.00 4.00

End of World War II, 50th Anniv. A220

No. 2954: a, P61 Black Widow. b, PT boat. c, B26 Marauder. d, Cruiser USS San Juan. e, US Gato class submarine. f, US destroyer.

No. 2955: a, Jan. 1945, Battle of Bulge is over. b, Sigfried Line is breached. c, Liberation of concentration camps. d, Operation "Manna," Allies drop food to starving Dutch. e, Old looking for snipers at end of Italian campaign. f, Newspaper headline announces Hitler's suicide. g, Soviet tanks pour into Berlin. h, U-858, first German warship to surrender in US waters.

No. 2956, $300, Battleship, aircraft carrier. No. 2957, $300, Top of Brandenburg Gate.

1995, July 6

2954 A220 $60 Sheet of 6, #a.-f. + label 6.00 6.00
2955 A220 $60 Sheet of 8, #a.-h. + label 8.00 8.00

Souvenir Sheets

2956-2957 A220 Set of 2 8.00 8.00

No. 2957 contains one 57x42mm stamp.

FAO, 50th Anniv. — A221

No. 2958: a, $35, Girl carrying sack on head. b, $60, Man carrying sack, woman sorting sacks. c, $200, Woman lifting sack.
$300, Pouring from ladle into bowl.

1995, July 6 Litho. *Perf. 14*

2958 A221 Strip of 3, #a.-c. 4.50 4.50

Souvenir Sheet

2959 A221 $300 multicolored 4.00 4.00

No. 2958 is a continuous design.

Rotary Intl., 90th Anniv. A222

Designs: $200, Paul Harris, Rotary emblem. $300, Old, new Rotary emblems.

1995, July 6

2960 A222 $200 multicolored 3.50 3.50

Souvenir Sheet

2961 A222 $300 multicolored 4.50 4.50

1995 Boy Scout Jamboree, Netherlands — A223

Slogan, emblem, and: $20, Campfire. $25, Scout, beach. $30, Hiking. $35, Snorkeling. $60, Natl. flag, scout salute. $200, Fishing from boat.
No. 2968, $300, Canoeing. No. 2969, $300, Camping.

1995, July 6

2962-2967 A223 Set of 6 6.00 6.00

Souvenir Sheets

2968-2969 A223 Set of 2 8.50 8.50

Queen Mother, 95th Birthday — A224

No. 2970: a, Drawing. b, Violet hat. c, Formal portrait. d, Green blue hat.
$325, As younger woman.

1995, July 6 *Perf. 13½x14*

2970 A224 $100 Strip or block of 4, #a.-d. 7.00 7.00

Souvenir Sheet

2971 A224 $325 multicolored 6.00 6.00

No. 2970 issued in sheets of 2.
Sheets of Nos. 2970 and 2971 exist with black border in margin with text "In Memoriam/1900-2002."

Holidays of the World A225

No. 2972: a, Thanksgiving, US. b, Christmas, Germany. c, Hanukkah, Israel. d, Easter, Spain. e, Carnivale, brazil. f, Bastill Day, France. g, Independence Day, India. h, St. Patrick's Day, Ireland.
$300, Chinese New Year, China.

1995, Aug. 8 Litho. *Perf. 14*

2972 A225 $60 Sheet of 8, #a.-h. 8.00 8.00

Souvenir Sheet

2973 A225 $300 multicolored 4.00 4.00

Marine Life A226

No. 2974, vert: a, Cocoa damselfish. b, Sergeant major. c, Beau gregory. d, Yellowtail damselfish.

No. 2975: a, $30, Butterflyfish. b, $35, Bluehead. c, $60, Yellow damselfish. d, $200, Clown wrasse.

No. 2976: a, $30, Lemon shark. b, $35, Green turtle. c, $60 Sawfish. d, $200, Stingray.

No. 2977, $60: a, Tiger shark. b, Needlefish. c, Horse-eye jack. d, Princess parrotfish. e, Yellowtail snapper. f, Spotted snake eel. g, Trunkfish. h, Cherubfish. i, French angelfish.

No. 2978, $60: a, Sei whale. b, Barracuda. c, Mutton snapper. d, Hawksbill turtle. e, Spanish hogfish. f, Queen angelfish. g, Porkfish. h, Trumpetfish. i, Electric ray.

No. 2979, $300, Carcharodon carcharias. No. 2980, $300, Dermochelys coriacea.

1995, Sept. 5 Litho. *Perf. 14*

2974 A226 $80 Strip of 4, #a.-d. 4.50 4.50

Sheets of 4, #a-d

2975-2976 A226 Set of 2 14.00 14.00

Sheets of 9, #a-i

2977-2978 A226 Set of 2 20.00 20.00

Souvenir Sheets

2979-2980 A226 Set of 2 8.00 8.00

No. 2974 was issued in sheets of 4.

Miniature Sheets

1996 Summer Olympics, Atlanta — A227

No. 2981 $60: a, Shot put. b, Relay. c, Balance beam. d, Cycling. e, Synchronized swimming. f, Hurdles. g, Pommel horse. h, Discus thrower, head down.

No. 2982, $60: a, Pole vault. b, Long jump. c, Track. d, Wrestling. e, Discus thrower, head up. f, Basketball. g, Boxing. h, Weight lifting.

No. 2983, $300, Long jump. No. 2984, $300, Runners.

1995, Oct. 2 Litho. *Perf. 14*
Sheets of 8, #a-h

2981-2982 A227 Set of 2 14.00 14.00

Souvenir Sheets

2983-2984 A227 Set of 2 8.00 8.00

Pocahontas Type of 1995
Miniature Sheets

Nos. 2985-2987: Various scenes from Disney animated film, horiz.

No. 2988, $325, Pocahontas behind tree branch, horiz. No. 2989, Pocahontas, Powhatan, horiz. No. 2990, $325, Pocahontas kneeling.

Perf. 14x13½, 13½x14 (#2990)
1995, Oct. 9 Litho.

2985 A218 $8 Sheet of 9, #a.-i. 3.50 3.50
2986 A218 $30 Sheet of 9, #a.-i. 11.50 11.50
2987 A218 $35 Sheet of 9, #a.-i. 15.00 15.00

Souvenir Sheets

2988-2990 A218 Set of 3 32.50 32.50

Fauna — A228

No. 2991: a, $35, House martin. b, $60. Hobby. c, $20, Sand martin (a). d, $200, Long-tailed skua (b).

No. 2992: a, Olive colobus. b, Violet-backed starling. c, Diana monkey. d, African palm civet. e, Giraffe, zebras. f, African linsang. g, Royal antelope (fawn). h, Royal antelope (adult, fawn) (g, i). i, Palm squirrel.

No. 2993, $300, Brush pig. No. 2994, $300, Chimpanzee.

1995, Oct. 18 Litho. *Perf. 14*

2991 A228 Block of 4, #a.-d. 4.50 4.50
2992 A228 $60 Sheet of 9, #a.-i. 7.50 7.50

Souvenir Sheets

2993-2994 A228 Set of 2 10.00 10.00

No. 2991 was issued in sheets of 16 stamps.

Queenstown Holy Mosque, Georgetown, Cent. — A229

1995, Dec. 1 Litho. *Perf. 14*

2995 A229 $60 multicolored 1.00 1.00

Christmas A230

Details or entire paintings, by Carracci: $25, The Angel of Annunciation. $30, Annunciation of the Virgin. $35, Assumption of the Virgin. $60, Baptism of Christ. $100, Madonna and Child. $300, Birth by the Virgin.

No. 3002, $325, Madonna and Ten Saints, by Fiorentino. No. 3003, $325, Mystical Marriage of St. Catherine, by Carracci.

1995, Dec. 4 *Perf. 13½x14*

2996-3001 A230 Set of 6 7.00 7.00

Souvenir Sheets

3002-3003 A230 Set of 2 9.00 9.00

Guyana Defense Force, 30th Anniv. — A231

1995, Dec. 7 *Perf. 14*

3004 A231 $6 Woman with gun .25 .25
3005 A231 $60 Man with gun .75 .75

For surcharge, see No. 4109.

John Lennon (1940-80) — A232

1995

3006 A232 $35 multicolored .75 .75

No. 3006 was issued in sheets of 16.

Nobel Prize Fund Established, Cent. — A233

No. 3007, $35: a, Henri Becquerel, physics, 1903. b, Igor Tamm, physics, 1958. c, Georges Köhler, medicine, 1984. d, Gerhard Domagk, medicine, 1939. e, Yasunari Kawabata, literature, 1968. f, Maurice Allais, economics, 1988. g, Aristide Briand, peace, 1926. h, Pavel Cherenkov, physics, 1958. i, Feodor Lynen, medicine, 1964.

No. 3008 $35: a, Adolf von Baeyer, chemistry, 1905. b, Hideki Yukawa, physics, 1949. c, George W. Beadle, medicine, 1958. d, Edwin M. McMillian, chemistry, 1951. e, Samuel C.C. Ting, physics, 1976. f, Saint-John Perse, literature, 1960. g, John F. Enders, medicine, 1954. h, Felix Bloch, physics, 1952. i, P.B. Medawar, medicine, 1960.

No. 3009, $35: a, Albrecht Kossel, medicine, 1910. b, Arthur H. Compton, physics, 1927. c, N.M. Butler, peace, 1931. d, Charles Laveran, medicine, 1907. e, George R. Minot, medicine, 1934. f, Henry H. Dale, medicine, 1936. g, Jacques Monod, medicine, 1965. h, Alfred Hershey, medicine, 1969. i, Pär Lagerkvist, literature, 1951.

No. 3010, $35: a, Francis Crick, medicine, 1962. b, Manne Siegbahn, physics, 1924. c, Eisaku Sato, peace, 1974. d, Robert Koch, medicine, 1905. e, Edgar D. Adrian, medicine, 1932. f, Erwin Neher, medicine, 1991. g, Henry Taube, chemistry, 1983. h, Norman Angell, peace, 1933. i, Robert Robinson, chemistry, 1947.

No. 3011 $35: a, Nikolai Basov, physics, 1964. b, Klas Arnoldson, peace, 1908. c, René Sully-Prudhomme, literature, 1901. d, Robert W. Wilson, physics, 1978. e, Hugo Theorell, medicine, 1955. f, Nelly Sachs, literature, 1966. g, Hans von Euler-Chelpin, chemistry, 1929. h, Mairead Corrigan, peace, 1976. i, Willis E. Lamb, Jr, physics, 1955.

No. 3012 $35: a, Norman F. Ramsey, physics, 1989. b, Chen Ning Yang, physics, 1957. c, Earl W. Sutherland, Jr., medicine, 1971. d, Paul Karrer, chemistry, 1937. e, Harmut Michel, chemistry, 1988. f, Richard Kuhn, chemistry, 1938. g, P.A.M. Dirac, physics, 1933. h, Victor Grignard, chemistry, 1912. i, Richard Willstätter, chemistry, 1915.

No. 3013, $300, Le Duc Tho, peace, 1973. No. 3014, $300, Yasunari Kawabata, literature, 1968. No. 3015, $300, Heinrich Böll, literature, 1972. No. 3016, $300, Henry Kissinger, peace, 1973. No. 3017, $300, Kenichi Fukui, chemistry, 1981. No. 3018, $300, Lech Walesa, peace, 1983.

1995, Dec. 20 Litho. *Perf. 14*

Sheets of 9, #a-i

3007-3012 A233 Set of 6 50.00 50.00

Souvenir Sheets

3013-3018 A233 Set of 6 30.00 30.00

Caribbean Development Bank, 25th Anniv. — A234

1995, Dec. 29 Litho. *Perf. 14*

3019 A234 $60 multicolored .75 .75

Marilyn Monroe (1926-62) A235

No. 3020, Various portraits. No. 3021, Portrait, horiz.

1995, Dec. 29 *Perf. 13½x14*

3020 A235 $60 Sheet of 9, #a.-i. 7.50 7.50

Souvenir Sheet

Perf. 14x13½

3021 A235 $300 multicolored 4.00 4.00

David Copperfield, Magician A236

Nos. 3022-3023, Various portraits, magic acts.

1995, Dec. 29 *Perf. 13½x14*

3022 A236 $60 Sheet of 9, #a.-i. 8.00 8.00

Souvenir Sheet

3023 A236 $300 multicolored 4.00 4.00

New Year 1996 (Year of the Rat) — A237

No. 3024 — Stylized rats: a, $20. b, $30. c, $50, light brown & multi. d, $100.

No. 3025: a, Like #3024a, b, Like #3024b. c, Like #3024c, darker brown & multi. d, Like #3024d.

No. 3026, Rat facing forward.

1996, Jan. 2 *Perf. 14½*

3024 A237 Block of 4, #a.-d. 3.00 3.00

Miniature Sheet

3025 A237 $50 Sheet of 4, #a.-d. 2.50 2.50

Souvenir Sheet

3026 A237 $150 multicolored 2.50 2.50

No. 3024 was issued in sheets of 16 stamps.

UNICEF, 50th Anniv. A238

No. 3027: a, Children, building in background. b, Man, boy, tree in background. c, Children behind tree. d, Man, children.

1996, Jan. 2 *Perf. 14*

3027 A238 $1100 Sheet of 4, #a.-d. *30.00 30.00*

No. 3027 is a continuous design.

Extreme speculation might have occurred with this issue.

Paintings by Peter Paul Rubens A239

Details or entire paintings: $6, The Garden of Love. $10, Two Sleeping Children. $20, All Saints Day. $25, Sacrifice of Abraham. $30, The Last Supper. $35, The Birth of Henry of Navarre. $40, Standing Female Saint Study. $50, $60, The Garden of Love, each diff. No. 0037, $200, The Martyrdom of St. Livinus. No. 3038, $200, Der Heilige Franz Von Paula. $300, The Union of Maria de Medici and Henry IV.

No. 3039, $325, The Three Crosses. No. 3040, $325, Decius Mus Addressing the Legions, horiz. No. 3041, $325, Triumph of Henry IV, horiz.

1996, Jan. 29 Litho. *Perf. 14*

3028-3038A A239 Set of 11 15.00 15.00

Souvenir Sheets

3039-3041 A239 Set of 3 15.00 15.00

Nos. 3039-3041 each contain one 57x85mm or 85x57mm stamp.

Miniature Sheets

A240

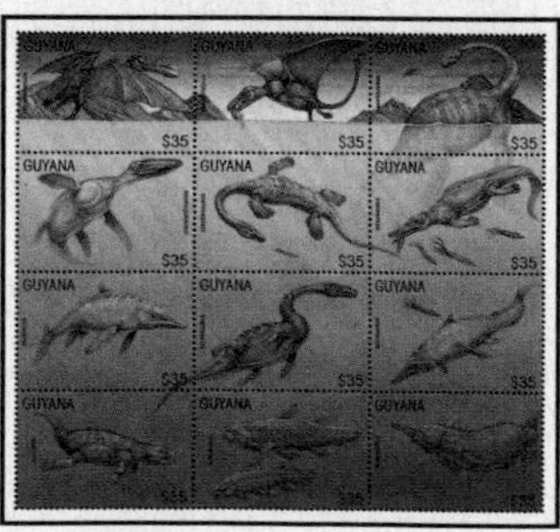

Prehistoric Animals — A241

No. 3042: a, Tarbosaurus. b, Hadrosaurus. c, Polacanthus. d, Psittacosaurus. e, Ornitholestes. f, Yangchuanosaurus. g, Scelidosaurus. h, Kentrosaurus. i, Coelophysis. j, Lesothosaurus. k, Plateosaurus. l, Staurikosaurus.

No. 3043, $35: a, Eudimorphodon. b, Criorynchus. c, Elasmosaurus. d, Rhomaleosaurus. e, Ceresiosaurus. f, Mesosaurus. g, Grendelius. h, Nothosaurus. i, Mixosaurus. j, Placodus. k, Coelacanth. l, Mosasaurus.

No. 3044, $35: a, Ornithomimus. b, Pteranodon. c, Rhamphorynchus. d, Ornitholestes. e, Brachiosaurus. f, Parasaurolophus. g, Ceratosaurus. h, Camarasaurus. i, Euoplocephalus. j, Scutellosaurus. k, Compsognathus. l, Stegoceras.

No. 3045, $35: a, Apatosaurus. b, Archaeopteryx. c, Dimorphodon. d, Deinonychus. e, Coelophysis. f, Tyrannosaurus. g, Triceratops. h, Anatosaurus. i, Saltasaurus. j, Allosaurus. k, Oviraptor. l, Stegosaurus.

No. 3046, $60: a, Heterodontosaurus (b). b, Compsognathus (c). c, Ornithomimus (b).

No. 3047, $60: a, Saurolophus. b, Muttaburrasaurus (a). c, Dicraeosaurus (b).

No. 3048, $300, Apatosaurus, allosaurus, horiz. No. 3049, $300, Tyrannosaurus rex.

No. 3050, $300, Quetzalcoatlus. No. 3051, $300, Lagosuchus. No. 3052, $300Struthiomimus.

1996, Feb. 12

3042 A240 $35 Sheet of 12, #a.-l. 6.00 6.00

Sheets of 12, #a-l

3043-3045 A241 Set of 3 20.00 20.00

Sheets of 3, #a-c

3046-3047 A240 Set of 2 6.00 6.00

Souvenir Sheets

3048-3049 A240 Set of 2 10.00 10.00
3050-3052 A241 Set of 3 15.00 15.00

Pandas — A242

No. 3053 — In tree: a, Lying on back, looking right. b, Arms, legs around branch. c, Paws holding onto tree. d, Sitting, looking left.

No. 3054 — On rocks by stream: a, Standing. b, Sitting, holding bamboo stick. c, Holding bamboo to mouth. d, Lying on stomach.

1996, Apr. 12 Litho. *Perf. 14*

3053 A242 $60 Sheet of 4, #a.-d. 4.00 4.00
3054 A242 $60 Sheet of 4, #a.-d. 4.00 4.00

China '96, 9th Asian Intl. Philatelic Exhibtion.

Mushrooms, Insects and Coral — A243

Designs: $20, Yellow morce, leaf beetle. $25, Green spored mushroom. $30, Leaf beetle, common mushroom. $35, Monarch caterpillars, pine cone mushroom.

No. 3059, $60: a, Green-beaded jelly club. b, Aspic puffball. c, Stalkless paxillus. d, Stout-stalked amanita.

No. 3060, $60: a, Fly agaric. b, Graying yellow russula, click beetle. c, Netted stinkhorn, housefly. d, Butterfly hunter, stropharia.

No. 3061, $60: a, Cockle-shell lentinus. b, Parasitic volvariella. c, Deadly lepiota. d, Shaggy-stalked boleta.

No. 3062: a, Armillauella mellea. b, Sealy vase chanterelle. c, Bitter pholiota. d, Flute white helvella. e, Fading scarlet waxy cap. f, Jask's lantern. g, Hygzocybe acutoconica. h, Mycena viscosa.

No. 3063, $300, Orange mycena. No. 3064, $300, Violet-branched coral, Red raspberry slime, yellow-tipped coral, horiz.

1996, May 3 Litho. *Perf. 14*

3055-3058 A243 Set of 4 3.50 3.50

Strips of 4, #a-d

3059-3061 A243 Set of 3 13.50 13.50
3062 A243 $60 Sheet of 8, #a.-h. 9.00 9.00

Souvenir Sheets

3063-3064 A243 Set of 2 9.00 9.00

Nos. 3059-3061 were issued in sheets of 8 stamps.

Deng Xiaoping, Chinese Communist Leader — A244

No. 3065: a, Painting inscription. b, With dignitaries, waving. c, Signing autograph. d, Waving.

$300, Wearing white shirt, vert.

1996 *Perf. 13*

3065 A244 $30 Strip or block of 4, #a.-d. 1.50 1.50

Souvenir Sheet

3066 A244 $300 multicolored 4.00 4.00

No. 3065 issued in sheets of 16 stamps.

Queen Elizabeth II, 70th Birthday A245

No. 3067: a, Portrait wearing blue dress. b, Wearing blue green dress, hat. c, On throne, opening Parliament.

$325, In ceremonial attire.

1996, May 3 Litho. *Perf. 13½x14*

3067 A245 $100 Strip of 3, #a.-c. 4.00 4.00

Souvenir Sheet

3068 A245 $325 multicolored 4.25 4.25

No. 3067 was issued in sheets of 9 stamps, with each strip having a different order.

Jerusalem, 3000th Anniv. — A246

No. 3069: a, $30. The Hulda Gates. b, $35, Old City, View from Mt. of Olives. c, $200, Absalom's Memorial, Kidron Valley.

$300, Children's Memorial.

1996 Litho. *Perf. 14*

3069 A246 Sheet of 3, #a.-c. 4.00 4.00

Souvenir Sheet

3070 A246 $300 multicolored 4.00 4.00

Birds — A247

No. 3071: a, Blue & yellow macaw. b, Andean condor. c, Crested eagle. d, White-tailed trogon. e, Toco toucan. f, Great horned owl. g, Andean cock-of-the-rock. h, Great curassow.

No. 3071I — Hummingbirds: j, Long-billed starthroat. k, Velvet-purple coronet. l, Racket-tailed coquette. m, Violet-tailed sylph. n, Broad-tailed hummingbird. o, Blue-tufted star-throat. p, White-necked jacobin. q, Ruby-throated hummingbird.

No. 3072, Ornate hawk eagle, horiz. No. 3073, Gould's violet-ear.

1996, July 10

3071 A247 $60 Sheet of 8, #a.-h. 6.00 6.00
3071I A247 $60 Sheet of 8, #j.-q. 6.00 6.00

Souvenir Sheets

3072 A247 $300 multicolored 4.50 4.50
3073 A247 $300 multicolored 4.50 4.50

Radio, Cent. A248

Entertainers: $20, Frank Sinatra. $35, Gene Autry. $60, Groucho Marx. $200, Red Skelton.

$300, Burl Ives.

1996, July 25

3074-3077 A248 Set of 4 4.00 4.00

Souvenir Sheet

3078 A248 $300 multicolored 4.00 4.00

1996 Summer Olympic Games, Atlanta A249

Designs: $20, Pancratium. $30, Olympic Stadium, 1956. $60, Leonid Spirin, 20k walk, 1956, vert. $200, Lars Hall, modern pentathlon, 1952, 1956, vert.

No. 3083, $50, vert.: a, Florence Griffith-Joyner. b, Ines Geissler. c, Nadia Comaneci. d, Tatiana Gutsu. e, Olga Korbut. f, Barbara Krause. g, Olga Bryzgina. h, Fanny Blankers-Koen. i, Irena Szewinska.

No. 3084, $50, vert.: a, Gerd Wessig. b, Jim Thorpe. c, Norman Read. d, Lasse Viren. e, Milt Campbell. f, Abebe Bikila. g, Jesse Owens. h, Viktor Saneev. i, Waldemer Cierpinski.

No. 3085, $50, vert.: a, Dietmar Schmidt. b, Pam Shriver. c, Zina Garrison. d, Hyun Jung-Hwa. e, Steffi Graf. f, Michael Jordan. g, Karch Kiraly. h, "Magic" Johnson. i, Ingolf Wiegert.

No. 3086, $50: a, Volleyball. b, Basketball. c, Tennis. d, Table tennis. e, Baseball. f, Handball. g, Field hockey. h, Water polo. i, Soccer.

No. 3087, $50, vert.: a, Cycling. b, Hurdles. c, High jump. d, Diving. e, Weight lifting. f, Canoeing. g, Wrestling. h, Gymnastics. i, Running.

No. 3088, $300, Carl Lewis, track and field gold medalist. No. 3089, $300, US defeats Korea for gold medal in baseball, 1988.

1996, July 25

3079-3082 A249 Set of 4 4.00 4.00

Sheets of 9, #a-i

3083-3087 A249 Set of 5 27.50 27.50

Souvenir Sheets

3088-3089 A249 Set of 2 8.00 8.00

Olymphilex '96 (No. 3088).

Disney Cartoons — A250

No. 3090 — Mickey outdoors: a, Mickey's Bait Shop. b, Ol' Mickey, The Lumbercamp Legend and Pluto the Yellow Dog. c, For All Men Are Equal Before Fish.

No. 3091, vert. — Super sports: a, BMX Championships. b, Goofy, Hockey Superstar. c, Malibu Surf City.

No. 3092, vert. — Nautical Mickey: a, The Path to Adventure is Shown in the Stars. b, Captain Mickey's Steamship School. c, Ahoy, Follow the Wind on Waves of Fortune.

No. 3093, $250, M. Mouse, ESQ, Lawman, vert.: No. 3094, $250, All Aboard, Ride the Great American Transcontinental Railroad. No. 3095, $250, Mouse and Pinkerton, Wild West Detective Agency, vert.

$300, Donald's Rock & Ice Mountaineers. $325, Guided by The Great Spirit, vert.

1996, July 26 *Perf. 14x13½, 13½x14*

3090 A250 $60 Strip of 3, #a.-c. 3.50 3.50
3091 A250 $80 Strip of 3, #a.-c. 5.00 5.00
3092 A250 $100 Strip of 3, #a.-c. 7.50 7.50

Souvenir Sheets

3093-3095 A250 Set of 3 20.00 20.00
3096 A250 $300 multi 6.50 6.50
3097 A250 $325 multi 7.00 7.00

Nos. 3090-3092 were issued in sheets of 9 stamps.

Disney Antique Toys — A251

No. 3098: a, Two-Gun Mickey. b, Wood-jointed Mickey doll. c, Donald Jack-in-the Box. d, Rocking Minnie. e, Fireman Donald Duck. f, Long-billed Donald Duck. g, Painted wood Mickey doll. h, Wind-up Jiminy Cricket.

No. 3099, $300, Mickey doll. No. 3100, $300, Carousel train.

1996, July 26 *Perf. 13½x14*

3098 A251 $6 Sheet of 8, #a.-h. 6.00 6.00

Souvenir Sheets

3099-3100 A251 Set of 2 14.00 14.00

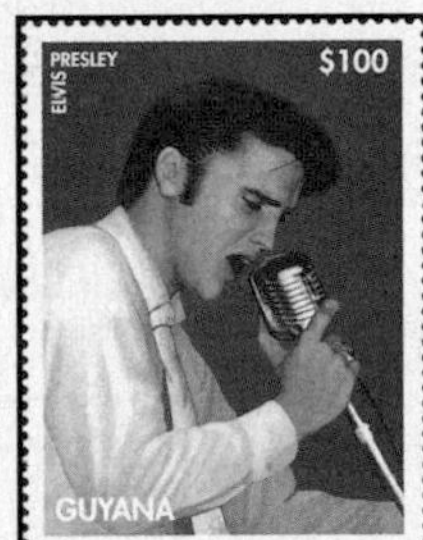

Elvis Presley's First "Hit" Year, 40th Anniv. A252

Various portraits.

1996, Sept. 8 Litho. *Perf. 13½x14*

3101 A252 $100 Sheet of 6, #a.-f. 9.00 9.00

Domestic Cats A253

No. 3102, $60: a, Birman. b, American curl. c, Turkish Angora. d, European shorthair. e, Persian. f, Scottish fold. g, Sphynx. h, Malayan. i, Cornish rex.

No. 3103, $60, vert: a, Norwegian forest. b, Russian shorthair. c, European shorthair. d, Birman. e, Ragdoll. f, Egyptian mau. g, Persian. h, Angora. i, Siamese.

No. 3104, $300, Maine coon, vert. No. 3105, $300, Himalayan.

1996, Sept. 18 *Perf. 14*

Sheets of 9, #a-i

3102-3103 A253 Set of 2 15.00 15.00

Souvenir Sheets

3104-3105 A253 Set of 2 9.00 9.00

Souvenir Sheet

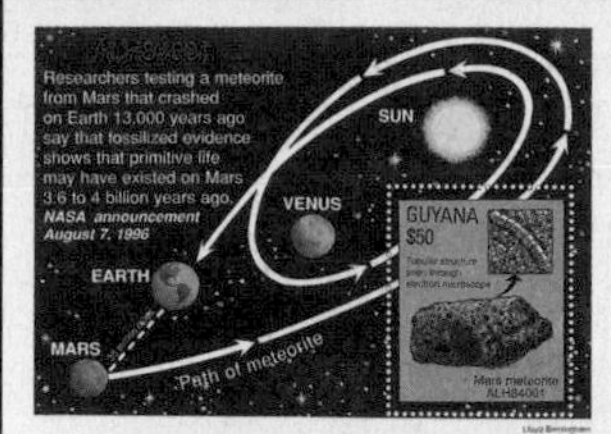

Mars Meteorite ALH84001 — A253a

1996, Oct. 7 Litho. *Perf. 14½x14¼*

3105A A253a $50 multi — —

Deep Ocean Exploration — A254

No. 3106: a, Goblin shark, coelacanth. b, Remote operated vehicle, JASON. c, Deep water invertebrates. d, Submarine NR1 (e). e, Giant squid (b, c, f, g, h, j, m). f, Sperm whale (b, c). g, Volcanic vents, submersible ALVIN. h, Air-recycling pressure suit, shipwreck. i, Bacteria survey, submersible SHINKAI 6500. j, Giant tube worms. k, Anglerfish. l, Six-gill shark (k). m. Autonomous underwater vehicle ABE. n, Viperfish. o, Swallower, hatchetfish.

$300, Sea anemone.

1996, Dec. 2 Litho. *Perf. 14*

3106 A254 $30 Sheet of 15, #a.-o. 6.50 6.50

Souvenir Sheet

3107 A254 $300 multicolored 4.00 4.00

Characters from Disney's Snow White in Christmas Scenes A255

Designs: $6, Snow White. $20, Doc. $25, Dopey, Sneezy. $30, Sleepy, Happy, Bashful. $35, Dopey, Santa. $60, Dopey, fireplace. $100, Dopey, Grumpy. $200, Dopey as Santa.

No. 3116, $300, Snow White looking at squirrel in box. No. 3117, $300, Dopey placing star on tree.

1996, Dec. 16 *Perf. 13½x14*

3108-3115 A255 Set of 8 14.00 14.00

Souvenir Sheets

3116-3117 A255 Set of 2 18.00 18.00

Marine Life A256

No. 3118: a, Red gorgonians. b, Plexaura homomalla, butterflyfish (a, c). c, Dendronephtbya. d, Common clownfish, anemone, mushroom coral (a). e, Anemone, horse-eyed jack (d, g-h). f, Slender snappers (c), splendid coral trout. g, Anemones. h, Brain coral, Indo-Pacific hard coral. i, Cup coral (f, h).

1996, Dec. 2 Litho. *Perf. 14*

3118 A256 $60 Sheet of 9, #a.-i. 9.00 9.00

New Year 1997 (Year of the Ox) — A257

No. 3119 — Denomination at: a, $20, LR. b, $30, LL. c, $35, UR. d, $50, UL.

No. 3120: a, Like #3119a. b, Like #3119b. c, Like #3119c.

$150, Ox, facing.

1997, Jan. 2 Litho. *Perf. 14½*

3119 A257 Block of 4, #a.-d. 3.00 3.00

3120 A257 $50 Sheet of 4, #a.-c. + #3119d 4.00 4.00

Souvenir Sheet

3121 A257 $150 multicolored 3.00 3.00

No. 3119 was issued in sheets of 16 stamps.

Mickey and Friends Celebrate Chinese Lunar New Year — A258

No. 3122: a, $6, Mickey. b, $20, Home visit. c, $25, Fortune lantern. d, $30, Silhouette. e, $35, Flower market. f, $60, Harmonious man, woman.

No. 3123: a, Red-pocket money. b, Lion dance. c, Calligraphy. d, Surplus every year. e, Fireworks. f, Ox.

$150, Mickey marching, vert. $200, Mickey, ox.

1997, Jan. 2 *Perf. 14x13½*

3122 A258 Sheet of 6, #a.-f. 4.00 4.00

3123 A258 $30 Sheet of 6, #a.-f. 4.50 4.50

Souvenir Sheets

Perf. 13½x14, 14x13½

3124 A258 $150 multicolored 4.00 4.00

3125 A258 $200 multicolored 4.50 4.50

Marine Life A259

No. 3126, $6, Angelfish. No. 3127, $6, Hyed snapper. $20, Box fish. $25, Golden damselfish. $35, Clown triggerfish. $200, Harlequin tuskfish.

$300, Caribbean flower coral.

1996 Litho. *Perf. 14*

3126-3131 A259 Set of 6 6.00 6.00

Souvenir Sheet

3132 A259 $300 multicolored 5.00 5.00

Hotel Tower, 50th Anniv. — A260

1996, Dec. 28

3133 A260 $30 multicolored .50 .50

For surcharge, see No. 4180.

Souvenir Sheet

The Summer Palace, Beijing — A261

1996, Apr. 12 Litho. *Perf. 13*

3134 A261 $60 multicolored 2.00 2.00

China '96. No. 3134 was not available until March 1997.

Transfer of Hong Kong — A262

No. 3135, $80: a, Tortoise. b, Dragon. c, Unicorn. d, Phoenix.

No. 3136, $80, vert.: a, Swallow & willow. b, Kingfisher & chrysanthemum. c, Crane & pine. d, Peacock & peony.

No. 3137, $80, vert.: a-d, Various kites.

No. 3138, vert.: a-b, Paintings of mountains and lakes.

1997, Feb. 12 *Perf. 14*

Sheets of 4 , #a-d

3135-3137 A262 Set of 3 15.00 15.00

3138 A262 $200 Sheet of 2, #a.-b. 6.00 6.00

Hong Kong '97. No. 3138 contains two 70x44mm stamps.

Motion Pictures, Cent. A263

No. 3139 — Movie star, World War II films: a, Burgess Meredith, "The Story of GI Joe." b, M.E. Clifton-James, "I Was Monty's Double." c, Audie Murphy, "To Hell and Back." d, Gary Cooper, "The Story of Dr. Wassell." e, James Mason, "The Desert Fox." f, Manart Kippen, "Mission to Moscow." g, Robert Taylor, "Above and Beyond." h, James Cagney, "The Gallant Hours." i, John Garfield, "Pride of the Marines."

$300, George C. Scott, "Patton," horiz.

1997, Feb. 21 *Perf. 13½x14*

3139 A263 $50 Sheet of 9, #a.-i. 10.00 10.00

Souvenir Sheet

Perf. 14x13½

3140 A263 $300 multicolored 5.00 5.00

Pres. John F. Kennedy (1917-63) — A264

1997, Mar. 14 Litho. *Perf. 14*

3141 A264 $50 blue 1.00 1.00

George Washington A265

Designs from works of art: No. 3142: a, Washington in battle. b, Washington taking oath. c, Washington Seated in Armchair, from engraving after Chappel. d, Col. Washington of Virginia Militia, by Charles W. Peale. e, George Washington, by Rembrandt Peale. f, Washington Addressing Constitutional Convention, by Junius Brutus Stearns. g, Washington on His Way to the Continental Congress. h, Washington on a White Charger, by John Faed. i, Washington as a Surveyor, from an engraving by G.R. Hall after Darley's drawing. j, Bas-relief of Washington Praying at Valley Forge. k, Death of Gen. Mercer at Battle of Princeton, by John Trumbull. l, Washington Taking Command of the Continental Army at Cambridge. m, George Washington, by Gilbert Stuart.

No. 3143: a, Washington Before the Battle of Trenton, by John Trumbull. b, Washington, His Family at Mt. Vernon, by Alonzo Chappel. c, Inauguration of Washington in New York City, by Chappel. d, Washington, by Adolph Ulrich Wertmuller. e, Washington Accepts His Commission as Commander-in-Chief, June 1775, Currier & Ives lithograph. f, Washington from a mezzotint by Sartain. g, On the Lawn at Mt. Vernon after the War. h, Washington Conversing with a Farmhand During the Baling Season with Nelly and Washington Custus Playing Nearby, from anonymous print after Junius Brutus Stearns. i, Nellie Custis' Wedding on Washington's Last Birthday, by Ogden. j, Washington Crossing the Delaware, by Leutze. k, Washington Receives Orders from Mortally Wounded Gen. Braddock at 1755 Battle of Monongahela. l, Washington Birthplace (supposed) on the Potomac, Currier & Ives lithograph. m, Washington at Yorktown, by James Peale.

1997, Mar. 14 Litho. *Perf. 14*

3142 Sheet of 13 12.50 12.50

a.-l. A265 $60 any single .75 .75

m. A265 $300 imperf. 3.00 3.00

3143 Sheet of 13 12.50 12.50

a.-l. A265 $60 any single .75 .75

m. A265 $300 imperf. 3.00 3.00

Nos. 3142m, 3143m are each 66x91mm and have simulated perforations.

No. 3142m exists perf. 14½.

Mushrooms A266

Designs: $6, Morchella hortensis. $20, Boletus chyrsenteron. $25, Hygrophorus agathosmus. $30, Cortinarius violaceus. $35, Acanthocystis geogenius. $60, Mycena polygramma. $200, Hebeloma radicosum. $300, Coprinus comatus.

No. 3152, $80: a, Coprinus picaceus. b, Stropharia umbonatescens. c, Paxillus involutus. d, Amanita inaurata. e, Lepiota rhacodes. f, Russula amoena.

No. 3153, $80: a, Volvaria volvacea. b, Psalliota augusta. c, Tricholoma aurantium. d, Pholiota spectabilis. e, Cortinarius armillatus. f, Agrocybe dura.
No. 3154, $300, Pholiota mutabilis. No. 3155, $300, Amanita muscaria.

1997, Apr. 2 Litho. *Perf. 14*
3144-3151 A266 Set of 8 10.50 10.50

Sheets of 6, #a-f
3152-3153 A266 Set of 2 16.00 16.00

Souvenir Sheets
3154-3155 A266 Set of 2 10.00 10.00

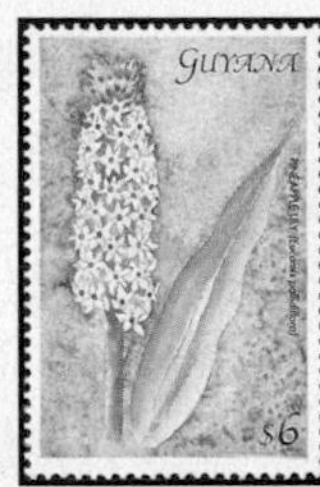
Flowers — A267

Designs: No. 3156, $6, Pineapple lily. No. 3157, $6, Blue columbine. $20, Petunia. $25, Lily of the Nile. $30, Bird of Paradise. $35, African daisy. $60, Cape daisy. $80, Gazania. $100, Cape water lily. $200, Insigne lady's slipper.
No. 3166: a, Monarch supperwart. b, Passion flower. c, Butterfly iris. d, Red-hot poker. e, Dir. G.T. Moore water lily. f, Superbissima painted tongue. g, Orchid. h, Annual chrysanthemum.
No. 3167: a, Tulips. b, Liatris. c, Roses. d, Gerber daisies. e, Sunflowers. f, Chrysanthemums.
No. 3168, Petunia.

1997, Apr. 2
3156-3165 A267 Set of 10 12.00 12.00
3166 A267 $60 Sheet of 8, #a.-h. 8.50 8.50
3167 A267 $80 Sheet of 6, #a.-f. 8.50 8.50

Souvenir Sheet
3168 A267 $300 multicolored 5.00 5.00

Deng Xiaoping (1904-97) — A268

1997, May 1
3169 A268 $100 shown 1.75 1.75

Souvenir Sheet
3170 A268 $150 Portrait, diff. 2.75 2.75

No. 3169 was issued in sheets of 3.

UNESCO, 50th Anniv. — A269

Designs: $20, Horyu-Ji, Japan. $25, Scandola Nature Reserve, France. $30, Great Wall Defenses, China. $35, Wurzburg, Germany. $60, Monastery of Batalha, Portugal. $200, Dubrovnik, Croatia.
No. 3177, $60, vert. — Sites in Germany: a, Cathedral of Aquisgran, Aachen. b, Cathedral at Trier. c, Column of Augusta Treveror, Trier. d, f, Residences, Wurzburg. e, Church interior, Wurzburg. g, House of the River at Inselstadt, Bamberg. h, Cathedral interior, Speyer.
No. 3178, $60, Sites in Greece, vert: No. 3178: a, Monastery of Thessaloniki. b, d, e, Monastery at Mystras. c, Church of Santa Sofia, Thessaloniki. f, City, Thessaloniki. g, Painting, Mystras. h, Museum of Byzantine Art, Thessaloniki.
No. 3179, $60, vert.: a, Monastery of Poblet Catalonia, Spain. b, Old City of Salamanca, Spain. c, Toledo, Spain. d, Cathedral of Florence, Italy. e, Tower of Pisa, Italy. f, g, h, Convent of Christ, Tomar, Portugal.

No. 3180, $80 — Sites in Japan: a, d, e, Horyu-Ji. b, c, Kyoto.
No. 3181, $80 — Sites in the Americas: a, Cuzco, Peru. b, Potosi, Bolivia. c, Fortress, San Lorenzo, Panama. d, Sangay Natl. Park, Ecuador. e, Los Glaciares Natl. Park, Argentina.
No. 3182, $80 — Sites in US: a, Monticello. b, Yosemite Natl. Park. c, Yellowstone Natl. Park. d, Olympic Natl. Park. e, Everglades.
No. 3183, $300, Mount Taishan Shrine, China. No. 3184, $300, Monastery of Batalha, Portugal. No. 3185, $300, Bamberg Cathedral (detail), Germany. No. 3186, $300, Monastery, Mount Athos, Greece.

1997, May 20
3171-3176 A269 Set of 6 9.00 9.00

Sheets of 8, #a-h + Label
3177-3179 A269 Set of 3 22.50 22.50

Sheets of 5
3180-3182 A269 Set of 3 17.50 17.50

Souvenir Sheets
3183-3186 A269 Set of 4 18.50 18.50

Queen Elizabeth II, Prince Philip, 50th Wedding Anniv. A270

No. 3187: a, Queen. b, Royal Arms. c, Wedding portrait. d, Queen, Prince. e, Broadlands House. f, Prince Philip.
$300, Queen Elizabeth II.

1997, May 20 Litho. *Perf. 14*
3187 A270 $60 Sheet of 6, #a.-f. 7.00 7.00

Souvenir Sheet
3188 A270 $300 multicolored 5.50 5.50

Paintings, by Hiroshige (1797-1858) A271

No. 3189: a, Oumayagashi. b, Ryogoku Ekoin & Moto-Yanagibashi Bridge. c, Pine of Success and Oumayagashi Asakusa River. d, Fireworks at Ryogoku. e, Dyers' Quarter, Kanda. f, Cotton-goods Lane, Odenma-cho.
No. 3190, $300, Suruga-cho. No. 3191, $300, Yatsukoji, inside Sujikai Gate.

1997, May 20 *Perf. 13½x14*
3189 A271 $80 Sheet of 6, #a.-f. 6.75 6.75

Souvenir Sheets
3190-3191 A271 Set of 2 10.00 10.00

Heinrich von Stephan (1831-97), Founder of UPU A272

No. 3192: a, Frieze of Roman post service. b, UPU emblem. c, Cable car, Boston, 1907.
$300, Von Stephan, Egyptian messenger.

1997, May 20 Litho. *Perf. 14*
3192 A272 $100 Sheet of 3, #a.-c. 8.00 8.00

Souvenir Sheet
3193 A272 $300 multicolored 9.00 9.00

PACIFIC 97.

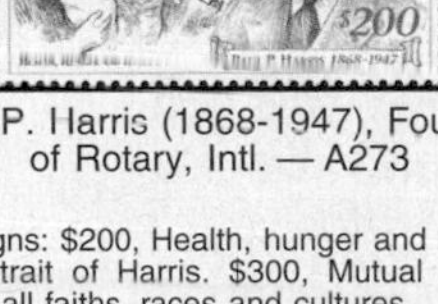
Paul P. Harris (1868-1947), Founder of Rotary, Intl. — A273

Designs: $200, Health, hunger and humanity, portrait of Harris. $300, Mutual respect among all faiths, races and cultures.

1997, May 20
3194 A273 $200 multicolored 2.75 2.75

Souvenir Sheet
3195 A273 $300 multicolored 4.25 4.25

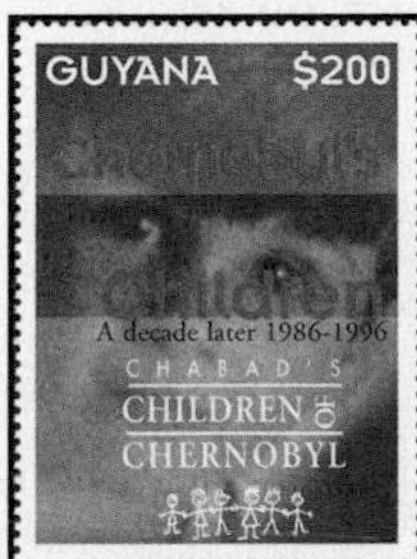
Chernobyl Disaster, 10th Anniv. A274

Designs: No. 3196, Chabad's Children of Chernobyl. No. 3197, UNESCO.

1997, May 20 *Perf. 13½x14*
3196 A274 $200 multicolored 3.00 3.00
3197 A274 $200 multicolored 3.00 3.00

Grimm's Fairy Tales — A275

Mother Goose — A276

Scenes from "Hansel & Gretel:" No. 3198: a, Hansel & Gretel in forest. b, Gingerbread house. c, Wicked witch. $500, Witch trying to capture Gretel, horiz.
$300, Rooster from "Cock-A-Doodle-Doo."

1997, May 20 *Perf. 13½x14*
3198 A275 $100 Sheet of 3, #a.-c. 5.50 5.50

Souvenir Sheets
Perf. 14, 14x13½
3199 A276 $300 multicolored 5.00 5.00
3200 A275 $500 multicolored 8.25 8.25

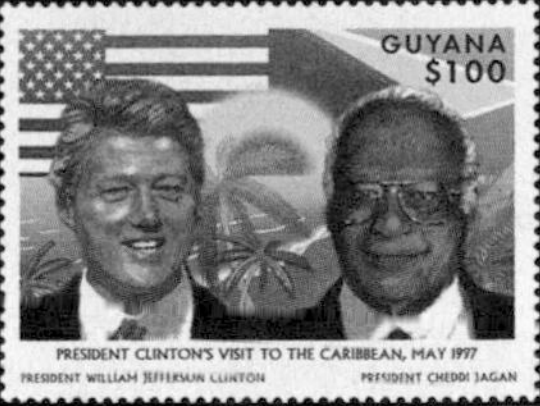
US Pres. Bill Clinton's Visit to Caribbean, May 1997 — A277

Designs: $30, Guyana Pres. Cheddi Jagan, Pres. Clinton, map of Caribbean, vert. $100, Clinton, Jagan, flags of US, Guyana, palm trees, beach.

Perf. 13½x14, 14x13½
1997, June 23
3201 A277 $30 multicolored .50 .50
3202 A277 $100 multicolored 1.50 1.50

Nos. 3201-3202 each issued in sheets of 9. See Nos. 3237-3238.

A278

1998 Winter Olympic Games, Nagano — A279

Medalists: $30, Georg Thoma. $35, Katja Seizinger. $60, Georg Hackl. $200, Katarina Witt.
No. 3207, $60: a, Gunda Niemann, 3000- & 5000-m speed skating, 1992. b, Tony Nash, Robin Dixon, 2-man bobsled, 1964. c, Switzerland 4-man bobsled, 1988. d, Piet Kleine, speed skating, 1976.
No. 3208, $60: a, Oksana Baiul, figure skating, 1994. b, Cathy Turner, 500-m short track speed skating, 1994. c, Brian Boitano, figure skating, 1988. d, Nancy Kerrigan, figure skating, 1994.
No. 3209: a, Markus Wasmeier. b, Jens Weissflog. c, Erhard Keller. d, Rosi Mittermaier. e, Gunda Niemann. f, Peter Angerer.
No. 3210, Swiss 4-Man bobsled team.
No. 3211, $300, Jean-Claude Killy, slalom, 1968. No. 3212, $300, Chen Lu, figure skating, 1992.

1997, July 1 *Perf. 14*
3203-3206 A278 Set of 4 4.75 4.75

Strips or Blocks of 4, #a-d
3207-3208 A279 Set of 2 12.00 12.00
3209 A278 $30 Sheet of 6, #a.-f. 3.00 3.00

Souvenir Sheets
3210 A278 $300 multicolored 6.00 6.00
3211-3212 A279 Set of 2 12.00 12.00

Nos. 3207-3208 issued in sheets of 8 stamps.

Souvenir Sheet

Return of Hong Kong to China — A280

Litho. & Embossed
1997, July 1 *Perf. 14*
3213 A280 $500 gold & multi 7.50 7.50

Domestic Cats A281

Designs, vert.: $30, Norwegian forest cat. $35, Oriental spotted tabby. $200, Asian smoke.

No. 3217: a, Abyssinian. b, Chocolate colorpoint shorthair. c, Silver tabby. d, Persian. e, Maine coon cat & kitten. f, Brown shaded Burmese. g, Persian kitten. h, Siamese. i, British shorthair.

$300, Manx, vert.

1997, July 29

3214-3216 A281 Set of 3 4.25 4.25
3217 A281 $60 Sheet of 9, #a.-i. 8.50 8.50

Souvenir Sheet

3218 A281 $300 multi 5.50 5.50

Birds A282

Designs: $25, Verdin. $30, Wood thrush, vert. $60, Rofous-sided towhee. $200, Pygmy nuthatch, vert.

No. 3223, $80: a, Groove-billed ani. b, Green honeycreeper. c, Toucanet. d, Wire-tailed manakin. e, Hoatzin. f, Tiger heron.

No. 3224, $80 — Hummingbirds: a, Magenta-throated woodstar. b, Long-tailed hermit. c, Red-footed plumeleteer. d, Anna's. e, White-tipped sicklebill. f, Fiery-throated.

No. 3225, $300, Pinnated bittern. No. 3226, $300, Keel-billed toucan.

1997, Aug. 12 Litho. *Perf. 14*

3219-3222 A282 Set of 4 6.00 6.00

Sheets of 6, #a-f

3223-3224 A282 Set of 2 16.00 16.00

Souvenir Sheets

3225-3226 A282 Set of 2 12.00 12.00

Dogs — A283

Designs: $20, Chihuahua. $25, Norfolk terrier. $60, Welsh terrier.

No. 3230: a, Shar-pei. b, Chihuahua. c, Chow chow. d, Sealyham terrier. e, Collie. f, German shorthair pointer. g, Bulldog. h, German shepherd. i, Old English sheepdog.

$300, Tibetan spaniel.

1997, July 29 Litho. *Perf. 14*

3227-3229 A283 Set of 3 3.75 3.75
3230 A283 $60 Sheet of 9, #a.-i. 8.50 8.50

Souvenir Sheet

3231 A283 $300 multicolored 5.50 5.50

Pres. Cheddi Jagan's 1st Election to Parliament, 50th Anniv. — A284

1997, Oct. 6 Litho. *Perf. 14*

3232 A284 $6 green & multi .25 .25
3233 A284 $30 pale yellow & multi 4.25 4.25

Nos. 3232-3233 each issued in sheets of 9.

Diana, Princess of Wales (1961-97) — A285

No. 3234: a-f, Various portraits.

No. 3235, $300, Wearing red dress. No. 3236, $300, With longer hair.

1997, Oct. 15

3234 A285 $80 Sheet of 6, #a-f 8.25 8.25

Souvenir Sheets

Perf. 14½

3235-3236 A285 Set of 2 10.00 10.00

Nos. 3235-3236 each contain one 34x52mm stamp.

US Pres. Bill Clinton's Visit Type of 1997

Designs: $6, Like #3201. No. 3238, Clinton, Jagan, flags, sun on horizon.

Perf. 13½x14, 14x13½

1997, Nov. 10

3237 A277 $6 multi .25 .25
3238 A277 $30 multi .50 .50

Nos. 3237-3238 each issued in sheets of 9. For surcharge, see No. 4115.

Souvenir Sheets

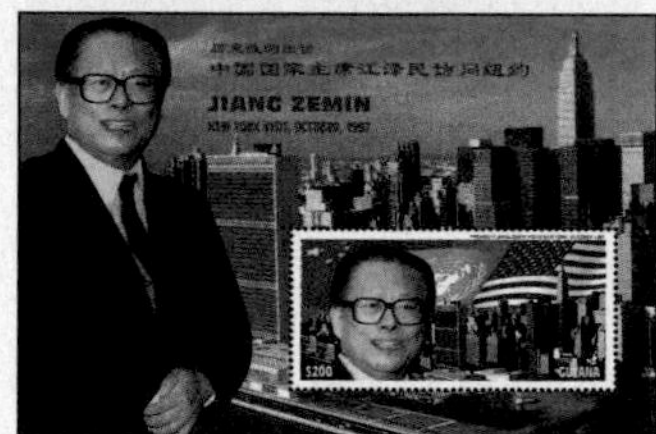

Chinese Pres. Jiang Zemin's Visit to New York — A286

Pres. Zemin, New York skyline, and: $200, Flags of China, UN, US. $300, Flags of China, US.

1997, Nov. 10 *Perf. 14*

3239 A286 $200 multicolored 3.00 3.00
3240 A286 $300 multicolored 4.50 4.50

Buildings in Guyana — A287

1997, Dec. 8 Litho. *Perf. 14*

3241 A287 $6 W. Fogarty #1 .25 .25
3242 A287 $30 Public building .60 .60

Christmas A288

Entire paintings, details, or sculptures: $25, $30, Diff. angels from The Triumph of Galatea, by Raphael. $35, Primavera, by Botticelli. $60, Angel Muscicians, by Agostino di Duccio, (bas relief). $100, From cover of Life Magazine, #1212, 1906. $200, Madonna and Saints, by Rosso Fiorentino.

No. 3249, $300, The Gardens of Love, by Rubens. No. 3250, $300, Cherubs, by Philippe de Champaigne.

1997, Dec. 8

3243-3248 A288 Set of 6 7.50 7.50

Souvenir Sheets

3249-3250 A288 Set of 2 12.00 12.00

Historical Events A289

Designs: No. 3251, $60, Explorers discover tomb of Tutankhamun, 1922. No. 3252, $60, Lincoln Memorial dedicated, Washington, DC, 1922. No. 3253, $60, Alexander Graham Bell dies, 1922. No. 3254, $60, Calvin Coolidge becomes President, 1923. No. 3255, $60, John L. Baird develops 1st experimental television, 1923. No. 3256, $60, Warren G. Harding dies, 1923. No. 3257, $60, First Winter Olympic Games, Chamonix, France, 1924. No. 3258, $60, Tennessee bans teaching of evolution in schools, 1925. No. 3259, $60, Chinese leader Sun Yat-Sen dies, 1925. No. 3260, $60, Robert Goddard launches 1st liquid fuel rocket, 1926. No. 3261, $60, Richard E. Byrd is 1st to fly over North Pole, 1926. No. 3262, $60, Sesquicentennial Exposition, Philadelphia, 1926.

1997. Dec. 8

3251-3262 A289 Set of 12 12.50 12.50

New Year 1998 (Year of the Tiger) — A290

No. 3263 — Various stylized tigers with denomination in: a, LR. b, LL. c, UR. d, UL.

$150, Tiger, red background.

1998, Jan. 5 Litho. *Perf. 14½*

3263 A290 $50 Sheet of 4, #a.-d. 5.00 5.00

Souvenir Sheet

3264 A290 $150 multicolored 4.25 4.25

Prehistoric Wildlife — A291

Designs: $25, Kentrosaurus. $30, Lesothosaurus. $35, Stegoceras. $60, Lagosuchus. $100, Herrerasaurus. $200, Iguanodon.

No. 3271, $55: a, Quetzalcoatlus (d). b, Pteranodon (a, c). c, Peteinosaurus. d, Criorhychus (g). e, Pterodaustro. f, Eudimorphodon. g, Archeopteryx. h, Dimorphodon. i, Sharovipteryx.

No. 3272, $55: a, Ceresiosaurus. b, Nothosaurus. c, Rhomaleosaurus. d, Grendelius. e, Mixosaurus. f, Mesosaurus. g, Placodus. h, Stethacanthus. i, Coelacanth.

No. 3273, $300, Styracosaurus, vert. No. 3274, $300, Yangchuanosaurus, vert.

1998, Feb. 23 Litho. *Perf. 14*

3265-3270 A291 Set of 6 7.00 7.00

Sheets of 9, #a-i

3271-3272 A291 Set of 2 16.00 16.00

Souvenir Sheets

3273-3274 A291 Set of 2 8.50 8.50

1998 World Cup Soccer Championships, France — A292

Group A: No. 3275, $30, Brazil. No. 3276, $30, Morocco. No. 3277, $30, Norway. No. 3278, $30, Scotland.

Group B: No. 3279, $30, Austria. No. 3280, $30, Cameroun. No. 3281, $30, Chile. No. 3282, $30, Italy.

Group C: No. 3283, $30, Denmark. No. 3284, $30, France. No. 3285, $30, Saudi Arabia. No. 3286, $30, South Africa.

Group D: No. 3287, $30, Bulgaria. No. 3288, $30, Nigeria. No. 3289, $30, Paraguay. No. 3290, $30, Spain.

Group E: No. 3291, $30, Belgium. No. 3292, $30, Holland. No. 3293, $30, S. Korea. No. 3294, $30, Mexico.

Group F: No. 3295, $30, Germany. No. 3296, $30, Iran. No. 3297, $30, US. No. 3298, $30, Yugoslavia.

Group G: No. 3299, $30, Colombia. No. 3300, $30, England. No. 3301, $30, Romania. No. 3302, $30, Tunisia.

Group H: No. 3303, $30, Argentina. No. 3304, $30, Croatia. No. 3305, $30, Jamaica. No. 3306, $30, Japan.

Japanese players, vert.: No. 3306A, $300, Okada. No. 3306B, $300, Nakata.

1998, Apr. 8 Litho. *Perf. 14x13½*

3275-3306 A292 Set of 32 14.00 14.00

Perf. 13½x14

Souvenir Sheets

3306A-3306B A292 Set of 2 8.50 8.50

Nos. 3275-3306 were each issued in sheets of 8 + 1 label.

For overprints see Nos. 3317-3324.

The Titanic A293

No. 3307: a, J. Bruce Ismay, managing director, White Star Line. b, Jack Phillips, radio operator. c, Margaret "Unsinkable Molly" Brown, passenger. d, Capt. Edward J. Smith. e, Frederick Fleet, lookout. f, Thomas Andrews, managing director of Harland and Wolff.

$300, Titanic sinking.

1998, June 17 Litho. *Perf. 14*

3307 A293 $80 Sheet of 6, #a.-f. 6.75 6.75

Souvenir Sheet

3308 A293 $300 multicolored 4.25 4.25

Sailing Ships A294

No. 3309, $80: a, Viking double-ended ship, 14th cent. b, Portuguese caravel. c, "Nina." d, Fannie, 1896. e, "Victoria," 1519. f, Arab sambook.

No. 3310, $80: a, "Dutch Fluyt." b, "Alastor." c, "Falcon." d, "Red Rover." e, "British Anglesey." f, "Archibald Russel."

No. 3311, $300, Oseberg ship. No. 3312, $300, "Half Moon," 1609.

1998, June 17 Litho. *Perf. 14*

Sheets of 6, #a-f

3309-3310 A294 Set of 2 13.50 13.50

Souvenir Sheets

3311-3312 A294 Set of 2 8.50 8.50

Diana, Princess of Wales (1961-97) — A295

Designs: No. 3313, $1500, Diana in black and brown fur trimmed hat and coat. No. 3314, $1500, Diana wearing suit and hat.

Litho. & Embossed

1998, Aug. 3 *Die Cut 7½*

3313-3314 A295 $1500 Set of 2 150.00

Queen Mother A296

1998, Aug. 4 *Perf. 13½*

3315 A296 $90 multicolored 1.40 1.40

CARICOM, 25th Anniv. — A297

1998, July 4 Litho. *Perf. 13½*

3316 A297 $20 multicolored .40 .40

Nos. 3275, 3282-3286, 3289, 3304 Ovptd. "FRANCE WINNERS" in Gold

1998, Aug. 20 Litho. *Perf. 14x13½*

3317 A292 $30 on #3275 .45 .45
3318 A292 $30 on #3282 .45 .45
3319 A292 $30 on #3283 .45 .45
3320 A292 $30 on #3284 .45 .45
3321 A292 $30 on #3285 .45 .45
3322 A292 $30 on #3286 .45 .45
3323 A292 $30 on #3289 .45 .45
3324 A292 $30 on #3304 .45 .45
Nos. 3317-3324 (8) 3.60 3.60

Nos. 3317-3324 were each issued in sheets of 8+label. Each sheet contains additional overprints in sheet margins.

National Hockey League Players — A298

No. 3325: a, Bryan Berard. b, Ray Bourque. c, Martin Brodeur. d, Pavel Bure. e, Chris Chelios. f, Sergei Fedorov. g, Peter Forsberg. h, Wayne Gretzky. i, Dominik Hasek. j, Brett Hull. k, Jarome Iginla. l, Jaromir Jagr. m, Paul Kariya. n, Saku Koivu. o, John LeClair. p, Brian Leetch. q, Eric Lindros. r, Patrick Marleau. s, Mark Messier. t, Mike Modano. u, Chris Osgood. v, Zigmund Palffy. w, Felix Potvin. x, Jeremy Roenick. y, Patrick Roy. z, Joe Sakic. aa, Sergei Samsonov. ab, Teemu Selanne. ac, Brendan Shanahan. ad, Ryan Smyth. ae, Jocelyn Thibault. af, Joe Thornton. ag, Keith Tkachuk. ah, John Vanbiesbrouck. ai, Steve Yzerman. aj, Dainius Zubrus.

1998, Apr. 1 Litho. *Perf. 13½*

3325 A298 $35 Sheet of 36, #a.-aj. 18.00 18.00

Aircraft A299

No. 3326, $80 — Military aircraft: a, A7K Corsair II. b, A6E Intruder. c, U2 Spy plane. d, Blackhawk. e, F-16. f, Phantom II.

No. 3327, $80 — Pioneers of aviation: a, Wright Brothers, 1903. b, Bleriot, 1911. c, Curtiss Jenny, 1919. d, Airship Schwaben, 1911. e, W-8B, 1923. f, DH-66, 1926.

No. 3328, $300, A-10 Warthog. No. 3329, $300HH-65A Dolphin.

1998, Sept. 28 *Perf. 14*

Sheets of 6, #a-f

3326-3327 A299 Set of 2 13.50 13.50

Souvenir Sheets

3328-3329 A299 Set of 2 8.50 8.50

Endangered Species — A300

Nos. 3330, $80, 3332, $300, Various pictures of the giant panda.

Nos. 3331, $80, 3333, $300, Various pictures of the mountain gorilla.

1998, Oct. 8 **Sheets of 6, a-f**

3330-3331 A300 Set of 2 17.00 17.00

Souvenir Sheets

3332-3333 A300 Set of 2 18.00 18.00

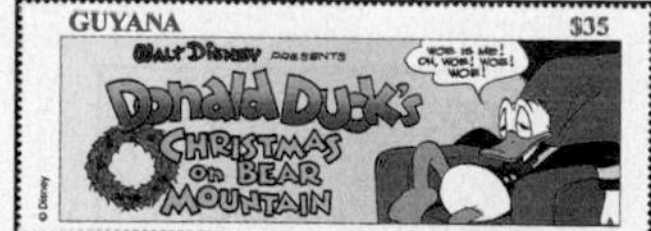

Donald Duck Adventures, Christmas on Bear Mountain — A301

No. 3334 — Cartoon panels: a, 1-8. b, 9-16. c, 17-24. d, 25-32. e, 33-40. f, 41-48. g, 49-56. h, 57-64. i, 65-72. j, 73-80. k, Pane of 2, Carl Barks, vert., bears and duck.

1998, Oct. 15 *Perf. 14x13½, 13½x14*

3334 Complete booklet 45.00 45.00
a.-j. A301 $35 Any pane of 4 2.75 2.75
k. A301 $300 Pane of 2 10.00 10.00

Disney's Uncle Scrooge, by Carl Barks, 50th anniv.

Organization of American States, 50th Anniv. A302

1998, Oct. 29 *Perf. 14*

3335 A302 $40 multicolored .55 .55

Ferrari Automobiles — A302a

No. 3335A: c, 212 Export. d, 410 Superamerica chassis. e, 125 S.

$300, 512 S Racer.

1998, Oct. 29 Litho. *Perf. 14*

3335A A302a $100 Sheet of 3, #c-e 5.00 5.00

Souvenir Sheet

3335B A302a $300 multi 5.00 5.00

No. 3335A contains three 39x25mm stamps.

Diana, Princess of Wales (1961-97) A303

No. 3336: a, Inscription panel at left. b, Panel at right.

1998, Oct. 29

3336 A303 $60 Horiz. pair, #a-b 2.00 2.00

Self-Adhesive

Serpentine Die Cut Perf. 11½

Sheet of 1

Size: 53x65mm

3336A A303 $300 Diana, buildings, bridge 65.00

No. 3336 was issued in sheets of 3 pairs.

Soaking in water may affect the multi-layer image of No. 3336A.

Issued: $60, 10/29; $300, 11/5/98.

Grand Prix Champion Racing Cars and Drivers — A304

No. 3337, $80: a, 1914 Grand Prix Mercedes, Christian Lautenschlager. b, 1930 Bugati Type 35B, P. Etancelin. c, 1934 Alfa Romeo P3, Louis Chiron. d, 1938 Mercedes Benz W154, Richard Seaman. e, 1938 Auto Union D Type, Tazio Nuvolari. f, 1951 Alfa Romeo 158, Juan Manuel Fangio.

No. 3338, $80: a, 1955 Mercedes Benz W196, Stirling Moss. b, 1960 Ferrari Dino 246, Phil Hill. c, 1966 Brabham-Repco BT19, Jack Brabham. d, 1970 Lotus Ford 72, John Miles. e, 1983 Renault RE40, Alain Prost. f, 1998 McLaren Mercedes MP4/13, David Coulthard.

No. 3339, $300, 1906 Grand Prix Renault, Ferenc Szisz. No. 3340, $300, 1956 Maserati 250F, Stirling Moss.

1998, Oct. 29 **Sheets of 6, #a-f**

3337-3338 A304 Set of 2 13.50 13.50

Souvenir Sheets

3339-3340 A304 Set of 2 8.50 8.50

Nos. 3339-3340 contain one 57x42mm stamp.

Tigger's Happy New Year — A304a

No. 3340A, vert. — Tigger: d, Giving gift to Winnie the Pooh. e, With fireworks. f, Giving flowers to Kanga. g, With Piglet. h, At door. i, With Eeyore.

No. 3340B, $300,Tigger beating drum. No. 3340C, $300, Tigger carrying staff for dragon.

1998, Oct. 29 Litho. *Perf. 13¼*

3340A A304a $60 Sheet of 6, #d-i 5.75 5.75

Souvenir Sheets

3340B-3340C A304a Set of 2 8.50 8.50

Gandhi — A305

No. 3341: a, Age 37, 1906. b, Age 77, 1946. c, Age 78, 1948. d, Age 77, 1947.

$300, Age 76, 1946, horiz.

1998, Oct. 29

3341 A305 $100 Sheet of 4, #a.-d. 5.50 5.50

Souvenir Sheet

3342 A305 $300 multicolored 4.25 4.25

No. 3341b-3341c are each 53x38mm.

Pablo Picasso A306

Paintings, details: $25, Sleeping Peasants, 1919. $60, Large Nude in Red Armchair, 1929, vert. $200, Sculpture, "Female Head," 1931, vert.

$300, Man and Woman, 1971, vert.

1998, Oct. 29 *Perf. 14½*

3343-3345 A306 Set of 3 4.00 4.00

Souvenir Sheet

3346 A306 $300 multicolored 4.50 4.50

Royal Air Force, 80th Anniv. A307

No. 3347, $100: a, Avro Lancaster B2. b, PBY-5A Catalina Amphibian. c, BAe Hawk TIA trainers (Red Arrows). d, Avro Lancaster, DeHavilland Mosquito.

No. 3348, $100: a, BAe Hawk TIA. b, C130 Hercules. c, Panavia Tornado GRI. d, BAe Hawk 200.

No. 3349 $150: a, BAe Nimrod RIP. b, Panavia Tornado F3 ADV. c, CH-47 Chinook helicopter. d, Panavia Tornado GRIA.

No. 3350, $200, Biplane, hawks in flight. No. 3351, $200, Eurofighter, Spitfire. No. 3352, $300, Eurofighters. No. 3353, $300, Head of hawk, hawk spreading wings, biplane. No. 3354, $300, Tiger Moth, Eurofighter. No. 3355, $300, Hawk spreading wings, biplane.

1998, Oct. 29 ***Perf. 14***

Sheets of 4, #a.-d.

3347-3349 A307 Set of 3 20.00 20.00

Souvenir Sheets

3350-3355 A307 Set of 6 22.50 22.50

1998 World Scout Jamboree, Chile — A308

No. 3356: a, James E. West, 1st scout executive with early Eagle Scouts. b, Pres. Kennedy greets Explorers, 51st Scouts anniv., 1961. c, Astronaut Walter Schirra receives a special merit badge, 1962.

1998, Oct. 29 **Litho.** ***Perf. 14***

3356 A308 $160 Sheet of 3, #a.-c. 7.00 7.00

Paintings by Eugene Delacroix (1798-1863) A309

No. 3357, $60: a, The Sultan of Morocco Receives the Count de Mornay. b, Armed Indian with a Gurkha Scimitar. c, Portrait presumed to be of the Singer Baroihet in Turkish Dress. d, Moroccan Notebook: Studies of Jewish Women. e, Arab Horseman Giving a Signal. f, Arab Cavalry Practicing a Charge. g, A Seated Moor. h, Jewish Woman in Traditional Dress.

No. 3358, $60: a, Corner of the Studio; the Stove. b, Room in the Apartment the Count de Mornay. c, Hamlet and Horatio in the Graveyard. d, George Sand. e, The Bride of Abydos. f, Elysian Fields. g, A Lioness Standing by a Tree. h, Monsieur Alfred Bruyas.

No. 3359, $300, Moroccan Jewish Wedding, horiz. No. 3360, $300, Death of Sardanapulus, horiz.

1998, Oct. 29 **Sheets of 8, #a.-h.**

3357-3358 A309 Set of 2 13.50 13.50

Souvenir Sheets

3359-3360 A309 Set of 2 8.50 8.50

Ferry and Flag of Guyana — A309a

1998, Oct. 31 **Litho.** ***Perf. 13¼x13¾***

Color of Ferry

3360A A309a $20 blue — —
3360B A309a $30 sepia — —

See Surinam Nos. 1148-1149.
For surcharge, see No. 4127.

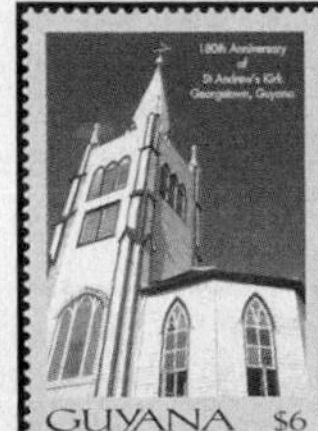

St. Andrew's Church, Georgetown, 180th Anniv. — A310

Various views of front of church: $6, $30, $60.

1998 **Litho.** ***Perf. 14***

3361-3363 A310 Set of 3 1.25 1.25

New Year 1999 (Year of the Rabbit) — A311

No. 3364 — Various stylized rabbits with denomination at: a, LR. b, LL. c, UR. d, UL. $150, Red background, Chinese inscription.

1999, Jan. 4 **Litho.** ***Perf. 14½***

3364 A311 $50 Sheet of 4, #a.-d. 3.00 3.00

Souvenir Sheet

3365 A311 $150 multicolored 2.25 2.25

Disney Characters in Sporting Activities A312

No. 3366, $80 — Skateboarding: a, Huey. b, Mickey. c, Dewey. d, Louie. e, Goofy. f, Donald.

No. 3367, $80 — Rollerblading: a, Minnie. b, Goofy. c, Daisy. d, Baby Duck. e, Donald. f, Mickey.

No. 3368, $80 — Skateboarding, rollerblading, red, white & blue background: a, Baby Duck. b, Daisy. c, Mickey. d, Goofy. e, Dewey. f, Donald.

No. 3369, $300, Dewey. No. 3370, $300, Daisy. No. 3371, $300, Goofy, horiz.

Perf. 13½x14, 14X13½

1999, Mar. 1 **Litho.**

Sheets of 6, #a-f

3366-3368 A312 Set of 3 25.00 25.00

Souvenir Sheets

3369-3371 A312 Set of 3 18.50 18.50

Mickey Mouse, 70th anniv.

Disney Characters in Trains — A313

No. 3372, $100 — 101 Dalmatians Express: a, Locomotive. b, Flatcar. c, Car with pillars. d, "Basket" car. e, Caboose.

No. 3373, $100 — Robin Hood Train: a, Engine. b, Marian, Robin Hood. c, Royal coach. d, Flatcar. e, Caboose.

No. 3374, $100 — Snow White, Diamond Mine Railroad: a, Engine. b, Flatcar. c, Snow White, Prince Charming. d, Passenger car. e, Pump car.

No. 3375, $100 — Little Mermaid Railroad: a, Engine. b, Fish holding pearls. c, Little Mermaid. d, Various marine life in car. e, "Bah Hum Bug!"

No. 3376: a, Dwarf from Diamond Mine Railroad driving locomotive. b, Dwarf on pump car.

No. 3377, $300, Bandits, Cruela De Vil. No. 3378, $300, Robin Hood, Bear. No. 3379, $300, Little Mermaid kissing Prince under mistletoe. No. 3380, $300, Little Mermaid holding starfish.

1999, Mar. 1 ***Perf. 13½x14***

Sheets of 5, #a-e

3372-3375 A313 Set of 4 36.00 36.00
3376 A313 $200 Sheet of 2, #a.-b. 9.00 9.00

Souvenir Sheets

3377-3380 A313 Set of 4 22.00 22.00

Caribbean Butterflies — A314

No. 3381, $80: a, Scarce Bamboo Page. b, Spicebush swallowtail. c, Isabella. d, The mosaic. e, Gulf fritillary. f, Figure-of-eight.

No. 3382, $80: a, Hewitson's blue hairstreak. b, Polydamas swallowtail. c, Common morpho. d, Blue-green reflector. e, Malachite. f, Grecian shoemaker.

No. 3383, $300, Giant swallowtail, vert. No. 3384, $300, Pipevine swallowtail, vert.

1999, Mar. 15 ***Perf. 14***

Sheets of 6, #a-f

3381-3382 A314 Set of 2 14.50 14.50

Souvenir Sheets

3383-3384 A314 Set of 2 9.00 9.00

Flowers A315

No. 3385, $60: a, Geranium. b, Oncidium macranthum. c, Bepi orchidglades. d, Sunflowers (2). e, Cattleya walkeriana. f, Cattleya frasquita. g, Helianthus maximilani (one). h, Paphiopedilum insigne sanderae, lily. i, Lily (2).

No. 3386, $60: a, Dendrobium nobile. b, Phalaenopsis schilleriana. c, Cymbidium alexette. d, Rhododendron. e, Phragmipedium besseae, laelia cinnabarina. f, Masdevallia veitchiana. g, Calochortus nuttallii. h, Brassolaeliocattleya pure gold. i, Laelia cinnabarina.

No. 3387: a, Leptotes bicolor, masdevallia ignea. b, Sophrolaeliocattleya, anguloa clowesii. c, Laelia pumila. d, Masdevallia ignea. e, Dendrobium phalaenopsis. f, Anguloa clowesii.

No. 3388, $300, Asocentrum miniatum, vert. No. 3389, $300, Iris pseudacorus.

1999, Mar. 15 **Litho.** ***Perf. 14***

Sheets of 9, #a-i

3385-3386 A315 Set of 2 16.00 16.00
3387 A315 $90 Sheet of 6, #a.-f. 7.50 7.50

Souvenir Sheet

3388-3389 A315 Set of 2 8.50 8.50

Akira Kurosawa (1910-98), Film Director — A316

No. 3390 — Films, vert.: a, "The Dream." b, "Rashomon." c, "Kagemusha." d, "Red Beard." e, "Seven Samurai." f, "Yojimbo."

No. 3391 — Portraits: a, Pointing. b, Hand on face. c, Standing. d, With camerman.

$300, Scene from "Dreams."

1999, Mar. 22

3390 A316 $80 Sheet of 6, #a.-f. 6.75 6.75
3391 A316 $130 Sheet of 4, #a.-d. 7.25 7.25

Souvenir Sheet

3392 A316 $300 multicolored 4.25 4.25

Mushrooms A317

Designs: $25, Coprinus atramentarius. $35, Hebeloma crustuliniforme. $100, Russula nigricans. $200, Tricholoma aurantium.

No. 3397, $60: a, Boletus aereus. b, Coprinus comatus. c, Inocybe godeyi. d, Morchella crassipes. e, Lepiota acutesquamosa. f, Amanita phalloides. g, Boletus spadiceus. h, Cortinarius collinitus. i, Lepiota procera.

No. 3398, $60: a, Russula ochroleuca. b, Hygrophorus hypotheius. c, Amanita rubescens. d, Boletus satanas. e, Amanita echinocephala. f, Amanita muscaria. g, Boletus badius. h, Hebeloma radicosum. i, Mycena polygramma.

No. 3399, $300, Lepiota acutequamoso. No. 3400, $300, Pluteus cervinus.

1999, May 6 **Litho.** ***Perf. 14***

3393-3396 A317 Set of 4 4.25 4.25

Sheets of 9, #a-i

Perf. 14½

3397-3398 A317 Set of 2 16.50 16.50

Souvenir Sheet

3399-3400 A317 Set of 2 9.00 9.00

Nos. 3397-3398 each contain nine 32x41mm stamps. Nos. 3399-3400 each contain one 32x41mm stamp.

Trains — A318

No. 3401, $80: a, Burlington Northern GP 39-2, 1974. b, CSX GP40-2, 1967. c, Erie Lackawana Railroad GP 9, 1956. d, Amtrak P 42 Genesis, 1993. e, Erie Railroad S-2, 1948. f, Pennsylvania Railroad S-1, 1947.

No. 3402, $80: a, Northern and Western #610, c. 1933. b, Pennsylvania Railroad M1B Mountain, 1930. c, Reading Railroad FP7A, 1951. d, New York Central 2-8-4, c. 1940. e, Union Pacific Challenger Big Boy, 1963. f, GP 15-15-1, 1956.

No. 3403, $80: a, Shinkansen Bullet 100 series, 1984, Japan. b, Ukranian Diesel ZMGR, 1983, Russia. c, Rhatische Bahn GE 6/6 II, Germany. d, Eurostar TGV, 1986, France. e, Atlantique TGV, 1989, France. f, Class 86-6, UK.

No. 3404, $80: a, Joseph Clark 0-4-0, 1868. b, Diamond Stack Bethel 4-4-0, 1863. c, New York Central #999, 1890. d, Boston & Maine Ballardville 0-4-0, 1876. e, Atlantic 4-4-0 Portland Rochester Railroad, 1863. f, America 4-4-0 Baltimore & Ohio Railroad, 1881.

Railroad pioneers: No. 3405, $300, George Stephen, vert. No. 3406, $300, Alfred de Glehn, vert. No. 3407, $300, George Nagelmackers, vert. No. 3408, $300, R.F. Trevithick, vert.

1999, May 10 ***Perf. 14***

Sheets of 6, #a.-f.

3401-3404 A318 Set of 4 29.00 29.00

Souvenir Sheets

3405-3408 A318 Set of 4 17.00 17.00

Australia '99 World Stamp Expo.

Wedding of Prince Edward and Sophie Rhys-Jones — A319

Various portraits: Nos. 3409, $150, 3411, $300, rose lilac sheet margin. Nos. 3410, $150, 3412, $300, yellow brown sheet margin.

1999, June 19 Litho. *Perf. 14¼*

Sheets of 4, #a.-d.

3409-3410 A319 Set of 2 17.00 17.00

Souvenir Sheets

3411-3412 A319 Set of 2 8.50 8.50

Nos. 3411-3412 are horiz.

Johann Wolfgang von Goethe (1749-1832), Poet — A320

No. 3413: a, Lynceus sings from the watch-tower. b, Portaits of Von Goethe and Friedrich von Schiller (1759-1805), poet. c, The fallen Icarus.

$300, Mephistopheles appears as salamander, vert.

1999, June 22 Litho. *Perf. 14*

3413 A320 $150 Sheet of 3, #a.-c. 6.25 6.25

Souvenir Sheet

3414 A320 $300 multicolored 4.25 4.25

IBRA '99, World Philatelic Exhibition, Nuremberg — A321

Designs: $60, Class E10 Bo-bo electric locomotive, BMW offices, Munich, 1952, vert. $200, Class 01, 4-6-2 steam express train, 1926.

1999, June 22

3415 A321 $60 multicolored .90 .90

3416 A321 $200 multicolored 2.75 2.75

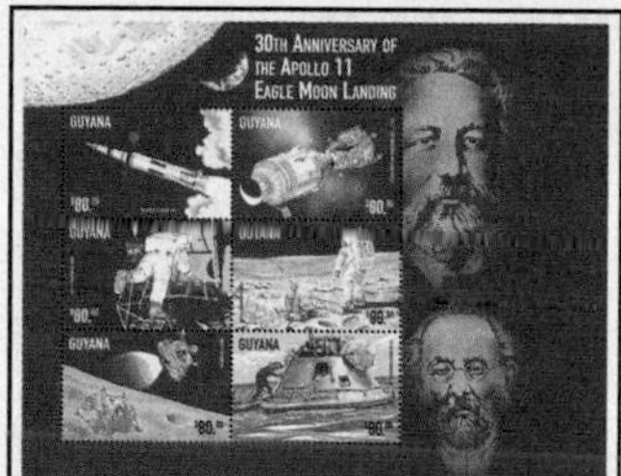

Apollo 11 Moon Landing, 30th Anniv. — A322

No. 3417, $80: a, Blast off. b, Command Module docked with Lunar Lander. c, First man on moon. d, Seismic experiments package. e, Back to the orbiter. f, Astronauts being picked up.

No. 3418, $80, vert: a, Sputnik, 1959, Konstantin Tsiolkovsky. b, Apollo 11 liftoff. c, On the moon. d, Collecting samples of lunar rocks. e, Apollo 11 Lunar Module. f, Splashdown.

No. 3419, $300, Salute to the flag. No. 3420, $300, Michael Collins.

1999, June 22 Sheets of 6, #a-f

3417-3418 A322 Set of 2 13.00 13.00

Souvenir Sheet

3419-3420 A322 Set of 2 8.50 8.50

Souvenir Sheets

PhilexFrance '99, World Philatelic Exhibition — A323

Designs: No. 3421, $300, Co-Co 7000 Class High Speed 1949-55. No. 3422, $300, 241-P Class 4-8-2 Express 1947-49.

1999, June 22

3421-3422 A323 Set of 2 9.00 9.00

Paintings by Hokusai (1760-1849) — A324

No. 3423, $80: a, Travelers Climbing a Mountain Path. b, Washing in a River. c, The Blind (eyes & mouth open). d, The Blind (eyes & mouth shut). e, Convolvulus and Tree-Frog. f, Fishermen Hauling a Net.

No. 3424, $80: a, Hibiscus and Sparrow. b, Hydrangea and Swallow. c, The Blind (eyes shut, mouth open). d, The Blind (eyes open, mouth shut). e, Irises. f, Lilies.

No. 3425, $300, Flowering Cherries at Mount Yoshino, vert. No. 3426, $300, A View of a Stone Causeway, vert.

1999, June 22 Litho. *Perf. 14x13¾*

Sheets of 6, #a-f

3423-3424 A324 Set of 2 13.50 13.50

Souvenir Sheets

Perf. 13¾x14

3425-3426 A324 Set of 2 8.50 8.50

Pope John Paul II — A325

1999, June 22 *Perf. 14*

3427 A325 $80 Sheet of 6, #a.-f. 7.50 7.50

John Glenn's Return to Space — A326

No. 3428: a, In space suit, 1962. b, After landing, 1962. c, As Senator. d, With helmet, 1998. e, Without helmet, 1998.

1999, June 22 *Perf. 14½x14¼*

3428 A326 $100 Sheet of 5, #a.-e. 7.00 7.00

Parrots and Parakeets — A327

No. 3429, $60: a, Hyacinth macaw. b, Blue and gold macaw. c, Blue-fronted Amazon parrot. d, Amazon parrot. e, Sun Conure. f, Tivi parakeet. g, Bavaria's conure. h, Fairy lorikeet.

No. 3430, $60: a, Marron macaw. b, Thick-billed parrot. c, Golden-crowned canuro. d, Yellow-naped macaw. e, Double yellow-headed parrot. f, Golden-fronted parakeet. g, Maroon-billed conure. h, Nanday conure.

No. 3431, $300, Jendaya conure, horiz. No. 3432, $300, Gray-cheeked parakeet.

1999, Aug. 3 *Perf. 14*

Sheets of 8, #a.-h.

3429-3430 A327 Set of 2 14.00 14.00

Souvenir Sheets

3431-3432 A327 Set of 2 8.50 8.50

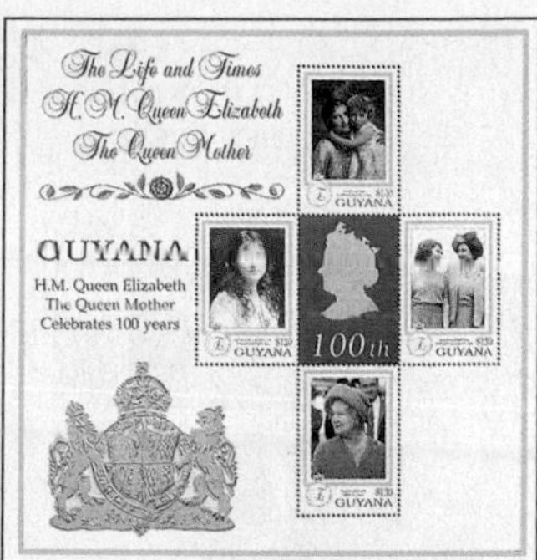

Queen Mother, 100th Birthday (in 2000) — A328

No. 3433: a, Duchess of York, Princess Elizabeth, 1928. b, Lady Elizabeth Bowles-Lyon, 1914. c, Queen Elizabeth, Princess Elizabeth, 1940. d, Queen Mother, Venice, 1984.

$400, Queen Mother, Canada, 1988.

1999, Aug. 4 Gold Frames

3433 A328 $130 Sheet of 4, #a.-d. + label 8.00 8.00

Souvenir Sheet

Perf. 13¾

3434 A328 $400 multicolored 5.50 5.50

No. 3434 contains one 38x50mm stamp. Margins of sheets are embossed.

See Nos. 3689-3690.

China Soccer League Superstars — A329

Nos. 3435a-3435g, 3436a-3436g, Various players. Nos. 3435h, 3436h, League emblem.

1999, Aug. 16 *Perf. 14½x14¼*

3435 A329 $50 Sheet of 8, #a.-h. 5.25 5.25

3436 A329 $60 Sheet of 8, #a.-h. 6.25 6.25

Rights of the Child — A330

No. 3437: a, Denomination at LL, flag at UR. b, Denomination at UL, flag at LL. c, Denomination at UL, flag at UR.

$300, Prince Talal.

1999, June 22 Litho. *Perf. 14*

3437 A330 $150 Sheet of 3, #a.-c. 5.50 5.50

Souvenir Sheet

3438 A330 $300 multicolored 4.00 4.00

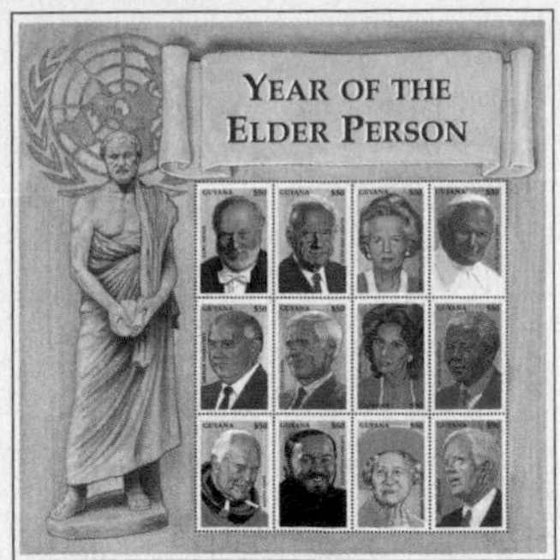

Intl. Year of the Elderly — A331

No. 3439: a, Kurt Masur. b, Rupert Murdoch. c, Margaret Thatcher. d, Pope John Paul II. e, Mikhail Gorbachev. f, Ted Turner. g, Sophia Loren. h, Nelson Mandela. i, John Glenn. j, Luciano Pavarotti. k, Queen Mother. l, Jimmy Carter.

No. 3440 — Ronald Reagan: a, As young man. b, In uniform. c, Feeding chimp. d, With campaign poster. e, With cowboy hat. f, With wine glass.

$300, Reagan in star.

1999, June 22 Litho. *Perf. 14*

3439	A331	$50 Sheet of 12, #a.-l.	8.50	8.50
3440	A331	$100 Sheet of 6, #a.-f.	7.00	7.00

Souvenir Sheet

3441	A331	$300 multicolored	3.50	3.50

Souvenir Sheet

Mei Lan Fang, Chinese Actor — A332

1999, Aug. 16 Litho. *Perf. 13¾*

3442	A332	$400 multicolored	4.50	4.50

First Balloon Flight Around the World — A333

No. 3443: a, Orbiter 3. b, Emblem. c, Bertrand Piccard. d, Brian Jones.

$300, Orbiter 3, flight path.

1999, Aug. 16 Litho. *Perf. 14*

3443	A333	$150 Sheet of 4, #a.-d.	7.25	7.25

Souvenir Sheet

3444	A333	$300 multicolored	4.00	4.00

The Kennedy Family A334

No. 3445: a, Jacqueline and John, Jr. b, John and John, Jr. c, John and Jacqueline. d, Jacqueline. e, John, Jr. and Caroline. f, John.

No. 3445G: h, John, Jr. as adult and child. i, John, Jr. and Jacqueline. j, John Jr.

1999, Oct. 4 Litho. *Perf. 13¾*

3445	A334	$80 Sheet of 6, #a.-f.	6.25	6.25
3445G	A334	$160 Sheet of 3, #h.-j.	5.75	5.75

Inter-American Development Bank, 40th Anniv. — A335

1999, Nov. 15 Litho. *Perf. 14*

3446	A335	$30 multicolored	.40	.40

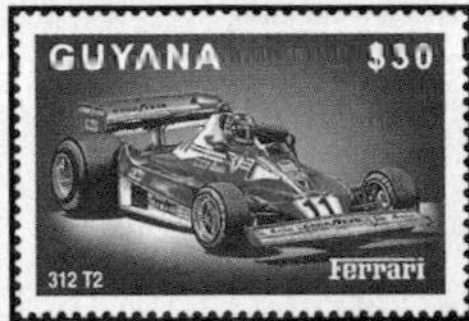

Ferrari Automobiles — A336

Designs: $30, 312 T2. $35, 553 F.1. $60, D 50. $200, 246 F.1. $300, 126/C2. $400, 312/B2.

1999 Litho. *Perf. 14*

3447-3452	A336	Set of 6	11.50	11.50

Sidney Sheldon, Novelist — A337

1999 Litho. *Perf. 14*

3453	A337	$80 multicolored	1.00	1.00

Issued in sheets of 4.

A338

No. 3454: a, During World War II. b, Wedding photo. c, As child. d, At coronation of George VI. e, In 1971. f, In 1991. g, in 1914. h, In 1988. i, At Royal Agricultural show. j, On 60th birthday.

$1,000, Portrait.

1999 Litho. *Perf. 12*

3454	A338	$60 Sheet of 10, #a.-j.	8.75	8.75

Imperf

Size: 51x76mm

3455	A338	$1000 multicolored	12.00	12.00

Sheets of No. 3454 exist with black border in margin with text "In Memoriam/1900-2002."

Queen Mother (b. 1900) — A339

Litho. & Embossed

1999, Aug. 4 *Die Cut Perf. 8¾*

3456	A339	$1500 gold & multi	*35.00*

Millennium A340

No. 3457, Founding of first university, 1088.

No. 3458 — Highlights of the 11th Century: a, Anasazi trade center. b, "Black Virgin." c, Seljuk warrior. d, Appearance of Halley's Comet. e, Battle of Hastings. f, William of Normandy crowned King of England. g, Power of the Fujiwara is checked. h, Holy Roman Emperor Henry IV. i, Muslims build Timbuktu. j, Like No. 3457. k, Gondolas come into use in Venice. l, El Cid. m, First crusade. n, Crusaders capture Jerusalem. o, Chinese statue of Guanyin. p, Rubiayat of Omar Khayyam (60x40mm). q, Syrian storage jar.

No. 3459 — Highlights of the 1910s: a, Manet and Post-impressionists show, Grafton Gallery, London. b, Standard Oil loses Supreme Court antitrust suit. c, Harriet Quimby, 1st female pilot in US d, US enters World War I. e, Titanic sinks. f, Pu Yi resigns as Chinese Emperor. g, Grand Central Station built in NYC. h, Assassination of Archduke Francis Ferdinand. i, Panama Canal opens. j, Lawrence of Arabia. k, Easter Uprising, Ireland. l, 1917 Russian Revolution. m, Execution of the Romanovs. n, Treaty of Versailles ends World War I. o, Influenza epidemic. p, Leo Tolstoy & Mark Twain die (60x40mm). q, Bauhaus opens, Weimar, Germany.

1999, Dec. 20 Litho. *Perf. 13¼x13*

3457	A340	$35 multi	.50	.50

Perf. 12¾x12½

3458	A340	$35 Sheet of 17, #a.-q.	7.50	7.50
3459	A340	$35 Sheet of 17, #a.-q., + label	7.50	7.50

Flowers — A341

No. 3460: Various flowers making up a photomosaic of Princess Diana.

No. 3461: Various details of paper money of the world making up a photomosaic of George Washington's portrait on $1 bill.

1999-2000 Litho. *Perf. 13¾*

3460	A341	$80 Sheet of 8, #a.-h.	12.00	12.00
3461	A341	$80 Sheet of 8, #a.-h.	10.00	10.00

Issued: No. 3460, 12/31; No. 3461, 3/27/00.

See Nos. 3568-3569.

LUNAR NEW YEAR

GUYANA $100 $100 GUYANA

GUYANA $100 $100 GUYANA

New Year 2000 (Year of the Dragon) — A342

No. 3462 — Dragons with denomination in: a, LR. b, LL. c, UR, d, UL.

$300, LR.

2000, Feb. 5 *Perf. 14¾*

3462	A342	$100 Sheet of 4, #a.-d.	5.00	5.00

Souvenir Sheet

3463	A342	$300 multi	3.50	3.50

A343

Automobiles — A344

No. 3464, $100: a, Nicholas Cugnot's steam-powered Fardier, 1769. b, Siegfried Marcus's motor carriage, 1875. c, Karl Benz's Velo, 1894. d, Virgilio Bordino's steam carriage, 1854. e, 1886 Benz. f, 1908 Ford Model T.

No. 3465, $100: a,1926 Duesenberg Model A Phaeton. b, 1927 Mercedes-Benz Model K. c, 1928, Rolls-Royce Phantom I limousine. d, 1935 Auburn 851 Speedster. e, 1936 Mercedes-Benz 540K Cabriolet B. f, 1949, Volkswagen Cabriolet Beetle.

No. 3466, $100: a, 1957 Ford Thunderbird. b, 1957 Jaguar XK150. c, 1968 Chevrolet Corvette Stingray. d, 1973 BMW 2002 Turbo. e, 1975 Porsche 911 Turbo. f, 1999 Volkswagen Beetle.

No. 3467, $100: a, 1886 Daimler motor car. b, 1898 Opel Luzman. c, 1899 Benz Landaulet coupe. d, 1892 Peugeot Vis-a-vis. e, 1886 Benz. f, 1894 Benz Velo, diff.

No. 3468, $100: a, 1896 Ford. b, 1903 De Dion-Bouton Populare. c, 1900 Adler. d, 1904 Vauxhall. e, 1908 Rolls-Royce Silver Ghost. f, 1908 Ford Model T, diff.

No. 3469, $400, 1904 Mercedes-Benz 60/70. No. 3470, $400, 1939 Mercedes-Benz Type 320 Cabriolet. No. 3471, $400, 1954 Mercedes-Benz 300SL Gullwing.

No. 3472, $400, 1904 Turner-Miesse. No. 3473, $400, 1910 Runabout.

2000, Mar. 13 Litho. *Perf. 13½*

Sheets of 6, #a.-f.

3464-3466 A343 Set of 3 22.00 22.00

Perf. 14

3467-3468 A344 Set of 2 14.00 14.00

Souvenir Sheets

Perf. 14½

3469-3471 A343 Set of 3 13.50 13.50

Perf. 14¼

3472-3473 A344 Set of 2 9.00 9.00

Size of stamps from Nos. 3463-3466, 41x25mm; from Nos. 3467-3468, 42x28mm.

No. 1341 Surcharged in Red

2000 ? Litho. Unwmk. *Perf. 14*

3473A A92 $6 on 25c #1341 —

Marine Life A345

Designs: $30, Lachnolaimus maximus. $35, Cyphoma gibbosum. $60, Trachinotus falcatus. $100, Bodianus pulchellus. $200, Anisotremus virginicus. $300, Etheostoma spectabile.

No. 3480, $80: a, Hypoplectrus indigo. b, Chlamys hastata. c, Sebastes rubrivinctus. d, Selene vomer. e, Marginella carnea. f, Phoca vitulina. g, Coryphaena hippurus. h, Epinephelus fulvus.

No. 3481, $80: a, Sphyraena barracuda. b, Saccopharynx sp. c, Chromodoris amoena. d, Makaira nigricans. e, Orcinus orca. f, Hippocampus reidi. g, Chelonia mydas. h, Emblemaria pandionis.

No. 3482, $80, vert.: a, Pterois volitans. b, Tursiops truncatus. c, Diplulmaris antarctica. d, Pomacanthus arcuatus. e, Aetobatus narinari. f, Carcharhinus amblyrhynchos. g, Sacura margaritacea. h, Octopus dolfeini.

No. 3483, $400, Asteroschema tenue, vert. No. 3484, $400, Apodichthys flavidus, vert. No. 3485, $400, Periclimenes pedersoni.

2000, May 15 *Perf. 14*

3474-3479 A345 Set of 6 8.50 8.50

Sheets of 8, #a.-h.

3480-3482 A345 Set of 3 25.00 25.00

Souvenir Sheets

3483-3485 A345 Set of 3 14.00 14.00

No. 3485 contains one 57x42mm stamp.

Souvenir Sheet

1999 Return of Macao to People's Republic of China — A346

No. 3486: a, Flag. b, Skyline.

2000, May 15

3486 A346 $150 Sheet of 2, #a.-b. 3.75 3.75

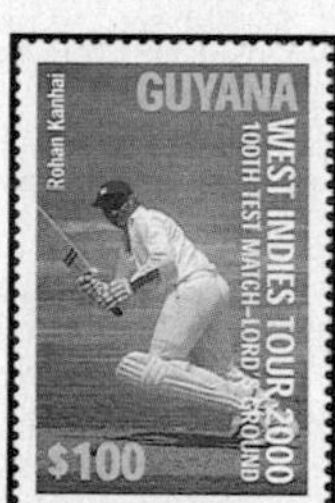

100th Test Match at Lord's Ground — A347

Designs: $100, Rohan Kanhai. $300, Clive Lloyd.

$400, Lord's Ground, horiz.

2000, May 15 Litho. *Perf. 14*

3487-3488 A347 Set of 2 5.00 5.00

Souvenir Sheet

3489 A347 $400 multi 5.25 5.25

Prince William, 18th Birthday — A348

No. 3490: a, With Prince Harry. b, Wearing sweater. c, In profile. d, In suit.

$400, In ski wear.

2000, May 15 *Perf. 14*

3490 A348 $100 Sheet of 4, #a-d 5.50 5.50

Souvenir Sheet

Perf. 13¾

3491 A348 $400 multi 5.25 5.25

No. 3490 contains four 28x42mm stamps. It exists imperf.

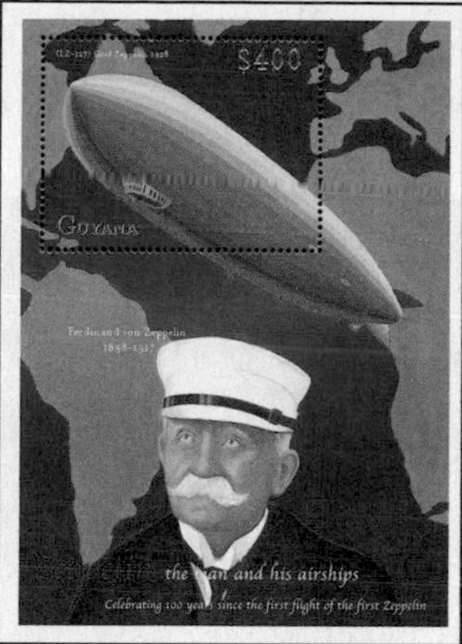

First Zeppelin Flight, Cent. — A349

No. 3492 — Ferdinand von Zeppelin and: a, LZ-1. b, LZ-2. c, LZ-9.

$400, LZ-127.

2000, May 15 *Perf. 14*

3492 A349 $200 Sheet of 3, #a-c 7.25 7.25

Souvenir Sheet

3493 A349 $400 multi 4.75 4.75

No. 3492 contains three 40x24mm stamps.

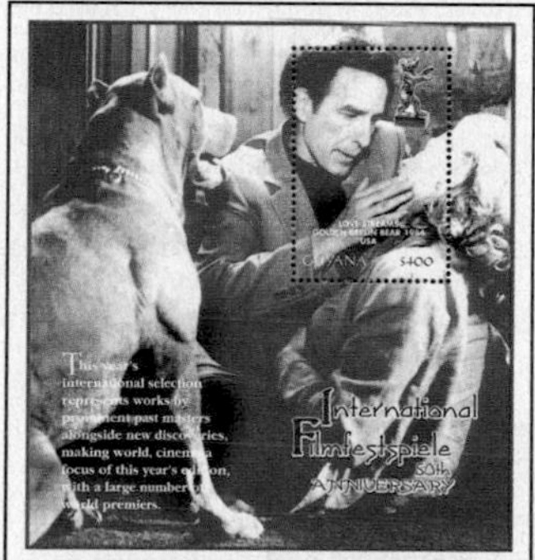

Berlin Film Festival, 50th Anniv. — A350

No. 3494: a, Das Boot Ist Voll. b, David. c, Hong Gao Liang (Red Sorghum). d, Die Ehe der Maria Braun. e, Edith Evans. f, Michel Simon.

$400, Love Streams.

2000, May 15

3494 A350 $100 Sheet of 6, #a-f 7.00 7.00

Souvenir Sheet

3495 A350 $400 multi 4.50 4.50

Apollo-Soyuz Mission, 25th Anniv. — A351

No. 3496: a, Vance D. Brand, Thomas P. Stafford. b, Apollo 18, docking adapter. c, Stafford, Valeri Kubasov.

$400, Stafford, Donald K. Slayton.

2000, May 15

3496 A351 $200 Sheet of 3, #a-c 7.25 7.25

Souvenir Sheet

3497 A351 $400 multi 4.50 4.50

Souvenir Sheets

2000 Summer Olympics, Sydney — A352

No. 3498: a, Henry Robert Pearce. b, Volleyball. c, Olympic Park, Montreal, and Canadian flag. d, Ancient Greek runners.

2000, May 15

3498 A352 $160 Sheet of 4, #a-d 7.50 7.50

Public Railways, 175th Anniv. — A353

No. 3499: a, Timothy Hackworth. b, Sans Pareil. c, Branhope Tunnel.

2000, May 15

3499 A353 $200 Sheet of 3, #a-c 7.00 7.00

Johann Sebastian Bach (1685-1750) — A354

2000, May 15

3500 A354 $400 multi 4.75 4.75

Souvenir Sheet

Albert Einstein (1879-1955) — A355

2000, May 15 Litho. *Perf. 14¼*

3501 A355 $400 multi 5.00 5.00

Space — A356

No. 3502, $100: a, Amsat IIIc. b, SRET. c, Inspector. d, Stardust. e, Temisat. f, Arsene.

No. 3503, $100, horiz.: a, Sun and Echo satellite (inscribed Apollo 11). b, Saturn, and-Pioneer. c, Moon and Apollo 11 (inscribed Echo satellite). d, Mars and Mars Explorer. e, Space Shuttle, Intl. Space Station. f, Halley's Comet and Giotto.

No. 3504, $100, horiz.: a, Cesar, Argentine, Spanish flags. b, Sirio 2, Italian flag. c, Taos S.80, French flag. d, Viking, Swedish flag. e, SCD 1, Brazilian flag. f, Offeq 1, Israeli flag.

No. 3505, $400, Clementine. No. 3506, $400, Solar Max, horiz.

2000, May 15 Litho. *Perf. 14*

Sheets of 6, #a-f

3502-3504 A356 Set of 3 22.00 22.00

Souvenir Sheets

3505-3506 A356 Set of 2 9.25 9.25

World Stamp Expo 2000, Anaheim.

The Three Stooges — A357

No. 3507: a, Shemp, Moe, Larry, man with glasses. b, Skeleton, Larry, Moe. c, Shemp. d, Stooges with fingers in mouths. e, Stooges reading book. f, Stooges attacking man. g, Stooges with candle. h, Stooges, man, fire bucket. i, Moe, Shemp, man in window.

No. 3508, $400, Moe in doorway. No. 3509, $400, Larry, skeleton.

2000, July 27 *Perf. 13¾*

3507 A357 $80 Sheet of 9, #a-i 8.75 8.75

Souvenir Sheets

3508-3509 A357 Set of 2 9.00 9.00

See Nos. 3542-3544.

Betty Boop — A358

No. 3510: a, In striped blouse. b, With shopping bags. c, On cushion. d, As belly dancer. e, In red lingerie. f, In cutoff shorts. g, With musical notes. h, In flowered pants. i, In black dress.

No. 3511, $400, In fur coat. No. 3512, $400, In polka dot bathing suit, with flamingos.

2000, July 27 *Perf. 13¾*

3510 A358 $80 Sheet of 9, #a-i 9.00 9.00

Souvenir Sheets

3511-3512 A358 Set of 2 9.00 9.00

See Nos. 3545-3552.

Third Annual Caribbean Media Conference A359

2000, Aug. 14 *Perf. 14*

3513 A359 $100 multi 1.25 1.25

European Soccer Championships — A360

No. 3514, $80, horiz.: a, Denmark. b, Germany. c, Italy. d, Netherlands. e, Portugal. f, Romania. g, Czech Republic. h, Norway.

No. 3515, $80, horiz.: a, Turkey. b, Slovenia. c, Yugoslavia. d, Sweden. e, Belgium. f, Spain. g, France. h, England.

No. 3516, $400, Jurgen Klinsmann. No. 3517, $400, Stefan Kuntz.

2000, Aug. 21 *Perf. 13¾*

Sheets of 8, #a-h, + label

3514-3515 A360 Set of 2 16.00 16.00

Souvenir Sheets

3516-3517 A360 Set of 2 9.50 9.50

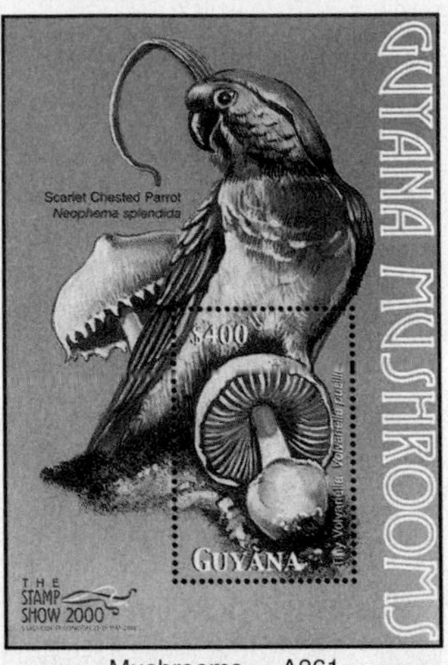

Mushrooms — A361

No. 3518, $100, horiz.: a, Sealy vase chanterelle. b, Caesar's mushroom. c, Green-headed jelly club. d, Salmon unicorn entoloma. e, White oysterette. f, Variable cort.

No. 3519, $100, horiz.: a, Coccora. b, Winter polypore. c, Turpentine waxy cap. d, Aeryginosa. e, Fly agaric. f, Honey mushroom.

No. 3520, $100, horiz: a, Salmon waxy cap. b, Shellfish-scented russula. c, Scarlet waxy cap. d, Stuntz's blue legs. e, Netted rhodotus. f, Indigo milky.

No. 3521, $400, Tiny volvariella. No. 3522, $400, Turkey tail, horiz. No. 3523, $400, Pinwheel marasmius, horiz.

2000, Oct. 4 *Perf. 14*

Sheets of 6, #a-f

3518-3520 A361 Set of 3 22.50 22.50

Souvenir Sheets

3521-3523 A361 Set of 3 14.00 14.00

The Stamp Show 2000, London.

A362

Flowers — A363

Designs: No. 3524, $35, Bougainvillea spectabilis. No. 3525, $60, Euphorbia milii. No. 3526, $200, Catharanthus roseus. No. 3527, $300, Ipomoea carnea.

No. 3528, $35, Russelia equisetiformis. No. 3529, $60, Sprekelia formosissima. No. 3530, $200, Passiflora quadrangularis. No. 3531, $300, Mirabilis jalapa.

No. 3532, $100: a, Lantana camara. b, Jatropha integerrima. c, Plumeria alba. d, Strelitzia reginae. e, Clerodendrum splendens. f, Thunbergia grandiflora.

No. 3533, $100, vert.: a, Cordia sebestena. b, Heliconia wagneriana. c, Dendrobium phalaenopsis. d, Passiflora caerulea. e, Oncidium nubigenum. f, Hibiscus rosa-sinensis.

No. 3534, $100: a, Ipomoea tricolor. b, Lantana camara (inscribed canara). c, Cantua buxifolia. d, Fuchsia. e, Eichornia crassipes. f, Cosmos sulphureus.

No. 3535, $100: a, Bignonia capreolata. b, Calceolaria herbeo-hybrida. c, Canna generalis. d, Bauhinia grandiflora. e, Amaranthus caudatus. f, Abutilon megapotamicum.

No. 3536, $400, Guzmania lingulata. No. 3537, $400, Cattleya granulosa, vert.

No. 3538, $400, Tacsonia van-volxemii. No. 3539, $400, Oeceoclades maculata.

2000, Oct. 30 *Perf. 14*

3524-3527 A362 Set of 4 6.75 6.75

3528-3531 A363 Set of 4 6.75 6.75

Sheets of 6, #a-f

3532-3533 A362 Set of 2 14.00 14.00

3534-3535 A363 Set of 2 14.00 14.00

Souvenir Sheets

3536-3537 A362 Set of 2 9.50 9.50

3538-3539 A363 Set of 2 9.50 9.50

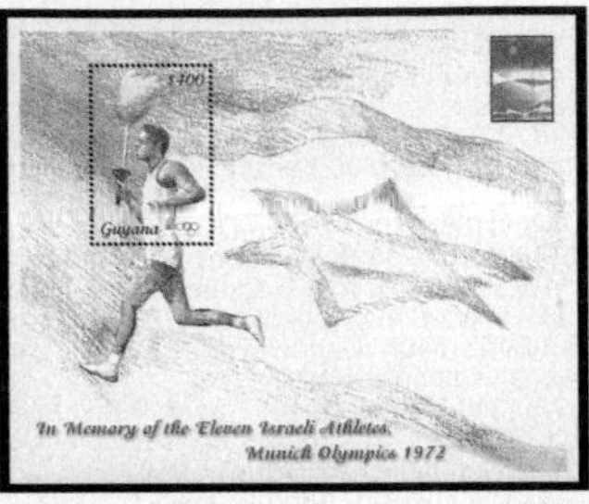

Munich Olympics Massacre — A364

No. 3540: a, Yaakov Springer. b, Andrei Schpitzer. c, Amitsur Shapira. d, David Berger. e, Ze'ev Friedman. f, Joseph Gottfreund. g, Moshe Weinberg. h, Kahat Shor. i, Mark Slavin. j, Eliezer Halfin. k, Joseph Romano. l, Poster of Munich Olympics.

2000, Oct. 30

3540 A364 $40 Sheet of 12, #a-l 7.00 7.00

Souvenir Sheet

3541 A364 $400 Torch bearer 5.50 5.50

Three Stooges Type of 2000

No. 3542: a, Moe with seltzer bottle, Shemp, Larry. b, As cave men trying to break rock. c, Moe with cow. d, Two women, Shemp, Moe. e, As cave men, seated. f, As cave men, Shemp holding large rock. g, Stooges wearing pith helmets. h, Stooges, picture frames. i, Stooges with fake beards.

No. 3543, $400, Larry, woman, vert. No. 3544, $400, Moe in plaid shirt, vert.

2000, July 27 Litho. *Perf. 13¾*

3542 A357 $80 Sheet of 9, #a-i 8.75 8.75

Souvenir Sheets

3543-3544 A357 Set of 2 9.00 9.00

Betty Boop Type of 2000

Souvenir Sheets

No. 3545, At football field. No. 3546, With tennis racquet. No. 3547, With ankh earrings, winking. No. 3548, With red swimsuit. No. 3549, As portrait of queen. No. 3550, As Can-can girl. No. 3551, Standing on shell. No. 3552, As Mona Lisa, horiz.

2000, July 27

3545-3552 A358 $400 Set of 8 40.00 40.00

I Love Lucy — A365

No. 3553: a, Lucy reading book. b, Ricky, Lucy with book. c, Ricky kissing Lucy. d, Lucy near window. e, Lucy grabbing Ethel. f, Ricky holding scarf, Lucy in bed. g, Ethel, Lucy, frying pan. h, Ricky with frying pan. i, Lucy, Ethel, coffee table.

No. 3554, $400, Lucy in pink robe. No. 3555, $400, Lucy with garbage can lid.

2000, July 27

3553 A365 $60 Sheet of 9, #a-i 6.75 6.75

Souvenir Sheets

3554-3555 A365 Set of 2 9.00 9.00

FIN. K. L — A366

No. 3556: a, Lee Hyo-Ri. b, Ok Ju-Hyun. c, Lee Jin. d, Lee Jin. e, Group. f, Sung Yu-Ri. g, Lee Hyo-Ri. h, Sung Yu-Ri. i, Ok Ju-Hyun. Nos. d, f, i, full color, others, sepia tone.

2000, Sept. 7 ***Perf. 13½***
3556 A366 $80 Sheet of 9, #a-i 9.00 9.00

Queen Mother, 100th Birthday — A367

2000, Dec. 1 ***Perf. 14***
3557 A367 $100 multi 1.40 1.40

Printed in sheets of 6.

Christmas — A368

$60, No. 3562b, Heads of 2 angels, org background. $90, No. 3562a, 2 full angels, bl background. $120, No. 3562c, Heads of 2 angels, bl background. No. 3561, $400, No. 3562d, 2 full angels, org background.
No. 3563, Baby Jesus, horiz.

2000, Dec. 18
3558-3561 A368 Set of 4 8.50 8.50
3562 A368 $180 Sheet of 4, #a-d 8.25 8.25

Souvenir Sheet

3563 A368 $400 multi 4.75 4.75

New Year 2001 (Year of the Snake) — A369

No. 3564: a, Green snake head. b, Red snake head. c, Blue snake head. d, Yellow snake head.
$250, Purple snake head, vert.

2001, Jan. 2 Litho. ***Perf. 13½x13***
3564 A369 $80 Sheet of 4, #a-d 4.25 4.25

Souvenir Sheet

Perf. 13x13½

3565 A369 $250 multi 3.00 3.00

Tourist Attractions — A370

Designs: No. 3566, $90, Prime Minister's residence. No. 3567, $90, Kaiteur Falls, vert.

2001, Jan. 30 ***Perf. 13¼***
3566-3567 A370 Set of 2 2.25 2.25

Flower Photomosaic Type of 1999

No. 3568, $80: Various photographs of flowers making up a photomosaic of the Queen Mother.
No. 3569, $100: Various photographs of religious sites making up a photomosaic of Pope John Paul II.

2001, Feb. 13 ***Perf. 13¾***

Sheets of 8, #a-h

3568-3569 A341 Set of 2 19.00 19.00

Souvenir Sheet

Chow Yun-Fat, Actor — A371

Background color: a, Blue green. b, Dark red. c, Olive brown. d, Red violet. e, Dark blue. f, Purple.

2001, Feb. 13 ***Perf. 13¾x13¼***
3570 A371 $60 Sheet of 6, #a-f 4.25 4.25

Pokémon — A372

No. 3571: a, Staryu. b, Seaking. c, Tentacool. d, Magikarp. e, Seadra. f, Goldeen.

2001, Feb. 13 ***Perf. 13¾***
3571 A372 $100 Sheet of 6, #a-f 7.50 7.50

Souvenir Sheet

3572 A372 $400 Horsea 4.50 4.50

Betty Boop Type of 2000

Designs: No. 3573, $400, In pink hat. No. 3574, $400, As singer on stage. No. 3575, $400, With red top and necklace, on beach. No. 3576, $400, In orange and black hat, horiz.

2001 ? Litho. ***Perf. 13¾***
3573-3576 A358 Set of 4 18.00 18.00

I Love Lucy Type of 2000

Designs: No. 3577, $400, Dressed like Carmen Miranda. No. 3578, $400, With blue hat and gloves. No. 3579, $400, As knife thrower's target. No. 3580, $400, At table, wearing blue hat. No. 3581, $400, Wearing glasses with thick black frames.

2001 ?
3577-3581 A365 Set of 5 22.50 22.50

A373

A374

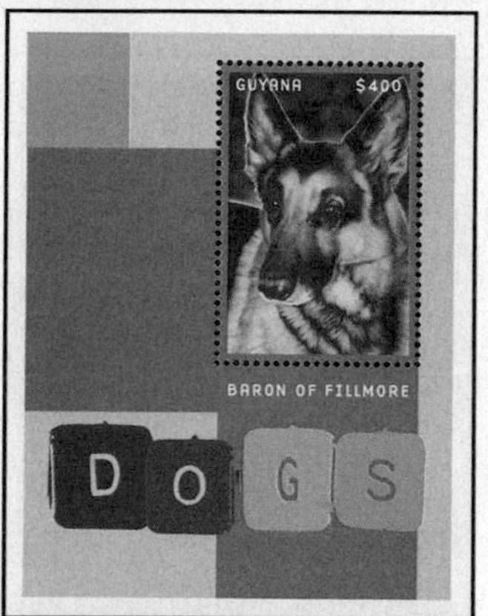
Cats and Dogs — A375

Designs: No. 3582, $35, Boxer. No. 3583, $60, Cinnamon ocicat. No. 3584, $100, Smooth dachshund. $300, White Manx.
No. 3586, $35, Chihuahua. No. 3587, $60, Persian tabby. No. 3588, $100, Colorpoint shorthair. $200, Cocker spaniel.
No. 3590 — Names of dogs (border color and location of denomination), $100: a, Pup (pink, bottom). b, Yogi (orange, bottom). c, Hooch (yellow, bottom) d, Huxley Blu (orange, top) e, Snowflake (yellow, top). f, Red (pink, top).
No. 3591 — Names of cats (border color and location of denomination), $100: a, Tom (orange, bottom). b, Puff (yellow, bottom). c, Jag (pink, bottom). d, Fritz (yellow, top). e, Smokey (pink, top). f, Thor, (orange, top).
No. 3592, $60: a, Devon rex. b, Egyptian mau. c, Turkish angora. d, Sphynx. e, Persian. f, American wirehair. g, Exotic shorthair. h, American curl.
No. 3593, $80: a, Airedale terrier. b, Greyhound. c, Afghan hound. d, Samoyed. e, Field spaniel. f, Scottish terrier. g, Brittany spaniel. h, Boston terrier.
No. 3594, $80: a, American shorthair. b, Somali. c, Singapura. d, Balinese. e, Egyptian mau. f, Scottish fold. g, Sphynx. h, Korat.
No. 3595, $80: a, Rottweiler. b, German shepherd. c, Bernese mountain dog. d, Sharpei. e, Dachshund. f, Jack Russell terrier. g, Boston terrier. h, Welsh corgi.
No. 3596, $400, Dalmatian. No. 3597, $400, Birman. No. 3598, $400, Abyssinian. No. 3599, $400, Beagle. No. 3600, $400, German shepeherd named Baron of Fillmore. No. 3601, $400, Cat named Spike.

2001, Mar. 1 ***Perf. 14***
3582-3585 A373 Set of 4 6.25 6.25
3586-3589 A374 Set of 4 5.25 5.25

Sheets of 6, #a-f

3590-3591 A375 Set of 2 16.00 16.00

Sheets of 8, #a-h

3592-3593 A373 Set of 2 15.00 15.00
3594-3595 A374 Set of 2 16.50 16.50

Souvenir Sheets

3596-3597 A373 Set of 2 9.50 9.50
3598-3599 A374 Set of 2 9.50 9.50
3600-3601 A375 Set of 2 9.50 9.50

Hong Kong 2001 Stamp Exhibition (Nos. 3592-3593, 3596-3597).

Souvenir Sheets

Hello Kitty — A376

Western children's stories with Hello Kitty characters: No. 3602, $400, Cinderella. No. 3603, $400, The Wizard of Oz. No. 3604, $400, Little Red Riding Hood. No. 3605, $400, Peter Pan. No. 3606, $400, Heidi. No. 3607, $400, Alice in Wonderland.
Oriental children's stories with Hello Kitty characters: No. 3608, $400, The Fishermen. No. 3609, $400, In the Snow. No. 3610, $400, Bamboo Princess. No. 3611, $400, Three in a Boat. No. 3612, $400, Up a Tree. No. 3613, $400, On a Bear.

2001, Mar. 28 Litho. ***Perf. 13¾***
3602-3613 A376 Set of 12 55.00 55.00

Phila Nippon '01, Japan — A377

Designs: No. 3614, $25, Hanaogi with Maidservant, by Eisho Chokosai. No. 3615, $25, Girl at a Hot Spring Resort, by Goyo Hashiguchi. No. 3616, $30, Morokoshi of the Echizenya, by Eiri Rekisentei. No. 3617, $30, Courtesan Receiving Letter of Invitation, by Harunobu Suzuki. No. 3618, $35, Two Girls on Their Way to or from the Bathhouse, by Suzuki. No. 3619, $35, Mother and Daughter on an Outing, by Hokusai. No. 3620, $60, Matron in Love, by Utamaro. No. 3621, $60, Girl and Frog, by Suzuki. No. 3622, $100, The Courtesan Midorigi, by Eisho Chokosai. No. 3623, $100, Three Beauties of High Fame, by Utamaro. No. 3624, $200, Maiko, by Bakusen Tsuchida. No. 3625, $200, Girl Breaking Off the Branch of a Flowering Tree, by Suzuki.
No. 3626 — Paintings by Jakuchu Ito (28x84mm): a, Insects, Reptiles and Amphibians at a Pond. b, Rose Mallows and Fowl. c, Rooster, Sunflower and Morning Glories. d, A Group of Roosters. e, Black Rooster and Nandina. f, Birds and Autumn Maples. g, Wagtail and Roses. h, Cockatoos in a Pine.
No. 3627 — Predominate features of sections of Procession to the Shugakuin Imperial Villa, by Sesshin Kakimoto (28x84mm): a, Bridge. b, High mountain, road and bridge. c, Large tree in foreground. d, Small island in foreground. e, Building at bottom. f, Building and large tree at bottom.
No. 3628 — Paintings of Women (28x84mm): a, Girls After the Bath, by Utamaro. b, Summer Evening on the River bank at Hama-cho, by Kiyonaga Torii. c, A Beauty in the Wind, by Ando Kaigetsudo. d, Sisters by Shoen Uemura. e, Kasamori Osen, by Suzuki.
No. 3629 — Details from Backstage at a Kabuki Theater, by Moronobu Hishikawa (30x38mm): a, Top of screen. b, Man with red kimono. c, Man with stringed instrument. e, Man on chair.
No. 3630, $400, Portrait of Senseki Takami, by Kazan Watanabe. No. 3631, $400, Fish and Octopus From the Colorful Realm of Living Beings, by Ito. No. 3632, $400, Woman Holding a Flower, by Hisako Kajiwara, horiz. No. 3633, $400, Palace of Immortals in an Autumn Valley, by Yako Okochi, horiz. No. 3634, $400, Wintry Sky, by Hosen Higashibara, horiz.

2001, June 18 ***Perf. 14***
3614-3625 A377 Set of 12 11.00 11.00
3626 A377 $80 Sheet of 8, #a-h 8.25 8.25

3627 A377 $100 Sheet of 6, #a-f 7.50 7.50
3628 A377 $120 Sheet of 5, #a-e 6.75 6.75
3629 A377 $160 Sheet of 4, #a-d 7.50 7.50

Sizes: 90x120mm, 120x90mm

Imperf

3630-3634 A377 Set of 5 22.50 22.50

Giuseppe Verdi (1813-1901), Opera Composer — A378

No. 3635: a, Verdi, score at LR. b, Actor, score from Rigoletto. c, Actor, score from Ernani. d, Verdi, scores at left.
$400, Verdi and scores.

2001, June 18 ***Perf. 14***
3635 A378 $160 Sheet of 4, #a-d 8.25 8.25

Souvenir Sheet

3636 A378 $400 multi 5.50 5.50

Toulouse-Lautrec Paintings — A379

No. 3637, horiz.: a, Maurice Joyant in the Baie de Somme. b, Monsieur Boileau. c, Monsieur, Madame and the Dog.
$300, Man from Monsieur, Madame and the Dog.

2001, June 18 ***Perf. 13¾***
3637 A379 $160 Sheet of 3, #a-c 5.50 5.50

Souvenir Sheet

3638 A379 $300 multi 5.25 5.25

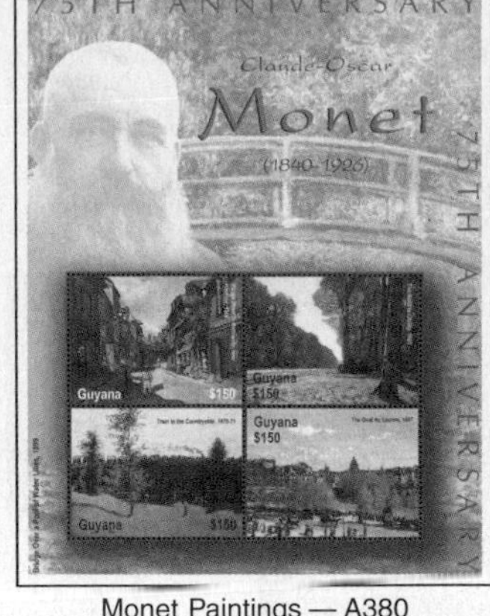

Monet Paintings — A380

No. 3639, horiz.: a, Village Street in Normandy, Near Honfleur. b, The Road to Chailly. c, Train in the Countryside. d, The Quai du Louvre.
$400, Flowering Garden.

2001, June 18
3639 A380 $150 Sheet of 4, #a-d 7.50 7.50

Souvenir Sheet

3640 A380 $400 multi 5.25 5.25

Queen Victoria (1819-1901) — A381

Pictures of Victoria from — No. 3641, $200: a, 1829. b, 1837. c, 1840. d, 1897 (with crown).
No. 3642, $200: a, 1850. b, 1843. c, 1859. d, 1897 (with hat).
No. 3643, $400, 1885 (with crown). No. 3644, $400, Undated.

2001, June 18 ***Perf. 14***

Sheets of 4, #a-d

3641-3642 A381 Set of 2 19.00 19.00

Souvenir Sheets

3643-3644 A381 Set of 2 9.50 9.50

Queen Elizabeth II, 75th Birthday — A382

No. 3645: a, Pink hat. b, Red hat. c, White hat. d, Tiara.

2001, June 18 ***Perf. 14***
3645 A382 $150 Sheet of 4, #a-d 7.50 7.50

Souvenir Sheet

Perf. 13¾

3646 A382 $400 shown 5.25 5.25

No. 3645 contains four 28x42mm stamps.

Photomosaic of Queen Elizabeth II — A383

2001, June 18 ***Perf. 14***
3647 A383 $80 multi .90 .90

Printed in sheets of 8, with and without inscription reading "In Celebration of the 50th Anniversary of H.M. Queen Elizabeth II's Accession to the Throne."

Flower Photomosaic Type of 1999-2000

No. 3648: Various pictures of American scenes making up a photomosaic of Pres. John F. Kennedy.

2001, June 18
3648 A341 $80 Sheet of 8, #a-h 7.50 7.50

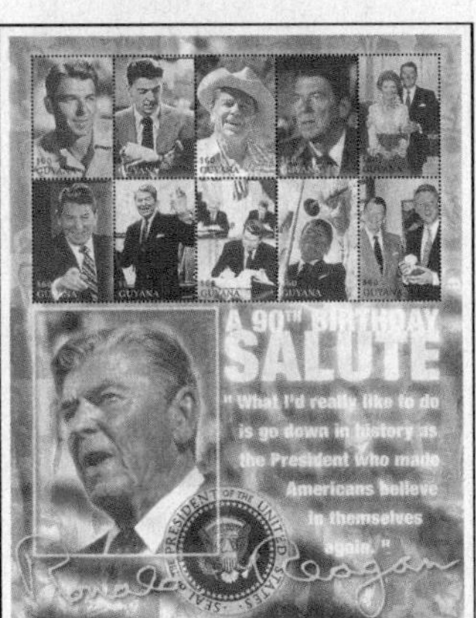

Pres. Ronald Reagan — A384

Reagan: a, In checked shirt. b, With Bonzo. c, With cowboy hat. d, With dark tie. e, With wife, Nancy. f, With striped tie. g, Waving. h, Signing treaty with Mikhail Gorbachev. i, With hammer and chisel. j, With Pres. Clinton.

2001, June 18
3649 A384 $60 Sheet of 10, #a-j 8.25 8.25

Betty Boop Type of 2000

Designs: No. 3650, $400, With swimsuit and sunglasses. No. 3651, $400, With lilac headdress. No. 3652, $400, With purple top and pirate's hat. No. 3653, $400, Dancing on radio, horiz.
No. 3654, $400, In orange and yellow polka dot swimsuit, holding gift. No. 3655, $400, Holding on to anchor. No. 3556, $400, In red bikini, surfing. No. 3557, $400, Wearing birthday hat, horiz.

2001 ***Perf. 13¾***
3650-3653 A358 Set of 4 18.00 18.00
3654-3657 A358 Set of 4 18.00 18.00

Historical Events Type of 1997

No. 3658: a, Securities and Exchange Commission formed, 1934. b, Herbert Hoover is elected president, 1928. c, The Jazz Singer is first talking movie, 1927. d, J. Edgar Hoover becomes director of FBI, 1924. e, Alexander Fleming discovers penicillin, 1928. f, FCC established to regulate broadcasting, 1934. g, Lindbergh becomes first to fly solo across Atlantic, 1927. h, Albert Einstein is awarded Nobel Prize for Physics, 1921. i, Hindenburg dies and Hitler becomes German Führer, 1934. j, Social Security Act provides safety for Americans, 1935. k, Earhart is first to fly solo from Hawaii to California, 1935. l, Marcus Garvey's prison sentence is commuted, 1927.

2001, Mar. 28 ***Perf. 14¼x14¾***
3658 A289 $60 Sheet of 12, #a-l 9.50 9.50

Prehistoric Animals — A385

Designs: $20, Allosaurus. $30, Opisthosaurus. $35, Pteranodon. $60, Cetiosaurus. $200, Archaeopteryx. $300, Parasaurolophus.
No. 3665, $100, horiz.: a, Alamosaurus. b, Archaeopteryx, diff. c, Pachycephalosaurus. d, Parasaurolophus, diff. e, Edmontosaurus. f, Triceratops.
No. 3666, $100, horiz.: a, Brachiosaurus and two palm trees. b, Dimorphodon. c, Coelophysis. d, Velociraptor. e, Antrodemus. f, Euparkeria.
No. 3667, $100, horiz.: a, Ichthyostega. b, Eryops. c, Ichthyosaur. d, Pliosaur. e, Dunklosteus. f, Eogyrinus.
No. 3668, $100, horiz.: a, Brachiosaurus and palm tree. b, Pteranodon, diff. c, Compsognathus. d, Corythosaurus. e, Allosaurus, diff. f, Torosaurus.
No. 3669, $400, Brachiosaurus, diff. No. 3670, $400, Torosaurus, diff., horiz. No. 3671, $400, Ichthyosaur, diff., horiz. No. 3672, $400, Pteranodon, diff., horiz.

2001, Oct. 15 ***Perf. 14***
3659-3664 A385 Set of 6 7.25 7.25

Sheets of 6, #a-f

3665-3668 A385 Set of 4 27.50 27.50

Souvenir Sheets

3669-3672 A385 Set of 4 18.00 18.00

Vegaspex (Nos. 3665-3672).

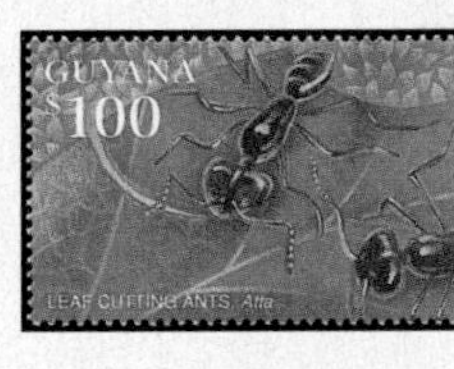

Animals of Tropical Rainforests A386

Designs: $35, Mandrill, vert. $100, Leaf cutting ants.
No. 3675, $80: a, Elephant. b, Impala. c, Leopard. d, Gray parrot. e, Hippopotamus. f, Pygmy chimp. g, African green python. h, Mountain gorilla.
No. 3676, $80: a, Three-toed sloth. b, Lion tamarin. c, Ringtail lemur. d, Sugar glider. e, Toucan. f, Trogons. g, Pygmy marmoset. h, Poison arrow frog.
No. 3677, $400, Tapir, vert. No. 3678, $400, Sable antelope, vert.

2001, Oct. 15
3673-3674 A386 Set of 2 1.50 1.50

Sheets of 8, #a-h

3675-3676 A386 Set of 2 14.50 14.50

Souvenir Sheets

3677-3678 A386 Set of 2 9.00 9.00

Tropical Birds — A387

No. 3679, $100, horiz.: a, Rainbow lorikeet. b, King bird of paradise. c, Yellow-chevroned parakeet. d, Masked lovebird. e, Scarlet ibis. f, Toco toucan.

No. 3680, $100, horiz.: a, Hyacinth macaw. b, Wire-tailed manakin. c, Scarlet macaw. d, Sun parakeet. e, Roseate spoonbill. f, Red-billed toucan.

No. 3681, $400, Eclectus parrot. No. 3682, $400, Sulfur-crested cockatoo.

2001, Oct. 15 Litho.

Sheets of 6, #a-f

3679-3680 A387 Set of 2 15.00 15.00

Souvenir Sheets

3681-3682 A387 Set of 2 11.00 11.00

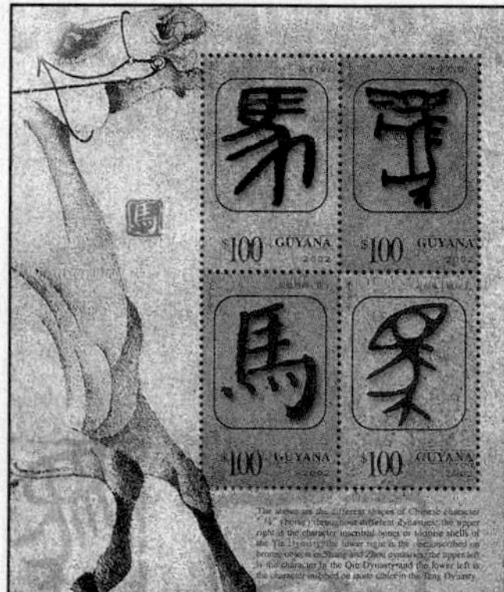

New Year 2002 (Year of the Horse) — A388

No. 3683 — Evolution of Chinese character for "horse": a, Two characters outside, one character inside parentheses at UR. b, Three characters outside, one character inside parentheses at UR. c, Four characters outside, one character inside parentheses at UR. d, Three characters outside, two characters inside parentheses at UR.

No. 3684 — Figure on horse: a, Denomination at UL. b, Denomination at UR.

2001, Oct. 15 ***Perf. 13***

3683 A388 $100 Sheet of 4, #a-d 6.50 6.50

Perf. 13¼

3684 A388 $150 Sheet of 2, #a-b 5.50 5.50

No. 3684 contains two 38x50mm stamps.

2002 World Cup Soccer Championships, Japan and Korea — A389

No. 3685, $100 — Posters from: a, 1950, and player. b, 1954, and Jules Rimet. c, 1958, Pelé and teammates. d, 1962, and Zito scoring goal. e, 1966, and English players celebrating. f, 1970, and Jairzinho.

No. 3686, $100 — Posters from: a, 1978, and Daniel Passarella. b, 1982, and Paolo Rossi. c, 1986, and Diego Maradona. d, 1990, and German players celebrating. e, 1994, and Brazilian players celebrating. f, 1998, and Zinedine Zidane.

No. 3687, $400, 1930 poster, head from Jules Rimet Trophy. No. 3688, $400, Head and globe from World Cup trophy.

2001, Dec. 26 ***Perf. 13¾x14¼***

Sheets of 6, #a-f

3685-3686 A389 Set of 2 14.00 14.00

Souvenir Sheets

Perf. 14¼

3687-3688 A389 Set of 2 9.00 9.00

Queen Mother Type of 1999 Redrawn

No. 3689: a, With Princess Elizabeth, 1928. b, Lady Elizabeth-Bowles Lyon, 1914. c, With Princess Elizabeth, 1950. d, In Venice, 1984. $400, In Canada, 1988.

2001, Dec. ***Perf. 14***

Yellow Orange Frames

3689 A328 $130 Sheet of 4, #a-d, + label 5.75 5.75

Souvenir Sheet

Perf. 13¾

3690 A328 $400 multi 4.50 4.50

Queen Mother's 101st birthday. No. 3690 contains one 38x50mm stamp with a bluer cast than that found on No. 3434. Sheet margins of Nos. 3689-3690 lack embossing and gold arms and frames found on Nos. 3433-3434.

I Love Lucy Type of 2000

Souvenir Sheets

Designs: No. 3691, $400, Lucy wearing leis, with hands up. No. 3692, $400, Lucy with checked shirt and apron, with mouth open.

2001 ? ***Perf. 13¾***

3691-3692 A365 Set of 2 9.00 9.00

Wedding of Netherlands Prince Willem-Alexander and Máxima Zorreguieta — A390

No. 3693: a, Couple (Máxima at left), flag colors at left. b, Couple (heads apart), flag colors at right. c, Couple (Máxima at right), flag colors at left. d, Couple (heads together), flag colors at right. e, Willem-Alexander. f, Máxima.

2002, Jan. 7 Litho. ***Perf. 14¾x14¼***

3693 A390 $120 Sheet of 6, #a-f 8.00 8.00

United We Stand — A391

2002, Feb. 6 ***Perf. 13½x13¼***

3694 A391 $200 multi 2.25 2.25

Printed in sheets of four.

Reign of Queen Elizabeth II, 50th Anniv. — A392

No. 3695: a, Blue hat. b, Feathered hat. c, Waving. d, With horse at right. $400, With horse at left.

2002, Feb. 6 ***Perf. 14½***

3695 A392 $150 Sheet of 4, #a-d 6.75 6.75

Souvenir Sheet

3696 A392 $400 multi 4.50 4.50

Flower Photomosaic Type of 1999-2000

No. 3697: Various science photographs making up a photomosaic of Albert Einstein.

2002, Feb. 25 ***Perf. 13¾***

3697 A341 $80 Sheet of 8, #a-h 7.25 7.25

Nobel Prizes, Cent. (in 2001) — A393

No. 3698, $100 — Chemistry laureates: a, Harold C. Urey, 1934. b, Willard F. Libby, 1960. c, Frederick Sanger, 1958 and 1980. d, Theodor Svedberg, 1926. e, Cyril N. Hinshelwood, 1956. f, Nikolai Semenov, 1956.

No. 3699, $100: a, Alexander Todd, Chemistry, 1957. b, John Steinbeck, Literature, 1962. c, Edward C. Kendall, Physiology or Medicine, 1950. d, Frederick G. Banting, Physiology or Medicine, 1923. e, Charles Nicolle, Physiology or Medicine, 1928. f, Charles Richet, Physiology or Medicine, 1913.

No. 3700, $400, International Red Cross, Peace, 1917. No. 3701, $400, John J. R. MacLeod, Physiology or Medicine, 1923. No. 3702, $400, Derek H. R. Barton, Chemistry, 1969.

2002, Feb. 25 ***Perf. 14***

Sheets of 6, #a-f

3698-3699 A393 Set of 2 13.50 13.50

Souvenir Sheets

3700-3702 A393 Set of 3 13.50 13.50

2002 Winter Olympics, Salt Lake City A394

Designs: No. 3703, $200, Skier. No. 3704, $200, Figure skater.

2002, July 1 Litho. ***Perf. 13¼x13½***

3703-3704 A394 Set of 2 4.50 4.50

a. Souvenir sheet, #3703-3704 4.50 4.50

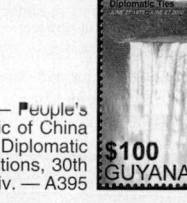

Guyana — People's Republic of China Diplomatic Relations, 30th Anniv. — A395

Designs: No. 3705, $100, Chinese flag, Kaieteur Falls, Guyana. No. 3706, $100, Guyanese flag, Great Wall of China.

2002, July 1 ***Perf. 14***

3705-3706 A395 Set of 2 2.25 2.25

Intl. Volunteers Year (in 2001) A396

Emblem, Guyanese flag and: $35, Person on ladder touching Guyana on map. $60, Map of Guyana and IVY emblem. $300, People.

2002, July 1

3707-3709 A396 Set of 3 4.50 4.50

Intl. Year of Ecotourism — A397

No. 3710: a, Owl. b, Waterfall and tourists. c, Baboon. d, Butterfly. e, Flower. f, Otter. $400, Leopard.

2002, July 1 ***Perf. 13¼x13***

3710 A397 $100 Sheet of 6, #a-f 6.75 6.75

Souvenir Sheet

3711 A397 $400 multi 4.50 4.50

Intl. Year of Mountains — A398

No. 3712: a, Devil's Tower, US. b, Schreckhorn, Switzerland. c, Mt. Rainier, US. d, Mt. Everest, Nepal and Tibet. No. 3713: Mt. McKinley, U.S.

2002, July 1 ***Perf. 13½x13¼***

3712 A398 $200 Sheet of 4, #a-d 14.00 14.00

Souvenir Sheet

3713 A398 $400 multi 7.00 7.00

See Nos. 3848-3851.

20th World Scout Jamboree, Thailand — A399

No. 3714: a, Environmental Science merit badge. b, Citizenship in the World merit badge. c, Life Saving merit badge.
$400, Mascot, Scout emblem.

2002, July 1
3714 A399 $200 Sheet of 3, #a-c 6.75 6.75

Souvenir Sheet

3715 A399 $400 multi 4.50 4.50

Flora and Fauna — A400

No. 3716, $100 — Butterflies: a, Sweet oil. b, Swallowtail. c, Southern white admiral. d, Prepona pheridamas. e, Plain tiger. f, Common eggfly.

No. 3717, $100 — Moths: a, Burgena varia. b, Lime hawkmoth. c, Spurge hawkmoth. d, Eligma laetipicta. e, Io moth. f, Pine hawkmoth.

No. 3718, $100 — Birds: a, Flycatcher. b, Barbary shrike. c, Red-faced mousebird. d, Red-footed booby. e, White-fronted goose. f, Great crested grebe.

No. 3719, $100 — Whales: a, Sperm. b, Pygmy sperm. c, Blue. d, Bottlenose. e, Killer. f, True's beaked.

No. 3720, $100, vert. — Orchids: a, Masdevallia tovarensis. b, Encyclia vitellina. c, Dendrobium nobile. d, Masdevallia falcata. e, Calanthe vestita. f, Brassolaeliacattleya Rising Sun.

No. 3721, $400, Zebra butterfly. No. 3722, $400, Callimorpha quadripuntaria. No. 3723, $400, Whiskered tern. No. 3724, $400, Beluga whale. No. 3725, $400, Brassavola nodosa.

2002, Aug. 7 ***Perf. 14***

Sheets of 6, #a-f

3716-3720 A400 Set of 5 47.50 47.50

Souvenir Sheets

3721-3725 A400 Set of 5 35.00 35.00

Elvis Presley (1935-77) A401

Designs: No. 3726, $60, In army uniform. No. 3727, $60, Singing.

2002, Aug. 16 ***Perf. 13¾***
3726-3727 A401 Set of 2 2.25 2.25

Each stamp was printed in a sheet of nine.

Popeye — A402

No. 3728: a, Popeye. b, Olive Oyl. c, Wimpy. d, Jeep. e, Swee'Pea and Olive Oyl. f, Swee'Pea.
$400, Popeye, diff.

2002, Oct. 7 ***Perf. 14***
3728 A402 $100 Sheet of 6, #a-f 8.50 8.50

Souvenir Sheet

3729 A402 $400 multi 6.50 6.50

New Year 2003 (Year of the Ram) — A403

Rams and background color of: a, Red. b, Orange. c, Bright pink. d, Yellow green.

2003, Jan. 27 Litho. ***Perf. 14¼x14½***
3730 A403 $100 Sheet of 4, #a-d 6.50 6.50

Pres. John F. Kennedy (1917-63) — A404

No. 3731, vert.: a, Pres. Kennedy, Presidential seal. b, Pres. Kennedy, Dr. Martin Luther King, Jr. c, Pres. Kennedy, space capsule. d, Pres. Kennedy, US flag, White House. e, Pres. Kennedy, map of Cuba, missile. f, Jacqueline and John F. Kennedy, Jr., US flag.
$400, Pres. Kennedy and wife, Jacqueline.

2003, Jan. 27 ***Perf. 14***
3731 A404 $100 Sheet of 6, #a-f 8.00 8.00

Souvenir Sheet

3732 A404 $400 multi 6.50 6.50

Pres. Ronald Reagan — A405

No. 3733, vert. — Pres. Reagan: a, And eagle. b, As actor. c, And Mt. Rushmore. d, And wife Nancy. e, And White House. f, Riding horse.
$400, With Mikhail Gorbachev.

2003, Jan. 27
3733 A405 $100 Sheet of 6, #a-f 8.00 8.00

Souvenir Sheet

3734 A405 $400 multi 7.00 7.00

Princess Diana (1961-97) — A406

No. 3735: a-f, Various depictions of Princess wearing tiaras or bridal veils.
$400, Wearing pink and yellow dress.

2003, Jan. 27
3735 A406 $100 Sheet of 6, #a-f 7.00 7.00

Souvenir Sheet

3736 A406 $400 multi 5.00 5.00

Paintings of Lucas Cranach the Elder (1472-1553) A407

Designs: $35, Portrait of a Man. $60, Portrait of a Woman. $100, Duchess Catherine of Mecklenburg. $200, Portrait of Duke Henry of Saxony.

No. 3741: a, The Virgin, c. 1518. b, The Virgin and Child Under the Apple Tree. c, The Virgin, c, 1535. d, The Virgin, c. 1525.
$400, The Virgin and Child Holding a Piece of Bread.

2003, June 17 Litho. ***Perf. 14¼***
3737-3740 A407 Set of 4 4.50 4.50
3741 A407 $150 Sheet of 4, #a-d 6.75 6.75

Souvenir Sheet

3742 A407 $400 multi 4.50 4.50

Art by Kunichika Toyohara (1835-1900) A408

Designs: $60, The Actor Shikan Nakamura IV. $80, The Actor Danjuro Ichikawa IX as Sukeroku, 1883. $100, The Actor Tatsunosuke Onoe. $300, The Actor Sadanji Ichikawa I as Kyusuke.

No. 3747: a, The Actor Sansho Kawarazaki as Watonai. b, The Actor Danjuro Ichikawa IX as Gongoru Kagemasa Kamakura. c, The Actor Sadanji Ichikawa I as Sadakuro. d, The Actor Danjuro Ichikawa IX as Sukeroku, 1898.
$400, The Actor Danjuro Ichikawa IX as Shukeigashira Kiyomasa Kato, horiz.

2003, June 17
3743-3746 A408 Set of 4 6.00 6.00
3747 A408 $150 Sheet of 4, #a-d 6.75 6.75

Souvenir Sheet

3748 A408 $400 multi 4.50 4.50

Paintings by Wassily Kandinsky (1866-1944) A409

Designs: $25, Tension in Red. $30, Black Accompaniment. $35, Calm Tension. $60, Hard and Soft. $100, Yellow Point, horiz. $300, Composition VIII, horiz.

No. 3755: a, Red Oval. b, On the White II. c, Mutual Agreement. d, Inclination.

No. 3756, $400, White Center, horiz. No. 3757, $400, Black Weft, horiz.

2003, June 17
3749-3754 A409 Set of 6 6.25 6.25
3755 A409 $150 Sheet of 4, #a-d 6.75 6.75

Size: 104x84mm

Imperf

3756-3757 A409 Set of 2 9.00 9.00

Caribbean Community, 30th Anniv. — A410

Anniversary emblem and: $20, Map of Guyana, vert. $60, Bank of Guyana Building. $100, Hands with torch, vert. $160, Stethoscope and AIDS ribbon, vert.

2003, July 7 ***Perf. 14***
3758-3761 A410 Set of 4 3.75 3.75

A411

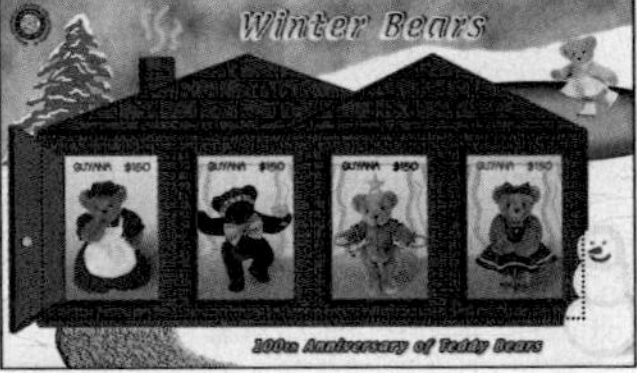

Teddy Bears, Cent. (in 2002) — A412

No. 3762 — Background color: a, Lilac. b, Dull greenish blue. c, Light blue. d, Dull yellow green. e, Dull blue green. f, Dull gray green. h, Gray. i, Dull green. j, Gray blue.

No. 3763 — Bear with: a, Red dress. b, Menorah. c, Christmas lights. d, Blue dress.

2003, Aug. 25
3762 A411 $80 Sheet of 9, #a-i 8.50 8.50
3763 A412 $150 Sheet of 4, #a-d 7.00 7.00

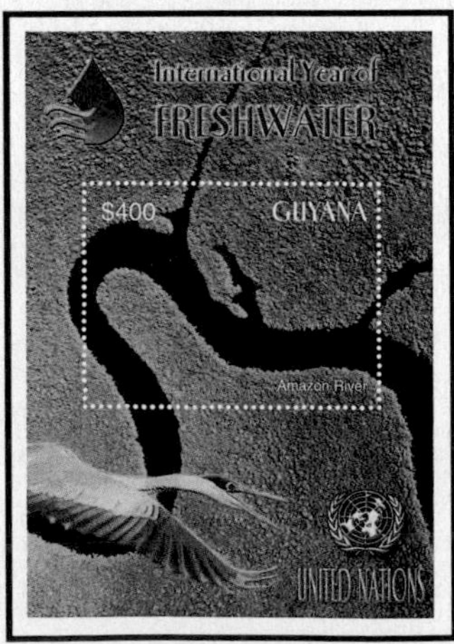

Intl. Year of Fresh Water — A413

No. 3764 — Kaieteur Falls: a, Top. b, Middle. c, Base.
$400, Amazon River.

2003, Aug. 25 ***Perf. 13¾***
3764 A413 $200 Sheet of 3, #a-c 8.25 8.25

Souvenir Sheet

3765 A413 $400 multi 6.00 6.00

Tour de France Bicycle Race, Cent. — A414

No. 3766: a, Jacques Anquetil, 1964. b, Felice Gimondi, 1965. c, Lucien Aimar, 1966. d, Roger Pingeon, 1967.
$400, Jan Janssen, 1968.

2003, Aug. 25 ***Perf. 13½x13***

3766 A414 $150 Sheet of 4, #a-d 7.25 7.25

Souvenir Sheet

3767 A414 $400 multi 5.00 5.00

Coronation of Queen Elizabeth II, 50th Anniv. — A415

No. 3768: a, Wearing tiara. b, Wearing dark blue dress. c, Wearing lilac dress.
$400, Wearing crown.

2003, Aug. 25 ***Perf. 14***

3768 A415 $200 Sheet of 3, #a-c 6.75 6.75

Souvenir Sheet

3769 A415 $400 multi 4.50 4.50

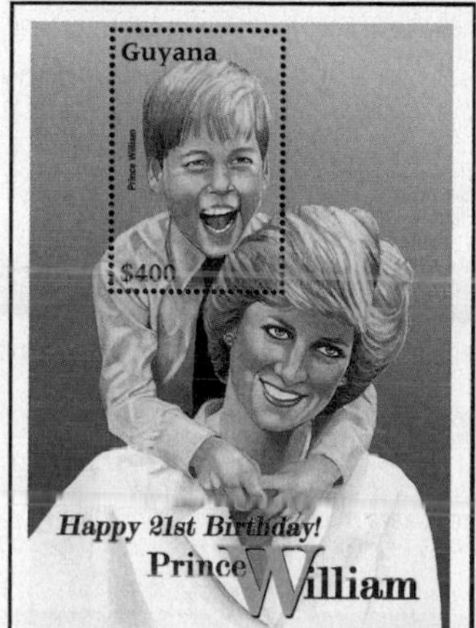

Prince William, 21st Birthday — A416

No. 3770: a, As toddler. b, As adult. c, As infant.
$400, As young boy.

2003, Aug. 25

3770 A416 $200 Sheet of 3, #a-c 7.00 7.00

Souvenir Sheet

3771 A416 $400 multi 5.50 5.50

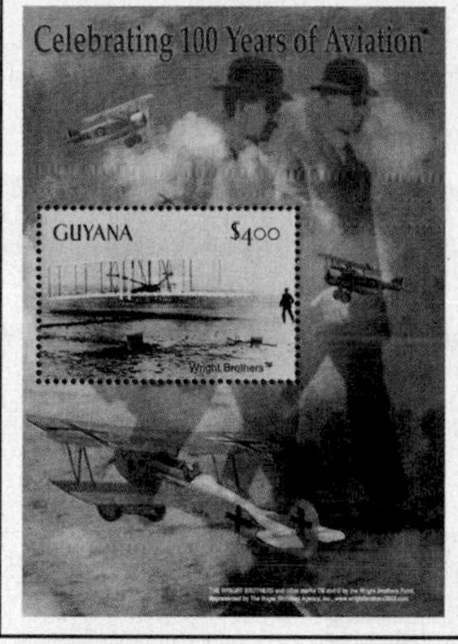

Powered Flight, Cent. — A417

Designs: $100, Airplane of Sir Alliot Verdon Roe. $160, Airplane of Samuel Franklin Cody.
No. 3772, $150: a, Wright Flyer. b, Spad 13. c, Sopwith F-1. d, Albatros D.II.
No. 3773, $150: a, Nieuport 17. b, S. E. 5a. c, D. H. 4. d, German biplane.
No. 3774, $400, Wright Flyer making first flight. No. 3775, $400, Fokker D.VIIs.

2003, Aug. 25

3771A A417 $100 multi 1.10 1.10
3771B A417 $160 multi 1.75 1.75

Sheets of 4, #a-d

3772-3773 A417 Set of 2 13.50 13.50

Souvenir Sheets

3774-3775 A417 Set of 2 10.00 10.00

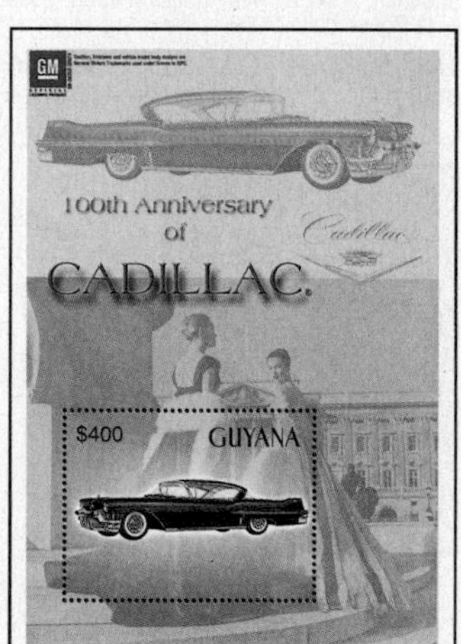

General Motors Automobiles — A418

No. 3776, $150 — Cadillacs: a, 1948 Sixty Special. b, 1966 Fleetwood Sixty Special. c, 1967 Eldorado. d, 1976 Eldorado convertible.
No. 3777, $150 — Corvettes: a, 1964 Stingray. b, 1963 Stingray. c, 1966 Stingray. 4. d, 1969.
No. 3778, $400, Undescribed Cadillac (1957 Coupe de Ville). No. 3779, $400, 1971 Corvette.

2003, Aug. 25 **Sheets of 4, #a-d**

3776-3777 A418 Set of 2 14.50 14.50

Souvenir Sheets

3778-3779 A418 Set of 2 9.50 9.50

Butterflies — A419

Designs: $20, Grecian shoemaker. $55, Clorinde. $80, Orange-barred sulphur. $100, Atala. $160, White peacock. $200, Polydamus swallowtail. $300, Giant swallowtail. $400, Banded king shoemaker. $500, Blue night. $1000, Orange theope. $2000, Small lacewing. $3000, Common morpho.

2003, Nov. 4 **Litho.** ***Perf. 13¼***

3780	A419	$20	multi	.30	.30
3781	A419	$55	multi	.85	.85
3782	A419	$80	multi	1.25	1.25
3783	A419	$100	multi	1.50	1.50
3784	A419	$160	multi	2.25	2.25
3785	A419	$200	multi	3.00	3.00
3786	A419	$300	multi	4.25	4.25
3787	A419	$400	multi	5.75	5.75
3788	A419	$500	multi	7.25	7.25
3789	A419	$1000	multi	13.50	13.50
3790	A419	$2000	multi	27.50	27.50
3791	A419	$3000	multi	40.00	40.00
	Nos. 3780-3791 (12)			107.40	107.40

Worldwide Fund for Nature (WWF) A420

No. 3792: a, Head of channel-billed toucan. b, Two toco toucans on branch. c, Channel-billed toucan on branch. d, Toco toucan and chick.

2003, Dec. 1 ***Perf. 14***

3792 Horiz. strip of 4, #a-d 5.00 5.00
a.-d. A420 $100 Any single 1.20 1.20
e. Souvenir sheet, 2 each #3792a-3792d 10.50 10.50

Mushrooms — A421

Designs: No. 3793, $20, Clitocybe gibba. No. 3794, $20, Clitocybe clavipes. $30, Calocybe carnea. $300, Marasmius.
No. 3797: a, Amanita spissa. b, Boletus aestivalis. c, Boletus rubellus. d, Clathrus archeri.
$400, Volvariella bombycina.

2003, Dec. 1

3793-3796 A421 Set of 4 4.50 4.50
3797 A421 $150 Sheet of 4, #a-d 7.25 7.25

Souvenir Sheet

3798 A421 $400 multi 5.75 5.75

Mammals A422

Designs: $25, Common tenrec. $60, Humboldt's woolly monkey, vert. $100, Gundi. $200, Harbor seal.
No. 3803: a, Prevost's squirrel. b, Mountain tapir. c, Sea otter. d, Indus dolphin.
$400, Peter's disk-winged bat, vert.

2003, Dec. 1

3799-3802 A422 Set of 4 4.25 4.25
3803 A422 $150 Sheet of 4, #a-d 6.75 6.75

Souvenir Sheet

3804 A422 $400 multi 4.50 4.50

Flowers — A423

Designs: $20, Begonia sedeni. $30, Dahlia. $35, Eschecholzia californica. $300, Lupinus perennis.
No. 3809: a, Agapanthus africanus. b, Hyacinth cultivars. c, Protea linearis. d, Hippestrum aulicum.
$400, Crocus sativus, horiz.

2003, Dec. 1

3805-3808 A423 Set of 4 4.25 4.25
3809 A423 $150 Sheet of 4, #a-d 6.75 6.75

Souvenir Sheet

3810 A423 $400 multi 5.00 5.00

Fish A424

Designs: $25, Regal tang. $60, Pajama tang. $100, Coral beauty. $200, Emperor angelfish.
No. 3815: a, High hat. b, Regal angelfish. c, Fire clown. d, Domino damselfish.
$400, Tomato clown.

2003, Dec. 1

3811-3814 A424 Set of 4 4.75 4.75
3815 A424 $150 Sheet of 4, #a-d 9.00 9.00

Souvenir Sheet

3816 A424 $400 multi 5.50 5.50

Guyana — Brazil Diplomatic Relations, 35th Anniv. A425

2003, Dec. 18

3817 A425 $20 multi .25 .25

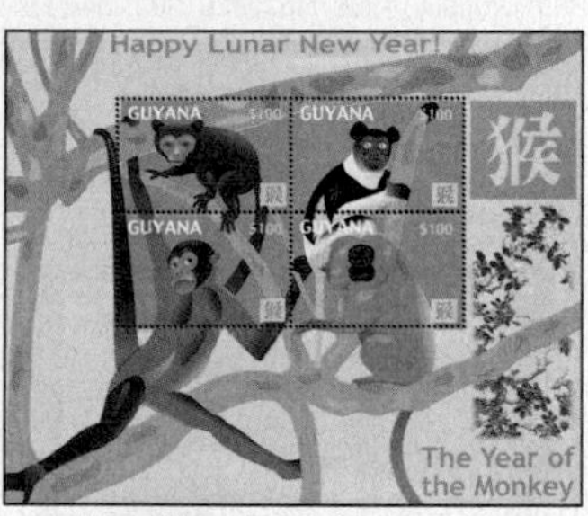

New Year 2004 (Year of the Monkey) — A426

No. 3818: a, Dark brown monkey with orange face. b, Dark brown and white monkey with brown face. c, Brown monkey. d, Orange monkey with black face.

2004, Jan. 5

3818 A426 $100 Sheet of 4, #a-d 4.75 4.75

Paintings by Tang Yin (1470-1524) — A427

No. 3819, vert.: a, Concubines of Emperor Shu. b, Lady. c, Untitled painting depicting woman. d, Untitled painting depicting landscape.
$400, Mountain Scene.

2004, Jan. 21 **Litho.** ***Perf. 13¼***

3819 A427 $150 Sheet of 4, #a-d 6.75 6.75

Souvenir Sheet

3820 A427 $400 multi 4.50 4.50

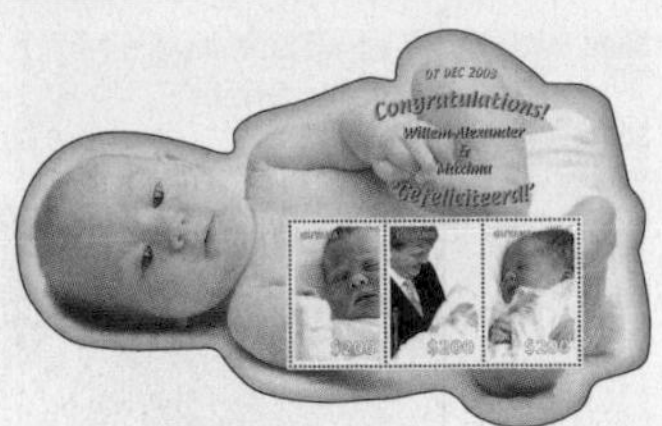

Birth of Princess Catherina Amalia of the Netherlands — A428

No. 3821: a, Princess, one hand shown. b, Princess and father, Prince Willem-Alexander. c, Princess, two hands shown.

2004, Feb. 15 *Perf. 14¼*
3821 A428 $200 Sheet of 3, #a-c 7.00 7.00

FIFA (Fédération Internationale de Football Association), Cent. — A429

World Cup championship teams: No. 3822, $80, Uruguay, 1930. No. 3823, $80, Italy, 1934. No. 3824, $80, Italy, 1938. No. 3825, $80, Uruguay, 1950. No. 3826, $80, Germany, 1954. No. 3827, $80, Brazil, 1958. No. 3828, $80, Brazil, 1962. No. 3829, $80, England, 1966. No. 3830, $80, Brazil, 1970.

2004, Feb. 16 *Perf. 13¼*
3822-3830 A429 Set of 9 8.25 8.25

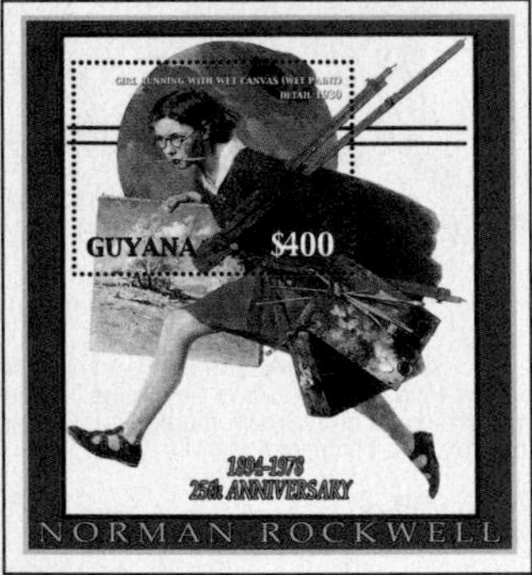

Paintings by Norman Rockwell (1894-1978) — A430

No. 3831, vert.: a, Doctor and Doll. b, Babysitter with Screaming Infant. c, Girl with Black Eye. d, Checkup.
$400, Girl Running with Wet Canvas (Wet Paint).

2004, Feb. 16 *Perf. 14¼*
3831 A430 $150 Sheet of 4, #a-d 6.75 6.75

Souvenir Sheet

3832 A430 $400 multi 4.50 4.50

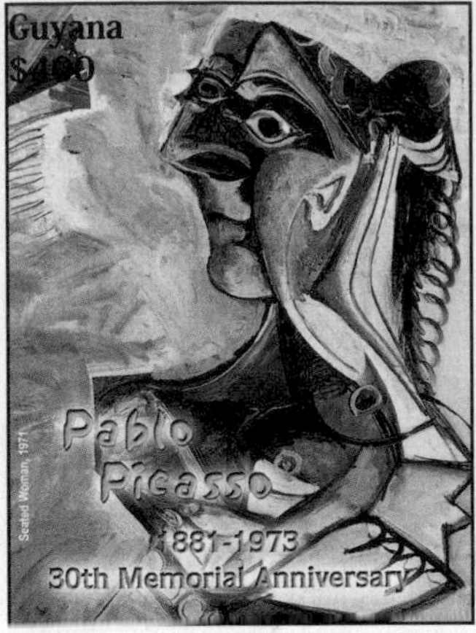

Paintings by Pablo Picasso (1881-1973) — A431

No. 3833: a, Woman in Yellow Hat. b, Seated Woman, 1962. c, Head of a Woman. d, Large Profile.
$400, Seated Woman, 1971.

2004, Feb. 16 *Perf. 14¼*
3833 A431 $150 Sheet of 4, #a-d 6.75 6.75

Imperf

3834 A431 $400 multi 4.50 4.50

No. 3833 contains four 38x50mm stamps.

Rembrandt Paintings A432

Designs: $35, A Woman Bathing. $60, Flora. $100, The Poet, Jan Hermansz Krul. $200, Portrait of a Young Man.
No. 3839: a, The Apostle James. b, The Apostle Bartholemew. c, The Evangelist Matthew Inspired by an Angel. d, The Apostle Peter Standing.
$400, Balaam and the Ass.

2004, Feb. 16 *Perf. 14¼*
3835-3838 A432 Set of 4 4.50 4.50
3839 A432 $150 Sheet of 4, #a-d 6.75 6.75

Souvenir Sheet

3840 A432 $400 multi 4.75 4.75

Paintings in the Hermitage, St. Petersburg, Russia — A433

Designs: $35, Mercury Giving Bacchus to Nymphs to Raise, by Laurent de La Hyre. $60, Satyr and Bacchante, by Nicolas Poussin, vert. $100, Parting of Abelard and Eloisa, by Angelica Kauffmann. $200, Pastoral Scene, by François Boucher.
No. 3845, vert.: a, The Union of Earth and Water, by Peter Paul Rubens. b, Hercules Between Love and Wisdom, by Pompeo Girolano Batoni. c, Innocence Choosing Love Over Wealth, by Pierre-Paul Prud'hon. d, Mars and Venus, by Joseph Marie Vien.
No. 3846, Allegory of Virtuous Life, by Hendrik Van Balen. No. 3847, Statue of Ceres, by Rubens, vert.

2004, Feb. 16 *Perf. 14¼*
3841-3844 A433 Set of 4 4.50 4.50
3845 A433 $150 Sheet of 4, #a-d 7.00 7.00

Imperf

Size: 77x55mm

3846 A433 $400 multi 5.50 5.50

Size: 56x77mm

3847 A433 $400 multi 5.50 5.50

Intl. Year of Mountains Type of 2002

Designs: $80, Mt. Kosciuszko, Australia. $100, Mt. Elbrus, Russia. $150, Mt. Vinson, Antarctica.
$400, Mt. Everest, Nepal.

2004 *Perf. 14*
3848-3850 A398 Set of 3 3.75 3.75

Souvenir Sheet

3851 A398 $400 multi 4.50 4.50

Miniature Sheet

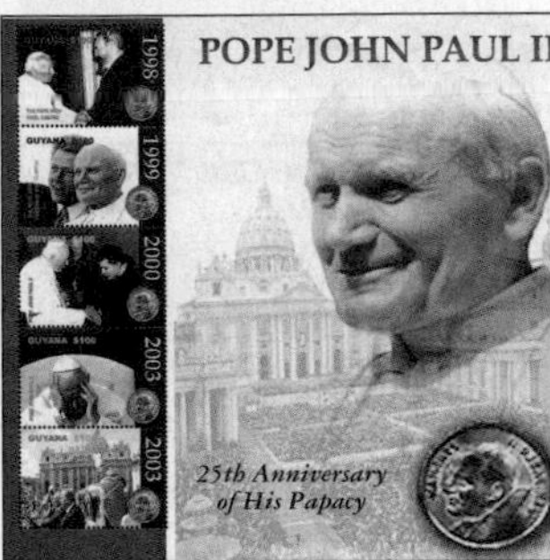

Election of Pope John Paul II, 25th Anniv. (in 2003) — A434

No. 3852: a, With Fidel Castro, 1998. b, With Pres. Bill Clinton, 1999. c, With bishop and man, 2000. d, With hands on head, 2003. e, In Popemobile, 2003.

2004, Sept. 27 **Litho.** *Perf. 14*
3852 A434 $100 Sheet of 5, #a-e 5.75 5.75

2004 Summer Olympics, Athens A435

Designs: $60, Poster for 1912 Stockholm Olympics. $80, High jump, 1932 Los Angeles Olympics, horiz. $100, Commemorative medal for 1932 Olympics. $200, Ancient Greek runners, horiz.

2004, Sept. 27 *Perf. 14¼*
3853-3856 A435 Set of 4 6.75 6.75

European Soccer Championships, Portugal — A436

No. 3857, vert.: a, Michel Platini. b, Luis Arconada. c, Bruno Bellone. d, Parc des Princes, Paris.
$400, 1984 France team.

2004, Sept. 27 **Litho.**
3857 A436 $150 Sheet of 4, #a-d 8.00 8.00

Souvenir Sheet

3858 A436 $400 multi 5.00 5.00

No. 3857 contains four 28x47mm stamps.

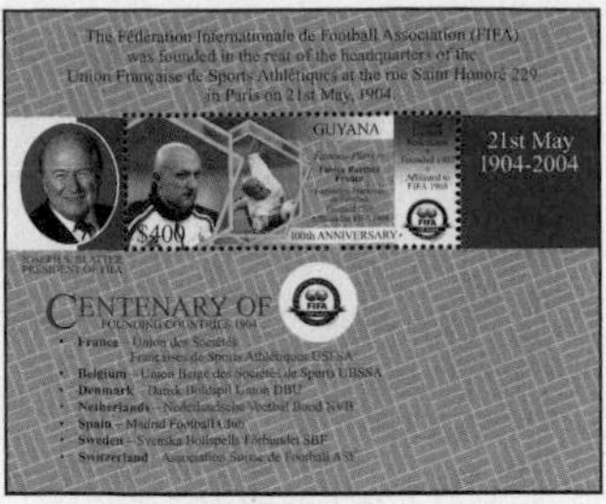

FIFA (Fédération Internationale de Football Association), Cent. — A437

No. 3859: a, Alf Ramsey. b, Pele. c, Lothar Matthaus. d, Dennis Bergkamp.
$400, Fabien Barthez.

2004, Sept. 27 *Perf. 12¾x12½*
3859 A437 $150 Sheet of 4, #a-d 7.00 7.00

Souvenir Sheet

3860 A437 $400 multi 5.00 5.00

A438

D-Day, 60th Anniv. — A439

No. 3861, $150: a, Operation Overlord begins. b, Troops in landing craft storm the beaches of Normandy. c, Troops deep behind enemy lines. d, Churchill announces landings a success.
No. 3862, $150: a, Royal Scots Fusiliers. b, 2nd Company, 101st Heavy Tank Battalion. c, Anti-tank gun of 7th Green Howards. d, 229th Engineer Combat Battalion.
No. 3863, $150, vert.: a, Michael Wittmann. b, Lt. Robert Edlin. c, CSM Stanley Hollis. d, Kurt Meyer.
No. 3864, vert.: a, Rear Admiral John L. Hall. b, Rear Admiral Carlton F. Bryant. c, General Dwight D. Eisenhower. d, General Hap Arnold.
No. 3865, $400, Tank battle, Cotentin Peninsula. No. 3866, $400, Seaforth Highlanders of Canada. No. 3867, $400, Sgt. Clifton Barker.
No. 3868, Major General Maxwell D. Taylor.

2004, Sept. 27 *Perf. 13½*

Sheets of 4, #a-d

3861-3863 A438 Set of 3 21.00 21.00
3864 A439 $150 Sheet of 4, #a-d 7.00 7.00

Souvenir Sheets

3865-3867 A438 Set of 3 15.00 15.00
3868 A439 $400 multi 5.00 5.00

A440

A441

A442

Locomotives — A443

No. 3869: a, Santa Fe Depot. b, LD Porta. c, D9000 Royal Scots Gray. d, TGV.

No. 3870, $150: a, Hercules 4-4-0. b, Sterling 8 ft Single Class 4-2-2. c, Class YP 4-6-2. d, Class 01.10 4-6-2.

No. 3871, $150: a, GWR King Class 4-6-0. b, 4500 Class 4-6-2. c, Class F 4-6-2. d, Class 231C 4-6-2.

No. 3872, $150: a, Western Railway, France, 1856. b, Dutch State Railway, 1880. c, Southern Railway, England, 1890. d, Madras and Southern Mahratta Railway, India, 1891.

No. 3873, $150: a, Baltimore and Ohio Railroad, US, 1856. b, Utica and Schenectady Railroad, US, 1837. c, Great Southern Railway, Spain, 1913. d, Victorian Government Railway, Australia, 1906.

No. 3874, $150: a, Shantung Railway, China, 1919. b, Great Indian Peninsula Railway, 1898. c, Cumberland Valley Railroad, US, 1851. d, Central Pacific Railroad, US, 1863.

No. 3875, $150: a, Great Northern Railway, Ireland, 1876. b, London and Northwestern Railways, 1873. c, Shanghai-Nanking Railway, China, 1910. d, London, Brighton and South Coast Railway, 1846.

No. 3876, $400, No. 999, 4-4-0. No. 3877, $400, Northumbrian 0-2-2, vert.

No. 3878, $400, Netherlands State Railway, 1888. No. 3879, $400, Austrian State Railway, 1868. No. 3880, $400, London, Midland and Scottish Railway, 1923. No. 3881, $400, Pennsylvania Railroad, 1848.

No. 3882, TGV Atlantique.

2004, Sept. 27 ***Perf. 13½***

3869 A440 $150 Sheet of 4, #a-d 7.00 7.00

Sheets of 4, #a-d

3870-3871 A441 Set of 2 14.00 14.00
3872-3875 A442 Set of 4 30.00 30.00

Souvenir Sheets

3876-3877 A441 Set of 2 10.00 10.00
3878-3881 A442 Set of 4 20.00 20.00
3882 A443 $400 multi 5.00 5.00

Souvenir Sheet

Deng Xiaoping (1904-97), Chinese Leader — A444

2004 ***Perf. 14***

3883 A444 $400 multi 4.75 4.75

South American Reptiles, Fish, Bats and Flowers — A445

No. 3884, $160 — Reptiles: a, Red-foot tortoise. b, Emerald tree boa. c, Green iguana. d, Cuvier's dwarf caiman.

No. 3885, $160 — Fish: a, Velvet cichlid. b, Freshwater sting ray. c, Splash tetra. d, Red piranha.

No. 3886, $160 — Bats: a, Mexican funnel-eared bat. b, Greater bulldog bat. c, Vampire bat. d, Doffroy's tailless bat.

No. 3887, $160, vert. — Flowers: a, Blue passion flower. b, Scarlet passion flower. c, Passion vine. d, Bromeliad flower.

No. 3888, $400, Eyelash viper. No. 3889, $400, Tambaqui, vert. No. 3890, $400, Short-tailed fruit bat, vert. No. 3891, $400, Epiphytic blueberry, vert.

Perf. 13¼x13½, 13½x13¼

2005, Jan. 10 **Litho.**

Sheets of 4, #a-d

3884-3887 A445 Set of 4 36.00 36.00

Souvenir Sheets

3888-3891 A445 Set of 4 19.50 19.50

New Year 2005 (Year of the Rooster) — A446

No. 3892: a, Rooster with dark feathers. b, Rooster with white feathers.

2005, Jan. 24 ***Perf. 12¾***

3892 A446 $50 Pair, #a-b 1.40 1.40

Printed in sheets containing two pairs.

Prehistoric Animals — A447

No. 3893, $150: a, Eustreptospondylus. b, Rhamphorhynchus. c, Utahraptor. d, Entelodonts.

No. 3894, $150: a, Moeritherium. b, Deinonychus. c, Ophthalmosaurus. d, Grendelius.

No. 3895, $150: a, Spinosaurus. b, Tarbosaurus. c, Coelophysis. d, Sinosauropteryx prima.

No. 3896, $400, Velociraptor babies. No. 3897, $400, Ophthalmosaurus baby. No. 3898, $400, Iguanodon bernissartensis, vert.

2005, Jan. 24 **Litho.** ***Perf. 12¾***

Sheets of 4, #a-d

3893-3895 A447 Set of 3 20.00 20.00

Souvenir Sheets

3896-3898 A447 Set of 3 15.00 15.00

Eddy Grant, Musician — A448

Designs: $20, Grant at UR. $80, Grant at UL.

No. 3901 — Portrait in: a, Blue. b, Yellow green. c, Blue violet. d, Red violet.

$400, Grant with guitar.

2005, Feb. 17 ***Perf. 12¾***

3899-3900 A448 Set of 2 1.25 1.25
3901 A448 $190 Sheet of 4, #a-d 9.75 9.75

Souvenir Sheet

3902 A448 $400 multi 4.75 4.75

Pope John Paul II (1920-2005) and Pres. Ronald Reagan (1911-2004) A449

2005, Aug. 12 **Litho.** ***Perf. 13½***

3903 A449 $300 multi 3.25 3.25

Battle of Trafalgar, Bicent. A450

Designs: $25, Vice-admiral Cuthbert Collingwood. $35, Admiral Horatio Nelson injured at Battle of Santa Cruz. $60, Nelson's funeral car arriving at St. Paul's Cathedral, horiz. $80, Nelson and Flag Captain Thomas M. Hardy. $100, First shots of Battle of Trafalgar, horiz. $300, British ship hoists signals to begin pincer movement.

$400, Nelson.

2005, Aug. 12 ***Perf. 13¼***

3904-3909 A450 Set of 6 6.50 6.50

Souvenir Sheet

Perf. 12

3910 A450 $400 multi 5.00 5.00

V-E Day, 60th Anniv. — A451

No. 3911, horiz.: a, Neville Chamberlain makes peace with Adolf Hitler, 1938. b, The Royal Air Force hits back. c, Victory, 1945.

$400, Netherlands #277.

2005, Aug. 12 ***Perf. 12¾***

3911 A451 $200 Sheet of 3, #a-c 7.25 7.25

Souvenir Sheet

3912 A451 $400 multi 5.00 5.00

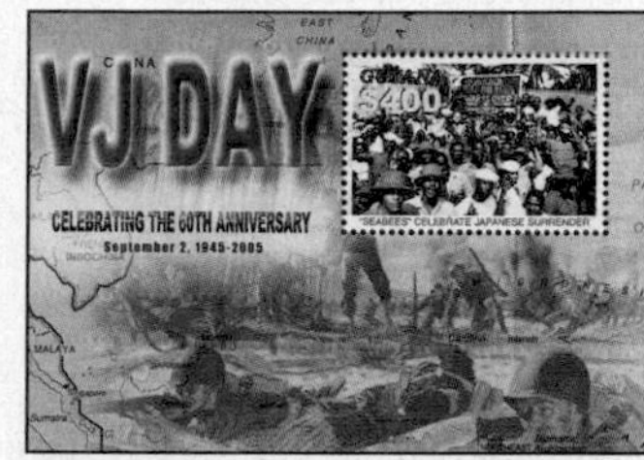

V-J Day, 60th Anniv. — A452

No. 3913: a, Japan attacks Pearl Harbor, 1941. b, Iwo Jima War Memorial, Harlington, Texas. c, Newspaper announcing Japanese surrender, 1945.

$400, Seebees celebrate Japanese surrender.

2005, Aug. 12

3913 A452 $200 Sheet of 3, #a-c 7.25 7.25

Souvenir Sheet

3914 A452 $400 multi 5.00 5.00

Rotary International, Cent. — A453

No. 3915: a, Dentist examining patient's mouth. b, 2005 Rotary President-elect Carl-Wilhelm Stenhammar. c, Rotary District of Guyana first couple.

$400, Homer Wood, founder of second Rotary Club.

2005, Aug. 12

3915 A453 $150 Sheet of 3, #a-c 6.25 6.25

Souvenir Sheet

3916 A453 $400 multi 4.75 4.75

Friedrich von Schiller (1759-1805), Writer — A454

Designs: $400, Schiller and Ludwig van Beethoven.

No. 3918: a, Schiller. b, Schiller and his house. c, Beethoven.

2005, Aug. 12
3917 A454 $400 multi 4.75 4.75

Souvenir Sheet

3918 A454 $200 Sheet of 3, #a-c 7.00 7.10

No. 3918 contains three 42x28mm stamps.

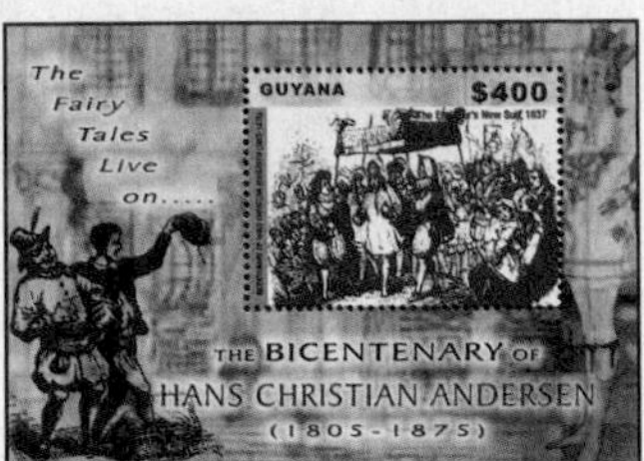

Hans Christian Andersen (1805-75), Author — A455

No. 3919: a, The Traveling Companion. b, The Shadow. c, The Drop of Water.
$400, The Emperor's New Suit.

2005, Aug. 12 ***Perf. 12¾***
3919 A455 $200 Sheet of 3, #a-c 7.00 7.00

Souvenir Sheet
Perf. 12

3920 A455 $400 multi 4.75 4.75

No. 3919 contains three 42x28mm stamps.

Jules Verne (1828-1905), Writer — A456

No. 3921, vert.: a, Verne. b, Book illustration. c, Space capsule as imagined by Verne. d, Space capsule.
$400, Man on the Moon.

2005, Aug. 12 ***Perf. 12¾***
3921 A456 $150 Sheet of 4, #a-d 6.50 6.50

Souvenir Sheet

3922 A456 $400 multi 5.00 5.00

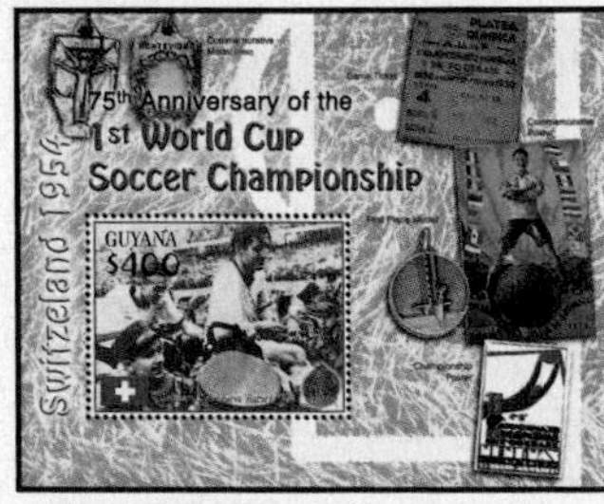

World Cup Soccer Championships, 75th Anniv. — A457

No. 3923: a, 1954 Germany team. b, Final goal in 1954 German victory over Hungary. c, Wankdorf Stadium. d, Helmut Rahn.
$400, German players celebrating victory.

2005, Aug. 12 ***Perf. 12***
3923 A457 $150 Sheet of 4, #a-d 8.00 8.00

Souvenir Sheet

3924 A457 $400 multi 4.75 4.75

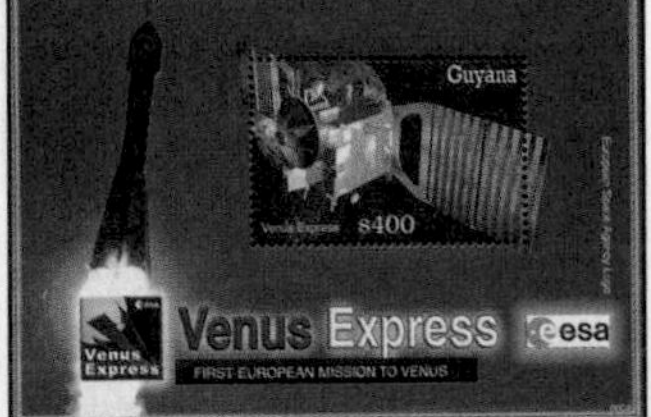

Space — A458

No. 3925: a, Luna 9 in space. b, Luna 9 capsule. c, Oceanus Procellarum region of Moon. d, Sergei Korolev. e, First images of the Moon. f, Launch of Molniya 8K78M rocket.

No. 3926, $200: a, Space Shuttle Discovery docked with International Space Station Destiny Laboratory, b, Astronaut Stephen K. Robinson attached to Canadarm 2. c, View of Discovery during docking operation. d, Discovery and stairway truck.

No. 3927, $200, vert.: a, First launch of Space Shuttle Columbia. b, Astronaut Robert C. Crippen. c, Astronaut John W. Young. d, Mission control.

No. 3928, $200, vert.: a, Launch vehicle MV-5 rocket. b, Hayabusa satellite. c, Composite color image of Itokawa asteroid. d, Projected return to Earth of satellite.

No. 3929, $400, Venus Express. No. 3930, $400, Lunar Reconnaissance Orbiter. No. 3931, $400, Calipso satellite. No. 3932, $400, Hayabusa satellite over Itokawa asteroid.

2006 **Litho.** ***Perf. 14***
3925 A458 $160 Sheet of 6, #a-f 12.50 12.50

Sheets of 4, #a-d

3926-3928 A458 Set of 3 28.00 28.00

Souvenir Sheets

3929-3932 A458 Set of 4 17.00 17.00

Issued: Nos. 3925, 3926, 3930, 7/10, Nos. 3928, 3932, 7/27.

Souvenir Sheet

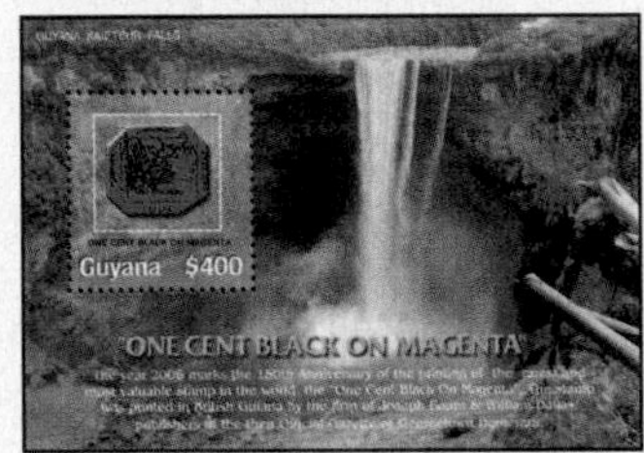

"Penny Magenta" Stamp, 150th Anniv. — A459

2006, July 27 ***Perf. 12x11½***
3933 A459 $400 multi 4.50 4.50

Souvenir Sheet

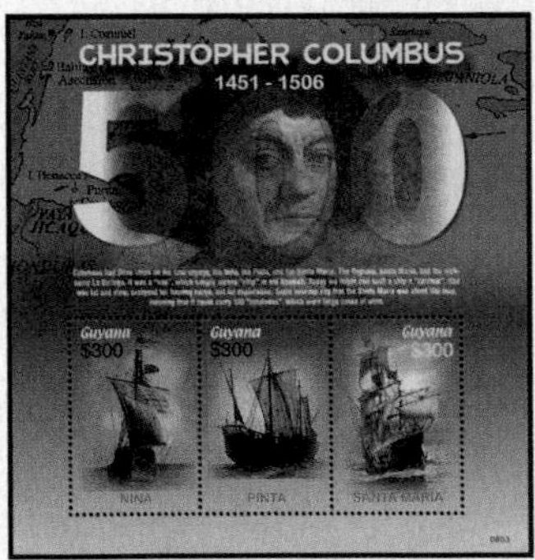

Christopher Columbus (1451-1506), Explorer — A460

No. 3934: a, Nina. b, Pinta. c, Santa Maria.

2006, July 27 ***Perf. 13¼***
3934 A460 $300 Sheet of 3, #a-c 11.00 11.00

Airships — A461

No. 3935: a, De Beers Zeppelin NT. b, Lockheed Martin LTA 2004. c, Strattelite concept airship.
$400, Skybus Airship.

2006, July 27 ***Perf. 13¼***
3935 A461 $200 Sheet of 3, #a-c 7.25 7.25

Souvenir Sheet

3936 A461 $400 multi 4.50 4.50

Rembrandt (1606-69), Painter — A462

No. 3937 — Details from The Music Makers: a, Man with viola. b, Woman with shawl. c, Man with harp. d, Woman with tiara.
$400, Old Man with a Jewelled Cross.

2006, July 27 ***Perf. 13¼***
3937 A462 $160 Sheet of 4, #a-d 8.25 8.25

Imperf

3938 A462 $400 shown 4.50 4.50

No. 3937 contains four 37x50mm stamps.

Queen Elizabeth II, 80th Birthday — A463

No. 3939: a, Queen and Guyana Parliament Building. b, Queen wearing black and white hat.
$400, Queen and flags of Guyana and Great Britain.

2006, July 27 ***Perf. 13¼***
3939 A463 $200 Pair, #a-b 4.50 4.50

Souvenir Sheet

3940 A463 $400 multi 5.25 5.25

No. 3939 printed in sheets containing two pairs.

Souvenir Sheet

2006 World Cup Soccer Championships, Germany — A464

No. 3941 — 2006 World Cup emblem, World Cup and: a, $80, Man in Japanese clothing. b, $100, Kemari players. c, $160, Tsu chu players. d, $300, People's Republic of China #2073.

2006, Sept. 14 **Litho.** ***Perf. 13¼***
3941 A464 Sheet of 4, #a-d 7.00 7.00

Betty Boop — A465

No. 3942, vert.: a, With top hat and cane. b, Holding mirror. c, Holding flower bouquet. d, In city. e, At microphone. f, Lifting dress.

No. 3943: a, Sitting with legs crossed. b, In car.

2006, Dec. 14 **Litho.** ***Perf. 14***
3942 A465 $100 Sheet of 6, #a-f 6.50 6.50

Souvenir Sheet

3943 A465 $200 Sheet of 2, #a-b 4.25 4.25

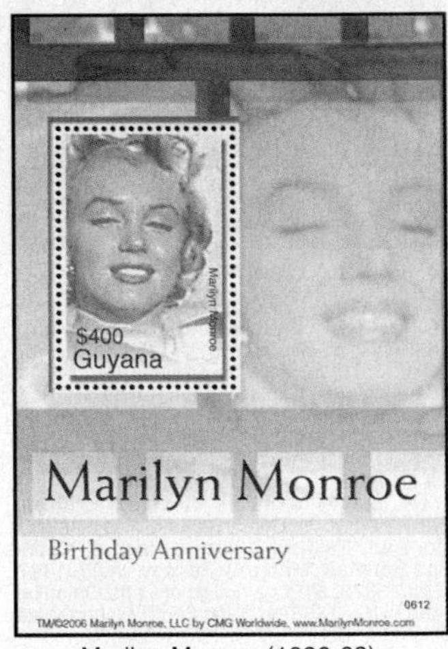

Marilyn Monroe (1926-62), Actress — A466

No. 3944: a, Wearing beret. b, Wearing red dress, horizontal post at both sides of neck. c, Wearing red dress, horizontal post at left of neck. d, With eyes closed.
$400, With eyes partially closed.

2007, Feb. 15 ***Perf. 13¼***
3944 A466 $200 Sheet of 4, #a-d 8.00 8.00

Souvenir Sheet

3945 A466 $400 multi 4.00 4.00

Dogs — A467

No. 3946: a, Papillon. b, Dogue de Bordeaux. c, Cavalier King Charles spaniel. d, Neapolitan mastiff.
$400, Basset hound.

2007, Feb. 15 ***Perf. 14***
3946 A467 $160 Sheet of 4, #a-d 6.50 6.50

Souvenir Sheet

3947 A467 $400 multi 4.00 4.00

Cats A468

Designs: $25, Chartreux. $35, Seal snowshoe. $60, Maine coon cat. $300, Turkish Angora.
$400, Blue Burmese, vert.

2007, Feb. 15
3948-3951 A468 Set of 4 4.25 4.25

Souvenir Sheet

3952 A468 $400 multi 4.00 4.00

Birds A469

Designs: $25, Summer tanager. $35, Gray-cheeked thrush. $60, Blackpoll warbler. $300, Thick-billed parrot.
No. 3957, vert.: a, Golden-tailed warbler. b, Blue-crowned parakeet. c, White-winged parakeet. d, Yellow-green vireo.
No. 3958, $400, Pacific golden plover, vert. No. 3959, $400, Bobolink, vert.

2007, Feb. 15
3953-3956 A469 Set of 4 4.25 4.25
3957 A469 $160 Sheet of 4, #a-d 6.50 6.50

Souvenir Sheets

3958-3959 A469 Set of 2 8.00 8.00

For overprint, see No. 4025.

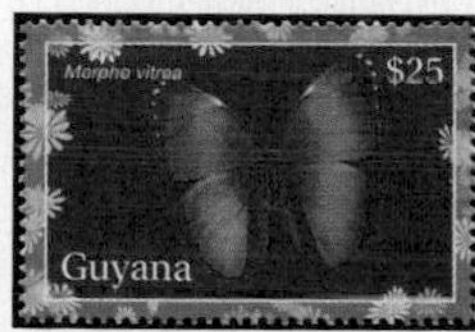

Butterflies A470

Designs: $25, Morpho vitrea. $35, Rothschildia hesperus. $60, Anaea nessus. $300, Dryas iulia.
No. 3964: a, Callithea sapphira. b, Prepona buckleyana. c, Lycorea pasinutia. d, Danaus eresimus.
No. 3965, $400, Cithaerias aurorina. No. 3966, $400, Eurytides protesilaus.

2007, Feb. 15
3960-3963 A470 Set of 4 4.25 4.25
3964 A470 $160 Sheet of 4, #a-d 6.50 6.50

Souvenir Sheets

3965-3966 A470 Set of 2 8.00 8.00

Orchids — A471

Designs: $25, Bletia florida. $35, Basiphyllaea corallicola. $60, Calopogon multiflorus. $300, Bletia purpurea.
No. 3971: a, Cypripedium acaule. b, Calopogon tuberosus. c, Calopogon pallidus. d, Bletia patula.
$400, Cypripodium reginae.

2007, Feb. 15
3967-3970 A471 Set of 4 4.25 4.25
3971 A471 $160 Sheet of 4, #a-d 6.50 6.50

Souvenir Sheet

3972 A471 $400 multi 4.00 4.00

Souvenir Sheet

New Year 2007 (Year of the Pig) — A472

No. 3973 — Pig at: a, $55, Right. b, $80, Left. c, $100, Right. d, $160, Left.

2007, Mar. 21 ***Perf. 13¼***
3973 A472 Sheet of 4, #a-d 4.00 4.00

Souvenir Sheet

Wolfgang Amadeus Mozart (1756-91), Composer — A473

No. 3974 — Mozart: a, In 1770. b, In 1762. c, Circa 1789. d, Portrait by Joseph Grassi.

2007, Mar. 21
3974 A473 $190 Sheet of 4, #a-d 7.50 7.50

Scouting, Cent. — A474

No. 3975, horiz.: a, Lord Robert Baden-Powell and dove. b, Scouts on raft. c, Scouts pulling tug-of-war rope.
$400, Dove and hand of Baden-Powell.

2007, Mar. 21
3975 A474 $180 Sheet of 3, #a-c 5.50 5.50

Souvenir Sheet

3976 A474 $400 multi 4.00 4.00

Souvenir Sheets

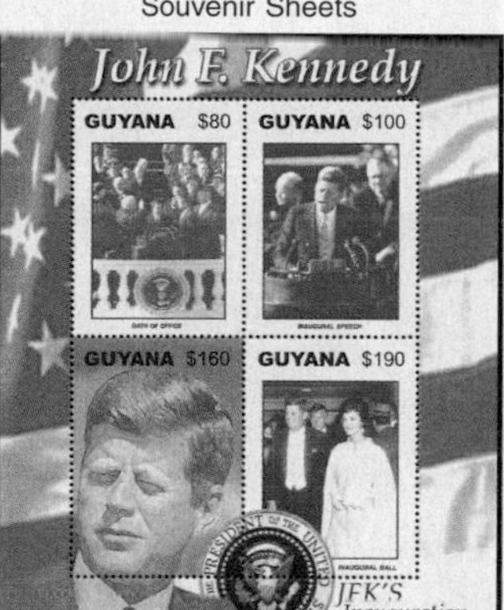

Pres. John F. Kennedy (1917-63) — A475

No. 3977: a, $80, Taking oath of office. b, $100, Giving inaugural speech. c, $160, Portrait. d, $190, With wife at inaugural ball.
No. 3978: a, $80, Peace Corps. b, $100, Space program. c, $160, Civil rights. d, $190, Portrait, diff.

2007, Mar. 21 ***Perf. 13¼***

Sheets of 4, #a-d

3977-3978 A475 Set of 2 10.50 10.50

Elvis Presley (1935-77) — A476

No. 3979, $160: a, Wearing glasses, blue panel at top. b, Without glasses, red background.
No. 3980, $160: a, Without glasses, orange panel at bottom. b, With glasses, red background.

2007, Mar. 21 ***Perf. 14***

Pairs, #a-b

3979-3980 A476 Set of 2 6.50 6.50

Nos. 3979-3980 each were printed in sheets containing two pairs.

2007 Cricket World Cup, West Indies — A477

Designs: $100, Cricket World Cup emblem, map and flag of Guyana. $200, Guyana cricket team, horiz.
$500, Cricket World Cup emblem.

2007, Mar. 28 ***Perf. 13¼***
3981-3982 A477 Set of 2 3.00 3.00

Souvenir Sheet

3983 A477 $500 multi 5.00 5.00

A478

Pope Benedict XVI — A479

2007, Apr. 17 **Litho.** ***Perf. 13¼***
3984 A478 $80 multi .80 .80

Litho. & Embossed

Serpentine Die Cut

Without Gum

3985 A479 $1500 multi 15.00 15.00

No. 3984 was printed in sheets of 8.

Concorde A480

No. 3986, $100: a, Concorde Prototype 002 and towing vehicle. b, Concorde Prototype 002 and stairway.
No. 3987, $100: a, Concorde and Royal Air Force Red Arrows. b, Concorde, Red Arrows and Queen Elizabeth 2.

2007, Apr. 17 **Litho.** ***Perf. 13¼***

Pairs, #a-b

3986-3987 A480 Set of 2 4.00 4.00

Nos. 3986-3987 were each printed in sheets containing 3 pairs.

Miniature Sheet

2008 Summer Olympics, Beijing — A481

No. 3988: a, Field hockey. b, Basketball. c, Judo. d, Shooting.

2008, Apr. 22 **Litho.** ***Perf. 13¼x13***
3988 A481 $100 Sheet of 4, #a-d 4.00 4.00

10th Caribbean Festival of Arts — A482

Map in: $20, Yellow and white, frame in red. $55, White, frame in green. $80, Yellow and white, frame in blue green. $160, Green, frame in white and yellow.

2008, Aug. 19 ***Perf. 14¼***
3989-3992 A482 Set of 4 3.25 3.25

Jesuits in Guyana, 150th Anniv. A483

Designs: $80, St. Stanislaus College. $100, Sacred Heart Church. $160, Father Cuthbert Cary-Elwes, missionary, and indigenous people.

2008. Aug. 25 Litho. ***Perf. 13x13¼***
3993-3995 A483 Set of 3 3.50 3.50

Souvenir Sheet

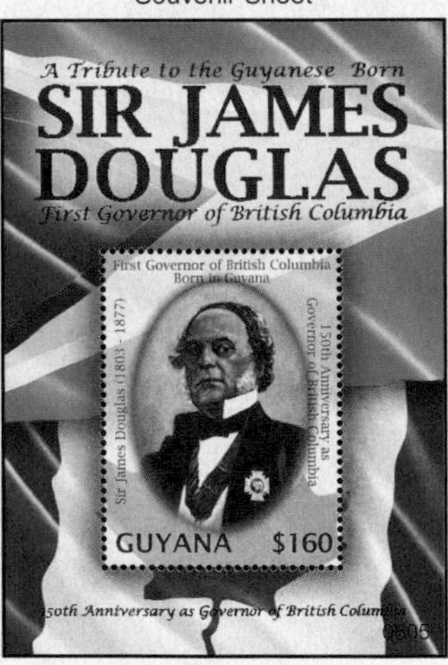

Sir James Douglas (1803-77), First Governor of British Columbia — A484

2008, Aug. 25 ***Perf. 13¼***
3996 A484 $160 multi 1.60 1.60

Peony A485

2009, Apr. 10 **Litho.**
3997 A485 $80 multi .80 .80

Printed in sheets of 8.

Miniature Sheet

Elvis Presley (1935-77) — A486

No. 3998 — Presley with: a, Red and blue jacket, bright yellow face, holding microphone. b, Brown jacket, holding microphone. c, White jacket and red shirt. d, Tan and white shirt. e, Gray face, holding microphone. f, With hand open.

2009, July 7 ***Perf. 12***
3998 A486 $160 Sheet of 6, #a-f 9.50 9.50

Miniature Sheet

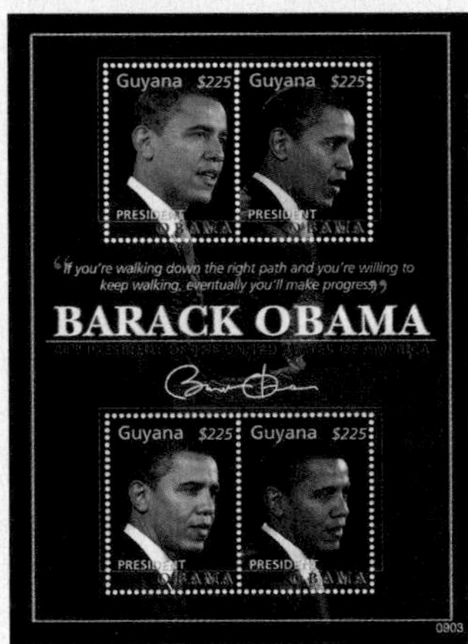

US Pres. Barack Obama — A487

No. 3999 — Pres. Obama with: a, Gray tie, with "O" on jacket and shirt collar and "B" on shirt collar and tie. b, Gray tie, with "O" on jacket and shirt collar and "B" on tie and jacket. c, Red tie. d, Gray tie, with "O" on jacket and "B" on tie and shirt collar.

2009, July 7
3999 A487 $225 Sheet of 4, #a-d 9.00 9.00

Miniature Sheet

China 2009 World Stamp Exhibition, Luoyang — A488

No. 4000 — Unnamed works of art by Wang Hui (1632-1717): a, Flowers. b, Mountain at right. c, Mountain at left in clouds, part of show emblem at LR. d, Mountain in center, part of show emblem at LL.

2009, Apr. 10 Litho. ***Perf. 12***
4000 A488 $100 Sheet of 4, #a-d 4.00 4.00

Miniature Sheet

Georgetown Rotary Club, 50th Anniv. — A489

No. 4001 — Map of Guyana, Rotary International emblem and: a, $80, 50th anniversary commemorative magazine. b, $80, Santa Claus visiting the elderly. c, $160, Poster showing people in wheelchairs. d, $160, Man and boy in front of canopy.

2009, July 22 ***Perf. 11½***
4001 A489 Sheet of 4, #a-d 4.75 4.75

Miniature Sheet

Ferrari Race Cars — A490

No. 4002: a, 1952 500 F2. b, 1953, 500 F2. c, 1958, 246 F1. d, 1976 312 T2.

2009, July 22 ***Perf. 14¼***
4002 A490 $200 Sheet of 4, #a-d 8.00 8.00

Souvenir Sheet

Takutu Bridge — A491

2009, Sept. 14 ***Perf. 13¼***
4003 A491 $400 multi 4.00 4.00

Scouting A492

Designs: No. 4004, $55, Parade for Guyana Scouting centenary. No. 4005, $55, Scout shooting arrow at 14th Caribbean Jamboree, vert. No. 4006, $80, Scout leader, Scout and tent. No. 4007, $80, Scouts lashing logs together. No. 4008, $160, Guyana Scouting Centenary emblem. No. 4009, $160, Emblem of 14th Caribbean Jamboree.

Perf. 14¾x14, 14x14¾

2009, Sept. 29
4004-4009 A492 Set of 6 5.75 5.75

Miniature Sheets

A493

Michael Jackson (1958-2009), Singer — A494

No. 4010: a, Wearing jacket with red collar. b, Wearing hat. c, Wearing black jacket, with microphone at mouth. d, Wearing red and black shirt, with microphone at mouth.

No. 4011: a, Facing forward, with microphone at mouth. b, Facing right, with microphone at waist. c, Facing left, with microphone at mouth. d, Facing forward with arms at side, with microphone at waist.

2009, Oct. 9 ***Perf. 11½x11¼***
4010 A493 $180 Sheet of 4, #a-d 7.25 7.25

Perf. 11¼x11½

4011 A494 $180 Sheet of 4, #a-d 7.25 7.25

Miniature Sheets

Teams in 2009 National Basketball Association Finals — A495

No. 4012, $90 — Los Angeles Lakers: a, Trevor Ariza. b, Shannon Brown. c, Jordan Farmar. d, Andrew Bynum. e, Kobe Bryant. f, Derek Fisher. g, Pau Gasol. h, Lamar Odom. i, Luke Walton.

No. 4013, $90 — Orlando Magic: a. Rafer Alston. b, Marcin Gortat. c, Rashard Lewis. d, Courtney Lee. e, Dwight Howard. f, Jameer Nelson. g, Mickael Pietrus. h, J. J. Redick. i, Hedo Türkoglu.

2009, Oct. 9 ***Perf. 14¼***

Sheets of 9, #a-i

4012-4013 A495 Set of 2 16.00 16.00

British Commonwealth, 60th Anniv. — A496

2009, Nov. 25 Litho. *Perf. 12x11½*
4014 A496 $60 multi .60 .60

Printed in sheets of 6.

Miniature Sheet

National Library, Cent. — A497

No. 4015: a, Building exterior, black and white photograph. b, Building exterior, color photograph. c, Interior, color photograph. d, Interior, black and white photograph.

2009, Dec. 15 *Perf. 11½x12*
4015 A497 $100 Sheet of 4, #a-d 4.00 4.00

Chinese Aviation, Cent. — A498

No. 4016: a, J-8II. b, J-11. c, J-10 with landing gear visible. d, J-10 with landing gear retracted.
$100, J-10, diff.

2009, Dec. 15 *Perf. 14*
4016 A498 $150 Sheet of 4, #a-d 6.00 6.00

Souvenir Sheet
Perf. 14¼
4017 A498 $100 multi 1.00 1.00

Aeropex 2009, Beijing. No. 4016 contains four 42x28mm stamps.

Pope Benedict XVI and Pope John Paul II — A499

No. 4018 — Pope Benedict XVI (while Cardinal) and Pope John Paul II with: a, Part of dome of St. Peter's Basilica at LL. b, Upper section of Basilica entablature at bottom. c, Columns of Basilica at bottom, with dark grayish yellow area next to denomination. d, As "c," with smaller light grayish yellow area next to denomination.

No. 4019: a, Pope Benedict XVI (while Cardinal). b, Pope John Paul II.

2009, Dec. 15 *Perf. 11½*
4018 A499 $200 Sheet of 4, #a-d 8.00 8.00

Souvenir Sheet
Perf. 11½x12
4019 A499 $400 Sheet of 2, #a-b 8.00 8.00

Miniature Sheet

Chinese Zodiac Animals — A500

No. 4020: a, Rat. b, Ox. c, Tiger. d, Rabbit. e, Dragon. f, Snake. g, Horse. h, Ram. i, Monkey. j, Cock. k, Dog. l, Pig.

2010, Jan. 4 *Perf. 12*
4020 A500 $45 Sheet of 12, #a-l 5.25 5.25

No. 661 Srchd.

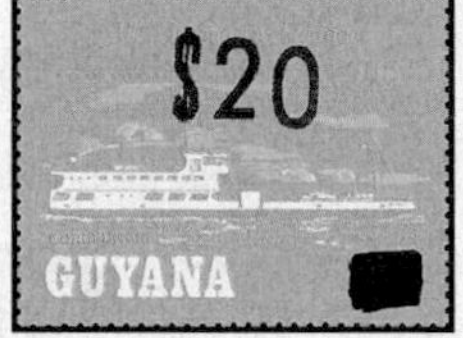

Method, Perf and Watermark As Before
2010
4020J A85 $20 on 30c #661 —

Obliterator is a marker line over old denomination.

Nos. 2316, 2363, 2932, 2935 and 2942A Handstamped Surcharged in Violet Black

Methods, Perfs and Watermarks As Before
2010

4020K	A215	$20 on $6 #2932	*40.00 40.00*
4020L	A215a	$20 on $6 #2942A	*40.00 40.00*
4020M	A125	$20 on $8.90 #2316	—
4020N	A129	$20 on $17.80 #2363	*90.00 90.00*
4020O	A215	$20 on $19 #2935	*40.00 40.00*

Obliterators are marker lines over old denominations.

No. 2942A Surcharged

2010 Method and Perf As Before
4020P A215a $20 on $6 #2942A *150.00 150.00*

Obliterator is a printed rectangle, which was augmented with a marker line when the rectangle missed the old denomination.

Miniature Sheet

Republic of Guyana, 40th Anniv. — A501

No. 4021: a, 2010 Republic Day emblem. b, Masqueraders. c, Mash float parade. d, Children's costume parade.

2010, Mar. 17 *Perf. 11½x12*
4021 A501 $80 Sheet of 4, #a-d 3.25 3.25

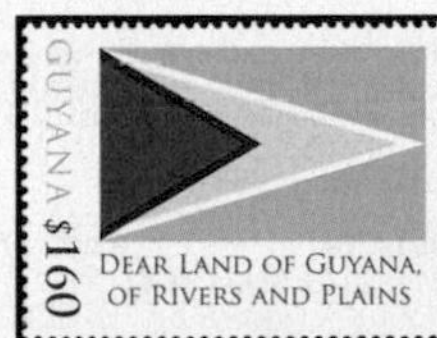

Personalizable Stamp — A502

2010, Apr. 26 Litho. *Perf. 14¾x14*
4022 A502 $160 gray & black 1.60 1.60

The image shown is generic. No. 4022 was available in sheets of 12 without any image ("Guyana $160" only), and vignette portions could be personalized.

Pope Benedict XVI — A503

Litho. & Embossed
2010, Apr. 26 *Die Cut Perf. 8½*
Without Gum
4023 A503 $2000 multi 20.00 20.00

Souvenir Sheet

Presidents of the United States and People's Republic of China — A504

No. 4024: a, Pres. Barack Obama. b, Pres. Hu Jintao.

2010, Apr. 26 Litho. *Perf. 11½*
4024 A504 $300 Sheet of 2, #a-b 6.00 6.00

No. 3957 Overprinted
Miniature Sheet

Methods and Perfs As Before
2010, Apr. 26
4025 A469 $160 Sheet of 4, #a-d 6.25 6.25

Miniature Sheets

Princess Diana (1961-97) — A505

No. 4026, $225 — Diana wearing: a, Tiara. b, Red and black hat. c, Blouse with red collar and cuffs. d, Sailor's hat.

No. 4027, $225 — Diana wearing: a, Black hat. b, Beige hat. c, White dress. d, Blue hat.

2010, Apr. 26 Litho. *Perf. 12*
Sheets of 4, #a-d
4026-4027 A505 Set of 2 18.00 18.00

Souvenir Sheets

A506

A507

A508

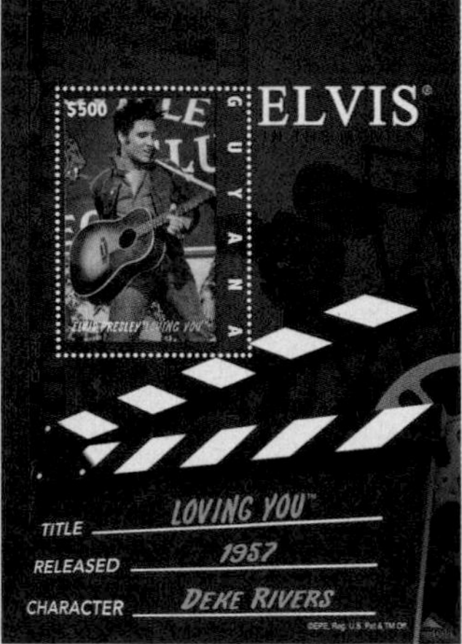

Elvis Presley (1935-77) — A509

2010, Apr. 26 ***Perf. 13¼***

4028	A506	$500	multi	5.00	5.00
4029	A507	$500	multi	5.00	5.00
4030	A508	$500	multi	5.00	5.00
4031	A509	$500	multi	5.00	5.00
	Nos. 4028-4031 (4)			20.00	20.00

Souvenir Sheet

New Year 2010 (Year of the Tiger) — A510

No. 4032 — Tiger with denomination in: a, Green. b, White.

2010, Jan. 4 **Litho.** ***Perf. 12***

4032 A510 $450 Sheet of 2, #a-b 9.00 9.00

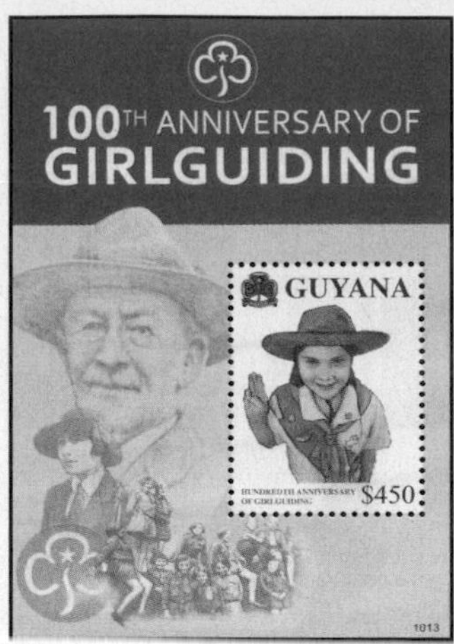

Girl Guides, Cent. — A511

No. 4033, horiz.: a, Three Girl Guides wearing rabbit ears. b, Two Girl Guides. c, Three Girl Guides wearing blue uniforms. d, Four Girl Guides holding rope.
$450, Girl Guide saluting.

2010, July 14 ***Perf. 11½x12***

4033 A511 $275 Sheet of 4, #a-d 11.00 11.00

Souvenir Sheet

Perf. 11¼x11½

4034 A511 $450 multi 4.50 4.50

Miniature Sheet

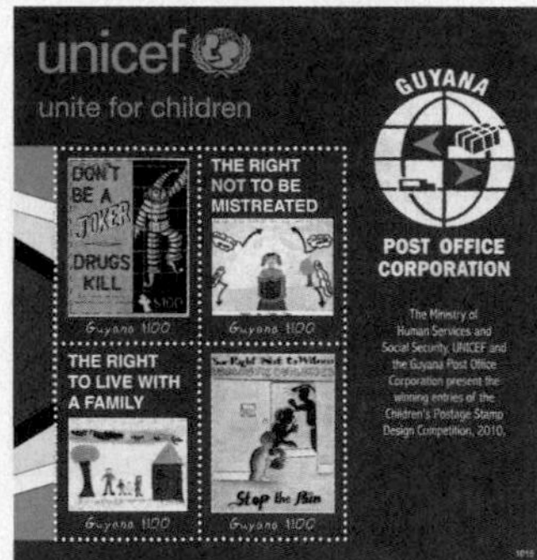

Winning Entries In Children's Postage Stamp Design Contest — A512

No. 4035 — Slogan: a, Don't Be a Joker - Drugs Kill. b, The Right Not to be Mistreated. c, The Right to Live With a Family. d, Your Right Not to Witness Domestic Violence.

2010, Sept. 2 ***Perf. 12***

4035 A512 $100 Sheet of 4, #a-d 4.00 4.00

Miniature Sheet

Porkknocker Day, 10th Anniv. — A513

No. 4036: a, Map of area near Bartica. b, Cyrilda de Jesus, female porkknocker (miner). c, Dick Manning, male porkknocker. d, Mazaruni diamonds and gold nuggets.

2010, Oct. 14

4036 A513 $100 Sheet of 4, #a-d 4.00 4.00

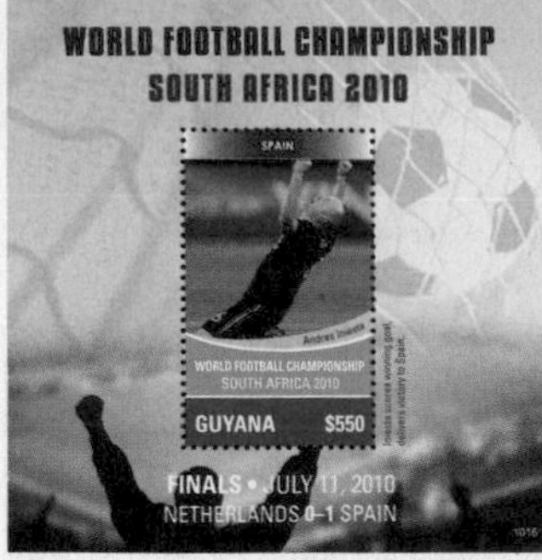

2010 World Cup Soccer Championships, South Africa — A514

No. 4037, $120: a, Joan Capdevila. b, Arjen Robben. c, Pedro. d, Gregory Van Der Wiel. e, Xabi Alonso. f, Wesley Sneijder.
No. 4038, $120: a, Dennis Aogo. b, Diego Forlan. c, Bastian Schweinsteiger. d, Martin Caceres. e, Stefan Kiessling. f, Maximiliano Pereira.
No. 4039, $550, Andres Iniesta. No. 4040, $550, Thomas Mueller.

2011, Feb. 21 **Litho.** ***Perf. 12***

Sheets of 6, #a-f

4037-4038 A514 Set of 2 14.00 14.00

Souvenir Sheets

4039-4040 A514 Set of 2 11.00 11.00

Miniature Sheets

Qin Shi Huang (259 B.C-210 B.C), First Emperor of China — A515

Deng Xiaoping (1904-97), Paramount Leader of People's Republic of China — A516

Jiang Zemin, President of People's Republic of China, 1993-2003 — A517

No. 4041: a, 21x22mm painting of Qin Shi Huang. b, Sculpture. c, 16x28 painting of Qin Shi Huang. d, Text.
No. 4042: Various photographs of Deng Xiaoping, as shown.
No. 4043: Various photographs of Jiang Zemin, as shown.

2011, Feb. 21

4041	A515	$150	Sheet of 4, #a-d	6.00	6.00
4042	A516	$150	Sheet of 4, #a-d	6.00	6.00
4043	A517	$150	Sheet of 4, #a-d	6.00	6.00
	Nos. 4041-4043 (3)			18.00	18.00

Beijing 2010 Intl. Stamp Exhibition.

Souvenir Sheet

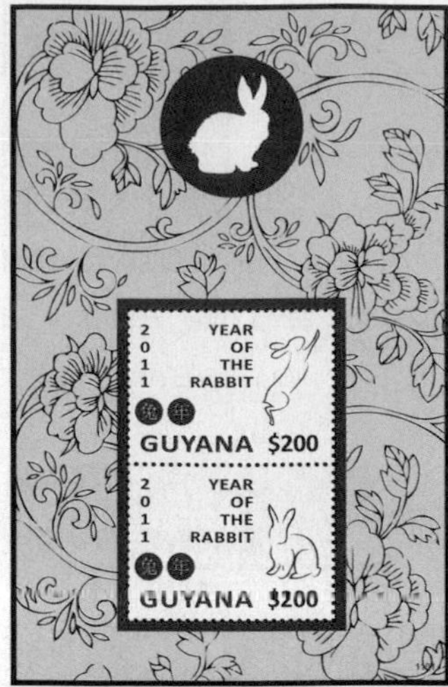

New Year 2011 (Year of the Rabbit) — A518

No. 4044 — Rabbit: a, Leaping. b, Sitting.

2011, Feb. 21 **Litho.** ***Perf. 12***

4044 A518 $200 Sheet of 2, #a-b 4.00 4.00

Christmas 2010 — A519

Paintings: $80, The Adoration of the Magi, by Hieronymus Bosch. $100, The Adoration of the Magi, by Peter Paul Rubens. $225, Madonna and Child, by Carlo Crivelli. $500, The Flight into Egypt, by Lucas Cranach the Elder.

2011, Mar. 9 **Litho.** ***Perf. 12¾x12½***

4045-4048 A519 Set of 4 9.00 9.00

Miniature Sheets

A520

Pope John Paul II (1920-2005) — A521

No. 4049: With "G" of "Guyana" on Papal Arms: a, Orange denomination, wearing vestments without clerical collar. b, Wearing white vestments and zucchetto. c, Wearing miter. d, Orange denomination, wearing vestments with clerical collar.
No. 4050: With "G" of Guyana to right of Papal Arms: a, Black denomination, praying. b, Wearing white vestments. c, Holding crucifix. d, White denomination, praying.

2011, Mar. 9 ***Perf. 13x13¼***
4049 A520 $225 Sheet of 4, #a-d 9.00 9.00
4050 A521 $225 Sheet of 4, #a-d 9.00 9.00

Text on Nos. 4049a-4049d is incorrectly placed on stamps.

A522

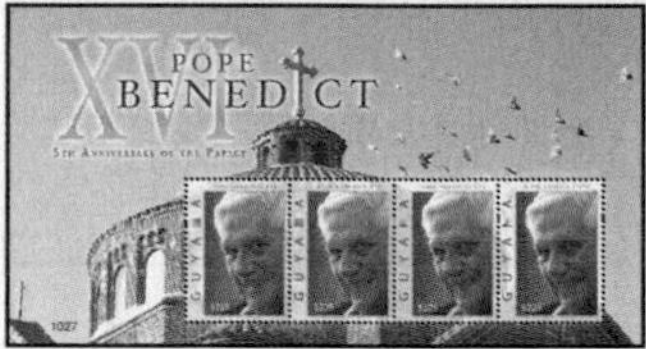

Pope Benedict XVI — A523

No. 4052: a, Blue sky at UL. b, Blue sky at UR. c, Part of bird above "XVI." d, Birds above "N" and last "A" in "Guyana."

2011, Mar. 9 ***Perf. 13x13¼***
4051 A522 $225 multi 2.25 2.25

Perf. 12

4052 A523 $225 Sheet of 4, #a-d 9.00 9.00

Souvenir Sheets

Popes and Their Coats of Arms — A524

No. 4053, $725: a, Pope Benedict XV (1854-1922). b, Arms of Pope Benedict XV.
No. 4054, $725: a, Pope Pius XI (1857-1939). b, Arms of Pope Pius XI.

2011, Mar. 9 **Litho.** ***Imperf.***
Sheets of 2, #a-b
Without Gum
4053-4054 A524 Set of 2 29.00 29.00

Miniature Sheets

Intl. Year of Astronomy (in 2009) — A525

No. 4055, $225: a, UNITEC-1. b, IKAROS. c, KSAT Negai. d, Waseda-sat 2.
No. 4056, $255: a, Phobos-Grunt arrival. b, Phobos-Grunt landing. c, Mars Reconnaissance Orbiter. d, Phobos-Grunt liftoff.

2011, Mar. 9 **Litho.** ***Perf. 13x13¼***
Sheets of 4, #a-d
4055-4056 A525 Set of 2 19.00 19.00

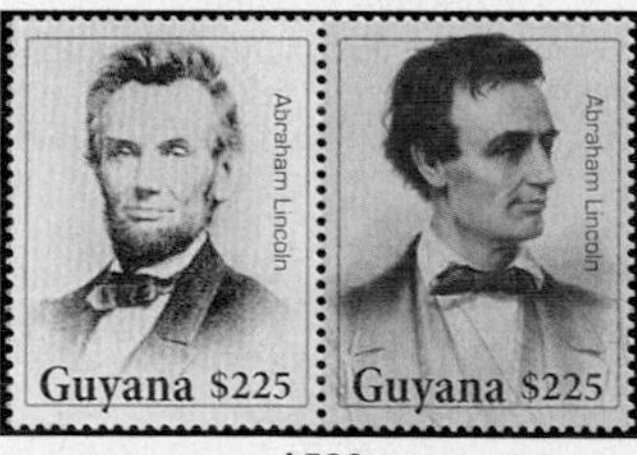

A526

U.S. Pres. Abraham Lincoln (1809-65) — A527

No. 4057 — Lincoln: a, With beard. b, Without beard.
No. 4058 — Background color above shoulder at right: a, Gray. b, Pink. c, Greenish gray. d, Lilac.

2011, Mar. 9 **Litho.** ***Perf. 13¼x13***
4057 A526 $225 Pair, #a-b 4.50 4.50

Perf. 12½

4058 A527 $225 Sheet of 4, #a-d 9.00 9.00

No. 4057 was printed in sheets containing two pairs.

Miniature Sheets

United States Civil War, 150th Anniv. — A528

No. 4059, $225 — Eagle, shield, Union and Confederate flags, Lieutenant Colonel John Pegram and Brigadier General William S. Rosecrans of Battle of Rich Mountain, July 11, 1861, and: a, Engagement at Rich Mountain. b, Battle of Rich Mountain (purple vignette). c, Battle of Rich Mountain (red brown vignette). d, Confederate prisoners.
No. 4060, $225 — Eagle, shield, Union and Confederate flags, Brigadier General James Longstreet and General Daniel Tyler of Battle of Blackburn's Ford, July 18, 1861, and: a, Blackburn's Ford. b, Members of Longstreet's brigade. c, Fairfax County Courthouse. d, Battle of Blackburn's Ford.
No. 4061, $225 — Eagle, shield, Union and Confederate flags, Brigadier General Joseph E. Johnston and Brigadier General Irvin McDowell of First Battle of Bull Run, July 21, 1861, and: a, First Battle of Bull Run. b, Confederate fortifications, Manassas. c, Union charge at Bull Run. d, Henry House in ruins.

2011, Apr. 4 ***Perf. 13 Syncopated***
Sheets of 4, #a-d
4059-4061 A528 Set of 3 27.00 27.00

Engagement of Prince William and Catherine Middleton
A529

Designs: No. 4062, Couple (black and white photo).
No. 4063 — Color photographs: a, Couple holding hands. b, Couple, Middleton wearing hat. c, Middleton. d, Prince William.
No. 4064 — Black-and-white photographs: a, Prince William. b, Middleton.
$450, Couple, Middleton at left.

2011, Apr. 4 ***Perf. 12***
4062 A529 $200 multi 2.00 2.00
4063 A529 $200 Sheet of 4, #a-d 8.00 8.00

Souvenir Sheets

Perf. 13 Syncopated

4064 A529 $225 Sheet of 2, #a-b 4.50 4.50
4065 A529 $450 multi 4.50 4.50

No. 4062 was printed in sheets of 4.

Mother Teresa (1910-97), Humanitarian
A530

2011, Apr. 4 ***Perf. 12***
4066 A530 $225 multi 2.25 2.25

Printed in sheets of 4.

Indipex 2011 Intl. Philatelic Exhibition, New Delhi — A531

No. 4067, $225 — Taj Mahal, Agra: a, Interior hallway. b, Large and small domes. c, Mausoleum, minarets and reflecting pool. d, Exterior wall and arches.
No. 4068, $225: a, Temple of Shiva, Varanasi. b, Ramnagar Fort. c, Kangra Valley. d, Khajuraho Temple.
$450, Statue of Lord Shiva.

Perf. 13 Syncopated
2011, Apr. 4 **Litho.**
Sheets of 4, #a-d
4067-4068 A531 Set of 2 17.50 17.50

Souvenir Sheet

Perf. 12¾

4069 A531 $450 multi 4.50 4.50

No. 4069 contains one 38x51mm stamp.

Worldwide Fund for Nature (WWF) — A532

No. 4070 — Bush dogs: a, Three at water hole. b, Four at water hole. c, Three in den. d, Head of adult.

2011, June 6 **Litho.** ***Perf. 13¼***
4070 Block of 4 6.00 6.00
a.-d. A532 $150 Any single 1.50 1.50
e. Souvenir sheet of 8, 2 each #4070a-4070d 12.00 12.00

Tenth World Cricket Cup Championships, India, Sri Lanka and Bangladesh — A533

Designs: $100, Shivnarine Chanderpaul. $150, Sardar Patel Stadium, Ahmedabad, India, horiz.
$300, Cricket World Cup.

2011, June 20 ***Perf. 12¾***
4071-4072 A533 Set of 2 2.50 2.50

Souvenir Sheet

Perf. 13 Syncopated

4073 A533 $300 multi 3.00 3.00

U.S. Pres. Barack Obama — A534

No. 4074, $225: a, Black background. b, Blue background.
No. 4075, $225: a, Bister background. b, Red background.

2011, June 20 ***Perf. 13 Syncopated***
Pairs, #a-b
4074-4075 A534 Set of 2 8.75 8.75

Nos. 4074-4075 each were printed in sheets containing two pairs.

A535

U.S. Pres. John F. Kennedy (1917-63) — A536

No. 4076: a, Head of Kennedy. b, Kennedy at lectern in stadium. c, Kennedy at lectern (black-and-white photo).
No. 4077: a, Kennedy and wife, Jacqueline (black-and-white photo). b, Kennedy presidential campaign button. c, Kennedy talking to person. d, Kennedy and wife (color photo).

2011, June 20 ***Perf. 13 Syncopated***
4076 A535 $175 Horiz. strip of 3, #a-c 5.25 5.25
4077 A536 $225 Sheet of 4, #a-d 8.75 8.75

No. 4076 was printed in sheet containing two strips.

Wedding of Prince William and Catherine Middleton — A537

No. 4078, $250 — Black-and-white photos of: a, Prince William. b, Couple. c, Procession in streets. d, Middleton.
No. 4079, $275, vert. — Color photos of: a, Couple holding hands (30x40mm. b, Couple in coach. c, Couple (60x40mm, with perforations in middle of stamp).
$500, Couple kissing, vert.

2011, Sept. 19 ***Perf. 12½x12***
4078 A537 $250 Sheet of 4, #a-d 10.00 10.00

Perf. 12x12½

4079 A537 $275 Sheet of 3, #a-c 8.25 8.25

Souvenir Sheet

Perf. 13¼

4080 A537 $500 multi 5.00 5.00

No. 4080 contains one 38x51mm stamp.

Souvenir Sheet

Visit to Germany of Pope Benedict XVI — A538

Litho. & Embossed

2011, Sept. 19 ***Microrouletted***

Without Gum

4081 A538 $3000 multi 30.00 30.00

Princess Diana (1961-97) — A539

No. 4082 — Princess Diana wearing: a, Pink hat and dress. b, White dress and veil. c, Striped sweater.

$450, Princess Diana wearing black hat, horiz.

2011, Oct. 12 Litho. ***Perf. 12x12½***

4082 A539 $275 Sheet of 3, #a-c 8.25 8.25

Souvenir Sheet

Perf. 13¼

4083 A539 $450 multi 4.50 4.50

No. 4083 contains one 51x38mm stamp.

Miniature Sheets

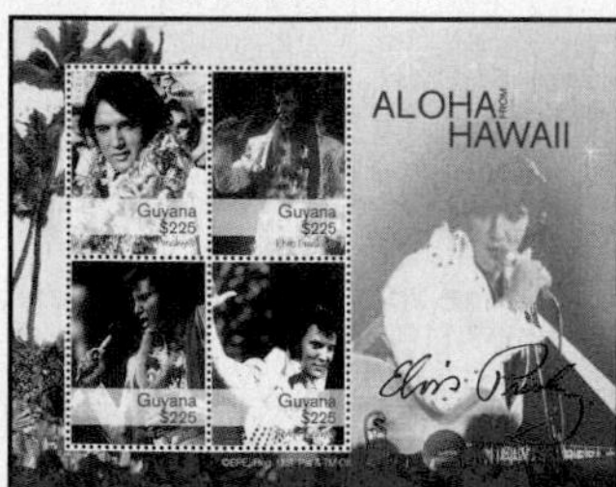

A540

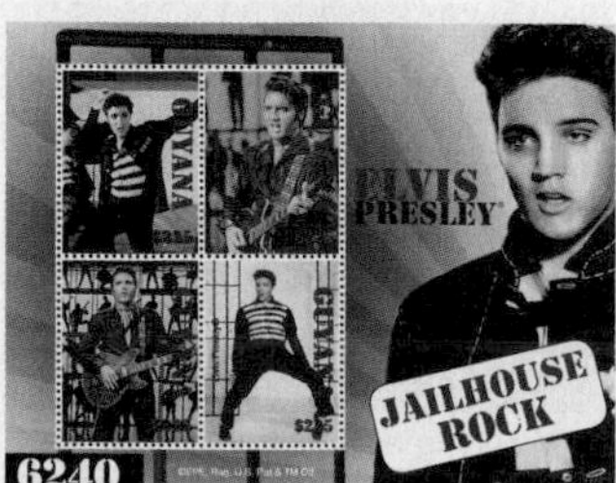

A541

Elvis Presley (1935-77) — A542

No. 4084 — Presley: a, Outdoors wearing leis. b, Holding microphone with hand even with his neck. c, Holding microphone with hand below his neck. d, Waving.

No. 4085 — Presley: a, With hand touching head. b, Playing guitar, figures in background out of focus. c, Playing guitar, figures in background in focus. d, Dancing, with jail bars in background.

No. 4086 — Presley albums: a, Viva Las Vegas. b, Elvis (curved lettering). c, Elvis (block letters in lights). d, I Got Stung.

No. 4087 — Presley albums: a, Blue Hawaii. b, Elvis' Gold Records. c, Elvis Presley. d, Moody Blue.

2011, Oct. 12 ***Perf. 12x12½***

4084 A540 $225 Sheet of 4, #a-d 9.00 9.00
4085 A541 $225 Sheet of 4, #a-d 9.00 9.00

Perf. 12½x12

4086 A542 $225 Sheet of 4, #a-d 9.00 9.00
4087 A542 $225 Sheet of 4, #a-d 9.00 9.00
Nos. 4084-4087 (4) 36.00 36.00

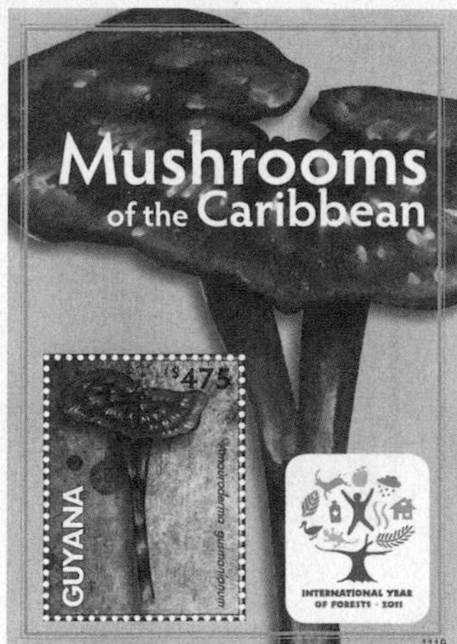

Mushrooms — A543

No. 4088: a, Pseudotulostoma volvata. b, Inocybe ayangannae. c, Amanita perphaea. d, Entoloma olivaceacoloratum. e, Panaeolus cyanescens. f, Tylopilus vinaceipallidus.

No. 4089: a, Boletellus dicymbophilus. b, Inocybe epidendron. c, Tylopilus pakaraimensis. d, Amanita aurantiobrunnea.

No. 4090, $475, Amauroderma gusmanianum. No. 4091, $475, Craterellus excelsus.

2011, Oct. 12 ***Perf. 11½***

4088 A543 $150 Sheet of 6, #a-f 9.00 9.00
4089 A543 $225 Sheet of 4, #a-d 9.00 9.00

Souvenir Sheets

4090-4091 A543 Set of 2 9.50 9.50

Intl. Year of Forests.

Miniature Sheet

Chinese Zodiac Animals — A544

No. 4092: a, Rat. b, Ox. c, Tiger. d, Rabbit. e, Dragon. f, Snake. g, Horse. h, Sheep. i, Monkey. j, Rooster. k, Dog. l, Boar.

Litho. With Foil Application

2012, Jan. 9 ***Perf. 13 Syncopated***

4092 A544 $50 Sheet of 12, #a-l 6.00 6.00

King Edward VIII (1894-1972) A545

King Edward VIII wearing: $300, Top hat. $700, Uniform, horiz.

2012, May 30 Litho. ***Perf. 12***

4093 A545 $300 multi 3.00 3.00
a. Inscribed "King Edward VIII" 3.00 3.00

Souvenir Sheet

4094 A545 $700 multi 7.00 7.00
a. Inscribed "King Edward VIII" 7.00 7.00

No. 4094 contains one 50x30mm stamp. Nos. 4093-4094 are incorrectly inscribed "King Edward XIII."

A546

Birds — A547

No. 4095, $160: a, Anhinga. b, Least grebe. c, Scarlet ibis. d, Neotropic cormorant.

No. 4096, $1.60: a, Northern caracara. b, Cocoi heron. c, Tricolored heron. d, Jabiru.

No. 4097, $400, Glossy ibis. No. 4098, $400, White-tailed kite, vert.

2012, May 30 ***Perf. 14***

Sheets of 4, #a-d

4095-4096 A546 Set of 2 13.00 13.00

Souvenir Sheets

Perf. 12

4097-4098 A547 Set of 2 8.00 8.00

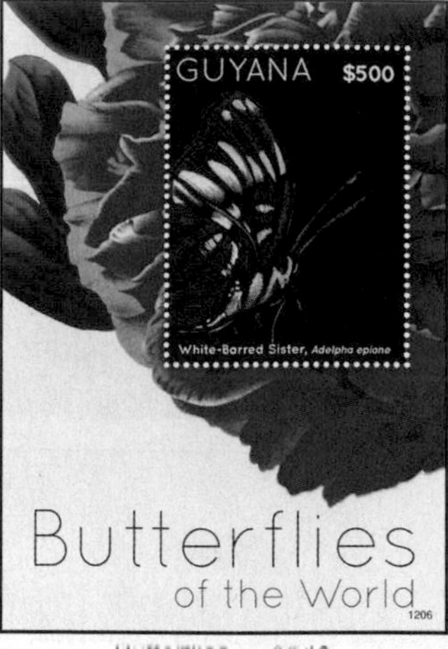

Butterflies — A548

No. 4099, $250, horiz.: a, Iphiclus sister. b, Gaudy altinote. c, Gulf fritillary. d, Tiger crescent.

No. 4100, $250, horiz.: a, Orange-banded gem. b, Red-barred amarynthis. c, Thesprotia sister. d, Orange-barred sister.

No. 4101, $500, White-barred sister. No. 4102, $500, Blue duskywing.

2012, May 30 ***Perf. 14***

Sheets of 4, #a-d

4099-4100 A548 Set of 2 20.00 20.00

Souvenir Sheets

Perf. 12½

4101-4102 A548 Set of 2 10.00 10.00

Nos. 4099-4100 each contain four 40x30mm stamps.

A549

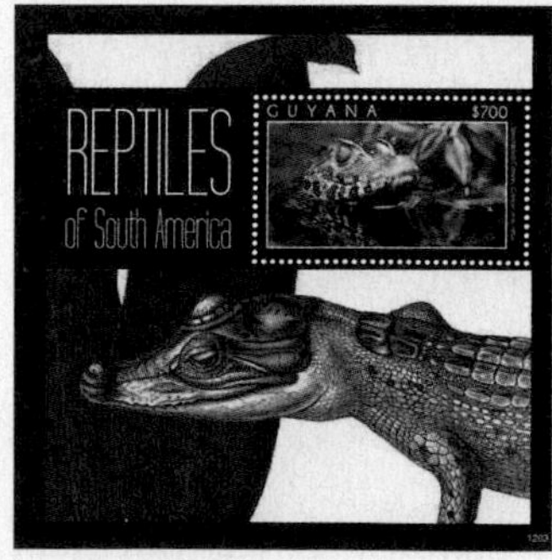

Reptiles — A550

No. 4103, $250: a, Giant tortoise. b, Caiman lizard. c, Marine iguana. d, Milk snake.

No. 4104, $250: a, Rainbow whiptail. b, Emerald tree boa. c, Green vine snake. d, Green iguana.

No. 4105, $700, Spectacled caiman. No. 4106, $700, Boa constrictor, vert.

2012, May 30 ***Perf. 14***

Sheets of 4, #a-d

4103-4104 A549 Set of 2 20.00 20.00

Souvenir Sheets

Perf. 12

4105-4106 A550 Set of 2 14.00 14.00

No. 4106 contains one 30x80mm stamp.

Nos. 70, 89, 2367, 2368, 2370, 2662, 2781, 2782, 2783, 2784, 2859, 2883, 2933, 3004, and 3238 Handstamp Surcharged in Violet Black Like No. 4020K

Methods, Perfs and Watermarks As Before

2012

4107 A7 $20 on 3c #70 *35.00 35.00*
4108 A14 $20 on 30c #89 *75.00 75.00*
4109 A231 $20 on $6 #3004 *45.00 45.00*
4110 A185 $20 on $6.40 #2781 *25.00 25.00*
4111 A185 $20 on $7.65 #2782 *25.00 25.00*
4112 A215 $20 on $8 #2933 —
4113 A185 $20 on $12.80 #2783 *25.00 25.00*
4114 A185 $20 on $15.30 #2784 *25.00 25.00*
4115 A277 $20 on $30 #3238 *75.00 75.00*

Miniature Sheet of 8, #a-h

4116 A203 $20 on $30 #2883 — —

Miniature Sheets of 12, #a-l

4117 A162 $20 on $30 #2662 — —
4118 A200 $20 on $35 #2859 — —

Miniature Sheets of 16, #a-p

4119 A129 $20 on $10 #2367 — —
4120 A129 $20 on $10 #2368 — —
4121 A129 $20 on $12.80 #2370 — —

Footnoted Disney Types of 1995 Surcharged Like No. 4020K in Violet Black

Methods and Perfs As Before

2012

Miniature Sheets of 8, #a-h, + Label

4122 A217 $20 on $5 #2917 foot-note — —
4123 A213 $20 on $5 #2918 foot-note — —

Miniature Sheet of 7, #a-g, + Label

4124 A213 $20 on $5 #2920 foot-note — —

Flower Type of 1971-76 Surcharged Like No. 4020K in Violet Black

4125 A28 $20 on 2c Yellow allamanda *75.00 75.00*
4126 A28 $20 on 8c Mazaruni Pride *75.00 75.00*
a. Pair, #4125-4126 — —

Nos. 4125-4126 were not issued without surcharge.

No. 3360B Surcharged Like No. 4020K

2012 Litho. *Perf. 13¼x13¾*

4127 A309a $20 on $30 #3360B *35.00 35.00*

Souvenir Sheet

Diplomatic Relations Between Guyana and People's Republic of China, 40th Anniv. — A552

No. 4128: a, Tiananmen, Beijing, China. b, Guyana International Conference Center.

2012, June 27 Litho. *Perf. 12½x12*

4128 A552 $350 Sheet of 2, #a-b 7.00 7.00

2012 Summer Olympics, London — A553

No. 4129 — Mascots: a, Wenlock (with torch). b, Mandeville (without torch).

2012, June 27 *Perf. 14*

4129 A553 $125 Horiz. pair, #a-b 2.50 2.50

No. 4129 was printed in sheets containing four pairs.

Orchids — A554

No. 4130: a, Ada aurantiaca. b, Cattleya labiata. c, Masdevallia haryana. d, Masdevallia davisii.
$700, Zygopetalum clayi.

2012, Aug. 28 *Perf. 13¾*

4130 A554 $250 Sheet of 4, #a-d 10.00 10.00

Souvenir Sheet

4131 A554 $700 multi 7.00 7.00

No. 357 Handstamp Surcharged Like No. 4020K

Method and Perf. As Before

2012 ?

4132 A8 $20 on 40c #357 *50.00 50.00*

Nos. 142 With "Revenue Only" Overprint, 445 and 506 Handstamp Surcharged in Black

2012 ? Litho.

4133 A28 $20 on 40c #142 with "Revenue Only" Overprint *40.00 40.00*
4134 A11 $20 on 40c #445 *65.00 65.00*
4135 A78 $20 on 40c on 2c #506 *65.00 65.00*

No. 2937 Surcharged

Method and Perf. As Before

2012 ?

4136 A215 $55 on $25 #2937 —

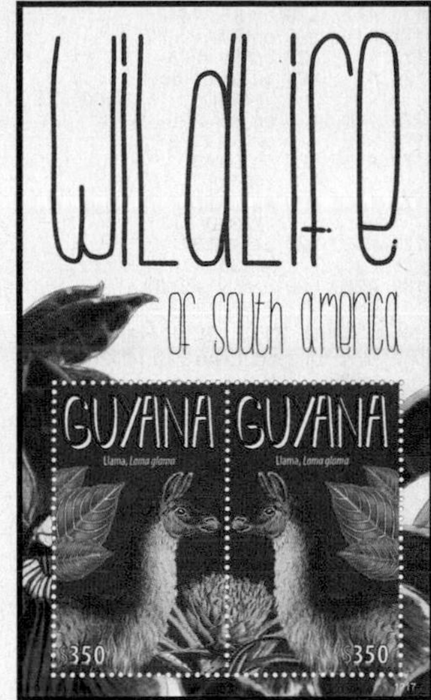

South American Wildlife — A555

No. 4137: a, Jaguar. b, Toucan. c, Chinchilla.
No. 4138: a, Llama facing right. b, Llama facing left.

2012, Oct. 23 Litho. *Perf. 12*

4137 A555 $300 Sheet of 3, #a-c 9.00 9.00

Souvenir Sheet

4138 A555 $350 Sheet of 2, #a-b 7.00 7.00

A556

Whales — A557

No. 4139: a, Killer whale. b, Humpback whale. c, Blue whale.
$700, Beluga whale.

2012, Oct. 23

4139 A556 $300 Sheet of 3, #a-c 9.00 9.00

Souvenir Sheet

4140 A557 $700 multi 7.00 7.00

Dolphins — A558

No. 4141, $300: a, Spinner dolphin. b, Atlantic spotted dolphin. c, Amazon River dolphin.
No. 4142, $300: a, Clymene dolphin. b, Dusky dolphin. c, White-sided dolphin.
No. 4143, $700, Common dolphin. No. 4144, $700, Bottlenose dolphin, vert.

Sheets of 3, #a-c

2012, Oct. 23 *Perf. 14, 12 (#4144)*

4141-4142 A558 Set of 2 18.00 18.00

Souvenir Sheets

4143-4144 A558 Set of 2 14.00 14.00

Shells — A559

No. 4145: a, Melampus coffeus coffeus. b, Nerita fulgurans. c, Nerita peloronta. d, Littorina nebulosa. e, Tectarius muricatus. f, Hyalina avena.
No. 4146: a, Cassis flammea. b, Liguus virgineus. c, Trigonostoma rugosum. d, Nerita virginea.
No. 4147, $500, Cymatium raderi. No. 4148, $500, Cassis madagascariensis.

2012, Oct. 23 *Perf. 13 Syncopated*

4145 A559 $175 Sheet of 6, #a-f 10.50 10.50
4146 A559 $225 Sheet of 4, #a-d 9.00 9.00

Souvenir Sheets

4147-4148 A559 Set of 2 10.00 10.00

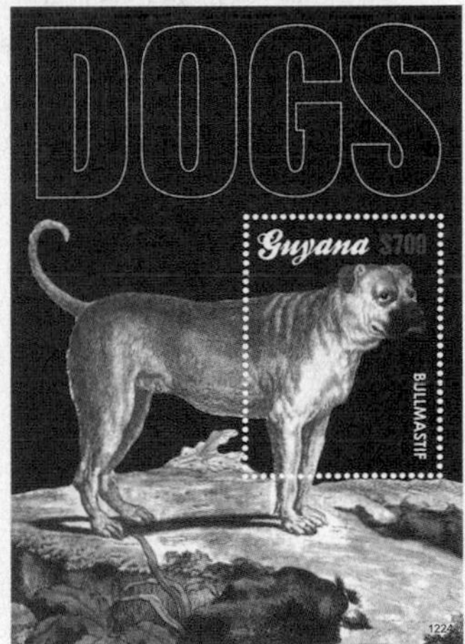

Dogs and Their Evolution — A560

No. 4149, horiz.: a, Gray wolf. b, Canaan dog. c, Maltese. d, Greyhound. e, Golden retriever.
No. 4150, horiz.: a, Coyote. b, Alaskan husky. c, Red fox. d, Yorkshire terrier.
No. 4151, $700, Bull mastiff. No. 4152, $700, Dalmatian.

2012, Oct. 23 *Perf. 12*

4149 A560 $225 Sheet of 5, #a-e 11.00 11.00
4150 A560 $250 Sheet of 4, #a-d 10.00 10.00

Souvenir Sheets

Perf. 14

4151-4152 A560 Set of 2 14.00 14.00

Completion of Painting of the Sistine Chapel Ceiling by Michelangelo, 500th Anniv. — A561

No. 4153, horiz. — Painting details: a, Joel. b, Daniel. c, The Libyan Sibyl.
No. 4154: a, Michelangelo. b, Detail of Ancestors of Christ.

2012, Oct. 29 *Perf. 12*
4153 A561 $225 Sheet of 3, #a-c 6.75 6.75

Souvenir Sheet

4154 A561 $350 Sheet of 2, #a-b 7.00 7.00

No. 4153 contains three 40x30mm stamps.

Miniature Sheets

Princess Diana (1961-97) — A562

No. 4155, $250 — Stamps with blue panels with Princess Diana: a, Holding flowers. b, Wearing white hat. c, Wearing tiara. b, Wearing beige hat with ribbon.

No. 4156, $250 — Stamps with yellow green panels with Princess Diana wearing: a, Red jacket and lei. b, Patterned dress and necklace. c, Jacket and tie. d, White jacket and leis.

Sheets of 4, #a-d

2012, Oct. 29 *Perf. 14, 12 (#4156)*
4155-4156 A562 Set of 2 20.00 20.00

Souvenir Sheets

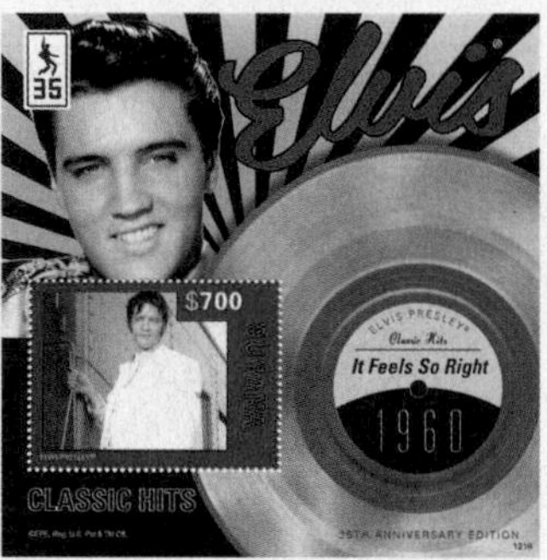

Elvis Presley (1935-77) — A563

Designs: No. 4157, $700, Color photograph of Presley, red frame with country name outlined in black. No. 4158, $700, Black-and-white photograph of Presley, red frame with country name outlined in white. No. 4159, $700, Color photograph of Presley, black frame. No. 4160, $700, Color photograph of Presley, gray frame. No. 4161, $700, Black-and-white photograph of Presley, purple frame.

2012, Oct. 29 *Perf. 12¾*
4157-4161 A563 Set of 5 35.00 35.00

Chinese Zodiac Animals — A564

Designs: No. 4162, $50, Rabbits. No. 4163, $50, Tiger.

2012, Dec. 5 *Perf. 13¼x13*
4162-4163 A564 Set of 2 1.00 1.00

Nos. 68, 136, 208, 231, 326, 328, 413Dg, 442, 1337-1339, 1987, 2360, 2361, 2652, 2728, 3133 Surcharged in Violet Black Like No. 4020K

Methods, Perfs and Watermarks As Before

2012
4164 A7 $20 on 1c #68 *35.00 35.00*
4165 A28 $20 on 5c #136 *50.00 50.00*
4166 A92 $20 on 25c #1337 —
4167 A92 $20 on 25c #1338 *150.00*
4168 A92 $20 on 25c #1339 — —
4169 A76 $20 on 30c #326 *85.00 85.00*
4170 A55 $20 on 35c #231 — —
4171 A72 $20 on 35c #442 — —
4172 A161 $20 on 80c #2652 —
4173 A48 $20 on $1 #208 — —
4174 A7 $20 on $1 on 6c #413Dg *25.00 25.00*
4175 A76 $20 on $3 #328 — —
4176 A66 $20 on $5 #1987 — —
4177 A176 $20 on $6.40 #2728 —
4178 A129 $20 on $8.90 #2360 —
4179 A129 $20 on $12.80 #2361 —
4180 A260 $20 on $30 #3133 —

Nos. 2369, 2372, 2858 Handstamp Surcharged Like No. 4020K

Methods and Perfs. As Before

2012 **Sheet of 16, #a-p**
4181 A129 $20 on $12.80 #2369 — —

Sheet of 16, #r-ag

4181Q A129 $20 on $12.80 #2372 — —

Sheet of 12, #a-l

4184 A200 $20 on $35 #2858 — —

No. 144 With "Revenue Only" Overprint and No. 520 Handstamp Surcharged Like No. 4133

Methods, Perfs and Watermarks As Before

2012-13 ?
4185 A28 $20 on 60c #144 with "Revenue Only" Overprint —
4186 A78 $20 on $1.70 on 3c #520 —

Nos. 72, 280, 283, 512 and 1340 Handstamp Surcharged Like No. 4020K

Methods, Perfs and Watermarks as Before

2012-13 ?
4187 A7 $20 on 6c #72 *25.00*
4188 A66 $20 on 10c #280 —
4189 A66 $20 on 25c #283 —
4190 A92 $20 on 25c #1340 —
4191 A78 $20 on 85c on 2c #512 —

Nos. 143 and 144 With "Revenue Only" Overprint, and Nos. 501, 526, 1337 and 1338 Handstamp Surcharged Like No. 4020J

Methods, Perfs and Watermarks As Before

2012-13 ?
4192 A78 $20 on 15c on 2c #501 —
4193 A92 $20 on 25c #1337 —
4194 A92 $20 on 25c #1338 —
4195 A28 $20 on 50c #143, "Revenue Only" Overprint —
4196 A28 $20 on 60c #144, "Revenue Only" Overprint —
4197 A78 $20 on $2.35 on 3c #526 —

Nos. 1341, 1467, 1468, 2362, 2934 Surcharged Like No. 4020K; and No. 1337 Surcharged Like No. 4020J

Methods, Perfs and Watermarks As Before

2012-13
4199 A92 $20 on 25c #1341 —
4200 A92 $20 on 25c #1467 *150.00*
4201 A92 $20 on 25c #1468 — —
4202 A129 $20 on $15.30 #2362 — —
4203 A92 $20 on 25c #1337 —
4204 A215 $20 on $15 #2934 —

Issued: No. 4201, 4204, 2012; Nos. 4199, 4200, 4202, 4203, 2013.

Nos. 1026, 1096, 1101, 1138, 1157 and 1163 Surcharged Like No. 4020K

Methods and Perfs. As Before

2012 ? **Unwmk.**
4205 A91 $20 on 75c #1026 (Series 1, Plate No. 5) — —
4206 A91 $20 on 75c #1096 (Series 1, Plate No. 55) — —
4207 A91 $20 on 75c #1101 (Series 1, Plate No. 60) — —
4208 A91 $20 on 75c #1138 (Series 1, Plate No. 83) — —
4209 A91 $20 on 75c #1157 (Series 1, Plate No. 92) — —
4210 A91 $20 on 75c #1163 (Series 1, Plate No. 95) — —

Miniature Sheet

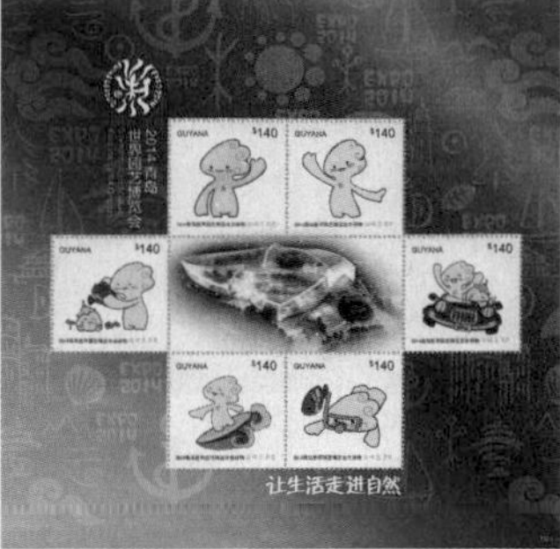

Intl. Horticultural Exposition, Qingdao, People's Republic of China — A565

No. 4211 — Mascot: a, Waving, hand raised at right. b, Waving, hand raised at left. c, Watering smaller mascot. d, With smaller mascot in automobile. e, Surfing. f, Snorkeling.

2013, Jan. 1 **Litho.** *Perf. 13¾*
4211 A565 $140 Sheet of 6, #a-f, + central label 8.25 8.25

World Environment Day — A566

No. 4212 — Various fish and marine life and parts of map depicting: a, North America and Eastern Asia. b, Oceania, Australia, and Antarctica. c, Antarctica, South America and Central America.

$710, Heart.

2013, Apr. 3 **Litho.** *Perf. 13*
4212 A566 $275 Sheet of 3, #a-c, + central label 7.75 7.75

Souvenir Sheet

Perf.

4213 A566 $710 multi 6.75 6.75

No. 4213 contains one 38mm diameter stamp.

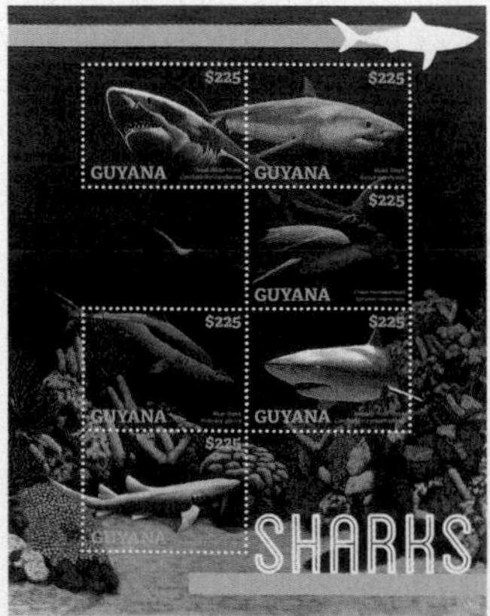

Sharks — A567

No. 4214: a, Great white shark. b, Mako shark. c, Great hammerhead shark. d, Blue shark. e, Blacktip reef shark. f, Nurse shark.

$710, Whale shark.

2013, Apr. 3 **Litho.** *Perf. 12*
4214 A567 $225 Sheet of 6, #a-f 13.00 13.00

Souvenir Sheet

4215 A567 $710 multi 6.75 6.75

No. 4215 contains one 80x30mm stamp.

Flowers — A568

No. 4216, $225: a, Asclepias curassavica. b, Passiflora tarminiana. c, Heliconia bihai. d, Aphelandra squarrosa.

No. 4217, $225: a, Bunchosia argentea. b, Strelitzia reginae. c, Aechmea chantinii. d, Acanthocereus tetragonus.

No. 4218, $710, Iris germanica, vert. No. 4219, $710, Fuchsia magellanica, vert.

2013, Apr. 3 **Litho.** *Perf. 13¾*

Sheets of 4, #a-d

4216-4217 A568 Set of 2 17.00 17.00

Souvenir Sheets

Perf. 12¾

4218-4219 A568 Set of 2 13.50 13.50

Nos. 4218 and 4219 each contain one 38x51mm stamp.

History of Art — A569

No. 4220, $275 — Mannerist paintings: a, Portrait of Ugolino Martelli, by Agnolo Bronzino. b, Sacrifice of Isaac, by Paolo Veronese. c, Ignudi, by Michelangelo.

No. 4221, $275 — Renaissance paintings of the Madonna: a, Madonna and Child, by Andrea del Verrocchio. b, Madonna, by Carlo Crivelli. c, Madonna, by Mathias Gothart Grünewald.

$710, Penitent Magdalene, by Tintoretto, horiz.

2013, Apr. 4 **Litho.** *Perf. 12¾*

Sheets of 3, #a-c

4220-4221 A569 Set of 2 15.50 15.50

Souvenir Sheet

4222 A569 $710 multi 6.75 6.75

A570

A571

A572

A573

A574

New Year 2013 (Year of the Snake) A575

Perf. 13 Syncopated

2013, Apr. 29 **Litho.**

4223 A570 $225 multi 2.25 2.25

Miniature Sheet

Perf. 13¼

4224 Sheet of 20, #4224a-4224d, 16 #4224e 16.00 16.00
- *a.* A571 $80 multi .80 .80
- *b.* A572 $80 multi .80 .80
- *c.* A573 $80 multi .80 .80
- *d.* A574 $80 multi .80 .80
- *e.* A575 $80 multi .80 .80

No. 4223 was printed in sheets of 4.

Miniature Sheet

Muhammad Ali, Boxer — A576

No. 4225 — Ali: a, With wrists taped. b, Wearing robe, both hands in boxing gloves. c, Close-up of face. d, Wearing robe, one hand in boxing glove visible.

Perf. 13 Syncopated

2013, Apr. 29 **Litho.**

4225 A576 $225 Sheet of 4, #a-d 9.00 9.00

Sinking of the Titanic, Cent. (in 2012) — A577

No. 4226 — Members of the Titanic's orchestra: a, W. Hartley. b, G. Krins. c, J. L. Hume. d, J. W. Woodward. e, P. C. Taylor. f, W. T. Brailey.
$700, Titanic, horiz.

2013, Apr. 29 **Litho.** ***Perf. 12***

4226 A577 $200 Sheet of 6, #a-f 12.00 12.00

Souvenir Sheet

4227 A577 $700 multi 7.00 7.00

No. 4227 contains one 80x30mm stamp.

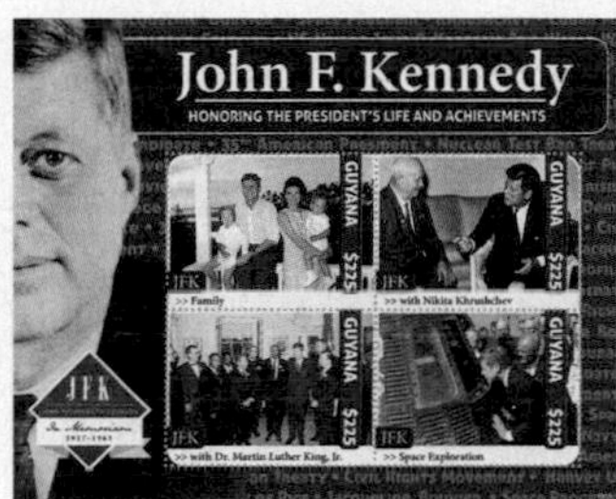

Pres. John F. Kennedy (1917-63) — A578

No. 4228 — Pres. Kennedy: a, With wife and children. b, Meeting Soviet Premier Nikita Khrushchev. c, Meeting with Dr. Martin Luther King, Jr., and others. d, Looking at recovered space capsule.
No. 4229, vert. — Campaign poster picturing: a, Kennedy. b, Lyndon B. Johnson.

2013, Apr. 29 **Litho.** ***Perf. 12½***

4228 A578 $225 Sheet of 4, #a-d 9.00 9.00

Souvenir Sheet

Perf. 14

4229 A578 $355 Sheet of 2, #a-b 7.00 7.00

No. 4229 contains two 30x40mm stamps.

Birds A579

No. 4230: a, Black-backed tanager. b, Golden-hooded tanager. c, Turquoise tanager. d, Burnished-buff tanager.
$710, Goldent tanager, vert.

2013, Apr. 29 **Litho.** ***Perf. 13¾***

4230 A579 $225 Sheet of 4, #a-d 9.00 9.00

Souvenir Sheet

Perf. 12½

4231 A579 $710 multi 7.00 7.00

No. 4231 contains one 38x51mm stamp.

Miniature Sheets

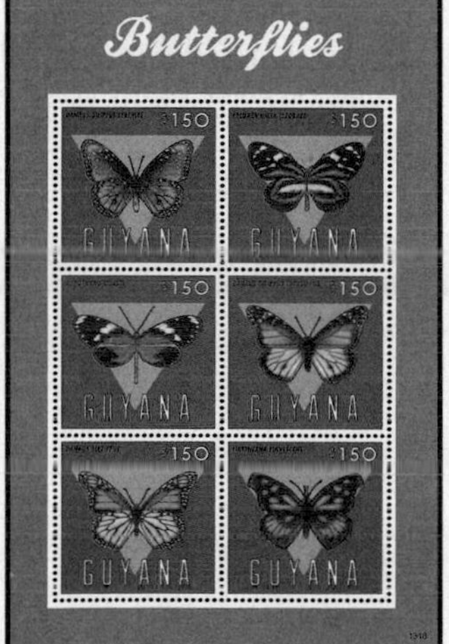

Butterflies — A580

No. 4232, $150: a, Danaus gilippus berenice. b, Lycorea halia cleobaea. c, Hypothyris lycaste. d, Danaus gilippus thersippus. e, Danaus plexippus. f, Libytheana fulvescens.
No. 4233, $200: a, Battus philenor orsua. b, Dismorphia eunoe desine. c, Dismorphia spio. d, Lieinix viridifascia. e, Lyropteryx lyra cleadas. f, Neophasia terlooii.

2013, Apr. 29 **Litho.** ***Perf. 13¾***

Sheets of 6, #a-f

4232-4233 A580 Set of 2 21.00 21.00

2009 Visit of Pope Benedict XVI to Israel — A581

2010 Visit of Pope Benedict XVI to Great Britain — A582

No. 4234 — Pope Benedict XVI: a, Touching Western Wall. b, Meeting Israeli President Shimon Peres. c, Behind microphones. d, Holding crucifix.
No. 4235 — Pope Benedict XVI: a, With Queen Elizabeth II and Prince Philip. b, Holding censer. c, Wearing miter. d, Holding chalice.
No. 4236, Pope Benedict XVI praying at Western Wall. No. 4237, Pope Benedict XVI and clergymen, British flag.

Perf. 13 Syncopated

2013, Apr. 29 **Litho.**

4234 A581 $225 Sheet of 4, #a-d 9.00 9.00
4235 A582 $225 Sheet of 4, #a-d 9.00 9.00

Souvenir Sheets

4236 A581 $710 multi 7.00 7.00
4237 A582 $710 multi 7.00 7.00

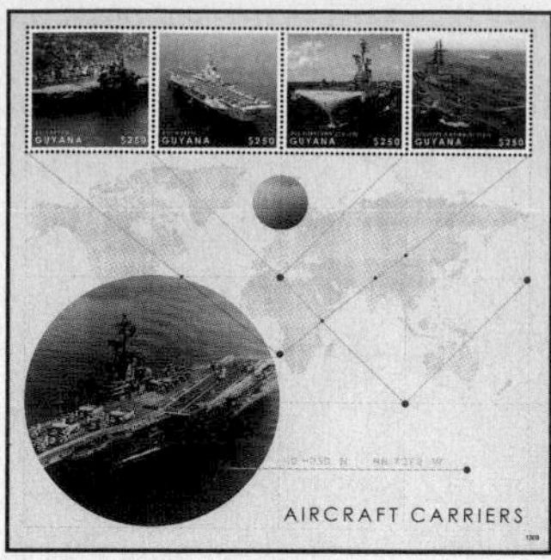

Aircraft Carriers — A583

No. 4238: a, Liaoning, People's Republic of China (previously Varyag, Russia). b, Foch, France. c, USS Yorktown, U.S. d, Giuseppe Garibaldi, Italy.
$700, Admiral Flota Sovetskogo Soyuza Kuznetsov, Russia, horiz.

2013, Apr. 29 Litho. *Perf. 13¾*
4238 A583 $250 Sheet of 4, #a-d 9.75 9.75

Souvenir Sheet
Perf. 12½
4239 A583 $700 multi 7.00 7.00

No. 4239 contains one 51x38mm stamp.

Miniature Sheets

A584

Exploration of Mars — A585

No. 4240: a, Mars Rover. b, Mars Spirit. c, Curiosity. d, Mars Reconnaissance Orbiter.
No. 4241: a, Mariner 4. b, Mariner 9. c, Phoenix. d, Odyssey.

Perf. 13 Syncopated
2013, Apr. 29 Litho.
4240 A584 $225 Sheet of 4, #a-d 9.00 9.00
4241 A585 $225 Sheet of 4, #a-d 9.00 9.00

Souvenir Sheet

Jigong Mountains, People's Republic of China — A586

2013, May 1 Litho. *Perf. 12*
4242 A586 $1000 multi 9.75 9.75

Constellations — A587

No. 4243, $250: a, Aries. b, Gemini. c, Leo. d, Scorpius.
No. 4244, $250: a, Cancer. b, Taurus. c, Capricornus. d. Pisces.
No. 4245, $700, Orion. No. 4246, $700, Pegasus.

2013, July 30 Litho. *Perf. 14*
Sheets of 4, #a-d
4243-4244 A587 Set of 2 20.00 20.00

Souvenir Sheets
4245-4246 A587 Set of 2 14.00 14.00

Caves of Thailand — A588

No. 4247: a, Temple at Phraya Nakhon Cave. b, Boat outside of entrance to cave at Phang Nga Bay. c, Phayanakorn Cave.
$710, Suwan Kuha Temple statue of Buddha in cave.

2013, Aug. 26 Litho. *Perf. 12½*
4247 A588 $275 Sheet of 3, #a-c 8.00 8.00

Souvenir Sheet
4248 A588 $710 multi 7.00 7.00

2013 Thailand World Stamp Exhibition, Bangkok.

Birth of Prince George of Cambridge — A589

No. 4249: a, Duchess of Cambridge holding Prince George. b, Duke of Cambridge holding Prince George. c, Duke and Duchess of Cambridge, Prince George.
$710, Duchess of Cambridge holding Prince George.

2013, Sept. 10 Litho. *Perf. 14*
4249 A589 $225 Sheet of 4, #4249a, 4249b, 2 #4249c 8.75 8.75

Souvenir Sheet
Perf. 12½
4250 A589 $710 multi 7.00 7.00

No. 4250 contains one 38x51mm stamp.

New Year 2014 (Year of the Horse) — A590

No. 4251 — Various horses with background color of: a, Light blue. b, Yellow. c, Pink. d, Pale orange. e, Lilac. f, Light green.
$710, Horse with yellow background.

2013, Oct. 10 Litho. *Perf. 14*
4251 A590 $200 Sheet of 6, #a-f 12.00 12.00

Souvenir Sheet
Perf. 12
4252 A590 $710 multi 7.00 7.00

Tourist Attractions in Brazil — A591

No. 4253: a, Mask from Le Roi Soleil Carnival. b, Old Colonial building. c, Ipanema Beach. d, Favela buildings. e, Tiled steps, Lapa, Rio de Janeiro. f, Toucan.
$710, Christ the Redeemer Statue, Rio de Janeiro, vert.

2013, Nov. 11 Litho. *Perf. 13¾*
4253 A591 $200 Sheet of 6, #a-f 12.00 12.00

Souvenir Sheet
Perf. 12½
4254 A591 $710 multi 7.00 7.00

Brasiliana 2013 Intl. Stamp Exhibition, Rio de Janeiro. No. 4254 contains one 38x51mm stamp.

Evangelical Lutheran Church in Guyana, 270th Anniv. — A592

Emblem and background color of: $20, Gray. $80, Light brown.

2013, Oct. 6 Litho. *Perf. 14*
4255-4256 A592 Set of 2 1.00 1.00

A593

Women in Aviation — A594

Designs: No. 4257, $20, Cheryl Moore, first female pilot in Guyana Defense Force. No. 4258, $20, Beverley Drake, first Guayanese commercial pilot. No. 4259, $80, Drake and Moore.
No. 4260 — Capt. Debra Gouveia, first female captain for a local airline: a, $80, Holding intercom. b, $80, Smiling. c, $150, Standing in front of airplane. d, $150, Leaning on airplane.

2013, Oct. 9 Litho. *Perf. 13¾*
4257-4259 A593 Set of 3 1.25 1.25
4260 A594 Sheet of 4, #a-d 4.50 4.50

Miniature Sheet

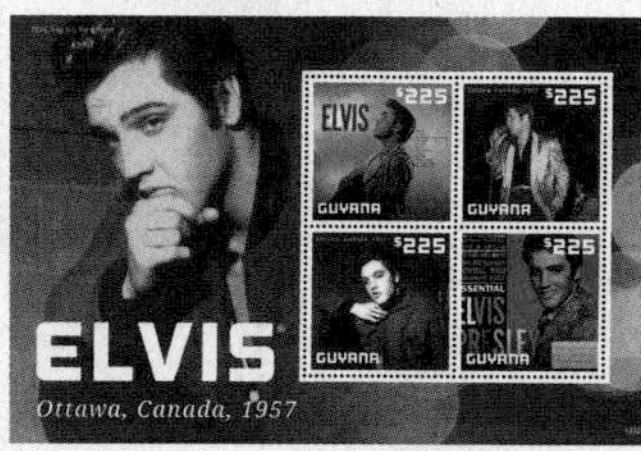

Elvis Presley (1935-77) — A595

No. 4261: a, Album cover with Presley playing guitar. b, Presley holding microphone at Ottawa concert, 1957. c, Presely wearing jacket. d, "Essential Elvis Presley" album cover.

2013, Dec. 2 Litho. *Perf. 13¾*
4261 A595 $225 Sheet of 4, #a-d 8.75 8.75

Christmas A596

Paintings: $20, Madonna, by Fra Angelico. $80, Madonna and Child, by Fra Filippo Lippi. $225, Merode Altarpiece, by Robert Campin. $550, Madonna, by Vitale da Bologna.
$710, Rest During the Flight to Egypt, by Joachim Patinir.

2013, Dec. 2 Litho. *Perf. 12½*
4262-4265 A596 Set of 4 8.50 8.50

Souvenir Sheet
4266 A596 $710 multi 7.00 7.00

Pres. Barack Obama — A597

Designs: No. 4268, $710, Pres. Obama with Israeli Prime Minister Benjamin Netanyahu, Israeli Pres. Shimon Peres and other men at Yad Vashem Holocaust Memorial, Jerusalem, horiz. No. 4269, $710, Pres. Obama on telephone in Oval Office.

2013, Dec. 9 Litho. *Perf. 14*
4267 A597 $225 multi 2.25 2.25

Souvenir Sheets

Perf. 12

4268-4269 A597 Set of 2 14.00 14.00

No. 4267 was printed in sheets of 4. No. 4269 contains one 30x50mm stamp.

A598

A599

Nelson Mandela (1918-2013), President of South Africa — A600

No. 4270 — Mandela: a, In suit and tie. b, Seated next to trophy. c, Seated.

No. 4271 — Mandela: a, In suit and tie, diff. b, With Olympic torch. c, Wearng patterned shirt.

$710, Mandela, diff. $1000, Mandela, diff.

2013, Dec. 15 Litho. *Perf. 13¾*
4270 A598 $200 Vert. strip of 3, #a-c 6.00 6.00
4271 A599 $200 Vert. strip of 3, #a-c 6.00 6.00

Souvenir Sheets

4272 A599 $710 multi 7.00 7.00

Imperf

4273 A600 $1000 multi 9.75 9.75

Nos. 4270 and 4271 each were printed in sheets containing two strips.

Cats — A601

No. 4274 — Cat breeds: a, Chartreaux. b, Bobtail. c, Siamese. d, Abyssinian.

$710, Ocicat.

2013, Dec. 23 Litho. *Perf. 14*
4274 A601 $225 Sheet of 4, #a-d 8.75 8.75

Souvenir Sheet

4275 A601 $710 multi 7.00 7.00

Reptiles — A602

No. 4276: a, Saban anole. b, Whiptail lizard. c, Barbados leaf-toed gecko. d, Anegada ground iguana.

$710, Dominican ground lizard.

2013, Dec. 23 Litho. *Perf. 13¾*
4276 A602 $225 Sheet of 4, #a-d 8.75 8.75

Souvenir Sheet

4277 A602 $710 multi 7.00 7.00

A603

New Year 2014 (Year of the Horse) — A604

2014, Jan. 2 Litho. *Perf. 13¾*
4278 A603 $180 multi 1.75 1.75
4279 A604 $180 multi 1.75 1.75

Nos. 4278 and 4279 were printed together in sheets of 8, containing 4 of each stamp, + a central label.

Miniature Sheets

A605

Mao Zedong (1893-1976), Chinese Communist Leader — A606

No. 4280 — Painting of Mao Zedong: a, Standing near chair. b, Wearing black coat, walking in snow. c, Wearing gray overcoat, holding cigarette. d, Wearign tan overcoat.

No. 4281: a, Mao Zedong with arm raised. b, Mao Zedong and table. c, Mao Zedong and Chinese flag. d, Mao Zedong at lectern with three microphones. e, Mao Zedong behind microphones holding picture of Chinese national emblem. f, Great Wall of China.

2014, Jan. 20 Litho. *Perf. 12*
4280 A605 $50 Sheet of 4, #a-d 2.00 2.00

Perf. 14

4281 A606 $50 Sheet of 6, #a-f 3.00 3.00

Souvenir Sheet

Elvis Presley (1935-77) — A607

2014, Jan. 20 Litho. *Imperf.*
4282 A607 $2000 multi 19.50 19.50

Sports of the Winter Olympics — A608

No. 4283: a, Speed skating. b, Curling. c, Ice dancing. d, Bobsledding. e, Ice hockey. f, Figure skating.

No. 4284, vert.: a, Biathlon. b, Snowboarding. c, Freestyle skiing. c, Alpine skiing.

2014, Feb. 26 Litho. *Perf. 14*
4283 A608 $200 Sheet of 6, #a-f 12.00 12.00

Perf. 12¾

4284 A608 $250 Sheet of 4, #a-d 9.75 9.75

No. 4284 contains four 38x51mm stamps. Inscription on No. 4284d is incorrect as stamp shows slalom skier.

Guinea Pigs — A609

No. 4285, $350: a, American (brown and white fur), denomination in brown. b, Skinny, denomination in green. c, Abyssinian (long brown and black fur, feet not visible), denomination in dark green. d, Teddy, denomination in yellow green.

No. 4286, $350: a, Teddy, denomination in brown. b, American, denomination in green. c, Skinny, denomination in dark green. d, Abyssinian, denomination in yellow green.

No. 4287, $350: a, American (gray animal), denomination in brown. b, Abyssinian (short brown and black fur, feet visible), denomination in green.

No. 4288, $500: a, Silkie. b, Teddy, diff.

2014, Feb. 26 Litho. *Perf. 13¾*

Sheets of 4, #a-d

4285-4286 A609 Set of 2 27.50 27.50

Souvenir Sheets

4287 A609 $350 Sheet of 2, #a-b 7.00 7.00
4288 A609 $500 Sheet of 2, #a-b 9.75 9.75

World War I, Cent. — A610

No. 4289, $350: a, Saint-Chomond tank, France. b, Mark IX tank, United Kingdom. c, Schneider CA1 tank, France. d, Medium Mark C tank, United Kingdom.

No. 4290, $350, vert.: a, Emperor Nicholas II of Russia. b, King Victor Emmanuel III of Italy. c, King Albert I of Belgium. d, U.S. Pres. Woodrow Wilson.

No. 4291: a, Renault FT tank, France. b, A7V tank, Germany.

No. 4292, vert.: a, French Prime Minister Aristide Briand. b, United Kingdom Prime Minister David Lloyd George.

2014, Feb. 26 Litho. *Perf. 14*

Sheets of 4, #a-d

4289-4290 A610 Set of 2 27.50 27.50

Souvenir Sheets

Perf. 12

4291 A610 $700 Sheet of 2, #a-b 13.50 13.50
4292 A610 $700 Sheet of 2, #a-b 13.50 13.50

Pope Francis — A611

No. 4293, $350 — Pope Francis: a, With Italian Prime Minister Enrico Letta. b, In front of black background. c, With hand raised. d, Wearing green vestments.

No. 4294, $350 — Pope Francis: a, At lectern. b, With Croatian President Ivo Josipovic. c, With Panamanian President Ricardo Alberto Martinelli Berrocal. d, Waving to crowd.

No. 4295, $700 — Pope Francis: a, With man in background. b, With arm raised.

No. 4296, $700 — Pope Francis: a, Holding crucifix. c, With Brazilian President Dilma Rousseff.

2014, Feb. 26 Litho. *Perf. 14*

Sheets of 4, #a-d

4293-4294 A611 Set of 2 27.50 27.50

Souvenir Sheets of 2, #a-b

Perf. 12½

4295-4296 A611 Set of 2 27.50 27.50

Nos. 4295 and 4296 each contain two 38x51mm stamps.

Chinese Space Program — A612

No. 4297: a, Shenzhou crew members, stars and satellite in background. b, Shenzhou crew members, Earth and Chinese flag in background. c, Shenzhou 5 mission patch.

No. 4298: a, View of China from space. b, Astronaut Jing Haipeng. c, Astronaut Liu Yang. d, Shenzhou 7 and Chinese flag.

No. 4299, $700, horiz.: a, Shenzhou 7 docking in space. b, Crew of Shenzhou 7 in space.

No. 4300, $700, horiz.: a, Astronaut Liu Wang. b, Earth and sunrise from space.

2014, Feb. 26 Litho. *Perf. 14*

4297 A612 $350 Sheet of 4, #4297a, 4297b, 2 #4297c 13.50 13.50

4298 A612 $350 Sheet of 4, #a-d 13.50 13.50

Souvenir Sheets of 2, #a-b

4299-4300 A612 Set of 2 27.50 27.50

Nos. 4299 and 4300 each contain two 51x38mm stamps.

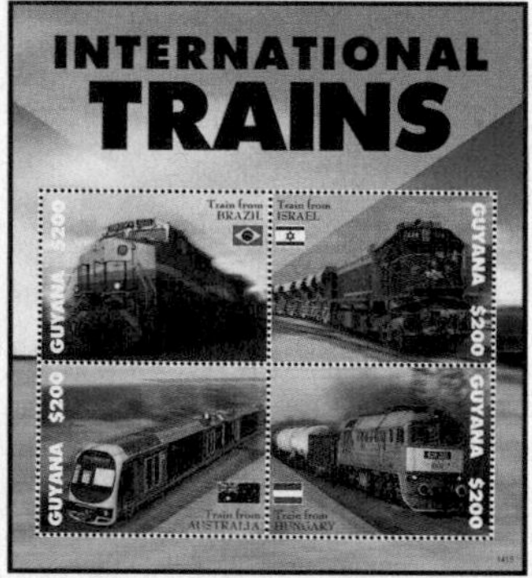

Trains and Flags — A613

No. 4301 — Train and flag from: a, Brazil. b, Israel. c, Australia. d, Hungary.

$710, Train and flag from Mexico.

2014, Mar. 5 Litho. *Perf. 12½*

4301 A613 $200 Sheet of 4, #a-d 7.75 7.75

Souvenir Sheet

4302 A613 $710 multi 7.00 7.00

Pink Flamingos — A614

No. 4303: a, Flamingo, no legs visible. b, Flamingo preening. c, Flamingo from front. d, Flamingo facing right.

No. 4304: a, Head of flamingo facing right. b, Head of flamingo facing left.

Perf. 13 Syncopated

2014, Mar. 10 Litho.

4303 A614 $200 Sheet of 4, #a-d 7.75 7.75

Souvenir Sheet

4304 A614 $400 Sheet of 2, #a-b 7.75 7.75

No. 4304 contains two 30x40mm stamps.

Characters From *Downton Abbey* Television Series — A615

No. 4305: a, Lady Edith Crawley. b, Tom Branson. c, Lady Rose MacClare. d, Lavinia Swire.

$800, Matthew Crawley and Lady Mary Crawley, horiz.

2014, Mar. 19 Litho. *Perf. 14*

4305 A615 $225 Sheet of 4, #a-d 8.75 8.75

Souvenir Sheet

4306 A615 $800 multi 7.75 7.75

Paintings by Henri de Toulouse-Lautrec (1864-1901) — A616

No. 4307, $200: a, Ambassadeurs — Aristide Bruant. b, Divan Japonais. c, Jane Avril. d, La Revue Blanche.

No. 4308, $200, horiz.: a, The Spanish Dancer. b, Vincent van Gogh. c, The Grand Tier. d, The Laundress.

No. 4309, $400: a, Moulin Rouge: La Goulue poster. b, The German Babylon.

No. 4310, $400: a, Moulin Rouge: La Goulue painting. b, Ball at the Moulin de la Galette.

2014, Mar. 24 Litho. *Perf. 12*

Sheets of 4 #a-d

4307-4308 A616 Set of 2 15.50 15.50

Souvenir Sheets of 2, #a-b

4309-4310 A616 Set of 2 15.50 15.50

Paintings — A617

No. 4311, $200: a, Mother and Child, by Gustav Klimt. b, Flowerpot with Chives, by Vincent van Gogh. c, Portrait of Bindo Altoviti, by Raphael.

No. 4312, $200: a, Dancer in Her Dressing Room, by Edgar Degas. b, The Garden of Earthly Delights, by Hieronymus Bosch. c, The Complain of the Watch, by Jean-Baptiste Greuze.

No. 4313, $800, The Music Lesson, by Johannes Vermeer. No. 4314, $800, Portrait of a Young Man, by Vincenzo Catena.

2014, Mar. 24 Litho. *Perf. 12½*

Sheets of 3, #a-c

4311-4312 A617 Set of 2 12.00 12.00

Size: 100x100mm

Imperf

4313-4314 A617 Set of 2 15.50 15.50

Worldwide Fund for Nature (WWF) — A618

Nos. 4315 and 4316 — Guiana spider monkey: a, Sitting on branch. b, With young. c, Climbing tree. d, Eating.

2014, Apr. 2 Litho. *Perf. 14*

4315 A618 $180 Block or vert. strip of 4, #a-d 7.00 7.00

4316 A618 $200 Block or vert. strip of 4, #a-d 7.75 7.75

Panama Canal, Cent. — A619

No. 4317: a, Construction, 1907. b, Gatun Lake. c, Construction, 1913. d, Map of Panama Canal.

No. 4318, horiz.: a, SS Ancon in Panama Canal, 1914. b, Centennial Bridge.

2014, May 12 Litho. *Perf. 12*

4317 A619 $200 Sheet of 4, #a-d 7.75 7.75

Souvenir Sheet

4318 A619 $400 Sheet of 2, #a-b 7.75 7.75

A620

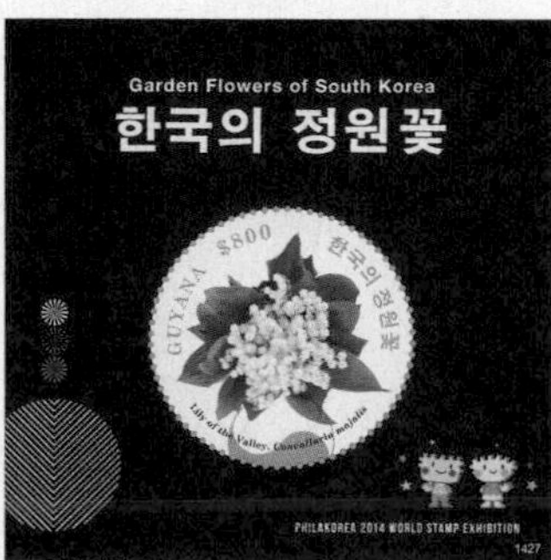

Korean Flowers — A621

No. 4319: a, Rhododendron. b, Tawny daylily. c, Hydrangea. d, Camellia. e, Magnolia. f, Daylily hybrid.

$800, Lily of the valley.

2014, May 12 Litho. *Perf. 13¾*

4319 A620 $200 Sheet of 6, #a-f 12.00 12.00

Souvenir Sheet

4320 A621 $800 multi 7.75 7.75

Philakorea 2014 World Stamp Exhibition, Seoul.

Wildlife A622

Designs: No. 4321, South American tapir. No. 4322, Squirrel monkey. No. 4323, Two-toed sloth. No. 4324, Giant anteater. No. 4325, Giant otter. No. 4326, Jaguar. No. 4327, Black caiman. No. 4328, Leatherback turtle. No. 4329, Red-billed toucan. No. 4330, Yellow-crowned Amazon. No. 4331, Purple honeycreeper. No. 4332, Scarlet macaw. No. 4333, Guianan cock-of-the-rock. No. 4334, Scarlet ibis. No. 4335, Black curassow. No. 4336, Harpy eagle. $130, Purple honeycreeper. $150, Red-billed toucan. $160, Scarlet ibis. $200, Black curassow.

2014, July 1 Litho. *Perf. 13¾*

4321 A622 $80 multi .80 .80
4322 A622 $80 multi .80 .80
4323 A622 $80 multi .80 .80
4324 A622 $80 multi .80 .80
4325 A622 $80 multi .80 .80
4326 A622 $80 multi .80 .80
4327 A622 $80 multi .80 .80
4328 A622 $80 multi .80 .80
4329 A622 $80 multi .80 .80
4330 A622 $80 multi .80 .80
4331 A622 $80 multi .80 .80
4332 A622 $80 multi .80 .80
4333 A622 $80 multi .80 .80
4334 A622 $80 multi .80 .80
4335 A622 $80 multi .80 .80
4336 A622 $80 multi .80 .80
4337 A622 $130 multi 1.25 1.25
4338 A622 $150 multi 1.50 1.50
4339 A622 $160 multi 1.60 1.60
4340 A622 $200 multi 2.00 2.00
Nos. 4321-4340 (20) 19.15 19.15

A623

A624

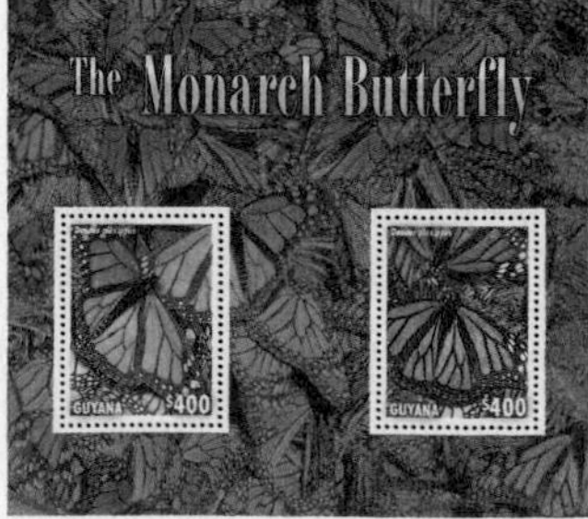

Monarch Butterflies — A625

No. 4341, $200 — Monarch butterfly with: a, Green foliage. b, Yellow flowers. c, Red flowers. d, Purple flower.

No. 4342, $200, vert.: a, Monarch butterfly caterpillar. b, Monarch butterfly chrysalis. c,

Monarch butterfly exiting chrysalis. d, Monarch butterfly on purple flower.

No. 4343 — Monarch butterfly on: a, White and purple flower. b, Orange red flower.

No. 4344: a, Monarch butterflies. b, Monarch butterflies, diff.

Perf. 12½x12, 12x12½

2014, July 1 Litho.

Sheets of 4, #a-d

4341-4342 A623 Set of 2 15.50 15.50

Souvenir Sheets

4343 A624 $400 Sheet of 2, #a-b 7.75 7.75

4344 A625 $400 Sheet of 2, #a-b 7.75 7.75

South American Animals — A626

No. 4345: a, Powis (black curassow). b, Gray-winged trumpeter. c, Poison arrow frog. d, Anole.

No. 4346, $750, Yellow-crowned Amazon. No. 4347, $750, Toco toucan.

2014, July 1 Litho. *Perf. 14*

4345 A626 $300 Sheet of 4, #a-d 12.00 12.00

Souvenir Sheets

Perf. 12½

4346-4347 A626 Set of 2 14.50 14.50

Nos. 4346 and 4347 each contain one 38x51mm stamp.

Souvenir Sheet

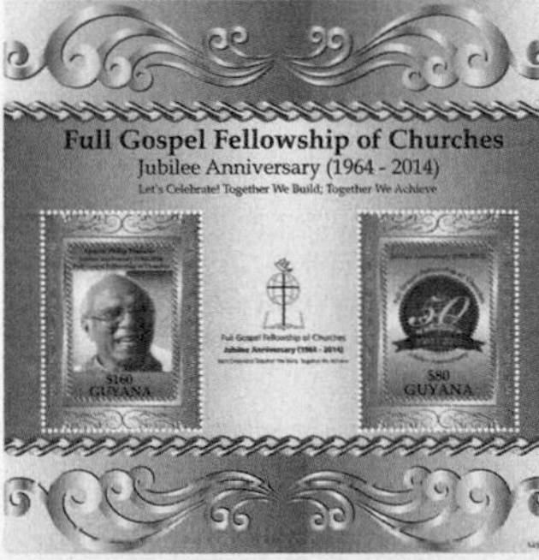

Full Gospel Fellowship of Churches, 50th Anniv. — A627

No. 4348: a, $80, 50th anniversary emblem. b, $160, Apostle Philip Mohabir.

2014, July 6 Litho. *Perf. 13¼*

4348 A627 Sheet of 2, #a-b 2.40 2.40

British Guiana No. 13, Map of Guyana — A628

British Guiana No. 13 — A630

British Guiana No. 13, Map of South America — A631

2014, Aug. 27 Litho. *Perf. 14*

4349 A628 $80 multi .80 .80

Souvenir Sheets

Perf. 13½x12½

4351 A630 $800 multi 7.75 7.75

Perf. 13¼

4352 A631 $800 multi 7.75 7.75

No. 4349 was printed in sheets of 12.

Miniature Sheet

British Guiana No. 13, World Map — A629

No. 4350 — Map depicting: a, North and Central America. b, Atlantic Ocean. c, Africa and Europe. d, Asia.

Perf. 13¼x12½

2014, Aug. 27 Litho.

4350 A629 $200 Sheet of 4, #a-d 7.75 7.75

Miniature Sheet

2014 World Cup Soccer Championships, Brazil — A632

No. 4353, $80 — Team from: a, Chile. b, Greece. c, Japan. d, Argentina. e, Belgium. f, Bosnia & Herzegovina. g, Brazil. h, Ivory Coast.

No. 4354, $80 — Team from: a, Costa Rica. b, Croatia. c, England. d, Algeria. e, Colombia. f, France. g, Germany. h, Ghana.

No. 4355, $80 — Team from: a, Honduras. b, Iran. c, Netherlands. d, Mexico. e, Nigeria. f, Cameroun. g, Portugal. h, South Korea.

No. 4356, $80 — Team from: a, Ecuador. b, Italy. c, Switzerland. d, Uruguay. e, Russia. f, United States. g, Australia. h, Spain.

2014, Sept. 4 Litho. *Perf. 12½*

Sheets of 8, #a-h, + Label

4353-4356 A632 Set of 4 25.00 25.00

Mei Lanfang (1894-1961), Chinese Opera Performer — A633

No. 4357 — Paintings of: a, Birds and flowers. b, Tree branch with buds and flowers. c, Mei Lanfang in costume. d, Pink flowers in vase. c, Fish and tree. d, Blue leaves and white flowers on branch in vase.

$800, Mei Lanfang in costume, diff.

2014, Sept. 4 Litho. *Perf. 12*

4357 A633 $200 Sheet of 6, #a-f 12.00 12.00

Souvenir Sheet

Perf. 12½

4358 A633 $800 multi 8.00 8.00

No. 4358 contains one 38x51mm stamp.

Chinese Art — A634

No. 4359 — Paintings by Zhang Daqian (1899-1983): a, Untitled abstract painting (60x40mm). b, Flower (Chinese text at UL, 30x40mm). c, Flower (Chinese text at UR, 30x40mm). d, Bird's Eye View of Mount Hehuan, diff. (60x40mm).

No. 4360, vert.: a, Wine container, Eastern Zhou Dynasty. b, Bottle with Immortal Zhongli Quan, Ming Dynasty. c, Stele with Buddha Dipankara, Northern Wei Dyansty. d, Buddha Vairocana, Tang Dynasty. e, Mirror back, Tang Dynasty. f, Tray, Yuan Dynasty.

No. 4361, $800, Painting of mountains by Wang Ximeng. No. 4262, $800, Painting of horse, by Xu Beihong, vert.

2014, Sept. 15 Litho. *Perf. 14*

4359 A634 $200 Sheet of 4, #a-d 8.00 8.00

4360 A634 $200 Sheet of 6, #a-f 12.00 12.00

Souvenir Sheets

Perf. 12

4361-4362 A634 Set of 2 16.00 16.00

Painting on No. 4359d is reversed and upside-down.

Miniature Sheet

University of Guyana, 50th Anniv. — A635

No. 4363: a, $80, Graduates facing left. b, $80, Two female graduates. c, $150, University building and pond. d, $150, University gate.

2014, Oct. 3 Litho. *Perf. 14*

4363 A635 Sheet of 4, #a-d 4.50 4.50

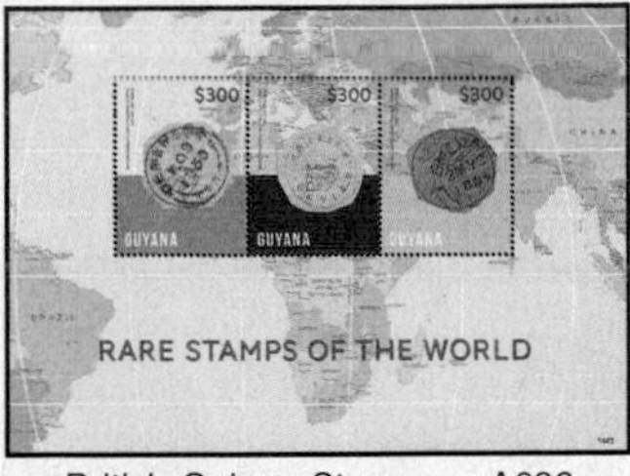

British Guiana Stamps — A636

No. 4364: a, British Guiana #2, map of Iberian Peninsula. b, British Guiana #4, map of Mediterranean Sea. c, British Guiana #5, map of Central Asia.

$800, British Guiana #1, map of Eastern Europe.

2014, Nov. 3 Litho. *Perf. 14*

4364 A636 $300 Sheet of 3, #a-c 8.75 8.75

Souvenir Sheet

Perf. 12

4365 A636 $800 multi 7.75 7.75

Fireflies — A637

No. 4366: a, Firefly facing right, denomination in black. b, Firefly facing left, denomination in black. c, Firefly facing left, denomination in white. d, Firefly facing right, denomination in white.

$800, Firefly, vert.

2014, Nov. 3 Litho. *Perf. 13¾*

4366 A637 $250 Sheet of 4, #a-d 9.75 9.75

Souvenir Sheet

Perf. 12½

4367 A637 $800 multi 7.75 7.75

No. 4367 contains one 38x51mm stamp.

Christmas A638

Paintings by Peter Paul Rubens: $160, The Circumcision of Christ. $200, The Ildefonso Altarpiece. $300, The Resurrection of Christ. $400, Madonna in a Garland of Flowers.

2014, Nov. 24 Litho. *Perf. 12½*

4368-4371 A638 Set of 4 10.50 10.50

Painting on No. 4371 is misidentified on stamp.

Souvenir Sheet

Guyana Defence Force, 50th Anniv. — A639

No. 4372 — Emblem and: a, $80, Helicopter. b, $80, Soldiers. c, $150, Headquarters.

2014, Nov. 11 Litho. *Perf. 12*
4372 A639 Sheet of 3, #a-c 3.00 3.00

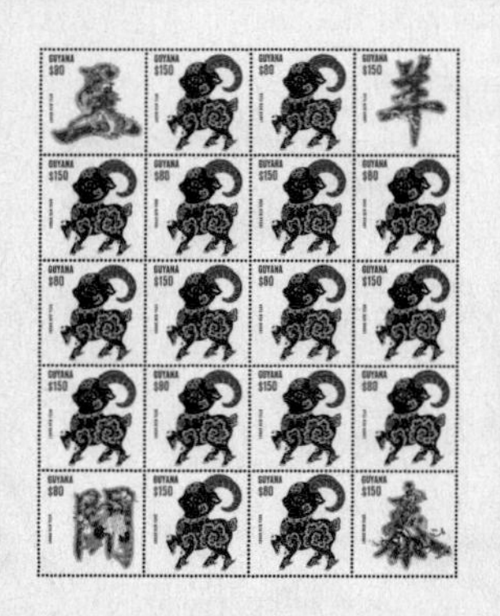

A640

A641

New Year 2015 (Year of the Ram) — A642

No. 4373: a, $80, Chinese character, butterfly, flowers, fish. b, $80, Chinese character, cranes, peaches, flowers. c, $80, Ram. d, $150, Chinese character, crane and flowers. e, Chinese character, birds on branch, flowers. f, $150, Ram.

No. 4374: a, Black ram standing. b, Red ram looking left. c, Black ram leaping. d, Red ram looking right.

No. 4375: a, Three rams. b, Man on ram facing right.

2014, Nov. 24 Litho. *Perf. 13¾*
4373 A640 Sheet of 20, #4373a, 4373b, 4373d, 4373e, 8 each #4373c, 4373f 22.50 22.50
4374 A641 $200 Sheet of 4, #a-d 7.75 7.75

Souvenir Sheet
Perf. 12
4375 A642 $400 Sheet of 2, #a-b 7.75 7.75

Miniature Sheet

Women in Aviation — A643

No. 4376 — Map and: a, $80, Jet and Paula McAdam. b, $80, Airplane and Sandra Persaud. c, $150, McAdam, Persaud, and propeller. d, $150, Persaud, McAdam and airport control tower.

2014, Dec. 7 Litho. *Perf. 12x12½*
4376 A643 Sheet of 4, #a-d 4.50 4.50

Prince George of Cambridge, 1st Birthday — A644

No. 4377, $250 — Denomination at UL: a, Duke and Duchess of Cambridge, Prince George. b, Duke of Cambridge holding Prince George, Prince George looking right. c, Duke of Cambridge holding Prince George, Prince George looking left. d, Prince George

No. 4378, $250 — Denomination at UR: a, Duchess of Cambridge holding Prince George. b, Duke and Duchess of Cambridge, Prince George, diff. c, Duke of Cambridge holding Prince George. d, Prince George, diff.

No. 4379, $800, Prince George, diff. No. 4380, $800, Duke and Duchess of Cambridge, Prince George, horiz.

Perf. 12x12½, 12½x12 (#4380)
2014, Dec. 16 Litho.
Sheets of 4, #a-d
4377-4378 A644 Set of 2 19.50 19.50

Souvenir Sheets
4379-4380 A644 Set of 2 15.50 15.50

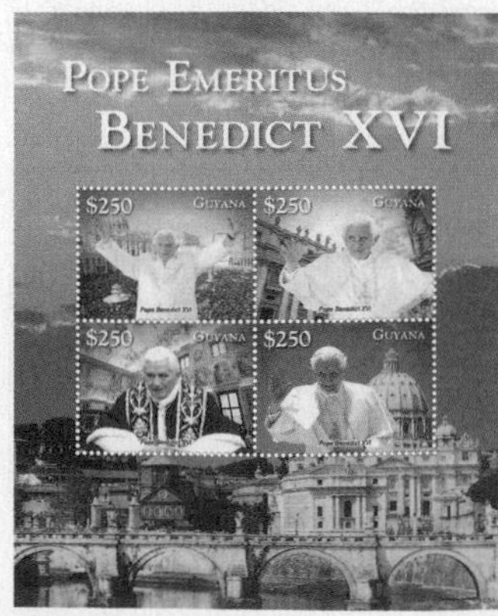

Pope Emeritus Benedict XVI — A645

No. 4381 — Pope Benedict XVI: a, With both arms waving, crowd in background. b, Waving, building and statue in background. c, Wearing red vestments. d, Waving, dome of St. Peter's Basilica in background.

$800, Pope Benedict XVI, vert.

2014, Dec. 31 Litho. *Perf. 12½x12*
4381 A645 $250 Sheet of 4, #a-d 9.75 9.75

Souvenir Sheet
Perf. 12x12½
4382 A645 $800 multi 7.75 7.75

Seagulls — A646

No. 4383, $300: a, Black-headed gull (70x35mm). b, California gull (35x35mm). c, Heermann's gull (35x35mm).

No. 4384, $300: a, Franklin's gull (35x70mm). b, Black-legged kittiwake (35x35mm). c, Glaucous-winged gull (35x35mm).

No. 4385, $800, Western gull, horiz. No. 4386, $800, Laughing gull, vert.

2015, Jan. 5 Litho. *Perf. 13¾*
Sheets of 3, #a-c
4383-4384 A646 Set of 2 17.50 17.50

Souvenir Sheets
Perf. 12
4385-4386 A646 Set of 2 15.50 15.50

No. 4385 contains one 50x30mm stamp. No. 4386 contains one 30x50mm stamp.

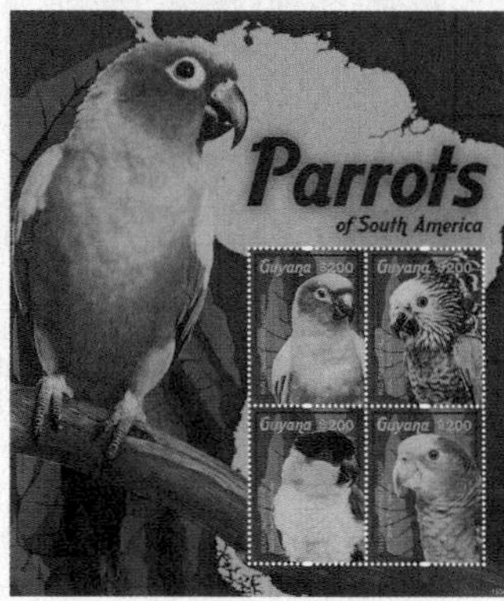

Parrots — A647

No. 4387, $200: a, Sun conure. b, Red-tailed Amazon. c, Black-headed caique. d, Yellow-crowned Amazon.

No. 4388, $200: a, Scarlet macaw. b, Lilacine Amazon. c, Jandaya parakeet. d, Blue-headed pionus.

No. 4389, $800, Blue-crowned parakeet. No. 4390, $800, Brown-hooded parrot, horiz.

Perf. 13 Syncopated
2015, Jan. 5 Litho.
Sheets of 4, #a-d
4387-4388 A647 Set of 2 15.50 15.50

Souvenir Sheets
4389-4390 A647 Set of 2 15.50 15.50

Personalizable Stamp — A647a

2015, Feb. 16 Litho. *Perf. 13¼*
4390A A647a $80 multi — —

No. 4390A could be personalized. The stamp shown has a handstamped personalization.

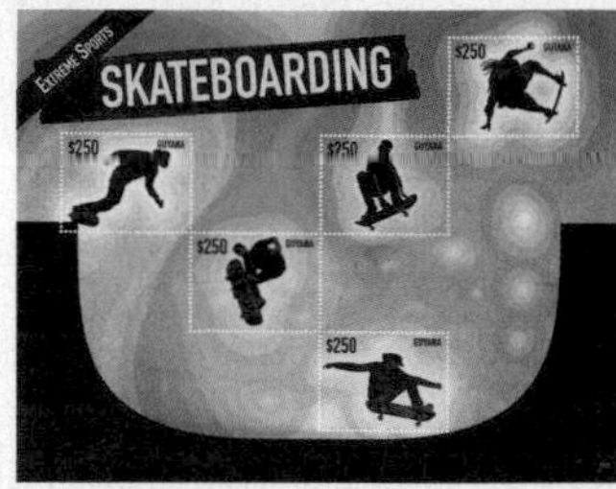

Skateboarding — A648

No. 4391 — Skateboarder: a, In air with hand near country name. b, On lip of vert ramp. c, In air touching skateboard. d, In air with hand on hip. e, In air with arms extended to sides.

$800, Skateboarder in air with right arm extended up next to denomination.

2015, Mar. 2 Litho. *Perf. 14*
4391 A648 $250 Sheet of 5, #a-e 12.50 12.50

Souvenir Sheet
Perf. 12
4392 A648 $800 multi 7.75 7.75

International Year of Light — A649

2015, Mar. 24 Litho. *Perf. 13¼*
4393 A649 $250 multi 2.40 2.40

Souvenir Sheet
4394 A649 $800 Earth, Sun at side 7.75 7.75

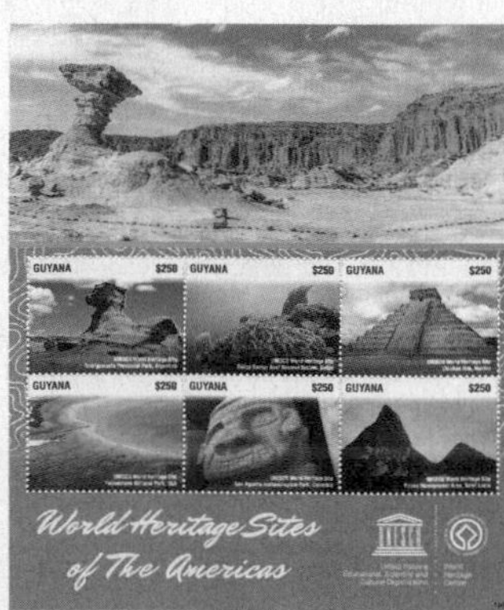

UNESCO World Heritage Sites in the Americas — A650

No. 4395: a, Ischigualasto Provincial Park, Argentina. b, Belize Barrier Reef Reserve System, Belize. c, Chichen Itza, Mexico. d, Yellowstone National Park, United States. e, San Agustín Archaeological Park, Colombia. f, Pitons Management Area, St. Lucia.

$800, Machu Picchu, Peru.

Perf. 12½x13¼

2015, Mar. 24 Litho.

4395 A650 $250 Sheet of 6, #a-f 14.50 14.50

Souvenir Sheet

4396 A650 $800 multi 7.75 7.75

Duke of Cambridge in People's Republic of China — A651

No. 4397: a, Duke of Cambridge seated. b, Chinese President Xi Jinping seated.

No. 4398, $800, Duke of Cambridge with Zhang Yaoguang in Forbidden City. No. 4399, $800, Duke of Cambridge with staff members of British Embassy in China. No. 4400, $800, Duke of Cambridge shaking hands with Pres. Xi Jinping, horiz.

2015, May 4 Litho. *Perf. 12*

4397 A651 $450 Sheet of 2, #a-b 8.75 8.75

Souvenir Sheets

4398-4400 A651 Set of 3 23.00 23.00

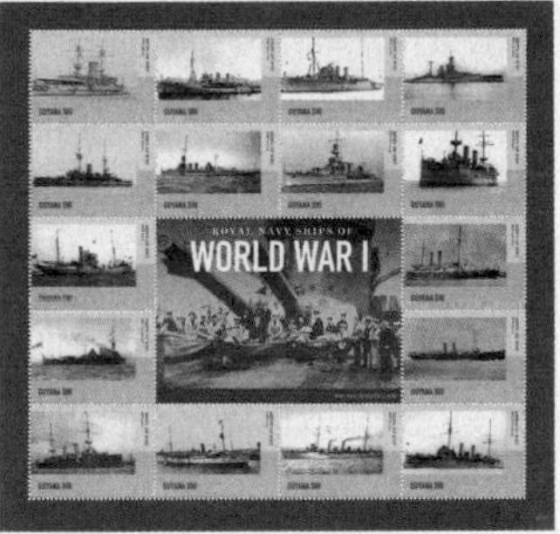

Royal Navy Ships of World War I — A652

No. 4401, $80: a, HMS Albion. b, HMS Anemone. c, HMS Azalea. d, HMS Barham. e, HMS Caesar. f, HMS Carlisle. g, HMS Coventry. h, HMS Eclipse. i, HMS Foyle. j, HMS Gibraltar. k, HMS Inconstant. l, HMS India. m, HMS Juno. n, HMS Odin. o, HMS Pelorus. p, HMS Proserpine.

No. 4402, $80: a, HMAS Sydney. b, HMS Achilles. c, HMS Africa. d, HMS Albemarle. e, HMS Bee. f, SS Empress. g, HMS Cumberland. h, HMS Bramble. i, HMS Argonaut. j, HMS Delhi. k, HMS Attentive. l, SS Ambrose. m, SS Lepanto. n, SS Knight Templar. o, HMS Suffolk. p, HMS Canopus.

2015, May 4 Litho. *Perf. 14*

Sheets of 16, #a-p, + Label

4401-4402 A652 Set of 2 25.00 25.00

Sir Winston Churchill (1874-1965) — A653

No. 4403 — Churchill: a, Standing near fence. b, With military officer. c, In automobile. d, At lectern.

$800, Churchill in automobile hoisting his hat in air on walking stick.

2015, June 20 Litho. *Perf. 14*

4403 A653 $250 Sheet of 4, #a-d 9.75 9.75

Souvenir Sheet

Perf. 12

4404 A653 $800 multi 7.75 7.75

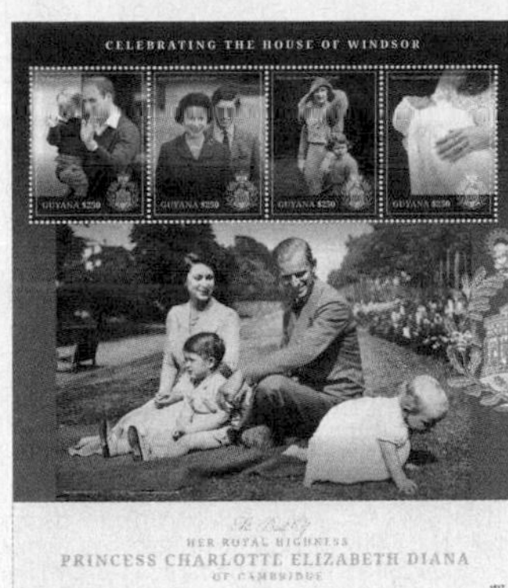

Birth of Princess Charlotte of Cambridge — A654

No. 4405: a, Duke of Cambridge holding Prince George. b, Queen Elizabeth II and Prince Charles. c, Queen Mother with Princess Elizabeth. d, Duchess of Cambridge holding Princess Charlotte.

$800, Duchess of Cambridge holding Princess Charlotte, diff.

2015, July 13 Litho. *Perf. 14*

4405 A654 $250 Sheet of 4, #a-d 9.75 9.75

Souvenir Sheet

Perf. 12

4406 A654 $800 multi 7.75 7.75

Miniature Sheets

Stamps of United Nations Countries — A655

No. 4407, $250: a, Burma (Myanmar) #1. b, Namibia #659. c, Nauru #1. d, Nepal #51. e, Netherlands #1. f, New Zealand #1.

No. 4408, $250: a, Nicaragua #1. b, Niger #1. c, Nigeria #1. d, Norway #1. e, Oman #1. f, Pakistan #1.

No. 4409, $250: a, Palau #1. b, Panama #1. c, Papua New Guinea #11. d, Paraguay #1. e, Peru #3. f, Philippines #6.

No. 4410, $250: a, Poland #1. b, Portugal #1. c, Qatar #1. d, Romania #22. e, Russia #1. f, Rwanda #1.

No. 4411, $250: a, Samoa #1a. b, San Marino #1. c, St. Thomas and Prince Islands (Sao Tome and Principe) #1. d, Saudi Arabia #138. e, Senegal #1. f, Serbia #1.

No. 4412, $250: a, Seychelles #1. b, Sierra Leone #1. c, Singapore #1. d, Slovakia #1. e, Slovenia #100. f, Solomon Islands #1.

No. 4413, $250: a, Somalia #1. b, South Africa #1. c, South Sudan #1. d, Spain #1. e, Ceylon (Sri Lanka) #1. f, St. Lucia #1.

No. 4414, $250: a, St. Vincent Grenadines #1. b, St. Kitts-Nevis # 1. c, Sudan #6. d, Suriname #3. e, Swaziland #1. f, Sweden #1.

2015, July 13 Litho. *Perf. 12½*

Sheets of 6, #a-f

4407-4414 A655 Set of 8 120.00 120.00

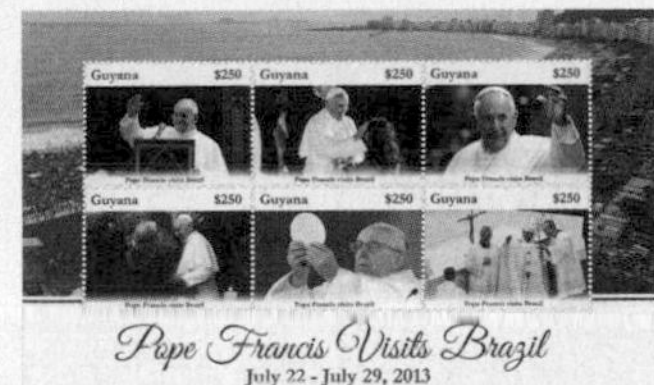

Visit of Pope Francis to Brazil — A656

No. 4415 — Pope Francis: a, At lectern, waving. b, Blessing girl. c, Waving. d, With priests. e, Holding eucharist. f, Holding cross.

$800, Pope Francis holding statue of Madonna of Aparecida, vert.

2015, Sept. 2 Litho. *Perf. 14*

4415 A656 $250 Sheet of 6, #a-f 15.00 15.00

Souvenir Sheet

Perf. 12

4416 A656 $800 multi 8.00 8.00

No. 4416 contains one 30x50mm stamp.

Miniature Sheet

Hand-in-Hand Insurance Company, 150th Anniv. — A657

No. 4417 — Building and: a, $80, Three people in street near lamp post, sepia-toned. b, $80, People lined up on sidewalk. c, $150, Other buildings, mauve & maroon photograph. d, Building in background, color photograph.

2015, Oct. 1 Litho. *Perf. 12½x12*

4417 A657 Sheet of 4, #a-d 4.50 4.50

Bank of Guyana, 50th Anniv. A658

Obverse and reverse of 2015 $5000 coin with background colors of: $80, Blue. $150, Green.

2015, Oct. 15 Litho. *Perf. 14*

4418-4419 A658 Set of 2 2.25 2.25

Christmas A659

Paintings by Fra Filippo Lippi: No. 4420, $80, Adoration of the Magi. No. 4421, $80, Madonna Enthroned with Saints. No. 4422, $150, Annunciation with Two Kneeling Donors. No. 4423, $150, Madonna with the Child and Two Angels.

2015, Nov. 2 Litho. *Perf. 12¾*

4420-4423 A659 Set of 4 4.50 4.50

Pope Benedict XVI — A660

No. 4424 — Pope Benedict XVI and candle with panel color of: a, $80, White. b, $140, Orange. c, $150, Dark blue.

$800, Pope Benedict with arms extended.

2015, Nov. 20 Litho. *Perf. 14*

4424 A660 Horiz. strip of 3, #a-c 3.75 3.75

Souvenir Sheet

Perf. 12

4425 A660 $800 multi 7.75 7.75

No. 4424 was printed in sheets containing two strips.

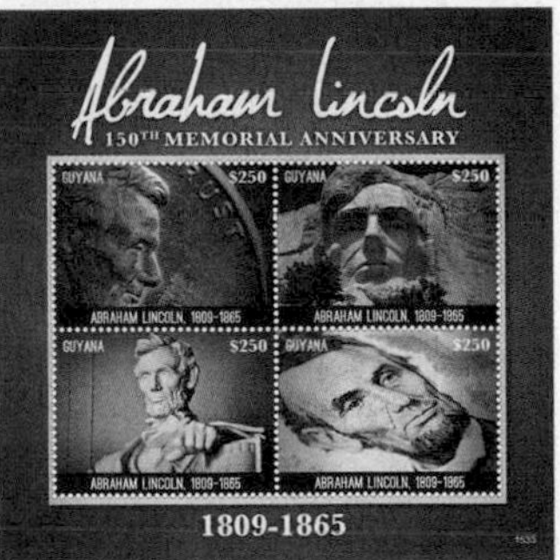

Pres. Abraham Lincoln (1809-65) — A661

No. 4426 — Lincoln as seen on: a, U.S. one-cent piece. b, Mount Rushmore. c, Lincoln Memorial statue. d, U.S. five-dollar bill.

$800, Lincoln Memorial statue.

2015, Dec. 21 Litho. *Perf. 14*

4426 A661 $250 Sheet of 4, #a-d 9.75 9.75

Souvenir Sheet

Perf. 12½

4427 A661 $800 multi 7.75 7.75

No. 4427 contains one 51x38mm stamp.

Visit of Pope Francis to New York City — A662

No. 4428 — Pope Francis: a, Looking to left, flags and sky in background. b, Waving, United Nations in background. c, As "a," waving. d, As "b," not waving. e, As "a," facing right. f, As "b," waving, mouth open.

$800, Pope Francis and flags, diff.

2015, Dec. 21 Litho. *Perf. 14*

4428 A662 $250 Sheet of 6, #a-f 14.50 14.50

Souvenir Sheet

Perf. 12

4429 A662 $800 multi 7.75 7.75

A663

A664

New Year 2016 (Year of the Monkey) — A665

No. 4430 — Background color: a, Beige. b, White.
No. 4431: a, Two monkeys. b, Monkey with fruit.
No. 4432: a, Like #4431a. b, Like #4431b.

2015, Dec. 21 Litho. *Perf. 13¾*

4430 A663 $80 Horiz. pair, #a-b 1.60 1.60
4431 A664 $100 Vert. pair, #a-b 2.00 2.00

Souvenir Sheet

4432 A665 $200 Sheet of 2, #a-b 4.00 4.00

Fruit Trees — A666

No. 4433: a, Acerolas. b, Cacao. c, Pomelos. d, Pomegranates.
No. 4434: a, Camu camus. b, Starfruit. c, Genipapos. d, Green lemons. e, Papayas. f, Common guavas.
$800, Bananas.

2015, Dec. 30 Litho. *Perf. 12*

4433 A666 $250 Sheet of 4, #a-d 9.75 9.75
4434 A666 $250 Sheet of 6, #a-f 14.50 14.50

Souvenir Sheet

Perf. 12½

4435 A666 $800 multi 7.75 7.75

No. 4435 contains one 38x51mm stamp.

Independence, 50th Anniv. (in 2016) — A667

Jaguar and "50" with denomination color of: $80, Bister. $130, Red brown. $150, Black. $200, Bister.

2015, Dec. 31 Litho. *Perf. 14*

4436-4439 A667 Set of 4 5.50 5.50

Queen Elizabeth II, Longest-Reigning British Monarch — A668

No. 4440 — Queen Elizabeth II wearing: a, Diamond diadem, panel at right. b, Diamond diadem, panel at left. c, Imperial state crown, panel at right. d, Imperial state crown, panel at left.
$800, Queen Elizabeth II in carriage.

2015, Dec. 31 Litho. *Perf. 14*

4440 A668 $250 Sheet of 4, #a-d 9.75 9.75

Souvenir Sheet

Perf. 12

4441 A668 $800 multi 7.75 7.75

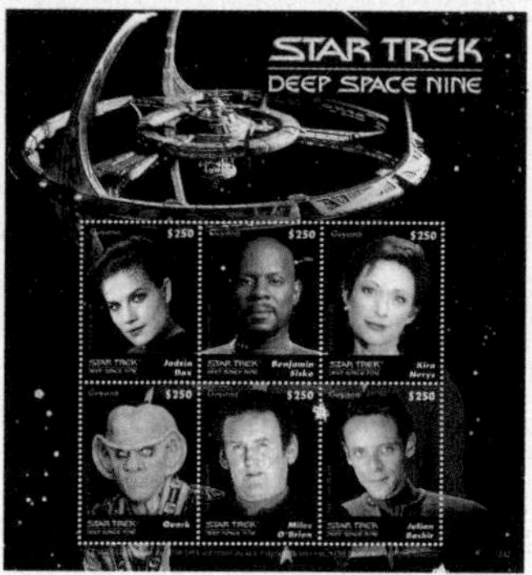

Characters From *Star Trek: Deep Space Nine* Television Series — A669

No. 4442: a, Jadzia Dax. b, Benjamin Sisko. c, Kira Nerys. d, Quark. e, Miles O'Brien. f, Julian Bashir.
$800, Dax and Sisko, horiz.

2015, Dec. 31 Litho. *Perf. 14*

4442 A669 $250 Sheet of 6, #a-f 14.50 14.50

Souvenir Sheet

4443 A669 $800 multi 7.75 7.75

No. 4443 contains one 80x30mm stamp.

Souvenir Sheets

Elvis Presley (1935-77) — A670

Designs: No. 4444, $800, Unique dance style. No. 4445, $800, A long train ride home. No. 4446, $800, Presley performing at Cynthia Milk Benefit Concert. No. 4447, $800, Family moves to Memphis, horiz. No. 4448, $1000, Presley reports to local draft board, horiz. No. 4449, $1000, Marquee on Memphian Theater, rented by Presley. No. 4450, $1000, Presley displaying honorary sherrif's badge. No. 4451, $1000, Presley meets Tom Jones in Las Vegas.

Perf. 12, 14 (#4446), 13x13¼ (#4448), 13¼x13 (#4449-4451)

2016 Litho.

4444-4451 A670 Set of 8 70.00 70.00

Issued: Nos. 4444-4447, 1/31; Nos. 4448-4451, 6/30.

Capybaras — A671

No. 4452: a, Bird on capybara. b, Capybara on grass, facing right. c, Capybara in water, facing right. d, Capybara in water, facing forward. e, Capybara in tall grass, facing left. f, Capybara standing on hillside.
$800, Five capybaras.

2016, Feb. 20 Litho. *Perf. 14*

4452 A671 $250 Sheet of 6, #a-f 14.50 14.50

Souvenir Sheet

Perf. 12

4453 A671 $800 multi 7.75 7.75

Miniature Sheets

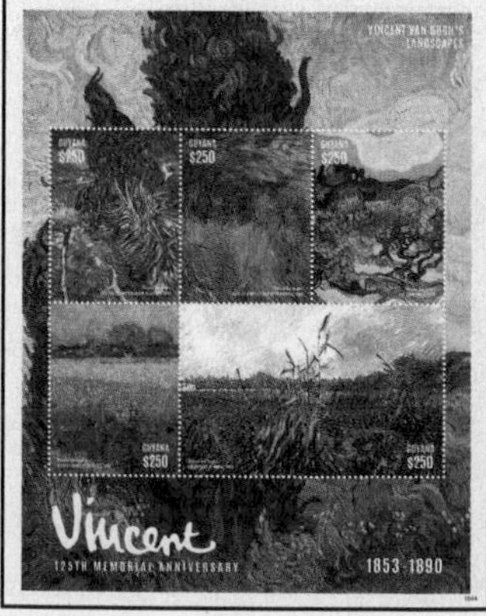

Paintings by Vincent van Gogh (1853-90) — A672

No. 4454, $250 — Landscapes: a, Doctor Gachet's Garden in Auvers, 1890 (38x51mm). b, Edge of a Wheatfield with Poppies, 1887 (38x51mm). c, The Olive Trees, 1889 (38x51mm). d, View of Arles with Irises, 1888 (38x51mm). e, Green Ears of Wheat, 1888 (76x51mm).
No. 4455, $250 — Self-portraits from: a, 1888 (38x51mm). b, 1889 (38x51mm). c, 1888 (with hat and pipe) (38x51mm). d, 1888 (with hat) (38x51mm). e, 1887 (76x51mm).

2016, Feb. 20 Litho. *Perf. 12½*

Sheets of 5, #a-e

4454-4455 A672 Set of 2 24.00 24.00

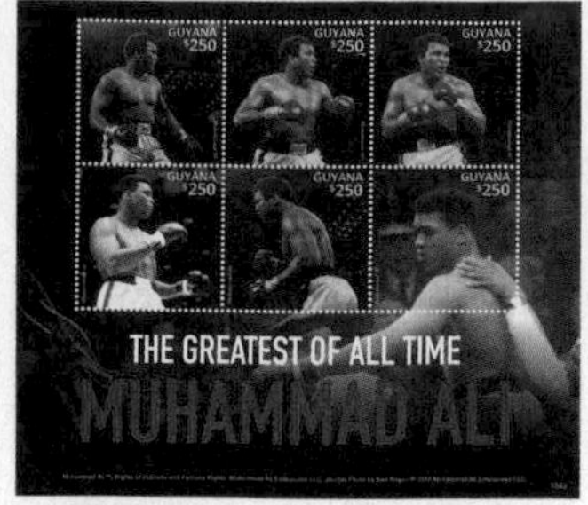

Muhammad Ali (1942-2016), Boxer — A673

No. 4456 — Various photographs of Ali in boxing ring, as shown.
$800, Ali throwing punch, horiz.

2016, Feb. 20 Litho. *Perf. 13¾*

4456 A673 $250 Sheet of 6, #a-f 14.50 14.50

Souvenir Sheet

Perf. 14

4457 A673 $800 multi 7.75 7.75

No. 4457 contains one 80x30mm stamp.

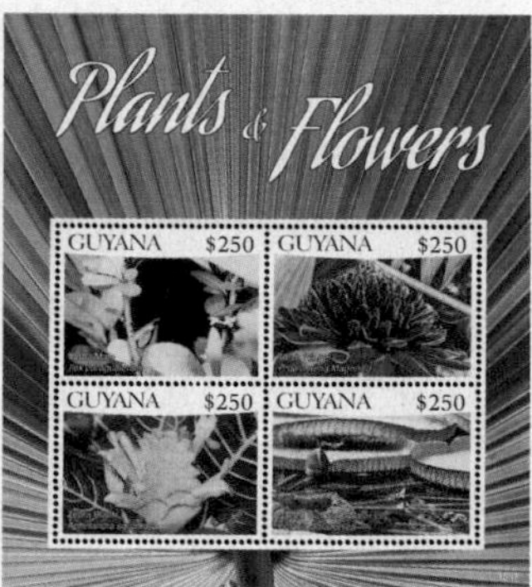

Plants and Flowers — A674

No. 4458: a, Yerba mate. b, Torch ginger. c, Zebra plant. d, Queen Victoria's water lily.
No. 4459: a, Bravo blue vein petunia. b, Cannonball tree. c, False bird-of-paradise. d, Pride of India. e, Pink banana flower. f, Red-flowering currant.
$800, Red pineapple flower.

2016, Feb. 20 Litho. *Perf. 14*

4458 A674 $250 Sheet of 4, #a-d 9.75 9.75
4459 A674 $250 Sheet of 6, #a-f 14.50 14.50

Souvenir Sheet

Perf. 12

4460 A674 $800 multi 7.75 7.75

Flowers — A675

Designs: $80, Catharanthus roseus. $130, Hibiscus. $150, Bougainvillea. $160, Queen Victoria's water lily. $200, Cannonball flower, horiz.

2016, Apr. 7 Litho. *Perf. 12*

4461-4465 A675 Set of 5 7.00 7.00

Independence, 50th anniv.

Independence, 50th Anniv. — A676

Designs: $80, Crowd. $130, Independence ceremony, May 26, 1966. $150, Fort Kyk-Over-Al, vert. $160, St. George's Cathedral, Georgetown, vert. $200, Flag of Guyana.

2016, Apr. 7 Litho. *Perf. 12½*
4466-4470 A676 Set of 5 7.00 7.00

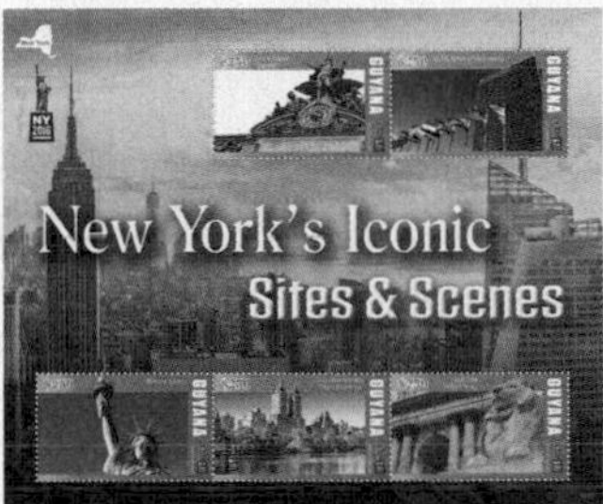

World Stamp Show 2016, New York — A677

No. 4471 — World Stamp Show emblem and New York City landmarks: a, Grand Central Terminal. b, United Nations Headquarters. c, Statue of Liberty. d, Jacqueline Kennedy Onassis Reservoir. e, New York Public Library.
$1000, Empire State Building and other buildings, vert.

2016, May 2 Litho. *Perf. 12*
4471 A677 $250 Sheet of 5, #a-e 12.50 12.50

Souvenir Sheet

4472 A677 $1000 multi 9.75 9.75

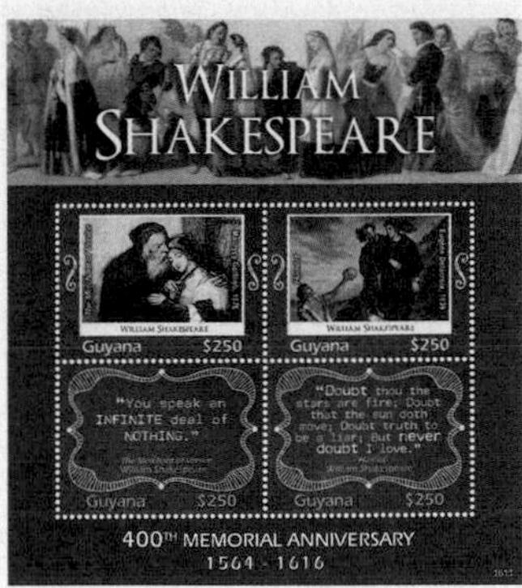

William Shakespeare (1564-1616), Writer — A678

No. 4473: a, Shylock and Jessica (characters from *The Merchant of Venice*), by Maurycy Gottlieb. b, Hamlet and Horation in the Graveyard (characters in *Hamlet*), by Eugène Delacroix. c, Line from *The Merchant of Venice*. d, Line from *Hamlet*.

No. 4474: a, The Wrestling Scene from *As You Like It*, by Francis Hayman. b, Scene from Shakespeare's *The Tempest*, by William Hogarth. c, The Revelation of Olivia's Betrothal from Act V, Scene I of *Twelfth Night*, by William Hamilton. d, Line from *As You Like It*. e, Line from *The Tempest*. f, Line from *Twelfth Night*.

$1000, The Reconciliation of the Montagues and the Capulets over the Dead Bodies of Romeo and Juliet, by Frederic Leighton.

2016, May 30 Litho. *Perf. 14*
4473 A678 $250 Sheet of 4, #a-d 9.75 9.75

Perf. 12

4474 A678 $250 Sheet of 6, #a-f 14.50 14.50

Souvenir Sheet

4475 A678 $1000 multi 9.75 9.75

No. 4475 contains one 50x30mm stamp.

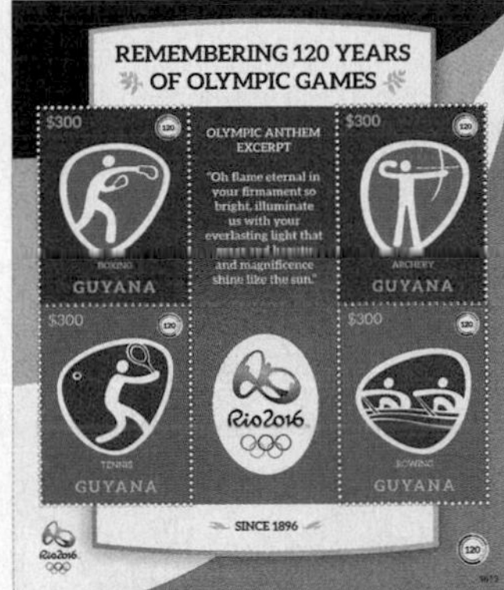

2016 Summer Olympics, Rio de Janeiro — A679

No. 4476, $300: a, Boxing. b, Archery. c, Tennis. d, Rowing.
No. 4477, $300: a, Handball. b, Weight lifting. c, Diving. d, Soccer.
No. 4478: a, Artistic gymnastics. b, Takashi Ono, Olympic gymnast.

2016, July 7 Litho. *Perf. 14*

Sheets of 4, #a-d

4476-4477 A679 Set of 2 23.50 23.50

Souvenir Sheet

Perf. 12½

4478 A679 $500 Sheet of 2, #a-b 9.75 9.75

No. 4478 contains two 38x51mm stamps.

A680

Queen Elizabeth II, 90th Birthday — A681

Various photographs of Queen Elizabeth II, as shown.

2016, July 25 Litho. *Perf. 14*
4479 A680 $250 Sheet of 6, #a-f 14.50 14.50

Souvenir Sheet

Perf.

4480 A681 $500 Sheet of 2, #a-b 9.75 9.75

Characters From *Star Trek: The Next Generation* Television Series — A682

No. 4481: a, Worf. b, William Riker. c, Data. d, Beverly Crusher. e, Geordi La Forge. f, Deanna Troi.
$1000, Captain Jean-Luc Picard.

2016, Aug. 29 Litho. *Perf. 12*
4481 A682 $250 Sheet of 6, #a-f 14.50 14.50

Souvenir Sheet

Perf. 12½

4482 A682 $1000 multi 9.75 9.75

No. 4482 contains one 38x51mm stamp.

ExoMars Mission to Mars — A683

No. 4483: a, ExoMars rover on Mars. b, NASA Deep Space Station 35. c, ExoMars trace gas orbiter, denomination at UR. d, ExoMars trace gas orbiter, denomination at LR.
$1000, Proton rocket over Earth, vert.

2016, Sept. 9 Litho. *Perf. 14*
4483 A683 $250 Sheet of 4, #a-d 9.75 9.75

Souvenir Sheet

Perf. 12

4484 A683 $1000 multi 9.75 9.75

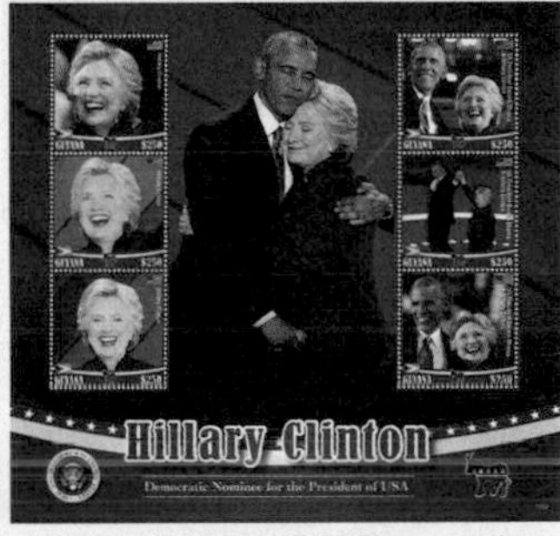

Hillary Clinton, 2016 Democratic Presidential Candidate — A684

No. 4485 — Various photographs of Secretary Clinton (#4485a, 4485c, 4485e) or Secretary Clinton and Pres. Barack Obama (#4485b, 4485d, 4485f), as shown.
$1000, Clinton and Obama, vert.

2016, Sept. 30 Litho. *Perf. 13¾*
4485 A684 $250 Sheet of 6, #a-f 15.00 15.00

Souvenir Sheet

Perf. 12½

4486 A684 $1000 multi 9.75 9.75

No. 4486 contains one 38x51mm stamp.

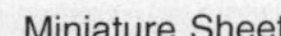

Miniature Sheet

Bauxite Mining in Guyana, Cent. — A685

No. 4487: a, $80, Kiln panorama. b, $140, Bauxite centennial emblem. c, $150, Mining of bauxite. d, $160, 1300 Dragline.

2016, Oct. 27 Litho. *Perf. 12½x12*
4487 A685 Sheet of 4, #a-d 5.25 5.25

National Day of Villages A686

Scenes depicting Exodus from Plantation Northbrook, 1839, with frame color of: $80, Bright green. $150, Orange vermilion.

2016, Nov. 7 Litho. *Perf. 12½x13¼*
4488-4489 A686 Set of 2 2.25 2.25

Worldwide Fund for Nature (WWF) — A687

No. 4490 — Giant armadillo: a, On ground, facing left. b, Facing forward. c, Climbing. d, Facing right.

2016, Nov. 17 Litho. *Perf. 14*
4490 A687 $400 Block of 4, #a-d 15.50 15.50
e. Miniature sheet of 8, 2 each #4490a-4490d 31.00 31.00

A688

A689

New Year 2017 (Year of the Rooster) — A690

No. 4491 — Rooster with background color of: a, Pale green. b, Light blue.

No. 4492: a, Rooster and Chinese character for "rooster." b, Rooster, fish and flowers.

2016, Dec. 5 Litho. *Perf. 13¾*

4491 A688 $250 Pair, #a-b 5.00 5.00

Souvenir Sheets

Perf. 12

4492 A689 $600 Sheet of 2, #a-b 12.00 12.00

Perf.

4493 A690 $800 multi 8.00 8.00

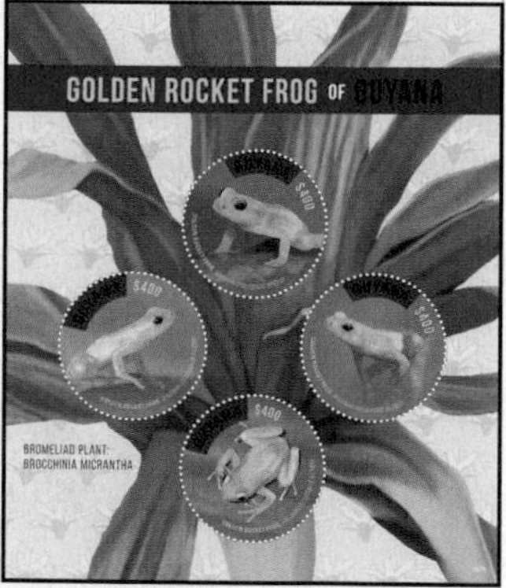

Golden Rocket Frog — A691

No. 4494: Various depictions of frog, as shown.

No. 4495: a, Two frogs. b, Tadpole.

2016, Dec. 30 Litho. *Perf.*

4494 A691 $400 Sheet of 4, #a-d 16.00 16.00

Souvenir Sheet

Perf. 12

4495 A691 $600 Sheet of 2, #a-b 12.00 12.00

No. 4495 contains two 64x32mm triangular stamps.

New Year 2017 (Year of the Rooster) — A692

Various roosters with number in LR corner of: No. 4496, $88, (3-1). No. 4497, $88, (3-2). No. 4498, $88, (3-3).

2017, Jan. 8 Litho. *Perf. 13¼x13*

4496-4498 A692 Set of 3 2.60 2.60

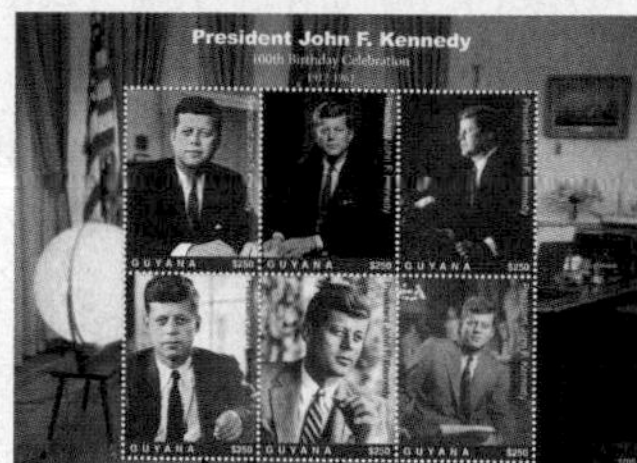

Pres. John F. Kennedy (1917-63) — A693

No. 4499 — Various photographs of Pres. Kennedy, as shown.

No. 4500 — Pres. Kennedy sitting: a, In rocking chair. b, In chair near window. c, On steps.

2017, Apr. 5 Litho. *Perf. 14*

4499 A693 $250 Sheet of 6, #a-f 14.50 14.50

Souvenir Sheet

4500 A693 $400 Sheet of 3, #a-c 11.50 11.50

Miniature Sheet

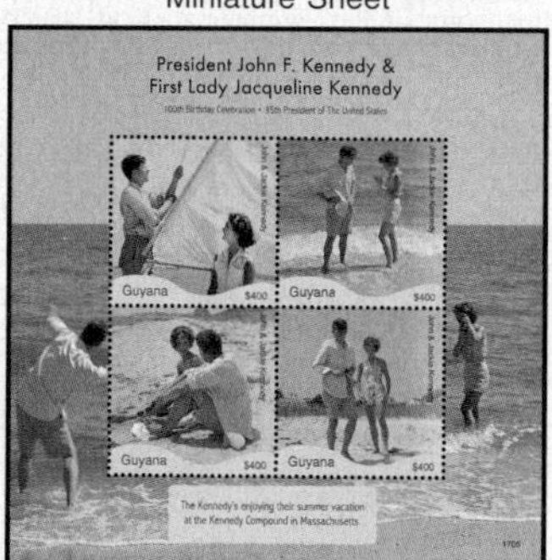

Pres. John F. Kennedy (1917-63), and Wife, Jacqueline (1929-94) — A694

No. 4501 — Pres. and Mrs. Kennedy: a, In sailboat. b, Standing in water. c, Sitting on beach. d, Standing on beach.

2017, Apr. 5 Litho. *Perf. 13¾*

4501 A694 $400 Sheet of 4, #a-d 15.50 15.50

Return of Hong Kong to China, 20th Anniv. — A695

Designs: No. 4502, $80, Deng Xiaoping, flag of People's Republic of China, doves and Hong Kong buildings (10-1). No. 4503, $80, Dove, Hong Kong buildings (10-2). No. 4504, $80, Flag of People's Republic of China, doves over Gate of Heavenly Peace, Beijing (10-3). No. 4505, $80, Buildings with decorations and signs (10-4). No. 4506, $80, Flag of Hong Kong and doves over buildings (10-5). No. 4507, $80, Flag of People's Republic of China and doves over Golden Bauhinia Statue (10-6). No. 4508, $80, Giant pandas, bamboo and Hong Kong Convention and Exhibition Center (10-7). No. 4509, $80, Doves and aerial view of Hong Kong (10-8). No. 4510, $80, Sleeping Beauty Castle, Hong Kong Disneyland, Hong Kong Film Awards Statue (10-9). No. 4511, $80, Ship and Hong Kong skyline (10-10).

2017, May 5 Litho. *Perf. 14*

4502-4511 A695 Set of 10 7.75 7.75

Miniature Sheet

Princess Diana (1961-97) — A696

No. 4512 — Princess Diana: a, $180, Wearing tiara (64x32mm). b, $200, Wearing white hat (64x32mm). c, $200, Wearing tiara, diff. (64x32mm). d, $200, Wearing beret with badge (64x32mm). e, $200, Without hat, black-and-white photograph (64x32mm). f, $200, Wearing sailor's cap (64x32mm). g, $200, As young woman (64x32mm). h, $200, Wearing wedding gown (64x32mm). i, $200, As young girl, black-and-white photograph (64x32mm). j, $200, As toddler, black-and-white photograph (64x32mm). k, $400, Wearing tiara, black-and-white phtotograph (64x64mm).

2017, June 7 Litho. *Perf. 12*

4512 A696 Sheet of 11, #a-k 23.00 23.00

Animals — A697

No. 4513: a, Moon jellyfish. b, Poison dart frog. c, Three-banded armadillo. d, Red bird-of-paradise.

$800, Reticulated giraffe, vert.

2017, Apr. 14 Litho. *Perf. 12¾*

4513 A697 $500 Sheet of 4, #a-d 19.50 19.50

Souvenir Sheet

4514 A697 $800 multi 7.75 7.75

Toucans — A698

No. 4515: a, Yellow-throated toucan. b, Toco toucan. c, Keel-billed toucan. d, White-throated toucan.

No. 4516, vert.: a, Keel-billed toucan, denomination in black, diff. b, Keel-billed toucan, denomination in white, diff.

2017, Aug. 7 Litho. *Perf. 12*

4515 A698 $400 Sheet of 4, #a-d 15.50 15.50

Souvenir Sheet

4516 A698 $600 Sheet of 2, #a-b 12.00 12.00

New Year 2018 (Year of the Dog) — A699

No. 4517, $400: a, Shih tzu. b, Chow chow.

No. 4518, $400: a, Pekingese. b, Chinese crested dog.

2017, Aug. 8 Litho. *Perf. 14*

Horiz. pairs, #a-b

4517-4518 A699 Set of 2 15.50 15.50

Nos. 4517-4518 were each printed in sheets containing two pairs.

Lions Clubs International, Cent. — A700

No. 4519: a, Yellow frame. b, Blue violet frame.

No. 4520, horiz.: a, Royal blue frame. b, Yellow frame.

2017, Sept. 11 Litho. *Perf. 12½*

4519 A700 $400 Pair, #a-b 7.75 7.75

Souvenir Sheet

Perf. 13¼

4520 A700 $600 Sheet of 2, #a-b 12.00 12.00

No. 4519 was printed in sheets containing two pairs. No. 4520 contains two 51x38mm stamps.

Sloths — A701

No. 4521: a, Hoffman's two-toed sloth, hanging with legs together. b, Brown-throated sloth. c, Adult and juvenile Brown-throated sloths. d, Hoffman's two-toed sloth, hanging with legs separated.

No. 4522, horiz. — Brown-throated sloth: a, With one paw visible and extended. b, Climbing tree. c, With front paw below head.

2017, Sept. 11 Litho. *Perf. 14*

4521 A701 $400 Sheet of 4, #a-d 15.50 15.50

Souvenir Sheet

4522 A701 $400 Sheet of 3, #a-c 12.00 12.00

Amazon Rainforest — A702

No. 4523: a, House on stilts. b, Fishing boats. c, Bend in river. d, Rainbow. e, Canoe and banks of tributary. d, Houses near river.

No. 4524: a, River and its banks. b, Water lilies. c, Tree in water.

2017, Nov. 22 Litho. *Perf. 14*
4523 A702 $250 Sheet of 6, #a-f 14.50 14.50

Souvenir Sheet

4524 A702 $400 Sheet of 3, #a-c 11.50 11.50

Miniature Sheet

World War II, 75th Anniv. — A703

No. 4525 — Posters inscribed: a, "I'm proud of you folks, too!" b,"Teamwork builds ships." c, "Buy Victory Bonds." d, "The Army needs lumber for crates and boxes." e, "Back 'em up with more metal." f, "Keep it coming!"

2017, Dec. 4 Litho. *Perf. 12½x13¼*
4525 A703 $400 Sheet of 6, #a-f 23.50 23.50

Jaguars — A704

No. 4526: a, Jaguar on tree branch. b, Head of jaguar facing forward. c, Jaguar with open mouth. d, Jaguar with torso at right.
$800, Jaguar, vert.

2017, Dec. 7 Litho. *Perf. 14*
4526 A704 $400 Sheet of 4, #a-d 15.50 15.50

Souvenir Sheet
Perf. 12¾

4527 A704 $800 multi 7.75 7.75

No. 4527 contains one 38x51mm stamp.

Wildlife of the Galapagos Islands — A705

No. 4528: a, Galapagos penguin. b, Magnificent frigatebird. c, Marine iguana. d, Blue-footed booby. e, Small ground finch. f, Galapagos sea lion.
$800, Giant tortoise.

2017, Dec. 26 Litho. *Perf. 14*
4528 A705 $250 Sheet of 6, #a-f 14.50 14.50

Souvenir Sheet
Perf. 12½

4529 A705 $800 multi 7.75 7.75

No. 4529 contains one 51x38mm stamp.

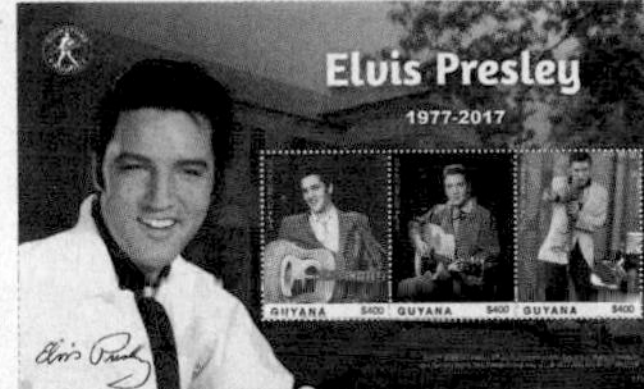

A706

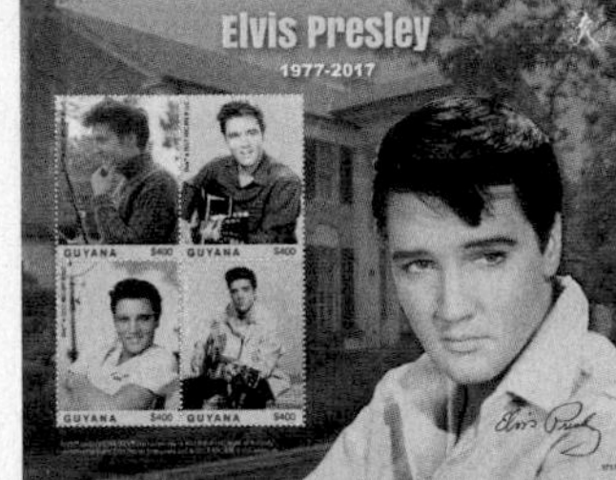

A707

Elvis Presley (1935-77) — A708

No. 4530 — Presley: a, With guitar slung over shoulder. b, Playing guitar. c, Holding microphone stand and pointing.

No. 4531 — Presley: a, Wearing turtleneck sweater. b, Wearing plaid shirt, playing guitar. c, With arms crossed. d, Sitting, playing guitar.

Inscriptions: No. 4532, $800, Elvis' only international concerts. No. 4533, $800, Record donation in support of acting colleagues. No. 4534, $800, Elvis' final movie - *Change of Habit*. No. 4535, $800, *G.I. Blues* - Elvis' most successful album.

2017, Dec. 26 Litho. *Perf. 14*
4530 A706 $400 Sheet of 3, #a-c 12.00 12.00
4531 A707 $400 Sheet of 4, #a-d 15.50 15.50

Souvenir Sheets
Perf. 12½

4532-4535 A708 Set of 4 31.00 31.00

Jaguarundis — A709

No. 4536 — Various photographs of jaguarundis with text at right in: a, $300, White. b, $300, Black. c, $500, White. d, $500, Black.

No. 4537, horiz. — Various photographs of jaguarundis: a, $550. b, $650.

2018, Jan. 24 Litho. *Perf. 14*
4536 A709 Sheet of 4, #a-d 15.50 15.50

Souvenir Sheet
Perf. 12½

4537 A709 Sheet of 2, #a-b 11.50 11.50

No. 4537 contains two 51x38mm stamps.

Birds — A710

No. 4538: a, $125, American flamingo. b, $225, Brown pelican. c, $325, Osprey. d, $525, Magnificent frigatebird.

No. 4539: a, $350, Scarlet ibis. b, $450, White-faced whistling duck. c, $550, Maguari stork.

2018, Jan. 24 Litho. *Perf. 14*
4538 A710 Sheet of 4, #a-d 11.50 11.50

Souvenir Sheet
Perf. 12

4539 A710 Sheet of 3, #a-c 13.00 13.00

Souvenir Sheet

Engagement of Prince Harry and Meghan Markle — A711

No. 4540 — Couple, with Prince Harry: a, Wearing scarf. b, Without scarf.

2018, Jan. 31 Litho. *Perf. 14*
4540 A711 $800 Sheet of 2, #a-b 11.50 11.50

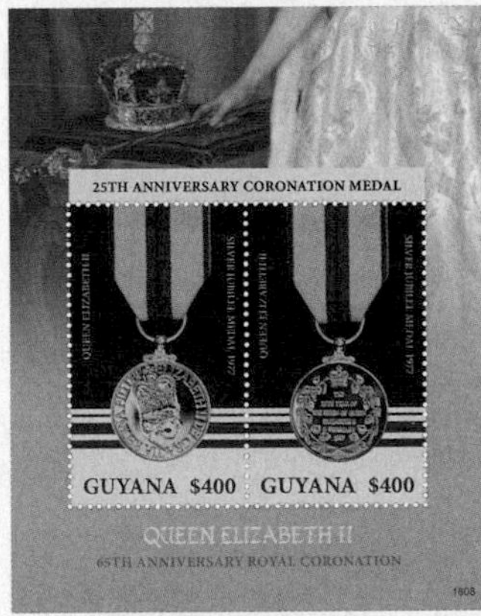

Coronation Anniversary Medals — A712

1953 Coronation Medal — A713

No. 4541, $400 — Dull pink bottom panel and side of 1977 Silver Jubilee medal showing: a, Head of Queen Elizabeth II. b, Crown, wreath and text.

No. 4542, $400 — Blue violet bottom panel and side of 2002 Golden Jubilee medal showing: a, Head of Queen Elizabeth II. b, Arms and dates.

No. 4543, $400 — Carmine red bottom panel and side of 2012 Diamond Jubilee medal showing: a, Head of Queen Elizabeth II. b, Crown, royal cypher and dates.

2018, Feb. 8 Litho. *Perf. 12*
Sheets of 2, #a-b

4541-4543 A712 Set of 3 23.00 23.00

Souvenir Sheet
Perf. 14

4544 A713 $800 multi 7.75 7.75

Souvenir Sheet

Kaieteur Falls — A714

No. 4545 — Various photographs: a, $300 (40x30mm). b, $400 (40x30mm). c, $500 (40x60mm).

2018, Mar. 14 Litho. *Perf. 14*
4545 A714 Sheet of 3, #a-c 12.00 12.00

Souvenir Sheet

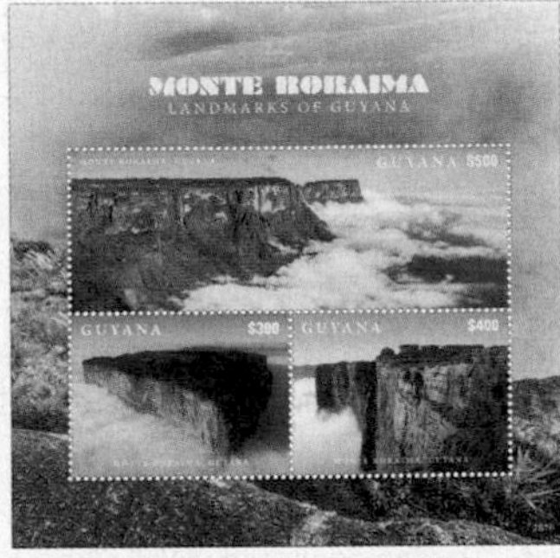

Mount Roraima — A715

No. 4546 — Various photographs: a, $300 (40x30mm). b, $400 (40x30mm). c, $500 (80x30mm).

2018, Mar. 14 Litho. *Perf. 14*
4546 A715 Sheet of 3, #a-c 12.00 12.00

Frogs — A716

No. 4547: a, $150, Three-striped poison frog. b, $200, Amazon milk frog. c, $250, Tiger-legged monkey frog. d, $300, Map tree frog. e, $350, Bumble bee poison dart frog. f, $400, Amazonian horned frog.
$800, Golden rocket frog.

2018, Mar. 14 Litho. *Perf. 14*
4547 A716 Sheet of 6, #a-f 16.00 16.00

Souvenir Sheet
Perf. 12½
4548 A716 $800 multi 8.00 8.00

No. 4548 contains one 51x38mm stamp.

Butterflies — A717

No. 4549: a, $200, Julia butterfly. b, $300, Cloudless sulphur butterfly. c, $400, Isabella tiger longwing butterfly. d, $500, Zebra mosaic butterfly.

No. 4550: a, $250, Red postman butterfly. b, $350, Lemon butterfly. c, $450, Doris longwing butterfly. d, $550, Malachite butterfly.

No. 4551, $400 — Emperor butterflies: a, On flower with wings closed. b, On rock with wings open.

2018, Mar. 14 Litho. *Perf. 12*
Sheets of 4, #a-d
4549-4550 A717 Set of 2 29.00 29.00

Souvenir Sheet
4551 A717 $400 Sheet of 2, #a-b 7.75 7.75

Miniature Sheet

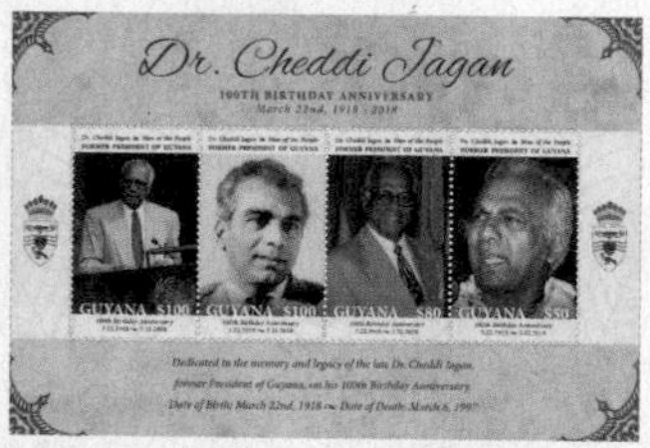

Pres. Cheddi Jagan (1918-97) — A718

No. 4552 — Various photogrpahs of Jagan in: a, $50, Black-and-white, looking left. b, $80, Color, flag in background. c, $100, Black-and-white, looking right. d, $100, Color, at podium.

2018, Mar. 16 Litho. *Perf. 12*
4552 A718 Sheet of 4, #a-d 3.25 3.25

Mao Zedong (1893-1976), Chairman of the Communist Party of China — A719

No. 4553 — Various photographs: a, $200. b, $300. c, $500.

$800, Mao Zedong at desk.

2018, Mar. 27 Litho. *Perf. 12*
4553 A719 Sheet of 3, #a-c 9.75 9.75

Souvenir Sheet
4554 A719 $800 multi 7.75 7.75

Souvenir Sheet

Fu Hao Owl-shaped Vessel From Yin Ruins, People's Republic of China — A720

2018, May 3 Litho. *Perf. 12*
4555 A720 $500 multi 4.75 4.75

Wildlife — A721

Designs: $25, Scarlet macaw. $80, Jaguar. $100, Black caiman. $140, Black curassow. $150, Red-billed toucan.

2018, June 7 Litho. *Perf. 12½*
4556-4560 A721 Set of 5 4.75 4.75

Miniature Sheet

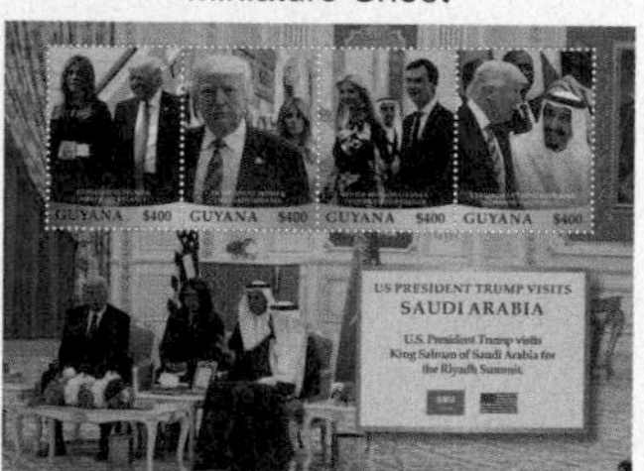

Visit of Pres. Donald Trump to Saudi Arabia — A722

No. 4561: a, Pres. Trump and wife, Melania, red panel at bottom. b, Pres. Trump and wife, blue panel at bottom. c, Ivanka Trump, Jared Kushner and King Salman. d, Pres. Trump and King Salman.

2018, July 13 Litho. *Perf. 12*
4561 A722 $400 Sheet of 4, #a-d 15.50 15.50

Hoatzins — A723

No. 4562 — Various photographs of hoatzins: a, $200 (40x30mm). b, $300 (40x30mm). c, $400 (40x60mm). d, $500 (40x60mm).

$850, Hoatzin, diff.

2018, July 13 Litho. *Perf. 14*
4562 A723 Sheet of 4, #a-d 13.50 13.50

Souvenir Sheet
Perf. 12
4563 A723 $850 multi 8.25 8.25

No. 4563 contains one 30x50mm stamp.

Miniature Sheets

A724

A725

Wedding of Prince Harry and Meghan Markle — A726

No. 4564: a, $400, Prince Harry. b, $400, Meghan Markle in wedding dress. c, $450, Couple in coach. d, $450, Couple in formal wear holding hands.

No. 4565: a, $400, Couple holding hands. b, $400, Prince Charles and bride's mother, Doria Ragland. c, $450, Prince Harry moving bride's veil. d, $450, Couple on wedding day.

No. 4566 — Royal brides in their wedding gowns: a, $400, Duchess of Cambridge. b, $400, Princess Diana of Wales. c, $450, Duchess of Sussex. d, $450, Queen Elizabeth II.

2018, July 13 Litho. *Perf. 12*
4564 A724 Sheet of 4, #a-d 16.50 16.50
4565 A725 Sheet of 4, #a-d 16.50 16.50
4566 A726 Sheet of 4, #a-d 16.50 16.50
Nos. 4564-4566 (3) 49.50 49.50

Elvis Presley (1935-77) — A727

2018, July 26 Litho. *Perf. 12*
4567 A727 $450 multi 4.50 4.50

No. 4567 was printed in sheets of 3.

Miniature Sheets

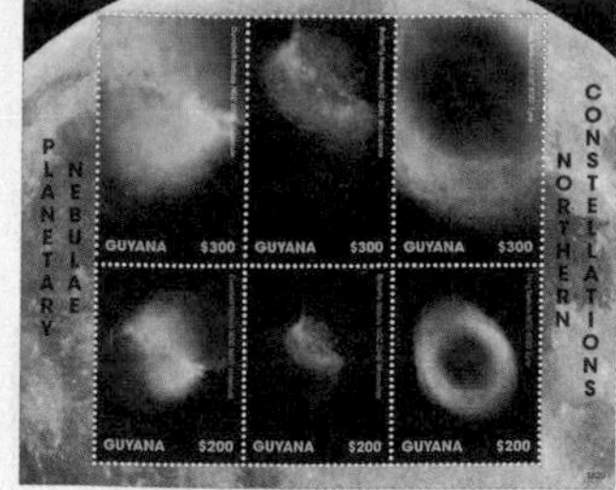

Nebulae — A728

No. 4568: a, $200, Dumbbell Nebula (30x40mm). b, $200, Butterfly Nebula (30x40mm). c, $200, Ring Nebula (30x40mm). d, $300, Dumbbell Nebula, diff. (30x50mm). e, $300, Butterfly Nebula, diff. (30x50mm). f, $300, Ring Nebula, diff. (30x50mm).

No. 4569: a, $200, Abell 31 (30x40mm). b, $200, Helix Nebula (30x40mm). c, $200, Little Ghost Nebula (30x40mm). d, $300, Abell 31, diff. (30x50mm). e, $300, Helix Nebula, diff. (30x50mm). f, $300, Little Ghost Nebula, diff. (30x50mm).

Perf. 14 ($200 stamps), 12x12x14x12 ($300 stamps)
2018, July 26 Litho.
Sheets of 6, #a-f
4568-4569 A728 Set of 2 29.00 29.00

Souvenir Sheet

Barbara Bush (1925-2018), First Lady of the United States — A729

No. 4570 — Mrs. Bush and: a, $400, Princess Diana (both standing, 40x30mm). b, $400, Princess Diana (both seated, 40x30mm). c, $500, Husband, Pres. George H. W. Bush, and Queen Elizabeth II (80x30mm).

2018, Aug. 5 Litho. *Perf. 14*
4570 A729 Sheet of 3, #a-c 12.50 12.50

Fish — A730

No. 4571: a, $250, Atlantic sailfish. b, $350, Blackfin tuna. c, $450, Atlantic bluefin tuna. d, $550, Dolphinfish.

$850, Atlantic blue marlin.

2018, Aug. 5 Litho. *Perf. 12*
4571 A730 Sheet of 4, #a-d 15.50 15.50

Souvenir Sheet
4572 A730 $850 multi 8.25 8.25

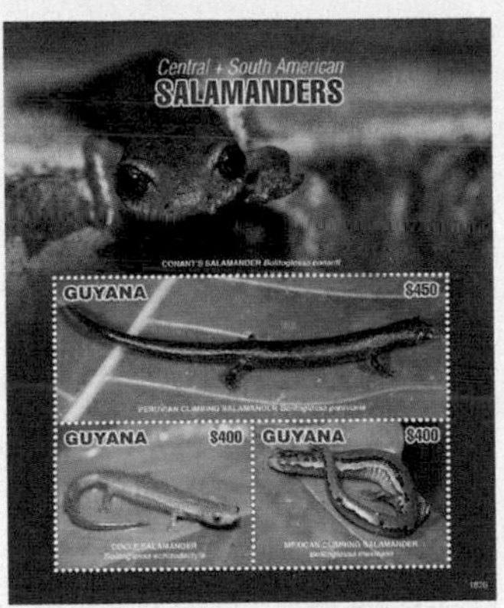

Salamanders — A731

No. 4573: a, $400, Cocle salamander (40x30mm). b, $400, Mexican climbing salamander (40x30mm). c, $450, Peruvian climbing salamander (80x30mm).
$820, Axolotl.

2018, Aug. 5 Litho. *Perf. 14*
4573 A731 Sheet of 3, #a-c 12.00 12.00

Souvenir Sheet

4574 A731 $820 multi 8.00 8.00

No. 4574 contains one 80x30mm stamp.

Mammals — A732

No. 4575: a, Head of Spectacled bear. b, Entire Spectacled bear. c, Head of Red brocket deer. d, Entire Red brocket deer. e, Head of Nine-banded armadillo. f, Entire Nine-banded armadillo.
$830, Spectacled bear, vert.

2018, Aug. 8 Litho. *Perf. 14*
4575 A732 $420 Sheet of 6, #a-f 24.00 24.00

Souvenir Sheet

Perf. 12

4576 A732 $830 multi 8.00 8.00

No. 4576 contains one 40x60mm stamp.

Miniature Sheets

Wild Cats — A733

No. 4577. a, $380, Oncilla. b, $400, Margay. c, $420, Ocelot. d, $440, Puma.
No. 4578, vert.: a, $380, Oncilla. b, $400, Margay. c, $420, Ocelot. d, $440, Puma.

2018, Aug. 8 Litho. *Perf. 12*

Sheets of 4, #a-d

4577-4578 A733 Set of 2 32.00 32.00

Miniature Sheet

New Year 2019 (Year of the Boar) — A734

No. 4579: a, Pink pig standing. b, Brown pig lying down. c, Pink pig lying down. d, Brown pig standing.

2018, Aug. 8 Litho. *Perf. 14*
4579 A734 $400 Sheet of 4, #a-d 15.50 15.50

Souvenir Sheet

New Year 2019 (Year of the Boar) — A736

2018, Sept. 8 Litho. *Perf. 13¾*
4582 A736 $800 multi 7.75 7.75

Relations Between Guyana and Brazil, 50th Anniv. A737

No. 4583 — Flags of Guyana and Brazil: a, $80. b, $200.

2018, Oct. 19 Litho. *Perf. 12½x12*
4583 A737 Vert. pair, #a-b 2.75 2.75

No. 4583 was printed in sheets containing 2 pairs.

Souvenir Sheet

Georgetown, 175th Anniv. — A738

2018, Oct. 29 Litho. *Perf. 13¼*
4584 A738 $80 multi .80 .80

A739

Atta Cephalotes — A740

Designs: $530, Queen leafcutter ant.
No. 4596: a, $200, Leafcutter ants carrying leafs (50x30mm). b, $400, Leafcutter ant carrying leaf on tree trunk (40x30mm). c, $400, Leafcutter ants and leaf (40x30mm). d, $400, Leafcutter ant and leaf (40x30mm).

2018, Nov. 20 Litho. *Perf. 14*
4585 A739 $530 multi 5.00 5.00

Miniature Sheet

Perf. 12

4586 A740 Sheet of 4, #a-d 13.50 13.50

No. 4585 was printed in sheets of 2.

Tanagers — A741

No. 4587: a, Silver-throated tanager. b, Silver-beaked tanager. c, Bay-headed tanager. d, Scarlet tanager. e, Golden-hooded tanager. f, Guira tanager.
No. 4588: a, $500, Speckled tanager facing right. b, $550, Speckled tanager facing left.

2018, Nov. 20 Litho. *Perf. 14*
4587 A741 $200 Sheet of 6, #a-f 11.50 11.50

Souvenir Sheet

4588 A741 Sheet of 2, #a-b 10.00 10.00

South American Tapirs — A742

No. 4589: a, Tapir's head facing right, no stripes visible. b, Tapir facing left. c, Head and striped neck of tapir facing right. d, Tapir facing forward.
No. 4590: a, $500, Tapir facing right. b, $550, Tapir facing right, diff.

2018, Nov. 20 Litho. *Perf. 14*
4589 A742 $300 Sheet of 4, #a-d 11.50 11.50

Souvenir Sheet

4590 A742 Sheet of 2, #a-b 10.00 10.00

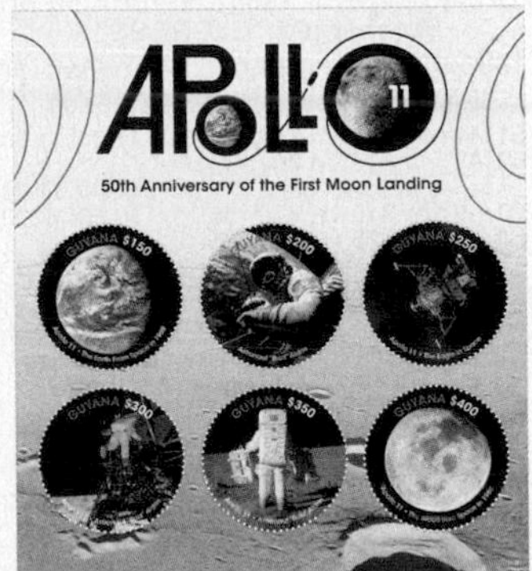

Flight of Apollo 11, 50th Anniv. (in 2019) — A743

No. 4591: a, $150, Picture of Earth from space. b, $200, Astronaut Edwin A. "Buzz" Aldrin. c, $250, Lunar Module. d, $300, Aldrin on ladder of Lunar Module. e, $350, Aldrin carryiing equipment on Moon. f, $400, Picture of Moon from space.
No. 4592: a, Plaque on Lunar Module. b, Eagle from mission patch.

2018, Nov. 20 Litho. *Perf.*
4591 A743 Sheet of 6, #a-f 16.00 16.00

Souvenir Sheet

Perf. 13¾

4592 A743 $600 Sheet of 2, #a-b 11.50 11.50

No. 4592 contains two 35x35mm stamps.

AIR POST STAMPS

No. 321 Surcharged in Blue "HUMAN RIGHTS / DAY / 1981 / 110 AIR"

1981, Nov. 14 *Perfs. as Before*
C1 A74 110c on $3 No. 321 3.00

For surcharge see No. 997.

Nos. 133, 136 and 146 Surcharged in Red, Black or Blue "AIR / Princess / of Wales / 1961-1982"

1982, June 25 *Perfs. as Before*

Printing Methods as Before

C2 A28 110c on 5c No. 136 (R) 3.00 1.00
C3 A28 220c on 1c No. 133 4.00 1.40
C4 A28 330c on $2 No. 146 (Bl) 4.00 1.60
Nos. C2-C4 (3) 11.00 4.00

For surcharges see Nos. 623, 785-787, 801, 804-804A, O19, O21, O30-O39.

No. 287 Surcharged in Dark Blue

Surcharges read: No. C5, "UNICEF / 1946-1986 / AIR"; No. C6, "UNESCO / 1946-1986 / AIR".

Perfs. as Before

1986, Oct. 24 Litho.
C5 A66 120c on $1 UNICEF 15.00 12.00
C6 A66 120c on $1 UNESCO 15.00 12.00
a. Pair, #C5-C6 30.00 24.00

Nos. 1026, 1095, 1096, 1096a, 1100, 1138, 1163 Surcharged "AIR"

1987-88 Litho. *Perf. 14*

Design A91

Plate Numbers in Parentheses

C7 75c on 25c No. 1100 (59) 13.50 1.50
C8 60c on No. 1095 (55) 11.00 10.00
C9 75c on No. 1026 (5) 1.25 .65

C10 75c on No. 1096 (55) 1.25 .65
a. 75c on No. 1096a
C11 75c on No. 1138 (83) 1.25 .65
C12 75c on No. 1163 (95) 1.25 .65

Issued: No. C7, 11/87; No. C8, 12/87; Nos. C9-C12, 8/88.

SPECIAL DELIVERY STAMPS

Orchid Type of 1985 Overprinted or Surcharged "EXPRESS"

1986-87 Litho. *Perf. 14*

Plate Numbers in Parentheses

E1 A91 $12 on #1372 (65) 11.00 11.00
E2 A91 $15 on 40c #1145 (86) 11.00 11.00
E3 A91(p) $15 on #E2 (86) 10.00 10.00
E4 A91 $25 on 25c like #1090 (53) 13.00 13.00
Nos. E1-E4 (4) 45.00

Issued: $12, $25, No. E2, 11/10. No. E3, 12/1987. No. E4 not issued without surcharge.

No. 1461c Surcharged "EXPRESS"

1986-87 Litho. *Imperf.*

E5 A96 $20 on 320c #1461c 10.00 10.00

No. E5 Ovptd. with Maltese Cross

1987, Mar. 3

E6 A96 $20 on No. E5 10.00 10.00

Orchid Type of 1985 Inscribed "Express"

1987-88 Litho. *Perf. 14*

Series 2

Plate Numbers in Parentheses

E7 A91 $15 like #1186 (11) 4.00 4.00
E8 A91 $20 like #1323 (93) 7.50 7.50
E9 A91 $25 like #1274 (63) 6.50 6.50
E10 A91 $45 like #1228 (35) 12.00 12.00
Nos. E7-E10 (4) 30.00 30.00

Issued: $45, 9/1; $15, 9/29; $25, 10/26; $20, 5/17/88.

No. "1461" Surcharged "EXPRESS / FORTY DOLLARS"

1987, Nov. *Perf. 14*

E11 A96 $40 on 320c No. 1461, imperf. btwn. 15.00 15.00

A five-pointed star appears between the lines of the surcharge on No. E11. See No. E14.

Nos. 1827e, 1830e Surcharged in Red "SPECIAL DELIVERY"

1988, Aug. 10 *Perf. 15*

E12 A100 $40 on $3.20 #1827e 12.00 12.00
E13 A100 $45 on $3.30 #1830e 12.00 12.00

See Nos. 2054b, 2056b.

Nos. "1461," 1822c Surcharged in Red "EXPRESS / FORTY DOLLARS"

1989, Mar. *Perf. 14*

E14 A96 $40 on 320c #1461, imperf. btwn. 7.00 7.00
E15 A96 $40 on 320c #1822c, imperf. btwn. 7.00 7.00

Butterflies Type of 1989 Inscribed "EXPRESS"

Souvenir Sheets

1989, Sept. 7 Litho. *Perf. 14*

E16 A115 $130 Phareas coeleste 7.75 7.75
E17 A115 $190 Papilio torquatus 12.50 12.50

For overprints see Nos. E19-E22, E24, E26-E27, E31.

Women in Space Type of 1989 Inscribed "EXPRESS"

Souvenir Sheets

1989, Nov. 8

E18 A116 $190 Valentina Tereshkova 5.00 5.00

For overprints see No. E23, E25, E28, E32.

Nos. E16-E17 Ovptd. with World Stamp Expo '89 Emblem

1989, Nov. 17

E19 A115 $130 on No. E16 7.00 7.00
E20 A115 $190 on No. E17 7.00 7.00

Nos. E16-E18 Ovptd. in Sheet Margin "Stamp World London 90" and Show Emblem

1990, May 3

E21 A115 $130 on No. E16
E22 A115 $190 on No. E17
E23 A116 $190 on No. E18
Nos. E21-E23 (3) 20.00

Nos. E17-E18 Ovptd. in Sheet Margin with Rotary Emblem and "ROTARY / INTERNATIONAL / 1905-1990"

1990, Mar.

E24 A115 $190 on No. E17
E25 A116 $190 on No. E18
Nos. E24-E25 (2) 22.50

Nos. E16-E18 Ovptd. in Sheet Margin "90th BIRTHDAY / H.M. THE / QUEEN MOTHER"

1990, June 8 Litho. *Perf. 14*

E26 A115 $130 on No. E16 7.75 7.75
E27 A115 $190 on No. E17 12.50 12.50
E28 A116 $190 on No. E18 12.50 12.50
Nos. E26-E28 (3) 32.75 32.75

Endangered Wildlife Type

Souvenir Sheets

1990, Nov. 6 Litho. *Perf. 14*

E29 A131 $130 Harpy eagle 7.00 7.00
E30 A131 $150 Ocelot 7.50 7.50

Nos. E29-E30 each contain one 43x57mm stamp.

Nos. E16, E18 Ovptd. in Sheet Margin with "BELGICA PHILATELIC / EXPOSITION 1990" and Scout, Lions, Rotary and Show Emblems

1990, June 2

E31 A115 $130 on No. E16 7.50 7.50
E32 A116 $190 on No. E18 7.50 7.50

No. E31 has Scout and Lions emblems. No. E32 has Scout and Rotary emblems.

POSTAGE DUE STAMPS

Type of British Guiana Inscribed "Guyana"

Perf. 13½x14

1967-68 Wmk. 314 Typo.

J2 D1 2c black ('68) 1.00 1.00
J3 D1 4c ultramarine .50 .50
J4 D1 12c carmine .75 .75
Nos. J2-J4 (3) 2.25 2.25

For surcharges see Nos. 897-898.

1973 Wmk. 364

J5 D1 1c green .35 *2.00*
J6 D1 2c black .35 *2.00*
J7 D1 4c ultramarine .35 *2.00*
J8 D1 12c carmine .40 *2.00*
Nos. J5-J8 (4) 1.45 8.00

For surcharges see Nos. 341-349, 658, 899-900.

OFFICIAL STAMPS

Nos. 74, 139, 141, 143-144, 146-147, 289A, 297, 300, 333, 395, 397, 401 Srchd. in Black, Red, or Black and Red

1981-82 *Perfs. as Before*

Printing Methods as Before

O1 A28 10c on 25c #141 (Bk & R) 4.00 2.25
O2 A8 15c on #74 10.00 2.00
O3 A28 15c on #139 13.50 1.00
O4 A28 30c on $2 #146 (Bk & R) 1.00 .50
O5 A28 50c on #143 (R) 2.00 .75
O6 A69 50c on #300 1.50 .40
O7 A28 60c on #144 (R) 1.50 .25
O8 A17 100c on #395 2.00 2.00
O9 A68 100c on $3 #297 (Bk & R) 5.00 .75
O10 A17 110c on #397 4.00 2.00
O11 A28 $1.10 on #333 (R)
O12 A28 125c on #401 (R) 4.50 .80
O13 A28 $2 on #146 (R) 12.50
O14 A28 $5 on #147 (R) 6.00 6.00
O15 A66 $10 on #289A 20.00

Issued: Nos. O1, O5, O7, O15, 6/8; Nos. O2, O4, O9, O11-O12, 7/1; No. O13, 7/12/82; others, 7/7.

Surcharge on Nos. O3, O6, O8, O10, O13-O14 have no obliterator. No. O11 is airmail.

Refer to 2nd paragraph in footnote following No. 147 for Nos. O1, O4-O5, O7 and O13.

For overprints and surcharges see No. 406, 425, 452, 454-456, 603, 618, 650, 817, 854, 861, 866, 933, 1378, 1381, 1384, 1387-1388.

Nos. 162, 256, 258, 282, 480, C2-C3 Srchd. in Blue or Black

1982 *Perfs. as Before*

Printing Methods as Before

O16 A66 20c on #282 10.00 1.25
O17 A33 40c on #162 3.00 1.50
O18 A60 40c on #256 2.00 1.00
O19 A28 110c on #C2 (Bk) 6.00 2.00
O20 A60 $2 on #258 18.00 3.50
O21 A28 220c on #C3 4.00 1.00
O22 A69 250c on #480 2.00 1.00
Nos. O16-O22 (7) 45.00

Issued: 110c, 9/15; others, 5/17. Nos. O19, O21 are airmail.

No. 481 Surcharged "OPS" Reading Up in Blue Violet or Blue Violet and Black

1984, Apr. 2 *Perfs. as Before*

O23 A66 150c on $5 6.00 3.00
O24 A66 200c on $5 6.50 3.25
O25 A66 225c on $5 (BV & Bk) 6.50 3.25
O25A A66 230c on $5 6.75 3.50
O26 A66 260c on $5 7.00 3.75
O27 A66 320c on $5 7.00 3.75
O28 A66 350c on $5 7.50 3.75
O29 A66 600c on $5 8.00 4.25
Nos. O23-O29 (8) 10.00 6.00

Nos. C2-C3 Surcharged "OPS" in Black and Blue, Black or Blue

1984, June 25 *Perfs. as Before*

O30 A28 25c on No. C2 (Bk)
O31 A28 30c on No. C2 1.00 .50
O32 A28 45c on No. C3 1.00 .50
O33 A28 55c on No. C2 (Bk) 1.25 .50
O34 A28 60c on No. C3 1.50 .60
O35 A28 75c on No. C3 2.00 .70
O36 A28 90c on No. C3 (Bl) 2.00 .70
O37 A28 120c on No. C3 2.25 .90
O38 A28 130c on No. C3 (Bl) 2.25 1.25
O39 A28 330c on No. C3 (Bl) 4.00 1.25
Nos. O30-O39 (10) 17.25

Overprint reads up on No. O39.

Orchid Type of 1985

Series 2

Plate Numbers in Parentheses

1987-88 Litho. Unwmk. *Perf. 14*

O40 A91 120c like #1250 (48) 1.50 .40
O41 A91 130c like #1322 (92) 1.50 .40
O42 A91 140c like #1229 (36) 1.00 .40
O43 A91 150c like #1242 (43) 1.50 .50
O44 A91 175c like #1221 (31) 1.00 .50
O45 A91 200c like #1271 (61) 1.50 .60
O46 A91 225c like #1213 (26) 1.50 .60
O47 A91 230c like #1283 (68) .75 .60
O48 A91 250c like #1268 (59) .75 .60
O49 A91 260c like #1284 (69) .75 .60
O50 A91 275c like #1319 (90) 1.75 .75
O51 A91 320c like #1292 (75) 1.75 .85
O52 A91 330c like #1208 (23) 2.00 1.00
O53 A91 350c like #1326 (95) 1.00 1.00
O54 A91 600c like #1285 (70) 1.50 1.50
O55 A91 $12 like #1286 (71) 2.50 2.50
O56 A91 $15 like #1308 (84) 3.00 3.00
Nos. O40-O56 (17) 25.25 15.80

Nos. O47, O53-O56 horiz.

Issued: Nos. O42, O44, O48, O49, 10/5/88; others, 10/5/87.

For overprints & surcharges see Nos. 1694, 1697, 1703, 1707, 1722-1726, 1728-1730.

PARCEL POST STAMPS

No. 145 Surcharged "PARCEL POST"

1981, June 8 Litho. *Perf. 13½*

Q1 A28 $15 on $1 No. 145 15.00 7.00
Q2 A28 $20 on $1 No. 145 15.00 10.00
Nos. Q1-Q2 (2) 38.00

For overprints see Nos. QO1-QO2.

No. 333 Surcharged "PARCEL POST" in Blue

1983, Jan. 15

Q3 A28 $12 on No. 333 13.00 2.00

For surcharge see No. 624.

No. 146 Surcharged "Parcel Post"

1983, Sept. 14

Q4 A28 $12 on $1.10 on $2 3.00 3.00

No. Q1 has a horizontal Royal Wedding / 1981 surcharge similar to No. 331. For overprint see No. QO5.

No. 255 Surcharged in Red

Surcharge reads: "TWENTY FIVE DOLLARS / PARCEL POST 25.00".

1985, Apr. 25 *Perf. 14*

Q5 A60 $25 on 35c No. 255 33.00 27.50

PARCEL POST OFFICIAL STAMPS

Nos. Q1-Q2 Overprinted "OPS" in Red

1981, June 8

QO1 A28 $15 on No. Q1 12.00 5.50
QO2 A28 $20 on No. Q2 13.00 8.50

For surcharges see Nos. 1389-1390.

No. 333 Surcharged in Blue

Surcharge reads: "OPS / 1982 / Parcel Post / $12.00".

1983, Jan. 15

QO3 A28 $12 on No. 333 115.00 20.00

No. QO3 Overprinted "OPS" in Black

1983, Aug. 22

QO4 A28 $12 on No. QO3 42.50 4.00

No. Q4 Overprinted "OPS" in Blue

1983, Nov. 3

QO5 A28 $12 on No. Q4 15.00 4.00

2018 Scott U.S. Minuteman Supplement

Announcing the 2018 Scott United States Minuteman supplement is now available for order. The largely popular Scott Minuteman 2018 supplement is printed on acid-free, heavy stock paper. The custom size paper will help display and highlight your newest additions. The pages will fit seamlessly into our metal-hinged 3-ring binders or the one-of-a-kind square 2-post binders for the collectors who like to keep it classic. Here are a few highlights for the 2018 Scott Minuteman supplement:

- All 2018 major stamp issues for the United States in 2018
- Scott numbers are displayed for easy identification
- Includes little narratives under the commemorative and definitive stamps
- A page(s) is provided for the Federal Duck stamps
- The precarious Hot Wheels stamps are displayed in a way that the collector decides on how to show them as singles or a sheet.

Item#		Retail	AA
180S018	Scott 2018 Minuteman Supplement	$22.99	$19.99

Bundle Today with the Scott Custom 2018 U.S. Mount Packs!

The 2018 U.S. Mount Packs are designed specifically for the 2018 Scott Minuteman supplement pages. These custom mounts will take the guessing out of mounting your 2018 stamps. Available in black or clear, so to fit in your existing album.

Item#		Retail	AA
180S018BB	Scott 2018 Minuteman Supplement + Black Custom Mounts	$69.98	**$47.98**
180S018BC	Scott 2018 Minuteman Supplement + Clear Custom Mounts	$69.95	**$47.98**

Visit www.AmosAdvantage.com

Call **800-572-6885**

Outside U.S. & Canada call: **(937) 498-0800**

Ordering Information: *AA prices apply to paid subscribers of Amos Media titles, or for orders placed online. Prices, terms and product availability subject to change. **Shipping & Handling:** U.S.: Orders total $0-$10.00 charged $3.99 shipping. U.S. Order total $10.01-$79.99 charged $7.99 shipping. U.S. Order total $80.00 or more charged 10% of order total for shipping. Taxes will apply in CA, OH, & IL. Canada: 20% of order total. Minimum charge $19.99 Maximum charge $200.00. Foreign orders are shipped via FedEx Intl. or USPS and billed actual freight.

Illustrated Identifier

This section pictures stamps or parts of stamp designs that will help identify postage stamps that do not have English words on them.

Many of the symbols that identify stamps of countries are shown here as well as typical examples of their stamps.

See the Index and Identifier for stamps with inscriptions such as "sen," "posta," "Baja Porto," "Helvetia," "K.S.A.", etc.

1. HEADS, PICTURES AND NUMERALS

GREAT BRITAIN

Great Britain stamps never show the country name, but, except for postage dues, show a picture of the reigning monarch.

Victoria

Edward VII George V Edward VIII

George VI

Elizabeth II

Some George VI and Elizabeth II stamps are surcharged in annas, new paisa or rupees. These are listed under Oman.

Silhouette (sometimes facing right, generally at the top of stamp)

The silhouette indicates this is a British stamp. It is not a U.S. stamp.

VICTORIA

Queen Victoria

INDIA

Other stamps of India show this portrait of Queen Victoria and the words "Service" (or "Postage") and "Annas."

AUSTRIA

YUGOSLAVIA

(Also BOSNIA & HERZEGOVINA if imperf.)

BOSNIA & HERZEGOVINA

Denominations also appear in top corners instead of bottom corners.

HUNGARY

Another stamp has posthorn facing left

BRAZIL

AUSTRALIA

Kangaroo and Emu

GERMANY

Mecklenburg-Vorpommern

SWITZERLAND

PALAU

2. ORIENTAL INSCRIPTIONS

CHINA

Any stamp with this one character is from China (Imperial, Republic or People's Republic). This character appears in a four-character overprint on stamps of Manchukuo. These stamps are local provisionals, which are unlisted. Other overprinted Manchukuo stamps show this character, but have more than four characters in the overprints. These are listed in People's Republic of China.

Some Chinese stamps show the Sun.

Most stamps of Republic of China show this series of characters.

Stamps with the China character and this character are from People's Republic of China. 人

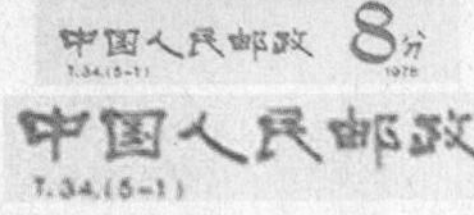

Calligraphic form of People's Republic of China

(一)	(二)	(三)	(四)	(五)	(六)
1	2	3	4	5	6
(七)	(八)	(九)	(十)	(一十)	(二十)
7	8	9	10	11	12

Chinese stamps without China character

REPUBLIC OF CHINA

PEOPLE'S REPUBLIC OF CHINA

Mao Tse-tung

MANCHUKUO

Temple

Emperor Pu-Yi

The first 3 characters are common to many Manchukuo stamps.

The last 3 characters are common to other Manchukuo stamps.

Orchid Crest

Manchukuo stamp without these elements

JAPAN

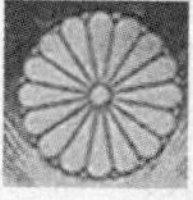

Chrysanthemum Crest

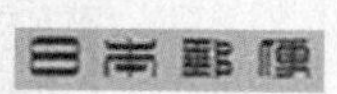

Country Name

Japanese stamps without these elements

The number of characters in the center and the design of dragons on the sides will vary.

RYUKYU ISLANDS

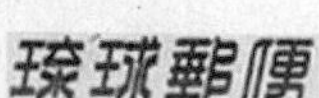

Country Name

PHILIPPINES (Japanese Occupation)

Country Name

NETHERLANDS INDIES (Japanese Occupation)

Indicates Japanese Occupation

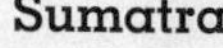

Java

Sumatra

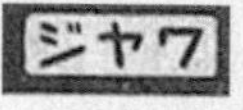

Country Name

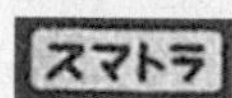

Country Name

Moluccas, Celebes and South Borneo

Country Name

NORTH BORNEO (Japanese Occupation)

Indicates Japanese Occupation

Country Name

MALAYA (Japanese Occupation)

Indicates Japanese Occupation

Country Name

BURMA

Union of Myanmar

ပြည်ထောင်စုမြန်မာနိုင်ငံတော်

Union of Myanmar

(Japanese Occupation)

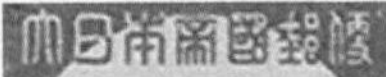

Indicates Japanese Occupation

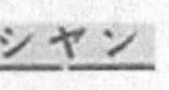

Country Name

Other Burma Japanese Occupation stamps without these elements

Burmese Script

KOREA

These two characters, in any order, are common to stamps from the Republic of Korea (South Korea) or of the People's Democratic Republic of Korea (North Korea).

This series of four characters can be found on the stamps of both Koreas. Most stamps of the Democratic People's Republic of Korea (North Korea) have just this inscription.

☯대한민국 우표

Indicates Republic of Korea (South Korea)

South Korean postage stamps issed after 1952 do not show currency expressed in Latin letters. Stamps wiith " HW," "HWAN," "WON," "WN," "W" or "W" with two lines through it, if not illustrated in listings of stamps before this date, are revenues. North Korean postage stamps do not have currency expressed in Latin letters.

Yin Yang appears on some stamps.

South Korean stamps show Yin Yang and starting in 1966, 'KOREA" in Latin letters

Example of South Korean stamps lacking Latin text, Yin Yang and standard Korean text of country name. North Korean stamps never show Yin Yang and starting in 1976 are inscribed "DPRK" or "DPR KOREA" in Latin letters.

THAILAND

Country Name

King Chulalongkorn

King Prajadhipok and Chao P'ya Chakri

3. CENTRAL AND EASTERN ASIAN INSCRIPTIONS

INDIA - FEUDATORY STATES

Alwar

Bhor

Bundi

Similar stamps come with different designs in corners and differently drawn daggers (at center of circle).

Dhar

Duttia

Faridkot

Hyderabad

Similar stamps exist with different central design which is inscribed "Postage" or "Post & Receipt."

Indore

Jammu & Kashmir

Text varies.

Jasdan

Jhalawar

Kotah

Size and text varies

Nandgaon

Nowanuggur

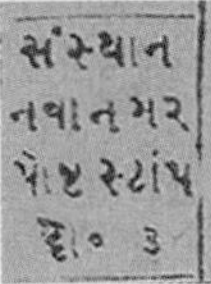

Poonch

Similar stamps exist in various sizes with different text

Rajasthan

Rajpeepla

Soruth

Tonk

BANGLADESH

বাংলাদেশ

Country Name

NEPAL

Similar stamps are smaller, have squares in upper corners and have five or nine characters in central bottom panel.

TANNU TUVA

ISRAEL

GEORGIA

This inscription is found on other pictorial stamps.

Country Name

ARMENIA

The four characters are found somewhere on pictorial stamps. On some stamps only the middle two are found.

4. AFRICAN INSCRIPTIONS

ETHIOPIA

5. ARABIC INSCRIPTIONS

١ ٢ ٣ ٤ ٥
1 2 3 4 5

٦ ٧ ٨ ٩ ٠
6 7 8 9 0

AFGHANISTAN

Many early Afghanistan stamps show Tiger's head, many of these have ornaments protruding from outer ring, others show inscriptions in black.

Arabic Script

Crest of King Amanullah

Mosque Gate & Crossed Cannons

The four characters are found somewhere on pictorial stamps. On some stamps only the middle two are found.

BAHRAIN

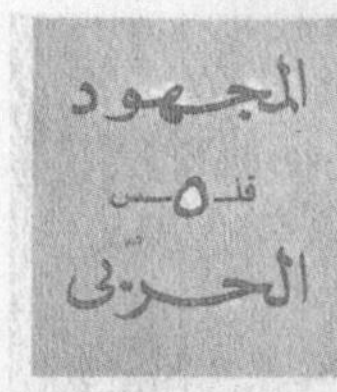

EGYPT

Postage

IRAN

Country Name

Royal Crown

Lion with Sword

Symbol

Emblem

IRAQ

JORDAN

LEBANON

Similar types have denominations at top and slightly different design.

LIBYA

Country Name in various styles

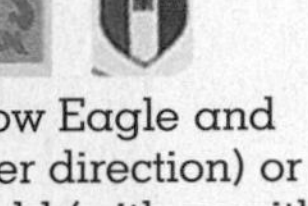

Other Libya stamps show Eagle and Shield (head facing either direction) or Red, White and Black Shield (with or without eagle in center).

Without Country Name

SAUDI ARABIA

Tughra (Central design)

Palm Tree and Swords

SYRIA

Arab Government Issues

THRACE

YEMEN

PAKISTAN

PAKISTAN - BAHAWALPUR

Country Name in top panel, star and crescent

TURKEY

Star & Crescent is a device found on many Turkish stamps, but is also found on stamps from other Arabic areas (see Pakistan-Bahawalpur)

Tughra (similar tughras can be found on stamps of Turkey in Asia, Afghanistan and Saudi Arabia)

Mohammed V

Mustafa Kemal

Plane, Star and Crescent

TURKEY IN ASIA

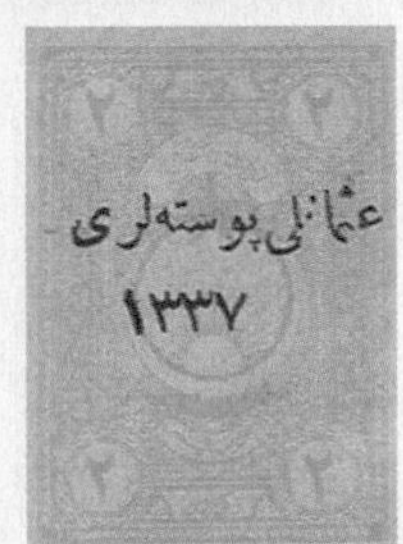

Other Turkey in Asia pictorials show star & crescent. Other stamps show tughra shown under Turkey.

6. GREEK INSCRIPTIONS

GREECE

Country Name in various styles (Some Crete stamps overprinted with the Greece country name are listed in Crete.)

Lepta

ΔΡΑΧΜΗ Drachma ΔΡΑΧΜΑΙ Drachmas ΛΕΠΤΟΝ Lepton

Abbreviated Country Name ΕΛΛ

Other forms of Country Name

No country name

CRETE

Country Name

Crete stamps with a surcharge that have the year "1922" are listed under Greece.

EPIRUS

Similar stamps have text above the eagle.

IONIAN IS.

7. CYRILLIC INSCRIPTIONS

RUSSIA

Postage Stamp Imperial Eagle

Postage in various styles

Abbreviation for Kopeck Abbreviation for Ruble Russia

Abbreviation for Russian Soviet Federated Socialist Republic RSFSR stamps were overprinted (see below)

Abbreviation for Union of Soviet Socialist Republics

This item is footnoted in Latvia

RUSSIA - Army of the North

"OKCA"

RUSSIA - Wenden

RUSSIAN OFFICES IN THE TURKISH EMPIRE

РОПиТ. These letters appear on other stamps of the Russian offices.

The unoverprinted version of this stamp and a similar stamp were overprinted by various countries (see below).

ARMENIA

BELARUS

FAR EASTERN REPUBLIC

Country Name

FINLAND

Circles and Dots on stamps similar to Imperial Russia issues

SOUTH RUSSIA

Country Name

BATUM

Forms of Country Name

TRANSCAUCASIAN FEDERATED REPUBLICS

Abbreviation for Country Name

KAZAKHSTAN

КАЗАКСТАН

COUNTRY NAME KYRGYZSTAN

КЫРГЫЗСТАН

КЫРГЫЗСТАН Country Name

ROMANIA

TAJIKISTAN

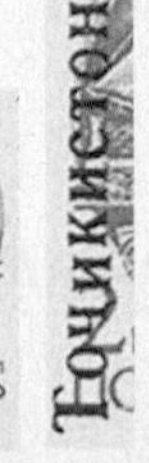

Country Name & Abbreviation

UKRAINE

Country Name in various forms

The trident appears on many stamps, usually as an overprint.

Abbreviation for Ukrainian Soviet Socialist Republic

WESTERN UKRAINE

Abbreviation for Country Name

AZERBAIJAN

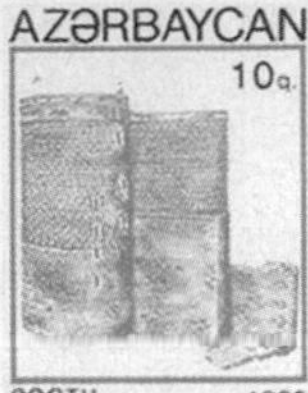

AZƏRBAYCAN

Country Name

А.С.С.Р. Abbreviation for Azerbaijan Soviet Socialist Republic

MONTENEGRO

ЦРНЕГОРЕ

ЦРНА ГОРА

Country Name in various forms

ЦР. ГОРЕ

Abbreviation for country name

No country name (A similar Montenegro stamp without country name has same vignette.)

SERBIA

СРПСКА СРБИЈА

Country Name in various forms

СРП. К.С.

Abbreviation for country name

No country name

MACEDONIA

МАКЕДОНИЈА

Country Name

МАКЕДОНСКИ
11 Октомври 1997

Different form of Country Name

SERBIA & MONTENEGRO

YUGOSLAVIA

ЈУГОСЛАВИЈА

Showing country name

No Country Name

BOSNIA & HERZEGOVINA (Serb Administration)

РЕПУБЛИКА СРПСКА

Country Name

РЕПУБЛИКЕ СРПСКЕ

Different form of Country Name

No Country Name

BULGARIA

Country Name Postage

Stotinka

СТОТИНКИ СТОТ.

Stotinki (plural) Abbreviation for Stotinki

Country Name in various forms and styles

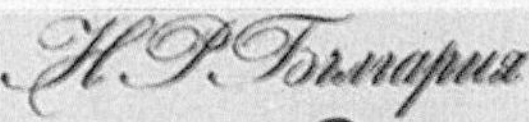

НРБългария

No country name

Abbreviation for Lev, leva

MONGOLIA

ТӨГРӨГ

Country name in one word Tugrik in Cyrillic

МОНГОЛ ШУУДАН МӨНГӨ

Country name in two words Mung in Cyrillic

Mung in Mongolian

Tugrik in Mongolian

Arms

No Country Name

INDEX AND IDENTIFIER

All page numbers shown are those in this Volume 3A.

Postage stamps that do not have English words on them are shown in the Illustrated Identifier.

Vols. 3A-3B Number Additions, Deletions & Changes

Number in 2019 Catalogue	Number in 2020 Catalogue
Georgia	
new	44a
new	45a
new	49b
Germany	
new	215a
new	243a
new	243b
new	244b
new	250b
new	252b
new	290a
new	290b
730a	deleted
new	B907a
Great Britain	
MH183c	deleted
MH193g	deleted
new	MH289B
new	MH393a
Isle of Man	
new	1435d
new	1435e
new	1435g
new	1435h
new	1435i
new	1547b
1435d	1435f
Guinea-Bissau	
new	1013
new	1014
new	1017
new	1019
new	1020
new	1024
new	1025
new	1026
new	1028
new	1029
new	1029A
Guyana	
new	1027a
new	1031a
new	1036a
new	1046a
new	1049a
new	1052a
new	1054a
new	1084a
new	1091a
new	1094a
new	1108a
new	2619E
Haiti	
new	J5a
new	J6a
new	J7a
new	J8a
new	J9a
Iraq	
new	29c
new	31c
new	33a
new	36c
new	39a
new	1469a
new	O39a

INDEX TO ADVERTISERS
2020 VOLUME 3A